Best Books for Children

Best Books for Children

Preschool Through Grade 6

8th Edition

Catherine Barr

John T. Gillespie

Children's and Young Adult Literature Reference Series
Catherine Barr, Series Editor

A Member of the Greenwood Publishing Group

Westport, Connecticut • London

Library of Congress Cataloging-in-Publication Data

Barr, Catherine, 1951-
 Best books for children : preschool through grade 6.— 8th ed. / by Catherine Barr and John T. Gillespie.
  p. cm. — (Children's and young adult literature reference series)
 Rev. ed. of: Best books for children / John T. Gillespie. 7th ed. 2002.
 Includes bibliographical references and index.
 ISBN 1-59158-085-4 (alk. paper)
 1. Children—Books and reading—United States. 2. Children's literature—Bibliography. 3. Best books—
United States. I. Gillespie, John Thomas, 1928– Best books for children. II. Title. III. Series.
Z1037.G48 2006
011.62—dc22   2005030882

British Library Cataloguing in Publication Data is available.

Library of Congress Catalog Card Number: 2005030882
ISBN: 1-59158-085-4

First published in 2006

Libraries Unlimited, 88 Post Road West, Westport, CT 06881
A Member of the Greenwood Publishing Group, Inc.
www.lu.com

Printed in the United States of America

The paper used in this book complies with the
Permanent Paper Standard issued by the National
Information Standards Organization (Z39.48–1984).

10 9 8 7 6 5 4 3 2 1

Contents

History and Geography

Recreation

Major Subjects Arranged Alphabetically

Preface

This is the eighth edition of *Best Books for Children*. The primary aim of this work, as with the earlier editions, is to provide a list of books recommended to satisfy both a child's recreational reading needs and the demands of a typical school curriculum. These recommendations are gathered from a number of sources, which are discussed on the following pages. For greatest depth, coverage has been limited to the age group from preschool children through readers in grade 6. Books that could be used with advanced sixth graders but are best suited to readers in grades 6 through 9 are listed in the companion volume *Best Books for Middle School and Junior High Readers* (Libraries Unlimited, 2004). It is suggested that this title be used to enrich collections for gifted fifth- and sixth-grade readers. A third volume, *Best Books for Senior High Readers* (Libraries Unlimited, 2004), covers grades 9 through 12.

Of the 26,958 titles in this eighth edition of *Best Books for Children*, 25,347 are individually numbered entries. The remaining 1,611 titles — those cited within the annotations — are additional recommended titles by the main entry author. More than one third of the 25,347 numbered entries are new to this edition.

In most cases, at least two recommendations were required from the sources consulted for a title to be considered for listing. However, a single recommendation could also make a title a candidate for inclusion. This was particularly true of nonfiction books in a series. The reviewing policies of many journals do not allow for the inclusion of all titles in a series. Some give little or no coverage to series books, while others review only representative titles or list titles without reviews. Where only a single recommendation was available, the reviewing history of the series was taken into consideration and books in the series were often examined and evaluated by the editor from copies supplied by the publisher. In these cases, such criteria as availability, currency, accuracy, usefulness, and relevance were applied.

Several sources were used to compile this annotated bibliography. At the outset, there was a thorough perusal and evaluation of the entries in the seventh (2002) edition of *Best Books for Children*. All out-of-print titles were dropped, as well as those that were considered no longer timely or suitable.

The other sources consulted were numerous and varied. The major tools were current reviewing periodicals, principally *Booklist*, *Bulletin of the Center for Children's Books*, *Horn Book*, *Horn Book Guide*, and *School Library Journal*.

It is hoped that this bibliography will be used in four different ways: (1) as a tool to evaluate the adequacy of existing collections; (2) as a book selection instrument for beginning and expanding collections; (3) as an aid for giving reading guidance to children; and (4) as a base for the preparation of bibliographies and reading lists. To increase the book's usefulness, particularly in the two latter areas, the chosen titles are arranged under broad interest areas or, as in the case of nonfiction works, by curriculum-oriented subjects rather than by the Dewey Decimal Classification System.

For example, a book on religious practices in colonial America might be cataloged under religion, but in this book it would be included with other books on "United States — Colonial Period." In this way, analogous titles that otherwise would be in separate sections are brought together and can be seen in relation to other books on the same broad topic.

In general, the titles that appear in the section Books for Younger Readers are those usually read to children or used in assisted-reading situations. The one exception in this section is the listing of "Books for Beginning Readers." This area contains books of fiction easy enough to be read by beginning readers; nonfiction beginning readers are integrated into the appropriate subject areas with mention in the annotation that the work is suitable for beginning readers. Interactive books, such as books containing tabs, pop-ups, or flaps, are integrated into appropriate sections but their annotations mention the nature of their format.

The "Imaginative Stories" section in the Picture Books area is divided into two categories: Fantasies and Imaginary Animals. The first contains both books that depict humans, usually children, in fanciful, unrealistic situations (many bordering on the supernatural) and books that include (as characters) such mythological beasts as dragons and unicorns. The Imaginary Animals category includes stories about anthropomorphized animals that engage in human activities (such as pigs going to school) and display human motivations and behavior.

Simple chapter books and similar nonfiction titles that bridge the reading abilities and interests of children in the upper primary grades and early middle grades are integrated into the appropriate sections for older readers and their annotations indicate that they are easily read.

In the Fiction for Older Readers areas, only general anthologies of short stories are included under "Short Stories and Anthologies." Collections of short stories on a single topic, such as sports stories, are found under that specific topic. In the fiction section labeled "Ethnic Groups," only those novels in which ethnicity is the central theme are included. Other novels that simply include members of minority groups are integrated into other more appropriate topical areas. Similarly, in the nonfiction Biography section under "African Americans," "Hispanic Americans," and "Native Americans," only those individuals who have been associated primarily with race-related activities are included. For example, a biography of Martin Luther King, Jr., would be found under "African Americans" but a life story of golfer Tiger Woods would be under sports biographies. Also in the nonfiction area, general books of science projects and experiments are found under "General Science — Experiments and Projects," but books of activities related to a specific area of science are included in that area.

Some types of books have been omitted from this bibliography. These include reference books such as dictionaries and encyclopedias, professional books (for example, other bibliographies), and such mass-market series as the Nancy Drew and Hardy Boys books, although individual libraries might wish to purchase them.

Special features that have been retained in this edition include a listing of "Major Subjects Arranged Alphabetically." This special list provides both the range of entry numbers and page numbers for the largest subject areas covered in the volume. Other features also continued are the International Standard Book Number (ISBN) for both hardcover and paperback editions, nonfiction series titles, and Dewey Decimal numbers for nonfiction titles. Also included are review citations for all books published and reviewed from 1985 through July 2005. These review citations will give librarians sources from which to obtain more detailed information about each of the books listed. The five sources are:

Booklist (BL)
Bulletin of the Center for Children's Books (BCCB)
Horn Book (HB)
Horn Book Guide (HBG)
Library Media Connection (LMC)
School Library Journal (SLJ)

The citing of only one review does not necessarily mean that the book received only a single recommendation; it might easily also have been listed in one or more of the other bibliographies consulted. Books without review citations or Dewey numbers are pre-1985 imprints and reprints of older recommended books recently brought back into print (the original publication date is indicated within the annotation if it was readily available).

An asterisk following a review citation denotes an outstanding recommendation from that source.

Entry Information

As in previous editions, titles in the main section of the book are assigned an entry number. The entry contains the following information where applicable: (1) author or editor; (2) title; (3) suitable grade levels; (4) adapter or translator; (5) indication of illustrations or illustrator's name (usually only for picture books); (6) series title for nonfiction books; (7) date of publication; (8) publisher and price of hardbound edition (LB=library binding); (9) ISBN of hardbound edition; (10) paperback (paper) publisher (if no publisher is listed, it is the same as the hardbound edition) and price; (11) ISBN of paperback edition; (12) number of pages; (13) annotation; (14) review citations; (15) Dewey Decimal number.

Indexes

Best Books for Children includes three indexes: author/illustrator, book title, and subject/grade level. Authors and illustrators are listed alphabetically by last name, followed by book titles and entry numbers; fiction titles are indicated by (F). In the Title Index, both main entry titles and internal titles cited within the annotation are included, all with entry numbers and (F) notations.

The Subject/Grade Level Index includes thousands of subject headings. Within each subject, entries are listed according to grade-level suitabilities. For example, under the subject Humorous Stories there may be numerous entry numbers given first for Primary (P) readers; then for the Primary-Intermediate (PI) group; for the Intermediate (I) group; for the Intermediate-Junior High (IJ) readers; and finally for all readers, covering grades from preschool through grade 8 (All). This will enable the professional to select the most appropriate titles for use. Biographical entries are listed in this index by the last name of the subject of the biography. The following codes are used to give approximate grade level:

P   (Primary) preschool through grade 3
PI (Primary-Intermediate) grades 2 through 4
I   (Intermediate) grades 4 through 6
IJ (Intermediate-Junior High) grades 5 through 8 (or in a few cases some higher grades)
All (All readers) preschool through grade 8 (or higher)

Specific, more exact grade-level suitabilities are given (parenthetically) for each book in its main text entry. To facilitate quick reference, all listings in all indexes refer the user to entry number, not page number.

Many people were involved in the preparation of this bibliography. I am especially grateful to my coauthor John Gillespie for his continuing contributions, to Barbara Ittner of Libraries Unlimited for her encouragement and support, and to Christine McNaull and Julie Miller, who make production of this large book possible.

Catherine Barr

Literature

Books for Younger Readers

Alphabet, Concept, and Counting Books

Alphabet Books

1 *ABC USA* (K–2). Illus. by Martin Jarrie. 2005, Sterling $14.95 (1-4027-1619-2). 32pp. A strikingly illustrated celebration of American culture and history, from alligator to Zydeco. (Rev: BL 2/15/05; SLJ 5/05) [421.1]

2 Agee, Jon. *Z Goes Home* (1–3). Illus. by author. 2003, Hyperion $16.95 (0-7868-1987-1). Offering much for both the visually and verbally inclined, this offbeat alphabet book follows the letter Z home after a day's work on the zoo sign. (Rev: HBG 4/04; SLJ 9/03)

3 Alda, Arlene. *Arlene Alda's ABC* (PS–K). Illus. 1993, Tricycle $12.95 (1-883672-01-5). 32pp. Objects turn into letters in this unusual alphabet book. (Rev: BL 1/1/94)

4 Allen, Susan, and Jane Lindaman. *Read Anything Good Lately?* (K–2). Illus. by Vicky Enright. 2003, Millbrook LB $22.90 (0-7613-2322-8). 32pp. From "an atlas at the airport to "the zodiac at the zoo," this alphabet book suggests places and ways to read. (Rev: BL 5/15/03; HBG 10/03; SLJ 7/03) [028]

5 Andreae, Giles. *K Is for Kissing a Cool Kangaroo* (K–1). Illus. by Guy Parker-Rees. 2003, Scholastic $15.95 (0-439-53126-8). A is for apple, but also aardvark, anteater, and ants in the action-packed illustrations in this rhyming alphabet book. (Rev: HBG 4/04; SLJ 12/03) [428.1]

6 Anglund, Joan Walsh. *In a Pumpkin Shell* (PS–2). Illus. by author. 1977, Harcourt paper $6.00 (0-15-644425-9). 32pp. A Mother Goose ABC book.

7 Anno, Mitsumasa. *Anno's Alphabet: An Adventure in Imagination* (PS–2). Illus. by author. 1992, HarperCollins paper $22.95 (0-06-443315-3). 64pp. A most unusual and distinctive alphabet book that shows the letters as pieces of rough-grained wood

and, on the opposite pages, objects beginning with that letter. An excellent introduction to art as well.

8 Aylesworth, Jim. *Naughty Little Monkeys* (PS–1). Illus. by Henry Cole. 2003, Dutton $15.99 (0-525-46940-0). When the (human) parents go out for the evening, their 26 little monkeys run riot — Andy making paper planes, Brooke bouncing, Carla eating cake, and so forth. (Rev: BL 9/1/03; HBG 4/04; SLJ 8/03)

9 Aylesworth, Jim. *Old Black Fly* (PS–2). Illus. by Stephen Gammell. 1992, Holt $16.95 (0-8050-1401-2). 32pp. A fun alphabet book that describes the 26 awful things Old Black Fly did one day. (Rev: BCCB 7–8/92; BL 2/15/92*; HB 5–6/92; SLJ 4/92*)

10 Azarian, Mary. *A Gardener's Alphabet* (K–2). Illus. by author. 2000, Houghton Mifflin $16.00 (0-618-03380-7). Stunning black woodcuts hand-tinted with watercolors are featured in this handsome alphabet book that uses words associated with gardens and gardening. (Rev: BCCB 9/00; BL 4/15/00; HBG 10/00; SLJ 6/00)

11 Baker, Leslie. *The Animal ABC* (PS–1). Illus. by author. 2003, Holt $15.95 (0-8050-6746-9). Delightful watercolors illustrate animals from Ant to Zebra. (Rev: BL 6/1–15/03; HBG 10/03; SLJ 5/03)

12 Beaton, Clare. *Zoe and Her Zebra* (PS). Illus. 1999, Barefoot $14.95 (1-902283-75-9). 32pp. A clever alphabet book in which children named for each letter of the alphabet (e.g., Alice, Ben) are chased by animals similarly arranged (e.g., alligator, bear). (Rev: BL 10/15/99; SLJ 12/99)

13 Berg, Cami. *D Is for Dolphin* (PS–3). Illus. by Janet Biondi. 1991, Windom $18.95 (1-879244-01-2). 56pp. In this alphabet book, every letter stands for a word associated with dolphins. (Rev: BCCB 6/91; BL 9/15/91; SLJ 7/91)

14 Bond, Michael. *Paddington Bear and the Busy Bee Carnival* (PS–1). Illus. by R. W. Alley. 1998, HarperCollins $12.95 (0-06-027765-3). 40pp. A pleasant picture book in which Paddington Bear enters a contest by listing all the things he sees that

begin with the letter *B*. (Rev: BL 5/15/98; HBG 10/98; SLJ 8/98)

15 Bonder, Dianna. *Accidental Alphabet* (K–2). Illus. by author. 2003, Whitecap $16.95 (1-55285-394-2). A bouncy rhyming text accompanies detailed illustrations. (Rev: SLJ 5/03)

16 Boynton, Sandra. *A Is for Angry: An Animal and Adjective Alphabet* (PS–K). Illus. 1987, Workman paper $6.95 (0-89480-507-X). 48pp. Adjectives are the focus of this alphabet book.

17 Bullard, Lisa. *Not Enough Beds!* (PS–K). Illus. by Joni Oeltjenbruns. 1999, Lerner $15.95 (1-57505-356-X). 32pp. In this alphabet book, family members must find unusual sleeping arrangements when they all arrive for Christmas. (Rev: BL 9/15/99; HBG 3/00; SLJ 10/99)

18 Bunting, Eve. *Girls A to Z* (K–3). Illus. by Suzanne Bloom. 2002, Boyds Mills $15.95 (1-56397-147-X). 32pp. An alphabet book filled with girls pretending to be grown-ups with interesting jobs (such as astronauts and gondoliers). (Rev: BL 9/15/02; HBG 3/03; SLJ 10/02)

19 Cahoon, Heather. *Word Play ABC* (1–3). Illus. by author. 1999, Walker LB $16.85 (0-8027-8684-7). 32pp. Each letter of the alphabet is accompanied by a pun or play on words; for example, for C, there is a picture of a crocodile in a pot and the word *crockpot*. (Rev: BCCB 7–8/99; BL 7/99; HBG 10/99; SLJ 4/99)

20 Capucilli, Alyssa Satin. *Mrs. McTats and Her Houseful of Cats* (PS–1). Illus. by Joan Rankin. 2001, Simon & Schuster $16.00 (0-689-83185-4). 32pp. Mrs. McTats adds alphabetically named stray cats (and one dog) to her household in this nicely illustrated and humorous book that teaches numbers as well. (Rev: BL 9/1/01; HBG 10/01; SLJ 8/01)

21 Carlson, Nancy. *ABC I Like Me!* (PS–1). Illus. 1997, Viking $14.99 (0-670-87458-2). 32pp. A little pig and his friends take a trip through the alphabet. (Rev: BL 4/1/97; SLJ 6/97)

22 Catalanotto, Peter. *Matthew A.B.C.* (PS–2). Illus. 2002, Simon & Schuster $14.95 (0-689-84582-0). 32pp. There is a Matthew for every letter of the alphabet in Mrs. Tuttle's class, and each boy has a special characteristic to match his letter. (Rev: BL 7/02; HB 7–8/02; HBG 10/02; SLJ 6/02)

23 Chaplin, Susan Gibbons. *I Can Sign My ABCs* (K–3). Illus. by Laura McCaul. 1986, Gallaudet Univ. $9.95 (0-930323-19-X). 56pp. The ABCs of sign language, with color illustrations. (Rev: BL 2/15/87)

24 Cheney, Lynne. *America: A Patriotic Primer* (2–4). 2002, Simon & Schuster $16.95 (0-689-85192-8). 40pp. The wife of the vice president presents an alphabet book for older children that outlines the virtues of America's democracy. (Rev: BCCB 3/02; BL 6/1–15/02; HBG 3/03; SLJ 7/02) [973]

25 Chesworth, Michael. *Alphaboat* (2–4). Illus. 2002, Farrar $16.00 (0-374-30244-8). 32pp. Spirited rhyming wordplay and cartoon illustrations take the crew of the Alphaboat on a lively journey in search of lost treasure. (Rev: BL 10/15/02; HBG 10/03; SLJ 9/02)

26 Chin-Lee, Cynthia. *A Is for Asia* (K–4). Illus. by Yumi Heo. 1997, Orchard LB $17.99 (0-531-33011-7). 32pp. A variety of topics, from geography to holidays, are covered in this unique alphabet book. (Rev: BCCB 5/97; BL 3/1/97; SLJ 4/97)

27 Chin-Lee, Cynthia, and Terri de la Pena. *A Is for the Americas* (2–4). Illus. by Enrique O. Sanchez. 1999, Orchard LB $16.99 (0-531-33194-6). 32pp. An alphabet book for older children that uses geographical and historical names — most of them associated with Hispanic and Native American culture. (Rev: BL 9/1/99; HBG 3/00; SLJ 10/99) [970]

28 Cline-Ransome, Lesa. *Quilt Alphabet* (PS–1). Illus. by James E. Ransome. 2001, Holiday House $17.95 (0-8234-1453-1). 32pp. In this alphabet picture book, the letters are incorporated into quilt squares and accompanied by riddles. (Rev: BL 9/1/01; HBG 3/02; SLJ 11/01) [811]

29 Crosbie, Michael J. *Arches to Zigzags: An Architecture ABC* (PS–3). Illus. by Kit Rosenthal and Steve Rosenthal. 2000, Abrams $18.95 (0-8109-4218-6). 32pp. In rhyme and illustrated with color photos from around America, this book uses architectural elements to introduce the alphabet (e.g., B is for balcony). (Rev: BCCB 12/00; BL 2/1/01; HBG 10/01; SLJ 12/00) [721]

30 Crowther, Robert. *My Pop-up Surprise ABC* (PS–K). Illus. by author. 1997, Orchard $16.95 (0-531-30038-2). A simple alphabet book that uses large, easily manipulated flaps and pull tabs. (Rev: SLJ 8/97)

31 Darling, Kathy. *ABC Cats* (K–3). Illus. by Tara Darling. 1998, Walker LB $16.85 (0-8027-8667-7). 32pp. Full-color photos of cats illustrate this charming alphabet book. (Rev: BL 11/1/98; HBG 10/99; SLJ 11/98)

32 Demarest, Chris L. *Alpha Bravo Charlie: The Military Alphabet* (K–3). Illus. 2005, Simon & Schuster $16.95 (0-689-86928-2). 40pp. From Alpha to Zulu, this large-format book introduces the military alphabet and corresponding U.S. Navy signal flag with many full-color illustrations of military scenes. (Rev: BL 5/15/05) [355]

33 Demarest, Chris L. *Firefighters A to Z* (PS–K). Illus. 2000, Simon & Schuster $16.95 (0-689-83798-4). 40pp. Beginning with "A is for Alarm," this is a large-format alphabet book showing fire fighters, their equipment, and their activities. (Rev: BL 7/00; HB 7–8/00; HBG 3/01; SLJ 12/00)

34 Dodd, Emma. *Dog's ABC: A Silly Story About the Alphabet* (PS–1). Illus. by author. 2002, Dutton $15.99 (0-525-46837-4). 32pp. Dog's day takes him through the alphabet with a series of events, each of which starts with a different letter. (Rev: BL 2/1/02; HBG 10/02; SLJ 2/02)

35 Dog Artlist Collection. *The Dog from Arf! Arf! to Zzzzzz* (PS–2). 2004, HarperCollins LB $15.89 (0-06-059858-1). "Fetch" and "Good dog" are just two of the dog-related entries in this alphabet book full of puppies. (Rev: SLJ 7/04)

4

36 Dugan, Joanne. *ABC NYC: A Book About Seeing New York City* (K–3). Photos by author. 2005, Abrams $14.95 (0-8109-5854-6). An urban ABC that introduces New York's sites, shapes, and sounds. (Rev: SLJ 6/05)

37 Edwards, Richard. *Amazing Animal Alphabet* (PS–1). Illus. 1999, Orchard $14.95 (0-531-30123-0). Arranged in alphabetical order, different animals are found hiding under flaps in this interactive book. (Rev: BL 12/15/99; SLJ 6/99)

38 Edwards, Wallace. *Alphabeasts* (PS–K). Illus. 2002, Kids Can $15.95 (1-55337-386-3). 32pp. Rhyming couplets caption lavish, full-page illustrations of animals from alligator to zebra. (Rev: BL 11/1/02; HBG 3/03; SLJ 12/02)

39 Ehlert, Lois. *Eating the Alphabet: Fruits and Vegetables from A to Z* (PS–1). Illus. by author. 1989, Harcourt $16.00 (0-15-224435-2); paper $5.95 (0-15-201036-X). 32pp. An eye-catching alphabet book. (Rev: BL 3/15/89; HB 5–6/89; SLJ 6/89)

40 Ernst, Lisa Campbell. *The Turn-Around, Upside-Down Alphabet Book* (PS–2). Illus. by author. 2004, Simon & Schuster $15.95 (0-689-85685-7). 32pp. Eye-catching graphics and an optical game make this alphabet book a good choice. (Rev: BL 6/1–15/04; HB 7–8/04) [428.1]

41 Ernst, Lisa Campbell. *The Turn-Around, Upside-down Alphabet Book* (PS–2). Illus. by author. 2004, Simon & Schuster $15.95 (0-689-86585-7). Each letter becomes three different objects as the book is turned; for example, the A is also a beak, an ice cream cone, and the point of a star. (Rev: HB 7–8/04; LMC 2/05; SLJ 8/04) [428.1]

42 Faulkenberry, Lauren. *What Do Animals Do on the Weekend? Adventures from A to Z* (K–3). Illus. by author. 2002, Novello Festival $17.95 (0-9708972-4-3). An alliterative approach to animal activities, where kangaroos kayak and penguins picnic, that also conveys factual information. (Rev: SLJ 10/02)

43 Fisher, Valorie. *Ellsworth's Extraordinary Electric Ears and Other Amazing Alphabet Anecdotes* (PS–2). 2003, Simon & Schuster $16.95 (0-689-85030-1). This fun-packed alphabet book introduces readers to 26 wildly diverse scenes and stories. (Rev: HBG 10/03; SLJ 7/03)

44 Fleming, Denise. *Alphabet Under Construction* (PS–2). Illus. 2002, Holt $16.95 (0-8050-6848-1). 32pp. An industrious mouse assembles an alphabet using actions that start with each letter. (Rev: BCCB 10/02; BL 8/02; HB 9–10/02; HBG 3/03; SLJ 9/02)

45 Floca, Brian. *The Racecar Alphabet* (PS–2). Illus. by author. 2003, Simon & Schuster $15.95 (0-689-85091-3). Sports cars, stock cars, Formula 1 — they're all included in this attractive, alliterative alphabet book. (Rev: HB 11–12/03; HBG 4/04; SLJ 11/03)

46 Frampton, David. *My Beastie Book of ABC: Rhymes and Woodcuts* (PS–3). Illus. by author. 2002, HarperCollins LB $15.89 (0-06-028824-8). Animals from A to Z are introduced with a letter, rhyme, and illustration. (Rev: BCCB 9/02; HBG 10/02; SLJ 5/02)

47 Geisert, Arthur. *Pigs from A to Z* (1–4). Illus. by author. 1986, Houghton Mifflin $17.95 (0-395-38509-1). 64pp. Complicated etchings hide letters, and it will take somewhat older-than-usual alphabet book readers to figure them out. (Rev: BL 11/15/86; HB 1–2/87; SLJ 12/86)

48 Gerstein, Mordicai. *The Absolutely Awful Alphabet* (1–3). Illus. 1999, Harcourt $15.00 (0-15-201494-2). 32pp. Using alliterative texts, each letter of the alphabet is introduced by a hideous monster. (Rev: BL 4/1/99; HBG 10/99; SLJ 5/99) [428.1]

49 Girnis, Meg. *A B C for You and Me* (PS–2). Illus. by Shirley Leamon Green. 2000, Whitman $14.95 (0-8075-0101-8). 32pp. Using photographs of children with Down syndrome, this alphabet book celebrates the beauty of all kinds of children. (Rev: BL 7/00; HB 5–6/00; HBG 10/00; SLJ 4/00)

50 Grassby, Donna. *A Seaside Alphabet* (1–3). Illus. by Susan Tooke. 2000, Tundra $19.95 (0-88776-516-5). Picture puzzles and nautical scenes featuring the seaside introduce the alphabet. (Rev: HBG 10/00; SLJ 6/00)

51 Gritz, Ona. *Tangerines and Tea: My Grandparents and Me* (PS–K). Illus. by Umi Heo. 2005, Abrams $15.95 (0-8109-5871-6). 32pp. An alliterative alphabet book featuring two preschoolers visiting their grandparents' farm. (Rev: BL 5/15/05)

52 Grossman, Bill. *My Little Sister Hugged an Ape* (K–3). Illus. by Kevin Hawkes. 2004, Knopf LB $18.99 (0-517-80018-7). A little girl hugs a variety of unlikely animals from apes to zebras. (Rev: HB 11–12/04; SLJ 11/04)

53 Haas, Jessie. *Appaloosa Zebra: A Horse Lover's Alphabet* (PS–3). Illus. by Margot Apple. 2002, HarperCollins LB $15.89 (0-688-17881-2). 40pp. This informative alphabet book for girls who love horses features a different breed for almost every letter. (Rev: BL 1/1–15/02; HBG 10/02; SLJ 2/02)

54 Hague, Kathleen. *Alphabears: An ABC Book* (PS–K). Illus. by Michael Hague. 1984, Holt paper $5.95 (0-8050-1637-6). 32pp. Twenty-six lovable bears are introduced, one for each letter.

55 Harrison, Ted. *A Northern Alphabet: A Is for Arctic* (K–2). Illus. by author. 1989, Tundra paper $7.95 (0-88776-233-6). 32pp. Scenes, people, and objects associated with the far north are used in this alphabet book. A reissue.

56 Hepworth, Cathi. *ANTics! An Alphabetical Anthology* (K–2). Illus. by author. 1992, Penguin Putnam LB $16.99 (0-399-21862-9). 32pp. This inventive picture book for older children features the names of people and concepts that contain the word "ant." (Rev: BL 5/15/92*; SLJ 7/92*)

57 Herzog, Brad. *H Is for Home Run: A Baseball Alphabet* (1–4). Illus. by Melanie Rose. 2004, Sleeping Bear $16.95 (1-58536-219-0). An alphabet book full of alliteration and baseball lore. (Rev: SLJ 8/04) [796.357]

58 Hoban, Tana. *26 Letters and 99 Cents* (PS–1). Illus. by author. 1987, Greenwillow $15.93 (0-688-06362-4). 32pp. An ABC and counting book combined by turning the book upside down. (Rev: BCCB 4/87; BL 3/1/87; SLJ 4/87)

59 Hobbie, Holly. *Toot and Puddle: Puddle's ABC* (PS–1). Illus. 2000, Little, Brown $14.95 (0-316-36593-9). 48pp. To teach Otto the turtle the alphabet, little pig Puddle paints 26 clever pictures that illustrate the letters. (Rev: BCCB 12/00; BL 9/15/00; HBG 3/01; SLJ 11/00)

60 Hopkins, Lee Bennett. *Alphathoughts: Alphabet Poems* (2–6). Illus. by Marla Baggetta. 2003, Boyds Mills $15.95 (1-56397-979-9). An alphabet book that can be used on several levels with brief verses that describe the chosen words. (Rev: BL 4/1/03; HBG 10/03; SLJ 3/03)

61 Horenstein, Henry. *A Is for . . .? A Photographer's Alphabet of Animals* (PS–3). Photos by author. 1999, Harcourt $16.00 (0-15-201582-5). An alphabet puzzle that shows a close-up photo of a part of an animal for each letter; the answers are in the back. (Rev: BCCB 11/99; HBG 3/00; SLJ 10/99) [591]

62 Howell, Theresa. *A Is for Airplane / A es para Avión* (PS–2). Illus. by David Brooks. 2003, Rising Moon $6.95 (0-87358-831-2). A bilingual alphabet book with bright illustrations. (Rev: SLJ 3/03)

63 Howell, Will C. *Zoo Flakes ABC* (PS–2). Illus. 2002, Walker LB $16.85 (0-8027-8827-0). 32pp. Clever cut-paper snowflakes depict the alphabet in animal forms — O is for Octopus, for example — and children will enjoy finding the elusive animals hidden in each flake. Also includes directions on making snowflake cutouts. (Rev: BL 12/1/02; HBG 3/03; SLJ 3/03) [736]

64 Howland, Naomi. *ABCDrive! A Car Trip Alphabet* (PS–1). Illus. 1994, Clarion $15.00 (0-395-66414-4). 32pp. An alphabet book that uses names of vehicles and terms connected with traveling. (Rev: BCCB 6/94; BL 4/15/94; SLJ 6/94)

65 Hughes, Shirley. *Alfie's ABC* (PS–1). Illus. 1998, Lothrop $16.00 (0-688-16126-X). 32pp. An alphabet book that uses children's favorite things (e.g., "S is for seaside, swimming, and sand castles") to introduce each letter. (Rev: BL 8/98*; HBG 3/99; SLJ 9/98)

66 Inkpen, Mick. *Kipper's A to Z: An Alphabet Adventure* (PS–2). Illus. 2001, Harcourt $16.95 (0-15-202594-4). 56pp. Arnold the pig and Kipper the dog find animals, sounds, and actions that run from A to Z. (Rev: BL 5/15/01; HBG 10/01; SLJ 6/01*)

67 Isadora, Rachel. *On Your Toes: A Ballet ABC* (PS–1). Illus. by author. 2003, Greenwillow LB $17.89 (0-06-050241-X). Eye-catching illustrations will grab readers, from Arabesque to Zipper. (Rev: HBG 10/03; SLJ 6/03) [792.8]

68 Jackson, Woody. *A Cow's Alfalfa-Bet* (PS–1). Illus. by author. 2003, Houghton Mifflin $15.00 (0-618-16599-1). Striking watercolors of New England countryside illustrate an interesting choice of alphabet words. (Rev: HBG 4/04; SLJ 9/03) [428.1]

69 Jay, Alison. *ABC: A Child's First Alphabet Book* (PS–2). Illus. by author. 2003, Dutton $15.99 (0-525-46951-6). Appealing illustrations accompany easily recognizable objects, starting with apple, balloon, and cow. (Rev: HBG 4/04; SLJ 9/03)

70 Jernigan, Gisela. *Agave Blooms Just Once* (2–4). Illus. by E. Wesley Jernigan. 1989, Harbinger paper $10.95 (0-943173-44-2). An alphabet book introducing the flora and fauna of the Sonoran Desert in rhyming verse. (Rev: BL 3/1/90)

71 Jirankova-Limbrick, Martina. *The Artful Alphabet* (PS–2). Illus. 2003, Candlewick $16.99 (0-7636-2187-0). 72pp. This highly visual alphabet book offers lots of interest for young eyes. (Rev: BL 2/1/04; HBG 4/04; SLJ 1/04) [428.1]

72 Johnson, Jean. *Firefighters A to Z* (PS–1). Illus. 1985, Walker LB $11.85 (0-8027-6590-4). 39pp. An alphabet book organized around the workings of a fire-fighting unit. Others in this series are: *Librarians A to Z* (1989); *Police Officers A to Z* (1986); *Postal Workers A to Z* (1987); *Teachers A to Z* (1987). (Rev: BL 3/1/86)

73 Johnson, Odette, and Bruce Johnson. *Apples, Alligators and Also Alphabets* (PS–K). Illus. 1992, Stoddart paper $3.95 (0-19-540906-X). 32pp. An inventive alphabet book with whimsical words and actions. (Rev: BL 4/15/91; SLJ 6/91)

74 Joyce, Susan. *ABC Animal Riddles* (K–3). Illus. by Doug DuBosque. 1998, Peel $13.95 (0-939217-51-1). 32pp. For each letter of the alphabet, there is a mystery animal whose identity can be determined from an accompanying rhyming riddle. (Rev: BL 7/99; HBG 10/99; SLJ 4/99) [818]

75 Joyce, Susan. *ABC Nature Riddles* (K–3). Illus. by Doug DuBosque. Series: ABC Riddles. 2000, Peel $13.95 (0-939217-53-8). An appealing book with an imaginative rhyming text and color drawings that presents a nature riddle for each letter of the alphabet. (Rev: HBG 3/01; SLJ 10/00)

76 Joyce, Susan. *Alphabet Riddles* (K–3). Illus. by Doug DuBosque. 1998, Peel $13.95 (0-939217-50-3). A rhyming riddle book with clues that include the first and last letters and characteristics of the answer. (Rev: BL 7/98; HBG 10/98; SLJ 6/98)

77 Kalman, Bobbie. *Christmas Long Ago from A to Z* (K–2). Series: AlphaBasiCs. 1999, Crabtree LB $14.97 (0-86505-385-5); paper $7.16 (0-86505-415-0). 31pp. An alphabet book that uses the symbols and activities associated with Christmas as a source for the letters. (Rev: SLJ 10/99)

78 Kalman, Maira. *What Pete Ate from A to Z* (1–3). Illus. 2001, Penguin Putnam $15.99 (0-399-23362-8). 40pp. Pete the dog eats everything in sight — all the way through the alphabet. (Rev: BL 9/1/01; HB 1–2/02; HBG 3/02; SLJ 9/01*)

79 Kellogg, Steven. *Aster Aardvark's Alphabet Adventures* (PS–3). Illus. 1987, Morrow paper $4.95 (0-688-11571-3). 40pp. The alphabet is interpreted through 26 vignettes, one to three pages long. (Rev: BL 9/1/87; HB 11–12/87; SLJ 12/87)

80 Kirk, David. *Miss Spider's ABC* (PS–3). Illus. 1998, Scholastic $16.95 (0-590-28279-4). 32pp. An ABC book in which a number of creatures, mainly bugs, prepare a surprise party for Miss Spider. (Rev: BL 12/1/98; HBG 3/99; SLJ 12/98)

81 Korman, Susan. *P Is for Philadelphia* (1–5). Illus. 2005, Temple Univ. $16.95 (1-59213-107-7). An alphabetical tour of a city full of diversity, with text on the left and illustrations by local schoolchildren on the right. (Rev: SLJ 6/05)

82 Krull, Kathleen. *M Is for Music* (PS–3). Illus. by Stacy Innerst. 2003, Harcourt $16.00 (0-15-201438-1). From anthem/accordion to zydeco/zither/zippy, Krull and Innerst provide a lively introduction to musical concepts. (Rev: HBG 4/04; SLJ 9/03)

83 Layne, Steven L. *Thomas's Sheep and the Great Geography Test* (1–3). Illus. by Perry Board. 1998, Pelican $14.95 (1-56554-274-6). In this alphabet book, Thomas sends four imaginary sheep on a worldwide trip, which involves a variety of activities such as acting in Australia and kayaking in Kenya. (Rev: HBG 10/98; SLJ 9/98)

84 Lear, Edward. *An Edward Lear Alphabet* (1–2). Illus. by Vladimir Radunsky. 1999, HarperCollins LB $14.89 (0-06-028114-6). 32pp. Introduces the nonsense alphabet of Edward Lear accompanied by droll illustrations. (Rev: BL 4/1/99; HBG 10/99; SLJ 6/99) [821]

85 Leopold, Niki Clark. *K Is for Kitten* (PS–2). Illus. by Susan Jeffers. 2002, Penguin Putnam $15.99 (0-399-23563-9). 32pp. An alphabet book about a girl and her kitten, with lovely artwork. (Rev: BL 9/15/02; HBG 3/03; SLJ 9/02) [811.6]

86 Lester, Mike. *A Is for Salad* (1–4). Illus. 2000, Penguin Putnam $9.99 (0-399-23388-1). 40pp. For children who already know their letters, this is a hilarious alphabet book that claims, for example, that L is for hair dryer and D is for remote control. (Rev: BCCB 7–8/00; BL 6/1–15/00*; HB 3–4/00; HBG 10/00; SLJ 4/00)

87 Leuck, Laura. *Jeepers Creepers: A Monstrous ABC* (PS–K). Illus. by David Parkins. 2003, Chronicle $15.95 (0-8118-3509-X). Twenty-six goofy monsters go through the typical daily routine of preschoolers. (Rev: BCCB 9/03; HBG 4/04; SLJ 12/03)

88 Lobel, Anita. *Away from Home* (PS–3). Illus. 1994, Greenwillow $15.89 (0-688-10355-3). 32pp. Each letter of the alphabet depicts a boy in a different place, e.g., Adam arrives in Amsterdam. (Rev: BCCB 9/94; BL 8/94; SLJ 10/94)

89 Lobel, Arnold. *On Market Street* (PS–1). Illus. by Anita Lobel. 1981, Greenwillow $16.89 (0-688-84309-3); Morrow paper $6.95 (0-688-08745-0). 40pp. A merry alphabet book with objects from apples to zippers.

90 MacDonald, Ross. *Achoo! Bang! Crash! The Noisy Alphabet* (K–3). Illus. by author. 2003, Millbrook LB $23.90 (0-7613-2900-5). From Achoo! to Zip! Zap! Zing! Zoom! this is a vigorous and noisy volume. (Rev: BL 11/1/03; HB 1–2/04; HBG 4/04; SLJ 12/03)

91 MacDonald, Suse. *Alphabatics* (PS–1). Illus. by author. 1986, Macmillan $17.95 (0-02-761520-0). 64pp. An alphabet book that forms a letter into part of the picture illustrating the sound of the letter, such as "m" as part of a mustache. (Rev: BL 12/15/86; SLJ 12/86)

92 McDonnell, Flora. *Flora McDonnell's ABC* (PS–K). Illus. 1997, Candlewick $16.99 (0-7636-0118-7). 32pp. A witty, delightful introduction to the alphabet using animals and fish engaging in zany activities. (Rev: BCCB 7–8/97; BL 4/15/97)

93 Marshall, Janet. *Look Once, Look Twice* (K–2). Illus. 1995, Ticknor $14.00 (0-395-71644-6). 64pp. A clever alphabet book that uses interesting patterns to introduce letters and words that begin with them. (Rev: BCCB 4/95; BL 2/1/95; HB 5–6/95; SLJ 4/95)

94 Martin, Bill, Jr., and John Archambault. *Chicka Chicka Boom Boom* (PS–2). Illus. by Lois Ehlert. 1989, Simon & Schuster $15.00 (0-671-67949-X). 32pp. The letters of the alphabet enjoy a series of adventures. (Rev: BL 10/15/89*; HB 1–2/90*; SLJ 11/89)

95 Martin, Mary Jane. *From Anne to Zach* (PS–K). Illus. by Michael Grejniec. 1996, Boyds Mills $15.95 (1-56397-573-4). This ABC book introduces the alphabet by using a lot of first names, both common and obscure. (Rev: SLJ 12/96)

96 Marzollo, Jean. *Baby's Alphabet* (PS). Photos by Nancy Sheehan. 2002, Millbrook $9.95 (0-7613-1643-4). Babies from a variety of backgrounds are shown from "All gone!" to "Zzzz." (Rev: HBG 3/03; SLJ 11/02)

97 Maurer, Donna. *Annie, Bea, and Chi Chi Dolores: A School Day Alphabet* (PS–4). Illus. by Denys Cazet. 1993, Orchard LB $16.99 (0-531-08617-8). A day in a kindergarten supplies the letters to introduce an alphabet. (Rev: BL 2/13/93; HB 7–8/93; SLJ 5/93)

98 Mayers, Florence Cassen. *Baseball ABC* (1–3). Illus. 1994, Abrams $12.95 (0-8109-1938-9). An unusual alphabet book that uses baseball terminology, equipment, teams, and players to introduce the ABCs. (Rev: SLJ 12/94)

99 Melmed, Laura Krauss. *Capital! Washington, D.C. from A to Z* (K–3). Illus. by Frane Lessac. 2003, HarperCollins LB $16.89 (0-688-17562-7). 48pp. Each letter of the alphabet introduces a different monument, museum, or other feature of Washington, D.C., in this book with folk-art-like illustrations. (Rev: BL 2/1/03; HBG 10/03; SLJ 1/03) [975.3]

100 Melmed, Laura Krauss. *New York, New York! The Big Apple from A to Z* (PS–2). Illus. by Frane Lessac. 2005, HarperCollins LB $17.89 (0-06-054876-2). From American Museum of Natural History to Bronx Zoo, this is a lively alphabetical guide to New York, full of factoids and interesting features, plus a useful map. (Rev: SLJ 6/05)

101 Merriam, Eve. *Where Is Everybody? An Animal Alphabet* (PS–3). Illus. by Diane De Groat. 1992, Simon & Schuster paper $14.95 (0-671-64964-7). 40pp. An alphabet book with many, many details in each picture. (Rev: BL 6/15/89; HB 7–8/89)

102 Micklethwait, Lucy, ed. *I Spy: An Alphabet in Art* (K–2). Illus. 1992, Greenwillow $19.00 (0-688-11679-5). 64pp. Young readers are asked to find objects in full-page reproductions of paintings.

(Rev: BCCB 2/93; BL 11/1/92; HB 1–2/93; SLJ 10/92)

103 Milich, Zoran. *The City ABC Book* (PS–2). Illus. 2001, Kids Can $15.95 (1-55074-942-0). 32pp. A Canadian photojournalist cleverly uses pictures of city structures to introduce the letters of the alphabet. (Rev: BCCB 3/01; BL 4/15/01; HB 7–8/01; HBG 10/01; SLJ 6/01)

104 Miller, Jane. *Farm Alphabet Book* (PS–K). Illus. 1987, Scholastic paper $2.99 (0-590-31991-4). 32pp. Photographs of farm life make an unusual ABC book.

105 Miranda, Anne. *Alphabet Fiesta: An English/ Spanish Alphabet Story* (PS–2). Illus. 2001, Turtle $18.95 (1-890515-29-9); paper $12.95 (1-890515-30-2). 54pp. The letters of the alphabet are introduced using Spanish and English words in this story of a zebra's birthday party. (Rev: BL 9/15/01; HBG 3/02; SLJ 1/02)

106 Moncure, Jane Belk. *My "a" Sound Box* (K–1). Illus. by Colin King. Series: New Sound Box Library. 2000, Child's World LB $21.36 (1-56766-767-8). 30pp. Many words beginning with the letter "a" are found and put in the "a" sound box. Others in this series are *My "c" Sound Box,"* and *My "d" Sound Box* (both 2000). (Rev: SLJ 3/01)

107 Most, Bernard. *A B C T-Rex* (PS–K). Illus. 2000, Harcourt $13.00 (0-15-202007-1). 32pp. A comical ABC book in which a suburban dinosaur eats his way through the alphabet. (Rev: BL 4/1/00; HBG 10/00; SLJ 4/00)

108 Murphy, Mary. *The Alphabet Keeper* (1–3). Illus. by author. 2003, Knopf LB $16.99 (0-375-92347-0). The letters escape the Alphabet Keeper and lead her a merry chase as they rearrange themselves to suit the circumstances. (Rev: BCCB 3/03; HBG 10/03; SLJ 3/03)

109 *Museum ABC: The Metropolitan Museum of Art* (K–3). Illus. 2002, Little, Brown $16.95 (0-316-07170-6). 60pp. The artwork is stunning in this simple alphabet book from the Metropolitan Museum of Art. (Rev: BL 11/15/02; HBG 3/03; SLJ 9/02) [708.147]

110 *My Big Alphabet Book* (PS–K). Series: Big Tab Board Books. 1999, DK $9.95 (0-7894-4681-2). An oversized board book that uses photos, drawings, and tabs to introduce the letters of the alphabet. (Rev: SLJ 2/00)

111 Napier, Matt. *Z Is for Zamboni: A Hockey Alphabet* (K–4). Illus. by Melanie Rose. 2002, Sleeping Bear $19.95 (1-58536-065-1). Historical highlights and facts about the game are presented in a simple A to Z using Canadian spellings. (Rev: SLJ 4/03)

112 Pallotta, Jerry. *The Frog Alphabet Book . . . and Other Awesome Amphibians* (PS–1). Illus. by Ralph Masiello. 1990, Charlesbridge $16.95 (0-88106-463-7); paper $6.95 (0-88106-462-9). 32pp. This alphabet book introduces amphibians and gives salient facts about different varieties. (Rev: BL 9/1/90)

113 Pallotta, Jerry. *The Skull Alphabet Book* (2–5). Illus. by Ralph Masiello. 2002, Charlesbridge $16.95 (0-88106-914-0); paper $7.95 (0-88106-915-9). 32pp. This unusual and challenging book features paintings of animal skulls from anteater to zebra, giving subtle verbal and visual clues to the identity of each animal. (Rev: BL 9/1/02; HBG 3/03; SLJ 7/02) [573.7]

114 Paul, Ann W. *Eight Hands Round: A Patchwork Alphabet* (1–4). Illus. by Jeanette Winter. 1991, HarperCollins LB $15.89 (0-06-024704-5). 32pp. An alphabet book that shows how the art of patchwork grew and why. (Rev: BCCB 7–8/91; BL 6/1/91; SLJ 7/91)

115 Pearson, Debora. *Alphabeep: A Zipping, Zooming ABC* (PS–K). Illus. by Edward Miller. 2003, Holiday House $16.95 (0-8234-1722-0). From "ambulance" to "zamboni," this is a celebration of moving vehicles and road signs. (Rev: HBG 4/04; SLJ 9/03)

116 Pelletier, David. *The Graphic Alphabet* (PS–2). Illus. 1996, Orchard $17.95 (0-531-36001-6). 32pp. Letters of the alphabet are pictured in various imaginative positions. (Rev: BCCB 12/96; BL 11/1/96; HB 11–12/96; SLJ 11/96)

117 Pinto, Sara. *The Alphabet Room* (PS). Illus. 2003, Bloomsbury $16.95 (1-58234-841-3). 56pp. Flaps lift to reveal a room that gradually fills up with all the items mentioned — apples, bowl, cat, and so forth. (Rev: BL 2/1/04*) [428.1]

118 Pratt, Kristin J. *A Swim Through the Sea* (PS–3). Illus. by author. 1994, Dawn $16.95 (1-883220-03-3); paper $7.95 (1-883220-04-1). An alphabet book in which Seamore the seahorse introduces a number of creatures from the deep. (Rev: SLJ 8/94)

119 Pratt, Kristin J. *A Walk in the Rainforest* (2–4). Illus. by author. 1992, Dawn $16.95 (1-878265-99-7); paper $7.95 (1-878265-53-9). 33pp. In this book written and illustrated by a high school student, plants and animals found in the rain forest are used to introduce the alphabet. (Rev: SLJ 7/92)

120 Press, Judy. *Alphabet Art: With A to Z Animal Art and Fingerplays* (PS–K). Illus. by Sue Dennen. Series: Little Hands Books. 1998, Williamson paper $12.95 (1-885593-14-7). 134pp. For teachers and parents, this book explains how to teach the alphabet using crafts, games, poems, and fingerplays. (Rev: SLJ 3/98)

121 Rash, Andy. *Agent A to Agent Z* (PS–2). Illus. 2004, Scholastic $16.95 (0-439-36882-0). 40pp. From A to Z, spies undertake often-ridiculous missions and end up in bizarre situations; an imaginatively illustrated, hard-boiled offering. (Rev: BL 1/1–15/04; HB 3–4/04; SLJ 2/04)

122 Rey, H. A. *Curious George Learns the Alphabet* (K–2). Illus. by author. 1963, Houghton Mifflin $14.95 (0-395-16031-6); paper $5.95 (0-395-13718-7). 72pp. George makes learning the alphabet a wonderful and amusing game.

123 Rose, Deborah L. *Into the A, B, Sea* (PS–3). Illus. by Steve Jenkins. 2000, Scholastic $15.95 (0-439-09696-0). 40pp. From anemones to zooplankton, this alphabet book cleverly explores all sorts of sea life. (Rev: BCCB 12/00; BL 9/15/00; HBG 10/01; SLJ 10/00) [591.77]

124 Rosenberg, Liz. *A Big and a Little Alphabet* (PS–1). Illus. by Vera Rosenberry. 1997, Orchard LB $16.99 (0-531-33050-8). 32pp. An ABC book that uses big and small animals to show the differences between upper and lowercase. (Rev: BL 11/1/97; HBG 3/98; SLJ 10/97)

125 Rumford, James. *There's a Monster in the Alphabet* (1–4). Illus. 2002, Houghton Mifflin $16.00 (0-618-22140-9). 40pp. An imaginative and complex alphabet book that looks at the origins of the letters, incorporating mythology and the Phoenician alphabet, with attractive Grecian-style illustrations. (Rev: BL 12/1/02; SLJ 10/02) [398.2]

126 Ryden, Hope. *ABC of Crawlers and Flyers* (2–4). Illus. 1996, Clarion $14.95 (0-395-72808-8). 32pp. Each letter of the alphabet introduces a different insect. (Rev: BL 9/15/96; SLJ 10/96)

127 Sandved, Kjell B. *The Butterfly Alphabet* (K–3). Illus. 1996, Scholastic $16.95 (0-590-48003-0). 72pp. In double-page spreads, the alphabet is introduced with breathtaking close-ups of wing patterns of butterflies and moths. (Rev: BL 3/15/96; SLJ 5/96)

128 Schafer, Kevin. *Penguins ABC* (PS–K). Photos by author. 2002, NorthWord $14.95 (1-55971-831-5). An alphabet book that will please penguin lovers. (Rev: SLJ 1/03)

129 Schnur, Steven. *Spring: An Alphabet Acrostic* (2–5). Illus. by Leslie Evans. 1999, Clarion $15.00 (0-395-82269-6). 32pp. Various aspects of spring are covered in this illustrated alphabet book that also uses acrostics. (Rev: BL 4/1/99; HBG 10/99; SLJ 4/99) [793.73]

130 Schnur, Steven. *Summer: An Alphabet Acrostic* (2–5). Illus. 2001, Clarion $15.00 (0-618-02372-0). 32pp. An alphabet book of poems about summer in which the first letter of each line of the poem combines in acrostic fashion to spell the name of the object described. (Rev: BL 3/15/01; HBG 10/01)

131 Schnur, Steven. *Winter: An Alphabet Acrostic* (PS–2). Illus. by Leslie Evans. 2002, Clarion $15.00 (0-618-02374-7). 32pp. Poetic acrostics for each letter of the alphabet are included in this beautifully illustrated follow-up to *Autumn* (1997), *Spring* (1999), and *Summer* (2001). (Rev: BCCB 11/02; BL 12/15/02; HBG 3/03; SLJ 11/02) [508.2]

132 Scillian, Devin. *P Is for Passport: A World Alphabet* (2–5). Illus. 2003, Sleeping Bear $19.95 (1-58536-157-7). Two dozen artists illustrated this alphabetical look at travel and at things that are part of the lives of people everywhere — B is for Bread, for example, and M is for music. (Rev: HBG 4/04; SLJ 3/04) [910]

133 Seeger, Laura Vaccaro. *The Hidden Alphabet* (PS). Illus. 2003, Roaring Brook $17.95 (0-7613-1941-7). 32pp. Inventive design keep readers alert as they search for the items behind the flaps that actually form parts of the relevant letters. (Rev: BL 2/1/04; HBG 4/04; SLJ 11/03) [428.1]

134 Seeley, Laura L. *The Book of Shadowboxes: A Story of the ABC's* (PS–3). Illus. 1990, Peachtree $16.95 (0-934601-65-8). Using objects in shadow-boxes as illustrations, the letters of the alphabet are introduced. (Rev: SLJ 4/91)

135 Seuss, Dr. *Dr. Seuss' ABC* (K–2). Illus. by author. 1963, Random $11.99 (0-394-90030-8). 72pp. A master author creates a strikingly popular alphabet book.

136 Shindler, Ramon, and Wojciech Graniczewski. *Found Alphabet* (1–3). Illus. 2005, Houghton Mifflin $16.00 (0-618-44232-4). 32pp. Brief verses and appealing photographs show found objects from airplane to zebra. (Rev: BL 6/1–15/05; SLJ 7/05)

137 Sierra, Judy. *There's a Zoo in Room 22* (PS–2). Illus. by Barney Saltzberg. 2000, Harcourt $16.00 (0-15-202033-0). 40pp. Miss Darling introduces an animal alphabet to her students including such pets as Claude the Cat, Katy Katydid, and Vincent Vulture. (Rev: BCCB 10/00; BL 8/00; HBG 3/01; SLJ 10/00)

138 Sloat, Teri. *Patty's Pumpkin Patch* (PS–2). Illus. 1999, Penguin Putnam $15.99 (0-399-23010-6). 32pp. From seed to pumpkin stand, this alphabet book presents the stages in the growth of a pumpkin and discusses all the creatures that visit the plant while it is growing. (Rev: BCCB 10/99; BL 9/1/99; HBG 3/00; SLJ 10/99)

139 Sobel, June. *B Is for Bulldozer: A Construction ABC* (PS–K). Illus. by Melissa Iwai. 2003, Harcourt $16.00 (0-15-202250-3). This appealing alphabet book focuses on the construction of a roller coaster, introducing a new tool, material, or piece of construction equipment for each letter of the alphabet. (Rev: HBG 10/03; SLJ 7/03)

140 *The Timbertoes ABC Alphabet Book* (PS–1). Illus. 1997, Boyds Mills $7.95 (1-56397-604-8). 32pp. The Timbertoes, a family of wooden figures, introduce the letters of the alphabet. (Rev: BL 3/1/97; SLJ 7/97)

141 Tobias, Tobi, ed. *A World of Words: An ABC of Quotations* (PS–3). Illus. by Peter Malone. 1998, Lothrop LB $15.93 (0-688-12130-6). 40pp. Poems and brief quotations are arranged alphabetically under such subjects as Animal, Book, Yard, and Zoo. (Rev: BL 10/1/98; HBG 3/99; SLJ 9/98) [811]

142 Turner, Priscilla. *The War Between the Vowels and the Consonants* (K–3). Illus. by Whitney Turner. 1996, Farrar $16.00 (0-374-38236-0). 30pp. Rivalry between vowels and consonants is used as a lively introduction to letters. (Rev: BL 12/1/96; SLJ 10/96)

143 Walton, Rick. *So Many Bunnies: A Bedtime ABC and Counting Book* (PS). Illus. by Paige Miglio. 1998, Lothrop LB $15.89 (0-688-13657-5). A combination ABC and counting book that is also a bedtime book because it tells how Mother Rabbit tucked her 26 babies in for the night. (Rev: HBG 10/98; SLJ 3/98)

144 Watson, Clyde. *Applebet: An ABC* (PS–2). Illus. by Wendy Watson. 1982, Farrar paper $5.95 (0-374-40427-5). 32pp. An alphabet book in which apples and a country fair provide the links from letter to letter.

145 Wethered, Peggy, and Ken Edgett. *Touchdown Mars! An ABC Adventure* (K–3). Illus. by Michael

Chesworth. 2000, Penguin Putnam $15.99 (0-399-23214-1). 40pp. In this alphabet picture book, nine children and a cat take off for a mission to Mars. (Rev: BCCB 6/00; BL 5/15/00; HBG 10/00; SLJ 10/00)

146 Willard, Nancy. *An Alphabet of Angels* (PS–3). Illus. 1994, Scholastic $16.95 (0-590-48480-X). 64pp. Using the alphabet as a framework, the artist creates and photographs pieces of sculpture that depict various angels. (Rev: BCCB 10/94; BL 9/15/94; SLJ 10/94)

147 Winter, Jeanette. *Calavera Abecedario: A Day of the Dead Alphabet Book* (K–3). Illus. 2004, Harcourt $16.00 (0-15-205110-4). 48pp. With a story about preparing for Mexico's Dia de los Muertos as a backdrop, Winter presents an alphabet celebrating the skeletons that mark the holiday. (Rev: BL 11/1/04; SLJ 5/05) [394.266]

148 Wisnewski, Andrea. *A Cottage Garden Alphabet* (2–4). Illus. 2003, Godine $18.95 (1-56792-229-5). 64pp. Beautiful cut-paper illustrations of a garden's bounty accompany each letter of the alphabet. (Rev: BL 2/15/03; HBG 10/03; SLJ 5/03) [635]

149 Wojtowycz, David. *Animal ABC* (K–1). Illus. by author. 2000, David & Charles $14.95 (1-86233-107-3). A host of animals from an athletic aardvark to a zig-zag zebra introduce the alphabet. (Rev: SLJ 9/00)

150 Wood, Audrey. *Alphabet Adventure* (PS–2). Illus. by Bruce Wood. 2001, Scholastic $15.95 (0-439-08069-X). 40pp. The 26 letters are on their way to teach a child the alphabet when they encounter some difficulties in this inventive book illustrated with glowing, computer-generated graphics. (Rev: BL 9/1/01; HBG 3/02; SLJ 9/01)

151 Wood, Audrey. *Alphabet Mystery* (PS–2). Illus. by Bruce Wood. 2003, Scholastic $15.95 (0-439-44337-7). When Little x disappears, the other 25 letters of the alphabet launch a search. (Rev: BL 12/1/03; HBG 4/04; SLJ 11/03)

152 Yorinks, Arthur. *The Alphabet Atlas* (1–4). Illus. by Adrienne Yorinks and Jeanyee Wong. 1999, Winslow $19.95 (0-890817-14-7). This alphabet book features countries of the world and, on each page, an illustration using different textiles in the shape of the country. (Rev: SLJ 7/99)

Concept Books

GENERAL

153 Aber, Linda Williams. *Grandma's Button Box* (K–1). Illus. by Page Eastburn O'Rourke. 2002, Kane paper $4.95 (1-57565-110-6). 32pp. When a young girl drops her grandmother's button box, she and her cousins try different ways of sorting them out in this simple concept launch. (Rev: BL 4/15/02)

154 Aliki. *Feelings* (K–2). Illus. 1984, Greenwillow $15.93 (0-688-03832-8); Morrow paper $4.95 (0-688-06518-X). 32pp. An introduction to various emotions.

155 Asquith, Ros. *Babies* (PS). Illus. by Sam Williams. 2003, Simon & Schuster $12.95 (0-689-85501-X). 24pp. A book of happy, busy babies, with a mirror on the last page so readers can view the best baby of all. (Rev: BCCB 10/02; BL 2/1/03; HBG 10/03; SLJ 3/03)

156 Baker, Alan. *Little Rabbits' First Time Book* (PS–K). Illus. 1999, Kingfisher $10.95 (0-7534-5220-0). 16pp. The activities of three bunnies throughout a day illustrate the passage of hours, which can be traced by using the movable hands on a clock. (Rev: BL 12/1/99; SLJ 2/00)

157 Barner, Bob. *Which Way to the Revolution? A Book About Maps* (1–3). Illus. by author. 1998, Holiday House $16.95 (0-8234-1352-7). In this concept book about maps, a little mouse informs Paul Revere that the British are coming. Together, they travel from Boston to Lexington, using a map to plot their journey. (Rev: HBG 10/98; SLJ 5/98)

158 Bauer, Marion Dane. *Toes, Ears, and Nose!* (PS). Illus. by Karen Katz. 2003, Simon & Schuster $5.99 (0-689-84712-2). In this colorful lift-the-flap title, preschoolers are introduced to various parts of the human body. (Rev: SLJ 6/03)

159 Beaton, Clare. *Daisy Gets Dressed* (PS–K). Illus. 2005, Barefoot $15.99 (1-84148-197-5). 24pp. A seek-and-find book that requires the reader to identify among many patterns the right pieces of clothing to complete Daisy's outfit. (Rev: BL 5/1/05)

160 Beaton, Clare. *How Big Is a Pig?* (PS–K). Illus. 2000, Barefoot $14.99 (1-84148-077-0). 32pp. Double-page spreads are used in this amusing book that illustrates opposites in animals — fast and slow dogs and quiet and jumpy frogs. (Rev: BL 10/1/00; HBG 3/01; SLJ 12/00)

161 Beeke, Tiphanie. *Roar Like a Lion! A First Book About Sounds* (PS). Illus. 2001, Sterling $7.95 (1-86233-143-X). 16pp. This fun-filled book about a mouse trying to find friends will have preschoolers making all kinds of jungle noises. (Rev: BL 3/1/02)

162 Berenstain, Stan, and Jan Berenstain. *Inside, Outside, Upside Down* (PS–1). Illus. by authors. 1968, Random LB $11.99 (0-394-91142-3). A bear has a brief trip that explains various concepts.

163 Bernhard, Durga. *Earth, Sky, Wet, Dry: A Book of Nature Opposites* (PS–2). Illus. 2000, Orchard LB $17.99 (0-531-33213-6). 40pp. Opposites are introduced using scenes from nature that demonstrate, for example, the difference between light and dark. (Rev: BL 2/1/00; HBG 10/00; SLJ 3/00)

164 Bernhard, Durga. *To and Fro, Fast and Slow* (PS–2). Illus. 2001, Walker LB $16.85 (0-8027-8783-5). 32pp. This clever, well-illustrated concept book uses a girl's visits to her mother's country home and her father's city apartment to show opposites. (Rev: BL 11/1/01; HBG 3/02; SLJ 9/01)

165 Blackstone, Stella. *Baby High, Baby Low* (PS). Illus. by Denise Fraifield and Fernando Azevedo. 1998, Holiday House $14.95 (0-8234-1345-4). 32pp. The author introduces the concept of opposites — such as high and low — using illustrations of activities involving babies of many races and their parents. (Rev: BL 12/1/98; HBG 3/99; SLJ 10/98)

166 Blackstone, Stella. *Can You See the Red Balloon?* (PS–K). Illus. by Debbie Harter. 1998, Orchard $14.95 (0-531-30077-3). A concept book that teaches color and shape identification through a series of double-page spreads filled with cartoon animals and objects. (Rev: HBG 10/99; SLJ 12/98)

167 Blackstone, Stella. *You and Me* (PS–1). Illus. by Giovanni Manna. 2000, Barefoot $15.99 (1-84148-263-3). 32pp. The author explores the concept of opposites using a boy and a girl on double-page spreads engaging in different activities. (Rev: BL 12/1/00; HBG 3/01; SLJ 12/00)

168 Burton, Jane. *My Kitten Friends* (PS). Illus. 2002, Simon & Schuster $5.99 (0-689-84767-X). 14pp. A concept board book that uses delightful pictures of kittens to illustrate behavior. Also use *My Puppy Friends* (2002). (Rev: BL 3/1/02)

169 Butler, John. *If You See a Kitten* (PS). Illus. by author. 2003, Peachtree $13.95 (1-56145-108-8). Cuddly kittens, pudgy pigs, and slithery snakes are among the animals introduced with suggested one-word responses — "Ahhh!" or "Yikes," for example. (Rev: BL 3/03; HBG 10/03; SLJ 5/03)

170 Carle, Eric. *From Head to Toe* (PS). Illus. 1997, HarperCollins LB $16.89 (0-06-023516-0). 32pp. Children make the same movements as animals in this concept book illustrated with lively collages. (Rev: BCCB 6/97; BL 4/15/97; SLJ 4/97) [613.7]

171 Carle, Eric. *My Very First Book of Words* (PS–1). Illus. by author. 1985, HarperCollins $2.95 (0-690-57368-5). 10pp. A nicely illustrated beginning word book, printed on heavy stock cards.

172 Carrier, Lark. *Do Not Touch* (1–3). Illus. by author. 1991, Picture Book paper $15.95 (0-88708-061-8). 28pp. A picture book with the concept of words within words. (Rev: BL 4/1/89)

173 Carter, David A. *More Bugs in Boxes* (PS–3). Illus. 1990, Simon & Schuster $13.95 (0-671-69577-0). A board book that explores the world of shapes and colors. (Rev: SLJ 8/90)

174 Cendrars, Blaise. *Shadow* (K–3). Trans. and illus. by Marcia Brown. 1982, Macmillan $17.00 (0-684-17226-7). 40pp. This Caldecott winner (1983) explores the mysterious world of shadows.

175 Charles, N. N. *What Am I? Looking Through Shapes at Apples and Grapes* (PS–K). Illus. by Leo Dillon and Diane Dillon. 1994, Scholastic $16.95 (0-590-47891-5). 36pp. Geometric shapes are used creatively to illustrate a number of clever riddles in this interactive book. (Rev: BL 11/15/94; SLJ 1/95)

176 Chesanow, Neil. *Where Do I Live?* (K–3). Illus. by Ann Iosa. 1995, Barron's paper $6.95 (0-8120-9241-4). 48pp. The concept of belonging is explored, from a room of one's own to being a part of the solar system. (Rev: BL 2/1/96) [910]

177 Clark, Emma Chichester. *Mimi's Book of Opposites* (PS). Illus. by author. Series: A Mimi Book. 2003, Charlesbridge $9.95 (1-57091-574-1). In this appealing concept book, Mimi the monkey and her little brother explore the world of opposites. (Rev: HBG 4/04; SLJ 11/03)

178 Cole, Joanna. *Sharing Is Fun* (PS). Illus. by Maxie Chambliss. 2004, HarperCollins $6.99 (0-06-050499-4). When Andrew's friends come to visit, his mother asks him to put away any toys he's not prepared to share. (Rev: SLJ 8/04)

179 Crews, Nina. *A High, Low, Near, Far, Loud, Quiet Story* (PS). Illus. 1999, Greenwillow LB $15.93 (0-688-16795-0). 24pp. The activities of a sister and younger brother are used to introduce a number of opposites. (Rev: BL 9/15/99; HBG 3/00; SLJ 12/99)

180 Crozon, Alain. *I Can Fly!* (PS–3). Illus. by author. Series: A Who Am I/What Am I Book. 1999, Chronicle $7.95 (0-8118-2407-1). This book contains pictures of 21 objects that can fly, such as a boomerang, a dandelion seed, and a superhero. For things on wheels use *I Can Roll* (1999). (Rev: SLJ 11/99)

181 Dale, Elizabeth. *How Long?* (PS–K). Illus. by Alan Marks. 1998, Orchard $14.95 (0-531-30101-X). 32pp. When a mouse mother postpones paying attention to her daughter for a minute or more, the little mouse wonders how long a minute is. (Rev: BL 10/1/98; HBG 3/99; SLJ 10/98)

182 Deegan, Kim. *My First Book of Opposites* (PS). Illus. 2002, Bloomsbury $7.95 (1-58234-756-5). 24pp. A sparkling introduction to opposites for preschoolers. (Rev: BL 8/02; SLJ 11/02) [428.1]

183 Dodd, Emma. *Dog's Colorful Day* (PS–K). Illus. 2001, Dutton $14.99 (0-525-46528-6). 32pp. A color and counting book that shows how a dog gains a number of unwanted spots on its coat including some chocolate, a grass stain, and a splat of red jam. (Rev: BL 2/15/01; HBG 10/01; SLJ 3/01)

184 Downing, Julie. *Where Is My Mommy?* (PS). Illus. by author. 2003, HarperCollins LB $16.89 (0-688-17825-1). Mommy is doing a variety of tasks — waking up baby rabbit, bringing baby bird some food — in this simple book. (Rev: HBG 10/03; SLJ 6/03)

185 Ellwand, David. *Clap Your Hands: An Action Book* (PS). Photos by author. 2002, Handprint $9.95 (1-929766-50-5). An oversized board book in which teddy bears stamp feet, touch toes, and so forth to the traditional song. (Rev: SLJ 7/02)

186 Emberley, Rebecca. *My Opposites / Mis Opuestos* (PS). 2000, Little, Brown $5.95 (0-316-23345-5). 20pp. A concept board book that introduces opposites in English and Spanish. (Rev: BCCB 12/00*; HBG 3/01; SLJ 9/00)

187 Falconer, Ian. *Olivia's Opposites* (PS). Illus. 2002, Simon & Schuster $6.99 (0-689-85088-3). 12pp. A simple board book featuring Olivia the pig that demonstrates the concept of opposites. (Rev: BL 7/02; HBG 10/02; SLJ 6/02)

188 Falwell, Cathryn. *Word Wizard* (K–3). Illus. 1998, Clarion $15.00 (0-395-85580-2). 32pp. In this picture book, Anna discovers the world of anagrams while eating a bowl of alphabet cereal, then she embarks on a series of adventures in which, for example, she turns an ocean into a canoe. (Rev: BL 5/15/98; HBG 10/98)

189 Fleming, Denise. *The Everything Book* (PS). Illus. 2000, Holt $18.95 (0-8050-6292-0). 64pp.

This book offers all sorts of information on topics ranging from the seasons and days of the week to parts of the body plus poems, songs, and games. (Rev: BCCB 10/00; BL 7/00; HBG 3/01; SLJ 10/00)

190 Ford, Miela. *What Color Was the Sky Today?* (PS–1). Illus. by Sally Noll. 1997, Greenwillow LB $14.93 (0-688-14559-0). 24pp. Using fewer than 100 words, this book introduces the concepts of colors, counting, time, and the weather. (Rev: BL 5/1/97; SLJ 3/97)

191 Fowler, Allan. *North, South, East, and West* (1–2). Illus. Series: Rookie Readers. 1993, Children's Book Pr. LB $18.50 (0-516-06011-2); Children's Book Pr. paper $4.95 (0-516-46011-0). 32pp. This is an introduction to the concept of directions for beginning readers in an attractive small format using many color photographs. (Rev: BL 9/1/93) [526]

192 Freymann, Saxton, and Joost Elffers. *Food for Thought: The Complete Book of Concepts for Growing Minds* (PS). Illus. 2005, Scholastic $14.95 (0-439-11018-1). 64pp. Colors, letters, numbers, opposites, and shapes are all introduced using the authors' signature fruits and vegetables. (Rev: BL 1/1–15/05; SLJ 3/05)

193 Gabriel, Nat. *Sam's Sneaker Squares* (1–2). Illus. by Ron Fritz. 2002, Kane paper $4.95 (1-57565-114-9). 32pp. In this concept book, Sam learns about measurements to determine the cost of mowing lawns. (Rev: BL 4/15/02)

194 Gibbons, Gail. *Playgrounds* (PS–1). Illus. by author. 1985, Holiday House LB $16.95 (0-8234-0553-2). 32pp. A concept book that shows young readers playground scenes that are familiar. (Rev: BCCB 6/85; BL 5/15/85; SLJ 5/85)

195 Gordon, Sharon. *Dirty Clean* (PS–2). Series: Bookworms: Just the Opposite. 2003, Benchmark LB $14.95 (0-7614-1569-6). 23pp. A primer in the contrast between things that are dirty and things that are clean and how they might get that way. (Rev: HBG 4/04; SLJ 3/04)

196 Gordon, Sharon. *Fast Slow* (PS–2). Series: Bookworms: Just the Opposite. 2003, Benchmark LB $14.95 (0-7614-1570-X). 23pp. The contrast between fast and slow is explored through various means of transportation, from rollerskates to cars. (Rev: HBG 4/04; SLJ 3/04)

197 Got, Yves. *Sam's Opposites* (PS). Illus. by author. 2003, Chronicle $9.95 (0-8118-4077-8). "Noisy/quiet," "careful/clumsy," and "sick/well" are among the opposites introduced by Sam the bunny. (Rev: HBG 4/04; SLJ 1/04) [428.1]

198 Got, Yves. *Sweet Dreams, Sam* (PS). Illus. 2000, Chronicle $8.95 (0-8118-2985-5). This interactive book uses different textures to explore the sense of touch, such as simulating the crinkly skin of an elephant. (Rev: BL 12/1/00)

199 Grejniec, Michael. *Good Morning, Good Night* (PS). Illus. 1997, North-South paper $6.95 (1-55858-704-7). 28pp. A concept book with basic vocabulary that demonstrates opposites. (Rev: BL 3/15/93; SLJ 8/93)

200 Grunwald, Lisa. *Now Soon Later* (PS). Illus. by Jane Johnson. 1996, Greenwillow $15.00 (0-688-13946-9). 24pp. Concepts involving time — like "now," "soon," and "later" — are explained through a girl's day-long activities. (Rev: BCCB 10/96; BL 7/96; SLJ 9/96)

201 Harper, Dan. *Telling Time with Big Mama Cat* (PS–2). Illus. by Barry Moser and Cara Moser. 1998, Harcourt $15.00 (0-15-201738-0). 28pp. Using a foldout clock with movable hands, young readers can trace the daily activities of Big Mama Cat while they learn to tell time. (Rev: BCCB 11/98; BL 8/98*; HBG 3/99; SLJ 12/98)

202 Harris, Pamela. *Hot, Cold, Shy, Bold* (PS–K). Illus. 1998, Kids Can $10.95 (1-55074-153-5). 32pp. A successful book of opposites that uses a rhyming text and color photos. (Rev: BL 3/15/98; HBG 10/98) [428.1]

203 Harris, Trudy. *Pattern Fish* (PS–1). Illus. by Anne Canevari Green. 2000, Millbrook LB $20.90 (0-7613-1712-0). This attractive concept book explores the world of patterns. (Rev: BCCB 9/00; HBG 10/01; SLJ 12/00)

204 Hartman, Gail. *As the Crow Flies: A First Book of Maps* (PS–1). Illus. by Harvey Stevenson. 1993, Aladdin paper $5.99 (0-689-71762-8). 32pp. The concept of maps is introduced by using the environments of different animals. (Rev: BL 3/1/91; HB 5–6/91; SLJ 3/91)

205 Heide, Florence Parry, et al. *It's About Time!* (PS–1). Illus. by Cathryn Falwell. 1999, Clarion $15.00 (0-395-86612-X). 32pp. Fourteen easy-to-read poems that deal with the concept of time. (Rev: BCCB 4/99; BL 3/15/99; HBG 10/99; SLJ 5/99) [811]

206 Herman, Gail. *Bad Luck Brad* (1–2). Illus. by Stephanie Roth. Series: Math Matters. 2002, Kane paper $4.95 (1-57565-112-2). 32pp. The concept of probability is explored when a series of misfortunes occur to Brad on a single day. (Rev: BL 5/1/02)

207 Hindley, Judy. *Ten Bright Eyes* (PS–1). Illus. by Alison Bartlett. 1998, Peachtree $14.95 (1-56145-173-8). As a mother bird roams the countryside looking for food for her young, the reader is introduced to numbers, shapes, and patterns as well as some related activities. (Rev: HBG 10/98; SLJ 11/98)

208 Hoban, Tana. *Black on White* (PS). Illus. 1993, Greenwillow $5.95 (0-688-11918-2). The photographs show black objects on a white background. A companion book is *White on Black* (1993). (Rev: HB 7–8/93; SLJ 8/93)

209 Hoban, Tana. *What Is That?* (PS). Illus. 1994, Greenwillow paper $5.95 (0-688-12920-X). 12pp. Using silhouettes, a number of common animals are pictured in this board book. Also use *Who Are They?* (1994). (Rev: BL 12/1/94; HB 11–12/94; SLJ 11/94)

210 Hoberman, Mary Ann. *A House Is a House for Me* (K–2). Illus. by Betty Fraser. 1978, Puffin paper $5.99 (0-14-050394-3). 48pp. This picture book explores the idea that various objects can serve as houses.

211 Hudson, Cheryl Willis. *Hands Can* (PS). Photos by John-Francis Bourke. 2003, Candlewick $14.99 (0-7636-1667-2). Bright colors and eye-catching photos draw readers into this display of movements and expressions made with hands. (Rev: BL 10/1/03; HBG 4/04; SLJ 12/03)

212 Jocelyn, Marthe. *A Day with Nellie* (PS). Illus. by author. 2002, Tundra $15.95 (0-88776-600-5). 24pp. Numbers, colors, the alphabet, and other concepts are introduced as readers follow preschooler Nellie through the activities of her ordinary day. (Rev: BL 12/1/02; HBG 3/03; SLJ 1/03)

213 Kassirer, Sue. *What's Next, Nina?* (1–3). Illus. by Page Eastburn O'Rourke. Series: Math Matters. 2001, Kane paper $4.95 (1-57565-106-8). 32pp. Nina must reconstruct a broken necklace of beads in this story that subtly but effectively introduces the concept of patterns. (Rev: SLJ 2/02)

214 Krauss, Ruth. *A Hole Is to Dig* (PS). Illus. by Maurice Sendak. 1952, HarperCollins $15.95 (0-06-023405-9); paper $5.95 (0-06-443205-X). 48pp. Child-perceived definitions, such as "the world is so you have something to stand on," complemented by whimsical drawings.

215 Kroll, Steven. *That Makes Me Mad!* (PS–1). Illus. by Christine Davenier. 2002, North-South LB $16.50 (1-58717-184-8). A newly illustrated edition of the 1976 story about Nina and everything that makes her mad. (Rev: HBG 3/03; SLJ 8/02)

216 Laden, Nina. *Grow Up!* (PS). Illus. 2003, Chronicle $6.95 (0-8118-3761-0). 26pp. A well-illustrated, rhyming board book about growing up in which a kitten becomes a cat, a puppy becomes a dog, a seedling become a tree, and so forth. (Rev: BL 5/15/03)

217 Landry, Leo. *Oh, Baby!* (PS). Illus. 2003, Little, Brown $12.95 (0-316-60732-0). 24pp. Tiny babies are shown in lots of unusual situations in this well-illustrated small picture book. (Rev: BL 5/15/03; HBG 10/03)

218 Llewellyn, Claire. *My First Book of Time* (PS–2). Illus. 1992, DK $14.95 (1-879431-78-5). 32pp. An oversize book with enticing photos and drawings provides an excellent introduction to the concept of time. (Rev: BCCB 7–8/92; BL 5/1/92; HB 7–8/92; SLJ 8/92) [529.7]

219 Maccarone, Grace. *Monster Math School Time* (K–2). Illus. by Margaret A. Hartelius. Series: Hello Math Reader. 1997, Scholastic $3.99 (0-590-30859-9). A beginning reader that teaches how to tell time through the antics of 12 monsters and their daily activities. (Rev: SLJ 1/98)

220 Mandel, Peter. *Boats on the River* (PS). Illus. by Edward Miller. 2004, Scholastic $6.99 (0-439-56415-8). Bright colors and simple shapes depict exciting scenes of boats, with descriptions of their functions, in this large-format board book. Also use *Planes at the Airport* (2004). (Rev: BL 4/15/04; SLJ 9/04) [623]

221 Manning, Linda. *Dinosaur Days* (PS–1). Illus. by Vlasta Van Kampen. 1994, Troll $12.95 (0-8167-3315-5). 32pp. Days of the week are intro-

duced by seven dinosaurs, each of which causes a household emergency. (Rev: BL 7/94; SLJ 8/94)

222 Marzollo, Jean. *I Spy School Days: A Book of Picture Riddles* (PS–2). Illus. by Walter Wick. Series: I Spy. 1995, Scholastic $12.95 (0-590-48135-5). 38pp. Riddles and puzzles using photographs are featured, each related to school activities. (Rev: BL 12/1/95; SLJ 10/95)

223 Matthias, Catherine. *Over-Under* (PS–1). Illus. by Gene Sharp. 1984, Children's Book Pr. paper $4.95 (0-516-42048-8). 32pp. Spatial concepts are explained in an easy-to-read format.

224 Milgrim, David. *My Friend Lucky* (PS–K). Illus. 2002, Simon & Schuster $12.00 (0-689-84253-8). 32pp. Through the everyday adventures of a boy and his dog, opposites such as wet and dry are explained. (Rev: BL 4/15/02; HBG 10/02; SLJ 2/02)

225 Minters, Frances. *Too Big, Too Small, Just Right* (PS–1). Illus. by Janie Bynum. 2001, Harcourt $13.00 (0-15-202157-4). 32pp. Opposites are introduced in clear examples and amusing illustrations. (Rev: BL 5/1/01; HBG 10/01; SLJ 4/01)

226 Modesitt, Jeanne. *Sometimes I Feel Like a Mouse: A Book About Feelings* (PS–1). Illus. by Robin Spowart. 1996, Scholastic paper $4.99 (0-590-44836-6). 32pp. Various emotions, like happy and proud, are pictured through poses of familar animals. (Rev: BL 10/1/92; SLJ 5/93)

227 Morris, Ann. *Play* (PS–3). Illus. 1998, Lothrop $15.00 (0-688-14551-3). 32pp. A concept book that shows children from different countries engaged in various play activities common to their cultures. (Rev: BL 5/15/98) [790.1]

228 Morris, Ann. *Teamwork* (PS–2). Illus. 1999, Lothrop LB $15.93 (0-688-16995-3). 32pp. The concept of teamwork is explored in a series of pictures depicting such activities as preschoolers playing soccer, Vietnam villagers harvesting rice, and dogs pulling a sled. (Rev: BL 12/1/99; HBG 3/00; SLJ 10/99) [302.3]

229 Morris, Ann. *Work* (PS–3). Illus. 1998, Lothrop $15.00 (0-688-14866-2). 32pp. Examples of activities from countries including Mexico, Israel, Egypt, Kenya, and Togo are used to explain the concept of work as it is performed around the world. (Rev: BL 5/15/98; HBG 10/98) [306.3]

230 Murphy, Chuck. *Chuck Murphy's Black Cat White Cat: A Pop-Up Book of Opposites* (K–2). Illus. 1998, Simon & Schuster $12.95 (0-689-81415-1). An interactive book that can be manipulated to produce opposites such as a black cat that turns into a white cat. (Rev: BL 1/1–15/99)

231 Murphy, Chuck. *Slide 'n Seek: Opposites* (PS–K). Illus. Series: Slide 'n Seek. 2001, Simon & Schuster $5.99 (0-689-84476-X). 12pp. Pull-tabs are used effectively to illustrate opposites in this small board book. (Rev: BL 12/15/01) [513]

232 Murphy, Mary. *If . . .* (PS–K). Illus. by author. 2000, Houghton Mifflin paper $4.95 (0-618-03399-8). In this flap book, a little penguin demonstrates cause and effect (e.g., if you plant a seed/a tree can grow). The concept of choice is explored in the companion volume *You Choose* (2000). (Rev: SLJ 6/00)

233 Murphy, Mary. *Some Things Change* (PS). Illus. 2001, Houghton Mifflin $9.95 (0-618-00334-7). 32pp. The concept of change is explored in this book about a young penguin, his teddy bear, and experiences they share — like a sunny day that becomes cloudy. (Rev: BL 3/15/01; HB 3–4/01; HBG 10/01; SLJ 3/01)

234 Murphy, Stuart J. *Game Time!* (2–3). Illus. by Cynthia Jabar. 2000, HarperCollins LB $15.89 (0-06-028025-5); paper $4.95 (0-06-446732-5). 33pp. The concept of measuring time — including weeks, days, hours, and seconds — is explored in this exciting tale of the Huskies, a girls' soccer team, and their big game. (Rev: HBG 3/01; SLJ 1/01)

235 Murphy, Stuart J. *The Greatest Gymnast of All* (PS–K). Illus. by Cynthia Jabar. Series: MathStart. 1998, HarperCollins LB $14.89 (0-06-027609-6); paper $4.95 (0-06-446718-X). 40pp. Using Zoe's gymnastics routine as a framework, the rhyming text introduces opposites, such as inside and outside, on and off, and high and low. (Rev: BL 12/1/98; HBG 3/99; SLJ 12/98) [516]

236 Murphy, Stuart J. *It's About Time!* (PS–2). Illus. Series: MathStart. 2005, HarperCollins $15.99 (0-06-055768-0); paper $4.99 (0-06-055769-9). 40pp. Introduces time-telling by linking everyday activities to the time of day; both analog and digital clocks are featured. (Rev: BL 3/1/05) [529]

237 Murphy, Stuart J. *Probably Pistachio* (1–3). Illus. by Marsha Winborn. Series: MathStart. 2001, HarperCollins LB $15.89 (0-06-028029-8); paper $4.95 (0-06-446734-1). 40pp. Throughout his day, Stuart makes predictions based on sound reasoning in this entertaining concept book about probability. (Rev: BL 2/15/01; HBG 10/01; SLJ 3/01) [519.2]

238 Murphy, Stuart J. *Rabbit's Pajama Party* (PS–K). Illus. by Frank Remkiewicz. Series: Math-Start. 1999, HarperCollins LB $15.89 (0-06-027617-7); paper $4.95 (0-06-446722-8). 40pp. Rabbit and friends enjoy a number of events in this concept book, which explains terms in sequencing such as *about, then,* and *when.* (Rev: BL 12/1/99; HBG 3/00; SLJ 9/99) [515]

239 Murphy, Stuart J. *Super Sand Castle Saturday* (1–3). Illus. by Julia Gorton. Series: MathStart. 1999, HarperCollins LB $15.89 (0-06-027613-4). The concept of measurement is introduced by three friends trying to determine who built the tallest sand castle with the longest moat and the longest wall. (Rev: HBG 10/99; SLJ 7/99)

240 Nilsen, Anna. *My Best Friends* (PS–K). Illus. by Emma Dodd. 2003, Gingham Dog $15.95 (0-7696-3159-2). Brightly colored cartoon characters illustrate the importance — and challenges — of friendship. (Rev: HBG 4/04; SLJ 1/04)

241 Parr, Todd. *The Daddy Book* (PS–K). Illus. 2002, Little, Brown $14.95 (0-316-60799-1). 32pp. A bright, simple book that points out the differences, and the similarities, between fathers. Also use the companion volume *The Mommy Book* (2002). (Rev: BL 3/15/02; HBG 10/02; SLJ 5/02)

242 Patilla, Peter. *Patterns* (2–4). Illus. Series: Math Links. 1999, Heinemann LB $19.95 (1-57572-967-9). 32pp. Different patterns are introduced in this concept book that uses double-page spreads and is arranged by order of difficulty. (Rev: BL 2/1/00; SLJ 12/99) [510]

243 Payne, Nina. *Four in All* (PS–3). Illus. by Adam Payne. 2001, Front Street $15.95 (1-886910-16-2). 32pp. A girl takes an imaginary journey in this richly illustrated, captivating verse for younger readers that uses four-word lines to present items that come in fours (such as north, east, south, and west) and is wonderfully illustrated by the author's son. (Rev: BCCB 12/01; BL 1/1–15/02; HBG 3/02; SLJ 12/01*)

244 Penner, Lucille R. *Where's That Bone?* (PS–2). Illus. by Lynn Adams. Series: Math Matters. 2000, Kane paper $4.95 (1-57565-097-5). 32pp. A dog forgets where he has buried his bones so Jill draws him a map in this concept book about distance and maps. (Rev: SLJ 2/01)

245 Penner, Lucille Recht. *X Marks the Spot!* (1–2). Illus. by Jerry Smath. 2002, Kane paper $4.95 (1-57565-111-4). 32pp. Brothers Leo and Jake learn to read charts to find treasures in their new hometown in this clever concept book. (Rev: BL 4/15/02)

246 Pollard, Nik. *The Tide* (PS–1). Illus. by author. 2002, Millbrook LB $22.90 (0-7613-2467-4). Rhythmic text and brightly colored illustrations convey the rising and falling tide and the sounds of the ocean. (Rev: HBG 10/02; SLJ 5/02)

247 Reidy, Hannah. *All Sorts of Clothes* (PS). Illus. by Emma Dodd. Series: All Sorts of Things. 2005, Picture Window LB $22.60 (1-4048-1063-3). 24pp. This toddler-friendly book helps little ones identify different articles of clothing. (Rev: BL 4/1/05)

248 Reidy, Hannah. *All Sorts of Noises* (PS). Illus. by Emma Dodd. Series: All Sorts of Things. 2005, Picture Window LB $22.60 (1-4048-1064-1). 24pp. Introduces noises of all kinds, from birds chirping to alarm clocks and street sounds. (Rev: SLJ 6/05)

249 Reiser, Lynn. *Ten Puppies* (PS–2). Illus. by author. 2003, Greenwillow LB $16.89 (0-06-008645-9). This brightly illustrated book introduces young readers to multiple concepts, including counting, colors, shapes, and sizes. (Rev: HB 5–6/03; HBG 10/03; SLJ 4/03)

250 Rex, Michael. *Truck Duck* (PS). Illus. by author. 2004, Penguin Putnam $9.99 (0-399-24009-8). Happy combinations of animals and forms of transportation — including a "Moose Caboose" and a "Blimb Chimp" — are shown in bright and detailed illustrations. (Rev: BL 1/1–15/04; SLJ 1/04)

251 Rose, Emma. *Pumpkin Faces: A Glowing Book You Can Read in the Dark!* (PS–K). Illus. by Judith Moffatt. 1997, Scholastic $6.95 (0-590-13454-X). A simple concept book that uses the faces of Halloween jack-o'-lanterns to express a variety of emotions. (Rev: SLJ 11/97)

252 Rotner, Shelley. *Lots of Feelings* (PS–1). Photos by author. 2003, Millbrook LB $21.90 (0-7613-2896-3). 24pp. Close-up photographs show children displaying a variety of emotions. (Rev: HBG 4/04; SLJ 4/04)

253 Rotner, Shelley. *Parts* (PS–1). Illus. 2001, Walker LB $17.85 (0-8027-8754-1). 32pp. Close-up shots of parts of everyday objects are accompanied by rhymes that give additional clues to the whole object that is revealed on the next page. (Rev: BCCB 6/01; BL 6/1–15/01; HBG 10/01; SLJ 5/01)

254 Sayre, April Pulley. *Shadows* (PS–1). Illus. by Harvey Stevenson. 2002, Holt $16.95 (0-8050-6059-6). 32pp. In this colorful picture book, a small boy and girl go to the seashore in search of shadows and find that everything has one. (Rev: BL 4/15/02; HBG 10/02; SLJ 6/02)

255 Schaefer, Lola M. *What's Up, What's Down?* (PS–2). Illus. by Barbara Bash. 2002, HarperCollins $15.99 (0-06-029757-3). 32pp. A fascinating and innovative approach that involves turning the book sideways and following arrows up and down to see the world from the point of view of various plants and animals. (Rev: BL 12/1/02; HBG 3/03; SLJ 1/03) [500]

256 Schwartz, David M. *If You Hopped Like a Frog* (K–4). Illus. by James Warhola. 1999, Scholastic $15.95 (0-590-09857-8). 32pp. This picture book discusses the concepts of ratio and proportion, using animal facts to explore topics such as relative strength. (Rev: BCCB 12/99; BL 11/15/99; HBG 3/00; SLJ 11/99) [513.2]

257 Sendak, Maurice. *The Nutshell Library* (PS–3). Illus. by author. 1962, HarperCollins $15.95 (0-06-025500-5). Miniature volumes include an alphabet book, *Alligators All Around,* and a counting book, *One Was Johnny* (both 1962).

258 Simon, Francesca. *Calling All Toddlers* (PS–K). Illus. by Susan Winter. 1999, Orchard $15.95 (0-531-30120-6). 33pp. In 16 verses, children are introduced to colors, shapes, movement, humor, and play. (Rev: BCCB 2/99; BL 4/15/99; HBG 10/99; SLJ 6/99)

259 Siomades, Lorianne. *Kangaroo and Cricket* (PS–1). Illus. by author. 1999, Boyds Mills $10.95 (1-56397-780-X). Two different animals on every page reveal how they are similar; for example, both dogs and squirrels bury things. (Rev: HBG 3/00; SLJ 12/99)

260 Slate, Joseph. *Miss Bindergarten Celebrates the 100th Day of Kindergarten* (PS–1). Illus. by Ashley Wolff. 1998, Dutton $15.99 (0-525-46000-4). 32pp. Superteacher Miss Bindergarten asks her students to bring 100 things to class to celebrate the 100th day of kindergarten in this combination alphabet and counting book. (Rev: BL 10/15/98; HBG 3/99; SLJ 9/98)

261 Spicer, Maggee, and Richard Thompson. *We'll All Go Flying* (PS–K). Illus. by Kim LaFave. 2002, Fitzhenry & Whiteside $16.95 (1-55041-698-7). Colors, shapes, sounds, and animals are all presented from the platform of a hot-air balloon in this counting book with movable flaps. (Rev: SLJ 12/02)

262 Spurr, Elizabeth. *Farm Life* (PS–1). Illus. by Steve Bjorkman. 2003, Holiday House $16.95 (0-8234-1777-8). 32pp. Basic colors and numbers one to ten are taught by exploring the buildings on a farm. (Rev: BL 3/15/03; HBG 10/03; SLJ 6/03)

263 Steggall, Susan. *On the Road* (PS–1). Illus. by author. 2005, Kane/Miller $14.95 (1-929132-70-0). A British import that introduces prepositions during a car trip that shows changing scenery and many other vehicles. (Rev: SLJ 4/05)

264 Steig, William. *Which Would You Rather Be?* (PS–2). Illus. by Harry Bliss. 2002, HarperCollins LB $15.89 (0-06-029654-2). 32pp. A boy and girl are given a series of choices about what they'd rather be (a dog or a cat; an elbow or a knee?). (Rev: BL 8/02; HBG 10/02; SLJ 6/02)

265 Swinburne, Stephen R. *What's Opposite?* (PS–1). Illus. 2000, Boyds Mills $15.95 (1-56397-881-4). 32pp. Using handsome photographs, this book explores the world of common opposites. (Rev: BL 9/1/00; HBG 3/01; SLJ 10/00)

266 Szekeres, Cyndy. *I Love My Busy Book* (PS–1). Illus. 1997, Scholastic $12.95 (0-590-69195-3). 48pp. Concepts like colors, manners, and parts of the body are introduced in double-page spreads. (Rev: BCCB 3/97; BL 2/1/97; SLJ 4/97)

267 Thomas, Shelley M. *Somewhere Today: A Book of Peace* (PS–3). Illus. by Eric Futran. 1998, Whitman $14.95 (0-8075-7545-3). 24pp. A book in which children and their activities illustrate the concepts of peaceful living, sharing, helping, and joining together. (Rev: BL 4/1/98; HBG 10/98; SLJ 8/98)

268 Tomczyk, Mary. *Shapes, Sizes and More Surprises!* (PS–1). Illus. by Loretta Braren. Series: Little Hands Early Learning Books. 1996, Williamson paper $12.95 (0-913589-95-0). 141pp. An activity book for youngsters filled with stories, puzzles, counting exercises, and games. (Rev: SLJ 10/96)

269 Van Fleet, Matthew. *One Yellow Lion* (PS). Illus. by author. 1992, Dial $9.99 (0-8037-1099-2). This book, with foldout pages and plenty of drawings of animals, presents the concepts of color and counting. (Rev: SLJ 9/92)

270 Walsh, Melanie. *My Beak, Your Beak* (PS). Illus. 2002, Houghton Mifflin $15.00 (0-618-15079-X). 32pp. Bright, simple illustrations complement text that finds differences and similarities between a host of animals in this book for very young readers. Also use *My Nose, Your Nose* (2002), which focuses on children. (Rev: BL 12/15/02; HBG 3/03; SLJ 10/02)

271 Webb, Steve. *Tanka Tanka Skunk!* (PS–1). Illus. by author. 2004, Scholastic $15.95 (0-439-57844-2). This story without a plot features rhythmic repetition of sounds and brightly colored cartoon animals. (Rev: SLJ 11/04)

272 Williams, Sue. *Let's Go Visiting* (PS–K). Illus. by Julie Vivas. 1998, Harcourt $15.00 (0-15-201823-9). 32pp. In this counting and color-identification book, a young child and his dog visit barnyard friends — one brown foal, two red calves, etc. (Rev: BL 11/1/98; HBG 3/99; SLJ 12/98)

273 Wilson-Max, Ken. *Wake Up, Sleep Tight* (PS–K). Illus. 1998, Scholastic $11.95 (0-590-76779-8). 16pp. Two simple board books in one — one about morning activities and the other about going to bed — are unified by a cutout clock with movable hands. Readers can change the clock to the hours mentioned in each rhyme. (Rev: BL 11/1/98)

274 Wojtowycz, David. *Can You Choo Choo?* (PS). Illus. by author. 2003, Scholastic $12.95 (0-439-39485-6). Preschoolers meet a variety of anthropomorphic vehicles and the noises they make. (Rev: HBG 4/04; SLJ 3/04)

275 Wormell, Christopher. *Teeth, Tales and Tentacles: An Animal Counting Book* (PS–3). 2004, Running Press $18.95 (0-7624-2100-2). 64pp. This clever animal-themed counting book operates on several levels, serving as an introduction to numbers for preschoolers, an overview of 20 different animal species from around the world, and a collection of fascinating facts and figures about those animals and their behavior. (Rev: BL 10/1/04*)

276 Yorke, Jane. *My First Spanish Number Book / Mi primer libro de numeros en espanol: A Bilingual Word Book* (PS–2). Illus. Series: My First Word Books. 2003, DK $16.99 (0-7894-9524-4). 48pp. Words, numbers, and basic math concepts are introduced in English and Spanish. (Rev: HBG 4/04; SLJ 12/03)

COLORS

277 Barry, Frances. *Duckie's Rainbow* (PS). Illus. by author. 2004, Candlewick $7.99 (0-7636-2066-1). Duckie passes many vivid colors as she hurries home in this fan-shaped board book with collage art. (Rev: SLJ 7/04) [813.6]

278 *Big Yellow Trucks and Diggers: Colors* (PS). 2003, Chronicle $6.95 (0-8118-4030-1). Colors are introduced through eye-catching photographs of appealing machines. (Rev: SLJ 1/04) [624]

279 Bown, Deni. *Color Fun* (PS). Illus. Series: Snapshot. 1995, DK $3.95 (0-7894-0230-0). 12pp. Colors are revealed by pulling tabs that open double-page spreads filled with objects of a particular color. (Rev: BL 1/1–15/96; SLJ 7/96) [701.85]

280 Brown, Margaret Wise. *My World of Color* (PS–K). Illus. by Loretta Krupinski. 2002, Hyperion LB $15.98 (0-7868-2519-7). 32pp. Two mouse artists introduce the colors of the rainbow plus white, black, brown, pink, and gray in a series of double-page spreads each of which contains a 4-line rhyme. (Rev: BL 5/1/02; HBG 10/02; SLJ 6/02)

281 Bryant-Mole, Karen. *Blue* (PS–1). Illus. Series: Images. 1996, Silver Pr. LB $10.95 (0-382-39590-5); paper $4.95 (0-382-39626-X). 24pp. A concept book that focuses on a single color and a variety of objects. Also use *Texture* (1996). (Rev: SLJ 1/97)

282 Carle, Eric. *Hello, Red Fox* (K–3). Illus. 1998, Simon & Schuster $16.00 (0-689-81775-4). 32pp. The author invites readers to experience a simple story by employing the phenomenon whereby staring at a color and then at a blank white page reveals a complementary color as if by magic. (Rev: BCCB 7–8/98; BL 4/1/98; HBG 10/98; SLJ 7/98)

283 Catalanotto, Peter. *Kitten Red, Yellow, Blue* (PS–K). Illus. 2005, Simon & Schuster $15.95 (0-689-86562-7). 32pp. Both colors and professions are introduced in this clever story that involves color-coding a batch of kittens according to their owners. (Rev: BL 2/15/05; SLJ 3/05)

284 Cousins, Lucy. *Maisy's Rainbow Dream* (PS). Illus. by author. 2003, Candlewick $16.99 (0-7636-2195-1). In a dream, Maisy the mouse explores the wonders of Rainbowland. (Rev: BL 12/1/03; SLJ 12/03)

285 Crowther, Robert. *Colors* (PS–K). Illus. by author. 2001, Candlewick $12.99 (0-7636-1404-1). Words on movable tabs are paired with bright double-page illustrations to introduce colors. (Rev: SLJ 7/01)

286 Edwards, Pamela Duncan. *Warthogs Paint: A Messy Color Book* (PS–K). Illus. by Henry Cole. 2001, Hyperion $14.99 (0-7868-0470-X). 32pp. When the warthogs decide to paint the kitchen, the primary colors soon get mixed up. (Rev: BL 6/1–15/01; HBG 3/02; SLJ 8/01)

287 Ehlert, Lois. *Color Farm* (PS–K). Illus. 1990, HarperCollins LB $15.89 (0-397-32441-3). 40pp. Various animals are pictured by using a number of different shapes and colors. (Rev: BL 11/15/90; HB 1–2/91; SLJ 11/90)

288 Ehlert, Lois. *Color Zoo* (PS–2). Illus. by author. 1989, HarperCollins LB $16.89 (0-397-32260-7). 32pp. How basic shapes can be combined to make familiar objects. (Rev: BL 5/15/89; SLJ 4/89)

289 Emberley, Rebecca. *My Colors / Mis Colores* (PS). 2000, Little, Brown $5.95 (0-316-23347-1). 20pp. A board book in English and Spanish introduces the basic colors. (Rev: BCCB 12/00*; HBG 3/01; SLJ 9/00)

290 Fox, Christyan, and Diane Fox. *What Color Is That, PiggyWiggy?* (PS–K). Illus. 2001, Handprint $5.95 (1-929766-17-3). 20pp. In this book about colors, PiggyWiggy dons articles of clothing of different hues until he becomes a perfect circus clown. (Rev: BL 4/1/01; SLJ 8/01)

291 Goldsen, Louise. *Colors* (K–2). Illus. by P. M. Valet and Sylvaine Perols. 1991, Scholastic paper $12.95 (0-590-45236-3). Through the use of clear acetate sheets, various colors are introduced and identified. (Rev: SLJ 5/92) [535.5]

292 Gunzi, Christiane. *My Very First Look at Colors* (PS–K). Illus. by Steve Gorton. Series: My Very First Look. 2001, Two-Can $8.95 (1-58728-236-4); paper $5.95 (1-58728-276-3). 24pp. A concept book that uses photographs of everyday objects to teach preschoolers about colors. (Rev: BL 2/15/02; HBG 10/02; SLJ 2/02) [535.6]

293 Harrison, Carlos. *Ruben's Rainbow / El Arco Iris de Ruben* (K–2). Illus. by Grizelle Paz. 2001, Globo Libros $15.95 (0-9706953-0-6). Ruben tumbles from a world of black and white into a world full of color in this bilingual text accompanied by a CD. (Rev: SLJ 1/02)

294 Hoban, Tana. *Colors Everywhere* (PS–K). Illus. 1995, Greenwillow $15.93 (0-688-12763-0). 32pp. A wordless picture book that identifies the colors found in each of the photographs used. (Rev: BCCB 3/95; BL 5/1/95; HB 7–8/95; SLJ 7/95)

295 Hoban, Tana. *Is It Red? Is It Yellow? Is It Blue?* (PS). Illus. 1978, Greenwillow $16.00 (0-688-84171-6); Morrow paper $4.95 (0-688-07034-5). 32pp. Without words, this picture book explains the concept of color.

296 Hoban, Tana. *Red, Blue, Yellow Shoe* (PS). Illus. by author. 1986, Greenwillow paper $5.95 (0-688-06563-5). 12pp. A very simple introduction to color in a board book. (Rev: BCCB 1/87; BL 10/15/86; HB 11–12/86)

297 Holm, Sharon Lane. *Zoe's Hats: A Book of Colors and Patterns* (PS–1). Illus. 2003, Boyds Mills $13.95 (1-59078-042-6). 32pp. Zoe has fun trying on all manner of hats in this simple book for the very young. (Rev: BL 2/1/03; HBG 10/03; SLJ 2/03)

298 Horacek, Petr. *Strawberries Are Red* (PS). Illus. by author. 2001, Candlewick $4.99 (0-7636-1461-0). Fruit and colors are introduced on brightly illustrated double-page spreads. Also use *What Is Black and White?* (2001). (Rev: SLJ 8/01)

299 Inkpen, Mick. *Kipper's Book of Colors* (PS). Illus. by author. 1999, Harcourt $4.95 (0-15-202285-6). This concept book about different colors features a lovable pup as a guide. (Rev: SLJ 10/99)

300 Jonas, Ann. *Color Dance* (PS–K). Illus. 1989, Greenwillow $15.93 (0-688-05991-0). 32pp. Dancers wave colored scarves and introduce various colors. (Rev: BL 8/89; SLJ 12/89)

301 Leuck, Laura. *Teeny, Tiny Mouse: A Book About Colors* (PS–1). Illus. by Pat Schories. 1998, BridgeWater $15.95 (0-8167-4547-1). A teeny, tiny mouse and her teeny, tiny child introduce the reader to colors as they list objects in their dollhouse. (Rev: HBG 10/98; SLJ 5/98)

302 Lionni, Leo. *Little Blue and Little Yellow* (PS–1). Illus. by author. 1959, Astor-Honor $13.00 (0-8392-3018-4). All the characters are blobs of color; an ingenious story intended to give the young child an awareness of color.

303 MacKinnon, Debbie. *Eye Spy Colors* (PS–K). Illus. by Anthea Sieveking. 1998, Charlesbridge $8.95 (0-88106-334-7). 24pp. Colors are introduced through a series of double-page spreads and peepholes. (Rev: BL 1/1–15/99; HBG 3/99)

304 Martin, Bill, Jr. *Brown Bear, Brown Bear, What Do You See?* (PS–1). Illus. by Eric Carle. 1992, Holt $15.95 (0-8050-1744-5). 32pp. This brightly illustrated easy-reader book first appeared in 1967 and is a fine introduction to colors. (Rev: BL 3/1/92; SLJ 5/92)

305 Milich, Zoran. *City Colors* (PS–1). Photos by author. 2004, Kids Can $14.95 (1-55337-542-4). Starting with basic colors (a red bus, a blue wall), the author works through a city's spectrum (from a green swing to a pink conduit) in this attractive concept book. (Rev: SLJ 5/04) [535.6]

306 Miller, Margaret. *I Love Colors* (PS–1). Illus. Series: Look Baby! 1999, Simon & Schuster $4.99 (0-689-82356-8). 14pp. In this board book about colors, babies are shown wearing different-colored headgear. (Rev: BL 8/99; SLJ 8/99)

307 Murphy, Chuck. *Color Surprises* (PS–1). Illus. 1997, Simon & Schuster paper $13.95 (0-689-81504-2). Introduces colors using flaps of the same color as the animal underneath. (Rev: BL 12/15/97)

308 Park, Linda Sue. *What Does Bunny See? A Book of Colors and Flowers* (PS). Illus. by Maggie Smith. 2005, Clarion $15.00 (0-618-23485-3). 32pp. Poppies, violets, primroses, and lilies are among the flowers Bunny sees in a colorful garden in this rhyming presentation of blossoms and their colors. (Rev: BL 3/1/05; SLJ 6/05)

309 Pinkney, Sandra L. *A Rainbow All Around Me* (PS–1). Illus. by Myles C. Pinkney. 2002, Scholastic $14.95 (0-439-30928-X). 40pp. Arresting photographs and simple text introduce colors and convey multicultural awareness. (Rev: BL 2/1/02; HBG 10/02; SLJ 3/02)

310 Robertson, Patrisha. *Cirque du Soleil: Parade of Colors* (K–4). Photos by Cirque du Soleil. 2003, Abrams $15.95 (0-8109-4515-0). 32pp. In this lushly illustrated concept book, young readers are introduced to colors in a parade of performers from the famed Cirque du Soleil. (Rev: HBG 4/04; SLJ 1/04)

311 Rodrigue, George. *Why Is Blue Dog Blue?* (PS–3). Illus. 2002, Stewart, Tabori & Chang $16.95 (1-58479-162-4). 40pp. The artist explains why he paints his dog different colors depending on the situation. (Rev: BL 6/1–15/02; HBG 10/02)

312 Rowe, Jeannette. *YoYo's Colors* (PS). Illus. by author. Series: YoYo. 2002, Tiger Tales $3.95 (1-58925-682-4). YoYo the yellow dog introduces preschoolers to other vividly colored creatures in this board book. Also use *YoYo's Numbers* and *YoYo's Toys* (both 2002). (Rev: SLJ 6/03)

313 Seeger, Laura Vaccaro. *Lemons Are Not Red* (PS–2). Illus. 2004, Roaring Brook $14.95 (1-59643-008-7). 32pp. Various objects introduce colors in this attractive small book that ends with a bedtime message. (Rev: BL 1/1–15/05)

314 Serfozo, Mary. *Who Said Red?* (PS–K). Illus. by Narahashi Keiko. 1988, Macmillan paper $5.99 (0-689-71592-7). 32pp. A little boy is looking for his lost kite in this picture book about colors. (Rev: BL 9/1/88; SLJ 1/89)

315 Seuss, Dr. *My Many Colored Days* (PS). Illus. by Steve Johnson and Lou Fancher. 1996, Knopf LB $17.99 (0-679-97597-7). 32pp. Various moods are linked with colors in this rhyming picture book. (Rev: BL 11/1/96; SLJ 12/96)

316 Shahan, Sherry. *Spicy Hot Colors / Colores Picantes* (PS–1). Illus. by Paula Barragan. 2004, August House $16.95 (0-87483-741-3). 24pp. Spicy-hot art and rhythmic descriptions introduce colors in both English and Spanish. (Rev: BL 9/15/04; SLJ 11/04) [535.6]

317 Shannon, George. *White Is for Blueberry* (PS–K). Illus. by Laura Dronzek. 2005, Greenwillow LB $16.89 (0-06-029276-8). 40pp. Plants and animals are linked to unexpected colors (for instance, crows are pink . . . when newly hatched from their eggs) in this lushly illustrated book. (Rev: BL 3/15/05; SLJ 5/05)

318 Siomades, Lorianne. *My Box of Color* (PS–1). Illus. by author. 1998, Boyds Mills $8.95 (1-56397-711-7). This book helps children explore their perceptions of color by presenting common objects in unusual colors and asking, for instance, whether a blue sun would be just as warm. (Rev: HBG 3/99; SLJ 11/98)

319 Swinburne, Stephen R. *What Color Is Nature?* (PS–K). Illus. 2002, Boyds Mills $15.95 (1-56397-967-5); paper $8.95 (1-59078-008-6). 32pp. Using bright photographs of children, animals, and plants, different colors are introduced. (Rev: BL 6/1–15/02; HBG 10/02)

320 Thompson, Richard, and Maggee Spicer. *We'll All Go Sailing* (PS–1). Illus. by Kim La Fave. 2001, Fitzhenry & Whiteside $16.95 (1-55041-662-6). 48pp. A concept book that introduces colors along with a variety of sea creatures. (Rev: BL 5/15/01; SLJ 7/01) [591.77]

321 Thong, Roseanne. *Red Is a Dragon: A Book of Colors* (PS–2). Illus. by Grace Lin. 2001, Chronicle $18.95 (0-8118-3177-9). 180pp. This concept book, a companion to *A Book of Shapes* (2000), is illustrated with Chinese American images. (Rev: BL 11/15/01; HBG 3/02; SLJ 1/02)

PERCEPTION

322 Ashbe, Jeanne. *What's Inside* (PS). Illus. by author. Series: Curious Nell. 2000, Kane/ Miller $9.95 (0-916291-97-9). This flap book explores the inside of things, such as a suitcase and a TV set — and examines three different stages of an unborn baby's development. (Rev: BCCB 6/00; HB 5–6/00; HBG 10/00; SLJ 5/00)

323 Becker, Bonny. *Tickly Prickly* (PS). Illus. by Shari Halpern. 1999, HarperCollins $9.95 (0-694-01239-4). 24pp. Using paper cutouts as illustrations, this book explores the sense of touch by describing how various objects and animals feel. (Rev: BL 7/99; HBG 10/99; SLJ 8/99)

324 Burns, Kate. *Jump Like a Frog!* (PS–K). Illus. 1999, David & Charles $6.95 (1-899607-35-8). 12pp. Five picture puzzles are found in this flap book, which asks young readers to find hidden animals. Also use *Snap like a Crocodile*. (Rev: BL 9/15/99; SLJ 10/99)

325 Carrier, Lark. *There Was a Hill . . .* (PS–1). Illus. by author. 1991, Picture Book paper $15.95 (0-907234-70-4). 40pp. An attractive picture book with a guessing game woven into the irresistible pages. (Rev: BL 9/15/85; SLJ 10/85)

326 Hoban, Tana. *Is It Rough? Is It Smooth? Is It Shiny?* (PS). Illus. by author. 1984, Greenwillow $17.95 (0-688-03823-9). 32pp. Textures are explored in a series of photographs.

327 Maclay, Elise. *The Forest Has Eyes* (PS–2). Illus. by Bev Doolittle. 1998, Greenwich Workshop $16.95 (0-86713-055-5). 32pp. Each of these nature paintings has a subject camouflaged within it (e.g., a snow pattern on a mountain is actually an eagle). (Rev: BL 10/15/98; SLJ 11/98) [970]

328 McMillan, Bruce. *Mouse View: What the Class Pet Saw* (PS–3). Illus. 1993, Holiday House LB $16.95 (0-8234-1008-0). 32pp. Familiar classroom sights are shown from a mouse's point of view. (Rev: BL 3/15/93*; SLJ 4/93)

329 Robert, Francois, and Jean Robert. *Find a Face* (PS–2). 2004, Chronicle $15.95 (0-8118-4338-6). Faces are everywhere in this inventive collection of photographs of objects ranging from light switches to shoe heels. (Rev: SLJ 8/04) [779]

330 Shaw, Charles. *It Looked Like Spilt Milk* (K–2). Illus. by author. 1947, HarperCollins LB $14.89 (0-06-025565-X); paper $5.95 (0-06-443159-2). 30pp. White material appears on each page, but its identity is not revealed until the end. Originally published in 1947.

SIZE AND SHAPE

331 Aber, Linda Williams. *Carrie Measures Up* (K–2). Illus. by Joy Allen. Series: Math Matters. 2001, Kane paper $4.95 (1-57565-100-9). 32pp. Carrie gets totally carried away measuring things around the house. (Rev: SLJ 6/01)

332 Adler, David A. *Shape Up! Fun with Triangles and Other Polygons* (2–5). Illus. by Nancy Tobin. 1998, Holiday House $15.95 (0-8234-1346-2). An introduction to shapes and angles, using household items such as pretzels, bread, and pencil and paper. (Rev: BCCB 9/98; HBG 10/98; SLJ 9/98)

333 Blackstone, Stella. *Bear in a Square* (PS–K). Illus. by Debbie Harter. 1998, Bearfoot $13.95 (1-901223-58-2). 32pp. This book is both an introduction to shapes and a counting book. (Rev: BL 10/1/98; SLJ 10/98)

334 Cohen, Caron L. *Where's the Fly?* (PS–3). Illus. by Nancy Barnet. 1996, Greenwillow $15.00 (0-688-14044-0). 32pp. Color pictures are used to explore the concepts of relative size and distance using, for example, closeups. (Rev: BCCB 4/96; BL 3/1/96; HB 7–8/96; SLJ 5/96)

335 Dotlich, Rebecca. *What Is a Triangle?* (PS). Illus. by Maria Ferrari. Series: Growing Tree. 2000, HarperCollins $9.95 (0-694-01392-7). 24pp. This simple reader introduces youngsters to a variety of objects — an ice cream cone and a slice of pizza, for example — that are shaped like triangles. (Rev: BL 12/15/00; HBG 3/01; SLJ 11/00) [516]

336 Dotlich, Rebecca. *What Is Round?* (PS). Illus. by Maria Ferrari. Series: Harper Growing Tree. 1999, HarperCollins $9.95 (0-694-01208-4). 24pp. The concept of roundness is explored in this picture book, which shows many objects that are round and others that are not. (Rev: BL 7/99; HBG 10/99; SLJ 4/99)

337 Dotlich, Rebecca. *What Is Square?* (PS). Photos by Maria Ferrari. Series: Harper Growing Tree. 1999, HarperCollins $9.95 (0-694-01207-6). All kinds of square objects are presented in this interactive concept book. (Rev: HBG 10/99; SLJ 8/99)

338 Emberley, Rebecca. *My Shapes / Mis Formas* (PS). 2000, Little, Brown $5.95 (0-316-23355-2). 20pp. Different shapes are introduced in English and Spanish in this board book. (Rev: BCCB 12/00*; HBG 3/01; SLJ 9/00)

339 Falwell, Cathryn. *Shape Space* (PS–2). Illus. 1992, Houghton Mifflin $14.95 (0-395-61305-1). 32pp. A cut-paper girl plays and builds with colorful cut-paper shapes. (Rev: BL 10/15/92; HB 1–2/93; SLJ 10/92)

340 Florian, Douglas. *A Pig Is Big* (PS–K). Illus. 2000, Greenwillow $15.95 (0-688-17125-7). 24pp. Using animals as subjects, this book explores the concept of comparative size. (Rev: BCCB 12/00*; BL 9/15/00; HB 11–12/00; HBG 3/01; SLJ 10/00)

341 Fox, Christyan, and Diane Fox. *What Shape Is That, PiggyWiggy?* (PS). Illus. by authors. 2002, Handprint $5.95 (1-929766-44-0). Shapes including squares, circles, arches, triangles, and diamonds are demonstrated as a pig and his teddy bear build a house in this board book. (Rev: SLJ 6/02)

342 Gordon, Sharon. *Big Small* (PS–2). Series: Bookworms: Just the Opposite. 2003, Benchmark LB $14.95 (0-7614-1568-8). 23pp. A young girl's various possessions are bigger than her little brother's in this exploration of the concept of size. (Rev: HBG 4/04; SLJ 3/04) [155.7]

343 Greene, Rhonda Gowler. *When a Line Bends . . . A Shape Begins* (PS–2). Illus. by James Kaczman. 1997, Houghton Mifflin $16.00 (0-395-78606-1). In this concept book, ten different shapes — including a circle, square, triangle, diamond, and heart — are introduced. (Rev: HBG 3/98; SLJ 10/97)

344 Gunzi, Christiane. *My Very First Look at Shapes* (PS–K). Illus. by Steve Gorton. Series: My Very First Look. 2001, Two-Can $8.95 (1-58728-238-0); paper $5.95 (1-58728-278-X). 24pp. Shapes are introduced using colorful photographs of easily recognized objects. Also use *My Very First Look at Sizes* (2001). (Rev: BL 2/15/02; HBG 10/02; SLJ 2/02) [516]

345 Hammersmith, Craig. *Patterns* (K–2). Series: Spyglass Books. 2003, Compass Point LB $18.60 (0-7565-0452-X). 24pp. Ideal for beginning readers, this brightly illustrated concept book shows how diverse arrangements of colors and shapes form recognizable patterns. (Rev: SLJ 10/03) [152.14]

346 Harris, Nicholas. *How Big?* (2–4). Illus. 2004, Gale/Blackbirch LB $19.96 (1-41030-068-4). 32pp. A fascinating exploration of relative size, comparing people, animals, and objects across spreads. Also use *How Tall?* (2004). (Rev: BL 1/1–15/04) [530.5]

347 Henkes, Kevin. *The Biggest Boy* (PS). Illus. by Nancy Tafuri. 1995, Greenwillow $14.93 (0-688-12830-0). 32pp. The concept of size is explored in this story of a youngster who dreams of being the biggest boy in the world. (Rev: BL 3/1/95; HB 5–6/95; SLJ 4/95)

348 Henkes, Kevin. *Circle Dogs* (PS–K). Illus. by Dan Yaccarino. 1998, Greenwillow LB $14.93 (0-688-15447-6). 32pp. Everyday circular shapes are explored in this picture book about a toddler and his two pet "circle" dachshunds. (Rev: BCCB 11/98; BL 9/15/98; HBG 3/99; SLJ 9/98)

349 Hoban, Tana. *Cubes, Cones, Cylinders, and Spheres* (PS–K). Illus. 2000, Greenwillow LB $15.89 (0-688-15326-7). 24pp. Delightful pictures introduce different shapes in everyday objects. (Rev: BCCB 12/00; BL 10/15/00; HBG 3/01; SLJ 10/00) [513]

350 Hoban, Tana. *Is It Larger? Is It Smaller?* (PS–1). Illus. by author. 1997, Morrow paper $4.95 (0-688-15287-2). 32pp. Effective photographs and design illustrate the concepts of large and small, without words. (Rev: BCCB 4/85; BL 3/15/85; SLJ 4/85)

351 Hoban, Tana. *Over, Under and Through and Other Spacial Concepts* (K–2). Illus. by author. 1973, Macmillan LB $17.00 (0-02-744820-7). 32pp. Spacial concepts are conveyed through brief text and photographs.

352 Hoban, Tana. *Shapes, Shapes, Shapes* (PS–1). Illus. by author. 1986, Greenwillow $15.89 (0-688-05833-7). 32pp. Eleven shapes are sought in the color photos. (Rev: BCCB 4/86; BL 3/1/86; HB 5–6/86)

353 Hoban, Tana. *So Many Circles, So Many Squares* (PS–1). Illus. 1998, Greenwillow $15.00 (0-688-15165-5). 32pp. In this wordless concept book, the author explores different things that are round or square. (Rev: BL 3/1/98; HB 7–8/98; HBG 10/98; SLJ 3/98) [516]

354 Hutchins, Pat. *Shrinking Mouse* (PS–K). Illus. 1997, Greenwillow $14.93 (0-688-13962-0). 32pp. A clever exploration of space and perspective using woodland animals and birds. (Rev: BL 2/15/97; SLJ 4/97*)

355 Jenkins, Steve. *Big and Little* (PS–2). Illus. 1996, Houghton Mifflin $14.95 (0-395-72664-6). 32pp. The concept of size is explored in this book that contrasts various animals. (Rev: BL 10/1/96; SLJ 10/96*)

356 Kalan, Robert. *Blue Sea* (K–3). Illus. by Donald Crews. 1979, Morrow paper $5.95 (0-688-11509-8). 24pp. Big fish and little fish in the sea convey the idea of size.

357 MacDonald, Suse. *Sea Shapes* (PS–K). Illus. 1994, Harcourt $13.95 (0-15-200027-5); paper $6.00 (0-15-201700-3). 32pp. Sea creatures and attractive collages are used to introduce a number of shapes. (Rev: BL 9/1/94; HB 11–12/94; SLJ 11/94)

358 MacKinnon, Debbie. *Eye Spy Shapes: A Peephole Book* (PS). Photos by Anthea Sieveking. 2000, Charlesbridge $8.95 (0-88106-135-2). In this interactive book, various shapes are introduced through a peephole guessing game. (Rev: HBG 10/01; SLJ 9/00)

359 Micklethwait, Lucy. *I Spy: Shapes in Art* (PS–2). 2004, Greenwillow $19.99 (0-06-073193-1). 40pp. A variety of shapes can be identified in beautiful reproductions of well-known works of art. (Rev: BL 8/04; SLJ 9/04) [701]

360 Montague-Smith, Ann. *First Shape Book* (PS–1). Illus. by Mandy Stanley. 2002, Kingfisher $12.95 (0-7534-5433-5). 47pp. Cartoon illustrations and a series of questions and games introduce shapes, mirror images, pairs, and size in a way that encourages identification, matching, and counting. (Rev: SLJ 7/02)

19

361 Murphy, Chuck. *Bow Wow: A Pop-Up Book of Shapes* (PS–3). Illus. 1999, Simon & Schuster $12.95 (0-689-82265-0). Each page features a particular shape, and when the shape is opened it reveals a pop-up surprise. (Rev: BCCB 9/99; BL 12/15/99)

362 Murphy, Chuck. *Slide 'n Seek: Shapes* (PS–K). Illus. Series: Slide 'n Seek. 2001, Simon & Schuster $5.99 (0-689-84477-8). 12pp. This small board book introduces shapes using pull-tabs and clear, bright illustrations. (Rev: BL 12/15/01) [513]

363 Murphy, Stuart J. *The Best Bug Parade* (PS–1). Illus. by Holly Keller. Series: MathStart. 1996, HarperCollins LB $15.89 (0-06-025872-1); paper $4.95 (0-06-446700-7). 33pp. A parade of bugs is used to introduce the concept of size. (Rev: BCCB 5/96; SLJ 6/96)

364 Murphy, Stuart J. *Circus Shapes* (PS). Illus. by Edward Miller. Series: MathStart. 1998, Harper-Collins LB $15.89 (0-06-027437-9). 40pp. Objects associated with the circus are pictured in this concept book that introduces various shapes. (Rev: BL 3/1/98; HBG 10/98; SLJ 4/98)

365 Murphy, Stuart J. *Let's Fly a Kite* (PS–3). Illus. by Brian Floca. 2000, HarperCollins LB $15.89 (0-06-028035-2); paper $4.95 (0-06-446737-6). 40pp. Geometry and symmetry in everyday life are the concepts explored in this picture book about two quarreling siblings. (Rev: BL 9/15/00; HBG 3/01; SLJ 11/00)

366 Myller, Rolf. *How Big Is a Foot?* (K–2). Illus. by author. 1991, Dell paper $3.99 (0-440-40495-9). The problem of relative sizes, humorously and imaginatively described.

367 Nathan, Cheryl, and Lisa McCourt. *The Long and Short of It* (K–2). Illus. by Cheryl Nathan. 1998, BridgeWater $15.95 (0-8167-4545-5). This book not only explores the concept of size but also introduces different animals to make valid comparisons. (Rev: HBG 10/98; SLJ 5/98)

368 Patilla, Peter. *Measuring* (2–4). Illus. Series: Math Links. 1999, Heinemann LB $19.95 (1-57572-965-2). 32pp. A clear, attractive presentation of concepts involved in measuring that uses a series of double-page spreads. (Rev: BL 2/1/00) [530.8]

369 Pollack, Pam, and Meg Belviso. *Chickens on the Move* (1–2). Illus. by Lynn Adams. 2002, Kane paper $4.95 (1-57565-113-0). 32pp. In this witty concept book, three children use 24 feet of fencing to create coops of different shapes to house their grandfather's three chickens. (Rev: BL 4/15/02)

370 Rau, Dana Meachen. *A Star in My Orange: Looking for Nature's Shapes* (PS–2). Illus. 2002, Millbrook LB $22.90 (0-7613-2414-3). 32pp. Through colorful photographs and simple text, this book explores shapes such as stars and spirals as they occur in nature. (Rev: BL 2/1/02; HBG 10/02; SLJ 5/02) [516]

371 Salzmann, Mary Elizabeth. *Circles* (PS–1). Series: What Shape Is It? 2000, ABDO LB $12.95 (1-57765-163-4). 24pp. A slim book that introduces circles and various objects that are circular in shape. Also use *Rectangles, Stars, Triangles* (all 2000). (Rev: HBG 10/00; SLJ 7/00)

372 Schlein, Miriam. *Round and Square* (PS–2). Illus. by Linda Bronson. 1999, Mondo $15.95 (1-57255-719-2). 32pp. With a rhyming text, this colorful picture book introduces the concepts of round and square. (Rev: BL 1/1–15/00)

373 Scott, Janine. *The Shape of Things* (K–2). Illus. Series: Spyglass Books. 2003, Compass Point LB $18.60 (0-7565-0453-8). 24pp. This photo-filled concept book introduces young readers to a wide array of different shapes, including circles, boxes, and stars. (Rev: SLJ 10/03) [516]

374 Scott, Janine. *Take a Guess: A Look at Estimation* (K–2). Illus. Series: Spyglass Books. 2003, Compass Point LB $18.60 (0-7565-0446-5). 24pp. This photo-filled volume introduces the concept of estimation and making approximations. (Rev: SLJ 12/03) [519.5]

375 Swinburne, Stephen R. *Lots and Lots of Zebra Stripes: Patterns in Nature* (PS–2). Illus. 1998, Boyds Mills $15.95 (1-56397-707-9). 32pp. Using wonderful photos, this book explores repeating patterns of lines and shapes and shows how they can be found in a number of objects great and small. (Rev: BL 9/15/98; HBG 3/99; SLJ 12/98) [778.9]

376 Thong, Roseanne. *Round Is a Mooncake* (PS–1). Illus. by Grace Lin. 2000, Chronicle $13.95 (0-8118-2676-7). 40pp. An Asian American girl looks at shapes she sees in her neighborhood in this book that explores circles, squares, and rectangles. (Rev: BL 12/1/00; HBG 3/01; SLJ 8/00)

377 Wells, Robert E. *Is a Blue Whale the Biggest Thing There Is?* (PS–3). Illus. 1993, Whitman LB $13.95 (0-8075-3655-5); paper $6.95 (0-8075-3656-3). 32pp. The concept of size is explored, first by comparing an elephant to the huge blue whale and ending with our galaxy being compared to the universe. (Rev: BCCB 11/93; BL 12/15/93; SLJ 1/94)

378 Wells, Robert E. *What's Smaller Than a Pygmy Shrew?* (1–4). Illus. 1995, Whitman LB $13.95 (0-8075-8837-7); paper $6.95 (0-8075-8838-5). 32pp. The concept of smallness is explored using examples from nature. (Rev: BL 8/95; SLJ 5/95)

Counting and Number Books

379 Adler, David A. *How Tall How Short How Far Away* (K–3). Illus. by Nancy Tobin. 1999, Holiday House $15.95 (0-8234-1375-6). Methods of measurement such as length, height, and distance are introduced in this attractive concept book. (Rev: BCCB 9/99; BL 4/1/99; HB 3–4/99; HBG 10/99; SLJ 4/99) [530.8]

380 Alda, Arlene. *Arlene Alda's 1 2 3* (PS–2). Illus. 1998, Tricycle $12.95 (1-883672-71-6). 24pp. Photographs of shapes that look like numbers, such as a 3 found in the curl of a banana peel, illustrate the numbers one to ten and back again. (Rev: BL 11/1/98; HB 11–12/98; HBG 3/99; SLJ 12/98)

381 Anderson, Lena. *Tea for Ten* (PS). Trans. from Swedish by Elisabeth Kallick Dyssegaard. Illus. by author. 2000, R&S $14.00 (91-29-64557-3). This rhyming counting book features a number of delightful animals including Hedgehog, Duck, Teddy, Frog, Pig, and Elephant. (Rev: HBG 10/00; SLJ 5/00)

382 Anno, Mitsumasa. *Anno's Counting Book: An Adventure in Imagination* (PS–K). Illus. by author. 1977, HarperCollins LB $16.89 (0-690-01288-8); paper $6.95 (0-06-443123-1). 32pp. An appealing book on numbers in which the same landscapes are used throughout; houses, birds, trees, and people are added as the seasons progress.

383 Appelt, Kathi. *Bat Jamboree* (PS–2). Illus. by Melissa Sweet. 1996, Morrow $15.93 (0-688-13883-7). A delightful counting book that focuses on the annual Bat Jamboree staged by some enterprising bats. (Rev: SLJ 9/96)

384 Appelt, Kathi. *Bats on Parade* (K–3). Illus. by Melissa Sweet. 1999, Morrow LB $15.93 (0-688-15666-5). 32pp. Basic multiplication is introduced in this story about a bat parade told with rhymes and peppy illustrations. (Rev: BL 4/1/99; HBG 10/99; SLJ 6/99)

385 Appelt, Kathi. *Rain Dance* (PS–1). Illus. by Emilie Chollat. 2001, HarperCollins $9.95 (0-694-01291-2). 24pp. A number of different animals enjoy playing in the rain in this simple counting book. (Rev: BL 4/1/01; HBG 3/02; SLJ 12/01)

386 Appelt, Kathi. *Toddler Two-Step* (PS). Illus. by Ward Schumaker. 2000, HarperCollins $9.95 (0-694-01244-0). A simple counting book that uses pictures of toddlers to count to ten and back again. (Rev: HBG 10/00; SLJ 7/00)

387 Baker, Keith. *Big Fat Hen* (PS–1). Illus. 1994, Harcourt $15.00 (0-15-292869-3). 32pp. A counting book that uses the rhyme "One, two, buckle my shoe" as a basis. (Rev: BL 4/1/94; SLJ 4/94)

388 Baker, Keith. *Quack and Count* (PS–1). Illus. 1999, Harcourt $14.00 (0-15-292858-8). 24pp. This book shows how to have fun with the number seven while counting ducks in various combinations to reach that number. (Rev: BL 10/15/99; HBG 3/00; SLJ 11/99)

389 Bang, Molly. *Ten, Nine, Eight* (PS–1). Illus. by author. 1983, Greenwillow $15.89 (0-688-00907-7); Morrow paper $5.95 (0-688-10480-0). 24pp. A counting-down book (from ten to one) involving an African American child going to bed. (Rev: BL 11/15/98)

390 Barrett, Judith. *I Knew Two Who Said Moo* (PS–1). Illus. by Daniel Moreton. 2000, Simon & Schuster $16.00 (0-689-82104-2). 32pp. Numbers from one to ten are introduced on double-page spreads with witty animal-oriented illustrations that entertain as well as instruct. (Rev: BCCB 7–8/00; BL 2/1/01; HBG 10/01; SLJ 10/00)

391 Barry, Frances. *Duckie's Ducklings: A One-to-Ten Counting Book* (PS). Illus. 2005, Candlewick $7.99 (0-7636-2514-0). 32pp. As Mother Duckie searches desperately for her ten ducklings, one by one, members of her brood line up directly behind her. (Rev: BL 2/15/05)

392 Bassede, Francine. *George's Store at the Shore* (PS). Illus. 1998, Orchard paper $14.95 (0-531-

30083-8). 32pp. In this delightful counting book, George the duck and Mary the cat go to the beach. (Rev: BL 2/15/98; HBG 10/98; SLJ 4/98)

393 Beaton, Clare. *One Moose, Twenty Mice* (PS–1). Illus. 1999, Barefoot $14.95 (1-902283-37-6). 32pp. A counting book containing different animals from one to 20, but posing the question "Where's the cat?" (Rev: BCCB 7–8/99; BL 5/15/99; SLJ 6/99)

394 Bennett, David. *One Cow Moo Moo!* (PS–2). Illus. by Andy Cooke. 1990, Holt $16.95 (0-8050-1416-0). In this cumulative story about farm animals and their sounds, counting skills are presented. (Rev: SLJ 12/90)

395 Blackstone, Stella. *Cleo's Counting Book* (PS). Illus. by Caroline Mockford. 2003, Barefoot $14.99 (1-84148-207-2). Cleo the cat counts what she sees in the great outdoors. (Rev: HBG 10/03; SLJ 9/03)

396 Bowen, Betsy. *Gathering: A Northwoods Counting Book* (K–4). Illus. by author. 1999, Houghton Mifflin $16.00 (0-395-98133-6); paper $5.95 (0-395-98134-4). This counting book shows preparations taken in the North for a long, hard winter, starting in the spring with planting a garden. (Rev: HBG 3/00; SLJ 9/99)

397 Brooks, Alan. *Frogs Jump: A Counting Book* (PS–1). Illus. by Steven Kellogg. 1996, Scholastic $15.95 (0-590-45528-1). 48pp. Madcap animals introduce basic numbers through unusual activities. (Rev: BL 10/15/96; SLJ 10/96)

398 Brooks, Bruce. *NBA by the Numbers* (K–3). Illus. 1997, Scholastic $10.95 (0-590-97578-1). 32pp. This book uses basketball terms to introduce the numbers 1–10, 20, 30, 40, and 50. (Rev: BL 3/1/97)

399 Brown, Ruth. *Ten Seeds* (PS–K). Illus. 2001, Knopf $14.95 (0-375-80697-0). 24pp. Ten seeds are planted at the beginning of this book, but their numbers gradually dwindle as a variety of characters plunder the bed. (Rev: BL 5/15/01; HB 9–10/01*; HBG 3/02; SLJ 7/01)

400 Brusca, Maria C., and Tona Wilson. *Three Friends: A Counting Book/Tres Amigos: Un Cuento para Contar* (PS–2). Illus. by Maria C. Brusca. 1995, Holt $15.95 (0-8050-3707-1). 32pp. Learning to count from one to ten in Spanish and English through watching the actions of a cowboy, a cowgirl, and a horse. (Rev: BL 11/15/95; SLJ 12/95)

401 Burns, Marilyn. *How Many Feet? How Many Tails? A Book of Math Riddles* (1–2). Illus. by Lynn Adams. 1996, Scholastic paper $3.99 (0-590-67360-2). 32pp. During a walk with Grandpa, a child learns about numbers in this easy-to-read book. (Rev: BL 2/1/97)

402 Burton, Katherine. *One Gray Mouse* (PS). Illus. by Kim Fernandes. 1997, Kids Can $9.95 (1-55074-225-6). 24pp. Different numbers of animals are presented in this pleasant picture book that teaches the concepts of counting and colors. (Rev: BL 11/15/97; SLJ 12/97) [513.2]

403 Butler, John. *While You Were Sleeping* (PS). Illus. 1999, Peachtree $15.95 (1-56145-211-4). 32pp. In this simple counting book a mother describes events that occurred while her child was asleep — such as the two mice that made a nest and the three bears that played chase. (Rev: BL 12/1/99; HBG 3/00; SLJ 12/99)

404 Cabrera, Jane. *Over in the Meadow* (PS). Illus. 2000, Holiday House $16.95 (0-8234-1490-6). 32pp. Readers learn numbers while naming animals and copying their actions in this fresh new treatment of the traditional counting song. (Rev: BCCB 5/00; BL 2/1/00; HBG 10/00; SLJ 4/00) [513.2]

405 Carle, Eric. *Roosters Off to See the World* (PS–K). Illus. by author. 1991, Picture Book $16.95 (0-88708-042-1). 28pp. In this counting book originally published in 1972, a rooster gathers together a group of animals to explore the world. Addition and subtraction are also introduced.

406 Catalanotto, Peter. *Daisy 1, 2, 3* (PS–1). Illus. by author. 2003, Simon & Schuster $15.95 (0-689-85457-9). Mrs. Tuttle, who has 20 Dalmatians — all called Daisy — in her obedience class, comes up with an ingenious way to tell them apart. (Rev: BL 11/1/03; HBG 4/04; SLJ 12/03)

407 Cato, Sheila. *Addition* (1–4). Illus. by Sami Sweeten. Series: A Question of Math Book. 1999, Carolrhoda LB $18.95 (1-57505-320-9). 32pp. Using cartoon characters and one addition problem per double-page spread, this book demonstrates the basic processes of addition. Also use *Subtraction* and *Counting and Numbers* (both 1999). (Rev: HBG 3/00; SLJ 11/99)

408 Cato, Sheila. *Division* (1–4). Illus. by Sami Sweeten. Series: A Question of Math Book. 1999, Carolrhoda LB $18.95 (1-57505-319-5). 32pp. Using a series of problems followed by clear answers and explanations, the principles of division are covered. Also use *Multiplication* (1999). (Rev: HBG 3/00; SLJ 11/99)

409 Cave, Kathryn. *One Child, One Seed: A South African Counting Book* (K–2). Photos by Gisele Wulfson. 2003, Holt $16.95 (0-8050-7204-7). 32pp. Cave interweaves basic counting skills with information about life in rural Natal in this innovative book that features beautiful photographs. (Rev: BL 5/1/03; HBG 10/03; SLJ 8/03) [513.2]

410 Chaconas, Dori. *One Little Mouse* (PS–K). Illus. by LeUyen Pham. 2002, Viking $15.99 (0-670-88947-4). 32pp. A little mouse searching for a new house visits other animals' homes before deciding that his own is best of all, in a rhyming text that teaches children to count up to ten and back down again. (Rev: BL 9/1/02; HBG 10/02; SLJ 8/02)

411 Chandra, Deborah. *Miss Mabel's Table* (PS–2). Illus. by Max Grover. 1994, Harcourt $14.95 (0-15-276712-6). 32pp. A counting book about Miss Mabel, her restaurant, and the food she serves. (Rev: BCCB 4/94; BL 3/15/94; SLJ 6/94)

412 Charles, Faustin. *A Caribbean Counting Book* (K–3). Illus. by Roberta Arenson. 1996, Houghton Mifflin $13.95 (0-395-77944-8). 32pp. Using Caribbean settings, this colorful counting book uses 12 rhymes from nine islands. (Rev: BCCB 5/96; BL 4/15/96; SLJ 6/96)

413 Cheng, Andrea. *Grandfather Counts* (PS–3). Illus. by Ange Zhang. 2000, Lee & Low $15.95 (1-58430-010-8). 32pp. In this unusual counting book, Helen, a little Chinese-American girl, and her grandfather count the cars on a passing train in both English and Chinese. (Rev: BL 12/15/00; HBG 3/01; SLJ 11/00)

414 Chorao, Kay. *Number One Number Fun* (PS–1). Illus. 1995, Holiday House LB $15.95 (0-8234-1142-7). 32pp. Simple arithmetic is highlighted through a series of clever rhymes involving addition and subtraction. (Rev: BCCB 2/95; BL 2/15/95; SLJ 3/95)

415 Christelow, Eileen, reteller. *Five Little Monkeys Jumping on the Bed* (PS–K). Illus. by Eileen Christelow. 1989, Ticknor $15.00 (0-89919-769-8); paper $5.95 (0-395-55701-1). An exuberant rendition of the favorite nursery rhyme. (Rev: BL 6/1/89)

416 Christelow, Eileen. *Five Little Monkeys Sitting in a Tree* (PS–K). Illus. 1991, Houghton Mifflin $15.00 (0-395-54434-3). 32pp. The numbers one through five are taught through the antics of five little monkeys. A sequel is: *Don't Wake Up Mama!* (1992). (Rev: BL 5/15/91; SLJ 8/91)

417 Clark, Emma Chichester. *Mimi's Book of Counting* (PS). Illus. by author. Series: A Mimi Book. 2003, Charlesbridge $9.95 (1-57091-573-3). In this appealing counting book, Mimi the monkey and her visiting grandmother find everyday household items that they count from one to ten. (Rev: HBG 4/04; SLJ 11/03)

418 Cleveland, David. *The April Rabbits* (PS–1). Illus. by Nurit Karlin. 1986, Scholastic paper $4.99 (0-590-42369-X). 32pp. The days of the month and a group of rabbits are used in this counting book. Reissue of a 1978 edition.

419 Coats, Lucy. *Down in the Daisies: A Baby Animal Counting Book* (PS–1). Illus. by Emily Bolam. 2003, Orion $16.95 (1-85881-513-4). This beautifully illustrated counting book spotlights baby animals and their mothers in all kinds of weather. (Rev: SLJ 10/03)

420 Coleman, Michael. *One, Two, Three, Oops!* (PS–K). Illus. by Gwyneth Williamson. 1999, Little Tiger $14.95 (1-888444-45-2). 32pp. When Mr. Rabbit begins to count his children, he has to work out which ones have been counted and which haven't. (Rev: BL 1/1–15/99; HBG 10/99; SLJ 3/99)

421 Cotten, Cynthia. *At the Edge of the Woods: A Counting Book* (PS–2). Illus. by Reg Cartwright. 2002, Holt $16.95 (0-8050-6354-4). 32pp. Gentle verse and bright, primitive paintings are used in this incremental tale of a forest day, in which one chipmunk, two young deer, and then more and more animals appear. (Rev: BL 12/1/02; HBG 3/03; SLJ 6/03)

422 Crews, Donald. *Ten Black Dots* (PS–K). Illus. by author. 1986, Greenwillow $15.89 (0-688-06068-4). 32pp. Dots form an integral part of this counting book, originally published in 1968, such as "five dots make buttons on a coat." (Rev: BL 3/1/86; SLJ 5/86)

423 Crowther, Robert. *My Pop-Up Surprise 123* (PS–K). Illus. by author. 1997, Orchard $16.95 (0-

531-30039-0). A simple counting book using easily manipulated flaps and pull tabs. (Rev: SLJ 8/97)

424 Crum, Shutta. *The Bravest of the Brave* (PS–1). Illus. by Tim Bowers. 2005, Knopf LB $17.99 (0-375-92637-2). A young skunk trying to be brave in the woods at night is frightened in turn by ghosts (owls), witches (porcupines), and so forth in this counting book with a happy ending. (Rev: SLJ 4/05)

425 Cuyler, Margery. *100th Day Worries* (K–2). Illus. by Arthur Howard. 2000, Simon & Schuster $16.00 (0-689-82979-5). 32pp. In this counting book, first-grader Jessica is asked to bring 100 objects to celebrate the 100th day of school. (Rev: BCCB 2/00; BL 11/1/99; HBG 10/00; SLJ 1/00)

426 Dahl, Michael. *Eggs and Legs: Counting by Twos* (PS–2). Illus. by Todd Ouren. Series: Know Your Numbers. 2005, Picture Window LB $22.60 (1-4048-0945-7). 24pp. Counting by twos to 20 is the focus of a lively story with bright cartoons and numerals hidden within the text and illustrations. Also use *Pie for Piglets: Counting by Twos* (2005). (Rev: SLJ 6/05)

427 Dahl, Michael. *One Big Building: A Counting Book About Construction* (PS–K). Illus. by Todd Ouren. Series: Know Your Numbers. 2004, Picture Window LB $22.60 (1-4048-0580-X). 24pp. "Fun Facts" about construction are included along with numbers from one to 12 — "one big plan" and "twelve stories tall." Also use *From the Garden: A Counting Book About Growing Food* (2004). (Rev: BL 4/1/04; SLJ 6/04) [513.2]

428 Dahl, Michael. *Pie for Piglets: Counting by Twos* (PS–K). Illus. Series: Know Your Numbers. 2005, Picture Window LB $22.60 (1-4048-0943-0). 24pp. An entertaining introduction to counting by two, with numbers hidden within the text and illustrations. Other titles in this series include *Hands Down: Counting by Fives* and *Lots of Ladybugs! Counting by Fives* (2005). (Rev: SLJ 6/05)

429 Deegan, Kim. *My First Book of Numbers* (PS). Illus. 2002, Bloomsbury $7.95 (1-58234-755-7). 24pp. A sparkling introduction to counting and numbers. (Rev: BL 8/02; SLJ 11/02) [513.2]

430 Demarest, Chris L. *Smokejumpers One to Ten* (PS–1). Illus. 2002, Simon & Schuster $17.00 (0-689-84120-5). 32pp. A counting book featuring courageous and hardworking parachuting fire fighters. (Rev: BCCB 7–8/02; BL 7/02; HBG 10/02; SLJ 7/02) [634.9]

431 De Regniers, Beatrice S. *So Many Cats!* (PS–1). Illus. by Ellen Weiss. 1985, Houghton Mifflin paper $6.95 (0-89919-700-0). 32pp. One by one, new cats arrive at the narrator's house, until there are 12. (Rev: BL 1/1/86; HB 11–12/85; SLJ 1/86)

432 deRubertis, Barbara. *A Collection for Kate* (1–2). Illus. by Gioia Fiammenghi. Series: Math Matters. 1999, Kane paper $4.95 (1-57565-089-4). 32pp. In this easy reader, Kate adds up her classmates' collections for a "collection week" at school and discovers that, when she combines her own small collections, she isn't far behind them after all. (Rev: BL 12/1/99; SLJ 1/00)

433 deRubertis, Barbara. *Count on Pablo* (1–2). Illus. by Rebecca Thornburgh. Series: Math Matters. 1999, Kane paper $4.95 (1-57565-090-8). 32pp. In this easy reader, a boy helps his grandmother gather, count, group, and package vegetables for market. (Rev: BL 12/1/99; SLJ 1/00)

434 deRubertis, Barbara. *Lulu's Lemonade* (1–3). Illus. by Paige Billin-Frye. Series: Math Matters. 2000, Kane paper $4.95 (1-57565-093-2). 32pp. In this easy-reader, Mattie and Martin learn measurements like teaspoons, cups, pints, etc., as they prepare a gallon of lemonade. (Rev: SLJ 6/00)

435 Dodd, Lynley. *Sniff-Snuff-Snap!* (K–2). Illus. by author. Series: Gold Star First Reader. 2000, Gareth Stevens LB $15.95 (0-8368-2677-9). 31pp. A beginning reader about a bossy warthog that is also a counting book. (Rev: SLJ 3/01)

436 Duke, Kate. *Twenty Is Too Many* (PS–2). Illus. 2000, Dutton $15.99 (0-525-42026-6). 48pp. The concept of subtraction is painlessly introduced using a shipload of 20 guinea pigs. (Rev: BL 7/00; HBG 3/01; SLJ 8/00)

437 Edwards, Pamela Duncan. *Roar! A Noisy Counting Book* (PS–2). Illus. by Henry Cole. 2000, HarperCollins LB $15.89 (0-06-028385-8). 32pp. A boisterous counting book involving animals, a jungle habitat, and lots of lions roaring. (Rev: BL 8/00; HBG 10/00; SLJ 6/00)

438 Ehlert, Lois. *Fish Eyes: A Book You Can Count On* (PS–K). Illus. 1990, Harcourt $14.95 (0-15-228050-2). 32pp. Compelling color and design introduce this counting book. (Rev: BL 3/1/90*; SLJ 5/90)

439 Emberley, Rebecca. *My Numbers / Mis Numeros* (PS). 2000, Little, Brown $5.95 (0-316-23350-1). 20pp. This counting board book introduces the numbers in both English and Spanish. (Rev: BCCB 12/00*; HBG 3/01; SLJ 9/00)

440 Ernst, Lisa Campbell. *Up to Ten and Down Again* (PS–K). Illus. by author. 1995, Morrow paper $4.95 (0-688-14391-1). 32pp. Beginning with "one duck is swimming," this simple counting book teaches numbers and tells a story. (Rev: BCCB 3/86; BL 3/1/86; SLJ 8/86)

441 Evans, Lezlie. *Can You Count Ten Toes? Count to 10 in 10 Different Languages* (PS–3). Illus. by Denis Roche. 1999, Houghton Mifflin $15.00 (0-395-90499-4). 32pp. Using double-page spreads, children from several countries count different objects from one to ten in their native language. (Rev: BL 3/15/99; HBG 10/99; SLJ 6/99) [513.2]

442 Falconer, Ian. *Olivia Counts* (PS). Illus. 2002, Simon & Schuster $6.99 (0-689-85087-5). 12pp. A simple board book featuring Olivia the pig with one beach ball, two bows, and so forth up to ten. (Rev: BCCB 6/02; BL 7/02; HBG 10/02; SLJ 6/02)

443 Falwell, Cathryn. *Feast for 10* (PS–K). Illus. 1993, Houghton Mifflin $15.00 (0-395-62037-6). 32pp. Using the common experience of shopping and preparing dinner, this book, which features an African American family, teaches youngsters the numbers from one to ten. (Rev: BCCB 6/93; BL 6/1–15/93; SLJ 6/93)

444 Falwell, Cathryn. *Turtle Splash! Countdown at the Pond* (PS–K). Illus. 2001, Greenwillow LB $15.89 (0-06-029463-9). 32pp. A rhythmic countdown to bedtime as one turtle after another — for a total of ten — splashes into a lake as evening comes closer and animals arrive at the water's edge. (Rev: BL 8/01; HBG 3/02; SLJ 9/01*)

445 Faulkner, Keith. *POP! Went Another Balloon! A Magical Counting Storybook* (PS–1). Illus. by Rory Tyger. 2003, Dutton $10.99 (0-525-47122-7). Toby the turtle is dismayed as, one by one, birds pop the ten balloons he's taking to his friend Tina. (Rev: HBG 10/03; SLJ 10/03)

446 Fearrington, Ann. *Who Sees the Lighthouse?* (K–3). Illus. by Giles Laroche. 2002, Penguin Putnam $15.99 (0-399-23703-8). 32pp. Lighthouses star in this counting book full of intricate, highly detailed illustrations. (Rev: BL 11/15/02; HBG 3/03; SLJ 10/02)

447 Flather, Lisa. *Ten Silly Dogs: A Countdown Story* (PS–K). Illus. 1999, Orchard $15.95 (0-531-30192-3). 32pp. Counting down from ten to one, this tale presents a number of dogs in various shapes and colors that one by one disappear from the action. (Rev: BL 9/15/99; HBG 3/00; SLJ 11/99)

448 Fleming, Denise. *Count!* (PS–K). Illus. by author. 1992, Holt $16.95 (0-8050-1595-7). Brightly colored animals and birds are used to introduce basic numbers. (Rev: SLJ 3/92)

449 Fox, Christyan, and Diane Fox. *Count to Ten, PiggyWiggy!* (PS–K). Illus. 2001, Handprint $5.95 (1-929766-18-1). 20pp. A counting book in which PiggyWiggy adds different numbers of ingredients to a mixing bowl to make a wonderful layer cake. (Rev: BL 4/1/01; SLJ 8/01)

450 French, Vivian. *One Ballerina Two* (PS–K). Illus. by Jan Ormerod. 1991, Lothrop $13.95 (0-688-10333-2). 32pp. The focus is on ballet in this simple counting book. (Rev: BCCB 12/91; BL 12/1/91; SLJ 12/91)

451 Freymann, Saxton, and Joost Elffers. *One Lonely Sea Horse* (PS–2). Illus. 2000, Scholastic $15.99 (0-439-11014-9). 32pp. Using various fruits and vegetables, photographs create a sea world of underwater creatures in this innovative counting book. (Rev: BCCB 7–8/00; BL 5/1/00; HBG 3/01; SLJ 7/00)

452 Friedman, Aileen. *The King's Commissioners* (K–2). Illus. by Susan Guevara. 1995, Scholastic $14.95 (0-590-48989-5). 40pp. In this sophisticated counting book, a king decides to take an inventory of his employees. (Rev: BCCB 2/95; BL 2/15/95; SLJ 3/95)

453 Fuller, Jill. *Springtime Addition* (PS–K). Series: Rookie Read-About Math. 2004, Children's Pr. LB $19.50 (0-516-24422-1). 31pp. A simple, colorful, and interesting introduction to addition featuring outdoor attractions. Also use *Toy Box Subtraction* and *A Garden Full of Sizes* (both 2004). (Rev: SLJ 3/05) [513.2]

454 Gardiner, Lindsey. *Good Night, Poppy and Max: A Bedtime Counting Book* (PS). Illus. by author. 2002, Little, Brown $6.95 (0-316-60122-5).

A board book in which Poppy and Max follow their bedtime routine, with one glass of milk, two cookies, and so on up to ten. (Rev: SLJ 3/03)

455 Geisert, Arthur. *Pigs from 1 to 10* (PS–2). Illus. by author. 1991, Houghton Mifflin $16.00 (0-395-58519-8). 32pp. In a series of hidden-picture illustrations, pigs search for a lost place and uncover the numbers zero to ten. (Rev: BL 11/1/92; HB 9–10/92*)

456 Giganti, Paul. *Each Orange Had Eight Slices* (PS–3). Illus. by Donald Crews. 1992, Greenwillow $15.89 (0-688-10429-0). This well-designed book challenges young readers to think analytically about what it portrays. (Rev: BCCB 4/92; BL 3/15/92; SLJ 3/92) [513.5]

457 Giganti, Paul. *How Many Snails?* (PS–K). Illus. by Donald Crews. 1988, Greenwillow $15.93 (0-688-06370-5). 24pp. A counting book that focuses on visual discrimination as well as numbers. (Rev: BL 8/88; SLJ 3/89)

458 Girnis, Meg. *1, 2, 3 for You and Me* (PS–1). Photos by Shirley Leamon Green. 2001, Whitman LB $14.95 (0-8075-6107-X). Smiling children with Down's syndrome are shown holding toys and everyday objects in this simple counting book. (Rev: HBG 10/01; SLJ 7/01)

459 Glass, Julie. *Counting Sheep* (1). Illus. by Mike Wohnoutka. Series: Step into Reading + Math. 2000, Random LB $11.99 (0-375-90619-3); paper $3.99 (0-375-80619-9). 32pp. In this easy-to-read counting book, a young boy starts counting sheep to get to sleep. The sheep are soon joined by kangaroos, monkeys, and bees. (Rev: BL 12/1/00; HBG 10/01)

460 Gorbachev, Valeri. *One Rainy Day* (PS–2). Illus. 2002, Penguin Putnam $15.99 (0-399-23628-7). 40pp. Pig escapes the rain under a tree and is joined by ten other animals also trying to stay dry. (Rev: BL 5/15/02; HBG 10/02; SLJ 8/02)

461 Grossman, Virginia. *Ten Little Rabbits* (PS–1). Illus. by Sylvia Long. 1991, Chronicle $13.95 (0-87701-552-X). 32pp. This counting book of rabbits dressed as Indians introduces the cultures of various American tribes. (Rev: BL 4/1/91; SLJ 6/91)

462 Gunzi, Christiane. *My Very First Look at Numbers* (PS–K). Illus. by Steve Gorton. Series: My Very First Look. 2001, Two-Can $8.95 (1-58728-237-2); paper $5.95 (1-58728-277-1). 24pp. Photographs of everyday objects are used to teach preschoolers about numbers. (Rev: BL 2/15/02; HBG 10/02; SLJ 2/02) [513.2]

463 Gustafson, Scott. *Scott Gustafson's Animal Orchestra: A Counting Book* (K–3). Illus. 1995, Greenwich Workshop $14.95 (0-86713-030-X). 32pp. An assembly of animals in tuxedo splendor. (Rev: BL 1/15/89; SLJ 2/89)

464 Guy, Ginger F. *¡Fiesta!* (PS–2). Illus. by René King Moreno. 1996, Greenwillow $15.00 (0-688-14331-8). Numbers are introduced in English and Spanish in this book about collecting articles to celebrate a Mexican fiesta. (Rev: SLJ 9/96)

465 Hague, Kathleen. *Ten Little Bears* (PS–K). Illus. by Michael Hague. 1999, Morrow LB $15.93 (0-688-16732-2). 24pp. In this counting book, ten little bears go out to play, but one by one they become separated. (Rev: BL 5/15/99; HBG 10/99)

466 Halls, Kelly M. *I Bought a Baby Chicken* (PS–1). Illus. by Karen Stormer Brooks. 2000, Boyds Mills $14.95 (1-56397-800-8). 32pp. In this comical counting book, a young girl and her family go out to buy some baby chickens. (Rev: BL 4/1/00; HBG 10/00; SLJ 7/00)

467 Harris, Trudy. *100 Days of School* (PS–K). Illus. by Beth Griffis Johnson. 1999, Millbrook LB $21.90 (0-7613-1271-4). 32pp. Various combinations of familiar objects are used to reach the number 100 in this innovative counting book. (Rev: BL 11/15/99; HBG 3/00; SLJ 11/99)

468 Harshman, Marc. *Only One* (PS–3). Illus. by Barbara Garrison. 1993, Dutton $15.99 (0-525-65116-0). 32pp. This counting book shows that a collective noun consists of several parts, for example, nine players make a baseball team. (Rev: BL 5/15/93)

469 Helakoski, Leslie. *The Smushy Bus* (K–2). Illus. by Sal Murdocca. 2002, Millbrook LB $22.90 (0-7613-1398-2). 32pp. Mr. Mathers, the clever bus driver, manages to fit 76 kids into a bus with four seats in this adventure combined with an early introduction to mathematical concepts. (Rev: BL 10/15/02; HBG 3/03; SLJ 11/02)

470 Helman, Andrea. *1, 2, 3 Moose: A Pacific Northwest Counting Book* (PS–2). Illus. by Art Wolfe. 1996, Sasquatch $15.95 (1-57061-078-9). 32pp. A one-to-20 counting book that employs the flora and fauna of the Pacific Northwest. (Rev: BL 11/1/96; SLJ 1/97) [428.1]

471 Hoban, Tana. *Count and See* (PS–K). Illus. 1972, Macmillan LB $17.00 (0-02-744800-2). 40pp. Beginning with numbers one to 15, then going to 100; clear photographs of familiar objects are easily recognized and fun to count.

472 Hoban, Tana. *Let's Count* (PS–1). Illus. 1999, Greenwillow $16.00 (0-688-16008-5). 40pp. Amazing photos are used in this counting book to highlight objects from one to 15, then by tens to 50, and finally to 100. (Rev: BL 9/15/99; HBG 3/00; SLJ 9/99) [513.2]

473 Hoban, Tana. *1, 2, 3* (PS). Illus. by author. 1985, Greenwillow paper $4.95 (0-688-02579-X). 12pp. Starting with one birthday cake, photos present objects in a baby's world. (Rev: BCCB 3/85; BL 3/15/85; SLJ 9/85)

474 Holland, Cheri. *Maccabee Jamboree: A Hanukkah Countdown* (PS). Illus. by Rosalyn Schanzer. 1998, Kar-Ben paper $4.95 (1-58013-019-4). Eight Maccabees play different Hanukkah games as one by one they disappear in this counting book. (Rev: SLJ 10/98)

475 Hughes, Shirley. *Alfie's 1-2-3* (PS). Illus. 2000, Lothrop $15.95 (0-688-17705-0). 32pp. Playful activities of a preschooler's day form the framework of this simple counting book. (Rev: BL 4/15/00; HBG 10/00; SLJ 5/00)

476 Hulme, Joy N. *Sea Squares* (K–3). Illus. by Carol Schwartz. 1993, Hyperion paper $5.95 (1-56282-520-8). 32pp. Children can visualize multi-

plication in this picture book with an underwater theme. (Rev: BL 12/1/91; SLJ 1/92) [513.5]

477 Hutchins, Pat. *One Hunter* (PS–2). Illus. by author. 1982, Morrow paper $4.95 (0-688-06522-8). 24pp. A counting book with a hunter and hidden African animals.

478 Hutchins, Pat. *Ten Red Apples* (PS–2). Illus. 2000, Greenwillow $23.95 (0-688-16797-7). 32pp. A charming counting book about a farmer and his apple crop. (Rev: BL 5/1/00; HBG 10/00; SLJ 5/00)

479 Inkpen, Mick. *Kipper's Book of Numbers* (PS). Illus. by author. 1999, Harcourt $4.95 (0-15-202286-4). A simple concept book in which youngsters are taught to count frogs, snails, and hedgehogs. (Rev: SLJ 10/99)

480 Jennings, Linda. *Nine Naughty Kittens* (PS–1). Illus. by Caroline Jayne Church. 1999, Little Tiger $14.95 (1-888444-62-2). A flap book that is also a counting book about kittens. (Rev: BCCB 1/00; HBG 3/00; SLJ 2/00)

481 Jocelyn, Marthe. *One Some Many* (PS–K). Illus. by Tom Slaughter. 2004, Tundra $11.95 (0-88776-675-7). A counting book in rhyme that creatively introduces the differences between "many," "few," "some," "none," and "more." (Rev: SLJ 6/04)

482 Jonas, Ann. *Splash!* (PS–1). Illus. 1995, Greenwillow $14.89 (0-688-11052-5). 24pp. Principles of addition and subtraction are shown by counting the animal life in and around a backyard pond. (Rev: BCCB 6/95; BL 6/1–15/95; HB 9–10/95; SLJ 6/95)

483 Kellogg, Steven. *Give the Dog a Bone* (K–3). Illus. 2000, North-South LB $15.88 (1-58717-002-7). 40pp. A riotous counting book that involves a grand total of 250 dogs (and one chicken). (Rev: BL 12/1/00; HBG 3/01; SLJ 11/00)

484 Kitamura, Satoshi. *When Sheep Cannot Sleep: The Counting Book* (PS–1). Illus. by author. 1986, Farrar paper $5.95 (0-374-48359-0). 32pp. Woolly the sheep can't sleep so he takes a walk — chasing one butterfly, watching two ladybugs, and so on. (Rev: BL 10/1/86; HB 11–12/86; SLJ 12/86)

485 Koller, Jackie F. *One Monkey Too Many* (PS–2). Illus. by Lynn Munsinger. 1999, Harcourt $16.00 (0-15-200006-2). 32pp. A raucous counting book — from one to six — about monkeys who cram themselves into places they shouldn't. (Rev: BCCB 5/99; BL 4/15/99; HB 3–4/99; HBG 10/99; SLJ 5/99)

486 Kusugak, Michael A. *My Arctic 1, 2, 3* (K–3). Illus. by Vladyana Krykorka. 1996, Annick $16.95 (1-55037-505-9); paper $6.95 (1-55037-504-0). Using Arctic animals as a focus, this counting book presents the numbers one through ten, 20, 100, and a million in both English and the Inuit language. (Rev: SLJ 5/97)

487 Lee, Huy Voun. *1, 2, 3, Go!* (PS–1). Illus. 2001, Holt $16.00 (0-8050-6205-X). 32pp. This introduction to Chinese numbers gives the Chinese characters for one to ten and for the words used to illustrate each number. (Rev: BL 2/1/01; HBG 10/01) [495.1]

488 Leedy, Loreen. *Fraction Action* (K–2). Illus. 1994, Holiday House LB $16.95 (0-8234-1109-5). 32pp. How to divide various objects and the meaning of fractions are explored in this simple, colorful arithmetic book. (Rev: BCCB 3/94; BL 3/15/94) [513.2]

489 Leedy, Loreen. *Subtraction Action* (1–3). Illus. 2000, Holiday House $16.95 (0-8234-1454-X). 32pp. In seven short chapters, Miss Prime and her class learn how to do subtraction. (Rev: BL 9/15/00; HBG 3/01; SLJ 9/00)

490 Le Sieg, Theo. *Wacky Wednesday* (PS–1). Illus. by George Booth. 1974, Random $11.99 (0-394-92912-8). 48pp. In this counting book, every page has a number of things out of place.

491 Lessac, Frane. *Island Counting 123* (PS–K). Illus. 2005, Candlewick $12.99 (0-7636-1960-4). 24pp. Set in the Caribbean, this counting book features warm island scenes. (Rev: BL 5/15/05)

492 Lesser, Carolyn. *Spots: Counting Creatures from Sky to Sea* (PS–1). Illus. by Laura Regan. 1999, Harcourt $16.00 (0-15-200666-4). 32pp. Spotted creatures such as jaguars, butterflies, and squids are used to introduce numbers from one to ten. (Rev: BCCB 5/99; BL 3/15/99; HBG 10/99; SLJ 4/99) [513.2]

493 Leuck, Laura. *One Witch* (PS). Illus. by S. D. Schindler. 2003, Walker LB $16.85 (0-8027-8861-0). A witch collects ingredients for a holiday stew from groups of friends in this Stone Soup story that allows readers to count up and down. (Rev: BL 9/1/03*; HBG 4/04; SLJ 8/03)

494 Lionel. *Peekaboo Babies* (PS–K). Illus. 1997, Orchard $12.95 (0-531-30016-1). 12pp. A counting book that uses tabs and flaps to find baby animals. (Rev: BL 12/15/97)

495 Lodge, Bernard. *How Scary!* (PS–K). Illus. 2001, Houghton Mifflin $15.00 (0-618-11547-1). 32pp. One growling giant, two dreadful dragons, and so on up to ten rattling robots all add up to a satisfying Halloween counting book. (Rev: BL 9/1/01; HBG 3/02; SLJ 9/01)

496 Long, Lynette. *Dealing with Addition* (1–3). 1998, Charlesbridge LB $15.95 (0-88106-269-3); paper $6.95 (0-88106-270-7). Playing cards are used to teach addition in this entertaining book. (Rev: HBG 10/98; SLJ 9/98)

497 Maccarone, Grace. *Monster Math Picnic* (1). Illus. by Margaret A. Hartelius. Series: Hello Math Reader. 1998, Scholastic paper $3.50 (0-590-37127-4). 24pp. Using ten monsters as subjects, this simple math book explores the various combinations of numbers that add up to ten. (Rev: BL 5/1/98; SLJ 7/98)

498 Maccarone, Grace. *Monster Money* (PS–1). Illus. by Margaret A. Hartelius. Series: Hello Reader! 1998, Scholastic paper $3.50 (0-590-12007-7). In this math concept book, several monsters learn how to count money when they go to a pet store to a buy a pet. (Rev: SLJ 2/99)

499 McCourt, Lisa. *The Rain Forest Counts!* (PS–1). Illus. by Cheryl Nathan. 1997, Troll $15.95 (0-8167-4388-6). 32pp. This rhyming counting book features the animals and plants of the rain forest. (Rev: BL 12/15/97; HBG 3/98; SLJ 11/97)

500 MacDonald, Elizabeth. *Mike's Kite* (PS–K). Illus. by Robert Kendall. 1993, Harcourt paper $11.40 (0-15-300320-0). 32pp. In this counting book, Mike and a number of bystanders get carried away on the tail of a kite. (Rev: BL 7/90; SLJ 9/90)

501 MacDonald, Suse. *Look Whooo's Counting* (PS–1). Illus. 2000, Scholastic $14.95 (0-590-68320-9). 32pp. While flying through the air and looking down on different groups of animals, little Owl learns to count from one to ten. (Rev: BL 10/15/00; HBG 3/01; SLJ 12/00)

502 McFarland, Lyn Rossiter. *Mouse Went Out to Get a Snack* (PS–1). Illus. by Jim McFarland. 2005, Farrar $16.00 (0-374-37672-7). One piece of cheese, two plump plums — these are just the first of the luxury items the mouse hopes to get back to his hole. (Rev: LMC 8-9/05*; SLJ 3/05)

503 McGrath, Barbara Barbieri. *The Baseball Counting Book* (PS–1). Illus. by Brian Shaw. 1999, Charlesbridge $15.95 (0-88106-332-0); paper $6.95 (0-88106-333-9). 32pp. Two Little League teams compete while the reader learns numbers from zero to 20. (Rev: BL 2/15/99; HBG 10/99; SLJ 3/99) [513.2]

504 McGrath, Barbara Barbieri. *The Cheerios Counting Book* (PS). Illus. by Rob Bolster and Frank Mazzola. 1998, Scholastic $10.95 (0-590-00321-6). 32pp. Using round cereal bits as objects to count, this book explains the numbers one to ten and then groups of ten up to 100. (Rev: BL 10/1/98; HBG 3/99; SLJ 9/98)

505 McMillan, Bruce. *Eating Fractions* (PS–2). Illus. 1991, Scholastic $15.95 (0-590-43770-4). 32pp. Challenging fractions at the beginning level. (Rev: BCCB 9/91; BL 8/91; SLJ 9/91*) [513.2]

506 McMillan, Bruce. *Jelly Beans for Sale* (PS–2). Illus. 1996, Scholastic $15.95 (0-590-86584-6). 32pp. Counting and basic math concepts are illustrated in this book about selling candies. (Rev: BCCB 10/96; BL 9/1/96; SLJ 10/96) [332.4]

507 McMillan, Bruce. *One, Two, One Pair!* (PS). Illus. 1996, Scholastic paper $4.95 (0-590-46082-X). 32pp. The concept of pairs is explored with sharp color images. (Rev: BCCB 2/91; BL 1/15/91; SLJ 2/91) [515.5]

508 Mannis, Celeste Davidson. *One Leaf Rides the Wind: Counting in a Japanese Garden* (PS–2). Illus. by Susan Kathleen Hartung. 2002, Viking $15.99 (0-670-03525-4). A Japanese girl counts the plants and objects in a traditional garden in this elegant book that also introduces haiku and the tea ceremony. (Rev: HBG 3/03; SLJ 10/02)

509 Marzollo, Jean. *Ten Cats Have Hats: A Counting Book* (PS–K). Illus. by David McPhail. 1994, Scholastic $6.95 (0-590-20656-7). A counting book that uses intriguing pictures containing unusual details to present numbers one to ten. (Rev: SLJ 11/94)

510 Melmed, Laura Krauss. *This First Thanksgiving Day: A Counting Story* (K–3). Illus. by Mark Buehner. 2001, HarperCollins LB $15.89 (0-688-14555-8). 32pp. Pilgrim and Indian children playfully prepare for the Thanksgiving feast in this rhyming counting book. (Rev: BL 9/1/01; HBG 3/02; SLJ 9/01)

511 Melville, Kirsty. *Splash! A Penguin Counting Book* (PS–1). Illus. by Jonathan Chester. 2001, Tricycle paper $5.95 (1-58246-042-6). 32pp. A slight story teaches counting from one to ten using charming penguins. (Rev: BL 1/1–15/01)

512 Merriam, Eve. *Ten Rosy Roses* (PS–1). Illus. by Julia Gorton. 1999, HarperCollins LB $14.89 (0-06-027888-9). 32pp. In this counting rhyme from ten down to one, children pick roses to make a bouquet for their teacher. (Rev: BCCB 4/99; BL 6/1–15/99; HBG 10/99; SLJ 6/99)

513 Michelson, Richard. *Ten Times Better* (PS–1). Illus. by Leonard Baskin. 2000, Marshall Cavendish $17.95 (0-7614-5070-X). 40pp. In this counting book, various animals brag about the number of appendages they have; for example, the squid is proud of his ten tentacles. (Rev: BCCB 1/01; BL 10/1/00; HBG 3/01; SLJ 10/00)

514 Milich, Zoran. *City 123* (PS–K). Illus. 2005, Kids Can $15.95 (1-55337-540-8). 32pp. City scenes — two yellow cabs, seven tall buildings — show numbers from one to ten. (Rev: BL 5/15/05; SLJ 5/05) [513.2]

515 Miller, Jane. *Farm Counting Book* (PS–1). Illus. by author. 1992, Simon & Schuster LB $5.95 (0-671-66552-9). 24pp. A counting book using photographs of farm animals.

516 Miller, Virginia. *Ten Red Apples: A Bartholomew Bear Counting Book* (PS–2). Illus. 2002, Candlewick $13.99 (0-7636-1901-9). 32pp. Bartholomew counts ten apples and ends up with apple pie in this colorful counting book. (Rev: BL 9/15/02; SLJ 11/02) [513.5]

517 Min, Laura. *Mrs. Sato's Hens* (1–2). Illus. by Benrei Huang. 1994, Scott Foresman $2.95 (0-673-36193-4). 8pp. In an easy-to-read counting book, every morning Mrs. Sato counts the eggs that her hens are laying. (Rev: BL 1/1/95)

518 Miranda, Anne. *Monster Math* (K–2). Illus. by Polly Powell. 1999, Harcourt $16.00 (0-15-201835-2). Introducing numbers that range from one to 50, this counting book tells of groups of monsters attending and leaving a birthday party. (Rev: HBG 3/00; SLJ 10/99)

519 Miranda, Anne. *Vroom, Chugga, Vroom-Vroom* (PS–1). Illus. by David Murphy. 1998, Turtle $15.95 (1-890515-07-8). 30pp. A number book in which race cars numbered one to 20 battle it out on the action-filled racetrack. (Rev: BL 5/1/98; HBG 10/98; SLJ 7/98)

520 Modesitt, Jeanne. *One, Two, Three Valentine's Day* (PS–1). Illus. by Robin Spowart. 2002, Boyds Mills $15.95 (1-56397-868-7). 32pp. A counting book in which Mr. Mouse takes valentine gifts to his friends, to one frog, two pigs, and so forth up to his ten little sons. (Rev: BL 1/1–15/03; HBG 3/03; SLJ 1/03)

521 Moore, Elaine. *Roly-Poly Puppies: A Counting Book* (PS–K). Illus. by Jacqueline Rogers. 1996, Scholastic $6.95 (0-590-46665-8). 32pp. The numbers one to ten are introduced through the antics of ten roly-poly puppies. (Rev: BL 9/15/96; SLJ 12/96)

522 Mora, Pat. *Uno, Dos, Tres: One, Two, Three* (PS–2). Illus. by Barbara Lavallee. 1996, Clarion $15.00 (0-395-67294-5). 43pp. The numbers one to ten are introduced in English and Spanish. (Rev: BL 6/1–15/96; HB 5–6/96; SLJ 4/96)

523 Morales, Yuyi. *Just a Minute: A Trickster Tale and Counting Book* (PS–2). Illus. by author. 2003, Chronicle $15.95 (0-8118-3758-0). This satisfying book combines counting — in both English and Spanish — and Spanish culture with Grandma's success in sending death away for another year. (Rev: BL 12/1/03*; HBG 4/04; SLJ 12/03) [398.2]

524 Mullins, Patricia. *One Horse Waiting for Me* (PS–1). Illus. 1998, Simon & Schuster paper $16.00 (0-689-81381-3). 32pp. All kinds of horses, even those from fantasies, appear in this handsome counting book. (Rev: BCCB 3/98; BL 3/1/98*; HBG 10/98; SLJ 5/98)

525 Murphy, Stuart J. *Divide and Ride* (PS–3). Illus. by George Ulrich. Series: MathStart. 1997, HarperCollins LB $15.89 (0-06-026777-1). 40pp. Concepts of division are illustrated by problems posed when 11 friends visit various carnival attractions. (Rev: BL 2/1/97; SLJ 3/97) [513.2]

526 Murphy, Stuart J. *Double the Ducks* (PS–1). Illus. by Valeria Petrone. Series: MathStart. 2003, HarperCollins LB $16.89 (0-06-028923-6); paper $4.99 (0-06-446249-8). 40pp. Simple addition and multiplication are explained as a young cowboy cares for five little ducks who bring friends and double his work. (Rev: BL 3/15/03; HBG 10/03) [513.2]

527 Murphy, Stuart J. *Earth Day-Hooray!* (1–3). Illus. by Renee Andriani. Series: MathStart. 2004, HarperCollins $15.99 (0-06-000127-5); paper $4.99 (0-06-000129-1). 40pp. Readers learn about the mathematical concept of sorting and about the benefits of recycling in this accessible and humorous book. (Rev: BL 1/1–15/04) [513]

528 Murphy, Stuart J. *A Fair Bear Share* (1–2). Illus. by John Speirs. Series: MathStart. 1998, HarperCollins LB $15.89 (0-06-027439-5). Bear cubs count out the food they have gathered into groups of ten in this simple math book. (Rev: BL 3/1/98; HBG 10/98; SLJ 5/98)

529 Murphy, Stuart J. *Henry the Fourth* (1–3). Illus. by Scott Nash. Series: MathStart. 1999, HarperCollins LB $15.89 (0-06-027611-8). 40pp. Ordinal numbers are introduced in this story of four performing dogs. (Rev: BL 4/15/99; HBG 10/99; SLJ 1/99) [513]

530 Murphy, Stuart J. *Jump, Kangaroo, Jump!* (1–3). Illus. by Kevin O'Malley. Series: MathStart. 1999, HarperCollins LB $15.89 (0-06-027615-0). 40pp. This book about 12 campers introduces simple division to young mathematicians. (Rev: BL 4/15/99; HBG 10/99; SLJ 2/99) [513.2]

531 Murphy, Stuart J. *The Penny Pot* (1–3). Illus. by Lynne W. Cravath. Series: MathStart. 1998, HarperCollins LB $14.89 (0-06-027607-X). 40pp. While Jessie tries different coin combinations to get enough money to have her face painted at the school fair, the reader learns about counting money and addition. (Rev: BL 12/15/98; HBG 3/99; SLJ 12/98) [513.2]

532 Nagel, Karen. *The Lunch Line* (2–4). Illus. by Jerry Zimmerman. 1996, Scholastic $3.99 (0-590-60246-2). 32pp. Kim has lost her lunch and must buy one in this simple book on calculation. (Rev: BL 2/1/97)

533 Napoli, Donna Jo, and Richard Chen. *How Hungry Are You?* (K–3). Illus. by Amy Walrod. 2001, Simon & Schuster $16.00 (0-689-83389-X). 32pp. Sharing becomes difficult (and requires some division) when too many friends arrive at an animals' picnic. (Rev: BL 9/15/01; HBG 3/02; SLJ 10/01)

534 Naylor, Phyllis Reynolds. *Ducks Disappearing* (PS–K). Illus. by Tony Maddox. 1997, Simon & Schuster $13.00 (0-689-31902-9). 30pp. A young child solves the mystery of missing ducklings in this counting book. (Rev: BCCB 2/97; BL 2/1/97; SLJ 3/97)

535 Newman, Leslea. *Dogs, Dogs, Dogs!* (PS–1). Illus. by Erika Oller. 2002, Simon & Schuster $16.00 (0-689-84492-1). A boisterous counting book full of appealing dogs that counts from one to ten and down again. (Rev: BL 10/02; SLJ 8/02)

536 Ochiltree, Dianne. *Cats Add Up! Math Activities by Marilyn Burns* (1–2). Illus. by Marcy Dunn-Ramsey. 1998, Scholastic paper $3.99 (0-590-12005-0). 40pp. In this easy-to-read counting book, a little girl starts with one cat and soon has ten. (Rev: BL 3/15/99)

537 Ochiltree, Dianne. *Ten Monkey Jamboree* (PS–2). Illus. by Anne-Sophie Lanquetin. 2001, Simon & Schuster $16.00 (0-689-83402-0). A counting book featuring a rambunctious bunch of monkeys, rhythmic and repetitive text that tells a lively story, and rich illustrations that use interesting perspectives. (Rev: HBG 3/02; SLJ 10/01)

538 Ochs, Carol P. *When I'm Alone* (PS–3). Illus. by Vicki Jo Redenbaugh. 1993, Carolrhoda LB $18.95 (0-87614-752-X). 32pp. In this counting book, various animals upset a girl's attempts to keep her part of the house tidy. (Rev: BL 2/1/93; SLJ 6/93)

539 O'Keefe, Susan Heyboer. *One Hungry Monster: A Counting Book in Rhyme* (PS–K). Illus. by Lynn Munsinger. 2001, Little, Brown $5.95 (0-316-60804-1). 16pp. A little boy tries to keep ten hungry monsters out of trouble. (Rev: BL 3/1/01)

540 Olson, K. C. *Construction Countdown* (PS–1). Illus. by David Gordon. 2004, Holt $14.95 (0-8050-6920-8). 32pp. Rhyming text and colorful illustrations of big construction trucks appear on double-page spreads, counting down from ten. (Rev: BL 5/15/04; SLJ 7/04) [629.22]

541 Olyff, Clotilde. *1 2 3 . . .* (PS–K). Illus. by author. 1994, Ticknor $13.95 (0-395-70736-6). A pop-up book that introduces numbers from one to the zero in ten, each in a different, attractive typeface. (Rev: SLJ 11/94)

542 *1 to 10 and Back Again: A Getty Museum Counting Book* (K–2). Photos by Jack Ross. Illus. by Nancy Ogami. 1999, Getty Museum $16.95 (0-89236-525-0). This counting book, which features French phases, cleverly uses the numbers one to ten as the furniture and items found in the Getty Museum are counted. (Rev: HBG 3/00; SLJ 7/99)

543 *One, Two, Skip a Few! First Number Rhymes* (PS–1). Illus. by Roberta Arenson. 1998, Barefoot $15.95 (1-901223-99-X). 32pp. Using different folk rhymes — like "one potato, two potato" — this energetic book covers numbers, counting, subtraction, and even some multiplication. (Rev: BL 12/1/98; SLJ 9/98) [398.8]

544 Ormerod, Jan. *Joe Can Count* (PS–3). Illus. 1993, Mulberry paper $3.95 (0-688-04588-X). 24pp. An African American toddler uses animals to count to ten. A reissue.

545 Packard, Edward. *Big Numbers* (1–4). Illus. by Sal Murdocca. 2000, Millbrook LB $22.40 (0-7613-1570-5). 32pp. This oversize book also deals with oversize numbers from one to ten to 100, 1,000, and then on to a million, billion, trillion, etc. (Rev: BCCB 3/00; BL 3/15/00; HBG 10/00; SLJ 4/00)

546 Pallotta, Jerry. *Ocean Counting: Odd Numbers* (PS–2). Illus. by Shennen Bersani. 2005, Charlesbridge $16.95 (0-88106-151-4); paper $6.95 (0-88106-150-6). 32pp. Facts about marine animals are interwoven into this lively counting book that concentrates on odd numbers. (Rev: BL 2/1/05; SLJ 3/05) [513.2]

547 Pallotta, Jerry. *Underwater Counting: Even Numbers* (1–3). Illus. by David Biedrzycki. 2001, Charlesbridge $16.95 (0-88106-952-3); paper $6.95 (0-88106-800-4). 32pp. A variety of underwater creatures are introduced in this counting book that gives even numbers from zero to 50. (Rev: BL 3/1/01; HBG 10/01)

548 Parker, Kim. *Counting in the Garden* (PS). Illus. 2005, Scholastic $16.95 (0-439-69452-3). 32pp. Colorful garden scenes shelter animals in groups from one to ten. (Rev: BL 6/1–15/05; SLJ 4/05)

549 Peek, Merle. *Roll Over! A Counting Song* (PS). Illus. by author. 1991, Houghton Mifflin paper $5.95 (0-395-58105-2). 32pp. A counting book from ten to one about animals in a bed.

550 Penner, Lucille R. *Lights Out!* (1–3). Illus. by Jerry Smath. Series: Math Matters. 2000, Kane paper $4.95 (1-57565-092-4). 32pp. The concept of subtraction is explored in this story about a girl who watches as the 32 lights outside her apartment go out. (Rev: SLJ 6/00)

551 Pinczes, Elinor J. *Inchworm and a Half* (PS–3). Illus. by Randall Enos. 2001, Houghton Mifflin $15.00 (0-395-82849-X). 32pp. The concept of fractions is explored in this amusing book about different-sized inchworms and the objects they measure. (Rev: BCCB 3/01; BL 3/15/01; HBG 10/01)

552 Pinczes, Elinor J. *One Hundred Hungry Ants* (K–3). Illus. by Bonnie Mackain. 1993, Houghton Mifflin $16.00 (0-395-63116-5). 32pp. Ants group and regroup on their march to a picnic site. (Rev: BL 3/1/93; SLJ 8/93)

553 Pinczes, Elinor J. *A Remainder of One* (PS–2). Illus. by Bonnie Mackain. 1995, Houghton Mifflin $15.00 (0-395-69455-8). 32pp. An arithmetic book that uses a parade of beetles before the queen as a focal point. (Rev: BL 3/1/95*; SLJ 5/95)

554 Pomerantz, Charlotte. *One Duck, Another Duck* (PS). Illus. by Jose Aruego and Ariane Dewey. 1984, Greenwillow $15.89 (0-688-03745-3). 24pp. Danny tries to count ducks but has problems.

555 Potter, Keith R. *Count Us In: A 1 to 10 Book* (PS–K). Illus. by Keith R. Potter and Jana Leo. Series: Doodlezoo. 1999, Chronicle $6.95 (0-8118-2064-5). Animal photos and cartoon creatures are used to introduce numbers from one to ten. (Rev: SLJ 10/99)

556 Prelutsky, Jack. *Halloween Countdown* (PS). Illus. by Dan Yaccarino. 2002, HarperCollins $6.99 (0-06-000512-2). Readers count the friendly looking ghosts in a boy's home in this board book. (Rev: BCCB 9/02; HBG 10/03; SLJ 10/02)

557 Rader, Laura. *Tea for Me, Tea for You* (PS). Illus. by author. 2003, HarperCollins LB $16.89 (0-06-008634-3). A piglet visits Swining's Tea Room to enjoy a solitary cup of tea but is soon joined by one friend after another until ten piglets are sitting at the table. (Rev: HBG 10/03; SLJ 11/03)

558 Raffi. *Five Little Ducks* (PS–1). Illus. by Jose Aruego and Ariane Dewey. 1988, Crown paper $5.99 (0-517-58360-7). 32pp. Mother Duck and her ducklings waddle "over the hills and far away" in this addition to the Songs to Read series. (Rev: BL 6/1/89; HB 5–6/89)

559 Rankin, Laura. *Swan Harbor: A Nature Counting Book* (PS–2). Illus. 2003, Dial $16.99 (0-8037-2561-2). 32pp. A counting book featuring 20 animals, plants, and other natural features of Swan Harbor, Maine. (Rev: BL 2/15/03; HBG 10/03; SLJ 4/03) [513.2]

560 Rathmann, Peggy. *10 Minutes till Bedtime* (K–2). Illus. 1998, Penguin Putnam $16.99 (0-399-23103-X). 46pp. A very active counting book involving a ten-minute countdown to bed for a little boy and ten mischievous hamsters numbered one through ten. (Rev: BCCB 12/98; BL 10/15/98; HB 9–10/98; HBG 3/99; SLJ 9/98)

561 Reidy, Hannah. *All Sorts of Numbers* (PS). Illus. by Emma Dodd. Series: All Sorts of Things. 2005, Picture Window LB $22.60 (1-4048-1062-5). 24pp. A bright introduction to numbers from one to five. (Rev: SLJ 6/05)

562 Rocklin, Joanne. *The Case of the Shrunken Allowance* (1–3). Illus. by Cornelius Van Wright and Ying-hwa Hu. Series: Hello Reader! 1999, Scholastic paper $3.99 (0-590-12006-9). The concept of money denominations and making change are introduced in a light plot about P. B.'s shrinking savings. (Rev: SLJ 3/99)

563 Rocklin, Joanne. *One Hungry Cat* (1–2). Illus. by Rowan Barnes-Murphy. Series: Hello Math Reader. 1997, Scholastic paper $3.99 (0-590-93972-6). A slapstick easy reader that introduces simple arithmetic by using cookies that a hungry cat enjoys eating. (Rev: BL 5/1/97; SLJ 7/97)

564 Root, Phyllis. *One Duck Stuck* (PS–1). Illus. by Jane Chapman. 1998, Candlewick $15.99 (0-7636-0334-1). 40pp. In this counting book that uses allit-

erative rhymes, different animals try to free a duck that gets stuck in the muck. (Rev: BL 4/1/98; HBG 10/98; SLJ 6/98)

565 Rose, Deborah Lee. *One Nighttime Sea* (PS–2). Illus. by Steve Jenkins. 2003, Scholastic $16.95 (0-439-33906-5). 40pp. This counting book uses rhyming text to introduce young readers to numbers from one to ten as well as common marine animals. (Rev: HBG 4/04; SLJ 9/03) [513.2]

566 Rose, Deborah Lee. *The Twelve Days of Kindergarten: A Counting Book* (PS–1). Illus. by Carey Armstrong-Ellis. 2003, Abrams $14.95 (0-8109-4512-6). The wonders of kindergarten are introduced along with numbers from one alphabet to 12 eggs. (Rev: HBG 4/04; SLJ 8/03) [372.21]

567 Roth, Susan L. *Night-Time Numbers: A Scary Counting Book* (PS–1). Illus. by author. Series: A Barefoot Beginner Book. 1999, Barefoot $15.95 (1-84148-001-0). Monsters and an angel are used to introduce the numbers one to ten in his book illustrated with collages. (Rev: SLJ 10/99)

568 Saul, Carol P. *Barn Cat* (PS–K). Illus. by Mary Azarian. 1998, Little, Brown $15.95 (0-316-76113-3). 32pp. In this counting book, Barn Cat sees all sorts of insects and animals, such as one green grasshopper and two brown crickets, before he discovers what he really wants — a saucer of milk. (Rev: BCCB 11/98; BL 9/15/98; HBG 3/99; SLJ 11/98)

569 Sayre, April Pulley, and Jeff Sayre. *One Is a Snail, Ten Is a Crab: A Counting by Feet Book* (PS–2). Illus. by Randy Cecil. 2003, Candlewick $15.99 (0-7636-1406-8). Readers count up to ten and then in multiples of ten to 100, using animal feet as units. (Rev: HBG 10/03; SLJ 7/03) [513.2]

570 Schaefer, Carole Lexa. *One Wheel Wobbles: A Homespun Counting Book* (PS–K). Illus. by Pierre Morgan. 2003, Candlewick $15.99 (0-7636-0472-0). 32pp. A country family's various means of transportation serve as the subject of this counting book. (Rev: BL 3/1/03; HBG 10/03; SLJ 5/03)

571 Schafer, Kevin. *Penguins 123* (PS–K). Photos by author. 2002, NorthWord $14.95 (1-55971-830-7). A counting book that will grab the attention of penguin lovers. (Rev: SLJ 1/03)

572 Schlein, Miriam. *More Than One* (PS–3). Illus. by Donald Crews. 1996, Greenwillow $14.93 (0-688-14103-X). 24pp. Using the concept of "one" as a framework, other numbers and groups of numbers are introduced. (Rev: BCCB 1/97; BL 11/1/96; SLJ 12/96) [513]

573 Schumaker, Ward. *In My Garden* (PS–1). Illus. 2000, Chronicle $13.95 (0-8118-2689-9). 32pp. A lively counting book that uses garden tools, plants, and outdoor creatures as props. (Rev: BL 7/00; HBG 10/00; SLJ 5/00)

574 Shea, Pegi Deitz, and Cynthia Weill. *Ten Mice for Tet* (PS–2). Illus. by To Ngoc Trang and Pham Vi t Dinh. 2003, Chronicle $15.95 (0-8118-3496-4). This handsome counting book introduces numbers one through ten plus the traditions of the Vietnamese New Year. (Rev: HBG 4/04; SLJ 12/03) [394.2]

575 Simon, Charnan. *One Happy Classroom* (1–2). Illus. by Rebecca M. Thornburgh. 1997, Children's Book Pr. LB $18.00 (0-516-20318-5). 32pp. An easy-to-read counting book that takes place in a classroom and involves counting from one to ten and back. (Rev: BL 5/1/97)

576 Singer, Marilyn. *Quiet Night* (PS–K). Illus. by John Manders. 2002, Clarion $15.00 (0-618-12044-0). 32pp. A riotous romp of a counting book in which the quiet of night turns into a symphony of animal noises. (Rev: BCCB 6/02; BL 3/15/02; HBG 10/02; SLJ 3/02)

577 Slater, Teddy. *Stay in Line* (1–2). Illus. 1996, Scholastic paper $3.99 (0-590-22713-0). 32pp. Children on a field trip learn various numerical ways of lining up. (Rev: BL 8/96)

578 Slaughter, Tom. *1 2 3* (PS–K). Illus. by author. 2003, Tundra $11.95 (0-88776-664-1). A cleverly designed counting book that introduces the numbers one through ten. (Rev: SLJ 11/03) [513.2]

579 Smith, Maggie. *Counting Our Way to Maine* (PS–2). Illus. 1995, Orchard LB $16.99 (0-531-08734-4). 32pp. Numbers from one to 20 are introduced by using a family's summer trip to Maine. (Rev: BCCB 3/95; BL 4/1/95; SLJ 5/95*)

580 Spanyol, Jessica. *Carlo Likes Counting* (PS–2). Illus. 2002, Candlewick $14.99 (0-7636-1774-1). 32pp. Carlo the giraffe counts from one to ten wherever he goes. (Rev: BL 10/1/02; HBG 3/03; SLJ 1/03)

581 Spowart, Robin. *Ten Little Bunnies* (PS). Illus. by author. 2001, Scholastic $7.95 (0-439-20863-7). A gentle counting book that can double as a bedtime story. (Rev: HBG 10/01; SLJ 8/01)

582 Swinburne, Stephen R. *Water for One, Water for Everyone: A Counting Book of African Animals* (PS–2). Illus. by Melinda Levine. 1998, Millbrook LB $21.40 (0-7613-0269-7); paper $6.95 (0-7613-0347-2). Animals, from one tortoise to ten elephants, come to an African watering hole in this simple counting book, which also gives the numbers in Swahili. (Rev: HBG 10/98; SLJ 6/98)

583 Swinburne, Stephen R. *What's a Pair? What's a Dozen?* (PS–1). Illus. 2000, Boyds Mills $15.95 (1-56397-827-X). 32pp. This advanced mathematical concept book introduces words and phrases such as even and odd, first and second, uni- and bi-, and baker's dozen. (Rev: BL 3/15/00; HBG 10/00; SLJ 4/00) [510]

584 Szekeres, Cyndy. *I Can Count 100 Bunnies: And So Can You!* (PS–1). Illus. 1999, Scholastic $12.95 (0-590-38361-2). 48pp. Wilbur counts 99 bunnies who come to welcome number 100 — Wilbur's new baby sister. (Rev: BL 1/1–15/99; HBG 10/99; SLJ 2/99)

585 Szekeres, Cyndy. *Learn to Count, Funny Bunnies* (PS). Illus. by author. 2000, Scholastic $6.99 (0-439-14994-0). In this board book, youngsters will learn to count to ten as the relatives of Wilbur Bunny arrive for his birthday party. (Rev: SLJ 5/00)

586 Tang, Greg. *Math Fables* (PS–1). Illus. by Heather Cahoon. 2004, Scholastic $16.95 (0-439-45399-2). 40pp. Groupings of numbers are shown

through rhyming stories with colorful art. (Rev: BL 2/1/04; SLJ 3/04) [513.2]

587 Thornhill, Jan, adapt. *Over in the Meadow* (PS–2). Illus. by Jan Thornhill. 2004, Maple Tree $16.95 (1-897066-08-2). Unusual illustrations add to the charm of this inventive rendition of a traditional counting song. (Rev: SLJ 1/05)

588 Tildes, Phyllis L. *Counting on Calico* (PS–K). Illus. 1995, Charlesbridge paper $6.95 (0-88106-862-4). 32pp. The features of a calico cat are used to introduce basic numbers, ending with 20 wet paw prints. (Rev: BL 6/1–15/95)

589 *The Timbertoes 123 Counting Book* (PS–1). Illus. 1997, Boyds Mills $7.95 (1-56397-627-7). 32pp. Basic numbers are introduced by the Timbertoes, a family of wooden figures, when they visit an apple orchard. (Rev: BL 3/1/97; SLJ 7/97)

590 *Toddler Two* (PS). Illus. by Winnie Cheon. 2000, Lee & Low $6.95 (1-58430-015-9). The concept of two is explored in this interactive board book with flaps and pop-ups. (Rev: SLJ 1/01)

591 Toft, Kim Michelle, and Allan Sheather. *One Less Fish* (K–3). Illus. 1998, Charlesbridge $15.95 (0-88106-322-3); paper $6.95 (0-88106-323-1). 32pp. Counting down from 12 to one, this book shows the perils fish face, including such threats as offshore oil drilling. (Rev: BL 7/98; HBG 10/98) [513.2]

592 Trinca, Rod, and Kerry Argent. *One Woolly Wombat* (PS–2). Illus. by Kerry Argent. 1985, Kane/Miller paper $6.95 (0-916291-10-3). 32pp. A charming one-to-14 counting book featuring Australian animals. (Rev: BL 7/85; HB 7–8/85; SLJ 9/85)

593 *Trucks and Diggers One to Ten: Counting* (PS). 2003, Chronicle $6.95 (0-8118-4029-8). Numbers are introduced through eye-catching photographs of appealing machines. (Rev: SLJ 1/04)

594 Wadsworth, Olive A. *Over in the Meadow: A Counting Rhyme* (PS–1). Illus. by Anna Vojtech. 2002, North-South $15.95 (0-7358-1596-8). 32pp. This classic nursery counting rhyme is given a fresh look with double-page spreads and stunning watercolors. (Rev: BL 4/15/02; HBG 10/02; SLJ 4/02)

595 Wallace, Nancy Elizabeth. *Count Down to Clean Up!* (PS–2). Illus. 2001, Houghton Mifflin $14.00 (0-618-10130-6). 32pp. Ten bunnies take a trip to the park, gathering supplies as they go, in this counting book with cut-paper artwork. (Rev: BL 9/15/01; HBG 3/02; SLJ 10/01)

596 Walsh, Ellen S. *Mouse Count* (PS–K). Illus. 1991, Harcourt $13.00 (0-15-256023-8). 32pp. In this counting book, ten little mice fall asleep unaware that a hungry snake is nearby. (Rev: BL 2/15/91; HB 5–6/91; SLJ 5/91*)

597 Walton, Rick. *One More Bunny: Adding from One to Ten* (PS–1). Illus. by Paige Miglio. 2000, Lothrop LB $15.89 (0-688-16848-5). 24pp. Readers participate in this counting book as they are asked to find bunnies in illustrations and add them up. (Rev: BL 4/15/00; HBG 10/00; SLJ 7/00)

598 Watson, Amy, et al. *The Folk Art Counting Book* (PS–2). Illus. 1992, Abrams $12.95 (0-8109-

3306-3). 40pp. Collections from the Rockefeller Folk Art Center in Williamsburg, Virginia, invite the younger reader to count to 20. (Rev: BL 6/15/92; SLJ 8/92) [745]

599 Wells, Robert. *Can You Count to a Googol?* (PS–1). Illus. 2000, Whitman $14.95 (0-8075-1060-2); paper $6.95 (0-8075-1061-0). 32pp. This counting book starts with one and moves to ten, 100, 1,000 until reaching a googol, the number one followed by 100 zeros. (Rev: BL 3/1/00; HBG 10/00; SLJ 5/00)

600 Williams, Rozanne Lanczak. *Adding* (PS–1). Illus. Series: I Can Do Math. 2004, Gareth Stevens LB $19.93 (0-8368-4108-5). 24pp. A question-and-answer format and abundant photographs introduce addition. Also use *Subtracting*, *Crayola Counting*, and *Learning About Coins* (all 2004).

601 Williams, Rozanne Lanczak. *The Coin Counting Book* (PS–3). Illus. 2001, Charlesbridge $16.95 (0-88106-325-8); paper $6.95 (0-88106-326-6). 32pp. This counting book uses coins to show how five pennies make a nickel and so on until the reader discovers the various combinations that make a dollar. (Rev: BL 3/1/01; HBG 10/01)

602 Wilson, Anna. *Over in the Grasslands* (PS–1). Illus. by Alison Bartlett. 2000, Little, Brown $14.95 (0-316-93910-2). 32pp. Using the African grasslands as a setting, animal mothers and their babies introduce numbers one to ten. (Rev: BL 10/1/00; HBG 3/01; SLJ 11/00)

603 Wilson, Karma. *A Frog in the Bog* (PS–2). Illus. by Joan Rankin. 2003, Simon & Schuster $16.95 (0-689-84081-0). A humorous counting book in which a hungry frog consumes progressively larger swamp snacks, including "one tick," "two fleas," "three flies," and "four slugs." (Rev: BL 11/1/03; HBG 4/04; SLJ 12/03)

604 Winter, Jeanette. *Josefina* (PS–3). Illus. 1996, Harcourt $15.00 (0-15-201091-2). 36pp. An original counting book that features the Mexican woman Josefina and her amazing collection of clay figures. (Rev: BCCB 10/96; BL 10/15/96*; SLJ 10/96)

605 Wojtowycz, David. *Animal Antics from 1 to 10* (PS). Illus. 2000, Holiday House $16.95 (0-8234-1552-X). 26pp. When readers visit Hotel 1 2 3, they are introduced to the numbers one to ten and some very unusual beasts like two tangoing toucans. (Rev: BL 10/15/00; HBG 3/01; SLJ 10/00)

606 Wong, Janet S. *Hide and Seek* (PS). Illus. by Margaret Chodos-Irvine. 2005, Harcourt $16.00 (0-15-204934-7). 40pp. Boy and dog rush off to hide while Dad counts to fsn. (Rev: BL 5/1/05; SLJ 4/05)

607 Yates, Philip. *Ten Little Mummies* (PS–2). Illus. by G. Brian Karas. 2003, Viking $15.99 (0-670-03641-2). Ten little mummies, "bored stiff" in their gloomy tomb, go outside to play, but, one by one, they disappear. (Rev: HB 9–10/03; HBG 4/04; SLJ 11/03)

608 Yektai, Niki. *Bears at the Beach: Counting 10 to 20* (PS–1). Illus. 1996, Millbrook LB $21.90 (0-7613-0047-3). 32pp. A wordless counting book that covers numbers from ten to 20. (Rev: BL 7/96; SLJ 6/96)

609 Zabar, Abbie. *55 Friends* (PS–3). Illus. by author. 1994, Hyperion $13.95 (0-7868-0021-6). In a fanciful text, animals from one to ten are introduced and then combined in various ways to reach 55. (Rev: SLJ 11/94)

610 Ziefert, Harriet. *A Dozen Ducklings Lost and Found* (K–2). Illus. by Donald Dreifuss. 2003, Houghton Mifflin $15.00 (0-618-14175-8). 32pp. While proudly parading her dozen ducklings through the barnyard, Mother Duck loses some in newly dug postholes. (Rev: BL 3/15/03; HBG 10/03; SLJ 3/03)

611 Ziefert, Harriet. *You Can't Buy a Dinosaur with a Dime: Problem-Solving in Dollars and Cents* (1–3). Illus. by Amanda Haley. 2003, Handprint $15.95 (1-929766-81-5). This bright and appealing introduction to addition and subtraction — and the virtues of saving — tells the story of Pete, who wants to buy a toy dinosaur. (Rev: SLJ 7/03) [513.2]

Bedtime Books and Nursery Rhymes

Bedtime Books

612 *All the Pretty Little Horses: A Traditional Lullaby* (PS–K). Illus. by Linda Saport. 1999, Clarion $14.00 (0-395-93097-9). 32pp. In this version of the classic lullaby, pictures from a bygone era depict an African American woman rocking her baby on a porch in the rural South. (Rev: BL 11/1/99; HBG 3/00; SLJ 12/99) [782.4]

613 Anastas, Margaret. *Mommy's Best Kisses* (PS). Illus. by Susan Winter. 2003, HarperCollins LB $16.89 (0-06-623606-1). Animal mothers kiss their babies in this charming book that ends with a human mother kissing her toddler good night. (Rev: HBG 4/04; SLJ 4/03)

614 Appelt, Kathi. *Bayou Lullaby* (PS–1). Illus. by Neil Waldman. 1995, Morrow LB $15.93 (0-688-12857-2). 40pp. A Cajun bedtime tale of a land ruled over by the king of the bullfrogs. (Rev: BL 3/15/95; SLJ 4/95*)

615 Appelt, Kathi. *Bubbles, Bubbles* (PS–K). Illus. by Fumi Kosaka. Series: Harper Growing Tree. 2001, HarperCollins $9.95 (0-694-01458-3). 24pp. Realistic illustrations and frothy verse portray a little girl enjoying her bedtime bath. (Rev: BL 10/1/01; HBG 10/02; SLJ 12/01)

616 Appelt, Kathi. *I See the Moon* (PS–K). Illus. by Debra R. Jenkins. 1997, Eerdmans $15.00 (0-8028-5118-5). 24pp. A bedtime book about a little girl all alone on the sea in a tiny boat. (Rev: BCCB 5/97; BL 3/15/97)

617 Apperley, Dawn. *Good Night, Sleep Tight, Little Bunnies* (PS). Illus. by author. 2002, Scholastic $9.95 (0-439-22525-6). A rhyming refrain and cartoon images depict young animals settling down for the night. (Rev: HBG 10/02; SLJ 5/02)

618 Arnold, Tedd. *Five Ugly Monsters* (PS–K). Illus. 1995, Scholastic $6.95 (0-590-22226-0). 24pp. Several groups of monsters interrupt a little boy's plans to go to sleep. (Rev: BCCB 10/95; BL 11/15/95; SLJ 12/95)

619 Arnold, Tedd. *Huggly Takes a Bath* (PS). Illus. 1999, Scholastic $15.95 (0-590-91820-6). 32pp. A naive little monster comes out from under the bed at night and, while exploring the bathroom, enjoys such delightful discoveries as bubble bath. (Rev: BL 2/1/99; HBG 10/99; SLJ 4/99)

620 Arquette, Kerry. *What Did You Do Today?* (PS–2). Illus. by Nancy Hayashi. 2002, Harcourt $16.00 (0-15-201414-4). 32pp. Many animals and one child describe their busy days in this rhyming picture book. (Rev: BL 5/15/02; HBG 10/02; SLJ 6/02)

621 Arro, Lena. *Good Night, Animals* (PS–1). Trans. by Joan Sandin. Illus. by Catarina Kruusval. 2002, Farrar $15.00 (91-29-65654-0). 28pp. A cumulative bedtime story in which two children who decide to camp out soon find their tent packed with animals. (Rev: BCCB 12/02; BL 12/15/02; HBG 3/03; SLJ 2/03)

622 Asch, Frank. *Good Night, Baby Bear* (PS). Illus. 1998, Harcourt $14.00 (0-15-200836-5). 32pp. Mother Bear has a hard time getting Baby Bear to bed down for the winter, particularly when he asks for the moon. (Rev: BL 7/98; HBG 3/99; SLJ 9/98)

623 Ballard, Robin. *Tonight and Tomorrow* (PS–K). Illus. 2000, Greenwillow $15.95 (0-688-16790-X). 24pp. As he goes to bed, a young boy imagines all the wonderful activities that are in store for him the next day. (Rev: BCCB 5/00; BL 4/15/00; HBG 10/00; SLJ 6/00)

624 Ballard, Robin. *When We Get Home* (PS–1). Illus. 1999, Greenwillow $16.00 (0-688-16168-5). 24pp. As a young girl drives home with her mother at night, she thinks of the comforting bedtime rituals that await her. (Rev: BL 4/1/99; HBG 10/99; SLJ 6/99)

625 Banks, Kate. *And If the Moon Could Talk* (PS–2). Illus. by Georg Hallensleben. 1998, Farrar $15.00 (0-374-30299-5). 32pp. At bedtime, a little girl's actions are duplicated in the outside world by a number of different animals. (Rev: BCCB 4/98; BL 2/15/98; HB 3–4/98*; HBG 10/98; SLJ 2/98*)

626 Banks, Kate. *Close Your Eyes* (PS). Illus. by Georg Hallensleben. 2002, Farrar $16.00 (0-374-31382-2). 40pp. A thoroughly enjoyable, dreamily illustrated story about a little tiger who doesn't want to fall asleep, and his mother's patient reassurances. (Rev: BL 10/15/02; HB 9–10/02; HBG 3/03; SLJ 7/02)

627 Banks, Kate. *The Night Worker* (PS–2). Illus. by Georg Hallensleben. 2000, Farrar $16.00 (0-374-35520-7). 40pp. Alex follows his Papa, a construction worker on the night shift, and helps him all night long until morning when he comes home to bed. (Rev: BCCB 7–8/00; BL 8/00*; HBG 3/01; SLJ 8/00)

628 Barger, Jan. *Bedtime, Nelly* (PS–K). Illus. by author. 2004, Charlesbridge $14.95 (1-58089-094-6). Nelly postpones sleep with a litany of good nights. (Rev: SLJ 8/04)

629 Bauer, Marion Dane. *Why Do Kittens Purr?* (PS–1). Illus. by Henry Cole. 2003, Simon & Schuster $15.95 (0-689-84179-5). 32pp. Charming rhymes answer a boy's questions about the world about him in a way that will set young ones' minds at ease. (Rev: BL 1/1–15/03; HBG 10/03; SLJ 3/03)

630 Beaton, Clare. *Mrs. Moon: Lullabies for Bedtime* (PS–1). Illus. by author. 2003, Barefoot $19.99 (1-84148-176-9). 48pp. This collection of lullabies and bedtime poetry includes many old favorites and is accompanied by a musical CD. (Rev: HBG 4/04; SLJ 1/04) [782.4]

631 Beaumont, Karen. *Baby Danced the Polka* (PS). Illus. by Jennifer Plecas. 2004, Dial $12.99 (0-8037-2587-6). Baby prefers dancing to sleeping in this lively bedtime book with flaps hiding stuffed animal dancing partners. (Rev: BL 2/15/04; HB 5–6/04; SLJ 6/04)

632 Beck, Andrea. *Elliot's Noisy Night* (PS–1). Illus. 2002, Kids Can $12.95 (1-55337-011-2). 32pp. Elliot the toy moose infects his friends with his fears about the noises at night and they all end up sleeping in Elliot's room. (Rev: BL 1/1–15/03; HBG 3/03)

633 Beck, Ian. *Home Before Dark* (PS–K). Illus. 2001, Scholastic $15.95 (0-439-17522-4). 32pp. A stuffed bear falls out of Lily's stroller in a park, but manages to find his way back home just in time to accompany Lily to bed. (Rev: BL 3/1/01; HBG 10/01; SLJ 3/01)

634 Bergman, Mara. *Musical Beds* (PS–1). Illus. by Marjolein Pottie. 2002, Simon & Schuster $14.95 (0-689-84463-8). 32pp. Three siblings spend the night scuttling from bed to bed, trying to relieve their various fears and discomforts in this appealing bedtime book. (Rev: BCCB 1/03; BL 10/15/02; HBG 3/03; SLJ 12/02)

635 Blomgren, Jennifer. *Where Do I Sleep? A Pacific Northwest Lullaby* (PS–2). Illus. by Andrea Gabriel. 2001, Sasquatch $15.95 (1-57061-258-7). 32pp. A peaceful bedtime book featuring animals native to the Pacific Northwest bedding down for the night. (Rev: BL 11/1/01; HBG 3/02; SLJ 11/01)

636 Boelts, Maribeth. *Looking for Sleepy* (PS). Illus. by Bernadette Pons. 2004, Whitman LB $14.95 (0-8075-0447-5). A bedtime picture book starring Little Bear and his patient father. (Rev: SLJ 4/04)

637 Bogan, Paulette. *Goodnight Lulu* (PS–2). Illus. by author. 2003, Bloomsbury $15.95 (1-58234-803-0). A mother hen reassures her chick that she will protect her from any potential dangers in this delightful bedtime book. (Rev: HBG 10/03; SLJ 7/03)

638 Bradley, Kimberly Brubaker. *Favorite Things* (PS–2). Illus. by Laura Huliska-Beith. 2003, Dial $16.99 (0-8037-2597-3). Matthew spins some fantastic tales when his mother asks him about his day as she tucks him into bed. (Rev: HBG 10/03; SLJ 8/03)

639 Bradman, Tony. *Daddy's Lullaby* (PS). Illus. by Jason Cockcroft. 2002, Simon & Schuster $16.95 (0-689-84295-3). 32pp. Late at night, a father tries to soothe his baby to sleep by quietly making his way around the house with the child in his arms. (Rev: BL 4/15/02; HBG 10/02; SLJ 5/02)

640 Branford, Henrietta. *Little Pig Figwort Can't Get to Sleep* (PS–K). Illus. by Claudio Munoz. 2002, Clarion $14.00 (0-618-15968-1). 32pp. When Little Pig Figwort can't sleep he sets out to find other creatures that have the same problem. (Rev: BCCB 5/02; BL 6/1–15/02; HBG 10/02; SLJ 7/02)

641 Brian, Janeen. *Where Does Thursday Go?* (PS–K). Illus. by Stephen M. King. 2002, Clarion $14.00 (0-618-21264-7). 32pp. A little bear and his friend search for Thursday, wondering where the day goes when nighttime comes, in this attractive book that makes a great bedtime story. (Rev: BL 3/1/02; HBG 10/02; SLJ 4/02)

642 Bright, Paul. *Under the Bed* (PS). Illus. by Ben Cort. 2004, Good Books $16.00 (1-56148-436-9). A boy is afraid of creatures under his bed, and it turns out they are also afraid of him in this book with amusing illustrations. (Rev: SLJ 8/04)

643 Brisson, Pat. *Star Blanket* (PS–1). Illus. by Erica Magnus. 2003, Boyds Mills $15.95 (1-56397-889-X). Laura's father tells her the familiar story of the time-worn, star-studded blanket on her bed. (Rev: HBG 4/04; SLJ 12/03)

644 Brown, Margaret Wise. *Goodnight Moon* (PS). Illus. by Clement Hurd. 1947, HarperCollins LB $14.89 (0-06-020706-X); paper $5.95 (0-06-443017-0). 32pp. A soothing go-to-sleep story. A pop-up book version is *The Goodnight Moon Room: A Pop-Up Book* (1985).

645 Brown, Margaret Wise. *Sheep Don't Count Sheep* (PS). Illus. by Benrei Huang. 2003, Simon & Schuster $14.95 (0-689-83346-6). 32pp. A little lamb can't get to sleep because there's too much going on in the field, so his mother tells him to count butterflies. (Rev: BL 1/1–15/03; HBG 10/03; SLJ 3/03)

646 Buchholz, Quint. *Sleep Well, Little Bear* (K–3). Trans. by Peter F. Neumeyer. Illus. 1994, Farrar $15.00 (0-374-37026-5). 33pp. At night, a toy bear thinks about the day just past and about the mysterious night outside. (Rev: BL 12/1/94; SLJ 12/94)

647 Bunting, Eve. *No Nap* (PS–1). Illus. by Susan Meddaugh. 1989, Houghton Mifflin $15.95 (0-89919-813-9). 28pp. Whenever bedtime is suggested, Susie says, "No nap." (Rev: BCCB 10/89; BL 9/15/89; HB 1–2/90; SLJ 10/89)

648 Bunting, Eve. *Too Many Monsters* (PS–3). Illus. by James Bernardin. 2001, Troll LB $15.95 (0-8167-7178-2). A mother tells her frightened son that monsters are afraid of ducks, and a great sound of quacking results. (Rev: HBG 3/02; SLJ 2/02)

649 Butler, John. *Hush, Little Ones* (PS). Illus. 2002, Peachtree $15.95 (1-56145-269-6). 32pp. A very visual bedtime book full of sleeping animals — birds in nests, monkeys up trees, a penguin between his father's feet. (Rev: BL 11/15/02; HBG 3/03; SLJ 10/02)

650 Capucilli, Alyssa Satin. *Little Spotted Cat* (PS–K). Illus. by Dan Andreasen. 2005, Dial $14.99 (0-8037-2692-9). 32pp. A traditional story book about a kitten who gets into all sorts of trouble when

his mother tells him that it's nap time. (Rev: BL 3/15/05; SLJ 6/05)

651 Carlstrom, Nancy White. *Swim the Silver Sea, Joshie Otter* (PS–K). Illus. by Ken Kuroi. 1997, Penguin Putnam paper $6.99 (0-698-11447-7). 40pp. At bedtime, a baby otter swims back to his mother and the love she gives him. (Rev: BL 4/1/93; SLJ 5/93)

652 Cazet, Denys. *Night Lights: 24 Poems to Sleep On* (PS–2). Illus. by author. 1997, Orchard LB $16.99 (0-531-33010-9). There are 24 bedtime rhymes in this nighttime collection; some are lullabies, others are amusing poems about animals at night. (Rev: SLJ 5/97)

653 Charlip, Remy. *Baby Hearts and Baby Flowers* (PS–K). Illus. by author. 2001, Greenwillow LB $15.89 (0-06-029592-9). Babies, puppies, and kittens are found "everywhere" in this gentle bedtime book. (Rev: HBG 10/02; SLJ 1/02)

654 Charlip, Remy. *Sleepytime Rhyme* (PS). Illus. 1999, Greenwillow $16.00 (0-688-16271-1). 24pp. In this bedtime book, a mother plays with her child while listing the body parts she loves. (Rev: BCCB 10/99; BL 11/15/99; HBG 3/00; SLJ 9/99)

655 Chislett, Gail. *Whump* (PS–1). Illus. by Vladyana Krykorka. 1992, Firefly paper $0.99 (1-55037-253-X). A little boy has trouble adjusting to his big new bed. (Rev: SLJ 3/90)

656 Cleary, Beverly. *Petey's Bedtime Story* (K–3). Illus. by David Small. 1993, Morrow LB $14.89 (0-688-10661-7). 32pp. Petey prolongs his bedtime rituals until his parents fall asleep from exhaustion. (Rev: BL 9/1/93; SLJ 2/94)

657 Cohen, Caron Lee. *Martin and the Giant Lion* (PS–K). Illus. by Elizabeth Sayles. 2002, Clarion $15.00 (0-618-04908-8). 32pp. After he is tucked into bed, Martin travels via his purple truck to a land where he plays with a family of lions. (Rev: BL 4/15/02; HBG 10/02; SLJ 7/02)

658 Cook, Sally. *Good Night Pillow Fight* (PS). Illus. by Laura Cornell. 2004, HarperCollins LB $16.89 (0-06-205190-3). Across a city, children and parents are shown in the usual struggles over bedtime, but eventually everyone seems to settle down. (Rev: BL 4/15/04*; SLJ 7/04)

659 Cowell, Cressida. *What Shall We Do with the Boo-Hoo Baby?* (PS–1). Illus. by Ingrid Godon. 2000, Scholastic $15.95 (0-439-15311-5). 32pp. Animals try different tactics to hush a crying baby and become so tired that they nap, which causes the baby to smile. (Rev: BCCB 2/01; BL 1/1–15/01; HBG 3/01; SLJ 3/01)

660 Crum, Shutta. *All on a Sleepy Night* (K–2). Illus. by Sylvie Daigneault. 2002, Stoddart $15.95 (0-7737-3315-9). 24pp. The sounds of his grandparents' house lull a young boy to sleep in this rhyming picture book. (Rev: BL 9/15/02; HBG 3/03; SLJ 5/02)

661 Cuneo, Mary L. *Mail for Husher Town* (PS–2). Illus. by Pamela Paparone. 2000, Greenwillow $15.95 (0-688-16525-7). 24pp. Julia, her cat, and three stuffed animals enjoy playing on the girl's green bedspread just before going to sleep. (Rev: BL 7/00; HBG 10/00; SLJ 6/00)

662 Davis, Kate. *I Hate to Go to Bed!* (PS–2). Illus. 1999, Harcourt $14.00 (0-15-201920-0). 36pp. A young girl tries all sorts of tricks to avoid going to sleep. (Rev: BL 10/15/99; HBG 3/00; SLJ 3/00)

663 deVries, Maggie. *How Sleep Found Tabitha* (PS–K). Illus. by Sheena Lott. 2002, Orca $16.95 (1-55143-193-9). 32pp. Pastel watercolor illustrations provide an excellent backdrop for this story of a sleepless child. (Rev: BL 8/02; HBG 10/02; SLJ 8/02)

664 Downey, Lynn. *Most Loved Monster* (PS–2). Illus. by Jack E. Davis. 2004, Dial $16.99 (0-8037-2728-3). Mama tucks in her four little monsters with fond words and praise for each. (Rev: SLJ 8/04)

665 Doyle, Malachy. *One, Two, Three O'Leary* (PS–2). Illus. by Will Hillenbrand. 2004, Simon & Schuster $15.95 (0-689-85513-3). A bouncy, noisy bedtime book full of traditional rhymes. (Rev: HB 1–2/05; SLJ 11/04)

666 Dragonwagon, Crescent. *Is This a Sack of Potatoes?* (PS–1). Illus. by Catherine Stock. 2002, Marshall Cavendish $16.95 (0-7614-5089-0). 32pp. Charlie hides under the covers at bedtime in this lift-the-flap book with charming watercolor illustrations. (Rev: BL 12/15/02; HBG 3/03; SLJ 11/02)

667 Dunbar, Joyce. *Tell Me Something Happy Before I Go to Sleep* (PS). Illus. by Debi Gliori. 1998, Harcourt $16.00 (0-15-201795-X). A young bunny has trouble getting to sleep until she begins thinking of all the nice things that will happen to her the next day. (Rev: HBG 3/99; SLJ 11/98)

668 Dyer, Jane. *Animal Crackers: A Delectable Collection of Pictures, Poems, and Lullabies for the Very Young* (PS). Illus. 1996, Little, Brown $17.95 (0-316-19766-1). 64pp. An immensely appealing collection of lullabies, poems, and nursery rhymes accompanied by muted illustrations. (Rev: BCCB 3/96; BL 4/15/96; SLJ 5/96)

669 Eduar, Gilles. *Dream Journey* (PS–K). Illus. by author. 1999, Orchard $15.95 (0-531-30202-4). While a little boy sleeps on his back, a camel travels through oceans, jungles, mountains, cities, and storms. (Rev: HBG 3/00; SLJ 12/99)

670 Eilenberg, Max. *Cowboy Kid* (PS–2). Illus. by Sue Heap. 2000, Candlewick $15.99 (0-7636-1058-5). 32pp. At bedtime, a little boy makes sure his stuffed toys also get a goodnight hug and kiss. (Rev: BCCB 9/00; BL 10/15/00; HBG 3/01; SLJ 7/00)

671 Emberley, Ed. *Go Away, Big Green Monster!* (PS–1). Illus. 1993, Little, Brown $15.95 (0-316-23653-5). 32pp. This toy book deals with a child's nighttime fears in a lighthearted way that will be both a joy and a comfort to young people. (Rev: BCCB 3/93; BL 4/15/93*; HB 7–8/93)

672 Engel, Diana. *Circle Song* (PS–1). Illus. 1999, Marshall Cavendish $15.95 (0-7614-5040-8). 32pp. A brief bedtime rhyme that evokes circles, including the moon. (Rev: BL 4/1/99; HBG 10/99; SLJ 6/99)

673 Faulkner, Keith. *The Scared Little Bear: A Not-Too-Scary Pop-up Book* (PS–2). Illus. by Jonathan Lambert. 2000, Scholastic $9.95 (0-531-30267-9).

A pop-up book in which a young bear discovers that the scary sounds he hears in the night are only his father snoring. (Rev: SLJ 2/01)

674 Fernandes, Eugenie. *Baby Dreams* (PS). Illus. by author. 1999, Stoddart $13.95 (0-7737-3139-3). An imaginative view of the images a sleeping baby might experience — being in a land of sleeping infants or being cradled on a rabbit's back. (Rev: SLJ 1/00)

675 Field, Eugene W. *Wynken, Blynken, and Nod* (PS–1). Illus. by David McPhail. 2004, Scholastic $15.95 (0-439-54303-7). 32pp. This large-format picture book casts three bunnies in the roles of Wynken, Blynken, and Nod for another retelling of the classic bedtime rhyme. (Rev: BL 2/1/04; SLJ 2/04) [811]

676 *Fishing for a Dream: Ocean Lullabies and Night Dreams* (PS–2). Ed. by Kate Kiesler. Illus. 1999, Clarion $16.00 (0-395-94149-0). 32pp. A collection of lullabies that focus on the nighttime sea and the images it evokes. (Rev: BL 12/15/99; HBG 3/00; SLJ 12/99) [782.4215]

677 Fox, Mem. *A Bedtime Story* (PS–2). Illus. by Elivia Savadier. 1996, Mondo $13.95 (1-57255-136-4). Polly and Bed Rabbit look forward to a bedtime story from their parents. (Rev: SLJ 12/96)

678 Fox, Mem. *Sleepy Bears* (PS–2). Illus. by Kerry Argent. 1999, Harcourt $16.00 (0-15-202016-0). 32pp. Mama Bear sings a different lullaby to each of her six cubs as they settle in for a winter's sleep. (Rev: BL 11/15/99; HBG 3/00; SLJ 10/99)

679 Fox, Mem. *Time for Bed* (PS). Illus. by Jane Dyer. 1993, Harcourt $16.00 (0-15-288183-2). 32pp. Various animals put their babies to sleep in this quiet bedtime book. (Rev: BCCB 10/93; BL 10/1/93; SLJ 10/93)

680 Frampton, David. *The Whole Night Through: A Lullaby* (PS–1). Illus. 2001, HarperCollins LB $15.89 (0-06-028826-4). 32pp. A boisterous little leopard is determined to stay awake. (Rev: BL 5/15/01; HBG 10/01; SLJ 6/01*)

681 Freedman, Claire. *Good Night, Sleep Tight* (PS–K). Illus. by Rory Tyger. 2003, Abrams $14.95 (0-8109-4513-4). In this heartwarming bedtime story, Grandma Bear gets little Archie to sleep when she tells him stories about putting his mother to bed. (Rev: BL 12/15/03; HBG 4/04; SLJ 12/03)

682 Freedman, Claire. *Hushabye Lily* (PS–1). Illus. by John Bendall-Brunello. 2003, Scholastic $15.95 (0-439-47106-0). A young bunny is kept awake by the many noises she hears in the farmyard. (Rev: HBG 4/04; SLJ 11/03)

683 Freedman, Claire. *Night-Night, Emily!* (PS). Illus. by Jane Massey. 2003, Tiger Tales $15.95 (1-58925-032-X). In this gentle bedtime story, little Emily is distressed when she can't find Mr. Teddy, her favorite stuffed animal; she tries substituting other stuffed toys, but she's unable to fall asleep until she discovers Mr. Teddy hidden beneath a pillow. (Rev: SLJ 1/04)

684 Gabriel, Andrea. *My Favorite Bear* (PS–1). Illus. 2003, Charlesbridge $15.95 (1-58089-038-5). 32pp. To get her little bear to sleep, a mother bear sings a song about different kinds of bears. (Rev: BL 2/15/03; HBG 10/03; SLJ 2/03)

685 Garelick, May. *Look at the Moon* (K–3). Illus. by Barbara Garrison. 1996, Mondo $14.95 (1-57255-142-9). 30pp. A young girl wonders if animals experience the same thrill of seeing moonlight as she does. (Rev: BL 11/15/96; SLJ 1/97)

686 Gay, Michel. *Zee Is Not Scared* (PS–2). Trans. from French by Marie Mianowski. Illus. by author. 2004, Clarion $15.00 (0-618-43931-5). 29pp. A little zebra can't settle down to sleep in this translation of a French story, and decides to dress up as a ghost and scare his parents. (Rev: SLJ 4/04)

687 George, Lindsay Barrett. *My Bunny and Me* (PS–2). Illus. 2001, Greenwillow LB $15.89 (0-688-16075-1). 32pp. A boy draws a bunny that comes to life and the two play together until the boy goes to bed and the bunny hops off into a field. (Rev: BL 1/1–15/01; HBG 10/01)

688 Gerber, Carole. *Firefly Night* (PS–3). Illus. by Marty Husted. 2000, Charlesbridge $16.95 (1-58089-051-2); paper $6.95 (1-58089-066-0). 32pp. Based on some lines from Longfellow's *Hiawatha*, this is the gentle story of a young Chippewa girl who is guided home at night by a firefly. (Rev: BL 11/1/00; HBG 3/01; SLJ 1/01)

689 Gerber, Carole. *Hush! A Gaelic Lullaby* (PS–2). Illus. by Marty Husted. 1997, Whispering Coyote $16.95 (1-879085-57-7). In this lullaby, an Irish family puts baby to bed while taking precautions against a storm that is approaching their farm. (Rev: HB 1–2, 3–4, 5–6/97; HBG 3/98; SLJ 1/98)

690 Gershator, Phillis. *The Babysitter Sings* (PS). Illus. by M lisande Potter. 2004, Holt $16.95 (0-8050-7199-7). Bright paintings of life in a warm island climate accompany a text derived from the lullabies of Africa, Spain, and the Caribbean. (Rev: HB 5–6/04; SLJ 7/04)

691 Gerstein, Mordicai. *Bedtime, Everybody!* (PS–2). Illus. 1996, Hyperion LB $13.49 (0-7868-2138-8). 32pp. Daisy has difficulty getting her many stuffed animals to go to bed. (Rev: BL 6/1–15/96; SLJ 6/96)

692 Gliori, Debi. *Debi Gliori's Bedtime Stories: Bedtime Tales with a Twist* (PS–2). Illus. 2002, DK $15.99 (0-7894-8861-2). 80pp. Old favorites such as "The Tortoise and the Hare" get surprising revisions in this amusing bedtime book. (Rev: BL 12/15/02; HBG 3/03; SLJ 2/03) [398.2]

693 Gliori, Debi. *Polar Bolero: A Bedtime Dance* (PS–2). Illus. 2001, Harcourt $16.00 (0-15-202436-0). 32pp. When it's too hot to sleep, a young polar bear heads to the place where they dance the Polar Bolero. (Rev: BL 5/1/01; HBG 10/01; SLJ 6/01)

694 Goodman, Joan E. *Bernard's Nap* (PS–1). Illus. by Dominic Catalano. 1999, Boyds Mills $14.95 (1-56397-728-1). 32pp. While trying to get Bernard, a baby elephant, to take his nap, the rest of his family nod off, but not Bernard — until he eventually gives in. (Rev: BL 3/15/99; HBG 10/99; SLJ 4/99)

695 Greenstein, Elaine. *Dreaming: A Countdown to Sleep* (PS–1). Illus. 2000, Scholastic $15.95 (0-439-06302-7). 32pp. With a text that involves counting down from ten to one, this picture book evokes a dreamy atmosphere before sleep comes. (Rev: BCCB 5/00; BL 2/1/00; HBG 3/01; SLJ 6/00)

696 Griffin, Sandra U. *Earth Circles* (PS–3). Illus. by author. 1989, Walker LB $13.85 (0-8027-6845-8). The circle of life from birth to death, including the need to sleep at the end of each day, is introduced as it appears in nature. (Rev: SLJ 11/89)

697 Hague, Kathleen. *Good Night, Fairies* (PS–3). Illus. by Michael Hague. 2002, North-South $15.95 (1-58717-134-1). 40pp. This magical bedtime book has a mother explaining to her child all the jobs performed by fairies. (Rev: BL 3/15/02; HBG 10/02)

698 Haines, Mike. *Countdown to Bedtime* (PS). Illus. by David Melling. 2001, Hyperion $12.99 (0-7868-0741-5). 16pp. A lift-the-flap book that accompanies a pair of young animals in their preparations for bed as a 10-minute deadline counts down. (Rev: BL 6/1–15/01; HBG 10/01; SLJ 7/01)

699 Harley, Bill. *Nothing Happened* (K–2). Illus. by Ann Miya. 1995, Tricycle $14.95 (1-883672-09-0). 32pp. Jack is determined to stay awake so he can share in all the exciting things he believes happen to his family when he is asleep. (Rev: BL 4/15/95; SLJ 6/95)

700 Harrison, Troon. *The Dream Collector* (PS–3). Illus. by Alan Daniel and Lea Daniel. 1999, Kids Can $15.95 (1-55074-437-2). 32pp. When the dream collector can't collect all the creatures left over from people's dreams because of a broken truck, little Zachary gives him a hand. (Rev: BL 3/1/99; HBG 10/99; SLJ 7/99)

701 Harshman, Marc. *All the Way to Morning* (PS–3). Illus. by Felipe Davalos. 1999, Marshall Cavendish $15.95 (0-7614-5042-4). 32pp. On a camping trip, a father tells his son what children in other countries such as Israel, Japan, and Kenya hear as they go to sleep at night. (Rev: BL 9/15/99; HBG 3/00; SLJ 11/99)

702 Hendry, Diana. *The Very Noisy Night* (PS–2). Illus. by Jane Chapman. 1999, Dutton $15.99 (0-525-46261-9). 36pp. Little Mouse can't sleep and wants to crawl into Big Mouse's bed but is rebuffed because his paws are too cold. (Rev: BL 12/1/99; HBG 3/00; SLJ 11/99)

703 Hest, Amy. *Kiss Good Night* (PS–1). Illus. by Anita Jeram. 2001, Candlewick $15.99 (0-7636-0780-0). 32pp. Sam, a little bear, cannot fall asleep without his mother's goodnight kiss. (Rev: BL 10/1/01; HBG 3/02; SLJ 11/01*)

704 Hines, Anna Grossnickle. *My Own Big Bed* (PS–K). Illus. by Mary Watson. 1998, Greenwillow $15.00 (0-688-15599-5). 24pp. At bedtime, a young girl enjoys her new, roomy bed, where Mommy and Daddy can sit next to her. (Rev: BL 10/15/98; HBG 3/99; SLJ 4/99)

705 Ho, Minfong. *Hush! A Thai Lullaby* (PS–3). Illus. by Holly Meade. 1996, Orchard LB $16.99 (0-531-08850-2). 32pp. In this lullaby, a mother quiets the animals, one by one, so that her baby can sleep. (Rev: BCCB 4/96; BL 4/15/96; HB 11–12/96; SLJ 3/96)

706 Hodge, Marie. *Are You Sleepy Yet, Petey?* (PS). Illus. by Renee Graef. 2005, Sterling $12.95 (1-4027-1265-0). A little boy in pajamas has trouble getting his puppy to go to sleep. (Rev: SLJ 6/05)

707 Hoellwarth, Cathryn C. *The Underbed* (PS–K). Illus. by Sibyl G. Grieg. 1990, Good Books $12.95 (0-934672-79-2). 24pp. Mother helps Tucker get rid of the monster he believes is under the bed. (Rev: BL 3/1/91; SLJ 7/91)

708 Hood, Thomas. *Before I Go to Sleep* (K–2). Illus. by Maryjane Begin. 1999, Morrow $16.00 (0-688-12424-0). In this 19th-century poem, a boy who is going to bed imagines what he would be doing if he were various animals such as a giraffe or mountain goat. (Rev: HBG 10/99; SLJ 6/99)

709 Hort, Lenny. *How Many Stars in the Sky?* (PS–1). Illus. by James E. Ransome. 1991, Morrow LB $15.93 (0-688-10104-6). 32pp. A boy and his father go out into the night to count the stars in the sky. (Rev: BCCB 6/91; BL 5/1/91; SLJ 5/91)

710 Hunter, Sally. *Humphrey's Bedtime* (PS–K). Illus. 2001, Holt $14.95 (0-8050-6903-8). 30pp. Little elephant Lottie watches her baby brother get ready for bed, proud that she's a big girl who can stay up later, but she tires eventually too. (Rev: BL 1/1–15/02; HBG 3/02; SLJ 2/02)

711 Hurd, Thacher. *Sleepy Cadillac: A Bedtime Tale* (PS–K). Illus. 2005, HarperCollins LB $16.89 (0-06-073021-8). 32pp. A dreamy story in which classic cars — a blue 1950s Cadillac convertible, in particular — take children off on soporific journeys. (Rev: BL 5/1/05; SLJ 5/05)

712 *Hush, Little Baby: A Traditional Lullaby* (PS). Illus. by Shari Halpern. 1997, North-South LB $15.88 (1-55858-808-6). 22pp. This lullaby is illustrated with fresh pictures that resemble parts of a quilt. (Rev: BL 10/15/97; HBG 3/98; SLJ 1/98)

713 James, Betsy. *The Dream Stair* (K–3). Illus. by Richard J. Watson. 1990, HarperCollins $13.95 (0-06-022787-7). 32pp. After Grandmother tucks her into bed, a little girl dreams of wandering "past clouds, past angels." (Rev: BL 3/1/90; SLJ 7/90)

714 Janovitz, Marilyn. *Maybe, My Baby* (PS). Illus. by author. 2003, North-South LB $16.50 (0-7358-1763-4). A wide variety of animal mothers try different methods to get their babies to sleep. (Rev: HBG 10/03; SLJ 6/03)

715 Jennings, Sharon. *No Monsters Here* (PS–K). Illus. by Ruth Ohi. 2004, Fitzhenry & Whiteside $14.95 (1-55041-787-8). 24pp. A young boy reassures his fearful father, checking there are no monsters under his father's bed before he settles down for the night. (Rev: BL 9/1/04; SLJ 10/04)

716 Jewell, Nancy. *Five Little Kittens* (PS). Illus. by Elizabeth Sayles. 1999, Clarion $9.95 (0-395-77517-5). 32pp. Five little kittens go through their daily routines and then contentedly fall asleep at the end of the day. (Rev: BL 8/99; HBG 3/00; SLJ 8/99)

717 Jewell, Nancy. *Sailor Song* (PS–1). Illus. by Stefano Vitale. 1999, Clarion $13.00 (0-395-82511-3). A lovely lullaby sung by a mother to her child that tells of a sailor's journey across sea and land to reach his snug house and waiting family. (Rev: HB 7–8/99; HBG 10/99; SLJ 5/99)

718 Jordan, Sandra. *Down on Casey's Farm* (PS–K). Illus. by author. 1996, Orchard LB $16.99 (0-531-08853-7). A bedtime book that introduces a number of farm animals through the fantasies of a young boy. (Rev: SLJ 10/96)

719 Kalman, Maira. *Hey Willy, See the Pyramids* (K–2). Illus. by author. 1988, Viking $16.99 (0-670-82163-2). 40pp. Sister Lulu tells a young boy an offbeat story about a woman and three cross-eyed dogs. (Rev: BL 2/1/89; SLJ 9/88)

720 Katz, Karen. *Counting Kisses* (PS). Illus. 2001, Simon & Schuster $14.00 (0-689-83470-5). 32pp. Every family member showers a baby with kisses until the young child peacefully drops off to sleep. (Rev: BCCB 2/01; BL 2/1/01; HBG 10/01; SLJ 2/01)

721 Kavanagh, Peter. *I Love My Mama* (PS–1). Illus. by Jane Chapman. 2003, Simon & Schuster $12.95 (0-689-85691-1). A mother elephant and her baby spend their day traversing the beautiful African landscape before settling down to sleep in the grass. (Rev: HBG 10/03; SLJ 4/03)

722 Koller, Jackie F. *No Such Thing* (K–3). Illus. by Betsy Lewin. 1997, Boyds Mills $14.95 (1-56397-490-8). 32pp. A monster and her son under the bed are undergoing the same comforting bedtime rituals as a real mother and son. (Rev: BCCB 3/97; BL 4/1/97; SLJ 6/97)

723 Kono, Erin Eitter. *Hula Lullaby* (PS–2). Illus. 2005, Little, Brown $15.99 (0-316-73591-4). 32pp. In her mother's lap, a Hawaiian girl listens to descriptions of the warm world around her until she falls asleep. (Rev: BL 5/1/05)

724 Lewis, Kim. *Good Night, Harry* (PS–K). Illus. by author. 2004, Candlewick $15.99 (0-7636-2206-0). Harry the elephant can't sleep, so Lulu and Ted — also soft toy animals — sit up with him until he drifts off. (Rev: SLJ 4/04)

725 Lindbergh, Reeve. *Our Nest* (PS–1). Illus. by Jill McElmurry. 2004, Candlewick $15.99 (0-7636-1286-3). 32pp. The comforts of all sorts of nests — from birds in trees to fish in water and boats in harbors — are celebrated in this gentle book. (Rev: BL 4/15/04*; SLJ 5/04)

726 Lindgren, Astrid. *I Don't Want to Go to Bed* (PS–1). Trans. by Barbara Lucas. Illus. by Ilon Wikland. 1988, Farrar $12.95 (91-29-59066-3). 32pp. Five-year-old Larry won't go to bed until Aunt Lottie gives him a pair of magic glasses. (Rev: BL 12/1/88; SLJ 4/89)

727 Loh, Morag. *Tucking Mommy In* (PS–1). Illus. by Donna Rawlins. 1988, Orchard paper $5.95 (0-531-07025-5). 40pp. Mommy falls asleep and the children tuck her in. (Rev: BCCB 9/88; BL 10/1/88; SLJ 10/88)

728 London, Jonathan. *Froggy Goes to Bed* (PS–K). Illus. by Frank Remkiewicz. 2000, Viking $15.99 (0-670-88860-5). 32pp. The nighttime rituals become so prolonged that Froggy's mother falls asleep before he does. (Rev: BL 3/1/00; HBG 10/00; SLJ 6/00)

729 Long, Sylvia. *Hush Little Baby* (PS–1). Illus. 1997, Chronicle $12.95 (0-8118-1416-5). 32pp. This song, a tender lullaby, focuses on the relationship between a mother and her baby bunny. (Rev: BL 6/1–15/97)

730 *Lullabies: An Illustrated Songbook* (PS–1). Illus. 1997, Harcourt $23.00 (0-15-201728-3). 96pp. Thirty-seven lullabies with simple piano accompaniment and guitar chords, as well as background information on each song. (Rev: BL 12/15/97; HBG 3/98; SLJ 1/98) [782]

731 *Lullaby Moons and a Silver Spoon* (PS–1). Ed. and illus. by Brooke Dyer. 2003, Little, Brown $15.95 (0-316-17474-2). 32pp. The bedtime rhymes collected here range from traditional favorites such as "Wynken, Blynken, and Nod" to more contemporary sleepy-time poems by writers including Nancy Willard and Eve Merriam. (Rev: BL 4/15/03; HBG 10/03; SLJ 5/03) [811.008]

732 Lum, Kate. *What! Cried Granny: An Almost Bedtime Story* (PS–K). Illus. by Adrian Johnson. 1999, Dial $14.99 (0-8037-2382-2). 32pp. While visiting his grandmother, Patrick puts her to work constructing a bed, knitting a blanket, making a pillow, etc., so he can go to bed properly. (Rev: BCCB 3/99; BL 5/1/99; HB 3–4/99; HBG 10/99; SLJ 3/99)

733 McBratney, Sam. *Guess How Much I Love You* (PS–K). Illus. by Anita Jeram. 1995, Candlewick $15.99 (1-56402-473-3). 32pp. In this bedtime book, a young rabbit tries to tell his father how much he loves him. (Rev: BL 3/15/95*; HB 7–8/95; SLJ 5/95)

734 McBratney, Sam. *You're All My Favorites* (PS–K). Illus. by Anita Jeram. 2004, Candlewick $15.99 (0-7636-2442-X). Three little bears worry that they are not good enough until they are reassured by their parents. (Rev: HB 9–10/04; SLJ 11/04)

735 McCain, Becky Ray. *Grandmother's Dreamcatcher* (K–2). Illus. by Stacey Schuett. 1998, Whitman $15.95 (0-8075-3031-X). 32pp. A young Chippewa boy goes to live with his grandmother, who cures him of having bad dreams by placing a dreamcatcher above his bed. (Rev: BL 10/1/98; HBG 3/99; SLJ 12/98)

736 McCourt, Lisa. *Good Night, Princess Pruney Toes* (PS). Illus. by Cyd Moore. 2001, Troll $15.95 (0-8167-5205-2). Sir Daddy helps to get his bouncy daughter, aka Princess Pruney Toes, ready for bed. (Rev: HBG 10/01; SLJ 5/01)

737 McCourt, Lisa. *I Love You, Stinky Face* (PS–K). Illus. by Cyd Moore. 1997, Troll $15.95 (0-8167-4392-4). 32pp. In this tender bedtime story, a young girl tests the limits of her mother's love with a series of questions like "Would you love me if I were a big scary ape?" (Rev: BL 10/15/97*; HBG 3/98; SLJ 10/97)

738 McCullough, Sharon Pierce. *Bunbun at Bedtime* (PS). Illus. 2001, Barefoot $14.99 (1-84148-438-5). 24pp. Bunbun dallies while his brother and sister get ready for bed until a scary noise prompts a burst of activity. (Rev: BL 10/1/01; HBG 3/02; SLJ 11/01)

739 MacDonald, Margaret Read. *Tuck-Me-In Tales: Bedtime Stories from Around the World* (PS–1). Illus. by Yvonne Davis. 1996, August House $19.95 (0-87483-461-9). 64pp. Five traditional bedtime stories from around the world are lavishly illustrated. (Rev: BL 10/1/96; SLJ 11/96) [398.2]

740 McDonald, Megan. *My House Has Stars* (PS–3). Illus. by Peter Catalanotto. 1996, Orchard LB $16.99 (0-531-08879-0). 32pp. Eight children from around the world tell about their homes in the evening and at night. (Rev: BCCB 11/96; BL 11/1/96; SLJ 10/96)

741 MacLachlan, Patricia. *Who Loves Me?* (PS). Illus. by Amanda Sheperd. 2005, HarperCollins LB $15.89 (0-06-027977-X). 40pp. A little girl and her cat check off all the people who love her. (Rev: BL 6/1–15/05; SLJ 5/05)

742 McMullan, Kate. *If You Were My Bunny* (PS–K). Illus. by David McPhail. 1996, Scholastic $7.95 (0-590-52749-5). 32pp. A bedtime book with lullabies sung by different loving animal mothers to their attentive offspring. (Rev: BL 5/1/96; HB 7–8/96)

743 McMullan, Kate. *Papa's Song* (PS–1). Illus. by Jim McMullan. 2000, Farrar $15.00 (0-374-35732-3). 32pp. Baby Bear has trouble going to sleep until Papa Bear takes him by boat onto a river where the rocking lulls him to sleep. (Rev: BL 2/15/00; HB 3–4/00; HBG 10/00; SLJ 5/00)

744 McMullen, Nigel. *It's Too Soon!* (PS). Illus. 2004, Simon & Schuster $14.95 (0-689-84248-1). 32pp. Little bunny Anna is reluctant to go to bed and makes lots of delaying demands of her grandfather. (Rev: BL 1/1–15/04; SLJ 3/04)

745 Mallat, Kathy. *Seven Stars More!* (PS). Illus. by author. 1998, Walker $14.95 (0-8027-8675-8). A counting book that is also a bedtime book about a little girl who counts objects to put herself to sleep. (Rev: HBG 3/99; SLJ 11/98)

746 Manushkin, Fran. *The Little Sleepyhead* (PS–1). Illus. by Leonid Gore. 2004, Dutton $16.99 (0-525-46956-7). A tired little boy tries to settle down to sleep with a variety of animals but can't find the right spot until he comes across a lamb. (Rev: SLJ 9/04)

747 Massie, Diane Redfield. *The Baby Beebee Bird* (PS–2). Illus. by Steven Kellogg. 2000, HarperCollins LB $15.89 (0-06-028084-0). 32pp. In this bedtime book, the animals in the zoo can't sleep at night because of the shrill cries of a newcomer, the nocturnal beebee bird. (Rev: BL 12/15/00; HBG 10/01; SLJ 9/00)

748 Melmed, Laura K. *Jumbo's Lullaby* (PS). Illus. by Henri Sorensen. 1999, Lothrop LB $15.93 (0-688-16996-1). 24pp. Mama Elephant tries to get her young child to sleep by describing how other animals go to bed. (Rev: BL 10/1/99; HBG 3/00; SLJ 9/99)

749 Millen, C. M. *Blue Bowl Down: An Appalachian Rhyme* (PS–1). Illus. by Holly Meade. 2004, Candlewick $16.99 (0-7636-1817-9). 32pp. Appealing cut-paper art and a lullaby rhyme depict an Appalachian mother and her toddler son step by step as they prepare bread dough for baking early the next morning. (Rev: BL 5/1/04; SLJ 9/04)

750 Mitton, Tony. *Goodnight Me, Goodnight You* (PS–1). Illus. by Mandy Sutcliffe. 2003, Little, Brown $14.95 (0-316-73880-8). A young brother and sister get ready for bed by quietly saying goodnight to everything in their world and to each other. (Rev: HBG 4/04; SLJ 2/04)

751 Moon, Nicola. *Tick-Tock, Drip-Drop! A Bedtime Story* (PS–K). Illus. by Eleanor Taylor. 2004, Bloomsbury $16.95 (1-58234-944-4). A clock, a dripping tap, and a purring cat are only three of the noises that disturb Mole and Rabbit as they try to go to sleep. (Rev: SLJ 11/04)

752 Morgan, Mary. *Sleep Tight, Little Mouse* (PS). Illus. by author. 2003, Knopf LB $14.99 (0-375-92308-X). 32pp. As he gets ready for bed, Little Mouse considers other options — such as a bird's nest or kangaroo's pouch — but decides that the best sleeping place is his own. (Rev: BL 5/15/03; HBG 10/03; SLJ 8/03)

753 Morrissey, Dean. *Ship of Dreams* (K–3). Illus. by author. 1994, Millpond: Abrams $17.95 (0-8109-3848-0). In this bedtime book, Joey takes off in his red wagon on a flight to see if the sandman really exists. (Rev: SLJ 12/94)

754 Mortensen, Denise Dowling. *Good Night Engines* (PS). Illus. by Melissa Iwai. 2003, Clarion $15.00 (0-618-13537-5). 32pp. At bedtime, a variety of forms of transport come to a halt and settle down for the night. (Rev: BL 12/15/03; HBG 4/04; SLJ 12/03)

755 Murray, Dennis. *The Stars Are Waiting* (PS–K). Illus. by Jacqueline Rogers. 1998, Marshall Cavendish $15.95 (0-7614-5024-6). 32pp. In this bedtime book, nighttime beckons all the animals of the forest to go to sleep and finally does the same to three young children in a neighboring farmhouse. (Rev: BL 8/98; HBG 10/98; SLJ 6/98)

756 Nakamura, Katherine Riley. *Song of Night: It's Time to Go to Bed* (PS). Illus. by Linnea Riley. 2002, Scholastic $15.95 (0-439-26678-5). 40pp. Animal parents help their beloved children get ready for bed in this charming bedtime book. (Rev: BL 2/1/02; HBG 10/02; SLJ 5/02)

757 Nobisso, Josephine. *The Moon's Lullaby* (PS–1). Illus. by Glo Coalson. 2001, Scholastic $15.95 (0-439-29312-X). 32pp. Muted watercolor illustrations complement this quiet tale of a yawn passed from one small baby to people across the world. (Rev: BL 1/1–15/02; HBG 3/02; SLJ 12/01)

758 O'Keefe, Susan Heyboer. *Good Night, God Bless* (PS–K). Illus. by Hideko Takahashi. 1999, Holt $15.95 (0-8050-6008-1). 32pp. A prayerful bedtime book in which a young boy, his family, some animals, and the whole town seek God's blessing. (Rev: BL 10/1/99; HBG 3/00; SLJ 10/99)

759 Ongman, Gudrun. *The Sleep Ponies* (PS–1). Illus. 2000, MindCastle $16.95 (0-9677204-0-0). 32pp. Dreaming children are able to ride sleep ponies and travel through wonderful landscapes in this soothing picture book. (Rev: BL 12/15/00)

760 Osofsky, Audrey. *Dreamcatcher* (PS–3). Illus. by Ed Young. 1992, Orchard LB $16.99 (0-531-08588-0). 32pp. An Ojibwa baby watches everyday events in his family's life and later sleeps peacefully. (Rev: BCCB 7–8/92; BL 2/15/92; SLJ 4/92)

761 Pank, Rachel. *Sonia and Barnie and the Noise in the Night* (PS–K). Illus. 1991, Scholastic paper $13.95 (0-590-44657-6). 32pp. Her cowardly cat may hide up in a tree, but brave and bossy Sonia takes on the "monster" who frightened them. (Rev: BL 6/1/91; SLJ 12/91)

762 Perl, Erica S. *Chicken Bedtime Is Really Early* (PS). Illus. by George Bates. 2005, Abrams $14.95 (0-8109-4926-1). 32pp. Baby farm animals — chicks, calves, bunnies, hamsters — turn in early to get some rest before the rooster crows in this bedtime picture book. (Rev: BL 3/15/05; SLJ 4/05)

763 Pitcher, Caroline. *The Winter Dragon* (K–2). Illus. by Sophy Williams. 2004, Lincoln $15.95 (1-84507-322-3). 36pp. Young Rory's dragon warms the winter nights, leaving the boy with memories of comfort and companionship when spring arrives. (Rev: BL 10/15/04; SLJ 1/05)

764 Plourde, Lynn. *Wild Child* (PS–3). Illus. by Greg Couch. 1999, Simon & Schuster $16.00 (0-689-81552-2). Mother Earth has a difficult time getting her child Autumn to go to sleep, but she does so just in time to welcome a new child, Winter. (Rev: HBG 3/00; SLJ 12/99)

765 Pumphrey, Jerome, and Jarrett Pumphrey. *Creepy Things Are Scaring Me* (K–2). Illus. by Rosanne Litzinger. 2003, HarperCollins LB $15.89 (0-06-028963-5). Children who grow fearful when the bedroom light goes out will find comfort in this charming story of a frightened young boy whose mother patiently reassures him that the nighttime shadows hold no terrors. (Rev: HBG 4/04; SLJ 9/03)

766 Raschka, Chris. *Can't Sleep* (PS–1). Illus. 1995, Orchard LB $15.99 (0-531-08779-4). 32pp. A young dog with insomnia takes comfort in having the moon watch over him until he goes to sleep. (Rev: BCCB 10/95; BL 9/15/95; SLJ 9/95*)

767 Raya-Norman, Faye. *Wolf Songs* (PS–2). Illus. by Richard Ziehler-Martin. 1999, Portunus $15.95 (1-886440-04-2). In this bedtime fantasy, young Matthew is led on a night walk by a silver wolf and is accompanied by a full moon, northern lights, and stars. (Rev: SLJ 2/00)

768 Robbins, Maria Polushkin. *Mother, Mother, I Want Another* (PS–2). Illus. by Jon Goodell. 2005, Knopf LB $16.99 (0-375-92588-0). 32pp. A newly illustrated edition of the bedtime story in which Mrs. Mouse misinterprets her son's request. (Rev: BL 2/15/05; SLJ 3/05)

769 Roberts, Bethany. *Gramps and the Fire Dragon* (PS–3). Illus. by Melissa Iwai. 2000, Clarion $15.00 (0-395-69849-9). 32pp. Not ready for bed, a boy and his grandfather dream of wild adventures as they conjure up pictures from the fireplace flames and, at last, doze off. (Rev: BL 1/1–15/01; HBG 3/01; SLJ 11/00)

770 Rock, Lois. *I Wish Tonight* (PS–2). Illus. by Anne Wilson. 2000, Good Books $16.00 (1-56148-315-X). In bed at night, a young boy wishes on a star and travels into a world of make-believe. (Rev: SLJ 12/00)

771 Roep, Nanda. *Kisses* (PS). Illus. by Marijke Ten Cate. 2002, Front Street $15.95 (1-886910-85-5). Goodnight kisses are the focus of this richly illustrated, gentle story. (Rev: HBG 3/03; SLJ 1/03)

772 Root, Phyllis. *Ten Sleepy Sheep* (PS–K). Illus. by Susan Gaber. 2004, Candlewick $15.99 (0-7636-1545-5). Ten little sheep, which can be distinguished by the ribbons around their necks, move from one place to another, always leaving one of their flock behind sound asleep. (Rev: HB 5–6/04; SLJ 4/04)

773 Roth, Carol. *Little Bunny's Sleepless Night* (PS–K). Illus. by Valeri Gorbachev. 1999, North-South LB $15.88 (0-7358-1070-2). 32pp. Little Bunny is lonely at night, so he tries sleeping with other animals. Each proves unsatisfactory (e.g., Bear snores), and so he returns home happily to his own bed. (Rev: BL 6/1–15/99; HBG 10/99; SLJ 7/99)

774 Rothstein, Gloria. *Sheep Asleep* (PS). Illus. by Lizzy Rockwell. 2003, HarperCollins LB $16.89 (0-06-029106-0). When sleep comes slowly to her young ones, the mother of 10 little sheep suggests counting — well, you know . . . . (Rev: HBG 10/03; SLJ 6/03)

775 Rydell, Katy. *Wind Says Good Night* (PS–1). Illus. by David Jorgensen. 1994, Houghton Mifflin $16.00 (0-395-60474-5). 42pp. This cumulative bedtime story tells how all the animals and birds cooperate so a little girl can go to sleep. (Rev: BCCB 5/94; BL 4/1/94; SLJ 4/94*)

776 Saltzberg, Barney. *Cornelius P. Mud, Are You Ready for Bed?* (PS). Illus. 2005, Candlewick $15.99 (0-7636-2399-7). 32pp. Asked many pre-bed questions ("Have you used the bathroom?"), Cornelius the pig blithely lies "yes" but the illustrations tell the truth. (Rev: BL 5/1/05; SLJ 3/05)

777 Sanroman, Susana. *Señora Reganona* (PS–3). Illus. by Domi. 1998, Douglas & McIntyre $14.95 (0-88899-320-X). 32pp. A child conquers her fear of the dark, which she calls "Señora Reganona," when she flies into the sky one night and makes a friend of the Señora. (Rev: BL 8/98; HBG 10/98; SLJ 9/98)

778 Schaefer, Carole L. *Down in the Woods at Sleepytime* (PS). Illus. by Vanessa Cabban. 2000, Candlewick $15.99 (0-7636-0843-2). 32pp. None of the animals in the woods is ready to go to bed, but when Grandma Owl shouts that it is story time everyone settles down. (Rev: BL 11/15/00; HBG 10/01; SLJ 11/00)

779 Schertle, Alice. *Good Night, Hattie, My Dearie, My Dove* (PS–1). Illus. by Ted Rand. 2002, Harper-Collins LB $15.89 (0-688-16023-9). 32pp. A sweet bedtime book about Hattie and the nine stuffed animals she wants to take to bed with her. (Rev: BL 4/1/02; HBG 10/02; SLJ 6/02)

780 Schotter, Roni. *Bunny's Night Out* (PS–1). Illus. by Margot Apple. 1989, Little, Brown $13.95 (0-316-77465-0). A bunny sneaks out at night and experiences adventures before coming home to his welcome bed. (Rev: SLJ 7/89)

781 Scotton, Rob. *Russell the Sheep* (PS–1). Illus. by author. 2005, HarperCollins LB $16.89 (0-06-059849-2). Russell can't sleep and counting doesn't work until he switches from stars to sheep. (Rev: SLJ 4/05)

782 Siegen-Smith, Nikki, comp. *A Pocketful of Stars: Poems About the Night* (K–3). Illus. by Emma Shaw-Smith. 1999, Barefoot $16.95 (1-902283-84-8). 40pp. An anthology of 21 short poems about the night and sleep by such poets as Walter de la Mare, Ogden Nash, and Ann Bonner. (Rev: SLJ 1/00) [811]

783 Spetter, Jung-Hee. *Lily and Trooper's Spring* (PS). Illus. 1999, Front Street $8.95 (1-886910-36-7). 32pp. Lily and her dog, Trooper, have a series of misadventures while attempting a quiet picnic in the country, and both of them need baths before bedtime. (Rev: BL 5/1/99; SLJ 7/99)

784 Spetter, Jung-Hee. *Lily and Trooper's Summer* (PS–K). Illus. 1999, Front Street $8.95 (1-886910-37-5). 32pp. Lily and her dog, Trooper, spend a wonderful day outdoors and then are so tired that they fall asleep on top of the covers. (Rev: BL 5/15/99; SLJ 7/99)

785 Spinelli, Eileen. *Kittycat Lullaby* (PS–K). Illus. by Anne Mortimer. 2001, Hyperion $14.99 (0-7868-0458-0). 32pp. A rambunctious kitten settles down after a long, busy day. (Rev: BL 8/01; HBG 3/02; SLJ 10/01)

786 Spinelli, Eileen. *Naptime, Laptime* (PS). Illus. by Melissa Sweet. 1995, Scholastic $6.95 (0-590-48510-5). 24pp. A child wonders where various animals sleep and then decides it's best on grandmother's lap. (Rev: BCCB 2/96; BL 12/1/95; SLJ 2/96)

787 Spinelli, Eileen. *What Do Angels Wear?* (PS–K). Illus. by Emily Arnold McCully. 2003, HarperCollins LB $16.89 (0-06-028887-6). In rhyming text, an inquisitive young girl and her mother discuss the nature of angels. (Rev: BL 11/1/03; HBG 4/04; SLJ 12/03)

788 Sproule, Gail. *Singing the Dark* (PS–2). Illus. by Sheena Lott. 2001, Fitzhenry & Whiteside $16.95 (1-55041-648-0). 40pp. Every night, Kaylie's mother sings a song "calling darkness" to greet the night, and Kaylie chimes in. (Rev: BL 12/15/01)

789 Steinbrenner, Jessica. *My Sleepy Room* (PS). Illus. by Elizabeth Wolf. 2004, Handprint $15.95 (1-59354-007-8). Bess's "sleepy room" is a comforting place where she reads, plays with toys, and sometimes sleeps. (Rev: SLJ 7/04)

790 Stevenson, James. *What's Under My Bed?* (1–3). Illus. by author. 1983, Greenwillow LB $15.93 (0-688-02327-4); Morrow paper $4.95 (0-688-09350-7). 32pp. A grandfather helps reduce his grandchildren's fears. A sequel is: *Worse Than Willy!* (1984).

791 Stickland, Paul. *Bears!* (PS–1). Illus. by author. 2001, Ragged Bear $15.95 (1-929927-34-7). A boy trying to go to sleep is disturbed by bears having a party. (Rev: HBG 10/02; SLJ 2/02)

792 Sutherland, Marc. *The Waiting Place* (PS–3). Illus. by author. 1998, Abrams $14.95 (0-8109-3994-0). 24pp. A bedroom becomes populated with a variety of objects and beings that enter through an open window in this unusual book about going to bed. (Rev: HBG 3/99; SLJ 3/99)

793 Szekeres, Cyndy. *The Deep Blue Sky Twinkles with Stars* (PS–K). Illus. 1998, Scholastic $12.95 (0-590-69198-8). 40pp. This bedtime book shows five young rabbits getting ready for bed and a story from Dad. (Rev: BL 2/15/98; HBG 10/98; SLJ 3/98)

794 Tafuri, Nancy. *I Love You, Little One* (PS–1). Illus. 1998, Scholastic $15.95 (0-590-92159-2). 32pp. In this bedtime story, different animal mothers try to tell their children how much they love them. (Rev: BL 2/1/98; HBG 10/98; SLJ 3/98)

795 Thomas, Joyce C. *Hush Songs: African American Lullabies* (PS). Illus. by Brenda Joysmith. 2000, Hyperion $15.99 (0-7868-0562-5). 48pp. A collection of ten African American lullabies with the words and full musical scores. (Rev: BL 12/15/00; HBG 10/01) [782.4]

796 Thompson, Lauren. *Little Quack's Bedtime* (PS–K). Illus. by Derek Anderson. 2005, Simon & Schuster $14.95 (0-689-86894-4). Mama Duck succeeds in getting four of her ducklings off to sleep, but Little Quack needs special attention. (Rev: SLJ 2/05)

797 Trapani, Iza. *Shoo Fly!* (PS–1). Illus. by author. 2000, Charlesbridge LB $15.95 (1-58089-052-0). This adaptation of a perky song concerns a little mouse and pesky fly and how they are both tucked in at night. (Rev: SLJ 1/01)

798 *Twilight Verses, Moonlight Rhymes* (PS). Ed. by Mary Joslin. Illus. by Liz Pichon. 1999, Augsburg $16.95 (0-8066-3885-0). 60pp. An anthology of nighttime rhymes that includes lullabies, nursery rhymes, and some prayers. (Rev: BL 12/15/99; HBG 3/00; SLJ 3/00) [821.008]

799 *Twinkle, Twinkle, Little Star* (PS). Illus. by Sylvia Long. 2001, Chronicle $13.95 (0-8118-2854-9). Watercolor illustrations show young animals greeting the first star before going home for the night in this rendition of the traditional lullaby. (Rev: HBG 3/02; SLJ 1/02)

800 Tyers, Jenny. *When It Is Night, When It Is Day* (PS–2). Illus. 1996, Houghton Mifflin $14.95 (0-395-71546-6). 32pp. The behavior of various animals at night is explored in this charming bedtime book. (Rev: BL 3/1/96; SLJ 4/96)

801 Waddell, Martin. *Can't You Sleep, Little Bear?* (PS). Illus. by Barbara Firth. 1992, Candlewick $15.99 (1-56402-007-X). 32pp. Even lanterns don't comfort Little Bear, who is scared of the dark, until Father Bear offers the comfort of his arms. (Rev: BCCB 4/92; BL 3/1/92*; SLJ 1/92*)

802 Wahl, Jan. *Elf Night* (1–3). Illus. by Peter Weevers. 2002, Carolrhoda $15.95 (1-57505-512-0). 32pp. A young boy spends a magical time with the fairy folk until he goes back to his bed. (Rev: BL 5/1/02; HBG 10/02; SLJ 5/02)

803 Wallace, John. *Anything for You* (PS–2). Illus. by Harry Horse. 2004, HarperCollins $15.99 (0-06-058129-8). At the end of the day, Little Charlie, a bear cub, lists all the things he'd do for his mother because he loves her. (Rev: SLJ 4/04)

804 Wallace, Nancy E. *Rabbit's Bedtime* (PS). Illus. by author. 1999, Houghton Mifflin $9.95 (0-395-98266-9). Before a youngster goes to sleep, he and his mother recall all the loving things they did together during the day. (Rev: HBG 3/00; SLJ 11/99)

805 Warnick, Elsa. *Bedtime* (PS–K). Illus. 1998, Harcourt $10.00 (0-15-201471-3). 28pp. This warmly illustrated picture book introduces all the small rituals associated with going to bed, such as using the potty and brushing one's teeth. (Rev: BL 8/98; HBG 3/99; SLJ 9/98)

806 *Weave Little Stars into My Sleep: Native American Lullabies* (2–4). Ed. by Neil Philip. Illus. by Edward S. Curtis. 2001, Clarion $16.00 (0-618-08856-3). 48pp. Fifteen Native American lullabies are accompanied by sepia-toned illustrations and background information. (Rev: BL 10/15/01; HBG 3/02; SLJ 11/01) [782.4215]

807 Welch, Willy. *Grumpy Bunnies* (PS–1). Illus. by Tammie Lyon. 2000, Charlesbridge $16.95 (1-58089-053-9); paper $6.95 (1-58089-060-1). 32pp. The day improves as it goes along for three little rabbits who go to bed looking forward to tomorrow. (Rev: HBG 10/00; SLJ 5/00)

808 Wells, Philip. *Daddy Island* (PS–K). Illus. by Niki Daly. 2001, Barefoot $15.99 (1-84148-197-1). 24pp. A boy imagines himself as all kinds of things — a crab, a wild storm, a rock — as he completes the mundane task of getting ready for bed. (Rev: BL 11/15/01; HBG 3/02; SLJ 12/01)

809 Wells, Rosemary. *Goodnight Max* (PS). Illus. by author. 2000, Viking $9.99 (0-670-88707-2). In this board book that contains touch-and-feel surprises Max the rabbit has to change his pajamas three times before he can get to sleep. (Rev: BL 6/1–15/03; HBG 10/03; SLJ 4/00)

810 Weninger, Brigitte. *It's Bedtime!* (PS–2). Trans. by Kathryn Grell. Illus. by Alan Marks. 2002, North-South LB $15.88 (0-7358-1603-4). 32pp. Ben is reluctant to go to sleep until he selects a scary toy to sleep with him and frighten away the monsters. (Rev: BL 7/02; HBG 10/02; SLJ 7/02)

811 Whybrow, Ian. *The Noisy Way to Bed* (PS–1). Illus. by Tiphanie Beeke. 2004, Scholastic $15.95 (0-439-55689-9). A little boy collects a parade of noisy farm animals on his way to bed. (Rev: SLJ 3/04)

812 Wild, Margaret. *Nighty Night!* (PS–1). Illus. by Kerry Argent. 2001, Peachtree $15.95 (1-56145-246-7). 32pp. Simple, rhythmic text and rich, humorous illustrations describe animal babies resisting their parents' efforts to put them to bed. (Rev: BCCB 9/01; BL 9/1/01; HBG 3/02; SLJ 9/01)

813 Wiles, Deborah. *One Wide Sky: A Bedtime Lullaby* (PS–K). Illus. by Tim Bowers. 2003, Harcourt $16.00 (0-15-202334-8). In this appealing bedtime and counting story, three children and two young squirrels enjoy the delights of the leafy backyard. (Rev: HBG 10/03; SLJ 6/03)

814 Winthrop, Elizabeth. *Asleep in a Heap* (PS–1). Illus. by Mary Morgan. 1993, Holiday House LB $15.95 (0-8234-0992-9). 32pp. Julia is much too busy to go to bed, but her antics send the rest of the family to sleep. (Rev: BL 11/15/93; SLJ 1/94)

815 Winthrop, Elizabeth. *Maggie and the Monster* (PS–K). Illus. by Tomie dePaola. 1987, Holiday House LB $15.95 (0-8234-0639-3); paper $5.95 (0-8234-0698-9). 32pp. Every single night a small girl monster comes into Maggie's room. (Rev: BL 4/1/87; SLJ 5/87)

816 Yolen, Jane. *How Do Dinosaurs Say Goodnight?* (PS–1). Illus. by Mark Teague. 2000, Scholastic $15.95 (0-590-31681-8). 40pp. A bedtime book that features all sorts of baby dinosaurs behaving like human children at bedtime. (Rev: BCCB 6/00; BL 4/1/00*; HBG 10/00; SLJ 6/00)

817 Yolen, Jane. *Time for Naps* (PS). Illus. by Hiroe Nakata. 2002, Simon & Schuster $7.99 (0-689-85057-3). This board book tells the story of a little girl putting her stuffed animals to bed. (Rev: SLJ 11/02)

818 Ziefert, Harriet. *Clara Ann Cookie, Go to Bed!* (PS–3). Illus. by Emily Bolam. 2000, Houghton Mifflin $15.00 (0-395-97381-3). 32pp. Clara Ann, who has been resisting her mother's efforts to put her to bed, gets the same treatment when her teddy bear refuses to accompany her when she finally gives in. (Rev: BL 9/1/00; HBG 3/01; SLJ 10/00)

819 Ziefert, Harriet. *Moonride* (PS–K). Illus. by Seymour Chwast. 2000, Houghton Mifflin $15.00 (0-618-00229-4). 32pp. A little boy accepts a ride from the moon and attends a night baseball game before he returns to his bed and sleep. (Rev: BL 3/15/00; HBG 10/00; SLJ 12/00)

Nursery Rhymes

820 Ada, Alma Flor, and F. Isabel Campoy. *Mama Goose: A Latino Nursery Treasury / Un Tesoro de Rimas Infantiles* (PS–2). Trans. by Tracey Heffernan. 2005, Hyperion LB $19.49 (0-7868-1953-7). 128pp. Spanish-language songs, rhymes, and childhood sayings, along with their English equivalents and watercolor illustrations. (Rev: BL 3/15/05) [398.8]

821 Ada, Alma Flor, and F. Isabel Campoy, sels. *Pio Peep! Traditional Spanish Nursery Rhymes* (PS–2). 2003, HarperCollins LB $16.89 (0-688-16020-4). 64pp. English-language adaptations retain the rhythm and poetry of these Spanish rhymes. (Rev: HBG 10/03; SLJ 7/03) [398.8]

822 Alter, Anna. *The Three Little Kittens* (PS–K). Illus. 2001, Holt $15.95 (0-8050-6471-0). 24pp. In this attractive and humorous version of the nursery rhyme, the three kittens recover their mittens from thieving mice. (Rev: BL 10/1/01; HBG 3/02; SLJ 11/01)

823 Aylesworth, Jim. *The Completed Hickory Dickory Dock* (PS–K). Illus. by Eileen Christelow. 1994, Aladdin paper $5.99 (0-689-71862-4). 32pp. The

"whole" story of what happened when the clock struck. (Rev: BL 10/1/90; SLJ 2/91) [811]

824 Beaton, Clare, comp. *Mother Goose Remembers* (PS). Illus. by Clare Beaton. 2000, Barefoot $16.99 (1-84148-073-8). 64pp. A highly appealing collection of 46 Mother Goose rhymes with pictures made of felt and other fabrics. (Rev: HBG 3/01; SLJ 9/00)

825 Beaton, Clare. *Playtime Rhymes for Little People* (PS–K). Illus. 2001, Barefoot $18.99 (1-84148-425-3). 64pp. Forty familiar children's rhymes are accompanied by embroidered collages. (Rev: BCCB 12/01; BL 10/15/01; HBG 3/02; SLJ 11/01) [398.8]

826 Beil, Karen M. *A Cake All for Me!* (PS–2). Illus. by Paul Meisel. 1998, Holiday House $16.95 (0-8234-1368-3). Using a nursery rhyme format, this is the story of Piggy who makes a cake and shares it with others. (Rev: HBG 3/99; SLJ 9/98)

827 Benjamin, Floella. *Skip Across the Ocean: Nursery Rhymes from Around the World* (PS–K). Illus. by Sheila Moxley. 1995, Orchard $15.95 (0-531-09455-3). 48pp. Thirty-two nursery rhymes from around the world, including several lullabies. (Rev: BL 10/1/95; SLJ 11/95)

828 *The Blue's Clues Nursery Rhyme Treasury* (PS–2). 2001, Simon & Schuster $15.95 (0-689-84682-7). A collection of classic rhymes with the addition of some Blue's Clues characters and colorful illustrations. (Rev: HBG 3/02; SLJ 1/02) [398.8]

829 Bornstein, Harry, and Karen L. Saulnier. *Nursery Rhymes from Mother Goose Told in Signed English* (K–2). Illus. by Patricia Peters and Linda C. Tom. 1993, Gallaudet Univ. $14.95 (0-930323-99-8). 41pp. Fourteen rhymes with signing symbols for the deaf. (Rev: SLJ 6/93) [398.8]

830 Boyle, Alison. *Twinkle, Twinkle, Little Star* (PS). Illus. 2000, David & Charles $10.95 (1-86233-111-1). In this interactive book using the familiar rhyme, a little star enters a house looking for a bear. (Rev: BL 12/1/00)

831 Brown, Marc. *Play Rhymes* (PS–1). Illus. 1993, Puffin paper $5.99 (0-140-54936-6). 32pp. There is humor, warmth, and coziness in these play rhymes. Also use: *Hand Rhymes* (1985). (Rev: BL 12/1/87; HB 11–12/87; SLJ 10/87) [398.8]

832 Brown, Ruth. *Ladybug, Ladybug* (PS–1). Illus. by author. 1992, Puffin paper $5.99 (0-14-054543-3). 32pp. An extended version of the Mother Goose rhyme. (Rev: BL 11/1/88) [398.8]

833 Cabrera, Jane. *Old Mother Hubbard* (PS). Illus. 2001, Holiday House $15.95 (0-8234-1659-3). 32pp. Old Mother Hubbard's dog is up to some new tricks in this colorful and imaginative rendition of the familiar nursery rhyme. (Rev: BCCB 11/01; BL 9/1/01; HBG 3/02; SLJ 1/02) [821.7]

834 Catalano, Dominic. *Hush! A Fantasy in Verse* (PS). Illus. by author. 2003, Gingham Dog $14.95 (1-57768-679-9). In this charming variation on the traditional nursery song/rhyme "Hush Little Baby," a father tries to comfort his young daughter after she wakes up from a bad dream. (Rev: HBG 4/04; SLJ 1/04)

835 Chapman, Jane. *Sing a Song of Sixpence: A Pocketful of Nursery Rhymes and Tales* (PS). 2004,

Candlewick $15.99 (0-7636-2545-0). 64pp. Striking acrylic artwork highlights this collection of familiar nursery rhymes and three fairy tales ("Goldilocks," "The Three Little Pigs," and "The Little Red Hen"). (Rev: BL 9/1/04; SLJ 10/04) [398.8]

836 *A Child's Treasury of Nursery Rhymes* (PS–K). Ed. by Kady MacDonald Denton. Illus. 1998, Kingfisher $17.95 (0-7534-5109-3). 96pp. An excellent collection of rhymes that includes old favorites plus tongue twisters, riddles, and limericks, all illustrated with joyous watercolors. (Rev: BCCB 1/99; BL 11/1/98; HBG 3/99; SLJ 11/98)

837 Crews, Nina. *The Neighborhood Mother Goose* (PS–2). Photos by author. 2004, Greenwillow LB $16.89 (0-06-051574-0). 63pp. "Mother" in this case is a real goose in a city park, and the illustrations portray urban youngsters and scenery. (Rev: HB 5–6/04; SLJ 1/04) [398.8]

838 Cummings, Pat. *My Aunt Came Back* (PS). Illus. by author. Series: Harper Growing Tree. 1998, HarperCollins $5.95 (0-694-01059-6). In this board book, featuring seven different rhymes, a little girl receives presents from her globe-trotting aunt. (Rev: HBG 10/98; SLJ 10/98)

839 Edwards, Pamela Duncan, retel. *Miss Polly Has a Dolly* (PS–1). Illus. by Elicia Castaldi. 2003, Penguin Putnam $15.99 (0-399-23857-3). A rhyming rope-jumping chant is expanded and set to music, with finger-play motions provided. (Rev: HBG 4/04; SLJ 11/03)

840 Edwards, Pamela Duncan. *The Neat Line: Scribbling Through Mother Goose* (PS–2). Illus. by Diana Cain Blumenthal. 2005, HarperCollins LB $16.89 (0-06-623971-0). 32pp. A baby scribble grows up to be a Neat Line and works its way into a book of nursery rhymes to help the familiar characters out of their predicaments. (Rev: BL 3/15/05; SLJ 5/05)

841 Foreman, Michael. *Michael Foreman's Mother Goose* (PS–K). Illus. by author. 1991, Harcourt $22.00 (0-15-255820-9). 160pp. A rewarding visual tour of nursery rhymes. (Rev: BL 9/15/91; SLJ 10/91*) [398.8]

842 Fyleman, Rose. *Mary Middling and Other Silly Folk: Nursery Rhymes and Nonsense Poems* (PS). Illus. by Katja Bandlow. 2004, Clarion $16.00 (0-618-38141-4). 28pp. Catchy rhymes first published in 1931 are revived in picture-book form with suitably silly illustrations. (Rev: BL 11/15/04; SLJ 9/04) [821]

843 Galdone, Paul. *Three Little Kittens* (2–4). Illus. by author. 1986, Houghton Mifflin $15.00 (0-89919-426-5); paper $5.95 (0-89919-796-5). 32pp. A lively reworking of the old nursery rhyme. (Rev: BL 10/1/86; SLJ 12/86) [398.8]

844 Hale, Sarah Josepha. *Mary Had a Little Lamb* (PS–1). Illus. by Salley Mavor. 1995, Orchard LB $16.99 (0-531-08725-5). 32pp. An effective version of the famous rhyme using collages for illustrations. (Rev: BCCB 5/95; BL 5/15/95; HB 3–4/95, 7–8/95, 11–12/95; SLJ 6/95*) [811]

845 Hallworth, Grace, ed. *Down by the River: Afro-Caribbean Rhymes, Games, and Songs for Children* (PS–1). Illus. by Caroline Binch. 1996, Scholastic $16.95 (0-590-69320-4). 40pp. More than 20 playground rhymes from the Caribbean are included in this joyful book illustrated with watercolors. (Rev: BCCB 1/97; BL 10/15/96; SLJ 12/96) [811]

846 Harper, Charise Mericle. *Itsy Bitsy the Smart Spider* (PS–2). Illus. by author. 2004, Dial $9.99 (0-8037-2901-4). This variation on the rhyme about the spider and the waterspout finds the spider working out ways to solve her problem. (Rev: SLJ 3/04)

847 Harper, Charise Mericle. *There Was a Bold Lady Who Wanted a Star* (PS–2). Illus. 2002, Little, Brown $15.95 (0-316-14673-0). 32pp. "The Little Old Lady Who Swallowed a Fly" is traded in for a modern lady who tries various modes of transport in her efforts to catch a star. (Rev: BCCB 11/02; BL 11/15/02; HBG 3/03; SLJ 9/02) [782]

848 Hayes, Sarah. *This Is the Bear* (PS). Illus. by Helen Craig. 1993, HarperCollins LB $11.89 (0-397-32171-6); Candlewick paper $2.50 (0-06-443103-7). 32pp. Written in "House That Jack Built" style, the story of the bear named Fred who is taken to the local dump and awaits rescue. A reissue. A sequel is *This Is the Bear and the Picnic Lunch* (1989). (Rev: BL 4/1/86; SLJ 9/86) [398.8]

849 *Hey Diddle Diddle* (PS–K). Illus. by Marilyn Janovitz. 1992, Hyperion LB $7.49 (1-56282-169-5). This book is illustrated with watercolors that humorously reproduce the old nursery rhyme. (Rev: SLJ 8/92) [398.8]

850 Hillenbrand, Will. *Here We Go Round the Mulberry Bush* (PS–K). Illus. by author. 2003, Harcourt $15.00 (0-15-202032-2). The familiar nursery rhyme forms the framework for this story of two shy young pigs facing the terrors of the first day at school. (Rev: HBG 4/04; SLJ 9/03)

851 Hoberman, Mary Ann. *Bill Grogan's Goat* (PS–3). Illus. by Nadine Bernard Westcott. 2002, Little, Brown $14.95 (0-316-36232-8). 32pp. The classic nonsense rhyme about Bill Grogan and the goat that is always in trouble is retold with clever illustrations. (Rev: BL 4/15/02; HBG 10/02; SLJ 4/02)

852 Honey, Elizabeth. *The Moon in the Man* (PS–1). Illus. by author. 2003, Allen & Unwin $15.95 (1-86508-455-7); paper $7.95 (1-86508-491-3). A collection of original nonsense rhymes and fingerplays. (Rev: SLJ 8/03)

853 *The House That Jack Built* (K–2). Illus. by Diana Mayo. 2001, Barefoot $15.99 (1-84148-251-X). Double-page illustrations in bold colors bring new life to the classic rhyme. (Rev: BL 10/15/01; HBG 3/02; SLJ 1/02) [398.8]

854 Hysom, Dennis. *Wooleycat's Musical Theater* (PS–1). Illus. by Christine Walker. Series: Wooleycat's Favorite Nursery Rhymes. 2003, Tortuga $18.95 (1-889910-25-2). 32pp. Ten nursery rhymes are retold with new twists (the cow that jumped over the moon becomes an astronaut, for instance) and set to music on an accompanying CD. (Rev: SLJ 4/04) [398.8]

855 Jackson, Alison. *If the Shoe Fits* (PS–1). Illus. by Karla Firehammer. 2001, Holt $16.95 (0-8050-

6466-4). 24pp. The old woman who lives in a shoe visits familiar nursery rhyme locations — Miss Muffet's teacup, a sock hanging from a clock — in search of a new home. (Rev: BCCB 3/02; BL 10/1/01; HBG 3/02; SLJ 12/01)

856 Janovitz, Marilyn. *Three Little Kittens* (PS–2). Illus. 2002, North-South LB $14.50 (0-7358-1643-3). 32pp. The adventures of the three little kittens in search of their mittens are shown in bright, appealing illustrations. (Rev: BL 10/1/02; HBG 3/03; SLJ 8/02) [398.8]

857 Jaques, Florence Page. *There Once Was a Puffin* (PS–K). Illus. by Shari Halpern. 2003, North-South LB $16.50 (0-7358-1771-5). A new edition of the nonsense rhyme about a puffin shaped like a muffin who is in need of some friends. (Rev: HBG 4/04; SLJ 11/03)

858 Kadair, Deborah Ousley. *There Was an Ol' Cajun* (K–3). Illus. by author. 2002, Pelican $14.95 (1-56554-917-1). Instead of a fly, the ol' Cajun swallows all manner of swamp life before coming across an alligator. (Rev: HBG 10/02; SLJ 12/02) [398.8]

859 Kirk, Daniel. *Jack and Jill* (K–2). Illus. by author. 2003, Penguin Putnam $15.99 (0-399-23553-1). In this new, expanded version of the classic nursery rhyme, Jack and Jill set off to fetch some water for their fish tank but discover a giant talking crocodile in the well. (Rev: BL 6/1–15/03; HBG 10/03; LMC 2/04; SLJ 11/03)

860 Linch, Tanya. *Three Little Kittens* (PS–K). Illus. by author. 2001, Gullane $12.95 (1-86233-204-5). The kittens' mittens are lost and dirtied, then found and washed, all with mother's forgiveness. (Rev: SLJ 1/02) [398.2]

861 Lobel, Arnold. *Whiskers and Rhymes* (PS–3). Illus. by author. 1985, Morrow paper $4.95 (0-688-08291-2). 48pp. Original nursery rhymes featuring cats in old-fashioned costumes. (Rev: BCCB 10/85; BL 9/15/85; SLJ 10/85) [398.8]

862 McMullan, Kate. *Baby Goose* (PS). Illus. by Pascal Lemaitre. 2004, Hyperion $15.99 (0-7868-0430-0). 34pp. Traditional nursery rhymes follow the hands around the clock and feature child-friendly adaptations and illustrations. (Rev: BL 11/15/04; SLJ 11/04) [398.8]

863 Marks, Alan, ed. *Over the Hills and Far Away: A Book of Nursery Rhymes* (PS–1). Illus. 1994, North-South $19.95 (1-55858-285-1). 97pp. Sixty of the most popular Mother Goose rhymes are contained in this well-designed volume. (Rev: BL 9/1/94*; SLJ 10/94) [398.8]

864 Marshall, James. *James Marshall's Mother Goose* (PS–1). Illus. by author. 1979, Farrar paper $6.95 (0-374-43723-8). 40pp. An ebullient, breezy treatment of traditional material. [398.8]

865 Martin, Bill, Jr. *"Fire! Fire!" Said Mrs. McGuire* (PS–K). Illus. by Richard Egielski. 1996, Harcourt $15.00 (0-15-227562-2). 32pp. With humorous illustrations, the traditional nursery rhyme is given a modern touch. (Rev: BCCB 4/96; BL 3/15/96; SLJ 6/96) [398.8]

866 *Michael Foreman's Playtime Rhymes* (PS–K). Illus. by Michael Foreman. 2002, Candlewick $18.99 (0-7636-1812-8). 108pp. An illustrated collection of traditional songs and rhymes, some familiar and some less well-known, that includes some activities. (Rev: HBG 3/03; SLJ 10/02) [398.8]

867 Montgomery, Michael G., and Wayne Montgomery. *Over the Candlestick: Classic Nursery Rhymes and the Real Stories Behind Them* (PS). Illus. by Michael G. Montgomery. 2002, Peachtree $16.95 (1-56145-259-9). 32pp. A large-format collection of classic nursery rhymes and a bit of the history behind them, with full-page illustrations. (Rev: BL 3/15/02; HBG 10/02; SLJ 6/02) [398.8]

868 Moses, Will. *Will Moses Mother Goose* (PS–1). Illus. by author. 2003, Philomel $17.99 (0-399-23744-5). 61pp. A whimsically illustrated collection of nursery rhymes and riddles, some well known and others less familiar. (Rev: HBG 4/04; SLJ 9/03) [398.8]

869 Mother Goose. *Gregory Griggs and Other Nursery Rhyme People* (PS–1). Illus. by Arnold Lobel. 1987, Macmillan paper $3.95 (0-688-07042-6). Out-of-the-ordinary nursery rhymes are included in this refreshingly different collection. Reissue of 1978 edition. [398.8]

870 Mother Goose. *Mother Goose: A Canadian Sampler* (PS–1). 1996, Groundwood $18.95 (0-88899-213-0). 63pp. Using illustrations from 29 of Canada's prominent picture book illustrators, this is a fine edition of Mother Goose rhymes. (Rev: SLJ 5/96)

871 Mother Goose. *Mother Goose: A Collection of Classic Nursery Rhymes* (PS–K). Illus. by Michael Hague. 1984, Holt $18.95 (0-8050-0214-6). 80pp. Forty-five nursery rhymes delicately illustrated. [398.8]

872 Mother Goose. *Mother Goose: A Sampler* (PS–K). Illus. 1996, Douglas & McIntyre $18.95 (0-88899-260-2). 64pp. Twenty-eight modern Canadian artists illustrate favorite rhymes from Mother Goose. (Rev: BL 6/1–15/96)

873 Mother Goose. *Real Mother Goose* (PS–3). Illus. by Blanche Fisher Wright. 1991, Checkerboard $12.95 (1-56288-041-1). 128pp. A reprint of the golden anniversary edition with introduction by May Hill Arbuthnot. [398.8]

874 Mother Goose. *The Real Mother Goose Clock Book* (PS–1). Illus. by Blanche Fisher Wright. 1991, Checkerboard $6.95 (1-56288-095-0). 22pp. Time-related rhymes and a clock with movable hands help children associate the clock with daily routines. [398.8]

875 Mother Goose. *Tomie dePaola's Mother Goose* (PS–1). Illus. by Tomie dePaola. 1985, Penguin Putnam $24.95 (0-399-21258-2). 127pp. Large format and lavish illustrations accompany these old favorites. (Rev: BCCB 11/85; BL 9/1/85; HB 1–2/86) [398.8]

876 *My First Action Rhymes* (PS). Illus. by Lynne W. Cravath. Series: Growing Tree. 2000, HarperCollins $9.95 (0-694-01418-4). 24pp. A collection of ten playful action rhymes that often point out parts of the body. (Rev: BL 10/15/00; HBG 10/01; SLJ 11/00) [811]

877 *My First Nursery Rhymes* (PS). Illus. by Bruce Whatley. Series: Growing Tree. 1999, Harper-Collins $9.95 (0-694-01205-X). 24pp. A joyous collection of ten favorite rhymes, including "Little Bo-Peep" and "Humpty Dumpty." (Rev: BL 2/1/99; HBG 10/99; SLJ 4/99) [398.8]

878 O'Brien, John. *The Farmer in the Dell* (PS–1). Illus. 2000, Boyds Mills $14.95 (1-56397-775-3). 40pp. Hilarious illustrations give new life to this favorite rhyme. (Rev: BL 11/1/00; HBG 3/01; SLJ 9/00) [782.42]

879 Opie, Iona, ed. *Here Comes Mother Goose* (PS). Illus. by Rosemary Wells. 1999, Candlewick $21.99 (0-7636-0683-9). 107pp. More than 50 well-known nursery rhymes are given fresh interpretations through clever new illustrations. (Rev: BCCB 12/99; BL 10/1/99*; HB 11–12/99; HBG 3/00; SLJ 10/99) [398.8]

880 Opie, Iona, ed. *My Very First Mother Goose* (PS). Illus. by Rosemary Wells. 1996, Candlewick $21.99 (1-56402-620-5). 108pp. A basic collection of 60 standard rhymes illustrated with imagination and charm. (Rev: BCCB 12/96; BL 9/1/96; HB 11–12/96; SLJ 10/96*) [398.8]

881 Ormerod, Jan. *Jan Ormerod's To Baby with Love* (PS). Illus. 1994, Lothrop $16.00 (0-688-12558-1). 40pp. Five catchy nursery rhymes that are attractively illustrated. (Rev: BL 8/94; SLJ 10/94)

882 Oxenbury, Helen. *The Helen Oxenbury Nursery Collection* (PS–1). Illus. 2004, Knopf LB $21.99 (0-375-92992-4). 96pp. This charming collection of poems, rhymes, and stories is drawn from previous books that are now out of print. (Rev: BL 12/1/04) [398.8]

883 Patz, Nancy, reteller. *Moses Supposes His Toeses Are Roses: And Seven Other Silly Old Rhymes* (K–3). Illus. by Nancy Patz. 1983, Harcourt paper $6.00 (0-15-255691-5). 32pp. Eight wonderful nonsense rhymes are well illustrated. [398.8]

884 Petersham, Maud, and Miska Petersham. *The Rooster Crows: A Book of American Rhymes and Jingles* (K–2). Illus. by authors. 1969, Macmillan LB $17.00 (0-02-773100-6). 64pp. Rope skipping, counting, and other game rhymes form the bulk of this jaunty collection. A reissue of the 1946 Caldecott Medal winner. [398.8]

885 Prelutsky, Jack. *Beneath a Blue Umbrella* (PS–2). Illus. by Garth Williams. 1990, Greenwillow $15.95 (0-688-06429-9). 64pp. A miscellany of 28 gaily illustrated rhymes by Mother Goose; good read-aloud material. (Rev: BCCB 3/90; HB 3–4/90; SLJ 6/90) [398.8]

886 *Ragged Bear's Nursery Rhymes* (PS–1). Ed. and illus. by Diz Wallis. 2001, Ragged Bear $19.95 (1-929927-36-3). 116pp. This collection of 100 nursery rhymes includes some that may be new to readers. (Rev: BL 2/15/02; HBG 3/02; SLJ 3/02) [398.8]

887 Sabuda, Robert. *Movable Mother Goose* (PS–1). 1999, Simon & Schuster $19.95 (0-689-81192-6). Pop-ups and flaps are used to illustrate this collec-

tion of favorite Mother Goose rhymes. (Rev: BL 12/15/99; HBG 3/00; SLJ 2/00)

888 Sayre, April Pulley. *Trout, Trout, Trout! A Fish Chant* (PS–2). Illus. by Trip Park. 2004, NorthWord $15.95 (1-55971-889-7). Bright cartoon illustrations complement this bouncy fish-related chant. (Rev: SLJ 7/04) [597.17]

889 Scanlon, Elizabeth Garton. *A Sock Is a Pocket for Your Toes: A Pocket Book* (PS–2). Illus. by Robin Preiss Glasser. 2004, HarperCollins $15.99 (0-06-029526-0). 32pp. This delightful rhyme book takes a broad brush to the concept of pockets — picturing a cave as a pocket for bears and ears as pockets for whispers. (Rev: BL 2/15/04; SLJ 2/04) [811]

890 Sewall, Marcia. *Animal Song* (PS–K). Illus. by author. 1988, Little, Brown $14.95 (0-316-78191-6). 128pp. An old chanting rhyme using animal names. (Rev: BL 3/15/88; SLJ 6–7/88) [398.8]

891 Sierra, Judy. *Monster Goose* (K–3). Illus. by Jack E. Davis. 2001, Harcourt $16.00 (0-15-202034-9). 56pp. Gruesome, gross, and goofy versions of familiar Mother Goose rhymes. (Rev: BCCB 12/01; BL 9/15/01; HBG 3/02; SLJ 9/01) [811]

892 Siomades, Lorianne. *Three Little Kittens* (PS–1). Illus. 2000, Boyds Mills $9.95 (1-56397-845-8). 32pp. The classic nursery rhyme is given a bright, mischievous treatment that involves both the kittens and some thieving mice. (Rev: BL 2/15/00; HBG 10/00; SLJ 4/00)

893 Spicer, Maggee, and Richard Thompson. *When They Are Up . . .* (PS–3). Illus. by Kirsti Anne Wakelin. 2004, Fitzhenry & Whiteside $14.95 (1-55041-707-X). This imaginative twist on the nursery song about the Duke of York's 10,000 men has them involved in such things as capturing armadillos and knitting socks; music and lyrics are appended. (Rev: SLJ 5/04) [811]

894 Stevens, Janet, and Susan Stevens Crummel. *And the Dish Ran Away with the Spoon* (K–3). Illus. 2001, Harcourt $17.00 (0-15-202298-8). 48pp. Familiar nursery rhymes are reworked with droll results. (Rev: BL 4/1/01*; HB 7–8/01; HBG 10/01; SLJ 5/01)

895 Still, James. *An Appalachian Mother Goose* (K–3). Illus. by Paul Johnson. 1998, Univ. Pr. of Kentucky $25.00 (0-8131-2070-5). 64pp. Familiar nursery rhymes are given an Appalachian flavor in these short poems by Kentucky's former poet laureate. (Rev: BL 3/1/99) [398.8]

896 Sutherland, Zena, ed. *The Orchard Book of Nursery Rhymes* (PS–1). Illus. by Faith Jaques. 1990, Orchard $22.95 (0-531-05903-0). 88pp. A collection of 72 familiar and lesser-known rhymes. (Rev: BCCB 10/90; BL 9/1/90; HB 1–2/91; SLJ 9/90*) [398.8]

897 *Sylvia Long's Mother Goose* (PS–K). Illus. by Sylvia Long. 1999, Chronicle $19.95 (0-8118-2088-2). 109pp. Animals, reptiles, and insects replace humans in the delightful illustrations featured in this Mother Goose anthology. (Rev: BCCB 12/99; BL 11/15/99; HBG 3/00; SLJ 12/99*) [398.8]

898 Taback, Simms. *This Is the House That Jack Built* (PS–2). Illus. 2002, Penguin Putnam $15.99 (0-399-23488-8). 32pp. An inventive, spirited take on the traditional nursery rhyme that focuses on the house and its contents. (Rev: BCCB 10/02; BL 10/1/02*; HB 11–12/02; HBG 3/03; SLJ 9/02*) [398.8]

899 Trapani, Iza, reteller. *Mary Had a Little Lamb* (PS–1). Illus. by Iza Trapani. 1998, Whispering Coyote $15.95 (1-58089-009-1). An expanded version of the nursery rhyme in which the little lamb has misadventures in a farmyard. (Rev: HBG 3/99; SLJ 11/98)

900 Unobagha, Uzo. *Off to the Sweet Shores of Africa* (PS). Illus. by Julia Cairns. 2000, Chronicle $16.95 (0-8118-2378-4). 56pp. Playful verses about African subjects are contained in this collection that seems inspired by Mother Goose. (Rev: BL 11/1/00; HBG 3/01; SLJ 10/00) [811]

901 Ward, Jennifer, and T. J. Marsh. *Somewhere in the Ocean* (PS–1). Illus. by Kenneth J. Spengler. 2000, Northland $15.95 (0-87358-748-0). 32pp. The nursery rhyme "Over in the Meadow" is changed so the setting is now the ocean and the animals are all sea creatures. (Rev: BL 4/1/00; HBG 10/00; SLJ 7/00)

902 Wells, Rosemary. *The Bear Went Over the Mountain* (PS). Illus. Series: Bunny Reads Back. 1998, Scholastic $4.99 (0-590-02910-X). 16pp. A board book that presents the familiar nursery rhyme with pictures showing a little bear leaving his mother, going over the mountain, and returning with a gift of flowers for her. (Rev: BL 12/15/98; HBG 3/99; SLJ 2/99)

903 Wells, Rosemary. *The Itsy-Bitsy Spider* (PS). Illus. Series: Bunny Reads Back. 1998, Scholastic $4.99 (0-590-02911-8). 16pp. The familiar nursery rhyme about a tiny spider climbing a waterspout is presented in a clever format in this board book. (Rev: BL 12/15/98; HBG 3/99; SLJ 2/99)

904 Winters, Jeanette. *The House That Jack Built* (PS–2). Illus. 2000, Dial $13.99 (0-8037-2524-8). 32pp. The old folk rhyme is retold in the form of a rebus puzzle with clever illustrations. (Rev: BCCB 7–8/00; BL 5/15/00; HBG 10/00; SLJ 5/00) [398.8]

905 Yolen, Jane, ed. *The Lap-Time Song and Play Book* (PS). Illus. by Margot Tomes. 1989, Harcourt $15.95 (0-15-243588-3). 32pp. A collection of 16 nursery games and songs with a history for each and simple piano arrangements. (Rev: BL 10/1/89; HB 11–12/89; SLJ 10/89) [782.42]

906 Zelinsky, Paul O. *Knick-Knack Paddywhack! A Moving Parts Book* (PS–3). Illus. 2002, Dutton $18.99 (0-525-46908-7). 8pp. This miracle of pull-tabs and flaps is a delicious combination of familiar, bouncy rhyme and counting song full of comedy and small details. (Rev: BCCB 2/03; BL 11/1/02; HB 1–2/03; HBG 3/03; SLJ 12/02) [782.42164]

907 Zemach, Margot. *Some from the Moon, Some from the Sun: Poems and Songs for Everyone* (K–3). Illus. 2001, Farrar $17.00 (0-374-39960-3). 48pp. A collection of traditional children's poems and rhymes illustrated by Caldecott Medal winner Margot Zemach. (Rev: BL 10/1/01; HB 9–10/01*; HBG 3/02; SLJ 8/01*) [398.8]

Stories Without Words

908 Aruego, Jose. *Look What I Can Do!* (K–2). Illus. by author. 1971, Macmillan paper $5.99 (0-689-71205-7). 32pp. An lmost wordless picture book about the antics that result when one caribou challenges another.

909 Bang, Molly. *The Grey Lady and the Strawberry Snatcher* (PS–1). Illus. by author. 1984, Macmillan $16.00 (0-02-708140-0). 48pp. The snatcher tries to get the strawberries from the Grey Lady.

910 Banyai, Istvan. *Zoom* (1–3). Illus. 1995, Viking $14.99 (0-670-85804-8). 64pp. A clever picture book that begins with small objects and zooms to larger perspectives. (Rev: BCCB 2/95; BL 2/1/95; SLJ 3/95)

911 Briggs, Raymond. *The Snowman* (K–3). Illus. by author. 1978, Random $17.00 (0-394-83973-0); paper $7.99 (0-394-88466-3). 32pp. A small boy has adventures with the snowman he has made.

912 Carle, Eric. *Do You Want to Be My Friend?* (PS–K). Illus. by author. 1971, HarperCollins LB $15.89 (0-690-01137-7); paper $6.95 (0-06-443127-4). 32pp. The end of an animal's tail appears on each page, and the child must guess the animal before turning the page to see the rest of it.

913 Crews, Donald. *Truck* (1–3). Illus. by author. 1980, Greenwillow $15.89 (0-688-84244-5); Morrow paper $4.95 (0-688-10481-9). 32pp. This picture book traces a truck trip from loading dock to its San Francisco destination.

914 Day, Alexandra. *Carl's Masquerade* (PS–1). Illus. 1992, Farrar $12.95 (0-374-31094-7). 32pp. Carl, the rottweiler baby-sitter, takes his young charge and follows its parents to a masquerade ball. (Rev: BCCB 12/92; BL 2/1/93; SLJ 11/92)

915 dePaola, Tomie. *The Hunter and the Animals: A Wordless Picture Book* (K–3). Illus. by author. 1981, Holiday House LB $16.95 (0-8234-0397-1); paper $6.95 (0-8234-0428-5). 32pp. A hunter lost in the forest is helped by the animals.

916 Goodale, Rebecca. *Island Dog* (PS–1). Illus. by author. 1999, Two Dog $17.95 (1-891090-03-8). In this wordless picture book, a dog spends a playful day on an island in Maine. (Rev: SLJ 1/00)

917 Louchard, Antonin. *Little Star* (K–2). Illus. by author. 2003, Hyperion $12.99 (0-7868-1939-1). This wordless book chronicles the transformation of a starfish into a heavenly star and back again into a starfish. (Rev: HBG 10/03; SLJ 5/03)

918 McCully, Emily Arnold. *Four Hungry Kittens* (PS–K). Illus. 2001, Dial $15.99 (0-8037-2505-1). 32pp. An engaging story about four hungry kittens on a farm who await their mother while she is out hunting for food. (Rev: BL 1/1–15/01; HBG 10/01; SLJ 3/01)

919 McCully, Emily Arnold. *Picnic* (PS–2). Illus. by author. 1984, HarperCollins LB $16.89 (0-06-

024100-4). 32pp. An eventful picnic for the mouse family.

920 McCully, Emily Arnold. *School* (PS–1). Illus. by author. 1987, HarperCollins LB $15.89 (0-06-024133-0); paper $5.95 (0-06-443233-5). 32pp. The littlest mouse decides to follow her siblings to school to see what it's like. (Rev: BL 9/1/87; SLJ 10/87)

921 Martin, Rafe. *Will's Mammoth* (K–2). Illus. by Stephen Gammell. 1989, Penguin Putnam $16.99 (0-399-21627-8). 32pp. A boy named Will travels back in time to when mammoths and saber-toothed tigers roamed the earth. (Rev: BCCB 11/89; BL 9/15/89; HB 3–4/90*; SLJ 10/89*)

922 Schories, Pat. *Breakfast for Jack* (PS–2). Illus. by author. 2004, Front Street $13.95 (1-932425-16-0). Jack the dog is very worried when his family leaves in the morning without giving him breakfast in this wordless book. Also use *Jack and the Missing Piece* (2004). (Rev: HB 1–2/05; SLJ 11/04)

923 Sis, Peter. *Dinosaur!* (PS–K). Illus. 2000, Greenwillow $14.95 (0-688-17049-8). 24pp. In this wordless book, the bath a boy takes with his toy dinosaur is suddenly transformed into a prehistoric scene where many dinosaurs are roaming in their native habitat. (Rev: BCCB 6/00; BL 3/15/00; HB 7–8/00; HBG 10/00; SLJ 6/00)

924 Tafuri, Nancy. *Junglewalk* (PS–K). Illus. by author. 1988, Greenwillow LB $15.93 (0-688-07183-X). 32pp. A bedtime story sends a young boy off to dreamland and adventures with a majestic tiger. (Rev: BL 3/1/88; HB 3–4/88)

925 Van Allsburg, Chris. *The Mysteries of Harris Burdick* (1–8). Illus. by author. 1984, Houghton Mifflin $17.95 (0-395-35393-9). 32pp. A group of pictures are presented and youngsters are asked to supply the stories.

926 Weitzman, Jacqueline Preiss. *You Can't Take a Balloon into the Metropolitan Museum* (K–3). Illus. by Robin P. Glasser. 1998, Dial $16.99 (0-8037-2301-6). 35pp. In this wordless picture book, a guard tends a balloon for a girl who is visiting the Metropolitan Museum of Art. When it gets loose, he chases it around Central Park and into the Plaza Hotel. (Rev: BL 11/15/98*; HB 11–12/98; HBG 3/99; SLJ 12/98)

927 Weitzman, Jacqueline Preiss. *You Can't Take a Balloon into the Museum of Fine Arts* (K–3). 2002, Dial $17.99 (0-8037-2570-1). 40pp. In this wordless book, a runaway balloon causes mishaps as it floats around the city of Boston. (Rev: BL 6/1–15/02*; HBG 10/02; SLJ 8/02)

928 Wiesner, David. *Free Fall* (PS–K). Illus. by author. 1988, Lothrop LB $17.89 (0-688-05584-2); paper $6.95 (0-688-10990-X). 32pp. An atlas falls from a boy's lap as he sleeps and opens his imagination to exotic places. (Rev: BCCB 5/88; BL 6/1/88; SLJ 6–7/88)

929 Wilson, April. *Magpie Magic: A Tale of Colorful Mischief* (PS–3). Illus. 1999, Dial $14.99 (0-8037-2354-7). 40pp. In this wordless book, a little boy draws simple pictures that come to life. (Rev: BL 4/15/99; HB 3–4/99; HBG 10/99; SLJ 4/99)

Picture Books

Imaginative Stories

FANTASIES

930 *The 20th Century Children's Book Treasury: Celebrated Picture Books and Stories to Read Aloud* (PS–3). Ed. by Janet Schulman. Illus. 1998, Knopf $40.00 (0-679-88647-8). 308pp. This anthology (a good introduction to children's literature for parents) condenses in size and shape 44 important picture books by such artists as Maurice Sendak, Wanda Gág, and Shirley Hughes. (Rev: BL 10/15/98; HB 11–12/98; HBG 3/99; SLJ 12/98)

931 Ada, Alma F. *Dear Peter Rabbit* (PS–1). Illus. by Leslie Tryon. 1994, Atheneum LB $16.00 (0-689-31850-2). 48pp. A number of fairy tale characters like Goldilocks and Peter Rabbit write letters to each other in this clever picture book. (Rev: BCCB 4/94; BL 5/1/94; SLJ 7/94*)

932 Ada, Alma F. *Yours Truly, Goldilocks* (PS–2). Illus. by Leslie Tryon. 1998, Simon & Schuster $16.00 (0-689-81608-1). 40pp. In this sequel to *Dear Peter Rabbit,* the letter-writing format continues with a series of letters exchanged by fairy-tale characters as they plan a housewarming party for the Three Little Pigs. (Rev: BL 5/1/98; HBG 10/98; SLJ 7/98)

933 Ada, Alma Flor. *With Love, Little Red Hen* (K–3). Illus. by Leslie Tryon. 2001, Simon & Schuster $16.00 (0-689-82581-1). 40pp. Little Red Hen writes to Hetty Henny about moving to the Hidden Forest, where her neighbors are other characters from children's stories. Third in a series including *Dear Peter Rabbit* (1994) and *Yours Truly, Goldilocks* (1998). (Rev: BL 9/15/01; HB 1–2/02; HBG 3/02; SLJ 10/01)

934 Agee, Jon. *The Incredible Painting of Felix Clousseau* (PS–3). Illus. by author. 1988, Farrar paper $4.95 (0-374-43582-0). 32pp. A very laid-back artist is oblivious to the havoc his paintings cause. (Rev: BCCB 11/88; BL 11/1/88; HB 1–2/89)

935 Ahlberg, Allan. *Shopping Expedition* (PS–1). Illus. by André Amstutz. 2005, Candlewick $16.99 (0-7636-2586-8). 32pp. A fanciful little girl describes how a shopping expedition goes dramatically awry in this story involving blizzards, floods, and jungles. (Rev: BL 5/1/05)

936 Ahlberg, Allan. *The Snail House* (K–3). Illus. by Gillian Tyler. 2001, Candlewick $13.99 (0-7636-0711-8). Grandma tells a story to her grandchildren about three youngsters who shrink in size until they can live in a snail house. (Rev: HB 5–6/01; HBG 10/01; SLJ 3/01)

937 Ajhar, Brian. *Home on the Range* (PS–1). 2004, Penguin Putnam $15.99 (0-8037-2918-9). 32pp. A city boy, yearning for wide, open spaces, is magically transported to the Wild West of his dreams. (Rev: BL 9/15/04)

938 Alborough, Jez. *My Friend Bear* (PS–1). Illus. 1998, Candlewick $16.99 (0-7636-0583-2). 32pp. Eddie hides a bear's toy teddy bear but gives it back to him when the two become fast friends. (Rev: BL 1/1–15/99; HBG 3/99; SLJ 12/98)

939 Alexander, Martha. *I'll Never Share You, Blackboard Bear* (PS). Illus. 2003, Candlewick $12.99 (0-7636-1590-0). 32pp. When Gloria and Stewart express an interest in Blackboard Bear, Alexander refuses to share, and it is up to Blackboard Bear to show Alexander how to be a good friend. (Rev: BL 1/1–15/04; HBG 4/04; SLJ 2/04)

940 Anderson, Bob. *Obo* (K–3). Illus. by author. 1999, Hampton Roads $16.00 (1-57174-123-2). 45pp. A young monkey who is enchanted with the song of a pretty little bird sets out to find the bird's home, which is known as Paradise. (Rev: SLJ 8/99)

941 Argueta, Manlio. *Magic Dogs of the Volcanoes: Los Perros Mágicos de los Volcanoes* (K–3). Illus. by Elly Simmons. 1990, Children's Book Pr. $14.95 (0-89239-064-6). 30pp. From El Salvador, this dual-language book tells the story of the magical dogs that live at the foot of volcanoes. (Rev: SLJ 2/91)

942 Armour, Peter. *Stop That Pickle!* (K–3). Illus. by Andrew Shachat. 1993, Houghton Mifflin $16.00 (0-395-66375-X). 32pp. The last pickle in the jar flees the deli and is pursued by a number of food items in this comic gem. (Rev: BL 1/1/94; SLJ 2/94)

943 Armstrong, Jennifer. *The Snowball* (K–1). Illus. by Jean Pidgeon. 1996, Random paper $3.99 (0-679-86444-X). 32pp. A snowball gathers up children as it rolls down a hill. (Rev: BL 2/1/97)

944 Ashforth, Camilla. *Willow by the Sea* (PS–1). Illus. 2002, Candlewick $12.00 (0-7636-1401-7). 32pp. A gentle story about gentle bear Willow having a lovely day with his friends at the seaside. Also use *Willow on the River* (2002). (Rev: BL 7/02; HBG 10/02; SLJ 7/02)

945 Ashman, Linda. *Rub-a-Dub Sub* (K–2). Illus. by Jeff Mack. 2003, Harcourt $16.00 (0-15-202658-4). Rhyming text complemented by vivid artwork follows a little boy on an underwater fantasy in a bright orange submarine. (Rev: HBG 10/03; SLJ 7/03)

946 Auch, Mary Jane. *The Easter Egg Farm* (PS–2). Illus. 1992, Holiday House LB $16.95 (0-8234-0917-1). 32pp. Humor and chaos infect a chicken ranch where the owner wears dangling earrings and trendy clothes and Pauline the hen lays "ugly" eggs. (Rev: BL 3/1/92*; SLJ 4/92)

947 Auch, Mary Jane. *Monster Brother* (PS–2). Illus. 1994, Holiday House LB $15.95 (0-8234-1095-1). 32pp. Rodney is visited by a monster every night, but his brother, Sidney, has a unique solution. (Rev: BCCB 11/94; BL 11/15/94; SLJ 11/94)

948 Avi. *Things That Sometimes Happen: Very Short Stories for Little Listeners* (PS). Illus. by Marjorie Priceman. 2002, Simon & Schuster $16.95 (0-689-83914-6). 40pp. Lively new illustrations enhance this collection of nine varied stories originally published in 1970. (Rev: BL 10/1/02; HBG 10/03; SLJ 11/02)

949 Aylesworth, Jim. *The Full Belly Bowl* (K–3). Illus. by Wendy A. Halperin. 1999, Simon & Schuster $16.00 (0-689-81033-4). 40pp. In this handsomely illustrated tale, an old man who is always

hungry is given a magical food bowl by a tiny creature he has saved from being eaten by a fox. (Rev: BCCB 12/99; BL 11/1/99*; HBG 3/00; SLJ 10/99)

950 Aylesworth, Jim. *My Sister's Rusty Bike* (K–3). Illus. by Richard Hull. 1996, Simon & Schuster $16.00 (0-689-31798-0). 32pp. A fantasy in which a boy meets unusual creatures as he travels American byways. (Rev: BL 11/15/96; SLJ 10/96)

951 Aylesworth, Jim. *The Tale of Tricky Fox* (PS–2). Illus. by Barbara McClintock. 2001, Scholastic $15.95 (0-439-09543-3). 32pp. Tricky Fox, who thinks he has caught a pig for dinner, is outwitted by an old woman who puts a ferocious bulldog in the fox's sack instead. (Rev: BCCB 3/01; BL 2/1/01; HB 3–4/01*; HBG 10/01; SLJ 3/01)

952 Babbitt, Natalie. *Elsie Times Eight* (PS–2). Illus. 2001, Hyperion $15.95 (0-7868-0900-0). 32pp. A hard-of-hearing fairy godmother mistakes "wait" for "eight" and multiplies her young charge, with challenging consequences. (Rev: BCCB 12/01; BL 11/15/01; HB 1–2/02; HBG 3/02; SLJ 11/01)

953 Bahrampour, Ali. *Otto: The Story of a Mirror* (K–3). Illus. by author. 2003, Farrar $16.00 (0-374-27078-3). TIred of his lackluster existence, Otto the mirror rebels and finds himself not only adventure but romance. (Rev: HB 3–4/03; HBG 10/03; SLJ 7/03)

954 Baicker, Karen. *Pea Pod Babies* (PS). Illus. by Sam Williams. 2003, Handprint $15.95 (1-59354-003-5). In this appealing rhyming story, three babies growing up in a pea pod resent their similarity and go their own ways. (Rev: BL 11/15/03; HBG 4/04; SLJ 12/03)

955 Bailey, Debbie. *Let's Pretend* (PS). Photos by Susan Huszar. Series: Talk-About-Books. 1999, Annick $5.95 (1-55037-558-X). In the color photos in this board book, children play by taking the roles of parents, doctors, cooks, monsters, firemen, and princesses. (Rev: SLJ 9/99)

956 Baker, Keith. *The Dove's Letter* (1–4). Illus. by author. 1993, Harcourt paper $5.95 (0-15-224134-5). 32pp. A dove finds an obviously lost letter and attempts to deliver it to the proper person. (Rev: BL 5/1/88; SLJ 7/88)

957 Baker, Keith. *The Magic Fan* (PS–2). Illus. 1989, Harcourt $14.95 (0-15-250750-7). 32pp. Village people don't like Yoshi's magic bridge until it saves them from a tidal wave. (Rev: BCCB 2/90; BL 11/1/89; HB 1–2/90; SLJ 10/89*)

958 Baker, Lisa. *Harold and the Purple Crayon: Dinosaur Days* (PS–1). Illus. Series: Harold and the Purple Crayon. 2002, HarperCollins $12.99 (0-06-000541-6). 40pp. Harold uses his crayon to journey to a jungle and play with dinosaurs. (Rev: BL 2/15/03; HBG 3/03; SLJ 1/03)

959 Balian, Lorna. *Humbug Witch* (1–3). Illus. by author. 1992, Humbug LB $14.95 (1-881772-24-1). 32pp. A little witch doesn't seem to get the hang of witchcraft.

960 Balian, Lorna. *Leprechauns Never Lie* (K–3). Illus. by author. 1994, Humbug LB $14.95 (1-881-77207-1). 32pp. Lazy Ninny Nanny is outwitted by a clever leprechaun.

961 Balian, Lorna. *Wilbur's Space Machine* (PS–1). Illus. 1990, Holiday House LB $19.95 (0-8234-0836-1). 32pp. Violet and Wilbur build a space machine to escape the world's pollution and an unwelcome guest, Googie. (Rev: BL 10/15/90; SLJ 2/91)

962 Bang, Molly. *Delphine* (PS–1). Illus. by author. 1988, Morrow $12.95 (0-688-05636-9). 32pp. Delphine takes a wild ride down the mountain to the post office where Gram's gift awaits her. (Rev: BCCB 10/88; HB 9–10/88; SLJ 9/88)

963 Bang, Molly. *The Paper Crane* (PS–1). 1985, Greenwillow paper $5.95 (0-688-07333-6). 32pp. A paper crane left by a thankful stranger leads to good fortune for a restaurant owner down on his luck. (Rev: BCCB 3/86; BL 1/15/86; HB 1–2/86)

964 Banks, Kate. *Alphabet Soup* (K–2). Illus. by Peter Sis. 1994, Knopf paper $5.99 (0-679-86723-6). 32pp. Instead of eating his alphabet soup, a little boy daydreams. (Rev: BL 11/1/88; SLJ 1/89)

965 Bannerman, Helen. *The Story of Little Babaji* (PS–1). Illus. by Fred Marcellino. 1996, Harper-Collins LB $14.89 (0-06-205065-6). 72pp. An excellent version of *Little Black Sambo,* now set in India and without racial slurs. (Rev: BL 9/1/96*; HB 9–10/96; SLJ 10/96)

966 Barrett, Judi. *Which Witch Is Which?* (PS–3). Illus. by Sharleen Collicott. 2001, Simon & Schuster $16.00 (0-689-82940-X). 32pp. Readers must study the illustrations to figure out which witch the rhyme on each spread describes. (Rev: BL 11/1/01; HBG 3/02; SLJ 9/01)

967 Barrett, Judith. *Cloudy with a Chance of Meatballs* (K–3). Illus. by Ron Barrett. 1978, Macmillan $16.00 (0-689-30647-4); paper $5.99 (0-689-70749-5). 32pp. In the land of ChewandSwallow, food falls from the skies.

968 Barrett, Judith. *Pickles to Pittsburgh: The Sequel to Cloudy with a Chance of Meatballs* (K–2). Illus. by Ron Barrett. 1997, Simon & Schuster $16.00 (0-689-80104-1). The people of the town of Chewandswallow take all their excess food and distribute it around the world — for example, eggplants to Ecuador and pickles to Pittsburgh. (Rev: HBG 3/98; SLJ 11/97)

969 Bartels, Alice L. *The Grandmother Doll* (PS–2). Illus. by Dusan Petricic. 2001, Annick LB $17.95 (1-55037-667-5); paper $6.95 (1-55037-666-7). Grandmother, mother, and Katy find ways to communicate their needs across the generations in this fantasy story. (Rev: HBG 10/01; SLJ 8/01)

970 Barwin, Gary. *The Magic Mustache* (K–3). Illus. by Stephane Jorisch. 1999, Annick LB $17.95 (1-55037-607-1); paper $6.95 (1-55037-606-3). In this fantasy, a nose who lives with his parents, two eyes, goes to market to trade a pair of eyeglasses for food. (Rev: SLJ 3/00)

971 Base, Graeme. *The Sign of the Seahorse: A Tale of Greed and High Adventure in Two Acts* (1–3). Illus. 1992, Abrams $19.95 (0-8109-3825-1). 48pp. A fable about undersea life that brings a lesson about the dangers of pollution. (Rev: BL 11/15/92; SLJ 11/92)

972 Bateman, Teresa. *Farm Flu* (PS–1). Illus. by Nadine Bernard Westcott. 2001, Whitman $15.95 (0-8075-2274-0). 32pp. In this humorous, rhyming story, a young boy who is in charge of the family farm while his mother is away must cope with a host of sick animals. (Rev: BL 4/1/01*; HBG 10/01; SLJ 4/01)

973 Bateman, Teresa. *Harp O' Gold* (PS–2). Illus. by Jill Weber. 2001, Holiday House $16.95 (0-8234-1523-6). 32pp. When Irish minstrel Tom trades his old harp for a new bright gold one owned by a leprechaun, he knows he has made a good exchange but still longs for his old harp. (Rev: BL 3/1/01; HBG 10/01)

974 Bateman, Teresa. *Leprechaun Gold* (PS–K). Illus. by Rosanne Litzinger. 1998, Holiday House $15.95 (0-8234-1344-6). 32pp. After Donald O'Dell refuses a gift of gold for saving a leprechaun's life, the little one devises a scheme to reward him. (Rev: BL 8/98; HB 7–8/98; HBG 10/98; SLJ 6/98)

975 Bateman, Teresa. *The Merbaby* (1–3). Illus. by Patience Brewster. 2001, Holiday House $16.95 (0-8234-1531-7). 32pp. A fisherman catches a merbaby and is rewarded when he returns it to the sea. (Rev: BCCB 9/01; BL 9/15/01; HBG 3/02; SLJ 1/02)

976 Bateson-Hill, Margaret. *Lao Lao of Dragon Mountain* (K–3). Illus. by Francesca Pelizzoli. 1998, Larousse $14.95 (1-84089-035-5). 32pp. The story of Lao Lao and her beautiful cutouts is told in English and Chinese. (Rev: BCCB 1/97; BL 12/15/96; SLJ 1/97)

977 Bauer, Marion Dane. *If You Had a Nose Like an Elephant's Trunk* (PS–3). Illus. by Susan Winter. 2001, Holiday House $16.95 (0-8234-1589-9). 32pp. A girl playfully imagines what she could do if she had the features or attributes of different animals. (Rev: BL 9/15/01; HBG 3/02; SLJ 9/01)

978 Baum, L. Frank. *The Wizard of Oz* (K–3). Illus. by Lisbeth Zwerger. 1996, North-South $19.95 (1-55858-638-5). 103pp. A Viennese artist reworks this classic tale with unusual, refreshing illustrations and an abridged text. (Rev: BL 10/15/96; SLJ 11/96*)

979 Baumgart, Klaus. *Laura's Secret* (PS–2). Trans. from German by Judy Waite. Illus. by author. 2003, Tiger Tales $16.95 (1-58925-031-1). Laura makes a wish on her secret star and soon the kite she and her younger brother Tommy made is flying high. (Rev: SLJ 1/04)

980 Beck, Andrea. *Elliot Digs for Treasure* (PS–2). Illus. 2001, Kids Can $12.95 (1-55074-806-8). 32pp. When stuffed toy Elliot Moose and his friends decide to dig for buried treasure they get stuck in the hole, and only persistence and cooperation can get them out. (Rev: BL 11/1/01; HBG 3/02; SLJ 11/01)

981 Beck, Andrea. *Elliot's Bath* (PS–1). Illus. 2001, Kids Can $12.95 (1-55074-802-5). 32pp. Elliot, a toy mouse, and Socks, a rag monkey, are looking forward to performing in the evening's talent show, but when they fall into a bathroom sink they become so soggy they are afraid they won't be able to perform. (Rev: BL 3/15/01; HBG 10/01)

982 Beck, Andrea. *Elliot's Emergency* (PS–2). Illus. 1998, Kids Can $12.95 (1-55074-441-0). 32pp. Elliot Moose, a stuffed toy, panics when he snags his fur on a nail. His friend Beaverton sews him up good as new. (Rev: BL 11/15/98; HBG 3/99; SLJ 12/98)

983 Beck, Ian. *Emily and the Golden Acorn* (K–2). Illus. 1992, Simon & Schuster paper $14.00 (0-671-75979-5). Emily's favorite oak tree is transformed into a sailing ship. (Rev: SLJ 11/92)

984 Beck, Ian. *Teddy's Snowy Day* (PS–K). Illus. 2002, Scholastic $15.95 (0-439-17520-8). 32pp. The simple story of a teddy bear who gets left out in the snow, has a wonderful time at first, and happily finds a ride home when he tires. (Rev: BL 10/1/02; HBG 3/03; SLJ 10/02)

985 Becker, Bonny. *Just a Minute* (PS–2). Illus. by Jack E. Davis. 2003, Simon & Schuster $15.95 (0-689-83374-1). In this whimsical tale, young Johnny MacGuffin imagines he's grown into an old man while waiting for his mother to return from a solo shopping foray. (Rev: HBG 4/04; SLJ 1/04)

986 Beeke, Jemma, and Tiphanie Beeke. *The Brand New Creature* (PS–2). 1998, Sterling $14.95 (1-899607-66-8). 32pp. When a young girl sets out to find a crocodile, she realizes that she doesn't know what a crocodile looks like, so she must ask the identity of a number of animals she meets. (Rev: BL 1/1–15/99; SLJ 6/99)

987 Bell, Cece. *Sock Monkey Goes to Hollywood: A Star Is Bathed* (PS–K). Illus. by author. 2003, Candlewick $13.99 (0-7636-1962-0). When Sock Monkey is nominated for an Oswald Award as Best Supporting Toy in a motion picture, he faces the challenge of getting clean enough to attend. (Rev: HBG 4/04; SLJ 12/03)

988 *Benjamin's First Book* (PS). Illus. 1997, Sterling $5.95 (0-8069-0389-9). 26pp. A board book that features photos of a delightful teddy bear named Benjamin. Also use *Benjamin's Toys* and *Shopping with Benjamin* (both 1997). (Rev: BL 2/1/98)

989 Berger, Barbara Helen. *A Lot of Otters* (PS). Illus. by author. 1997, Philomel $16.99 (0-399-22910-8). At night, a toddler climbs into a cardboard box with his book and sails off into waters filled with fun-loving otters. (Rev: HBG 3/98; SLJ 9/97*)

990 Bergman, Mara. *Snip Snap! What's That?* (PS–2). Illus. by Nick Maland. 2005, Greenwillow $15.99 (0-06-077754-0). 32pp. When an alligator creeps into their apartment, three children frighten him back into a manhole in this picture book with a refrain made for shouting. (Rev: BL 3/1/05; SLJ 6/05)

991 Berkeley, Laura. *The Seeds of Peace* (K–3). Illus. by Alison Dexter. 1999, Barefoot LB $15.95 (1-84148-007-X). An old hermit tries to show an unhappy, wealthy merchant how he can plant the seeds of peace within himself. (Rev: SLJ 1/00)

992 Berkeley, Laura. *The Spirit of the Maasai Man* (K–3). Illus. 2000, Barefoot $16.95 (1-902283-74-0). 32pp. When animals in a zoo hear the song of the Maasai Man they remember their natural homes. (Rev: BL 3/15/00; SLJ 7/00)

993 Bertrand, Lynne. *Granite Baby* (K–2). Illus. by Kevin Hawkes. 2005, Farrar $16.00 (0-374-32761-0). 40pp. A tall tale set in New Hampshire about five giant sisters who learn to care for a tiny baby one of them carves from granite. (Rev: BL 4/1/05; SLJ 4/05)

994 Birchmore, Daniel A. *The White Curtain* (PS–2). Illus. by Gail Lucas. 1997, Cucumber Island Storytellers $15.95 (1-887813-09-8). Gusts of wind blow a white curtain outdoors, where it can enjoy exploring the world. (Rev: SLJ 2/98)

995 Blackstone, Stella. *An Island in the Sun* (K–3). Illus. by Nicoletta Ceccoli. 2002, Barefoot $15.99 (1-84148-193-9). 24pp. A boy in a small sailboat visits an island where he plays with a polka-dot dog before taking him home at night. (Rev: BL 5/1/02; HBG 10/02; SLJ 7/02)

996 Bloom, Becky. *Mice Make Trouble* (K–2). Illus. by Pascal Biet. 2000, Orchard LB $16.99 (0-531-33253-5). 32pp. When he uses his sister's magical pencils, everything that Henry draws comes to life, including six mischievous mice. (Rev: BL 4/1/00; HBG 10/00; SLJ 3/00)

997 Bloom, Suzanne. *Piggy Monday: A Tale About Manners* (PS–1). Illus. 2001, Whitman $15.95 (0-8075-6529-6). 40pp. Mrs. Hubbub's class has turned into pigs and it's up to the Pig Lady to transform them back into children by teaching them some manners. (Rev: BL 8/01; HBG 3/02; SLJ 1/02)

998 Bluitgen, Kåre. *A Boot Fell from Heaven* (PS–2). Illus. by Chiara Carrer. 2003, Kane/Miller $15.95 (1-929132-45-X). When God travels to Earth to retrieve a boot He's dropped, He gets little help from the planet's inhabitants until he comes across a little boy. (Rev: BL 5/15/03; SLJ 6/03)

999 Boesky, Amy. *Planet Was* (K–3). Illus. by Nadine Bernard Westcott. 1990, Little, Brown $14.95 (0-316-10084-6). 32pp. Young Prince Hierre introduces change into the life of Planet Was. (Rev: BL 12/1/90; SLJ 1/91)

1000 Bornstein, Ruth. *The Dancing Man* (K–4). Illus. 1998, Clarion $15.00 (0-395-83429-5). 32pp. In this tale set in a poor village near the Baltic Sea, a boy finds a pair of magical shoes and spends his life dancing in them to produce happiness and joy for others. (Rev: BL 4/15/98; HBG 10/98; SLJ 6/98)

1001 Bowen, Anne. *Tooth Fairy's First Night* (K–2). Illus. by on Berkeley. 2005, Carolrhoda $15.95 (1-57505753-0). A young tooth fairy finds her first assignment more taxing than she expected. (Rev: SLJ 6/05)

1002 Bradman, Tony. *Midnight in Memphis* (1–2). Illus. by Martin Chatterton. Series: Blue Bananas. 2001, Crabtree LB $14.97 (0-7787-0848-9); paper $4.46 (0-7787-0894-2). 48pp. After a UFO damages their pyramid in Egypt, Mommy Mummy and her mummy family hire some ladies to repair it in this humorous fantasy. (Rev: BL 5/1/02; SLJ 8/02)

1003 Breathed, Berkeley. *Edwurd Fudwupper Fibbed Big: Explained by Fannie Fudwupper* (K–3). Illus. by author. 2000, Little, Brown $15.95 (0-316-10675-5). A boy's constant fibbing gets him into serious trouble particularly when it causes the arrival of an angry monster from space. (Rev: HBG 3/01; SLJ 11/00)

1004 Brenner, Barbara. *What the Elephant Told* (PS–K). Illus. by Akemi Gutierrez. 2003, Holt $15.95 (0-8050-6442-7). A young boy and an elephant share a day in the park and discover they have a great deal in common. (Rev: BL 5/15/03; HBG 10/03; SLJ 7/03)

1005 Brett, Jan. *Trouble with Trolls* (PS–3). Illus. 1992, Penguin Putnam $16.99 (0-399-22336-3). 32pp. In this Scandinavian-type tale, Treva has trouble with trolls when they try to steal her dog Tuffi. (Rev: BCCB 12/92; BL 9/1/92*; SLJ 9/92)

1006 Briggs, Raymond. *Jim and the Beanstalk* (PS–2). Illus. by author. 1997, Penguin Putnam paper $5.99 (0-698-11577-5). 40pp. A humorous, fast-moving sequel to the well-known tale.

1007 Brisson, Pat. *Tap-Dance Fever* (PS–2). Illus. by Nancy Cote. 2005, Boyds Mills $15.95 (1-59078-290-9). 32pp. Annabelle Applegate's non-stop tap dancing annoys her neighbors — until the day her tapping charms the rattlesnakes. (Rev: BL 3/1/05; SLJ 3/05)

1008 Brooks, Nigel, and Abigail Horner. *Country Mouse Cottage: How We Lived a Hundred Years Ago* (PS–2). Illus. 2000, Walker $15.95 (0-8027-8752-5). 32pp. In England circa 1900, Edward Country Mouse takes the reader on a tour of his rural house including the kitchen, laundry room, bed, bathroom, and even the schoolroom. (Rev: BCCB 12/00; BL 3/1/01; HBG 3/01; SLJ 12/00)

1009 Brown, Calef. *Tippintown: A Guided Tour* (PS–2). Illus. by author. 2003, Houghton Mifflin $15.00 (0-618-14972-4). This rollicking, brightly illustrated story, told in rhyme, transports young readers to the magical world of Tippintown, where the guide has an elephant's trunk and the gargoyles play games. (Rev: HBG 10/03; SLJ 5/03)

1010 Brown, Jeff. *Flat Stanley* (1–3). Illus. by Tomi Ungerer. 1964, HarperCollins LB $15.89 (0-06-020681-0). 64pp. A falling bulletin board flattens Stanley so he is only one-half-inch thick.

1011 Brown, Jeff. *Invisible Stanley* (2–3). Illus. by Steve Bjorkman. 1996, HarperCollins paper $4.25 (0-06-442029-9). 81pp. When Stanley suddenly becomes invisible, he performs many humanitarian acts, including foiling a bank robbery. (Rev: SLJ 12/96)

1012 Brown, Kerry Hannula. *Tupag the Dreamer* (PS–3). Illus. by Linda Saport. 2001, Marshall Cavendish $15.95 (0-7614-5076-9). Banished from his long-ago village at a time when all was dark and cold, lazy Tupag meets Raven the creator and is accorded his one wish, for a season of light. (Rev: HBG 10/01; SLJ 5/01)

1013 Brown, Marc. *Witches Four* (PS–1). Illus. by author. 1980, Parents LB $5.95 (0-8193-1014-X). 48pp. Four witches lose their magic hats, which are found by four homeless cats.

1014 Brown, Margaret Wise. *The Fierce Yellow Pumpkin* (PS–1). Illus. by Richard Egielski. 2003, HarperCollins LB $16.89 (0-06-024481-X). A tiny pumpkin yearns to grow up to be fierce, like the scarecrow, and eventually gets his wish. (Rev: HBG 4/04; SLJ 8/03)

1015 Brown, Margaret Wise. *The Little Scarecrow Boy* (PS–K). Illus. by David Diaz. 1998, HarperCollins LB $15.89 (0-06-026290-7). 40pp. When his father tells him to wait until he is older before going into the field to scare crows, the little scarecrow disobeys and ventures out — with unexpected results. (Rev: BL 9/1/98; HB 11–12/98; HBG 3/99; SLJ 11/98)

1016 Brown, Margaret Wise. *Mouse of My Heart: A Treasury of Sense and Nonsense* (PS). Illus. by Loretta Krupinski. 2001, Hyperion LB $20.49 (0-7868-2546-4). 179pp. This handsome book full of lovely illustrations contains more than 50 stories and poems grouped into categories such as Adventure, Nature, and Nonsense. (Rev: HBG 10/01; SLJ 6/01)

1017 Browne, Anthony. *My Dad* (PS–3). Illus. 2001, Farrar $16.00 (0-374-35101-5). 32pp. A little boy imagines all the things his dad could do if he wanted — walk on a tightrope or sing in the opera, for example. (Rev: BL 3/1/01; HBG 10/01)

1018 Brumbeau, Jeff. *The Quiltmaker's Journey* (K–3). Illus. by Gail de Marken. 2005, Scholastic $17.95 (0-439-51219-0). 56pp. Readers find out what prompted a young girl to become the Quiltmaker in this prequel to *The Quiltmaker's Gift* (1999); with bright quilt-themed illustrations. (Rev: BL 3/1/05; SLJ 4/05)

1019 Bryan, Sean. *A Boy and His Bunny* (PS–1). Illus. by Tom Murphy. 2005, Arcade $14.95 (1-55970-725-9). A boy wakes up with a bunny on his head but allays his mother's concerns with the reassurance that this will in no way limit his activities. (Rev: SLJ 6/05)

1020 Buehner, Caralyn. *Snowmen at Night* (PS). Illus. by Mark Buehner. 2002, Penguin Putnam $15.99 (0-8037-2550-7). 32pp. Captivating illustrations and breezy text put snowmen into action (sledding, playing baseball, and drinking iced cocoa), revealing why snowmen look so tuckered out in the mornings. (Rev: BL 10/15/02; HBG 3/03; SLJ 10/02)

1021 Buffett, Jimmy, and Savannah Buffett. *The Jolly Mon* (2–5). Illus. by Lambert Davis. 1988, Harcourt $16.00 (0-15-240530-5). 32pp. The story of Jolly Mon in the Caribbean whose musical voice gains him a magical guitar. (Rev: BCCB 6/88; BL 4/1/88; SLJ 7/88)

1022 Buffett, Jimmy, and Savannah Buffett. *Trouble Dolls* (K–3). Illus. by Lambert Davis. 1991, Harcourt $16.00 (0-15-290790-4). 32pp. Four tiny dolls come alive to help a young girl search for her missing father. (Rev: BL 3/15/91; SLJ 6/91)

1023 Bunting, Eve. *Ducky* (PS–2). Illus. by David Wisniewski. 1997, Clarion $15.00 (0-395-75185-3). 32pp. A yellow plastic duck has many adventures when he is washed overboard from an ocean liner. (Rev: BL 8/97; HB 11–12/97; HBG 3/98; SLJ 9/97)

1024 Bunting, Eve. *Night of the Gargoyles* (PS–3). Illus. by David Wiesner. 1994, Clarion $14.95 (0-395-66553-1). 28pp. A horror story in which gargoyles come alive at night. (Rev: BCCB 11/94; BL 10/1/94; SLJ 10/94*)

1025 Bunting, Eve. *Riding the Tiger* (2–4). Illus. by David Frampton. 2001, Clarion $16.00 (0-395-79731-4). 32pp. In this picture-book fantasy about the abuse of power, a young boy realizes how frightening he can become when he rides through town on the back of a ferocious tiger. (Rev: BL 3/1/01*; HBG 10/01; SLJ 3/01)

1026 Burningham, John. *The Magic Bed* (PS). Illus. by author. 2003, Knopf LB $18.99 (0-375-92423-X). Georgie chooses an antique bed to replace his crib and soon finds his nights are full of magical adventures. (Rev: HBG 4/04; SLJ 10/03)

1027 Burningham, John. *Mr. Grumpy's Outing* (PS–K). Illus. 2001, Holt $6.95 (0-8050-6629-2). 20pp. A board-book version of the tale of Mr. Grumpy and the animals he takes for a trip down the river. (Rev: BL 4/1/01; HBG 3/02)

1028 Burns, Marilyn. *The Greedy Triangle* (K–3). Illus. by Gordon Silveria. 1995, Scholastic $15.95 (0-590-48991-7). 40pp. A little triangle is tired of his shape and becomes a quadrilateral. (Rev: BCCB 3/95; BL 2/1/95; SLJ 3/95)

1029 Bursik, Rose. *Amelia's Fantastic Flight* (PS–3). Illus. 1994, Holt paper $6.95 (0-8050-3386-6). 32pp. Amelia flies from country to country in the plane she has built, returning home in time for dinner. (Rev: BL 3/1/92)

1030 Butterworth, Nick. *The Rescue Party* (PS–1). Illus. by author. 1993, Little, Brown $14.95 (0-316-11923-7). A park keeper enjoys playing with his animal buddies until a young rabbit falls down a well. (Rev: SLJ 2/94)

1031 Carle, Eric. *Draw Me a Star* (PS–2). Illus. 1992, Penguin Putnam $16.99 (0-399-21877-7). 36pp. The story of creation is told through the artist's drawings of various objects. (Rev: BCCB 12/92; BL 9/15/92; SLJ 10/92)

1032 Carle, Eric. *Little Cloud* (PS–K). Illus. 1996, Penguin Putnam $15.95 (0-399-23034-3). 32pp. A little cloud transforms itself into a variety of shapes and finally produces rain. (Rev: BL 4/1/96; HB 5–6/96; SLJ 5/96)

1033 Carle, Eric. *Papa, Please Get the Moon for Me* (PS–K). Illus. by author. 1986, Picture Book $19.00 (0-88708-026-X). 32pp. A little girl's father gets a high ladder to climb to the moon, but has to admit it's too large to bring home. (Rev: BL 6/1/86; SLJ 8/86)

1034 Carle, Eric. *10 Little Rubber Ducks* (PS–1). Illus. 2005, HarperCollins LB $20.89 (0-06-074076-0). 36pp. Ten rubber ducks fall off a ship and float off in different directions; the tenth is adopted by a mother duck despite the fact that it can only squeak, not quack. (Rev: BL 5/1/05; SLJ 1/05)

1035 Carlstrom, Nancy White. *The Way to Wyatt's House* (PS–K). Illus. by Mary Morgan. 2000, Walker LB $16.85 (0-8027-8742-8). 32pp. Two quiet children have a loud and lovely time visiting with friend Wyatt and all the animals on his farm. (Rev: BL 9/1/00; HBG 3/01; SLJ 10/00)

1036 Carmack, Lisa Jobe. *Philippe in Monet's Garden* (PS–1). Illus. by Lisa Canney Chesaux. 1998, Museum of Fine Arts, Boston $10.95 (0-87846-456-5). 24pp. A frog escapes to Monet's Giverny garden where he gives the artist some tips and inspiration. (Rev: BL 1/1–15/99; HBG 3/99)

1037 Carr, Jan. *Big Truck and Little Truck* (PS–3). Illus. by Ivan Bates. 2000, Scholastic $15.95 (0-439-07177-1). 32pp. On Farley's farm, Little Truck remembers everything Big Truck has taught him and is able to save himself after sliding into a ditch. (Rev: BL 11/15/00; HBG 3/01; SLJ 11/00)

1038 Carrick, Carol. *Patrick's Dinosaurs on the Internet* (1–2). Illus. by David Milgrim. 1999, Clarion $16.00 (0-395-50949-1). 32pp. A dinosaur appears on young Patrick's computer screen and then whisks the boy off to a distant planet where the dinosaurs now live. (Rev: BL 12/1/99; HBG 3/00; SLJ 9/99)

1039 Carroll, Lewis. *Alice's Adventures in Wonderland* (K–6). Illus. by Robert Sabuda. 2003, Simon & Schuster $24.95 (0-689-84743-2). 12pp. Dazzling — but perhaps delicate — pop-ups adorn this faithful adaptation of Lewis Carroll's classic story. (Rev: BL 3/15/04; HB 11–12/03; HBG 4/04; SLJ 11/03)

1040 Carter, Anne. *From Poppa* (K–3). Illus. by Kasia Charko. 2001, Lobster $16.95 (1-894222-02-4). 32pp. A girl and her grandfather make an enchanted duck decoy. (Rev: BL 10/1/01)

1041 Carter, Anne. *Tall in the Saddle* (K–2). Illus. by David McPhail. 1999, Orca $14.95 (1-55143-154-8). 32pp. As a boy walks down a modern city street, everything becomes transformed into a scene from the Wild West. (Rev: BL 9/1/99; HBG 3/00; SLJ 9/99)

1042 Chambers, Catherine. *The Elephants' Ears* (PS–1). Illus. by Caroline Mockford. 2000, Barefoot $15.95 (1-84148-052-5). 32pp. A story about brother and sister elephants that explains why the ears of the elephants are different in India and in Africa. (Rev: BL 4/1/00; SLJ 4/00)

1043 Charles, Veronika M. *Stretch, Swallow and Stare* (K–4). Illus. by Veronika Martenova Charles. 1999, Stoddart $16.95 (0-7737-3098-2). A young boy finds his sister with the help of three female companions, each of whom possesses an unusual power. (Rev: SLJ 1/00)

1044 Charlip, Remy, and Burton Supree. *Mother Mother I Feel Sick Send for the Doctor Quick Quick Quick* (PS–K). Illus. 2001, Tricycle $15.95 (1-58246-043-4). 48pp. A boy who complains of being sick is operated on and objects including a teapot and a bicycle are removed from his stomach. (Rev: BL 3/1/01; HBG 10/01)

1045 Child, Lauren. *Who's Afraid of the Big Bad Book?* (K–3). Illus. by author. 2003, Hyperion $16.99 (0-7868-0926-4). While reading his favorite book of fairy tales, young Herb falls asleep and awakes to find himself in the middle of a fairy tale world in which the characters scold him for treating their book badly. (Rev: BCCB 1/04; BL 1/1–15/04; HBG 4/04; SLJ 12/03)

1046 Chrismer, Melanie. *Phoebe Clappsaddle and the Tumbleweed Gang* (K–3). Illus. by Virginia M. Roeder. 2002, Pelican $14.95 (1-56554-966-X). Talented young Phoebe gets the best of a gang of mean cowpokes in this tall tale set in the Old West. (Rev: HBG 3/03; SLJ 1/03)

1047 Christiana, David. *The First Snow* (PS–3). Illus. 1996, Scholastic $15.95 (0-590-22855-2). 32pp. Aunt Arctica persuades Mother Nature to let Winter come into her kingdom. (Rev: BL 2/1/97; SLJ 2/97)

1048 Chwast, Seymour. *Harry, I Need You!* (1–3). Illus. by author. 2002, Houghton Mifflin $15.00 (0-618-17917-8). Harry is an imaginative child who conjures up all sorts of scenarios when his mother calls for him. (Rev: SLJ 9/02)

1049 Cibula, Matt. *What's Up With You, Taquandra Fu?* (K–2). Illus. by Brian Strassburg. 1997, Zino $16.95 (1-55933-212-3). Taquandra Fu is an odd-ball, but when she tries to become conventional she prefers her old, erratic self. (Rev: SLJ 4/98)

1050 Clark, Emma C. *Catch That Hat!* (K–2). Illus. 1990, Little, Brown $12.95 (0-316-14496-7). 28pp. A rhymed story about the adventures of a runaway hat. (Rev: BL 5/15/90*; SLJ 8/90)

1051 Clark, Emma C. *I Love You, Blue Kangaroo!* (PS–2). Illus. 1999, Doubleday $15.95 (0-385-32638-6). 32pp. When Lily loses interest in her Blue Kangaroo, it switches its loyalties to Lily's younger brother. (Rev: BL 1/1–15/99; HBG 10/99; SLJ 3/99)

1052 Clement, Rod. *Just Another Ordinary Day* (K–3). Illus. by author. 1997, HarperCollins LB $15.89 (0-06-027667-3). A clever picture book from Australia in which ordinary daily occurrences are pictured in very extraordinary ways with outlandish characters. (Rev: BCCB 9–8/97; SLJ 6/97*)

1053 Clerk, Jessica. *The Wriggly, Wriggly Baby* (PS). Illus. by Laura Rankin. 2002, Scholastic $16.95 (0-590-96067-9). 32pp. A squirmy baby slithers through a number of fantastic adventures in this rollicking tale. (Rev: BL 10/1/02; HBG 3/03; SLJ 9/02)

1054 Clibbon, Meg. *Imagine You're a Mermaid!* (K–4). Illus. by Lucy Clibbon. Series: Imagine This! 2003, Annick $19.95 (1-55037-791-4); paper $7.95 (1-55037-790-6). A pun-filled book all about mermaids and what they're really like. (Rev: SLJ 3/04)

1055 Coffelt, Nancy. *Dogs in Space* (PS–2). Illus. 1993, Harcourt $14.95 (0-15-200440-8). 32pp. High-flying dogs visit one planet after another. (Rev: BL 2/15/93; SLJ 4/93)

1056 Coffelt, Nancy. *Tom's Fish* (PS–2). Illus. 1994, Harcourt $13.95 (0-15-200587-0). 32pp. Tom can't understand why his pet goldfish, Jessie, swims

upside down. (Rev: BL 3/15/94; HB 9–10/93; SLJ 5/94)

1057 Cole, Babette. *Princess Smartypants Rules* (1–3). Illus. Series: Princess Smartypants. 2005, Penguin Putnam $15.99 (0-399-24349-6). 32pp. A superbaby turns Princess Smartypants' world upside-down in this zany tale that includes dragons, an evil count, and a prince. (Rev: BL 3/1/05; SLJ 3/05)

1058 Cole, Brock. *Larky Mavis* (PS–3). Illus. 2001, Farrar $16.00 (0-374-34365-9). 32pp. Eccentric Larky Mavis finds a baby inside a peanut, which she calls Heart's Delight and cares for despite universal disdain. (Rev: BCCB 9/01; BL 7/01; HB 9–10/01*; HBG 3/02; SLJ 8/01)

1059 Cole, Joanna. *Golly Gump Swallowed a Fly* (PS–3). Illus. by Bari Weissman. 1982, Parents $5.95 (0-8193-1069-7). 48pp. A new version of "The Old Woman Who Swallowed a Fly" story.

1060 Collins, Ross. *Busy Night* (PS–2). Illus. 2002, Bloomsbury $15.95 (1-58234-750-6). 32pp. Ben's bedroom gets crowded when the Sandman, the Tooth Fairy, a "thing under the bed," and Santa Claus all come to visit. (Rev: BL 7/02)

1061 Colon, Raul. *Orson Blasts Off!* (PS–2). Illus. 2004, Simon & Schuster $15.95 (0-689-84278-3). 40pp. When Orson's computer crashes, bringing an end to his computer games, he winds up on a dream journey to such places as the North Pole and the moon in this imaginatively written and illustrated book. (Rev: BL 2/1/04*; SLJ 4/04)

1062 Compton, Kenn, and Joanne Compton. *Granny Greenteeth and the Noise in the Night* (PS–2). Illus. by Kenn Compton. 1993, Holiday House LB $14.95 (0-8234-1051-X). In this humorous cumulative tale, Granny Greenteeth tries to get help to discover what is making the noise that comes from under her bed. (Rev: SLJ 3/94)

1063 Conover, Chris. *The Lion's Share* (PS–3). Illus. 2000, Farrar $16.00 (0-374-39974-3). 40pp. When young Prince Leo visits King Otto of a rival kingdom he discovers that Otto's greatest treasure is his book-filled palace and the ability to read. (Rev: BL 3/15/00; HBG 10/00; SLJ 5/00)

1064 Conrad, Pam. *The Tub People* (PS–2). Illus. by Richard Egielski. 1989, HarperCollins $15.00 (0-060-21340-X); paper $6.95 (0-06-443306-4). 32pp. In this fantasy, wooden figures who enjoy playing in the tub are swept down the drain. (Rev: BCCB 11/89; BL 8/89; HB 11–12/89*; SLJ 12/89)

1065 Coplestone, Lis. *Noah's Bed* (PS–2). Illus. by Jim Coplestone. 2004, Frances Lincoln $14.95 (1-84507-002-X). Frightened by the torrential rainstorm, various animals sneak one by one into bed with Noah, Mrs. Noah, and grandson Eber. (Rev: SLJ 6/04)

1066 Coppinger, Tom. *Curse in Reverse* (PS–2). Illus. by Dirk Zimmer. 2003, Simon & Schuster $16.95 (0-689-83096-3). A childless couple is kind to Agnezza the witch and the two are delighted when they discover the true meaning of the curse she bestowed upon them. (Rev: HB 9–10/03; HBG 4/04; SLJ 7/03)

1067 Corey, Shana. *First Graders from Mars: Episode 4 — Tera, Star Student* (K–2). Illus. by Mark Teague. 2003, Scholastic $15.95 (0-439-26634-3); paper $4.50 (0-439-45219-8). 29pp. Purple-haired Tera discovers bossiness is unwelcome in her first-grade Martian classroom. (Rev: HBG 4/04; SLJ 8/03)

1068 Corey, Shana. *First Graders from Mars: Episode 3 — Nergal and the Great Space Race* (1–3). Illus. by Mark Teague. 2002, Scholastic paper $4.50 (0-439-42443-2). 32pp. It's Health Week on Mars, and Nergal isn't looking forward to the space race. (Rev: SLJ 1/03)

1069 Corey, Shana. *First Graders from Mars: Episode 2 — The Problem with Pelly* (K–2). Illus. by Mark Teague. 2002, Scholastic $14.95 (0-439-26632-7); paper $4.50 (0-439-36784-0). 32pp. This silly book with a serious message tells the story of Pelly, a foreigner to Mars, who is self-conscious because she doesn't look like her Martian classmates. (Rev: BL 2/15/02; HBG 10/02; SLJ 4/02)

1070 Coristine, Philip. *Serena and the Wild Doll* (K–3). Illus. by Julia Gukova. 2000, Annick LB $19.95 (1-55037-649-7); paper $6.95 (1-55037-648-9). 32pp. Serena, a proper doll who lives in an attic, is joined by a wild doll in a tattered dress and a fox, and the three venture out to see the city. (Rev: BL 2/15/01; HBG 3/01; SLJ 11/00)

1071 Cotten, Cynthia. *Snow Ponies* (K–3). Illus. by Jason Cockcroft. 2001, Holt $15.95 (0-8050-6063-4). Snow ponies released by Old Man Winter turn the world white everywhere they roam. (Rev: HBG 3/02; SLJ 12/01)

1072 Cowan, Catherine, trans. and adapt. *My Life with the Wave: Based on the Story by Octavio Paz* (K–3). Illus. by Mark Buehner. 1997, Lothrop LB $15.89 (0-688-12661-8). At the seashore, a boy captures a wave and takes it home, with unfortunate results. (Rev: HB 9–10/97; HBG 3/98; SLJ 8/97*)

1073 Cowen-Fletcher, Jane. *Farmer Will* (PS). Illus. 2001, Candlewick $14.99 (0-7636-0988-9). 32pp. Young Will's toy animals become real when they get outside, and they all play together until they're tired. (Rev: BL 7/01; HBG 10/01; SLJ 7/01)

1074 Cowley, Joy. *Mrs. Wishy-Washy's Farm* (PS–1). Illus. by Elizabeth Fuller. 2003, Philomel $15.99 (0-399-23872-7). Obsessed with cleanliness, Mrs. Wishy-Washy decides it's time to scrub all the animals on the farm; to escape their date with the tub, her cow, duck, and pig run off, only to find themselves in loads of trouble and longing to be reunited with their master. (Rev: HBG 10/03; SLJ 7/03)

1075 Cowley, Joy. *Singing Down the Rain* (K–2). Illus. by Jan S. Gilchrist. 1997, HarperCollins LB $14.00 (0-06-027603-7). 32pp. Fantasy and reality blend in this story about a young girl, a drought, and a tiny woman who is a "rain singer." (Rev: BL 11/15/97; SLJ 10/97)

1076 Cowley, Joy. *The Wishing of Biddy Malone* (1–3). Illus. by Christopher Denise. 2004, Penguin Putnam $15.99 (0-399-23404-7). 40pp. Biddy makes three wishes when she strays into a faerie vil-lage, but comes to realize that the handsome young man did not promise to grant them. (Rev: BL 1/1–15/04; SLJ 3/04)

1077 Cox, Judy. *The West Texas Chili Monster* (1–4). Illus. by John O'Brien. 1998, BridgeWater $15.95 (0-8167-4546-3). Attracted to a chili cook-off, a creature from outer space samples a lot of different chilies but chooses Mama's as the best. (Rev: HBG 10/98; SLJ 6/98)

1078 Coy, John. *Vroomaloom: Zoom* (PS–K). Illus. by Joe Cepeda. 2000, Crown $15.95 (0-517-80009-8). 24pp. Because little Carmela can't sleep, her father takes her on a wild joyride that involves driving through farmlands, cities, swamps, seashores, and many other areas. (Rev: BCCB 1/01; BL 12/1/00; HBG 3/01; SLJ 10/00)

1079 Creech, Sharon. *Fishing in the Air* (K–3). Illus. by Chris Raschka. 2000, HarperCollins LB $15.89 (0-06-028112-X). 32pp. A highly imaginative fantasy in which objects seen by a boy and his father on a fishing trip change into images inspired by Chagall and Picasso. (Rev: BL 11/1/00; HBG 3/01; SLJ 9/00)

1080 Crew, Gary. *Pig on the Titanic: A True Story* (K–2). Illus. by Bruce Whatley. 2005, HarperCollins LB $16.89 (0-06-052306-9). 32pp. A music-box pig named Maxixe describes the sinking of the *Titanic* and how his music keeps up the spirits of the children in his lifeboat in this compelling story based on reality. (Rev: BL 6/1–15/05; SLJ 5/05)

1081 Crews, Nina. *I'll Catch the Moon* (PS–K). Illus. by author. 1996, Greenwillow $14.89 (0-688-14135-8). A mood piece in which a young boy fantasizes about climbing to the moon and circling the earth. (Rev: BCCB 5/96; HB 5–6/96; SLJ 5/96)

1082 Crummel, Susan Stevens. *All in One Hour* (PS–1). Illus. by Dorothy Donohue. 2003, Marshall Cavendish $16.95 (0-7614-5129-3). 32pp. Paper-cut collage illustrations tell a "This Is the House That Jack Built" type story featuring a mouse, a cat, a dog, a dogcatcher, a robber, and a police officer. (Rev: BL 3/15/03; HBG 10/03; SLJ 5/03)

1083 Cullen, Lynn. *Little Scraggly Hair: A Dog on Noah's Ark* (PS–3). Illus. by Jacqueline Rogers. 2003, Holiday House $16.95 (0-8234-1772-7). With an Appalachian flair, this tells the story of Noah's ark and as a bonus explains why dogs have wet noses. (Rev: BCCB 2/04; BL 11/1/03; HBG 4/04; SLJ 12/03)

1084 Cuyler, Margery. *Big Friends* (PS–1). Illus. by Ezra Tucker. 2004, Walker $16.95 (0-8027-8886-6). 32pp. Big Hasuni's lonely life on an African mountaintop ends when he encounters a giant woman. (Rev: BL 4/15/04; SLJ 4/04)

1085 Cuyler, Margery. *The Biggest, Best Snowman* (PS–2). Illus. by Will Hillenbrand. 1998, Scholastic $15.95 (0-590-13922-3). 32pp. Little Nell is always left out of family activities because she is told she is too small, but her animal friends give her the confidence to build the biggest snowman ever. (Rev: BCCB 12/98; BL 12/15/98; HBG 3/99; SLJ 4/99)

1086 Czernecki, Stefan. *Zorah's Magic Carpet* (K–3). Illus. by author. 1996, Hyperion LB $15.49

(0-7868-2066-7). In this tale set in Morocco, a young woman weaves a magic carpet that takes her to exotic places that she later weaves into other carpets. (Rev: HB 7–8/96; SLJ 4/96)

1087 Daniels, Teri. *G-Rex* (K–2). Illus. by Tracey Campbell Pearson. 2000, Orchard LB $17.99 (0-531-33243-8). A boy turns himself into a dinosaur so he can get more attention at home. (Rev: HBG 3/01; SLJ 10/00)

1088 Davol, Marguerite W. *How Snake Got His Hiss* (PS–3). Illus. by Mercedes McDonald. 1996, Orchard LB $15.99 (0-531-08768-9). 32pp. Not only does this tale tell how a snake got its hiss but also how the hyena got its spots and the lion its mane. (Rev: BCCB 4/96; BL 4/15/96; SLJ 3/96)

1089 Davol, Marguerite W. *The Loudest, Fastest, Best Drummer in Kansas* (PS–2). Illus. by Cat B. Smith. 2000, Orchard LB $16.99 (0-531-33191-1). 32pp. In this tall tale, Maggie proves that the loud noises she makes on her drums can have beneficial results. (Rev: BL 3/15/00; HBG 10/00; SLJ 5/00)

1090 Davol, Marguerite W. *The Paper Dragon* (PS–3). Illus. by Robert Sabuda. 1997, Simon & Schuster $18.00 (0-689-31992-4). 60pp. This story set in China tells how Mi Fei accomplishes his task of putting a destructive dragon to sleep. (Rev: BL 10/15/97*; HBG 3/98; SLJ 11/97)

1091 Davol, Marguerite W. *The Snake's Tales* (2–4). Illus. by Yumi Heo. 2002, Scholastic $15.95 (0-439-31769-X). 32pp. In this absorbing and cheerful story inspired by a traditional Seneca tale, the first storyteller is a wily snake who persuades children to swap food for stories. (Rev: BL 1/1–15/03; HBG 3/03; SLJ 9/02)

1092 Deacon, Alexis. *Beegu* (K–2). Illus. by author. 2003, Farrar $16.00 (0-374-30667-2). Stranded on Earth after her spaceship crashes, Beegu, an appealing yellow alien, finds acceptance from small earthlings but is driven away at every turn by adults. (Rev: HBG 4/04; SLJ 11/03)

1093 Deedy, Carmen A. *The Library Dragon* (K–2). Illus. by Michael P. White. 1994, Peachtree $16.95 (1-56145-091-X). The new librarian is a real firebreathing dragon who in time learns to trust children with her books. (Rev: BCCB 2/95; SLJ 12/94)

1094 Dematons, Charlotte. *Let's Go* (K–3). Illus. 2001, Front Street $15.95 (1-886910-65-0). 32pp. A young boy's trip to the corner store turns into a magical adventure. (Rev: BL 5/15/01; HBG 10/01; SLJ 10/01)

1095 Dematons, Charlotte. *Looking for Cinderella* (PS–3). Illus. 1996, Front Street $15.95 (1-886910-13-8). 32pp. In an old windmill, Hilda encounters many fairy tale characters, including Hansel and Gretel and Tom Thumb. (Rev: BCCB 10/96; BL 9/15/96; SLJ 1/97)

1096 Demi. *Liang and the Magic Paintbrush* (2–4). Illus. by author. 1980, Holt paper $5.95 (0-8050-0801-2). 32pp. A boy in old China finds that everything he dreams comes to life.

1097 dePaola, Tomie. *Big Anthony: His Story* (PS–3). Illus. 1998, Penguin Putnam $16.99 (0-399-23189-7). 32pp. Klutzy Big Anthony goes out on his own to earn his fortune and finds himself at the door of the Italian witch Strega Nona. (Rev: BL 11/15/98; HBG 3/99; SLJ 11/98)

1098 dePaola, Tomie. *Bill and Pete* (K–2). Illus. by author. 1996, Penguin Putnam paper $5.99 (0-698-11400-0). 32pp. Pete is a toothbrush (alias a bird) who helps young Bill in a series of world misadventures.

1099 dePaola, Tomie. *Jamie O'Rourke and the Pooka* (PS–3). Illus. 2000, Penguin Putnam $16.99 (0-399-23467-5). 32pp. A humorous original folktale about the laziest man in Ireland and the strange donkey-like beast, the pooka, that helps clean his house. (Rev: BL 1/1–15/00; HBG 10/00; SLJ 3/00)

1100 dePaola, Tomie. *Sing, Pierrot, Sing: A Picture Book in Mime* (PS–2). Illus. by author. 1983, Harcourt paper $3.95 (0-15-274989-6). 32pp. A group of children comfort Pierrot at his loss of Columbine.

1101 dePaola, Tomie. *Strega Nona Meets Her Match* (K–2). Illus. 1993, Penguin Putnam $15.95 (0-399-22421-1). 34pp. Strega Amelia comes to town and takes away business from the town's other witch, Strega Nona. (Rev: BCCB 12/93; BL 11/1/93; HB 11–12/93)

1102 dePaola, Tomie. *Strega Nona Takes a Vacation* (K–3). Illus. 2000, Penguin Putnam $16.99 (0-399-23562-0). 32pp. While Strega Nona is away on vacation, Big Anthony uses too many bath crystals and creates enough soapsuds to flow into town. (Rev: BL 10/15/00; HBG 3/01; SLJ 10/00)

1103 dePaola, Tomie. *The Unicorn and the Moon* (PS–3). Illus. 1994, Silver Burdett LB $18.95 (0-382-24658-6). 32pp. When the moon becomes trapped between two mountains, a unicorn tries to rescue it. (Rev: BL 1/1/95)

1104 Desimini, Lisa. *Moon Soup* (PS–3). Illus. 1993, Hyperion LB $15.49 (1-56282-464-3). 32pp. An unusual man concocts a brew he calls moon soup and flies to the moon to eat it. (Rev: BL 11/1/93; SLJ 1/94)

1105 Desimini, Lisa. *Sun and Moon: A Giant Love Story* (PS–3). Illus. 1999, Scholastic $16.95 (0-590-18720-1). 40pp. An enchanting fable about the growing love between a girl and a boy whose heads are literally in the clouds. (Rev: BCCB 1/99; BL 1/1–15/99; HBG 10/99; SLJ 3/99)

1106 De Varennes, Monique. *The Sugar Child* (K–2). Illus. by Leonid Gore. 2004, Simon & Schuster $16.95 (0-689-85244-4). A marzipan girl named Matine sheds tears and turns into a real girl in this story set in French Canada but based on a Russian tale. (Rev: BL 12/1/04; SLJ 11/04)

1107 Devlin, Wende, and Harry Devlin. *Old Black Witch!* (K–3). Illus. by Harry Devlin. 1992, Macmillan $13.95 (0-02-729185-5). 32pp. When Nicky and his mother buy an old house, they find a witch living in the chimney. (Rev: BL 11/15/92)

1108 Dillon, Jana. *Lucky O'Leprechaun Comes to America* (PS–1). Illus. by author. 2000, Pelican $14.95 (1-56554-816-7). A fantasy in which Lucky O'Leprechaun gets caught in the luggage of three Irish immigrant girls and is forced to travel with them to America. (Rev: HBG 10/01; SLJ 1/01)

1109 Diterlizzi, Tony. *Jimmy Zangwow's Out-of-This-World Moon Pie Adventure* (K–2). Illus. by author. 2000, Simon & Schuster $16.00 (0-689-82215-4). When Jimmy's mother refuses to give him a Moon Pie, the young boy travels to the moon to get his own. (Rev: BCCB 5/00; HBG 10/00; SLJ 4/00)

1110 Diterlizzi, Tony. *Ted* (PS–1). Illus. by author. 2001, Simon & Schuster $16.00 (0-689-83235-4). A young boy succeeds in getting his father's attention through a lively imaginary friend. (Rev: BCCB 2/01; HBG 10/01; SLJ 4/01)

1111 Dollinger, Renate. *The Rabbi Who Flew: A Grandma Hanne Sheyne Story* (K–3). Illus. 2000, Booksmythe $18.00 (0-945585-20-9). 48pp. When a rabbi gains the power to fly, his friends realize that he has holes in his shoes and devise a plan to mend them. (Rev: BL 2/1/01)

1112 Donaldson, Julia. *Room on the Broom* (K–3). Illus. by Axel Scheffler. 2001, Dial $15.99 (0-8037-2657-0). 32pp. A witch's animal friends cleverly save her from a dragon in this rhyming tale featuring entertaining illustrations. (Rev: BCCB 9/01; BL 9/1/01; HBG 3/02; SLJ 9/01)

1113 Donaldson, Julia. *The Spiffiest Giant in Town* (PS–1). Illus. by Axel Scheffler. 2003, Dial $15.99 (0-8037-2848-4). 32pp. George, the giant, buys a new set of clothing but ends up giving it all away to animal friends in need. (Rev: BL 3/1/03; HBG 10/03; SLJ 3/03)

1114 Donnelly, Liza. *Dinosaur Beach* (PS–2). Illus. by author. 1991, Scholastic paper $2.50 (0-685-43744-2). A boy and his dog spend a lovely day playing with the dinosaurs at a beach. (Rev: SLJ 7/89)

1115 Donnelly, Liza. *Dinosaur Garden* (PS–3). Illus. 1991, Scholastic paper $3.25 (0-590-43172-2). 32pp. Rex's seedlings sprout into a tropical jungle that is soon home to plant-eating dinosaurs. (Rev: BL 4/15/90; SLJ 3/90)

1116 Dorros, Arthur. *Abuela* (K–2). Illus. by Elisa Kleven. 1991, Dutton $16.99 (0-525-44750-4). 40pp. Rosalba and her grandmother fly over New York City in her imagination. (Rev: BCCB 9/92; BL 10/15/91*; HB 11–12/91*; SLJ 10/91)

1117 Dorros, Arthur. *The Fungus That Ate My School* (1–4). Illus. by David Catrow. 2000, Scholastic $15.95 (0-590-47704-8). 32pp. A science experiment goes awry and a fungus takes over a school in this psychedelic fantasy. (Rev: BCCB 7–8/00; BL 6/1–15/00; HB 3–4/00; HBG 10/00; SLJ 4/00)

1118 Doucet, Sharon Arms. *Alligator Sue* (K–2). Illus. by Anne Wilsdorf. 2003, Farrar $17.00 (0-374-30218-9). When a hurricane sweeps Sue away from her houseboat home in a Louisiana swamp, she finds herself adopted by a very large family of alligators. (Rev: HBG 4/04; SLJ 9/03)

1119 Doyle, Charlotte. *You Can't Catch Me* (PS–1). Illus. by Rosanne Litzinger. 1998, HarperCollins $9.95 (0-694-01038-3). In a hide-and-seek series of pictures, various animals are playfully caught by their pursuers in the same way that a little girl is captured by her mother in a loving embrace. (Rev: HBG 10/98; SLJ 7/98)

1120 Doyle, Malachy. *Antonio on the Other Side of the World, Getting Smaller* (K–3). Illus. by Carll Cneut. 2003, Candlewick $15.99 (0-7636-2173-0). During a visit to his grandmother "on the other side of the world," Antonio unaccountably begins to shrink and continues to get smaller and smaller until he gets back home to mom. (Rev: BCCB 12/03; BL 10/15/03; HBG 4/04; SLJ 12/03)

1121 Doyle, Malachy. *The Bold Boy* (PS–K). Illus. by Jane Ray. 2001, Candlewick $15.99 (0-7636-1624-9). 40pp. A modern folktale about a wicked child who claims property as his own until the townspeople rebel . . . but at the end it seems the whole story is ready to repeat in typical circular fashion. (Rev: BL 12/15/01; HB 9–10/01; HBG 3/02; SLJ 1/02)

1122 Doyle, Malachy. *Hungry! Hungry! Hungry!* (K–3). Illus. by Paul Hess. 2001, Peachtree $15.95 (1-56145-241-6). A young boy asks a "ghastly goblin" many questions about his size and other scary features. (Rev: BCCB 4/01; HBG 10/01; SLJ 7/01)

1123 Drawson, Blair. *Flying Dimitri* (K–3). Illus. 1997, Orchard $14.95 (0-531-30037-4). 40pp. A fantasy in which a young boy flies to Mars to save a princess but is happy to get home, where his father tucks him into bed. (Rev: BL 12/15/97; HBG 3/98; SLJ 4/98)

1124 Drawson, Blair. *Mary Margaret's Tree* (K–3). Illus. 1996, Orchard LB $16.99 (0-531-08871-5). 32pp. In this fantasy, Mary Margaret views the change of seasons from atop a tree that she has planted. (Rev: BL 10/1/96; SLJ 10/96)

1125 Drescher, Henrik. *The Boy Who Ate Around* (K–3). Illus. 1994, Hyperion LB $15.49 (0-7868-2011-X). 40pp. When young Mo objects to the family dinner fare, he turns into a ravenous warthog that eats everything in sight. (Rev: BL 11/1/94; SLJ 10/94)

1126 Drescher, Henrik. *Simon's Book* (PS–1). Illus. by author. 1983, Lothrop paper $5.95 (0-688-10484-3). 32pp. A frightening monster chases Simon through the pages of his drawing pad.

1127 Drury, Tim. *When I'm Big* (K–2). Illus. by Nila Aye. 1999, Orchard $15.95 (0-531-30189-3). Confined to their home because of rain, a young brother and sister think of all the things they will do when they grow up. (Rev: HBG 3/00; SLJ 12/99)

1128 Dunbar, Joyce. *Magic Lemonade* (1–2). Illus. by Jan McCafferty. Series: Blue Bananas. 2001, Crabtree LB $14.97 (0-613-52875-1); paper $4.46 (0-7497-4645-9). 48pp. Bossy Zoe proves to be a difficult but imaginative playmate in this amusing fantasy. (Rev: BL 5/1/02)

1129 Dunbar, Joyce. *Shoe Baby* (PS). Illus. by Polly Dunbar. 2005, Candlewick $15.99 (0-7636-2779-8). 32pp. A baby has a lovely time traveling about in a shoe in this nicely illustrated book. (Rev: BL 6/1–15/05)

1130 Dunbar, Polly. *Flyaway Katie* (PS–1). 2004, Candlewick $14.99 (0-7636-2366-0). 40pp. Young Katie decides to enliven her day with color, not only in her clothes but on her body, in this whimsical tale. (Rev: BL 6/1–15/04; SLJ 9/04)

1131 Duquennoy, Jacques. *The Ghosts' Trip to Loch Ness* (PS–2). Illus. by author. 1996, Harcourt $11.00 (0-15-201440-3). A quartet of ghosts travels to Scotland for a glimpse of the Loch Ness monster in this amusing fantasy. (Rev: BCCB 10/96; SLJ 10/96)

1132 Dyer, Sarah. *Five Little Fiends* (K–3). Illus. 2002, Bloomsbury $15.95 (1-58234-751-4). 32pp. In this unusual picture book, the little fiends of the title emerge from statues to steal parts of the environment, until they realize the error of their ways. (Rev: BL 9/1/02; SLJ 9/02)

1133 Eaton, Deborah, and Susan Halter. *No One Told the Aardvark* (PS–2). Illus. by Jim Spence. 1997, Charlesbridge paper $6.95 (0-88106-871-3). In this humorous story, a young boy thinks of all the advantages there would be if he were different animals. (Rev: SLJ 6/97)

1134 Edwards, Pamela Duncan. *Dear Tooth Fairy* (PS–2). Illus. by Marie-Louise Fitzpatrick. 2003, HarperCollins LB $16.89 (0-06-623973-7). Six-year-old Claire, concerned that she still has all her teeth, writes a letter to the Tooth Fairy; much to her surprise, the Tooth Fairy writes back with some reassuring advice. (Rev: HBG 4/04; SLJ 1/04)

1135 Edwards, Pamela Duncan. *The Leprechaun's Gold* (PS–2). Illus. by Henry Cole. 2004, Harper-Collins LB $16.89 (0-06-623975-3). 32pp. Young Tom's determination to become the finest harpist in Ireland is foiled by leprechauns. (Rev: BL 1/1–15/04; SLJ 2/04)

1136 Edwards, Pamela Duncan. *Rude Mule* (K–1). Illus. by Barbara Nascimbeni. 2002, Holt $15.95 (0-8050-7007-9). A young host teaches a rude mule a thing or two about manners. (Rev: HBG 3/03; SLJ 8/02)

1137 Egan, Tim. *Distant Feathers* (K–3). Illus. 1998, Houghton Mifflin $15.00 (0-395-85808-9). 32pp. A giant bird taps on Sedrick Van Pelt's window and asks for bread in this humorous picture book. (Rev: BL 3/15/98; HBG 10/98; SLJ 5/98)

1138 Egielski, Richard. *Buz* (PS–2). Illus. 1995, HarperCollins LB $15.89 (0-06-023567-5). 32pp. A bug that is eaten accidently by a boy finally finds an escape route via the boy's ear. (Rev: BCCB 10/95; BL 8/95; SLJ 9/95)

1139 Elliott, George. *The Boy Who Loved Bananas* (PS–2). Illus. by Andrej Krystoforski. 2005, Kids Can $14.95 (1-55337-744-3). After watching the monkeys at the zoo, Matthew vows only to eat bananas, which is fine until he morphs into a monkey himself. (Rev: SLJ 6/05)

1140 Elya, Susan Middleton. *Fairy Trails: A Story Told in English and Spanish* (PS). Illus. by Mercedes McDonald. 2005, Bloomsbury $16.95 (1-58234-927-4). 32pp. On their way to their aunt's house, Miguel and Maria meet a variety of fairy-tale characters — Aladdin, Cinderella, and so forth — in a rhyming text sprinkled with Spanish words and names. (Rev: BL 5/15/05)

1141 Esterl, Arnica. *Okino and the Whales* (K–3). Illus. by Marek Zawadzki. 1995, Harcourt $16.00 (0-15-200377-0). 32pp. A mother tells her son the story of how his great-great-grandmother rescued her daughter from the underwater kingdom of Iwa. (Rev: BL 10/15/95; SLJ 1/96)

1142 Eyles, Heather. *Well, I Never!* (K–2). Illus. by Terry Ross. 1990, Overlook $11.95 (0-87951-383-7). Polly complains to her mother that there are monsters in her room — and she's right. (Rev: BCCB 3/90; SLJ 3/90)

1143 Fancher, Lou, adapt. *The Velveteen Rabbit* (PS–2). Illus. by Steve Johnson and Lou Fancher. 2002, Simon & Schuster $16.95 (0-689-84134-5). With appealing illustrations and very readable text, Fancher retells the story of a stuffed rabbit that becomes real. (Rev: HBG 3/03; SLJ 12/02)

1144 Feiffer, Jules. *The House Across the Street* (PS–2). Illus. 2002, Hyperion $15.95 (0-7868-0910-8). 32pp. Cartoon-style illustrations show the house across the street, where a boy's imaginary self doesn't have to obey his parents and can do whatever he wants — like eating with his elbows on the table and even putting a swimming pool in the bedroom. (Rev: BCCB 1/03; BL 12/1/02; HBG 3/03; SLJ 2/03)

1145 Fernandes, Eugenie. *Sleepy Little Mouse* (PS–K). Illus. by Kim Fernandes. 2000, Kids Can $12.95 (1-55074-701-0). 24pp. When Little Mouse cries at nap time, she produces so many tears that her bed floats down a river and into the sea where she is found by sea creatures. (Rev: BL 10/1/00; HBG 3/01)

1146 Fitzpatrick, Marie-Louise. *I'm a Tiger, Too!* (PS–1). Illus. 2002, Millbrook LB $22.90 (0-7613-2410-0). 32pp. A young boy plays with various animals in different locales but after they each leave him, he makes friends with a boy his own age. (Rev: BL 4/15/02; HBG 10/02; SLJ 6/02)

1147 Fleischman, Paul. *The Animal Hedge* (K–3). Illus. by Bagram Ibatoulline. 2003, Candlewick $16.99 (0-7636-1606-0). Drought forces a farmer and his three sons to move into a modest home surrounded by a hedge that has seems to have amazing powers of prediction. (Rev: HBG 4/04; SLJ 10/03)

1148 Fleischman, Paul. *Sidewalk Circus* (K–3). Illus. by Kevin Hawkes. 2004, Candlewick $15.99 (0-7636-1107-7). 32pp. Triggered by posters advertising an upcoming circus, a young girl's imagination transforms the events of everyday life into a dizzying series of colorful circus performances. (Rev: BL 4/15/04*; HB 5–6/04; SLJ 7/04)

1149 Fleischman, Paul. *Weslandia* (K–3). Illus. by Kevin Hawkes. 1999, Candlewick $15.99 (0-7636-0006-7). 40pp. In this offbeat fantasy, unconventional Wesley cultivates magical seeds that serve as the basis of a new civilization. (Rev: BCCB 7–8/99; BL 7/99*; HB 3–4/99; HBG 10/99; SLJ 6/99)

1150 Florczak, Robert. *Yikes!!!* (PS). Illus. by author. 2003, Scholastic $15.95 (0-590-05043-5). A young child encounters some fearsome creatures on an imaginary journey and utters suitable cries of dismay. (Rev: BL 11/15/03; HBG 4/04; SLJ 12/03)

1151 Florian, Douglas. *Monster Motel* (PS–1). Illus. 1993, Harcourt $13.95 (0-15-255320-7). Many of the 13 poems that are presented deal with monsters who live in a motel. (Rev: SLJ 6/93)

1152 Foreman, Michael. *Hello World* (PS). Illus. by author. 2003, Candlewick $16.99 (0-7636-2112-9). Rich illustrations and a poetic text depict a teddy bear and a toddler who gather a flock of fellow travelers — cats, puppies, frogs, ducks — as they set off to view the world. (Rev: HBG 4/04; SLJ 1/04)

1153 Foreman, Michael. *Jack's Fantastic Voyage* (K–3). Illus. 1992, Harcourt $14.95 (0-15-239496-6). 32pp. Jack doubts that his grandfather really had the adventures he claims until one night the two experience together an equally amazing voyage. (Rev: BL 11/15/92; SLJ 11/92)

1154 Fox, Frank G. *Jean Laffite and the Big Ol' Whale* (2–3). Illus. by Scott Cook. 2003, Farrar $16.00 (0-374-33669-5). 32pp. A tall tale about the infamous pirate ingeniously dislodging a whale trapped in the Mississippi River. (Rev: BL 2/15/03; HB 5–6/03; HBG 10/03; SLJ 4/03)

1155 Fox, Mem. *Feathers and Fools* (1–4). Illus. by Nicholas Wilton. 1996, Harcourt $16.00 (0-15-200473-4). An antiwar allegory about the rivalry between peacocks and swans. (Rev: SLJ 7/96)

1156 Fox, Mem. *The Magic Hat* (PS–1). Illus. by Tricia Tusa. 2002, Harcourt $16.00 (0-15-201025-4). 32pp. A magic hat transforms the people on whose heads it lands into a variety of different animals in this charming fantasy. (Rev: BCCB 7–8/02; BL 4/15/02; HBG 10/02; SLJ 4/02)

1157 Fox, Mem. *The Straight Line Wonder* (K–4). Illus. by Marc Rosenthal. 1997, Mondo $14.95 (1-57255-206-9). 24pp. Three straight lines are dear friends until one of them wants to change its shape. (Rev: BL 10/15/97; HBG 3/98; SLJ 1/98)

1158 Frascino, Edward. *Nanny Noony and the Magic Spell* (PS–3). Illus. by author. 1988, Pippin $15.95 (0-945912-00-5). 32pp. How the spell on the farm is undone. (Rev: BL 11/15/88; SLJ 1/89)

1159 Frazier, Craig. *Stanley Goes for a Drive* (PS–3). Illus. by author. 2004, Chronicle $15.95 (0-8118-4429-3). Out for a drive in his pickup on a hot summer day, Stanley milks a spotted cow, tosses the milk to the sky, and enjoys the resulting clouds and rain; the simple text is enhanced by wonderful illustrations. (Rev: SLJ 9/04)

1160 Freeman, Don. *A Rainbow of My Own* (K–3). Illus. by author. 1966, Puffin paper $5.99 (0-14-050328-5). 32pp. A boy's search for a rainbow ends in his own home.

1161 Freymann, Saxton, and Joost Elffers. *Gus and Button* (PS–3). 2001, Scholastic $15.95 (0-439-11015-7). 32pp. This tale about a bland-colored mushroom boy and his mushroom dog on a quest to find a colorful place that contrasts with their life is artfully illustrated with computer-enhanced photographs of vegetables. (Rev: BL 11/15/01; HBG 3/02; SLJ 12/01)

1162 Fuge, Charles. *I Know a Rhino* (PS). Illus. 2002, Sterling $12.95 (1-4027-0137-3). 32pp. This captivating rhyming fantasy about a little girl's imaginary adventures with animals is enriched by amusing illustrations, including a portrayal of a genteel rhino pouring tea. (Rev: BL 12/1/02; SLJ 2/03)

1163 Gackenbach, Dick. *Barker's Crime* (PS–2). Illus. 1996, Harcourt $15.00 (0-15-200628-1). 32pp. Greedy Mr. Gobble takes Barker the dog to court for inhaling the aroma of the miser's meals. (Rev: BL 3/1/96; SLJ 7/96)

1164 Gackenbach, Dick. *Harry and the Terrible Whatzit* (PS–2). Illus. by author. 1979, Houghton Mifflin $15.00 (0-395-28795-2); paper $6.95 (0-89919-223-8). 32pp. Harry follows his mother into the dark cellar to confront the terrible two-headed Whatzit.

1165 Galdone, Paul. *The Magic Porridge Pot* (K–3). Illus. by author. 1976, Houghton Mifflin $16.00 (0-395-28805-3). 32pp. The familiar tale of the magic pot that produces porridge but runs amuck when the words that stop it are forgotten.

1166 Gay, Marie-Louise. *On My Island* (PS–1). Illus. 2001, Groundwood $16.95 (0-88899-396-X). 32pp. In this fantasy set on an island, a young boy who shares his home with a variety of animals claims nothing ever happens, but the opposite is true. (Rev: BL 3/15/01)

1167 Gebhard, Wilfried. *What Eddie Can Do* (PS–1). Illus. 2004, Kane/Miller $15.95 (1-929132-60-3). 32pp. Eddie doesn't have time to learn to tie his shoelaces as he's too busy enjoying his elaborate imaginary adventures; shoelace tying instructions included. (Rev: BL 3/1/04; SLJ 7/04)

1168 Gershator, David, and Phillis Gershator. *Palampam Day* (PS–2). Illus. by Enrique O. Sanchez. 1997, Marshall Cavendish $15.95 (0-7614-5002-5). 32pp. Set in the West Indies, this story tells about a boy who is suddenly having conversations with all sorts of objects, like a coconut, a dog, and a bowl of bananas. (Rev: BL 8/97; HBG 3/98; SLJ 9/97)

1169 Gerstein, Mordicai. *Carolinda Clatter!* (PS–2). Illus. 2005, Roaring Brook $16.95 (1-59643-063-X). 40pp. When Carolinda Clatter is born, her penchant for noise threatens the whole town of Pupickton, which is perched atop a sleeping giant's stomach. (Rev: BL 6/1–15/05)

1170 Getz, David. *Floating Home* (1–3). Illus. by Michael Rex. 1997, Holt $15.95 (0-8050-4497-3). 32pp. When teacher wants Maxine to see her home in a new way, she becomes an astronaut to see it from space. (Rev: BCCB 5/97; BL 5/1/97; SLJ 5/97)

1171 Gillerlain, Gayle, reteller. *The Reverend Thomas's False Teeth* (K–3). Illus. by Dena Schutzer. 1995, BridgeWater $14.95 (0-8167-3303-1). When the Reverend Thomas's false teeth fall into deep water, Gracie thinks of an ingenious way to retrieve them. (Rev: SLJ 12/95)

1172 Gilliland, Judith Heide. *Not in the House, Newton!* (PS–3). Illus. by Elizabeth Sayles. 1995, Clarion $15.00 (0-395-61195-4). 32pp. When Newton draws objects using his magical red crayon, they jump off the pages. (Rev: BL 12/15/95; SLJ 1/96)

1173 Gillmor, Don. *Yuck, a Love Story* (K–4). Illus. by Marie-Louise Gay. 2000, Stoddart $14.95 (0-7737-3218-7). Austin Grouper develops a crush on the girl next door and, to prove his love, lassos the moon as a gift. (Rev: SLJ 11/00)

1174 Gilman, Phoebe. *The Gypsy Princess* (PS–3). Illus. 1997, Scholastic $15.95 (0-590-86543-9). 32pp. Cinnamon tires of being a princess and longs for the gypsy life. (Rev: BCCB 3/97; BL 2/1/97; SLJ 3/97)

1175 Ginsburg, Mirra. *Where Does the Sun Go at Night?* (PS–1). Illus. by Jose Aruego and Ariane Dewey. 1980, Morrow paper $4.95 (0-688-07041-8). 32pp. A question-and-answer format is used in this adaptation of an Armenian song.

1176 Glassman, Peter. *My Working Mom* (K–3). Illus. by Tedd Arnold. 1994, Morrow $15.93 (0-688-12260-4). This working mom is different from others because she is a practicing witch. (Rev: BCCB 5/94; SLJ 8/94)

1177 Goennel, Heidi. *I Pretend* (PS). Illus. 1995, Morrow LB $15.93 (0-688-13593-5). 32pp. A child imagines wonderful adventures out of commonplace events. (Rev: BL 4/1/95; SLJ 6/95)

1178 Gogol, Nikolai. *Sorotchintzy Fair* (1–4). Trans. by Daniel Reynolds. Illus. by Gennady Spirin. 1991, Godine $16.95 (0-87923-879-8). 24pp. Based on a Gogol story, this is a tale about a young girl who falls in love with a stranger she meets at a county fair. (Rev: BCCB 6/92; BL 5/15/91; HB 9–10/91; SLJ 8/91)

1179 Goldin, David. *Go-Go-Go!* (PS–3). Illus. 2000, Abrams $16.95 (0-8109-4141-4). 32pp. Maurice hopes to win the great bicycle race on his bike, Red Lightning, but he is slowed down when he picks up passengers including an elephant, a monkey, and a musician. (Rev: BL 12/1/00; HBG 3/01; SLJ 9/00)

1180 Gollub, Matthew. *Ten Oni Drummers* (K–4). Illus. by Kazuko Stone. 2000, Lee & Low $15.95 (1-58430-011-6). Ten Japanese oni, or goblins, come to a boy's house and scare away his spooky dreams in this fantasy that also introduces Japanese numbers from one to ten. (Rev: HBG 3/01; SLJ 1/01)

1181 Goode, Diane. *Tiger Trouble!* (PS–2). Illus. 2001, Scholastic $15.95 (0-439-20866-1). 40pp. Lily the tiger's continued residence in Jack's apartment building is at risk until she foils a burglar in this story set in New York in the early 1900s. (Rev: BL 10/1/01; HBG 3/02; SLJ 12/01)

1182 Gottfried, Maya. *Last Night I Dreamed a Circus* (PS–3). Illus. by Robert Rahway Zakanitch. 2003, Knopf $15.95 (0-375-82388-3). 32pp. The sights of a dream circus, described in picturesque language. (Rev: BL 2/1/03; HBG 10/03; SLJ 5/03)

1183 Graham, Bob. *Jethro Byrd, Fairy Child* (PS–2). Illus. 2002, Candlewick $15.99 (0-7636-1772-5). 32pp. Young Annabelle becomes friends with a fairy, Jethro Byrd, who is invisible to everyone else. (Rev: BCCB 10/02; BL 5/1/02; HBG 10/02; SLJ 6/02*)

1184 Graham, Bob. *Max* (PS–2). Illus. 2000, Candlewick $15.99 (0-7636-1138-7). 32pp. Born of superhero parents, Max has inherited all the family traditions as well as a superhero suit, but he still doesn't know how to fly. (Rev: BCCB 1/01; BL 11/1/00; HBG 3/01; SLJ 9/00)

1185 Gralley, Jean. *The Moon Came Down on Milk St* (PS–1). Illus. by author. 2004, Holt $16.95 (0-8050-7266-7). A variety of community workers rush to help when the moon falls out of the sky and breaks into pieces. (Rev: SLJ 11/04)

1186 Grambling, Lois G. *This Whole Tooth Fairy Thing's Nothing But a Big Rip-off!* (K–2). Illus. by Thomas Payne. 2002, Marshall Cavendish $15.95 (0-7614-5104-8). Little Hippo and the Tooth Fairy come to an agreement when she arrives late for the appropriate exchange. (Rev: HBG 10/02; SLJ 7/02)

1187 Grambling, Lois G. *The Witch Who Wanted to Be a Princess* (K–2). Illus. by Judy Love. 2002, Charlesbridge LB $15.95 (1-58089-062-8). Young witch Bella longs to be a princess, but witches are now endangered and are forbidden from transforming themselves. (Rev: HBG 3/03; SLJ 8/02)

1188 Graves, Keith. *Frank Was a Monster Who Wanted to Dance* (PS–2). Illus. 1999, Chronicle $12.95 (0-8118-2169-2). 26pp. Frank, a monster, dances so strenuously at a theater that his head becomes undone and he loses his brains. (Rev: BCCB 6/99; BL 7/99; HBG 3/00; SLJ 7/99)

1189 Gray, Libba M. *Is There Room on the Feather Bed?* (PS–1). Illus. by Nadine Bernard Westcott. 1997, Orchard $16.95 (0-531-30013-7). 32pp. On a rainy night, animals ask to be allowed to share the comfortable feather bed of a farm couple. (Rev: BL 3/1/97; SLJ 4/97)

1190 Greban, Tanguy. *Sarah So Small* (PS). Illus. by Quentin Greban. 2004, Milk & Cookies $16.95 (0-689-03594-2). 32pp. Three-year-old Sarah shrinks rapidly after swallowing a magic pearl that her father stole from a visiting witch named Hazel. (Rev: BL 1/1–15/05; SLJ 10/04)

1191 Greene, Rhonda Gowler. *Eek! Creak! Snicker, Sneak* (PS–1). Illus. by Joseph A. Smith. 2002, Simon & Schuster $16.00 (0-689-83047-5). Two children give monsters Bugbear and Bugaboo a scare of their own. (Rev: BCCB 3/02; HBG 10/02; SLJ 2/02)

1192 Greenspun, Adele Aron. *Bunny and Me* (PS). Illus. 2000, Scholastic $9.95 (0-439-14700-X). 40pp. A baby and bunny enjoy playing together; when the bunny goes away, the baby is heartbroken until he reappears. (Rev: BL 3/15/00; HBG 10/00; SLJ 4/00)

1193 Grey, Mini. *Traction Man Is Here!* (PS–2). Illus. 2005, Knopf LB $17.99 (0-375-93191-0). 32pp. A little boy's action figure sets off on adventures all around the house as the boy uses household objects for imaginative play. (Rev: BL 3/1/05; SLJ 6/05)

1194 Grindley, Sally. *Mucky Duck* (PS). Illus. by Neal Layton. 2003, Bloomsbury $13.95 (1-58234-821-9). Oliver Dunkley enjoys spending time with Mucky Duck, who lives in a pond behind Oliver's house and who seems to create mess wherever she goes. (Rev: HBG 10/03; SLJ 7/03)

1195 Grindley, Sally. *Polar Skater* (PS–2). Illus. by Heli Hieta. 2004, Lobster $15.95 (1-894222-88-1). A little girl gains confidence on her ice skates and she leaves her father to skim through a fanciful polarscape full of arctic animals. (Rev: SLJ 1/05)

1196 Grobler, Piet. *Hey, Frog!* (PS–K). Illus. 2002, Front Street $15.95 (1-886910-84-7). 32pp. Humorous illustrations and fast-reading text tell the story of a greedy frog who drinks all the water on the African savannah, leaving the other thirsty animals to plot their revenge, including the tickly eels. (Rev: BL 1/1–15/03; HB 1–2/03; HBG 3/03; SLJ 1/03)

1197 Gruelle, Johnny. *Raggedy Ann Stories* (PS–3). Illus. 1993, Macmillan LB $16.00 (0-02-737585-4). 96pp. This story features the lovable rag doll. A reissue. Also use: *Raggedy Andy Stories* (1993).

1198 Gurney, John Steven. *Dinosaur Train* (PS–1). Illus. 2002, HarperCollins LB $16.89 (0-06-029246-6). 32pp. Dinosaurs and trains: young Jesse combines his two favorite things in a wonderful, fanciful dream. (Rev: BL 11/15/02; HBG 3/03; SLJ 12/02)

1199 Guthrie, Donna. *The Witch Who Lives Down the Hall* (PS–2). Illus. by Amy Schwartz. 1985, Harcourt $12.95 (0-15-298610-3). 32pp. A young boy thinks his new high-rise neighbor is a witch, and proves it when the two of them fly above the city on her magic carpet. (Rev: BCCB 1/86; BL 9/15/85; SLJ 10/85)

1200 Haas, Irene. *A Summertime Song* (PS–3). Illus. 1997, Simon & Schuster paper $16.00 (0-689-50549-3). 32pp. A frog presents a little girl with a magic paper hat that shrinks her so she is able to attend a birthday party with little animals like a mouse and an inchworm. (Rev: BL 5/15/97; HB 5–6/97; SLJ 6/97)

1201 Hachler, Bruno. *Snow Ravens* (PS–2). Trans. from German by Marianne Martens. Illus. by Birte Muller. 2002, North-South LB $16.50 (0-7358-1690-5). One raven wants to try making a snow angel like the children, while the other two are too busy complaining about winter. (Rev: HBG 3/03; SLJ 2/03)

1202 Hachler, Bruno. *What Does My Teddy Bear Do All Day?* (PS–K). Trans. by Charise Myngheer. Illus. by Birte Muller. 2004, Minedition $14.99 (0-698-40003-8). While a little girl spies on her teddy bear, wondering what he does all day, she fails to notice what her other toys are getting up to. (Rev: SLJ 1/05)

1203 Hamilton, Richard. *Polly's Picnic* (K–1). Illus. by Sophy Williams. 2003, Bloomsbury $16.95 (1-58234-819-7). In rhyming narrative and strikingly lovely illustrations, author Richard Hamilton and illustrator Sophy Williams sketch this charming story of Polly, whose riverside picnic is ruined by greedy animals who then seek a way to make amends. (Rev: HBG 10/03; SLJ 8/03)

1204 Harker, Lesley. *Annie's Ark* (PS–2). Illus. by author. 2002, Scholastic $15.95 (0-439-36823-5). Noah's granddaughter is so busy looking after the animals on the ark that she can't find time for herself. (Rev: HBG 3/03; SLJ 1/03)

1205 Harley, Bill. *Sarah's Story* (K–2). Illus. by Eve Aldridge. 1996, Tricycle $15.95 (1-883672-20-1). Sarah has some amazing adventures when she visits an ant colony. (Rev: BCCB 3/97; SLJ 1/97)

1206 Harris, Peter. *Ordinary Audrey* (PS–2). Illus. by David Runert. 2001, ME Media $14.95 (1-58925-014-1). 32pp. When 5-year-old Deadwood Deb, a dangerous cowgirl, isn't around to defend her town against invading outlaws, her timid twin sister Audrey must take her place in this tale set in the Wild West. (Rev: BCCB 2/02; BL 2/15/02)

1207 Harrison, Carlos. *Ruben's Jungle / La selva de Ruben* (PS–2). Illus. by Grizelle Paz. 2003, Globo Libros $16.95 (0-9706953-1-4). Ruben visits the jungle in this appealing bilingual story, packaged with an audio CD. (Rev: SLJ 7/03)

1208 Harrison, David L. *The Animals' Song* (PS–K). Illus. by Chris L. Demarest. 1997, Boyds Mills $14.95 (1-56397-144-5). 32pp. When a little girl and boy play their flute and drum, all the animals join in. (Rev: BCCB 6/97; BL 4/1/97; SLJ 3/97)

1209 Heidbreder, Robert. *I Wished for a Unicorn* (PS–3). Illus. by Kady M. Denton. 2000, Kids Can $14.95 (1-55074-543-3). 32pp. A young girl's dog is transformed into a unicorn and together they travel into a magic land. (Rev: BCCB 5/00; BL 4/15/00; HBG 10/00; SLJ 8/00)

1210 Hendrick, Mary J. *If Anything Ever Goes Wrong at the Zoo* (PS–2). Illus. by Jane Dyer. 1993, Harcourt $15.00 (0-15-238007-8). 32pp. When the zoo floods, Leslie and her mother make room in their home and yard for the animals. (Rev: BL 6/1–15/93; SLJ 7/93*)

1211 Henkes, Kevin. *Oh!* (PS). Illus. by Laura Dronzek. 1999, Greenwillow LB $14.93 (0-688-17054-4). 24pp. A delightful picture book that depicts how children and a variety of animals react to a fresh fall of snow. (Rev: BCCB 10/99; BL 10/1/99*; HBG 3/00; SLJ 10/99)

1212 Herrera, Juan Felipe. *Super Cilantro Girl / La Supernina del Cilantro* (K–3). Illus. by Honorio Robledo Tapia. 2003, Children's Book Pr. $16.95 (0-89239-187-1). 30pp. Transformed into a giant green superheroine, 8-year-old Esmeralda Sinfronteras uses her newfound powers to rescue her mother, who can't return to the United States without a green card. (Rev: HBG 4/04; SLJ 12/03)

1213 Hicks, Barbara Jean. *Jitterbug Jam: A Monster Tale* (1–3). Illus. by Alexis Deacon. 2005, Farrar $16.00 (0-374-33685-7). 40pp. A monster is frightened by the little boy under his bed in this picture book with amusing artwork. (Rev: BL 3/1/05)

1214 Highet, Alistair. *The Yellow Train* (K–3). Illus. by Francois Roca. 2000, Creative $17.95 (1-56846-128-3). 40pp. Theo and Grandpa travel back in time and embark on a magical journey through unspoiled landscapes as they ride the Yellow Train with Grandpa at the controls. (Rev: BL 12/15/00; HBG 3/01; SLJ 12/00)

1215 Hindley, Judy. *Rosy's Visitors* (K–3). Illus. by Helen Craig. 2002, Candlewick $14.99 (0-7636-1769-5). 32pp. Rosy finds herself a new home in a hollow of a tree and there she is visited by a number of animals. (Rev: BL 5/1/02; HBG 10/02; SLJ 8/02)

1216 Hobbs, Will. *Beardream* (1–4). Illus. by Jill Kastner. 1997, Simon & Schuster $16.00 (0-689-31973-8). 32pp. When a great bear fails to reappear in the spring, a boy climbs into the mountains to look for it. (Rev: BL 4/15/97; SLJ 4/97)

1217 Hoberman, Mary Ann. *Miss Mary Mack* (PS). Illus. by Nadine Bernard Westcott. 2001, Little, Brown $5.95 (0-316-36642-0). 24pp. This bouncy board book presents a clapping rhyme that features Miss Mary Mack and her pet elephant. (Rev: BL 2/15/01; HBG 3/02)

1218 Hoffman, Alice. *Horsefly* (K–3). Illus. by Steve Johnson and Lou Fancher. 2000, Hyperion $15.99 (0-7868-0367-3). 48pp. Jewel cures her fear of horses when she cares for a foal and, as an added bonus, learns that her pet can fly. (Rev: BL 12/1/00; HBG 3/01; SLJ 10/00)

1219 Holwitz, Peter. *Stick Kid* (PS–2). Illus. by author. 2003, Philomel $13.99 (0-399-24163-9). A stick figure child comes to life and grows up in this imaginative story with rhyming text. (Rev: SLJ 4/04)

1220 Horn, Emily. *Excuse Me . . . Are You a Witch?* (PS–3). Illus. by Pawel Pawlak. 2003, Charlesbridge LB $15.95 (1-58089-093-8). Having read that witches favor black cats as companions, Herbert the black kitten searches long and hard for a witch but is about to give up when a class of aspiring witches adopts him. (Rev: HBG 4/04; SLJ 8/03)

1221 Horn, Sandra Ann. *The Dandelion Wish* (PS–K). Illus. by Jason Crockcroft. 2000, DK $15.95 (0-7894-6326-1). 32pp. When they blow all the seeds off a dandelion with one breath, Sam and Jo get their wish: a carnival comes to their quiet meadow. (Rev: BL 8/00; HBG 3/01; SLJ 12/00)

1222 Hort, Lenny. *We're Going on Safari* (PS–2). Illus. by Tom Arma. 2002, Abrams $12.95 (0-8109-0574-4). 32pp. This photographic expedition with rhyming chant pairs costumed babies with real animal equivalents in various habitats. (Rev: BL 11/1/02; HBG 3/03; SLJ 11/02)

1223 Howard, Arthur. *Hoodwinked* (PS–1). Illus. 2001, Harcourt $16.00 (0-15-202656-8). 32pp. Mitzi the witch has trouble finding a suitable pet and ends up with an unlikely choice. (Rev: BCCB 9/01; BL 9/1/01; HB 1–2/02; HBG 3/02; SLJ 9/01*)

1224 Hubbard, Patricia. *My Crayons Talk* (PS–1). Illus. by G. Brian Karas. 1996, Holt $15.95 (0-8050-3529-X). 32pp. Crayons in a box unite to produce a series of colorful pictures. (Rev: BCCB 5/96; BL 4/1/96; SLJ 5/96)

1225 Hughes, Shirley. *Stories by Firelight* (K–3). Illus. 1993, Lothrop $16.00 (0-688-04568-5). 64pp. This collection of stories, many of which are fantasies, explore wintry themes and are linked by poems. (Rev: BL 12/1/93; SLJ 1/94)

1226 Hughes, Ted. *How the Whale Became and Other Stories* (PS–3). Illus. by Jackie Morris. 2000, Orchard $25.00 (0-531-30303-9). 96pp. From the great English poet, this is a collection of creation fables explaining how individual creatures, such as the whale, owl, and cat, came to be. (Rev: BCCB 12/00; BL 12/1/00*; HBG 10/01; SLJ 11/00)

1227 Huntington, Amy. *One Monday* (PS–1). Illus. 2001, Scholastic $16.95 (0-439-29304-9). 32pp. A blustery wind blows through Annabelle's farm, causing mayhem for the animals who live there. (Rev: BL 2/1/02; HBG 3/02; SLJ 12/01)

1228 Hurd, Thacher. *Moo Cow Kaboom!* (PS–2). Illus. by author. 2003, HarperCollins LB $16.89 (0-06-050502-8). A cow is abducted by an alien cowboy named Zork, but she puts up such resistance that she's soon sent back home. (Rev: HB 5–6/03; HBG 10/03; SLJ 6/03)

1229 Hurst, Margaret M. *Grannie and the Jumbie: A Caribbean Tale* (K–3). Illus. by author. 2001, HarperCollins LB $15.89 (0-06-623633-9). A spirited young Caribbean boy ignores his grandmother's warnings about the supernatural, and Jumbie the bogeyman comes to grab him. (Rev: HBG 3/02; SLJ 2/02)

1230 Hutchins, Hazel. *It's Raining, Yancy and Bear* (PS). Illus. by Ruth Ohi. 1998, Annick $15.95 (1-55037-529-6); paper $5.95 (1-55037-528-8). Yancy, a young boy, and his stuffed friend, Bear, change places, visit a museum with Grandfather, and later plant a garden. (Rev: SLJ 1/99)

1231 Hutchins, Pat. *The Very Worst Monster* (K–2). Illus. by author. 1985, Greenwillow $16.88 (0-688-04011-X); paper $4.95 (0-688-07816-8). 32pp. A monster family has a new addition, and Hazel is not happy with her new baby brother. (Rev: BCCB 4/85; HB 5–6/87; SLJ 5/85)

1232 Ichikawa, Satomi. *La La Rose* (PS). Illus. 2004, Penguin Putnam $15.99 (0-399-24029-2). 40pp. Atmospheric illustrations draw readers into the adventures of a pink stuffed rabbit who is separated from her young owner in Paris's Luxembourg Gardens. (Rev: BL 1/1–15/04; SLJ 2/04)

1233 Inkpen, Mick. *Nothing* (PS–K). Illus. 1998, Orchard $14.95 (0-531-30076-5). 32pp. A stuffed toy that is left behind when a family moves finds a new home with the help of a cat. (Rev: BCCB 3/98; BL 3/15/98; HBG 10/98; SLJ 6/98)

1234 Inns, Christopher. *Help!* (PS–K). Illus. by author. 2004, Frances Lincoln $14.95 (1-84507-004-6). The blue rabbit Dr. Hopper and brown dog Nurse Barker from *Next! Please* go on emergency calls to help other toy animals. (Rev: SLJ 6/04)

1235 Inns, Christopher. *Next! Please* (PS–K). Illus. by author. 2001, Tricycle $14.95 (1-58246-038-8). A blue rabbit doctor and brown dog nurse spend their days at the toy hospital mending other stuffed animals, healing them with kind words when repairs are not possible. (Rev: HBG 10/01; SLJ 5/01)

1236 Ishinabe, Fusako. *Spring Snowman* (PS–1). Illus. 1991, Garrett LB $14.60 (0-944483-83-6). 32pp. Animals in the forest find that when spring comes their snowman disappears. (Rev: BL 5/1/91)

1237 Jackson, Shelley. *Sophia: The Alchemist's Dog* (1–3). Illus. 2002, Simon & Schuster $17.95 (0-689-84279-1). 48pp. Although the alchemist has failed to turn lead into gold, the king praises his wonderful artwork and neither realizes that the alchemist's dog has got the recipe right. (Rev: BL 10/1/02; HBG 3/03; SLJ 10/02)

1238 Jackson, Shirley. *9 Magic Wishes* (K–2). Illus. by Miles Hyman. 2001, Farrar $16.00 (0-374-35525-8). 32pp. The grandson of the author has illustrated in soft-focus pastels this new edition of the story first published in 1963 about a little girl who is offered nine wishes but doesn't need the last one. (Rev: BL 12/15/01; HBG 3/02; SLJ 10/01)

1239 James, Simon. *Sally and the Limpet* (PS–1). Illus. 1991, Macmillan $13.95 (0-689-50528-0). At the beach, Sally finds a shell that attaches itself to her. (Rev: HB 3–4/91; SLJ 6/91)

1240 Jandl, Ernst. *Next Please* (PS–K). Illus. by Norman Junge. 2003, Penguin Putnam $14.99 (0-399-23758-5). In a story that combines a little suspense with a large final dose of reassurance, broken toys wait for their turn to go through the closed door. (Rev: HB 9–1003; HBG 4/04; LMC 11/03; SLJ 11/03)

1241 Jeffers, Susan. *My Pony* (K–3). Illus. by author. 2003, Hyperion $15.99 (0-7868-1995-2). A young girl who cannot have the horse she wants draws pictures of one, and it carries her on fantastic adventures. (Rev: HBG 4/04; SLJ 11/03)

1242 Johnson, Paul B. *Bearhide and Crow* (K–3). Illus. 2000, Holiday House $16.95 (0-8234-1470-1). 32pp. When Amos, a happy-go-lucky farmer, gets cheated by shifty Sam, Crow helps him get even. (Rev: BCCB 5/00; BL 4/1/00; HBG 10/00; SLJ 5/00)

1243 Johnson, Paul B. *The Cow Who Wouldn't Come Down* (K–2). Illus. 1993, Orchard LB $16.99 (0-531-08631-3). 32pp. Miss Rosemary has problems getting her cow back to earth once it learns how to fly. (Rev: BCCB 7–8/93; BL 2/1/93; HB 5–6/93; SLJ 5/93*)

1244 Johnson, Paul B. *A Perfect Pork Stew* (K–2). Illus. 1998, Orchard $15.95 (0-531-30070-6). 32pp. In this original Baba Yaga tale, a witch mistakes some dirt for a pig and makes a stew of it that gives her a tummy ache. (Rev: BL 3/15/98; HBG 10/98; SLJ 4/98)

1245 Johnston, Tony. *Go Track a Yak!* (K–3). Illus. by Tim Raglin. 2003, Simon & Schuster $15.95 (0-689-83789-5). A yak saves the day when a wicked witch who has advised yak milk to save a starving child returns to claim the child as her own. (Rev: BCCB 9/03; HBG 4/04; SLJ 11/03)

1246 Jonas, Ann. *The Trek* (PS–1). Illus. by author. 1985, Morrow paper $4.95 (0-688-08742-6). 32pp. A young girl imagines she is trekking through a dangerous jungle on her way to school. (Rev: BCCB 3/86; BL 11/15/85; SLJ 10/85)

1247 Jonell, Lynne. *Mommy Go Away!* (PS). Illus. by Petra Mathers. 1997, Penguin Putnam $12.99 (0-399-23001-7). 25pp. In this role-reversal fantasy, Christopher makes his bossy mother so tiny that he can lecture her as she does him. (Rev: BL 10/15/97; HB 9–10/97; HBG 3/98; SLJ 12/97)

1248 Jones, Ursula. *The Witch's Children* (PS–2). Illus. by Russell Ayto. 2003, Holt $16.95 (0-8050-7205-5). Underdeveloped spell-casting skills get

three siblings into quite a lot of trouble in the park. (Rev: HB 7–8/03; HBG 10/03; SLJ 7/03)

1249 Jorg, Sabine. *Mina and the Bear* (1–4). Trans. by Charise Neugebauer. Illus. by Alexander Reichstein. 1999, North-South LB $15.88 (0-7858-1037-0). Mina's health is endangered because of her intense longing for a teddy bear, so after a bear story from the doctor, she becomes a bear. (Rev: BL 4/1/99)

1250 Joslin, Mary. *The Shore Beyond* (K–3). Illus. by Alison Jay. 2000, Good Books $16.00 (1-56148-316-8). 28pp. In this parable about the journey through life, two girls weave willows into boats so they can explore the world beyond their homes. (Rev: BL 12/1/00; SLJ 2/01)

1251 Joslin, Mary. *The Tale of the Heaven Tree* (K–3). Illus. by Meilo So. 1999, Eerdmans $16.00 (0-8028-5190-8). In this story, a small child hears a voice from the Maker to help save Earth by planting trees. (Rev: BL 10/1/99; HBG 3/00; SLJ 3/00)

1252 Joyce, William. *Rolie Polie Olie* (PS–K). Illus. 1999, HarperCollins LB $15.89 (0-06-027164-7). 48pp. A whimsical story about a day in the life of Rolie Polie Olie, a round, robotlike creature, and his family as they perform chores and have fun. (Rev: BCCB 10/99; BL 11/1/99; HBG 3/00; SLJ 10/99)

1253 Joyce, William. *Sleepy Time Olie* (PS–K). Illus. 2001, HarperCollins LB $15.89 (0-06-029614-3). 48pp. This brightly colored, rollicking picture book about space-kid Olie (first seen in *Rolie Polie Olie* [1999] and *Snowie Rolie* [2000]) finds him building a laugh-ray to fix his grandfather's broken smile. (Rev: BL 11/15/01; HBG 3/02; SLJ 10/01)

1254 Jukes, Mavis. *You're a Bear* (PS–2). Illus. by Steve Johnson and Lou Fancher. 2003, Knopf LB $18.99 (0-375-90267-8). A young girl dons a furry hooded jacket and pretends to be a bear. (Rev: BL 12/1/03; HBG 4/04; SLJ 12/03)

1255 Kadono, Eiko. *Grandpa's Soup* (1–3). Illus. by Satomi Ichikawa. 1999, Eerdmans $16.00 (0-8028-5195-9). 32pp. Grandpa tries to duplicate the soup that Grandma used to make, and with each new try he attracts more animals to sample his creation. (Rev: BL 12/1/99; HBG 3/00; SLJ 2/00)

1256 Kane, Tracy. *Fairy Houses* (K–3). Illus. by author. 2001, Great White Dog Picture Co. $15.95 (0-9708104-5-8). Kristen builds a fairy house that attracts many animals but will fairies ever come? (Rev: SLJ 1/02)

1257 Karim, Roberta. *This Is a Hospital, Not a Zoo!* (K–3). Illus. by Sue Truesdell. 1998, Clarion $15.00 (0-395-72070-2). 48pp. When nurses and doctors want to poke or prod young Filbert MacFee, he simply turns himself into a wild animal like a penguin or giraffe. (Rev: BL 3/1/98)

1258 Karlin, Nurit. *The Tooth Witch* (PS–K). Illus. by author. 1985, HarperCollins LB $13.89 (0-397-32120-1). 32pp. The story of Abra Cadabra and how she becomes the first Tooth Fairy. (Rev: BCCB 10/85; BL 6/15/85; SLJ 9/86)

1259 Kastner, Jill. *Princess Dinosaur* (PS–K). Illus. 2001, Greenwillow LB $15.89 (0-688-17046-3). 32pp. An action-filled picture book about the adventures of Princess Dinosaur and her friends Cowboy Tex, a toy, and Bettina, a doll. (Rev: BCCB 5/01; BL 4/15/01; HBG 10/01; SLJ 5/01)

1260 Keats, Ezra Jack. *Regards to the Man in the Moon* (PS–1). Illus. by author. 1987, Macmillan paper $5.99 (0-689-71160-3). 32pp. Lewis and his friend visit outer space via their imaginations. Originally published in 1981.

1261 Keens-Douglas, Richardo. *The Miss Meow Pageant* (K–3). Illus. by Marie Lafrance. 1998, Annick LB $16.95 (1-55037-537-7); paper $6.95 (1-55037-536-9). Henrietta, a teacher, adopts a stray cat she names Sparrow and decides to enter her pet in "The Miss Meow Pageant." (Rev: SLJ 1/99)

1262 Keller, Laurie. *The Scrambled States of America* (K–3). Illus. 1998, Holt $16.95 (0-8050-5802-8). In this lighthearted introduction to the 50 states, Kansas and Nebraska decide to have a party where the states exchange places, but complications occur when, for example, Minnesota gets a sunburn while Florida is freezing. (Rev: BCCB 10/98; BL 1/1–15/99; HBG 3/99; SLJ 11/98)

1263 Kelley, Marty. *Fall Is Not Easy* (PS–K). Illus. 1998, Zino $12.95 (1-55933-234-4). 32pp. In the fall of the year, a tree tries out new colors and designs for its leaves, including red-and-white stripes, polka dots, and rainbow faces. (Rev: BL 1/1–15/99)

1264 Kellogg, Steven. *The Missing Mitten Mystery* (PS–1). Illus. 2000, Dial $15.99 (0-8037-2566-3). 32pp. In this reworking of the 1974 title, a little girl sets off with her dog Oscar to find a lost mitten and discovers it is acting as the heart of a snowman. (Rev: BL 10/15/00*; HBG 3/01)

1265 Kellogg, Steven. *Ralph's Secret Weapon* (PS–3). Illus. by author. 1983, Dial paper $3.95 (0-8037-0307-4). 32pp. Ralph's bassoon playing is so bad, his aunt thinks it will charm a bothersome sea monster.

1266 Kelly, Mij. *William and the Night Train* (PS–1). Illus. by Alison Jay. 2001, Farrar $16.00 (0-374-38437-1). 32pp. William and his mother are the only normal-looking people on the train to Tomorrow; the others have tiny heads and huge bodies and the cargo consists of different animals and unusual objects. (Rev: BL 2/15/01*; HBG 10/01; SLJ 3/01)

1267 Kennedy, Kim. *Pirate Pete* (K–3). Illus. by Doug Kennedy. 2002, Abrams $15.95 (0-8109-4356-5). 32pp. Pete and his parrot share a series of swashbuckling adventures after he steals a treasure map from a queen. (Rev: BL 6/1–15/02; HBG 10/02)

1268 Ketteman, Helen. *Bubba, The Cowboy Prince: A Fractured Texas Tale* (K–3). Illus. by James Warhola. 1997, Scholastic $15.95 (0-590-25506-1). 32pp. A Western version of the Cinderella story in which a cow is the fairy godmother. (Rev: BL 12/1/97; HBG 3/98)

1269 Ketteman, Helen. *Heat Wave* (K–3). Illus. by Scott Goto. 1998, Walker LB $16.85 (0-8027-8645-6). 32pp. In this hilarious fantasy, a heat wave gets stuck on a rural weather vane causing a great

upheaval for plants and animals. (Rev: BL 2/1/98; HBG 10/98; SLJ 3/98)

1270 Ketteman, Helen. *Luck with Potatoes* (1–3). Illus. by Brian Floca. 1995, Orchard LB $15.99 (0-531-08773-5). 32pp. A tall tale about a farmer who finds his lost cows in the giant potatoes he has been growing. (Rev: BL 10/1/95; SLJ 10/95)

1271 Khalsa, Dayal Kaur. *Green Cat* (PS–K). Illus. 2002, Tundra $14.95 (0-88776-586-6). 24pp. This posthumous offering tells the tale of a brother and sister who bicker over the space in their room, until a big green cat shows them just how crowded the room can get. (Rev: BL 3/15/02; HBG 10/02; SLJ 5/02)

1272 Khoza, Valanga. *Gezani and the Tricky Baboon* (K–2). Illus. by Sally Rippin. 2003, Allen & Unwin $14.95 (1-86508-720-3). This "pourquoi" picture book (from Australia, but set in Africa) tells the story of why the baboon has a naked backside. (Rev: SLJ 3/04)

1273 Kimmel, Eric A. *A Cloak for the Moon* (PS–3). Illus. by Katya Krenina. 2001, Holiday House $16.95 (0-8234-1493-0). 32pp. A tailor heads for China in search of material for a cloak for the moon, and earns a luminous thread as a reward for a good deed. (Rev: BCCB 4/01; BL 7/01; HBG 10/01; SLJ 5/01)

1274 Kimmel, Eric A. *The Erie Canal Pirates* (K–3). Illus. by Andrew Glass. 2002, Holiday House $16.95 (0-8234-1657-7). 32pp. A humorous tale about a captain battling pirates on the Erie Canal, using the traditional folk song as a base. (Rev: BCCB 11/02; BL 10/15/02; HBG 3/03; SLJ 11/02)

1275 Kimmel, Eric A. *Grizz!* (PS–3). Illus. by Andrew Glass. 2000, Farrar $17.00 (0-374-36824-4). 288pp. Cowboy Lucky Doolin makes a pact with the devil that he will gain great wealth if he doesn't bathe, shave, or change his clothes for seven years. (Rev: BL 5/1/00; HBG 9/00; SLJ 3/00)

1276 Kimmel, Eric A. *Pumpkinhead* (1–3). Illus. by Steve Haskamp. 2001, Winslow $15.95 (1-890817-33-3). Pumpkinhead sets off on a quest to find out if everyone in the world has a pumpkin head, only to be turned off course by a pair of pesky squirrels. (Rev: HBG 3/02; SLJ 9/01)

1277 Kimmel, Eric A. *Robin Hook, Pirate Hunter!* (PS–3). Illus. by Michael Dooling. 2001, Scholastic $15.95 (0-590-68199-0). 32pp. A teenage superhero dressed like Robin Hood thwarts pirates with the help of other children and some animals. (Rev: BL 1/1–15/01; HBG 10/01; SLJ 3/01)

1278 Kimmel, Eric A. *The Tale of Ali Baba and the Forty Thieves: A Story from the Arabian Nights* (1–3). Illus. by Will Hillenbrand. 1996, Holiday House LB $15.95 (0-8234-1258-X). 30pp. Ali Baba and the story of his amazing treasure trove are covered in colorful prose. (Rev: BCCB 2/97; BL 12/1/96; SLJ 12/96)

1279 King, Stephen Michael. *Milli, Jack, and the Dancing Cat* (PS–3). Illus. by author. 2004, Philomel $14.99 (0-399-24240-6). Milli makes plain shoes for plain people until Jack and the Dancing Cat offer her dancing lessons if she'll make them fancy boots. (Rev: SLJ 4/04)

1280 Kinsey-Warnock, Natalie. *The Fiddler of the Northern Lights* (K–3). Illus. by Leslie Bowman. 1996, Dutton $15.99 (0-525-65215-9). 32pp. A fantasy set in the far North about a fiddler whose music makes the northern lights dance. (Rev: BL 11/15/96; SLJ 11/96)

1281 Kinsey-Warnock, Natalie. *On a Starry Night* (PS–1). Illus. by David McPhail. 1994, Orchard LB $16.99 (0-531-08670-4). 32pp. When her father throws her into the air, a young girl visits the stars before returning to his arms. (Rev: BL 2/1/94; HB 7–8/94; SLJ 5/94)

1282 Kipling, Rudyard. *How the Camel Got His Hump* (K–3). Illus. by Lisbeth Zwerger. 2001, North-South LB $15.88 (0-7358-1483-X). 24pp. The classic Kipling story is complemented by beautiful new, detailed illustrations. (Rev: BL 12/1/01; HBG 3/02; SLJ 12/01)

1283 Kipling, Rudyard. *Rikki-Tikki-Tavi* (1–3). Illus. by Lambert Davis. 1992, Harcourt $18.00 (0-15-267015-7). 44pp. A mongoose overcomes snakes that live in the garden of an English family in India. (Rev: BL 9/15/92)

1284 Kirk, Daniel. *Moondogs* (K–2). Illus. 1999, Penguin Putnam $15.99 (0-399-23128-5). 32pp. When Willy's parents decide that he needs a dog, the young boy constructs a spaceship and goes to the moon to get one. (Rev: BL 3/15/99; HB 3–4/99; HBG 10/99; SLJ 3/99)

1285 Kirkpatrick, Karey. *Disney's James and the Giant Peach* (K–3). Illus. by Lane Smith. 1996, Disney LB $16.89 (0-7868-5039-6). 48pp. A simplified retelling of Roald Dahl's work, aimed at the primary grades. (Rev: BCCB 6/96; BL 5/1/96)

1286 Kitamura, Satoshi. *Me and My Cat?* (K–3). Illus. 2000, Farrar $16.00 (0-374-34906-1). 40pp. A wrongfully administered witch's curse results in Nicholas changing bodies with his cat Leonardo. (Rev: BCCB 5/00; BL 3/1/00; HB 3–4/00; HBG 10/00; SLJ 3/00)

1287 Kleven, Elisa. *The Dancing Deer and the Foolish Hunter* (K–3). Illus. 2002, Dutton $16.99 (0-525-46832-3). 32pp. A hunter captures a dancing deer, but discovers she can't dance without the music of the birds in this tale about nature's reciprocity. (Rev: BL 2/15/02; HBG 10/02; SLJ 4/02)

1288 Kleven, Elisa. *The Paper Princess* (K–2). Illus. 1994, Dutton $15.99 (0-525-45231-1). 32pp. A paper princess created by a little girl flies over the city and learns about life. (Rev: BL 7/94; SLJ 6/94*)

1289 Kleven, Elisa. *The Paper Princess Finds Her Way* (PS–1). Illus. by author. 2003, Dutton $15.99 (0-525-46911-7). Ignored by the now-grown girl who made her, a paper princess flies off in search of new adventures. (Rev: HBG 4/04; SLJ 10/03)

1290 Knutson, Kimberley. *Jungle Jamboree* (PS–1). Illus. 1998, Marshall Cavendish $15.95 (0-7614-5032-7). 32pp. In this rainy day fantasy, a group of children who are confined to the house have an imaginary jungle adventure. (Rev: BL 9/1/98; HBG 3/99; SLJ 11/98)

1291 Komaiko, Leah. *My Perfect Neighborhood* (K–2). Illus. by Barbara Westman. 1990, Harper-Collins $13.95 (0-06-023287-0). 32pp. In jiving rhymes, a young girl surveys her most unusual neighborhood. (Rev: BL 3/1/90; SLJ 8/90)

1292 Kraft, Erik. *Chocolatina* (1–4). Illus. by Denise Brunkus. 1998, BridgeWater $15.95 (0-8167-4544-7). A humorous story about a girl who is turned into her favorite food, chocolate, and finds that she prefers to eat it rather than be it. (Rev: HBG 10/98; SLJ 5/98)

1293 Krauss, Ruth. *Bears* (PS–K). Illus. by Maurice Sendak. 2005, HarperCollins LB $15.89 (0-06-075716-7). 24pp. Sendak's colorful and expressive art enhance and extend the very brief text of the 1948 original about teddy bears in all kinds of situations. (Rev: BL 6/1–15/05; SLJ 6/05)

1294 Krauss, Ruth. *The Carrot Seed* (K–1). Illus. by Crockett Johnson. 1945, HarperCollins LB $14.89 (0-06-023351-6); paper $5.95 (0-06-443210-6). 24pp. A young boy is convinced that the seeds he plants will grow, in spite of his family's doubts.

1295 Kroll, Steven. *The Candy Witch* (PS–1). Illus. by Marylin Hafner. 1979, Scholastic paper $2.50 (0-590-44509-X). 32pp. A family of witches perform good work except for the youngest, who undoes their work.

1296 Krudop, Walter Lyon. *The Man Who Caught Fish* (K–3). Illus. 2000, Farrar $16.00 (0-374-34786-7). 32pp. Set in ancient Thailand, this is the story of a greedy king who wants more than his legal share of the fish caught by a master fisherman. (Rev: BL 2/15/00; HB 3–4/00; HBG 10/00; SLJ 4/00)

1297 Krulik, Nancy. *Anyone But Me* (2–4). Illus. by John and Wendy. Series: Katie Kazoo, Switcheroo. 2002, Grosset paper $3.99 (0-448-42653-6). 80pp. Katie, who can change at will, becomes a hamster and transforms a bully who is scared of hamsters into a nice person. In *Out to Lunch* (2002), she becomes a cafeteria worker and improves the food. (Rev: SLJ 5/02)

1298 Lairla, Sergio. *Abel and the Wolf* (K–4). Trans. from German by Marianne Martens. Illus. by Alessandra Roberti. 2004, North-South LB $16.50 (0-7358-1903-3). Despite their early rivalry, Abel and the wolf become fast friends in this story that incorporates many familiar elements. (Rev: SLJ 6/04)

1299 Landalf, Helen. *The Secret Night World of Cats* (PS–1). Illus. by Mark Rimland. 1998, Smith & Kraus $16.95 (1-57525-117-5). 32pp. When Amanda's cat goes missing one night, the little girl ventures into a forest where she encounters many cats and is finally reunited with her own beloved pet. (Rev: BL 9/15/98; HBG 3/99; SLJ 9/98)

1300 Landry, Leo. *The Snow Ghosts* (PS–2). Illus. by author. 2003, Houghton Mifflin $9.95 (0-618-19655-2). Playful snow ghosts live in the far, far north. (Rev: BCCB 11/03; HBG 4/04; SLJ 11/03)

1301 Langley, Jonathan. *Missing!* (PS–K). Illus. 2000, Marshall Cavendish $15.95 (0-7614-5078-5). 32pp. Lupin the cat, not realizing that it is school vacation, sets off to meet preschooler Daisy and is disturbed when the child doesn't appear. (Rev: BCCB 11/00; BL 9/1/00; HBG 3/01; SLJ 9/00)

1302 Larson, Kirby. *The Magic Kerchief* (PS–3). Illus. by Rosanne Litzinger. 2000, Holiday House $15.95 (0-8234-1473-6). 32pp. Griselda, an old grump whose bluntness alienates everyone, dons a magic kerchief that allows her only to say nice things. (Rev: BL 8/00; HB 9–10/00; HBG 3/01; SLJ 10/00)

1303 Lasky, Kathryn. *The Gates of the Wind* (PS–3). Illus. by Janet Stevens. 1995, Harcourt $15.00 (0-15-204264-4). Even though she is living a comfortable life, Gamma Lee decides one day to set out with her donkey to explore the Gates of the Wind. (Rev: SLJ 10/95)

1304 Lawler, Janet. *If Kisses Were Colors* (PS–1). Illus. by Alison Jay. 2003, Dial $15.99 (0-8037-2617-1). 32pp. A fanciful series of characterizations of kisses — as colors, pebbles, comets, flowers, and more — are accompanied by appealing illustrations. (Rev: BL 3/1/03; HBG 10/03; SLJ 3/03)

1305 Lawson, Janet. *Audrey and Barbara* (K–2). Illus. 2002, Simon & Schuster $13.95 (0-689-83896-4). 32pp. A little girl and her reluctant cat take a pretend voyage to India in a bathtub. (Rev: BL 9/15/02; HB 5–6/02; HBG 10/02; SLJ 7/02)

1306 Leedahl, Shelley A. *The Bone Talker* (PS–2). Illus. by Bill Slavin. 2000, Red Deer $15.95 (0-88995-214-0). 32pp. To help cheer up elderly Grandmother Bones, a little girl gets her to begin making a quilt that later becomes a patchwork of fields across the Great Plains. (Rev: BL 4/15/00)

1307 Leedy, Loreen. *Follow the Money!* (1–3). Illus. 2002, Holiday House $16.95 (0-8234-1587-2). 32pp. George, a newly minted quarter, has a busy day from delivery at the bank through many adventures to his eventual return to the bank. (Rev: BCCB 4/02; BL 4/15/02*; HBG 10/02; SLJ 5/02)

1308 Leedy, Loreen. *How Humans Make Friends* (1–4). Illus. 1996, Holiday House $15.95 (0-8234-1223-7). 32pp. Zork, an extraterrestrial, learns about human behavior, the nature of friendship, and the importance of sharing. (Rev: BL 4/1/96; SLJ 7/96)

1309 Leedy, Loreen. *The Potato Party and Other Troll Tales* (PS–2). Illus. by author. 1989, Holiday House LB $14.95 (0-8234-0761-6). 32pp. A delightful collection of seven original stories about trolls. (Rev: SLJ 12/89)

1310 Le Guin, Ursula K. *A Ride on the Red Mare's Back* (PS–2). Illus. by Julie Downing. 1992, Orchard LB $17.99 (0-531-08591-0). 48pp. This original fairy tale tells how a girl rescues her brother from the trolls. (Rev: BCCB 10/92; BL 6/15/92; HB 3–4/93; SLJ 9/92*)

1311 Leonard, Marie. *Tibili: The Little Boy Who Didn't Want to Go to School* (K–3). Illus. by Andree Prigent. 2002, Kane $15.95 (1-929132-20-4). 36pp. An African child is reluctant to start school but, when the animals show him how impor-

tant reading is, he changes his mind. (Rev: BL 6/1–15/02; HBG 10/02; SLJ 4/02)

1312 Lerner, Harriet, and Susan Goldhor. *Franny B. Kranny, There's a Bird in Your Hair!* (PS–3). Illus. by Helen Oxenbury. 2001, HarperCollins LB $15.89 (0-06-029503-1). 40pp. A bird settles in Franny's hair when her overabundant locks are put up for a special occasion, and she refuses to dislodge it. (Rev: BCCB 9/01; BL 6/1–15/01; HB 7–8/01; HBG 10/01; SLJ 6/01)

1313 Leslie, Amanda. *Who's That Scratching at My Door? A Peekaboo Riddle Book* (PS–K). Illus. by author. 2001, Handprint $12.95 (1-929766-19-X). A young boy is looking for a friend, but the animals that keep showing up at the door (actually, under the flap) are never quite right until a puppy turns up. (Rev: HBG 10/01; SLJ 7/01)

1314 Lester, Helen. *Pookins Gets Her Way* (PS–1). Illus. by Lynn Munsinger. 1990, Houghton Mifflin paper $7.95 (0-395-53965-X). 32pp. Pookins gets nasty if she doesn't get her own way, but she learns a lesson in self-indulgence from a gnome. (Rev: BL 4/15/87; SLJ 8/87)

1315 Lester, Helen. *Princess Penelope's Parrot* (PS–1). Illus. by Lynn Munsinger. 1996, Houghton Mifflin $14.95 (0-395-78320-8). 32pp. A browbeaten parrot gets revenge on a bossy princess. (Rev: BCCB 1/97; BL 9/1/96; HB 1–12/96; SLJ 10/96)

1316 Lester, Helen. *The Wizard, the Fairy and the Magic Chicken* (K–2). Illus. by Lynn Munsinger. 1983, Houghton Mifflin $16.00 (0-395-33885-9); paper $6.95 (0-395-47945-2). 32pp. Three friends are in competition with their magic tricks.

1317 Lester, Julius. *Shining* (K–3). Illus. by John Clapp. 2003, Harcourt $17.00 (0-15-200773-3). Shunned by her fellow villagers because she refuses to speak, Shining eventually finds her voice and becomes the leader of her people. (Rev: BCCB 12/03; HBG 4/04; SLJ 11/03)

1318 Leuck, Laura. *My Creature Teacher* (K–2). Illus. by Scott Nash. 2004, HarperCollins LB $16.89 (0-06-029695-X). A most unnatural teacher rules over the classroom of the narrator in this funny/spooky/gross combination. (Rev: SLJ 7/04)

1319 Leuck, Laura. *My Monster Mama Loves Me So* (PS). Illus. by Mark Buehner. 1999, Lothrop LB $15.93 (0-688-16867-1). A slight, humorous tale in which a little monster tells the ways his mother loves him — like attending his beastball games. (Rev: HBG 3/00; SLJ 1/00)

1320 Levert, Mireille. *An Island in the Soup* (PS). Illus. 2001, Groundwood $15.95 (0-88899-403-6). 32pp. Victor of the Noodle experiences great danger while traveling through his soup. (Rev: BL 7/01; HBG 10/01; SLJ 6/01)

1321 Levine, Gail Carson. *Betsy Who Cried Wolf!* (PS–2). Illus. by Scott Nash. 2002, HarperCollins LB $15.89 (0-06-028764-0). 40pp. A wolf tries to outwit the new shepherd, 8-year-old Betsy, but she manages to make him an ally. (Rev: BCCB 10/02; BL 7/02; HBG 10/02; SLJ 6/02)

1322 Lewis, Kim. *Here We Go, Harry* (PS). Illus. by author. 2005, Candlewick $15.99 (0-7636-2549-3).

Three stuffed animals — Lulu the lamb, Ted the bear, and Harry the elephant — climb a hill and try to fly. (Rev: SLJ 3/05)

1323 Lia, Simone. *Billy Bean's Dream* (PS–3). Illus. by author. 2000, David & Charles $15.95 (1-86233-260-6). Billy, a jelly bean, longs to travel into space and nearly gets his wish in this zany tale with bold illustrations. (Rev: SLJ 4/01)

1324 Light, Steve. *The Shoemaker Extraordinaire* (PS–1). Illus. 2003, Abrams $14.95 (0-8109-4236-4). 32pp. The tale of Hans Crispin, who makes magical shoes for a giant named Barefootus. (Rev: BL 3/15/03; HBG 4/04; SLJ 7/03)

1325 Lillegard, Dee. *Tiger, Tiger* (PS–2). Illus. by Susan Guevara. 2002, Penguin Putnam $16.99 (0-399-22633-8). 32pp. Dramatic illustrations add to this exciting story, in which lonely Pocu finds a magic feather in the hot jungle and uses it and his imagination to create a tiger — a very hungry tiger. (Rev: BL 1/1–15/03; HBG 3/03; SLJ 12/02)

1326 Lindenbaum, Pija. *Bridget and the Gray Wolves* (PS–2). Illus. 2001, Farrar $14.00 (91-29-65395-9). 24pp. Timid little Bridget always expects the worst, but when she becomes surrounded by wolves she surprisingly becomes leader of the pack in this humorous reversal full of funny lupines. (Rev: BCCB 9/01; BL 12/15/01; HBG 3/02; SLJ 11/01)

1327 Lindenbaum, Pija. *Bridget and the Moose Brothers* (PS–1). Trans. from Swedish by Kjersti Board. Illus. by author. 2004, R&S $16.00 (91-29-66046-7). Bridget wants a baby brother or sister, but what she gets instead is a trio of uncouth moose. (Rev: SLJ 5/04)

1328 Lindenbaum, Pija. *Bridget and the Muttonheads* (PS–2). Trans. by Kjersti Board. Illus. 2002, Farrar $16.00 (91-29-65650-8). 28pp. Little Bridget, on vacation with her parents and bored by the pool, wanders off to find an adventure of her own in this imaginative tale. (Rev: BL 8/02; HB 11–12/02; HBG 3/03; SLJ 1/03)

1329 Lindgren, Astrid. *Most Beloved Sister* (2–4). Trans. by Elisabeth Kallick Dyssegaard. Illus. by Hans Arnold. 2002, Farrar $15.00 (91-29-65502-1). 28pp. When her baby brother is born, Barbara's imaginary twin sister, Lalla-Lee, comes to her rescue and the two have a day of magical adventures together in this vividly illustrated story that was originally published a half-century ago. (Rev: BL 7/02; HBG 10/02; SLJ 8/02)

1330 Loki. *Jake Greenthumb* (PS–2). Illus. by Jason Gaillard. 2002, Mondo $15.95 (1-59034-186-4). 32pp. Jake's thumb is so green that the plants he is looking after threaten to take over his room. (Rev: HBG 10/02; SLJ 9/02)

1331 Long, Melinda. *How I Became a Pirate* (PS–3). Illus. by David Shannon. 2003, Harcourt $16.00 (0-15-201848-4). The charms of a life aboard a pirate ship wane as Jeremy Jacob realizes he misses bedtime stories and goodnight kisses. (Rev: HBG 4/04; SLJ 9/03)

1332 Loomis, Christine. *Astro Bunnies* (PS–K). Illus. by Ora Eitan. 2001, Penguin Putnam $15.99 (0-399-23175-7). 32pp. A simple, short story that tells of a bunny's trip into outer space. (Rev: BCCB 2/01; BL 2/15/01; HB 1–2/01; HBG 10/01; SLJ 2/01)

1333 Lowell, Susan. *The Bootmaker and the Elves* (K–4). Illus. by Tom Curry. 1997, Orchard LB $17.99 (0-531-33044-3). 32pp. The old folktale is given a new setting, the Old West, and a new subject, cowboy boots. (Rev: BL 9/15/97; HB 11–12/97; HBG 3/98; SLJ 11/97)

1334 Lyon, George E. *The Outside Inn* (K–3). Illus. by Vera Rosenberry. 1991, Orchard paper $6.95 (0-531-07086-7). 32pp. All kinds of creatures seek their food, while in the foreground youngsters prepare a "pretend" meal. (Rev: BL 7/91; SLJ 9/91)

1335 Lyons, Dana. *The Tree* (PS–2). Illus. by David Danioth. 2002, Illumination Arts $16.95 (0-9701907-1-9). An 800-year-old Douglas fir describes its life in simple verse and worries that its future is threatened. (Rev: SLJ 10/02)

1336 McAllister, Angela. *Harry's Box* (K–2). Illus. by Jenny Jones. 2003, Bloomsbury $16.95 (1-58234-772-7). Young Harry's cardboard box is transformed into many more appealing places to play — a store, a pirate ship, and an underwater cave, to name just a few. (Rev: HBG 4/04; SLJ 10/03)

1337 McCarthy, Meghan. *The Adventures of Patty and the Big Red Bus* (PS–2). Illus. by author. 2005, Knopf LB $14.99 (0-375-92939-8). A little girl and her younger sister pilot a big red bus up mountains, underwater, to put out a fire, to a circus, and finally to the moon. (Rev: LMC 3/05; SLJ 3/05)

1338 McClements, George. *Jake Gander, Storyville Detective: The Case of the Greedy Granny* (1–3). 2002, Hyperion $15.99 (0-7868-0662-1). The humorous story of Jake's efforts to solve a mystery surrounding Red R. Hood's grandmother. (Rev: HBG 3/03; SLJ 9/02)

1339 McClintock, Barbara. *Dahlia* (PS–2). Illus. 2002, Farrar $16.00 (0-374-31678-3). 32pp. When Charlotte is given a frilly doll named Dahlia, she includes her in her tomboy adventures in this picture book set in the Victorian age. (Rev: BCCB 10/02; BL 9/1/02; HB 9–10/02*; HBG 3/03; SLJ 11/02*)

1340 McCloskey, Kevin. *Mrs. Fitz's Flamingos* (PS–2). Illus. 1992, Lothrop LB $13.93 (0-688-10475-4). 32pp. To brighten the view from her windows, Mrs. Fitz places plastic flamingos on her neighbor's roof. (Rev: BL 4/15/92; SLJ 6/92)

1341 MacDonald, Amy. *Quentin Fenton Herter III* (K–3). Illus. by Giselle Potter. 2002, Farrar $16.00 (0-374-36170-3). 32pp. Quentin Fenton Herter III is a good boy who's plagued by a not-so-good "shadow," Quentin Fenton Three. (Rev: BCCB 9/02; BL 5/15/02; HB 5–6/02; HBG 10/02; SLJ 5/02)

1342 McDonald, Megan. *Ant and Honey Bee: What a Pair!* (PS–2). Illus. by G. Brian Karas. 2005, Candlewick $13.99 (0-7636-1265-0). 32pp. Ant and Honey Bee set off happily for the costume party, but rain ruins their efforts and they must improvise hastily. (Rev: BL 2/15/05; SLJ 4/05)

1343 MacDonald, Ross. *Another Perfect Day* (K–2). Illus. 2002, Millbrook LB $22.90 (0-7613-2659-6). 32pp. Jack hits the new day on the run — exercising with alligators, catching the train in his hands — but then his world seems to start changing; his suit is now a tutu, his airplane is now a tricycle . . . and when he wakes up in bed it all becomes clear. (Rev: BL 11/1/02; HBG 3/03; SLJ 9/02)

1344 McDonnell, Flora. *Giddy-up! Let's Ride!* (K–3). Illus. 2002, Candlewick $16.99 (0-7636-1778-4). 32pp. Different kinds of horses and other beasts carry a variety of riders — such as a princess, a fairy, a goatherd, and a rajah — in this delightful fantasy. (Rev: BCCB 10/02; BL 5/1/02; HBG 10/02; SLJ 7/02)

1345 McElmurry, Jill. *Mad About Plaid* (K–2). Illus. 2000, HarperCollins LB $14.89 (0-688-16952-X). 32pp. Madison Pratt finds a magical plaid purse that turns everything the same plaid pattern. (Rev: BL 4/1/00; HBG 10/00; SLJ 5/00)

1346 MacGill-Callahan, Sheila. *The Last Snake in Ireland: A Story About St. Patrick* (PS–2). Illus. by Will Hillenbrand. 1999, Holiday House $15.95 (0-8234-1425-6). 32pp. The last snake in Ireland eludes St. Patrick and finds himself a resident of Loch Ness. (Rev: BCCB 3/99; BL 3/15/99; HBG 10/99; SLJ 3/99)

1347 McGuirk, Leslie. *Snail Boy* (PS–2). Illus. by author. 2003, Candlewick $15.99 (0-7636-1259-6). Eye-catching art highlights this offbeat story of a huge snail seeking a safe haven with a young boy. (Rev: HBG 10/03; SLJ 9/03)

1348 McKissack, Patricia, and Onawumi Jean Moss. *Precious and the Boo Hag* (K–2). Illus. by Krysten Brooker. 2005, Simon & Schuster $16.95 (0-689-85194-4). 40pp. Precious, stuck home alone with a stomachache when her mother and brother must leave, resists multiple attempts by the Boo Hag to gain entry to the house. (Rev: BL 2/1/05; SLJ 3/05)

1349 McMillan, Bruce. *Ghost Doll* (K–1). Illus. by author. 1997, Apple Island paper $10.00 (0-934313-01-6). 32pp. Chrissy changes a ghost doll into the real thing.

1350 McMillan, Bruce. *The Remarkable Riderless Runaway Tricycle* (K–3). Illus. by author. 1985, Apple Island paper $10.00 (0-934313-00-8). 48pp. A tricycle, unwilling to be consigned to the dump, sets out on its own trip. This reissued picture book was first published in 1978 and contains black-and-white photographs.

1351 McMullan, Kate. *I Stink!* (PS–3). Illus. by James McMullan. 2002, HarperCollins LB $15.89 (0-06-029849-9). 40pp. In this boldly illustrated picture book, a garbage truck describes its activities during its nightly rounds. (Rev: BCCB 6/02; BL 6/1–15/02; HB 5–6/02*; HBG 10/02; SLJ 5/02)

1352 McNaughton, Janet. *Brave Jack and the Unicorn* (K–3). Illus. by Susan Tooke. 2005, Tundra $15.95 (0-88776-677-3). 32pp. Drawing on traditional Newfoundland tales, this is the story of Jack, who is sent off in search of his older brothers and succeeds in finding them — as well as a wife —

with the help of plants and animals that reward him with magical gifts. (Rev: BL 6/1–15/05)

1353 McNeil, Florence, and David McPhail. *Sail Away* (PS–2). Illus. by David McPhail. 2000, Orca $15.95 (1-55143-147-5). 32pp. Nautical terms are explained in this picture book about a boy dressed as a pirate who, with his animal friends, sails a pirate ship. (Rev: BCCB 10/00; BL 10/1/00; HBG 3/01; SLJ 12/00)

1354 McPhail, David. *Edward and the Pirates* (PS–3). Illus. 1997, Little, Brown $15.95 (0-316-56344-7). 32pp. The pirates that Edward is reading about come alive and kidnap him. (Rev: BCCB 7–8/97; BL 4/15/97; SLJ 5/97)

1355 McPhail, David. *Edward in the Jungle* (PS–3). Illus. 2002, Little, Brown $15.95 (0-316-56391-9). 32pp. While reading about Tarzan, Edward is transported to Africa where he is saved from a menacing crocodile by the Lord of the Jungle. (Rev: BCCB 4/02; BL 4/1/02; HBG 10/02; SLJ 3/02)

1356 McPhail, David. *The Party* (PS–1). Illus. 1990, Little, Brown $14.95 (0-316-56330-7). 32pp. A little boy and his stuffed toys have a party after Dad falls asleep. (Rev: BL 10/1/90; SLJ 11/90)

1357 McQueen, John Troy. *A World Full of Monsters* (PS–3). Illus. by Marc Brown. 2001, HarperCollins LB $15.89 (0-06-029770-0). 32pp. Today, there are few monsters and they mainly do helpful tasks at night, but they used to be plentiful and do much more, according to this amusing picture book. (Rev: BL 9/15/01; HBG 3/02)

1358 Madden, Don. *The Wartville Wizard* (K–3). Illus. by author. 1986, Macmillan paper $5.99 (0-689-71667-2). 32pp. An old man who picks up litter is given the "power over trash" by Mother Nature in this tale about littering. (Rev: BL 11/1/86; SLJ 1/87)

1359 Madinaveitia, Horacio. *Sir Robert's Little Outing* (K–3). Illus. 1992, Wonder Well LB $13.95 (1-879567-01-6); paper $7.95 (1-879567-00-8). 30pp. An oafish knight, Sir Robert, sets out on a quest to win the fair Princess Dorothea. (Rev: BL 1/1/93)

1360 Magnier, Thierry. *Isabelle and the Angel* (PS–3). Illus. by Georg Hallensleben. 2000, Chronicle $14.95 (0-8118-2526-4). 36pp. When the little angel in Isabelle's favorite painting at the art galley comes to life, she gets a magical tour of the museum. (Rev: BL 12/1/00; HBG 3/01; SLJ 12/00)

1361 Mahy, Margaret. *Simply Delicious!* (K–3). Illus. by Jonathan Allen. 1999, Orchard $15.95 (0-531-30181-8). 32pp. As Mr. Minky bicycles home with a super ice-cream cone for his son, he attracts a number of jungle beasts who follow him for a taste. (Rev: BL 9/1/99; HB 9–10/99; HBG 3/00; SLJ 9/99)

1362 Maizlish, Lisa. *The Ring* (PS–1). Illus. 1996, Greenwillow $15.00 (0-688-14217-6). 24pp. A magic ring turns winter to summer and allows a boy to fly over New York City. (Rev: BL 6/1–15/96; HB 7–8/96; SLJ 5/96)

1363 Maloney, Peter, and Felicia Zekauskas. *Bronto Eats Meat* (PS–3). Illus. by authors. 2003, Dial $16.99 (0-8037-2791-7). A young brontosaurus accidentally swallows a little boy, giving Bronto a severe stomachache and three choices for how to expel the foreign object. (Rev: HBG 10/03; SLJ 7/03)

1364 Maloney, Peter, and Felicia Zekauskas. *The Magic Hockey Stick* (K–3). Illus. 1999, Dial $12.99 (0-8037-2476-4). 40pp. When her mother buys Wayne Gretzky's hockey stick at an auction, a young hockey player notices that, although her game improves by using the magic stick, Gretzky's declines. (Rev: BL 12/1/99; HBG 10/00; SLJ 10/99)

1365 Marciano, John Bemelmans. *There's a Dolphin in the Grand Canal* (K–2). Illus. 2005, Viking $15.99 (0-670-05987-0). 40pp. Bored despite the fact that he lives in Venice, Luca gets a thrilling ride over the city on the back of a dolphin. (Rev: BL 6/1–15/05)

1366 Martin, Jacqueline B. *Higgins Bend Song and Dance* (1–4). Illus. by Brad Sneed. 1997, Houghton Mifflin $16.00 (0-395-67583-9). Simon Henry vows to use any method possible to catch Oscar, a wily catfish. (Rev: HBG 3/98; SLJ 9/97)

1367 Marzollo, Jean. *Snow Angel* (PS–2). Illus. by Jacqueline Rogers. 1995, Scholastic $14.95 (0-590-48748-5). In this fantasy, a little girl is taken on a flight by a snow angel on a wintry day. (Rev: SLJ 12/95)

1368 Masini, Beatrice. *A Brave Little Princess* (K–3). Illus. by Octavia Monaco. 2000, Barefoot $15.99 (1-84148-267-6). 32pp. A tiny princess doesn't look her age so she goes out into the world to prove that she is stronger and braver than she looks. (Rev: BL 10/1/00; HBG 3/01; SLJ 2/01)

1369 Mayer, Mercer. *Shibumi and the Kitemaker* (2–4). Illus. 1999, Marshall Cavendish $18.95 (0-7614-5054-8). 48pp. An original folktale about an emperor's daughter who is shocked at the peasants' living conditions in her father's kingdom and wants him to do something about it. (Rev: BL 10/15/99; HBG 10/00; SLJ 9/99)

1370 Mayhew, James. *Katie and the Mona Lisa* (K–3). Illus. 1999, Orchard $15.95 (0-531-30177-X). 32pp. In the company of Mona Lisa, Katie enters several famous Renaissance paintings to regain Mona Lisa's famous smile. (Rev: BCCB 9/99; BL 9/1/99; HBG 3/00; SLJ 12/99)

1371 Mayhew, James. *Katie and the Sunflowers* (K–3). Illus. 2001, Scholastic $15.95 (0-531-30325-X). 32pp. Katie's museum escapades continue with a romp through Van Gogh, Gauguin, and Cezanne canvases that involves sunflowers, still lifes, and a chase through a cafe. (Rev: BL 6/1–15/01; HBG 10/01; SLJ 7/01)

1372 Mayhew, James. *Katie Meets the Impressionists* (PS–2). Illus. 1999, Orchard $15.95 (0-531-30151-6). 32pp. While visiting an art galley with her Grandma, Katie becomes so involved with the work of the Impressionists that she enters the paintings of Renoir, Monet, and Degas. (Rev: BL 4/1/99; HBG 10/99; SLJ 3/99)

1373 Mayhew, James. *Katie's Sunday Afternoon* (1–3). Illus. 2005, Scholastic $16.95 (0-439-60678-0). 32pp. Katie literally dives into the paintings of the Pointillists during a visit to the museum with her grandmother. (Rev: BL 3/1/05; SLJ 2/05)

1374 Mayhew, James. *Secret in the Garden: A Peek-Through Book* (K–3). Illus. by author. 2003, Scholastic $15.95 (0-439-40435-5). Sophie finds a number of treasures when a robin gives her the key to a secret garden in this book that uses die-cut holes effectively. (Rev: HBG 10/03; SLJ 3/03)

1375 Meddaugh, Susan. *Cinderella's Rat* (K–2). Illus. 1997, Houghton Mifflin $15.00 (0-395-86833-5). 32pp. An amusing picture book that tells what happened to the rat that was turned into Cinderella's coachman. (Rev: BL 10/1/97; HB 9–10/97; HBG 3/98; SLJ 10/97*)

1376 Meddaugh, Susan. *Harry on the Rocks* (PS–2). Illus. 2003, Houghton Mifflin $15.00 (0-618-27603-3). 32pp. Stranded on an island, Harry befriends its only other inhabitant, a dragon. (Rev: BL 2/15/03; HBG 10/03; SLJ 5/03)

1377 Meddaugh, Susan. *Martha Blah Blah* (PS–2). Illus. 1996, Houghton Mifflin $14.95 (0-395-79755-1). 32pp. Martha the dog, who talks after eating alphabet soup, finds her vocabulary constricted when the soup company reduces the letters in each can. (Rev: BCCB 12/96; BL 9/15/96; HB 11–12/96; SLJ 11/96*)

1378 Medearis, Angela Shelf. *The Ghost of Sifty Sifty Sam* (K–3). Illus. by Jacqueline Rogers. 1997, Scholastic $14.95 (0-590-48290-4). 32pp. A chef named Dan uses his cooking to tame a ghost whose wailings have made a house unfit for living. (Rev: BL 12/1/97; HBG 3/98; SLJ 11/97)

1379 Melling, David. *The Kiss That Missed* (PS–2). Illus. by author. 2002, Barron's $14.95 (0-7641-5451-6). A royal kiss goes astray and must be retrieved from a spooky forest full of dangers. (Rev: HBG 3/03; SLJ 12/02)

1380 Meyer, Eleanor Walsh. *The Keeper of Ugly Sounds* (PS–2). Illus. by Vlad Guzner. 1998, Winslow $16.95 (1-890817-02-3). 32pp. A young boy is responsible for stuffing bad noises caused by unpleasant acts into bags and sending them out to sea — a chore that he comes to find disagreeable. (Rev: BL 12/1/98; SLJ 1/99)

1381 Milord, Susan. *The Ghost on the Hearth* (PS–2). Illus. by Lydia Dabcovich. 2003, Vermont Folklife Center $15.95 (0-916718-18-2). 32pp. A well-illustrated ghost story set in early 19th-century Quebec, in which a young girl returns from the dead to the house in which she worked. (Rev: BL 2/1/04; HBG 4/04; SLJ 12/03)

1382 Min, Willemien. *Peter's Patchwork Dream* (PS–K). Illus. 1999, Barefoot $15.95 (1-902283-45-7). 26pp. Peter, who is sick in bed, enters the world of his patchwork quilt and is soon traveling through fields, orchards, and across the sea. (Rev: BL 5/1/99; SLJ 6/99)

1383 Mitchell, Adrian. *Nobody Rides the Unicorn* (1–4). Illus. by Stephen Lambert. 2000, Scholastic $16.95 (0-439-11204-4). 32pp. An evil king tricks a young girl into capturing the unicorn, but when she realizes what has happened she is able to free him.

(Rev: BCCB 2/00; BL 4/15/00; HBG 10/00; SLJ 1/01)

1384 Modarressi, Mitra. *Yard Sale!* (K–3). Illus. 2000, DK $15.95 (0-7894-2651-X). 32pp. When Mr. Flotsam holds a yard sale to dispose of magical items he has collected, the buyers end up turning the town topsy-turvy. (Rev: BL 3/1/00; HBG 10/00; SLJ 7/00)

1385 Morris, Bob. *Crispin the Terrible* (PS–3). Illus. by Dasha Ziborova. 2000, Callaway $17.95 (0-935112-44-8). 32pp. Crispin the cat feels unappreciated and dreams how his life would be if he had a new identity, like Crispin the Explorer or Crispin the Country Cat. (Rev: BL 1/1–15/01; HBG 10/01; SLJ 12/00)

1386 Morrow, Tara Jaye. *Just Mommy and Me* (PS). Illus. by Katy Bratun. 2004, HarperCollins LB $13.89 (0-06-000725-7). Told in rhyme, with an imaginative graphic layout, this is the story of a little boy who thinks about what fun it would be if he and his mother were monkeys. (Rev: SLJ 4/04)

1387 Munsch, Robert. *Mud Puddle* (PS–2). Illus. by Sami Suomalainen. 1996, Annick LB $16.95 (1-55037-469-9); paper $5.95 (1-55037-468-0). 32pp. Jule Ann is attacked by a mud puddle every time she leaves her house. (Rev: BL 4/1/96)

1388 Murphy, Stuart J. *A Pair of Socks* (PS–1). Illus. by Lois Ehlert. 1996, HarperCollins LB $15.89 (0-06-025880-2). 40pp. A sock sets out to find its lost mate. (Rev: BL 10/1/96; SLJ 12/96)

1389 Muth, Jon J. *The Three Questions: Based on a Story by Leo Tolstoy* (PS–3). Illus. 2002, Scholastic $16.95 (0-439-19996-4). 32pp. A conversation-starter about a boy who finds the answers to his philosophical questions in an act of kindness. (Rev: BL 3/15/02; HBG 10/02; SLJ 6/02)

1390 Namioka, Lensey. *The Hungriest Boy in the World* (K–3). Illus. by Aki Sogabe. 2001, Holiday House $16.95 (0-8234-1542-2). 32pp. A little Japanese boy swallows a hunger monster that causes the boy to eat everything in sight. (Rev: BL 4/1/01; HB 5–6/01; HBG 10/01; SLJ 4/01)

1391 Napoli, Donna Jo. *Albert* (K–2). Illus. by Jim LaMarche. 2001, Harcourt $16.00 (0-15-201572-8). 32pp. When Albert, a reclusive man, sticks a hand out of his apartment window, two cardinals build a nest in it and Albert must stay in this position until the birds' eggs hatch. (Rev: BL 3/1/01; HBG 10/01)

1392 Nash, Scott. *Tuff Fluff: The Case of Duckie's Missing Brain* (1–3). Illus. 2004, Candlewick $16.99 (0-7636-1882-9). 32pp. Tuff Fluff, a stuffed toy rabbit detective, takes on a tough assignment when he agrees to look into the mysterious disappearance of Duckie's brain. (Rev: BL 5/1/04; SLJ 7/04)

1393 Nesbit, E. *The Book of Beasts* (K–3). Illus. by Inga Moore. 2001, Candlewick $16.99 (0-7636-1579-X). When a new young king opens the Book of Beasts and releases the animals therein, a Red Dragon starts to wreak havoc. (Rev: HBG 3/02; SLJ 12/01)

1394 Newman, Leslea. *Cats, Cats, Cats!* (PS–2). Illus. by Erika Oller. 2001, Simon & Schuster $16.00 (0-689-83077-7). 32pp. When Mrs. Brown goes to bed at night, her 60 cats knit, eat, read, write, perform, and party. (Rev: BCCB 3/01; BL 2/15/01; HBG 10/01; SLJ 3/01)

1395 Nickle, John. *The Ant Bully* (PS–1). Illus. 1999, Scholastic $14.95 (0-590-39591-2). 32pp. Lucas terrorizes the ants in his backyard until they shrink him and put him on trial. (Rev: BCCB 2/99; BL 2/1/99; HB 1–2/99; HBG 10/99; SLJ 3/99)

1396 Nickle, John. *TV Rex* (K–3). Illus. 2001, Scholastic $15.95 (0-439-12043-8). 40pp. Rex crawls inside the TV set to fix it and soon finds he has become part of a series of different programs including a wrestling show and a soap opera. (Rev: BCCB 3/01; BL 1/1–15/01; HBG 10/01)

1397 Nightingale, Sandy. *Cider Apples* (K–3). Illus. 1996, Harcourt $15.00 (0-15-201244-3). 32pp. Fairies help a young girl and her grandmother save an ailing apple tree. (Rev: BL 9/1/96; SLJ 11/96)

1398 Nightingale, Sandy. *A Giraffe on the Moon* (PS). Illus. 1992, Harcourt $13.95 (0-15-230950-0). 32pp. A fine visual feast in a picture book that begins "I didn't expect to see . . ." (Rev: BL 2/15/92*; SLJ 3/92)

1399 Nimmo, Jenny. *Pig on a Swing* (PS). Illus. by Caroline Uff. 2003, Hodder $16.95 (0-340-85241-0). Bored at the playground, a little boy conjures up a menagerie of creatures to keep him company. (Rev: SLJ 1/04)

1400 Nolen, Jerdine. *Big Jabe* (1–4). Illus. by Kadir Nelson. 2000, Lothrop LB $15.89 (0-688-13663-X). 32pp. An original tall tale about a man of unusual strength who could lead slaves to freedom. (Rev: BCCB 9/00; BL 4/1/00; HB 7–8/00; HBG 10/00; SLJ 6/00)

1401 Nolen, Jerdine. *Harvey Potter's Balloon Farm* (K–3). Illus. by Mark Buehner. 1994, Morrow $15.95 (0-688-07887-7). 32pp. In this tall tale, a little girl learns all the secrets of trade when she visits Harvey's balloon farm and discovers how they are grown. (Rev: BL 4/15/94; HB 7–8/94; SLJ 5/94)

1402 Nolen, Jerdine. *Hewitt Anderson's Great Big Life* (K–3). Illus. by Kadir Nelson. 2005, Simon & Schuster $16.95 (0-689-86866-9). Born into a family of giants, little Hewitt fails to develop properly, but despite his diminutive size he constantly proves his worth. (Rev: BL 3/1/04; SLJ 5/05)

1403 Nolen, Jerdine. *Raising Dragons* (PS–2). Illus. by Elise Primavera. 1998, Harcourt $16.00 (0-15-201288-5). 32pp. An African American child raises a dragon named Hank on her parents' farm and teaches him to perform useful chores. Eventually, though, she must take him to a land where he will be with his own kind. (Rev: BCCB 6/98; BL 4/1/98; HB 3–4/98; HBG 10/98; SLJ 4/98)

1404 Nolen, Jerdine. *Thunder Rose* (K–3). Illus. by Kadir Nelson. 2003, Harcourt $16.00 (0-15-216472-3). Born during a fierce thunderstorm, Thunder Rose is an African American child of extraordinary talent and magical ability in this vividly illustrated story set in the West. (Rev: HBG 4/04; SLJ 9/03)

1405 Norling, Beth. *The Stone Baby* (K–2). Illus. by author. 2003, Lothian $18.95 (0-7344-0353-4). A little girl protects a stone baby through a series of adventures, including encounters with wild animals and pirates. (Rev: SLJ 5/04)

1406 Novak, Matt. *No Zombies Allowed* (K–2). Illus. by author. 2002, Simon & Schuster $16.95 (0-689-84130-2). Witch Wizzle and Witch Woddle are busy crossing names off their monster party guest list because of bad behavior the year before. (Rev: BCCB 9/02; HB 9–10/02; HBG 3/03; SLJ 8/02)

1407 Noyes, Deborah. *It's Vladimir!* (K–3). Illus. by Christopher Mills. 2001, Marshall Cavendish $15.95 (0-7614-5071-8). 32pp. A young vampire is impatient to learn how to turn into a bat. (Rev: BL 10/15/01; HBG 3/02; SLJ 10/01)

1408 O'Brien, John. *Poof!* (PS–2). Illus. by author. 1999, Boyds Mills $14.95 (1-56397-815-6). A sleepy wizard and his wife avoid daily chores by waving their magic wands; "Poof!" they solve each problem. (Rev: HBG 3/00; SLJ 11/99)

1409 O'Connor, George. *Kapow!* (PS–2). Illus. by author. 2004, Simon & Schuster $14.95 (0-689-86718-2). Switching easily between real life and fantasy, this is the story of a boy who morphs into a superhero called American Eagle. (Rev: SLJ 8/04)

1410 Oliviero, Jamie. *Som See and the Magic Elephant* (1–3). Illus. by Jo'Anne Kelly. 1995, Hyperion $14.95 (0-7868-0025-9). 32pp. Before Som See's great aunt dies, she wants to touch a white elephant. With the help of magical powers, Som See is eventually able to grant her wish. (Rev: BL 5/1/95; SLJ 5/95)

1411 Olson, Mary W. *An Alligator Ate My Brother* (PS–2). Illus. by Tammie Lyon. 2000, Boyds Mills $15.95 (1-56397-803-2). 32pp. Paul can't convince his parents that an alligator has just eaten baby brother Jimmy. (Rev: BCCB 12/00; BL 12/1/00; HBG 3/01; SLJ 11/00)

1412 Olson, Mary W. *Nice Try, Tooth Fairy* (PS–1). Illus. by Katherine Tillotson. 2000, Simon & Schuster $15.00 (0-689-82422-X). When a girl asks the Tooth Fairy to return her tooth so she can show it to her grandfather, a mistake is made and a hippo's tooth is brought. (Rev: HBG 10/00; SLJ 11/00)

1413 O'Malley, Kevin. *Once Upon a Cool Motorcycle Dude* (3–5). Illus. by Kevin O'Malley and others. 2005, Walker LB $17.85 (0-8027-8949-8). 32pp. Together, a boy and a girl compose a story, both using their favorite themes, resulting in a funny combination of superheroes and princesses. (Rev: BL 3/15/05)

1414 Oram, Hiawyn. *In the Attic* (PS–K). Illus. by Satoshi Kitamura. 1985, Holt paper $5.95 (0-8050-0780-6). 32pp. A little boy climbs his fire engine ladder into his attic, where he has exciting adventures, even though, as his mother tells him, "we don't have an attic." (Rev: BCCB 3/85; BL 6/15/85; SLJ 10/85)

1415 Oram, Hiawyn. *Rubbaduck and Ruby Roo* (PS–1). Illus. by David Lucas. 2005, Boyds Mills $15.95 (1-59078-356-5). 32pp. Rubbaduck is angry when rag doll Ruby Roo eats up everything in his kitchen and trades away his coat, but all ends well

when Ruby's magic turns to gold. (Rev: BL 3/1/05; SLJ 3/05)

1416 Ordal, Stina Langlo. *Princess Aasta* (PS). Illus. 2002, Bloomsbury $16.95 (1-58234-783-2). 32pp. Princess Aasta's polar bear friend, acquired through a letter to the newspaper, takes her on an entertaining trip to the North Pole. (Rev: BCCB 1/03; BL 11/15/02; SLJ 1/03)

1417 Ormerod, Jan. *Miss Mouse's Day* (PS–K). Illus. 2001, HarperCollins LB $14.89 (0-688-16334-3). 32pp. A toddler's day from getting up to a goodnight kiss and cuddle is described by her best friend, a doll named Miss Mouse. (Rev: BL 3/15/01*; HB 3–4/01; HBG 10/01; SLJ 3/01)

1418 Osborne, Mary Pope. *Mummies in the Morning* (1–4). Illus. 1993, Random LB $11.99 (0-679-92424-8); paper $3.99 (0-679-82424-3). 72pp. Jack and Annie time-travel to ancient Egypt to help a queen find a copy of the Book of the Dead. (Rev: BL 4/1/94)

1419 Packard, Mary. *We Are Monsters* (K–1). Illus. by John Magine. 1996, Scholastic $3.99 (0-590-68995-9). 32pp. At nighttime, terrible monsters are afraid that children are hiding under their beds in this book with removable flashcards. (Rev: BL 2/1/97)

1420 Palatini, Margie. *Piggie Pie!* (K–3). Illus. by Howard Fine. 1995, Clarion $15.00 (0-395-71691-8). 32pp. Gritch the Witch is off to Old MacDonald's farm in search of eight plump pigs for her favorite pie. (Rev: BL 9/1/95*; SLJ 11/95*)

1421 Palatini, Margie. *Zak's Lunch* (K–3). Illus. by Howard Fine. 1998, Clarion $15.00 (0-395-81674-2). 32pp. When faced with a simple ham-and-cheese sandwich for lunch, Zak dreams of owning his own restaurant, where he will have delicious, forbidden foods every day. (Rev: HBG 10/98; SLJ 6/98)

1422 Palazzo, Tony. *Magic Crayon* (PS–2). Illus. by author. 1967, Lion LB $12.95 (0-87460-089-8). Imaginative fun for very young readers.

1423 Papineau, Lucie. *Gontrand and the Crescent Moon* (K–4). Trans. from French by David Homel. Illus. by Alain Reno. 1999, Dominique & Friends paper $8.95 (1-894363-15-9). Set in prehistoric times, this is the story of how the moon was formed in order to guide a group of lost children home. (Rev: SLJ 2/00)

1424 Paraskevas, Betty. *The Tangerine Bear* (PS–2). Illus. by Michael Paraskevas. 1997, HarperCollins LB $14.00 (0-06-205147-4). 32pp. Toy Tangerine Bear wants to become part of a family, but nobody wants him because his smile was sewn on upside down. (Rev: BL 11/1/97)

1425 Parnall, Peter. *Spaces* (1–3). Illus. 1993, Millbrook LB $22.90 (1-56294-336-7). 32pp. A fantastic view of what unusual creatures and thoughts can fill all sorts of spaces. (Rev: BL 12/1/93; SLJ 12/93)

1426 Partridge, Elizabeth, adapt. *Kogi's Mysterious Journey* (K–3). Illus. by Aki Sogabe. 2003, Dutton $17.99 (0-525-47078-6). In medieval Japan, Kogi, an artist frustrated by his inability to truly capture the natural beauty around him, is temporarily transformed into a fish, an experience that charges his paintings with a new vitality. (Rev: HBG 4/04; SLJ 11/03)

1427 Passen, Lisa. *The Incredible Shrinking Teacher* (K–3). 2002, Holt $15.95 (0-8050-6452-4). 32pp. Strict teacher Irma Birnbaum gets her just desserts when she faces a series of indignities after being shrunk. (Rev: BL 6/1–15/02; HBG 10/02; SLJ 5/02)

1428 Paterson, Katherine. *Celia and the Sweet, Sweet Water* (1–4). Illus. by Vladimir Vagin. 1998, Clarion $15.00 (0-395-91324-1). 32pp. On a quest to get some sweet water to help cure her mother's ills, Celia and her talking dog set out to find the village her mother comes from. (Rev: BL 9/1/98; HBG 3/99; SLJ 9/98)

1429 Paterson, Katherine. *The King's Equal* (2–5). Illus. by Vladimir Vagin. 1992, HarperCollins LB $16.89 (0-06-022497-5). 64pp. An arrogant king learns humility when the bride he wants does not want him. (Rev: BCCB 1/93; BL 7/92; SLJ 9/92*)

1430 Pawagi, Manjusha. *The Girl Who Hated Books* (K–3). Illus. by Leanne Franson. 1999, Beyond Words $14.95 (1-896764-11-8). 24pp. When nonreader Meena accidentally frees a lot of book characters, such as Humpty Dumpty and Ali Baba, from the pages of their books, she has to read the whole family library to find where they belong. (Rev: BL 11/1/99; SLJ 6/99)

1431 Peet, Bill. *Big Bad Bruce* (K–3). Illus. by author. 1982, Houghton Mifflin $16.00 (0-395-25150-8); paper $7.95 (0-395-32922-1). Bruce encounters a witch and is shrunk to the size of a chipmunk.

1432 Peet, Bill. *The Caboose Who Got Loose* (K–3). Illus. by author. 1980, Houghton Mifflin $16.00 (0-395-14805-7); paper $7.95 (0-395-28715-4). 48pp. When Katy Caboose is jarred loose from the rest of the train, she gets her wish to be a "cabin in the trees," free from noise and smoke.

1433 Peet, Bill. *Jennifer and Josephine* (1–3). Illus. by author. 1980, Houghton Mifflin paper $7.95 (0-395-29608-0). Jennifer, an old touring car, and her friend Josephine the cat, are driven through several adventures by a reckless driver.

1434 Pelletier, Andrew. *Sixteen Miles to Spring* (K–3). Illus. by Katya Krenina. 2002, Whitman $15.95 (0-8075-7388-4). 32pp. A fanciful explanation of spring in which two friends travel from south to north each year, starting at Christmas and spreading seeds as they go. (Rev: BCCB 4/02; BL 5/1/02; HBG 10/02; SLJ 6/02)

1435 Pendziwol, Jean, and Martine Gourbault. *No Dragons for Tea: Fire Safety for Kids (and Dragons)* (PS–1). Illus. 1999, Kids Can $14.95 (1-55074-569-7). 32pp. A young girl's pet dragon sneezes, and her experiences with the ensuing blaze teach fire safety to readers. (Rev: BCCB 4/99; BL 2/1/99; HBG 10/99; SLJ 4/99)

1436 Perry, Sarah. *If . . .* (K–4). Illus. 1995, Getty Museum $16.95 (0-89236-321-5). 46pp. Using a number of unconventional statements beginning with "if," this imaginative book presents a series of eyecatching, ingenious pictures to illustrate each phrase. (Rev: BCCB 1/96; BL 10/15/95*; HBG 9/99; SLJ 2/96)

1437 Persun, Morgan Reed. *No Pets Allowed* (PS–2). Illus. by Timothy Banks. 1998, Journey Bks. paper $5.49 (1-57924-077-1). 30pp. Every time Percy speaks the name of an animal, that creature appears, until his apartment is jammed. (Rev: SLJ 2/99)

1438 Pienkowski, Jan. *Pizza! A Yummy Pop-up* (PS). Illus. by author. 2002, Candlewick $12.99 (0-7636-1626-5). Lots of food noises accompany the varied and elaborate pop-ups presented here. (Rev: SLJ 4/02)

1439 Pilkey, Dav. *Ricky Ricotta's Giant Robot* (2–4). Illus. by Martin Ontiveros. 2000, Scholastic $16.95 (0-590-30719-3). 111pp. Ricky Ricotta, a tiny mouse, is a victim of bullying until he becomes friends with a large robot who protects him. (Rev: BCCB 5/00; HBG 10/00; SLJ 4/00)

1440 Pilkey, Dav. *Ricky Ricotta's Giant Robot vs. the Mutant Mosquitoes from Mercury* (1–3). Illus. by Martin Ontiveros. 2000, Scholastic paper $3.99 (0-590-30722-3). 127pp. Ricky the mouse and his robot friend fight extraterrestrial insects and an evil robot. (Rev: SLJ 10/00)

1441 Pilkey, Dav. *Ricky Ricotta's Mighty Robot vs. the Stupid Stinkbugs from Saturn* (2–4). Illus. by Martin Ontiveros. 2003, Scholastic $16.95 (0-439-37644-0); paper $3.99 (0-439-37645-9). 125pp. After the evil Sergeant Stinkbug kidnaps his cousin Lucy, Ricky Ricotta, stalwart mouse, and his trusty robot friend come to the rescue. (Rev: HBG 4/04; SLJ 1/04)

1442 Pilkey, Dav. *When Cats Dream* (PS–3). Illus. 1992, Orchard LB $16.99 (0-531-08597-X). 32pp. Cats' dreams are more fun and more colorful than their reality. (Rev: BCCB 9/92; BL 8/92; HB 3–4/93; SLJ 9/92*)

1443 Pinkney, Brian. *Cosmo and the Robot* (PS–3). Illus. 2000, Greenwillow LB $15.89 (0-688-15941-9). 32pp. Cosmo, who is growing up on Mars, saves his sister from the clutches of a robot that has gone haywire. (Rev: BCCB 5/00; BL 7/00; HB 7–8/00; HBG 10/00; SLJ 6/00)

1444 Plourde, Lynn. *Spring's Sprung* (PS–1). Illus. by Greg Couch. 2002, Simon & Schuster $16.00 (0-689-84229-5). March, April, and May are querulous siblings who test Mother Earth's patience in this ode to spring. (Rev: HBG 10/02; SLJ 3/02)

1445 Plourde, Lynn. *Winter Waits* (K–2). Illus. by Greg Couch. 2001, Simon & Schuster $16.00 (0-689-83268-0). 32pp. Father Time is too busy to play with his son Little Winter, but when the boy shows him how he has covered the world with beautiful snow, Father Time rewards him with a round of play. (Rev: BL 12/15/00; HBG 10/01; SLJ 1/01)

1446 Polacco, Patricia. *Appelemando's Dreams* (PS–2). Illus. 1991, Penguin Putnam $15.95 (0-399-21800-9). 32pp. Appelemando teaches the townspeople that they should never question the importance of dreams. (Rev: BL 10/15/91; SLJ 9/91)

1447 Polacco, Patricia. *Babushka's Doll* (PS–2). Illus. 1990, Simon & Schuster $16.95 (0-671-68343-8). 32pp. Natasha, a pest, learns her lesson when a doll comes alive and begins nagging. (Rev: BCCB 11/90; BL 9/15/90*; HB 1–2/91; SLJ 11/90)

1448 Polacco, Patricia. *Rechenka's Eggs* (K–2). Illus. by author. 1988, Penguin Putnam $16.99 (0-399-21501-8). 32pp. Old Babushka saves a wild goose, and when her decorated eggs are broken, the goose repays her kindness by laying her own decorated eggs. (Rev: BCCB 6/88; BL 4/1/88; SLJ 5/88)

1449 Poydar, Nancy. *Cool Ali* (PS–1). Illus. 1996, Simon & Schuster paper $13.00 (0-689-80755-4). 26pp. Ali cools her neighborhood by drawing items that suggest moderate temperatures. (Rev: BCCB 10/96; BL 8/96; HB 9–10/96; SLJ 9/96)

1450 Preston, Tim. *The Lonely Scarecrow* (K–3). Illus. by Maggie Kneen. 1999, Dutton $14.99 (0-525-46080-2). 32pp. A scarecrow is unhappy that he frightens away animals and birds, but when winter comes, he is transformed into a snowman loved by all creatures. (Rev: BCCB 11/99; BL 10/1/99; HBG 3/00; SLJ 1/00)

1451 Pulver, Robin. *Punctuation Takes a Vacation* (1–3). Illus. by Lynn Rowe Reed. 2003, Holiday House $16.95 (0-8234-1687-9). 32pp. Punctuation marks take offense at a teacher's comment and disappear, leaving children unable to write properly. (Rev: BL 3/1/03; HB 5–6/03; HBG 10/03; SLJ 4/03)

1452 Pyle, Howard. *Bearskin* (1–4). Illus. by Trina S. Hyman. 1997, Morrow $15.93 (0-688-09838-X). 48pp. An abandoned youngster is cared for by a bear and grows up to be a dragon-slaying hero. (Rev: BL 11/1/97*; HB 9–10/97; HBG 3/98; SLJ 8/97*)

1453 Rascal. *Oregon's Journey* (K–3). Illus. by Louis Joos. 1994, Troll $15.95 (0-8167-3305-8). 40pp. A dwarf and a performing bear leave the circus and head west to Oregon and freedom. (Rev: BCCB 6/94; BL 4/15/94*; SLJ 8/94)

1454 Rassmus, Jens. *Farmer Enno and His Cow* (1–5). Trans. by Dominic Barth. Illus. by author. 1998, Orchard $14.95 (0-531-30081-1). Farmer Enno denies his obsessive dream to buy a ship and become a sailor until his wise cow gives him some sound advice. (Rev: HBG 10/98; SLJ 4/98)

1455 Ratnett, Michael. *Monster Train* (K–3). Illus. by June Goulding. 2000, Orchard $15.95 (0-531-30293-8). This interactive book uses pop-ups and other devices to illustrate a ride on a monster train with passengers like Frankenstein. (Rev: BL 12/1/00)

1456 Ray, Mary L. *Pumpkins: A Story for a Field* (K–4). Illus. by Barry Root. 1992, Harcourt $15.00 (0-15-252252-2). 32pp. A farmer reaches an agreement with a vacant field and together they grow a bumper crop of pumpkins. (Rev: BL 10/15/92; HB 11–12/92; SLJ 3/93)

1457 Ray, Mary Lyn. *All Aboard!* (PS–2). Illus. by Amiko Hirao. 2002, Little, Brown $14.95 (0-316-73507-8). 32pp. The rabbit named Mr. Barnes, who appears to be traveling alone, belongs in fact to the little girl on the same train. (Rev: BL 11/1/02; HBG 3/03; SLJ 10/02)

1458 Rees, Douglas. *Grandy Thaxter's Helper* (1–3). Illus. by S. D. Schindler. 2004, Simon & Schuster $15.95 (0-689-83020-3). Grandy Thaxter succeeds in wearing out the Grim Reaper in this story set in colonial times. (Rev: BCCB 10/04; HB 11–12/04; SLJ 11/04)

1459 Rex, Michael. *My Freight Train* (PS–K). Illus. 2002, Holt $15.95 (0-8050-6682-9). 32pp. A little boy segues from playing with his toy train to a day as engineer of a real freight train, and explains every detail of the train and his duties. (Rev: BL 11/15/02; HBG 3/03; SLJ 11/02)

1460 Reynolds, Adrian. *Pete and Polo's Big School Adventure* (PS–K). Illus. 2000, Orchard $15.95 (0-531-30275-X). 32pp. Pete is certain that all will go well on the first day of school but Polo, his stuffed polar bear, isn't so sure. (Rev: BL 9/1/00; HBG 10/01; SLJ 12/00)

1461 Reynolds, Adrian. *Pete and Polo's Farmyard Adventure* (PS–K). Illus. 2002, Scholastic $16.95 (0-439-30913-1). 32pp. A boy named Pete and his toy polar bear search for missing ducks after they discover the pond has dried up. (Rev: BL 8/02; HBG 10/02; SLJ 7/02)

1462 Richardson, Judith B. *Old Winter* (PS–1). Illus. by R. W. Alley. 1996, Orchard LB $16.99 (0-531-08883-9). 32pp. Old Winter is so angry at people criticizing his season that he decides to remain in the North although spring is scheduled to arrive. (Rev: BCCB 12/96; BL 10/1/96; SLJ 12/96)

1463 Ringgold, Faith. *Tar Beach* (PS–2). Illus. 1991, Crown LB $18.99 (0-517-58031-4). 32pp. A little girl on the rooftop of her apartment building dreams of soaring over New York City. (Rev: BCCB 3/91; BL 1/1/91; HB 5–6/91*; SLJ 2/91*)

1464 Roberts, Bethany. *May Belle and the Ogre* (PS–2). Illus. by Marsha Winborn. Series: Dutton Easy Reader. 2003, Dutton $14.99 (0-525-46855-2). 48pp. Plucky but solitary May Belle befriends an ogre in this winning easy-reader. (Rev: HBG 10/03; SLJ 7/03)

1465 Roberts, Bethany. *Monster Manners* (PS–2). Illus. by Andrew Glass. 1996, Clarion $15.00 (0-395-69850-2). 32pp. A rhyming book that explains basic manners with brilliantly colored illustrations and the antics of three often misbehaving monsters. (Rev: SLJ 4/96)

1466 Roberts, David, and Corina Fletcher. *Ghoul School* (K–4). Illus. 2000, Abrams $17.95 (0-8109-4140-6). A pop-up book about a school run by Ms. Vampira where strange things take place, like eating worms for lunch. (Rev: BL 12/1/00)

1467 Robertson, M. P. *The Egg* (K–2). Illus. by author. 2001, Penguin Putnam $15.99 (0-8037-2546-9). When the egg that George has cared for hatches and a little dragon emerges, George must assume a motherly role and teach his adopted child how to do dragon things like fly, breath fire, and slay knights. (Rev: BCCB 2/01; HBG 10/01; SLJ 1/01*)

1468 Robinson, Fay. *Where Did All the Dragons Go?* (PS–3). Illus. by Victor Lee. 1996, Troll $15.95 (0-8167-3808-4). 32pp. All kinds of dragons swirl about in the pages of this unusual picture book. (Rev: BL 12/15/96)

1469 Robinson, Fiona. *The Useful Moose: A Truthful, Moose-full Tale* (K–2). Illus. by author. 2004, Abrams $14.95 (0-8109-4925-3). Always fond of moose, Molly's affection deepens when a trio visits her apartment and helps her with household chores. (Rev: SLJ 1/05)

1470 Robinson, Sue. *Bear in the Barnyard* (PS–2). Illus. by Tony Morris. 2004, Good Books $16.00 (1-56148-430-X). A teddy bear thinks he's ready for farm life but gets some surprises. (Rev: SLJ 9/04)

1471 Robinson, Tim. *Tobias, the Quig and the Rumplenut Tree* (PS–4). Illus. by author. 2000, Winslow $16.95 (1-890817-20-1). In this fantasy, Tobias must free the quig, an unusual bird, so the bird can spread seeds of the rumplenut tree. (Rev: HBG 10/00; SLJ 10/00)

1472 Robledo, Honorio. *Nico Visits the Moon* (PS–2). Illus. 2001, Cinco Puntos $15.95 (0-938317-57-1). 32pp. Baby Nico floats to the moon when he grabs a bunch of balloons intended to hang things out of his reach. (Rev: BL 11/1/01; HBG 3/02; SLJ 12/01)

1473 Robles, Anthony D. *Lakas and the Manilatown Fish / Si Lakas at ang Isdang Manilatown* (K–3). Trans. by Eloisa D. de Jesus and Magdalena de Guzman. Illus. by Carl Angel. 2003, Children's Book Pr. $16.95 (0-89239-182-0). 32pp. In this whimsical bilingual (English and Tagalog) story, a young Filipino boy and his father race through the streets of San Francisco in pursuit of a fish that can talk, jump, and play. (Rev: HB 5–6/03; HBG 10/03; SLJ 10/03)

1474 Rohmann, Eric. *Pumpkinhead* (PS–1). Illus. by author. 2003, Knopf LB $16.99 (0-375-92416-7). Otho, a little boy with a pumpkin for a head, has an amazing adventure as his head is passed from bat to fish to squid to fisherman, and eventually home to his parents to be rejoined to his body. (Rev: HBG 4/04; SLJ 7/03)

1475 Root, Phyllis. *Aunt Nancy and Old Man Trouble* (K–2). Illus. by David Parkins. 1996, Candlewick $16.99 (1-56402-374-8). 32pp. Aunt Nancy outwits Old Man Trouble by posing a question he can't answer. (Rev: BCCB 3/96; BL 5/1/96; HB 9–10/96; SLJ 5/96)

1476 Root, Phyllis. *Grandmother Winter* (PS–2). Illus. by Beth Krommes. 1999, Houghton Mifflin $15.00 (0-395-88399-7). 32pp. When Grandmother Winter shakes out her quilt and causes a snowfall, all nature responds to the coming of winter. (Rev: BCCB 10/99; BL 11/15/99; HB 9–10/99; HBG 3/00; SLJ 9/99)

1477 Root, Phyllis. *Rosie's Fiddle* (K–3). Illus. by Kevin O'Malley. 1997, Lothrop LB $15.93 (0-688-12853-X). 32pp. Rosie O'Grady is challenged by the devil to engage in a fiddling contest in this somewhat scary picture book. (Rev: BCCB 4/97; BL 4/15/97; SLJ 4/97)

1478 Rosenberg, Liz. *The Carousel* (K–3). Illus. by Jim LaMarche. 1995, Harcourt $16.00 (0-15-200853-5). 32pp. Two girls discover that the horses

of the carousel in the park have come alive. (Rev: BCCB 12/95; BL 11/15/95; SLJ 1/96*)

1479 Roth, Susan L. *Grandpa Blows His Penny Whistle Until the Angels Sing* (PS–3). Illus. 2001, Barefoot $16.99 (1-84148-247-1). 40pp. Using his penny whistle, Grandpa calls on angels to awaken Little Boy James, his grandson, who has fallen from a church roof. (Rev: BL 4/1/01; HBG 10/01; SLJ 5/01*)

1480 Rumford, James. *The Nine Animals and the Well* (1–3). Illus. 2003, Houghton Mifflin $16.00 (0-618-30915-2). 32pp. Nine animals bear birthday gifts for the raja (three almond cakes, four sugar cones), each worried that his gift is not good enough, in this combination of charming text and counting book. (Rev: BL 7/03; HB 5–6/03; HBG 10/03; SLJ 6/03)

1481 Ryan, Pam Munoz. *Mice and Beans* (PS–2). Illus. by Joe Cepeda. 2001, Scholastic $15.95 (0-439-18303-0). 32pp. Readers get a mouse's perspective in this story of mice helping Rosa Maria prepare for her grandchild's birthday celebration that interweaves Spanish expressions. (Rev: BCCB 10/01; BL 9/15/01; HBG 3/02; SLJ 10/01)

1482 Ryder, Joanne. *Rainbow Wings* (K–4). Illus. by Victor Lee. 2000, HarperCollins LB $15.98 (0-688-14129-3). 40pp. This fantasy in which children get wings to fly also presents the different kinds of wings found in nature such as those of an owl and a monarch butterfly. (Rev: BL 5/1/00; HBG 10/00; SLJ 5/00)

1483 Ryder, Joanne. *The Snail's Spell* (K–2). Illus. by Lynne Cherry. 1992, Puffin paper $5.99 (0-14-050891-0). 32pp. A little boy knows how a snail feels when he shrinks to that size. Originally published in 1982.

1484 Rylant, Cynthia. *Cat Heaven* (PS–3). Illus. 1997, Scholastic $15.95 (0-590-10054-8). 40pp. A picture book about the activities in cat heaven. (Rev: BL 9/1/97; HBG 3/98; SLJ 10/97)

1485 Rylant, Cynthia. *The Great Gracie Chase: Stop That Dog!* (PS–1). Illus. by Mark Teague. 2001, Scholastic $15.95 (0-590-10041-6). 40pp. Gracie Rose decides to break the rules and take a walk by herself, causing a frantic neighborhood search when she seems to be lost. (Rev: BCCB 3/01; BL 2/15/01; HBG 10/01)

1486 Rylant, Cynthia. *Little Whistle* (PS–K). Illus. by Tim Bowers. 2001, Harcourt $14.00 (0-15-201087-4). 32pp. Little Whistle, a guinea pig who lives in a toy store, loves the nights when all the toys come to life and he can play with them. (Rev: BL 2/15/01; HBG 10/01)

1487 Rylant, Cynthia. *Scarecrow* (K–3). Illus. by Lauren Stringer. 1998, Harcourt $16.00 (0-15-201084-X). 40pp. A gentle scarecrow tells about his contented life, how he appreciates nature, and of his many animal friends. (Rev: BCCB 6/98; BL 4/1/98; HBG 10/98; SLJ 4/98)

1488 Sabuda, Robert. *The Blizzard's Robe* (K–3). Illus. 1999, Simon & Schuster $16.00 (0-689-31988-6). 32pp. In return for the kindness of the people, the monster Blizzard gives them the Northern Lights to illuminate the winter darkness. (Rev: BL 11/15/99; HBG 3/00; SLJ 10/99)

1489 Sage, Angie. *Molly and the Birthday Party* (PS–1). Illus. by author. 2001, Peachtree $9.95 (1-56145-248-3). Fuzzy, green Molly goes to Olly's birthday party but is reluctant to hand over his present. She also appears in *Molly at the Dentist* (2001). (Rev: HBG 3/02; SLJ 11/01)

1490 Saltzberg, Barney. *This Is a Great Place for a Hot Dog Stand* (1–3). Illus. 1995, Hyperion LB $15.49 (0-7868-2057-8). 32pp. The hot dog stand that the monster Izzy operates is threatened by the construction of a super shopping mall. (Rev: BL 4/15/95; SLJ 5/95)

1491 Sandburg, Carl. *The Wedding Procession of the Rag Doll and the Broom Handle and Who Was in It* (1–3). Illus. by Harriet Pincus. 1978, Harcourt paper $6.00 (0-15-695487-5). 32pp. Illustrated edition of one of the Rootabaga Stories.

1492 Sanfield, Steve. *The Girl Who Wanted a Song* (K–3). Illus. by Stephen T. Johnson. 1996, Harcourt $16.00 (0-15-200969-8). Through contact with a lost Canada goose, orphaned Marici finds that she has a distinctive song to sing, like the birds and animals around her. (Rev: SLJ 7/97)

1493 Sasso, Sandy Eisenberg. *God Said Amen* (1–3). Illus. by Avi Katz. 2000, Jewish Lights $16.95 (1-58023-080-6). Two children are able to settle the differences between their two kingdoms so that each kingdom can profit from the strengths of the other. (Rev: SLJ 3/01)

1494 Say, Allen. *River Dream* (1–3). Illus. by author. 1988, Houghton Mifflin $14.95 (0-395-48294-1); paper $6.95 (0-395-65749-0). 32pp. In a dream, Mark learns you don't need to kill fish to enjoy fishing. (Rev: HB 11–12/88)

1495 Schaap, Martine. *Mop to the Rescue* (PS–K). Illus. by Alex de Wolf. 1999, Front Street $15.95 (0-8126-0167-X). 40pp. Seven short stories for the very young about a lovable sheepdog named Mop. (Rev: BL 5/1/99; HBG 10/99; SLJ 11/99)

1496 Schaap, Martine. *Mop's Backyard Concert* (PS–1). Illus. by Alex de Wolf. Series: Mop and Family. 2000, McGraw-Hill $12.95 (1-57768-892-9). 30pp. Twins Julie and Justin lose their dog Mop in a park only to find him singing in a six-piece band. Also enjoy *Mop's Treasure Hunt*. (Rev: BCCB 1/01; HBG 3/01; SLJ 3/01)

1497 Schachner, Judith Byron. *Yo, Vikings!* (K–3). Illus. 2002, Dutton $16.99 (0-525-46889-7). 32pp. In this fantasy, a girl imagines that she is a Viking and when a Viking ship arrives for her, she takes several of her friends on a high adventure. (Rev: BL 6/1–15/02; HBG 10/02; SLJ 8/02)

1498 Schanzer, Rosalyn. *Davy Crockett Saves the World* (K–3). Illus. 2001, HarperCollins LB $16.89 (0-688-16992-9). 32pp. Davy Crockett is called upon to battle Halley's Comet in this tall tale rich with colorful illustrations. (Rev: BCCB 2/02; BL 11/15/01; HBG 10/02; SLJ 8/01)

1499 Scheer, Julian. *By the Light of the Captured Moon* (PS–3). Illus. by Ronald Himler. 2001, Holiday House $16.95 (0-8234-1624-0). 32pp. Billy

captures the moon but soon finds he can't hide it and must let it go again. (Rev: BL 5/1/01; HBG 10/01; SLJ 3/01)

1500 Schertle, Alice. *The Skeleton in the Closet* (1–3). Illus. by Curtis Jobling. 2003, HarperCollins LB $16.89 (0-688-17739-5). In this amusing twist on the usual spine-chilling skeleton story, a young boy describes a nighttime visit from a skeleton who wants to borrow some clothes. (Rev: HB 11–12/03; HBG 4/04; SLJ 9/03)

1501 Schneider, Christine M. *Horace P. Tuttle, Magician Extraordinaire* (K–3). Illus. 2001, Walker $15.95 (0-8027-8788-6). 32pp. Horace's magic act is in trouble when his animal and human assistants become disgruntled. (Rev: BL 9/15/01; HBG 3/02; SLJ 10/01)

1502 Schneider, Howie. *Chewy Louie* (PS–1). Illus. 2000, Rising Moon $15.95 (0-87358-765-0). 32pp. Louie can't stop chewing things, but when he starts on the family car and the house, his family must act to stop him. (Rev: BL 8/00; HBG 10/00; SLJ 11/00)

1503 Schnitzlein, Danny. *The Monster Who Ate My Peas* (1–4). Illus. by Matt Faulkner. 2001, Peachtree $15.95 (1-56145-216-5). A demanding monster asks for a boy's prize possessions in return for eating his peas. (Rev: HBG 3/02; SLJ 1/02)

1504 Schubert, Ingrid, and Dieter Schubert. *Abracadabra* (PS–1). Illus. 1997, Front Street $15.95 (1-886910-17-0). 32pp. Macrobius the Magician delights in causing confusion by having animals exchange body parts. (Rev: BL 7/97)

1505 Schwab, Eva. *Robert and the Robot* (PS–K). Illus. 2001, Front Street $15.95 (1-886910-59-6). 32pp. An alien robot helps Robert clean up his room as a thank you for providing him with batteries. (Rev: BL 7/01; HBG 10/01; SLJ 5/01)

1506 Schwartz, Roslyn. *The Mole Sisters and the Piece of Moss* (PS–K). Illus. by author. Series: The Mole Sisters. 1999, Annick LB $14.95 (1-55037-583-0); paper $4.95 (1-55037-582-2). The mole sisters find an unhappy piece of moss and take it on an adventure. Also use *The Mole Sisters and the Rainy Day* (1999). (Rev: SLJ 2/00)

1507 Schwarz, Michelle. *The Best Restaurant in the World* (K–2). Illus. by Roland Harvey. 2004, Dutton $15.99 (0-525-47149-9). 32pp. The kid-friendly culinary delights — chocolate castles and so forth — at the Super Sailing Sea Restaurant fill a young boy's imagination. (Rev: BL 5/15/04; SLJ 10/04)

1508 Schwarz, Viviane. *The Adventures of a Nose* (PS–3). Illus. by Joel Stewart. 2002, Candlewick $14.99 (0-7636-1674-5). 32pp. Suitably imaginative artwork accompanies this tale of a nose longing to find a place where he fits in. (Rev: BL 3/15/02; HBG 10/02; SLJ 5/02)

1509 Scieszka, Jon. *The Good, the Bad and the Goofy* (2–5). Illus. by Lane Smith. 1992, Viking $14.99 (0-670-84380-6). 70pp. There are many near escapes when Joe, Fred, and Sam are taken back in time to 1868 and the days of the Chisholm Trail. (Rev: SLJ 7/92)

1510 Scruggs, Afi-Odelia. *Jump Rope Magic* (PS–4). Illus. by David Diaz. 2000, Scholastic $16.95 (0-

590-69327-1). 40pp. This picture book incorporates a number of jump rope rhymes into the story of friends who love skipping rope in spite of a neighbor who hates to hear the noise. (Rev: BCCB 6/00; BL 2/1/00; HBG 10/00; SLJ 4/00)

1511 Seibold, J. Otto, and V. L. Walsh. *Penguin Dreams* (K–3). Illus. 1999, Chronicle $13.95 (0-8118-2558-2). 32pp. A penguin dreams of a fabulous flight he would like to take into outer space and through the ocean depths. (Rev: BL 9/15/99; HBG 3/00; SLJ 1/00)

1512 Sendak, Maurice. *Maurice Sendak's Really Rosie* (1–4). Illus. by author. 1975, HarperCollins paper $11.95 (0-06-443138-X). 48pp. A book based on the TV presentation, including seven songs used in the program.

1513 Sendak, Maurice. *Outside Over There* (PS–3). Illus. by author. 1981, HarperCollins paper $8.95 (0-06-443185-1). 40pp. Goblins steal Ira's baby sister and leave another made of ice.

1514 Sendak, Maurice. *Where the Wild Things Are* (K–3). Illus. by author. 1988, HarperCollins LB $16.89 (0-06-025493-9); paper $6.95 (0-06-443178-9). 48pp. The few moments' wild reverie of a small unruly boy who has been sent supperless to his room. Caldecott Medal winner, 1964.

1515 Seuss, Dr. *The 500 Hats of Bartholomew Cubbins* (K–2). Illus. by author. 1989, Random $15.99 (0-394-94484-4). 48pp. What happened when Bartholomew couldn't take his hat off before the king.

1516 Seuss, Dr. *And to Think That I Saw It on Mulberry Street* (K–3). Illus. by author. 1989, Random LB $15.99 (0-394-94494-1). 32pp. A rhyme about what Marco saw on Mulberry Street.

1517 Seuss, Dr. *Bartholomew and the Oobleck* (K–2). Illus. by author. 1949, Random LB $12.99 (0-394-90075-8). What happens when sticky green stuff begins falling instead of snow? Also use: *McElligot's Pool* (1947).

1518 Seuss, Dr. *The Butter Battle Book* (K–2). Illus. by author. 1984, Random LB $14.99 (0-394-96580-9). 48pp. A warning about the nuclear arms race in words and pictures.

1519 Seuss, Dr. *On Beyond Zebra!* (K–2). Illus. by author. 1955, Random LB $16.99 (0-394-90084-7). A nonsense alphabet that begins after Z.

1520 Shannon, Margaret. *The Red Wolf* (PS–3). Illus. by author. 2002, Houghton Mifflin $15.00 (0-618-05544-4). Locked up in her tower, Roseulpin receives a box full of wool for her seventh birthday and knits herself a liberating disguise. (Rev: BCCB 5/02; HBG 10/02; SLJ 5/02)

1521 Shaw-MacKinnon, Margaret. *Tiktala* (1–3). Illus. by Laszlo Gal. 1996, Holiday House $15.95 (0-8234-1221-0). 32pp. In this fantasy, an Inuit girl gains sufficient knowledge and wisdom to become a soapstone carver. (Rev: BL 7/96; HB 7–8/96; SLJ 5/96)

1522 Shields, Carol Diggory. *Colors* (1–3). Illus. by Svjetlan Junakovic. Series: Animagicals. 2000, Handprint $9.95 (1-929766-04-1). 24pp. Poems, riddles, illustrations, and flaps are used imaginative-

ly to present colors. Also use in a similar format: *Music* (2000). (Rev: BL 1/1–15/01; HBG 3/01; SLJ 12/00)

1523 Shields, Carol Diggory. *Food Fight!* (PS–2). Illus. by Doreen Gay-Kassel. 2002, Handprint $15.95 (1-929766-29-7). Pun-filled fun for the contents of the kitchen while the humans are asleep. (Rev: HBG 3/03; SLJ 10/02)

1524 Shields, Carol Diggory. *On the Go* (PS–2). Illus. by Svjetlan Junakovic. Series: Animagicals. 2001, Handprint $9.95 (1-929766-14-9). This tall, narrow book uses rhyming riddles, illustrations, and flaps to tickle young imaginations about animal movements. Also use *Patterns* (2001). (Rev: HBG 10/01; SLJ 8/01)

1525 Shulevitz, Uri. *What Is a Wise Bird Like You Doing in a Silly Tale Like This?* (K–4). Illus. 2000, Farrar $16.00 (0-374-38300-6). 40pp. A delightful picture book that contains three intertwining stories involving an emperor, his twin brother, and a very smart bird named Lou. (Rev: BL 8/00*; HB 9–10/00; HBG 3/01; SLJ 8/00)

1526 Siddals, Mary M. *I'll Play With You* (PS–1). Illus. by David Wisniewski. 2000, Clarion $14.00 (0-395-90373-4). 28pp. Children invite various aspects of the natural world like the sun and clouds to come and play with them. (Rev: BCCB 12/00; BL 10/1/00; HBG 3/01; SLJ 11/00)

1527 Silverman, Erica. *Big Pumpkin* (PS–1). Illus. by S. D. Schindler. 1992, Macmillan $16.00 (0-02-782683-X). 32pp. A witch gets help from several friends, including a ghost, a vampire, and a bat, to pick a huge pumpkin in her garden. (Rev: BL 9/1/92; HB 3–4/93; SLJ 9/92)

1528 Silverman, Erica. *Gittel's Hands* (K–3). Illus. by Deborah N. Lattimore. 1996, Troll $14.95 (0-8167-3798-3). 32pp. A beggar, who is the prophet Elijah in disguise, helps a young girl fashion objects from a silver coin. (Rev: BL 5/15/96; HB 7–8/96; SLJ 6/96)

1529 Sis, Peter. *Ballerina!* (PS–K). Illus. 2001, Greenwillow $14.95 (0-688-17944-4). 24pp. In this fantasy, little Terry acts out her dreams of being the "best ballerina of all." (Rev: BCCB 5/01; BL 4/1/01; HBG 10/01; SLJ 4/01)

1530 Sis, Peter. *Fire Truck* (PS–K). Illus. 1998, Greenwillow $14.95 (0-688-15878-1). 24pp. A young boy becomes so obsessed with fire trucks that he becomes one. Only the lure of pancakes can bring him back to his little-boy body. (Rev: BCCB 1/99; BL 9/15/98; HB 9–10/98; HBG 3/99; SLJ 9/98)

1531 Sis, Peter. *Madlenka* (PS–3). Illus. 2000, Farrar $17.00 (0-374-39969-7). 48pp. When Madlenka finds she has a loose tooth, she wanders through her culturally diverse neighborhood telling everyone about her condition in this, at times surreal, picture book. (Rev: BCCB 10/00; BL 9/1/00; HB 9–10/00; HBG 3/01; SLJ 10/00)

1532 Sis, Peter. *Madlenka's Dog* (PS–2). Illus. 2002, Farrar $17.00 (0-374-34699-2). 40pp. A flap book in which many of Madlenka's friends imagine what her invisible dog looks like. (Rev: BCCB 6/02; BL 4/1/02*; HB 3–4/02*; HBG 10/02; SLJ 4/02*)

1533 Slangerup, Erik Jon. *Dirt Boy* (PS). Illus. by John Manders. 2000, Whitman $15.95 (0-8075-4424-8). 32pp. Fister enjoys playing in the muck with a giant, but when the giant begins to threaten him, Fister runs home for safety and a welcome bath. (Rev: BCCB 5/00; BL 3/1/00; HBG 10/00; SLJ 4/00)

1534 Sloat, Teri. *Farmer Brown Shears His Sheep: A Yarn About Wool* (PS–K). Illus. by Nadine Bernard Westcott. 2000, DK $15.95 (0-7894-2637-4). 24pp. After the sheep have been shorn of their wool, they get so cold that Farmer Brown has to knit each one a sweater. (Rev: BL 10/15/00; HB 9–10/00; HBG 3/01; SLJ 10/00)

1535 Smee, Nicola. *The Tusk Fairy* (PS–K). Illus. by author. 1994, BridgeWater paper $3.95 (0-8167-3312-0). When Lizzie's toy elephant begins to unravel, she places it under her pillow, hoping for a visit from the tusk fairy. (Rev: SLJ 8/94)

1536 Smith, Dana Kessimakis. *A Wild Cowboy* (PS–1). Illus. by Laura Freeman. 2004, Hyperion $14.99 (0-7868-1931-6). 32pp. With a vivid imagination and his little brother as a trusty sidekick, a young boy turns a visit to grandma's house into a cowboy adventure. (Rev: BL 4/1/04; SLJ 5/04)

1537 Smith, Jos. A. *Circus Train* (PS–3). Illus. 2001, Abrams $17.95 (0-8109-4148-1). 38pp. Young Timothy helps a stranded circus train by asking the elephants to fill the railroad cars with air, allowing the train to float to its destination. (Rev: BL 4/1/01; HBG 10/01; SLJ 4/01)

1538 Smith, Lane. *The Happy Hocky Family* (K–4). Illus. by author. 1993, Viking $13.99 (0-670-85206-6). 60pp. A parody on basal readers that features the Hocky family and the flat repetitious writing style that satirizes the dull Dick and Jane readers. (Rev: SLJ 9/93*)

1539 Smith, Lane. *Pinocchio the Boy; or, Incognito in Collidi* (K–3). Illus. 2002, Viking $16.99 (0-670-03585-8). 48pp. What happens after Pinocchio is turned into a real boy is the subject of this inventive picture book. (Rev: BL 8/02; HB 9–10/02; HBG 3/03; SLJ 9/02*)

1540 Smith, Linda. *Mrs. Biddlebox* (PS–2). Illus. by Marla Frazee. 2002, HarperCollins LB $17.89 (0-06-029782-4). 32pp. Mrs. Biddlebox is having a bad day and decides to cook it away, making a cake of the various components — gloom, fog, sky, and so on — and eating the result before happily greeting the night. (Rev: BCCB 1/03; BL 11/15/02; HB 11–12/02; HBG 3/03; SLJ 10/02)

1541 Smith, Stu. *Goldilocks and the Three Martians* (PS–2). Illus. by Michael Garland. 2004, Dutton $15.99 (0-525-46972-9). In search of a planet that's just right, Goldilocks investigates a house on Mars. (Rev: SLJ 8/04)

1542 Sorel, Edward. *Johnny on the Spot* (K–4). Illus. 1998, Simon & Schuster $16.00 (0-689-81293-0). 32pp. When Johnny's ancient radio starts receiving tomorrow's news, he becomes an overnight sensation. (Rev: BL 8/98; HBG 3/99; SLJ 11/98)

1543 Spalding, Andrea. *It's Raining, It's Pouring* (PS–3). Illus. by Leslie Elizabeth Watts. 2001, Orca $15.95 (1-55143-186-6). 32pp. A little girl sets out into the clouds on a thundery day to find the old man mentioned in the song and he rewards her kindness by stopping the storm. (Rev: BL 10/1/01; HBG 10/02; SLJ 9/01)

1544 Spalding, Andrea. *Sarah May and the New Red Dress* (K–3). Illus. by Janet Wilson. 1999, Orca $14.95 (1-55143-117-3). A little girl wants a red dress and with the help of the West Wind, she gets her wish. (Rev: BL 2/1/99; HBG 10/99; SLJ 6/99)

1545 Sperring, Mark. *Find-a-Saurus* (PS–1). Illus. by Alexandra Steele-Morgan. 2003, Scholastic $15.95 (0-439-53162-4). Despite his mother's insistence that all dinosaurs are extinct, Marty is convinced that the creatures are just good at hiding, so he sets off to find one. (Rev: HBG 4/04; SLJ 1/04)

1546 Sperring, Mark. *Wanda's First Day* (K–2). Illus. by Kate Pope. 2004, Scholastic $15.95 (0-439-62773-7). 32pp. On her first day in a new school, Wanda, a youthful witch, finds herself the only pupil of her kind in a classroom full of fairies. (Rev: BL 8/04; SLJ 7/04)

1547 Spinelli, Eileen. *City Angel* (PS–K). Illus. by Kyrsten Brooker. 2005, Dial $16.99 (0-8037-2821-2). 32pp. An urban angel (African American with a white gown and wings) goes about her daily tasks of watching over and caring for the people and animals of a busy city. (Rev: BL 1/1–15/05; SLJ 2/05)

1548 Spinelli, Eileen. *Sophie's Masterpiece: A Spider's Tale* (PS–2). Illus. by Jane Dyer. 2001, Simon & Schuster $16.00 (0-689-80112-2). 32pp. As her last project, an unappreciated spider named Sophie weaves a beautiful baby blanket for a pregnant woman. (Rev: BL 4/15/01*; HB 7–8/01; HBG 10/01; SLJ 5/01)

1549 Stadler, John. *What's So Scary?* (1–3). Illus. by author. 2001, Scholastic $16.95 (0-531-30301-2). The animals portrayed in a book are upset with the illustrator and decide to take over the story themselves in this humorous and unusual picture book. (Rev: HBG 10/01; SLJ 8/01)

1550 Steig, William. *Caleb and Kate* (PS–3). Illus. by author. 1977, Farrar paper $5.95 (0-374-41038-0). 32pp. Because he constantly quarrels with his wife, Caleb is transformed into a dog by a witch.

1551 Steig, William. *Wizzil* (K–4). Illus. by Quentin Blake. 2000, Farrar $16.00 (0-374-38466-5). 32pp. A rollicking story about Wizzil the witch and her revenge for almost being killed by farmer DeWitt Frimp. (Rev: BCCB 10/00; BL 10/1/00*; HB 7–8/00; HBG 3/01; SLJ 8/00)

1552 Stephens, Helen. *Blue Horse* (PS–K). Illus. 2003, Scholastic $15.95 (0-439-43178-6). 32pp. Shy Tilly is new in town and lonely until her stuffed animal, Blue Horse, advises her to befriend a girl in the park. (Rev: BL 3/15/03; HBG 10/03; SLJ 3/03)

1553 Stewart, Sarah. *The Money Tree* (PS). Illus. by David Small. 1991, Farrar $16.00 (0-374-35014-0). 32pp. Miss McGillicuddy's pleasant life is interrupted when a strange tree begins blooming with paper money. (Rev: BCCB 12/91*; BL 10/15/91; HB 1–2/92; SLJ 1/92)

1554 Stewig, John W. *Clever Gretchen* (K–3). Illus. by Patricia Wittmann. 2000, Marshall Cavendish $15.95 (0-7614-5066-1). 32pp. In order to win the bride of his choice, young Hans must promise to obey a goat-footed man after a period of seven years. (Rev: BL 9/15/00; HBG 3/01; SLJ 10/00)

1555 Stockton, Frank R. *The Bee-Man of Orn* (1–3). Illus. by P. J. Lynch. 2004, Candlewick $17.99 (0-7636-2239-7). 48pp. The century-old children's fantasy about an old beekeeper who seeks his true origins is newly illustrated in a large-format picture book. (Rev: BL 2/15/04*; SLJ 3/04)

1556 Stone, Phoebe. *When the Wind Bears Go Dancing* (PS–1). Illus. 1997, Little, Brown $15.95 (0-316-81701-5). 32pp. While the wind makes noises outside, a little girl dreams of dancing with five white bears in the midnight sky. (Rev: BL 1/1–15/98; HBG 3/98; SLJ 1/98)

1557 Strom, Maria Diaz. *Rainbow Joe and Me* (1–3). Illus. 1999, Lee & Low $15.95 (1-880000-93-8). 32pp. In this picture book, using African American characters, a blind musician shows painter Eloise how he creates colors through his music. (Rev: BL 11/15/99; HBG 3/00; SLJ 11/99)

1558 Sturges, Philemon. *Crocky Dilly* (1–4). Illus. by Paige Miglio. 1998, Museum of Fine Arts, Boston $14.95 (0-87846-458-1). 32pp. This story tells how, in ancient Egypt, the crocodile became known as the Queen of the Nile. (Rev: BL 4/1/99; SLJ 5/99)

1559 Sturgis, Alexander. *Dan's Angel: A Detective's Guide to the Language of Paintings* (PS–3). Illus. by Lauren Child. 2003, Kane/Miller $16.95 (1-929132-47-6). Young Dan likes mysteries and is pleased when Fra Angelico's Angel Gabriel steps out of "The Annunciation" and helps him to find the stories hidden within the famous paintings. (Rev: HBG 4/04; SLJ 11/03)

1560 Suen, Anastasia. *Raise the Roof!* (PS–1). Illus. by Elwood H. Smith. 2003, Viking $15.99 (0-670-89282-3). 32pp. A house is constructed despite a dog's "help" in this picture book with cartoon-like, stylized illustrations. (Rev: BCCB 2/03; BL 2/15/03; HB 3–4/03; HBG 10/03; SLJ 2/03)

1561 Sunami, Kitoba. *How the Fisherman Tricked the Genie* (K–2). Illus. by Amiko Hirao. 2002, Simon & Schuster $16.00 (0-689-83399-7). 40pp. A tale within a tale about a fisherman who releases an angry genie from a bottle. (Rev: BL 8/02; HB 9–10/02; HBG 3/03; SLJ 8/02)

1562 Sutherland, Marc. *MacMurtrey's Wall* (1–3). Illus. 2001, Abrams $16.95 (0-8109-4494-4). 28pp. MacMurtrey the giant is accustomed to being the greatest, but discovers he is no match for the sea when he tries to capture it behind a wall. (Rev: BL 11/15/01; HBG 3/02; SLJ 2/02)

1563 Taravant, Jacques. *The Little Wing Giver* (2–4). Trans. by Nina Ignatowicz. Illus. by Peter Sis. 2001, Holt LB $14.95 (0-8050-6412-5). 32pp. A little boy sent to Earth by God distributes wings to any creature who wants them, and in the end gets

a pair of his own, giving God the idea for angels. (Rev: BL 11/15/01; HBG 3/02; SLJ 11/01)

1564 Tavares, Matt. *Zachary's Ball* (K–4). Illus. 2000, Candlewick $15.99 (0-7636-0730-4). 32pp. Young Zachary is magically transported to the pitcher's mound at Boston's Fenway Park, where his next pitch will determine the outcome of an exciting game. (Rev: BCCB 5/00; BL 4/15/00; HBG 10/00; SLJ 8/00)

1565 Taylor, Alastair. *Swollobog* (1–3). Illus. 2001, Houghton Mifflin $15.00 (0-618-04348-9). 32pp. Swollobog, an ugly dog who eats everything, meets her match when she swallows a helium balloon and takes off. (Rev: BL 3/15/01; HBG 10/01)

1566 Tazewell, Charles. *The Littlest Angel* (PS–3). Illus. by Paul Micich. 1991, Ideals $16.95 (0-8249-8516-8). 32pp. A young angel in heaven keeps getting into trouble because there is nothing to do. (Rev: BL 9/15/91; SLJ 10/98)

1567 Teague, Mark. *The Secret Shortcut* (PS–3). Illus. 1996, Scholastic $15.95 (0-590-67714-4). 32pp. Pirates, space aliens, and a plague of frogs are only three of the obstacles that prevent Wendell and Floyd from getting to school on time. (Rev: BL 9/15/96; SLJ 11/96)

1568 Thayer, Jane. *Gus Loves His Happy Home* (PS–2). Illus. by Seymour Fleishman. 1989, Shoe String LB $17.50 (0-208-02249-X). With time on his hands, Gus the Friendly Ghost goes for a ride on the tail of a kite. (Rev: BL 2/15/90; SLJ 2/90)

1569 Thomas, Frances. *One Day, Daddy* (PS). Illus. by Ross Collins. 2001, Hyperion $15.99 (0-7868-0732-6). Little Monster weighs the future — will he be an explorer? — but worries that he won't be able to take his parents with him. (Rev: BCCB 10/01; HBG 3/02; SLJ 9/01)

1570 Thomas, Peggy. *Joshua the Giant Frog* (K–3). Illus. by Cat Bowman Smith. 2005, Pelican $15.95 (1-58980-267-5). A huge green frog turns out to be very useful in this tall tale set on the Erie Canal, as he pulls barges and deepens the canal. (Rev: SLJ 4/05)

1571 Thompson, Richard. *The Follower* (PS–3). Illus. by Martin Springett. 2000, Fitzhenry & Whiteside $15.95 (1-55041-532-8). 32pp. A picture-book poem about a witch who is being followed by a creature that the reader can detect hidden in the illustrations. (Rev: BL 12/15/00; SLJ 12/00)

1572 Tibo, Gilles. *Simon and the Snowflakes* (PS–1). Illus. 1991, Tundra paper $4.95 (0-88776-274-3). 24pp. Young Simon likes to count snowflakes as they come down. (Rev: BL 12/15/88; SLJ 4/89)

1573 Timmers, Leo. *Happy with Me* (K–2). Illus. 2002, Tallfellow/Smallfellow $16.95 (1-931290-08-3). 32pp. After considering the ups and downs of being different animals, a little boy decides he's happy being himself in this colorful picture book. (Rev: BL 7/02)

1574 Tompert, Ann. *Grandfather Tang's Story* (K–3). Illus. by Robert Andrew Parker. 1990, Crown LB $17.99 (0-517-57272-9). 32pp. As a Chinese grandfather tells his granddaughter a tale about two foxes, he arranges Chinese puzzles to form the animals' shapes. (Rev: BCCB 4/90; BL 4/15/90; SLJ 5/90)

1575 Trottier, Maxine. *Dreamstones* (K–3). Illus. by Stella East. 2000, Stoddart $14.95 (0-7737-3191-1). 22pp. Fantasy and reality blend in this story about a boy who is spending the winter in the Far North with his father and is helped by a mysterious stranger when he gets lost. (Rev: BL 7/00; SLJ 8/00)

1576 Tulloch, Shirley. *Who Made Me?* (PS–1). Illus. by Cathie Felstead. 2000, Augsburg $16.99 (0-8066-4045-6). 32pp. Different jungle animals give different answers to a little black girl who asks "Who made me?" And she discovers that all of them are correct. (Rev: BL 4/15/00; HBG 10/00; SLJ 8/00)

1577 Turner, Ann. *Secrets from the Dollhouse* (PS–3). Illus. by Raul Colon. 2000, HarperCollins LB $15.89 (0-06-024567-0). 32pp. This is the story, told in free verse, of a family that inhabits a doll house and how their lives are controlled by the Girl, Boy, and Cat who play with them. (Rev: BL 1/1–15/00*; HBG 10/00; SLJ 2/00)

1578 Tzannes, Robin. *Professor Puffendorf's Secret Potions* (K–4). Illus. by Korky Paul. 1992, Checkerboard $16.95 (1-56288-267-8). 36pp. A scientist's secret potions are used in her absence by her lazy assistant, Slag. (Rev: BL 2/1/93)

1579 Ungerer, Tomi. *Tortoni Tremolo: The Cursed Musician* (K–3). Illus. 1998, Roberts Rinehart $16.95 (1-57098-226-0). 32pp. A fantasy about a musician whose musical notes turn into edible nuggets. (Rev: BL 1/1–15/99; HBG 10/99)

1580 U'Ren, Andrea. *Pugdog* (PS–3). Illus. 2001, Farrar $16.00 (0-374-36149-5). 32pp. When Mike discovers that his dog, Pug, is female he begins treating her differently and that makes Pug miserable. (Rev: BL 3/1/01; HBG 10/01)

1581 Uribe, Veronica. *Buzz, Buzz, Buzz* (PS–1). Trans. by Veronica Uribe and Elisa Amado. Illus. by Gloria Calderon. 2001, Douglas & McIntyre $15.95 (0-88899-430-3). 32pp. A brother and sister disturbed by an annoying mosquito seek help from the animals in the jungle. (Rev: BL 7/01; HBG 10/01; SLJ 8/01)

1582 Vainio, Pirkko. *The Dream House* (K–3). Trans. by J. Alison James. Illus. by author. 1997, North-South LB $15.88 (1-55858-750-0). The land on which Lucas is building his dream house is so small that he must stack the rooms. (Rev: HBG 3/98; SLJ 1/98)

1583 Van Allsburg, Chris. *Bad Day at Riverbend* (K–3). Illus. 1995, Houghton Mifflin $17.95 (0-395-67347-X). 32pp. This book, set in the Old West, is about a strange light that freezes everything that it touches. (Rev: BCCB 9/95; BL 10/15/95; SLJ 10/95)

1584 Van Allsburg, Chris. *Ben's Dream* (2–4). Illus. by author. 1982, Houghton Mifflin $16.95 (0-395-32084-4). 32pp. Ben dreams that he is in a flood and passing the great landmarks of the world.

1585 Van Allsburg, Chris. *Jumanji* (1–4). Illus. by author. 1981, Houghton Mifflin $17.95 (0-395-

30448-2). A board game that two children play brings out a jungle world. Caldecott Medal winner, 1982.

1586 Van Allsburg, Chris. *Just a Dream* (K–3). Illus. 1990, Houghton Mifflin $17.95 (0-395-53308-2). 48pp. Walter, who doesn't recycle his trash, takes a trip into the future and finds the situation bleak. (Rev: BCCB 11/90; BL 10/15/90; HB 1–2/91; SLJ 12/90)

1587 Van Allsburg, Chris. *The Stranger* (K–2). Illus. by author. 1986, Houghton Mifflin $18.00 (0-395-42331-7). 32pp. Farmer Bailey hits a man with his car and brings him home. Autumn is unaccountably delayed until the strange man departs. (Rev: BL 10/1/86; HB 11–12/86; SLJ 11/86)

1588 Van Allsburg, Chris. *The Widow's Broom* (K–2). Illus. 1992, Houghton Mifflin $17.95 (0-395-64051-2). 32pp. In this tale of good and evil, a witch's broom falls from the sky with the witch still on it. (Rev: BCCB 10/92*; BL 9/15/92*; HB 1–2/93; SLJ 11/92*)

1589 Van Allsburg, Chris. *The Wretched Stone* (K–3). Illus. 1991, Houghton Mifflin $17.95 (0-395-53307-4). 32pp. A magical stone that some sailors find turns them into monkeys. (Rev: BCCB 11/91; BL 10/1/91; HB 1–2/92*; SLJ 11/91)

1590 Van Allsburg, Chris. *Zathura: A Space Adventure* (K–3). Illus. 2002, Houghton Mifflin $18.00 (0-618-25396-3). 32pp. Twenty years after the publication of *Jumanji*, this sequel rockets Danny and Walter Budwing off to an exciting adventure on the planet Zathura. (Rev: BL 11/15/02; HB 11–12/02; HBG 3/03; SLJ 11/02)

1591 Van Camp, Richard. *A Man Called Raven* (K–3). Illus. by George Littlechild. 1997, Children's Book Pr. $15.95 (0-89239-144-8). A man appears to two boys who have injured a raven and tells them the story of the terrible consequences that befell a man who did the same thing. (Rev: SLJ 6/97)

1592 Vande Velde, Vivian. *Troll Teacher* (PS–3). Illus. by Mary Jane Auch. 2000, Holiday House $16.95 (0-8234-1503-1). 32pp. Elizabeth and her classmates can't convince anyone that their new teacher, Miss Turtledove, is really a mean old troll. (Rev: BL 11/15/00; HBG 3/01; SLJ 10/00)

1593 Van Dusen, Chris. *Down to the Sea with Mr. Magee* (K–4). Illus. 2000, Chronicle $13.95 (0-8118-2499-3). 32pp. Mr. Magee and his little dog, Dee, are shipwrecked with a playful whale and find themselves on top of a huge spruce tree. (Rev: BCCB 5/00; BL 6/1–15/00; HBG 10/00; SLJ 5/00)

1594 Van Dusen, Chris. *If I Built a Car* (K–2). Illus. 2005, Dutton $15.99 (0-525-47400-5). 32pp. Wonderful parodies of 1950s concepts of the future illustrate a boy's over-the-top plans to redesign the boring family car. (Rev: BL 5/15/05)

1595 Varvasovszky, Laszlo. *Henry in Shadowland* (1–4). Illus. 1990, Godine $17.95 (0-87923-785-6). Henry enters his shadow-box theater world to find the king of Shadowland. (Rev: SLJ 2/91)

1596 Vaughan, Marcia. *Dorobo the Dangerous* (K–2). Illus. by Kazuko Stone. Series: Animal Fair. 1994, Silver Burdett LB $14.95 (0-382-24070-7);

paper $4.95 (0-382-24453-2). This fantasy with a Japanese setting tells how a young girl sets out to find the culprit that is stealing her fish. (Rev: SLJ 1/95)

1597 Vaughan, Richard Lee. *Eagle Boy: A Pacific Northwest Native Tale* (PS–3). Illus. by Lee Christiansen. 2000, Sasquatch $16.95 (1-57061-171-8). 32pp. When Eagle Boy is left behind by his people, the eagles with whom he has shared his fishing catch bring him food. (Rev: BL 1/1–15/01; HBG 10/01; SLJ 12/00)

1598 Vesey, Amanda. *The Princess and the Frog* (K–3). Illus. by author. 1985, Little, Brown $14.95 (0-316-90036-2). 32pp. Unlike the Grimm Brothers' tale, this frog remains a frog even after the princess's kiss. (Rev: BCCB 5/85; HB 3–4/86; SLJ 1/86)

1599 Vigna, Judith. *Boot Weather* (PS–K). Illus. by author. 1989, Whitman LB $14.95 (0-8075-0837-3). 32pp. Kim puts on her boots to play in the snow and imagines all sorts of exciting adventures. (Rev: BCCB 2/89; BL 3/1/89; SLJ 5/89)

1600 Vivian, Bart. *Imagine* (1–3). Illus. 1998, Beyond Words $14.95 (1-885223-72-2). 32pp. This book invites daydreamers to think about what everyday objects could become and what the future might bring — with a little imagination. (Rev: BL 10/1/98; HBG 3/99; SLJ 12/98)

1601 Vulliamy, Clara. *Small* (PS–K). Illus. 2002, Clarion $15.00 (0-618-19459-2). 32pp. When Tom has an overnight visit with his grandmother, he forgets his stuffed mouse, Small, but Small manages to make his way to Granny's. (Rev: BCCB 4/02; BL 4/15/02; HBG 10/02; SLJ 4/02)

1602 Waddell, Martin. *Tom Rabbit* (PS). Illus. by Barbara Firth. 2001, Candlewick $15.99 (0-7636-1089-5). 32pp. When his owner doesn't come to retrieve him, the little stuffed animal named Tom Rabbit is certain he has been abandoned. (Rev: BL 3/1/01; HBG 10/01)

1603 Wagerin, Walter. *Probity Jones and the Fear Not Angel* (PS–2). Illus. by Tim Ladwig. 1996, Augsburg $16.99 (0-8066-2992-4). 32pp. When Probity is too sick to appear in a Christmas pageant, an angel takes her to witness what she is missing. (Rev: BL 12/15/96)

1604 Waldman, Neil. *The Starry Night* (PS–2). Illus. 1999, Boyds Mills $15.95 (1-56397-736-2). 32pp. Bernard takes an artist named Vincent around New York City to find a suitable scene to paint, and in turn, Vincent takes Bernard to the Museum of Modern Art and shows him *Starry Night* before disappearing. Could it have been Vincent van Gogh? (Rev: BCCB 1/00; BL 11/1/99; HBG 3/00; SLJ 10/99)

1605 Walter, Mildred P. *Brother to the Wind* (K–2). Illus. by Leo Dillon and Diane Dillon. 1985, Lothrop LB $15.93 (0-688-03812-3). 32pp. A folk-like tale set in Africa about a boy who wants to fly. (Rev: BCCB 3/85; HB 7–8/85; SLJ 5/85)

1606 Walton, Rick. *Noah's Square Dance* (PS–3). Illus. by Thor Wickstrom. 1995, Lothrop $16.00 (0-688-11186-6). 32pp. Noah acts as caller during a square dance involving the animals on his ark. (Rev: BL 9/1/95; SLJ 10/95)

1607 Ward, Helen. *The Dragon Machine* (2–3). Illus. by Wayne Anderson. 2003, Dutton $15.99 (0-525-47114-6). 32pp. Dragons that are only visible to George dog his footsteps until he decides to fly them home in a flying machine. (Rev: BL 3/15/03; HBG 10/03; SLJ 7/03)

1608 Ward, Helen. *The Tin Forest* (K–3). Illus. by Wayne Anderson. 2001, Dutton $17.99 (0-525-46787-4). 36pp. A lush, colorful garden blooms from a dreary junkyard of tin, thanks to the efforts of one old man. (Rev: BL 9/15/01; HBG 3/02; SLJ 10/01)

1609 Ward, Nick. *Farmer George and the Hungry Guests* (PS–K). Illus. 2001, Pavilion $14.95 (1-86205-436-3). 32pp. Farmer George investigates his missing breakfast ingredients and finds that four hungry foxes have helped themselves. (Rev: BL 4/15/01)

1610 Warner, Sunny. *Madison Finds a Line* (PS–2). Illus. by author. 1999, Houghton Mifflin $15.00 (0-395-88508-6). 32pp. Madison and her cat, Caspar, follow a piece of rope and enter a fantasy land of wonder and adventure. (Rev: HBG 3/00; SLJ 1/00)

1611 Warnes, Tim. *Happy Birthday, Dotty!* (PS–1). Illus. by author. 2003, Tiger Tales $15.95 (1-58925-026-5). Dotty the dog is having a birthday, but her friends are nowhere to be found; after noticing a trail of arrows, she follows them to one gift after another and, finally, to a gathering of friends all ready to celebrate with her. (Rev: SLJ 4/03)

1612 Wayland, April Halprin. *To Rabbittown* (PS–1). Illus. by Robin Spowart. 1989, Scholastic paper $3.95 (0-590-44777-7). 32pp. A poem about a girl and her pet rabbit and their journey. (Rev: BL 2/1/89; SLJ 4/89)

1613 Weatherby, Mark A. *My Dinosaur* (PS–1). Illus. 1997, Scholastic paper $15.95 (0-590-97203-0). 32pp. A little girl travels through the night sky with her dinosaur before returning to bed. (Rev: BCCB 5/97; BL 3/1/97; SLJ 3/97)

1614 Weeks, Sarah. *Angel Face* (PS–1). Illus. by David Diaz. 2002, Simon & Schuster $17.95 (0-689-83302-4). 32pp. When a little boy wanders away, his mother enlists a crow to help find him. (Rev: BL 2/1/02; HBG 10/02; SLJ 3/02)

1615 Weilerstein, Sadie R. *K'tonton's Sukkot Adventure* (PS–3). Illus. by Joe Boddy. 1993, Jewish Publication Soc. $12.95 (0-8276-0502-1). A tiny boy disobeys his father and attends Sukkot services in the synagogue by hiding in a small box. (Rev: SLJ 3/94)

1616 Welling, Peter J. *Andrew McGroundhog and His Shady Shadow* (1–3). Illus. by author. 2001, Pelican $14.95 (1-56554-711-X). Andrew McGroundhog's shadow is cold and wants Andrew to hibernate for the winter. (Rev: HBG 10/01; SLJ 8/01)

1617 Wells, Rosemary. *The Small World of Binky Braverman* (PS–2). Illus. by Richard Egielski. 2003, Viking $15.99 (0-670-03636-6). A now-grown Binky Braverman, attending the funeral of his Aunt Fran, recalls a magical summer visit to her home in

Memphis years earlier. (Rev: BCCB 12/03; BL 10/1/03; HBG 4/04; SLJ 11/03)

1618 Westcott, Nadine Bernard. *The Giant Vegetable Garden* (PS–K). Illus. by author. 1981, Little, Brown $14.95 (0-316-93129-2); paper $4.95 (0-316-93130-6). 32pp. A mayor gets his town's residents to grow large vegetables.

1619 Wheeler, Lisa. *Avalanche Annie: A Not-So-Tall Tale* (K–2). Illus. by Kurt Cyrus. 2003, Harcourt $16.00 (0-15-216735-8). The diminutive Annie Halfpint lassos an avalanche that threatens the residents of Yoohoo Valley in northern Michisota. (Rev: BL 10/15/03; HBG 4/04; SLJ 12/03)

1620 Whelan, Gloria. *The Miracle of Saint Nicholas* (PS–3). Illus. by Judith G. Brown. 1997, Ignatius $14.95 (1-883937-18-3). 32pp. After the end of Communism, a young Russian boy who vows to clean up his local church is helped by a miracle. (Rev: BL 11/1/97; HBG 3/98)

1621 White, Amanda. *Sand Sister* (PS–1). Illus. by Yuyi Morales. 2004, Barefoot $16.99 (1-84148-617-5). 32pp. A lonely little girl draws a figure in the sand that promptly comes to life only to disappear after a happy day together, but the girl's sadness is alleviated by the news that she will soon have a sibling of her own. (Rev: BL 3/15/04; SLJ 10/04)

1622 Whybrow, Ian. *Harry and the Snow King* (PS–K). Illus. by Adrian Reynolds. 1999, Sterling $14.95 (1-899607-85-4). 32pp. After his tiny snow king melts, Harry is comforted when there is a fresh fall of snow and the yard is full of snow kings. (Rev: BL 7/99; SLJ 6/99)

1623 Whybrow, Ian. *Sammy and the Dinosaurs* (PS–2). Illus. by Adrian Reynolds. 1999, Orchard $15.95 (0-531-30207-5). A charming fantasy about a young boy's attachment to his toy dinosaurs and how he accidentally lost and recovered them. (Rev: BCCB 9/99; HB 9–10/99; HBG 3/00; SLJ 9/99)

1624 Whybrow, Ian. *Sammy and the Robots* (PS–1). Illus. by Adrian Reynolds. 2001, Scholastic $15.95 (0-531-30327-6). Sammy's robot is off being mended and when Sammy's grandmother must go into the hospital, Sammy realizes she needs a robot to look after her. (Rev: HBG 10/01; SLJ 7/01)

1625 Whybrow, Ian. *Sissy Button Takes Charge!* (PS–2). Illus. by Olivia Villet. 2002, Scholastic $15.95 (0-439-12870-6). 32pp. Sissy isn't good at cleaning up despite her mother's reminders, but when she goes on an imaginary picnic with her teddy bears she finds the mess they make quite frustrating. (Rev: BL 12/1/02; HBG 3/03; SLJ 12/02)

1626 Wiesner, David. *June 29, 1999* (PS–3). Illus. 1992, Houghton Mifflin $15.95 (0-395-59762-5). 32pp. Holly sends small growing vegetables into space in balloons and reaps a fantastic harvest. (Rev: BCCB 11/92; BL 10/15/92; HB 1–2/93*; SLJ 11/92*)

1627 Wiesner, David. *Sector 7* (K–4). Illus. 1999, Clarion $16.00 (0-395-74656-6). 48pp. In an almost wordless fantasy, a young boy who enjoys drawing is taken to a cloud terminal where clouds are hoping they will be made into new exciting shapes. (Rev:

BCCB 1/00*; BL 9/15/99; HB 9–10/99; HBG 3/00; SLJ 9/99)

1628 Wild, Margaret. *Midnight Babies* (PS–K). Illus. by Ann James. 2001, Clarion $15.00 (0-618-10412-7). 32pp. At night, Baby Brenda slips past sleeping Mom and Dad and heads for the Midnight Cafe where the dancing is about to begin. (Rev: BL 2/15/01*; HBG 10/01)

1629 Wild, Margaret. *The Pocket Dogs* (PS–K). Illus. by Stephen M. King. 2001, Scholastic $15.95 (0-439-23973-7). 32pp. Little dogs Biff and Buff are carried around in the pockets of their master's coat, but Biff slips through a hole in his pocket and finds he is lost in a huge grocery store. (Rev: BCCB 3/01; BL 2/1/01*; HBG 10/01)

1630 Willard, Nancy. *Pish, Posh, Said Hieronymus Bosch* (K–3). Illus. by Leo Dillon and Diane Dillon. 1991, Harcourt $22.00 (0-15-262210-1). 32pp. Willard's fanciful poem introduces readers to the strange world of grotesque creatures created by Hieronymus Bosch. (Rev: BCCB 12/91; BL 11/15/91; SLJ 12/91*) [811]

1631 Willard, Nancy. *The Sorcerer's Apprentice* (1–4). Illus. by Leo Dillon and Diane Dillon. 1993, Scholastic $16.95 (0-590-47329-8). 32pp. Sylvia, the sorcerer's apprentice, is overcome when she is directed to make clothes for the many creatures found in the magician's house. (Rev: BCCB 1/94; BL 11/1/93; SLJ 1/94)

1632 Williams, Arlene. *Dragon Soup* (K–3). Illus. by Sally J. Smith. 1996, H. J. Kramer $15.95 (0-915811-63-4). 32pp. Tonlu visits the Cloud Dragons to get help in avoiding an arranged marriage. (Rev: BL 7/96; SLJ 6/96)

1633 Williams, Linda. *The Little Old Lady Who Was Not Afraid of Anything* (PS–1). Illus. by Megan Lloyd. 1986, HarperCollins LB $15.89 (0-690-04586-7); paper $5.95 (0-06-443183-5). 32pp. The scary tale of a little old woman who comes upon two big shoes in the forest going clomp clomp all by themselves. (Rev: BCCB 10/86; BL 10/1/86; SLJ 1/87)

1634 Willis, Jeanne. *The Boy Who Thought He Was a Teddy Bear* (PS–2). Illus. by Susan Varley. 2002, Peachtree $15.95 (1-56145-270-X). Three bears bring up a little boy as if he were their own. (Rev: HBG 3/03; SLJ 12/02)

1635 Willis, Jeanne. *Do Little Mermaids Wet Their Beds?* (PS–1). Illus. by Penelope Jossen. 2001, Whitman $15.95 (0-8075-1668-6). 32pp. With a little help from a mermaid, 4-year-old Cecelia stops wetting her bed. (Rev: BL 6/1–15/01; HBG 3/02; SLJ 5/01)

1636 Wilson, Gina. *Grandma's Bears* (K–2). Illus. by Paul Howard. 2004, Candlewick $15.99 (0-7636-2518-3). 40pp. With some trepidation, young Nat pays a visit to Grandma's house, which she shares with a number of large — but good-natured — bears. (Rev: BL 2/1/05)

1637 Wilson, Gina. *Ignis* (3–5). Illus. by P. J. Lynch. 2001, Candlewick $16.99 (0-7636-1623-0). 40pp. Ignis the dragon who can't shoot flame tries other lifestyles — as hippo, parrot, and child — before he finally finds his spark atop a volcano. (Rev: BL 12/15/01; HBG 3/02; SLJ 12/01)

1638 Wilson, Sarah. *George Hogglesberry: Grade School Alien* (K–2). Illus. by Chad Cameron. 2002, Tricycle $14.95 (1-58246-063-9). 38pp. George comes from planet Frollop II, and he just can't seem to get things right in second grade. (Rev: HBG 3/03; SLJ 12/02)

1639 Wilson-Max, Ken. *Max's Starry Night* (PS–1). Illus. 2001, Hyperion $14.99 (0-7868-0553-6). 32pp. Max, a little boy, and his friends — an elephant named Blue and a pig named Little Pink — look at the night sky and wish upon a star. (Rev: BL 1/1–15/01; HBG 10/01; SLJ 3/01)

1640 Winch, John. *The Old Man Who Loved to Sing* (PS–3). Illus. 1996, Scholastic paper $5.99 (0-590-22641-X). 40pp. The animals in the valley are unhappy when their neighbor, an old man, stops serenading them. (Rev: BL 4/15/96; HB 7–8/96; SLJ 4/96)

1641 Winch, John. *The Old Woman Who Loved to Read* (PS–1). Illus. 1997, Holiday House $16.95 (0-8234-1281-4); paper $6.95 (0-8234-1348-9). 32pp. An old woman buys a farmhouse in which to retire and read, but she finds unexpected chores awaiting her. (Rev: BL 3/1/97; SLJ 5/97)

1642 Winnick, Karen B. *Barn Sneeze* (PS–1). Illus. 2002, Boyds Mills $15.95 (1-56397-948-9). 32pp. The animals in Sue's barn are sneezing, so Sue brings them some tea — and sneezes too. (Rev: BL 5/15/02; HBG 10/02; SLJ 6/02)

1643 Winthrop, Elizabeth. *A Very Noisy Girl* (PS–K). Illus. by Ellen Weiss. 1991, Holiday House LB $14.95 (0-8234-0858-2). When Elizabeth's mother asks her to be quiet, Elizabeth responds by turning herself into a dog. (Rev: SLJ 5/91)

1644 Wisniewski, David. *Tough Cookie* (K–3). Illus. 1999, Lothrop $16.00 (0-688-15337-2). 32pp. A parody on hard-boiled detective novels, this story involves Tough Cookie, his former girlfriend, Pecan Sandy, and Cookie's old partner, Chips, who has been badly hurt by Fingers. (Rev: BL 11/1/99; HBG 3/00; SLJ 9/99)

1645 Wolff, Ferida. *Seven Loaves of Bread* (K–4). Illus. by Katie Keller. 1993, Morrow LB $15.93 (0-688-11112-2). 32pp. Rose does a poor job when she takes over the bread-baking chores that Milly has to abandon because of illness. (Rev: BL 9/15/93; SLJ 11/93*)

1646 Wolff, Patricia R. *The Toll-Bridge Troll* (PS–2). Illus. by Kimberly B. Root. 1995, Harcourt $15.00 (0-15-277665-6). 24pp. Trigg outwits a troll who demands a toll for crossing the bridge that leads to Trigg's school. (Rev: BL 4/15/95; HB 9–10/95; SLJ 6/95)

1647 Wood, Audrey. *The Bunyans* (K–3). Illus. by David Shannon. 1996, Scholastic $15.95 (0-590-48089-8). 32pp. Meet the rest of the Bunyan family, including two gigantic children. (Rev: BCCB 1/97; BL 9/15/96; SLJ 12/96*)

1648 Wood, Audrey. *Elbert's Bad Word* (PS–1). Illus. by author. 1988, Harcourt $15.00 (0-15-225320-3). 32pp. A bad word flies into Elbert's mouth, which gets him in trouble, so he goes to the local wizard for help. (Rev: BL 10/1/88; HB 1–2/89; SLJ 10/88)

1649 Wood, Audrey. *The Rude Giants* (PS–3). Illus. 1993, Harcourt $13.95 (0-15-269412-9). 32pp. Clever Gerda convinces two dirty, ugly, rude giants to clean up the castle before they eat everybody. (Rev: BCCB 6/93; BL 3/1/93*; SLJ 5/93)

1650 Wood, Audrey. *When the Root Children Wake Up* (2–4). Illus. by Ned Bittinger. 2002, Scholastic $16.95 (0-590-42517-X). 32pp. Elegant artwork complements this superb retelling of an early 20th-century German tale about the seasons. (Rev: BCCB 7–8/02; BL 2/15/02; HBG 10/02; SLJ 5/02)

1651 Wood, Audrey, and Mark Teague. *The Flying Dragon Room* (PS–3). Illus. 1996, Scholastic $14.95 (0-590-48193-2). 32pp. With a set of tools he has been given, young Patrick creates a fantastic home, complete with a friendly dinosaur. (Rev: BL 4/1/96*; SLJ 3/96)

1652 Wood, Audrey, and Don Wood. *Piggies* (PS–K). Illus. by Don Wood. 1991, Harcourt $16.00 (0-15-256341-5). 32pp. Fingers can become piggies in this imaginative book with elaborate artwork. (Rev: BCCB 4/91*; BL 3/1/91*; SLJ 5/91*)

1653 Woodruff, Elvira. *The Wing Shop* (PS–2). Illus. by Stephen Gammell. 1991, Holiday House LB $16.95 (0-8234-0825-6). 32pp. In an effort to get back to the street where he once lived, Matthew tries to fly with a variety of wings. (Rev: BCCB 6/91; BL 3/15/91; HB 5–6/91; SLJ 11/91)

1654 Wormell, Chris. *The Big Ugly Monster and the Little Stone Rabbit* (PS–2). Illus. by author. 2004, Knopf LB $17.99 (0-375-92891-X). When a very ugly and lonely monster dies, the place where he lived bursts into bloom. (Rev: BCCB 9/04; SLJ 9/04)

1655 Yaccarino, Dan. *The Birthday Fish* (PS–K). Illus. 2005, Holt $16.95 (0-8050-7493-7). 32pp. Although she was about to throw away the goldfish she received for her birthday instead of the hoped-for pony, Cynthia decides to keep it when it speaks to her. (Rev: BL 5/15/05)

1656 Yaccarino, Dan. *The Lima Bean Monster* (K–3). Illus. by Adam McCauley. 2001, Walker LB $16.85 (0-8027-8777-0). 32pp. Sammy buries unwanted lima beans in a vacant lot, with monstrous results. (Rev: BL 9/1/01; HBG 3/02; SLJ 9/01)

1657 Yaccarino, Dan. *Zoom! Zoom! Zoom! I'm Off to the Moon* (PS–K). Illus. 1997, Scholastic $15.95 (0-590-95610-8). 32pp. A little boy boards his red rocket for a trip to the moon and back. (Rev: BL 11/15/97; HB 9–10/97; HBG 3/98; SLJ 12/97)

1658 Yen, Clara. *Why Rat Comes First: A Story of the Chinese Zodiac* (PS–1). Illus. by Hideo C. Yoshida. 1991, Children's Book Pr. $14.95 (0-89239-072-7). 32pp. The story of how the 12 years in the Chinese calendar were named after particular animals. (Rev: BL 9/15/91; SLJ 10/91)

1659 Yep, Laurence. *The City of Dragons* (K–3). Illus. by Jean Tseng and Mou-Sien Tseng. 1995, Scholastic $14.95 (0-590-47865-6). 32pp. A boy's very sad face moves dragons to shed tears of pearls. (Rev: BL 11/15/95; SLJ 11/95)

1660 Yorinks, Arthur. *Company's Going* (2–4). Illus. by David Small. 2001, Hyperion $15.99 (0-7868-0415-7). 40pp. In this sequel to *Company's Coming* (2000), the meatball-loving aliens who visited Shirley and Moe on Earth take the elderly couple to their own planet to cater a wedding. (Rev: BCCB 1/02; BL 1/1–15/02; HB 1–2/02*; HBG 3/02; SLJ 2/02)

1661 Yorinks, Arthur. *Louis the Fish* (PS–2). Illus. by Richard Egielski. 1980, Farrar paper $5.95 (0-374-44598-2). 32pp. The story of an unhappy man who is turned into a fish.

1662 Yorinks, Arthur. *Tomatoes from Mars* (1–4). Illus. by Mort Drucker. 1999, HarperCollins $14.95 (0-06-205070-2). Bedlam reigns in Washington when the sky is suddenly filled with saucers containing tomatoes from Mars. (Rev: HBG 3/00; SLJ 1/00)

1663 Ziefert, Harriet. *Squarehead* (PS–2). Illus. by Todd McKie. 2001, Houghton Mifflin $16.00 (0-618-08378-2). Squarehead George is only happy around square shapes until his dreams show him a curving moon and a big, round earth. (Rev: HBG 10/01; SLJ 5/01)

1664 Zimmerman, Andrea, and David Clemesha. *Digger Man* (PS–K). Illus. by authors. 2003, Holt $15.95 (0-8050-6628-4). A little boy fantasizes about using his big yellow digger to create a park where he and his younger brother can play. (Rev: BL 9/1/03; HBG 4/04; SLJ 12/03)

1665 Hughes, Vi. *Aziz the Storyteller* (K–3). Illus. by Stefan Czernecki. 2002, Crocodile $15.95 (1-56656-456-5). Aziz, a lover of storytelling, trades the family's donkey for a special carpet, which proves worthwhile despite his father's ire. (Rev: HBG 10/02; SLJ 11/02)

1666 Heap, Sue. *What Shall We Play?* (K–3). Illus. 2002, Candlewick $13.99 (0-7636-1685-0). 32pp. Lily May, who possesses the ability to fly, finally persuades her friends to join her in a game of playing fairies. (Rev: BCCB 7–8/02; BL 6/1–15/02; HBG 10/02; SLJ 4/02)

IMAGINARY ANIMALS

1667 Ada, Alma F. *Friend Frog* (K–2). Illus. by Lori Lohsteter. 2000, Harcourt $16.00 (0-15-201522-1). Field Mouse is so in awe of Frog's ability to jump, croak, and swim that he wonders if they can ever be friends. (Rev: HBG 10/00; SLJ 5/00)

1668 Adams, Jean Ekman. *Clarence Goes Out West and Meets a Purple Horse* (K–2). Illus. 2000, Rising Moon $15.95 (0-87358-753-7). 32pp. Smoky, a purple horse, introduces a tenderfoot piglet named Clarence to all the fun of line dancing, card playing, and other cowboy pleasures. (Rev: BL 4/1/00; HBG 10/00; SLJ 6/00)

1669 Agee, Jon. *Milo's Hat Trick* (PS–2). Illus. 2001, Hyperion $15.95 (0-7868-0902-7). 32pp. Milo isn't much of a magician until he meets a bear who knows hat tricks. (Rev: BL 7/01; HB 5–6/01*; HBG 10/01; SLJ 5/01*)

1670 Alborough, Jez. *Captain Duck* (PS–1). Illus. by author. 2003, HarperCollins $15.99 (0-06-052123-6). Duck, whose madcap exploits were previously seen in *Fix-It Duck* (2000) and *Duck in the Truck* (2002), is back, this time taking Frog and Sheep for a bumpy ride in Goat's boat. (Rev: HBG 10/03; SLJ 7/03)

1671 Alborough, Jez. *Duck in the Truck* (PS–K). Illus. 2000, HarperCollins $14.95 (0-06-028685-7). 40pp. In this humorous tale, Duck's truck becomes stuck in the muck, and he needs the help of Frog, Sheep, and Goat to become unstuck. (Rev: BL 12/15/99; HBG 10/00)

1672 Alborough, Jez. *Duck's Key, Where Can It Be?* (PS–1). Illus. by author. 2005, Kane/Miller $14.95 (1-929132-72-7). The frog who has Duck's key asks readers not to tell; readers lift flaps to find where frog is hiding. (Rev: SLJ 3/05)

1673 Alborough, Jez. *Fix-It Duck* (PS–K). Illus. 2002, HarperCollins $15.95 (0-06-000699-4). 40pp. A hilarious romp that begins when Duck sets out to fix what he believes is a leaky roof. (Rev: BL 4/1/02; HBG 10/02; SLJ 5/02)

1674 Alborough, Jez. *Hug* (PS–1). Illus. by author. 2000, Candlewick $14.99 (0-7636-1287-1). Bob, a tiny chimp, longs for a hug like he sees other animals getting and finally his mother appears and satisfies his wish. (Rev: HBG 3/01; SLJ 12/00)

1675 Alborough, Jez. *Some Dogs Do* (PS–2). Illus. by author. 2003, Candlewick $15.99 (0-7636-2201-X). In this whimsical tale told in rhyming verse, a puppy named Sid takes flight on his way to school one day. (Rev: HBG 4/04; SLJ 12/03)

1676 Alborough, Jez. *Where's My Teddy?* (PS–1). Illus. 1992, Candlewick $16.99 (1-56402-048-7). 32pp. Eddie loses his teddy bear and retraces his steps in the forest trying to find him. (Rev: BCCB 9/92*; BL 10/1/92; SLJ 8/92)

1677 Alexander, Sue. *There's More . . . Much More* (PS–1). Illus. by Patience Brewster. 1987, Harcourt $12.95 (0-15-200605-2). 32pp. A squirrel helps a little girl to fill a flower basket and understand the beauties of the forest. (Rev: BL 11/15/87; SLJ 12/87)

1678 Alter, Anna. *Estelle and Lucy* (PS–K). Illus. 2001, Greenwillow LB $14.89 (0-688-17883-9). 24pp. Estelle, a kitten, shows her younger sister, Lucy, a mouse, all the things that older children can do that younger ones are forbidden to do. (Rev: BL 4/1/01*; HBG 10/01; SLJ 7/01)

1679 Alter, Anna. *Francine's Day* (PS–K). Illus. by author. 2003, Greenwillow LB $16.89 (0-06-623937-0). Francine the fox is a reluctant student and would rather stay in bed than get up and get ready, but she dutifully goes about her daily schedule, finding moments of enjoyment in spite of herself. (Rev: HBG 4/04; SLJ 9/03)

1680 Anastas, Margaret. *A Hug for You* (PS). Illus. by Susan Winter. 2005, HarperCollins LB $16.89 (0-06-623614-2). A simple story in which a duckling shows the value of hugs. (Rev: SLJ 3/05)

1681 Anaya, Rudolfo A. *Roadrunner's Dance* (K–3). 2000, Hyperion $15.99 (0-7868-0254-5).

32pp. The bully Snake is defeated when Desert Woman creates Roadrunner, who is able to get the best of Snake through his unique dance. (Rev: BCCB 12/00; BL 12/15/00; HBG 3/01; SLJ 9/00)

1682 Anderson, Peggy Perry. *Let's Clean Up!* (PS–2). Illus. 2002, Houghton Mifflin $15.00 (0-618-19602-1). 32pp. Rhyming text tells the story of little frog Joe, who can't resist messing up the room his mother just cleaned. (Rev: BL 3/1/02; HBG 10/02; SLJ 4/02)

1683 Andreae, Giles. *Cock-a-doodle-doo! Barnyard Hullabaloo* (PS). Illus. by David Wotjowycz. 2000, Little Tiger $14.95 (1-888444-75-4). 32pp. Sing-song verses describe the activities of some farmyard animals and the sounds they make. (Rev: BL 3/15/00; HBG 10/00; SLJ 5/00)

1684 Andreae, Giles. *Heaven Is Having You* (PS). Illus. by Vanessa Cabban. 2002, Tiger Tales $14.95 (1-58925-016-8). Grandma Bear sees heaven all around her, especially when Little Bear is with her. (Rev: SLJ 7/02)

1685 Andreae, Giles. *Love Is a Handful of Honey* (PS–1). Illus. by Vanessa Cabban. 1999, Little Tiger $14.95 (1-888444-58-4). 32pp. The daily activities of a little bear, depicted in gentle watercolors, express the joy of childhood and the wonder of love. (Rev: BL 12/1/99; HBG 3/00; SLJ 11/99)

1686 Andreasen, Dan. *A Special Day for Mommy* (PS–1). Illus. 2004, Simon & Schuster $15.95 (0-689-84977-X). 40pp. A piglet tries to make Mother's Day special for her mom but in the process creates a mess that Mom will have to tidy up in the end. (Rev: BL 4/1/04; SLJ 7/04)

1687 Andreasen, Dan. *With a Little Help from Daddy* (PS–K). Illus. by author. 2003, Simon & Schuster $15.95 (0-689-84565-0). A bright blue elephant learns many basic lessons from his father — how to shake hands and how to make a bed, for example. (Rev: HBG 10/03; SLJ 5/03)

1688 Anholt, Laurence. *Chimp and Zee* (PS–2). Illus. by Catherine Anholt. 2001, Penguin Putnam $16.99 (0-8037-2671-6). Chimp and Zee become separated from Mumkey when they hide in a basket of bananas that is resting on top of an elephant, not a rock. (Rev: HBG 3/02; SLJ 10/01)

1689 Appelt, Kathi. *The Alley Cat's Meow* (PS–K). Illus. by Jon Goddell. 2002, Harcourt $16.00 (0-15-201980-4). 32pp. A pair of "hep cats" is depicted in cool verse and flowing acrylics as they meet at the Alley Cat's Meow jazz club, fall in love, and dance their way to fame. (Rev: BL 1/1–15/03; HBG 3/03; SLJ 10/02)

1690 Appelt, Kathi. *Bats Around the Clock* (K–2). Illus. by Melissa Sweet. 2000, HarperCollins LB $15.89 (0-688-16470-6). 32pp. During a 12-hour dance marathon, bats engage in dancing the Shrug, Jitterbug, Twist, and other strenuous jigs. (Rev: BL 5/1/00; HBG 10/00; SLJ 6/00)

1691 Appelt, Kathi. *Oh, My Baby, Little One* (PS–K). Illus. by Jane Dyer. 2000, Harcourt $16.00 (0-15-200041-0). 32pp. When baby bird goes off to school, Mama misses her and begins to worry about

her well-being. (Rev: BL 3/1/00; HBG 10/00; SLJ 4/00)

1692 Apperley, Dawn. *Don't Wake the Baby* (PS–2). Illus. by author. 2001, Bloomsbury $16.95 (0-7475-5003-4). A young squirrel tries unsuccessfully to keep quiet so as not to disturb her sleeping sibling. (Rev: SLJ 12/01)

1693 Apperley, Dawn. *Flip and Flop* (PS–K). Illus. 2001, Scholastic $12.95 (0-439-28892-4). 32pp. Little penguin Flop wants to do everything his big brother Flip does, but must find someone else to play with when big brother goes off with a friend. (Rev: BL 1/1–15/02; HBG 3/02; SLJ 3/02)

1694 Apperley, Dawn. *Hello Little Chicks* (PS). Illus. by author. 2000, David & Charles $3.95 (1-86233-181-2). This board book uses rhymes and watercolor paintings to describe the activities of little chicks. Also use: *Hello Little Ducks, Hello Little Lamb,* and *Hello Little Piglet* (all 2000). (Rev: SLJ 2/01)

1695 Araki, Mie. *The Perfect Tail: A Fred and Lulu Story* (PS–1). Illus. by author. 2004, Chronicle LB $14.95 (0-8118-4266-5). Fred the rabbit, envious of other animals' tails, tries to enhance his own until Lulu the rhinoceros reassures him that his own is just perfect. (Rev: SLJ 9/04)

1696 Archer, Dosh, and Mike Archer. *Looking After Little Ellie* (PS–K). Illus. 2005, Bloomsbury $15.95 (1-58234-971-1). 32pp. Six mice agree to baby-sit a baby elephant and find this more challenging than they had expected, especially when it comes to diaper changing. (Rev: BL 2/15/05; SLJ 4/05)

1697 Ardalan, Hayde. *Milton* (K–3). Illus. by author. 2000, Chronicle $7.95 (0-8118-2762-3). An amusing tale about a cat named Milton who is very impressed with himself and his attributes. (Rev: HBG 10/00; SLJ 5/00)

1698 Armstrong, Alan. *Whittington* (5–8). Illus. by S. D. Schindler. 2005, Random LB $16.99 (0-375-92864-2). 208pp. Happy to have found a place to live, Whittington the cat regales the other barnyard animals with tales of his famous forebears. (Rev: BL 5/15/05)

1699 Arno, Iris Hiskey. *The Secret of the First One Up* (K–2). Illus. by Renee Graef. 2003, NorthWord $15.95 (1-55971-867-6). Young groundhog Lila is the first in her family to awaken after a long winter's sleep and learns about the importance of her shadow. (Rev: SLJ 12/03)

1700 Arnold, Katya. *Duck, Duck, Goose?* (PS–1). Illus. 1997, Holiday House $15.95 (0-8234-1296-2). 32pp. Goose tries in vain to improve her appearance by swapping body parts with other animals. (Rev: BL 7/97; HB 9–10/97; SLJ 9/97)

1701 Arnold, Katya, reteller. *Me Too! Two Small Stories About Small Animals* (PS). Illus. by Katya Arnold. 2000, Holiday House $15.95 (0-8234-1483-3). Two gentle animal stories that are translations from the work of Vladimir Suteev. (Rev: HB 3–4/00; HBG 10/00; SLJ 3/00)

1702 Arnold, Katya. *Meow!* (PS–K). Illus. 1998, Holiday House $16.95 (0-8234-1361-6). 32pp. While searching for the animal who says "meow," a puppy encounters a number of different animals, each of whom produces its own distinctive sound. (Rev: BCCB 7–8/98; BL 4/15/98; HBG 10/98; SLJ 5/98)

1703 Arnold, Marsha Diane. *Prancing, Dancing Lily* (PS–2). Illus. by John Manders. 2004, Dial $16.99 (0-8037-2823-9). Lily the cow may soon be the leader of her herd, but first she sets off on a long journey to gain experience; cartoon illustrations add to the fun. (Rev: SLJ 3/04)

1704 Arnosky, Jim. *Armadillo's Orange* (PS–2). Illus. by author. 2003, Penguin Putnam $15.99 (0-399-23412-8). Armadillo's burrow is clearly marked by a large orange, until the day it's moved by a gust of wind and the solitary young animal must rely on his neighbors to guide him home. (Rev: HBG 10/03; SLJ 7/03)

1705 Arrhenius, Peter. *The Penguin Quartet* (K–3). Illus. by Ingela Peterson. 1998, Carolrhoda $14.95 (1-57505-252-0). Four dapper penguins — soon to be dads — find it boring waiting for their eggs to hatch, so they pack them up and go to New York where they become the popular Penguin Quartet. (Rev: HBG 3/99; SLJ 11/98)

1706 Aruego, Jose, and Ariane Dewey. *Rockabye Crocodile* (PS–1). Illus. by authors. 1988, Morrow paper $4.95 (0-688-12333-3). 32pp. A retelling of a Philippine fable concerning two elderly boars, one kind, one mean, and their treatment from a mother crocodile. (Rev: BL 9/15/88; HB 9–10/88; SLJ 12/88)

1707 Asch, Devin, and Frank Asch. *Baby Duck's New Friend* (PS–K). Illus. 2001, Harcourt $15.00 (0-15-202257-0). 32pp. When Baby Duck wanders away to the seashore, he discovers he can fly and get home by himself. (Rev: BL 3/15/01; HBG 10/01)

1708 Asch, Frank. *Baby Bird's First Nest* (PS–2). Illus. by author. 1999, Harcourt $14.00 (0-15-201726-7). When Baby Bird falls out of her nest, Little Frog helps her back after a series of adventures. (Rev: HBG 10/99; SLJ 6/99)

1709 Asch, Frank. *Just Like Daddy* (PS–1). Illus. by author. 1984, Simon & Schuster paper $5.99 (0-671-66457-3). 32pp. Fatherhood is explained by a bear and his dad in this warm, humorous book. Another Bear story is: *Milk and Cookies* (Parents Magazine Pr. 1982).

1710 Asch, Frank. *Moondance* (PS–K). Illus. 1993, Scholastic $12.95 (0-590-45487-0). 32pp. Bear wants to dance with the moon, but doesn't feel worthy of the honor. (Rev: BL 2/15/93; SLJ 6/93)

1711 Asch, Frank. *Mr. Maxwell's Mouse* (2–4). Illus. by Devin Asch. 2004, Kids Can $15.95 (1-55337-486-X). 32pp. To celebrate a promotion, Mr. Maxwell, a well-dressed and self-important cat, visits his favorite restaurant and unwisely orders raw mouse. (Rev: BL 10/1/04; SLJ 9/04*)

1712 Asch, Frank. *Sand Cake* (K–2). Illus. by author. 1979, Parents LB $5.95 (0-8193-0986-9). 48pp. On the beach, Papa Bear makes a sand cake.

1713 Asch, Frank, and Vladimir Vagin. *Dear Brother* (K–3). Illus. 1992, Scholastic $13.95 (0-590-

43107-2). 32pp. Two mouse brothers read letters from two ancestors that prove how important a brother can be. (Rev: BCCB 2/92; BL 6/15/92; SLJ 4/92)

1714 Asch, Frank, and Vladimir Vagin. *Insects from Outer Space* (PS–2). Illus. by Vladimir Vagin. 1995, Scholastic $14.95 (0-590-45489-7). 32pp. Insects from outer space and their earthling counterparts enjoy each other at the Bug Ball. (Rev: BL 2/1/95; SLJ 4/95)

1715 Ashman, Linda. *Can You Make a Piggy Giggle?* (PS–K). Illus. by Henry Cole. 2002, Dutton $12.99 (0-525-46881-1). 32pp. While trying in vain to make a pig laugh, a boy draws giggles from other farm animals in this funny picture book with cartoon-style illustrations. (Rev: BCCB 4/02; BL 7/02; HBG 10/02; SLJ 6/02)

1716 Asquith, Ros. *Mrs Pig's Night Out* (PS–2). Illus. by Selina Young. 2003, Hodder $17.95 (0-340-81707-0). Mrs. Pig's youngsters take full advantage of Mom's night out despite Mr. Pig's presence. (Rev: BL 5/15/03; SLJ 8/03)

1717 Atkins, Jeannine. *Robin's Home* (PS–1). Illus. by Candace Whitman. 2001, Farrar $16.00 (0-374-36337-4). 32pp. Little Robin is so happy in the nest that he doesn't want to leave it, but in time he learns to fly and the sky becomes his home. (Rev: BL 3/15/01; HBG 10/01)

1718 Auch, Mary Jane. *Bantam of the Opera* (K–3). Illus. 1997, Holiday House LB $16.95 (0-8234-1312-8). 32pp. Luigi, a bantam rooster with a huge voice, gets his chance at the Cosmopolitan Opera Company. (Rev: BL 10/1/97; HBG 3/98; SLJ 10/97*)

1719 Auch, Mary Jane. *Bird Dogs Can't Fly* (PS–1). Illus. 1993, Holiday House LB $15.95 (0-8234-1050-1). 32pp. Blue, a bird dog, nurses an injured goose back to health. (Rev: BL 10/15/93; SLJ 12/93)

1720 Auch, Mary Jane. *Eggs Mark the Spot* (PS–3). Illus. 1996, Holiday House $16.95 (0-8234-1242-3). 32pp. A hen copies onto her eggs some portraits painted by famous artists. (Rev: BL 3/15/96; SLJ 5/96)

1721 Auch, Mary Jane. *Hen Lake* (PS–3). Illus. 1995, Holiday House LB $16.95 (0-8234-1188-5). 32pp. The hen Poulette stages her own ballet and also gets the best of snooty Mr. Peacock. (Rev: BL 8/95; SLJ 10/95)

1722 Auch, Mary Jane. *Peeping Beauty* (PS–3). Illus. 1993, Holiday House LB $16.95 (0-8234-1001-3). 32pp. Poulette the hen decides she wants to be a ballerina. (Rev: BL 3/1/93; SLJ 4/93*)

1723 Auch, Mary Jane. *Poultrygeist* (PS–1). Illus. by Mary Jane Auch and Herm Auch. 2003, Holiday House $16.95 (0-8234-1756-5). Upset by the noise made by rowdy roosters Rudy and Ralph, Clarissa the cow and Sophie the pig dress up as a spooky "poultrygeist." (Rev: HBG 4/04; SLJ 9/03)

1724 Auch, Mary Jane. *Souperchicken* (K–2). Illus. by Herm Auch. 2003, Holiday House $16.95 (0-8234-1704-2). 32pp. Talented hen Henrietta saves her aunts from the "Souper Soup Co." truck on their way to what they think is a free vacation, but is in fact the soup pot. (Rev: BL 3/15/03; HBG 10/03; SLJ 5/03)

1725 Axelrod, Amy. *Pigs in the Pantry: Fun with Math and Cooking* (PS–2). Illus. by Sharon McGinley-Nally. 1997, Simon & Schuster $14.00 (0-689-80665-5). 40pp. The story of Mr. Pig's disastrous cooking spree, with some added math facts about measuring ingredients. (Rev: BCCB 5/97; BL 3/1/97; SLJ 4/97)

1726 Axelrod, Amy. *Pigs on a Blanket* (K–3). Illus. by Sharon McGinley-Nally. 1996, Simon & Schuster paper $14.00 (0-689-80505-5). 32pp. Unforeseen problems cause delays for a pig family that wants to spend a day at the beach. (Rev: BL 5/15/96; SLJ 6/96)

1727 Axelrod, Amy. *Pigs Will Be Pigs* (K–3). Illus. by Sharon McGinley-Nally. 1994, Four Winds paper $14.00 (0-02-765415-X). 40pp. To finance a dinner out, the pig family engages in a money hunt around the house. (Rev: BCCB 2/94; BL 2/15/94; SLJ 5/94*)

1728 Aylesworth, Jim. *Aunt Pitty Patty's Piggy* (PS–K). Illus. by Barbara McClintock. 1999, Scholastic $15.95 (0-590-89987-2). 32pp. A delightful cumulative tale involving Aunt Pitty Patty's efforts to get her pig home and the many animals she asks for help. (Rev: BCCB 12/99; BL 9/15/99*; HB 9–10/99; HBG 3/00; SLJ 10/99)

1729 Baker, Alan. *Little Rabbits' First Farm Book* (PS). Illus. 2001, Kingfisher $11.95 (0-7534-5352-5). 29pp. Four rabbits complete chores on a farm, introducing children to facts about various animals through illustrations, informational sidebars, and games at the end of the book. (Rev: BL 11/15/01; HBG 10/02; SLJ 2/02)

1730 Baker, Keith. *Who Is the Beast?* (K–2). Illus. 1990, Harcourt $14.95 (0-15-296057-0). 32pp. A tiger tries to make the other jungle animals less afraid of him. (Rev: BL 9/1/90; HB 11–12/90; SLJ 11/90)

1731 Baker, Leslie. *You Bad Dog!* (PS–2). Illus. by author. 2003, Dutton $15.99 (0-525-47127-8). Bridget, a gentle Rottweiler, is tired of getting blamed for the mischief of her friend, Lulu the terrier, so she goes to the movies alone, hoping for a little peace and quiet; when Lulu shows up and causes a ruckus, Bridget flees but turns back after deciding that having a good friend is worth the trouble it entails. (Rev: HBG 4/04; SLJ 7/03)

1732 Baker, Liza. *I Love You Because You're You* (K–3). Illus. by David McPhail. 2001, Scholastic $9.95 (0-439-20638-3). 32pp. In rhyming text, a mother fox reassures her child that her love for him will endure through his many moods and feelings. (Rev: BL 1/1–15/02; HBG 3/02; SLJ 11/01)

1733 Bancroft, Catherine, and Hannah C. Gruenberg. *Felix's Hat* (K–3). Illus. by Hannah C. Gruenberg. 1993, Macmillan LB $14.95 (0-02-708325-X). 32pp. Felix Frog cannot be consoled when he loses his favorite possession, an orange hat. (Rev: BL 3/15/93; SLJ 7/93)

1734 Bang, Molly. *Goose* (PS–3). Illus. 1996, Scholastic $10.95 (0-590-89005-0). 40pp. After hatching from her egg, Duckling finds a surrogate family with a group of woodchucks. (Rev: BCCB 12/96; BL 9/15/96*; HB 11–12/96; SLJ 11/96*)

1735 Bang-Campbell, Monika. *Little Rat Rides* (2–4). Illus. by Molly Bang. 2004, Harcourt $15.00 (0-15-204667-4). 48pp. Although she has long dreamed of riding a horse, just as her father once did, Little Rat is consumed by misgivings when the opportunity to ride finally arrives. (Rev: BL 5/1/04; HB 5–6/04; SLJ 5/04)

1736 Banks, Kate. *The Turtle and the Hippopotamus: A Rebus Book* (PS–1). Illus. by Tomek Bogacki. 2002, Farrar $16.50 (0-374-37885-1). 32pp. In this rebus book, a turtle attempts to imitate other animals in his quest to cross a river and avoid a scary-looking hippo. (Rev: BL 8/02; HB 5–6/02; HBG 10/02; SLJ 8/02)

1737 Barbero, Maria. *The Bravest Mouse* (K–1). Trans. from French by Sibylle Kazeroid. Illus. by author. 2002, North-South LB $16.50 (0-7358-1709-X). A little mouse who is embarrassed by his birthmark gains self-confidence when he bests a nasty cat. (Rev: HBG 3/03; SLJ 1/03)

1738 Barnes, Laura T. *Ernest and the Big Itch* (K–3). Illus. by Carol A. Camburn. 2002, Barnesyard $15.95 (0-9674681-2-4). 32pp. Two birds help Ernest, a donkey, find a new place to scratch his itch. (Rev: BL 5/15/02; SLJ 9/02)

1739 Barnes, Laura T. *Teeny Tiny Ernest* (PS–K). Illus. by Carol A. Camburn. 2000, Barnesyard $15.95 (0-9674681-1-6). 32pp. Ernest, a miniature donkey, tries different methods to look taller but the other animals tell him that they never noticed that he was small because beauty comes from within. (Rev: BL 11/15/00; SLJ 3/01)

1740 Baronian, Jean-Baptiste. *Will You Still Love Me?* (PS–2). Illus. by Noris Kern. 2001, Chronicle $15.95 (0-8118-3319-4). Polar bear cub Polo seeks reassurance that his parents still love him in this beautifully illustrated book. (Rev: HBG 3/02; SLJ 11/01)

1741 Barringer, William. *Gregory and Alexander* (K–1). Illus. by Kim LaFave. 2003, Orca $16.95 (1-55143-252-8). An unlikely friendship between a mouse named Gregory and a caterpillar named Al is the focus of this gentle story. (Rev: HBG 10/03; SLJ 9/03)

1742 Barroux. *Where's Mary's Hat?* (PS–1). Illus. by author. 2003, Viking $15.99 (0-670-03601-3). Mary the cow is distraught when she can't find her favorite hat; during her search she finds lots of other animals have interesting headwear. (Rev: HBG 10/03; SLJ 6/03)

1743 Base, Graeme. *Jungle Drums* (PS–2). Illus. 2004, Abrams $18.95 (0-8109-5044-8). 40pp. A diminutive warthog named Ngiri Mdogo makes his mark when he acquires magical drums in this brightly illustrated, oversize book. (Rev: BL 9/1/04; SLJ 10/04)

1744 Bass, Jules. *Herb, the Vegetarian Dragon* (K–3). Illus. by Debbie Harter. 1999, Barefoot LB

$15.95 (1-902283-36-8). Herb, a gentle vegetarian dragon, is wrongfully accused of people-eating and escapes death only with the help of a brave girl. (Rev: SLJ 7/99)

1745 Bassede, Francine. *A Day with the Bellyflops* (PS–2). Illus. by author. 2000, Orchard LB $15.99 (0-531-33242-X). Constant interruptions by her three piglets prevent Mrs. Bellyflop from getting her work done. (Rev: HBG 10/00; SLJ 3/00)

1746 Bate, Lucy. *Little Rabbit's Loose Tooth* (PS–K). Illus. by Diane De Groat. 1975, Crown paper $6.99 (0-517-55122-5). 32pp. Little Rabbit loses her first tooth and makes the most of it in this beguiling story.

1747 Bateman, Teresa. *Fluffy: The Scourge of the Sea* (PS–2). Illus. by Michael Chesworth. 2005, Charlesbridge $14.95 (1-58089-099-7). 32pp. Despite his dandified appearance, poodle Fluffy wins his captors' respect when seized by a pack of canine pirates. (Rev: BL 1/1–15/05; SLJ 3/05)

1748 Bateman, Teresa. *Hunting the Daddyosaurus* (PS–K). Illus. by Benrei Huang. 2002, Whitman $15.95 (0-8075-1433-0). 32pp. A brother and sister dinosaur parade around the house looking for their father and finally find him in his easy chair. (Rev: BL 5/1/02; HBG 10/02; SLJ 3/02)

1749 Bates, Ivan. *All By Myself* (PS–1). Illus. 2000, HarperCollins $14.95 (0-06-028585-0). 32pp. Maya, an elephant, tries to be an independent food gatherer but can't reach the juicy leaves the way her mother can. (Rev: BL 4/1/00; HBG 10/00)

1750 Bauer, Marion Dane. *Frog's Best Friend* (1–2). Illus. by Diane D. Hearn. 2002, Holiday House $14.95 (0-8234-1501-5). 32pp. Frog wants Turtle to be his exclusive best friend but Turtle also wants to be friends with Squirrel, Bird, and Otter. (Rev: BL 5/1/02; HBG 10/02; SLJ 6/02)

1751 Baumgart, Klaus. *Where Are You, Little Green Dragon?* (PS–2). Illus. by author. 1993, Hyperion $12.95 (1-56282-344-2); paper $4.95 (0-7868-1073-4). 32pp. The Little Green Dragon with his friendly fly share many adventures. (Rev: SLJ 8/93)

1752 Beaton, Clare. *How Loud Is a Lion?* (PS). Illus. 2002, Barefoot $14.99 (1-84148-896-8). 24pp. Elegant, stylish animals are introduced in this book for toddlers that asks, "How loud is a lion?" (Rev: BL 4/1/02; HBG 10/02; SLJ 6/02)

1753 Beaumont, Karen. *Duck, Duck, Goose! (A Coyote's on the Loose!)* (PS–1). Illus. by Jose Aruego and Ariane Dewey. 2004, HarperCollins $15.99 (0-06-050802-7). 32pp. Fear of a coyote in their midst (in fact, a dirty bunny) spreads through the farmyard animals like wildfire. (Rev: BL 3/1/04; SLJ 2/04)

1754 Bechtold, Lisze. *Edna's Tale* (PS–2). Illus. 2001, Houghton Mifflin $15.00 (0-618-09164-5). 32pp. Edna's tail is her pride and joy and the cat is mortified when she arrives at a party covered in foliage. (Rev: BL 5/1/01; HBG 10/01; SLJ 6/01)

1755 Beck, Scott. *Pepito the Brave* (PS–1). Illus. by author. 2001, Dutton $12.99 (0-525-46524-3). Other animals teach Pepito, a little red bird, how to hop, swim, run, burrow, and climb before he has the courage to try to fly. (Rev: HBG 10/01; SLJ 2/01)

1756 Bedard, Michael. *Sitting Ducks* (K–4). Illus. 1998, Penguin Putnam $15.99 (0-399-22847-0). 40pp. When a little inhabitant of the Colossal Duck Factory discovers that he and his fellows are being fattened to feed the local alligators, he must sound the alarm and rescue all the ducks. (Rev: BCCB 10/98; BL 12/1/98; HBG 3/99; SLJ 10/98)

1757 Bedford, David. *Big Bears Can!* (K–2). Illus. by Gaby Hansen. 2001, Tiger Tales $14.95 (1-58925-006-0). Big Bear has to babysit his little brother but can't resist his sibling's taunts, with messy results. (Rev: SLJ 8/01)

1758 Bedford, David. *The Copy Crocs* (PS–2). Illus. by Emily Bolam. 2004, Peachtree $15.95 (1-56145-304-8). Crocodile's friends follow him everywhere he goes and copy whatever he does. (Rev: SLJ 3/04)

1759 Bedford, David. *Shaggy Dog and the Terrible Itch* (PS–2). Illus. by Gwyneth Williamson. 2001, Barron's $12.95 (0-7641-5391-9). Poor Shaggy Dog can't reach his back and needs scratching help from friends, and, it turns out, a good bath. (Rev: HBG 3/02; SLJ 1/02)

1760 Bedford, David. *Touch the Sky, My Little Bear* (PS–K). Illus. by Jane Chapman. 2001, Handprint $15.95 (1-929766-20-3). 32pp. A little polar bear wonders what it would be like to be big like his mother. (Rev: BL 4/15/01; HBG 10/01; SLJ 5/01)

1761 Bengamin, Alan. *Curious Critters: A Pop-Up Menagerie* (PS–1). Illus. by David A. Carter. 1998, Simon & Schuster $16.95 (0-689-81586-7). Pull a flap and strange new animals like a kangarooster perform in this interactive book. (Rev: BL 1/1–15/99)

1762 Benjamin, A. H. *It Could Have Been Worse* (PS–K). Illus. by Tim Warnes. 1998, Little Tiger $14.95 (1-888444-26-6). 28pp. After suffering a series of accidents, Mouse thinks he is having an unlucky day, but each misadventure has actually saved him from his natural enemies. (Rev: BL 5/15/98; HBG 10/98)

1763 Berenstain, Stan, and Jan Berenstain. *The Berenstain Bears in the Dark* (PS–2). Illus. by authors. 1982, Random paper $3.25 (0-394-85443-8). 32pp. Brother and Sister Bear in one of a very large series of books.

1764 Bergman, Tamar. *Where Is?* (PS–1). Illus. by Rutu Modan. 2002, Houghton Mifflin $15.00 (0-618-09539-X). 24pp. A young kitten who is left with his grandparents spends the day wondering where his mother has gone. (Rev: BL 12/15/02; HBG 3/03; SLJ 9/02)

1765 Berkes, Marianne. *Marsh Music* (K–3). Illus. by Robert Noreika. 2000, Millbrook LB $21.90 (0-7613-1850-X). 32pp. From dawn to dusk, the world is alive with the sound of frogs making music in this amusing book about marsh life, nature, and song. (Rev: BL 12/1/00; HBG 3/01; SLJ 12/00)

1766 Berkner, Laurie. *Victor Vito and Freddie Vasco: Two Polar Bears on a Mission to Save the Klondike Cafe!* (PS–2). Illus. by Henry Cole. 2004, Scholastic $16.95 (0-439-42914-5). A pair of polar bears from Alaska travel around the United States looking for new dishes to serve at their Klondike Cafe. (Rev: SLJ 3/04)

1767 Berliner, Franz. *Wildebeest* (PS–1). Illus. by Lilian Brogger. 1991, Ideals $13.95 (0-8249-8488-9). 32pp. When a wildebeest changes his nature, he gets a new name — gnu. (Rev: BL 1/15/92)

1768 Best, Cari. *Montezuma's Revenge* (PS–2). Illus. by Diane Palmisciano. 1999, Orchard LB $16.99 (0-531-33198-9). 32pp. To show his owner's family his worth, the dog Montezuma switches places with Wild Bill, a dog from the wrong side of the tracks. (Rev: BL 11/15/99; HBG 3/00; SLJ 11/99)

1769 Bingham, Mindy. *Minou* (1–3). Illus. by Itoko Maeno. 1987, Advocacy $14.95 (0-911655-36-0). 64pp. When Minou loses her home in Paris, a smart cat named Celeste grooms her to become a mouser at Notre Dame. (Rev: BL 9/1/87; SLJ 6–7/87)

1770 Birchall, Mark. *Rabbit's Wooly Sweater* (PS–K). Illus. by author. 2001, Carolrhoda LB $15.95 (1-57505-465-5). When little Rabbit's new sweater is washed, it shrinks to become the perfect size for Mr. Cuddles, the stuffed toy that is Rabbit's best friend. (Rev: HBG 10/01; SLJ 3/01)

1771 Bishop, Gavin. *Stay Awake, Bear!* (PS–1). Illus. by author. 2000, Orchard LB $16.99 (0-531-33249-7). Old Bear and his neighbor decide that hibernation is a waste of time and so decide to stay awake all winter. (Rev: HBG 10/00; SLJ 3/00)

1772 Bjorkman, Steve. *Supersnouts!* (PS–1). Illus. 2004, Holiday House $16.95 (0-8234-1810-3). 32pp. A young pig named Hamlet gets a chance to join the Superhero Pig Patrol in this pun- and action-packed story. (Rev: BL 4/1/04; SLJ 5/04)

1773 Blackaby, Susan. *Rembrandt's Hat* (PS–3). 2002, Houghton Mifflin $15.00 (0-618-11452-1). Rembrandt the bear has lost his hat and tries many inventive substitutes before finding one that suits him. (Rev: BCCB 5/02; BL 4/15/02; HBG 10/02; SLJ 7/02)

1774 Blackstone, Stella. *Bear About Town* (PS). Illus. by Debbie Harter. 2000, Barefoot $13.95 (1-902283-57-0). A bear walks through town and sees new sights and visits new places each day of the week. (Rev: SLJ 7/00)

1775 Blackstone, Stella. *Bear at Home* (PS–K). Illus. by Debbie Harter. 2001, Barefoot $14.99 (1-84148-436-9). Bear and his cat take readers on a tour of Bear's brightly colored house; a floor plan is provided. (Rev: HBG 3/02; SLJ 10/01)

1776 Blackstone, Stella. *Bear in Sunshine* (PS–K). Illus. by Debbie Harter. 2001, Barefoot $14.99 (1-84148-321-4). 24pp. Bear is a cheerful character who makes the best of the weathers. (Rev: BL 5/15/01; HBG 10/01; SLJ 6/01)

1777 Blackstone, Stella. *Bear's Busy Family* (PS–1). Illus. by Debbie Harter. 1999, Barefoot $13.95 (1-902283-90-2). 32pp. This book about members of a young bear's family can be used to introduce the names and relationships in an extended family. (Rev: BL 9/15/99; SLJ 8/99)

1778 Blackstone, Stella. *Cleo in the Snow* (PS). Illus. by Caroline Mockford. 2002, Barefoot $14.99 (1-84148-951-4). A kitten sensibly decides that a warm spot in front of the fire is more fun than sledding. (Rev: HBG 3/03; SLJ 11/02)

1779 Blackstone, Stella. *Cleo on the Move* (K–2). Illus. by Caroline Mockford. Series: Cleo the Cat. 2002, Barefoot $14.99 (1-84148-898-4). Cleo the cat and Caspar the dog are moving to a new house. (Rev: HBG 3/03; SLJ 10/02)

1780 Blackstone, Stella. *There's a Cow in the Cabbage Patch* (PS–1). Illus. by Clare Beaton. 2001, Barefoot $14.99 (1-84148-333-8). 32pp. All the farm animals seem to be in the wrong places until the sound of the dinner bell straightens them out. (Rev: BCCB 4/01; BL 4/15/01; HBG 10/01; SLJ 5/01)

1781 Blackwood, Mary. *Derek the Knitting Dinosaur* (PS–2). Illus. by Kerry Argent. 1990, Carolrhoda LB $15.95 (0-87614-400-8); paper $5.95 (0-87614-540-3). 32pp. This dinosaur prefers to knit woolly socks and sweaters rather than terrorize the neighborhood like his uncivilized siblings. (Rev: BL 7/90; SLJ 7/90)

1782 Blood, Charles L., and Martin Link. *The Goat in the Rug* (K–2). Illus. by Nancy Winslow Parker. 1990, Simon & Schuster paper $5.99 (0-689-71418-1). 40pp. How a Navajo rug is made, from the goat Geraldine's point of view.

1783 Bloom, Becky. *Crackers* (K–2). Illus. by Pascal Biet. 2001, Scholastic $15.95 (0-531-30326-8). Crackers the cat has a good relationship with mice and therefore has trouble finding a job until he finds one that suits him perfectly. (Rev: HBG 10/01; SLJ 8/01)

1784 Bloom, Suzanne. *A Splendid Friend, Indeed* (PS–2). Illus. 2005, Boyds Mills $15.95 (1-59078-286-0). 32pp. Goose is talkative and outgoing, while Bear is quiet and introverted, but somehow the two manage to strike up a lasting friendship. (Rev: BL 2/15/05; SLJ 5/05)

1785 Bodnar, Judit Z. *Tale of a Tail* (PS–2). Illus. by John Sandford. 1998, Lothrop LB $15.93 (0-688-12175-6). 48pp. When Bear asks to share Fox's catch of fresh fish, Fox suggests he catch his own by hanging his tail in the water as bait. The water freezes, encasing Bear's tail in ice, but Bear thinks of an ingenious solution. (Rev: BCCB 11/98; BL 10/1/98*; HBG 3/99; SLJ 11/98)

1786 Boelts, Maribeth. *Big Daddy, Frog Wrestler* (PS–2). Illus. by Benrei Huang. 2000, Whitman $14.95 (0-8075-0717-2). 32pp. Curtis, a frog, is proud that Big Daddy is a championship wrestler, but when his father leaves to fight in a big tournament his son's pride turns to loneliness. (Rev: BL 3/1/00; HBG 10/00; SLJ 3/00)

1787 Boelts, Maribeth. *Dry Days, Wet Nights* (PS–K). Illus. by Kathy Parkinson. 1994, Whitman LB $14.95 (0-8075-1723-2); paper $5.95 (0-8075-1724-0). 32pp. Little Bunny, who is out of diapers during the day, is upset when he wets the bed at night. (Rev: BCCB 4/94; BL 5/1/94; SLJ 4/94)

1788 Boelts, Maribeth. *You're a Brother, Little Bunny!* (PS–K). Illus. by Kathy Parkinson. 2001, Whitman $14.95 (0-8075-9446-6). 32pp. Little Bunny's parents help him to adjust when the arrival of his baby brother doesn't quite meet his expectations. (Rev: BL 12/1/01; HBG 3/02; SLJ 1/02)

1789 Bogacki, Tomek. *Cat and Mouse in the Night* (PS–1). Illus. 1998, Farrar $16.00 (0-374-31190-0). 32pp. Cat and Mouse venture out at night, and their initial fear turns to wonder when a ghostly owl shows them the moon and the stars. (Rev: BL 8/98; HBG 3/99; SLJ 9/98)

1790 Bogacki, Tomek. *The Story of a Blue Bird* (PS–1). Illus. 1998, Farrar $15.00 (0-374-37197-0). 32pp. The story of a young bird who ventures out of the nest alone and learns to fly before returning to tell his brother and sister of his adventure. (Rev: BL 5/1/98; HBG 10/98)

1791 Bond, Felicia. *Tumble Bumble* (PS–K). Illus. 1996, Front Street $13.95 (1-886910-15-4). 32pp. A simple rhyme about the adventures of a bug that goes for a walk. (Rev: BL 11/15/96; SLJ 10/96)

1792 Bond, Michael. *Paddington Bear* (PS–2). Illus. by R. W. Alley. 1998, HarperCollins $12.95 (0-06-027854-4). 32pp. A simple version of the first Paddington story in which the bear meets the Brown family in Paddington Station. (Rev: BL 1/1–15/99; HBG 3/99)

1793 Bond, Michael. *Paddington Bear All Day* (PS). Illus. by R. W. Alley. 1998, HarperCollins $5.95 (0-694-00893-1). 14pp. In this board book for the very young, the reader is introduced to Paddington Bear and his daily schedule — from getting up in the morning to going to bed at night. (Rev: BL 4/1/98)

1794 Bond, Michael. *Paddington Bear Goes to Market* (PS). Illus. by R. W. Alley. 1998, HarperCollins $5.95 (0-694-00891-5). 14pp. In this board book about Paddington Bear, our furry hero visits the local market and buys buns from the bakery for himself and a friend. (Rev: BL 4/1/98)

1795 Bond, Michael. *Paddington Bear in the Garden* (PS–2). Illus. by R. W. Alley. 2002, HarperCollins $12.95 (0-06-029696-8). 32pp. When Paddington finds that a pile of concrete has been placed on his garden plot, he decides to create a rock garden. (Rev: BL 4/15/02; HBG 10/02)

1796 Bonning, Tony. *Another Fine Mess* (PS–2). Illus. by Sally Hobson. 1998, Little Tiger $14.95 (1-888444-43-6). 32pp. Fox unloads a mess of trash into Badger's living room, but it eventually ends up back at Fox's front door. (Rev: BL 11/15/98; HBG 3/99; SLJ 2/99)

1797 Bornstein, Ruth. *Little Gorilla* (PS). Illus. by author. 1986, Houghton Mifflin $15.00 (0-395-28773-1); paper $5.95 (0-89919-421-4). 32pp. Even though Little Gorilla grows into a big gorilla, everyone still loves him.

1798 Bos, Burny. *Alexander the Great* (PS–2). Illus. by Hans De Beer. 2000, North-South LB $15.88 (0-7358-1344-2). 32pp. Alexander, a mouse, disguises himself in a bear costume to fool the mouse-catching house cat, but when he ventures out for food the cat captures him and mistakenly thinks he is one of her kittens. (Rev: BL 12/15/00; HBG 10/01; SLJ 12/00)

1799 Bos, Burny. *Leave It to the Molesons!* (2–4). Trans. by J. Alison James. Illus. by Hans De Beer.

1995, North-South LB $13.88 (1-55858-432-3). 46pp. Six episodes in the life of a mole family as told from the son's point of view. A sequel to *Meet the Molesons* (1994). (Rev: BL 3/1/96; SLJ 3/96)

1800 Bosschaert, Greet. *Teenie Bird and How She Learned to Fly* (PS–1). Illus. 2001, Abrams $12.95 (0-8109-3586-4). 32pp. Teenie Bird is afraid of flying but keeps trying until she is a success. (Rev: BL 3/1/01; HBG 10/01; SLJ 3/01)

1801 Bottner, Barbara. *The Scaredy Cats* (PS–2). Illus. by Victoria Chess. 2003, Simon & Schuster $14.95 (0-689-83786-0). Mr. and Mrs. Scaredy Cat allow their lives to be governed by fear until Baby Scaredy Cat suggests that they may be missing out on some good things as well as the bad. (Rev: HB 3–4/03; HBG 10/03; SLJ 4/03)

1802 Bourgeois, Paulette. *Franklin and the Thunderstorm* (PS–K). Illus. by Brenda Clark. 1998, Kids Can $10.95 (1-55074-403-8). Unlike his animal friend, Franklin Tortoise is afraid of thunderstorms until the wise old owl tells him what causes them. (Rev: HBG 10/98; SLJ 7/98)

1803 Bourgeois, Paulette. *Franklin Goes to the Hospital* (PS–3). Illus. by Brenda Clark. 2000, Kids Can $10.95 (1-55074-732-0). 32pp. Franklin the turtle's shell is cracked during a soccer game and he must go to the hospital for an operation. (Rev: BL 6/1–15/00; HBG 10/00)

1804 Bourgeois, Paulette. *Franklin's Bad Day* (K–2). Illus. by Brenda Clark. 1997, Scholastic paper $4.50 (0-590-69332-8). Franklin the turtle misses his friend Otter so much that he makes a scrapbook to send to her. (Rev: SLJ 5/97)

1805 Bourgeois, Paulette. *Franklin's Classic Treasury* (PS–K). Illus. by Brenda Clark. 1999, Kids Can $15.95 (1-55074-742-8). 128pp. This book contains four previously published books about Franklin the little turtle. (Rev: BL 12/1/99; HBG 3/00)

1806 Bourgeois, Paulette. *Franklin's Classic Treasury, Volume II* (PS–K). Illus. by Brenda Clark. 2000, Kids Can $15.95 (1-55074-813-0). 128pp. A collection of four delightful stories about Franklin the turtle that were originally published separately. (Rev: BL 5/1/00; HBG 10/00)

1807 Bourgeois, Paulette. *Franklin's Friendship Treasury* (PS–K). Illus. by Brenda Clark. 2000, Kids Can $15.95 (1-55074-872-6). 120pp. This is an anthology of four previously published stories about Franklin the turtle including *Franklin Has a Sleepover* (1996), *Franklin's Bad Day* (1996) and *Franklin's Secret Club* (1998). (Rev: BL 12/15/00; HBG 3/01)

1808 Bourgeois, Paulette, and Sharon Jennings. *Franklin's Class Trip* (PS–1). Illus. by Brenda Clark. 1999, Kids Can $10.95 (1-55074-470-4). 32pp. When his class visits a natural history museum, Franklin the turtle is afraid that there will be live dinosaurs. (Rev: BL 3/1/99; HBG 10/99; SLJ 5/99)

1809 Boxall, Ed. *Francis the Scaredy Cat* (PS). Illus. 2002, Candlewick $14.99 (0-7636-1767-9). 32pp. A quiet, carrot-loving cat named Francis conquers his secret fears when he believes he must rescue his friend. (Rev: BL 12/15/02; HBG 3/03; SLJ 9/02)

1810 Bradman, Tony. *A Goodnight Kind of Feeling* (PS–1). Illus. by Clive Scruton. 1998, Holiday House $15.95 (0-8234-1351-9). 32pp. A young cat spends a wonderful day walking in the park, going on an amusement park ride, and having a bath. (Rev: BL 6/1–15/98; HBG 10/98; SLJ 6/98)

1811 Brandenberg, Franz. *Nice New Neighbors* (K–2). Illus. by Aliki. 1990, Scholastic paper $2.75 (0-590-44117-5). 56pp. A family of mouse children generously include their neighbors, who formerly spurned them, when they decide to give a play — The Three Blind Mice.

1812 Braun, Sebastien. *I Love My Daddy* (PS). Illus. by author. 2004, HarperCollins $12.99 (0-06-054311-6). The story of Baby Bear's day and all the things he does with his father. (Rev: SLJ 4/04)

1813 Breese, Gillian, and Tony Langham. *The Amazing Adventures of Teddy Tum Tum* (PS–1). Illus. by Patrick Lowry. 1992, Arcade $11.95 (1-55970-185-4). 32pp. A teddy bear tells the other toys in the playroom about his adventures. (Rev: BL 6/15/92; SLJ 11/92)

1814 Brett, Jan. *Armadillo Rodeo* (PS–2). Illus. 1995, Penguin Putnam $16.99 (0-399-22803-9). 32pp. Nearsighted Bo, an armadillo, has fun when he wanders onto the Curly H Ranch. (Rev: BCCB 10/95; BL 9/15/95; SLJ 10/95)

1815 Brett, Jan. *Berlioz Bear* (K–3). Illus. 1991, Penguin Putnam $14.95 (0-399-22248-0). 32pp. Berlioz, a bear, is mystified by a strange buzz coming from his bass fiddle. (Rev: BL 9/15/91; HB 11–12/91; SLJ 10/91*)

1816 Brett, Jan. *Comet's Nine Lives* (PS–3). Illus. 1996, Penguin Putnam $16.99 (0-399-22931-0). 30pp. Comet, a white cat, has many adventures on Nantucket Island until finding a permanent home in a lighthouse. (Rev: BL 10/15/96; SLJ 12/96)

1817 Brett, Jan. *Fritz and the Beautiful Horses* (K–3). Illus. by author. 1987, Houghton Mifflin $16.00 (0-395-30850-X); paper $5.95 (0-395-45356-9). 32pp. Pony Fritz is ostracized by the other horses and leads a lonely life.

1818 Brett, Jan. *The Hat* (PS–3). Illus. 1997, Penguin Putnam $16.99 (0-399-23101-3). 32pp. When a red wool stocking is blown onto the head of Hedgie the hedgehog, he maintains that it is his new hat. (Rev: BL 9/1/97*; HBG 3/98; SLJ 9/97)

1819 Brett, Jan. *Hedgie's Surprise* (PS–1). Illus. 2000, Penguin Putnam $16.99 (0-399-23477-2). 32pp. Henny wants to have family but a hungry troll named Tomten keeps stealing her eggs until she gets help from Hedgie the hedgehog. (Rev: BCCB 10/00; BL 9/1/00; HBG 3/01; SLJ 9/00)

1820 Brett, Jan. *Town Mouse, Country Mouse* (PS–3). Illus. 1994, Penguin Putnam LB $16.99 (0-399-22622-2). 32pp. A town cat and a country owl, both of whom enjoy mice for dinner, decide to change places. (Rev: BL 9/1/94; SLJ 9/94)

1821 Brewster, Patience. *Rabbit Inn* (PS–K). Illus. 1991, Little, Brown $14.95 (0-316-10747-6). Two rabbits run an inn and their guests help to spruce up the place. (Rev: SLJ 7/91)

1822 Bridges, Margaret Park. *Now What Can I Do?* (PS–K). Illus. by Melissa Sweet. 2001, North-South LB $15.88 (1-58717-047-7). 32pp. A mother raccoon turns her son's chores into pure entertainment. (Rev: BL 7/01; HBG 3/02; SLJ 8/01)

1823 Bridges, Margaret Park. *Will You Take Care of Me?* (PS–2). Illus. by Melissa Sweet. 1998, Morrow LB $15.93 (0-688-15195-7). 32pp. A mother kangaroo assures her baby that she will always care for him, regardless of the circumstances — even if he turns into a star or a field of flowers. (Rev: BL 8/98; HBG 3/99; SLJ 12/98)

1824 Bridwell, Norman. *Clifford's Good Deeds* (PS–1). Illus. by author. 1985, Scholastic paper $3.25 (0-590-44292-9). 32pp. Clifford is a large shaggy dog whose efforts to be helpful result in comic mishaps. Also use: *Clifford Takes a Trip* (1985); *Clifford's Tricks* (1986); *Clifford the Big Red Dog* (1988); *Clifford the Small Red Puppy* (1990); *Clifford at the Circus* (1985); *Clifford Goes to Hollywood* (1986).

1825 Bright, Paul. *Quiet!* (PS–2). Illus. by Guy Parker-Rees. 2003, Scholastic $15.95 (0-439-54512-9). When it's time for Baby Leo's nap, Papa Lion warns the jungle creatures that he will eat any animal who wakes the baby up, but in the ensuing quiet Papa finds himself getting very, very hungry. (Rev: HBG 4/04; SLJ 12/03)

1826 Brimner, Larry. *Cat on Wheels* (PS–3). Illus. by Mary Peterson. 2000, Boyds Mills $15.95 (1-56397-747-8). 32pp. A cat imagines what it would be like to travel through town on an orange skateboard with bright blue wheels. (Rev: BL 12/1/00; HBG 3/01; SLJ 11/00)

1827 Brimner, Larry Dane. *The Littlest Wolf* (PS–2). Illus. by Jose Aruego and Ariane Dewey. 2002, HarperCollins LB $15.89 (0-06-029040-4). His father offers constant comfort as Little Wolf, the runt of the pack, worries that he can't run, jump, roll, and pounce like the other youngsters. (Rev: BCCB 7–8/02; HBG 10/02; SLJ 5/02)

1828 Brock, Betty. *No Flying in the House* (2–4). Illus. by Wallace Tripp. 1970, HarperCollins paper $4.95 (0-06-440130-8). A small dog seeks shelter for herself and her human friends.

1829 Brodzinsky, Anne Braff. *The Mulberry Bird: An Adoption Story*. Rev. ed. (K–4). Illus. by Diane Stanley. 1996, Perspectives $16.00 (0-944934-15-3). 47pp. The process of adoption is the subject of this book about a little bird whose mother can't care for him and so she allows another bird couple to take her place. (Rev: SLJ 11/96)

1830 Brooks, Erik. *The Practically Perfect Pajamas* (1–3). Illus. 2000, Winslow $16.95 (1-890817-22-8). 32pp. Percy the polar bear is made fun of by his peers because of his red, star-studded pajamas, but he is cold and miserable without them. (Rev: BL 5/15/00; HBG 10/00; SLJ 5/00)

1831 Brown, Jo. *Hoppity Skip Little Chick* (PS). Illus. by author. 2005, Tiger Tales $15.95 (1-58925-045-1). Little Chick has fun with the other animals on the farm, but he is thrilled to discover that he has some siblings of his own. (Rev: SLJ 5/05)

1832 Brown, Jo. *Where's My Mommy?* (PS–K). Illus. by author. 2002, Tiger Tales $14.95 (1-58925-019-2). A crocodile baby seeking its mother is humorously persuaded that it's not a monkey, an elephant, a donkey, a tiger, or a zebra. (Rev: SLJ 7/02)

1833 Brown, Ken. *Nellie's Knot* (PS–K). Illus. 1993, Macmillan LB $13.95 (0-02-714930-7). 32pp. In order not to forget something, a young elephant ties a knot in her trunk, but then she can't remember why. (Rev: BL 4/15/93)

1834 Brown, Ken. *The Scarecrow's Hat* (PS–1). Illus. 2001, Peachtree $15.95 (1-56145-240-8). 32pp. Through a series of barters and exchanges a resourceful chicken finally gets what she wants, the scarecrow's hat. (Rev: BL 3/15/01; HBG 10/01)

1835 Brown, Ken. *What's the Time, Grandma Wolf?* (PS–2). Illus. 2001, Peachtree $15.95 (1-56145-250-5). 32pp. All the animals in the woods are wary of Grandma Wolf, but curiosity keeps pulling them closer in this suspenseful story that turns out well in the end. (Rev: BL 7/01; HBG 3/02; SLJ 9/01)

1836 Brown, Marc. *Arthur, It's Only Rock 'n' Roll* (1–3). Illus. 2002, Little, Brown $15.95 (0-316-11854-0). 32pp. Arthur the aardvark's friend Francine starts a band, U Stink, that is invited to play with the successful Backstreet Boys. (Rev: BL 11/1/02; HBG 3/03; SLJ 12/02)

1837 Brown, Marc. *Arthur Lost and Found* (PS–K). Illus. 1998, Little, Brown $15.95 (0-316-10912-6). 32pp. In a balanced tale of fun and caution, Arthur and his pal Buster get lost on the wrong side of town. (Rev: BL 12/1/98; HBG 3/99; SLJ 1/99)

1838 Brown, Marc. *Arthur Meets the President* (PS–3). Illus. 1991, Little, Brown $15.95 (0-316-11265-8). 32pp. Arthur the aardvark writes a prize-winning essay that takes him to Washington to meet the president. Also use: *Arthur's Pet Business* (1990); *Arthur Babysits* (1992). (Rev: BL 5/1/91; HB 7–8/91; SLJ 7/91)

1839 Brown, Marc. *Arthur Writes a Story* (PS–3). Illus. 1996, Little, Brown $15.95 (0-316-10916-9). 32pp. Arthur's classmates embellish the simple story of how he got his puppy. (Rev: BL 9/15/96; SLJ 9/96)

1840 Brown, Marc. *Arthur's Chicken Pox* (PS–3). Illus. by author. Series: Arthur Adventure. 1994, Little, Brown $15.95 (0-316-11384-0). When Arthur gets chicken pox, nobody can console him about his lost trip to the circus. (Rev: HB 5–6/94; SLJ 6/94*)

1841 Brown, Marc. *Arthur's Computer Disaster* (PS–1). Illus. 1997, Little, Brown $15.95 (0-316-11016-7). 32pp. Arthur disobeys his mother and plays with the computer, with unfortunate results. (Rev: BL 9/15/97; HB 11–12/97; HBG 3/98; SLJ 10/97)

1842 Brown, Marc. *Arthur's Family Treasury* (PS–1). Illus. 2000, Little, Brown $18.95 (0-316-12147-9). 96pp. Three previously published books about Arthur the aardvark (*Arthur's Birthday*,

Arthur's Family Vacation, and *Arthur's Baby*) are included in this entertaining anthology. (Rev: BL 6/1–15/00; HBG 10/00)

1843 Brown, Marc. *Arthur's First Sleepover* (K–3). Illus. 1994, Little, Brown $15.95 (0-316-11445-6). 32pp. Arthur Aardvark and his friends are fooled into thinking that space aliens have landed. (Rev: BCCB 11/94; BL 10/1/94; SLJ 10/94)

1844 Brown, Marc. *Arthur's Mystery Envelope* (K–3). 1998, Little, Brown $12.95 (0-316-11546-0); paper $3.95 (0-316-11547-9). 56pp. When Arthur the aardvark is given a letter to deliver to his parents by his principal, he is so fearful of its contents that he wonders if he should conveniently lose it. (Rev: HBG 10/98; SLJ 6/98)

1845 Brown, Marc. *Arthur's New Puppy* (PS–1). Illus. 1993, Little, Brown $15.95 (0-316-11355-7). 32pp. Arthur the aardvark teaches his new puppy a few basic manners. (Rev: BL 12/1/93; SLJ 2/94)

1846 Brown, Marc. *Arthur's Teacher Moves In* (PS–1). Illus. 2000, Little, Brown $15.95 (0-316-11979-2). 32pp. After Arthur invites his teacher to stay at his home until his roof is repaired, the aardvark is labeled teacher's pet by the other students. (Rev: BL 11/1/00; HBG 3/01; SLJ 1/01)

1847 Brown, Marc. *Arthur's Underwear* (PS–1). Illus. 1999, Little, Brown $15.95 (0-316-11012-4). 32pp. Arthur experiences the ultimate embarrassment when his pants rip and reveal his underwear. (Rev: BL 1/1–15/00; HBG 3/00)

1848 Brown, Marc. *D.W. Rides Again!* (PS–3). Illus. 1993, Little, Brown $15.95 (0-316-11356-5). 32pp. D.W. the aardvark learns how to ride a bike from her older brother, Arthur. (Rev: BL 11/1/93; HB 9–10/93; SLJ 12/93)

1849 Brown, Marc. *D.W. the Picky Eater* (PS–2). Illus. 1995, Little, Brown $14.95 (0-316-10957-6). 32pp. The little aardvark, D.W., is a picky eater who gradually discovers what she is missing. (Rev: BL 2/1/95; HB 7–8/95; SLJ 3/95*)

1850 Brown, Marc. *D.W. Thinks Big* (PS–3). Illus. 1993, Little, Brown $15.95 (0-316-11305-0). 24pp. An aardvark feels left out at the wedding where her brother is ring bearer and her cousin is the flower girl. (Rev: BL 3/15/93; HB 5–6/93; SLJ 5/93)

1851 Brown, Marc. *D.W.'s Library Card* (PS–2). Illus. by author. 2001, Little, Brown $14.95 (0-316-11013-2). Arthur the aardvark teaches little sister D.W. how to look after — and enjoy — library books. (Rev: HBG 3/02; SLJ 12/01)

1852 Brown, Marc. *D.W.'s Lost Blankie* (PS). Illus. 1998, Little, Brown $13.95 (0-316-10914-2). 24pp. Arthur's little sister, D.W., is inconsolable when she loses her beloved blankie. Luckily, Mom knows where to find it. (Rev: BL 5/15/98; HBG 10/98; SLJ 5/98)

1853 Brown, Marc, and Laurie Krasny Brown. *The Bionic Bunny Show* (2–3). Illus. by Marc Brown. 1984, Little, Brown $14.95 (0-316-11120-1); paper $5.95 (0-316-10992-4). 32pp. An ordinary rabbit becomes a super TV star thanks to makeup magic.

1854 Brown, Marc, and Stephen Krensky. *Perfect Pigs: An Introduction to Manners* (K–2). Illus. by authors. 1983, Little, Brown paper $6.95 (0-316-11080-9). 32pp. Pig people show the basics of good manners.

1855 Brown, Margaret Wise. *The Runaway Bunny* (PS–K). Illus. by Clement Hurd. 1972, Harper-Collins LB $14.89 (0-06-020766-3); paper $5.95 (0-06-443018-9). 40pp. With nine colorful illustrations, this new edition of an old favorite is a charming story of mother bunny's love for her restless youngster, who keeps trying to escape but is always found.

1856 Brown, Margaret Wise. *Sailor Boy Jig* (PS–K). Illus. by Dan Andreasen. 2002, Simon & Schuster $16.00 (0-689-83348-2). 32pp. A sailor puppy dances the jig, catches his supper, and gets ready for bed in this previously unpublished rhyme. (Rev: BL 3/15/02; HBG 10/02; SLJ 6/02)

1857 Brown, Margaret Wise. *Where Have You Been?* (PS–1). Illus. by Leo Dillon and Diane Dillon. 2004, HarperCollins LB $16.89 (0-06-028379-3). In rhythmic verse with appealing illustrations, an owl asks various animals where they have been. (Rev: BL 5/1/04; HB 5–6/04; SLJ 6/04)

1858 Browne, Anthony. *Piggybook* (K–2). Illus. by author. 1990, Knopf paper $7.99 (0-679-80837-X). 32pp. Mrs. Piggot walks out when her family turns into real pigs and takes her for granted. (Rev: BCCB 10/86; BL 10/1/86; SLJ 10/86)

1859 Bruce, Lisa. *Fran's Friend* (PS–2). Illus. by Rosalind Beardshaw. 2003, Bloomsbury $15.95 (1-58234-777-8). 32pp. Fred the dog tries unsuccessfully to help Fran with her craft project. (Rev: BL 3/1/03; HBG 10/03; SLJ 5/03)

1860 Brug, Sandra Gilbert. *Soccer Beat* (1–3). Illus. by Elisabeth Moseng. 2003, Simon & Schuster $15.95 (0-689-84580-4). 32pp. Two teams of unlikely creatures play a lively soccer match portrayed with eye-catching cartoon illustrations and rhyming narrative. (Rev: BL 9/1/03; HBG 4/04; SLJ 8/03)

1861 Bruss, Deborah. *Book! Book! Book!* (PS–K). Illus. by Tiphanie Beeke. 2001, Scholastic $15.95 (0-439-13525-7). 40pp. A crew of bored animals head to the library and try to make the librarian understand. (Rev: BCCB 2/01; BL 5/15/01; HBG 10/01; SLJ 5/01)

1862 Buehner, Caralyn. *Superdog: The Heart of a Hero* (PS–1). Illus. by Mark Buehner. 2004, Harper-Collins $15.99 (0-06-623620-7). 32pp. Dexter, a determined dachshund, is successful in his bid to become a superhero and even manages to rescue his former nemesis, Cleevis the tomcat. (Rev: BL 4/1/04; SLJ 2/04)

1863 Bunting, Eve. *Can You Do This, Old Badger?* (PS–2). Illus. by LeUyen Pham. 2000, Harcourt $15.00 (0-15-201654-6). 32pp. A conversation between an old badger and a young badger shows the differences in age and knowledge and how one can learn from the other. (Rev: BL 3/15/00; HBG 10/00; SLJ 3/00)

1864 Bunting, Eve. *Little Bear's Little Boat* (PS). Illus. by Nancy Carpenter. 2003, Clarion $12.00 (0-395-97462-3). 32pp. Little Bear is devoted to his boat, but when he grows too big for it he happily turns it over to a smaller bear. (Rev: HBG 10/03; SLJ 8/03)

1865 Bunting, Eve. *The Wedding* (K–2). Illus. by Iza Trapani. 2003, Charlesbridge LB $15.95 (1-58089-040-7). Miss Brindle Cow gives many animals a ride to a wedding, and surprises them on arrival with the announcement that she is the bride. (Rev: HBG 4/04; SLJ 8/03)

1866 Bush, John. *The Fish Who Could Wish* (PS–2). Illus. by Korky Paul. 1991, Kane/Miller $13.95 (0-916291-35-9); paper $6.95 (0-916291-48-0). The adventures of a fish whose wishes always come true. (Rev: SLJ 8/91)

1867 Buzzeo, Toni. *Dawdle Duckling* (PS–2). Illus. by Margaret Spengler. 2003, Dial $15.99 (0-8037-2731-3). A daydreaming duckling tries the patience of his mother in this appealing picture book with lyric text and rich artwork. (Rev: BL 5/15/03; HBG 10/03; SLJ 4/03)

1868 Buzzeo, Toni. *Ready or Not, Dawdle Duckling* (PS–2). Illus. by Margaret Spengler. Series: Dawdle Duckling. 2005, Dial $15.99 (0-8037-2959-6). 32pp. Dawdle, a slightly eccentric duckling, doesn't quite get the point of hide-and-seek. (Rev: BL 3/1/05; SLJ 3/05)

1869 Bynum, Janie. *Altoona Baboona* (PS–K). 1999, Harcourt $13.00 (0-15-201860-3). 32pp. In this enjoyable fantasy, Altoona Baboona is bored on her dune-a and searches for adventure in a hot air balloon-a. (Rev: HBG 10/99; SLJ 4/99)

1870 Bynum, Janie. *Altoona Up North* (PS–3). Illus. by author. 2001, Harcourt $14.00 (0-15-202313-5). Altoona Baboona, Raccoon-a, and Loon-a travel to the cold north for an adventurous visit with Auntie. (Rev: HBG 3/02; SLJ 10/01)

1871 Bynum, Janie. *Pig Enough* (PS–1). Illus. by author. 2003, Harcourt $16.00 (0-15-216582-7). Willy the guinea pig's assertions that he is big enough to be a Pig Scout are met with ridicule until he proves his true worth. (Rev: HBG 4/04; SLJ 9/03)

1872 Cabrera, Jane. *Dog's Day* (PS–K). Illus. 2000, Orchard $12.95 (0-531-30262-8). 32pp. Dog has a fine day swinging on the trees with Monkey and playing games with other animal friends but best of all is having fun with his dad. (Rev: BL 2/1/00; HBG 10/00; SLJ 3/00)

1873 Cabrera, Jane. *The Lonesome Polar Bear* (PS–2). Illus. by author. 2003, Random $13.95 (0-375-82410-3). A polar bear cub searches desperately for a friend; a friendly snow cloud tries to help by providing lots of snow creatures for the cub to enjoy, but these quickly melt away. (Rev: HBG 4/04; SLJ 1/04)

1874 Calhoun, Mary. *Cross-Country Cat* (K–2). Illus. by Erick Ingraham. 1979, Morrow paper $5.95 (0-688-06519-8). 40pp. A Siamese cat named Henry sets out on a cross-country skiing adventure.

1875 Calhoun, Mary. *Hot-Air Henry* (PS–4). Illus. by Erick Ingraham. 1981, Morrow paper $5.95 (0-688-04068-3). 40pp. Siamese cat Henry sneaks into the basket of a hot-air balloon.

1876 Cameron, C. C. *One for Me, One for You* (PS–1). Illus. by Grace Lin. 2003, Millbrook LB $22.90 (0-7613-2807-6). 32pp. A young hippo and alligator learn about sharing and fairness. (Rev: BL 3/15/03; HBG 10/03; SLJ 6/03)

1877 Cannon, Janell. *Crickwing* (1–4). Illus. 2000, Harcourt $16.00 (0-15-201790-9). 48pp. Crickwing, a starving cockroach-artist, joins forces with some plucky leafcutter ants to rout a group of voracious army ants in this gripping story set in a rain forest. (Rev: BL 10/15/00*; HBG 3/01; SLJ 11/00)

1878 Cannon, Janell. *Little Yau* (K–2). Illus. 2002, Harcourt $16.00 (0-15-201791-7). 56pp. Yau, a cat-like "Fuzzhead," searches for a cure to help her ailing friend Trupp in this sequel to *Trupp* (1995). (Rev: BL 9/15/02; HBG 3/03)

1879 Cannon, Janell. *Stellaluna* (PS–3). Illus. 1993, Harcourt $16.00 (0-15-280217-7). 48pp. Stellaluna, a fruit bat, is separated from her mother and raised by birds. (Rev: BL 4/1/93; SLJ 6/93)

1880 Cannon, Janell. *Trupp: A Fuzzhead Tale* (K–2). Illus. 1995, Harcourt $15.00 (0-15-200130-1). 48pp. After a narrow escape in the big city, Trupp, a catlike animal, decides to go back to his cave in the cliffs. (Rev: BCCB 5/95; BL 4/15/95; SLJ 7/95)

1881 Cannon, Janell. *Verdi* (K–3). Illus. 1997, Harcourt $16.00 (0-15-201028-9). 48pp. A baby python named Verdi has fun and adventures when he travels alone in the rain forest. (Rev: BCCB 6/97; BL 4/15/97; SLJ 5/97)

1882 Capucilli, Alyssa Satin. *Only My Dad and Me* (PS–1). Illus. by Tiphanie Beeke. 2003, HarperCollins $6.99 (0-694-52584-7). A young bunny and his father find amusing things to do outside during each of the seasons. (Rev: SLJ 5/03)

1883 Capucilli, Alyssa Satin. *What Kind of Kiss?* (PS–1). Illus. by Hiroe Nakata. 2001, HarperCollins $6.95 (0-694-01573-3). 12pp. Different kinds of kisses are introduced in this question-and-answer book about a loving bear family that contains foldouts on each double-page spread. (Rev: BL 4/1/02; SLJ 12/01)

1884 Carle, Eric. *The Grouchy Ladybug* (PS–K). Illus. by author. 1977, HarperCollins $15.00 (0-690-01391-4). 48pp. A grouchy ladybug, who is looking for a fight, challenges every insect and animal she meets regardless of size. Brilliantly illustrated in collage, the pages vary in size with the size of the animal.

1885 Carle, Eric. *The Mixed-Up Chameleon* (PS–2). Illus. by author. 1984, HarperCollins LB $15.89 (0-690-04397-X); paper $6.95 (0-06-443162-2). 32pp. A new edition of the story of a chameleon who finally decides to be himself.

1886 Carle, Eric. *"Slowly, Slowly, Slowly," Said the Sloth* (K–3). Illus. by author. 2002, Philomel $16.99 (0-399-23954-5). A sloth explains to a variety of jungle animals the reasons why he likes to take things easy in this beautifully illustrated book. (Rev: HBG 3/03; SLJ 9/02)

1887 Carle, Eric. *The Very Busy Spider* (PS–K). Illus. by author. 1989, Penguin Putnam $19.99 (0-399-21166-7). 32pp. A spider spins its web in this striking picture book. Also use the story of a crab that outgrows his shell in: *A House for Hermit Crab* (1991, Picture Book). (Rev: BCCB 5/85; BL 6/1/85; SLJ 5/85)

1888 Carle, Eric. *The Very Clumsy Click Beetle* (PS–1). Illus. 1999, Penguin Putnam $21.99 (0-399-23201-X). 32pp. A click beetle learns to use its life-saving device of clicking to turn over when it is on its back, but only in the nick of time. (Rev: BL 10/1/99; HBG 3/00; SLJ 11/99)

1889 Carle, Eric. *The Very Lonely Firefly* (PS–1). Illus. 1995, Penguin Putnam $22.99 (0-399-22774-1). 32pp. A little firefly searches for some of his own kind but is confused by such lights as candles and fireworks. (Rev: BCCB 7–8/95; BL 5/15/95; HB 9–10/95; SLJ 8/95)

1890 Carle, Eric. *The Very Quiet Cricket* (PS–1). Illus. 1990, Penguin Putnam $21.99 (0-399-21885-8). 48pp. A newly hatched cricket has a problem getting his wings to chirp. (Rev: BCCB 11/90; BL 10/1/90; HB 1–2/91; SLJ 12/90)

1891 Carle, Eric, and Kazuo Iwamura. *Where Are You Going? To See My Friend!* (K–2). Illus. 2003, Scholastic $19.95 (0-439-41659-0). 40pp. A dog asks various animals to come and meet his friend in this charming and inventive bilingual English-Japanese picture book. (Rev: BL 1/1–15/03; HB 5–6/03; HBG 10/03; SLJ 3/03)

1892 Carlson, Nancy. *Harriet and the Garden* (PS–1). Illus. by author. 1982, Carolrhoda LB $15.95 (0-87614-184-X). 32pp. Harriet, a childlike dog, has several simple adventures. Others in the series are: *Harriet and the Roller Coaster; Harriet and Walt; Harriet's Recital* (all 1982).

1893 Carlson, Nancy. *Harriet and the Roller Coaster* (PS–2). Illus. 2003, Carolrhoda $15.95 (1-57505-053-6). 32pp. A 20th-anniversary edition of the classic story about Harriet's courage and George's unexpected lack of it. (Rev: BL 1/1–15/04; HBG 4/04)

1894 Carlson, Nancy. *How About a Hug?* (PS–K). Illus. 2001, Viking $15.99 (0-670-03506-8). 32pp. A pig family awards hugs in a variety of circumstances. (Rev: BL 7/01; HBG 3/02; SLJ 12/01)

1895 Carlson, Nancy. *I Like Me!* (PS–K). Illus. by author. 1988, Puffin paper $5.99 (0-14-050819-8). 32pp. An exuberant book that teaches how to appreciate oneself. (Rev: BL 6/15/88; SLJ 9/88)

1896 Carlson, Nancy. *Look Out, Kindergarten, Here I Come! / ¡Preparate Kindergarten! Alla voy!* (PS–3). Trans. by Teresa Mlawer. Illus. 2004, Viking $15.99 (0-670-03673-0). 32pp. A bilingual story about Henry the mouse's ambivalence toward his first day of kindergarten. (Rev: BL 3/1/04; SLJ 9/04)

1897 Carlson, Nancy. *Loudmouth George and the Cornet* (PS–2). Illus. by author. 1983, Carolrhoda LB $15.95 (0-87614-214-5). 32pp. George, a rabbit, gets dismissed from the school band. Others in the series are: *Loudmouth George and the Big Race; Loudmouth George and the Fishing Trip; Loud-*

mouth George and the New Neighbors; Loudmouth George and the Sixth-Grade Bully (all 1983).

1898 Carlson, Nancy. *Smile a Lot!* (PS–2). Illus. 2002, Carolrhoda $15.95 (0-87614-869-0). 32pp. A happy frog greets the challenges of daily life — going to the dentist, spelling tests — with a big smile and a happy attitude. (Rev: BL 9/15/02; HBG 3/03; SLJ 10/02)

1899 Carmichael, Clay. *Lonesome Bear* (PS–K). Illus. 2001, North-South $13.95 (1-55858-967-8). 48pp. Bear can't find his owner, but meets two other lonely animals and they try to comfort each other. (Rev: BL 7/01; HBG 10/01; SLJ 8/01)

1900 Carr, Jan. *Swine Divine* (PS–1). Illus. by Robert Bender. 1999, Holiday House $15.95 (0-8234-1434-5). 32pp. Rosie the pig is honored to be photographed in a bonnet and tutu by Mr. Porkpie, but she would rather be on the farm rolling in the mud and eating her swill. (Rev: BL 3/1/99; HBG 10/99; SLJ 6/99)

1901 Carrick, Carol. *What Happened to Patrick's Dinosaurs?* (K–2). Illus. by Donald Carrick. 1988, Houghton Mifflin $16.00 (0-89919-406-0); paper $5.95 (0-89919-797-3). Patrick explains to his young brother his theory of how dinosaurs disappeared: they left by spaceship. (Rev: HB 8–9/86; SLJ 5/86)

1902 Casad, Mary Brooke. *Bluebonnet at the Marshall Train Depot* (2–4). Illus. by Benjamin Vincent. 1999, Pelican $14.95 (1-56554-311-4). Bluebonnet, an armadillo, visits a museum that was once a train depot and learns something about Texas's railroad history. (Rev: SLJ 3/00)

1903 Casanova, Mary. *One-Dog Canoe* (PS–1). Illus. by Ard Hoyt. 2003, Farrar $16.50 (0-374-35638-6). 32pp. A girl and her dog are crowded out when other animals decide to pile into their canoe. (Rev: BL 2/15/03; HBG 10/03; SLJ 3/03)

1904 Catalano, Dominic. *Mr. Basset Plays* (K–3). Illus. 2003, Boyds Mills $15.95 (1-59078-007-8). 32pp. Reginald E. Basset, a hound of means, realizes that money isn't everything. (Rev: BL 3/1/03; HBG 10/03; SLJ 3/03)

1905 Catalanotto, Peter. *Dylan's Day Out* (PS–2). Illus. 1989, Watts LB $16.99 (0-531-08429-9). 32pp. Dylan, a bored dalmatian, escapes for a day of freedom. (Rev: BL 10/1/89; SLJ 11/89)

1906 Catchpool, Michael. *Where There's a Bear, There's Trouble!* (PS–2). Illus. by Vanessa Cabban. 2002, ME Media $14.95 (1-58925-002-2). 32pp. Geese and mice follow a bouncy bear in search of honey and all goes well until they arrive at a hive full of threatening bees. (Rev: BL 12/1/02)

1907 Cauley, Lorinda Bryan. *The Trouble with Tyrannosaurus Rex* (PS–2). Illus. by author. 1988, Harcourt paper $7.00 (0-15-290881-1). 32pp. The story of how Duckbill and Ankylosaurus scare away Tyrannosaurus Rex, the terror of the forest. (Rev: BL 4/1/88; SLJ 9/88)

1908 Caumartin, Francois. *Now You See Them, Now You Don't* (PS–2). Trans. from French by David Homel. Illus. by author. 1996, Firefly paper $4.95 (1-55209-007-8). 20pp. Whimsical illustrations show animals trying to disguise themselves in different ways to fool Simon the hunter. (Rev: SLJ 1/97)

1909 Cave, Katherine. *Henry's Song* (PS–K). Illus. by Sue Hendra. 2000, Eerdmans $16.00 (0-8028-5198-3). 26pp. When the other animals objects to the quality of Henry's singing voice, the Maker encourages them to sing together in harmony. (Rev: BL 4/15/00; HBG 10/00; SLJ 9/00)

1910 Cazet, Denys. *A Fish in His Pocket* (PS–2). Illus. by author. 1987, Orchard paper $5.95 (0-531-07021-2). 32pp. Russell the bear causes the death of a fish — accidentally — in this story of who is responsible when an accident ends in death. (Rev: BL 8/87; SLJ 12/87)

1911 Cazet, Denys. *Nothing at All* (PS–1). Illus. 1994, Orchard LB $16.99 (0-531-08672-0). 32pp. A humorous picture book about silly farm animals and a scarecrow that has a mouse in his pants. (Rev: BCCB 7–8/94; BL 3/1/94; SLJ 5/94)

1912 Chadwick, Tim. *Cabbage Moon* (PS–1). Illus. by Piers Harper. 1994, Orchard $15.95 (0-531-06827-7). 32pp. A bunny travels to the moon and finds that it is a big, juicy, green cabbage. (Rev: BL 6/1–15/94; SLJ 4/94)

1913 Charles, Faustin, and Michael Terry. *The Selfish Crocodile* (PS–2). Illus. 1999, Little Tiger $14.95 (1-888444-56-8). 32pp. A selfish crocodile won't allow any animals in his river until a little mouse helps him and he realizes the value of friendship. (Rev: BL 6/1–15/99)

1914 Chataway, Carol. *The Perfect Pet* (PS–2). Illus. by Greg Holfeld. 2002, Kids Can $14.95 (1-55337-178-X). Pigs Hamlet, Pygmalion, and Podge are seeking the perfect pet, and find one through a process of elimination. (Rev: HBG 10/02; SLJ 7/02)

1915 Chen, Chih-Yuan. *Guji Guji* (PS–3). Illus. by author. 2004, Kane/Miller $15.95 (1-929132-67-0). Guji Guji, a crocodile raised by a duck, faces difficult decisions when he grows to maturity. (Rev: SLJ 11/04)

1916 Cherry, Lynne. *The Armadillo from Amarillo* (K–3). Illus. 1994, Harcourt $16.00 (0-15-200359-2). 32pp. Sasparillo the armadillo wanders the earth and travels on a space shuttle to find out where he fits into the grand scheme of things. (Rev: BL 3/1/94; SLJ 4/94)

1917 Cherry, Lynne. *How Groundhog's Garden Grew* (PS–3). Illus. 2003, Scholastic $15.95 (0-439-32371-1). 40pp. Squirrel shows Groundhog how to plant a garden, with delicious results come harvest time. (Rev: BL 2/1/03; HBG 10/03; SLJ 2/03)

1918 Cherry, Lynne. *Who's Sick Today?* (PS–K). Illus. by author. 1998, Harcourt paper $6.00 (0-152-01886-7). 24pp. Showing such novelties as a "snake with an ache" or a "small red fox with chicken pox." (Rev: BL 5/15/88; HB 5–6/88; SLJ 7/88)

1919 Child, Lauren. *That Pesky Rat* (K–3). Illus. 2002, Candlewick $15.99 (0-7636-1873-X). 32pp. A rat wants to be a pet — like his spoiled cat and rabbit friends — and finally finds a nearsighted owner who thinks he's a cat. (Rev: BL 9/1/02; HBG 3/03; SLJ 8/02)

1920 Chorao, Kay. *The Cats Kids* (PS–K). Illus. 1998, Holiday House $16.95 (0-8234-1405-1). 48pp. Three simple tales about three sibling kittens present experiences typical of brothers and sisters everywhere. (Rev: BL 11/1/98; HBG 3/99; SLJ 11/98)

1921 Chorao, Kay. *Pig and Crow* (PS–2). Illus. 2000, Holt $16.95 (0-8050-5863-X). 32pp. Pig gets help for his loneliness from Crow, who tries several ways to rid Pig of the blues. (Rev: BL 7/00*; HB 5–6/00; HBG 10/00; SLJ 6/00)

1922 Christelow, Eileen. *Five Little Monkeys Wash the Car* (PS–1). Illus. 2000, Clarion $15.00 (0-395-92566-5). 33pp. Mama, a monkey, gets help from her five little monkeys when she decides to sell the rickety old family car. (Rev: BL 5/1/00; HBG 10/00; SLJ 5/00)

1923 Christelow, Eileen. *Five Little Monkeys with Nothing to Do* (PS–1). Illus. 1996, Clarion $15.00 (0-395-75830-0). 36pp. Five little monkeys prepare for their Grandma Bessie's visit. (Rev: BCCB 12/96; BL 9/1/96; SLJ 11/96)

1924 Christelow, Eileen. *The Great Pig Escape* (PS–1). Illus. 1994, Clarion $14.95 (0-395-66973-1). 32pp. On their way to be sold at market, some pigs escape and disguise themselves as humans. (Rev: BL 9/15/94; SLJ 11/94)

1925 Christelow, Eileen. *The Great Pig Search* (K–3). Illus. 2001, Clarion $15.00 (0-618-04910-X). 32pp. Farmer Bert and his wife Ethel travel to Florida to search in vain for their runaway pigs, who evade them by donning hilarious disguises. (Rev: BL 9/1/01; HB 3–4/02; HBG 10/02; SLJ 9/01*)

1926 Christelow, Eileen. *Jerome Camps Out* (PS–3). Illus. 1998, Clarion $16.00 (0-395-75831-9). 32pp. On a camping trip, alligator Jerome gets even with the camp bully, Buster, who has put Jerome's clothes in a tree. (Rev: BL 4/15/98; HBG 10/98; SLJ 6/98)

1927 Christelow, Eileen. *The Robbery at the Diamond Dog Diner* (PS–1). Illus. by author. 1988, Houghton Mifflin paper $6.95 (0-89919-722-1). 32pp. Some zany goings-on at the Diamond Dog Diner when Glenda Feathers announces that jewel thieves are in town. (Rev: BCCB 10/86; BL 11/1/86; SLJ 2/86)

1928 Church, Caroline Jayne. *One Smart Goose* (PS–2). Illus. 2005, Scholastic $16.95 (0-439-68765-9). 32pp. A clever goose uses camouflage to hide from a fox, earning the respect of his fellow geese. (Rev: BL 3/1/05; SLJ 5/05)

1929 Churchill, Vicki. *Sometimes I Like to Curl Up in a Ball* (PS). Illus. by Charles Fuge. 2001, Sterling $12.95 (1-86233-253-3). Wombat is a lively preschooler who tackles all kinds of activities with gusto. (Rev: SLJ 1/02)

1930 Clement, Gary. *The Great Poochini* (PS–2). Illus. by author. 1999, Groundwood $15.95 (0-88899-331-5). By day he is Jack, an ordinary dog, but at night he becomes the Great Poochini, the famous canine opera singer whose important role is *Dog Giovanni*. (Rev: SLJ 12/99*)

1931 Clements, Andrew. *Big Al and Shrimpy* (PS–2). Illus. by Yoshi. 2002, Simon & Schuster $16.95 (0-689-84247-3). Little Shrimpy gets the chance to reward Big Al's kindness by helping him get his fin free. (Rev: HBG 3/03; SLJ 11/02)

1932 Clements, Andrew. *Circus Family Dog* (PS–2). Illus. by Sue Truesdell. 2000, Clarion $15.00 (0-395-78648-7). 32pp. When a new, active dog joins the circus, old Grumps must learn a new trick to keep up. (Rev: BCCB 7–8/00; BL 6/1–15/00; HBG 10/00; SLJ 8/00)

1933 Cocca-Leffler, Maryann. *Bravery Soup* (PS–1). Illus. 2002, Whitman $15.95 (0-8075-0870-5). 32pp. Carlin the raccoon is afraid of everything until Bear, who is making bravery soup, helps him conquer his fears. (Rev: BL 4/15/02; HBG 10/02; SLJ 3/02)

1934 Coffey, Maria. *A Cat in a Kayak* (K–2). Illus. by Eugenie Fernandes. 1998, Annick LB $16.95 (1-55037-509-1); paper $6.95 (1-55037-508-3). Cat Teelo leaves his house in an effort to escape the noisy animals his young master brings there, but he finds that in the long run home is best. (Rev: SLJ 7/98)

1935 Cole, Babette. *Hurrah for Ethelyn* (K–3). Illus. 1991, Little, Brown $14.95 (0-316-15189-0). 32pp. A rat named Ethelyn bests the school bully, Tina Toerat. (Rev: BL 9/1/91; SLJ 3/92)

1936 Cole, Babette. *Lady Lupin's Book of Etiquette* (PS–3). Illus. by author. 2002, Peachtree $14.95 (1-56145-257-2). Lady Lupin sets about teaching her puppies proper behavior (don't bark with your mouth full, and so forth). (Rev: HBG 10/02; SLJ 7/02)

1937 Collington, Peter. *Clever Cat* (K–3). Illus. by author. 2000, Knopf $15.95 (0-375-80477-3). Tibs is such a clever cat that his owners send him out to find a job so he can become self-sufficient. (Rev: BCCB 10/00; BL 8/00; HB 9–10/00; HBG 3/01; SLJ 8/00*)

1938 Cooper, Helen. *Pumpkin Soup* (PS–2). Illus. 1999, Farrar $15.00 (0-374-36164-9). 32pp. Cat, Squirrel, and Duck change duties during the traditional ritual of making pumpkin soup — with confusing results. (Rev: BL 9/1/99; HBG 3/00; SLJ 9/99)

1939 Coulman, Valerie. *Sink or Swim* (K–2). Illus. by Roge Girard. 2003, Lobster $15.95 (1-894222-54-7). Another adventure for Ralph the cow — this time, with help from his friends, he learns to swim. (Rev: SLJ 5/04)

1940 Cousins, Lucy. *Go, Maisy, Go!* (PS). Illus. by author. 2003, Candlewick $8.99 (0-7636-2118-8). Maisy the mouse tries her hand at transportation in this lift-the-flap board book. (Rev: SLJ 4/03)

1941 Cousins, Lucy. *Jazzy in the Jungle* (PS). Illus. by author. 2002, Candlewick $14.99 (0-7636-1903-5). Flaps and die cuts enhance the excitement as Mama JoJo searches the jungle for her baby, Jazzy. (Rev: SLJ 12/02)

1942 Cousins, Lucy. *Maisy at the Farm* (PS–1). Illus. by author. 1998, Candlewick $12.99 (0-7636-0576-X). In this interactive book with tabs and flaps, a little mouse visits a farm and helps with the chores. (Rev: SLJ 10/98)

1943 Cousins, Lucy. *Maisy Goes Swimming* (PS). Illus. 1990, Little, Brown $13.95 (0-316-15834-8). Maisy, a mouse, goes to a swimming pool in this book that contains many flaps and tabs. Also use: *Maisy Goes to Bed* (1990). (Rev: BCCB 10/90*; SLJ 9/90)

1944 Cousins, Lucy. *Maisy Goes to School* (PS–K). Illus. 1992, Candlewick $13.99 (1-56402-085-1). Maisy, a little mouse, enjoys all the various activities when she attends preschool. Also use: *Maisy Goes to the Playground* (1992). (Rev: SLJ 11/92)

1945 Cousins, Lucy. *Where Are Maisy's Friends?* (PS). Illus. by author. 2000, Candlewick $4.99 (0-7636-1119-0). A flap board book in which the reader is asked to play hide-and-seek with Maisy, a mouse, and her friends by lifting the flaps. Also use: *Where Does Maisy Live?* (2000). (Rev: SLJ 12/00)

1946 Cowley, Joy. *The Mouse Bride* (PS–1). Illus. by David Christiana. 1995, Scholastic $13.95 (0-590-47503-7). 32pp. A tiny mouse sets out to find a husband and after many rejections finds the mouse of her dreams. (Rev: BCCB 11/95; BL 1/1–15/96; SLJ 11/95)

1947 Cox, Judy. *Rabbit Pirates: A Tale of the Spinach Main* (PS–3). Illus. by Emily Arnold McCully. 1999, Harcourt $16.00 (0-15-201832-8). 32pp. Two elderly rabbits run a restaurant in Provence, France, where they remember their past experiences together. (Rev: BL 10/15/99; HBG 3/00; SLJ 10/99)

1948 Cresp, Gael. *The Tale of Gilbert Alexander Pig* (PS–2). Illus. 2000, Barefoot $15.95 (1-84148-215-3). 32pp. A clever little pig who realizes that the wolf could be a serious threat reaches an agreement with him so they can help each other. (Rev: BL 3/15/00; SLJ 8/00)

1949 Crimi, Carolyn. *Tessa's Tip-Tapping Toes* (PS–2). Illus. by Marsha Gray Carrington. 2002, Scholastic $16.95 (0-439-31768-1). 32pp. A dancing mouse and a singing cat decide they can no longer stifle their talents, and soon have the whole household joining in. (Rev: BL 3/1/02; HBG 10/02)

1950 Cronin, Doreen. *Click, Clack, Moo: Cows That Type* (PS–3). Illus. by Betsy Lewin. 2000, Simon & Schuster $15.00 (0-689-83213-3). 32pp. In this humorous tale, barnyard animals go on strike for better working conditions including electric blankets for cold nights. (Rev: BCCB 9/00; BL 4/1/00; HB 3–4/00; HBG 10/00)

1951 Cronin, Doreen. *Diary of a Worm* (PS–1). Illus. by Harry Bliss. 2003, HarperCollins LB $16.89 (0-06-000151-8). Presented in the form of a diary, this amusing title features a young earthworm who muses about the pros and cons of life as a worm. (Rev: HB 11–12/03; HBG 4/04; SLJ 10/03)

1952 Cronin, Doreen. *Duck for President* (K–3). Illus. by Betsy Lewin. 2004, Simon & Schuster $15.95 (0-689-86377-2). Bored with his life, Duck arranges and wins an election to replace Farmer Brown as head of the farm and then winds up running the country; voting problems and Duck's campaign techniques add to the fun for adults. (Rev: SLJ 3/04)

1953 Cronin, Doreen. *Giggle, Giggle, Quack* (PS–1). Illus. by Betsy Lewin. 2002, Simon & Schuster $15.00 (0-689-84506-5). 32pp. A hilarious cartoon story about novice Bob and his attempts to care for some farm animals in spite of the intervention of bossy Duck. (Rev: BCCB 6/02; BL 4/15/02; HB 5–6/02; HBG 10/02; SLJ 6/02)

1954 Crum, Shutta. *Fox and Fluff* (PS–1). Illus. by John Bendall-Brunello. 2002, Whitman $15.95 (0-8075-2544-8). 32pp. A chick with an identity crisis thinks a fox is his papa in this amusing tale for young readers. (Rev: BL 10/15/02; HB 1–2/03; HBG 3/03; SLJ 12/02)

1955 Crume, Marion. *Do You See Mouse?* (PS–2). Illus. by Normand Chartier. 1995, Silver Pr. LB $18.95 (0-382-24683-7); paper $5.95 (0-382-24685-3). Visual clues are used so the reader can enter into the animals' game of hide-and-seek. (Rev: SLJ 7/95)

1956 Crunk, Tony. *Grandpa's Overalls* (PS–1). Illus. by Scott Nash. 2001, Scholastic $15.95 (0-531-30321-7). 32pp. When Grandpa's overalls run away, he is left unable to work; but then Grandma's nightie takes off too, and the whole neighborhood (all dogs) gives chase. (Rev: BCCB 5/01; BL 8/01; HBG 10/01; SLJ 7/01)

1957 *Curious George and the Puppies* (PS–K). Illus. 1998, Houghton Mifflin $12.00 (0-395-91217-2); paper $3.95 (0-395-91215-6). 24pp. This is one of a new series of eight books about the mischievous monkey. Other titles include *Curious George Goes to a Movie, Curious George Makes Pancakes,* and *Curious George's Dream*. (Rev: BL 11/15/98; HBG 3/99)

1958 Currey, Anna. *Tickling Tigers* (PS–K). Illus. 1996, Barron's $12.95 (0-8120-6594-8); paper $5.95 (0-8120-9594-4). 32pp. Hannibal, a little mouse, narrowly escapes capture by several tigers whom he has enraged. (Rev: BL 10/15/96)

1959 Curtiss, A. B. *In the Company of Bears* (K–2). Illus. by Barbara Stone. 1994, Oldcastle LB $18.95 (0-932529-72-0). Humorous illustrations depict polar bears engaging in many human activities. (Rev: SLJ 9/94)

1960 Cushman, Doug. *Mystery at the Club Sandwich* (1–4). Illus. by author. 2004, Clarion $15.00 (0-618-41969-1). 30pp. In this entertaining hard-boiled detective story, elephant sleuth Nick Trunk — who works for peanuts — investigates the disappearance of Maggie Trouble's lucky marbles. (Rev: SLJ 1/05)

1961 Cusimano, Maryann K. *You Are My I Love You* (PS–2). Illus. by Satomi Ichikawa. 2001, Penguin Putnam $15.99 (0-399-23392-X). 32pp. Rhyming text and warm illustrations celebrate the relationship between mother and baby teddy bears during a day's activities. (Rev: BL 5/1/01; HBG 10/01; SLJ 5/01)

1962 Cutler, Jane. *Rose and Riley* (K–2). Illus. by Thomas F. Yezerski. 2005, Farrar $15.00 (0-374-36340-4). 48pp. Little vole Rose tends to expect the worst in all situations, but her friend Riley the groundhog is always there to allay her concerns. (Rev: BCCB 3/05; SLJ 3/05)

1963 Dahl, Roald. *The Enormous Crocodile* (K–3). Illus. by Quentin Blake. 1978, Puffin paper $3.99 (0-140-36556-7). 48pp. Animals band together to save a group of children from becoming a crocodile's lunch.

1964 Dallas-Conte, Juliet. *Cock-a-Moo-Moo* (PS–1). Illus. by Alison Bartlett. 2002, Little, Brown $15.95 (0-316-60505-0). 32pp. In spite of being mocked by other barnyard animals because of the sounds he makes, Rooster is able to warn them of a fox attack by using his voice. (Rev: BCCB 4/02; BL 6/1–15/02; HBG 10/02; SLJ 5/02)

1965 Dans, Peter E. *Perry's Baltimore Adventure: A Bird's-Eye View of Charm City* (K–3). Illus. by Kim Harrell. 2003, Tidewater $11.95 (0-87033-540-5). This beautifully illustrated tale of a peregrine falcon family also introduces readers to Baltimore's major attractions. (Rev: SLJ 8/03)

1966 Daugherty, James. *Andy and the Lion* (1–4). Illus. by author. 1938, Puffin paper $5.99 (0-14-050277-7). 80pp. A popular, modern version of the story of Androcles and the lion.

1967 Davenier, Christine. *Leon and Albertine* (PS–1). Illus. 1998, Orchard $15.95 (0-531-30072-2). 32pp. Leo, a pig, is attracted to Albertine, a chicken who is decidedly not interested. (Rev: BCCB 3/98; BL 2/1/98; HBG 10/98; SLJ 3/98*)

1968 Davies, Gill. *Tiny's Big Wish* (PS–1). Illus. by Rachael O'Neill. 2001, Sterling $12.95 (0-8069-7839-2). In this quiet tale, a little elephant is reassured that he will indeed grow bigger. (Rev: HBG 3/02; SLJ 2/02)

1969 Davies, Gill. *Wilbur Waited* (PS–K). Illus. by Rachael O'Neill. 2001, Sterling $12.95 (0-8069-7843-0). 32pp. A little tiger is jealous of the attention his parents give his new baby sister. (Rev: BL 3/15/02; HBG 3/02)

1970 Davis, Katie. *Party Animals* (PS–2). Illus. by author. 2002, Harcourt $15.00 (0-15-216675-0). A tiny blue ant feels left out of preparations for a festive party. (Rev: HBG 3/03; SLJ 12/02)

1971 Davis, Katie. *Who Hops?* (PS–1). Illus. 1998, Harcourt $13.00 (0-15-201839-5). 36pp. A nonsense book in which a variety of animals perform impossible feats, such as cows hopping like frogs. (Rev: BL 9/15/98; HBG 3/99; SLJ 9/98)

1972 Davol, Marguerite W. *Batwings and the Curtain of Night* (PS–4). Illus. by Mary GrandPré. 1997, Orchard $15.95 (0-531-30005-6). 32pp. In order to get more light, some nocturnal animals decide to pull back the curtain of night in this creation story. (Rev: BCCB 4/97; BL 4/15/97; SLJ 4/97)

1973 Day, Alexandra. *Carl Goes to Daycare* (PS–2). Illus. 1993, Farrar $12.95 (0-374-31093-9). 32pp. In an emergency, Carl the rottweiler has to take care of youngsters at a day care center. (Rev: BCCB 11/93; BL 12/15/93; SLJ 12/93)

1974 Day, Alexandra. *Carl's Afternoon in the Park* (2–6). Illus. 1991, Farrar $12.95 (0-374-31109-9). 32pp. Carl, a rottweiler, is placed in charge of a puppy and a toddler while Mom goes for tea with a friend in the park. (Rev: BCCB 11/91; BL 10/15/91; SLJ 11/91)

1975 Day, Alexandra. *Carl's Christmas* (PS–K). Illus. 1990, Farrar $12.95 (0-374-31114-5). 32pp. On Christmas Eve, Carl, a big black dog, takes the baby he is caring for out to greet the world. (Rev: BCCB 10/90; BL 11/1/90)

1976 Day, Alexandra. *Follow Carl!* (PS–2). Illus. 1998, Farrar $12.95 (0-374-34380-2). 32pp. Carl, the enterprising rottweiler, and a group of children play follow-the-leader. The children soon find themselves rolling in the grass, fetching sticks, and chasing a squirrel. (Rev: BL 8/98; HBG 3/99)

1977 Day, Alexandra. *Frank and Ernest on the Road* (PS–3). Illus. 1994, Scholastic $14.95 (0-590-45048-4). 48pp. Highway slang is introduced as Frank the bear and Ernest the elephant hit the road in a truck. (Rev: BCCB 3/94; BL 12/15/93*; SLJ 2/94*)

1978 Day, Alexandra. *Frank and Ernest Play Ball* (K–4). Illus. 1990, Scholastic $12.95 (0-590-42548-X). 48pp. The intrepid bear and elephant temporarily manage a baseball team. (Rev: BCCB 6/90; BL 3/1/90; SLJ 2/90)

1979 Day, David. *King of the Woods* (K–2). Illus. by Ken Brown. 1993, Four Winds LB $13.95 (0-02-726361-4). A little wren defeats all the stronger animals in the forest and claims as her own the golden apple she has found. (Rev: SLJ 3/94)

1980 Day, Nancy Raines. *Double Those Wheels* (PS–2). Illus. by Steve Haskamp. 2003, Dutton $15.99 (0-525-46853-6). A pizza-delivering, accident-prone monkey progressively increases the size of his delivery vehicle from a unicycle to a train with 64 wheels. (Rev: HBG 4/04; SLJ 8/03)

1981 Deacon, Alexis. *Slow Loris* (PS–2). Illus. 2002, Kane $15.95 (0-916291-27-1). 32pp. During the day Loris the lion is lethargic, but at night he leads a secret life. (Rev: BCCB 5/02; BL 6/1–15/02)

1982 De Beer, Hans. *Leonardo's Dream* (K–3). Trans. by Marisa Miller. 2004, North-South LB $16.50 (0-7358-1927-0). Leonardo is a penguin with a yearning to fly. (Rev: SLJ 2/05)

1983 De Beer, Hans. *Little Polar Bear and the Big Balloon* (K–2). Trans. from German by Rosemary Lanning. Illus. by author. 2002, North-South LB $16.50 (0-7358-1533-X). Little polar bear Lars and a puffin friend take a trip in a brightly colored hot-air balloon. (Rev: HBG 3/03; SLJ 11/02)

1984 De Beer, Hans. *Little Polar Bear Finds a Friend* (PS–2). 1990, North-South $13.95 (1-55858-092-1). 32pp. A clever walrus is able to help Lars, a polar bear, escape captors. (Rev: BL 11/15/90; SLJ 2/91)

1985 De Beer, Hans. *Oh No, Ono!* (PS–2). Trans. from German by Marianne Martens. Illus. by author. 2004, North-South LB $16.50 (0-7358-1938-6). Ono, an irrepressible piglet, has a series of amusing farmyard misadventures. (Rev: SLJ 9/04)

1986 De Brunhoff, Jean. *The Story of Babar, the Little Elephant* (PS). Illus. by author. 1937, Random LB $5.99 (0-394-90575-X). A time-tested reading favorite about the little French elephant. (Rev: HBG 3/03)

1987 De Brunhoff, Laurent. *Babar and the Succotash Bird* (PS–1). Illus. 2000, Abrams $16.95 (0-8109-5700-0). 32pp. Alexander, Babar the elephant's son, encounters a magical bird that squawks "Succotash" and gives him the power of flight. (Rev: BL 12/1/00; HBG 3/01; SLJ 12/00)

1988 De Brunhoff, Laurent. *Babar's Museum of Art* (K–3). Illus. by author. 2003, Abrams $16.95 (0-8109-4597-5). 44pp. Babar and Celeste set up an art museum in Celesteville's abandoned train station and fill it with works of art from their personal collection — which boasts pachyderm versions of many classics. (Rev: HBG 4/04; SLJ 11/03)

1989 Degen, Bruce. *Daddy Is a Doodlebug* (PS–1). Illus. 2000, HarperCollins LB $15.89 (0-06-028416-1). 40pp. A little bug and his dad spend a fine day together. (Rev: BL 6/1–15/00; HBG 10/00; SLJ 4/00)

1990 Degen, Bruce. *Jamberry* (PS–1). Illus. by author. 1983, HarperCollins LB $15.89 (0-06-021417-1). 32pp. A boy and a bear collect berries for jam.

1991 Degen, Bruce. *Sailaway Home* (PS–K). Illus. 1996, Scholastic $14.95 (0-590-46443-4). 32pp. A little pig imagines all sorts of adventures that could take place aboard his toy boat. (Rev: BL 8/96; SLJ 3/96)

1992 De Groat, Diane. *Good Night, Sleep Tight, Don't Let the Bedbugs Bite!* (PS–K). Illus. 2002, North-South LB $15.88 (1-58717-129-5). 32pp. Gilbert's spooky first night at camp reveals that other campers are just as fearful as he. (Rev: BL 7/02; HB 7–8/02; HBG 10/02; SLJ 8/02)

1993 De Groat, Diane. *Liar, Liar, Pants on Fire* (K–2). Illus. 2003, North-South LB $16.50 (1-58717-215-1). 32pp. Gilbert the opossum, playing George Washington in the school play, learns a lesson about being honest. (Rev: BL 2/15/03; HBG 10/03; SLJ 5/03)

1994 Delaney, Michael. *Birdbrain Amos* (3–5). Illus. 2002, Penguin Putnam $14.99 (0-399-23614-7). 160pp. Amos the hippopotamus hires a tick bird, Kumba, to rid him of a bug problem but finds only additional irritation when Kumba builds a nest on his head. (Rev: BCCB 4/02; BL 4/1/02*; HB 3–4/02; HBG 10/02; SLJ 4/02)

1995 Demarest, Chris L. *Honk!* (PS–1). Illus. by author. 1998, Boyds Mills $9.95 (1-56397-221-2). Using flaps, different animals and the sounds they make are revealed in this story about a lost duck. (Rev: HBG 3/99; SLJ 10/98)

1996 Denim, Sue. *The Dumb Bunnies* (K–2). Illus. by Dav Pilkey. 1994, Scholastic $13.95 (0-590-47708-0). 32pp. The story of the three dumb bunnies and their hectic misadventures. (Rev: BL 1/15/94; SLJ 3/94)

1997 Denim, Sue. *The Dumb Bunnies Go to the Zoo* (1–3). Illus. by Dav Pilkey. 1997, Scholastic $14.95 (0-590-84735-X). 32pp. The three Dumb Bunnies go to the zoo, where they create havoc. (Rev: BL 4/1/97; SLJ 3/97)

1998 Denim, Sue. *Make Way for Dumb Bunnies* (1–3). Illus. by Dav Pilkey. 1996, Scholastic $12.95 (0-590-58286-0). 32pp. A slapstick tale about the misadventures of an unthinking rabbit family. (Rev: BL 2/1/96; SLJ 3/96)

1999 Denslow, Sharon P. *Big Wolf and Little Wolf* (PS–K). Illus. by Cathie Felstead. 2000, Greenwillow $15.95 (0-688-16174-X). 32pp. Little Wolf is frightened by strange noises coming from the bushes and discovers it is his mother playing a trick on him. (Rev: BCCB 7–8/00; BL 5/1/00; HBG 10/00; SLJ 5/00)

2000 Depalma, Mary Newell. *The Strange Egg* (PS–2). Illus. by author. 2001, Houghton Mifflin $15.00 (0-618-09507-1). A monkey has to explain to a small bird that it is sitting on an orange. (Rev: HBG 10/01; SLJ 5/01)

2001 dePaola, Tomie. *Bill and Pete Go Down the Nile* (K–3). Illus. by author. 1987, Penguin Putnam $15.95 (0-399-21395-3); paper $5.99 (0-698-11401-9). 32pp. A crocodile and a bird in a delightful romp down the Nile. (Rev: BL 5/1/87; SLJ 9/87)

2002 dePaola, Tomie. *Bill and Pete to the Rescue* (PS–2). Illus. 1998, Penguin Putnam $15.99 (0-399-23208-7). 48pp. Pete the Crocodile and his friend Bill, a bird, help save Pete's cousin, little Jane Allison, from the hands of Bad Guy's Big Bad Brother. (Rev: BCCB 7–8/98; BL 5/15/98; SLJ 5/98)

2003 dePaola, Tomie. *Bonjour, Mr. Satie* (1–3). Illus. 1991, Penguin Putnam $15.95 (0-399-21782-7). 32pp. Mr. Satie, a cat, tells his niece and nephew about exciting experiences in the art salons of Paris. (Rev: BCCB 3/91; BL 3/1/93)

2004 dePaola, Tomie. *Four Friends in Autumn* (PS–2). Illus. by author. 2004, Simon & Schuster $14.95 (0-689-85980-5). In this tale adapted from *Four Stories for Four Seasons* (1980), four friends — Missy Cat, Mistress Pig, Master Dog, and Mister Frog — gather for dinner at Mistress Pig's house. (Rev: SLJ 11/04)

2005 dePaola, Tomie. *Four Stories for Four Seasons* (2–3). Illus. by author. 1994, Simon & Schuster paper $6.95 (0-671-88633-9). 48pp. Dog, Cat, Frog, and Pig are involved in activities for each season in this reissued picture book. Also use: *Michael Bird Boy* (1987).

2006 dePaola, Tomie. *The Knight and the Dragon* (1–3). Illus. by author. 1998, Penguin Putnam $16.99 (0-399-20707-4); paper $5.99 (0-698-11623-2). An inexperienced knight and an inexperienced dragon prepare themselves to do battle.

2007 dePaola, Tomie. *Little Grunt and the Big Egg: A Prehistoric Fairy Tale* (PS–3). Illus. 1990, Holiday House LB $16.95 (0-8234-0730-6). 32pp. Little Grunt adopts a pet dinosaur named George. (Rev: BL 4/1/90)

2008 dePaola, Tomie. *Meet the Barkers: Morgan and Moffat Go to School* (PS–1). Illus. 2001, Penguin Putnam $13.99 (0-399-23708-9). 32pp. Terrier siblings Morgie and Moffie have always been different — Moffie is smart, Morgie gregarious — and these characteristics hold true when they start school. (Rev: BL 6/1–15/01; HBG 3/02; SLJ 8/01)

2009 dePaola, Tomie. *A New Barker in the House* (PS–2). Illus. Series: The Barkers. 2002, Penguin Putnam $13.99 (0-399-23865-4). 32pp. When the Barker family adopts Spanish-speaking Marcos, twins Morgie and Moffie try hard to make him feel comfortable in this book full of Spanish words and charming art. (Rev: BL 7/02; HBG 10/02; SLJ 6/02)

2010 dePaola, Tomie. *T-Rex Is Missing!* (1–2). Illus. by author. 2002, Grosset LB $13.89 (0-448-42882-2); paper $3.99 (0-448-42870-9). 32pp. The disappearance of a toy dinosaur causes a major falling out between two animal friends. (Rev: HBG 10/03; SLJ 2/03)

2011 dePaola, Tomie. *Trouble in the Barkers' Class* (K–2). Illus. by author. 2003, Penguin Putnam $14.99 (0-399-24164-7). Moffie and Morgie Barker, twin terriers, are disappointed when the newcomer to their class, Carole Anne, turns out to be an ill-tempered bully. (Rev: HBG 4/04; SLJ 10/03)

2012 Desimini, Lisa. *Dot the Fire Dog* (PS–3). Illus. 2001, Scholastic $15.95 (0-439-23322-4). 40pp. Dot the Dalmatian rescues a kitten while helping her fire fighter owners put out a fire. (Rev: BL 10/1/01; HB 11–12/01; HBG 3/02; SLJ 12/01)

2013 De Vries, Anke. *My Elephant Can Do Almost Anything* (PS–1). Illus. by Ilja Walraven. 1996, Front Street $14.95 (1-886910-06-5). A boy's imaginary playmate, an elephant, is upset when the boy goes to school. (Rev: BCCB 6/96; HB 7–8/96; SLJ 6/96)

2014 De Vries, Anke. *Piggy's Birthday Dream* (PS). Illus. by Jung-Hee Spetter. 1997, Front Street $14.95 (1-886910-21-9). 32pp. Piggy is so shy that she doesn't tell any of the barnyard animals it's her birthday, but they plan their own surprise for her. (Rev: BL 11/15/97; HBG 3/98; SLJ 11/97)

2015 Dewan, Ted. *Bing: Get Dressed* (PS). Illus. by author. Series: Bing Bunny. 2004, Random $5.95 (0-385-75020-X). Bing gets dressed with supervision and advice from Flop in this bright, small-format book. Also use *Bing: Paint Day* (2004). (Rev: BL 2/15/04; SLJ 7/04)

2016 Dewan, Ted. *Bing: Go Picnic* (PS). Illus. 2005, Random $5.99 (0-375-75056-0). 24pp. Bing the bunny and stuffed animal Flop plan a picnic outdoors but are rained out and must set up indoors instead. Also use *Make Music* (2005). (Rev: BL 5/1/05)

2017 Dickson, Louise. *The Vanishing Cat* (PS–2). Illus. by Pat Cupples. 2001, Kids Can $14.95 (1-55337-026-0); paper $6.95 (1-55074-836-X). 39pp. Detective dogs Lu and Clancy suspect that a cruise ship magician, a cat, is up to no good. (Rev: HBG 3/02; SLJ 12/01)

2018 Dierssen, Andreas. *Timid Timmy* (K–2). Trans. from German by Marianne Martens. Illus. by Felix Scheinberger. 2003, North-South LB $16.50 (0-7358-1812-6). Timmy the hare discovers that honesty, although scary, can have its rewards. (Rev: HBG 4/04; SLJ 8/03)

2019 DiPucchio, Kelly. *What's the Magic Word?* (PS–K). Illus. by Marsha Winborn. 2005, HarperCollins LB $16.89 (0-06-000579-3). 32pp. Blown by the wind, poor Little Bird lands in different animal homes; happily, he ends up back in his nest when he uses the magic word, "please." (Rev: BL 3/1/05; SLJ 5/05)

2020 Dockray, Tracy. *My Bunny Diary: By Dora Cottontail* (K–3). Illus. 2002, North-South $15.95 (1-58717-118-X). 40pp. Dora, a tomboy bunny, records in her diary the ups and downs of her friendship with Ally. (Rev: BL 4/1/02; HBG 10/02)

2021 Dodd, Emma. *Dog's Noisy Day: A Story to Read Aloud* (PS–K). Illus. 2003, Dutton $14.99 (0-525-47015-8). 32pp. Dog tries to imitate the sounds he hears around the farm, from a rooster's crow to a bee's buzz. (Rev: BL 2/15/03; HBG 10/03; SLJ 3/03)

2022 Dodds, Dayle Ann. *The Kettles Get New Clothes* (PS–2). Illus. by Jill McElmurry. 2002, Candlewick $15.99 (0-7636-1091-7). 32pp. A rhyming tale about a family of dogs who make their yearly pilgrimage to town to buy new clothes, only to find the clothes in the shop are now much fancier than they'd like. (Rev: BL 12/15/02; HB 1–2/03; HBG 3/03; SLJ 12/02)

2023 Dohaney, Rainy. *Tinka* (PS–2). Illus. by author. 2003, Simon & Schuster $15.95 (0-689-85261-4). Tinka, a diminutive sheep, finds comfort in her friendship with a crow named Sooty, who helps her to prove that being small has its advantages. (Rev: BL 6/1–15/03; HBG 4/04; SLJ 5/03)

2024 Donaldson, Julia. *The Gruffalo* (PS–3). Illus. by Axel Scheffler. 1999, Dial $15.99 (0-8037-2386-5). 32pp. A mouse frightens away his animal enemies with tales of a make-believe monster, the gruffalo, but unfortunately for him a real gruffalo appears. (Rev: BL 7/99; HBG 10/99; SLJ 8/99)

2025 Donaldson, Julia. *The Snail and the Whale* (PS–3). Illus. by Axel Scheffler. 2004, Dial $16.99 (0-8037-2922-7). A tiny snail, anxious to see the world, attaches itself to a humpback whale, and the two enjoy rhythmic, rhyming travels. (Rev: SLJ 2/04)

2026 Donohue, Dorothy. *Veggie Soup* (PS–3). Illus. 2000, Winslow $15.95 (1-890817-21-X). 40pp. When Miss Bun, a rabbit, decides to create her own veggie soup, each of her friends brings a different ingredient. (Rev: BL 11/15/00; HBG 3/01; SLJ 10/00)

2027 Doray, Malika. *One More Wednesday* (PS–3). Trans. by Suzanne Freeman. Illus. 2001, Greenwillow LB $15.89 (0-06-029590-2). 48pp. A young animal misses his grandmother when she dies but comes to realize that his memories of their good times bring comfort. (Rev: BL 6/1–15/01; HBG 10/01; SLJ 7/01)

2028 Dorros, Arthur. *City Chicken* (PS–2). Illus. by Henry Cole. 2003, HarperCollins LB $16.89 (0-06-028483-8). 40pp. Adventurous city chicken Henrietta takes a trip to the country, encounters an industrial egg farm, and gladly returns to her quiet city life. (Rev: BCCB 2/03; BL 3/15/03; HB 3–4/03; HBG 10/03; SLJ 2/03)

2029 Dotlich, Rebecca Kai. *Grandpa Loves* (PS–K). Illus. by Kathryn Brown. 2005, HarperCollins LB

$16.89 (0-06-029406-X). 32pp. A young pig describes all the things her grandfather loves — billiards, backpacking, flipping pancakes, and so forth. (Rev: BL 6/1–15/05; SLJ 5/05)

2030 Dotlich, Rebecca Kai. *Mama Loves* (PS–1). Illus. by Kathryn Brown. 2004, HarperCollins $14.99 (0-06-029407-8). 32pp. A tally of all the things that Mama Pig loves to do with her baby daughter. (Rev: BL 3/1/04)

2031 Doughty, Rebecca. *You Are to Me* (PS–1). Illus. by author. 2004, Penguin Putnam $12.99 (0-399-24176-0). A peach-colored pig uses unusual metaphors to express affection for a lavender-gray rabbit. (Rev: BL 1/1–15/04; SLJ 1/04)

2032 Dubanevich, Arlene. *Pig William* (PS–1). Illus. by author. 1985, Simon & Schuster LB $14.95 (0-02-733200-4). 32pp. Pig William is such a dawdler that his brothers leave without him for a picnic. (Rev: BCCB 12/85; BL 1/15/86)

2033 Duffield, Katy S. *Farmer McPeepers and His Missing Milk Cows* (K–3). Illus. by Steve Gray. 2003, Rising Moon $15.95 (0-87358-825-8). When Farmer McPeepers's dairy cows steal his eyeglasses, he looks for them all day while his cows have a great day off; the illustrations provide the fun. (Rev: HBG 4/04; SLJ 10/03)

2034 Dunbar, Joyce. *A Chick Called Saturday* (PS–1). Illus. by Brita Granstrom. 2003, Eerdmans $16.00 (0-8028-5260-2). Saturday, an inquisitive chick, is disappointed in life until he discovers that he's got a real talent for crowing. (Rev: HBG 4/04; SLJ 8/03)

2035 Dunbar, Joyce. *Eggday* (PS–K). Illus. by Jane Cabrera. 1999, Holiday House $15.95 (0-8234-1510-4). 32pp. Dora the Duck declares that tomorrow is Eggday and that each animal, including the horse and pig, should bring their eggs. (Rev: BL 4/1/99; HB 5–6/99; HBG 10/99; SLJ 7/99)

2036 Dunbar, Joyce. *The Love-Me Bird* (PS–3). Illus. by Sophie Fatus. 2004, Scholastic $15.95 (0-439-47431-0). 32pp. A little pink bird in a polka-dot dress gets no response to her cries of "Love me!" until she changes her tune. (Rev: BL 2/15/04; SLJ 1/04)

2037 Dunbar, Joyce. *Tell Me What It's Like to Be Big* (K–3). Illus. by Debi Gliori. 2001, Harcourt $16.00 (0-15-202564-2). 32pp. Detailed, vivid images illustrate the story of Willa the rabbit, who is frustrated because she is too little to reach the food on the table. (Rev: BL 12/15/01; HBG 3/02; SLJ 9/01)

2038 Duncan, Lois. *I Walk at Night* (PS–3). Illus. by Steve Johnson and Lou Fancher. 2000, Viking $15.99 (0-670-87513-9). 32pp. Told from a cat's point of view, this story describes the feline's independent life. (Rev: BCCB 2/00; BL 2/1/00; HBG 10/00; SLJ 3/00)

2039 Dunrea, Olivier. *Gossie and Gertie* (PS). Illus. 2002, Houghton Mifflin $9.95 (0-618-17676-4). 32pp. A little gosling named Gossie learns a lesson in individuality when her best friend Gertie no longer wants to do everything she does. Also use

Gossie (2002). (Rev: BL 8/02; HB 1–2/03*; HBG 3/03; SLJ 9/02*)

2040 Dunrea, Olivier. *Ollie* (PS–1). Illus. by author. 2003, Houghton Mifflin $9.95 (0-618-33928-0). Goslings Gossie and Gertie grow impatient waiting for their sibling Ollie to hatch from his egg. (Rev: HBG 4/04; SLJ 7/03)

2041 Dunrea, Olivier. *Ollie the Stomper* (PS). Illus. by author. 2003, Houghton Mifflin $9.95 (0-618-33930-2). Ollie, the contrary gosling who refused to emerge from his egg in *Ollie* (2003), first decides he wants boots and then that he needs a swim instead. (Rev: HBG 4/04; SLJ 7/03)

2042 Dyer, Jane. *Little Brown Bear Won't Go to School* (PS). Illus. by author. 2003, Little, Brown $15.95 (0-316-19685-1). Little Brown Bear doesn't like the idea of school until he tries his hand at a few working alternatives. (Rev: HBG 4/04; SLJ 8/03)

2043 Dyer, Jane. *Little Brown Bear Won't Take a Nap!* (PS–1). Illus. 2002, Little, Brown $15.95 (0-316-19764-5). 32pp. Little Bear, reluctant to lie down and hibernate, takes a train ride south with a flock of geese, who help him to get back home when he changes his mind. (Rev: BL 9/15/02; HBG 3/03; SLJ 9/02)

2044 Eduar, Gilles. *Jooka Saves the Day* (PS–2). Trans. by Dominic Barth. Illus. 1997, Orchard $15.95 (0-531-30036-6). 40pp. Jooka tries to be like all the crocodiles in the rain forest, but it is impossible because he is really a dragon. (Rev: BL 12/1/97; HB 9–10/97; HBG 3/98; SLJ 9/97)

2045 Edvall, Lilian. *The Rabbit Who Didn't Want to Go to Sleep* (PS). Trans. from Swedish by Elisabeth Kallick Dyssegaard. Illus. by Sara Gimbergsson. 2004, R&S $15.00 (91-29-66001-7). The little rabbit just doesn't want to go to sleep . . . there are still cars to race. (Rev: SLJ 6/04)

2046 Edwards, Pamela Duncan. *Clara Caterpillar* (PS–1). Illus. by Henry Cole. 2001, HarperCollins LB $15.89 (0-06-028996-1). 32pp. In this alliterative story, vain Catisha grows into a beautiful crimson butterfly but her allure makes her vulnerable and she needs help from plain Clara, the cabbage butterfly. (Rev: BL 7/01; HBG 10/01; SLJ 6/01)

2047 Edwards, Pamela Duncan. *Little Brown Hen's Shower* (PS–K). Illus. by Darcia LaBrosse. 2002, Hyperion $15.99 (0-7868-0467-X). 32pp. A hilarious tale about Little Brown Hen who opens up a big umbrella for herself and a small one for her egg because she is going to a baby shower. (Rev: BL 4/1/02; SLJ 7/02)

2048 Edwards, Pamela Duncan. *Livingstone Mouse* (PS–2). Illus. by Henry Cole. 1996, HarperCollins LB $15.89 (0-06-025870-5). 32pp. A mouse decides that China would be a nice place for him to build his nest. (Rev: BL 10/1/96; SLJ 9/96)

2049 Edwards, Pamela Duncan. *McGillycuddy Could!* (PS). Illus. by Sue Porter. 2005, HarperCollins LB $15.89 (0-06-029002-1). Kangaroo McGillycuddy's ability to hop, jump, bounce, and kick fails to impress the other animals at the farm. (Rev: BCCB 2/05; HB 3–4/05; SLJ 3/05)

2050 Edwards, Pamela Duncan. *Slop Goes the Soup: A Noisy Warthog Word Book* (PS). Illus. by Henry Cole. 2001, Hyperion $14.99 (0-7868-0469-6). 28pp. The warthogs are at it again, this time making dinner and making lots of (onomatopoeic) noise. (Rev: BL 10/15/01; HBG 3/02; SLJ 12/01)

2051 Edwards, Richard. *Copy Me, Copycub* (PS–K). Illus. by Susan Winter. 1999, HarperCollins $14.95 (0-06-028570-2). 32pp. From spring to winter hibernation, this book tells of a year in the life of a mother bear and the little child she calls Copycub because he repeats everything she does. (Rev: BL 9/1/99; HBG 3/00; SLJ 12/99)

2052 Edwards, Roland. *Tigers* (PS–K). Illus. by Judith Riches. 1992, Morrow LB $14.93 (0-688-11686-8). 32pp. A child imagines hearing a pride of playful tigers just beyond the bedroom door. (Rev: BL 2/1/93; SLJ 12/92)

2053 Egan, Tim. *Burnt Toast on Davenport Street* (K–2). Illus. 1997, Houghton Mifflin $14.95 (0-395-79618-0). 32pp. A fly — who has granted Arthur, a dog, three wishes — gets the wishes mixed up in this hilarious fantasy. (Rev: BL 4/15/97; SLJ 5/97*)

2054 Egan, Tim. *A Mile from Ellington Station* (K–3). Illus. 2001, Houghton Mifflin $15.00 (0-618-00393-2). 32pp. Preston, a bear who is a checkers champion, is beaten by a multitalented dog from France named Marley, so Preston claims Marley is a sorcerer. (Rev: BL 4/15/01; HBG 10/01; SLJ 5/01)

2055 Egan, Tim. *Serious Farm* (K–3). Illus. by author. 2003, Houghton Mifflin $15.00 (0-618-22694-X). Farmer Fred takes life too seriously and his livestock decides to get him to lighten up. (Rev: HB 9–10/03; HBG 4/04; SLJ 10/03)

2056 Egielski, Richard. *Slim and Jim* (PS–3). Illus. 2002, HarperCollins LB $15.89 (0-06-028353-X). 40pp. An orphaned rat named Slim is saved from a world of crime through the intervention of Jim, a mouse-boy. (Rev: BCCB 9/02; BL 5/1/02*; HB 7–8/02; HBG 10/02; SLJ 5/02)

2057 Ehlert, Lois. *Mole's Hill* (PS–2). Illus. 1994, Harcourt $15.00 (0-15-255116-6). 32pp. Fox demands that Mole move from her hill, but she is able to outwit him and remain. (Rev: BCCB 4/94; BL 3/15/94; HB 7–8/94; SLJ 5/94)

2058 Ehlert, Lois. *Nuts to You!* (PS–2). Illus. 1993, Harcourt $16.00 (0-15-257647-9). A rural squirrel shows how he gathers food in the big city. (Rev: BL 3/1/93; HB 3–4/93; SLJ 4/93)

2059 Ehlert, Lois. *Top Cat* (PS–1). Illus. 1998, Harcourt $16.00 (0-15-201739-9). 40pp. Top Cat resents the arrival of a new striped kitten in his household, but soon they become friends. (Rev: BL 8/98; HBG 3/99; SLJ 9/98)

2060 Eilenberg, Max. *Squeak's Good Idea* (PS–K). Illus. by Patrick Benson. 2001, Candlewick $14.99 (0-7636-1591-9). 48pp. Young elephant Squeak believes in being prepared and takes piles of clothes and a basketful of food when he sets off for a trip into the backyard. (Rev: BL 12/15/01; HB 1–2/02; HBG 3/02; SLJ 12/01)

2061 Elliott, Laura Malone. *Hunter's Best Friend at School* (PS–1). Illus. by Lynn Munsinger. 2002, HarperCollins LB $17.89 (0-06-000231-X). 32pp. Hunter's mother offers guidance when Hunter explains that he doesn't really enjoy being naughty but wants to stay friends with mischievous fellow raccoon Stripes. (Rev: BCCB 10/02; BL 10/1/02; HBG 3/03; SLJ 9/02)

2062 Ellwand, David, and Ruth Ellwand. *Midas Mouse* (PS–2). Photos by David Ellwand. 2000, Lothrop $14.95 (0-688-16745-4). 32pp. Midas Mouse gets his wish and everything he touches turns to gold, but he realizes he has problems when his cheese is inedible. (Rev: BL 10/1/00; HBG 3/01; SLJ 11/00)

2063 Elya, Susan Middleton. *Eight Animals Bake a Cake* (2–4). Illus. by Lee Chapman. 2002, Penguin Putnam $15.99 (0-399-23468-3). 32pp. Too many animals almost spoil the cake in this appealing picture book that introduces Spanish words and includes a recipe for pineapple upside-down cake. (Rev: BL 7/02; HBG 3/03; SLJ 8/02)

2064 Elya, Susan Middleton. *Eight Animals on the Town* (1–3). Illus. by Lee Chapman. 2000, Penguin Putnam $15.99 (0-399-23437-3). 32pp. English and Spanish words are mixed in this delightful story about eight animals who head into town for dinner. (Rev: BCCB 1/01; BL 12/1/00; HBG 3/01; SLJ 9/00)

2065 Elya, Susan Middleton. *Eight Animals Play Ball* (1–3). Illus. by Lee Chapman. 2003, Penguin Putnam $15.99 (0-399-23569-8). The eight animals from Elya's earlier books go to the park and start a baseball game in a charming mix of English and Spanish. (Rev: HBG 10/03; SLJ 3/03)

2066 Emberley, Ed. *Thanks, Mom* (PS–1). Illus. by author. 2003, Little, Brown $15.95 (0-316-24022-2). A tiny mouse is chased by a variety of circus animals when he snatches a chunk of cheese, but his intrepid mother rescues him just in time. (Rev: HBG 10/03; SLJ 5/03)

2067 Emmett, Jonathan. *Bringing Down the Moon* (PS–2). Illus. by Vanessa Cabban. 2001, Candlewick $15.99 (0-7636-1577-3). 24pp. Little Mole tries to capture the moon from the sky. (Rev: BL 2/1/02; HBG 3/02; SLJ 1/02)

2068 Emmett, Jonathan. *Dinosaurs After Dark* (PS). Illus. by Curtis Jobling. 2002, HarperCollins $14.99 (0-00-198375-X). Little Bobby investigates a strange noise one night and comes across a herd of lively dinosaurs. (Rev: BCCB 3/02; SLJ 6/02)

2069 Emmett, Jonathan. *No Place Like Home* (PS–1). Illus. by Vanessa Cabban. 2005, Candlewick $15.99 (0-7636-2554-X). Mole's friends all recommend new homes for him, but each has disadvantages, so Mole decides to return underground. (Rev: SLJ 3/05)

2070 Emmett, Jonathan. *Ruby in Her Own Time* (PS–1). Illus. by Rebecca Harry. 2004, Scholastic $15.95 (0-439-57915-5). 32pp. Ruby the duckling is the smallest and slowest of her siblings and continues to take life at her own pace even as an adult. (Rev: BL 2/15/04; SLJ 3/04)

2071 Eriksson, Eva. *A Crash Course for Molly* (PS–2). Trans. by Elisabeth Kallick Dyssegaard.

Illus. Series: Molly. 2005, Farrar $16.00 (91-29-66156-0). 32pp. It's mishap after mishap when Molly the pig practices riding her bike at the park. (Rev: BL 4/1/05; SLJ 6/05)

2072 Ernst, Lisa Campbell. *When Bluebell Sang* (K–3). Illus. by author. 1989, Macmillan paper $5.99 (0-689-71584-6). 40pp. Bluebell the cow finds that life behind the footlights isn't all it's cracked up to be. (Rev: BL 3/1/89; SLJ 4/89)

2073 Ezra, Mark. *The Frightened Little Owl* (PS–K). Illus. by Gavin Rowe. 1997, Interlink $14.95 (1-56656-264-3). 32pp. Fearful Little Owl takes her first flight in order to find her mother and discovers that she likes it. (Rev: BL 6/1–15/97; SLJ 7/97)

2074 Ezra, Mark. *The Hungry Otter* (PS–2). Illus. by Gavin Rowe. 1996, Crocodile $14.95 (1-56656-216-3). When Little Otter saves a crow from a fox, the crow, in turn, helps the otter by breaking holes in the ice so that the animal can fish. (Rev: SLJ 4/97)

2075 Falconer, Ian. *Olivia* (PS–K). Illus. 2000, Simon & Schuster $16.00 (0-689-82953-1). 40pp. An outstanding picture book about Olivia, a delightful little pig, who is a bundle of energy and talent. (Rev: BCCB 11/00*; BL 8/00*; HBG 3/01; SLJ 9/00)

2076 Falconer, Ian. *Olivia . . . and the Missing Toy* (PS–1). Illus. by author. 2003, Simon & Schuster $16.95 (0-689-85291-6). When her favorite stuffed animal mysteriously disappears, Olivia the pig turns sleuth in this story with witty illustrations. (Rev: BL 9/1/03*; HBG 4/04; SLJ 10/03)

2077 Falconer, Ian. *Olivia Saves the Circus* (PS–1). Illus. 2001, Simon & Schuster $16.00 (0-689-82954-X). 32pp. Olivia, the little pig full of talented energy, describes how she took over each and every role when the circus was hit by a rash of earaches. (Rev: BCCB 11/01; BL 8/01; HB 11–12/01; HBG 3/02; SLJ 10/01)

2078 Faulkner, Keith. *The Long-Nosed Pig* (PS–K). Illus. by Jonathan Lambert. 1998, Dial $12.99 (0-8037-2296-6). An interactive pop-up book about a long-nosed pig that has an accident in which it is flattened. (Rev: BL 12/15/97; HBG 10/98; SLJ 8/98)

2079 Faulkner, Keith. *The Wide-Mouthed Frog* (PS–1). Illus. by Jonathan Lambert. 1996, Dial $12.99 (0-8037-1875-6). 14pp. An interactive book that pictures a variety of animals and their eating habits. (Rev: BL 2/1/96; SLJ 4/96)

2080 Fearnley, Jan. *Billy Tibbies Moves Out!* (PS–1). Illus. 2004, HarperCollins $15.99 (0-06-054650-6). 32pp. Learning to share is the theme of this well-illustrated book in which Billy Tibbles, a cat, is unhappy about his younger brother sharing his room. (Rev: BL 2/15/04; SLJ 3/04)

2081 Fearnley, Jan. *A Perfect Day for It* (PS–1). Illus. by author. 2002, Harcourt $16.00 (0-15-216634-3). Bear leads a growing parade of animals to the top of the mountain, each following for a different reason. (Rev: HBG 3/03; SLJ 12/02)

2082 Feiffer, Jules. *Bark, George* (PS–3). Illus. 1999, HarperCollins LB $14.89 (0-06-205186-5). 32pp. When puppy George is asked to bark by his mother, he manages to produce a range of animal sounds including a "meow" and a "moo," but never an "arf." (Rev: BCCB 11/99; BL 8/99*; HBG 3/00; SLJ 9/99)

2083 Fernandes, Eugenie. *Busy Little Mouse* (PS–K). Illus. by Kim Fernandes. 2002, Kids Can $12.95 (1-55074-776-3). 24pp. Joyful, three-dimensional art is used to illustrate this lighthearted tale of various farm animals who play together. (Rev: BL 4/15/02)

2084 Fierstein, Harvey. *The Sissy Duckling* (2–4). Illus. by Henry Cole. 2002, Simon & Schuster $16.00 (0-689-83566-3). 40pp. Young Elmer is branded a sissy because of his feminine ways, but he later shows everyone how really special he is. (Rev: BCCB 7–8/02; BL 6/1–15/02*; HBG 10/02; SLJ 5/02)

2085 Finn, Isobel. *The Very Lazy Ladybug* (PS–1). Illus. by Jack Tickle. 2001, Tiger Tales $14.95 (1-58925-007-9). This ladybug is so lazy that she can't be bothered to fly and hops rides with a variety of animals instead, until she is finally forced to take to the air. (Rev: BCCB 5/01; SLJ 7/01)

2086 Flack, Marjorie. *Ask Mr. Bear* (PS–1). Illus. by author. 1968, Macmillan $14.00 (0-02-735390-7); paper $5.99 (0-02-043090-6). 32pp. To find a present for his mother's birthday, Danny asks a variety of animals for suggestions, with little success until he meets Mr. Bear.

2087 Fleming, Denise. *Lunch* (PS–K). Illus. 1992, Holt $16.95 (0-8050-1636-8). 30pp. A mouse samples all the goodies on a banquet table and gets fatter and fatter. (Rev: BCCB 12/92; BL 11/1/92; HB 1–2/93; SLJ 12/92*)

2088 Fleming, Denise. *Mama Cat Has Three Kittens* (PS–K). Illus. 1998, Holt $15.95 (0-8050-5745-5). 32pp. Two of Mama Cat's kittens are well behaved, but the third, Boris, just loves to nap. (Rev: BCCB 12/98; BL 11/15/98; HBG 3/99; SLJ 11/98)

2089 Fleming, Denise. *Time to Sleep* (PS–1). Illus. 1997, Holt $16.95 (0-8050-3762-4). 32pp. In this cumulative tale, Bear passes along the information that winter is on the way. (Rev: BL 10/1/97; HBG 3/98; SLJ 11/97)

2090 Floyd, Madeleine. *Captain's Purr* (PS–K). Illus. by author. 2003, Harcourt $16.00 (0-15-204939-8). When night falls, Captain the cat leaves his comfortable home by the river and sets off to visit his sweetheart. (Rev: BL 9/1/03; HBG 4/04; SLJ 11/03)

2091 Fontenot, Mary Alice. *Clovis Crawfish and Echo Gecko* (PS–2). Illus. by Julie Dupr Buckner. 2003, Pelican $14.95 (1-56554-708-X). In bayou country, Lizette Lizard introduces Clovis Crawfish and his friends to Echo Gecko, a shy little lizard who would like to learn French; a Cajun glossary is appended. (Rev: HBG 10/03; SLJ 5/03)

2092 Fontes, Justine Korman. *Signs of Spring* (K–2). Illus. by Rob Hefferan. 2002, Mondo $14.95 (1-59034-189-9). 24pp. On their way to school, Lucy, a mouse, and Zack, a chipmunk, gather signs of spring for show-and-tell. (Rev: BL 6/1–15/02; HBG 10/02; SLJ 8/02)

2093 Ford, Miela. *On My Own* (PS). Photos by author. 1999, Greenwillow $5.95 (0-688-16452-8). A board book illustrated with photographs about a polar bear cub who wants to be able to play on his own. (Rev: SLJ 7/99)

2094 Fox, Christyan, and Diane Fox. *Astronaut PiggyWiggy* (PS). Illus. by authors. 2002, Handprint $9.95 (1-929766-41-6). PiggyWiggy looks through his telescope and pictures himself blasting off and visiting distant places. (Rev: HBG 10/02; SLJ 7/02)

2095 Fox, Christyan, and Diane Fox. *Bathtime PiggyWiggy* (PS–K). Illus. 2001, Handprint $12.95 (1-929766-32-7). 24pp. PiggyWiggy's imagination takes him on underwater adventures in the bathtub. (Rev: BL 2/1/02; SLJ 1/02)

2096 Fox, Christyan, and Diane Fox. *Fire Fighter PiggyWiggy* (PS–K). Illus. 2001, Handprint $9.95 (1-929766-16-5). 24pp. PiggyWiggy has ideas of what he would do as a fire fighter but at the same time he recognizes that a real fire fighter would be needed in an emergency. (Rev: BL 5/1/01; HBG 10/01; SLJ 5/01)

2097 Fox, Christyan, and Diane Fox. *Goodnight PiggyWiggy* (PS). Illus. by authors. 2000, Handprint $12.95 (1-929766-06-8). Using a different flap to explore each career, a pig wonders what he will do when he grows up. (Rev: BL 12/1/00; HBG 10/01; SLJ 12/00)

2098 Fox, Christyan, and Diane Fox. *Pirate PiggyWiggy* (PS). Illus. by authors. 2003, Handprint $11.95 (1-929766-76-9). After an adventure on the seven seas, PiggyWiggy and his friends are happy to find loot in the picnic basket. (Rev: SLJ 6/03)

2099 Fox, Mem. *Hattie and the Fox* (PS–K). Illus. by Patricia Mullins. 1987, Macmillan $16.00 (0-02-735470-9); paper $5.99 (0-689-71611-7). 32pp. A cumulative tale about a big black hen who spies a fox in the farmyard. (Rev: BL 3/15/87; HB 5–6/87; SLJ 5/87)

2100 Fox, Mem. *Hunwick's Egg* (PS–2). Illus. by Pamela Lofts. 2005, Harcourt $16.00 (0-15-216318-2). 32pp. A kindly bandicoot adopts and cares for an egg that is actually a stone in this strikingly illustrated book that shows the plants and animals of Australia's desert habitat. (Rev: BL 2/15/05; SLJ 3/05)

2101 Fox, Mem. *Koala Lou* (PS–2). Illus. by Pamela Lofts. 1989, Harcourt $15.00 (0-15-200502-1). 32pp. A young koala named Koala Lou finds that her mother is too busy with her younger children to shower the same affection on her as before. (Rev: BL 11/15/89; HB 11–12/89; SLJ 1/90)

2102 Fox, Mem. *Possum Magic* (K–2). Illus. by Julie Vivas. 1990, Harcourt $15.00 (0-15-200572-2); paper $6.00 (0-15-263224-7). 32pp. Grandmother Opossum makes Hush invisible, and then forgets how she did it in this tale from Down Under. (Rev: BL 12/1/87; SLJ 12/87)

2103 Fox, Mem. *Where Is the Green Sheep?* (PS–1). Illus. by Judy Horacek. 2004, Harcourt $15.00 (0-15-204907-X). A beginning reader in rhyme featuring sheep in all kinds of activities, with the added fillip of a search for the green sheep. (Rev: HB 5–6/04; SLJ 4/04)

2104 France, Anthony. *From Me to You* (K–1). Illus. by Tiphanie Beeke. 2004, Candlewick $15.99 (0-7636-2255-9). An anonymous letter pulls Rat out of his despondent slump, and he applies the same tactic when Bat is feeling low. (Rev: BL 1/1–15/04; SLJ 1/04)

2105 Frascino, Edward. *Nanny Noony and the Dust Queen* (PS–3). Illus. 1990, Pippin LB $15.95 (0-945912-09-9). 32pp. Nanny Noony must grapple with a powerful sorceress, the Dust Queen. (Rev: BL 6/15/90; SLJ 9/90)

2106 Fraser, Mary Ann. *I.Q. Goes to the Library* (PS–3). Illus. by author. 2003, Walker LB $16.85 (0-8027-8878-5). I.Q., the school mouse, wants to get a library card but faces a few obstacles along the way. (Rev: HBG 4/04; SLJ 11/03)

2107 Freedman, Claire. *Dilly Duckling* (PS–1). Illus. by Jane Chapman. 2004, Simon & Schuster $15.95 (0-689-86772-7). 32pp. Dilly the duckling is distraught when one of her feathers blows away, but relieved when her mother explains that the shedding is natural. (Rev: BL 3/1/04; SLJ 4/04)

2108 Freedman, Claire. *Where's Your Smile, Crocodile?* (PS–K). Illus. by Sean Julian. 2001, Peachtree $16.95 (1-56145-251-3). Kyle the crocodile can't seem to smile, no matter how hard others try to amuse him, until he comes across a sad little lion and tries in turn to cheer him up. (Rev: HBG 3/02; SLJ 11/01)

2109 Freeman, Don. *Bearymore* (K–3). Illus. by author. 1979, Puffin paper $4.99 (0-14-050279-3). 40pp. A circus bear must build a new act, but he hibernates instead.

2110 Freeman, Don. *Corduroy* (PS–1). Illus. by author. 1968, Puffin paper $5.99 (0-14-050173-8). 32pp. The amusing story of a toy bear whose one missing button from his green corduroy overalls almost costs him the opportunity of belonging to someone. A sequel is: *A Pocket for Corduroy* (1978).

2111 Freeman, Don. *Dandelion* (K–2). Illus. by author. 1964, Puffin paper $5.99 (0-14-050218-1). 48pp. A vain lion goes to a barber shop before a party and makes himself unrecognizable to his friends.

2112 Freeman, Don. *Gregory's Shadow* (PS–1). Illus. 2000, Viking $15.99 (0-670-89328-5). 32pp. Gregory Groundhog doesn't want to be separated from his shadow nor does he want six more weeks of winter — what a dilemma! (Rev: BL 1/1–15/01; HBG 3/01; SLJ 2/01)

2113 Freeman, Don. *Manuelo the Playing Mantis* (K–2). Illus. 2004, Viking $15.99 (0-670-03684-6). 32pp. Manuelo the praying mantis longs to make music but is frustrated in his efforts until a clever spider helps him construct a cello. (Rev: BL 4/15/04; SLJ 4/04)

2114 French, Jackie. *Diary of a Wombat* (K–2). Illus. by Bruce Whatley. 2003, Clarion $14.00 (0-618-38136-8). A wombat relates her daily life in her diary; most entries deal with eating and sleeping until some friendly humans arrive. (Rev: HBG 4/04; SLJ 8/03)

2115 French, Jackie. *Too Many Pears!* (PS–1). Illus. by Bruce Whatley. 2003, Star Bright $16.95 (1-932065-47-4). Pamela the cow develops a real love for pears in this humorously illustrated picture book. (Rev: HBG 4/04; SLJ 11/03)

2116 Friedman, Jim. *The Mysterious Misadventures of Foy Rin Jin: A Decidedly Dysfunctional Dragon* (K–3). Illus. by Patti Stren. 1999, HarperCollins LB $15.89 (0-06-028551-6). Because he breathes water instead of fire, an unhappy dragon leaves his conventional colleagues and finds happiness with humans. (Rev: HBG 3/00; SLJ 1/00)

2117 Fries, Claudia. *A Pig Is Moving In!* (PS–2). Illus. 2000, Orchard LB $16.99 (0-531-33307-8). 32pp. A fox, a hen, and a hare are mistaken when they jump to the conclusion that, because their new neighbor is a pig, he will be dirty and messy. (Rev: BL 12/15/00; HBG 3/01; SLJ 9/00)

2118 Froehlich, Margaret W. *That Kookoory!* (1–3). Illus. by Marla Frazee. 1995, Harcourt $15.00 (0-15-277650-8). 40pp. This picture book tells of the confrontation between a prideful rooster and his arch enemy the weasel. (Rev: BCCB 5/95; BL 4/15/95; HB 7–8/95; SLJ 5/95)

2119 Fuge, Charles. *My Dad!* (PS–K). Illus. by author. 2003, Sterling $12.95 (1-4027-0707-X). A little bear scares away his playmates, one by one, by boasting about his father's fearsomeness, then finds himself all alone in the forest. (Rev: HBG 4/04; SLJ 4/04)

2120 Futterer, Kurt. *Emile* (PS–2). Trans. by Bronwen Gray Sepcht and Ingrid MacGillis. Illus. by Ralf Futterer. 2004, MacAdam/Cage $17.95 (1-931561-95-8). 32pp. Emile, a white cat who lives in a pristine home, finds himself covered in color after a visit to van Gogh's studio and his new appearance inspires his owners to adopt a brighter life. (Rev: BL 1/1–15/05)

2121 Galloway, Ruth. *Fidgety Fish* (PS–3). Illus. by author. 2001, Tiger Tales $14.95 (1-58925-012-5). A rambunctious little fish is sent out to swim until he's tired, and ignores warnings to stay away from Big Fish. (Rev: SLJ 2/02)

2122 Gantos, Jack. *Back to School for Rotten Ralph* (PS–3). Illus. by Nicole Rubel. 1998, HarperCollins LB $14.89 (0-06-027532-4). 40pp. When Sarah starts school, leaving her cat, Rotten Ralph, alone, he decides to wear a disguise and pretend to be her new school friend. (Rev: BL 8/98; HBG 3/99; SLJ 10/98)

2123 Gantos, Jack. *Practice Makes Perfect for Rotten Ralph* (1–3). Illus. by Nicole Rubel. Series: Rotten Ralph Rotten Reader. 2002, Farrar $15.00 (0-374-36356-0). 48pp. In this easy reader, Rotten Ralph the cat gets a few lessons about jealousy and cheating when he visits the carnival with Sarah and his cousin Percy wins all the prizes. (Rev: BL 3/1/02; HB 5–6/02; HBG 10/02; SLJ 3/02)

2124 Gantos, Jack. *Rotten Ralph* (K–3). Illus. by Nicole Rubel. 1976, Houghton Mifflin $16.00 (0-395-24276-2); paper $6.95 (0-395-29202-6). 48pp. Ralph is truly a nasty cat — mean and disruptive —

until he is reformed under unusual circumstances. A sequel is: *Worse Than Rotten, Ralph* (1982).

2125 Gantos, Jack. *Wedding Bells for Rotten Ralph* (PS–1). Illus. by Nicole Rubel. 1999, HarperCollins LB $14.89 (0-06-027534-0). 40pp. Ralph the red cat is up to his usual rotten tricks; this time he spoils a wedding at which his owner, Sarah, is a flower girl. (Rev: BL 6/1–15/99; HBG 10/99; SLJ 6/99)

2126 Gardner, Sally. *The Countess's Calamity* (K–3). Illus. by author. Series: Tales from the Box. 2003, Bloomsbury $14.95 (1-58234-812-X); paper $6.95 (1-58234-855-3). 124pp. When five little dolls are left abandoned in a box in the park, Mr. and Mrs. Mouse adopt them; four of the dolls seem delighted by the Mouses' hospitality, but one, named Countess, remains cold and aloof until she's rescued from a hungry cat by the mouse couple and the other dolls. (Rev: HBG 10/03; SLJ 8/03)

2127 Garland, Michael. *Last Night at the Zoo* (K–3). Illus. 2001, Boyds Mills $15.95 (1-56397-759-1). 32pp. The animals at the zoo are bored, so they break out and head for a night at Club Boogie. (Rev: BL 7/01; HBG 3/02; SLJ 5/01)

2128 Gavril, David. *Hector and the Noisy Neighbor* (PS–2). Illus. by author. 2004, Dial $12.99 (0-8037-2808-5). Hector the rabbit and his new neighbor, a pig called Rutherford, have opposing opinions about noise but find a life together in their apartment building. (Rev: SLJ 3/04)

2129 Gay, Michel. *Zee* (PS–2). Illus. by author. 2003, Clarion $15.00 (0-618-38148-1). 29pp. Desperate to wake his parents so he can snuggle with them in bed, Zee, a zebra toddler, decides that perhaps a little coffee might nudge them into wakefulness so that he can join them. (Rev: HBG 4/04; SLJ 8/03)

2130 Geisert, Arthur. *The Giant Ball of String* (K–3). Illus. 2002, Houghton Mifflin $16.00 (0-618-13221-X). 32pp. The children (piglets, actually) of Rumpus Ridge, Wisconsin, devise a clever scheme to reclaim their town's giant ball of string, which a nearby town has taken captive. (Rev: BL 9/15/02; HBG 3/03; SLJ 9/02)

2131 Geisert, Arthur. *Mystery* (2–4). Illus. by author. 2003, Houghton Mifflin $16.00 (0-618-27293-3). 32pp. The illustrations are the focus of this story about a little pig who investigates the theft of paintings from the art museum. (Rev: HBG 4/04; SLJ 10/03)

2132 George, Lindsay Barrett. *The Secret* (PS–2). Illus. by author. 2005, HarperCollins LB $16.89 (0-06-029600-3). 32pp. Mr. Snail whispers his secret to a mouse, who whispers it to a beetle, who passes it on to a turtle, and so forth until the secret ("I love you") finally makes it to Miss Snail. (Rev: BL 3/1/04; SLJ 5/05)

2133 Geras, Adele. *My Wishes for You* (PS–1). Illus. by Cliff Wright. 2002, Simon & Schuster $15.95 (0-689-85333-5). 32pp. Kindhearted rabbit parents wish good things for their child in this bucolic, beautifully illustrated picture book. (Rev: BL 12/15/02; HBG 3/03; SLJ 12/02)

2134 Gershator, David, and Phillis Gershator. *Moon Rooster* (K–3). Illus. by Megan Halsey. 2001, Marshall Cavendish $15.95 (0-7614-5092-0). A young rooster persists in crowing at the moon despite human annoyance. (Rev: HBG 3/02; SLJ 12/01)

2135 Gershator, Phillis. *When It Starts to Snow* (K–2). Illus. by Martin Matje. 1998, Holt $15.95 (0-8050-5404-9). 32pp. Various animals and birds express in simple rhymes their reactions to the falling snow. (Rev: BCCB 12/98; BL 11/15/98; HBG 3/99; SLJ 11/98)

2136 Gerstein, Mordicai, and Susan Y. Harris. *Daisy's Garden* (PS–3). Illus. 1995, Hyperion LB $15.49 (0-7868-2080-2). 32pp. A year in the life of a garden tended by rabbits, mice, groundhogs, goats, and other animals. (Rev: BL 7/95; SLJ 4/95)

2137 Gibbs, Lynne. *Quiet as a Mouse* (PS–2). Illus. by Melanie Mitchell. Series: Growing Pains. 2003, Gingham Dog $12.95 (1-57768-481-8). Painfully shy, Molly the mouse very reluctantly agrees to accompany her gregarious sisters to a party, but once there her shyness melts away and she ends up being the life of the party. (Rev: HBG 4/04; SLJ 8/03)

2138 Gibbs, Lynne. *Schooltime for Sammy* (PS–K). Illus. by Melanie Mitchell. Series: Growing Pains. 2003, Gingham Dog $12.95 (1-57768-482-6); paper $4.95 (1-57768-931-3). Sammy the chimp prefers to play in the treetops of his jungle home until he hears about all the fun he missed at school. (Rev: HBG 4/04; SLJ 1/04)

2139 Ginsburg, Mirra. *Across the Stream* (PS–2). Illus. by Nancy Tafuri. 1982, Greenwillow $15.93 (0-688-01206-X); Morrow paper $4.95 (0-688-10477-0). 24pp. Mother hen saves her three chicks from the fox.

2140 Ginsburg, Mirra, trans. *The Chick and the Duckling* (PS–K). Adapted from the Russian by V. Suteyev. Illus. by Jose Aruego and Ariane Dewey. 1988, Simon & Schuster paper $4.95 (0-689-71226-X). 32pp. A duck and a chick who hatch at the same time become constant companions.

2141 Gliori, Debi. *Can I Have a Hug?* (PS). Illus. 2002, Scholastic $5.95 (0-439-27602-0). 8pp. In this oversize board book, a bear is so anxious for a hug he's ready to cuddle up to a hive of bees. Also use *Tickly Under There* (2002). (Rev: BL 6/1–15/02)

2142 Gliori, Debi. *Flora's Blanket* (PS). Illus. 2001, Scholastic $15.95 (0-531-30305-5). 32pp. Flora, a young bunny, cannot sleep because her favorite blanket has disappeared. (Rev: BL 5/15/01; HBG 10/01; SLJ 7/01*)

2143 Gliori, Debi. *Flora's Surprise!* (PS–2). Illus. by author. 2003, Scholastic $15.95 (0-439-45590-1). Flora, a young rabbit, plants a brick in the hope that it will grow into a house. (Rev: BCCB 3/03; HBG 10/03; SLJ 3/03)

2144 Gliori, Debi. *Mr. Bear Says, Are You There, Baby Bear? A Lift-the-Flap Book* (PS). Illus. by author. 1999, Orchard $9.95 (0-531-30182-6). Movable flaps are used in this story about Papa Bear's search for his missing child. (Rev: SLJ 1/00)

2145 Gliori, Debi. *Mr. Bear to the Rescue* (PS–1). Illus. 2000, Orchard $15.95 (0-531-30276-8). 32pp. When bunny Flora is missing, Mr. Bear loads his tools into his carriage and sets off to help. (Rev: BL 11/15/00; HBG 10/01; SLJ 11/00)

2146 Gliori, Debi. *Mr. Bear's New Baby* (PS). Illus. 1999, Orchard $15.95 (0-531-30152-4). 32pp. Small Bear discovers that the new baby will stop crying if the family cuddles together. (Rev: BL 2/1/99; HBG 10/99; SLJ 3/99)

2147 Gliori, Debi. *Mr. Bear's Vacation* (PS–1). Illus. 2000, Orchard $15.95 (0-531-30255-5). 32pp. Mr. and Mrs. Bear and their two small children go on an accident-filled camping trip. (Rev: BL 5/15/00; HBG 10/00; SLJ 3/00)

2148 Gliori, Debi. *No Matter What* (PS–K). Illus. 1999, Harcourt $16.00 (0-15-202061-6). 32pp. Small, a young fox, tests the love that Large feels for him through a series of questions to determine the extent of this love. (Rev: BL 11/15/99; HBG 3/00; SLJ 11/99)

2149 Gliori, Debi. *Penguin Post* (PS–2). Illus. 2002, Harcourt $16.00 (0-15-216765-X). 40pp. While his parents take the day off to tend their ready-to-hatch egg, Milo the penguin takes over their mail route and has a variety of amusing adventures. (Rev: BL 12/15/02; HBG 3/03; SLJ 11/02)

2150 Gliori, Debi. *Where Did That Baby Come From?* (PS–2). Illus. 2005, Harcourt $16.00 (0-15-205373-5). 32pp. A tiger cub wonders where his new sibling came from — a store? outer space? the zoo? — but happily accepts his presence in the end. (Rev: BL 3/1/05; SLJ 4/05)

2151 Godwin, Laura. *The Best Fall of All* (K–1). Illus. by Jane Chapman. 2002, Simon & Schuster $14.95 (0-689-84713-0). 32pp. Honey the cat and Happy the dog learn to have fun in the fallen leaves. (Rev: BL 12/1/02; HBG 3/03; SLJ 10/02)

2152 Goldsmith, Howard. *Sleepy Little Owl* (PS–1). Illus. by Denny Bond. 1997, McGraw-Hill $12.95 (0-07-024543-6). 30pp. Through a series of daytime adventures, a young owl realizes that he is a nocturnal creature. (Rev: SLJ 2/98)

2153 Gollub, Matthew. *Gobble, Quack, Moon* (PS–2). Illus. by Judy Love. 2002, Tortuga $18.95 (1-889910-20-1). 32pp. Katie the cow and her barnyard friends hop on a rocket ship and spend a happy time on the moon. (Rev: BL 6/1–15/02)

2154 Gollub, Matthew. *The Jazz Fly* (PS–2). Illus. by Karen Hanke. 2000, Tortuga $17.95 (1-889910-17-1). 32pp. A bouncy book with an accompanying CD about a hip fly, his jazz talk, and his job in a club as a drummer. (Rev: BL 8/00; SLJ 8/00)

2155 Goodman, Joan Elizabeth. *Bernard Goes to School* (PS–K). Illus. by Dominic Catalano. 2001, Boyds Mills $15.95 (1-56397-958-6). 32pp. Although he feels shy at first, Bernard the elephant eventually is able to say goodbye to his parents on his first day of preschool. (Rev: BCCB 9/01; BL 10/1/01; HBG 3/02; SLJ 8/01)

2156 Goodman, Joan Elizabeth. *Bernard Wants a Baby* (PS–K). Illus. by Dominic Catalano. 2004, Boyds Mills $15.95 (1-59078-088-4). Although he has expressed a wish for siblings, young elephant Bernard is uncertain when triplets arrive. (Rev: SLJ 7/04)

2157 Gorbachev, Valeri. *The Big Trip* (PS–2). Illus. 2004, Penguin Putnam $15.99 (0-399-23965-0). 32pp. Goat throws a wet blanket on his friend Pig's vacation plans when he questions the safety of every possible form of transportation. (Rev: BL 5/1/04; SLJ 3/04)

2158 Gorbachev, Valeri. *Chicken Chickens Go to School* (PS). Illus. by author. 2003, North-South LB $16.50 (0-7358-1767-7). A teacher helps the two timid chickens to overcome their anxieties about their first day at school. (Rev: HBG 4/04; SLJ 9/03)

2159 Gorbachev, Valeri. *Nicky and the Fantastic Birthday Gift* (PS–1). Illus. by author. 2000, North-South LB $15.88 (0-7358-1379-5). As a birthday present for his mother, Nicky the rabbit not only draws a picture as his siblings do, but also makes up an elaborate story to go with it. (Rev: HBG 3/01; SLJ 11/00)

2160 Gorbachev, Valeri. *Peter's Picture* (PS–1). Illus. 2000, North-South LB $15.88 (1-55858-966-X). 32pp. Peter the bear gets too much praise from other adults about his painting of a flower, but his parents know exactly how to please their son and put it in a frame. (Rev: BL 4/15/00; HBG 10/00; SLJ 6/00)

2161 Gorbachev, Valeri. *That's What Friends Are For* (PS–1). Illus. 2005, Philomel $15.99 (0-399-23966-9). 32pp. When Goat sees Pig crying, he imagines all kinds of disasters that might explain the situation. (Rev: BL 5/15/05)

2162 Gorbachev, Valeri. *Whose Hat Is It?* (PS–K). Illus. by author. 2004, HarperCollins LB $15.89 (0-06-053435-4). A turtle patiently seeks the owner of a pink hat found swept away by the wind. (Rev: SLJ 7/04)

2163 Goss, Linda. *The Frog Who Wanted to Be a Singer* (K–3). Illus. by Cynthia Jabar. 1996, Orchard LB $16.99 (0-531-08745-X). 40pp. Scorned by both frogs and birds because he wants to sing, a young frog astounds everyone with his talent. (Rev: BCCB 4/96; BL 4/15/96*; SLJ 5/96)

2164 Got, Yves. *Where's Sam?* (PS). Illus. by author. 2003, Chronicle $10.95 (0-8118-3764-5). Sam the bunny and his friends enjoy a costume party in this bright, large-format flap book. (Rev: HBG 10/03; SLJ 6/03)

2165 Graham, Margaret B. *Be Nice to Spiders* (PS–2). Illus. by author. 1967, HarperCollins LB $15.89 (0-06-022073-2). 32pp. Helen, Billy's pet spider, makes all the animals at the zoo happy when she spins webs and catches flies for them.

2166 Gralley, Jean. *Very Boring Alligator* (PS). Illus. 2001, Holt $15.95 (0-8050-6328-5). 32pp. A boring alligator just won't go away — until a little girl makes up her mind to get rid of him. (Rev: BL 9/15/01; HBG 3/02; SLJ 10/01)

2167 Grant, Nicola. *Don't Be So Nosy, Posy!* (PS–1). Illus. by Tim Warnes. 2004, Tiger Tales $15.95 (1-58925-036-2). Piglet Posy is insatiably curious and

pokes her nose into everybody's business; eventually this annoying trait pays off. (Rev: SLJ 4/04)

2168 Gray, Kes. *Cluck O'clock* (PS–3). Illus. by Mary McQuillan. 2004, Holiday House $16.95 (0-8234-1809-X). 32pp. Time plays an important role in this chicken-themed story that counts off the hours from first light — four "o'cluck" — until midnight. (Rev: BL 4/1/04; SLJ 3/04)

2169 Gray, Kes. *The Get Well Soon Book* (PS–1). Illus. by Mary McQuillan. 2000, Millbrook LB $21.90 (0-7613-1922-0). 32pp. An entertaining picture book that tells how different animals can have accidents and illnesses — Cynthia centipede sprains 98 ankles playing field hockey and Danny the Dalmatian breaks out in stripes. (Rev: BL 12/15/00; HBG 3/01; SLJ 2/01)

2170 Gray, Kes. *Our Twitchy* (PS–1). Illus. by Mary McQuillan. 2003, Holt $15.95 (0-8050-7454-6). When Twitchy the rabbit wonders why his parents don't look like him, his adoptive mother and father — a cow and horse — explain that they love him just the way he is. (Rev: HBG 4/04; SLJ 12/03)

2171 Gray, Libba M. *Small Green Snake* (PS–1). Illus. by Holly Meade. 1994, Orchard LB $16.99 (0-531-08694-1). 32pp. A disobedient garter snake wanders away from home and finds himself a prisoner in a jelly jar. (Rev: BL 9/15/94*; SLJ 9/94)

2172 Greene, Rhonda Gowler. *Barnyard Song* (PS–1). Illus. by Robert Bender. 1997, Simon & Schuster $14.00 (0-689-80758-9). 40pp. A variation of the "Old MacDonald" rhyme in which barnyard animals lose their voices because of bad cases of the flu. (Rev: BL 8/97; HBG 3/98; SLJ 9/97*)

2173 Greene, Rhonda Gowler. *Firebears: The Rescue Team* (PS–2). Illus. by Dan Andreasen. 2005, Holt $15.95 (0-8050-7010-9). 32pp. The bears of Fire Station Number Eight have a busy day responding to calls ranging from a kitten stuck in a tree to a blazing store. (Rev: BL 6/1–15/05)

2174 Greene, Rhonda Gowler. *Jamboree Day* (PS–2). Illus. by Jason Wolff. 2001, Scholastic $15.95 (0-439-29310-3). A festive, colorful crew of animals enjoys a toe-tapping jamboree. (Rev: HBG 3/02; SLJ 1/02)

2175 Greene, Stephanie. *Not Just Another Moose* (K–3). Illus. by Andrea Wallace. 2000, Marshall Cavendish $15.95 (0-7614-5061-0). A year in the life of Hildy, a pig, and Moose, who worries his antlers won't grow back in the spring. (Rev: HBG 10/00; SLJ 5/00)

2176 Grigg, Carol. *The Singing Snowbear* (PS–K). Illus. by author. 1999, Houghton Mifflin $15.00 (0-395-94223-3). Snowbear learns the song that the whale sings and the two entertain all the creatures of the Arctic. (Rev: HBG 3/00; SLJ 1/00)

2177 Grindley, Sally. *No Trouble at All* (PS–1). Illus. by Eleanor Taylor. 2002, Bloomsbury $15.95 (1-58234-757-3). 32pp. As Grandfather ruminates about the good behavior of his grandcubs, the two little bears are making mischief throughout the house. (Rev: BL 8/02; SLJ 7/02)

2178 Grindley, Sally. *What Are Friends For?* (PS–1). Illus. by Penny Dann. 1998, Kingfisher $14.95 (0-

7534-5108-5). 32pp. The friendship between Figgy, a young fox, and Jefferson Bear is threatened when Figgy wants to play and Jefferson doesn't. (Rev: BL 4/15/98; HBG 10/98; SLJ 8/98)

2179 Grubb, Lisa. *Happy Dog!* (PS–2). Illus. by author. 2003, Philomel $16.99 (0-399-23707-0). On a rainy day, Jack Cat paints himself a new friend, Happy Dog, and the two have many happy adventures. (Rev: HBG 10/03; SLJ 6/03)

2180 Grubb, Lisa. *Happy Dog Sizzles!* (PS–1). Illus. 2004, Penguin Putnam $15.99 (0-399-24193-0). 32pp. Bright illustrations add to the humor in this story of Happy Dog and Jack Cat entering an invention contest. (Rev: BL 5/1/04; SLJ 6/04)

2181 Guarino, Deborah. *Is Your Mama a Llama?* (PS–K). Illus. by Steven Kellogg. 1989, Scholastic $14.95 (0-590-41387-2). 32pp. A pleasing study of who belongs to whom, as a koala and her baby clutch each other or an opossum ambles off with babies aboard her back. (Rev: BCCB 11/89; BL 10/1/89; SLJ 10/89)

2182 Guest, C. Z. *Tiny Green Thumbs* (PS–1). Illus. by Loretta Krupinski. 2000, Hyperion $15.99 (0-7868-0516-1). Tiny Bun and Little Mouse show how to plant and grow a little garden with directions for cultivating vegetables like carrots, green beans, corn, and cucumbers. (Rev: HBG 10/00; SLJ 3/00)

2183 Gugler, Laurel Dee. *There's a Billy Goat in the Garden* (PS–1). Illus. by Clare Beaton. 2003, Barefoot $14.99 (1-84148-089-4). 32pp. A tiny bee chases a billy goat from the garden after the dog, pig, donkey, cow, and horse are unsuccessful. (Rev: BL 3/15/03; HBG 10/03; SLJ 4/03)

2184 Gutman, Anne. *Gaspard and Lisa at the Museum* (PS–1). Illus. by Georg Hallensleben. 2001, Knopf $9.95 (0-375-81117-6). 32pp. Young animals Gaspard and Lisa have an adventure during their class trip to the Museum of Natural History. Also use *Gaspard in the Hospital* (2001). (Rev: BL 11/15/01; HBG 3/02; SLJ 11/01)

2185 Gutman, Anne. *Gaspard at the Seashore* (PS). Illus. by Georg Hallensleben. 2002, Knopf $9.95 (0-375-81118-4). 32pp. Little Gaspard dreams of daring water sports at the seashore, but is afraid because he can't swim. (Rev: BL 8/02; HBG 10/02; SLJ 5/02)

2186 Gutman, Anne. *Lisa in New York* (PS). Illus. by Georg Hallensleben. 2002, Knopf $9.95 (0-375-81119-2). 32pp. Lisa gets lost while visiting her uncle, who lives in New York City. (Rev: BL 8/02; HBG 10/02; SLJ 5/02)

2187 Gutman, Anne, and Georg Hallensleben. *Gaspard on Vacation* (PS–1). Illus. 2001, Knopf $9.95 (0-375-81115-X). 32pp. Gaspard, a black rabbit, is on vacation with his family in Venice where he causes havoc by racing around the canals in a kayak. (Rev: BL 2/1/01*; HB 5–6/01; HBG 10/01)

2188 Gutman, Anne, and Georg Hallensleben. *Lisa's Airplane Trip* (PS–1). Illus. 2001, Knopf $9.95 (0-375-81114-1). 32pp. Lisa, a small white rabbit, enjoys the thrill of traveling alone on an airplane for the first time, particularly when she in taken into the cockpit. (Rev: BL 2/1/01; HB 5–6/01; HBG 10/01)

2189 Hadithi, Mwenye. *Hot Hippo* (PS–3). Illus. by Adrienne Kennaway. 1986, Little, Brown LB $14.95 (0-316-33722-6). A folktale-like story of Hot Hippo, who longed to live in the water, and the god of everything, who wanted him to live on land. (Rev: BL 12/1/86; HB 1–2/87; SLJ 2/87)

2190 Hafner, Marylin. *Molly and Emmett's Surprise Garden* (K–2). Illus. by author. 2001, McGraw-Hill $12.95 (1-57768-895-3). 30pp. When Molly and Emmett the cat are planting a garden, Emmett opens all the packets at the same time and the seeds get all mixed up. (Rev: HBG 10/01; SLJ 8/01)

2191 Hall, Martin. *Charlie and Tess* (PS–2). Illus. by Catherine Walters. 1996, Little Tiger $14.95 (1-888444-06-1). 28pp. An orphaned lamb that has been raised by a farmer's family later saves his flock on a snowy night. (Rev: BL 4/15/97; SLJ 3/97)

2192 Hall, Nancy Christen. *Mouse at Night* (PS–K). Illus. by Buket Erdogan. 2000, Orchard $14.95 (0-531-30260-1). 32pp. At night in Miss Bumbly's house, a mouse emerges from its hole and engages in all sorts of activities, including preparing breakfast for Miss Bumbly. (Rev: BL 5/1/00; HBG 10/00; SLJ 4/00)

2193 Hanel, Wolfram. *Little Elephant Runs Away* (PS–2). Trans. from German by J. Alison James. Illus. by Cristina Kadmon. 2001, North-South LB $15.88 (0-7358-1445-7). When Little Elephant runs away to the sea, he's ashamed to admit that he's lost and pretends to be ill instead. (Rev: HBG 10/01; SLJ 4/01)

2194 Hanel, Wolfram. *Little Elephant's Song* (PS–K). Trans. from German by J. Alison James. Illus. by Cristina Kadmon. 2000, North-South LB $15.88 (0-7358-1298-5). A young elephant learns many skills including how to trumpet. (Rev: HBG 10/00; SLJ 7/00)

2195 Harley, Bill. *Sitting Down to Eat* (K–3). Illus. by Kitty Harvill. 1996, August House $15.95 (0-87483-460-0). In this cumulative tale, a boy invites so many animals into his house that it explodes. (Rev: SLJ 1/97)

2196 Harris, Lee. *Never Let Your Cat Make Lunch for You* (K–2). Illus. by Debbie Tilley. 1999, Tricycle $12.95 (1-883672-80-5). 24pp. Although at times the images produced are somewhat gross (e.g., mouse sandwiches), this is a humorous tale of why cats can't prepare proper meals for humans. (Rev: BL 10/15/99; HBG 3/00; SLJ 12/99)

2197 Harrison, David L. *A Farmer's Garden: Rhymes for Two Voices* (PS–1). Illus. by Arden Johnson-Petrov. 2000, Boyds Mills $15.95 (1-56397-776-1). 32pp. A farmer's dog asks various animals and plants what they like best about the farmer's garden and what they do there. (Rev: BL 9/1/00; HBG 10/01; SLJ 11/00)

2198 Harrison, Joanna. *Dear Bear* (PS–2). Illus. 1994, Carolrhoda LB $16.61 (0-87614-839-9). 32pp. Katie is afraid of the bear that lives under the stairs and writes him a letter about her fear. (Rev: BCCB 1/95; BL 1/1/95; SLJ 2/95*)

2199 Harter, Debbie. *The Animal Boogie* (PS–2). Illus. by author. 2000, Barefoot $14.99 (1-84148-094-0). A rhythmic text adds to the fun of seeing various animals boogie-ing to lively music. (Rev: HBG 10/01; SLJ 12/00)

2200 Hartman, Bob. *Grumblebunny* (PS–3). Illus. by David Clark. 2003, Penguin Putnam $15.99 (0-399-23780-1). Eternal optimists, Cuddlemop, Sweetsnuffle, and Pretty are sweet in temperament and quite unlike their cousin Grumblebunny, whose sour disposition is a constant; when all four bunnies are snatched by a hungry wolf for soup makings, the three sweet bunnies begin to appreciate the advantages of being grumpy now and then. (Rev: HBG 10/03; SLJ 7/03)

2201 Haseley, Dennis. *Photographer Mole* (K–3). Illus. by Juli Kangas. 2004, Dial $16.99 (0-8037-2924-3). Traditional illustrations grace this story of a mole photographer who feels, despite his success, that there is something missing from his pictures. (Rev: SLJ 7/04)

2202 Haseley, Dennis. *A Story for Bear* (K–3). Illus. by Jim LaMarche. 2002, Harcourt $16.00 (0-15-200239-1). 32pp. Although he doesn't understand the words she is saying, a young bear responds to the stories a woman reads to him. (Rev: BL 5/1/02; HBG 10/02; SLJ 3/02)

2203 Hassett, John, and Ann Hassett. *Charles of the Wild* (PS–K). Illus. 1997, Houghton Mifflin $14.95 (0-395-78575-8). 32pp. A timid little dog has some tame encounters that he interprets as exciting adventures. (Rev: BL 4/1/97; SLJ 5/97)

2204 Hayes, Geoffrey. *Patrick and the Big Bully* (K–2). Illus. by author. 2001, Hyperion $15.99 (0-7868-0717-2). Little bear Patrick deals with a bully by pretending to be a dragon. (Rev: HBG 3/02; SLJ 1/02)

2205 Hayes, Geoffrey. *Patrick at the Circus* (PS–2). Illus. by author. Series: The Adventures of Patrick Brown. 2002, Hyperion $15.99 (0-7868-0716-4). Little bear Patrick's father takes the place of the clown at the circus. (Rev: HBG 10/02; SLJ 7/02)

2206 Heal, Gillian. *Grandpa Bear's Fantastic Scarf* (K–3). Illus. 1997, Beyond Words $14.95 (1-885223-41-2). 30pp. A young bear learns about life's meaning through studying the colors in his grandpa's scarf, a visual record of his life. (Rev: BL 4/1/97; SLJ 7/97)

2207 Heide, Florence Parry, and Sylvia Van Clief. *That's What Friends Are For* (PS–2). Illus. by Holly Meade. 2003, Candlewick $15.99 (0-7636-1397-5). 40pp. Poor Theodore the elephant has hurt his leg and gets totally useless advice from most of the animals in the forest. (Rev: BL 3/15/03; HBG 10/03; SLJ 5/03)

2208 Heller, Nicholas. *Elwood and the Witch* (PS–1). Illus. by Joseph A. Smith. 2000, Greenwillow LB $16.99 (0-688-16946-5). 32pp. Elwood the pig gets on a witch's broom by mistake and doesn't know how to land it. (Rev: BL 8/00; HBG 3/01; SLJ 9/00)

2209 Helmer, Diana Star. *The Cat Who Came for Tacos* (PS–2). 2003, Whitman LB $14.95 (0-8075-5106-6). Flynn the cat is invited into the home of Senor Tom and Senora Rosa where he enjoys a meal of tuna tacos and learns some valuable lessons about table manners. (Rev: HBG 4/04; SLJ 9/03)

2210 Henkes, Kevin. *Chrysanthemum* (PS–1). Illus. 1991, Greenwillow $15.89 (0-688-09700-6). 32pp. Other mouse children make fun of Chrysanthemum's name until her music teacher helps out. (Rev: BCCB 10/92; BL 8/91; HB 9–10/91*; SLJ 9/91*)

2211 Henkes, Kevin. *Julius, the Baby of the World* (PS–3). Illus. 1990, Greenwillow $15.89 (0-688-08944-5). 32pp. Lilly, a girl mouse, has a fit of jealousy when her baby brother gets all the attention in the family. (Rev: BCCB 11/90; BL 11/1/90; HB 1–2/91*; SLJ 10/90*)

2212 Henkes, Kevin. *Julius's Candy Corn* (PS). Illus. by author. 2003, Greenwillow $6.99 (0-06-053789-2). Julius the mouse has been forbidden to touch the 10 cupcakes, so he decides to count the candy corns on their tops instead, and it's easier to count in your mouth . . . . (Rev: HBG 4/04; SLJ 8/03)

2213 Henkes, Kevin. *Kitten's First Full Moon* (PS). Illus. by author. 2004, Greenwillow LB $16.89 (0-06-058829-2). A kitten mistakes the moon for a bowl of milk and is determined to lap it up. Caldecott Medal winner, 2005. (Rev: BL 2/15/04*; HB 5–6/04; SLJ 4/04)

2214 Henkes, Kevin. *Owen* (PS). Illus. 1993, Greenwillow $15.89 (0-688-11450-4). 24pp. Owen, a mouse, loves his fuzzy yellow blanket more than anything. (Rev: BL 8/93*)

2215 Henkes, Kevin. *Owen's Marshmallow Chick* (PS). Illus. 2002, Greenwillow $6.95 (0-06-001012-6). 24pp. Little Owen the mouse loves all the candy in his Easter basket, most especially the marshmallow chick. (Rev: BCCB 2/02; BL 1/1–15/02; HBG 10/02; SLJ 2/02)

2216 Henkes, Kevin. *Sheila Rae, the Brave* (PS–1). Illus. by author. 1987, Greenwillow $15.89 (0-688-07156-2); Puffin paper $3.95 (0-14-050835-X). 32pp. Sheila Rae, a mouse, fears nothing until she takes the wrong way home. (Rev: BL 9/1/87; SLJ 9/87)

2217 Henkes, Kevin. *Sheila Rae's Peppermint Stick* (PS). 2001, HarperCollins $6.95 (0-06-029451-5). 24pp. Mouse Sheila Rae is tormenting her sister with tricky challenges when she falls and breaks the prized peppermint stick in half, prompting her to share it forthwith. (Rev: HB 9–10/01*; HBG 3/02; SLJ 12/01*)

2218 Henkes, Kevin. *A Weekend with Wendell* (PS–1). Illus. by author. 1986, Greenwillow $15.93 (0-688-06326-8); Morrow paper $5.95 (0-688-14024-6). 32pp. Wendell makes his weekend stay seem like a year to Sophie Mouse, until they have a meeting of the minds. (Rev: BCCB 10/86; BL 9/1/86; SLJ 10/86)

2219 Henkes, Kevin. *Wemberly Worried* (PS–1). Illus. 2000, Greenwillow $15.95 (0-688-17027-7). 32pp. Wemberly, a little mouse girl, is a real worrywart until she makes a new friend at school who makes the world look less scary. (Rev: BCCB 9/00; BL 8/00; HB 9–10/00; HBG 3/01; SLJ 8/00)

2220 Henkes, Kevin. *Wemberly's Ice-Cream Star* (PS). Illus. by author. 2003, Greenwillow $6.99 (0-06-050405-6). Wemberly the mouse finds a solution to her ice cream conundrum: if she gets two bowls and waits until it melts, it won't drip and she can share with her stuffed rabbit. (Rev: HBG 10/03; SLJ 5/03)

2221 Hest, Amy. *Don't You Feel Well, Sam?* (PS–2). Illus. by Anita Jeram. 2002, Candlewick $15.99 (0-7636-1009-7). A gentle story about a little bear who doesn't want to take his cough medicine at first. (Rev: BL 11/15/02*; HBG 3/03; SLJ 9/02)

2222 Hest, Amy. *Guess Who, Baby Duck!* (PS–K). Illus. by Jill Barton. 2004, Candlewick $14.99 (0-7636-1981-7). When Baby Duck has a cold, her grandfather brings an album of pictures to cheer her up. (Rev: SLJ 5/04)

2223 Hest, Amy. *Make the Team, Baby Duck!* (PS–1). Illus. by Jill Barton. 2002, Candlewick $16.99 (0-7636-1541-2). 32pp. Baby Duck, afraid to swim but yearning to be part of the swim team, gains confidence through Grandpa's encouragement. (Rev: BL 8/02; HBG 3/03; SLJ 9/02)

2224 Hest, Amy. *You Can Do It, Sam* (PS–K). Illus. by Anita Jeram. 2003, Candlewick $15.99 (0-7636-1934-5). Sam the bear and his mother bake cakes for their neighbors, and Sam makes the deliveries all by himself. (Rev: HBG 4/04; SLJ 10/03)

2225 Hill, Eric. *Spot at Home* (PS). Illus. by author. Series: Little Spot Board Books. 1991, Penguin Putnam $3.99 (0-399-21774-6). 14pp. This board book features the everyday adventures of the lovable dog Spot. (Rev: BL 6/15/91)

2226 Hill, Eric. *Spot Goes to a Party* (PS–1). Illus. by author. 1992, Penguin Putnam $12.99 (0-399-22409-2). In this lift-the-flap book, Spot the dog dresses as a cowboy to go to a costume party. (Rev: SLJ 9/92)

2227 Hill, Eric. *Spot Goes to the Park* (PS–1). Illus. by author. 1991, Penguin Putnam $12.99 (0-399-21833-5). In this book with easily lifted flaps, Spot the dog enjoys a day in the park playing with his friends. (Rev: SLJ 12/91)

2228 Hill, Eric. *Spot's Baby Sister* (PS). Illus. by author. 1989, Penguin Putnam $12.99 (0-399-21640-5). In a lift-the-flap format, this is the story of Spot the dog and his little sister. (Rev: SLJ 11/89)

2229 Hillenbrand, Will. *Down by the Station* (PS–2). Illus. 1999, Harcourt $15.00 (0-15-201804-2). 40pp. Inspired by the song "Down by the Station," this joyful picture book depicts a train that is taking baby animals to a children's zoo. (Rev: BL 10/15/99; HB 11–12/99; HBG 3/00; SLJ 10/99)

2230 Hillerman, Tony. *Buster Mesquite's Cowboy Band* (PS–2). Illus. by Ernest Franklin. 2001, Buffalo Medicine $15.95 (0-914001-11-6). 32pp. The artwork is the highlight of this story about a burro who loses his job and starts a band with other musically inclined animals. (Rev: BL 11/1/01)

2231 Hindley, Judy. *Do Like a Duck Does!* (PS–K). Illus. by Ivan Bates. 2002, Candlewick $14.99 (0-7636-1668-0). 40pp. A mama duck out-foxes a fox in this charming, brightly illustrated picture book. (Rev: BCCB 4/02; BL 3/1/02; HBG 10/02)

2232 Hines, Anna Grossnickle. *Which Hat Is That?* (PS). Illus. by LeUyen Pham. 2002, Harcourt $15.00 (0-15-216477-4). 36pp. This guessing game challenges readers to name the activity that matches the little mouse's hat, with answers under the flaps. (Rev: BL 11/15/02; HBG 3/03; SLJ 12/02)

2233 Hines, Anna Grossnickle. *Whose Shoes?* (PS–1). Illus. by LeUyen Pham. 2001, Harcourt $14.00 (0-15-201773-9). A bouncy story of a young mouse who likes to try on other people's shoes and listen to the different sounds they make. (Rev: HBG 3/02; SLJ 8/01)

2234 Hissey, Jane. *Little Bear Lost* (PS–K). Illus. 1994, Sandvick paper $9.99 (1-881445-44-5). 32pp. Just when the picnic is about to begin, Little Bear is missing. (Rev: BL 11/1/89)

2235 Hobbie, Holly. *Toot and Puddle* (PS–1). Illus. by author. 1997, Little, Brown $14.95 (0-316-36552-1). While one globe-trotting pig sees the world, his friend stays at home, enjoying life's simple pleasures. (Rev: HBG 3/98; SLJ 12/97)

2236 Hobbie, Holly. *Toot and Puddle: I'll Be Home for Christmas* (PS–2). Illus. by author. 2001, Little, Brown $15.95 (0-316-36623-4). While Puddle the pig has been eagerly preparing for Toot's return from a trip to Scotland, Toot is spared from a disappointing delay when a sleigh mysteriously picks him up and wafts him home to a happy reunion. (Rev: HBG 3/02; SLJ 10/01)

2237 Hobbie, Holly. *Toot and Puddle: Top of the World* (PS–2). Illus. 2002, Little, Brown $15.95 (0-316-36513-0). 32pp. Toot and Puddle, the friendly pigs, visit France and Nepal before deciding that home beckons. Also use *Toot and Puddle: Charming Opal* (2003). (Rev: BL 10/1/02; HBG 3/03)

2238 Hobbie, Holly. *Toot and Puddle: You Are My Sunshine* (PS–2). Illus. by author. 1999, Little, Brown $14.95 (0-316-36562-9). In this story about friendship, two little piglets, Tulip and Puddle, try to cheer up their friend Toot, who is feeling blue. (Rev: BCCB 9/99; HBG 3/00; SLJ 8/99)

2239 Hobbs, Will. *Howling Hill* (K–3). Illus. by Jill Kastner. 1998, Morrow LB $15.93 (0-688-15430-1). 40pp. Hanni, a wolf cub, gets lost and must rely on a bear to help her home in this survival story. Hanni also learns how to howl like the rest of her family. (Rev: BL 9/1/98; HBG 3/99; SLJ 10/98)

2240 Hogrogian, Nonny. *The Tiger of Turkestan* (K–3). Illus. 2002, Hampton Roads $16.95 (1-57174-308-1). 32pp. After his wise grandmother's death, Little Tiger examines his purpose in life and eventually becomes a dancing tiger in this beautifully illustrated picture book. (Rev: BL 1/1–15/03; HBG 3/03; SLJ 4/03)

2241 Holabird, Katherine. *Angelina and Henry* (PS–2). Illus. by Helen Craig. 2002, Pleasant Co. $12.95 (1-58485-523-1). 32pp. A scary episode tests the mettle of mouse Angelina Ballerina and her cousin Henry when they get lost in the woods during a storm. (Rev: BL 10/1/02; HBG 3/03; SLJ 10/02)

2242 Honigsberg, Peter Jan. *Armful of Memories* (K–2). Illus. by Tony Morse. 2002, RDR $17.95 (1-57143-089-X). 32pp. Newbery Mole sells all of his deceased grandparents' possessions in order to get rich, but soon realizes his memories are worth more than money. (Rev: BL 1/1–15/02; HBG 10/02)

2243 Hooper, Meredith. *Dogs' Night* (K–4). Illus. by Allan Curless and Mark Burgess. 2000, Millbrook LB $21.90 (0-7613-1824-0). 32pp. The dogs in the National Gallery in London leave their paintings once a year for a party, but on this occasion they get mixed up and enter the wrong paintings in this hilarious picture book. (Rev: BL 3/15/00; HBG 10/00; SLJ 7/00)

2244 Hoopes, Lyn Littlefield. *My Own Home* (PS–2). Illus. by Ruth Richardson. 1991, HarperCollins $13.95 (0-06-022570-X). A lost little owl is looking for his home. (Rev: SLJ 6/91)

2245 Horn, Peter. *The Best Father of All* (PS–K). Trans. from German by J. Alison James. Illus. by Cristina Kadmon. 2003, North-South LB $16.50 (0-7358-1680-8). In this appealing father-and-son story, a turtle dad tells his son about the things that various animal fathers do to support and encourage their children; in the end the turtle boy decides his dad is the best of them all. (Rev: HBG 10/03; SLJ 8/03)

2246 Horning, Sandra. *The Giant Hug* (PS–2). Illus. by Valeri Gorbachev. 2005, Knopf LB $17.99 (0-375-92477-9). 40pp. Owen the pig sends his grandmother a giant hug that must be passed from person to person by mail workers across the country. (Rev: BL 1/1–15/05; SLJ 2/05)

2247 Horowitz, Dave. *Soon Baboon Soon* (PS–2). Illus. by author. 2005, Penguin Putnam $14.99 (0-399-24268-6). Baboons, chimpanzees, and other apes gather together for a drum show in this picture book with a distinct rhythm. (Rev: SLJ 4/05)

2248 Horse, Harry. *Little Rabbit Lost* (PS–2). Illus. 2002, Peachtree $15.95 (1-56145-273-4). 32pp. Detailed watercolors set the scene as Little Rabbit's birthday trip to RabbitWorld is almost ruined when he gets lost. (Rev: BL 12/1/02; HBG 3/03; SLJ 10/02)

2249 Howard, Arthur. *Cosmo Zooms* (PS–2). Illus. 1999, Harcourt $15.00 (0-15-201788-7). 32pp. Cosmo, a black-and-white dog, accidentally discovers a hidden talent when he falls asleep on a skateboard and begins a fateful trip through town. (Rev: BL 11/1/99; HBG 3/00; SLJ 9/99)

2250 Howe, James. *Horace and Morris But Mostly Dolores* (PS–2). Illus. by Amy Walrod. 1999, Simon & Schuster $16.00 (0-689-31874-X). 32pp. Three mice — two boys and a girl — decide to join unisex clubs, but in time they leave them for a day of exploring together. (Rev: BCCB 3/99; BL 2/15/99*; HBG 10/99; SLJ 3/99)

2251 Howe, James. *Horace and Morris Join the Chorus / But What About Dolores?* (PS–1). Illus. by Amy Walrod. 2002, Simon & Schuster $16.95 (0-

689-83939-1). 32pp. Dolores is so miserable at being left out of the chorus that she writes a sad poetic letter to the Moustro, which is then set to music, gaining her a reputation as a songwriter plus a place in the chorus. (Rev: BL 11/15/02; HB 1–2/03; HBG 3/03; SLJ 11/02)

2252 Howe, James. *I Wish I Were a Butterfly* (PS–2). Illus. by Ed Young. 1987, Harcourt $17.00 (0-15-200470-X). 28pp. Cricket thinks he's ugly; then a butterfly hears his music and wishes he were a cricket. (Rev: BL 11/1/87; SLJ 11/87)

2253 Huneck, Stephen. *Sally Goes to the Farm* (PS–2). Illus. 2002, Abrams $17.95 (0-8109-4498-7). 40pp. Sally the dog visits a farm and has a wonderful time with Molly and other animal friends in this picture book with simple text and large, bold pictures that add to the story. (Rev: BL 7/02; HBG 10/02; SLJ 7/02)

2254 Hunter, Anne. *Possum and the Peeper* (K–2). Illus. by author. 1998, Houghton Mifflin $15.00 (0-395-84631-5). Other animals join Possum in his search to find the origin of the peeping sound he hears. (Rev: BL 6/1–15/98; HBG 10/98; SLJ 3/98*)

2255 Hunter, Anne. *Possum's Harvest Moon* (PS–1). Illus. 1996, Houghton Mifflin $15.00 (0-395-73575-0). 32pp. Possum is so inspired by the autumn that he throws a party for his animal friends. (Rev: BCCB 10/96; BL 9/1/96*; HB 9–10/96; SLJ 8/96*)

2256 Hunter, Sally. *Humphrey's Corner* (PS–1). Illus. by author. 2001, Holt $14.95 (0-8050-6786-8). Young elephant Humphrey can't find anywhere in the house to settle down and play, until his mother shows him the cozy kitchen where she will be. (Rev: HBG 3/02; SLJ 10/01)

2257 Hurd, Thacher. *Art Dog* (PS–3). Illus. 1996, HarperCollins LB $15.89 (0-06-024425-9). 32pp. Arthur, a canine museum guard with artistic abilities, solves the mystery of the missing painting, the *Mona Woofa*. (Rev: BCCB 2/96; BL 1/1–15/96; SLJ 2/96)

2258 Hurd, Thacher. *Mama Don't Allow: Starring Miles and the Swamp Band* (PS–1). Illus. by author. 1984, HarperCollins LB $15.89 (0-06-022690-0); paper $5.95 (0-06-443078-2). 40pp. The Swamp Band finds that the only audience that likes them is the alligator.

2259 Hurd, Thacher. *Mystery on the Docks* (1–3). Illus. by author. 1983, HarperCollins paper $6.95 (0-06-443058-8). 32pp. Ralph, an opera lover, rescues his favorite singer from rat-kidnappers.

2260 Hutchins, Pat. *Good-Night, Owl!* (PS–K). Illus. by author. 1972, Macmillan LB $16.00 (0-02-745900-4). 32pp. Owl is kept awake by animal noises as various animals perch on a branch of his tree; but when darkness falls, owl has his turn and wakes everyone with his screeches.

2261 Hutchins, Pat. *Little Pink Pig* (PS–1). Illus. 1994, Greenwillow $16.00 (0-688-12014-8). 32pp. Little Pig fails to heed his mother's call for bedtime because he is busy chasing a butterfly. (Rev: BL 4/1/94; HB 5–6/94; SLJ 5/94)

2262 Hutchins, Pat. *Rosie's Walk* (K–2). Illus. by author. 1968, Macmillan LB $16.00 (0-02-745850-

4); paper $5.99 (0-02-043750-1). 32pp. Rosie the hen miraculously escapes capture by a fox.

2263 Hutchins, Pat. *We're Going on a Picnic!* (PS–1). Illus. 2002, Greenwillow LB $15.89 (0-688-16800-0). 32pp. Hen, Duck, and Goose set off for a picnic, but find their food has mysteriously disappeared in this terrific tale for young readers. (Rev: BCCB 7–8/02; BL 3/1/02; HBG 10/02; SLJ 3/02)

2264 Hutchins, Pat. *What Game Shall We Play?* (PS–K). Illus. 1995, Morrow paper $4.95 (0-688-13573-0). 24pp. Duck and Frog ask several of their animal friends what game they should play. (Rev: BCCB 10/90; BL 10/15/90; HB 11–12/90; SLJ 9/90*)

2265 Inkpen, Mick. *The Great Pet Sale* (PS–1). Illus. 1999, Orchard $14.95 (0-531-30130-3). 16pp. At a pet store sale, a rat, priced at only one cent, hopes that a young boy will choose him. (Rev: BL 4/15/99; HBG 10/99; SLJ 7/99)

2266 Inkpen, Mick. *Kipper* (PS–K). Illus. 1992, Talman $15.95 (1-85430-333-3). 32pp. When Kipper the dog cleans his basket and gets rid of his toys, he finds it is impossible to be as comfortable as he was before. (Rev: BL 4/1/92; SLJ 5/92)

2267 Inkpen, Mick. *Kipper and Roly* (PS–1). Illus. 2001, Harcourt $13.95 (0-15-216344-1). 32pp. Kipper the dog gets to keep the hamster he bought for his friend Pig's birthday. (Rev: BL 9/15/01; HBG 3/02; SLJ 9/01)

2268 Inkpen, Mick. *Kipper's Monster* (PS–K). Illus. by author. 2002, Harcourt $13.95 (0-15-216614-9). Kipper the pup and pal Tiger retreat to Tiger's bedroom after scaring themselves in their tent. (Rev: HBG 10/02; SLJ 7/02)

2269 Inkpen, Mick. *Kipper's Rainy Day* (PS–K). Illus. by author. 2001, Harcourt paper $5.95 (0-15-216351-4). Kipper the dog enjoys the rain and wonders which of his friends also like it, in this book with flaps that provide answers to questions. Also use *Kipper's Sunny Day* (2001). (Rev: SLJ 10/01)

2270 Inkpen, Mick. *Kipper's Snowy Day* (PS–K). Illus. by author. 1996, Harcourt $14.00 (0-15-201362-8). Two dogs enjoy a day's activities on a snowy day, including making a giant snow dog. (Rev: SLJ 12/96)

2271 Inkpen, Mick. *Picnic* (PS–K). Illus. by author. Series: Little Kipper. 2001, Harcourt paper $4.95 (0-15-216319-0). Kipper and Tiger, two dogs, encounter problems before settling down to have a happy picnic. The same characters also appear in *Thing!* (2001). (Rev: SLJ 3/01)

2272 Irbinskas, Heather. *How Jackrabbit Got His Very Long Ears* (K–3). Illus. by Kenneth J. Spengler. 1994, Northland LB $15.95 (0-87358-566-6). 32pp. When Jackrabbit fails to follow the instructions of the Great Spirit, he is given big ears so that he can hear better. (Rev: BL 6/1–15/94)

2273 Itaya, Satoshi. *Buttons and Bo* (K–3). Trans. by Marianne Martens. Illus. by author. 2004, North-South LB $16.50 (0-7358-1884-3). Lost in the forest, a bear and his younger brother learn about each other's strengths. (Rev: SLJ 8/04)

2274 Jackson, Chris. *The Gaggle Sisters River Tour* (PS–2). Illus. 2002, Lobster $16.95 (1-894222-58-X). 32pp. Sadie the duck is the star of the show on the river, until her hat is ruined and sister Dorothy, the behind-the-scenes toiler, saves the day. (Rev: BL 12/15/02; SLJ 1/03)

2275 Jackson, Chris. *The Gaggle Sisters Sing Again* (K–2). Illus. by author. 2003, Lobster $15.95 (1-894222-56-3). The singing geese of *The Gaggle Sisters River Tour* (2002) are seen in four humorous vignettes with watercolor cartoon illustrations. (Rev: SLJ 12/03)

2276 James, Simon. *Little One Step* (PS–2). Illus. 2003, Candlewick $15.99 (0-7636-2070-X). 32pp. When the youngest duck gets tired, his siblings encourage him to persevere. (Rev: BL 3/15/03; HBG 10/03; SLJ 4/03)

2277 Jennings, Linda. *Scramcat* (PS–2). Illus. by Rhian N. James. 1994, Crocodile $13.95 (1-56656-137-X). A stray cat that is shunned by everyone suddenly becomes popular when it foils a robbery. (Rev: SLJ 11/94)

2278 Jennings, Sharon. *Priscilla and Rosy* (PS–2). Illus. by Linda Hendry. 2001, Fitzhenry & Whiteside $15.95 (1-55041-676-6). 32pp. Detailed illustrations complement this story of two rat best friends, in which Priscilla deals with competing invitations and finally recognizes that friendship is most important. (Rev: BL 12/15/01; SLJ 1/02)

2279 Jennings, Sharon. *Priscilla's Paw de Deux* (K–3). Illus. by Linda Hendry. 2002, Fitzhenry & Whiteside $14.95 (1-55041-718-5). 36pp. Priscilla the rat sneaks into a dance studio after hours to practice ballet, only to meet up with a menacing cat. (Rev: BL 12/15/02; SLJ 2/03)

2280 Jeram, Anita. *All Together Now* (PS–K). Illus. by author. 2000, Candlewick $13.99 (0-7636-0846-7). Mommy Rabbit and Bunny are joined by Little Duckling and Miss Mouse to make a very special family. (Rev: HBG 10/00; SLJ 2/00)

2281 Jeram, Anita. *Bill's Belly Button* (PS–1). Illus. 1991, Little, Brown $14.95 (0-316-46114-8). 32pp. Bill, an elephant, becomes alarmed when he discovers he does not have a belly button. (Rev: BL 9/15/91; SLJ 10/91)

2282 Jeram, Anita. *I Love My Little Storybook* (PS–K). Illus. 2002, Candlewick $12.99 (0-7636-1698-2). 32pp. A little bunny explains how much he loves his story book and all the characters and situations it contains. (Rev: BL 6/1–15/02; HBG 10/02; SLJ 8/02)

2283 Jeschke, Susan. *Perfect the Pig* (K–2). Illus. by author. 1981, Scholastic paper $6.95 (0-8050-4704-2). 40pp. The adventures of a winged pig named Perfect.

2284 Johansen, Hanna. *Henrietta and the Golden Eggs* (1–3). Trans. by John S. Barrett. Illus. by Kathi Bhend. 2002, Godine $16.95 (1-56792-210-4). 64pp. The story of Henrietta, a chicken with dreams of freedom, is told with intricate pen-and-ink drawings. (Rev: BL 3/15/03; HBG 10/03)

2285 Johansen, K. V. *Pippin Takes a Bath* (PS–1). Illus. by Bernice Lum. 1999, Kids Can $12.95 (1-

55074-627-8). 32pp. Pippin the dog refuses to take a bath until he has an encounter with a skunk. (Rev: BL 11/15/99; HBG 3/00; SLJ 11/99)

2286 Johnson, D. B. *Henry Builds a Cabin* (PS–3). Illus. 2002, Houghton Mifflin $15.00 (0-618-13201-5). 32pp. A sensible bear called Henry convinces his friends that a Thoreau-style cabin, and the great outdoors, is all that he needs to be happy. (Rev: BCCB 5/02; BL 3/15/02*; HB 7–8/02; HBG 10/02; SLJ 3/02)

2287 Johnson, D. B. *Henry Climbs a Mountain* (K–3). Illus. by author. 2003, Houghton Mifflin $15.00 (0-618-26902-9). In this third picture book based on the life of Thoreau, Henry the bear is jailed for nonpayment of taxes and escapes into the scenery he has drawn on the wall, joining a stranger who is traveling north to freedom. (Rev: BL 10/1/03*; HBG 4/04; SLJ 9/03)

2288 Johnson, D. B. *Henry Hikes to Fitchburg* (PS–3). Illus. 2000, Houghton Mifflin $15.00 (0-395-96867-4). 32pp. Henry the bear decides to take a nature walk to Fitchburg while his friend will ride the train in this amusing take-off on Thoreau's attitudes and his New England circle. (Rev: BCCB 7–8/00; BL 4/15/00*; HB 5–6/00; HBG 10/00; SLJ 6/00)

2289 Johnson, Gillian. *My Sister Gracie* (PS–3). Illus. by author. 2000, Tundra $16.95 (0-88776-514-9). Fabio, a dog, wants a thoroughbred brother to play with but his family adopts a female mutt from the pound. (Rev: HBG 3/01; SLJ 12/00)

2290 Johnson, Jane. *Are You Ready for Bed?* (PS–K). Illus. by Gaby Hansen. 2002, Tiger Tales $14.95 (1-58925-017-6). Just as exhausted Mrs. Rabbit gets one child off to sleep, another wakes up. (Rev: SLJ 12/02)

2291 Johnson, Paul B. *The Pig Who Ran a Red Light* (PS–2). Illus. 1999, Orchard LB $16.99 (0-531-33136-9). 32pp. Gertrude the cow, who is being mimicked by George the pig, solves the problem by acting like a pig. (Rev: BL 5/1/99; HBG 10/99; SLJ 3/99)

2292 Johnson, Paul Brett. *The Goose Who Went Off in a Huff* (PS–1). Illus. 2001, Scholastic $15.95 (0-531-30317-9). 40pp. Magnolia the goose starts acting oddly when she is overwhelmed by a maternal urge. (Rev: BL 5/15/01; HBG 10/01; SLJ 7/01)

2293 Johnston, Tony. *Chicken in the Kitchen* (PS). Illus. by Eleanor Taylor. 2005, Simon & Schuster $15.95 (0-689-85641-5). 32pp. A chicken wreaks havoc in a kitchen as she searches for a suitable nest in which to lay her eggs. (Rev: BL 1/1–15/05; SLJ 5/05)

2294 Johnston, Tony. *The Chizzywink and the Alamagoozlum* (PS–3). Illus. by Robert Bender. 1998, Holiday House $16.95 (0-8234-1359-4). 32pp. A humorous tale about several animals trying to prevent a giant mosquito (or chizzywink) from entering their house and eating their maple syrup (the alamagoozlum). (Rev: BL 6/1–15/98; HBG 10/98; SLJ 6/98)

2295 Johnston, Tony. *The Iguana Brothers: A Tale of Two Lizards* (PS–2). Illus. by Mark Teague.

1995, Scholastic $15.95 (0-590-47468-5). 32pp. Dom and Tom, iguana brothers, have many differences but remain best friends. (Rev: BCCB 7–8/95; BL 1/15/95*; SLJ 4/95)

2296 Johnston, Tony. *The Worm Family* (1–3). Illus. by Stacy Innerst. 2004, Harcourt $16.00 (0-15-205011-6). The seven Worms, long and skinny and very proud of their essential worminess, nevertheless find it diffcult to locate welcoming neighbors. (Rev: BCCB 9/04; SLJ 2/05)

2297 Jones, Carol. *What's the Time, Mr. Wolf?* (PS–3). Illus. 1999, Houghton Mifflin $15.00 (0-395-95800-8). 32pp. Mr. Wolf invites a number of his tasty friends to a special dinner, but they are aware of his hidden purpose in this book that uses flaps to anticipate plot developments. (Rev: BL 9/15/99; HBG 3/00; SLJ 12/99)

2298 Jones, Elisabeth. *Sunshine and Storm* (PS–K). Illus. by James Coplestone. 2001, Ragged Bear $14.95 (1-929927-27-4). 32pp. Attention-grabbing, expressive art accompanies a story of a temporary rift in the friendship between a dog and cat. (Rev: BL 6/1–15/01; HBG 10/01; SLJ 8/01)

2299 Jorgensen, Gail. *Gotcha!* (PS–1). Illus. by Kerry Argent. 1997, Scholastic $15.95 (0-590-96208-6). 32pp. Bertha the bear creates mayhem when she chases a fly that has eyes on her birthday cake. (Rev: BCCB 4/97; BL 2/1/97; SLJ 3/97)

2300 Joyce, William. *Bently and Egg* (PS–3). Illus. 1992, HarperCollins $15.95 (0-06-020385-4); paper $5.95 (0-06-443352-8). Bently, a frog, is asked to egg-sit for his friend the duck. (Rev: BCCB 3/92; BL 1/1/92; HB 3–4/92; SLJ 4/92*)

2301 Joyce, William. *The Leaf Men and the Brave Good Bugs* (PS–3). Illus. 1996, HarperCollins LB $16.89 (0-06-027238-4). 40pp. The good bugs in a garden join to help restore an old woman's sickly rosebush. (Rev: BL 10/1/96; SLJ 10/96)

2302 Judes, Marie-Odile. *Max, the Stubborn Little Wolf* (K–3). Trans. by Joan Robins. Illus. by Martine Bourre. 2001, HarperCollins $14.95 (0-06-029417-5). 32pp. When Max, a young wolf, states that he wants to become a florist, his father, who thinks this is an occupation unsuitable for a macho wolf, tries to change his son's mind. (Rev: BL 2/1/01; HBG 10/01; SLJ 3/01)

2303 Kaczman, James. *A Bird and His Worm* (PS–2). Illus. 2002, Houghton Mifflin $15.00 (0-618-09460-1). 32pp. A bird and his friend, a worm, learn a lesson about strangers in their travels south. (Rev: BCCB 12/02; BL 9/15/02; HBG 3/03; SLJ 9/02)

2304 Kalan, Robert. *Moving Day* (PS–1). Illus. by Yossi Abolafia. 1996, Greenwillow $14.93 (0-688-13949-3). 32pp. A hermit crab sets out to find a new home. (Rev: BL 6/1–15/96; SLJ 7/96)

2305 Kalman, Maira. *Ooh-La-La (Max in Love)* (PS–4). Illus. 1991, Viking $16.99 (0-670-84163-3). 32pp. Max the dog falls for Crepes Suzette, a dalmatian, in fascinating Paris. (Rev: BL 10/15/91; SLJ 11/91)

2306 Kaminsky, Jef. *Poppy and Ella: Three Stories About Two Friends* (PS–1). Illus. by author. 2000, Hyperion LB $15.49 (0-7868-2447-6). Using cartoons as illustrations, this book describes the exploits of two birds who are friends. (Rev: BCCB 9/00; HBG 10/00; SLJ 7/00)

2307 Kangas, Juli. *The Surprise Visitor* (PS–2). Illus. by author. 2005, Dial $16.99 (0-8037-2989-8). A mouse called Edgar Small tries to return a little blue egg to its rightul owner. (Rev: SLJ 3/05)

2308 Kasza, Keiko. *Don't Laugh, Joe!* (PS–1). Illus. 1997, Penguin Putnam $15.99 (0-399-23036-X). 32pp. A young opossum has an unusual problem: He can't stop giggling while playing dead. (Rev: BL 8/97; SLJ 6/97)

2309 Kasza, Keiko. *The Mightiest* (1–3). Illus. 2001, Penguin Putnam $15.99 (0-399-23586-8). 32pp. Lion, Bear, and Elephant argue about who among them is the mightiest, but they are all outdone by an old woman. (Rev: BL 9/1/01; HBG 3/02; SLJ 11/01)

2310 Kasza, Keiko. *A Mother for Choco* (PS–1). Illus. 1992, Penguin Putnam LB $15.99 (0-399-21841-6). 32pp. A little bird sets out to find his mother and is adopted by a kindly bear. (Rev: BCCB 4/92; BL 3/15/92; HB 5–6/92; SLJ 4/92*)

2311 Kasza, Keiko. *My Lucky Day* (K–2). Illus. by author. 2003, Penguin Putnam $15.99 (0-399-23874-3). A hungry fox can't believe his luck when a piglet comes knocking, but the little pig has many sensible suggestions and in the end the fox is too tired to eat. (Rev: HB 9–10/03; HBG 4/04; SLJ 9/03)

2312 Katz, Avner. *Tortoise Solves a Problem* (K–3). Illus. 1993, HarperCollins LB $12.89 (0-06-020799-X). 32pp. While searching for a new house, the tortoise invents the tortoise shell. (Rev: BL 1/15/93)

2313 Kaufmann, Nancy. *Bye, Bye!* (PS). Illus. by Jung-Hee Spetter. 2003, Front Street $14.95 (1-886910-95-2). On the first day of school, Daddy stays with his piglet son until the teacher makes him leave. (Rev: HBG 4/04; SLJ 10/03)

2314 Keller, Holly. *Farfallina and Marcel* (PS–K). Illus. 2002, HarperCollins LB $17.89 (0-06-623933-8). 32pp. A gosling and a caterpillar, best friends, need time to find each other again when they become a goose and a butterfly. (Rev: BL 9/15/02; HBG 3/03; SLJ 10/02)

2315 Keller, Holly. *Geraldine and Mrs. Duffy* (PS–K). Illus. 2000, Greenwillow LB $15.89 (0-688-16888-4). 32pp. It takes some doing but new babysitter Mrs. Duffy gradually wins over hostile Geraldine, a little pig, and her brother Willy. (Rev: BL 10/1/00; HBG 3/01; SLJ 8/00)

2316 Keller, Holly. *Geraldine's Big Snow* (PS–K). Illus. by author. 1988, Greenwillow $15.89 (0-688-07514-2). 24pp. Young Geraldine, a pig, eagerly awaits the first snow. (Rev: BL 8/88; HB 11–12/88; SLJ 2/89)

2317 Keller, Holly. *Geraldine's Blanket* (PS–2). Illus. by author. 1988, Morrow paper $4.95 (0-688-07810-9). 32pp. A little pig named Geraldine becomes extremely attached to a blanket her aunt gave her.

2318 Keller, Holly. *Pearl's New Skates* (PS–2). Illus. 2005, Greenwillow LB $16.89 (0-06-056281-1). 24pp. Pearl the rabbit is delighted with her new ice skates but finds them surprisingly difficult to use. (Rev: BL 1/1–15/05; SLJ 2/05)

2319 Keller, Holly. *What a Hat!* (PS). Illus. by author. 2003, Greenwillow LB $16.89 (0-06-051480-9). Rabbit siblings Henry and Wizze have opposite reactions to Cousin Newton's attachment to his orange hat. (Rev: HB 11–12/03; HBG 4/04; SLJ 10/03)

2320 Kelley, True. *Blabber Mouse* (1–3). Illus. 2001, Dutton $15.99 (0-525-46742-4). 32pp. Blabber Mouse's classmates finally are forced to devise a solution to stop his chatter when he reminds teacher that she forgot to assign homework. (Rev: BL 12/1/01; HBG 3/02; SLJ 10/01)

2321 Kellogg, Steven, reteller. *Chicken Little* (1–3). Illus. by Steven Kellogg. 1985, Morrow paper $4.95 (0-688-07045-0). 32pp. A wacky version of the old favorite. (Rev: BCCB 11/85; BL 9/1/85; SLJ 10/85)

2322 Kellogg, Steven. *The Mysterious Tadpole: 25th Anniversary Edition* (PS–2). Illus. 2002, Dial $16.99 (0-8037-2788-7). 36pp. This anniversary edition brings a slightly longer text and new illustrations to the story of the tadpole that won't stop growing. (Rev: BL 11/1/02; HBG 3/03)

2323 Kellogg, Steven. *A Penguin Pup for Pinkerton* (PS–2). Illus. 2001, Dial $15.99 (0-8037-2536-1). 32pp. Pinkerton the Great Dane fantasizes that a football is an egg with hilarious consequences in this detailed and humorously illustrated story. (Rev: BL 9/1/01; HB 9–10/01; HBG 3/02; SLJ 8/01*)

2324 Kennedy, X. J. *Elympics* (PS–3). Illus. by Graham Percy. 1999, Penguin Putnam $15.99 (0-399-23249-4). 32pp. This large-format book tells how the Olympic Games would be played if all the participants were elephants. (Rev: BCCB 1/00; BL 3/1/00; HBG 3/00; SLJ 9/99)

2325 Kent, Jack. *Joey* (PS–2). Illus. by author. 1987, Simon & Schuster $11.95 (0-671-66459-X). 32pp. Joey, a young kangaroo, is not allowed out of his mother's pouch, so he invites his friends in.

2326 Kern, Noris. *I Love You with All My Heart* (PS–K). Illus. 1998, Chronicle $14.95 (0-8118-2031-9). 32pp. Several Arctic animals tell a polar bear cub how their mothers love them. (Rev: BL 4/15/98; HBG 10/98; SLJ 8/98)

2327 Ketteman, Helen. *Armadillo Tattletale* (K–3). Illus. by Keith Graves. 2000, Scholastic $15.95 (0-590-99723-8). 32pp. In this original folktale, Armadillo's ears are cut down to a proper size to stop him from hearing — and passing on — gossip. (Rev: BCCB 11/00; BL 12/15/00; HBG 3/01; SLJ 9/00)

2328 Kettner, Christine. *An Ordinary Cat* (PS–K). Illus. 1991, HarperCollins LB $13.89 (0-06-023173-4). 32pp. Inwardly, William is not the ordinary cat that everyone sees. (Rev: BL 1/1/91; SLJ 12/91)

2329 Kilaka, John. *Fresh Fish: A Tale from Tanzania* (K–3). Illus. by author. 2005, Groundwood $16.95 (0-88899-656-X). 28pp. Despite Sokwe Chimpanzee's generosity, Dog steals fish from him and is put on trial by the other animals; he is sentenced, makes his penance, and all is forgiven. (Rev: BCCB 6/05; SLJ 6/05)

2330 Kinerk, Robert. *Clorinda* (PS–2). Illus. by Steven Kellogg. 2003, Simon & Schuster $15.95 (0-689-86449-3). After a very brief stint as a performer, Clorinda the cow heads back to the farm and there shares her knowledge of ballet. (Rev: BL 11/1/03; HBG 4/04; SLJ 11/03)

2331 King, Bob. *Sitting on the Farm* (PS–1). Illus. by Bill Slavin. 1992, Scholastic paper $7.99 (0-590-73979-2). 32pp. In successive verses of a silly song, a young girl calls on animals to remove a bug from her knee. (Rev: BL 2/1/92; SLJ 8/92)

2332 Kirk, David. *Little Miss Spider* (PS–1). Illus. 1999, Scholastic $12.95 (0-439-08389-3). 32pp. After hatching, Little Miss Spider sets out to find her mother and is helped by a kindly green beetle named Betty. (Rev: BL 12/1/99; HBG 3/00; SLJ 11/99)

2333 Kirk, David. *Little Miss Spider at Sunny Patch School* (PS–K). Illus. by author. 2000, Scholastic $12.95 (0-439-08727-9). Miss Spider starts school and soon finds she is failing leaf chewing, flying, and stinging but gains high marks in climbing and spinning. (Rev: HBG 3/01; SLJ 9/00)

2334 Kirk, David. *Little Pig, Biddle Pig* (PS). Illus. Series: Biddle Books. 2001, Scholastic $9.95 (0-439-30575-6). 32pp. Little Pig's desire to remain clean wins her no friends in the pig pen. (Rev: BL 1/1–15/02; HBG 3/02; SLJ 11/01)

2335 Kirk, David. *Miss Spider's New Car* (PS–2). Illus. 1997, Scholastic $16.95 (0-590-30713-4). 32pp. Miss Spider and her husband, Holley, go shopping for a car and become the victims of a nefarious car dealer. (Rev: BL 11/1/97; HBG 3/98; SLJ 1/98)

2336 Kirk, David. *Miss Spider's Tea Party* (PS–3). Illus. 1994, Scholastic $16.95 (0-590-47724-2). 32pp. No one wants to accept Miss Spider's invitation to tea for fear of being eaten. (Rev: BL 1/15/94; SLJ 6/94)

2337 Kirk, David. *Miss Spider's Wedding* (K–4). Illus. 1995, Scholastic $16.95 (0-590-56866-3). 40pp. Miss Spider finds she is very wrong when she thinks handsome Spiderus Reeves is "Mr. Right." A sequel to *Miss Spider's Tea Party* (1993). (Rev: BL 10/1/95; SLJ 10/95)

2338 Kleven, Elisa. *Sun Bread* (PS–1). Illus. 2001, Dutton $16.99 (0-525-46674-6). 32pp. Longing for sun, the baker makes a sun-shaped loaf so enticing that the animals cheer up and sun breaks through the clouds. (Rev: BL 5/1/01; HBG 10/01; SLJ 6/01)

2339 Knowles, Sheena. *Edwina the Emu* (PS–1). Illus. by Rod Clement. 1997, HarperCollins paper $6.95 (0-06-443483-4). At the zoo, Edwina the emu leaves her husband to tend their eggs while she goes out looking for a job. (Rev: SLJ 9/97)

2340 Koehler, Phoebe. *Making Room* (PS–1). Illus. 1993, Macmillan LB $14.95 (0-02-750875-7). 48pp. A large dog makes room in his household for a woman, a baby, and a cat. (Rev: BL 3/15/93; SLJ 8/93)

2341 Kolar, Bob. *Racer Dogs* (PS–2). Illus. 2003, Dutton $15.99 (0-525-45939-1). 32pp. Dogs zoom racecars around a track and end up in a jumbled pileup in this funny picture book. (Rev: BL 2/1/03; HBG 10/03; SLJ 3/03)

2342 Koller, Jackie French. *Baby for Sale* (PS–2). Illus. by Janet Pedersen. 2002, Marshall Cavendish $16.95 (0-7614-5106-4). 32pp. Rabbit Peter, fed up with his baby sister, tries to sell her to the neighbors but finally decides to keep her when he realizes that he loves her. (Rev: BL 9/1/02; HBG 3/03; SLJ 9/02)

2343 Komoda, Beverly. *The Too Hot Day* (PS–K). Illus. 1991, HarperCollins $14.89 (0-06-021612-3). 32pp. Mama and her bunny family try to escape the heat through a variety of activities. (Rev: BL 5/15/91; SLJ 8/91)

2344 Komoda, Beverly. *The Winter Day* (PS–1). Illus. 1991, HarperCollins $13.95 (0-06-023301-X). 32pp. The Hopper children, a group of rabbits, are enjoying the snow until a bully named Spike spoils their fun. (Rev: BL 12/1/91; SLJ 1/92)

2345 Kopelke, Lisa. *Excuse Me!* (K–2). Illus. 2003, Simon & Schuster $15.95 (0-689-85111-1). 32pp. Frog, a notorious burper, discovers (after living among other belchers) that it's better to be polite. (Rev: BL 2/15/03; HBG 10/03; SLJ 4/03)

2346 Kopelke, Lisa. *Tissue, Please!* (PS–1). Illus. by author. 2004, Simon & Schuster $15.95 (0-689-86248-2). Frog has a very runny nose and discovers that tissues do serve a purpose. (Rev: SLJ 11/04)

2347 Kortepeter, Paul. *The Hugs and Kisses Contest* (PS–1). Illus. by Susan Wheeler. 2002, Dutton $14.99 (0-525-46531-6). 28pp. A sweet story about a brother and sister rabbit who compete for the most hugs and kisses from their mother in a single day. (Rev: BL 4/1/02; HBG 10/02; SLJ 3/02)

2348 Koscielniak, Bruce. *Geoffrey Groundhog Predicts the Weather* (PS–1). Illus. 1995, Houghton Mifflin $15.00 (0-395-70933-4). 32pp. When Geoffrey Groundhog emerges from his hole on Groundhog Day, he finds he is part of a media event. (Rev: BCCB 11/95; BL 10/15/95; SLJ 10/95)

2349 Kovalski, Maryann. *Brenda and Edward* (PS–2). Illus. 1997, Kids Can $14.95 (0-919964-77-X). 32pp. Two dogs who adore each other are separated until, years later, a series of coincidences brings them back together. (Rev: BL 10/15/97; SLJ 9/97)

2350 Kovalski, Maryann. *Omar on Ice* (PS–2). Illus. 1999, Fitzhenry & Whiteside $13.95 (1-55041-507-7). 32pp. Omar, a young bear, learns he can produce beautiful pictures on the ice when he whirls and swirls while skating. (Rev: BL 10/15/99)

2351 Kovalski, Maryann. *Queen Nadine* (K–2). Illus. by author. 1998, Orca $14.95 (1-55143-093-2). When a farmer sells his cows to raise corn, he decides to keep Nadine, the dreamy loner of his herd. (Rev: HBG 3/99; SLJ 12/98)

2352 Kranendonk, Anke. *Just a Minute* (PS–K). Illus. by Jung-Hee Spetter. 1998, Front Street $14.95 (1-886910-29-4). 32pp. Every time Piggy wants attention, mama says "Just a minute," little knowing what mischief her son is up to in the meantime. (Rev: BL 4/15/98; HBG 10/98; SLJ 7/98)

2353 Kraus, Robert. *Big Squeak, Little Squeak* (PS–1). Illus. by Kevin O'Malley. 1996, Orchard LB $16.99 (0-531-08774-3). 32pp. Two little mice outwit Mr. Kit Kat, the owner of the local cheese store, who is intent on capturing them. (Rev: BL 10/15/96; SLJ 10/96)

2354 Kraus, Robert. *Herman the Helper* (PS–K). Illus. by Jose Aruego and Ariane Dewey. 1987, Simon & Schuster paper $6.99 (0-671-66270-8). Herman, a green octopus, helps his many friends with his many arms. A reissued title, as are: *Another Mouse to Feed* and *Milton the Early Riser* (both 1987).

2355 Kraus, Robert. *Leo the Late Bloomer* (PS–K). Illus. by Jose Aruego. 1971, HarperCollins LB $15.89 (0-87807-043-5). 32pp. Leo, a lion, is just a late bloomer, as Mother tells Father, but Father is worried. Finally Leo blooms — he can read, write, and eat neatly. A beguiling, humorous story.

2356 Kraus, Robert. *Mouse in Love* (PS–2). Illus. by Jose Aruego and Ariane Dewey. 2000, Orchard LB $16.99 (0-531-33297-7). 32pp. Mouse searches high and low for the mouse of his dreams and finds that she lives next door. (Rev: BCCB 11/00; BL 9/15/00; HBG 3/01; SLJ 8/00)

2357 Kraus, Robert. *Whose Mouse Are You?* (PS–1). Illus. by Jose Aruego. 1970, Macmillan paper $5.99 (0-689-71142-5). 32pp. A young mouse is asked eight questions by his family — which should delight young children who are asked similar questions by their families.

2358 Krischanitz, Raoul. *Nobody Likes Me!* (K–2). Trans. by Rosemary Lanning. Illus. 1999, North-South LB $15.88 (0-7358-1055-9). A lonely dog, shunned by other animals, is accepted after he becomes friends with a respected fox. (Rev: BL 4/15/99; HBG 10/99)

2359 Kroll, Virginia. *Busy, Busy Mouse* (PS). Illus. by Fumi Kosaka. 2003, Viking $15.99 (0-670-03527-0). A mouse gets ready for bed just as its human counterparts are getting up in this entertaining juxtaposition of quite different lives. (Rev: HBG 10/03; SLJ 8/03)

2360 Krosoczka, Jarrett J. *Punk Farm* (PS–2). Illus. 2005, Knopf LB $17.99 (0-375-92429-9). 40pp. When the farmer's away, the animals play a rock version of "Old MacDonald Had a Farm." (Rev: BL 5/1/05)

2361 Kudrna, C. Imbior. *To Bathe a Boa* (PS). Illus. by author. 1986, Carolrhoda LB $15.95 (0-87614-306-0); paper $5.95 (0-87614-490-3). A little boy hunts high and low for his boa, who doesn't want a bath. (Rev: BL 1/1/87; SLJ 2/87)

2362 Kvasnosky, Laura McGee. *Frank and Izzy Set Sail* (PS–1). Illus. 2004, Candlewick $15.99 (0-7636-2146-3). 32pp. Frank, a reclusive bear, and Izzy, an adventurous rabbit, manage to have a great time on a overnight jaunt to Crescent Island despite their differences in temperament. (Rev: BL 5/15/04; SLJ 6/04)

2363 Kvasnosky, Laura McGee. *See You Later, Alligator* (PS–K). Illus. 1995, Harcourt $10.00 (0-15-200301-0). 24pp. Popular sayings are used to describe a little alligator's day at school. (Rev: BL 9/15/95; SLJ 11/95)

2364 Laden, Nina. *Bad Dog* (K–4). Illus. by author. 2000, Walker $15.95 (0-8027-8747-9); paper $16.85 (0-8027-8748-7). After a series of amusing adventures, Bad Dog finds he is in jail. (Rev: BCCB 10/00; HBG 3/01; SLJ 9/00)

2365 Laden, Nina. *Roberto: The Insect Architect* (2–4). Illus. 2000, Chronicle $15.95 (0-8118-2465-9). 40pp. A termite named Roberto achieves his dream of being an architect by planning and building a shelter for homeless bugs. (Rev: BCCB 12/00; BL 11/15/00; HBG 3/01)

2366 Laden, Nina. *When Pigasso Met Mootisse* (K–2). Illus. 1998, Chronicle $15.95 (0-8118-1121-2). 40pp. Two painters, Pigasso, a pig, and Mootisse, a bull, become rivals in the art world in this takeoff on the Picasso-Matisse feud. (Rev: BL 11/1/98; HBG 3/99; SLJ 11/98)

2367 Laguna, Sofie. *Too Loud Lily* (PS–1). Illus. by Kerry Argent. 2004, Scholastic $14.95 (0-439-57913-9). 32pp. A little hippopotamus who just can't help being loud finds that her booming voice is a hit with the school's new drama teacher. (Rev: BL 2/15/04; SLJ 3/04)

2368 Lakin, Patricia. *Clarence the Copy Cat* (PS–2). Illus. by John Manders. 2002, Doubleday LB $17.99 (0-385-90854-7). 32pp. Clarence the cat is a pacifist and won't catch mice, which makes it difficult for him to find a home until he discovers the library, but even there a mouse finally turns up and causes much hilarity. (Rev: BL 11/1/02; HBG 3/03; SLJ 10/02)

2369 Lakin, Patricia. *Snow Day!* (PS–1). Illus. by Scott Nash. 2002, Dial $15.99 (0-8037-2642-2). 32pp. There's a twist to this story of four crocodiles playing in the snow — they're all school principals. (Rev: BL 11/15/02; HBG 3/03; SLJ 11/02)

2370 Landstrom, Olof, and Lena Landstrom. *Boo and Baa at Sea* (PS). Illus. 1997, Farrar $7.95 (91-29-63921-2). 26pp. In this simple reading book, Boo and Baa get stuck when they take out a rowboat. Also use *Boo and Baa on a Cleaning Spree* (1997). (Rev: BL 7/97; SLJ 7/97)

2371 Landstrom, Olof, and Lena Landstrom. *Boo and Baa in a Party Mood* (PS). Trans. by Joan Sandin. Illus. 1996, Farrar paper $7.95 (91-29-63918-2). 22pp. In this simple picture book, two young sheep, Boo and Baa, prepare for a friend's birthday party. Also use *Boo and Baa in Windy Weather* (1996). (Rev: BL 11/1/96)

2372 Landstrom, Olof, and Lena Landstrom. *Boo and Baa in the Woods* (PS–K). Illus. 2000, Farrar $7.95 (91-29-64754-1). 28pp. Boo and Baa, two sheep, are disappointed when they can't find berries to pick, but some ants accidentally show them a spot where berries are abundant. Also use *Boo and Baa Get Wet* (2000). (Rev: BL 11/15/00; HBG 3/01; SLJ 9/00)

2373 Langreuter, Jutta. *Little Bear Brushes His Teeth* (PS–K). Illus. by Vera Sobat. 1997, Millbrook LB $21.40 (0-7613-0190-9); paper $7.95 (0-7613-0230-1). 32pp. Little Bear pretends he is a soldier fighting bacteria when he brushes his teeth. Also use *Little Bear Goes to Kindergarten* (1997). (Rev: BL 2/1/97; SLJ 7/97)

2374 Lansky, Vicki. *It's Not Your Fault, KoKo Bear: A Read-Together Book for Parents and Young Children During Divorce* (PS–2). Illus. by Jane Prince. 1998, Book Peddlers $10.95 (0-916773-46-9); paper $5.99 (0-916773-47-7). When KoKo Bear's parents divorce, the cub goes through the emotions associated with it: anger, guilt, confusion, and sadness. (Rev: HBG 10/98; SLJ 6/98)

2375 Larios, Julie Hofstrand. *On the Stairs* (PS–1). Illus. by Mary Hofstrand Cornish. 1999, Front Street $15.95 (1-886910-34-0). 32pp. Using rhyming verse, this book portrays two mice and the fun they have naming each of the 12 steps on their stairs. (Rev: BL 12/15/99; HBG 3/00; SLJ 12/99)

2376 Lasky, Kathryn. *Science Fair Bunnies* (K–2). Illus. by Marylin Hafner. 2000, Candlewick $15.99 (0-7636-0729-0). 32pp. Clyde, a bunny, uses a loose tooth as the basis of a show-stealing science fair project. (Rev: BL 7/00; HBG 10/00; SLJ 7/00)

2377 Lasky, Kathryn. *Tumble Bunnies* (K–2). Illus. by Marylin Hafner. 2005, Candlewick $15.99 (0-7636-2265-6). Clyde, a bunny who never seems to get picked for the team, is pleased to discover the pleasure of individual events such as trampoline. (Rev: SLJ 4/05)

2378 Lass, Bonnie, and Philemon Sturges. *Who Took the Cookies from the Cookie Jar?* (PS–K). Illus. by Ashley Wolff. 2000, Little, Brown $14.95 (0-316-82016-4). 32pp. A little skunk, dressed as a cowboy, becomes a detective and inquires of various animals who stole the cookies from the cookie jar. (Rev: BCCB 12/00; BL 10/15/00; HBG 3/01; SLJ 10/00)

2379 Lavis, Steve. *Little Mouse Has a Party* (PS). Illus. by author. Series: Ragged Bears Ready Readers. 2000, Ragged Bear $6.95 (1-929927-11-8). Little Mouse spends a week getting ready for his party, which will take place on Sunday, in this simple text with one sentence per page. Also use *Little Mouse Has a Friend* (2000). (Rev: HBG 10/01; SLJ 6/01)

2380 Lawrence, John. *This Little Chick* (PS–K). Illus. 2002, Candlewick $15.99 (0-7636-1716-4). 32pp. A little chick learns the many languages of the barnyard as he visits his animal friends. (Rev: BCCB 4/02; BL 2/1/02; HBG 10/02; SLJ 3/02*)

2381 Layton, Neal. *Hot Hot Hot* (K–3). Illus. by author. 2004, Candlewick $15.99 (0-7636-2148-X). A lighthearted story about a pair of woolly mammoths, Oscar and Arabella, and how they try to keep cool when summer suddenly comes in the middle of the Ice Age. (Rev: HB 7–8/04; SLJ 6/04)

2382 Leaf, Munro. *The Story of Ferdinand* (K–4). Illus. by Robert Lawson. 1936, Puffin paper $6.99 (0-14-050234-3). 72pp. The classic story of the bull who wants only to sit and smell flowers.

2383 Lebrun, Claude. *Little Brown Bear Does Not Want to Eat* (PS). Illus. by Daniele Bour. Series: Little Brown Bear Books. 1996, Children's Book Pr. LB $12.00 (0-531-07823-2); paper $3.50 (0-531-17823-7). A simple book about a childhood problem and its solution. Also use *Little Brown Bear Is Growing Up* and *Little Brown Bear Wants to Be Read To* (both 1996). (Rev: SLJ 9/96)

2384 Lee, Ho Baek. *While We Were Out* (PS–1). Illus. by author. 2003, Kane/Miller $15.95 (1-929132-44-1). An adventurous white rabbit finds herself home alone and decides to try some of the luxuries of human life. (Rev: BL 4/15/03*; HB 7–8/03; HBG 10/03; SLJ 6/03)

2385 Leedy, Loreen. *The Furry News: How to Make a Newspaper* (1–4). Illus. 1990, Holiday House LB $16.95 (0-8234-0793-4). 32pp. Big Bear becomes disgusted with his local newspaper and decides to publish his own. (Rev: BCCB 5/90; BL 5/1/90)

2386 Leedy, Loreen. *The Great Trash Bash* (K–2). Illus. 1991, Holiday House LB $16.95 (0-8234-0869-8). Mayor Hippo discovers that his town has too much trash. (Rev: SLJ 5/91)

2387 Leedy, Loreen. *The Monster Money Book* (2–4). Illus. 1992, Holiday House LB $16.95 (0-8234-0922-8). 32pp. Sarah joins a monster club and learns about various denominations of money. (Rev: BCCB 3/92; BL 3/15/92; SLJ 6/92)

2388 Leedy, Loreen. *Pingo the Plaid Panda* (PS–K). Illus. by author. 1989, Holiday House LB $13.95 (0-8234-0727-6). 32pp. A panda whose fur is plaid feels he is not liked because he is different. (Rev: SLJ 7/89)

2389 LeGuin, Ursula. *Tom Mouse* (K–3). Illus. by Julie Downing. 2002, Millbrook LB $22.90 (0-7613-2663-4). 40pp. A mouse with wanderlust finds a traveling companion in an elderly African American woman when he boards a train bound for the unknown. (Rev: BCCB 5/02; BL 3/15/02; HB 5–6/02; HBG 10/02; SLJ 5/02)

2390 L'Engle, Madeleine. *The Other Dog* (PS–1). Illus. by Christine Davenier. 2001, North-South $15.95 (1-58717-040-X). 48pp. An older dog wonders why the family has adopted another dog and why the newcomer seems to be getting special attention. (Rev: BL 3/1/01; HBG 10/01)

2391 Lerman, Rory S. *Charlie's Checklist* (PS–2). Illus. by Alison Bartlett. 1997, Orchard paper $14.95 (0-531-30001-3). 32pp. When Charlie the puppy places a want ad to find a new home in the city, his young country master is forlorn at the thought of him leaving. (Rev: BCCB 6/97; BL 6/1–15/97; SLJ 5/97)

2392 Leslie, Amanda. *Are Chickens Stripy? A Lift-the-Flap Book* (PS). Illus. by author. 2000, Handprint $4.95 (1-929766-09-2). A flap book that describes the behavior of various animals in an amusing way. Also use *Do Crocodiles Moo?* (2000). (Rev: SLJ 12/00)

2393 Lester, Helen. *Hooway for Wodney Wat* (PS–2). Illus. by Lynn Munsinger. 1999, Houghton Mifflin $15.00 (0-395-92392-1). 32pp. A humorous story about Wodney Wat and his problems pronouncing the letter *r*. (Rev: BL 5/1/99; HB 7–8/99; HBG 10/99; SLJ 5/99)

2394 Lester, Helen. *Listen, Buddy* (PS–3). Illus. by Lynn Munsinger. 1995, Houghton Mifflin $15.00 (0-395-72361-2). 32pp. Buddy, a daydreaming rabbit, gets into serious trouble because he can't pay attention. (Rev: BL 10/15/95; SLJ 11/95)

2395 Lester, Helen. *Me First* (PS–3). Illus. by Lynn Munsinger. 1992, Houghton Mifflin $14.95 (0-395-58706-9). 32pp. Pinkerton the pig is so pushy that he will do anything to be first. (Rev: BL 10/1/92; HB 11–12/92; SLJ 10/92*)

2396 Lester, Helen. *A Porcupine Named Fluffy* (PS–K). Illus. by Lynn Munsinger. 1986, Houghton Mifflin $16.00 (0-395-36895-2); paper $6.95 (0-395-52018-5). Fluffy's ridiculous name leads to a friendship with a rhino, with another ridiculous name — Hippo. (Rev: BL 4/15/86; SLJ 8/86)

2397 Lester, Helen. *Score One for the Sloths!* (PS–3). Illus. by Lynn Munsinger. 2001, Houghton Mifflin $15.00 (0-618-10857-2). 32pp. A school full of sleepy sloths faces closure for its low test scores and it's up to a new student called Sparky to save the day. (Rev: BL 8/01; HB 9–10/01; HBG 3/02; SLJ 10/01)

2398 Lester, Helen. *Something Might Happen* (PS). Illus. by Lynn Munsinger. 2003, Houghton Mifflin $15.00 (0-618-25406-4). 32pp. Afraid of almost everything, Twitchly Fidget the lemur hides in his lonely hut until his Aunt Bridget dispels his fears and reveals a new way to live. (Rev: HBG 4/04; SLJ 9/03)

2399 Lester, Helen. *Tacky and the Emperor* (PS–3). Illus. by Lynn Munsinger. 2000, Houghton Mifflin $15.00 (0-395-98210-4). 32pp. Tacky, a penguin, gets royal treatment when he puts on a fancy suit that is actually the emperor's robes. (Rev: BL 8/00; HBG 3/01; SLJ 11/00)

2400 Lester, Helen. *Tacky in Trouble* (PS–1). Illus. by Lynn Munsinger. 1998, Houghton Mifflin $15.00 (0-395-86113-6). 32pp. Tacky, a fearless penguin, lands on a tropical isle after an ice-surfing spree and becomes a centerpiece in the kitchen of one of the island's elephants. (Rev: BCCB 5/98; BL 4/1/98; HBG 10/98; SLJ 5/98)

2401 Lester, Helen. *Tacky the Penguin* (PS–3). Illus. by Lynn Munsinger. 1988, Houghton Mifflin $15.00 (0-395-45536-7); paper $5.95 (0-395-56233-3). 32pp. Most penguins wear black, but Tacky prefers Hawaiian shirts and checkered bow ties. (Rev: BCCB 4/88; BL 4/1/88)

2402 Lester, Helen. *Tackylocks and the Three Bears* (K–2). Illus. by Lynn Munsinger. 2002, Houghton Mifflin $15.00 (0-618-22490-4). 32pp. Tacky the penguin adds his own personal touches to his role as Goldilocks, much to the delight of his audience. (Rev: BCCB 12/02; BL 10/1/02; HBG 3/03; SLJ 9/02)

2403 Lester, Helen. *Three Cheers for Tacky* (K–2). Illus. by Lynn Munsinger. 1994, Houghton Mifflin $14.95 (0-395-66841-7). 32pp. Tacky the Penguin has the spirit but not the skill to function in a cheer-leading competition. (Rev: BL 2/15/94; HB 9–10/94; SLJ 5/94)

2404 Lester, Julius. *Ackamarackus: Julius Lester's Sumptuously Silly Fantastically Funny Fables* (PS–3). Illus. by Emilie Chollat. 2001, Scholastic $17.95 (0-590-48913-5). 48pp. Six humorous, inventive tales featuring such animal characters as Bernard the Bee, Adalbert the Alligator, and Ellen the Eagle. (Rev: BCCB 3/01; BL 2/1/01; HBG 10/01; SLJ 3/01)

2405 Lester, Robin, and Helen Lester. *Wuzzy Takes Off* (PS). Illus. by Miko Imai. 1995, Candlewick $8.95 (1-56402-498-9). 32pp. Wuzzy, a teddy bear, confuses an ordinary playground with being on the moon. (Rev: BL 2/1/96)

2406 Lesynski, Loris. *Night School* (1–3). Illus. 2001, Annick LB $18.95 (1-55037-585-7); paper $5.95 (1-55037-584-9). 32pp. Being a night owl, Eddie likes the idea of Night School until he realizes that many of the students are not like him. (Rev: BL 6/1–15/01; HBG 10/01)

2407 Lewis, Kevin. *My Truck Is Stuck!* (PS–K). Illus. by Daniel Kirk. 2002, Hyperion $14.99 (0-7868-0534-X). 40pp. When their dump truck gets stuck, the two dogs hauling a load of bones seek help, in this amusing, brightly illustrated book with a teasing subplot and some basic counting reminders. (Rev: BL 11/1/02; HBG 3/03; SLJ 10/02)

2408 Lewis, Paeony. *I'll Always Love You* (PS). Illus. by Penny Ives. 2002, Tiger Tales paper $5.95 (1-58925-360-4). Alex Bear's mother is disappointed when he behaves badly but always forgives him and says she'll love him. (Rev: SLJ 8/02)

2409 Lewis, Rob. *Brothers and Sisters* (PS–1). Illus. by author. 2005, Hodder $16.99 (0-340-86600-4). The good and the bad side of having siblings are presented in the two halves of this book about young rabbits. (Rev: SLJ 4/05)

2410 Lewis, Rob. *Friends* (PS–2). Illus. 2001, Holt $16.95 (0-8050-6691-8). 32pp. Little rabbit Oscar has trouble making new friends until he accepts that everyone is different in this beginning reader with attractive, cartoonlike illustrations. (Rev: BL 11/15/01; HBG 3/02; SLJ 12/01)

2411 Lewison, Wendy C. *Shy Vi* (PS–K). Illus. by Stephen J. Smith. 1993, Simon & Schuster paper $14.00 (0-671-76968-5). 28pp. A little mouse named Violet is so shy that she can't speak above a whisper. (Rev: BL 5/1/93; SLJ 7/93)

2412 Leznoff, Glenda. *Pigmalion* (K–2). Illus. by Rachel Berman. 2002, Tradewind $15.95 (1-896580-20-3). Little pig Juliet is a skilled singer, actor, and dancer but so shy that she must rehearse in private when she's chosen for the part of Eliza Piglittle. (Rev: SLJ 8/02)

2413 Lidz, Jane. *Zak: The One-of-a-Kind Dog* (PS–2). Photos by author. 1997, Abrams paper $12.95 (0-8109-3995-9). Zak, a mixed-breed dog, wonders about his ancestors and concludes that whoever they were, he is one of a kind. (Rev: BL 4/15/98; HBG 3/98; SLJ 3/98)

2414 Liersch, Anne. *A House Is Not a Home* (K–3). Illus. by Christa Unzner. 1999, North-South LB

$15.88 (0-7358-1157-1). 32pp. Bossy Badger alienates all the other woodland creatures, but when winter comes he is lonely and asks if he can join them in their cozy home. (Rev: BL 11/1/99; HBG 3/00; SLJ 11/99)

2415 Lies, Brian. *Hamlet and the Magnificent Sandcastle* (K–3). Illus. 2001, Moon Mountain $15.95 (0-9677929-2-4). 32pp. Hamlet the pig and his porcupine friend Quince are stranded on Hamlet's giant sandcastle when the tide comes in. (Rev: BL 1/1–15/02; SLJ 6/01)

2416 Lillegard, Dee. *The Big Bug Ball* (PS–K). Illus. by Rex Barron. 1999, Penguin Putnam LB $15.99 (0-399-23121-8). A rhyming tale about various insects who stage some jazzy entertainment in a city park. (Rev: HBG 10/99; SLJ 7/99)

2417 Lin, Grace. *Okie-Dokie, Artichokie!* (K–2). Illus. by author. 2003, Viking $14.99 (0-670-03623-4). Relations initially are strained between Marklee the monkey and his new downstairs neighbor, Artichoke the giraffe. (Rev: BL 9/1/03; HBG 4/04; SLJ 11/03)

2418 Lin, Grace. *Olvina Flies* (PS–1). Illus. 2003, Holt $15.95 (0-8050-6711-6). 32pp. Olvina, a hen, is reluctant to take her first airplane ride but finds a friend in a fellow traveler, a penguin. (Rev: BL 2/1/03; HB 5–6/03; HBG 10/03; SLJ 4/03)

2419 Lindgren, Barbro. *Benny's Had Enough!* (PS–K). Trans. by Elisabeth Kallick Dyssegaard. Illus. by Olof Landstrom. 1999, Farrar $14.00 (91-29-64563-8). 28pp. A little piglet runs away but finds that life outside his comfortable home is difficult. (Rev: BL 10/15/99; HB 11–12/99; HBG 3/00; SLJ 12/99)

2420 Lionni, Leo. *Alexander and the Wind-Up Mouse* (K–2). Illus. by author. 1969, Pantheon paper $5.99 (0-394-82911-5). 32pp. Alexander, a real mouse, envies Willy, a toy, windup mouse, who is loved and cuddled.

2421 Lionni, Leo. *The Biggest House in the World* (PS–2). Illus. by author. 1968, Knopf paper $5.99 (0-394-82740-6). 32pp. A young snail, desiring a larger shell, receives fatherly advice and decides that small accommodations are an asset in regaining his mobility.

2422 Lionni, Leo. *Fish Is Fish* (K–2). Illus. by author. 1970, Knopf paper $5.99 (0-394-82799-6). 32pp. A fable about a fish who learns from a frog how to be happy just being himself.

2423 Lionni, Leo. *Frederick* (PS–2). Illus. by author. 1967, Knopf LB $18.99 (0-394-91040-0); paper $5.99 (0-394-82614-0). 40pp. A field mouse appears to be ignoring the coming of winter, but actually he is not.

2424 Lionni, Leo. *The Greentail Mouse* (PS–2). Illus. 2003, Knopf $15.95 (0-375-82399-9). 32pp. A reissue of a 1973 picture book that tells the story of field mice who must learn to trust each other again. (Rev: BL 1/1–15/03; HBG 10/03)

2425 Lionni, Leo. *Inch by Inch* (PS–2). Illus. by author. 1962, Astor-Honor $19.00 (0-8392-3010-9). When the birds demand that he measure the length

of a nightingale's song, this clever, captive inchworm inches his way to freedom.

2426 Lionni, Leo. *Matthew's Dream* (K–3). Illus. 1995, Random paper $5.99 (0-679-87318-X). With his imagination, Matthew, a little mouse, can turn his dismal home into something stunning. (Rev: BCCB 3/91; BL 1/1/91; SLJ 4/91*)

2427 Lionni, Leo. *Swimmy* (PS–1). Illus. by author. 1963, Pantheon LB $18.99 (0-394-91713-8); Knopf paper $5.99 (0-394-82620-5). 40pp. A remarkable little fish instructs the rest of his school in the art of protection — swim in the formation of a gigantic fish! Beautiful, full-color illustrations.

2428 Lithgow, John. *Marsupial Sue* (K–3). Illus. by Jack E. Davis. 2001, Simon & Schuster $17.95 (0-689-84394-1). Sue the kangaroo is unhappy with her fate and wishes she were another kind of animal. (Rev: HBG 3/02; SLJ 11/01)

2429 Lithgow, John. *Micawber* (PS–2). Illus. by C. F. Payne. 2002, Simon & Schuster LB $17.95 (0-689-83341-5). An art-loving squirrel spends a summer in the country mastering brushes and colors, and returns triumphantly to New York to open a gallery above the Central Park carousel in this book/CD combination. (Rev: HBG 3/03; SLJ 9/02)

2430 Livingston, Irene. *Finklehopper Frog Cheers* (PS–1). Illus. by Brian Lies. 2005, Tricycle $14.95 (1-58246-138-4). Finklehopper Frog and his rabbit friend Ruby both have fears about attending the town picnic. (Rev: BL 3/1/04; SLJ 5/05)

2431 Lobel, Arnold. *Fables* (2–4). Illus. by author. 1980, HarperCollins LB $15.89 (0-06-023974-3); paper $6.95 (0-06-443046-4). 48pp. An Americanized Aesop with excellent illustrations. Caldecott Medal winner, 1981.

2432 Lodge, Bernard. *Tanglebird* (PS–1). Illus. 1997, Houghton Mifflin $14.95 (0-395-84543-2). 32pp. Tanglebird searches for material so that he can make a nest as tidy as those of other birds. (Rev: BL 3/1/97; SLJ 4/97)

2433 London, Jonathan. *"Eat!" Cried Little Pig* (PS). Illus. by Delphine Durand. 2003, Dutton $15.99 (0-525-46906-0). Little Pig has a healthy appetite and makes a horrible mess as he eats until he learns a new word: neat. (Rev: HBG 4/04; SLJ 12/03)

2434 London, Jonathan. *Froggy Eats Out* (PS–1). Illus. by Frank Remkiewicz. 2001, Viking $15.99 (0-670-89686-1). 32pp. Froggy's family tries to take him to a real restaurant, but despite his best intentions Froggy fails to behave and they end up eating fast food after all. (Rev: BL 6/1–15/01; HBG 10/01; SLJ 8/01)

2435 London, Jonathan. *Froggy Gets Dressed* (PS–1). Illus. by Frank Remkiewicz. 1992, Viking $15.99 (0-670-84249-4). Froggy gets so exhausted dressing and undressing to play in the snow that he decides to sleep for the winter. (Rev: SLJ 9/92)

2436 London, Jonathan. *Froggy Goes to School* (PS–K). Illus. by Frank Remkiewicz. 1996, Viking $15.99 (0-670-86726-8). 32pp. Froggy is embarrassed to find himself at school in his underwear. (Rev: BL 6/1–15/96; SLJ 8/96)

2437 London, Jonathan. *Froggy Goes to the Doctor* (PS–2). Illus. by Frank Remkiewicz. 2002, Viking $15.99 (0-670-03857-5). 32pp. Froggy's visit (without underwear) to the doctor is amusing for all concerned. (Rev: BL 1/1–15/03)

2438 London, Jonathan. *Froggy Learns to Swim* (PS–1). Illus. by Frank Remkiewicz. 1995, Viking $15.99 (0-670-85551-0). After his mother teaches him to swim and he learns how to use flippers and a snorkel, Froggy doesn't want to leave the water. (Rev: SLJ 1/96)

2439 London, Jonathan. *Froggy Plays in the Band* (PS–2). Illus. by Frank Remkiewicz. 2002, Viking $15.99 (0-670-03532-7). The members of Froggy's marching band must remember one thing — not to stop for anything! (Rev: BCCB 4/02; HBG 10/02; SLJ 4/02)

2440 London, Jonathan. *Froggy Plays Soccer* (PS–1). Illus. by Frank Remkiewicz. 1999, Viking $15.99 (0-670-88257-7). 32pp. Froggy is a failure during the soccer game to win the City Cup until he gets a reminder from Dad and kicks the winning goal. (Rev: BL 3/1/99; HBG 10/99; SLJ 3/99)

2441 London, Jonathan. *Froggy's Day with Dad* (K–3). Illus. by Frank Remkiewicz. 2004, Viking $15.99 (0-670-03596-3). Froggy and Dad have a pleasant day together despite some bumps along the way. (Rev: SLJ 6/04)

2442 London, Jonathan. *Froggy's First Kiss* (PS–2). Illus. by Frank Remkiewicz. 1998, Viking $14.99 (0-670-87064-1). When Frogilina responds to Froggy's advances with a big kiss, the young swain retreats in panic. (Rev: BCCB 4/98; HBG 10/98; SLJ 3/98)

2443 London, Jonathan. *Let's Go, Froggy!* (PS–2). Illus. by Frank Remkiewicz. 1994, Viking $15.99 (0-670-85055-1). Preparations for a picnic so exhaust Froggy and his father that they are too tired to travel and decide to have their picnic on the patio. (Rev: SLJ 5/94)

2444 Lorenz, Lee. *A Weekend in the City* (PS–2). Illus. 1991, Pippin $15.95 (0-945912-15-3). 32pp. Pig and Duck search for some common ground with friend Moose when they propose a visit to the city for his birthday. (Rev: BCCB 11/91; BL 1/1/92; SLJ 12/91)

2445 Loupy, Christopher. *Hugs and Kisses* (PS–K). Illus. by Eve Tharlet. 2002, North-South LB $15.88 (0-7358-1485-6). 36pp. Hugs the puppy wants to find out what kisses are all about in this charmingly illustrated story for preschoolers. (Rev: BL 2/1/02; HBG 10/02)

2446 Low, Joseph. *Mice Twice* (K–3). Illus. by author. 1986, Macmillan paper $5.99 (0-689-71060-7). 32pp. Cat invites Mouse to dinner but Mouse brings along Dog. Reissue of 1980 publication.

2447 Lowell, Susan. *The Three Little Javelings* (PS–3). Illus. by Jim Harris. 1992, Northland LB $15.95 (0-87358-542-9). 32pp. This Americanized version of the "Three Little Pigs" features a coyote instead of the wolf. (Rev: BL 1/1/93)

2448 Lozoff, Bo. *The Wonderful Life of a Fly Who Couldn't Fly* (PS–2). Illus. by Beth Stover. 2002, Hampton Roads $17.95 (1-57174-286-7). A young fly with a wise mother learns to accept life without wings. (Rev: HBG 3/03; SLJ 2/03)

2449 Lund, Deb. *Dinosailors* (K–2). Illus. by Howard Fine. 2003, Harcourt $16.00 (0-15-204609-7). 40pp. Six dinosaurs set out to sea with humorous results told in rhyming verse. (Rev: BL 9/1/03; HBG 4/04; SLJ 9/03)

2450 Lund, Jillian. *Two Cool Coyotes* (K–3). Illus. 1999, Dutton $15.99 (0-525-46151-5). 32pp. When coyote Frank's best buddy Angelina moves away, he is lost until he finds a new friend. (Rev: BL 9/15/99; HBG 3/00; SLJ 10/99)

2451 Lyon, David. *The Runaway Duck* (K–3). Illus. by author. 1985, Lothrop paper $4.95 (0-688-07334-4). 32pp. Egbert, a wooden duck, is tied to a car bumper, but when the string breaks his adventure really begins. (Rev: BCCB 5/85; BL 6/15/85; SLJ 5/85)

2452 McAllister, Angela. *Barkus, Sly and the Golden Egg* (K–2). Illus. by Sally Anne Lambert. 2002, Bloomsbury $15 (1-58234-764-6). Three crafty chickens plan a clever escape from two dastardly foxes and alert the townspeople to the foxes' thieving ways. (Rev: SLJ 9/02)

2453 McAllister, Angela. *The Little Blue Rabbit* (PS–K). Illus. by Jason Cockcroft. 2003, Bloomsbury $16.95 (1-58234-834-0). Blue Rabbit, a plush toy, is devoted to his Boy and becomes very depressed when Boy goes missing. (Rev: HBG 4/04; SLJ 7/03)

2454 Macaulay, David. *Why the Chicken Crossed the Road* (K–3). Illus. by author. 1987, Houghton Mifflin $16.00 (0-395-44241-9); paper $6.95 (0-395-58411-6). 32pp. Readers will enjoy the humor of this chain reaction set off when one chicken crosses the road. (Rev: BCCB 11/87; BL 10/15/87; SLJ 12/87)

2455 McCarty, Peter. *Little Bunny on the Move* (PS–K). Illus. 1999, Holt $15.95 (0-8050-4620-8). 32pp. A snow white bunny sets out on a long journey to find a home. (Rev: BCCB 11/99; BL 12/15/99; HBG 3/00; SLJ 12/99*)

2456 McCarty, Peter. *T Is for Terrible* (PS–K). Illus. by author. 2004, Holt $15.95 (0-8050-7404-X). A Tyrannosaurus with low self-esteem decides that his behavior just comes naturally. (Rev: SLJ 8/04)

2457 McCaughrean, Geraldine. *Unicorns! Unicorns!* (K–2). Illus. by Sophie Windham. 1997, Holiday House LB $15.95 (0-8234-1319-5). 32pp. Because they are busy helping other animals, two unicorns fail to get on Noah's ark. (Rev: BL 11/15/97; HBG 3/98; SLJ 10/97)

2458 McClintock, Barbara. *Molly and the Magic Wishbone* (PS–3). Illus. 2001, Farrar $16.00 (0-374-34999-1). 32pp. Molly the kitten is given a magic wishbone and wisely uses it to make a very important wish for her little sister in this fairy tale whose illustrations reveal its Dickensian origin. (Rev: BL 9/1/01; HB 1–2/02; HBG 3/02; SLJ 10/01)

2459 McCullough, Sharon Pierce. *Bunbun at the Fair* (PS). Illus. by author. 2002, Barefoot $14.99 (1-84148-900-X). Bunbun, a mischievous little rabbit, goes missing at the fair and his siblings search for him. (Rev: HBG 3/03; SLJ 12/02)

2460 McCully, Emily Arnold. *First Snow* (PS–K). Illus. by author. 2004, HarperCollins LB $16.89 (0-06-623853-6). This new edition adds words and larger illustrations to the simple portrait of a family of mice on a wintry day, whose littlest member is initially scared of sledding. (Rev: SLJ 1/04)

2461 McCully, Emily Arnold. *Monk Camps Out* (PS–1). Illus. 2000, Scholastic $15.95 (0-439-09976-5). 32pp. Mouse parents help their son Monk to set up his tent in the backyard and then wait up during the night wondering if their son will become frightened and lonely and want to come back in. (Rev: BL 5/15/00; HB 3–4/00; HBG 10/00; SLJ 4/00)

2462 McCully, Emily Arnold. *Speak Up, Blanche!* (K–3). Illus. 1991, HarperCollins LB $14.89 (0-06-024228-0). 32pp. The sheep Eva drops granddaughter Blanche off to apprentice at the theatrical bears theater. (Rev: BL 9/1/91*; SLJ 9/91)

2463 MacDonald, Alan. *Beware of the Bears!* (K–3). Illus. by Gwyneth Williamson. 1998, Little Tiger $14.95 (1-888444-28-2). 32pp. After Goldilocks makes a mess of the bears' house, they get even by making a mess in a house they mistakenly believe to be hers. (Rev: BL 5/15/98; HBG 10/98)

2464 MacDonald, Alan. *The Pig in a Wig* (PS–1). Illus. by Paul Hess. 1999, Peachtree $15.95 (1-56145-197-5). Peggoty is made to feel ugly by other farm animals but she accepts her appearance when she sees her adoring pig mother with her little baby. (Rev: HBG 3/00; SLJ 12/99)

2465 MacDonald, Amy. *The Spider Who Created the World* (PS–3). Illus. by G. Brian Karas. 1996, Orchard LB $16.99 (0-531-08855-3). 32pp. To find a place to lay her egg, Nobb the spider creates the earth with fire and water in this original creation story. (Rev: BCCB 5/96; BL 4/15/96; HB 9–10/96; SLJ 3/96)

2466 MacDonald, Margaret Read. *Pickin' Peas* (PS–3). Illus. by Pat Cummings. 1998, HarperCollins LB $14.89 (0-06-027970-2). 32pp. Little Girl uses various tactics to prevent Mr. Rabbit from picking the peas in her garden. (Rev: BL 7/98; HBG 10/98; SLJ 10/98)

2467 McDonald, Megan. *Penguin and Little Blue* (PS–1). Illus. by Katherine Tillotson. 2003, Simon & Schuster $15.95 (0-689-84415-8). Penguin and Little Blue perform at a water park in San Francisco, but when the show goes on the road, they jump at the chance to return to the Antarctic and their friends. (Rev: BL 11/1/03; HBG 4/04; LMC 3/04; SLJ 11/03)

2468 MacDonald, Suse. *Elephants on Board* (PS–1). Illus. 1999, Harcourt $15.00 (0-15-200951-5). 32pp. When their truck breaks down, ten elephants try to commandeer another vehicle, with humorous results. (Rev: BL 3/15/99; HBG 10/99; SLJ 6/99)

2469 MacDonald, Suse. *Here a Chick, Where a Chick?* (PS). Illus. by author. 2004, Scholastic $10.95 (0-439-45594-4). Flaps reveal a variety of

barnyard animals in this lively tale with a repeating rhyme. (Rev: SLJ 6/04)

2470 McElligott, Matthew. *Absolutely Not* (K–2). Illus. by author. 2004, Walker LB $17.85 (0-8027-8889-0). 32pp. Two bug friends on a walk perceive things quite differently — where one sees a log, the other sees a dog, for example. (Rev: SLJ 4/04)

2471 McGeorge, Constance W. *Boomer's Big Surprise* (PS–2). Illus. by Mary Whyte. 1999, Chronicle $14.95 (0-8118-1977-9). 32pp. At first, Boomer the golden retriever is jealous of his new sibling, but Baby and he begin playing together and soon become buddies. (Rev: BL 5/1/99; HBG 10/99; SLJ 6/99)

2472 McGuire, Leslie. *Brush Your Teeth, Please* (PS–K). Illus. by Jean Pidgeon. Series: Joshua Morris Books. 1993, Reader's Digest $10.99 (0-89577-474-7). A pop-up book with movable "toothbrushes" in an animal story designed to get kids to brush their teeth. (Rev: SLJ 9/93)

2473 McKee, David. *Elmer and the Kangaroo* (PS–K). Illus. 2000, HarperCollins $14.95 (0-688-17951-7). 32pp. Elmer, a patchwork elephant, helps a kangaroo newly arrived in the forest to gain confidence about his jumping ability. (Rev: BL 5/15/00; HBG 10/00; SLJ 5/00)

2474 McKee, David. *Elmer and the Lost Teddy Bear* (PS–K). Illus. 1999, Lothrop $15.00 (0-688-16912-0). 32pp. Elmer, the patchwork elephant, helps Baby Elephant who is sad because he has lost his teddy bear. (Rev: BL 6/1–15/99; HBG 10/99; SLJ 7/99)

2475 McKee, David. *Elmer in the Snow* (PS–1). Illus. by author. 1995, Lothrop $13.00 (0-688-14596-5). In this picture book, a patchwork elephant takes some other elephants to snow-covered mountains so they will appreciate the meaning of cold. (Rev: SLJ 12/95)

2476 McKee, David. *I Can Too!* (PS). Illus. by author. 1997, Lothrop $15.95 (0-688-15547-2). In this pop-up book, an elephant takes a walk in the jungle and confronts a variety of animals with different talents. (Rev: HBG 3/98; SLJ 1/98)

2477 McKee, David. *Zebra's Hiccups* (PS–3). Illus. 1993, Simon & Schuster paper $14.00 (0-671-79440-X). Zebra begins to hiccup so violently that he begins to lose his stripes. (Rev: SLJ 6/93)

2478 McLaren, Chesley. *Zat Cat: A Haute Couture Tail* (K–3). Illus. 2002, Scholastic $16.95 (0-439-27316-1). 40pp. A cat who shreds the offerings at a Parisian fashion show becomes a designer sensation. (Rev: BL 3/1/02; HBG 10/02; SLJ 4/02)

2479 McLellan, Stephanie Simpson. *The Chicken Cat* (PS–1). Illus. by Sean Cassidy. 2000, Fitzhenry & Whiteside $14.95 (1-55041-531-X). 40pp. Merlin, a kitten, learns to fly and takes his friend Guinevere, a hen, for a ride. (Rev: BL 7/00; SLJ 12/00)

2480 McLeod, Emilie W. *The Bear's Bicycle* (PS–2). Illus. by David McPhail. 1986, Little, Brown paper $5.95 (0-316-56206-8). 32pp. A small boy and his teddy bear have an exciting bicycle ride as he gives the bear safety lessons. When the bear, grown to

2481 McMullan, Kate. *Pearl and Wagner: Three Secrets* (K–2). Illus. by R. W. Alley. 2004, Dial $14.99 (0-8037-2574-4). 48pp. Pearl the rabbit and Wagner the mouse share secrets during trips to an ice cream factory and a birthday party at an amusement park. (Rev: BL 5/15/04; SLJ 5/04)

2482 McNulty, Faith. *The Elephant Who Couldn't Forget* (1–3). Illus. by Marc Simont. 1980, HarperCollins $11.95 (0-06-024145-4). 64pp. A moral lesson about an elephant who was unable to forgive and forget. Reissue of 1980 publication.

2483 McPhail, David. *The Bear's Toothache* (PS–K). Illus. by author. 1972, Little, Brown paper $5.95 (0-316-56325-0). 32pp. A very funny story of a little boy's attempt to help extract a bear's tooth and rid him of his toothache.

2484 McPhail, David. *Big Brown Bear's Up and Down Day* (PS). Illus. by author. 2003, Harcourt $16.00 (0-15-216407-3). Big Brown Bear is not at all happy when Rat tries to trick him out of his slipper, but in time the two become friends who share. (Rev: BCCB 10/03; BL 11/03; HBG 4/04; SLJ 11/03)

2485 McPhail, David. *The Blue Door: A Fox and Rabbit Story* (K–2). Illus. by John O'Connor. 2001, Fitzhenry & Whiteside $15.95 (1-55041-647-2). Fox and Rabbit set off to visit Fox's storytelling uncle in the city, but all they know about his whereabouts is that he has a blue door. (Rev: SLJ 2/02)

2486 McPhail, David. *Drawing Lessons from a Bear* (PS–2). Illus. 2000, Little, Brown $14.95 (0-316-56345-5). 32pp. An old bear reminisces about his life as a cub and how he decided to devote his life to drawing and teaching others the love of drawing. (Rev: BCCB 3/00; BL 2/15/00; HBG 10/00; SLJ 5/00)

2487 McPhail, David. *Emma in Charge* (PS–K). Illus. 2005, Dutton $12.99 (0-525-47411-0). 24pp. Emma the young bear puts her dolls through their paces as they attend school, go to the doctor, and to the zoo. (Rev: BL 5/15/05; SLJ 6/05)

2488 McPhail, David. *Emma in Charge* (PS–K). Illus. by author. 2005, Dutton $12.99 (0-525-47411-0). The young bear has a busy day shepherding her toys through school — math, spelling, music, recess — followed by a checkup and a trip to the "zoo." (Rev: SLJ 6/05)

2489 McPhail, David. *The Glerp* (PS–3). Illus. 1994, Silver Burdett LB $18.95 (0-382-24668-3); paper $5.95 (0-382-24670-6). 32pp. The glerp, a snail-like animal that eats everything, meets its match when it tries to swallow an elephant. (Rev: BL 2/1/95; SLJ 4/95)

2490 McPhail, David. *Lost!* (PS–K). Illus. 1990, Little, Brown $14.95 (0-316-56329-3). 32pp. A young boy tries to help a bear get home from the big city. (Rev: BL 4/1/90; HB 5–6/90; SLJ 6/90)

2491 McPhail, David. *Mole Music* (PS–3). Illus. 1999, Holt $15.95 (0-8050-2819-6). 32pp. Mole, who lives underground, attracts a large aboveground audience when he becomes a superb violinist. (Rev: BCCB 5/99; BL 2/15/99; HBG 10/99; SLJ 4/99)

2492 McPhail, David. *Pig Pig Gets a Job* (PS–1). Illus. 1990, Dutton $14.99 (0-525-44619-2). 32pp. Pig Pig thinks of exotic ways to make some money. (Rev: BL 11/15/90; HB 11–12/90)

2493 McPhail, David. *Pigs Aplenty, Pigs Galore!* (PS–3). Illus. 1993, Dutton $15.99 (0-525-45079-3). 32pp. An unsuspecting man is suddenly surrounded by hordes of pigs in various costumes engaged in a variety of activities. (Rev: BL 4/1/93*; SLJ 7/93*)

2494 Mahoney, Daniel J. *The Saturday Escape* (K–2). Illus. 2002, Clarion $14.00 (0-618-13326-7). 32pp. Three friends shirk their chores in order to make it to library story time. (Rev: BL 3/15/02; HB 5–6/02; HBG 10/02; SLJ 3/02)

2495 Maitland, Barbara. *The Bear Who Didn't Like Honey* (PS–K). Illus. by Odilon Moraes. 1997, Orchard $14.95 (0-531-09546-0). 32pp. Little Bear hides his fears with a series of excuses but later demonstrates that he has unexpected courage. (Rev: BCCB 5/97; BL 2/15/97; SLJ 5/97)

2496 Mallat, Kathy. *Brave Bear* (PS–K). Illus. 1999, Walker $14.95 (0-8027-8704-5). 24pp. A bear cub helps a baby bluebird that has fallen from its nest, by climbing the tree to put the bird back in its home. (Rev: BL 12/1/99; HB 9–10/99; HBG 3/00; SLJ 9/99)

2497 Mallat, Kathy. *Just Ducky* (PS). Illus. 2002, Walker LB $16.85 (0-8027-8825-4). 24pp. Ducky has no luck convincing Frog, Mouse, or Bee to play with him, so he plays with his own reflection in a pond in this colorful picture book. (Rev: BL 9/1/02; HBG 3/03; SLJ 11/02)

2498 Mallat, Kathy. *Mama Love* (PS–2). Illus. by author. 2004, Walker LB $16.85 (0-8027-8904-8). A tender mother-and-child story told in rhyme and starring chimpanzees is enhanced by rich illustrations. (Rev: SLJ 3/04)

2499 Mammano, Julie. *Rhinos Who Play Baseball* (2–3). Illus. by author. 2003, Chronicle $13.95 (0-8118-3605-3). The energetic rhinos have fun while introducing baseball moves and terms. (Rev: HBG 10/03; SLJ 4/03)

2500 Mammano, Julie. *Rhinos Who Play Soccer* (PS–3). Illus. 2001, Chronicle $12.95 (0-8118-2779-8). 32pp. Soccer fans will welcome this jargon-filled story of Rhinos versus All-Stars. (Rev: BL 7/01; HBG 10/01; SLJ 7/01)

2501 Mammano, Julie. *Rhinos Who Skateboard* (K–4). Illus. by author. 1999, Chronicle $12.95 (0-8118-2356-3). A batch of happy rhinos enjoy skateboarding as they fly through the air and invent a whole new vocabulary. (Rev: SLJ 8/99)

2502 Mammano, Julie. *Rhinos Who Snowboard* (K–3). Illus. by author. 1997, Chronicle $11.95 (0-8118-1715-6). Snowboarding rhinos introduce the slang connected with the sport. (Rev: SLJ 3/98)

2503 Mammano, Julie. *Rhinos Who Surf* (PS–2). Illus. by author. 1996, Chronicle $12.95 (0-8118-1000-3). A group of rhinos go surfing in this action-packed, humorous picture book. (Rev: SLJ 7/96*)

2504 Mangan, Anne. *The Smallest Bear* (PS–K). Illus. by Joanne Moss. 1998, Crocodile $14.95 (1-56656-266-X). A small bear finds a hive filled with honey, and his paws are just tiny enough to fit inside. (Rev: HBG 10/98; SLJ 7/98)

2505 Markes, Julie. *I Can't Talk Yet, but When I Do . . .* (PS–2). Illus. by Laura Rader. 2003, Harper-Collins LB $16.89 (0-06-009922-4). A baby mouse thinks of all the things for which he would thank his older sister if only he could talk. (Rev: HBG 10/03; SLJ 5/03)

2506 Marshall, James. *George and Martha* (PS–1). Illus. by author. 1972, Houghton Mifflin $16.00 (0-395-16619-5); paper $6.95 (0-395-19972-7). 48pp. The friendship of two hippos leads to some very humorous situations. Also use the sequels: *George and Martha Encore* (1973); *George and Martha Rise and Shine* (1977); *George and Martha One Fine Day* (1982); *George and Martha Back in Town* (1984); *George and Martha Tons of Fun* (1986).

2507 Marshall, James. *George and Martha Round and Round* (K–2). Illus. by author. 1988, Houghton Mifflin $13.95 (0-395-46763-2); paper $6.95 (0-395-58410-8). 48pp. Five stories about hippos George and Martha. (Rev: BCCB 9/88; BL 9/15/88; SLJ 9/88)

2508 Marshall, James. *Swine Lake* (K–3). Illus. by Maurice Sendak. 1999, HarperCollins LB $15.89 (0-06-205172-5). 40pp. A wolf becomes so engrossed by a performance of *Swine Lake* that he forgets to choose one of the porkers for his next meal. (Rev: BCCB 7–8/99; BL 5/1/99*; HB 7–8/99; HBG 10/99; SLJ 7/99)

2509 Marshall, James. *Yummers Too: The Second Course* (PS–1). Illus. by author. 1990, Houghton Mifflin paper $6.95 (0-395-53967-6). 32pp. Emily Pig has trouble earning back the money when she eats the profits at Eugene's Popsicle business. (Rev: BL 10/1/86; SLJ 11/86)

2510 Martin, Bill, Jr. *A Beasty Story* (PS–3). Illus. by Steven Kellogg. 1999, Harcourt $16.00 (0-15-201683-X). 40pp. Four mice explore a dark, dark house to find the beast they know lives inside. (Rev: BL 9/15/99; HBG 3/00; SLJ 9/99)

2511 Martin, Bill, Jr. *Chicken Chuck* (PS–2). Illus. by Steven Salerno. 2000, Winslow $16.95 (1-890817-31-7). When Chicken Chuck eats a blue seed, a blue feather sprouts from his forehead and he becomes the hit of the barnyard. (Rev: HBG 10/00; SLJ 6/00)

2512 Martin, Bill, Jr., and John Archambault. *Barn Dance!* (PS–2). Illus. by Ted Rand. 1986, Holt $16.95 (0-8050-0089-5); paper $6.95 (0-8050-0799-7). 32pp. The animals are holding a lively barn dance on a full-moon night. (Rev: BL 1/15/87; SLJ 2/87)

2513 Martin, Bill, Jr., and Michael Sampson. *The Little Squeegy Bug* (K–2). Illus. by Patrick Corrigan. 2001, Winslow $16.95 (1-890817-90-2). 32pp. A little bug becomes a firefly with help and persistence. (Rev: BCCB 1/02; BL 9/1/01; HBG 10/02; SLJ 9/01)

2514 Martin, David. *Piggy and Dad Go Fishing* (PS–2). Illus. by Frank Remkiewicz. 2005, Candlewick $14.99 (0-7636-2506-X). Piggy is a sensitive soul and can't bring himself to put a worm on a hook or keep a fish once he has caught it. (Rev: SLJ 5/05)

2515 Martin, Linda. *When Dinosaurs Go to School* (PS–1). Illus. 1999, Chronicle $13.95 (0-8118-2089-0). 32pp. A series of rhymes follow a pair of young dinosaurs through a typical day at school. (Rev: BL 9/1/99; HBG 3/00; SLJ 7/99)

2516 Massie, Elizabeth, and Barbara Spilman Lawson. *Jambo, Watoto! Hello, Children!* (K–2). Illus. by Marsha Heatwole. 1998, Creative Arts $15.95 (0-9642712-3-0). Four young cheetahs remember their mother's advice and, when she goes out hunting, they stay put in their hiding place in spite of being tempted to come out by other animals. (Rev: SLJ 1/99)

2517 Mathers, Petra. *Lottie's New Friend* (PS–3). Illus. 1999, Simon & Schuster $15.00 (0-689-82014-3). 32pp. Herbie the duck feels threatened when friend Lottie cultivates a glamorous new arrival, Dodo, but soon the three become friends. (Rev: BL 7/99; HBG 10/99; SLJ 3/99)

2518 Maybarduk, Linda. *James the Dancing Dog* (PS–3). Illus. by Gillian Johnson. 2004, Tundra $15.95 (0-88776-619-6). 24pp. The whimsical tale of a beagle that longs to dance and eventually enjoys a moment of balletic glory. (Rev: BL 11/15/04)

2519 Meade, Holly. *John Willy and Freddy McGee* (PS–1). Illus. 1998, Marshall Cavendish $15.95 (0-7614-5033-5). 32pp. John Willy and Freddy McGee, two guinea pigs, escape from their cage and have fun in the pockets of a pool table until the balls begin dropping on them. (Rev: BCCB 1/99; BL 9/1/98; HB 1–2/99; HBG 3/99; SLJ 9/98)

2520 Meddaugh, Susan. *The Best Place* (PS–2). Illus. 1999, Houghton Mifflin $15.00 (0-395-97994-3). 32pp. A wolf who has sold his comfortable home to a family of rabbits so he can see the world soon regrets his decision. (Rev: BCCB 12/99; BL 11/1/99; HBG 3/00; SLJ 9/99)

2521 Meddaugh, Susan. *Hog-Eye* (K–2). Illus. 1995, Houghton Mifflin $14.95 (0-395-74276-5). 32pp. A female pig outwits a fox who has problems reading his recipe for pig soup. (Rev: BCCB 10/95; BL 9/1/95; SLJ 10/95*)

2522 Meddaugh, Susan. *Martha and Skits* (PS–2). Illus. 2000, Houghton Mifflin $15.00 (0-618-05776-5). 32pp. Martha, the talking dog, has her paws full taking care of a young pup named Skits who loves to catch Frisbees. (Rev: BCCB 11/00; BL 6/1–15/00; HBG 3/01; SLJ 8/00)

2523 Meddaugh, Susan. *Martha Calling* (PS–3). Illus. 1994, Houghton Mifflin $14.95 (0-395-69825-1). 30pp. Martha, the talking dog, must disguise herself as a human to circumvent the "No Dogs Allowed" rule at the Come-On-Inn. (Rev: BCCB 9/94; BL 10/1/94*; HB 11–12/94; SLJ 11/94*)

2524 Meddaugh, Susan. *Martha Speaks* (PS–3). Illus. 1992, Houghton Mifflin $15.00 (0-395-63313-

120

3). 32pp. Helen feeds her dog alphabet soup, and suddenly she can talk! (Rev: BCCB 11/92*; BL 9/1/92*; HB 1–2/93*; SLJ 12/92)

2525 Meddaugh, Susan. *Martha Walks the Dog* (PS–3). Illus. 1998, Houghton Mifflin $15.00 (0-395-90494-3). 32pp. Martha, the talking dog, uses kindness, the ultimate weapon, to tame a mean dog who is her new neighbor. (Rev: BCCB 12/98; BL 9/1/98; HB 11–12/98; HBG 3/99; SLJ 10/98)

2526 Meddaugh, Susan. *Perfectly Martha* (PS–2). Illus. 2004, Houghton Mifflin $16.00 (0-618-37857-X). 32pp. Martha the talking dog is rightly suspicious about the claims of the Perfect Pup Institute. (Rev: BL 3/15/04; SLJ 4/04)

2527 Meddaugh, Susan. *Tree of Birds* (PS–1). Illus. 1990, Houghton Mifflin $16.00 (0-395-53147-0). 32pp. When Harry nurses Sally, an injured bird, back to health, her friends arrive to make sure Harry doesn't keep her as a pet. (Rev: BCCB 3/90; BL 4/1/90; HB 9–10/90; SLJ 4/90)

2528 Meeuwissen, Tony. *Remarkable Animals: 1,000 Amazing Amalgamations* (PS–1). Illus. 1998, Orchard $15.95 (0-531-30066-8). Ten animals, including an alligator and rhinoceros, are divided into three sections, and flipping through the pages creates strange new animals. (Rev: BCCB 5/98; BL 1/1–15/99; HB 7–8/98; HBG 10/98; SLJ 4/98)

2529 Meres, Jonathan. *The Big Bad Rumor* (K–2). Illus. by Jacqueline East. 2000, Orchard $14.95 (0-531-30292-X). The rumor that a big bad wolf is coming gets garbled as the news is passed from one farm animal to another. (Rev: HBG 3/01; SLJ 11/00)

2530 Milford, Susan. *Willa the Wonderful* (PS–2). Illus. 2003, Houghton Mifflin $15.00 (0-618-27522-3). 32pp. When Willa, a little pink pig, chooses a fairy princess as her favorite career, her teacher and classmates are initially unimpressed. (Rev: BL 3/15/03; HBG 10/03; SLJ 6/03)

2531 Miller, Edna. *Mousekin's Family* (1–3). Illus. by author. 1972, Prentice Hall LB $9.95 (0-13-604462-X). 32pp. Complications occur when a little white-footed mouse mistakenly believes she has found a relative. Other titles in the series are: *Mousekin's Close Call* (1980); *Mousekin's Fables* (1982).

2532 Miller, Ruth. *The Bear on the Bed* (PS–2). Illus. by Bill Slavin. 2002, Kids Can $15.95 (1-55337-036-8). A boisterous bear takes over a little girl's cabin at camp, with consequences sure to please children if not adults. (Rev: HBG 10/02; SLJ 7/02)

2533 Mitton, Tony. *Dinosaurumpus!* (PS). Illus. by Guy Parker-Rees. 2003, Scholastic $15.95 (0-439-39514-3). 32pp. Party with the dinosaurs in this joyous, energetic picture book with vivid, comical illustrations showing the dancing dinos in all their scaly glory. (Rev: BL 1/1–15/03; HBG 10/03; SLJ 3/03)

2534 Mitton, Tony. *Down by the Cool of the Pool* (PS–2). Illus. by Guy Parker-Rees. 2002, Scholastic $15.95 (0-439-30915-8). A group of animals dance and leap around the pool until they all fall in — and

continue to party in the water. (Rev: HBG 10/02; SLJ 7/02)

2535 Mitton, Tony. *The Tale of Tales* (PS–2). Illus. by Peter Bailey. 2004, Random $15.95 (0-385-75016-1). 112pp. A group of animals making their way to Volcano Valley to hear "the tale of tales" recount their own favorite stories as they travel. (Rev: BL 4/15/04; SLJ 4/04)

2536 Modesitt, Jeanne. *Mama, If You Had a Wish* (PS–K). Illus. by Robin Spowart. 1993, Simon & Schuster paper $16.00 (0-671-75437-8). 30pp. When questioned by her son, a bunny mother says she only wants him to be his natural self. (Rev: BL 7/93; SLJ 8/93)

2537 Moers, Hermann. *Rufus and Max* (PS–2). Trans. from German by Kathryn Grell. Illus. by Philippe Goossens. 2003, North-South LB $16.50 (0-7358-1798-7). In this delightful German import, young canine friends Rufus and Max engage in a playful game of make-believe, building a castle from which they can rule all that they survey. (Rev: HBG 10/03; SLJ 9/03)

2538 Montanari, Eva. *The Crocodile's True Colors* (K–3). Illus. 2002, Watson-Guptill $14.95 (0-8230-2435-0). 32pp. Young readers learn about art forms — cubism, expressionism, and so forth — through this story of animals learning to draw. (Rev: BL 12/1/02; HBG 3/03; SLJ 11/02)

2539 Montes, Marisa. *Egg-Napped!* (PS–1). Illus. by Marsha Winborn. 2002, HarperCollins LB $15.89 (0-06-028951-1). 32pp. Mr. and Mrs. Gabbler Goose are in a panic when their egg goes missing in this humorous, rhyming adventure. (Rev: BL 2/15/02; HBG 10/02; SLJ 3/02)

2540 Moodie, Fiona. *Noko and the Night Monster* (PS–K). Illus. 2001, Marshall Cavendish $15.95 (0-7614-5093-9). 32pp. The friends of Takadu the aardvark band together to rid him of his fear of the Night Monster in this nicely illustrated, appealing story. (Rev: BL 12/1/01; HBG 3/02; SLJ 12/01)

2541 Moon, Nicola. *Mouse Tells the Time* (K–1). Illus. by Anthony Morris. 2003, Pavilion $16.95 (1-84365-000-2). Mouse searches for a more efficient way to mark the passage of time in this nicely illustrated book that includes a foldout page showing four clocks that indicate key hours of the day. (Rev: SLJ 6/03)

2542 Mora, Pat. *Delicious Hullabaloo: Pachanga deliciosa* (PS–1). Illus. by Francisco Mora. 1999, Arte Publico $14.95 (1-55885-246-8). 32pp. In this bilingual book, lizards, armadillos, and other exotic animals enjoy dancing at a desert dinner party. (Rev: BL 5/1/99; HBG 3/99; SLJ 3/99)

2543 Morgan, Michaela. *Brave, Brave Mouse* (PS–K). Illus. by Michelle Cartlidge. 2004, Whitman $15.95 (0-8075-0869-1). 32pp. Little Mouse fights his many fears by silently repeating rhymes that reinforce his inner strength. (Rev: BL 1/1–15/05; SLJ 11/04)

2544 Morgan, Michaela. *Helpful Betty Solves a Mystery* (PS–2). Illus. by Moira Kemp. Series: On My Own. 1994, Carolrhoda LB $18.60 (0-87614-832-1). While traveling through the jungle helping friends, Betty, a hippo, solves the mystery of a missing egg. Also use *Helpful Betty to the Rescue* (1994). (Rev: BCCB 9/94; SLJ 10/94)

2545 Morrison, Toni, and Slade Morrison. *The Book of Mean People* (PS). Illus. by Pascal Lemaitre. 2002, Hyperion LB $17.49 (0-7868-2471-9). 48pp. Cartoon-style rabbit children learn the different ways in which people can be mean. (Rev: BCCB 1/03; BL 10/15/02; HBG 3/03; SLJ 11/02)

2546 Morton, Jane, and Ted Dreier. *Moozie's Kind Adventure* (K–2). Illus. by Jane Royse. Series: Moozie Adventures. 1999, Best Friends $14.95 (0-9662268-1-X). Moozie, a gentle cow, saves some ducklings who are endangered by a herd of stampeding cows. (Rev: SLJ 1/00)

2547 Moss, Miriam. *Bare Bear* (PS–2). Illus. by Mary McQuillan. 2005, Holiday House $16.95 (0-8234-1934-7). 32pp. Busby the bear finds himself bare after the wind blows his clothes off a clothesline; during his search to find the garments he meets some oddly dressed animals and an ogre. (Rev: BL 3/15/05; SLJ 3/05)

2548 Moss, Miriam. *Don't Forget I Love You* (PS–2). Illus. by Anna Currey. 2004, Dial $15.99 (0-8037-2920-0). 32pp. A mother bear and her son have a difficult morning when they get off to a late start. (Rev: BL 1/1–15/04; SLJ 2/04)

2549 Moss, Miriam. *I'll Be Your Friend, Smudge!* (PS–2). Illus. by Lynne Chapman. 2002, Gullane $12.95 (1-86233-207-X). Young mouse Smudge is crying because she has no friends when Hare turns up and befriends her. Also use *Smudge's Grumpy Day, It's My Turn, Smudge!*, and *A New House for Smudge* (all 2002). (Rev: SLJ 8/02)

2550 Moss, Miriam. *The Snow Bear* (PS–1). Illus. by Maggie Kneen. 2001, Dutton $15.99 (0-525-46658-4). Winter scenes and spare, poetic text depict a polar bear cub who gets help from other animals in his search for his mother. (Rev: HBG 3/02; SLJ 10/01)

2551 Most, Bernard. *Cock-A-Doodle-Moo!* (PS–1). Illus. 1996, Harcourt paper $13.00 (0-15-201252-4). 32pp. When a rooster develops a voice problem, a cow tries to help out. (Rev: BL 9/1/96; SLJ 12/96)

2552 Most, Bernard. *The Cow That Went Oink* (PS–1). Illus. 1990, Harcourt $13.00 (0-15-220195-5). A cow and a pig are ridiculed because they aren't the same as other farm animals. (Rev: HB 7–8/90; SLJ 12/90)

2553 Most, Bernard. *If the Dinosaurs Came Back* (1–3). Illus. by author. 1978, Harcourt $16.00 (0-15-238020-5); paper $6.00 (0-15-238021-3). 32pp. All the things that might happen if dinosaurs came back to the world.

2554 Moyer, Marshall M. *Rollo Bones, Canine Hypnotist* (K–4). Illus. 1998, Tricycle $14.95 (1-883672-65-1). 32pp. Rollo Bones, an amazing dog who can hypnotize people, realizes that he must hypnotize his master to keep him in line. (Rev: BL 6/1–15/98; HBG 10/98; SLJ 7/98)

2555 Mozelle, Shirley. *The Pig Is in the Pantry, the Cat Is on the Shelf* (PS–1). Illus. by Jennifer Plecas. 2000, Clarion $15.00 (0-395-78627-4). 32pp. When

farmer McDuffel goes to town leaving the farmhouse door open, the animals take over, singing, cooking, taking baths, and making a big mess. (Rev: BL 8/00; HBG 10/00; SLJ 5/00)

2556 Muller, Birte. *Giant Jack* (PS–3). Trans. by J. Alison James. Illus. 2002, North-South LB $15.88 (0-7358-1621-2). 32pp. Jack, a rat, discovers why he feels different from his sisters: He was adopted into a mouse family. (Rev: BL 5/15/02; HBG 10/02; SLJ 7/02)

2557 Muller, Robin. *Hickory, Dickory, Dock* (K–2). Illus. by Suzanne Duranceau. 1994, Scholastic $15.95 (0-590-47278-X). 32pp. A cat throws a party with unexpected guests in this book with a rhyme for each hour of the day. (Rev: BL 5/1/94; SLJ 5/94)

2558 Murphy, Kelly. *The Boll Weevil Ball* (K–2). Illus. by author. 2002, Holt $15.95 (0-8050-6712-4). A little beetle is out of his depth at a dance until he makes friends with a pretty firefly. (Rev: HBG 3/03; SLJ 9/02)

2559 Murphy, Mary. *I Am an Artist* (PS). Illus. by author. 2000, Houghton Mifflin $4.95 (0-618-03401-3). In this appealing board book, a little penguin plays at being a nurse, cowboy, and model. The same penguin is featured in *I Make A Cake* (2000). (Rev: SLJ 6/00)

2560 Murphy, Mary. *I Like It When . . .* (PS). Illus. 1997, Harcourt $10.95 (0-15-200039-9). 32pp. A small penguin tells her mother of her favorite things that they do together. (Rev: BL 4/1/97; SLJ 5/97)

2561 Murphy, Mary. *Koala and the Flower* (PS–2). Illus. 2002, Millbrook LB $21.90 (0-7613-2674-X). 32pp. A curious little koala discovers the wonders of the library, with artwork that becomes more exciting as the story progresses. (Rev: BL 8/02; HBG 10/02; SLJ 9/02)

2562 Murray, Marjorie Dennis. *Don't Wake up the Bear!* (PS–2). Illus. by Patricia Wittmann. 2003, Marshall Cavendish $14.95 (0-7614-5107-2). A number of woodland creatures find refuge from the icy blasts of winter in the cozy cave of a hibernating bear. (Rev: HBG 4/04; SLJ 11/03)

2563 Murray, Marjorie Dennis. *Little Wolf and the Moon* (PS–2). Illus. by Stacey Schuett. 2002, Marshall Cavendish $16.95 (0-7614-5100-5). A little wolf asks many thoughtful questions about the nature of the moon. (Rev: HBG 3/03; SLJ 12/02)

2564 Muth, Jon J. *Zen Shorts* (K–3). Illus. 2005, Scholastic $16.95 (0-439-33911-1). 40pp. A beautifully illustrated introduction to Zen thinking through Stillwater the panda, who tells three children meaningful stories that make them see the world and each other in new ways. (Rev: BL 3/1/05; SLJ 2/05)

2565 Myers, Walter Dean. *The Blues of Flats Brown* (K–3). Illus. by Nina Laden. 2000, Holiday House $16.95 (0-8234-1480-9). 32pp. Two junkyard dogs, the musical Flats Brown and his friend Caleb, escape their mean owner — who wants to make them fighting dogs — by means of Flats' great blues playing. (Rev: BCCB 2/00; BL 3/1/00*; HBG 10/00; SLJ 3/00)

2566 Neugebauer, Charise. *The Real Winner* (K–2). Illus. by Barbara Nascimbeni. 2000, North-South LB $15.88 (0-7358-1253-5). An overly competitive raccoon named Rocky learns how to relax and love life by following the example of a kind young hippo. (Rev: HBG 10/00; SLJ 7/00)

2567 Newman, Jeff. *Reginald* (PS–3). Illus. by author. 2003, Doubleday LB $17.99 (0-385-90862-8). Despite the animosity of his animal neighbors, Reginald the bull loves his life in the Amazon rain forest. (Rev: HBG 4/04; SLJ 12/03)

2568 Newman, Leslea. *Pigs, Pigs, Pigs!* (PS–2). Illus. by Erika Oller. 2003, Simon & Schuster $15.95 (0-689-84979-6). 32pp. A town joyfully welcomes a group of pigs with feasting and dancing in this rhyming picture book. Also use *Dogs, Dogs, Dogs* (2002) and *Cats, Cats, Cats* (2001). (Rev: BL 2/15/03; HBG 10/03; SLJ 2/03)

2569 Newman, Leslea. *Where Is Bear?* (PS). Illus. by Valeri Gorbachev. 2004, Harcourt $16.00 (0-15-204936-3). Bear disappears during a forest animals' game of hide-and-seek. (Rev: SLJ 11/04)

2570 Newman, Marjorie. *Mole and the Baby Bird* (2–4). Illus. by Patrick Benson. 2002, Bloomsbury $16.95 (1-58234-784-0). 32pp. Little Mole rescues a baby bird and, with a little help from his grandfather, learns that wild things need to be free. (Rev: BCCB 11/02; BL 10/15/02; SLJ 12/02)

2571 Newsome, Jill. *Night Walk* (PS–K). Illus. by Claudio Munoz. 2003, Clarion $15.00 (0-618-32458-5). 32pp. Flute, a cat, and Daisy, a dog, take a nighttime walk with their owner and encounter both friends and foes. (Rev: BL 2/15/03; HBG 4/04; SLJ 4/03)

2572 Newton, Jill. *Bored! Bored! Bored!* (PS). Illus. 2002, Bloomsbury $15.95 (1-58234-760-3). 32pp. Claude the shark finds a way to alleviate his boredom with gardening. (Rev: BL 8/02; SLJ 9/02)

2573 Newton, Jill. *Gordon in Charge* (PS–K). Illus. by author. 2003, Bloomsbury $15.95 (1-58234-823-5). Newcomer Gordon the Goose challenges Gordon the Goat for leadership of the farmyard. (Rev: HBG 4/04; SLJ 10/03)

2574 Nimmo, Jenny. *Something Wonderful* (PS–2). Illus. by Debbie Boon. 2001, Harcourt $16.00 (0-15-216486-3). 32pp. Little Hen feels ordinary in comparison with the others until she proudly becomes a mother. (Rev: BL 9/15/01; HBG 3/02; SLJ 9/01)

2575 Nivola, Claire A. *The Forest* (K–3). Illus. 2002, Farrar $16.00 (0-374-32452-2). 32pp. A young mouse conquers his fear of the forest as he leaves his cozy house and sets off to enter this mysterious place. (Rev: BL 4/15/02; HBG 10/02; SLJ 6/02)

2576 Nolan, Lucy. *A Fairy in a Dairy* (PS–2). Illus. by Laura J. Bryant. 2003, Marshall Cavendish $16.95 (0-7614-5130-7). Decked out in a pink tutu, Pixie the cow brings dairy magic to the town of Buttermilk Hollow, which finds itself in dire financial straits. (Rev: HBG 4/04; SLJ 11/03)

2577 Norac, Carl. *I Love You So Much* (PS–1). Illus. by Claude K. Dubois. 1998, Doubleday $9.95 (0-385-32512-6). Lola the hamster is looking for the proper occasion to tell her famiy that she loves them. (Rev: HBG 10/98; SLJ 2/98)

2578 Nordholm, Gayle. *The Rainbow Tiger* (PS–1). Illus. by Jennifer Frohwerk. 2002, Hara $16.95 (1-883697-52-2). 40pp. After his wish is granted, a tiger regrets that he asked to exchange his stripes for the colors of a peacock. (Rev: BL 5/1/02)

2579 Novak, Matt. *Jazzbo and Googy* (PS–K). Illus. by author. 2000, Hyperion LB $15.49 (0-7868-2340-2). Googy, a little bear, has problems making friends until he saves Jazzbo's teddy from a mud puddle. (Rev: BCCB 9/00; HBG 10/00; SLJ 6/00)

2580 Novak, Matt. *Mouse TV* (PS–3). Illus. 1994, Orchard LB $17.99 (0-531-08706-9). 32pp. When their TV breaks down, a mouse family, all of whom are TV addicts, must find new ways to amuse themselves. (Rev: BCCB 10/94; BL 9/1/94; SLJ 10/94*)

2581 Novak, Matt. *Newt* (PS–2). Illus. by author. Series: I Can Read. 1996, HarperCollins LB $15.89 (0-06-024502-6). 48pp. A sportily dressed salamander has three easy-to-read adventures in this book about discovering friendship. (Rev: BCCB 2/96; SLJ 7/96)

2582 Numeroff, Laura. *The Chicken Sisters* (PS–2). Illus. by Sharleen Collicott. 1997, HarperCollins LB $14.89 (0-06-026680-5). 32pp. The three Chicken Sisters mistakenly believe that they have mastered many of the arts. (Rev: BL 5/1/97*; SLJ 5/97)

2583 Numeroff, Laura. *If You Give a Moose a Muffin* (PS–2). Illus. by Felicia Bond. 1991, HarperCollins LB $15.89 (0-06-024406-2). 32pp. This circular tale begins with a moose being lured to a boy's house to receive a muffin. (Rev: BCCB 9/91; BL 7/91; SLJ 12/91*)

2584 Numeroff, Laura. *If You Give a Mouse a Cookie* (PS–K). Illus. by Felicia Bond. 1985, HarperCollins LB $14.89 (0-06-024587-5). 32pp. A little mouse asks for a variety of things until the floor is a clutter of goods. (Rev: BCCB 7/85; BL 6/1/85; HBG 10/01; SLJ 5/85)

2585 Numeroff, Laura. *If You Give a Pig a Pancake* (PS–1). Illus. by Felicia Bond. 1998, HarperCollins LB $14.89 (0-06-026687-2). 32pp. Giving a pig a pancake leads from one consequence to another until we get back to a new plate of pancakes. (Rev: BCCB 6/98; BL 5/15/98; HBG 10/98; SLJ 7/98)

2586 Numeroff, Laura. *If You Take a Mouse to School* (PS–1). Illus. by Felicia Bond. 2002, HarperCollins LB $15.89 (0-06-028329-7). The adventurous mouse has a wonderful day at school. (Rev: BCCB 10/02; HBG 3/03; SLJ 9/02)

2587 Numeroff, Laura. *If You Take a Mouse to the Movies* (PS–1). Illus. by Felicia Bond. 2000, HarperCollins LB $15.89 (0-06-027868-4). 40pp. A charming picture book that recounts the many amusing consequences of taking a mouse to a movie. (Rev: BCCB 12/00; BL 12/1/00; HBG 10/01)

2588 Numeroff, Laura. *What Mommies Do Best / What Daddies Do Best* (PS–1). Illus. by Lynn Munsinger. 1998, Simon & Schuster $13.00 (0-689-80577-2). 40pp. In these two stories the reader discovers that both parents do all of the activities pictured — making snowmen, reading stories, watching the sunset — equally well. (Rev: BL 4/1/98; HBG 3/99; SLJ 4/98)

2589 Numeroff, Laura, and Nate Evans. *Sherman Crunchley* (PS–3). Illus. by Tim Bowers. 2003, Dutton $15.99 (0-525-47130-8). Canine police officer Sherman Crunchley, of Biscuit City, likes nothing about his job except the hat. (Rev: HBG 4/04; SLJ 12/03)

2590 Nunez, Marisa. *Camilla the Zebra* (PS). Trans. from Spanish by Susana Lopez Rubio. Illus. by Oscar Villan. Series: Books for Dreaming. 2003, Kalandraka $14.95 (84-95730-39-1). Camilla the zebra is heartbroken when a gust of wind blows away seven of her stripes but pleased when her friends offer inventive replacements. (Rev: SLJ 11/03)

2591 Oates, Joyce Carol. *Come Meet Muffin!* (PS–2). Illus. by Mark Graham. 1998, Ecco $18.00 (0-88001-556-X). 32pp. Muffin, a wise young cat, guides two lost fawns back to their mother but has problems finding his way back home. (Rev: BL 8/98; HBG 3/99; SLJ 1/99)

2592 Oates, Joyce Carol. *Where Is Little Reynard?* (1–3). Illus. by Mark Graham. 2003, HarperCollins LB $16.89 (0-06-029583-X). Little Reynard is the runt of the litter of kittens and his diminutive size has made him shy and withdrawn, but all that changes for the better after a confidence-boosting frolic with some friendly young foxes. (Rev: HBG 4/04; SLJ 9/03)

2593 O'Callahan, Jay. *Herman and Marguerite: An Earth Story* (K–3). Illus. by Laura O'Callahan. 1996, Peachtree $15.95 (1-56145-103-7). An earthworm that wants to explore aboveground is almost burned by the sun until a caterpillar rescues it. (Rev: SLJ 7/96)

2594 Oh, Jiwon. *Cat and Mouse: A Delicious Tale* (PS–2). Illus. by author. 2003, HarperCollins LB $15.89 (0-06-052744-7). The bonds of friendship between Cat and Mouse threaten to fray when Cat receives a cookbook that features delicious mouse-based recipes. (Rev: HB 5–6/03; HBG 10/03; SLJ 9/03)

2595 O'Keefe, Susan Heyboer. *Love Me, Love You* (PS). Illus. by Robin Spowart. 2001, Boyds Mills $15.95 (1-56397-837-7). 32pp. A simple but beautifully rendered story about a mother rabbit and baby engaged in everyday activities. (Rev: BL 4/15/01; HBG 10/01; SLJ 4/01)

2596 O'Malley, Kevin. *Bud* (K–3). Illus. 2000, Walker LB $16.85 (0-8027-8719-3). 32pp. When a storm ruins the garden of young Bud, a rhino, his grandfather helps him set things straight. (Rev: BCCB 6/00; BL 4/1/00; HBG 10/00; SLJ 6/00)

2597 O'Malley, Kevin. *Leo Cockroach . . . Toy Tester* (PS–2). Illus. 1999, Walker LB $16.85 (0-8027-8690-1). 32pp. Leo Cockroach feels he is unappreciated as a prize toy tester, so he decides to move on. (Rev: BCCB 6/99; BL 4/15/99; HBG 10/99; SLJ 4/99)

2598 O'Malley, Kevin. *Little Buggy* (PS–2). Illus. 2002, Harcourt $16.00 (0-15-216339-5). 32pp. Two earthbound slugs watch a young ladybug learning to fly, making caustic comments all the while in this cheerful tale of perseverance. (Rev: BL 10/1/02; HBG 3/03; SLJ 9/02)

2599 O'Malley, Kevin. *Little Buggy Runs Away* (PS–K). Illus. by author. 2003, Harcourt $16.00 (0-15-216550-9). Little Buggy, upset after a fight with Big Buggy, runs away from home. (Rev: BL 11/15/03; HBG 4/04; SLJ 11/03)

2600 Oram, Hiawyn. *Badger's Bad Mood* (PS–3). Illus. by Susan Varley. 1998, Scholastic $15.95 (0-590-18920-4). 32pp. In order to get Badger out of his blue funk, his animal friends arrange an awards ceremony to honor him for being a true friend. (Rev: BCCB 5/98; BL 5/15/98; HBG 10/98; SLJ 8/98)

2601 Oram, Hiawyn. *The Wrong Overcoat* (PS–1). Illus. by Mark Birchall. 2000, Carolrhoda $15.95 (1-57505-453-1). 32pp. In spite of compliments about the new coat his mother bought him, little Chimp dislikes it and takes it back to the store for a replacement. (Rev: BL 7/00; HBG 10/00; SLJ 6/00)

2602 Ormerod, Jan. *If You're Happy and You Know It!* (PS). Illus. by Lindsey Gardiner. 2003, Star Bright $15.95 (1-932065-07-5); paper $5.95 (1-932065-10-5). 32pp. Animals demonstrate ways to show happiness in this update of the classic song. (Rev: BL 3/15/03; HBG 10/03; SLJ 5/03)

2603 Ormerod, Jan. *When an Elephant Comes to School* (PS–2). Illus. 2005, Scholastic $16.95 (0-439-73967-5). 32pp. An elephant's first day at school is made easier by thoughtful actions on the part of other students. (Rev: BL 6/1–15/05)

2604 Ormondroyd, Edward. *Broderick* (PS–3). Illus. by John Larrecq. 1969, Houghton Mifflin LB $5.75 (0-686-86580-4). 40pp. Broderick, a mouse, loves to chew books, but one night he stops chewing and reads one. The book is on surfing, and it changes his life!

2605 Palatini, Margie. *Bad Boys* (K–2). Illus. by Henry Cole. 2003, HarperCollins LB $16.89 (0-06-000103-8). Willy and Wally Wolf, on the run from the Three Little Pigs and Little Red Riding Hood, dress up in sheep's clothing in the hope of fooling Trudie Ewe and Meryl Sheep. (Rev: BCCB 11/03; BL 11/15/03; HBG 4/04; LMC 3/04; SLJ 11/03)

2606 Palatini, Margie. *Earthquack!* (PS–1). Illus. by Barry Moser. 2002, Simon & Schuster $15.95 (0-689-84280-5). 32pp. The barnyard becomes alarmed, Henny-Penny-style, when the animals feel what they think is an earthquake in this rhyming tale. (Rev: BCCB 7–8/02; BL 7/02; HBG 10/02; SLJ 6/02)

2607 Palatini, Margie. *Stinky Smelly Feet: A Love Story* (PS–3). Illus. by Ethan Long. 2004, Dutton $15.99 (0-525-47201-0). Love between ducks Douglas and Dolores prevails despite Douglas's extremely smelly feet. (Rev: BCCB 6/04; SLJ 6/04)

2608 Parker, Mary Jessie. *Wild and Woolly* (PS–2). Illus. by Shannon McNeill. 2005, Dutton $15.99 (0-525-47276-2). 32pp. A sheep, used to life on the farm, meets a wild ram and they begin an unlikely friendship in this nicely illustrated picture book. (Rev: BL 3/15/05; SLJ 3/05)

2609 Parr, Todd. *The Best Friends Book* (K–2). Illus. by author. 2000, Little, Brown $5.95 (0-316-69201-8). A small book that humorously explains the nature of friendship using funny drawings of humans and animals. Also use the equally funny *Zoo Do's and Don'ts* (2000). (Rev: HBG 10/00; SLJ 8/00)

2610 Parr, Todd. *Otto Goes to Bed* (PS–K). Illus. by author. 2003, Little, Brown $9.95 (0-316-73873-5). The title character, a yellow dog with one red ear and one blue ear, does everything he can to put off going to bed, but his attitude changes when he discovers how much fun he can have in his dreams. (Rev: HBG 10/03; SLJ 7/03)

2611 Parr, Todd. *Otto Goes to the Beach* (PS–K). Illus. by author. 2003, Little, Brown $9.95 (0-316-73870-0). Otto, a most unusually colored dog, goes to the beach in search of friends and after rejections by an ill-tempered crab and a surfing cat finally finds a kindred spirit in a purple poodle with a pink coiffure. (Rev: HBG 10/03; SLJ 7/03)

2612 Partis, Joanne. *Stripe* (PS–1). Illus. 2000, Lerner $14.95 (1-57505-450-7). 32pp. Stripe, a curious little tiger, disobeys his parents and wanders alone into the jungle with near-disastrous results. (Rev: BL 4/15/00; HBG 10/00; SLJ 7/00)

2613 Partis, Joanne. *Stripe's Naughty Sister* (PS). Illus. by author. 2002, Carolrhoda LB $15.95 (0-87614-466-0). The tiger cub's baby sister spoils his games with his friends and exhausts him into the bargain. (Rev: HBG 10/02; SLJ 4/02)

2614 Paterson, Brian. *Zigby Camps Out* (PS–2). Illus. by author. 2003, HarperCollins $12.99 (0-06-052921-0). Zigby the zebra convinces Bertie Bird and McMeer the meerkat to join him on a camping trip that turns into more of an adventure than they'd bargained for. (Rev: HBG 10/03; SLJ 7/03)

2615 Paterson, Brian. *Zigby Hunts for Treasure* (PS–2). Illus. by author. 2003, HarperCollins $12.99 (0-06-052922-9). On a canoeing trip with friends Bertie Bird and McMeer the meerkat, Zigby the zebra finds a map in a bottle, and together the three friends embark on a search for treasure. (Rev: HBG 10/03; SLJ 7/03)

2616 Paul, Ann Whitford. *Little Monkey Says Good Night* (PS–K). Illus. by David Walker. 2003, Farrar $16.00 (0-374-34609-7). 32pp. Before going to bed, Little Monkey goes into the circus tent to say goodnight to all the performers. (Rev: BL 3/15/03; HBG 10/03; SLJ 7/03)

2617 Paxton, Tom. *The Jungle Baseball Game* (K–3). Illus. by Karen L. Schmidt. 1999, Morrow LB $15.93 (0-688-13980-9). 40pp. A picture-book version of the song about the baseball game between champion monkeys and bumbling hippos. (Rev: BL 5/1/99; HBG 10/99; SLJ 4/99)

2618 Payne, Emmy. *Katy No-Pocket* (PS–1). Illus. by H. A. Rey. 1973, Houghton Mifflin $17.00 (0-395-17104-0); paper $5.95 (0-395-13717-9). 32pp.

Until Katy finds an apron with pockets, she is very sad, for she has no way to carry her baby.

2619 Payne, Tony, and Jan Payne. *The Hippo-Not-Amus* (K–2). Illus. by Guy Parker-Rees. 2004, Scholastic $15.95 (0-439-56418-2). Portly is a disaffected hippo and he explores a variety of other physical possibilities. (Rev: SLJ 9/04)

2620 Pearson, Tracey Campbell. *Bob* (PS–K). Illus. 2002, Farrar $16.00 (0-374-39957-3). 32pp. Bob the rooster's wide-ranging animal vocabulary — he can meow, moo, and ribbet with the best of them — succeeds in scaring off a fox. (Rev: BL 11/15/02; HBG 3/03; SLJ 8/02)

2621 Pearson, Tracey Campbell. *Myrtle* (PS). Illus. 2004, Farrar $15.00 (0-374-35157-0). 32pp. Cowed by the mean new neighbor, Myrtle the mouse gains courage when her aunt returns from safari and tells her about confronting lions. (Rev: BL 1/1–15/04; SLJ 5/04)

2622 Peet, Bill. *Cock-a-Doodle Dudley* (PS–3). Illus. 1990, Houghton Mifflin $16.00 (0-395-55331-8). 48pp. Dudley takes credit for making the sun rise. (Rev: BCCB 10/90; BL 9/15/90; HB 11–12/90; SLJ 11/90)

2623 Peet, Bill. *Cowardly Clyde* (K–2). Illus. by author. 1984, Houghton Mifflin paper $7.95 (0-395-36171-0). 48pp. A horse named Clyde quivers in fear at the thought of fighting a dragon with his master, Sir Galavant. Other titles by this author and publisher are: *Ant and the Elephant* (1980); *The Luckiest One of All* (1985); *No Such Things* (1985); *Pamela Camel* (1986); *Farewell to Shady Glade* (1991).

2624 Peet, Bill. *Eli* (1–3). Illus. by author. 1984, Houghton Mifflin paper $8.95 (0-395-36611-9). 48pp. An old lion is saved from hunters by playing dead. Others by Bill Peet and published by Houghton are: *Hubert's Hair-Raising Adventure* (1959); *Ella* (1964); *Chester the Worldly Pig* (1978); *Kermit the Hermit* (1980); *Cyrus the Unsinkable Sea Serpent* (1982).

2625 Peet, Bill. *The Gnats of Knotty Pine* (K–3). Illus. by author. 1984, Houghton Mifflin $16.00 (0-395-21405-X); paper $7.95 (0-395-36612-7). The tiny gnats help save the animals of Knotty Pine at hunting time.

2626 Peet, Bill. *Whingdingdilly* (2–4). Illus. by author. 1977, Houghton Mifflin $16.00 (0-395-24729-2); paper $7.95 (0-395-31381-3). Scamp, tired of leading a dog's life, is transformed by a witch. Some others by this author and publisher are: *The Spooky Tail of Prewitt Peacock* (1973); *Merle the High Flying Squirrel* (1974); *Fly, Homer, Fly* (1979); *Randy's Dandy Lions* (1979); *Huge Harold* (1982); *How Droofus the Dragon Lost His Head* (1983); *The Pinkish, Purplish, Bluish Egg* (1984).

2627 Peet, Bill. *Zella, Zack, and Zodiac* (PS–1). Illus. 1986, Houghton Mifflin $16.00 (0-395-41069-X); paper $7.95 (0-395-52207-2). 32pp. The tale of Zack, an ostrich adopted by Zella the zebra, and Zella's colt Zodiac, whom Zack saves. (Rev: BCCB 6/86; BL 3/16/86; SLJ 5/86)

2628 Peguero, Leone. *Lionel and Amelia* (PS–1). Illus. by Adrian Peguero and Gerard Peguero. 1996, Mondo paper $4.95 (1-57255-197-6). 30pp. The mice, who want to be friends, copy each other's ways but decide it's best to be natural. (Rev: BL 1/1–15/97)

2629 Perry, Phyllis J. *The Secret of the Silver Key* (2–4). Illus. by Ron Lipking. Series: Fribble Mouse Library Mystery. 2003, Upstart paper $16.95 (1-93214-603-2). 90pp. Fribble uses the library to help solve the mystery of an old chest his grandparents have given him. (Rev: SLJ 3/04)

2630 Peters, Lisa Westberg. *Cold Little Duck, Duck, Duck* (PS–1). Illus. by Sam Williams. 2000, Greenwillow LB $15.89 (0-688-16179-0). 32pp. A duck who finds that her pond is still frozen over imagines all the wonders of spring and, before she knows it, spring arrives. (Rev: BL 5/15/00; HB 7–8/00; HBG 10/00)

2631 Peters, Lisa Westberg. *We're Rabbits!* (PS–1). Illus. by Jeff Mack. 2004, Harcourt $16.00 (0-15-204671-2). 32pp. A gardener tries to negotiate with three rabbits, offering without success selected carrot substitutes. (Rev: BL 3/15/04)

2632 Petty, Dini. *The Queen, the Bear, and the Bumblebee* (K–2). Illus. by Rose Cowles. 2001, Beyond Words $15.95 (1-58270-036-2). When given three wishes, the Queen and the Bear are quick with desires but Bumblebee is quite happy as he is. (Rev: HBG 10/01; SLJ 8/01)

2633 Pfister, Marcus. *The Rainbow Fish* (PS–2). Trans. by J. Alison James. Illus. 1992, North-South LB $18.88 (1-55858-010-7). 28pp. Rainbow Fish feels superior to those plain fish that surround him until he finds that sharing brings happiness. (Rev: BL 1/1/93; SLJ 11/92)

2634 Pfister, Marcus. *Rainbow Fish and the Big Blue Whale* (PS–K). Trans. by J. Alison James. Illus. 1998, North-South LB $18.88 (0-7358-1010-9). 32pp. Rainbow Fish and his friends are afraid that a whale who arrives in their area will eat all the krill and then eat them. (Rev: BL 9/15/98; HBG 3/99; SLJ 9/98)

2635 Pfister, Marcus. *The Rainbow Fish Board Book* (PS). Illus. 1996, North-South $9.95 (1-55858-536-2). 12pp. A board book version of the tale first published in 1993 of the lovely rainbow fish and his quest for friends. (Rev: BL 3/15/96)

2636 Pfister, Marcus. *Rainbow Fish to the Rescue!* (PS–1). Illus. 1995, North-South LB $18.88 (1-55858-487-0). 32pp. When Rainbow Fish and his friends face a shark attack, the group accepts a new striped fish into the circle. This is the sequel to *Rainbow Fish* (1992). (Rev: BL 9/15/95; SLJ 9/95)

2637 Pichon, Liz. *The Very Ugly Bug* (PS–2). Illus. by author. 2005, Tiger Tales $15.95 (1-58925-048-6). The very ugly bug is afraid that she doesn't have her friends' ability to fly, or to hide, or to disguise herself in order to avoid being eaten. (Rev: BCCB 5/05; SLJ 5/05)

2638 Piepmeier, Charlotte. *Lucy's Journey to the Wild West: A True Story* (1–3). Illus. by Sally Blakemore. 2002, Azro $19.95 (1-929115-07-5).

40pp. Lucy the Labrador relates the new sights as her owners move to New Mexico from North Carolina in this story that comes with a map of the trip. (Rev: BL 2/15/03; SLJ 6/03)

2639 Piers, Helen. *Who's in My Bed?* (PS). Illus. by Dave Saunders. 1999, Marshall Cavendish $15.95 (0-7614-5046-7). 21pp. Farm animals displace one another when taking over sleeping places in this picture book that uses flaps to tell its story. (Rev: BCCB 7–8/99; BL 4/15/99; HB 5–6/99; HBG 10/99; SLJ 7/99)

2640 Pilkey, Dav. *Dog Breath: The Horrible Trouble with Hally Tosis* (PS–2). Illus. 1994, Scholastic $14.95 (0-590-47466-9). 32pp. Hally Tosis, a dog with terrible breath, uses his affliction to capture two burglars. (Rev: BL 9/15/94; HB 11–12/94; SLJ 1/95)

2641 Pilkey, Dav. *The Moonglow Roll-o-Rama* (PS–3). Illus. 1995, Orchard LB $16.99 (0-531-08726-3). 32pp. Some animals steal off at night to a magical roller skating rink, which is why they sleep during the day. (Rev: BCCB 3/95; BL 2/1/95; SLJ 3/95)

2642 Pin, Isabel. *The Seed* (PS–3). Illus. 2001, North-South LB $15.88 (0-7358-1408-2). 32pp. Two teams of beetles vie for the prize of a cherry tree, envisioning future orchards. (Rev: BL 5/15/01; HBG 10/01; SLJ 7/01)

2643 Pinkwater, Daniel. *Bad Bears and a Bunny: An Irving and Muktuk Story* (K–2). Illus. by Jill Pinkwater. 2005, Houghton Mifflin $16.00 (0-618-33926-4). 32pp. Irving and Muktuk, the two naughty polar bears who live in a New Jersey zoo, come up against one tough rabbit. (Rev: BL 2/15/05; SLJ 3/05)

2644 Pinkwater, Daniel. *Bad Bears in the Big City: An Irving and Muktuk Story* (K–3). Illus. by Jill Pinkwater. 2004, Houghton Mifflin $16.00 (0-618-25208-8). 32pp. In a sequel to *Two Bad Bears* (2001), the unrepentant duo, now confined to their quarters at a New Jersey zoo, break out and embark on a muffin hunt. (Rev: BL 3/1/04; SLJ 4/04)

2645 Pinkwater, Daniel. *Bongo Larry* (1–3). Illus. by Jill Pinkwater. 1998, Marshall Cavendish $14.95 (0-7614-5020-3). 32pp. Groovy Larry the polar bear takes up the bongo drums and lands in jail for playing them in a park after curfew. (Rev: BL 7/98; HBG 10/98; SLJ 5/98)

2646 Pinkwater, Daniel. *Ice Cream Larry* (PS–3). Illus. by Jill Pinkwater. 1999, Marshall Cavendish $15.95 (0-7614-5043-2). 32pp. Larry the polar bear gets into trouble when he gobbles up 250 pounds of ice cream. (Rev: BCCB 6/99; BL 4/1/99; HBG 10/99; SLJ 5/99)

2647 Pinkwater, Daniel. *Irving and Muktuk: Two Bad Bears* (PS–3). Illus. by Jill Pinkwater. 2001, Houghton Mifflin $15.00 (0-618-09334-6). 32pp. Two polar bears plot to steal the main attraction from a town's blueberry muffin festival. (Rev: BL 9/15/01; HBG 3/02; SLJ 9/01)

2648 Pinkwater, Daniel. *Young Larry* (K–3). Illus. by Jill Pinkwater. 1997, Marshall Cavendish $14.95 (0-7614-5004-1). 32pp. Larry, a polar bear, gets his first job being a lifeguard. Also use *At the Hotel, Larry* (1997). (Rev: BL 9/1/97; HBG 3/98; SLJ 10/97*)

2649 Polisar, Barry L. *The Trouble with Ben* (PS–3). Illus. by David Clark. 1992, Rainbow $14.95 (0-938663-13-5). 32pp. A young bear annoys his human classmates by indulging in bearlike activities. (Rev: BL 6/1/92; SLJ 7/92)

2650 Posthuma, Sieb. *Benny* (PS–1). Illus. 2003, Kane $15.95 (1-929132-43-3). 32pp. A dog's sniffing ability is impaired when he comes down with a cold. (Rev: BCCB 3/03; BL 2/15/03; HB 7–8/03; HBG 10/03; SLJ 8/03)

2651 Potter, Beatrix. *The Complete Adventures of Peter Rabbit* (K–3). Illus. by author. 1982, Puffin paper $7.99 (0-14-050444-3). 96pp. An omnibus of the Peter Rabbit stories.

2652 Potter, Beatrix. *The Tales of Peter Rabbit and Benjamin Bunny* (1–2). Adapted by Sindy McKay. Illus. by author. Series: We Both Read. 1998, Treasure Bay $7.99 (1-891327-01-1). Two texts, one for parents and the other for children, face each other in this version that uses the original illustrations. (Rev: SLJ 3/99)

2653 Prater, John. *Hold Tight!* (PS). Illus. by author. Series: Baby Bear Books. 2003, Barron's paper $5.95 (0-7641-2304-1). Baby Bear convinces Grandbear to take a break from his laundry chores, and the two enjoy fantasy time together. (Rev: SLJ 6/03)

2654 Prater, John. *On Top of the World* (PS). Illus. 1998, Mondo $15.95 (1-57255-649-8). Four stuffed animals sneak out one night for some fun on a playground slide. (Rev: BL 2/1/99; HBG 3/99)

2655 Pratt, Pierre. *Car* (PS). Illus. by author. 2001, Candlewick $4.99 (0-7636-1390-8). Cheerful board-book characters Olaf the elephant and Venus the mouse introduce readers to single words in spreads of bold, appealing art. Also use *Park*, *Shopping*, and *Home*. (Rev: SLJ 11/01)

2656 Price, Mathew. *Don't Worry, Alfie* (PS). Illus. by Emma C. Clark. 1999, Orchard $9.95 (0-531-30127-3). In this tab book, a mother assures her bear-cub son, Alfie, that she will protect him. Also use *Where's Alfie?* (1999). (Rev: SLJ 7/99)

2657 Price, Mathew. *Patch Finds a Friend* (PS–K). Illus. by Emma C. Clark. 2000, Orchard $5.95 (0-531-30264-4). A tab book in which Patch, a little spotted puppy, makes friends with a small, gray cat. Also use *Patch and the Rabbits* (2000). (Rev: SLJ 5/00)

2658 Provencher, Rose-Marie. *Mouse Cleaning* (PS–2). Illus. by Bernadette Pons. 2001, Holt $15.95 (0-8050-6240-8). Lazy Grandma Twilly, a squirrel, becomes obsessed with house cleaning when she finds a mouse. (Rev: HBG 10/01; SLJ 7/01)

2659 Pryor, Bonnie. *The Porcupine Mouse* (PS–2). Illus. by Maryjane Begin. 1988, Morrow $15.93 (0-688-07154-6). 32pp. Louie and Dan don't heed Mama Mouse's warnings when they go off to find a home of their own. (Rev: BL 3/1/88; SLJ 9/88)

2660 Puttock, Simon. *Big Bad Wolf Is Good* (PS–K). Illus. by Lynne Chapman. 2002, Sterling $12.95 (0-8069-0027-X). A sad and lonely wolf who wants to make friends finds that hardly anyone trusts him. (Rev: HBG 3/03; SLJ 8/02)

2661 Puttock, Simon. *A Story for Hippo: A Book About Loss* (1–4). Illus. by Alison Bartlett. 2001, Scholastic $15.95 (0-439-26219-4). 32pp. When old, wise Hippo dies, Monkey is disconsolate but learns to find comfort in sharing memories of his old friend. (Rev: BL 12/1/01; HBG 3/02; SLJ 11/01)

2662 Quackenbush, Robert. *Henry's Awful Mistake* (PS–2). Illus. by author. 1981, Parents LB $5.95 (0-8193-1040-9). 48pp. Henry, a duck, tries to rid his horse of an ant. A sequel is: *Henry's Important Date* (1982).

2663 Quackenbush, Robert. *Lost in the Amazon: A Miss Mallard Mystery* (2–4). Illus. 1990, Pippin LB $15.95 (0-945912-11-0). Miss Mallard, the detective duck, is off on another case, this one in Brazil. (Rev: SLJ 1/91)

2664 Radunsky, Vladimir. *One: A Nice Story About an Awful Braggart* (PS–2). Illus. by author. 2003, Viking $16.99 (0-670-03564-5). 32pp. Six, the sixth of nine armadillo siblings and the only one who is pink rather than green, expresses at every opportunity his belief that he is No. 1 in all important respects. (Rev: HBG 4/04; SLJ 10/03)

2665 Radunsky, Vladimir. *Ten* (K–2). Illus. 2002, Viking $16.99 (0-670-03563-7). 32pp. Humorous, giddy artwork draws the reader into this story of newlyweds Mr. and Mrs. Armadillo, who love each other and welcome the simultaneous arrival of 10 babies called One, Two, Three, and so forth. (Rev: BL 11/15/02; HBG 3/03; SLJ 9/02)

2666 Rand, Gloria. *Willie Takes a Hike* (1–3). Illus. by Ted Rand. 1996, Harcourt $15.00 (0-15-200272-3). 32pp. In spite of his elaborate preparations, Willie the mouse gets lost on a hiking trip. (Rev: BL 4/1/96; SLJ 6/96)

2667 Rankin, Joan. *First Day* (PS). 2002, Simon & Schuster $16.95 (0-689-84563-4). 32pp. A young puppy has many misgivings about starting school but loves it when he gets there. (Rev: BL 6/1–15/02; HBG 3/03)

2668 Raschka, Chris. *Arlene Sardine* (K–2). Illus. by author. 1998, Orchard LB $16.99 (0-531-33111-3). The whimsical story of Arlene's two-year life, from her birth in a fjord to her final resting place in a can. (Rev: BCCB 9/98; HBG 3/99; SLJ 9/98)

2669 Raschka, Chris. *The Blushful Hippopotamus* (PS–K). Illus. by author. 1996, Orchard LB $16.99 (0-531-08882-0). Young Roosevelt Hippopotamus can't control his blushing and is ridiculed by his sister. (Rev: HB 9–10/96; SLJ 9/96)

2670 Rathmann, Peggy. *Good Night, Gorilla* (PS–1). Illus. 1994, Penguin Putnam $14.99 (0-399-22445-9). 40pp. After the zookeeper says good night to his animals, a playful gorilla lets them out of their cages. (Rev: BCCB 5/94; BL 7/94; HB 7–8/94; SLJ 7/94)

2671 Reich, Janet. *Gus and the Green Thing* (PS–2). Illus. by author. 1993, Walker LB $9.85 (0-8027-8253-1). A dog named Gus follows a leaf from the bleak city into the countryside and finds a new green world. (Rev: SLJ 10/93)

2672 Reiser, Lynn. *Little Clam* (PS–1). Illus. 1998, Greenwillow LB $14.93 (0-688-15909-5). 32pp. Little Clam shows that he can protect himself when he is attacked first by a seagull, then a sea star, and finally a conch. (Rev: BL 8/98; HB 9–10/98; HBG 3/99; SLJ 11/98)

2673 Rex, Michael. *Dunk Skunk* (PS–K). Illus. by author. 2005, Penguin Putnam $10.99 (0-399-24281-3). Athletic animals with rhyming names — Goal Mole, Hurdle Turtle — are shown in action. (Rev: SLJ 4/05)

2674 Rey, H. A. *Cecily G. and the Nine Monkeys* (K–2). Illus. by author. 1974, Houghton Mifflin $16.00 (0-395-18430-4); paper $5.95 (0-395-50651-4). 32pp. A lonely giraffe and nine homeless monkeys share some uproarious adventures.

2675 Rey, H. A. *Curious George* (K–4). Illus. by author. 1941, Houghton Mifflin $14.95 (0-395-15993-8); paper $5.95 (0-395-15023-X). 56pp. A small monkey finds himself in difficulties due to his mischievous curiosity. Also use by the same author: *Curious George Takes a Job* (1947); *Curious George Rides a Bike* (1952); *Curious George Gets a Medal* (1957).

2676 Rey, H. A., and Margaret Rey. *Whiteblack the Penguin Sees the World* (PS–2). Illus. 2000, Houghton Mifflin $15.00 (0-618-07389-2). 32pp. A well-crafted plot about a penguin who leaves Penguinland for a series of adventures that include hatching two ostrich eggs. (Rev: BL 11/1/00; HBG 3/01; SLJ 11/00)

2677 Rey, Margaret. *Curious George Flies a Kite* (K–2). Illus. by H. A. Rey. 1973, Houghton Mifflin $15.00 (0-395-16965-8); paper $5.95 (0-395-25937-1). 80pp. More predicaments are encountered by this fun-loving monkey. Also use by the same author: *Curious George Goes to the Hospital* (1973).

2678 Richardson, John. *Grunt* (PS–K). Illus. by author. 2002, Clarion $15.00 (0-618-15974-6). The runt of the litter of piglets, Wee-skin-and-bones, runs away from the scorn of his siblings and meets a kindly boar who's into positive thinking. (Rev: BCCB 6/02; HBG 10/02; SLJ 5/02)

2679 Riddell, Chris. *Platypus* (PS). Illus. 2002, Harcourt $15.00 (0-15-216493-6). 32pp. Clean, simple illustrations and cheerful text tell the story of a platypus who mistakenly adds a shell — with a hermit crab inside — to his collection of special things. (Rev: BL 3/1/02; HBG 10/02; SLJ 6/02)

2680 Riddell, Chris. *Platypus and the Birthday Party* (PS). Illus. by author. 2003, Harcourt $16.00 (0-15-204753-0). Platypus, with the help of his friend Echidna, throws a birthday party for Bruce, his favorite stuffed animal. (Rev: HBG 4/04; SLJ 12/03)

2681 Riddell, Chris. *Platypus and the Lucky Day* (PS–1). Illus. by author. 2002, Harcourt $15.00 (0-15-216723-4). Mishaps are succeeded by happy discoveries in Platypus's lucky day. (Rev: HBG 3/03; SLJ 11/02)

2682 Riley, Linnea. *Mouse Mess* (PS–2). Illus. 1997, Scholastic $15.95 (0-590-10048-3). 32pp. While the human family is asleep upstairs, a messy mouse is creating havoc downstairs in a search for food. (Rev: BL 10/1/97; HBG 3/98; SLJ 11/97*)

2683 Ripper, Georgie. *Brian and Bob: The Tale of Two Guinea Pigs* (PS–2). Illus. by author. 2003, Hyperion $15.99 (0-7868-1925-1). Guinea pigs Brian and Bob are miserable when they are separated, then overjoyed when it turns out they have been adopted by the same family. (Rev: HBG 4/04; SLJ 12/03)

2684 Rix, Jamie. *Giddy Goat* (PS–2). Illus. by Lynne Chapman. 2003, Gingham Dog $14.95 (0-7696-3161-4). The inspiring story of Giddy, a mountain goat who shuns the heights favored by his family until the plight of a lamb lost in the mountains helps him conquer his fears. (Rev: HBG 4/04; SLJ 12/03)

2685 Roberts, Bethany. *Rosie to the Rescue* (PS). Illus. by Kay Chorao. 2003, Holt $15.95 (0-8050-6486-9). Rosie the squirrel waits anxiously for her parents and imagines what she would do to save them if they were in peril. (Rev: BL 5/15/03; HBG 10/03; SLJ 7/03)

2686 Roche, Denis. *Little Pig Is Capable* (PS–2). Illus. 2002, Houghton Mifflin $15.00 (0-395-91368-3). 32pp. Little Pig's parents treat him like a baby until he saves his scouting troop from a suspiciously hairy new scoutmaster. (Rev: BL 3/1/02; HB 5–6/02; HBG 10/02; SLJ 8/02)

2687 Roche, Denis. *Mim, Gym, and June* (PS–2). Illus. by author. 2003, Houghton Mifflin $15.00 (0-618-15254-7). Mim, a second-grate cat who is small for her age, and June, a third-grade bully, become friends after each displays prowess. (Rev: HBG 10/03; SLJ 4/03)

2688 Rockwell, Anne. *Chip and the Karate Kick* (K–2). Illus. by Paul Meisel. 2004, HarperCollins LB $15.89 (0-06-028446-3). 40pp. Chip the rabbit is so eager to earn a belt in karate that he almost loses sight of the martial art's true spirit. (Rev: BL 5/1/04; SLJ 6/04)

2689 Rockwell, Norman. *Willie Was Different* (1–3). Illus. by author. 1994, Berkshire House $16.95 (0-936399-61-9). After achieving world renown as a composer, Willie the wood thrush decides it is best to return to his forest home. (Rev: SLJ 12/94)

2690 Roddie, Shen. *You're Too Small!* (PS–2). Illus. by Steve Lavis. 2004, Tiger Tales $15.95 (1-58925-038-9); paper $6.95 (1-58925-385-X). A little mouse finds that his small size can be a big advantage. (Rev: SLJ 6/04)

2691 Rohmann, Eric. *My Friend Rabbit* (PS–1). 2003, Roaring Brook paper $5.95 (1-596430-80-X). 32pp. Mouse is in the pilot's seat when Rabbit launches his toy airplane, which promptly gets stuck in a tree. Caldecott Medal Winner, 2003.

2692 Rong, Yu. *A Lovely Day for Amelia Goose* (PS). Illus. by author. 2004, Candlewick $14.99 (0-

7636-2309-1). Eye-catching illustrations draw readers into a simple story of a goose greeting friends and playing at the pond. (Rev: SLJ 6/04)

2693 Root, Barry. *Gumbrella* (PS–1). Illus. 2002, Penguin Putnam $15.99 (0-399-23347-4). 32pp. Gumbrella the elephant efficiently nurses her animal patients back to health, but then refuses to let them go. (Rev: BCCB 12/02; BL 11/15/02; HB 9–10/02; HBG 3/03; SLJ 11/02)

2694 Root, Phyllis. *Oliver Finds His Way* (PS–2). Illus. by Christopher Denise. 2002, Candlewick $14.99 (0-7636-1383-5). 40pp. Oliver, a little bear, chases a leaf until he gets lost but soon figures out how to return to Mama and Papa in this autumn picture book. (Rev: BCCB 12/02; BL 9/15/02; HB 1–2/03; HBG 3/03; SLJ 10/02)

2695 Rosoff, Meg. *Meet Wild Boars* (PS–2). Illus. by Sophie Blackall. 2005, Holt $15.95 (0-8050-7488-0). 32pp. Wild boars Morris, Boris, Horace, and Doris make for very impolite house guests in this outrageously funny picture book. (Rev: BL 3/15/05)

2696 Ross, Tony. *Centipede's 100 Shoes* (PS–1). Illus. by author. 2003, Holt $15.95 (0-8050-7298-5). Young readers will find some valuable math lessons in this charming tale of a young centipede who decides he needs some shoes to protect his many feet; his mother buys 50 pairs, only to discover that there are 58 shoes left over after the little creature has been fully shod. (Rev: HBG 10/03; SLJ 6/03)

2697 Ross, Tony. *Silly Silly* (PS–K). Illus. by author. 1999, Andersen $19.95 (0-86264-740-1). A silly book about two silly characters, a mouse and a goose, who agree to a contest to see who can tell the silliest story. (Rev: SLJ 2/00)

2698 Rotenberg, Lisa. *Rodeo Pup* (PS–2). Illus. 1998, Firefly LB $14.95 (1-55209-245-3). 32pp. Told by his young owner, this is the story of Rodeo Pup, a feisty dalmatian who becomes so famous he eventually has his own Web site. (Rev: BL 9/15/98; SLJ 11/98)

2699 Roth, Carol. *The Little School Bus* (2–4). Illus. by Pamela Paparone. 2002, North-South LB $15.50 (0-7358-1647-6). 32pp. This romp of a read-aloud will have kids chanting along as silly animals board a bus and ride around town. (Rev: BCCB 9/02; BL 8/02; HBG 3/03; SLJ 7/02)

2700 Roth, Susan L. *It's Still a Dog's New York: A Book of Healing* (K–3). Illus. by author. 2001, National Geographic $12.00 (0-7922-7050-9). In this sequel to *It's a Dog's New York* (2001), New York dogs Pepper and Rover discuss their feelings about September 11, 2001. (Rev: HBG 10/02; SLJ 6/02)

2701 Roth, Susan L. *My Love for You All Year Round* (PS). Illus. by author. 2003, Dial $14.99 (0-8037-2796-8). A big white mouse expresses her affection for a little brown mouse, introducing the months of the year and a lot of vocabulary into the bargain. (Rev: BL 12/1/03; HBG 4/04; SLJ 12/03)

2702 Rowe, Jeannette. *YoYo Goes Next Door* (PS–1). Illus. by author. 2003, Tiger Tales paper $5.95 (1-58925-368-X). In this delightful lift-the-flap picture book, YoYo the yellow dog visits the homes of several neighborhood friends, enjoying a special adventure at each stop. (Rev: SLJ 8/03)

2703 Rowe, Jeannette. *YoYo Goes to the Park* (PS–1). Illus. by author. 2003, Tiger Tales paper $5.95 (1-58925-369-8). In this colorfully illustrated lift-the-flap book, YoYo, a yellow dog with one red ear and one blue ear, visits the park and has fun feeding the ducks, riding his scooter, playing on the slide and swings, and flying a kite. (Rev: SLJ 8/03)

2704 Rowe, John. *Monkey Trouble* (K–2). Illus. by John A. Rowe. 1999, North-South LB $15.88 (0-7358-1034-6). A monkey who never listens is taken on an adventure by the wind and has difficulty finding his way home. (Rev: HBG 3/00; SLJ 10/99)

2705 Rowe, John. *Smudge* (PS–2). Illus. 1997, North-South LB $16.88 (1-55858-789-6). 36pp. Smudge, a rat, tries a number of surrogate animal families but finds his own is best. (Rev: BL 12/1/97; HBG 3/98; SLJ 11/98)

2706 Rowinski, Kate. *Ellie Bear and the Fly-Away Fly* (PS–2). Illus. by Dawn Peterson. 1993, Down East $14.95 (0-89272-335-1). On a fishing trip with her uncle, L. L. Bear, Ellie Bear catches a trout but decides to spare its life. (Rev: SLJ 4/94)

2707 Rubel, Nicole. *Grody's Not So Golden Rules* (K–2). Illus. by author. 2003, Harcourt $16.00 (0-15-216241-0). Grody the dog is disdainful of the rules imposed on him by grown-ups and makes up his own, with some predictably smelly results. (Rev: HBG 10/03; SLJ 7/03)

2708 Rudolph, Marguerita. *Grey Neck* (PS–3). Illus. by Leslie Shuman Kranz. 1988, Stemmer $13.95 (0-88045-068-1). 32pp. Grey Neck can't leave for the yearly journey south because of a broken wing. (Rev: BL 6/1/88; SLJ 9/88)

2709 Ruelle, Karen Gray. *Mother's Day Mess* (1–2). Illus. 2003, Holiday House $14.95 (0-8234-1773-5); paper $4.95 (0-8234-1781-6). 32pp. Kittens Harry and Emily make great plans for Mother's Day, but somehow they don't quite succeed. (Rev: BL 3/1/03; HBG 10/03; SLJ 3/03)

2710 Rumford, James. *Calabash Cat and His Amazing Journey* (K–3). Illus. by author. 2003, Houghton Mifflin $16.00 (0-618-22423-8). Calabash Cat, searching for the point where the world ends, travels farther and farther afield with different animals serving as his guide for each leg of the journey. (Rev: HB 11–12/03; HBG 4/04; SLJ 9/03)

2711 Rusackas, Francisca. *I Love You All Day Long* (PS). Illus. by Priscilla Burris. 2002, HarperCollins LB $13.89 (0-06-050277-0). 32pp. A little pig, upset that he won't be with his mother at school, is reassured when his mother tells him that she loves him "all day long." (Rev: BL 2/1/03; HBG 3/03; SLJ 2/03)

2712 Rush, Christopher. *Venus Peter Saves the Whale* (1–3). Illus. by Mairi Hedderwick. 1992, Pelican $14.95 (0-88289-928-7). 26pp. On an isolated Scottish island, seagulls want a young boy to save a stranded whale. (Rev: BL 6/1/92)

2713 Rylant, Cynthia. *Bunny Bungalow* (PS–K). Illus. by Nancy Hayashi. 1999, Harcourt $13.00 (0-

15-201092-0). 32pp. A rabbit family transforms a ramshackle cottage into a lovely home with imagination, work, and love. (Rev: BL 4/15/99; HBG 10/99; SLJ 6/99)

2714 Rylant, Cynthia. *The Lighthouse Family: The Storm* (1–3). Illus. by Preston McDaniels. 2002, Simon & Schuster $14.95 (0-689-84880-3). 80pp. Pandora the lighthouse keeper cat has a lonely life until Seabold the dog arrives in a storm, only to be followed later by three baby mice, who join the happy and growing family. Also use *The Lighthouse Family: The Eagle* (2004). (Rev: BL 11/15/02; HBG 3/03; SLJ 11/02)

2715 Rylant, Cynthia. *Little Whistle's Dinner Party* (PS–K). Illus. by Tim Bowers. Series: Little Whistle. 2001, Harcourt $14.00 (0-15-201079-3). 32pp. Little Whistle the guinea pig has a dinner party for his friends in the toy store in this simple story enhanced by detailed, appealing paintings. (Rev: BL 10/1/01; HBG 3/02; SLJ 10/01)

2716 Rylant, Cynthia. *Little Whistle's Medicine* (PS–1). Illus. by Tim Bowers. 2002, Harcourt $15.00 (0-15-201086-6). 32pp. Lovable guinea pig Little Whistle searches the toy store where he lives to find a remedy for his friend Soldier's headache. (Rev: BL 3/1/02; HBG 10/02; SLJ 4/02)

2717 Rylant, Cynthia. *Poppleton Has Fun* (PS–1). Illus. by Mark Teague. 2000, Scholastic $15.95 (0-590-84839-9); paper $3.99 (0-590-84841-0). 56pp. This book in the Poppleton Pig series contains three short stories about sharing. (Rev: BL 11/15/00; HBG 3/01; SLJ 12/00)

2718 Rylant, Cynthia. *Thimbleberry Stories* (PS–2). Illus. by Maggie Kneen. 2000, Harcourt $15.00 (0-15-201081-5). 64pp. A beautifully illustrated book that contains four short stories about Nigel Chipmunk who lives on peaceful Thimbleberry Lane. (Rev: BCCB 9/00; BL 5/1/00; HBG 10/00; SLJ 5/00)

2719 Sacre, Antonio. *The Barking Mouse* (PS–1). Illus. by Alfredo Aguirre. 2003, Whitman LB $14.95 (0-8075-0571-4). A mouse mother impresses her family with her barking abilities when a cat threatens them in this attractively illustrated retelling of a Cuban tale. (Rev: HBG 10/03; SLJ 6/03)

2720 Saller, Carol. *Pug, Slug, and Doug the Thug* (K–2). Illus. by Vicki Jo Redenbaugh. 1994, Carolrhoda LB $19.95 (0-87614-803-8). 32pp. In this Western tale, a young boy captures three outlaws when he accidentally starts a chain of events that prove to be their downfall. (Rev: BL 4/1/94)

2721 Salley, Coleen. *Epossumondas* (PS–3). Illus. by Janet Stevens. 2002, Harcourt $16.00 (0-15-216748-X). 40pp. A bumbling little possum can't seem to get anything right in this uproarious adaptation of a classic Louisiana tale. (Rev: BCCB 10/02; BL 8/02; HB 11–12/02; HBG 3/03; SLJ 9/02*)

2722 Saltzberg, Barney. *Crazy Hair Day* (K–3). Illus. by author. 2003, Candlewick $15.99 (0-7636-1954-X). Stanley the hamster, who sports spikily colorful hair, is mortified to learn that it's School Picture Day, not Crazy Hair Day. (Rev: HBG 4/04; SLJ 12/03)

2723 Sampson, Michael, and Mary Beth Sampson. *Star of the Circus* (PS–K). Illus. 1997, Holt $14.95 (0-8050-4284-9). 32pp. Each of a group of egocentric animals thinks that he or she is the star of the circus. (Rev: BL 4/1/97; SLJ 3/97)

2724 Samuels, Jenny. *A Nose Like a Hose* (PS). Illus. by author. 2003, Scholastic $12.95 (0-439-37303-4). In whimsical rhyming text, a young elephant considers all the advantages enjoyed by a creature with "a nose like a hose." (Rev: HBG 10/03; SLJ 10/03)

2725 Sardegna, Jill. *The Roly-Poly Spider* (PS–K). Illus. by Tedd Arnold. 1994, Scholastic $13.95 (0-590-47119-8). 32pp. A fat spider uses age-old devices like flattery to lure insect meals into its web. (Rev: BL 11/15/94; SLJ 1/95)

2726 Scamell, Ragnhild. *Three Bags Full* (K–1). Illus. by Sally Hobson. 1993, Orchard $14.95 (0-531-05486-1). 26pp. Millie the sheep gives so much of her wool to her friends that she begins to feel the cold. (Rev: BL 7/93)

2727 Scarry, Richard. *Pie Rats Ahoy!* (K–1). Illus. by author. Series: Step into Reading. 1994, Random LB $11.99 (0-679-94760-4); paper $3.99 (0-679-84760-X). 32pp. Uncle Willy hides inside a model of a crocodile to capture pirates who are frightening the residents of Busytown Bay. (Rev: SLJ 9/94)

2728 Schachner, Judith Byron. *The Grannyman* (PS–3). Illus. 1999, Dutton $15.99 (0-525-46122-1). 32pp. In this fantasy an old cat fondly remembers all his activities as a youngster including stalking wildebeest and playing Bach. (Rev: BCCB 1/00; BL 3/15/00; HBG 3/00; SLJ 11/99)

2729 Schaefer, Carole Lexa. *Full Moon Barnyard Dance* (PS–K). Illus. by Christine Davenier. 2003, Candlewick $15.99 (0-7636-1878-0). The animals at the dance inadvertently switch partners when clouds block out the moon. (Rev: HBG 4/04; SLJ 11/03)

2730 Schindel, John. *What Did They See?* (PS–K). Illus. by Doug Cushman. 2003, Holt $14.95 (0-8050-6167-3). Raccoon makes an exciting discovery in Elvis Grundoon's Antiques and Curiosities Shop, and she can't wait to share it with her friends, Beaver, Porcupine, and Otter. (Rev: HBG 10/03; SLJ 8/03)

2731 Schlein, Miriam. *Little Raccoon's Big Question* (PS–1). Illus. by Ian Schoenherr. 2004, HarperCollins $15.99 (0-06-052116-3). 32pp. A gentle story with evocative illustrations in which a playful Little Raccoon asks his mother when she loves him most. (Rev: BL 4/15/04; SLJ 3/04)

2732 Schubert, Ingrid, and Dieter Schubert. *Bear's Egg* (PS–2). Illus. 1999, Front Street $15.95 (1-886910-46-4). 32pp. When Bear becomes the owner of some untended goose eggs, he faces such problems as hatching the eggs and teaching the young goslings how to survive. (Rev: BL 10/1/99; HBG 3/00; SLJ 11/99)

2733 Schubert, Ingrid, and Dieter Schubert. *Beaver's Lodge* (PS). Illus. 2001, Front Street $15.95 (1-

886910-68-5). 32pp. While Beaver is ill, Bear and Hedgehog build him a house but forget to give it a door. (Rev: BL 7/01; HBG 10/01; SLJ 5/01)

2734 Schubert, Ingrid, and Dieter Schubert. *There's a Hole in My Bucket* (PS–2). Illus. 1998, Front Street $15.95 (1-886910-28-6). 32pp. Bear and his friend Hedgehog try to repair a hole in a bucket so that Bear can water his flowers. Fortunately the rain comes and solves their problems. (Rev: BL 5/15/98; HBG 10/98; SLJ 7/98)

2735 Schubert, Ingrid, and Dieter Schubert. *There's Always Room for One More* (PS–1). Illus. by authors. 2002, Front Street $15.95 (1-886910-77-4). A butterfly adds the final ounce that tips over the raft bearing Beaver, Badger, Bear, Hedgehog, Mole, and Hare. (Rev: HBG 10/02; SLJ 4/02)

2736 Schuurmans, Hilde. *Sidney Won't Swim* (PS–K). Illus. by author. 2001, Charlesbridge LB $15.95 (0-57091-476-1). A young dog doesn't want to take swimming lessons until his friends show him how much fun it can be. (Rev: SLJ 2/01)

2737 Schwartz, Henry. *How I Captured a Dinosaur* (PS–K). Illus. by Amy Schwartz. 1989, Orchard paper $5.95 (0-531-07028-X). 32pp. Liz discovers a dinosaur on a camping trip and takes him home. (Rev: BCCB 2/89; BL 2/1/89; SLJ 4/89)

2738 Schwartz, Roslyn. *The Mole Sisters and the Blue Egg* (PS–K). Illus. 2001, Annick LB $14.95 (1-55037-705-1); paper $4.95 (1-55037-704-3). 32pp. The energetic Mole sisters aren't sure what they're seeking, but they have a great time on their quest and discover their quarry is a beautiful blue eggshell that makes a perfect swing. Also use *The Mole Sisters and the Moonlit Night* (2001). (Rev: BL 12/15/01)

2739 Schwartz, Roslyn. *The Mole Sisters and the Busy Bees* (PS). 2000, Annick $4.95 (1-55037-663-2); paper $4.95 (1-55037-662-4). 32pp. A small book in which two mole sisters watch bees as they go about their work. Also use *The Mole Sisters and the Wavy Wheat* (2000). (Rev: SLJ 11/00)

2740 Schwartz, Roslyn. *The Mole Sisters and the Cool Breeze* (PS–K). Illus. 2002, Annick LB $14.95 (1-55037-771-X); paper $4.95 (1-55037-770-1). 32pp. The engaging Mole sisters use leaves as fans on a hot day with amusing consequences in this small book. Also use *The Mole Sisters and the Question* (2002). (Rev: BL 1/1–15/03; HBG 3/03; SLJ 1/03)

2741 Sebastian, John. *J.B.'s Harmonica* (K–3). Illus. by Garth Williams. 1993, Harcourt $13.95 (0-15-240091-5). 32pp. A young bear is so bad at playing the harmonica that the neighbors complain. (Rev: BL 3/15/93; SLJ 4/93)

2742 Segal, Lore. *More Mole Stories and Little Gopher, Too* (PS). Illus. by Sergio Ruzzier. Series: Mole. 2005, Farrar $16.00 (0-374-35026-4). 40pp. Mole and his grandmother have a loving relationship, but that doesn't mean that Mole doesn't ever cause her trouble in these short stories. A companion to *Why Mole Shouted and Other Stories* (2004). (Rev: BL 3/1/05; SLJ 4/05)

2743 Segal, Lore. *Why Mole Shouted and Other Stories* (PS). Illus. by Sergio Ruzzier. 2004, Farrar $16.00 (0-374-38417-7). Four short stories share the loving relationship between little Mole and his grandmother. (Rev: SLJ 4/04)

2744 Selkowe, Valrie M. *Happy Birthday to Me!* (PS–K). Illus. by John Sandford. 2001, Harper-Collins LB $15.89 (0-688-16680-6). 32pp. A young rabbit finds a key that leads him to a roomful of characters who sing his favorite song. (Rev: BL 8/01; HBG 10/01; SLJ 6/01)

2745 Sellers, Heather. *Spike and Cubby's Ice Cream Island Adventure* (PS–2). Illus. by Amy L. Young. 2004, Holt $16.95 (0-8050-6910-0). Spike and Cubby, two dogs, are sailing to the grand opening of Ice Cream Island when a huge storm blows up. (Rev: SLJ 11/04)

2746 Serwacki. *Doorknob the Rabbit and the Carnival of Bugs* (PS–2). Illus. by author. 2005, Tricycle $14.95 (1-58246-143-0). Doorknob foolishly opens the door without checking who's there and in come 6,000 bugs; Doorknob's efforts to get rid of them include mice, who move in too, followed by cats, who also show no signs of leaving. (Rev: SLJ 5/05)

2747 Seuss, Dr. *Horton Hears a Who!* (K–3). Illus. by author. 1954, Random LB $16.99 (0-394-90078-2). The children's favorite elephant discovers a whole town of creatures so small that they live on a speck of dust. Other titles by Dr. Seuss: *Horton Hatches the Egg* (1940); *If I Ran the Zoo* (1950); *If I Ran the Circus* (1956); *Yertle the Turtle and Other Stories* (1958).

2748 Shah, Idries. *The Silly Chicken* (K–3). Illus. by Jeff Jackson. 2000, Hoopoe $17.00 (1-883536-19-7). 32pp. An amusing story about a chicken who convinces the inhabitants of a town that the earth is going to swallow them up. (Rev: BL 12/15/00; SLJ 3/01)

2749 Shannon, David. *Duck on a Bike* (PS–1). Illus. 2002, Scholastic $15.95 (0-439-05023-5). 40pp. A funny tale about a duck who dares to ride a bike, and the reactions of his farm-animal friends. (Rev: BCCB 3/02; BL 2/15/02; HB 3–4/02; HBG 10/02; SLJ 3/02*)

2750 Shannon, George. *Heart to Heart* (PS–3). Illus. by Steve Bjorkman. 1995, Houghton Mifflin $14.00 (0-395-72773-1). 32pp. Squirrel prepares a unique valentine for his friend Mole that celebrates all the good times they have had together. (Rev: BL 11/15/95; SLJ 11/95)

2751 Shannon, George. *Lizard's Guest* (K–2). Illus. by Jose Aruego and Ariane Dewey. 2003, Greenwillow LB $16.89 (0-06-009084-7). When Lizard accidentally stomps on Skunk's toes while singing and dancing, the barely-injured Skunk plays on the tiny reptile's conscience, winning from Lizard a promise to wait on Skunk hand and foot until his injuries heal. (Rev: HBG 10/03; SLJ 6/03)

2752 Shannon, George. *Lizard's Home* (K–2). Illus. by Jose Aruego and Ariane Dewey. 1999, Greenwillow LB $15.93 (0-688-16003-4). 32pp. Lizard devises a plan to win back his favorite resting place

— a rock that has been taken over by Snake. (Rev: BL 10/1/99; HBG 3/00; SLJ 9/99)

2753 Shannon, George. *Tippy-Toe Chick, Go!* (PS–K). Illus. by Laura Dronzek. 2003, Harper-Collins LB $16.89 (0-06-029824-3). 32pp. Little Chick is a dreamer, but she saves the day when a dog threatens Mother Hen and her brood. (Rev: BCCB 3/03; BL 1/1–15/03; HB 1–2/03*; HBG 10/03; SLJ 2/03)

2754 Shannon, George. *Wise Acres* (K–2). Illus. by Deborah Zemke. 2004, Handprint $15.95 (1-59354-041-8). The animals on Wise Acres farm are presented in three stories — of a lost tambourine, a lonely ram, and an aging turkey worried about his wrinkles. (Rev: SLJ 7/04)

2755 Shannon, Margaret. *Gullible's Troubles* (PS–3). Illus. 1998, Houghton Mifflin $15.00 (0-395-83933-5). 32pp. A humorous story about an innocent little guinea pig named Gullible who is tricked and teased but wins out in the end. (Rev: BCCB 7–8/98; BL 4/1/98; HB 7–8/98; HBG 10/98; SLJ 5/98)

2756 Sharkey, Niamh. *The Ravenous Beast* (PS–2). Illus. by author. 2003, Candlewick $16.99 (0-7636-2182-X). In this fantastical but reassuringly upbeat tale, the Ravenous Beast, a dinosaur-like creature, takes on all challengers to the title of "hungriest animal of all." (Rev: HBG 4/04; SLJ 12/03)

2757 Sharmat, Marjorie W. *I'm Terrific* (PS–1). Illus. by Kay Chorao. 1977, Holiday House LB $15.95 (0-8234-0282-7); paper $5.95 (0-8234-0955-4). 32pp. An amusing story of a bear cub who thinks he is marvelous and insists on telling everyone so.

2758 Sharmat, Marjorie W. *Tiffany Dino Works Out* (PS–3). Illus. by Nate Evans. 1995, Simon & Schuster paper $15.00 (0-689-80309-5). 32pp. Tiffany Dino becomes upset with her weight and decides to do something about it. (Rev: BL 11/15/95; SLJ 12/95)

2759 Sharmat, Mitchell. *Gregory, the Terrible Eater* (PS–3). Illus. by Jose Aruego and Ariane Dewey. 1980, Macmillan $16.00 (0-02-782250-8); Scholastic paper $4.99 (0-590-43350-4). 32pp. Gregory, a young goat, prefers a diet of fruit and vegetables to paper, shoes, and clothing.

2760 Shaw, Nancy. *Sheep Take a Hike* (PS–1). Illus. by Margot Apple. 1994, Houghton Mifflin $13.95 (0-395-68394-7). 32pp. When they get lost in the woods, a flock of sheep find their way home because of bits of wool left on bushes. (Rev: BL 9/15/94; HB 11–12/94; SLJ 9/94*)

2761 Shields, Carol Diggory. *The Bugliest Bug* (PS–2). Illus. by Scott Nash. 2002, Candlewick $15.99 (0-7636-0784-3). On her way to the Bugliest Bug Contest, Damselfly Dilly recognizes that the judges are really spiders in disguise. (Rev: HBG 10/02; SLJ 5/02)

2762 Shih, Bernadette L. *Ling Ling: The Most Beautiful Giant Panda in the World* (K–1). Illus. by Dionysia. 1999, Opal Bks. $16.95 (1-902587-04-9). Ling Ling, a panda, seeks reassurance from other animals that she is the most beautiful panda in the world. (Rev: SLJ 10/99)

2763 Sierra, Judy. *Counting Crocodiles* (PS–1). Illus. by Will Hillenbrand. 1997, Harcourt $16.00 (0-15-200192-1). 40pp. A hungry monkey wants bananas from a neighboring island, but she is afraid that crocodiles will catch her if she tries to swim. (Rev: BL 9/1/97; HBG 3/98; SLJ 10/97)

2764 Sierra, Judy. *Good Night Dinosaurs* (PS–1). Illus. by Victoria Chess. 1996, Clarion $15.00 (0-395-65016-X). 32pp. Stylized drawings of dinosaurs portray them in humorous day-to-day activities, such as snoozing in the mud and sucking on baby bottles. (Rev: BCCB 3/96; BL 1/1–15/96; HB 7–8/96; SLJ 4/96)

2765 Sierra, Judy. *Preschool to the Rescue* (PS–K). Illus. by Will Hillenbrand. 2001, Harcourt $15.00 (0-15-202035-7). 32pp. A group of animal preschoolers come to the rescue of a pizza van and other vehicles that are stuck in a huge mud puddle. (Rev: BCCB 4/01; BL 4/15/01; HB 5–6/01; HBG 10/01; SLJ 5/01)

2766 Simmons, Jane. *Come Along, Daisy!* (PS). Illus. 1998, Little, Brown $12.95 (0-316-79790-1). 32pp. Daisy, a duckling, becomes distracted by the pond life around her, gets lost, and decides not to stray again after her mother finds her. (Rev: BCCB 9/98; BL 6/1–15/98*; HBG 10/98; SLJ 8/98)

2767 Simmons, Jane. *Daisy and the Egg* (PS–K). Illus. 1999, Little, Brown $12.95 (0-316-79747-2). 32pp. Duckling Daisy decides to help out by sitting on an egg and is happy when it hatches and a baby duckling appears. (Rev: BL 2/15/99; HB 5–6/99; HBG 10/99; SLJ 7/99)

2768 Simmons, Jane. *Daisy Says "Here We Go 'Round the Mulberry Bush"* (PS). Illus. by author. 2002, Little, Brown $7.95 (0-316-79811-8). Duckling Daisy enjoys dancing along to the song until it's time for bed in this board book. Also use *Daisy Says "If You're Happy and You Know It"* (2002). (Rev: SLJ 8/02)

2769 Simmons, Jane. *Daisy's Hide-and-Seek: A Lift-the-Flap Book* (PS). Illus. by author. 2001, Little, Brown $9.95 (0-316-79616-6). Daisy the duck searches for Pip, a baby duck, all over the place before finding him tucked under his mother's wing in this book with flaps to lift. (Rev: SLJ 4/01)

2770 Simmons, Jane. *Quack, Daisy, QUACK!* (PS–K). Illus. 2002, Little, Brown $13.95 (0-316-79587-9). 32pp. Daisy the duck and her little brother Pip visit their aunt in the country, where Daisy loses her mother in a crowded duck pond. (Rev: BL 3/1/02; HBG 10/02; SLJ 3/02)

2771 Simmons, Steven J. *Percy to the Rescue* (PS–3). Illus. by Kim Howard. 1998, Charlesbridge $15.95 (0-88106-390-8). 32pp. Percy, a blue pigeon who visits the tourist sites in London daily, helps rescue two boys who are trapped on an island in a park lake. (Rev: BL 8/98; HBG 3/99)

2772 Simon, Francesca. *Hugo and the Bully Frogs* (PS–1). Illus. by Caroline Jayne Church. 1999, David & Charles $14.95 (1-86233-093-X). Poor Hugo, a little frog, is intimidated by three big bullies in his pond until he gets help from a duck. (Rev: SLJ 3/00)

2773 Simon, Francesca. *Where Are You?* (PS). Illus. by David Melling. 1998, Peachtree $12.95 (1-56145-179-7). 32pp. Harry, a little dog, follows his interest in food while in a supermarket. When he becomes separated from Grandpa, though, he experiences the fear of being lost. (Rev: BL 12/1/98; HBG 3/99; SLJ 5/99)

2774 Simont, Marc. *The Goose That Almost Got Cooked* (K–2). Illus. 1997, Scholastic $15.95 (0-590-69075-2). 40pp. A Canada goose is happy to leave the flock and join some white geese on a farm until she realizes that in this situation she might become somebody's dinner. (Rev: BL 11/1/97; HBG 3/98; SLJ 8/97*)

2775 Slate, Joseph. *Miss Bindergarten Plans a Circus with Kindergarten* (PS–2). Illus. by Ashley Wolff. 2002, Dutton $16.99 (0-525-46884-6). Miss Bindergarten and her alphabetical charges each have a role to play in the circus. (Rev: HBG 3/03; SLJ 12/02)

2776 Slate, Joseph. *Story Time for Little Porcupine* (PS–3). Illus. by Jacqueline Rogers. 2000, Marshall Cavendish $15.95 (0-7614-5073-4). 32pp. At bedtime Papa and Little Porcupine trade stories similar to folktales, like Papa's story on how a trickster moon got the best of Big Porcupine. (Rev: BL 10/15/00; HBG 3/01; SLJ 10/00)

2777 Smith, Mary Ann, and Katie Smith Milway. *Cappuccina Goes to Town* (PS–2). Illus. by Eugenie Fernandes. 2002, Kids Can $15.95 (1-55074-807-6). Cappuccina goes shopping, and all the shopkeepers seem oblivious to the fact that she's a cow. (Rev: HBG 10/02; SLJ 8/02)

2778 Snow, Alan. *The Truth About Cats* (K–4). Illus. 1996, Little, Brown $14.95 (0-316-80282-4). 32pp. With great daring, this book reveals that cats are really aliens from the Planet Nip. A companion to *How Dogs Really Work!* (1993). (Rev: BL 4/15/96; SLJ 3/96)

2779 Soto, Gary. *Chato Goes Cruisin'* (PS–2). Illus. by Susan Guevara. 2005, Penguin Putnam $16.99 (0-399-23974-X). 32pp. Disappointed to find themselves on a dog-only cruise, Chato and Novio Boy, cool cats from LA, nonetheless set off in search for help when the dogs all fall ill. (Rev: BL 5/1/05; SLJ 6/05)

2780 Soto, Gary. *Chato's Kitchen* (PS–3). Illus. by Susan Guevara. 1995, Penguin Putnam $16.99 (0-399-22658-3). 32pp. In his Los Angeles barrio home, the cat Chato extends an invitation to some mice to come to dinner. (Rev: BL 3/1/95; HB 9–10/95; SLJ 7/95*)

2781 Spanyol, Jessica. *Carlo Likes Reading* (PS–K). Illus. 2001, Candlewick $14.95 (0-7636-1550-1). 32pp. The sink, a frog, his toothbrush — everything in Carlo's world has a label, and the bright yellow giraffe loves to read them. (Rev: BL 11/1/01; HBG 3/02; SLJ 10/01)

2782 Spelman, Cornelia Maude. *When I Care About Others* (K–2). Illus. by Kathy Parkinson. Series: The Way I Feel. 2002, Whitman LB $14.95 (0-8075-8889-X). 24pp. Readers are encouraged to be kind to others through the simple story of a little bear shown treating others as he likes to be treated. (Rev: BL 7/02; HBG 10/02; SLJ 7/02)

2783 Spelman, Cornelia Maude. *When I Feel Angry* (PS–1). Illus. by Nancy Cote. 2000, Whitman $14.95 (0-8075-8888-1). 32pp. A young bunny finds that he can deal in a number of ways with the anger he sometimes feels: by resting, crying, exercising, or asking for help. (Rev: BL 3/15/00; HBG 10/00; SLJ 4/00)

2784 Spelman, Cornelia Maude. *When I Feel Sad* (PS–2). Illus. by Kathy Parkinson. Series: The Way I Feel. 2002, Whitman LB $14.95 (0-8075-8891-1). A guinea pig describes what makes her feel sad. (Rev: HBG 3/03; SLJ 1/03)

2785 Spelman, Cornelia Maude. *When I Feel Scared* (PS–K). Illus. by Kathy Parkinson. Series: The Way I Feel. 2002, Whitman LB $14.95 (0-8075-8890-3). 24pp. A little bear talks about his fears, how some fears help him survive, and how others are unnecessary. (Rev: BL 4/15/02; HBG 10/02; SLJ 7/02)

2786 Spinelli, Eileen. *Bath Time* (PS). Illus. by Janet Pedersen. 2003, Marshall Cavendish $14.95 (0-7614-5117-X). 32pp. A little penguin has lots of fun preparing for and then having his bath. (Rev: BL 3/15/03; HBG 10/03; SLJ 6/03)

2787 Spinelli, Eileen. *Six Hogs on a Scooter* (PS–1). Illus. by Scott Nash. 2000, Orchard LB $16.99 (0-531-33212-8). 40pp. After a series of mishaps, six hogs arrive at the opera house so late that the performance is over and they must wait until the next day for a ride home. (Rev: BL 3/1/00; HBG 10/00; SLJ 4/00)

2788 Spinelli, Eileen. *Something to Tell the Grandcows* (PS–2). Illus. by Bill Slavin. 2004, Eerdmans $16.00 (0-8028-5236-X). 32pp. Hoping to have a story to impress her grandcows, Emmadine the cow signs up to join Byrd's 1933 expedition to the South Pole. (Rev: BL 4/1/04; SLJ 3/04)

2789 Spinelli, Eileen. *Three Pebbles and a Song* (PS–2). Illus. by S. D. Schindler. 2003, Dial $16.99 (0-8037-2528-0). Moses, a young mouse, is distracted by the world around him and fails to collect the supplies his family needs, but Mama, Papa, and sister Missy have taken care of this and he is able to entertain them with his own discoveries. (Rev: HBG 4/04; SLJ 9/03)

2790 Spinelli, Jerry. *My Daddy and Me* (PS–K). Illus. by Seymour Chwast. 2003, Knopf $15.95 (0-375-80606-7). 40pp. A dog son describes all the joys of his life with his father. (Rev: BL 3/1/03; HBG 10/03; SLJ 6/03)

2791 Spohn, Kate. *By Word of Mouse* (PS–2). Illus. by author. 2004, Bloomsbury $16.95 (1-58234-867-7). A field mouse who likes living in the big blue home of two artist sisters encourages her relatives to join here there. (Rev: BCCB 11/04; SLJ 7/04)

2792 Spohn, Kate. *Dog and Cat Make a Splash* (PS–2). Illus. by author. Series: Viking Easy-to-Read. 1997, Viking $13.99 (0-670-87178-8). 31pp. Four gentle stories about Dog and his best friend, Cat. (Rev: SLJ 6/97)

2793 Spohn, Kate. *Turtle and Snake's Valentine's Day* (PS–1). Illus. by author. Series: Viking Easy-to-Read. 2003, Viking $13.99 (0-670-03613-7). 30pp. Best friends Turtle and Snake each busily plan a Valentine's Day surprise for the other. (Rev: BL 1/1–15/04; HBG 4/04; SLJ 1/04)

2794 Spurling, Margaret. *Bilby Moon* (PS–2). Illus. by Danny Snell. 2001, Kane $14.95 (1-929132-06-9). 32pp. Bilby wonders where the moon has gone and is eventually reassured that it will come back. (Rev: BL 5/1/01; HBG 10/01)

2795 Spurr, Elizabeth. *A Pig Named Perrier* (K–3). Illus. by Martin Matje. 2002, Hyperion $15.99 (0-7868-0302-9). 32pp. When movie star Marabella discovers that her spoiled pet pig, Perrier, enjoys playing in the mud, she takes him to a spa for mud baths. (Rev: BCCB 9/02; BL 4/15/02; HBG 10/02; SLJ 7/02)

2796 Stadler, Alexander. *Beverly Billingsly Borrows a Book* (PS–2). Illus. 2002, Harcourt $16.00 (0-15-202510-3). 32pp. Beverly is thrilled to have her own library card, until she hears some scary rumors about what happens to children with overdue books. (Rev: BL 3/15/02; HBG 3/03; SLJ 4/02)

2797 Stadler, Alexander. *Beverly Billingsly Takes a Bow* (K–2). Illus. by author. 2003, Harcourt $16.00 (0-15-216816-8). A last-minute case of the jitters keeps Beverly from winning one of the lead roles in the school play, but on opening night she comes to the rescue when the star performer suffers from her own stage fright. (Rev: HBG 10/03; SLJ 4/03)

2798 Stadler, Alexander. *Beverly Billingsly Takes the Cake* (PS–2). Illus. 2005, Harcourt $16.00 (0-15-205357-3). 32pp. When Beverly's attempts to make a perfect cake are foiled, her mother helps her come up with a solution. (Rev: BL 4/1/05; SLJ 4/05)

2799 Stadler, John. *Catilda* (PS). Illus. 2003, Simon & Schuster $16.95 (0-689-84728-9). 32pp. Kitten Catilda's parents discuss her lost teddy bear in the text while the illustrations show Catilda on a long and perilous journey to retrieve the lost toy from the torch of the Statue of Liberty. (Rev: BCCB 3/03; BL 1/1–15/03; HBG 10/03; SLJ 2/03)

2800 Stanley, Mandy. *Lettice: The Dancing Rabbit* (PS–K). Illus. 2002, Simon & Schuster $14.95 (0-689-84797-1). 32pp. A little bunny named Lettice longs to be a ballerina like a human child. (Rev: BL 2/1/02; HBG 10/02; SLJ 4/02)

2801 Steig, William. *Doctor De Soto* (K–3). Illus. by author. 1982, Farrar $16.00 (0-374-31803-4). A mouse dentist outwits a fox.

2802 Steig, William. *Farmer Palmer's Wagon Ride* (K–2). Illus. by author. 1992, Farrar paper $4.95 (0-374-42268-0). Farmer Palmer, a pig, and the hired hand, a donkey, have a disastrous ride home from the market in this engaging nonsensical bit of fun.

2803 Steig, William. *Gorky Rises* (1–3). Illus. by author. 1986, Farrar paper $4.95 (0-374-42784-4). 32pp. A frog named Gorky concocts a formula that sends him on a magical journey.

2804 Steig, William. *Solomon the Rusty Nail* (K–2). Illus. by author. 1985, Farrar paper $6.95 (0-374-46903-2). 32pp. A rabbit's ability to change himself into a rusty nail whenever he wishes leads him to

some interesting adventures and keeps him away from the prowling cat. (Rev: BCCB 3/86; BL 1/1/86; SLJ 2/86)

2805 Steig, William. *Sylvester and the Magic Pebble* (K–3). Illus. by author. 1988, Simon & Schuster paper $5.99 (0-671-66269-4). 32pp. A donkey who collects pebbles finds a red stone that will grant wishes — and off Sylvester goes on a series of adventures. Caldecott Medal winner, 1970.

2806 Steig, William. *Tiffky Doofky* (K–2). Illus. by author. 1978, Farrar paper $3.95 (0-374-47748-5). A canine garbage collector awaits a fortune-teller's prophecy to come true.

2807 Steinberg, Laya. *Thesaurus Rex* (PS–3). Illus. by Debbie Harter. 2003, Barefoot $15.99 (1-84148-042-8). Readers follow Thesaurus Rex, a little turquoise-colored dinosaur, through a typical, vocabulary-expanding day of junior dino antics. (Rev: HBG 4/04; LMC 2/04; SLJ 12/03)

2808 Stenmark, Victoria. *The Singing Chick* (PS–K). Illus. by Randy Cecil. 1999, Holt $15.95 (0-8050-5255-0). 32pp. A circular tale about small to large animals who eat each other — until they are all spit out by a bear. (Rev: BCCB 2/99; BL 3/15/99; HB 5–6/99; HBG 10/99; SLJ 5/99)

2809 Stephens, Helen. *Ahoyty-Toyty* (K–2). Illus. by author. 2004, Random LB $16.99 (0-385-75040-4). Two dogs learn about social classes while on a cruise. (Rev: SLJ 6/04)

2810 Stevens, Janet, and Susan Stevens Crummel. *Cook-a-Doodle-Doo!* (PS–3). Illus. 1999, Harcourt $17.00 (0-15-201924-3). 48pp. A group of farm animals are happy to help Big Brown Rooster prepare strawberry shortcake in this delightful farce. (Rev: BCCB 7–8/99; BL 4/15/99*; HB 5–6/99; HBG 10/99; SLJ 4/99)

2811 Stevens, Janet, and Susan Stevens Crummel. *Jackalope* (K–3). Illus. by Janet Stevens. 2003, Harcourt $17.00 (0-15-216736-6). 56pp. A wild and wacky multilayered story of a jackrabbit who wants to be scary and his fairy godrabbit's humorous efforts to oblige. (Rev: BL 3/15/03; HBG 10/03; SLJ 7/03)

2812 Stevenson, James. *The Castaway* (2–4). Illus. 2002, HarperCollins LB $15.89 (0-688-16966-X). 32pp. Hubie, a young mouse, falls from a dirigible onto a desert island where he meets a fellow castaway, Leo, a porcupine. (Rev: BL 6/1–15/02; HB 7–8/02; HBG 10/02; SLJ 5/02)

2813 Stevenson, James. *Flying Feet* (1–3). Illus. 2004, Greenwillow $15.99 (0-06-051975-4). 48pp. The animal residents of Mud Flat become dance crazy when a team of (larcenous) traveling tap dancers comes to town. (Rev: BL 2/1/04; SLJ 3/04)

2814 Stevenson, James. *Heat Wave at Mud Flat* (K–2). Illus. 1997, Greenwillow $14.93 (0-688-14206-0). 32pp. During a very hot, dry period, a rainmaker visits Mud Flat and the animal inhabitants react in different ways. (Rev: BL 5/15/97; HB 7–8/97; SLJ 5/97*)

2815 Stevenson, James. *The Most Amazing Dinosaur* (PS–3). Illus. 2000, Greenwillow LB $15.89 (0-688-16433-1). 32pp. When Wilfred, a rat, takes refuge from a snowstorm in a natural history museum, he is given a tour by other resident creatures. (Rev: BL 7/00; HBG 10/00; SLJ 6/00)

2816 Stevenson, James. *Mud Flat Spring* (PS–2). Illus. 1999, Greenwillow LB $14.93 (0-688-15773-4). 40pp. In nine short stories, the various animals of Mud Flat greet the spring. (Rev: BL 5/1/99; HBG 10/99; SLJ 3/99)

2817 Stewart, Paul. *A Little Bit of Winter* (PS–K). Illus. by Chris Riddell. 1999, HarperCollins $12.95 (0-06-028278-9). 24pp. Before Hedgehog hibernates, he asks Rabbit to save him a bit of winter, and Rabbit obliges by saving a snowball. (Rev: BL 3/1/99; HBG 10/99; SLJ 3/99)

2818 Stewart, Paul. *Rabbit's Wish* (PS–1). Illus. by Chris Riddell. 2001, HarperCollins $12.95 (0-06-029518-X). 32pp. Rabbit and Hedgehog get a chance to play together — a rare event, since Hedgehog sleeps during the day. (Rev: BL 10/15/01; HBG 10/01; SLJ 7/01)

2819 Stickland, Paul. *Dinosaur Stomp: A Monster Pop-Up* (PS–K). Illus. 1996, Dutton $15.99 (0-525-45591-4). This pop-up book involves dancing dinosaurs. (Rev: BL 12/15/96; SLJ 2/97)

2820 Stickland, Paul, and Henrietta Stickland. *Dinosaur Roar!* (PS–K). Illus. 1994, Dutton $13.99 (0-525-45276-1). 32pp. In this tale about two dinosaurs, several antonyms are introduced. (Rev: BL 10/1/94; SLJ 1/95)

2821 Stock, Catherine. *A Spree in Paree* (PS–2). Illus. 2004, Holiday House $16.95 (0-8234-1720-4). 32pp. Monsieur Monmouton is persuaded to take his farm animals to Paris, where they act like crass tourists and generally have a great time throwing their weight around. (Rev: BL 3/15/04; SLJ 5/04)

2822 Stoeke, Janet Morgan. *Minerva Louise and the Red Truck* (PS–1). Illus. 2002, Dutton $14.99 (0-525-46909-5). 32pp. The silly hen Minerva Louise gets taken for a ride in the farm truck and, as usual, misinterprets everything she sees. (Rev: BL 12/1/02; HB 11–12/02; HBG 3/03; SLJ 9/02)

2823 Stojic, Manya. *Rain* (PS–1). Illus. 2000, Crown LB $15.89 (0-517-80086-1). 32pp. All the animals in the hot, dry African savanna sense the coming of a welcome rainstorm. (Rev: BCCB 7–8/00; BL 7/00; SLJ 5/00)

2824 Stoltz, Mary. *Belling the Tiger* (2–4). Illus. by Pierre Pratt. 2004, Running Press $15.95 (0-7624-1889-3). 32pp. This is a newly illustrated edition of the 1961 Newbery Honor Book about two young mice charged with the daunting task of putting a bell on the household cat; the print is very small for this age group. (Rev: BL 9/1/04; SLJ 9/04)

2825 Stone, Kazuko G. *Aligay Saves the Stars* (PS–1). Illus. 1991, Scholastic $13.95 (0-590-44382-8). An alligator is sent into space to retrieve the boomerang he threw too high. (Rev: SLJ 1/92)

2826 Sturges, Philemon. *This Little Pirate* (PS–K). Illus. by Amy Walrod. 2005, Dutton $15.99 (0-525-46440-9). 40pp. Colorful illustrations and humorous text follow two bands of pig pirates fighting over a box until they become so tired they declare a truce

and settle down to enjoy its contents. (Rev: BL 6/1–15/05)

2827 Sturges, Philemon. *Waggers* (PS–3). Illus. by Jim Ishikawa. 2005, Dutton $16.99 (0-525-47116-2). This story of why dogs wag their tails involves the interference of a crafty cat. (Rev: SLJ 3/05)

2828 Suteyev, V. *Mushroom in the Rain* (K–2). Trans. by Mirra Ginsburg. Illus. by Jose Aruego and Ariane Dewey. 1987, Macmillan paper $5.99 (0-689-71441-6). 32pp. An ant huddled under a mushroom in the rain makes room for a variety of animals. A reissued 1974 book.

2829 Sweeney, Joan. *Once upon a Lily Pad: Froggy Love in Monet's Garden* (PS–2). Illus. by Kathleen Fain. 1995, Chronicle $9.95 (0-8118-0868-8). 32pp. Two married frogs, Hector and Henrietta, play in Monet's lily pond at Giverny, France, and pose for the artist. (Rev: BL 1/1–15/96; SLJ 2/96)

2830 Sykes, Julie. *Dora's Eggs* (PS). Illus. by Jane Chapman. 1997, Little Tiger $14.95 (1-888444-09-6). Dora the hen is disappointed when none of the animals pay attention to her first eggs; but when they hatch, it is a different matter. (Rev: HBG 3/98; SLJ 12/97)

2831 Sykes, Julie. *I Don't Want to Take a Bath* (PS–1). Illus. by Tim Warnes. 1997, Little Tiger $14.95 (1-888444-20-7). 32pp. Little Tiger avoids taking a bath by running into the jungle to play with friends. (Rev: BL 12/1/97; HBG 3/98)

2832 Sykes, Julie. *Little Tiger's Big Surprise!* (PS–K). Illus. by Tim Warnes. 1999, Little Tiger $14.95 (1-888444-52-5). Little Tiger runs away when he is told he will soon have a little brother or sister but, when he returns, he is delighted with the new baby. (Rev: HBG 3/00; SLJ 2/00)

2833 Sykes, Julie. *Smudge* (PS–K). Illus. by Jane Chapman. 1998, Little Tiger $14.95 (1-888444-44-4). 32pp. When Smudge, a dog, and his friends are caught in a rainstorm, they try to get into a house for shelter, but their attempts fail — until Smudge gets a winning idea. (Rev: BL 10/15/98; HBG 3/99; SLJ 10/98)

2834 Sykes, Julie. *Wait for Me, Little Tiger!* (PS–1). Illus. by Tim Warnes. 2001, Tiger Tales $14.95 (1-58925-009-5). Little Tiger reluctantly takes his annoying little sister out to play, and of course she disappears. (Rev: SLJ 7/01)

2835 Symes, Ruth Louise. *The Sheep Fairy: When Wishes Have Wings* (PS–1). Illus. by David Sim. 2003, Scholastic $15.95 (0-439-53168-3). 32pp. Wendy Woolcoat rescues a fairy in distress, is granted one wish, and finds herself saving her flock from a wolf. (Rev: BL 10/1/03; HBG 4/04; LMC 2/04; SLJ 12/03)

2836 Tafuri, Nancy. *Goodnight, My Duckling* (PS). Illus. 2005, Scholastic $16.95 (0-439-39881-9). 32pp. A turtle comes to the rescue of a straggler duckling. (Rev: BL 1/1–15/05; SLJ 4/05)

2837 Tafuri, Nancy. *Have You Seen My Duckling?* (PS–2). Illus. by author. 1984, Greenwillow $16.89 (0-688-02798-9); Morrow paper $5.95 (0-688-10994-2). 24pp. Mother Duck asks a number of animals if they have seen her missing duckling.

2838 Tafuri, Nancy. *Silly Little Goose!* (PS). Illus. 2001, Scholastic $15.95 (0-439-06304-3). 32pp. When a silly little goose discovers that every place she wants for her nest is already occupied, she finds a farmer's hat and decides it is the perfect place to lay her eggs. (Rev: BL 2/1/01; HBG 10/01)

2839 Tafuri, Nancy. *Where Did Bunny Go?* (PS). 2001, Scholastic $15.95 (0-439-16959-3). 32pp. Bunny disappears during a game of hide-and-seek and his friends worry that he is angry until he returns to reassure them of his friendship in this gentle story. (Rev: BL 12/1/01; HBG 3/02; SLJ 12/01)

2840 Tafuri, Nancy. *You Are Special, Little One* (PS–1). Illus. by author. 2003, Scholastic $16.95 (0-439-39879-7). Six different animal babies ask their parents about the qualities that make them special. (Rev: HBG 4/04; SLJ 10/03)

2841 Takao, Yuko. *A Winter Concert* (K–2). Illus. by author. 1997, Millbrook LB $18.40 (0-7613-0301-4). As a mouse listens to a concert, his black-and-white world slowly becomes one of color. (Rev: HBG 3/98; SLJ 1/98)

2842 Talley, Linda. *Thank You, Meiling* (K–3). Illus. by Itoko Maeno. 1999, MarshMedia $16.95 (1-55942-118-5). 30pp. A young duck learns about courtesy and Chinese traditions as she accompanies a boy on his preparations for the Chinese Moon Festival celebration. (Rev: SLJ 3/00)

2843 Taylor, Eleanor. *Beep, Beep, Let's Go!* (PS). Illus. 2005, Bloomsbury $15.95 (1-58234-973-8). 32pp. Various animals use various forms of transport to get to the beach, where they have a wonderful time. (Rev: BL 5/1/05)

2844 Taylor, Thomas. *The Loudest Roar* (PS–3). Illus. by author. 2003, Scholastic $15.95 (0-439-50130-X). The animals of the jungle decide to teach a noisy young tiger a lesson. (Rev: HBG 10/03; SLJ 3/03)

2845 Teague, Mark. *Dear Mrs. LaRue: Letters from Obedience School* (K–3). Illus. 2002, Scholastic $15.95 (0-439-20663-4). 32pp. Poor Ike LaRue sends pitiful letters home to his owner, complaining about the conditions at doggy school, but the pictures belie his words. (Rev: BL 11/1/02; HBG 3/03; SLJ 9/02)

2846 Teague, Mark. *Pigsty* (PS–3). Illus. 1994, Scholastic $14.95 (0-590-45915-5). 32pp. Even messy Wendell, a pig, resents his friends creating chaos in his room. (Rev: BL 9/15/94; SLJ 10/94*)

2847 Tekavec, Heather. *Storm Is Coming!* (PS–1). Illus. by Margaret Spengler. 2002, Dial $14.99 (0-8037-2626-0). 32pp. A group of frightened animals bunch together in the barn, anticipating the arrival of Storm and comforted by the fact that the howling wind, flashing light, and rain will scare him away. (Rev: BL 3/1/02; HBG 10/02; SLJ 3/02)

2848 Tekavec, Heather. *What's That Awful Smell?* (PS–2). Illus. by Margaret Spengler. 2004, Dial $15.99 (0-8037-2660-0). A bad smell in the barn has the animals searching for its source, which turns out not to be the piglet they first suspect. (Rev: HB 7–8/04; SLJ 4/04)

2849 Testa, Fulvio. *Time to Get Out* (PS–K). Illus. by author. 1993, Tambourine LB $13.93 (0-688-12908-9). A cumulative story about a boy and several animals that join forces to track down a loud noise they hear on a tropical island. (Rev: SLJ 10/93)

2850 Tharlet, Eve. *Nancy, the Little Gosling* (PS–1). Trans. by Charise Myngheer. Illus. by author. 2005, Minedition $14.99 (0-698-40008-9). A gosling who wants to be a butterfly researcher when she grows up has trouble learning some goose basics. (Rev: SLJ 2/05)

2851 Theobald, Joseph. *Marvin Wanted More!* (PS–3). Illus. by author. 2003, Bloomsbury $16.95 (0-7475-5631-8). Marvin is a sheep with an uncontrollable appetite, and the consequences just grow and grow. (Rev: SLJ 9/03)

2852 Thompson, Lauren. *Mouse's First Day of School* (PS). Illus. by Buket Erdogan. 2003, Simon & Schuster $12.95 (0-689-84727-0). Mouse finds many items of interest when he finds his way into the classroom in this small book with large, bold type. (Rev: HBG 4/04; SLJ 9/03)

2853 Thompson, Lauren. *Mouse's First Spring* (PS). Illus. by Buket Erdogan. 2005, Simon & Schuster $12.95 (0-689-85838-8). 32pp. Mouse and his mother playfully identify spring flora and fauna in this rhyming picture book. (Rev: BL 3/1/05; SLJ 4/05)

2854 Thompson, Lauren. *Mouse's First Summer* (PS–1). Illus. by Buket Erdogan. 2004, Simon & Schuster $12.95 (0-689-85835-3). Mouse experiences the joys of summer with companion Minka. (Rev: SLJ 6/04)

2855 Thomson, Pat. *Drat That Fat Cat* (PS–1). Illus. by Ailie Busby. 2003, Scholastic $15.95 (0-439-47195-8). In this bright and bouncy cumulative tale, a very fat cat grows even fatter as, one by one, he consumes virtually everything he encounters. (Rev: BCCB 1/04; BL 1/1–15/04; HB 1–2/04; HBG 4/04; SLJ 12/03)

2856 Tompert, Ann. *The Hungry Black Bag* (PS–1). Illus. by Jacqueline Chwast. 1999, Houghton Mifflin $15.00 (0-395-89418-2). 32pp. A goat, who robs animals selling their goods in a market, finally gets his comeuppance. (Rev: BL 5/15/99; HBG 10/99; SLJ 5/99)

2857 Tompert, Ann. *Just a Little Bit* (PS–K). Illus. by Lynn Munsinger. 1993, Houghton Mifflin $16.00 (0-395-51527-0). 32pp. In this cumulative tale, several animals try to help Mouse balance the scales when he tries to seesaw with Elephant. (Rev: BL 11/1/93; HB 9–10/93; SLJ 12/93)

2858 Tompert, Ann. *Nothing Sticks Like a Shadow* (PS–3). Illus. by Lynn Munsinger. 1988, Houghton Mifflin paper $7.95 (0-395-47950-9). 32pp. Rabbit tries to get rid of his shadow.

2859 Trivizas, Eugene. *The Three Little Wolves and the Big Bad Pig* (K–4). Illus. by Helen Oxenbury. 1993, Macmillan $17.00 (0-689-50569-8). 32pp. In this role-reversal story, three wolves are menaced by a big, bad pig who knocks their house down with a sledgehammer when huffing and puffing won't do the trick. (Rev: BCCB 9/93; BL 9/1/93; SLJ 12/93*)

2860 Tryon, Leslie. *Patsy Says* (K–3). Illus. 2001, Simon & Schuster $16.00 (0-689-82297-9). 40pp. With parents' night approaching at school, Patsy Pig, a teacher's helper, tries to give her class lessons in etiquette. (Rev: BL 4/15/01; HBG 10/01; SLJ 5/01)

2861 Turnbull, Ann. *Too Tired* (K–2). Illus. by Emma C. Clark. 1994, Harcourt $13.95 (0-15-200549-8). 32pp. There is a crisis on the ark when Noah discovers that the sloths are too tired to board. (Rev: BL 3/15/94; SLJ 4/94)

2862 *Turtle's Race with Beaver: A Traditional Seneca Story* (1–3). Illus. by Jose Aruego and Ariane Dewey. 2003, Penguin Putnam $15.99 (0-8037-2852-2). 32pp. Turtle and Beaver compete for ownership of a pond in this variant on a Seneca Indian tale that resembles Aesop's story of the tortoise and the hare. (Rev: BL 9/15/03; HBG 4/04; SLJ 10/03)

2863 Tyson, Leigh Ann. *An Interview with Harry the Tarantula* (PS–3). Illus. by Henrik Drescher. 2003, National Geographic $15.95 (0-7922-5122-9). A spoof talk-show in which Harry Spyder reveals to Katy Did some of the details of a frightening experience with a human, conveying factual information on tarantulas in the process. (Rev: HBG 4/04; SLJ 12/03)

2864 Umansky, Kaye. *A Chair for Baby Bear* (PS–1). Illus. by Chris Fisher. 2004, Barron's $12.95 (0-7641-5789-2). Baby Bear returns home from an unsuccessful search for a suitable chair to find a package from Goldilocks. (Rev: SLJ 2/05)

2865 Ungerer, Tomi. *Crictor* (PS–2). Illus. by author. 1958, HarperCollins paper $5.95 (0-06-443044-8). 32pp. A boa constrictor becomes the hero of a small French town after he captures a burglar.

2866 Ungerer, Tomi. *Flix* (2–4). Illus. by author. 1998, Roberts Rinehart $16.95 (1-57098-161-2). When Cotza, a cat, gives birth to a dog, she and her husband are startled but raise young Flix to be their pride and joy. (Rev: HBG 3/99; SLJ 9/98)

2867 Vail, Rachel. *Over the Moon* (K–2). Illus. by Scott Nash. 1998, Orchard $15.95 (0-531-30068-4). 32pp. A creative monkey director is adapting the rhyme "Hey Diddle Diddle" for the stage but has problems getting the cow to jump over the moon. (Rev: BL 9/15/98; HBG 3/99; SLJ 9/98)

2868 Vainio, Pirkko. *The Best of Friends* (PS–K). Illus. 2000, North-South LB $15.88 (0-7358-1151-2). 32pp. Although Hare and Bear are very different, they become good friends in this gentle story. (Rev: BL 6/1–15/00; HBG 10/00; SLJ 6/00)

2869 Valckx, Catharina. *Lizette's Green Sock* (PS–K). Illus. 2005, Clarion $15.00 (0-618-45298-2). 32pp. A little bird is thrilled to find a single green sock, and sports it on her foot before moving it to her head. (Rev: BL 5/1/05; SLJ 5/05)

2870 Van Allsburg, Chris. *Two Bad Ants* (1–4). Illus. by author. 1988, Houghton Mifflin $17.95 (0-395-48668-8). 32pp. The story of two adventure-some ants. (Rev: BCCB 12/88; BL 10/1/88; SLJ 11/88)

2871 Van Laan, Nancy. *Scrubba Dub* (PS–1). Illus. by Bernadette Pons. 2003, Simon & Schuster $15.95 (0-689-84459-X). 32pp. A baby rabbit has lots of fun in the bath in this rhyming picture book. (Rev: BL 2/15/03; HBG 10/03; SLJ 4/03)

2872 Van Laan, Nancy. *Tickle Tum!* (PS). Illus. by Bernadette Pons. 2001, Simon & Schuster $14.95 (0-689-83143-9). 32pp. It takes patience, creativity, and lots of energy to get food into the mouth of obstinate Baby Rabbit. (Rev: BL 2/1/01; HBG 10/01; SLJ 3/01)

2873 Varley, Susan. *Badger's Parting Gifts* (1–4). Illus. by author. 1984, Morrow paper $5.95 (0-688-11518-7). 32pp. After initial grief, the animals retain happy memories of their dead friend, Badger. (Rev: SLJ 1/00)

2874 Vaughan, Marcia. *Kissing Coyotes* (K–4). Illus. by Kenneth J. Spengler. 2002, Rising Moon $15.95 (0-87358-814-2). Jack Rabbit's boasting gets out of hand and his animal friends require that he follow through on his claims. (Rev: SLJ 2/03)

2875 Vaughan, Marcia. *Snap!* (PS–2). Illus. by Sascha Hutchinson. 1996, Scholastic $14.95 (0-590-60377-9). 32pp. A young kangaroo plays with other Australian animals until a crocodile spoils their fun. (Rev: BL 7/96; SLJ 4/96)

2876 Verboven, Agnes. *Ducks Like to Swim* (PS). Illus. by Anne Westerduin. 1997, Orchard $13.95 (0-531-30054-4). 32pp. Mother Duck quacks for rain so that her babies can go swimming. (Rev: BL 9/1/97; HBG 3/98; SLJ 9/97)

2877 Voake, Charlotte. *Pizza Kittens* (PS–2). Illus. 2002, Candlewick $15.99 (0-7636-1622-2). 40pp. Three little kittens and their parents try to solve the problem of different eating preferences and behaviors. (Rev: BCCB 6/02; BL 5/1/02; HBG 10/02; SLJ 5/02*)

2878 Vrombaut, An. *Clarabella's Teeth* (PS). Illus. by author. 2003, Clarion $14.00 (0-618-33379-7). Clarabella the crocodile misses out on all the fun with her friends because she's busy brushing her teeth. (Rev: HBG 10/03; SLJ 4/03)

2879 Waber, Bernard. *An Anteater Named Arthur* (PS–2). Illus. by author. 1967, Houghton Mifflin $16.00 (0-395-20336-8); paper $5.95 (0-395-25936-3). 48pp. A mother anteater despairs of her son Arthur, who has problems very much like those of a young boy.

2880 Waber, Bernard. *Bearsie Bear and the Surprise Sleepover Party* (PS–K). Illus. 1997, Houghton Mifflin $15.00 (0-395-86450-X). 40pp. A number of animals are given shelter for the night; but when the porcupine tries to bed down, everybody leaves. (Rev: BL 10/1/97; HB 9–10/97; HBG 3/98; SLJ 10/97)

2881 Waber, Bernard. *Bernard* (K–3). Illus. by author. 1986, Houghton Mifflin paper $8.95 (0-395-42648-0). 48pp. When his owners quarrel over his custody, Bernard, a dog, leaves home.

2882 Waber, Bernard. *Evie and Margie* (PS–2). Illus. by author. 2003, Houghton Mifflin $15.00 (0-

618-34124-2). 32pp. The friendship of young hippos Evie and Margie is tested when both try out for the leading role in a school play. (Rev: HB 9–10/03; HBG 4/04; SLJ 10/03)

2883 Waber, Bernard. *Fast Food! Gulp! Gulp!* (PS–2). Illus. by author. 2001, Houghton Mifflin $15.00 (0-618-14189-8). 32pp. Hungry customers gobble food at such a rate that the cook eventually quits, preferring the pace of a health-food restaurant. (Rev: HBG 10/02; SLJ 9/01*)

2884 Waber, Bernard. *Funny, Funny Lyle* (PS–1). Illus. by author. 1987, Houghton Mifflin $16.00 (0-395-43619-2); paper $5.95 (0-395-60287-4). 40pp. Felicity, mother of Lyle the crocodile, is picked up for shoplifting, but finds her true calling as a nurse. (Rev: BL 8/87; SLJ 12/87)

2885 Waber, Bernard. *The House on East 88th Street* (K–2). Illus. by author. 1973, Houghton Mifflin $14.95 (0-395-18157-7); paper $5.95 (0-395-19970-0). 48pp. Adventures of a pet crocodile (Lyle) who lives with a family in a New York City brownstone. Other books about Lyle by the same author and publisher: *Lyle, Lyle, Crocodile* (1965); *Lyle and the Birthday Party* (1966); *Lyle Finds His Mother* (1974); *Lovable Lyle* (1977).

2886 Waber, Bernard. *Ira Says Goodbye* (K–2). Illus. 1988, Houghton Mifflin $15.00 (0-395-48315-8); paper $5.95 (0-395-58413-2). 40pp. Ira is sad because his best friend is moving away. (Rev: BCCB 10/88; BL 9/1/88; SLJ 9/88)

2887 Waber, Bernard. *A Lion Named Shirley Williamson* (PS–2). Illus. 1996, Houghton Mifflin $15.95 (0-395-80979-7). 40pp. The other lions in the zoo are jealous of the special attention given to the lion named Shirley Williamson. (Rev: BL 9/1/96*; SLJ 12/96*)

2888 Waber, Bernard. *Lyle at the Office* (PS–3). Illus. 1994, Houghton Mifflin $14.95 (0-395-70563-0). 46pp. Lyle becomes very popular when he spends a day helping out in Mr. Primm's office. (Rev: BL 6/1–15/94; SLJ 9/94*)

2889 Waber, Bernard. *The Mouse That Snored* (PS–3). Illus. 2000, Houghton Mifflin $15.00 (0-395-97518-2). 32pp. A mouse who has a terrible snore moves into a house where everyone hates noise so much they won't even eat celery. (Rev: BL 8/00; HB 11–12/00; HBG 3/01; SLJ 10/00)

2890 Waber, Bernard. *The Snake: A Very Long Love Story* (PS). Illus. by author. 1978, Houghton Mifflin LB $7.95 (0-685-02310-9). A long trip brings the snake back home again.

2891 Waber, Bernard. *You Look Ridiculous, Said the Rhinoceros to the Hippopotamus* (K–2). Illus. by author. 1973, Houghton Mifflin $17.95 (0-395-07156-9); paper $5.95 (0-395-28007-9). 32pp. The hippopotamus is discontented with her shape and imagines herself with many of the appendages of neighboring animals.

2892 Waddell, Martin. *Good Job, Little Bear* (PS). Illus. by Barbara Firth. 1999, Candlewick $15.99 (0-7636-0736-3). 32pp. While on a walk, Little Bear tries some dangerous stunts, but Big Bear is always

there to save him. (Rev: BL 8/99; HB 3–4/99; HBG 10/99; SLJ 5/99)

2893 Waddell, Martin. *Harriet and the Crocodiles* (1–3). Illus. by Mark Burgess. 1984, Little, Brown $11.95 (0-316-91622-6). Harriet loses her pet crocodile and sets out to find him.

2894 Waddell, Martin. *Hi, Harry! The Moving Story of How One Slow Tortoise Slowly Made a Friend* (PS). Illus. by Barbara Firth. 2003, Candlewick $14.99 (0-7636-1802-0). 56pp. Harry wants to make friends but all the other animals are in too much of a rush until he thinks of Sam Snail. (Rev: BL 3/1/03; HB 3–4/03*; HBG 10/03; SLJ 4/03)

2895 Waddell, Martin. *Mimi and the Dream House* (PS–2). Illus. by Leo Hartas. 1998, Candlewick paper $3.99 (0-7636-0387-5). A little mouse named Mimi constructs the house of her dreams. (Rev: BL 4/15/98; SLJ 7/98)

2896 Waddell, Martin. *Owl Babies* (PS–1). Illus. by Patrick Benson. 1992, Candlewick $15.99 (1-56402-101-7). 32pp. Three small owls, left alone by their mother, wonder if she is coming back. (Rev: BL 12/1/92; HB 3–4/93; SLJ 12/92)

2897 Waddell, Martin. *Webster J. Duck* (PS–1). Illus. by David Parkins. 2001, Candlewick $13.99 (0-7636-1506-4). 32pp. Webster J. Duck has hatched, but has trouble finding his mother. (Rev: BL 11/15/01; HBG 3/02; SLJ 7/01)

2898 Wagner, Jenny. *Motor Bill and the Lovely Caroline* (K–3). Illus. by Ron Brooks. 1995, Ticknor $14.95 (0-395-71547-4). 32pp. Bill, a donkey, is happy when Caroline, a goat, agrees to go riding with him. (Rev: BL 1/15/95; SLJ 4/95)

2899 Wagner, Karen. *Bravo, Mildred and Ed!* (PS–3). Illus. by Janet Pedersen. 2000, Walker $17.85 (0-8027-8734-7); paper $17.85 (0-8027-8735-5). Although mice Mildred and Ed enjoy doing things together, they also learn to be independent in this charming tale. (Rev: HBG 3/01; SLJ 9/00)

2900 Wagner, Karen. *A Friend Like Ed* (PS–1). Illus. by Janet Pedersen. 1998, Walker LB $16.85 (0-8027-8663-4). 32pp. Mouse Mildred is getting tired of her friend Ed's antics, but once she cultivates the friendship of bossy, overbearing Pearl instead, she decides that Ed isn't so bad after all. (Rev: BL 9/15/98; HBG 3/99; SLJ 11/98)

2901 Wahl, Jan. *Rabbits on Mars* (PS–3). Illus. by Kimberly Schamber. 2003, Lerner $15.95 (1-57505-511-2). 32pp. Three rabbits who are tired of dodging traffic and dogs set off for Mars, which they imagine to be full of carrots. (Rev: BL 3/15/03; HBG 10/03; SLJ 7/03)

2902 Wahl, Jan. *Three Pandas* (PS–1). Illus. by Naava. 2000, Boyds Mills $15.95 (1-56397-749-4). 32pp. Three little pandas have a series of misadventures when they explore beyond their bamboo forest; so they decide to head back home. (Rev: BL 2/15/00; HBG 10/00; SLJ 5/00)

2903 Wallace, Karen. *City Pig* (PS–3). Illus. by Lydia Monks. 2000, Orchard $15.95 (0-531-30252-0). 32pp. Elegant, sophisticated Dolores, a pig, finds her big-city existence unsatisfying and exchanges it for life with country pigs who enjoy simple things. (Rev: BL 2/15/00; HBG 10/00; SLJ 3/00)

2904 Wallace, Nancy E. *Apples, Apples, Apples* (K–2). Illus. 2000, Winslow $15.95 (1-890817-19-8). 40pp. When a rabbit family goes to an orchard to pick apples, they learn a lot about the fruit, the varieties, and how they grow. (Rev: BL 10/15/00; HBG 3/01; SLJ 9/00)

2905 Wallace, Nancy E. *A Taste of Honey* (PS–2). Illus. 2000, Winslow $16.95 (1-890817-51-1). 32pp. Little bear Lily asks Poppy where honey comes from, and his answers trace the story of honey from the jar back to the bees. (Rev: BL 2/15/01; HBG 10/01)

2906 Wallace, Nancy Elizabeth. *Baby Day!* (PS). Illus. 2003, Houghton Mifflin $9.95 (0-618-27576-2). 32pp. A baby rabbit and mother spend a happy day together in this board book with cut-paper illustrations. (Rev: BL 2/15/03; HBG 10/03; SLJ 3/03)

2907 Wallace, Nancy Elizabeth. *Pumpkin Day!* (PS–2). Illus. 2002, Marshall Cavendish $16.95 (0-7614-5128-5). 32pp. A rabbit family visits a pumpkin farm to learn how they grow, before picking some for carving and eating. (Rev: BCCB 10/02; BL 8/02; HBG 3/03; SLJ 11/02)

2908 Wallace, Nancy Elizabeth. *Seeds! Seeds! Seeds!* (K–3). Illus. 2004, Marshall Cavendish $16.95 (0-7614-5159-5). 40pp. A package from Grandpa gets Buddy Bear involved in a variety of activities involving seeds. (Rev: BL 4/15/04; SLJ 6/04)

2909 Walsh, Ellen S. *For Pete's Sake* (PS–1). Illus. 1998, Harcourt $15.00 (0-15-200324-X). Pete is an alligator who thinks he is a flamingo just like all his feathered friends — until he accidentally meets some other alligators. (Rev: BL 10/15/98; HB 11–12/98; HBG 3/99; SLJ 11/98)

2910 Walsh, Ellen S. *Hop Jump* (PS–1). Illus. 1993, Harcourt $13.95 (0-15-292871-5). 32pp. Most of the other frogs enjoy hopping, but Betsy prefers to dance. (Rev: BL 11/1/93; HB 11–12/93; SLJ 10/93)

2911 Walsh, Ellen S. *Mouse Paint* (PS–K). Illus. 1989, Harcourt $14.00 (0-15-256025-4). 32pp. Three mice paint themselves as camouflage and find they like their new look. (Rev: BL 5/15/89; HB 7–8/89; SLJ 9/89)

2912 Walsh, Ellen S. *Samantha* (PS–1). Illus. 1996, Harcourt $14.00 (0-15-252264-6). 32pp. Samantha, a mouse, doesn't want to become too dependent on the protection that her fairy godmother gives her. (Rev: BCCB 6/96; BL 2/15/96; SLJ 5/96)

2913 Walsh, Ellen Stoll. *Dot and Jabber and the Big Bug Mystery* (PS–1). Illus. by author. 2003, Harcourt $15.00 (0-15-216518-5). Dot and Jabber, mouse detectives, use their sleuthing skills to find out why the insects they've been watching all seem to be disappearing. (Rev: HBG 4/04; SLJ 11/03)

2914 Walsh, Ellen Stoll. *Dot and Jabber and the Great Acorn Mystery* (PS–2). Illus. 2001, Harcourt $15.00 (0-15-202602-9). 40pp. Mouse sleuths Dot and Jabber investigate who moved the acorn that grew into a little oak tree. (Rev: BL 10/1/01; HBG 3/02; SLJ 9/01)

2915 Walsh, Ellen Stoll. *Dot and Jabber and the Mystery of the Missing Stream* (K–2). Illus. by author. 2002, Harcourt $15.00 (0-15-216512-6). Readers will learn a little science and logic from this story of two mice investigating why a stream has dried up. (Rev: HBG 3/03; SLJ 11/02)

2916 Walton, Rick. *Bertie Was a Watchdog* (PS–1). Illus. by Arthur Robins. 2002, Candlewick $10.99 (0-7636-1385-1). Bertie the dog doesn't look fierce, but he's smart. (Rev: HBG 10/02; SLJ 8/02)

2917 Walton, Rick. *Bunnies on the Go: Getting from Place to Place* (PS–2). Illus. by Paige Miglio. 2003, HarperCollins LB $16.89 (0-06-029186-9). 32pp. Rhyming text and illustrations with visual clues make a guessing game out of this story of a bunny family's vacation on boats, trains, bicycles, and other forms of transportation. (Rev: BL 1/1–15/03; HBG 10/03; SLJ 3/03)

2918 Walton, Rick. *Herd of Cows! Flock of Sheep! Quiet! I'm Tired! I Need My Sleep!* (K–2). Illus. by Julie Olson. 2002, Gibbs Smith $15.95 (1-58685-153-5). Bright illustrations and expressive language follow animals through their elaborate efforts to rescue Farmer Bob from the flood. (Rev: HBG 3/03; SLJ 9/02)

2919 Walton, Rick. *Once There Was a Bull . . . (frog)* (K–3). Illus. by Greg Hally. 1995, Gibbs Smith $15.95 (0-87905-652-5). 32pp. This clever story about a bullfrog searching for his lost hop uses the splitting of compound words to create different perceptions. (Rev: BL 12/15/95)

2920 Ward, Helen. *The Rooster and the Fox: A Tale from Chaucer* (K–3). Illus. 2003, Millbrook LB $24.90 (0-7613-2920-X). 40pp. "The Nun's Priest's Tale" about the proud rooster and the wily fox is adapted here in an effective tale using elegant, readable text and realistic watercolor art that makes the various animals come to life. (Rev: BCCB 2/03; BL 1/1–15/03; HBG 10/03; SLJ 10/04)

2921 Ward, Nick. *Come On, Baby Duck!* (PS–1). Illus. by author. 2004, Good Books $16.00 (1-56148-447-4). A baby duck is too scared to swim until his teddy falls in. (Rev: SLJ 11/04)

2922 Wardlaw, Lee. *The Chair Where Bear Sits* (PS–K). Illus. by Russell Benfanti. 2001, Winslow $14.95 (1-890817-85-6). 56pp. Eye-catching illustrations tell the cumulative tale, in the vein of "The House That Jack Built," of a baby bear who delights in the commotion caused by spilled juice. (Rev: BL 11/15/01; SLJ 2/02)

2923 Waring, Richard. *Hungry Hen* (PS). Illus. by Caroline Jayne Church. 2002, HarperCollins $14.95 (0-06-623880-3). 32pp. A greedy fox waits for a hen to grow fatter, but gets a surprise when he finally tries to eat her in this suspenseful and beautiful presentation. (Rev: BCCB 3/02; BL 1/1–15/02; HBG 10/02; SLJ 1/02*)

2924 Waterton, Betty. *A Salmon for Simon* (K–3). Illus. by Ann Blades. 1991, Salem paper $14.95 (0-88899-107-X). 32pp. A small Canadian Indian has a great adventure with a live salmon.

2925 Watson, Richard Jesse. *The Magic Rabbit* (PS–1). Illus. 2005, Scholastic $15.95 (0-590-

47964-4). 40pp. A white rabbit pops out of a hat and discovers that he's got some pretty amazing magical abilities, but somehow all this isn't much fun without a friend to share it. (Rev: BL 1/1–15/05; SLJ 4/05)

2926 Watt, Melanie. *Leon the Chameleon* (PS–K). Illus. 2001, Kids Can $14.95 (1-55074-867-X). 32pp. Leon's color changes clash with the background, leaving him embarrassed and lonely. (Rev: BL 4/1/01; HBG 3/02; SLJ 4/01)

2927 Watts, Bernadette. *Harvey Hare: Postman Extraordinaire* (PS–K). Illus. 1997, North-South LB $15.88 (1-55858-688-1). 32pp. Because Harvey Hare is such a devoted mail carrier, his friends give him a present to solve his problems with the weather. (Rev: BL 3/15/97; SLJ 3/97)

2928 Weaver, Katie McAllaster. *Bill in a China Shop* (PS–2). Illus. by Tim Raglin. 2003, Bloomsbury $16.95 (1-58234-832-4). Bill is a bull who is fond of good china but has trouble gaining entry to shops. (Rev: BL 12/1/03; HBG 4/04; SLJ 12/03)

2929 Weaver, Tess. *Opera Cat* (2–4). Illus. by Andrea Wesson. 2002, Clarion $15.00 (0-618-09635-3). 32pp. Alma the cat rescues her mistress, the opera diva Madame SoSo, by singing the solos when Madame SoSo comes down with laryngitis in this humorous book with lovely illustrations. (Rev: BL 10/1/02; SLJ 12/02)

2930 Weeks, Sarah. *I'm a Pig* (PS–2). Illus. by Holly Berry. 2005, HarperCollins LB $16.89 (0-06-074344-1). Appealing illustrations accompany a pig's expressions of happiness with her life and herself. (Rev: SLJ 5/05)

2931 Weeks, Sarah. *My Somebody Special* (PS–2). Illus. by Ashley Wolff. 2002, Harcourt $16.00 (0-15-202561-8). 40pp. An encouraging story about animal preschoolers who enjoy their class but are happy to be picked up by their loved ones at the end of the day. (Rev: BL 8/02; HBG 10/02; SLJ 5/02)

2932 Weeks, Sarah. *Two Eggs, Please* (PS–1). Illus. by Betsy Lewin. 2003, Simon & Schuster $15.95 (0-689-83196-X). Differing tastes are clearly — and amusingly — shown as an assortment of animal customers order eggs prepared in various ways. (Rev: HB 9–10/03; HBG 4/04; SLJ 6/04)

2933 Wegman, William. *My Town* (K–4). Illus. 1998, Hyperion $16.95 (0-7868-0410-6). 40pp. Weimaraner Chip discovers that he can use the photos he has taken around town for a school report on community helpers. (Rev: BL 12/1/98; HBG 3/99; SLJ 1/99)

2934 Weigelt, Udo. *Alex Did It!* (K–2). Trans. from German by J. Alison James. Illus. by Cristina Kadmon. 2002, North-South LB $15.88 (0-7358-1579-8). Three young hares are merrily blaming a fictitious Alex for their various misdeeds when they come across a real Alex. (Rev: HBG 10/02; SLJ 7/02)

2935 Weigelt, Udo. *Bear's Last Journey* (PS–2). Trans. from German by Sibylle Kazeroid. Illus. by Cristina Kadmon. 2003, North-South LB $16.50 (0-7358-1800-2). When Bear sickens and dies, his ani-

mal neighbors must come to terms with the loss of their friend. (Rev: HBG 10/03; SLJ 10/03)

2936 Weigelt, Udo. *It Wasn't Me!* (1–3). Illus. by Julia Gukova. 2001, North-South LB $15.88 (0-7358-1524-0). 32pp. Mouse jumps to conclusions when he accuses Raven, the confessed thief of *Who Stole the Gold* (2000), of stealing Ferret's raspberries. (Rev: BL 1/1–15/02; HBG 10/02; SLJ 2/02)

2937 Weigelt, Udo. *The Wild Wombat* (PS–1). Trans. from German by Kathryn Grell. Illus. by Anne-Katrin Piepenbrink. 2002, North-South LB $16.50 (0-7358-1512-7). As the news of a wombat's arrival is passed from animal to animal at the zoo, the descriptions of him become more and more fearsome. (Rev: HBG 3/03; SLJ 12/02)

2938 Weiss, Ellen. *Babar Goes to School* (K–2). Illus. 2003, Abrams $9.95 (0-8109-4582-7). Babar the elephant goes to school with his three children and finds the experience exhausting in this story with illustrations that resemble the originals. (Rev: SLJ 4/04)

2939 Weiss, Leatie. *My Teacher Sleeps in School* (K–2). Illus. by Ellen Weiss. 1985, Puffin paper $5.99 (0-14-050559-8). 32pp. Because their teacher is always there, two elephant children believe their teacher lives in school.

2940 Wells, Rosemary. *Felix and the Worrier* (PS–2). Illus. by author. 2003, Candlewick $12.99 (0-7636-1405-X). Felix the guinea pig starts to fret about all sorts of things when a strange yellow creature called the Worrier begins bothering him. (Rev: HBG 4/04; SLJ 10/03)

2941 Wells, Rosemary. *Felix Feels Better* (PS). Illus. 2001, Candlewick $12.99 (0-7636-0639-1). 32pp. Guinea pig Felix feels so ill the day after eating too much that his mother takes him to the doctor. (Rev: BCCB 6/01; BL 5/1/01; HBG 10/01; SLJ 5/01)

2942 Wells, Rosemary. *Mama, Don't Go!* (PS–2). Illus. by Jody Wheeler and Rosemary Wells. Series: Yoko and Friends School Days. 2001, Hyperion $9.99 (0-7868-0720-2); paper $3.99 (0-7868-1526-4). 31pp. The characters from *Yoko* return as kitten Yoko starts school and refuses to be without her mother. (Rev: HBG 3/02; SLJ 1/02)

2943 Wells, Rosemary. *Max Cleans Up* (PS–3). Illus. 2000, Viking $15.99 (0-670-89218-1). 32pp. Max's idea of cleaning up his room is to stuff everything into the front pocket of his overalls in this story about a delightful rabbit. (Rev: BL 2/1/01; HBG 10/01; SLJ 12/00)

2944 Wells, Rosemary. *Only You* (PS–K). Illus. by author. 2003, Viking $14.99 (0-670-03634-X). A baby bear tells his mother how important she is to him. (Rev: HBG 10/03; SLJ 5/03)

2945 Wells, Rosemary. *Only You / Solo Tu* (PS–K). Trans. by Teresa Mlawer. Illus. 2004, Viking $14.99 (0-670-03692-7). 24pp. In brightly illustrated English and Spanish, a bear and her young child go about their daily life. (Rev: BL 1/1–15/04; SLJ 4/04)

2946 Wells, Rosemary. *Read Me a Story* (K–2). Illus. by Jody Wheeler and Rosemary Wells. Series:

Yoko and Friends School Days. 2002, Hyperion $9.99 (0-7868-0727-X); paper $3.99 (0-7868-1533-7). 31pp. Little kitten Yoko is afraid to reveal her reading ability in case her mother stops reading her bedtime stories. (Rev: HBG 3/03; SLJ 12/02)

2947 Wells, Rosemary. *Read to Your Bunny* (PS). Illus. by author. 1998, Scholastic $7.95 (0-590-30284-1). Using a cast of bunnies, the author shows that reading can be fun anywhere. (Rev: BL 5/1/98; HBG 10/98; SLJ 3/98)

2948 Wells, Rosemary. *Ruby's Beauty Shop* (PS–K). Illus. 2002, Viking $15.99 (0-670-03553-X). 32pp. Max the bunny gets a beauty makeover from his big sister Ruby and her friend Louise — and then Max does his own. (Rev: BCCB 11/02; BL 8/02; HBG 3/03; SLJ 10/02)

2949 Wells, Rosemary. *The School Play* (PS–2). Illus. by Jody Wheeler and Rosemary Wells. Series: Yoko and Friends School Days. 2001, Hyperion $9.99 (0-7868-0721-0); paper $3.99 (0-7868-1527-2). 31pp. Yoko isn't pleased to find she's won the role of a cavity in the school play about hygiene. (Rev: HBG 3/02; SLJ 1/02)

2950 Wells, Rosemary. *Timothy Goes to School* (PS–K). Illus. 2000, Viking $15.99 (0-670-89182-7). 40pp. Timothy the raccoon fails to fit in during his first day at school until he meets Violet, another outsider. (Rev: BL 6/1–15/00; HBG 3/01)

2951 Wells, Rosemary. *Timothy's Tales from Hilltop School* (PS–1). Illus. by Rosemary Wells and Jody Wheeler. 2002, Viking $16.99 (0-670-03554-8). 64pp. Timothy the raccoon deals with bullies, teasing, a birthday party, and other experiences in this collection of six stories. (Rev: BCCB 10/02; HB 1–2/03; HBG 3/03; SLJ 10/02)

2952 Weninger, Brigitte. *Davy, Help! It's a Ghost!* (K–2). Trans. from German by J. Alison James. Illus. by Eve Tharlet. 2002, North-South LB $16.50 (0-7358-1688-3). Davy and his rabbit siblings create their own monsters to frighten off the ghosts. (Rev: HBG 3/03; SLJ 10/02)

2953 Weninger, Brigitte. *The Elf's Hat* (K–3). Trans. by J. Alison James. Illus. by John A. Rowe. 2000, North-South LB $15.88 (0-7358-1255-1). 36pp. When an elf loses his hat in the forest, a lot of small animals use it as a home. (Rev: BL 5/1/00; HBG 10/00; SLJ 7/00)

2954 Weninger, Brigitte. *What Have You Done, Davy?* (PS–2). Trans. by Rosemary Lanning. Illus. by Eve Tharlet. 1996, North-South LB $15.88 (1-55858-582-6). 32pp. Davy, a young rabbit, is having a terrible day and leaves a trail of destruction wherever he goes. (Rev: BL 4/15/96; SLJ 7/96)

2955 Weninger, Brigitte. *Why Are You Fighting, Davy?* (1–3). Trans. by Rosemary Lanning. Illus. by Eve Tharlet. 1999, North-South LB $15.88 (0-7358-1074-5). 32pp. Davy the rabbit quarrels with his best friend and later makes up when he gets tired of being alone. (Rev: BL 11/1/99; HBG 3/00; SLJ 11/99)

2956 Weninger, Brigitte. *Will You Mind the Baby, Davy?* (K–3). Illus. by Eve Tharlet. 1997, North-South LB $15.88 (1-55858-732-2). 32pp. Davy the

bunny finds that his baby sister needs a strong older brother to help and protect her. (Rev: BL 5/15/97; SLJ 7/97)

2957 Wheeler, Lisa. *Old Cricket* (PS–2). Illus. by Ponder Goembel. 2003, Simon & Schuster $16.95 (0-689-84510-3). Old Cricket pleads a string of ailments to avoid having to get to work, but an encounter with a hungry crow finally sets him straight. (Rev: BL 5/15/03; HBG 10/03; SLJ 5/03)

2958 Wheeler, Lisa. *One Dark Night* (PS–K). Illus. by Ivan Bates. 2003, Harcourt $16.00 (0-15-202318-6). In this mildly spooky adventure tale with a twist at the end, told in rhyme, Mouse and Mole confront the menaces of the night as they traverse the forest and swamp. (Rev: HBG 10/03; SLJ 6/03)

2959 Wheeler, Lisa. *Porcupining: A Prickly Love Story* (PS–1). Illus. by Janie Bynum. 2003, Little, Brown $14.95 (0-316-98912-6). A lonely porcupine tries unsuccessfully to woo a succession of animals before finding the right one. (Rev: HBG 10/03; SLJ 1/03)

2960 Wheeler, Lisa. *Sailor Moo: Cow at Sea* (1–3). Illus. by Ponder Goembel. 2002, Simon & Schuster $16.95 (0-689-84219-8). 32pp. A rhyming, humorous picture book about a young cow who longs to have a life at sea and ends up on a cattle barge turned pirate ship. (Rev: BL 5/1/02; HBG 3/03; SLJ 8/02)

2961 Whippo, Walt. *Little White Duck* (PS–3). Illus. by Joan Paley. 2000, Little, Brown $13.95 (0-316-03227-1). 32pp. The old song about Little White Duck and other animals enjoying a pond is given a fresh treatment with vibrant collage illustrations. (Rev: BCCB 5/00; BL 2/1/00; HBG 10/00; SLJ 4/00)

2962 White, Carolyn. *The Adventure of Louey and Frank* (PS–1). Illus. by Laura Dronzek. 2001, Greenwillow LB $14.89 (0-688-16605-9). 24pp. Louey, a rabbit, and Frank, a bear, encounter a large object on a boating adventure that turns out to be a whale. (Rev: BCCB 3/01; BL 1/1–15/01; HBG 10/01; SLJ 3/01)

2963 White, Kathryn. *When They Fight* (PS–K). Illus. by Cliff Wright. 2000, Winslow $14.95 (1-890817-46-5). 32pp. A young badger is terrorized and runs away when his parents quarrel. (Rev: BL 4/15/00; HBG 3/01; SLJ 6/00)

2964 Whybrow, Ian. *Harry and the Dinosaurs Say "Raahh!"* (PS–1). Illus. by Adrian Reynolds. 2004, Random $14.95 (0-375-82542-8). A new adventure for Harry and his magical dinosaurs, this one involving a trip to the dentist with a tyrannosaurus for company. (Rev: HB 5–6/04; SLJ 3/04)

2965 Whybrow, Ian. *Little Wolf's Book of Badness* (2–4). Illus. by Tony Ross. 1999, Carolrhoda LB $12.95 (1-57505-410-8). 132pp. In this hilarious story, Little Wolf is too well behaved so he is sent to Cunning College to learn how to be bad. (Rev: HBG 3/00; SLJ 11/99)

2966 Whybrow, Ian. *Parcel for Stanley* (PS–2). Illus. by Sally Hobson. 1998, Levinson $14.95 (1-899607-53-6). A simple story in which a rabbit, who has a sorry reputation, shines after he learns a few magic tricks. (Rev: SLJ 3/99)

2967 Whybrow, Ian. *Wish, Change, Friend* (PS–K). Illus. by Tiphanie Beeke. 2002, Simon & Schuster $16.00 (0-689-84930-3). 32pp. Three words — wish, change, and friend — transform Little Pig's life in this gentle story that is an ode to the power of books. (Rev: BCCB 2/02; BL 2/15/02; HBG 10/02; SLJ 1/02)

2968 Wickstrom, Lois. *Oliver: A Story About Adoption* (PS–3). Illus. by Priscilla Marden. 1991, Our Child Pr. $14.95 (0-9611872-5-5). When lizard Oliver receives a reprimand from his adoptive father, he thinks his real parents would behave differently. (Rev: SLJ 2/92)

2969 Wiesner, David. *Tuesday* (PS–2). Illus. 1991, Houghton Mifflin $17.00 (0-395-55113-7). 32pp. Frogs have a wonderful time on Tuesday. Will the pigs have as great a time one week later? Caldecott Medal winner, 1992. (Rev: BCCB 5/91; BL 5/1/91; SLJ 5/91*)

2970 Wild, Margaret. *Fox* (1–3). Illus. by Ron Brooks. 2001, Kane $14.95 (1-929132-16-6). 40pp. A somewhat dark portrayal of the friendship between a one-eyed dog and an injured magpie, this book set in the Australian bush introduces concepts including grief, cruelty, and self-acceptance. (Rev: BL 11/15/01; HBG 3/02; SLJ 12/01)

2971 Wild, Margaret. *Kiss Kiss!* (PS–2). Illus. by Bridget Strevens-Marzo. 2004, Simon & Schuster $12.95 (0-689-86279-2). A baby hippo sets off on his morning stroll through the jungle without first kissing his mother. (Rev: BL 1/1–15/04; SLJ 1/04)

2972 Wild, Margaret. *Piglet and Mama* (PS–K). Illus. by Stephen Michael King. 2005, Abrams $14.95 (0-8109-5869-4). 32pp. Poor piglet searches all over the farm for his mama, leading to a joyous reunion. (Rev: BL 3/1/05; SLJ 6/05)

2973 Wild, Margaret. *Tom Goes to Kindergarten* (PS–1). Illus. by David Legge. 2000, Whitman $15.95 (0-8075-8012-0). 32pp. Mr. and Mrs. Panda overstay their welcome when they accompany their son Tom on his first day in school. (Rev: BL 5/1/00; HBG 10/00; SLJ 4/00)

2974 Wilhelm, Hans. *Anook the Snow Princess* (PS–2). Illus. by author. 2003, Barron's $12.95 (0-7641-5600-4). Loosely based on Shakespeare's *King Lear,* this enchanting animal tale tells of Anook, a polar bear princess, whose sisters sabotage her plan to present her father with a magical gift; banished, Anook is adopted by a pack of wolves and years later returns to claim her rightful place as queen. (Rev: HBG 4/04; SLJ 1/04)

2975 Wilhelm, Hans. *Hello Sun!* (PS–2). Illus. by author. 2003, Carolrhoda LB $15.95 (1-57505-348-9). Quentin, a hedgehog, is a mostly nocturnal creature, so he is completely enchanted when he first sees the rays of the sun; he decides to build a tree house so he will have the best possible view of the sun and, despite some teasing from a fox, gets the job done in record time. (Rev: HBG 4/04; SLJ 1/04)

2976 Wilhelm, Hans. *More Bunny Trouble* (PS–1). Illus. by author. 1989, Scholastic paper $4.99 (0-

590-41590-5). 32pp. Ralph is tapped to baby-sit his bunny sister, but he lets her get out of sight and lost. (Rev: BL 3/1/89; SLJ 5/89)

2977 Wilhelm, Hans. *The Royal Raven* (PS–3). Illus. 1996, Scholastic $15.95 (0-590-54337-7). 32pp. A raven named Crawford tries to become special by changing his appearance. (Rev: BL 3/15/96; SLJ 7/96)

2978 Wilhelm, Hans. *Tyrone the Horrible* (PS–2). Illus. by author. 1988, Scholastic paper $4.99 (0-590-41472-0). 32pp. Tyrone the terrible bully dinosaur is making Boland's prehistoric life a misery. (Rev: BL 9/1/88; SLJ 12/88)

2979 Willans, Tom. *Wait! I Want to Tell You a Story* (K–4). Illus. by author. 2005, Simon & Schuster $15.95 (0-689-87166-X). Using a traditional delaying tactic, a series of animals about to be eaten cry "Wait! I want to tell you a story." (Rev: BCCB 3/05; HB 5–6/05; SLJ 5/05)

2980 Williams, Barbara. *Albert's Impossible Toothache* (K–2). Illus. by Doug Cushman. 2003, Candlewick $15.99 (0-7636-1723-7). 40pp. Albert the turtle calls his sore toe toothache, causing some confusion. (Rev: BL 3/15/03; HBG 10/03; SLJ 6/03)

2981 Williams, Garth. *Benjamin's Treasure* (PS–1). Illus. by Rosemary Wells and Garth Williams. 2001, HarperCollins LB $15.89 (0-06-028741-1). 32pp. When Benjamin, a rabbit, is shipwrecked on a deserted island, he finds a treasure chest but realizes his greatest treasure is his wife back home. (Rev: BL 2/15/01; HBG 10/01)

2982 Williams, Sue. *Dinnertime!* (PS–K). Illus. by Kerry Argent. 2002, Harcourt $16.00 (0-15-216471-5). 32pp. A fox hunts six fat rabbits in this exciting animal fantasy with a happy ending. (Rev: BCCB 4/02; BL 4/1/02*; HBG 10/02; SLJ 5/02)

2983 Willis, Jeanne. *Misery Moo* (PS–2). Illus. by Tony Ross. 2005, Holt $16.95 (0-8050-7672-7). Misery Moo won't be cheered despite a little lamb's best efforts, so he gives up and goes off in a state of depression of his own. (Rev: BL 5/15/04; SLJ 6/05)

2984 Willis, Jeanne. *Never Too Little to Love* (PS–K). Illus. by Jan Fearnley. 2004, Candlewick $10.99 (0-7636-2267-2). 32pp. Too-Little, a tiny mouse, climbs on successively higher objects in an attempt to reach his lady love in this well-designed, tall book. (Rev: BL 2/1/05)

2985 Willis, Jeanne. *Tadpole's Promise* (K–4). Illus. by Tony Ross. 2005, Simon & Schuster $15.95 (0-689-86524-4). A caterpillar and a tadpole declare undying love and promise that neither of them will ever change. (Rev: BCCB 7-8/05; SLJ 5/05)

2986 Willner-Pardo, Gina. *Spider Storch, Rotten Runner* (2–3). Illus. by Nick Sharratt. 2001, Whitman LB $11.95 (0-8075-7594-1). 83pp. In this beginning chapter book, Spider dreads the Third-Grade Olympics because he can't run fast and must take part in the relay race. (Rev: HBG 3/02; SLJ 12/01)

2987 Wilson, Karma. *Bear Snores On* (PS–1). Illus. by Jane Chapman. 2002, Simon & Schuster $16.00 (0-689-83187-0). 40pp. On a cold winter night, animals gather in a sleeping bear's cave to share food and warmth in this charming story told in rhyme. (Rev: BL 1/1–15/02; HBG 10/02; SLJ 1/02*)

2988 Wilson, Karma. *Bear Wants More* (PS–2). Illus. by Jane Chapman. 2003, Simon & Schuster $16.95 (0-689-84509-X). When spring comes, Bear wakes up and is extremely hungry. (Rev: BCCB 3/03; BL 4/15/03; HBG 10/03; SLJ 2/03)

2989 Wilson, Karma. *Dinos on the Go!* (PS). Illus. by Laura Rader. 2004, Little, Brown $15.99 (0-316-73811-5). A lively story, full of jokes, about dinosaurs in a variety of forms of transport on their way to a major dino reunion. (Rev: SLJ 9/04)

2990 Wilson, Karma. *Hilda Must Be Dancing* (PS–2). Illus. by Suzanne Watts. 2004, Simon & Schuster $15.95 (0-689-84788-2). Hilda the hippo shakes the ground when she dances through the jungle, disturbing her neighbors. (Rev: SLJ 3/04)

2991 Wilson, Karma. *Sakes Alive! A Cattle Drive* (K–3). Illus. by Karla Firehammer. 2005, Little, Brown $15.99 (0-316-98841-3). 32pp. Cows Molly and Mabel steal the farmer's truck and take off on an exciting "cattle drive." (Rev: BL 5/1/05)

2992 Wilson, Karma. *Sweet Briar Goes to Camp* (K–2). Illus. by LeUyen Pham. 2005, Dial $16.99 (0-8037-2971-5). 32pp. With the help of Sweet Briar the skunk, Petal the porcupine is soon feeling comfortable and welcome at day camp. (Rev: BL 5/1/05; SLJ 6/05)

2993 Wilson, Karma. *Sweet Briar Goes to School* (K–1). Illus. by LeUyen Pham. 2003, Dial $16.99 (0-8037-2767-4). On her first day at school Sweet Briar the skunk has trouble making friends with her classmates, who are put off by the little skunk's distinctive smell; when a marauding wolf runs off with a student, Sweet Briar saves the day by using her skunk scent to repel the creature, winning the gratitude and friendship of her classmates. (Rev: HBG 4/04; SLJ 8/03)

2994 Winthrop, Elizabeth. *Bear and Roly-Poly* (K–3). Illus. by Patience Brewster. 1996, Holiday House $15.95 (0-8234-1197-4). 32pp. Nora brings Bear a baby sister in the form of Roly-Poly panda. (Rev: BL 3/1/96; SLJ 5/96)

2995 Winthrop, Elizabeth. *Dumpy La Rue* (PS–1). Illus. by Betsy Lewin. 2001, Holt $15.95 (0-8050-6385-4). 32pp. Piggy Dumpy La Rue won't take no for an answer when his family and other barnyard animals tell him it isn't proper for pigs to dance. (Rev: BL 3/15/01; HBG 10/01)

2996 Wise, William. *Christopher Mouse: The Tale of a Small Traveler* (3–5). Illus. by Patrick Benson. 2004, Bloomsbury $15.95 (1-58234-878-2). 152pp. Christopher Mouse, who learned his mother's lessons well, relates with humor and intelligence the ups and downs of his varied life. (Rev: BL 4/1/04*; SLJ 6/04)

2997 Wishinsky, Frieda. *Give Maggie a Chance* (K–2). Illus. by Dean Griffiths. 2002, Fitzhenry & Whiteside $15.95 (1-55041-682-0). 32pp. Maggie is an imaginative little cat who is terrified of public speaking and resents Kimberly's self-confidence in front of the class. (Rev: SLJ 12/02)

2998 Wisniewski, David. *Sumo Mouse* (PS–3). Illus. 2002, Chronicle $16.95 (0-8118-3492-1). 32pp. Giant slapstick superhero Sumo Mouse comes to the rescue of kidnapped Tokyo mice in a complex plot that combines lots of action, comedy, and drama. (Rev: BCCB 1/03; BL 1/1–15/03; HBG 3/03; SLJ 12/02)

2999 Wollman, Jessica. *Andrew's Bright Blue T-Shirt* (PS–2). Illus. by Ana L. Escriva. 2002, Doubleday $14.95 (0-385-74616-4). 32pp. A young fox named Andrew dreams of playing soccer and wears his brother's hand-me-down soccer T-shirt every day, until he tragically grows out of it — and his brother says he's now old enough to play. (Rev: BL 10/1/02; HBG 3/03; SLJ 10/02)

3000 Wood, A. J. *The Little Penguin* (PS–2). Illus. by Stephanie Boey. 2002, Dutton $15.99 (0-525-47023-9). 32pp. A visually appealing, tender book about a young, fuzzy penguin who longs for his father's refined look. (Rev: BL 10/15/02; HBG 3/03; SLJ 12/02)

3001 Wood, Audrey. *Jubal's Wish* (PS–3). Illus. by Don Wood. 2000, Scholastic $15.95 (0-439-16964-X). 32pp. Jubal wants his friends to join him on a picnic but they are too busy to attend in this story about friendship. (Rev: BL 12/1/00; HBG 3/01; SLJ 10/00)

3002 Wood, Audrey. *Little Penguin's Tale* (PS–2). Illus. 1989, Harcourt $13.95 (0-15-246475-1). 32pp. Little Penguin's escapades result in his being swallowed by a whale. (Rev: BL 11/15/89)

3003 Wood, Audrey. *Oh My Baby Bear!* (PS–1). Illus. 1990, Harcourt $13.95 (0-15-257698-3). 32pp. Baby Bear gradually learns to take care of himself. (Rev: BL 11/1/90; SLJ 11/90)

3004 Wood, Audrey. *Silly Sally* (PS). Illus. 1992, Harcourt $16.00 (0-15-274428-2). 32pp. This delightful nonsense book tells of Silly Sally and her trip into town walking backwards and upside down. (Rev: BCCB 6/92; BL 3/15/92*; SLJ 4/92)

3005 Wood, Douglas. *What Dads Can't Do* (PS–2). Illus. by Doug Cushman. 2000, Simon & Schuster $14.00 (0-689-82620-6). An amusing picture book in which a baby dinosaur lists all the things that regular people can do but dads can't, like crossing the street without holding hands or reading a book by themselves. (Rev: HBG 10/00; SLJ 5/00)

3006 Wood, Douglas. *What Moms Can't Do* (PS). Illus. by Doug Cushman. 2001, Simon & Schuster $14.00 (0-689-83358-X). A young dinosaur helps his mother with all her chores but there is one thing he can't duplicate and that is her love for him. (Rev: HBG 10/01; SLJ 3/01)

3007 Wood, Douglas. *What Teachers Can't Do* (PS–2). Illus. by Doug Cushman. 2002, Simon & Schuster $14.95 (0-689-84644-4). 32pp. A young dinosaur looks at all the silly and odd things teachers can't do — be late for school, add 2 + 2, for example. (Rev: BL 8/02; HBG 3/03; SLJ 10/02)

3008 Wood, Jakki. *Never Say Boo to a Goose!* (PS). Illus. by Clare Beaton. 2002, Barefoot $14.99 (1-84148-255-2). 24pp. Tiger the kitten ignores his mother's warning and sets off to find out what happens when he says "boo!" to a goose, if only he can find one. (Rev: BL 12/1/02; HBG 3/03; SLJ 11/02)

3009 Woods, Noah. *Tom Cat* (PS–2). Illus. by author. 2004, Random LB $16.99 (0-375-92497-3). Tom Cat has identity problems until he learns how to "meow." (Rev: SLJ 8/04)

3010 Woodworth, Viki. *Daisy the Dancing Cow* (PS–3). Illus. by author. 2003, Boyds Mills $15.95 (1-59078-059-0). Daisy, last seen in *Daisy the Firecow* (2001), is relegated to a backstage job at the theater until a dancer is injured. (Rev: HBG 4/04; SLJ 10/03)

3011 Woodworth, Viki. *Daisy the Firecow* (PS–1). Illus. 2001, Boyds Mills $15.95 (1-56397-934-9). 32pp. Daisy the cow is bored on the farm and becomes a fire station's mascot. (Rev: BL 7/01; HBG 10/01)

3012 Wormell, Christopher. *Puff-Puff, Chugga-Chugga* (PS–2). Illus. 2001, Simon & Schuster $15.00 (0-689-83986-3). 32pp. A tiny train gets overloaded when it picks up a walrus, a bear, and an elephant. (Rev: BL 2/15/01; HBG 10/01)

3013 Wormell, Mary. *Hilda Hen's Scary Night* (PS–K). Illus. 1996, Harcourt $14.00 (0-15-200990-6). 32pp. In the morning, Hilda Hen sets out to find the creatures that had frightened her the night before. (Rev: BL 9/15/96; SLJ 10/96)

3014 Wormell, Mary. *Hilda Hen's Search* (PS–1). Illus. 1994, Harcourt $13.95 (0-15-200069-0). 32pp. Hilda Hen wanders the barnyard looking for a suitable place to lay her eggs. (Rev: BL 12/1/94; SLJ 11/94)

3015 Wright, Betty R. *Pet Detectives* (PS–3). Illus. by Kevin O'Malley. 1999, BridgeWater LB $15.95 (0-8167-4952-3). When a burglar breaks into their home, Kitty, a cat, and Belle, a dog, decide that they must work together to catch him. (Rev: SLJ 5/99)

3016 Yaccarino, Dan. *Unlovable* (PS–1). Illus. by author. 2002, Holt $15.95 (0-8050-6321-8). 32pp. A puppy who is teased unmercifully about his funny looks befriends a dog he can't see — and who can't see him — on the other side of the fence. (Rev: BL 11/15/01; HBG 10/02; SLJ 1/02)

3017 Yee, Brenda Shannon. *Hide and Seek* (PS–K). Illus. by Debbie Tilley. 2001, Scholastic $15.95 (0-531-30302-0). 32pp. A mouse finds he enjoys playing hide-and-seek with the woman of the house. (Rev: BL 5/15/01; HBG 10/01; SLJ 7/01)

3018 Yee, Patrick. *Winter Rabbit* (PS). Illus. by author. 1994, Viking $13.99 (0-670-85353-6). A bear and a squirrel build a huge snow bunny before they begin their winter sleep. (Rev: SLJ 7/94)

3019 Yee, Wong H. *Big Black Bear* (PS–K). Illus. 1993, Houghton Mifflin $15.00 (0-395-66359-8). 32pp. An ill-mannered young bear who bullies a little girl gets a severe bawling out from his mother. (Rev: BL 11/1/93; SLJ 10/93)

3020 Yee, Wong H. *Fireman Small: Fire Down Below!* (K–2). Illus. by Wong Herbert Yee. 2001, Houghton Mifflin $15.00 (0-618-00707-5). Children will learn safety tips while reading this charming story of a very small fireman who rescues the occu-

pants of a hotel. (Rev: HB 11–12/01; HBG 3/02; SLJ 10/01)

3021 Yee, Wong H. *Hamburger Heaven* (PS–2). Illus. by author. 1999, Houghton Mifflin $15.00 (0-395-87548-X). When it appears that the diner at which she works might close, Pinky Pig designs a new menu to save her job. (Rev: HBG 10/99; SLJ 5/99)

3022 Yee, Wong H. *Here Come Trainmice!* (PS). 2000, Houghton Mifflin $4.95 (0-395-98401-7). 14pp. This board book describes the different cars of a train, all of which are populated by expressive mice, and all the parts of a train ride. A companion volume about trucks is *Hooray for Truckmice!* (2000). (Rev: SLJ 11/00)

3023 Yee, Wong H. *Mrs. Brown Went to Town* (PS–2). Illus. 1996, Houghton Mifflin $14.95 (0-395-75282-5). 32pp. A group of domestic animals move into Mrs. Brown's house when the woman is sent to the hospital. (Rev: BL 4/1/96; SLJ 7/96)

3024 Yee, Wong H. *The Officer's Ball* (PS–2). Illus. 1997, Houghton Mifflin $14.95 (0-395-81182-1). 32pp. While carrying out his duties as a police officer, Sergeant Hippo practices his newly learned dance steps for the big officers ball. (Rev: BL 3/15/97; SLJ 5/97)

3025 Yolen, Jane. *How Do Dinosaurs Get Well Soon?* (PS–1). Illus. by Mark Teague. 2003, Scholastic $15.95 (0-439-24100-6). 40pp. Humorous, full-color illustrations are coupled with rhyming text to show giant young dinosaurs who must learn how to behave while ill (taking medicine, resting, and so forth). (Rev: BL 1/1–15/03*; HB 3–4/03; HBG 10/03; SLJ 2/03)

3026 Yolen, Jane. *Off We Go!* (PS–K). Illus. by Laurel Molk. 2000, Little, Brown $12.95 (0-316-90228-4). 32pp. A bouncy picture book about several animals, all of whom are on their way to visit their grandmothers. (Rev: BCCB 3/00; BL 3/15/00; HBG 10/00; SLJ 5/00)

3027 Yolen, Jane. *Picnic with Piggins* (K–3). Illus. by Jane Dyer. 1988, Harcourt paper $7.00 (0-15-261535-0). 32pp. Piggins, the pig butler, solves the mystery of the missing Rexy, one of the children of the house. Also use the first story about the Reynard butler, *Piggins* (1987); and *Piggins and the Royal Wedding* (1989). (Rev: BCCB 5/88; BL 4/1/88; HB 7–8/88)

3028 Yorinks, Arthur. *Hey, Al* (2–4). Illus. 1986, Farrar $17.00 (0-374-33060-3); paper $5.95 (0-374-42985-5). 32pp. Eddie the dog wants to change his life, but when a bird takes him and Al the janitor to a bird-inhabited island, Eddie isn't quite so sure. Caldecott Medal winner, 1987. (Rev: BL 1/1/87; SLJ 3/87)

3029 Young, Selina. *Big Dog and Little Dog Go Sailing* (1–2). Series: Blue Bananas. 2001, Crabtree $14.97 (0-7787-0845-4); paper $4.46 (0-7787-0891-8). 48pp. When they go boating, two individualistic dogs experience some amazing adventures including an encounter with a whale. (Rev: BL 5/1/02)

3030 Zalben, Jane Breskin. *Don't Go!* (PS–K). Illus. 2001, Clarion $15.00 (0-618-07250-0). 32pp. A gentle story of a young elephant who is comforted to have his stuffed toy with him on his first day of preschool. (Rev: BL 8/01; HBG 3/02; SLJ 9/01)

3031 Zalben, Jane Breskin. *Pearl Plants a Tree* (PS–2). Illus. 1995, Simon & Schuster paper $14.00 (0-689-80034-7). 32pp. A little lamb learns from her grandfather and plants an apple seed that later sprouts. (Rev: BL 11/15/95; SLJ 1/96)

3032 Zane, Alexander. *The Wheels on the Race Car* (PS–K). Illus. by James Warhola. 2005, Scholastic LB $14.95 (0-439-59080-9). In an exciting, action-packed combination of bright illustrations and compelling verse, rambunctious animals pilot racecars around a track, stopping for fill-ups and tune-ups. (Rev: BL 2/1/05; LMC 8-9/05; SLJ 3/05)

3033 Ziefert, Harriet. *Animal Music* (PS–1). Illus. by Donald Saaf. 1999, Houghton Mifflin $15.00 (0-395-95294-8). 48pp. Several animal musicians perform in two shows — one a marching band concert and the other a country jamboree. (Rev: BL 10/15/99; HBG 3/00; SLJ 10/99)

3034 Ziefert, Harriet. *Egad Alligator!* (PS–3). Illus. by Todd McKie. 2002, Houghton Mifflin $16.00 (0-618-14171-5). 40pp. Little Gator doesn't understand why people are afraid of him until he experiences fear himself when he sits on a python. (Rev: BCCB 9/02; BL 4/15/02; HBG 10/02; SLJ 4/02)

3035 Ziefert, Harriet. *Murphy Meets the Treadmill* (PS–1). Illus. by Emily Bolam. 2001, Houghton Mifflin $16.00 (0-618-11357-6). 32pp. Murphy the dog must lose weight, and a treadmill does the trick in this funny book with expressive, cartoonlike illustrations. (Rev: BL 9/1/01; HBG 3/02; SLJ 10/01)

3036 Ziefert, Harriet. *Pumpkin Pie* (PS–K). Illus. by Donald Dreifuss. 2000, Houghton Mifflin $15.00 (0-618-04883-9). 32pp. A troublemaking goat named Pumpkin Pie causes problems because of her bad behavior at a county fair. (Rev: BL 12/1/00; HBG 3/01; SLJ 10/00)

3037 Zimmerman, Andrea, and David Clemesha. *Fire! Fire! Hurry! Hurry!* (PS–2). Illus. by Karen Barbour. 2003, Greenwillow LB $16.89 (0-06-029760-3). The animals in the firehouse are eager to enjoy their spaghetti dinner, but they are constantly disturbed by alarm calls. (Rev: HBG 10/03; SLJ 4/03)

3038 Zolotow, Charlotte. *Mr. Rabbit and the Lovely Present* (PS–3). Illus. by Maurice Sendak. 1977, HarperCollins paper $5.95 (0-06-443020-0). 32pp. A little girl meets Mr. Rabbit, and together they find the perfect birthday gift for her mother.

Realistic Stories

ADVENTURE STORIES

3039 Ahlberg, Allan. *It Was a Dark and Stormy Night* (K–3). Illus. by Janet Ahlberg. 1994, Viking $13.99 (0-670-85159-0). 32pp. A young captive of robbers escapes in the confusion caused by their acting out a story that he has told them. (Rev: BCCB 7–8/94; BL 5/1/94)

3040 Arnold, Marsha Diane. *The Bravest of Us All* (PS–3). Illus. by Brad Sneed. 2000, Dial $15.99 (0-8037-2409-8). 32pp. When a tornado comes, young Ruby Jane helps her older sister to take shelter. (Rev: BCCB 6/00; BL 5/1/00; HBG 10/00; SLJ 5/00)

3041 Axtell, David. *We're Going on a Lion Hunt* (PS–1). Illus. 2000, Holt $15.95 (0-8050-6159-2). 32pp. In this variation on the familiar chant, two African girls go out on a lion hunt. (Rev: BCCB 5/00; BL 2/15/00; HBG 10/00; SLJ 5/00)

3042 Bailey, Linda. *When Addie Was Scared* (1–3). Illus. by Wendy Bailey. 1999, Kids Can $14.95 (1-55074-431-3). 32pp. Though Addie is a fearful, timid child, she summons up great courage to frighten off a hawk when it attacks her grandmother's chickens. (Rev: BL 11/15/99; HBG 3/00; SLJ 11/99)

3043 Beard, Darleen Bailey. *Twister* (PS–3). Illus. by Nancy Carpenter. 1999, Farrar $16.00 (0-374-37977-7). 32pp. While two children hide in a cellar near their trailer home during a tornado, their mother ventures out to help an elderly neighbor. (Rev: BL 2/1/99; HBG 10/99; SLJ 3/99)

3044 Blades, Ann. *Back to the Cabin* (K–3). Illus. 1997, Orca paper $6.95 (1-55143-051-7). 32pp. Activities like swimming and fishing take the place of TV watching when two brothers spend a summer in a cabin by a lake. (Rev: BL 6/1–15/97)

3045 Brown, Don. *Alice Ramsey's Grand Adventure* (K–3). Illus. 1997, Houghton Mifflin $15.00 (0-395-70127-9). 32pp. The story of Alice Ramsey's cross-country automobile trip in 1909. (Rev: BL 9/15/97; HB 11–12/97; HBG 3/98; SLJ 9/97*) [917.3]

3046 Bunting, Eve. *Trouble on the T-Ball Team* (PS–2). Illus. by Irene Trivas. 1997, Clarion $13.95 (0-395-66060-2). 32pp. Members of Linda's T-ball team are mysteriously losing things. (Rev: BCCB 4/97; BL 3/1/97; SLJ 5/97)

3047 Burningham, John. *Mr. Gumpy's Motor Car* (K–3). Illus. by author. 1976, HarperCollins LB $17.89 (0-690-00799-X). 48pp. Mr. Gumpy takes his daughter and an assortment of animals for a ride in the country in his old-fashioned touring car. Companion to: *Mr. Gumpy's Outing* (Holt 1995).

3048 Caines, Jeannette. *Just Us Women* (PS–2). Illus. by Pat Cummings. 1984, HarperCollins paper $5.95 (0-06-443056-1). 32pp. A little African American girl is looking forward to a car ride she is going to take with her aunt.

3049 Caple, Kathy. *Hillary to the Rescue* (PS–3). Illus. 2000, Carolrhoda $14.95 (1-57505-420-5). 32pp. Hillary overdresses for her drama club winter outing but finds that these clothes are useful when she has to seek help after the group's bus breaks down. (Rev: BL 11/15/00; HBG 3/01; SLJ 12/00)

3050 Carrick, Carol. *Left Behind* (PS–2). Illus. by Donald Carrick. 1988, Houghton Mifflin $16.60 (0-89919-535-0). 32pp. On a class visit to the city aquarium, Christopher gets left behind at the subway stop. (Rev: BCCB 9/88; BL 9/15/88; HB 9–10/88)

3051 Carrick, Carol. *Sleep Out* (K–2). Illus. by Donald Carrick. 1982, Houghton Mifflin paper $6.95 (0-89919-083-9). 32pp. Christopher has an unsettling experience when he spends his first night outdoors in his sleeping bag. Another title by the same author: *Ben and the Porcupine* (1985).

3052 Carter, Anne Laurel. *Under a Prairie Sky* (PS–3). Illus. by Alan Daniel and Lea Daniel. 2002, Orca $16.95 (1-55143-226-9). 32pp. A Canadian boy gets a taste of being a Mountie when he rescues his younger brother from a coming storm. (Rev: BL 5/15/02; HBG 10/02; SLJ 6/02)

3053 Cleary, Beverly. *The Real Hole* (PS–1). Illus. by DyAnne DiSalvo-Ryan. 1986, Morrow paper $4.95 (0-688-14741-0). 32pp. Four-year-old Jimmy digs a big hole and puts it to good use. A reissue of the 1960 edition.

3054 Cowley, Joy. *The Video Shop Sparrow* (2–4). Illus. by Gavin Bishop. 1999, Boyds Mills $15.95 (1-56397-826-1). 32pp. Two youngsters, noticing that a sparrow is trapped in a store that will be closed for two weeks, try to get help in rescuing the bird. (Rev: BL 12/1/99; HBG 3/00; SLJ 12/99)

3055 Crews, Donald. *Sail Away* (PS–3). Illus. 1995, Greenwillow LB $15.93 (0-688-11054-1). 32pp. A family weathers a storm in their sailboat. (Rev: BCCB 4/95; BL 4/1/95; HB 9–10/95; SLJ 5/95*)

3056 Demas, Corinne. *Hurricane!* (K–3). Illus. by Lenice U. Strohmeier. 2000, Marshall Cavendish $15.95 (0-7614-5052-1). 32pp. Inspired by Hurricane Bob of 1991, this picture book tells how a little girl and her family prepare for, experience, and survive a hurricane on Cape Cod. (Rev: BL 3/1/00; HBG 10/00; SLJ 4/00)

3057 Elya, Susan Middleton. *Say Hola to Spanish at the Circus* (PS–4). Illus. by Loretta Lopez. Series: Say Hola to Spanish. 2000, Lee & Low $15.95 (1-880000-92-X). 32pp. Using English and about 70 Spanish words, this brightly illustrated book combines the two languages in an introduction to the fun and excitement of the circus. (Rev: BL 7/00; HBG 10/00; SLJ 7/00)

3058 Enderle, Judith R., and Stephanie G. Tessler. *Nell Nugget and the Cow Caper* (K–2). Illus. by Paul Yalowitz. 1996, Simon & Schuster paper $15.00 (0-689-80502-0). In this humorous Western tale, Nell Nugget sets out to find the culprit who has rustled her favorite cow, Goldie. (Rev: BCCB 5/96; HB 9–10/96; SLJ 7/96)

3059 English, Karen. *Big Wind Coming!* (PS–2). Illus. by Cedric Lucas. 1996, Whitman LB $14.95 (0-8075-0726-1). 32pp. A severe windstorm and its effects on an African American family as seen through the eye of the young daughter. (Rev: BCCB 1/97; BL 10/15/96; SLJ 11/96)

3060 Feiffer, Jules. *I Lost My Bear* (PS–2). Illus. by author. 1998, Morrow LB $15.93 (0-688-15148-5). A young girl plays detective when she discovers that her favorite toy is missing. (Rev: BCCB 6/98; BL 4/1/98; HB 3–4/98*; HBG 10/98; SLJ 3/98)

3061 Fleming, Candace. *When Agnes Caws* (PS–2). Illus. by Giselle Potter. 1999, Simon & Schuster $16.00 (0-689-81471-2). 40pp. A girl noted for her

birdcalls is sent to the Himalayas to find the pink-headed duck, little realizing that the villainous Colonel Pittsnap is following her. (Rev: BCCB 2/99; BL 2/15/99; HB 3–4/99; HBG 10/99)

3062 Fox, Mem. *Tough Boris* (PS–3). Illus. by Kathryn Brown. 1994, Harcourt $16.00 (0-15-289612-0). 32pp. Boris is a rough and tough pirate, but when his parrot dies, he cries. (Rev: BL 3/1/94; HB 5–6/94; SLJ 5/94)

3063 Funke, Cornelia. *Pirate Girl* (K–2). Illus. by Kerstin Meyer. 2005, Scholastic $15.95 (0-439-71672-1). 32pp. A band of pirates meet their match when they kidnap young Molly. (Rev: BL 6/1–15/05)

3064 George, Jean Craighead. *Cliff Hanger* (1–3). Illus. by Wendell Minor. 2002, HarperCollins LB $15.89 (0-06-000261-1). Young Axel must climb a cliff to rescue his dog in this suspenseful story that conveys a lot of information about mountain climbing and the dangers involved. (Rev: BCCB 7–8/02; HBG 10/02; SLJ 12/02)

3065 Gerrard, Roy. *Wagons West!* (K–2). Illus. 1996, Farrar $15.00 (0-374-38249-2). 32pp. A rollicking tall tale about Buckskin Dan, leader of a wagon train headed west in the 1840s. (Rev: BCCB 2/96; BL 3/15/96; SLJ 3/96*)

3066 Gershator, Phillis. *Tiny and Bigman* (K–3). Illus. by Lynne W. Cravath. 1999, Marshall Cavendish $15.95 (0-7614-5044-0). 32pp. On their Caribbean island, Miss Tiny, who is married to Mr. Bigman, vows that, in spite of an oncoming hurricane, she will remain home to have her baby. (Rev: BCCB 12/99; BL 10/15/99; HBG 3/00; SLJ 11/99)

3067 Graham, Georgia. *The Strongest Man This Side of Cremona* (PS–3). Illus. 1998, Northern Lights $15.95 (0-88995-182-9). 32pp. Young Matthew and his dad seek shelter when a tornado approaches their farm on the Canadian prairie. (Rev: BL 2/1/99; SLJ 5/99)

3068 Haynes, Max. *Dinosaur Island* (PS–2). Illus. 1991, Lothrop $13.95 (0-688-10329-4). 32pp. Maddy and Bing travel in a land where dinosaurs are hidden in the pictures. (Rev: BL 10/1/91; SLJ 1/92)

3069 Jam, Teddy. *The Fishing Summer* (K–3). Illus. by Ange Zhang. 1997, Douglas & McIntyre $12.95 (0-88899-285-8). 32pp. A boy stows away on his uncle's fishing boat and works hard to learn the family trade. (Rev: BL 9/15/97; SLJ 2/98)

3070 Jane, Pamela. *The Big Monkey Mix-up* (1–4). Illus. by Cathy Bobak. 1997, Avon paper $3.99 (0-380-78951-5). 65pp. A simple mystery that revolves around a missing monkey and Benjamin's desire to lose at least one of his baby teeth. (Rev: SLJ 1/98)

3071 Jezek, Alisandra. *Miloli's Orchids* (K–3). Illus. by Yoshi Miyake. 1991, Raintree LB $22.83 (0-8172-2784-9). 31pp. Written by a youngster, this story set in Hawaii tells of a young girl's attempts to save orchids from a volcano. (Rev: SLJ 6/91)

3072 Johnson, Scott. *I Can't Wait Until I'm Old Enough to Hunt with Dad* (1–3). Illus. by Karen Johnson. 1995, Deer Pond $14.95 (1-887251-56-1). 32pp. A young boy accompanies his father on a bow-and-arrow deer hunt. (Rev: BL 2/1/96)

146

3073 Keats, Ezra Jack. *Maggie and the Pirate* (1–3). Illus. by author. 1987, Scholastic paper $4.95 (0-590-44852-8). 32pp. Maggie tries to find the kidnapper of her pet cricket. A reissue of the 1979 edition.

3074 Kimmel, Eric A. *Four Dollars and Fifty Cents* (2–4). Illus. by Glen Rounds. 1990, Holiday House LB $16.95 (0-8234-0817-5). 32pp. To get out of paying a bad debt, cowboy Shorty Long pretends to be dead. (Rev: BL 9/15/90; HB 1–2/91*; SLJ 11/90)

3075 Kinsey-Warnock, Natalie. *The Summer of Stanley* (PS–3). Illus. by Donald Gates. 1997, Dutton $14.99 (0-525-65177-2). 32pp. Stanley, the family goat, changes from pest to hero when he helps save a boy who has fallen into a river. (Rev: BL 7/97; SLJ 6/97)

3076 Lamm, C. Drew. *Pirates* (K–3). Illus. by Stacey Schuett. 2001, Hyperion $15.99 (0-7868-0392-4). 30pp. Ellery reads her little brother Max a book about pirates, intending to scare the pants off him, but in the end it's Max who has the last laugh in a story sure to elicit goosebumps. (Rev: BCCB 1/02; BL 11/1/01; HBG 3/02; SLJ 11/01)

3077 Lasky, Kathryn. *Marven of the Great North Woods* (K–4). Illus. by Kevin Hawkes. 1997, Harcourt $16.00 (0-15-200104-2). 48pp. During the 1918 flu epidemic, 10-year-old Marven is sent to a logging camp in Minnesota, where he has to assume many adult responsibilities. (Rev: BL 12/15/97; HB 11–12/97; HBG 3/98; SLJ 10/97)

3078 Look, Lenore. *Ruby Lu, Brave and True* (1–3). Illus. by Anne Wilsdorf. 2004, Simon & Schuster $15.95 (0-689-84907-9). 112pp. Ruby, a Chinese American 8-year-old, deals with family, school, and cultural problems in this appealing book with a glossary of terms. (Rev: BL 1/1–15/04; SLJ 2/04)

3079 Lumry, Amanda, and Laura Hurwitz. *Amazon River Rescue* (K–4). Illus. by Sarah McIntyre. Series: Adventures of Riley. 2004, Eaglemont Pr. $15.95 (0-9662257-9-1). Riley and Alice come across animals including a jaguar when they get lost in the Amazon; lots of sidebars supply factual information. (Rev: SLJ 11/04)

3080 Maguire, Gregory. *Crabby Cratchitt* (PS–3). Illus. by Andrew Glass. 2000, Clarion $15.00 (0-395-60485-0). 32pp. Crabby Cratchitt, who can't stand the clucking of her hen, decides to solve the problem by having a chicken dinner, until she sees the hen's nest filled with eggs. (Rev: BL 9/1/00; HBG 3/01; SLJ 8/00)

3081 Martin, Bill, Jr., and John Archambault. *The Ghost-Eye Tree* (K–3). Illus. by Ted Rand. 1985, Holt $16.95 (0-8050-0208-1); paper $6.95 (0-8050-0947-7). 32pp. A brother and sister are sent to fetch a pail of milk on a spooky night past the Ghost-Eye Tree. (Rev: BL 12/15/85; HB 1–2/86; SLJ 2/86)

3082 Martin, Bill, Jr., and John Archambault. *White Dynamite and Curly Kidd* (1–3). Illus. by Ted Rand. 1986, Holt paper $6.95 (0-8050-1018-1). 48pp. A nervous fan carries on a conversation with a bull rider who is about to break out of the chute on White Dynamite. (Rev: BL 7/86; SLJ 4/86)

3083 Mayhew, James. *Miranda the Explorer: A Magical Round-the-World Adventure* (1–3). Illus. by author. 2003, Orion $16.95 (1-84255-000-4); paper $8.95 (1-84255-280-5). Another adventure for the plucky Miranda of *Miranda the Castaway*, this time involving a perilous round-the-world trip by hot-air balloon, sprinkled with foreign words and images. (Rev: BL 1/1–15/04; SLJ 6/04)

3084 O'Connor, Jane. *Amy's (Not So) Great Camp-Out* (1–3). Illus. by Laurie S. Long. 1993, Penguin Putnam paper $5.99 (0-448-40166-5). 64pp. A superactive girl gets sick when her Brownie troop goes on a camping trip. Also use *Corrie's Secret Pal* (1993). (Rev: BL 1/1/94)

3085 Rex, Michael. *My Fire Engine* (K–2). Illus. 1999, Holt $15.95 (0-8050-5391-3). 28pp. The young narrator joins a fire-engine crew and participates in answering an alarm that saves a family from a burning house. (Rev: BL 3/15/99; HBG 10/99; SLJ 5/99)

3086 Rosen, Michael J. *We're Going on a Bear Hunt* (PS–2). Illus. by Helen Oxenbury. 1989, Macmillan $17.00 (0-689-50476-4). 40pp. The storytelling favorite is re-created with expansive pictures that capture the enthusiasm of the story. (Rev: BCCB 9/89; BL 8/89*; HB 11–12/89*; SLJ 8/89*)

3087 Rylant, Cynthia. *Tulip Sees America* (PS–3). Illus. by Lisa Desimini. 1998, Scholastic $15.95 (0-590-84744-9). 32pp. A young man and his dog travel across the United States and find a place by the sea in Oregon where they want to stay. (Rev: BL 3/15/98; HBG 10/98; SLJ 4/98)

3088 Scott, Ann H. *Cowboy Country* (1–3). Illus. by Ted Lewin. 1993, Clarion $14.95 (0-395-57561-3). 40pp. A hardworking cowhand takes a young boy on an overnight trip to show him what life on the range really is. (Rev: BCCB 11/93; BL 9/1/93; HB 11–12/93; SLJ 9/93*)

3089 Seymour, Tres. *We Played Marbles* (K–3). Illus. by Dan Andreasen. 1998, Orchard LB $16.99 (0-531-33074-5). 32pp. The Civil War battle that took place at Fort Craig, Kentucky, unfolds as two boys play an innocent game on its site. (Rev: BL 2/15/98; HBG 10/98; SLJ 3/98)

3090 Steig, William. *Brave Irene* (K–2). Illus. by author. 1986, Farrar $17.00 (0-374-30947-7). 32pp. The incredible adventures of Irene, who sets out in a snowstorm to deliver the duchess's new dress for the ball. (Rev: BCCB 12/86; BL 11/1/86; HB 11–12/86)

3091 Stevenson, James. *"Could Be Worse!"* (K–3). Illus. by author. 1977, Morrow paper $4.95 (0-688-07035-3). 32pp. Grandpa's response to minor catastrophes is always the same.

3092 Stutson, Caroline. *Cowpokes* (PS–2). Illus. by Daniel San Souci. 1999, Lothrop $15.00 (0-688-13973-6). 24pp. Takes the reader through an action-packed day spent by high-spirited cartoon cowboys riding, roping, eating, making mistakes, and bedding down at night. (Rev: BL 9/15/99; HBG 3/00; SLJ 9/99)

3093 Sullivan, Silky. *Grandpa Was a Cowboy* (K–3). Illus. by Bert Dodson. 1996, Orchard LB

$16.99 (0-531-08861-8). 32pp. A young orphan is intrigued by the tales his grandfather spins about his career as a cowboy. (Rev: BL 4/1/96; SLJ 4/96)

3094 Swanson, Diane. *The Balloon Sailors* (2–4). Illus. by Krystyna Lipka-Sztarballo. 2003, Annick LB $15.95 (1-55037-809-0). A family in a kingdom divided by a guarded stone wall decides to fly over it in a hot-air balloon; a postscript likens the situation to Berlin after World War II. (Rev: SLJ 3/04)

3095 Van Allsburg, Chris. *The Garden of Abdul Gasazi* (K–3). Illus. by author. 1979, Houghton Mifflin $17.95 (0-395-27804-X). 32pp. Young Alan wanders into the garden of a retired magician with unexpected results.

3096 Wallace, Ian. *A Winter's Tale* (K–3). Illus. 1997, Douglas & McIntyre $15.95 (0-88899-286-6). 32pp. A gentle outdoor adventure in which Abigail is taken camping by her father and brother to celebrate her ninth birthday. (Rev: BL 10/15/97; SLJ 12/97)

3097 Ward, Helen. *The Boat* (1–3). Illus. by Ian Andrew. 2005, Simply Read $16.95 (1-894965-18-3). 32pp. When flooding threatens an old man and his menagerie of animals, it is a young boy who tries to save them all. (Rev: BL 6/1–15/05)

3098 Ward, Lynd. *The Biggest Bear* (K–3). Illus. by author. 1952, Houghton Mifflin $16.00 (0-395-14806-5); paper $6.95 (0-395-15024-8). 88pp. Johnny wanted a bearskin on his barn so he went looking for the biggest bear. Caldecott Medal winner, 1953.

3099 Wheeler, Lisa. *Seadogs: An Epic Ocean Operetta* (PS–2). Illus. by Mark Siegel. 2004, Simon & Schuster $16.95 (0-689-85689-X). 40pp. In Victorian times, a little girl dog enjoys going to an operetta about and starring seagoing dogs in this comic-book-style story for the youngest readers. (Rev: BL 2/1/04; HB 3–4/04; SLJ 3/04)

3100 Wiesner, David. *Hurricane* (1–3). Illus. 1990, Houghton Mifflin $16.00 (0-395-54382-7). 32pp. Two boys take refuge in their hideout in a tree during a hurricane watch. (Rev: BCCB 11/90; BL 12/15/90; HB 1–2/91; SLJ 10/90*)

3101 Williams, Vera B. *Three Days on a River in a Red Canoe* (K–3). Illus. by author. 1981, Greenwillow $15.89 (0-688-84307-7); Morrow paper $5.95 (0-688-04072-1). 32pp. A little girl describes a canoe trip with her cousins and their mother.

3102 Zagwin, Deborah Turney. *The Sea House* (K–3). Illus. 2002, Tricycle $15.95 (1-58246-030-2). 32pp. Clee and her brother have an adventure on their uncle's boat. (Rev: BL 4/1/02; HBG 10/02; SLJ 6/02)

COMMUNITY AND EVERYDAY LIFE

3103 Adorjan, Carol. *I Can! Can You?* (PS–K). Illus. by Miriam Nerlove. 1990, Whitman LB $13.95 (0-8075-3491-9). 24pp. A little girl tells about the skills she has mastered. (Rev: BL 12/15/90; SLJ 2/91)

3104 Agassi, Martine. *Hands Are Not for Hitting* (PS–1). Illus. by Marieka Heinlen. 2000, Free Spirit paper $10.95 (1-57542-077-5). 35pp. This book preaches the lesson that there are better things for

hands to do than hurting other people. (Rev: SLJ 2/01)

3105 Albee, Sarah. *Clever Trevor* (1–3). Illus. by Paige Billin-Frye. Series: Science Solves It! 2003, Kane paper $4.99 (1-57565-123-8). 32pp. When a gang of bullies invades the playground, clever Trevor uses scientific principles to outsmart them. (Rev: SLJ 6/03)

3106 Aliki. *All By Myself!* (PS–K). Illus. 2000, HarperCollins LB $14.89 (0-06-028930-9). 32pp. A picture book that shows a boy going through a typical day and engaging in such activities as practicing a violin, taking a bath, brushing his teeth, and pulling on socks. (Rev: BL 11/1/00; HB 9–10/00; HBG 3/01; SLJ 9/00)

3107 Aliki. *Hello! Good-bye!* (PS–2). Illus. 1996, Greenwillow $14.89 (0-688-14334-2). 32pp. The many ways of saying "hello" and "good-bye" around the world. (Rev: BCCB 12/96; BL 7/96; SLJ 9/96)

3108 Allen, Kathryn Madeline. *This Little Piggy's Book of Manners* (PS–1). Illus. by Nancy Wolff. 2003, Holt $15.95 (0-8050-6769-8). Bright illustrations demonstrate both good and bad behavior on the part of a number of little piggies. (Rev: HBG 4/04; SLJ 11/03)

3109 Allen, Kit. *Slide, Already!* (PS–2). Illus. 2005, Houghton Mifflin $12.00 (0-618-49643-2). 32pp. A simple story about the fears and joys involved in a boy's first experience on a slide. (Rev: BL 6/1–15/05)

3110 Antoine, Héloïse. *Curious Kids Go to Preschool: Another Big Book of Words* (PS). Illus. by Ingrid Godon. 1996, Peachtree $13.95 (1-56145-129-0). An introduction to preschool experiences through defining such words as *school bus*, *backpack*, and *lunch box*. (Rev: SLJ 11/96)

3111 Appelt, Kathi. *The Best Kind of Gift* (K–2). Illus. by Paul Brett Johnson. 2003, HarperCollins LB $17.89 (0-688-15393-3). In this heartwarming tale of Appalachia, Jory Timmons find that he has gifts to offer despite his small size. (Rev: HBG 10/03; SLJ 6/03)

3112 Appelt, Kathi. *Incredible Me!* (PS–K). Illus. by G. Brian Karas. 2003, HarperCollins LB $16.89 (0-06-028623-7). 32pp. A little girl dances and plays while proudly listing all the traits that make her special. (Rev: BL 2/15/03; HBG 10/03; SLJ 2/03)

3113 Appelt, Kathi. *Watermelon Day* (PS–3). Illus. by Dale Gottlieb. 1996, Holt $15.95 (0-8050-2304-6). Young Jesse grows impatient waiting for her watermelon to grow sufficiently so that it can be eaten when her pappy declares it is a watermelon day. (Rev: BCCB 1/96; SLJ 6/96)

3114 Armstrong-Ellis, Carey. *Prudy's Problem and How She Solved It* (K–2). Illus. 2002, Abrams $14.95 (0-8109-0569-8). 32pp. Unconventional Prudy collects everything until her room is so full that a single gum wrapper causes it to explode. (Rev: BL 12/15/02; HBG 3/03; SLJ 10/02)

3115 Arnold, Tedd. *Even More Parts: Idioms from Head to Toe* (1–3). Illus. by author. 2004, Dial $15.99 (0-8037-2938-3). In this entertaining sequel to *Parts* (1997) and *More Parts* (2001), the boy given to literal interpretations of idioms — "I lost my head" — is ready to go to school. (Rev: SLJ 1/05)

3116 Arnold, Tedd. *More Parts* (1–4). Illus. by author. 2001, Dial $15.99 (0-8037-1417-3). A young boy is terrified by phrases that seem to threaten survival such as "laugh your head off" and "give him a hand." (Rev: BCCB 9/01; HBG 3/02; SLJ 9/01)

3117 Atkins, Jeannine. *Get Set! Swim!* (K–3). Illus. by Hector Viveros Lee. 1998, Lee & Low $15.95 (1-880000-66-0). 32pp. Jessenia's mother and brother attend her swim meet, and swimming reminds Jessenia of her mother's home in Puerto Rico. (Rev: BL 5/15/98; HBG 10/98; SLJ 5/98)

3118 Ayres, Katherine. *Matthew's Truck* (PS). Illus. by Hideko Takahashi. 2005, Candlewick $8.99 (0-7636-2269-9). 24pp. A toddler-friendly board book about a little boy imagining himself the driver of his toy dump truck. (Rev: BL 3/1/05)

3119 Baer, Edith. *This Is the Way We Eat Our Lunch: A Book About Children Around the World* (PS–3). Illus. by Steve Bjorkman. 1995, Scholastic $14.95 (0-590-46887-1). 32pp. A visit to lunchtime in nine states, two Canadian provinces, and 11 other countries, with accompanying recipes and food facts. (Rev: BCCB 9/95; BL 9/15/95; SLJ 9/95)

3120 Baer, Gene. *Thump, Thump, Rat-a-Tat-Tat* (PS–K). Illus. by Lois Ehlert. 1991, HarperCollins paper $4.95 (0-064-43265-3). 32pp. Re-creates the sights and sounds of a marching band. (Rev: BCCB 2/90; BL 11/1/89*; HB 9–10/89*; SLJ 1/90)

3121 Baicker, Karen. *Tumble Me Tumbily* (PS). Illus. by Sam Williams. 2002, Handprint $15.95 (1-929766-61-0). 36pp. Three rhymes — two bouncy ones for waking up and eating, and a quieter one for bedtime — are decorated by illustrations that introduce a vast cast of characters. (Rev: BL 11/1/02; HBG 3/03; SLJ 4/03)

3122 Baicker, Karen. *You Can Do It Too!* (PS). Illus. by Ken Wilson-Max. 2005, Handprint $13.95 (1-59354-080-9). 24pp. A girl encourages her little brother to do as she is doing. (Rev: BL 6/1–15/05)

3123 Bailey, Linda. *The Best Figure Skater in the Whole Wide World* (PS–2). Illus. by Alan Daniel and Lea Daniel. 2001, Kids Can $15.95 (1-55074-879-3). Lizzy dreams of becoming a world-class figure skater, but has to accept being cast as a tree. (Rev: HBG 3/02; SLJ 12/01)

3124 Baker, Jeannie. *Home* (K–3). Illus. 2004, Greenwillow $15.99 (0-06-623935-4). 32pp. Without a single word, Baker tells a compelling story of the value of conservation and environmental action. (Rev: BL 3/15/04*; HB 3–4/04; SLJ 3/04)

3125 Baker, Jeannie. *Window* (2–4). Illus. 1991, Greenwillow $16.89 (0-688-08918-6). 24pp. The changes from a rural to an urban setting are traced in the changes seen through a window. (Rev: BCCB 3/91; BL 4/15/91; HB 5–6/91; SLJ 3/91*)

3126 Ballard, Robin. *Good-bye, House* (PS–K). Illus. 1994, Greenwillow $13.93 (0-688-12526-3). 24pp. Before she moves, a little girl says good-bye

to each room in her old home. (Rev: BL 3/15/94; HB 7–8/94; SLJ 6/94)

3127 Ballard, Robin. *My Day, Your Day* (PS–K). Illus. 2001, Greenwillow LB $14.89 (0-06-029187-7). 32pp. This book about day care shows a picture of children engaging in various group activities on one page and, facing it, a picture of parents at work doing similar things. (Rev: BL 1/1–15/01; HBG 10/01)

3128 Bang, Molly. *Yellow Ball* (PS–1). Illus. 1991, Morrow LB $15.93 (0-688-06315-2). 24pp. The yellow ball over the sea on the jacket becomes the focus of a game of catch. (Rev: BCCB 4/91; BL 3/1/91*; SLJ 5/91)

3129 Banks, Kate. *The Great Blue House* (PS–2). Illus. by Georg Hallensleben. 2005, Farrar $16.00 (0-374-32769-6). 40pp. A vacation house sits quiet and empty during the winter — or is it? Inviting illustrations show animal movements and house noises. (Rev: BL 6/1–15/05)

3130 Barber, Barbara E. *Allie's Basketball Dream* (PS–3). Illus. by Darryl Ligasan. 1996, Lee & Low $15.95 (1-880000-38-5). 32pp. When she receives her first basketball, Allie perseveres until she is able to shoot a basket. (Rev: BCCB 2/97; BL 1/1–15/97; SLJ 11/96)

3131 Barber, Barbara E. *Saturday at The New You* (PS–3). Illus. by Anna Rich. 1994, Lee & Low $14.95 (1-880000-06-7). 32pp. Shauna, an African American girl, has fun on Saturdays helping at her mother's beauty shop. (Rev: BCCB 12/94; BL 12/1/94; SLJ 1/95)

3132 Barron, Rex. *Showdown at the Food Pyramid* (PS–2). Illus. by author. 2004, Penguin Putnam $15.99 (0-399-23715-1). The foods of the pyramid battle over their positions until chaos ensues and a new, sensible structure is needed. (Rev: SLJ 7/04)

3133 Barton, Byron. *Building a House* (PS–2). Illus. by author. 1981, Greenwillow LB $16.93 (0-688-84291-7); Morrow paper $4.95 (0-688-09356-6). 32pp. The stages of building a house are simply presented.

3134 Bartone, Elisa. *American Too* (PS–3). Illus. by Ted Lewin. 1996, Lothrop LB $15.93 (0-688-13279-0). 40pp. An Italian American girl dresses as the Statue of Liberty for the Festival of San Gennaro in New York City. (Rev: BCCB 12/96; BL 8/96; SLJ 12/96)

3135 Bateson-Hill, Margaret. *Shota and the Star Quilt* (PS–3). Illus. by Christine Fowler. 1998, Zero to Ten $14.95 (1-84089-021-5). 32pp. Shota, a Lakota girl, and her friend Esther persuade their landlord not to tear down their apartment building, by showing him a star quilt that celebrates their apartment home. (Rev: BL 2/1/99; HBG 3/99)

3136 Beaumont, Karen. *I Like Myself!* (PS–1). Illus. by David Catrow. 2004, Harcourt $16.00 (0-15-202013-6). Bright illustrations enliven the humorous verse about a girl who likes herself both inside and out. (Rev: BCCB 7/04; SLJ 7/04)

3137 Bennett, William J., ed. *The Children's Book of Virtues* (PS–3). Illus. by Michael Hague. 1995, Simon & Schuster $21.00 (0-684-81353-X). 111pp.

Stories, poems, and fables illustrate ten virtues in this collection based on the concepts used in the adult *Book of Virtues*. (Rev: BL 1/1–15/96) [808.8]

3138 Bertram, Debbie, and Susan Bloom. *The Best Time to Read* (K–2). Illus. by Michael Bloom. 2005, Random LB $16.99 (0-375-93025-6). 32pp. The whole family — even the dog — seems to have better things to do than listen to a little boy read. (Rev: BL 5/15/05)

3139 Best, Cari. *Red Light, Green Light, Mama and Me* (PS–2). Illus. by Niki Daly. 1995, Orchard LB $16.99 (0-531-08752-2). 32pp. Lizzie spends an exciting day with her mother, who is a children's librarian in a big downtown library. (Rev: BCCB 9/95; BL 9/1/95; SLJ 10/95)

3140 Birdseye, Tom. *Airmail to the Moon* (K–2). Illus. by Stephen Gammell. 1988, Holiday House LB $15.95 (0-8234-0683-0); paper $6.95 (0-8234-0754-3). 32pp. Motor-mouth Ora Mae vows to "send to the moon" the one who stole her tooth. (Rev: BL 3/15/88; HB 5–6/88; SLJ 5/88)

3141 Blackstone, Stella. *Baby Rock, Baby Roll* (PS–1). Illus. by Denise and Fernando. 1997, Holiday House LB $13.95 (0-8234-1311-X). 32pp. Three children from different races bounce through a day's activities. (Rev: BL 9/1/97; HBG 3/98; SLJ 10/97)

3142 Blackstone, Stella. *Making Minestrone* (K–3). Illus. by Nan Brooks. 2000, Barefoot $15.99 (1-84148-211-0). 32pp. A group of multiethnic kids get together under the supervision of a lonely boy to make a fine batch of minestrone soup. (Rev: BL 10/1/00; HBG 3/01; SLJ 10/00)

3143 Bogart, Jo Ellen. *Jeremiah Learns to Read* (K–3). Illus. by Laura Fernandez. 1999, Orchard $15.95 (0-531-30190-7). 32pp. An elderly farmer named Jeremiah is taught to read by the local teacher and children in a one-room school, and in exchange he shares with them some of his animal lore. (Rev: BL 9/15/99; HBG 3/00; SLJ 10/99)

3144 Borden, Louise. *Albie the Lifeguard* (PS–3). Illus. by Elizabeth Sayles. 1993, Scholastic $14.95 (0-590-44585-5). 32pp. Albie is not a confident swimmer, but in his backyard he fantasizes about being a lifeguard. (Rev: BL 3/15/93; SLJ 6/93)

3145 Bourgeois, Paulette. *Big Sarah's Little Boots* (PS–1). Illus. by Brenda Clark. 1992, Scholastic paper $4.95 (0-590-42623-0). 32pp. Preschooler Sarah can't understand why her favorite yellow boots have shrunk. (Rev: BL 1/1/90; SLJ 11/89)

3146 Boynton, Sandra. *Hey! Wake Up!* (PS). Illus. by author. 2000, Workman $6.95 (0-7611-1976-0). A board book about morning activities like yawning, stretching, breakfast, and getting dressed. Also use *Pajama Time!* (2000). (Rev: SLJ 2/01)

3147 Brandenberg, Alexa. *Ballerina Flying* (PS–2). Illus. 2002, HarperCollins LB $15.89 (0-06-029550-3). 40pp. Mina pretends she is flying during her ballet class in this book that features names, pronunciations, and drawings of ballet steps and positions. (Rev: BL 7/02; HBG 10/02)

3148 Brandenberg, Alexa. *I Am Me!* (PS). Illus. by author. 1996, Harcourt $12.00 (0-15-200974-4).

After toddlers mention a number of careers they are interested in, they engage in activities related to each. (Rev: SLJ 12/96)

3149 Bregoli, Jane. *The Goat Lady* (2–4). Illus. by author. 2004, Tilbury House $16.95 (0-88448-260-X). Wonderful paintings enhance this story of an elderly French Canadian woman who was not accepted by the people of her Massachusetts town because she raised goats and failed to fit in. (Rev: SLJ 3/05) [759.13]

3150 Brennan, Linda Crotta. *Marshmallow Kisses* (PS–1). Illus. by Mari Takabayashi. 2000, Houghton Mifflin $15.00 (0-395-73872-5). 32pp. Various summer activities — swinging on a porch and playing in the sand — are described in pictures and simple words. (Rev: BL 3/15/00; HBG 10/00; SLJ 3/00)

3151 Brenner, Barbara. *Good Morning, Garden* (K–3). Illus. by Denise Ortakales. 2004, NorthWord $15.95 (1-55971-888-9). Attractive illustrations show a young girl greeting the flowers, plants, insects, and animals in her garden. (Rev: SLJ 6/04)

3152 Brisson, Pat. *The Summer My Father Was Ten* (PS–3). Illus. by Andrea Shine. 1998, Boyds Mills $15.95 (1-56397-435-5). A father tells his daughter while they plant a garden together of the guilt he felt when, as a child, he vandalized a neighbor's garden. (Rev: BCCB 5/98; BL 2/1/98*; HBG 10/98; SLJ 4/98)

3153 Brooks, Erik. *Octavius Bloom and the House of Doom* (1–3). Illus. by author. 2003, Whitman LB $14.95 (0-8075-5820-6). In this detective story told in rhyming verse, Octavius Bloom, new boy in town, decides to investigate mysterious Priscilla O'Moore's ramshackle shed. (Rev: HBG 10/03; SLJ 6/03)

3154 Brown, Laurie Krasny, and Marc Brown. *Visiting the Art Museum* (K–3). Illus. 1992, Dutton paper $6.99 (0-140-54820-3). 32pp. An introduction to the art museum, sometimes an overpowering place for young children. (Rev: BCCB 10/86; BL 9/15/86; SLJ 10/86)

3155 Brown, Marc, and Stephen Krensky. *Dinosaurs, Beware! A Safety Guide* (PS–2). Illus. by authors. 1984, Little, Brown paper $7.95 (0-316-11219-4). 32pp. Sixty safety tips are illustrated with drawings of dinosaurs.

3156 Brown, Margaret Wise. *Another Important Book* (PS–1). Illus. by Chris Raschka. 1999, HarperCollins LB $15.89 (0-06-026283-4). 32pp. In a series of rhymes, this book identifies important achievements and developments in the first six years of a child's life. (Rev: BCCB 1/00; BL 10/15/99; HB 9–10/99; HBG 3/00; SLJ 9/99)

3157 Brown, Margaret Wise. *Red Light, Green Light* (PS–K). Illus. by Leonard Weisgard. 1994, Scholastic paper $4.95 (0-590-44559-6). 40pp. This introduction to traffic signs was first published in 1944.

3158 Brown, Margaret Wise. *Robin's Room* (PS–2). Illus. by Steve Johnson and Lou Fancher. 2002, Hyperion $14.99 (0-7868-0602-8). 32pp. Robin becomes a model child after his wishes about redecorating his room are granted. (Rev: BCCB 9/02; BL 4/15/02; HBG 10/02)

3159 Brownlow, Mike. *The Big White Book with Almost Nothing in It* (PS–1). Illus. by author. 2001, Ragged Bear $13.95 (1-929927-24-X). As the reader turns the apparently almost blank pages, flaps, folds, and die-cut holes soon reveal a whole cast of cartoon circus characters. (Rev: SLJ 10/01)

3160 Bunting, Eve. *Peepers* (K–3). Illus. by James E. Ransome. 2001, Harcourt $16.00 (0-15-260297-6). 32pp. Two brothers come to appreciate the beauty of the fall colors so admired by the tourists, or "Leaf Peepers," who visit their New England town. (Rev: BL 9/1/01; HBG 3/02; SLJ 10/01)

3161 Bunting, Eve. *The Pumpkin Fair* (PS–2). Illus. by Eileen Christelow. 1997, Clarion $15.00 (0-395-70060-4). 32pp. All of the activities and fun of an autumn pumpkin fair are here, including the pumpkin-judging contests. (Rev: BL 11/1/97; HBG 3/98; SLJ 9/97)

3162 Bunting, Eve. *Smoky Night* (K–3). Illus. by David Diaz. 1994, Harcourt $16.00 (0-15-269954-6). 32pp. Two families, one Korean American and the other African American, reach out to one another during the terrible Los Angeles riots. Caldecott Medal winner, 1995. (Rev: BCCB 3/94; BL 3/1/94; HB 5–6/94; SLJ 5/94*)

3163 Burleigh, Robert. *I Love Going Through This Book* (PS–K). Illus. by Dan Yaccarino. 2001, HarperCollins $15.95 (0-06-028805-1). 32pp. This boisterous excursion through a book, courtesy of a young boy and animal friends, introduces young readers to the parts of a book and the fun of reading. (Rev: BCCB 6/01; BL 6/1–15/01; HBG 10/01; SLJ 6/01)

3164 Burleigh, Robert. *Messenger, Messenger* (PS–3). Illus. by Barry Root. 2000, Simon & Schuster $16.00 (0-689-82103-4). 32pp. Presents the daily life of a bike messenger in a big city as he travels from slums to skyscrapers and returns home at night to his apartment and a striped orange cat. (Rev: BCCB 11/00; BL 5/15/00*; HBG 10/00; SLJ 6/00)

3165 Burton, Virginia Lee. *The Little House* (1–3). Illus. by author. 1978, Houghton Mifflin $14.95 (0-395-18156-9); paper $5.95 (0-395-25938-X). Story of a little house in the country that over the years witnesses change and progress. Caldecott Medal winner, 1943. (Rev: HBG 10/03)

3166 Caines, Jeannette. *I Need a Lunch Box* (PS–K). Illus. by Pat Cummings. 1988, HarperCollins LB $16.89 (0-06-020985-2); paper $5.95 (0-06-443341-2). 32pp. Mama says no to a lunch box for a little boy who hasn't yet started school. (Rev: BL 9/15/88; SLJ 12/88)

3167 Capucilli, Alyssa Satin. *The Potty Book for Boys* (PS). 2000, Barron's $5.95 (0-7641-5232-7). 32pp. The male narrator explains how he receives his own potty, how he sits on it, and how he is rewarded if successful. The same story from a girl's point of view is in *The Potty Book for Girls* (2000). (Rev: SLJ 9/00)

3168 Carlson, Nancy. *There's a Big, Beautiful World Out There!* (K–2). Illus. 2002, Viking $15.99 (0-670-03580-7). 32pp. Written just after September 11, 2001, this book uses cheery illustrations and a chatty approach to potential terrors to reassure children that anxieties are normal and the world is still a good place. (Rev: BL 10/1/02; HBG 3/03; SLJ 11/02)

3169 Carlstrom, Nancy White. *The Snow Speaks* (PS–2). Illus. by Jane Dyer. 1992, Little, Brown $15.95 (0-316-12861-9). 32pp. Children enjoy the various aspects of a snowstorm in the country from the first flakes to the coming of the snowplows. (Rev: BL 9/15/92)

3170 Carney, Margaret. *At Grandpa's Sugar Bush* (PS–3). Illus. by Janet Wilson. 1998, Kids Can $15.95 (1-55074-341-4). 32pp. During his spring vacation, a young boy visits his grandparents on their Ontario farm and assists them in making maple syrup. (Rev: BL 4/1/98; HBG 10/98; SLJ 4/98)

3171 Carter, Anne Laurel. *My Home Bay* (PS). Illus. by Alan Daniel and Lea Daniel. Series: Northern Lights Books for Children. 2004, Red Deer $17.95 (0-88995-284-1). When her family moves clear across Canada from Vancouver to Nova Scotia, young Gwyn is initially disdainful of her new surroundings. (Rev: BL 2/1/04; SLJ 8/04)

3172 Carter, Don. *Send It!* (PS–2). Illus. by author. 2003, Millbrook LB $19.90 (0-7613-2573-5). A good choice for beginning readers, this appealing story tracks a package from wrapping to post office to transportation to delivery at a birthday party. (Rev: BL 12/15/03; HBG 4/04; SLJ 12/03)

3173 Caseley, Judith. *On the Town: A Community Adventure* (K–3). Illus. 2002, HarperCollins LB $15.89 (0-06-029585-6). 32pp. For a school assignment, Charlie and his mother visit people and places in the neighborhood but, afterward, Charlie realizes that home is best. (Rev: BL 4/15/02; HBG 10/02; SLJ 5/02)

3174 Catalanotto, Peter. *Emily's Art* (K–3). Illus. 2001, Simon & Schuster $16.00 (0-689-83831-X). 32pp. Emily is so disappointed when her picture doesn't win the art contest that she says she'll never paint again. (Rev: BCCB 9/01; BL 7/01; HBG 10/01; SLJ 6/01*)

3175 Charlip, Remy, and Lillian Moore. *Hooray for Me!* (PS–2). Illus. by Vera B. Williams. 1996, Tricycle $14.95 (1-883672-43-0). 36pp. A new edition of an old favorite that explores a child's relationships. (Rev: BL 11/15/96)

3176 Chinn, Karen. *Sam and the Lucky Money* (PS–2). Illus. by Cornelius Van Wright and Ying-hwa Hu. 1995, Lee & Low $15.95 (1-880000-13-X). Sam decides that the money he has received at Chinese New Year would be best used by giving it to a poor stranger. (Rev: SLJ 12/95)

3177 Chorao, Kay. *Little Farm by the Sea* (K–3). Illus. 1998, Holt $15.95 (0-8050-5053-1). 32pp. In this large-format picture book, a group of children watch farm activities throughout the year. (Rev: BCCB 7–8/98; BL 5/15/98; HB 3–4/98; HBG 10/98; SLJ 6/98)

3178 Clary, Margie Willis. *A Sweet, Sweet Basket* (K–4). Illus. by Dennis L. Brown. 1995, Sandlapper

$15.95 (0-87844-127-1). 40pp. An older woman explains to her granddaughter how baskets are woven from the sweetgrass that grows in South Carolina. (Rev: BL 9/1/95)

3179 Clements, Andrew. *Workshop* (PS–1). Illus. by David Wisniewski. 1999, Clarion $16.00 (0-395-85579-9). As a young apprentice becomes involved in the creation of a carousel, all of the tools of the woodworker are introduced. (Rev: BCCB 7–8/99; BL 4/15/99*; HBG 10/99; SLJ 5/99) [621.9]

3180 Cocca-Leffler, Maryann. *Bus Route to Boston* (PS–2). Illus. 2000, Boyds Mills $15.95 (1-56397-723-0). 32pp. The author-illustrator recalls the thrill of living outside Boston and taking trips by bus into the big city to shop and see the sights. (Rev: BL 2/1/00; HBG 10/00; SLJ 4/00)

3181 Cohn, Diana. *¡Sí, Se Puede! / Yes, We Can! Janitor Strike in L.A.* (PS–3). Illus. by Francisco Delgado. 2002, Cinco Puntos $15.95 (0-938317-66-0). 32pp. Mexican American boy Carlitos supports his janitor mother in seeking to start a union, in this bilingual picture book based on a Los Angeles strike in 2000. (Rev: BL 10/1/02; HBG 3/03; SLJ 11/02*)

3182 Cole, Henry. *Jack's Garden* (PS–4). Illus. 1995, Greenwillow $16.00 (0-688-13501-3). 24pp. In this cumulative tale, the plants and insects found in Jack's garden are introduced. (Rev: BCCB 5/95; BL 4/1/95; HB 5–6/95; SLJ 5/95)

3183 Cole, Joanna. *My Big Boy Potty Book* (PS). Illus. by Maxie Chambliss. 2000, HarperCollins $5.95 (0-688-17042-0). 32pp. In this reassuring picture book, Michael is told that he will succeed in potty training because practice makes perfect. The female counterpart is *My Big Girl Potty Book* (2000). (Rev: BL 2/1/01; HBG 3/01; SLJ 11/00)

3184 Coleman, Evelyn. *To Be a Drum* (K–3). Illus. by Aminah Robinson. 1998, Whitman LB $16.95 (0-8075-8006-6). 32pp. Daddy Wes tells two children about the history of African Americans and their struggles as revealed in the rhythm of drumbeats. (Rev: BL 2/15/98; HBG 10/98; SLJ 5/98)

3185 Collier, Bryan. *Uptown* (PS–3). Illus. 2000, Holt $15.95 (0-8050-5721-8). 32pp. A young boy points out the sights and delights of Harlem — shopping on 125th Street and going to a jazz club. (Rev: BCCB 11/00; BL 6/1–15/00; HBG 10/00; SLJ 7/00)

3186 Cook, Lisa Broadie. *Martin MacGregor's Snowman* (K–2). Illus. by Adam McCauley. 2003, Walker LB $17.85 (0-8027-8859-9). Martin spends the winter trying to create alternatives to snow, and is rewarded on April Fool's Day with an actual storm. (Rev: HBG 4/04; SLJ 10/03)

3187 Cooper, Elisha. *Ballpark* (K–2). Illus. 1998, Greenwillow $15.00 (0-688-15755-6). 40pp. An active day at a ballpark is outlined in this colorful picture book that highlights everyone's participation, from groundskeepers and concession workers to fans and players. (Rev: BCCB 3/98; BL 4/1/98; HB 7–8/98; HBG 10/98)

3188 Cooper, Elisha. *Country Fair* (PS–2). Illus. 1997, Greenwillow $15.00 (0-688-15531-6). 40pp. The activities associated with a country fair are pic-

tured. (Rev: BL 9/15/97; HB 9–10/97; HBG 3/98; SLJ 9/97)

3189 Copeland, Cynthia L. *What Are You Waiting For?* (K–1). Illus. by Mike Gordon. Series: Silly Millies. 2003, Millbrook LB $17.90 (0-7613-2804-1). 31pp. As a young boy surveys the site for a new playground, he approaches construction workers as they arrive and urges them to get busy. (Rev: HBG 10/03; SLJ 6/03)

3190 Coulman, Valerie. *I Am a Ballerina* (PS–1). Illus. by Sandra Lamb. 2004, Lobster $15.95 (1-894222-91-1). 32pp. The engaging tale of aspiring ballerina Molly. (Rev: BL 2/1/05; SLJ 3/05)

3191 Cousins, Lucy. *Maisy's Pop-Up Playhouse* (2–5). Illus. 1995, Candlewick $19.99 (1-56402-635-3). 16pp. Pop-ups reveal the contents of Maisy's playhouse. (Rev: BL 2/1/96)

3192 Cox, Judy. *Now We Can Have a Wedding!* (PS–2). Illus. by DyAnne DiSalvo-Ryan. 1998, Holiday House LB $15.95 (0-8234-1342-X). 32pp. The narrator goes from apartment to apartment in her building and sees that everyone is making a different national dish to bring to her sister's wedding. (Rev: BL 2/15/98; HBG 10/98; SLJ 3/98)

3193 Crews, Donald. *Carousel* (PS–2). Illus. by author. 1982, Greenwillow $15.93 (0-688-00909-3). 32pp. A ride on a carousel is described in pictures and text.

3194 Crews, Donald. *Night at the Fair* (K–2). Illus. 1998, Greenwillow $14.93 (0-688-11484-9). 24pp. Game booths, food concessions, and the Ferris wheel are only three of the attractions at a country fair that are highlighted in this engaging book. (Rev: BCCB 6/98; BL 3/1/98; HB 5–6/98; HBG 10/98; SLJ 4/98)

3195 Crews, Donald. *Shortcut* (PS–3). Illus. 1992, Greenwillow $15.93 (0-688-06437-X). 32pp. Seven children follow a railroad track back home as the train gets closer and closer. (Rev: BCCB 10/92*; BL 10/15/92*; HB 1–2/93*; SLJ 11/92)

3196 Crews, Nina. *One Hot Summer Day* (PS–K). Illus. 1995, Greenwillow $14.89 (0-688-13394-0). 24pp. Using collages, the author illustrates the many activities associated with a hot summer's day. (Rev: BCCB 6/95; BL 6/1–15/95; HB 7–8/95; SLJ 6/95)

3197 Crews, Nina. *Snowball* (PS–1). Illus. 1997, Greenwillow $14.89 (0-688-14929-4). 24pp. This is the story of an African American child in a city and how she gets her wish for snow. (Rev: BL 12/1/97; HBG 3/98; SLJ 9/97)

3198 Cummins, Julie. *Country Kid, City Kid* (K–2). Illus. by Ted Rand. 2002, Holt $16.95 (0-8050-6467-2). Ben's life on the farm and Jody's life in the city are contrasted on facing pages. (Rev: HBG 3/03; SLJ 11/02)

3199 Curtis, Carolyn. *I Took the Moon for a Walk* (PS–2). Illus. by Alison Jay. 2004, Barefoot $16.99 (1-84148-611-6). 32pp. A young boy enjoys a nighttime stroll around his neighborhood with the moon as his companion; antique-looking panoramic illustrations add to the dreamlike text. (Rev: BL 4/1/04; SLJ 6/04)

3200 Curtis, Jamie Lee. *I'm Gonna Like Me: Letting Off a Little Self-Esteem* (1–3). Illus. by Laura Cornell. 2002, HarperCollins LB $17.89 (0-06-028762-4). 32pp. Humorous, detailed illustrations and rhyming text show a boy and girl taking turns liking themselves. (Rev: BL 10/1/02; HBG 3/03; SLJ 10/02)

3201 Cutler, Jane. *Common Sense and Fowls* (3–5). Illus. by Lynne Barasch. 2005, Farrar $16.00 (0-374-32262-7). 136pp. In this sequel to *Family Dinner* (1995), Rachel and Brian try to alleviate a dispute and improve communication by offering Mrs. Krnc styrofoam vowels and Mr. Gioai styrofoam consonants. (Rev: SLJ 3/05)

3202 Cuyler, Margery. *From Here to There* (PS–3). Illus. by Yu Cha Pak. 1999, Holt $16.95 (0-8050-3191-X). 32pp. A little girl describes where she lives in an ever-widening address — from town to county to state and so on. (Rev: BL 6/1–15/99; HBG 10/99; SLJ 5/99)

3203 Cuyler, Margery. *Please Say Please! Penguin's Guide to Manners* (PS–2). Illus. by Will Hillenbrand. 2004, Scholastic $15.95 (0-590-29224-2). A lesson in manners, taught with bad examples from a dinner party at Penguin's house. (Rev: HB 5–6/04; SLJ 4/04)

3204 Danis, Naomi. *Walk with Me* (PS). Illus. by Jacqueline Rogers. Series: Story Corner. 1995, Scholastic $6.95 (0-590-45855-8). A mother and her preschool daughter combine a pleasant outdoor walk with some nature study. (Rev: SLJ 8/95)

3205 Danneberg, Julie. *First Day Jitters* (K–4). Illus. by Judy Love. 2000, Charlesbridge $16.95 (1-58089-054-7). 32pp. A little girl imagines all the terrible things that could happen to her on her first day of school, but is pleasantly surprised with the real thing. (Rev: BL 3/15/00; HBG 10/00; SLJ 5/00)

3206 Davies, Sarah. *Happy to Be Girls* (K–2). Illus. by Jenny Mattheson. 2005, Penguin Putnam $14.99 (0-399-23983-9). 32pp. A simple rhyming celebration of girlhood, showing diverse girls in varied situations. (Rev: BL 5/1/05; SLJ 6/05)

3207 Davis, Jill. *My Busy Day* (PS–K). Illus. by Jill Kastner. 2004, Penguin Putnam $15.99 (0-670-05891-2). 32pp. Colorful art and rhyming couplets the everyday life of a young girl. (Rev: BL 11/1/04)

3208 Delton, Judy. *My Mom Made Me Go to Camp* (1–3). Illus. by Lisa McCue. 1993, Dell paper $2.99 (0-440-40838-5). 32pp. Archie, who does not want to attend summer camp, gradually changes his mind. (Rev: BL 1/1/91; SLJ 2/91)

3209 Derby, Sally. *My Steps* (PS–1). Illus. by Adjoa J. Burrowes. 1996, Lee & Low $15.95 (1-880000-40-7). 32pp. An African American city child tells what a wonderful playground her front steps can be. (Rev: BL 10/15/96; SLJ 10/96)

3210 Desimini, Lisa. *Policeman Lou and Policewoman Sue* (K–2). Illus. by author. 2003, Scholastic $15.95 (0-439-40888-1). Policeman Lou and Policewoman Sue work together to keep the residents of their community safe; tips for children are included at the end. (Rev: BL 5/15/03; HBG 4/04; SLJ 6/03)

3211 Devine, Monica. *Carry Me, Mama* (PS–1). Illus. by Pauline Paquin. 2002, Stoddart $15.95 (0-7737-3317-5). A beautifully illustrated story of a mother gently persuading her child to walk further and further. (Rev: HB 5–6/02; HBG 10/02; SLJ 7/02)

3212 Diouf, Sylviane A. *Bintou's Braids* (PS–2). Illus. by Shane W. Evans. 2001, Chronicle $14.95 (0-8118-2514-0). 40pp. A little girl yearns for long, beautiful braids in this story featuring daily life and customs in a West African village. (Rev: BCCB 11/01; BL 11/15/01; HB 1–2/02; HBG 3/02; SLJ 1/02)

3213 DiSalvo-Ryan, DyAnne. *Grandpa's Corner Store* (K–3). Illus. 2000, HarperCollins LB $15.89 (0-688-16717-9). 40pp. When Grandpa decides to sell his grocery store, Lucy devises a plan to get him to change his mind. (Rev: BL 5/1/00; HBG 10/00; SLJ 7/00)

3214 DiSalvo-Ryan, DyAnne. *Spaghetti Park* (K–2). Illus. 2002, Holiday House $16.95 (0-8234-1682-8). 32pp. A haven for down-and-outs is transformed into a popular neighborhood park with a lively bocce court. (Rev: BL 11/15/02; HBG 3/03; SLJ 1/03)

3215 *Do Skyscrapers Touch the Sky? First Questions and Answers About the City* (PS–K). Illus. 1994, Time-Life $14.95 (0-7835-0886-7). 48pp. Obvious questions about city life — like "What's under the street?" — are answered in well-illustrated double-page spreads. (Rev: BL 2/1/95) [307.76]

3216 Doherty, Berlie. *Coconut Comes to School* (PS–2). Illus. by Ivan Bates. 2003, HarperCollins $17.95 (0-00-710433-2). The simple story of Coconut the donkey and how she rescues the teacher who had previously failed to appreciate her. (Rev: SLJ 9/03)

3217 Dooley, Norah. *Everybody Bakes Bread* (K–3). Illus. by Peter J. Thornton. 1996, Carolrhoda LB $15.95 (0-87614-864-X). 40pp. On an errand for her mother, Carrie sees her neighbors bake a variety of breads in this sequel to *Everybody Cooks Rice* (1991). (Rev: BL 3/1/96; SLJ 4/96)

3218 Dragonwagon, Crescent. *And Then It Rained . . .: And Then the Sun Came Out . . .* (PS–4). Illus. by Diane Greenseid. 2003, Simon & Schuster $17.95 (0-689-81884-X). Begin at one end of this book and you get a story of a rainy day that eventually tries people's patience; flip the book over and the sun is out and life is quite different. (Rev: BL 6/1–15/03; HBG 10/03; SLJ 5/03)

3219 Driscoll, Laura. *The Blast Off Kid* (1–2). Illus. by Rebecca Thornburgh. Series: Math Matters. 2003, Kane paper $4.95 (1-57565-130-0). 32pp. Jim hopes to collect 10,000 Blast Off Bar wrappers so he can win a trip to space camp, and it is his skill in grouping them that makes it possible to keep track. (Rev: SLJ 1/04)

3220 Duncan, Debbie. *When Molly Was in the Hospital: A Book for Brothers and Sisters of Hospitalized Children* (PS–2). Illus. by Nina Ollikainen. Series: MiniMed. 1994, Rayve $12.95 (1-877810-44-4). The experiences of a young girl whose younger sister faces major surgery and the many conflicting emotions she feels. (Rev: SLJ 3/95)

3221 Dunrea, Olivier. *It's Snowing!* (PS). Illus. 2002, Farrar $16.00 (0-374-39992-1). 32pp. In a remote, cold place, mother and baby venture out into the snowy night, have fun sledding and creating sculptures, and then head back into the warmth. (Rev: BL 11/15/02; HB 9–10/02; HBG 3/03; SLJ 10/02)

3222 Edwards, Michelle, and Phyllis Root. *What's That Noise?* (PS). Illus. by Paul Meisel. 2002, Candlewick $15.99 (0-7636-1350-9). Two young boys try to be brave as the spooky sounds and shadows of night surround them. (Rev: HBG 3/03; SLJ 12/02)

3223 Edwards, Richard. *Fly with the Birds: A Word and Rhyme Book* (PS–K). Illus. by Satoshi Kitamura. 1996, Orchard $12.95 (0-531-09491-X). In this flap book, a child narrates her day, from waking up to bedtime and dreamland. (Rev: SLJ 3/96)

3224 Ehlert, Lois. *Circus* (PS–2). Illus. 1992, HarperCollins $15.95 (0-060-20252-1). 40pp. The razzle-dazzle of the circus is translated into the relative quiet of the picture-book experience. (Rev: BL 1/1/92; HB 3–4/92; SLJ 4/92) [791.3]

3225 Ehlert, Lois. *Growing Vegetable Soup* (PS–K). Illus. by author. 1987, Harcourt $15.00 (0-15-232575-1); paper $6.00 (0-15-232580-8). 40pp. Father and child plant seeds and sprouts "to grow vegetable soup." Also use: *Planting a Rainbow* (1988). (Rev: BL 3/1/87; SLJ 3/87)

3226 Ehlert, Lois. *Leaf Man* (PS–2). Illus. 2005, Harcourt $16.00 (0-15-205304-2). 40pp. An imaginative story about autumn leaves. (Rev: BL 6/1–15/05)

3227 Ehlert, Lois. *Market Day: A Story Told with Folk Art* (PS–2). Illus. 2000, Harcourt $16.00 (0-15-202158-2). 36pp. This picture book depicts a day when the farmers load their trucks with goods and go to the market to buy and sell, and work and play. (Rev: BCCB 7–8/00; BL 5/15/00; HBG 10/00; SLJ 7/00)

3228 Ehrlich, Fred. *Does a Panda Go to School?* (PS–K). Illus. by Emily Bolam. Series: Early Experiences. 2003, Handprint $10.95 (1-59354-017-5). Bright illustrations fill this small-format, question-and-answer explanation of some of the differences between animals and children. Also use the similarly humorous *Does a Yak Get a Haircut?* (Rev: SLJ 2/04) [372.21]

3229 Ellis, Sarah. *Next Stop!* (PS–K). Illus. by Ruth Ohi. 2000, Fitzhenry & Whiteside $13.95 (1-55041-539-5). 32pp. Little Claire helps the bus driver by calling out the names of the streets and the special attractions found at each stop. (Rev: BL 12/1/00; SLJ 1/01)

3230 Ernst, Lisa Campbell. *Bear's Day* (PS). Illus. by author. 2000, Viking $5.99 (0-670-89115-0). A board book that shows a toddler playing with a teddy bear. The same child plays with a cat in *Cat's Play* (2000). (Rev: BCCB 4/00; BL 10/1/00; SLJ 7/00)

3231 Esbensen, Barbara J. *Jumping Day* (PS–1). Illus. by Maryann Cocca-Leffler. 1999, Boyds Mills $9.95 (1-56397-709-5). 24pp. A delightful look at a girl at play as she skips her way to school. (Rev: HBG 10/99; SLJ 4/99)

3232 Evans, Lezlie. *Sometimes I Feel Like a Storm Cloud* (PS–1). Illus. by Marsha Gray Carrington. 1999, Mondo $15.95 (1-57255-621-8). 32pp. A girl's moods are expressed in a series of similes that capture her feelings. (Rev: BL 12/15/99)

3233 Fair, Sylvia. *The Bedspread* (K–2). Illus. by author. 1982, Morrow $17.00 (0-688-00877-1). 32pp. Two old ladies decide to embroider their bedspreads.

3234 Farrell, John. *It's Just a Game* (K–3). Illus. by John E. Cymerman. 1999, Boyds Mills $15.95 (1-56397-785-0). 32pp. Even though they lose every game but one, and in spite of parents who are overcompetitive, a group of kids enjoy playing on their soccer team. (Rev: BL 12/1/99; HBG 3/00; SLJ 11/99)

3235 Field, Rachel. *General Store* (PS–1). Illus. by Nancy Winslow Parker. 1988, Little, Brown $15.95 (0-316-28163-8). 24pp. A poem that extols the charms of the old-fashioned store. Another version has illustrations by Giles Laroche (1988, Little, Brown). (Rev: BCCB 5/88; BL 3/1/88; HB 5–6/88)

3236 Fitz-Gibbon, Sally. *On Uncle John's Farm* (1–3). Illus. by Brian Deines. 2005, Fitzhenry & Whiteside $15.95 (1-55041-691-X); paper $8.95 (1-55041-886-6). A gentle story of a little girl's busy day on the farm. (Rev: BL 3/1/04; SLJ 5/05)

3237 Fitz-Gibbon, Sally. *Two Shoes, Blue Shoes, New Shoes!* (PS–1). Illus. by Farida Zaman. 2002, Fitzhenry & Whiteside $14.95 (1-55041-729-0). 32pp. This colorfully illustrated picture book focuses on a child's joy and excitement about a new pair of shoes. (Rev: SLJ 4/03)

3238 Fitzgerald, Joanne. *This Is Me and Where I Am* (PS–2). Illus. 2004, Fitzhenry & Whiteside $14.95 (1-55041-819-X). 32pp. A young child gradually focuses in on his small point in the universe and then expands his view again. (Rev: BL 10/1/04; SLJ 11/04)

3239 Flanagan, Alice K. *A Busy Day at Mr. Kang's Grocery Store* (1–2). Illus. by Christine Osinski. Series: Our Neighborhood. 1996, Children's Book Pr. LB $19.50 (0-516-20047-X). 32pp. Everyday activities in a neighborhood grocery store are pictured and introduced in a simple text. (Rev: BL 1/1–15/97) [381]

3240 Flanagan, Alice K. *Call Mr. Vasquez, He'll Fix It!* (1–2). Illus. by Christine Osinski. Series: Our Neighborhood. 1996, Children's Book Pr. LB $19.50 (0-516-20045-3). 32pp. The activities of a neighborhood repairman are introduced in simple text and pictures. (Rev: BL 1/1–15/97) [647]

3241 Flanagan, Alice K. *Learning Is Fun with Mrs. Perez* (PS–1). Illus. Series: Our Neighborhood. 1998, Children's Book Pr. LB $19.50 (0-516-20774-1). 32pp. A brief text and large color photographs introduce youngsters to the work of Mrs. Perez, a Cuban immigrant who teaches a bilingual kindergarten in Chicago. (Rev: BL 6/1–15/98; HBG 10/98) [370.117]

3242 Flanagan, Alice K. *Ms. Davison, Our Librarian* (1–2). Illus. by Christine Osinski. Series: Our Neighborhood. 1996, Children's Book Pr. LB $20.00 (0-516-20009-7); paper $6.95 (0-516-26060-X). 32pp. The activities and duties of a librarian are described and pictured. (Rev: BL 1/1–15/97; SLJ 2/97) [021]

3243 Flattinger, Hubert. *Stormy Night* (PS–1). Trans. from German by J. Alison James. Illus. by Nathalie Duroussy. 2002, North-South LB $16.50 (0-7358-1667-0). A reassuring story with the message that even if it's dark and stormy, all will be well. (Rev: HBG 3/03; SLJ 2/03)

3244 Fleischman, Sid. *The Scarebird* (PS–2). Illus. by Peter Sis. 1988, Greenwillow $15.89 (0-688-07318-2). 32pp. An old farmer named Lonesome John puts up a headless scarecrow to scare the birds, but then decides to give the scarecrow a head. (Rev: BCCB 9/88; BL 9/15/88; SLJ 9/88)

3245 Fleming, Denise. *Where Once There Was a Wood* (PS–2). Illus. 1996, Holt $16.95 (0-8050-3761-6). 32pp. A piece of land is described as it was before a housing development changed it. (Rev: BCCB 3/96; BL 5/1/96; SLJ 6/96)

3246 Fletcher, Ralph. *The Circus Surprise* (PS–2). Illus. by Vladimir Vagin. 2001, Clarion $15.00 (0-395-98029-1). 32pp. Despite all his training, Nick panics when he gets lost at the circus. (Rev: HBG 10/01; SLJ 6/01)

3247 Flynn, Kitson. *Carrot in My Pocket* (PS). Illus. by Denise Ortakales. 2001, Moon Mountain $15.95 (0-9677929-6-7). A young farm boy describes in verse a day looking for a lost carrot, and names the animals and farm implements he encounters. (Rev: HBG 3/02; SLJ 2/02)

3248 Ford, Christine. *Snow!* (PS). Illus. by Candace Whitman. Series: Growing Tree. 1999, Harper-Collins $9.95 (0-694-01199-1). 24pp. For the very young, this is a rhyming story about a brother and sister who spend a snowy day outdoors with their dad and pet dog. (Rev: BL 1/1–15/00; HBG 3/00; SLJ 12/99)

3249 Ford, Miela. *My Day in the Garden* (PS–3). Illus. by Anita Lobel. 1999, Greenwillow LB $15.93 (0-688-15542-1). 24pp. Little girls at home on a rainy day use their imaginations and the costumes they find to create an indoor garden. (Rev: BCCB 3/99; BL 5/1/99; HBG 10/99; SLJ 5/99)

3250 Freeman, Mylo. *Potty!* (PS). Illus. by author. 2002, Tricycle $13.95 (1-58246-070-1). All the animals of the jungle try out a potty, but it's a small child's bottom that fits it properly. (Rev: HBG 10/02; SLJ 4/02)

3251 French, Vivian. *Oh No, Anna!* (PS). Illus. by Alex Ayliffe. 1997, Peachtree $14.95 (1-56145-125-8). A flap book that chronicles a number of minor household accidents that befall Anna. (Rev: HBG 3/98; SLJ 12/97)

3252 Friedman, Laurie. *A Style All Her Own* (PS–1). Illus. by Sharon Watts. 2004, Carolrhoda $15.95 (1-57505-599-6). Isabelle Ashley Parker McBride likes to dress in her own style, even when she's asked to be a flower girl, but her aunt manages to negotiate a compromise. (Rev: SLJ 4/05)

3253 Gammell, Stephen. *Ride* (PS–1). Illus. 2001, Harcourt $16.00 (0-15-202682-7). 32pp. A squabble between siblings in the back seat is taking on momentous proportions when Mom offers sustenance and the hostilities are abandoned . . . temporarily? (Rev: BCCB 3/01; BL 5/1/01; HB 5–6/01; HBG 10/01; SLJ 5/01)

3254 Gardella, Tricia. *Blackberry Booties* (PS–2). Illus. by Glo Coalson. 2000, Orchard LB $16.99 (0-531-33184-9). 32pp. Mikki Jo works hard picking blackberries and then uses bartering techniques to get a pair of booties made for her newborn cousin. (Rev: BCCB 4/00; BL 3/15/00; HBG 10/00; SLJ 5/00)

3255 Gardella, Tricia. *Casey's New Hat* (PS–1). Illus. by Margot Apple. 1997, Houghton Mifflin $14.95 (0-395-72035-4). 32pp. Casey has trouble finding a new hat that she likes and finally settles for an old one that Grandpa no longer wants. (Rev: BL 4/15/97; SLJ 4/97)

3256 Garland, Sarah. *Eddie's Garden and How to Make Things Grow* (K–3). 2004, Lincoln $15.95 (1-84507-015-1). 40pp. Instructions on growing the plants follow the appealing story of siblings Eddie and Lily, who start their own vegetable garden with their mother's help. (Rev: BL 6/1–15/04; SLJ 7/04)

3257 Garland, Sarah. *Ellie's Breakfast* (PS). Illus. by author. 2001, Red Fox paper $8.95 (0-09-969261-9). Father and Ellie do their morning chores — feeding the animals and collecting the eggs. (Rev: SLJ 3/02)

3258 Garland, Sherry. *The Summer Sands* (PS–1). Illus. by Robert J. Lee. 1995, Harcourt $15.00 (0-15-282492-8). 32pp. Children and their parents use their old Christmas trees to act as a windbreak to form new sand dunes. (Rev: BL 4/15/95; SLJ 6/95)

3259 Gauch, Patricia Lee. *Tanya and the Red Shoes* (PS–2). Illus. by Satomi Ichikawa. 2002, Penguin Putnam $16.99 (0-399-23314-8). 40pp. Young ballet dancer Tanya finds out that graduating to toe shoes isn't everything she thought it would be. (Rev: BL 3/1/02; HB 5–6/02; HBG 10/02; SLJ 3/02)

3260 Gay, Marie-Louise. *Stella, Princess of the Sky* (PS). Illus. 2004, Groundwood $15.95 (0-88899-601-2). 32pp. Red-headed Stella is happy to answer younger brother Sam's questions about the sky. (Rev: BL 11/1/04; SLJ 10/04)

3261 Gay, Marie-Louise. *Stella, Queen of the Snow* (PS–1). Illus. 2000, Douglas & McIntyre $15.95 (0-88899-404-4). 32pp. Little Sam discovers the wonders of snow when his boisterous big sister takes him out to play in it. (Rev: BCCB 1/01; BL 11/1/00; HBG 3/01; SLJ 10/00)

3262 Gay, Marie-Louise. *Stella, Star of the Sea* (PS–K). Illus. 1999, Douglas & McIntyre $15.95 (0-88899-337-4). 32pp. While at the seashore, Sam delays taking a plunge into the water by asking his older sister, Stella, a multitude of questions. (Rev: BCCB 5/99; BL 5/15/99; SLJ 8/99)

3263 Geisert, Bonnie. *Desert Town* (K–3). Illus. by Arthur Geisert. 2001, Houghton Mifflin $16.00 (0-395-95387-1). 32pp. A year in a desert town is traced in this book that allows the readers to explore homes in cutaway views. (Rev: HB 3–4/01; HBG 10/01; SLJ 3/01)

3264 Geisert, Bonnie. *Mountain Town* (1–3). Illus. by Arthur Geisert. 2000, Houghton Mifflin $16.00 (0-395-95390-1). 32pp. A series of vignettes portray life in a mountain town during different seasons. (Rev: BL 3/15/00; HBG 10/00; SLJ 4/00)

3265 Geisert, Bonnie. *River Town* (1–3). Illus. by Arthur Geisert. 1999, Houghton Mifflin $16.00 (0-395-90891-4). 32pp. This picture book depicts a small river town over a year's time, during which the river floods and threatens to destroy the community. (Rev: BCCB 6/99; BL 7/99; HBG 10/99; SLJ 5/99) [307.72]

3266 Geisert, Bonnie, and Arthur Geisert. *Prairie Town* (1–3). Illus. 1998, Houghton Mifflin $16.00 (0-395-85907-7). 32pp. Brief text and detailed etchings colored with washes cover a year in the life of a small Midwestern town. Specific events and sites are illustrated as well as panoramic views of the entire town. (Rev: BL 4/1/98; HB 5–6/98; HBG 10/98; SLJ 4/98)

3267 George, Kristine O'Connell. *Book!* (PS). Illus. by Maggie Smith. 2001, Clarion $9.95 (0-395-98287-1). 32pp. A toddler finds great joy in his first picture book in this engaging package of friendly text and lively illustrations. (Rev: BL 12/1/01; HBG 3/02; SLJ 10/01) [811]

3268 Gerber, Carole. *Blizzard* (PS–K). Illus. by Marty Husted. 2001, Charlesbridge $15.95 (1-58089-064-4). 32pp. A boy describes in verse the delight of being cozy and warm inside while a winter storm rages outside. (Rev: BL 9/15/01; HBG 3/02; SLJ 10/01)

3269 Gibbons, Gail. *Fire! Fire!* (PS–2). Illus. by author. 1984, HarperCollins LB $15.89 (0-690-04416-X); paper $6.95 (0-06-446058-4). 40pp. The various ways a fire is fought.

3270 Gibbons, Gail. *How a House Is Built* (PS–K). Illus. 1990, Holiday House LB $16.95 (0-8234-0841-8). 32pp. A good introduction to the construction of a wood frame house. (Rev: BL 10/15/90; SLJ 10/90) [690]

3271 Glaser, Linda. *Our Big Home: An Earth Poem* (2–3). Illus. by Elisa Kleven. 2000, Millbrook LB $21.90 (0-7613-1650-7). 32pp. Some of the common joys of life — such as water, dirt, sun, moon, wind, sky, dark, and the fact one is alive — are celebrated with outstanding illustrations. (Rev: BL 5/15/00; HBG 10/00; SLJ 4/00)

3272 Godwin, Laura. *The Flower Girl* (PS–3). Illus. by John Wallace. 2000, Hyperion $12.99 (0-7868-0408-4). A description of a wedding from the flower girl's point of view. (Rev: SLJ 2/01)

3273 Gold, August. *Where Does God Live?* (PS–1). Illus. by Matthew J. Perlman. 2001, Skylight Paths paper $7.95 (1-893361-39-X). 32pp. With help from her parents, a little girl who wonders where God

lives begins to see evidence of him all around her. (Rev: BL 10/1/01)

3274 Gomi, Taro. *Everyone Poops* (PS). Trans. by Amanda M. Stinchecum. Illus. Series: Can You Believe It! 1993, Kane/Miller $11.95 (0-916291-45-6). 28pp. This book shows that all animals poop and that this is a natural part of life. (Rev: BCCB 4/93; BL 5/15/93) [612]

3275 Gomi, Taro. *My Friends* (PS–K). Illus. 1995, Chronicle paper $5.95 (0-811-81237-5). 36pp. A little girl talks about all the things she's learned from her friends, such as jumping from her dog. (Rev: BL 7/90; SLJ 7/90)

3276 Good, Merle, and Dan Boltz. *Dan's Pants: The Adventures of Dan, the Fabric Man* (K–3). Illus. by Cheryl Benner. 2000, Good Books $16.00 (1-56148-307-9). Dan and his wife Fran sell fabrics, and over the years Fran sews many patches from different bolts of cloth to mend Dan's pants. (Rev: SLJ 12/00)

3277 Graham, Bob. *Rose Meets Mr. Wintergarten* (PS–2). Illus. by author. 1992, Candlewick $14.95 (1-56402-039-8). 32pp. When her ball goes over Mr. Wintergarten's fence, Rose is able to find out what her neighbor is really like. (Rev: BCCB 7–8/92; BL 5/15/92; HB 5–6/92; SLJ 8/92)

3278 Grahn, Geoffrey. *What's Going on in There?* (K–3). Illus. by author. 2005, Scholastic $14.95 (0-439-57495-1). Readers must take time to examine each spread and identify what is really taking place in Grahnville (the pizza cook is really assembling a dinosaur, for example). (Rev: SLJ 3/05)

3279 Gray, Libba M. *When Uncle Took the Fiddle* (PS–2). Illus. by Lloyd Bloom. 1999, Orchard $15.95 (0-531-30137-0). 32pp. Although it's bedtime, an Appalachian family and their neighbors come to life when Uncle picks up his fiddle and starts to play. (Rev: BCCB 11/99; BL 9/15/99; HBG 3/00; SLJ 11/99)

3280 Gray, Rita. *Nonna's Porch* (PS–2). Illus. by Terry Widener. 2004, Hyperion $15.99 (0-7868-1613-9). On her porch, Nonna knits a blanket that depicts the summer scene. (Rev: SLJ 11/04)

3281 Greenfield, Eloise. *Big Friend, Little Friend* (PS). Illus. by Jan S. Gilchrist. 1991, Writers & Readers $4.95 (0-86316-204-5). 12pp. This is one of a series of board books about the everyday activities of some African American children. Also use: *Daddy and I; I Make Music;* and *My Doll, Keshia* (all 1991). (Rev: BL 12/15/91; SLJ 12/91)

3282 Greenfield, Eloise. *Water, Water* (PS). Illus. by Jan S. Gilchrist. 1999, HarperCollins $9.95 (0-694-01247-5). 24pp. A young boy experiences the wonder of water by wading, fishing, drinking, and simply watching it. (Rev: BL 8/99; HBG 3/00; SLJ 10/99)

3283 Gregory, Nan. *Amber Waiting* (PS–1). Illus. by Kady MacDonald Denton. 2003, Red Deer $17.95 (0-88995-258-2). When Dad is late — as always — picking Amber up from kindergarten, the little girl imagines ways to get even. (Rev: BL 5/15/03*; SLJ 7/03)

3284 Grejniec, Michael. *What Do You Like?* (K–2). Illus. 1995, North-South paper $6.95 (1-55858-417-X). 32pp. A boy and a girl like the same things, but in different ways. (Rev: BL 8/92; SLJ 1/93)

3285 Griffin, Kitty, and Kathy Combs. *Cowboy Sam and Those Confounded Secrets* (PS–2). Illus. by Mike Wohnoutka. 2001, Clarion $15.00 (0-618-08854-7). 32pp. Sam keeps the town's secrets under his 10-gallon hat, but it eventually becomes full. (Rev: HBG 3/02; SLJ 12/01)

3286 Grimes, Nikki. *Come Sunday* (PS–3). Illus. by Michael Bryant. 1996, Eerdmans $15.00 (0-8028-5108-8); paper $7.50 (0-8028-5134-7). 32pp. Young Latasha finds that going to church on Sunday is an exciting adventure. (Rev: BCCB 3/97; BL 6/1–15/96*; SLJ 6/97)

3287 Gundersheimer, Karen. *Find Cat, Wear Hat* (PS). Illus. 1995, Scholastic $5.95 (0-590-48061-8). 24pp. A beginner's book in which each page explains in two words the accompanying picture. Similar in scope is the author's *Splish Splash, Bang Crash* (1995). (Rev: BL 1/15/95; SLJ 9/95)

3288 Haas, Jessie. *Hurry!* (PS–2). Illus. by Joseph A. Smith. 2000, Greenwillow $15.95 (0-688-16889-2). 24pp. Nora and her grandparents work hard loading hay onto a horse-drawn wagon just before the rains come. (Rev: BL 5/15/00; HB 7–8/00; HBG 10/00; SLJ 6/00)

3289 Hamanaka, Sheila. *All the Colors of the Earth* (PS–2). Illus. 1994, Morrow $15.89 (0-688-11132-7). 32pp. A collection of paintings that show children of various ethnic backgrounds together having fun. (Rev: BCCB 10/94; BL 9/1/94; HB 11–12/94; SLJ 8/94*)

3290 Hamilton, Kersten. *Firefighters to the Rescue!* (PS–2). Illus. by Rich Davis. 2005, Viking $15.99 (0-670-03503-3). 32pp. Fire fighters rush to a house fire in this story that also shows their routine and the fire station. (Rev: BL 5/15/05)

3291 Hamm, Diane J. *Laney's Lost Momma* (PS–1). Illus. by Sally G. Ward. 1991, Whitman LB $14.95 (0-8075-4340-3). 32pp. Mother and daughter are reunited after Laney loses her mother in a department store. (Rev: BL 1/1/92; SLJ 12/91)

3292 Harper, Charise Mericle. *When I Grow Up* (K–2). Illus. by author. 2001, Chronicle $14.95 (0-8118-2905-7). "Adventurous" and "generous" are only two of the 14 characteristics that children aspire to in this appealing picture book. (Rev: HBG 10/01; SLJ 7/01)

3293 Harper, Jessica. *Nora's Room* (PS–1). Illus. by Lindsay Harper duPont. 2001, HarperCollins LB $15.89 (0-06-029137-0). 32pp. Everyone in the family wonders what's making the incredible noise coming from Nora's room. (Rev: BL 7/01; HBG 10/01; SLJ 7/01)

3294 Hatkoff, Craig, and Juliana Lee Hatkoff. *Good-Bye, Tonsils* (PS–3). Illus. by Marilyn Mets. 2001, Viking $15.99 (0-670-89775-2). 32pp. In detail, with illustrations, Juliana Hatkoff describes having her tonsils out and how she felt before and after. (Rev: BL 8/01; HBG 10/01; SLJ 8/01)

3295 Hautzig, David. *At the Supermarket* (PS–2). Illus. 1994, Orchard LB $17.99 (0-531-08682-8). 32pp. An hour-by-hour account that describes in pictures and text what happens during a single day in a modern supermarket. (Rev: BL 3/15/94; SLJ 5/94) [381]

3296 Havill, Juanita. *Jamaica's Find* (PS–1). Illus. by Anne S. O'Brien. 1986, Houghton Mifflin $16.00 (0-395-39376-0); paper $5.95 (0-395-45357-7). 32pp. Jamaica finds a stuffed dog, which she brings home, but her parents make her return to the park where she found it, and where she also finds its true owner. Also use: *Jamaica Tag-Along* (1989). (Rev: BCCB 5/86; BL 4/1/86; SLJ 8/86)

3297 Hayes, Joe. *A Spoon for Every Bite* (PS–3). Illus. by Rebecca Leer. 1996, Orchard LB $17.99 (0-531-08799-9). 32pp. A poor couple fools a rich neighbor into spending his fortune for spoons. (Rev: BCCB 4/96; BL 3/15/96; SLJ 4/96)

3298 Hayes, Sarah. *Eat Up, Gemma* (PS–1). Illus. by Jan Ormerod. 1988, Lothrop $16.00 (0-688-08149-5). 32pp. Gemma is at the stage where food is mostly a toy. (Rev: BCCB 9/88; BL 9/1/88; HB 11–12/88)

3299 Hayles, Marsha. *Pajamas Anytime* (PS). Illus. by Hiroe Nakata. 2005, Penguin Putnam $15.99 (0-399-23871-9). 32pp. A celebration of pajamas as the ultimate comfort clothing, at all times of the year. (Rev: BL 2/1/05; SLJ 3/05)

3300 Hegi, Ursula. *Trudi and Pia* (1–3). Illus. by Giselle Potter. 2003, Simon & Schuster $16.95 (0-689-84683-5). 40pp. Trudi, a dwarf, meets another dwarf at the circus and feels less alone. (Rev: BL 3/1/03; HBG 10/03; SLJ 3/03)

3301 Heide, Florence Parry. *Some Things Are Scary* (PS–1). Illus. by Jules Feiffer. 2000, Candlewick $15.99 (0-0736-1222-7). 40pp. This is a book about everyday things that young children might find scary — being hugged by a huge adult or finding out that your best friend's best friend isn't you. (Rev: BL 10/15/00*; SLJ 1/01*)

3302 Helldorfer, M. C. *Got to Dance* (PS). Illus. by Hiroe Nakata. 2004, Doubleday LB $17.99 (0-385-90865-2). A young girl with a lot of energy loves to dance in this story set in a city in the heat of summer. (Rev: SLJ 8/04)

3303 Henkes, Kevin. *Good-bye, Curtis* (PS–K). Illus. by Marisabina Russo. 1995, Greenwillow $14.89 (0-688-12828-9). 24pp. After 42 years of service, mailcarrier Curtis makes his last rounds. (Rev: BL 10/15/95; HB 11–12/95; SLJ 10/95)

3304 Hennessy, B. G. *Because of You* (PS–2). Illus. by Hiroe Nakata. 2005, Candlewick $15.99 (0-7636-1926-4). 24pp. A picture book focusing on what children can do to serve others and to make the world a better place. (Rev: BL 3/1/05)

3305 Heo, Yumi. *One Afternoon* (PS–1). Illus. 1994, Orchard $15.95 (0-531-06845-5). 32pp. A mother and her son discover on a big-city walk that everything from a jackhammer to a cash register makes its own distinctive sound. (Rev: BL 8/94; HB 11–12/94; SLJ 11/94)

3306 Herrera, Juan Felipe. *Grandma and Me at the Flea / Los Meros Meros Remateros* (2–4). Illus. by

Anita De Lucio-Brock. 2002, Children's Book Pr. $15.95 (0-89239-171-5). 32pp. A bilingual story about a boy named Juanito who helps his grandmother at a California flea market. (Rev: BL 4/1/02; HBG 10/02)

3307 Hershenhorn, Esther. *Chicken Soup by Heart* (K–3). Illus. by Rosanne Litzinger. 2002, Simon & Schuster $16.95 (0-689-82665-6). 32pp. Rudie and his mother make chicken soup with some special additives for Mrs. Gittel, Rudie's elderly neighbor and babysitter. (Rev: BCCB 1/03; BL 9/1/02; HBG 3/03; SLJ 11/02)

3308 Hesse, Karen. *Come On, Rain!* (K–2). Illus. by Jon J. Muth. 1999, Scholastic $15.95 (0-590-33125-6). 32pp. A delightful book about a group of children who enjoy a cloudburst during a sweltering day in the big city. (Rev: BCCB 4/99; BL 2/1/99; HB 7–8/99; HBG 10/99; SLJ 3/99)

3309 Hest, Amy. *The Purple Coat* (K–2). Illus. by Amy Schwartz. 1992, Macmillan paper $5.99 (0-689-71634-6). 32pp. This year Gabrielle wants a purple coat instead of the navy blue coat she always wears, and Grandpa the tailor comes up with an ingenious solution. (Rev: BL 9/1/86; HB 1–2/87; SLJ 11/86)

3310 High, Linda O. *Barn Savers* (PS–3). Illus. by Ted Lewin. 1999, Boyds Mills $15.95 (1-56397-403-7). 32pp. A boy and his father dismantle a barn to save it from bulldozers and salvage its parts for new uses. (Rev: BL 11/1/99*; HBG 3/00; SLJ 11/99)

3311 High, Linda O. *Beekeepers* (K–2). Illus. by Doug Chayka. 1998, Boyds Mills $14.95 (1-56397-486-X). 32pp. A little girl, under the guidance of her grandfather, engages in the many activities involved in bee-keeping, including gathering the honey. (Rev: BCCB 4/98; BL 5/15/98; HBG 3/99; SLJ 6/98)

3312 Hill, Frances. *The Bug Cemetery* (PS–1). Illus. by Vera Rosenberry. 2002, Holt $16.95 (0-8050-6370-6). A bug-cemetery-lemonade-stand-business turns serious when Billy's cat dies. (Rev: HBG 10/02; SLJ 4/02)

3313 Hines, Anna Grossnickle. *What Can You Do in the Snow?* (PS). Illus. by Thea Kliros. 1999, Greenwillow $5.95 (0-688-16078-6). This small board book filled with watercolor paintings shows multicultural children building snowmen and engaging in other winter activities. Also use *What Can You Do in the Wind?* (1999). (Rev: HBG 10/99; SLJ 6/99)

3314 Hines, Anna Grossnickle. *What Can You Do in the Sun?* (PS). Illus. by Thea Kliros. 1999, Greenwillow $5.95 (0-688-16080-8). 20pp. Several experiences that are associated with being in the sun are joyfully presented in this board book. A companion book is *What Can You Do in the Wind?* (Rev: BL 6/1–15/99; HBG 10/99; SLJ 6/99)

3315 Hoban, Julia. *Amy Loves the Rain* (PS–K). Illus. by Lillian Hoban. 1989, HarperCollins $9.95 (0-06-022357-X). 24pp. Amy sits in her car seat as they go to pick up Daddy in the rain. Also use: *Amy Loves the Sun* (1988). (Rev: BL 4/15/89; HB 7–8/89)

3316 Hoban, Julia. *Amy Loves the Snow* (PS). Illus. by Lillian Hoban. 1989, HarperCollins $9.95 (0-06-022361-8). 24pp. A simple text that dramatizes the fun youngsters have in the snow. (Rev: BL 10/1/89; SLJ 10/89)

3317 Hooks, Bell. *Be Boy Buzz* (PS–K). Illus. by Chris Raschka. 2002, Hyperion $16.99 (0-7868-0814-4). 32pp. Spare, rhythmic text and clear, lively images celebrate the energetic joy of being an African American boy. (Rev: BCCB 12/02; BL 11/1/02; HBG 3/03; SLJ 12/02)

3318 Hopkinson, Deborah. *Band of Angels: A Story Inspired by the Jubilee Singers* (2–4). Illus. by Raul Colon. 1999, Simon & Schuster $16.00 (0-689-81062-8); paper $6.99 (0-689-84897-0). The fictionalized story of Ella Sheppard and the Fisk University Jubilee Singers. (Rev: BL 2/15/03)

3319 Houghton, Eric. *The Crooked Apple Tree* (PS–2). Illus. by Caroline Gold. 1999, Barefoot LB $15.95 (1-902283-59-7). A year in the life of a young brother and sister as they play imaginative games around an old apple tree as the seasons change. (Rev: SLJ 7/99)

3320 Hubbell, Patricia. *Black All Around!* (PS–2). Illus. by Don Tate. 2003, Lee & Low $16.95 (1-58430-048-5). 32pp. An African American girl looks around to discover that the world is full of lovely things that are black, such as a lake at night and her Momma's cheek. (Rev: BL 2/15/03; HBG 10/03; SLJ 5/03)

3321 Hubbell, Patricia. *Sidewalk Trip* (PS–K). Illus. by Mari Takabayashi. 1999, HarperCollins $9.95 (0-694-01174-6). 24pp. Mother and daughter take a walk in the neighborhood and encounter pigeons, dogs, and an ice-cream truck. (Rev: BL 9/15/99; HBG 10/99; SLJ 7/99)

3322 Hudson, Cheryl W., and Bernette G. Ford. *Bright Eyes, Brown Skin* (PS). Illus. by George Ford. 1990, Just Us $12.95 (0-940975-10-6). 24pp. This book features four African American children on a typical day in preschool. (Rev: BL 12/1/90*; SLJ 1/91)

3323 Hughes, Shirley. *Two Shoes, New Shoes* (PS). Illus. by author. 1986, Lothrop paper $4.95 (0-688-04207-4). 24pp. A rhyming board book about clothes. (Rev: BL 12/15/86; HB 1–2/87; SLJ 12/86)

3324 Humphries, Tudor. *Hiding* (PS–K). Illus. 1997, Orchard $14.95 (0-531-30056-0). 32pp. After she has been scolded by her mother, a little girl goes into hiding until she becomes lonely. (Rev: BL 12/1/97; HBG 3/98; SLJ 3/98)

3325 Hurd, Thacher. *Zoom City* (PS). Illus. by author. 1998, HarperCollins $5.95 (0-694-01057-X). A board book that contains bright, action-filled illustrations of cars zooming around. (Rev: HBG 10/98; SLJ 6/98)

3326 Hurwitz, Johanna. *New Shoes for Silvia* (PS–3). Illus. by Jerry Pinkney. 1993, Morrow $15.93 (0-688-05287-8). 32pp. Silvia finds all sorts of uses for her new shoes until her feet are big enough for her to wear them. (Rev: BCCB 11/93; BL 10/15/93; HB 11–12/93; SLJ 10/93)

3327 Hutchins, Pat. *The Doorbell Rang* (K–2). Illus. by author. 1986, Greenwillow $15.93 (0-688-05252-5); Morrow paper $4.95 (0-688-09234-9). 24pp. Every time the doorbell rings, it means more of Ma's cookies are eaten, which leaves less for Victoria and Sam — until Grandma arrives with a package. (Rev: BCCB 3/86; BL 6/15/86; SLJ 4/86)

3328 Intrater, Roberta G. *Smile!* (PS). Photos by Roberta Grobel Intrater. Series: Babyfaces. 1997, Scholastic $4.95 (0-590-05899-1). In this board book, a toddler responds to a photographer's requests. Also use *Peek-a-Boo!* (1997). (Rev: SLJ 2/98)

3329 Ireland, Karin. *Don't Take Your Snake for a Stroll* (K–2). Illus. by David Catrow. 2003, Harcourt $16.00 (0-15-202361-5). In rhyming verse and colorful artwork, a young boy is warned about the consequences of taking unusual pets on a variety of different outings. (Rev: BL 5/15/03; HBG 10/03; SLJ 10/03)

3330 Isaacs, Gwynne L. *While You Are Asleep* (PS–2). Illus. by Cathi Hepworth. 1991, Walker LB $13.85 (0-8027-6986-1). 32pp. This picture book describes the intersecting lives of several people who work at night. (Rev: BL 9/1/91; SLJ 8/91)

3331 Isadora, Rachael. *Lili at Ballet* (K–3). Illus. 1993, Penguin Putnam LB $16.99 (0-399-22423-8). 32pp. A lovely picture book of a child's dance experiences. (Rev: BCCB 4/93; BL 2/1/93*; HB 5–6/93; SLJ 3/93)

3332 Isadora, Rachel. *Not Just Tutus* (K–3). Illus. 2003, Penguin Putnam $13.99 (0-399-23603-1). 40pp. The author uses her personal knowledge of ballet school to convey the magic and hardships of a young dancer's life in this book that combines rhyming text and watercolor art that will attract young ballet fans. (Rev: BL 1/1–15/03; HBG 10/03; SLJ 4/03)

3333 Isadora, Rachel. *Peekaboo Morning* (PS–K). Illus. 2002, Penguin Putnam $15.99 (0-399-23602-3). 32pp. An African American toddler plays peekaboo with friends, relatives, and family pets in this delightful book for preschoolers. (Rev: BCCB 7–8/02; BL 3/1/02; HBG 10/02; SLJ 7/02)

3334 Jabar, Cynthia. *Bored Blue? Think What You Can Do!* (PS–1). Illus. 1991, Little, Brown $14.95 (0-316-43458-2). 32pp. This book suggests all sorts of activities for bored kids, some of them in the world of fantasy, in rhyming text. (Rev: BL 4/1/91; SLJ 6/91)

3335 Jacobs, Paul Dubois, and Jennifer Swender. *My Subway Ride* (K–3). Illus. by Selina Alko. 2004, Gibbs Smith $15.95 (1-58685-357-0). New York City's subway comes alive in the rhythmic text and bright illustrations that depict landmark sites. (Rev: SLJ 9/04)

3336 Jakob, Donna. *Tiny Toes* (PS–1). Illus. by Mireille Levert. 1995, Hyperion LB $14.49 (0-7868-2009-8). 32pp. Toes engage in a variety of activities, including dancing. (Rev: BL 4/1/95; SLJ 6/95)

3337 Jarman, Julia. *Big Red Tub* (PS–K). Illus. by Adrian Reynolds. 2004, Scholastic $14.95 (0-439-

67232-5). 32pp. This bath-time book full of color and adventure features little Stan and Stella plus a cast of non-human characters. (Rev: BL 1/1–15/05)

3338 Jenkins, Emily. *My Favorite Thing (According to Alberta)* (PS–2). Illus. by AnnaLaura Cantone. 2004, Simon & Schuster $15.95 (0-689-84975-3). Alberta's likes and dislikes are well-defined, and her favorite thing is — of course — herself. (Rev: HB 7–8/04; SLJ 9/04)

3339 Jenness, Aylette. *Come Home with Me: A Multicultural Treasure Hunt* (1–4). Photos by Max Belcher. Illus. by Laura DeSantis. Series: Kids Bridge. 1993, New Pr. $16.95 (1-56584-064-X). 48pp. A treasure hunt that introduces four cultural groups represented in various neighborhoods in Boston. (Rev: SLJ 4/94)

3340 Jennings, Sharon. *Into My Mother's Arms* (PS–K). Illus. by Ruth Ohi. 2000, Fitzhenry & Whiteside $14.95 (1-55041-533-6). 32pp. A mother and her daughter spend a busy day, starting with breakfast, continuing with activities like going shopping, and finally coming home to bed. (Rev: BL 5/15/00; SLJ 7/00)

3341 Johnson, Angela. *The Leaving Morning* (PS–2). Illus. by David Soman. 1996, Orchard paper $5.95 (0-531-07072-7). 32pp. All the sorrow and anticipation of a move are captured in this picture of a family saying good-bye to their home and friends. (Rev: BL 9/1/92; HB 9–10/92; SLJ 9/92)

3342 Johnson, Angela. *Rain Feet* (PS). Illus. by Rhonda Mitchell. 1994, Orchard $4.95 (0-531-06849-8). 12pp. A little African American boy enjoys splashing through puddles in this board book. Also use *Mama Birds, Baby Birds* (1994). (Rev: BL 12/1/94; HB 9–10/94; SLJ 1/95)

3343 Johnson, Angela. *Shoes Like Miss Alice's* (PS–K). Illus. by Ken Page. 1995, Orchard LB $16.99 (0-531-08664-X). 32pp. Sally resents her baby-sitter Miss Alice until she sees her wide assortment of shoes. (Rev: BL 3/15/95; SLJ 7/95)

3344 Johnson, Paul B. *Farmers' Market* (PS–2). 1997, Orchard LB $16.99 (0-531-33014-1). 32pp. On Saturdays during the summer, Laura and her family sell their produce at the Farmers' Market in Lexington, Kentucky. (Rev: BCCB 4/97; BL 3/15/97; SLJ 6/97)

3345 Johnston, Tony. *The Quilt Story* (PS–2). Illus. by Tomie dePaola. 1996, Penguin Putnam paper $5.99 (0-698-11368-3). 32pp. The star of this book is the quilt, which gives fun, warmth, and comfort to two generations. (Rev: BCCB 7/85; BL 8/85; SLJ 9/85)

3346 Jordan, June. *Kimako's Story* (K–3). Illus. by Kay Burford. 1991, Houghton Mifflin paper $3.95 (0-395-60338-2). 42pp. Seven-year-old Kimako explores her neighborhood.

3347 *The Jump at the Sun Treasury: An African American Picture Book Collection* (PS–3). Illus. 2001, Hyperion $15.99 (0-7868-0754-7). 205pp. An anthology of seven previously published picture books with African American themes. (Rev: BL 2/15/02; HBG 3/02)

3348 Kalman, Maira. *Next Stop Grand Central* (K–3). Illus. 1999, Penguin Putnam LB $15.99 (0-399-22926-4). 32pp. All the excitement and turmoil of rush hour at Grand Central Station — the busiest railroad station in the world, where half a million people converge every day — is captured in this intriguing picture book. (Rev: BCCB 3/99; BL 12/15/98*; HB 5–6/99; HBG 10/99; SLJ 2/99)

3349 Katz, Karen. *The Colors of Us* (PS–1). Illus. 1999, Holt $15.95 (0-8050-5864-8). 32pp. Lena discovers that her friends and neighbors are all delicious shades of brown like the foods she enjoys, including peanut butter and chocolate cupcakes. (Rev: BCCB 12/99; BL 9/15/99; HBG 3/00; SLJ 9/99)

3350 Katz, Karen. *Twelve Hats for Lena: A Book of Months* (PS–3). Illus. by author. 2002, Simon & Schuster $16.95 (0-689-84873-0). Lena creates hats that are suitable for each month of the year, and hat-making directions are included. (Rev: HBG 3/03; SLJ 10/02)

3351 Kesselman, Wendy. *Sand in My Shoes* (PS–3). Illus. by Ronald Himler. 1995, Hyperion LB $15.49 (0-7868-2045-4). 32pp. At the end of summer, a little girl says good-bye to the beach she loves but still retains little remembrances like sand in her shoes. (Rev: BL 6/1–15/95; SLJ 7/95)

3352 Killion, Bette. *Just Think!* (PS–K). Illus. by Linda Bronson. Series: Harper Growing Tree. 2001, HarperCollins $9.95 (0-694-01315-3). 24pp. Mom's admonitions to hurry or to slow down prompt vivid images in her daughter's mind. (Rev: BL 12/15/01; HBG 3/02)

3353 King, Stephen M. *Emily Loves to Bounce* (PS–K). Illus. by author. 2003, Philomel $15.99 (0-399-23886-7). Emily bounces wherever she can, in brief rhyming text and lively illustrations. (Rev: HBG 10/03; SLJ 3/03)

3354 Kinsey-Warnock, Natalie. *A Farm of Her Own* (K–2). Illus. by Kathleen Kolb. 2001, Dutton $15.99 (0-525-46507-3). 32pp. Emma enjoys summer at Sunnyside Farm so much that when she grows up she buys the farm herself. (Rev: BCCB 6/01; BL 7/01; HBG 10/01; SLJ 6/01)

3355 Knutson, Kimberley. *Beach Babble* (PS–K). Illus. 1998, Marshall Cavendish $15.95 (0-7614-5026-2). 32pp. The sounds of a day at the beach are re-created in this picture book illustrated with collage artwork. (Rev: BL 6/1–15/98; HBG 10/98; SLJ 7/98)

3356 Koller, Jackie F. *Bouncing on the Bed* (PS). Illus. by Anna Grossnickle Hines. 1999, Orchard LB $16.99 (0-531-33138-5). 32pp. A description by a toddler of all the fun things in a typical day, such as bouncing on the bed, sliding down the stairs, and snuggling down at bedtime. (Rev: BL 2/1/99; HBG 10/99; SLJ 4/99)

3357 Koski, Mary. *Impatient Pamela Calls 9-1-1* (PS–K). Illus. by Dan Brown. 1998, Trellis LB $15.95 (0-9663281-9-1). 32pp. Impatient Pamela learns a number of skills and puts them to use calling 911 when her neighbor Martin begins choking. (Rev: BL 12/1/98)

3358 Krasilovsky, Phyllis. *The Very Little Boy* (PS–1). Illus. by Karen Gundersheimer. 1992, Scholastic paper $4.95 (0-590-44762-9). In this book that describes development, a young boy grows physically and is able to accomplish more skills. (Rev: SLJ 12/92)

3359 Krebs, Laurie. *The Beeman* (PS–2). Illus. by Melissa Iwai. 2002, National Geographic $16.95 (0-7922-7224-2). 32pp. A beekeeper gives his granddaughter a tour of the hives and the process of extracting honey, then the two enjoy muffins and honey. (Rev: BL 10/1/02; HBG 3/03; SLJ 9/02)

3360 Kroll, Virginia. *Boy, You're Amazing!* (1–3). Illus. by Sachiko Yoshikawa. 2004, Whitman $15.95 (0-8075-0868-3). 32pp. In this appealing companion to *Girl, You're Amazing,* Kroll celebrates in rhyming text the unique character traits and abilities of boys. (Rev: BL 4/15/04; SLJ 5/04)

3361 Kroll, Virginia. *Girl, You're Amazing!* (K–3). Illus. by Melisande Potter. 2001, Whitman $15.95 (0-8075-2930-3). 32pp. This picture book is a pep talk that tells girls they can do anything they want and be anyone they wish. (Rev: BL 4/1/01; HBG 10/01; SLJ 4/01)

3362 Kunhardt, Edith. *I'm Going to Be a Police Officer* (PS–2). Illus. 1995, Scholastic paper $3.25 (0-590-25485-5). 32pp. An average day in a small-town police officer's day as seen through the eyes of his two children, who spend time with him at the police station. (Rev: BL 1/1–15/96)

3363 Kuskin, Karla. *The Philharmonic Gets Dressed* (1–4). Illus. by Marc Simont. 1982, HarperCollins $15.95 (0-06-023622-1); paper $5.95 (0-06-443124-X). 48pp. One hundred and five musicians are across town getting ready for a big concert.

3364 Laden, Nina. *Ready, Set, Go!* (PS). Illus. by author. 2000, Chronicle $6.95 (0-8118-2601-5). An interactive book in which cut-out circles reveal activities that are viewed completely when the page is turned. (Rev: SLJ 9/00)

3365 Larios, Julie. *Have You Ever Done That?* (PS–3). Illus. by Anne Hunter. 2001, Front Street $15.95 (1-886910-49-9). Rhythmic questions stir a child's imagination and reveal his dreamlike views of the world around him. (Rev: HBG 3/02; SLJ 12/01)

3366 Lawrence, Mary. *What's That Sound?* (1–3). Illus. by Lynn Adams. Series: Science Solves It! 2002, Kane paper $4.99 (1-57565-118-1). 32pp. Tim's older sister Amy shrugs off every spooky sound he hears, and scientific sidebars explain how each one was made. (Rev: SLJ 10/02)

3367 Leghorn, Lindsay. *Proud of Our Feelings* (PS–2). Illus. by author. 1995, Magination $11.95 (0-945354-68-1). A little girl demonstrates the various emotions that her friends feel, like friendliness, sadness, happiness, silliness, and anger. (Rev: SLJ 4/96)

3368 Lester, Alison. *When Frank Was Four* (PS–2). Illus. 1996, Houghton Mifflin $15.00 (0-395-74275-7). 32pp. Double-page spreads reveal many activities that a group of Australian children engage in from infancy to school age. A sequel to *Clive Eats*

Alligators (1986). (Rev: BL 2/15/96; HB 5–6/96; SLJ 4/96)

3369 Levert, Mireille. *Lucy's Secret* (PS–1). Illus. 2004, Douglas & McIntyre $16.95 (0-88899-566-0). 32pp. Lucy is eager for her seeds to grow into plants, but Anna Zinnia explains the need for patience. (Rev: BL 3/15/04; SLJ 4/04)

3370 Levy, Constance. *The Story of Red Rubber Ball* (PS–K). Illus. by Hiroe Nakata. 2004, Harcourt $16.00 (0-15-216589-4). A simple, rhythmic story about a ball left in a park and the various animals that take a look at it. (Rev: SLJ 7/04)

3371 Lewin, Ted. *Big Jimmy's Kum Kau Chinese Take Out* (K–3). Illus. 2001, HarperCollins LB $16.89 (0-688-16027-1). 40pp. This fast-paced, realistically illustrated book shows a typical day at a busy Chinese restaurant in Brooklyn, as told by the proprietors' young son. (Rev: BCCB 1/02; BL 1/1–15/02; HBG 3/02; SLJ 4/02)

3372 Lewis, Kim. *The Shepherd Boy* (PS–2). Illus. 1990, Macmillan LB $13.95 (0-02-758581-6). 32pp. A young boy who longs to be a shepherd like his father practices on a toy lamb. (Rev: BL 12/1/90; SLJ 12/90)

3373 Lewis, Paeony. *No More Cookies!* (PS–K). Illus. by Brita Granström. 2005, Scholastic $16.95 (0-439-68332-7). 32pp. Florence is very inventive in her efforts to get at the cookie jar. (Rev: BL 5/1/05; SLJ 5/05)

3374 Lin, Grace. *Dim Sum for Everyone* (PS–K). Illus. 2001, Knopf $14.95 (0-375-81082-x). 32pp. Text and appealing illustrations show an Asian family enjoying a meal at a dim sum restaurant in Chinatown. (Rev: BL 6/1–15/01; HBG 3/02; SLJ 7/01)

3375 Lin, Grace. *Fortune Cookie Fortunes* (K–2). Illus. 2004, Knopf $15.95 (0-375-81521-X). 32pp. The fortune cookies that follow a meal are the focus of this story featuring the family from *Dim Sum for Everyone* (2001). (Rev: BL 2/15/04; SLJ 6/04)

3376 Lomas Garza, Carmen. *In My Family / En Mi Familia* (1–4). Illus. 1996, Children's Book Pr. $15.95 (0-89239-138-3). 32pp. In 13 paintings labeled bilingually, the artist portrays his childhood in Kingsville, Texas. (Rev: BL 11/1/96; HB 11–12/96)

3377 London, Jonathan. *The Candystore Man* (K–3). Illus. by Kevin O'Malley. 1998, Lothrop $16.00 (0-688-13241-3). 24pp. A hip candy store owner in Bayonne, New Jersey, takes a young boy on a jazzy tour of the neighborhood and teaches him how to become a part of it. (Rev: BL 11/15/98; HBG 3/99; SLJ 10/98)

3378 London, Jonathan. *Sun Dance Water Dance* (K–3). Illus. by Greg Couch. 2001, Dutton $15.99 (0-525-46682-7). 40pp. Poetic text and bright pictures capture the charms of summer. (Rev: BL 8/01; HBG 10/01; SLJ 7/01)

3379 London, Jonathan. *When the Fireflies Come* (K–2). Illus. by Terry Widener. 2003, Dutton $15.99 (0-525-45404-7). Poetic prose and colorful illustrations celebrate the delights of a summer night. (Rev: HBG 10/03; SLJ 6/03)

3380 Loomis, Christine. *In the Diner* (PS–1). Illus. by Nancy Poydar. 1994, Scholastic $14.95 (0-590-46716-6). 32pp. Lots of action words in short sentences are used to describe the hustle and bustle of a diner. (Rev: BL 4/15/94; SLJ 5/94)

3381 Loomis, Christine. *Rush Hour* (PS–2). Illus. by Mari Takabayashi. 1996, Houghton Mifflin $15.95 (0-395-69129-X). 32pp. Catchy rhymes and lively illustrations show what working parents do after they leave home in the morning. (Rev: BL 7/96; SLJ 9/96)

3382 Ludy, Mark. *The Grump* (2–4). Illus. by author. 2000, Green Pastures $16.95 (0-9664276-1-0). Lydia, a little deaf girl, is able to reform the village grump through small acts of kindness. (Rev: SLJ 2/01)

3383 Lukasewich, Lori. *The Night Fire* (PS–1). Illus. by author. 2001, Stoddart $15.95 (0-7737-3296-9). Rhyming couplets and bright illustrations follow fire fighters through a nighttime blaze. (Rev: SLJ 1/02)

3384 Lunn, Janet. *Come to the Fair* (K–2). Illus. by Gilles Pelletier. 1997, Tundra $15.95 (0-88776-409-6). The Martin family prepares for a visit to the county fair and spends an enjoyable day there. (Rev: HBG 3/98; SLJ 2/98)

3385 Lyon, George E. *Come a Tide* (PS–2). Illus. by Stephen Gammell. 1990, Orchard LB $16.99 (0-531-08454-X). 32pp. Grandma knows the tide will rise after a four-day deluge. (Rev: BL 2/1/90*; HB 3–4/90; SLJ 6/90*)

3386 Lyon, George E. *Who Came Down That Road?* (K–3). Illus. by Peter Catalanotto. 1992, Orchard paper $5.95 (0-531-07073-5). 32pp. The story of a road through history. (Rev: BL 9/1/92; SLJ 10/92)

3387 Lyon, George Ella. *Weaving the Rainbow* (K–2). Illus. by Stephanie Anderson. 2004, Simon & Schuster $15.95 (0-689-85169-3). 40pp. A well-illustrated, step-by-step picture-book story of an artist who raises sheep, shears the wool, processes it, and finally produces a woven work of art. (Rev: BL 2/15/04; SLJ 2/04)

3388 McAllister, Angela. *Be Good, Gordon* (PS–2). Illus. by Tim Archbold. 2002, Bloomsbury paper $8.95 (0-7475-5580-X). Young Gordon is taken aback when his new babysitter wants to do all the things he's forbidden to enjoy. (Rev: SLJ 1/03)

3389 Macaulay, David. *Shortcut* (K–4). Illus. 1995, Houghton Mifflin $15.95 (0-395-52436-9). 64pp. The lives of six people cross in a series of different stories. The author also uses this method of overlapping storytelling in *Black and White* (1990). (Rev: BCCB 9/95; BL 10/15/95; HB 3–4/95; SLJ 9/95*)

3390 McCarty, Peter. *Baby Steps* (PS–K). Illus. 2000, Holt $16.00 (0-8050-5953-9). 32pp. Using clear pencil illustrations, this book traces the growth of baby Suki from one day old to her first steps at one year old. (Rev: BCCB 10/00; BL 10/1/00; HBG 3/01; SLJ 10/00)

3391 McClements, George. *The Last Badge* (1–3). Illus. 2005, Hyperion $16.99 (0-7868-0956-6). 40pp. In this takeoff of Boy Scout achievements, Grizzly Scout Samuel is determined to get the much-sought-after Moon Frog Badge. (Rev: BL 5/15/05)

3392 McCoy, Glenn. *Penny Lee and Her TV* (PS–3). Illus. by author. 2002, Hyperion $15.99 (0-7868-0661-3). Once separated from her beloved TV, Penny Lee is fascinated by everything that's going on in the world. (Rev: BCCB 6/02; HBG 10/02; SLJ 6/02)

3393 McDonald, Megan. *The Potato Man* (K–3). Illus. by Ted Lewin. 1991, Orchard LB $16.99 (0-531-08514-7). 32pp. Grampa recalls the time when his neighborhood was regularly visited by peddlers, including the potato man. (Rev: BCCB 2/91; BL 1/15/91*; HB 5–6/91)

3394 McGee, Marni. *Wake Up, Me!* (PS–2). Illus. by Sam Williams. 2002, Simon & Schuster $17.00 (0-689-83163-3). 40pp. As a child goes through his morning rituals, he must continually remind the parts of his body to "wake up." (Rev: BL 6/1–15/02; HBG 10/02; SLJ 5/02)

3395 McGrath, Bob. *Uh Oh! Gotta Go! Potty Tales from Toddlers* (PS). Illus. by Shelley Dieterichs. 1996, Barron's $5.95 (0-8120-6564-6). About 20 children describe different potty experiences in this unusual book that will help in toilet training. (Rev: SLJ 1/97) [613]

3396 McGregor, Merideth. *Cowgirl* (PS–1). Illus. 1992, Walker LB $15.85 (0-8027-8171-3). 32pp. Simple, direct text describes the routines of life on a present-day ranch. (Rev: BCCB 2/93; BL 10/1/92; SLJ 12/92) [636.2]

3397 McKee, David. *The Conquerors* (K–3). Illus. by author. 2004, Handprint $16.95 (1-59354-078-7). The ruler of a large country conquers neighboring nations "so they can be like us" but fails to recognize that the culture sometimes flows in the other direction. (Rev: BCCB 1/05; HB 1–2/05; SLJ 2/05)

3398 MacKinnon, Debbie. *My Day* (PS–K). Illus. by Anthea Sieveking. 1999, Little, Brown $7.95 (0-316-64898-1). Everyday activities of children are pictured in this interactive book that uses tabs to show action. (Rev: BL 12/15/99)

3399 MacLean, Kole. *Even Firefighters Hug Their Moms* (PS–K). Illus. by Mike Reed. 2002, Dutton $15.99 (0-525-46996-6). 32pp. A young boy is so immersed in his elaborate role-playing (as fire fighter, police officer, doctor) that he's too busy to give his mother the requested hug. (Rev: BL 11/15/02; HBG 3/03; SLJ 10/02)

3400 McLerran, Alice. *Roxaboxen* (K–3). Illus. by Barbara Cooney. 1991, Lothrop LB $15.93 (0-688-07593-2). 32pp. The story of children in the desert who fashion an imaginary town. (Rev: BCCB 3/91*; BL 2/15/91*; HB 3–4/91; SLJ 2/91*)

3401 McMenemy, Sarah. *Jack's New Boat* (PS–K). Illus. 2005, Candlewick $15.99 (0-7636-2477-2). 32pp. With bright collage-and-gouache illustrations, this is the story of young Jack's new toy boat, which is lost almost as soon as he gets it but luckily is later found. (Rev: BL 5/1/05)

3402 McPhail, David. *Farm Morning* (PS–K). Illus. by author. 1985, Harcourt $15.95 (0-15-227299-2); paper $7.00 (0-15-227300-X). 32pp. A little girl and

her father do early-morning farm chores. (Rev: BCCB 12/85; BL 11/15/85; HB 11–12/85)

3403 McPhail, David. *The Teddy Bear* (PS–2). Illus. 2002, Holt $15.95 (0-8050-6414-1). 32pp. A young boy generously gives his teddy bear to a homeless man who has become attached to it. (Rev: BL 5/1/02*; HBG 10/02; SLJ 6/02)

3404 Maestro, Betsy. *Taxi: A Book of City Words* (PS–1). Illus. by Giulio Maestro. 1989, Houghton Mifflin paper $6.95 (0-395-54811-X). A taxi picks up and drops off people over the city and introduces new words. (Rev: BL 4/15/89; SLJ 4/89)

3405 Mahy, Margaret. *Down the Dragon's Tongue* (PS–3). Illus. by Patricia MacCarthy. 2000, Orchard $15.95 (0-531-30272-5). 32pp. When Mr. Prospero, a very proper gentleman, takes his twin children to a playground, he falls in love with riding the slide known as the Dragon's Tongue. (Rev: BL 7/00; HBG 3/01; SLJ 12/00)

3406 Maisner, Heather. *Time to See the Doctor* (PS). Illus. by Kristina Stephenson. Series: First Time Stories. 2004, Kingfisher paper $5.95 (0-7534-5737-7). 24pp. Although he has a fever and sore ears, Ben won't let the doctor near him until his older sister shows that it's OK. (Rev: BL 1/1–15/05)

3407 Manushkin, Fran. *Let's Go Riding in Our Strollers* (2–4). Illus. by Benrei Huang. 1993, Hyperion LB $14.49 (1-56282-391-4). 32pp. In a big city, two children enjoy all the excitement of being taken out for a ride by their mothers in their strollers. (Rev: BL 6/1–15/93)

3408 Martin, Bill, Jr., and John Archambault. *Here Are My Hands* (PS). Illus. by Ted Rand. 1987, Holt $15.95 (0-8050-0328-2). 32pp. Children indicate body parts, such as a boy pointing to a bandaged knee, which is for "falling down." (Rev: BL 7/87; SLJ 6–7/87)

3409 Martin, Bill, Jr., and John Archambault. *Listen to the Rain* (PS–2). Illus. by James Endicott. 1988, Holt $15.95 (0-8050-0682-6). 32pp. A rhyming story about rain with double-page watercolors. (Rev: SLJ 10/88)

3410 Martin, Bill, Jr., and John Archambault. *Up and Down on the Merry-Go-Round* (PS–1). Illus. by Ted Rand. 1988, Holt paper $4.95 (0-8050-1638-4). 32pp. A full-color merry-go-round whirls its delighted passengers in rhyming cadence. (Rev: BL 6/15/88; HB 7–8/88)

3411 Martin, David. *We've All Got Bellybuttons!* (PS–K). Illus. by Randy Cecil. 2005, Candlewick $15.99 (0-7636-1775-X). Cartoon animals explore their bodies and ask the reader to mimic their movements (clapping, closing eyes, opening mouths, and so forth). (Rev: BCCB 2/05; SLJ 2/05)

3412 Mathers, Petra. *Dodo Gets Married* (K–3). Illus. 2001, Simon & Schuster $16.00 (0-689-83018-1). 32pp. Captain Vince, who has lost a leg in a helicopter mission, is helped by his helicopter buddies to woo and win neighbor Dodo. (Rev: BL 4/15/01; HBG 10/01; SLJ 5/01)

3413 Mathers, Petra. *Lottie's New Beach Towel* (PS–2). Illus. 1998, Simon & Schuster $15.00 (0-689-81606-5). 32pp. Lottie shows her ingenuity when she puts her new beach towel to a variety of uses, including making an improvised sail and shaping it into a veil for a bride. (Rev: BL 6/1–15/98; HB 5–6/98; HBG 10/98; SLJ 6/98)

3414 Meadows, Michelle. *The Way the Storm Stops* (PS). Illus. by Rosanne Litzinger. 2003, Holt $16.95 (0-8050-6595-4). When a fierce thunderstorm frightens a young girl, her mother comforts and reassures her. (Rev: HBG 4/04; SLJ 12/03)

3415 Medearis, Angela Shelf. *Dancing with the Indians* (K–3). Illus. by Samuel Byrd. 1991, Holiday House LB $16.95 (0-8234-0893-0). 32pp. A young African American girl and her family attend a pow-wow of the Oklahoma Seminoles. (Rev: BCCB 11/91; BL 12/1/91; SLJ 1/92)

3416 Medearis, Angela Shelf. *Poppa's New Pants* (K–3). Illus. by John Ward. 1995, Holiday House LB $15.95 (0-8234-1155-9). 32pp. Shortening father's new pants to fit him causes a minor family crisis. (Rev: BCCB 7–8/95; BL 6/1–15/95; SLJ 6/95)

3417 Meyers, Susan. *Everywhere Babies* (PS). Illus. by Marla Frazee. 2001, Harcourt $16.00 (0-15-202226-0). 32pp. A charming representation of the first year of a baby's life with a rhyming text and watercolors showing babies being fed and playing games like peek-a-boo. (Rev: BL 3/1/01; HB 5–6/01*; HBG 10/01)

3418 Miller, Margaret. *Baby Food* (PS). Illus. 2000, Simon & Schuster $5.99 (0-689-83190-0). 14pp. This charming board book is filled with pictures of children eating. Toddlers and babies prepare for different activities in the companion work *Get Ready, Baby* (2000). (Rev: BL 7/00)

3419 Miller, Virginia. *On Your Potty!* (PS). Illus. 2000, Candlewick $5.99 (0-7636-1268-5). 18pp. At first Ba, a little bear, insists that he doesn't have to use the potty, but soon he changes his mind in this board book. (Rev: BL 11/15/00; HBG 3/01)

3420 Miranda, Anne. *Baby-Sit* (PS). Illus. by Dorothy Stott. 1990, Little, Brown $9.95 (0-316-57454-6). The activities of two children and their baby-sitter are portrayed. (Rev: SLJ 10/90)

3421 Miranda, Anne. *To Market, To Market* (K–2). Illus. by Janet Stevens. 1997, Harcourt $16.00 (0-15-200035-6). 36pp. A wildly funny picture book about market day misunderstandings. (Rev: BL 11/1/97; HB 11–12/97; HBG 3/98; SLJ 1/98)

3422 Mitchell, Lori. *Different Just Like Me* (K–3). Illus. 1999, Charlesbridge LB $15.95 (0-88106-975-2). 32pp. April's experiences during the week, when she meets new people, help her appreciate her much-anticipated weekend visit with her Grammie. (Rev: BL 3/1/99; HBG 10/99; SLJ 3/99)

3423 Moore, Lilian. *While You Were Chasing a Hat* (PS–K). Illus. by Rosanne Litzinger. 2001, HarperCollins $9.95 (0-694-01342-0). 24pp. This book explores all the things that the wind can do on a spring day such as causing a flag to furl and trees to bend. (Rev: BL 4/1/01; HBG 10/01; SLJ 1/02)

3424 Mora, Pat. *Maria Paints the Hills* (K–3). Illus. by Maria Hesch. 2002, Museum of New Mexico paper $9.95 (0-89013-410-3). 32pp. A simple story

and stunning folk-art illustrations capture the life of a little girl in New Mexico. (Rev: BL 12/15/02; HBG 3/03)

3425 Mora, Pat. *Tomas and the Library Lady* (PS–3). Illus. by Raul Colon. 1997, Knopf LB $18.99 (0-679-90401-8). 40pp. The story of a migrant boy who finds a special place that welcomes and helps him: the library. (Rev: BL 8/97; HBG 3/98; SLJ 10/97)

3426 Morris, Ann. *Hats, Hats, Hats* (PS–1). Illus. by Ken Heyman. 1989, Morrow paper $6.95 (0-688-12274-4). 32pp. A full-color display of varieties of hats. Also use: *Bread, Bread, Bread* (1989). (Rev: BL 4/15/89; SLJ 5/89)

3427 Morris, Ann. *Houses and Homes* (PS–1). Illus. 1992, Lothrop LB $16.93 (0-688-10169-0). 32pp. A fascinating look at how houses are built around the world. (Rev: BCCB 12/92; BL 10/1/92)

3428 Morton, Christine. *Picnic Farm* (PS–K). Illus. by Sarah Barringer. 1998, Holiday House LB $15.95 (0-8234-1332-2). After touring a farm, a little girl and boy have a picnic using some of its produce, like eggs, bread, butter, and fruit. (Rev: HBG 10/98; SLJ 3/98)

3429 Moss, Lloyd. *Our Marching Band* (PS–3). Illus. by Diana C. Bluthenthal. 2001, Penguin Putnam $15.99 (0-399-23335-0). 32pp. Silly rhyming text and exuberant cartoon watercolors portray a group of children practicing, and then performing, in a marching band. (Rev: BL 8/01; SLJ 8/01)

3430 Moss, Marissa. *Mel's Diner* (PS–3). Illus. 1994, Troll $13.95 (0-8167-3460-7). 32pp. Mabel, an African American child, loves to help out at her parents' diner. (Rev: BL 10/1/94; SLJ 12/94)

3431 Mould, Wendy. *Ants in My Pants* (PS–K). Illus. 2001, Clarion $15.00 (0-618-09640-X). 32pp. Jacob wants to play with his trains and comes up with inventive ways to delay getting dressed to go shopping. (Rev: BL 8/01; HBG 3/02; SLJ 9/01)

3432 Munsch, Robert. *Ribbon Rescue* (PS–1). Illus. by Eugenie Fernandes. 1999, Scholastic $11.95 (0-590-89012-3). 32pp. A Mohawk girl named Jillian is so helpful to all the members of a wedding party that they make her the flower girl. (Rev: BL 7/99; HBG 10/99; SLJ 6/99)

3433 Nash, Margaret. *Secret in the Mist* (PS–2). Illus. by Stephen Lambert. 1999, Sterling $14.95 (1-899607-98-6). 32pp. A young boy secretly plants a seed and watches it grow both day and night. Finally, his secret is revealed when a beautiful sunflower appears. (Rev: BL 6/1–15/99; SLJ 9/99)

3434 Nikola-Lisa, W. *America: My Land, Your Land, Our Land* (K–3). Illus. 1997, Lee & Low $15.95 (1-880000-37-7). 32pp. A handsome picture book that shows many of the contrasts that are present in the United States. (Rev: BL 9/1/97; SLJ 7/97)

3435 Nikola-Lisa, W. *Summer Sun Risin'* (PS–1). Illus. by Don Tate. 2002, Lee & Low $16.95 (1-58430-034-5). A gentle story of a young African American boy's busy day on the farm — looking after the animals, plowing, picnicking, fishing, and bedtime stories. (Rev: HBG 10/02; SLJ 5/02)

3436 Noble, Sheilagh. *More!* (PS). Illus. 2000, Zero to Ten $9.95 (1-84089-127-0). 24pp. A sweet story about a mother and a daughter enjoying a walk in the park. (Rev: BL 1/1–15/01)

3437 Noonan, Julia. *Bath Day* (PS). Illus. by author. Series: Puppy and Me. 2000, Scholastic $6.99 (0-439-11492-6). A slight story about a little girl who plays in her wading pool with her dog. Also use *Breakfast Time* (2000). (Rev: HBG 10/00; SLJ 8/00)

3438 Norling, Beth. *Little School* (PS). Illus. by author. 2003, Kane/Miller $15.95 (1-929132-42-5). Norling traces 20 ethnically diverse preschoolers through their day in this inventive and enthralling volume. (Rev: SLJ 6/03)

3439 Nunes, Susan. *The Last Dragon* (PS–3). Illus. by Chris K. Soentpiet. 1995, Clarion $15.00 (0-395-67020-9). 32pp. A Chinese American boy named Peter gets everyone in Chinatown to help him repair a ten-man dragon he has purchased. (Rev: BL 5/1/95; SLJ 5/95)

3440 Nye, Naomi Shihab. *Baby Radar* (PS). Illus. by Nancy Carpenter. 2003, Greenwillow LB $16.89 (0-688-15949-4). The world is seen from the low-down viewpoint of a toddler in a stroller on a fine fall day. (Rev: HBG 4/04; SLJ 9/03)

3441 O'Book, Irene. *Maybe My Baby* (PS). Photos by Paula Hible. 1998, HarperCollins $5.95 (0-694-00872-9). A simple board book in which babies wear a series of job-related hats to help toddlers identify different careers. (Rev: SLJ 6/98)

3442 O'Connell, Rebecca. *The Baby Goes Beep* (PS). Illus. by Ken Wilson-Max. 2003, Millbrook LB $21.90 (0-7613-2867-X). A busy toddler learns about various sounds as he goes about his daily routines. (Rev: BCCB 10/03; BL 11/1/03; HB 1–2/04; HBG 4/04; SLJ 12/03)

3443 O'Garden, Irene. *The Scrubbly-Bubbly Car Wash* (PS–2). Illus. by Cynthia Jabar. 2003, HarperCollins LB $16.89 (0-06-029486-8). A bouncing rhyme takes a father and two children on a ride through the car wash. (Rev: BCCB 3/03; BL 4/1/03; HBG 4/04; SLJ 3/03)

3444 Ohi, Ruth. *Pants Off First!* (PS). Illus. Series: Early Bird Boardbook. 2001, Fitzhenry & Whiteside $6.95 (1-55041-667-7). 16pp. As a little boy undresses, he puts his clothes on his pets in this humorous story that ends with a twist. (Rev: BL 7/01)

3445 O'Neill, Alexis. *Estela's Swap* (K–3). Illus. by Enrique O. Sanchez. 2002, Lee & Low $16.95 (1-58430-044-2). 32pp. Colorful illustrations accompany this story of Estela, a Hispanic girl who wants to sell a music box to earn money for dance lessons. (Rev: BL 12/15/02; HBG 3/03; SLJ 10/02)

3446 Osborne, Mary Pope. *Rocking Horse Christmas* (PS–3). Illus. by Ned Bittinger. 1997, Scholastic $15.95 (0-590-92955-0). 32pp. A young boy has many adventures on his favorite toy, a wooden rocking horse, but in time he outgrows it. (Rev: BL 10/1/97; HBG 3/98; SLJ 10/97)

3447 Oxenbury, Helen. *Pig Tale* (K–2). Illus. 2005, Simon & Schuster $16.95 (1-4169-0277-5). 32pp. Two pigs, Briggs and his wife Bertha, are thrilled

when they become rich but soon find that money isn't everything after all. (Rev: BL 5/15/05)

3448 Oxenbury, Helen. *Tom and Pippo Go Shopping* (PS). Illus. by author. 1989, Macmillan paper $5.95 (0-689-71278-2). 14pp. The toddler and his toy monkey on a new adventure. Also use: *Tom and Pippo in the Garden; Tom and Pippo See the Moon; Tom and Pippo's Day* (all 1989). (Rev: BL 3/15/89; HB 5–6/89)

3449 Page, Debra. *Orcas Around Me: My Alaskan Summer* (K–3). Illus. by Leslie Bowman. 1997, Whitman LB $15.95 (0-8075-6137-1). 40pp. A boy observes the wildlife of the north Pacific coast while he helps on the salmon boats operated by his parents. (Rev: BL 8/97; HBG 3/98; SLJ 9/97) [639.2]

3450 Pallotta, Jerry. *Going Lobstering* (PS–2). Illus. by Rob Bolster. 1990, Charlesbridge $16.95 (0-88106-475-0); paper $7.95 (0-88106-474-2). 32pp. A boy and his sister spend a fascinating day on a lobster boat. (Rev: BL 12/1/90)

3451 Parr, Todd. *The Feel Good Book* (PS–2). Illus. by author. 2002, Little, Brown $14.95 (0-316-07206-0). A list of things that make you feel good is illustrated with lively art. (Rev: HBG 3/03; SLJ 10/02)

3452 Parr, Todd. *It's Okay to Be Different* (PS–2). Illus. by author. 2001, Little, Brown $14.95 (0-316-66603-3). Readers learn that it's OK to be adopted, to wear glasses, to have an unusual nose, to lose a race — and to have a pet worm. (Rev: HBG 3/02; SLJ 10/01)

3453 Patricelli, Leslie. *Blankie* (PS). 2005, Candlewick $6.99 (0-7636-2363-6). 24pp. A toddler-friendly board book about a child and a much-loved blanket. (Rev: BL 4/1/05)

3454 Paul, Ann W. *Shadows Are About* (PS–2). Illus. by Mark Graham. 1992, Scholastic paper $13.95 (0-590-44842-0). 32pp. A brother and sister accompanied by their shadows explore the world around them. (Rev: BL 7/92; SLJ 4/92)

3455 Perez, Amada Irma. *My Very Own Room / Mi propio cuartito* (1–3). Illus. by Maya Christina Gonzalez. 2000, Children's Book Pr. $15.95 (0-89239-164-2). 32pp. A bilingual story about a young Mexican American girl who is looking for a little privacy in her crowded home. (Rev: BCCB 11/00; BL 7/00; HB 11–12/00; HBG 3/01; SLJ 8/00)

3456 Pilkey, Dav. *The Paperboy* (PS–1). Illus. 1996, Orchard LB $15.99 (0-531-08856-1). 32pp. This book reflects the thoughts of a young boy when he makes early-morning rounds on his paper route with his dog. (Rev: BCCB 3/96; BL 3/1/96*; HB 7–8/96; SLJ 3/96*)

3457 Pinkney, Andrea Davis. *Fishing Day* (PS–2). Illus. by Shane W. Evans. 2003, Hyperion LB $16.49 (0-7868-2614-2). In the pre-civil rights South, African American Reenie shares her fishing secrets with a white boy who's having little luck. (Rev: BCCB 1/04; BL 11/15/03; HBG 4/04; SLJ 12/03)

3458 Pinkney, Sandra L. *Shades of Black: A Celebration of Our Children* (PS–2). Illus. by Myles C. Pinkney. 2000, Scholastic $14.95 (0-439-14892-8).

40pp. This book of beautiful photographs shows children whose skin is of various shades of black and whose eyes and hair also show a diversity. (Rev: BCCB 1/01; BL 11/1/00; HBG 3/01; SLJ 12/00)

3459 Piumini, Roberto. *Doctor Me Di Cin* (2–4). Illus. by Piet Grobler. 2001, Front Street $15.95 (1-886910-67-7). A crafty Chinese doctor eventually succeeds in luring a pallid prince outside to get some fresh air. (Rev: HBG 3/02; SLJ 10/01)

3460 Plourde, Lynn. *Snow Day* (PS–1). Illus. by Hideko Takahashi. 2001, Simon & Schuster $16.00 (0-689-82600-1). There's plenty of onomatopoeia in this celebration of the activities that take place on a snowy day. (Rev: HBG 10/02; SLJ 1/02)

3461 Pocock, Rita. *Annabelle and the Big Slide* (PS). Illus. 1989, Harcourt $10.95 (0-15-200407-6). 32pp. Annabelle summons up her courage to climb the ladder and zoom down the playground slide. (Rev: BL 1/1/90; HB 11–12/89; SLJ 12/89)

3462 Polacco, Patricia. *Aunt Chip and the Great Triple Creek Dam Affair* (K–3). Illus. 1996, Penguin Putnam $15.95 (0-399-22943-4). 32pp. Because of television, a whole town forgets how to read until Aunt Chip, the town librarian, intervenes. (Rev: BCCB 6/96; BL 4/15/96; SLJ 5/96*)

3463 Pollak, Barbara. *Our Community Garden* (PS–3). Illus. by author. 2004, Beyond Words $15.95 (1-58270-109-1). A group of children tend the vegetables in their plots and enjoy a feast at harvest time. (Rev: SLJ 11/04)

3464 Prosek, James. *A Good Day's Fishing* (2–4). Illus. 2004, Simon & Schuster $15.95 (0-689-85327-0). 40pp. A child sorts through his fishing tackle, describing the value of various pieces of equipment and what they can catch. (Rev: BL 2/15/04; SLJ 5/04)

3465 Purmell, Ann. *Apple Cider Making Days* (PS–2). Illus. by Joanne Friar. 2002, Millbrook LB $21.90 (0-7613-2364-3). 32pp. Making cider is a family activity in this colorful book with detailed illustrations of the process. (Rev: BL 12/1/02; HBG 3/03; SLJ 1/03)

3466 Quinsey, Mary Beth. *Why Does That Man Have Such a Big Nose?* (PS–1). Illus. by Wilson Chan. 1986, Parenting LB $16.95 (0-943990-25-4); paper $5.95 (0-943990-24-6). 32pp. Explaining some of the physical differences among people and how or why they happen. (Rev: BL 1/1/87; SLJ 12/86)

3467 Ransom, Candice. *The Big Green Pocketbook* (PS–1). Illus. by Felicia Bond. 1993, HarperCollins LB $16.89 (0-06-020849-X). 32pp. At every stop during a day of errands with her mother, a little girl is given something for her empty pocketbook. (Rev: BL 7/93; SLJ 7/93)

3468 Raschka, Chris. *Ring! Yo?* (PS–2). Illus. 2000, DK $15.95 (0-7894-2614-5). 38pp. A boy on the phone reacts in various ways to what he hears during a telephone conversation and the reader must use his imagination to guess what is causing these strange emotional reactions. At the end, the author suggests what the other person might have said.

(Rev: BCCB 4/00; BL 3/15/00*; HB 3–4/00; HBG 10/00; SLJ 5/00)

3469 Rau, Dana Meachen. *Ways to Go* (K–1). Illus. by Jane Conteh-Morgan. 2001, Compass Point LB $18.60 (0-7565-0071-0). 24pp. Minimal text and appealing illustrations portray a choice of modes of transport. (Rev: SLJ 10/01) [388]

3470 Ray, Mary L. *Red Rubber Boot Day* (PS). Illus. by Lauren Stringer. 2000, Harcourt $16.00 (0-15-213756-4). 32pp. Told from a child's point of view, this book gives details on the indoor and outdoor activities that are possible on a rainy day. (Rev: BL 3/15/00; HBG 10/00; SLJ 4/00)

3471 Reichert, Amy. *While Mama Had a Quick Little Chat* (K–3). Illus. by Alexandra Boiger. 2005, Simon & Schuster $15.95 (0-689-85170-7). 40pp. Rose's mother is on the phone for ages, and Rose, who is supposed to be getting ready for bed, is unable to stop hordes of visitors from taking over their home. (Rev: BL 6/1–15/05)

3472 Rice, David L. *Because Brian Hugged His Mother* (PS–3). Illus. by K. Dyble Thompson. 1999, Dawn $16.95 (1-883220-90-4); paper $7.95 (1-883220-89-0). 32pp. The hug that Brian gives his mother produces a string of kindnesses throughout the community. (Rev: BL 8/99; HBG 10/99)

3473 Richmond, Marianne. *Hooray for You! A Celebration of "You-ness"* (PS–2). Illus. by author. 2001, Waldman $15.95 (0-931674-44-1). Differences in cultures, characteristics, and goals are all shown to be of value. (Rev: HBG 3/02; SLJ 1/02)

3474 Robbins, Ken. *Make Me a Peanut Butter Sandwich (and a Glass of Milk)* (PS–3). Illus. 1992, Scholastic $14.95 (0-590-43550-7). 32pp. Photos and minimal text tell how a favorite snack for children gets to the table. (Rev: BCCB 10/92; BL 9/1/92) [641]

3475 Roberts, Bethany. *The Wind's Garden* (PS–1). Illus. by Melanie Hope Greenberg. 2001, Holt $15.95 (0-8050-6367-6). 32pp. A little girl and the wind each plant their gardens, and they grow in their different ways. (Rev: BL 6/1–15/01; HBG 10/01; SLJ 5/01)

3476 Rockwell, Anne. *Long Ago Yesterday* (PS–K). Illus. 1999, Greenwillow $16.00 (0-688-14411-X). 24pp. Ten two-page short stories about the everyday life experiences of children. (Rev: BL 11/15/99; HBG 3/00; SLJ 10/99)

3477 Roddie, Shen. *Toes Are to Tickle* (PS). Illus. by Kady M. Denton. 1997, Tricycle $13.95 (1-883672-49-X). 24pp. A playful picture book that gives pleasant definitions to common articles, like "A tree is to hide behind." (Rev: BL 6/1–15/97; SLJ 9/97)

3478 Rogers, Paul. *Tiny* (K–3). Illus. by Korky Paul. 2002, Kane paper $7.95 (1-929132-26-3). A twist on the house, street, town, country, continent progression that moves out from a flea to a star. (Rev: SLJ 8/02)

3479 Rollings, Susan. *New Shoes, Red Shoes* (PS–K). Illus. 2000, Orchard $15.95 (0-531-30268-7). 32pp. Bouncy rhymes are used in this slight story about the fun of going to pick out a new pair of shoes. (Rev: BL 2/1/00; HBG 10/00; SLJ 5/00)

3480 Roop, Peter, and Connie Roop. *A City Album* (2–3). Illus. Series: Long Ago and Today. 1998, Heinemann LB $13.95 (1-57572-600-9). 24pp. Using old and new photographs, this work compares city life today, when people ride subway trains, buses, cars, and bicycles, with city life a century ago, when people walked or rode horses. (Rev: BL 12/15/98) [307.76]

3481 Roop, Peter, and Connie Roop. *A School Album* (2–3). Illus. 1998, Heinemann LB $13.95 (1-57572-603-3). 24pp. Using double-page spreads and historic and modern photos, schools of 100 years ago are compared to schools today. (Rev: BL 12/15/98) [372.97]

3482 Roosa, Karen. *Beach Day* (PS–K). Illus. by Maggie Smith. 2001, Clarion $15.00 (0-618-02923-0). 32pp. Lively art and detailed illustrations depict a day at the beach for a group of multicultural children. (Rev: BL 5/1/01; HBG 10/01; SLJ 4/01)

3483 Rose, Emma. *Ballet Magic: A Pop-up Book* (PS–1). Illus. by Jan Palmer. 1996, Scholastic $12.95 (0-590-26242-4). 12pp. Various ballet positions and movements are shown in this pop-up book. (Rev: BL 12/15/96)

3484 Rosenberg, Liz. *Eli's Night-Light* (PS–1). Illus. by Joanna Yardley. 2001, Scholastic $15.95 (0-531-30316-0). 32pp. When his light burns out, a brave little boy appreciates the glow from the clock, headlights passing, and above all the shining stars. (Rev: BL 6/1–15/01; HBG 10/01; SLJ 8/01)

3485 Rosenberry, Vera. *Run, Jump, Whiz, Splash* (PS–2). Illus. by author. 1999, Holiday House $15.95 (0-8234-1378-0). A simple but lyrical account of the activities of two children throughout the seasons of a year. (Rev: HBG 3/00; SLJ 9/99)

3486 Rosenberry, Vera. *Vera Goes to the Dentist* (PS–3). Illus. 2002, Holt $16.95 (0-8050-6668-3). 32pp. Vera is so frightened by her first trip to the dentist that she runs out of the office, but she is finally caught and becomes calm enough to finish the examination. (Rev: BL 4/1/02; HBG 10/02; SLJ 5/02)

3487 Rosenberry, Vera. *Vera Rides a Bike* (K–2). Illus. 2004, Holt $16.95 (0-8050-7125-3). 32pp. Vera makes the daunting transition from a tricycle to a two-wheeler. (Rev: BL 5/15/04; HB 5–6/04; SLJ 7/04)

3488 Rosenberry, Vera. *When Vera Was Sick* (PS–K). Illus. 1998, Holt $15.95 (0-8050-5405-7). 24pp. This book chronicles all the problems of being sick and confined to one's room until the magical day when you're well again. (Rev: BCCB 1/99; BL 11/15/98; HB 9–10/98; HBG 3/99; SLJ 12/98)

3489 Rosenthal, Amy Krouse. *Little Pea* (PS–2). Illus. by Jen Corace. 2005, Chronicle $12.95 (0-8118-4658-X). Little Pea is a happy child until it comes to meals, when he struggles through the candy courses waiting with anticipation for the dessert of spinach. (Rev: BL 3/1/04; SLJ 5/05)

3490 Ross, Tony. *Wash Your Hands!* (PS–2). Illus. by author. 2000, Kane/Miller paper $6.95 (1-929132-01-8). A young girl learns that it is important to wash your hands after playing and before eating food if you want to stay healthy and avoid bad germs. (Rev: HBG 3/01; SLJ 3/01)

3491 Rotner, Shelley, and Sheila Kelly. *Feeling Thankful* (PS–2). Illus. 2000, Millbrook LB $20.90 (0-7613-1918-2). 24pp. This simple photo-essay enumerates the many things, such as a family or a pet, for which children can be thankful. (Rev: BL 12/1/00; HBG 3/01; SLJ 12/00) [179]

3492 Rotner, Shelley, and Ken Kreisler. *Citybook* (PS–K). Illus. by Shelley Rotner. 1994, Orchard LB $16.99 (0-531-08687-9). 32pp. Ken explains why he loves visiting the city in this picture book filled with color photos of big-city life and sights. (Rev: BL 2/15/94; HB 5–6/94; SLJ 3/94)

3493 Rounds, Glen. *Cowboys* (PS–1). Illus. 1991, Holiday House LB $16.95 (0-8234-0867-1). 32pp. A day in the life of a cowboy is described in sparse text and shown in complementary illustrations. (Rev: BCCB 4/91; BL 6/1/91; SLJ 5/91)

3494 Rubel, Nicole. *No More Vegetables!* (K–2). Illus. 2002, Farrar $16.00 (0-374-36362-5). 32pp. Picky eater Ruthie boycotts all vegetables until her mother asks her to help in the garden. (Rev: BL 12/15/02; HBG 3/03; SLJ 8/02)

3495 Russell, Barbara Timberlake. *The Remembering Stone* (PS–2). Illus. by Claire B. Cotts. 2004, Farrar $16.00 (0-374-36242-4). 32pp. Rich illustrations heighten the appeal of this story of young Ana, who dreams of returning to her family's native Costa Rica and who is herself surrounded by others with dreams. (Rev: BL 2/15/04; SLJ 4/04)

3496 Russell, Joan Plummer. *Aero and Officer Mike: Police Partners* (2–4). Illus. by Kris Turner Sinnenberg. 2001, Boyds Mills $15.95 (1-56397-931-4). 32pp. Aero is Officer Mike's police dog, and the two of them are shown working together in this book of photographs and text. (Rev: BL 9/15/01; HBG 3/02; SLJ 12/01) [363.2]

3497 Russo, Marisabina. *Mama Talks Too Much* (PS–2). Illus. 1999, Greenwillow $16.00 (0-688-16411-0). 32pp. On the way to the supermarket, Celeste is impatient with her mother's stops to chat with friends until Celeste meets Mrs. Castro's new puppy, Jake. (Rev: BCCB 9/99; BL 12/1/99; HBG 3/00; SLJ 9/99)

3498 Ruurs, Margriet. *When We Go Camping* (PS–3). Illus. by Andrew Kiss. 2001, Tundra $14.95 (0-88776-476-2). 32pp. The joys of camping are brought to life in this detailed, realistically illustrated story of siblings on a camping trip with their parents. (Rev: BL 12/15/01; HBG 10/01; SLJ 7/01)

3499 Ryan, Pam Munoz. *Mud Is Cake* (PS–1). Illus. by David McPhail. 2002, Hyperion $15.99 (0-7868-0501-3). A brother and sister enjoy playful fantasies, such as a stick becoming a wand and a porch becoming a stage. (Rev: BL 6/1–15/02; HBG 10/02; SLJ 5/02)

3500 Rylant, Cynthia. *Appalachia: The Voices of Sleeping Birds* (PS–3). Illus. by Barry Moser. 1991, Harcourt $17.00 (0-15-201605-8). 32pp. A loving book in simple text and art about remembering Appalachia. (Rev: BCCB 6/91; BL 2/1/91*; HB 9–10/91*; SLJ 4/91*) [974]

3501 Rylant, Cynthia. *Let's Go Home: The Wonderful Things About a House* (PS–3). Illus. by Wendy A. Halperin. 2002, Simon & Schuster $16.00 (0-689-82326-6). 32pp. A delightful look at different types of houses and their interiors. (Rev: BL 4/15/02*; HBG 10/02; SLJ 6/02) [392.3]

3502 Rylant, Cynthia. *Mr. Griggs' Work* (PS–2). Illus. by Julie Downing. 1989, Orchard paper $6.95 (0-531-07037-9). 32pp. Mr. Griggs, who works at the post office, loves his job. (Rev: BCCB 2/89; BL 2/1/89; HB 3–4/89)

3503 Sabuda, Robert. *Cookie Count: A Tasty Pop-Up* (PS–1). Illus. 1997, Simon & Schuster $19.95 (0-689-81191-8). 12pp. Pop-ups involving food are featured in this book, including an amazing gingerbread house. (Rev: BL 12/15/97; HBG 10/98)

3504 Salat, Cristina. *Peanut's Emergency* (K–2). Illus. by Tammie Lyon. 2002, Charlesbridge $16.95 (1-57091-440-0); paper $6.95 (1-57091-441-9). 32pp. Peanut seeks help when her mother is late picking her up from school in this story about what to do in an "emergency." (Rev: BL 9/15/02; HBG 3/03)

3505 Sayre, April Pulley. *It's My City! A Singing Map* (PS–1). Illus. by Denis Roche. 2001, Greenwillow LB $15.89 (0-688-16916-3). A little girl doesn't need directions because she has made up her own onomatopoeic song that describes the route. (Rev: HB 11–12/01; HBG 3/02; SLJ 10/01)

3506 Schaap, Martine. *Mop and the Birthday Picnic* (PS–1). Illus. by Alex de Wolf. Series: Mop and Family. 2001, McGraw-Hill $12.95 (1-57768-882-1). 30pp. Mop the dog eats all the hot dogs at the birthday party for twins Julie and Justin. They also have a good time in *Mop's Mountain Adventure* (2000). (Rev: HBG 10/01; SLJ 10/01)

3507 Schaefer, Carole Lexa. *Someone Says* (PS–K). Illus. by Pierr Morgan. 2003, Viking $15.99 (0-670-03664-1). A group of young schoolchildren enjoy themselves with creative play. (Rev: HBG 4/04; SLJ 11/03)

3508 Schertle, Alice. *All You Need for a Snowman* (PS–K). Illus. by Barbara Lavallee. 2002, Harcourt $16.00 (0-15-200789-X). 32pp. As the text describes the essentials for making a successful snowman, a group of children are shown building two gigantic examples. (Rev: BCCB 1/03; BL 11/15/02; HB 11–12/02; HBG 3/03; SLJ 12/02)

3509 Schick, Eleanor. *I Am: I Am a Dancer* (PS–1). Illus. by author. 2002, Marshall Cavendish $15.95 (0-7614-5097-1). A girl in a leotard imitates animals, clouds, and a dreamer. (Rev: HBG 10/02; SLJ 1/03)

3510 Schneider, Christine M. *Saxophone Sam and His Snazzy Jazz Band* (PS–3). Illus. 2002, Walker LB $17.85 (0-8027-8810-6). 32pp. A tuneful tale with a catchy beat and inventive illustrations about siblings who track a jazz tune through their house until they find the source in the attic. (Rev: BL 12/1/02; HBG 3/03; SLJ 11/02)

3511 Schotter, Roni. *Captain Bob Sets Sail* (PS–2). Illus. by Joe Cepeda. 2000, Simon & Schuster $16.00 (0-689-82081-X). 32pp. A boy named Captain Bob turns his bath into an exciting affair on the Soapy Seas with his mother acting as the great Sea Hand. (Rev: BCCB 9/00; BL 7/00; HBG 10/00; SLJ 5/00)

3512 Schotter, Roni. *Captain Bob Takes Flight* (K–2). Illus. by Joe Cepeda. 2003, Simon & Schuster $15.95 (0-689-83388-1). 32pp. Cleaning his room becomes quite enjoyable when Bob pretends he's a pilot and his mother cooperatively acts as the control tower. (Rev: BL 3/15/03; HBG 10/03; SLJ 5/03)

3513 Schotter, Roni. *Dreamland* (K–2). Illus. by Kevin Hawkes. 1996, Orchard LB $16.99 (0-531-08858-8). 40pp. Theo's fanciful drawings of strange inventions become real when his uncle creates an amusement park. (Rev: BL 4/1/96; SLJ 4/96*)

3514 Schotter, Roni. *Nothing Ever Happens on 90th Street* (PS–2). Illus. by Kyrsten Brooker. 1997, Orchard LB $17.99 (0-531-08886-3). 32pp. Eva's writing assignment changes how her neighborhood acts and interacts. (Rev: BL 3/1/97; SLJ 3/97*)

3515 Schwartz, Amy. *A Glorious Day* (PS). Illus. by author. 2004, Simon & Schuster $16.95 (0-689-84802-1). Readers watch the various residents of a city apartment building going about their daily life. (Rev: HB 5–6/04; SLJ 4/04)

3516 Schwartz, Amy. *Some Babies* (PS–K). Illus. 2000, Orchard $15.95 (0-531-30287-3). 32pp. A mother obliges when her child wants to hear about other babies by telling stories about activities like playing on a slide or sitting in strollers. (Rev: BL 12/15/00; HB 9–10/00; HBG 3/01; SLJ 10/00)

3517 Schwartz, Amy. *What James Likes Best* (PS). Illus. 2003, Simon & Schuster $16.95 (0-689-84059-4). 32pp. This oversize book contains four stories about preschooler James, who likes expeditions. (Rev: BCCB 3/03; BL 3/1/03*; HB 5–6/03; HBG 10/03; SLJ 3/03)

3518 Scott, Ann H. *Brave as a Mountain Lion* (K–3). Illus. by Glo Coalson. 1996, Clarion $14.95 (0-395-66760-7). 32pp. Spider, a Shoshone boy, gets help from his family to conquer his fears, but it is from watching a real spider that he gets real help. (Rev: BCCB 2/96; BL 3/15/96; SLJ 4/96)

3519 Scrimger, Richard. *Princess Bun Bun* (PS–K). Illus. by Gillian Johnson. 2002, Tundra $12.95 (0-88776-543-2). Winifred and her family are off to visit Uncle Dave in the Castle Apartments, a name that conjures moats and monsters until Uncle Dave sets them right. (Rev: HBG 10/02; SLJ 7/02)

3520 Sears, William, et al. *You Can Go to the Potty* (PS). Illus. by Renee W. Andriani. 2002, Little, Brown $12.95 (0-316-78888-0). 32pp. This introduction to toilet training is designed for adults to read with children, combining text for the young with sidebars for the adults. (Rev: BL 11/15/02; HBG 3/03; SLJ 11/02)

3521 Seuss, Dr. *Oh, the Places You'll Go!* (PS–3). Illus. 1990, Random LB $17.99 (0-679-90527-8). This book of advice for youngsters tells them that in spite of problems, they can succeed. (Rev: BL 1/1/90*; SLJ 3/90)

3522 Seymour, Tres. *The Smash-up Crash-up Derby* (K–2). Illus. by S. D. Schindler. 1995, Orchard LB $16.99 (0-531-08731-X). 32pp. A boy and members of his family enjoy the fall fair, particularly the demolition derby. (Rev: BCCB 3/95; BL 2/1/95; SLJ 3/95)

3523 Shannon, Terry Miller, and Timothy Warner. *Tub Toys* (PS–1). Illus. by Lee Calderon. 2002, Tricycle $14.95 (1-58246-066-3). A little boy gets ready for bath time by collecting all his toys. (Rev: HBG 3/03; SLJ 2/03)

3524 Sharratt, Nick, and Stephen Tucker. *The Time It Took Tom* (PS–2). Illus. by Nick Sharratt. 2000, Little Tiger $14.95 (1-888444-63-0). It takes three weeks to restore the living room to normal after Tom goes wild with a can of red paint. (Rev: HBG 10/00; SLJ 3/00)

3525 Shea, Pegi Deitz. *I See Me!* (PS). Illus. by Lucia Washburn. Series: Growing Tree. 2000, HarperCollins $7.95 (0-694-01278-5). 16pp. In this board book for the very young, a toddler notices her reflection in a mirror, on the back of a metal spoon, on the television screen, and in her mother's sunglasses. (Rev: BL 5/15/00)

3526 Shelby, Anne. *Homeplace* (PS–2). Illus. by Wendy A. Halperin. 1995, Orchard LB $17.99 (0-531-08732-8). 32pp. A grandmother tells her grandchild about the history of her family and the old homestead. (Rev: BCCB 5/95; BL 2/15/95; SLJ 4/95*)

3527 Shelby, Anne. *The Someday House* (PS–2). Illus. by Rosanne Litzinger. 1996, Orchard LB $16.99 (0-531-08860-X). 32pp. Three children imagine living in a variety of different houses and settings. (Rev: BL 3/1/96; SLJ 4/96)

3528 Shulevitz, Uri. *Snow* (PS). Illus. 1998, Farrar $16.00 (0-374-37092-3). 32pp. A young child is able to see the beauty in a single snowflake whereas the more sophisticated adults cannot. (Rev: BCCB 1/99; BL 10/15/98*; HB 1–2/99; HBG 3/99; SLJ 12/98)

3529 Siddals, Mary M. *Millions of Snowflakes* (PS). Illus. by Elizabeth Sayles. 1998, Clarion $13.00 (0-395-71531-8). 25pp. Using cool pastel drawings and a spare, rhyming text, this playful story describes all the things one can do in the snow, such as making angels and catching snowflakes. (Rev: BL 11/1/98; HBG 3/99; SLJ 9/98)

3530 Siegelson, Kim L. *Dancing the Ring Shout!* (PS–3). Illus. by Lisa Cohen. 2003, Hyperion $15.99 (0-7868-0453-X). Toby, an African American boy in the rural South, isn't sure what he can contribute to the traditional call-and-response ring shout. (Rev: BL 12/1/03; HBG 4/04; SLJ 12/03)

3531 Simon, Seymour. *Fighting Fires* (PS–2). Illus. Series: SeeMore Readers. 2002, North-South $13.95 (1-58717-168-6); paper $3.95 (1-58717-169-4). 32pp. An eye-catching book for preschoolers and early readers about fire fighters and their equipment. (Rev: BL 8/02; HBG 3/03; SLJ 7/02) [628.9]

3532 Singer, Marilyn. *Block Party Today!* (K–2). Illus. by Stephanie Roth. 2004, Knopf LB $18.99 (0-375-92216-4). 32pp. After a jump rope dispute, the lure of the block party in her Brooklyn neighborhood prompts Lola to make up with her friends. (Rev: BL 5/15/04; SLJ 5/04)

3533 Singer, Marilyn. *Fred's Bed* (PS). Illus. by JoAnn Adinolfi. 2001, HarperCollins $9.95 (0-694-01451-6). Fred wants a new bed and his teasing mother offers him all kinds of choices — an eagle's nest, a rabbit hole, and so forth. (Rev: HBG 10/01; SLJ 12/01)

3534 Siomades, Lorianne. *A Place to Bloom* (PS). Illus. by author. 1997, Boyds Mills $7.95 (1-56397-656-0). A collection of random thoughts about attitudes, likes, dislikes, and emotions, all expressed in catchy rhymes. (Rev: HBG 3/98; SLJ 9/97)

3535 Skultety, Nancy. *From Here to Here* (PS–K). Illus. by Tammie Lyon. 2005, Boyds Mills $15.95 (1-59078-092-2). 32pp. Farmer Dibble asks for a new road and he gets just that, with its construction and all the equipment involved well documented. (Rev: BL 5/15/05; SLJ 5/05)

3536 Slegers, Liesbet. *Kevin Goes to School* (PS). Illus. by author. 2002, Kane $7.95 (1-929132-31-X). A small-format book in which a toddler deals in simple language with his first day at school. Also use *Kevin Goes to the Hospital*, *Kevin Spends the Night*, and *Kevin Takes a Trip*. (Rev: HBG 3/03; SLJ 3/03)

3537 Smith, Cynthia Leitich. *Jingle Dancer* (PS–2). Illus. by Cornelius Van Wright and Ying-hwa Hu. 2000, Morrow LB $15.89 (0-688-16242-8). 32pp. Jenna, a Native American girl, gathers metal jingles to sew onto her dress so she can make pleasant sounds when she dances in the next powwow. (Rev: BCCB 7–8/00; BL 5/15/00; HBG 10/00; SLJ 7/00)

3538 Smith, Dana Kessimakis. *A Brave Spaceboy* (PS–2). Illus. by Laura Freeman. 2005, Hyperion $15.99 (0-7868-0933-7). On moving day, a boy and his younger sibling invest an empty box with spaceship powers and imagine themselves exploring the stars. (Rev: BL 3/1/04; HB 3–4/04; SLJ 5/05)

3539 Spetter, Jung-Hee. *Lily and Trooper's Fall* (PS–K). Illus. 1999, Front Street $8.95 (1-886910-38-3). 32pp. Lily and her fun-loving dog Trooper enjoy such fall activities as jumping in a pile of leaves. Also use *Lily and Trooper's Winter* (1999). (Rev: BL 12/1/99; HBG 3/00; SLJ 10/99)

3540 Spier, Peter. *People* (2–4). Illus. by author. 1980, Doubleday $16.95 (0-385-13181-X); paper $12.95 (0-385-24469-X). 48pp. A view of people's varying life-styles and ways of life.

3541 Spinelli, Eileen. *Rise the Moon* (PS–2). Illus. by Raul Colon. 2003, Dial $16.99 (0-8037-2601-5). 40pp. Glowing moonlit illustrations and poetic text introduce moonstruck characters — a wolf who calls to the night, a sailor swaying to sleep, an artist painting. (Rev: BL 1/1–15/03*; HBG 10/03; SLJ 4/03)

3542 Spinelli, Eileen. *A Safe Place Called Home* (K–2). Illus. by Christy Hale. 2001, Marshall Cavendish $15.95 (0-7614-5085-8). 32pp. A boy is glad to know that home is at the end of a scary walk during which dogs bark and a bully looks threatening. (Rev: BCCB 9/01; BL 10/1/01; HBG 3/02; SLJ 2/02)

3543 Steen, Sandra, and Susan Steen. *Car Wash* (PS–1). Illus. by G. Brian Karas. 2001, Penguin Putnam $15.99 (0-399-23369-5). 32pp. Two twins and their dad experience the fun and excitement of going through a car wash. (Rev: BCCB 1/01*; BL 1/1–15/01; HBG 10/01; SLJ 1/01)

3544 Stevens, Jan Romero. *Carlos Digs to China / Carlos Excava Hasta la China* (K–2). Trans. by Mario Lamo-Jimenez. Illus. by Jeanne Arnold. 2001, Rising Moon LB $15.95 (0-87358-764-2). A bilingual story in which Carlos decides to dig to China so that he can taste all that wonderful food. (Rev: HBG 10/01; SLJ 6/01)

3545 Stevens, Janet, and Susan Stevens Crummel. *Plaidypus Lost* (PS–1). Illus. by Janet Stevens. 2004, Holiday House $16.95 (0-8234-1561-9). 40pp. A little girl keeps finding and losing the platypus the Grandma made from an old plaid shirt. (Rev: BL 3/15/04; SLJ 5/04)

3546 Stevenson, James. *July* (K–3). Illus. by author. 1990, Greenwillow LB $12.88 (0-688-08823-6). 32pp. The author recalls his childhood and the fun he had going to the beach with his grandparents. (Rev: BL 5/1/90; HB 5–6/90; SLJ 3/90*) [741]

3547 Stevenson, James. *Popcorn* (2–5). Illus. 1998, Greenwillow $15.00 (0-688-15261-9). 64pp. Daily life in a small seaside town is captured in a series of quiet, moving poems illustrated with exquisite watercolors. (Rev: BCCB 4/98; BL 5/1/98*; HB 5–6/98; HBG 10/98; SLJ 5/98)

3548 Stewart, Sarah. *The Library* (K–3). Illus. by David Small. 1995, Farrar $16.00 (0-374-34388-8). 32pp. The life story of a woman who loved reading books so much that eventually a library was named after her. (Rev: BCCB 5/95; BL 3/15/95; HB 7–8/95; SLJ 9/95)

3549 Stock, Catherine. *Island Summer* (K–2). Illus. 1999, Lothrop $16.00 (0-688-12780-0). 32pp. After a cold winter, an island springs back to life when the summer residents arrive, only to become quiet again when they leave in the fall. (Rev: BL 10/15/99; HBG 3/00; SLJ 9/99)

3550 Strickland, Michael R. *Haircuts at Sleepy Sam's* (PS–2). Illus. by Keaf Holliday. 1998, Boyds Mills $15.95 (1-56397-562-9). Although two African American brothers have a note from their mother for the barber telling him how to cut their hair, the barber, Sam, gives them the cut they want. (Rev: BL 10/15/98; HBG 3/99; SLJ 11/98)

3551 Stuve-Bodeen, Stephanie. *We'll Paint the Octopus Red* (PS–2). Illus. by Pam DeVito. 1998, Woodbine $14.95 (1-890627-06-2). 28pp. A young girl thinks of all the things that she and her new baby brother can do together. When she is told that he has Down syndrome, she maintains that they still will do those things, though now each activity might take a little longer. (Rev: BL 9/15/98; HBG 3/99; SLJ 12/98)

3552 Swanson, Susan Marie. *The First Thing My Mama Told Me* (K–2). Illus. by Christine Davenier. 2002, Harcourt $16.00 (0-15-201075-0). 40pp.

Seven-year-old Lucy loves her name, and in this book recalls the ways her name has been special to her throughout her childhood. (Rev: BL 7/02; HBG 10/02; SLJ 8/02)

3553 Swift, Fran. *Old Blue Buggy* (PS–2). Illus. by Carol Thompson. 2003, Dutton $15.99 (0-525-45766-6). A blue buggy gives Henry and his mother many happy memories and they are pleased when they see the buggy is still getting use. (Rev: HBG 10/03; SLJ 7/03)

3554 Takabayashi, Mari. *I Live in Brooklyn* (1–2). Illus. 2004, Houghton Mifflin $16.00 (0-618-30899-7). 32pp. Michelle, 6, lives in Brooklyn and describes the routines of her life there. (Rev: BL 2/15/04; HB 7–8/04; SLJ 4/04)

3555 Tarpley, Natasha A. *Bippity Bop Barbershop* (PS–1). Illus. by E. B. Lewis. 2002, Little, Brown $15.95 (0-316-52284-8). 32pp. Miles accompanies his father to the local barbershop for his first haircut. (Rev: BCCB 3/02; BL 2/15/02; HBG 10/02; SLJ 2/02)

3556 Tarpley, Natasha A. *I Love My Hair!* (PS–1). Illus. by E. B. Lewis. 1998, Little, Brown $15.95 (0-316-52275-9). 32pp. A young African American girl has fun creating different styles with her hair. (Rev: BCCB 4/98; BL 2/15/98; HBG 10/98; SLJ 2/98)

3557 Terasaki, Todd. *Ghosts for Breakfast* (2–4). Illus. by Shelly Shinjo. 2002, Lee & Low $16.95 (1-58430-046-9). 32pp. The Troublesome Trio informs Farmer Tanaka that there are ghosts in his field, so the farmer investigates, only to find that the ghosts are daikon radishes hanging to dry. (Rev: BL 1/1–15/03; HBG 3/03; SLJ 10/02)

3558 Testa, Fulvio. *The Visit* (K–2). Trans. from German by Marianne Martens. Illus. by author. 2002, North-South LB $16.50 (0-7358-1685-9). A city boy is introduced to the joys of the countryside. (Rev: HBG 3/03; SLJ 1/03)

3559 Thomas, Joyce C. *Cherish Me!* (PS–K). Illus. by Nneka Bennett. Series: Harper Growing Tree. 1998, HarperCollins $9.95 (0-694-01097-9). The concept of healthy self-esteem is explored in this poem celebrating the life of an African American child. (Rev: BL 1/1–15/99; HBG 3/99; SLJ 12/98)

3560 Thomas, Joyce C. *You Are My Perfect Baby* (PS). Illus. by Nneka Bennett. Series: Harper Growing Tree. 1999, HarperCollins $5.95 (0-694-01096-0). In this board book, an African American mother and her baby engage in simple activities that show off the wonders of the little one's body, like his twinkling toes. (Rev: SLJ 8/99)

3561 Thompson, Carol. *Baby Days* (PS). Illus. 1991, Macmillan $15.95 (0-02-789235-1). 48pp. Illustrates a number of activities that toddlers can engage in from waking to bedtime. (Rev: BL 12/1/91; SLJ 1/92)

3562 Tibo, Gilles. *Shy Guy* (PS–3). Trans. from German by Sibylle Kazeroid. Illus. by Pef. 2002, North-South LB $16.50 (0-7358-1711-1). Shy Greg finds that his goldfish gives him confidence. (Rev: HBG 3/03; SLJ 1/03)

3563 Tildes, Phyllis Limbacher. *Billy's Big-Boy Bed* (PS). Illus. by author. 2002, Charlesbridge LB $15.95 (1-57091-475-3). Billy gets a new, big bed but prefers to remain in his crib for the time being. (Rev: HBG 10/02; SLJ 3/02)

3564 Tresselt, Alvin. *Wake Up, City!* (PS–K). Illus. by Carolyn Ewing. 1990, Lothrop LB $13.88 (0-688-08653-5). 32pp. Pictures activities in the city from daybreak until the work day begins. (Rev: BCCB 9/90; BL 5/1/90; SLJ 8/90)

3565 Tresselt, Alvin. *White Snow Bright Snow* (K–3). Illus. by Roger Duvoisin. 1988, Lothrop LB $15.89 (0-688-51161-9); Morrow paper $5.95 (0-688-08294-7). Small-town snowfall is chronicled in this reissued Caldecott Medal winner of 1948.

3566 Turner, Nancy Byrd. *When Young Melissa Sweeps* (PS–3). Illus. by Debrah Santini. 1998, Peachtree $15.95 (1-56145-157-6). 30pp. First published in 1927, this poem captures a young girl's joy and enthusiasm as she dances with her broom while cleaning the house. (Rev: BL 5/1/98; HBG 10/98)

3567 Turner, Sandy. *Grow Up* (K–3). Illus. by author. 2003, HarperCollins LB $16.89 (0-06-000954-3). A child muses about the many career possibilities open to him — lion tamer, sub commander, nurse, environmental activist, and numerologist, to name just a few — all shown in witty illustrations. (Rev: HBG 10/03; SLJ 8/03)

3568 Tusa, Tricia. *Bunnies in My Head* (PS–2). Illus. 1998, Univ. of Texas. M. D. Anderson Cancer Center $20.00 (0-9664551-8-5). 32pp. Using a brief story line, this book reproduces the artwork created by children at the Anderson Cancer Center in Houston, Texas. (Rev: BL 2/1/99; SLJ 2/99)

3569 Uff, Caroline. *Lulu's Busy Day* (PS–K). Illus. 2000, Walker $14.95 (0-8027-8716-9). 24pp. A little girl named Lulu engages in such activities as coloring, playing ball, swinging in a park, eating dinner, and going to bed. (Rev: BL 3/1/00; HBG 10/00; SLJ 5/00)

3570 Van Der Meer, Mara. *Can We Play? A Pop-up, Lift-the-Flap Story About the Days of the Week* (PS–K). Illus. by Mara Van Der Meer and Ron Van Der Meer. 2002, Abrams $14.95 (0-8109-0379-2). A little girl anticipates Sunday, when everyone says they'll be free to play. (Rev: SLJ 10/02)

3571 Van Rossum, Heleen. *Will You Carry Me?* (PS). Illus. by Peter van Harmelen. 2005, Kane/Miller $15.95 (1-929132-74-3). A creative mother makes the walk home from the park much more interesting than if Thomas had simply been carried. (Rev: SLJ 6/05)

3572 Van Wert, Faye. *Empty Pockets* (PS–1). Illus. by author. 2000, Greene Bark $16.95 (1-88085-161-X). When Stevie's mother discovers a frog in his dresser drawer, she puts a stop to his hobby of bringing home everything he finds. (Rev: SLJ 3/01)

3573 Walton, Rick. *How Can You Dance?* (PS–K). Illus. by Ana Lopez-Escriva. 2001, Penguin Putnam $13.99 (0-399-23229-X). 32pp. A celebration of dance, in which a little boy and his mother swing to the rhythm of the text. (Rev: BCCB 7–8/01; BL 6/1–15/01; HBG 10/01; SLJ 7/01)

3574 Walton, Rick. *A Very Hairy Scary Story* (K–3). Illus. by David Clark. 2004, Penguin Putnam $15.99 (0-399-23858-1). On her way home later than promised, a girl sees lots of scary things in the night. (Rev: SLJ 8/04)

3575 Warner, Sunny. *The Moon Quilt* (K–4). Illus. 2001, Houghton Mifflin $15.00 (0-618-05583-5). 32pp. An old woman and her cat spend happy times together until death claims them both after satisfying lives. (Rev: BL 4/15/01; HBG 10/01; SLJ 4/01)

3576 Weatherford, Carole Boston. *Jazz Baby* (PS). Illus. by Laura Freeman. 2002, Lee & Low $11.95 (1-58430-039-6). A crew of ethnically diverse youngsters dances to the beat of a lively rhyme and jazz instruments. (Rev: HBG 10/02; SLJ 6/02)

3577 Weeks, Sarah. *If I Were a Lion* (PS–1). Illus. by Heather M. Solomon. 2004, Simon & Schuster $15.95 (0-689-84836-6). 40pp. A little girl who has been criticized for her "wild" behavior goes on the defensive and imagines what truly wild behavior would involve. (Rev: BL 3/15/04; SLJ 4/04)

3578 Weeks, Sarah. *Paper Parade* (PS–2). Illus. by Ed Briant. 2004, Simon & Schuster $15.95 (0-689-85607-5). A little girl who can't join in the parade going on outside creates her own with scissors and paper. (Rev: HB 7–8/04; SLJ 6/04)

3579 Weidt, Maryann N. *Daddy Played Music for the Cows* (PS–3). Illus. by Henri Sorensen. 1995, Lothrop LB $14.93 (0-688-10058-9). 32pp. Life on a farm is recorded in this story of a girl who grows from baby to school age in this environment. (Rev: BL 10/1/95; SLJ 10/95)

3580 Wellington, Monica. *Ana cultiva manzanas / Apple Farmer Annie* (PS–2). Illus. by author. 2004, Dutton LB $10.99 (0-525-47252-5). The Spanish translation appears in large type above the smaller-type English original about a happy apple farmer. (Rev: BL 9/04; SLJ 9/04)

3581 Wellington, Monica. *Apple Farmer Annie* (PS–2). Illus. 2001, Dutton $14.99 (0-525-46727-0). 32pp. Annie is busy picking, sorting, selling, and baking her apples in this picture book that includes apple recipes. (Rev: BL 9/1/01; HBG 3/02; SLJ 8/01)

3582 Wellington, Monica. *Firefighter Frank* (PS–1). Illus. by author. 2002, Dutton $14.99 (0-525-47021-2). A day in the life of a fire fighter, from simple tasks like shopping and looking after equipment to responding to an emergency. (Rev: HBG 3/03; SLJ 1/03)

3583 Wells, Rosemary. *Bingo* (PS). Illus. by author. Series: Bunny Reads Back. 1999, Scholastic $4.95 (0-590-02913-4). A variation on this familiar song makes Bingo a female in this enchanting board book. (Rev: SLJ 7/99)

3584 Weninger, Brigitte. *Ragged Bear* (PS–2). Trans. from German by Marianne Martens. Illus. by Alan Marks. 1996, North-South LB $15.88 (1-55858-663-6). After poor Teddy is abused by his owner and left in the park, he is adopted by a more caring child. (Rev: SLJ 12/96)

3585 Wickstrom, Sylvie. *I Love You, Mister Bear* (PS–1). Illus. by author. 2004, HarperCollins LB

$15.89 (0-06-029332-2). Young Sosha rescues a dilapidated stuffed bear from a yard sale and takes it home for some special care and love. (Rev: BL 1/1–15/04; SLJ 1/04)

3586 Wilcox, Brad. *Hip, Hip, Hooray for Annie McRae!* (PS–1). Illus. by Julie Hansen Olson. 2001, Gibbs Smith $15.95 (1-58685-058-X). Annie McRae has a healthy self-confidence and when her parents and teachers forget to praise her one day, she simply does it herself. (Rev: HBG 3/02; SLJ 10/01)

3587 Willems, Mo. *Don't Let the Pigeon Drive the Bus!* (PS). Illus. by author. 2003, Hyperion $12.99 (0-7868-1988-X). A pigeon with ambitions, right now to drive the school bus, is shown in attitudes that preschoolers will instantly recognize. Caldecott Honor Book, 2004. (Rev: BL 9/1/03*; HB 7–8/03; HBG 10/03; SLJ 5/03)

3588 Willems, Mo. *Time to Pee!* (PS). Illus. by author. 2003, Hyperion $12.99 (0-7868-1868-9). This useful guide to toilet training is enlivened by illustrations of tiny mice carrying signs with helpful advice and words of reassurance. (Rev: HBG 4/04; SLJ 12/03) [649]

3589 Williams, Sherley A. *Working Cotton* (PS–2). Illus. by Carole Byard. 1992, Harcourt $14.95 (0-15-299624-9). 32pp. A migrant child laborer tells of her daylong work in the fields. (Rev: BCCB 10/92; BL 9/1/92*; HB 11–12/93; SLJ 11/92)

3590 Williams, Sue. *I Went Walking* (PS–K). Illus. by Julie Vivas. 1990, Harcourt $13.95 (0-15-200471-8). 32pp. This book involves guessing the identity of animals hidden in pictures during a boy's afternoon walk. (Rev: BCCB 12/92; BL 9/1/90*; HB 11–12/90; SLJ 10/90*)

3591 Williams, Vera B. *Cherries and Cherry Pits* (K–3). Illus. by author. 1986, Greenwillow $16.93 (0-688-05146-4); Morrow paper $5.95 (0-688-10478-9). 40pp. Three tales and pictures from young Bidemmi, a black girl, about giving, loving, and making art. (Rev: BL 10/15/86; HB 9–10/86; SLJ 10/86)

3592 Williams, Vera B., and Jennifer Williams. *Stringbean's Trip to the Shining Sea* (2–4). Illus. by Vera B. Williams. 1988, Greenwillow $15.89 (0-688-07162-7); Scholastic paper $5.99 (0-590-44851-X). 48pp. A journey from Kansas to the West Coast, with Stringbean sending postcards along the way, which make up a kind of photo album. (Rev: BCCB 5/88; BL 3/1/88; SLJ 3/88)

3593 Wilson, Sarah. *Hocus Focus* (2–3). Illus. by Amy Wummer. Series: Science Solves It. 2004, Kane paper $4.90 (1-57565-136-X). 32pp. Jack and Gina, one near-sighted and the other far-sighted, decide to work together rather than wear glasses and suffer taunts; an eye chart and scientific information are appended. (Rev: BL 3/15/04; SLJ 6/04)

3594 Wilson-Max, Ken. *Flush the Potty* (PS). Illus. by author. 2000, Scholastic $7.95 (0-439-17325-6). An effective interactive board book that makes the noise of a flushing toilet to mark the successful transition from diapers to potty. (Rev: SLJ 2/01)

3595 Winthrop, Elizabeth. *Shoes* (PS–K). Illus. by William Joyce. 1986, HarperCollins LB $16.89 (0-06-026592-2); paper $5.95 (0-06-443171-1). 32pp. Rhyming verse about shoes and feet. (Rev: BL 10/1/86; HB 1–2/87; SLJ 12/86)

3596 Wishinsky, Frieda. *Nothing Scares Us* (PS–2). Illus. by Neal Layton. 2000, Carolrhoda LB $15.95 (1-57505-490-6). Two dear friends who think they are fearless discover that each has a secret, hidden fear. (Rev: BCCB 10/00; HBG 3/01; SLJ 11/00)

3597 Wolfe, Frances. *One Wish* (PS–1). 2004, Tundra $15.95 (0-88776-662-5). 32pp. A young girl dreams of having a cottage by the sea in this gentle story with detailed oil paintings. (Rev: BL 6/1–15/04; SLJ 6/04)

3598 Wolfe, Frances. *Where I Live* (PS–1). Illus. 2001, Tundra $14.95 (0-88776-529-7). 32pp. A little girl describes where she lives (the seaside) and her activities there. (Rev: BCCB 5/01; BL 5/1/01; HBG 10/01; SLJ 4/01)

3599 Wolff, Nancy. *Tallulah in the Kitchen* (K–2). Illus. 2005, Holt $16.95 (0-8050-7463-5). 32pp. Tallulah, a cat, and her sidekicks crocodile Freddie and pig Roxie whip up some pancakes and impart information about cooking in general. (Rev: BL 6/1–15/05)

3600 Wong, Janet S. *Buzz* (PS–K). Illus. by Margaret Chodos-Irvine. 2000, Harcourt $15.00 (0-15-201923-5). 32pp. A young child lists all the things in his house that make a buzzing sound, like a bee and his father's electric razor. (Rev: BCCB 7–8/00; BL 7/00; HB 5–6/00; SLJ 5/00)

3601 Wong, Olive. *From My Window* (PS–K). Illus. by Anna Rich. 1995, Silver Pr. LB $15.95 (0-382-24665-9); paper $5.95 (0-382-24667-5). A young boy notices several changes in his neighborhood as snow falls. (Rev: SLJ 9/95)

3602 Wood, Audrey. *The Napping House Wakes Up* (PS–2). Illus. by Don Wood. 1994, Harcourt $17.95 (0-15-200890-X). 20pp. All sorts of actions take place in this interactive version of the popular picture book. (Rev: BL 11/15/94; SLJ 11/94)

3603 Wood, Douglas. *A Quiet Place* (K–3). Illus. by Dan Andreasen. 2002, Simon & Schuster $16.95 (0-689-81511-5). 32pp. A boy searches for a secluded place to be alone with his thoughts, far from the noise and bustle of the city. (Rev: BL 2/15/02; HBG 10/02; SLJ 7/02)

3604 Woodruff, Elvira. *Can You Guess Where We're Going?* (PS–3). Illus. by Cynthia Fisher. 1998, Holiday House $15.95 (0-8234-1387-X). Gramps gives clues to his grandson as to their destination — a place filled with excitement, adventure, and entertainment — which turns out to be the local library. (Rev: HBG 3/99; SLJ 1/99)

3605 Wyeth, Sharon D. *Something Beautiful* (PS–3). Illus. by Chris K. Soentpiet. 1998, Doubleday $16.95 (0-385-32239-9). 32pp. In spite of the squalor and poverty around her, a small African American girl is able to find some things of beauty in her neighborhood. (Rev: BCCB 12/98; BL 9/15/98; HBG 3/99; SLJ 12/98)

3606 Yashima, Taro. *Umbrella* (PS–1). Illus. by author. 1958, Puffin paper $5.99 (0-14-050240-8). 32pp. A 3-year-old Japanese American girl, born in New York City, longs for a rainy day so she can use her new blue umbrella and red rubber boots.

3607 Yee, Wong H. *Fireman Small* (PS–K). Illus. 1994, Houghton Mifflin $15.00 (0-395-68987-2). 28pp. Every time Fireman Small tries to sleep, he must respond to another emergency. (Rev: BL 2/1/95; SLJ 12/94)

3608 Yee, Wong H. *Tracks in the Snow* (PS). Illus. by Wong Herbert Yee. 2003, Holt $15.95 (0-8050-6771-X). A simple story, told in rhyming text, about a young girl who traces tracks in the snow to see who made them and finally realizes she made them herself the day before. (Rev: BL 12/1/03; HB 11–12/03; HBG 4/04; SLJ 12/03)

3609 Yim, Natasha. *Otto's Rainy Day* (PS). Illus. by Pamela R. Levy. 2000, Charlesbridge LB $15.95 (1-57091-400-1). 32pp. While Mom is trying to get work done on her home computer, little Otto craves attention and is constantly getting into trouble. (Rev: BL 6/1–15/00; HBG 10/01; SLJ 8/00)

3610 Young, Amy. *Belinda in Paris* (PS–2). Illus. 2005, Viking $15.99 (0-670-03693-5). 32pp. Belinda, the big-footed ballerina, arrives in Paris for a big performance only to discover that her specially made pointe shoes are on their way to Pago Pago. (Rev: BL 1/1–15/05; SLJ 4/05)

3611 Young, Amy. *Belinda the Ballerina* (PS–2). Illus. 2003, Viking $15.99 (0-670-03549-1). 32pp. Belinda is rejected by ballet judges because of her huge feet, and she sadly abandons dance until a band arrives at Fred's Fine Food and her feet can't resist. (Rev: BL 3/1/03; HBG 10/03; SLJ 3/03)

3612 Zolotow, Charlotte. *The Beautiful Christmas Tree* (PS–2). Illus. by Yan Nascimbene. 1999, Houghton Mifflin $15.00 (0-395-91365-9). 32pp. A man, who has moved into an old brownstone and planted a tree in front of his new home, is not accepted by any of his neighbors except a young boy who, along with him, enjoys watching the tree grow strong and beautiful. (Rev: BL 12/1/99; HBG 3/00; SLJ 10/99)

3613 Zolotow, Charlotte. *I Like to Be Little* (K–3). Illus. by Erik Blegvad. 1987, HarperCollins paper $5.95 (0-06-443248-3). 32pp. The advantages of being small are explored in this 1966 picture book originally titled *I Want to Be Little*.

FAMILY STORIES

3614 Ackerman, Karen. *Song and Dance Man* (K–3). Illus. by Stephen Gammell. 1988, Knopf LB $16.99 (0-394-99330-6); paper $6.99 (0-679-81995-9). 32pp. Up in the attic, Grandpa shows three children what it's like to be a song-and-dance man. Caldecott Medal winner, 1989. (Rev: BCCB 11/88; BL 10/1/88; HB 11–12/88)

3615 Ada, Alma Flor. *I Love Saturdays y Domingos* (PS–3). Illus. by Elivia Savadier. 2002, Simon & Schuster $16.95 (0-689-31819-7). 32pp. A little girl visits Grandma and Grandpa on Saturday and Abuelito and Abuelita on Sunday in this multicul-

tural story that incorporates Spanish words and phrases. (Rev: BL 2/1/02; HBG 10/02; SLJ 1/02)

3616 Adler, David A. *It's a Baby, Andy Russell* (3–5). Illus. by Leanne Franson. 2005, Harcourt $14.00 (0-15-216742-0). 128pp. Andy and his sister Rachel are glad that the new baby is arriving but worried about coexisting with Aunt Janet while their mother is in hospital. (Rev: BL 5/15/05; SLJ 3/05)

3617 Adoff, Arnold. *Black Is Brown Is Tan* (K–3). Illus. by Emily Arnold McCully. 1973, HarperCollins $15.00 (0-060-20083-9). 32pp. A story in rhyme, which needs to be read aloud for greater understanding, depicts the warmth and companionship of an interracial family.

3618 Alexander, Martha. *Where Does the Sky End, Grandpa?* (PS). Illus. by author. 1992, Harcourt $12.95 (0-15-295603-4). In this gentle story, a young girl walks through the pastures with her grandfather. (Rev: SLJ 7/92)

3619 Alexander, Sue. *One More Time, Mama* (PS–2). Illus. by David Soman. 1999, Marshall Cavendish $15.95 (0-7614-5051-3). 32pp. A mother tells her daughter of the long wait she had through three seasons — spring, summer, and fall — until the little girl was born. (Rev: BL 11/15/99; HBG 3/00; SLJ 11/99)

3620 Aliki. *Welcome, Little Baby* (PS–K). Illus. by author. 1987, Greenwillow $16.00 (0-688-06810-3). 24pp. Addressed to the newborn child and celebrating the innocence of the infant. (Rev: BL 3/1/87; SLJ 6–7/87)

3621 Allen, Janet. *Best Little Wingman* (K–3). Illus. by Jim Postier. 2005, Boyds Mills $15.95 (1-59078-197-X). Janny is happy to help her father plowing the roads in rural Maine. (Rev: SLJ 3/05)

3622 Altman, Linda Jacobs. *Singing with Momma Lou* (2–5). Illus. by Larry Johnson. 2002, Lee & Low $16.95 (1-58430-040-X). 32pp. Tamika uses photograph albums to help her grandmother, who suffers from Alzheimer's disease, remember some of her past. (Rev: BL 5/15/02; HBG 10/02; SLJ 6/02)

3623 Amado, Elisa. *Cousins* (1–4). Illus. by Luis Garay. 2004, Groundwood $16.95 (0-88899-459-1). The narrator is a little girl who has difficulty living in two cultures — her extended family is of different ethnic backgrounds. (Rev: SLJ 5/04) [813]

3624 Anderson, Laurie Halse. *The Big Cheese of Third Street* (PS–2). Illus. by David Gordon. 2002, Simon & Schuster $16.00 (0-689-82464-5). 32pp. Benny is the only tiny member of a giant-sized family but he gets a chance to shine at the annual block party's greased-pole climb. (Rev: BCCB 3/02; BL 12/1/01; HBG 10/02; SLJ 2/02)

3625 Andreae, Giles. *There's a House Inside My Mommy* (PS–1). Illus. by Vanessa Cabban. 2002, Whitman $15.95 (0-8075-7853-3). 32pp. Rhythmic text and simple illustrations show a young boy's impressions of the baby growing inside his mother. (Rev: BL 11/1/02; HBG 3/03; SLJ 11/02)

3626 Anholt, Catherine, and Laurence Anholt. *Big Book of Little Children* (PS–K). Illus. by authors. 2003, Candlewick $15.99 (0-7636-2210-9). 79pp. Spreads bearing bright watercolor-and-ink illustrations include words, phrases, or rhymes about little children and their feelings and activities. (Rev: HBG 4/04; SLJ 1/04)

3627 Anholt, Laurence. *Sophie and the New Baby* (PS–1). Illus. by Catherine Anholt. 2000, Whitman $15.95 (0-8075-7550-X). 32pp. A story that stretches over several seasons about a little girl waiting for a sibling to be born and then adjusting to her baby brother. (Rev: BL 9/15/00; HBG 3/01; SLJ 11/00)

3628 Argueta, Jorge. *Xochitl and the Flowers / Xochitl, la nina de las flores* (K–3). Illus. by Carl Angel. 2003, Children's Book Pr. $16.95 (0-89239-181-2). 31pp. Newly arrived in San Francisco from their native El Salvador, Xochitl Flores and her family have problems adapting to their new home but find joy in the flowers they grow and sell. (Rev: BL 12/1/03; HBG 4/04; SLJ 12/03)

3629 Armas, Teresa. *Remembering Grandma / Recordando a Abuela* (1–3). Trans. by Gabriela Baeza Ventura. Illus. by Pauline Rodriguez Howard. 2003, Pi-ata $14.95 (1-55885-344-8). Lorena brings comfort to her grandfather when they share her dead grandmother's prized belongings in this appealing bilingual story. (Rev: BL 5/15/03; SLJ 7/03)

3630 Asquith, Ros. *My Do It!* (PS). Illus. by Sam Williams. 2000, DK paper $5.95 (0-7894-5648-6). An enjoyable flap book in which a little boy insists that he do a lot of chores that his mother would ordinarily do. (Rev: SLJ 10/00)

3631 Austin, Heather. *Visiting Aunt Sylvia's: A Maine Adventure* (K–2). Illus. by author. 2002, Down East $15.95 (0-89272-523-0). A young narrator looks back at happy times at Aunt Sylvia's cabin in rural Maine — stacking wood, skiing, roasting marshmallows, swimming in the summer, and other seasonal memories. (Rev: HBG 10/03; SLJ 2/03)

3632 Axelrod, Amy. *My Last Chance Brother* (2–4). Illus. by Jack E. Davis. 2002, Dutton $15.99 (0-525-46659-2). 32pp. Max is irritated by his big brother Gordon's silly antics, but at the last minute decides to give Gordon one last chance. (Rev: BL 7/02; HBG 3/03; SLJ 9/02)

3633 Ayres, Katherine. *A Long Way* (PS–1). Illus. by Tricia Tusa. 2003, Candlewick $15.99 (0-7636-1047-X). A young girl sets off to deliver a gift to her neighboring grandmother, imagining the box she carries has turned into a car, a boat, a plane, and a subway train. (Rev: HBG 10/03; SLJ 5/03)

3634 Baca, Ana. *Chiles for Benito / Chiles para Benito* (K–3). Trans. by Jose Juan Colin. Illus. by Anthony Accardo. 2003, Piñata $14.95 (1-55885-389-8). In New Mexico, Cristina hears stories about her ancestor's magic seeds as she and her grandmother string red chiles to dry. (Rev: BL 12/15/03; SLJ 12/03)

3635 Ballard, Robin. *I Used to Be the Baby* (PS–K). Illus. 2002, HarperCollins LB $15.89 (0-06-029587-2). 24pp. A little boy helps take care of his toddler brother but still expects to spend time on his mother's lap. (Rev: BL 5/1/02; HBG 10/02; SLJ 5/02)

3636 Ballard, Robin. *When I Am a Sister* (PS–K). Illus. 1998, Greenwillow $15.00 (0-688-15397-6). 24pp. Kate wonders if she will still be welcome when she visits her father and stepmother after their new baby arrives. (Rev: BL 3/1/98; HBG 10/98; SLJ 4/98)

3637 Barbour, Karen. *Little Nino's Pizzeria* (PS–2). Illus. by author. 1990, Harcourt paper $6.00 (0-15-246321-6). 32pp. When his father's business turns big, Tony is only in the way. (Rev: BL 9/15/87; SLJ 11/87)

3638 Barclay, Jane. *Going on a Journey to the Sea* (PS–1). Illus. by Doris Barrette. 2002, Lobster $16.95 (1-894222-34-2). 32pp. A boy and his sister spend a pleasant day at the beach in this rhyming picture book. (Rev: BL 5/15/02; SLJ 8/02)

3639 Barnwell, Ysaye M. *No Mirrors in My Nana's House* (PS–3). Illus. by Synthia Saint James. 1998, Harcourt $18.00 (0-15-201825-5). 32pp. The idea that people can find beauty in humble surroundings and can rise above a demeaning environment is presented in this picture book about an African American family. (Rev: BL 9/15/98; HBG 3/99; SLJ 10/98)

3640 Barrett, John M. *Daniel Discovers Daniel* (2–3). Illus. by Joe Servello. 1980, Human Sciences $16.95 (0-87705-423-1). 32pp. Daniel tries to satisfy his father's need for a sports-minded son.

3641 Battle-Lavert, Gwendolyn. *The Music in Derrick's Heart* (PS–3). Illus. by Colin Bootman. 2000, Holiday House $16.95 (0-8234-1353-5). 32pp. The power of music is explored in this gentle story about a young African American boy who is learning to play the harmonica by taking lessons from his uncle Booker T. (Rev: BCCB 3/00; BL 2/15/00*; HBG 10/00; SLJ 3/00)

3642 Bauer, Marion Dane. *The Very Best Daddy of All* (PS–K). Illus. by Leslie Wu. 2004, Simon & Schuster $12.95 (0-689-84178-7). Pastel paintings and rhyming text show how fathers — animal, bird, and human — care for the well-being of their offspring. (Rev: SLJ 6/04)

3643 Bea, Holly. *Bless Your Heart* (PS–K). Illus. by Kim Howard. 2001, H. J. Kramer $15.00 (0-915811-94-4). 32pp. A mother offers many blessings to her children as they enjoy a colorful day by the sea. (Rev: BL 10/1/01; HBG 3/02)

3644 Beardshaw, Rosalind. *Grandpa's Surprise* (PS). 2004, Bloomsbury $15.95 (1-58234-934-7). 32pp. Grandpa builds Stanley a boxcar in this gentle story with vivid illustrations presented in an oversize format. Also use *Grandma's Beach* (Bloomsbury, 2004), in which Grandma rescues the day. (Rev: BL 8/04; SLJ 8/04)

3645 Behrens, June. *Fiesta!* (1–3). Illus. by Scott Taylor. 1978, Children's Book Pr. LB $4.95 (0-516-48815-5). 32pp. The fun of celebrating a Mexican American family holiday — Cinco de Mayo.

3646 Bertram, Debbie. *The Best Place to Read* (PS–1). Illus. by Michael Garland. 2003, Random $14.95 (0-375-82293-3). 32pp. The poor protagonist searches for a good spot to settle down and read his new book, and eventually finds the perfect place with his mother. (Rev: BL 1/1–15/03; HBG 10/03; SLJ 5/03)

3647 Bertrand, Diane Gonzales. *The Empanadas That Abuela Made / Las empanadas que hacía la abuela* (K–2). Trans. by Gabriela Baeza Ventura. Illus. by Alex Pardo DeLange. 2003, Piñata $14.95 (1-55885-388-X). Presented in the form of a cumulative rhyme, this bilingual tale suitable for beginning and ESL readers follows Abuela step-by-step as she prepares her popular pumpkin empanadas. (Rev: SLJ 12/03)

3648 Bertrand, Diane Gonzales. *Family, Familia* (1–4). Trans. by Julia Mercedes Castilla. Illus. by Pauline Rodriguez Howard. 1999, Piñata $14.95 (1-55885-269-7). A bilingual book in which Daniel Gonzalez enjoys a Tex-Mex feast when he goes to a family reunion in San Antonio. (Rev: HBG 3/00; SLJ 9/99)

3649 Bertrand, Diane Gonzales. *Sip, Slurp, Soup, Soup / Caldo, Caldo, Caldo* (K–3). Illus. by Alex P. DeLange. 1997, Piñata $14.95 (1-55885-183-6). A simple bilingual book about a family making soup. (Rev: HBG 3/98; SLJ 8/97)

3650 Birdseye, Tom. *A Regular Flood of Mishap* (PS–3). Illus. by Megan Lloyd. 1994, Holiday House LB $16.95 (0-8234-1070-6). 32pp. In spite of accidentally causing a number of disasters, Ima Bean finds she is still wanted by her family. (Rev: BL 3/15/94; SLJ 3/94)

3651 Birdseye, Tom. *Waiting for Baby* (PS–K). Illus. by Loreen Leedy. 1991, Holiday House LB $14.95 (0-8234-0892-2). 32pp. A young boy eagerly awaits an arrival in the family and later is happy with his baby brother. (Rev: BL 1/1/91; SLJ 11/91)

3652 Biro, Maureen Boyd. *Walking with Maga* (PS–3). Illus. by Joyce Wheeler. 2001, All About Kids $16.95 (0-9700863-4-2). 32pp. A young girl accompanies her beloved grandmother Maga on walks, finding joy in what they see and the people they meet. (Rev: BL 12/15/01; HBG 3/03; SLJ 7/02)

3653 Blake, Robert J. *The Perfect Spot* (PS–3). Illus. 1992, Penguin Putnam $16.99 (0-399-22132-8). 32pp. A boy and his father spend a wonderful day together in the woods. (Rev: BL 3/15/92; SLJ 7/92)

3654 Bogart, Jo Ellen. *Gifts* (PS–2). Illus. by Barbara Reid. 1996, Scholastic $15.95 (0-590-55260-0). 44pp. A joyful picture book in which a grandmother presents her granddaughter with a variety of imaginative gifts. (Rev: BL 2/1/96; SLJ 3/96*)

3655 Bond, Rebecca. *Just Like a Baby* (PS–2). Illus. 1999, Little, Brown $14.95 (0-316-10416-7). 32pp. Everyone in the family contributes to preparing a cradle for the new baby, and the baby responds by sleeping happily in it. (Rev: BCCB 9/99; BL 9/15/99; HBG 3/00; SLJ 9/99)

3656 Bosak, Susan V. *Something to Remember Me By* (PS–3). Illus. by Laurie McGaw. 1997, Communication Project $15.95 (1-896232-01-9). 32pp. This touching story about the loving relationship between a girl and her grandmother that lasts until the girl is grown and the old lady dies. (Rev: BL 11/1/97; SLJ 12/97)

3657 Bourgeois, Paulette. *Oma's Quilt* (PS–3). Illus. by Stephane Jorisch. 2001, Kids Can $15.95 (1-55074-777-0). 32pp. Grumpy Oma hates her new life in a nursing home, so granddaughter Emily and her mother decide to make her a special quilt. (Rev: BCCB 12/01; BL 12/15/01; HBG 3/02; SLJ 11/01)

3658 Bowen, Anne. *How Did You Grow So Big, So Soon?* (PS–2). Illus. by Marni Backer. 2003, Carolrhoda LB $15.95 (0-87614-024-X). A little boy and his mother, on the eve of his starting school, talk about his life so far. (Rev: HBG 4/04; SLJ 3/04)

3659 Bowen, Anne. *I Loved You Before You Were Born* (PS–K). Illus. by Greg Shed. 2001, HarperCollins LB $15.89 (0-06-028721-7). 32pp. A grandmother tells her new grandchild how much she looked forward to the baby's birth. (Rev: BL 7/01; HBG 10/01; SLJ 7/01)

3660 Boyd, Lizi. *I Love Mommy* (PS). Illus. by author. 2004, Candlewick $8.99 (0-7636-2216-8). A frog mother and child spend a happy day together in this simple, attractive book. Also use *I Love Daddy* (2004), about a similarly happy day. (Rev: SLJ 6/04)

3661 Boyden, Linda. *The Blue Roses* (K–3). Illus. by Amy Cordova. 2002, Lee & Low $16.95 (1-58430-037-X). 32pp. When her beloved grandfather dies, Rosalie remembers the lessons he taught her in the garden. (Rev: BCCB 9/02; BL 5/15/02; HBG 10/02; SLJ 6/02)

3662 Braun, Sebastien. *I Love My Mommy* (PS). Illus. by author. 2004, HarperCollins $12.99 (0-06-054310-8). An oversized format, large print, and bright colors enhance this look at relationships between mothers and children, using animals as the storytellers. (Rev: SLJ 4/04)

3663 Bridges, Margaret Park. *Am I Big or Little?* (PS–2). Illus. by Tracy Dockray. 2000, North-South LB $14.88 (1-58717-020-5). 32pp. A loving relationship between mother and child is shown as they discuss the ways in which the girl is big and the ways in which she is little. (Rev: BL 10/1/00; HBG 3/01; SLJ 9/00)

3664 Bridges, Margaret Park. *If I Were Your Father* (PS–K). Illus. by Kady M. Denton. 1999, Morrow $16.00 (0-688-15192-2). 32pp. A little boy and his father talk about fantastic things they could do together, such as shaving with whipped cream. (Rev: BL 8/99; HBG 10/99; SLJ 5/99)

3665 Bridges, Margaret Park. *If I Were Your Mother* (PS–K). Illus. by Kady M. Denton. 1999, Morrow $16.00 (0-688-15190-6). 32pp. While talking with her mother, a little girl imagines that their roles are reversed. (Rev: BL 8/99; HBG 10/99; SLJ 5/99)

3666 Brillhart, Julie. *When Daddy Came to School* (PS). Illus. 1995, Whitman LB $13.95 (0-8075-8878-4). 32pp. On his third birthday, a little boy is delighted when his father visits his nursery school. (Rev: BL 3/1/95; SLJ 5/95)

3667 Brisson, Pat. *Hobbledy-Clop* (PS–K). Illus. by Maxie Chambliss. 2003, Boyds Mills $15.95 (1-56397-888-1). In the repetitive style of an old Irish folktale, this is the story of Brendan O'Doyle's visit to his grandmother, accompanied by a growing troop of animals. (Rev: HBG 10/03; SLJ 2/03)

3668 Broach, Elise. *What the No-Good Baby Is Good For* (PS). Illus. by Abby Carter. 2005, Penguin Putnam $15.99 (0-399-23877-8). 32pp. John is fed up with his new baby sister and wants her just to go away, but when his mother agrees and starts to pack a bag he begins to have doubts. (Rev: BL 5/15/05; SLJ 6/05)

3669 Brown, Alan. *Nikki and the Rocking Horse* (PS–2). Illus. by Peter Utton. 1999, HarperCollins paper $9.95 (0-00-664517-8). Nikki's mother can't afford the rocking horse her daughter wants, so she makes one in a woodworking class. (Rev: SLJ 2/00)

3670 Brown, Marc. *D.W., Go to Your Room!* (PS–K). Illus. 1999, Little, Brown $13.95 (0-316-10905-3). 32pp. D.W. is sent to her room for grabbing a toy from her baby sister, but soon after, she is won over by her young sister's smile. (Rev: BL 6/1–15/99; HBG 10/99; SLJ 7/99)

3671 Browne, Anthony. *My Mom* (PS–2). Illus. 2005, Farrar $16.00 (0-374-35098-1). 32pp. The mom in this book with clever illustrations is sometimes frazzled, sometimes dazzling, but always her child's hero. (Rev: BL 3/1/05; SLJ 6/05)

3672 Brutschy, Jennifer. *Just One More Story* (K–2). Illus. by Cat B. Smith. 2002, Scholastic $16.95 (0-439-31767-3). Austin and his parents travel the country living in a trailer, and every night Austin gets one story, until they spend a night at Uncle Rory's two-story house. (Rev: BCCB 7–8/02; HB 7–8/02; HBG 10/02; SLJ 7/02)

3673 Buck, Nola. *How a Baby Grows* (PS). Illus. by Pamela Paparone. 1998, HarperCollins $5.95 (0-694-00873-7). This nicely illustrated book depicts the various activities in which babies can participate — seeing, speaking, hearing, and sharing. (Rev: HBG 10/98; SLJ 7/98)

3674 Buckley, Helen E. *Grandfather and I* (PS–1). Illus. by Jan Ormerod. 1994, Lothrop $16.00 (0-688-12533-6). 24pp. A young boy describes the fine times he has with his grandfather walking around the neighborhood. Also use *Grandmother and I* (1994). (Rev: BL 2/15/94; HB 7–8/94; SLJ 4/94*)

3675 Bunting, Eve. *A Day's Work* (K–3). Illus. by Ronald Himler. 1994, Clarion $15.00 (0-395-67321-6). 32pp. A young Mexican American boy must act as guardian and interpreter for his grandfather, newly arrived from Mexico and looking for work. (Rev: BCCB 10/94; BL 11/1/94; SLJ 1/95)

3676 Bunting, Eve. *Flower Garden* (PS–1). Illus. by Kathryn Hewitt. 1994, Harcourt $16.00 (0-15-228776-0). 32pp. A girl and her father create a window box of flowers as a birthday present for her mother. (Rev: BL 2/15/94*; HB 5–6/94; SLJ 4/94*)

3677 Bunting, Eve. *Jin Woo* (PS–3). Illus. by Chris K. Soentpiet. 2001, Clarion $16.00 (0-395-93872-4). 32pp. David is uncertain about his new little brother who is arriving from Korea, but the child, Jin Woo, soon wins his heart. (Rev: BL 3/15/01; HBG 10/01)

3678 Bunting, Eve. *The Memory String* (K–3). Illus. by Ted Rand. 2000, Clarion $15.00 (0-395-86146-2). 32pp. Laura begins to accept her stepmother, Jane, after Jane helps Laura search for lost buttons from her collection, each of which is associated with a member of her family. (Rev: BL 8/00; HBG 3/01; SLJ 8/00)

3679 Bunting, Eve. *My Big Boy Bed* (PS). Illus. by Maggie Smith. 2003, Clarion $15.00 (0-618-17742-6). 32pp. A 3-year-old boy celebrates his graduation from crib to "big boy bed" and thinks of all the new possibilities it opens to him. (Rev: HBG 4/04; SLJ 11/03)

3680 Bunting, Eve. *A Picnic in October* (K–3). Illus. by Nancy Carpenter. 1999, Harcourt $16.00 (0-15-201656-2). 32pp. As usual, Grandma has her birthday party on Ellis Island, so she can relive her arrival in America many years before. (Rev: BL 10/15/99; HBG 3/00; SLJ 10/99)

3681 Bunting, Eve. *Sunshine Home* (K–3). Illus. by Diane De Groat. 1994, Clarion $16.00 (0-395-63309-5). 32pp. Timmie is unhappy when he visits his grandmother in her nursing home for the first time. (Rev: BCCB 4/94; BL 3/15/94; SLJ 4/94)

3682 Bunting, Eve. *The Wall* (K–2). Illus. by Ronald Himler. 1990, Houghton Mifflin $15.00 (0-395-51588-2). 32pp. A picture book on the subject of the Vietnam Veterans War Memorial. (Rev: BCCB 7–8/92; BL 4/1/90*; HB 7–8/90; SLJ 5/90*)

3683 Bunting, Eve. *The Wednesday Surprise* (PS–2). Illus. by Donald Carrick. 1989, Houghton Mifflin $16.00 (0-89919-721-3); paper $5.95 (0-395-54776-8). 32pp. Anna is proudest of Grandma's surprise — Grandma has learned to read, and Anna has taught her. (Rev: BCCB 3/89; BL 3/1/89; SLJ 6/89)

3684 Burrowes, Adjoa J. *Grandma's Purple Flowers* (PS–3). Illus. 2000, Lee & Low $15.95 (1-880000-73-3). 32pp. A young African American girl grieves after her beloved grandmother's death but gains acceptance when, in the spring, her grandmother's flowers bloom. (Rev: BL 11/1/00; HBG 3/01; SLJ 12/00)

3685 Buzzeo, Toni. *The Sea Chest* (2–4). Illus. by Mary GrandPré. 2002, Dial $16.99 (0-8037-2703-8). 32pp. An elderly aunt tells her niece, who is eagerly awaiting an adopted sister, about the girl her family found in a sea chest and adopted many years ago. (Rev: BL 9/15/02; HBG 3/03; SLJ 8/02)

3686 Caines, Jeannette. *Abby* (PS–1). Illus. by Steven Kellogg. 1973, HarperCollins paper $5.95 (0-06-443049-9). 32pp. Abby, a little African American girl, is adopted and enjoys hearing about the day she became part of her warm, loving family.

3687 Campbell, Louisa. *Phoebe's Fabulous Father* (K–2). Illus. by Bridget S. Taylor. 1996, Harcourt $14.00 (0-15-200996-5). Phoebe has always respected her cello-playing father; but when she finds out how much of his music he has sacrificed for his family, she grows to love him more. (Rev: BCCB 11/96; SLJ 12/96)

3688 Campos, Tito. *Muffler Man / El Hombre Mofle* (K–3). Illus. by Lamberto Alvarez and Beto Alvarez. 2001, Arte Publico $14.95 (1-55885-318-9). 32pp.

Young Mexican Chuy Garcia and his mother are finally able to follow Chuy's father to the United States, where Chuy persuades his father to indulge his artistic abilities. (Rev: BL 12/15/01; SLJ 1/02)

3689 Carlson, Nancy. *My Family Is Forever* (PS–1). Illus. 2004, Viking $15.99 (0-670-03650-1). 32pp. A young Asian girl muses about families and considers the characteristics she shares with her adoptive Caucasian parents: "I'm a good cook like my dad, and a wonderful dancer like my mom." (Rev: BL 4/1/04; SLJ 3/04)

3690 Carlstrom, Nancy White. *Before You Were Born* (PS–2). Illus. by Linda Saport. 2002, Eerdmans $17.00 (0-8028-5185-1). 32pp. This exceptional story inspired by Psalm 139 celebrates the bond between parents and children. (Rev: BL 2/1/02; HBG 10/02; SLJ 6/02)

3691 Carney, Margaret. *The Biggest Fish in the Lake* (K–3). Illus. by Janet Wilson. 2001, Kids Can $15.95 (1-55074-720-7). 32pp. A young girl describes her happy experiences fishing with her grandfather. (Rev: BL 7/01; HBG 10/01; SLJ 7/01)

3692 Carpenter, Mary Chapin. *Halley Came to Jackson* (K–2). Illus. by Dan Andreasen. 1998, HarperCollins $15.95 (0-06-025400-9). 40pp. This picture book spans a lifetime, beginning with a baby being shown Halley's comet by her father in Jackson, Mississippi, and ending with her as an old woman on the same porch looking at the same sight 80 years later. (Rev: BL 10/15/98; HBG 3/99)

3693 Carrick, Carol. *Valentine* (PS–2). Illus. by Paddy Bouma. 1995, Clarion $15.00 (0-395-66554-X). 29pp. In spite of a loving grandmother, Heather misses her mother when she goes to work. (Rev: BL 4/1/95; SLJ 5/95)

3694 Carter, Don. *Heaven's All-Star Jazz Band* (PS–2). Illus. 2002, Knopf LB $17.99 (0-375-91571-0). 40pp. A grandson fondly imagines his grandfather hanging out in heaven with his favorite jazz greats, in this lively account with 3-D art and a jazzy beat. (Rev: BCCB 2/03; BL 11/15/02; HBG 3/03; SLJ 11/02)

3695 Carter, Donna Renee. *Music in the Family* (K–2). Illus. by Cortrell J. Harris. 1995, Lindsey $15.95 (1-885242-01-8). 30pp. Oliver is crushed when the family tells him that he doesn't play his saxophone well enough to join them in an international music competition. (Rev: SLJ 2/96)

3696 Caseley, Judith. *Sisters* (PS–2). Illus. by author. 2004, Greenwillow LB $16.89 (0-06-051047-1). Melissa and her newly adopted sister take turns telling the story of their growing relationship. (Rev: SLJ 4/04)

3697 Catalanotto, Peter. *The Painter* (PS–2). Illus. by author. Series: Richard Jackson Books. 1995, Orchard LB $16.99 (0-531-08765-4). A joyous picture book that celebrates a loving relationship between a girl and her artist-father. (Rev: SLJ 9/95*)

3698 Cates, Karin. *The Secret Remedy Book: A Story of Comfort and Love* (PS–2). Illus. by Wendy Anderson Halperin. 2003, Scholastic $16.95 (0-439-35226-6). 32pp. Auntie Zep produces the perfect remedy for Lolly's homesickness. (Rev: HBG 4/04; SLJ 8/03)

3699 Cazet, Denys. *Dancing* (PS–1). Illus. 1995, Orchard LB $16.99 (0-531-08766-2). 32pp. The crying of his baby brother drives Alex out of the house onto the porch, where he is comforted by his father. (Rev: BL 9/15/95; SLJ 9/95)

3700 Chall, Marsha Wilson. *Sugarbush Spring* (PS–1). Illus. by Jim Daly. 2000, Lothrop LB $15.93 (0-688-14908-1). A little girl in Minnesota tells about the annual collection of sap from the family sugar bush and how the sap is turned into syrup. (Rev: BL 1/1–15/04; HBG 10/00; SLJ 3/00)

3701 Cheng, Andrea. *Goldfish and Chrysanthemums* (PS–2). Illus. by Michelle Chang. 2003, Lee & Low $16.95 (1-58430-057-4). To cheer up her Chinese-born grandmother, Nancy builds a fishpond and borders it with chrysanthemums, just like Ni Ni had as a child. (Rev: HBG 10/03; SLJ 6/03)

3702 Cheng, Andrea. *When the Bees Fly Home* (PS–2). Illus. by Joline McFadden. 2002, Tilbury House $16.96 (0-88448-238-3). 32pp. A boy who lacks self-confidence finds he has an unsuspected talent as he works to help his bee-keeping family in this novel that includes plenty of bee facts and lovely watercolors. (Rev: BL 7/02; HBG 3/03)

3703 Choi, Sook N. *Halmoni and the Picnic* (K–3). Illus. by Karen M. Dugan. 1993, Houghton Mifflin $14.95 (0-395-61626-3). 24pp. A grandmother newly arrived from Korea has difficulty adjusting to New York City. (Rev: BL 8/93)

3704 Clements, Andrew. *Because Your Daddy Loves You* (PS–K). Illus. by R. W. Alley. 2005, Clarion $16.00 (0-618-00361-4). 32pp. A daddy is shown helping a child in many ways in this picture book that celebrates the everyday things fathers do. (Rev: BL 3/1/05)

3705 Cohen, Barbara. *Molly's Pilgrim*. Rev. ed. (1–4). Illus. by Daniel Duffy. 1998, Lothrop $15.00 (0-688-16279-7); paper $3.99 (0-688-16280-0). 32pp. The mother of a Russian immigrant girl makes her child a pilgrim doll modeled on herself, a modern-day pilgrim. (Rev: BL 11/15/98; HBG 3/99)

3706 Cohen, Caron Lee. *Everything Is Different at Nonna's House* (PS). Illus. by Hiroe Nakata. 2003, Clarion $16.00 (0-618-07335-3). 32pp. A little city boy delights in his grandparents' farm far from the hustle-bustle of his urban home. (Rev: HBG 10/03; SLJ 7/03)

3707 Cohen, Miriam. *My Big Brother* (PS–2). Illus. by Ronald Himler. 2004, Star Bright $15.95 (1-59572-007-3). 40pp. When the older brother he idolizes joins the army, a young African American boy assumes the "big brother" role for his younger sibling. (Rev: BL 1/1–15/05)

3708 Cole, Brock. *Fair Monaco* (K–3). Illus. by author. 2004, Front Street $16.95 (1-932425-07-1). An anxiety-ridden grandmother struggles to look after her three girl grandchildren and the power of the girls' dreams makes their lives brighter. (Rev: SLJ 1/05)

3709 Cole, Joanna. *I'm a Big Brother* (PS–1). Illus. by Maxie Chambliss. 1997, Morrow $5.95 (0-688-14507-8). 32pp. Babies and their activities and needs are introduced in terms a big brother can understand. A companion volume that covers the same material is *I'm a Big Sister* (1997). (Rev: BL 3/1/97; SLJ 4/97)

3710 Collins, Pat Lowery. *Come Out, Come Out!* (PS). Illus. by Dee Huxley. 2005, Penguin Putnam $15.99 (0-399-23977-4). 32pp. Unhappy Hildy hides in a pile of leaves as her family searches for her. (Rev: BL 2/1/05; SLJ 4/05)

3711 Cooke, Trish. *Full, Full, Full, of Love* (PS–1). Illus. by Paul Howard. 2003, Candlewick $15.99 (0-7636-1851-9). 32pp. A young boy enjoys a family dinner at his grandmother's house in this happy, cozy picture book. (Rev: BCCB 3/03; BL 2/15/03; HBG 10/03; SLJ 2/03)

3712 Cooney, Barbara. *Island Boy* (2–4). Illus. by author. 1988, Puffin paper $5.99 (0-14-050756-6). 40pp. The life of Matthias Tibbetts of Tibbetts Island, Maine, who sails the world and returns home to raise his own family. (Rev: BCCB 10/88; BL 10/1/88; SLJ 10/88)

3713 Cooper, Melrose. *Gettin' Through Thursday* (1–3). Illus. by Nneka Bennett. 1998, Lee & Low $15.95 (1-880000-67-9). In this sweet story of a single-parent African American family, Mama is proud that her third-grade son makes the honor roll, but the family is too poor to have a celebration. (Rev: HBG 10/99; SLJ 1/99)

3714 Corey, Dorothy. *Will There Be a Lap for Me?* (PS–1). Illus. by Nancy Poydar. 1992, Whitman LB $13.95 (0-8075-9109-2). 24pp. When her mother's lap becomes smaller because she is expecting a baby, Lyle misses her favorite place to sit and be loved. (Rev: BL 3/1/92; SLJ 6/92)

3715 Coville, Bruce. *The Lapsnatcher* (PS–2). Illus. by Marissa Moss. 1997, Troll $15.95 (0-8167-4233-2). 32pp. The thing that a boy dislikes most about the family's new baby is that it takes up all the room on his mother's lap. (Rev: BL 6/1–15/97; SLJ 7/97)

3716 Cowell, Cressida. *Don't Do That, Kitty Kilroy!* (PS–K). Illus. by author. 2000, Orchard $15.95 (0-531-30209-1). Kitty's mother agrees to let her rambunctious daughter do her own thing for a day, with predictable results. (Rev: HBG 10/00; SLJ 3/00)

3717 Cowen-Fletcher, Jane. *Mama Zooms* (PS–1). Illus. 1994, Scholastic $19.95 (0-590-72848-2); paper $4.99 (0-590-45775-6). 32pp. Mama's "zooming machine" turns out to be her wheelchair. (Rev: BL 4/15/93; SLJ 5/93)

3718 Cox, Judy. *My Family Plays Music* (PS–1). Illus. by Elbrite Brown. 2003, Holiday House $16.95 (0-8234-1591-0). A young girl from a multiracial musical family introduces each person and the instrument and kind of music played. (Rev: HBG 4/04; SLJ 10/03)

3719 Coy, John. *Night Driving* (PS–3). Illus. by Peter McCarty. 1996, Holt $14.95 (0-8050-2931-1). 28pp. A young boy takes his first long nighttime car ride with his father. (Rev: BCCB 12/96; BL 9/1/96; HB 9–10/96; SLJ 10/96)

3720 Coy, John. *Two Old Potatoes and Me* (K–2). Illus. by Carolyn Fisher. 2003, Knopf LB $17.99 (0-375-92180-X). A young girl and her recently divorced father grow potatoes together in this well-illustrated book that includes a recipe for mashed potatoes. (Rev: HBG 10/03; SLJ 6/03)

3721 Coyle, Carmela LaVigna. *Do Princesses Wear Hiking Boots?* (PS–1). Illus. by Mike Gordon. 2003, Rising Moon $15.95 (0-87358-828-2). In this charming tale, presented in rhyming text, a little girl asks her mother what princesses are like and discovers, to her surprise, that they're not all that different from her. (Rev: SLJ 8/03)

3722 Crews, Donald. *Bigmama's* (PS–2). Illus. 1991, Greenwillow $15.89 (0-688-09951-3). 32pp. A family's annual summer trip to grandparents' house in the country is a celebration of childhood memories. (Rev: BCCB 11/91*; BL 11/15/91*; HB 9–10/91; SLJ 10/91) [921]

3723 Crum, Shutta. *My Mountain Song* (K–3). Illus. by Ted Rand. 2004, Clarion $16.00 (0-618-15970-3). 32pp. Brenda Gail collects favorite memories to make her very own song in this story set in her great-grandparents' home in the Kentucky highlands. (Rev: BL 5/1/04; SLJ 6/04)

3724 Cummings, Pat. *Angel Baby* (PS–2). Illus. 2000, Lothrop LB $15.89 (0-688-14822-0). 24pp. Amanda Lynn, who has to take care of her baby brother, knows he isn't the angel baby everyone thinks he is. (Rev: BCCB 7–8/00; BL 6/1–15/00; HBG 10/00; SLJ 6/00)

3725 Curtis, Jamie Lee. *Tell Me Again About the Night I Was Born* (PS–1). Illus. by Laura Cornell. 1996, HarperCollins LB $15.89 (0-06-024529-8). 40pp. A young girl gleefully fills in all the details about what happened on the night she was born. (Rev: BCCB 1/97; BL 10/15/96; SLJ 10/96*)

3726 Curtis, Marci. *Big Brother, Little Brother* (K–3). Illus. 2004, Dial $12.99 (0-8037-2870-0). 40pp. As this photoessay shows, brothers comes in all shapes, sizes, colors, and temperaments. (Rev: BL 5/15/04; SLJ 7/04)

3727 Cutler, Jane. *Darcy and Gran Don't Like Babies* (PS–1). Illus. by Susannah Ryan. 1993, Scholastic $14.95 (0-590-44587-1). 32pp. Darcy dislikes babies, particularly her new baby sister, and finds comfort with her grandmother. (Rev: BCCB 10/93; BL 12/1/93; HB 11–12/93; SLJ 11/93*)

3728 Czech, Jan M. *The Coffee Can Kid* (PS–2). Illus. by Maurie J. Manning. 2002, Child Welfare League of America paper $9.95 (0-87868-821-8). 24pp. Six-year-old Annie asks her father to retell the story of her birth in Asia and her adoption. (Rev: BL 7/02; SLJ 7/02)

3729 Daly, Niki. *Old Bob's Brown Bear* (PS–1). Illus. 2002, Farrar $16.00 (0-374-35612-2). 32pp. Emma feels her grandfather isn't giving his new teddy bear enough attention and takes the toy on a joyous spree, but other interests eventually intervene and Grandpa is pleased to get his teddy back. (Rev: BL 10/1/02; HBG 3/03; SLJ 11/02)

3730 D'Antonio, Nancy. *Our Baby from China: An Adoption Story* (PS–2). Illus. 1997, Whitman LB

$13.95 (0-8075-6162-2). 24pp. The story of a couple's journey to China, where they adopt a little girl, and their trip home with the baby. (Rev: BL 3/1/97; SLJ 6/97)

3731 D'Arc, Karen Scourby. *"My Grandmother Is a Singing Yaya"* (PS–2). Illus. by Diane Palmisciano. 2001, Scholastic $15.95 (0-439-29309-X). 32pp. A little girl is afraid she will be embarrassed at a Grandparents' Day picnic by her grandmother, who is given to bursting into song at odd moments. (Rev: BL 1/1–15/02; HBG 3/02; SLJ 11/01)

3732 Davol, Marguerite W. *Black, White, Just Right!* (PS–1). Illus. by Irene Trivas. 1993, Whitman LB $14.95 (0-8075-0785-7). 32pp. A child with mixed-race parentage enjoys the many differences she sees in her parents, not only their color. (Rev: BL 11/1/93)

3733 Deedy, Carmen A. *Agatha's Feather Bed: Not Just Another Wild Goose Story* (PS–2). Illus. by Laura L. Seeley. 1991, Peachtree $14.95 (1-56145-008-1). 32pp. Agatha is ashamed when she learns that six geese are featherless so she could have a featherbed. (Rev: BL 6/1/91; SLJ 9/91)

3734 Demas, Corinne. *Nina's Waltz* (K–3). Illus. by Deborah Lanino. 2000, Orchard LB $17.99 (0-531-33281-0). When wasp stings prevent Nina's father from playing the fiddle in a competition, she steps in to take his place. (Rev: HBG 3/01; SLJ 11/00)

3735 dePaola, Tomie. *The Baby Sister* (PS–1). Illus. 1996, Penguin Putnam $16.99 (0-399-22908-6). 32pp. When Tommy's mother has a baby, his grandmother comes to stay. (Rev: BL 3/15/96; HB 5–6/96; SLJ 5/96)

3736 dePaola, Tomie. *Tom* (K–2). Illus. 1993, Penguin Putnam LB $15.95 (0-399-22417-3). 32pp. A picture book about the special relationship between the author/artist and his grandfather. (Rev: BCCB 5/93; BL 1/15/93*; HB 7–8/93*; SLJ 4/93)

3737 dePaola, Tomie. *Watch Out for the Chicken Feet in Your Soup* (K–2). Illus. by author. 1974, Simon & Schuster $12.95 (0-685-35587-X); paper $5.95 (0-685-35588-8). 32pp. Joey is a little embarrassed to take his friend Eugene to his old-fashioned Italian grandmother's for a visit, but in spite of her strange foreign ways, both boys pronounce the visit a great success.

3738 Dodd, Anne W. *The Story of the Sea Glass* (K–2). Illus. by Mary Beth Owens. 1999, Down East $15.95 (0-89272-416-1). 32pp. A young girl and her grandmother revisit the seaside house where Nana used to live, and this visit inspires memories of past events. (Rev: BL 2/1/00; HBG 3/00; SLJ 3/00)

3739 Doyle, Charlotte. *Twins!* (PS–K). Illus. by Julia Gorton. 2003, Penguin Putnam $10.99 (0-399-23718-6). 32pp. Twin girls play, splash, share, and enjoy a day together in this rhyming picture book. (Rev: BL 2/15/03; HBG 10/03; SLJ 3/03)

3740 Duble, Kathleen Benner. *Pilot Mom* (PS–3). Illus. by Alan Marks. 2003, Charlesbridge LB $15.95 (1-57091-555-5). Jenny's mother, an Air Force pilot, is due to leave on a mission to Europe and the two make preparations for her departure. (Rev: HBG 4/04; SLJ 1/04)

3741 Dunbar, James. *When I Was Young: One Family Remembers 300 Years of History* (PS–2). Illus. by Martin Remphry. 1999, Carolrhoda LB $15.95 (1-57505-359-4). Josh hears about his family and traces its history back to the 1600s with glimpses of 7-year-old children through the ages. (Rev: HBG 3/00; SLJ 9/99)

3742 Duncan, Alice Faye. *Honey Baby Sugar Child* (PS). Illus. by Susan Keeter. 2005, Simon & Schuster $15.95 (0-689-84678-9). 32pp. An African American mother expresses love for her toddler in reassuring colloquial text accompanied by warm illustrations. (Rev: BL 2/1/05; SLJ 3/05)

3743 Dupasquier, Philippe. *A Sunday with Grandpa* (PS–2). Illus. by author. 1999, Andersen $19.95 (0-86264-791-6). A sunny picture book from England about a young girl who visits her loving grandfather in the countryside. (Rev: SLJ 7/99)

3744 Dwyer, Mindy. *Quilt of Dreams* (1–3). Illus. 2000, Graphic Arts Center $15.95 (0-88240-522-5); paper $8.95 (0-88240-521-7). 32pp. Katy wants to finish the quilt that her grandmother began before her death. (Rev: BL 3/15/01; HBG 10/01; SLJ 1/01)

3745 Ellis, Sarah. *Big Ben* (PS–1). Illus. by Kim LaFave. 2001, Fitzhenry & Whiteside $15.95 (1-55041-679-0). 32pp. Preschooler Ben feels left out when he doesn't get a report card like his older siblings, until they create one especially for him. (Rev: BL 1/1–15/02; HB 3–4/02; HBG 10/02; SLJ 2/02)

3746 Elya, Susan Middleton. *Oh No, Gotta Go!* (PS–1). Illus. by G. Brian Karas. 2003, Penguin Putnam $14.99 (0-399-23493-4). A young girl's outing turns into a frantic search for a bathroom in this amusing book that introduces several Spanish words and phrases into the poetic text. (Rev: HBG 10/03; SLJ 7/03)

3747 Emmons, Chip. *Sammy Wakes His Dad* (PS–2). Illus. by Shirley Venit Anger. 2002, Star Bright $13.95 (1-887734-87-2). Sammy's father is now wheelchair-bound, but Sammy asks him to come fishing anyway. (Rev: HBG 10/02; SLJ 8/02)

3748 English, Karen. *Speak English for Us, Marisol!* (PS–3). Illus. by Enrique O. Sanchez. 2000, Whitman $14.95 (0-8075-7554-2). 32pp. Marisol, a young Latin American girl, often acts as a translator to help various members of her family. (Rev: BL 9/15/00; HBG 3/01; SLJ 9/00)

3749 Ericsson, Jennifer A. *She Did It!* (PS). Illus. by Nadine Bernard Westcott. 2002, Farrar $16.00 (0-374-36776-0). 32pp. The artwork is detailed and witty in this story about four sisters who giggle and fight their way through their day, with their mother all the while asking, "Who did it?" (Rev: BL 2/15/02; HBG 10/02; SLJ 3/02)

3750 Evans, Lezlie. *If I Were the Wind* (PS–1). Illus. by Victoria Lisi. 1997, Ideals $14.95 (1-57102-096-9). 32pp. A mother says that even if she is changed by enchantment into other objects she will still protect and love her young daughter. (Rev: BL 8/97; SLJ 6/97)

3751 Fazio, Brenda Lena. *Grandfather's Story* (PS–3). Illus. 1996, Sasquatch $15.95 (1-57061-028-2). 32pp. In a Japanese setting, this story tells how a grandfather teaches his young grandson about life. (Rev: BL 11/15/96; SLJ 3/97)

3752 Fearnley, Jan. *A Special Something* (PS–K). Illus. 2000, Hyperion $15.99 (0-7868-0589-7). 32pp. A little girl wonders what is inside her mother's big tummy and is surprised when a baby joins the family. (Rev: BCCB 9/00; BL 7/00; HBG 10/00; SLJ 8/00)

3753 Feiffer, Jules. *The Daddy Mountain* (PS–1). Illus. 2004, Hyperion $15.95 (0-7868-0912-4). 32pp. Feiffer charts the progress of a little girl as she climbs her dad as though he were a jungle gym. (Rev: BL 5/1/04; HB 5–6/04; SLJ 6/04)

3754 Finkelstein, Ruth. *Big Like Me! A New Baby Story* (PS–K). Illus. by Esther Touson. 2001, Hachai $9.95 (1-929628-04-8). 32pp. Benny has just learned some basic skills from his older brother when a new baby joins his Orthodox Jewish family. (Rev: BL 8/01; HBG 3/02; SLJ 1/02)

3755 Fisher, Iris L. *Katie-Bo: An Adoption Story* (PS–3). Illus. by Miriam Schaer. 1988, Adama $12.95 (0-915361-91-4). The story of Katie-Bo, who is coming from Korea to join her new family, told through the eyes of a young boy. (Rev: BL 5/15/88; SLJ 8/88)

3756 Fisher, Valorie. *My Big Brother* (PS–K). Illus. 2002, Simon & Schuster $14.95 (0-689-84327-5). 40pp. The amazing feats of one big brother, from the point of view of his baby sibling. (Rev: BCCB 7–8/02; BL 9/15/02; HBG 3/03; SLJ 7/02)

3757 Fisher, Valorie. *My Big Sister* (PS–1). Photos by author. 2003, Simon & Schuster $14.95 (0-689-85479-X). A baby's comical view of his big sister is enhanced by the effective photographs. (Rev: HBG 4/04; SLJ 11/03)

3758 Fleischman, Paul. *Lost! A Story in String* (1–4). Illus. by C. B. Mordan. 2000, Holt $15.95 (0-8050-5583-5). 30pp. When the electricity goes off during a storm, Grandmother entertains her little granddaughter with an adventure story. (Rev: BCCB 10/00; BL 7/00; HBG 10/00; SLJ 6/00)

3759 Fleming, Candace. *Smile, Lily!* (PS–1). Illus. by Yumi Heo. 2004, Simon & Schuster $15.95 (0-689-83548-5). 32pp. Graphically illustrated, this is a charming tale about a baby who won't stop crying despite the entreaties of all her family — until her brother intervenes. (Rev: BL 1/1–15/04; HB 3–4/04; SLJ 3/04)

3760 Fletcher, Ralph. *Grandpa Never Lies* (PS–2). Illus. by Harvey Stevenson. 2000, Clarion $15.00 (0-395-79770-5). 32pp. A little girl has a special relationship with her grandparents and when her grandmother dies, the little girl and Grandpa mourn together. (Rev: BL 12/15/00; HBG 3/01; SLJ 11/00)

3761 Fournier Le Ray, Anne-Laure. *Grandparents!* (PS–K). Illus. by Roser Capdevila. 2003, Kane/Miller $10.95 (1-929132-46-8). A gentle look at grandparents and the ways in which they differ and are the same. (Rev: SLJ 6/03)

3762 Fowler, Susi G. *Beautiful* (PS–2). Illus. by Jim Fowler. 1998, Greenwillow $15.00 (0-688-15111-6). 32pp. Uncle George, who is dying from an incurable illness, teaches his young nephew the joys of gardening and how to nurture the lives of plants. (Rev: BL 4/1/98; HBG 10/98; SLJ 6/98)

3763 Fox, Mem. *Sophie* (K–3). Illus. by Aminah Robinson. 1994, Harcourt $13.95 (0-15-277160-3). 32pp. The story of the love shared by a girl and her grandfather from her birth to his death. (Rev: BCCB 11/94; BL 10/1/94; SLJ 11/94)

3764 Fox, Mem. *Whoever You Are* (K–3). Illus. by Leslie Staub. 1997, Harcourt $16.00 (0-15-200787-3). 32pp. A reassuring book for children that tells them that regardless of their situations, there are toher like them all over the world. (Rev: BL 10/1/97; HBG 3/98; SLJ 10/97)

3765 French, Vivian. *Oliver's Fruit Salad* (PS–2). Illus. by Alison Bartlett. 1998, Orchard $14.95 (0-531-30087-0). 32pp. Oliver remembers how he helped his grandfather pick fruit in his garden, and this helps him enjoy the fruit salad he prepares with his mother and grandparents. (Rev: BCCB 10/98; BL 10/15/98; HBG 3/99; SLJ 9/98)

3766 French, Vivian, and Alex Ayliffe. *Not Again, Anna!* (PS). Illus. 1998, Sterling $14.95 (1-899607-96-X). 24pp. In this book with foldout pages, Little Anna learns to care for her stuffed bunny in the same way her mother cares for her. (Rev: BL 1/1–15/99; SLJ 3/99)

3767 Friedman, Ina R. *How My Parents Learned to Eat* (2–4). Illus. by Allen Say. 1987, Houghton Mifflin $15.00 (0-395-35379-3); paper $5.95 (0-395-44235-4). 32pp. John, an American, and Aiko, a Japanese girl, learn each other's eating habits.

3768 Fruisen, Catherine Myler. *My Mother's Pearls* (PS–3). Illus. 2000, Cedco $12.95 (0-7683-2177-8). 32pp. A little girl tells about the six generations of women in her family who have worn the family heirloom string of pearls. (Rev: BL 8/00; HBG 3/01)

3769 Furgang, Kathy. *Flower Girl* (PS–2). Illus. by Harley Jessup. 2003, Viking $15.99 (0-670-88950-4). 40pp. Anna's reluctance to participate in her aunt's wedding is overcome by enchantment with the preparations. (Rev: BCCB 3/03; BL 2/1/03; HBG 10/03; SLJ 2/03)

3770 Galindo, Mary Sue. *Icy Watermelon / Sandia fria* (PS–3). Illus. by Pauline Rodriguez Howard. 2000, Arte Publico $14.95 (1-55885-306-5). 32pp. In this bilingual English and Spanish book, three Latino children share stories and jokes with their parents and grandparents on a porch where they are eating watermelon. (Rev: BL 12/15/00; SLJ 1/01)

3771 Garden, Nancy. *Molly's Family* (PS–2). Illus. by Sharon Wooding. 2004, Farrar $16.00 (0-374-35002-7). 32pp. Although hurt by a classmate's remark about the makeup of her family — "no one has two mommies" — Molly comes to see that families come in all sorts of packages. (Rev: BL 4/15/04; HB 7–8/04; SLJ 5/04)

3772 Gardner, Sally. *Mama, Don't Go Out Tonight* (PS–K). Illus. 2002, Bloomsbury $16.95 (1-58234-

790-5). 32pp. This colorful story, in simple dialogue and vivid drawings, describes a young girl's fears when her mother is going out for the evening and then shows the fine time both mother and daughter have in the end. (Rev: BL 1/1–15/03; SLJ 12/02)

3773 Garland, Sherry. *My Father's Boat* (K–4). Illus. by Ted Rand. 1998, Scholastic $15.95 (0-590-47867-2). A family story in which a Vietnamese American fisherman and his son head out to sea on their shrimp boat, and the man, remembering his childhood, hopes one day to take his son to meet his grandfather in Vietnam. (Rev: BCCB 9/98; HBG 10/98; SLJ 7/98)

3774 Garrett, Ann. *Keeper of the Swamp* (2–4). Illus. by Karen Chandler. 1999, Turtle $16.95 (1-890515-12-4). A poignant story about a young boy who makes a special trip with his dying grandfather to a swamp to feed an alligator that the grandfather had saved from poachers. (Rev: HBG 3/00; SLJ 7/99)

3775 Gay, Marie-Louise. *Good Morning, Sam* (PS–1). Illus. 2003, Douglas & McIntyre $14.95 (0-88899-528-8). 32pp. Preschooler Sam's efforts to dress himself are hindered by his dog and helped by his big sister. (Rev: BL 3/15/03; HB 7–8/03; HBG 10/03; SLJ 4/03)

3776 George, Kristine O'Connell. *Up!* (PS). Illus. by Niroe Nakata. 2005, Clarion $15.00 (0-618-06489-3). 32pp. A little girl and her daddy enjoy a day at the park in this rhyming picture book. (Rev: BL 3/1/05; SLJ 3/05)

3777 Gewing, Lisa. *Mama, Daddy, Baby and Me* (PS). Illus. by Donna Larimer. 1989, Spirit $14.95 (0-944296-04-1). 32pp. In simple rhymes, a youngster responds to a new baby in the house. (Rev: BL 12/1/89; SLJ 12/89)

3778 Gilchrist, Jan Spivey. *Indigo and Moonlight Gold* (K–3). Illus. 1993, Black Butterfly $13.95 (0-86316-210-X). 32pp. A tender moment between a mother and child is described in moving prose and beautiful oil paintings. (Rev: BCCB 2/94; BL 3/1/94; SLJ 5/94)

3779 Gillard, Denise. *Music from the Sky* (PS–1). Illus. by Stephen Taylor. 2001, Douglas & McIntyre $15.95 (0-88899-311-0). 32pp. A music-loving young African American girl spends time with her grandpa, who makes her a flute so she can make her own music. (Rev: BL 2/15/01; HBG 10/01)

3780 Gilles, Almira Astudillo. *Willie Wins* (PS–3). Illus. by Carl Angel. 2001, Lee & Low $16.00 (1-58430-023-X). 32pp. Willie isn't much interested in his father's stories of his youth in the Philippines, but when he needs a money bank for a school project, the coconut alkansiya his father gives him has a surprise in it. (Rev: BL 5/1/01; HBG 10/01; SLJ 6/01)

3781 Gilmore, Rachna. *A Gift for Gita* (2–3). Illus. by Alice Priestley. 2002, Tilbury House paper $7.95 (0-88448-239-1). 24pp. When Gita's father is offered a job back in their native India, the immigrant family must make a choice. (Rev: BL 9/15/02)

3782 Glassman, Peter. *My Dad's Job* (1–3). Illus. by Timothy Bush. 2003, Simon & Schuster $15.95 (0-689-82890-X). Based on his father's remarks about his job, a young boy imagines that Dad's workplace must be loads of fun; he convinces his father to take him to work with him one day and, to everyone's surprise, decides that life at the office is even more fun than he had imagined. (Rev: HBG 10/03; SLJ 9/03)

3783 Godfrey, Jan. *Sam's New Baby* (PS–1). Illus. by Jane Coulson. 1998, Abingdon $12.95 (0-687-09570-0). 24pp. Sam discovers that everyone's fingerprints are different. After his baby sister is born, he examines her fingers through a magnifying glass and realizes that she, too, is a unique being. (Rev: BL 9/15/98)

3784 Good, Merle. *Reuben and the Blizzard* (K–3). Illus. by P. Buckley Moss. 1995, Good Books $14.95 (1-56148-184-X). 32pp. Young Reuben and his Amish family weather a blizzard and help a neighbor get to the hospital. (Rev: BL 1/1–15/96; SLJ 4/96)

3785 Good, Merle. *Reuben and the Quilt* (PS–3). Illus. by P. Buckley Moss. 1999, Good Books $16.00 (1-56148-234-X). 32pp. To help with a neighbor's medical bills, an Amish family sews a quilt, but when it is stolen before the auction, they create an unusual plan for its recovery. (Rev: BL 6/1–15/99; SLJ 6/99)

3786 Gove, Doris. *My Mother Talks to Trees* (K–3). Illus. by Marilynn H. Mallory. 1999, Peachtree $14.95 (1-56145-166-5). 32pp. At first, a little girl finds walking with her mother an embarrassing experience because her mother talks to the trees, but eventually the girl changes her mind and begins talking to a sapling in her yard. (Rev: BL 5/1/99; HBG 10/99; SLJ 7/99)

3787 Graham, Bob. *Spirit of Hope* (PS–3). Illus. 1996, Mondo $14.95 (1-57255-202-6). 30pp. The Fairweathers face a crisis when they are told to vacate their home. (Rev: BL 12/1/96; SLJ 3/97)

3788 Grambling, Lois G. *Daddy Will Be There* (PS–K). Illus. by Walter Gaffney-Kessell. 1998, Greenwillow $15.00 (0-688-14983-9). 24pp. Even though a little girl engages in many different activities, like playing with her friends, she is happy with the assurance that sooner or later she will be reunited with her father. (Rev: BL 5/15/98; HBG 10/98; SLJ 6/98)

3789 Grambling, Lois G. *Grandma Tells a Story* (PS–1). Illus. by Fred Willingham. 2001, Charlesbridge LB $15.95 (1-58089-057-1). Two grandparents are overjoyed to learn that a longed-for grandchild is on its way in this gentle story with bright illustrations. (Rev: HBG 10/01; SLJ 7/01)

3790 Gray, Kes. *Baby on Board* (PS–2). Illus. by Sarah Nayler. 2004, Simon & Schuster $15.95 (0-689-86572-4). 32pp. A young girl awaiting the arrival of a new sibling reports in entertaining "news flashes" on the changes in her mother over nine months of pregnancy. (Rev: BL 5/15/04; SLJ 7/04)

3791 Gray, Libba M. *My Mama Had a Dancing Heart* (PS–3). Illus. by Raul Colon. 1995, Orchard LB $16.99 (0-531-08770-0). 32pp. Evocative pictures are used to illustrate a series of imaginative experiences shared by a mother and daughter in each of the seasons. (Rev: BL 9/15/95*; SLJ 9/95*)

3792 Greene, Rhonda Gowler. *At Grandma's* (PS–1). Illus. by Karla Firehammer. 2003, Holt $15.95 (0-8050-6336-6). Welcoming illustrations accompany this story of a child's overnight visit to Grandma's house. (Rev: BL 6/1–15/03*; HBG 10/03; SLJ 7/03)

3793 Greenfield, Eloise. *First Pink Light* (PS–1). Illus. by Jan S. Gilchrist. 1991, Writers & Readers $13.95 (0-86316-207-X). A young African American boy waits in a rocking chair to greet his father, who has been away for a year. (Rev: BL 12/15/91; SLJ 1/92)

3794 Greenfield, Eloise. *Grandpa's Face* (K–3). Illus. by Floyd Cooper. 1988, Philomel $16.99 (0-399-21525-5); Penguin Putnam paper $6.99 (0-698-11381-0). 32pp. Tamika worries about her grandfather's reactions. (Rev: BL 11/15/88; HB 3–4/89; SLJ 11/88)

3795 Greenfield, Eloise. *She Come Bringing Me That Little Baby Girl* (K–2). Illus. by John Steptoe. 1990, HarperCollins paper $6.95 (0-06-443296-3). 32pp. Kevin resents all the attention the new baby is getting; most of all he resents the fact that she is a girl.

3796 Greenspun, Adele Aron, and Joanie Schwarz. *Grandparents Are the Greatest Because . . .* (PS Up). Photos by Adele Aron Greenspun. 2003, Dutton $12.99 (0-525-47131-6). This photographic ode to the relationship between grandchildren and their grandparents is filled with images of multicultural family groups, each of which is accompanied by a brief quote from a grandparent or grandchild. (Rev: HBG 4/04; SLJ 8/03)

3797 Guest, Elissa. *Iris and Walter and Baby Rose* (PS–K). Illus. by Christine Davenier. 2002, Harcourt $14.00 (0-15-202120-5). 44pp. Iris can't wait to be a big sister, until the baby arrives and isn't what Iris expected at all. (Rev: BL 3/15/02; HBG 10/02; SLJ 4/02)

3798 Gurley, Nan. *Twice Yours: A Parable of God's Gift* (K–3). Illus. by Bill Farnsworth. 2002, Zondervan $14.99 (0-310-70194-5). 40pp. A grandfather tells his grandson a story relating to the words of the apostle Peter. (Rev: BL 2/1/02)

3799 Guthrie, Donna. *Grandpa Doesn't Know It's Me: A Family Adjusts to Alzheimer's Disease* (K–3). Illus. by Katy K. Arnsteen. 1986, Human Sciences paper $10.95 (0-89885-308-7). The story of Lizzie, who adores her grandfather, and the tragedy of her grandfather's Alzheimer's disease. (Rev: BCCB 7–8/86; BL 8/86)

3800 Hanrahan, Brendan. *My Sisters Love My Clothes* (PS–2). Illus. by Lise Stork. 1992, Perry Heights Pr. $12.95 (0-9630181-0-8). 32pp. Young Louie has a smart wardrobe, but his sisters keep borrowing his clothes. (Rev: BCCB 4/92; BL 9/1/92)

3801 Hanson, Mary. *The Difference Between Babies and Cookies* (PS–K). Illus. by Debbie Tilley. 2002, Harcourt $16.00 (0-15-202406-9). 32pp. A new sister finds out that babies aren't quite as sweet as Mom told her. (Rev: BL 3/1/02; HBG 10/02; SLJ 5/02)

3802 Harper, Jessica. *I Like Where I Am* (PS–2). Illus. by G. Brian Karas. 2004, Penguin Putnam $15.99 (0-399-23479-9). 32pp. A little boy faces the trauma of moving in this playfully illustrated book with a happy ending. (Rev: BL 2/15/04; SLJ 3/04)

3803 Harper, Jessica. *Lizzy's Do's and Don'ts* (1–3). Illus. by Lindsay Harper duPont. 2002, Harper-Collins LB $15.89 (0-06-623861-7). 40pp. Cartoon art helps to convey the messages of this book, in which a mother and daughter realize they say "don't" to each other far too often. (Rev: BL 3/15/02; HBG 10/02; SLJ 7/02)

3804 Harris, Robie H. *Don't Forget to Come Back!* (PS–2). Illus. by Harry Bliss. 2004, Candlewick $15.99 (0-7636-1782-2). 40pp. A little girl strongly protests her parents' departure for the evening but ends up having a delightful time with the baby-sitter; a newly illustrated version of a 1978 title. (Rev: BL 3/1/04; HB 3–4/04; SLJ 3/04)

3805 Harris, Robie H. *Happy Birth Day!* (PS–2). Illus. by Michael Emberley. 1996, Candlewick $16.99 (1-56402-424-5). 32pp. A baby's first day after birth is caught in text, narrated by the young parents, and paintings. (Rev: BL 5/1/96*; SLJ 12/96*)

3806 Harris, Robie H. *Hello Benny! What It's Like to Be a Baby* (PS–3). Illus. by Michael Emberley. 2002, Simon & Schuster $16.95 (0-689-83257-5). 40pp. Following a baby's life from birth to first birthday, this book combines a fictional storyline with lots of factual information about babies in general. (Rev: BCCB 11/02; BL 10/15/02; HB 11–12/02; HBG 3/03; SLJ 9/02)

3807 Harris, Robie H. *Hi New Baby!* (PS–3). Illus. by Michael Emberley. 2000, Candlewick $16.99 (0-7636-0539-5). 32pp. Narrated by the father, this is the tender story of a young girl's first meeting with her new baby brother. (Rev: BL 10/1/00; HBG 3/01; SLJ 11/00)

3808 Harshman, Marc. *Roads* (PS–2). 2002, Marshall Cavendish $16.95 (0-7614-5112-9). 32pp. A thoughtful picture book about traveling from a child's perspective. (Rev: BL 10/15/02; HBG 3/03; SLJ 9/02)

3809 Haskins, Francine. *I Remember "121"* (PS–3). Illus. 1991, Children's Book Pr. $14.95 (0-89239-100-6). 32pp. This is an autobiographical sketch of the artist growing up in an African American neighborhood in Washington, D.C. (Rev: BL 12/15/91; SLJ 3/92) [973]

3810 Haughton, Emma. *Rainy Day* (PS–1). Illus. by Angelo Rinaldi. 2000, Lerner $15.95 (1-57505-452-3). A boy and his father spend a day together and must find a way to work around the rain. (Rev: BL 3/1/03; HBG 9/00; SLJ 8/00)

3811 Hausherr, Rosmarie. *Celebrating Families* (PS–2). Illus. 1997, Scholastic $16.95 (0-590-48937-2). 32pp. Different kinds of families are pictured in this photo-essay. (Rev: BL 3/1/97; SLJ 3/97)

3812 Havill, Juanita. *Treasure Map* (PS–2). Illus. by Elivia Savadier. 1992, Houghton Mifflin $15.00 (0-395-57817-5). 32pp. Alicia hears the story of how her great-grandmother left Mexico and came to the United States. (Rev: BL 3/1/92; SLJ 6/92)

3813 Hawxhurst, Joan C. *Bubbe and Gram: My Two Grandmothers* (PS–3). Illus. by Jane K. Bynum. 1996, Dovetail $12.95 (0-9651284-2-3). 32pp. From his two grandmothers — one Jewish, the other Christian — a young girl learns about and accepts two ways of worship. (Rev: BL 1/1–15/97)

3814 Hayles, Marsha. *He Saves the Day* (PS–1). Illus. by Lynne W. Cravath. 2002, Penguin Putnam $15.99 (0-399-23363-6). An imaginative little boy plays by himself, emerging victorious from a variety of expeditions until his mother must in turn save the day. (Rev: BCCB 3/02; HBG 10/02; SLJ 4/02)

3815 Haynes, Max. *Grandma's Gone to Live in the Stars* (PS–2). Illus. 2000, Whitman $15.95 (0-8075-3026-3). 32pp. In this simple luminous book about death, Grandma, who is dying, hovers over the things and people she loves, including her sleeping family, to say goodbye. (Rev: BL 12/1/00*; HBG 3/01; SLJ 12/00)

3816 Hazen, Barbara S. *If It Weren't for Benjamin (I'd Always Get to Lick the Icing Spoon)* (PS–2). Illus. by Laura Hartman. 1979, Human Sciences paper $10.95 (0-89885-172-6). 32pp. A younger sibling recounts the reasons for his sense of injustice.

3817 Hearne, Betsy. *Seven Brave Women* (K–3). Illus. by Bethanne Andersen. 1997, Greenwillow $14.89 (0-688-14503-5). 24pp. The narrator introduces seven creative, courageous women in her family who made their quiet but important marks on history, from the Revolutionary War to the present. (Rev: BL 6/1–15/97; HB 9–10/97; HBG 3/98; SLJ 9/97)

3818 Henderickson, Karen. *Baby and I Can Play and Fun with Toddlers* (PS–K). Illus. by Marina Megale. 1990, Parenting LB $17.95 (0-943990-57-2); paper $7.95 (0-943990-56-4). 56pp. This book tells preschoolers how to play safely with young babies. (Rev: BL 9/1/90) [649.64]

3819 Henderson, Kathy. *And the Good Brown Earth* (PS). Illus. by author. 2004, Candlewick $15.99 (0-7636-2301-6). A well-illustrated story about Joe and his grandmother enjoying all four seasons in the garden. (Rev: SLJ 4/04)

3820 Henkes, Kevin. *Shhhh* (PS–1). Illus. 1989, Greenwillow $15.89 (0-688-07986-5). 24pp. A little girl wakes up the whole household with her horn. (Rev: BL 8/89; SLJ 1/90)

3821 Heo, Yumi. *Father's Rubber Shoes* (PS–3). Illus. 1995, Orchard LB $16.99 (0-531-08723-9). 32pp. Yungsu's father tells his lonely son why the family has moved to the United States. (Rev: BL 9/15/95; HB 11–12/95; SLJ 11/95)

3822 Heo, Yumi. *One Sunday Morning* (PS–1). Illus. 1999, Orchard LB $16.99 (0-531-33156-3). 32pp. Minho dreams that he and his father spend a day in the park experiencing its sights and sounds.

(Rev: BCCB 5/99; BL 4/1/99; HB 3–4/99; HBG 10/99; SLJ 4/99)

3823 Herman, Charlotte. *The Memory Cupboard: A Thanksgiving Story* (PS–2). Illus. by Ben F. Stahl. 2003, Whitman LB $15.95 (0-8075-5055-8). Katie is upset when she breaks her grandmother's gravy boat, but Grandma shows her that memories are more important than possessions. (Rev: BL 9/1/03; HBG 4/04; SLJ 11/03)

3824 Hesse, Karen. *Poppy's Chair* (K–3). Illus. by Kay Life. 1993, Macmillan LB $14.95 (0-02-743705-1). 32pp. Leah learns from her grandmother how to accept her grandfather's death. (Rev: BL 3/15/93; SLJ 7/93)

3825 Hickman, Martha W. *Robert Lives with His Grandparents* (1–3). Illus. by Tim Hinton. 1995, Whitman LB $14.95 (0-8075-7084-2). 32pp. Robert, who lives with his grandparents, is embarrassed at the thought that his grandmother will be coming to school on parents' day. (Rev: BL 2/1/96; SLJ 1/96)

3826 High, Linda Oatman. *Winter Shoes for Shadow Horse* (PS–3). Illus. by Ted Lewin. 2001, Boyds Mills $15.95 (1-56397-472-X). 32pp. A boy shoes a horse for the very first time under the watchful eye of his blacksmith father. (Rev: BL 9/1/01; HBG 3/02; SLJ 10/01)

3827 Himmelman, John. *Wanted: Perfect Parents* (K–2). Illus. 1993, BridgeWater $13.95 (0-8167-3028-8). 32pp. Gregory realizes that perfect parents are those who can tuck him in lovingly at night. (Rev: BL 10/15/93; SLJ 8/93)

3828 Hines, Anna Grossnickle. *Daddy Makes the Best Spaghetti* (PS–K). Illus. by author. 1986, Houghton Mifflin paper $5.95 (0-89919-794-9). The story of the warm relationship between a father and son as they spend time together doing things at home. (Rev: BL 3/1/86; HB 9–10/86; SLJ 5/86)

3829 Hines, Anna Grossnickle. *My Grandma Is Coming to Town* (PS–K). Illus. by Melissa Sweet. 2003, Candlewick $13.99 (0-7636-1237-5). 24pp. When grandma visits Albert for the first time since he was a baby, he is shy and hides while grandma waits patiently. (Rev: BL 3/15/03; HBG 10/03; SLJ 7/03)

3830 Hines, Anna Grossnickle. *When We Married Gary* (PS–1). Illus. 1996, Greenwillow $15.00 (0-688-14276-1). 28pp. Two young sisters adjust to Gary, their new stepfather, when their mother remarries. (Rev: BL 3/1/96; HB 7–8/96; SLJ 5/96)

3831 Holman, Sandy Lynne. *Grandpa, Is Everything Black Bad?* (PS–3). Illus. by Lela Kometiani. 1998, Culture C.O.-O.P. $18.95 (0-9644655-0-7). 32pp. A child named Montsho thinks that black is often associated with things that are bad, but his beloved grandfather assures him that black is beautiful. (Rev: BL 1/1–15/99; SLJ 12/98)

3832 Hooks, Bell. *Homemade Love* (PS). Illus. by Shane W. Evans. 2002, Hyperion $16.99 (0-7868-0643-5). 32pp. An African American girl revels in the love of her supportive parents in this brightly illustrated book. (Rev: BCCB 2/03; BL 2/1/03; HBG 3/03; SLJ 12/02)

3833 Hooks, William H. *The Mighty Santa Fe* (K–3). Illus. by Angela T. Thomas. 1993, Macmillan LB $14.95 (0-02-744432-5). 32pp. William is overjoyed to find that his grandmother shares his enthusiasm for model trains. (Rev: BL 11/15/93)

3834 Hopkinson, Deborah. *Bluebird Summer* (1–3). Illus. by Bethanne Andersen. 2001, Greenwillow LB $15.89 (0-688-17399-3). 32pp. Two young children and their grieving grandfather start a garden project as a tribute to their grandmother, who has recently died. (Rev: BL 4/15/01; HBG 10/01; SLJ 5/01)

3835 Houston, Gloria. *My Great-Aunt Arizona* (K–4). Illus. by Susan C. Lamb. 1992, HarperCollins LB $15.89 (0-06-022607-2). 32pp. The story of the author's great-aunt, who was born in the Appalachians and lived there until the age of 93. (Rev: BCCB 4/92; BL 1/1/92; SLJ 3/92) [371.1]

3836 Howard, Elizabeth F. *What's in Aunt Mary's Room?* (PS–2). Illus. by Cedric Lucas. 1996, Clarion $14.95 (0-395-69845-6). 32pp. Aunt Flossie explains the importance in the life of this African American family of the book stored in Aunt Mary's room, the family Bible. A sequel to *Aunt Flossie's Hats (and Crab Cakes Later)* (1991). (Rev: BL 2/15/96; SLJ 5/96)

3837 Howard, Elizabeth F. *When Will Sarah Come?* (PS–K). Illus. by Nina Crews. 1999, Greenwillow LB $15.93 (0-688-16181-2). 24pp. On Sarah's first day at school, younger brother Jonathan waits impatiently for her return. (Rev: BCCB 10/99; BL 10/15/99; HBG 3/00; SLJ 9/99)

3838 Howard, Elizabeth Fitzgerald. *Flower Girl Butterflies* (PS–2). Illus. by Christiane Kromer. 2004, Greenwillow $15.99 (0-688-17809-X). 32pp. Sarah is scared of being a flower girl until she actually starts down the aisle. (Rev: BL 3/1/04; SLJ 4/04)

3839 Howe, James. *Kaddish for Grandpa in Jesus' Name Amen* (K–2). Illus. by Catherine Stock. 2004, Simon & Schuster $16.95 (0-689-80185-8). 32pp. Five-year-old Emily, a Jewish girl, finds her own way to mourn the death of her Christian grandfather. (Rev: BL 5/15/04; SLJ 7/04)

3840 Hru, Dakari. *Tickle Tickle* (PS). Illus. by Ken Wilson-Max. 2002, Millbrook LB $21.90 (0-7613-2468-2). 32pp. A small child tells in rhyme how much he loves to be tickled by Papa. (Rev: BL 5/15/02; HBG 10/02; SLJ 8/02)

3841 Hughes, Shirley. *Annie Rose Is My Little Sister* (PS–1). Illus. 2003, Candlewick $15.99 (0-7636-1959-0). 32pp. Alfie's descriptions of his little sister Annie Rose's daily activities are accompanied by appealingly detailed pastel illustrations. (Rev: BL 3/1/03; HBG 10/03; SLJ 4/03)

3842 Hughes, Shirley. *The Big Alfie and Annie Rose Storybook* (2–3). Illus. by author. 1989, Lothrop $18.00 (0-688-07672-6). 64pp. Stories, poems, and eye-catching artwork featuring Alfie and his little sister. (Rev: BCCB 4/89; BL 3/15/89; HB 5–6/89)

3843 Hughes, Shirley. *The Big Alfie Out of Doors Storybook* (PS–2). Illus. 1992, Lothrop $17.00 (0-688-11428-8). 64pp. Four-year-old Alfie has four happy experiences with different members of his family. (Rev: BCCB 10/92*; BL 10/15/92; HB 1–2/93; SLJ 10/92)

3844 Hume, Stephen Eaton. *Red Moon Follows Truck* (PS–3). Illus. by Leslie Elizabeth Watts. 2001, Orca $16.95 (1-55143-218-8). 32pp. A boy narrates his family's move across the country and their adventures along the way, particularly those of Gypsy the dog. (Rev: BL 1/1–15/02; HBG 3/02; SLJ 2/02)

3845 Hundal, Nancy. *Camping* (PS–3). Illus. by Brian Deines. 2002, Fitzhenry & Whiteside $16.95 (1-55041-668-5). 32pp. Luminous illustrations form the backdrop for a young girl's discovery that camping in the wilderness has its delights after all. (Rev: BL 12/1/02; SLJ 11/02)

3846 Hurwitz, Johanna. *Russell's Secret* (PS–3). Illus. by Heather Maione. 2001, HarperCollins $14.95 (0-688-17574-0). 32pp. Pre-schooler Russell envies his baby sister until his mother agrees to treat him just like a baby for a day. (Rev: BL 1/1–15/02; HBG 10/02; SLJ 1/02)

3847 Hutchins, Hazel. *I'd Know You Anywhere* (PS). Illus. by Ruth Ohi. 2002, Annick LB $19.95 (1-55037-747-7); paper $7.95 (1-55037-746-9). 24pp. A father reassures his son that he'd know him no matter how he was disguised in this book for very young readers. (Rev: BL 12/15/02; HBG 3/03; SLJ 4/03)

3848 Hutchins, Pat. *Titch* (K–3). Illus. by author. 1971, Macmillan paper $5.99 (0-689-71688-5). 32pp. Titch, the youngest in the family, enjoys a moment of triumph. A sequel is: *You'll Soon Grow into Them, Titch* (1983, Greenwillow).

3849 Igus, Toyomi. *Two Mrs. Gibsons* (K–3). Illus. by Daryl Wells. 1996, Children's Book Pr. $14.95 (0-89239-135-9). 32pp. The two Mrs. Gibsons in a young girl's life are her mother and her grandmother. (Rev: BCCB 5/96; BL 5/15/96; SLJ 10/96)

3850 Igus, Toyomi. *When I Was Little* (K–3). Illus. by Higgins Bond. 1992, Just Us $14.95 (0-940975-32-7). 32pp. Noel finds it hard to believe there was no television and other things he takes for granted when his African American grandfather was growing up. (Rev: BL 3/1/93)

3851 Jacobs, Kate. *A Sister's Wish* (K–2). Illus. by Nancy Carpenter. 1996, Hyperion LB $15.49 (0-7868-2112-4). A little girl longs to have a sister of her own but later realizes that being a good sister to her brothers is nice, too. (Rev: SLJ 7/96)

3852 Jagtenberg, Yvonne. *Jack's Kite* (K–2). Illus. by author. 2004, Roaring Brook LB $22.90 (0-7613-2904-4). Jack has a kite but he is waiting — and waiting — for his father to come and show him how to fly it. (Rev: HB 1–2/05; SLJ 2/05)

3853 Jenkins, Emily. *Daffodil* (PS–2). Illus. by Tomek Bogacki. 2004, Farrar $16.00 (0-374-31676-7). 32pp. Rose, Violet, and Daffodil are triplets, and their mother likes to dress them in clothes that match their names until Daffodil rebels and the trio finally get to choose their own clothes. (Rev: BL 3/15/04; HB 5–6/04; SLJ 5/04)

3854 Jenkins, Emily. *Five Creatures* (PS–K). Illus. by Tomek Bogacki. 2001, Farrar $16.00 (0-374-32341-0). 32pp. Child-like drawings are used in this book that describes the everyday activities of a family and their two cats in an entertaining format that is also an exercise in reasoning. (Rev: BCCB 2/01; BL 3/15/01*; HB 3–4/01*; HBG 10/01)

3855 Jennings, Sharon. *The Bye-Bye Pie* (1–3). Illus. by Ruth Ohi. 1999, Fitzhenry & Whiteside $13.95 (1-55041-405-4). 32pp. Chocolate pies are on the menu as two brothers, Alfie and Joey, make preparations for a surprise party for Grandma. (Rev: BL 11/15/99)

3856 Johnson, Angela. *The Aunt in Our House* (PS–3). Illus. by David Soman. 1996, Orchard LB $16.99 (0-531-08852-9). 32pp. An aunt brings new life and interesting talents during a visit to her brother's biracial family. (Rev: BL 3/1/96; SLJ 4/96)

3857 Johnson, Angela. *Do Like Kyla* (PS–1). Illus. by James E. Ransome. 1990, Orchard $15.95 (0-531-05852-2); paper $6.95 (0-531-07040-9). 32pp. The younger of two sisters imitates the older sibling all day long. (Rev: BL 2/15/90; SLJ 4/90)

3858 Johnson, Angela. *One of Three* (PS–K). Illus. by David Soman. 1991, Orchard $15.95 (0-531-05955-3); paper $5.95 (0-531-07061-1). 32pp. A young African American girl remembers the good times growing up with two older sisters. (Rev: BL 7/91; SLJ 10/91)

3859 Johnson, Angela. *Tell Me a Story, Mama* (PS–1). Illus. by David Soman. 1989, Orchard paper $6.95 (0-531-07032-8). 32pp. An African American mother and daughter reminisce about childhood. (Rev: BCCB 2/89; BL 4/1/89; SLJ 3/89)

3860 Johnson, Angela. *The Wedding* (K–2). Illus. by David Soman. 1999, Orchard LB $17.99 (0-531-33139-3). Through the eyes of young Daisy, the reader experiences all the excitement of the preparations for her sister's wedding. (Rev: BCCB 3/99; HBG 10/99; SLJ 3/99)

3861 Johnson, Angela. *When I Am Old with You* (PS–2). Illus. by David Soman. 1990, Orchard LB $16.99 (0-531-08484-1); paper $6.95 (0-531-07035-2). 32pp. A young African American boy daydreams of all the things he and his grandfather can do when the youngster grows older. (Rev: BL 9/1/90; SLJ 9/90*)

3862 Johnson, Dinah. *Sunday Week* (PS–3). Illus. by Tyrone Geter. 1999, Holt $15.95 (0-8050-4911-8). 32pp. The days of the week are explored through the activities of an African American family, climaxing on Sunday when faith, family, and food take over. (Rev: BCCB 6/99; BL 2/15/99; HB 3–4/99; HBG 10/99; SLJ 6/99)

3863 Johnson, Dolores. *Grandma's Hands* (1–3). Illus. by author. 1998, Marshall Cavendish $15.95 (0-7614-5025-4). Initially unhappy at having to live with his grandmother on her farm, a young African American boy grows to love her and her home. (Rev: HBG 10/98; SLJ 5/98)

3864 Johnston, Tony. *Fishing Sunday* (PS–4). Illus. by Barry Root. 1996, Morrow $16.00 (0-688-13458-0). 32pp. A young boy is embarrassed by his grandfather's eccentric behavior during a fishing expedition. (Rev: BL 5/15/96; SLJ 6/96)

3865 Johnston, Tony. *Uncle Rain Cloud* (PS–3). Illus. by Fabricio Vandenbroeck. 2001, Charlesbridge $15.95 (0-88106-371-1). 32pp. A touching picture about Carlos' cranky Uncle Tomas who becomes animated and happy only when telling stories about his homeland, Mexico, and its culture. (Rev: BL 2/15/01*; HBG 10/01)

3866 Jolin, Dominique. *It's Not Fair!* (PS–3). Illus. by author. 1996, Crossing Pr. $14.95 (0-89594-780-3). A patient father listens as his daughter complains that her friends have more than she does and then reminds her that she has him. (Rev: SLJ 8/96)

3867 Jonell, Lynne. *Let's Play Rough!* (PS–1). Illus. by Ted Rand. 2000, Penguin Putnam $13.99 (0-399-23039-4). 32pp. An episodic picture book that depicts the different games that a little boy plays with his dad. (Rev: BL 2/1/00; HBG 10/00; SLJ 3/00)

3868 Jonell, Lynne. *Mom Pie* (PS–2). Illus. by Petra Mathers. 2001, Penguin Putnam $12.99 (0-399-23422-5). 32pp. While Mom is busy preparing for company, Christopher and his young brother amuse themselves. (Rev: BL 3/15/01; HB 1–2/01; HBG 10/01)

3869 Joosse, Barbara M. *Ghost Wings* (PS–3). Illus. by Giselle Potter. 2001, Chronicle $15.95 (0-8118-2164-1). 40pp. A young Mexican girl revisits the spot where she and her now-dead grandmother used to watch migrating monarch butterflies. (Rev: BCCB 7–8/01; BL 4/15/01; HBG 10/01; SLJ 5/01)

3870 Joosse, Barbara M. *I Love You the Purplest* (PS–1). Illus. by Mary Whyte. 1996, Chronicle $15.95 (0-8118-0718-5). 32pp. Two young brothers compete for the attention of their mother, who demonstrates that she loves them equally. (Rev: BL 10/15/96; SLJ 5/97)

3871 Joosse, Barbara M. *Mama, Do You Love Me?* (PS–2). Illus. by Barbara Lavallee. 1991, Chronicle $14.95 (0-87701-759-X). An Eskimo girl asks her mother if she will still be loved even when she is naughty. (Rev: BCCB 12/91; HB 11–12/91; SLJ 11/91)

3872 Joosse, Barbara M. *Nikolai, the Only Bear* (PS–K). Illus. by Renata Liwska. 2005, Philomel $15.99 (0-399-23884-0). A misfit bear who has lived in a Russian orphanage for several years is finally adopted by an American couple who are bear-friendly. (Rev: SLJ 4/05)

3873 Joslin, Mary. *The Goodbye Boat* (PS–2). Illus. by Claire St Louis Little. 1999, Eerdmans $15.00 (0-8028-5186-X). 28pp. As a metaphor for death, a grandmother leaves her family behind and goes on a long sea journey. (Rev: BL 5/1/99; HBG 10/99; SLJ 6/99)

3874 Jukes, Mavis. *Like Jake and Me* (2–3). Illus. by Lloyd Bloom. 1987, Knopf paper $7.99 (0-394-89263-1). 32pp. Alex and his stepfather explore the meaning of fear.

3875 Juster, Norton. *The Hello, Goodbye Window* (PS–2). Illus. by Chris Raschka. 2005, Hyperion

$15.95 (0-7868-0914-0). 32pp. A little girl enjoys visiting Nanna and Poppy's house and looking out their special window. (Rev: BL 3/15/05; SLJ 3/05)

3876 Kallok, Emma. *Gem* (K–3). Illus. by Joel Bower. 2001, Tricycle $14.95 (1-58246-027-2). 32pp. A saxophone-playing neighbor welcomes a new baby into the world with her own special song. (Rev: BL 6/1–15/01; HBG 3/02; SLJ 4/01)

3877 Kaplan, John. *Mom and Me* (PS–1). Illus. 1996, Scholastic $10.95 (0-590-47294-1). 32pp. In photographs and text, three children talk about their mothers and what these maternal bonds mean to them. (Rev: BL 3/1/96; SLJ 4/96) [306]

3878 Katz, Karen. *Over the Moon: An Adoption Tale* (PS–1). Illus. 1997, Holt $16.95 (0-8050-5013-2). 32pp. A husband and wife prepare for the baby they are going to adopt. (Rev: BL 9/1/97; HBG 3/98; SLJ 9/97)

3879 Keillor, Garrison. *Daddy's Girl* (PS). Illus. by Robin Preiss Glasser. 2005, Hyperion $16.99 (0-7868-1986-3). Four stories in verse celebrate the strong connection between father and daughter; Keillor sings the verses on the accompanying CD. (Rev: SLJ 4/05)

3880 Kirk, Daniel. *Snow Family* (PS–3). Illus. 2000, Hyperion $14.99 (0-7868-0304-5). 32pp. When Jacob realizes that the snow children have no parents, he creates a snow mother and father to make a snow family. (Rev: BL 9/1/00*; HBG 3/01; SLJ 9/00)

3881 Komaiko, Leah. *Just My Dad and Me* (K–3). Illus. by Jeffrey Greene. Series: Laura Geringer Books. 1995, HarperCollins LB $15.89 (0-06-024574-3). A young girl's dream of spending a day alone with her father is dashed when a carload of relatives arrives. (Rev: SLJ 7/95*)

3882 Koutsky, Jan Dale. *My Grandma, My Pen Pal* (2–4). Illus. 2002, Boyds Mills $15.95 (1-56397-118-6). 24pp. The story of a granddaughter's relationship with her grandmother, in the form of a treasured scrapbook. (Rev: BL 5/15/02; HBG 10/02; SLJ 6/02)

3883 Kovalski, Maryann. *Take Me Out to the Ball Game* (PS–2). 2004, Fitzhenry & Whiteside $15.95 (1-55041-897-1). 32pp. The familiar lyrics to "Take Me Out ot the Ball Game" form the framework for this picture-book story of two young sisters' exciting excursion to Yankee Stadium with their grandmother. (Rev: BL 8/04; SLJ 10/04)

3884 Kraus, Robert. *Little Louie the Baby Bloomer* (PS–2). Illus. by Jose Aruego. 1998, HarperCollins LB $15.89 (0-06-026294-X). 32pp. Leo is worried about his younger brother, who can't do anything right. (Rev: BL 3/15/98; HBG 10/98; SLJ 7/98)

3885 Krauss, Ruth. *You're Just What I Need* (PS). Illus. by Julia Noonan. 1998, HarperCollins $14.95 (0-06-027514-6). 32pp. A sentimental picture book in which a mother wonders what the strange bundle could be under the blankets in her bed, knowing, of course, that it is her young child playing a game of hide-and-seek. (Rev: BL 7/98; HBG 10/98; SLJ 7/98)

3886 Kroll, Virginia. *She Is Born: A Celebration of Daughters* (K–3). Illus. by John Rowe. 2000, Beyond Words $15.95 (1-885223-94-3). 32pp. This happy book introduces a baby girl into the world with examples of how she will be lovingly treated. (Rev: BL 7/00; HBG 10/00; SLJ 8/00)

3887 Kurtz, Jane. *Faraway Home* (PS–3). Illus. by E. B. Lewis. 2000, Harcourt $16.00 (0-15-200036-4). 32pp. In this moving family story, a young African American girl has to adjust to the fact that her father must return home to Ethiopia to care for his sick mother. (Rev: BCCB 5/00; BL 2/15/00*; HBG 10/00; SLJ 4/00)

3888 Kurtz, Jane. *In the Small, Small Night* (PS–2). Illus. by Rachel Isadora. 2005, Greenwillow LB $17.89 (0-06-623813-7). 32pp. Abena tells her little brother, Kofi, stories from Ghana, their homeland, to help him fall asleep and to calm his fears about adjusting to their new country. (Rev: BL 3/15/05; SLJ 2/05)

3889 Kurtz, Jane. *Rain Romp: Stomping Away a Grouchy Day* (PS–1). Illus. by Dyanna Wolcott. 2002, HarperCollins LB $17.89 (0-06-029806-5). 32pp. A little girl's mood matches the stormy sky outside until she joins her parents in a dance in the rain. (Rev: BL 9/15/02; HBG 3/03; SLJ 9/02)

3890 Kuskin, Karla. *I Am Me* (PS–2). Illus. by Dyanna Wolcott. 2000, Simon & Schuster $14.00 (0-689-81473-9). 32pp. Although a young girl realizes that she resembles other members of her family (she has her mother's green eyes, for example), she is, nevertheless, a distinct individual. (Rev: BL 6/1–15/00; HBG 10/00; SLJ 7/00)

3891 Lach, William. *Baby Loves* (PS). 2003, Simon & Schuster $12.95 (0-689-85340-8). Mother-and-child paintings by Mary Cassatt are paired with two-word chants in this simple, small book. (Rev: BL 6/1–15/03; HBG 10/03; SLJ 5/03)

3892 Lakin, Patricia. *Dad and Me in the Morning* (K–3). Illus. by Robert G. Steele. 1994, Whitman LB $14.95 (0-8075-1419-5). 32pp. A deaf boy and his father communicate their feelings to each other as they watch a sunrise. (Rev: BL 4/1/94; SLJ 6/94)

3893 Laminack, Lester L. *The Sunsets of Miss Olivia Wiggins* (K–4). Illus. by Constance R. Bergum. 1998, Peachtree $15.95 (1-56145-139-8). 32pp. Although it appears that Miss Olivia Wiggins, an Alzheimer's disease sufferer, does recognize her daughter and great-grandson when they visit her at a nursing home, inwardly she is recalling pleasant times from the past. (Rev: BL 5/1/98; HBG 10/98; SLJ 7/98)

3894 Lane, Lindsey. *Snuggle Mountain* (PS). Illus. by Melissa Iwai. 2003, Clarion $15.00 (0-618-04328-4). 31pp. Lttle Emma conjures up all sorts of fantasies as she climbs to the top of Snuggle Mountain (her parents' bed). (Rev: HBG 10/03; SLJ 4/03)

3895 Langley, Karen. *Shine* (K–2). Illus. by Jonathan Langley. 2002, Marshall Cavendish $15.95 (0-7614-5127-7). Jimmy worries that his busy father won't come to see him as the star of Bethlehem. (Rev: HBG 3/03; SLJ 1/03)

3896 Lasky, Kathryn. *Before I Was Your Mother* (PS–2). Illus. by LeUyen Pham. 2003, Harcourt $16.00 (0-15-201464-0). 40pp. Ruby's mother tells Ruby tales about her own childhood and her friends and activities. (Rev: BL 3/15/03; HBG 10/03; SLJ 5/03)

3897 Lasky, Kathryn. *Lucille Camps In* (PS–1). Illus. by Marylin Hafner. 2003, Knopf LB $16.99 (0-517-80042-X). Young Lucille is downcast when her older brother and sister go off on a camping trip with their father, but her spirits pick up when she and her mother have an indoor camping adventure at home. (Rev: HBG 10/03; SLJ 7/03)

3898 Lasky, Kathryn, and Jane Kamine. *Mommy's Hands* (PS–K). Illus. by Darcia LaBrosse. 2002, Hyperion $15.99 (0-7868-0280-4). 32pp. Three children — one Asian, one Caucasian, and one African American — describe what they like about their mothers' hands. (Rev: BL 6/1–15/02; HBG 10/02; SLJ 7/02)

3899 Lears, Laurie. *Becky the Brave: A Story About Epilepsy* (PS–3). Illus. by Gail Piazza. 2002, Whitman LB $14.95 (0-8075-0601-X). Sarah admires her older sister Becky's confidence and composure, but Becky has not been brave enough to tell her classmates about her epilepsy. (Rev: HBG 10/02; SLJ 5/02)

3900 Lears, Laurie. *Megan's Birthday Tree: A Story About Open Adoption* (K–3). Illus. by Bill Farnsworth. 2005, Whitman $15.95 (0-8075-5036-1). 32pp. Megan worries that she will be forgotten when her birth mother, Kendra, moves to a new house, but she is reassured that they will still see one another. (Rev: BL 3/1/05; SLJ 6/05)

3901 LeBox, Annette. *Wild Bog Tea* (K–3). Illus. by Harvey Chan. 2001, Groundwood $16.95 (0-88899-406-0). 32pp. A man's gentle remembrances of childhood with his grandfather include walks through the bogs and marshes of Labrador. (Rev: BL 12/15/01; HBG 3/02; SLJ 9/01)

3902 Lee, Spike, and Tonya Lewis Lee. *Please, Baby, Please* (K–2). Illus. by Kadir Nelson. 2002, Simon & Schuster $16.95 (0-689-83233-8). 32pp. An appealing picture book by movie director Spike Lee and his producer wife that shows a mother continually pleading with her toddler to behave, until at bedtime it's the little one who begs for a goodnight kiss. (Rev: BCCB 2/03; BL 12/1/02; HBG 3/03; SLJ 12/02)

3903 Leedy, Loreen. *Who's Who in My Family?* (PS–1). Illus. 1995, Holiday House LB $16.95 (0-8234-1151-6). 32pp. Family relationships and the words used to describe them are the subject of this book on all kinds of families. (Rev: BCCB 3/95; BL 3/1/95; SLJ 4/95)

3904 Legge, David. *Bamboozled* (PS–3). Illus. 1995, Scholastic $14.95 (0-590-47989-X). 32pp. A surreal presentation of a girl's visit to her grandfather's house. (Rev: BCCB 3/95; BL 1/15/95; HB 11–12/95; SLJ 3/95*)

3905 Leighton, Audrey O. *A Window of Time* (K–3). Illus. by Rhonda Kyrias. 1995, NADIA $15.95 (0-9636335-1-1). 32pp. Shawn is troubled by his grandfather's frequent loss of memory and mental confusion. (Rev: BL 2/1/96)

3906 Lemieux, Margo. *The Fiddle Ribbon* (1–3). Illus. by Francis Livingston. 1996, Silver Burdett LB $22.00 (0-382-39096-2); paper $5.95 (0-382-39098-9). Jennie learns to play the fiddle and brother Jimmy enjoys folk dancing during the summer they spend on their grandparent's farm. (Rev: SLJ 9/96)

3907 Levine, Abby. *Daddies Give You Horsey Rides* (PS–1). Illus. by John Bendall-Brunello. 2004, Whitman $15.95 (0-8075-1429-2). 32pp. Animal fathers display the varied ways in which they add value to their children's lives in this simple book with a lively rhyme and humorous illustrations. (Rev: BL 3/15/04; SLJ 5/04)

3908 Levy, Janice. *Abuelito Eats with His Fingers* (1–3). Illus. by Layne Johnson. 1999, Eakin $14.95 (1-57168-177-9). Tina is ashamed of her crude, peasantlike grandfather, but one day she discovers they share a love of art. (Rev: HBG 3/00; SLJ 9/99)

3909 Lewis, Cynthia C. *Dilly's Big Sister Diary* (2–4). Illus. by Cynthia Copeland Lewis. 1998, Millbrook LB $19.90 (0-7613-0414-2). Eight-year-old Dilly is given a diary by her parents to chronicle the development of her new younger brother, Matthew. (Rev: HBG 3/99; SLJ 2/99)

3910 Lewis, Rob. *Hide-and-Seek with Grandpa* (1–3). Illus. by author. 1997, Mondo paper $4.50 (1-57255-226-3). 48pp. Young Finley is always surprised at his Grandpa Bear's vim and vigor. Also use *Grandpa Comes to Stay* (1997). (Rev: SLJ 8/97)

3911 Lin, Grace. *Kite Flying* (K–3). 2002, Knopf $14.95 (0-375-81520-1). 32pp. A Chinese girl describes the family ritual of making and flying kites. (Rev: BL 6/1–15/02; HBG 10/02; SLJ 7/02)

3912 Lin, Grace. *The Ugly Vegetables* (K–2). Illus. 1999, Charlesbridge LB $15.95 (0-88106-336-3). 32pp. A Chinese American girl is disappointed in the dullness of her family garden compared with the lovely flowers she sees in other gardens — until harvest time when her mother makes a delicious soup from all the unusual Chinese vegetables. (Rev: BL 9/15/99; HB 9–10/99; HBG 3/00; SLJ 9/99)

3913 Lindahl, Inger. *Bertil and the Bathroom Elephants* (PS–K). Trans. from Swedish by Elisabeth Kallick Dyssegaard. Illus. by Eva Lindstrom. 2003, R&S $15.00 (91-29-65944-2). Three-year-old Bertil starts to believe that his invented elephants really do exist under the bathtub and refuses to use the bathroom at all. (Rev: HB 9–10/03; HBG 4/04; SLJ 12/03)

3914 Lindbergh, Reeve. *My Hippie Grandmother* (PS–2). Illus. by Abby Carter. 2003, Candlewick $15.99 (0-7636-0671-5). 24pp. A little girl talks about her grandmother, who went to Woodstock and has a flower power poster. (Rev: BL 3/1/03; HBG 10/03; SLJ 4/03)

3915 Lindbergh, Reeve. *The Visit* (K–3). Illus. by Wendy Andersen Halperin. 2005, Dial $16.99 (0-8037-1189-1). 40pp. Rhyming couplets and eye-catching artwork evoke two sisters' enjoyment of a visit to the farm of their aunt and uncle. (Rev: BL 2/15/05; SLJ 3/05)

3916 Lo, Ginnie. *Mahjong All Day Long* (PS–2). Illus. by Beth Lo. 2005, Walker LB $17.85 (0-8027-8942-0). 32pp. The game of mahjong is important in a Chinese family's rituals and enjoyment of life. (Rev: BL 2/15/05; SLJ 5/05)

3917 Lobel, Anita. *Potatoes, Potatoes* (K–3). Illus. 2004, Greenwillow LB $16.89 (0-06-051818-9). 40pp. A new edition of a 1967 picture book about two brothers whose mother teaches them to make peace. (Rev: BL 1/1–15/04)

3918 Lohans, Alison. *Waiting for the Sun* (K–2). Illus. by Marilyn Mets and Peter Ledwon. 2002, Red Deer $16.95 (0-88995-240-X). After a lot of anticipation, Mollie is disappointed at first by the sight of her new baby brother. (Rev: SLJ 7/02)

3919 Long, Earlene. *Gone Fishing* (PS–2). Illus. by Richard Brown. 1987, Houghton Mifflin paper $5.95 (0-395-44236-2). 32pp. A loving story of a boy's fishing trip with his father.

3920 Look, Lenore. *Love as Strong as Ginger* (K–4). Illus. by Stephen T. Johnson. 1999, Simon & Schuster $15.00 (0-689-81248-5). 40pp. A young Chinese American girl goes to visit a cannery in the Seattle area where her grandmother, a recent immigrant, has to work backbreaking hours to earn a living. (Rev: BL 10/15/99*; HB 5–6/99; HBG 10/99; SLJ 7/99)

3921 Loomis, Christine. *Across America, I Love You* (K–2). Illus. by Kate Kiesler. 2000, Hyperion LB $16.49 (0-7868-2314-3). Different landscapes and different seasons are used to illustrate the lasting relationship between mother and daughter. (Rev: HBG 3/01; SLJ 7/00)

3922 Louie, Therese On. *Raymond's Perfect Present* (K–2). Illus. by Suling Wang. 2002, Lee & Low $16.95 (1-58430-055-8). 32pp. A tender story about a boy who can't afford flowers for his sick mother, but instead plants seeds. (Rev: BL 10/15/02; HBG 3/03; SLJ 11/02)

3923 Lyon, George E. *Five Live Bongos* (PS–1). Illus. by Jacqueline Rogers. 1994, Scholastic $15.95 (0-590-46654-2). 40pp. Five brothers and sisters make so much noise indoors that they are banished to the garage. (Rev: BL 10/15/94; SLJ 10/94)

3924 McCaughrean, Geraldine. *My Grandmother's Clock* (K–3). Illus. by Stephen Lambert. 2002, Clarion $15.00 (0-618-21695-2). 32pp. A grandmother explains to her young granddaughter how she tells time: by relying on life's rhythms, rather than on clocks. (Rev: BL 9/15/02; HB 1–2/03; HBG 3/03; SLJ 9/02)

3925 McCloskey, Robert. *One Morning in Maine* (1–3). Illus. by author. 1952, Puffin paper $5.99 (0-14-050174-6). An exciting day, the loss of Sal's first tooth, is realistically recaptured by this fine storyteller and in the large, extraordinary blue-pencil drawings of Penobscot Bay. Also use: *Blueberries for Sal* (1948).

3926 McCormick, Wendy. *The Night You Were Born* (PS–2). Illus. by Sophy Williams. 2000, Peachtree $15.95 (1-56145-225-4). 32pp. While waiting for news of the arrival of a sibling, Jamie listens to a story about the night he was born. (Rev: BL 1/1–15/01; HBG 3/01; SLJ 12/00)

3927 McCourt, Lisa. *I Miss You, Stinky Face* (PS–K). Illus. by Cyd Moore. 1999, Troll $15.95 (0-8167-5647-3). 32pp. A youngster's anxiety about his mother getting home causes a series of "what ifs," such as "What if the airplane forgets to fly?" (Rev: BL 4/15/99; SLJ 5/99)

3928 McCourt, Lisa. *The Most Thankful Thing* (PS–1). Illus. by Cyd Moore. 2003, Troll LB $15.95 (0-8167-7721-7). A young girl wonders what her mother is most thankful for as they page through a scrapbook. (Rev: HBG 4/04; SLJ 8/03)

3929 McCully, Emily Arnold. *The Orphan Singer* (PS–3). Illus. 2001, Scholastic $16.95 (0-439-19274-9). 32pp. A poor family leaves a talented daughter at an orphanage where she will receive the best vocal training possible. (Rev: BCCB 2/02; BL 11/15/01; HB 9–10/01; HBG 3/02; SLJ 11/01*)

3930 McCutcheon, John. *Happy Adoption Day!* (PS–2). Illus. by Julie Paschkis. 1996, Little, Brown $15.95 (0-316-55455-3). 32pp. In simple rhymes, the story of an American family's adoption of an Asian child is told. (Rev: BL 12/1/96; SLJ 11/96) [782.42]

3931 McFarlane, Sheryl. *Waiting for the Whales* (PS–3). Illus. by Ron Lightburn. 1991, Orca paper $6.95 (0-920501-96-6). 32pp. On his lonely island an old man and his granddaughter await the sighting of the summer whales. (Rev: BL 5/15/93; SLJ 6/93)

3932 MacLachlan, Patricia. *Mama One, Mama Two* (1–3). Illus. by Ruth Bornstein. 1982, HarperCollins LB $15.89 (0-06-024082-2). 32pp. Maudie is told why she has two mothers in this gentle story of a foster home.

3933 MacLachlan, Patricia. *The Sick Day* (PS–1). Illus. by Jane Dyer. 2001, Doubleday $12.95 (0-385-32150-3). 32pp. Emily's father takes care of her when she gets sick but the next day, when he catches the bug, it's Emily's turn to play nurse. (Rev: BL 2/15/01; HBG 10/01)

3934 MacLachlan, Patricia. *Through Grandpa's Eyes* (1–3). Illus. by Deborah Kogan Ray. 1980, HarperCollins LB $15.89 (0-06-024043-1); paper $5.95 (0-06-443041-3). 48pp. John's blind grandfather shares with him the special way he sees and moves in the world.

3935 McMahon, Patricia, and Conor Clarke McCarthy. *Just Add One Chinese Sister* (PS–2). Illus. by Karen A. Jerome. 2005, Boyds Mills $16.95 (1-56397-989-6). 32pp. A moving journal chronicles a family's adoption of a little girl from China in alternating entries by the adoptive mother and initially reluctant big brother Conor. (Rev: BL 2/1/05; SLJ 2/05) [362.73]

3936 McMillan, Bruce. *Step by Step* (PS). Illus. by author. 1990, Apple Island LB $15.00 (0-688-07234-8). 28pp. Photos trace Evan from four months until he becomes a fast walker at 14 months. (Rev: BL 9/1/87; HB 11–12/87; SLJ 9/87)

3937 Mahy, Margaret. *A Busy Day for a Good Grandmother* (PS–3). Illus. by Margaret Chamberlain. 1993, Macmillan $14.95 (0-689-50595-7). 32pp. Mrs. Oberon is an unconventional grandmother who rides skateboards and fights vultures and alligators. (Rev: BL 10/15/93; SLJ 9/93)

3938 Maloney, Peter, and Felicia Zekauskas. *His Mother's Nose* (K–3). Illus. 2001, Dial $15.99 (0-8037-2545-0). 40pp. Percival learns that he is special even if many of his traits and features were inherited from family members. (Rev: BL 9/1/01; HBG 3/02; SLJ 10/01)

3939 Manning, Mick, and Brita Granström. *Supermom* (PS–K). Illus. 2001, Whitman $15.95 (0-8075-7666-2). 32pp. Using both humans and animals as subjects, this book explores the many tasks that mothers perform. (Rev: BL 3/15/01; HBG 10/01)

3940 Manson, Ainslie. *Ballerinas Don't Wear Glasses* (PS–3). Illus. by Dean Griffiths. 2000, Orca $15.95 (1-55143-158-0). 32pp. In this warm family story, older brother Ben must help his little sister Alison prepare for her dance recital. (Rev: BL 12/1/00; HBG 3/01; SLJ 8/00)

3941 Mario, Heidi Stetson. *I'd Rather Have an Iguana* (PS–1). Illus. 1999, Charlesbridge $14.95 (0-88106-357-6). 32pp. Big sister doesn't want to have a baby brother, but one day when they are alone, she changes her mind. (Rev: BL 1/1–15/99; HBG 10/99; SLJ 4/99)

3942 Martin, C. L. G. *Three Brave Women* (K–2). Illus. by Peter Elwell. 1991, Macmillan $16.00 (0-02-762445-5). 32pp. Caitlin finds she is afraid of spiders, and her grandmother tells her of her private fears. (Rev: BL 5/1/91; SLJ 5/91)

3943 Martin, Jacqueline Briggs. *The Water Gift and the Pig of the Pig* (K–2). Illus. by Linda S. Wingert-er. 2003, Houghton Mifflin $15.00 (0-618-07436-8). When the pig that is an important part of their family history disappears, Isabel discovers that — like her grandfather — she has the ability to locate precious things. (Rev: HB 5–6/03; HBG 10/03; SLJ 6/03)

3944 Maslac, Evelyn Hughes. *Finding a Job for Daddy* (PS–3). Illus. by Kay Life. 1996, Whitman LB $13.95 (0-8075-2437-9). 32pp. Laura tries to cheer up her father, who is out of work. (Rev: BL 4/1/96)

3945 Masurel, Claire. *Two Homes* (PS–K). Illus. by Kady M. Denton. 2001, Candlewick $14.99 (0-7636-0511-5). 40pp. Young Alex takes a matter-of-fact attitude to his two homes, one with his mother, the other with his father. (Rev: BL 6/1–15/01; HBG 10/01; SLJ 8/01)

3946 Matze, Claire Sidhom. *The Stars in My Geddoh's Sky* (PS–3). Illus. by Bill Farnsworth. 1999, Whitman $14.95 (0-8075-5332-8). An Arab grandfather (geddoh) from Palestine comes to the U.S. to visit the family of his grandson, Alex. (Rev: BL 5/15/99; HBG 10/99; SLJ 5/99)

3947 Mauner, Claudia, and Elisa Smalley. *Zoe Sophia's Scrapbook: An Adventure in Venice* (1–4). Illus. by Claudia Mauner. 2003, Chronicle $14.95 (0-8118-3606-1). Nine-year-old Zoe Sophia, accompanied by her dachshund Mickey, explores the wonders of Venice during a visit to her Great-Aunt

Dorothy in this picture book for older readers using a diary format. (Rev: BL 5/15/03; HBG 10/03; SLJ 8/03)

3948 May, Kathy L. *Molasses Man* (PS–3). Illus. by Felicia Marshall. 2000, Holiday House $16.95 (0-8234-1438-8). 32pp. Seen through the eyes of a young African American boy, this is the story of how his family makes molasses under the supervision of Grandpa, the Molasses Man. (Rev: BL 10/1/00; HBG 3/01; SLJ 10/00)

3949 Melmed, Laura Krauss. *A Hug Goes Around* (PS–k). Illus. by Betsy Lewin. 2002, HarperCollins LB $15.89 (0-688-14681-8). 32pp. In spite of minor disasters, a family muddles through because they can comfort each other with hugs. (Rev: BL 6/1–15/02)

3950 Mennen, Ingrid. *One Round Moon and a Star for Me* (PS–1). Illus. by Niki Daly. 1994, Orchard LB $16.99 (0-531-08654-2). 32pp. In this tale that takes place in Lesotho, a young boy needs reassurance when a new baby arrives in the family. (Rev: BCCB 4/94; BL 2/15/94; SLJ 9/94)

3951 Michaels, William. *Clare and Her Shadow* (PS–1). Illus. by author. 1991, Shoe String LB $16.50 (0-208-02301-1). While on a walk with her grandmother, Clare discovers her shadow. (Rev: SLJ 2/92)

3952 Michelson, Rich. *Too Young for Yiddish* (K–4). Illus. by Neil Waldman. 2002, Charlesbridge $15.95 (0-88106-118-2). 32pp. A young boy wants his grandfather to teach him the Yiddish language in this poignant tale that is part history, part family story. (Rev: BL 3/1/02; HBG 10/02; SLJ 3/02)

3953 Millen, C. M. *The Low-Down Laundry Line Blues* (PS–3). Illus. by Christine Davenier. 1999, Houghton Mifflin $15.00 (0-395-87497-1). 32pp. A little girl is cheered up when her younger sister uses their laundry line as a skipping rope. (Rev: BL 4/15/99; HB 3–4/99; HBG 10/99; SLJ 5/99)

3954 Miller, Margaret. *Baby Faces* (PS). Illus. 1998, Simon & Schuster $4.99 (0-689-81911-0). 14pp. A board book in which babies' faces are used to illustrate different moods and attitudes. (Rev: BL 7/98; HBG 10/98; SLJ 7/98)

3955 Miller, Margaret. *What's on My Head?* (PS). Illus. 1998, Simon & Schuster $4.99 (0-689-81912-9). 14pp. In this board book, babies wear such unusual headgear as a firefighter's hat, beanbag animals, and a rubber duck. (Rev: BL 7/98; HBG 10/98; SLJ 7/98)

3956 Miller, William. *A House by the River* (K–2). Illus. by Cornelius Van Wright. 1997, Lee & Low $15.95 (1-880000-48-2). 32pp. Belinda is afraid that her house will get flooded if heavy rains come, but her mother tells her about how the house has been a safe haven through the years. (Rev: BL 5/15/97; HB 7–8/97; SLJ 7/97)

3957 Miller, William. *Zora Hurston and the Chinaberry Tree* (PS–3). Illus. by Cornelius Van Wright and Ying-hwa Hu. 1994, Lee & Low $15.95 (1-880000-14-8); paper $6.95 (1-880000-33-4). 32pp. A picture book that explores the trauma experienced by the author Zora Hurston when her beloved mother died when the girl was only nine. (Rev: BL 10/15/94; SLJ 12/94) [813]

3958 Minchella, Nancy. *Mama Will Be Home Soon* (PS). Illus. by Keiko Narahashi. 2003, Scholastic $15.95 (0-439-38491-5). Lili doesn't want her mother to leave and worries about finding her again, but her mother reassures her, telling Lili to watch for Mama's yellow hat. (Rev: HBG 10/03; SLJ 8/03)

3959 Mitchell, Rhonda. *The Talking Cloth* (PS–2). Illus. 1997, Orchard LB $16.99 (0-531-33004-4). 32pp. When Amber drapes her aunt's cloth from Ghana around herself, she pretends she is an Ashanti princess. (Rev: BCCB 6/97; BL 2/15/97; SLJ 7/97)

3960 Molk, Laurel. *When You Were Just a Heartbeat* (PS–1). Illus. 2004, Little, Brown $16.95 (0-316-57980-7). 32pp. Gentle watercolor illustrations highlight a mother's joy as she tells her newborn about the new life growing within her against the backdrop of the changing seasons. (Rev: BL 5/1/04; SLJ 7/04)

3961 Monk, Isabell. *Blackberry Stew* (PS–2). Illus. by Janice Lee Porter. 2005, Carolrhoda $15.95 (1-57505-605-4). 32pp. Hope learns that she can keep her grandfather alive in her memory in this story of a warm African American family. (Rev: BL 2/1/05; SLJ 6/05)

3962 Monk, Isabell. *Family* (PS–2). Illus. by Janice L. Porter. 2001, Carolrhoda $15.95 (1-57505-485-X). 32pp. Celebrates the fun and food of an African American family reunion (complete with recipes). (Rev: BL 2/15/01; HBG 10/01)

3963 Monk, Isabell. *Hope* (K–3). Illus. by Janice L. Porter. 1999, Carolrhoda LB $15.95 (1-57505-230-X). Hope's great aunt Poogee tells the little girl that she should be proud of her biracial background and that her white father and African American mother represent two important cultures. (Rev: HBG 10/99; SLJ 6/99)

3964 Montanari, Eva. *Tiff, Taff, and Lulu* (K–2). Illus. by author. 2004, Houghton Mifflin $16.00 (0-618-40238-1). Three monster sisters put aside their differences when their mother is injured in an accident. (Rev: SLJ 9/04)

3965 Mora, Pat. *Pablo's Tree* (PS–3). Illus. by Cecily Lang. 1994, Macmillan paper $16.00 (0-02-767401-0). 32pp. Ever since his daughter adopted young Pablo, grandfather decorates a tree on the anniversary of the boy's arrival. (Rev: BCCB 9/94; BL 11/1/94; HB 11–12/94)

3966 Morrow, Tara Jaye. *Mommy Loves Her Baby / Daddy Loves His Baby: A Mommy/Daddy Flipbook* (PS). Illus. by Tiphanie Beeke. 2003, HarperCollins LB $16.89 (0-06-029078-1). In this sentimental paean to parental love, a mother and father separately compare the love for their baby to things that animals love, as in Mommy saying she loves the infant like "fishies love the seas, like the monkeys love bananas and the squirrels love the trees." (Rev: HB 5–6/03; HBG 10/03; SLJ 7/03)

3967 Newman, Leslea. *Felicia's Favorite Story* (PS–1). Illus. by Adriana Romo. 2003, Two Lives paper $9.95 (0-9674468-5-6). 24pp. Felicia, who was born in Guatemala, loves to hear her adoptive parents — two women — tell her how she came to be a member of their family. (Rev: SLJ 10/03)

3968 Nielsen-Fernlund, Susin. *Mormor Moves In* (PS–1). 2004, Orca $16.95 (1-55143-291-9). Astrid has a hard time adapting to the arrival of her bereaved Swedish grandmother. (Rev: SLJ 11/04)

3969 Norac, Carl. *My Daddy Is a Giant* (PS). Illus. by Ingrid Godon. 2005, Clarion $16.00 (0-618-44399-1). 32pp. Eye-catching illustrations draw readers into this simple story of a boy who idolizes his father. (Rev: BL 6/1–15/05; SLJ 5/05)

3970 Numeroff, Laura. *What Grandmas Do Best / What Grandpas Do Best* (PS–K). Illus. by Lynn Munsinger. 2000, Simon & Schuster $14.00 (0-689-80552-7). 40pp. This is an upside-down book that if read one way shows children happy with their grandmothers and, when turned over, shows similar scenes with grandfathers. (Rev: BL 11/15/00; HBG 3/01; SLJ 10/00)

3971 O'Callahan, Jay. *Orange Cheeks* (PS–2). Illus. by Patricia Raine. 1993, Peachtree $15.95 (1-56145-073-1). 40pp. A young boy tries not to create trouble when he visits his grandmother. (Rev: BL 7/93)

3972 O'Hair, Margaret. *Twin to Twin* (PS). Illus. by Thierry Courtin. 2003, Simon & Schuster $15.95 (0-689-84494-8). Toddler twins — brother and sister — are shown going about their daily lives in a friendly text and lively illustrations. (Rev: BL 6/1–15/03; HBG 10/03; SLJ 5/03)

3973 Okimoto, Jean Davies, and Elaine M. Aoki. *The White Swan Express: A Story About Adoption* (K–3). Illus. by Meilo So. 2002, Clarion $16.00 (0-618-16453-7). 32pp. This story alternates between adoptive parents in North America and the children awaiting adoption in China, with information on the legalities of adopting children and on China's policies on childbirth. (Rev: BL 11/1/02; HBG 3/03; SLJ 2/03)

3974 Older, Effin. *My Two Grandmothers* (PS–1). Illus. by Nancy Hayashi. 2000, Harcourt $16.00 (0-15-200785-7). 32pp. Lily loves her two very different grandmothers and spends Hanukkah with Bubbe Silver in her big city apartment and Christmas with Grammy Lane on her farm. (Rev: BL 10/15/00; HBG 3/01; SLJ 10/00)

3975 Ormerod, Jan. *Who's Whose?* (K–3). Illus. 1998, Lothrop LB $15.93 (0-688-14679-1). 32pp. A delightful, breezy account of the members of three families, their activities, and how they help one another. (Rev: BL 3/15/98; HBG 10/98; SLJ 4/98)

3976 Ostrow, Vivian. *My Brother Is from Outer Space: The Book of Proof* (K–3). Illus. by Eric Brace. 1996, Whitman $14.95 (0-8075-5325-5). 32pp. Alex is convinced that his young brother is really an alien from outer space. (Rev: BCCB 5/96; BL 4/1/96; SLJ 6/96)

3977 Ovenell-Carter, Julie. *The Butterflies' Promise* (K–3). Illus. by Kitty Macaulay. 1999, Annick LB $15.95 (1-55037-567-9); paper $5.95 (1-55037-566-0). When Milly's grandfather goes to a nursing home, the little girl thinks of a way to bring his beloved garden to him. (Rev: HBG 10/99; SLJ 10/99)

3978 Pak, Soyung. *Dear Juno* (PS–2). Illus. by Susan Kathleen Hartung. 1999, Viking $15.99 (0-670-88252-6). 32pp. Although he can't read Korean, Juno is able to piece together clues about the contents of the letter he has received from his grandmother in Seoul. (Rev: BCCB 1/00; BL 11/15/99; HBG 3/00; SLJ 12/99)

3979 Palatini, Margie. *Goldie Is Mad* (PS–K). Illus. by author. 2001, Hyperion LB $15.49 (0-7868-2490-5). Goldie doesn't like her baby brother at all, but when she imagines him gone she finds she might miss him. (Rev: HBG 3/02; SLJ 7/01)

3980 Paradis, Susan. *My Daddy* (PS–1). Illus. 1998, Front Street $15.95 (1-886910-30-8). 32pp. A wonderful picture book about a boy's admiration for his father, who can perform such wonders as riding a two-wheeled bike and finding his way home from work alone. (Rev: BL 7/98*; HBG 10/98; SLJ 1/99)

3981 Paradis, Susan. *My Mommy* (PS–1). Illus. 2002, Front Street $15.95 (1-886910-73-1). 32pp. Radiant, cheery illustrations that feature sly peeks at wild animals accompany a little girl's simple list of the reasons she loves her mother. (Rev: BL 1/1–15/03; HBG 3/03; SLJ 1/03)

3982 Parr, Todd. *The Family Book* (PS–2). Illus. by author. 2003, Little, Brown $15.95 (0-316-73896-4). Families of all kinds are celebrated in bright, humorous illustrations. (Rev: HBG 4/04; SLJ 12/03)

3983 Partridge, Elizabeth. *Whistling* (PS–2). Illus. by Anna Grossnickle Hines. 2003, Greenwillow LB $16.89 (0-06-050236-3). A beautifully illustrated portrait of the close relationship between a father and son as they enjoy a camping trip. (Rev: HBG 10/03; SLJ 4/03)

3984 Patrick, Denise Lewis. *Ma Dear's Old Green House* (PS–2). Illus. by Sonia Lynn Sadler. 2004, Just Us $16.95 (0-940975-55-6). 32pp. A young African American girl recalls the joys of a summer spent at her grandmother's house in the South. (Rev: BL 2/1/05; SLJ 1/05)

3985 Patrick, Denise Lewis. *Red Dancing Shoes* (PS–2). Illus. by James E. Ransome. 1993, Morrow $15.89 (0-688-10393-6). Grandma gives her young granddaughter a new pair of dancing shoes. (Rev: BL 3/1/93; SLJ 3/93)

3986 Patrick, Jean L. S. *If I Had a Snowplow* (PS–1). Illus. by Karen M. Dugan. 2001, Boyds Mills $14.95 (1-56397-746-X). A loving boy tells his mother what he would do for her if he had various objects (a truck, a tractor, a bulldozer). (Rev: HBG 3/02; SLJ 12/01)

3987 Pearson, Debora. *Leo's Tree* (PS–K). Illus. by Nora Hilb. 2004, Annick LB $19.95 (1-55037-845-7); paper $5.95 (1-55037-844-9). Leo and the linden tree planted when he was a baby grow together; when sister Sophie arrives, another sapling is added. (Rev: SLJ 6/04)

3988 Pellegrini, Nina. *Families Are Different* (PS–3). Illus. 1991, Holiday House LB $16.95 (0-8234-0887-6). 32pp. Two adopted Korean girls gradually

adjust to their new American family. (Rev: BL 12/15/91; SLJ 10/91)

3989 Pelton, Mindy L. *When Dad's at Sea* (PS–1). Illus. by Robert Grantt Steele. 2004, Whitman $15.95 (0-8075-6339-0). 32pp. Emily learns to deal with feelings of loss and fear during the six months her father is deployed at sea as a Navy pilot. (Rev: BL 3/15/04; SLJ 7/04)

3990 Perkins, Lynne Rae. *The Broken Cat* (PS–2). Illus. 2002, Greenwillow LB $15.89 (0-06-029264-4). 32pp. While Frank waits with his injured cat at the vet's office, his mother, aunt, and grandmother distract him with a story about the time his mother broke her arm. (Rev: BL 3/15/02; HB 5–6/02*; HBG 10/02; SLJ 6/02)

3991 Pham, LeUyen. *Big Sister, Little Sister* (PS–2). Illus. 2005, Hyperion $15.99 (0-7868-5182-1). 40pp. The tensions between younger and older sisters are captured in simple text and lively illustrations. (Rev: BL 6/1–15/05)

3992 Plourde, Lynn. *Dad, Aren't You Glad?* (PS–2). Illus. by Amy Wummer. 2005, Dutton $12.99 (0-525-47362-9). A little boy tries to give his father a treat by taking over his chores, with predictable consequences. (Rev: SLJ 3/05)

3993 Plourde, Lynn. *Thank You, Grandpa* (K–3). Illus. by Jason Cockcroft. 2003, Dutton $15.99 (0-525-46992-3). 32pp. When a girl's grandfather dies, she uses what she learned on their nature walks together to say good-bye. (Rev: BL 2/15/03; HBG 10/03; SLJ 4/03)

3994 Polacco, Patricia. *My Ol' Man* (1–3). Illus. 1995, Penguin Putnam $16.99 (0-399-22822-5). 32pp. Two youngsters enjoy the stories that their traveling-salesman father tells when he comes home. (Rev: BL 4/1/95; SLJ 5/95)

3995 Polacco, Patricia. *My Rotten Redheaded Older Brother* (K–3). Illus. 1994, Simon & Schuster $16.00 (0-671-72751-6). 30pp. A young girl engages in a fierce rivalry with her brother in spite of an underlying love. (Rev: BL 9/15/94; SLJ 10/94*)

3996 Polacco, Patricia. *Thunder Cake* (PS–3). Illus. 1990, Penguin Putnam $15.95 (0-399-22231-6). 32pp. A grandmother helps her young granddaughter conquer her fears of electrical storms by eating Thunder Cake. (Rev: BCCB 3/90; BL 2/15/90*; HB 3–4/90; SLJ 3/90*)

3997 Polacco, Patricia. *When Lightning Comes in a Jar* (2–4). Illus. 2002, Penguin Putnam $16.99 (0-399-23164-1). 40pp. An autobiographical remembrance of fun, games, and traditions at family reunions. (Rev: BL 8/02; HBG 10/02; SLJ 6/02)

3998 Pomerantz, Charlotte. *The Chalk Doll* (PS–1). Illus. by Frane Lessac. 1989, HarperCollins paper $6.95 (0-06-443333-1). 32pp. Rose is sick, and Mother tells her stories of her Jamaican girlhood. (Rev: BL 5/15/89; HB 7–8/89)

3999 Porter-Gaylord, Laurel. *I Love My Daddy Because . . .* (PS–K). Illus. by Ashley Wolff. 1991, Dutton $7.99 (0-525-44624-9). 24pp. Reasons for loving one's father are illustrated through both human and animal examples. A companion volume is *I Love My Mommy Because . . .* (Rev: BCCB 2/91; BL 4/15/91; SLJ 1/92)

4000 Pow, Tom. *Tell Me One Thing, Dad* (PS–1). Illus. by Ian Andrew. 2004, Candlewick $15.99 (0-7636-2474-8). 32pp. To postpone the moment when her bedroom light will be turned off for the night, young Molly asks her father about a variety of real and imaginary creatures. (Rev: BL 4/1/04*; SLJ 6/04)

4001 Prigger, Mary Skillings. *Aunt Minnie and the Twister* (PS–2). Illus. by Betsy Lewin. 2002, Clarion $15.00 (0-618-11136-0). 32pp. Aunt Minnie and her nine nieces and nephews run to the root cellar to escape a twister that turns their house completely around. (Rev: BL 2/15/02; HB 5–6/02; HBG 10/02; SLJ 4/02)

4002 Prigger, Mary Skillings. *Aunt Minnie McGranahan* (PS–2). Illus. by Betsy Lewin. 1999, Clarion $15.00 (0-395-82270-X). 32pp. Minnie McGranahan accepts nine orphaned nieces and nephews into her household, and although she regulates their schedules, there is always time for fun. (Rev: BCCB 5/99; BL 5/1/99; HBG 10/99; SLJ 5/99)

4003 Pringle, Laurence. *Bear Hug* (K–3). Illus. by Kate S. Palmer. 2003, Boyds Mills $15.95 (1-56397-876-8). Jesse and Becky go camping with Dad and really hope to see a bear. (Rev: HBG 10/03; SLJ 2/03)

4004 Pryor, Bonnie. *The Dream Jar* (K–4). Illus. by Mark Graham. 1996, Morrow LB $15.93 (0-688-13062-3). 32pp. In turn-of-the-century New York City, a young immigrant girl helps her family by teaching them English. (Rev: BL 3/1/96; HB 7–8/96; SLJ 3/96)

4005 Rahaman, Vashanti. *Read for Me, Mama* (PS–1). Illus. 1997, Boyds Mills $14.95 (1-56397-313-8). 32pp. An African American boy hopes that his mother, a hotel maid, will have time to read a story to him. (Rev: BCCB 3/97; BL 2/15/97; SLJ 4/97)

4006 Rand, Gloria. *The Cabin Key* (K–3). Illus. by Ted Rand. 1994, Harcourt $15.00 (0-15-213884-6). 32pp. A young girl tells about the wonderful things she loves about the family's log cabin in the mountains. (Rev: BCCB 10/94; BL 11/1/94; SLJ 11/94)

4007 Rau, Dana Meachen. *Yahoo for You* (K–1). Illus. by Cary Pilo. 2002, Compass Point LB $18.60 (0-7365-0177-6). 32pp. Grandma likes to engage in all sorts of activities with her cute granddaughter but draws the line at going on a roller coaster. (Rev: BL 5/1/02)

4008 Raven, Margot Theis. *Circle Unbroken* (PS–3). Illus. by E. B. Lewis. 2004, Farrar $16.00 (0-374-31289-3). A grandmother teaches her granddaughter how to make Gullah baskets and tells her about her African heritage. (Rev: BL 5/15/04; SLJ 4/04)

4009 Ray, Deborah Kogan. *Lily's Garden* (K–2). Illus. 2002, Millbrook LB $21.90 (0-7613-2653-7). 32pp. Lily's grandparents have moved to California, and as the seasons pass in Maine Lily thinks about them while working in her garden. (Rev: BL 10/1/02; HBG 3/03; SLJ 11/02)

4010 Regan, Dian C. *Daddies* (PS). Illus. by Mary Morgan. 1996, Scholastic $5.95 (0-590-47973-3). 32pp. Children engage in a variety of activities with their fathers. (Rev: BL 6/1–15/96; SLJ 7/96)

4011 Reid, Barbara. *The Party* (PS–3). Illus. 1999, Scholastic $15.95 (0-590-97801-2). 32pp. The narrator and her young sister are wary of going to a family gathering, but when the games start, so does the fun. (Rev: BL 5/1/99; HBG 10/99; SLJ 5/99)

4012 Reid, Margarette S. *The Button Box* (K–3). Illus. by Sarah Chamberlain. 1990, Dutton $14.99 (0-525-44590-0). 24pp. A boy imagines interesting stories behind the different buttons in his grandmother's button box. (Rev: BCCB 3/90; BL 4/15/90; SLJ 9/90)

4013 Reiser, Lynn. *Cherry Pies and Lullabies* (PS–1). Illus. 1998, Greenwillow $16.00 (0-688-13391-6). 40pp. A girl shows how four generations in her family have given and received love while continuing treasured family traditions. (Rev: BL 3/1/98; HB 5–6/98; HBG 10/98; SLJ 9/98)

4014 Reynolds, Peter. *Ish* (PS–2). Illus. 2004, Candlewick $14.00 (0-7636-2344-X). 32pp. Ramon is an aspiring young artist who nearly quits when his older brother belittles his work; fortunately, his little sister has better taste. (Rev: BL 11/1/04; SLJ 1/05*)

4015 Ries, Lori. *Super Sam!* (PS–1). 2004, Charlesbridge $14.95 (1-58089-041-5). When he dons a blankie cape, Sam becomes a superhero and his toddler brother Petey is full of awe. (Rev: SLJ 9/04)

4016 Rockwell, Anne. *Father's Day* (PS–2). Illus. by Lizzy Rockwell. 2005, HarperCollins LB $15.89 (0-06-051378-0). 40pp. A class of children write books about their fathers, showing the wide diversity of family situations. (Rev: BL 5/15/05; SLJ 5/05)

4017 Rockwell, Anne. *Pumpkin Day, Pumpkin Night* (PS–1). Illus. by Megan Halsey. 1999, Walker LB $16.85 (0-8027-8697-9). 32pp. A young boy and his mother carve a pumpkin face, bake pies, and toast pumpkin seeds in this engaging picture book. (Rev: BL 9/1/99; HBG 3/00; SLJ 10/99)

4018 Root, Phyllis. *The Name Quilt* (PS–1). Illus. by Margot Apple. 2003, Farrar $16.00 (0-374-35484-7). 32pp. When Sadie stays at Grandma's, she sleeps under a patchwork quilt embroidered with names and listens to Grandma's stories about these relatives. (Rev: BL 3/15/03; HBG 10/03; SLJ 5/03)

4019 Rosenberg, Liz. *The Silence in the Mountains* (1–3). Illus. by Chris K. Soentpiet. 1999, Orchard LB $16.99 (0-531-33084-2). 32pp. Iskander and his family must leave their war-torn country and find peace in America. (Rev: BL 2/1/99; HBG 10/99; SLJ 7/99)

4020 Rosenberg, Liz. *We Wanted You* (PS–3). Illus. by Peter Catalanotto. 2002, Millbrook LB $23.90 (0-7613-2661-8). An adopted son and his parents look back fondly at their anticipation of his arrival and his early life. (Rev: HBG 10/02; SLJ 4/02)

4021 Rosenberry, Vera. *The Growing-Up Tree* (K–1). Illus. by author. 2003, Holiday House $16.95 (0-8234-1718-2). An apple tree planted when he was a baby plays an important role throughout

Alfred's life. (Rev: BL 1/1–15/04; HBG 4/04; SLJ 10/03)

4022 Ross, Lillian. *Buba Leah and Her Paper Children* (1–4). Illus. by Mary Morgan. 1991, Jewish Publication Soc. $17.95 (0-8276-0375-4). 32pp. The "paper children" to which Great-Aunt Buba Leah refers turn out to be her real children, who sailed to America to build a better life. (Rev: BL 1/1/92; SLJ 1/92)

4023 Rouss, Sylvia. *My Baby Brother* (K–2). Illus. by Liz Goulet Dubois. 2002, Jonathan David $14.95 (0-8246-0445-8). 24pp. Sarah, a young Jewish girl, initially resists the description of her new baby brother as a "miracle." (Rev: BL 10/1/02)

4024 Russo, Marisabina. *The Big Brown Box* (PS–1). Illus. 2000, Greenwillow $15.95 (0-688-17096-X). 32pp. Sam uses a big brown box to imagine all sorts of objects and when his younger brother gets a smaller brown box the two pretend the boxes are space ships. (Rev: BL 5/1/00; HBG 10/00; SLJ 5/00)

4025 Russo, Marisabina. *Come Back, Hannah!* (PS). Illus. 2001, HarperCollins LB $15.89 (0-688-17384-5). 32pp. Hannah is an excellent crawler and exhausts her mother as she scoots around the house getting into everything. (Rev: BL 8/01; HBG 10/01; SLJ 7/01)

4026 Russo, Marisabina. *The Trouble with Baby* (PS–1). Illus. by author. 2003, Greenwillow LB $16.89 (0-06-008925-3). Siblings Hannah and Sam have always had a good time playing together, but when Hannah gets a new doll named Baby, Sam gets jealous and refuses to play; eventually Hannah comes up with a solution that brings sister and brother together again. (Rev: HBG 10/03; SLJ 6/03)

4027 Ryder, Joanne. *My Father's Hands* (PS–3). Illus. by Mark Graham. 1994, Morrow LB $15.93 (0-688-09190-3). 32pp. A little girl watches her father work the soil with his hands and is fascinated by the many tiny animals he finds in the garden. (Rev: BL 10/1/94; SLJ 9/94)

4028 Saenz, Benjamin Alire. *A Gift from PapaDiego* (K–4). Illus. by Geronimo Garcia. 1998, Cinco Puntos paper $10.95 (0-938317-33-4). 40pp. Little Diego wants a Superman suit so he can fly to Mexico to visit with his beloved grandfather. When that fails, his disappointment is lessened by the news that his grandfather is coming to visit. (Rev: BL 5/1/98; HB 7–8/98)

4029 Sandburg, Carl. *The Huckabuck Family and How They Raised Popcorn in Nebraska and Quit and Came Back* (K–3). Illus. by David Small. 1999, Farrar $16.00 (0-374-33511-7). 40pp. This story, part of the author's *Rootabaga Stories,* tells of the Huckabuck family, their trials and tribulations, travels, and eventual return to their farm. (Rev: BCCB 9/99; BL 9/15/99; HB 9–10/99; HBG 3/00; SLJ 8/99)

4030 Santucci, Barbara. *Anna's Corn* (PS–3). Illus. by Lloyd Bloom. 2002, Eerdmans $16.00 (0-8028-5119-3). 32pp. Anna misses her grandfather after his death, especially the times they spent walking

together in the cornfield. (Rev: BL 10/1/02; HBG 3/03; SLJ 2/03)

4031 Sasso, Sandy Eisenberg. *For Heaven's Sake* (K–3). Illus. by Kathryn Kunz Finney. 1999, Jewish Lights $16.95 (1-58023-054-7). 32pp. Young Isaiah wonders where heaven is and discovers, through his wise grandmother, that it is all around you. (Rev: BL 10/1/99; SLJ 1/00)

4032 Say, Allen. *Grandfather's Journey* (PS–3). Illus. by author. 1993, Houghton Mifflin $16.95 (0-395-57035-2). 32pp. An autobiographical story that chronicles the passages of generations of the author's family as they moved between Japan and the United States. Winner of the 1994 Caldecott Medal. (Rev: BL 7/93*; SLJ 9/98)

4033 Say, Allen. *The Lost Lake* (2–4). Illus. 1989, Houghton Mifflin $16.00 (0-395-50933-5). 32pp. Realizing that he is not paying sufficient attention to his son, Dad takes him on a camping trip. (Rev: BCCB 1/90; BL 10/1/89; HB 1–2/90; SLJ 12/89*)

4034 Schertle, Alice. *Down the Road* (PS–3). Illus. by E. B. Lewis. 1995, Harcourt $16.00 (0-15-276622-7). 40pp. Hetty accidentally breaks the eggs that she has been carefully carrying from the store for her family's breakfast. (Rev: BCCB 12/95; BL 9/15/95*; SLJ 4/96)

4035 Schindel, John. *Dear Daddy* (K–3). Illus. by Dorothy Donohue. 1995, Whitman LB $13.95 (0-8075-1531-0). 32pp. Jesse longs to see his dad, who lives miles away. Finally, in a telephone conversation, they plan for a summer visit. (Rev: BL 5/1/95; SLJ 5/95)

4036 Schindel, John. *Frog Face: My Little Sister and Me* (PS–1). Illus. by Janet Delaney. 1998, Holt $14.95 (0-8050-5546-0). Photos show the conflicting emotions that a preschooler feels about her new baby sister: delighted one minute and jealous the next. (Rev: BL 11/1/98; HB 9–10/98; HBG 3/99; SLJ 11/98)

4037 Schlein, Miriam. *The Story About Me* (PS–1). Illus. by Kristina Stephenson. 2004, Whitman $15.95 (0-8075-7631-X). 32pp. A grandmother tells her granddaughter about all the anticipation and happiness that preceded the little girl's birth. (Rev: BL 5/1/04; SLJ 5/04)

4038 Schlessinger, Laura C., and Martha L. Lambert. *Why Do You Love Me?* (PS–1). Illus. by Paul Meisel. 1999, HarperCollins $15.95 (0-06-027866-8). 40pp. A reassuring story in which a mother tells her young son that in spite of his mischievous behavior she still loves him. (Rev: HBG 10/99; SLJ 4/99)

4039 Schotter, Roni. *In the Piney Woods* (1–3). Illus. by Kimberly B. Root. 2003, Farrar $16.00 (0-374-33623-7). 32pp. Rebirth and renewal are themes in this gentle story about a little girl called Ella, her aging grandfather, and their beloved woods. (Rev: BL 7/03; HBG 10/03; SLJ 4/03)

4040 Schwartz, Amy. *A Teeny Tiny Baby* (PS–1). Illus. 1994, Orchard LB $17.99 (0-531-08668-2). 32pp. A teeny tiny baby tells about all the things he likes and dislikes about his status. (Rev: BCCB 9/94; BL 7/94*; SLJ 9/94*)

4041 Scrimger, Richard. *Eugene's Story* (PS–1). Illus. by Gillian Johnson. 2003, Tundra $15.95 (0-88776-544-0). Eugene triumphs over his bossy big sister in this imaginative tale. (Rev: HBG 4/04; SLJ 3/04)

4042 Segal, Lore. *Tell Me a Mitzi* (K–2). Illus. by Harriet Pincus. 1982, Farrar paper $5.95 (0-374-47502-4). 40pp. Three hilarious stories about the antics of a city family: a mad trip to Grandma's house, coming down with a cold, and a meeting with the president.

4043 Selway, Martina. *Don't Forget to Write* (PS–2). Illus. 1992, Ideals $12.95 (0-8249-8543-5). 28pp. On a visit to Grandad's farm, Rosie writes letters daily to her mother. (Rev: BL 6/1/92; SLJ 8/92)

4044 Shannon, David. *No, David!* (PS–K). Illus. 1998, Scholastic $14.95 (0-590-93002-8). 32pp. It seems that everything young David does is met with a "No!" from his mother, but in spite of her criticism, he knows she loves him. (Rev: BCCB 9/98; BL 9/1/98; HBG 3/99; SLJ 8/98)

4045 Shannon, David. *Oh, David! A Diaper David Book* (PS). Illus. by author. 2005, Scholastic $6.99 (0-439-68881-7). In a board book prequel to the preschool David, we see the toddler unrolling toilet paper, refusing food, and filling his diaper, before a last cuddle with his long-suffering mother. Also use *Oops! A Diaper David Book* (2005). (Rev: BCCB 3/05; SLJ 3/05)

4046 Shapiro, Jody Fickes. *Up, Up, Up! It's Apple-Picking Time* (K–3). Illus. by Kitty Harvill. 2003, Holiday House $16.95 (0-8234-1610-0). Author Jody Fickes Shapiro beautifully evokes all the color and wonder of autumn and harvest in this story of a family's visit to the apple farm of Grandma and Grandpa. (Rev: HBG 4/04; SLJ 9/03)

4047 Sherkin-Langer, Ferne. *When Mommy Is Sick* (PS–2). Illus. by Kay Life. 1995, Whitman $12.95 (1-8075-8894-6). 32pp. A first-person narrative about the emptiness a young girl feels when her mother is hospitalized. (Rev: BL 3/15/95; SLJ 5/95)

4048 Shields, Carol Diggory. *Lucky Pennies and Hot Chocolate* (PS–2). Illus. by Hiroe Nakata. 2000, Dutton $13.99 (0-525-46450-6). 32pp. A little boy is looking forward to a visit from his favorite person who turns out to be his grandfather. (Rev: BCCB 9/00; BL 8/00; HBG 3/01; SLJ 9/00)

4049 Shough, Carol Gandee. *All the Mamas: A True Love Story for Mothers and Daughters of All Ages* (K–2). Illus. 1998, Summerhouse $16.95 (1-887714-29-4). 32pp. The never-ending cycle of mother love is traced in one family as a contemporary mother holds and kisses her baby, just as her mother did to her and just as preceding generations of mothers held and kissed their babies. (Rev: BL 8/98; SLJ 9/98)

4050 Shough, Carol Gandee. *All the Papas: A True Love Story for Fathers and Their Children* (K–4). Illus. by author. 1999, Summerhouse $16.95 (1-887714-36-7). 32pp. Based on the author's family history, this book pictures eight generations of fathers and their loving relationships with their families. (Rev: SLJ 7/99)

4051 Showers, Paul. *The Listening Walk* (K–2). Illus. by Aliki. 1991, HarperCollins LB $15.89 (0-06-021638-7). A boy and his father listen to the sounds around them as they walk. (Rev: SLJ 7/91)

4052 Shulevitz, Uri. *The Treasure* (K–2). Illus. by author. 1979, Farrar $16.00 (0-374-37740-5); paper $5.95 (0-374-47955-0). 32pp. A man discovers that the most valuable things in life are usually found at home.

4053 Shulman, Mark. *Stella the Star* (PS–2). Illus. by Vincent Nguyen. 2004, Walker $16.95 (0-8027-8894-7). 32pp. After the big buildup, it's a surprise when it turns out that Stella's role is as a heavenly star, not the leading lady in her school production. (Rev: BL 4/15/04; SLJ 5/04)

4054 Singer, Marilyn. *Didi and Daddy on the Promenade* (PS–K). Illus. by Marie-Louise Gay. 2001, Clarion $14.00 (0-618-04640-2). 32pp. Didi and her father love to walk and play on Sunday mornings on the Brooklyn Heights Promenade that overlooks the Manhattan skyline. (Rev: BCCB 4/01; BL 4/1/01; HBG 10/01; SLJ 5/01)

4055 Singer, Marilyn. *The One and Only Me* (PS–K). Illus. by Nicole Rubel. 2000, HarperCollins $9.95 (0-694-01279-3). A little girl explains how she is like various members of her extended family in this charming family story illustrated with brightly colored cartoons. (Rev: HBG 10/00; SLJ 7/00)

4056 Slier, Deborah. *Hello Baby* (PS). Illus. 1988, Checkerboard $2.95 (1-56288-087-X). 12pp. A board book that shows basic actions, such as sitting and crying, for the toddler. Also use: *Baby's Words; Busy Baby* (both 1988). (Rev: BCCB 7–8/88; BL 7/88)

4057 Smalls, Irene. *Kevin and His Dad* (PS–1). Illus. by Michael Hays. 1999, Little, Brown $15.95 (0-316-79899-1). 32pp. An African American boy and his dad spend a day together — first helping around the house, then playing baseball, and going to a movie. (Rev: BCCB 5/99; BL 2/15/99; HBG 10/99; SLJ 5/99)

4058 Smith, Patricia. *Janna and the Kings* (PS–2). Illus. by Aaron Boyd. 2003, Lee & Low $16.95 (1-58430-088-4). Janna, a young African American girl, hesitantly returns to the barbershop her grandfather loved before he died. (Rev: BL 11/15/03; HBG 4/04; SLJ 11/03)

4059 Smith, Will. *Just the Two of Us* (PS–1). Illus. by Kadir Nelson. 2001, Scholastic $16.95 (0-439-08792-9). 32pp. Smith uses his song "Just the Two of Us" as the foundation for this celebration of a father's love for his son. (Rev: BL 7/01; HBG 10/01; SLJ 6/01)

4060 Smothers, Ethel Footman. *Auntee Edna* (K–3). Illus. by Wil Clay. 2001, Eerdmans $16.00 (0-8028-5154-1). Tokee doesn't look forward to staying the night with elderly Auntee Edna but has a wonderful time. (Rev: HBG 10/01; SLJ 8/01)

4061 Smythe, Anne. *Islands* (K–2). Illus. by Laszlo Gal. 1996, Douglas & McIntyre $14.95 (0-88899-238-6). 32pp. A mother and a daughter skate across a frozen lake to three small islands and examine wildlife in this quiet picture book. (Rev: BL 12/1/96)

4062 Soto, Gary. *If the Shoe Fits* (PS–3). Illus. by Terry Widener. 2002, Penguin Putnam $15.99 (0-399-23420-9). 32pp. Rigo, who is sick of wearing hand-me-downs, gets a new pair of loafers for his ninth birthday. (Rev: BCCB 3/02; BL 1/1–15/02; HB 7–8/02; HBG 10/02; SLJ 1/02)

4063 Spalding, Andrea. *The Most Beautiful Kite in the World* (PS–2). Illus. by Leslie Watts. 2003, Fitzhenry & Whiteside $14.95 (1-55041-716-9). Jenny is disappointed when her father gives her a homemade kite, but she forgets her pique as she learns to add enhancements. (Rev: SLJ 8/03)

4064 Spinelli, Eileen. *When Mama Comes Home Tonight* (PS–1). Illus. by Jane Dyer. 1998, Simon & Schuster $14.00 (0-689-81065-2). 32pp. A touching picture book that describes the activities that a mother and child engage in when the two are reunited after Mother gets home from work. (Rev: BL 7/98*; HBG 3/99; SLJ 11/98)

4065 Spinelli, Eileen. *While You Are Away* (PS–1). Illus. by Renee Graef. 2004, Hyperion $15.99 (0-7868-0972-8). 32pp. Three children of different ethnicities wonder how their parents — overseas on military duty — are doing, and share their own ways of finding comfort. (Rev: BL 3/15/04; SLJ 4/04)

4066 Springer, Susan Woodward. *Seldovia Sam and the Very Large Clam* (2–4). Illus. by Amy Meissner. Series: Seldovia Sam. 2003, Alaska Northwest paper $6.95 (0-88240-570-5). 64pp. Another adventure for Sam and his dog in Alaska, this time involving a perilous search for a giant clam. (Rev: SLJ 4/04)

4067 Steptoe, John. *Baby Says* (PS). Illus. by author. 1988, Lothrop LB $15.89 (0-688-07424-3). 32pp. An almost wordless picture book catching the exchange between a baby and a big brother. (Rev: BL 4/1/88; HB 7–8/88; SLJ 3/88)

4068 Steptoe, John. *Stevie* (PS–2). Illus. by author. 1969, HarperCollins paper $6.95 (0-06-443122-3). 32pp. A small African American boy eloquently expresses his resentment at having to share his possessions and mother with a temporary younger boarder who becomes "kinda like a little brother"; illustrated in bold line and color.

4069 Stevenson, Harvey. *Grandpa's House* (PS–1). Illus. by author. 1994, Hyperion LB $15.49 (1-56282-589-5). A simple text is used with effective pictures to convey the fine time young Woody has during a visit with his grandfather. (Rev: SLJ 6/94)

4070 Stewart, Sarah. *The Friend* (1–3). Illus. by David Small. 2004, Farrar $16.00 (0-374-32463-8). Belle, daughter of wealthy and distant parents, and Bea, African American housekeeper, spend much of their time together at the family's house on the beach. (Rev: BL 8/04; SLJ 8/04)

4071 Stilz, Carol C. *Grandma Buffalo, May and Me* (K–3). Illus. by Constance R. Bergum. 1995, Sasquatch $14.95 (1-57061-015-0). 32pp. Poppy visits parts of Montana where her great-grandmother once lived and does the same things her ancestor

did, like plant an apple tree and feed the buffalo. (Rev: BL 10/1/95; SLJ 12/95)

4072 Stoeke, Janet Morgan. *Waiting for May* (K–3). Illus. by author. 2005, Dutton $16.99 (0-525-47098-0). A family adopting a girl from China waits impatiently for the journey there to begin. (Rev: SLJ 6/05)

4073 Taylor, Ann. *Baby Dance* (PS). Illus. by Marjorie van Heerden. Series: Harper Growing Tree. 1999, HarperCollins $5.95 (0-694-01206-8). In this board book, an African American dad and his baby daughter play to a series of catchy rhymes. (Rev: BCCB 5/99; SLJ 3/99)

4074 Thomas, Eliza. *The Red Blanket* (PS–2). Illus. by Joe Cepeda. 2004, Scholastic $15.95 (0-439-32253-7). 32pp. This endearing tale of a young woman's journey to China to adopt a child is based on events from the author's life. (Rev: BL 5/15/04; SLJ 7/04)

4075 Thomas, Elizabeth. *Green Beans* (PS–2). Illus. by Vicki Jo Redenbaugh. 1992, Carolrhoda LB $15.95 (0-87614-708-2). 32pp. Gramma, who is trying too hard to make her green beans grow, lets granddaughter Dorothea take over. (Rev: BCCB 2/93; BL 9/15/92; SLJ 1/93)

4076 Thomas, Jane Resh. *Saying Good-bye to Grandma* (2–4). Illus. by Marcia Sewall. 1988, Houghton Mifflin paper $7.95 (0-395-54779-2). 40pp. Seven-year-old Suzie attends Grandma's funeral. (Rev: BL 10/15/88; HB 9–10/88; SLJ 2/89)

4077 Thomas, Joyce Carol. *Joy* (PS–K). Illus. by Pamela Johnson. 2001, Hyperion $6.99 (0-7868-0750-4). An African American woman tells her child of her love in this charming board book. (Rev: SLJ 2/02)

4078 Thomas, Naturi. *Uh-oh! It's Mama's Birthday!* (PS–3). Illus. by Keinyo White. 1997, Whitman LB $13.95 (0-8075-8268-9). 24pp. An African American boy gives his mother what she really wants on her birthday: a big hug. (Rev: BL 2/15/97; HB 3–4/97; SLJ 5/97)

4079 Thompson, Mary. *My Brother Matthew* (K–4). Illus. 1992, Woodbine $14.95 (0-933149-47-6). 28pp. The family member who adjusts best to the baby who is born with physical problems is young David. (Rev: BL 2/15/93; SLJ 6/92)

4080 Tiffault, Benette W. *A Quilt for Elizabeth* (1–4). Illus. by Mary McConnell. 1992, Centering paper $8.95 (1-56123-034-0). After Elizabeth accepts her father's death, she and her grandmother begin a quilt using patches of his clothing. (Rev: SLJ 8/92)

4081 Tobias, Tobi. *Wishes for You* (PS–K). Illus. by Henri Sorensen. 2003, HarperCollins LB $16.89 (0-688-10839-3). Sentences beginning with "I hope" express dreams adults have for children. (Rev: BL 5/15/03; HBG 10/03; SLJ 6/03)

4082 Tompert, Ann. *Will You Come Back for Me?* (PS). Illus. by Robin Kramer. 1988, Whitman LB $14.95 (0-8075-9112-2); paper $5.95 (0-8075-9113-0). 32pp. Her mother must go to work and the little girl must go to day care, but she worries that her mother won't come back for her. (Rev: BCCB 12/88; BL 11/1/88; SLJ 1/89)

4083 Torres, Leyla. *The Kite Festival* (1–3). Illus. 2004, Farrar $16.00 (0-374-38054-6). 32pp. When Fernando and his family find themselves at a kite festival without a kite, they make one from scratch and end up winning a prize. (Rev: BL 2/15/04; SLJ 7/04)

4084 Torres, Leyla. *Liliana's Grandmothers* (PS–2). Illus. 1998, Farrar $16.00 (0-374-35105-8). 32pp. Liliana compares the lives of her two grandmothers — one lives nearby in America and the other lives in another country and speaks only Spanish. (Rev: BL 7/98; HBG 3/99; SLJ 3/99)

4085 Tunnell, Michael O. *Mailing May* (K–3). Illus. by Ted Rand. 1997, Morrow LB $15.89 (0-688-12879-3). 32pp. Unable to afford a rail ticket, May's father sends her parcel post to visit her grandmother. (Rev: BL 8/97; HB 9–10/97; HBG 3/98; SLJ 9/97)

4086 Van Leeuwen, Jean. *Sorry* (K–3). Illus. by Brad Sneed. 2001, Penguin Putnam $15.99 (0-8037-2261-3). 32pp. A row over oatmeal leads to a life-long rift between two neighboring brothers and their descendants until their great-grandchildren discover a very useful word. (Rev: BCCB 9/01; BL 6/1–15/01; HBG 10/01; SLJ 5/01)

4087 Velasquez, Eric. *Grandma's Records* (K–3). Illus. 2001, Walker LB $17.85 (0-8027-8761-4). 32pp. A young boy enjoys summers full of Latin music with his grandmother in Spanish Harlem in this novel based on the author's own memories. (Rev: BL 5/15/01; HBG 10/01; SLJ 9/01)

4088 Vestergaard, Hope. *Driving Daddy* (PS–1). Illus. by Thierry Courtin. 2003, Dutton $6.99 (0-525-47032-8). 24pp. A small-format book in which a little boy gets to ride on his father's shoulders. (Rev: BL 3/1/03; HBG 10/03; SLJ 3/03)

4089 Vigil-Pinon, Evangelina. *Marina's Muumuu / El Muumuu de Marina* (2–5). Illus. by Pablo Torrecilla. 2001, Arte Publico $14.95 (1-55885-350-2). 32pp. A bilingual story about a girl named Marina who dreams of wearing a colorful, tropical muumuu like those from her grandmother's home. (Rev: BL 1/1–15/02; SLJ 1/02)

4090 Viorst, Judith. *Alexander and the Terrible, Horrible, No Good, Very Bad Day* (K–3). Illus. by Ray Cruz. 1972, Macmillan LB $14.00 (0-689-30072-7); paper $4.99 (0-689-71173-5). Alexander wakes up to a bad day and things get progressively worse as the hours wear on, until he thinks he may escape it all and go to Australia.

4091 Viorst, Judith. *Alexander, Who's Not (Do You Hear Me? I Mean It!) Going to Move* (PS–3). Illus. by Robin P. Glasser. 1995, Simon & Schuster LB $15.00 (0-689-31958-4). 42pp. Alexander of bad-day fame, faces another crisis when he adamantly refuses to move to the family's new home. (Rev: BCCB 11/95; BL 8/95*; SLJ 10/95*)

4092 Viorst, Judith. *I'll Fix Anthony* (PS–3). Illus. by Arnold Lobel. 1969, Macmillan paper $4.99 (0-689-71202-2). 32pp. A young boy has a field day planning revenge on an older brother.

4093 Waboose, Jan B. *Firedancers* (1–4). Illus. by C. J. Taylor. 2000, Stoddart $14.95 (0-7737-3138-5). 32pp. A young Ojibwa girl visits Smooth Rock Island at night and joins her grandmother as a Firedancer. (Rev: BL 7/00)

4094 Wahl, Jan. *Mabel Ran Away with the Toys* (PS–2). Illus. by Liza Woodruff. 2000, Charlesbridge $16.95 (1-58089-059-8); paper $6.95 (1-58089-067-9). Little Mabel has problems adjusting when a new baby disrupts her schedule. (Rev: HBG 3/01; SLJ 9/00)

4095 Waldherr, Kris. *Harvest* (PS–1). Illus. 2001, Walker LB $16.85 (0-8027-8793-2). 32pp. A girl and her mother harvest and prepare fruits and vegetables from the garden in order to prepare for winter in this simple yet memorable autumn story. (Rev: BL 11/15/01; HBG 3/02; SLJ 11/01)

4096 Wallace, John. *Monster Toddler* (PS–1). Illus. by author. 2003, Hyperion $15.99 (0-7868-1996-0). Timothy, described as the "sweetest boy in all the world," puts on a monster suit and promptly runs out of control, wrecking things at every turn until his sister Charlotte finally calms him down. (Rev: HBG 10/03; SLJ 8/03)

4097 Walvoord, Linda. *Razzamadaddy* (PS–1). Illus. by Sachiko Yoshikawa. 2004, Marshall Cavendish $14.95 (0-7614-5158-7). A father and son enjoy a day at the beach, depicted in rhyming text and vivid illustrations. (Rev: SLJ 7/04)

4098 Weninger, Brigitte. *Davy in the Middle* (PS). Illus. by Eve Tharlet. 2004, North-South LB $16.50 (0-7358-1934-3). Middle child Davy feels out of sorts — he is too small to go hiking with his older brother and too big to play with the little ones, although he seems to be just right for babysitting. (Rev: SLJ 8/04)

4099 Weston, Martha. *Apple Juice Tea* (PS–K). Illus. 1994, Clarion $14.95 (0-395-65480-7). 32pp. Polly scarcely remembers her grandmother; but when they are reunited, they have a great time together. (Rev: BL 11/1/94; SLJ 9/94)

4100 Weston, Tamson. *Hey, Pancakes!* (PS–1). Illus. by Stephen Gammell. 2003, Harcourt $16.00 (0-15-216502-9). Rhyming verse and mixed-media artwork portray three siblings energetically cooking up a sloppy batch of pancakes. (Rev: HBG 4/04; SLJ 9/03)

4101 Whelan, Gloria. *Jam and Jelly by Holly and Nelly* (K–2). Illus. by Gijsbert van Frankenhuyzen. 2002, Sleeping Bear $17.95 (1-58536-109-7). 48pp. A captivating story of a mother's determination to buy her daughter a coat so she can go to school in the cold. (Rev: BL 12/15/02; SLJ 1/03)

4102 Whybrow, Ian. *A Baby for Grace* (PS–1). Illus. by Christian Birmingham. 1998, Kingfisher $14.95 (0-7534-5142-5). 32pp. Everything that a young girl tries to do to be helpful around the house, including holding the new baby, is greeted with the same response, "No, Grace." (Rev: BL 10/1/98; HBG 3/99; SLJ 1/99)

4103 Wild, Margaret. *All the Better to See You With!* (K–3). Illus. by Pat Reynolds. 1993, Whitman LB $14.95 (0-8075-0284-7). 32pp. A girl who is always outshone by her four brothers and sisters gains attention when she needs glasses. (Rev: BL 7/93; SLJ 8/93)

4104 Wild, Margaret. *Our Granny* (PS–1). Illus. by Julie Vivas. 1994, Ticknor $14.95 (0-395-67023-3). 32pp. All kinds of grandmothers from the glamorous and kinky to cuddly and plain are celebrated in this lively picture book. (Rev: BCCB 5/94; BL 1/15/94*; HB 5–6/94; SLJ 4/94*)

4105 Wild, Margaret. *Remember Me* (PS–2). Illus. by Dee Huxley. 1995, Whitman LB $14.95 (0-8075-6934-8). 32pp. In spite of her increasing forgetfulness, Grandma remembers the good times she spent with Ellie, her granddaughter. (Rev: BL 2/1/96; SLJ 1/96)

4106 Willhoite, Michael. *Daddy's Roommate* (PS–2). Illus. 1990, Alyson paper $10.95 (1-55583-118-4). 32pp. After his parents' divorce, a young boy finds that his father has a male partner and on weekends the boy enjoys visiting the two of them. (Rev: BCCB 2/91; BL 3/1/91; SLJ 4/91)

4107 Williams, Karen Lynn. *Circles of Hope* (PS–K). Illus. by Linda Saport. 2005, Eerdmans $16.00 (0-8028-5276-9). 32pp. In Haiti, a boy called Facile struggles to grow a tree as a gift for his new baby sister, finally building a protective circle of stones. (Rev: BL 5/15/05; SLJ 4/05)

4108 Williams, Vera B. *A Chair for My Mother* (PS–2). Illus. by author. 1982, Greenwillow $15.93 (0-688-00915-8). 32pp. After fire destroys their home, Rose and her mother and grandmother save to buy a nice new chair. Two sequels are: *Something Special for Me* (1983); *Music, Music for Everyone* (1984).

4109 Williams, Vera B. *Lucky Song* (PS–K). Illus. 1997, Greenwillow $14.93 (0-688-14460-8). 24pp. Evie is a lucky girl because all of her wants and needs are satisfied by her loving family. (Rev: BL 10/1/97*; HB 9–10/97; HBG 3/98; SLJ 8/97*)

4110 Willis, Jeanne. *Don't Let Go!* (PS–2). Illus. by Tony Ross. 2003, Penguin Putnam $16.99 (0-399-24008-X). In this touching story of a girl's relationship with her father, Megan is anxious to learn how to ride a bike so she can easily travel to her father's house from the home where she lives with her mother, but she's also a little nervous about this new experience; Dad patiently works with his daughter until she's ready to take off on her own. (Rev: HBG 10/03; SLJ 6/03)

4111 Wilson, Karma. *Mama Always Comes Home* (PS). Illus. by Brooke Dyer. 2005, HarperCollins LB $16.89 (0-06-057506-9). A mother tells her child that she will always come home, using animal stories as reassuring examples. (Rev: SLJ 5/05)

4112 Wilson, Sarah. *Big Day on the River* (PS–2). Illus. by Randy Cecil. 2003, Holt $16.95 (0-8050-6787-6). Young Willie's plans for a carefree rafting trip are almost ruined by her overly solicitous extended family. (Rev: BL 6/1–15/03; HBG 10/03; SLJ 4/03)

4113 Winch, John. *Keeping Up with Grandma* (PS–3). Illus. 2000, Holiday House $16.95 (0-8234-1563-5). 32pp. Grandma wants to start mountain climbing, whitewater canoeing, and hot-air ballooning but she and Grandpa later decide that their usual quiet life is better. (Rev: BL 11/15/00; HBG 3/01; SLJ 11/00)

4114 Wing, Natasha L. *Jalapeno Bagels* (PS–2). Illus. by Robert Casilla. 1996, Simon & Schuster $15.00 (0-689-80530-6). 32pp. Pablo, who comes from a racially mixed family, finds his life is enriched by both cultures. (Rev: BL 6/1–15/96; SLJ 7/96)

4115 Winthrop, Elizabeth. *I'm the Boss!* (PS–1). Illus. by Mary Morgan. 1994, Holiday House LB $15.95 (0-8234-1113-3). 32pp. Julia is tired of being bossed around and wants her chance to be a dictator. (Rev: BL 5/1/94; SLJ 7/94)

4116 Winthrop, Elizabeth. *Promises* (1–3). Illus. by Betsy Lewin. 2000, Clarion $16.00 (0-395-82272-6). 32pp. Sarah's mother is very ill with cancer and the young girl misses the good times they had before she became sick. (Rev: BL 6/1–15/00; HBG 10/00; SLJ 6/00)

4117 Winthrop, Elizabeth. *Squashed in the Middle* (K–3). Illus. by Pat Cummings. 2005, Holt $16.95 (0-8050-6497-4). 32pp. Middle child Daisy gets her family's attention when she goes to a friend's house all on her own. (Rev: BL 4/1/05; SLJ 6/05)

4118 Wolff, Ashley. *Me Baby, You Baby* (PS). Illus. by author. 2004, Dutton $14.99 (0-525-46952-4). This book follows two toddlers (a white girl and a black boy) and their mothers through a busy day, including a visit to the zoo. (Rev: BL 3/1/04*; HB 3–4/04; SLJ 3/04)

4119 Wood, Douglas. *Grandad's Prayers of the Earth* (K–3). Illus. by P. J. Lynch. 1999, Candlewick $16.99 (0-7636-0660-X). 32pp. A boy and his grandfather talk about prayer, and after the old man's death, the boy remembers his gentle ways and his loving faith. (Rev: BL 12/1/99; HBG 3/00; SLJ 1/00)

4120 Woodson, Jacqueline. *Visiting Day* (K–2). Illus. by James E. Ransome. 2002, Scholastic $15.95 (0-590-40005-3). 32pp. This is a gentle family story of a little African American girl's visit to her father in prison. (Rev: BCCB 12/02; BL 11/1/02; HB 11–12/02; HBG 3/03; SLJ 9/02)

4121 Woodtor, Dee Parmer. *Big Meeting* (K–3). Illus. by Dolores Johnson. 1996, Simon & Schuster $16.00 (0-689-31993-9). 32pp. A celebration of a down-home family reunion is chronicled in this joyous book. (Rev: BL 9/1/96; SLJ 9/96)

4122 Wyse, Lois, and Molly Rose Goldman. *How to Take Your Grandmother to the Museum* (1–3). Illus. by Marie-Louise Gay. 1998, Workman $12.95 (0-7611-0990-0). 48pp. When a young boy discovers that his grandmother has never been to New York City's American Museum of Natural History, he takes her on his own special guided tour. (Rev: BL 1/1–15/99; HBG 3/99; SLJ 12/98)

4123 Yektai, Niki. *Triplets* (PS–2). Illus. 1998, Millbrook LB $21.40 (0-7613-0351-0). 32pp. This lively picture book explores the rivalry among three siblings and its humorous consequences. (Rev: BL 5/15/98; HBG 10/98; SLJ 8/98)

4124 Yolen, Jane. *Grandma's Hurrying Child* (PS–K). Illus. by Kay Chorao. 2005, Harcourt $16.00 (0-15-201813-1). Grandma tells Maddy how she rushed by train to be there for Maddy's birth. (Rev: BL 2/1/04; HBG 4/04; SLJ 4/05)

4125 Zagwyn, Deborah Turney. *Apple Batter* (K–3). Illus. 1999, Tricycle $14.95 (1-883672-92-9). 32pp. Loretta plants and cares for three apple trees while her young son develops an interest in baseball in this picture book that ends with both interests converging. (Rev: BL 1/1–15/00; HBG 3/00; SLJ 12/99)

4126 Zalben, Jane Breskin. *Baby Babka, the Gorgeous Genius* (K–4). Illus. by Victoria Chess. 2004, Clarion $15.00 (0-618-23489-6). 38pp. Beryl is disappointed when the new baby is another boy, but Uncle Morty has a solution. (Rev: SLJ 11/04)

4127 Zamorano, Ana. *Let's Eat!* (PS–2). Illus. by Julie Vivas. 1997, Scholastic $15.95 (0-590-13444-2). 32pp. A loving Spanish family enjoys Mama's food even more when she returns home from the hospital with baby Rosa. (Rev: BCCB 4/97; BL 5/15/97; SLJ 4/97*)

4128 Ziefert, Harriet. *Clara Ann Cookie* (PS–1). Illus. by Emily Bolam. 1999, Houghton Mifflin $15.00 (0-395-92324-7). 32pp. After waking, Clara Ann is in a terrible mood until Mom makes a game of getting dressed and preparing to face the world. (Rev: BL 3/1/99; HBG 10/99; SLJ 4/99)

4129 Ziefert, Harriet. *My Friend Grandpa* (K–3). Illus. by Robert Wurzburg. 2004, Blue Apple $15.95 (1-59354-063-9). A celebration of the close relationship Emma shares with her grandfather and the happy times they spend in the country. (Rev: SLJ 11/04)

4130 Ziefert, Harriet. *A New Coat for Anna* (K–3). Illus. by Anita Lobel. 1986, Knopf paper $6.99 (0-394-89861-3). 40pp. It's been a long time since Anna has had a new coat, and her mother vows to get one for her in this story of post-World War II Europe. (Rev: BCCB 3/87; BL 12/15/86; SLJ 12/86)

4131 Ziefert, Harriet. *31 Uses for a Mom* (PS–K). Illus. by Rebecca Doughty. 2003, Penguin Putnam $12.99 (0-399-23862-X). 32pp. Moms turn out to be fairly useful things in this list that covers a wide range of attributes. (Rev: BL 1/1–15/03; HBG 10/03; SLJ 3/03)

4132 Ziefert, Harriet. *Waiting for Baby* (PS–K). Illus. by Emily Bolan. 1998, Holt $13.95 (0-8050-5929-6). After weeks of suspense, Max gets so tired of waiting for his brother to be born that he goes out to play and then, of course, the blessed event occurs. (Rev: BL 12/15/98; HBG 3/99; SLJ 5/99)

4133 Zisk, Mary. *The Best Single Mom in the World: How I Was Adopted* (PS–K). Illus. by author. 2001, Whitman LB $14.95 (0-8075-0666-4). A little girl and her mother tell the tale of her adoption across the sea. (Rev: HBG 3/02; SLJ 1/02)

4134 Zolotow, Charlotte. *The Poodle Who Barked at the Wind* (PS–1). Illus. by Valerie Coursen. 2002, Holt $16.95 (0-8050-6306-4). 32pp. Updated illustrations grace this new edition of the charming book about a father who comes to understand why the family poodle barks. (Rev: BL 1/1–15/03; HBG 3/03; SLJ 11/02)

4135 Zolotow, Charlotte. *The Quarreling Book* (K–2). Illus. by Arnold Lobel. 1963, HarperCollins paper $5.95 (0-06-443034-0). 32pp. Father's failure to kiss mother one morning triggers a series of quarrels, but the pet dog sets things right. Also use: *The Hating Book* (1969).

4136 Zolotow, Charlotte. *Some Things Go Together* (PS–1). Illus. by Ashley Wolff. Series: Harper Growing Tree. 1999, HarperCollins $9.95 (0-694-01197-5). Family love is pictured in this tender story about belonging that is also suitable as a bedtime book. (Rev: HBG 10/99; SLJ 3/99)

4137 Zolotow, Charlotte. *William's Doll* (PS–3). Illus. by William Pene du Bois. 1972, HarperCollins LB $15.89 (0-06-027048-9); paper $5.95 (0-06-443067-7). 32pp. William wanted a doll, much to his father's dismay; but when Grandma comes to visit she presents William with a doll, saying that now he will have an opportunity to practice being a good father.

4138 Zweibel, Alan. *Our Tree Named Steve* (1–3). Illus. by David Catrow. 2005, Penguin Putnam $14.99 (0-399-23722-4). A sad story about a beloved tree knocked down by a storm. (Rev: BL 2/1/04; SLJ 4/05)

FRIENDSHIP STORIES

4139 Aliki. *We Are Best Friends* (K–3). Illus. by author. 1982, Morrow paper $5.95 (0-688-07037-X). 32pp. Robert is at a loss when his best friend moves away.

4140 Appelt, Kathi. *Bubba and Beau, Best Friends* (PS–K). Illus. by Arthur Howard. 2002, Harcourt $16.00 (0-15-202060-8). 32pp. Bubba, a little boy, and Beau, his puppy, are unhappy when the smelly blanket they love is washed and now smells of soap. (Rev: BCCB 4/02; BL 4/1/02; HBG 10/02; SLJ 7/02)

4141 Baker, Roberta. *Lizard Walinsky* (K–2). Illus. by Debbie Tilley. 2004, Little, Brown $15.95 (0-316-07331-8). Lizard, a girl who prefers dinosaurs to dolls, gets along well with Spider, but when first grade comes around he must go to a different school and Lizard must find a new friend. (Rev: SLJ 6/04)

4142 Beaumont, Karen. *Being Friends* (PS–2). Illus. by Joy Allen. 2002, Dial $15.99 (0-8037-2529-9). 32pp. Two girls, best friends despite their different personalities, have fun together in this rhyming picture book. (Rev: BL 9/15/02; HBG 10/02; SLJ 7/02)

4143 Blake, Quentin. *Fantastic Daisy Artichoke* (PS–1). Illus. by author. 2001, Red Fox paper $11.00 (0-09-940006-5). Rhythmic text and bright, lively drawings tell the story of the fun two children had when they met their friend Daisy. (Rev: SLJ 10/01)

4144 Bluthenthal, Diana Cain. *Matilda the Moocher* (PS–2). Illus. 1997, Orchard LB $16.99 (0-531-33003-6). 32pp. Libby gets tired of her friend Matilda's constant borrowing of her possessions and money. (Rev: BL 3/15/97; SLJ 5/97)

4145 Bottner, Barbara. *Rosa's Room* (PS–1). Illus. by Beth Spiegel. 2004, Peachtree $15.95 (1-56145-302-1). 32pp. Rosa's room in her new house seems strangely empty until she finds a friend to share it. (Rev: BL 4/1/04; SLJ 5/04)

4146 Brown, Laurie Krasny. *How to Be a Friend: A Guide to Making Friends and Keeping Them* (K–3). Illus. by Marc Brown. 1998, Little, Brown $14.95 (0-316-10913-4). 32pp. Using humanlike dinosaurs as subjects, this practical guide shows how to make friends and keep their friendship. (Rev: BL 10/15/98; HB 11–12/98; HBG 3/99; SLJ 9/98)

4147 Carlson, Nancy. *My Best Friend Moved Away* (PS–K). Illus. 2001, Viking $15.99 (0-670-89498-2). 32pp. A little girl is sad as she remembers the good times she shared with the girl next door. (Rev: BL 4/1/01; HBG 10/01; SLJ 6/01)

4148 Carlstrom, Nancy White. *Blow Me a Kiss, Miss Lilly* (K–2). Illus. by Amy Schwartz. 1990, Harper-Collins LB $15.89 (0-06-021013-3). 32pp. The story of a special friendship between an elderly lady and little Sara. (Rev: BCCB 5/90; BL 4/15/90; HB 5–6/90; SLJ 7/90)

4149 Carmi, Giora. *A Circle of Friends* (K–2). Illus. by author. 2003, Star Bright $15.95 (1-932065-00-8). In this heartwarming, wordless picture book, a young boy unknowingly sets in motion a circle of kindness when he shares his muffin with a homeless man he finds sleeping on a park bench. (Rev: HBG 4/04; SLJ 1/04)

4150 Carr, Jan. *Frozen Noses* (PS–K). Illus. by Dorothy Donohue. 1999, Holiday House $15.95 (0-8234-1462-0). 32pp. Collage illustrations and an interesting text are used to describe three friends having fun outdoors on a cold winter's day. (Rev: BL 9/15/99; HBG 3/00; SLJ 9/99)

4151 Carter, Anne Laurel. *Circus Play* (K–2). Illus. by Joanne Fitzgerald. 2002, Orca $16.95 (1-55143-225-0). 32pp. A young boy whose mom is a trapeze artist tries to dampen the other children's dreams about circus life, but eventually realizes it's more fun to join in. (Rev: BL 12/1/02; HBG 3/03)

4152 Davies, Sally J. K. *When William Went Away* (K–3). Illus. 1999, Carolrhoda $15.95 (1-57505-303-9). 32pp. When Matthew's best friend William moves away, the boy is lost until Mary moves in next door, and William finds out that girls can also be friends. (Rev: BL 8/99; HBG 3/00; SLJ 7/99)

4153 Edwards, Nancy. *Glenna's Seeds* (K–2). Illus. by Sarah K. Hoctor. 2001, Child & Family $9.95 (0-87868-788-2). Glenna gives away a packet of marigold seeds and thereby starts off a chain of kind events that involves all the people on the block. (Rev: SLJ 4/01)

4154 English, Karen. *Neeny Coming, Neeny Going* (PS–3). Illus. by Synthia Saint James. 1996, Troll $14.95 (0-8167-3796-7). 32pp. Two friends are reunited on an island off the coast of South Carolina but can't resume their relationship. (Rev: BL 5/15/96; HB 7–8/96; SLJ 7/96)

4155 Failing, Barbara Larmon. *Lasso Lou and Cowboy McCoy* (PS–2). Illus. by Tedd Arnold. 2003, Dial $16.99 (0-8037-2578-7). McCoy's 10-gallon

hat is not enough to turn him into a cowboy, but Lasso Lou is patient and helps him to learn the ropes. (Rev: HBG 4/04; SLJ 10/03)

4156 Fox, Mem. *Wilfrid Gordon McDonald Partridge* (K–2). Illus. by Julie Vivas. 1989, Kane/Miller $13.95 (0-916291-04-9); paper $7.95 (0-916291-26-X). 32pp. The heartwarming story of the boy with four names who collects memorabilia in a box to take to his friend with four names in a nursing home because he has heard she is losing her memory. (Rev: BL 2/15/86; HB 1–2/86; SLJ 2/86)

4157 Greenfield, Eloise. *Me and Neesie* (PS–2). Illus. by Jan Spivey Gilchrist. 2005, HarperCollins LB $16.89 (0-06-000702-8). A 30th-anniversary edition of the classic story about an African American girl, Janell, and her imaginary friend. (Rev: SLJ 1/05)

4158 Havill, Juanita. *Brianna, Jamaica, and the Dance of Spring* (PS–3). Illus. by Anne S. O'Brien. 2002, Houghton Mifflin $16.00 (0-618-07700-6). 32pp. Asian American Brianna longs to play the role of butterfly in the dance recital. (Rev: BL 3/15/02; HBG 10/02; SLJ 4/02)

4159 Havill, Juanita. *Jamaica and Brianna* (PS–1). Illus. by Anne S. O'Brien. 1993, Houghton Mifflin $16.00 (0-395-64489-5). 32pp. Jamaica is upset when her friend, Brianna, makes fun of her hand-me-down boots. (Rev: BCCB 11/93; BL 10/15/93; HB 11–12/93; SLJ 10/93)

4160 Havill, Juanita. *Jamaica's Blue Marker* (PS–1). Illus. by Anne S. O'Brien. 1995, Houghton Mifflin $16.00 (0-395-72036-2). 32pp. Jamaica feels annoyance toward a classmate until she finds out he is moving. (Rev: BCCB 10/95; BL 7/95; SLJ 1/96)

4161 Henkes, Kevin. *Chester's Way* (PS–2). Illus. by author. 1988, Greenwillow $15.89 (0-688-07608-4). 32pp. Chester and Wilson are best friends and will have nothing to do with new girl Lilly, until she bails them out of trouble. (Rev: BL 9/1/88; HB 9–10/88; SLJ 9/88)

4162 Hilton, Nette. *Andrew Jessup* (K–3). Illus. by Cathy Wilcox. 1993, Ticknor $13.95 (0-395-66900-6). 32pp. Andrew was a wonderful, considerate friend; and when he moves away, his buddy is convinced that no one can take his place. (Rev: BL 12/15/93; SLJ 10/93)

4163 Jahn-Clough, Lisa. *Alicia's Best Friends* (PS–1). Illus. 2003, Houghton Mifflin $15.00 (0-618-23951-0). 32pp. Alicia must find a solution when her four close friends insist she choose one as her best friend. (Rev: BL 3/15/03; HBG 10/03; SLJ 3/03)

4164 Jahn-Clough, Lisa. *Missing Molly* (PS). Illus. 2000, Houghton Mifflin $15.00 (0-618-00980-9). 32pp. In a hide-and-seek game with Simon, Molly pretends to be missing while making an appearance in a disguise to fool her friend. (Rev: BL 2/1/00; HBG 10/00; SLJ 4/00)

4165 Jahn-Clough, Lisa. *My Friend and I* (PS). Illus. 1999, Houghton Mifflin $15.00 (0-395-93545-8). 32pp. A little girl and her friend quarrel after one of their toys breaks, but soon they make up. (Rev: BL 4/15/99; HBG 10/99; SLJ 5/99)

4166 Jahn-Clough, Lisa. *Simon and Molly Plus Hester* (PS–K). Illus. 2001, Houghton Mifflin $15.00 (0-618-08220-4). 32pp. The relationship between two best friends changes when a third playmate joins them. (Rev: BL 9/1/01; HBG 3/02; SLJ 9/01)

4167 Jam, Teddy. *The Stoneboat* (1–3). Illus. by Ange Zhang. 1999, Douglas & McIntyre $15.95 (0-88899-368-4). 32pp. In this Canadian story, a boy and his older brother save the life of their cranky neighbor and gradually break down the barriers of race and prejudice that separate them. (Rev: BCCB 12/99; BL 1/1–15/00; HBG 10/00; SLJ 1/00)

4168 Jones, Rebecca C. *Matthew and Tilly* (PS–2). Illus. by Beth Peck. 1995, Puffin paper $5.99 (0-14-055640-0). 32pp. Matthew, a white boy, and Tilly, a black girl, resume their close friendship after an argument. (Rev: BL 1/15/91; SLJ 3/91)

4169 Keats, Ezra Jack. *Goggles!* (K–3). Illus. by author. 1987, Macmillan paper $4.95 (0-689-71157-3). 40pp. Dachshund Willie outmaneuvers some neighborhood bullies trying to confiscate the motorcycle goggles found by Peter. Bold collage paintings perfectly capture inner-city neighborhood scenes.

4170 Keats, Ezra Jack. *Whistle for Willie* (PS–1). Illus. by author. 1964, Puffin paper $5.99 (0-14-050202-5). After many false starts, Peter at last learns to whistle.

4171 King, Stephen M. *Henry and Amy (Right-Way-Round and Upside Down)* (PS–1). Illus. 1999, Walker LB $16.85 (0-8027-8687-1). 32pp. Henry, who can't get anything right, meets Amy, who never makes mistakes, and they become friends. (Rev: BL 6/1–15/99; HBG 10/99; SLJ 6/99)

4172 Kline, Suzy. *Horrible Harry and the Ant Invasion* (2–4). Illus. by Frank Remkiewicz. 1989, Viking $13.99 (0-670-82469-0). 64pp. Horrible Harry becomes class monitor for the ant farm. (Rev: BL 12/1/89; SLJ 3/90)

4173 Kroll, Virginia. *Pink Paper Swans* (K–4). Illus. by Nancy L. Clouse. 1994, Eerdmans $15.00 (0-8028-5081-2). 32pp. In this account of how Janetta Jackson began helping Mrs. Tsujimoto, an origami expert, there are instructions for making a pink swan. (Rev: BCCB 10/94; BL 7/94; SLJ 8/94)

4174 Lachtman, Ofelia Dumas. *Tina and the Scarecrow Skins / Tina y las Pieles de Espantapajaros* (2–5). 2002, Arte Publico $14.95 (1-55885-373-1). 32pp. A story, told in both English and Spanish, of Tina and her friend Little Bell, who dresses oddly and makes up strange words, but ends up saving the day (and the tamales). (Rev: BL 2/15/03; SLJ 3/03)

4175 Lester, Alison. *Tessa Snaps Snakes* (K–2). Illus. by author. 1991, Houghton Mifflin paper $13.95 (0-685-52551-1). In double-page spreads, seven little children reveal their secrets and pet dislikes. (Rev: HB 11–12/91; SLJ 12/91)

4176 Lonborg, Rosemary. *Helpin' Bugs* (PS–2). Illus. by Diane R. Houghton. 1995, Little Friend $14.95 (0-9641285-2-7). 32pp. Lonely Hanna finds happiness helping her neighbor Douglas create a bug village. (Rev: BL 1/1–15/96; SLJ 2/96)

4177 Lyon, George E. *Together* (PS–2). Illus. by Vera Rosenberry. 1989, Orchard $15.95 (0-531-05831-X); paper $5.95 (0-531-07047-6). 32pp. Short poems explore the meaning of togetherness and friendship. (Rev: BL 9/15/89; HB 11–12/89; SLJ 9/89) [811]

4178 McBratney, Sam. *I'm Sorry* (PS–2). Illus. by Jennifer Eachus. 2000, HarperCollins $15.95 (0-06-028686-5). 40pp. Two best friends part after having a violent quarrel but the boy feels very sad at losing his friend and wonders if she feels sad too. (Rev: BL 8/00; HBG 10/00; SLJ 6/00)

4179 McCormick, Wendy. *Daniel and His Walking Stick* (PS–2). Illus. by Constance R. Bergum. 2005, Peachtree $15.95 (1-56145-330-7). On a trip to the country, Jesse meets a friend of her dead grandfather and the two become good friends, taking daily walks and talking about nature. (Rev: SLJ 5/05)

4180 McDonald, Megan. *Reptiles Are My Life* (K–2). Illus. by Paul Johnson. 2001, Scholastic $15.95 (0-439-29306-5). 32pp. Emily's arrival spoils the friendship between Maggie and Amanda until Amanda defends the other two and the three become inseparable. (Rev: HBG 3/02; SLJ 8/01)

4181 Munson, Derek. *Enemy Pie* (K–3). Illus. by Tara Calahan King. 2000, Chronicle $14.95 (0-8118-2778-X). A young boy is nice to a boy he doesn't like and ends up having a good time. (Rev: BCCB 1/01; HBG 3/01; SLJ 12/00)

4182 Okimoto, Jean Davies. *Dear Ichiro* (K–2). Illus. by Doug Keith. 2002, Kumagai $16.95 (1-57061-373-7). 32pp. Grampa's comments about the end of hostile feelings between Americans and Japanese make Henry reconsider his recent rupture with his friend Oliver. (Rev: BL 11/15/02; HBG 3/03; SLJ 3/03)

4183 Polacco, Patricia. *The Bee Tree* (K–3). Illus. 1993, Penguin Putnam $16.99 (0-399-21965-X). 32pp. After gathering honey from the bee tree with his granddaughter, Grampa explains that sweet things also can be found in books. (Rev: BL 3/1/93; HB 5–6/93; SLJ 6/93*)

4184 Polacco, Patricia. *Mrs. Katz and Tush* (K–4). Illus. 1992, Bantam $15.00 (0-553-08122-5). 32pp. A lonely Jewish widow is befriended by an African American boy who brings her a kitten to love. (Rev: BCCB 7–8/92; BL 4/15/92; HB 11–12/92; SLJ 7/92)

4185 Potter, Giselle. *Chloë's Birthday . . . and Me* (PS–3). Illus. by author. 2004, Simon & Schuster $15.95 (0-689-86230-X). In this sequel to *The Year I Didn't Go to School* (2002), Potter describes her jealous feelings on her younger sister's fifth birthday, celebrated in France; artwork and ephemera add to the atmosphere. (Rev: BCCB 7/04; HB 7–8/04; SLJ 7/04)

4186 Raschka, Chris. *Yo! Yes?* (K–4). Illus. 1993, Orchard LB $16.99 (0-531-08619-4). 32pp. This picture book consists of a conversation between two boys, one white, one African American. (Rev: BCCB 4/93; BL 3/15/93; HB 5–6/93; SLJ 5/93*)

4187 Redbank, Tennant. *Which Way, Wendy?* (1–3). Illus. by Rebecca Thornburgh. Series: Social Studies Connects. 2005, Kane paper $4.99 (1-57565-147-5). 32pp. New girl Wendy makes some friends by reading and returning a map they lost; ends with a page on how to read maps. (Rev: BL 3/1/05)

4188 Reynolds, Marilynn. *A Present for Mrs. Kazinski* (PS–3). Illus. by Lynn Smith-Ary. 2001, Orca $15.95 (1-55143-196-3). 32pp. Frank is thrilled that Mrs. Kazinski likes the gift he chooses for her 80th birthday. (Rev: BL 10/15/01; HBG 3/02)

4189 Rodman, Mary Ann. *My Best Friend* (PS–2). Illus. by E. B. Lewis. 2005, Viking $15.99 (0-670-05989-7). 32pp. Lily, 6, is crushed when Tamika, one of the girls she sees each week at the pool, doesn't want to be best friends. (Rev: BL 3/15/05; SLJ 5/05)

4190 Ryan, Pam Munoz. *A Box of Friends* (K–2). Illus. by Mary Whyte. 2003, Gingham Dog $14.95 (1-57768-420-6). Annie's grandmother helps her put together a box of memories, to cheer her after a move to a new house. (Rev: HBG 10/03; SLJ 9/03)

4191 Schotter, Roni. *Captain Snap and the Children of Vinegar Lane* (K–3). Illus. by Marcia Sewall. 1989, Orchard paper $5.95 (0-531-07038-7). 32pp. A bitter old man frightens the children away with his snapping fingers, until one day they discover he is ill. (Rev: BL 5/1/89; SLJ 5/89)

4192 Schubert, Ingrid, and Dieter Schubert. *Wild Will* (K–2). Illus. 1994, Carolrhoda LB $19.95 (0-87614-816-X). 32pp. Gradually, young Frank breaks down the hostility that a retired pirate feels toward people. (Rev: BL 9/15/94; SLJ 8/94)

4193 Shriver, Maria. *What's Wrong with Timmy?* (K–3). Illus. by Sandra Spieled. 2001, Little, Brown $14.95 (0-316-23337-4). 48pp. Eight-year-old Kate makes friends with Timmy, a boy who is mentally retarded, and wonders what it feels like to be Timmy. (Rev: BL 10/1/01; HBG 3/02; SLJ 1/02)

4194 Slaughter, Hope. *A Cozy Place* (PS–K). Illus. by Susan Torrence. 1991, Red Hen LB $15.95 (0-931093-13-9). 32pp. Two girls discover that it is each other's presence that makes a place cozy. (Rev: BL 6/1/91)

4195 Snihura, Ulana. *I Miss Franklin P. Shuckles* (K–3). Illus. by Leanne Franson. 1998, Annick LB $15.95 (1-55037-517-2); paper $5.95 (1-55037-516-4). When school starts, Molly decides to drop Franklin as a friend, but when she does she realizes how much she misses him. (Rev: SLJ 6/98)

4196 Starkman, Neal. *The Riddle* (K–2). Illus. by Ellen Sasaki. 1990, Comprehensive Health paper $10.00 (0-935529-13-6). 50pp. When a class assignment matches them together, Maria and a shy boy named Pete become friends. (Rev: BL 9/1/90)

4197 Steptoe, John. *Creativity* (PS–3). Illus. by E. B. Lewis. 1997, Clarion $15.95 (0-395-68706-3). 32pp. An African American boy wonders why a new class member who is as dark-skinned as himself can only speak Spanish. (Rev: BL 2/15/97; SLJ 4/97)

4198 Stone, Phoebe. *Go Away, Shelley Boo!* (1–3). Illus. by author. 1999, Little, Brown $15.95 (0-316-81677-9). A young girl imagines that her new neighbor next door is a real hellion, but she turns

out to be a great friend. (Rev: HBG 3/00; SLJ 11/99)

4199 Stroud, Bettye. *Down Home at Miss Dessa's* (PS–3). Illus. by Felicia Marshall. 1996, Lee & Low $14.95 (1-880000-39-3). 32pp. When Miss Dessa is injured, neighborhood children help her in this story of African Americans in the South. (Rev: BCCB 12/96; BL 12/15/96; SLJ 1/97)

4200 Sullivan, Sarah. *Root Beer and Banana* (PS). Illus. by Greg Shed. 2005, Candlewick $16.99 (0-7636-1748-2). 32pp. A gentle story about a new friendship made over ice pops on a hot day in the South. (Rev: BL 5/1/05)

4201 Viorst, Judith. *Rosie and Michael* (1–3). Illus. by Lorna Tomei. 1974, Macmillan $15.00 (0-689-30439-0); paper $4.99 (0-689-71272-3). 40pp. In spite of the many tricks they play on one another, Rosie and Michael are still friends.

4202 Vizurraga, Susan. *Miss Opal's Auction* (1–3). Illus. by Mark Graham. 2000, Holt $16.00 (0-8050-5891-5). As an auctioneer sells Miss Opal's possessions before she enters a retirement apartment, a young white girl remembers all the great times she and her elderly African American friend shared. (Rev: HBG 3/01; SLJ 11/00)

4203 Von Konigslow, Andrea Wayne. *Bing and Chutney* (PS–K). Illus. by author. 1999, Annick LB $16.95 (1-55037-609-8); paper $5.95 (1-55037-608-X). Two female friends separate to seek their own fortunes and, after each is successful, they are reunited. (Rev: SLJ 1/00)

4204 Waber, Bernard. *Gina* (PS–3). Illus. 1995, Houghton Mifflin $14.95 (0-395-74279-X). 32pp. Gina's skill at baseball helps her make friends when she moves to a new neighborhood in Queens where there are just boys. (Rev: BL 9/15/95; SLJ 10/95)

4205 Wallace, Ian. *The Naked Lady* (K–3). Illus. 2002, Millbrook LB $23.90 (0-7613-2660-X). 40pp. A young boy is initially shocked by a statue of a naked lady but through a friendship with the sculptor learns to appreciate it and develops his own artistic ambitions. (Rev: BL 12/1/02; HBG 3/03; SLJ 11/02)

4206 Wallace, Nancy E. *Paperwhite* (PS–1). Illus. 2000, Houghton Mifflin $14.00 (0-618-04283-0). 32pp. In spite of their age differences, Lucy and neighbor Miss Mamie enjoy each other's company and engage in such activities as planting narcissus bulbs for the spring. (Rev: BCCB 11/00; BL 11/15/00; HBG 3/01; SLJ 10/00)

4207 Whitcomb, Mary E. *Odd Velvet* (K–3). Illus. by Tara Calahan King. 1998, Chronicle $13.95 (0-8118-2004-1). 32pp. Because she dresses and behaves differently than other children in her school, Velvet is ignored by them, but gradually they change their ways. (Rev: BCCB 1/99; BL 11/1/98; HBG 3/99; SLJ 1/99)

4208 Wiles, Deborah. *Freedom Summer* (K–3). Illus. by Jerome Lagarrigue. 2001, Simon & Schuster $16.00 (0-689-83016-5). 32pp. Set in the South during desegregation, this is the story of the friendship between John Henry Waddell, an African American boy, and the narrator, who is white. (Rev:

BCCB 2/01; BL 2/15/01; HB 5–6/01; HBG 10/01; SLJ 2/01)

4209 Woloson, Eliza. *My Friend Isabelle* (PS–1). Illus. by Bryan Gough. 2003, Woodbine House $14.95 (1-890627-50-X). Charlie describes his friendship with Isabelle, a girl with Down syndrome, emphasizing that the differences between them (he's tall, she's short; he's fast, she's slow) help to make their relationship even more rewarding. (Rev: HBG 4/04; SLJ 12/03)

4210 Woodson, Jacqueline. *The Other Side* (K–3). Illus. by E. B. Lewis. 2001, Penguin Putnam $16.99 (0-399-23116-1). 32pp. The story of a white girl and a black girl who form a friendship despite the barrier between their houses. (Rev: BCCB 2/01; BL 2/15/01*; HBG 10/01; SLJ 1/01)

4211 Yee, Brenda Shannon. *Sand Castle* (PS–2). Illus. by Thea Kliros. 1999, Greenwillow $15.00 (0-688-16194-4). As Jen builds a sandcastle, other children come to help and add distinctive parts in this story about cooperation and friendship. (Rev: HB 7–8/99; HBG 10/99; SLJ 6/99)

4212 Yezerski, Thomas F. *Together in Pinecone Patch* (K–4). Illus. 1998, Farrar $16.00 (0-374-37647-6). 32pp. Two poor immigrant children, one from Poland and the other from Ireland, meet and fall in love and marry. (Rev: BL 2/1/98; HBG 10/98; SLJ 3/98)

4213 Ziefert, Harriet. *39 Uses for a Friend* (PS–3). Illus. by Rebecca Doughty. 2001, Penguin Putnam $11.99 (0-399-23616-3). 32pp. Clever pictures humorously illustrate the roles friends can play — alarm clock, napkin, hairdresser, and so on. (Rev: BL 12/1/01; HBG 3/02; SLJ 12/01)

4214 Zolotow, Charlotte. *I Know a Lady* (PS–2). Illus. by James Stevenson. 1984, Morrow paper $4.95 (0-688-11519-5). 24pp. Sally loves a kind old lady who lives in the neighborhood.

HUMOROUS STORIES

4215 Ackerman, Karen. *Bean's Big Day* (K–4). Illus. by Paul Mombourquette. 2004, Kids Can $15.95 (1-55337-444-4). Someone in the small early-20th-century town of Bean, Pennsylvania, is going to be chosen to be in a movie in this story told by an 8-year-old narrator called Cricket. (Rev: SLJ 5/04)

4216 Addy, Sharon Hart. *When Wishes Were Horses* (PS–3). Illus. by Brad Sneed. 2002, Houghton Mifflin $15.00 (0-618-13166-3). 32pp. Zeb's wishes for horses spiral out of control as each wish is granted, causing great crowding and confusion in an Old West town. (Rev: BL 12/1/02; SLJ 11/02)

4217 Ahlberg, Allan. *The Adventures of Bert* (PS–2). Illus. by Raymond Briggs. 2001, Farrar $16.00 (0-374-30092-5). 32pp. Five short tales about a silly man named Bert, who always seems to get into trouble. (Rev: BCCB 9/01; BL 9/1/01; HB 7–8/01*; HBG 3/02; SLJ 8/01)

4218 Ahlberg, Allan. *A Bit More Bert* (PS–2). Illus. by Raymond Briggs. 2002, Farrar $16.00 (0-374-32489-1). 32pp. The appealing Bert goes about daily life, meets other Berts, looks for his lost dog

Bert, and generally bumbles around in a friendly, funny way. (Rev: BCCB 11/02; BL 11/1/02; HB 9–10/02*; HBG 3/03; SLJ 11/02)

4219 Ahrens, Robin Isabel. *Dee and Bee* (PS–1). Illus. by Amanda Haley. 2000, Winslow $14.95 (1-890817-26-0). 32pp. Identical twin sisters often switch identities to fool their friends and family and, sometimes, even the reader. (Rev: BL 4/15/00)

4220 Alarcon, Karen Beaumont. *Louella Mae, She's Run Away!* (PS–2). Illus. by Rosanne Litzinger. 1997, Holt $15.95 (0-8050-3532-X). 32pp. In this merry barnyard romp a farm family turns out in full force to have a search when the mysterious Louella Mae is missing. (Rev: BL 6/1–15/97; HB 5–6/97; SLJ 5/97)

4221 Alda, Arlene. *Hurry Granny Annie* (K–3). Illus. by Eve Aldridge. 1999, Tricycle $14.95 (1-883672-72-4). 32pp. A long entourage, including granddaughter Ruthie, other children, and some animals, follows Granny, who is in a hurry to catch the sunset. (Rev: BL 8/99; HBG 3/00; SLJ 1/00)

4222 Allard, Harry. *The Stupids Have a Ball* (K–3). Illus. by James Marshall. 1984, Houghton Mifflin $18.00 (0-395-26497-9); paper $5.95 (0-395-36169-9). The whole Stupid family decides to celebrate when the children bring home terrible report cards from school. Two others in the series: *The Stupids Step Out* (1974); *The Stupids Die* (1981).

4223 Allard, Harry. *The Stupids Take Off* (K–3). Illus. by James Marshall. 1989, Houghton Mifflin $16.00 (0-395-50068-0). 32pp. The irresistible noodleheads set off on a fourth adventure, this time to avoid a visit from Uncle Carbuncle. (Rev: BCCB 10/89; BL 10/1/89; SLJ 10/89)

4224 Andreae, Giles. *Pants* (PS–2). Illus. by Nick Sharratt. 2003, Random $12.95 (0-385-75014-5). Cartoon-style illustrations highlight a rambunctious look at undergarments of all patterns and sizes. (Rev: HBG 4/04; SLJ 11/03)

4225 Appelt, Kathi. *Bubba and Beau Meet the Relatives* (PS–2). Illus. by Arthur Howard. 2004, Harcourt $16.00 (0-15-216630-0). 32pp. Newly clean, Baby Bubba and Beau the dog greet the arriving relatives before heading straight back to the mudhole, this time with baby Arlene in tow. (Rev: BL 3/15/04; HB 7–8/04; SLJ 5/04)

4226 Asch, Frank. *Monsieur Saguette and His Baguette* (PS–1). Illus. by author. 2004, Kids Can $14.95 (1-55337-461-4). A loaf of French bread assists in all sorts of adventures in this humorous Parisian romp. (Rev: SLJ 6/04)

4227 Ashman, Linda. *To the Beach!* (PS). Illus. by Nadine Bernard Wescott. 2005, Harcourt $16.00 (0-15-216490-1). 32pp. So many things are forgotten that the anticipated day at the beach ends up being a day in the backyard. (Rev: BL 5/1/05; SLJ 6/05)

4228 Auch, Mary Jane. *The Princess and the Pizza* (K–2). Illus. by Mary Jane Auch and Herm Auch. 2002, Holiday House $16.95 (0-8234-1683-6). In a fractured fairy tale, Paulina easily wins the contest for the prince's hand, but prefers instead to open a Pizza Palace. (Rev: BCCB 3/02; HBG 10/02; SLJ 5/02)

4229 Baehr, Patricia. *Mouse in the House* (PS–1). Illus. by Laura Lydecker. 1994, Holiday House LB $15.95 (0-8234-1102-8). When a mouse moves into Mrs. Teapot's house, she tries a number of unsuccessful ploys to get rid of it. (Rev: SLJ 9/94)

4230 Baker, Keith. *Hide and Snake* (PS–K). Illus. 1991, Harcourt $15.00 (0-15-233986-8). 32pp. A snake hides in each of the double-page spreads depicting everyday life. (Rev: BL 11/15/91; SLJ 12/91*)

4231 Barrett, Judith. *Animals Should Definitely Not Wear Clothing* (PS–1). Illus. by Ron Barrett. 1970, Macmillan $13.95 (0-689-20592-9); paper $5.99 (0-689-70807-6). 32pp. Humorous idea expressed in brief text and comic drawings. A sequel is: *Animals Should Definitely Not Act Like People* (Simon & Schuster 1988).

4232 Barton, Byron. *Wee Little Woman* (PS–K). Illus. 1995, HarperCollins LB $14.89 (0-06-023388-5). 32pp. The milk that a wee woman gets from her wee cow is stolen by a cat. (Rev: BCCB 6/95; BL 7/95; SLJ 8/95*)

4233 Bartram, Simon. *Man on the Moon: A Day in the Life of Bob* (1–3). Illus. by author. 2002, Candlewick $16.99 (0-7636-1897-7). Bob is custodian of the moon, and his daily tasks include clearing litter, entertaining tourists, and selling souvenirs. (Rev: HBG 3/03; SLJ 10/02)

4234 Bell, Cece. *Sock Monkey Boogie-Woogie: A Friend Is Made* (PS–2). Illus. 2004, Candlewick $14.99 (0-7636-2392-X). 32pp. Sock Monkey creates the dance partner of his dreams — out of argyle socks — in this energetic romp about a Big Celebrity Dance. (Rev: BL 1/1–15/05; SLJ 1/05)

4235 Best, Cari. *When Catherine the Great and I Were Eight!* (PS–2). Illus. by Giselle Potter. 2003, Farrar $16.00 (0-374-39954-9). One thing after another goes wrong when 8-year-old Sara and her Russian grandmother set off for the beach in this sequel to *Three Cheers for Catherine the Great* (1999). (Rev: HB 9–10/03; HBG 4/04; SLJ 9/03)

4236 Birdseye, Tom, and Debbie H. Birdseye. *She'll Be Comin' Round the Mountain* (K–3). Illus. by Andrew Glass. 1994, Holiday House LB $15.95 (0-8234-1032-3). 32pp. A variation on the old song that tells about a group of mountain folk who are awaiting Tootie's comin' round the mountain for a visit. (Rev: BL 7/94; SLJ 9/94)

4237 Bishop, Claire Huchet. *Five Chinese Brothers* (1–3). Illus. by Kurt Wiese. 1988, Penguin Putnam paper $5.99 (0-698-11357-8). 64pp. Physically identical in every way, each of the five Chinese brothers has one distinguishing trait that saves the lives of all of them.

4238 Blake, Quentin. *Mrs. Armitage: Queen of the Road* (PS–2). Illus. by author. 2003, Peachtree $15.95 (1-56145-287-4). The adventurous Mrs. Armitage and her dog set off in an old jalopy and take it in their stride when it starts losing parts and winds up a mere skeleton of a car. (Rev: HBG 4/04; SLJ 10/03)

4239 Bloom, Suzanne. *The Bus for Us* (PS–K). Illus. 2001, Boyds Mills $10.95 (1-56397-932-2). 32pp. A humorous story that describes children waiting to be picked up on the first day of school. (Rev: BL 3/15/01*; HBG 10/01)

4240 Bock, Lee. *Oh, Crumps! / Ay, caramba!* (PS–2). Trans. by Eida de la Vega. Illus. by Morgan Midgett. 2003, Raven Tree LB $16.95 (0-9720192-4-3). 32pp. A humorous tale, in both English and Spanish, about an exhausted farmer trying to keep up with his never-ending tasks and "repair the cow, climb the fence, milk the hay, and mow the silo." (Rev: HBG 10/03; SLJ 7/03)

4241 Bourgeois, Paulette. *Too Many Chickens!* (PS–3). Illus. by Bill Slavin. 1990, General Dist. Services paper $4.95 (1-550-74067-9). 32pp. A gift of chicken eggs to a class of elementary school children brings unexpected results. (Rev: BL 8/91; SLJ 6/91)

4242 Bradman, Tony. *Michael* (PS–3). Illus. by Tony Ross. 1998, Trafalgar paper $9.95 (0-86264-759-2). 32pp. Brainy Michael won't pay attention in class; he just wants to learn about spacecraft. (Rev: BL 1/15/91; SLJ 3/91)

4243 Broadley, Leo. *Pedro the Brave* (PS–2). Illus. by Holly Swain. 2002, ME Media $14.95 (1-58925-024-9). 32pp. Clever Pedro outwits the wolf that plans to eat him and his animal friends by feeding the wolf Pedro's special (fiery) hot sauce. (Rev: BCCB 2/03; BL 12/1/02; SLJ 4/03)

4244 Brown, Marc. *Arthur and the Crunch Cereal Contest* (2–4). Illus. 1998, Little, Brown $12.95 (0-316-11552-5); paper $3.95 (0-316-11553-3). 64pp. Arthur tries to compose a winning entry for the Crunch Cereal Jingle Contest, but it is his young sister, D. W., who supplies the inspiration. (Rev: BL 11/1/98; HBG 10/98; SLJ 10/98)

4245 Brown, Margaret Wise. *The Dirty Little Boy* (K–2). Illus. by Steven Salerno. 2001, Winslow $16.95 (1-890817-52-X). First published in 1939 under a different title, this is the story of a little boy who tries to get clean by imitating animals' baths. (Rev: HBG 10/01; SLJ 5/01)

4246 Brown, Ruth. *The Big Sneeze* (PS–K). Illus. by author. 1997, Morrow paper $4.95 (0-688-15282-1). 32pp. A fly lands on a farmer's nose; he sneezes, and havoc breaks out in the barnyard. (Rev: BCCB 2/86; BL 9/15/85; SLJ 10/85)

4247 Brumbeau, Jeff. *Miss Hunnicutt's Hat* (K–3). Illus. by Gail de Marcken. 2003, Scholastic $16.95 (0-439-31895-5). 48pp. Miss Hunnicutt strongly defends her right to wear a chicken on her hat for the visit of the queen. (Rev: BL 1/1–15/03; HBG 10/03; SLJ 3/03)

4248 Bunting, Eve. *My Backpack* (PS–K). Illus. 1997, Boyds Mills $14.95 (1-56397-433-9). 32pp. A young boy thinks he is doing everyone a favor when he gathers a lot of objects around the house and stores them in his backpack for safekeeping. (Rev: BL 5/1/97; SLJ 4/98)

4249 Butler, Dorothy. *Another Happy Tale* (PS–2). Illus. by John Hurford. 1992, Crocodile $12.95 (0-940793-88-1). Mabel and Ned are so ill prepared to bring up their baby girl that they accidentally sell her as part of a litter of pigs. (Rev: SLJ 4/92)

4250 Byars, Betsy. *The Golly Sisters Go West* (1–3). Illus. by Sue Truesdell. 1986, HarperCollins LB $15.89 (0-06-020884-8); paper $3.95 (0-06-444132-6). 64pp. In six stories, two adventurous women take on frontier life and the Wild West. (Rev: BCCB 11/86)

4251 Calmenson, Stephanie. *The Frog Principal* (PS–2). Illus. by Denise Brunkus. 2001, Scholastic $15.95 (0-590-37070-7). 32pp. A magician turns a school principal into a frog in this humorous story with colorful illustrations. (Rev: BL 9/15/01; HBG 3/02; SLJ 10/01)

4252 Carrick, Carol. *Big Old Bones: A Dinosaur Tale* (PS–3). Illus. by Donald Carrick. 1992, Houghton Mifflin paper $6.95 (0-395-61582-8). 32pp. Professor Potts finds a bunch of old bones to take back East to assemble. (Rev: BL 3/1/89; HB 5–6/89; SLJ 5/89)

4253 Carrier, Lisa, and Lenore Hart. *T. Rex at Swan Lake* (PS–1). Illus. by Chris Demarest. 2004, Dutton $15.99 (0-525-47717-4). A dinosaur skeleton tired of being on display in a museum decides to try her hand at ballet. (Rev: BL 8/04; SLJ 8/04)

4254 Cates, Karin. *A Far-Fetched Story* (PS–2). Illus. by Nancy Carpenter. 2002, HarperCollins LB $15.89 (0-688-15939-7). 32pp. All the members of Grandmother's family, including the baby, have different far-fetched reasons why they came home with no firewood in this newfangled folktale. (Rev: BL 2/15/02; HBG 10/02; SLJ 1/02)

4255 Cecil, Randy. *One Dark and Dreadful Night* (K–3). Illus. by author. 2004, Holt $16.95 (0-8050-6779-5). A cast of optimistic children make their own edits to Maestro Von Haughty's gloomy adaptations of three traditional fairy tales. (Rev: SLJ 8/04)

4256 Charlip, Remy. *Little Old Big Beard and Big Young Little Beard* (PS). Illus. by author Rettenmund and Tamara Rettenmund. 2003, Marshall Cavendish $16.95 (0-7614-5142-0). Two bearded cowboys embark on a search for their missing cow, but they are so inept that the cow has to find them. (Rev: HBG 4/04; SLJ 10/03)

4257 Charlip, Remy. *Why I Will Never Ever Ever Ever Have Enough Time to Read This Book* (K–3). Illus. by Jon J. Muth. 2000, Tricycle $14.95 (1-58246-018-3). 40pp. A humorous book about a little girl who has so many things to do, like homework and calling friends, that she will never to able to finish the big book that is always at her side. (Rev: BL 1/1–15/01; HBG 3/01; SLJ 9/00)

4258 Child, Lauren. *Clarice Bean, Guess Who's Babysitting?* (1–4). Illus. by author. 2001, Candlewick $16.99 (0-7636-1373-8). While her firefighter Uncle Ted is looking after Clarice and her siblings, their pet guinea pig escapes in this uproarious picture book. (Rev: HBG 10/01; SLJ 3/01*)

4259 Child, Lauren. *I Am Not Sleepy and I Will Not Go to Bed* (PS–3). Illus. 2001, Candlewick $16.99 (0-7636-1570-6). 32pp. Charlie tries to get his imaginative little sister to go to bed. (Rev: BL 8/01; HBG 3/02; SLJ 9/01)

4260 Child, Lauren. *I Want a Pet* (PS–1). Illus. 1999, Tricycle $13.95 (1-883672-82-1). 24pp. A hilarious story about a family that cannot agree on the perfect pet. (Rev: BL 4/15/99; HB 5–6/99; HBG 10/99; SLJ 5/99)

4261 Child, Lauren. *I Will Never Not Ever Eat a Tomato* (PS–2). Illus. by author. 2000, Candlewick $15.99 (0-7636-1188-3). Charlie gets his fussy little sister to eat by calling the food by exotic names. (Rev: HBG 3/01; SLJ 11/00)

4262 Child, Lauren. *What Planet Are You From, Clarice Bean?* (K–3). Illus. 2002, Candlewick $16.99 (0-7636-1696-6). 32pp. The delightful Clarice Bean joins her family in supporting her brother in his efforts to save a neighborhood tree. (Rev: BCCB 3/02; BL 4/15/02; HBG 10/02; SLJ 3/02*)

4263 Chodos-Irvine, Margaret. *Ella Sarah Gets Dressed* (PS). Illus. by author. 2003, Harcourt $16.00 (0-15-216413-8). Toddler Ella Sarah will not accept the fashion advice of her family, preferring to dress herself in vivid attire for her tea party. Caldecott Honor Book, 2004. (Rev: BL 6/1–15/03*; HBG 10/03; SLJ 7/03)

4264 Christelow, Eileen. *The Five-Dog Night* (PS–3). Illus. 1993, Clarion $14.95 (0-395-62399-5). 36pp. On cold nights, cranky old Ezra finds an unusual use for his five pet dogs. (Rev: BL 9/15/93; SLJ 10/93)

4265 Cibula, Matt. *The Contrary Kid* (2–4). Illus. by Brian Strassburg. 1995, Zino $16.95 (1-55933-177-1). 32pp. Cartoons and rhymes are used to tell about the antics of a kooky kid who revels in being different. (Rev: BL 1/1–15/96; SLJ 7/96)

4266 Clarke, Gus. *Nothing But Trouble* (PS–2). Illus. by author. 1998, Andersen paper $9.95 (0-86264-841-6). Maisie's day begins with her baby brother rudely wakening her, and her mother spilling cereal on her head — then things go from bad to worse. (Rev: SLJ 3/99)

4267 Clement, Rod. *Grandpa's Teeth* (PS–3). Illus. 1998, HarperCollins $15.95 (0-06-027671-1). 32pp. When Grandpa's false teeth are stolen, a nationwide search is begun. (Rev: BL 2/15/98; HBG 10/98; SLJ 3/98*)

4268 Clements, Andrew. *Double Trouble in Walla Walla* (1–3). Illus. by Sal Murdocca. 1997, Millbrook LB $21.90 (0-7613-0306-5). A girl is sent to the principal's office when she can't stop speaking in hyphenated words, like mish-mash. (Rev: HBG 3/98; SLJ 1/98)

4269 Clifford, Rowan. *Rodeo Ron and His Milkshake Cows* (K–2). Illus. 2005, Knopf LB $17.99 (0-375-93195-3). 32pp. When Rodeo Ron rides into the town of Cavity with his four cows of different hues, the soda bar owners challenge him to a shake-off — milkshakes vs. soft drinks — with the children as judges. (Rev: BL 6/1–15/05)

4270 Colandro, Lucille. *There Was a Cold Lady Who Swallowed Some Snow!* (PS–2). Illus. by Jared Lee. 2003, Scholastic paper $5.95 (0-439-47109-5). 32pp. This twist on the familiar story has the old lady devouring everything a strange combination of items, but when everything comes back out, there's the makings of a snowman. (Rev: BL 2/1/04)

4271 Cole, Brock. *Buttons* (K–3). Illus. 2000, Farrar $16.00 (0-374-31001-7). 32pp. When their father bursts his buttons, three daughters set out separately to bring him new ones, in this charming, humorous tale. (Rev: BCCB 3/00; BL 2/15/00*; HB 3–4/00; HBG 10/00; SLJ 4/00)

4272 Collins, Ross. *Alvie Eats Soup* (PS–2). Illus. 2002, Scholastic $15.95 (0-439-27260-2). 32pp. Alvie will only eat soup, and his parents despair when his gourmet chef grandmother arrives for a visit. (Rev: BL 11/1/02; HBG 3/03; SLJ 10/02)

4273 Corbett, Elizabeth T. *Three Wise Old Women* (PS–2). Illus. by Yu-Mei Han. 2004, Dutton $15.99 (0-525-47230-4). 32pp. Jaunty illustrations high-light the nonsensical nature of this 19th-century rhyme. (Rev: BL 1/1–15/04; HB 5–6/04; SLJ 2/04)

4274 Cronin, Doreen. *Wiggle* (PS–K). Illus. by Scott Menchin. 2005, Simon & Schuster $12.95 (0-689-86375-6). 40pp. A playful dog urges children to wiggle their way through the day. (Rev: BL 5/1/05; SLJ 6/05)

4275 Cuyler, Margery. *Skeleton Hiccups* (2–4). Illus. by S. D. Schindler. 2002, Simon & Schuster $14.95 (0-689-84770-X). 32pp. A skeleton tries to rid him-self of a bad case of hiccups and is finally scared out of them by looking in the mirror. (Rev: BCCB 9/02; BL 9/15/02; HB 9–10/02; HBG 3/03; SLJ 10/02)

4276 Cuyler, Margery. *That's Good! That's Bad!* (PS–K). Illus. by David Catrow. 1993, Holt paper $6.95 (0-8050-2954-0). 32pp. A boy's red balloon whisks him aloft for a series of adventures. (Rev: BCCB 12/91; BL 12/1/91; SLJ 11/91)

4277 Cuyler, Margery. *That's Good! That's Bad! In the Grand Canyon* (K–3). Illus. by David Catrow. 2002, Holt $16.95 (0-8050-5975-X). 32pp. A boy visiting the Grand Canyon has some "BAD" (but funny) close calls before he catches up with his grandmother. (Rev: BL 5/15/02; HBG 10/02; SLJ 6/02)

4278 Defelice, Cynthia. *Old Granny and the Bean Thief* (K–2). Illus. by Cat Bowman Smith. 2003, Farrar $16.00 (0-374-35614-9). When a thief steals some of Old Granny's beans and the sheriff is out of town, she enlists the help of a motley crew, includ-ing an alligator and a cactus. (Rev: HB 9–10/03; HBG 4/04; SLJ 9/03)

4279 Defelice, Cynthia. *The Real, True Dulcie Campbell* (PS–2). Illus. by R. W. Alley. 2002, Far-rar $16.00 (0-374-36220-3). 32pp. Dulcie lives on a farm but fancies herself a princess, switched at birth. (Rev: BCCB 12/02; BL 8/02; HBG 3/03; SLJ 9/02)

4280 Defelice, Cynthia. *Willy's Silly Grandma* (K–3). Illus. by Shelley Jackson. 1997, Orchard LB $16.99 (0-531-33012-5). Willy's Grandma spouts a lot of silly superstitions, but she is right in telling Willy not to go by the Old Swamp at night. (Rev: BCCB 6/97; HB 5–6/97; SLJ 4/97*)

4281 Delton, Judy. *Blue Skies, French Fries* (2–3). Illus. by Alan Tiegreen. 1988, Dell paper $3.99 (0-440-40064-3). 80pp. The Pee Wee scouts earn badges. Also use: *Lucky Dog Days; Peanut Butter Pilgrims; Camp Ghost-Away* (all 1988). (Rev: BL 2/15/89)

4282 dePaola, Tomie. *Helga's Dowry: A Troll Love Story* (K–2). Illus. by author. 1977, Harcourt paper $6.00 (0-15-640010-3). 32pp. Helga cannot marry Lars because she has no dowry, but this humorous account tells how she acquires one.

4283 dePaola, Tomie. *Pancakes for Breakfast* (PS–2). Illus. by author. 1978, Harcourt $14.95 (0-15-259455-8); paper $5.00 (0-15-670768-3). 32pp. The trials and travails of a country woman who decides to make some pancakes.

4284 Derby, Sally. *King Kenrick's Splinter* (K–3). Illus. by Leonid Gore. 1994, Walker LB $15.85 (0-8027-8323-6). 32pp. King Kenrick is afraid to have a splinter removed from his big toe. (Rev: BL 11/1/94; SLJ 1/95)

4285 De Regniers, Beatrice S. *May I Bring a Friend?* (PS–2). Illus. by Beni Montresor. 1971, Macmillan LB $16.95 (0-689-20615-1); paper $5.99 (0-689-71353-3). 48pp. The king and queen invite a small boy to tea, and each time he goes, he takes a friend — a seal, a hippopotamus, and several lions. Calde-cott Medal winner, 1965.

4286 Dodds, Dayle Ann. *Sing, Sophie!* (PS–1). Illus. by Rosanne Litzinger. 1997, Candlewick $15.99 (0-7836-0131-4). 32pp. Everyone ignores Sophie's singing talent except her baby brother, who prefers it to the sound of thunder. (Rev: BL 5/15/97; SLJ 6/97)

4287 Dodds, Dayle Ann. *Where's Pup?* (PS–K). Illus. by Pierre Pratt. 2003, Dial $12.99 (0-8037-2744-5). A clown makes the rounds of his fellow circus performers in a frantic search for his missing puppy; a final fold-out page reveals the pup's loca-tion atop a pyramid of acrobats. (Rev: HB 3–4/03*; HBG 10/03; SLJ 7/03)

4288 Dorros, Arthur. *When the Pigs Took Over* (PS–3). Illus. by Diane Greenseid. 2002, Dutton $15.99 (0-525-42030-4). 32pp. A pair of New Mex-ican brothers stars in a comic cumulative tale sprin-kled with Spanish phrases. (Rev: BL 2/1/02; HBG 10/02; SLJ 2/02)

4289 Downey, Lynn. *Sing, Henrietta! Sing!* (PS–3). Illus. by Tony Sansevero. 1997, Ideals $14.95 (1-57102-103-5). George loves his dear friend Henriet-ta, but he finds her singing earsplitting. (Rev: SLJ 7/97)

4290 Dragonwagon, Crescent. *The Bat in the Dining Room* (1–4). Illus. by S. D. Schindler. 1997, Mar-shall Cavendish $15.95 (0-7614-5007-6). 32pp. When a bat causes havoc after flying into the crowded dining room, Melissa gently coaxes the creature out. (Rev: BL 10/1/97; HBG 3/98; SLJ 9/97)

4291 Dyer, Heather. *Tina and the Penguin* (K–2). Illus. by Mireille Levert. 2002, Kids Can $14.95 (1-55074-947-1). 32pp. Tina fails in her elaborate efforts to keep her penguin secret in this humorous story with funny illustrations. (Rev: BL 1/1–15/03; HBG 3/03; SLJ 11/02)

4292 Egan, Tim. *Chestnut Cove* (PS–3). Illus. 1995, Houghton Mifflin $16.00 (0-395-69823-5). 32pp. A once-happy community becomes divided when people compete to grow the biggest watermelon. (Rev: BL 3/15/95; HB 11–12/95; SLJ 3/95*)

4293 Egan, Tim. *The Trial of Cardigan Jones* (K–3). Illus. by author. 2004, Houghton Mifflin $16.00 (0-618-40237-3). Although he only sniffed the pie, Cardigan, a moose who is clumsy with his antlers, is put on trial for theft. (Rev: BCCB 10/04; SLJ 9/04)

4294 Elliott, David. *Hazel Nutt, Mad Scientist* (K–2). Illus. by True Kelley. 2003, Holiday House $16.95 (0-8234-1711-5). Mad scientist Hazel Nutt wins over frightened villagers with the strange creatures she creates in her lab — singer Dracula-la-la and piano-monster combo Frankensteinway. (Rev: HBG 4/04; SLJ 3/04)

4295 Elya, Susan Middleton. *Cowboy Jose* (K–1). Illus. by Tim Raglin. 2005, Penguin Putnam $15.99 (0-399-23570-1). 32pp. In bouncy rhyming English and Spanish, a poor Mexican cowboy seeks the money to impress Rosita but in the end decides to spend it on his faithful horse. (Rev: BL 2/1/05; SLJ 4/05)

4296 Emmett, Jonathan. *Someone Bigger* (PS–1). Illus. by Adrian Reynolds. 2004, Clarion $16.00 (0-618-44397-5). 32pp. Dad says Sam is too little to handle the kite, it needs someone bigger; and of course so it proves as a whole string of people and animals are pulled into the air until Sam acts to save the day. (Rev: BL 3/1/04; SLJ 5/04)

4297 English, Karen. *Just Right Stew* (PS–1). Illus. by Anna Rich. 1998, Boyds Mills $15.95 (1-56397-487-8). Friends and relatives offer advice concerning ingredients as Victoria's mother and aunt try to prepare oxtail soup. (Rev: BL 2/15/98; HBG 10/98; SLJ 3/98)

4298 Ernst, Lisa Campbell. *Stella Louella's Runaway Book* (PS–2). Illus. 1998, Simon & Schuster $16.00 (0-689-81883-1). 40pp. Stella Louella traces the whereabouts of her lost library book by questioning various townspeople who have read it and passed it along. (Rev: BCCB 12/98; BL 8/98; HBG 3/99; SLJ 9/98)

4299 Esbaum, Jill. *Stink Soup* (1–4). Illus. by Roger Roth. 2004, Farrar $16.00 (0-374-37252-7). While on vacation at grandmother's farm, Willie keeps misbehaving (and letting older sister Annabelle take the blame) — until he encounters a skunk. (Rev: SLJ 3/04)

4300 Everitt, Betsy. *Mean Soup* (PS–1). Illus. 1992, Harcourt $16.00 (0-15-253146-7). 32pp. Horace gets rid of his nasty thoughts and feelings by throwing them into a pot and making mean soup. (Rev: BL 3/15/92*; SLJ 7/92)

4301 Feiffer, Jules. *By the Side of the Road* (2–4). 2002, Hyperion $15.95 (0-7868-0908-6). 64pp. A boy becomes so fed up with being bossed around by his dad that he decides to set out on his own. (Rev: BCCB 9/02; BL 6/1–15/02*; HBG 10/02; SLJ 5/02)

4302 Fleming, Candace. *Muncha! Muncha! Muncha!* (PS–2). Illus. by G. Brian Karas. 2002, Simon & Schuster $16.00 (0-689-83152-8). 32pp. Mr.

McGreely goes to great lengths to defend his vegetable garden from a group of clever rabbits in this hilarious story. (Rev: BCCB 3/02; BL 1/1–15/02; HBG 10/02; SLJ 2/02*)

4303 Fox, Mem. *Guess What?* (PS–2). Illus. by Vivienne Goodman. 1990, Harcourt $15.00 (0-15-200452-1). 32pp. Through a series of questions, a strange lady, who is a witch, is introduced. (Rev: BL 9/1/90; HB 11–12/91; SLJ 11/90)

4304 Fox, Mem. *Shoes from Grandpa* (PS–K). Illus. by Patricia Mullins. 1992, Orchard paper $6.95 (0-531-07031-X). 32pp. A cumulative story about buying clothes for a growing Jessie. (Rev: BL 2/15/90; HB 3–4/90; SLJ 4/90*)

4305 Freeman, Don. *Mop Top* (K–2). Illus. by author. 1978, Puffin paper $5.99 (0-14-050326-9). 48pp. Moppy changes his mind about a haircut after being mistaken for a floor mop by a nearsighted shopper.

4306 French, Vivian. *Oliver's Milk Shake* (PS–1). Illus. by Alison Bartlett. 2001, Scholastic $15.95 (0-531-30304-7). 32pp. Oliver's aunt sees the picky eater drinking orange soda for breakfast and puts Oliver through a busy day of pro-milk orientation before he explains her mistake. (Rev: BL 8/01; HBG 10/01; SLJ 6/01)

4307 French, Vivian. *Oliver's Vegetables* (PS–2). Illus. by Alison Bartlett. 1995, Orchard $14.95 (0-531-09462-6). 32pp. Longing for some French fries, Oliver promises to eat anything he finds in his Grandpa's vegetable garden, hoping to find potatoes. (Rev: BL 9/15/95; SLJ 10/95)

4308 French, Vivian, and Alex Ayliffe. *Let's Go, Anna!* (PS). 2000, David & Charles $14.95 (1-86233-074-3). 32pp. A flap book that relates Anna's hilarious misadventures during a shopping trip and at the same time gives youngsters a chance to count to five and learn the concept of size. (Rev: BL 1/1–15/01; SLJ 3/01)

4309 Frienz, D. J. *Where Will Nana Go Next? An Illustrated Tour of 19 Places to Go and Things to Do Across America and the World* (PS–1). Illus. by Sean Garber. 1999, Howling at the Moon $15.95 (0-9654333-0-7). Feisty Nana and her dog Spike visit some of America's tourist sights, in this book illustrated with bright, humorous cartoons. (Rev: SLJ 8/99)

4310 Gage, Wilson. *My Stars, It's Mrs. Gaddy: The Three Mrs. Gaddy Stories* (1–4). Illus. by Marylin Hafner. 1991, Greenwillow $15.95 (0-688-10514-9). 96pp. Mrs. Gaddy has a number of humorous adventures on her farm. (Rev: BL 10/15/91; HBG 4/04; SLJ 1/04)

4311 Garrison, Susan. *How Emily Blair Got Her Fabulous Hair* (K–3). Illus. by Marjorie Priceman. 1995, Troll $14.95 (0-8167-3496-8). 32pp. Emily longs to have curly hair but settles for arranging her straight locks into braids. (Rev: BL 1/1–15/96; SLJ 1/96)

4312 Geringer, Laura. *A Three Hat Day* (PS–1). Illus. by Arnold Lobel. 1985, HarperCollins LB $15.89 (0-06-021989-0); paper $5.95 (0-06-443157-6). 32pp. R. R. Pottle the Third is a gentleman who loves hats in this tale of loneliness and finding someone who cares. (Rev: BCCB 1/86; BL 9/15/85; HB 11–12/85)

4313 Gibbons, Faye. *The Day the Picture Man Came* (K–2). Illus. by Sherry Meidell. 2003, Boyds Mills $16.95 (1-56397-161-5). 32pp. The members of the Howard family prepare to have their picture taken by a traveling photographer in this funny story set in the Georgia mountains. (Rev: BL 2/15/03; HBG 10/03; SLJ 3/03)

4314 Gibbons, Faye. *Emma Jo's Song* (K–3). Illus. by Sherry Meidell. 2001, Boyds Mills $15.95 (1-56397-935-7). 32pp. Emma Jo is the hit of the family reunion when she sings a duet with a howling dog. (Rev: BL 4/1/01; HBG 10/01; SLJ 5/01)

4315 Gibbons, Faye. *Mama and Me and the Model T* (PS–3). Illus. by Ted Rand. 1999, Morrow LB $15.93 (0-688-15299-6). 40pp. In this delightful sequel to *Mountain Wedding,* Mama shows that it's not just the menfolk who can drive the new Model T around the farm. (Rev: BL 11/15/99; HB 3/00; SLJ 11/99)

4316 Gibbons, Faye. *Mountain Wedding* (K–4). Illus. by Ted Rand. 1996, Morrow $16.89 (0-688-11349-4). 40pp. A series of humorous mishaps delay the wedding of widow Searcy and widower Long. (Rev: BCCB 9/96; BL 4/1/96; HB 5–6/96; SLJ 4/96)

4317 Gill-Brown, Vanessa. *Rufferella* (K–3). Illus. by Mandy Stanley. 2001, Scholastic $12.95 (0-439-25617-8). 32pp. Diamante transforms her dog into Rufferella, who reaches great heights as a singer until meeting her downfall, a plateful of sausages. (Rev: BL 8/01; HBG 10/01; SLJ 8/01)

4318 Golembe, Carla. *Dog Magic* (PS–2). Illus. 1997, Houghton Mifflin $15.00 (0-395-81662-9). 32pp. Molly Gail thinks that the new slippers she received for her birthday have magically cured her fear of dogs. (Rev: BL 11/1/97; HBG 3/98; SLJ 9/97)

4319 Goode, Diane. *Monkey Mo Goes to Sea* (PS–1). Illus. 2002, Scholastic $15.95 (0-439-26681-5). 40pp. Young Bertie and his monkey, Mo, are invited to dine aboard a 1920s luxury liner, where Mo's attempts to "act like a gentleman" have riotous consequences. (Rev: BL 3/15/02*; HB 3–4/02; HBG 10/02; SLJ 3/02)

4320 Gosney, Joy. *Naughty Parents* (PS). Illus. by author. 2000, Millbrook LB $21.90 (0-7613-1823-2). In this humorous tale of role reversal, a little girl must take care of her parents when they spend an afternoon in the park, including finding them at the "Missing Parents Booth." (Rev: HBG 10/00; SLJ 5/00)

4321 Gottlieb, Dale. *Where Jamaica Go?* (PS–1). Illus. 1996, Orchard LB $15.99 (0-531-08875-8). 32pp. In Afro-Caribbean jargon, Jamaica travels downtown, to the beach, and on a trip in her father's van. (Rev: BL 10/1/96; SLJ 11/96)

4322 Grambling, Lois G. *Can I Have a Stegosaurus, Mom? Can I? Please!?* (PS–1). Illus. by H. Lewis. 1995, Troll $15.95 (0-8167-3386-4). 32pp. A boy points out all the advantages of having a dinosaur

for a pet, including eating all his distasteful vegetables. (Rev: BCCB 12/94; BL 1/15/95; SLJ 6/95)

4323 Graves, Keith. *Loretta: Ace Pinky Scout* (1–2). Illus. 2002, Scholastic $16.95 (0-439-36831-6). 40pp. Loretta discovers that not everyone can be perfect when she fails to earn her marshmallow toasting badge in this bright and silly spoof about scouting. (Rev: BL 10/15/02; HBG 3/03; SLJ 12/02)

4324 Gray, Kes. *Billy's Bucket* (PS–1). Illus. by Garry Parsons. 2003, Candlewick $15.99 (0-7636-2127-7). Billy sees rich underwater life in a new bucket — sharks, submarines, maybe a mermaid — and he forbids his parents to use it; unfotunately, his father needs to wash the car. (Rev: HBG 10/03; SLJ 6/03)

4325 Greenberg, David. *Snakes!* (PS–1). Illus. by Lynn Munsinger. 2004, Little, Brown $15.95 (0-316-32076-5). 32pp. A boy and his dog face an invasion of snakes in this funny story in rhythmic, rhyming verse. (Rev: BL 5/15/04; HB 5–6/04; SLJ 5/04)

4326 Greene, Carol. *The Golden Locket* (K–3). Illus. by Marcia Sewall. 1992, Harcourt $13.95 (0-15-231220-X); paper $5.00 (0-15-201008-4). 32pp. Miss Teaberry's generosity leads to amusing complications in this picture book. (Rev: BCCB 7–8/92; BL 4/1/92; HB 5–6/92; SLJ 5/92)

4327 Griffin, Kitty, and Kathy Combs. *The Foot-Stomping Adventures of Clementine Sweet* (K–2). Illus. by MikeWohnoutka. 2004, Clarion $15.00 (0-618-24746-7). 32pp. The feisty Clementine Sweet makes her presence felt in her Texas town. (Rev: BL 3/1/04; SLJ 3/04)

4328 Grossman, Bill. *Timothy Tunny Swallowed a Bunny* (PS–2). Illus. by Kevin Hawkes. 2001, HarperCollins $14.95 (0-06-028010-7). 32pp. Eighteen nonsense poems explore comic situations, such as the boy who grew a new nose every year. (Rev: BCCB 2/01; BL 2/15/01; HB 3–4/01*; HBG 10/01; SLJ 3/01)

4329 Gulbis, Stephen. *Cowgirl Rosie and Her Five Baby Bison* (PS–2). Illus. 2001, Little, Brown $12.95 (0-316-60230-2). 24pp. Cowgirl Rosie sets out to find the villain who stole her five baby bison on the trip into town. (Rev: BL 5/15/01; SLJ 5/01)

4330 Halperin, Wendy A. *When Chickens Grow Teeth* (K–3). Illus. 1996, Orchard LB $16.99 (0-531-08876-6). 32pp. Confined to bed because of an accident, Toine makes himself useful by hatching some chicken eggs. (Rev: BL 10/15/96; SLJ 9/96)

4331 *Hannah Mae O'Hannigan's Wild West Show* (1–2). Illus. by Lisa Campbell Ernst. 2003, Simon & Schuster $16.95 (0-689-85191-X). 40pp. Citified Hannah Mae has dreams of becoming a cowgirl; she practices day and night (on a herd of hamsters), and her skills are remarkable when she finally makes it out West. (Rev: BL 8/03; HB 7–8/03; HBG 10/03; SLJ 7/03)

4332 Harper, Jamie. *Don't Grown-Ups Ever Have Fun?* (PS–2). Illus. by author. 2003, Little, Brown $15.95 (0-316-14664-1). The three laid-back children in this humorous story like their lives of leisure and can't see why their parents won't relax. (Rev: HBG 10/03; SLJ 4/03)

4333 Harper, Jo. *Outrageous, Bodacious Boliver Boggs!* (2–3). Illus. by JoAnn Adinolfi. 1996, Simon & Schuster paper $16.00 (0-689-80504-7). Boliver Boggs invents a number of outrageous stories to explain why he is late for school. (Rev: SLJ 4/96)

4334 Harris, Peter. *Perfect Prudence* (1–3). Illus. by Deborah Allwright. 2003, Gingham Dog $15.95 (1-57768-437-0). So perfect is Prudence that she ends up with not only every role in the school play but all the backstage jobs as well; in the end, however, it becomes clear, despite Prudence's valiant efforts, that it's too big a job for just one person. (Rev: HBG 10/03; SLJ 8/03)

4335 Hartman, Bob. *The Wolf Who Cried Boy* (PS–2). Illus. by Tim Raglin. 2002, Penguin Putnam $15.99 (0-399-23578-7). 32pp. The cautionary tale is turned inside-out in this humorous story in which a wolf spots a pack of boy scouts. (Rev: BCCB 7–8/02; BL 7/02; HB 5–6/02; HBG 10/02; SLJ 6/02)

4336 Hartry, Nancy. *Jocelyn and the Ballerina* (PS–3). Illus. by Linda Hendry. 2000, Fitzhenry & Whiteside $14.95 (1-55041-649-9). 32pp. Jocelyn is so attached to her tutu that she puts it on under the beautiful pink dress she has to wear to a wedding. (Rev: BL 12/15/00; SLJ 1/01)

4337 Hassett, Ann. *Mouse in the House* (PS–2). Illus. by John Hassett. 2004, Houghton Mifflin $15.00 (0-618-35317-8). 32pp. Nana Quimby's discovery of a mouse in the house leads to even greater headaches as family members introduce one animal after another to rid the dwelling of an unwelcome guest. (Rev: BL 4/15/04*; HB 5–6/04; SLJ 3/04)

4338 Hassett, John, and Ann Hassett. *Cat Up a Tree* (PS–2). Illus. 1998, Houghton Mifflin $15.00 (0-395-88415-2). 32pp. As the number of cats increases in a tree outside her house, Nana Quimby tries several sources for help, starting with the firehouse and the police station and ending with the post office and the library, but finally she has do something about it herself. (Rev: BCCB 11/98; BL 10/15/98*; HBG 3/99; SLJ 10/98)

4339 Hebson, Denny. *Robots Everywhere* (PS–2). Illus. by Todd Hoffman. 2004, Walker $15.95 (0-8027-8892-0). 32pp. Robots are indeed everywhere — shopping, having their hair done (by blowtorch), getting rusty at the beach, and applying oil for "sensitive tin." (Rev: BL 3/15/04; SLJ 4/04)

4340 Himmelman, John. *Lights Out!* (K–2). Illus. 1995, Troll $13.95 (0-8167-3450-X). 32pp. A humorous story about the terrible creatures the six Badger Scouts believe await them at summer camp. (Rev: BL 4/1/95; SLJ 8/95)

4341 Hoberman, Mary Ann. *The Seven Silly Eaters* (PS–3). Illus. by Marla Frazee. 1997, Harcourt $16.00 (0-15-200096-8). 40pp. A humorous picture book about Mrs. Peters and her brood of picky eaters. (Rev: BCCB 5/97; BL 3/1/97; HB 5–6/97; SLJ 3/97)

4342 Hoberman, Mary Ann. *There Once Was a Man Named Michael Finnegan* (PS–1). Illus. by Nadine Bernard Westcott. 2001, Little, Brown $14.95 (0-316-36301-4). 32pp. This is a wacky collection of simple nonsense verses about poor Michael Finnegan and his dog. (Rev: BCCB 4/01; BL 4/1/01; HBG 10/01; SLJ 5/01)

4343 Hoff, Syd. *Arturo's Baton* (PS–3). Illus. 1995, Clarion $13.95 (0-395-71020-0). 32pp. When a famous conductor loses his favorite baton, he no longer can perform. (Rev: BL 9/1/95; SLJ 9/95)

4344 Howard, Arthur. *Serious Trouble* (PS–2). Illus. by author. 2003, Harcourt $16.00 (0-15-202664-9). Despite his serious parents, Prince Ernest is determined to become a jester, and he shows some talent at this when he coaxes a laugh from a three-headed dragon and thereby saves the kingdom. (Rev: HB 11–12/03; HBG 4/04; SLJ 11/03)

4345 Hubbell, Patricia. *Pots and Pans* (PS). Illus. by Diane De Groat. 1998, HarperCollins $9.95 (0-694-01072-3). Baby clears out the kitchen cupboards, producing chaos and a mad clattering as the child bangs away at the pots and pans. (Rev: BCCB 9/98; BL 8/98; HBG 10/98; SLJ 6/98)

4346 Huliska-Beith, Laura. *The Book of Bad Ideas* (K–3). Illus. by author. 2000, Little, Brown $14.95 (0-316-08748-3). A humorous book of bad ideas — like jumping off the high dive to show off your new bathing suit. (Rev: BCCB 11/00; HBG 3/01; SLJ 9/00)

4347 Hutchins, Pat. *Don't Forget the Bacon!* (K–3). Illus. by author. 1976, Morrow paper $4.95 (0-688-08743-4). 32pp. A young boy mixes up the shopping list on a trip to the grocery store.

4348 Inkpen, Mick. *Billy's Beetle* (PS–2). Illus. 1992, Harcourt $13.95 (0-15-200427-0). 32pp. Even with the help of a trained dog, Billy is not able to find his lost beetle. (Rev: BL 4/15/92; SLJ 8/92)

4349 Isaacs, Anne. *Swamp Angel* (K–4). Illus. by Paul O. Zelinsky. 1994, Dutton $15.99 (0-525-45271-0). 40pp. Angelica Longrider is a true tall-tale heroine because, among her many accomplishments, she is able to lasso a tornado. (Rev: BCCB 11/94; BL 10/15/94*; SLJ 12/94*)

4350 Jackson, Alison. *The Ballad of Valentine* (K–3). Illus. by Tricia Tusa. 2002, Dutton $16.99 (0-525-46720-3). 32pp. This parody of "My Darling, Clementine" stars a comic Valentine performing everyday tasks in her cabin while an admirer tries and fails to send her expressions of love. (Rev: BCCB 1/03; BL 11/15/02; SLJ 12/02)

4351 Jackson, Ellen. *Scatterbrain Sam* (K–3). Illus. by Matt Faulkner. 2001, Charlesbridge $15.95 (0-88106-394-0). 32pp. In this tall-tale adaptation of a Welsh story, Scatterbrain Sam seeks a cure for his brain and in the process finds true love. (Rev: BL 8/01; HBG 3/02; SLJ 7/01)

4352 Jam, Teddy. *The Charlotte Stories* (1–3). Illus. by Harvey Chan. 1996, Groundwood $14.95 (0-88899-210-6). 48pp. Charlotte is a candid 7-year-old who can't avoid trouble because of her open, honest nature. (Rev: SLJ 12/96)

4353 Johnson, Arden. *The Lost Tooth Club* (K–2). Illus. by author. 1998, Tricycle $13.95 (1-883672-55-4). Olivia tries various methods to lose her loose front tooth, so she can join the exclusive Lost Tooth Club. (Rev: HBG 10/98; SLJ 6/98)

4354 Johnson, Doug. *Never Ride Your Elephant to School* (PS–3). Illus. by Abby Carter. 1995, Holt $16.95 (0-8050-2880-3). 32pp. This cautionary tale describes all the catastrophes that can occur when you take an elephant to school. (Rev: BL 9/15/95; SLJ 12/95)

4355 Johnson, Paul B. *Mr. Persnickety and Cat Lady* (K–2). Illus. by Paul Johnson. 2000, Orchard LB $16.99 (0-531-33283-7). A humorous story about Mr. Persnickety who tries to get rid of his neighbor's 37 cats until his house is infested with mice. (Rev: BCCB 7–8/00; HBG 3/01; SLJ 11/00)

4356 Jonas, Ann. *Round Trip* (PS–4). Illus. by author. 1983, Morrow paper $4.95 (0-688-09986-6). 32pp. A book to read forward, backward, and then upside down.

4357 Jonas, Ann. *Watch William Walk* (PS–K). Illus. 1997, Greenwillow $14.89 (0-688-14175-7). 24pp. An alphabet adventure in which the entire story is told with words that begin with *w*. (Rev: BL 4/1/97; HB 7–8/97; SLJ 4/97)

4358 Kelley, Marty. *The Rules* (K–3). Illus. by author. 2000, Zino $12.95 (1-55933-284-0). Though the text offers many important dos and don'ts, the pictures show children humorously breaking each of the rules. (Rev: BL 9/15/03; HBG 4/04; SLJ 12/00)

4359 Ketteman, Helen. *The Great Cake Bake* (1–3). Illus. by Matt Collins. 2005, Walker LB $17.85 (0-8027-8952-8). 32pp. Donna Rae's efforts at cake baking all have disastrous results, but the mayor proposes anyway and next year, Donna Rae will be a judge. (Rev: BL 6/1–15/05; SLJ 5/05)

4360 Ketteman, Helen. *Shoeshine Whittaker* (1–3). Illus. by Scott Goto. 1999, Walker LB $16.85 (0-8027-8715-0). 32pp. In Mudville, Shoeshine guarantees how long his shine will last — and lives to regret it. (Rev: BL 10/15/99; HBG 3/00; SLJ 10/99)

4361 Kimmel, Eric A. *I Took My Frog to the Library* (PS–K). Illus. by Blanche Sims. 1992, Puffin paper $5.99 (0-14-050916-X). 32pp. A number of different animals create havoc when they visit the library. (Rev: BL 2/15/90; SLJ 3/90)

4362 Kinerk, Robert. *Timothy Cox Will Not Change His Socks* (PS–2). Illus. by Stephen Gammell. 2005, Simon & Schuster $16.95 (0-689-87181-3). 32pp. Tim is a determined boy and manages to go a month or so without changing his socks, despite a great deal of opposition. (Rev: BL 5/1/05; SLJ 6/05)

4363 Kiser, Kevin. *Buzzy Widget* (1–4). Illus. by John O'Brien. 1999, Marshall Cavendish $15.95 (0-7614-5057-2). Buzzy, a compulsive inventor, creates mechanical helpmates including CHEF, MAID, and WIFE. (Rev: HBG 3/00; SLJ 10/99)

4364 Koller, Jackie French. *Horace the Horrible: A Knight Meets His Match* (PS–3). Illus. by Jackie Urbanovic. 2003, Marshall Cavendish $16.95 (0-7614-5150-1). The humorous tale of Horace's knightly efforts to entertain his unhappy niece, the Princess Minuette. (Rev: BCCB 12/03; HBG 4/04; SLJ 11/03)

4365 Koren, Edward. *Very Hairy Harry* (PS–2). Illus. by author. 2003, HarperCollins LB $16.89 (0-06-050908-2). The *New Yorker* cartoonist offers the story of Harry, a hairy guy who thinks he wants to be even hairier. (Rev: HBG 4/04; LMC 2/04; SLJ 11/03)

4366 Krosoczka, Jarrett J. *Baghead* (PS–2). Illus. 2002, Knopf $15.95 (0-375-81566-X). 40pp. Confounding the skeptics, Josh succeeds in spending a day with a paper bag over his head, but his reason for doing so remains hidden until the end. (Rev: BL 11/15/02; HBG 3/03; SLJ 10/02)

4367 Laden, Nina. *Peek-a-Who?* (PS). Illus. by author. 2000, Chronicle $6.95 (0-8118-2602-3). A board book that uses die-cut windows so the reader can play a game of peek-a-boo. (Rev: SLJ 7/00)

4368 Lattimore, Deborah N. *The Lady with the Ship on Her Head* (PS–2). Illus. 1990, Harcourt $14.95 (0-15-243525-5). 32pp. In 18th-century France, Madame Pompenstance is unaware that a ship has landed on her hair. (Rev: BL 3/15/90; SLJ 6/90)

4369 Lawston, Lisa. *A Pair of Red Sneakers* (PS–2). Illus. by B. B. Sams. 1998, Orchard LB $16.99 (0-531-33104-0). 32pp. Miles imagines all the wonderful things he could do with a new pair of red sneakers, only to discover the store is out of them. (Rev: BL 10/1/98; HBG 3/99; SLJ 9/98)

4370 Lester, Helen. *It Wasn't My Fault* (PS–1). Illus. by Lynn Munsinger. 1985, Houghton Mifflin $16.00 (0-395-35629-6). 32pp. Nerdy Murdley Gurdson tries to discover why an ostrich laid an egg on his head. (Rev: BCCB 6/85; BL 3/1/85; SLJ 5/85)

4371 Levitin, Sonia. *A Single Speckled Egg* (K–3). Illus. by John Larrecq. 1976, Houghton Mifflin $6.95 (0-87466-074-2). 40pp. Three foolish farmers are outwitted by their wives in this ridiculous tale told in the folk tradition.

4372 Lithgow, John. *The Remarkable Farkle McBride* (K–2). Illus. by C. F. Payne. 2000, Simon & Schuster $16.00 (0-689-83340-7). Farkle McBride tires of each musical instrument he tries until he realizes he was born to become a conductor. (Rev: BCCB 6/00; HBG 3/01; SLJ 9/00)

4373 Ljungkvist, Laura. *Toni's Topsy-Turvy Telephone Day* (K–3). Illus. 2001, Abrams $15.95 (0-8109-4486-3). 32pp. Telephone interference scrambles Toni's potluck invitations and her friends turn up with extra guests instead of food. (Rev: BL 6/1–15/01; HBG 10/01; SLJ 5/01)

4374 Lobel, Arnold. *Ming Lo Moves the Mountain* (PS–3). Illus. by author. 1982, Morrow paper $5.95 (0-688-10995-0). 32pp. A humorous tale about a man's attempt to move a mountain away from his house.

4375 London, Sara. *Firehorse Max* (PS–1). Illus. 1997, HarperCollins LB $14.00 (0-06-205095-8). 32pp. Grandpa Lev's new horse, a former horse at the firehouse, has a behavioral problem when fire bells ring. (Rev: BL 10/1/97; SLJ 10/97)

4376 Lord, John Vernon. *The Giant Jam Sandwich* (PS–2). Illus. by author. 1987, Houghton Mifflin $17.00 (0-395-16033-2); paper $5.95 (0-395-44237-0). A rhymed verse about the citizens of Itching Down who make a giant jam sandwich to attract wasps.

4377 Loredo, Elizabeth. *Giant Steps* (PS–2). Illus. by Barry Root. 2004, Penguin Putnam $16.99 (0-399-23491-8). 32pp. Five goofy giants play "giant steps," striding all over the globe and providing lessons in geography as they go along. (Rev: BL 2/1/04; SLJ 3/04)

4378 Low, Alice. *Aunt Lucy Went to Buy a Hat* (PS–1). Illus. by Laura Huliska-Beith. 2004, HarperCollins $15.99 (0-06-008971-7). 32pp. An imaginative and well-illustrated story told in rhyme about forgetful Aunt Lucy's search for a hat. (Rev: BL 2/1/04; SLJ 3/04)

4379 Lucas, David. *Halibut Jackson* (PS–1). Illus. 2004, Knopf $16.95 (0-375-82690-4). 32pp. Shy Halibut aims to be invisible and wears clothes intended to blend in to his surroundings, but he misinterprets a royal invitation and attracts a lot of attention. (Rev: BL 2/1/04; SLJ 3/04)

4380 Luciani, Brigitte. *Those Messy Hempels* (PS–2). Trans. from German by J. Alison James. 2004, North-South LB $16.50 (0-7358-1910-6). An exceptionally untidy family has trouble finding the whisk needed to bake a cake. (Rev: SLJ 9/04)

4381 Lum, Kate. *Princesses Are Not Quitters!* (PS–3). Illus. by Sue Hellard. 2003, Bloomsbury $16.95 (1-58234-762-X). Three bored princesses trade places with their servants for a day, giving the royal trio a new appreciation for the efforts of those who labor on their behalf. (Rev: BL 6/1–15/03; HBG 10/03; SLJ 5/03)

4382 McCarthy, Megan. *Show Dog* (K–2). Illus. 2004, Viking $15.99 (0-670-03688-9). 40pp. Witty illustrations underline the humor in this story of two dog opposites competing for the same prize. (Rev: BL 1/1–15/04; SLJ 3/04)

4383 McCloskey, Robert. *Burt Dow, Deep-Water Man* (K–3). Illus. by author. 1963, Puffin paper $5.99 (0-14-050978-X). 64pp. The humorous tale of an old Maine fisherman who caught a whale by the tail and then used a multicolored Band-Aid to cover the hole.

4384 McCloskey, Robert. *Lentil* (K–3). Illus. by author. 1940, Puffin paper $5.99 (0-14-050287-4). 64pp. Tale of a boy who can't carry a tune, yet learns to play the harmonica.

4385 McCully, Emily Arnold. *Popcorn at the Palace* (K–3). Illus. 1997, Harcourt $16.00 (0-15-277699-0). 40pp. The Ferris family is considered odd by Illinois neighbors in the mid-1800s because they go to England to demonstrate corn popping for the queen. (Rev: BL 9/15/97; HBG 3/98; SLJ 10/97)

4386 MacDonald, Amy. *Cousin Ruth's Tooth* (PS–1). Illus. by Marjorie Priceman. 1996, Houghton Mifflin $16.00 (0-395-71253-X). 32pp. When Ruth loses a tooth, the whole family mounts a search to find it. (Rev: BCCB 6/96; BL 4/1/96; SLJ 5/96)

4387 McDonald, Megan. *Beetle McGrady Eats Bugs!* (PS–2). Illus. by Jane Manning. 2005, HarperCollins LB $16.89 (0-06-001355-9). Beetle is an adventurous soul and for Fun with Food Week declares that she will eat an ant. (Rev: BL 3/1/04; SLJ 5/05)

4388 McEvoy, Greg. *The Ice Cream King* (K–3). Illus. by author. 1998, Stoddart $13.95 (0-7737-3069-9). After graduating from King School, Lionel finds there are few openings, so he compromises and becomes an ice-cream seller known as "The Ice Cream King." (Rev: SLJ 12/98)

4389 Mangas, Brian. *Follow That Puppy!* (PS–2). Illus. by R. W. Alley. 1991, Simon & Schuster paper $12.95 (0-671-70780-9). When Puppy escapes his elderly owner while out for a walk, an exciting chase occurs. (Rev: SLJ 11/91)

4390 Manning, Maurie J. *The Aunts Go Marching* (PS–1). Illus. 2003, Boyds Mills $15.95 (1-59078-026-4). 32pp. Aunts (rather than the usual ants) march to town in this version of the familiar children's song. (Rev: BL 2/1/03; HB 5–6/03; HBG 10/03; SLJ 4/03)

4391 Martchenko, Michael. *Ma, I'm a Farmer* (1–3). Illus. by author. 2003, Annick LB $18.95 (1-55037-697-7); paper $5.95 (1-55037-696-9). Computer geek-turned-farmer, Fred soon discovers that rural life is not quite as stress-relieving as he had hoped, so he decides to apply his technological know-how to agrarian problems, with hilarious consequences. (Rev: SLJ 1/04)

4392 Martin, Bill, Jr. *The Maestro Plays* (PS–K). Illus. by Vladimir Radunsky. 1994, Holt $15.95 (0-8050-1746-1). 38pp. A circus setting is used to show all the different instruments the maestro plays. (Rev: BCCB 12/94; BL 11/1/94; SLJ 11/94*)

4393 Martin, Bill, Jr., and Michael Sampson. *Little Granny Quarterback* (K–3). Illus. by Michael Chesworth. 2001, Boyds Mills $15.95 (1-56397-930-6). A zany story in which Granny Whiteoak, a star football player in her day, saves her team from defeat. (Rev: HBG 3/02; SLJ 12/01)

4394 Marx, Patricia. *Meet My Staff* (K–2). Illus. by Roz Chast. 1998, HarperCollins $14.95 (0-06-027484-0). 40pp. Young Walter has his staff do all the things he hates, such as eating revolting vegetables, but what happens when the staff takes a day off? (Rev: BCCB 12/98; BL 8/98; HBG 3/99; SLJ 12/98)

4395 Marzollo, Jean. *I Spy Funhouse: A Book of Picture Riddles* (PS–3). Photos by Walter Wick. 1993, Scholastic $12.95 (0-590-46293-8). 40pp. This entertaining book consists of a series of picture puzzles involving an amusement park fun house and of a series of rhyming word clues. (Rev: BL 5/15/93; SLJ 4/93) [793]

4396 Mazer, Anne. *The No-Nothings and Their Baby* (PS–3). Illus. by Ross Collins. 2000, Scholastic $15.95 (0-590-68049-8). 40pp. Three goofy stories about Mr. and Mrs. No-Nothing and their misguided efforts to bring up a baby. (Rev: BL 1/1–15/01; HBG 3/01; SLJ 11/00)

4397 Most, Bernard. *Whatever Happened to the Dinosaurs?* (1–3). Illus. by author. 1984, Harcourt $16.00 (0-15-295295-0); paper $4.95 (0-15-295296-9). 32pp. Fantastic explanations to the title question.

4398 Munsch, Robert. *Alligator Baby* (PS–2). Illus. by Michael Martchenko. 1997, Scholastic $10.95 (0-590-21101-3). 29pp. An amusing story about overwrought parents who bring different baby animals home from the zoo, thinking each is their child. (Rev: HBG 3/98; SLJ 11/97)

4399 Munsch, Robert. *Andrew's Loose Tooth* (1–2). Illus. by Michael Martchenko. 1998, Scholastic $10.95 (0-590-21102-1). 32pp. Even the Tooth Fairy who arrives on her motorcycle can't dislodge Andrew's stubborn loose tooth. (Rev: BCCB 7–8/98; BL 3/15/98; HBG 10/98; SLJ 5/98)

4400 Munsch, Robert. *Get Out of Bed!* (PS–2). Illus. by Alan Daniel and Lea Daniel. 1998, Scholastic $10.95 (0-590-76977-4). 32pp. Because she has watched television all night, Amy can't get out of bed in the morning, so her family takes her to school in her bed, with humorous results. (Rev: BL 9/15/98; HBG 3/99; SLJ 9/98)

4401 Munsch, Robert. *More Pies!* (PS–2). Illus. by Michael Martchenko. 2002, Scholastic $13.95 (0-439-18773-7). 26pp. A very hungry Samuel isn't satisfied with his mother's huge breakfast and enters a pie-eating contest, only to arrive home victorious and find that pies are on the menu for lunch. (Rev: BCCB 1/03; HBG 3/03; SLJ 3/03)

4402 Munsch, Robert. *Munschworks: The First Munsch Collection* (PS–3). Illus. by Michael Martchenko. 1998, Annick $19.95 (1-55037-523-7). 128pp. This omnibus volume includes five of Robert Munsch's popular picture books, including *The Paper Bag Princess, David's Father,* and *Thomas' Snowsuit.* (Rev: BL 1/1–15/99)

4403 Munsch, Robert. *Munschworks 2: The Second Munsch Treasury* (PS–2). Illus. by Michael Martchenko and Helene Desputeaux. 1999, Annick $19.95 (1-55037-553-9). 136pp. This anthology contains five of Robert Munsch's picture books including *Purple, Green and Yellow, Pigs,* and *Something Good.* (Rev: BL 1/1–15/00; HBG 3/00)

4404 Munsch, Robert. *Stephanie's Ponytail* (1–3). Illus. by Michael Martchenko. 1996, Firefly $16.95 (1-55037-485-0); paper $5.95 (1-55037-484-2). Stephanie is annoyed when every one of her style changes is copied by class members and her teacher. (Rev: SLJ 11/96)

4405 Munsch, Robert. *Up, Up, Down* (PS–3). Illus. by Michael Martchenko. 2001, Scholastic $11.95 (0-439-18770-2). 28pp. Although her parents tell her not to, Anna persists in climbing on things. (Rev: HBG 3/02; SLJ 8/01)

4406 Munsch, Robert, and Michael Kusugak. *Munschworks 3: The Third Munsch Treasury* (PS–2). Illus. by Vladyana Krykorka and Michael Martchenko. 2000, Annick $19.95 (1-55037-633-0). 144pp. A large book that is a compilation of five of Munsch's previously published picture books including *Stephanie's Ponytail* (1986), *Angela's Airplane* (1988), and *A Promise Is a Promise* (1988). (Rev: BL 2/1/01; HBG 10/01) [813]

4407 Myers, Lynne B., and Christopher Myers. *Turnip Soup* (PS–2). Illus. by Katie Keller. 1994, Hyperion LB $14.49 (1-56282-446-5). 32pp. George is afraid that there is a Komodo dragon in his basement, and he is right. (Rev: BL 11/15/94; SLJ 2/95)

4408 Neitzel, Shirley. *Our Class Took a Trip to the Zoo* (PS–2). Illus. by Nancy Winslow Parker. 2002, HarperCollins LB $15.89 (0-688-15544-8). 32pp. A humorous rebus story about a boy's mishaps on a class trip to the zoo. (Rev: BL 3/15/02; HBG 10/02; SLJ 6/02)

4409 Nikola-Lisa, W. *Can You Top That?* (K–3). Illus. by Hector Viveros Lee. 2000, Lee & Low $15.95 (1-880000-99-7). 32pp. A group of children try to outdo each other by naming the strange animals they have at home, but a young African American tops them all by claiming he can produce an elephant — and he can, a little stuffed one. (Rev: BL 9/15/00; HBG 10/01; SLJ 12/00)

4410 Noble, Trinka Hakes. *Jimmy's Boa and the Bungee Jump Slam Dunk* (K–3). Illus. by Steven Kellogg. 2003, Dial $16.99 (0-8037-2600-7). Jimmy and his pet boa constrictor create havoc when they visit the school gym, where dance lessons are taking place. (Rev: HBG 4/04; SLJ 9/03)

4411 Noble, Trinka Hakes. *Meanwhile, Back at the Ranch* (PS–1). Illus. by Tony Ross. 1987, Puffin paper $5.99 (0-14-054564-6). 32pp. A humorous Western adventure concerning Rancher Hicks and his drive into Sleepy Gulch for some excitement. (Rev: BL 4/1/87; SLJ 5/87)

4412 Nolan, Lucy. *The Lizard Man of Crabtree County* (K–3). Illus. by Jill Kastner. 1999, Marshall Cavendish $15.95 (0-7614-5049-1). 32pp. A young boy, who dresses up as a bush, causes a commotion when he is mistaken for the Lizard Man. (Rev: BCCB 10/99; BL 11/15/99; HBG 3/00; SLJ 10/99)

4413 Nolen, Jerdine. *Plantzilla* (1–3). Illus. by David Catrow. 2002, Harcourt $16.00 (0-15-202412-3). 32pp. Third-grader Mortimer takes charge of the classroom plant, nicknamed Plantzilla, for the summer, and peculiar things begin to happen. (Rev: BCCB 11/02; BL 10/15/02; HBG 3/03; SLJ 9/02)

4414 Novak, Matt. *The Pillow War* (PS–2). Illus. 1998, Orchard LB $16.99 (0-531-33048-6). 32pp. Millie and Fred have a pillow fight over who will sleep with Sam the dog, but Sam has other plans. (Rev: BL 2/15/98; HBG 10/98; SLJ 3/98)

4415 Novak, Matt. *Too Many Bunnies* (PS–K). Illus. by author. 2005, Roaring Brook $7.95 (1-59643-038-9). Enhanced by a die-cut format, this is the story of five overcrowded bunnies who spy an invitingly empty hole across the field and one by one hop over there only to find they are no better off. (Rev: BCCB 2/05; HB 3–4/05; SLJ 6/05)

4416 Oller, Erika. *The Cabbage Soup Solution* (PS–2). Illus. 2004, Dutton $15.99 (0-525-47005-0). 32pp. Old Elsie's cats solve the mystery of who has been tampering with the cabbage crop — rabbits. (Rev: BL 2/15/04; SLJ 2/04)

4417 O'Neill, Alexis. *Loud Emily* (PS–3). Illus. by Nancy Carpenter. 1998, Simon & Schuster $16.00 (0-689-81078-4). 40pp. Although her family abhors their daughter's booming voice, Emily finds many uses for it, such as serenading whales and saving endangered ships at sea. (Rev: BCCB 10/98; BL 10/15/98; HBG 3/99; SLJ 10/98)

4418 Oppenheim, Shulamith Levey. *What Is the Full Moon Full Of?* (PS–2). Illus. by Cyd Moore. 1997, Boyds Mills $14.95 (1-56397-479-7). 32pp. Every one of the animals has a different answer when Jonas asks what the moon is full of. (Rev: BL 12/1/97; HBG 3/98; SLJ 12/97)

4419 Palatini, Margie. *Bedhead* (K–3). Illus. by Jack E. Davis. 2000, Simon & Schuster $16.00 (0-689-82397-5). No one can tame Oliver's wild hair and so he must wear his trusty blue baseball hat to school. (Rev: BCCB 10/00; HBG 3/01; SLJ 7/00)

4420 Palatini, Margie. *The Perfect Pet* (PS–2). Illus. by Bruce Whatley. 2003, HarperCollins LB $16.89 (0-06-000109-7). When Elizabeth's parents reject every suggestion for a new pet, the young girl adopts a tiny bug that she names Doug. (Rev: BL 7/03; HBG 10/03; SLJ 5/03)

4421 Parkinson, Curtis. *Emily's Eighteen Aunts* (PS–2). Illus. by Andrea Wayne von Konigslow. 2003, Fitzhenry & Whiteside $15.95 (0-7737-3336-1). 32pp. Feeling neglected with a new baby in the house, Emily advertises for an aunt and ends up with 18. (Rev: BL 2/15/03; SLJ 4/03)

4422 Parnell, Robyn. *My Closet Threw a Party* (PS–2). Illus. by Jimmy Pickering. 2005, Sterling $14.95 (1-4027-1298-7). A little girl finds an inventive way of explaining the total mess in her closet. (Rev: BL 5/1/04; SLJ 6/05)

4423 Patschke, Steve. *The Spooky Book* (K–3). Illus. by Matt McElligott. 1999, Walker LB $16.85 (0-8027-8693-6). 32pp. Two children, in separate houses, don't realize that they are reading scary books about each other and their spooky homes. (Rev: BCCB 9/99; BL 10/15/99; HBG 3/00; SLJ 11/99)

4424 Peters, Lisa Westberg. *Purple Delicious Blackberry Jam* (PS–3). Illus. by Barbara McGregor. 1992, Arcade $14.95 (1-55970-167-6). 32pp. Two children persuade their grandmother to make blackberry jam, but the results are not as expected. (Rev: BL 12/1/92; SLJ 3/93)

4425 Pinkwater, Daniel. *The Big Orange Splot* (K–2). Illus. by author. 1992, Scholastic paper $4.99 (0-590-44510-3). 32pp. A cumulative story about the effects of dropping a can of orange paint on the roof of Mr. Plumbean's house.

4426 Pinkwater, Daniel. *The Picture of Morty and Ray* (1–3). Illus. by Jack E. Davis. 2003, HarperCollins LB $16.89 (0-06-623786-6). 32pp. Afterr watching *The Portrait of Dorian Gray*, Morty and Ray use crayons to create a self-portrait and then misbehave in hopes of seeing it change. (Rev: BL 9/15/03; HBG 4/04; SLJ 9/03)

4427 Pinkwater, Daniel. *Rainy Morning* (PS–2). Illus. by Jill Pinkwater. 1999, Simon & Schuster $16.00 (0-689-81143-8). 32pp. During a rainstorm, Mr. and Mrs. Submarine open their kitchen to all sorts of creatures, and soon it is filled with everything from a wildebeest to Ludwig van Beethoven and the U.S. Marine Band. (Rev: BCCB 3/99; BL 3/1/99; HBG 10/99; SLJ 3/99)

4428 Plourde, Lynn. *Pigs in the Mud in the Middle of the Rud* (PS–2). Illus. by John Schoenherr. 1997, Scholastic $15.95 (0-590-56863-9). A farm family in their Model T Ford can't budge because of the animals in their way, including some pigs wallowing in the mud. (Rev: BCCB 2/97; SLJ 3/97*)

4429 Polacco, Patricia. *The Graves Family* (K–3). Illus. by author. 2003, Philomel $16.99 (0-399-24034-9). The townspeople steer a wide berth around the spooky Graves family's blood-red house until a decorating guru gives the Graves' home his stamp of approval. (Rev: HBG 4/04; SLJ 9/03)

4430 Polacco, Patricia. *In Enzo's Splendid Gardens* (1–4). Illus. 1997, Penguin Putnam $16.99 (0-399-23107-2). 32pp. A cumulative tale of chaos in an outdoor Italian restaurant begun by an innocent bee. (Rev: BL 8/97; SLJ 5/97)

4431 Polisar, Barry L. *Don't Do That! A Child's Guide to Bad Manners, Ridiculous Rules, and Inadequate Etiquette*. Rev. ed. (K–4). Illus. by David Clark. 1995, Rainbow $14.95 (0-938663-20-8). An irreverent book of manners that, for example, tells how to pick one's nose properly in public. (Rev: SLJ 8/95)

4432 Pomerantz, Charlotte. *Serena Katz* (K–2). Illus. by R. W. Alley. 1992, Macmillan LB $13.95 (0-02-774901-0). 32pp. The Duncan family visits the amazing, multitalented Serena Katz of New York City. (Rev: BCCB 6/92; BL 4/15/92; SLJ 6/92)

4433 Porte, Barbara Ann. *Chickens! Chickens!* (PS–2). Illus. by Greg Henry. 1995, Orchard LB $15.99 (0-531-08727-1). 32pp. A humorous tale of a man who achieves fame through his many paintings of chickens. (Rev: BCCB 4/95; BL 2/1/95; HB 3–4/95; SLJ 4/95)

4434 Poydar, Nancy. *Mailbox Magic* (PS–2). Illus. 2000, Holiday House $15.95 (0-8234-1525-2). 32pp. Will, who longs to get mail, collects box tops to send away for a cereal bowl. (Rev: BL 6/1–15/00; HBG 10/01; SLJ 9/00)

4435 Priest, Robert. *The Old Pirate of Central Park* (PS–2). Illus. 1999, Houghton Mifflin $15.00 (0-395-90505-2). 32pp. Old Pirate launches a replica of his ship, the *Laughing Dog,* in Central Park's sailboat pond, only to find that a retired queen wants to do the same with her ocean liner, the S.S. *Uppity Princess.* (Rev: BCCB 9/99; BL 4/1/99; HBG 10/99; SLJ 6/99)

4436 Proimos, James. *The Loudness of Sam* (K–3). Illus. 1999, Harcourt $13.00 (0-15-202087-X). 32pp. Sam likes to do everything in a big way, and soon his aunt, whom he is visiting, is behaving the same way. (Rev: BCCB 4/99; BL 7/99; HBG 10/99; SLJ 5/99)

211

4437 Provencher, Rose-Marie. *Slithery Jake* (PS). Illus. by Abby Carter. 2004, HarperCollins LB $16.89 (0-06-623821-8). 32pp. Sid's snake goes missing, causing much ado. (Rev: BL 1/1–15/04; SLJ 3/04)

4438 Pulver, Robin. *Axle Annie* (PS–3). Illus. by Tedd Arnold. 1999, Dial $15.99 (0-8037-2096-3). 32pp. Shifty Rhodes and friends conspire to get extra ice and snow on a steep hill so that the school bus, driven by Axle Annie, will not be able to make it and there will be, at long last, a snow day in Burskyville. (Rev: BL 2/15/00; HBG 3/00; SLJ 10/99)

4439 Pulver, Robin. *Mrs. Toggle's Zipper* (K–2). Illus. by R. W. Alley. 1990, Macmillan LB $13.95 (0-02-775451-0). 32pp. When Mrs. Toggle's zipper gets stuck, everyone at her school tries to help her out of her coat. (Rev: BCCB 3/90; BL 3/1/90; SLJ 5/90)

4440 Radunsky, Vladimir, and Eugenia Radunsky. *Yucka Drucka Droni* (1–3). Illus. 1998, Scholastic $15.95 (0-590-09837-3). 40pp. A European tale that is a tongue twister about three brothers who marry three sisters and have children with strange names. (Rev: BCCB 7–8/98; BL 2/1/98; HBG 10/98; SLJ 3/98*)

4441 Ransom, Jeanie Franz. *Grandma U* (K–2). Illus. by Lucy Corvino. 2002, Peachtree $15.95 (1-56145-214-9). Molly McCool goes to Grandma University to prepare for an impending arrival in this entertaining tale. (Rev: HBG 3/03; SLJ 12/02)

4442 Rathmann, Peggy. *The Day the Babies Crawled Away* (K–2). Illus. by author. 2003, Penguin Putnam $16.99 (0-399-23196-X). A picture book with effective oversize illustrations and a simple story about a toddler who comes to the rescue after babies crawl away from their preoccupied parents. (Rev: BCCB 12/03; BL 9/15/03; HB 9–10/03; HBG 4/04; LMC 3/04; SLJ 11/03)

4443 Reiss, Mike. *The Great Show-and-Tell Disaster* (1–4). Illus. by Mike Cressy. 2001, Price Stern Sloan $13.99 (0-8431-7680-6). All kinds of words are turned into anagrams with unfortunate consequences in this humorous, oversized book. (Rev: HBG 3/02; SLJ 1/02)

4444 Robart, Rose. *The Cake That Mack Ate* (PS–K). Illus. by Maryann Kovalski. 1991, Little, Brown paper $5.95 (0-316-74891-9). A cumulative tale featuring a festive party table. (Rev: BL 3/1/87; SLJ 6–7/87)

4445 Robinson, Bruce. *The Obvious Elephant* (PS–2). Illus. by Sophie Windham. 2002, Bloomsbury $15.95 (1-58234-769-7). 32pp. Townspeople are mystified by the appearance of an elephant, unsure of what it is or does, until a small boy sets them straight. (Rev: BL 9/15/02; SLJ 8/02)

4446 Root, Phyllis. *Rattletrap Car* (PS–K). Illus. by Jill Barton. 2001, Candlewick $15.99 (0-7636-0919-6). 32pp. A hilarious picture book in which a family uses ingenious means to repair their old car, such as using a beach ball for a tire. (Rev: BL 4/1/01; HBG 10/01; SLJ 6/01)

4447 Roth, Roger. *Fishing for Methuselah* (PS–3). Illus. 1998, HarperCollins $14.95 (0-06-027592-8). 32pp. Each of two great rivals in the North Country vows that he will catch the biggest fish in the lake, Methuselah, during the annual Winter Carnival. (Rev: BCCB 11/98; BL 11/15/98; HBG 3/99; SLJ 12/98)

4448 Ryan-Lush, Geraldine. *Hairs on Bears* (K–3). Illus. by Normand Cousineau. 1994, Annick LB $14.95 (1-55037-351-X); paper $4.95 (1-55037-352-8). A humorous picture book about the problems caused when the family pooch begins to shed his hair. (Rev: SLJ 12/94)

4449 Saenz, Benjamin Alire. *Grandma Fina and Her Wonderful Umbrellas / La Abuelita Fina y Sus Sombrillas Maravillosas* (K–2). Trans. by Pilar Herrera. Illus. by Geronimo Garcia. 1999, Cinco Puntos $15.95 (0-938317-46-6). 31pp. In this bilingual book, Grandma Fina is given a total on nine new umbrellas on her birthday, but she knows exactly what to do with each of them. (Rev: HBG 3/00; SLJ 10/99)

4450 Sage, James. *Farmer Smart's Fat Cat* (PS–2). Illus. by Russell Ayto. 2002, Chronicle $14.95 (0-8118-3502-2). 32pp. When Farmer Boast, Farmer Bluster, and Farmer Smart face a mouse problem, the first two come up with inventive but ineffective strategies, while Farmer Smart quietly gets a cat. (Rev: BL 7/02; HBG 10/02; SLJ 7/02)

4451 Saltzberg, Barney. *Where, Oh, Where Is My Underwear? A Pop-Up Book* (PS–K). Illus. 1994, Hyperion $9.95 (1-56282-694-8). 12pp. A search for underwear leads to great fun pulling tabs and lifting flaps in this interactive book. (Rev: BL 11/15/94)

4452 Samuels, Barbara. *Aloha, Dolores* (PS–2). Illus. 2000, DK $15.95 (0-7894-2508-4). 32pp. A humorous story in which a young girl goes to great lengths to make sure her cat wins a trip to Hawaii. (Rev: BL 3/1/00; HBG 10/00; SLJ 4/00)

4453 SanAngelo, Ryan. *Spaghetti Eddie* (PS–2). Illus. by Jackie Urbanovic. 2002, Boyds Mills $15.95 (1-56397-974-8). 32pp. Eddie uses his favorite food — spaghetti — to help a neighbor with broken shoelaces, to fashion a fishing net, and even to stop a robbery. (Rev: BL 8/02; HBG 3/03; SLJ 9/02)

4454 Savadier, Elivia. *No Haircut Today!* (PS–K). Illus. 2005, Roaring Brook $15.95 (1-59643-046-X). 32pp. Dominic definitely does not want to have his hair cut. (Rev: BL 5/1/05; SLJ 6/05)

4455 Sayre, April Pulley. *Noodle Man: The Pasta Superhero* (K–3). Illus. by Stephen Costanza. 2002, Scholastic $16.95 (0-439-29307-3). 40pp. Al Dente saves his family's business when the pasta machine he invents helps him perform heroic feats all over town in this pun-filled tale. (Rev: BL 2/15/02; HBG 10/02; SLJ 3/02)

4456 Scheer, Julian. *Rain Makes Applesauce* (K–2). Illus. by Marvin Bileck. 1964, Holiday House $16.95 (0-8234-0091-3). 36pp. A series of silly statements nonsensically presented and accompanied by humorous detailed pictures.

4457 Schneider, Christine M. *Picky Mrs. Pickle* (K–2). Illus. by author. 1999, Walker LB $16.85 (0-8027-8703-7). Mrs. Pickle has a pickle fetish and her stubborn niece tries to introduce her to other tastes. (Rev: HBG 3/00; SLJ 9/99)

4458 Schnetzler, Pattie. *Widdermaker* (K–4). Illus. by Rick Sealock. 2002, Carolrhoda LB $15.95 (0-87614-647-7). On their way to capture a pesky longhorn called the Widdermaker, Cowpoke Pete and his steed Desert Rose create the Painted Desert and Monument Valley in this zany tall tale. (Rev: HBG 3/03; SLJ 11/02)

4459 Scieszka, Jon. *Baloney (Henry P.)* (1–4). Illus. by Lane Smith. 2001, Viking $15.99 (0-670-89248-3). 32pp. A small green alien comes up with a humdinger of an excuse for being late to school in this story full of humor. (Rev: BCCB 5/01; BL 5/15/01*; HB 5–6/01; HBG 10/01; SLJ 5/01)

4460 Scieszka, Jon. *The Stinky Cheese Man: And Other Fairly Stupid Tales* (2–6). Illus. by Lane Smith. 1992, Viking $16.99 (0-670-84487-X). 56pp. Lots of fun with fractured fairy tales. (Rev: BCCB 10/92*; BL 9/1/92; HB 11–12/92*; HBG 10/02; SLJ 9/92*)

4461 Sendak, Maurice. *Chicken Soup with Rice: A Book of Months* (K–3). Illus. by author. 1962, HarperCollins LB $15.89 (0-06-025535-8). 48pp. A rhyming story that takes one through each of the months with the always suitable chicken soup with rice.

4462 Seuss, Dr., and Jack Prelutsky. *Hooray for Diffendoofer Day!* (K–4). Illus. by Lane Smith. 1998, Knopf LB $18.99 (0-679-99008-9). 56pp. With this story about an unusual teacher named Miss Bonkers, Prelutsky and Smith complete the sketches Dr. Seuss left when he died in 1991. (Rev: BCCB 6/98; BL 5/1/98; HBG 10/98; SLJ 6/98)

4463 Seymour, Tres. *I Love My Buzzard* (K–3). Illus. by S. D. Schindler. 1994, Orchard LB $16.99 (0-531-08669-0). 32pp. Mom gives up and decides to leave when her young son's menagerie grows and grows. (Rev: BL 1/15/94; SLJ 4/94)

4464 Seymour, Tres. *Too Quiet for These Old Bones* (PS–1). Illus. by Paul Johnson. 1997, Orchard LB $16.99 (0-531-33052-4). 32pp. To their surprise, four children discover that Granny doesn't really want the quiet they expect and instead would like to make a racket. (Rev: BL 11/15/97; HBG 3/98; SLJ 10/97)

4465 Shannon, David. *David Gets in Trouble* (PS–1). Illus. 2002, Scholastic $15.95 (0-439-05022-7). 32pp. David of *No, David* (1998) and *David Goes to School* (1999) denies any responsibility for the trouble he causes — until bedtime, when he finally apologizes to Mom. (Rev: BL 9/15/02; HB 1–2/03; HBG 3/03; SLJ 9/02*)

4466 Shannon, David. *The Rain Came Down* (PS–2). Illus. 2000, Scholastic $15.95 (0-439-05021-9). 32pp. Rain creates chaos in a big city as every living thing reacts in surprise. (Rev: BCCB 12/00; BL 10/15/00; HB 9–10/00; HBG 3/01; SLJ 10/00)

4467 Sharmat, Marjorie W. *Gila Monsters Meet You at the Airport* (PS–2). Illus. by Byron Barton. 1980, Macmillan $16.00 (0-02-782450-0); paper $4.95 (0-689-71383-5). 32pp. A young boy imagines all sorts of horrible things about his move from New York City.

4468 Sharratt, Nick. *Shark in the Park!* (PS–1). Illus. 2002, Random $14.95 (0-385-75008-0). 24pp. A boy peering through his telescope at the park thinks he sees sharks everywhere, but each turn of the page shows readers the real object — a black cat's ear or a bird's wing. (Rev: BL 9/1/02; HBG 3/03; SLJ 12/02)

4469 Simms, Laura. *Rotten Teeth* (K–3). Illus. by David Catrow. 1998, Houghton Mifflin $15.00 (0-395-82850-3). 32pp. Melissa has many things she could bring to school for show-and-tell, such as the alligator that lives in her family's doghouse. But her final choice is so disgusting that she will be remembered forever in the school's history. (Rev: BCCB 12/98; BL 9/1/98; HBG 3/99; SLJ 9/98)

4470 Sloat, Teri. *The Thing That Bothered Farmer Brown* (PS–1). Illus. by Nadine Bernard Westcott. 1995, Orchard LB $16.99 (0-531-08733-6). 32pp. A pesky mosquito keeps Farmer Brown and all the farm animals awake. (Rev: BL 2/1/95; SLJ 3/95)

4471 Sloat, Teri. *This Is the House That Was Tidy and Neat* (PS–1). Illus. by R. W. Alley. 2005, Holt $16.95 (0-8050-6921-6). 32pp. A father arrives home to find his house in havoc, and it all started with a cookie. (Rev: BL 5/1/05)

4472 Slobodkina, Esphyr. *Caps for Sale* (K–3). Illus. by author. 1947, HarperCollins LB $15.89 (0-06-025778-4); paper $5.95 (0-06-443143-6). 48pp. When some monkeys engage in a bit of monkey business, the cap peddler must use his imagination to retrieve his wares.

4473 Slonim, David. *Oh, Ducky! A Chocolate Calamity* (K–2). Illus. by author. 2003, Chronicle $15.95 (0-8118-3562-6). Cartoon-style illustrations highlight this wacky tale about a candy factory worker who loses his beloved rubber ducky in the chocolate machine. (Rev: HBG 10/03; SLJ 4/03)

4474 Spence, Rob, and Amy Spence. *Clickety Clack* (PS–1). Illus. by Margaret Spengler. 1999, Viking $15.99 (0-670-87946-0). 32pp. Each of the passengers picked up by a little black train makes so much noise that Driver Zack must take stern measures. (Rev: BL 7/99; HBG 10/99; SLJ 8/99)

4475 Stadler, John. *The Cats of Mrs. Calamari* (PS–2). Illus. 1997, Orchard $15.95 (0-531-30020-X). 32pp. When Mrs. Calamari discovers that her new landlord hates cats, she must think of unusual ways to save her large brood. (Rev: BL 3/1/97*; SLJ 5/97)

4476 Stadler, John. *Take Me Out to the Ball Game: A Pop-Up Book* (PS–3). Illus. by author. 2005, Simon & Schuster $12.95 (0-689-85917-1). An elaborate pop-up book with lots of humorous and informative details about baseball itself and the culture surrounding it, with a cast of animal characters preparing for a game at Howler Stadium. (Rev: SLJ 6/05)

4477 Stanley, Diane. *Raising Sweetness* (PS–3). Illus. by G. Brian Karas. 1999, Penguin Putnam

$15.99 (0-399-23225-7). 32pp. The kindly sheriff of Possum Trot adopts Sweetness and seven other orphans, and to show her appreciation, Sweetness arranges a reunion between the sheriff and his girlfriend. (Rev: BCCB 2/99; BL 2/15/99; HB 3–4/99; HBG 10/99; SLJ 1/99*)

4478 Stanley, Diane. *Saving Sweetness* (PS–3). Illus. by G. Brian Karas. 1996, Penguin Putnam $16.99 (0-399-22645-1). 32pp. After she runs away from an orphanage, Sweetness must save the sheriff who has been trying to catch her. (Rev: BCCB 11/96; BL 1/1–15/97*; HB 9–10/96; SLJ 11/96*)

4479 Steig, William. *The Amazing Bone* (K–2). Illus. by author. 1983, Farrar $17.00 (0-374-30248-0). 32pp. A bone that talks saves a piglet from being eaten by a fox in this nonsensical and witty story.

4480 Steig, William. *Pete's a Pizza* (PS–K). Illus. 1998, HarperCollins $13.95 (0-06-205157-1). 32pp. Pete is in a terrible mood until his parents pretend he is a pizza and begin kneading him, tossing him in the air, and sprinkling him with flour. (Rev: BL 10/1/98*; HB 9–10/98; HBG 3/99; SLJ 11/98)

4481 Steig, William. *Potch and Polly* (1–3). Illus. by Jon Agee. 2002, Farrar $16.00 (0-374-36090-1). 32pp. Potch, born under a happy angel, falls in love with Polly Pumpernickel, but a series of unfortunate incidents mar the romance, and the happy angel must intervene to help the lovers unite in this charmingly illustrated book. (Rev: BL 9/1/02; HBG 3/03; SLJ 8/02*)

4482 Stevens, Jan R. *Carlos and the Skunk: Carlos y el Zorrillo* (1–4). Illus. by Jeanne Arnold. 1997, Northland LB $15.95 (0-87358-591-7). 32pp. A bilingual book in which Carlos tangles with a skunk. (Rev: BL 5/15/97; HBG 3/98)

4483 Stevenson, James. *Yard Sale* (2–4). Illus. 1996, Greenwillow $14.89 (0-688-14127-7). 32pp. All of the creatures of Mud Flat participate in an unusual yard sale. (Rev: BL 3/15/96; HB 7–8/96; SLJ 7/96*)

4484 Stuart, Chad. *The Ballymara Flood* (PS–3). Illus. by George Booth. 1996, Harcourt $15.00 (0-15-205698-X). 40pp. A boy's innocent bath time ritual ends in a flood. (Rev: BL 4/1/96; SLJ 6/96)

4485 Tafuri, Nancy. *This Is the Farmer* (PS). Illus. 1994, Morrow $16.95 (0-688-09468-6). 24pp. A series of amusing cause-and-effect situations begin when a farmer gives a good-morning kiss to his wife. (Rev: BL 5/15/94; HB 9–10/94; SLJ 5/94)

4486 Teague, Mark. *Baby Tamer* (PS–3). Illus. 1997, Scholastic $15.95 (0-590-67712-8). 32pp. Amanda, the new baby-sitter, proves unflappable when tested by the Eggmont children. (Rev: BL 8/97; HBG 3/98; SLJ 10/97)

4487 Thompson, Kay. *Eloise Takes a Bawth* (PS–3). Illus. by Hilary Knight. 2002, Simon & Schuster $17.95 (0-689-84288-0). 80pp. The effervescent Eloise ignores Nanny's warnings about her "bawth" and the resulting flood succeeds in making more realistic the Venetian Masked Ball taking place below. (Rev: BL 12/1/02; HB 1–2/03; HBG 3/03; SLJ 12/02)

4488 Thomson, Pat. *The Squeaky, Creaky Bed* (PS–K). Illus. by Niki Daly. 2003, Doubleday LB

$17.99 (0-385-90856-3). In this cumulative tale, a young boy who can't fall asleep in his noisy bed is offered another comforting animal each successive night; of course, when he finally gets a new bed, the quiet keeps him awake. (Rev: BL 5/15/03; HBG 10/03; SLJ 9/03)

4489 Viorst, Judith. *Super-Completely and Totally the Messiest* (K–4). Illus. by Robin P. Glasser. 2001, Simon & Schuster $16.00 (0-689-82941-8). 32pp. Olivia describes the antics of her baby sister, who deserves the title "The Messiest." (Rev: BL 2/1/01; HBG 10/01; SLJ 3/01)

4490 Waber, Bernard. *Do You See a Mouse?* (PS–1). Illus. 1995, Houghton Mifflin $14.95 (0-395-72292-6). 32pp. Every one of the characters in this humorous picture book fails to see the mouse that is apparent to the reader. (Rev: BL 4/1/95; HB 7–8/95; SLJ 9/95)

4491 Wallace, Ian. *The True Story of Trapper Jack's Left Big Toe* (1–3). Illus. 2002, Millbrook LB $24.90 (0-7613-2405-4). 40pp. In this wild romp set in the Yukon, Josh sets out to find the amputated toe of Trapper Jack that is supposedly preserved in an old tobacco tin. (Rev: BCCB 7–8/02; BL 6/1–15/02; HB 5–6/02; HBG 10/02; SLJ 4/02)

4492 Walsh, Melanie. *Do Pigs Have Stripes?* (PS–1). Illus. 1996, Houghton Mifflin $12.95 (0-395-73976-4). 40pp. Nonsensical questions about animals (like the title) produce equally entertaining answers. (Rev: BL 3/1/96; HB 5–6/96; SLJ 4/96)

4493 Walter, Virginia. *"Hi, Pizza Man!"* (PS–2). Illus. by Ponder Goembel. 1995, Orchard LB $16.99 (0-531-08735-2). 32pp. Vivian wonders what sort of messenger will deliver the pizza that she and her mother have ordered. (Rev: BL 1/15/95; HB 3–4/95; SLJ 3/95)

4494 Walton, Rick. *Suddenly, Alligator! An Adverbial Tale* (1–4). Illus. by Jim Bradshaw. 2004, Gibbs Smith $15.95 (1-58685-313-9). Full of adverbs, this is the story of a boy whose well-worn socks are so aromatic they cause an alligator to pass out. (Rev: SLJ 11/04)

4495 Weeks, Sarah. *Mrs. McNosh Hangs Up Her Wash* (PS–K). Illus. by Nadine Bernard Westcott. 1998, HarperCollins $9.95 (0-694-01076-6). 24pp. On wash day, Mrs. McNosh gets carried away and begins hanging out such items as the newspaper, the dog, and the phone to dry. (Rev: BCCB 5/98; BL 4/15/98; HBG 10/98; SLJ 7/98)

4496 Weeks, Sarah. *Oh My Gosh, Mrs McNosh!* (PS–1). Illus. by Nadine Bernard Westcott. 2002, HarperCollins LB $15.89 (0-06-008858-3). 32pp. Mrs. McNosh suffers a series of misadventures when her dog George breaks free from his leash and she chases him through town. (Rev: BCCB 5/02; BL 5/1/02; HBG 10/02; SLJ 6/02)

4497 Weigel, Jeff. *Atomic Ace (He's Just My Dad)* (1–3). Illus. 2004, Whitman $15.95 (0-8075-3216-9). 32pp. A boy downplays the problems of having a superhero father in this humorous story. (Rev: BL 3/1/04; SLJ 5/04)

4498 Westcott, Nadine Bernard. *Peanut Butter and Jelly: A Play Rhyme* (PS–K). Illus. by author. 1987,

Puffin paper $5.99 (0-14-054852-1). 32pp. A play rhyme describes the making of this food that is a children's favorite. (Rev: BL 10/1/87; SLJ 9/87)

4499 Whatley, Bruce, and Rosie Smith. *Captain Pajamas* (PS–2). Illus. by Bruce Whatley. 2000, HarperCollins LB $15.89 (0-06-026614-7). 32pp. Late one night Brian believes that aliens have landed, but the sounds he hears are only his dog trying to get into the fridge. (Rev: BCCB 9/00; BL 5/15/00; HBG 10/00; SLJ 6/00)

4500 Wheeler, Lisa. *Bubble Gum, Bubble Gum* (PS–1). Illus. by Laura Huliska-Beith. 2004, Little, Brown $15.95 (0-316-98894-4). 32pp. In bouncy rhyming verse and bold illustrations, a number of different animals become snared by a big gob of bubble gum in the middle of the road. (Rev: BL 5/15/04; SLJ 5/04)

4501 White, Linda. *Too Many Pumpkins* (PS–2). Illus. by Megan Lloyd. 1996, Holiday House LB $16.95 (0-8234-1245-8). 28pp. Rebecca Estelle, who hates pumpkins, finds she has a bumper crop in her garden. (Rev: BCCB 12/96; BL 9/15/96; SLJ 11/96)

4502 White, Linda Arms. *Comes a Wind* (PS–3). Illus. by Tom Curry. 2000, DK $15.95 (0-7894-2601-3). 32pp. In this tall tale, two fiercely competitive brothers learn to cooperate when their mother gets blown away by a mighty Texas wind. (Rev: BCCB 3/00; BL 3/15/00; HBG 10/00; SLJ 5/00)

4503 Williams, Vera B. *"More More More," Said the Baby: 3 Love Stories* (PS). Illus. 1990, Greenwillow $15.89 (0-688-09174-1). 32pp. All the ways that parents and grandparents play with youngsters are portrayed in this humorous picture book. (Rev: BCCB 10/90; BL 10/1/90; HB 11–12/90; SLJ 10/90*)

4504 Willis, Jeanne. *I Want to Be a Cowgirl* (PS–2). Illus. by Tony Ross. 2002, Holt $14.95 (0-8050-6997-6). 24pp. A city girl dreams of forsaking her dolls and tea parties for life as a cowgirl. (Rev: BL 3/15/02; HBG 10/02; SLJ 7/02)

4505 Winthrop, Elizabeth. *Dancing Granny* (PS–2). Illus. by Salvatore Murdocca. 2003, Marshall Cavendish $16.95 (0-7614-5141-2). Granny has a grand time at the party at the zoo, dancing with many animals, including a fetching bear. (Rev: HBG 4/04; SLJ 10/03)

4506 Wood, Audrey. *King Bidgood's in the Bathtub* (PS–2). Illus. by Don Wood. 1985, Harcourt $16.00 (0-15-242730-9). 32pp. No one can get the king out of his bathtub, until the young page thinks of pulling the plug. (Rev: BCCB 1/86; BL 10/1/85; SLJ 11/85)

4507 Wood, Audrey. *The Napping House* (PS–2). Illus. by Don Wood. 1984, Harcourt $16.00 (0-15-256708-9). 32pp. A cumulative story about all the members of a household taking a nap except for a flea.

4508 Zemach, Kaethe. *Just Enough and Not Too Much* (PS–2). Illus. by author. 2003, Scholastic $16.95 (0-439-37724-2). Simon the Fiddler has acquired too much stuff, so he throws a party and requires the guests to take a chair, hat, and toy home with them. (Rev: HBG 4/04; SLJ 10/03)

4509 Ziefert, Harriet. *I Swapped My Dog* (PS–1). Illus. by Emily Bolam. 1998, Houghton Mifflin $15.00 (0-395-89159-0). 32pp. A cumulative story about a man who swaps each animal he receives for what he thinks is a better one, but ends up with his original faithful dog. (Rev: BL 3/1/98; HB 7–8/98; HBG 10/98; SLJ 5/98)

4510 Ziefert, Harriet. *Someday We'll Have Very Good Manners* (PS–3). Illus. by Chris L. Demarest. 2001, Penguin Putnam $15.99 (0-399-23558-2). 32pp. A merry book juxtaposing future proper behavior with current boorishness. (Rev: BL 2/15/01; HBG 10/01; SLJ 2/01)

4511 Zimelman, Nathan. *How the Second Grade Got $8,205.50 to Visit the Statue of Liberty* (K–3). Illus. by Bill Slavin. 1992, Whitman LB $14.95 (0-8075-3431-5). 32pp. Second-graders try to raise money for a field trip, with humorous results. (Rev: BL 9/15/92)

NATURE AND SCIENCE

4512 Allan, Nicholas. *Where Willy Went: The Big Story of a Little Sperm!* (PS–1). Illus. 2005, Knopf LB $17.99 (0-375-93030-2). 32pp. An unusual and appealing overview of the human reproductive process, in which Willy, a sperm who has spent his life polishing his swimming skills, triumphs over his competitors and fertilizes the egg. (Rev: BL 2/1/05; SLJ 3/05)

4513 Anderson, David A. *The Rebellion of Humans: An African Spiritual Journey* (K–4). Illus. by Claude Joachim. 1994, Sights $18.95 (0-9629978-6-2). 32pp. This ecological tale tells about an African tribe that forgets the lessons of the past and creates a wasteland by destroying the forests. A sequel to *The Origin of Life on Earth* (1992). (Rev: BL 10/1/94)

4514 Asch, Frank. *The Earth and I* (PS–2). Illus. 1994, Harcourt $15.00 (0-15-200443-2). 32pp. A young boy shares many thoughts and activities with his friend the earth. (Rev: BL 1/15/95; HBG 4/04; SLJ 10/94)

4515 Asch, Frank. *Like a Windy Day* (K–2). Illus. by Frank Asch and Devin Asch. 2002, Harcourt $15.00 (0-15-216376-X). 32pp. A little girl thinks about all the neat things the wind can do and imagines herself playing with the personified wind that floats overhead. (Rev: BL 10/1/02; HBG 3/03; SLJ 10/02)

4516 Asch, Frank. *The Sun Is My Favorite Star* (PS–1). Illus. 2000, Harcourt $15.00 (0-15-202127-2). 32pp. A little girl sings the praises of the sun and the light that it gives her. (Rev: BL 11/1/00; HBG 3/01; SLJ 10/00)

4517 Aschenbrenner, Gerald. *Jack, the Seal and the Sea* (1–4). Illus. by author. 1988, Silver Burdett LB $12.95 (0-382-09985-0); paper $4.95 (0-382-09986-9). 30pp. Jack rescues a seal who leads him to bountiful fishing grounds. (Rev: BL 1/15/89; SLJ 3/89)

4518 Atwell, Debby. *River* (K–3). Illus. 1999, Houghton Mifflin $15.00 (0-395-93546-6). 32pp. This book describes the changes that occur to an American river over time, and the reader gets an antipollution lesson along the way. (Rev: BL 11/1/99; HBG 3/00; SLJ 11/99)

4519 Baillie, Marilyn. *Nose to Toes* (PS–1). Illus. by Marisol Sarrazin. 2001, Boyds Mills $15.95 (1-56397-319-7). Bright, clean illustrations and simple text show children exploring their similarities to different animals. (Rev: HBG 3/02; SLJ 10/01)

4520 Baker, Sanna Anderson. *Mississippi Going North* (K–3). Illus. by Bill Farnsworth. 1996, Whitman LB $15.95 (0-8075-5164-3). A picture book about a family that explores the northern part of the Mississippi River by canoe and sees many animals and birds. (Rev: SLJ 10/96)

4521 Bang, Molly. *Common Ground: The Water, Earth, and Air We Share* (PS–3). Illus. 1997, Scholastic $12.95 (0-590-10056-4). 32pp. A parable in which villagers misuse their grazing areas points out the modern environmental problem of wasting the earth's resources. (Rev: BL 10/1/97*; HB 11–12/97; HBG 3/98; SLJ 10/97)

4522 Banks, Kate. *Gift from the Sea* (PS–3). Illus. by Georg Hallensleben. 2001, Farrar $16.00 (0-374-32566-9). 40pp. This book traces the past of an ancient rock that a boy finds on the beach. (Rev: BL 4/15/01; HB 5–6/01; HBG 10/01; SLJ 6/01)

4523 Baskwill, Jane. *Somewhere* (PS–1). Illus. by Trish Hill. 1996, Mondo $13.95 (1-57255-131-3). A simple rhyme and drawings of simple outdoor scenes are used to introduce the beauty and variety of nature. (Rev: HBG 4/04; SLJ 5/96)

4524 Bauer, Marion. *Clouds* (PS–1). Illus. by John Wallace. Series: Ready-to-Read. 2004, Simon & Schuster LB $11.89 (0-689-85440-4). 32pp. For beginning readers, this is an atttractive introduction to three common types of clouds — cirrus, stratus, and cumulus. Also use *Rain* (2004). (Rev: BL 2/1/04; SLJ 5/04) [551.57]

4525 Bauer, Marion Dane. *When I Go Camping with Grandma* (PS–2). Illus. by Allen Garns. 1995, Troll $15.95 (0-8167-3448-8). 32pp. A mood piece that lovingly describes a camping trip with a child and grandmother. (Rev: BL 1/1/95; SLJ 4/95)

4526 Below, Halina. *Chestnut Dreams* (PS–1). Illus. by author. 2000, Fitzhenry & Whiteside $14.95 (1-55041-545-X). 40pp. The life cycle of a horse chestnut tree is explored in this picture book that shows a girl and her grandmother enjoying and observing the tree through several seasons. (Rev: SLJ 1/01)

4527 Bess, Clayton. *The Truth About the Moon* (K–3). Illus. by Rosekrans Hoffman. 1983, Houghton Mifflin paper $6.95 (0-395-64371-6). 48pp. A young African boy hears both realistic and fanciful explanations for the moon. (Rev: SLJ 1/04)

4528 Borden, Louise. *Caps, Hats, Socks, and Mittens: A Book About the Four Seasons* (PS–K). Illus. by Lillian Hoban. 1989, Scholastic paper $4.99 (0-590-44872-2). Children are introduced to the uniqueness of each season. (Rev: BL 2/15/89; SLJ 4/89)

4529 Brandt, Keith. *Wonders of the Seasons* (1–3). Illus. by James Watling. 1982, Troll LB $17.25 (0-89375-580-X); paper $3.50 (0-89375-581-8). 32pp. A simple introduction to the four seasons and the characteristics of each.

4530 Brinckloe, Julie. *Fireflies!* (PS–1). Illus. by author. 1986, Simon & Schuster paper $4.99 (0-689-71055-0). 32pp. A boy catches fireflies one evening, but when their light grows dim, he releases them. (Rev: BL 5/1/85; HB 9–10/85; SLJ 4/85)

4531 Brown, Margaret Wise. *Wait Till the Moon Is Full* (PS–1). Illus. by Garth Williams. 1948, HarperCollins paper $5.95 (0-06-443222-X). 32pp. The fears of night are dispelled in this tender story about raccoons.

4532 Buchanan, Ken. *This House Is Made of Mud* (PS–1). Illus. by Libba Tracy. 1994, Northland LB $14.95 (0-87358-593-3); paper $6.95 (0-87358-580-1). 32pp. A child describes his adobe house in the Sonoran Desert and the plants and animal life around it. (Rev: BL 9/15/91)

4533 Bunting, Eve. *Anna's Table* (K–2). Illus. by Taia Morley. 2003, NorthWord $15.95 (1-55971-841-2). 32pp. Anna collects treasures that she finds — such as mouse bones, dead butterflies — and keeps them on her nature table. (Rev: BL 3/15/03; SLJ 10/03)

4534 Bunting, Eve. *Butterfly House* (K–2). Illus. by Greg Shed. 1999, Scholastic $15.95 (0-590-84884-4). 32pp. A young girl and her grandfather rescue a caterpillar and observe it change into a butterfly. (Rev: BL 6/1–15/99; HBG 10/99; SLJ 4/99)

4535 Bunting, Eve. *Secret Place* (K–3). Illus. by Ted Rand. 1996, Clarion $15.00 (0-395-64367-8). 32pp. A young boy finds a place in the city where wildlife still exists. (Rev: BL 9/1/96; SLJ 9/96)

4536 Bunting, Eve. *Someday a Tree* (PS–3). Illus. by Ronald Himler. 1993, Houghton Mifflin $15.00 (0-395-61309-4). 32pp. In spite of attention from friends, a sick tree continues to die. (Rev: BL 3/1/93; SLJ 5/93)

4537 Bunting, Eve. *Sunflower House* (PS–2). Illus. by Kathryn Hewitt. 1996, Harcourt $15.00 (0-15-200483-1). 32pp. A boy plants some sunflower seeds and witnesses the dramatic miracle of plant growth. (Rev: BL 4/1/96; SLJ 5/96)

4538 Cannon, Annie. *The Bat in the Boot* (PS–2). Illus. 1996, Orchard LB $16.99 (0-531-08795-6). 32pp. Two children nurture a baby bat until its mother comes to rescue it. (Rev: BL 4/1/96; SLJ 6/96)

4539 Carle, Eric. *The Tiny Seed* (K–2). Illus. by author. 1991, Picture Book $16.00 (0-88708-015-4). 32pp. A tiny seed travels by the wind, survives all sorts of perils, and grows into a flower. A reissue.

4540 Carlstrom, Nancy White. *What Does the Sky Say?* (K–2). Illus. by Tim Ladwig. 2001, Eerdmans $17.00 (0-8028-5208-4). 32pp. A poetic celebration of the sky and all its changing features. (Rev: BCCB 7–8/01; BL 7/01; HBG 10/01; SLJ 12/01)

4541 Carr, Jan. *Dappled Apples* (PS–1). Illus. by Dorothy Donohue. 2001, Holiday House $15.95 (0-8234-1583-X). 32pp. Cut-paper collages and rhyming text celebrate autumn as three children and a dog enjoy themselves. (Rev: BL 10/1/01; HBG 3/02; SLJ 9/01)

4542 Carr, Jan. *Splish, Splash, Spring* (PS–1). Illus. by Dorothy Donohue. 2001, Holiday House $15.95

(0-8234-1578-3). 32pp. It is spring and young playmates and a dog enjoy all its pleasures — playing in the rain, digging for worms, and flying kites. (Rev: BL 4/1/01; HBG 10/01; SLJ 5/01)

4543 Cash, Megan Montague. *What Makes the Seasons?* (PS–2). Illus. by author. 2003, Viking $15.99 (0-670-03598-X). A young African American girl and her cat experience the charms of each of the four seasons. (Rev: HBG 4/04; SLJ 10/03)

4544 Cherry, Lynne. *The Great Kapok Tree: A Tale of the Amazon Rain Forest* (K–3). Illus. 1990, Harcourt $16.00 (0-15-200520-X). 32pp. A carefully researched picture book of the Amazon rain forest. (Rev: BL 3/15/90; HB 5–6/90; SLJ 5/90)

4545 Christian, Peggy. *If You Find a Rock* (1–3). Illus. by Barbara Hirsch Lember. 2000, Harcourt $16.00 (0-15-239339-0). 32pp. This book illustrated with photographs tells of the varieties and purposes of rocks, such as rocks for skipping across ponds or for hiding little creatures. (Rev: BCCB 7–8/00; BL 4/1/00; HBG 10/00; SLJ 4/00)

4546 Cole, Henry. *I Took a Walk* (PS–K). Illus. 1998, Greenwillow $15.00 (0-688-15115-9). 28pp. A boy narrates his walk through woods and a meadow, by a stream and a pond, as he observes an assortment of animals, plants, and insects. (Rev: BCCB 3/98; BL 5/1/98; HB 5–6/98; HBG 10/98; SLJ 5/98)

4547 Cole, Henry. *On the Way to the Beach* (PS–3). Illus. by author. 2003, Greenwillow $15.99 (0-688-17515-5). On the fold-out illustrations, readers look for a variety of plant and animal life — a snowy egret, a terrapin, a prickly pear — as they follow a young girl on a walk to the beach. (Rev: BL 5/15//3; HBG 10/03; SLJ 5/03)

4548 Condra, Estelle. *See the Ocean* (K–2). Illus. by Linda Crockett-Blassingame. 1994, Ideals $14.95 (1-57102-005-5). 32pp. A blind girl, using her inner feelings, is the first to detect the ocean. (Rev: BL 10/15/94; SLJ 10/94)

4549 Crumpacker, Bunny. *Alexander's Pretending Day* (PS–K). Illus. by Dan Andreasen. 2005, Dutton $15.99 (0-525-46936-2). 32pp. Alexander plays "what if" and his mother always responds with a reassuring answer. (Rev: BL 2/15/05; SLJ 4/05)

4550 Deady, Kathleen W. *All Year Long* (PS–2). Illus. by Linda Bronson. 2004, Carolrhoda $15.95 (1-57505-537-6). 32pp. A young girl explains how changes in her family's activities signal the arrival of a new season. (Rev: BL 4/15/04; SLJ 4/04)

4551 Demunn, Michael. *The Earth Is Good: A Chant in Praise of Nature* (PS–1). Illus. by Jim McMullan. 1999, Scholastic $15.95 (0-590-35010-2). Accompanied by her puppy, a little girl explores the earth, including mountains, fields, an ocean, and forests. (Rev: HBG 10/99; SLJ 8/99)

4552 dePaola, Tomie. *Charlie Needs a Cloak* (PS–1). Illus. by author. 1982, Simon & Schuster paper $5.95 (0-671-66467-0). The facts about cloth making are humorously presented in this story of Charlie, a shepherd.

4553 dePaola, Tomie. *The Cloud Book* (K–3). Illus. by author. 1975, Holiday House LB $15.95 (0-

8234-0259-2); paper $6.95 (0-8234-0531-1). 32pp. The ten most common clouds, along with related myths and sayings.

4554 dePaola, Tomie. *The Quicksand Book* (1–3). Illus. by author. 1977, Holiday House LB $15.95 (0-8234-0291-6); paper $6.95 (0-8234-0532-X). 32pp. Science is both informative and entertaining in this story of Jungle Girl, who falls into a patch of quicksand.

4555 Desimini, Lisa, et al. *All Year Round* (PS–1). Illus. 1997, Scholastic $15.95 (0-590-36097-3). 32pp. Four artists have contributed their illustrations and short poems to this book about the seasons. (Rev: BL 12/15/97; HBG 3/98)

4556 Dixon, Ann. *Winter Is* (PS–2). Illus. by Mindy Dwyer. 2002, Alaska Northwest $15.95 (0-88240-543-8); paper $8.95 (0-88240-554-6). 32pp. Three youngsters' joy in a snowy winter is shown in flowing watercolors and bouncy rhymes as the children make snow angels, watch the northern lights, and view winter wildlife from their dogsled. (Rev: BL 1/1–15/03; HBG 3/03)

4557 Dorros, Arthur. *Feel the Wind* (PS–2). Illus. by author. 1989, HarperCollins LB $15.89 (0-690-04741-X); paper $4.95 (0-06-445095-3). 32pp. Defining what causes the wind to blow. (Rev: BL 4/1/89; SLJ 6/89)

4558 Dunn, Judy. *The Little Rabbit* (K–2). Illus. by Phoebe Dunn. 1980, Random paper $3.25 (0-394-84377-0). 32pp. A real rabbit family is introduced in photographs.

4559 Dunn, Phoebe. *Farm Animals* (PS). Illus. by author. 1984, Random $3.99 (0-394-86254-6). 28pp. An introduction to more than 15 farm animals.

4560 Dussling, Jennifer. *Picky Peggy* (1–3). Illus. by Lynn Adams. Series: Science Solves It. 2004, Kane paper $4.99 (1-57565-138-6). 32pp. Peggy is a picky eater, but — with the help of her pet duckling — she learns the importance of a balanced diet; solid scientific information is woven into the story. (Rev: BL 2/15/04; SLJ 6/04)

4561 Dussling, Jennifer. *Rainbow Mystery* (1–3). Illus. by Barry Gott. Series: Science Solves It. 2002, Kane paper $4.99 (1-57565-119-X). 32pp. Annie and Mike solve a mystery (rainbows on a wall) by discovering a science concept (prisms). (Rev: BL 9/15/02)

4562 Easwaran, Eknath. *The Monkey and the Mango: Stories of My Granny* (K–2). Illus. by Ilka Jerabek. 1996, Nilgiri Pr. $14.95 (0-915132-82-6). 29pp. In the southern Indian state of Kerala, a grandmother tells her grandson a number of stories that tell about the wonders of nature, creation, and humankind's relation to all creatures. (Rev: HBG 4/04; SLJ 8/96)

4563 Ehlert, Lois. *Feathers for Lunch* (PS–2). Illus. 1990, Harcourt $16.00 (0-15-230550-5). 32pp. A wide variety of American birds are introduced by way of a cat's stalking activities. (Rev: BCCB 1/91; BL 9/1/90; HB 11–12/90*; HBG 4/04; SLJ 12/90)

4564 Ehlert, Lois. *In My World* (PS–1). Illus. 2002, Harcourt $15.00 (0-15-216269-0). 40pp. Die-cut shapes are used to present various flora and fauna and other phenomena of nature in this impressive picture book. (Rev: BL 5/1/02*; HB 7–8/02; HBG 10/02; SLJ 5/02)

4565 Ehlert, Lois. *Pie in the Sky* (PS–2). Illus. 2004, Harcourt $16.00 (0-15-216584-3). 40pp. A well-designed and well-illustrated book about a "pie tree" that supplies cherries for the birds and animals as well as fruit for pie; a recipe is included. (Rev: BL 2/15/04; HB 7–8/04; SLJ 4/04)

4566 Ehlert, Lois. *Red Leaf, Yellow Leaf* (PS–2). Illus. 1991, Harcourt $16.00 (0-15-266197-2). 32pp. A child tells of buying, planting, and caring for a sugar maple tree. (Rev: BCCB 10/91; BL 10/1/91*; HB 11–12/91*; SLJ 11/91)

4567 Elliott, David. *Evangeline Mudd and the Golden-Haired Apes of the Ikkinasti Jungle* (2–4). Illus. by Andr a Wesson. 2004, Candlewick $15.99 (0-7636-1876-4). 196pp. Eight-year-old heroine Evangeline finds herself deeply involved in foiling a plot to destroy the rain forest. (Rev: SLJ 3/04)

4568 Erdrich, Lise. *Bears Make Rock Soup and Other Stories* (2–4). Illus. by Lisa Fifield. 2002, Children's Book Pr. $16.95 (0-89239-172-3). 32pp. A collection of short stories and art depicting the Native American connection to animals and the earth. (Rev: BCCB 1/03; BL 8/02; HBG 3/03; SLJ 9/02)

4569 Ernst, Lisa Campbell. *Wake Up, It's Spring!* (PS–K). Illus. 2004, HarperCollins LB $16.89 (0-06-008986-5). 32pp. The arrival of a warm spring sun is celebrated as plants, animals, and people bask in its rays. (Rev: BL 1/1–15/04; SLJ 2/04)

4570 Evans, Lezlie. *Rain Song* (PS–1). Illus. by Cynthia Jabar. 1995, Houghton Mifflin $14.95 (0-395-69865-0). 32pp. Two girls enjoy the sounds and the excitement of a rainstorm. (Rev: BCCB 3/95; BL 3/15/95; SLJ 7/95)

4571 Fife, Dale H. *Empty Lot* (K–3). Illus. by Jim Arnosky. 1996, Sierra Club paper $6.95 (0-871-56859-4). Harry realizes that his empty country lot is actually alive with all kinds of wildlife. (Rev: SLJ 8/91)

4572 Fisher, Aileen. *The Story Goes On* (PS–3). Illus. by Mique Moriuchi. 2005, Roaring Brook $16.95 (1-59643-037-0). A circular nature tale in which a seed sprouts and grows, a bug finds it appetizing, a frog eats the bug, and so forth through the shooting of a hawk to the final enrichment of the soil. (Rev: SLJ 6/05)

4573 Fisher, Leonard Everett. *Sky, Sea, the Jetty, and Me* (1–3). Illus. 2001, Marshall Cavendish $15.95 (0-7614-5082-3). 32pp. A young narrator at the seashore experiences the excitement and violence of a sudden storm. (Rev: BL 3/15/01; HBG 10/01)

4574 Fitch, Sheree. *No Two Snowflakes* (K–3). Illus. by Janet Wilson. 2001, Orca $16.95 (1-55143-206-4). 32pp. A boy in colder climes describes snow to his pen pal in the tropics. (Rev: BL 3/1/02; HBG 3/02; SLJ 1/02)

4575 Flatharta, Antoine Ó. *Hurry and the Monarch* (PS–2). Illus. by Meilo So. 2005, Knopf LB $16.99 (0-375-93003-5). 40pp. A tortoise called Hurry and

a migrating butterfly pause to reflect on their differences in this attractive book that addresses the realities of the insect and animal worlds. (Rev: BL 5/15/05)

4576 Fleming, Denise. *In the Small, Small Pond* (PS–K). Illus. 1993, Holt $16.95 (0-8050-2264-3); paper $6.95 (0-8050-5983-0). 30pp. In a series of collages, a frog views a year of changing seasons in a small pond. (Rev: BL 9/1/93; HB 9–10/93; SLJ 9/93*)

4577 Fletcher, Ralph. *Twilight Comes Twice* (K–2). Illus. by Kate Kiesler. 1997, Clarion $15.00 (0-395-84826-1). 32pp. In radiant illustrations, the author describes two times of day: the evening at twilight and dawn, when twilight colors are again present. (Rev: BL 10/15/97; HBG 3/98; SLJ 10/97)

4578 Fletcher, Ralph J. *Hello, Harvest Moon* (K–3). Illus. by Kate Kiesler. 2004, Houghton Mifflin $16.00 (0-618-16451-0). 32pp. The glow of the harvest moon shines over the peaceful neighborhood in this gentle book. (Rev: BL 9/1/03; HBG 4/04; SLJ 9/03)

4579 Franklin, Kristine L. *The Gift* (PS–2). Illus. by Barbara Lavallee. 1999, Chronicle $14.95 (0-8118-0447-X). In this sea story set in the Pacific Northwest, a young fisherman throws the Chinook salmon he has just caught back into the ocean to be food for a passing pod of killer whales. (Rev: HBG 3/00; SLJ 1/00)

4580 Frasier, Debra. *On the Day You Were Born* (K–2). Illus. 1991, Harcourt $16.00 (0-15-257995-8). 32pp. The wonders of nature and the interdependence of all living things are celebrated in this book that introduces science in a personalized way. (Rev: BL 6/15/91; SLJ 6/91*)

4581 Frasier, Debra. *Out of the Ocean* (PS–3). Illus. 1998, Harcourt $16.00 (0-15-258849-3). 40pp. A mother and her child explore the many gifts that the ocean can give, such as a seashell or pelican feathers. (Rev: BL 4/15/98; HBG 10/98; SLJ 8/98)

4582 Frazier, Craig. *Stanley Mows the Lawn* (PS–2). Illus. by author. 2005, Chronicle $15.95 (0-8118-4846-9). Stanley and a snake come face to face as Stanley mows the lawn. (Rev: SLJ 5/05)

4583 Gackenbach, Dick. *Mighty Tree* (PS). Illus. 1992, Harcourt $13.95 (0-15-200519-6). 32pp. This large picture book presents the uses and wonder of trees. (Rev: BL 4/1/92; SLJ 6/92) [582.16]

4584 Gay, Marie-Louise. *Stella, Fairy of the Forest* (PS–1). Illus. 2002, Groundwood $15.95 (0-88899-448-6). 32pp. The energetic Stella of the signature red hair answers her little brother Sam's many questions about nature. (Rev: BCCB 3/02; BL 3/15/02; HBG 10/02; SLJ 6/02*)

4585 George, Kristine O'Connell. *Hummingbird Nest: A Journal of Poems* (K–4). Illus. by Barry Moser. 2004, Harcourt $16.00 (0-15-202325-9). 48pp. George conveys the magic of watching a hummingbird raise a family in these short poems partnered by watercolors. (Rev: BL 2/1/04*; SLJ 4/04)

4586 George, Lindsay Barrett. *In the Snow: Who's Been Here?* (PS–1). Illus. 1995, Greenwillow

$16.89 (0-688-12321-X). 40pp. On their way to go sledding, two children discover clues showing that various animals are present in this nature book that supplies interesting explanations. (Rev: BL 12/1/95; SLJ 12/95)

4587 George, William T. *Box Turtle at Long Pond* (2–3). Illus. by Lindsay B. George. 1989, Greenwillow LB $15.89 (0-688-08185-1). 24pp. Box Turtle ambles out from a rotting log on Long Pond at the beginning of the day. (Rev: BL 9/1/89; SLJ 10/89*)

4588 Gibbons, Gail. *The Reasons for Seasons* (K–3). Illus. 1995, Holiday House LB $16.95 (0-8234-1174-5). 32pp. The seasons, their causes, and the changes they produce are introduced. (Rev: BL 4/1/95; SLJ 5/95) [525]

4589 Gibbons, Gail. *The Seasons of Arnold's Apple Tree* (PS–1). Illus. by author. 1984, Harcourt $15.00 (0-15-271246-1); paper $6.00 (0-15-271245-3). 32pp. Arnold's apple tree is useful in all seasons.

4590 Glaser, Linda. *It's Spring* (PS–1). Illus. by Susan Swan. Series: Celebrate the Seasons. 2002, Millbrook LB $21.90 (0-7613-1760-0). 32pp. A boy enjoys a spring day and muses on the changing seasons. Also use *It's Fall* (2001), *It's Winter* (2002), and *It's Summer!* (2003). (Rev: BL 5/15/02; HBG 10/02; SLJ 3/02)

4591 Glaser, Omri. *Round the Garden* (K–3). Illus. by Byron Glaser and Sandra Higashi. 2000, Abrams $15.95 (0-8109-4137-6). 34pp. This easily read text explains the water cycle through the journey of a tear that eventually becomes a drop of rain that helps an onion grow. (Rev: BCCB 11/00; BL 6/1–15/00; HBG 10/00; SLJ 5/00)

4592 Godkin, Celia. *When the Giant Stirred: Legend of a Volcanic Island* (K–3). Illus. 2002, Fitzhenry & Whiteside $17.95 (1-55041-683-9). 40pp. A handsomely illustrated story of a people who must leave a lush island when its volcano erupts, with a clear description of the natural cycle of renewal. (Rev: BL 11/1/02; SLJ 12/02)

4593 Haas, Jessie. *Sugaring* (PS–2). Illus. by Joseph A. Smith. 1996, Greenwillow $15.00 (0-688-14200-1). 24pp. The stages of making maple sugar and syrup are examined when Nora decides to help her grandfather in this late winter ritual. A sequel to *Mowing* (1994) and *No Foal Yet* (1995). (Rev: BL 11/15/96; SLJ 10/96)

4594 Hader, Berta, and Elmer Hader. *The Big Snow* (PS–3). Illus. by authors. 1972, Macmillan LB $17.00 (0-02-737910-8); paper $6.95 (0-689-71757-1). 48pp. How all the little animals of a country hillside survive a heavy winter storm. Caldecott Medal winner, 1949.

4595 Hague, Kathleen. *Calendarbears: A Book of Months* (PS–1). Illus. by Michael Hague. 1997, Holt $14.95 (0-8050-3818-3). 32pp. Twelve engaging bears highlight activities associated with each of the months. (Rev: BL 3/15/97; SLJ 7/97)

4596 Hall, Zoe. *The Apple Pie Tree* (PS–2). Illus. by Shari Halpern. 1996, Scholastic $15.95 (0-590-62382-6). 32pp. The changes that occur to an apple tree during one year are described by two sisters. (Rev: BCCB 12/96; BL 10/1/96; SLJ 12/96)

4597 Hall, Zoe. *Fall Leaves Fall!* (PS). Illus. by Shari Halpern. 2000, Scholastic $15.95 (0-590-10079-3). 40pp. In autumn, two children play with leaves and engage in activities like kicking them, comparing their shapes, and raking them into piles. (Rev: BL 12/15/00; HBG 3/01; SLJ 9/00)

4598 Hall, Zoe. *The Surprise Garden* (PS–1). Illus. by Shari Halpern. 1998, Scholastic $15.95 (0-590-10075-0). 32pp. A charming book in which children plant seeds and tend their gardens until the plants grow into marvelous vegetables. (Rev: BCCB 3/98; BL 1/1–15/98; HBG 10/98; SLJ 3/98)

4599 Hargrove, Linda. *Wings Across the Moon* (PS). Illus. by Joung Un Kim. Series: Harper Growing Tree. 2001, HarperCollins $9.95 (0-694-01280-7). 24pp. A mother and child watch the moon's passage and the animals that make their appearance at night. (Rev: BL 4/15/01; HBG 10/01; SLJ 1/02)

4600 Haskins, Lori. *Butterfly Fever* (1–3). Illus. by Jerry Smath. Series: Science Solves It. 2004, Kane paper $4.99 (1-57565-134-3). 32pp. Fourth-grader Ellie discovers that her new town is a destination for migrating monarch butterflies, and with her classmates she learns all about them. (Rev: BL 2/15/04; SLJ 6/04)

4601 Hayward, Linda. *Monster Bug* (1–2). Illus. by Diane Palmisciano. Series: Science Solves It! 2004, Kane paper $4.99 (1-57565-135-1). 32pp. Scared the day before by the image of a monster bug, Kyle realizes the nature of shadows and plots revenge with an even more frightening sight. (Rev: SLJ 6/04)

4602 Henkes, Kevin. *So Happy!* (1–3). Illus. by Anita Lobel. 2005, Greenwillow LB $16.89 (0-06-056484-9). 32pp. Everything changes for a bored little boy in the Southwest when the rain comes. (Rev: BL 2/1/05; SLJ 3/05)

4603 Hoberman, Mary Ann. *Right Outside My Window* (K–2). Illus. by Nicholas Wilton. 2002, Mondo $15.95 (1-59034-194-5). 24pp. Simple two-line rhymes describe the beautiful changing views through the four seasons. (Rev: BL 8/02; HBG 10/02; SLJ 11/02)

4604 Hoberman, Mary Ann. *Whose Garden Is It?* (PS–1). Illus. by Jane Dyer. 2004, Harcourt $16.00 (0-15-202631-2). 40pp. The gardener, the plants, the creatures of the garden, and the sun and the rain all come forward to claim credit to the title question as elderly Mrs. McGee and a young child stroll admiringly through it. (Rev: BL 4/15/04; SLJ 5/04)

4605 Hort, Lenny. *We're Going on a Treasure Hunt* (PS–1). Photos by Tom Arma. 2003, Abrams $12.95 (0-8109-4654-8). In this delightful voyage of underwater exploration, which features the work of photographer Tom Arma, readers follow a baby decked out in snorkeling gear as he hunts for treasure beneath the surface of the sea. (Rev: HBG 4/04; SLJ 1/04)

4606 *How Big Is the Ocean? First Questions and Answers About the Beach* (PS–3). Illus. Series: First Questions and Answers. 1994, Time-Life $14.95 (0-7835-0897-2). 48pp. Basic questions about the ocean — such as "Why is it blue?" — are answered in this picture book. (Rev: BL 3/1/95; HBG 4/04; SLJ 1/04) [508]

4607 Howell, Will C. *I Call It Sky* (K–3). Illus. by John Ward. 1999, Walker LB $16.85 (0-8027-8678-2). Concepts of weather are explored as children play through snow, rain, fog, and other weather phenomena. (Rev: BL 5/1/99; HBG 10/99; SLJ 6/99)

4608 Hubbell, Patricia. *Hurray for Spring!* (PS–K). Illus. by Taia Morley. 2005, North Word $15.95 (1-55971-913-3). 32pp. A little boy describes the many joys of spring in accessible first-person rhyming text. (Rev: BL 5/15/05; SLJ 4/05)

4609 Hughes, Shirley. *Out and About* (PS–1). Illus. 1988, Lothrop $16.00 (0-688-07690-4). 48pp. A colorful journey through the seasons in a picture book of poems. (Rev: BCCB 6/88; BL 3/15/88; SLJ 5/88)

4610 Jackson, Ellen. *Brown Cow, Green Grass, Yellow Mellow Sun* (K–2). Illus. by Victoria Raymond. 1995, Hyperion LB $14.89 (0-7867-2006-3). 32pp. The process of getting milk from a cow and turning it into butter is the subject of this picture book illustrated with photos of objects made from modeling clay. (Rev: BL 6/1–15/95; SLJ 5/95)

4611 James, Simon. *The Birdwatchers* (PS–1). Illus. 2002, Candlewick $15.99 (0-7636-1676-1). 32pp. A young girl accompanies her grandfather on a bird-watching expedition in this book filled with dramatic watercolor illustrations. (Rev: BCCB 6/02; BL 8/02; HBG 10/02; SLJ 5/02*)

4612 Johnston, Tony. *Desert Song* (K–3). Illus. by Ed Young. 2000, Sierra Club $15.95 (0-87156-491-2). 32pp. A lyrical volume that describes the sights and sounds of the desert in a book-length poem filled with glowing illustrations. (Rev: BL 10/1/00*; SLJ 12/00)

4613 Johnston, Tony. *Isabel's House of Butterfies* (K–3). Illus. by Susan Guevara. 2003, Sierra Club $15.95 (0-87156-409-2). When financial problems seem likely to doom her beloved oyamel tree — which each winter attracts thousands of migrating butterflies — Isabel, an 8-year-old Mexican girl, comes up with a plan. (Rev: HBG 4/04; SLJ 12/03)

4614 Johnston, Tony. *The Whole Green World* (PS–1). Illus. by Elisa Kleven. 2005, Farrar $15.00 (0-374-38400-2). A little girl and her dog plant seeds and enjoy the results in this rhyming verse presented within detailed circular illustrations. (Rev: SLJ 4/05)

4615 Jones, Betty, comp. *A Child's Seasonal Treasury* (PS–2). Illus. by Betty Jones. 1997, Tricycle $22.95 (1-883672-30-9). 136pp. For each of the seasons, a collection of poems, songs, fingerplays, and activities. (Rev: SLJ 10/97)

4616 Joosse, Barbara M. *Snow Day!* (K–2). Illus. by Jennifer Plecas. 1995, Clarion $14.95 (0-395-66588-4). 31pp. Activities to engage in on a snow day are pictured, including a family snow fight. (Rev: SLJ 9/95*)

4617 Karas, G. Brian. *Atlantic* (PS–3). Illus. 2002, Penguin Putnam $15.99 (0-399-23632-5). 32pp. In this first-person narrative, the Atlantic Ocean tells what and where it is, how people view it, and how it

is affected by the moon and sun. (Rev: BCCB 4/02; BL 4/15/02*; HBG 10/02; SLJ 6/02)

4618 Keats, Ezra Jack. *The Snowy Day* (PS–1). Illus. by author. 1962, Puffin paper $5.99 (0-14-050182-7). 40pp. A young African American boy's delight during his first snowfall. Caldecott Medal winner, 1963.

4619 Killion, Bette. *The Same Wind* (2–5). Illus. by Barbara B. Falk. 1992, HarperCollins LB $14.89 (0-06-021051-6). 32pp. The many kinds of winds and their uses are explored in this picture book. (Rev: BL 1/1/93)

4620 Kinsey-Warnock, Natalie. *When Spring Comes* (K–2). Illus. by Stacey Schuett. 1993, Dutton $16.99 (0-525-45008-4). 32pp. Looking out on a winter landscape, a young girl remembers all the activities connected with spring. (Rev: BL 3/1/93; SLJ 4/93)

4621 Kreger, Claire. *Cheese* (2–4). Illus. Series: From Start to Finish. 2003, Gale/Blackbirch $19.95 (1-56711-380-X). 32pp. A close look at cheese, starting with the animal producing the required milk and continuing through the entire manufacturing and quality-control process. (Rev: BL 5/15/03) [637]

4622 Kroll, Virginia. *The Seasons and Someone* (K–3). Illus. by Tatsuro Kiuchi. 1994, Harcourt $15.00 (0-15-271233-X). 32pp. In this exquisite picture book, a little Eskimo girl watches the changes of seasons from her Northern home. (Rev: BL 12/1/94; SLJ 1/95*)

4623 Kurtz, Jane, and Christopher Kurtz. *Water Hole Waiting* (PS–3). Illus. by Lee Christiansen. 2002, HarperCollins LB $15.89 (0-06-029851-0). 32pp. A picture book about animals taking turns drinking at an African water hole. (Rev: BCCB 6/02; BL 5/15/02; HBG 10/02; SLJ 5/02*)

4624 Lakin, Patricia. *Hurricane!* (1–3). Illus. by Vanessa Lubach. 2000, Millbrook LB $21.90 (0-7613-1616-7). 32pp. A girl and her father make preparations to withstand Hurricane Bob and after the storm has passed survey the damage. (Rev: BL 10/15/00; HBG 3/01; SLJ 1/01)

4625 LaMarche, Jim. *The Raft* (2–4). Illus. 2000, HarperCollins LB $15.89 (0-688-13978-7). 40pp. Nicky is unhappy spending the summer with his grandmother in the country until he learns the joy of camping outdoors and the wonders of the animal life around him. (Rev: BCCB 7–8/00; BL 5/1/00; HBG 10/00; SLJ 5/00)

4626 Lawson, Julie. *Midnight in the Mountains* (K–3). Illus. by Sheena Lott. 1998, Orca $14.95 (1-55143-113-0). After spending her first day in the mountains during winter, a young girl who is too excited to sleep thinks about all the fun she had that day, like making snow angels. (Rev: HBG 3/99; SLJ 1/99)

4627 Leedy, Loreen. *Blast Off to Earth! A Look at Geography* (PS–3). Illus. 1992, Holiday House LB $16.95 (0-8234-0973-2). 32pp. An alien teacher and his students take a class trip to Earth. (Rev: BL 11/1/92; SLJ 1/93) [910]

4628 Levine, Evan. *Not the Piano, Mrs. Medley!* (PS–2). Illus. by S. D. Schindler. 1991, Watts LB $16.99 (0-531-08556-2). 32pp. Mrs. Medley, Max, and Word the dog pack just about everything — except bathing suits — to go to the beach. (Rev: BL 7/91*; HB 9–10/91; SLJ 11/91*)

4629 Lewis, J. Patrick. *Earth and Me: Our Family Tree* (K–4). Illus. by Christopher Canyon. Series: A Sharing Nature with Children Book. 2002, Dawn $16.95 (1-58469-031-3); paper $7.95 (1-58469-030-5). Rich artwork and lyric text introduce animals of all kinds — and one boy — appreciating the beauty and bounty of their environment. (Rev: HBG 10/02; SLJ 4/02)

4630 Lewis, Richard. *In the Space of the Sky* (PS–2). Illus. by Debra Frasier. 2002, Harcourt $16.00 (0-15-253150-5). 24pp. A poetic introduction to the universe that covers both the external and internal worlds. (Rev: BL 5/1/02; HBG 10/02; SLJ 5/02)

4631 Lindbergh, Reeve. *North Country Spring* (K–2). Illus. by Liz Sivertson. 1997, Houghton Mifflin $15.95 (0-395-82819-8). 32pp. Vivid rhyming couplets and expressive paintings evoke the changes that spring brings to the northern United States. (Rev: BL 5/15/97; SLJ 4/97)

4632 Locker, Thomas. *Walking with Henry: Based on the Life and Works of Henry David Thoreau* (2–4). Illus. 2002, Fulcrum $17.95 (1-55591-355-5). 32pp. A fictionalized account of Henry David Thoreau as he hikes through the wilderness, describing his beliefs about man's relationship with nature. (Rev: BL 12/1/02; HBG 3/03; SLJ 1/03) [818]

4633 London, Jonathan. *Dream Weaver* (PS–2). Illus. by Rocco Baviera. 1998, Harcourt $16.00 (0-15-200944-2). 32pp. A boy watches a spider on its web and later dreams of weaving his own web to catch falling stars. (Rev: BL 4/1/98; HBG 10/98; SLJ 7/98)

4634 London, Jonathan. *Giving Thanks* (K–2). Illus. by Gregory Manchess. 2003, Candlewick $16.99 (0-7636-1680-X). 32pp. On a walk in the country, a father individually thanks the things of nature — from insects to trees to the sun and moon — and his young son, at first, thinks this is an odd thing to do. (Rev: BL 2/1/04; HBG 4/04; SLJ 1/04)

4635 London, Jonathan. *Park Beat: Rhymin' Through the Seasons* (PS–3). Illus. by Woodleigh Hubbard. 2001, HarperCollins LB $15.89 (0-688-13995-7). Snappy verses and detailed illustrations with changing perspectives describe how a park changes with the seasons. (Rev: HBG 10/01; SLJ 5/01)

4636 Luke, Melinda. *Green Dog* (1–3). Illus. by Jane Manning. Series: Science Solves It. 2002, Kane paper $4.99 (1-57565-115-7). 32pp. Teddy investigates the cause of murky water in the goldfish bowl and discovers algae. (Rev: BL 9/15/02)

4637 Maass, Robert. *When Autumn Comes* (PS–2). Illus. 1990, Holt paper $6.95 (0-8050-2349-6). 32pp. What people do as autumn progresses, with large, handsome photos. (Rev: BL 10/1/90; SLJ 9/90) [508]

4638 Maass, Robert. *When Summer Comes* (K–2). Illus. 1993, Holt paper $5.95 (0-8050-4706-9). 30pp. In this tribute to the joys of summer, many of the activities associated with this season are pictured in photographs. (Rev: BL 6/1–15/93; SLJ 6/93) [508]

4639 McCloskey, Robert. *Time of Wonder* (1–4). Illus. by author. 1957, Puffin paper $5.99 (0-14-050201-7). 64pp. Full-color watercolors illustrate this poetic text describing a summer on the Maine coast and the hurricane that hits it. Caldecott Medal winner, 1958.

4640 McCurdy, Michael. *Hannah's Farm: The Seasons on an Early American Homestead* (1–3). Illus. by author. 1988, Holiday House LB $12.95 (0-8234-0700-4). 32pp. The seasons are presented on this 19th-century farm in Massachusetts. (Rev: BL 11/15/88; SLJ 2/89)

4641 McNulty, Faith. *Orphan: The Story of a Baby Woodchuck* (K–3). Illus. by Darby Morrell. 1992, Scholastic $11.95 (0-590-43838-7). 48pp. The author befriends a baby woodchuck on her Rhode Island farm and then realizes she must teach it to return to the wild. (Rev: BL 4/15/92; SLJ 9/92) [599.32]

4642 Maestro, Betsy. *Snow Day* (PS–2). Illus. by Giulio Maestro. 1992, Scholastic paper $4.95 (0-590-46083-8). 32pp. While families stay home because of the heavy snow, snow removal crews are doing their job. (Rev: BCCB 10/89; BL 11/1/89; SLJ 1/90) [628]

4643 Major, Beverly. *Over Back* (1–3). Illus. by Thomas B. Allen. 1993, HarperCollins LB $14.89 (0-06-020287-4). A young African American girl takes the reader on a nature tour behind her house. (Rev: BL 2/1/93; SLJ 3/93)

4644 Marshall, Janet. *A Honey of a Day* (PS–1). Illus. 2000, Greenwillow $23.95 (0-688-16917-1). 24pp. A pleasant story about an outdoor wedding is used to introduce and picture 28 lovely flowers including sweet william and black-eyed susan. (Rev: BL 7/00; HBG 10/00; SLJ 5/00)

4645 Michels, Tilde. *What a Beautiful Day!* (PS–2). Illus. by Thomas Muller. 1992, Carolrhoda LB $18.95 (0-87614-739-2). 32pp. On a beautiful summer morning, young Peter enjoys nature as he walks in the woods. (Rev: BL 1/15/93; SLJ 4/93)

4646 Milton, Joyce. *Honeybees* (1–3). Illus. by Pete Mueller. Series: All Aboard Science Reader. 2003, Grosset LB $13.89 (0-448-43142-4); paper $3.99 (0-448-42846-6). 48pp. An accessible introduction to honeybees for beginning readers, including information on how their community works and where honey comes from. (Rev: BL 5/15/03; HBG 10/03) [595.79]

4647 Mockford, Caroline. *What's This?* (PS–1). Illus. 2000, Barefoot $15.95 (1-84148-018-5). 32pp. This simple picture book describes the cultivation and growth of a sunflower seed and plant by a little girl and brown bird. (Rev: BL 5/1/00; SLJ 8/00) [631.5]

4648 Mora, Pat. *Listen to the Desert / Oye al Desierto* (PS–2). Illus. by Francisco Mora. 1994, Clarion $16.00 (0-395-67292-9). Using double-page spreads, this book in English and Spanish introduces the animals and sounds found in a Southwestern desert. (Rev: HBG 4/04; SLJ 10/94) [574.5]

4649 Nidey, Kelli. *When Autumn Falls* (PS–1). Illus. by Susan Swan. 2004, Whitman LB $15.95 (0-8075-0490-4). Falling leaves, apples, and temperatures are just some of the features of autumn highlighted. (Rev: SLJ 9/04)

4650 O'Malley, Kevin. *Straight to the Pole* (PS–3). Illus. by author. 2003, Walker LB $16.85 (0-8027-8868-8). A little boy struggles melodramatically through a snowstorm, and just when all hope seems to be lost, two sled-riding friends appear to tell him that school's been canceled for the day. (Rev: HBG 4/04; SLJ 11/03)

4651 Otten, Charlotte F. *January Rides the Wind: A Book of Months* (PS–2). Illus. by Todd L. W. Doney. 1997, Lothrop LB $15.93 (0-688-12557-3). 32pp. Short poems and evocative paintings capture the essence of the outdoor world during each month of the year. (Rev: BL 10/15/97*; HBG 3/98; SLJ 10/97)

4652 Pallotta, Jerry. *Dory Story* (PS–4). Illus. by David Biedrzycki. 2000, Charlesbridge $15.95 (0-88106-075-5). 32pp. An ocean food chain from krill-eating plankton to huge orcas eating tuna is explored in this story of a boy's imaginary dory trip into the depths. (Rev: BL 2/1/00*; HBG 10/00; SLJ 3/00)

4653 Peet, Bill. *The Wump World* (1–3). Illus. by author. 1981, Houghton Mifflin $16.00 (0-395-19841-0); paper $6.95 (0-395-31129-2). An animal parable in which pollution and the waste of natural resources are the main themes.

4654 Perkins, Lynne Rae. *Snow Music* (PS–2). Illus. by author. 2003, Greenwillow LB $16.89 (0-06-623958-3). A simple, musical story of a boy searching for his runaway dog in the snow, showing the tracks of deer, rabbits, squirrels. (Rev: BCCB 12/03; BL 9/1/03; HB 11–12/03; HBG 4/04; LMC 3/04; SLJ 11/03)

4655 Peters, Lisa Westberg. *The Sun, the Wind, and the Rain* (K–3). Illus. by Ted Rand. 1988, Holt paper $6.95 (0-8050-1481-0). 48pp. The creation and evolution of mountains using the analogy of a little girl at the beach. (Rev: BL 10/15/88; HB 11–12/88; HBG 4/04; SLJ 10/88)

4656 Petit, Genevieve. *The Seventh Walnut* (K–3). Illus. by Joelle Boucher. 1992, Wellington $13.95 (0-922984-10-7). 32pp. The story of how a walnut, dropped on the ground, grows into a tree; translated from the French. (Rev: BCCB 10/92; BL 12/1/92) [574]

4657 Prelutsky, Jack. *It's Snowing! It's Snowing!* (1–4). Illus. by Jeanne Titherington. 1984, Greenwillow $17.93 (0-688-01513-1). 48pp. A few story poems on the experiences and joys of winter. (Rev: BL 1/1–15/04; SLJ 1/04)

4658 Ravishankar, Anushka. *Tiger on a Tree* (PS–2). Illus. by Pulak Biswas. 2004, Farrar $15.00 (0-374-37555-0). In this impressively illustrated chanting tale from India, villagers capture a tiger and then wonder what they should do with it — in the end, they let it go. (Rev: HB 5–6/04; SLJ 3/04)

4659 Ray, Mary L. *Mud* (PS–2). Illus. by Lauren Stringer. 1996, Harcourt $16.00 (0-15-256263-X). In the period between winter and spring, it is the season of mud, and this book joyfully explores it. (Rev: HBG 4/04; SLJ 6/96*)

4660 Riha, Susanne. *Animals and the Seasons: The Cycle of Nature* (1–3). Trans. from German by Annette Betz. Illus. by author. 2000, Blackbirch $17.95 (1-56711-429-6). 30pp. This book of stunning illustrations and text takes the reader through the four seasons and depicts the flora and fauna of each. (Rev: HBG 10/00; SLJ 9/00)

4661 Rockwell, Anne. *The Storm* (K–3). Illus. by Robert Sauber. 1994, Hyperion LB $16.49 (0-7868-2013-6). The morning after a violent storm hits their coastal home, a young girl and her mother walk the beach and view all the accumulated debris. (Rev: SLJ 11/94)

4662 Root, Phyllis. *If You Want to See a Caribou* (PS–2). Illus. by Jim Meyer. 2004, Houghton Mifflin $16.00 (0-618-39314-5). 32pp. Set on a wooded island in Lake Superior, this gentle book celebrates the caribou in poetry and woodblock images. (Rev: BL 4/15/04; SLJ 4/04)

4663 Rosenberry, Vera. *Who Is in the Garden?* (PS–2). Illus. 2001, Holiday House $16.95 (0-8234-1529-5). 32pp. A little boy tours a garden and finds such wonders as wrens in a birch tree, a snake in a grape vine, and a turtle under the rhubarb. (Rev: BL 3/1/01; HBG 10/01) [577.5]

4664 Rotner, Shelley, and Steve Calcagnino. *The Body Book* (PS–K). Illus. 2000, Orchard LB $16.99 (0-531-33256-X). 32pp. As well as pointing out the different parts of the body, this picture book shows that people are basically the same even though they come in different sizes, shapes, and colors. (Rev: BL 3/1/00; HBG 10/00; SLJ 5/00) [611]

4665 Rucki, Ani. *When the Earth Wakes* (PS–1). Illus. 1998, Scholastic $15.95 (0-590-05951-3). 32pp. The text describes the changes that occur in the spring, and the pictures show a bear cub and its mother waking up and entering the world again. (Rev: BL 3/1/98; HBG 10/98; SLJ 3/98)

4666 Ryan, Pam M. *Hello Ocean* (PS–2). Illus. by Mark Astrella. 2001, Charlesbridge $16.95 (0-88106-987-6); paper $6.95 (0-88106-988-4). 32pp. A young girl who is visiting an ocean beach describes how this experience affects her senses. (Rev: BL 3/1/01*; HBG 10/01)

4667 Ryder, Joanne. *Each Living Thing* (PS–3). Illus. by Ashley Wolff. 2000, Harcourt $16.00 (0-15-201898-0). 32pp. In a gentle, rhyming text, the author cautions readers to respect and protect all living things. (Rev: BL 4/15/00; HBG 10/00; SLJ 4/00)

4668 Ryder, Joanne. *Earthdance* (K–4). Illus. by Norman Gorbaty. 1996, Holt $16.95 (0-8050-2678-9). 32pp. The earth and its wonders are celebrated in this brief poem with accompanying drawings. (Rev: BCCB 7–8/96; BL 4/1/96; SLJ 5/96*) [811]

4669 Ryder, Joanne. *A Fawn in the Grass* (PS–K). Illus. by Keiko Narahashi. 2001, Holt $16.95 (0-8050-6236-X). 32pp. A child's sense of wonder is conveyed in this quiet picture book about a pre-schooler's walk in a meadow, where he sees such sights as a fawn, insects, squirrels, worms, a hawk, and a mole. (Rev: BL 3/1/01; HBG 10/01)

4670 Ryder, Joanne. *The Waterfall's Gift* (1–3). Illus. by Richard J. Watson. 2001, Sierra Club $15.95 (0-87156-579-X). A young girl visits a waterfall in the woods and marvels at the beauties of nature. (Rev: HBG 3/02; SLJ 8/01)

4671 Rylant, Cynthia. *In November* (PS–2). Illus. by Jill Kastner. 2000, Harcourt $16.00 (0-15-201076-9). 32pp. Lovely oil paintings and poetic language are used to evoke November atmosphere and activities, including a Thanksgiving feast and the coming of winter. (Rev: BL 9/1/00*; HBG 3/01; SLJ 9/00)

4672 Rylant, Cynthia. *This Year's Garden* (PS–K). Illus. by Mary Szilagyi. 1984, Macmillan paper $4.95 (0-689-71122-0). 32pp. A year in the garden in drawings and gentle text.

4673 Rylant, Cynthia. *The Whales* (PS–3). Illus. 1996, Scholastic $15.95 (0-590-58285-2). 40pp. The behavior and thoughts of whales are depicted in words and illustrations. (Rev: BL 4/1/96; HBG 4/04; SLJ 3/96)

4674 Sanders, Scott R. *Meeting Trees* (PS–2). Illus. by Robert Hynes. 1997, National Geographic $16.00 (0-7922-4140-1). During a walk in the woods with his father, a boy learns to identify a number of trees by their shapes, bark, and leaves. (Rev: HBG 3/98; SLJ 7/97)

4675 Schnur, Steven. *Spring Thaw* (K–3). Illus. by Stacey Schuett. 2000, Viking $15.99 (0-670-87961-4). 32pp. A poetic picture book that depicts signs of spring in a rural setting. (Rev: BL 3/1/00; HBG 10/00; SLJ 2/00)

4676 Seuling, Barbara. *Spring Song* (PS–K). Illus. by Greg Newbold. 2001, Harcourt $16.00 (0-15-202317-8). 32pp. Questions and answers are used in this lovely book that depicts spring and animal activities associated with it. (Rev: BL 4/15/01; HBG 10/01; SLJ 5/01)

4677 Seuss, Dr. *The Lorax* (K–3). Illus. by author. 1971, Random LB $16.99 (0-394-92337-5). 64pp. The Lorax, a little brown creature, has tried in vain to ward off pollution and ecological blight, but Onceler, who wanted the trees for his business, would not heed the warning.

4678 Shea, Pegi Deitz. *New Moon* (PS–1). Illus. by Cathryn Falwell. 1996, Boyds Mills $14.95 (1-56397-410-X). 24pp. Vinnie and her big brother explore the various phases of the moon. (Rev: BL 1/1–15/97; SLJ 10/96)

4679 Shetterly, Susan Hand. *Shelterwood* (K–3). Illus. by Rebecca Haley McCall. 1999, Tilbury House $16.95 (0-88448-210-3). 40pp. Set in Maine, this picture book shows the lessons a girl learned from her grandfather about nature and how to preserve the earth's riches. (Rev: BL 3/1/00; SLJ 3/00)

4680 Siddals, Mary M. *Tell Me a Season* (PS–K). Illus. by Petra Mathers. 1997, Clarion $12.95 (0-395-71021-9). 26pp. A cheerful picture book that explores the seasons and describes each in terms of colors. (Rev: BCCB 7–8/97; BL 4/1/97; SLJ 5/97)

4681 Spinelli, Eileen. *Here Comes the Year* (PS–1). Illus. by Keiko Narahashi. 2002, Holt $16.95 (0-8050-6685-3). 32pp. Each of the months is personified in this picture book that explains the changes in nature during a single year. (Rev: BCCB 4/02; BL 5/1/02; HBG 10/02; SLJ 6/02)

4682 Sturges, Philemon. *I Love Bugs!* (PS–2). Illus. by Shari Halpern. 2005, HarperCollins LB $14.89 (0-06-056169-6). 32pp. A young boy in search of bugs finds them all around in this rhyming picture book that includes bug facts. (Rev: BL 3/1/05; SLJ 4/05)

4683 Stynes, Barbara W. *Walking with Mama* (PS–K). Illus. 1997, Dawn $14.95 (1-883220-56-4); paper $6.95 (1-883220-57-2). 24pp. A nature walk through the forest with his mother is described by a toddler. (Rev: BL 9/15/97)

4684 Sweetland, Nancy. *God's Quiet Things* (PS–K). Illus. by Rick Stevens. 1994, Eerdmans $15.00 (0-8028-5082-0). 32pp. Quiet things in nature, like butterflies flying, are celebrated in this thoughtful picture book. (Rev: BL 1/1/95; SLJ 1/95)

4685 Swope, Sam. *Gotta Go! Gotta Go!* (PS–2). Illus. by Sue Riddle. 2000, Farrar $12.00 (0-374-32757-2). 32pp. The story of the caterpillar who turns into a monarch butterfly and travels three thousand miles from the U.S. to Mexico because he's "gotta go." (Rev: BCCB 5/00; BL 3/1/00*; HB 5–6/00; HBG 10/00; SLJ 5/00)

4686 Tafuri, Nancy. *Snowy Flowy Blowy: A Twelve Months Rhyme* (PS–2). Illus. by author. 1999, Scholastic $15.95 (0-590-18973-5). The months of the year are presented in double-page spreads with illustrations that picture the seasons. (Rev: HBG 3/00; SLJ 10/99)

4687 Tamar, Erika. *The Garden of Happiness* (PS–3). Illus. by Barbara Lambase. 1996, Harcourt $16.00 (0-15-230582-3). 40pp. Marisol's seed, planted in a New York City cracked sidewalk, grows into a huge sunflower. (Rev: BL 7/96*; SLJ 5/96)

4688 Taylor, Joanne. *Full Moon Rising* (1–3). Illus. by Susan Tooke. 2002, Tundra $16.95 (0-88776-548-3). An attractive, poetic introduction to the full moons of the year. (Rev: HBG 3/03; SLJ 12/02) [523.3]

4689 Taylor, Theodore. *Hello, Arctic!* (PS–2). Illus. by Margaret Chodos-Irvine. 2002, Harcourt $16.00 (0-15-201577-9). 40pp. A simple text and dramatic illustrations show the changing Arctic seasons and the animals and plants found there. (Rev: BL 10/1/02; HBG 3/03; SLJ 11/02)

4690 Titherington, Jeanne. *Pumpkin Pumpkin* (PS–1). Illus. by author. 1986, Greenwillow $16.89 (0-688-05696-2); Morrow paper $4.95 (0-688-09930-0). 24pp. A simple, rhythmic picture book about the facts of plant life. (Rev: BCCB 3/86; BL 3/15/86; SLJ 4/86)

4691 Tresselt, Alvin. *Hide and Seek Fog* (K–2). Illus. by Roger Duvoisin. 1965, Lothrop LB $15.93 (0-688-51169-4); Morrow paper $5.95 (0-688-07813-3). 32pp. Pastel watercolors quietly reflect obscure seashore scenes as the mysterious, deepening fog rolls in from the sea.

4692 Tresselt, Alvin. *Rain Drop Splash* (K–3). Illus. by Leonard Weisgard. 1946, Morrow paper $4.95 (0-688-09352-3). 28pp. How the raindrops form a puddle that grows from pond to river and finally joins the sea.

4693 Udry, Janice May. *A Tree Is Nice* (PS). Illus. by Marc Simont. 1957, HarperCollins LB $15.89 (0-06-026156-0); paper $5.95 (0-06-443147-9). 32pp. The many delights to be had in, with, or under a tree: picking apples, raking leaves, swinging, or just sitting in the shade. Caldecott Medal winner, 1957.

4694 verDorn, Bethea. *Day Breaks* (PS–3). Illus. by Thomas Graham. 1992, Arcade $14.95 (1-55970-187-0). A gentle picture book that presents various scenes of morning as it is experienced across the United States. (Rev: SLJ 9/92)

4695 Waboose, Jan B. *Morning on the Lake* (K–3). Illus. by Karen Reczuch. 1998, Kids Can $15.95 (1-55074-373-2). 32pp. Three stories about an Ojibwa grandfather and his young grandson, their walks in a forest, and the mystical bond they feel with nature. (Rev: BL 3/15/98; HBG 10/98; SLJ 5/98)

4696 Walker, Rob D. *Once upon a Cloud* (K–3). Illus. by Matt Mahurin. 2005, Scholastic $16.95 (0-439-68879-5). 40pp. The author explores all the possibilities of what clouds might be, from cotton candy to puffs of pipe smoke, in lighthearted rhyme with imaginative illustrations. (Rev: BL 3/1/05; SLJ 3/05)

4697 Wallace, Nancy Elizabeth. *Leaves! Leaves! Leaves!* (PS–2). Illus. by author. 2003, Marshall Cavendish $16.95 (0-7614-5140-4). Buddy Bear and his mother observe the dramatic changes in leaves and trees over the course of the seasons. (Rev: HBG 4/04; SLJ 9/03)

4698 Wellington, Monica. *Zinnia's Flower Garden* (K–2). Illus. by author. 2005, Dutton $14.99 (0-525-47368-8). An informative tour of gardens and gardening, in the company of Zinnia and her animal friends. (Rev: SLJ 2/05)

4699 Weninger, Brigitte. *Precious Water: A Book of Thanks* (PS–1). Illus. by Anne Moller. 2002, North-South LB $13.88 (0-7358-1514-3). 32pp. A young girl and her cat explore the uses, sources, and nature of water. (Rev: BL 4/15/02; HBG 10/02; SLJ 5/02)

4700 Wood, Audrey. *Birdsong* (PS–2). Illus. by Robert Florczak. 1997, Harcourt $16.00 (0-15-200014-3). 32pp. An impressive picture book that identifies a state bird and a flower through the experiences of children in different parts of the United States. (Rev: BL 10/1/97; HBG 3/98; SLJ 10/97)

4701 Yerxa, Leo. *Last Leaf First Snowflake to Fall* (K–3). Illus. 1994, Orchard LB $14.99 (0-531-08674-7). 32pp. Two Indians explore the country-side and canoe across a pond in this picture book that explores the coming of winter. (Rev: BL 10/1/94; SLJ 12/94)

4702 Yolen, Jane. *Harvest Home* (K–2). Illus. by Greg Shed. 2002, Harcourt $16.00 (0-15-201819-0). 32pp. An earthy ode to harvest time, written in verse and complemented by glowing illustrations. (Rev: BL 10/15/02; HBG 3/03; SLJ 11/02)

4703 Yorinks, Arthur. *Happy Bees!* (PS–1). Illus. by Carey Armstrong-Ellis. 2005, Abrams $15.95 (0-8109-5866-X). A buzzing group of happy bees enjoy themselves while causing havoc among humans and animals. (Rev: SLJ 4/05)

OTHER TIMES, OTHER PLACES

4704 Ackerman, Karen. *Araminta's Paint Box* (K–3). Illus. by Betsy Lewin. 1998, Aladdin paper $5.99 (0-689-82091-7). 32pp. The Darling family is heading west to California by wagon. (Rev: BCCB 3/90; BL 2/1/90; SLJ 3/90)

4705 Adams, Jeanie. *Going for Oysters* (K–3). Illus. by author. 1993, Whitman LB $15.95 (0-8075-2978-8). A picture book that uses a simple story to introduce Australian aboriginal life by depicting life in a native outback community. (Rev: SLJ 1/94)

4706 Addy, Sharon Hart. *Right Here on This Spot* (PS–3). Illus. 1999, Houghton Mifflin $15.00 (0-395-73091-0). 32pp. This book focuses on a single piece of land and what happened on that spot from prehistoric times to the present. (Rev: BL 10/15/99; HBG 3/00; SLJ 11/99)

4707 Adler, David A. *The Babe and I* (PS–2). Illus. by Terry Widener. 1999, Harcourt $16.00 (0-15-201378-4). 32pp. During the Great Depression, the young narrator sells newspapers on the street, and one day Babe Ruth buys a paper from him. (Rev: BCCB 6/99; BL 3/15/99*; HB 3–4/99; HBG 10/99; SLJ 5/99)

4708 Alakija, Polly. *Catch That Goat!* (PS–2). Illus. by author. 2002, Barefoot $16.99 (1-84148-908-5). Young Ayoka's goat runs amok in the market in this beautifully illustrated story set in Nigeria. (Rev: HBG 3/03; SLJ 12/02)

4709 Alda, Arlene. *Morning Glory Monday* (PS–2). Illus. by Maryann Kovalski. 2003, Tundra $17.95 (0-88776-620-X). To lift the spirits of her mother, who is homesick for Italy, a young girl plants morning glory seeds in the window boxes of her family's early-20th-century New York City tenement, and the vines spread to brighten the whole community. (Rev: BL 1/1–15/04; HBG 4/04; SLJ 11/03)

4710 Alexander, Sue. *Behold the Trees* (K–3). Illus. by Leonid Gore. 2001, Scholastic $16.95 (0-590-76211-7). 48pp. This picture book is about the trees of Israel, how the forests were cut down years ago, and how people began planting trees after World War I. (Rev: BCCB 3/01; BL 3/1/01*; HBG 10/01; SLJ 3/01)

4711 Aliki. *Marianthe's Story: Painted Words / Spoken Memories* (K–3). Illus. by author. 1998, Greenwillow LB $15.93 (0-688-15662-2). In this book combining two stories, the first tells how Mari, a young immigrant girl, expresses herself in her paintings; in the second, Mari relates life in her native land. (Rev: BCCB 1/99; HB 9–10/98; HBG 3/99; SLJ 10/98)

4712 Alrawi, Karim. *The Girl Who Lost Her Smile* (1–4). Illus. by Stefan Czernecki. 2000, Winslow $16.95 (1-890817-17-1). 40pp. A Middle Eastern tale about a young girl who has lost her smile and is told she will only get it back when a great artist paints a picture she likes. (Rev: BL 11/1/00; HBG 3/01; SLJ 12/00)

4713 Ancona, George. *Fiesta Fireworks* (1–3). Photos by author. 1998, Lothrop LB $15.93 (0-688-14818-2). A photo-essay describing a feast day in the city of Tultepec, Mexico, where some of the world's greatest fireworks are made. (Rev: BL 4/1/98; HB 5–6/98; HBG 10/98; SLJ 3/98)

4714 Anholt, Laurence. *Camille and the Sunflowers: A Story About Vincent van Gogh* (PS–3). Illus. 1994, Barron's $14.95 (0-8120-6409-7). 32pp. Young Camille befriends the artist van Gogh when he comes to paint in his village in the Netherlands. (Rev: BL 12/1/94; SLJ 2/95)

4715 Anholt, Laurence. *The Magical Garden of Claude Monet* (PS–3). Illus. 2003, Barren's $14.95 (0-7641-5574-1). 32pp. Julie and her dog spend a day with Impressionist painter Claude Monet in this fictionalized look at the artist's later work, with illustrations echoing Monet's style. (Rev: BL 2/15/04; HBG 4/04; SLJ 5/04)

4716 Arcellana, Francisco. *The Mats* (K–4). Illus. by Hermes Alegre. 1999, Kane/Miller $13.95 (0-916291-86-3). 24pp. A tender story about a Philippine family whose father returns home and brings a gift for each member of the group, including those children who have died. (Rev: BL 5/1/99; HBG 10/99; SLJ 9/99)

4717 Arnold, Marsha Diane. *The Pumpkin Runner* (K–3). Illus. by Brad Sneed. 1998, Dial $15.99 (0-8037-2124-2). 32pp. Based on a true story, this picture book tells of a 61-year-old Australian farmer who eats pumpkins for energy and wins a footrace against younger, better-trained opponents. (Rev: BCCB 11/98; BL 11/1/98; HBG 3/99; SLJ 12/98)

4718 Atwell, Debby. *Barn* (PS–3). Illus. 1996, Houghton Mifflin $15.95 (0-395-78568-5). 32pp. Events in the life of a barn, from its erection in the late 1700s to the present day. (Rev: BL 10/1/96; SLJ 8/96*)

4719 Avi. *Finding Providence: The Story of Roger Williams* (2–3). Illus. by James Watling. 1997, HarperCollins LB $15.89 (0-06-025294-4). 48pp. An easy-to-read book that tells, through the eyes of Roger Williams's daughter, the story of Williams's Boston trial and escape to the wilderness. (Rev: BCCB 3/97; BL 2/1/97; HB 5–6/97; SLJ 3/97)

4720 Baker, Jeannie. *The Story of Rosy Dock* (K–3). Illus. 1995, Greenwillow $14.89 (0-688-11493-8). 32pp. In the outback of Australia, the plant ecology is disturbed when settlers introduce rosy dock, a plant with distinctive red seedpods. (Rev: BCCB 3/95; BL 4/1/95*; SLJ 5/95) [508.94]

4721 Bania, Michael. *Kumak's House: A Tale of the Far North* (PS–2). Illus. 2002, Alaska Northwest $15.95 (0-88240-540-3); paper $8.95 (0-88240-541-1). 32pp. In this story packed with details about Arctic life, Kumak finds his house really feels quite large when all the animals he has taken in finally leave. (Rev: BL 9/1/02; HBG 10/02; SLJ 1/03)

4722 Banim, Lisa. *American Dreams* (2–3). Illus. Series: Stories of the States. 1993, Silver Moon LB $14.95 (1-881889-34-3). 80pp. In this story set in

California, the friendship between Jeannie and Amy, a Japanese American girl, is shattered when World War II breaks out. (Rev: SLJ 12/93)

4723 Barren, T. A. *High as a Hawk: A Brave Girl's Historic Climb* (1–4). Illus. by Ted Lewin. 2004, Penguin Putnam $16.99 (0-399-23704-6). 32pp. In 1905, an 8-year-old girl climbs more than 14,000 feet to the top of Longs Peak in Colorado; panoramic illustrations enhance this story based on truth. (Rev: BL 3/1/04; SLJ 5/04)

4724 Bartone, Elisa. *Peppe the Lamplighter* (2–4). Illus. by Ted Lewin. 1993, Lothrop LB $15.89 (0-688-10269-7); Morrow paper $4.95 (0-688-15469-7). 32pp. The story of an immigrant Italian boy who is a lamplighter in turn-of-the-century New York City. (Rev: BCCB 5/93; BL 4/15/93; SLJ 7/93)

4725 Bauld, Jane Scoggins. *Journey of the Third Seed* (K–2). Illus. by Cynthia G. Darr. 2001, Eakin $16.95 (1-57168-428-X); paper $9.95 (1-57168-429-8). Three lotus seeds lost at sea a thousand years ago resurface, and the third seed journeys to America where lotus blossoms from the plant now flourish. (Rev: HBG 10/01; SLJ 7/01)

4726 Baylor, Byrd. *One Small Blue Bead* (1–4). Illus. by Ronald Himler. 1992, Macmillan $16.00 (0-684-19334-5). 32pp. A story of an early tribe of cave dwellers in the American Southwest. First published in 1965. (Rev: BL 3/1/92; SLJ 4/92)

4727 Bell, Lili. *The Sea Maidens of Japan* (K–4). Illus. by Erin M. Brammer. 1997, Ideals $14.95 (1-57102-095-0). 32pp. A Japanese girl who is afraid of diving is expected to become an ama — a woman who dives to the ocean floor to harvest seafood. (Rev: BCCB 5/97; BL 6/1–15/97; SLJ 6/97)

4728 Bemelmans, Ludwig. *Madeline* (PS–3). Illus. by author. 1987, Viking $16.99 (0-670-81667-1). 32pp. The unforgettable Madeline in a pop-up-book format. (Rev: BL 11/15/87)

4729 Bemelmans, Ludwig, and John Bemelmans Marciano. *Madeline in America and Other Holiday Tales* (PS–3). Illus. 1999, Scholastic $19.95 (0-590-03910-5). This Madeline tale was completed by the author's grandson. The book also contains a few other short stories, including one about Christmas. (Rev: BL 11/15/99; HBG 10/00; SLJ 2/00)

4730 Benchley, Nathaniel. *Sam the Minuteman* (2–4). Illus. by Arnold Lobel. 1969, HarperCollins LB $15.89 (0-06-020480-X); paper $3.95 (0-06-444107-5). 64pp. An easy-to-read book that gives information on the way of life at the beginning of the Revolution.

4731 Beskow, Elsa. *Pelle's New Suit* (PS–3). Illus. by author. 1989, Gryphon $15.95 (0-86315-092-6). 16pp. A Swedish story of the steps in getting a new suit for a small boy, from shearing the lamb to tailoring.

4732 Bildner, Phil. *Shoeless Joe and Black Betsy* (2–4). Illus. by C. F. Payne. 2002, Simon & Schuster $17.00 (0-689-82913-2). 40pp. Mixed-media illustrations complement this tale about Shoeless Joe Jackson and Ol' Charlie, the man who fashioned the bat known as Black Betsy. (Rev: BL 2/15/02; HBG 10/02; SLJ 4/02)

4733 Bildner, Phil. *The Shot Heard 'Round the World* (2–4). Illus. by C. F. Payne. 2005, Simon & Schuster $16.95 (0-689-86273-3). 32pp. The story of the fateful (for baseball fans) summer of 1951, when the Giants beat the Brooklyn Dodgers in a playoff, accompanied by nostalgic artwork. (Rev: BL 3/1/05; SLJ 5/05) [796.357]

4734 Blos, Joan W. *The Heroine of the Titanic: A Tale Both True and Otherwise of the Life of Molly Brown* (1–4). Illus. by Tennessee Dixon. 1991, Morrow $16.00 (0-688-07546-0). 40pp. A picture-book biography of the boisterous survivor of the Titanic who later became a Colorado legend. (Rev: BCCB 9/91; BL 8/91; SLJ 9/91)

4735 Booth, David. *The Dust Bowl* (K–4). Illus. by Karen Reczuch. 1997, Kids Can $16.95 (1-55074-295-7). 32pp. A story about a poor Canadian farm family living in a Western dust bowl during the 1930s. (Rev: BL 9/1/97; SLJ 12/97)

4736 Brace, Steve. *From Beans to Batteries* (PS–2). Illus. by Annie Kubler. Series: One World. 1999, Child's Play paper $6.99 (0-85953-799-4). Village life in Peru is depicted in this tale about a boy who walks to a market to trade beans for batteries to use in his radio. (Rev: SLJ 6/99)

4737 Bradby, Marie. *Momma, Where Are You From?* (PS–3). Illus. by Chris K. Soentpiet. 2000, Orchard LB $17.99 (0-531-33105-9). 32pp. At her daughter's request, an African American woman describes her life in the rural South during segregation. (Rev: BCCB 3/00; BL 2/15/00; HBG 10/00; SLJ 4/00)

4738 Bradby, Marie. *More Than Anything Else* (K–3). Illus. by Chris K. Soentpiet. 1996, Orchard LB $16.99 (0-531-08764-6). 32pp. A fictionalized account of the childhood of Booker T. Washington, told in a picture book format. (Rev: BL 7/95; SLJ 11/95*)

4739 Brett, Jan. *Daisy Comes Home* (K–3). Illus. 2002, Penguin Putnam $16.99 (0-399-23618-X). 32pp. Detailed artwork complements this tale, set in China, of a put-upon chicken named Daisy who is washed down the river, and the resolute young owner who rescues her. (Rev: BCCB 3/02; BL 3/15/02*; HBG 10/02; SLJ 3/02)

4740 Bridges, Shirin Yim. *Ruby's Wish* (K–2). Illus. by Sophie Blackall. 2002, Chronicle $15.95 (0-8118-3490-5). 32pp. Ruby is an intelligent girl from a wealthy Chinese family who aspires to go to university at a time when few girls were educated, and to her surprise gets her wish. (Rev: BCCB 10/02; BL 11/15/02; HBG 3/03; SLJ 2/03)

4741 Bunting, Eve. *Gleam and Glow* (1–4). Illus. by Peter Sylvada. 2001, Harcourt $16.00 (0-15-202596-0). 32pp. A Bosnian mother and children flee their home leaving two precious golden fish in the pond and later return from a refugee camp to find their home ruined but the pond full of golden fish. (Rev: BCCB 12/01; BL 12/15/01; HBG 3/02; SLJ 9/01)

4742 Bunting, Eve. *Going Home* (K–3). Illus. by David Diaz. 1996, HarperCollins LB $15.89 (0-06-026297-4). 32pp. Carlos and his family leave their adopted home in California to visit their original home in Mexico. (Rev: BCCB 12/96; BL 10/1/96; SLJ 9/96)

4743 Bunting, Eve. *I Have an Olive Tree* (PS–3). Illus. by Karen Barbour. 1999, HarperCollins LB $16.98 (0-06-027574-X). Sophia, a Greek American girl, and her mother go to Greece to revisit their family home and the olive tree that Sophia's grandfather planted before he died. (Rev: BCCB 5/99; BL 5/15/99; HB 7–8/99; HBG 10/99; SLJ 5/99)

4744 Bunting, Eve. *Market Day* (PS–2). Illus. by Holly Berry. 1996, HarperCollins LB $15.89 (0-06-025368-1). 32pp. Market day in a small Irish town is an exciting event, particularly when the young narrator is given a penny by her father to spend. (Rev: BL 2/15/96*; SLJ 4/96)

4745 Bunting, Eve. *So Far from the Sea* (K–4). Illus. by Chris K. Soentpiet. 1998, Clarion $15.00 (0-395-72095-8). 32pp. A young Japanese-American girl and her family visit the former internment camp of Manzanar and recall the family's hardships and experiences during their imprisonment from 1942 to the end of World War II. (Rev: BCCB 7–8/98; BL 5/1/98; HB 5–6/98; HBG 10/98; SLJ 6/98)

4746 Burke, Timothy R. *Tugboats in Action* (PS–2). Illus. 1993, Whitman LB $15.95 (0-8075-8112-7). 32pp. Life aboard a tugboat on its journey on the Buffalo River to Lake Erie. (Rev: BCCB 12/93; BL 10/15/93; SLJ 1/94)

4747 Burleigh, Robert. *Lookin' for Bird in the Big City* (2–4). Illus. by Marek Los. 2001, Harcourt $16.00 (0-15-202031-4). A young Miles Davis searches for saxophonist Charlie "Bird" Parker in this fictionalized picture book set in 1940s New York City. (Rev: BL 2/15/03; HBG 10/01; SLJ 6/01)

4748 Burleigh, Robert. *The Secret of the Great Houdini* (2–4). Illus. by Leonid Gore. 2002, Simon & Schuster $16.95 (0-689-83267-2). 40pp. Sam and his uncle watch in suspense as Houdini performs an amazing escape in this fictional account mixed with biography and a message of self-esteem. (Rev: BL 7/02; HBG 3/03; SLJ 7/02)

4749 Bynum, Eboni, and Roland Jackson. *Jamari's Drum* (K–4). 2004, Groundwood $16.95 (0-88899-531-8). Jamari has always loved the sound of the great village drum, but when he takes over its drumming he neglects his duty and disaster nearly ensues. (Rev: HB 1–2/05; SLJ 11/04)

4750 Capatti, Bérénice. *Klimt and His Cat* (1–3). Illus. by Octavia Monaco. 2005, Eerdmans $18.00 (0-8028-5282-3). 40pp. Klimt's cat, Katze, describes his interesting life with the artist in this book full of beautiful illustrations. (Rev: BL 2/1/05)

4751 Castaneda, Omar S. *Abuela's Weave* (K–3). Illus. by Enrique O. Sanchez. 1993, Lee & Low $15.95 (1-880000-00-8). 32pp. In Guatemala, a young girl and her grandmother take their handicrafts to sell at a fiesta. (Rev: BL 8/93; SLJ 7/93)

4752 Celenza, Anna Harwell. *Bach's Goldberg Variations* (K–3). Illus. by JoAnn E. Kitchel. 2005, Charlesbridge $19.95 (1-57091-510-5). 32pp. This story of the Bach variations that helped a young man win a job as harpsichordist to a count includes a CD of the music. (Rev: BL 5/15/05)

4753 Celenza, Anna Harwell. *The Heroic Symphony* (K–4). Illus. by JoAnn E. Kitchel. 2004, Charlesbridge $19.95 (1-57091-509-1). Watercolor illustrations enliven this detailed story of Beethoven's "Eroica" symphony and how he struggled to complete it despite his increasing deafness. (Rev: SLJ 3/04)

4754 Chall, Marsha Wilson. *Prairie Train* (K–3). Illus. by John Thompson. 2003, HarperCollins LB $16.89 (0-688-13434-3). A young girl details her first train trip — a visit to Grandma in St. Paul, Minnesota — and the passing scenery of the early 20th century. (Rev: HBG 4/04; LMC 4/04; SLJ 12/03)

4755 Chamberlin, Mary, and Rich Chamberlin. *Mama Panya's Pancakes: A Village Tale from Kenya* (K–3). Illus. by Julia Cairns. 2005, Barefoot $16.99 (1-84148-139-4). Mama Panya is worried she won't have enough pancakes for all the people her son Adika has invited, but all the guests bring their own contributions and there is plenty to go round in this story set in Kenya. (Rev: BL 3/1/04; SLJ 5/05)

4756 Chanin, Michael. *The Chief's Blanket* (PS–4). Illus. by Kim Howard. 1998, H. J. Kramer $14.95 (0-915811-78-2). 32pp. Using Navajo life during the 1800s as a background, this picture book tells how a young Indian girl weaves a blanket to buy horses so her grandmother will be able to travel in comfort. (Rev: BL 4/15/98; SLJ 7/98)

4757 Chen, Chih-Yuan. *On My Way to Buy Eggs* (PS). Illus. by author. 2003, Kane/Miller $15.95 (1-929132-49-2). In this import from Taiwan, a little girl on her way to buy eggs finds delights and adventure all around her. (Rev: HBG 4/04; SLJ 10/03)

4758 Cheripko, Jan. *Brother Bartholomew and the Apple Grove* (1–3). Illus. by Kestutis Kasparavicius. 2004, Boyds Mills $15.95 (1-59078-096-5). 32pp. Brother Stephen believes he can do a better job of looking after the orchard than old Brother Bartholomew, but he soon learns the dangers of pride. (Rev: BL 3/1/04; SLJ 4/04)

4759 Cherry, Lynne, and Mark J. Plotkin. *The Shaman's Apprentice* (K–4). Illus. 1998, Harcourt $16.00 (0-15-201281-8). 40pp. In the Amazon rain forest, young Kamanya hopes to become his tribe's new shaman, but new diseases brought in by foreigners challenge the powers of his traditional medicines. (Rev: BL 4/1/98; HBG 10/98; SLJ 5/98)

4760 Choi, Yangsook. *Peach Heaven* (K–2). Illus. 2005, Farrar $16.00 (0-374-35761-7). 32pp. A Korean girl and her grandmother rejoice when peaches from a mountaintop orchard rain down on their house during a storm. (Rev: BL 3/15/05)

4761 Claverie, Jean. *Little Lou* (2–3). Illus. 1990, Creative Ed. $22.60 (0-88682-329-3). 48pp. Little Lou describes how he was introduced to blues music when he was a child in the thirties. (Rev: BL 4/15/91)

4762 Collier, Mary Jo, and Peter Collier. *The King's Giraffe* (1–3). Illus. by Stephane Poulin. 1996, Simon & Schuster $16.00 (0-689-80679-5). 40pp. In 1826, the pasha of Egypt sent the King of France an unusual gift: a giraffe. (Rev: BCCB 3/96; BL 6/1–15/96; SLJ 3/96)

4763 Compestine, Ying Chang. *The Story of Chopsticks* (K–3). Illus. by YongSheng Xuan. 2001, Holiday House $16.95 (0-8234-1526-0). 32pp. An inventive tale of the origin of chopsticks that includes a lesson in table manners and a simple recipe. (Rev: BL 1/1–15/02; HBG 10/02; SLJ 12/01)

4764 Compestine, Ying Chang. *The Story of Kites* (K–3). Illus. by YongSheng Xuan. 2003, Holiday House $16.95 (0-8234-1715-8). Those irrepressible Kang brothers try a variety of methods of scaring the birds away from the rice fields before succeeding by inventing kites. (Rev: BL 4/15/03; HBG 10/03; SLJ 5/03)

4765 Compestine, Ying Chang. *The Story of Noodles* (1–3). Illus. by YongSheng Xuan. 2002, Holiday House $16.95 (0-8234-1600-3). 32pp. The inventive Kang brothers of *The Story of Chopsticks* return to help their mother in the emperor's cooking contest. (Rev: BCCB 2/03; BL 11/1/02; HBG 3/03; SLJ 11/02)

4766 Compestine, Ying Chang. *The Story of Paper* (K–3). Illus. by YongSheng Xuan. 2003, Holiday House $16.95 (0-8234-1705-0). Disciplined for inattentiveness in class, the resourceful Kang brothers search for a way to redeem themselves and end up inventing paper. (Rev: BL 12/15/03; HBG 4/04; SLJ 11/03)

4767 Connor, Leslie. *Miss Bridie Chose a Shovel* (1–4). Illus. by Mary Azarian. 2004, Houghton Mifflin $16.00 (0-618-30564-5). 32pp. Miss Birdie makes a wise decision when she chooses a shovel rather than a keepsake to take from Ireland to her new life in America in 1856. (Rev: BL 3/1/04*; SLJ 5/04)

4768 Cooney, Barbara. *Hattie and the Wild Waves: A Story from Brooklyn* (1–5). Illus. 1990, Viking $15.99 (0-670-83056-9). 40pp. A re-creation of a young girl's life growing up in turn-of-the-century Brooklyn and Manhattan. (Rev: BCCB 12/90*; BL 11/1/90*; HB 1–2/91*; SLJ 12/90)

4769 Cordsen, Carol Foskett. *The Milkman* (PS–2). Illus. by Douglas B. Jones. 2005, Dutton $15.99 (0-525-47208-8). 32pp. In a former, easier time, Mr. Plimpton delivers milk and eggs and a great deal more — gifts, cards, and lost puppies, for example. (Rev: BL 5/1/05)

4770 Corey, Shana. *Players in Pigtails* (PS–3). Illus. by Rebecca Gibbon. 2003, Scholastic $16.95 (0-439-18305-7). Corey tells the story of a fictional character named Katie Casey who helps start the All-American Girls Professional Baseball League during World War II. (Rev: BL 3/1/04; HBG 10/03; SLJ 4/03)

4771 Corey, Shana. *You Forgot Your Skirt, Amelia Bloomer!* (1–3). Illus. by Chesley McLaren. 2000, Scholastic $16.95 (0-439-07819-9). The story of

Amelia Bloomer, how she founded a newspaper, worked for women's rights, and started a dress craze. (Rev: BCCB 2/00; BL 2/1/00*; HBG 10/00; SLJ 3/00)

4772 Corpi, Lucha. *Where Fireflies Dance* (K–4). Illus. by Mira Reisberg. 1997, Children's Book Pr. $15.95 (0-89239-145-6). 32pp. The author remembers everyday incidents in her life growing up in a Mexican town. (Rev: BL 1/1–15/98; HBG 3/98; SLJ 12/97)

4773 Cowcher, Helen. *Whistling Thorn* (PS–3). Illus. 1993, Scholastic $14.95 (0-590-47299-2). 40pp. A nonfiction account of why the thorn trees of Africa's grasslands whistle when the wind blows through them. (Rev: BL 10/15/93; SLJ 10/93) [583]

4774 Cowen-Fletcher, Jane. *It Takes a Village* (PS–1). Illus. 1994, Scholastic $15.95 (0-590-46573-2). 32pp. Yemi realizes that all the townspeople are concerned when her young brother wanders off at market time in this book that explores life in a West African village. (Rev: BL 1/1/94; SLJ 3/94)

4775 Cutler, Jane. *The Cello of Mr. O* (1–4). Illus. by Greg Couch. 1999, Dutton $15.99 (0-525-46119-1). 32pp. In a war-torn city where food is scarce and all the men are at the front, there is a tiny ray of hope from the music that Mr. O plays in the town square every day. (Rev: BCCB 12/99; BL 12/15/99*; HBG 3/00; SLJ 11/99)

4776 da Costa, Deborah. *Snow in Jerusalem* (K–3). Illus. by Ying-hwa Hu and Cornelius Van Wright. 2001, Whitman $15.95 (0-8075-7521-6). 30pp. A Jewish boy and a Muslim boy find a way to peacefully resolve a disagreement about a cat in this picture book set in Jerusalem. (Rev: BL 10/15/01; HBG 3/02; SLJ 12/01)

4777 Daly, Niki. *Once Upon a Time* (PS–K). Illus. 2003, Farrar $16.00 (0-374-35633-5). 40pp. Sarie overcomes her fear of reading aloud by reading to her aunt in this picture book set in South Africa. (Rev: BL 2/15/03; HB 5–6/03; HBG 10/03; SLJ 5/03)

4778 Daly, Niki. *What's Cooking, Jamela?* (PS–2). Illus. 2001, Farrar $16.00 (0-374-35602-5). 32pp. Vibrant illustrations capture the colors of a black South African township in this tale of little Jamela, whose pet chicken is in peril. (Rev: BCCB 1/02; BL 11/1/01; HB 9–10/01; HBG 3/02; SLJ 10/01)

4779 Day, Marie. *Quennu and the Cave Bear* (K–3). Illus. by author. 1999, Owl $17.95 (1-895688-86-8); paper $6.95 (1-895688-87-6). 32pp. A young girl conquers her fear of cave bears and paints one on the wall during a prehistoric ceremony; includes accurate information about cave art. (Rev: HBG 10/99; SLJ 5/99)

4780 Delgado, María Isabel. *Chave's Memories / Los Recuerdos de Chave* (PS–3). Illus. by Yvonne Symank. 1996, Piñata $14.95 (1-55885-084-8). A bilingual picture book in which a woman recalls her trips as a child from Brownsville, Texas, to her grandparents' ranch in northern Mexico. (Rev: SLJ 12/96)

4781 Demas, Corinne. *The Boy Who Was Generous with Salt* (K–3). Illus. by Michael Hays. 2002, Marshall Cavendish $15.95 (0-7614-5099-8). As cook aboard a fishing vessel in 1850, Ned plots to get home in time for his ninth birthday. (Rev: HBG 10/02; SLJ 5/02)

4782 Demi. *The Greatest Power* (K–3). Illus. 2004, Simon & Schuster $19.95 (0-689-84503-0). 40pp. Ping, introduced in *The Empty Pot* (1990), invites all the children in his empire to consider what might be the greatest power in the world, with interesting results. (Rev: BL 2/1/04; SLJ 3/04)

4783 dePaola, Tomie. *Pascual and the Kitchen Angels* (PS–2). Illus. 2004, Penguin Putnam $16.99 (0-399-24214-7). 32pp. The patron saint of cooks is introduced in a charming story of a boy who communes with the animals and requires the help of angels when asked to make a meal. (Rev: BL 1/1–15/04; SLJ 2/04)

4784 Dillon, Jana. *Sasha's Matrioshka Dolls* (K–3). Illus. by Deborah N. Lattimore. 2003, Farrar $16.00 (0-374-37387-6). 32pp. A story of a box maker in old Moscow, who makes the first nesting Russian dolls for his granddaughter. (Rev: BL 3/15/03; HBG 10/03; SLJ 7/03)

4785 Dorros, Arthur. *Julio's Magic* (K–2). Illus. by Ann Grifalconi. 2005, HarperCollins LB $16.89 (0-06-029005-6). 32pp. Julio, a young Mexican wood-carver, helps his elderly teacher, Iluminado, to create the winning entry for the annual wood-carving contest. (Rev: BL 1/1–15/05; SLJ 1/05)

4786 Drummond, Allan. *Casey Jones* (K–3). Illus. 2001, Farrar $16.00 (0-374-31175-7). 32pp. Inspired by railroading in the 1800s, this is the story of Casey, his fateful trip, and the fiery wreck that was his train. (Rev: BL 2/15/01; HBG 10/01)

4787 Drummond, Allan. *Liberty!* (1–4). Illus. 2002, Farrar $17.00 (0-374-34385-3). 40pp. An unnamed boy narrates the story of the unveiling of the Statue of Liberty in 1886, in this tale based on fact. (Rev: BL 3/15/02*; HBG 10/02; SLJ 5/02)

4788 Edwards, Pamela Duncan. *Barefoot: Escape on the Underground Railroad* (K–4). Illus. by Henry Cole. 1997, HarperCollins LB $15.89 (0-06-027138-8). 32pp. The birds and other animals in a forest seem to work together to help an escaped slave. (Rev: BL 2/15/97; SLJ 2/97*)

4789 Emberley, Rebecca. *Taking a Walk / Caminando: A Book in Two Languages/Una Libra en Dos Lenguas* (1–3). Illus. 1994, Little, Brown paper $6.95 (0-316-23471-0). 32pp. Bright artwork and simple phrases introduce Spanish to English readers, and vice versa. Also use the bilingual *My House/Mi Casa* (1990). (Rev: BL 6/15/90; HB 9–10/90; SLJ 8/90)

4790 Erdrich, Louise. *The Range Eternal* (K–3). Illus. by Steve Johnson. 2002, Hyperion $15.99 (0-7868-0220-0). 32pp. An adult woman buys an antique Range Eternal woodstove, which brings back warm memories of her childhood in the mountains when the stove was the focal point of the kitchen. (Rev: BCCB 12/02; BL 10/1/02; HBG 3/03; SLJ 10/02)

4791 Ernst, Lisa Campbell. *Sam Johnson and the Blue Ribbon Quilt* (K–3). Illus. by author. 1983, Lothrop LB $15.89 (0-688-01517-4); Morrow paper $4.95 (0-688-11505-5). 32pp. The men and the women vie for honors in the quilting contest.

4792 Esbaum, Jill. *Ste-e-e-eamboat A-comin'!* (K–4). Illus. by Adam Rex. 2005, Farrar $16.00 (0-374-37236-5). 40pp. The excitement of the arrival of the packet *S. L. Clemens* at sleepy towns on the Mississippi in 1867 is portrayed in rhyming verse and beautiful realistic illustrations. (Rev: SLJ 3/05)

4793 Faulkner, Matt. *The Pirate Meets the Queen* (K–3). Illus. 2005, Philomel $15.99 (0-399-24038-1). 32pp. Granny O'Malley, the 16th-century Irish pirate, tells her life story and describes her showdown with Queen Elizabeth I over the capture of Granny's son Toby. (Rev: BL 5/15/05; SLJ 6/05)

4794 Feder, Paula K. *The Feather-Bed Journey* (K–3). Illus. by Stacey Schuett. 1995, Whitman LB $15.95 (0-8075-2330-5). 32pp. Grandma tells her grandchildren how her favorite feather pillow was once part of a large feather bed that kept her warm in a Jewish ghetto during World War II. (Rev: BCCB 12/95; BL 10/15/95; SLJ 11/95)

4795 Feeney, Stephanie. *A Is for Aloha* (PS–K). Photos by Jeff Reese. 1985, Univ. of Hawaii Pr. $11.95 (0-8248-0722-7). A simple introduction to Hawaii and its many cultures.

4796 Fitzpatrick, Marie-Louise. *You, Me and the Big Blue Sea* (PS–2). Illus. 2002, Millbrook LB $22.90 (0-7613-2806-8). 32pp. A little boy and his mother have different memories of a sea voyage they took when he was a toddler, in this richly illustrated book set in the 19th century. (Rev: BL 12/1/02; HBG 3/03; SLJ 11/02)

4797 Fleming, Candace. *Boxes for Katje* (K–3). Illus. by Stacey Dressen-McQueen. 2003, Farrar $16.00 (0-374-30922-1). Based on actual events, this is a heartwarming story of an Indiana town's efforts to help Dutch people suffering from severe postwar shortages in 1945. (Rev: HB 9–10/03; HBG 4/04; SLJ 9/03)

4798 Francis, David "Panama", and Bob Reiser. *David Gets His Drum* (K–2). Illus. by Eric Velasquez. 2002, Marshall Cavendish $16.95 (0-7614-5088-2). 32pp. African American jazz musician "Panama" Francis loved music from a young age and here tells the sad story of his first drum. (Rev: BL 11/15/02; HBG 3/03; SLJ 10/02)

4799 Freschet, Gina. *Naty's Parade* (K–2). Illus. 2000, Farrar $16.00 (0-374-35500-2). 32pp. Naty, dressed in a big mouse costume, gets lost during the Mexican Guelaguetza parade but the sounds and smells lead her back to it. (Rev: BL 5/15/00; HBG 10/00; SLJ 3/00)

4800 Frew, Andrew W. *The Invisible Seam* (2–4). Illus. by Jun Matsuoka. 2003, Moon Mountain $15.95 (1-931659-02-8). 32pp. Realistic watercolor illustrations complement the gentle early-20th-century story of Michi, an apprentice seamstress whose expertise causes conflict with her co-workers. (Rev: BL 6/1–15/03; HBG 10/03; SLJ 4/04)

4801 Friedman, Robin. *The Silent Witness: A True Story of The Civil War* (K–3). Illus. by Claire A. Nivola. 2005, Houghton Mifflin $16.00 (0-618-44230-8). A touching story about the young owner of a rag doll that was present at the surrender of the Confederacy in 1865; the girl never saw it after that day but it is now on display in Appomattox. (Rev: BCCB 6/05; HB 5–6/05; SLJ 6/05)

4802 Fuchs, Bernie. *Ride Like the Wind: A Tale of the Pony Express* (K–4). Illus. by author. 2004, Scholastic $16.95 (0-439-26645-9). 32pp. The fictional adventures of young Pony Express rider Johnny Free and his pony JennySoo are augmented by historical material. (Rev: SLJ 3/04)

4803 Funke, Cornelia. *The Princess Knight* (PS–2). Trans. by Anthea Bell. Illus. by Kerstin Meyer. 2004, Scholastic $15.95 (0-439-53630-8). 32pp. Princess Violetta can joust, ride, and use a sword as well as her older brothers, so when her father wants to give her away as a tournament prize on her 16th birthday, she dons a disguise and takes part in the contest herself. (Rev: BL 2/1/04*; SLJ 3/04)

4804 Garaway, Margaret K. *Ashkii and His Grandfather* (K–3). Illus. by Harry Warren. 1995, Old Hogan $14.95 (0-963-88517-0); paper $8.95 (0-963-88516-2). 33pp. A young Navajo boy helps his grandfather at summer sheep camp. (Rev: BL 3/1/90)

4805 Garay, Luis. *The Kite* (K–2). Illus. 2002, Tundra $14.95 (0-88776-503-3). 32pp. Francisco, a Latin American boy who must help support his family after his father's death, dreams of having a kite. (Rev: BL 8/02; HBG 10/02; SLJ 12/02)

4806 Garay, Luis. *Pedrito's Day* (K–3). Illus. 1997, Orchard $14.95 (0-531-09522-3). 32pp. Pedrito, a Mexican boy, is heartbroken when he loses the money he had saved to buy a bicycle. (Rev: BL 3/1/97; SLJ 4/97)

4807 Geeslin, Campbell. *Elena's Serenade* (1–3). Illus. by Ana Juan. 2004, Simon & Schuster $16.95 (0-689-84908-7). 40pp. Elena proves her father wrong and succeeds in blowing magnificent pieces of glass in this story set in Mexico. (Rev: BL 3/1/04; SLJ 3/04)

4808 George, Jean Craighead. *Nutik and Amaroq Play Ball* (K–2). Illus. by Ted Rand. 2001, HarperCollins $15.95 (0-06-028166-9). 40pp. Amaroq, an Eskimo boy, discovers that his wolf Nutik's sense of direction is better when they head home after playing football. (Rev: BL 5/15/01; HBG 10/01; SLJ 7/01)

4809 George, Jean Craighead. *Nutik, the Wolf Pup* (PS–3). Illus. by Ted Rand. 2001, HarperCollins LB $15.89 (0-06-028165-0). 40pp. Amaroq nurses a wolf pup back to health and then must give him up and return him to the pack. (Rev: BL 2/1/01; HBG 10/01; SLJ 3/01)

4810 Germein, Katrina. *Big Rain Coming* (PS–2). Illus. by Bronwyn Bancroft. 2000, Clarion $15.00 (0-618-08344-8). 32pp. In the Australian Outback where it gets very hot, every living creature is waiting for the rain that Old Joseph claims is on its way. (Rev: BL 8/00; HBG 3/01; SLJ 9/00)

4811 Gerstein, Mordicai. *The Mountains of Tibet* (K–3). Illus. by author. 1989, HarperCollins paper $6.95 (0-06-443211-4). 32pp. A woodcutter spends his life in a Tibetan valley in this story of reincarnation. (Rev: BL 11/15/87; HB 11–12/87; SLJ 11/87)

4812 Glass, Andrew. *Bewildered for Three Days: As to Why Daniel Boone Never Wore His Coonskin Cap* (2–3). Illus. 2000, Holiday House $16.95 (0-8234-1446-9). 32pp. After several hair-raising adventures including spending a night in a hollow log with a mother raccoon, Daniel Boone swears off wearing his coonskin cap forever. (Rev: BCCB 11/00; BL 9/1/00; HBG 10/01; SLJ 10/00)

4813 Goble, Paul. *Death of the Iron Horse* (K–2). Illus. by author. 1993, Simon & Schuster paper $5.99 (0-689-71686-9). 32pp. Rail sabotage from the Indian point of view, set in 1867. (Rev: BCCB 4/87; BL 4/1/87; HB 5–6/87)

4814 Goodman, Susan E. *Cora Frear: A True Story* (2–3). Illus. by Doris Ettlinger. Series: Brave Kids. 2002, Simon & Schuster LB $11.89 (0-689-84330-5); paper $3.99 (0-689-84329-1). 51pp. A 10-year-old and her doctor father are surrounded by a prairie fire in the late 19th century. (Rev: HBG 10/02; SLJ 8/02)

4815 Graham, Christine. *When Pioneer Wagons Rumbled West* (PS–2). Illus. by Sherry Meidell. 1998, Deseret $14.95 (1-57345-272-6). 26pp. This picture book illustrates the hardships faced by Mormon families and the importance of prayer in their lives as they journeyed to settle land for their new home in Utah. (Rev: BL 9/15/98; SLJ 12/98)

4816 Green, Norma B. *The Hole in the Dike* (K–2). Illus. by Eric Carle. 1975, Scholastic paper $4.95 (0-590-46146-X). 32pp. Brilliant illustrations accompany this simple retelling of the Mary Mapes Dodge story of the boy who put his finger in the dike and saved his Dutch town.

4817 Greenwood, Mark. *The Legend of Moondyne Joe* (K–3). Illus. by Frane Lessac. 2002, Cygnet $19.95 (1-876268-70-0). Moondyne Joe, a legendary Australian figure who arrived there as a convict in the mid-1800s, was known for his ability to escape from jail. (Rev: SLJ 1/03)

4818 Guarnieri, Paolo. *A Boy Named Giotto* (K–3). Trans. by Jonathan Galassi. Illus. by Bimba Landmann. 1999, Farrar $17.00 (0-374-30931-0). 32pp. A fictional story about how the painter Giotto found his profession through the teachings of the master artist Cimabue. (Rev: BCCB 1/00*; BL 12/15/99; HBG 3/00; SLJ 10/99)

4819 Hall, Donald. *Ox-Cart Man* (K–3). Illus. by Barbara Cooney. 1979, Puffin paper $6.99 (0-14-050441-9). 40pp. The cycle of production and sale of goods in 19th-century New England is pictured in human terms. Caldecott Medal winner, 1980.

4820 Hanson, Regina. *The Face at the Window* (1–3). Illus. by Linda Saport. 1997, Clarion $14.95 (0-395-78625-8). 32pp. A little girl in Jamaica is afraid of the old neighbor lady until her parents take the youngster to meet her. (Rev: BCCB 5/97; BL 6/1–15/97; SLJ 6/97)

4821 Hanson, Regina. *A Season for Mangoes* (PS–2). Illus. by Eric Velasquez. 2005, Clarion $15.00 (0-618-15972-X). 32pp. Sareen, a young Jamaican girl, struggles to find the confidence to address the mourners at her beloved grandmother's wake, or "sit-up." (Rev: BL 2/1/05; SLJ 5/05)

4822 Harper, Jo, and Josephine Harper. *Prairie Dog Pioneers* (PS–3). Illus. by Craig Spearing. 1998, Turtle $16.95 (1-890515-10-8). 48pp. This historical adventure story tells of the experiences of Mae Dean and her family as they travel by covered wagon to their new home in the Texas panhandle. (Rev: BL 9/15/98; HBG 3/99; SLJ 10/98)

4823 Hartfield, Claire. *Me and Uncle Romie: A Story Inspired by the Life and Art of Romare Bearden* (K–3). Illus. by Jerome Lagarrigue. 2002, Dial $16.99 (0-8037-2520-5). 40pp. James enjoys spending time with his uncle, the Harlem Renaissance artist Romare Bearden, in this picture book with reproductions of the artist's work. (Rev: BL 2/15/03; HBG 3/03; SLJ 12/02)

4824 Hazen, Barbara Shook. *Katie's Wish* (PS–2). Illus. by Emily Arnold McCully. 2002, Dial $15.99 (0-8037-2478-0). 32pp. Beautiful, impressionistic illustrations and powerful narrative enhance this book about a girl named Katie, who survives the Irish potato famine and travels to America to reunite with her Da. (Rev: BL 10/15/02; HBG 3/03; SLJ 9/02)

4825 Heide, Florence Parry, and Judith Heide Gilliland. *Sami and the Time of the Troubles* (1–4). Illus. by Ted Lewin. 1992, Houghton Mifflin $15.95 (0-395-55964-2). 40pp. This compelling picture book shows a modern Beirut family caught up in the horrors of war. (Rev: BL 4/1/92*; HB 7–8/92; SLJ 5/92*)

4826 Hershenhorn, Esther. *Fancy That* (K–3). Illus. by Megan Lloyd. 2003, Holiday House $16.95 (0-8234-1605-4). In the 1840s, a young orphan named Pip travels the countryside trying to earn money as a portrait painter, but his realistic style fails to please his customers. (Rev: BL 9/15/03; HBG 4/04; SLJ 11/03)

4827 Hidaka, Masako. *Girl from the Snow Country* (K–2). Trans. by Amanda Mayer Stinchecum. Illus. 1986, Kane/Miller $13.95 (0-916291-06-5). 32pp. Her wish comes true when Mi-chan makes snow bunnies and needs something to make red eyes. (Rev: BL 2/1/87; SLJ 1/87)

4828 High, Linda Oatman. *The Girl on the High-Diving Horse: An Adventure in Atlantic City* (2–4). Illus. by Ted Lewin. 2003, Philomel $16.99 (0-399-23649-X). It's 1936 and young Ivy Cordelia longs to ride one of the horses that dive into a tank of water on the boardwalk in Atlantic City. (Rev: BCCB 2/03; BL 4/15/03; HBG 10/03; SLJ 2/03)

4829 Hines, Gary. *Thanksgiving in the White House* (1–3). 2003, Holt $15.95 (0-8050-6530-X). 32pp. When President Abraham Lincoln proclaims Thanksgiving a national holiday in 1863, Tad, the chief executive's son, must scramble to save his pet turkey from the chopping block. (Rev: BL 9/1/03; HBG 4/04; SLJ 9/03)

4830 Hoberman, Mary Ann. *Yankee Doodle* (PS–2). Illus. by Nadine Bernard Westcott. Series: Sing-Along. 2004, Little, Brown $15.95 (0-316-14551-3). 32pp. In picture-book form with bouncing verses, this is a whimsical rendition of the story of Yankee, a young man in a gentler time and place who joins forces with a young lady, her pet poodle, a toad, and a rooster to open a restaurant; music is provided on the endpapers along with activities. (Rev: BL 4/15/04; SLJ 6/04) [782.42]

4831 Hoffman, Mary. *Boundless Grace* (PS–3). Illus. by Caroline Binch. 1995, Dial $16.99 (0-8037-1715-6). 32pp. Grace's father sends airplane tickets for her to visit him in Gambia and meet his new family. (Rev: BCCB 6/95; BL 4/15/95; HB 7–8/95; SLJ 5/95*)

4832 Hoffman, Mary. *The Color of Home* (PS–3). Illus. by Karin Littlewood. 2002, Penguin Putnam $15.99 (0-8037-2841-7). 32pp. A young Somalian boy who has emigrated to America to escape civil war has trouble adjusting to his new life until he is able to paint pictures of his fears and hopes. (Rev: BCCB 10/02; BL 10/15/02; HBG 3/03; SLJ 9/02)

4833 Homan, Lynn M., and Thomas Reilly. *The Tuskegee Airmen Story* (K–3). Illus. by Rosalie M. Shepherd. 2002, Pelican $14.95 (1-58980-005-2). 32pp. A grandfather tells of his days as a Tuskegee Airman during World War II. (Rev: BL 2/15/03; HBG 3/03)

4834 Hong, Lily T. *The Empress and the Silkworm* (PS–3). Illus. 1995, Whitman LB $16.95 (0-8075-2009-8). 32pp. A Chinese empress uses the silk threads she finds when she discovers the cocoons of silkworms to make a robe for the emperor. (Rev: BCCB 12/95; BL 9/15/95; SLJ 11/95)

4835 Hopkinson, Deborah. *Maria's Comet* (1–3). Illus. by Deborah Lanino. 1999, Simon & Schuster $16.00 (0-689-81501-8). 32pp. A fictionalized story of astronomer Maria Mitchell's childhood in the early 1800s. (Rev: BCCB 1/00; BL 9/15/99; HBG 3/00; SLJ 10/99)

4836 Hopkinson, Deborah. *Saving Strawberry Farm* (PS–2). Illus. by Rachel Isadora. 2005, Greenwillow LB $17.89 (0-688-17401-9). 32pp. During the Depression, young Davy plays a key role in helping Miss Elsie to save her strawberry farm. (Rev: BL 5/1/05)

4837 Hopkinson, Deborah. *Under the Quilt of Night* (K–2). Illus. by James E. Ransome. 2002, Simon & Schuster $16.00 (0-689-82227-8). 40pp. A young slave girl describes her dangerous escape through the Underground Railroad. (Rev: BCCB 2/02; BL 2/15/02; HB 7–8/02; HBG 10/02; SLJ 1/02*)

4838 Howard, Ellen. *The Log Cabin Church* (K–3). Illus. by Ronald Himler. 2002, Holiday House $16.95 (0-8234-1740-9). 32pp. Elviery initially questions her Michigan frontier community's desire to build a church in this sequel to *The Log Cabin Quilt* (1996) and *The Log Cabin Christmas* (2000). (Rev: BL 10/1/02; HBG 3/03; SLJ 10/02)

4839 Howard, Ellen. *The Log Cabin Quilt* (K–3). Illus. by Ronald Himler. 1996, Holiday House LB $16.95 (0-8234-1247-4). 28pp. Quilting scraps help chink the holes in a log cabin in this story of Western pioneers. (Rev: BCCB 10/96; BL 12/15/96; SLJ 10/96)

4840 Hughes, Monica. *A Handful of Seeds* (K–3). Illus. by Luis Garay. 1996, Orchard $14.95 (0-531-09498-7). 32pp. When Concepcion moves from the country to the city, she brings some seeds with her to start a garden in the barrio. (Rev: BCCB 6/96; BL 4/1/96; SLJ 3/96)

4841 Hurst, Carol Otis. *Rocks in His Head* (K–3). Illus. by James Stevenson. 2001, Greenwillow LB $15.89 (0-06-029404-3). 32pp. A man pursues his interest in rock collecting from childhood through raising a family in the Depression until he succeeds in turning a hobby into a career. (Rev: BCCB 12/01; BL 6/1–15/01; HB 7–8/01; HBG 10/01; SLJ 6/01)

4842 Iijima, Geneva Cobb. *The Way We Do It in Japan* (K–3). Illus. by Paige Billin-Frye. 2002, Whitman $14.95 (0-8075-7822-3). 32pp. When Gregory's family moves to Japan, he learns about the differences between Japanese and American culture. (Rev: BCCB 3/02; BL 5/15/02; HBG 10/02; SLJ 4/02)

4843 Isadora, Rachel. *Bring on That Beat* (PS–2). Illus. by author. 2002, Penguin Putnam $15.99 (0-399-23232-X). 32pp. In this rhyming, rhythmic ode to jazz set in 1930s Harlem, a band plays on a street corner and a crowd gathers to listen. (Rev: BCCB 1/02; BL 2/15/02; HBG 10/02; SLJ 1/02)

4844 Johnson, Angela. *I Dream of Trains* (PS–2). Illus. by Loren Long. 2003, Simon & Schuster $16.95 (0-689-82609-5). A young African American boy working in the cotton fields of the Mississippi Delta dreams of riding away to a better life on a locomotive driven by the legendary Casey Jones. (Rev: HBG 4/04; SLJ 10/03)

4845 Johnson, Angela. *Just Like Josh Gibson* (PS–2). Illus. by Beth Peck. 2004, Simon & Schuster $15.95 (0-689-82628-1). 32pp. Negro Leagues legend Josh Gibson is a source of inspiration in this story about an African American girl who finds success at baseball in the 1940s. (Rev: BL 2/15/04; SLJ 3/04)

4846 Johnson, Angela. *The Rolling Store* (K–3). Illus. by Peter Catalanotto. 1997, Orchard LB $16.99 (0-531-33015-X). 32pp. A young African American girl tells her friend about the traveling store in a truck that used to visit their community during her grandfather's childhood. (Rev: BCCB 5/97; BL 2/15/97; SLJ 4/97)

4847 Johnson, Dinah. *Quinnie Blue* (PS–2). Illus. by James E. Ransome. 2000, Holt $16.95 (0-8050-4378-0). 32pp. An African American girl imagines what life was like when her grandmother was growing up. (Rev: BL 4/15/00; HBG 10/00; SLJ 6/00)

4848 Johnston, Tony. *Sunsets of the West* (1–3). Illus. by Ted Lewin. 2002, Penguin Putnam $16.99 (0-399-22659-1). 32pp. A picture book that describes a family's journey westward by covered wagon and their day-to-day life. (Rev: BL 6/1–15/02; HBG 10/02; SLJ 7/02)

4849 Joosse, Barbara M. *Lewis and Papa: Adventure on the Santa Fe Trail* (2–4). Illus. by Jon Van Zyle. 1998, Chronicle $14.95 (0-8118-1959-0). 40pp.

During an adventurous wagon-train journey across the Great Plains with his father, young Lewis learns that sometimes being afraid and crying are natural parts of life. (Rev: BL 6/1–15/98; HBG 10/98; SLJ 10/98)

4850 Jungman, Ann. *The Most Magnificent Mosque* (1–4). Illus. by Shelley Fowles. 2004, Frances Lincoln $15.95 (1-84507-012-7). A beautiful mosque in Cordoba, Spain, is saved from destruction through the combined support of three friends — a Christian, a Jew, and a Muslim — who played in its gardens when they were young. (Rev: SLJ 9/04)

4851 Kahn, Rukhsana. *Ruler of the Courtyard* (K–1). Illus. by R. Gregory Christie. 2003, Viking $15.99 (0-670-03583-1). 32pp. Saba overcomes her fear of chickens after facing up to a snake in this story set in Pakistan. (Rev: BL 2/15/03; HB 3–4/03; HBG 10/03; SLJ 2/03)

4852 Kalman, Maira. *Sayonara, Mrs. Kackleman* (K–3). Illus. 1989, Viking $16.99 (0-670-82945-5). 40pp. Japan is introduced through the wild and woolly adventures of an American tourist. (Rev: BCCB 11/89; BL 11/15/89; SLJ 1/90)

4853 Karim, Roberta. *Kindle Me a Riddle* (K–2). Illus. by Bethanne Andersen. 1999, Greenwillow LB $15.93 (0-688-16204-5). 40pp. In frontier America, a family traces the origins of their simple pioneer home and its contents, such as the candles that were once beeswax. (Rev: BL 9/1/99; HBG 3/00; SLJ 1/00)

4854 Kay, Verla. *Covered Wagons, Bumpy Trails* (PS–3). Illus. by S. D. Schindler. 2000, Penguin Putnam $15.99 (0-399-22928-0). A rhyming tale with excellent paintings that depicts the hardships and triumphs of a pioneer family and their journey to California. (Rev: HB 1–2/01; HBG 3/01; SLJ 11/00)

4855 Kay, Verla. *Gold Fever* (K–3). Illus. by S. D. Schindler. 1999, Penguin Putnam $15.99 (0-399-23027-0). 32pp. A young man encounters many obstacles while traveling to the California Gold Rush but, when he doesn't find gold, must go home disappointed. (Rev: BL 1/1–15/99; HB 3–4/99; HBG 10/99; SLJ 3/99)

4856 Kay, Verla. *Homespun Sarah* (K–3). Illus. by Ted Rand. 2003, Penguin Putnam $15.99 (0-399-23417-9). 32pp. Eighteenth-century Pennsylvania farm life is introduced as readers follow Sarah through a typical day. (Rev: BL 3/1/03; HBG 10/03; SLJ 6/03)

4857 Kay, Verla. *Orphan Train* (K–2). Illus. by Ken Stark. 2003, Penguin Putnam $15.99 (0-399-23613-9). This rhyming introduction to the Orphan Train experience includes many historical details and realistic oil paintings. (Rev: HBG 10/03; SLJ 6/03)

4858 Kay, Verla. *Tattered Sails* (K–3). Illus. by Dan Andreasen. 2001, Penguin Putnam $15.99 (0-399-23345-8). 32pp. A description of the difficult voyage of three Pilgrim children and their parents on their way to America in search of a better life. (Rev: BL 10/15/01; HBG 3/02; SLJ 9/01)

4859 Keefer, Janice Kulyk. *Anna's Goat* (2–4). Illus. by Janet Wilson. 2001, Orca $15.95 (1-55143-153-

X). 32pp. Based on a true story, a nanny goat helps ease the pain and loneliness of two refugee children. (Rev: BL 3/15/01; HBG 10/01)

4860 Kellerhals-Stewart, Heather. *Brave Highland Heart* (PS–1). Illus. by Werner Zimmerman. 1999, Stoddart $15.95 (0-7737-3099-0). 32pp. A little Scottish girl fears she will be denied permission to go the ceilidh, a traditional Scottish party that will be held in the family barn, but her father allows her to stay up and enjoy the fun and dancing. (Rev: BL 8/99; SLJ 6/99)

4861 Ketcham, Sallie. *Bach's Big Adventure* (PS–3). Illus. by Timothy Bush. 1999, Orchard LB $17.99 (0-531-33140-7). 32pp. Ten-year-old Bach journeys to Hamburg to hear the man who is supposedly the greatest organist in the world. (Rev: BCCB 5/99; BL 4/1/99; HBG 10/99; SLJ 6/99)

4862 Khan, Rukhsana. *The Roses in My Carpets* (1–4). Illus. by Ronald Himler. 1998, Holiday House $15.95 (0-8234-1399-3). 32pp. A young Afghan boy who lives in a refugee camp dreams of freedom and a place without bombs or warfare as he learns to weave carpets. (Rev: BL 11/15/98; HBG 3/99; SLJ 11/98)

4863 Khan, Rukhsana. *Silly Chicken* (PS–2). Illus. by Yunmee Kyong. 2005, Viking $15.99 (0-670-05912-9). 32pp. A young Pakistani girl named Rani is jealous of her mother's affection for the family chicken. (Rev: BL 1/1–15/05; SLJ 4/05)

4864 Kinsey-Warnock, Natalie. *From Dawn till Dusk* (K–3). Illus. by Mary Azarian. 2002, Houghton Mifflin $16.00 (0-618-18655-7). 40pp. The author describes her childhood on a Vermont farm, contrasting the hard work with the resulting benefits as she details the different activities throughout the year. (Rev: BL 11/15/02; HBG 3/03; SLJ 10/02)

4865 Kinsey-Warnock, Natalie. *Nora's Ark* (K–3). Illus. by Emily Arnold McCully. 2005, HarperCollins LB $16.89 (0-06-029517-1). 32pp. The house that Grandpa is building up on the hill proves useful after all when the storms come in this story based on flooding in Vermont in 1927. (Rev: BL 5/15/05)

4866 Kirk, Connie Ann. *Sky Dancers* (1–3). Illus. by Christy Hale. 2004, Lee & Low $16.95 (1-58430-162-7). 32pp. John Cloud, a young Mohawk boy, is overwhelmed by New York City and by the skill and daring of his steelworker father, laboring far above the ground on the Empire State Building. (Rev: BL 11/15/04; SLJ 1/05)

4867 Koscielniak, Bruce. *Hear, Hear, Mr. Shakespeare: Story, Illustrations, and Selections from Shakespeare's Plays* (1–4). Illus. by author. 1998, Houghton Mifflin $15.00 (0-395-87495-5). In Stratford-on-Avon, Shakespeare must suddenly write a play for a troupe of visiting players, and Queen Elizabeth is very impressed. (Rev: HBG 10/98; SLJ 5/98)

4868 Krensky, Stephen. *Dangerous Crossing: The Revolutionary Voyage of John and John Quincy Adams* (2–4). Illus. by Greg Harlin. 2005, Dutton $16.99 (0-525-46966-4). 32pp. This book based on diary accounts and including powerful watercolor paintings brings to life the perilous 1778 voyage of young John Quincy and his father aboard the *Boston*. (Rev: BL 3/1/05; SLJ 2/05)

4869 Krishnaswami, Uma. *Chachaji's Cup* (K–3). Illus. by Soumya Sitaraman. 2003, Children's Book Pr. $16.95 (0-89239-178-2). 32pp. Neel, an Indian boy living in the United States, listens to his great-uncle Chachaji's Hindu legends and his stories of the hardships and dangers he faced as a child refugee during the partition of India and Pakistan in 1947. (Rev: BL 3/15/03; HBG 10/03; SLJ 6/03)

4870 Krishnaswami, Uma. *Monsoon* (PS–2). Illus. by Jamel Akib. 2003, Farrar $16.00 (0-374-35015-9). A young girl in India and her family await the arrival of the monsoon rains in this attractive picture book full of Indian culture, with informative back matter. (Rev: BCCB 1/04; BL 9/1/03; HBG 4/04; LMC 3/04; SLJ 12/03)

4871 Kroeger, Mary Kay, and Louise Borden. *Paperboy* (K–4). Illus. by Ted Lewin. 1996, Clarion $16.95 (0-395-64482-8). 32pp. In 1927 Cincinnati, a young paperboy has trouble selling his newspapers when boxing champ Jack Dempsey loses the prizefight. (Rev: BCCB 3/96; BL 3/15/96; HB 9–10/96; SLJ 8/96*)

4872 Kroll, Virginia. *Especially Heroes* (3–5). Illus. by Tim Ladwig. 2003, Eerdmans $16.00 (0-8028-5221-1). 32pp. The narrator remembers an incident in 1962, when her father reacted to an attack on a black woman in their neighborhood. (Rev: BL 2/1/03; HBG 10/03; SLJ 4/03)

4873 Kroll, Virginia. *Sweet Magnolia* (1–3). Illus. by Laura Jacques. 1995, Charlesbridge paper $6.95 (0-88106-414-9). When Denise visits her grandmother, a naturalist, in Louisiana, she learns about the flora and fauna of the swamps and tastes Cajun food. (Rev: SLJ 2/96)

4874 Kusugak, Michael A. *Arctic Stories* (2–4). Illus. by Vladyana Krykorka. 1998, Annick $18.95 (1-55037-452-4); paper $6.95 (1-55037-453-2). 40pp. Three stories about an Inuit girl growing up in a village around northern Hudson Bay are simply told with full-page watercolors. (Rev: BL 11/1/98; SLJ 3/99)

4875 Kyuchukov, Hristo. *My Name Was Hussein* (1–3). Illus. by Allan Eitzen. 2004, Boyds Mills $15.95 (1-56397-964-0). 32pp. Based on the author's childhood experiences, this sobering tale looks at persecution of a Roma group in Bulgaria. (Rev: BL 4/15/04; SLJ 4/04)

4876 Lamorisse, Albert. *The Red Balloon* (1–3). Illus. by author. 1967, Doubleday $16.95 (0-385-00343-9); paper $10.95 (0-385-14297-8). 45pp. Pascal possesses a magic balloon that leads him on a tour of Paris, and he must defend the balloon from a gang of boys bent on bursting it.

4877 Lanteigne, Helen. *The Seven Chairs* (K–3). Illus. by Maryann Kovalski. 1998, Orchard $14.95 (0-531-30110-9). 32pp. A picture book that traces the history of seven chairs that were carved by a woodworker in England several centuries ago. (Rev: BL 9/1/98; HBG 3/99; SLJ 11/98)

4878 Lawlor, Laurie. *Old Crump: The True Story of a Trip West* (1–3). Illus. by John Winch. 2002, Holiday House $16.95 (0-8234-1608-9). 32pp. The members of a wagon train and their ox, Old Crump, find themselves lost in Death Valley in 1850. (Rev: BL 3/15/02; HBG 10/02; SLJ 6/02)

4879 Lawson, Julie. *Arizona Charlie and the Klondike Kid* (K–3). Illus. by Kasia Charko. 2003, Orca $16.95 (1-55143-250-1). Young Ben, an aspiring Gold Rush entertainer, finds the stage more alarming than he expected but shows his mettle when he encounters a thief. (Rev: HBG 10/03; SLJ 9/03)

4880 Lawson, Julie. *Emma and the Silk Train* (1–5). Illus. by Paul Mombourquette. 1998, Kids Can $15.95 (1-55074-388-0). 32pp. When a train carrying bales of silk is derailed, Emma joins the search for the lost silk, finds a bale, and gets stuck on a small island. Based on the true story of a "silker" derailment in 1927. (Rev: BL 11/1/98; HBG 3/99; SLJ 10/98)

4881 Lawson, Julie. *The Klondike Cat* (1–3). Illus. by Paul Mombourquette. 2002, Kids Can $15.95 (1-55337-013-9). 32pp. Noah doesn't get in trouble for bringing his cat on the journey to the Klondike in 1896 because it turns out that mousers are in great demand. (Rev: BL 11/15/02; HBG 3/03; SLJ 1/03)

4882 Lee, Jeanne M. *Bitter Dumplings* (K–3). Illus. 2002, Farrar $16.00 (0-374-39966-2). 32pp. An orphaned girl, an old woman, and an escaped slave come to depend on one another in 15th-century China. (Rev: BCCB 5/02; BL 5/15/02; HB 5–6/02; HBG 10/02; SLJ 5/02)

4883 Lees, Stewart. *Runaway Jack* (2–4). 2004, Barron's $14.95 (0-7641-5712-4). 32pp. An informative afterword and striking illustrations add depth to this picture-book story of a slave boy's separation from, and eventual reunion with, his family. (Rev: BL 11/15/04)

4884 Leiner, Katherine. *Mama Does the Mambo* (K–3). Illus. by Edel Rodriguez. 2001, Hyperion $15.99 (0-7868-0646-X). 40pp. After Sofia's father dies, Sofia is worried that her mother will never dance again in this story set in Havana, Cuba. (Rev: BCCB 12/01; BL 11/1/01; HB 1–2/02*; HBG 3/02; SLJ 11/01)

4885 Lester, Alison. *Ernie Dances to the Didgeridoo* (PS–2). Illus. 2001, Houghton Mifflin $15.00 (0-618-10442-9). 32pp. Ernie is away in aborigine territory in northern Australia for a year, and sends each of his six friends a letter about each of the six seasons and his various activities. (Rev: BL 5/15/01; HBG 10/01; SLJ 4/01)

4886 Lester, Alison. *My Farm* (K–4). Illus. 1994, Houghton Mifflin $14.95 (0-395-68193-6). 32pp. The author recalls her childhood on an Australian farm — the chores, the cattle, and the joy of receiving a palomino pony at Christmas. (Rev: BCCB 7–8/94; BL 7/94; SLJ 9/94*) [630]

4887 Le Tord, Bijou. *A Bird or Two: A Story About Henri Matisse* (K–3). Illus. 1999, Eerdmans $17.00 (0-8028-5184-3). 32pp. Using Matisse-like paintings, this picture book tells about the artist and the south of France that he loved. (Rev: BL 11/15/99; HBG 3/00; SLJ 2/00)

4888 Levine, Ellen. *The Tree That Would Not Die* (1–4). Illus. by Ted Rand. 1995, Scholastic $14.95 (0-590-43724-0). 32pp. The story of the 400-year-old Treaty Oak in Texas and the important historical events that it witnessed. (Rev: BCCB 10/95; BL 11/1/95*; SLJ 12/95) [813]

4889 Levitin, Sonia. *Boom Town* (PS–3). Illus. by Cat B. Smith. 1998, Orchard LB $17.99 (0-531-33043-5). 40pp. In Gold Rush California, Amanda gets rich making wonderful gooseberry pies. A companion to *Nine for California* (1996). (Rev: BCCB 5/98; BL 2/15/98; HB 3–4/98; HBG 10/98; SLJ 3/98)

4890 Levitin, Sonia. *Taking Charge* (K–3). Illus. by Cat B. Smith. 1999, Orchard LB $17.99 (0-531-33149-0). 32pp. In this story about a California pioneer family, young Amanda must take over caring for baby Nathan after their mother is called away on an emergency. (Rev: BL 4/15/99; HB 3–4/99; HBG 10/99; SLJ 4/99)

4891 Lewin, Hugh. *Jafta* (K–3). Illus. by Lisa Kopper. 1983, Lerner paper $4.95 (0-87614-494-6). 24pp. There are six volumes in this set that are about a black South African child and his father. Others are: *Jafta's Father* (1983); *Jafta's Mother* (1983); *Jafta: The Journey* (1984); *Jafta: The Town* (1984); *Jafta and the Wedding* (1988).

4892 Lewin, Ted. *The Storytellers* (K–3). Illus. 1998, Lothrop $16.00 (0-688-15178-7). 40pp. In the ancient Moroccan city of Fez, Abdul and his grandfather wander through the colorful streets until they find a suitable spot to entertain people with their intriguing stories. (Rev: BL 4/1/98; HBG 10/98; SLJ 4/98)

4893 Lewis, Rose. *I Love You Like Crazy Cakes* (PS–3). Illus. by Jane Dyer. 2000, Little, Brown $14.95 (0-316-52538-3). 32pp. The author, an American, presents a fictional account of her trip to China to adopt a baby girl. (Rev: BL 9/1/00; HBG 10/01; SLJ 10/00)

4894 Lieberman, Syd. *The Wise Shoemaker of Studena* (K–3). Illus. by Martin Lemelman. 1994, Jewish Publication Soc. $15.95 (0-8276-0509-9). 32pp. Samuel learns not to judge people by their appearances when he offends the disreputable-looking wise man Yossi. (Rev: BL 10/15/94)

4895 Lindgren, Astrid. *The Tomten* (PS–2). Illus. by Harald Wiberg. 1997, Penguin Putnam paper $5.99 (0-698-11591-0). 32pp. The friendly troll speaks in Tomten language only animals and children understand. By the same author, illustrator, and publisher: *The Tomten and the Fox* (1989).

4896 Lindsey, Kathleen D. *Sweet Potato Pie* (1–3). Illus. by Charlotte Riley-Webb. 2003, Lee & Low $16.95 (1-58430-061-2). When foreclosure threatens the farm, Sadie, an 8-year-old African American girl, pitches in with the rest of her family to sell sweet potato pies. (Rev: BL 9/15/03; HBG 4/04; SLJ 12/03)

4897 Lipp, Frederick. *The Caged Birds of Phnom Penh* (PS–3). Illus. by Ronald Himler. 2001, Holiday House $16.95 (0-8234-1534-1). 32pp. Ary, an 8-year-old girl living in Cambodia, tests the proverb that says "letting a caged bird go free makes wishes come true." (Rev: BCCB 4/01; BL 4/1/01; HBG 3/02; SLJ 5/01)

4898 Littlesugar, Amy. *Freedom School, Yes!* (PS–3). Illus. by Floyd Cooper. 2001, Penguin Putnam $16.99 (0-399-23006-8). 40pp. Based on fact, this is the story of volunteers who came South during the civil rights struggle in 1964 and set up "freedom schools." (Rev: BCCB 2/01; BL 2/15/01; HBG 10/01; SLJ 1/01)

4899 London, Jonathan. *Ali, Child of the Desert* (K–4). Illus. by Ted Lewin. 1997, Lothrop LB $15.93 (0-688-12561-1). 32pp. Ali and his camel, Jabad, survive in the desert after a terrible dust storm separates them from the rest of their party. (Rev: BCCB 6/97; BL 3/1/97; SLJ 5/97)

4900 London, Jonathan. *Hurricane!* (K–3). Illus. by Henri Sorensen. 1998, Lothrop $16.00 (0-688-12977-3). 32pp. Two boys experience the fierceness of a hurricane when it strikes their Puerto Rico home. (Rev: BL 8/98; HBG 3/99; SLJ 1/99)

4901 London, Jonathan. *What the Animals Were Waiting For* (K–3). Illus. by Paul Morin. 2002, Scholastic $16.95 (0-439-33630-9). 32pp. An African boy watches animals wait for rain during the dry "Months of Hunger." (Rev: BCCB 6/02; BL 5/15/02; HBG 10/02; SLJ 5/02)

4902 Lyon, George E. *Dreamplace* (K–4). Illus. by Peter Catalanotto. 1993, Orchard $15.95 (0-531-05466-7); paper $6.95 (0-531-07101-4). 32pp. A poetic text about a girl who sees the 800-year-old site of the Anasazi and dreams of when the tribe lived there long ago. (Rev: BCCB 3/93; BL 3/15/93*; HB 3–4/93; SLJ 3/93*)

4903 McBrier, Page. *Beatrice's Goat* (K–3). Illus. by Lori Lohstoeter. 2001, Simon & Schuster $16.00 (0-689-82460-2). 40pp. Beatrice longs to attend school in her Ugandan village, and when her family gets a goat from an aid organization, it provides enough income to send her there. (Rev: BCCB 2/01; BL 2/15/01; HBG 10/01; SLJ 2/01)

4904 McCully, Emily Arnold. *Beautiful Warrior: The Legend of the Nun's Kung Fu* (K–4). Illus. 1998, Scholastic $16.95 (0-590-37487-7). 40pp. In this beautiful picture book, two women learn kung fu and use it in different ways in 17th-century China. (Rev: BCCB 3/98; BL 2/1/98; SLJ 2/98*)

4905 McCully, Emily Arnold. *Mirette and Bellini Cross Niagara Falls* (PS–3). Illus. 2000, Penguin Putnam $15.99 (0-399-23348-2). 32pp. A thrilling adventure story in which young Mirette and her guardian, the high-wire-artist, Bellini, come to the States for the ultimate stunt, crossing Niagara Falls on a wire. (Rev: BCCB 1/01; BL 11/15/00; HBG 10/01; SLJ 11/00)

4906 McCully, Emily Arnold. *Mirette on the High Wire* (PS–2). Illus. 1992, Penguin Putnam $16.99 (0-399-22130-1). 32pp. Set in Paris 100 years ago, this is the story of how a young girl helps a high-wire performer regain his courage. Caldecott Medal winner, 1993. (Rev: BCCB 10/92*; BL 11/15/92; SLJ 10/92)

4907 MacDonald, Suse. *Nanta's Lion: A Search and Find Adventure* (PS–1). Illus. 1995, Morrow $15.00 (0-688-13125-5). 24pp. An interactive book about an African girl who sets out to find the lion that has been stealing cattle from her village. (Rev: BL 4/15/95; SLJ 5/95)

4908 MacKall, Dandi Daley. *Silent Dreams* (K–4). Illus. by Karen A. Jerome. 2003, Eerdmans $16.00 (0-8028-5200-9). In the early 1900s, a trip to the silent movies is a great experience for young Camilla, who lives in a cardboard box with her homeless aunt. (Rev: HBG 10/03; SLJ 4/03)

4909 McKay, Lawrence, Jr. *Caravan* (1–4). Illus. by Darryl Ligasan. 1995, Lee & Low $14.95 (1-880000-23-7). A boy tells about going on his first caravan through the mountains in Afghanistan to trade his family's furs for grain. (Rev: SLJ 12/95)

4910 McKissack, Patricia. *Goin' Someplace Special* (K–3). Illus. by Jerry Pinkney. 2001, Simon & Schuster $16.00 (0-689-81885-8). 40pp. Young Tricia Ann sets off on her first journey by herself and must navigate the South of the 1950s, working out where an African American is allowed to go. (Rev: BCCB 9/01; BL 8/01; HB 11–12/01; HBG 3/02; SLJ 9/01)

4911 McKissack, Patricia. *Ma Dear's Aprons* (PS–3). Illus. by Floyd Cooper. 1997, Simon & Schuster $16.00 (0-689-81051-2). 32pp. During the early 1900s in Alabama, Ma Dear must support her family by doing domestic work. (Rev: BCCB 6/97; BL 2/15/97; HBG 5–6/97; SLJ 6/97)

4912 MacLachlan, Patricia. *Three Names* (K–3). Illus. by Alexander Pertzoff. 1991, HarperCollins LB $16.89 (0-06-024036-9). 32pp. A boy repeats the stories that his great-grandfather told him of growing up in pioneer days. (Rev: BCCB 1/92; BL 8/91; HB 9–10/91; SLJ 7/91)

4913 Madrigal, Antonio H. *Erandi's Braids* (PS–3). Illus. by Tomie dePaola. 1999, Penguin Putnam $15.99 (0-399-23212-5). 32pp. Erandi, a young member of a poor 1950s Mexican family, reluctantly decides to sell her beautiful hair to help her family. (Rev: BL 1/1–15/99*; HBG 10/99; SLJ 2/99)

4914 Mannis, Celeste Davidson. *The Queen's Progress: An Elizabethan Alphabet* (2–4). Illus. by Bagram Ibatoulline. 2003, Viking $16.99 (0-670-03612-9). 48pp. Lavishly illustrated, this stunning picture book tracks the "royal progress" of Queen Elizabeth I and her entourage as they make their annual journey across the English countryside; the book is organized alphabetically with relevant facts and trivia supplied for each letter, as in "A for Adventure" and "T for Treason." (Rev: BL 4/1/03; HBG 10/03; SLJ 5/03) [942.05]

4915 Manson, Ainslie. *A Dog Came, Too: A True Story* (1–3). Illus. by Ann Blades. 1993, Macmillan $13.95 (0-689-50567-1). 32pp. In a fictionalized format, this is the story of the dog that accompanied explorer Alexander Mackenzie across Canada to the Pacific Ocean. (Rev: BCCB 3/93; BL 5/1/93; SLJ 2/04) [917.1]

4916 Manson, Ainslie. *Just Like New* (1–4). Illus. by Karen Reczuch. 1996, Douglas & McIntyre $14.95 (0-88899-228-9). 32pp. During World War II, a Canadian girl sends her favorite doll to a deprived English youngster at Christmas. (Rev: BCCB 1/97; BL 11/15/96; SLJ 12/96)

4917 Medearis, Angela Shelf. *Rum-a-Tum-Tum* (PS–3). Illus. by James E. Ransome. 1997, Holiday House LB $16.95 (0-8234-1143-5). 32pp. All the color, excitement, and sound of a market in the French Quarter of New Orleans at the turn of the century are captured in this picture book. (Rev: BCCB 7–8/97; BL 5/1/97; SLJ 7/97)

4918 Meisel, Paul. *Zara's Hats* (PS–2). Illus. 2003, Dutton $15.99 (0-525-45465-9). 32pp. When Zara's hat-making father must travel abroad in search of feathers, Zara sells beautiful hats of her own making in this story set in turn-of-the-20th-century New York. (Rev: BL 2/15/03; HBG 10/03; SLJ 2/03)

4919 Melmed, Laura K. *Little Oh* (K–4). Illus. by Jim LaMarche. 1997, Lothrop LB $15.93 (0-688-14209-5). 32pp. In this story set in Japan, a potter makes an origami girl come to life. (Rev: BL 9/1/97; HB 9–10/97; HBG 3/98; SLJ 11/97*)

4920 Millen, C. M. *A Symphony for the Sheep* (K–3). Illus. by Mary Azarian. 1996, Houghton Mifflin $14.95 (0-395-76503-X). 32pp. The old-fashioned way of making woolen clothes is shown in this rhyme set in the Irish countryside. (Rev: BCCB 12/96; BL 8/96; SLJ 1/97)

4921 Miller, William. *The Bus Ride* (PS–1). Illus. by John Ward. 1998, Lee & Low $15.95 (1-880000-60-1). 32pp. Set in the segregated South during the 1950s, this picture book tells of the consequences faced by a young girl when she dares to sit in the front of a bus. (Rev: BL 8/98; HBG 3/99; SLJ 10/98)

4922 Miller, William. *The Piano* (K–3). Illus. by Susan Keeter. 2000, Lee & Low $15.95 (1-880000-98-9). 32pp. In the segregated South in the early 1900s, music-loving Tia is taught to play the piano by the elderly woman for whom she cleans house. (Rev: BCCB 10/00; BL 7/00; HBG 10/00; SLJ 7/00)

4923 Miller, William. *Rent Party Jazz* (1–4). Illus. by Charlotte Riley-Webb. 2001, Lee & Low $16.95 (1-58430-025-6). 32pp. A young African American boy named Sonny and an old jazz musician named Smilin' Jack throw a rent party to help Sonny's mother in 1930s New Orleans. (Rev: BL 11/15/01; HBG 3/02; SLJ 11/01)

4924 Miller, William. *Richard Wright and the Library Card* (K–4). Illus. by Gregory Christie. 1997, Lee & Low $15.95 (1-880000-57-1). 32pp. In this story based on fact, African American Richard Wright, growing up in the segregated South, borrows books from the all-white library by pretending he is taking them to his white boss. (Rev: BCCB 3/98; BL 12/1/97; HBG 3/98; SLJ 2/98)

4925 Mollel, Tololwa M. *My Rows and Piles of Coins* (PS–3). Illus. by E. B. Lewis. 1999, Clarion $15.00 (0-395-75186-1). 32pp. Saruni, a Tanzanian boy, scrimps and saves to buy a bicycle, so he can help his mother with her chores. (Rev: BCCB 10/99; BL 8/99; HBG 3/00; SLJ 8/99)

4926 Montes, Marisa. *Juan Bobo Goes to Work* (PS–3). Illus. by Joe Cepeda. 2000, HarperCollins LB $15.89 (0-688-16234-7). 32pp. A charming story — set in Puerto Rico and using many Spanish words and phrases — about Juan Bobo who makes a rich girl laugh and is rewarded with a ham every Sunday. (Rev: BL 2/1/01; HBG 3/01; SLJ 10/00)

4927 Morrow, Barbara Olenyik. *A Good Night for Freedom* (K–4). Illus. by Leonard Jenkins. 2004, Holiday House $16.95 (0-8234-1709-3). 32pp. In 1839, young Hallie helps two runaway slave girls despite her father's warnings not to do so. (Rev: BL 3/1/04; SLJ 2/04)

4928 Myers, Tim. *Basho and the Fox* (K–3). Illus. by Oki S. Han. 2000, Marshall Cavendish $15.95 (0-7614-5068-8). 32pp. Basho, Japan's famous haiku poet, meets a fox who promises not to eat the poet's cherries if he can produce a poem that the fox thinks is worthy. (Rev: BL 9/15/00; HB 9–10/00; HBG 3/01; SLJ 10/00)

4929 Namioka, Lensey. *The Laziest Boy in the World* (K–3). Illus. by YongSheng Xuan. 1998, Holiday House $16.95 (0-8234-1330-6). 32pp. A humorous story about a Chinese boy who is so lazy he washes alternate sides of his face each day, and the thief who makes him change his ways. (Rev: BL 11/1/98; HBG 3/99; SLJ 10/98)

4930 Nelson, S. D. *The Star People: A Lakota Story* (PS–2). Illus. by author. 2003, Abrams $14.95 (0-8109-4584-3). When two Lakota siblings, Sister Girl and Young Wolf, wander far from home and encounter a multitude of dangers, they are guided to safety by the Star People, the spirits of the Old Ones. (Rev: HBG 4/04; SLJ 9/03)

4931 Nelson, Vaunda Micheaux. *Almost to Freedom* (1–3). Illus. by Colin Bootman. Series: Carolrhoda Picture Books Ser. 2003, Carolrhoda $15.95 (1-57505-342-X). 40pp. This moving story, narrated by the rag doll of a slave child, describes how the child, Lindy, and her family escape to freedom on the Underground Railroad. (Rev: BL 9/15/03; HBG 4/04; SLJ 12/03)

4932 Nobisso, Josephine. *The Weight of a Mass: A Tale of Faith* (K–3). Illus. by Katalin Szegedi. 2002, Gingerbread House $17.95 (0-940112-09-4); paper $9.95 (0-940112-10-8). In a land where most people have abandoned their faith, an old woman reveals the power of the Mass. (Rev: HBG 3/03; SLJ 1/03)

4933 Noguchi, Rick, and Deneen Jenks. *Flowers from Mariko* (K–3). Illus. by Michelle Reiko Kumata. 2001, Lee & Low $16.95 (1-58430-032-9). 32pp. When Mariko's Japanese American family is released from an internment camp after World War II, they must work to rebuild the life they lost. (Rev: BL 11/1/01; HBG 3/02; SLJ 11/01)

4934 Noyes, Deborah. *Hana in the Time of the Tulips* (K–3). Illus. by Bagram Ibatoulline. 2004, Candlewick $16.99 (0-7636-1875-6). 40pp. When her father is swept up in the tulip mania gripping 17th-century Holland, young Hana seeks to regain

his attention; the illustrations evoke paintings by Rembrandt. (Rev: BL 11/1/04; SLJ 10/04)

4935 Olaleye, Isaac. *Bikes for Rent!* (PS–3). Illus. by Chris L. Demarest. 2001, Scholastic $16.95 (0-531-30290-3). 32pp. A hard-working Nigerian boy who loves bicycles must prove that he is responsible enough to take care of a new one. (Rev: BCCB 6/01; BL 8/01; HBG 10/01; SLJ 7/01)

4936 Olaleye, Isaac. *Lake of the Big Snake: An African Rain Forest Adventure* (K–3). Illus. by Claudia Shepard. 1998, Boyds Mills $15.95 (1-56397-096-1). In this story set in an African rain forest, two boys disobey their mothers, wander away from home, and encounter a giant snake. (Rev: BL 10/15/98; HBG 3/99; SLJ 11/98)

4937 Olofsson, Helena. *The Little Jester* (K–3). Illus. 2002, R&S $16.00 (91-29-65499-8). 28pp. French monks reluctantly open the doors of the monastery to a jester, who then performs a miracle. (Rev: BL 3/15/02; HBG 10/02; SLJ 5/02)

4938 Oppenheim, Shulamith Levey. *Ali and the Magic Stew* (PS–3). Illus. by Winslow Pels. 2002, Boyds Mills $15.95 (1-56397-869-5). 32pp. In this Persian tale, a proud, spoiled merchant's son learns humility when he must beg for coins to save his father's life. (Rev: BCCB 5/02; BL 4/15/02; HBG 10/02; SLJ 4/02)

4939 Oppenheim, Shulamith Levey. *Yanni Rubbish* (K–3). Illus. by Doug Chayka. 1999, Boyds Mills $15.95 (1-56397-668-4). 28pp. Yanni, a young Greek trash collector, is embarrassed when his friends make fun of him and his dusty wagon, until he and his mother paint and decorate his cart so it becomes the pride of the town. (Rev: BL 3/1/99; HBG 10/99; SLJ 8/99)

4940 Orr, Katherine. *My Grandpa and the Sea* (K–3). Illus. 1990, Carolrhoda LB $19.95 (0-87614-409-1). 32pp. When Grandpa loses his fishing business to modern-day fishermen, he finds a new way of earning a living. (Rev: BCCB 11/90; BL 10/1/90)

4941 Osborne, Mary Pope. *New York's Bravest* (K–3). Illus. by Steve Johnson and Lou Fancher. 2002, Knopf LB $17.99 (0-375-92196-6). 32pp. A dramatically illustrated tribute to Mose Humphreys, a brave New York fire fighter who died while saving lives in the 1840s. (Rev: BCCB 9/02; BL 7/02; HB 11–12/02; HBG 3/03; SLJ 9/02*)

4942 Pace, Lorenzo. *Jalani and the Lock* (PS–K). Illus. 2001, Rosen $15.95 (0-8239-9700-6). 32pp. A young African boy named Jalani, who spends years as a slave, passes the lock from his chains on to his grandchildren. (Rev: BL 2/15/01)

4943 Pacilio, V. J. *Ling Cho and His Three Friends* (1–3). Illus. by Scott Cook. 2000, Farrar $16.00 (0-374-34545-7). 32pp. A clever picture book about a prosperous Chinese farmer who wants to share his wealth with his neighbors without injuring their pride. (Rev: BL 3/1/00; HBG 10/00; SLJ 5/00)

4944 Pak, Soyung. *A Place to Grow* (K–2). Illus. by Marcelino Truong. 2002, Scholastic $16.95 (0-439-13015-8). 32pp. An Asian immigrant explains through metaphor his journey from a war-torn homeland to a safe place as he and his daughter plant seeds together in the garden. (Rev: BL 10/15/02; HB 1–2/03; HBG 3/03; SLJ 11/02)

4945 Panahi, H. L. *Bebop Express* (K–2). Illus. by Steve Johnson. 2005, HarperCollins LB $16.89 (0-06-057191-8). 32pp. Rhythm and atmosphere make this a jazzy train trip from New York to New Orleans. (Rev: BL 6/1–15/05)

4946 Park, Frances, and Ginger Park. *Good-Bye, 382 Shin Dang Dong* (1–3). Illus. by Yangsook Choi. 2002, National Geographic $16.95 (0-7922-7985-9). Jangmi is sad to leave Korea and her friends and move to Massachusetts. (Rev: HBG 3/03; SLJ 10/02)

4947 Park, Frances, and Ginger Park. *The Royal Bee* (K–3). Illus. by Christopher Zhong-Yuan Zhang. 2000, Boyds Mills $15.95 (1-56397-614-5). A simple tale about a poor Korean boy growing up in the the late 19th century and his efforts to get an education so he can lift himself and his mother out of poverty. (Rev: HBG 10/00; SLJ 4/00)

4948 Park, Frances, and Ginger Park. *Where on Earth Is My Bagel?* (K–3). Illus. by Grace Lin. 2001, Lee & Low $16.00 (1-58430-033-7). A Korean boy hungry for a bagel sends a message to New York by pigeon but only receives a recipe in return, which his local baker is happy to make in this book full of bagel shapes. (Rev: HBG 3/02; SLJ 9/01)

4949 Park, Linda Sue. *The Firekeeper's Son* (K–3). Illus. by Julie Downing. 2004, Clarion $16.00 (0-618-13337-2). 40pp. In the early 19th-century Korea, a young boy must take his father's place and light the bonfire that is part of the signal system; beautiful watercolor illustrations complement the picture-book story. (Rev: BL 2/1/04; SLJ 5/04)

4950 Partridge, Elizabeth. *Oranges on Golden Mountain* (K–3). Illus. by Aki Sogabe. 2001, Dutton $16.99 (0-525-46453-0). 40pp. Jo Lee is sent to live with an uncle who is a fisherman on the California coast and there the little boy often dreams of China and his mother. (Rev: BCCB 2/01; BL 1/1–15/01; HBG 3/02; SLJ 3/01)

4951 Patz, Nancy. *Who Was the Woman Who Wore the Hat?* (3–6). Illus. 2003, Dutton $14.99 (0-525-46999-0). 48pp. The hat, part of the exhibit in the Jewish Historical Museum in Amsterdam, inspires the author to reflect on what the woman who wore it was like. (Rev: BL 2/15/03; HBG 10/03; SLJ 3/03)

4952 Pilegard, Virginia Walton. *The Warlord's Beads* (K–3). Illus. by Nicolas Debon. 2001, Pelican $14.95 (1-56554-863-9). 32pp. In this story set in China, a boy invents a primitive abacus to help his father keep track of the warlord's riches. (Rev: BL 2/1/02; HBG 3/02; SLJ 2/02)

4953 Pilegard, Virginia Walton. *The Warlord's Fish* (PS–2). Illus. by Nicolas Debon. 2002, Pelican $14.95 (1-56554-964-3). 32pp. A tale set in ancient China that explores the history of the compass. (Rev: BL 2/1/03; HBG 3/03; SLJ 2/03)

4954 Pilegard, Virginia Walton. *The Warlord's Puzzle* (K–3). Illus. by Nicolas Debon. 2000, Pelican $14.95 (1-56554-495-1). 32pp. A handsome tile given to a Chinese warlord is broken into various geometric shapes and only a simple peasant can

solve the puzzle and put it together again. (Rev: BL 4/1/00; HBG 10/00; SLJ 6/00)

4955 Polacco, Patricia. *Babushka Baba Yaga* (PS–3). Illus. 1993, Penguin Putnam $15.95 (0-399-22531-5). In this reversal of the traditional Russian folklore, the witch Baba Yaga is really a kindly grandmother named Babushka. (Rev: BL 8/93)

4956 Polacco, Patricia. *The Butterfly* (K–4). Illus. 2000, Penguin Putnam $16.99 (0-399-23170-6). 32pp. Based on a true story, this picture book tells of a little girl growing up in France during World War II who becomes aware that her family is hiding a Jewish family in the cellar. (Rev: BCCB 6/00; BL 4/1/00; HBG 10/00; SLJ 5/00)

4957 Porte, Barbara Ann. *Ma Jiang and the Orange Ants* (K–3). Illus. by Annie Cannon. 2000, Orchard LB $17.99 (0-531-33241-1). 32pp. Ma Jiang devises an unusual way to catch carnivorous "orange" ants to sell to fruit growers for pest control. (Rev: BL 10/15/00; HBG 3/01; SLJ 12/00)

4958 Pryor, Bonnie. *The House on Maple Street* (PS–1). Illus. by Beth Peck. 1987, Morrow paper $5.95 (0-688-12031-8). 32pp. Chris and Jenny find a small china cup and begin a kind of history exploration from the house on Maple Street. (Rev: BL 4/1/87; SLJ 5/87)

4959 Pushker, Gloria Teles. *Toby Belfer Visits Ellis Island* (PS–1). Illus. by Judith Hierstein. Series: Toby Belfer. 2003, Pelican $14.95 (1-58980-117-2). 32pp. Toby learns about her Jewish heritage from her great-grandmother, and then visits the museum on Ellis Island. (Rev: BL 1/1–15/04; HBG 4/04)

4960 Rabin, Staton. *Casey Over There* (K–3). Illus. by Greg Shed. 1994, Harcourt $14.95 (0-15-253186-6). 32pp. In this picture book, Aubrey's brother is fighting in the trenches, while he is growing up in Brooklyn during World War I. (Rev: BL 3/15/94; SLJ 5/94)

4961 Radunsky, Vladimir. *Manneken Pis: A Simple Story of a Boy Who Peed on a War* (K–2). Illus. 2002, Simon & Schuster $15.95 (0-689-83193-5). 32pp. The statue of Menneken Pis in Brussels is the inspiration for this tale of a frightened little boy who stops a war by relieving himself on the combatants. (Rev: BL 10/15/02; HB 9–10/02; HBG 3/03; SLJ 12/02) [398.249]

4962 Ransom, Candice. *Liberty Street* (PS–3). Illus. by Eric Velasquez. 2003, Walker LB $17.85 (0-8027-8871-8). Despite the loss this will cause her, Kezia's mother encourages the young slave to learn to read and arranges for her to escape to freedom. (Rev: BCCB 3/04; BL 11/1/03; HBG 4/04; SLJ 12/03)

4963 Ransom, Candice. *The Promise Quilt* (K–3). Illus. by Ellen Beier. 1999, Walker LB $16.85 (0-8027-8695-2). 32pp. In this picture book set in the South during the Civil War, Addie loses her father when he joins General Lee and his fight for "the cause." (Rev: BL 11/1/99; HBG 3/00; SLJ 11/99)

4964 Ransom, Candice F. *Rescue on the Outer Banks* (1–3). Illus. by Karen Ritz. 2002, Carolrhoda LB $21.27 (0-87614-460-1); paper $6.95 (0-87614-815-1). 48pp. A 10-year-old boy narrates the true story of an 1896 sea rescue by an African American lifeboat crew, a feat that was officially recognized 100 years later. (Rev: HBG 10/02; SLJ 4/02)

4965 Rappaport, Doreen, and Lyndall Callan. *Dirt on Their Skirts: The Story of the Young Women Who Won the World Championship* (PS–3). Illus. by E. B. Lewis. 2000, Dial $16.99 (0-8037-2042-4). 40pp. A fictionalized account of the 1946 championship game of the All-American Girls Professional Baseball League. (Rev: BCCB 2/00; BL 1/1–15/00; HBG 10/00; SLJ 3/00)

4966 Ray, Mary L. *Basket Moon* (K–3). Illus. by Barbara Cooney. 1999, Little, Brown $15.95 (0-316-73521-3). 32pp. A 19th-century boy is embarrassed when townspeople call him and his father, a basket weaver, "hillbillies," but gradually he is able to reaffirm the love he feels for his dad. (Rev: BCCB 9/99; BL 6/1–15/99; HB 11–12/99; HBG 3/00; SLJ 9/99)

4967 Reddix, Valerie. *Dragon Kite of the Autumn Moon* (K–3). Illus. by Jean Tseng. 1992, Lothrop LB $13.93 (0-688-11031-2). 32pp. When Grandfather becomes sick, Tad-Tin must fly his kite alone in this tale set in Formosa. (Rev: BL 5/15/92; SLJ 8/92)

4968 Reiser, Lynn. *Tortillas and Lullabies: Tortillas y cancioncitas* (PS–3). Illus. by Corazones Valientes. 1998, Greenwillow $16.00 (0-688-14628-7). 40pp. Three generations of Latin American women are depicted in this bilingual story of how love and gifts have been exchanged in a family through the years. (Rev: BL 4/1/98; HB 5–6/98; SLJ 4/98)

4969 Reynolds, Marilynn. *The Name of the Child* (1–3). Illus. by Don Kilby. 2002, Orca $16.95 (1-55143-221-8). 32pp. Nervous young Lloyd is sent to the country during the 1918 flu epidemic for his safety, but ends up having to take charge in the midst of a storm. (Rev: BL 1/1–15/03; HBG 3/03; SLJ 1/03)

4970 Richardson, Jean. *The Courage Seed* (2–3). Illus. by Pat Finney. 1993, Eakin $14.95 (0-89015-902-5). 71pp. When her parents are killed, a young Navajo girl is fearful that she will lose her tribal ways when she goes to live with an aunt in Houston. (Rev: SLJ 2/94)

4971 Ringgold, Faith. *Cassie's Word Quilt* (K–3). Illus. 2002, Knopf $13.95 (0-375-81200-8). 32pp. This simple wordbook uses a quilt pattern of pictures to introduce the daily life of Cassie, a little girl living in New York City in 1939. (Rev: BL 3/1/02; HBG 10/02; SLJ 2/02)

4972 Roop, Peter, and Connie Roop. *Buttons for General Washington* (2–3). Illus. by Peter E. Hanson. 1986, Carolrhoda LB $21.27 (0-87614-294-3); paper $5.95 (0-87614-476-8). 48pp. Based on incidents from the life of John Darragh, this is the story of a 14-year-old boy who carries secret messages to George Washington hidden in his coat buttons during the Revolution. (Rev: BCCB 12/86; BL 12/1/86)

4973 Ryan, Pam M. *Amelia and Eleanor Go for a Ride: Based on a True Story* (2–4). Illus. by Brian Selznick. 1999, Scholastic $16.95 (0-590-96075-X). 40pp. An interesting, if exaggerated, variation on the story of Amelia Earhart and Eleanor Roosevelt's shared plane ride. (Rev: BL 10/15/99; HBG 3/00; SLJ 9/99)

4974 Saltzman, David. *The Jester Has Lost His Jingle* (1–3). Illus. 1995, Jester $20.00 (0-9644563-0-3). 64pp. A jester who is out of work because he isn't funny sets out to discover laughter in the world. (Rev: BL 10/15/95; SLJ 10/95)

4975 Sandin, Joan. *The Long Way to a New Land* (1–3). Illus. by author. 1981, HarperCollins paper $3.95 (0-06-444100-8). 64pp. An easy-to-read account of a Swedish family's journey to New York in the late 1860s.

4976 Say, Allen. *The Bicycle Man* (K–3). Illus. by author. 1982, Houghton Mifflin $11.95 (0-685-05704-6); paper $5.95 (0-395-50652-2). 48pp. Two American soldiers in Japan put on a show for a school.

4977 Schick, Eleanor. *Navajo Wedding Day: A Dine Marriage Ceremony* (1–3). Illus. 1999, Marshall Cavendish $15.95 (0-7614-5031-9). 40pp. A realistic picture book that describes a marriage ceremony in Navajo country. (Rev: BL 4/15/99; HBG 10/99; SLJ 4/99)

4978 Scott, Ann H. *On Mother's Lap* (PS–K). Illus. by Glo Coalson. 1992, Houghton Mifflin $15.00 (0-395-58920-7); paper $6.95 (0-395-62976-4). 32pp. A warm, tender story of an Eskimo family and of a young boy's realization that there is enough room on mother's lap for both him and his sister.

4979 Seabrooke, Brenda. *The Boy Who Saved the Town* (2–4). Illus. by Howard M. Burns. 1990, Tidewater $7.95 (0-87033-405-0). 28pp. This legend tells how the town of St. Michaels escaped bombardment by the British in the War of 1812. (Rev: BL 9/1/90; HBG 4/04; SLJ 2/04)

4980 Shank, Ned. *The Sanyasin's First Day* (K–3). Illus. by Catherine Stock. 1999, Marshall Cavendish $15.95 (0-7614-5055-6). 32pp. The lives of several people intersect in this story set in modern India about a holy man who begs on the streets and is given alms by a child. (Rev: BL 10/1/99; HBG 3/00; SLJ 11/99)

4981 Siebert, Diane. *Rhyolite: The True Story of a Ghost Town* (2–4). Illus. by David Frampton. 2003, Clarion $16.00 (0-618-09673-6). 32pp. Woodcut illustrations and simple narrative verse chronicle the brief history of Rhyolite, Nevada, a gold-mining town that enjoyed a brief heyday in the early 1900s. (Rev: BL 4/15/03; HB 7–8/03; HBG 10/03; SLJ 5/03) [811]

4982 Siemiatycki, Jack, and Avi Slodovnick. *The Hockey Card* (1–3). Illus. by Doris Barrette. 2002, Lobster $16.95 (1-894222-65-2). 32pp. Uncle Jack tells his nephew about an exciting game during recess many years ago in which he bet everything on his treasured Maurice "The Rocket" Richard card. (Rev: BL 1/1–15/03)

4983 Silvano, Wendi. *Just One More* (K–3). Illus. by Ricardo Gamboa. 2002, All About Kids $16.95 (0-9700863-7-7). Young Hector protests every time another body is added to the overcrowded bus in this story set in the Andes. (Rev: HBG 3/03; SLJ 9/02)

4984 Simon, Norma. *All Kinds of Children* (PS–K). Illus. by Diane Paterson. 1999, Whitman $15.95 (0-8075-0281-2). 32pp. This book emphasizes how children around the world have different lifestyles and homes but similar needs. (Rev: BL 3/15/99; HBG 10/99; SLJ 6/99) [305.23]

4985 Slate, Joseph. *The Great Big Wagon That Rang: How the Liberty Bell Was Saved* (PS–2). Illus. by Craig Spearing. 2002, Marshall Cavendish $16.95 (0-7614-5108-0). 32pp. The story of a farmer's role in saving the Liberty Bell from the British. (Rev: BL 11/1/02; HBG 3/03; SLJ 11/02)

4986 Smalls, Irene. *Don't Say Ain't* (1–3). Illus. by Colin Bootman. 2003, Charlesbridge $15.95 (1-57091-381-1). 32pp. A gifted African American student attending an integrated school in 1957 learns to "speak proper" when appropriate. (Rev: BL 2/15/03; HBG 10/03; SLJ 3/03)

4987 Sorel, Edward, and Cheryl Carlesimo. *The Saturday Kid* (K–3). Illus. 2000, Simon & Schuster $18.00 (0-689-82399-1). 32pp. Set in New York City in a different era, this picture book tells how Leo gets the best of the bully Morty when he plays the violin and meets the mayor, two events that Morty and his parents are surprised to see in a newsreel at the local movie theater. (Rev: BL 12/15/00; HBG 3/01; SLJ 9/00)

4988 Spinelli, Eileen. *Summerbath Winterbath* (K–3). Illus. by Elsa Warnick. 2001, Eerdmans $16.00 (0-8028-5179-7). 32pp. Althea enjoys both summer and winter baths, which are very different in this early-1900s setting. (Rev: BL 5/15/01; HBG 10/01; SLJ 7/01)

4989 Stanley, Diane. *Joining the Boston Tea Party* (2–4). Illus. by Holly Berry. 2001, HarperCollins LB $15.89 (0-06-027068-3). 48pp. Twins Liz and Lenny travel back in time to take part in the Boston Tea Party in this picture book that also contains nonfiction historical material. (Rev: BL 9/15/01; HB 11–12/01; HBG 3/02; SLJ 8/01)

4990 Stanley, Sanna. *Monkey for Sale* (PS–K). Illus. 2002, Farrar $17.00 (0-374-35017-5). 32pp. Lively illustrations bring to life the story of two girls in the Congo who decide to buy a captured monkey and set it free in the jungle. (Rev: BCCB 2/03; BL 12/1/02; HBG 3/03; SLJ 12/02)

4991 Stark, Ken. *Oh, Brother!* (1–3). Illus. 2003, Penguin Putnam $15.99 (0-399-23766-6). 32pp. The author fondly recalls his childhood in Illinois through text and pictures. (Rev: BL 2/1/03; HBG 10/03; SLJ 4/03)

4992 Steig, William. *When Everybody Wore a Hat* (K–3). Illus. 2003, HarperCollins LB $18.89 (0-06-009701-9). 40pp. Steig looks back at the Bronx of 1916 — the year he was 8 years old. (Rev: BL 5/1/03; HB 5–6/03; HBG 10/03; SLJ 5/03) [813.5]

4993 Stevens, Jan R. *Carlos and the Cornfield / Carlos y la Milpa de Maiz* (K–3). Illus. by Jeanne Arnold. 1995, Northland LB $14.95 (0-87358-596-8). 32pp. Carlos learns some truths about gardening when he plants corn to earn enough money to buy a pocketknife. (Rev: BL 9/1/95; SLJ 9/95)

4994 Stewart, Sarah. *The Gardener* (K–3). Illus. by David Small. 1997, Farrar $16.00 (0-374-32517-0). 40pp. During the Depression, a little girl is sent off to live with a cold, somber uncle, but gradually she wins him over. (Rev: BL 6/1–15/97; HB 11–12/97; HBG 3/98; SLJ 8/97*)

4995 Stewig, John W. *Making Plum Jam* (K–2). Illus. by Kevin O'Malley. 2002, Hyperion $15.99 (0-7868-0460-2). 32pp. A boy visiting his three eccentric aunts regrets the fact that they poach plums from a neighboring farm to make jam. (Rev: BCCB 7–8/02; BL 8/02; HBG 10/02; SLJ 6/02)

4996 Stock, Catherine. *Gugu's House* (1–3). Illus. 2001, Clarion $14.00 (0-618-00389-4). 32pp. Set in Zimbabwe, this is the story of a loving grandmother whose talents include creating paintings and sculptures, as well as telling stories to granddaughter Kukamba. (Rev: BL 2/15/01*; HBG 10/01)

4997 Stowell, Penelope. *The Greatest Potatoes* (1–3). Illus. by Sharon Watts. 2005, Hyperion $15.99 (0-7868-5113-9). 40pp. Based on real events, this is the amazing story of Cornelius Vanderbilt, George Crum (a cook in Saratoga, New York), and the invention of the potato chip. (Rev: BL 6/1–15/05)

4998 Stroud, Bettye. *The Leaving* (K–3). Illus. by Cedric Lucas. 2001, Marshall Cavendish $15.95 (0-7614-5067-X). 32pp. Five years after emancipation, a young girl helps her parents escape from bondage. (Rev: BL 2/15/01; HBG 10/01)

4999 Stroud, Bettye. *The Patchwork Path: A Quilt Map to Freedom* (K–3). Illus. by Erin Susanne Bennett. 2005, Candlewick $15.99 (0-7636-2423-3). 32pp. On her way with her father to Canada and freedom, 10-year-old slave Hannah thinks of the quilt her mother used to teach her the necessary code. (Rev: BL 2/1/05; SLJ 1/05)

5000 Stuve-Bodeen, Stephanie. *Babu's Song* (PS–2). Illus. by Aaron Boyd. 2003, Lee & Low $16.95 (1-58430-058-2). Set in Tanzania, this heart-warming story tells of the close relationship between Babu and his mute grandfather and the choices they must make about possessions and expenditures. (Rev: BL 6/1–15/03; HBG 10/03; SLJ 12/03)

5001 Stuve-Bodeen, Stephanie. *Elizabeti's Doll* (PS–1). Illus. by Christy Hale. 1998, Lee & Low $15.95 (1-880000-70-9). 32pp. In Tanzania, Elizabeti lacks a doll to copy her mother's activities with her new baby, so the little girl uses a rock instead. (Rev: BL 10/1/98; HB 11–12/98; HBG 3/99; SLJ 9/98)

5002 Stuve-Bodeen, Stephanie. *Mama Elizabeti* (1–3). Illus. by Christy Hale. 2000, Lee & Low $15.95 (1-58430-002-7). 32pp. Set in contemporary Tanzania, this story involves Elizabeti and her problems caring for her toddler brother. (Rev: BCCB 9/00; BL 8/00; HB 7–8/00; HBG 10/00; SLJ 7/00)

5003 Sweeney, Joan. *Bijou, Bonbon and Beau: The Kittens Who Danced for Degas* (K–3). Illus. by Leslie Wu. 1998, Chronicle $12.95 (0-8118-1975-2). Three kittens are saved by artist Edgar Degas when the stage manager threatens to throw them out of the theater that they have called home. (Rev: BCCB 7–8/98; BL 7/98; HBG 10/98; SLJ 6/98)

5004 Sweeney, Joan. *Suzette and the Puppy: A Story About Mary Cassatt* (PS–3). Illus. by Jennifer Heyd Wharton. 2000, Barron's $12.95 (0-7641-5294-7). A fictionalized story of a little French girl and how Mary Cassatt came to paint her as the "Little Girl in a Blue Armchair." (Rev: SLJ 1/01)

5005 Tarbescu, Edith. *Annushka's Voyage* (PS–3). Illus. by Lydia Dabcovich. 1998, Clarion $15.00 (0-395-64366-X). 32pp. A picture book that depicts the experiences of two young Jewish girls, Anya and her young sister, Tanya, when they leave their village in Russia to join their father in America. (Rev: BL 9/1/98; HBG 3/99; SLJ 12/98)

5006 Taulbert, Clifton L. *Little Cliff and the Cold Place* (K–2). Illus. by E. B. Lewis. 2002, Dial $16.99 (0-8037-2558-2). 32pp. Little Cliff lives in Mississippi in the 1950s and longs to go to the Arctic, so his great-grandfather comes up with a compromise — a fishing expedition at the icehouse. (Rev: BL 11/1/02; HBG 3/03; SLJ 9/02)

5007 Taulbert, Clifton L. *Little Cliff's First Day of School* (PS–3). Illus. by E. B. Lewis. 2001, Dial $15.99 (0-8037-2557-4). 32pp. Little Cliff, an African American child, is terrified of going to school in this story set in the South of the 1950s. (Rev: BL 5/15/01; HB 7–8/01; HBG 10/01; SLJ 6/01)

5008 Tavares, Matt. *Mudball* (K–3). Illus. 2005, Candlewick $15.99 (0-7636-2387-3). 32pp. The entertaining story of a baseball game long ago that, thanks to a mud puddle, gained renown for the game's shortest home run. (Rev: BL 3/1/05; SLJ 3/05)

5009 Taylor, Debbie. *Sweet Music in Harlem* (1–3). Illus. by Frank Morrison. 2004, Lee & Low $16.95 (1-58430-165-1). 32pp. A famous 1958 photograph inspired this story about young C.J. scrambling to find his jazz-playing uncle's hat for a photo shoot and in the process attracting some of Harlem's most notable jazzmen, who want to join in. (Rev: BL 5/1/04; SLJ 7/04)

5010 Taylor, Joanne. *Making Room* (1–3). Illus. by Peter Rankin. 2004, Tundra $15.95 (0-88776-651-X). In 1800s Nova Scotia, a man gradually adds to his one-room house as his family grows. (Rev: SLJ 11/04)

5011 Tchana, Katrin, and Louise T. Pami. *Oh, No, Toto!* (K–3). Illus. by Colin Bootman. 1997, Scholastic $15.95 (0-590-46585-6). 32pp. Toto, a young African boy, tastes exotic Cameroon food when his mother takes him to the market. (Rev: BCCB 3/97; BL 3/1/97; SLJ 3/97)

5012 Thaxter, Celia. *Celia's Island Journal* (PS–3). Illus. by Loretta Krupinski. 1992, Little, Brown $15.95 (0-316-83921-3). 32pp. The author's life on White Island off the New England coast. (Rev: BL 12/1/92; HB 11–12/92; SLJ 10/92) [974.1]

5013 Thermes, Jennifer. *When I Was Built* (2–3). Illus. by author. 2001, Holt $16.95 (0-8050-6532-6). 32pp. An 18th-century house serves as the narrator

for this book comparing the lives of the colonial family that once lived there with the family of today. (Rev: BL 1/1–15/02; HBG 3/02; SLJ 12/01)

5014 Thong, Roseanne. *The Wishing Tree* (PS–2). Illus. by Connie McLennan. 2004, Shen's $16.95 (1-885008-26-0). 30pp. After years of visits to the Wishing Tree, Ming turns his back on the annual tradition when his grandmother dies. (Rev: BL 2/1/05)

5015 Tompert, Ann. *The Pied Piper of Peru* (K–2). Illus. by Kestutis Kasparavicius. 2002, Boyds Mills $15.95 (1-56397-949-7). 32pp. A 16th-century Peruvian saint tries to rid the priory of a colony of mice in this story about Saint Martin de Porres. (Rev: BCCB 4/02; BL 3/15/02; HBG 10/02) [270.6]

5016 Tran, Truong. *Going Home, Coming Home / Ve Nha Tham Que Hu'O'Ng* (1–3). Illus. by Ann Phong. 2003, Children's Book Pr. $16.95 (0-89239-179-0). 32pp. Eight-year-old Vietnamese American Ami Chi visits the homeland of her parents in this poignant bilingual tale. (Rev: BL 9/1/03; SLJ 9/03)

5017 Trottier, Maxine. *Flags* (1–4). Illus. by Paul Morin. 1999, Stoddart $16.95 (0-7737-3136-9). When their Japanese American neighbor, Mr. Hiroshi, is sent to an internment camp after Pearl Harbor, Mary saves some stones and some bulbs from his garden to start one of her own. (Rev: SLJ 3/00)

5018 Trottier, Maxine. *Little Dog Moon* (K–5). Illus. by Laura Fernandez and Rick Jacobson. 2000, Stoddart $14.95 (0-7737-3220-9). Moon, a young Tibetan terrier, helps guide two Tibetan children across the border to freedom in Nepal. (Rev: SLJ 3/01)

5019 Trottier, Maxine. *Prairie Willow* (K–3). Illus. by Laura Fernandez and Rick Jacobson. 1998, Stoddart $15.95 (0-7737-3067-2). 24pp. After the harvest, Emily, who lives with her family in a sod house on the Canadian prairie, is allowed to choose a gift for herself. She buys a weeping willow tree, which she and her family nurture for many years. (Rev: BL 9/15/98; SLJ 2/99)

5020 Trottier, Maxine. *The Walking Stick* (K–3). Illus. by Annouchka Gravel Galouchko. 1999, Stoddart $15.95 (0-7737-3101-6). A story about a walking stick fashioned by a Buddhist monk in Vietnam for a young boy who carries it throughout his life, even when he must leave his native land and come to America. (Rev: SLJ 9/99)

5021 Uhlberg, Myron. *Dad, Jackie, and Me* (2–5). Illus. by Colin Bootman. 2005, Peachtree $16.95 (1-56145-329-3). In Brooklyn in 1947, a boy and his deaf father admire Jackie Robinson's baseball prowess. (Rev: BCCB 5/05; BL 8/05; SLJ 5/05)

5022 Ulmer, Mike. *The Gift of the Inuksuk* (PS–2). Illus. by Melanie Rose. 2004, Sleeping Bear $17.95 (1-58536-214-X). 32pp. This sparely worded, original pourquoi tale offers an explanation for the *Inuksuk*, sculptures of piled stones, that dot the Arctic landscape. (Rev: BL 1/1–15/05; SLJ 4/05)

5023 U'Ren, Andrea. *Mary Smith* (PS–2). Illus. by author. 2003, Farrar $16.00 (0-374-34842-1). The colorful story of a day in the life of pre-alarm-clock

Mary Smith, who uses a peashooter to wake the people of her town; an afterword gives historical context. (Rev: HB 9–10/03; HBG 4/04; SLJ 9/03)

5024 Van Leeuwen, Jean. *The Amazing Air Balloon* (1–3). Illus. by Marco Ventura. 2003, Penguin Putnam $16.99 (0-8037-2258-3). 32pp. Based on a true event, this is a 13-year-old boy's fictionalized first-person account of the first American ascent in a hot-air balloon in 1784. (Rev: BL 1/1–15/03; HBG 10/03; SLJ 3/03)

5025 Van West, Patricia E. *The Crab Man* (1–3). Illus. by Cedric Lucas. 1998, Turtle $15.95 (1-890515-08-6). 40pp. A young Jamaican boy must decide whether or not he should continue to sell her mit crabs after he discovers that they are being cruelly treated. (Rev: BL 10/1/98; HBG 3/99; SLJ 11/98)

5026 Vaughan, Marcia. *The Secret to Freedom* (K–3). Illus. by Larry Johnson. 2001, Lee & Low $16.95 (1-58430-021-3). 32pp. Great Aunt Lucy talks about her days as a slave and the secret quilt code that directed her brother Albert and other slaves on the road to freedom. (Rev: BL 6/1–15/01; HBG 10/01; SLJ 6/01)

5027 Vaughan, Marcia. *Up the Learning Tree* (K–3). Illus. by Derek Blanks. 2003, Lee & Low $16.95 (1-58430-049-3). A schoolteacher risks everything to help a brave young slave gain an education. (Rev: BL 11/1/03; HBG 4/04; SLJ 11/03)

5028 Von Ahnen, Katherine. *Charlie Young Bear* (2–3). Illus. by Paulette L. Lambert. Series: Council for Indian Education. 1994, Roberts Rinehart paper $4.95 (1-57098-001-2). 42pp. After the U.S. government agrees on a cash settlement with the Mesquakie Indians in 1955, Charlie Young Bear hopes his share will be a bike. (Rev: SLJ 4/95)

5029 Wallace, Ian. *Mavis and Merna* (K–3). Illus. 2005, Douglas & McIntyre $16.95 (0-88899-647-0). 40pp. Gully's, the general store in her 1960s Canadian town, has always been one of Mavis's favorite places, and when owner Joe Gully dies, Mavis becomes friends with his widow even though the store is closed. (Rev: BL 5/1/05; SLJ 6/05)

5030 Wallner, Alexandra. *Sergio and the Hurricane* (K–3). Illus. 2000, Holt $16.00 (0-8050-6203-3). 32pp. Sergio learns about the destructive power of a hurricane when it hits the Puerto Rican town in which he lives. (Rev: BCCB 10/00; BL 9/15/00; HBG 3/01; SLJ 11/00)

5031 Walton, Rick. *Dance, Pioneer, Dance!* (K–3). Illus. by Brad Teare. 1998, Deseret $14.95 (1-57345-243-2). 28pp. Brigham Young calls a square dance in which humans and animals take part. His whimsical verses recall the journey of the first Mormons to Utah in 1847. (Rev: BL 9/15/98; SLJ 8/98)

5032 Ward, Leila. *I Am Eyes Ni Macho* (PS–1). Illus. by Nonny Hogrogian. 1987, Scholastic paper $3.95 (0-590-40990-5). 32pp. A new day and all of nature's wonders are greeted by a Kenyan child. A reissue of the 1978 edition.

5033 Warner, Sunny. *The Magic Sewing Machine* (PS–3). Illus. 1997, Houghton Mifflin $16.00 (0-395-82747-7). 32pp. Two orphaned children take

their sewing machine to the orphanage in this story set in Dickensian London. (Rev: BL 9/15/97; HBG 3/98; SLJ 9/97)

5034 Waterton, Betty. *Pettranella* (K–3). Illus. by Ann Blades. 1991, Firefly paper $4.95 (0-88899-108-8). 32pp. An immigrant girl grows flowers from seeds she brought from Europe.

5035 Watkins, Sherrin. *Green Snake Ceremony* (PS–2). Illus. by Kim Doner. Series: The Greyfeather. 1996, Council Oak $17.95 (0-933031-89-0). Neither a Shawnee girl nor the green snake that lives under the porch want to participate in the traditional snake ceremony that involves the young girl putting the snake in her mouth. (Rev: SLJ 12/96)

5036 Watson, Mary. *The Butterfly Seeds* (K–4). Illus. 1995, Morrow LB $15.93 (0-688-14133-1). 32pp. Jake, a new immigrant to the US, plants seeds his grandfather back home gave him in a window-box in his tenement building. (Rev: BL 9/1/95; SLJ 11/95)

5037 Watson, Pete. *The Market Lady and the Mango Tree* (K–3). Illus. by Mary Watson. 1994, Morrow $14.00 (0-688-12970-6). 32pp. When Market Lady places nets around the mango tree so that children will have to buy the fruit rather than pick it from the ground, she realizes that this is an act of selfishness. (Rev: BL 2/15/94; SLJ 6/94)

5038 Weeks, Sarah. *Piece of Jungle* (PS–1). Illus. by Suzanne Duranceau. 1999, HarperCollins $15.95 (0-06-028409-9). 32pp. Through song lyrics (found on the accompanying cassette), young children are introduced to a rain forest and the plants and animals found there. (Rev: BL 8/99)

5039 Wellington, Monica. *Crepes by Suzette* (PS–2). Illus. 2004, Dutton $15.99 (0-525-46934-6). 32pp. A collage of ephemera and photographs create an intriguing backdrop to this simple story about Suzette, who sells crepes on the streets of Paris. (Rev: BL 1/1–15/04; SLJ 3/04)

5040 Wenberg, Michael. *Elizabeth's Song* (1–4). Illus. by Cornelius Van Wright. 2002, Beyond Words $15.95 (1-58270-069-9). 32pp. The fictionalized story of African American folk singer Elizabeth Cotton, 11-year-old author of "Freight Train Comin'." (Rev: BL 2/15/03; HBG 10/03)

5041 Wiebe, Rudy. *Hidden Buffalo* (1–3). Illus. by Michael Lonechild. 2004, Red Deer $17.95 (0-88995-285-X). 32pp. Based on a traditional tale, this book tells how a dream inspires the starving Cree people to brave dangers and journey to the Badlands in search of buffalo herds. (Rev: BL 3/1/04; SLJ 7/04)

5042 Williams, Karen L. *Painted Dreams* (PS–1). Illus. by Catherine Stock. 1998, Lothrop LB $15.93 (0-688-13902-7). 40pp. Set in the slums of Haiti, this picture book tells of little Ti Marie, who finds some discarded paints in an artist's trash and, with his help, cultivates her artistic talent. (Rev: BL 9/15/98; HBG 3/99; SLJ 10/98)

5043 Williams, Karen L. *When Africa Was Home* (PS–2). Illus. by Floyd Cooper. 1991, Orchard LB $16.99 (0-531-08525-2). 32pp. A white boy is so at home in Africa with his black friends that he feels lost when he has to go to America. (Rev: BCCB 2/92; BL 1/15/91*; SLJ 4/91)

5044 Williams, Laura E. *Torch Fishing with the Sun* (K–3). Illus. by Fabricio Vandenbroeck. 1999, Boyds Mills $15.95 (1-56397-685-4). 32pp. Young Makoa's grandfather tells him that he uses the sun as a torch while he fishes, but the boy has doubts when others claim that the old man actually buys his catch from another fisherman. (Rev: BL 3/15/99; HBG 10/99; SLJ 6/99)

5045 Willow, Diane. *At Home in the Rain Forest* (PS–3). Illus. by Laura Jacques. 1991, Charlesbridge $15.95 (0-88106-485-8). 32pp. The flora and fauna of the Amazon rain forest are explored in text and color paintings. (Rev: BL 6/1/91) [574]

5046 Wilson, Budge. *A Fiddle for Angus* (K–3). Illus. by Susan Tooke. 2001, Tundra $16.95 (0-88776-500-9). 32pp. Angus decides to learn to play the fiddle in this story set in Nova Scotia. (Rev: BL 10/15/01; HBG 3/02; SLJ 10/01)

5047 Winnick, Karen B. *Mr. Lincoln's Whiskers* (1–3). Illus. 1996, Boyds Mills $15.95 (1-56397-485-1). 32pp. A young girl writes to Lincoln to suggest that he would gain votes if he grew whiskers. (Rev: BL 12/15/96; SLJ 1/97)

5048 Winnick, Karen B. *Sybil's Night Ride* (K–3). Illus. 2000, Boyds Mills $15.95 (1-56397-697-8). 32pp. This picture book re-creates the historic ride of 16-year-old Sybil Ludington who, during the American Revolution, raced on her horse to warn her father's troops that the British were burning Danbury, New York. (Rev: BL 3/1/00; HBG 10/00)

5049 Winter, Jeanette. *Elsina's Clouds* (PS–3). Illus. 2004, Farrar $16.00 (0-374-32118-3). 40pp. In Basotho tradition, Elsina paints the outside walls of her house, decorating them with bright colors and scenes of nature. (Rev: BL 3/1/04; HB 3–4/04; SLJ 4/04)

5050 Winter, Jeanette. *Follow the Drinking Gourd* (K–3). Illus. by author. 1988, Knopf paper $5.99 (0-679-81997-5). 48pp. The story of Peg Leg Pete who helps slaves escape to the North. (Rev: BCCB 1/89; BL 12/15/88; SLJ 5/89)

5051 Winter, Jeanette. *Niño's Mask* (K–3). Illus. 2003, Dial $15.99 (0-8037-2807-7). 40pp. Niño makes his own mask to wear at a Mexican village fiesta in this picture book sprinkled with Spanish words. (Rev: BCCB 3/03; BL 2/1/03; HB 3–4/03; HBG 10/03; SLJ 12/03)

5052 Wisniewski, David. *Rain Player* (K–3). Illus. 1991, Houghton Mifflin $17.00 (0-395-55112-9). 32pp. Young Pik challenges the rain god in this story based on Mayan folklore. (Rev: BCCB 11/91; BL 10/15/91*; HB 1–2/92; SLJ 10/91)

5053 Wittmann, Patricia. *Buffalo Thunder* (K–4). Illus. by Bert Dodson. 1997, Marshall Cavendish $15.95 (0-7614-5001-7). 32pp. A young boy and his family share many adventures when they travel west in their prairie schooner. (Rev: BL 9/15/97; HBG 3/98; SLJ 9/97)

5054 Wong, Janet S. *The Trip Back Home* (PS–2). Illus. by Bo Jia. 2000, Harcourt $16.00 (0-15-200784-9). 32pp. The food and fun involved when

the author visited her grandparents in rural Korea when she was a child are recalled in this tender story of family love. (Rev: BL 11/15/00; HBG 3/01; SLJ 12/00)

5055 Woodruff, Elvira. *The Memory Coat* (K–4). Illus. by Michael Dooling. 1999, Scholastic $15.95 (0-590-67717-9). 32pp. This story of a Jewish family's migration from Russia to America focuses on Rachel and her orphaned cousin, Grisha. (Rev: BL 1/1–15/99; HBG 10/99; SLJ 3/99)

5056 Wright, Courtni C. *Jumping the Broom* (K–3). Illus. by Gershom Griffith. 1994, Holiday House LB $15.95 (0-8234-1042-0). A picture book set in the days of slavery about the marriage celebration known as "jumping the broom." (Rev: BCCB 7–8/94; SLJ 4/94)

5057 Yacowitz, Caryn. *Pumpkin Fiesta* (PS–1). Illus. by Joe Cepeda. 1998, HarperCollins $14.95 (0-06-027658-4). 32pp. Foolish Fernando tries by fair and foul means to rob Old Juana of the glory of winning the fiesta's special prize for her extraordinary pumpkins, but justice triumphs. (Rev: BL 9/1/98; HB 11–12/98; HBG 3/99; SLJ 9/98)

5058 Yaroshevskaya, Kim. *Little Kim's Doll* (K–3). Illus. by Luc Melanson. 1999, Groundwood $14.95 (0-88899-353-6). Growing up in Communist Russia during the 1930s, young Kim longs for a doll but her parents want to give her a more practical gift like a toy rifle. (Rev: SLJ 8/99)

5059 Yezerski, Thomas F. *A Full Hand* (PS–2). Illus. 2002, Farrar $16.00 (0-374-42502-7). 32pp. Nine-year-old Asa accompanies his captain father on a canal boat trip, during which he learns a lot about canals. (Rev: BCCB 12/02; BL 1/1–15/03; HBG 3/03; SLJ 9/02)

5060 Yin. *Coolies* (K–4). Illus. by Chris K. Soentpiet. 2001, Penguin Putnam $16.99 (0-399-23227-3). 40pp. The experiences of two Chinese brothers who migrate to America to work on the Transcontinental Railroad reveal the courage and integrity of these Chinese Americans and the racism they endured. (Rev: BCCB 2/01; BL 2/1/01; HB 3–4/01; HBG 10/01; SLJ 3/01)

PERSONAL PROBLEMS

5061 Adams, Eric J., and Kathleen Adams. *On the Day His Daddy Left* (1–3). Illus. by Layne Johnson. 2000, Whitman $14.95 (0-8075-6072-3). Danny worries that his parents' divorce is his fault. (Rev: BL 3/1/03; HBG 3/01; SLJ 12/00)

5062 Allen, Debbie. *Dancing in the Wings* (K–3). Illus. by Kadir Nelson. 2000, Dial $16.99 (0-8037-2501-9). 32pp. Sassy is afraid that she is too tall and lanky to become a ballerina, but a Russian ballet master chooses her to dance in a festival. (Rev: BCCB 11/00; BL 11/15/00; HBG 3/01; SLJ 9/00)

5063 Altman, Linda Jacobs. *Amelia's Road* (PS–3). Illus. by Enrique O. Sanchez. 1993, Lee & Low $15.95 (1-880000-04-0). 32pp. Amelia, the daughter of migrant workers, cries every time her father takes out a map because it means her family will move again. (Rev: BL 9/15/93; SLJ 12/93)

5064 Bahr, Mary. *If Nathan Were Here* (K–2). Illus. by Karen A. Jerome. 2000, Eerdmans $16.00 (0-8028-5187-8). 32pp. A boy imagines all the things he could do if Nathan were there but, as the reader learns, Nathan is dead and his friend misses him. (Rev: BL 4/15/00; HBG 10/00; SLJ 8/00)

5065 Bang, Molly. *When Sophie Gets Angry — Really, Really Angry* (PS–3). Illus. 1999, Scholastic $15.95 (0-590-18979-4). 40pp. This book describes in drawings and text what happens to Sophie when she becomes angry. (Rev: BCCB 4/99; BL 2/1/99; HBG 10/99; SLJ 1/99*)

5066 Barron, T. A. *Where Is Grandpa?* (PS–3). Illus. by Chris K. Soentpiet. 2000, Penguin Putnam $15.99 (0-399-23037-8). 32pp. A young boy believes his dead grandfather is enjoying all the beauties of nature that he loved. (Rev: BL 5/1/00; HBG 10/00; SLJ 2/00)

5067 Bateman, Teresa. *Hamster Camp: How Harry Got Fit* (K–3). Illus. by Nancy Cote. 2005, Whitman $15.95 (0-8075-3139-1). 32pp. Harry, an indolent boy with a craving for unhealthy foods, accompanies his pet to Hamster Camp, where Harry is promptly transformed into a hamster and learns to eat properly. (Rev: BL 5/15/05)

5068 Battle-Lavert, Gwendolyn. *Off to School* (K–3). Illus. by Gershom Griffith. 1995, Holiday House LB $15.95 (0-8234-1185-0). 32pp. A migrant worker's child, Wezielee, longs to go to school but must stay at the camp and cook for the laborers. (Rev: BL 10/15/95; SLJ 1/96)

5069 Baumgart, Klaus. *Don't Be Afraid, Tommy* (PS–1). Illus. by author. 1998, Little Tiger $14.95 (1-888444-32-0). Tommy learns to conquer his own fears when he is given a toy dog and told to teach him not to be afraid. (Rev: HBG 10/98; SLJ 7/98)

5070 Bernstein, Sharon C. *A Family That Fights* (PS–3). Illus. by Karen Ritz. 1991, Whitman LB $13.95 (0-8075-2248-1). 32pp. A quiet story that deals with three children who live in a family where the father hits their mother and threatens them when he is angry. (Rev: BL 11/15/91; SLJ 2/92)

5071 Best, Cari. *Getting Used to Harry* (PS–3). Illus. by Diane Palmisciano. 1996, Orchard LB $16.99 (0-531-08794-8). 32pp. Cynthia gradually adjusts to her mother's new husband, Harry the shoe man. (Rev: BCCB 10/96; BL 11/1/96; SLJ 10/96)

5072 Bond, Rebecca. *When Marcus Moore Moved In* (PS–2). Illus. by author. 2003, Little, Brown $15.95 (0-316-10458-2). Vibrant illustrations bring to life this story of Marcus, who is uncertain of his new city neighborhood until he meets Kate. (Rev: BL 5/15/03; HBG 10/03; SLJ 8/03)

5073 Bottner, Barbara. *Bootsie Barker Bites* (PS–3). Illus. by Peggy Rathmann. 1992, Penguin Putnam $15.95 (0-399-22125-5). 32pp. The young narrator stands just so much from bully Bootsie Barker and finally stands up for herself. (Rev: BCCB 9/92; BL 10/1/92*; HB 3–4/93; SLJ 2/93*)

5074 Bower, Gary. *Ivy's Icicle: Forgiving Others* (K–4). Illus. by Jan Bower. Series: Thinking of Others. 2002, Tyndale $14.99 (0-8423-7417-5). Ivy's heart becomes like an icicle when Dustin breaks her

new doll, but she is gently persuaded that grudges are a bad thing. (Rev: SLJ 3/03)

5075 Brandt, Amy. *Benjamin Comes Back / Benjamin regresa* (PS–K). 2000, Child Care Books for Kids paper $11.95 (1-884834-79-5). 32pp. A bilingual book about day care in which Benjamin misses his mother so much that he needs to be reassured that she will be coming for him after school. (Rev: SLJ 10/00)

5076 Brown, Tricia. *Someone Special, Just Like You* (PS–2). Photos by Fran Ortiz. 1984, Holt $16.95 (0-8050-0481-5). 64pp. A book that shows that children are children even if they are handicapped.

5077 Bulla, Clyde Robert. *The Chalk Box Kid* (2–3). Illus. by Thomas B. Allen. 1987, Random LB $11.99 (0-394-99102-8); paper $3.99 (0-394-89102-3). 64pp. Miffed because Uncle Max is sharing his room, Gregory sets out to explore his new neighborhood. (Rev: BCCB 9/87; BL 12/1/87; SLJ 12/87)

5078 Bunnett, Rochelle. *Friends in the Park* (PS–K). Illus. by Carl Sahlhoff. 1993, Checkerboard $7.95 (1-56288-347-X). 32pp. In this book of photographs and text, disabled kids are shown enjoying all the activities that youngsters like. (Rev: BL 4/15/93) [305.9]

5079 Bunting, Eve. *The Days of Summer* (PS–3). Illus. by William Low. 2001, Harcourt $16.00 (0-15-201840-9). 32pp. In this moving picture book, a girl and her younger sister are bewildered when their grandparents divorce. (Rev: BL 4/1/01; HBG 10/01; SLJ 5/01)

5080 Bunting, Eve. *Fly Away Home* (K–3). Illus. by Ronald Himler. 1991, Houghton Mifflin $16.00 (0-395-55962-6). 32pp. The airport serves as a home for two homeless people — a boy and his father. (Rev: BCCB 5/92; BL 4/1/91*; HB 7–8/91; SLJ 6/91*)

5081 Bunting, Eve. *On Call Back Mountain* (1–3). Illus. by Barry Moser. 1997, Scholastic $15.95 (0-590-25929-6). Two young brothers adjust to the death of an elderly man who has worked as a fire spotter in a tower close to their home. (Rev: SLJ 3/97)

5082 Burnett, Frances Hodgson. *A Little Princess* (K–2). Illus. by Barbara McClintock. 2000, HarperCollins LB $16.89 (0-06-029010-2). 32pp. A retelling in a shortened form of Burnett's beloved classic story of a privileged child who turned pauper and back again. (Rev: BL 1/1–15/01; HBG 3/01)

5083 Canfield, Jack, and Mark V. Hansen. *Chicken Soup for Little Souls: The Best Night Out with Dad* (K–4). Illus. by Bert Dodson. Series: Chicken Soup for Little Souls. 1997, Health Communications $14.95 (1-55874-508-4). 32pp. This slight story teaches the value of being unselfish and giving to others. Also use *Chicken Soup for Little Souls: The Goodness Gorilla* and *Chicken Soup for Little Souls: The Never-Forgotten Doll* (1997). (Rev: BL 11/15/97; HBG 3/98; SLJ 1/98)

5084 Carlson, Nancy. *Arnie and the New Kid* (PS–2). Illus. 1992, Puffin paper $5.99 (0-14-050945-3). 32pp. When Arnie has an accident, he realizes what life is like for newcomer Philip, who is confined to a wheelchair. (Rev: BCCB 5/90; BL 5/15/90)

5085 Carr, Jan. *Dark Day, Light Night* (PS–2). Illus. by James E. Ransome. 1996, Hyperion LB $15.49 (0-7868-2014-4). 32pp. When 'Manda claims there is nothing in the world she really likes, Aunt Ruby compiles a list of her own favorite things. (Rev: BL 2/15/96; HB 5–6/96; SLJ 6/96)

5086 Carrick, Carol. *Patrick's Dinosaurs* (PS–3). Illus. by Donald Carrick. 1983, Houghton Mifflin $15.00 (0-89919-189-4); paper $5.95 (0-89919-402-8). 32pp. Patrick is frightened when his brother tells him about dinosaurs.

5087 Carter, Dorothy. *Bye, Mis' Lela* (K–3). Illus. by Harvey Stevenson. 1998, Farrar $16.00 (0-374-31013-0). 32pp. An African American girl must cope with the death of her beloved baby sitter, Mis' Lela. (Rev: BL 2/15/98; HBG 10/98; SLJ 3/98)

5088 Caseley, Judith. *Priscilla Twice* (K–2). Illus. 1995, Greenwillow LB $14.93 (0-688-13306-1). 32pp. After her parents divorce, Priscilla finds that she now has two of everything, including two sets of clothes. (Rev: BL 8/95; SLJ 9/95)

5089 Cave, Kathryn. *You've Got Dragons* (K–3). Illus. by Nick Maland. 2003, Peachtree $16.95 (1-56145-284-X). Young Ben explains about the dragons he gets when in stressful situations, and what he does to get rid of them. (Rev: BCCB 11/03; BL 10/15/03; HBG 4/04; SLJ 12/03)

5090 Child, Lauren. *Clarice Bean, That's Me* (PS–2). Illus. by author. 1999, Candlewick $16.99 (0-7636-0961-7). Clarice Bean's house is so crowded that she hopes she will be sent to her room as a punishment so she can be alone for a while. (Rev: HBG 3/00; SLJ 12/99)

5091 Clark, Emma Chichester. *What Shall We Do, Blue Kangaroo?* (PS–1). Illus. by author. 2003, Doubleday LB $17.99 (0-385-90866-0). Lily is delighted to realize she doesn't have to depend on adults for things to do, but glad that stuffed toy Blue Kangaroo is still around to help. (Rev: BL 5/15/03; HB 9–10/03; HBG 4/04; SLJ 7/03)

5092 Clifton, Lucille. *One of the Problems of Everett Anderson* (PS–3). Illus. by Ann Grifalconi. 2001, Holt $16.95 (0-8050-5201-1). 24pp. Everett turns to his mother for advice when he becomes concerned about his classmate Greg, who is often bruised and seems troubled. (Rev: BL 9/15/01; HBG 3/02; SLJ 10/01)

5093 Cohn, Janice. *Molly's Rosebush* (PS–2). Illus. by Gail Owens. 1994, Whitman LB $14.95 (0-8075-5213-5). 32pp. Grandma helps Molly get over her grief at the loss of her mother's baby by miscarriage. (Rev: BL 1/15/95; SLJ 3/95)

5094 Cooper, Helen. *Tatty Ratty* (PS–K). Illus. 2002, Farrar $16.00 (0-374-37386-8). 32pp. When Molly accidentally leaves her favorite stuffed animal on the bus, she is comforted by thoughts of the grand adventures he is having. (Rev: BL 2/15/02; HBG 10/02; SLJ 4/02)

5095 Cosby, Bill. *The Day I Was Rich* (1–3). Illus. by Varnette P. Honeywood. Series: Little Bill. 1999, Scholastic $15.95 (0-590-52172-1); paper $3.99 (0-590-52173-X). In this beginning chapter book, Little Bill discovers that the object he found is not a diamond but only a glass paperweight. Also use *The Worst Day of My Life* (1999). (Rev: HBG 3/00; SLJ 2/00)

5096 Cowley, Joy. *Big Moon Tortilla* (PS–3). Illus. by Dyanne Strongbow. 1998, Boyds Mills $14.95 (1-56397-601-3). When Marta Enos has a bad day at home on the Papago reservation in southern Arizona, her grandmother tells her a traditional tale to help her cope with problems. (Rev: BL 10/15/98; HBG 10/99; SLJ 11/98)

5097 Crary, Elizabeth. *I'm Frustrated* (PS–1). Illus. by Jean Whitney. 1992, Parenting LB $16.95 (0-943990-65-3). 30pp. In this slim book, a child is faced with a difficult situation and must work through his feelings. Others in this series are: *I'm Mad; I'm Proud* (both 1992). (Rev: SLJ 6/92)

5098 Cristaldi, Kathryn. *Samantha the Snob* (1–3). Illus. by Denise Brunkus. Series: Step into Reading. 1994, Random LB $11.99 (0-679-94640-3); paper $3.99 (0-679-84640-9). 48pp. Everyone thinks that the new girl in their class is a snob and showoff, but her birthday party shows that they are wrong. (Rev: SLJ 11/94)

5099 Curtis, Jamie Lee. *Today I Feel Silly: And Other Moods That Make My Day* (PS–2). Illus. by Laura Cornell. 1998, HarperCollins $14.95 (0-06-024560-3). 32pp. In this lighthearted picture book, the young narrator describes how she feels on different days and the ways she copes with emotional ups and downs. (Rev: BL 10/15/98; HBG 3/99; SLJ 12/98)

5100 Czech, Jan M. *An American Face* (PS–2). Illus. by Frances Clancy. 2000, Child & Family paper $8.95 (0-87868-718-1). 32pp. Korean-born Jessie believes that when he becomes an American citizen he will get a new face like his adoptive American parents. (Rev: BL 5/15/00; SLJ 8/00)

5101 Davies, Sally J. K. *Why Did We Have to Move Here?* (K–3). Illus. 1997, Carolrhoda $15.95 (1-57505-046-3). 32pp. After William and his family move to a new home, he has difficulty making friends. (Rev: BL 12/15/97; HBG 3/98)

5102 dePaola, Tomie. *Now One Foot, Now the Other* (K–3). Illus. by author. 1981, Penguin Putnam $13.95 (0-399-20774-0). 48pp. Bobby helps his grandfather recover from a stroke.

5103 dePaola, Tomie. *Oliver Button Is a Sissy* (K–3). Illus. by author. 1979, Harcourt $14.00 (0-15-257852-8); paper $6.00 (0-15-668140-4). 48pp. People think Oliver is a sissy until he shines in a talent show as a fine tap dancer.

5104 Edwards, Becky. *My Brother Sammy* (PS–2). Illus. by David Armitage. 1999, Millbrook LB $21.90 (0-7613-1417-2). An older boy has troubles adjusting to the erratic behavior of his autistic younger brother, Sammy. (Rev: HBG 10/99; SLJ 7/99)

5105 Ehrlich, H. M. *Gotcha, Louie!* (PS–K). Illus. by Emily Bolam. 2002, Houghton Mifflin $15.00 (0-618-19549-1). 32pp. Young Louie gets lost in the tall grass close to the beach, but his mother very cleverly finds him. (Rev: BL 4/15/02; HBG 10/02; SLJ 4/02)

5106 Ehrlich, H. M. *Louie's Goose* (PS–3). Illus. by Emily Bolam. 2000, Houghton Mifflin $15.00 (0-618-03023-9). 32pp. Louie is so attached to his stuffed goose, Rosie, that, although it is falling apart and needs constant repair, he can't part with it. (Rev: BL 3/1/00; HBG 10/00; SLJ 3/00)

5107 Ellis, Sarah. *Ben Over Night* (PS–2). Illus. by Kim LaFave. 2005, Fitzhenry & Whiteside $16.95 (1-55041-807-6). 32pp. Peter's house is only across the street, but even though Ben loves to play there, he's scared to stay there overnight. (Rev: BL 5/1/05; SLJ 6/05)

5108 Elya, Susan Middleton. *Home at Last* (K–3). Illus. by Felipe Davalos. 2002, Lee & Low $16.95 (1-58430-020-5). 32pp. Ana, who has recently arrived from Mexico with her family, helps persuade her mother to attend English-language classes. (Rev: BCCB 9/02; BL 5/1/02; HBG 10/02; SLJ 7/02)

5109 Fernandes, Eugenie. *A Difficult Day* (K–2). Illus. 1999, Kids Can $14.95 (0-921103-17-4). 32pp. Poor Melinda has a bad day and a temper tantrum, but it ends with cookies and hugs from an understanding mom. (Rev: BL 5/15/99; HBG 10/99)

5110 Figueredo, D. H. *When This World Was New* (PS–3). Illus. by Enrique O. Sanchez. 1999, Lee & Low $15.95 (1-880000-86-5). 32pp. Danilito leaves his warm Caribbean island to migrate with his parents to the U.S., and there he has many unsettling experiences but one outstanding joy — seeing the city transformed by snow. (Rev: BL 6/1–15/99; HBG 10/99; SLJ 7/99)

5111 Fine, Edith Hope. *Under the Lemon Moon* (K–3). Illus. by René King Moreno. 1999, Lee & Low $15.95 (1-880000-69-5). 32pp. Young Rosalinda learns to cope with loss when a thief steals all the lemons from her pet tree and damages it as well. (Rev: BL 5/15/99; HBG 10/99; SLJ 4/99)

5112 Fleming, Virginia. *Be Good to Eddie Lee* (K–3). Illus. by Floyd Cooper. 1993, Penguin Putnam $16.99 (0-399-21993-5). 30pp. Eddie Lee, a boy with Down's syndrome, teaches his neighbor, Christy, to look at the world differently. (Rev: BL 1/15/94; SLJ 2/94)

5113 Fox, Mem. *Harriet, You'll Drive Me Wild!* (PS). Illus. by Marla Frazee. 2000, Harcourt $16.00 (0-15-201977-4). 32pp. Harriet is such a pest that her usually patient mother begins to shout at her but then they kiss and make up. (Rev: BCCB 6/00; BL 3/1/00; HB 3–4/00; HBG 10/00; SLJ 4/00)

5114 Frame, Jeron Ashford. *Yesterday I Had the Blues* (K–2). Illus. by R. Gregory Christie. 2003, Tricycle $14.95 (1-58246-084-1). A young African American boy, who's suffered a bout of the blues, ponders the varied moods of his family members and assigns each a color; vibrant illustrations add to the engaging text. (Rev: HBG 4/04; SLJ 10/03)

5115 Fraustino, Lisa Rowe. *The Hickory Chair* (PS–3). Illus. by Benny Andrews. 2001, Scholastic $15.95 (0-590-52248-5). 32pp. Although Louis was born blind, he seems to have a sixth sense. For example, after his beloved grandmother dies, it is Louis who finds her notes about the disposal of her property. (Rev: BCCB 3/01*; BL 3/1/01; HBG 10/01; SLJ 2/01)

5116 Freymann, Saxton, and Joost Elffers. *How Are You Peeling? Foods with Moods* (PS–1). Illus. 1999, Scholastic $15.95 (0-439-10431-9). 48pp. Collages of fruits and vegetables are used to portray human emotions. (Rev: BL 2/1/00; HBG 3/00; SLJ 1/00) [152.4]

5117 Gauch, Patricia L. *Presenting Tanya, the Ugly Duckling* (PS–3). Illus. by Satomi Ichikawa. 1999, Penguin Putnam $16.99 (0-399-23200-1). 32pp. Dancing the lead in *The Ugly Duckling* gives Tanya the confidence she needs to turn from an awkward dancer into a graceful swan. (Rev: BL 7/99*; HBG 10/99; SLJ 6/99)

5118 Gehret, Jeanne. *The Don't-Give-Up-Kid and Learning Differences* (K–3). Illus. by Sandra A. DePauw. 1992, Verbal Images paper $9.95 (0-884-28110-9). 32pp. A first-grader receives special attention to help his dyslexia. (Rev: BL 6/1/90)

5119 Gifaldi, David. *Ben, King of the River* (K–3). Illus. by Layne Johnson. 2001, Whitman $14.95 (0-8075-0635-4). 32pp. An older boy is afraid his disabled brother will spoil the family's first camping trip. (Rev: BL 3/1/01; HBG 10/01)

5120 Giff, Patricia Reilly. *Ronald Morgan Goes to Bat* (PS–3). Illus. by Susanna Natti. 1988, Puffin paper $5.99 (0-14-050669-1). 32pp. Ronald is so bad a batter that he closes his eyes when the ball comes, but his spirit is unbeatable. Also use: *Watch Out, Ronald Morgan!* (1985). (Rev: BL 6/1/88; HB 9–10/88; SLJ 9/88)

5121 Gilbert, Jane. *Indescribably Arabella* (PS–2). Illus. by author. 2003, Simon & Schuster $15.95 (0-689-85321-1). Arabella Anastasia is ambitious but unsuccessful until an elderly couple take her under their wings and nurture her artistic flair. (Rev: HBG 10/03; SLJ 6/03)

5122 Glenn, Sharlee. *Keeping Up with Roo* (K–2). Illus. by Dan Andreasen. 2004, Penguin Putnam $14.99 (0-399-23480-2). 32pp. As Gracie grows up, she gradually comes to recognize that her beloved Aunt Roo has limited mental abilities. (Rev: BL 1/1–15/04; SLJ 3/04)

5123 Gomi, Taro. *I Lost My Dad* (PS–2). Illus. 2001, Kane/Miller $12.95 (0-916291-04-2). 32pp. This book explores a young boy's panic and fear when he is separated from his dad in a large department store. (Rev: BL 3/1/01)

5124 Grifalconi, Ann. *Tiny's Hat* (K–3). Illus. by author. 1999, HarperCollins LB $14.89 (0-06-027655-X). When Tiny's father, a blues player, goes away, the little girl dons her daddy's big black hat and begins to sing the blues. (Rev: HBG 10/99; SLJ 1/99)

5125 Grimm, Edward. *The Doorman* (K–3). Illus. by Ted Lewin. 2000, Orchard LB $17.99 (0-531-33280-2). 32pp. Residents in a New York City apartment building mourn the death of the doorman who meant so much to them. (Rev: BCCB 7–8/00; BL 7/00; HBG 3/01; SLJ 10/00)

5126 Gunning, Monica. *A Shelter in Our Car* (K–3). Illus. by Elaine Pedlar. 2004, Children's Book Pr. $16.95 (0-89239-183-8). 32pp. Jamaican-born Zettie and her mother live in the backseat of their car while they try to make a real life for themselves. (Rev: BL 4/1/04)

5127 Hanson, Regina. *The Tangerine Tree* (PS–3). Illus. by Harvey Stevenson. 1995, Clarion $14.95 (0-395-68963-5). 32pp. Ida's Jamaican family is torn apart when her father must become a migrant worker in New York City. (Rev: BL 7/95; SLJ 9/95)

5128 Harris, Robie H. *Goodbye Mousie* (PS). Illus. by Jan Ormerod. 2001, Simon & Schuster $16.00 (0-689-83217-6). 32pp. With help from his parents, a young boy comes to terms with the death of his pet mouse. (Rev: BCCB 10/01; BL 9/1/01; HBG 3/02; SLJ 9/01)

5129 Harrison, Troon. *Aaron's Awful Allergies* (PS–1). Illus. by Eugenie Fernandes. 1998, Kids Can $12.95 (1-55074-299-X). Aaron is unhappy when he has to get rid of his pets because of his allergies. (Rev: HBG 10/98; SLJ 3/98)

5130 Harshman, Marc. *The Storm* (K–3). Illus. by Mark Mohr. 1995, Dutton $15.99 (0-525-65150-0). 32pp. Wheelchair-bound Jonathan finds himself in the path of a deadly tornado. (Rev: BL 5/1/95; SLJ 7/95)

5131 Heide, Florence Parry, and Roxanne H. Pierce. *Oh, Grow Up!* (K–4). Illus. by Nadine Bernard Westcott. 1996, Orchard LB $16.99 (0-531-08771-9). 32pp. Humorous verses and imaginative drawings illustrate everyday problems in growing up, such as dealing with brothers and sisters. (Rev: BCCB 3/96; BL 3/1/96; SLJ 4/96)

5132 Heitler, Susan M. *David Decides About Thumbsucking: A Motivating Story for Children and an Informative Guide for Parents* (PS–3). Illus. by Paula Singer. 1996, Reading Matters paper $13.95 (0-9614780-2-0). 52pp. This photo-essay concentrates on David and his decision to give up his thumb sucking. (Rev: BL 11/1/85; SLJ 2/86)

5133 Henley, Karyn. *Gram's Song* (PS–3). Illus. by Bill Farnsworth. 2003, Tyndale $14.99 (0-8423-7669-0). 32pp. This illustrated story with a Christian focus is designed to help children cope with the death of someone they love. (Rev: SLJ 3/04)

5134 Holcomb, Nan. *Andy Finds a Turtle* (K–3). Illus. by Dot Yoder. Series: Turtle Books. 1992, Jason LB $14.95 (0-944727-13-1); paper $8.95 (0-944727-02-6). 32pp. The story of Andy, a young boy with cerebral palsy. Two other books about children with physical problems are: *Danny and the Merry-Go-Round* and *How about a Hug* (both 1992). All three are reissues.

5135 Hopkins, Beverly H. *Changes: My Family and Me* (PS–2). Illus. by Sarah K. Hoctor. 1999, Child & Family $8.95 (0-87868-723-8). As seen through the eyes of the oldest child in a family, this account tells of the changes that a family experiences when parents divorce, remarry, and have both stepchildren and children of their own. (Rev: SLJ 6/99)

5136 Howard, Arthur. *The Hubbub Above* (K–2). Illus. by author. 2005, Harcourt $16.00 (0-15-204592-9). Sydney is very happy living on the 52nd floor of Ivory Towers until elephant neighbors called the Kabooms move in and destroy her peace. (Rev: SLJ 5/05)

5137 Howard, Elizabeth F. *Virgie Goes to School with Us Boys* (K–2). Illus. by E. B. Lewis. 2000, Simon & Schuster $16.00 (0-689-80076-2). 32pp. Virgie, youngest in a family of boys, vows that she will accompany her brothers when they walk the seven miles to school every Monday morning. (Rev: BCCB 2/00; BL 11/1/99*; HBG 10/00; SLJ 3/00)

5138 Hru, Dakari. *Joshua's Masai Mask* (K–3). Illus. by Anna Rich. 1993, Lee & Low $14.95 (1-880000-02-4). 32pp. By playing the kalimba, an African musical instrument, in his school's talent show, Joshua gains self-esteem. (Rev: BL 4/1/93)

5139 Hughes, Shirley. *Alfie and the Birthday Surprise* (PS–K). Illus. 1998, Lothrop $16.00 (0-688-15187-6). 32pp. Alfie, an English toddler, helps his neighbors adjust to the death of their pet cat, Smoky. (Rev: BCCB 3/98; BL 3/1/98; HB 5–6/98; HBG 10/98; SLJ 3/98)

5140 Hutchins, Hazel. *Believing Sophie* (K–3). Illus. by Dorothy Donohue. 1995, Whitman LB $14.95 (0-8075-0625-7). 32pp. Sophie is falsely accused of stealing cough drops from her local store. (Rev: BL 9/1/95; SLJ 1/96)

5141 Isadora, Rachael. *Ben's Trumpet* (K–3). Illus. by Rachel Isadora. 1979, Greenwillow $16.95 (0-688-80194-3); Morrow paper $6.95 (0-688-10988-8). 32pp. A young African American boy dreams of becoming a trumpet player and eventually is taken to a jazz club by a musician.

5142 Isherwood, Shirley. *Flora the Frog* (K–3). Illus. by Anna C. Leplar. 2000, Peachtree $16.95 (1-56145-223-8). 32pp. Flora is so upset at playing a frog in the class play, that she throws away the frog costume that her mother and aunt have made. (Rev: BCCB 11/00; BL 9/15/00; HBG 3/01; SLJ 10/00)

5143 Jennings, Patrick. *The Lightning Bugs* (2–4). Illus. by Anna Alter. 2003, Holiday House $15.95 (0-8234-1673-9). 55pp. Ike and his sister Mem join their friends in catching lightning bugs, but Ike becomes distressed when there is cruelty involved. (Rev: HBG 4/04; SLJ 8/03)

5144 Jimenez, Francisco. *La Mariposa* (K–3). Illus. by Simon Silva. 1998, Houghton Mifflin $16.00 (0-395-81663-7). 40pp. Francisco becomes adept at drawing butterflies and, as a gesture of reconciliation, offers one of his drawings to the boy who beat him up on the playground. (Rev: BL 3/1/99; HBG 3/99; SLJ 11/98)

5145 Johnston, Tony. *That Summer* (K–3). Illus. by Barry Moser. 2002, Harcourt $16.00 (0-15-201585-X). 32pp. A boy remembers the summer his brother Joey died, when he dealt with his grief by helping his grandmother make a quilt to memorialize Joey's life. (Rev: BCCB 9/02; BL 5/15/02; HBG 10/02; SLJ 5/02)

5146 Jonell, Lynne. *When Mommy Was Mad* (PS–1). Illus. by Petra Mathers. 2002, Penguin Putnam $13.99 (0-399-23433-0). 32pp. Robbie is upset because Mommy seems angry in this book with stick-figure illustrations. (Rev: BCCB 9/02; BL 5/15/02; HBG 10/02; SLJ 6/02)

5147 Joosse, Barbara M. *Stars in the Darkness* (K–3). Illus. by R. Gregory Christie. 2002, Chronicle $14.95 (0-8118-2168-4). 28pp. A boy becomes involved in a gang, prompting his mother and brother to join in neighborhood peace walks. (Rev: BCCB 9/02; BL 5/15/02; HBG 10/02; SLJ 8/02)

5148 Jordan, Deloris, and Roslyn M. Jordan. *Salt in His Shoes: Michael Jordan in Pursuit of a Dream* (K–4). Illus. by Kadir Nelson. 2000, Simon & Schuster $16.95 (0-689-83371-7). 32pp. A fictionalized tale about a youthful Michael Jordan whose mother (the author) encourages him to pursue his basketball dreams even though he's the shortest boy on the team. (Rev: BL 2/1/01; HBG 3/01)

5149 Joslin, Sesyle. *What Do You Say, Dear?* (1–3). Illus. by Maurice Sendak. 1958, HarperCollins LB $15.89 (0-06-023074-6); paper $5.95 (0-06-443112-6). 48pp. Humorous handbook on manners for young ladies and gentlemen of 6 to 8. Also use: *What Do You Do, Dear?* (1958).

5150 Karkowsku, Nancy. *Grandma's Soup* (PS–3). Illus. by Shelly O. Haas. 1989, Kar-Ben paper $5.95 (0-930494-99-7). Several grandchildren gradually adjust to the fact that their grandmother has Alzheimer's disease. (Rev: SLJ 12/89)

5151 Keats, Ezra Jack. *Louie* (PS–K). Illus. by author. 1983, Greenwillow $14.89 (0-688-02383-5). 32pp. Louie, a silent child, makes his first friend, a puppet, and is allowed to keep it for his very own.

5152 Kelley, Marty. *Winter Woes* (PS–2). Illus. by author. 2005, Zino $12.95 (1-55933-306-5). A little boy imagines in humorous detail the myriad dangers that might befall him should he go out into the snow. (Rev: SLJ 4/05)

5153 Kibbey, Marsha. *My Grammy: A Book About Alzheimer's Disease* (1–3). Illus. by Karen Ritz. 1988, Carolrhoda paper $4.95 (0-87614-544-6). 32pp. Eight-year-old Amy and her family must cope with Grammy's worsening Alzheimer's disease. (Rev: BL 7/88; SLJ 10/88)

5154 Klassen, Heather. *I Don't Want to Go to Justin's House Anymore* (PS–2). Illus. by Beth Jepson. 1999, Child & Family paper $6.95 (0-87868-724-6). Collin witnesses child abuse at friend Justin's house, and gets his mother to promise to get help. (Rev: SLJ 3/00)

5155 Kolbisen, Irene M. *Wiggle-Butts and Up-Faces* (PS–K). Illus. by Sandy D. Zmolek. 1989, I Think I Can LB $14.95 (1-877863-00-9). 32pp. Ingrid's young brother is afraid of taking beginner swimming lessons. (Rev: BL 12/1/89)

5156 Krauss, Ruth. *A Very Special House* (PS–K). Illus. by Maurice Sendak. 1953, HarperCollins LB $17.89 (0-06-023456-3). 32pp. A little boy tells what it would be like in his very special house — no one would ever say "Stop, Stop."

5157 Krisher, Trudy. *Kathy's Hats: A Story of Hope* (PS–3). Illus. by Nadine Bernard Westcott. 1992, Whitman LB $14.95 (0-8075-4116-8). 32pp. When Kathy undergoes chemotherapy for cancer, she finds a new reason to wear her hats. (Rev: BCCB 10/92; BL 10/1/92; SLJ 6/91)

5158 Kroll, Virginia. *Brianna Breathes Easy: A Story About Asthma* (1–3). Illus. by Jayoung Cho. 2005, Whitman $1.00 (0-8075-0880-2). 32pp. Brianna learns she has asthma and how to control it in this informative story that will ease the fears of children with this condition. (Rev: BL 3/1/05)

5159 Kruszka, Bonnie J. *Eating Gluten-Free with Emily: A Story for Children with Celiac Disease* (PS–1). Illus. by Richard S. Cihlar. 2004, Woodbine $14.95 (1-890627-62-3). Emily learns to avoid foods that will cause digestive problems. (Rev: SLJ 4/05)

5160 Lachner, Dorothea. *Danny, the Angry Lion* (PS–K). Trans. by J. Alison James. Illus. by Gusti. 2000, North-South $15.95 (0-7358-1386-8). 32pp. A charming story about a boy who storms out of the house in a fit of anger and how he gradually calms down. (Rev: BL 12/15/00; HBG 3/01; SLJ 11/00)

5161 Lagercrantz, Rose, and Samuel Lagercrantz. *Is It Magic?* (K–3). Trans. by Paul Norlen. Illus. by Eva Eriksson. 1991, R&S $13.95 (91-29-59182-1). Young Pete and Cilla are in love until the class bully steps in. (Rev: SLJ 3/91)

5162 Lampert, Emily. *A Little Touch of Monster* (PS–1). Illus. by Melanie Kroupa. 1986, Little, Brown LB $12.95 (0-316-51287-7). 32pp. No one listens to Parker, so he turns into a bit of a monster; then they listen to him too much, granting almost his every wish. (Rev: BCCB 5/86; BL 3/15/86; HB 5–6/86)

5163 Lasker, Joe. *Nick Joins In* (K–3). Illus. by author. 1980, Whitman LB $14.95 (0-8075-5612-2). 32pp. Wheelchair-bound Nicky wonders what will happen to him when he goes to a regular school.

5164 Lears, Laurie. *Ian's Walk: A Story About Autism* (2–3). Illus. by Karen Ritz. 1998, Whitman $14.95 (0-8075-3480-3). 32pp. Narrator Julie and her sister Tara take their autistic younger brother, Ian, for a walk. Although they are disturbed by his unusual reactions to events and have ambivalent feelings toward him, they show their love by rescuing him when he wanders away. (Rev: BL 4/1/98; HB 5–6/98; HBG 10/98; SLJ 9/98)

5165 Leary, Mary. *Karate Girl* (K–2). Illus. by author. 2003, Farrar $16.00 (0-374-33977-5). Determined to protect her younger brother from the bullies who've been harassing him, a girl enrolls in karate school, where she not only learns martial arts skills but also develops a new self-confidence. (Rev: BL 12/15/03; HBG 4/04; SLJ 11/03)

5166 Leonetti, Mike. *The Goalie Mask* (2–4). Illus. by Shayne Letain. Series: Hockey Heroes. 2004, Raincoast $15.95 (1-55192-703-9). A young player learns from his grandfather about the invention of the mask that protects players' faces from hockey pucks. (Rev: SLJ 2/05)

5167 Levy, Janice. *Totally Uncool* (K–3). Illus. by Chris Monroe. 1998, Carolrhoda $15.95 (1-57505-306-3). 32pp. Alex is not impressed with Elizabeth, Dad's new girlfriend, until Elizabeth helps cure her headaches and designs a prize-winning costume for her. (Rev: BCCB 2/99; BL 2/15/99; HBG 10/99; SLJ 3/99)

5168 Lichtenheld, Tom. *What Are You So Grumpy About?* (K–3). Illus. 2003, Little, Brown $15.95 (0-316-59236-6). 32pp. Humorous double-spread cartoons show situations that could provoke a bad temper. (Rev: BL 3/15/03; HBG 10/03; SLJ 4/03)

5169 Lindgren, Barbro. *Sam's Ball* (PS). Illus. by Eva Eriksson. 1983, Morrow paper $6.95 (0-688-02359-2). 32pp. A book in which a toddler shares his toy with a kitty. Four others in this series are: *Sam's Car; Sam's Cookie; Sam's Teddy Bear* (all 1982); *Sam's Bath* (1983).

5170 Litchfield, Ada B. *Words in Our Hands* (2–4). Illus. by Helen Cogancherry. 1980, Whitman LB $14.95 (0-8075-9212-9). Michael describes his life with his deaf parents.

5171 Lobby, Ted. *Jessica and the Wolf: A Story for Children Who Have Bad Dreams* (PS–1). Illus. by Tennessee Dixon. 1990, Brunner $11.95 (0-945354-22-3); paper $8.95 (0-945354-21-5). 32pp. Parents help their daughter when she has a recurring nightmare about a wolf. (Rev: BL 9/1/90)

5172 London, Jonathan. *The Lion Who Has Asthma* (PS–2). Illus. by Nadine Bernard Westcott. 1992, Whitman LB $14.95 (0-8075-4559-7). In his imagination, asthmatic Sean becomes a variety of animals to suit different situations. (Rev: SLJ 6/92)

5173 Lottridge, Celia B. *Something Might Be Hiding* (PS–K). Illus. by Paul Zwolak. 1996, Douglas & McIntyre $14.95 (0-88899-176-2). 24pp. A child feels the stress of moving to a new house. (Rev: BL 8/96; SLJ 6/96)

5174 McCourt, Lisa. *Chicken Soup for Little Souls: The New Kid and the Cookie Thief* (K–2). Illus. by Mary O. Young. Series: Chicken Soup for Little Souls. 1998, Health Communications $14.95 (1-55874-588-2). 32pp. Julie mistakenly thinks that the boy next to her on the school bus has eaten her cookies and forces herself to apologize. (Rev: BL 2/1/99; HBG 3/99; SLJ 12/98)

5175 McCully, Emily Arnold. *Mouse Practice* (PS–3). Illus. 1999, Scholastic $15.95 (0-590-68220-2). 32pp. Monk lacks the necessary skills to play baseball with the big kids until he figures out a way to improve his skills. (Rev: BCCB 2/99; BL 4/15/99; HB 3–4/99; HBG 10/99; SLJ 3/99)

5176 McKay, Hilary. *There's a Dragon Downstairs* (PS–2). Illus. by Amanda Harvey. 2005, Simon & Schuster $16.95 (0-689-86774-3). 32pp. Sophie conquers her fear of nighttime noises first by dressing up to scare them away, then by discovering their source. (Rev: BL 3/1/05; SLJ 4/05)

5177 McKissack, Patricia. *The Honest-to-Goodness Truth* (PS–3). Illus. by Giselle Potter. 2000, Simon & Schuster $16.00 (0-689-82668-0). 32pp. When Libby tells the honest truth to her friends and classmates, she finds that she can hurt their feelings. (Rev: BCCB 2/00; BL 12/15/99; HBG 10/00; SLJ 1/00)

5178 MacLean, Christine Kole. *Everybody Makes Mistakes* (PS–2). Illus. by C. B. Decker. 2005, Dutton $15.99 (0-525-47225-8). 32pp. Jack has goofed and seeks to justify his mistake by using excuses he's heard from adults. (Rev: BL 5/15/05)

5179 McNamara, Margaret. *The Pumpkin Patch* (PS–1). Illus. by Mike Gordon. Series: Robin Hill School. 2003, Simon & Schuster LB $11.89 (0-689-85875-2); paper $3.99 (0-689-85874-4). 32pp. Katie's classmates laugh at her pumpkin, saying it's too small, but it's just the right size for a pie. (Rev: HBG 4/04; SLJ 10/03)

5180 Magorian, Michelle. *Who's Going to Take Care of Me?* (PS–K). Illus. by James G. Hale. 1990, HarperCollins $13.95 (0-06-024105-5). 32pp. When Eric's older sister starts school, he wonders who will take care of him. (Rev: BL 11/15/90; HB 1–2/91; SLJ 12/90)

5181 Mauser, Pat Rhoads. *Patti's Pet Gorilla* (2–4). Illus. by Diane Palmisciano. 1991, Avon paper $2.95 (0-380-71039-0). 64pp. Patti wants to impress her classmates at show-and-tell, so she tells them she has a pet gorilla. (Rev: BCCB 9/87; BL 3/15/87; SLJ 8/87)

5182 Mayer, Mercer. *You're the Scaredy-Cat* (K–2). Illus. by author. 1991, Rain Bird paper $5.95 (1-879920-01-8). 40pp. Two young boys decide to spend the night camping out in the backyard.

5183 Medearis, Angela Shelf. *Annie's Gifts* (K–3). Illus. by Anna Rich. 1995, Just Us $14.95 (0-940975-30-0); paper $6.95 (0-940975-31-9). Annie is upset because everyone in her family except her is musically talented. (Rev: BCCB 4/95; SLJ 9/95)

5184 Miller, Elizabeth I. *Just Like Home: Como en Mi Tierra* (PS–3). Illus. by Mira Reisberg. 1999, Whitman $14.95 (0-8075-4068-4). 32pp. A Hispanic girl gradually fits into American life in this bilingual picture book. (Rev: BL 12/1/99; HBG 3/00; SLJ 12/99)

5185 Miller, Kathryn Ann. *Did My First Mother Love Me? A Story for an Adopted Child* (K–3). Illus. by Jami Moffett. 1994, Morning Glory $12.95 (0-930934-85-7); paper $5.95 (0-930934-84-9). 47pp. A girl learns the reasons why her real mother put her up for adoption and is comforted by this knowledge. (Rev: SLJ 7/94)

5186 Miller, William. *Night Golf* (1–3). Illus. by Cedric Lucas. 1999, Lee & Low $15.95 (1-880000-79-2). This is the story of an African American boy in the late 1950s, the prejudice he encounters when he wants to play golf on an all-white course, and how he perseveres and overcomes this problem. (Rev: HBG 10/99; SLJ 6/99)

5187 Millman, Isaac. *Moses Goes to a Concert* (K–4). Illus. 1998, Farrar $16.00 (0-374-35067-1). 40pp. This picture book, written in both English and American Sign Language, portrays the everyday experiences of a deaf child, Moses, and of a special occasion when he and his classmates go to a concert. (Rev: BL 4/15/98*; HBG 10/98; SLJ 4/98)

5188 Millman, Isaac. *Moses Goes to School* (PS–3). Illus. 2000, Farrar $16.00 (0-374-35069-8). 32pp. This story, written in both English and sign language, tells how Moses and his friends learn at their special school for the deaf. (Rev: BL 8/00; HBG 3/01; SLJ 8/00)

5189 Millman, Isaac. *Moses Goes to the Circus* (PS–2). Illus. by author. 2003, Farrar $16.00 (0-374-35064-7). Moses, who is deaf, and his family go to a circus for vision- and hearing-impaired children. (Rev: BL 4/15/03; HBG 10/03; SLJ 3/03)

5190 Mochizuki, Ken. *Baseball Saved Us* (2–4). Illus. by Dom Lee. 1993, Lee & Low $15.95 (1-880000-01-6). 32pp. A Japanese American boy gains acceptance playing an excellent game of baseball learned while an internee during World War II. (Rev: BCCB 5/93; BL 4/15/93; HB 7–8/93; SLJ 6/93)

5191 Monnier, Miriam. *Just Right!* (PS–K). Illus. 2001, North-South LB $15.88 (0-7358-1522-4). 32pp. A little girl is told she's too big to do some things and too little to do others. (Rev: BL 11/1/01; HBG 3/02; SLJ 11/01)

5192 Montenegro, Laura Nyman. *A Bird About to Sing* (1–3). Illus. 2003, Houghton Mifflin $15.00 (0-618-18865-7). 32pp. Natalie overcomes her reluctance to read her poems to others after attending a poetry reading. (Rev: BL 2/15/03; HBG 10/03; SLJ 4/03)

5193 Mora, Pat. *The Rainbow Tulip* (PS–4). Illus. by Elizabeth Sayles. 1999, Viking $15.99 (0-670-87291-1). 32pp. A Mexican American child feels torn between her family traditions and the alien Anglo world, but she learns through experience that it is all right to be different. (Rev: BCCB 12/99; BL 11/1/99; HBG 3/00; SLJ 11/99)

5194 Munsch, Robert, and Saoussan Askar. *From Far Away* (K–3). Illus. by Michael Martchenko. 1995, Firefly LB $16.95 (1-55037-397-8); paper $5.95 (1-55037-396-X). 24pp. Saoussan, a war refugee, has problems adjusting to her new home in Canada. (Rev: BL 1/1–15/96; SLJ 3/96)

5195 Napoli, Donna Jo. *Flamingo Dream* (K–3). Illus. by Cathie Felstead. 2002, HarperCollins LB $15.89 (0-688-17863-4). 32pp. A young narrator suffers the loss of her beloved father to cancer. (Rev: BL 4/15/02; HB 7–8/02; HBG 10/02; SLJ 5/02)

5196 Ness, Evaline. *Sam, Bangs and Moonshine* (K–2). Illus. by author. 1966, Holt $15.95 (0-8050-0314-2); paper $6.95 (0-8050-0315-0). 48pp. A little girl learns to distinguish truth from "moonshine" only after her cat and playmate nearly meet tragedy. Caldecott Medal winner, 1967.

5197 Newman, Leslea. *Saturday Is Pattyday* (PS–3). Illus. by Annette Hegel. 1993, New Victoria LB $14.95 (0-934678-52-9); paper $6.95 (0-934678-51-0). 24pp. Frankie is unhappy when her two moms break up and one moves to her own apartment. (Rev: BCCB 11/93; BL 11/1/93)

5198 Newsome, Jill. *Dream Dancer* (PS–2). Illus. by Claudio Munoz. 2002, HarperCollins LB $15.89 (0-06-001322-2). 48pp. A ballerina doll given to her by her grandmother helps Lily through her long recovery after an injury leaves her unable to dance. (Rev: BL 1/1–15/02; HBG 10/02; SLJ 3/02)

5199 Old, Wendie C. *Stacy Had a Little Sister* (PS–2). Illus. by Judith Friedman. 1995, Whitman LB $14.95 (0-8075-7598-4). 32pp. When Stacy's baby sister dies of SIDS, she feels confused and guilty. (Rev: BCCB 5/95; BL 1/1/95; SLJ 2/95)

5200 Paterson, Katherine. *The Smallest Cow in the World* (PS–2). Illus. by Jane Brown. 1991, HarperCollins LB $14.89 (0-06-024691-X); paper $3.95 (0-06-444164-4). 64pp. When he and his family move to another farm, Marvin misses Rosie, the cow he left behind. (Rev: BCCB 1/92*; BL 9/15/91; HB 9–10/91; SLJ 1/92*)

5201 Peacock, Carol Antoinette. *Mommy Far, Mommy Near: An Adoption Story* (K–2). Illus. by Shawn Costello Brownell. 2000, Whitman $14.95 (0-8075-5234-8). 32pp. In spite of her loving Caucasian American family, Elizabeth, an adopted Chinese girl, sometimes wonders why her real mother gave her up and why there wasn't enough room for her in China. (Rev: BL 3/15/00; HBG 10/00; SLJ 5/00)

5202 Peterson, Jeanne Whitehouse. *I Have a Sister, My Sister Is Deaf* (1–3). Illus. by Deborah Kogan Ray. 1977, HarperCollins LB $15.89 (0-06-024702-9); paper $5.95 (0-06-443059-6). 32pp. About a young girl's adjustment to deafness.

5203 Polacco, Patricia. *Thank You, Mr. Falker* (K–4). Illus. 1998, Penguin Putnam $15.99 (0-399-23166-8). 40pp. Based on the author's personal experiences, this is the story of Trisha, who was able to draw beautifully but hid the fact that she couldn't read until she got special help in the fifth grade. (Rev: BCCB 6/98; BL 5/1/98; HBG 10/98; SLJ 6/98)

5204 Pollack, Eileen. *Whisper Whisper Jesse, Whisper Whisper Josh: A Story About AIDS* (K–4). Illus. by Bruce Gilfoy. 1992, Advantage LB $16.95 (0-9624828-4-6); paper $5.95 (0-9624828-3-8). 32pp. Jesse's uncle, Josh, who is dying of AIDS, comes to stay with Jesse's family. (Rev: BL 3/15/93)

5205 Ransom, Jeanie Franz. *I Don't Want to Talk About It* (K–3). Illus. by Kathryn Kunz Finney. 2000, Magination $14.95 (1-55798-664-9); paper $8.95 (1-55798-703-3). 28pp. A young girl whose parents are divorcing talks about her feelings and means of coping. (Rev: SLJ 2/01)

5206 Raschka, Chris. *Waffle* (PS–2). Illus. 2001, Simon & Schuster $16.00 (0-689-83838-7). 40pp. Waffle, a champion worrier and procrastinator, manages to overcome his failings. (Rev: BCCB 5/01; BL 5/15/01; HB 5–6/01; HBG 10/01; SLJ 5/01)

5207 Rathmann, Peggy. *Ruby the Copycat* (K–3). Illus. 1991, Scholastic $14.95 (0-590-43747-X). 32pp. At first, Angela is flattered when a new girl, Ruby, copies everything she does; then it becomes annoying. (Rev: BL 11/15/91; SLJ 1/92*)

5208 Recorvits, Helen. *My Name Is Yoon* (K–2). Illus. by Gabi Swiatkowska. 2003, Farrar $16.00 (0-374-35114-7). 32pp. Yoon, a Korean immigrant child, is unhappy in America until she begins to feel at home in her new and different surroundings. (Rev: BL 3/15/03; HBG 10/03; SLJ 5/03)

5209 Reynolds, Marilynn. *Goodbye to Griffith Street* (K–2). Illus. by Renn Benoit. 2004, Orca $16.95 (1-55143-285-4). It snows on John's last day on Griffith Street (his parents are getting divorced and he and his mother must move), and John decides to leave his friends and neighbors with the gift of snow angels and stars. (Rev: SLJ 1/05)

5210 Reynolds, Marilynn. *The Magnificent Piano Recital* (K–3). Illus. by Laura Fernandez and Rick Jacobson. 2001, Orca $15.95 (1-55143-180-7). 32pp. When Arabella moves to a new town, she feels lonely and unwanted until she triumphs at a piano recital. (Rev: BL 3/1/01; HBG 10/01)

5211 Robberecht, Thierry. *Angry Dragon* (PS–2). Illus. by Philippe Goossens. 2004, Clarion $15.00 (0-618-47430-7). 32pp. A little boy pictures himself transformed into a fire-breathing dragon every time his anger gets out of control. (Rev: BL 1/1–15/05)

5212 Rodriguez, Bobbie. *Sarah's Sleepover* (1–3). Illus. by Mark Graham. 2000, Viking $15.99 (0-670-87750-6). 32pp. Sarah, who is blind, helps her visiting cousins by leading them to safety when the lights go out. (Rev: BL 4/1/00; HBG 10/00; SLJ 5/00)

5213 Rodriguez, Luis J. *America Is Her Name* (2–4). Illus. by Carlos Vazquez. 1998, Curbstone $15.95 (1-880684-40-3). Lonely in her barrio home in Chicago, America Soliz learns to express herself in poetry. (Rev: HBG 10/98; SLJ 9/98)

5214 Rosenberry, Vera. *Vera Runs Away* (PS–3). Illus. 2000, Holt $16.00 (0-8050-6267-X). 32pp. Vera feels so underappreciated at home when she receives a straight-A report card that she decides to run away. (Rev: BL 10/15/00; HBG 3/01; SLJ 11/00)

5215 Rotner, Shelley, and Sheila Kelly. *Something's Different* (K–3). Illus. 2002, Millbrook LB $22.90 (0-7613-1923-9). 32pp. A boy tries to understand his parents' marital problems. (Rev: BL 3/1/02; HBG 10/02; SLJ 8/02)

5216 Say, Allen. *Allison* (PS–3). Illus. 1997, Houghton Mifflin $17.00 (0-395-85895-X). 32pp. Little Allison, an Asian girl, is upset when she learns that she has been adopted by her Caucasian parents. (Rev: BL 12/15/97*; HBG 3/98; SLJ 10/97)

5217 Say, Allen. *Emma's Rug* (PS–3). Illus. 1996, Houghton Mifflin $16.95 (0-395-74294-3). 32pp. Emma is inconsolable when she loses the rug that has been the inspiration for her art. (Rev: BCCB 11/96; BL 10/1/96; HB 9–10/96; SLJ 9/96)

5218 Schick, Eleanor. *Mama* (K–3). Illus. 2000, Marshall Cavendish $15.95 (0-7614-5060-2). 32pp. A mother's death and the ensuing sorrow, acceptance, and cherishing of memories are the subjects of this picture book, seen through a young daughter's eyes. (Rev: BL 2/15/00; HBG 10/00; SLJ 5/00)

5219 Schotter, Roni. *Missing Rabbit* (PS–2). Illus. by Cyd Moore. 2002, Clarion $15.00 (0-618-03432-3). 32pp. After her parents divorce, Kara finds a toy rabbit is an anchor in her movements between two homes. (Rev: BL 5/1/02; HBG 10/02; SLJ 4/02)

5220 Schotter, Roni. *Room for Rabbit* (PS–2). Illus. by Cyd Moore. 2003, Clarion $15.00 (0-618-18183-0). 32pp. Kara finds that her father's new wife is taking up too much space and uses her rabbit as her

spokesperson. (Rev: BL 3/1/03; HBG 10/03; SLJ 4/03)

5221 Sendak, Maurice. *Pierre: A Cautionary Tale in Five Chapters and a Prologue* (K–3). Illus. by author. 1962, HarperCollins LB $15.89 (0-06-025965-5). 48pp. The story about a young boy whose motto is "I don't care."

5222 Senisi, Ellen B. *All Kinds of Friends, Even Green!* (K–4). Photos by author. 2002, Woodbine $14.95 (1-890627-35-6). Wheelchair-bound Zaki chooses a neighbor's iguana for his school assignment, because the plucky animal manages to cope despite missing toes. (Rev: HBG 10/03; SLJ 11/02)

5223 Shange, Ntozake. *White Wash* (PS–2). Illus. by Michael Sporn. 1997, Walker $15.95 (0-8027-8490-9). Helene-Angel and her brother are attacked by a group of white thugs who cover her face with white paint and traumatize her so much that she doesn't want to return to school. (Rev: HBG 3/98; SLJ 5/98)

5224 Shannon, David. *A Bad Case of Stripes* (1–3). Illus. 1998, Scholastic $15.95 (0-590-92997-6). 32pp. Camilla's desire to please and be popular causes her some problems. (Rev: BCCB 3/98; BL 1/1–15/98; HBG 10/98; SLJ 3/98)

5225 Shavick, Andrea. *You'll Grow Soon, Alex* (PS–1). Illus. by Russell Ayto. 2000, Walker $15.95 (0-8027-8736-3). 32pp. Alex tries everything including diet and exercise to hasten his growth but later decides that being tall has its disadvantages. (Rev: BL 10/15/00; HBG 10/01; SLJ 10/00)

5226 Shin, Sun Yung. *Cooper's Lesson* (PS–3). Trans. by Min Paek. Illus. by Kim Cogan. 2004, Children's Book Pr. $16.95 (0-89239-193-6). 32pp. Cooper's mother is Korean and his father is white, resulting in some confusion for the young boy; the story is told in English and Korean. (Rev: BL 3/15/04*; SLJ 5/04)

5227 Simon, Norma. *I Wish I Had My Father* (2–4). Illus. by Arieh Zeldich. 1983, Whitman LB $13.95 (0-8075-3522-2). 32pp. A young boy wishes his divorced father was back with him.

5228 Smalls, Irene. *Because You're Lucky* (PS–3). Illus. by Michael Hays. 1997, Little, Brown $15.95 (0-316-79867-3). 32pp. A young boy goes to live with his aunt's family and arouses the hostility of his cousin. (Rev: BL 9/1/97; HBG 3/98; SLJ 10/97)

5229 Smothers, Ethel Footman. *The Hard-Times Jar* (1–3). Illus. by John Holyfield. 2003, Farrar $16.00 (0-374-32852-8). 32pp. Emma, the dark-skinned daughter of migrant workers, finds the strength to face her new third-grade classroom in Pennsylvania, and learns to appreciate reading and books. (Rev: BL 8/03; HBG 4/04; SLJ 10/03)

5230 Spalding, Andrea, and Janet Wilson. *Me and Mr. Mah* (PS–2). Illus. 2000, Orca $14.95 (1-55143-168-8). Ian misses his father after his parents divorce but finds a friend and kindred spirit in Mr. Mah, a neighbor who misses his family in China. (Rev: BL 3/1/03; HBG 9/00; SLJ 3/00)

5231 Spelman, Cornelia Maude. *After Charlotte's Mom Died* (K–2). Illus. by Judith Friedman. 1996, Whitman LB $13.95 (0-8075-0196-4). 32pp. Charlotte feels conflicting emotions, such as anger and fear, as she adjusts to her mother's death. (Rev: BL 4/15/96; SLJ 8/96)

5232 Spelman, Cornelia Maude. *Mama and Daddy Bear's Divorce* (PS–1). Illus. by Kathy Parkinson. 1998, Whitman $13.95 (0-8075-5221-6). 32pp. Though animals are used as characters, this is a realistic story about the effects of divorce. It offers the comforting message that love continues even through separation. (Rev: BL 12/1/98; HBG 3/99; SLJ 9/98)

5233 Spelman, Cornelia Maude. *When I Feel Jealous* (PS–1). Illus. by Kathy Parkinson. Series: The Way I Feel Books. 2003, Whitman LB $14.95 (0-8075-8886-5). A little bear talks about the sorts of things that make her jealous and what she does to cope with such feelings. (Rev: HBG 4/04; SLJ 10/03)

5234 Spinelli, Eileen. *Wanda's Monster* (K–2). Illus. by Nancy Hayashi. 2002, Whitman $15.95 (0-8075-8656-0). 32pp. Granny is the only one who believes there's a monster in Wanda's closet, but points out that it can't be much fun for the monster. (Rev: BL 12/1/02; HB 1–2/03; HBG 3/03; SLJ 10/02)

5235 Stadler, Alexander. *Lila Bloom* (K–2). Illus. 2004, Farrar $16.00 (0-374-34474-4). 40pp. Lila's been having a horrible day and a trip to ballet class only threatens to make matters worse, but Lila surprises herself with her dancing. (Rev: BL 4/1/04; SLJ 6/04)

5236 Stauffacher, Sue. *Harry Sue* (5–8). 2005, Knopf LB $17.99 (0-375-93274-7). 272pp. Both her parents are in prison and 11-year-old Harry Sue Clotkin acts as tough as she can in the face of a difficult life with her grandmother. (Rev: BL 5/1/05)

5237 Steig, William. *Spinky Sulks* (K–3). Illus. 1988, Farrar paper $4.95 (0-374-46990-3). 32pp. Spinky is a first-class sulker but is forced to reconsider his position. (Rev: BCCB 12/88; BL 1/15/89; HB 3–4/89)

5238 Stein, Sara Bonnett. *About Dying* (1–3). Illus. by author. 1974, Walker $10.95 (0-8027-6172-0); paper $8.95 (0-8027-7223-4). 48pp. Sensitive portrayal of the death of a bird and of a grandfather. Also use: *About Handicaps* (1974); *Making Babies* (1974); *About Phobias; The Adopted One; On Divorce* (all 1979).

5239 Stolz, Mary. *Storm in the Night* (K–3). Illus. by Pat Cummings. 1988, HarperCollins LB $15.89 (0-06-025913-2); paper $5.95 (0-06-443256-4). 32pp. Grandfather tells Thomas, a young African American boy, of a time when he was afraid, in order to calm the child's fears about a dark, stormy night. (Rev: BL 2/1/88; HB 7–8/88; SLJ 3/88)

5240 Tarpley, Natasha Anastasia. *Joe-Joe's First Flight* (PS–2). Illus. by E. B. Lewis. 2003, Knopf $15.95 (0-375-81053-6). 40pp. In the 1920s, young Joe-Joe dreams of flying a plane but fears that, as an African American, he won't be allowed to. (Rev: BL 2/15/04; HBG 10/03; SLJ 7/03)

5241 Thompson, Mary. *Andy and His Yellow Frisbee* (1–3). Illus. by author. 1996, Woodbine $14.95 (0-933149-83-2). The story of an autistic child as

seen through the eyes of a young classmate. (Rev: SLJ 1/97)

5242 Vail, Rachel. *Sometimes I'm Bombaloo* (PS–2). Illus. by Yumi Heo. 2002, Scholastic $15.95 (0-439-08755-4). 32pp. Katie is a mostly-good kid who sometimes turns into an angry "Bombaloo." (Rev: BCCB 4/02; BL 2/1/02; HBG 10/02; SLJ 3/02)

5243 Verniero, Joan C. *You Can Call Me Willy: A Story for Children About AIDS* (K–3). Illus. by Verdon Flory. Series: Books to Help Parents Help Their Children. 1995, Magination paper $8.95 (0-945354-60-6). A touching story of a third-grader who has AIDS and the intolerance and misunderstandings she faces at school. (Rev: SLJ 9/95)

5244 Vigna, Judith. *I Wish Daddy Didn't Drink So Much* (PS). Illus. by author. 1988, Whitman paper $5.95 (0-8075-3526-5). 32pp. A Christmas story told by a little girl whose father is an alcoholic. (Rev: BL 10/1/88; SLJ 1/89)

5245 Vigna, Judith. *Saying Goodbye to Daddy* (K–2). Illus. 1991, Whitman LB $14.95 (0-8075-7253-5). 32pp. When her father is killed in a car accident, Clare goes through the phases of grieving. (Rev: BL 2/1/91; SLJ 3/91)

5246 Viorst, Judith. *The Tenth Good Thing About Barney* (K–2). Illus. by Erik Blegvad. 1971, Macmillan $14.00 (0-689-20688-7); paper $4.99 (0-689-71203-0). 32pp. At a backyard funeral, a little boy tries to think of ten good things to say about his cat, Barney — but can come up with only nine.

5247 Waber, Bernard. *Ira Sleeps Over* (PS–2). Illus. by author. 1973, Houghton Mifflin $15.00 (0-395-13893-0); paper $5.95 (0-395-20503-4). 48pp. When Ira is invited to sleep overnight at Reggie's house, he wants to go, but should he or shouldn't he take along his teddy bear?

5248 Watts, Jeri Hanel. *Keepers* (K–3). Illus. by Felicia Marshall. 1997, Lee & Low $15.95 (1-880000-58-X). 32pp. Kenyon feels guilty because he has bought a baseball glove with the money intended for Grandmother's 90th birthday present. (Rev: BL 1/1–15/98; HBG 3/98; SLJ 1/98)

5249 Weiss, Ellen. *The Nose Knows* (1–3). Illus. by Margeaux Lucas. Series: Science Solves It! 2002, Kane paper $4.99 (1-57565-120-3). 32pp. Peter's acute nose is useful when everyone has a cold in this story that interweaves scientific facts. (Rev: SLJ 1/03)

5250 Williams, Sherley A. *Girls Together* (PS–3). Illus. by Synthia Saint James. 1999, Harcourt $16.00 (0-15-230982-9). 32pp. Set in a California housing project, this moving picture book describes the harsh living conditions that a migrant child faces every day. (Rev: BCCB 5/99; BL 2/15/99; HB 3–4/99; HBG 10/99; SLJ 6/99)

5251 Willis, Jeanne. *Susan Laughs* (PS–K). Illus. 2000, Holt $15.00 (0-8050-6501-6). 32pp. Susan is presented in a series of activities — laughing, singing, and swimming, for example — and on the last page is shown in her wheelchair. (Rev: BCCB 10/00; BL 8/00; HBG 3/01; SLJ 11/00)

5252 Winton, Tim. *The Deep* (PS–2). Illus. by Karen Louise. 2000, Tricycle $14.95 (1-58246-024-8). 32pp. Alice is afraid to swim in the deep water near her home until some playful dolphins help her to overcome her fears. (Rev: BL 5/15/00; HBG 10/00; SLJ 7/00)

5253 Wishinsky, Frieda. *Each One Special* (PS–2). Illus. by H. Werner Zimmermann. 1999, Orca $14.95 (1-55143-122-X). 32pp. When a creative cake decorator is fired from his job, he takes up a related field — sculpting. (Rev: BL 1/1–15/99; HBG 10/99; SLJ 7/99)

5254 Woodson, Jacqueline. *Our Gracie Aunt* (K–3). Illus. by Jon J. Muth. 2002, Hyperion $15.99 (0-7868-0620-6). 32pp. Johnson and his sister Beebee experience different emotions when they are taken in by their aunt after their mother abandons them. (Rev: BCCB 9/02; BL 9/1/02; HBG 3/03; SLJ 12/02)

5255 Woodson, Jacqueline. *Sweet, Sweet Memory* (K–3). Illus. by Floyd Cooper. 2001, Hyperion $14.99 (0-7868-0241-3). 32pp. Even though Grandpa is dead and she grieves for him, a young African American girl follows his advice that life must go on. (Rev: BL 2/15/01; HBG 10/01)

5256 Zolotow, Charlotte. *The Three Funny Friends* (PS–2). Illus. by Linda Bronson. 2003, Running Press $15.95 (0-7624-1553-3). A lonely young girl, who has just moved to a new town, comforts herself with three imaginary friends — Guy-Guy, Bickerina, and Mr. Dobie — until a real-life friend comes along. (Rev: SLJ 12/03)

REAL AND ALMOST REAL ANIMALS

5257 Abercrombie, Barbara. *Bad Dog, Dodger!* (1–3). Illus. by Adam Gustavson. 2002, Simon & Schuster $14.95 (0-689-83782-8). 40pp. Fearful that he might lose his pup because of the dog's bad behavior, Sam decides to give Dodger some obedience lessons. (Rev: BL 4/1/02; HBG 10/02; SLJ 11/02)

5258 Abley, Mark. *Ghost Cat* (PS–K). Illus. by Karen Reczuch. 2001, Groundwood $16.95 (0-88899-433-8). 32pp. Elderly Miss Wilkinson depends on her cat for companionship and is bereft when he becomes ill and dies, but comforted when the rose bush she plants on his grave blooms. (Rev: HBG 3/02; SLJ 9/01)

5259 Adlerman, Daniel. *Africa Calling: Nighttime Falling* (PS–1). Illus. by Kimberly Adlerman. 1996, Whispering Coyote $15.95 (1-879085-98-4). 32pp. A young girl tries to imagine her stuffed animals in their native African habitats. (Rev: BL 10/1/96; SLJ 9/96)

5260 Appelt, Kathi. *Where, Where Is Swamp Bear?* (PS–1). Illus. by Megan Halsey. 2002, HarperCollins LB $15.89 (0-688-17103-6). 32pp. A young Louisiana boy called Pierre goes fishing with his Granpere, but the boy's main preoccupation is looking for the elusive Swamp Bear and learning about the bear's life. (Rev: BL 2/15/02; HBG 10/02; SLJ 1/02*)

5261 Araki, Mie. *Kitten's Big Adventure* (PS). Illus. 2005, Harcourt $15.00 (0-15-216738-2). 40pp. A small kitten enjoys chasing a butterfly but is quick to hurry back to its mother's side. (Rev: BL 5/1/05; SLJ 6/05)

5262 Archambault, John. *The Birth of a Whale* (K–2). Illus. by Janet Skiles. 1996, Silver Burdett LB $18.95 (0-382-39566-2). 48pp. In rhythmic verse and watercolor illustrations, the birth of a humpback whale is chronicled. (Rev: BL 3/15/96; SLJ 3/96) [599.5]

5263 Arnosky, Jim. *Coyote Raid in Cactus Canyon* (K–2). Illus. by author. 2005, Penguin Putnam $15.99 (0-399-23413-6). A rattlesnake scares off the coyotes that have been plaguing the smaller animals in Cactus Canyon. (Rev: SLJ 3/05)

5264 Arnosky, Jim. *Little Lions* (PS). Illus. 1998, Penguin Putnam $15.99 (0-399-22944-2). 32pp. A simple picture book that reports on the playful activities of two mountain lion cubs and their ever-watchful mother. (Rev: BL 3/1/98; HBG 10/98; SLJ 3/98)

5265 Arnosky, Jim. *Raccoon on His Own* (PS–2). Illus. by author. 2001, Penguin Putnam $15.99 (0-399-22756-3). A curious baby raccoon is carried off in a wooden boat. (Rev: BCCB 7–8/01; HBG 10/01; SLJ 5/01)

5266 Arnosky, Jim. *Turtle in the Sea* (PS–2). Illus. 2002, Penguin Putnam $15.99 (0-399-22757-1). 32pp. A sea turtle survives the dangers surrounding her in the ocean. (Rev: BL 9/1/02; HBG 3/03; SLJ 8/02)

5267 Arrigoni, Patricia. *Harpo: The Baby Harp Seal* (2–3). Illus. 1995, Travel Publishers $16.95 (0-9625468-8-7). 32pp. Harpo, a baby harp seal, is rescued by a little girl when he is separated from his mother. (Rev: BL 2/1/96)

5268 Asch, Frank. *The Last Puppy* (PS–2). Illus. by author. 1989, Simon & Schuster paper $4.95 (0-671-66687-8). 32pp. An enchanting story of the puppy born last in a large litter.

5269 Ashman, Linda. *Castles, Caves, and Honeycombs* (PS–K). Illus. by Lauren Stringer. 2001, Harcourt $16.00 (0-15-202211-2). 32pp. Animal homes — nests, shells, dens, or hollow logs — are pictured in drawings and rhyming verse. (Rev: BL 3/15/01*; HB 7–8/01; HBG 10/01)

5270 Austin, Patricia. *The Cat Who Loved Mozart* (1–3). Illus. by Henri Sorenson. 2001, Holiday House $16.95 (0-8234-1535-X). 32pp. Nine-year-old Jennifer adopts a stray cat that resists her affection until it hears her practicing for a piano recital. (Rev: BL 5/1/01; HBG 10/01; SLJ 6/01)

5271 Banks, Kate. *Baboon* (PS–K). Illus. by Georg Hallensleben. 1997, Farrar $14.00 (0-374-30474-2). 32pp. A mother introduces her baby baboon to the intricacies of the great world. (Rev: BCCB 4/97; BL 3/1/97*; HB 5–6/97; SLJ 3/97)

5272 Banks, Kate. *The Cat Who Walked Across France* (PS–2). Illus. by Georg Hallensleben. 2004, Farrar $16.00 (0-374-39968-9). 40pp. A French cat who has been uprooted after the death of his owner decides to head back to the house he loves; beautiful paintings document his long and difficult journey. (Rev: BL 3/15/04; HB 3–4/04; SLJ 3/04)

5273 Barner, Bob. *Fish Wish* (PS–K). Illus. 2000, Holiday House $16.95 (0-8234-1482-5). 32pp. Collages are used to illustrate this fanciful picture book about a boy who dreams of being a fish and encountering all the creatures in a coral reef. (Rev: BL 2/1/00; HBG 10/00; SLJ 5/00)

5274 Bartoletti, Susan Campbell. *Nobody's Diggier Than a Dog* (PS–K). Illus. by Beppe Giacobbe. 2005, Hyperion $15.99 (0-7868-1824-7). 40pp. In this energetic companion to *Nobody's Nosier Than a Cat,* dogs are shown in typically doggy situations. (Rev: BL 1/1–15/05; SLJ 2/05)

5275 Bartoletti, Susan Campbell. *Nobody's Nosier Than a Cat* (PS–3). Illus. by Beppe Giacobbe. 2003, Hyperion $15.99 (0-7868-1614-7). Humorous illustrations and lively rhymes depict the physical and behavioral characteristics of cats. (Rev: BL 11/1/03; HBG 4/04; SLJ 12/03)

5276 Barton, Byron. *Bones, Bones, Dinosaur Bones* (PS–K). Illus. 1990, HarperCollins LB $15.89 (0-690-04827-0). 32pp. Paleontologists collect a number of bones and reconstruct a dinosaur. (Rev: BL 10/15/90; HB 11–12/90*; SLJ 9/90)

5277 Base, Graeme. *The Water Hole* (PS–1). Illus. 2001, Abrams $18.95 (0-8109-4568-1). 30pp. Part counting book, part introduction to animal species, and part overview of the water cycle, this richly illustrated picture book shows various animals — from one rhino to ten kangaroos — gathering at a water hole. (Rev: BL 10/1/01; HBG 3/02; SLJ 12/01)

5278 Beames, Margaret. *Night Cat* (K–4). Illus. by Sue Hitchcock. 2003, Scholastic $15.95 (0-439-38576-8). Menacing creatures and a shower of rain persuade Oliver the cat of the benefits of home. (Rev: HBG 4/04; SLJ 9/03)

5279 Becker, John. *Mugambi's Journey* (K–3). Illus. by Mark Clapsadle. 2004, Gingham Dog $14.95 (0-7696-3167-3). A cheetah cub called Mugambi shows his courage on the Serengeti Plain. (Rev: SLJ 11/04)

5280 Berenzy, Alix. *Sammy: The Classroom Guinea Pig* (PS–2). Illus. 2005, Holt $16.95 (0-8050-4024-2). 32pp. Lots of information about guinea pigs is conveyed as Ms. B.'s class investigates why Sammy is making so much noise. (Rev: BL 5/15/05)

5281 Berkes, Marianne. *Marsh Morning* (2–4). Illus. by Robert Noreika. 2003, Millbrook LB $22.90 (0-7613-2568-9). 32pp. Watercolor illustrations and short rhymes tell the stories of 15 species of birds and their morning songs. (Rev: BL 3/15/03; HBG 10/03; SLJ 4/03)

5282 Bernard, Robin. *Juma and the Honey Guide* (PS–3). Illus. by Nneka Bennett. 1996, Dillon LB $18.95 (0-382-39162-4); paper $5.95 (0-382-39164-0). 32pp. A young African boy and his father share a honeycomb with a small bird that has led them to the beehive. (Rev: BL 8/96; SLJ 8/96)

5283 Best, Cari. *Goose's Story* (PS–3). Illus. by Holly Meade. 2002, Farrar $16.00 (0-374-32750-5). 32pp. A young girl witnesses how an injured goose copes with his disability and tries to survive though left behind by the flock. (Rev: BCCB 9/02; BL 5/1/02*; HB 5–6/02; HBG 10/02; SLJ 7/02)

5284 Blackstone, Stella. *Secret Seahorse* (PS–2). Illus. by Clare Beaton. 2004, Barefoot $14.99 (1-84148-704-X). 32pp. A fast-moving seahorse weaves in and out of sight through the coral reefs and caves beneath the sea. (Rev: BL 4/15/04; SLJ 1/05)

5285 Blackstone, Stella. *Who Are You, Baby Kangaroo?* (PS–K). Illus. by Clare Beaton. 2004, Barefoot $14.99 (1-84148-217-X). A puppy determined to find out the word for a baby kangaroo travels far and wide asking other animals. (Rev: SLJ 11/04)

5286 Blades, Ann. *Mary of Mile 18* (K–3). Illus. 2001, Tundra $14.95 (0-88776-581-5). 48pp. This 30th anniversary reissue of the classic story of a Canadian girl who takes in a part-wolf pup has a larger format and slight redesign. (Rev: BL 10/15/01; HBG 10/02)

5287 Blake, Robert J. *Akiak: A Tale from the Iditarod* (PS–3). Illus. 1997, Penguin Putnam $16.99 (0-399-22798-9). 32pp. An aging sled dog named Akiak participates in the Iditarod sled race for the last time. (Rev: BL 9/1/97; HBG 3/98; SLJ 9/97*)

5288 Blake, Robert J. *Carousel Cat* (K–3). Illus. by author. 2005, Philomel $16.99 (0-399-23382-2). The cat who kept Dan company as he ran the carousel becomes a hero. (Rev: SLJ 3/05)

5289 Blake, Robert J. *Fledgling* (PS–3). Illus. 2000, Penguin Putnam $15.99 (0-399-23321-0). 32pp. A fledgling kestrel spends an exciting day in New York City when he takes his first flight. (Rev: BL 12/15/00; HB 1–2/01; HBG 3/01; SLJ 10/00)

5290 Blake, Robert J. *Togo* (2–4). Illus. 2002, Penguin Putnam $16.99 (0-399-23381-4). 48pp. Blake's brilliantly illustrated story is a gripping tribute to Togo, the dog that should have got credit for the famous serum run during the diphtheria epidemic in Nome in 1925. (Rev: BL 9/15/02; HBG 3/03; SLJ 9/02*)

5291 Blanc, Esther S. *Berchick* (1–3). Illus. by Tennessee Dixon. 1989, Volcano $14.95 (0-912078-81-2). Mama takes care of a colt found beside its dead mother. (Rev: SLJ 11/89)

5292 Bloom, Suzanne. *No Place for a Pig* (K–3). Illus. by author. 2003, Boyds Mills $15.95 (1-59078-047-7). When her apartment becomes too small for her rapidly growing pig, Ms. Taffy's neighbors come to the rescue. (Rev: BL 1/1–15/04; HBG 4/04; SLJ 11/03)

5293 Bloxam, Frances. *Little Tom Turkey* (PS–2). Illus. by Jim Sollers. 2005, Down East $15.95 (0-89272-671-7). In rhyming verse with dollops of humor and fact, Bloxam tells the story of an appealing and ambitious young wild turkey. (Rev: SLJ 6/05)

5294 Bogan, Paulette. *Spike in the Kennel* (PS–1). Illus. 2001, Penguin Putnam $12.99 (0-399-23594-9). 32pp. Spike the dog must spend a night at the kennel and hates it at first. (Rev: BL 7/01; HBG 10/01; SLJ 6/01)

5295 Bogan, Paulette. *Spike in Trouble* (PS–2). Illus. by author. 2003, Penguin Putnam $13.99 (0-399-23765-8). Sent to obedience school for misdeeds he didn't commit, Spike the dog enjoys the experience anyway and returns home to uncover the real culprit. (Rev: HBG 10/03; SLJ 5/03)

5296 Boyd, Lizi. *Black Dog Gets Dressed* (PS). Illus. by author. 2003, Candlewick $11.99 (0-7636-1980-9). A young boy dresses his black Labrador in human clothes and, to complete the role reversal, dons a black dog costume himself. (Rev: HBG 4/04; SLJ 9/03)

5297 Bradford, Karleen. *You Can't Rush a Cat* (2–3). Illus. by Leslie Elizabeth Watts. 2003, Orca $16.95 (1-55143-247-1). 32pp. Jessica helps her grandfather coax a shy stray kitten out of the bushes in this charming story. (Rev: BL 2/1/04; HBG 4/04; SLJ 2/04)

5298 Broome, Errol. *Drusilla the Lucky Duck* (3–4). Illus. by Sharon Thompson. 2003, Annick $16.95 (1-55037-799-X); paper $4.95 (1-55037-798-1). 72pp. The story of young Carrie and her pet duckling Drusilla, and how Carrie races to save Drusilla from becoming someone's dinner. (Rev: SLJ 3/04)

5299 Brown, Margaret Wise. *Big Red Barn* (PS–1). Illus. by Felicia Bond. 1989, HarperCollins LB $15.95 (0-06-020749-3). 32pp. The big red barn contains lots and lots of animals and their offspring. (Rev: BL 3/1/89; SLJ 6/89)

5300 Brown, Margaret Wise. *Bumble Bee* (PS). Illus. by Victoria Raymond. Series: Harper Growing Tree. 1999, HarperCollins $5.95 (0-694-01749-3). This 1959 poem about an active bumblebee is now in a board book format with bright illustrations. (Rev: SLJ 7/99)

5301 Brown, Margaret Wise. *The Good Little Bad Little Pig* (PS–1). Illus. by Dan Yaccarino. 2002, Hyperion LB $16.49 (0-7868-2514-6). A little boy gets the pig he wants in this simple story with charming illustrations. (Rev: HBG 3/03; SLJ 11/02)

5302 Brown, Margaret Wise. *Wheel on the Chimney* (PS–3). Illus. by Tibor Gergely. 1954, Harper-Collins LB $13.00 (0-397-30296-7). 32pp. Hungarian storks return each spring from Africa to nest on farmers' chimneys. A 1955 Caldecott Honor Book.

5303 Brown, Tricia. *Groucho's Eyebrows* (K–2). Illus. by Barbara Lavallee. 2003, Alaska Northwest $15.95 (0-88240-556-X). Enticing illustrations grace this story of an Alaskan girl named Kristie and her white cat with magnificent black eyebrows. (Rev: HBG 4/04; SLJ 6/04)

5304 Buck, Nola. *Oh, Cats!* (PS–1). Illus. by Nadine Bernard Westcott. 1997, HarperCollins LB $12.89 (0-06-025374-6). 32pp. A little girl tries to befriend three very independent cats. (Rev: BL 11/15/96; SLJ 2/97)

5305 Bunting, Eve. *Red Fox Running* (PS–3). Illus. by Wendell Minor. 1993, Houghton Mifflin $15.95 (0-395-58919-3). 30pp. A story about a hungry fox that hunts until it kills a bobcat to bring home to his family. (Rev: BL 11/15/93; SLJ 12/93)

5306 Bunting, Eve. *Whales Passing* (PS–2). Illus. by Lambert Davis. 2003, Scholastic $15.95 (0-590-60358-2). A gentle — and fact-filled — story of a boy being introduced by his father to the wonders of orcas and nature in general. (Rev: HBG 10/03; SLJ 6/03)

5307 Burningham, John. *Hey! Get Off Our Train* (K–3). Illus. 1990, Crown paper $7.99 (0-517-88204-3). 48pp. A boy's dream takes him on a train trip around the world where he sees environmental dangers. (Rev: BCCB 4/90; BL 5/15/90; HB 5–6/90; SLJ 5/90)

5308 Bushey, Jeanne. *A Sled Dog for Moshi* (K–3). Illus. by Germaine Arnaktauyok. 1994, Hyperion LB $15.49 (1-56282-632-8). 40pp. A sled dog saves two Inuit children during a storm. (Rev: BL 1/15/95; SLJ 1/95)

5309 Bushnell, Jack. *Sky Dancer* (K–3). Illus. by Jan Ormerod. 1996, Lothrop LB $15.93 (0-688-05289-4). 32pp. Jenny tries to save a red-tailed hawk from being shot by local farmers. (Rev: BL 9/15/96; SLJ 9/96)

5310 Butler, John. *Pi-Shu, the Little Panda* (K–2). Illus. 2001, Peachtree $15.95 (1-56145-242-4). 32pp. The daily activities of a baby panda named Pi-shu are recounted in this picture book that also gives information on why this is an endangered species. (Rev: BL 3/15/01; HBG 10/01)

5311 Buzzeo, Toni. *Little Loon and Papa* (PS–2). Illus. by Margaret Spengler. 2004, Dial $15.99 (0-8037-2958-8). Despite his father's patient advice, Little Loon is having trouble learning to dive until outside pressures force him to take the plunge. (Rev: SLJ 6/04)

5312 Calmenson, Stephanie. *Perfect Puppy* (PS–1). Illus. by Thomas F. Yezerski. 2001, Houghton Mifflin $15.00 (0-618-01139-0). 32pp. A puppy aspires to be the perfect pet in this charming tale about unconditional love and what it takes to train an animal. (Rev: BL 3/1/02; HBG 3/02; SLJ 3/02)

5313 Campbell, Rod. *Dear Zoo* (PS). Illus. by author. 1983, Puffin paper $4.95 (0-317-62180-7). 22pp. A youngster keeps sending back the pets requested from a zoo until a puppy arrives.

5314 Capucilli, Alyssa Satin. *Inside a Barn in the Country: A Rebus Read-Along Story* (PS–K). Illus. by Tedd Arnold. 1995, Scholastic $10.95 (0-590-46999-1). 32pp. Using simple verses, this game book also teaches the sounds that animals make. (Rev: BL 1/15/95; SLJ 4/95)

5315 Carle, Eric. *Does a Kangaroo Have a Mother, Too?* (PS–1). Illus. 2000, HarperCollins LB $16.89 (0-06-028767-5). 32pp. In this simple book about wildlife, 12 young animals are presented along with their mothers. (Rev: BCCB 4/00; BL 1/1–15/00; HBG 10/00; SLJ 4/00) [591.3]

5316 Carle, Eric. *Have You Seen My Cat?* (PS–2). Illus. by author. 1991, Picture Book $16.00 (0-88708-054-5). A small boy loses his cat, sees many other felines, and returns home to find that his cat has had kittens. A reissue of a 1973 title.

5317 Carle, Eric. *Mister Seahorse* (PS–3). Illus. 2004, Penguin Putnam $16.99 (0-399-24269-4). 40pp. Imaginative tissue-paper collages with occasional overlays show Mr. Seahorse as he keeps vigil over Mrs. Seahorse's eggs in his pouch and encounters other marine fathers who play a role in caring for their young. (Rev: BL 4/1/04*; SLJ 5/04)

5318 Carle, Eric. *The Very Hungry Caterpillar* (PS–2). Illus. by author. 1981, Penguin Putnam $19.99 (0-399-20853-4). 32pp. A caterpillar eats a great deal and then spins its cocoon.

5319 Carrick, Carol. *Mothers Are Like That* (PS–1). Illus. by Paul Carrick. 2000, Clarion $15.00 (0-395-88351-2). 32pp. This tender picture book shows how various animals keep their offspring clean including a human mother and child. (Rev: BL 3/15/00; HB 3–4/00; HBG 10/00; SLJ 5/00)

5320 Carrick, Carol. *The Polar Bears Are Hungry* (PS–2). Illus. by Paul Carrick. 2002, Clarion $15.00 (0-618-15962-2). 32pp. A polar bear mother finds it more and more difficult to feed her cubs as spring and summer arrive, in this fictional presentation that will prompt discussion of human impact on animals. (Rev: BL 10/15/02; HBG 3/03; SLJ 11/02)

5321 Chekhov, Anton. *Kashtanka* (K–3). Illus. by Gennady Spirin. 1995, Gulliver $16.00 (0-15-200539-0). In this story set in 19th-century Russia, a lost dog is found by a circus performer. (Rev: SLJ 12/95)

5322 Chitwood, Suzanne Tanner. *Wake Up, Big Barn!* (PS–1). Illus. 2002, Scholastic $15.95 (0-439-26627-0). 40pp. Farm animals are introduced in lively collage in this rhythmic book for preschoolers. (Rev: BL 2/1/02; HBG 10/02; SLJ 4/02)

5323 Chorao, Kay. *Grayboy* (PS–2). Illus. 2002, Holt $16.95 (0-8050-6411-7). 32pp. This book about two children who rescue an injured seagull expertly weaves nature facts with fiction. (Rev: BL 8/02; HBG 10/02; SLJ 7/02)

5324 Christian, Peggy. *Chocolate, a Glacier Grizzly* (K–3). Illus. by Carol Cottone-Kolthoff. 1997, Benefactory $12.95 (1-882728-63-7). 32pp. The story of a female grizzly bear in Glacier National Park from her birth to the birth of her own cubs years later. (Rev: SLJ 11/97)

5325 Cimarusti, Marie Torres. *Peek-a-Moo!* (PS). Illus. by Stephanie Peterson. 1998, Dutton $9.99 (0-525-46083-7). A flap book that introduces seven familiar farm animals and the sounds they make. (Rev: SLJ 11/98)

5326 Clark, Emma Chichester. *Up in Heaven* (PS–2). Illus. by author. 2004, Doubleday LB $17.99 (0-385-90871-7). Daisy, Arthur's beloved dog, dies and goes to heaven, where she sends him reassuring dreams and interests him in getting a new puppy. (Rev: HB 3–4/04; SLJ 3/04)

5327 Clarke, Jane. *Only Tadpoles Have Tails* (PS–2). Illus. by Jane Gray. Series: Flying Foxes. 2004, Crabtree LB $14.97 (0-7787-1484-5); paper $4.46 (0-7787-1530-2). 46pp. Kicky the frog is embarrassed about his tadpole tail until it helps him swim fast enough to escape piranhas. (Rev: SLJ 8/04)

5328 Clements, Andrew. *Naptime for Slippers* (PS–1). Illus. by Janie Bynum. 2005, Dutton $12.99 (0-525-47287-8). 32pp. Slippers the puppy is active and interested in everything going on around him, so much so that he misses naptime and is exhausted

when it's time for a walk. (Rev: BL 2/1/05; SLJ 2/05)

5329 Clements, Andrew. *Slippers at Home* (PS–2). Illus. by Janie Bynum. 2004, Dutton $14.99 (0-525-47138-3). 32pp. Slippers is a happy puppy who enjoys the differences among his human family members. (Rev: SLJ 1/05)

5330 Clements, Andrew. *Tara and Tiree, Fearless Friends: A True Story* (K–2). Illus. by Ellen Beier. Series: Pets to the Rescue. 2002, Simon & Schuster LB $15.00 (0-689-82917-5). 32pp. Jim's dogs work together to rescue him when he falls through the ice. (Rev: HBG 3/03; SLJ 3/03)

5331 Coffelt, Nancy. *Good Night, Sigmund* (PS–1). Illus. 1992, Harcourt $13.95 (0-15-200464-5). 40pp. The artwork is a show stealer in this story of a young boy and his pet cat. (Rev: BL 2/15/92; SLJ 5/92)

5332 Coffey, Maria. *A Cat Adrift* (PS–1). Illus. by Eugenie Fernandes. 2002, Annick LB $18.95 (1-55037-727-2); paper $6.95 (1-55037-726-4). 32pp. Teelo the cat makes friends with a little girl and her grandfather when they rescue him from the ocean. (Rev: BL 7/02; HBG 10/02; SLJ 8/02)

5333 Cohen, Barbara S. *Forever Friends* (PS–2). Illus. by Dorothy Louise Hall. 2002, Tallfellow/Smallfellow $16.95 (1-931290-12-1). 32pp. Petey the dog describes all he does for his owner, Skip, in this playful picture book. (Rev: BL 7/02)

5334 Collard, Sneed B., III. *Butterfly Count* (1–3). Illus. by Paul Kratter. 2002, Holiday House $16.95 (0-8234-1607-0). 32pp. Amy's great-great-grandmother gave her prairie land to help restore the regal fritillary butterfly to its rightful home, and now Amy awaits its return. (Rev: BL 4/1/02; HBG 10/02; SLJ 6/02)

5335 Cooper, Elisha. *Magic Thinks Big* (PS–1). Illus. 2004, Greenwillow LB $15.89 (0-06-058165-4). 32pp. Readers are invited into the musings of an imaginative but idle tabby cat named Magic. (Rev: BL 5/15/04; HB 5–6/04; SLJ 4/04)

5336 Cooper, Susan. *Frog* (K–3). Illus. by Jane Browne. 2002, Simon & Schuster $17.00 (0-689-84302-X). 32pp. Joe learns how to swim by watching a frog that has fallen into the family pool. (Rev: BCCB 7–8/02; BL 6/1–15/02; HB 7–8/02; HBG 10/02; SLJ 6/02)

5337 Cowcher, Helen. *Jaguar* (K–2). Illus. 1997, Scholastic $15.95 (0-590-29937-9). 32pp. When an armed hunter finally corners the jaguar that has been killing his cattle, he is so enthralled by its beauty that he cannot shoot it. (Rev: BL 10/15/97; HBG 3/98; SLJ 8/97)

5338 Crum, Shutta. *Click!* (K–2). Illus. by John Beder. 2003, Fitzhenry & Whiteside $14.95 (1-55005-074-5). 24pp. A nicely illustrated story told in parallel about a boy and his mother (who are wildlife photographers) and a bear and her cub. (Rev: BL 2/15/04; SLJ 2/04)

5339 Cutler, Jane. *Mr. Carey's Garden* (K–3). Illus. by G. Brian Karas. 1996, Houghton Mifflin $14.95 (0-395-68191-X). 32pp. Eveyone offers free advice on how Mr. Carey can rid his garden of snails. (Rev: BL 3/15/96; HB 5–6/96; SLJ 5/96)

5340 Dalgliesh, Alice. *The Bears on Hemlock Mountain* (1–4). Illus. by Helen Sewell. 1990, Macmillan paper $4.99 (0-689-71604-4). 64pp. Jonathan ventured over the mountain by himself after dark and discovered the reality of bear existence!

5341 Davenport, Zoe. *Animals* (PS). Illus. 1995, Ticknor $5.95 (0-395-71537-7). 16pp. A simple concept book that introduces vocabulary related to various animals. (Rev: BL 2/1/95; SLJ 8/95) [599]

5342 Davies, Nicola. *Bat Loves the Night* (PS–3). Illus. by Sarah Fox-Davies. 2001, Candlewick $15.99 (0-7636-1202-2). 32pp. All about one bat's busy night, with color illustrations and bat facts throughout. (Rev: BCCB 12/01; BL 9/1/01; HBG 3/02; SLJ 9/01)

5343 Davis, Katie. *Who Hoots?* (PS–K). Illus. 2000, Harcourt $14.00 (0-15-202312-7). 36pp. This fun book delightfully presents animals that hoot, buzz, squeak, roar, and quack, and those that don't. (Rev: BL 10/1/00; HBG 3/01; SLJ 12/00)

5344 De Cock, Nicole. *The Girl and the Elephant* (K–2). Illus. by author. 2004, Tricycle $15.95 (1-58246-133-3). A girl misses the elephant when he leaves the zoo and decides to go to Africa in pursuit. (Rev: SLJ 11/04)

5345 Dennard, Deborah. *Bullfrog at Magnolia Circle* (K–4). Illus. by Kristin Kest. Series: Smithsonian Backyard. 2002, Soundprints $15.95 (1-931465-04-5); paper $5.95 (1-931465-39-8). 32pp. A young bullfrog who has reached maturity looks for a stretch of bayou to call his own in this accurate portrayal of a bullfrog's life. (Rev: HBG 3/03; SLJ 12/02)

5346 Dewey, Jennifer Owings. *Once I Knew a Spider* (K–2). Illus. by Jean Cassels. 2002, Walker LB $17.85 (0-8027-8701-0). 32pp. A woman — first pregnant, then a new mother — watches a spider's transitions as it weaves a web and lays eggs in this book that features fine close-up illustrations of the spider. (Rev: BL 9/15/02; HBG 10/02; SLJ 10/02)

5347 DiSalvo-Ryan, DyAnne. *A Dog Like Jack* (PS–2). Illus. 1999, Holiday House $15.95 (0-8234-1369-1). 32pp. Mike and his dog Jack share many years together, and when the dog dies, Mike grieves but learns to celebrate his friend's life. (Rev: BL 3/1/99; HBG 10/99; SLJ 4/99)

5348 Disher, Garry. *Switch Cat* (PS–2). Illus. by Andrew McLean. 1995, Ticknor $14.95 (0-395-71643-8). 32pp. Two very different girls have equally mismatched cats as pets. (Rev: BL 3/15/95; SLJ 3/95*)

5349 Dixon, Ann. *Blueberry Shoe* (PS–3). Illus. by Evon Zerbetz. 1999, Alaska Northwest $15.95 (0-88240-518-7); paper $8.95 (0-88240-519-5). 32pp. Several Alaskan animals are introduced in this story of a lost red sneaker and how each of the animals that finds it changes it. (Rev: BL 10/15/99; HBG 3/00; SLJ 12/99)

5350 Dodds, Dayle Ann. *Hello, Sun!* (PS–K). Illus. by Sachiko Yoshikawa. 2005, Dial $9.99 (0-8037-2895-6). 32pp. A little girl and her cat choose

clothes for the day, but the weather keeps changing. (Rev: BL 6/1–15/05; SLJ 6/05)

5351 Doherty, Berlie. *Paddiwak and Cozy* (PS–1). Illus. by Alison Bartlett. 1999, Orchard $14.95 (0-531-30180-X). 32pp. Instant dislike develops when new cat Cozy is introduced into Sally's house and meets Paddiwak, the cat-in-residence. (Rev: BL 8/99; HBG 3/00; SLJ 10/99)

5352 Doner, Kim. *Buffalo Dreams* (K–4). 1999, Graphic Arts $16.95 (1-55868-475-1); paper $9.95 (1-55868-476-X). 40pp. When her little brother angers the mother of a rare white buffalo, Sarah must summon up the courage to rescue him. (Rev: BL 1/1–15/00; HBG 3/00; SLJ 2/00)

5353 Doyle, Malachy. *Cow* (PS–3). Illus. by Angelo Rinaldi. 2002, Simon & Schuster $17.00 (0-689-84462-X). 40pp. Realistic paintings and a simple text follow a cow through a typical day beginning with morning milking. (Rev: BL 6/1–15/02; HBG 3/03; SLJ 7/02)

5354 Doyle, Malachy. *Sleepy Pendoodle* (PS–1). Illus. by Julie Vivas. 2002, Candlewick $12.99 (0-7636-1561-7). 32pp. A humorous story based on an Irish folktale about a girl who can't remember the right words to wake up her sleeping puppy. (Rev: BL 4/15/02; HBG 10/02; SLJ 3/02)

5355 Doyle, Malachy. *Storm Cats* (PS–1). Illus. by Stuart Trotter. 2002, Simon & Schuster $15.95 (0-689-84464-6). A storm brings two neighboring children, and their cats, together. (Rev: HBG 3/03; SLJ 10/02)

5356 Doyle, Malachy. *Well, a Crocodile Can! Flip-up Flaps and Pop-up Tricks* (PS–K). Illus. by Britta Teckentrup. 1999, Millbrook $12.95 (0-7613-1032-0). Pop-ups and flaps are used to show a variety of different animals performing amazing tricks that are true to their nature — like an elephant wiggling its ears. (Rev: SLJ 3/00)

5357 Dunbar, Joyce. *Four Fierce Kittens* (PS–K). Illus. by Jakki Wood. 1992, Scholastic $13.95 (0-590-45535-4). 32pp. Four kittens think they are fierce but cannot frighten the other farm animals. (Rev: BL 6/1/92; SLJ 4/92)

5358 Dunn, Judy. *The Little Puppy* (PS–K). Illus. by Phoebe Dunn. 1984, Random paper $3.25 (0-394-86595-2). 32pp. The story of a little boy who must care for his first puppy.

5359 Edwards, Becky. *My Cat Charlie* (K–3). Illus. by David Armitage. 2001, Bloomsbury $17.95 (0-7475-4465-4). A little girl and her beloved cat must separate when her family moves to an apartment. (Rev: SLJ 12/01)

5360 Edwards, Pamela Duncan. *Muldoon* (PS–K). Illus. by Henry Cole. 2002, Hyperion $14.99 (0-7868-0360-6). 32pp. Muldoon, a dog, is convinced that he "works" for the West family — but he's actually a much-loved pet. (Rev: BL 2/15/03; HBG 3/03; SLJ 12/02)

5361 Erlbruch, Wolf. *Mrs. Meyer the Bird* (PS–2). Illus. 1997, Orchard LB $15.99 (0-531-33017-6). 32pp. Mrs. Meyer is a born worrier until she finds an injured bird to take care of and take her mind off her problems. (Rev: BCCB 5/97; BL 4/1/97; SLJ 4/97)

5362 Ets, Marie Hall. *Play with Me* (PS–K). Illus. by author. 1955, Puffin paper $5.99 (0-14-050178-9). 32pp. A little girl finds a playmate among the meadow creatures when she finally learns to sit quietly and not frighten them.

5363 Faulkner, Keith. *David Dreaming of Dinosaurs* (K–2). Illus. by Jonathan Lambert. 1992, Fantasy $13.00 (1-56021-182-2). 12pp. David dreams of dinosaurs and they appear in foldout illustrations. (Rev: BL 11/15/92)

5364 Fine, Anne. *Ruggles* (PS–2). Illus. by Ruth Brown. 2004, Andersen paper $7.95 (1-84270-212-2). 32pp. Ruggles the dog revels in the time he spends rambling around the neighborhood. (Rev: BL 5/1/04)

5365 Flack, Marjorie. *Angus and the Ducks* (K–2). Illus. by author. 1997, Farrar paper $5.95 (0-374-40385-6). 40pp. Angus, the Scottish terrier, and his amusing adventures. Other titles in this series are: *Angus and the Cat* and *Angus Lost* (both 1989).

5366 Fleming, Denise. *Barnyard Banter* (PS–1). Illus. 1994, Holt $16.95 (0-8050-1957-X). 32pp. All the farm animals greet Goose with their appropriate sounds as she tours the farmyard. (Rev: BCCB 5/94; BL 5/1/94; HB 5–6/94; SLJ 5/94*)

5367 Fleming, Denise. *Buster* (PS–1). Illus. by author. 2003, Holt $15.95 (0-8050-6279-3). The idyllic life of Buster the dog is threatened by the arrival of Betty the kitten, but when he runs away and gets lost, it's Betty who comes to the rescue. (Rev: HB 9–10/03; HBG 4/04; SLJ 9/03)

5368 Fleming, Denise. *In the Tall, Tall Grass* (PS–1). Illus. 1991, Holt $16.95 (0-8050-1635-X). 32pp. An excellent story-hour book in which a caterpillar munches through the tall, tall grass, watching nature along the way. (Rev: BL 10/1/91*; HB 1–2/92*; SLJ 9/91*)

5369 Ford, Miela. *Bear Play* (PS–1). Illus. 1995, Greenwillow $14.89 (0-688-13833-0). 24pp. The antics of two playful polar bear cubs are captured in a simple text and large color photographs. (Rev: BL 1/1–15/96; SLJ 11/95)

5370 Ford, Miela. *Mom and Me* (PS–3). Illus. 1998, Greenwillow $15.00 (0-688-15889-7). 24pp. Using amazing photographs, this simple picture book depicts the playful antics of a mother polar bear and her cub. (Rev: BL 8/98; HBG 3/99; SLJ 9/98)

5371 Foreman, Michael. *Saving Sinbad!* (PS–2). Illus. 2002, Kane $15.95 (1-929132-34-4). 32pp. The story of an exciting boat rescue in a seaside village, told and illustrated from a dog's point of view. (Rev: BL 12/15/02; HBG 3/03)

5372 Fox, Mem. *Zoo-Looking* (PS–1). Illus. by Candace Whitman. 1996, Mondo $14.95 (1-57255-010-4). 28pp. Flora is happy when the animals at the zoo seem to look back at her. (Rev: BCCB 7–8/96; BL 6/1–15/96; SLJ 7/96)

5373 Freedman, Claire. *Gooseberry Goose* (PS–2). Illus. by Vanessa Cabban. 2003, Tiger Tales $15.95 (1-58925-030-3). Gooseberry the gosling practices his flying techniques in preparation for migration

south, while animals are busy getting ready for the coming of winter. (Rev: SLJ 12/03)

5374 Freedman, Claire. *One Magical Morning* (PS). Illus. by Louise Ho. 2005, Good Books $16.00 (1-56148-472-5). A mother bear and her baby watch morning arrive and the animals waking up. (Rev: SLJ 5/05)

5375 French, Vivian. *Caribou Journey* (1–3). Illus. by Lisa Flather. Series: Fantastic Journeys. 2001, Zero to Ten $15.95 (1-84089-216-1). 32pp. Animal migration is explored in this story about a pregnant caribou, Ragged Ear, and the herd's annual march to the calving grounds. (Rev: BL 4/1/02; SLJ 12/01)

5376 French, Vivian. *Swallow Journey* (K–3). Illus. by Karin Littlewood. Series: Fantastic Journeys. 2001, Zero to Ten $15.95 (1-84089-215-3). 32pp. Dramatic watercolor illustrations accompany this account of the migration of swallows from England to southern Africa. (Rev: BL 1/1–15/02)

5377 French, Vivian. *Whale Journey* (K–3). Illus. by Lisa Flather. 1998, Zero to Ten $14.95 (1-84089-022-3). 32pp. Beginning with his birth, this book traces the journey north to Alaskan waters of gray whale Little Grey and his mother and a friend. (Rev: BL 1/1–15/99; HBG 3/99)

5378 Freymann, Saxton, and Joost Elffers. *Baby Food* (PS–1). Illus. by authors. 2003, Scholastic $12.95 (0-439-11017-3). The food sculptors who created *Dog Food* (2002) offer a gallery of baby animals carved from a wide variety of fruits and vegetables. (Rev: HBG 4/04; SLJ 11/03) [641.8]

5379 Freymann, Saxton, and Joost Elffers. *Dog Food* (PS–3). Illus. 2002, Scholastic $12.95 (0-439-11016-5). 32pp. Clever canine sculptures made entirely of fruits and vegetables fill the pages of this picture book by the authors of *How Are You Peeling?* (1991). (Rev: BL 10/15/02; HBG 3/03; SLJ 9/02) [736]

5380 Friedman, Mel, and Ellen Weiss. *Kitten Castle* (K–3). Illus. by Lynn Adams. 2001, Kane paper $4.95 (1-57565-103-3). 32pp. Anna and her friend Tom use everyday items to build a castle for four lively kittens in this book that introduces shapes. (Rev: SLJ 9/01)

5381 Gag, Wanda. *Millions of Cats* (PS–1). Illus. by author. 1996, Penguin Putnam paper $5.99 (0-698-11363-2). 112pp. A wonderful picture book about an old man looking for a cat who suddenly finds himself with millions. (Rev: HBG 4/04; SLJ 3/04)

5382 Galvin, Laura Gates. *Bumblebee at Apple Tree Lane* (1–3). Illus. by Kristin Kest. 2000, Soundprints $15.95 (1-56899-820-1). 31pp. This fictional account of the queen bumblebee follows her life from waking from hibernation in the spring to crawling underground when winter approaches. (Rev: HBG 3/01; SLJ 3/01)

5383 Galvin, Laura Gates. *River Otter at Autumn Lane* (PS–2). Illus. by Christopher Leeper. 2002, Soundprints $15.95 (1-931465-62-2); paper $6.95 (1-931465-70-3). 32pp. A fictional introduction to the behavior, diet, and habitat of a mother otter and her young, with appealing realistic paintings. (Rev: BL 2/1/03)

5384 Gay, Marie-Louise. *Good Night Sam* (PS–1). Illus. by author. 2003, Groundwood $14.95 (0-88899-530-X). As preschooler Sam and his older sister Stella search for their missing dog, readers will see the dog hidden in each picture. (Rev: HBG 4/04; SLJ 11/03)

5385 George, Jean Craighead. *Frightful's Daughter* (1–3). Illus. by Daniel San Souci. 2002, Dutton $16.99 (0-525-46907-9). 32pp. Sam Gribley (of *My Side of the Mountain* and its sequels) must rescue a chick of the falcon he calls Frightful. (Rev: BL 9/1/02; HBG 3/03; SLJ 9/02)

5386 George, Jean Craighead. *Look to the North: A Wolf Pup Diary* (K–4). Illus. by Lucia Washburn. 1997, HarperCollins LB $15.89 (0-06-023640-X). 32pp. A description of a year in the lives of three wolf cubs and how they adjust to each of the seasons. (Rev: BL 4/15/97; SLJ 4/97)

5387 George, Lindsay Barrett. *Around the World: Who's Been Here?* (K–3). Illus. 1999, Greenwillow LB $15.93 (0-688-15269-4). 40pp. Different animals are introduced in this question-and-answer game involving a trip around the world and a series of different locales. (Rev: BL 8/99; HB 3–4/99; HBG 10/99; SLJ 4/99)

5388 George, Twig C. *Seahorses* (K–3). 2003, Millbrook LB $24.90 (0-7613-2869-6). 32pp. Seahorses and their lives are presented in eye-catching illustrations and poetic but informative text. (Rev: HBG 4/04; SLJ 4/04) [597]

5389 Gibbel, Mark. *Oh, Harry!* (PS). Illus. by Sarah Massini. 2003, Holt $15.95 (0-8050-6851-1). Everyone's sleep is interrupted when Harry, a newly adopted kitten, tries out all the beds in turn. (Rev: HBG 4/04; SLJ 10/03)

5390 Gill, Shelley. *Alaska's Three Bears* (PS–2). Illus. by Shannon Cartwright. 1990, Paws Four $15.95 (0-934007-10-1); paper $8.95 (0-934007-11-X). 32pp. In a folklike tale, three types of Alaskan bears — polar bears, black bears, and grizzlies — are introduced. (Rev: BL 3/1/91)

5391 Gill, Shelley. *Big Blue* (1–3). Illus. by Ann Barrow. 2003, Charlesbridge LB $15.95 (1-57091-352-8). In this delightful tale based on a real-life experience of the author, a young girl's dream of swimming with a blue whale is fulfilled when her mother takes her on a trip to Baja California in Mexico. (Rev: HBG 4/04; SLJ 8/03)

5392 Gliori, Debi. *The Snow Lambs* (PS–3). Illus. 1996, Scholastic $15.95 (0-590-20304-5). 40pp. Young Sam worries about the safety of the family's sheepdog during severe winter weather. (Rev: BCCB 2/97; BL 11/15/96*; SLJ 10/96)

5393 Godwin, Laura. *What the Baby Hears* (PS). Illus. by Mary Morgan. 2002, Hyperion $15.99 (0-7868-0560-9). 32pp. A charming story that describes the various sounds that baby animals hear from their parents. (Rev: BL 5/1/02; HBG 10/02; SLJ 6/02)

5394 Golembe, Carla. *Annabelle's Big Move* (PS–1). Illus. 1999, Houghton Mifflin $12.00 (0-395-91543-0). 32pp. When the family she lives with moves, Annabelle the dog is confused and a little frightened by all the activity, including being put in a crate that

goes on an airplane. (Rev: BL 4/15/99; HBG 10/99; SLJ 5/99)

5395 Goodhart, Pippa. *Pudgy: A Puppy to Love* (PS–1). Illus. by Caroline Jayne Church. 2003, Scholastic $15.95 (0-439-45699-1). Lucy is a sad little girl until one day in the woods she meets a lonely puppy named Pudgy. (Rev: HBG 10/03; SLJ 4/03)

5396 Graham, Bob. *"Let's Get a Pup!" Said Kate* (PS–K). Illus. 2001, Candlewick $14.99 (0-7636-1452-1). 32pp. A little girl and her parents come home from the shelter with a lovely puppy but then return to get an older dog too. (Rev: BCCB 9/01; BL 7/01; HB 9–10/01; HBG 3/02; SLJ 7/01)

5397 Graham-Yooll, Liz. *Timothy Tib* (PS–2). Illus. 2001, Ragged Bear $15.95 (1-929927-25-8). 32pp. A celebration of a cat's life and the pleasure the cat brings to the narrator. (Rev: BL 5/15/01; HBG 10/01; SLJ 7/01)

5398 Greenberg, David T. *Skunks!* (K–4). Illus. by Lynn Munsinger. 2001, Little, Brown $15.95 (0-316-32606-2). For those who are not overly sensitive to strong smells, this is a witty account of all sorts of things you definitely do not want to do with a skunk. (Rev: HBG 10/01; SLJ 8/01)

5399 Grindley, Sally. *Little Elephant Thunderfoot* (K–2). Illus. by John Butler. 1999, Peachtree $15.95 (1-56145-180-0). After his grandmother is killed by poachers in an African savanna, Little Elephant must find a new home and adjust to a new herd. (Rev: HBG 3/00; SLJ 2/00)

5400 Grindley, Sally. *Little Sibu: An Orangutan Tale* (PS–2). Illus. by John Butler. 1999, Peachtree $15.95 (1-56145-196-7). Little Sibu is now 7 and his mother must force him to leave her and live on his own as other male orangutans do. (Rev: HBG 10/99; SLJ 5/99)

5401 Grindley, Sally. *Polar Star* (K–3). Illus. by John Butler. 1998, Peachtree $15.95 (1-56145-181-9). A beautifully illustrated story about Polar Star, her cubs, and their activities in the cold land they call home. (Rev: HBG 3/99; SLJ 12/98)

5402 Grooms, Molly. *We Are Bears* (PS–1). Illus. by Lucia Guarnotta. 2000, NorthWord $12.95 (1-55971-747-5). 32pp. A mother bear takes her two cubs out on a nature walk. (Rev: BL 12/15/00)

5403 Guthrie, Arlo. *Mooses Come Walking* (PS–K). Illus. by Alice M. Brock. 1995, Chronicle $11.95 (0-8118-1051-8). 32pp. A picture book that gives advice to youngsters when moose come visiting at night. (Rev: BL 12/15/95)

5404 Haas, Jessie. *No Foal Yet* (1–3). Illus. by Joseph A. Smith. 1995, Greenwillow LB $15.93 (0-688-12956-9). 24pp. Nora becomes impatient waiting for her horse Bonnie to give birth; but when it finally happens, no one is around. (Rev: BL 5/15/95; HB 5–6/95; SLJ 6/95)

5405 Hacking, Norm. *When Cats Go Wrong* (K–4). Illus. by Cynthia Nugent. 2005, Raincoast $16.95 (1-55192-729-2). A young boy describes a house that has been trashed by a naughty kitten in this picture book with vibrant illustrations and an accompanying CD of the tango-inspired song. (Rev: BL 3/1/04; SLJ 5/05)

5406 Hale, Irina. *The Naughty Crow* (K–3). Illus. 1992, Macmillan LB $14.95 (0-689-50546-9). 32pp. In a story set in czarist Russia, a naughty crow is banished from the household that has adopted him. (Rev: BL 11/5/92; SLJ 10/92)

5407 Harjo, Joy. *The Good Luck Cat* (PS–3). Illus. by Paul Lee. 2000, Harcourt $16.00 (0-15-232197-7). Having used up eight of her nine lives, Woogie, a cat, disappears and everyone fears the worse. (Rev: BCCB 4/00; BL 6/1–15/03; HBG 10/00; SLJ 4/00)

5408 Harper, Dan. *Sit, Truman!* (PS). Illus. by Cara Moser and Barry Moser. 2001, Harcourt $16.00 (0-15-202616-9). 32pp. Truman, a drooling mastiff, is affectionately chastised for his antics throughout the day in this humorously illustrated volume. (Rev: BL 9/15/01; HBG 3/02; SLJ 10/01)

5409 Harper, Isabelle. *My Cats Nick and Nora* (PS–1). Illus. by Barry Moser. 1995, Scholastic $14.95 (0-590-47620-3). 32pp. Isabelle and cousin Emmie spend every Sunday taking care of the family pets, Nick and Nora. A sequel to *My Dog Rosie* (1994). (Rev: BL 10/1/95; SLJ 10/95)

5410 Harper, Isabelle. *Our New Puppy* (PS–1). Illus. by Barry Moser. 1996, Scholastic $14.95 (0-590-56926-0). 32pp. Rosie gradually grows to love the family's new puppy. (Rev: BL 9/1/96; SLJ 10/96)

5411 Harshman, Terry Webb. *Bessie's Bed* (PS–2). Illus. by Sharon Hawkins Vargo. Series: Silly Millies. 2003, Millbrook LB $17.90 (0-7613-2742-8). 32pp. In this cumulative tale for beginning readers, a variety of creatures climb into Bessie's bed on a stormy night, but they all make too much noise for sleep. (Rev: HBG 4/04; SLJ 3/04)

5412 Harvey, Amanda. *Dog Days: Starring Otis* (PS–1). Illus. 2003, Doubleday $15.95 (0-385-74621-0). 32pp. Poor Otis the dog feels so neglected when a new kitten arrives that he runs away from home, only to find he misses his young mistress. A sequel is *Dog Gone: Starring Otis* (2004). (Rev: BL 1/1–15/03; HBG 10/03; SLJ 2/03)

5413 Hazen, Barbara S. *Tight Times* (2–3). Illus. by Trina S. Hyman. 1979, Puffin paper $5.99 (0-14-050442-7). 32pp. A child is allowed to keep a stray kitten even though there are hard times in the household.

5414 Heiligman, Deborah. *Fun Dog, Sun Dog* (K–3). Illus. by Tim Bowers. 2005, Marshall Cavendish $14.95 (0-7614-5162-5). 32pp. Tinka, an energetic golden retriever, and her boy enjoy a day at the beach, described in catchy rhymes. (Rev: BL 5/1/05; SLJ 5/05)

5415 Helmer, Marilyn. *Fog Cat* (PS–2). Illus. by Paul Mombourquette. 1999, Kids Can $14.95 (1-55074-460-7). 32pp. Hannah manages, in foggy weather, to get a wild cat to come indoors — but only long enough to have her litter and leave again. (Rev: BL 3/15/99; HBG 10/99; SLJ 5/99)

5416 Helmer, Marilyn. *Mr. McGratt and the Ornery Cat* (PS–3). Illus. by Martine Gourbault. 1999, Kids Can $14.95 (1-55074-564-6). At first Mr. McGratt

wants to get rid of the cat that has moved in but, in time, he realizes he has found the perfect pet. (Rev: HBG 3/00; SLJ 12/99)

5417 Henderson, Kathy. *Dog Story* (PS–K). Illus. 2005, Bloomsbury $16.99 (0-7475-5071-9). 32pp. Jo eventually gets the dog she wants, but only after she has been offered various substitutes — a mouse, a cat, a brother, and so forth. (Rev: BL 2/15/05; SLJ 4/05)

5418 Herriot, James. *Blossom Comes Home* (1–3). Illus. by Ruth Brown. 1988, St. Martin's paper $6.95 (0-312-09131-1). 32pp. Farmer Dakin is sad to sell Blossom the cow, but happy when she escapes and returns home. (Rev: BL 12/1/88; HB 1–2/89)

5419 Herriot, James. *Moses the Kitten* (PS–3). Illus. by Peter Barrett. 1984, St. Martin's paper $6.95 (0-312-06419-5). 32pp. The story of a stray black kitten and how it was saved.

5420 Herriot, James. *Smudge, the Little Lost Lamb* (1–3). Illus. by Ruth Brown. 1991, St. Martin's $12.95 (0-312-06404-7). 32pp. Smudge, a new twin lamb, gets into trouble when he pushes under the fence and goes free. (Rev: BL 1/15/92)

5421 Heyman, Anita. *Gretchen the Bicycle Dog* (K–3). Photos by author. Illus. 2003, Dutton $14.99 (0-525-47066-2). Like many dachshunds, Gretchen hurts her back and can no longer run and play, so her loving family gets her a special cart attachment that allows her to carry on with life. (Rev: HBG 10/03; SLJ 3/03)

5422 Himler, Ronald. *Six Is So Much Less Than Seven* (K–2). Illus. by author. 2002, Star Bright $16.95 (1-887734-91-0). An old man mourns the death of his cat, which leaves him with only six. (Rev: HBG 10/02; SLJ 12/02)

5423 Himmelman, John. *Pipaluk and the Whales* (PS–2). Illus. by author. 2002, National Geographic $16.95 (0-7922-8217-5). The fascinating story, based on reality, of villagers who worked for months to save thousands of beluga whales trapped in winter ice. (Rev: HBG 10/02; SLJ 9/02)

5424 Hindley, Judy. *Does a Cow Say Boo?* (PS–1). Illus. by Brita Granström. 2002, Candlewick $15.99 (0-7636-1718-0). 32pp. Animal sounds are explored in this tour around a farm. (Rev: BCCB 10/02; BL 6/1–15/02; HBG 10/02; SLJ 9/02)

5425 Hirschi, Ron. *No, No, Jack* (PS–1). Illus. by Pierre Pratt. 2002, Dial $10.99 (0-8037-2612-0). 32pp. A mischievous dog named Jack makes off with the family's things and hides them in the closet in this charming open-the-flap book. (Rev: BL 1/1–15/02; HBG 10/02; SLJ 7/02)

5426 Hirschi, Ron. *What Is a Cat?* (PS–K). Illus. by Linda Q. Younker. 1991, Walker LB $14.85 (0-8027-8123-3). 32pp. An attractive book for young browsers to enjoy. (Rev: BL 1/15/92; SLJ 11/91) [599.7]

5427 Hirschi, Ron. *What Is a Horse?* (PS–2). Illus. by Linda Q. Younker and Ron Hirschi. 1989, Walker LB $12.85 (0-8027-6877-6). 32pp. This introduction includes material on structure, habits, and uses of the horse. Also use: *Where Do Horses Live?* (1989). (Rev: BL 8/89; SLJ 1/90) [636.1]

5428 Hirschi, Ron. *Where Do Cats Live?* (PS–K). Illus. by Linda Q. Younker. 1991, Walker LB $14.85 (0-8027-8110-1). 32pp. A visually appealing book that shows cats living alone, together, indoors, outdoors, everywhere. (Rev: BL 1/15/92; SLJ 11/91) [636.8]

5429 Hiscock, Bruce. *Coyote and Badger: Desert Hunters of the Southwest* (2–4). Illus. 2001, Boyds Mills $15.95 (1-56397-848-2). 32pp. Coyote and Badger discover that each can use the other's talents to make hunting more efficient. (Rev: BL 4/15/01; HBG 10/01; SLJ 7/01)

5430 Hobbs, Leigh. *Old Tom's Holiday* (K–3). Illus. by author. 2004, Peachtree $16.95 (1-56145-316-1). Angela Throgmorton believes she left her cat at home but she is lonely on holiday and is thrilled to find out that he came along after all. (Rev: SLJ 11/04)

5431 Hollenbeck, Kathleen M. *Islands of Ice: The Story of a Harp Seal* (PS–3). Illus. by John Paul Genzo. Series: Smithsonian Backyard. 2001, Smithsonian Institution $15.95 (1-56899-965-8). 32pp. This fictional story about a harp seal focuses on true facts about the animal's life and habitat. (Rev: BL 2/1/02)

5432 Holsonback, Anita. *Monkey See, Monkey Do: An Animal Exercise Book for You!* (PS–K). Illus. by Leo Timmers. 1997, Millbrook LB $20.90 (0-7613-0260-3). Each page features an animal in its natural habitat along with a drawing of a boy and girl who mimic the way the creature moves and a verse. (Rev: HBG 3/98; SLJ 1/98)

5433 Horowitz, Ruth. *Crab Moon* (K–4). Illus. by Kate Kiesler. 2000, Candlewick $15.99 (0-7636-0709-6). 32pp. During the first full moon in June, Daniel and his mother go down to the beach to watch the horseshoe crabs fertilize and bury their eggs. (Rev: BL 8/00; HBG 10/00; SLJ 5/00)

5434 Houk, Randy. *Chessie, the Travelin' Man* (K–3). Illus. by Paula Bartlett. 1997, Benefactory $12.95 (1-882728-56-4). 32pp. The story of a Florida manatee and his trips from the South to Port Judith, Rhode Island, in 1994 and 1995. (Rev: SLJ 11/97)

5435 Hubbell, Patricia. *Bouncing Time* (PS). Illus. by Melissa Sweet. 2000, HarperCollins LB $15.89 (0-688-17377-2). 32pp. A delightful rhyming poem about a mother with a child in a backpack who visit a zoo and watch the animals at play. (Rev: BCCB 5/00; BL 4/1/00; HBG 10/00; SLJ 7/00)

5436 Huneck, Stephen. *Sally Goes to the Beach* (K–3). Illus. 2000, Abrams $17.95 (0-8109-4186-4). 38pp. Simple color woodcuts are used to illustrate this dog's-eye view of a day at the beach. (Rev: BCCB 11/00; BL 5/15/00; HBG 10/00; SLJ 6/00)

5437 Huneck, Stephen. *Sally Goes to the Mountains* (PS–1). Illus. by author. 2001, Abrams $17.95 (0-8109-4485-5). Sally the black Lab has a wonderful dream in which she goes to the mountains and meets all kinds of animals. (Rev: HBG 10/01; SLJ 7/01)

5438 Huneck, Stephen. *Sally Goes to the Vet* (PS–2). Illus. 2004, Abrams $17.95 (0-8109-4813-3). 32pp. Sally, a good-natured black Labrador, finds that a visit to the vet's office can be fun. (Rev: BL 5/15/04; SLJ 11/04)

5439 Hutchins, Hazel. *One Dark Night* (PS–2). Illus. by Susan Kathleen Hartung. 2001, Viking $15.99 (0-670-89246-7). 32pp. With help from a little boy, a mother cat brings her kittens into safety during a storm. (Rev: BCCB 7–8/01; BL 5/15/01; HB 7–8/01; HBG 10/01; SLJ 6/01)

5440 Hutchins, Hazel. *One Duck* (K–2). Illus. by Ruth Ohi. 1999, Annick LB $18.95 (1-55037-561-X); paper $6.95 (1-55037-560-1). A duck whose nest is in the way of an oncoming tractor is helped by a considerate farmer. (Rev: HBG 3/00; SLJ 10/99)

5441 Isadora, Rachael. *A South African Night* (PS–K). Illus. 1998, Greenwillow $14.89 (0-688-11390-7). 24pp. As the people of Johannesburg go home after a day's work and prepare for bed, many of the animals in the Kruger National Park begin their nocturnal activities. (Rev: BCCB 4/98; BL 2/15/98; HBG 10/98; SLJ 8/98)

5442 Jagtenberg, Yvonne. *Jack's Rabbit* (PS–1). Illus. 2003, Millbrook $15.95 (0-7613-1544-5). 32pp. Jack's rabbit escapes while Jack is trying to draw him and Jack hunts for him all over the place. (Rev: BL 3/1/03)

5443 Jennings, Sharon. *Bearcub and Mama* (PS). Illus. by Melanie Watt. 2005, Kids Can $15.95 (1-55337-556-1). 32pp. Bearcub has learned well from his mother, and when he is separated from her in a storm, he knows what to do. (Rev: BL 2/15/05)

5444 Johnson, Herschel. *A Visit to the Country* (1–3). Illus. by Romare Bearden. 1989, HarperCollins $13.95 (0-06-022849-0). 32pp. Mike nurses an injured cardinal back to health but knows he must return it to the wild. (Rev: BL 9/15/89; SLJ 12/89)

5445 Johnson, Paul B., and Celeste Lewis. *Lost* (PS–2). Illus. by Paul Johnson. 1996, Orchard LB $16.99 (0-531-08851-0). 32pp. While camping out in Arizona's Tonto National Forest, a young girl's dog wanders off and gets lost. (Rev: BCCB 3/96; BL 4/1/96; SLJ 4/96*)

5446 Johnston, Tony. *The Barn Owls* (PS–3). Illus. by Deborah Kogan Ray. 2000, Charlesbridge $15.95 (0-88106-981-7). 32pp. Eloquent pictures and text describe the activities of a family of barn owls. (Rev: BL 2/15/00; HBG 10/00; SLJ 3/00)

5447 Johnston, Tony. *Desert Dog* (K–3). Illus. by Robert Weatherford. 2001, Sierra Club $15.95 (0-87156-979-5). 32pp. A goat-herding dog offers a portrait of his life in verse. (Rev: BL 1/1–15/02; HBG 3/02; SLJ 11/01)

5448 Jonas, Ann. *Bird Talk* (K–2). Illus. 1999, Greenwillow LB $14.93 (0-688-14173-0). 32pp. About 65 different species of birds comment on a garden being seeded, with each bird identified by name at the back of this imaginative nature book. (Rev: BCCB 5/99; BL 6/1–15/99; HBG 10/99; SLJ 4/99)

5449 Jonas, Ann. *Two Bear Cubs* (1–3). Illus. by author. 1982, Greenwillow $15.93 (0-688-01408-9). 24pp. A mother bear shepherds her two cubs through some everyday adventures.

5450 Joosse, Barbara M. *Bad Dog School* (K–3). Illus. by Jennifer Plecas. 2004, Clarion $15.00 (0-618-13331-3). 32pp. After going to obedience school, formerly over-zesty puppy Zippy becomes too restrained and his family decides to untrain him a bit. (Rev: SLJ 9/04)

5451 Joosse, Barbara M. *Nugget and Darling* (K–3). Illus. by Sue Truesdell. 1997, Clarion $14.95 (0-395-64571-9). 32pp. The dog Nugget becomes jealous when his young mistress pays attention to a stray kitten. (Rev: BL 3/1/97; SLJ 4/97)

5452 Kasperson, James. *Little Brother Moose* (PS–3). Illus. by Karlyn Holman. 1995, Dawn paper $7.95 (1-883220-33-5). 32pp. A young moose who wanders into town finds his way home by following migrating geese. (Rev: BL 7/95; SLJ 10/95)

5453 Kawata, Ken. *Animal Tails* (PS–K). Illus. by Masayuki Yabuuchi. 2001, Kane $13.95 (1-929132-05-0). Readers guess which animal each colorful tail should be attached to, before turning the page and finding the answer. (Rev: HBG 10/01; SLJ 6/01) [573.998]

5454 Kerr, Judith. *Goodbye Mog* (K–3). Illus. by author. 2003, HarperCollins $17.95 (0-00-714968-9). Mog the cat dies early in this book but lingers around in spirit to watch over her family's recovery and acceptance of a new kitten. (Rev: SLJ 4/03)

5455 Ketteman, Helen. *Grandma's Cat* (PS–K). Illus. by Marsha Winborn. 1996, Houghton Mifflin $16.00 (0-395-73094-5). 32pp. A little girl has trouble befriending her grandmother's independent cat. (Rev: BL 4/1/96; SLJ 5/96)

5456 Kimmel, Haven. *Orville: A Dog Story* (K–3). Illus. by Robert Andrew Parker. 2003, Clarion $15.00 (0-618-15955-X). 32pp. A moving story about a stray dog trying to find a comfortable home. (Rev: BCCB 11/03; BL 9/15/03; HBG 4/04; LMC 1/04; SLJ 11/03)

5457 King, Deborah. *The Flight of the Snow Geese* (K–2). Illus. 1998, Orchard $15.95 (0-531-30088-9). 32pp. In verses accompanied by watercolor paintings, the author tells of the annual journey of snow geese from their tundra home to warmer climates. (Rev: BL 9/15/98; HBG 3/99; SLJ 11/98)

5458 Kirk, David. *Little Bird, Biddle Bird* (PS–K). Illus. by author. 2001, Scholastic $9.95 (0-439-26092-2). Little Bird must learn to find his own food, and remembers his mother's advice as he forages. (Rev: HBG 10/01; SLJ 7/01)

5459 Kirk, David. *Little Bunny, Biddle Bunny* (PS). Illus. by author. 2002, Scholastic $9.95 (0-439-33819-0). A gentle story of a little rabbit's adventures in sunny meadows. (Rev: HBG 10/02; SLJ 4/02)

5460 Koralek, Jenny. *Cat and Kit* (PS–2). Illus. by Patricia MacCarthy. 1995, Hyperion LB $14.49 (0-7868-2030-6). 32pp. Cat rescues Kit, but in time the young kitten returns to the wild where he belongs. (Rev: BL 7/95; SLJ 9/95)

5461 Kotzwinkle, William, and Glenn Murray. *Walter the Farting Dog* (K–3). Illus. by Audrey Colman. 2001, Frog $14.95 (1-58394-053-7). 32pp. Poor Walter's flatulence almost causes his new family to return him to the pound, until he uses his unique "gift" to save them from burglars. (Rev: BL 2/15/02)

5462 Kotzwinkle, William, and Glenn Murray. *Walter the Farting Dog: Trouble at the Yard Sale* (K–3). Illus. by Audrey Colman. 2004, Dutton $15.99 (0-525-47217-7). 32pp. Walter proves himself a hero in this grossly amusing second book about his flatulent tendencies. (Rev: BL 4/15/04; SLJ 4/04)

5463 Krebs, Laurie. *We're Sailing to Galapagos: A Week in the Pacific* (PS–3). Illus. by Grazia Restelli. 2005, Barefoot $16.99 (1-84148-902-6). During a visit to the Galapagos, readers are introduced to the various animals found there, with informative text following a rhyming story. (Rev: SLJ 5/05)

5464 Kroll, Steven. *Patches Lost and Found* (K–3). Illus. by Barry Gott. 2001, Winslow $16.95 (1-890817-53-8). 32pp. Jenny loves to draw pictures but can't write stories, so she draws pictures of her pet hamster and fills in the words of a story afterward. (Rev: BL 3/1/01*; HBG 10/01)

5465 Kroll, Steven. *A Tale of Two Dogs* (PS–1). Illus. by Mike Reed. 2004, Marshall Cavendish $16.95 (0-7614-5161-7). 32pp. When the Morrisons return puppy Morgan to the pound and come home with a less unruly dog, are they really further ahead? (Rev: BL 4/15/04; SLJ 7/04)

5466 Kroll, Virginia. *Motherlove* (PS–2). Illus. by Lucia Washburn. 1998, Dawn $16.95 (1-883220-81-5); paper $7.95 (1-883220-80-7). In rhyming text, the role of mothers in the animal kingdom is explored with paintings of various animal mothers and their offspring. (Rev: HBG 3/99; SLJ 3/99) [591.56]

5467 Kuiper, Nannie. *Bailey the Bear Cub* (PS–K). Trans. from Dutch by J. Alison James. Illus. by Jeska Verstegen. 2002, North-South LB $15.88 (0-7358-1625-5). A sensible bear mother helps her cub overcome his anxieties and learn to catch his own dinner. (Rev: HBG 10/02; SLJ 5/02)

5468 Kuskin, Karla. *So, What's It Like to Be a Cat?* (PS–2). Illus. by Betsy Lewin. 2005, Simon & Schuster $15.95 (0-689-84733-5). 32pp. A self-confident cat happily answers in graceful lyrics the questions posed by a young interviewer. (Rev: BL 5/1/05)

5469 Kutner, Merrily. *Down on the Farm* (PS). Illus. by Will Hillenbrand. 2004, Holiday House $16.95 (0-8234-1721-2). Barnyard animals are introduced in bouncy rhymes and lots of caws, honks, and oinks. (Rev: SLJ 3/04)

5470 Labatt, Mary. *Sam Gets Lost* (PS). Trans. and illus. by Marisol Sarrazin. Series: Kids Can Read. 2004, Kids Can paper $3.95 (1-55337-563-7). 32pp. Puppy Sam gets lost — and then found — in this simple story. Also use *Sam Goes to School* (2004). (Rev: BL 7/04)

5471 Lang, Glenna. *Looking Out for Sarah* (PS–3). Illus. 2001, Charlesbridge $15.95 (0-88106-647-8). 32pp. Based on a true story, this book presents a typical day in the life of a blind woman through the eyes of her guide dog, Perry. (Rev: BL 11/1/01; HB 9–10/01; HBG 3/02; SLJ 9/01)

5472 Lange, Willem. *John and Tom* (K–3). Illus. by Burt Dodson. Series: Family Heritage. 2001, Vermont Folklife Center $14.95 (0-916718-17-4). 32pp. A young logger named John is pinned beneath a tree and is rescued by his horse in this based-in-truth tale set in 1950s Vermont. (Rev: BL 11/1/01; SLJ 12/01)

5473 Lawson, Julie. *Bear on the Train* (PS–2). Illus. by Brian Deines. 1999, Kids Can $14.95 (1-55074-560-3). 32pp. Bear enters the hopper of a train to eat some grain and becomes so comfortable that he hibernates there all winter. (Rev: BL 10/15/99; HBG 3/00; SLJ 11/99)

5474 Lechner, John. *A Froggy Fable* (PS–2). Illus. 2005, Candlewick $14.99 (0-7636-2123-4). 32pp. Accepting change is the message of this fable about a frog who is dismayed when his cozy home under a rock is disturbed. (Rev: BL 6/1–15/05; SLJ 5/05)

5475 Lee, Chinlun. *Good Dog, Paw!* (PS–2). Illus. 2004, Candlewick $15.99 (0-7636-2178-1). 40pp. Paw, the much loved dog of April the veterinarian, recounts the events of a typical day. (Rev: BL 4/15/04; HB 5–6/04; SLJ 8/04)

5476 Leedy, Loreen. *Mapping Penny's World* (PS–2). Illus. 2000, Holt $17.00 (0-8050-6178-9). 32pp. Using her newly learned map skills, Penny draws maps of the territory covered by her pet boxer, Lisa. (Rev: BCCB 9/00; BL 7/00; HBG 3/01; SLJ 9/00)

5477 Lesser, Carolyn. *Great Crystal Bear* (K–3). Illus. by William Noonan. 1996, Harcourt $15.00 (0-15-200667-2). 32pp. The author pictures how polar bears survive their hostile environment. (Rev: BL 5/1/96; SLJ 6/96)

5478 Levy, Elizabeth. *The Cool Ghoul Mystery* (2–4). Illus. by Mordicai Gerstein. Series: Fletcher Mysteries. 2003, Simon & Schuster LB $11.89 (0-689-86160-5); paper $3.99 (0-689-86159-1). 59pp. Dog detective Fletcher and his companion, a flea called Jasper, delve into a mystery while on a snowboarding vacation with their human family in this well-illustrated volume. (Rev: HBG 4/04; SLJ 3/04)

5479 Lewin, Ted. *Nilo and the Tortoise* (K–3). Illus. by author. 1999, Scholastic $16.95 (0-590-69004-0). Young Nilo is stranded overnight on one of the Galapagos Islands and shares sleeping quarters with a giant tortoise. (Rev: BL 8/99; SLJ 4/99)

5480 Lewis, Kim. *Little Baa* (PS–K). Illus. 2001, Candlewick $15.99 (0-7636-1447-5). 32pp. When Little Baa disappears, Ma sets off in search and is eventually helped by a young shepherd and his dog. (Rev: BL 5/1/01; HBG 10/01; SLJ 6/01)

5481 Lewis, Wendy A. *In Abby's Hands* (1–4). Illus. by Marilyn Mets and Peter Ledwon. 2004, Red Deer $17.95 (0-88995-282-5). Abby is home alone when her Labrador retriever goes into labor, and she gains confidence as she offers the dog comfort and aid. (Rev: SLJ 3/04)

5482 Lindgren, Barbro. *Julia Wants a Pet* (K–2). Trans. from Swedish by Elisabeth Kallick Dyssegaard. Illus. by Eva Eriksson. 2003, R&S $15.00 (91-29-65940-X). Seven-year-old Julia travels far and wide in her search for the perfect pet. (Rev: HB 9–10/03; HBG 4/04; SLJ 11/03)

5483 Lindgren, Barbro. *Rosa: Perpetual Motion Machine* (PS–2). Illus. by Eva Eriksson. 1996, Douglas & McIntyre $14.95 (1-55054-241-9). 32pp. A mischievous pup breaks her lease, runs away, and gets lost. (Rev: BL 6/1–15/96; SLJ 7/96)

5484 Lobel, Arnold. *The Rose in My Garden* (PS–3). Illus. by Anita Lobel. 1984, Morrow paper $6.95 (0-688-12265-5). 40pp. A cumulative tale that starts with a bee sleeping on a rose.

5485 London, Jonathan. *Baby Whale's Journey* (1–3). Illus. by Jon Van Zyle. 1999, Chronicle $14.95 (0-8118-2496-9). 35pp. A poetic introduction to the life of a sperm whale from its birth through weaning to final acceptance by the pod as they feed on a giant squid. (Rev: BL 11/1/99; HBG 3/00; SLJ 1/00)

5486 London, Jonathan. *Crunch Munch* (PS). Illus. by Michael Rex. 2001, Harcourt $13.00 (0-15-202603-7). Simple double-page spreads look at the noises animals make when they eat. (Rev: HBG 10/01; SLJ 4/01)

5487 London, Jonathan. *Mustang Canyon* (PS–2). Illus. by Daniel San Souci. 2002, Candlewick $15.99 (0-7636-1554-4). 40pp. An exciting story about Little Pinto the mustang and his desert herd, followed by a glossary and information on the history of the horse in America. (Rev: BL 12/1/02; HBG 3/03; SLJ 8/03)

5488 London, Jonathan. *Sled Dogs Run* (K–2). Illus. by Jonathan Van Zyle. 2005, Walker LB $17.85 (0-8027-8958-7). 32pp. A girl describes how she raises three Siberian husky pups, training them to be sled dogs. (Rev: BL 6/1–15/05; SLJ 5/05)

5489 London, Jonathan. *Wiggle Waggle* (PS). Illus. by Michael Rex. 1999, Harcourt $13.00 (0-15-201940-5). 32pp. Using double-page spreads, this book amusingly explains how various animals walk. (Rev: BL 5/15/99; HBG 10/99; SLJ 6/99)

5490 Losordo, Stephen. *Cow Moo Me* (PS). Illus. by Jane Conteh-Morgan. Series: Harper Growing Tree. 1998, HarperCollins $5.95 (0-694-01108-8). In a series of two-page spreads, common animals engage in humorous activities with accompanying rhyming text. (Rev: BL 12/15/98; SLJ 2/99)

5491 Luthardt, Kevin. *Larabee* (PS–1). Illus. 2004, Peachtree $15.95 (1-56145-300-5). 32pp. Larabee, an amiable puppy who likes to help deliver the mail, longs to receive a letter of his own. (Rev: BL 3/15/04; SLJ 4/04)

5492 Luthardt, Kevin. *Peep!* (PS–2). Illus. by author. 2003, Peachtree $15.95 (1-56145-046-4). A young boy and a hatchling duck become fast friends; when the bird eventually flies away, the youngster is sad until one day, on a walk, he hears a "mew." (Rev: BL 5/03; HB 7–8/03; HBG 10/03; SLJ 5/03)

5493 Lyon, George E. *Ada's Pal* (PS–1). Illus. by Marguerite Casparian. 1996, Orchard LB $16.99 (0-531-08878-2). 32pp. Ada pines away when her companion, the other dog in the family, dies. (Rev: BL 9/15/96; SLJ 9/96)

5494 Lyon, George E. *A Traveling Cat* (PS–1). Illus. by Paul Johnson. 1998, Orchard $15.95 (0-531-30102-8). 32pp. A little girl cares for a stray cat and tends to her litter. When the cat later disappears, the girl realizes that she is a born traveler. (Rev: BL 11/15/98; HB 11–12/98; HBG 3/99; SLJ 9/98)

5495 Macaulay, David. *Angelo* (K–3). Illus. 2002, Houghton Mifflin $16.00 (0-618-16826-5). 48pp. An Italian artist and a wounded pigeon share an unlikely friendship in this beautifully illustrated picture book that gives a bird's-eye view of Rome. (Rev: BCCB 6/02; BL 7/02; HB 5–6/02; HBG 10/02; SLJ 5/02)

5496 McCarty, Peter. *Hondo and Fabian* (PS–K). Illus. 2002, Holt $16.95 (0-8050-6352-8). 32pp. Captivating illustrations and simple text portray a day in the life of two family pets, Hondo the dog and Fabian the cat. Caldecott Honor Book, 2003. (Rev: BL 2/15/02; HBG 10/02; SLJ 6/02)

5497 McDonald, Megan. *Insects Are My Life* (PS–2). Illus. by Paul Johnson. 1995, Orchard LB $16.99 (0-531-08724-7). 32pp. No one seems to understand Amanda's fascination with insects. (Rev: BCCB 4/95; BL 3/1/95; HB 3–4/95; SLJ 3/95*)

5498 McDonald, Megan. *Whoo-oo Is It?* (PS–1). Illus. by S. D. Schindler. 1992, Orchard LB $16.99 (0-531-08574-0). 32pp. A mother owl oversees the hatching of her egg in this book that explores the sounds of the night. (Rev: BL 2/1/92; HB 5–6/92; SLJ 4/92)

5499 McFarland, Lyn Rossiter. *Widget* (PS–1). Illus. by Jim McFarland. 2001, Farrar $16.00 (0-374-38428-2). 32pp. Preschoolers will love the charming illustrations and humorous story about a stray dog who pretends to be a cat in order to fit in at his new home. (Rev: BL 11/1/01; HBG 3/02; SLJ 8/01*)

5500 McFarland, Lyn Rossiter. *Widget and the Puppy* (PS–2). Illus. by Jim McFarland. 2004, Farrar $16.00 (0-374-38429-0). Widget the dog falls asleep while babysitting a puppy and it is the six cats of the household that save the day, although they get none of the praise. (Rev: SLJ 9/04)

5501 McFarlane, Sheryl. *This Is the Dog* (PS–2). Illus. by Chrissie Wysotski. 2003, Fitzhenry & Whiteside $14.95 (1-55041-551-4). Rhythmic text and striking illustrations highlight this story of a wayward golden retriever puppy. (Rev: SLJ 10/03)

5502 McGeorge, Constance W. *Boomer Goes to School* (PS–K). Illus. by Mary Whyte. 1996, Chronicle $14.95 (0-8118-1117-4). 32pp. Boomer, a golden retriever, becomes a hero during show-and-tell when he visits his young master's school. (Rev: BL 4/15/96; SLJ 7/96)

5503 McGeorge, Constance W. *Boomer's Big Day* (PS–2). Illus. by Mary Whyte. 1994, Chronicle $14.95 (0-8118-0526-3). 32pp. Boomer, a dog, is a bystander as the family prepares to move, but even-

tually he is transported to his new home. (Rev: BL 7/94)

5504 McGraw, Sheila. *Pussycats Everywhere!* (PS–2). Illus. by author. 2000, Firefly LB $19.95 (1-55209-346-8); paper $6.95 (1-55209-348-4). When Karen's cat wanders away and she places lost-cat posters everywhere, 37 cats are brought to her house. (Rev: HBG 3/01; SLJ 12/00)

5505 McHenry, E. B. *Poodlena* (PS–1). Illus. 2004, Bloomsbury $16.95 (1-58234-824-3). 32pp. Poodlena, a pampered pink poodle, takes pains to preserve her pristine appearance until an encounter with a playful canine persuades her that she's been missing out on a lot of fun. (Rev: BL 5/1/04; SLJ 11/04)

5506 McKenna, Virginia. *Back to the Blue* (K–3). Illus. by Ian Andrew. Series: Born Free Wildlife Book/Templar Book. 1998, Millbrook LB $21.40 (0-7613-0409-6). Based on fact, these are accounts of real animal rescue and relocation projects run by the conservation charity Born Free Foundation. (Rev: BL 8/98; HBG 10/98; SLJ 3/98)

5507 McLellan, Stephanie Simpson. *Leon's Song* (PS–3). Illus. by Dianna Bonder. 2004, Fitzhenry & Whiteside $15.95 (1-55041-813-0). Leon, a 40-year-old frog who lacks a sense of fulfillment, comes into his own when he alerts the pond creatures to the presence of danger. (Rev: SLJ 1/05)

5508 MacLeod, Elizabeth. *I Heard a Little Baa* (PS). Illus. by Louise Phillips. 1998, Kids Can $7.95 (1-55074-496-8). 24pp. An animal guessing game in which different animal riddles-in-rhyme are solved by unfolding pages. (Rev: HBG 3/99; SLJ 12/98)

5509 McMenemy, Sarah. *Waggle* (PS–2). Illus. by author. 2003, Candlewick $14.99 (0-7636-2059-9). A little girl's efforts to find the perfect name for her new puppy are related in simple, lively text and bright illustrations. (Rev: BL 5/15/03; HBG 10/03; SLJ 8/03)

5510 McMillan, Bruce. *Gletta the Foal* (PS–2). Illus. 1998, Marshall Cavendish $14.95 (0-7614-5039-4). 32pp. An Icelandic foal tells her own story as she plays with other horses, adjusts to her family, and experiences new emotions. Captivating photos accompany the imaginative text. (Rev: BL 9/15/98; HBG 3/99; SLJ 12/98)

5511 McNulty, Faith. *The Lady and the Spider* (K–3). Illus. by Bob Marstall. 1986, HarperCollins $15.00 (0-06-024191-8); paper $5.95 (0-06-443152-5). 48pp. The reader enters the small world of the spider, who lives on a head of lettuce in a garden and feels part of it. (Rev: BL 3/15/86; SLJ 9/86)

5512 McNulty, Faith. *A Snake in the House* (K–4). Illus. by Ted Rand. 1994, Scholastic $14.95 (0-590-44758-0). 32pp. A captured garter snake escapes in a boy's house and eventually is successful in getting back to his pond. (Rev: BCCB 2/94; BL 5/1/94; SLJ 3/94)

5513 Madrigal, Antonio H. *Blanca's Feather* (1–4). Illus. by Gerardo Suzan. 2000, Rising Moon $15.95 (0-87358-743-X). 32pp. On Saint Francis of Assisi's Day, Rosalia can't find her hen to take to church to be blessed and brings one of her feathers instead. (Rev: BL 4/15/00; HBG 10/00; SLJ 7/00)

5514 Mahy, Margaret. *Dashing Dog!* (PS–2). Illus. by Sarah Garland. 2002, HarperCollins LB $15.89 (0-06-000457-6). 32pp. Rhyming verse and lively illustrations present a poodle's day at the beach, during which the rambunctious pup ruins his nice hairdo, chases birds and Frisbees . . . and rescues the baby. (Rev: BL 10/1/02; HBG 3/03; SLJ 9/02)

5515 Mallat, Kathy. *Trouble on the Tracks* (PS–K). Illus. 2001, Walker LB $16.85 (0-8027-8773-8). 24pp. A train is derailed by trouble — then it's revealed that Trouble is a cat, and the train is a toy. (Rev: BL 9/1/01; HBG 3/02; SLJ 9/01)

5516 Maltbie, P. I. *Picasso and Minou* (PS–2). Illus. by Pau Estrada. 2005, Charlesbridge $15.95 (1-57091-620-9). 32pp. Minou, a cat of strong artistic tastes who lives with Picasso, is pleased when the artist leaves his Blue Period in this beautifully illustrated picture book that blends fact and fiction. (Rev: BL 2/15/05; SLJ 4/05)

5517 Marsh, T. J., and Jennifer Ward. *Way Out in the Desert* (PS–2). Illus. by Kenneth J. Spengler. 1998, Rising Moon $15.95 (0-87358-687-5). 32pp. Using double-page spreads, familiar animals of the desert are presented in a delightful takeoff on "Over in the Meadow." (Rev: BCCB 5/98; HBG 10/98; SLJ 6/98)

5518 Martin, Ann M. *Leo the Magnificat* (K–3). Illus. by Emily Arnold McCully. 1996, Scholastic $15.95 (0-590-48498-2). 32pp. A nomadic cat finds a home in a community church. (Rev: BCCB 12/96; BL 9/1/96; SLJ 11/96)

5519 Martin, Bill, Jr. *Panda Bear, Panda Bear, What Do You See?* (PS–2). Illus. by Eric Carle. 2003, Holt $15.95 (0-8050-1758-5). Ten endangered animals — including the bald eagle, red wolf, and black panther — are introduced in Martin and Carle's familiar format. (Rev: HBG 4/04; SLJ 8/03)

5520 Martin, Bill, Jr. *Polar Bear, Polar Bear, What Do You Hear?* (PS–K). Illus. by Eric Carle. 1991, Holt $15.95 (0-8050-1759-3). 32pp. Animal sounds from ten different animals are featured in this picture book. (Rev: BCCB 12/91; BL 11/15/91; HB 1–2/92; SLJ 11/91*)

5521 Martin, Jacqueline B. *Washing the Willow Tree Loon* (2–4). Illus. by Nancy Carpenter. 1995, Simon & Schuster $16.00 (0-689-80415-6). 40pp. A fictionalized account of how an oil-slicked loon is saved by a woman who, with others, tries to save animals after an oil barge hits a bridge. (Rev: BL 12/15/95; HB 9–10/95; SLJ 10/95)

5522 Marzollo, Jean. *Mama Mama* (PS). Illus. by Laura Regan. Series: Harper Growing Tree. 1999, HarperCollins $5.95 (0-694-01245-9). This board book celebrates the tender mother-child relations that exist with such animals as a lioness, leopard, chimpanzee, panda, elephant, and sea otter. (Rev: SLJ 11/99)

5523 Masurel, Claire. *A Cat and a Dog* (PS–1). Illus. by Bob Kolar. 2001, North-South $13.95 (1-55858-949-X). 32pp. A warring cat and dog suddenly realize they each have different skills and can help each other. (Rev: BCCB 5/01; BL 6/1–15/01; HBG 10/01; SLJ 7/01)

5524 Masurel, Eric. *Un gato y un perro / A Cat and a Dog* (PS–1). Trans. by Andres Antreasyan. Illus. by Bob Kolar. 2003, North-South paper $6.95 (0-7358-1784-7). A cat and dog, normally antagonistic toward each other, decide to band together to solve each other's problems in this bilingual tale. (Rev: BL 3/1/04)

5525 Mayhew, James. *Cluck, Cluck Who's There?* (PS). Illus. by Caroline Jayne Church. 2004, Scholastic $9.95 (0-439-57737-3). The transformation of Hattie's three eggs into tiny chicks is detailed in nicely illustrated lift-the-flap pages. (Rev: SLJ 2/04)

5526 Meade, Holly. *A Place to Sleep* (PS–2). Illus. 2001, Marshall Cavendish $15.95 (0-7614-5096-3). 32pp. Facts about where and how different animals sleep, playfully conveyed through colorful illustrations and amusing text. (Rev: BCCB 12/01; BL 9/1/01; HBG 3/02; SLJ 9/01)

5527 Meggs, Libby Phillips. *Go Home! The True Story of James the Cat* (K–3). Illus. 2000, Whitman $15.95 (0-8075-2975-3). 32pp. This picture book, based on a true story, chronicles the plight of a lost cat that survives in a hostile environment through a winter and into late summer. (Rev: BL 3/1/00; HBG 10/00; SLJ 8/00)

5528 Meunier, Brian. *Pipiolo and the Roof Dogs* (PS–2). Illus. by Perky Edgerton. 2003, Dutton $16.99 (0-525-47128-6). Young Lupe and her canine companion Pipiolo feel sorry for the "roof dogs" that never touch the ground, and Pipiolo decides to take action. (Rev: HBG 4/04; SLJ 10/03)

5529 Meyers, Susan. *Puppies! Puppies! Puppies!* (PS–2). Illus. by David Walker. 2005, Abrams $15.95 (0-8109-5856-2). 32pp. Cute, cuddly puppies, doing everything that puppies love to do, are the focus of this picture book featuring endearing artwork. (Rev: BL 4/1/05)

5530 Middleton, Charlotte. *Do You Still Love Me?* (PS–K). Illus. by author. 2003, Candlewick $15.99 (0-7636-2254-0). When Anna gets a new pet — a baby chameleon called Pequito — Dudley the dog is unhappy and left out until he rescues the newcomer from a cat and gains a new role. (Rev: HBG 4/04; SLJ 9/03)

5531 Miller, Edna. *Patches Finds a New Home* (K–2). Illus. by author. 1989, Simon & Schuster paper $12.95 (0-671-66266-X). 40pp. A mother cat searches for a new home for herself and her kittens. (Rev: BL 6/15/89; SLJ 6/89)

5532 Miller, Ruth. *I Went to the Bay* (PS–1). Illus. by Martine Gourbault. 1999, Kids Can $12.95 (1-55074-498-4). 24pp. A young boy searches above and below water for frogs but finds only a variety of other marine animals. (Rev: BL 3/15/99; HBG 10/99; SLJ 6/99) [629]

5533 Minshull, Evelyn. *Eaglet's World* (PS–2). Illus. by Andrea Gabriel. 2002, Whitman $15.95 (0-8075-8929-2). 32pp. An eaglet ventures first from his egg and then from his nest in this story about growth and independence. (Rev: BL 3/1/02; HBG 10/02; SLJ 5/02)

5534 Mitchell, Adrian, and Daniel Pudles. *Twice My Size* (PS–1). Illus. 1999, Millbrook LB $21.40 (0-7613-1423-7). 32pp. A series of animals each introduces another animal friend that is bigger than it is. (Rev: BL 4/15/99; HBG 10/99; SLJ 6/99)

5535 Mockford, Caroline. *Cleo the Cat* (PS). Illus. by author. 2000, Barefoot $14.99 (1-84148-259-5). A charming story about a cat named Cleo who finds a home and a friend. (Rev: HBG 3/01; SLJ 12/00)

5536 Mockford, Caroline. *Come Here, Cleo!* (PS–1). Illus. by author. 2001, Barefoot $14.99 (1-84148-329-X). A cat has simple adventures such as climbing a tree and chasing a butterfly. (Rev: HBG 10/01; SLJ 4/01)

5537 Nethery, Mary. *Mary Veronica's Egg* (PS–2). Illus. by Paul Yalowitz. 1999, Orchard LB $16.99 (0-531-33134-2). 32pp. Mary Veronica finds a large egg that, to her delight, later hatches into a duckling. (Rev: BCCB 2/99; BL 7/99; HBG 10/99; SLJ 3/99)

5538 Newman, Leslea. *The Best Cat in the World* (PS–2). Illus. by Ronald Himler. 2004, Eerdmans $16.00 (0-8028-5252-1). 32pp. Mourning for his dead cat Charlie, Victor is reluctant to bring a new kitten into his life. (Rev: BL 1/1–15/04; SLJ 2/04)

5539 Nicholls, Judith. *Billywise* (PS–2). Illus. by Jason Cockcroft. 2002, Bloomsbury $16.95 (1-58234-778-6). A mother owl urges her owlet to leave the nest and fly. (Rev: SLJ 10/02)

5540 Ochiltree, Dianne. *Pillow Pup* (PS–1). Illus. by Mireille D'Allance. 2002, Simon & Schuster $14.95 (0-689-83408-X). 32pp. Puppy Maggie and her owner enjoy a friendly pillow fight. (Rev: BL 5/15/02; HBG 10/02)

5541 O'Connor, Jane, and Jessie Hartland. *The Perfect Puppy for Me!* (1–3). Illus. by Jessie Hartland. 2003, Viking $15.99 (0-670-03614-5). A young boy who loves dogs researches the breeds that will be available on his birthday, conveying lots of information along with the endearing story. (Rev: BL 5/15/03; HBG 10/03; SLJ 7/03)

5542 Okimoto, Jean D. *Blumpoe the Grumpoe Meets Arnold the Cat* (PS–3). Illus. by Howie Schneider. 1990, Little, Brown $13.95 (0-316-63811-0). 32pp. In an accommodating hotel, a grumpy old man is offered a cat to keep him company. (Rev: BL 5/15/90; HB 7–8/90; SLJ 7/90)

5543 Orr, Katherine. *Story of a Dolphin* (K–4). Illus. 1993, Carolrhoda LB $15.95 (0-87614-777-5). 32pp. Tourists on a Caribbean island mistreat the dolphin that Laura and her father have grown to love and understand. (Rev: BL 9/15/93; SLJ 10/93)

5544 Park, Linda Sue. *Mung-Mung: A Foldout Book of Animal Sounds* (PS). Illus. by Diane Bigda. 2004, Charlesbridge $9.95 (1-57091-486-9). This guessing game for preschoolers involves animal sounds in several languages — first the onomatopoeic sound in lettering, then, overleaf, a drawing of the animal who makes it. (Rev: SLJ 6/04) [418]

5545 Parker, Marjorie Blain. *Jasper's Day* (1–3). Illus. by Janet Wilson. 2002, Kids Can $15.95 (1-55074-957-9). 32pp. A touching but realistic story of a family's last day with their pet dog, before he is put to sleep. (Rev: BL 12/15/02; HBG 3/03; SLJ 1/03)

5546 Partridge, Elizabeth. *Moon Glowing* (K–2). Illus. by Joan Paley. 2002, Dutton $16.99 (0-525-46873-0). 32pp. Rich, textured illustrations and simple verses present a simple introduction to hibernation, as animals prepare for the winter, gathering food and finding shelters. (Rev: BL 12/1/02; HBG 3/03; SLJ 11/02*)

5547 Patent, Dorothy Hinshaw. *Baby Horses* (PS–1). Illus. by William Muñoz. 1991, Carolrhoda LB $22.60 (0-87614-690-6). 56pp. A new edition presenting the first months of a foal's life in simple text and color photos. (Rev: BL 1/1/92) [636.1]

5548 Pennac, Daniel. *Dog* (3–5). Trans. by Sarah Adams. 2004, Candlewick $15.99 (0-7636-2421-7). 192pp. Dog, long homeless, thinks his life may finally be changing for the better when he's adopted by a young girl named Plum, but things don't go nearly as smoothly as he'd hoped. (Rev: BL 5/15/04; SLJ 8/04)

5549 Penner, Lucille R. *Dinosaur Babies* (PS–1). Illus. by Peter Barrett. Series: Step into Reading. 1991, Random paper $3.99 (0-679-81207-5). 32pp. An easily read introduction to dinosaurs and their babies in large type with many illustrations. (Rev: BL 2/1/92; SLJ 1/92) [567.9]

5550 Perrow, Angeli. *Lighthouse Dog to the Rescue* (K–3). Illus. by Emily Harris. 2000, Down East $15.95 (0-89272-487-0). 32pp. Based on a real incident in Maine during the 1930s, a dog that lives in a lighthouse brings a mail boat's captain safely home during a terrible blizzard. (Rev: BL 3/1/01; HBG 10/01)

5551 Pfeffer, Wendy. *Mallard Duck at Meadow View Pond* (PS–3). Illus. by Taylor Oughton. Series: Smithsonian Backyard. 2001, Smithsonian Institution $15.95 (1-56899-956-9). 32pp. This fictional story about a duck focuses on true facts about the animal's life and habitat. (Rev: BL 2/1/02)

5552 Pilkey, Dav. *Dogzilla* (K–3). Illus. 1993, Harcourt $13.00 (0-15-223944-8); paper $7.00 (0-15-223945-6). 32pp. Using retouched photos of the author's pets as illustrations, this zany story tells of Dreadful Dogzilla, whose breath could send everyone running. Also use *Kat Kong* (1993). (Rev: BL 9/1/93; SLJ 12/93)

5553 Pitcher, Caroline. *The Time of the Lion* (PS–3). Illus. by Jackie Morris. 1998, Beyond Words $15.95 (1-885223-83-8). 32pp. In an African savanna, Joseph becomes friendly with a lion whose cubs are later saved by Joseph's father. (Rev: BL 1/1–15/99; HBG 3/99; SLJ 12/98)

5554 Plowden, Sally Hartmam. *Turtle Tracks* (PS–2). Illus. by Tee Plowden. 2002, PCF $14.95 (0-9679016-6-9). 32pp. At the beach one day, a girl learns all about sea turtles in this book that includes turtle facts and wildlife resources. (Rev: BL 7/02)

5555 Polacco, Patricia. *Mrs. Mack* (K–4). Illus. 1998, Penguin Putnam $16.99 (0-399-23167-6). 40pp. Drawing on incidents in the author's childhood, this is the story of Mrs. Mack, who allowed the author to work around horses and gain self-confidence. (Rev: BL 11/15/98; HBG 3/99; SLJ 12/98)

5556 Politi, Leo. *Song of the Swallows* (K–3). Illus. by author. 1987, Macmillan LB $15.00 (0-684-18831-7); paper $5.99 (0-689-71140-9). 32pp. Juan rings the mission's bells to welcome the swallows back to San Juan Capistrano. Caldecott Medal winner, 1950.

5557 Porte, Barbara Ann. *Tale of a Tadpole* (PS–3). Illus. by Annie Cannon. 1997, Orchard LB $16.99 (0-531-33049-4). 32pp. Francine watches the changes that occur to a tadpole until it becomes a toad. (Rev: BL 8/97; HBG 3/98; SLJ 9/97)

5558 Posey, Lee. *Night Rabbits* (PS–3). Illus. by Michael G. Montgomery. 1999, Peachtree $15.95 (1-56145-164-9). 32pp. A little girl who can't get to sleep watches the rabbits on the lawn, but in the morning she's always ready for her father's arms. (Rev: BL 5/1/99; HBG 10/99; SLJ 5/99)

5559 Preller, James. *Cardinal and Sunflower* (PS–2). Illus. by Huy Voun Lee. 1998, HarperCollins $14.95 (0-06-026222-2). 32pp. Sunflower seeds scattered during the winter by a mother and daughter feed a pair of cardinals. They raise a family the following spring and feed on a sunflower that has grown from one of the overlooked seeds. (Rev: BL 6/1–15/98; HBG 10/98; SLJ 6/98)

5560 Pringle, Laurence. *Naming the Cat* (K–3). Illus. by Katherine Potter. 1997, Walker LB $16.85 (0-8027-8622-7). 32pp. A family ponders what the best name would be for their new cat. After watching its escapades, they decide to call him Lucky. (Rev: BL 10/1/97; HBG 3/98; SLJ 11/97)

5561 Provensen, Alice. *A Day in the Life of Murphy* (PS–2). Illus. by author. 2003, Simon & Schuster $16.95 (0-689-84884-6). Murphy, a fun-loving terrier who lives on a farm, describes a typical day in his life. (Rev: BL 5/15/03; HB 7–8/03; HBG 10/03; SLJ 7/03)

5562 Raff, Courtney Granet. *Giant of the Sea: A Story of a Sperm Whale* (PS–2). Illus. by Shawn Gould. 2002, Soundprints $15.95 (1-931465-72-X); paper $6.95 (1-931465-80-0). 32pp. A fictional look at the behavior, diet, and habitat of a mother sperm whale and her young, with attractive illustrations that often show the animal's perspective. (Rev: BL 2/1/03)

5563 Rand, Gloria. *A Home for Spooky* (K–4). Illus. by Ted Rand. 1998, Holt $15.95 (0-8050-4611-9). 32pp. Annie shares her school lunch with a stray dog she names Spooky and eventually gets permission to bring the dog home. Based on a true story. (Rev: BL 4/1/98; HBG 10/98; SLJ 6/98)

5564 Rand, Gloria. *Little Flower* (PS–1). Illus. by R. W. Alley. 2002, Holt $16.95 (0-8050-6480-X). 32pp. Miss Pearl takes a fall and is saved in a unique way by her potbellied pig, Little Flower. (Rev: BL 3/15/02; HBG 10/02; SLJ 8/02)

5565 Rand, Gloria. *Mary Was a Little Lamb* (PS–1). Illus. by Ted Rand. 2004, Holt $16.95 (0-8050-6816-3). 32pp. Based on truth, this is the story of a lovable lamb named Mary who becomes such a dis-

traction that she is banished to a petting zoo. (Rev: BL 4/15/04; SLJ 6/04)

5566 Rathmann, Peggy. *Officer Buckle and Gloria* (PS–2). Illus. 1995, Penguin Putnam $16.99 (0-399-22616-8). 32pp. A police dog named Gloria steals the show when Officer Buckle gives a presentation on safety to local school children. Caldecott Medal winner, 1996. (Rev: BCCB 10/95; BL 11/1/95*; HB 11–12/95; HBG 4/04; SLJ 9/95*)

5567 Rice, Eve. *Sam Who Never Forgets* (PS–1). Illus. by author. 1977, Morrow paper $5.95 (0-688-07335-2). 32pp. Sam, the zookeeper, feeds all the animals each day, but one day there appears to be nothing for the elephant.

5568 Richardson, Justin, and Peter Parnell. *And Tango Makes Three* (PS–2). Illus. by Henry Cole. 2005, Simon & Schuster $14.95 (0-689-87845-1). 32pp. This warm story of two male penguins who prefer each other's company to that of females and who together raise a chick called Tango is based on a true story. (Rev: BL 5/15/05)

5569 Robertus, Polly M. *The Dog Who Had Kittens* (PS–2). Illus. by Janet Stevens. 1991, Holiday House LB $16.95 (0-8234-0860-4). 32pp. Baxter, a basset hound, decides that he can help raise the new family of Eloise the cat. (Rev: BL 3/15/91; SLJ 5/91)

5570 Roome, Diana Reynolds. *The Elephant's Pillow* (PS–2). Illus. by Jude Daly. 2003, Farrar $16.00 (0-374-32015-2). Sing Lo, the pampered son of a wealthy Peking merchant, soothes the grumpy Imperial Elephant and in the process learns something about himself. (Rev: BL 1/1–15/04; HBG 4/04; SLJ 11/03)

5571 Rosen, Michael. *Howler* (PS–2). Illus. by Neal Layton. 2004, Bloomsbury $15.95 (1-58234-851-0). Rover the dog, last seen in *Rover* (1999), cannot understand the changes taking place in his home, until the new baby arrives. (Rev: SLJ 8/04)

5572 Rostoker-Gruber, Karen. *Rooster Can't Cock-a-Doodle-Doo* (PS–2). Illus. by Paul Rátz de Tagyos. 2004, Dial $15.99 (0-8037-2877-8). All the animals band together to wake Farmer Ted when the rooster has a sore throat. (Rev: HB 7–8/04; SLJ 7/04)

5573 Rotner, Shelley, and Cheo Garcia. *Pick a Pet* (PS–1). Illus. 1999, Orchard LB $16.99 (0-531-33147-4). 32pp. Using alliteration, this story involves Patty's search for a pet, such as a freckled frog, or a plump pig, or even one of the fanciful creatures Patty imagines. (Rev: BL 7/99; HBG 10/99; SLJ 4/99)

5574 Rounds, Glen. *Once We Had a Horse* (K–2). Illus. 1996, Holiday House $15.95 (0-8234-1241-5). 32pp. One summer, a boy and his sister learn to ride a gentle farm horse. (Rev: BL 6/1–15/96; SLJ 7/96*)

5575 Rounds, Glen. *Wild Horses* (1–4). Illus. 1993, Holiday House LB $14.95 (0-8234-1019-6). 32pp. The lives of wild horses in the West are explored in text and beautiful drawings. (Rev: BL 4/1/93) [599.72]

5576 Roy, Ron. *Three Ducks Went Wandering* (PS–1). Illus. by Paul Galdone. 1987, Ticknor paper $5.96 (0-89919-494-X). Three ducks are oblivious to the dangers all around them when they take a walk.

5577 Royston, Angela. *Baby Animals* (PS). Illus. by Andrew Aloof. Series: Eye Openers. 1992, Macmillan paper $8.99 (0-689-71563-3). 24pp. Numerous photographs in color help introduce a variety of baby animals to preschoolers. (Rev: BL 8/92; SLJ 10/92) [599]

5578 Royston, Angela. *Jungle Animals* (PS–2). Illus. by Martine Blaney and Dave Hopkins. Series: Eye Openers. 1991, Macmillan $8.99 (0-689-71519-6). 21pp. A number of jungle animals are introduced. (Rev: BL 9/15/91; SLJ 1/92) [581]

5579 Ruepp, Krista. *Runaway Pony* (PS–2). Illus. by Ulrike Heyne. 2005, North-South $15.95 (0-7358-1985-8). 32pp. Anna's pony, Prince, is back home from the herd, but Anna must work to regain his trust when he is spooked by a loud tractor in this sequel to *The Winter Pony* (2002). (Rev: BL 6/1–15/05)

5580 Ruepp, Krista. *Winter Pony* (K–3). Illus. by Ulrike Heyne. 2002, North-South LB $16.50 (0-7358-1692-1). 32pp. Anna worries about her pony, Prince, when he is sent to summer pasture in this story set in northern Iceland. (Rev: BL 1/1–15/03; HBG 3/03; SLJ 12/02)

5581 Rush, Ken. *What About Emma?* (PS–3). Illus. 1996, Orchard LB $16.99 (0-531-08884-7). 32pp. Even though her farm family must sell their stock to survive, Sue is allowed to keep her favorite cow, Emma. (Rev: BL 9/1/96; SLJ 9/96)

5582 Ryder, Joanne. *Come Along, Kitten* (PS). Illus. by Susan Winter. 2003, Simon & Schuster $15.95 (0-689-83164-1). A big, laid-back dog with a protective bent and a curious kitten enjoy exploring together. (Rev: HBG 4/04; SLJ 7/03)

5583 Rylant, Cynthia. *The Bookshop Dog* (PS–K). Illus. 1996, Scholastic $15.95 (0-590-54331-8). 40pp. A dog named Martha Jane becomes the mascot at her owner's bookshop. (Rev: BL 9/1/96; SLJ 9/96)

5584 Rylant, Cynthia. *Dog Heaven* (PS–1). Illus. 1995, Scholastic $15.95 (0-590-41701-0). 32pp. In dog heaven, dogs run and play and wait for their absent friends. (Rev: BCCB 10/95; BL 8/95; HBG 4/04; SLJ 10/95)

5585 Rylant, Cynthia. *The Old Woman Who Named Things* (PS–3). Illus. by Kathryn Brown. 1996, Harcourt $16.00 (0-15-257809-9). 32pp. An old lady who only names things that will outlive her doesn't name the pup she adopts. (Rev: BL 5/1/96*; HB 5–6/98; SLJ 10/96*)

5586 Sackett, Hannah Kate. *Animal Faces at Night* (2–4). Illus. by Martin Camm. Series: Animal Faces. 2003, McGraw-Hill $16.95 (1-57768-427-3). 32pp. A lesson in 13 creatures that live by night and sleep by day, from the luna moth to the nocturnal rhinoceros. (Rev: HBG 4/04; SLJ 3/04) [591.5]

5587 Sackett, Hannah Kate. *Animal Faces in the Forest* (2–4). Illus. by Martin Camm. Series: Animal Faces. 2003, McGraw-Hill $16.95 (1-57768-428-1). 32pp. Thirteen forest animals, from beetles to beavers, are pictured and described, with explanations of how facial characteristics help the animal to survive. (Rev: HBG 4/04; SLJ 3/04) [591]

5588 Sáez Castán, Javier. *The Three Hedgehogs* (K–3). Illus. by Javier Saez Caston. 2004, Groundwood $15.95 (0-88899-595-4). 32pp. In this colorfully illustrated tale told in two acts, three hungry hedgehogs steal apples from an orchard and must undergo a trial. (Rev: SLJ 7/04)

5589 Salerno, Steven. *Little Tumbo* (PS–2). Illus. by author. 2003, Marshall Cavendish $14.95 (0-7614-5136-6). Little Tumbo is a very small elephant and his squeaks initially fail to raise an alarm, but when he is captured for a second time he manages a full-blown trumpet. (Rev: HBG 4/04; SLJ 12/03)

5590 Sampson, Michael, and Bill Martin, Jr. *Caddie the Golf Dog* (PS–3). Illus. by Floyd Cooper. 2002, Walker LB $17.85 (0-8027-8818-1). 32pp. Jennifer's parents finally give permission for a dog too late for her to keep her beloved stray, but in a happy turn of events she ends up with the puppy of that very stray. (Rev: BL 12/1/02; HBG 3/03; SLJ 12/02)

5591 Sayre, April Pulley. *Crocodile Listens* (PS–3). Illus. by JoEllen M. Stammen. 2001, Greenwillow LB $15.89 (0-688-16505-2). A hungry crocodile mother waits attentively, ignoring all the other animals, for her babies to be ready to hatch in this engaging story that includes information about the Nile crocodile. (Rev: BCCB 10/01; HBG 3/02; SLJ 10/01)

5592 Sayre, April Pulley. *Dig, Wait, Listen* (PS–2). Illus. by Barbara Bash. 2001, Greenwillow LB $15.89 (0-688-16615-6). 32pp. A desert-dwelling spadefoot toad is alert for the sound of rain, and when it comes she emerges from under the surface to mate, lay her eggs, and watch her young hatch and grow. (Rev: BL 6/1–15/01; HB 7–8/01; HBG 10/01; SLJ 6/01)

5593 Scamell, Ragnhild. *Wish Come True Cat* (K–2). Illus. by Gaby Hansen. 2001, Barron's $13.95 (0-7641-5392-7). A little girl comes to love a scruffy cat who turns up after she had wished for a cute kitten. (Rev: HBG 3/02; SLJ 1/02)

5594 Schachner, Judy. *Skippyjon Jones* (K–3). Illus. by author. 2003, Dutton $15.99 (0-525-47134-0). Young readers will fall in love with Skippyjon Jones, a rambunctious Siamese kitten who would rather play at being a bird or dog than accept his true identity as a cat. (Rev: HBG 4/04; SLJ 1/04)

5595 Schaefer, Lola M. *Arrowhawk* (2–3). Illus. by Gabi Swiatkowska. 2004, Holt $16.95 (0-8050-6371-4). 32pp. Based on real events, this is a beautifully illustrated story, told from the bird's point of view, of a young red-tailed hawk that was nursed back to health after being shot by an arrow. (Rev: BL 5/15/04; SLJ 5/04)

5596 Schaeffer, Carole Lexa. *Cool Time Song* (PS). Illus. by Pierr Morgan. 2005, Viking $15.99 (0-670-05928-5). 32pp. Savanna animals enjoy the cool of the evening after a hot day in this beautifully illustrated picture book with a message about caring for natural resources. (Rev: BL 3/1/05; SLJ 4/05)

5597 Schindel, John. *Busy Penguins* (PS). Illus. by Jonathan Chester. 2000, Tricycle $6.95 (1-58246-016-7). 20pp. A board book that shows penguins in various activities — jumping, sliding, diving, bumping, and even pooping. (Rev: BL 3/15/00; SLJ 8/00)

5598 Schuch, Steve. *A Symphony of Whales* (1–4). Illus. by Peter Sylvada. 1999, Harcourt $16.00 (0-15-201670-8). 32pp. Based on fact, this is the story of a Siberian girl whose ability to reproduce the song of the whales helps save a group of Beluga whales trapped in a bay. (Rev: BCCB 11/99; BL 1/1–15/00; HBG 3/00; SLJ 11/99)

5599 Schulman, Janet. *A Bunny for All Seasons* (PS–K). Illus. by Meilo So. 2003, Knopf $9.95 (0-375-82256-9). 32pp. A gentle story of a bunny enjoying a wonderful garden full of food, meeting another rabbit, getting cozy for the winter, and the pair returning to the garden with their young in the spring. (Rev: BL 3/1/03; HBG 10/03; SLJ 2/03)

5600 Seymour, Tres. *Hunting the White Cow* (PS–3). Illus. by Wendy A. Halperin. 1993, Orchard LB $17.99 (0-531-08646-1). 32pp. After a white cow has escaped from the farm, several people try unsuccessfully to catch her. (Rev: BCCB 10/93; BL 9/1/93; HB 11–12/93; SLJ 12/93*)

5601 Shapiro, Arnold L. *Mice Squeak, We Speak* (PS–K). Illus. by Tomie dePaola. 1997, Penguin Putnam $13.99 (0-399-23202-8). 32pp. Three friends introduce the different sounds made by a variety of animals. (Rev: BL 9/15/97*; HBG 3/98; SLJ 10/97)

5602 Shaw, Nancy. *Raccoon Tune* (PS–2). Illus. by Howard Fine. 2003, Holt $15.95 (0-8050-6544-X). A family of raccoons have a splendid (and noisy) time raiding trash cans and feasting on a surprise haul of trout. (Rev: HBG 10/03; SLJ 7/03)

5603 Sheehan, Patty. *Shadow and the Ready Time* (K–3). Illus. by Itoko Maeno. 1994, Advocacy $14.95 (0-911655-13-1). 38pp. A wolf cub is raised by an older, lame wolf when he is separated from his pack. (Rev: SLJ 12/94)

5604 Simmie, Lois. *Mister Got To Go and Arnie* (K–3). Illus. by Cynthia Nugent. 2002, Raincoast $15.95 (1-55192-494-3). A competition for territory between a male terrier and a cat is solved when the dog is distracted by a pretty female terrier. (Rev: SLJ 8/02)

5605 Simmons, Jane. *Ebb and Flo and the Baby Seal* (PS–2). Illus. 2002, Simon & Schuster $16.00 (0-689-84368-2). 32pp. A dog named Ebb helps reunite a baby seal with its mother. (Rev: BL 1/1–15/02; HBG 10/02; SLJ 3/02*)

5606 Simon, Norma. *Fire Fighters* (PS–K). Illus. by Pamela Paparone. 1995, Simon & Schuster paper $14.00 (0-689-80280-3). 32pp. A day in the life of firefighters who are actually dalmatians. (Rev: BL 9/15/95; SLJ 12/95)

5607 Simon, Norma. *Oh, That Cat!* (K–3). Illus. by Dora Leder. 1986, Whitman LB $13.95 (0-8075-5919-9). 32pp. Max may be obnoxious in some

ways, but he's special too. (Rev: BL 4/15/86; SLJ 8/86)

5608 Simont, Marc. *The Stray Dog* (PS–3). Illus. 2001, HarperCollins LB $15.89 (0-06-028934-1). 32pp. A family goes back to a picnic ground to bring home the stray dog they saw the week before in this tender animal story. Caldecott Honor Book, 2002. (Rev: BCCB 3/01; BL 1/1–15/01; HBG 10/01; SLJ 2/01)

5609 Singer, Marilyn. *Good Day, Good Night* (PS–2). Illus. by Ponder Goembel. 1998, Marshall Cavendish $15.95 (0-7614-5018-1). An interesting book that describes, in rhyme, how various animals spend their days and nights. (Rev: BCCB 7–8/98; HBG 10/98; SLJ 6/98)

5610 Sis, Peter. *Komodo!* (PS–2). Illus. 1993, Greenwillow $15.89 (0-688-11584-5). 32pp. On a trip to Indonesia, a young boy encounters the animal he has been fascinated with, the Komodo dragon. (Rev: BCCB 6/93; BL 4/15/93*; HB 5–6/93*; SLJ 7/93*)

5611 Slier, Deborah. *Farm Animals* (PS). Illus. 1988, Checkerboard $2.95 (1-56288-084-5). 12pp. Farm creatures for the toddler to admire. (Rev: BCCB 7–8/88; BL 7/88)

5612 Smith, Charles R. *Loki and Alex: The Adventures of a Dog and His Best Friend* (K–3). Illus. 2001, Dutton $14.99 (0-525-46700-9). 32pp. The events of a day are narrated from the perspectives of a young African American boy and his dog, using color for the boy's comments and black and white for the dog's. (Rev: BL 6/1–15/01; HBG 10/01; SLJ 7/01)

5613 Smith, Maggie. *Desser the Best Ever Cat* (PS–1). Illus. 2001, Knopf $14.95 (0-375-81056-0). 32pp. An engaging picture book arranged like a scrapbook of memories that tells the life story of a family's beloved cat from the day he was adopted as a stray. (Rev: BL 2/15/01; HBG 10/01)

5614 Spirin, Gennady. *Martha* (PS–K). Illus. by author. 2005, Philomel $14.99 (0-399-23980-4). Spirin's son brings to their home in Moscow a crow with a broken wing and insists that they keep it alive. (Rev: BCCB 4/05; BL 7/05; SLJ 4/05)

5615 Stockdale, Susan. *Some Sleep Standing Up* (PS–K). Illus. 1996, Simon & Schuster paper $13.00 (0-689-80509-8). 32pp. Two-page spreads illustrate the ways in which various animals sleep. (Rev: BL 9/1/96; SLJ 4/96) [591.52]

5616 Stojic, Manya. *Snow* (PS–K). Illus. 2002, Knopf $15.95 (0-375-82348-4). 32pp. Lush acrylics and spare but rhythmic text show animals preparing for the coming of winter. (Rev: BL 12/1/02; HBG 3/03; SLJ 12/02)

5617 Swanson, Diane. *Animals Can Be So Sleepy* (PS–K). Illus. 2001, Sterling $10.95 (1-55054-837-9). 24pp. Each spread in this simple picture book features a sleeping animal on one page and a short poem about it on the other. (Rev: BL 1/1–15/02)

5618 Tafuri, Nancy. *Mama's Little Bears* (PS). Illus. 2002, Scholastic $15.95 (0-439-27311-0). 40pp. Under Mama's watchful eye, three curious little bear cubs explore their surroundings. (Rev: BL 3/1/02; HB 3–4/02; HBG 10/02; SLJ 4/02)

5619 Taha, Karen T. *Hotdog on TV* (PS–2). Illus. by Hideko Takahashi. Series: Dial Easy-to-Read. 2005, Dial $14.99 (0-8037-2933-2). 40pp. Hotdog, a dachshund, is so appealing that a new variety of ice cream is invented for him to advertise on TV. (Rev: BL 6/1–15/05)

5620 Tan, Amy. *The Chinese Siamese Cat* (1–4). Illus. by Gretchen Schields. 1994, Macmillan paper $16.95 (0-02-788835-5). 32pp. A Chinese tale that explains how cats got their markings. (Rev: BL 10/1/94; SLJ 11/94)

5621 Taylor, Livingston. *Can I Be Good?* (PS–3). Illus. by Ted Rand. 1993, Harcourt $15.00 (0-15-200436-X). 32pp. Though he claims he is trying to be good, a golden retriever seems to be always causing confusion and disorder. (Rev: BL 9/15/93; SLJ 10/93)

5622 Taylor, Mark. *The Frog House* (PS–2). Illus. by Barbara Garrison. 2004, Dutton $15.99 (0-525-46174-4). 32pp. Appealing art draws the reader into this simple story of a tree frog that is attracted to an apple-shaped birdhouse. (Rev: BL 1/1–15/04; SLJ 3/04)

5623 Thompson, Colin. *Unknown* (2–3). Illus. by Anna Pignataro. 2000, Walker LB $16.85 (0-8027-8731-2). 32pp. A small stray dog labeled "Unknown" in the animal shelter is able to warn the keeper about a dangerous fire. (Rev: BCCB 5/00; BL 5/1/00; HBG 10/00; SLJ 7/00)

5624 Thompson, Lauren. *Little Quack* (PS–K). Illus. by Derek Anderson. 2003, Simon & Schuster $14.95 (0-689-84723-8). 32pp. Five little ducklings follow their mother — the last very reluctantly — into the pond in this charming picture book. (Rev: BL 2/1/03; HBG 10/03; SLJ 6/03)

5625 Tildes, Phyllis L. *Animals: Black and White* (PS–2). Illus. by author. 1996, Charlesbridge paper $6.95 (0-88106-959-0). This picture puzzle book consists of guessing games in which several black-and-white animals describe themselves and show parts of their bodies before their identities are revealed. (Rev: SLJ 1/97)

5626 Tildes, Phyllis Limbacher. *Calico's Curious Kittens* (PS). Illus. 2003, Charlesbridge $16.95 (1-57091-511-3); paper $6.95 (1-57091-512-1). 32pp. Calico's kittens are full of mischief, but as cute as can be. (Rev: BL 2/1/03; HBG 10/03; SLJ 2/03)

5627 Timmel, Carol Ann. *Tabitha: The Fabulous Flying Feline* (PS–1). Illus. by Laura Kelly. 1996, Walker paper $16.85 (0-8027-8449-6). 32pp. Tabitha the cat remains undiscovered for 13 days in the cargo hold of a large airplane. (Rev: BL 10/15/96; SLJ 11/96)

5628 Townsend, Una Belle. *Grady's in the Silo* (1–4). Illus. by Bob Artley. 2003, Pelican $14.95 (1-58980-098-2). Based on a real-life event, this is an entertaining story about Grady, a cow that gets stuck in a silo while trying to avoid an injection. (Rev: HBG 10/03; SLJ 5/03)

5629 Tsubakiyama, Margaret. *Mei-Mei Loves the Morning* (PS–3). Illus. by Cornelius Van Wright and Ying-hwa Hu. 1999, Whitman $15.95 (0-8075-5039-6). In modern, urban China, Mei-Mei and her grandfather participate in the family's daily routines, such as feeding the bird, eating breakfast, going to the park, and shopping at the market. (Rev: BCCB 5/99; BL 3/15/99; HBG 10/99; SLJ 5/99)

5630 Van Camp, Richard. *What's the Most Beautiful Thing You Know About Horses?* (K–3). Illus. by George Littlechild. 1998, Children's Book Pr. $15.95 (0-89239-154-5). A little child living in Canada's Northwest Territories asks about the beauty of horses. (Rev: HBG 3/99; SLJ 10/98)

5631 Van Laan, Nancy. *When Winter Comes* (PS–2). Illus. by Susan Gaber. 2000, Simon & Schuster $16.00 (0-689-81778-9). As a family walks through the woods during an early snowfall, they wonder about the animals cope during the winter; the illustrations reveal the answers. (Rev: HBG 3/01; SLJ 11/00)

5632 Vargo, Vanessa. *Zebra Talk* (PS–1). Illus. 1991, Child's Play paper $5.99 (0-85953-395-6). 20pp. A mother zebra explains how life was years ago when thousands of zebras roamed the plains of Africa. (Rev: BL 3/1/91)

5633 Vernick, Audrey Glassman, and Ellen Glassman Gidaro. *Bark and Tim: A True Story of Friendship Based on the Paintings of Tim Brown* (K–3). Illus. by Tim Brown. 2003, Overmountain $14.95 (1-57072-271-4). This charming story, based on the Mississippi childhood of African American folk artist Tim Brown, tells about a young boy's loving relationship with a dog named Bark. (Rev: HBG 4/04; SLJ 1/04)

5634 Voake, Charlotte. *Ginger Finds a Home* (PS–K). Illus. by author. 2003, Candlewick $15.99 (0-7636-1999-X). In this prequel to *Ginger* (1997), Ginger is a homeless young cat barely eking out an existence until a sweet young girl begins to feed him and eventually lures him into her home and heart. (Rev: BL 7/03*; HBG 10/03; SLJ 6/03)

5635 Waddell, Martin. *It's Quacking Time!* (PS–K). Illus. by Jill Barton. 2005, Candlewick $15.99 (0-7636-2738-0). 32pp. Young Duckling learns a lot about nature as his family waits for a new egg to hatch. (Rev: BL 2/1/05; SLJ 4/05)

5636 Waddell, Martin. *A Kitten Called Moonlight* (PS–1). Illus. by Christian Birmingham. 2001, Candlewick $15.99 (0-7636-1176-X). 32pp. A young girl and her mother recall how they found a stray white kitten and brought it home to be their pet. (Rev: BL 4/1/01; HBG 10/01; SLJ 4/01)

5637 Waddell, Martin. *Snow Bears* (PS–2). Illus. by Sarah Fox-Davies. 2002, Candlewick $14.99 (0-7636-1906-X). 32pp. A cozy, well-illustrated tale about a mother bear and her three cubs at play. (Rev: BCCB 2/03; BL 12/15/02; HB 1–2/03; HBG 10/03; SLJ 1/03)

5638 Walsh, Alice. *Heroes of the Isle aux Morts* (PS–3). Illus. by Geoff Butler. 2001, Tundra $14.95 (0-88776-501-7). 32pp. Based on truth, this is the story of a dramatic rescue at sea in 1832, in which a Newfoundland dog plays a major role. (Rev: BL 6/1–15/01; HBG 10/01; SLJ 10/01)

5639 Walsh, Melanie. *Do Donkeys Dance?* (PS). Illus. 2000, Houghton Mifflin $15.00 (0-618-00330-4). 40pp. Using questions and answers, this simple picture book reveals the distinctive qualities of various animals. (Rev: BCCB 4/00; BL 4/15/00; HB 7–8/00; HBG 10/00; SLJ 4/00)

5640 Ward, Helen. *Old Shell, New Shell: A Coral Reef Tale* (K–3). Illus. 2002, Millbrook LB $24.90 (0-7613-2708-8). 40pp. A hermit crab seeks a bigger home in this boldly illustrated tale, which also includes a detailed key identifying life on a coral reef. (Rev: BL 1/1–15/02; HBG 10/02; SLJ 2/02)

5641 Warnes, Tim. *Mommy Mine* (PS). Illus. by Jane Chapman. 2005, HarperCollins $15.99 (0-06-058947-7). 32pp. Contrasting mothers and their babies — mice and elephants, for example — are juxtaposed in bright pictures with a simple rhyme. (Rev: BL 5/15/05)

5642 Warrick, Karen Clemens. *If I Had a Tail* (PS–2). Illus. by Sherry Neidigh. 2001, Rising Moon LB $15.95 (0-87358-781-2). 32pp. An amusing picture book in which the tails of various animals and their uses are explored. (Rev: BL 4/1/01; HBG 10/01; SLJ 6/01)

5643 Weller, Frances W. *Riptide* (PS–3). Illus. by Robert J. Blake. 1990, Penguin Putnam $15.95 (0-399-21675-8). 32pp. A dog named Riptide acts as a lifeguard on Cape Cod. (Rev: BL 3/15/90*; HB 7–8/90; HBG 4/04; SLJ 4/90*)

5644 Weller, Frances Ward. *The Day the Animals Came: A Story of Saint Francis Day* (PS–2). Illus. by Loren Long. 2003, Philomel $16.99 (0-399-23630-9). The blessing of the animals at the Cathedral of St. John the Divine in New York City makes a young Caribbean girl named Ria feel more at home. (Rev: BL 10/1/03; HBG 4/04; SLJ 11/03)

5645 Wells, Rosemary. *McDuff and the Baby* (PS–1). Illus. by Susan Jeffers. 1997, Hyperion LB $12.89 (0-7868-2258-9). 24pp. McDuff, a terrier, loses status when a new baby arrives in his home. (Rev: BL 9/15/97; HBG 3/98; SLJ 10/97)

5646 Wells, Rosemary. *McDuff's Wild Romp* (PS). Illus. by Susan Jeffers. Series: McDuff Stories. 2005, Hyperion $9.99 (0-7868-1930-8). 32pp. The adorable West Highland terrier ends up in disgrace after a scrap with a cat over a piece of turkey. (Rev: BL 6/1–15/05; SLJ 4/05)

5647 West, Jim, and Marshall Izen. *The Dog Who Sang at the Opera* (1–3). Illus. by Erika Oller. 2004, Abrams $16.95 (0-8109-4928-8). 32pp. A Russian wolfhound's operatic debut ends ignominiously in this story based on a real incident. (Rev: BL 1/1–15/05; SLJ 2/05)

5648 Wheeler, Lisa. *Sixteen Cows* (PS–2). Illus. by Kurt Cyrus. 2002, Harcourt $16.00 (0-15-202676-2). 32pp. After their herds of cows mingle when a dividing fence is blown down, Cowboy Gene and Cowgirl Sue decide they should also, and so they get married. (Rev: BL 6/1–15/02; HBG 10/02; SLJ 4/02)

5649 White, Amanda. *Rip and Rap* (PS). Illus. by Debbie Harter. 2002, Barefoot $14.99 (1-84148-944-1). Sheepdog puppies Rip and Rap become indistinguishable when Rap gets covered in mud. (Rev: HBG 3/03; SLJ 1/03)

5650 White, Kathryn. *The Nutty Nut Chase* (PS–3). Illus. by Vanessa Cabban. 2004, Good Books $16.00 (1-56148-446-6). Two quarrelsome squirrels are among the animals much surprised by a disappearing nut. (Rev: SLJ 1/05)

5651 Wieler, Diana. *To the Mountains by Morning* (K–3). Illus. by Ange Zhang. 1996, Douglas & McIntyre $14.95 (0-88899-227-0). 32pp. Knowing she is going to be disposed of because of her age, Old Bailey the mare runs away. (Rev: BL 7/96; SLJ 6/96)

5652 Wildsmith, Brian, and Rebecca Wildsmith. *Wake Up, Wake Up!* (PS–1). Illus. 1993, Harcourt $6.95 (0-15-200685-0). 16pp. One by one, the animals wake up until, finally, the farmer also wakes up to feed them. (Rev: BL 3/15/93)

5653 Willis, Nancy Carol. *Raccoon Moon* (PS–2). Illus. 2002, Birdsong $15.95 (0-9662761-2-4); paper $6.95 (0-9662761-3-2). 32pp. Three raccoon cubs are born and grow up in this wonderfully illustrated introduction to a raccoon's lifecycle. (Rev: BL 12/15/02; SLJ 1/03)

5654 Wilson, Sarah. *A Nap in a Lap* (PS). Illus. by Akemi Gutierrez. 2003, Holt $15.95 (0-8050-6973-X). A little girl and her dog observe the diverse places and ways in which various animals nap before heading home where, the child herself takes a nap on her mother's lap. (Rev: BL 1/1–15/04; SLJ 1/04)

5655 Wojtowycz, David. *Can You Moo?* (PS). Illus. by author. 2003, Scholastic $12.95 (0-439-39483-X). 32pp. An introduction to animal noises for the youngest readers. (Rev: HBG 4/04; SLJ 3/04)

5656 Wolf, Erica. *Brave Little Raccoon* (PS–K). Illus. 2005, Holt $16.95 (0-8050-7408-2). 32pp. Lost in the forest, Little Raccoon is more than a little scared and is happy to discover that her mother has never been far away. (Rev: BL 5/1/05)

5657 Wood, Ellen. *Hundreds of Fish* (1–4). Illus. by Monique Felix. 2000, Creative $17.95 (1-56846-162-3). 40pp. The food chain is explored in this picture book set in Alaska about a young girl who, while ice fishing, catches a pike that she saw eating three ducklings months before. (Rev: HBG 10/00; SLJ 9/00)

5658 Yaccarino, Dan. *So Big!* (PS). Illus. 2001, HarperCollins $7.95 (0-694-01509-1). 12pp. This book explores the sizes of various baby animals through a series of fold-up flaps. (Rev: BL 1/1–15/01)

5659 Yang, James. *Joey and Jet* (PS–2). Illus. 2004, Simon & Schuster $15.95 (0-689-86923-6). 32pp. A boy and a dog have fun with a ball in this attractive volume that highlights the use of prepositions. (Rev: BL 1/1–15/05)

5660 Yolen, Jane. *Hoptoad* (PS–K). Illus. by Karen Lee Schmidt. 2003, Harcourt $16.00 (0-15-216352-2). In this simple, appealing tale told in rhyming text, a man and his son stop their camper to rescue a toad from a dangerous trip across the road. (Rev: BL 5/15/03; HBG 10/03; SLJ 6/03)

5661 Yolen, Jane. *Owl Moon* (PS–2). Illus. by John Schoenherr. 1987, Penguin Putnam $16.99 (0-399-21457-7). 32pp. Winner of the 1988 Caldecott Medal, this is the poetic story of a little girl and her father on an owl adventure in winter. (Rev: BL 12/15/87; SLJ 12/87)

5662 Zagwyn, Deborah Turney. *Turtle Spring* (PS–1). Illus. 1998, Tricycle $15.95 (1-883672-53-8). 32pp. Clee is happy to have a pet turtle to play with instead of her baby brother. Over the winter, though, she thinks the turtle has died, and she comes to love her brother. In spring, Clee's turtle wakes from its hibernation and she has both brother and turtle to love. (Rev: BL 7/98*; HBG 10/98; SLJ 8/98)

5663 Ziefert, Harriet. *Birdhouse for Rent* (PS–K). Illus. by Donald Dreifuss. 2001, Houghton Mifflin $15.00 (0-618-04881-2). A birdhouse is used by bees and chipmunks before Mrs. Chickadee moves in, lays her eggs, and sees her chicks hatch. (Rev: HBG 3/02; SLJ 9/01)

5664 Ziefert, Harriet. *One Smart Skunk* (PS–3). Illus. by Santiago Cohen. 2004, Blue Apple $15.95 (1-59354-064-7). Rebecca the skunk's life under the deck becomes unbearable as she suffers from a combination of moth balls and rap music. (Rev: SLJ 1/05)

5665 Zimmerman, Andrea, and David Clemesha. *My Dog Toby* (PS–2). Illus. by True Kelley. 2000, Harcourt $15.00 (0-15-202014-4). 32pp. The little girl who owns Toby is convinced that he is a bright dog and Toby proves she is right. (Rev: BCCB 6/00; BL 5/1/00*; HBG 10/00; SLJ 5/00)

SCHOOL STORIES

5666 Allard, Harry. *Miss Nelson Has a Field Day* (1–3). Illus. by James Marshall. 1985, Houghton Mifflin $15.00 (0-395-36690-9); paper $5.95 (0-395-48654-8). 32pp. The plucky Miss Nelson gets a losing football team into shape. (Rev: BCCB 7/85; BL 5/15/85; HB 5–6/85)

5667 Allard, Harry. *Miss Nelson Is Missing!* (K–2). Illus. by James Marshall. 1985, Houghton Mifflin $16.00 (0-395-25296-2); paper $5.95 (0-395-40146-1). When Miss Nelson's students in Room 207 misbehave, she disappears and is replaced by a martinet. A sequel is: *Miss Nelson Is Back* (1985).

5668 Aseltine, Lorraine. *First Grade Can Wait* (K–2). Illus. by Virginia Wright-Frierson. 1988, Whitman LB $13.95 (0-8075-2451-4). 32pp. At 6, Luke isn't mature enough to start school, so his parents decide to hold him out for a year. (Rev: BL 3/15/88; SLJ 7/88)

5669 Ashley, Bernard. *Cleversticks* (PS–1). Illus. by Derek Brazell. 1995, Crown paper $6.99 (0-517-88332-5). 32pp. Ling Sung is a nobody at school until he reveals he can use chopsticks. (Rev: BCCB 7–8/92; BL 11/15/92; SLJ 3/93)

5670 Bateman, Teresa. *The Bully Blockers Club* (PS–3). Illus. by Jackie Urbanovic. 2004, Whitman LB $15.95 (0-8075-0918-3). Lotty Raccoon is determined not to put up with being bullied by classmate Grant Grizzly, so she starts an anti-bully club. (Rev: SLJ 11/04)

5671 Best, Cari. *Shrinking Violet* (K–3). Illus. by Giselle Potter. 2001, Farrar $16.00 (0-374-36882-1). 40pp. Shy Violet has her moment in the limelight when she's cast in an offstage speaking role. (Rev: BCCB 10/01; BL 8/01; HB 9–10/01; HBG 3/02; SLJ 8/01*)

5672 Boelts, Maribeth. *Little Bunny's Preschool Countdown* (PS). Illus. by Kathy Parkinson. 1996, Whitman LB $14.95 (0-8075-4582-1). 32pp. LB, a rabbit, begins to dread his first day at preschool. (Rev: BL 9/15/96; SLJ 11/96)

5673 Boelts, Maribeth. *When It's the Last Day of School* (K–2). Illus. by Hanako Wakiyama. 2004, Penguin Putnam $15.99 (0-399-23498-5). 32pp. Full of anticipation about summer vacation, James vows to be on his best behavior on the very last day of school. (Rev: BL 4/15/04; SLJ 4/04)

5674 Bogacki, Tomek. *Circus Girl* (K–2). Illus. 2001, Farrar $17.00 (0-374-31291-5). 32pp. When the circus comes to town, a young member attends the local school and surprises the students by befriending an outcast. (Rev: BL 7/01; HBG 3/02; SLJ 10/01)

5675 Brandt, Amy. *When Katie Was Our Teacher / Cuando Katie era nuestra maestra* (PS–K). 2000, Child Care Books for Kids $11.95 (1-884834-78-7). 32pp. In this bilingual book about day care, Katie and her friends miss their teacher when she leaves. (Rev: SLJ 10/00)

5676 Brown, Marc. *D.W.'s Guide to Preschool* (PS). Illus. by author. 2003, Little, Brown $15.95 (0-316-12069-3). D. W., Arthur's little sister, offers advice on virtually every aspect of preschool life, covering such important topics as bathroom breaks, circle time, and snack time. (Rev: HBG 4/04; SLJ 12/03)

5677 Bunting, Eve. *My Special Day at Third Street School* (K–3). Illus. by Suzanne Bloom. 2004, Boyds Mills $15.95 (1-59078-075-2). 32pp. A boy explains in engaging detail the class preparations for an author visit by Amanda Drake — and the successes of the day itself. (Rev: BL 3/15/04*; SLJ 3/04)

5678 Bunting, Eve. *Our Teacher's Having a Baby* (K–2). Illus. by Diane De Groat. 1992, Houghton Mifflin $15.00 (0-395-60470-2). 32pp. Mrs. Neal explains to her class that she is going to have a baby, and together they prepare for the event. (Rev: BL 9/15/92; HB 5–6/04; SLJ 3/93)

5679 Carlson, Nancy. *Henry's 100 Days of Kindergarten* (PS–K). Illus. 2005, Viking $15.99 (0-670-05977-3). 32pp. When the 100th day of kindergarten arrives, the teacher has collected 100 jellybeans, and Henry the mouse brings his 100-year-old great-grandmother to school. (Rev: BL 3/15/05; SLJ 2/05)

5680 Carlson, Nancy. *Hooray for Grandparents' Day!* (PS–2). Illus. 2000, Viking $15.99 (0-670-88876-1). 32pp. Arnie has no grandparents to bring to school on Grandparents' Day and he feels left out. (Rev: BL 6/1–15/00; HBG 3/01; SLJ 8/00)

5681 Carlson, Nancy. *Look Out Kindergarten, Here I Come!* (PS–K). Illus. 1999, Viking $15.99 (0-670-88378-6). 32pp. Henry is excited about his first day in kindergarten, particularly after he makes a new friend. (Rev: BL 6/1–15/99; HBG 10/99; SLJ 7/99)

5682 Carlstrom, Nancy White. *Giggle-Wiggle Wake Up!* (PS–1). Illus. by Melissa Sweet. 2003, Knopf LB $17.99 (0-375-91350-5). Lively wordplay accompanies Sammy through a Monday morning and arrival at preschool. (Rev: HBG 4/04; SLJ 12/03)

5683 Carter, Alden R. *Dustin's Big School Day* (K–2). Illus. by Dan Young and Carol S. Carter. 1999, Whitman $14.95 (0-8075-1741-0). 32pp. Photographs are used to document Dustin's day in school, when a ventriloquist visits as a special treat. (Rev: BCCB 3/99; BL 4/15/99; HBG 10/99; SLJ 6/99)

5684 Caseley, Judith. *Bully* (PS–3). Illus. 2001, Greenwillow LB $15.89 (0-688-17868-5). 32pp. Mickey's parents give him good advice when his friend Jack turns into an unfriendly bully. (Rev: BCCB 6/01; BL 5/15/01; HBG 10/01; SLJ 6/01)

5685 Caseley, Judith. *Field Day Friday* (PS–2). Illus. 2000, Greenwillow LB $15.89 (0-688-16762-4). 32pp. At his school's field day, Mickey's sneaker comes off during the 50-yard dash and the wretched youngster comes in last. (Rev: BL 5/1/00; HBG 10/00; SLJ 5/00)

5686 Chapra, Mimi. *Amelia's Show-and-Tell Fiesta / Amelia y la fiesta de "muestra y cuenta"* (K–2). Illus. by Martha Aviles. 2004, HarperCollins LB $15.89 (0-06-050256-8). When she gets to school, Amelia worries that her Cuban fiesta dresses are not suitable for show-and-tell in this book with lively English text and a more pedestrian Spanish translation. (Rev: SLJ 9/04)

5687 Chardiet, Bernice, and Grace Maccarone. *The Best Teacher in the World* (PS–2). Illus. by G. Brian Karas. 1991, Scholastic paper $2.50 (0-590-43307-5). 32pp. Bunny is selected by her favorite teacher to run an errand. (Rev: BL 1/1/90; SLJ 10/90)

5688 Choi, Yangsook. *The Name Jar* (PS–3). Illus. 2001, Knopf LB $18.99 (0-375-90613-4). 32pp. Unhei's classmates offer ideas for a new American name, but Unhei eventually decides to keep her own. (Rev: BL 12/15/01; HBG 3/02; SLJ 11/01)

5689 Cocca-Leffler, Maryann. *Mr. Tanen's Tie Trouble* (K–3). Illus. by author. 2003, Whitman LB $14.95 (0-8075-5305-0). Mr. Tanen the school principal puts his collection of wondrous ties up for auction when he discovers the playground has no funds. (Rev: BL 6/03; SLJ 5/03)

5690 Cocca-Leffler, Maryann. *Mr. Tanen's Ties* (PS–2). Illus. 1999, Whitman LB $14.95 (0-8075-5301-8). 32pp. Mr. Tanen wears different ties to school each day to mark various occasions, but Mr. Apple, the superintendent of schools, doesn't like it. (Rev: BL 5/15/99; HBG 10/99; SLJ 3/99)

5691 Cohen, Miriam. *Will I Have a Friend?* (PS–2). Illus. by Lillian Hoban. 1967, Macmillan paper $4.99 (0-689-71333-9). 32pp. Jim, a kindergartner, lives out the actual concern that small children have about finding a friend on the first day of school. By the same author and publisher: *No Good in Art* (1980); *So What?* (1982); *Jim's Dog Muffins* (1986); *Jim Meets the Thing* (1989).

5692 Conlin, Susan, and Susan L. Friedman. *All My Feelings at Preschool: Nathan's Day* (PS–K). Illus. by Kathryn M. Smith. 1991, Parenting LB $16.95 (0-943990-61-0); paper $6.95 (0-943990-60-2). 32pp. This picture book describes a day in the life of Nathan at his nursery school. (Rev: BL 6/1/91)

5693 Corey, Shana. *First Graders from Mars: Episode 1 — Horus's Horrible Day* (K–2). Illus. by Mark Teague. 2001, Scholastic $14.95 (0-439-26220-8); paper $4.50 (0-439-31955-2). 32pp. Horus, a Martian lad, is having a horrible time getting used to first grade until he meets another scared student. (Rev: BL 8/01; HBG 3/02; SLJ 9/01)

5694 Couric, Katie. *The Blue Ribbon Day* (K–2). Illus. by Marjorie Priceman. 2004, Doubleday $15.95 (0-385-50142-0). Carrie O'Toole is disappointed when she fails to make the Brookhaven School soccer team. (Rev: SLJ 1/05)

5695 Couric, Katie. *The Brand New Kid* (K–2). Illus. by Marjorie Priceman. 2000, Doubleday $15.95 (0-385-50030-0). Lazlo S. Gasky is unhappy and friendless at his new school, until a classmate decides to help him. (Rev: SLJ 2/01)

5696 Creech, Sharon. *A Fine, Fine School* (K–3). Illus. by Harry Bliss. 2001, HarperCollins LB $15.89 (0-06-027737-8). 32pp. A wonderfully illustrated, very funny story about a school principal who just doesn't know when to quit. (Rev: BL 8/01; HBG 3/02; SLJ 8/01)

5697 Cuyler, Margery. *Stop, Drop, and Roll* (K–3). Illus. by Arthur Howard. 2001, Simon & Schuster $16.00 (0-689-84355-0). 32pp. Jessica agonizes over her role in a play for Fire Prevention Week. (Rev: BCCB 11/01; BL 9/15/01; HBG 3/02; SLJ 10/01)

5698 Daniels, Teri. *The Feet in the Gym* (K–3). Illus. by Travis Foster. 1999, Winslow $15.95 (1-890817-12-4). 32pp. The humorous story of how a poor school custodian tries to keep the school clean, in spite of different groups of children, each producing its own terrible mess. (Rev: BL 7/99; SLJ 6/99)

5699 Danneberg, Julie. *First Year Letters* (K–3). Illus. by Judy Love. 2003, Charlesbridge $16.95 (1-58089-084-9); paper $6.95 (1-58089-085-7). 32pp. Letters exchanged by a fictional new teacher and her students reveal how they learn together during the course of a school year. (Rev: BL 2/1/03; HBG 10/03)

5700 Davis, Gibbs. *The Other Emily* (K–2). Illus. by Linda Shute. 1990, Harcourt paper $4.95 (0-395-54947-7). 32pp. Emily loves her name until she encounters another Emily in her class.

5701 dePaola, Tomie. *The Art Lesson* (K–3). Illus. by author. 1989, Penguin Putnam $16.99 (0-399-21688-X). 32pp. Tommy just keeps on drawing and drawing and drawing. (Rev: BCCB 3/89; BL 3/1/89; SLJ 4/89)

5702 dePaola, Tomie. *Stagestruck* (PS–2). Illus. 2005, Penguin Putnam $16.99 (0-399-24338-0).

32pp. When Tommy fails to win the starring role in his kindergarten production of Peter Rabbit, he decides to steal the show anyway, and ends up apologizing. (Rev: BL 1/1–15/05; SLJ 1/05)

5703 Driscoll, Laura. *Lila the Fair* (1–3). Illus. by Blanche Sims. 2005, Kane paper $4.99 (1-57565-148-3). 32pp. Lila calls herself "fair" because of her abilities as a peacemaker, which she exercises often as a middle child. (Rev: BL 3/1/05)

5704 Edwards, Becky. *My First Day at Nursery School* (PS–1). Illus. by Anthony Flintoft. 2002, Bloomsbury $15.95 (1-58234-761-1). 32pp. A reassuring tale of a child's first day at nursery school. (Rev: BL 8/02; SLJ 8/02)

5705 Ely, Lesley. *Looking After Louis* (1–3). Illus. by Polly Dunbar. 2004, Whitman $15.95 (0-8075-4746-8). 32pp. Through the eyes of a little girl, this story looks at the experiences of an autistic boy and his treatment by his classmates. (Rev: BL 4/15/04; SLJ 4/04)

5706 Fain, Moira. *Snow Day* (K–3). Illus. 1996, Walker LB $16.85 (0-8027-8410-0). 32pp. Maggie Murphy escapes a school punishment when a snow day is declared the following day. (Rev: BCCB 10/96; BL 10/15/96; SLJ 10/96*)

5707 Falwell, Cathryn. *David's Drawings* (PS–2). Illus. 2001, Lee & Low $16.00 (1-58430-031-0). 32pp. Collages of cut-paper and fabric illustrate this story of how one boy's drawing of a bare tree becomes a classroom's cooperative masterpiece. (Rev: BL 11/15/01; HBG 10/02; SLJ 10/01)

5708 Finchler, Judy. *Miss Malarkey Doesn't Live in Room 10* (K–3). Illus. by Kevin O'Malley. 1995, Walker LB $15.85 (0-8027-8387-2). 32pp. A young boy is convinced that his teacher lives at school until she moves into his apartment building. (Rev: BL 11/15/95; SLJ 12/95)

5709 Finchler, Judy. *Miss Malarkey Won't Be In Today* (1–3). Illus. by Kevin O'Malley. 1998, Walker LB $16.85 (0-8027-8653-7). 32pp. Miss Malarkey is too sick to go to school, but she worries about the reception different substitute teachers will get. When she returns, she is surprised to find out who took her place. (Rev: BL 9/1/98; HBG 3/99; SLJ 10/98)

5710 Finchler, Judy. *Testing Miss Malarkey* (1–4). Illus. by Kevin O'Malley. 2000, Walker LB $16.85 (0-8027-8737-8). 32pp. A humorous story in which kids are being prepared for standardized tests that they eventually pass with flying colors. (Rev: BL 10/1/00)

5711 Finchler, Judy. *You're a Good Sport, Miss Malarkey* (K–3). Illus. by Kevin O'Malley. 2002, Walker LB $16.85 (0-8027-8816-5). 32pp. When Miss Malarkey takes the job of soccer coach, she finds she must give the parents a lesson in sportsmanship. (Rev: BL 10/15/02; HBG 3/03; SLJ 10/02)

5712 French, Simon. *Guess the Baby* (PS–1). Illus. by Donna Rawlins. 2002, Clarion $14.00 (0-618-25989-9). 32pp. Classmates bring in their baby pictures and try to guess who's who. (Rev: BL 12/15/02; HBG 3/03; SLJ 12/02)

5713 Giff, Patricia Reilly. *Today Was a Terrible Day* (2–3). Illus. by Susanna Natti. 1980, Puffin paper $5.99 (0-14-050453-2). 32pp. Ronald is having a terrible day until his teacher writes him an understanding note. (Rev: SLJ 3/04)

5714 Gutman, Dan. *Mr. Klutz Is Nuts!* (2–3). Illus. by Jim Paillot. Series: My Weird School. 2004, HarperCollins LB $15.89 (0-06-050703-9); paper $3.99 (0-06-050702-0). 96pp. The school principal is an eccentric character who uses unusual incentives in this humorous easy chapter book that will appeal to reluctant readers. (Rev: SLJ 11/04)

5715 Harris, Robie H. *I Am Not Going to School Today!* (PS–K). Illus. by Jan Ormerod. 2003, Simon & Schuster $16.95 (0-689-83913-8). All the worries of the first day of school are captured in this story that ends happily. (Rev: HBG 4/04; SLJ 7/03)

5716 Hathorn, Libby. *Freya's Fantastic Surprise* (1–3). Illus. by Sharon Thompson. 1989, Scholastic $12.95 (0-590-42442-4). 32pp. Freya makes up so many surprises at News Time in school that her classmates become hostile. (Rev: HB 3–4/89)

5717 Havill, Juanita. *Jamaica and the Substitute Teacher* (PS–3). Illus. by Anne S. O'Brien. 1999, Houghton Mifflin $15.00 (0-395-90503-6). 32pp. Jamaica is so ashamed of cheating on a spelling test that she can't cope with the guilt and decides to confess. (Rev: BL 2/15/99; HB 5–6/99; HBG 10/99; SLJ 5/99)

5718 Henkes, Kevin. *Lilly's Purple Plastic Purse* (PS–K). Illus. 1996, Greenwillow $14.89 (0-688-12898-X). 32pp. Lilly runs afoul of her teacher, Mr. Slinger, whom she adores. A sequel to *Julius, the Baby of the World* (1990). (Rev: BCCB 10/96; BL 8/96*; HB 9–10/96; SLJ 8/96*)

5719 Howe, James. *When You Go to Kindergarten* (PS–1). Photos by Betsy Imershein. 1994, Morrow LB $15.93 (0-688-12913-7). 48pp. With color photos and a simple text, this book tells what a child can expect when he or she goes to kindergarten. (Rev: BL 9/1/94; SLJ 9/94) [372.21]

5720 Howlett, Bud. *I'm New Here* (K–4). Illus. 1993, Houghton Mifflin $16.00 (0-395-64049-0). 32pp. A photo-essay about a fifth-grader from El Salvador and her first experiences in an American school. (Rev: BL 10/1/93; SLJ 9/93)

5721 Jocelyn, Marthe. *Hannah's Collections* (PS–K). Illus. 2000, Dutton $14.99 (0-525-46442-5). 24pp. Hannah is facing a dilemma choosing which of her collections — buttons, feathers, or rings — she should share with her class. (Rev: BL 9/15/00*; HBG 3/01; SLJ 10/00)

5722 Johnson, Dolores. *My Mom Is My Show-and-Tell* (K–3). Illus. 1999, Marshall Cavendish $15.95 (0-7614-5041-6). 32pp. Brian, an African American boy who is the class clown, is anxious about his mother's visit on Parents' Day. (Rev: BL 4/15/99; HBG 10/99; SLJ 5/99)

5723 Johnson, Doug. *Substitute Teacher Plans* (1–3). Illus. by Tammy Smith. 2002, Holt $16.95 (0-8050-6520-2). 32pp. An exhausted teacher mixes up the instructions for her substitute with her list of things to do on her day off, sending her students on an adventure. (Rev: BL 9/15/02; HBG 3/03; SLJ 8/02)

5724 Karas, G. Brian. *The Class Artist* (K–3). Illus. 2001, Greenwillow LB $15.89 (0-688-17815-4). 32pp. A boy struggles with an art assignment until his teacher suggests that he draw a picture of how he feels. (Rev: BCCB 9/01; BL 11/15/01; HBG 3/02; SLJ 9/01)

5725 Kirk, Daniel. *Lunchroom Lizard* (K–2). Illus. by author. 2004, Penguin Putnam $15.99 (0-399-24178-7). An escaped gecko called Gil wanders through the school cafeteria seemingly oblivious to the hubbub taking place around him. (Rev: SLJ 8/04)

5726 Kline, Suzy. *Horrible Harry and the Dragon War* (1–3). Illus. by Frank Remkiewicz. 2002, Viking $13.99 (0-670-03559-9). 64pp. Harry and classmate Song Lee quarrel over a school project on dragons but finally become friends again. (Rev: BL 6/1–15/02; HBG 3/03; SLJ 8/02)

5727 Kline, Suzy. *Horrible Harry Goes to the Moon* (2–3). Illus. by Frank Remkiewicz. 2000, Viking $13.99 (0-670-88764-1). 64pp. In this story about Horrible Harry, Miss Mackle's third-grade class decides to hold a bake sale to buy a used telescope. (Rev: HBG 10/00; SLJ 2/00)

5728 Layton, Neal. *The Sunday Blues: A Book for Schoolchildren, Schoolteachers, and Anybody Else Who Dreads Monday Mornings* (K–2). Illus. 2002, Candlewick $15.99 (0-7636-1975-2). 40pp. Steve, who dreads returning to school all day Sunday, finds, come Monday, that it isn't so bad. (Rev: BCCB 10/02; BL 9/15/02; HBG 3/03; SLJ 12/02)

5729 Lehn, Barbara. *What Is a Teacher?* (K–2). Photos by Carol Krauss. 2000, Millbrook LB $19.90 (0-7613-1713-9). The characteristics of a good teacher are acted out in a series of captioned photos showing children in the teacher's role. (Rev: HBG 3/01; SLJ 1/01)

5730 Lovell, Patty. *Stand Tall, Molly Lou Melon* (K–3). Illus. by David Catrow. 2001, Penguin Putnam $14.99 (0-399-23416-0). First-grader Molly Lou's grandmother has told her to believe in herself, and Molly Lou puts this successfully into action when she moves to a new school and must deal with the bully. (Rev: BCCB 10/01; HBG 3/02; SLJ 10/01)

5731 McCain, Becky Ray. *Nobody Knew What to Do: A Story About Bullying* (K–3). Illus. by Todd Leonardo. 2001, Whitman $14.95 (0-8075-5711-0). 32pp. When a boy sees bullies bothering one of his classmates, he decides to ask the teacher for help. (Rev: BL 5/15/01; HBG 10/01; SLJ 5/01)

5732 McCourt, Lisa. *It's Time for School, Stinky Face* (PS–1). Illus. by Cyd Moore. 2000, Troll $15.95 (0-8167-6961-3). 32pp. A little boy who is wildly imagining the worst things that could happen to him on his first day at school is reassured by his mother. (Rev: BL 10/15/00; HBG 3/01; SLJ 10/00)

5733 McGhee, Alison. *Countdown to Kindergarten* (PS–K). Illus. by Harry Bliss. 2002, Harcourt $16.00 (0-15-202516-2). 32pp. A soon-to-be kindergartner fears starting school because she's heard

that, among other things, you must be able to tie your shoes. (Rev: BCCB 10/02; BL 8/02; HBG 3/03; SLJ 9/02)

5734 McGhee, Alison. *Mrs. Watson Wants Your Teeth* (K–2). Illus. by Harry Bliss. 2004, Harcourt $16.00 (0-15-204931-2). A rumor that her teacher is a 300-year-old alien with a purple tongue and a liking for baby teeth scares a first grader on her first day of school. (Rev: SLJ 9/04)

5735 MacKall, Dandi Daley. *First Day* (PS–K). Illus. by Tiphanie Beeke. 2003, Harcourt $16.00 (0-15-216577-0). Told in rhyming text, this story of a little girl's first day of school is a good choice for children facing the transition from family room to classroom. (Rev: HBG 4/04; SLJ 9/03)

5736 Moon, Nicola. *Something Special* (K–2). Illus. by Alex Ayliffe. 1997, Peachtree $14.95 (1-56145-137-1). 32pp. Charlie decides to bring his new baby sister to school for a special show-and-tell. (Rev: BL 6/1–15/97; SLJ 6/97)

5737 Morgenstern, Susie. *It Happened at School: Two Tales* (3–5). Trans. by Gillian Rosner. Illus. by Serge Bloch. 2005, Viking $14.99 (0-670-06022-4). 112pp. Two light, humorous stories show a slice of life in French elementary schools. (Rev: BL 6/1–15/05)

5738 Moss, Marissa. *Regina's Big Mistake* (PS–2). Illus. 1990, Houghton Mifflin $16.00 (0-395-55330-X). 32pp. At first, Regina is unable to get an inspiration for an art assignment, but gradually the drawing takes shape. (Rev: BCCB 10/90; BL 11/1/90; SLJ 1/91)

5739 Moss, Miriam. *Scritch Scratch* (1–3). Illus. by Delphine Durand. 2002, Scholastic $16.95 (0-439-36835-9). It's the teacher's head that harbors the first louse, and the teacher has nobody to comb it out. (Rev: BCCB 11/02; HBG 3/03; SLJ 10/02)

5740 Moss, Miriam. *Wibble Wobble* (K–2). Illus. by Joanna Mockler. 2001, ME Media $14.95 (1-58925-013-3). 32pp. William is elated to lose his first tooth, and when it goes missing he enlists the help of the class to find it. (Rev: BL 2/1/02; SLJ 11/01)

5741 Munsch, Robert. *We Share Everything!* (PS–1). Illus. by Michael Martchenko. 1999, Scholastic $11.95 (0-590-89600-8). 32pp. In kindergarten, the high jinks of Amanda and Jeremiah prove to be too much for their long-suffering teacher. (Rev: BCCB 11/99; BL 9/1/99; HBG 3/00; SLJ 9/99)

5742 Musgrave, Susan, and Marie-Louise Gay. *Dreams Are More Real than Bathtubs* (K–3). Illus. 1999, Orca $14.95 (1-55143-107-6). 32pp. A little girl shares her thoughts about her family, her pet stuffed lion, fears, and starting first grade. (Rev: BL 7/99; HBG 10/99; SLJ 8/99)

5743 Nobisso, Josephine. *In English of Course* (2–4). Illus. by Dasha Ziborova. 2002, Gingerbread House $16.95 (0-940112-07-8); paper $8.95 (0-940112-08-6). 32pp. Young Josephine, a new immigrant from Italy, manages to communicate with her New York City classmates despite her limited knowledge of English. (Rev: BL 2/15/03; HBG 3/03; SLJ 2/03)

5744 O'Malley, Kevin. *Humpty Dumpty Egg-Splodes* (2–4). Illus. 2001, Walker LB $16.85 (0-8027-8757-6). 32pp. A father who's reading a story to his son's class changes it to something much more exciting when the teacher leaves the room, elaborating extensively on the Humpty Dumpty story. (Rev: BCCB 5/01; BL 7/01; HBG 10/01; SLJ 6/01)

5745 O'Neill, Alexis. *The Recess Queen* (PS–1). Illus. by Laura Huliska-Beith. 2002, Scholastic $15.95 (0-439-20637-5). 32pp. Mean Jean, the recess queen, has a change in attitude when the new girl at school asks her to play in this brightly illustrated, energetic tale. (Rev: BCCB 3/02; BL 3/1/02; HBG 10/02; SLJ 3/02)

5746 Pak, Soyung. *Sumi's First Day of School Ever* (PS–1). Illus. by Joung Un Kim. 2003, Viking $15.99 (0-670-03522-X). Sumi, a little Korean girl, is afraid on her first day of school, but the kindness of a teacher and friendliness of a classmate make her feel more comfortable. (Rev: HB 7–8/03; HBG 4/04; SLJ 8/03)

5747 Park, Barbara. *Junie B., First Grader: One Man Band* (1–3). Illus. by Denise Brunkus. Series: Junie B. Jones. 2003, Random LB $13.99 (0-375-92522-8). 87pp. Junie B. debuts as a cheerleader in this entry in the popular series. Also use *Shipwrecked* (2004). (Rev: HBG 4/04; SLJ 3/04)

5748 Perez, L. King. *First Day in Grapes* (1–3). Illus. by Robert Casilla. 2002, Lee & Low $16.95 (1-58430-045-0). 32pp. Chico, the son of migrant workers, starts third grade in yet another school with trepidation, but his first day goes well despite bullies and a surly bus driver. (Rev: BL 11/15/02; HBG 3/03; SLJ 10/02)

5749 Plourde, Lynn. *Pajama Day* (PS–2). Illus. by Thor Wickstrom. 2005, Dutton $16.99 (0-525-47355-6). 40pp. When Drew A. Blank shows his inventiveness when he arrives at school unprepared for Pajama Day. (Rev: BL 1/1–15/05; SLJ 2/05)

5750 Plourde, Lynn. *School Picture Day* (K–2). Illus. by Thor Wickstrom. 2002, Dutton $16.99 (0-525-46886-2). 40pp. Josephina Caroleena Wattasheena's curious nature causes calamity at her school on picture day. (Rev: BL 8/02; HBG 3/03; SLJ 7/02)

5751 Polacco, Patricia. *Mr. Lincoln's Way* (K–3). Illus. 2001, Penguin Putnam $16.99 (0-399-23754-2). 40pp. A school principal uses a bully's interest in birds to teach him about tolerance and kindness. (Rev: BL 9/1/01; HBG 3/02; SLJ 8/01)

5752 Poydar, Nancy. *Bunny Business* (PS–3). Illus. by author. 2003, Holiday House $16.95 (0-8234-1771-9). Harry turns out to be a good listener despite his fellow students' low opinion. (Rev: HBG 10/03; SLJ 4/03)

5753 Poydar, Nancy. *First Day, Hooray!* (PS–1). Illus. 1999, Holiday House $15.95 (0-8234-1437-X). 32pp. Young Ivy Green is worried about her first day at school, but so are others involved in the school's opening, including the bus driver and the principal. (Rev: BL 10/15/99; HBG 3/00; SLJ 8/99)

5754 Poydar, Nancy. *Last Day, Hooray!* (K–2). Illus. 2004, Holiday House $16.95 (0-8234-1807-3).

32pp. With visions of summer dancing in their heads, students and staff celebrate the final day of the school year. (Rev: BL 4/15/04; SLJ 4/04)

5755 Poydar, Nancy. *Snip, Snip . . . Snow!* (PS–1). Illus. 1997, Holiday House LB $15.95 (0-8234-1328-4). 32pp. Sophie is so disappointed at the lack of snow that she persuades her teacher to let the class make paper snowflakes. (Rev: BL 11/1/97; HBG 3/98; SLJ 10/97)

5756 Pulver, Robin. *Author Day for Room 3T* (K–3). Illus. by Chuck Richards. 2005, Clarion $16.00 (0-618-35406-9). 32pp. It's Author Day and the class has been eagerly anticipating someone "new and different," so when a chimp turns up (the librarian is very near-sighted), they are not taken aback. (Rev: BL 5/1/05; SLJ 4/05)

5757 Radabaugh, Melinda. *Going to School* (PS–1). Series: First Time. 2003, Heinemann LB $18.50 (1-4034-0227-2). 24pp. A reassuring, simple introduction to what happens during a typical day at school. (Rev: HBG 10/03; SLJ 6/03) [372.12]

5758 Reiser, Lynn. *Earthdance* (PS–3). Illus. 1999, Greenwillow LB $15.93 (0-688-16327-0). 32pp. While Terra is at school preparing for a show, her astronaut mother is traveling to the end of the universe. (Rev: BL 12/1/99; HBG 3/00; SLJ 10/99)

5759 Reynolds, Peter H. *The Dot* (K–2). Illus. by author. 2003, Candlewick $14.00 (0-7636-1961-2). A young girl who is sure she can't draw finds success when she heeds her teacher's advice to "make a mark and see where it takes you." (Rev: HBG 4/04; SLJ 11/03)

5760 Rockwell, Anne. *Career Day* (PS–K). Illus. by Lizzy Rockwell. 2000, HarperCollins $14.95 (0-06-027565-0). 32pp. During Mrs. Madoff's classroom Career Day presentations, ten children introduce a parent or grandparent who talks about his or her occupation. (Rev: BL 5/1/00; HBG 10/00; SLJ 7/00)

5761 Rockwell, Anne. *100 School Days* (K–1). Illus. by Lizzy Rockwell. 2002, HarperCollins LB $14.89 (0-06-029145-1). 40pp. Mrs. Madoff's class celebrates the 100th day of school by bringing in hundreds of snacks and they donate the 100 pennies that have been amassed to a needy town. (Rev: BCCB 10/02; BL 9/15/02; HBG 3/03; SLJ 9/02)

5762 Rockwell, Anne. *Welcome to Kindergarten* (PS–K). Illus. 2001, Walker LB $16.85 (0-8027-8746-0). 32pp. A little boy at a kindergarten open house thinks the building is much too big until he learns about all the interesting things he will be doing there. (Rev: BL 6/1–15/01; HBG 10/01; SLJ 5/01)

5763 Rogers, Jacqueline. *Tiptoe into Kindergarten* (PS–1). Illus. 1999, Scholastic $10.95 (0-590-46653-4). 32pp. A preschooler steals into her brother's kindergarten class and soon becomes part of the activities. (Rev: BL 8/99; HBG 3/00; SLJ 9/99)

5764 Rosenberry, Vera. *Vera's First Day of School* (PS–1). Illus. 1999, Holt $15.95 (0-8050-5936-9). 32pp. On her first day of school, Vera gets confused, and when she finds the school doors closed, she runs home where her mother comforts her.

(Rev: BL 9/15/99; HB 9–10/99; HBG 3/00; SLJ 9/99)

5765 Rousaki, Maria. *Unique Monique* (PS–2). Illus. by Polina Papanikolaou. 2003, Kane/Miller $15.95 (1-929132-51-4). Monique experiments with various ways to enhance her drab school uniform, but they all meet with the principal's disapproval until she thinks of her teeth. (Rev: HBG 4/04; SLJ 11/03)

5766 Russo, Marisabina. *I Don't Want to Go Back to School* (PS–2). Illus. 1994, Greenwillow $15.89 (0-688-04602-9). 32pp. A little boy worries about his reception when he returns to school after summer vacation. (Rev: BL 9/1/94; SLJ 7/94*)

5767 Rylant, Cynthia. *The Ticky-Tacky Doll* (PS–1). Illus. by Harvey Stevenson. 2002, Harcourt $16.00 (0-15-201078-5). 32pp. A little girl, sad to leave her doll behind when she goes to school, is cheered when her grandmother makes her a smaller doll to take with her. (Rev: BL 9/1/02; HBG 3/03; SLJ 11/02)

5768 Saltzberg, Barney. *Show-and-Tell* (K–3). Illus. 1994, Hyperion LB $15.49 (0-7868-2016-0). 32pp. Young Phoebe's parents always interfere with her school plans and create something grand out of a simple assignment. (Rev: BL 10/15/94; SLJ 10/94)

5769 Schwartz, Amy. *Annabelle Swift, Kindergartner* (PS–K). Illus. by author. 1988, Orchard paper $6.95 (0-531-07027-1). 32pp. A good match of art and text tells the story of Annabelle, who finds that school isn't as much fun as she had thought — until it's time to count the milk money. (Rev: BCCB 5/88; BL 2/1/88; HB 3–4/88)

5770 Schwartz, Amy. *Begin at the Beginning: A Little Artist Learns About Life* (PS–2). Illus. 2005, HarperCollins LB $16.89 (0-06-000112-7). 40pp. Sara struggles to pick a subject and get started on her art fair project. (Rev: BL 5/15/05)

5771 Scieszka, Jon. *Math Curse* (1–4). Illus. by Lane Smith. 1995, Viking $16.99 (0-670-86194-4). 32pp. All sorts of math problems and riddles, from the practical to the absurd are presented in this school story. (Rev: BCCB 10/95; BL 11/1/95*; HB 11–12/95; SLJ 9/95*)

5772 Senisi, Ellen B. *Kindergarten Kids* (PS–K). Illus. 1994, Scholastic paper $2.50 (0-590-47614-9). 32pp. A photo-essay that describes a typical day in a kindergarten class in Schenectady, New York. (Rev: BL 11/1/94) [372.21]

5773 Shannon, David. *David Goes to School* (PS–K). Illus. 1999, Scholastic $14.95 (0-590-48087-1). 32pp. David, an imaginative nonconformist, has difficulty doing the right thing when he begins school. (Rev: BCCB 1/00; BL 8/99*; HBG 3/00; SLJ 9/99)

5774 Shaw, Mary. *Brady Brady and the Big Mistake* (K–3). Illus. by Chuck Temple. 2003, Stoddart paper $4.95 (0-7737-6304-X). The entertaining, sports-based adventures of Brady Brady and the Ice Hogs continue. Also use *Brady Brady and the Singing Tree* and *Brady Brady and the Twirlin' Torpedo* (both 2003). (Rev: SLJ 8/03)

5775 Shaw, Mary. *Brady Brady and the Great Rink* (1–3). Illus. by Chuck Temple. Series: Brady Brady. 2002, Stoddart paper $4.95 (0-7737-6224-8). Brady builds a skating rink in his backyard that comes in handy when the school's power fails. Also use *Brady Brady and the Runaway Goalie* (2002). (Rev: SLJ 10/02)

5776 Slate, Joseph. *Miss Bindergarten Has a Wild Day in Kindergarten* (PS–2). Illus. by Ashley Wolff. 2005, Dutton $16.99 (0-525-47084-0). Miss Bindergarten and her students are having a wild day as water spills, hats fly, and butterflies are set free — a fine finale. (Rev: SLJ 2/05)

5777 Slate, Joseph. *Miss Bindergarten Stays Home from Kindergarten* (PS–2). Illus. by Ashley Wolff. 2000, Dutton $16.99 (0-525-46396-8). Miss Bindergarten catches the flu and has to stay home; progressively the students and even the substitute, Mr. Tusky, are also infected. (Rev: HBG 3/01; SLJ 11/00)

5778 Slate, Joseph. *Miss Bindergarten Takes a Field Trip* (PS–K). Illus. by Ashley Wolff. 2001, Dutton $16.99 (0-525-46710-6). 32pp. Miss Bindergarten takes her kindergartners on an interesting field trip that subtly introduces all sorts of shapes. (Rev: BL 10/1/01; HBG 3/02; SLJ 9/01)

5779 Stuve-Bodeen, Stephanie. *Elizabeti's School* (PS–1). Illus. by Christy Hale. 2002, Lee & Low $16.95 (1-58430-043-4). 32pp. Elizabeti tackles her first day at school and comes home to tell her loving family all about it in this story set in Tanzania. (Rev: BCCB 12/02; BL 9/15/02; HB 11–12/02; HBG 3/03; SLJ 9/02)

5780 Tanner, Suzy-Jane. *Tinyflock Nursery School* (PS–K). Illus. by author. 2004, HarperCollins $6.99 (0-06-055723-0). The first day of school is traumatic for Baabaara, but toward the end she begins to see its charms. (Rev: SLJ 8/04)

5781 Tester, Sylvia Root. *We Laughed a Lot, My First Day of School* (PS–1). Illus. by Frances Hook. 1979, Child's World LB $14.95 (0-685-55556-9). A Mexican American boy has an unexpectedly pleasant first day at school.

5782 Tolstoy, Leo. *Philipok* (PS–3). Illus. by Gennady Spirin. 2000, Penguin Putnam $16.99 (0-399-23482-9). 32pp. Philipok is too young to attend school but he decides to go anyway in this story adapted from Tolstoy by Ann Beneduce. (Rev: BL 12/1/00; HBG 3/01; SLJ 1/01)

5783 Uegaki, Chieri. *Suki's Kimono* (K–3). Illus. by St phane Jorisch. 2003, Kids Can $15.95 (1-55337-084-8). Undeterred by her older sisters' opposition, young Suki proudly wears her favorite garment — a kimono — on the first day of school. (Rev: HBG 4/04; SLJ 12/03)

5784 Veldkamp, Tjibbe. *The School Trip* (PS–3). Illus. by Philip Hopman. 2001, Front Street $15.95 (1-886910-70-7). 32pp. Afraid of attending school, Davy opts to build his own, and when he adds wheels the fun really starts. (Rev: BL 8/01; HBG 10/01; SLJ 7/01)

5785 Weston, Carrie. *Lucky Socks* (K–3). Illus. by Charlotte Middleton. 2002, Penguin Putnam $14.99 (0-8037-2741-0). 32pp. Kevin can't find his "lucky" yellow socks to wear to school for field day, but discovers that even when things don't go quite right, the day can still be special. (Rev: BL 2/15/02; HBG 10/02; SLJ 3/02)

5786 Wheatley, Nadia. *Luke's Way of Looking* (K–4). Illus. by Matt Ottley. 2001, Kane $15.95 (1-929132-18-2). Appealing illustrations extend this story of a young boy who doesn't match his art teacher's expectations. (Rev: HBG 3/02; SLJ 6/02)

5787 Williams, Suzanne. *The Marvelous Mind of Matthew McGhee, Age 8: Master of Minds?* (1–3). Illus. by Abby Carter. Series: Ready-for-Chapters. 2004, Simon & Schuster paper $3.99 (0-689-86336-5). 64pp. Third-grader Matthew thinks he may be able to influence what his friends are thinking about, but discovers that this can lead to problems. (Rev: SLJ 3/04)

5788 Willis, Jeanne. *I Hate School* (K–3). Illus. by Tony Ross. 2004, Simon & Schuster $15.95 (0-689-86523-6). Honor Brown really truly doesn't like school and explains exactly why with great flights of rhyming fancy. (Rev: SLJ 8/04)

5789 Winkler, Henry, and Lin Oliver. *I Got a "D" in Salami* (3–5). Illus. 2003, Grosset $12.99 (0-448-43233-1); paper $4.99 (0-448-43163-7). 167pp. When Hank Zipzer gets three Ds on his report card, he goes to great lengths to keep this bad news from his parents. (Rev: HBG 4/04; SLJ 10/03)

5790 Yashima, Taro. *Crow Boy* (K–3). Illus. by author. 1955, Puffin paper $5.99 (0-14-050172-X). 40pp. Distinguished picture book about a shy little Japanese boy who feels like an outsider at school.

5791 Ziefert, Harriet. *Schools Have Learn* (PS–2). Illus. by Amanda Haley. 2004, Blue Apple $15.95 (1-59354-056-6). Inventive wordplay — "good-byes have hugs, backpacks have lugs" — accompanies children through a typical day. (Rev: BCCB 12/04; SLJ 2/05)

TRANSPORTATION AND MACHINES

5792 Anderson, Catherine. *Fire Truck Factory* (PS–2). Illus. Series: Read and Learn. 2005, Heinemann LB $14.45 (1-4034-6162-7). 24pp. The construction of a fire truck is shown in clear photographs and short, simple sentences. (Rev: BL 5/1/05; SLJ 5/05) [629.225]

5793 Baer, Edith. *This Is the Way We Go to School* (PS–2). Illus. by Steve Bjorkman. 1994, Scholastic paper $5.99 (0-590-49443-0). 40pp. How children around the world go to school is told in rhyming couplets. (Rev: BCCB 10/90; BL 10/1/90; SLJ 7/90*) [629]

5794 Barton, Byron. *Airport* (PS–1). Illus. by author. 1982, HarperCollins LB $14.89 (0-690-04169-1); paper $5.95 (0-06-443145-2). 32pp. Common sights at an airport, reproduced in drawings and text.

5795 Barton, Byron. *My Car* (PS). Illus. 2001, Greenwillow LB $14.89 (0-06-029625-9). 40pp. Sam shows readers his car, describing its features, its many uses, and how he drives it. (Rev: BL 7/01; HB 11–12/01*; HBG 3/02; SLJ 8/01)

5796 Bell, Babs. *The Bridge Is Up!* (PS). Illus. by Rob Hefferan. 2004, HarperCollins LB $13.89 (0-06-053794-9). A colorfully illustrated cumulative tale about a long line of vehicles (driven by various animals) all waiting to cross a drawbridge. (Rev: SLJ 3/04)

5797 *Bikes, Cars, Trucks and Trains* (PS–1). Illus. 1997, Scholastic $19.95 (0-590-47653-X). Overlays are used to explore the interiors of cars and other vehicles. Also use *Boats and Ships* (1997). (Rev: BL 12/15/97) [388.09]

5798 Booth, Philip. *Crossing* (1–4). Illus. by Bagram Ibatoulline. 2001, Candlewick $16.99 (0-7636-1420-3). 40pp. Excellent gouache artwork accompanies a rhythmic, lyrical poem featuring townspeople watching a period freight train pass. (Rev: BL 11/15/01; HBG 3/02; SLJ 11/01) [811]

5799 Borden, Louise. *The Neighborhood Trucker* (PS–2). Illus. by Sandra Speidel. 1997, Scholastic paper $3.95 (0-590-46037-4). 32pp. A boy is entranced with trucks, particularly a cement truck driven by Slim. (Rev: BCCB 12/90; BL 9/1/90; SLJ 10/90)

5800 Brown, Margaret Wise. *Two Little Trains* (PS–K). Illus. by Diane Dillon. 2001, HarperCollins $15.95 (0-06-028376-9). 40pp. Using double-page spreads, this book shows two parallel journeys, one by a streamlined diesel train as it travels across the country and the other by a toy train as it moves around a house. (Rev: BL 4/15/01*; HB 5–6/01*; HBG 10/01; SLJ 5/01)

5801 Burton, Virginia Lee. *Mike Mulligan and His Steam Shovel* (1–3). Illus. by author. 1939, Houghton Mifflin LB $11.95 (0-395-06681-6); paper $5.95 (0-395-25939-8). Thrilling race against time as Mike Mulligan and his steam shovel dig a cellar in one day. Also use: *Katy and the Big Snow* (1973).

5802 Collicut, Paul. *This Car* (PS–1). Illus. 2002, Farrar $15.00 (0-374-39965-4). 32pp. All types of cars, from toys to high-performance vehicles, are the subjects of this colorful picture book by the author and illustrator of *This Boat* (2001), *This Plane* (2000), and *This Train* (1999). (Rev: BL 8/02; HBG 3/03; SLJ 8/02)

5803 Cowley, Joy. *The Rusty, Trusty Tractor* (K–2). Illus. by Olivier Dunrea. 1999, Boyds Mills $14.95 (1-56397-565-3). 40pp. In spite of a tractor salesman's dire predictions, Micah's grandfather's 50-year-old tractor takes the old man through another season on the farm. (Rev: BCCB 3/99; BL 3/15/99; HBG 10/99; SLJ 5/99)

5804 Crews, Donald. *Bicycle Race* (PS–K). Illus. by author. 1985, Greenwillow $15.89 (0-688-05172-3). 24pp. A counting book that features 12 bicyclists in yellow numbered helmets, with a flat tire added for drama. (Rev: BL 9/15/85; SLJ 11/85)

5805 Crews, Donald. *Flying* (PS). Illus. by author. 1986, Greenwillow $15.93 (0-688-04319-4); Morrow paper $5.95 (0-688-09235-7). 32pp. Brief text and full-color art highlight this study in movement as a plane takes off, flies over different landscapes, and lands. (Rev: BL 9/1/86; SLJ 10/86)

5806 Crews, Donald. *Freight Train / Tren de carga* (PS–2). Trans. by M. J. Infante. Illus. by author. 2003, Greenwillow $15.99 (0-06-056202-1). A lively bilingual book version of the 1979 Caldecott Honor Book showing a multicolored freight train as it makes its journey through tunnels, over bridges, and around big cities. (Rev: HBG 4/04; SLJ 12/03)

5807 Crews, Donald. *Inside Freight Train* (PS). Illus. 2001, HarperCollins $9.95 (0-688-17087-0). 12pp. A well-designed board book that makes Crews's famous 1978 book interactive by using split pages that slip sideways to reveal smaller pages. (Rev: BL 12/15/00*; HBG 10/01)

5808 Crews, Donald. *School Bus* (PS–1). Illus. by author. 1984, Greenwillow $15.89 (0-688-02808-X); Morrow paper $5.95 (0-688-12267-1). 32pp. Many kinds of school buses pick up children for school.

5809 Delafosse, Claude. *Tools* (PS–1). Trans. from French by Wendy Barish. Illus. by Daniel Moignot. Series: First Discovery. 1999, Scholastic $12.95 (0-439-04404-9). This book covers such common tools as pliers, wall anchors, saws, and hammers. (Rev: HBG 3/00; SLJ 1/00)

5810 Downs, Mike. *The Noisy Airplane Ride* (PS–2). Illus. by David Gordon. 2003, Tricycle $14.95 (1-58246-091-4). 32pp. Computer-generated graphics combine with rhyming narrative to take the mystery out of air travel. (Rev: BL 4/1/03; HBG 10/03; SLJ 8/03) [387.7]

5811 Eick, Jean. *Bulldozers* (PS). Series: Big Machines at Work. 1999, Child's World LB $13.95 (1-56766-525-X). 32pp. This book for the very young introduces (in text and photos) bulldozers, their functions, and their parts. (Rev: BL 4/15/98; HBG 10/99; SLJ 6/99) [629]

5812 Eick, Jean. *Concrete Mixers* (PS). Series: Big Machines at Work. 1999, Child's World LB $13.95 (1-56766-527-6). 32pp. The basics of concrete mixers, how they work, and their fundamental parts are described in simple text and photographs. (Rev: BL 4/15/98; HBG 10/99; SLJ 6/99) [629]

5813 Englart, Mindi Rose. *Helicopters* (2–4). Illus. Series: From Start to Finish. 2003, Gale/Blackbirch $19.95 (1-56711-478-4). 32pp. A picture-book look at how helicopters are built — from design through manufacture to flight testing — with features on key figures and machines. (Rev: BL 5/15/03) [629.133]

5814 Frazee, Marla. *Roller Coaster* (PS–1). Illus. by author. 2003, Harcourt $16.00 (0-15-204554-6). A young boy who is just tall enough to ride the giant coaster for the first time has a breath-taking experience. (Rev: HB 5–6/03; HBG 10/03; SLJ 7/03)

5815 Gibbons, Faye. *Full Steam Ahead* (K–3). Illus. by Sherry Meidell. 2002, Boyds Mills $15.95 (1-56397-858-X). 32pp. Sammy and his family experience the excitement of seeing the first train to roll through their home town in Georgia. (Rev: BL 4/1/02; HBG 10/02; SLJ 7/02)

5816 Gibbons, Gail. *Boat Book* (PS–1). Illus. by author. 1983, Holiday House LB $16.95 (0-8234-0478-1); paper $5.95 (0-8234-0709-8). 32pp. An illustration of all sorts of boats in simple drawings.

5817 Gibbons, Gail. *Emergency!* (PS–1). Illus. 1994, Holiday House LB $16.95 (0-8234-1128-1). 32pp. This picture book shows how a number of people are saved through the use of such vehicles as fire engines, Coast Guard boats, and police cars. (Rev: BCCB 11/94; BL 10/15/94; SLJ 11/94) [363.3]

5818 Gibbons, Gail. *New Road!* (K–2). Illus. by author. 1983, HarperCollins LB $15.89 (0-690-04343-0). 32pp. The process of road construction from start to finish.

5819 Gramatky, Hardie. *Little Toot* (K–3). Illus. by author. 1939, Penguin Putnam $16.99 (0-399-22419-X); paper $6.99 (0-698-11576-7). 96pp. Little Toot, son of the mightiest tug in the harbor, had no ambition until he became a hero during a raging storm.

5820 Hennessy, B. G. *Road Builders* (PS–1). Illus. by Simms Taback. 1994, Viking $14.99 (0-670-83390-8). 32pp. A picture book that shows how different kinds of machines and vehicles are used in building a road. (Rev: BL 5/1/94; SLJ 9/94) [625.7]

5821 Hill, Lee S. *Get Around in the City* (1–3). Series: Get Around Book. 1999, Carolrhoda LB $15.95 (1-57505-307-1). 32pp. An attractive, practical book that depicts in photos and text different kinds of urban transportation including cars, buses, gondolas, and elephants. A companion volume is *Get Around in the Country* (1999). (Rev: HBG 10/99; SLJ 7/99) [629.04]

5822 Hill, Lee Sullivan. *Earthmovers* (2–3). Illus. Series: Pull Ahead Books. 2002, Lerner LB $22.60 (0-8225-0689-0); paper $5.95 (0-8225-0603-3). 32pp. A small-format book for younger readers about how earthmovers and their drivers accomplish their tasks. Also use *Trains* (2002). (Rev: BL 8/02; HBG 3/03; SLJ 10/02)

5823 Hoban, Tana. *Construction Zone* (PS–1). Illus. 1997, Greenwillow $15.89 (0-688-12285-X). 32pp. Thirteen construction machines like the bulldozer, backhoe, and forklift are introduced in pictures and a simple text. (Rev: BCCB 4/97; BL 4/1/97; SLJ 3/97) [624]

5824 Hundal, Nancy. *Number 21* (PS–3). Illus. by Brian Denes. 2001, Fitzhenry & Whiteside $16.95 (1-55041-543-3). 32pp. Three children are excited to see Dad's new dump truck, especially when he fills the dump box with water to make an instant swimming pool. (Rev: BL 8/01; SLJ 4/01)

5825 Imershein, Betsy. *Trucks* (PS). Illus. 2000, Simon & Schuster $4.99 (0-689-82887-X). 14pp. This board book gives information about eight different trucks. (Rev: BCCB 9/00; BL 6/1–15/00; HBG 10/00)

5826 Johnson, Angela. *Those Building Men* (1–4). Illus. by Barry Moser. 2001, Scholastic $16.95 (0-590-66521-9). 32pp. This poem pays tribute to builders and construction workers who move earth for canals, lay steel for railroads, and cut down trees for building. (Rev: BCCB 2/01; BL 2/1/01; HBG 10/01; SLJ 3/01)

5827 Jorgensen, Norman. *The Call of the Osprey* (K–3). Illus. by Brian Harrison-Lever. 2004, Fremantle Arts Centre $22.50 (1-920731-85-7). A young boy named Tom and a retired sea captain lovingly restore a steamboat, which Tom then inherits, in a simple story full of sea lore. (Rev: SLJ 2/05)

278

5828 Katz, Bobbi. *Truck Talk: Rhymes on Wheels* (PS–1). Illus. 1997, Scholastic $10.95 (0-590-69328-X). 32pp. Each of the trucks pictured — e.g., tow trucks, ambulances, and garbage trucks — describes its function in its own words. (Rev: BL 4/1/97; SLJ 3/97) [811]

5829 Kuklin, Susan. *All Aboard! A True Train Story* (PS–1). Illus. 2003, Scholastic $16.95 (0-439-45583-9). 32pp. An eye-catching visit to the Durango & Silverton narrow-gauge steam railway in Colorado, with minimal text. (Rev: BL 2/1/04; HBG 4/04; SLJ 12/03)

5830 Lenski, Lois. *The Little Fire Engine* (PS). Illus. 2002, Random $6.99 (0-375-82263-1). 30pp. An abridged, colorful board-book version of the 1940s classic about a fireman and his engine rescuing the inhabitants from a house fire. Also use *The Little Train* (2002). (Rev: BL 12/1/02; HBG 3/03)

5831 Lewis, Kevin. *The Lot at the End of My Block* (PS–2). Illus. by Reg Cartwright. 2001, Hyperion LB $16.49 (0-7868-2512-X). Using a rhyme similar to "The House That Jack Built" a young boy tells how an empty lot is transformed into an apartment building. (Rev: HBG 10/01; SLJ 3/01)

5832 Liebman, Dan. *I Want to Be a Mechanic* (K–2). Series: I Want to Be. 2003, Firefly LB $14.95 (1-55297-695-5); paper $3.99 (1-55297-693-9). A photo-filled inside look at a day in the life of an auto mechanic. (Rev: SLJ 8/03) [629.28]

5833 Lyon, David. *The Biggest Truck* (PS–1). Illus. by author. 1988, Lothrop LB $13.88 (0-688-05514-1). 32pp. Jim the truck driver goes to work when everyone else is going to bed. (Rev: BL 11/1/88; SLJ 1/89)

5834 Maccarone, Grace. *Cars! Cars! Cars!* (PS). Illus. by David A. Carter. 1995, Scholastic $6.95 (0-590-47572-X). 24pp. The concept of different styles, colors, and models of cars is introduced in this very simple picture book. (Rev: BL 1/15/95; SLJ 12/95)

5835 McGough, Roger. *Until I Met Dudley: How Everyday Things Really Work* (K–4). Illus. by Chris Riddell. 1997, Walker $15.95 (0-8027-8623-5). An amusing story that explains how five common appliances, like a toaster, work. (Rev: HBG 3/98; SLJ 11/97)

5836 McMullan, Kate. *I'm Mighty!* (PS–2). Illus. by Jim McMullan. 2003, HarperCollins LB $16.89 (0-06-009291-2). A feisty little tugboat proves that size is not an indicator of power. (Rev: BCCB 12/03; BL 11/1/03; HB 11–12/03; HBG 4/04; SLJ 11/03)

5837 Maestro, Betsy, and Ellen DelVecchio. *Big City Port* (PS–2). Illus. by Giulio Maestro. 1984, Macmillan LB $14.95 (0-02-762110-3); Scholastic paper $4.95 (0-590-41577-8). 32pp. A picture book that shows activities in a big-city port.

5838 Mayo, Margaret. *Emergency!* (PS–1). Illus. by Alex Ayliffe. 2002, Carolrhoda $14.95 (0-87614-922-0). 32pp. Arresting artwork details emergency vehicles and their uses in this exciting, large-format picture book. (Rev: BL 8/02; HBG 3/03; SLJ 10/02)

5839 Miranda, Anne. *Beep! Beep!* (PS). Illus. by David Murphy. 1999, Turtle $15.95 (1-890515-14-

0). All kinds of vehicles are shown in this picture book about a boy who imagines that he is riding in each of them. (Rev: HBG 3/00; SLJ 6/99)

5840 Moignot, Daniel. *Fire Fighting* (PS–1). Trans. from French by Wendy Barish. Illus. by author. Series: First Discovery. 1999, Scholastic $12.95 (0-439-04403-0). Using one sentence per page, this simple account introduces fire fighting equipment such as trucks, ladders, and protective clothing. (Rev: HBG 3/00; SLJ 1/00)

5841 Mott, Evelyn Clarke. *Steam Train Ride* (PS–K). Illus. 1991, Walker LB $14.85 (0-8027-6996-9). A delightful ride for train lovers on Engine 89. (Rev: BL 5/15/91; SLJ 8/91) [625.2]

5842 Neitzel, Shirley. *I'm Taking a Trip on My Train* (PS–1). Illus. by Nancy Winslow Parker. 1999, Greenwillow LB $14.93 (0-688-15834-X). 32pp. A boy pretends he is an engineer on his toy train in this picture book, which uses rebus drawings to introduce parts of a train and a freight yard. (Rev: BL 4/15/99; HBG 10/99; SLJ 3/99)

5843 Parker, Neal Evan. *Captain Annabel* (PS–4). Illus. by Emily Harris. 2005, Down East $15.95 (0-89272-653-9). Encouraged by her father, Annabel has always loved sailing, and she grows up to be a tugboat captain. (Rev: SLJ 5/05)

5844 Piper, Watty. *The Little Engine That Could* (K–2). Illus. by George Hauman and Doris Hauman. 1930, Penguin Putnam $7.99 (0-448-40520-2). 48pp. Little Engine saves the day. (Rev: HBG 4/04; SLJ 3/04)

5845 Relf, Patricia. *Tonka Big Book of Trucks* (PS–3). Illus. by Thomas La Padula. 1996, Scholastic $12.95 (0-590-84572-1). 48pp. Double-page spreads are used to describe a variety of trucks and their drivers. (Rev: BL 10/1/96; SLJ 9/96) [629.2]

5846 Rex, Michael. *My Race Car* (PS–2). Illus. 2000, Holt $15.95 (0-8050-6101-0). 32pp. In this fantasy, a young boy imagines being on a racetrack in his car and, after checking the car, participating in an exciting race at top speed. (Rev: BCCB 9/00; BL 5/1/00; HBG 10/00; SLJ 7/00) [629.228]

5847 Richards, Laura E. *Jiggle Joggle Jee!* (PS). Illus. by Sam Williams. 2001, HarperCollins LB $15.89 (0-688-17833-2). 32pp. A newly illustrated version of an early-20th-century fantasy poem about a train. (Rev: BL 7/01; HBG 10/01; SLJ 5/01)

5848 Rotner, Shelley. *Wheels Around* (PS–1). Illus. 1995, Houghton Mifflin $13.95 (0-395-71815-5). 32pp. All kinds of wheeled vehicles from fire and mail trucks to small trailers and wheelchairs are featured. (Rev: BL 11/1/95; SLJ 10/95) [621.8]

5849 Siebert, Diane. *Train Song* (PS–2). Illus. by Mike Wimmer. 1990, HarperCollins LB $16.89 (0-690-04728-2). 32pp. This poem portrays trains as they travel across America. (Rev: BCCB 12/90; BL 10/1/90; SLJ 9/90*)

5850 Sis, Peter. *Trucks Trucks Trucks* (PS). Illus. 1999, Greenwillow $14.95 (0-688-16276-2). 24pp. Matt enters an imaginary world where he operates a number of massive trucks and oversees their many operations. (Rev: BCCB 5/99; BL 6/1–15/99; HB 5–6/99; HBG 10/99; SLJ 5/99)

5851 Stickland, Paul. *Truck Jam* (PS–K). Illus. 2000, Ragged Bear $16.95 (1-929927-03-7). A pop-up book whose pages are filled with dump trucks, tow trucks, and pickups. (Rev: BL 12/1/00)

5852 Sturges, Philemon. *I Love Planes!* (PS–1). Illus. by Shari Halpern. 2003, HarperCollins LB $14.89 (0-06-028899-X). 32pp. A little boy imagines taking flight in an airplane, a balloon, a spaceship, and more. Also use *I Love Trains!* (2001). (Rev: BL 2/1/03; HBG 10/03; SLJ 3/03)

5853 Todd, Mark. *Monster Trucks!* (PS). Illus. by author. 2003, Houghton Mifflin $15.00 (0-618-18208-X). Bright spreads with cartoon illustrations introduce 14 types of heavy vehicles and the work they do. (Rev: HBG 4/04; SLJ 10/03)

5854 Weatherby, Brenda. *The Trucker* (PS–2). Illus. by Mark Alan Weatherby. 2004, Scholastic $15.95 (0-439-39877-0). 32pp. A little boy dreams he's driving a tractor-trailer in this well-illustrated book, and wakes to find that he's been riding along in his father's big rig. (Rev: BL 2/15/04; SLJ 4/04)

5855 Wilson-Max, Ken. *Little Green Tow Truck* (PS–2). Illus. 1997, Scholastic paper $14.95 (0-590-89802-7). 14pp. Tabs and flaps are featured in this book about the parts and uses of tow trucks. Also use *Big Red Fire Truck* (1997). (Rev: BL 12/15/97) [629]

5856 Wilson-Max, Ken. *Little Red Plane* (PS–1). Illus. 1995, Scholastic $14.95 (0-590-43008-4). 14pp. By pulling tabs, the reader can make this airplane perform all sorts of stunts. (Rev: BL 2/1/96)

5857 Ziefert, Harriet. *Train Song* (PS). Illus. by Donald Saaf. 2000, Orchard $14.95 (0-531-30204-0). 32pp. A little boy watches a freight train go by and sees the contents of all the cars: logs, pigs, ducks, cows, and so on. (Rev: BL 4/1/00; HBG 10/00; SLJ 4/00)

5858 Zimmerman, Andrea, and David Clemesha. *Dig!* (PS–K). Illus. by Marc Rosenthal. 2004, Harcourt $16.00 (0-15-216785-4). Mr. Rally and his dog, Lightning, really enjoy digging — with a backhoe or without. (Rev: BL 5/15/04; SLJ 7/04)

Stories About Holidays and Holy Days

GENERAL AND MISCELLANEOUS

5859 *The 11th Commandment: Wisdom from Our Children* (PS–3). Illus. 1996, Jewish Lights $16.95 (1-879045-46-X). 48pp. The results of a survey of a group of children from different faiths who were asked to suggest an 11th commandment. (Rev: BL 10/1/96) [170]

5860 Barker, Margot. *What Is Martin Luther King, Jr. Day?* (K–2). Illus. by Matthew Bates. Series: Understanding Holidays. 1990, Children's Book Pr. paper $4.95 (0-516-43784-4). 48pp. Two white classmates learn from their African American friends who Martin Luther King, Jr., was and why we celebrate his birthday. (Rev: SLJ 2/91) [921]

5861 Bauer, Marion Dane. *My Mother Is Mine* (PS–1). Illus. by Peter Elwell. 2001, Simon & Schuster $13.00 (0-689-82267-7). Soft pastel illustrations and gentle verses celebrate the relationship between mother and child as a little girl works on a card for Mother's Day. (Rev: HBG 10/01; SLJ 4/01)

5862 Bertrand, Diane Gonzales. *Uncle Chente's Picnic / El Picnic de Tío Chente* (K–2). Trans. by Julia Mercedes Castilla. Illus. by Pauline Rodriguez Howard. 2001, Piñata $14.95 (1-55885-337-5). Uncle Chente arrives for a Fourth of July picnic, but plans must be changed when there is a huge storm. (Rev: SLJ 1/02)

5863 Bouchard, David. *The Dragon New Year: A Chinese Legend* (PS–3). Illus. by Zhong-Yang Huang. 1999, Peachtree $16.95 (1-56145-210-6). 32pp. A Chinese grandmother explains to her frightened grandchild the origin of the noisy Dragon Dance at New Year's and how it was intended to frighten a real dragon who lived at the bottom of the sea. (Rev: BL 9/1/99; HBG 3/00; SLJ 11/99)

5864 Bourgeois, Paulette. *Franklin's Holiday Treasury* (PS–1). Illus. by Brenda Clark. 2002, Kids Can $15.95 (1-55337-045-7). 128pp. Four holiday adventures of Franklin the turtle are gathered here: Halloween, Thanksgiving, Christmas, and Valentine's Day. (Rev: BL 1/1–15/03; HBG 3/03)

5865 Brown, Marc. *Arthur's April Fool* (PS–2). Illus. by author. 1985, Little, Brown $15.95 (0-316-11196-1); paper $5.95 (0-316-11234-8). 32pp. Arthur is afraid he will forget his magic tricks prepared for the April Fools' Day show.

5866 Bunting, Eve. *The Mother's Day Mice* (PS–1). Illus. by Jan Brett. 1986, Houghton Mifflin $15.00 (0-89919-387-0); paper $5.95 (0-89919-702-7). Three little mice go out to seek presents for Mother's Day; the smallest one brings home a song he heard a human sing. (Rev: BCCB 4/86; BL 4/1/86; SLJ 3/86)

5867 Bunting, Eve. *A Perfect Father's Day* (PS–1). Illus. by Susan Meddaugh. 1993, Houghton Mifflin paper $5.95 (0-395-66416-0). 32pp. Susie plans a perfect time for her father on Father's Day. (Rev: BL 4/15/91; SLJ 5/91)

5868 Bunting, Eve. *St. Patrick's Day in the Morning* (PS–2). Illus. by Jan Brett. 1983, Houghton Mifflin $15.00 (0-395-29098-8); paper $5.95 (0-89919-162-2). 32pp. Jamie is too small to parade to the top of the hill with the rest of his family, so he rises early and has a St. Patrick's Day adventure of his own.

5869 Carrier, Roch. *A Happy New Year's Day* (2–4). Illus. by Gilles Pelletier. 1991, Tundra $14.95 (0-88776-267-0). This is a happy recollection of a New Year's Day spent in a French Canadian town during World War II. (Rev: SLJ 2/92)

5870 Chin, Steven A. *Dragon Parade: A Chinese New Year Story* (PS–3). Illus. by Mou-Sien Tseng. 1993, Raintree LB $22.83 (0-8114-7215-9). 32pp. This is a fictionalized account of the Chinese immigrant Noram Ah Sing, who started the first big New Year's Parade in San Francisco. (Rev: BL 5/1/93; SLJ 7/93)

5871 Compestine, Ying Chang. *The Runaway Rice Cake* (PS–3). Illus. by Tungwai Chau. 2001, Simon & Schuster $16.95 (0-689-82972-8). 40pp. As part of the Chinese New Year's Eve celebration, Mooma

Chang cooks a rice cake that comes to life and runs away. (Rev: BL 2/1/01; HBG 3/02; SLJ 2/01)

5872 dePaola, Tomie. *The Lady of Guadalupe* (K–3). Illus. by author. 1980, Holiday House LB $16.95 (0-8234-0373-4); paper $8.95 (0-8234-0403-X). 48pp. The legend of the patron saint of Mexico is retold in this excellent picture book.

5873 Dillon, Jana. *Lucky O'Leprechaun* (K–2). Illus. by author. 1998, Pelican $14.95 (1-56554-333-5). On St. Patrick's Day weekend, Meg and Sean are determined to catch the leprechaun that lives under a thorn bush in the garden. (Rev: HBG 3/99; SLJ 1/99)

5874 English, Karen. *Nadia's Hands* (K–4). Illus. by Jonathan Weiner. 1999, Boyds Mills $15.95 (1-56397-667-6). 32pp. A Pakistani American girl learns to appreciate the rich traditions of marriage in her faith when she is asked to be a flower girl at her aunt's wedding. (Rev: BCCB 4/99; BL 3/1/99; HBG 10/99; SLJ 4/99)

5875 Ford, Juwanda G. *K Is for Kwanzaa: A Kwanzaa Alphabet Book* (K–3). Illus. by Ken Wilson-Max. 1997, Scholastic $10.95 (0-590-92200-9). 32pp. Arranged alphabetically various objects, customs, and rituals connected with Kwanzaa are introduced. (Rev: BL 9/1/97; HBG 3/98; SLJ 10/97) [394.261]

5876 French, Vivian. *A Present for Mom* (PS). Illus. by Dana Kubick. 2002, Candlewick $13.99 (0-7636-1587-0). 32pp. Stanley, a young cat, finds that the best gift for Mother's Day is a box of kisses. (Rev: BL 5/1/02; HBG 10/02; SLJ 5/02)

5877 Freschet, Gina. *Beto and the Bone Dance* (K–3). Illus. 2001, Farrar $16.00 (0-374-31720-8). 32pp. The spirit of Beto's grandmother visits him on the Day of the Dead in this picture book set in Mexico. (Rev: BCCB 12/01; BL 10/15/01; HBG 3/02; SLJ 10/01)

5878 Garcia, Aurora Col-n. *Cinco de Mayo* (1–3). Series: Holiday Histories. 2003, Heinemann LB $22.79 (1-4034-3501-4). 32pp. The annual celebration marking Mexico's battlefield victory over French forces on May 5, 1862, is explained for younger readers in this well-illustrated book. (Rev: SLJ 5/04) [394.262]

5879 Ghazi, Suhaib Hamid. *Ramadan* (K–4). Illus. by Omar Rayyan. 1996, Holiday House $16.95 (0-8234-1254-7). 32pp. The Islamic month of Ramadan, with its fasting and prayers, as seen through the eyes of a young boy. (Rev: BCCB 12/96; BL 10/1/96; SLJ 10/96) [297]

5880 Gower, Catherine. *Long-Long's New Year* (K–3). Illus. by He Zhihong. 2005, Tuttle $16.95 (0-8048-3666-3). 32pp. Long-Long and his grandfather sell cabbages at the market to raise money for the upcoming Spring Festival, also known as Chinese New Year. (Rev: BL 2/15/05; SLJ 6/05)

5881 Johnston, Tony. *Day of the Dead* (K–4). Illus. by Jeanette Winter. 1997, Harcourt $14.00 (0-15-222863-2). 56pp. A Mexican family makes preparations for the holiday Day of the Dead and celebrates it festively. (Rev: BL 9/15/97; HBG 3/98; SLJ 9/97)

5882 Katz, Karen. *My First Kwanzaa* (PS). Illus. by author. 2003, Holt $14.95 (0-8050-7077-X). Double-page spreads with colorful illustrations introduce the seven days of Kwanzaa and the associated traditions. (Rev: HBG 4/04; SLJ 10/03) [394.2]

5883 Keep, Richard. *Clatter Bash! A Day of the Dead Celebration* (K–3). Illus. by author. 2004, Peachtree $15.95 (1-56145-322-6). After the people leave the graveyards, the skeletons emerge and have a party, enjoying the food left behind for them. (Rev: SLJ 2/05)

5884 Kimmelman, Leslie. *Happy 4th of July, Jenny Sweeney!* (PS–1). Illus. by Nancy Cote. 2003, Whitman LB $15.95 (0-8075-3152-9). Young Jenny observes the Fourth of July celebrations of her ethnically diverse community. (Rev: BL 5/15/03; HBG 10/03; SLJ 7/03)

5885 Kroll, Steven. *It's Groundhog Day!* (PS–2). Illus. by Jeni Bassett. 1987, Scholastic paper $3.25 (0-590-44669-X). 32pp. Godfrey Groundhog will not see his shadow come February 2, and this very much upsets Roland Raccoon, who owns a ski lodge. (Rev: BL 10/15/87; SLJ 11/87)

5886 Kroll, Steven. *Mary McLean and the St. Patrick's Day Parade* (1–3). Illus. by Michael Dooling. 1991, Scholastic $15.95 (0-590-43701-1). 32pp. A young Irish girl newly arrived in the United States is visited by a leprechaun on St. Patrick's Day. (Rev: BCCB 2/91; BL 1/1/91; SLJ 6/91)

5887 Levy, Janice. *The Spirit of Tio Fernando: A Day of the Dead Story/El Espiritu de Tio Fernando: Una Historia del Dia de los Muertos* (1–3). Trans. by Teresa Mlawer. Illus. by Morella Fuenmayor. 1995, Whitman $14.95 (0-8075-7585-2); paper $6.95 (0-8075-7586-0). 32pp. On the Day of the Dead, Nando remembers his Uncle Fernando, who died six months before. (Rev: BL 11/15/95; SLJ 11/95)

5888 Low, William. *Chinatown* (K–1). Illus. 1997, Holt paper $15.95 (0-8050-4214-8). 32pp. At Chinese New Year's, a boy and his grandmother take a tour through their Chinatown. (Rev: BL 9/15/97; HBG 3/98; SLJ 9/97)

5889 Luenn, Nancy. *A Gift for Abuelita: Celebrating the Day of the Dead / Un regalo para Abuelita: En celebración del Día de los Muertos* (K–3). Illus. by Robert Chapman. 1998, Rising Moon $15.95 (0-87358-688-3). 32pp. Told in English and Spanish, this picture book relates Rosita's tribute to her grandmother on the Day of the Dead. (Rev: BCCB 1/99; BL 3/15/99; HBG 3/99; SLJ 3/99)

5890 Medearis, Angela Shelf. *Seven Spools of Thread: A Kwanzaa Story* (K–3). Illus. by Daniel Minter. 2000, Whitman $15.95 (0-8075-7315-9). 40pp. An original folktale that takes place in a Ghanaian village and effectively introduces the seven principles of Kwanzaa. (Rev: BL 9/15/00; HBG 3/01)

5891 Moore, Elizabeth, and Alice Couvillon. *Mimi and Jean-Paul's Cajun Mardi Gras* (1–3). Illus. by Marilyn C. Rougelot. 1996, Pelican $14.95 (1-56554-069-7). The unique Courir (Run) de Mardi

Gras celebrated in Cajun country is experienced by a young girl. (Rev: SLJ 3/96)

5892 Moorman, Margaret. *Light the Lights! A Story About Celebrating Hanukkah and Christmas* (K–3). Illus. 1994, Scholastic $12.95 (0-590-47003-5). 32pp. This book celebrates the spirit of both Christmas and Hanukkah and shows similarities in these holidays and their traditions. (Rev: BL 8/94) [394.26]

5893 Nolan, Janet. *The St. Patrick's Day Shillelagh* (2–4). Illus. by Ben F. Stahl. 2002, Whitman $15.95 (0-8075-7344-2). 32pp. On his trip from Ireland to America during the potato famine, Fergus carved a beautiful shillelagh that is passed from generation to generation. (Rev: BL 1/1–15/03; HBG 3/03; SLJ 12/02)

5894 O'Donnell, Elizabeth Lee. *Patrick's Day* (K–2). Illus. by Jacqueline Rogers. 1994, Morrow $15.00 (0-688-07853-2). 32pp. When Patrick, who is growing up in an Irish village, realizes that St. Patrick's Day is not in his honor, he becomes very grumpy. (Rev: BL 4/1/94; SLJ 5/94)

5895 Patrick, Diane. *Family Celebrations* (2–5). Illus. by Michael Bryant. 1993, Silver Moon LB $14.95 (1-881889-04-1). 62pp. Portrays a variety of family gatherings that are associated with such occasions as birth, marriage, and death as they are observed in many cultures. (Rev: BL 6/1–15/93) [392]

5896 Roberts, Bethany. *Fourth of July Mice!* (PS–1). Illus. by Doug Cushman. Series: Holiday Mice. 2004, Clarion $13.00 (0-618-31367-4). 32pp. The family of mice featured in other holiday titles celebrate Independence Day in fine style. (Rev: BL 5/15/04)

5897 Rockwell, Anne. *Mother's Day* (PS–1). Illus. by Lizzy Rockwell. 2004, HarperCollins $14.99 (0-06-051374-8). 40pp. Looking forward to Mother's Day, the children in Mrs. Madoff's classroom explain how they will celebrate the occasion. (Rev: BL 2/15/04; SLJ 3/04)

5898 Sasso, Sandy Eisenberg. *A Prayer for the Earth: The Story of Naamah, Noah's Wife* (PS–2). Illus. by Bethanne Andersen. 1997, Jewish Lights $16.95 (1-879045-60-5). 32pp. Noah's wife, Naamah, is given the job of bringing samples of each of the earth's plants into Noah's Ark. (Rev: BCCB 7–8/97; BL 2/15/97; SLJ 6/97)

5899 Schnetzler, Pattie. *Earth Day Birthday* (PS–4). Illus. by Chad Wallace. Series: Sharing Nature with Children. 2004, Dawn $16.95 (1-58469-053-4); paper $8.95 (1-58469-054-2). Set to the melody of "The Twelve Days of Christmas," the lyrics in this attractively illustrated song showcase 12 animal species from different parts of the world; information on Earth Day follows the text. (Rev: SLJ 7/04) [782.42]

5900 Shragg, Karen I. *A Solstice Tree for Jenny* (K–3). Illus. by Heidi Schwabacher. 2001, Prometheus paper $12.00 (1-57392-930-1). 50pp. Jenny wants to know why her family doesn't celebrate any religious holidays. (Rev: BL 12/15/01)

5901 Swartz, Nancy Sohn. *In Our Image: God's First Creatures* (PS–2). Illus. by Melanie Hall. 1998, Jewish Lights $16.95 (1-879045-99-0). 32pp. Several animals reveal characteristics that God would want humans to possess, such as the bravery of the tiger and the gentleness of the lamb. (Rev: BL 10/1/98; HBG 3/99; SLJ 3/99) [296.3]

5902 Tucker, Kathy. *The Leprechaun in the Basement* (PS–2). Illus. by John Sandford. 1999, Whitman $18.95 (0-8075-4450-7). 32pp. On St. Patrick's Day, Michael meets a leprechaun and the two learn a lesson from each other about relationships. (Rev: BL 1/1–15/99; HBG 10/99; SLJ 12/98)

5903 Vaughan, Marcia. *The Dancing Dragon* (K–2). Illus. by Stanley Wong Hoo Foon. 1996, Mondo paper $5.95 (1-57255-134-8). In rhyming couplets, a Chinese American child describes preparations for Chinese New Year celebrations, including the dragon parade. (Rev: SLJ 12/96)

5904 Whitehead, Kathy. *Looking for Uncle Louie on the 4th of July* (K–3). Illus. by Pablo Torrecilla. 2005, Boyds Mills $15.95 (1-59078-061-2). 32pp. On the 4th of July in Texas, young Joe watches the parade, waiting with bated breath for the arrival of his Uncle Louie's spectacular car. (Rev: BL 5/15/05; SLJ 5/05)

5905 Wojciechowski, Susan. *A Fine St. Patrick's Day* (K–2). Illus. by Tom Curry. 2004, Random LB $16.99 (0-375-92386-1). In this magical St. Patrick's Day story, the townspeople of Tralee are rewarded for a good deed and win the annual decorating contest against neighboring Tralah. (Rev: SLJ 1/04)

5906 Wong, Janet. *Apple Pie Fourth of July* (PS–2). Illus. by Margaret Chodos-Irvine. 2002, Harcourt $16.00 (0-15-202543-X). 40pp. A young Chinese American girl working in her parents' grocery is convinced no one will want to eat their Chinese food on the Fourth of July. (Rev: BL 8/02; HBG 10/02; SLJ 5/02)

5907 Wong, Janet S. *This Next New Year* (PS–3). Illus. by Yangsook Choi. 2000, Farrar $16.00 (0-374-35503-7). 32pp. A little boy who is half Korean prepares to celebrate Chinese New Year and describes the traditional and modern customs involved. (Rev: BCCB 9/00; BL 9/15/00; HB 11–12/00; HBG 3/01; SLJ 10/00)

BIRTHDAYS

5908 Bailey, Debbie. *Happy Birthday* (PS). Photos by Susan Huszar. Series: Talk-About-Books. 1999, Annick $5.95 (1-55037-559-8). In this board book, full-color illustrations are used to show different ways of celebrating children's birthdays. (Rev: SLJ 9/99)

5909 Barker, Marjorie. *Magical Hands* (2–4). Illus. by Yoshi. 1989, Picture Book $16.00 (0-88708-103-7). 28pp. William does his friends' work, hoping they will think it is magic, and then finds that his work is done too! (Rev: BL 2/1/90)

5910 Beck, Andrea. *Elliot Bakes a Cake* (PS–1). Illus. 1999, Kids Can $12.95 (1-55074-443-7). 32pp. Elliot Moose and his stuffed toy friends converge on the kitchen to bake a birthday cake for their pal Lionel Lion. (Rev: BL 10/1/99; HBG 3/00; SLJ 12/99)

5911 Bertrand, Diane Gonzales. *The Last Doll / La Ultima Muneca* (PS–3). Illus. by Anthony Accardo. 2001, Arte Publico $14.95 (1-55885-290-5). 32pp. A special doll dressed in white lace is chosen to be a gift for Teresa at her *quinceanera* coming-of-age party. (Rev: BL 10/1/01; SLJ 4/01)

5912 Best, Cari. *Three Cheers for Catherine the Great!* (PS–3). Illus. by Giselle Potter. 1999, DK $16.95 (0-7894-2622-6). Sara decides that the perfect birthday present for her Russian grandmother would be to help her learn to read and write English. (Rev: BCCB 1/00; BL 9/15/99*; HB 11–12/99; HBG 3/00; SLJ 8/99)

5913 Brown, Marc. *Arthur's Birthday* (K–2). Illus. 1989, Little, Brown $15.95 (0-316-11073-6); paper $5.95 (0-316-11074-4). Muffy is upset to learn that Arthur's birthday is the same day as hers. (Rev: BL 4/15/89; HB 5–6/89)

5914 Brown, Tricia. *Hello, Amigos!* (K–2). Illus. by Fran Ortiz. 1992, Holt paper $7.95 (0-8050-1891-3). 48pp. The anticipation and excitement of Frankie Valdez's birthday. (Rev: BCCB 1/87; BL 12/15/86; SLJ 4/87)

5915 Butler, Dorothy. *My Brown Bear Barney at the Party* (PS–2). Illus. by Elizabeth Fuller. 2001, Greenwillow LB $15.89 (0-688-17549-X). 24pp. At Barney Hinkel's birthday party his little sister claims that Barney Bear is hers, much to the consternation of the toy's real owner. (Rev: BL 2/1/01; HBG 10/01; SLJ 2/01)

5916 Cameron, Ann. *Julian, Dream Doctor* (2–4). Illus. by Ann Strugnell. Series: Stepping Stone. 1990, Random LB $11.99 (0-679-90524-3); paper $3.99 (0-679-80524-9). 40pp. In this warm story of an African American family, Julian wants to discover Dad's idea of a dream birthday present. (Rev: BCCB 3/90; BL 5/15/90; HB 9–10/90; SLJ 7/90)

5917 Capucilli, Alyssa Satin. *Happy Birthday, Biscuit!* (PS). Illus. by Pat Schories. Series: I Can Read. 1999, HarperCollins LB $12.89 (0-06-028361-0). 24pp. A frisky puppy named Biscuit enjoys a birthday romp with his friends in this book for beginning readers. (Rev: BL 6/1–15/99; HBG 10/99; SLJ 6/99)

5918 Carle, Eric. *The Secret Birthday Message* (PS–1). Illus. by author. 1972, HarperCollins LB $15.89 (0-690-72348-2); paper $6.95 (0-06-443099-5). 26pp. In a brightly illustrated picture book with intriguing cutouts, a little boy has to decipher the coded message to find his birthday present.

5919 Chavarria-Chairez, Becky. *Magda's Pinata Magic / Magda y el Piñata Magica* (K–3). Trans. by Gabriela Baeza Ventura. Illus. by Anne Vega. 2001, Arte Publico $14.95 (1-55885-320-0). 32pp. Gabriel is upset by the idea of destroying his birthday pinata, so his sister Magda comes up with a solution in this bilingual picture book. (Rev: BL 10/15/01; SLJ 1/02)

5920 Chavarria-Chairez, Becky. *Magda's Tortillas / Las tortillas de Magda* (K–2). Trans. by Julia Mer-

cedes Castilla. Illus. by Anne Vega. 2000, Piñata $14.95 (1-55885-286-7). On her birthday, Magda produces tortillas in different shapes in this bilingual book. (Rev: SLJ 10/00)

5921 Cohen, Caron Lee. *Happy to You!* (PS). Illus. by Rosanne Litzinger. 2001, Clarion $15.00 (0-618-04229-6). 32pp. Little Daniel says "Happy to you!" to everything he sees after hearing the song "Happy Birthday to You" in this rhyming picture book. (Rev: BL 9/15/01; HBG 3/02; SLJ 9/01)

5922 Cutler, Jane. *The Birthday Doll* (PS–1). Illus. by Hiroe Nakata. 2004, Farrar $16.00 (0-374-30719-9). 32pp. Tradition triumphs over glitz in this story of a young girl receiving two very different presents on her birthday. (Rev: BL 1/1–15/04; SLJ 3/04)

5923 Day, Alexandra. *Carl's Birthday* (PS–2). Illus. 1995, Farrar $12.95 (0-374-31144-7). 32pp. In this almost wordless picture book, Madeline and her beloved Rottweiler, Carl, secretly help prepare a surprise birthday party for the dog. (Rev: BL 1/1–15/96; SLJ 12/95)

5924 De Groat, Diane. *Happy Birthday to You, You Belong in a Zoo* (PS–1). Illus. 1999, Morrow $15.00 (0-688-16544-3). 32pp. Gilbert wants to get even with bully Lewis by giving him a dumb gift at his birthday party, but Mom saves the day. (Rev: BL 8/99; HBG 3/00; SLJ 10/99)

5925 Dickinson, Rebecca. *Monster Cake* (PS–3). Illus. by author. 2000, Scholastic paper $5.99 (0-439-06752-9). Monster children make a delicious birthday cake for their mother that consists of worms, slugs, and bugs. (Rev: SLJ 3/01)

5926 Dominguez, Kelli Kyle. *The Perfect Pinata / La Piñata Perfecta* (PS–2). Trans. by Teresa Mlawer. Illus. by Diane Patterson. 2002, Whitman $14.95 (0-8075-6495-8). 32pp. This bilingual text describes Marisa's reluctance to break her beautiful sixth-birthday pinata and her parents' happy solution. (Rev: BL 4/15/02; HBG 10/02)

5927 Dorflinger, Carolyn. *Tomorrow Is Mom's Birthday* (PS–1). Illus. by Iza Trapani. 1994, Whispering Coyote $14.95 (1-879085-84-4). 32pp. Tyler thinks of all sorts of things to give to his mother on her birthday, but he decides to paint a family portrait. (Rev: BCCB 4/94; BL 5/1/94)

5928 Edmiston, Jim. *The Emperor Who Forgot His Birthday* (PS–1). Illus. by author. Series: A Barefoot Beginner Book. 1999, Barefoot $14.95 (1-84148-015-0). An emperor wakes up and finds that his cat, family, and servants are all missing, little knowing that they are preparing a surprise birthday party for him. (Rev: SLJ 12/99)

5929 Estes, Kristyn Rehling. *Manuela's Gift* (K–2). Illus. by Claire B. Cotts. 1999, Chronicle $15.95 (0-8118-2085-8). Manuela dreams of having a beautiful yellow dress but, when she doesn't receive it because her family is poor, she gradually accepts the situation. (Rev: BL 6/1–15/99; HBG 10/99; SLJ 10/99)

5930 Falwell, Cathryn. *Butterflies for Kiri* (K–3). Illus. by author. 2003, Lee & Low $16.95 (1-58430-100-7). Kiri, a young Japanese-American girl, overcomes her initial frustrations as she struggles to make sense of the origami kit she's received as a birthday gift. (Rev: BL 5/15/03; HBG 10/03; SLJ 5/03)

5931 Fox, Mem. *Night Noises* (PS–2). Illus. by Terry Denton. 1989, Harcourt $16.00 (0-15-200543-9); paper $4.95 (0-15-257421-2). 32pp. An old lady's dog becomes agitated at the commotion he hears outside while the woman sleeps, which turns out to be relatives arriving for a surprise ninetieth birthday party. (Rev: BL 11/15/89; HB 11–12/89*; SLJ 9/89*)

5932 Giff, Patricia Reilly. *Happy Birthday, Ronald Morgan!* (2–3). Illus. by Susanna Natti. 1988, Puffin paper $5.99 (0-14-050668-3). 32pp. The day goes from bad to worse for Ronald, but ends up delightfully with a surprise birthday party. (Rev: BL 10/15/86; SLJ 4/87)

5933 Graham, Bob. *Oscar's Half Birthday* (PS–K). Illus. 2005, Candlewick $16.99 (0-7636-2699-6). 32pp. A happy interracial family goes to the park to celebrate little Oscar's birthday. (Rev: BL 5/1/05)

5934 Griffith, Helen V. *How Many Candles?* (K–3). Illus. by Sonja Lamut. 1999, Greenwillow $16.00 (0-688-16258-4). 24pp. Different animals help celebrate Robbie's tenth birthday, although each realizes that its life cycle span differs from that of humans. (Rev: BL 10/15/99; HBG 3/00; SLJ 9/99)

5935 Hershenhorn, Esther. *There Goes Lowell's Party!* (K–3). Illus. by Jacqueline Rogers. 1998, Holiday House LB $15.95 (0-8234-1313-6). In this tale set in the Ozarks, Lowell is afraid that rain will spoil his birthday party. (Rev: BCCB 4/98; HBG 10/98; SLJ 3/98)

5936 Hest, Amy. *Nana's Birthday Party* (K–4). Illus. by Amy Schwartz. 1993, Morrow $15.95 (0-688-07497-9). 32pp. Maggie wants to write a story for her grandmother for her birthday, but she lacks the inspiration. (Rev: BL 8/93*)

5937 Hobbie, Holly. *Toot and Puddle: A Present for Toot* (PS–1). Illus. 1998, Little, Brown $12.95 (0-316-36556-4). 32pp. Puddle, a pig, is in a quandary about buying a birthday present for friend Toot, another pig. (Rev: BL 11/1/98; HBG 3/99; SLJ 10/98)

5938 Howe, James. *Creepy-Crawly Birthday* (PS–3). Illus. by Leslie Morrill. 1991, Morrow LB $13.88 (0-688-09688-3). 48pp. Toby's pet dog and cat have an unexpected surprise for him at his birthday party. (Rev: BL 11/15/91; SLJ 11/91)

5939 Hutchins, Pat. *Happy Birthday, Sam* (1–3). Illus. by author. 1978, Morrow paper $5.95 (0-688-10482-7). 32pp. Sam is disappointed on his birthday morning to discover that he hasn't grown at all.

5940 Hutchins, Pat. *It's My Birthday* (PS–2). 1999, Greenwillow LB $14.93 (0-688-09664-6). 32pp. Monster Billy acts so selfishly about his birthday presents that he finds it difficult to get anyone to play with him. (Rev: BL 6/1–15/99; HBG 10/99; SLJ 3/99)

5941 Kulling, Monica. *Edgar Badger's Balloon Day* (K–3). Illus. by Carol O'Malia. 1997, Mondo paper $4.50 (1-57255-220-4). 46pp. Edgar Badger is afraid that his friends have forgotten that his birthday is approaching. (Rev: SLJ 1/98)

5942 Lodge, Bernard. *Mouldylocks* (K–3). Illus. 1998, Houghton Mifflin $15.00 (0-395-90945-7). 32pp. Mouldylocks, a witch, attends her surprise birthday party, where she plays such games as Snakes and Ladders with real snakes and ladders. When things get out of hand, she has to use her new book of spells to turn her guests back into themselves. (Rev: BL 9/1/98; HBG 3/99; SLJ 10/98)

5943 Look, Lenore. *Henry's First-Moon Birthday* (PS–3). Illus. by Yumi Heo. 2001, Simon & Schuster $16.00 (0-689-82294-4). 40pp. Young Jen, a Chinese American girl, helps her grandmother in the preparation of her young brother's first-moon birthday party. (Rev: BCCB 3/01; BL 4/1/01*; HBG 10/01; SLJ 6/01*)

5944 Lopez, Loretta. *The Birthday Swap* (PS–3). Illus. 1997, Lee & Low $15.95 (1-880000-47-4). 32pp. A young Mexican American girl enjoys the annual reunion of family from both sides of the border, when everyone comes to celebrate her older sister's birthday. (Rev: BCCB 6/97; BL 5/1/97; SLJ 6/97)

5945 McCourt, Lisa, adapt. *Della Splatnuk, Birthday Girl* (K–3). Illus. by Pat G. Porter. Series: Chicken Soup for Little Souls. 1999, Health Communications $14.95 (1-55874-600-5). Carrie realizes how cruel her classmates are when she is the only one to attend Della's birthday party because the others think she is weird. (Rev: BL 5/1/99; HBG 10/99; SLJ 9/99)

5946 McLarey, Kristina Thermaenius, and Myra McLarey. *When You Take a Pig to a Party* (PS–3). Illus. by Marjory Wunsch. 2000, Orchard LB $16.99 (0-531-33257-8). 32pp. When Adelaide is invited to Ethan's birthday party she makes the mistake of bringing her pet pig, Sherman, along. (Rev: BL 4/15/00; HBG 10/00; SLJ 4/00)

5947 Moon, Nicola. *Happy Birthday, Amelia* (K–2). Illus. by Jenny Jones. 2000, Pavilion $17.95 (1-86205-208-5). 32pp. On her birthday, Amelia follows clues that take her around her farmyard home and eventually to the orchard where everyone is waiting for her party to begin. (Rev: BL 7/00)

5948 Mueller, Virginia. *Monster's Birthday Hiccups* (PS–K). Illus. by Lynn Munsinger. 1992, Whitman LB $13.95 (0-8075-5267-4). 24pp. Monster cures his hiccups at his birthday party by blowing out the candles on his cake and granting his own wish. (Rev: BL 1/15/92)

5949 Oram, Hiawyn. *Badger's Bring Something Party* (PS–2). Illus. by Susan Varley. 1995, Lothrop $15.00 (0-688-14082-3). 32pp. Mole feels out of place at Badger's birthday party because he didn't have a gift to bring. A prequel to *Badger's Parting Gifts* (1984). (Rev: BL 4/15/95; HB 5–6/95; SLJ 7/95)

5950 Pfister, Marcus. *Make a Wish, Honey Bear!* (PS–K). Illus. 1999, North-South LB $15.88 (0-7358-1244-6). 32pp. When it's time to blow out the candles on his birthday cake, Honey Bear doesn't know what to wish for, so everyone in the family offers a suggestion. (Rev: BL 11/1/99; HBG 3/00; SLJ 11/99)

5951 Polacco, Patricia. *Some Birthday!* (K–3). Illus. 1991, Simon & Schuster paper $16.00 (0-671-72750-8). 32pp. Patricia thinks everyone has forgotten about her sixth birthday, until the surprise comes in the evening. (Rev: BL 1/1/92*; SLJ 10/91)

5952 Pomerantz, Charlotte. *The Birthday Letters* (K–3). Illus. by JoAnn Adinolfi. 2000, Greenwillow LB $15.89 (0-688-16336-X). Tom decides to disinvite Emilia from his dog's birthday party when he learns she is going to bring her pet gerbils. (Rev: HBG 10/00; SLJ 6/00)

5953 Rose, Deborah Lee. *Birthday Zoo* (PS–2). Illus. by Lynn Munsinger. 2002, Whitman $15.95 (0-8075-0776-8). 32pp. A little boy is treated to a rollicking birthday party hosted by the animals at the zoo in this rhyming picture book. (Rev: BL 9/15/02; HB 11–12/02; HBG 3/03; SLJ 10/02)

5954 Roth, Susan L. *Happy Birthday Mr. Kang* (2–4). Illus. 2001, National Geographic $16.95 (0-7922-7723-6). 32pp. When Mr. Kang's grandson Sam asks if the old man's hua mei bird wants its freedom, Mr. Kang releases it with surprising results in this birthday story. (Rev: BL 1/1–15/01; HBG 10/01; SLJ 2/01)

5955 Scamell, Ragnhild. *Toby's Doll's House* (PS–3). Illus. by Adrian Reynolds. 1999, Levinson $14.95 (1-86233-026-3). Toby takes all the boxes in which his birthday gifts were packed and turns them into the doll's house that he really wanted. (Rev: SLJ 9/99)

5956 Segal, Lore. *Morris the Artist* (PS–2). Illus. by Boris Kulikov. 2003, Farrar $16.00 (0-374-35063-9). Morris, an aspiring artist, takes a gift of a paint set to Benjamin's birthday party but finds he cannot part with it and eventually opens it up himself. (Rev: HBG 4/04; SLJ 6/03)

5957 Shaw, Nancy. *Sheep in a Shop* (PS–1). Illus. by Margot Apple. 1991, Houghton Mifflin $14.00 (0-395-53681-2). 32pp. Five sheep are a little short of cash when they shop for a present for a friend. (Rev: HB 5–6/91*; SLJ 2/91)

5958 Soto, Gary. *Chato and the Party Animals* (PS–3). Illus. by Susan Guevara. 2000, Penguin Putnam $15.99 (0-399-23159-5). 32pp. Because he is from a pound, Novio Boy doesn't know his birthday, so Chato the Cat organizes a special surprise birthday party for him. (Rev: BL 8/00; HBG 3/01; SLJ 7/00)

5959 Spinelli, Eileen. *In My New Yellow Shirt* (PS). Illus. by Hideko Takahashi. 2001, Holt $15.95 (0-8050-6242-4). 32pp. A birthday boy sees lots of potential in his new yellow shirt, despite his friend's dismissal of the gift. (Rev: BCCB 9/01; BL 6/1–15/01; HBG 3/02; SLJ 8/01)

5960 Starr, Meg. *Alicia's Happy Day* (PS–1). Illus. by Ying-hwa Hu. 2003, Star Bright $15.95 (1-887724-85-6). 32pp. Alicia's birthday is a happy, special day thanks to her friends, neighbors, and family. (Rev: BL 2/1/03)

5961 Stevens, Jan R. *Carlos and the Carnival: Carlos y la Feria* (K–3). Illus. by Jeanne Arnold. 1999, Northland $15.95 (0-87358-733-2). 32pp. In this bilingual book, Carlos receives some money for his birthday but does not need his father's advice about spending it wisely. (Rev: BL 8/99; HBG 3/00; SLJ 7/99)

5962 Uff, Caroline. *Happy Birthday, Lulu!* (PS). Illus. 2000, Walker $14.95 (0-8027-8751-7). 24pp. Lulu celebrates her birthday in many ways, receiving cards, opening presents, getting a special phone call from Grandpa, and having a big party. (Rev: BL 12/1/00)

5963 Wallace, John. *Tiny Rabbit Goes to a Birthday Party* (PS–K). Illus. 2000, Holiday House $16.95 (0-8234-1489-2). 32pp. Tiny Rabbit is worried about going to his first birthday party but, when he has a good time, he starts to make plans for his own party. (Rev: BL 2/1/00; HBG 10/00; SLJ 4/00)

5964 Wallace, Nancy E. *Tell-A-Bunny* (PS–1). Illus. 2000, Winslow $15.95 (1-890817-29-5). 32pp. When bunnies phone each other about a surprise birthday party, the message gets garbled as it is passed from one bunny to another. (Rev: BL 5/15/00; HBG 10/00; SLJ 5/00)

5965 Wardlaw, Lee. *Bow-Wow Birthday* (PS–3). Illus. by Arden Johnson-Petrov. 1998, Boyds Mills $15.95 (1-56397-489-4). A humorous story about a group of children who hold a birthday party for an ancient dog who only wants to sleep in his favorite closet. (Rev: BCCB 4/98; BL 3/1/98; HBG 10/98; SLJ 5/98)

5966 Weninger, Brigitte. *Happy Birthday, Davy!* (PS–2). Trans. by Rosemary Lanning. Illus. by Eve Tharlet. 2000, North-South LB $15.88 (0-7358-1346-9). 32pp. Bunny Davy gets his birthday wish — having people pay attention to him — when his grandparents come to visit. (Rev: BL 12/15/00; HBG 3/01; SLJ 12/00)

5967 Whittington, Mary K. *The Patchwork Lady* (K–2). Illus. by Jane Dyer. 1991, Harcourt $13.95 (0-15-259580-5). A woman whose house and dress look like a patchwork quilt decides to hold a birthday party for herself. (Rev: SLJ 6/91)

5968 Wright, Betty Ren. *The Blizzard* (PS–2). Illus. by Ronald Himler. 2003, Holiday House $16.95 (0-8234-1656-9). It's Billy's birthday and a snowstorm means his cousins can't come to celebrate, but his disappointment disappears when a full-blown blizzard means his whole class must spend the night at his house. (Rev: BL 7/03*; HBG 4/04; SLJ 10/03)

CHRISTMAS

5969 Aliki. *Christmas Tree Memories* (PS–2). Illus. 1991, HarperCollins LB $14.89 (0-06-020008-1). 32pp. This is a remembrance of Christmases past and the activities associated with celebrations years ago. (Rev: BL 7/91; HB 11–12/91)

5970 Arnold, Katya. *The Adventures of Snowwoman* (PS–3). Illus. 1998, Holiday House $15.95 (0-8234-1390-X). 32pp. Children build Snowwoman to take a message to Santa to bring them a tree. (Rev: BL 12/1/98; HBG 3/99; SLJ 3/99)

5971 Auch, Mary Jane. *The Nutquacker* (K–3). Illus. 1999, Holiday House $16.95 (0-8234-1524-4).

32pp. Clara the duck wanders off to find something called "Christmas," which she hears is on its way, only to find that Christmas is a time for being with people who love you. (Rev: BL 11/1/99; HBG 3/00; SLJ 10/99)

5972 Augustin, Barbara. *Antonella and Her Santa Claus* (PS–1). Illus. by Gerhard Lahr. 2001, Kane $14.95 (1-929132-13-1). 40pp. An Italian girl's Christmas wish is granted when Hungarian children find the balloon she has sent to Santa. (Rev: BL 10/15/01; HBG 3/02; SLJ 10/01)

5973 Autry, Gene, and Oakley Haldeman. *Here Comes Santa Claus* (PS–1). Illus. by Bruce Whatley. 2002, HarperCollins LB $18.89 (0-06-028269-X). 32pp. The 1947 song coauthored by Gene Autry forms the basis of this picture book that follows parallel stories of Santa's preparations and a family readying for his arrival. (Rev: BL 10/1/02; HBG 3/03; SLJ 10/02)

5974 Barry, Robert. *Mr. Willowby's Christmas Tree* (PS–2). Illus. 2000, Doubleday $15.95 (0-385-32721-8). 32pp. A Christmas tree makes the rounds of seven different homes. In each case it is chopped down a little to fit the house, until the last part is so small that three little mice find it just right. (Rev: BL 9/1/00; HBG 10/01)

5975 Bauer, Marion Dane. *Christmas in the Forest* (2–3). Illus. 1998, Holiday House $15.95 (0-8234-1371-3). 48pp. The spirit of Christmas pervades the animal kingdom and makes friends out of traditional enemies in this beginning reader. (Rev: BL 12/1/98; HBG 3/99; SLJ 10/98)

5976 Baumgart, Klaus. *Laura's Christmas Star* (1–3). Trans. from German by Judy Waite. Illus. by author. 1999, Little Tiger $16.95 (1-888444-59-2). Facing a treeless Christmas, young Laura finds a small, raggedy tree in the street and brings it home. (Rev: HBG 3/00; SLJ 10/99)

5977 Beck, Andrea. *Elliot's Christmas Surprise* (PS–1). Illus. by author. Series: An Elliot Moose Story. 2003, Kids Can $12.95 (1-55337-474-6); paper $5.95 (1-55337-661-7). Elliot, the stuffed moose, scrambles to get Christmas gifts for all his friends after he receives a big red box. (Rev: HBG 4/04; SLJ 10/03)

5978 Becker, Bonny. *The Christmas Crocodile* (PS–1). Illus. by David Small. 1998, Simon & Schuster $16.00 (0-689-81503-4). 40pp. Alice Jayne finds a crocodile under the Christmas tree. He destroys the family's Christmas by eating all the presents and ruining the living room, but order is restored when they take him to a petting zoo. (Rev: BL 9/1/98; HBG 3/99; SLJ 10/98)

5979 Berger, Barbara Helen. *The Donkey's Dream* (K–3). Illus. by author. 1985, Penguin Putnam $16.95 (0-399-21233-7). 32pp. The story of a donkey who at Christmas time carried "a lady full of heaven" to a stable. (Rev: HB 11–12/85; SLJ 10/85)

5980 Bodkin, Odds. *The Christmas Cobwebs* (PS–3). Illus. by Terry Widener. 2001, Harcourt $16.00 (0-15-201459-4). 32pp. A poor family must sell the treasured Christmas ornaments brought from Germany, but spiders spin beautiful webs to take their place on the tree. (Rev: BCCB 11/01; BL 9/15/01; HBG 3/02; SLJ 10/01)

5981 Bond, Michael. *Paddington Bear and the Christmas Surprise* (K–2). Illus. by R. W. Alley. 1997, HarperCollins $11.95 (0-694-00897-4). Paddington's visit with his family to a department store at Christmas is not the joyful occasion he had hoped for. (Rev: BL 9/15/97; SLJ 10/97)

5982 Borden, Louise. *Just in Time for Christmas* (1–4). Illus. by Ted Lewin. 1994, Scholastic $14.95 (0-590-45355-6). 32pp. Christmas time for Will in Kentucky is a happy time except that he is fearful that Great Gram is becoming too forgetful. (Rev: BL 8/94)

5983 Boynton, Sandra. *Bob: And 6 More Christmas Stories* (PS–K). Illus. by author. 1999, Simon & Schuster $7.99 (0-689-82568-4). A humorous book that consists of seven double-page stories about animals celebrating Christmas. (Rev: SLJ 10/99)

5984 Brett, Jan. *Christmas Trolls* (K–3). Illus. 1993, Penguin Putnam LB $16.99 (0-399-22507-2). 32pp. Treva discovers that the mysterious disappearance of objects from her house is the work of trolls. (Rev: BL 7/93)

5985 Brett, Jan. *The Wild Christmas Reindeer* (K–2). Illus. 1990, Penguin Putnam $16.99 (0-399-22192-1). 32pp. Santa has a whole new crew of wild reindeer that might not want to work on Christmas Eve. (Rev: BL 9/15/90*)

5986 Brown, Elizabeth Ferguson. *Coal Country Christmas* (PS–2). Illus. by Harvey Stevenson. 2003, Boyds Mills $15.95 (1-59078-020-5). A bittersweet Christmas story about a young girl visiting her grandmother's home in Pennsylvania's depressed coal country. (Rev: HBG 4/04; SLJ 10/03)

5987 Brown, Marc. *Arthur's Christmas* (K–2). Illus. by author. 1984, Little, Brown $15.95 (0-316-11180-5). Arthur, an anteater, has a series of Christmas adventures.

5988 Buck, Nola. *Santa's Short Suit Shrunk: And Other Christmas Tongue Twisters* (1–3). Illus. by Sue Truesdell. Series: I Can Read. 1997, HarperCollins LB $14.89 (0-06-026663-5). 32pp. A grab bag of tongue twisters about Christmas topics like shopping, feasting, and opening presents. (Rev: BL 9/15/97; HB 11–12/97; HBG 3/98; SLJ 10/97)

5989 Bunting, Eve. *Christmas Cricket* (PS–2). Illus. by Timothy Bush. 2002, Clarion $15.00 (0-618-06554-7). 32pp. A cricket perched among the branches of a Christmas tree is heartened to hear his chirping described as an angel's song. (Rev: BL 9/15/02; HBG 3/03; SLJ 10/02)

5990 Bunting, Eve. *The Day Before Christmas* (1–3). Illus. by Beth Peck. 1992, Houghton Mifflin $16.00 (0-89919-866-X). 32pp. Allie's grandfather takes her to see The Nutcracker, just as he had taken her deceased mother. (Rev: BL 11/1/92; HB 11–12/92)

5991 Bunting, Eve. *December* (K–3). Illus. by David Diaz. 1997, Harcourt $16.00 (0-15-201434-9). 40pp. A miracle occurs when a homeless mother and her son allow an old lady to sleep in their cardboard home at Christmas time. (Rev: BL 9/1/97*; HBG 3/98; SLJ 10/97*)

5992 Bunting, Eve. *Night Tree* (PS–3). Illus. by Ted Rand. 1991, Harcourt $13.95 (0-15-257425-5). 32pp. On the night before Christmas, a family drives into the woods and decorates a tree. (Rev: BCCB 10/91; BL 9/15/91; HB 11–12/91)

5993 Bunting, Eve. *We Were There: A Nativity Story* (PS–3). Illus. by Wendell Minor. 2001, Clarion $16.00 (0-395-82265-3). 32pp. A variety of creatures including the rat, spider, toad, and snake claim they too were present at Jesus' birth. (Rev: BL 9/1/01; HBG 3/02; SLJ 10/01)

5994 Byrd, Robert. *Saint Francis and the Christmas Donkey* (K–4). Illus. 2000, Dutton $15.99 (0-525-46480-8). 40pp. Saint Francis tells a donkey two stories to make him feel better about his lot in life; one about the donkey that carried Mary to Bethlehem. (Rev: BCCB 11/00; BL 9/1/00*; HB 11–12/00; HBG 3/01)

5995 Calhoun, Mary. *A Shepherd's Gift* (PS–2). Illus. by Raul Colon. 2001, HarperCollins LB $15.89 (0-688-15177-9). 32pp. An orphan boy and a lamb make a visit to a stable, where they find baby Jesus and his family. (Rev: BCCB 11/01; BL 9/1/01; HBG 3/02; SLJ 10/01)

5996 Carle, Eric. *Dream Snow* (PS–1). Illus. 2000, Philomel $21.99 (0-399-23579-5). 32pp. In this counting book set at Christmastime, a farmer dreams that a gentle snow covers all his animals. (Rev: BCCB 10/00; BL 9/1/00; HBG 3/01)

5997 Carlson, Lori M. *Hurray for Three Kings' Day!* (PS–3). Illus. by Ed Martinez. 1999, Morrow LB $15.93 (0-688-16240-1). 32pp. The traditional Latin American holiday is the setting for this story about Anita and her older brothers, who dress as the Christmas kings and carry make-believe gifts around the town. (Rev: BL 9/1/99; HBG 3/00; SLJ 10/99)

5998 Carlson, Nancy. *Harriet and George's Christmas Treat* (PS–2). Illus. 2001, Carolrhoda $15.95 (1-57505-506-6). 32pp. Harriet and George try unsuccessfully to avoid eating Mrs. Hoozit's Christmas fruitcake. (Rev: BL 10/1/01; HBG 3/02; SLJ 10/01)

5999 Catalano, Dominic. *Santa and the Three Bears* (PS–K). Illus. 2000, Boyds Mills $15.95 (1-56397-864-4). 32pp. Mama, Papa, and Baby Bear seek shelter in Santa's house while he is out delivering gifts and the three intruders wreak mayhem before falling asleep. (Rev: BL 9/1/00; HBG 3/01)

6000 Chmielarz, Sharon. *Down at Angel's* (PS–3). Illus. by Jill Kastner. 1994, Ticknor $14.95 (0-395-65993-0). 32pp. At Christmas time, two children and their mother deliver a box of goodies to their friend, a woodcarver named Angel. (Rev: BCCB 12/94; BL 8/94; HB 11–12/94)

6001 Chorao, Kay. *The Christmas Story* (PS–3). Illus. 1996, Holiday House LB $16.95 (0-8234-1251-2). 28pp. The biblical account of Christmas from the King James version is illustrated in Renaissance-like paintings. (Rev: BL 9/1/96)

6002 Clements, Andrew. *Bright Christmas: An Angel Remembers* (PS–3). Illus. by Kate Kiesler. 1996, Clarion $16.00 (0-395-72096-6). 30pp. The Christmas story as seen through the eyes of an angel. (Rev: BCCB 11/96; BL 9/1/96; SLJ 4/04)

6003 Climo, Shirley. *The Cobweb Christmas* (K–3). Illus. by Joe Lasker. 1982, HarperCollins LB $15.89 (0-690-04216-7); paper $5.95 (0-06-443110-X). 32pp. Spiders turn Tante's Christmas tree into a glistening thing of beauty.

6004 Coffey, Tim. *Christmas at the Top of the World* (PS). Illus. by author. 2003, Whitman LB $15.95 (0-8075-5762-5). Little Reindeer, joined by his mother and other animals, travels to the North Pole to find his father and see the wonders "at the top of the world." (Rev: HBG 4/04; SLJ 10/03)

6005 Conrad, Pam. *The Tub People's Christmas* (PS–K). Illus. by Richard Egielski. 1999, HarperCollins LB $15.89 (0-06-026029-7). 32pp. Small wooden toys named the Tub People are confused when they become ornaments on a Christmas tree. (Rev: BL 9/1/99; HBG 3/00; SLJ 10/99)

6006 Corrin, Sara, and Stephen Corrin, eds. *Round the Christmas Tree* (K–4). Illus. by Jill Bennett. 1983, Puffin paper $3.95 (0-317-62263-3). Sixteen stories, many of them fairy tales, about Christmas.

6007 Currey, Anna. *Truffle's Christmas* (PS–1). Illus. 2000, Orchard $15.95 (0-531-30266-0). 32pp. Truffle, a mouse, is sorry he asked Santa for a hula hoop for Christmas because he knows the family needs a new blanket more. (Rev: BL 9/15/00; HBG 3/01)

6008 Czernecki, Stefan, and Timothy Rhodes. *Pancho's Pinata* (PS–2). Illus. by Stefan Czernecki. 1992, Hyperion $14.95 (1-562-82277-2); paper $4.95 (0-786-81007-6). 40pp. The fanciful story of how the first pinata was invented, in the village of San Miguel. (Rev: BL 11/1/92) [398.2]

6009 D'Allance, Mireille. *Bear's Christmas Star* (PS–1). Illus. 2000, Simon & Schuster $12.95 (0-684-83826-3). 28pp. Bear wants to help trim the Christmas tree but Papa says he is just too small; however, at the end, it takes both of them to put the star on the top of the tree. (Rev: BL 11/1/00)

6010 De Groat, Diane. *Jingle Bells, Homework Smells* (K–2). Illus. 2000, HarperCollins LB $15.99 (0-688-17544-9). 32pp. Around the Christmas holiday season, Gilbert the possum puts off doing his school assignment until it is too late. (Rev: BL 9/1/00; HBG 3/01)

6011 dePaola, Tomie, ed. *The Clown of God* (K–3). Illus. by Tomie dePaola. 1978, Harcourt $16.00 (0-15-219175-5); paper $7.00 (0-15-618192-4). 45pp. On Christmas Eve, a juggler gives to a statue of Christ his only possession, the gift of his art.

6012 dePaola, Tomie. *Country Angel Christmas* (PS–1). Illus. 1995, Penguin Putnam $16.95 (0-399-22817-9). 32pp. Three little angels think they have been forgotten in the preparations for Christmas, but St. Nicholas comes to the rescue. (Rev: BCCB 11/95; BL 9/15/95)

6013 dePaola, Tomie. *An Early American Christmas* (K–2). Illus. by author. 1987, Holiday House $16.95 (0-8234-0617-2); paper $6.95 (0-8234-0979-1). 32pp. What it might have been like for a German family of long ago to move to a New England village where most of the people did not celebrate Christmas. (Rev: BCCB 11/87; BL 9/1/87)

6014 dePaola, Tomie, reteller. *The Legend of Old Befana* (PS–3). Illus. by Tomie dePaola. 1980, Harcourt $16.00 (0-15-243816-5); paper $6.00 (0-15-243817-3). 32pp. The legend of the old lady who is still searching for the Christ child.

6015 dePaola, Tomie. *Merry Christmas, Strega Nona* (PS–3). Illus. by author. 1986, Harcourt $16.00 (0-15-253183-1); paper $7.00 (0-15-253184-X). 32pp. Strega Nona is worried because her helper Big Anthony doesn't seem to be helping her to prepare for Christmas at all. (Rev: BL 11/1/86; HB 11–12/86)

6016 dePaola, Tomie. *The Night of Las Posadas* (K–4). Illus. 1999, Penguin Putnam $15.99 (0-399-23400-4). 32pp. During the festival of Las Posadas, a Spanish custom that celebrates the search for shelter by Joseph and Mary, a miracle occurs in this fantasy set in Santa Fe, New Mexico. (Rev: BL 9/1/99; HBG 3/00; SLJ 10/99)

6017 Donnelly, Liza. *Dinosaurs' Christmas* (PS–2). Illus. 1994, Scholastic paper $2.99 (0-590-44798-X). 32pp. Rex and his dog Bones travel by dinosaur to the North Pole just before Christmas. (Rev: BL 7/91)

6018 Dooley, Norah. *Everybody Serves Soup* (2–4). Illus. by Peter J. Thornton. 2000, Carolrhoda $15.95 (1-57505-422-1). 40pp. When Carrie tastes her neighbors' soups, she gets an idea for a unique Christmas present for her mother. (Rev: BL 1/1–15/01; HBG 3/01)

6019 Dunbar, Joyce. *This Is the Star* (K–3). Illus. by Gary Blythe. 1996, Harcourt $16.00 (0-15-200851-9). 36pp. A cumulative tale using the story of the Nativity as a framework. (Rev: BL 9/1/96; HBG 4/04; SLJ 4/04)

6020 Dunrea, Olivier. *Bear Noel* (PS–2). Illus. 2000, Farrar $16.00 (0-374-39990-5). 32pp. On Christmas Eve, Hare, Fox, Wolf, and other animals await the arrival of Bear Noel and the wonderful things he will bring. (Rev: BCCB 11/00; BL 9/1/00; HBG 3/01)

6021 Evans, Richard Paul. *The Light of Christmas* (K–2). Illus. by Daniel Craig. 2002, Simon & Schuster $16.95 (0-689-83468-3). 32pp. A boy called Alexander does a good deed and is rewarded with the special right to light the flame on Christmas Eve. (Rev: BL 10/1/02; HBG 3/03; SLJ 10/02)

6022 Facklam, Margery. *Only a Star* (K–3). Illus. by Nancy Carpenter. 1996, Eerdmans $15.00 (0-8028-5122-3). 32pp. The Christmas star magically transforms all creatures and objects that it illuminates. (Rev: BL 10/15/96; SLJ 10/96*)

6023 Falwell, Cathryn. *Christmas for 10* (PS–K). Illus. 1998, Clarion $15.00 (0-395-85581-0). 32pp. A Christmas counting book that shows an African American family engaged in a number of holiday activities. (Rev: BL 9/1/98; HBG 3/99; SLJ 10/98)

6024 Faulkner, Keith. *Santa's Surprise: A Pop-up Storybook* (PS–K). Illus. by Jonathan Lambert. 2003, Dial $12.99 (0-8037-2903-0). In this beautifully illustrated pop-up book, Santa searches desperately for his red-nosed reindeer but is hampered by his failing vision. (Rev: SLJ 10/03)

6025 Fearnley, Jan. *Little Robin's Christmas* (K–2). Illus. 1998, Little Tiger $14.95 (1-888444-40-1). 32pp. When Little Robin gives away all of his vests to shivering animals, Santa Claus gives him a new red one for Christmas and also gives him a new name, Little Robin Redbreast. (Rev: BL 9/15/98; HBG 3/99; SLJ 10/98)

6026 Fearrington, Ann. *Christmas Lights* (PS–2). Illus. 1996, Houghton Mifflin $15.95 (0-395-71036-7). 32pp. On Christmas night, a family drives around the city to see all the Christmas lights. (Rev: BL 9/1/96; SLJ 4/04)

6027 Foreman, Michael. *Cat in the Manger* (PS–3). Illus. 2001, Holt $16.95 (0-8050-6677-2). 24pp. A cat is displaced from his bed to make room for a baby in the manger. (Rev: BCCB 11/01; BL 9/15/01; HBG 3/02; SLJ 10/01)

6028 Fox, Mem. *Wombat Divine* (PS–3). Illus. by Kerry Argent. 1996, Harcourt $15.00 (0-15-201416-0). 32pp. A sleepy wombat gets to play baby Jesus in the Christmas Nativity play. (Rev: BL 10/15/96; SLJ 10/96*)

6029 Gackenbach, Dick. *Claude the Dog: A Christmas Story* (K–3). Illus. by author. 1984, Houghton Mifflin paper $5.95 (0-89919-124-X). 32pp. Claude gives away all his presents but gets an even better one from his master. A related title is: *What's Claude Doing?* (1984).

6030 Gammell, Stephen. *Wake Up, Bear . . . It's Christmas!* (PS–1). Illus. by author. 1981, Morrow paper $4.95 (0-688-09934-3). 32pp. A bear is afraid he will sleep through Christmas.

6031 Gantos, Jack. *Rotten Ralph's Rotten Christmas* (K–2). Illus. by Nicole Rubel. 1984, Houghton Mifflin $15.00 (0-395-35380-7); paper $4.95 (0-395-45685-1). 32pp. This miserable cat is determined that Sarah's Christmas will also be miserable.

6032 Garland, Michael. *Christmas Magic* (PS–3). Illus. 2001, Dutton $16.99 (0-525-46797-1). 32pp. Arresting artwork shows how Emily's Christmas Eve was a night of real enchantment. (Rev: BCCB 11/01; BL 9/1/01; HBG 3/02; SLJ 10/01)

6033 Gibbons, Gail. *Santa Who?* (K–4). Illus. 1999, Morrow LB $15.93 (0-688-15529-4). 32pp. This book traces the legend of Santa Claus — from Saint Nicholas in Europe, the bringing of Sinter Cleas to America by the Dutch, and its evolution in modern times. (Rev: BCCB 10/99; BL 9/1/99; HBG 3/00; SLJ 10/99)

6034 Gillmor, Don. *The Christmas Orange* (K–2). Illus. by Marie-Louise Gay. 1999, Stoddart $15.95 (0-7737-3100-8). 32pp. When Anton receives only an orange for Christmas, he sues Santa for breach of promise. (Rev: BL 1/1–15/00)

6035 Gliori, Debi. *What Can I Give Him?* (PS–3). Illus. 1998, Holiday House $15.95 (0-8234-1392-6). 32pp. Using double-page spreads — one depicting a contemporary girl with her loving family at Christmastime and the other a poor servant girl in the stable where Jesus was born — this book explores the

288

question of what one should give as a loving present. (Rev: BL 9/1/98; HBG 3/99; SLJ 10/98)

6036 Godwin, Laura. *Happy Christmas, Honey!* (K–1). Illus. by Jane Chapman. 2002, Simon & Schuster $14.95 (0-689-84714-9). 32pp. Honey the kitten makes a mess of all the Christmas preparations, so Happy the dog assigns her to help him wait for Santa to arrive in this beginning reader. (Rev: BL 11/1/02; HBG 3/03; SLJ 10/02)

6037 Greenfield, Monica. *Waiting for Christmas* (PS–1). Illus. by Jan S. Gilchrist. 1996, Scholastic $15.95 (0-590-52700-2). 32pp. An African American brother and sister look forward to the excitement of Christmas. (Rev: BL 9/1/96)

6038 Gutman, Anne. *Gaspard and Lisa's Christmas Surprise* (PS–K). Illus. by Georg Hallensleben. Series: The Misadventures of Gaspard and Lisa. 2002, Knopf $9.95 (0-375-82229-1). Gaspard and Lisa, young animals, set out to make a raincoat for their teacher. (Rev: HBG 3/03; SLJ 10/02)

6039 Hague, Michael. *The Perfect Present* (PS–1). Illus. 1996, Morrow $16.00 (0-688-10880-6). 48pp. Jack, a rabbit, goes to Big Bear's Toy Shoppe to find a Christmas present for his girlfriend. (Rev: BL 9/1/96; SLJ 4/04)

6040 Hall, Katy, and Lisa Eisenberg. *Ho Ho Ho, Ha Ha Ha: Holly-arious Christmas Knock-Knock Jokes* (1–3). Illus. by Stephen Carpenter. 2001, HarperCollins paper $6.95 (0-694-01362-5). A collection of Christmas jokes with punch lines under the flaps. (Rev: SLJ 10/01)

6041 Harvey, Brett. *My Prairie Christmas* (1–3). Illus. by Deborah Kogan Ray. 1990, Holiday House LB $16.95 (0-8234-0827-2). 32pp. Young Eleanor wonders what sort of Christmas her pioneering family can have in their new Dakota home. (Rev: BCCB 11/90; BL 10/1/90)

6042 Hayes, Sarah. *Happy Christmas, Gemma* (PS–1). Illus. by Jan Ormerod. 1986, Lothrop $15.00 (0-688-06508-2). 32pp. Christmas is warmly celebrated by this Jamaican immigrant family. (Rev: BCCB 11/86; BL 11/15/86; HB 11–12/86)

6043 Hayles, Marsha. *The Feathered Crown* (K–2). Illus. by Bernadette Pons. 2002, Holt $16.95 (0-8050-6421-4). 32pp. In this Nativity story told in rhyming text, mother birds fly from near and far to feather baby Jesus' "nest." (Rev: BL 9/1/02; HBG 3/03; SLJ 10/02)

6044 Heath, Amy. *Sofie's Role* (PS–2). Illus. 1992, Macmillan LB $14.95 (0-02-743505-9). 36pp. On the day before Christmas, a young girl helps her parents in their bakery. (Rev: BCCB 12/92; BL 7/92)

6045 Herman, John. *One Winter's Night* (K–2). Illus. by Leo Dillon and Diane Dillon. 2003, Philomel $16.99 (0-399-23418-7). A cow about to give birth finds shelter in the stable where Mary and Joseph are expecting their baby. (Rev: HBG 4/04; SLJ 10/03)

6046 High, Linda O. *A Christmas Star* (K–3). Illus. by Ronald Himler. 1997, Holiday House LB $15.95 (0-8234-1301-2). 32pp. Stolen gifts are miraculously returned to a church in this Christmas tale set dur-

ing the Depression. (Rev: BL 9/1/97; HBG 3/98; SLJ 10/97)

6047 High, Linda Oatman. *The Last Chimney of Christmas Eve* (PS–2). Illus. by Kestutis Kasparavicius. 2001, Boyds Mills $15.95 (1-56397-804-0). 32pp. Nicholas, a chimney sweep, repays a kind stranger by growing up to be Santa Claus. (Rev: BL 9/15/01; HBG 3/02; SLJ 10/01)

6048 Hoban, Lillian. *Arthur's Christmas Cookies* (1–2). Illus. by author. 1972, HarperCollins LB $15.89 (0-06-022368-5); paper $3.95 (0-06-444055-9). 64pp. What can Arthur give his parents for Christmas? Christmas cookies such as he learned to bake in Cub Scouts are the answer, but a hilarious mix-up occurs when salt is used instead of sugar.

6049 Hodges, Margaret. *Silent Night: The Song and Its Story* (PS–3). Illus. by Tim Ladwig. 1997, Eerdmans $17.00 (0-8028-5138-X). 32pp. A dramatic retelling of the 1818 creation of this much-loved Christmas carol. (Rev: BL 9/1/97; HBG 3/98; SLJ 10/97)

6050 Hooks, William H. *The Legend of the Christmas Rose* (K–4). Illus. by Richard A. Williams. 1999, HarperCollins LB $14.89 (0-06-027103-5). 32pp. Dorothy has no presents to offer the infant Jesus, but an angel provides her with the flower now known as the Christmas Rose. (Rev: BL 9/1/99; HBG 3/00)

6051 Hooper, Maureen Brett. *Silent Night: A Christmas Carol Is Born* (1–3). Illus. by Kasi Kubiak. 2001, Boyds Mills $15.95 (1-56397-782-6). 32pp. The fictionalized story behind the carol "Silent Night." (Rev: BL 9/15/01; HBG 3/02; SLJ 10/01)

6052 Horn, Sandra Ann. *Babushka* (K–3). Illus. by Sophie Fatus. 2002, Barefoot $16.99 (1-84148-353-2). 32pp. In this version of a Russian tale, Babushka travels to visit the newly born Christ child, but gives away the gifts she brought to needy people along the way. (Rev: BL 12/15/02; HBG 3/03; SLJ 10/02)

6053 Howard, Ellen. *The Log Cabin Christmas* (K–3). Illus. by Ronald Himler. 2000, Holiday House $16.95 (0-8234-1381-0). 32pp. Set in Michigan during pioneer times, Elvirey and her family are afraid there will be no Christmas now that Mam's dead, but the young girl decides she can save the day. (Rev: BCCB 11/00; BL 11/15/00; HBG 3/01)

6054 Hudson, Cheryl W. *Hold Christmas in Your Heart: African-American Songs, Poems, and Stories for the Holidays* (K–2). Illus. 1995, Scholastic $10.95 (0-590-48024-3). 32pp. Poems, stories, and songs from African American authors are found in this fine anthology. (Rev: BL 9/15/95)

6055 Hughes, Langston. *Carol of the Brown King* (PS–3). Illus. by Ashley Bryan. 1998, Simon & Schuster $16.00 (0-689-81877-7). 32pp. A colorful picture book that presents six short poems about Christmas — five by Langston Hughes plus one poem he translated from a Puerto Rican Christmas card. (Rev: BL 9/1/98; HB 9–10/98; HBG 3/99; SLJ 10/98) [811]

6056 Hurd, Thacher. *Santa Mouse and the Ratdeer* (PS–1). Illus. 1998, HarperCollins $14.95 (0-06-027694-0). 40pp. Santa Mouse has a bad day when he can't find his clothes and his sleigh crashes, but little Rosie Mouse comes to the rescue. (Rev: BL 11/1/98; HBG 10/99; SLJ 10/98)

6057 Inkpen, Deborah. *Harriet and the Little Fat Fairy* (PS–1). Illus. by author. 2002, Barron's $11.95 (0-7641-5562-8). Emily's hamster disappears inside the Christmas tree, but Santa responds to Emily's request for help. (Rev: HBG 3/03; SLJ 10/02)

6058 Jeffs, Stephanie. *Christopher Bear's First Christmas* (PS–K). Illus. by Jacqui Thomas. Series: Christopher Bear. 2002, Augsburg $5.99 (0-8066-4349-8). 29pp. Joe and his bear participate in the preschool's presentation of the first Christmas. (Rev: SLJ 10/02)

6059 Jimenez, Francisco. *The Christmas Gift: El regalo de Navidad* (K–4). Illus. by Claire B. Cotts. 2000, Houghton Mifflin $15.00 (0-395-92869-9). 32pp. In this bilingual book, Panchito is disappointed because there is no money to buy him the red ball he wants for Christmas. (Rev: BCCB 12/00; BL 9/1/00; HBG 3/01)

6060 Johnston, Tony. *A Kenya Christmas* (K–2). Illus. by Leonard Jenkins. 2003, Holiday House $16.95 (0-8234-1623-2). A Kenya man tells his grandchilden about a wondrous Christmas from his past, involving snow made from chicken feathers and a Santa carried on an elephant. (Rev: HBG 4/04; SLJ 10/03)

6061 Joosse, Barbara M. *A Houseful of Christmas* (PS–2). Illus. by Betsy Lewin. 2001, Holt $14.95 (0-8050-6391-9). 32pp. Granny's pets must adapt when Christmas comes and her house fills up with relatives. (Rev: BL 10/1/01; HBG 3/02; SLJ 10/01)

6062 Joyce, William. *Snowie Rolie* (PS–2). Illus. 2000, HarperCollins $15.95 (0-06-029285-7). 40pp. When the snowman Rolie the robot builds begins to melt, he whisks it off to leave it in safety with Santa Claus. (Rev: BL 9/1/00; HBG 10/01)

6063 Kasparavicius, Kestutis. *The Bear Family's World Tour Christmas* (K–2). Illus. by author. 2002, Abrams $14.95 (0-8109-0573-6). The Bear Family sets off by hot-air balloon to visit relatives around the world. (Rev: HBG 3/03; SLJ 10/02)

6064 Kastner, Jill. *Merry Christmas, Princess Dinosaur!* (PS). Illus. 2002, HarperCollins LB $17.89 (0-06-000472-X). 32pp. Princess Dinosaur is so excited by the prospect of Santa's visit that she falls asleep in the Christmas tree. (Rev: BL 9/1/02; HBG 3/03; SLJ 10/02)

6065 Katz, Karen. *Counting Christmas* (PS). Illus. by author. 2003, Simon & Schuster $14.95 (0-689-84925-7). Counting from 10 down to one, this holiday book features double-page spreads full of Christmas details. (Rev: HBG 4/04; SLJ 10/03)

6066 Kennedy, Pamela. *A Christmas Carol* (K–3). Illus. by Carol Heyer. 1995, Ideals $14.95 (1-57102-047-0). 32pp. With vibrant paintings and a simple text, the classic story is retold for a young audience. (Rev: BL 11/15/95)

6067 Knowlton, Laurie L. *The Nativity: Mary Remembers* (K–3). Illus. by Kasi Kubiak. 1998, Boyds Mills $14.95 (1-56397-714-1). 32pp. The story of the Nativity is retold through the eyes of Mary, who wonders how she could have been chosen to bear the child who will be the Messiah. (Rev: BCCB 11/98; BL 9/15/98; HBG 10/99; SLJ 10/98)

6068 Kroeber, Theodora. *A Green Christmas* (K–3). Illus. by John Larrecq. 1967, Houghton Mifflin $6.95 (0-87466-047-5). Children new to California discover that Santa Claus will visit places without snow.

6069 Krupinski, Loretta. *Christmas in the City* (PS–2). Illus. 2002, Hyperion $15.99 (0-7868-0834-9). 40pp. This beautifully illustrated book tells the tale of Mr. and Mrs. Mouse and their Christmas trip to New York during which they explore the city and Mrs. Mouse gives birth in a manger. (Rev: BL 9/15/02; HBG 3/03; SLJ 10/02)

6070 Kvasnosky, Laura McGee. *Zelda and Ivy One Christmas* (K–3). Illus. 2000, Candlewick $15.99 (0-7636-1000-3). 48pp. The fox sisters and their recently widowed neighbor prepare for Christmas by baking gingerbread cookies and looking through catalogs for presents. (Rev: BCCB 12/00; BL 11/15/00; HB 11–12/00; HBG 3/01)

6071 Landa, Norbert. *Little Bear's Christmas* (PS–K). Illus. by Marlis Scharff-Kniemeyer. 1999, Little Tiger $14.95 (1-888444-60-6). 32pp. Little Bear sets the alarm clock so he will not hibernate through Christmas and miss seeing Santa Claus. (Rev: BL 10/1/99; HBG 3/00; SLJ 10/99)

6072 Leeson, Christine. *The Magic of Christmas* (PS–3). Illus. by Gaby Hansen. 2001, ME Media $14.95 (1-58925-011-7). 30pp. In this charming picture book, Molly Mouse and her brothers and sisters decorate a Christmas tree with help from forest friends usually considered enemies. (Rev: BL 9/15/01; SLJ 10/01)

6073 Lewis, J. Patrick. *The Snowflake Sisters* (PS–2). Illus. by Lisa Desimini. 2003, Simon & Schuster $16.95 (0-689-85029-8). Crystal and Ivory, two snowflake siblings, find themselves in New York and settle on a snowman in Central Park in this Christmas-related story with wonderful collage illustrations. (Rev: HBG 4/04; SLJ 10/03)

6074 Lobato, Arcadio. *The Secret of the North Pole* (PS–K). Illus. by author. 2002, McGraw-Hill $15.00 (1-56189-309-9). A polar bear discovers how Santa manages to deliver all the presents on Christmas Eve. (Rev: HBG 3/03; SLJ 10/02)

6075 McCaughrean, Geraldine. *How the Reindeer Got Their Antlers* (1–3). Illus. by Heather Holland. 2000, Holiday House $16.95 (0-8234-1562-7). 32pp. The reindeer is ashamed of its twisted antlers, until Santa uses them to save the day when his sleigh slips on ice. (Rev: BL 9/1/00; HBG 3/01)

6076 McDonald, Megan. *Tundra Mouse: A Storyknife Tale* (PS–2). Illus. by S. D. Schindler. 1997, Orchard LB $16.99 (0-531-33047-8). 32pp. Tundra Mouse and House Mouse think they are doing people a favor when they tidy up by stripping a Christmas tree of its ornaments, little knowing it's the night before Christmas. (Rev: BL 1/1–15/98; HBG 3/98; SLJ 10/97)

6077 McGovern, Ann. *The Lady in the Box* (K–3). Illus. by Marni Backer. 1997, Turtle $14.95 (1-890515-01-9). 32pp. At Christmas time, two youngsters help a homeless woman who is living over a hot-air vent. (Rev: BL 9/1/97; SLJ 10/97)

6078 McKay, Hilary. *Was That Christmas?* (PS–2). Illus. by Amanda Harvey. 2002, Simon & Schuster $16.00 (0-689-84765-3). 32pp. Bella is crushed when Santa's visit to her preschool doesn't live up to her expectations, but all is well come Christmas morning. (Rev: BCCB 11/02; BL 9/1/02; HB 11–12/02*; HBG 3/03; SLJ 10/02)

6079 McPhail, David. *Henry Bear's Christmas* (K–2). Illus. by author. 2003, Simon & Schuster $16.95 (0-689-82198-0). 40pp. Despite unwise expenditures on raffle tickets, Henry Bear and Stanley, his raccoon friend, have a happy Christmas and a beautifully decorated, albeit puny, tree. (Rev: HBG 4/04; SLJ 10/03)

6080 McQuade, Jacqueline. *Christmas with Teddy Bear* (PS–K). Illus. 1996, Dial $13.99 (0-8037-2075-0). 32pp. Christmas traditions like carol singing are introduced through the activities of a teddy bear. (Rev: BL 9/1/96)

6081 Manushkin, Fran. *The Perfect Christmas Picture* (PS–3). Illus. by Karen Ann Weinhaus. 1980, HarperCollins $11.95 (0-06-024068-7). 64pp. An easily read story of Mr. Green, who wants to photograph his family for a Christmas picture.

6082 Marzollo, Jean. *I Spy Christmas: A Book of Picture Riddles* (PS–3). Illus. by Walter Wick. 1992, Scholastic $12.95 (0-590-45846-9). 40pp. Full-color photos illustrate 13 scenes of Christmas. (Rev: BCCB 11/92; BL 11/1/92) [793.73]

6083 Mathers, Petra. *Herbie's Secret Santa* (PS–2). Illus. Series: Lottie's World. 2002, Simon & Schuster $15.95 (0-689-83550-7). 32pp. Herbie the duck feels dreadful about stealing a Christmas cookie, so his friend Lottie, a hen, helps him set things right. (Rev: BL 9/1/02; HBG 3/03; SLJ 10/02)

6084 May, Robert L. *Rudolph the Red-Nosed Reindeer: The Original Story of Rudolph* (K–3). Illus. by David Wenzel. 2001, Grosset $9.99 (0-448-42534-3). The original text of Rudolph is presented with new illustrations that convey a warm, nostalgic feeling. (Rev: HBG 3/02; SLJ 10/01)

6085 Medearis, Angela Shelf. *Poppa's Itchy Christmas* (PS–1). Illus. by John Ward. 1998, Holiday House $15.95 (0-8234-1298-9). 32pp. George, an African American youngster, is not happy with the scarf and red long underwear he receives for Christmas, but when he falls through the ice while trying out his new skates, they are the two items that help save his life. (Rev: BL 9/1/98; HBG 10/99; SLJ 10/98)

6086 Mendez, Phil. *The Black Snowman* (K–4). Illus. by Carole Byard. 1989, Scholastic $15.95 (0-590-40552-7). 48pp. An African American learns a little about his heritage from a snowman that comes to life. (Rev: BCCB 11/89; BL 10/1/89; SLJ 9/89)

6087 Menotti, Gian Carlo. *Amahl and the Night Visitors* (K–3). Illus. by Michele Lemieux. 1986, Morrow LB $19.88 (0-688-05427-7). 64pp. A lavish edition of the story of this touching opera. (Rev: BCCB 10/86; HB 11–12/86)

6088 Modesitt, Jeanne. *Little Bunny's Christmas Tree* (PS–K). Illus. by Robin Spowart. 2003, Simon & Schuster $12.95 (0-689-84342-9). Little Bunny and the rest of the family take care in selecting a Christmas tree. (Rev: HBG 4/04; SLJ 10/03)

6089 Moeri, Louise. *Star Mother's Youngest Child* (PS–2). Illus. by Trina S. Hyman. 1975, Houghton Mifflin $14.95 (0-395-21406-8); paper $5.95 (0-395-29929-2). 48pp. An old woman and a star child celebrate Christmas.

6090 Moore, Clement C. *The Night Before Christmas: A Goblin Tale* (PS–3). Illus. by Jacqueline Rogers. 2003, Dial $16.99 (0-8037-2785-2). This offbeat retelling moves the action from a typical family home to the snake-infested den of a goblin family. (Rev: HBG 4/04; SLJ 10/03)

6091 Moore, Clement Clarke. *The Night Before Christmas* (PS–3). Illus. by Raquel Jaramillo. 2001, Simon & Schuster $18.95 (0-689-84053-5). 40pp. The familiar Christmas rhyme, presented in the style of a family photo album. (Rev: BCCB 11/02; BL 9/1/01; HBG 3/02; SLJ 10/01)

6092 Morrissey, Dean. *The Christmas Ship* (K–4). Illus. 2000, HarperCollins LB $16.89 (0-06-028576-1). 40pp. On Christmas Eve, toy maker Sam Thatcher helps Santa by delivering toys from his boat, which soars through the night sky. (Rev: BL 10/1/00; HBG 3/01)

6093 Moses, Will. *Silent Night* (1–4). Illus. 1997, Penguin Putnam $16.99 (0-399-23100-5). 40pp. Using the words of the carol as chapter headings, this is the story of a family's exciting Christmas in rural Vermont. (Rev: BL 9/1/97; HBG 3/98; SLJ 10/97)

6094 Murphy, Mary. *Little Owl and the Star: A Christmas Story* (PS–K). Illus. by author. 2003, Candlewick $12.99 (0-7636-2268-0). Little Owl follows a star and witnesses the Nativity. (Rev: HB 11–12/03; HBG 4/04; SLJ 10/03)

6095 *My First Christmas Board Book* (PS). Series: DK My First Book. 1999, DK $6.95 (0-7894-4735-5). A simple board book that introduces the symbols and meaning of Christmas with material on a manger, animals of the stable, and so on. (Rev: SLJ 10/99)

6096 Neugebauer, Charise. *Santa's Gift* (PS–2). Illus. by Barbara Nascimbeni. 1999, North-South LB $15.88 (0-7358-1146-6). 32pp. With the help of his only friend, Humphrey the hippo, selfish kitten Timmy learns at Christmastime that it is as much fun to give as to receive. (Rev: BL 9/1/99; HBG 3/00; SLJ 10/99)

6097 O'Brien, John. *Mother Hubbard's Christmas* (K–2). Illus. 1996, Boyds Mills $14.95 (1-56397-139-9). 28pp. This hilarious variation on the standard nursery rhyme tells how Mother Hubbard prepares for Christmas. (Rev: BL 10/15/96)

6098 Oppenheim, Joanne. *The Miracle of the First Poinsettia: A Mexican Christmas Story* (K–2). Illus. by Fabian Negrin. 2003, Barefoot $16.99 (1-84148-245-5). Young Juanita has no money to give to the church so she follows the advice of a stone angel and gathers weeds, which are miraculously transformed into the beautiful scarlet blossoms of a poinsettia. (Rev: HBG 4/04; SLJ 10/03)

6099 Page, Josephine. *Little Lamb's Christmas* (PS). Illus. by David Milgrim. 2003, Scholastic $7.99 (0-439-52464-4). Little Lamb, alerted to the birth of Jesus by an angel, joins shepherds on their journey to the lowly stable where the wondrous event has just occurred. (Rev: SLJ 10/03)

6100 Palatini, Margie. *Moosletoe* (PS–1). Illus. by Henry Cole. 2000, Hyperion $15.99 (0-7868-0567-6). 32pp. The moose with the remarkable mustache allows it to be decked with ornaments to preserve the spirit of the Christmas season. (Rev: BL 9/1/00; HBG 3/01)

6101 Parish, Peggy. *Merry Christmas, Amelia Bedelia* (1–2). Illus. by Lynn Sweat. 1986, Greenwillow $15.89 (0-688-06102-8); Avon paper $3.99 (0-380-70325-4). 64pp. Christmas fun with silly Amelia Bedelia, the maid with nonsensical assumptions. (Rev: BCCB 10/86; BL 10/1/86)

6102 Parker, Toni Trent. *Snowflake Kisses and Gingerbread Smiles* (PS–2). Photos by Earl Anderson. 2002, Scholastic $6.95 (0-439-33872-7). Photographs of seasonal items and African American children emphasize the delights of Christmas. (Rev: HBG 3/03; SLJ 10/02)

6103 Paterson, Katherine. *Marvin's Best Christmas Present Ever* (1–2). Illus. by Jane Brown. 1997, HarperCollins LB $14.89 (0-06-027160-4). 48pp. Marvin is so happy with the Christmas wreath he has made for the family's trailer door that he doesn't want to take it down. (Rev: BL 9/1/97; HB 11–12/97; HBG 3/98; SLJ 10/97*)

6104 Pilkey, Dav. *Dragon's Merry Christmas* (1–2). Illus. 1991, Orchard LB $16.99 (0-531-08557-0). 48pp. The Christmas tree that Dragon finds in the forest is too perfect to cut down. (Rev: BL 7/91)

6105 Pinkney, Andrea Davis. *Mim's Christmas Jam* (PS–3). Illus. by Brian Pinkney. 2001, Harcourt $16.00 (0-15-201918-9). 32pp. Pap, digging subway tunnels in New York in the early 20th century, can't be home for Christmas, so Mim sends him homemade jam that fills Pap's boss with Christmas spirit. (Rev: BCCB 11/01; BL 9/15/01; HBG 3/02; SLJ 10/01)

6106 Pinkwater, Daniel. *Wolf Christmas* (PS–3). Illus. by Jill Pinkwater. 1998, Marshall Cavendish $15.95 (0-7614-5030-0). 32pp. On the longest night of the year, three wolf pups are taken by their Uncle Louis to see a human village and witness how this other animal species acts during their winter holidays. (Rev: BL 9/1/98; HBG 3/99; SLJ 10/98)

6107 Polacco, Patricia. *The Trees of the Dancing Goats* (PS–3). Illus. 1996, Simon & Schuster $16.00 (0-689-80862-3). 32pp. A Jewish family delivers Christmas trees to needy Christian families. (Rev: BL 11/1/96; SLJ 2/97)

6108 Polacco, Patricia. *Uncle Vova's Tree* (K–2). Illus. 1989, Penguin Putnam $15.95 (0-399-21617-0). 32pp. Old Christmas customs are described when a young girl spends Christmas with elderly Russian relatives. (Rev: BL 9/15/89; HB 11–12/89)

6109 Polacco, Patricia. *Welcome Comfort* (K–3). Illus. by author. 1999, Philomel LB $16.99 (0-399-23169-2). Welcome Comfort, an overweight foster child, gets a special surprise at Christmas. (Rev: BCCB 11/99; HBG 3/00; SLJ 10/99)

6110 Prater, John. *Is It Christmas?* (PS–K). Illus. by author. 2003, Barron's $13.95 (0-7641-5668-3). Grandbear and Baby Bear prepare for the coming of Christmas. (Rev: HBG 4/04; SLJ 10/03)

6111 Price, Moe. *The Reindeer Christmas* (K–3). Illus. by Atsuko Morozumi. 1993, Harcourt $15.95 (0-15-266199-9). 32pp. A delightful Christmas story that tells why Santa decided that reindeer should be the animals to pull his sleigh. (Rev: BL 9/15/93)

6112 Primavera, Elise. *Auntie Claus* (PS–2). Illus. 1999, Harcourt $16.00 (0-15-201909-X). 40pp. Sophie Crinkle follows her Aunt Claus to a snowy land and there discovers that her relative is the real force behind Christmas. (Rev: BCCB 12/99; BL 9/1/99; HBG 3/00; SLJ 10/99)

6113 Primavera, Elise. *Auntie Claus and the Key to Christmas* (K–2). 2002, Harcourt $16.00 (0-15-202441-7). 40pp. Christopher, trying to get on Santa's "bad" list, journeys to the North Pole and becomes a believer after meeting the bad boys and girls on the list. (Rev: BCCB 11/02; BL 9/15/02; HBG 3/03; SLJ 10/02)

6114 Pulver, Robin. *Christmas for a Kitten* (PS–2). Illus. by Layne Johnson. 2003, Whitman LB $15.95 (0-8075-1151-X). Santa adopts a tiny abandoned kitten that has been having a tough time. (Rev: HBG 4/04; SLJ 10/03)

6115 Quattlebaum, Mary. *The Shine Man: A Christmas Story* (K–4). Illus. by Tim Ladwig. 2001, Eerdmans $17.00 (0-8028-5181-9). 32pp. A hobo receives a heavenly reward when he shines a boy's shoes on Christmas Eve. (Rev: BL 9/1/01; HBG 3/02; SLJ 10/01)

6116 Rader, Laura. *Who'll Pull Santa's Sleigh Tonight?* (PS–1). Illus. by author. 2003, HarperCollins LB $13.89 (0-06-008089-2). Santa fears he won't be able to make his annual Christmas rounds when all his reindeer come down with the flu. (Rev: HBG 4/04; SLJ 10/03)

6117 Rahaman, Vashanti. *O Christmas Tree* (K–3). Illus. by Frane Lessac. 1996, Boyds Mills $14.95 (1-56397-237-9). 26pp. Anslem has problems believing in a traditional Christmas with snow and Christmas trees in his Caribbean home. (Rev: BCCB 11/96; BL 9/1/96*)

6118 Ransom, Candice. *The Christmas Dolls* (K–3). Illus. by Moira Fain. 1998, Walker LB $16.85 (0-8027-8661-8). 32pp. Claire is sad because her father will be absent for Christmas. She is comforted by helping her mother repair dolls to give to poor children and by making a rag doll that she will give her mother on Christmas morning. (Rev: BL 9/1/98; HBG 3/99; SLJ 10/98)

6119 Ransom, Candice. *One Christmas Dawn* (K–3). Illus. by Peter M. Fiore. 1996, Troll $15.95 (0-

8167-3384-8). 32pp. In 1917 Appalachia, a young girl awaits the promised arrival of her father for Christmas. (Rev: BL 10/15/96)

6120 Reiss, Mike. *Santa Claustrophobia* (2–5). Illus. by David Catrow. 2002, Price Stern Sloan $10.99 (0-8431-7756-X). Santa is suffering from claustrophobia and Doc Holiday recommends some time off. (Rev: BCCB 12/02; HBG 3/03; SLJ 10/02)

6121 Repchuk, Caroline. *The Snow Tree* (PS–1). Illus. by Josephine Martin. 1997, Dutton $15.99 (0-525-45903-0). 32pp. Animals offer to a little bear many colorful objects to decorate his Christmas tree. (Rev: BL 9/1/97; HBG 3/98)

6122 Rosenberg, Liz. *On Christmas Eve* (PS–K). Illus. by John Clapp. 2002, Millbrook LB $21.90 (0-7613-2707-X). 40pp. A little boy worries that Santa won't be able to find him when his family must spend Christmas Eve at a motel. (Rev: BCCB 10/02; BL 9/15/02; HBG 3/03; SLJ 10/02)

6123 Rowlands, Avril. *The Christmas Sheep and Other Stories* (2–4). Illus. by Rosslyn Moran. 2001, Good Books $16.00 (1-56148-336-2). 48pp. Four stories about the animals that were part of the first Christmas. (Rev: BL 9/15/01; SLJ 10/01)

6124 Rylant, Cynthia. *Christmas in the Country* (K–2). Illus. by Diane Goode. 2002, Scholastic $15.95 (0-439-07334-0). 32pp. A story of a loving family's beautiful white Christmas, full of tradition and celebration. (Rev: BL 9/15/02; HB 11–12/02; HBG 3/03; SLJ 10/02)

6125 Rylant, Cynthia. *Little Whistle's Christmas* (K–2). Illus. by Tim Bowers. 2003, Harcourt $16.00 (0-15-204590-2). Little Whistle, the guinea pig who lives in a toy store, and his toy friends discover the true meaning of Christmas. (Rev: HBG 4/04; SLJ 10/03)

6126 Rylant, Cynthia. *Mr. Putter and Tabby Bake the Cake* (1–3). Illus. by Arthur Howard. 1994, Harcourt $13.00 (0-15-200205-7); paper $6.00 (0-15-200214-6). 44pp. Mr. Putter bakes a Christmas cake for his neighbor, Mrs. Teaberry, in this easily read book. (Rev: BL 10/15/94; HB 9–10/94; SLJ 12/94)

6127 Rylant, Cynthia. *Silver Packages: An Appalachian Christmas Story* (K–3). Illus. by Chris K. Soentpiet. 1997, Orchard LB $16.99 (0-531-33051-6). 32pp. At Christmas time, a young doctor tries to repay an Appalachian community for the gifts that were given to him in the past. (Rev: BL 9/1/97; HBG 3/98; SLJ 10/97)

6128 Say, Allen. *Tree of Cranes* (PS–3). Illus. 1991, Houghton Mifflin $17.95 (0-395-52024-X). 32pp. A Japanese woman brings a tree indoors because it reminds her of the Christmas she spent years ago in California. (Rev: BCCB 9/91*; BL 9/15/91; HB 11–12/91*)

6129 Shannon, David. *The Amazing Christmas Extravaganza* (K–3). Illus. 1995, Scholastic $15.95 (0-590-48090-1). 32pp. A parable about Mr. Merriweather and how he alienates his neighbors at Christmas time. (Rev: BL 9/15/95)

6130 Sierra, Judy. *'Twas the Fright Before Christmas* (PS). Illus. by Will Hillenbrand. 2002, Harcourt $16.00 (0-15-201805-0). A humorous cumulative tale of woes affecting the residents of a haunted house. (Rev: HBG 3/03; SLJ 10/02)

6131 Slate, Joseph. *The Secret Stars* (PS–2). Illus. by Felipe Davalos. 1998, Marshall Cavendish $15.95 (0-7614-5027-0). 32pp. On the Night of the Three Kings holiday, the weather in New Mexico is so bad that Pepe and Sila worry that the kings will not be able to deliver their presents. (Rev: BL 9/15/98; HBG 3/99; SLJ 10/98)

6132 Soto, Gary. *Too Many Tamales* (PS–1). Illus. by Ed Martinez. 1993, Penguin Putnam $15.95 (0-399-22146-8). 32pp. A Hispanic child enthusiastically enters into the cooking and other rituals that surround her family's celebration of Christmas. (Rev: BCCB 10/93; BL 9/15/93; HB 11–12/93)

6133 Speirs, John. *The Little Boy's Christmas Gift* (PS–3). Illus. 2001, Abrams $16.95 (0-8109-4399-9). 32pp. A boy's gift to the Holy Family is a decorated tree in this lavishly illustrated picture book. (Rev: BL 10/15/01; HBG 3/02)

6134 Spirin, Gennady. *The Christmas Story: According to the Gospels of Matthew and Luke from the King James Bible* (1–6). Illus. 1998, Holt $19.95 (0-8050-5292-5). 32pp. A beautifully illustrated version of the Nativity that incorporates verses from the Gospels of Matthew and Luke from the King James version of the Bible. (Rev: BL 11/15/98; HBG 3/99; SLJ 10/98) [232.9]

6135 Spowart, Robin. *Inside, Outside Christmas* (PS). Illus. 1998, Holiday House $15.95 (0-8234-1370-5). 32pp. Using double-page spreads and short rhyming phrases, this picture book depicts inside and outside activities of a loving mouse family at Christmas. (Rev: BL 9/1/98; HBG 3/99; SLJ 10/98)

6136 Stevenson, James. *Christmas at Mud Flat* (1–3). Illus. 2000, HarperCollins LB $15.89 (0-688-17302-0). 48pp. It's a week before Christmas and everyone in Mud Flat is making hasty preparations for the big event. (Rev: BCCB 11/00; BL 9/1/00; HBG 3/01)

6137 Strand, Keith. *Grandfather's Christmas Tree* (PS–3). Illus. by Thomas Locker. 1999, Harcourt $16.00 (0-15-201821-2). 32pp. A lovely Christmas story about a pioneer family who are saved from having to chop down their last spruce tree for firewood and, thus, are able to save a pair of geese that have taken shelter in it. (Rev: BL 9/1/99; HBG 3/00; SLJ 10/99)

6138 Sykes, Julie. *Hurry, Santa!* (PS–K). Illus. by Tim Warnes. 1998, Little Tiger $14.95 (1-888444-37-1). 32pp. Santa oversleeps and Christmas Eve becomes a big rush, rush, rush to get everything done in time. (Rev: BL 9/1/98; HBG 3/99; SLJ 10/98)

6139 Tafuri, Nancy. *The Donkey's Christmas Song* (PS). Illus. 2002, Scholastic $16.95 (0-439-27313-7). 32pp. A donkey is reluctant to add his braying to the manger lullaby. (Rev: BL 9/15/02; HBG 3/03; SLJ 10/02)

6140 Taylor, Jane. *Twinkle, Twinkle Little Star* (PS). Illus. by Lesley Harker. 2001, Scholastic $15.95 (0-439-29656-0). 24pp. Two children follow a star to the baby Jesus in this unique interpretation of the classic poem. (Rev: BL 11/15/01; HBG 3/02; SLJ 10/01)

6141 Tews, Susan. *The Gingerbread Doll* (K–3). Illus. by Megan Lloyd. 1993, Clarion $16.00 (0-395-56438-7). 32pp. Starting as a poor youngster during the Great Depression when she gets a gingerbread doll, Rebecca finds that her Christmas presents change as her family gets more prosperous. (Rev: BL 9/1/93)

6142 Thayer, Jane. *The Puppy Who Wanted a Boy* (1–3). Illus. by Lisa McCue. 1986, Morrow paper $5.95 (0-688-08293-9). 48pp. Petey the puppy doesn't get a boy for Christmas as he wished, but he does find 50 boys in a Home for Boys to whom he can give his love. (Rev: BL 4/1/86; SLJ 5/86)

6143 Thompson, Kay. *Eloise at Christmastime* (PS–3). Illus. by Hilary Knight. 199, Simon & Schuster $17.50 (0-689-83039-4). A reissue of the book about the little girl who lives in the Plaza Hotel in New York City and her adventures at Christmas. (Rev: BL 11/15/99; HBG 3/00)

6144 Thomson, Pat. *Beware of the Aunts!* (PS–2). Illus. by Emma C. Clark. 1992, Macmillan $14.95 (0-689-50538-8). Nine unusual aunts and Christmas gift giving are the subjects of this humorous book. (Rev: SLJ 7/92)

6145 Trivas, Irene. *Emma's Christmas* (PS–4). Illus. 1988, Orchard paper $6.95 (0-531-07022-0). 32pp. When Emma, the farmer's daughter, declines the prince's offer of marriage, he begins to send her gifts. (Rev: BCCB 10/88; BL 9/15/88; HB 11–12/88)

6146 Tudor, Tasha. *Corgiville Christmas* (K–2). Illus. by author. 2003, Front Street $15.95 (1-932425-00-4). Corgiville, a 1920s New England village populated by corgis, cats, rabbits, and other animals, is buzzing with activity as its residents prepare for the Christmas holiday. (Rev: HBG 4/04; SLJ 10/03)

6147 Turner, Sandy. *Silent Night* (2–4). Illus. 2001, Simon & Schuster $16.00 (0-689-84156-6). 32pp. An inventive and skillfully illustrated story of a dog that barks madly to alert his owners that Santa has arrived, to no avail. (Rev: BL 10/1/01; HB 11–12/01; HBG 3/02; SLJ 10/01*)

6148 Van Allsburg, Chris. *The Polar Express* (K–2). Illus. by author. 1985, Houghton Mifflin $18.95 (0-395-38949-6). 32pp. Whisked aboard the Polar Express to the North Pole on Christmas Eve, a young boy gets to receive the first gift of Christmas. Caldecott Medal winner, 1986. (Rev: BCCB 10/85; BL 10/1/85; SLJ 10/85)

6149 Waber, Bernard. *Lyle at Christmas* (K–3). Illus. 1998, Houghton Mifflin $16.00 (0-395-91304-7). 48pp. At Christmastime, Lyle, the lovable crocodile, tries to cheer up Mr. Grumps, who is in the dumps, by finding his beloved cat, Loretta. (Rev: BL 9/1/98; HB 11–12/98; HBG 3/99; SLJ 10/98)

6150 Wallner, Alexandra. *An Alcott Family Christmas* (K–2). Illus. 1996, Holiday House LB $15.95 (0-8234-1265-2). 30pp. A fictionalized account of how Louisa May Alcott's family might have observed Christmas as the March family did in *Little Women*. (Rev: BL 9/1/96)

6151 Walsh, Vivian, and J. Otto Seibold. *Olive, the Other Reindeer* (1–3). Illus. 1997, Chronicle $13.95 (0-8118-1807-1). 32pp. A little dog believes that she is really a reindeer and heads to the North Pole to give Santa a hand. (Rev: BL 10/15/97; HBG 3/98)

6152 Ward, Helen. *The Animals' Christmas Carol* (PS–3). Illus. 2001, Millbrook LB $23.90 (0-7613-2408-9). 40pp. A beautifully illustrated book based on the Christmas carol "The Friendly Beasts," in which animals bring gifts to baby Jesus in the manger. (Rev: BCCB 11/01; BL 9/15/01; HBG 3/02)

6153 Wells, Rosemary. *McDuff's New Friend* (PS–K). Illus. by Susan Jeffers. 1998, Hyperion $12.95 (0-7868-0386-X). In this sweet tale, McDuff, a terrier, and his owner dig a tunnel after a severe snowstorm and find Santa stuck in a snowdrift. (Rev: BL 12/1/98; HBG 3/99; SLJ 10/98)

6154 Wells, Rosemary. *Morris's Disappearing Bag* (PS–1). Illus. 1999, Viking $15.99 (0-670-88721-8). 40pp. A young rabbit is disappointed with the stuffed bear he gets for Christmas but is delighted with another present that contains a Disappearing Bag. (Rev: BL 1/1–15/00; HBG 3/00)

6155 Weninger, Brigitte. *A Letter to Santa Claus* (K–3). Trans. by Sibylle Kazeroid. Illus. by Anne Moller. 2000, North-South LB $15.88 (0-7358-1360-4). 32pp. A sweet tale about a poor boy whose letter to Santa is answered in an amazing way. (Rev: BL 9/1/00; HBG 3/01)

6156 Wild, Margaret. *Thank You, Santa* (PS–3). Illus. by Kerry Argent. 1992, Scholastic $12.95 (0-590-45805-1). 32pp. After Christmas, a young girl in Australia begins a correspondence with Santa Claus. (Rev: BCCB 11/92; BL 11/1/92)

6157 Williams, Sam. *Teddy Bears Trim the Tree* (PS–K). Illus. by Jacqueline McQuade. 2000, Scholastic $14.95 (0-439-19285-4). An interactive book about a group of teddy bears who find a Christmas tree, bring it in, and decorate it in time for Santa's arrival. (Rev: BL 12/1/00)

6158 Winthrop, Elizabeth. *Bear's Christmas Surprise* (PS–2). Illus. by Patience Brewster. 1991, Holiday House LB $14.95 (0-8234-0888-4). 32pp. While playing hide-and-seek, Bear accidentally discovers some Christmas presents hidden in a closet and opens them. (Rev: BL 9/15/91)

6159 Wolff, Patricia Rae. *A New Improved Santa* (K–3). Illus. by Lynne W. Cravath. 2002, Scholastic $15.95 (0-439-35249-5). Santa spends the year on self-improvement — diet, exercise, new hairstyle — only to find the children prefer him the old way. (Rev: BCCB 11/02; HBG 3/03; SLJ 10/02)

6160 Wood, Audrey. *The Christmas Adventure of Space Elf Sam* (PS–3). Illus. by Bruce Robert Wood. 1998, Scholastic $15.95 (0-590-03143-0). 40pp. When families from Earth colonize outer space, Santa Claus needs help to perform his Christmas Eve duties. (Rev: BL 9/1/98; HBG 3/99; SLJ 10/98)

6161 Wood, Audrey. *A Cowboy Christmas: The Miracle at Lone Pine Ridge* (PS–4). Illus. by Robert

Florczak. 2001, Simon & Schuster $19.95 (0-689-82190-5). 48pp. Christmas becomes a special time for young Evan after he rescues cowboy Cully, who then marries his mother. (Rev: BL 9/1/01; HBG 3/02; SLJ 10/01)

6162 Wood, Don, and Audrey Wood. *Merry Christmas, Big Hungry Bear!* (PS–2). Illus. 2002, Scholastic $15.95 (0-439-32092-5). 48pp. Little Mouse decides to share his Christmas with Big Hungry Bear, who never gets any presents. (Rev: BCCB 11/02; BL 9/15/02; HBG 3/03; SLJ 10/02)

6163 Wood, Douglas. *What Santa Can't Do* (PS–2). Illus. by Doug Cushman. 2003, Simon & Schuster $15.95 (0-689-86171-0). In this whimsical Christmas tale, readers will learn about the many things that humans can — and Santa can't — do; Santa is depicted as a cheery green dinosaur dressed in the traditional regalia of old Saint Nick. (Rev: HBG 4/04; SLJ 10/03)

6164 Wright, Cliff. *Santa's Ark* (K–3). Illus. 1997, Millbrook LB $22.40 (0-7613-0314-6). 36pp. Different animals from around the world stow away in Santa's sleigh when he makes his stops. (Rev: BL 12/15/97; HBG 3/98; SLJ 10/97)

6165 Yin. *Dear Santa, Please Come to the 19th Floor* (1–3). Illus. by Chris Soentpiet. 2002, Philomel $16.99 (0-399-23636-8). Willy asks Santa for a special present for his friend Carlos, who is in a wheelchair and living in poverty. (Rev: HBG 3/03; SLJ 10/02)

6166 Zagwyn, Deborah Turney. *The Winter Gift* (K–3). Illus. 2000, Tricycle $15.95 (1-883672-93-7). 32pp. Grandma is selling all her furniture before moving into an apartment, but she gives her piano to her grandchildren to continue the tradition of playing it at Christmas. (Rev: BL 9/1/00*; HBG 3/01)

6167 Ziefert, Harriet. *Home for Navidad* (PS–3). Illus. by Santiago Cohen. 2003, Houghton Mifflin $15.00 (0-618-34976-6). Ten-year-old Rosa, who lives with her grandmother and uncle in Mexico, hopes her mother will finally make it back from New York to spend Christmas with them. (Rev: HB 9–10/03; HBG 4/04; SLJ 10/03)

EASTER

6168 Berlin, Irving. *Easter Parade* (PS–1). Illus. by Lisa McCue. 2003, HarperCollins LB $16.89 (0-06-029126-5). 32pp. Father Rabbit and his behatted young daughter parade down the street with all the other finely dressed animals in this cheerful rendition of the famous Irving Berlin song. (Rev: BL 3/15/03; HBG 4/04; SLJ 2/03) [782.42164]

6169 Bishop, Adela. *The Easter Wolf* (PS–2). Illus. by Carole Dzapla. 1991, Dot $12.95 (0-9625620-1-7). 28pp. When he is saved from drowning by the Easter Rabbit, a hungry wolf reforms. (Rev: BL 3/15/91)

6170 Bostrom, Kathleen Long. *Sunrise Hill: An Easter Story of Faith, Inspiration, and Courage* (K–3). Illus. by Rick Johnson. 2004, Zondervan $14.99 (0-310-70508-8). 32pp. Despite the loss of their church, the people of a 19th-century farming community celebrate a special Easter service on Sunrise Hill, affirming their faith in rebirth. (Rev: BL 3/1/04)

6171 Denim, Sue. *The Dumb Bunnies' Easter* (K–2). Illus. by Dav Pilkey. 1995, Scholastic $12.95 (0-590-20241-3). 32pp. The Dumb Bunnies have a very distorted view of what to expect from the Easter Bunny. (Rev: BL 2/1/95; SLJ 2/95)

6172 Devlin, Wende, and Harry Devlin. *Cranberry Easter* (PS–3). Illus. by Harry Devlin. 1990, Macmillan LB $15.00 (0-02-729935-X). In the town of Cranberryport, friends help each other and the result is a happy Easter. (Rev: SLJ 3/90)

6173 Elschner, Geraldine. *The Easter Chick* (PS–2). Trans. by Marianne Martens. Illus. by Alexandra Junge. 2004, North-South $15.95 (0-7358-1855-X). 32pp. The fact that Easter is a movable feast is underlined in this story in which an owl helps a mother hen to schedule the hatching of her chick. (Rev: BL 3/1/04; SLJ 5/04)

6174 Friedrich, Priscilla, and Otto Friedrich. *The Easter Bunny That Overslept* (PS–1). Illus. by Adrienne Adams. 1983, Morrow paper $4.95 (0-688-07038-8). 40pp. Santa Claus helps a tardy Easter Bunny who has trouble getting up on time.

6175 Friedrich, Priscilla, and Otto Friedrich. *The Easter Bunny That Overslept* (PS–2). Illus. by Donald Saaf. 2002, HarperCollins LB $14.89 (0-06-029646-1). 32pp. In this bright new version of a 1950s classic, the Easter Bunny oversleeps and discovers that no one wants Easter eggs on the Fourth of July or Halloween. (Rev: BL 2/15/02; HBG 10/02; SLJ 1/02)

6176 Gibbons, Gail. *Easter* (PS–2). Illus. by author. 1989, Holiday House LB $16.95 (0-8234-0737-3); paper $6.95 (0-8234-0866-3). 32pp. Biblical, pagan, and modern aspects of the holiday are described. (Rev: BL 4/1/89; SLJ 3/89)

6177 Heyward, DuBose. *The Country Bunny and the Little Gold Shoes* (K–3). Illus. by Marjorie Flack. 1939, Houghton Mifflin $15.00 (0-395-15990-3); paper $5.95 (0-395-18557-2). 48pp. Cottontail, the mother of 21 bunnies, finally realizes her great ambition to be an Easter Bunny.

6178 Houselander, Caryll. *Petook: An Easter Story* (K–3). Illus. by Tomie dePaola. 1988, Holiday House LB $16.95 (0-8234-0681-4). 32pp. The rooster, Petook, and a simple story of Easter. (Rev: BL 4/15/88; SLJ 5/88)

6179 Nerlove, Miriam. *Easter* (PS–1). Illus. 1989, Whitman paper $4.95 (0-8075-1872-7). 24pp. This major religious holiday is described in rhyming text. (Rev: BL 1/15/90; SLJ 4/90)

6180 Polacco, Patricia. *Chicken Sunday* (PS–3). Illus. 1992, Penguin Putnam $15.95 (0-399-22133-6). 32pp. Three youngsters of different races and religions unite to help Miss Eula have a good Easter. (Rev: BCCB 7–8/92; BL 3/15/92*; SLJ 5/92*)

6181 Tegen, Katherine. *The Story of the Easter Bunny* (PS–1). Illus. by Sally Anne Lambert. 2005, HarperCollins LB $13.89 (0-06-050712-8). 40pp. A pet white rabbit takes over the Easter preparations — basket weaving, candy making, and egg coloring

— when the elderly couple who own him become too old to continue. (Rev: BL 2/1/05; SLJ 2/05)

6182 Weigelt, Udo. *The Easter Bunny's Baby* (PS–2). Trans. by Alison James. 2001, North-South LB $15.88 (0-7358-1443-0). 32pp. Easter Bunny receives an egg that hatches into a baby ostrich. (Rev: BL 4/1/01; HBG 10/01; SLJ 4/01)

6183 Wiencirz, Gerlinde. *Teddy's Easter Secret* (PS–2). Trans. by J. Alison James. Illus. by Giuliano Lunelli. 2001, North-South LB $15.88 (0-7358-1358-2). 32pp. During an excursion in the woods, Teddy, a stuffed toy, meets the Easter Bunny and brings home some colored eggs for his young owner. (Rev: BL 3/15/01; HBG 10/01)

6184 Zolotow, Charlotte. *The Bunny Who Found Easter* (PS–2). Illus. by Helen Craig. 1998, Houghton Mifflin $15.00 (0-395-86265-5). 32pp. A new edition of the story about a bunny who wanders through a year searching for Easter so he can enjoy the company of other bunnies. The 1959 edition is illustrated by Betty Peterson. (Rev: BL 3/1/98; HBG 3/99; SLJ 9/98)

HALLOWEEN

6185 Adams, Georgie. *The Three Little Witches Storybook* (PS–3). Illus. by Emily Bolam. 2002, Hyperion $15.99 (0-7868-0824-1). 32pp. Young witches Zara, Ziggy, and Zoe have magical fun in these eight short, brightly illustrated stories that make good Halloween reading. (Rev: BL 9/1/02; HBG 3/03; SLJ 12/02)

6186 Behn, Harry. *Halloween* (2–3). 2003, Cheshire Studio Books $15.95 (0-7358-1609-3). 32pp. Three children costumed as a devil, skeleton, and witch find trick-or-treating can become very spooky as the evening progresses. (Rev: BL 9/1/03; HBG 4/04; SLJ 8/03)

6187 Bridwell, Norman. *Clifford's Halloween* (PS–1). Illus. by author. 1970, Scholastic paper $2.99 (0-590-44287-2). 32pp. Halloween adventures of a big red dog.

6188 Broyles, Anne. *Shy Mama's Halloween* (2–4). Illus. by Leane Morin. 2000, Tilbury House $16.95 (0-88448-218-9). 40pp. Recently arrived from Russia, Anya and her siblings are taken out on Halloween by their mother and suddenly feel more at home in their new country. (Rev: BL 11/15/00; HBG 3/01; SLJ 1/01)

6189 Bullard, Lisa. *Trick-or-Treat on Milton Street* (K–2). Illus. by Joni Oeltjenbruns. 2001, Carolrhoda LB $15.95 (1-57505-158-3). Charley gets a big surprise on Halloween that makes him look at his new neighborhood in quite a different way. (Rev: HBG 3/02; SLJ 9/01)

6190 Bunting, Eve. *The Bones of Fred McFee* (K–3). Illus. by Kurt Cyrus. 2002, Harcourt $16.00 (0-15-202004-7). 32pp. A toy skeleton hung in a tree makes Halloween particularly eerie for a brother and sister, and the local animals. (Rev: BCCB 10/02; BL 9/1/02; HBG 3/03; SLJ 9/02)

6191 Bunting, Eve. *Scary, Scary Halloween* (PS–1). Illus. by Jan Brett. 1986, Houghton Mifflin $15.00 (0-89919-414-1); paper $5.95 (0-89919-799-X).

32pp. A scary poem tells of a parade of creatures on Halloween night. (Rev: BCCB 9/86; BL 9/1/86; HB 11–12/86)

6192 Carlson, Nancy. *Harriet's Halloween Candy* (PS–K). Illus. by author. 1982, Carolrhoda LB $15.95 (0-87614-182-3); Lerner paper $4.95 (0-87614-850-X). 32pp. A childlike dog overeats on Halloween candy.

6193 Caseley, Judith. *Witch Mama* (PS–2). Illus. 1996, Greenwillow LB $14.93 (0-688-14458-6). 32pp. On Halloween, Mama becomes Witch Mama, but she still cares for her two children. (Rev: BL 9/1/96; SLJ 8/96)

6194 Cazet, Denys. *Never Poke a Squid* (PS–2). Illus. 2000, Orchard LB $17.99 (0-531-33279-9). 32pp. When the school principal pins an award on the Halloween squid costume that Arnie and friend Raymond are wearing, ink pours out — to the delight of all the first-grade kids. (Rev: BCCB 9/00; BL 9/1/00; HBG 3/01; SLJ 9/00)

6195 Costello, David. *Here They Come!* (K–3). Illus. by author. 2004, Farrar $15.00 (0-374-33051-4). Goblins congregate for the annual Halloween party, eager for thrills. (Rev: SLJ 11/04)

6196 Crimi, Carolyn. *Boris and Bella* (K–2). Illus. by Gris Grimly. 2004, Harcourt $15.00 (0-15-202528-6). 32pp. Messy monster Bella Lagrossi and her fastidious neighbor Boris Kleanitoff find they have something in common in this entertaining Halloween tale full of wordplay. (Rev: BL 1/1–15/05; SLJ 9/04)

6197 Cushman, Doug. *Aunt Eater's Mystery Halloween* (1–2). Illus. Series: I Can Read. 1998, HarperCollins LB $14.89 (0-06-027804-8). 64pp. Four short mysteries about Halloween are solved by Aunt Eater, the anteater who dresses like Sherlock Holmes. (Rev: BL 9/1/98; HBG 3/99; SLJ 10/98)

6198 De Groat, Diane. *Trick or Treat, Smell My Feet* (PS–3). Illus. 1998, Morrow LB $14.93 (0-688-15767-X). 32pp. Gilbert takes his sister's Halloween costume to the school parade instead of his own by mistake and finds that he has to dress as a ballerina instead of a Martian space pilot. (Rev: BL 9/1/98; HBG 3/99; SLJ 10/98)

6199 Druce, Arden. *Halloween Night* (PS–K). Illus. by David Wenzel. 2001, Rising Moon $14.95 (0-87358-797-9); paper $6.95 (0-87358-762-6). 32pp. Rhyming riddles about a spooky Halloween night are accompanied by illustrations that suit the mood and contain clues. (Rev: BCCB 9/01; BL 9/1/01; HBG 3/02; SLJ 9/01)

6200 Egan, Tim. *The Experiments of Doctor Vermin* (K–3). Illus. 2002, Houghton Mifflin $15.00 (0-618-13224-4). 32pp. Sheldon the pig stumbles into Dr. Vermin's spooky mansion on Halloween night, but finds refuge with the wolves next door in this amusing story. (Rev: BL 9/1/02; HBG 3/03; SLJ 10/02)

6201 *Five Little Pumpkins* (PS). Illus. by Dan Yaccarino. 1998, HarperCollins $5.95 (0-694-01177-0). 16pp. A board book that illustrates the old rhyme about five little pumpkins sitting on a gate. (Rev: BL 12/15/98; HBG 3/99; SLJ 2/99)

6202 Fleming, Denise. *Pumpkin Eye* (1–3). Illus. 2001, Holt $15.95 (0-8050-6681-0). 32pp. Lightly scary Halloween excitement is captured in rhyming text and inventive artwork. (Rev: BCCB 10/01; BL 9/15/01; HBG 3/02; SLJ 9/01)

6203 Glassman, Miriam. *Halloweena* (K–2). Illus. by Victoria Roberts. 2002, Simon & Schuster $15.95 (0-689-82825-X). 40pp. Hepzibah, a witch, has trouble raising Halloweena, a baby girl, in this picture book with detailed and clever illustrations. (Rev: BCCB 10/02; BL 9/1/02; HBG 3/03; SLJ 9/02)

6204 Gralley, Jean. *Hogula: Dread Pig of Night* (PS–1). Illus. 1999, Holt $15.95 (0-8050-5700-5). 32pp. A Halloween story about Hogula, a vampire pig, who lives on Grimey Pork Chop Hill and likes to snort on human necks. (Rev: BCCB 10/99; BL 11/15/99; HBG 3/00; SLJ 11/99)

6205 Greene, Carol. *The 13 Days of Halloween* (PS–3). Illus. by Tim Raglin. 2000, Troll $15.95 (0-8167-6965-6). 32pp. A dapper ghoul tries to woo his friend with such gifts as a vulture in a dead tree in this take-off on the Christmas carol. (Rev: BL 9/1/00; HBG 10/01; SLJ 9/00)

6206 Hall, Zoe. *It's Pumpkin Time!* (K–3). Illus. by Shari Halpern. 1994, Scholastic $14.95 (0-590-47833-8). This picture book describes how two children plant a pumpkin seed and care for it so that it will be useful at Halloween. (Rev: SLJ 11/94)

6207 Hautzig, Deborah. *Little Witch's Big Night* (1–2). Illus. by Marc Brown. 1984, Random paper $3.99 (0-394-86587-1). 48pp. Little Witch has a better Halloween than she expected.

6208 Hennessy, B. G. *Corduroy's Halloween: A Lift-the-Flap Book* (PS–K). Illus. by Lisa McCue. 1995, Viking $11.99 (0-670-86193-6). Flaps that lift add surprise to this story of how a little bear spends his Halloween. (Rev: SLJ 10/95)

6209 Hoban, Lillian. *Arthur's Halloween Costume* (1–3). Illus. by author. 1984, HarperCollins LB $15.89 (0-06-022391-X); paper $3.95 (0-06-444101-6). 64pp. Arthur is annoyed because no one understands his Halloween costume.

6210 Holub, Joan. *Boo Who? A Spooky Lift-the-Flap Book* (PS–1). Illus. by author. Series: Spooky Lift-the-Flap Book. 1997, Scholastic $6.95 (0-590-05905-X). Rhymes and flaps are used to introduce the objects and creatures associated with Halloween. (Rev: SLJ 10/97)

6211 Hubbard, Patricia. *Trick or Treat Countdown* (PS). Illus. by Michael Letzig. 1999, Holiday House $15.95 (0-8234-1367-5). A simple counting rhyme goes from one to 12 and back again, using Halloween symbols and general spookiness. (Rev: BCCB 10/99; BL 9/1/99; HBG 3/00; SLJ 9/99)

6212 Hubbell, Patricia. *Boo! Halloween Poems and Limericks* (K–4). Illus. by Jeff Spackman. 1998, Marshall Cavendish $15.95 (0-7614-5023-8). 32pp. Witty original poems and limericks about Halloween are presented with suitably lurid illustrations. (Rev: BL 9/1/98; HBG 3/99; SLJ 9/98) [811]

6213 Hulme, Joy N. *Eerie Feary Feeling: A Hairy Scary Pop-Up Book* (K–2). Illus. by Paul Ely. 1998, Orchard $13.95 (0-531-30086-2). Cats, bats, witches, ghosts, and ghouls are all featured in this interactive pop-up book. (Rev: SLJ 12/98)

6214 Hutchins, Pat. *Which Witch Is Which?* (PS–K). Illus. 1989, Greenwillow $15.89 (0-688-06358-6). 24pp. Identical twins dress as witches on Halloween. (Rev: BL 9/1/89; SLJ 8/89*)

6215 Jane, Pamela. *Monster Mischief* (PS–1). Illus. by Vera Rosenberry. 2001, Simon & Schuster $16.00 (0-689-80471-7). 32pp. Monsters settle for candy when their Halloween stew is ruined. (Rev: BCCB 9/01; BL 9/1/01; HBG 3/02; SLJ 9/01)

6216 Johnston, Tony. *The Vanishing Pumpkin* (PS–2). Illus. by Tomie dePaola. 1996, Penguin Putnam paper $5.99 (0-698-11414-0). 32pp. An old man and an old woman set out on Halloween to find their pumpkin.

6217 Johnston, Tony. *Very Scary* (PS–K). Illus. by Douglas Florian. 1995, Harcourt $14.00 (0-15-293625-4). 32pp. When a girl carves a pumpkin into a jack-o'-lantern, it shouts "Boo" and frightens everyone. (Rev: BL 9/15/95; SLJ 11/95)

6218 Keats, Ezra Jack. *The Trip* (1–3). Illus. by author. 1978, Greenwillow $15.93 (0-688-84123-6); Morrow paper $5.95 (0-688-07328-X). 32pp. Halloween proves to be a time when Louis isn't lonely anymore.

6219 Kraus, Robert. *How Spider Saved Halloween* (K–3). Illus. by author. 1988, Scholastic paper $2.99 (0-590-42117-4). 32pp. Spider saves the fun of Halloween by creating an ingenious disguise.

6220 Kroll, Steven. *The Biggest Pumpkin Ever* (PS–2). Illus. by Jeni Bassett. 1984, Holiday House LB $16.95 (0-8234-0505-2); Scholastic paper $2.50 (0-590-41113-6). 32pp. Two mice hope to grow the largest pumpkin ever for Halloween.

6221 Lasky, Kathryn. *Porkenstein* (PS–2). Illus. by David Jarvis. 2002, Scholastic $15.95 (0-590-62380-X). 40pp. Porkenstein, a huge mutant pig created to seek revenge on the Big Bad Wolf, gobbles him up on Halloween. (Rev: BCCB 10/02; BL 9/15/02; HBG 3/03; SLJ 9/02)

6222 Lattimore, Deborah N. *Cinderhazel: The Cinderella of Halloween* (PS–2). Illus. 1997, Scholastic $15.95 (0-590-20232-4). 32pp. A parody on the famous fairy tale, with a feminist twist and a Halloween setting. (Rev: BL 9/1/97; HBG 3/98; SLJ 10/97)

6223 Leedy, Loreen. *The Dragon Halloween Party* (PS–2). Illus. by author. 1986, Holiday House paper $5.95 (0-8234-0765-9). 32pp. Ten children and their mother Ma Dragon get ready for their Halloween party, in short rhyming verse. (Rev: BL 9/15/86; SLJ 12/86)

6224 Leedy, Loreen. *2 x 2=Boo! A Set of Spooky Multiplication Stories* (1–4). Illus. 1995, Holiday House LB $16.95 (0-8234-1190-7). 32pp. Halloween creatures and objects are used in a series of scary stories to demonstrate the principles of multiplication. (Rev: BL 9/15/95; SLJ 11/95)

6225 Levine, Abby. *This Is the Pumpkin* (PS–K). Illus. by Paige Billin-Frye. 1997, Whitman LB $13.95 (0-8075-7886-X). 24pp. All of the fun and excitement of Halloween, first at school then trick-or-treating, is captured in a catchy cumulative verse. (Rev: BL 9/1/97; HBG 3/98; SLJ 9/97)

6226 Lewis, Kevin. *The Runaway Pumpkin* (PS–2). Illus. by S. D. Schindler. 2003, Scholastic $15.95 (0-439-43974-4). A giant pumpkin on the rampage is finally brought under control in this Halloween story with a repetitive chorus. (Rev: HBG 4/04; SLJ 10/03)

6227 London, Jonathan. *Froggy's Halloween* (PS–1). Illus. by Frank Remkiewicz. 1999, Viking $15.99 (0-670-88449-9). 32pp. Froggy decides to dress as the Frog Prince on Halloween and looks so handsome that, to his dismay, Frogilina wants to kiss him. (Rev: BL 9/1/99; HBG 3/00; SLJ 9/99)

6228 Martin, Bill, Jr., and John Archambault. *The Magic Pumpkin* (PS–2). Illus. by Robert J. Lee. 1989, Holt $15.95 (0-8050-1134-X). 32pp. A carved pumpkin proves to be a menace to the young narrator in this scary story. (Rev: BL 9/1/89; SLJ 12/89)

6229 Mayr, Diane. *Littlebat's Halloween Story* (PS–1). Illus. by Gideon Kendall. 2001, Whitman $14.95 (0-8075-7629-8). 32pp. Littlebat loves story time but his mother tells him he must remain hidden until he can make an appearance without scaring the children. (Rev: BL 9/1/01; HBG 3/02; SLJ 9/01)

6230 Meddaugh, Susan. *The Witches' Supermarket* (PS–3). Illus. 1991, Houghton Mifflin $13.95 (0-395-57034-4). 32pp. On Halloween, Helen finds herself in a strange supermarket offering such goodies as scum milk and bug bars. (Rev: BCCB 9/91; BL 8/91; SLJ 11/91)

6231 Melmed, Laura Krauss. *Fright Night Flight* (PS–2). Illus. by Henry Cole. 2002, HarperCollins LB $17.89 (0-06-029702-6). 32pp. A witch and her friends set off on jet-fueled brooms for a trick-or-treat spree, warning readers in rhyme that they're the next stop. (Rev: BL 9/1/02; HBG 3/03; SLJ 9/02)

6232 Mills, Claudia. *Gus and Grandpa and the Halloween Costume* (2–3). Illus. by Catherine Stock. Series: Gus and Grandpa. 2002, Farrar $15.00 (0-374-32816-1). 48pp. It's Grandpa who solves Gus's Halloween costume crisis, producing a Mounties uniform that Gus's father wore when he was a boy. (Rev: BL 9/1/02; HBG 3/03)

6233 Mitton, Tony. *Spooky Hour* (PS–2). Illus. by Guy Parker-Rees. 2004, Scholastic $16.95 (0-439-60373-0). A bouncy Halloween book featuring witches, ghosts, skeletons, and other characters on their way to a great feast. (Rev: SLJ 8/04)

6234 Nikola-Lisa, W. *Shake Dem Halloween Bones* (PS–2). Illus. by Mike Reed. 1997, Houghton Mifflin $16.00 (0-395-73095-3). 32pp. Fairy tale characters shake, rattle, and roll at a super Halloween party. (Rev: BL 10/1/97; HBG 3/98)

6235 O'Malley, Kevin. *Velcome* (2–4). Illus. 1997, Walker LB $16.95 (0-8027-8629-4). 32pp. A picture book of jokes and scary stories for Halloween that are narrated by a host who "velcomes" you into his house. (Rev: BL 9/1/97; HBG 3/98; SLJ 9/97)

6236 Palatini, Margie. *Broom Mates* (K–3). Illus. by Howard Fine. 2003, Hyperion $15.99 (0-7868-0418-1). A premature visit from her sister, Mag the Hag, threatens to ruin Halloween festivities for Gritch the Witch in this romp full of puns. (Rev: HBG 4/04; SLJ 9/03)

6237 Parish, Herman. *Happy Haunting, Amelia Bedelia* (K–2). Illus. by Lynn Sweat. 2004, Greenwillow LB $16.89 (0-06-051894-4). 64pp. Amelia Bedelia is supposed to be helping Mr. and Mrs. Rogers with their Halloween party. (Rev: SLJ 8/04)

6238 Passen, Lisa. *Attack of the 50-Foot Teacher* (K–3). Illus. 2000, Holt $16.00 (0-8050-6100-2). 32pp. Miss Birmbaum assigns homework on Halloween but, after an encounter with space aliens and a visit with her principal, she realizes that nobody gives homework on a holiday like this. (Rev: BL 11/15/00; HBG 3/01; SLJ 12/00)

6239 Pilkey, Dav. *The Hallo-Wiener* (PS–2). Illus. 1995, Scholastic $14.95 (0-590-41703-7). 32pp. At Halloween, Oscar the dachshund earns a change in his nickname from Wiener Dog to Hero Sandwich. (Rev: BCCB 10/95; BL 9/15/95; SLJ 10/95*)

6240 Polacco, Patricia. *Picnic at Mudsock Meadow* (K–3). Illus. 1992, Penguin Putnam $15.95 (0-399-21811-4). 32pp. During the Halloween festivities, William is a failure until he has courage enough to investigate a scary swamp. (Rev: BL 11/15/92; HB 11–12/92; SLJ 10/92)

6241 Pollack, Pam, and Meg Belviso. *Halloween Night on Shivermore Street* (PS–2). Illus. by Randy DuBurke. 2004, Chronicle $15.95 (0-8118-3946-X). Three children enjoy a masquerade ball until the clock strikes 13. (Rev: SLJ 8/04)

6242 Poydar, Nancy. *The Perfectly Horrible Halloween* (PS–3). Illus. 2001, Holiday House $16.95 (0-8234-1592-9). 32pp. Arnold successfully improvises for the Halloween contest after forgetting his costume. (Rev: BL 9/1/01; HBG 3/02; SLJ 9/01)

6243 Reiner, Carl. *Tell Me a Scary Story . . . But Not Too Scary!* (PS–2). Illus. by James Bennett. 2003, Little, Brown $18.95 (0-316-83329-0). In this suspenseful Halloween tale, a curious boy finds more than he bargained for when he goes exploring in the basement of a mysterious neighbor. (Rev: HBG 4/04; SLJ 10/03)

6244 Rex, Michael. *Brooms Are for Flying!* (PS). Illus. by author. 2000, Holt $16.00 (0-8050-6410-9). A pretty little witch leads a group of kids in Halloween costumes in simple appropriate exercises like showing the skeleton how to shake one's bones. (Rev: BL 9/1/03; HB 9–10/00; HBG 3/01; SLJ 9/00)

6245 Roberts, Bethany. *Halloween Mice!* (PS–1). Illus. by Doug Cushman. 1995, Clarion $13.00 (0-395-67064-0). 32pp. At Halloween, a group of mice turn the tables and frighten a cat. (Rev: BL 9/15/95; SLJ 9/95)

6246 Ross, Eileen. *The Halloween Showdown* (K–2). Illus. by Lynn Rowe Reed. 1999, Holiday House $15.95 (0-8234-1395-0). At Halloween, Grandmother Katt enlists the help of her animal friends to save a kitty that has been stolen by a witch named Grizzorka. (Rev: BCCB 10/99; HBG 3/00; SLJ 9/99)

6247 Roy, Ron. *The Bald Bandit* (2–4). Illus. by John S. Gurney. Series: A to Z Mysteries. 1997, Random LB $11.99 (0-679-98449-6); paper $3.99 (0-679-88449-1). 70pp. A short Halloween story about three youngsters who are trying to find a videotape of a bank robbery. (Rev: HBG 3/98; SLJ 1/98)

6248 Ruelle, Karen Gray. *Spookier Than a Ghost* (1–2). Illus. 2001, Holiday House $14.95 (0-8234-1667-4). 32pp. Kitten Emily's Halloween costume doesn't turn out quite as she had hoped, but she and brother Harry still have fun trick-or-treating in this easy reader. (Rev: BL 9/15/01; HBG 3/02; SLJ 9/01)

6249 Rylant, Cynthia. *Moonlight: The Halloween Cat* (PS–K). Illus. by Melissa Sweet. 2003, HarperCollins LB $15.89 (0-06-029712-3). Moonlight the black cat serves as tour guide for this non-spooky celebration of Halloween. (Rev: HBG 4/04; SLJ 9/03)

6250 Saltzberg, Barney. *The Problem with Pumpkins: A Hip and Hop Story* (PS–1). Illus. 2001, Harcourt $14.00 (0-15-202489-1). 40pp. Hip (a hippo) and her best friend Hop (a rabbit) argue about what they should be for Halloween. (Rev: BL 9/15/01; HBG 3/02; SLJ 9/01)

6251 Serfozo, Mary. *Plumply, Dumply Pumpkin* (PS–1). Illus. by Valeria Petrone. 2001, Simon & Schuster $12.95 (0-689-83834-4). 32pp. Rhyming text and bright illustrations show little tiger Peter's search for the perfect pumpkin to carve into a jack-o'-lantern. (Rev: BL 9/1/01; HBG 3/02; SLJ 9/01)

6252 Shaw, Nancy. *Sheep Trick or Treat* (PS–1). Illus. by Margot Apple. 1997, Houghton Mifflin $14.00 (0-395-84168-2). 32pp. Sheep in costumes go trick-or-treating at Halloween and have unexpected adventures. (Rev: BL 9/1/97; HB 9–10/97; HBG 3/98; SLJ 9/97)

6253 Sierra, Judy. *The House That Drac Built* (K–2). Illus. by Will Hillenbrand. 1995, Harcourt $14.00 (0-15-200015-1). 40pp. Halloween misadventures occur to a number of animals in the house that Drac built. (Rev: BCCB 10/95; BL 9/15/95; SLJ 9/95)

6254 Smalls, Irene. *Jenny Reen and the Jack Muh Lantern* (PS–3). Illus. by Keinyo White. 1996, Simon & Schuster $16.00 (0-689-31875-8). 32pp. Jenny Reen, a slave child, is frightened by a wild creature she sees in the woods in this Halloween tale. (Rev: BCCB 12/96; BL 9/1/96; SLJ 12/96)

6255 Spirn, Michele. *A Know-Nothing Halloween* (1–2). Illus. Series: I Can Read. 2000, HarperCollins LB $15.99 (0-06-028186-6). 48pp. Four friends and a dog named Floris learn some Halloween tricks and scare themselves in this book for beginning readers. (Rev: BL 9/1/00)

6256 Tegen, Katherine. *Dracula and Frankenstein Are Friends* (PS–2). Illus. by Doug Cushman. 2003, HarperCollins LB $16.89 (0-06-000116-X). The bonds of friendship between Frankenstein and Dracula are severely strained when the two host competing parties on Halloween. (Rev: HBG 4/04; SLJ 9/03)

6257 Thompson, Lauren. *Mouse's First Halloween* (PS–K). Illus. by Buket Erdogan. 2000, Simon & Schuster $12.95 (0-689-83176-5). 32pp. On his first Halloween, Mouse has a few scary adventures. (Rev: BL 9/1/00; HBG 3/01; SLJ 8/00)

6258 Todd, Mark. *What Will You Be for Halloween?* (PS–2). Illus. 2001, Houghton Mifflin $9.95 (0-618-08803-2). 32pp. Brief, rhymed text accompanies pictures of children dressed in Halloween costumes. (Rev: BL 9/1/01; HBG 3/02; SLJ 9/01)

6259 Updike, David. *An Autumn Tale* (2–4). Illus. by Robert Andrew Parker. 1988, Pippin $15.95 (0-945912-02-1). 40pp. A magical Halloween tale of young Homer and his dog Sophocles. (Rev: BCCB 5/89; BL 10/15/88; SLJ 11/88)

6260 Vaughan, Marcia. *We're Going on a Ghost Hunt* (PS–3). Illus. by Ann Schweninger. 2001, Harcourt $15.00 (0-15-202353-4). 32pp. A light-hearted rhyming Halloween story of two children who go out hunting for a ghost, only to become frightened and run home. (Rev: BL 9/15/01; HBG 3/02; SLJ 9/01)

6261 Walton, Rick. *Mrs. McMurphy's Pumpkin* (PS–3). Illus. by Delana Bettoli. 2004, HarperCollins $8.99 (0-06-053409-5). An uppity pumpkin challenges an unafraid Mrs. Murphy. (Rev: SLJ 8/04)

6262 West, Kipling. *A Rattle of Bones: A Halloween Book of Collective Nouns* (K–2). Illus. 1999, Orchard $15.95 (0-531-30196-6). 32pp. In a series of rhyming couplets, collective nouns are effectively introduced to describe groups of creatures associated with Halloween, such as a cloud of bats, a venom of spiders, and a wake of vultures. (Rev: BL 9/1/99; HBG 3/00; SLJ 9/99)

6263 Weston, Martha. *Tuck's Haunted House* (PS–2). Illus. 2002, Clarion $14.00 (0-618-15966-5). 32pp. Tuck the pig stages a haunted house for his friends, and his little sister Bunny adds to the scariness of Halloween. (Rev: BL 9/1/02; HBG 3/03; SLJ 10/02)

6264 Wiencirz, Gerlinde. *Teddy's Halloween Secret* (PS–2). Trans. from German by J. Alison James. Illus. by Giuliano Lunelli. 2001, North-South LB $15.88 (0-7358-1531-3). Paul's animal friends are so successful in creating his Halloween costume that nobody recognizes him. (Rev: HBG 3/02; SLJ 9/01)

6265 Williams, Suzanne. *The Witch Casts a Spell* (PS–2). Illus. by Barbara Olsen. 2002, Dial $14.99 (0-8037-2646-5). 32pp. Spookily costumed children at a Halloween party dance along to this song, sung to the tune of "The Farmer in the Dell." (Rev: BL 9/1/02; HBG 3/03)

6266 Winters, Kay. *The Teeny Tiny Ghost* (PS–1). Illus. by Lynn Munsinger. 1997, HarperCollins LB $14.89 (0-06-025684-2). 32pp. A tiny ghost passes the test of not being frightened on Halloween. (Rev: BL 9/1/97; HBG 3/98; SLJ 11/97)

6267 Winters, Kay. *The Teeny Tiny Ghost and the Monster* (K–3). Illus. by Lynn Munsinger. 2004, HarperCollins LB $15.89 (0-06-028885-X). The teeny tiny ghost is surprised to win the Make a

Monster contest with his creation made from junk. (Rev: SLJ 8/04)

6268 Winters, Kay. *Whooo's Haunting the Teeny Tiny Ghost?* (PS–1). Illus. by Lynn Munsinger. 1999, HarperCollins $14.95 (0-06-027358-5). 32pp. The teeny tiny ghost finds that someone is haunting his house and later discovers that it is his cousin practicing his haunting techniques. (Rev: BL 9/1/99; HBG 3/00; SLJ 9/99)

6269 Winthrop, Elizabeth. *Halloween Hats* (1–3). Illus. by Sue Truesdell. 2002, Holt $15.95 (0-8050-6386-2). 32pp. Amusing illustrations add to the fun as children try on all sorts of hats for Halloween trick-or-treating. (Rev: BL 9/15/02; HBG 3/03; SLJ 10/02)

6270 Yolen, Jane. *Child of Faerie, Child of Earth* (K–3). Illus. by Jane Dyer. 1997, Little, Brown $15.95 (0-316-96897-8). 32pp. On Halloween, a little girl is transported to a magical fairy land but, in time, realizes that she must go home. (Rev: BL 1/1–15/98; HBG 3/98; SLJ 1/98)

6271 Ziefert, Harriet. *On Halloween Night* (PS–2). Illus. by Renee W. Andriani. 2001, Puffin paper $5.99 (0-14-056820-4). Emily's costume grows in "The House That Jack Built" fashion as her whole family pitches in to help. (Rev: SLJ 9/01)

6272 Zolotow, Charlotte. *A Tiger Called Thomas* (PS–2). Illus. by Diana Cain Bluthenthal. 2003, Hyperion $15.99 (0-7868-0517-X). A new edition, with new illustrations, of the story about shy young Thomas who gains courage in his new neighborhood when he dresses up as a tiger for Halloween. (Rev: HBG 4/04; SLJ 9/03)

JEWISH HOLY DAYS

6273 Adler, David A. *Chanukah in Chelm* (K–3). Illus. by Kevin O'Malley. 1997, Lothrop LB $15.89 (0-688-09953-X). 32pp. A bumbling synagogue keeper is the central character in this story set at Hanukkah. (Rev: BL 9/1/97; HB 9–10/97; HBG 3/98; SLJ 10/97*)

6274 Biers-Ariel, Matt. *Solomon and the Trees* (K–3). Illus. by Esti Silverberg-Kiss. 2001, UAHC $12.95 (0-8074-0749-6). 32pp. King Solomon rues the day that he inadvertently allowed his forest to be cut down to build the Temple, in the legend said to have inspired the Jewish holiday of Tu Bish'vat. (Rev: BL 8/01)

6275 Bunting, Eve. *One Candle* (2–3). Illus. by K. Wendy Popp. 2002, HarperCollins LB $17.89 (0-06-028116-2). 32pp. Grandma brings a potato to the family Hanukkah celebration in remembrance of her time in a World War II concentration camp. (Rev: BL 9/1/02; HBG 3/03; SLJ 10/02)

6276 Carter, David A. *Chanukah Bugs: A Pop-Up Celebration* (PS–K). Illus. by author. 2002, Simon & Schuster $10.95 (0-689-81860-2). Flaps that resemble gift boxes open to reveal the "Shammash Bug," the "Dizzy Dreidel Bug," and so forth, one for each of the eight nights. (Rev: SLJ 10/02)

6277 Cohen, Barbara. *Here Come the Purim Players!* (K–3). Illus. by Shoshana Mekibel. 1998, UAHC $12.95 (0-8074-0645-7). In medieval Prague, the Jews in the ghetto celebrate Purim at the rabbi's house with a performance of the story of Esther. (Rev: SLJ 6/98)

6278 Gelman, Rita G. *Queen Esther Saves Her People* (K–3). Illus. by Frane Lessac. 1998, Scholastic $15.95 (0-590-47025-6). 40pp. A personalized account of the Jewish girl Esther and how she saved her people at the court of the Persian king. (Rev: BCCB 3/98; BL 3/1/98; HBG 10/98; SLJ 2/98) [222]

6279 Glaser, Linda. *The Borrowed Hanukkah Latkes* (K–3). Illus. by Nancy Cote. 1997, Whitman LB $15.95 (0-8075-0841-1). 32pp. Gradually, Rachel persuades the family's neighbor Mrs. Greenberg to join them for Hanukkah. (Rev: BL 9/1/97; HBG 3/98; SLJ 10/97)

6280 Gold-Vukson, Marji. *The Colors of My Jewish Year* (PS). Illus. by Madeline Wikler. 1998, Kar-Ben $4.95 (1-58013-011-9). This concept book introduces the colors of the rainbow (plus a few others) while describing the Jewish holidays associated with each. (Rev: SLJ 11/98)

6281 Goldin, Barbara D. *The World's Birthday: A Rosh Hashanah Story* (PS–3). Illus. by Jeanette Winter. 1990, Harcourt $13.95 (0-15-299648-6). 32pp. On Rosh Hashanah, the celebration of the birth of the world, Daniel wants to invite the world over to its birthday party. (Rev: BL 9/1/90; HB 11–12/90; SLJ 2/91)

6282 Greenberg, Melanie H. *Blessings: Our Jewish Ceremonies* (PS–3). Illus. 1995, Jewish Publication Soc. $16.95 (0-8276-0540-4). 32pp. Various ceremonies and rituals connected with the Jewish faith are explained. (Rev: BL 2/1/96) [296.4]

6283 Groner, Judye, and Madeline Wikler. *All About Hanukkah: In Story and Song*. Rev. ed. (K–3). Illus. by Kinny Kreiswirth. 1999, Kar-Ben paper $12.95 (1-58013-057-7). 32pp. This story on the origins of Hanukkah tells of struggles of the Jewish people of 2000 years ago to regain their religious freedom by opposing the power of a Syrian king. (Rev: SLJ 10/99) [286]

6284 Hall, Katy, and Lisa Eisenberg. *Hanukkah Ha-Has: Knock-Knock Jokes That Are a Latke Fun* (1–3). Illus. by Stephen Carpenter. Series: A Lift-the-Flap Knock-Knock Book. 2001, HarperCollins paper $6.95 (0-694-01361-7). Punch lines under the flaps make for groaning suspense in this collection that is illustrated with a family enjoying latkes and dreidel games. (Rev: SLJ 10/01) [818]

6285 Howland, Naomi. *Latkes, Latkes, Good to Eat: A Chanukah Story* (PS–1). Illus. 1999, Clarion $15.99 (0-395-89903-6). 32pp. As a reward for helping an old lady, Sadie is given a magic frying pan, which will produce as many latkes at Hanukkah as she wants. (Rev: BL 9/1/99; HBG 3/00; SLJ 10/99)

6286 Howland, Naomi. *The Matzah Man: A Passover Story* (PS–1). Illus. 2002, Clarion $15.00 (0-618-11750-4). 32pp. Matzah Man attempts to escape the Passover seder in this version of the story of the gingerbread boy filled with familiar Jewish references. (Rev: BL 2/15/02; HBG 10/02; SLJ 3/02)

6287 Jules, Jacqueline. *Clap and Count! Action Rhymes for the Jewish New Year* (PS). Illus. by Sally Springer. 2001, Kar-Ben $17.95 (1-58013-067-4). 56pp. Nursery rhymes and finger plays with a Jewish twist take children through the holidays and holy days of the Jewish year. (Rev: BL 11/1/01)

6288 Kimmel, Eric A. *Asher and the Capmakers: A Hanukkah Story* (K–3). Illus. by Will Hillenbrand. 1993, Holiday House LB $15.95 (0-8234-1031-5). 32pp. Asher has many adventures when he sets out to borrow an egg for the family's latkes. (Rev: BL 7/93)

6289 Kimmel, Eric A. *The Chanukkah Guest* (PS–2). Illus. by Giora Carmi. 1990, Holiday House LB $16.95 (0-8234-0788-8); paper $6.95 (0-8234-0978-3). 32pp. Bubba Brayna is making potato latkes for the rabbi. (Rev: BCCB 12/90; BL 9/15/90*)

6290 Kimmel, Eric A. *Hershel and the Hanukkah Goblins* (K–3). Illus. by Trina S. Hyman. 1989, Holiday House LB $16.95 (0-8234-0769-1). 32pp. In this tale set in Eastern Europe, Hershel is looking forward to Hanukkah until he finds that the synagogue is haunted by goblins. (Rev: BCCB 10/89; BL 9/1/89; HB 1–2/90)

6291 Kimmel, Eric A. *The Magic Dreidels: A Hanukkah Story* (PS–3). Illus. by Katya Krenina. 1996, Holiday House LB $16.95 (0-8234-1256-3). 28pp. In this Hanukkah story, Jacob receives a magic dreidel from a goblin. (Rev: BCCB 11/96; BL 9/1/96)

6292 Kimmel, Eric A. *When Mindy Saved Hanukkah* (PS–2). Illus. by Barbara McClintock. 1998, Scholastic $15.95 (0-590-37136-3). 32pp. Mindy and Zayde, members of the miniature Klein family who live in the historic Eldridge Street Synagogue in New York, evade the huge synagogue cat and bring home a Hanukkah candle, showing that they are as brave as the heroes of old, the Maccabees. (Rev: BCCB 1/99; BL 9/1/98; HBG 3/99; SLJ 10/98)

6293 Kimmel, Eric A. *Zigazak! A Magical Hanukkah Night* (PS–4). Illus. by Jon Goodell. 2001, Doubleday $15.95 (0-385-32652-1). 32pp. A rabbi outwits two playful devils who are disrupting a small town's Hanukkah celebration. (Rev: BCCB 10/01; BL 10/1/01; HBG 3/02; SLJ 10/01)

6294 Kimmelman, Leslie. *The Runaway Latkes* (PS). Illus. by Paul Yalowitz. 2000, Whitman $15.95 (0-8075-7176-8). 32pp. In this humorous Hanukkah version of "The Gingerbread Man," three latkes jump out of the pan and roll off to see the town. (Rev: BL 9/1/00; HBG 3/01)

6295 Kimmelman, Leslie. *Sound the Shofar! A Story for Rosh Hashanah and Yom Kippur* (PS–1). Illus. by John Himmelman. 1998, HarperCollins $12.95 (0-06-027501-4). 32pp. A young girl describes the family's activities during Rosh Hashanah and Yom Kippur while her uncle blows the ram's horn, known as the shofar. (Rev: BL 10/1/98; HBG 3/99; SLJ 1/99)

6296 Kobre, Faige. *A Sense of Shabbat* (PS–K). Illus. 1990, Torah $14.95 (0-933873-44-1). 32pp. This Jewish holiday is shown from a preschooler's sensory perspective. (Rev: BCCB 3/91; BL 1/1/91) [296.4]

6297 Kress, Camille. *Purim!* (PS). Illus. by author. 1999, UAHC $5.95 (0-8074-0654-6). A brief text and quiet illustrations depict a group of children acting out the story of Purim. (Rev: SLJ 8/99)

6298 Kress, Camille. *Tot Shabbat* (PS). Illus. 1996, UAHC $5.95 (0-8074-0607-4). 7pp. In this simple board book, the Jewish Sabbath is introduced. (Rev: BL 2/1/97; SLJ 9/97)

6299 Krulik, Nancy. *Is It Hanukkah Yet?* (K–1). Illus. by DyAnne DiSalvo-Ryan. Series: Step into Reading. 2000, Random $3.99 (0-375-80286-X). 48pp. This easy-to-read book follows the last-minute preparations for Hanukkah and the first night's activities as seen through the eyes of a little girl. (Rev: BL 9/1/00)

6300 Lanton, Sandy. *Lots of Latkes: A Hanukkah Story* (K–3). Illus. by Vicki Jo Redenbaugh. 2003, Lerner $14.95 (1-58013-091-7); paper $6.95 (1-58013-061-5). Despite the fact that everyone brought latkes instead of the varied spread that had been planned, the guests at Rivka Leah's Hanukkah party have a wonderful time. (Rev: HBG 4/04; SLJ 10/03)

6301 Levine, Abby. *This Is the Dreidel* (PS–2). Illus. by Paige Billin-Frye. 2003, Whitman LB $14.95 (0-8075-7884-3). Simple rhyming couplets and bright illustrations show Max and his younger sister Ruth preparing for and participating in the fun of Hanukkah. (Rev: HBG 4/04; SLJ 10/03)

6302 Levine, Abby. *This Is the Matzah* (PS–2). Illus. by Paige Billin-Frye. 2005, Whitman $15.95 (0-8075-7885-1). 32pp. Max and his sister Ruth help their parents prepare for the Seder celebration in this introduction to the traditions of Passover told in rhyming couplets. (Rev: BL 2/15/05; SLJ 5/05)

6303 Manushkin, Fran. *The Matzah That Papa Brought Home* (PS–1). Illus. by Ned Bittinger. 1995, Scholastic $14.95 (0-590-47146-5). 32pp. A cumulative tale that introduces symbols associated with Passover. (Rev: BL 1/15/95; SLJ 2/95)

6304 Medoff, Francine. *The Mouse in the Matzah Factory* (K–3). Illus. by Nicole In den Bosch. 2003, Kar-Ben paper $6.95 (1-58013-048-8). 32pp. A curious mouse follows a harvest of wheat from field to mill to bakery, where it is made into matzohs for Passover. (Rev: BL 3/15/03; SLJ 10/03)

6305 Melmed, Laura K. *Moishe's Miracle: A Hanukkah Story* (K–3). Illus. by David Slonim. 2000, HarperCollins LB $15.98 (0-688-14683-X). 32pp. Moishe's generosity at Hanukkah results in a gift of a magical pan that makes pancakes for all. (Rev: BL 9/1/00; HB 9–10/00; HBG 3/01)

6306 Michelson, Richard. *Grandpa's Gamble* (PS–4). Illus. by Barry Moser. 1999, Marshall Cavendish $15.95 (0-7614-5034-3). 32pp. At Passover, Grandpa, a Jewish immigrant of many years ago, regrets that he lied and cheated to get ahead and tells how he changed his wicked ways. (Rev: BCCB 4/99; BL 3/15/99; HBG 10/99; SLJ 6/99)

6307 Modesitt, Jeanne. *It's Hanukkah!* (PS–1). Illus. by Robin Spowart. 1999, Holiday House $15.95 (0-8234-1451-5). A family of mice enjoy all the activities associated with Hanukkah, including lighting the Menorah and eating latkes. (Rev: HBG 3/00; SLJ 10/99)

6308 Nerlove, Miriam. *Hanukkah* (PS–1). Illus. 1989, Whitman paper $5.95 (0-8075-3142-1). 24pp. A brief history and explanation of the customs and activities of Hanukkah in verse. (Rev: BL 7/89; SLJ 9/89)

6309 Nerlove, Miriam. *Passover* (PS–1). Illus. 1989, Whitman LB $13.95 (0-8075-6360-9). 24pp. A description of this Jewish holy day in rhyming text. (Rev: BL 1/15/90; SLJ 4/90)

6310 Nerlove, Miriam. *Purim* (PS–1). Illus. 1992, Whitman LB $13.95 (0-8075-6682-9). 24pp. Watercolors and simple text explain the joyful observance of Purim. (Rev: BL 1/1/92; SLJ 9/92)

6311 Nerlove, Miriam. *Shabbat* (PS–1). Illus. 1998, Whitman $13.95 (0-8075-7324-8). 24pp. Using a simple rhyming text and gentle watercolors, this book shows how a happy, traditional family observes Shabbat, the Jewish Sabbath, both at home and at the synagogue. (Rev: BL 10/1/98; HBG 3/99; SLJ 10/98) [296.4]

6312 Newman, Leslea. *Matzo Ball Moon* (PS–3). Illus. by Elaine Greenstein. 1998, Clarion $15.00 (0-395-71530-X). 32pp. At Passover, all of Eleanor's family enjoy the matzo balls of her grandmother, Bubbe, and when Eleanor opens the door to welcome the prophet Elijah, she sees a full moon and imagines it to be another of Bubbe's yummy creations. (Rev: BL 4/1/98; HBG 10/98; SLJ 6/98)

6313 Newman, Leslea. *Runaway Dreidel!* (PS–2). Illus. by Krysten Brooker. 2002, Holt $17.95 (0-8050-6237-8). 32pp. A rhyming fantasy about a dreidel that takes off, zooming into space to become a star. (Rev: BCCB 11/02; BL 9/1/02; HBG 3/03; SLJ 10/02)

6314 Oberman, Sheldon. *By the Hanukkah Light* (1–4). Illus. by Neil Waldman. 1997, Boyds Mills $15.95 (1-56397-658-7). 32pp. As Rachel and her grandfather polish the menorah at Hanukkah, he tells her about the Holocaust and its meaning for the Jewish people. (Rev: BL 9/1/97*; HBG 3/98; SLJ 10/97)

6315 Olswanger, Anna. *Shlemiel Crooks* (2–4). Illus. by Paula Goodman Koz. 2005, NewSouth paper $14.95 (1-58838-165-X). 36pp. Based on a true incident, this humorous story tells of the hapless thieves who plan to steal Reb Elias's special Passover wine. (Rev: BL 5/15/05; SLJ 6/05)

6316 Portnoy, Mindy A. *Matzah Ball: A Passover Story* (PS–3). Illus. by Katherine J. Kahn. 1994, Kar-Ben paper $6.95 (0-929371-69-0). While attending a baseball game during Passover, Aaron meets an elderly man (Elijah perhaps?) who tells him about Jewish fans going to games at Ebbets Field. (Rev: SLJ 8/94)

6317 Pushker, Gloria Teles. *Toby Belfer and the High Holy Days* (K–3). Illus. by Judith Hierstein. Series: Toby Belfer. 2001, Pelican $14.95 (1-56554-765-9). 32pp. Toby explains the meaning of the Jewish holidays of Rosh Hashanah and Yom Kippur to her friend Donna. (Rev: BL 10/1/01; HBG 3/02; SLJ 1/02)

6318 Rosen, Michael J. *Our Eight Nights of Hanukkah* (K–3). Illus. by DyAnne DiSalvo-Ryan. 2000, Holiday House $16.95 (0-8234-1476-0). 32pp. The activities of a Jewish family are chronicled as they celebrate the eight nights of Hanukkah. (Rev: BL 9/1/00; HBG 3/01)

6319 Rothenberg, Joan. *Inside-Out Grandma* (K–3). Illus. 1995, Hyperion LB $15.49 (0-7868-2092-6). 32pp. A circuitous story about the relationship between a grandmother wearing her clothes inside out and making potato pancakes at Hanukkah. (Rev: BCCB 11/95; BL 9/15/95)

6320 Rouss, Sylvia A. *Sammy Spider's First Passover* (PS–K). Illus. by Katherine J. Kahn. 1995, Kar-Ben paper $6.95 (0-929371-82-8). A pleasant story about a little spider that watches the Shapiro family make preparations for Passover. (Rev: SLJ 7/95)

6321 Rouss, Sylvia A. *Sammy Spider's First Rosh Hashanah* (PS–1). Illus. by Katherine J. Kahn. 1996, Kar-Ben paper $6.95 (0-929371-99-2). Mother Spider explains to her son Sammy the holiday customs and symbols associated with the Jewish New Year. (Rev: SLJ 5/97)

6322 Rouss, Sylvia A. *Sammy Spider's First Shabbat* (K–2). Illus. by Katherine J. Kahn. 1998, Kar-Ben $14.95 (1-58013-007-0); paper $5.95 (1-58013-006-2). Sammy Spider observes the Shapiro family's preparations for the Shabbat, including braiding the challah. (Rev: SLJ 6/98)

6323 Silverman, Erica, adapt. *When the Chickens Went on Strike: A Rosh Hashanah Tale* (K–3). Illus. by Matthew Trueman. 2003, Dutton $15.99 (0-525-46862-5). Adapted from a tale by Sholom Aleichem, this amusing story tells how the chickens of a small Russian village protest the Jewish New Year ritual of Kapores, in which a chicken is held over the head of believers to absolve them of guilt. (Rev: HB 7–8/03; HBG 4/04; SLJ 9/03)

6324 Simpson, Lesley. *The Shabbat Box* (PS–1). Illus. by Nicole In den Bosch. 2001, Kar-Ben paper $6.95 (1-58013-027-5). 32pp. Ira must come up with a solution when he loses the treasured class Shabbat box on his way home from school. (Rev: BL 10/1/01; SLJ 12/01)

6325 Snyder, Carol. *God Must Like Cookies, Too* (PS–1). Illus. by Beth Glick. 1993, Jewish Publication Soc. $16.95 (0-8276-0423-8). 32pp. A young girl attends a Shabbat service at temple and looks forward to the three cookies she has been promised after the service. (Rev: BL 1/15/94; SLJ 10/93)

6326 Spinner, Stephanie. *It's a Miracle: A Hanukkah Storybook* (K–2). Illus. by Jill McElmurry. 2003, Simon & Schuster $16.95 (0-689-84493-X). Owen lights the candles each night of the holiday and his Grandma Karen tells a story of Jewish family life. (Rev: HBG 4/04; SLJ 10/03)

6327 Stillerman, Marci. *Nine Spoons: A Chanukah Story* (K–2). Illus. by Pesach Gerber. 1998, Hachai $11.95 (0-922613-84-2). In a Nazi concentration camp, Raizel shows her ingenuity by fashioning a menorah out of nine spoons so that Hanukkah can be celebrated. (Rev: HB 1–2/99; HBG 3/99; SLJ 10/98)

6328 Topek, Susan Remick. *A Costume for Noah: A Purim Story* (PS–K). Illus. by Sally Springer. 1996, Kar-Ben $13.95 (0-929371-91-7); paper $5.95 (0-929371-90-9). Traditional terms and customs are introduced in this simple story of a boy preparing with his friends to celebrate Purim. (Rev: SLJ 5/96)

6329 Topek, Susan Remick. *Shalom Shabbat: A Book for Havdalah* (PS). Illus. by Shelly Schonebaum Ephraim. 1998, Kar-Ben $4.95 (1-58013-010-0). This simple board book celebrates the ceremony of Havdalah that takes place at the end of the Jewish Sabbath. (Rev: SLJ 2/99)

6330 Ungar, Richard. *Rachel's Gift* (K–3). Illus. 2003, Tundra $16.95 (0-88776-616-1). 32pp. With humor and style, Ungar describes a Chelm family's preparations for its Passover seder. (Rev: BL 5/1/03; HBG 10/03; SLJ 5/03)

6331 Vorst, Rochel Groner. *The Sukkah That I Built* (PS–2). Illus. by Elizabeth Victor-Elsby. 2002, Hachai $9.95 (1-929628-07-2). 26pp. A young boy (with help from his family) builds a sukkah — a temporary structure used in the celebration of Sukkot — to the refrain of "The House that Jack Built." (Rev: BL 10/1/02; HBG 3/03)

6332 Weilerstein, Sadie R. *K'tonton's Yom Kippur Kitten* (K–2). Illus. by Joe Boddy. 1995, Jewish Publication Soc. $12.95 (0-8276-0541-2). 36pp. K'tonton learns the true meaning of Yom Kippur when he tries to blame a kitten for the problems he has created. (Rev: BL 11/15/95; SLJ 3/96)

6333 Wilkowski, Susan. *Baby's Bris* (PS–1). Illus. by Judith Friedman. 1999, Karben $16.95 (1-58013-052-6); paper $6.95 (1-58013-053-4). 32pp. A young girl grows to love her baby brother particularly through an understanding of the bris ceremony when the boy is circumcised. (Rev: BL 1/1–15/00; HBG 3/00; SLJ 1/00)

6334 Yorinks, Arthur. *The Flying Latke* (1–3). Photos by Paul Colin and Arthur Yorinks. Illus. by William Steig. 1999, Simon & Schuster $16.95 (0-689-82597-8). A humorous Hanukkah story about a quarrel that results in a latke flying over New Jersey and a family being trapped for eight days and nights. (Rev: BCCB 11/99; HBG 3/00; SLJ 10/99)

6335 Zalben, Jane Breskin. *Happy New Year, Beni* (PS–3). Illus. 1993, Holt $13.95 (0-8050-1961-8). 28pp. A tender picture book showing an extended Jewish family celebrating the New Year. (Rev: BL 7/93)

6336 Zalben, Jane Breskin. *Pearl's Passover: A Family Celebration Through Stories, Recipes, Crafts, and Songs* (K–3). Illus. 2002, Simon & Schuster $16.00 (0-689-81487-9). 48pp. A lamb named Pearl and her family prepare for Passover in

this volume that interweaves fictional characters with recipes, crafts, and basic information about the holiday. (Rev: BL 2/15/02; HB 3–4/02; HBG 10/02; SLJ 2/02)

6337 Zolkower, Edie Stoltz. *Too Many Cooks: A Passover Parable* (PS–2). Illus. by Shauna Mooney Kawasaki. 2000, Kar-Ben paper $5.95 (1-58013-063-1). At Passover, everyone in the family decides to add a special ingredient to Bubbie's charoses for the seder. (Rev: SLJ 12/00)

THANKSGIVING

6338 Bateman, Teresa. *A Plump and Perky Turkey* (PS–2). Illus. by Jeff Shelly. 2001, Winslow $15.95 (1-890817-91-0). 40pp. Pete the turkey cleverly escapes hungry townspeople on Thanksgiving. (Rev: BCCB 11/01; BL 9/1/01; HBG 3/02; SLJ 9/01)

6339 Brown, Marc. *Arthur's Thanksgiving* (K–3). Illus. by author. 1983, Little, Brown paper $5.95 (0-316-11232-1). 32pp. Arthur is made director of his class Thanksgiving play.

6340 Bunting, Eve. *How Many Days to America? A Thanksgiving Story* (2–4). Illus. by Beth Peck. 1988, Houghton Mifflin $16.00 (0-89919-521-0); paper $5.95 (0-395-54777-6). 32pp. A family flees oppression on a Caribbean island and heads for the United States. (Rev: BL 11/1/88; SLJ 10/88)

6341 Bunting, Eve. *A Turkey for Thanksgiving* (PS–1). Illus. by Diane De Groat. 1991, Houghton Mifflin $15.00 (0-89919-793-0). 32pp. After bringing a live turkey home at Thanksgiving, Mr. and Mrs. Moose decide to have a vegetarian meal. (Rev: BCCB 9/91; BL 10/1/91; SLJ 9/91)

6342 Capucilli, Alyssa Satin. *Happy Thanksgiving, Biscuit!* (PS). Illus. by Pat Schories. 1999, HarperCollins paper $6.95 (0-694-01221-1). In this flap book, Biscuit, an endearing puppy, enjoys the fuss surrounding Thanksgiving. (Rev: SLJ 12/99)

6343 Cazet, Denys. *Minnie and Moo and the Thanksgiving Tree* (1–2). Illus. 2000, DK $12.95 (0-7894-2654-4); paper $3.95 (0-7894-2655-2). 418pp. At Thanksgiving, Minnie and Moo help the animals (starting with the turkeys) escape by hiding them in a tree only to discover that the farmer and his family are vegetarians. (Rev: BL 9/1/00; HB 9–10/00; HBG 3/01; SLJ 9/00)

6344 Corey, Shana. *Millie and the Macy's Parade* (PS–2). Illus. by Brett Helquist. 2002, Scholastic $16.95 (0-439-29754-0). 40pp. Millie, a Polish American girl whose father works for Mr. Macy, comes up with a great idea: a Thanksgiving Day parade. (Rev: BL 9/1/02; HBG 3/03; SLJ 10/02)

6345 Cowley, Joy. *Gracias, the Thanksgiving Turkey* (PS–2). Illus. by Joe Cepeda. 1996, Scholastic $15.95 (0-590-46976-2). 32pp. A New York City boy dreads Thanksgiving, when his pet turkey, Gracias, will be killed. (Rev: BCCB 11/96; BL 9/1/96; SLJ 12/96)

6346 Dalgliesh, Alice. *The Thanksgiving Story* (K–3). Illus. by Helen Sewell. 1988, Macmillan $16.00 (0-684-18999-2); paper $5.99 (0-689-71053-4). 32pp. This reissued 1954 Caldecott Honor Book tells of the Hopkins family's experiences from the Mayflower voyage to the first Thanksgiving.

6347 De Groat, Diane. *We Gather Together . . . Now Please Get Lost!* (PS–2). Illus. 2001, North-South LB $15.88 (1-58717-096-5). 32pp. Gilbert and his animal classmates take an entertaining, mishap-filled field trip to Pilgrim Town. (Rev: BL 9/1/01; HBG 3/02; SLJ 8/01)

6348 Geisert, Arthur. *Nursery Crimes* (PS–3). Illus. 2001, Houghton Mifflin $16.00 (0-618-06487-7). 32pp. Turkey-shaped topiaries have gone missing, and the family of pigs who created them must figure out how to expose the thief. (Rev: BCCB 9/01; BL 11/15/01; HBG 3/02; SLJ 11/01)

6349 Gibbons, Gail. *Thanksgiving Is . . .* (PS–2). Illus. by author. 2004, Holiday House $16.95 (0-8234-1849-9). Brief text introduces the holiday and its relation to harvest time, Pilgrims, and Native Americans. (Rev: SLJ 9/04) [394.2]

6350 Goode, Diane. *Thanksgiving Is Here!* (PS–2). Illus. by author. 2003, HarperCollins LB $16.89 (0-06-051589-9). An appealing portrait of an extended family gathering for its annual Thanksgiving feast. (Rev: HBG 4/04; SLJ 9/03)

6351 Greene, Rhonda Gowler. *The Very First Thanksgiving Day* (PS–2). Illus. by Susan Gaber. 2002, Simon & Schuster $15.95 (0-689-83301-6). 40pp. The story of the first Thanksgiving, told in rhyme and accompanied by lovely paintings. (Rev: BL 9/15/02; HBG 3/03; SLJ 10/02)

6352 Jackson, Alison. *I Know an Old Lady Who Swallowed a Pie* (PS–2). Illus. by Judith Byron Schachner. 1997, Dutton $15.99 (0-525-45645-7). 32pp. This favorite folk song is given a new twist by using foods associated with Thanksgiving. (Rev: BL 9/1/97; HBG 3/98; SLJ 11/97)

6353 Jennings, Sharon. *Franklin's Thanksgiving* (PS–1). Illus. by Brenda Clark. Series: Franklin. 2001, Kids Can $10.95 (1-55074-798-3). 32pp. Franklin the turtle's family Thanksgiving dinner becomes so overcrowded that the feast is moved outdoors. (Rev: BL 9/15/01; HBG 3/02; SLJ 9/01)

6354 Kimmelman, Leslie. *Round the Turkey: A Grateful Thanksgiving* (2–4). Illus. by Nancy Cote. 2002, Whitman $15.95 (0-8075-7131-8). 32pp. The members of a family gathered for Thanksgiving take turns giving thanks, in rhyme. (Rev: BL 9/15/02; HBG 3/03; SLJ 9/02)

6355 Kroll, Steven. *Oh, What a Thanksgiving!* (K–2). Illus. by S. D. Schindler. 1988, Scholastic paper $3.95 (0-590-40616-7). 32pp. David imagines himself at Plymouth in 1620. (Rev: BL 9/15/88; SLJ 9/88)

6356 Milgrim, David. *Thank You, Thanksgiving* (PS–K). Illus. by author. 2003, Clarion $9.95 (0-618-27466-9). 32pp. A little girl walks through town expressing in simple words her thanks to all the animals and objects that enrich her life. (Rev: HBG 4/04; SLJ 9/03)

6357 Pomeranc, Marion Hess. *The Can-Do Thanksgiving* (K–2). Illus. by Nancy Cote. 1998, Whitman $14.95 (0-8075-1054-8). 32pp. Through a school food drive and a contribution of a can of peas, Dee

is chosen to help serve a Thanksgiving meal and, there, meets a new friend. (Rev: BL 11/1/98; HBG 3/99; SLJ 9/98)

6358 Rael, Elsa Okon. *Rivka's First Thanksgiving* (PS–3). Illus. by Maryann Kovalski. 2001, Simon & Schuster $16.00 (0-689-83901-4). 32pp. Young Rivka challenges a rabbi when he says that Jews should not celebrate Thanksgiving in this story set in early 1900s New York. (Rev: BCCB 11/01; BL 9/15/01; HBG 3/02; SLJ 11/01)

6359 Roberts, Bethany. *Thanksgiving Mice!* (PS–1). Illus. by Doug Cushman. 2001, Clarion $13.00 (0-618-12040-8). 32pp. Mice put on a play about the trials of the Pilgrims and the first Thanksgiving. (Rev: BL 9/1/01; HBG 3/02; SLJ 9/01)

6360 Rockwell, Anne. *Thanksgiving Day* (PS–K). Illus. by Lizzy Rockwell. 1999, HarperCollins LB $14.89 (0-06-028388-2). 40pp. In a series of double-page spreads, a preschooler and his classmates perform a short play that tells what they have learned about the first Thanksgiving and the Pilgrims. (Rev: BL 9/1/99; HBG 3/00; SLJ 10/99)

6361 Roop, Peter, and Connie Roop. *Let's Celebrate Thanksgiving* (1–4). Illus. by Gwen Connelly. 1999, Millbrook LB $19.90 (0-7613-0973-X); paper $5.95 (0-7613-0429-0). 32pp. An easy-to-read explanation of Thanksgiving's origination and how it is celebrated, along with some related jokes and projects. (Rev: BL 9/15/99; HBG 3/00; SLJ 11/99) [394.2649]

6362 Ruelle, Karen G. *The Thanksgiving Beast Feast* (1–2). Illus. 1999, Holiday House $14.95 (0-8234-1511-2). 32pp. At Thanksgiving, Harry Cat and his sister, Emily, decide to show their thanks by preparing food for the birds, squirrels, and chipmunks in their neighborhood. (Rev: BL 9/1/99; HB 9–10/99; HBG 3/00; SLJ 9/99)

6363 Scheer, Julian. *A Thanksgiving Turkey* (PS–3). Illus. by Ronald Himler. 2001, Holiday House $16.95 (0-8234-1674-7). 32pp. A boy learns to know his grandfather and Virginia farm life in a beautifully illustrated and sensitive story that culminates with the capture and release of a wild turkey. (Rev: BCCB 10/01; BL 9/1/01; HBG 3/02; SLJ 9/01)

6364 Spinelli, Eileen. *Thanksgiving at the Tappletons'* (PS–3). Illus. by Megan Lloyd. 2003, HarperCollins LB $15.89 (0-06-008671-8). Everything seems to be going wrong as the Tappletons, a family of wolves, prepare for their Thanksgiving feast. (Rev: HBG 4/04; SLJ 9/03)

6365 Spirn, Michele. *The Know-Nothings Talk Turkey* (1–2). Illus. Series: I Can Read. 2000, HarperCollins $14.95 (0-06-028183-9). 48pp. In his easy-to-read book, four friends and their dog Floris decide to serve a turkey at Thanksgiving so they invite one to their dinner. (Rev: BL 9/1/00; HBG 3/01; SLJ 10/00)

6366 Willey, Margaret. *Thanksgiving with Me* (PS–2). Illus. by Lloyd Bloom. 1998, HarperCollins $14.95 (0-06-027113-2). 32pp. While her mother describes each of her six brothers, a little girl waits with great anticipation for the arrival of her uncles at Thanksgiving time. (Rev: BCCB 11/98; BL 9/1/98; HBG 3/99; SLJ 9/98)

VALENTINE'S DAY

6367 Bond, Felicia. *The Day It Rained Hearts* (PS–K). 2001, HarperCollins LB $14.89 (0-06-001078-9). 63pp. When it rains hearts, Cornelia catches them and makes unique, individualized valentines for her friends. (Rev: BL 12/1/01; HBG 3/02)

6368 Bunting, Eve. *The Valentine Bears* (K–3). Illus. by Jan Brett. 1983, Houghton Mifflin $15.00 (0-89919-138-X); paper $5.95 (0-89919-313-7). 32pp. Mr. and Mrs. Bear decide not to sleep through Valentine's Day this year.

6369 Capucilli, Alyssa Satin. *Biscuit's Valentine's Day* (PS). Illus. by Pat Schories. 2000, HarperCollins $6.95 (0-694-01222-X). 20pp. While his young owner is preparing for Valentine's Day, Biscuit the dog is engaged in all sorts of activities that are revealed when the reader lifts the flaps in this interactive book. (Rev: BL 2/15/01)

6370 Carr, Jan. *Sweet Hearts* (PS–2). Illus. by Dorothy Donohue. 2002, Holiday House $16.95 (0-8234-1732-8). 32pp. Elaborately constructed collage valentines star in this story in which a little panda creates and decorates paper hearts for his parents. (Rev: BL 12/1/02; HBG 3/03; SLJ 11/02)

6371 Gantos, Jack. *Rotten Ralph's Rotten Romance* (PS–1). Illus. by Nicole Rubel. 1997, Houghton Mifflin $14.95 (0-395-73978-0). 32pp. Rotten Ralph decides to be completely unlovable on Valentine's Day. (Rev: BL 11/15/96; SLJ 2/97)

6372 Gregory, Valiska. *A Valentine for Norman Noggs* (PS–2). Illus. by Marsha Winborn. 1999, HarperCollins LB $14.89 (0-06-027657-6). 32pp. Hamster Norman faces possible trouble when he ignores the threats of bullies Richard and Arthur and delivers a valentine to Wilhemina. (Rev: BCCB 2/99; BL 4/1/99; HBG 10/99; SLJ 1/99)

6373 Hoban, Lillian. *Silly Tilly's Valentine* (K–2). Illus. by author. Series: I Can Read. 1998, HarperCollins LB $14.89 (0-06-027401-8). 47pp. Tilly the mole is so excited about a snowfall that she forgets it is Valentine's Day. (Rev: HBG 10/98; SLJ 2/98)

6374 Lexau, Joan M. *Don't Be My Valentine: A Classroom Mystery* (1–2). Illus. by Syd Hoff. 1999, HarperCollins $14.95 (0-06-028239-8). 64pp. In this easy-to-read book, Amy Lou keeps butting into Sam's affairs, so he sends her a not-so-nice valentine that, unfortunately, is received by his teacher. (Rev: BL 3/15/99; HBG 10/99)

6375 Modell, Frank. *One Zillion Valentines* (PS–2). Illus. by author. 1987, Morrow paper $4.95 (0-688-07329-8). 32pp. Milton and Marvin distribute their homemade hearts to the neighborhood.

6376 Poydar, Nancy. *Rhyme Time Valentine* (PS–3). Illus. 2002, Holiday House $16.95 (0-8234-1684-4). 32pp. Poor little Ruby is dismayed when the valentines she made are blown away by a strong wind. (Rev: BL 1/1–15/03; HBG 3/03; SLJ 11/02)

6377 Roberts, Bethany. *Valentine Mice!* (PS–K). Illus. by Doug Cushman. 1998, Clarion $13.00 (0-395-77518-3). 32pp. A group of mice are so busy delivering valentines in a snowy forest that they don't realize the smallest one of them is missing. (Rev: BL 12/15/97; HBG 10/98; SLJ 1/98)

6378 Rockwell, Anne. *Valentine's Day* (K–2). Illus. by Lizzy Rockwell. 2000, HarperCollins LB $14.89 (0-06-028515-X). 40pp. Mrs. Madoff's class make and send valentines to their friend, Michido, who is back in Japan and, on Valentine's Day, a package arrives from her filled with origami valentines. (Rev: BL 1/1–15/01)

6379 Roop, Peter, and Connie Roop. *Let's Celebrate Valentine's Day* (2–4). Illus. by Katy K. Arnsteen. Series: Let's Celebrate. 1999, Millbrook LB $19.90 (0-7613-0972-1); paper $5.95 (0-7913-0428-2). 32pp. Discusses the origins of Valentine's Day, describes how it is celebrated, and includes many related jokes and riddles. (Rev: BL 2/15/99; HBG 10/99; SLJ 4/99) [394.2618]

6380 Ruelle, Karen G. *Snow Valentines* (1–2). Illus. Series: Holiday House Readers. 2000, Holiday House $14.95 (0-8234-1533-3). 32pp. A book for beginning readers that describes how two little cats solve the problem of what to get their parents for Valentine's Day. (Rev: BL 7/00; HBG 10/01; SLJ 9/00)

Books for Beginning Readers

6381 Aboff, Marcie. *The Giant Jelly Bean Jar* (K–2). Illus. by Paige Billin-Frye. Series: Puffin Easy-to-Read. 2004, Penguin Putnam LB $13.99 (0-525-47236-3). 32pp. Ben is too shy to speak up, even when he knows the answer that will win the jar of candy. (Rev: BL 2/1/04; SLJ 9/04)

6382 Adler, David A. *Bones and the Cupcake Mystery* (K–2). Illus. by Barbara Johansen Newman. 2005, Viking $13.99 (0-670-05939-0). 32pp. Boy detective Jeffrey Bones investigates what happened to a classmate's spinach noodle cupcake. (Rev: BL 2/15/05; SLJ 6/05)

6383 Adler, David A. *Young Cam Jansen and the Baseball Mystery* (1–2). Illus. by Susanna Natti. Series: A Viking Easy-to-Read Book. 1999, Viking $13.99 (0-670-88481-2). 32pp. Cam Jansen, the girl with the amazing memory, tackles the problem of a missing baseball. (Rev: BL 10/1/99; HBG 10/99; SLJ 6/99)

6384 Adler, David A. *Young Cam Jansen and the Dinosaur Game* (1–2). Illus. 1996, Viking $13.99 (0-670-86399-8). 32pp. Cam discovers that a boy has cheated in order to win a prize. (Rev: BCCB 5/96; BL 8/96; SLJ 7/96)

6385 Adler, David A. *Young Cam Jansen and the Double Beach Mystery* (K–2). Illus. by Susanna Natti. Series: Viking Easy-to-Read. 2002, Viking $13.99 (0-670-03531-9). 32pp. An easy-to-read mystery involving Cam and her friend Eric and mysterious doings on the beach. (Rev: BL 5/1/02; HBG 10/02; SLJ 6/02)

6386 Adler, David A. *Young Cam Jansen and the Library Mystery* (K–2). Illus. by Susanna Natti.

2001, Viking $13.99 (0-670-89281-5). 32pp. Cam is determined to find her father's missing shopping list. (Rev: BL 5/1/01; HBG 10/01)

6387 Adler, David A. *Young Cam Jansen and the New Girl Mystery* (PS–2). Illus. by Susanna Natti. 2004, Viking $13.99 (0-670-05915-3). 32pp. When Jennifer, the new girl in school, disappears, Cam sets out to track her down. (Rev: BL 5/1/04)

6388 Adler, David A. *Young Cam Jansen and the Pizza Shop Mystery* (1–2). Illus. by Susanna Natti. Series: Easy-to-Read. 2000, Viking $13.99 (0-670-88861-3). 32pp. Cam Jansen uses her photographic memory to determine who stole her jacket and why in this book for beginning readers. (Rev: BL 4/15/00; HBG 10/00; SLJ 5/00)

6389 Ahlberg, Allan. *The Ghost Train* (1–2). Illus. by André Amstutz. Series: Funnybones. 1992, Morrow paper $3.95 (0-688-11659-0). 32pp. Three skeletons known as the Funnybones take a train ride to a ghost town. (Rev: BL 10/1/92)

6390 Albee, Sarah. *The Dragon's Scales* (1–2). Illus. by John Manders. Series: Step into Reading + Math. 1998, Random LB $11.99 (0-679-98381-3); paper $3.99 (0-679-88381-9). 48pp. While telling an exciting story about a clever girl who outwits a dragon, this book also explains the concept of weights and measures. (Rev: BL 7/98)

6391 Albert, Shirley. *Doll Party* (1–2). Illus. by Amy Flynn. 1994, Penguin Putnam paper $3.99 (0-448-40182-7). 32pp. An easy-to-read book about Becky and her new doll. (Rev: BL 1/1/95)

6392 Alexander, Sue. *World Famous Muriel and the Magic Mystery* (2–3). Illus. by Marla Frazee. 1990, HarperCollins LB $12.89 (0-690-04789-4). 32pp. Muriel, known for her tightrope walking and incredible smarts, is after a missing magician. (Rev: BL 3/15/90; SLJ 7/90)

6393 Allen, Laura J. *Rollo and Tweedy and the Ghost at Dougal Castle* (1–2). Illus. Series: I Can Read. 1992, HarperCollins LB $15.89 (0-06-020107-X). 64pp. A mouse detective and his assistant catch the ghost that is haunting a Scottish castle. (Rev: BCCB 9/92*; BL 6/15/92; HB 9–10/92; SLJ 10/92)

6394 Alphin, Elaine Marie. *Dinosaur Hunter* (1–2). Illus. by Don Bolognese. Series: I Can Read Book 4 Ser. 2003, HarperCollins LB $16.89 (0-06-028304-1). 48pp. After discovering dinosaur bones on his family's Wyoming ranch in the late 19th century, Ned foils the attempts of a fossil hunter to swindle him out of them. (Rev: BL 9/1/03; HBG 4/04; SLJ 12/03)

6395 Armstrong, Jennifer. *Sunshine, Moonshine* (1–2). Illus. by Lucia Washburn. 1997, Random paper $3.99 (0-679-86442-3). 32pp. A busy day in the life of a young boy is chronicled in this easy-to-read book. (Rev: BL 5/1/97; SLJ 8/97)

6396 Augustyn, Brian. *Batman: The Mad Hatter* (1–3). Illus. by Rick Burchett. Series: Scholastic Reader. 2004, Scholastic paper $3.99 (0-439-47098-6). 40pp. Hats are disappearing all over Gotham in this Batman story for beginning readers featuring bright comic-book illustrations. (Rev: SLJ 8/04)

6397 Backstein, Karen. *The Blind Men and the Elephant* (1–2). Illus. by Annie Mitra. 1992, Scholastic paper $3.50 (0-590-45813-2). 48pp. The Indian folktale about the blind men who each see the nature of the elephant in a different way. (Rev: BL 3/1/93) [398.2]

6398 Bader, Bonnie. *Benny the Big Shot Goes to Camp* (1–2). Illus. by Shari Warren. Series: All Aboard Reading. 2003, Grosset LB $13.89 (0-448-43141-6); paper $3.99 (0-448-42894-6). 48pp. Benny's bragging fails to impress his campmates and they steal his "blankie." (Rev: BL 5/15/03; HBG 10/03)

6399 Baker, Alan. *Little Rabbits' First Word Book* (PS). Illus. 1996, Kingfisher $10.95 (0-7534-5020-8). 40pp. For beginning readers, basic words are given for everyday objects. (Rev: BL 11/1/96) [428.1]

6400 Baker, Barbara. *Digby and Kate and the Beautiful Day* (1–2). Illus. by Marsha Winborn. Series: Dutton Easy Reader. 1998, Dutton $13.99 (0-525-45855-7). 48pp. In this easy reader, dog Digby and cat Kate find that, like all true friends, they sometimes have their differences. (Rev: BL 2/1/98; HBG 10/98; SLJ 3/98*)

6401 Baker, Barbara. *N-O Spells No!* (1–3). Illus. by Nola L. Malone. 1993, Scholastic paper $3.99 (0-590-44186-8). 64pp. In this book illustrated with cartoons, there are five short stories about Annie and her big brother. (Rev: BL 6/1/91; SLJ 8/91)

6402 Baker, Keith. *Little Green* (PS–1). Illus. 2001, Harcourt $16.00 (0-15-292859-6). 32pp. In this easy reader, a boy is fascinated by the behavior of a hummingbird. (Rev: BCCB 4/01; BL 4/15/01; HBG 10/01; SLJ 4/01)

6403 Baker, Keith. *Lucky Days with Mr. and Mrs. Green* (K–2). Illus. by author. 2005, Harcourt $16.00 (0-15-216500-2). 72pp. Mr. Green looks for his wife's lost pearls, guesses the number of gumballs in a jar, and enters a singing contest in the three stories in this chapter book. (Rev: BCCB 4/05; HB 5–6/05; SLJ 3/05)

6404 Baker, Keith. *Meet Mr. and Mrs. Green* (PS–2). Illus. by author. 2002, Harcourt $16.00 (0-15-216506-1). Alligator couple Mr. and Mrs. Green enjoy camping, going to the fair, and an agreeable outlook on life. (Rev: HBG 3/03; SLJ 11/02)

6405 Baker, Keith. *More Mr. and Mrs. Green* (PS–2). Illus. by author. 2004, Harcourt $16.00 (0-15-216494-4). 68pp. Mr. and Mrs. Green — a likeable pair of alligators — star in three new adventures for new readers. (Rev: SLJ 3/04)

6406 Bang-Campbell, Monika. *Little Rat Sets Sail* (2–3). Illus. by Molly Bang. 2002, Harcourt $14.00 (0-15-216297-6). 48pp. In this beginning chapter book, Little Rat shows great courage as she takes sailing lessons from Buzzy Bear. (Rev: BCCB 5/02; BL 4/1/02; HB 7–8/02*; HBG 10/02; SLJ 6/02)

6407 Bauer, Marion Dane. *Bear's Hiccups* (1–2). Illus. by Diane D. Hearn. Series: Holiday House Readers. 1998, Holiday House $14.95 (0-8234-1339-X). 48pp. A group of animals demands to know if Bear, a grouch who wants to dominate the forest pond, is responsible for the disappearance of Frog. (Rev: BCCB 6/98; BL 5/1/98; HBG 10/98; SLJ 6/98)

6408 Bauer, Marion Dane. *Turtle Dreams* (1–2). Illus. by Diane D. Hearn. Series: Holiday House Readers. 1997, Holiday House LB $14.95 (0-8234-1322-5). 48pp. In this easy reader, Turtle goes to sleep for the winter and finds that he has wonderful dreams. (Rev: BL 2/1/98; HBG 3/98; SLJ 1/98)

6409 Bechtold, Lisze. *Buster, the Very Shy Dog* (2). Illus. 1999, Houghton Mifflin $16.00 (0-395-85008-8). 48pp. An easy reader about how shy puppy Buster adjusts to his new home and to Phoebe, an older dog. (Rev: BCCB 3/99; BL 5/15/99; HB 7–8/99; HBG 10/99; SLJ 5/99)

6410 Benchley, Nathaniel. *A Ghost Named Fred* (1–3). Illus. by Ben Shecter. 1968, HarperCollins LB $15.89 (0-06-020474-5). 64pp. To get out of the rain, George enters an empty house and meets Fred, an absentminded ghost.

6411 Benchley, Nathaniel. *Oscar Otter* (K–2). Illus. by Arnold Lobel. 1966, HarperCollins LB $15.89 (0-06-020472-9); paper $3.95 (0-06-444025-7). 64pp. Hilarious words and pictures describe Oscar's fun on the long and perilous slide he builds to get to his pool.

6412 Bernstein, Margery. *My Brother, the Pest* (1–2). Illus. by Dorothy Handelman. Series: Real Kids Readers. 1999, Millbrook LB $16.90 (0-7613-2055-5); paper $3.99 (0-7613-2080-6). 32pp. A rhyming story of sibling rivalry involving two sisters who quarrel and make up. (Rev: BL 5/15/99; SLJ 8/99)

6413 Black, Sonia. *Hanging Out with Mom* (1–2). Illus. by George Ford. 2000, Scholastic paper $3.99 (0-590-86636-2). 32pp. A beginning reader about a day that an African American boy and his mother spend in the park. (Rev: BL 10/1/00)

6414 Blackstone, Stella. *Bear on a Bike* (PS–1). Illus. by Debbie Harter. Series: A Barefoot Beginner Book. 1999, Barefoot $13.95 (1-901223-49-3). A bear, accompanied by a young African American boy, takes off in a variety of vehicles to see the world and its wonders. (Rev: SLJ 3/99)

6415 Blair, Eric, retel. *Belling the Cat: A Retelling of Aesop's Fable* (K–3). Illus. by Dianne Silverman. Series: Read-It! Readers Fairy Tales. 2004, Picture Window LB $18.60 (1-4048-0321-1). 24pp. A simple retelling for beginning readers, with brief material on Aesop and on the nature of a fable. Also use *The Shoemaker and His Elves: A Retelling of the Grimms' Fairy Tale*. (Rev: SLJ 8/04)

6416 Bonsall, Crosby. *Mine's the Best* (1–2). Illus. by author. 1997, HarperCollins paper $3.75 (0-064-44213-6). 32pp. Two small boys discover they have identical balloons, and then begins the argument — whose is the best?

6417 Bonsall, Crosby. *Piggle* (1–2). Illus. by author. 1973, HarperCollins LB $15.89 (0-06-020580-6). 64pp. Homer goes in search of someone to play games with and finds Bear, who enjoys "Piggle" with him. This rhyming spree of nonsense words will please beginning readers. (Rev: HBG 10/02)

6418 Bonsall, Crosby. *Tell Me Some More* (1–3). Illus. by Fritz Siebel. 1961, HarperCollins LB $15.89 (0-06-020601-2). 64pp. Andrew introduces his friend to the magic of the library.

6419 Bonsall, Crosby. *Who's a Pest?* (1–3). Illus. by author. 1962, HarperCollins LB $15.89 (0-06-020621-7); paper $3.95 (0-06-444099-0). 64pp. Even though his four sisters, a lizard, a rabbit, and a chipmunk insist that he's a pest, Homer refuses to believe it. (Rev: HBG 10/02)

6420 Bonsall, Crosby. *Who's Afraid of the Dark?* (1–3). Illus. by author. 1980, HarperCollins LB $15.89 (0-06-020599-7); paper $3.95 (0-06-444071-0). 32pp. A little boy talks about how Stella, his dog, is afraid of the dark. (Rev: HBG 10/02)

6421 Bottner, Barbara. *Bootsie Barker Ballerina* (1–2). Illus. by G. Brian Karas. 1997, HarperCollins LB $14.89 (0-06-027101-9). 40pp. Bootsie Barker gets her comeuppance when she tries to bully everyone in her ballet class, including the teacher. (Rev: BL 5/1/97; SLJ 6/97)

6422 Bottner, Barbara. *Two Messy Friends* (K–2). Illus. by author. Series: Hello Reader! 1999, Scholastic paper $3.50 (0-590-63285-X). In this beginning reader, two very different friends accommodate their differences because they value their friendship. (Rev: SLJ 8/99)

6423 Bottner, Barbara, and Gerald Kruglik. *Pish and Posh* (K–2). Illus. by Barbara Bottner. Series: I Can Read. 2004, HarperCollins LB $16.89 (0-06-051417-5). 46pp. Irrepressible Posh ignores careful Pish's advice and leaps straight into *The Fairy Handbook*, casting spells without heed. (Rev: SLJ 1/04)

6424 Bowdish, Lynea. *Thunder Doesn't Scare Me!* (K–1). Illus. by John Wallace. Series: Rookie Readers. 2001, Children's Book Pr. $18.00 (0-516-22151-5). 32pp. A small square book about a little girl and her dog who try to be brave during a thunderstorm. (Rev: BL 7/01)

6425 Brenner, Barbara. *Wagon Wheels* (1–3). Illus. by Don Bolognese. 1993, HarperCollins LB $15.89 (0-06-020669-1); paper $3.95 (0-06-444052-4). 64pp. The adventures of an African American family in Kansas in the 1870s.

6426 Bridwell, Norman. *Clifford Makes a Friend* (1). Illus. Series: Hello Reader! 1998, Scholastic paper $3.50 (0-590-37930-5). 32pp. Clifford, the beloved shaggy dog, meets a boy and, after copying his actions, becomes his friend. (Rev: BL 3/15/99)

6427 Brill, Marlene T. *Allen Jay and the Underground Railroad* (1–2). Illus. by Janice L. Porter. Series: On My Own. 1993, Carolrhoda LB $21.27 (0-87614-776-7); paper $5.95 (0-87614-605-1). 48pp. This story, which is based on fact, tells how a young Quaker child helped a slave to freedom. (Rev: BL 7/93; SLJ 8/93)

6428 Brimner, Larry. *Cats!* (1). Illus. by Tom Payne. 2000, Children's Book Pr. $15.00 (0-516-22010-1); paper $4.95 (0-516-27075-3). 24pp. After a little girl lets nine cats into her room, they oblige by playing with her in this book for beginning readers. (Rev: BL 2/15/01)

6429 Brimner, Larry. *Cowboy Up!* (PS–2). Illus. by Susan Miller. Series: Rookie Readers. 1999, Children's Book Pr. LB $17.00 (0-516-21199-4). 31pp. A beginning reader that tells, in simple text and pictures, of a cowboy's day at the rodeo. (Rev: HBG 10/99; SLJ 8/99)

6430 Brimner, Larry. *Dinosaurs Dance* (PS–K). Series: Rookie Readers. 1998, Children's Book Pr. LB $17.00 (0-516-20752-0). 32pp. Gaily colored cartoons show dinosaurs performing a series of dances in this beginning reader. (Rev: HBG 10/98; SLJ 7/98)

6431 Brisson, Pat. *Hot Fudge Hero* (1–3). Illus. by Diana C. Bluthenthal. 1997, Holt $15.95 (0-8050-4551-1). 73pp. A simple chapter book about the adventures of Bertie, a likable second-grade kid, who always gets a hot fudge sundae when he succeeds in his endeavors. (Rev: BCCB 6/97; BL 4/1/97; HB 7–8/97; SLJ 7/97)

6432 Brisson, Pat. *Little Sister, Big Sister* (2–3). Illus. 1999, Holt $15.95 (0-8050-5887-7). 56pp. Two sisters, Zelda and Ivy, are sometimes friends and sometimes enemies in these four stories for beginning readers. (Rev: BCCB 3/99; BL 4/15/99; HBG 10/99; SLJ 7/99)

6433 Brown, Marc. *There's No Place Like Home* (1–3). Illus. Series: Step into Reading. 1991, Parents $5.00 (0-8193-1125-1). 40pp. In this easy reader, various kinds of homes are introduced in verse. (Rev: BL 12/1/91)

6434 Brown, Margaret Wise. *I Like Stars* (1). Illus. by Joan Paley. Series: Road to Reading. 1998, Golden Books paper $3.99 (0-307-26105-0). 32pp. A little rabbit leaves his bed and joins in play with a frog, a bird, and a mouse in this easy-to-read book. (Rev: BL 3/15/99)

6435 Brust, Beth Wagener. *The Great Tulip Trade* (K–2). Illus. by Jenny Mattheson. Series: Step into Reading. 2005, Random LB $11.99 (0-375-92573-2); paper $3.99 (0-375-82573-8). 48pp. In tulip-crazy 1636 Holland, Anna refuses to trade her most cherished bloom even in exchange for gold and diamonds. (Rev: BL 6/1–15/05)

6436 Buck, Nola. *Sid and Sam* (PS–K). Illus. Series: My First I Can Read Book. 1996, HarperCollins LB $14.89 (0-06-025372-X). 32pp. Sid's song is so long that his friend Sam says, "So long." (Rev: BCCB 7–8/96; BL 8/96; SLJ 6/96)

6437 Bulla, Clyde Robert. *Daniel's Duck* (1–3). Illus. by Joan Sandin. 1979, HarperCollins LB $15.89 (0-06-020909-7); paper $3.95 (0-06-444031-1). 64pp. In this story for beginning readers, a young boy is hurt when people make fun of his wood carving of a duck.

6438 Burke, Jennifer S. *Cloudy Days* (PS–1). Series: Weather Report. 2000, Children's Book Pr. LB $13.50 (0-516-23117-0); paper $4.95 (0-516-23042-5). 24pp. In this beginning reader, a young girl decides what she will do and wear on a cloudy day. Also use *Sunny Days* (2000). (Rev: SLJ 3/01)

6439 Burnard, Damon. *Dave's Haircut* (K–3). Illus. by author. 2003, Dutton $10.99 (0-525-46967-2). 45pp. Unable to see any longer, Dave decides to cut

his own hair — with such disastrous results that he finally has to visit a barber. (Rev: HB 7–8/03; HBG 4/04; SLJ 8/03)

6440 Byars, Betsy. *Ant Plays Bear* (1–3). Illus. by Marc Simont. 1997, Viking $13.99 (0-670-86776-4). 32pp. An easy-to-read book that explores in four stories the relationship between a boy and his younger brother, Ant. (Rev: BL 9/1/97*; HB 7–8/97; HBG 3/98; SLJ 6/97)

6441 Byars, Betsy. *The Golly Sisters Ride Again* (1–3). Illus. by Sue Truesdell. 1994, HarperCollins LB $15.89 (0-06-021564-X). 64pp. Easily read stories about the Golly sisters, who run a traveling show in the old West. (Rev: BCCB 6/94; BL 4/1/94; HB 7–8/94; SLJ 6/94*)

6442 Byars, Betsy. *My Brother, Ant* (1–3). Illus. by Marc Simont. 1996, Viking $13.99 (0-670-86664-4). 32pp. A charming, amusing, easy chapter book in which a boy details some of the antics of his younger brother, Anthony — Ant, for short. (Rev: BL 1/1–15/96*; HB 7–8/96; SLJ 4/96)

6443 Calmenson, Stephanie. *My Dog's the Best!* (1–2). Illus. by Marcy Ramsey. 1997, Scholastic $3.99 (0-590-33072-1). 32pp. An easy-to-read book in which a number of children tell why they think their dog is best. (Rev: BL 2/1/98)

6444 Cameron, Ann. *Julian's Glorious Summer* (2–3). Illus. by Dora Leder. 1987, Random paper $3.99 (0-394-89117-1). 64pp. Troubles begin for Julian when he lies because he is afraid to ride a bike. Also use two other stories about the ups and downs of this warm African American family: *More Stories Julian Tells* (Knopf 1986); *Julian, Secret Agent* (Random 1988). (Rev: BCCB 12/87; BL 12/15/87; SLJ 12/87)

6445 Caple, Kathy. *The Friendship Tree* (1–2). Illus. Series: Holiday House Readers. 2000, Holiday House $14.95 (0-8234-1376-4). 32pp. Blanche and Otis are sheep in this easy reader that consists of four stories about trees and forests. (Rev: BL 2/15/00; HB 7–8/00; HBG 10/00; SLJ 4/00)

6446 Caple, Kathy. *Well Done, Worm!* (K–1). Illus. Series: Brand New Reader. 2000, Candlewick $10.99 (0-7636-1146-8). 32pp. Four very short stories featuring a lovable worm are contained in this beginning reader. (Rev: BL 10/1/00; HBG 3/01; SLJ 3/01)

6447 Caple, Kathy. *Worm Gets a Job* (PS–2). Illus. by author. 2004, Candlewick $15.99 (0-7636-1694-X). Worm's efforts to earn money for painting supplies have unexpected consequences. (Rev: SLJ 7/04)

6448 Cappetta, Cynthia. *Chairs, Chairs, Chairs!* (PS–2). Illus. by Rick Stromoski. Series: Rookie Readers. 1999, Children's Book Pr. LB $17.00 (0-516-21542-6). 31pp. A beginning reader that introduces different kinds of chairs, their sizes and shapes, and tells where they can be found. (Rev: HBG 10/99; SLJ 8/99)

6449 Capucilli, Alyssa Satin. *Bathtime for Biscuit* (1). Illus. by Pat Schories. 1998, HarperCollins LB $12.89 (0-06-027938-9). 32pp. A simple story about the problems a little boy has getting his little dog,

Biscuit, into the bath. (Rev: BL 11/1/98; HBG 3/99; SLJ 10/98)

6450 Capucilli, Alyssa Satin. *Biscuit* (K–1). Illus. 1996, HarperCollins LB $14.89 (0-06-026198-6). 32pp. A dog named Biscuit tries to make his wants known. (Rev: BL 8/96; SLJ 7/96)

6451 Capucilli, Alyssa Satin. *Biscuit Finds a Friend* (1–2). Illus. by Pat Schories. 1997, HarperCollins LB $14.89 (0-06-027413-1). 24pp. In this easy reader, a puppy named Biscuit finds a lost baby duckling. (Rev: BL 5/1/97; SLJ 6/97)

6452 Capucilli, Alyssa Satin. *Biscuit Goes to School* (K–1). Illus. by Pat Schories. Series: My First I Can Read Book. 2002, HarperCollins LB $16.89 (0-06-028683-0). 32pp. Biscuit the puppy follows his girl to school in this book for beginning readers. (Rev: BL 8/02; HBG 3/03)

6453 Capucilli, Alyssa Satin. *Biscuit Wants to Play* (PS–K). Illus. by Pat Schories. Series: My First I Can Read Book. 2001, HarperCollins LB $12.89 (0-06-028070-0). 32pp. Biscuit returns, and this time he wants to make friends with two reluctant kittens. (Rev: BL 11/1/01; HBG 10/01; SLJ 4/01)

6454 Capucilli, Alyssa Satin. *Biscuit's New Trick* (K–1). Illus. by Pat Schories. Series: I Can Read. 2000, HarperCollins $12.95 (0-06-028067-0). 32pp. A little girl thinks she is a failure at trying to get Biscuit, a puppy, to fetch a ball in this simple beginner's story. (Rev: BL 4/15/00; HBG 10/00; SLJ 6/00)

6455 Capucilli, Alyssa Satin. *Inside a Zoo in the City: A Rebus Read-Along Story* (PS–K). Illus. by Tedd Arnold. 2000, Scholastic $11.95 (0-590-99715-7). 32pp. Told with pictures that substitute for the names of various animals, this simple rebus book tells how the animals in a zoo actually live in apartments and have to get up in the morning and go to work like other people. (Rev: BL 12/15/00; HBG 10/01; SLJ 3/01)

6456 Carter, Candace. *Sid's Surprise* (PS–K). Illus. by Joung Un Kim. Series: Green Light Reader. 2005, Harcourt $12.95 (0-15-205183-X); paper $3.95 (0-15-205182-1). 32pp. This easy chapter book features a little snake who is thrilled to finally have a rattle — just like the big snakes. (Rev: BL 3/1/05)

6457 Cazet, Denys. *Elvis the Rooster Almost Goes to Heaven* (PS–3). Illus. by author. Series: I Can Read. 2003, HarperCollins LB $16.89 (0-06-000501-7). 48pp. Elvis, the rooster from the Minnie and Moo series, falls into a panic when he fails to crow one morning and must be restored to normal by his friends. (Rev: HBG 10/03; SLJ 5/03)

6458 Cazet, Denys. *Minnie and Moo: The Night Before Christmas* (K–2). Illus. Series: An I Can Read Book. 2002, HarperCollins LB $17.89 (0-06-623753-X). 48pp. Cows Minnie and Moo decide to dress up as Santa and Mrs. Claus and, accompanied by chickens and a rooster disguised as reindeer, set off to deliver the farmer's presents in this humorous takeoff of the well-known poem. Also use *Minnie and Moo and the Attack of the Easter Bunnies*

(2004). (Rev: BL 10/1/02; HB 11–12/02; HBG 3/03; SLJ 10/02)

6459 Cazet, Denys. *Minnie and Moo: The Night of the Living Bed* (1–2). Illus. by author. Series: I Can Read Book 3 Ser. 2003, HarperCollins LB $16.89 (0-06-000503-3). 48pp. It's Halloween, and cows Minnie and Moo team up to collect as much chocolate as possible. (Rev: BL 9/1/03; HBG 4/04; SLJ 9/03)

6460 Cazet, Denys. *Minnie and Moo: Will You Be My Valentine?* (PS–2). Illus. Series: An I Can Read Book. 2002, HarperCollins LB $16.89 (0-06-623755-6). 48pp. Some feelings are hurt when Minnie and Moo's valentines end up with the wrong recipients in this humorous easy reader. (Rev: BL 1/1–15/03; HB 1–2/03; HBG 3/03; SLJ 2/03)

6461 Cazet, Denys. *Minnie and Moo and the Musk of Zorro* (1–2). Illus. 2000, DK $12.95 (0-7894-2652-8); paper $3.95 (0-7894-2653-6). 48pp. Minnie and Moo, cows who are best friends, masquerade as Zorro to save the farm from a fox in this book for beginning readers. (Rev: BL 12/1/00; HB 9–10/00; HBG 3/01; SLJ 11/00)

6462 Cazet, Denys. *Minnie and Moo Go Dancing* (1–2). Illus. 1998, DK $12.95 (0-7894-2515-7); paper $3.95 (0-7894-2536-X). 48pp. In this easy reader, unexpected things happen when cows Minnie and Moo dress up to go dancing. (Rev: BCCB 9/98; BL 7/98; HBG 3/99; SLJ 11/98)

6463 Cazet, Denys. *Minnie and Moo Go to Paris* (1–2). Illus. 1999, DK $12.95 (0-7894-2595-5). 48pp. Two fun-loving cows commandeer a tour bus that takes them to China, Paris, and a safari park. Also use *Minnie and Moo Save the Earth* (1999). (Rev: BCCB 10/99; BL 12/1/99; HBG 3/00)

6464 Cazet, Denys. *Minnie and Moo Go to the Moon* (1–2). Illus. 1998, DK $12.95 (0-7894-2516-5); paper $3.95 (0-7894-2537-8). 48pp. Two cows, Minnie and Moo, have an exciting adventure after Moo decides she would like to drive a tractor. (Rev: BCCB 9/98; BL 7/98; HB 9–10/98; HBG 3/99; SLJ 11/98)

6465 Cazet, Denys. *Minnie and Moo Meet Frankenswine* (1–2). Illus. by author. Series: An I Can Read Book. 2001, HarperCollins LB $14.89 (0-06-623749-1). 46pp. Cows Minnie and Moo investigate the monster that is terrifying the farm animals. (Rev: HBG 3/02; SLJ 9/01)

6466 Cazet, Denys. *The Octopus* (1–3). Illus. Series: I Can Read. 2005, HarperCollins LB $16.89 (0-06-051089-7). 48pp. Barney the puppy is miserable with chicken pox, so Grandpa tells him an elaborate tall tale about his triumph over an octopus. (Rev: BL 1/1–15/05; SLJ 1/05)

6467 Chaconas, Dori. *Cork and Fuzz* (K–2). Illus. by Lisa McCue. 2005, Viking $13.99 (0-670-03602-1). 32pp. Cork and Fuzz, a muskrat and a possum, both bored and lonely, try to overlook their differences and find a common interest. (Rev: SLJ 5/05)

6468 Charles, Veronika M. *Don't Go into the Forest!* (2–3). Illus. by Leanne Franson. Series: Easy-to-Read Spooky Tales. 2001, Stoddart paper $5.95 (0-7737-6190-X). 56pp. Young boys tell each other scary stories while they contemplate entering a forest at night. (Rev: SLJ 1/02)

6469 Charles, Veronika M. *Don't Open the Door!* (2–3). Illus. by Leanne Franson. 2001, Stoddart paper $5.95 (0-7737-6137-3). 56pp. During a sleepover at the narrator's house, the guests enjoy telling each other scary stories. (Rev: BL 4/15/01; SLJ 9/01)

6470 Cleary, Beverly. *Muggie Maggie* (2–3). Illus. by Kay Life. 1990, Avon paper $4.95 (0-380-71087-0). 80pp. Third-grader Maggie decides that learning to write is not necessary for a girl who can use a computer. (Rev: BCCB 6/90; BL 3/15/90; HB 11–12/90; SLJ 6/90)

6471 Clements, Andrew. *Dolores and the Big Fire: A True Story* (1–2). Illus. by Ellen Beier. Series: Pets to the Rescue. 2002, Simon & Schuster $15.00 (0-689-82916-7). 32pp. Dolores, a cat who is afraid of the dark, manages to save her master when their house catches fire. (Rev: BL 6/1–15/02; HBG 10/02; SLJ 5/02)

6472 Clements, Andrew. *Pets to the Rescue: Brave Norman* (1–2). Illus. by Ellen Beier. Series: Ready-to-Read. 2001, Simon & Schuster $15.00 (0-689-82914-0). 32pp. A blind dog rescues a drowning girl in this book for beginning readers. (Rev: BL 11/1/01; HBG 3/02; SLJ 2/02)

6473 Clements, Andrew. *Ringo Saves the Day! A True Story* (K–3). Illus. by Ellen Beier. 2001, Simon & Schuster $15.00 (0-689-82915-9). 32pp. Ringo the cat — named for his affection for drumming — alerts his owners to a broken gas pipe in their backyard. (Rev: HBG 3/02; SLJ 9/01)

6474 Clifford, Eth. *Flatfoot Fox and the Case of the Missing Schoolhouse* (2–3). Illus. by Brian Lies. 1997, Houghton Mifflin $15.00 (0-395-81446-4). 48pp. An easy read in which Flatfoot Fox and sidekick Secretary Bird foil the schemes of Wacky Weasel. (Rev: BL 3/15/97; SLJ 4/97)

6475 Clifford, Eth. *Flatfoot Fox and the Case of the Nosy Otter* (2–4). Illus. by Brian Lies. 1992, Houghton Mifflin $15.00 (0-395-60289-0). 32pp. Flatfoot Fox is hot on the trail of Nosy, Mrs. Chatterbox Otter's missing son. Also use: *Flatfoot Fox and the Case of the Missing Eye* (1991). (Rev: BCCB 11/92; BL 9/1/92; SLJ 9/92)

6476 Cocca-Leffler, Maryann. *Ice-Cold Birthday* (K–1). Illus. Series: All Aboard Reading. 1992, Penguin Putnam paper $3.95 (0-448-40380-3). 32pp. A young girl has a delightful birthday in spite of a power blackout. (Rev: BL 10/1/92; SLJ 9/92)

6477 Coerr, Eleanor. *The Big Balloon Race* (1–3). Illus. by Carolyn Croll. 1992, HarperCollins LB $15.89 (0-06-021353-1); paper $3.95 (0-06-444053-2). 64pp. Arill and her mother fly their balloon in a suspenseful race.

6478 Coerr, Eleanor. *Buffalo Bill and the Pony Express* (2–4). Illus. by Don Bolognese. 1995, HarperCollins LB $15.89 (0-06-023373-7). 64pp. Billy outsmarts some Indians and scares off a pack of wolves in this easily read adventure. (Rev: BCCB 4/95; BL 4/15/95; HB 7–8/95; SLJ 5/95)

6479 Coerr, Eleanor. *Chang's Paper Pony* (1–3). Illus. by author. 1988, HarperCollins LB $15.89 (0-06-021329-9); paper $3.95 (0-06-444163-6). 64pp. A young Chinese boy longs for a pony in the California Gold Rush days. (Rev: BL 7/88; SLJ 12/88)

6480 Coerr, Eleanor. *The Josefina Story Quilt* (1–3). Illus. by Bruce Degen. 1986, HarperCollins LB $15.89 (0-06-021349-3); paper $3.95 (0-06-444129-6). 64pp. Faith's sorrow at the death of her pet hen during their trip west to California is softened by the quilt she sews in remembrance. (Rev: BCCB 5/86; BL 3/15/86; SLJ 5/86)

6481 Cohen, Caron L. *How Many Fish?* (1–2). Illus. by S. D. Schindler. Series: My First I Can Read Book. 1998, HarperCollins paper $12.95 (0-06-027713-0). 32pp. A fish is trapped under a child's upside-down pail, but later it is freed in this easy-to-read adventure. (Rev: BL 2/1/98; HBG 10/98; SLJ 2/98)

6482 Cole, Joanna. *Bully Trouble* (1–3). Illus. by Marylin Hafner. 1989, Random paper $3.99 (0-394-84949-3). 48pp. Two friends concoct a plan to get even with a bully. (Rev: BL 2/1/90; SLJ 2/90)

6483 Cole, Joanna. *The Missing Tooth* (1–3). Illus. by Marylin Hafner. 1989, Random paper $3.99 (0-394-89279-8). 48pp. Arlo is upset when best friend Robby loses a second tooth and he doesn't. (Rev: BL 3/1/89; SLJ 5/89)

6484 Cole, Joanna. *Norma Jean, Jumping Bean* (1–3). Illus. 1987, Random paper $3.99 (0-394-88668-2). 48pp. Norma Jean, a kangaroo child, stops jumping when her feelings are ruffled, until field day at school. (Rev: BCCB 6/87; BL 6/1/87; SLJ 6–7/87)

6485 Cole, Joanna, and Stephanie Calmenson, eds. *Ready . . . Set . . . Read! The Beginning Reader's Treasury* (K–2). Illus. 1990, Doubleday $17.95 (0-385-41416-1). 144pp. This is an easily read collection of stories by such writers as Dr. Seuss and Maurice Sendak. (Rev: BL 12/1/90; SLJ 9/90*)

6486 Collicott, Sharleen. *Mildred and Sam and Their Babies* (PS–2). Illus. Series: I Can Read! 2005, HarperCollins LB $16.89 (0-06-058112-3). 48pp. For beginning readers, this is a simple story about eight baby mice growing up in a safe and loving home. (Rev: BL 5/15/05)

6487 Conford, Ellen. *Annabel the Actress, Starring in Hound of the Barkervilles* (2–4). Illus. by Renee W. Andriani. 2002, Simon & Schuster LB $15.00 (0-689-84734-3). 96pp. Annabel's acting career is almost sabotaged by a slobbering dog, a ruined costume, and other nuisances. Also use *Annabel the Actress Starring in Camping It Up* (2004). (Rev: BCCB 10/02; BL 7/02; HBG 3/03; SLJ 7/02)

6488 Cooper, Susan. *The Magician's Boy* (2–4). Illus. by Serena Riglietti. 2005, Simon & Schuster $15.95 (0-689-87622-X). 112pp. The Boy, apprenticed to a master magician, is dispatched to find a missing puppet and in the course of his search ends up in a land filled with characters from familiar fairy tales and nursery rhymes. (Rev: BL 1/1–15/05; SLJ 3/05)

6489 Cosby, Bill. *One Dark and Scary Night* (K–2). Illus. by Varnette P. Honeywood. Series: Little Bill. 1999, Scholastic $15.95 (0-590-51475-X); paper $3.99 (0-590-51476-8). In this beginning reader, Little Bill learns to conquer his fears concerning noises he hears in the night. (Rev: HBG 10/99; SLJ 7/99)

6490 Cosby, Bill. *Shipwreck Saturday* (2–4). Illus. Series: Little Bill. 1998, Scholastic $13.95 (0-590-16400-7); paper $3.99 (0-590-95620-5). 40pp. Although Little Bill's boat is destroyed on its first voyage, a friend uses its parts for a kite. (Rev: BL 5/15/98; SLJ 6/98)

6491 Cosby, Bill. *Super-Fine Valentine* (2–4). Illus. Series: Little Bill. 1998, Scholastic $13.95 (0-590-16401-5); paper $3.99 (0-590-95622-1). 40pp. Using eye-catching artwork, this is the simple story of Little Bill who is reluctant to give his friend Mia a Valentine until some of his other friends give her one first. (Rev: BL 5/15/98; SLJ 6/98)

6492 Cottle, Joan. *Emily's Shoes* (1). Illus. 1999, Children's Book Pr. LB $17.50 (0-516-21585-X). 32pp. In this simple reader, Emily imagines all sorts of activities that she can engage in, along with the shoes that each would require. (Rev: BL 10/1/99)

6493 Cottringer, Anne. *Movie Magic: A Star Is Born* (2–4). Illus. by Roger Stewart. Series: Eyewitness Reader. 1999, DK $12.95 (0-7894-4009-1); paper $3.95 (0-7894-4008-3). 48pp. In this easy reader, which uses color photos to show the movie-making process, a young African American girl gets a part in a science fiction movie. (Rev: SLJ 8/99)

6494 Cowley, Joy. *Agapanthus Hum and Major Bark* (K–2). Illus. by Jennifer Plecas. 2001, Penguin Putnam $13.99 (0-399-23322-9). 48pp. In this easy-to-read chapter book, Agapanthus Hum enters her dog, Major Bark, in a dog show where he wins as the dog with the smallest eyes. (Rev: BCCB 3/01; BL 2/15/01; HBG 10/01; SLJ 2/01)

6495 Cowley, Joy. *Agapanthus Hum and the Angel Hoot* (PS–2). Illus. by Jennifer Plecas. Series: Agapanthus Hum. 2003, Penguin Putnam $13.99 (0-399-23344-X). 48pp. When Agapanthus Hum loses a tooth, she finds she can make a special sound her father calls an "angel hoot." (Rev: BCCB 3/03; BL 2/15/03; HBG 10/03; SLJ 2/03)

6496 Cox, Phil Roxbee. *Ted in a Red Bed* (K–1). Illus. by Stephen Cartwright. Series: Easy Words to Read. 1999, EDC paper $7.95 (0-7460-3023-1). 16pp. A beginning reader with flaps about a bear who buys a bed and falls asleep on it in the store. (Rev: SLJ 12/99)

6497 Coxe, Molly. *Big Egg* (1–2). Illus. 1997, Random LB $11.99 (0-679-98126-8); paper $3.99 (0-679-88126-3). 32pp. For the beginning reader, this story tells what happens after Hen finds a huge egg among her little ones. (Rev: BL 5/1/97)

6498 Coxe, Molly. *Hot Dog* (1). Illus. Series: Road to Reading. 1998, Golden Books paper $3.99 (0-307-26101-8). 32pp. A dog who is trying to fight the heat, irritates a cat, skunk, pig, and others in this beginning reader. (Rev: BCCB 2/99; BL 3/15/99)

6499 Cristaldi, Kathryn. *Baseball Ballerina* (1–3). Illus. by Abby Carter. Series: Step into Reading. 1992, Random paper $3.99 (0-679-81734-4). 48pp. A young girl who loves baseball is afraid that her friends will find out she is taking ballet lessons. (Rev: BCCB 6/92; BL 6/1/92; SLJ 9/92)

6500 Cristaldi, Kathryn. *Princess Lulu Goes to Camp* (1–2). Illus. by Heather H. Maione. 1997, Penguin Putnam paper $3.99 (0-448-41125-3). 48pp. An easy reader about the obnoxious Princess Lulu at a summer camp. (Rev: BL 8/97; SLJ 12/97)

6501 Cushman, Doug. *Aunt Eater Loves a Mystery* (1–2). Illus. by author. 1987, HarperCollins LB $15.89 (0-06-021327-2); paper $3.95 (0-06-444126-1). 64pp. Grandmotherly Aunt Eater, an anteater, loves to solve mysteries. (Rev: BL 10/1/87; SLJ 12/87)

6502 Cushman, Doug. *Aunt Eater's Mystery Vacation* (1–2). Illus. 1992, HarperCollins LB $15.89 (0-06-020514-8). 64pp. Amateur detective Aunt Eater finds mystery and adventure on what was promised to be a relaxing cruise. (Rev: BL 4/1/92; SLJ 6/92)

6503 Cushman, Doug. *Inspector Hopper's Mystery Year* (1–3). Illus. by author. Series: I Can Read. 2003, HarperCollins LB $16.89 (0-06-008963-6). 64pp. Grasshopper Inspector Hopper and his assistant, McBugg, are kept busy throughout the year with seasonal mysteries to solve. (Rev: HBG 10/03; SLJ 5/03)

6504 Cutler, Jane. *Rose and Riley Come and Go* (K–2). Illus. by Thomas F. Yezerski. 2005, Farrar $15.00 (0-374-36341-2). 48pp. Friends Rose, a tiny vole, and Riley, a lively groundhog, make discoveries about nature in three episodic stories for beginning readers that feature silly wordplay and detailed illustrations. (Rev: BL 6/1–15/05)

6505 Danziger, Paula. *Get Ready for Second Grade, Amber Brown* (1–3). Illus. by Tony Ross. 2002, Penguin Putnam $12.99 (0-399-23607-4). 48pp. Amber's concerns about the new second-grade teacher turn out to be unfounded in this prequel for beginning readers. (Rev: BL 11/1/02; HBG 10/02; SLJ 7/02)

6506 Danziger, Paula. *It's a Fair Day, Amber Brown* (1–3). Illus. by Tony Ross. 2002, Penguin Putnam $12.99 (0-399-23606-6). 48pp. Amber and her family spend an enjoyable day at the fair despite some arguments and Amber getting lost. (Rev: BL 11/1/02; HBG 10/02; SLJ 7/02)

6507 Danziger, Paula. *It's Justin Time, Amber Brown* (1–3). Illus. by Tony Ross. 2001, Penguin Putnam $12.99 (0-399-23470-5). 48pp. In this beginning reader, Amber Brown, age 7, gets her wish of a watch for her birthday now that she has learned to tell the time. (Rev: HBG 10/01; SLJ 3/01)

6508 Danziger, Paula. *Orange You Glad It's Halloween, Amber Brown?* (1–3). Illus. by Tony Ross. 2005, Penguin Putnam $13.99 (0-399-23471-3). 48pp. In addition to planning for Halloween, Amber has concerns about school and family life in this easy-reader that also features her best friend Justin. (Rev: BL 5/15/05)

6509 Danziger, Paula. *What a Trip, Amber Brown* (K–3). Illus. by Tony Ross. Series: A Is for Amber. 2001, Penguin Putnam $12.99 (0-399-23469-1). 48pp. Amber and Justin enjoy an on-again off-again friendship on a vacation in the "Poke a nose." (Rev: HBG 10/01; SLJ 4/01)

6510 Davis, Tim. *Mice of the Westing Wind: Book One* (2–3). Illus. by author. 1998, Journey Bks. paper $6.49 (1-57924-065-8). 114pp. Two mouse spies, Charles and Oliver, join a group out to capture a crew of pirate sea dogs who have escaped from prison. Also use *The Mouse of the Westing Wind: Book Two* (1998). (Rev: SLJ 5/99)

6511 Delacre, Lulu. *Rafi and Rosi* (1–3). Illus. by author. Series: I Can Read. 2004, HarperCollins LB $16.89 (0-06-009896-1). 63pp. Tree frogs Rafi — who has an inventive mind — and younger sister Rosi enjoy mild adventures in Puerto Rico, brightly illustrated with cartoon-like drawings. (Rev: SLJ 3/04)

6512 Delton, Judy. *Cookies and Crutches* (1–2). Illus. by Alan Tiegreen. 1988, Dell paper $3.99 (0-440-40010-4). 80pp. Molly and her friends find out that baking at home isn't quite as easy as it looks. (Rev: BL 6/1/88)

6513 Denslow, Sharon Phillips. *Georgie Lee* (2–4). Illus. by Lynne Rae Perkins. 2002, HarperCollins LB $15.89 (0-688-17941-X). 96pp. When J.D. visits his grandmother on her farm, they have great times together and with Grandma's intelligent cow, Georgie Lee. (Rev: BCCB 6/02; BL 7/02; HB 7–8/02; HBG 10/02; SLJ 5/02)

6514 dePaola, Tomie. *Hide-and-Seek All Week* (1–2). Illus. Series: The Barkers. 2001, Penguin Putnam LB $13.89 (0-448-42617-X); paper $3.99 (0-448-42545-9). 32pp. Moffie and Morgie and friends decide they want to play hide-and-seek during recess, but can't decide on the rules. (Rev: BL 2/1/02; HBG 3/02; SLJ 2/02)

6515 dePaola, Tomie. *Kit and Kat* (1–2). Illus. 1994, Penguin Putnam paper $3.99 (0-448-40748-5). 32pp. Three easily read stories about the everyday adventures of Kit and Kat, the Kitten Kids. (Rev: BL 1/1/95)

6516 deRubertis, Barbara. *Deena's Lucky Penny* (1–2). Illus. by Joan Holub and Cynthia Fisher. Series: Math Matters. 1999, Kane paper $4.95 (1-57565-091-6). 32pp. This easy reader introduces the simple arithmetic of counting money, through the story of a young girl who saves to buy her mother a birthday present. (Rev: BL 12/1/99)

6517 Dobkin, Bonnie. *Everybody Says* (1–2). Illus. by Keith Neely. 1993, Children's Book Pr. LB $18.00 (0-516-02019-6). 32pp. In this easy-to-read book, a young boy's opinions differ from those of everyone else. (Rev: BL 12/1/93)

6518 Dodd, Lynley. *Hairy Maclary and Zachary Quack* (PS–2). Illus. by author. Series: Gold Star First Reader. 2000, Gareth Stevens LB $15.95 (0-8368-2676-0). 31pp. Harry the dog has a joyful day playing with Zachary Quack in this delightful first reader. Also use, in the same series, *Sniff-Snuff-*

Snap! (2000), the story of a bossy wart hog. (Rev: SLJ 2/01)

6519 Donnelly, Judy. *The Titanic: Lost . . . and Found* (2–4). Illus. by Keith Kohler. 1987, Random paper $3.99 (0-394-88669-0). 48pp. In a simple account the author describes the sinking of the Titanic and its rediscovery. (Rev: BCCB 6/87; BL 6/1/87; SLJ 6–7/87)

6520 Donnelly, Judy. *Tut's Mummy: Lost . . . and Found* (2–3). Illus. by James Watling. 1988, Random paper $3.99 (0-394-89189-9). 48pp. The story of the 20th-century discovery of King Tut's tomb. (Rev: BL 10/1/88; SLJ 10/88)

6521 Dotlich, Rebecca. *Away We Go!* (PS). Illus. by Dan Yaccarino. Series: Growing Tree. 2000, HarperCollins $9.95 (0-694-01393-5). 24pp. All kinds of vehicles — from a school bus and jumbo jet to a wheelchair and sled — are pictured along with people in motion in this easy-to-read book. (Rev: BL 9/1/00; HBG 3/01; SLJ 11/00)

6522 Dubowski, Cathy E. *Pirate School* (1–3). Illus. by Mark Dubowski. Series: All Aboard Reading. 1996, Grosset paper $3.95 (0-448-41132-6). 48pp. An easy-to-read adventure about a boy who attends pirate school. (Rev: SLJ 4/97)

6523 Dubowski, Cathy E., and Mark Dubowski. *Snug Bug* (PS–1). Illus. 1995, Penguin Putnam paper $3.99 (0-448-40849-X). 32pp. An easily read book about a little bug that prepares for bed. (Rev: BL 7/95)

6524 Duey, Kathleen. *Moonsilver: The Unicorn's Secret #1* (2–4). Illus. by Omar Rayyan. 2001, Simon & Schuster paper $3.99 (0-689-84269-4). 80pp. This alluring fantasy tale for younger readers introduces a young girl who finds a mysterious white mare with a scar on its forehead. (Rev: BL 1/1–15/02; SLJ 12/01)

6525 Duey, Kathleen. *The Mountains of the Moon* (2–4). Illus. by Omar Rayyan. Series: Ready-for-Chapters Unicorn's Secret. 2002, Simon & Schuster LB $11.89 (0-689-85137-5); paper $3.99 (0-689-84272-4). 80pp. The fourth episode in the continuing magical story of Heart and her unicorns, for beginning readers. Also use the third book in the series, *The Silver Bracelet* (2002). (Rev: BL 9/1/02; HBG 3/03)

6526 Duey, Kathleen. *The Sunset Gates* (2–4). Illus. by Omar Rayyan. Series: Unicorn's Secret. 2002, Simon & Schuster LB $11.89 (0-689-85347-5); paper $3.99 (0-689-85346-7). 80pp. The adventures of Heart Avamir, who is on the run in an effort to save two unicorns, continue in this easy-reader as she travels with gypsies and learns to read. Also use *True Heart* (2003). (Rev: BL 3/1/03; HBG 10/03)

6527 Duffey, Betsy. *How to Be Cool in the Third Grade* (1–3). Illus. by Janet Wilson. 1993, Viking $13.99 (0-670-84798-4). 80pp. Robbie wants to be a "cool dude" at school, but circumstances — including a run-in with the class bully — thwart his plans. (Rev: BCCB 10/93; BL 9/1/93; SLJ 9/93)

6528 Durant, Alan. *Brown Bear Gets in Shape* (K–2). Illus. by Annabel Hudson. Series: I Am Reading. 2004, Kingfisher paper $3.95 (0-7534-

5797-0). 45pp. Brown Bear is determined to get in shape, and tries copying Bunny and Chimp's diet and exercise regimens. (Rev: SLJ 8/04)

6529 Dussling, Jennifer. *Fair Is Fair!* (1–2). Illus. by Diane Palmisciano. Series: Math Matters. 2003, Kane paper $4.95 (1-57565-131-9). 32pp. Marco's skill with bar graphs helps him persuade his father to raise his allowance. (Rev: SLJ 2/04)

6530 Eastman, P. D. *Are You My Mother?* (1–3). Illus. by author. 1960, Random LB $13.99 (0-394-90018-9). 64pp. A bird falls from the nest and looks for its mother.

6531 Eastman, Patricia. *Sometimes Things Change* (K–1). Illus. by Seymour Fleishman. 1983, Children's Book Pr. LB $18.00 (0-516-02044-7); paper $4.95 (0-516-42044-5). 32pp. A story of how things in nature change.

6532 Eaton, Deborah. *The Rainy Day Grump* (K–2). Illus. by Dorothy Handelman. Series: Real Kids Readers. 1998, Millbrook LB $16.90 (0-7613-2018-0); paper $3.99 (0-7613-2043-1). 32pp. In this easy reader illustrated by color photographs, Rosie tries to amuse her brother Clay who is grumpy because it's raining and he can't go out to play. (Rev: BL 11/1/98)

6533 Ehrlich, Amy. *Bravo, Kazam!* (PS–K). Illus. by Barney Saltzberg. Series: Brand New Readers. 2002, Candlewick $12.99 (0-7636-1315-0); paper $4.99 (0-7636-1316-9). 40pp. In this beginning reader illustrated with cartoons, a rabbit is chased by a pack of magical cards. (Rev: BL 4/15/02)

6534 Elste, Joan. *True Blue* (2–3). Illus. by DyAnne DiSalvo-Ryan. 1996, Penguin Putnam paper $3.99 (0-448-41264-0). 48pp. J.D. worries when his faithful dog Blue disappears. (Rev: BL 11/15/96)

6535 Erickson, John R. *Hank the Cowdog: The Case of the Haystack Kitties* (2–3). Illus. by Gerald L. Holmes. Series: Hank the Cowdog. 1998, Gulf $14.95 (0-87719-338-X). 113pp. Hank's many adventures on the ranch include being threatened by a bull and saving a family of kittens. (Rev: SLJ 11/98)

6536 Finch, Margo. *The Lunch Bunch* (K–2). Photos by Dorothy Handelman. Series: Real Kids Readers. 1998, Millbrook LB $16.90 (0-7613-2005-9); paper $3.99 (0-7613-2030-X). 32pp. A new girl at school searches for friends in this enjoyable beginning reader. (Rev: SLJ 7/98)

6537 Fine, Anne. *The Jamie and Angus Stories* (2–4). Illus. by Penny Dale. 2002, Candlewick $15.99 (0-7636-1862-4). 112pp. Jamie and toy bull Angus have a variety of gentle adventures in these six stories for beginning chapter book readers. (Rev: BCCB 10/02; BL 11/15/02; HB 1–2/03*; HBG 3/03; SLJ 9/02)

6538 Floyd, Lucy. *A Place for Nicholas* (PS–2). Illus. by David McPhail. Series: Green Light Reader. 2005, Harcourt paper $3.95 (0-15-205149-X). 24pp. Nicholas longs for a space of his own in this reprint of a 1997 title. (Rev: BL 2/15/05)

6539 Ford, Bernette. *Don't Hit Me!* (K–1). Illus. by Gary Grier. Series: Just for You! 2004, Scholastic paper $3.99 (0-439-56860-9). 32pp. A simple easy-

reader story about friends agreeing to disagree, featuring African Americans. Also use *Hurry Up!!* (2004). (Rev: SLJ 1/05)

6540 Ford, Juwanda G. *Shop Talk* (K–3). Illus. by Jim Hoston. Series: Just for You! 2004, Scholastic paper $3.99 (0-439-56873-0). 32pp. A simple easy-reader story about a visit to the barbershop, featuring African Americans. (Rev: SLJ 1/05)

6541 Ford, Juwanda G. *Sunday Best* (K–3). Illus. by Colin Bootman. Series: Just for You! 2004, Scholastic paper $3.99 (0-439-56854-4). 32pp. An African American family enjoys a weekend together. (Rev: SLJ 1/05)

6542 Freschet, Gina. *Up and at 'Em with Winnie and Ernst* (PS–2). Illus. Series: Winnie and Ernst. 2005, Farrar $15.00 (0-374-38446-0). 48pp. Their second chapter book finds Winnie and Ernst, a possum and an otter, very busy having adventures. (Rev: BL 3/1/05; SLJ 3/05)

6543 Gantos, Jack. *Rotten Ralph Helps Out: A Rotten Ralph Reader* (1–2). Illus. by Nicole Rubel. 2001, Farrar $14.00 (0-374-36355-2). 48pp. Ralph the rotten cat helps — or rather hinders — Sarah with her project on ancient Egypt. (Rev: BL 7/01; HB 9–10/01; HBG 3/02; SLJ 8/01)

6544 Garcia, Carolyn. *Moonboy* (PS–2). Illus. by author. 1999, Beyond Words $15.95 (1-885223-81-1). Because of his unusual appearance, Moonboy is shunned by all except a boy named Ed, who wants him as a friend. (Rev: HBG 3/00; SLJ 8/99)

6545 Gelman, Rita G. *Pizza Pat* (PS–1). Illus. by Will Terry. Series: Step into Reading. 1999, Random LB $11.99 (0-679-99134-4); paper $3.99 (0-679-89134-X). 25pp. An easy reader that consists of a joyful cumulative rhyme about the ingredients in a pizza. (Rev: HBG 10/99; SLJ 9/99)

6546 George, Olivia. *My Birthday Cake* (K–2). Illus. by Martha Avil s. Series: My First Reader. 2005, Children's Pr. LB $17.50 (0-516-25178-3). 31pp. A birthday girl tries to make her own cake, covering it with blue icing, in this book for beginning readers with a list of words. (Rev: SLJ 5/05)

6547 Ghigna, Charles. *Mice Are Nice* (1). Illus. by Jon Goodell. Series: Step into Reading. 1999, Random LB $11.99 (0-679-98929-3); paper $3.99 (0-679-88929-9). 32pp. In a pet store, a small mouse tells a little girl why mice make the best pets compared with other animals. (Rev: BL 10/1/99; HBG 3/00)

6548 Gibala-Broxholm, Scott. *Scary Fright, Are You All Right?* (K–3). Illus. 2002, Dial $14.99 (0-8037-2588-4). 48pp. Scary Fright, a little monster, alarms her parents by acting too much like a human girl. (Rev: BL 9/15/02; HBG 3/03; SLJ 8/02)

6549 Giff, Patricia Reilly. *The Beast in Ms. Rooney's Room* (2–4). Illus. by Blanche Sims. 1984, Dell paper $4.50 (0-440-40485-1). 80pp. A volume in the Kids of the Polk Street School series. Another title is: *Fish Face* (1984).

6550 Giff, Patricia Reilly. *Garbage Juice for Breakfast* (2–3). Illus. by Blanche Sims. 1989, Bantam paper $3.99 (0-440-40207-7). 156pp. Dawn hopes to beat her rival at finding the hidden treasure at summer camp. (Rev: BL 12/15/89)

6551 Giff, Patricia Reilly. *In the Dinosaur's Paw* (2–4). Illus. by Blanche Sims. 1985, Dell paper $3.99 (0-440-44150-1). 80pp. The Polk Street School kids in the month of February. Also use: *The Candy Corn Contest* (1984); *December Secrets* (1984); *The Valentine Star* (1985); *All about Stacy* (1988). (Rev: BL 4/15/85)

6552 Giff, Patricia Reilly. *Next Stop, New York City! The Polk Street Kids on Tour* (2–4). Illus. by Blanche Sims. Series: Polk Street Special. 1997, Dell paper $3.99 (0-440-41362-1). 119pp. When Ms. Rooney and the Polk Street crowd visit New York City, Emily Arrow is upset because she has been dubbed an expert on the Big Apple, but she really knows nothing about it. (Rev: SLJ 10/97)

6553 Giff, Patricia Reilly. *Purple Climbing Days* (1–3). Illus. by Blanche Sims. 1985, Bantam paper $3.99 (0-440-47309-8). 80pp. Richard "Beast" Best of the Polk Street School is afraid to climb the floor-to-ceiling rope in gym. Two others in this series are: *Lazy Lions, Lucky Lambs; Snaggle Doodles* (both 1985). (Rev: BL 8/85; SLJ 11/85)

6554 Giff, Patricia Reilly. *Sunny-Side Up* (1–3). Illus. by Blanche Sims. 1986, Dell paper $3.99 (0-440-48406-5). 74pp. The Polk Street School kids are in summer school and have to deal with Matthew's announcement that he is moving away. Another in this series is: *Spectacular Stone Soup* (1989). (Rev: BL 10/1/86; SLJ 3/87)

6555 Gikow, Louise A. *A Day with Daddy* (PS–2). Illus. by Gustavo Mazali. Series: My First Reader. 2004, Children's Pr. LB $17.50 (0-516-24410-8). 31pp. Daddy is the one exhausted by a day out in this rhyming book for beginning readers with cartoon illustrations and a word list. (Rev: SLJ 7/04)

6556 Graham, Bob. *Tales from the Waterhole* (K–3). Illus. by author. 2004, Candlewick $16.99 (0-7636-2324-5). 62pp. The animals of the savannah enjoy playing around the waterhole — soccer, skateboarding, and so forth — in this series of five short stories for beginning readers. (Rev: SLJ 7/04)

6557 Greco, Francesca. *Gideon* (2–4). Illus. by author. 2003, Star Bright $16.95 (1-932065-02-4). Poor Gideon the chameleon — always invisible to his jungle neighbors — comes into his own when he warns them of an approaching tiger. (Rev: HBG 10/03; SLJ 5/03)

6558 Greene, Carol. *Hi, Clouds* (K–2). Illus. by Gene Sharp. 1983, Children's Book Pr. LB $18.00 (0-516-02036-6); paper $4.95 (0-516-42036-4). 32pp. Two children see many objects in clouds in this easy-to-read book. Two others in this series are: *Ice Is . . . Whee!; Shine, Sun!* (both 1983).

6559 Greene, Stephanie. *Owen Foote, Super Spy* (2–4). Illus. by Martha Weston. 2001, Clarion $14.00 (0-618-11752-0). 90pp. Owen and his friends spy on their elementary-school principal in this funny adventure. (Rev: BL 1/1–15/02; HB 11–12/01; HBG 3/02; SLJ 10/01)

6560 Griffith, Helen V. *Alex and the Cat* (2–3). Illus. 1997, Greenwillow $15.00 (0-688-15241-4). 56pp. Contains seven charming short stories about the adventures of Alex the dog and his cat friend. (Rev: BL 10/15/97; HBG 3/98; SLJ 10/97)

6561 Grimes, Nikki. *A Day With Daddy* (K–2). Illus. by Nicole Tadgell. Series: Just for You! 2004, Scholastic paper $3.99 (0-439-56850-1). 32pp. An African American who lives with his mother looks forward to an outing with his father in this easy-reader. (Rev: BL 10/15/04; SLJ 2/05)

6562 Grimes, Nikki. *Wild, Wild Hair* (1–2). Illus. by George Ford. Series: Hello Reader! 1997, Scholastic $3.99 (0-590-26590-3). A young African American girl dreads Monday, when her hair is braided, in this easy-to-read book. (Rev: BL 5/1/97; SLJ 4/97)

6563 Guest, Elissa Haden. *Iris and Walter: The School Play* (K–2). Illus. by Christine Davenier. Series: Iris and Walter. 2003, Harcourt $15.00 (0-15-216481-2). 44pp. Iris and Walter are excited to have roles in the school play, but when the big day finally arrives, Iris is sick. Also use *Iris and Walter: Lost and Found* (2004). (Rev: HB 5–6/03; HBG 10/03; SLJ 4/03)

6564 Guest, Elissa Haden. *Iris and Walter: The Sleepover* (K–1). Illus. by Christine Davenier. 2002, Harcourt $14.00 (0-15-216487-1). 44pp. Iris can't wait for the sleepover at Walter's house, but when it arrives she can't sleep and has to be taken home to bed. (Rev: BL 11/1/02; HBG 3/03; SLJ 10/02)

6565 Guest, Elissa Haden. *Iris and Walter and Cousin Howie* (1–3). Illus. by Christine Davenier. 2003, Harcourt $15.00 (0-15-216695-5). 44pp. Best pals Iris and Walter look forward to a visit from Walter's cousin Howie, but the reality proves disappointing, especially for Iris. (Rev: BCCB 2/04; BL 9/15/03; HBG 4/04; SLJ 12/03)

6566 Guest, Elissa Haden. *Iris and Walter and the Field Trip* (1–3). Illus. by Christine Davenier. 2005, Harcourt $15.00 (0-15-205014-0). 44pp. Despite his teacher's warnings to stay together, Walter is so entranced by the coral reef exhibit at the aquarium that the class has to go back to get him. (Rev: BL 5/15/05; SLJ 6/05)

6567 Guest, Elissa Haden. *Iris and Walter, True Friends* (2–4). Illus. 2001, Harcourt $14.00 (0-15-202121-3). 44pp. The first two chapters tell the story of Iris, Walter, and their experiences with a lively horse; the last two are school episodes in which Iris must conquer fears and Walter doesn't want to be known as Walt. (Rev: BCCB 9/01; BL 5/1/01; HBG 10/01; SLJ 5/01)

6568 Guilfoile, Elizabeth. *Nobody Listens to Andrew* (1–3). Illus. by Mary Stevens. 1957, Modern Curriculum paper $5.10 (0-8136-5959-0). The reaction of Andrew's elders when he tells them there is a bear in his bed.

6569 Haddix, Margaret Peterson. *Say What?* (2–4). Illus. by lames Bernardin. 2004, Simon & Schuster $12.95 (0-689-86255-5). 96pp. Sukie is much confused when her parents start talking nonsense, and she and her siblings retaliate in kind when they discover their parents' real motive. (Rev: BL 2/15/04; SLJ 2/04)

6570 Hall, Katy, and Lisa Eisenberg. *Ribbit Riddles* (2). Illus. by Robert Bender. 2001, Dial $13.99 (0-8037-2525-6). 40pp. A simple book of funny riddles for beginning readers. Also use *Sheepish Riddles* (1996) and *Kitty Riddles* (2000). (Rev: BL 4/15/01; HBG 10/01; SLJ 7/01)

6571 Hall, Kirsten. *At the Carnival* (K–1). Illus. by Laura Rader. 1996, Scholastic $3.99 (0-590-68994-0). 32pp. An easy reader that uses detachable pages and a trip to the carnival to introduce language. (Rev: BL 2/1/97)

6572 Hanel, Wolfram. *Old Mahony and the Bear Family* (1–3). Trans. by Rosemary Lanning. Illus. 1997, North-South LB $13.88 (1-55858-714-4). 46pp. Old Mahony enjoys salmon fishing with Big Bill the bear; but when Bill's family appears, he wonders about their future together. (Rev: BL 9/15/97; SLJ 7/97)

6573 Harrison, David L. *Johnny Appleseed: My Story* (1–2). Illus. by Mike Wohnoutka. Series: Step Into Reading. 2001, Random LB $11.99 (0-375-91247-9); paper $3.99 (0-375-81247-4). 48pp. Johnny Appleseed tells the story of his life to a pioneer family. (Rev: BL 2/1/02; HBG 3/02) [634]

6574 Haskins, Lori. *Ducks in Muck* (K–1). Illus. by Valeria Petrone. Series: Step into Reading. 2000, Random paper $3.99 (0-679-89166-8). 32pp. A simple humorous tale about ducks that escape from trucks stuck in muck. (Rev: BL 4/15/00; HBG 10/00; SLJ 2/01)

6575 Hautzig, Deborah. *Little Witch Goes to School* (K–3). Illus. by Sylvie Wickstrom. Series: Step into Reading. 1998, Random paper $3.99 (0-679-88738-5). 47pp. When she promises to be bad, Little Witch is allowed to go to school, where she breaks her promise by being a good and cooperative student. (Rev: SLJ 1/99)

6576 Hautzig, Deborah. *The Nutcracker Ballet* (1–3). Illus. by Carolyn Ewing. 1992, Random paper $3.99 (0-679-82385-9). 48pp. In a simple narrative, this is the story of the Nutcracker. (Rev: BL 12/1/92)

6577 Hayes, Geoffrey. *The Secret of Foghorn Island* (2–3). Illus. by author. 1988, Random paper $3.99 (0-394-89614-9). 48pp. Otto and Uncle Tooth investigate four shipwrecks on the island. (Rev: BL 10/1/88; SLJ 12/88)

6578 Hayward, Linda. *What Homework?* (1–3). Illus. by Page Eastburn O'Rourke. 2002, Kane paper $4.99 (1-57565-116-5). 32pp. Andy succeeds in completing his assignment in the nick of time. (Rev: SLJ 11/02)

6579 Head, Judith. *Mud Soup* (1–2). Series: Step into Reading. 2003, Random LB $11.99 (0-375-81087-0). 48pp. In this charming cross-cultural tale for beginning readers, Josh learns from a Latina friend that different doesn't mean bad. (Rev: BL 8/03; HBG 4/04)

6580 Heling, Kathryn, and Deborah Hembrook. *Mouse Makes Magic* (K–1). Illus. by Patrick Joseph. Series: Step into Reading. 2002, Random LB $11.99 (0-375-92184-2); paper $3.99 (0-375-82184-8). 32pp. A mouse magician enjoys changing the mid-

dle vowels in three-letter words. (Rev: HBG 3/03; SLJ 1/03)

6581 Heling, Kathryn, and Deborah Hembrook. *Mouse Makes Words: A Phonics Reader* (1–2). Illus. by Patrick Joseph. Series: Step into Reading. 2002, Random paper $3.99 (0-375-81399-3). 32pp. By changing the first letter in a series of words, new words are formed in this beginning reader. (Rev: BL 4/1/02; HBG 10/02; SLJ 7/02)

6582 Herman, Gail. *Double-Header* (1–2). Illus. by Jerry Smath. 1993, Penguin Putnam paper $3.95 (0-448-40157-6). 32pp. Monsters Bob and Rob, who share the same body, but with two heads, discuss their dilemma. (Rev: BL 12/1/93; SLJ 2/94)

6583 Herman, Gail. *My Dog Talks* (PS–2). Illus. by Ron Fritz. Series: Hello Reader! 1995, Scholastic paper $3.99 (0-590-22196-5). A beginning reader that describes the bond between a boy and his dog as so close that they seem to talk to each other. (Rev: SLJ 9/95)

6584 Herman, R. A. *Pal the Pony* (1–2). Illus. 1996, Penguin Putnam paper $3.99 (0-448-41257-8). 32pp. A pony named Pal shows his true talents at a rodeo. (Rev: BL 8/96; SLJ 7/96)

6585 Hill, Eric. *Spot Goes to School* (PS). Illus. by author. 1984, Penguin Putnam paper $12.99 (0-399-21073-3). 22pp. A book that tells the story of a young dog. Two others in this series are: *Spot's First Walk* (1981); *Spot's Birthday Party* (1982).

6586 Hill, Susan. *Ruby Bakes a Cake* (K–3). Illus. by Margie Moore. Series: An I Can Read. 2004, HarperCollins LB $16.89 (0-06-008976-8). 28pp. Ruby, a raccoon, consults her friends before making a cake and includes all the ingredients they suggest. (Rev: SLJ 6/04)

6587 Hill, Susan. *Ruby Paints a Picture* (PS–K). Illus. by Margie Moore. Series: I Can Read! 2005, HarperCollins LB $16.89 (0-06-008980-6). 32pp. At her friends' requests, Ruby the raccoon adds them to the picture she is painting, but at first they do not like the results. (Rev: BL 5/15/05)

6588 Himmelman, John. *The Animal Rescue Club* (1–3). Illus. by author. Series: An I Can Read Book. 1998, HarperCollins LB $14.89 (0-06-027409-3). 46pp. In this easy reader, members of the Animal Rescue Club take a number of creatures in distress to a hospital and later return them to their natural habitats. (Rev: HBG 10/98; SLJ 6/98)

6589 Himmelman, John. *The Clover County Carrot Contest* (1–2). Illus. 1991, Silver Burdett paper $3.50 (0-671-69641-6). 48pp. Each member of a family of inventive bears tries to grow the best carrot. Also use: *The Super Camper Caper* (1991). (Rev: BL 6/1/91; SLJ 10/91)

6590 Hindley, Judy. *Princess Rosa's Winter* (1–2). Illus. by Margaret Chamberlain. Series: I Am Reading. 2005, Kingfisher paper $3.95 (0-7534-5859-4). 48pp. Princess Rosa and her family remember what they enjoy about winter when Hoda the jester entertains them in their castle. (Rev: BL 3/15/05)

6591 Hoban, Lillian. *Arthur's Back to School Day* (1–2). Illus. Series: I Can Read. 1996, HarperCollins LB $15.89 (0-06-024956-0). 48pp. Arthur and friends are confused by a lunch box mix-up on the first day at school. (Rev: BL 9/15/96; SLJ 9/96)

6592 Hoban, Lillian. *Arthur's Birthday Party* (1–2). Illus. 1999, HarperCollins $14.95 (0-06-027798-X). 64pp. As expected at Arthur's birthday party, all his friends perform amazing gymnastic tricks, but Arthur wins the best all-round gymnast award. (Rev: BL 3/15/99; HB 1–2/99; HBG 10/99; SLJ 2/99)

6593 Hoban, Lillian. *Arthur's Loose Tooth* (1–3). Illus. by author. 1985, HarperCollins LB $15.89 (0-06-022354-5); paper $3.95 (0-06-444093-1). 64pp. Brave Arthur the chimp is afraid of blood, so how does he get rid of his loose tooth in order to eat taffy apples? (Rev: BL 10/15/85; HB 11–12/85; SLJ 12/85)

6594 Hoban, Lillian, and Phoebe Hoban. *Ready . . . Set . . . Robot!* (2–3). Illus. by Lillian Hoban. 1982, HarperCollins $11.95 (0-06-022345-6). 64pp. A robot, Sol-1, competes in a space race.

6595 Hoban, Russell. *Bedtime for Frances* (1–2). Illus. by Garth Williams. 1960, HarperCollins LB $13.89 (0-06-022351-0); paper $5.95 (0-06-443451-6). 32pp. Frances, a badger, tries every familiar trick to tease her way past bedtime. Others in the series: *Bread and Jam for Frances* (1965); *A Bargain for Frances* (1970).

6596 Hoban, Russell. *Best Friends for Frances* (1–2). Illus. by Lillian Hoban. 1969, HarperCollins LB $15.89 (0-06-022328-6); paper $5.95 (0-06-443008-1). 32pp. When friend Albert decides that he must exclude girls from his "wondering day" and baseball game, Frances chooses younger sister Gloria as a companion. Also use: *A Baby Sister for Frances* (1964).

6597 Hoff, Syd. *Barkley* (1–3). Illus. by author. 1975, HarperCollins LB $15.89 (0-06-022448-7). 32pp. An easily read story about a forcibly retired, aging circus dog.

6598 Hoff, Syd. *Barney's Horse* (1–3). Illus. by author. 1987, HarperCollins LB $15.89 (0-06-022450-9); paper $3.95 (0-06-444142-3). 32pp. Barney the peddler and his horse delight children, but elevated trains soon begin to rumble overhead. (Rev: BCCB 11/87; BL 10/1/87)

6599 Hoff, Syd. *Danny and the Dinosaur* (K–2). Illus. by author. 1958, HarperCollins LB $15.89 (0-06-022466-5); paper $3.95 (0-06-444002-8). 64pp. Danny wanted to play and so did the dinosaur. What could have been more natural than for them to leave the museum together? Also from the same author and publisher: *Sammy the Seal* (1959).

6600 Hoff, Syd. *Danny and the Dinosaur Go to Camp* (1–3). Illus. 1996, HarperCollins LB $15.89 (0-06-026440-3). 32pp. At summer camp, a dinosaur provides transportation for tired boys and girls. (Rev: BL 8/96; SLJ 6/96)

6601 Hoff, Syd. *Grizzwold* (1–2). Illus. by author. 1963, HarperCollins LB $15.89 (0-06-022481-9); paper $3.95 (0-06-444057-5). 64pp. After foresters have destroyed his home, a bear sets out to find a new one.

6602 Hoff, Syd. *Happy Birthday, Danny and the Dinosaur!* (1–3). Illus. 1995, HarperCollins LB $15.89 (0-06-026438-1). 32pp. Danny invites his friend the dinosaur to his birthday party in this easy-to-read book. (Rev: BCCB 10/95; BL 10/1/95; SLJ 9/95)

6603 Hoff, Syd. *The Lighthouse Children* (1–2). Illus. Series: I Can Read. 1994, HarperCollins LB $15.89 (0-06-022959-4). 32pp. After a storm destroys their lighthouse, two children must leave the seagulls they feed in this easy-to-read book. (Rev: BL 2/1/94; SLJ 4/94)

6604 Hoff, Syd. *Mrs. Brice's Mice* (PS–2). Illus. by author. 1988, HarperCollins LB $15.89 (0-06-022452-5); paper $3.95 (0-06-444145-8). 32pp. Mrs. Brice has 25 mice — one is an individualist. (Rev: BCCB 12/88; BL 12/1/88; SLJ 4/89)

6605 Hoff, Syd. *Sammy the Seal* (K–1). Illus. Series: I Can Read. 2000, HarperCollins LB $14.89 (0-06-028546-X). 64pp. After wandering from the zoo, a small seal discovers there is no place like home. (Rev: BL 12/1/99; HBG 10/00)

6606 Hoff, Syd. *Stanley* (1–3). Illus. by author. 1992, HarperCollins LB $15.89 (0-06-022536-X); paper $3.95 (0-06-444010-9). 64pp. A caveman finds a new home in this inventive tale.

6607 Holub, Joan. *The Garden That We Grew* (K–2). Illus. by Hiroe Nakata. Series: Viking Easy-to-Read. 2001, Viking $13.99 (0-670-89799-X). 32pp. Children plant pumpkin seeds, tend the plant, harvest the full-grown pumpkins, eat the resulting pies and cookies, and make Halloween faces. (Rev: BL 7/01; HB 7–8/01*; HBG 3/02; SLJ 8/01)

6608 Hood, Susan. *I Am Mad!* (PS–1). Photos by Dorothy Handelman. Series: Real Kids Readers. 1999, Millbrook LB $16.90 (0-7613-2061-X); paper $3.99 (0-7613-2086-5). 28pp. For very beginning readers, this is a simple story of a bullying older sister. (Rev: SLJ 1/00)

6609 Hood, Susan. *Meet Trouble* (PS–1). Illus. by Kristina Stephenson. Series: First Friends First Readers. 2001, Grosset paper $3.99 (0-448-42455-X). Trouble the cat didn't come by his name by accident, and lives up to it in the first of the two stories in this humorous book. (Rev: SLJ 12/01)

6610 Hood, Susan. *The New Kid* (K–1). Illus. by Dorothy Handelman. Series: Real Kids Readers. 1998, Millbrook LB $16.90 (0-7613-2014-8); paper $3.99 (0-7613-2039-3). 32pp. Sid, a newcomer at school, acts strangely because he is uncomfortable, but one boy, who understands the situation, makes the effort to become his friend. (Rev: BL 11/1/98; SLJ 1/99)

6611 Hood, Susan. *Pup and Hound in Trouble* (PS–1). Illus. by Linda Hendry. Series: Kids Can Read. 2005, Kids Can $14.95 (1-55337-676-5); paper $3.95 (1-55337-677-3). 32pp. Pup and Hound get into trouble on the farm in this rhyming easy reader. (Rev: BL 3/1/05; SLJ 6/05)

6612 Hood, Susan. *Pup and Hound Stay Up Late* (K–1). Illus. by Linda Hendry. 2005, Kids Can $14.95 (1-55337-678-1); paper $3.95 (1-55337-679-X). 32pp. Hound spends his time trying to keep Pup out of trouble in this rhyming easy-reader. (Rev: SLJ 6/05)

6613 Hooks, Gwendolyn. *The Mystery of the Missing Dog* (K–3). Illus. by Nancy Devard. Series: Just for You! 2004, Scholastic paper $3.99 (0-439-56864-1). 32pp. Alex, an African American boy, searches his apartment looking for his dog in this easy-reader. Also use *Three's a Crowd* (2004), about jealousy. (Rev: SLJ 1/05)

6614 Hooks, Gwendolyn. *Nice Wheels* (K–2). Illus. by Renee Andriani. Series: My First Reader. 2005, Children's Pr. LB $17.50 (0-516-25179-1). 31pp. The new boy in class has a wheelchair in this book for beginning readers with a list of words. (Rev: SLJ 5/05)

6615 Hooks, William H. *Mr. Big Brother* (1–2). Illus. by Kate Duke. Series: Bank Street Ready-to-Read. 1999, Gareth Stevens $14.95 (0-8368-2417-2). 32pp. Eli is looking forward to having a new baby brother; when the baby arrives and it is a girl, Eli needs some time to adjust. (Rev: BL 2/15/00; HBG 10/00; SLJ 9/99)

6616 Horowitz, Ruth. *Big Surprise in the Bug Tank* (1–3). Illus. by Joan Holub. Series: Dial Easy-to-Read. 2005, Dial $14.99 (0-8037-2874-3). 46pp. The two boys first seen in *Breakout at the Bug Lab* (2001) adopt two giant cockroaches from the mother's lab and, of course, the population soon expands from two. (Rev: BCCB 1/05; HB 5–6/05; SLJ 2/05)

6617 Horowitz, Ruth. *Breakout at the Bug Lab* (1–2). Illus. by Joan Holub. Series: Dial Easy-to-Read. 2001, Dial $13.99 (0-8037-2510-8). 48pp. Two boys try to find Max the cockroach, one of the bugs that their mother studies at a nature lab. (Rev: BCCB 7–8/01; BL 4/15/01; HB 7–8/01; HBG 10/01; SLJ 4/01*)

6618 Howe, James. *Pinky and Rex and the New Baby* (K–3). Illus. by Melissa Sweet. 1994, Avon paper $3.99 (0-380-12083-3). 48pp. Rex and her best friend are nervous about the new baby Rex's parents are planning to adopt. (Rev: BL 3/1/93; SLJ 6/93)

6619 Howe, James. *Pinky and Rex Get Married* (K–3). Illus. by Melissa Sweet. 1990, Simon & Schuster LB $11.95 (0-685-58512-3). 48pp. Two young friends, a 7-year-old girl and a boy named Pinky, are so close that they decide to get married. Also use: *Pinky and Rex* (1990). (Rev: BCCB 4/90; BL 4/15/90*; HB 3–4/90; SLJ 5/90)

6620 Howe, James. *The Vampire Bunny* (1–3). Illus. by Jeff Mack. 2004, Simon & Schuster $14.95 (0-689-85724-1). 41pp. Chester the cat and Harold the dog disagree over whether the baby bunny they have found is a vampire in this adaptation for beginning readers. (Rev: SLJ 6/04)

6621 Hudson, Wade. *Jamal's Busy Day* (PS–1). Illus. by George Ford. 1991, Just Us LB $12.95 (0-940975-21-1); paper $6.95 (0-940975-24-6). Jamal, an African American boy, prepares with his parents for a busy day — he will spend his at school and they at work. (Rev: SLJ 2/92)

6622 Hudson, Wade. *The Two Tyrones* (K–3). Illus. by Mark Page. 2004, Scholastic paper $3.99 (0-439-

56866-8). 32pp. School is starting and it turns out there will be two Tyrones this year. (Rev: SLJ 1/05)

6623 Hurwitz, Johanna. *The Adventures of Ali Baba Bernstein* (2–4). Illus. 1985, Morrow $16.95 (0-688-04161-2); Avon paper $4.95 (0-380-72349-2). 96pp. Episodes in the life of David Bernstein, an 8-year-old who changes what he thinks is his boring name. Also use: *Hurray for Ali Baba Bernstein* (1989). (Rev: BCCB 6/85; BL 5/15/85; HB 5–6/85)

6624 Hurwitz, Johanna. *Oh No, Noah!* (2–4). Illus. by Mike Reed. 2002, North-South $14.95 (1-58717-133-3). 128pp. Eight-year-old Noah finds it's not so hard to make friends in his new neighborhood in this beginning chapter book. (Rev: HBG 10/02; SLJ 5/02)

6625 Hutchins, Hazel. *Robyn's Art Attack* (K–3). Illus. by Yvonne Cathcart. Series: First Novels. 2002, Formac paper $3.99 (0-88780-564-7). 59pp. Robyn's classmates expect a boring day when she chooses an art gallery for their field trip. (Rev: SLJ 1/03)

6626 Inches, Alison. *Corduroy Writes a Letter* (K–2). Illus. by Allan Eitzen. Series: Viking Easy-to-Read. 2002, Viking $13.99 (0-670-03548-3). 32pp. Corduroy the teddy bear and Lisa, an African American girl, find out how much they can accomplish by writing letters. Also use *Corduroy's Garden* (2002). (Rev: BL 1/1–15/03; HBG 3/03)

6627 Jacobson, Jennifer Richard. *Winnie Dancing on Her Own* (2–3). Illus. by Alissa Imre Geis. 2001, Houghton Mifflin $15.00 (0-618-13287-2). 96pp. Her father helps clumsy 8-year-old Winnie when she tries to take up ballet to be with her best friends. (Rev: BCCB 11/01; BL 9/15/01; HBG 3/02; SLJ 12/01)

6628 Jane, Pamela. *Milo and the Flapjack Fiasco* (K–3). Illus. by Meredith Johnson. 2004, Mondo $13.95 (1-59336-113-0). 32pp. Milo and his sister Sam try to make flapjacks for the visiting teacher in this easy-reader. (Rev: SLJ 6/04)

6629 Jarman, Julia. *The Magic Backpack* (PS–2). Illus. by Adriano Gon. Series: Flying Foxes. 2004, Crabtree LB $14.97 (0-7787-1487-X); paper $4.46 (0-7787-1533-7). 48pp. Josh forgets to bring a key ingredient for the class cake, but fortunately his magic backpack flies him to a cocoa plantation in Ghana. (Rev: SLJ 8/04)

6630 Jennings, Patrick. *The Tornado Watches: An Ike and Mem Story* (2–5). Illus. by Anna Alter. 2002, Holiday House $15.95 (0-8234-1672-0). 64pp. A young boy named Ike fears his family is in danger after a tornado warning causes them to spend the night in their basement. (Rev: BL 8/02; HB 1–2/03; HBG 3/03; SLJ 12/02)

6631 Jennings, Patrick. *The Weeping Willow* (2–4). Illus. by Anna Alter. 2002, Holiday House $15.95 (0-8234-1671-2). 56pp. Friends Ike and Buzzy decide to build a tree house, only to find themselves embroiled in arguments. (Rev: BL 12/15/02; HB 1–2/03*; HBG 3/03; SLJ 2/03)

6632 Johansen, K. V. *Pippin and the Bones* (PS–2). Illus. by Bernice Lum. 2000, Kids Can $12.95 (1-55074-629-4). 32pp. For beginning readers, this is the story of a dog named Pippin who digs up some huge bones that his master gives to the museum. (Rev: BL 8/00; HBG 10/00; SLJ 8/00)

6633 Johnson, Crockett. *Harold and the Purple Crayon* (K–2). Illus. by author. 1958, HarperCollins paper $5.95 (0-06-443022-7). 64pp. A little boy draws all of the things necessary for him to go for a walk. Three sequels are: *Harold's Trip to the Sky* (1957); *Harold's Circus* (1959); *A Picture for Harold's Room* (1960).

6634 Johnston, Tony. *Alien and Possum Hanging Out* (2–3). Illus. by Tony Diterlizzi. 2002, Simon & Schuster $15.00 (0-689-83836-0). 48pp. Three stories about the continuing unlikely friendship between a robot-like alien and a possum. (Rev: HBG 10/02; SLJ 8/02)

6635 Johnston, Tony. *The Bull and the Fire Truck* (1–2). Illus. by R. W. Alley. 1996, Scholastic $3.99 (0-590-47597-5). 32pp. An easily read book about how a community accommodates a bull that hates the color red. (Rev: BL 2/1/97)

6636 Johnston, Tony. *Sparky and Eddie: The First Day of School* (1–2). Illus. by Susannah Ryan. Series: Hello Reader! 1997, Scholastic $13.95 (0-590-47978-4); paper $3.99 (0-590-47979-2). 32pp. In this easy reader, friends Sparky and Eddie decide that they won't start school if they can't be in the same rooms. (Rev: BL 8/97; HBG 3/98; SLJ 9/97)

6637 Johnston, Tony. *Sparky and Eddie: Wild, Wild Rodeo* (1–2). Illus. by Susannah Ryan. Series: Hello Reader! 1998, Scholastic $13.95 (0-590-47984-9). 40pp. Two friends, Sparky and Eddie, are crushed when their class doesn't win the school rodeo contests, such as roping teddy bears. (Rev: BL 5/1/98; HBG 10/98; SLJ 5/98)

6638 Jordan, Sandra. *Frog Hunt* (PS–1). Illus. 2002, Millbrook LB $22.90 (0-7613-2652-9). 32pp. An easily read book about two boys and the animal life they encounter when they go into a freshwater pond looking for frogs. (Rev: BL 6/1–15/02; HBG 10/02; SLJ 4/02)

6639 Karlin, Nurit. *The Fat Cat Sat on the Mat* (1–2). Illus. 1996, HarperCollins LB $14.89 (0-06-026674-0). 32pp. A witch's rat can't budge a cat from a favorite resting place, the mat. (Rev: BCCB 10/96; BL 9/15/96; SLJ 12/96)

6640 Keenan, Sheila. *More or Less a Mess* (1–2). Illus. by Patrick Girouard. Series: Hello Math Reader. 1997, Scholastic $3.99 (0-590-60248-9). When a girl is told by her mother to tidy up her room, she doesn't know where to begin, so she puts everything under the covers of her bed. (Rev: BL 5/1/97)

6641 Kerrin, Jessica Scott. *Martin Bridge, Ready for Takeoff!* (2–4). Illus. by Joseph Kelly. 2005, Kids Can $14.95 (1-55337-688-9). 120pp. Martin must deal with typical third-grade dilemmas in this three-chapter book with pencil illustrations. (Rev: BL 3/15/05; SLJ 5/05)

6642 Kessler, Leonard. *Here Comes the Strikeout* (1–2). Illus. by author. 1992, HarperCollins LB $15.89 (0-06-023156-4); paper $3.95 (0-06-444011-7). 64pp. Bobby always strikes out at bat until his friend Willie helps him to improve his game. Two

other sports stories by the same author and publisher are: *Kick, Pass and Run* (1966); *Last One in Is a Rotten Egg* (1969). (Rev: BL 12/1/92)

6643 Kettner, Christine. *Oliver Cat on Planet B* (1–2). Series: Dutton Easy Reader. 2003, Penguin Putnam $15.99 (0-525-47094-8). 48pp. A young cat named Oliver stars in the three adventures in this easy-reader, which involve playing with a friend, building a spaceship, and a magical fishing trip. (Rev: BL 7/03; HBG 10/03; SLJ 7/03)

6644 Kline, Suzy. *Horrible Harry and the Locked Closet* (2–4). Illus. by Frank Remkiewicz. 2004, Viking $13.99 (0-670-05944-7). 80pp. Bored after four days of indoor recess and not completely diverted by their study of volcanoes, Horrible Harry and other students in Miss Mackle's class investigate what's behind a locked closet door. (Rev: BL 5/1/04; SLJ 11/04)

6645 Kline, Suzy. *Horrible Harry and the Mud Gremlins* (2–4). Illus. by Frank Remkiewicz. Series: Horrible Harry. 2003, Viking $13.99 (0-670-03617-X). 64pp. Horrible Harry encourages his classmates to break a school rule and go under the playground fence to see fungi with his mini-microscope. (Rev: BL 3/15/03; HBG 10/03)

6646 Kline, Suzy. *Horrible Harry Goes to Sea* (2–4). Illus. by Frank Remkiewicz. 2001, Viking $13.99 (0-670-03516-5). 64pp. After hearing a student's story of an ancestor who sailed on the *Titanic*, the teacher arranges a class riverboat trip and many humorous adventures ensue. (Rev: BL 12/1/01; HBG 3/02; SLJ 11/01)

6647 Krensky, Stephen. *Arthur and the Seventh-Inning Stretcher* (2–4). Illus. Series: Arthur Good Sports. 2001, Little, Brown $13.95 (0-316-11861-3); paper $3.95 (0-316-12094-4). 64pp. Binky feels left out when he can't play baseball because of an injury. (Rev: BL 5/15/01; HBG 3/02)

6648 Krensky, Stephen. *Buster's Dino Dilemma* (1–3). Illus. by Marc Brown. Series: A Marc Brown Arthur Chapter Book. 1998, Little, Brown paper $3.95 (0-316-11560-6). 58pp. Based on scripts used in the PBS series, this easy chapter book involves Arthur and a fossil he has found during a school field trip. Also use *Locked in the Library!* (1998). (Rev: HBG 10/98; SLJ 11/98)

6649 Krensky, Stephen. *Lionel at School* (K–2). Illus. by Susanna Natti. Series: Easy-to-Read. 2000, Dial $13.99 (0-8037-2457-8). 48pp. The four easy-to-read stories in this book about Lionel focus on his experiences at school. (Rev: BL 10/1/00; HBG 3/01; SLJ 9/00)

6650 Krensky, Stephen. *Lionel's Birthday* (1–3). Illus. by Susanna Natti. Series: Dial Easy-to-Read. 2003, Penguin Putnam $13.99 (0-8037-2752-6). 48pp. In this ninth easy-reader about Lionel, he prepares for an upcoming birthday and buries a time capsule. (Rev: BL 7/03; HBG 4/04; SLJ 10/03)

6651 Krensky, Stephen. *My Loose Tooth* (1). Illus. by Hideko Takahashi. Series: Step into Reading. 1999, Random LB $11.99 (0-679-98847-5). 32pp. In this easily read story, a young boy discovers, while brushing his teeth, that he has a loose tooth, and soon he can't forget it. (Rev: BL 3/15/99; HBG 10/99; SLJ 8/99)

6652 Krensky, Stephen. *We Just Moved!* (1–2). Illus. by Larry DiFiori. Series: Hello Reader! 1998, Scholastic paper $3.50 (0-590-33127-2). 32pp. Set during the Middle Ages, this humorous story tells of a young boy's move to a new castle and how this compares with a change of homes in modern times. (Rev: BL 7/98)

6653 Kueffner, Sue. *Our New Baby* (PS–1). Illus. by Dorothy Stott. Series: All-Star Readers. 1999, Reader's Digest paper $3.99 (1-57584-292-0). 31pp. A beginning reader about the upheaval caused by the arrival of a new baby as seen by her older sister. (Rev: SLJ 7/99)

6654 Kurt, Kemal. *Mixed-Up Journey to Magic Mountain* (2–4). Trans. from German by Marianne Martens. Illus. by Wolfgang Slawski. 2002, North-South LB $13.88 (0-7358-1633-6). 58pp. Marco the magician's inability to spell causes all sorts of problems. (Rev: HBG 10/02; SLJ 4/02)

6655 Labatt, Mary. *Pizza for Sam* (PS–1). Illus. by Marisol Sarrazin. Series: Kids Can Read. 2003, Kids Can $14.95 (1-55337-329-4); paper $3.95 (1-55337-331-6). 32pp. Sam does not want to eat dog food and greets a pizza with joy. (Rev: BL 3/1/03; HBG 10/03; SLJ 5/03)

6656 Labatt, Mary. *Sam Finds a Monster* (PS–2). Illus. by Marisol Sarrazin. Series: Kids Can Read. 2003, Kids Can $14.95 (1-55337-351-0); paper $3.95 (1-55337-352-9). 32pp. A lovable puppy named Sam tries to track down a monster she believes has escaped from the television into her owners' house. (Rev: HBG 10/03; SLJ 5/03)

6657 Lachtman, Ofelia Dumas. *Pepita Finds Out / Lo Que Pepita Descubre* (1–3). Trans. by Carolina Villarroel. Illus. by Alex P. DeLange. 2002, Piñata $14.95 (1-55885-375-8). Pepita frets because she can't find a suitable subject for her school report in this novel with the English text above the Spanish. (Rev: HBG 10/03; SLJ 3/03)

6658 Landry, Leo. *Sea Surprise* (2–4). Illus. 2005, Holt $15.95 (0-8050-6645-4). 64pp. The planning for Eel's surprise party involves lots of underwater suspense. (Rev: BL 5/15/05)

6659 Larson, Kirby. *Cody and Quinn, Sitting in a Tree* (2–3). Illus. 1996, Holiday House $14.95 (0-8234-1227-X). 64pp. Cody is teased by a bully because of his friendship with a girl, Quinn. (Rev: BCCB 9/96; BL 4/1/96; SLJ 4/96)

6660 Laurence, Daniel. *Captain and Matey Set Sail* (K–2). Illus. by Claudio Munoz. Series: An I Can Read Book. 2001, HarperCollins LB $14.89 (0-06-028957-0). 64pp. Two pirates bicker constantly about everything — what to call their parrot, what to do with the treasure if they ever find it, which song to sing while scrubbing the deck, and so forth. (Rev: BCCB 9/01; BL 7/01; HB 1–2/02; HBG 3/02; SLJ 11/01)

6661 Lavis, Steve. *Little Mouse Has a Busy Day* (PS–K). Illus. by author. 2000, Ragged Bear $6.95 (1-929766-10-X). This book for beginning readers traces the hour-by-hour activities of Little Mouse

from getting up at 8 A.M. to bedtime at 6. Also use *Little Mouse Has an Adventure.* (Rev: SLJ 1/01)

6662 Lawlor, Laurie. *The Worst Kid Who Ever Lived on Eighth Avenue* (1–2). Illus. by Cynthia Fisher. 1998, Holiday House $14.95 (0-8234-1350-0). 48pp. Mary Lou and her friends are convinced that big bad Leroy is up to no good when he buries a large bag in his backyard. (Rev: BL 5/1/98; HBG 10/98; SLJ 4/98)

6663 Leonard, Marcia. *Best Friends* (PS–1). Photos by Dorothy Handelman. Series: Real Kids Readers. 1999, Millbrook LB $16.90 (0-7613-2064-4); paper $3.99 (0-7613-2089-X). 30pp. In this simple story for very beginning readers that is illustrated with photographs, two girls describe their similarities and differences. (Rev: SLJ 1/00)

6664 Leonard, Marcia. *Dan and Dan* (PS–1). Photos by Dorothy Handelman. Series: Real Kids Readers. 1998, Millbrook LB $16.90 (0-7613-2003-2); paper $3.99 (0-7613-2028-8). 31pp. A beginning reader that tells of the loving relationship between a young boy and his namesake and grandfather. (Rev: SLJ 6/98)

6665 Leonard, Marcia. *Get the Ball, Slim* (1). Illus. by Dorothy Handelman. Series: Real Kids Readers. 1998, Millbrook LB $16.90 (0-7613-2000-8); paper $3.99 (0-7613-2025-3). 32pp. Using photographs for illustrations, this simple reader tells about African American twins Tim and Jim and their dog Slim. (Rev: BL 5/1/98; HBG 10/98; SLJ 6/98)

6666 Leonard, Marcia. *I Like Mess* (1). Illus. by Dorothy Handelman. Series: Real Kids Readers. 1998, Millbrook LB $16.90 (0-7613-2002-4); paper $3.99 (0-7613-2027-X). 32pp. In this simple reader illustrated with photographs, a young girl tries to please her mother by cleaning up the mess she has created. (Rev: BL 5/1/98; SLJ 6/98)

6667 Leonard, Marcia. *My Pal Al* (PS–1). Photos by Dorothy Handelman. Series: Real Kids Readers. 1998, Millbrook LB $16.90 (0-7613-2001-6); paper $3.99 (0-7613-2026-1). 31pp. A beginning reader that describes how a little African American girl loves her favorite toy. (Rev: SLJ 6/98)

6668 Leonard, Marcia. *No New Pants!* (1). Illus. by Dorothy Handelman. Series: Real Kids Readers. 1999, Millbrook LB $16.90 (0-7613-2063-6); paper $3.99 (0-7613-2088-1). 32pp. A young African American child doesn't want to go shopping for pants with his mother, but he enjoys getting a pair of hand-me-downs from his brother. (Rev: BL 12/1/99; HBG 3/00)

6669 Le Sieg, Theo. *Ten Apples Up on Top* (K–2). Illus. 1961, Random LB $11.99 (0-394-90019-7). 72pp. Three bears try to pile apples on their heads in this nonsense story. Also from the same author and publisher: *I Wish That I Had Duck Feet* (1965); *Eye Book* (1968).

6670 Levinson, Nancy S. *Clara and the Bookwagon* (1–2). Illus. by Carolyn Croll. 1988, HarperCollins LB $15.89 (0-06-023838-0); paper $3.95 (0-06-444134-2). 64pp. A real-life story about a young girl who wants to read despite her father's objections. (Rev: BL 4/1/88; SLJ 7/88)

6671 Levinson, Nancy Smiler. *Prairie Friends* (2–4). Illus. by Stacey Schuett. Series: An I Can Read Book. 2003, HarperCollins LB $16.89 (0-06-028002-6). 64pp. Betsy is thrilled when a girl her age moves into the neighborhood, but the city girl takes time to adapt to her new surroundings in this story that includes lots of interesting facts about prairie life in the middle 1800s. (Rev: BL 1/1–15/03; HBG 10/03; SLJ 3/03)

6672 Levy, Elizabeth. *The Creepy Computer Mystery* (2–3). Illus. by Denise Brunkus. 1996, Scholastic paper $3.99 (0-590-60322-1). 48pp. The trio Invisible Ink solves the mystery of the online intruder. (Rev: BL 9/15/96)

6673 Levy, Elizabeth. *A Hare-Raising Tail* (2–5). Illus. by Mordicai Gerstein. Series: Ready-for-Chapters. 2002, Simon & Schuster paper $3.99 (0-689-84626-6). 64pp. Fletcher the basset hound finds a new home with Jill, and all goes well until Jill takes him to school for show-and-tell. (Rev: BL 9/1/02; HBG 10/02; SLJ 1/03)

6674 Levy, Elizabeth. *The Karate Class Mystery* (2–4). Illus. by Denise Brunkus. 1996, Scholastic $3.99 (0-590-60323-X). 48pp. A mystery in which Justin's karate belt disappears and the culprit must be caught. (Rev: BL 2/1/97)

6675 Levy, Elizabeth. *The Mystery of the Missing Dog* (2–3). Illus. 1995, Scholastic paper $3.99 (0-590-47484-7). 44pp. Invisible Chip loses his invisible dog, Max, but solves a mystery with the help of friends Justin and Charlene. (Rev: BL 1/1–15/96)

6676 Levy, Elizabeth. *Parents' Night Fright* (2–4). Illus. by Denise Brunkus. 1998, Scholastic paper $3.99 (0-590-60324-8). 48pp. When Charlene's prize-winning story disappears, she and buddies Justin, who is deaf, and the invisible Chip set out to solve the mystery. (Rev: BL 7/98; SLJ 9/98)

6677 Levy, Elizabeth. *Take Two, They're Small* (2–4). Illus. by Mark Elliott. 2002, HarperCollins LB $15.89 (0-06-028593-1). 86pp. As she enters fourth grade, Eve isn't pleased to find she'll have to deal with her irritating, younger twin sisters in this sequel to *Big Trouble in Little Twinsville* (2001). (Rev: BL 4/1/03; HBG 3/03; SLJ 1/03)

6678 Lewin, Betsy. *Wiley Learns to Spell* (PS–1). Illus. by author. Series: Hello Reader! 1998, Scholastic paper $3.50 (0-590-10835-2). In this easy reader, Wiley, a mischievous monster, makes words out of an armload of colorful block letters. (Rev: SLJ 2/99)

6679 Lewis, Rob. *Grandpa at the Beach* (2–3). Illus. 1998, Mondo paper $4.50 (1-57255-552-1). 47pp. A grandfather bear and his grandson, Finley, investigate the reports that a beach house contains a monster and discover it is only Dad. (Rev: BL 7/98)

6680 Lewis, Rob. *Too Much Trouble for Grandpa* (2–3). Illus. 1998, Mondo paper $4.50 (1-57255-551-3). 47pp. Grandpa Bear brings home things he believes will not cause problems, such as a cat and a girlfriend, but in each case he is wrong. (Rev: BL 7/98)

6681 Little, Jean. *Emma's Magic Winter* (1–2). Illus. by Jennifer Plecas. 1998, HarperCollins $14.95 (0-06-025389-4). 64pp. Though Emma is basically very shy, she is brave enough to make a good friend of Sally, the new girl next door. (Rev: BCCB 10/98; BL 11/1/98; HB 9–10/98*; HBG 3/99; SLJ 10/98)

6682 Little, Jean. *Emma's Yucky Brother* (1–2). Illus. by Jennifer Plecas. Series: I Can Read. 2001, HarperCollins LB $14.89 (0-06-028349-1). 64pp. In this book for beginning readers, Emma has mixed feelings when her family adopts a 4-year-old boy. (Rev: BL 12/1/00; HBG 10/01; SLJ 1/01)

6683 Lobel, Arnold. *Frog and Toad Are Friends* (K–2). Illus. by author. 1970, HarperCollins LB $15.89 (0-06-023958-1); paper $3.90 (0-06-444020-6). 64pp. Two new friends for the independent reader. Three sequels are: *Frog and Toad Together* (1972); *Frog and Toad All Year* (1976); *Days with Frog and Toad* (1979).

6684 Lobel, Arnold. *Grasshopper on the Road* (1–2). Illus. by author. 1978, HarperCollins LB $15.89 (0-06-023962-X); paper $3.95 (0-06-444094-X). 64pp. A series of short stories, each with a vital message.

6685 Lobel, Arnold. *Mouse Soup* (1–2). Illus. by author. 1977, HarperCollins LB $15.89 (0-06-023968-9); paper $3.95 (0-06-444041-9). 64pp. When Mouse is caught by Weasel, who plans to use him for soup, he convinces his captor that "mouse soup must be mixed with stones to make it taste really good."

6686 Lobel, Arnold. *Mouse Tales* (1–2). Illus. by author. 1972, HarperCollins LB $15.89 (0-06-023942-5); paper $3.95 (0-06-444013-3). 64pp. Seven bedtime stories told by Papa Mouse to his seven sons. Lively little drawings add to the humor.

6687 Lobel, Arnold. *Owl at Home* (1–2). Illus. by author. 1975, HarperCollins LB $15.89 (0-06-023949-2); paper $3.95 (0-06-444034-6). 64pp. Five stories dealing with the humorous and bungling attempts of Owl to be helpful.

6688 Lobel, Arnold. *Small Pig* (K–2). Illus. by author. 1969, HarperCollins LB $15.89 (0-06-023932-8); paper $3.95 (0-06-444120-2). 64pp. A dirty little pig in a search for mud ends up in cement.

6689 Lobel, Arnold. *Uncle Elephant* (K–3). Illus. by author. 1981, HarperCollins LB $15.89 (0-06-023980-8); paper $3.95 (0-06-444104-0). 64pp. A nephew and uncle elephant form a friendship.

6690 Lopshire, Robert. *Put Me in the Zoo* (1–3). Illus. by author. 1960, Beginner Books $7.99 (0-394-80017-6). 72pp. An unusual dog thinks he should be in the zoo, but his talents really mean he should be in a circus.

6691 Lunn, Carolyn. *A Whisper Is Quiet* (1–2). Illus. by Clovis Martin. 1989, Children's Book Pr. LB $18.00 (0-516-02087-0); paper $4.95 (0-516-42087-9). 32pp. A concept book introduces opposites. (Rev: BL 3/1/89)

6692 Maccarone, Grace. *The Gym Day Winner* (PS–1). Illus. 1996, Scholastic paper $3.99 (0-590-26263-7). 32pp. A youngster finds a sport at which he excels. (Rev: BL 8/96; SLJ 1/97)

6693 Maccarone, Grace. *I Shop with My Daddy* (1). Illus. by Denise Brunkus. Series: Hello Reader! 1998, Scholastic paper $3.50 (0-590-50196-8). 32pp. A little girl and her father go shopping, and as a last item, he allows her something sweet — a frozen yogurt. (Rev: BL 7/98)

6694 Maccarone, Grace. *The Lunch Box Surprise* (1). Illus. by Betsy Lewin. 1995, Scholastic paper $3.99 (0-590-26267-X). 32pp. First-grader Sam is surprised at school when he finds that his mother hasn't packed his lunch. (Rev: BL 1/1–15/96)

6695 Maccarone, Grace. *My Tooth Is About to Fall Out* (1–2). Illus. by Betsy Lewin. 1995, Scholastic $3.99 (0-590-48376-5). 32pp. An easy-to-read book about the problems of having a loose tooth. (Rev: BL 7/95)

6696 Maccarone, Grace. *Recess Mess* (1–2). Illus. by Betsy Lewin. Series: Hello Reader! 1996, Scholastic paper $3.99 (0-590-73878-X). 32pp. Sam has trouble determining which bathroom is for boys in this easily read school story. (Rev: BL 2/1/97)

6697 McCully, Emily Arnold. *The Grandma Mix-Up* (1–3). Illus. by author. 1988, HarperCollins LB $15.89 (0-06-024202-7); paper $3.95 (0-06-444150-4). 64pp. Two grandmothers with very different ways arrive to baby-sit. (Rev: BL 12/1/89; SLJ 3/89)

6698 McCully, Emily Arnold. *Grandmas at Bat* (1–2). Illus. 1993, HarperCollins paper $3.95 (0-06-444193-8). 64pp. Pip's two grandmothers, last-minute replacements, coach his baseball team. (Rev: BL 3/1/93; HB 7–8/93; SLJ 6/93)

6699 McDonald, Megan. *Beezy and Funnybone* (1–2). Illus. by Nancy Poydar. Series: Beezy. 2000, Orchard LB $15.99 (0-531-33211-X); paper $4.95 (0-531-07161-8). 48pp. A book for beginning readers that contains three simple stories about a little girl and her dog Funnybone. (Rev: BL 7/00; HBG 10/00; SLJ 9/00)

6700 McDonald, Megan. *Beezy at Bat* (1–2). Illus. by Nancy Poydar. 1998, Orchard LB $14.99 (0-531-33085-0). 48pp. In this, the third book about Beezy, she plays baseball, exchanges riddles with Gran, and scares a friend with a snake. (Rev: BL 11/1/98; HBG 3/99; SLJ 9/98)

6701 McDonald, Megan. *Beezy Magic* (2–4). Illus. by Nancy Poydar. 1997, Orchard LB $14.99 (0-531-33064-8). 48pp. Three easily read short stories involving carrot-haired Beezy, her family, and her dog. (Rev: BL 7/98; HBG 10/98; SLJ 4/98)

6702 McDonald, Megan. *Shining Star* (1–3). Series: Step into Reading. 2003, Random $11.99 (0-307-46340-0); paper $3.99 (0-307-26340-1). 48pp. Star and her best friend Blister find varied uses for duck tape in this book for beginning readers. (Rev: BL 7/03; HBG 4/04)

6703 McDonald, Megan. *Stink: The Incredible Shrinking Kid* (2–4). Illus. by Peter H. Reynolds. Series: Judy Moody. 2005, Candlewick $12.99 (0-7636-2025-4). 112pp. Stink, Judy Moody's younger brother, is convinced he's shrinking and decides to make the best of it in this beginning chapter book. (Rev: BL 3/1/05; SLJ 4/05)

6704 McKay, Sindy. *Ben and Becky in the Haunted House* (1–3). Illus. by Meredith Johnson. Series: We Both Read. 1999, Treasure Bay $7.99 (1-891327-14-3); paper $3.99 (1-891327-18-6). The story of two children who are forced to spend a night in a haunted house is told with two texts, one for adults and the other for beginning readers. (Rev: SLJ 11/99)

6705 McKenna, Colleen O'Shaughnessy. *Doggone . . . Third Grade!* (2–3). Illus. by Stephanie Roth. 2002, Holiday House $15.95 (0-8234-1696-8). 80pp. Third-grader Gordie comes up with a trick for his dog to perform in the class talent show. (Rev: BL 7/02; HBG 10/02; SLJ 7/02)

6706 McKenna, Colleen O'Shaughnessy. *Third Grade Ghouls* (2–4). Illus. by Stephanie Roth. 2001, Holiday House $15.95 (0-8234-1652-6). 80pp. This simple beginning chapter book finds third-grader Gordie searching for the perfect costume to wear for the Halloween parade. (Rev: BL 1/1–15/02; HBG 10/02; SLJ 2/02)

6707 McKissack, Patricia. *Monkey-Monkey's Trick: Based on an African Folk Tale* (1–3). Illus. by Paul Meisel. 1988, Random paper $3.99 (0-394-89173-2). 48pp. Monkey-Monkey needs help building his new house in this amusing fable. (Rev: BL 3/1/89)

6708 McKissack, Patricia. *Tippy Lemmey* (2–4). Illus. by Susan Keeter. Series: Ready-for-Chapters. 2003, Simon & Schuster paper $3.99 (0-689-85019-0). 64pp. Mischievous Tippy the dog is a source of annoyance to Leandra and her friends, but when the pup is kidnapped, they come to his rescue in this story set in Tennessee in 1951. (Rev: BCCB 3/03; BL 1/1–15/03; HB 3–4/03; HBG 10/03; SLJ 1/03)

6709 McKissack, Patricia, and Fredrick McKissack. *Messy Bessey's Family Reunion* (K–1). Illus. by Dana Regan. Series: Rookie Readers. 2000, Children's Book Pr. LB $18.00 (0-516-20830-6); paper $4.95 (0-516-26552-0). 32pp. In this easy reader, Messy Bessey is so upset at the mess she and her relatives have made at an outdoor picnic that she organizes them into a clean-up squad. (Rev: BL 12/1/00)

6710 McKissack, Patricia, and Fredrick McKissack. *Messy Bessey's Holidays* (PS–2). Illus. by Dana Regan. Series: Rookie Readers. 1999, Children's Book Pr. LB $17.00 (0-516-20829-2). 30pp. In this beginning reader, a child bakes cookies for her friends for Hanukkah, Christmas, and Kwanzaa. (Rev: HBG 10/99; SLJ 8/99)

6711 McKissack, Patricia, and Fredrick McKissack. *Miami Makes the Play* (2–4). Illus. Series: Road to Reading. 2001, Golden Books paper $3.99 (0-307-26505-6). 92pp. Miami and friends head for baseball camp for a summer of fun and play but must make some decisions, such as whether to support a coed team. (Rev: BL 5/1/01; HBG 10/01)

6712 McNamara, Margaret. *The Counting Race* (PS–1). Illus. by Mike Gordon. Series: Ready-to-Read. 2003, Simon & Schuster LB $11.89 (0-689-85540-0); paper $3.99 (0-689-85539-7). 31pp. The concept of counting by twos is introduced in this easy-reader story about first graders at Robin Hill School. (Rev: HBG 4/04; SLJ 7/03)

6713 McNamara, Margaret. *One Hundred Days (Plus One)* (K–3). Illus. by Mike Gordon. Series: Robin Hill School. 2003, Simon & Schuster LB $11.89 (0-689-85536-2); paper $3.99 (0-689-85535-4). 32pp. Hannah is miserable when she misses the 100th day of school, for which she has been collecting buttons, but gets a happy surprise when she returns to class. (Rev: HBG 10/03; SLJ 4/03)

6714 McPhail, David. *A Bug, a Bear, and a Boy* (1–2). Illus. 1998, Scholastic paper $3.50 (0-590-14904-0). 32pp. A young boy spends an enjoyable day with his two companions, a bear and a bug. (Rev: BL 11/1/98)

6715 McPhail, David. *The Day the Sheep Showed Up* (1–2). Illus. Series: Hello Reader! 1998, Scholastic paper $3.50 (0-590-84910-7). 32pp. An uproarious farce in which the other animals try to find out what sort of being is a sheep after it unexpectedly joins the farm community. (Rev: BL 5/1/98)

6716 McPhail, David. *A Girl, a Goat, and a Goose* (1). Illus. 2000, Scholastic paper $3.99 (0-439-09978-1). 32pp. Three good friends — a girl, a goose, and a goat — share four amiable adventures in this book for beginning readers. (Rev: BL 12/1/00)

6717 McPhail, David. *The Great Race* (1–2). Illus. Series: Hello Reader! 1998, Scholastic paper $3.50 (0-590-84909-3). 32pp. In this humorous easy reader, the animals have a race and, in spite of many mistakes, end together — each one a winner! (Rev: BL 5/1/98)

6718 McPhail, David. *Piggy's Pancake Parlor* (1–3). Illus. 2002, Dutton $15.99 (0-525-45930-8). 48pp. A pig and a fox open a pancake parlor using the farmer's secret recipe in this charming beginning chapter book. (Rev: BCCB 7–8/02; BL 8/02; HBG 10/02; SLJ 6/02)

6719 McPhail, David. *Rick Is Sick* (PS–1). Illus. Series: Green Light Readers. 2004, Harcourt $11.95 (0-15-205091-4). 24pp. Bunny Jack finds Rick the bear sick in bed and does what he can to help in this simple story for very early readers. (Rev: BL 3/15/04; SLJ 5/04)

6720 McPhail, David. *Snow Lion* (PS–2). Illus. by author. 1983, Parents LB $5.00 (0-8193-1098-0). 48pp. A lion finds it's too hot for him to stay in the jungle.

6721 Maitland, Barbara. *The Bookstore Valentine* (K–2). Illus. by David LaRochelle. Series: Dutton Easy Reader. 2002, Dutton $13.99 (0-525-46913-3). 32pp. Cobweb the ghost-bookstore cat and the bookstore mice plot to get the shop's owner and his new assistant involved in a romantic relationship. (Rev: BCCB 1/03; BL 1/1–15/03; HBG 3/03; SLJ 12/02)

6722 Marshall, Edward. *Three by the Sea* (1–3). Illus. by James Marshall. 1981, Puffin paper $3.99 (0-14-037004-8). 48pp. Three friends, Lolly, Spider, and Sam, tell stories by the seashore.

6723 Marshall, James. *Fox Outfoxed* (2–3). Illus. 1992, Viking paper $3.99 (0-14-038113-9). 48pp. Three easily read stories about Fox and how his careful plans misfire. (Rev: BCCB 4/92; BL 4/1/92; HB 7–8/92; SLJ 5/92*)

6724 Martin, David. *Three Little Bears* (PS–2). Illus. by Akemi Gutierrez. Series: Brand New Readers. 2004, Candlewick $12.99 (0-7636-2349-0). 40pp. Three young bears enjoy swimming, ice cream, snow, and dancing in this easy-reader. (Rev: SLJ 1/05)

6725 Marzollo, Jean. *I Am an Apple* (PS–1). Illus. by Judith Moffatt. Series: Hello Reader! 1997, Scholastic $3.99 (0-590-37223-8). A beginning reader that details the life of an apple from flower to fruit to market to table. (Rev: SLJ 1/98)

6726 Marzollo, Jean. *I'm a Caterpillar* (K–2). Illus. by Judith Moffatt. Series: Hello Reader! 1997, Scholastic $3.50 (0-590-84779-1). A beginning reader that presents, in story form, the life cycle of a caterpillar. (Rev: SLJ 11/97)

6727 Marzollo, Jean. *Once upon a Springtime* (1–2). Illus. by Jacqueline Rogers. Series: Hello Reader! 1998, Scholastic paper $3.50 (0-590-46017-X). 30pp. A fawn and its mother stay together during the first year of its life and observe humans and their comparable annual activities. (Rev: BL 5/1/98)

6728 Marzollo, Jean. *Soccer Cousins* (2–4). Illus. by Irene Trivas. Series: Hello Reader! 1997, Scholastic $3.99 (0-590-74254-X). 32pp. In this easy-to-read book David is afraid that he is not a good soccer player, but he is thrilled with the invitation to go to Mexico to see his cousin play. (Rev: BL 2/1/98; SLJ 6/98)

6729 Marzollo, Jean. *Soccer Sam* (1–2). Illus. by Blanche Sims. 1987, Random paper $3.99 (0-394-88406-X). 48pp. Marco from Mexico spends a year with his friend Sam in the United States, and the boys organize a soccer team. (Rev: BL 8/87; SLJ 9/87)

6730 Marzollo, Jean, et al. *Football Friends* (1–2). Illus. by True Kelley. Series: Hello Reader! 1997, Scholastic $3.99 (0-590-38395-7). 32pp. Freddy becomes so angry with his friend Mark when they choose teams for playing football that he begins using his fists and feet in this easy-to-read sports book. (Rev: BL 2/1/98; SLJ 3/98)

6731 Marzollo, Jean, and Dan Marzollo. *Basketball Buddies* (1–2). Illus. by True Kelley. 1998, Scholastic paper $3.99 (0-590-38401-5). 32pp. Although Paul is tall he is not a good basketball player, but with his teammate's help, he improves. (Rev: BL 3/15/99; SLJ 4/99)

6732 Mason, Jane B. *Hellow, Two-Wheeler!* (1–2). Illus. by David Monteith. 1995, Penguin Putnam paper $3.95 (0-448-40853-8). 48pp. A boy accidentally learns to ride his bike without its training wheels. (Rev: BL 7/95)

6733 Masters, Anthony. *Ricky's Rat Gang* (1–3). Illus. by Chris Fisher. Series: I Am Reading. 2004, Kingfisher paper $3.95 (0-7534-5800-4). 41pp. Three mice plot to drive bullying rats from the supermarket storeroom in this book for beginning readers. (Rev: SLJ 9/04)

6734 Masurel, Claire. *That Bad, Bad Cat* (1). Illus. by True Kelley. Series: All Aboard Reading. 2002, Penguin Putnam $13.89 (0-448-42665-X); paper $3.99 (0-448-42622-6). 32pp. The family cat is always misbehaving, but when he fails to show up for dinner everyone misses him. (Rev: BL 6/1–15/02; HBG 10/02)

6735 Matthias, Catherine. *I Love Cats* (K–1). Illus. by Tom Dunnington. 1983, Children's Book Pr. LB $18.00 (0-516-02041-2); paper $4.95 (0-516-42041-0). 32pp. The narrator likes many things, but cats are best.

6736 Mayfield, Sue. *Shoot!* (1–2). Illus. by Ken Cox. Series: Blue Bananas. 2001, Crabtree LB $14.97 (0-7787-0847-0); paper $4.46 (0-7787-0893-4). 48pp. Shoot the dog, the team mascot, helps Jamie and his friends win the soccer game. (Rev: SLJ 7/02)

6737 Medearis, Angela Shelf. *Here Comes the Snow* (1). Illus. 1996, Scholastic paper $3.99 (0-590-26266-1). 32pp. Kids enjoy all of the fun of a first snowfall. (Rev: BL 8/96; SLJ 9/96)

6738 Medearis, Angela Shelf. *Singing for Dr. King* (K–3). Illus. by Cornelius Van Wright and Ying-hwa Hu. Series: Just for You! 2004, Scholastic paper $3.99 (0-439-56855-2). 32pp. An African American third grader becomes involved in civil rights in this easy-reader. (Rev: SLJ 1/05)

6739 Meister, Cari. *My Pony Jack* (PS–K). Illus. by Amy Young. Series: Viking Easy-to-Read. 2005, Viking $13.99 (0-670-05917-X). 32pp. In simple rhyming couplets suitable for beginning readers, Lacy talks about her pony and how she grooms him. (Rev: BL 5/1/05)

6740 Meister, Cari. *Skinny and Fats, Best Friends* (K–2). Illus. by Steve Bjorkman. Series: Holiday House Reader. 2002, Holiday House $14.95 (0-8234-1692-5). 32pp. Skinny, a rabbit, and Fats, a pig, enjoy spending time fishing, making marshmallows, and building rockets. (Rev: HBG 3/03; SLJ 10/02)

6741 Meister, Cari. *Tiny Goes to the Library* (1). Illus. by Rich Davis. 2000, Viking $13.89 (0-670-88556-8). 32pp. Tiny, an enormous dog, helps his young master by pulling home the wagon that the boy has overfilled with library books. (Rev: BCCB 7–8/00; BL 4/15/00; HBG 10/00; SLJ 7/00)

6742 Meister, Cari. *Tiny the Snow Dog* (K–1). Illus. by Rich Davis. 2001, Viking $13.99 (0-670-89117-7). Giant Tiny the dog hides in the snow from his young owner, who can't see him despite many visual clues. (Rev: BL 11/1/01; HBG 3/02; SLJ 10/01)

6743 Meister, Cari. *Tiny's Bath* (K–1). Illus. by Rich Davis. 1999, Viking $13.89 (0-670-87962-2). 32pp. A boy tries to give his huge dog a bath but finds he has to use the backyard pool. (Rev: BCCB 4/99; BL 3/15/99; HB 5–6/99; HBG 10/99; SLJ 5/99)

6744 Meister, Cari. *When Tiny Was Tiny* (1). Illus. by Rich Davis. Series: Easy-to-Read. 1999, Viking LB $13.89 (0-670-88058-2). 32pp. A simple story about a boy and his dog, Tiny, who is no longer so. (Rev: BL 10/1/99; HBG 3/00; SLJ 12/99)

6745 Milgrim, David. *Ride Otto Ride!* (K–1). Illus. 2002, Simon & Schuster $14.95 (0-689-84417-4). 32pp. An easy-to-read book about the adventures of a robot named Otto and his animal friends. Also use *See Otto* (2002). (Rev: BL 9/15/02; HBG 3/03; SLJ 3/03)

6746 Milgrim, David. *See Pip Point* (PS–1). Illus. Series: Ready-to-Read. 2003, Simon & Schuster $14.95 (0-689-85116-2). 32pp. A simple book for beginning readers about a mouse named Pip and his adventures with a balloon. (Rev: BL 2/1/03; HBG 10/03)

6747 Miller, Sara S. *Cat in the Bag* (1). Illus. by Benton Mahan. Series: Rookie Readers. 2001, Children's Book Pr. $18.00 (0-516-22014-4). 32pp. While trying to pack, a little girl must keep chasing her cat out of her suitcase in this easy reader. (Rev: BL 11/1/01)

6748 Miller, Sara S. *Three More Stories You Can Read to Your Cat* (1–3). Illus. by True Kelley. 2002, Houghton Mifflin $15.00 (0-618-11035-6). 48pp. These simple, playful stories are about cats who face such problems as wanting to come inside during a snow storm and finding entertainment on a particularly boring birthday. (Rev: BL 4/15/02; HBG 10/02; SLJ 5/02)

6749 Miller, Sara S. *Three More Stories You Can Read to Your Dog* (2–3). Illus. 2000, Houghton Mifflin $15.00 (0-395-92293-3). 48pp. Three amusing easy-to-read stories that will amuse children, even if they don't have a dog. (Rev: BL 3/15/00; HBG 10/00; SLJ 4/00)

6750 Miller, Sara S. *Three Stories You Can Read to Your Cat* (1–3). Illus. by True Kelley. 1997, Houghton Mifflin $13.95 (0-395-78831-5). 48pp. An easy-to-read book about Kelley's playful, adventurous cat. (Rev: BL 3/1/97; SLJ 5/97)

6751 Miller, Sara S. *Three Stories You Can Read to Your Dog* (2–4). Illus. by True Kelley. 1995, Houghton Mifflin $15.00 (0-395-69938-X). 42pp. Three easy-to-read stories that feature a muddle-headed dog that doesn't know how to behave. (Rev: BCCB 3/95; BL 4/15/95; SLJ 4/95)

6752 Miller, Sara S. *Three Stories You Can Read to Your Teddy Bear* (1–3). Illus. by True Kelley. 2004, Houghton Mifflin $15.00 (0-618-30397-9). 48pp. In this companion to *Three Stories You Can Read to Your Cat* (1993) and *Three Stories You Can Read to Your Dog* (1995), three entertaining stories are designed to be read to a teddy bear. (Rev: BL 3/1/04; SLJ 6/04)

6753 Mills, Claudia. *Gus and Grandpa and Show-and-Tell* (1–2). Illus. by Catherine Stock. Series: Gus and Grandpa. 2000, Farrar $13.00 (0-374-32819-6). 48pp. Gus doesn't shine at show-and-tell until he brings his grandfather to school to talk about history in this delightful easy-to-read story. (Rev: BL 10/1/00; HBG 3/01; SLJ 8/00)

6754 Mills, Claudia. *Gus and Grandpa Go Fishing* (1–3). Illus. by Catherine Stock. Series: Gus and Grandpa Ser. 2003, Farrar $15.00 (0-374-32815-3). 48pp. Grandpa shows Gus how to fish in this installment in the long-running series. (Rev: BL 9/1/03; HBG 4/04; SLJ 10/03)

6755 Milton, Joyce. *Whales: The Gentle Giants* (2–3). Illus. by Alton Langford. 1989, Random paper $3.99 (0-394-89809-5). 48pp. A sailor named Brendan steps on the back of a whale. (Rev: BL 6/1/89)

6756 Minarik, Else Holmelund. *Little Bear* (K–2). Illus. by Maurice Sendak. 1957, HarperCollins LB $15.89 (0-06-024241-8); paper $3.95 (0-06-444004-4). 64pp. Humorous adventure stories of Mother Bear and Little Bear. Others in the series: *Little Bear's Friend* (1960); *Little Bear's Visit* (1961); *A Kiss for Little Bear* (1968).

6757 Minarik, Else Holmelund. *No Fighting, No Biting!* (PS–3). Illus. by Maurice Sendak. 1958, HarperCollins LB $15.89 (0-06-024291-4); paper $3.95 (0-06-444015-X). 64pp. Light-foot and Quick-foot, two little alligators, teach Rosa and Willy a lesson.

6758 Moffatt, Judith. *Who Stole the Cookies?* (1–2). Illus. 1996, Penguin Putnam paper $3.99 (0-448-41127-X). 32pp. A cast of animal characters ask who stole the cookies in this rhyming first reader. (Rev: BL 8/96; SLJ 9/96)

6759 Moore, Lilian. *Little Raccoon* (2–4). Illus. by Doug Cushman. 2002, Holt $15.95 (0-8050-6543-1). 64pp. A beginning reader that contains three stories about a little raccoon who is becoming independent. (Rev: BL 4/1/02; HBG 10/02)

6760 Morris, Kim. *Molly in the Middle* (2–3). Illus. by Dorothy Handelman. Series: Real Kids Readers. 1999, Millbrook LB $17.90 (0-7613-2059-8); paper $3.99 (0-7613-2084-9). 48pp. Molly, a middle child, decides that if she can't be the youngest or oldest, she will be the "est" in some other way, such as being the loudest or funniest. (Rev: BL 5/15/99; SLJ 8/99)

6761 Namm, Diane. *Guess Who?* (PS–2). Illus. by David Sheldon. Series: My First Reader. 2004, Children's Pr. LB $17.50 (0-516-24412-4). 31pp. Potential visitors are the subject of this rhyming book for beginning readers with cartoon illustrations and a word list. (Rev: SLJ 7/04)

6762 Napoli, Donna Jo, and Robert Furrow. *Sly the Sleuth and the Pet Mysteries* (2–4). Illus. by Heather Maione. Series: Sly the Sleuth. 2005, Dial $15.99 (0-8037-2993-6). 96pp. Sylvia (a.k.a. "Sly the Sleuth") solves her friends' pet mysteries in this illustrated easy reader, the first in a series. (Rev: BL 3/1/05)

6763 Nelson, Vaunda Micheaux. *Ready? Set. Raymond!* (K–1). Illus. by Derek Anderson. Series: Step into Reading. 2002, Random LB $11.99 (0-375-91363-7); paper $3.99 (0-375-81363-2). 32pp. Raymond, an appealing African American boy, "does things fast," including making a friend and running a race, in this collection of three short, nicely illustrated stories. (Rev: BL 9/15/02; HBG 3/03; SLJ 12/02)

6764 Nixon, Joan Lowery. *Gus and Gertie and the Lucky Charms* (2–4). Illus. by Diane De Groat. 2002, North-South LB $14.88 (1-58717-100-7). 48pp. Gus and Gertie solve a mystery at the Ani-

mals' Winter Olympics in this beginning chapter book. (Rev: BL 1/1–15/02; SLJ 1/02)

6765 Nodset, Joan L. *Come Here, Cat* (K–3). Illus. by Steven Kellogg. 1973, HarperCollins $10.00 (0-06-024557-3). 32pp. A young girl chases a cat around her house and onto the roof in this simple but enjoyable story.

6766 Nodset, Joan L. *Go Away, Dog* (1–2). Illus. by Paul Meisel. 1997, HarperCollins LB $12.89 (0-06-027503-0). 32pp. A boy finds that he can't get rid of the dog that is following him in this easy-to-read book. (Rev: BL 8/97; HBG 3/98; SLJ 10/97)

6767 Nodset, Joan L. *Who Took the Farmer's Hat?* (1–2). Illus. by Fritz Siebel. 1963, HarperCollins LB $15.89 (0-06-024566-2); paper $6.95 (0-06-443174-6). 32pp. When the wind blows away the farmer's hat, all of the animals think they saw it.

6768 Nolen, Jerdine. *Max and Jax in Second Grade* (1–3). Illus. by Karen L. Schmidt. 2002, Harcourt $14.00 (0-15-201668-6). 44pp. In this easily read chapter book, brother and sister crocodile twins, who have different interests, join forces to help each other. (Rev: BL 6/1–15/02; HBG 10/02; SLJ 4/02)

6769 Noonan, Julia. *Hare and Rabbit: Friends Forever* (1–2). Illus. by author. 2000, Scholastic paper $3.99 (0-439-08753-8). Hare and Rabbit share a house and enjoy three simple adventures together. (Rev: SLJ 11/00)

6770 O'Brien, Claire. *Barn Party* (1–3). Illus. by Tim Archbold. Series: I Am Reading. 2005, Kingfisher paper $3.95 (0-7534-5854-3). 48pp. Rooster's social snobbery backfires when the other animals boycott his exclusive party and throw one of their own. (Rev: BL 5/15/05)

6771 O'Connor, Jane. *Kate Skates* (PS–1). Illus. by DyAnne DiSalvo-Ryan. 1995, Penguin Putnam paper $3.99 (0-448-40935-6). 48pp. Tiny Jen easily learns to skate on her double blades, but older sister Kate has problems with her grownup single blades. (Rev: BL 1/1–15/96; SLJ 5/96)

6772 O'Connor, Jane. *Molly the Brave and Me* (1–3). Illus. by Sheila Hamanaka. 1990, Random paper $3.99 (0-394-84175-1). 48pp. Molly seems fearless, but in time of trouble Beth leads the way. (Rev: BCCB 6/90; BL 6/1/90; SLJ 8/90)

6773 O'Connor, Jane. *Nina, Nina Ballerina* (PS–1). Illus. by DyAnne DiSalvo-Ryan. 1993, Penguin Putnam paper $3.99 (0-448-40511-3). 32pp. When Nina breaks her arm, she worries that she will not be able to perform in her ballet class show. (Rev: BL 7/93; SLJ 8/93)

6774 O'Connor, Jane. *The Teeny Tiny Woman* (K–2). Illus. by R. W. Alley. 1986, Random $11.99 (0-394-98320-3); paper $3.99 (0-394-88320-9). 32pp. The familiar folktale retold. By the same author, another easy reader, *Sir Small and the Dragonfly* (1988). (Rev: BL 12/1/86)

6775 Osborne, Mary Pope. *Dinosaurs Before Dark* (1–2). Illus. by Sal Murdocca. 1992, Random LB $11.99 (0-679-92411-6). 68pp. Jack and his sister time-travel to the days of the dinosaurs. (Rev: BL 10/1/92; SLJ 9/92)

6776 Packard, Mary. *The Very Bad Day* (PS–2). Illus. by Joy Allen. 2004, Children's Pr. LB $17.50 (0-516-24415-9). 31pp. Things do not start off well for the young heroine of this rhyming book for beginning readers, with cartoon illustrations and a word list. (Rev: SLJ 7/04)

6777 Packard, Mary. *When I Am Big* (PS–1). Illus. by Laura Rader. Series: All-Star Readers. 1999, Reader's Digest paper $3.99 (1-57584-294-7). 31pp. A beginning reader about a young boy's dreams of the future and achieving athletic glory. (Rev: SLJ 7/99)

6778 Papademetriou, Lisa. *My Pen Pal, Pat* (1–3). Photos by Dorothy Handelman. Series: Real Kids Readers. 1998, Millbrook LB $17.90 (0-7613-2023-7); paper $3.99 (0-7613-2048-2). 45pp. Two pen pals named Pat finally meet and discover that one is a boy and the other a girl. (Rev: HBG 3/99; SLJ 12/98)

6779 Papademetriou, Lisa. *You're in Big Trouble, Brad!* (1–3). Photos by Dorothy Handelman. Series: Real Kids Readers. 1998, Millbrook LB $17.90 (0-7613-2022-9); paper $3.99 (0-7613-2047-4). 44pp. When Brad is called to the principal's office, he thinks that he is facing big trouble, but actually he just forgot his lunch. (Rev: SLJ 12/98)

6780 Parish, Herman. *Amelia Bedelia 4 Mayor* (2–3). Illus. 1999, Greenwillow $15.00 (0-688-16721-7). 48pp. The literal-minded housekeeper decides to throw her hat in the ring (and does just that!) when she plans to run for mayor. (Rev: BL 8/99; HBG 3/00; SLJ 9/99)

6781 Parish, Herman. *Bravo, Amelia Bedelia!* (1–3). Illus. by Lynn Sweat. 1997, Greenwillow $11.95 (0-688-15155-8). 40pp. Literal-minded Amelia Bedelia creates havoc at a school concert in this beginning reader. (Rev: BL 5/1/97; SLJ 4/97)

6782 Parish, Herman. *Calling Doctor Amelia Bedelia* (PS–2). Illus. by Lynn Sweat. Series: Amelia Bedelia. 2002, HarperCollins LB $17.89 (0-06-001422-9). 64pp. When Amelia Bedelia helps out in a doctor's office for the day, she wreaks such havoc that only ice cream can save the day. (Rev: BL 8/02; HB 11–12/02; HBG 3/03; SLJ 8/02)

6783 Parish, Peggy. *Amelia Bedelia* (1–3). Illus. by Fritz Siebel. 1992, HarperCollins LB $15.89 (0-06-020187-8); paper $3.95 (0-06-444155-5). 64pp. The adventures of a literal-minded housekeeper, in a newly illustrated edition. Other series titles are: *Amelia Bedelia and the Surprise Shower* (1966); *Thank You, Amelia Bedelia* (1993).

6784 Parish, Peggy. *Amelia Bedelia Goes Camping* (2–4). Illus. by Lynn Sweat. 1985, Greenwillow $16.00 (0-688-04057-8); Avon paper $3.99 (0-380-70067-0). 56pp. Amelia's camping trip is the occasion for all kinds of mistakes. Also use: *Amelia Bedelia's Family Album* (1988). (Rev: BCCB 7/85; BL 3/15/85; SLJ 5/85)

6785 Parish, Peggy. *No More Monsters for Me!* (K–3). Illus. by Marc Simont. 1981, HarperCollins LB $15.89 (0-06-024658-8); paper $3.95 (0-06-444109-1). 64pp. A young girl wants to keep a monster for a pet.

6786 Parish, Peggy. *Play Ball, Amelia Bedelia* (1–3). Illus. by Wallace Tripp. 1972, HarperCollins LB $14.89 (0-06-024656-1); paper $3.95 (0-06-444205-5). 64pp. Amelia Bedelia has trouble with baseball lingo. Other series titles are: *Come Back, Amelia Bedelia* (1971); *Teach Us, Amelia Bedelia* (1977, Greenwillow); *Amelia Bedelia Helps Out* (1979, Greenwillow); *Amelia Bedelia and the Baby* (1981, Greenwillow).

6787 Parish, Peggy. *Scruffy* (1–2). Illus. by Kelly Oechsli. 1988, HarperCollins LB $15.89 (0-06-024660-X); paper $3.95 (0-06-444137-7). 64pp. A small boy learns how to choose and care for his first pet — a kitten. (Rev: BL 2/1/88; SLJ 7/88)

6788 Park, Barbara. *Junie B., First Grader (at Last!)* (2–3). Illus. by Denise Brunkus. 2001, Random LB $13.99 (0-375-81516-3). 96pp. When her best friend deserts her and she finds out she needs glasses, Junie B. Jones discovers that first grade is not what she expected. (Rev: BL 11/15/01; HBG 3/02; SLJ 1/02)

6789 Park, Barbara. *Junie B. Jones Has a Monster Under Her Bed* (2–3). Illus. by Denise Brunkus. Series: Stepping Stone. 1997, Random $11.99 (0-679-96697-8). 80pp. An easy reader in which little Junie is convinced that an invisible monster lives under her bed. Also use *Junie B. Jones Is Not a Crook* (1997). (Rev: HB 7–8/97; SLJ 11/97)

6790 Park, Barbara. *Junie B. Jones Loves Handsome Warren* (1–2). Illus. by Denise Brunkus. 1996, Random LB $11.99 (0-679-96696-X); paper $3.99 (0-679-86696-5). 71pp. Junie falls in love with a new boy in her kindergarten class in this easy-to-read book. (Rev: BL 2/1/97)

6791 Parker, Marjorie Blain. *Hello, Freight Train!* (PS–K). Illus. by Bob Kolar. Series: Scholastic Reader. 2005, Scholastic paper $3.99 (0-439-59891-5). 32pp. A dog tells his puppy about the different types of wagons on the passing freight train. (Rev: BL 5/15/05)

6792 Partridge, Elizabeth. *Annie and Bo and the Big Surprise* (1–2). Illus. by Martha Weston. 2002, Dutton $13.99 (0-525-46728-9). 48pp. Bo surprises his best friend Annie with a cake in this story about friendship and affection for beginning readers. (Rev: BL 11/1/01; HBG 10/02)

6793 Pearson, Susan. *Eagle-Eye Ernie Comes to Town* (2–3). Illus. by Gioia Fiammenghi. 1990, Simon & Schuster paper $11.95 (0-671-70564-4). 70pp. Ernestine earns the admiration of her classmates when she solves the mystery of items missing from lunch bags. (Rev: BCCB 12/92; BL 10/1/90; SLJ 4/91)

6794 Pearson, Susan. *The Green Magician Puzzle* (1–3). Illus. by Gioia Fiammenghi. 1991, Simon & Schuster paper $11.95 (0-671-74054-7). 88pp. Ernie and her classmates must solve a series of riddles to become the Green Magicians of the Earth Day parade. (Rev: SLJ 12/91)

6795 *Pet Stories: You Don't Have to Walk* (1–2). Illus. 2000, North-South LB $14.88 (1-58717-032-9); paper $3.99 (1-58717-031-0). 64pp. A book for beginning readers that features stories and excerpts from well-known easy-to-read books like Cynthia Rylant's Henry and Mudge stories. A companion book is *School Stories: Your Dog Didn't Eat* (2000). (Rev: BL 7/00; HBG 3/01)

6796 Petrie, Catherine. *Joshua James Likes Trucks* (PS–1). Illus. by Jerry Warshaw. 1982, Children's Book Pr. paper $4.95 (0-516-43525-6). 32pp. A description of all the trucks that Joshua likes.

6797 Phillips, Joan. *My New Boy* (K–2). Illus. by Lynn Munsinger. 1986, Random paper $3.99 (0-394-88277-6). 32pp. A pet store puppy searches for just the right owner. Also use: *Lucky Bear* (1986). (Rev: BCCB 1/87; BL 12/1/86)

6798 Phillips, Sally Kahler. *Cake Cake Cake Pie* (PS–K). Illus. Series: Step into Reading. 2004, Random LB $11.99 (0-375-92929-0); paper $3.99 (0-375-82929-6). 32pp. A young boy is about to tuck into dessert when a black cat comes on the scene, creating colorful havoc. (Rev: BL 2/1/05)

6799 Pilkey, Dav. *Big Dog and Little Dog Making a Mistake* (PS–K). Illus. by author. Series: A Big Dog and Little Dog Book. 1999, Harcourt $5.95 (0-15-200354-1). This board book for beginning readers tells what happens when two doggy friends mistake a skunk for a kitten. (Rev: SLJ 6/99)

6800 Pinkwater, Daniel. *Mush's Jazz Adventure* (2–4). Illus. by Jill Pinkwater. Series: Ready-for-Chapters. 2002, Simon & Schuster LB $11.89 (0-689-84576-6); paper $3.99 (0-689-84572-3). 37pp. Mush, an alien dog, tells the story of her arrival on Earth and how she and three other animals saved a dance hall owner from robbers in this entertaining and improbable beginning chapter book. (Rev: HBG 3/03; SLJ 2/03)

6801 Pinkwater, Daniel. *Second-Grade Ape* (2–3). Illus. by Jill Pinkwater. Series: Hello Reader! 1998, Scholastic paper $3.99 (0-590-37261-0). 48pp. Young Flash Fleetwood mistakes a gorilla hiding in the bushes for a cat and takes him home as a pet. (Rev: BL 5/1/98; SLJ 9/98)

6802 Platt, Kin. *Big Max* (1–2). Illus. by Robert Lopshire. Series: I Can Read. 1992, HarperCollins LB $15.89 (0-06-024751-7); paper $3.95 (0-06-444006-0). 64pp. A modest detective unravels the case of the king's missing elephant in this newly illustrated I Can Read Book.

6803 Pomerantz, Charlotte. *The Outside Dog* (1–3). Illus. by Jennifer Plecas. 1993, HarperCollins LB $15.89 (0-06-024783-5). 64pp. An easy-reader that tells how Marisol gradually breaks down her grandfather's opposition to having a dog as a pet. (Rev: BCCB 10/93; BL 9/15/93*; SLJ 11/93*)

6804 Porte, Barbara Ann. *Harry in Trouble* (1–3). Illus. by Yossi Abolafia. 1989, Dell paper $4.99 (0-440-80210-5). 48pp. Harry's third library card has disappeared! (Rev: BCCB 2/89; BL 3/1/89; SLJ 3/89)

6805 Proimos, James. *Johnny Mutton, He's So Him!* (PS–3). Illus. by author. 2003, Harcourt $16.00 (0-15-216760-9). 42pp. Young readers will be delighted with this collection of amusing stories about the adventures of Johnny Mutton, a sheep in boy's clothing. (Rev: HB 5–6/03; HBG 10/03; SLJ 8/03)

6806 Proimos, James. *Mutton Soup: More Adventures of Johnny Mutton* (2–4). Illus. 2004, Harcourt $16.00 (0-15-216772-2). 48pp. In these five graphic-novel-style stories, Johnny Mutton — the lamb adopted by humans — gets etiquette lessons, goes on the rollercoast, and has other adventures. (Rev: BL 3/1/04; HB 3–4/04; SLJ 4/04)

6807 *The Random House Book of Easy-to-Read Stories* (K–2). Illus. 1993, Random $19.95 (0-679-83438-9). 252pp. Easy-to-read stories from 16 authors, including Dr. Seuss, the Berenstains, and P. D. Eastman. (Rev: BCCB 1/94; BL 2/1/94; HBG 10/01; SLJ 3/94)

6808 Ransom, Candice. *Danger at Sand Cave* (1–3). Illus. by Den Schofield. Series: On My Own History. 2000, Carolrhoda LB $21.27 (1-57505-379-9); paper $5.95 (1-57505-454-X). 46pp. A fictitious 10-year-old boy helps in the unsuccessful efforts to rescue Floyd Collins from a cave in 1925. (Rev: HB 7–8/00; HBG 10/00; SLJ 8/00)

6809 Rau, Dana Meachen. *A Box Can Be Many Things* (1–2). Illus. by Paige Billin-Frye. Series: Rookie Readers. 1997, Children's Book Pr. LB $18.00 (0-516-20317-7). 32pp. Two children rescue a big box from the garbage and use it in many imaginative ways in this beginning reader. (Rev: BL 5/1/97)

6810 Rau, Dana Meachen. *Chilly Charlie* (K–1). Illus. by Martin Lemelman. Series: Rookie Readers. 2001, Children's Book Pr. $15.00 (0-516-22210-4); paper $4.95 (0-516-27288-8). 24pp. Charlie feels that he is getting cold and needs a hug to keep him warm. (Rev: BL 4/15/01)

6811 Rau, Dana Meachen. *In the Yard* (K–1). Illus. by Elizabeth Wolf. Series: Compass Point Early Reader. 2001, Compass Point LB $18.60 (0-7565-0116-4). 24pp. A brief, simple text and bold illustrations depict an African American family enjoying their backyard. (Rev: SLJ 2/02)

6812 Rau, Dana Meachen. *Lots of Balloons* (K–1). Illus. by Jayoung Cho. 2001, Compass Point LB $18.60 (0-7565-0117-2). 24pp. A little girl wants balloons of various colors, comparing each to a familiar item. (Rev: SLJ 2/02)

6813 Rau, Dana Meachen. *Purple Is Best* (1). Illus. by Mik Cressy. Series: Rookie Readers. 1999, Children's Book Pr. LB $17.50 (0-516-21638-4). 32pp. Sue who loves blue and Fred who paints in red get together and produce purple in this easy reader. (Rev: BL 12/1/99)

6814 Rau, Dana Meachen. *Shoo, Crow! Shoo!* (1). Illus. by Mary Galan Rojas. Series: Compass Point Early Reader. 2001, Compass Point LB $18.60 (0-7565-0072-9). 24pp. Two children make a scarecrow from old clothes, hay, and a pumpkin. (Rev: BL 7/01; SLJ 8/01)

6815 Ritchie, Alison. *Horrible Haircut* (1–2). Illus. by Ian Newsham. Series: Blue Bananas. 2001, Crabtree LB $14.97 (0-7787-0844-6); paper $4.46 (0-7787-0890-X). 45pp. Lucy and her mother make a deal — if Lucy doesn't like the cut her mother gives her, she gets to cut her mother's hair — in this book for fluent beginning readers. (Rev: SLJ 7/02)

6816 Robins, Joan. *Addie Meets Max* (1–3). Illus. by Sue Truesdell. 1985, HarperCollins $9.95 (0-06-025063-1). 32pp. Addie is sure she won't like her new neighbor until mother invites him in for pizza. Also use: *Addie Runs Away* (1989). (Rev: BCCB 5/85; BL 4/15/85; SLJ 5/85)

6817 Rocklin, Joanne. *This Book Is Haunted* (K–2). Illus. by JoAnn Adinolfi. 2002, HarperCollins LB $17.89 (0-06-028457-9). 46pp. A selection of not-very-frightening Halloween stories for beginning readers. (Rev: BCCB 10/02; HBG 3/03; SLJ 9/02)

6818 Roop, Peter, and Connie Roop. *Keep the Lights Burning, Abbie* (1–3). Illus. by Peter E. Hanson. 1985, Carolrhoda LB $21.27 (0-87614-275-7); paper $5.95 (0-87614-454-7). 40pp. The true story of Abbie Burgess, who keeps the lighthouse lights ablaze for four storm-filled weeks while her father is on the mainland. (Rev: BCCB 1/86; BL 1/15/86) [387.1]

6819 Ross, Alice, and Kent Ross. *The Copper Lady* (1–3). Illus. by Leslie Bowman. 1997, Carolrhoda LB $21.27 (0-87614-934-4). 48pp. An easy-to-read book about a young Parisian who watches the construction of the Statue of Liberty and stows away on the ship that is taking it to the United States. (Rev: BCCB 7–8/97; BL 8/97; HB 5–6/04; SLJ 9/97)

6820 Roy, Ron. *Kidnapped at the Capital* (2–4). Illus. by Liza Woodruff. Series: Capital Mysteries. 2002, Golden Books LB $11.99 (0-307-46514-4); paper $3.99 (0-307-26514-5). 80pp. A mystery takes K.C. Corcoran and Marshall Li on a lively hunt through Washington, D.C. (Rev: BL 9/1/02)

6821 Ruelle, Karen Gray. *April Fool!* (1–2). Series: Holiday House Reader. 2002, Holiday House $14.95 (0-8234-1686-0). 32pp. Two little kittens try to come up with April Fool's jokes to play on their parents and each other. (Rev: BL 2/1/02; HBG 10/02; SLJ 6/02)

6822 Ruelle, Karen Gray. *The Crunchy, Munchy Christmas Tree* (1–2). Illus. by author. Series: Holiday House Readers Ser. 2004, Holiday House $14.95 (0-8234-1787-5). 32pp. Kitten siblings Harry and Emily's find a way to entertain themselves when their Christmas plans are disrupted by a snowstorm. (Rev: BL 9/1/03; HBG 4/04; SLJ 10/03)

6823 Ruelle, Karen Gray. *Easter Egg Disaster* (1–2). Illus. Series: Holiday House Reader. 2004, Holiday House $14.95 (0-8234-1806-5). 32pp. In four short chapters suitable for beginning readers, kittens Harry and Emily have various misadventures with eggs. (Rev: BL 3/15/04; SLJ 4/04)

6824 Ruelle, Karen Gray. *Easy as Apple Pie: A Harry and Emily Adventure* (K–2). Illus. by author. Series: Holiday House Reader. 2002, Holiday House $14.95 (0-8234-1759-X). 32pp. Kittens Harry and Emily have different reactions when invited to pick apples with their grandparents. (Rev: BL 8/02; HBG 3/03; SLJ 10/02)

6825 Rylant, Cynthia. *The Case of the Climbing Cat* (1–2). Illus. by G. Brian Karas. Series: High Rise Private Eyes. 2000, Greenwillow LB $14.89 (0-688-16309-2). 48pp. An easy-to-read mystery in which Bunny, a rabbit, and Jack, a raccoon, help a neigh-

bor find her stolen binoculars. Also use *The Case of the Missing Monkey* (2000). (Rev: BCCB 11/00; BL 10/1/00; HBG 3/01; SLJ 8/00)

6826 Rylant, Cynthia. *Henry and Mudge and Annie's Good Move* (2–3). Illus. by Suçie Stevenson. 1998, Simon & Schuster $14.00 (0-689-81174-8). 40pp. Henry and his dog Mudge are both excited to hear that Henry's cousin, Annie, is going to move next door. (Rev: BL 7/98; HBG 3/99; SLJ 10/98)

6827 Rylant, Cynthia. *Henry and Mudge and Mrs. Hopper's House* (K–2). Illus. by Carolyn Bracken. Series: Ready-to-Read. 2003, Simon & Schuster $14.95 (0-689-81153-5). 40pp. Henry is apprehensive about spending the evening at his babysitter's dark, gloomy house, but when he arrives with his dog Mudge, he finds the house full of music and clothes to dress up in. Also use *Henry and Mudge and the Funny Lunch* (2004). (Rev: BL 3/15/03; HBG 10/03)

6828 Rylant, Cynthia. *Henry and Mudge and the Great Grandpas* (K–2). Illus. by Suçie Stevenson. Series: Ready-to-Read. 2005, Simon & Schuster $14.95 (0-689-81170-5). 40pp. Henry and Mudge the dog visit Great Grandpa Bill, and all the other grandpas at his house. (Rev: BL 5/1/05)

6829 Rylant, Cynthia. *Henry and Mudge and the Starry Night* (1). Illus. by Suçie Stevenson. Series: Ready-to-Read. 1998, Simon & Schuster $14.00 (0-689-81175-6). 48pp. Henry, his dog Mudge, and Henry's parents go camping where they witness such wonders as a deer, a waterfall, a rainbow, and a starry night. (Rev: BL 5/1/98; HBG 10/98; SLJ 4/98)

6830 Rylant, Cynthia. *Henry and Mudge and the Tall Tree House* (K–2). Illus. by Carolyn Bracken. Series: Ready-to-Read. 2002, Simon & Schuster $14.95 (0-689-81173-X). 40pp. Uncle Jake builds Henry a great tree house but Mudge the dog can't climb up to it so the tree house is eventually moved to Henry's bedroom. (Rev: BL 1/1–15/03; HBG 10/03; SLJ 2/03)

6831 Rylant, Cynthia. *Henry and Mudge and Their Snowman Plan: The Nineteenth Book of Their Adventures* (1–2). Illus. by Suçie Stevenson. Series: Ready-to-Read. 1999, Simon & Schuster $14.00 (0-689-81169-1). 40pp. After a snowstorm, Henry and his dog Mudge entry a snowman-building competition and win third prize. (Rev: BL 10/1/99; HBG 3/00; SLJ 3/00)

6832 Rylant, Cynthia. *Henry and Mudge in the Family Trees* (1–2). Illus. by Suçie Stevenson. 1997, Simon & Schuster $14.00 (0-689-81179-9). 48pp. In this easy reader, Henry is afraid that his new relatives won't like his dog, Mudge. (Rev: BL 8/97; HBG 3/98; SLJ 9/97)

6833 Rylant, Cynthia. *The High-Rise Private Eyes: The Case of the Sleepy Sloth* (1–2). Illus. by G. Brian Karas. Series: High-Rise Private Eyes. 2002, HarperCollins LB $16.89 (0-06-009099-5). 48pp. Bunny and Jack solve a mystery for their friend Ramon in this fifth installment in the humorous, easy-to-read series with cartoon illustrations. (Rev: BL 9/15/02; HBG 3/03; SLJ 12/02)

6834 Rylant, Cynthia. *The High-Rise Private Eyes: The Case of the Troublesome Turtle* (2–4). Illus. 2001, Greenwillow LB $14.89 (0-688-16311-4). 48pp. Bunny Brown and her partner Jack Jones, a raccoon, investigate the disappearance of some balloons. (Rev: BL 5/15/01; HB 5–6/01; HBG 10/01; SLJ 7/01)

6835 Rylant, Cynthia. *Mr. Putter and Tabby Catch the Cold* (K–2). Illus. by Arthur Howard. 2002, Harcourt $14.00 (0-15-202414-X). 44pp. Tabby tries to help Mr. Putter cope with his cold, but it takes neighbor Mrs. Teaberry and her dog Zeke to provide the necessary comfort. (Rev: BL 11/1/02; HBG 3/03; SLJ 10/02)

6836 Rylant, Cynthia. *Mr. Putter and Tabby Feed the Fish* (2–4). Illus. by Arthur Howard. 2001, Harcourt $14.00 (0-15-202408-5). 44pp. Taking home three goldfish turns out to be a mistake when Tabby the cat develops a "fish problem." (Rev: BL 5/1/01; HBG 10/01; SLJ 5/01*)

6837 Rylant, Cynthia. *Mr. Putter and Tabby Fly the Plane* (1–2). Illus. by Arthur Howard. 1997, Harcourt $11.00 (0-15-256253-2); paper $5.95 (0-15-201060-2). 44pp. For beginning readers, this humorous story tells about Mr. Putter's purchase of a radio-controlled biplane. Also use *Mr. Putter and Tabby Row the Boat* (1997). (Rev: BL 4/1/97; SLJ 4/97)

6838 Rylant, Cynthia. *Mr. Putter and Tabby Pick the Pears* (1–3). Illus. by Arthur Howard. 1995, Harcourt $13.00 (0-15-200245-6); paper $6.00 (0-15-200246-4). 44pp. Mr. Putter experiments with an alternative method to harvest pears from his tree. (Rev: BL 1/1–15/96; SLJ 10/95)

6839 Rylant, Cynthia. *Mr. Putter and Tabby Pour the Tea* (1–2). Illus. by Arthur Howard. 1994, Harcourt $13.00 (0-15-256255-9); paper $5.95 (0-15-200901-9). 44pp. Lonely Mr. Putter finds a friend when he adopts a cat from the local pound. Also use *Mr. Putter and Tabby Walk the Dog* (1994). (Rev: BL 2/1/94; HB 5–6/94; SLJ 4/94)

6840 Rylant, Cynthia. *Mr. Putter and Tabby Stir the Soup* (K–2). Illus. by Arthur Howard. 2003, Harcourt $14.00 (0-15-202637-1). Mr. Putter and Tabby go next door to Mrs. Teaberry's house to make soup, but her dog Zeke makes this difficult. (Rev: HBG 4/04; SLJ 10/03)

6841 Rylant, Cynthia. *Mr. Putter and Tabby Take the Train* (1–2). Illus. by Arthur Howard. 1998, Harcourt $13.00 (0-15-201786-0). 44pp. Mr. Putter and Mrs. Teaberry decide to take a train ride with their pets, but they learn that animals are not allowed on the train. (Rev: BL 11/1/98; HBG 3/99; SLJ 9/98)

6842 Rylant, Cynthia. *Mr. Putter and Tabby Toot the Horn* (1–3). Illus. by Arthur Howard. 1998, Harcourt $13.00 (0-15-200244-8). 44pp. Elderly Mr. Putter heeds the advice of his neighbor, Mrs. Teaberry, and joins a band with amusing results. (Rev: BL 5/1/98; HBG 10/98; SLJ 4/98)

6843 Rylant, Cynthia. *Mr. Putter and Tabby Write the Book* (K–2). Illus. by Arthur Howard. 2004, Harcourt $14.00 (0-15-200241-3). Mr. Putter has

every intention of writing a novel, but naps, snacks, and procrastination get in the way. (Rev: SLJ 9/04)

6844 Rylant, Cynthia. *Poppleton* (1–2). Illus. by Mark Teague. 1997, Scholastic $15.95 (0-590-84782-1). 48pp. Poppleton the pig has three adventures, including one in which he helps a friend take his medicine. (Rev: BL 2/1/97; SLJ 3/97)

6845 Rylant, Cynthia. *Poppleton and Friends* (1–3). Illus. by Mark Teague. 1997, Scholastic $15.95 (0-590-84786-4). 48pp. Three stories about the friendship of Poppleton pig with his buddies Hudson and Cherry Sue. (Rev: BL 8/97; HBG 3/98; SLJ 9/97)

6846 Rylant, Cynthia. *Poppleton Everyday* (PS–2). Illus. by Mark Teague. 1998, Scholastic $14.95 (0-590-84845-3). 48pp. A beginning reader that presents Poppleton the pig in three humorous stories about his misadventures. (Rev: BCCB 4/98; HBG 10/98; SLJ 5/98)

6847 Rylant, Cynthia. *Poppleton Forever* (1–2). Illus. by Mark Teague. 1998, Scholastic $14.95 (0-590-84843-7). 56pp. In this easy reader, Poppleton the pig and friend Cherry Pie, a llama, share three adventures — one involving getting Poppleton's newly planted tree to grow. (Rev: BL 7/98; HBG 3/99; SLJ 9/98)

6848 Rylant, Cynthia. *Poppleton in Fall* (1–2). Illus. by Mark Teague. 1999, Scholastic $14.95 (0-590-84789-9); paper $3.99 (0-590-84794-5). 56pp. In these three episodes, Poppleton Pig is always helped out of troubling situations by his dear friend Cherry Sue, the llama. (Rev: BL 10/15/99; HBG 3/00; SLJ 9/99)

6849 Rylant, Cynthia. *Poppleton in Spring* (K–2). Illus. by Mark Teague. Series: Poppleton. 1999, Scholastic paper $3.99 (0-590-84822-4). 48pp. Three adventures involving the popular pig, Poppleton, and his springtime activities. (Rev: HBG 10/99; SLJ 3/99)

6850 Rylant, Cynthia. *Poppleton in Winter* (1–3). Illus. by Mark Teague. 2001, Scholastic paper $3.99 (0-590-84838-0). 48pp. Poppleton the pig worries about icicles, tries his hand at sculpting, and has a surprise birthday party. (Rev: BCCB 12/01; HBG 3/02; SLJ 10/01)

6851 Rylant, Cynthia. *Puppy Mudge Wants to Play* (PS–K). Illus. by Suçie Stevenston. Series: Ready-to-Read Puppy Mudge. 2005, Simon & Schuster $14.95 (0-689-83984-7). 32pp. Puppy Mudge finally succeeds in distracting Henry from his book and getting him to play. (Rev: BL 5/15/05)

6852 Sachar, Louis. *Marvin Redpost: Kidnapped at Birth?* (1–3). Illus. by Neal Hughes. Series: Stepping Stone. 1992, Random LB $11.99 (0-679-91946-5); paper $3.99 (0-679-81946-0). 68pp. Marvin Redpost secretly believes that he is the kidnapped son of the king. (Rev: BCCB 10/92; BL 12/1/92; SLJ 3/93)

6853 Sadler, Marilyn. *The Parakeet Girl* (1–3). Illus. by Roger Bollen. Series: Step into Reading. 1997, Random paper $3.99 (0-679-87289-2). 48pp. Emma is happy with her parakeet until her brother also gets one in this easy reader. (Rev: BCCB 7–8/97; BL 5/1/97; SLJ 9/97)

6854 Scarry, Richard. *Mr. Fixit's Magnet Machine* (1–2). Illus. Series: Ready-to-Read. 1998, Simon & Schuster paper $3.99 (0-671-81624-3). 32pp. When Huckle, Lowly, and Mr. Frumble notice metal objects flying into the air, they trace this phenomenon to Mr. Fixit's new magnet machine. (Rev: BL 7/98)

6855 *Scary Stories to Read When It's Dark* (1–3). Illus. Series: Reading Rainbow Reader. 2000, North-South LB $14.88 (1-58717-036-1); paper $3.99 (1-58717-035-3). 64pp. Seven easy-to-read scary stories by such writers as Arnold Lobel, Betsy Byars, and Alvin Schwartz. (Rev: BL 10/1/00; HBG 3/01)

6856 Schade, Susan, and Jon Buller. *Toad on the Road* (1). Illus. 1992, Random paper $3.99 (0-679-82689-0). 32pp. Toad and his friends go out in his car for a series of pleasant experiences. (Rev: BL 6/15/92)

6857 Scheffler, Ursel. *Be Brave, Little Lion!* (1–3). Illus. 2000, North-South LB $13.88 (0-7358-1265-9). 48pp. In this beginning reader, lion cub Lea learns that being afraid is often beneficial when she wanders away to explore on her own. (Rev: BL 6/1–15/00; HBG 10/00)

6858 Scherer, Jeffrey. *One Snowy Day* (1–2). Illus. 1997, Scholastic $3.50 (0-590-74240-X). 32pp. When snow arrives, a bear, kitten, and deer come together to build a snowman. (Rev: BL 2/1/98)

6859 Schwartz, Alvin. *Busy Buzzing Bumblebees and Other Tongue Twisters* (1–3). Illus. by Paul Meisel. 1992, HarperCollins LB $15.89 (0-06-025269-3). 64pp. A collection of nonsensical tongue twisters, illustrated with watercolors, for beginning readers. (Rev: BL 4/1/92; SLJ 6/92) [818]

6860 Schwartz, Alvin. *Ghosts! Ghostly Tales from Folklore* (K–2). Illus. by Victoria Chess. 1991, HarperCollins LB $15.89 (0-06-021797-9); paper $3.95 (0-06-444170-9). 64pp. Contains a number of suspenseful ghost stories written for the beginning reader. (Rev: BCCB 9/91; BL 9/15/91; HB 9–10/91; SLJ 9/91)

6861 Schwartz, Alvin. *I Saw You in the Bathtub and Other Folk Rhymes* (1–3). Illus. by Syd Hoff. 1989, HarperCollins paper $3.95 (0-06-444151-2). 64pp. An amusing assortment of folk rhymes. Also use: *All of Our Noses Are Here and Other Noodle Tales* (1985). (Rev: BCCB 4/89; BL 3/1/89; SLJ 5/89)

6862 Serfozo, Mary. *A Head Is for Hats* (1–2). Illus. by Katy Bratun. 2000, Scholastic paper $3.99 (0-439-09909-9). 32pp. Using simple, easy-to-read verses, this book explains what ears, eyes, noses, mouths, hands, and feet are for. (Rev: BL 10/1/00)

6863 Seuss, Dr. *The Cat in the Hat* (1–3). Illus. by author. 1957, Random LB $11.99 (0-394-90001-4). 72pp. The story of the fabulous cat that came to visit one rainy day when Mother was away. Also from the same author and publisher: *The Cat in the Hat Comes Back!* (1958); *Foot Book* (1968).

6864 Seuss, Dr. *Green Eggs and Ham* (K–3). Illus. by author. 1960, Random $11.99 (0-394-90016-2). 72pp. A charming nonsense book.

6865 Seuss, Dr. *Hop on Pop* (1–2). Illus. by author. 1963, Random LB $11.99 (0-394-90029-4). 72pp. One of the many entertaining, controlled vocabulary stories of Dr. Seuss. Also use: *One Fish, Two Fish, Red Fish, Blue Fish* (1960); *Fox in Socks* (1965).

6866 Seuss, Dr. *I Am Not Going to Get Up Today!* (1–2). Illus. by James Stevenson. 1987, Random LB $11.99 (0-394-99217-2). 48pp. A rhyming story about a little boy who refuses to get up in the morning. (Rev: BL 12/1/87)

6867 Seuss, Dr. *I Can Lick Thirty Tigers Today and Other Stories* (K–3). Illus. by author. 1969, Random $14.95 (0-394-80094-X). The Cat in the Hat tells three zany stories.

6868 Seuss, Dr. *I Can Read with My Eyes Shut!* (1–2). Illus. by author. 1978, Random LB $11.99 (0-394-93912-3). The Cat in the Hat tells us of all the joys of reading.

6869 Seuss, Dr. *Oh Say Can You Say?* (1–3). Illus. by author. 1979, Random LB $11.99 (0-394-94255-8). Tongue-twisting verses presented by a variety of imaginative creatures.

6870 Sharmat, Marjorie W. *Nate the Great* (1–3). Illus. by Marc Simont. 1986, Dell paper $4.50 (0-440-46126-X). 48pp. Nate, a boy detective, puts on his Sherlock Holmes outfit and sets out confidently to solve the mystery of the missing painting. Other titles in the series: *Nate the Great Goes Undercover* (1977); *Nate the Great and the Lost List* (1976); *Nate the Great and the Phony Clue* (1981); *Nate the Great and the Sticky Case* (1981); *Nate the Great and the Missing Key* (1981); *Nate the Great and the Snowy Trail* (1982).

6871 Sharmat, Marjorie W. *Nate the Great and the Fishy Prize* (1–3). Illus. by Marc Simont. 1988, Dell paper $4.50 (0-440-40039-2). Nate the Great and his dog Sludge solve the mystery of the stolen prize. Also use: *Nate the Great Stalks Stupidweed* (1986); *Nate the Great Goes Down in the Dumps* (1989). (Rev: BL 8/85; SLJ 9/85)

6872 Sharmat, Marjorie W. *Nate the Great and the Monster Mess* (1–3). Illus. by Martha Weston. 1999, Delacorte $14.95 (0-385-32114-7). 45pp. In this beginning reader mystery, Nate and his dog, Sludge, set out to find his mother's missing recipe for monster cookies. (Rev: HBG 3/00; SLJ 12/99)

6873 Sharmat, Marjorie W., and Craig Sharmat. *Nate the Great and the Tardy Tortoise* (1–3). Illus. by Marc Simont. 1995, Delacorte $13.95 (0-385-32111-2). 48pp. Using a trail of half-eaten plants as a guide, Nate the Great is able to return a lost turtle to its owner. (Rev: BL 10/1/95; SLJ 10/95)

6874 Sharmat, Marjorie W., and Mitchell Sharmat. *Nate the Great: San Francisco Detective* (1–3). Illus. by Martha Weston. 2000, Delacorte LB $15.99 (0-385-90000-7). 48pp. Nate the Great and his dog Sludge solve the mystery of a lost joke book in this easy-reader. (Rev: BL 7/00; HBG 10/01)

6875 Sharmat, Marjorie W., and Mitchell Sharmat. *Nate the Great and the Big Sniff* (1–2). Illus. by Martha Weston. 2001, Delacorte $13.95 (0-385-32604-1). 48pp. Boy detective Nate the Great has lost his faithful sidekick, Sludge, outside a department store in this latest installment of the beginning chapter-book series. (Rev: BL 11/1/01; HBG 3/02; SLJ 10/01)

6876 Sharmat, Marjorie W., and Mitchell Sharmat. *Nate the Great on the Owl Express* (1–3). Illus. by Martha Weston. 2003, Delacorte LB $16.99 (0-385-90102-X). 47pp. Yet another case for young detective Nate and beginning readers, this one involving a pet owl who needs an escort on a perilous train trip. (Rev: HBG 4/04; SLJ 3/04)

6877 Shaw, Nancy. *Sheep in a Jeep* (K–2). Illus. by Margot Apple. 1986, Houghton Mifflin $14.00 (0-395-41105-X); paper $4.95 (0-395-47030-7). 32pp. Silly sheep in a silly tale; they fall down, Jeep and all, and land in a muddy pool. Also use: *Sheep on a Ship* (1989). (Rev: BL 9/15/86; HB 11–12/86)

6878 Shaw, Nancy. *Sheep Out to Eat* (PS–1). Illus. by Margot Apple. 1992, Houghton Mifflin $14.00 (0-395-61128-8). 32pp. Several sheep are asked to leave a tea shop after they misbehave in this amusing story in rhyme. (Rev: BL 9/15/92; SLJ 9/92)

6879 Shea, George. *First Flight: The Story of Tom Tate and the Wright Brothers* (2–3). Illus. by Don Bolognese. Series: I Can Read. 1997, HarperCollins LB $15.89 (0-06-024504-2). 48pp. A fictional account of a boy who is a friend of Orville and Wilbur Wright and participates in their flights. (Rev: BL 11/15/96; HB 3–4/97; SLJ 1/97)

6880 Shreeve, Elizabeth. *Hector Springs Loose* (2–4). Illus. by Pamela Levy. Series: The Adventures of Hector Fuller. 2004, Simon & Schuster LB $11.89 (0-689-86418-3); paper $3.99 (0-689-86414-0). 67pp. Hector the wumblebug loses his home to a flea circus and goes off in search of a new one in this work for new chapter-book readers. (Rev: SLJ 3/04)

6881 Sierra, Judy. *Coco and Cavendish: Circus Dogs* (1–2). Illus. by Paul Meisel. Series: Step into Reading. 2003, Random LB $11.99 (0-375-92237-7); paper $4.99 (0-375-82237-2). 48pp. Two privileged circus dogs are put out of work by mechanical replacements but prove their worth in a new career. (Rev: BL 1/1–15/04; HBG 4/04)

6882 *Silly Stories to Tickle Your Funny Bone* (1–2). Illus. Series: Reading Rainbow Reader. 2000, North-South LB $14.88 (1-58717-034-5); paper $3.99 (1-58717-033-7). 64pp. This is an excellent collection of previously published simple, humorous stories for beginning readers by such writers as James Marshall, Cynthia Rylant, and Arnold Lobel. (Rev: BL 12/1/00; HBG 10/01)

6883 Silverman, Erica. *Cowgirl Kate and Cocoa* (PS–2). Illus. by Betsy Lewin. 2005, Harcourt $15.00 (0-15-202124-8). 48pp. Four easy-to-read chapters about the fun-filled friendship between a cowgirl and her talking horse. (Rev: BL 3/1/05; SLJ 3/05)

6884 Simon, Charnan. *Come! Sit! Speak!* (PS–2). Illus. by Bari Weissman. Series: Rookie Readers. 1997, Children's Book Pr. LB $18.00 (0-516-20397-5). 32pp. A humorous beginning reader about a girl who wanted a puppy but got a baby sister instead. (Rev: HBG 3/98; SLJ 2/98)

6885 Simon, Charnan. *I Like to Win!* (PS–1). Photos by Dorothy Handelman. Series: Real Kids Readers. 1999, Millbrook LB $16.90 (0-7613-2062-8); paper $3.99 (0-7613-2087-3). 31pp. An African American girl and boy resolve their differences about winning at board games in this book for the very beginning reader. (Rev: SLJ 1/00)

6886 Simon, Charnan. *Mud!* (1). Illus. by Dorothy Handelman. Series: Real Kids Readers. 1999, Millbrook LB $16.90 (0-7613-2051-2); paper $3.99 (0-7613-2076-8). 32pp. Color photographs are used to illustrate this easy-to-read story about three boys playing in the mud. (Rev: BL 5/15/99)

6887 Singer, Bill. *The Fox with Cold Feet* (K–2). Illus. by Dennis Kendrick. 1980, Parents LB $5.95 (0-8193-1022-0). 48pp. A fox sets out to get a pair of boots to help cure his cold feet.

6888 Singer, Marilyn. *Solomon Sneezes* (PS–1). Illus. by Brian Floca. Series: Harper Growing Tree. 1999, HarperCollins $9.95 (0-694-01748-5). In this beginning reader, Solomon Snorkel's sneezes are so powerful they can knock down skiers and topple a giant. (Rev: HBG 3/00; SLJ 9/99)

6889 Skofield, James. *Detective Dinosaur* (1–3). Illus. 1996, HarperCollins LB $14.89 (0-06-024908-0). 48pp. Three uncomplicated mysteries are included in this easily read book. (Rev: BL 8/96; SLJ 8/96)

6890 Slaughter, Hope. *Buckley and Wilberta* (2–3). Illus. Series: I'm Reading Now. 1996, Red Hen LB $14.95 (0-931093-15-5). 64pp. Two friends, Buckley the Hedgehog and Wilberta Rabbit, are featured in four stories. (Rev: BL 4/1/96)

6891 Smath, Jerry. *Pretzel and Pop's Closetful of Stories* (2–3). Illus. 1991, Silver Burdett LB $7.95 (0-671-72231-X). 64pp. Pop rabbit tells his daughter Pretzel stories about her relatives. (Rev: BL 12/1/91)

6892 Smith, Janice Lee. *Jess and the Stinky Cowboys* (1–2). Illus. by Lisa Thiesing. Series: Dial Easy-to-Read. 2004, Dial $14.99 (0-8037-2641-4). 48pp. Deputy Sheriff Jess has to stand up to some smelly cowboys who refuse to take a bath in this humorous story in which all the characters are anthropomorphic dogs. (Rev: BL 2/15/04; SLJ 2/04)

6893 Smith, Janice Lee. *Wizard and Wart in Trouble* (1–2). Illus. by Paul Meisel. Series: I Can Read. 1998, HarperCollins LB $14.89 (0-06-027762-9). 48pp. Wizard and his dog Wart straighten out problems with the use of magic spells. (Rev: BL 5/1/98; HBG 10/98; SLJ 6/98)

6894 Spohn, Kate. *Dog and Cat Shake a Leg* (K–1). Illus. 1996, Viking $13.99 (0-670-86758-6). 32pp. Dog and Cat share many everyday activities and have good times in this easily read book. (Rev: BL 1/1–15/96; SLJ 4/96)

6895 Spohn, Kate. *Turtle and Snake's Day at the Beach* (K–1). Illus. by author. Series: Viking Easy-to-Read. 2003, Viking $13.99 (0-670-03628-5). 32pp. Turtle and Snake need help from their friends as they tackle a sand-building contest in this easy-reader. (Rev: HBG 10/03; SLJ 7/03)

6896 Spohn, Kate. *Turtle and Snake's Spooky Halloween* (PS–1). Illus. by author. 2002, Viking $13.99 (0-670-03560-2). 32pp. Turtle and Snake plan a really good Halloween party and follow their checklist. (Rev: HBG 3/03; SLJ 9/02)

6897 Stadler, John. *The Adventures of Snail at School* (1–2). Illus. 1993, HarperCollins LB $15.89 (0-06-021042-7). 64pp. Snail has an unexpected adventure when he volunteers to pick up books at the school library. (Rev: BL 9/15/93)

6898 Stamper, Judith. *The Wild Leaf Ride* (PS–2). Illus. by Carolyn Bracken. Series: Scholastic Reader. 2004, Scholastic paper $3.99 (0-439-56998-5). Ms. Frizzle's students have an exciting time on the Magic School Bus as they set off in search of a leaf in this book for beginning readers. (Rev: SLJ 3/05)

6899 Stamper, Judith B. *Breakfast at Danny's Diner: A Book About Multiplication* (K–2). Illus. by Chris Demarest. Series: All Aboard Math. 2003, Grosset LB $13.89 (0-448-43266-8); paper $3.99 (0-448-43210-2). 45pp. Basic multiplication skills are conveyed in this entertaining book about two youngsters helping out at their uncle's diner. (Rev: BL 1/1–15/04; HBG 4/04; SLJ 3/04)

6900 Stamper, Judith B. *Five Goofy Ghosts* (2–3). Illus. by Tim Raglin. Series: Hello Reader! 1997, Scholastic $3.99 (0-590-92152-5). 32pp. Five horror stories that are also humorous are contained in this simple beginning reader. (Rev: BL 2/1/98)

6901 Stamper, Judith B. *Space Race* (K–1). Illus. by Jerry Zimmerman. Series: Hello Reader! 1999, Scholastic paper $3.50 (0-590-76267-2). An easy reader that introduces imaginative space vehicles and alien-type characters. (Rev: SLJ 9/99)

6902 Stamper, Judith B. *Tic-Tac-Toe: Three in a Row* (K–1). Illus. by Ken Wilson-Max. Series: Hello Math Reader. 1998, Scholastic paper $3.50 (0-590-39963-2). This book explains, in a beginning-reader format with a simple story, how one can always win at tic-tac-toe. (Rev: BL 11/1/98; SLJ 7/98)

6903 Standiford, Natalie. *The Bravest Dog Ever: The True Story of Balto* (1–3). Illus. by Donald Cook. 1989, Random paper $3.99 (0-394-89695-5). 48pp. In easy-to-read format, this is the true story of an amazing dog who guided a sled team carrying medicine to Nome, Alaska. (Rev: BCCB 1/90; BL 2/1/90; SLJ 2/90) [636.7]

6904 Stanley, George E. *Ghost Horse* (1–3). Illus. by Ann Barrow. Series: Road to Reading. 2000, Golden Books paper $3.99 (0-307-26500-5). 69pp. With the help of a new friend, Emily solves the mystery of a ghost horse she spies from her bedroom window. (Rev: SLJ 3/01)

6905 Stanley, George E. *Snake Camp* (1–2). Illus. by Jared Lee. Series: Road to Reading. 2000, Golden Books $10.99 (0-307-46406-7); paper $3.99 (0-307-26406-8). 32pp. In this easy-reader, Stevie mistakenly is sent to a snake camp instead of a computer camp and, unfortunately, Stevie is terrified of snakes. (Rev: BL 12/1/00; HBG 3/01)

6906 Stern, Maggie. *George and Diggety* (2–3). Illus. 2000, Orchard LB $15.99 (0-531-33295-0).

48pp. A humorous, easy-to-read book about a good-hearted kid named George and his dog Diggety. (Rev: BL 9/1/00; HB 9–10/00; HBG 3/01)

6907 Stern, Maggie. *Singing Diggety* (1–3). Illus. by Blanche Sims. 2001, Scholastic $14.95 (0-531-30318-7); paper $4.95 (0-531-07179-0). 46pp. George and his naughty dog Diggety have further humorous adventures as they go to dog school, enter costume contests, and perform for show-and-tell. (Rev: BCCB 10/01; HB 9–10/01; HBG 3/02; SLJ 8/01)

6908 Stevenson, James. *Mud Flat April Fool* (1–3). Illus. 1998, Greenwillow $15.89 (0-688-15164-7). 48pp. A humorous book for beginning readers in which the animal residents of Mud Flat have fun playing jokes on April Fools' Day. (Rev: BL 2/15/98; HB 5–6/98; HBG 10/98; SLJ 3/98)

6909 Suen, Anastasia. *Willie's Birthday* (K–2). Illus. by Allan Eitzen. 2001, Viking $13.99 (0-670-88943-1). 32pp. A beginning reader in which mayhem results when Peter invites his friends and their pets to help celebrate the birthday of his dachshund, Willie. (Rev: HBG 10/01; SLJ 3/01)

6910 Suen, Anastasia, and Ezra Jack Keats. *The Clubhouse* (K–2). Illus. by Allan Eitzen. Series: Viking Easy-To-Read. 2002, Viking $13.99 (0-670-03537-8). 32pp. Peter, an African American boy, and his friends find a pile of wood and build a place to play. (Rev: BL 4/15/02; HBG 10/02; SLJ 8/02)

6911 Suen, Anastasia, and Ezra Jack Keats. *Loose Tooth* (K–2). Illus. by Allan Eitzen. 2002, Viking $13.99 (0-670-03536-X). 32pp. Young Peter wants to keep his loose tooth in place at least until after the class photo has been taken. (Rev: BL 4/15/02; HBG 10/02; SLJ 4/02)

6912 Sullivan, Paula. *Todd's Box* (PS–1). Illus. by Nadine Bernard Westcott. Series: Green Light Readers. 2004, Harcourt $11.95 (0-15-205093-0). 24pp. Todd ignores his mother's scolding and continues to pick up items of interest, presenting them all to her once they are on the bus. (Rev: BL 3/15/04; SLJ 5/04)

6913 Swanson, June. *I Pledge Allegiance* (1–3). Illus. by Rick Hanson. 1990, Carolrhoda LB $21.27 (0-87614-393-1). 40pp. The difficult words in the Pledge of Allegiance are explained and its history is traced. (Rev: BCCB 6/90; BL 6/1/90; SLJ 7/90) [323.6]

6914 Sweeney, Jacqueline. *Critter Day* (K–2). Series: We Can Read! 2000, Marshall Cavendish $21.36 (0-7614-1119-4). After a day of games, each animal has won one of the events. Also use *Molly's Store*, *Homesick*, and *What About Bettie*, all in the same series for beginning readers (all 2000). (Rev: HBG 3/01; SLJ 11/00)

6915 Tafuri, Nancy. *Spots, Feathers, and Curly Tails* (PS). Illus. by author. 1988, Greenwillow $15.93 (0-688-07537-1). 32pp. A concept book that makes a mystery of identifying familiar animals from the barnyard. (Rev: BL 8/88; HB 11–12/88; SLJ 12/88)

6916 Tafuri, Nancy. *Will You Be My Friend?* (PS–K). Illus. 2000, Scholastic $15.95 (0-590-63782-7).

32pp. In this easy reader, a young bunny and his friends help Bird rebuild his home when his nest is ruined in a rainstorm. (Rev: BL 1/1–15/00; HBG 10/00; SLJ 3/00)

6917 Taylor, Sean. *Small Bad Wolf* (K–2). Illus. by Jan Lewis. Series: I Am Reading. 2004, Kingfisher paper $3.95 (0-7534-5801-2). 45pp. Small Bad Wolf wants to emulate his father, but his father's lessons leave something to be desired. (Rev: SLJ 8/04)

6918 Taylor-Butler, Christine. *Ah-Choo* (K–2). Illus. by Carol Koeller. Series: My First Reader. 2005, Children's Pr. LB $17.50 (0-516-25175-9). 31pp. A girl at home with a cold finds ways to amuse herself in this book for beginning readers with a list of words. (Rev: SLJ 5/05)

6919 Thiesing, Lisa. *The Viper* (K–2). Illus. Series: Dutton Easy Reader. 2002, Dutton $13.99 (0-525-46892-7). 32pp. In this hilarious mystery, Peggy the Pig gets scared when she gets a phone call from "zee Viper." (Rev: BL 5/1/02; HBG 3/03; SLJ 8/02*)

6920 Thomas, Shelley M. *Get Well, Good Knight* (K–2). Illus. by Jennifer Plecas. Series: Dutton Easy Reader. 2002, Dutton $13.99 (0-525-46914-1). 48pp. The Good Knight rides off on a quest to cure three little dragons with horrible colds, in this appealing easy reader. (Rev: BCCB 12/02; BL 1/1–15/03; HB 9–10/02; HBG 3/03; SLJ 11/02)

6921 Thomas, Shelley M. *Good Night, Good Knight* (1–3). Illus. by Jennifer Plecas. Series: Dutton Easy Reader. 2000, Dutton $13.99 (0-525-46326-7). 48pp. A gentle knight discovers three young dragons who want to be tucked in for the night in this charming bedtime book for beginning readers. (Rev: BCCB 2/00; BL 2/15/00; HBG 10/00; SLJ 3/00)

6922 Tidd, Louise Vitellaro. *The Best Pet Yet* (K–2). Photos by Dorothy Handelman. Series: Real Kids Readers. 1998, Millbrook LB $16.90 (0-7613-2006-7); paper $3.99 (0-7613-2031-8). 32pp. A boy selects his first pet in this beginning reader with photographs. (Rev: HBG 10/98; SLJ 7/98)

6923 Tidd, Louise Vitellaro. *I'll Do It Later* (1–2). Illus. by Dorothy Handelman. Series: Real Kids Readers. 1999, Millbrook LB $16.90 (0-7613-2066-0); paper $3.99 (0-7613-2091-1). 32pp. In this easy reader, a snow day provides a lazy boy with a reprieve from submitting a school assignment. (Rev: BL 12/1/99; SLJ 11/99)

6924 Tidd, Louise Vitellaro. *Let Me Help!* (1–2). Illus. by Dorothy Handelman. Series: Real Kids Readers. 1999, Millbrook LB $16.90 (0-7613-2067-9); paper $3.99 (0-7613-2092-X). 32pp. In spite of Tara's good intentions, her efforts to help her father always end disastrously. (Rev: BL 10/1/99; HBG 3/00)

6925 Tidd, Louise Vitellaro. *Lost and Found* (PS–2). Photos by Dorothy Handelman. Series: Real Kids Readers. 1998, Millbrook LB $16.90 (0-7613-2020-2); paper $3.99 (0-7613-2045-8). 31pp. Using engaging photos and double-page spreads, this easy-reader tells about the search for a lost sneaker. (Rev: SLJ 1/99)

6926 Turner, Ann. *Dust for Dinner* (1–2). Illus. by Robert Barrett. 1995, HarperCollins LB $15.89 (0-06-023377-X). 64pp. An easy-to-read book about an Oklahoma family ruined by drought and the Depression. (Rev: BCCB 9/95; BL 7/95; SLJ 10/95)

6927 Vail, Rachel. *Mama Rex and T: Homework Trouble* (2–4). Illus. by Steve Bjorkman. 2002, Scholastic $14.95 (0-439-40628-5); paper $4.99 (0-439-42616-2). 32pp. Mama Rex and T, a young dinosaur, finish the project he's neglected in this challenging beginning chapter book. Also use *Mama Rex and T: The Horrible Play Date* (2002), about friendship. (Rev: HBG 3/03; SLJ 10/02)

6928 Vail, Rachel. *Mama Rex and T: The Reading Champion* (1–3). Illus. by Steve Bjarkman. 2004, Scholastic paper $3.99 (0-439-57822-1). A young dinosaur initially has trouble reading in this appealing easy-reader. (Rev: SLJ 8/04)

6929 Van Laan, Nancy. *Moose Tales* (1–2). Illus. by Amy Rusch. 1999, Houghton Mifflin $15.00 (0-395-90863-9). 48pp. An easy chapter book that involves Moose and his adventures with friend Beaver. (Rev: BL 10/15/99; HBG 3/00; SLJ 12/99)

6930 Van Leeuwen, Jean. *Amanda Pig and the Awful, Scary Monster* (K–2). Illus. by Ann Schweninger. 2003, Penguin Putnam $13.99 (0-8037-2766-6). 48pp. Amanda Pig finally succeeds in conquering her fear of monsters in this easy-reader. (Rev: HB 7–8/03; HBG 10/03; SLJ 7/03)

6931 Van Leeuwen, Jean. *Amanda Pig and the Really Hot Day* (K–2). Illus. by Ann Schweninger. Series: Dial Easy-to-Read. 2005, Dial $14.99 (0-8037-2887-5). 48pp. Four episodic easy-reader stories show Amanda Pig and her family coping with hot weather. (Rev: BL 6/1–15/05)

6932 Van Leeuwen, Jean. *Oliver the Mighty Pig* (PS–2). Illus. by Ann Schweninger. Series: Dial Easy-to-Read. 2004, Dial $14.99 (0-8037-2886-7). 48pp. Oliver really enjoys the superhero powers imparted by his Mighty Pig cape, and feels very weak while it's in the wash in this easy-reader. (Rev: BL 3/1/04; SLJ 3/04)

6933 Viorst, Judith. *Alexander, Who Used to Be Rich Last Sunday* (K–2). Illus. by Ray Cruz. 1978, Macmillan LB $16.00 (0-689-30602-4); paper $4.99 (0-689-71199-9). 32pp. Alexander spends his dollar gift foolishly penny by penny. (Rev: SLJ 6/04)

6934 Wallace, Carol. *One Nosy Pup* (PS–2). Illus. by Steve Bjorkman. Series: Holiday House Reader. 2005, Holiday House $16.95 (0-8234-1917-7). 40pp. A beagle puppy discovers a new friend, Charlie the hamster, in the kitchen of his owners' new house. (Rev: BL 3/1/05; SLJ 4/05)

6935 Wallace, Karen. *A Bed for the Winter* (PS–3). Series: DK Reader. 2000, DK $12.95 (0-7894-5706-7); paper $3.95 (0-7894-5707-5). 32pp. In this beginning reader, a dormouse searches for a winter home and sees other animals doing the same thing. (Rev: HBG 3/01; SLJ 1/01)

6936 Walsh, Vivian. *Gluey: A Snail Tale* (K–3). Illus. by J. Otto Seibold. 2002, Harcourt $15.00 (0-15-216620-3). 48pp. Celerina the rabbit moves into Gluey the snail's home, believing it to be abandoned, and hosts a disastrous party in this complex tale for beginning readers. (Rev: BL 10/15/02; HBG 3/03; SLJ 12/02)

6937 Weeks, Sarah. *Splish, Splash!* (1). Illus. by Ashley Wolff. 1999, HarperCollins $12.95 (0-06-027892-7). 32pp. In his bathtub, Chub the fish is joined by many friends who want to frolic with him. (Rev: BL 3/15/99; HBG 10/99; SLJ 2/99)

6938 Weiss, Ellen. *Twins Go to Bed* (PS–1). Illus. by Sam Williams. Series: Ready-to-Read. 2004, Simon & Schuster LB $11.89 (0-689-86518-X); paper $3.99 (0-689-86517-1). Sleepy siblings prepare for the night in this book for beginning readers. Also use *Twins Have a Fight* (2004). (Rev: SLJ 8/04)

6939 West, Colin. *Moose and Mouse* (K–2). Illus. by author. Series: I Am Reading. 2004, Kingfisher paper $3.95 (0-7534-5715-6). 45pp. Moose and mouse are friends despite their differences. (Rev: SLJ 8/04)

6940 Weston, Martha. *Cats Are Like That* (1–2). Illus. 1999, Holiday House LB $14.95 (0-8234-1419-1). 32pp. Fuzzy the cat is jealous when Dot begins showering her attentions on her new pet fish. (Rev: BL 3/15/99; HBG 10/99; SLJ 6/99)

6941 Weston, Martha. *Jack and Jill and Big Dog Bill: A Phonics Reader* (1). Illus. Series: Early Step into Reading. 2002, Random LB $11.99 (0-375-91248-7); paper $3.99 (0-375-81248-2). 32pp. Two small children, Jack and Jill, along with their dog, try to slide down a snow-covered hillside on their sled with amusing results in this easy reader. (Rev: BL 4/15/02; HBG 10/02; SLJ 7/02)

6942 Weston, Martha. *Space Guys* (K–1). Illus. Series: Holiday House Readers. 2000, Holiday House $14.95 (0-8234-1487-6). 32pp. A group of space travelers spend a riotous night in an average American home in this science fiction easy-reader. (Rev: BL 4/15/00; HBG 10/00; SLJ 5/00)

6943 Wetterer, Margaret K. *Kate Shelley and the Midnight Express* (2–3). Illus. by Karen Ritz. 1990, Carolrhoda LB $21.27 (0-87614-425-3). 48pp. Based on a true story, the tale of a young girl who saved a train from disaster. (Rev: BCCB 11/90; BL 9/15/90; SLJ 1/91)

6944 Wheeler, Lisa. *Who's Afraid of Granny Wolf?* (1–2). Illus. by Frank Ansley. 2004, Simon & Schuster $14.95 (0-689-84952-4). 47pp. Traditional enemies — the wolf and the pig — are best of friends in this humorous original story. (Rev: SLJ 8/04)

6945 Wilhelm, Hans. *I Lost My Tooth!* (PS–1). Illus. by author. Series: Hello Reader! 1999, Scholastic

paper $3.50 (0-590-64230-8). A little puppy plans to leave his loose tooth for the Tooth Fairy when it falls out, but he accidentally swallows it. (Rev: SLJ 9/99)

6946 Wilhelm, Hans. *It's Too Windy!* (1). 2000, Scholastic paper $3.99 (0-439-10849-7). 32pp. An easy-to-read book about a shaggy white dog who saves a baby when its stroller rolls away. (Rev: BL 7/00)

6947 Willis, Jeanne. *Be Quiet, Parrot!* (1–2). Illus. by Mark Birchall. 2000, Carolrhoda $7.95 (1-57505-492-2). 32pp. In this beginning reader, a noisy parrot interrupts everyone and everything with his constant talking. Also use *Take Turns, Penguin!* (2000), an additional story about sharing and selfishness. (Rev: BL 12/1/00; HBG 3/01; SLJ 1/01)

6948 Wiseman, Bernard. *Barber Bear* (2–3). Illus. by author. 1987, Little, Brown paper $11.95 (0-316-94859-4). 48pp. Puns aplenty in this story of Barber Bear. (Rev: BL 8/87; SLJ 8/87)

6949 Wiseman, Bernard. *Morris and Boris at the Circus* (1–2). Illus. by author. 1988, HarperCollins LB $15.89 (0-06-026478-0); paper $3.95 (0-06-444143-1). 64pp. Two friends, a moose and a bear, attend the circus. Also use: *Morris Goes to School* (1983). (Rev: BL 12/1/88; SLJ 2/89)

6950 Wishinsky, Frieda. *A Bee in Your Ear* (2–4). Illus. by Louise-Andree Laliberte. 2005, Orca paper $4.99 (1-55143-324-9). 64pp. Kate must contend with spelling-bee pressure, a bully named Violet, and problems with her friend Jake in this beginning chapter book. (Rev: BL 3/15/05)

6951 Wishinsky, Frieda. *Just Mabel* (1–3). Illus. by Sue Heap. Series: I Am Reading. 2004, Kingfisher paper $3.95 (0-7534-5742-3). 45pp. Mabel finds a way to stop the teasing about her name and her clothes in this book for beginning readers. (Rev: SLJ 9/04)

6952 Ziefert, Harriet. *I'm Going to New York to Visit the Lions* (K–3). Illus. by Tanya Roitman. Series: I'm Going to Read! 2005, Sterling $11.95 (1-4027-2076-9). Nate and Kate meet the lions outside New York's Public Library in this book for beginning readers that highlights new vocabulary across the top of each page. (Rev: SLJ 5/05)

6953 Ziefert, Harriet. *Toes Have Wiggles Kids Have Giggles* (K–3). Illus. by Rebecca Doughty. 2002, Penguin Putnam $13.99 (0-399-23617-2). 32pp. Clever wordplays and amusing rhymes introduce readers to what words can do. (Rev: BL 6/1–15/02)

Fiction for Older Readers

6954 Adler, C. S. *Always and Forever Friends* (5–7). 1990, Avon paper $3.99 (0-380-70687-3). 176pp. Wendy, at 11, is having a painful struggle making new friends after Meg moves away until she meets Honor, who is African American and very hesitant about accepting Wendy. (Rev: BCCB 4/88; BL 4/1/88; SLJ 4/88)

6955 Adler, C. S. *The Magic of the Glits* (5–7). Illus. by Ati Forberg. 1987, Avon paper $2.50 (0-380-70403-X). 96pp. Jeremy, age 12, takes care of 7-year-old Lynette for the summer. A reissue of the 1979 edition. Also use *Some Other Summer* (1988).

6956 Agell, Charlotte. *Welcome Home or Someplace Like It* (5–8). 2003, Holt $16.95 (0-8050-7083-4). 240pp. In her notebook (number 27), Aggie records her arrival with her brother at their grandfather's home in Maine and their experiences getting to know the town and its residents. (Rev: BCCB 1/04; BL 11/15/03; HBG 3/02; SLJ 11/03)

6957 Alcock, Vivien. *The Trial of Anna Cotman* (5–8). 1990, Houghton Mifflin paper $6.95 (0-395-81649-1). 160pp. Anna finds that the secret society to which she belongs is gradually becoming an instrument of terror. (Rev: SLJ 2/90)

6958 Alcott, Louisa May. *The Quiet Little Woman: A Christmas Story* (4–7). Illus. by C. Michael Dudash. 1999, Honor Bks. $14.99 (1-56292-616-0). 128pp. A collection of three sentimental Christmas stories in a small-format volume. (Rev: BL 5/15/99; SLJ 10/99)

6959 Anderson, M. T. *The Serpent Came to Gloucester* (2–4). Illus. by Bagram Ibatoulline. 2005, Candlewick $16.99 (0-7636-2038-6). 40pp. In poetic narrative, Anderson tells, from the point of view of a young boy, the story of continued sightings of a supposed sea serpent on the coast of Massachusetts in 1817. (Rev: BL 6/1–15/05; SLJ 6/05)

6960 Atinsky, Steve. *Tyler on Prime Time* (5–7). 2002, Delacorte $14.95 (0-385-72917-0). 176pp. Tyler has the time of his life when he auditions for a part in a TV show and learns about show business backstage and the problems involved. (Rev: BCCB 9/02; BL 5/1/02; HBG 10/02; SLJ 8/02)

6961 Bauer, Marion Dane. *On My Honor* (5–7). 1986, Houghton Mifflin $15.00 (0-89919-439-7); Dell paper $4.99 (0-440-46633-4). 96pp. A powerful story in which 12-year-old Joel faces telling his parents that his friend Tony has drowned in the river they promised never to swim. (Rev: BCCB 10/86; BL 9/1/86; SLJ 11/86)

6962 Bernard, Virginia. *Eliza Down Under: Going to Sydney* (5–8). Series: Going To. 2000, Four Corners paper $7.95 (1-893577-02-3). 96pp. This novel deals with Eliza's adventures in Australia when she accompanies her mother to the 2000 Olympic Games in Sydney. (Rev: SLJ 3/00)

6963 Björk, Christina. *Vendela in Venice* (4–7). Illus. 1999, R&S $18.00 (91-29-64559-X). 93pp. Vendela travels to Venice with her father and falls in love with the enchanting city, describing its many attractions. (Rev: BL 11/15/99; HB 11–12/99; HBG 3/00; SLJ 1/00)

6964 Blatchford, Claire H. *Nick's Secret* (5–7). 2000, Lerner LB $17.95 (0-8225-0743-9). 168pp. When 13-year-old Nick, who is deaf, is summoned to a motel by Darryl Smythe and his gang of vandals, the boy knows he is in for trouble. (Rev: BL 9/15/00; HBG 3/01; SLJ 12/00)

6965 Blumenthal, Deborah. *Ice Palace* (K–4). Illus. by Ted Rand. 2003, Clarion $16.00 (0-618-15960-6). 32pp. In Saranac Lake, NY, a 10-year-old girl and her father watch as prisoners — including her uncle — from a nearby correctional facility construct a massive ice palace that will be the centerpiece of the town's annual winter carnival. (Rev: HBG 4/04; SLJ 10/03)

6966 Bradby, Marie. *Once upon a Farm* (2–5). Illus. by Ted Rand. 2002, Scholastic $16.95 (0-439-31766-5). A farm boy recalls in simple rhyming verse the beauty and pleasures of a rural life before the city started to encroach on the country. (Rev: HBG 10/02; SLJ 3/02)

6967 Brinson, Cynthia L. *Seeing Sugar* (3–4). 2003, Penguin Putnam $15.99 (0-670-03646-3). 96pp. Kate's new eyeglasses give the fourth grader a whole new outlook on life. (Rev: BL 7/03; HBG 10/03; SLJ 8/03)

6968 Brontë, Charlotte. *Jane Eyre* (6–8). Illus. by Kathy Mitchell. 1983, Penguin Putnam $16.99 (0-448-06031-0); Bantam paper $4.95 (0-553-21140-4). 576pp. The immortal love story of Jane and Mr. Rochester.

6969 Brooks, Bruce. *Everywhere* (5–8). 1990, HarperCollins LB $16.89 (0-06-020729-9). 80pp. Eleven-year-old Dooley, who is African American, helps a 10-year-old white boy live through the emotional trauma of waiting to see if his beloved grandfather will recover from a heart attack. (Rev: BCCB 10/90; BL 10/15/90*; SLJ 9/90*)

6970 Buchanan, Jane. *The Berry-Picking Man* (3–5). Illus. by Leslie Bowman. 2003, Farrar $15.00 (0-374-40610-3). 96pp. Although upset at first by her mother's kindness to a former mental patient, 9-year-old Meggie is pleased when her family includes him in their Christmas festivities. (Rev: BL 8/03; HBG 4/04; SLJ 6/03)

6971 Butcher, Kristin. *The Runaways* (5–8). 1998, Kids Can $16.95 (1-55074-413-5). During an unsuccessful attempt to run away from home, young Nick Battle meets Luther, a homeless man, and through this friendship gains insights into poverty in America. (Rev: BL 4/15/98; HBG 10/98; SLJ 4/98)

6972 Byars, Betsy. *The Pinballs* (5–7). 1977, HarperCollins LB $16.89 (0-06-020918-6). 144pp. Three misfits in a foster home band together to help lessen their problems.

6973 Carey, Elizabeth Doyle. *Summer Begins* (4–6). Series: Callahan Cousins. 2005, Little, Brown $10.99 (0-316-73690-2). 272pp. Four 12-year-old girl cousins spend the summer at their grandmother's house on Gull Island, enjoying the social life and coping with family problems. (Rev: BL 6/1–15/05)

6974 Carlson, Ron. *The Speed of Light* (4–7). 2003, HarperCollins LB $16.89 (0-06-029825-1). 288pp. Baseball, science experiments, and the mysteries of the universe occupy Larry and his two best friends during the summer before junior high. (Rev: BL 8/03; HBG 4/04; SLJ 7/03)

6975 Carlyle, Carolyn. *Mercy Hospital: Crisis!* (5–8). 1993, Avon paper $3.50 (0-380-76846-1). 128pp. Three friends volunteer at a local hospital. (Rev: SLJ 7/93)

6976 Chocolate, Deborah M. *NEATE to the Rescue!* (4–7). 1992, Just Us paper $3.95 (0-940975-42-4). 98pp. A 13-year-old African American girl and her friends help out when her mother's seat on the local council is put in doubt by a racist. (Rev: BCCB 3/93; BL 3/15/93)

6977 Clements, Andrew. *The School Story* (4–7). Illus. 2001, Simon & Schuster $16.00 (0-689-82594-3). 160pp. Two 12-year-old girls tackle the task of getting a book by a new author published.

(Rev: BCCB 7–8/01; BL 6/1–15/01; HB 7–8/01; HBG 10/01; SLJ 6/01)

6978 Clements, Andrew. *A Week in the Woods* (4–8). 2002, Simon & Schuster $16.95 (0-689-82596-X). 208pp. Mark, a lonely 5th grader, and a forceful teacher test each other — and Mark's survival skills — on a weeklong camping trip. (Rev: BCCB 1/03; BL 10/1/02; HBG 3/03; SLJ 11/02)

6979 Cole, Sheila. *The Canyon* (4–6). 2002, HarperCollins LB $15.89 (0-06-029496-5). 144pp. A California sixth-grader named Zach fights to preserve the canyon near his home when he discovers it is targeted for development. (Rev: BL 8/02; HBG 10/02; SLJ 6/02)

6980 Colfer, Eoin. *Benny and Omar* (5–8). 2001, O'Brien paper $7.95 (0-86278-567-7). 240pp. Benny, a young Irish lad, has trouble adjusting to his new life in Tunisia until he befriends Omar, a local orphan without a home, and the two have some exciting and amusing adventures. (Rev: BL 8/01; SLJ 12/01)

6981 Conrad, Pam. *Our House: The Stories of Levittown* (4–7). Illus. by Brian Selznick. 1995, Scholastic paper $14.95 (0-590-46523-6). 96pp. A series of fictional vignettes trace the history of the middle-class community of Levittown, New York. (Rev: BCCB 12/95; BL 1/1–15/96; HB 11–12/95; SLJ 11/95)

6982 Creech, Sharon. *Granny Torrelli Makes Soup* (4–6). Illus. by Chris Raschka. 2003, HarperCollins LB $16.89 (0-06-029291-1). 160pp. Food, warmth, and wisdom blend as 12-year-old Rosie spends time with her grandmother and talks about her blind friend Bailey and other life experiences. (Rev: BL 9/1/03*; HB 11–12/03; HBG 4/04; SLJ 8/03*)

6983 Dahl, Roald. *Matilda* (4–8). Illus. by Quentin Blake. 1998, Puffin paper $6.99 (0-14-130106-6). 224pp. Superbright 1st-grader Matilda deals with the evil school principal Miss Trunchbutt. (Rev: BCCB 10/88; HB 1–2/89; SLJ 10/88)

6984 Danziger, Paula, and Ann M. Martin. *Snail Mail No More* (5–7). 2000, Scholastic paper $16.95 (0-439-06335-3). 336pp. Two 13-year-old friends correspond by e-mail and reveal funny, thought-provoking experiences that involve family and social problems. (Rev: BCCB 4/00; BL 3/15/00; HBG 10/00; SLJ 3/00)

6985 Deans, Sis. *Every Day and All the Time* (5–8). 2003, Holt $16.95 (0-8050-7337-X). 240pp. Twelve-year-old Emily is still haunted by her brother's death and she resists the idea of selling the family house in which they all lived together. (Rev: BL 9/1/03; HBG 4/04; SLJ 12/03)

6986 Donahue, John. *Till Tomorrow* (5–7). 2001, Farrar $16.00 (0-374-37580-1). 176pp. When his family moves to a U.S. Army base in France in the early 1960s, Terry befriends an unpopular boy, with surprising results. (Rev: BCCB 11/01; BL 9/15/01; HBG 3/02; SLJ 9/01)

6987 Dowell, Frances O'Roark. *Where I'd Like to Be* (5–8). 2003, Simon & Schuster $15.95 (0-689-84420-4). 232pp. Maddie, a foster child living in a children's home, reveals her longing for a real home to a new friend. (Rev: BL 5/15/03; HBG 4/04; SLJ 4/03)

6988 Dunlop, Eileen. *Finn's Search* (4–7). 1994, Holiday House $14.95 (0-8234-1099-4). 128pp. Two Scottish boys try to save a gravel pit from local developers. (Rev: BCCB 12/94; BL 10/1/94; SLJ 10/94)

6989 Eduar, Gilles. *Gigi and Zachary's Around-the-World Adventure: A Seek-and-Find Game* (2–4). Illus. by author. 2003, Chronicle $16.95 (0-8118-3909-5). Young readers follow Gigi the giraffe and Zachary the zebra on a trip to far-flung countries, learning about exotic destinations and searching for specific items in the accompanying illustrations. (Rev: HBG 10/03; SLJ 6/03)

6990 Fletcher, Ralph. *Flying Solo* (5–8). 1998, Clarion $15.00 (0-395-87323-1). This novel answers the question, "What would a 6th-grade class do if their substitute teacher fails to appear and they are left alone for a whole day?" (Rev: BCCB 9/98; BL 8/98*; HB 11–12/98; HBG 3/99; SLJ 10/98)

6991 Frank, Lucy. *Lucky Stars* (4–7). 2005, Simon & Schuster $16.95 (0-689-85933-3). 304pp. Kira, a talented singer with a feisty character, arrives in New York City to find that her father has plans that don't fit in with her own. (Rev: BL 5/15/05)

6992 Gantos, Jack. *Heads or Tails: Stories from the Sixth Grade* (5–8). 1994, Farrar $16.00 (0-374-32909-5). 176pp. A collection of eight unusual short stories about 6th-grader Jack, a born survivor who overcomes amazing obstacles in this book set in Fort Lauderdale. (Rev: BCCB 7–8/94; HB 7–8/94; SLJ 6/94*)

6993 Gantos, Jack. *Jack on the Tracks: Four Seasons of Fifth Grade* (5–7). 1999, Farrar $16.00 (0-374-33665-2). 192pp. An episodic novel (the fourth about Jack Henry) in which Jack, a preadolescent, has several innocent adventures while growing up. (Rev: BCCB 9/99; BL 9/1/99; HB 11–12/99; HBG 3/00; SLJ 10/99)

6994 Gantos, Jack. *Jack's Black Book* (5–8). 1997, Farrar $16.00 (0-374-33662-8). In this third semiautobiographical novel, Jack is living in Florida with his family, tries to build a coffin for his dead dog, hopes to improve his writing skills, and is sent to a vocational training school. (Rev: BL 10/15/97; BR 3–4/98; HBG 3/98; SLJ 10/97)

6995 Garden, Nancy. *Meeting Melanie* (4–7). 2002, Farrar $16.00 (0-374-34943-6). 208pp. Melanie's mother doesn't want Melanie to get friendly with the "natives" on the Maine island where they're spending the summer, but Melanie and Allie become fast allies nonetheless. (Rev: BCCB 1/03; BL 12/1/02; HBG 3/03; SLJ 9/02)

6996 Graves, Bonnie. *Taking Care of Trouble* (3–5). Illus. by Robin P. Glasser. 2002, Dutton $14.99 (0-525-46830-7). 112pp. In this beginning chapter book, Joel is worried about passing his emergency preparedness drill until he's called on to babysit a kid nicknamed Trouble, and realizes he can handle anything. (Rev: BCCB 6/02; BL 3/15/02; HBG 10/02; SLJ 4/02)

6997 Greene, Constance C. *A Girl Called Al* (5–7). Illus. by Byron Barton. 1991, Puffin paper $5.99 (0-14-034786-0). 128pp. The friendship between two 7th graders and their apartment building superintendent is humorously and deftly recounted.

6998 Greenwald, Sheila. *Rosy Cole's Worst Ever, Best yet Tour of New York City* (3–5). 2003, Farrar $16.00 (0-374-36349-8). 128pp. Rosy takes her cousin on a tour of New York City and, despite her plans constantly going awry, the two have wonderful adventures. (Rev: BL 7/03; HB 7–8/03; HBG 4/04; SLJ 11/03)

6999 Gregory, Deborah. *Wishing on a Star* (5–8). Series: The Cheetah Girls. 1999, Hyperion paper $3.99 (0-7868-1384-9). 120pp. A light novel about five girls in New York City who form a singing group, the Cheetah Girls, and are soon signed up for an important gig. (Rev: SLJ 1/00)

7000 Griffin, Adele. *Witch Twins at Camp Bliss* (2–5). 2002, Hyperion $15.99 (0-7868-0763-6). 128pp. Luna and Claire, twin witches first seen in *Witch Twins* (2001), are off to Camp Bliss, where (in addition to typical camp activities) they search for a "rebel witch." (Rev: BCCB 7–8/02; BL 7/02; HBG 10/02; SLJ 6/02)

7001 Grunwell, Jeanne Marie. *Mind Games* (5–8). 2003, Houghton Mifflin $15.00 (0-618-17672-1). 144pp. Six very different 7th graders get to know each other as they collaborate on a science fair project in this inventive novel sprinkled with press clippings and project notes. (Rev: BL 5/15/03; HB 5–6/03; HBG 10/03; LMC 10/03; SLJ 5/03)

7002 Hall, Katy, and Lisa Eisenberg. *The Paxton Cheerleaders: Go for It, Patti!* (4–7). 1994, Simon & Schuster paper $3.50 (0-671-89490-X). 137pp. Four 7th-grade girls from different backgrounds make the cheerleading team in their junior high school. (Rev: BL 2/1/95)

7003 Hamilton, Richard. *Violet and the Mean and Rotten Pirates* (2–4). Illus. by Sam Hearn. 2004, Bloomsbury $16.95 (0-613-84722-9); paper $6.95 (1-58234-866-9). 288pp. Vile — short for Violet — helps a band of pirates to go straight and start a circus. (Rev: BL 7/03)

7004 Hansen, Joyce. *The Gift-Giver* (4–7). 1980, Houghton Mifflin paper $6.95 (0-89919-852-X). 128pp. Doris forms a friendship with a quiet boy, Amir.

7005 Hapka, Catherine. *Supernova* (4–7). Series: Star Power. 2004, Simon & Schuster paper $4.99 (0-689-86787-5). 136pp. With her album topping the pop charts, 14-year-old Star Calloway should be enjoying success, but her happiness is marred by the continuing disappearance of her family. The sequel is *Always Dreamin'* (2004). (Rev: SLJ 8/04)

7006 Hathaway, Barbara. *Missy Violet and Me* (3–5). 2004, Houghton Mifflin $15.00 (0-618-37163-X). 112pp. Stories of growing up in a southern town in the 1930s are told from the viewpoint of an 11-year-old girl. (Rev: BL 2/15/04; SLJ 5/04)

7007 Hazen, Lynn E. *Mermaid Mary Margaret* (3–5). Illus. 2004, Bloomsbury $14.95 (1-58234-869-3). 87pp. Aspiring mermaid Mary Margaret, 11, keeps a diary of her adventures on a cruise through the Greek islands with her recently widowed grandmother. (Rev: SLJ 9/04)

7008 Henkes, Kevin. *Olive's Ocean* (5–8). 2003, Greenwillow LB $16.89 (0-06-053544-X). 224pp. During a summer at the beach, Martha, an aspiring writer, wrestles with a classmate's sudden death, has her first whiff of romance, and gets to know her family and herself better. Newbery Honor Book, 2004. (Rev: BL 9/1/03*; HB 11–12/03*; HBG 4/04; SLJ 8/03*)

7009 Hiaasen, Carl. *Hoot* (5–8). 2002, Knopf $15.95 (0-375-82181-3). 272pp. Roy Eberhart, the new kid in Coconut Cove, finds himself embroiled in a battle to save some owls. Newbery Honor Book, 2003. (Rev: BCCB 11/02; BL 10/15/02; HB 11–12/02; HBG 3/03; SLJ 8/02)

7010 Hirsch, Odo. *Hazel Green* (3–6). 2003, Bloomsbury $15.95 (1-58234-820-0). 188pp. The title character in this appealing tale takes on the adult establishment in her community as she fights for the right of children to march in the annual Frogg Day parade. (Rev: BL 6/1–15/03; HBG 10/03; SLJ 6/03)

7011 Hobbs, Valerie. *Stefan's Story* (5–8). 2003, Farrar $16.00 (0-374-37240-3). 176pp. Wheelchair-bound Stefan, 13, visits his friend Carolina in Oregon, where an environmental dispute is splitting the community in two. A sequel to *Carolina Crow Girl* (1999). (Rev: BL 9/15/03; HBG 4/04; SLJ 8/03)

7012 Holt, Kimberly Willis. *When Zachary Beaver Came to Town* (5–9). 1999, Holt $16.95 (0-8050-6116-9). 227pp. Thirteen-year-old Toby Wilson learns the value of love and friendship when he gets to know Zachary Beaver, a 643-pound teen who has been abandoned by his guardian. (Rev: BCCB 12/99; BL 9/15/99; HB 11–12/99; HBG 3/00; SLJ 11/99*)

7013 Honeycutt, Natalie. *Josie's Beau* (5–7). 1988, Avon paper $2.95 (0-380-70524-9). 128pp. Beau's mother doesn't want him fighting, so Josie offers to say she's the one who fights — but the lie backfires. (Rev: BCCB 12/87; BL 12/1/87; SLJ 12/87)

7014 Hossack, Sylvie. *Green Mango Magic* (4–7). 1999, Avon $14.00 (0-380-97613-7). 128pp. Maile, who lives alone with her grandmother in Hawaii since her father abandoned her, finds a friend in Brooke, from Seattle, who is a recovering cancer patient. (Rev: BCCB 12/98; BL 5/1/99; HBG 10/99; SLJ 2/99)

7015 Howe, James. *The Misfits* (5–8). 2001, Simon & Schuster $16.00 (0-689-83955-3). 288pp. A group of 7th-grade social misfits challenge the so-called norms at their school by running for student council and instituting a no-names-calling day. (Rev: BCCB 1/02; BL 11/15/01; HB 11–12/01; HBG 3/02; SLJ 11/01)

7016 Hudson, Wade. *Anthony's Big Surprise* (5–7). Series: NEATE. 1998, Just Us paper $3.95 (0-940975-42-6). 89pp. Interracial tensions erupt in junior high school when some African American students are suspended and Anthony, who is also trying to cope with a family crisis, must deal with both problems. (Rev: SLJ 6/99)

7017 Hughes, Monica, sel. *What If? Amazing Stories* (5–10). 1998, Tundra paper $6.95 (0-88776-458-4). 199pp. Fourteen fantasy and science fiction short stories by noted Canadian writers are included in this anthology, plus a few related poems. (Rev: BL 2/15/99; SLJ 6/99)

7018 Jennings, Patrick. *The Beastly Arms* (5–7). 2001, Scholastic paper $16.95 (0-439-16589-X). 288pp. A dreamy 6th grader who pictures animals in everything he sees, discovers a world of real beasts when he and his mother move to the Beastly Arms. (Rev: BCCB 10/01; BL 5/1/01; HB 7–8/01; HBG 10/01; SLJ 4/01)

7019 Jennings, Richard W. *The Great Whale of Kansas* (5–9). 2001, Houghton Mifflin $15.00 (0-618-10228-0). 160pp. When a boy finds a prehistoric whale fossil in his backyard, the discovery brings unexpected consequences. (Rev: HB 9–10/01; HBG 3/02; SLJ 8/01)

7020 Johnson, Angela. *Violet's Music* (PS–2). Illus. 2004, Dial $16.99 (0-8037-2740-2). 32pp. Violet has always loved music and is thrilled when she finally meets some kindred spirits. (Rev: BL 3/15/04; SLJ 2/04)

7021 Jones, Diana Wynne. *Unexpected Magic: Collected Stories* (5–10). 2004, Greenwillow $16.99 (0-06-055533-5). An exciting anthology of 16 tales of mystery and magic by a master of fantasy. (Rev: BL 4/15/04; SLJ 9/04)

7022 Jukes, Mavis. *Getting Even* (5–7). 1988, Knopf paper $4.50 (0-679-86570-5). 160pp. Maggie seems unable to stop the nasty pranks of classmate Corky, and receives differing advice from her divorced parents. (Rev: BCCB 5/88; BL 4/1/88; SLJ 5/88)

7023 Jung, Reinhardt. *Bambert's Book of Missing Stories* (5–8). Trans. from German by Anthea Bell. Illus. by Peter Allen. 2004, Knopf LB $16.99 (0-375-92997-5). 124pp. A reclusive dwarf named Bambert writes 11 tales and sends them out on hot-air balloons, hoping they will be enhanced by their finders and sent back. (Rev: SLJ 11/04)

7024 Kelly, Katy. *Lucy Rose: Big on Plans* (3–4). Illus. by Adam Rex. 2005, Delacorte LB $14.99 (0-385-90235-2). 141pp. It's the summer before fourth grade and Lucy Rose writes in her diary about her many happy plans, but also about her parents' separation and the unfriendly new girl who has moved into the neighborhood. (Rev: SLJ 6/05)

7025 Kherdian, David. *The Revelations of Alvin Tolliver* (5–7). 2001, Hampton Roads paper $7.95 (1-57174-255-7). 48pp. Twelve-year-old Alvin is fascinated with nature and the great outdoors, and finds some unusual adult friends who introduce him to nature's charms. (Rev: BL 12/1/01; SLJ 3/02)

7026 Kimmel, Elizabeth Cody. *Lily B. on the Brink of Cool* (4–8). 2003, HarperCollins LB $16.89 (0-06-000587-4). 240pp. Lily Blennerhassett, 13 and an aspiring author who keeps a diary, has been spending a very boring summer and is easily seduced by the allure of the LeBlanc family and their active and sophisticated way of life. (Rev: BL 12/1/03; HBG 4/04; SLJ 10/03)

7027 Kline, Lisa Williams. *The Princesses of Atlantis* (5–7). 2002, Cricket $16.95 (0-8126-2855-1). 184pp. Twelve-year-old Arlene experiences ups and downs in her friendship with Carly, with whom she is writing a novel about two princesses. (Rev: BL 4/15/02; HBG 10/02; SLJ 7/02)

7028 Koertge, Ron. *The Heart of the City* (5–7). 1998, Orchard LB $16.99 (0-531-33078-8). 144pp. Apprehensive about moving to the big city of Los Angeles, 10-year-old Joy soon finds a friend in a young African American girl and together they fight the takeover of an abandoned house by hoods. (Rev: BCCB 4/98; BL 4/1/98; HBG 10/98)

7029 Konigsburg, E. L. *The Outcasts of 19 Schuyler Place* (4–8). 2004, Simon & Schuster $16.95 (0-689-86636-4). 304pp. Rescued from summer camp by aging uncles, Margaret is dismayed to find that their prized garden sculptures are endangered in this absorbing, amusing, and thought-provoking novel. (Rev: BL 12/15/03*; HB 3–4/04; SLJ 1/04*)

7030 Konigsburg, E. L. *The View from Saturday* (5–7). 1996, Simon & Schuster $16.00 (0-689-80993-X). 163pp. A complicated tale about four 6th-graders who are contestants in an Academic Bowl competition. Newbery Medal winner, 1997. (Rev: BCCB 11/96; BL 10/15/96; SLJ 9/96*)

7031 Korman, Gordon. *The Twinkle Squad* (5–7). 1992, Scholastic paper $13.95 (0-590-45249-5). 160pp. A bossy, insecure 6th grader and a defender of weaker kids are sentenced to the school's Special Discussion Group. (Rev: BCCB 11/92; BL 9/15/92; SLJ 9/92)

7032 Koss, Amy Goldman. *The Cheat* (5–8). 2003, Dial $16.99 (0-8037-2794-1). 144pp. When three 8th-graders are caught cheating on a geography test, they have to make difficult decisions — do they reveal their source? (Rev: BCCB 2/03; BL 1/1–15/03; HBG 10/03; SLJ 1/03)

7033 Lantz, Francess Lin. *The Day Joanie Frankenhauser Became a Boy* (4–6). 2005, Dutton $15.99 (0-525-47437-4). 208pp. When she moves to a new school and finds her name has been listed as John, Joanie decides to try life as a boy. (Rev: BL 6/1–15/05)

7034 Lewis, Maggie. *Morgy Coast to Coast* (3–5). Illus. by Michael Chesworth. 2005, Houghton Mifflin $15.00 (0-618-44896-9). 80pp. Morgy describes life at school and at home — hockey, the trumpet, and a retired greyhound figure large — through narrative and emails to his friend in California in this sequel to *Morgy Makes His Move* (2002). (Rev: BL 6/1–15/05; SLJ 5/05)

7035 Littman, Sarah Darer. *Confessions of a Closet Catholic* (4–7). 2005, Dutton $15.99 (0-525-47365-3). 193pp. Since she made friends with Mac, a Catholic girl, 11-year-old Justine has been questioning her Jewish faith. (Rev: SLJ 1/05)

7036 Lubar, David. *Hidden Talents* (5–9). 1999, Tor $16.95 (0-312-86646-1). 224pp. Five misfits, who are attending the last-resort Edgeview Alternative School, become friends and discover extrasensory talents they can use against the school bully. (Rev: BL 9/15/99; HBG 10/99; SLJ 11/99)

7037 McDonald, Megan. *Judy Moody Declares Independence* (2–4). Illus. by Peter Reynolds. 2005, Candlewick $15.99 (0-7636-2361-X). 150pp. A visit to historic sites in Boston provokes a spirited uprising against various parental rules and requirements. (Rev: BL 6/1–15/05)

7038 McGuigan, Mary Ann. *Where You Belong* (5–8). 1997, Simon & Schuster $16.95 (0-689-81250-7). 176pp. In 1963 in the Bronx, a lonely white girl growing up in poverty forms a friendship with an African American girl. (Rev: BCCB 5/97; BL 6/1–15/97; BR 11–12/97; SLJ 7/97)

7039 McKenna, Colleen O'Shaughnessy. *Camp Murphy* (5–7). 1993, Scholastic paper $13.95 (0-590-45807-8). 160pp. It's harder than it looks when Collette and friends decide to run a week-long day camp for the neighborhood kids. (Rev: BCCB 3/93; BL 3/15/93; SLJ 4/93)

7040 MacLachlan, Patricia, and Emily MacLachlan. *Painting the Wind* (1–4). Illus. by Katy Schneider. 2003, HarperCollins LB $16.89 (0-06-029799-9). A young boy spends a summer watching and learning as a number of painters capture diverse scenes on his island; at the end the budding artist challenges himself to paint the wind. (Rev: BL 8/03; HBG 10/03; SLJ 5/03)

7041 Martin, Jacqueline Briggs. *On Sand Island* (PS–2). Illus. by David A. Johnson. 2003, Houghton Mifflin $16.00 (0-618-23151-X). Ten-year-old Carl, who lives on an island in Lake Superior, dreams of having a boat and, with the help of the community, he succeeds in building one. (Rev: BCCB 10/03; BL 8/03; HBG 4/04; LMC 3/04; SLJ 11/03)

7042 Mason, Jane. *Bella Baxter Inn Trouble* (2–4). Illus. by John Shelley. 2005, Simon & Schuster paper $3.99 (0-689-86280-6). 80pp. Seven-year-old Bella is proud to be able to contribute when her family buys an old house, planning to turn it into an inn. (Rev: BL 5/15/05)

7043 Morgan, Melissa J. *Natalie's Secret* (4–6). Series: Camp Confidential. 2005, Grosset paper $4.99 (0-448-43737-6). 160pp. Eleven-year-old Natalie is a city girl and finds adjusting to camp challenging, especially when her famous father is arriving and she will have to tell her new friends the truth. (Rev: SLJ 4/05)

7044 Moss, Marissa. *Madame Amelia Tells All* (3–6). Illus. 2001, Pleasant Co. paper $5.95 (1-58485-305-0). 112pp. Amelia approaches the role of fortune-teller with her usual, entertaining inventiveness. (Rev: BL 8/01; SLJ 7/01)

7045 O'Connor, Barbara. *Me and Rupert Goody* (5–7). 1999, Farrar $15.00 (0-374-34904-5). 112pp. Set in Appalachia, this novel deals with the problems of young Jennalee, how she becomes friendly with the local store owner, and how this friendship is endangered when the owner's son moves into town. (Rev: BCCB 10/99; BL 11/1/99; HB 9–10/99; HBG 3/00; SLJ 10/99)

7046 Petrie, Kathye Fetsko. *Flying Jack* (K–3). Illus. by Paula J. Mahoney. 2003, Boyds Mills $15.95 (1-56397-971-3). This heartwarming tale recounts the story of Jack, who has dreamed of flying since he was a small boy. (Rev: HBG 4/04; SLJ 10/03)

7047 Quattlebaum, Mary. *Jackson Jones and Mission Greentop* (3–6). 2004, Delacorte LB $17.99 (0-385-90139-9). 101pp. Jackson Jones was initially unenthused about his vegetable garden, but once it is threatened he realizes its value. (Rev: BCCB 9/04; HB 9–10/04; SLJ 11/04)

7048 Radunsky, Vladimir, and Chris Raschka. *Table Manners* (1–4). Illus. 2001, Candlewick $16.99 (0-7636-1453-X). 32pp. Dudunya and Chester illustrate proper dining etiquette in this merry book of manners for younger readers. (Rev: BCCB 12/01; BL 1/1–15/02; HBG 3/02; SLJ 11/01)

7049 Rallison, Janette. *Playing the Field* (5–7). 2002, Walker $16.95 (0-8027-8804-1). 180pp. Thirteen-year-old McKay's friend Tony urges him to pursue pretty Serena, but McKay is more interested in friendship than romance. (Rev: BCCB 7–8/02; BL 5/15/02; HBG 10/02; SLJ 4/02)

7050 Romain, Trevor. *Under the Big Sky* (4–7). Illus. 2001, HarperCollins LB $14.89 (0-06-029495-7). 48pp. Encouraged by his grandfather, a young boy searches far and wide for the secret of life. (Rev: BL 8/01; HBG 10/01; SLJ 8/01)

7051 Rylant, Cynthia. *God Went to Beauty School* (4–8). 2003, HarperCollins LB $16.89 (0-06-009434-6). 64pp. God indulges in a lot of mortal activities, some fairly wacky, in this collection of thought-provoking poems. (Rev: BL 8/03; HB 7–8/03*; HBG 10/03; SLJ 6/03)

7052 Sachs, Marilyn. *The Bears' House* (4–7). Illus. by Louis Glanzman. 1987, Avon paper $2.99 (0-380-70582-6). 80pp. A poor girl escapes from reality by living in a fantasy in her classroom. A reissue of the 1971 edition.

7053 Schmidt, Gary D. *The Great Stone Face* (2–5). Illus. by Bill Farnsworth. 2002, Eerdmans $16.00 (0-8028-5194-0). 32pp. The Great Stone Face in this beautifully illustrated picture-book retelling of Nathaniel Hawthorne's story may be more familiar as the (now-lost) "Old Man of the Mountains." (Rev: BL 10/1/02; HBG 3/03; SLJ 11/02)

7054 Shura, Mary Francis. *The Josie Gambit* (5–7). 1986, Avon paper $2.50 (0-380-70497-8). 160pp. Josie's friend Tory behaves in an inexplicable way to his new friend Greg. (Rev: BCCB 5/86; SLJ 9/86)

7055 Smallcomb, Pam. *Camp Buccaneer* (2–4). Illus. by Tom Lichtenheld. 2002, Simon & Schuster LB $15.00 (0-689-84383-6); paper $3.99 (0-689-84384-4). 64pp. A beginning chapter book about a girl who learns all about piracy — and herself — from the denizens of Camp Buccaneer. (Rev: BL 6/1–15/02; HBG 10/02; SLJ 6/02)

7056 Smith, Anne Warren. *Tails of Spring Break* (4–6). 2005, Whitman $15.95 (0-8075-6358-7). 128pp. Things don't go well for Katie and her little brother when they decide to start a pet-sitting business. (Rev: BL 5/15/05; SLJ 5/05)

7057 Snyder, Zilpha Keatley. *The Magic Nation Thing* (4–7). 2005, Delacorte LB $17.99 (0-385-90107-0). 192pp. Abby O'Mally, 13, has the ability

to read minds and find lost objects but this doesn't help her to bring her parents back together. (Rev: BL 5/1/05)

7058 Stolz, Mary. *The Bully of Barkham Street* (4–8). Illus. by Leonard Shortall. 1963, HarperCollins paper $5.95 (0-06-440159-6). 224pp. Eleven-year-old Martin goes through a typical phase of growing up — feeling misunderstood. Also use *A Dog on Barkham Street* (1960).

7059 Talbott, Hudson. *Safari Journal* (3–6). Illus. by author. 2003, Harcourt $18.00 (0-15-216393-X). 64pp. Twelve-year-old Carey is not happy when his aunt drags him off for a two-week safari in East Africa, but once he arrives he is enchanted by the new people, customs, and sights and records them all in his diary. (Rev: HBG 10/03; SLJ 4/03)

7060 Thomas, Frances. *Polly's Absolutely Worst Birthday Ever* (2–4). 2003, Delacorte $14.95 (0-385-73025-X). 96pp. In her diary, 9-year-old Polly confides in detail the disappointments and triumphs of her life. (Rev: BL 7/03; HBG 10/03; SLJ 11/03)

7061 Thompson, Lauren. *One Riddle, One Answer* (3–6). Illus. by Linda S. Wingerter. 2001, Scholastic $15.95 (0-590-31335-5). Beautiful illustrations set a Persian mood for this tale of a mathematically inclined sultan's daughter who sets a riddle intended to find the perfect husband. (Rev: BCCB 4/01; HBG 10/01; SLJ 4/01)

7062 Thompson, Richard. *The Night Walker* (K–3). Illus. by Martin Springett. 2002, Fitzhenry & Whiteside $16.00 (1-55041-672-3). A tense tale about a young boy out walking near dark who suspects he's being followed by the Night Walker. (Rev: BL 9/1/03; SLJ 4/03)

7063 Vail, Rachel. *If You Only Knew* (4–7). Series: Friendship Ring. 1998, Scholastic paper $14.95 (0-590-03370-0). 240pp. In this book shaped like a CD, Zoe Grandon, a 7th grader, gives up a boy she likes to pursue a friendship. (Rev: BCCB 10/98; BL 10/15/98; HBG 3/99; SLJ 10/98)

7064 Vail, Rachel. *Not That I Care* (4–7). Series: Friendship Ring. 1998, Scholastic paper $14.95 (0-590-03476-6). 240pp. For a classroom presentation on 10 items that reveal who you are, Morgan Miller remembers crucial incidents in her life but, in her final report, glosses over the truth. (Rev: BCCB 12/98; BL 11/15/98; HBG 3/99; SLJ 12/98)

7065 Vail, Rachel. *Please, Please, Please* (4–7). Series: Friendship Ring. 1998, Scholastic paper $14.95 (0-590-00327-5). 288pp. CJ Hurley has to overcome a controlling mother in order to hang out with her friends in this book shaped like a CD. (Rev: BCCB 10/98; BL 10/15/98; HBG 3/99; SLJ 12/98)

7066 Van Draanen, Wendelin. *Flipped* (5–8). 2001, Knopf $14.95 (0-375-81174-5). 212pp. In 2nd grade Julianna was infatuated with Bryce, but now, six years later, the situation is reversed in this story told from each viewpoint in alternating chapters. (Rev: BCCB 1/02; BL 12/15/01; HBG 3/02; SLJ 11/01*)

7067 Van Draanen, Wendelin. *Swear to Howdy* (5–7). 2003, Knopf LB $17.99 (0-375-92505-8). 144pp. Twelve-year-olds Rusty and Joey enjoy their inventive escapades until one of their pranks causes the death of Joey's sister and they must examine their pledge of silence. (Rev: BCCB 2/04; BL 10/1/03*; HBG 4/04; SLJ 11/03)

7068 Vaupel, Robin. *My Contract with Henry* (5–8). 2003, Holiday House $17.95 (0-8234-1701-8). 192pp. An 8th-grade Thoreau project brings a group of outsider students together as they learn about the environment, the simple life, and each other. (Rev: BL 7/03; HBG 10/03; SLJ 7/03)

7069 Voigt, Cynthia. *Bad Girls in Love* (5–8). Series: Bad Girls. 2002, Simon & Schuster $15.95 (0-689-82471-8). 240pp. Margalo falls in love with a popular boy and Michelle (Mikey) has a crush on a teacher in this fourth book of the series. (Rev: BCCB 10/02; BL 8/02; HB 9–10/02; HBG 3/03; SLJ 7/02)

7070 Voigt, Cynthia. *It's Not Easy Being Bad* (5–7). 2000, Simon & Schuster $16.00 (0-689-82473-4). 256pp. Seventh-graders Mikey and Margalo, who have reputations for being bad, come up with several plans for getting in with the popular set at school. (Rev: BCCB 12/00*; BL 11/15/00; HB 1–2/01; HBG 3/01; SLJ 11/00)

7071 Waysman, Dvora. *Back of Beyond: A Bar Mitzvah Journey* (5–7). Illus. 1996, Pitspopany paper $4.95 (0-943706-54-8). 140pp. On a trip to Australia, a 12-year-old Jewish boy becomes involved in the Aborigine culture and witnesses a ritual of manhood similar to a bar mitzvah. (Rev: SLJ 5/96)

7072 Weatherford, Carole Boston. *Princeville: The 500-Year Flood* (3–5). Illus. by Douglas Alvord. 2001, Coastal Carolina LB $14.95 (1-928556-32-9). 32pp. An African American family in North Carolina is forced to leave home as the waters caused by Hurricane Floyd rise. (Rev: BL 2/15/02)

7073 Weston, Carol. *Melanie in Manhattan* (3–6). 2005, Knopf LB $17.99 (0-375-93028-0). 266pp. Romance — with Miguel, who is coming from Spain to visit — and friendship with Cecily preoccupy the thoughts of fifth grader Melanie. (Rev: SLJ 1/05)

7074 Williams, Marcia. *Charles Dickens and Friends* (3–6). Illus. 2002, Candlewick $17.99 (0-7636-1905-1). 48pp. Williams uses a graphic novel style to retell five works by Dickens, weaving in era-accurate artwork and acute commentary. (Rev: BL 10/15/02; HBG 3/03; SLJ 2/03)

7075 Wittlinger, Ellen. *Gracie's Girl* (4–7). 2000, Simon & Schuster $16.95 (0-689-82249-9). 192pp. Bess and her best friend Ethan, both middle schoolers, get involved with a homeless old lady. (Rev: BCCB 2/01; BL 9/15/00; HBG 3/01; SLJ 11/00)

7076 Wojciechowski, Susan. *Beany Goes to Camp* (2–4). Illus. by Susanna Natti. 2002, Candlewick $15.99 (0-7636-1615-X). 110pp. Beany (Bernice) has to go to camp for a week, whether she likes it or not, in this beginning chapter book. (Rev: BCCB 7–8/02; BL 7/02; HBG 10/02; SLJ 5/02)

7077 Yep, Laurence. *Angelfish* (4–6). 2001, Penguin Putnam $16.99 (0-399-23041-6). 224pp. Robin has won a starring role in *Beauty and the Beast* and at the same time must start working for a man who seems to treat her just like the Beast. (Rev: BL 5/15/01; HBG 10/01; SLJ 6/01)

Adventure and Mystery

7078 Abbott, Kate. *Mystery at Echo Cliffs* (4–6). Illus. by Faith DeLong. 1994, Red Crane paper $11.95 (1-878610-37-6). 183pp. After the death of their parents, two Navajo youngsters move back to the reservation, where they help track down a gang of pottery thieves. (Rev: SLJ 12/94)

7079 Adams, W. Royce. *Me and Jay* (5–8). 2001, Rairarubia paper $10.99 (1-58832-021-9). 125pp. Two 13-year-olds meet with trouble at every turn when they venture into forbidden territory in search of a hidden pond. (Rev: BL 1/1–15/02)

7080 Adler, David A. *Andy Russell, NOT Wanted by the Police* (3–5). Illus. by Leanne Franson. 2001, Harcourt $14.00 (0-15-216474-X). 128pp. Andy and Tamika solve the mystery of an intruder at a neighbor's house in this beginning chapter book. (Rev: BL 1/1–15/02; HBG 3/02; SLJ 1/02)

7081 Adler, David A. *Cam Jansen and the Barking Treasure Mystery* (2–4). Illus. 1999, Viking $13.99 (0-670-88516-9). 64pp. Cam and her best friend solve the mystery of a missing dog. (Rev: BL 10/15/99; HBG 3/00; SLJ 12/99)

7082 Adler, David A. *Cam Jansen and the Birthday Mystery* (2–4). Illus. 2000, Viking $13.99 (0-670-88877-X). 64pp. In this beginning chapter book, Cam, with her photographic memory, solves the mystery of who stole her grandparents' luggage at the airport. (Rev: BL 11/1/00; HBG 3/01; SLJ 1/01)

7083 Adler, David A. *Cam Jansen and the Catnapping Mystery* (2–3). Illus. 1998, Viking $13.99 (0-670-88044-2). 47pp. Cam Jansen, super girl detective, helps police track down the thief who posed as a bellhop and stole an elderly woman's luggage and pet cat from the Royal Hotel. (Rev: BL 11/15/98; HBG 3/99; SLJ 1/99)

7084 Adler, David A. *Cam Jansen and the First Day of School Mystery* (2–4). Illus. by Susanna Natti. 2002, Viking $13.99 (0-670-03575-0). 64pp. Cam's great memory comes into play when her teacher is arrested and taken away on the first day of school. (Rev: BL 12/1/02; HBG 3/03; SLJ 1/03)

7085 Adler, David A. *Cam Jansen and the Ghostly Mystery* (2–4). Illus. 1996, Viking $12.99 (0-670-86872-8). 64pp. Cam Jansen and her friend Eric are involved in the robbery of a ticket booth at a rock concert. (Rev: BL 1/1–15/97; HBG 3/98; SLJ 12/96)

7086 Adler, David A. *Cam Jansen and the Mystery at the Haunted House* (2–4). Illus. by Susanna Natti. 1992, Viking $13.99 (0-670-83419-X). 58pp. Cam uses her photographic memory to uncover the thief who stole her aunt's wallet at an amusement park. (Rev: BL 4/1/92; SLJ 4/92)

7087 Adler, David A. *Cam Jansen and the Mystery of the Chocolate Fudge Sale* (2–4). Illus. by Susanna Natti. 1993, Viking $11.99 (0-670-84968-5).

64pp. Cam springs into action when she spots a suspicious woman around a vacant house. (Rev: BL 10/15/93; SLJ 9/93)

7088 Adler, David A. *Cam Jansen and the Scary Snake Mystery* (2–4). Illus. 1997, Viking $13.99 (0-670-87517-1). 64pp. Cam solves a mystery in which her mother's video camera is stolen after it had been used to photograph someone's pet snake. (Rev: BL 11/15/97; SLJ 12/97)

7089 Adler, David A. *Cam Jansen and the School Play Mystery* (2–4). Illus. 2001, Viking $13.99 (0-670-89280-7). 64pp. Readers already familiar with Cam's exploits will enjoy this story in which Cam uses her photographic memory to solve the mystery of the missing admission money while her friends act onstage in a play about Honest Abe. (Rev: BL 8/01; HBG 3/02; SLJ 1/02)

7090 Adler, David A. *Cam Jansen and the Tennis Trophy Mystery* (2–4). Illus. by Susanna Natti. Series: Cam Jansen. 2003, Viking $13.99 (0-670-03643-9). 56pp. In this 23rd adventure for young detective Cam Jansen, a teacher falls under suspicion in the theft of a tennis trophy. (Rev: HBG 4/04; SLJ 3/04)

7091 Adler, David A. *Cam Jansen and the Triceratops Pops Mystery* (2–4). Illus. 1995, Viking $13.99 (0-670-86027-1). 64pp. Cam and her friend Eric solve the mystery of the missing CDs. (Rev: BL 11/1/95; SLJ 12/95)

7092 Adler, David A. *Parachuting Hamsters and Andy Russell* (2–4). Illus. 2000, Harcourt $14.00 (0-15-202185-X). 144pp. A beginning chapter book in which Andy Russell solves the mystery of the parachuting hamsters when he visits his friend Tamika's aunt and uncle in a big city apartment building. (Rev: BL 11/1/00; HBG 10/01; SLJ 10/00)

7093 Aiken, Joan. *Midwinter Nightingale* (5–8). Series: Wolves Chronicles. 2003, Delacorte $15.95 (0-385-73081-0). 224pp. Dido Twite and Simon, Duke of Battersea, continue their adventures in this eighth installment in the series, protecting a dying king, searching for a missing coronet, and defeating an evil baron. (Rev: BL 6/1–15/03; HBG 10/03; SLJ 6/03)

7094 Aiken, Joan. *The Wolves of Willoughby Chase* (4–6). Illus. by Pat Marriott. 1987, Dell paper $4.99 (0-440-49603-9). 168pp. A Victorian melodrama about two little girls who outwit their wicked governess-guardian. A reissue of the 1963 edition. Two sequels are: *Black Hearts in Battersea* (1981) and *Nightbirds on Nantucket* (1969).

7095 Alexander, Lloyd. *Gypsy Rizka* (4–7). 1999, Puffin paper $5.99 (0-14-130980-6). 176pp. A delightful adventure story featuring Rizka, a young gypsy who lives alone in her wagon and becomes involved in a series of hilarious situations with the neighboring townspeople. (Rev: BL 3/15/99*; HB 3–4/99; HBG 10/99; SLJ 3/99)

7096 Alexander, Lloyd. *The Xanadu Adventure* (5–8). 2005, Button $16.99 (0-525-47371-8). 160pp. Vesper Holly, accompanied by friends and guardians, sets off for Asia Minor to search for an artifact in the ancient city of Troy but soon finds herself in the

clutches of her nemesis, Dr. Desmond Helvitius. (Rev: BL 2/1/05; SLJ 2/05)

7097 Allison, Jennifer. *Gilda Joyce: Psychic Investigator* (5–7). 2005, Dutton $10.99 (0-525-47375-0). 336pp. Thirteen-year-old Gilda Joyce and a new friend, Juliet, look into the suicide of Juliet's aunt in this richly layered mystery. (Rev: BL 5/1/05)

7098 Anastasio, Dina. *The Case of the Glacier Park Swallow* (4–7). Illus. 1994, Roberts Rinehart paper $6.95 (1-879373-85-8). 80pp. Juliet, who wants to be a veterinarian, stumbles upon a drug-smuggling ring in this tightly knit mystery. (Rev: BL 12/1/94; SLJ 10/94)

7099 Anastasio, Dina. *The Case of the Grand Canyon Eagle* (5–8). Series: Juliet Stone Environmental Mystery. 1994, Roberts Rinehart paper $6.95 (1-879373-84-X). 73pp. In this ecological mystery, 17-year-old Juliet Stone investigates the disappearance of eagle eggs. (Rev: SLJ 10/94)

7100 Anderson, Janet S. *The Last Treasure* (5–7). 2003, Dutton $17.99 (0-525-46919-2). 256pp. A whole family becomes immersed in a saga of intrigue and suspense that reaches back into the 19th century. (Rev: BL 3/15/03; HBG 4/04; SLJ 6/03*)

7101 Anderson, Mary. *Suzy's Secret Snoop Society* (4–6). 1990, Avon paper $2.95 (0-380-75917-9). 112pp. Two new friends accidentally uncover a criminal plot. (Rev: BL 12/15/90)

7102 Andrews, Jean F. *The Secret in the Dorm Attic* (3–5). 1990, Gallaudet Univ. paper $4.95 (0-930323-66-1). 100pp. At a school for the deaf, some boys uncover stolen jewels and become the victims of a kidnapping. (Rev: BL 10/1/90)

7103 Armstrong, Jennifer, and Nancy Butcher. *The Kindling* (5–9). Series: Fire-Us. 2002, HarperCollins LB $15.89 (0-06-029411-6). 224pp. In 2007, after a virus has killed the adults, a small band of children join together in a Florida town and try to carry on with life. (Rev: BCCB 6/02; BL 4/15/02; HBG 10/02; SLJ 10/02)

7104 Avi. *Captain Grey* (5–8). 1993, Morrow paper $4.95 (0-688-12234-5). 160pp. In 1783, young Kevin is captured by pirates. A reissue.

7105 Avi. *The Christmas Rat* (4–7). 2000, Simon & Schuster $16.00 (0-689-83842-5). 144pp. Eric finds that he is on the side of the rat that is hiding in a basement storage area and is being hunted by a mysterious exterminator. (Rev: BCCB 10/00; BL 9/1/00; HB 11–12/00; HBG 3/01)

7106 Avi. *Who Stole the Wizard of Oz?* (4–6). Illus. by Derek James. 1990, McKay paper $4.99 (0-394-84992-2). 128pp. Several books disappear from the Chickertown Library book sale.

7107 Babbitt, Natalie. *Goody Hall* (4–6). Illus. by author. 1986, Farrar paper $4.95 (0-374-42767-4). 176pp. Gothic mystery told with suspense and humor, centering around the magnificent home of the Goody family.

7108 Babbitt, Natalie. *Kneeknock Rise* (4–7). Illus. by author. 1970, Farrar paper $5.95 (0-374-44260-6). 96pp. Young Egan sets out bravely to see the mysterious people-eating Megrimum.

7109 Balliett, Blue. *Chasing Vermeer* (5–8). Illus. by Brett Helquist. 2004, Scholastic $16.95 (0-439-37294-1). 272pp. Petra and Calder, brainy 12-year-old classmates at the University of Chicago Lab School, join forces to find out what happened to a missing Vermeer painting. (Rev: BL 4/1/04*; HB 7–8/04; SLJ 7/04)

7110 Banks, Kate. *Howie Bowles, Secret Agent* (2–3). Illus. 1999, Farrar $15.00 (0-374-33500-1). 96pp. In this easy chapter book, Howie Banks decides to become a secret agent to solve the mystery of who is putting gum in the school's water fountains. (Rev: BCCB 12/99; BL 12/15/99; HB 11–12/99; HBG 3/00; SLJ 10/99)

7111 Bartholomew, Lois Thompson. *The White Dove* (5–8). 2000, Houghton Mifflin $15.00 (0-618-00464-5). 208pp. In this adventure story set in a mythical kingdom, Princess Tasha escapes from the evil Com and must undertake a dangerous mission to help overthrow the tyrant. (Rev: BL 3/1/00; HBG 10/00; SLJ 5/00)

7112 Bartlett, Susan. *The Seal Island Seven* (2–4). Illus. by Tricia Tusa. 2002, Viking $15.99 (0-670-03533-5). 70pp. In this beginning chapter book, Pru and her friends investigate who is destroying the fairy houses that are a Seal Island tradition. (Rev: BCCB 10/02; HBG 3/03; SLJ 10/02)

7113 Barton, Byron. *I Want to Be an Astronaut* (2–4). Illus. by author. 1988, HarperCollins LB $15.89 (0-690-04744-4); paper $6.95 (0-06-443280-7). 32pp. Simple text explains a child's desire to go into outer space. (Rev: BCCB 10/88; BL 5/15/88; SLJ 5/88)

7114 Base, Graeme. *The Eleventh Hour: A Curious Mystery* (4–6). Illus. 1989, Abrams $18.95 (0-8109-0851-4). 32pp. An elaborate picture-book mystery written in verse. (Rev: BL 11/1/89; SLJ 2/90)

7115 Blades, Ann. *A Boy of Tache* (3–5). Illus. 1995, Tundra paper $5.95 (0-88776-350-2). A novel of life in Tache, an Indian reservation in northwest Canada, which focuses on a young boy and a trapping expedition.

7116 Blatchford, Claire H. *Nick's Mission* (4–6). 1995, Lerner LB $19.95 (0-8225-0740-4). 144pp. A hearing-impaired boy happens on a gang of smugglers who are illegally bringing macaws into the United States from Mexico. (Rev: BL 11/15/95; SLJ 10/96)

7117 Bledsoe, Lucy Jane. *The Antarctic Scoop* (4–7). 2003, Holiday House $16.95 (0-8234-1792-1). 168pp. In this fast-paced adventure story, 12-year-old Victoria, a shy girl with ambitious dreams, wins a trip to Antarctica but discovers during her travels that the real goal of the contest sponsor is to develop and exploit the icy continent. (Rev: BL 1/1–15/04; HBG 4/04; SLJ 1/04)

7118 Bledsoe, Lucy Jane. *Tracks in the Snow* (3–6). 1997, Holiday House paper $15.95 (0-8234-1309-8). 96pp. A survival story about two girls caught in the woods during a violent snowstorm. (Rev: BL 8/97; HBG 3/98; SLJ 7/97)

7119 Bodett, Tom. *Williwaw* (5–8). 1999, Random paper $5.50 (0-375-80687-3). The story of two

youngsters — 13-year-old September Crane and her 12-year-old brother Ivan — and their life in the wilds of Alaska, where they are often left alone by their fisherman father. (Rev: BCCB 6/99; BL 4/1/99; HBG 10/99; SLJ 5/99)

7120 Bonners, Susan. *Above and Beyond* (5–7). 2001, Farrar $16.00 (0-374-30018-6). 151pp. Jerry makes a new friend and discovers the truth about an incident that took place many years ago. (Rev: BCCB 12/01; HBG 10/02; SLJ 10/01)

7121 Brittain, Bill. *Dr. Dredd's Wagon of Wonders* (4–6). Illus. by Andrew Glass. 1987, HarperCollins LB $15.89 (0-06-020714-0). 160pp. Set in a remote New England town. Dr. Dredd comes to Coven Tree to cure the drought and causes havoc in this spooky tale. (Rev: SLJ 8/87)

7122 Brittain, Bill. *Who Knew There'd Be Ghosts?* (4–6). Illus. by Michele Chessare. 1985, Harper-Collins paper $4.95 (0-06-440224-X). 128pp. Tommy, the narrator, relates how he discovers ghosts Essie and Horace and how they help him solve a mystery. (Rev: BL 6/1/85; HB 7–8/85; SLJ 5/85)

7123 Bruchac, Joseph. *Skeleton Man* (5–9). 2001, HarperCollins LB $16.89 (0-06-029076-5). 128pp. After her parents' disappearance, 6th-grader Molly, a Native American, must escape from the spooky man claiming to be her great-uncle. (Rev: BCCB 9/01; BL 9/1/01; HBG 3/02; SLJ 8/01*)

7124 Buckey, Sarah Masters. *Gangsters at the Grand Atlantic* (4–6). Illus. by Douglas Fryer. Series: History Mysteries. 2003, Pleasant Co. paper $6.95 (1-58485-719-6). 176pp. Emily, 12, has a brush with gangsters in this story full of suspense set in 1925 Philadelphia and at the Jersey Shore. (Rev: BL 5/15/03; HBG 10/03)

7125 Bunting, Eve. *Coffin on a Case* (4–6). 1992, HarperCollins $14.95 (0-06-020273-4). 108pp. The daughter of a woman who has disappeared enlists the aid of a private detective's son to find her. (Rev: BCCB 11/92; BL 10/1/92; SLJ 10/92)

7126 Bunting, Eve. *Someone Is Hiding on Alcatraz Island* (5–8). 1986, Berkley paper $4.99 (0-425-10294-7). 144pp. A boy and a young woman ranger are trapped by a gang of thugs on Alcatraz. (Rev: BL 7/88)

7127 Burns, Laura J., and Melinda Metz. *The Case of the Prank That Stank* (5–8). Series: Wright and Wong. 2005, Penguin Putnam $9.99 (1-59514-014-X). 192pp. Agatha Wong is a lively extrovert, while Orville — who has Asperger's syndrome — longs for peace and tranquility, but the two are close friends and together investigate a mystery. (Rev: BL 5/1/05)

7128 Butler, Dori Hillestad. *Do You Know the Monkey Man?* (5–7). 2005, Peachtree $14.95 (1-56145-340-4). 224pp. After a psychic says that her twin sister — believed drowned 10 years before — is not dead at all, 13-year-old Samantha sets off with a friend to investigate. (Rev: BL 5/1/05; SLJ 6/05)

7129 Cadwallader, Sharon. *Cookie McCorkle and the Case of the Emerald Earrings* (3–5). Illus. by Patrick Chapin. 1991, Avon paper $2.95 (0-380-

76098-3). 128pp. Ten-year-old Cookie and her dog Moriarity solve a mystery in the Holmesian manner. Followed by: *Cookie McCorkle and the Case of the Polka-Dot Safecracker* (1991). (Rev: BL 9/15/91)

7130 Capeci, Anne. *Danger: Dynamite!* (3–6). Illus. by Paul Casale. Series: Cascade Mountain Railroad Mysteries. 2003, Peachtree $12.95 (1-56145-288-2). 127pp. In this engaging mystery tale set in the 1920s, 10-year-old Billy and his best friend Finn investigate the mysterious disappearance of a crate of dynamite. (Rev: HBG 4/04; SLJ 1/04)

7131 Capeci, Anne. *Ghost Train* (3–5). Illus. by author. Series: Cascade Mountain Railroad Mysteries. 2004, Peachtree $12.95 (1-56145-324-2). 144pp. Billy, Finn, and Dannie are instrumental in preventing a train robbery in this fast-paced mystery full of historical detail. (Rev: SLJ 1/05)

7132 Casanova, Mary. *Moose Tracks* (4–6). 1995, Hyperion LB $15.49 (0-7868-2035-7). 128pp. During a moose hunt, Seth and friend Matt stumble onto a pair of dangerous poachers. (Rev: BCCB 7–8/95; BL 7/95; SLJ 6/95)

7133 Cavanagh, Helen. *Panther Glade* (5–8). 1993, Simon & Schuster paper $16.00 (0-671-75617-6). Bill spends a summer in Florida with his great-aunt Cait. He's afraid of the Everglades and alligators, but he comes to appreciate Indian history and crafts. (Rev: BL 6/1–15/93; SLJ 6/93)

7134 Christian, Mary Blount. *Sebastian (Super Sleuth) and the Copycat Crime* (3–5). 1993, Macmillan LB $13.00 (0-02-718211-8). 64pp. Sebastian the dog detective once again comes to the rescue and this time solves the mystery of the stolen manuscript. (Rev: BL 1/1/94; SLJ 3/94)

7135 Clifford, Eth. *Help! I'm a Prisoner in the Library* (3–5). Illus. by George Hughes. 1979, Houghton Mifflin $16.00 (0-395-28478-3); Scholastic paper $4.50 (0-590-44351-8). 112pp. Two youngsters are locked in a library after it closes. Two sequels are: *The Dastardly Murder of Dirty Pete* (1981); *Just Tell Me When We're Dead!* (1983).

7136 Clifford, Eth. *Scared Silly* (3–5). Illus. by George Hughes. 1989, Scholastic paper $2.75 (0-590-42382-7). 128pp. Mary Rose and Jo-Beth encounter a mysterious Walk-Your-Way-Around-the-World Museum. (Rev: BCCB 4/88; BL 4/1/88; SLJ 6–7/88)

7137 Coleman, Michael. *Weirdo's War* (5–8). 1998, Orchard paper $16.95 (0-531-30103-6). Noted for being the class misfit, Daniel is paired with Tozer, his nemesis, on a class excursion in this life-or-death survival story. (Rev: BCCB 11/98; BL 8/98; BR 5–6/99; HB 9–10/98*; HBG 3/99; SLJ 10/98)

7138 Comino, Sandra. *The Little Blue House* (4–7). 2003, Douglas & McIntyre $15.95 (0-88899-504-0). 155pp. Young Cintia and her friend Bruno investigate why an abandoned house in their small town in Argentina turns blue for one day each year in this suspenseful novel that contains some violence. (Rev: BL 2/15/04)

7139 Conford, Ellen. *A Case for Jenny Archer* (2–4). Illus. by Diane Palmisciano. 1990, Little, Brown paper $4.50 (0-316-15352-4). Jenny, who longs to become a detective, inadvertently foils a burglary. (Rev: BL 1/15/89; SLJ 3/89)

7140 Creech, Sharon. *The Wanderer* (5–9). Illus. by David Diaz. 2000, HarperCollins LB $16.89 (0-06-027731-9). 288pp. In this Newbery Honor Book, 13-year-old Sophie, her two cousins, and three uncles sail across the Atlantic to England in a 45-foot yacht. (Rev: BCCB 4/00*; BL 4/1/00; HB 5–6/00; HBG 10/00; SLJ 4/00*)

7141 Crossman, David A. *The Mystery of the Black Moriah* (5–8). Series: A Bean and Ab Mystery. 2002, Down East $16.95 (0-89272-536-2). 234pp. The ever-curious Bean and Ab become caught up in a mystery adventure involving pirates, kidnappers, and a legendary ghost. (Rev: HBG 3/03; SLJ 12/02)

7142 Crossman, David A. *The Secret of the Missing Grave* (5–8). Series: A Bean and Ab Mystery. 1999, Down East $16.95 (0-89272-456-0). 184pp. Two girls investigate a haunted house and become involved in a mystery concerning a missing treasure and stolen paintings in this fast-paced novel set in Maine. (Rev: HBG 3/00; SLJ 1/00)

7143 Cushman, Doug. *The Mystery of the Monkey's Maze* (1–4). Illus. 1999, HarperCollins LB $14.89 (0-06-027720-3). 32pp. After receiving threatening notes, Dr. Irene A. Tann, who is in Borneo on the trail of a flower that will cure hiccups, asks Seymour Sleuth and his sidekick Abbott Moggs to crack the case. (Rev: BL 6/1–15/99; HBG 10/99; SLJ 5/99)

7144 Deedy, Carmen A. *The Secret of Old Zeb* (2–3). Illus. by Michael P. White. 1997, Peachtree $16.95 (1-56145-115-0). An adventure novel in which Uncle Walter tells his niece about a summer when he found that his next-door neighbor was building a ship in his basement. (Rev: HBG 3/98; SLJ 3/98)

7145 Defelice, Cynthia. *Death at Devil's Bridge* (5–8). 2000, Farrar $16.00 (0-374-31723-2). 181pp. This mystery, set on Martha's Vineyard, tells of 13-year-old Ben Daggett and his investigation of the death of a teenager suspected of dealing in drugs. (Rev: BCCB 9/00; BL 8/00; HBG 3/01; SLJ 9/00)

7146 Defelice, Cynthia. *The Missing Manatee* (5–8). 2005, Farrar $16.00 (0-374-31257-5). 192pp. Skeet Waters sets out to solve the mystery of a murdered manatee he finds near his Florida home. (Rev: BL 3/1/05; SLJ 6/05)

7147 Defoe, Daniel. *Robinson Crusoe* (3–6). Illus. by N. C. Wyeth. Series: Scribner Storybook Classic. 2003, Simon & Schuster $18.95 (0-689-85104-9). 51pp. This abridged version makes Defoe's classic tale accessible to younger readers while retaining much of the excitement of the original. (Rev: HBG 10/03; SLJ 4/03)

7148 Delaney, Mark. *The Protester's Song* (5–9). Series: Misfits, Inc. 2001, Peachtree paper $5.95 (1-56145-244-0). 214pp. Four teens keep themselves busy investigating an incident that occurred during riots in Ohio in 1970 and, in a subplot, try to stop the new principal from removing books from the library. (Rev: SLJ 8/01)

343

7149 Delaney, Mark. *The Vanishing Chip* (5–8). Series: Misfits, Inc. 1998, Peachtree paper $5.95 (1-56145-176-2). 188pp. Four teens who don't fit in at school investigate the disappearance of the world's most powerful computer chip. (Rev: BL 12/15/98; SLJ 2/99)

7150 Demers, Barbara. *Willa's New World* (5–8). 2000, Coteau paper $6.95 (1-55050-150-X). 192pp. An adventure story set in Canada around 1800 in which 15-year-old Willa is sent to a trading post on Hudson's Bay. (Rev: BL 9/15/00; SLJ 9/00)

7151 Disher, Garry. *Ratface* (5–9). 1994, Ticknor $14.95 (0-395-69451-5). Kidnapped by a racist Australian cult known as the White League, Max, Christina, and Stefan escape captivity and are pursued by Ratface, a cult deputy. (Rev: BL 11/1/94; SLJ 12/94)

7152 Draper, Sharon M. *Lost in the Tunnel of Time* (3–6). Illus. by Michael Bryant. Series: Ziggy and the Black Dinosaurs. 1996, Just Us paper $6.00 (0-940975-63-7). 96pp. While exploring tunnels used by the Underground Railroad, boys are trapped underground when one of the tunnels collapses. (Rev: SLJ 8/96)

7153 Draper, Sharon M. *Shadows of Caesar's Creek* (3–5). Series: Ziggy and the Black Dinosaurs. 1997, Just Us paper $6.00 (0-940975-76-9). 91pp. A group of African American kids get lost in a state park and are rescued by a Shawnee chief. (Rev: SLJ 6/98)

7154 Duey, Kathleen, and Karen A. Bale. *Flood: Mississippi, 1927* (4–6). Series: Survival! 1998, Simon & Schuster paper $3.99 (0-689-82116-6). 169pp. Two children living on the banks of the Mississippi set out to rescue their hard-earned, hidden money before it is swept away in a flood. (Rev: SLJ 12/98)

7155 Dygard, Thomas J. *River Danger* (5–9). 1998, Morrow $15.99 (0-688-14852-2). 151pp. An adventure story in which an older and younger brother happen on a car-theft ring while on a canoe trip in Arkansas. (Rev: BL 3/15/98; BR 11–12/98; HBG 10/98; SLJ 5/98)

7156 Easley, Maryann. *I Am the Ice Worm* (4–6). 1996, Boyds Mills $15.95 (1-56397-412-6). 127pp. A California girl is rescued by Inupiats when she is stranded in Alaska after a plane crash. (Rev: BL 10/15/96; SLJ 11/96)

7157 Easton, Kelly. *Canaries and Criminals* (3–6). 2003, Candlewick $15.99 (0-7636-1928-0). 118pp. This fast-paced follow-up to *Trouble at Betts Pets* (2002) has young Aaron involved with a mysterious turtle. (Rev: HBG 4/04; SLJ 4/04)

7158 Easton, Patricia H. *A Week at the Fair: A Country Celebration* (2–5). Photos by Herb Ferguso. 1995, Millbrook LB $20.90 (1-56294-527-0). A week's activities at a county fair in western Pennsylvania are seen through the eyes of a 12-year-old girl. (Rev: SLJ 2/96)

7159 Eden, Alexandra. *Holy Smoke: A Bones and Duchess Mystery* (5–7). 2004, Alien A. Knoll $16.00 (1-888310-46-4). 112pp. Ex-cop Bones Fatzinger and Verity Buscador, a 12-year-old girl

with Asperger's syndrome, work together to track down the person responsible for setting fire to a local church. (Rev: BL 5/1/04)

7160 Ellis, Mary. *Lily Dragon* (3–5). Illus. by Rachael Phillips. 2001, HarperCollins paper $7.50 (0-00-675458-9). 139pp. Lily sets off on a trip to visit her mother's family in China, determined to hunt for the hidden treasure she's heard about so often. (Rev: SLJ 8/01)

7161 Elmer, Robert. *Far from the Storm* (4–7). Series: Young Underground. 1995, Bethany House paper $5.99 (0-55661-377-6). 174pp. At the end of World War II, Danish twins Peter and Elise set out to find the culprit who set their uncle's boat on fire. (Rev: BL 2/15/96)

7162 Elmer, Robert. *Follow the Star* (5–8). Series: Young Underground. 1997, Bethany House paper $5.99 (1-55661-660-0). 178pp. In post–World War II Denmark, Henrik believes that his mother is being held captive by the Russians, who believe she is a spy. (Rev: SLJ 2/98)

7163 Emerson, Kathy L. *The Mystery of the Missing Bagpipes* (5–7). 1991, Avon paper $2.95 (0-380-76138-6). 128pp. Kim tries to find the real culprit when a young boy is wrongfully accused of stealing a set of ancient bagpipes and some precious daggers. (Rev: BL 9/15/91)

7164 Emerson, Scott. *The Case of the Cat with the Missing Ear: From the Notebooks of Edward R. Smithfield, D.V.M.* (5–7). 2003, Simon & Schuster LB $15.95 (0-689-85861-2). This canine takeoff of the Sherlock Holmes format features Yorkshire terrier Samuel Blackthorne and his sidekick and chronicler Dr. Edward Smithfield, who investigate mysteries with humor and deductive prowess. (Rev: BCCB 10/02; BL 12/1/03; HBG 4/04; SLJ 3/04)

7165 Engh, M. J. *The House in the Snow* (4–6). Illus. 1990, Scholastic paper $2.75 (0-590-42658-3). 144pp. Orphan Benjamin lands in a house of robbers who have cloaks that make them invisible. With the help of the other boys, he plans to take over the house. (Rev: BL 11/1/87; SLJ 9/87)

7166 Erickson, John R. *Discovery at Flint Springs* (5–8). 2004, Viking $16.99 (0-670-05946-3). 192pp. In 1927, 14-year-old Riley and his younger brother Coy join in an exciting search for archaeological sites on their Texas ranch. (Rev: BL 2/1/05; SLJ 12/04)

7167 Ericson, Helen. *Harriet Spies Again* (4–6). 2002, Delacorte LB $17.99 (0-385-90022-8). 230pp. This well-done continuation of the tales of Louise Fitzhugh's *Harriet the Spy* has the junior sleuth investigating her caretaker's sudden bout of sadness. (Rev: BCCB 4/02; BL 3/15/02; HB 5–6/02; HBG 10/02; SLJ 5/02)

7168 Ewing, Lynne. *Drive-By* (5–8). 1996, HarperCollins paper $4.99 (0-06-440649-0). When Tito's brother is killed in a gang-related shooting, he is bullied and threatened by the gang to reveal where his brother hid a cache of stolen money. (Rev: SLJ 8/96)

7169 Falcone, L. M. *The Mysterious Mummer* (5–7). 2003, Kids Can $16.95 (1-55337-376-6). 192pp.

When Joey, 13, arrives in Newfoundland to spend Christmas with his aunt, he finds some very mysterious goings-on. (Rev: HBG 4/04; SLJ 10/03)

7170 Fama, Elizabeth. *Overboard* (4–8). 2002, Cricket $15.95 (0-8126-2652-4). 176pp. Fourteen-year-old Emily struggles to save her own life and that of a boy named Isman when a ferry sinks off the coast of Sumatra. (Rev: BCCB 6/02; BL 7/02; HBG 10/02; SLJ 7/02)

7171 Farley, Carol. *The Case of the Haunted Health Club* (4–6). 1991, Avon paper $2.95 (0-380-75918-7). 112pp. Two sisters solve a mystery involving a health club. (Rev: BL 3/15/91)

7172 Farley, Carol. *The Case of the Vanishing Villain* (5–6). Illus. 1986, Avon paper $2.95 (0-380-89959-0). 80pp. A 10-year-old solves the mystery of an escaped convict's disappearance. Also use *Mystery of the Melted Diamonds* (1986); *The Case of the Lost Lookalike* (1988). (Rev: BL 9/15/86; SLJ 11/86)

7173 Ferguson, Dwayne J. *Case of the Missing Ankh* (2–4). Series: Kid Caramel. 1997, Just Us paper $4.50 (0-940975-71-8). 59pp. Two junior detectives solve the mystery of the stolen museum treasure. (Rev: SLJ 9/97)

7174 Ferguson, Dwayne J. *Kid Caramel, Private Investigator: The Werewolf of PS 40* (3–5). Series: Kid Caramel. 1998, Just Us paper $4.50 (0-940975-82-3). 68pp. When animals begin to disappear from his town, Kid Caramel and his sidekick, Earnie, set out to find the culprit. (Rev: SLJ 3/99)

7175 Fields, T. S. *Danger in the Desert* (5–7). 1997, Rising Moon $12.95 (0-87358-666-2); paper $6.95 (0-87358-664-6). 126pp. A survival story about two boys who endure great hardships when they are left without food or supplies in the desert. (Rev: HBG 3/98; SLJ 11/97)

7176 Fienberg, Anna. *Horrendo's Curse* (3–6). Illus. by Kim Gamble. 2002, Annick $18.95 (1-55037-773-6); paper $6.95 (1-55037-772-8). 160pp. Twelve-year-old Horrendo, whose curse is an inability to say anything cruel although surrounded by rude foul-mouths, manages to persuade his pirate kidnappers that politeness is the best policy. (Rev: BL 12/1/02; HBG 10/03; SLJ 2/03)

7177 Figley, Marty Rhodes. *The Schoolchildren's Blizzard* (1–3). Illus. by Shelley O. Haas. Series: On My Own History. 2004, Carolrhoda LB $27.93 (1-57505-586-1). 48pp. A teacher rescues 16 students after the roof of the school is blown off during a severe blizzard in 1888 in this story based on a Nebraska storm. (Rev: BL 3/1/04)

7178 Fleischman, Paul. *The Half-a-Moon Inn* (5–7). Illus. by Kathryn Jacobi. 1991, HarperCollins paper $4.99 (0-06-440364-5). 96pp. A young mute boy sets out to find his mother in a violent snowstorm.

7179 Fleischman, Sid. *Disappearing Act* (4–6). 2003, Greenwillow LB $16.89 (0-06-051963-0). 144pp. Twelve-year-old Kevin and his older sister Holly, recently orphaned, flee to California in a vain attempt to elude a mysterious stalker and find themselves in challenging and suspenseful situations

among eccentric characters on Venice Beach. (Rev: BL 6/1–15/03; HB 5–6/03; HBG 10/03; SLJ 5/03)

7180 Fleischman, Sid. *The Ghost in the Noonday Sun* (5–7). Illus. by Warren Chappell. 1989, Greenwillow $16.00 (0-688-08410-9); Scholastic paper $3.50 (0-590-43662-7). 144pp. This pirate story features all the standard ingredients — a shanghaied boy, a villainous captain, and buried treasure. (Rev:)

7181 Fleischman, Sid. *The Giant Rat of Sumatra or Pirates Galore* (4–6). Illus. by John Hendrix. 2005, Greenwillow LB $16.89 (0-06-074239-9). 208pp. In a fast-paced adventure, 12-year-old cabin boy Edmund Amos Peters, who's been shipwrecked and captured by pirates, arrives in mid-19th-century San Diego to find his adventures are not over. (Rev: BL 2/1/05; SLJ 1/05)

7182 Fleischman, Sid. *The Whipping Boy* (5–7). Illus. 1986, Greenwillow $16.99 (0-688-06216-4); Troll paper $4.95 (0-8167-1038-4). 96pp. Prince Brat and his whipping boy, Jemmy, who takes the blame for all the bad things the prince does, find their roles reversed when they meet up with CutWater and Hold-Your-Nose Billy. Newbery Medal winner, 1987. (Rev: BCCB 3/86; BL 3/1/86; SLJ 5/86)

7183 Frels, Merry Hassell. *Simmering Secrets of Weeping Mary* (4–7). 2005, Longhorn Creek paper $9.95 (0-9714358-9-8). 120pp. Twelve-year-old Duty (short for Deuteronomy) Devilrow investigates the death of her cousin Nehemiah and the mystery of her own heritage. (Rev: BL 5/1/05)

7184 Galbraith, Kathryn O. *Something Suspicious* (4–6). 1987, Avon paper $2.50 (0-380-70253-3). 128pp. Lizzie and her friend Ivy are on the trail of the bank robber known as the Green Pillowcase Bandit. (Rev: BCCB 1/86; BL 10/1/85)

7185 Garden, Nancy. *The Case of the Stolen Scarab* (4–6). Illus. by Danamarie Hosler. Series: Candlestone Inn Mystery. 2004, Two Lives paper $8.95 (0-9674468-7-2). 205pp. Nikki and Travis, with their mothers, have only just arrived at their new inn when a mystery presents itself — a scarab has been stolen and the thief may be in the area. (Rev: SLJ 3/05)

7186 Garland, Michael. *Mystery Mansion: A Look Again Book* (2–4). Illus. by author. 2001, Dutton $15.99 (0-525-46675-4). Aunt Jeanne leaves young Tommy a series of rhyming notes that send him (and the reader) on a detecting tour of her mansion and its abundance of wildlife. (Rev: HBG 3/02; SLJ 9/01)

7187 Garland, Sherry. *The Silent Storm* (4–7). 1993, Harcourt $14.95 (0-15-274170-4). 240pp. Alyssa, who has lost both of her parents in a violent storm and has become mute because of the trauma, hears that another hurricane is approaching. (Rev: BCCB 4/93; BL 6/1–15/93; SLJ 7/04)

7188 George, Jean Craighead. *Julie of the Wolves* (5–8). Illus. by John Schoenherr. 1974, Harper-Collins LB $16.89 (0-06-021944-0); paper $5.99 (0-06-440058-1). 180pp. Julie (Inuit name, Miyax) begins a trek across frozen Alaska and is saved only by the friendship of a pack of wolves. Newbery Medal winner, 1973.

7189 George, Jean Craighead. *Julie's Wolf Pack* (5–7). Illus. Series: Julie of the Wolves. 1997, HarperCollins LB $17.89 (0-06-027407-7). 208pp. Kapu, leader of the pack, is captured by researchers in this continuing story of Julie and her wolf friends. (Rev: BL 9/1/97; BR 1–2/98; HBG 3/98; SLJ 9/97)

7190 George, Jean Craighead. *The Talking Earth* (6–8). 1983, HarperCollins LB $15.89 (0-06-021976-9); paper $4.95 (0-06-440212-6). 160pp. A young Seminole girl spends three months in the Everglades alone.

7191 George, Jean Craighead. *Tree Castle Island* (4–7). Illus. 2002, HarperCollins LB $16.89 (0-06-000255-7). 240pp. A boy tests his survival skills in the Okefenokee Swamp, and meets the twin he never knew he had, in this tale rich in details about the setting. (Rev: BL 3/15/02; HBG 10/02; SLJ 5/02)

7192 George, Twig C. *Swimming with Sharks* (4–6). Illus. 1999, HarperCollins LB $13.89 (0-06-027758-0). 96pp. Sarah and her grandfather, a shark expert, are on the trail of a "finner" — someone who cuts off sharks' fins and leaves them to die. (Rev: BL 7/99; HBG 10/99; SLJ 7/99)

7193 Gerson, Corrine. *My Grandfather the Spy* (5–7). 1990, Walker $14.95 (0-8027-6955-1). 120pp. When a man arrives on the family farm in Vermont with a briefcase full of money, Danny suspects his grandfather is a spy. (Rev: BL 6/15/90; SLJ 8/90)

7194 Giff, Patricia Reilly. *Kidnap at the Catfish Cafe* (2–4). Illus. 1998, Viking $13.99 (0-670-88180-5). 63pp. When Minnie finds both a cat named Max and an amber ring, she finds she has two cases to solve in this witty mystery. (Rev: BL 11/1/98; HBG 3/99; SLJ 1/99)

7195 Gilson, Jamie. *Soccer Circus: Featuring Hobie Hanson* (4–6). Illus. by Dee deRosa. 1993, Lothrop $15.00 (0-688-12021-0). 148pp. On a harmless overnight soccer trip, Hobie manages to get into a great deal of trouble. (Rev: BL 4/1/93; SLJ 6/93)

7196 Givner, Joan. *Ellen Fremedon* (5–7). 2004, Groundwood $15.95 (0-88899-557-1). 176pp. When her family seeks to block a proposed housing development, 12-year-old Ellen Fremedon, an aspiring novelist, must set aside her summer project to cope with the repercussions. (Rev: BL 11/15/04)

7197 Godden, Rumer. *The Rocking Horse Secret* (4–6). Illus. by Juliet Stanwell Smith. 1988, Puffin paper $3.95 (0-317-69650-5). 64pp. Tibby solves many problems when she finds a will hidden in a rocking horse.

7198 Gorman, Carol. *Jennifer-the-Jerk Is Missing* (4–6). 1994, Simon & Schuster $15.00 (0-671-86578-1). 135pp. Amy wonders whether Malcolm, her baby-sitting charge, is telling the truth about seeing a kidnapping. (Rev: BCCB 5/94; BL 6/1–15/94; SLJ 6/94)

7199 Gourley, Catherine, ed. *Read for Your Life: Tales of Survival from the Editors of Read Magazine* (5–8). Series: Best of Read. 1998, Millbrook paper $5.95 (0-7613-0344-8). This is a collection of excellent survival stories from 50 years of *Read,* a literary magazine for middle and high school students. (Rev: BL 8/98)

7200 Greene, Stephanie. *Owen Foote, Frontiersman* (2–4). Illus. 1999, Clarion $14.00 (0-395-61578-X). 96pp. In this beginning chapter book, Owen and his pal Joseph must rescue their tree fort from two older boys who threaten to destroy it. (Rev: BL 10/15/99; HB 9–10/99; HBG 3/00; SLJ 10/99)

7201 Grossman, David, and Beotsi Rozenberg. *Duel* (4–7). 2004, Bloomsbury $15.95 (1-58234-930-4). 112pp. In 1966 Jerusalem, 12-year-old David turns detective to find out what happened to the valuable painting his best friend, a 70-year-old man, is accused of stealing. (Rev: BL 9/1/04; SLJ 8/04)

7202 Grover, Wayne. *Dolphin Freedom* (3–5). Illus. 1999, Greenwillow $15.00 (0-688-16010-7). 112pp. Diver Wayne Grover tries to save dolphins that are the target of a poaching ring working off the coast of Florida. (Rev: BL 5/15/99; HBG 10/99; SLJ 6/99)

7203 Gutman, Dan. *Shoeless Joe and Me* (4–7). Series: Baseball Card Adventure. 2002, HarperCollins LB $16.89 (0-06-029254-7). 144pp. Thirteen-year-old Joe travels back in time to remedy the 1919 Black Sox scandal and save Shoeless Joe's reputation. (Rev: BL 1/1–15/02; HBG 10/02; SLJ 3/02)

7204 Hahn, Mary D. *Following the Mystery Man* (5–7). 1988, Avon paper $4.99 (0-380-70677-6). 192pp. Madigan is certain that her grandmother's new boarder is none other than her missing father. (Rev: BL 3/15/88; HB 7–8/88; SLJ 4/88)

7205 Hahn, Mary D. *The Spanish Kidnapping Disaster* (5–7). 1991, Houghton Mifflin $16.00 (0-395-55696-1); Avon paper $4.50 (0-380-71712-3). 132pp. Felix is tagging along on her mother's honeymoon in Spain and is not having a good time. (Rev: BCCB 5/91; BL 3/15/91; SLJ 5/91)

7206 Hamilton, Virginia. *The House of Dies Drear* (5–8). Illus. by Eros Keith. 1984, Macmillan $17.00 (0-02-742500-2); paper $4.99 (0-02-043520-7). 256pp. First-rate suspense as history professor Small and his young son Thomas investigate their rented house, formerly a station on the Underground Railroad, unlocking the secrets and dangers from attitudes dating back to the Civil War.

7207 Hamilton, Virginia. *The Mystery of Drear House* (5–7). 1987, Greenwillow $16.95 (0-688-04026-8); Scholastic paper $4.50 (0-590-95627-2). 224pp. The story of Thomas Small and the threat to the treasure of Drear House. The final installment in the saga of this station on the Underground Railroad. (Rev: BCCB 5/87; BL 6/15/87; SLJ 6–7/87)

7208 Harding, Donal. *The Leaving Summer* (4–6). 1996, Morrow $15.00 (0-688-13893-4). 177pp. An 11-year-old boy and his aunt hide an injured escaped convict in their basement and nurse him back to health in this coming-of-age story. (Rev: BCCB 9/96; SLJ 4/96)

7209 Harlow, Joan Hiatt. *Star in the Storm* (4–7). Illus. 2000, Simon & Schuster $16.00 (0-689-

82905-1). 160pp. This novel, set in Newfoundland in 1912, tells how a girl and her dog save a ship full of stranded passengers. (Rev: BCCB 3/00; BL 1/1–15/00; HB 3–4/00; HBG 10/00; SLJ 4/00)

7210 Harrison, Ted. *Children of the Yukon* (2–4). Illus. by author. 1977, Tundra paper $6.95 (0-88776-163-1). Life in present-day Yukon with a little historical material.

7211 Haugaard, Erik C. *Under the Black Flag* (5–7). 1994, Roberts Rinehart paper $8.95 (1-879373-63-7). 170pp. Fourteen-year-old William is captured by the pirate Blackbeard and held for ransom in this 18th-century yarn. (Rev: BL 4/1/94; HB 9–10/94; SLJ 5/94)

7212 Hausman, Gerald. *Castaways: Stories of Survival* (5–8). 2003, Greenwillow LB $16.89 (0-06-008599-1). 160pp. True stories of shipwreck survivors inspired these six tales of endurance and good fortune. (Rev: BL 9/15/03; HBG 10/03; SLJ 6/03)

7213 Hawks, Robert. *The Richest Kid in the World* (4–8). 1992, Avon paper $2.99 (0-380-76241-2). 136pp. Josh is kidnapped and taken to the estate of billionaire Grizzle Welch. (Rev: SLJ 5/92)

7214 Hayes, Daniel. *The Trouble with Lemons* (5–8). 1991, Random paper $5.99 (0-449-70416-5). Tyler, 14, has all kinds of problems — allergies, asthma, and nightmares — and then he finds a dead body. (Rev: BL 5/1/91; SLJ 6/91)

7215 Hearne, Betsy. *Who's in the Hall? A Mystery in Four Chapters* (2–4). Illus. 2000, Greenwillow LB $15.89 (0-688-16262-2). 32pp. Three different sets of kids in the same apartment building are troubled by a stranger who knocks at their doors asking to be let in. (Rev: BCCB 1/01; BL 9/15/00; HBG 3/01; SLJ 8/00)

7216 Heisel, Sharon E. *Wrapped in a Riddle* (4–6). 1993, Houghton Mifflin $14.95 (0-395-65026-7). 140pp. When a series of unexplained events occur at her grandmother's bed-and-breakfast, Miranda becomes a sleuth intent on solving the mysteries. (Rev: BCCB 11/93; BL 10/1/93; SLJ 2/94)

7217 Henderson, Aileen K. *The Summer of the Bonepile Monster* (3–5). Illus. 1995, Milkweed $15.95 (1-57131-603-5); paper $6.95 (1-57131-602-7). 140pp. Hollis changes into a self-reliant young man during a summer spent in the country during which he solves a community mystery. (Rev: BCCB 7–8/95; BL 5/1/95; SLJ 7/95)

7218 Herndon, Ernest. *The Secret of Lizard Island* (3–5). 1994, HarperCollins paper $5.99 (0-310-38251-3). 128pp. Through a misunderstanding, Eric, a typical 12-year-old, is sent to a South Pacific island where scientists are growing huge lizards. (Rev: BL 9/1/94)

7219 Hesse, Karen. *Stowaway* (5–8). Illus. 2000, Simon & Schuster $17.95 (0-689-83987-1). 319pp. Told by an 11-year-old stowaway, this adventurous sea story tells of Captain Cook's two-and-a-half-year voyage around the world beginning in 1768. (Rev: BL 12/15/00; HB 1–2/01; HBG 3/01; SLJ 11/00)

7220 Heyes, Eileen. *O'Dwyer and Grady Starring In: Acting Innocent* (4–6). 2002, Simon & Schuster paper $4.99 (0-689-84911-7). 128pp. Billy and Virginia, child actors in the 1930s, find that their friend Chubby Muldoon is accused of murdering an actress. (Rev: BL 5/1/02; SLJ 3/02)

7221 Heyes, Eileen. *O'Dwyer and Grady Starring in Tough Act to Follow* (4–7). Illus. by Eric Bowman. Series: O'Dwyer and Grady. 2003, Simon & Schuster paper $4.99 (0-689-84920-6). 176pp. Young actors Billy and Virginia stumble into a mystery while searching for props for a show in this action-packed story set in the 1930s. (Rev: BL 5/15/03; SLJ 7/03)

7222 Hildick, E. W. *The Purloined Corn Popper* (4–6). 1997, Marshall Cavendish $14.95 (0-7614-5010-6). 160pp. In this new mystery series, Tim Kowalski and his friend investigate the disappearance of a corn popper that contained Mrs. Kowalski's money. Also use *Sneak Thief* (1997). (Rev: BL 1/1–15/98; HBG 10/98; SLJ 2/98)

7223 Hilgartner, Beth. *A Murder for Her Majesty* (5–8). 1986, Houghton Mifflin paper $5.95 (0-395-61619-0). 256pp. Alice disguises herself as a boy to escape her father's murderers. (Rev: BCCB 9/86; SLJ 10/86)

7224 Hobbs, Will. *Down the Yukon* (5–8). 2001, HarperCollins LB $16.89 (0-06-029540-6). 208pp. In this sequel to *Jason's Gold*, Jason decides to compete in a race to the new gold fields in Alaska. (Rev: BL 4/1/01; HBG 10/01; SLJ 5/01)

7225 Hobbs, Will. *Jackie's Wild Seattle* (5–8). 2003, HarperCollins LB $16.89 (0-06-051631-3). 192pp. In the aftermath of September 11, 2001, Shannon, 14, and her younger brother spend an exciting and healing summer in Seattle with their animal rescuer uncle. (Rev: BL 6/1–15/03; HBG 4/04; SLJ 5/03)

7226 Hobbs, Will. *Jason's Gold* (5–9). 1999, Morrow $16.99 (0-688-15093-4). 192pp. In this sharply realistic novel, 15-year-old Jason leaves Seattle in 1897 and, with a dog he has saved, heads for the Klondike and gold. (Rev: BL 8/99; HB 9–10/99; HBG 3/00; SLJ 11/99)

7227 Hobbs, Will. *Wild Man Island* (5–9). 2002, HarperCollins LB $15.89 (0-06-029810-3). 192pp. An adventure story in which 14-year-old Andy becomes stranded on a remote Alaska island, faces many dangers, and tests his dead archaeologist father's theories about the earliest prehistoric immigrants to America. (Rev: BL 4/15/02; HB 7–8/02; HBG 10/02; SLJ 5/02)

7228 Hol, and Hamel. *To Scratch a Thief* (3–5). Illus. by Brad Weinman. 2004, HarperCollins LB $15.89 (0-06-052983-0). 131pp. Mr. Stink, international feline agent, gets help from animal friends in his efforts to track a killer and a thief. (Rev: SLJ 2/05)

7229 Hopper, Nancy J. *Ape Ears and Beaky* (4–7). 1987, Avon paper $2.50 (0-380-70270-3). 112pp. Scott and Beaky solve the mystery of the robberies in a condominium.

7230 Horowitz, Anthony. *Stormbreaker* (5–9). Series: Alex Rider Adventure. 2001, Philomel

$16.99 (0-399-23620-1). 208pp. Fourteen-year-old Alex becomes embroiled in dangerous undercover exploits when his MI6 uncle is murdered. (Rev: BCCB 9/01; BL 9/1/01; HBG 10/01; SLJ 6/01)

7231 Horowitz, Anthony. *Three of Diamonds* (5–8). 2005, Philomel $16.99 (0-399-24157-4). 240pp. Tim and Nick succeed in solving crimes despite Tim's blunderings in these three fast-paced and entertaining mystery stories full of wordplay. (Rev: BL 5/15/05; SLJ 5/05)

7232 Howard, Milly. *The Case of the Dognapped Cat* (2–4). Illus. 1997, Bob Jones Univ. paper $6.49 (0-89084-936-6). 144pp. Three Florida youngsters call themselves Crimebusters and, in this adventure, solve the mystery of a cat that has been kidnapped. (Rev: BL 1/1–15/98)

7233 Howe, James. *Dew Drop Dead: A Sebastian Barth Mystery* (4–7). 1990, Macmillan $16.00 (0-689-31425-6). 160pp. A group of boys discover a corpse, but by the time the police arrive it has disappeared. (Rev: BL 3/1/90; SLJ 4/90)

7234 Hunt, L. J. *The Abernathy Boys* (5–7). 2004, HarperCollins LB $16.89 (0-06-029259-8). 208pp. Young Bud and Temple Abernathy survive an eventful journey through the desert in this fictionalized version of a real expedition in the early 20th century. (Rev: BL 1/1–15/04; SLJ 3/04)

7235 Hyde, Dayton O. *Mr. Beans* (5–7). 2000, Boyds Mills $14.95 (1-56397-866-0). 160pp. In a small town in Oregon in the early 1940s, bully Mugsy wrongfully accuses a tame bear of attacking him, and timid Chirp frees the bear and takes off with him on a wilderness journey. (Rev: BL 11/15/00; HBG 10/01; SLJ 1/01)

7236 Hyland, Hilary. *The Wreck of the Ethie* (4–7). Illus. by Paul Bachem. 1999, Peachtree paper $7.95 (1-56145-198-3). 115pp. Told through the eyes of two youngsters, this is a novelization of a true incident in which a dog saved passengers after their ship sank off the coast of Newfoundland. (Rev: SLJ 4/00)

7237 Jam, Teddy. *ttuM* (2–4). Illus. by Harvey Chan. Series: A Charlotte Novel. 1999, Groundwood $14.95 (0-88899-373-0); paper $5.95 (0-88899-374-9). 109pp. In this beginning chapter book, a little girl who speaks to her dog, ttuM, in reverse, solves a mystery about a strange person in black seen canoeing on the village lake. (Rev: SLJ 3/00)

7238 Jennings, Patrick. *The Bird Shadow: An Ike and Mem Story* (2–4). Illus. by Anna Alter. 2001, Holiday House $15.95 (0-8234-1670-4). 55pp. Ike and little sister Mem end up making a new friend when they dare to investigate a spooky old house. (Rev: HBG 10/02; SLJ 3/02)

7239 Johnson, Annabel, and Edgar Johnson. *The Grizzly* (5–7). Illus. by Gilbert Riswold. 1964, HarperCollins paper $4.95 (0-06-440036-0). 194pp. A perceptive story of a father-son relationship in which David, on a camping trip, saves his father's life when a grizzly bear attacks.

7240 Johnson, Rodney. *The Secret of Dead Man's Mine* (5–7). Illus. by Jill Thompson. Series: Rinnah Two Feathers Mystery. 2001, Uglytown paper $12.00 (0-9663473-3-1). 241pp. Rinnah Two Feathers and two friends set out to solve the mystery of a suspicious stranger and find themselves in danger. (Rev: SLJ 9/01)

7241 Joosse, Barbara M. *Alien Brain Fryout* (2–5). Illus. Series: Wild Willy Mystery. 2000, Clarion $15.00 (0-395-68964-3). 96pp. When the behavior of the neighborhood bully changes radically for the better, Willie and his friends think he might be under the control of extraterrestrials. (Rev: BL 9/15/00; HBG 3/01; SLJ 9/00)

7242 Joosse, Barbara M. *Ghost Trap: A Wild Willie Mystery* (3–5). Illus. 1998, Clarion $15.00 (0-395-66587-6). 69pp. An easily read mystery about three friends, Willie, Kyle, and Lucy, and mysterious happenings that occur in a house formerly owned by an amateur detective and now the home of Kyle and his family. (Rev: BCCB 7–8/98; BL 6/1–15/98; HB 7–8/98; HBG 10/98; SLJ 6/98)

7243 Karas, Phyllis. *For Lucky's Sake* (5–8). 1997, Avon paper $3.99 (0-380-78647-8). In this mystery with an animal rights theme, Benjy investigates a fire in which two greyhounds rescued from a research lab are killed. (Rev: BL 10/1/97)

7244 Karr, Kathleen. *Bone Dry* (5–8). 2002, Hyperion $15.99 (0-7868-0776-8). 240pp. Young Matthew assists phrenologist Asa B. Cornwall in a hunt for the skull of Alexander the Great in this action-packed adventure story, a sequel to *Skullduggery* (2000). (Rev: BCCB 10/02; BL 9/15/02; HBG 10/03; SLJ 8/02)

7245 Keene, Carolyn. *Where's Nancy?* (4–7). Series: Nancy Drew Super Mystery. 2005, Simon & Schuster paper $4.99 (0-4169-0034-9). 176pp. Nancy herself is missing in this first installment of a new series. (Rev: BL 5/1/05)

7246 Kehret, Peg. *Don't Tell Anyone* (4–7). 2000, Dutton $15.99 (0-525-46388-7). 144pp. After Megan sees a hit-and-run accident, she receives a threatening message in this adventure that also contains forgery, arson, and a kidnapping. (Rev: BCCB 5/00; BL 8/00; HBG 10/00; SLJ 4/00)

7247 Kehret, Peg. *Earthquake Terror* (4–7). 1998, Puffin paper $4.99 (0-14-038343-3). 144pp. A violent earthquake strikes the small island on which 12-year-old Jonathan is alone with his younger sister, Abby. (Rev: BCCB 3/96; BL 1/1–15/96; SLJ 2/96)

7248 Kehret, Peg. *Searching for Candlestick Park* (5–8). 1997, Dutton $14.99 (0-525-65256-6). 160pp. An adventure story about a boy who sets out from Seattle to find his father in San Francisco. (Rev: BL 8/97; BR 3–4/98; HBG 3/98; SLJ 9/97)

7249 Kehret, Peg. *The Stranger Next Door* (4–6). 2002, Dutton $15.99 (0-525-46829-3). 160pp. Twelve-year-old Alex discovers who's behind a spate of vandalism and arson in his new neighborhood, with the help of his feline friend Pete. (Rev: BL 2/1/02; HBG 10/02; SLJ 3/02)

7250 Kelleher, D. V. *Defenders of the Universe* (3–6). Illus. by Jane Brown. 1993, Houghton Mifflin $16.00 (0-395-60515-6). 128pp. Rachel is asked to join a crime-fighting club at her new school. (Rev: BL 3/15/93; SLJ 4/93)

7251 King-Smith, Dick. *Harry's Mad* (4–6). Illus. 1990, Macmillan $15.95 (0-7451-1101-7); Knopf paper $4.99 (0-679-88688-5). Mad the talking parrot is stolen, but the sharp-witted bird finally makes it back home. (Rev: BCCB 5/87; BL 7/87; SLJ 5/87)

7252 Kingman, Lee. *The Luck of the Miss L* (5–7). 1986, Houghton Mifflin $12.95 (0-685-11813-4). 160pp. Alec faces obstacles at every turn as he practices rowing for the Junior Rowers Race. (Rev: BCCB 9/86; BL 8/86; HB 5–6/86)

7253 Klise, Kate. *Trial by Jury Journal* (5–8). Illus. by M. Sarah Klise. 2001, HarperCollins LB $16.89 (0-06-029541-4). 256pp. When she is given the opportunity to serve as her state's first juvenile juror, 12-year-old Lily's sleuthing skills solve a murder mystery and save the day. (Rev: BCCB 4/01; BL 9/1/01; HB 5–6/01; HBG 10/01; SLJ 6/01)

7254 Konigsburg, E. L. *Silent to the Bone* (5–9). 2000, Simon & Schuster $16.00 (0-689-83601-5). 272pp. A mystery story filled with suspense about a baby who's been dropped and a 13-year-old suspect who has lost his ability to speak. (Rev: BL 8/00*; HB 11–12/00; HBG 3/01; SLJ 9/00)

7255 Korman, Gordon. *Chasing the Falconers* (4–7). 2005, Scholastic paper $5.99 (0-439-65136-0). 144pp. In this fast-paced adventure, Aiden and Meg Falconer must evade pursuers as they work to gather evidence that will prove their parents' innocence of treason. (Rev: BL 5/15/05)

7256 Kotzwinkle, William. *Trouble in Bugland: A Collection of Inspector Mantis Mysteries* (6–8). Illus. by Joe Servello. 1996, Godine paper $14.95 (1-56792-070-5). 160pp. An all-insect cast in a takeoff on Sherlock Holmes mysteries. A reissue.

7257 Krupinski, Loretta. *Lost in the Fog* (3–4). Illus. 1990, Little, Brown $14.95 (0-316-07462-4). 32pp. When their boat loaded with geese overturns, Mother Tipton thinks of a novel plan to save herself and Willie. (Rev: BL 5/1/90)

7258 Labatt, Mary. *The Ghost of Captain Briggs* (3–5). Illus. by Troy Hill-Jackson. Series: Sam, Dog Detective. 1999, Kids Can $12.95 (1-55074-638-3); paper $4.95 (1-55074-636-7). 116pp. Jenny learns to read the thoughts of sheepdog Samantha, and together they investigate a haunted house. Also use *Spying on Dracula* (1999). (Rev: HBG 3/00; SLJ 2/00)

7259 Lachtman, Ofelia Dumas. *Call Me Consuelo* (4–6). 1997, Arte Publico paper $9.95 (1-55885-187-9). 147pp. Consuelo, a recent arrival in Los Angeles, becomes involved in finding the criminals who are committing mysterious local robberies. (Rev: SLJ 7/97)

7260 Landon, Lucinda. *Meg Mackintosh and the Mystery at the Medieval Castle: A Solve-It-Yourself Mystery* (3–6). Illus. by author. 1989, Little, Brown paper $4.95 (0-316-51376-8). 64pp. While Meg and her class visit a castle, a jewel-encrusted chalice is stolen. Also use: *Meg Mackintosh and the Case of the Curious Whale Watch* (1987). (Rev: BL 6/15/89)

7261 Landon, Lucinda. *Meg Mackintosh and the Mystery at the Soccer Match* (3–6). Illus. by author.

Series: Solve-It-Yourself Mystery. 1997, Secret Passage paper $4.95 (1-888695-05-6). 48pp. Detective Meg and her soccer team are competing for a gold medal that suddenly disappears from the awards table. (Rev: SLJ 3/98)

7262 Landon, Lucinda. *Meg Mackintosh and the Mystery in the Locked Library: A Solve-It-Yourself Mystery* (3–6). Illus. 1996, Secret Passage paper $4.95 (1-888695-04-8). 48pp. Along with Meg Mackintosh, readers are asked to solve the mystery of the stolen rare book. (Rev: BL 2/1/93; SLJ 3/93)

7263 Lawrence, Caroline. *The Assassins of Rome* (5–8). Series: Roman Mysteries. 2003, Millbrook LB $22.90 (0-7613-2605-7). 163pp. In this fast-paced historical thriller, Flavia Gemina and her friends Nubia, Lupus, and Jonathan travel to Rome in an attempt to foil an assassination attempt. (Rev: BL 1/1–15/04; HBG 4/04; SLJ 1/04)

7264 Lawrence, Caroline. *The Secrets of Vesuvius* (4–6). 2002, Millbrook LB $22.90 (0-7613-2603-0). 192pp. Clever teen detective Flavia and her friends continue to solve mysteries in ancient Rome in this sequel to *The Thieves of Ostia* (2002) in which Pliny makes a cameo appearance and Vesuvius erupts. (Rev: BL 11/1/02; HBG 3/03; SLJ 11/02)

7265 Leavey, Peggy Dymond. *The Deep End Gang* (3–7). 2003, Napoleon paper $7.95 (0-929141-89-X). 125pp. Twelve-year-old Martin joins forces with two friends to investigate suspicious events at a deserted house in his neighborhood. (Rev: SLJ 9/03)

7266 Leonhardt, Alice. *Return of the Gypsy Witch* (5–7). 2003, Simon & Schuster paper $4.99 (0-689-85527-3). 176pp. An exciting mystery featuring two detecting sisters and five very valuable comic books. (Rev: BL 5/1/03; SLJ 4/03)

7267 Leroux, Gaston. *The Phantom of the Opera* (3–6). Illus. by Paul Jennis. 1989, Random paper $3.99 (0-394-83847-5). 48pp. An abridgment of this horror story about a defaced man who lives in the depths of an opera house. (Rev: SLJ 1/90)

7268 Levin, Betty. *Shadow-Catcher* (4–7). 2000, Greenwillow $15.95 (0-688-17862-6). 160pp. In Maine during the 1890s, young Jonathan Capewell has the opportunity to act the detective in a local mystery and behave like the heroes in the dime novels he reads. (Rev: BL 5/15/00*; HB 7–8/00; HBG 10/00; SLJ 6/00)

7269 Levin, Betty. *Shoddy Cove* (5–7). 2003, Greenwillow LB $16.89 (0-06-052272-0). 144pp. Clare, 12, is working at a living-history museum when she meets two strange children and must solve two mysteries from different centuries. (Rev: BL 7/03; HBG 10/03; SLJ 6/03)

7270 Levy, Elizabeth. *Frankenstein Moved In on the Fourth Floor* (2–4). Illus. by Mordicai Gerstein. 1979, HarperCollins paper $4.95 (0-06-440122-7). 64pp. Is the strange Mr. Frank really Frankenstein? A sequel is: *Dracula Is a Pain in the Neck* (1983).

7271 Lisle, Janet T. *A Message from the Match Girl* (4–6). Series: Investigators of the Unknown. 1995, Orchard LB $16.99 (0-531-08787-5). 128pp. Georgina and Poco wonder if the messages and mementos that Walter is receiving from the past are genuine. (Rev: BCCB 11/95; BL 10/1/95; SLJ 10/95*)

7272 Little, Kimberly Griffiths. *Enchanted Runner* (5–7). 1999, Avon $15.00 (0-380-97623-4). 160pp. Twelve-year-old Kendall, who is half Native American, hopes to excel in running as his ancestors did, and is given an unusual opportunity to test himself. (Rev: BCCB 9/99; BL 9/1/99; HBG 3/00; SLJ 12/99)

7273 Lloyd, Emily. *Catch of the Day: The Case of the Helpless Humpbacks* (4–6). Series: Kinetic City Super Crew. 1997, McGraw-Hill paper $4.25 (0-07-006390-7). 166pp. The Kinetic City Super Crew faces opposition from some fishermen when its members try various methods to discourage whales from swimming into fishing nets off the coast of Nova Scotia. (Rev: SLJ 7/98)

7274 Lloyd, Emily. *Forest Slump: The Case of the Pilfered Pine Needles* (3–5). 1997, McGraw-Hill paper $4.25 (0-07-006388-5). 150pp. Using a message from science as a basis, this novel tells how four youngsters solve the mystery of who has stolen the pine needles from the forest floor. (Rev: BL 2/15/98; SLJ 4/98)

7275 Lourie, Peter. *The Lost Treasure of Captain Kidd* (5–8). Illus. 1996, Shawangunk Pr. paper $10.95 (1-885482-03-5). 136pp. Friends Killian and Alex set out to discover Captain Kidd's treasure buried on the banks of the Hudson River centuries ago. (Rev: BL 2/15/96; SLJ 6/96)

7276 McClain, Margaret S. *Bellboy: A Mule Train Journey* (4–6). Illus. by Sara Brown Stuart. 1989, New Mexico Publg. $17.95 (0-9622468-1-6). 192pp. A young boy takes a job leading a mule train into isolated towns in northern California in the 1870s. (Rev: BL 3/1/90)

7277 Machado, Ana Maria. *From Another World* (4–7). Illus. by Lucia Brandao. 2005, Douglas & McIntyre $15.95 (0-88899-597-0). 128pp. Spending a night in an outbuilding of an old farmhouse, Mariano and his three friends meet the ghost of a 19th-century slave girl and promise to help in this story set in Brazil. (Rev: BL 5/1/05; SLJ 6/05)

7278 Mahy, Margaret. *Clancy's Cabin* (3–5). Illus. by Barbara Steadman. 1995, Overlook $14.95 (0-87951-592-9). 95pp. Two brothers and a sister spend a summer in a cabin in New Zealand and have great adventures, one of which involves finding a treasure. (Rev: SLJ 1/96)

7279 Mahy, Margaret. *The Pirate Uncle* (3–6). Illus. 1995, Overlook $14.95 (0-87951-555-4). 128pp. Nick and sister Caroline vacation with Uncle Ludovic, a pirate who is trying to reform. (Rev: BCCB 5/95; BL 4/15/95; SLJ 5/95)

7280 Mahy, Margaret. *Tangled Fortunes* (4–6). Illus. 1994, Delacorte $14.95 (0-385-32066-3). 105pp. The friendship between a brother and sister is explored in this mystery set in New Zealand. (Rev: BL 10/1/94; SLJ 11/94*)

7281 Maifair, Linda Lee. *The Case of the Bashed-Up Bicycle* (2–4). 1996, Zondervan paper $3.99 (0-310-20736-3). 64pp. Tomboy Darcy solves the mystery of who stripped down her brother's new

bicycle. Also use *The Case of the Nearsighted Neighbor* (1996). (Rev: BL 11/15/96)

7282 Markham, Marion M. *The April Fool's Day Mystery* (2–4). Illus. by Pau Estrada. 1991, Avon paper $3.50 (0-380-71716-6). 42pp. The detective twins Kate and Micky Dixon try to clear the name of Billy Wade, wrongfully accused of putting a snake in the school cafeteria's flour bin. (Rev: BL 7/91; SLJ 9/91)

7283 Markham, Marion M. *The Halloween Candy Mystery* (2–4). Illus. by Emily Arnold McCully. 1982, Avon paper $2.95 (0-380-70965-1). 48pp. The Dixon twins and their brother solve the mystery of a Halloween thief. Another mystery is: *The Christmas Present Mystery* (1984).

7284 Markham, Marion M. *The Thanksgiving Day Parade Mystery* (3–4). Illus. 1986, Avon paper $2.95 (0-380-70967-8). 48pp. Twins Kate and Mickey track down the disappearance of the school band on the way to the Macy's Thanksgiving Day Parade. Also use: *The Birthday Party Mystery* (1989). (Rev: BCCB 11/86; BL 9/15/86; SLJ 11/86)

7285 Martin, Les. *Humbug* (5–8). Series: X-Files. 1996, HarperCollins paper $3.95 (0-06-440627-X). Even for veteran FBI agents Fox Mulder and Dana Scully, the murder of "The Alligator Man" is bizarre. (Rev: SLJ 6/96)

7286 Martin, Terri. *A Family Trait* (5–7). 1999, Holiday House $15.95 (0-8234-1467-1). 156pp. In this fast-paced story, Iris, 11 years old and incurably curious, has a number of mysteries to solve while trying to finish a book report. (Rev: BL 10/1/99; HBG 3/00; SLJ 10/99)

7287 Matas, Carol. *Rosie in Los Angeles: Action!* (3–6). 2004, Simon & Schuster paper $4.99 (0-689-85716-0). 128pp. An action story set in California in the early 20th century and starring the same lively young Rosie as two earlier books. (Rev: SLJ 3/04)

7288 Mazer, Harry. *Snow Bound* (5–7). 1987, Dell $20.25 (0-8446-6240-2); paper $5.50 (0-440-96134-3). Tony and Cindy survive for several days after being trapped in a snow storm. (Rev: BL 9/1/89)

7289 Meacham, Margaret. *Oyster Moon* (3–6). Illus. by Marcy Ramsey. 1996, Cornell Maritime paper $9.95 (0-87033-459-X). 112pp. Anna, who is able to communicate through telepathy with her twin brother, Toby, receives messages indicating that he is in danger. (Rev: SLJ 11/96)

7290 Medearis, Angela Shelf. *The Spray-Paint Mystery* (3–5). 1996, Scholastic paper $3.99 (0-590-48474-5). 102pp. A young African American third-grader sets out to find the culprit who is spray-painting a wall in his school. (Rev: BL 2/15/97; SLJ 4/97)

7291 Mitchell, Marianne. *Finding Zola* (5–8). 2003, Boyds Mills $16.95 (1-59078-070-1). 144pp. A 13-year-old girl in a wheelchair investigates the disappearance of an elderly woman who has been staying with her. (Rev: BL 5/15/03; HBG 10/03; SLJ 2/03)

7292 Mitchell, Marianne. *Firebug* (5–8). 2004, Boyds Mills $16.95 (1-59078-170-8). 164pp. Twelve-year-old Haley investigates a suspicious fire at her Uncle Jake's Arizona ranch. (Rev: BL 3/15/04; SLJ 2/04)

7293 Mitchell, Nancy. *Global Warning: Attack on the Pacific Rim!* (5–8). Illus. by Darren Wiebe and Ryan T. Fong. Series: The Changing Earth Trilogy. 1999, Lightstream paper $5.95 (1-892713-02-0). 191pp. A thrilling adventure story about Jenny Powers, a wheelchair-bound youngster, who must warn the authorities of an impending biological disaster at her school. (Rev: SLJ 10/99)

7294 Morpurgo, Michael. *Kensuke's Kingdom* (4–7). 2003, Scholastic paper $16.95 (0-439-38202-5). 176pp. A boy washed onto a seemingly deserted island finds a friend in a Japanese solider who has lived there since World War II. (Rev: BL 2/15/03; HB 5–6/03; HBG 10/03; SLJ 3/03)

7295 Mundis, Hester. *My Chimp Friday* (4–7). 2002, Simon & Schuster $16.00 (0-689-83837-9). 176pp. Rachel and her family grow to love their new pet, a chimp named Friday, but when kidnappers try to steal Friday, Rachel realizes he is not an ordinary chimp. (Rev: BL 6/1–15/02; HBG 10/02; SLJ 6/02)

7296 Murphy, Elspeth C. *The Mystery of the Dancing Angels* (2–5). Illus. 1995, Bethany House paper $3.99 (1-55661-408-X). 64pp. The Three Cousins Detective Club sets out to solve the mystery involving a 4-year-old distant cousin and a family riddle. (Rev: BL 10/1/95; SLJ 9/95)

7297 Murphy, Elspeth C. *The Mystery of the Haunted Lighthouse* (2–4). Illus. by Joe Nordstrom. Series: Three Cousins Detective Club. 1995, Bethany House paper $3.99 (1-55661-411-X). 64pp. The Three Cousins Detective Club visits an abandoned lighthouse and decides it is haunted. (Rev: BL 12/15/95)

7298 Murphy, Elspeth C. *The Mystery of the Hobo's Message* (2–4). Illus. 1995, Bethany House paper $3.99 (1-55661-409-8). 64pp. Five youngsters use coded messages to foil a plot by developers to take over property dishonestly. (Rev: BL 10/15/95; SLJ 11/95)

7299 Murphy, T. M. *The Secrets of Code Z* (4–8). Series: A Belltown Mystery. 2001, J. N. Townsend paper $9.95 (1-880158-33-7). 144pp. Orville Jacques becomes embroiled in a fast-paced mystery involving CIA cover-ups, a death powder, and an evil Russian. (Rev: BL 5/15/01; SLJ 7/01)

7300 Murphy, T. M. *The Secrets of Cranberry Beach* (5–8). Series: A Belltown Mystery. 1996, Silver Burdett paper $4.95 (0-382-39303-1). After an encounter with the murderer that almost costs him his life, amateur detective 16-year-old Orville Jacques solves a baffling crime. (Rev: SLJ 1/97)

7301 Murrow, Liza Ketchum. *The Ghost of Lost Island* (4–6). 1991, Holiday House $15.95 (0-8234-0874-4). 176pp. Gabe and his sister try to solve the mystery of a drowned dairymaid on Lost Island. (Rev: BCCB 5/91; BL 4/15/91; SLJ 5/91)

7302 Napoli, Donna Jo. *North* (4–7). 2004, Greenwillow $15.99 (0-06-057987-0). 352pp. Twelve-year-old Alvin, an African American boy fascinated by explorer Matthew Henson, sets off for the Arctic and, with the help of several adults along the way,

makes the long and complex journey safely. (Rev: BL 3/1/04; SLJ 5/04)

7303 Napoli, Donna Jo. *Three Days* (4–6). 2001, Dutton $15.99 (0-525-46790-4). 176pp. A harrowing story full of advice on keeping safe in which 11-year-old Jackie is kidnapped on a trip to Italy after her father dies at the wheel of their car. (Rev: BCCB 11/01; BL 10/1/01; HB 9–10/01; HBG 3/02; SLJ 8/01*)

7304 Napoli, Donna Jo. *Trouble on the Tracks* (5–7). 1997, Scholastic paper $14.95 (0-590-13447-7). 190pp. Zach and his younger sister are embroiled in an Australian adventure involving smugglers and survival in a desert. (Rev: BCCB 3/97; BL 2/1/97; SLJ 3/97)

7305 Naylor, Phyllis Reynolds. *Bernie Magruder and the Bats in the Belfry* (4–7). 2003, Simon & Schuster $16.95 (0-689-85066-2). 144pp. Bernie is investigating a bat with a fatal bite; could it be connected to the fact that the bells in the belfry are annoyingly stuck on the same tune? (Rev: BL 1/1–15/03; HBG 10/03; SLJ 4/03)

7306 Naylor, Phyllis Reynolds. *Peril in the Bessledorf Parachute Factory* (4–6). 2000, Simon & Schuster $16.00 (0-689-82539-0). 148pp. In this Bessledorf Hotel adventure, Bernie Magruder tries to marry off his sister so he can have her room. (Rev: BL 1/1–15/00; HBG 3/01; SLJ 2/00)

7307 Naylor, Phyllis Reynolds. *The Treasure of Bessledorf Hill* (3–5). 1998, Simon & Schuster $15.00 (0-689-81337-6). 136pp. In this Bessledorf mystery, Bernie decides to follow clues he hopes will lead to buried treasure. (Rev: BL 1/1–15/98; HB 7/04; HBG 10/98; SLJ 3/98)

7308 Newman, Robert. *The Case of the Baker Street Irregular: A Sherlock Holmes Story* (4–6). 1984, Macmillan paper $4.95 (0-689-70766-5). Young Andrew unexpectedly finds himself teamed up with Sherlock Holmes.

7309 Nickerson, Sara. *How to Disappear Completely and Never Be Found* (4–8). Illus. by Sally Wern Comport. 2002, HarperCollins LB $15.89 (0-06-029772-7). 288pp. Two youngsters with problems, 12-year-old Margaret and her friend Boyd, explore a deserted mansion and solve the mystery of the supernatural terrors it supposedly contains. (Rev: BCCB 5/02; BL 4/1/02; HB 7–8/02; HBG 10/02; SLJ 4/02)

7310 Nixon, Joan Lowery. *Ghost Town* (4–7). 2000, Delacorte $14.95 (0-385-32681-5). 149pp. This collection of stories combines the author's flair for writing mysteries with an interest in the Wild West. (Rev: BL 9/1/00; HBG 3/01; SLJ 10/00)

7311 Nixon, Joan Lowery. *The Trap* (5–8). 2002, Delacorte LB $17.99 (0-385-90063-5). 192pp. A gripping mystery in which 16-year-old Julie investigates deaths and missing jewelry, and faces danger herself. (Rev: BL 9/15/02; HBG 3/03; SLJ 9/02)

7312 Nolan, Peggy. *The Spy Who Came in from the Sea* (4–8). 1999, Pineapple $14.95 (1-56164-186-3). 129pp. In this adventure story set in World War II Florida, 14-year-old Frank, who has a reputation for lying, is not believed when he claims to have seen a

German sub off the coast. (Rev: HBG 3/00; SLJ 1/00)

7313 Obrist, Jurg. *Case Closed?! 40 Mini-Mysteries for You to Solve* (2–5). Illus. 2003, Millbrook LB $22.90 (0-7613-2739-8). 80pp. Readers help young detectives Daisy and Ridley solve mysteries involving puzzles, codes, and other challenges. (Rev: BL 2/15/04; HBG 4/04; SLJ 2/04)

7314 O'Dell, Scott. *Black Star, Bright Dawn* (5–8). 1988, Houghton Mifflin $17.00 (0-395-47778-6); Fawcett paper $6.50 (0-449-70340-1). 144pp. An Inuit girl decides to run the 1,197-mile sled dog race called the Iditarod. (Rev: BCCB 6/88; BL 4/1/88; BR 9–10/88; SLJ 5/88)

7315 O'Dell, Scott. *Island of the Blue Dolphins* (5–8). 1960, Houghton Mifflin $16.00 (0-395-06962-9); Dell paper $6.50 (0-440-43988-4). 192pp. An Indian girl spends 18 years alone on an island off the coast of California in the 1800s. Newbery Medal winner, 1961. A sequel is *Zia* (1976). (Rev: BL 3/1/88)

7316 Otis, James. *Toby Tyler: Or Ten Weeks with a Circus* (4–6). 1981, Buccaneer LB $25.95 (0-89966-363-X); Dover paper $2.00 (0-486-29349-1). 152pp. A perennial favorite about a subject popular with most children.

7317 Parkinson, Curtis. *Storm-Blast* (4–8). 2003, Tundra paper $7.95 (0-88776-630-7). 156pp. On a sailing trip in the Caribbean, three teens become stranded in a small dinghy and must use their resources to survive. (Rev: SLJ 10/03)

7318 Patneaude, David. *The Last Man's Reward* (5–8). 1996, Whitman LB $14.95 (0-8075-4370-5). 185pp. In this adventure, a group of boys agree to a pact rewarding the last to leave the neighborhood. (Rev: BL 6/1–15/96; SLJ 7/96)

7319 Patneaude, David. *Someone Was Watching* (5–8). Illus. by Paul Micich. 1993, Whitman LB $14.95 (0-8075-7531-3). 221pp. Chris and his friend disobey parental orders and fly to Florida to rescue Chris's younger sister from kidnappers. (Rev: SLJ 7/93)

7320 Paulsen, Gary. *Brian's Winter* (5–9). 1996, Delacorte $15.95 (0-385-32198-8). In a reworking of the ending of *Hatchet,* in which Brian Robeson is rescued after surviving a plane crash, this novel tells what would have happened had Brian had to survive a harsh winter in the wilderness. (Rev: BL 12/15/95; BR 5–6/96; SLJ 2/96)

7321 Paulsen, Gary. *Escape from Fire Mountain* (4–6). Series: Culpepper Adventure. 1995, Dell paper $3.99 (0-440-41025-8). 67pp. An adventure story in which a young girl faces incredible challenges to rescue two lost children. (Rev: SLJ 7/95)

7322 Penn, Audrey. *Mystery at Blackbeard's Cove* (5–8). Illus. by Joshua Miller. 2004, Tanglewood $14.95 (0-9749303-1-8). 360pp. The death of Mrs. McNemmish, a descendant of Blackbeard the pirate, sets in motion a series of adventures for four young residents of Okracoke Island. (Rev: BL 1/1–15/05)

7323 Philbrick, Rodman. *The Young Man and the Sea* (5–6). 2004, Scholastic $16.95 (0-439-36829-4). 192pp. With a nod to Hemingway, this is the story of Skiff, a 12-year-old boy living in Maine, who seeks to solve his problems by catching a giant bluefin tuna. (Rev: BL 1/1–15/04; HB 3–4/04; SLJ 2/04)

7324 Pilling, Ann. *The Year of the Worm* (5–7). 2000, Lion paper $7.50 (0-7459-4294-6). 172pp. Lonely Peter Wrigley, who is mourning his father's death, gets his chance to become a hero when he uncovers a group of birds'-nest poachers in this English novel set in the Lake District. (Rev: SLJ 3/01)

7325 Ransome, Arthur. *Swallows and Amazons* (4–7). Illus. by author. 1985, Godine paper $14.95 (0-87923-573-X). 352pp. These adventures of the four Walker children have been read for many years. A reissue. Others in the series *Swallowdale* (1985); *Peter Duck* (1987).

7326 Ransome, Arthur. *Winter Holiday* (4–7). Illus. by author. 1989, Godine paper $14.95 (0-87923-661-2). Further adventures of the Swallows and Amazons. A reissue. A sequel is *Coot Club.*

7327 Rau, Dana Meachen. *One Giant Leap* (3–5). Illus. by Thomas Buchs. Series: Odyssey. 1996, Smithsonian Institution $14.95 (1-56899-343-9); paper $5.95 (1-58899-344-7). 32pp. The first moon landing is described in a fictional account in which a young boy believes he is Neil Armstrong. (Rev: BL 10/15/96)

7328 Reiche, Dietlof. *Ghost Ship* (5–8). Trans. by John Brownjohn. 2005, Scholastic $16.95 (0-439-59704-8). 336pp. A suspenseful adventure featuring ghosts, piracy, buried treasure, and romance between 12-year-old Vicki and a boy on vacation in her seaside town. (Rev: BL 5/15/05)

7329 Repp, Gloria. *Mik-Shrok* (4–8). Illus. by Jim Brooks. 1998, Bob Jones Univ. paper $6.49 (1-57924-069-0). 133pp. A married missionary couple journey to a remote Alaska village in 1950, where they begin their work and, in time, acquire a dog team led by Mik-Shrok. (Rev: BL 3/1/99)

7330 Riehecky, Janet. *The Mystery of the Missing Money* (4–6). Illus. 1996, Forest House LB $12.95 (1-56674-087-8); paper $5.95 (1-56674-701-2). 120pp. Twins Karen and Kyle investigate strange lights and noises in an empty old house. (Rev: BL 7/96; SLJ 7/96)

7331 Riehecky, Janet. *The Mystery of the UFO* (4–6). Illus. 1996, Forest House LB $12.95 (1-56674-088-6); paper $6.95 (1-56674-702-3). 128pp. Rumors of UFO sightings bring twins Karen and Kyle to a campground to investigate. (Rev: BL 7/96; SLJ 7/96)

7332 Roberts, Willo Davis. *Baby-Sitting Is a Dangerous Job* (5–7). 1987, Fawcett paper $6.50 (0-449-70177-8). 192pp. Darcy tries to cope with three bratty children, but a kidnapping puts her and her charges in the hands of three dangerous men. (Rev: BCCB 3/85; BL 5/1/85; SLJ 5/85)

7333 Roberts, Willo Davis. *Hostage* (4–7). Illus. 2000, Simon & Schuster $16.00 (0-689-81669-3). 144pp. When she returns home unexpectedly from school, Kaci is taken hostage, along with a snoopy neighbor, by a gang of thieves. (Rev: BCCB 2/00; BL 2/1/00; HBG 3/01; SLJ 2/00)

7334 Robinson, Mary. *The Amazing Valvano and the Mystery of the Hooded Rat* (4–6). 1990, Avon paper $2.75 (0-380-70713-6). 168pp. Maria's plans for her great magic act go astray when Lester the rat is stolen. (Rev: BL 6/15/88; SLJ 4/88)

7335 Rocklin, Joanne. *Sonia Begonia* (4–6). Illus. by Julie Downing. 1986, Avon paper $2.50 (0-380-70307-6). 96pp. Sonia Begley wants to follow in her family's footsteps and open her own business, which she does with some amusing results. (Rev: BCCB 3/86; BL 3/15/86; SLJ 5/86)

7336 Rogo, Thomas Paul. *A Surfrider's Odyssey* (5–8). Illus. by author. 1999, Bess Pr. $19.95 (1-57306-082-8). 64pp. Set in the 1940s, this old-fashioned novel tells how a boy teaches himself to surf and later becomes a hero when he rescues a woman whose sailboat has capsized. (Rev: HBG 10/99; SLJ 8/99)

7337 Roy, Ron. *The Deadly Dungeon* (2–4). Illus. by John S. Gurney. Series: A to Z Mysteries. 1998, Random LB $11.99 (0-679-98755-X); paper $3.99 (0-679-88755-5). 86pp. Dink, Josh, and Ruth Rose uncover a mystery when they travel to Maine to visit a castle. (Rev: SLJ 10/98)

7338 Roy, Ron. *The Goose's Gold* (2–4). Illus. by John S. Gurney. Series: Stepping Stone. 1999, Random paper $3.99 (0-679-89078-5). 86pp. An easy chapter book mystery in which three young sleuths overhear a man planning a robbery and set out to foil his plot. (Rev: BL 10/15/99; HBG 10/99; SLJ 7/99)

7339 Ruckman, Ivy. *Night of the Twisters* (4–6). 1984, HarperCollins LB $15.89 (0-690-04409-7); paper $4.95 (0-06-440176-6). 160pp. An 11-year-old boy witnesses a series of tornadoes that destroy his Nebraska town.

7340 Ruckman, Ivy. *Spell It M-U-R-D-E-R* (4–6). 1994, Bantam paper $3.50 (0-553-48175-4). 160pp. Two girls stumble upon a murderer when they try to escape from a summer camp they detest. (Rev: BL 7/94; SLJ 8/94)

7341 Sachar, Louis. *Holes* (5–8). 1998, Farrar $16.00 (0-374-33265-7). 240pp. This Newbery Award-winning novel describes unfortunate Stanley Yelnats's stay at a juvenile detention home after he has been wrongfully found guilty of stealing a pair of sneakers. (Rev: HB 9–10/98*; HBG 3/99; SLJ 9/98*)

7342 Scieszka, Jon. *Knights of the Kitchen Table* (3–5). Illus. by Lane Smith. 1991, Viking $14.99 (0-670-83622-2). 64pp. The Time Warp Trio hangs out with Lancelot and his pals. Also use: *The Not-So-Jolly Roger* (1991). (Rev: BCCB 7–8/91; BL 5/1/91; SLJ 8/91*)

7343 Seidler, Tor. *Brainboy and the Deathmaster* (4–7). 2003, HarperCollins LB $17.89 (0-06-029182-6). 320pp. Recently orphaned in a fire, Darryl, a 12-year-old video game expert, finds himself in a shelter run by a man who plans to exploit the children's technological knowhow. (Rev: BL 9/15/03; HBG 4/04; SLJ 10/03)

7344 Selznick, Brian. *The Boy of a Thousand Faces* (4–7). Illus. 2000, HarperCollins $14.95 (0-06-026265-6). 48pp. Ten-year-old Alonzo King has a fixation on horror movies and makeup disguises, both of which help him when the The Beast comes to town. (Rev: BL 9/15/00; HBG 3/01; SLJ 9/00)

7345 Shands, Linda. *Wild Fire* (4–6). 2001, Revell paper $5.99 (0-8007-5746-7). 176pp. Wakara, a 15-year-old of American Indian and Irish parentage, is still mourning her mother's death when she and her brother become trapped by a forest fire. (Rev: BL 5/1/01)

7346 Shearer, Alex. *Sea Legs* (4–6). 2005, Simon & Schuster $15.95 (0-689-87143-0). 320pp. Twins Clive and Eric stow away on the cruise sip where their father works and end up fighting pirates in this entertaining story. (Rev: BL 3/15/05; SLJ 3/05)

7347 Shura, Mary Francis. *Don't Call Me Toad!* (4–6). Illus. by Jacqueline Rogers. 1987, Avon paper $2.95 (0-380-70496-X). Jane and Dinah have a rocky relationship at first and become involved in a mystery about robberies that sweep a town. (Rev: BCCB 7–8/87; BL 5/15/87; SLJ 4/87)

7348 Simon, Seymour. *The On-Line Spaceman and Other Cases* (3–6). Illus. 1997, Morrow $15.00 (0-688-14433-0). 96pp. Using deduction and an advanced knowledge of science, 12-year-old Einstein Anderson solves ten short mysteries. (Rev: BL 5/1/97; SLJ 4/97)

7349 Skurzynski, Gloria, and Alane Ferguson. *Buried Alive* (4–7). Series: Mysteries in Our National Parks. 2003, National Geographic $15.95 (0-7922-6966-7); paper $5.95 (0-7922-6968-3). 146pp. A hit man and an avalanche are only two of the challenges Jack and Ashley face while on vacation with their parents in Denali National Park. (Rev: HBG 10/03; SLJ 12/03)

7350 Skurzynski, Gloria, and Alane Ferguson. *Cliff-Hanger* (4–7). 1999, National Geographic $15.95 (0-7922-7036-3). 152pp. In Mesa Verde National Park, the Landon family encounters two problems — a foster care girl named Lucky, who is deceitful, and a rampaging cougar. (Rev: BL 4/15/99; HBG 10/99; SLJ 5/99)

7351 Skurzynski, Gloria, and Alane Ferguson. *Deadly Waters* (4–7). Illus. Series: Mysteries in Our National Parks. 1999, National Geographic $15.95 (0-7922-7037-1). 160pp. The Landon kids — Jack, Ashley, and foster brother, Bridger — travel to the Florida Everglades where their parents are investigating the mysterious deaths of some manatees. (Rev: BL 10/15/99; HBG 3/00; SLJ 10/99)

7352 Skurzynski, Gloria, and Alane Ferguson. *Ghost Horses* (4–6). Illus. Series: National Parks Mystery. 2000, National Geographic $15.95 (0-7922-7055-X). 152pp. Horses that are behaving strangely, a flash flood, and interpersonal conflicts are three of the elements in this mystery story set in Utah's Zion National Park. (Rev: BL 12/15/00; HBG 3/01; SLJ 11/00)

7353 Skurzynski, Gloria, and Alane Ferguson. *The Hunted* (5–8). Illus. Series: Mysteries in Our National Parks. 2000, National Geographic $15.95

(0-7922-7053-3). 160pp. The Landon family sets out to discover why young grizzly bears are disappearing from Glacier National Park. (Rev: BL 6/1–15/00; HBG 10/00; SLJ 8/00)

7354 Skurzynski, Gloria, and Alane Ferguson. *Rage of Fire* (4–6). Illus. Series: National Parks Mystery. 1998, National Geographic $15.95 (0-7922-7035-5). 160pp. While visiting Devastation Trail in Hawaii Volcanoes National Park, Jack Landon, his sister, and their friend, a Vietnamese youngster, realize they are being stalked by a mysterious woman in red. (Rev: BL 6/1–15/98; HBG 10/98; SLJ 7/98)

7355 Skurzynski, Gloria, and Alane Ferguson. *Wolf Stalker* (5–8). Series: Mysteries in Our National Parks. 1997, National Geographic $15.00 (0-7922-7034-7). Three youngsters solve the mystery of who is killing the wolves of Yellowstone Park. (Rev: BR 3–4/98; HBG 3/98; SLJ 1/98)

7356 Smith, Roland. *Cryptid Hunters* (5–8). 2005, Hyperion $15.99 (0-7868-5161-9). 352pp. Thirteen-year-old twins Marty and Grace find themselves in an action-packed adventure in the Congo. (Rev: BL 2/1/05; SLJ 5/05)

7357 Smith, Roland. *Jaguar* (5–8). 1997, Hyperion $16.49 (0-7868-2226-0). 192pp. When Jake visits his zoologist father at a jaguar preserve in Brazil, he gets involved in a mystery and, at one point, must survive alone in the Amazon jungle. A sequel to *Thunder Cave*. (Rev: BL 5/15/97; BR 1–2/98; SLJ 6/97)

7358 Snicket, Lemony. *The Ersatz Elevator* (3–6). Illus. Series: A Series of Unfortunate Events. 2001, HarperCollins LB $14.89 (0-06-028889-2). 266pp. Count Olaf soon finds the Baudelaire orphans at their new home, chez Mr. and Mrs. Squalor. (Rev: BL 8/01; HBG 10/01; SLJ 8/01)

7359 Snicket, Lemony. *The Hostile Hospital* (4–6). Illus. by Brett Helquist. Series: A Series of Unfortunate Events. 2001, HarperCollins LB $9.89 (0-06-028891-4). 272pp. The Baudelaire children face danger and intrigue in their quest to find out more about their dead parents. (Rev: BL 10/15/01; HBG 3/02; SLJ 11/01)

7360 Snicket, Lemony. *The Miserable Mill* (4–6). Series: A Series of Unfortunate Events. 2000, HarperCollins LB $14.89 (0-06-028315-7). 128pp. The unfortunate Baudelaire orphans are forced to work in a lumber mill in this entertaining segment of the ongoing melodrama set in mock-Victorian times. (Rev: BL 5/1/00; HBG 10/00; SLJ 7/00)

7361 Snicket, Lemony. *The Slippery Slope* (3–5). Illus. by Brett Helquist. 2003, HarperCollins LB $14.89 (0-06-029641-0). 337pp. In this episode in the continuing saga, Violet and Klaus get help from a stranger as they seek to free Sunny from the clutches of Count Olaf and find the "last safe place." (Rev: BL 1/1–15/04; HBG 4/04; SLJ 1/04)

7362 Snicket, Lemony. *The Vile Village* (3–6). Illus. Series: A Series of Unfortunate Events. 2001, HarperCollins LB $14.89 (0-06-028890-6). 272pp. Aphorisms abound as a village decides to raise three children and takes on the Baudelaire orphans. (Rev: BL 8/01; HBG 3/02; SLJ 8/01)

7363 Sobol, Donald J. *Encyclopedia Brown and the Case of the Disgusting Sneakers* (3–5). Illus. by Gail Owens. 1990, Morrow $15.95 (0-688-09012-5). 68pp. Ten new cases just as hard to solve and as much fun as previous brainteasers. (Rev: BCCB 12/90; BL 9/15/90; SLJ 1/91)

7364 Sobol, Donald J. *Encyclopedia Brown and the Case of the Jumping Frogs* (4–6). Illus. 2003, Delacorte $14.95 (0-385-72931-6). 96pp. The 10-year-old sleuth cracks another bunch of not-so-easy cases in this new entry in a long series. (Rev: BL 2/1/04; HBG 4/04)

7365 Sobol, Donald J. *Encyclopedia Brown and the Case of the Mysterious Handprints* (3–5). Illus. 1985, Morrow $16.00 (0-688-04626-6). 96pp. Matching wits with the 10-year-old sleuth in ten more crime cases. Also use: *Encyclopedia Brown and the Case of the Secret Pitch* (1978, Bantam); *Encyclopedia Brown Lends a Hand* (1979, Dutton); *Encyclopedia Brown and the Case of the Treasure Hunt* (1988). (Rev: BL 11/15/85; SLJ 2/86)

7366 Sobol, Donald J. *Encyclopedia Brown, Boy Detective* (3–5). Illus. by Leonard Shortall and Lillian Brandi. 1979, Bantam paper $4.50 (0-553-15724-8). 96pp. Ten-year-old Leroy Brown opens his own detective agency and solves ten crimes. Some sequels are: *Encyclopedia Brown and the Case of the Dead Eagles* (1977); *Encyclopedia Brown Finds the Clues; Encyclopedia Brown Gets His Man; Encyclopedia Brown Keeps the Peace* (all 1979); *Encyclopedia Brown Sets the Pace* (1984).

7367 Soto, Gary. *Crazy Weekend* (4–7). 1994, Scholastic paper $13.95 (0-590-47814-1). 143pp. Two boys are being pursued by some crooks in this fast-moving adventure story. (Rev: BCCB 7–8/94; SLJ 3/94)

7368 Sperry, Armstrong. *Call It Courage* (5–8). Illus. by author. 1968, Macmillan $16.95 (0-02-786030-2); paper $4.99 (0-689-71391-6). 96pp. The "Crusoe" theme is interwoven with this story of a Polynesian boy's courage in facing the sea he feared. Newbery Medal winner, 1941.

7369 Spirn, Michele. *The Bridges in London: Going to London* (5–7). Series: Going To. 2000, Four Corners paper $7.95 (1-893577-00-7). 96pp. When two sisters fly to London with their parents, they become involved in a mystery when they find a suitcase full of knives. (Rev: SLJ 3/00)

7370 Springer, Nancy. *Lionclaw* (5–8). Series: Tales of Rowan Hood. 2002, Penguin Putnam $16.99 (0-399-23716-X). 128pp. Gentle, music-loving Lionel abandons his timidity when Rowan Hood is captured, but, despite his newfound courage, his father still refuses to accept him in this sequel to *Rowan Hood: Outlaw Girl of Sherwood Forest* (2001). (Rev: BL 10/1/02; HBG 10/03; SLJ 10/02)

7371 Springer, Nancy. *Outlaw Princess of Sherwood* (4–7). Series: Tales of Rowan Hood. 2003, Penguin Putnam $16.99 (0-399-23721-6). 160pp. The third installment of this series features Princess Ettarde, whose father has hatched a dastardly plot to lure Etty away from Sherwood Forest. (Rev: BL 12/1/03; HBG 4/04; SLJ 9/03)

7372 Springer, Nancy. *Rowan Hood: Outlaw Girl of Sherwood Forest* (4–7). Series: Tales of Rowan Hood. 2001, Penguin Putnam $16.99 (0-399-23368-7). 208pp. A young girl finds adventure when she journeys to Sherwood Forest to find the father she doesn't know, Robin Hood. (Rev: BL 4/15/01; HBG 10/01; SLJ 7/01)

7373 Springer, Nancy. *Wild Boy: A Tale of Rowan Hood* (3–6). 2004, Penguin Putnam $16.99 (0-399-24015-2). 160pp. Rook, part of Robin Hood's merry band of outlaws, finds himself torn between vengeance and compassion when the son of his father's killer is captured. (Rev: BL 5/15/04; SLJ 8/04)

7374 Stanley, George. *The Case of the Dirty Clue* (2–4). Illus. by Salvatore Murdocca. Series: Ready-for-Chapters. 2003, Aladdin LB $11.89 (0-689-86358-6). 80pp. Misty's bike has been run over, and the Third-Grade Detectives and their ex-spy teacher sweep into action, regarding soil samples as a key clue. (Rev: BL 2/1/04; HBG 4/04)

7375 Stanley, George E. *The Clue of the Left-Handed Envelope* (2–3). Illus. by Sal Murdocca. Series: Third-Grade Detectives. 2000, Simon & Schuster paper $3.99 (0-689-82194-8). 80pp. Noelle and Todd together with the other third graders and their teacher, Mr. Merlin, unmask the identity of the person who has sent Amber Lee a secret-admirer letter. (Rev: BCCB 12/00; SLJ 2/01)

7376 Steiner, Barbara. *Foghorn Flattery and the Dancing Horses* (4–6). 1991, Avon paper $2.95 (0-380-76147-5). 108pp. Carly and brother Foghorn travel to Vienna and encounter a mystery. (Rev: BL 6/15/91)

7377 Stem, Jacqueline. *The Cellar in the Woods* (4–6). 1997, Eakin $14.95 (1-57168-115-9). 145pp. In East Texas, three cousins explore a deserted house and encounter danger. (Rev: SLJ 1/98)

7378 Stengel, Joyce A. *Mystery of the Island Jewels* (5–8). 2002, Simon & Schuster paper $4.99 (0-689-85049-2). 199pp. On a cruise to Martinique with her father and new stepfamily, 14-year-old Cassie and new friend Charles uncover a mystery. (Rev: SLJ 6/02)

7379 Stevenson, James. *The Bones in the Cliff* (4–7). 1995, Greenwillow $15.99 (0-688-13745-8). 128pp. Pete is sure that a hit man is stalking his father at their home on Cutlass Island. (Rev: BCCB 6/95; BL 5/1/95*; SLJ 4/95)

7380 Stevenson, James. *The Unprotected Witness* (4–7). 1997, Greenwillow $15.00 (0-688-15133-7). 176pp. In this sequel to *The Bones in the Cliff*, Pete and his friend Rootie try to unravel the mystery of where a treasure is buried by seeking cludes in a letter from Pete's dead father. (Rev: BL 10/1/97*; HB 11–12/97; HBG 3/98; SLJ 9/97)

7381 Stine, R. L. *The Wrong Number* (5–9). 1990, Pocket paper $4.99 (0-671-69411-1). While making a crank telephone call, a teenager hears a murder being committed. (Rev: SLJ 6/90)

7382 Stolz, Mary. *Casebook of a Private (Cat's) Eye* (3–5). Illus. 1999, Front Street $14.95 (0-8126-2650-8). 128pp. Eileen O'Kelly, a cat detective from Boston, solves a number of short mysteries in

this novel set in 1912. (Rev: BCCB 6/99; BL 4/15/99; HBG 10/99; SLJ 6/99)

7383 Stray, P. J. *Secrets of the Mayan Ruins* (4–6). Series: Passport to Mystery. 1995, Silver Burdett LB $13.95 (0-382-24704-3); paper $4.95 (0-382-24705-1). 139pp. Three teenagers join forces to solve the mystery of the stolen Mayan artifacts in this mystery set in Mexico. (Rev: SLJ 9/95)

7384 Strickland, Brad. *The Tower at the End of the World* (4–6). Series: Lewis Barnavelt. 2001, Dial $16.99 (0-8037-2620-1). 144pp. Lewis Barnavelt is back, this time solving a spooky mystery (and thereby saving the world) while vacationing in Michigan with his uncle and their friends. (Rev: BL 9/1/01; HBG 3/02; SLJ 9/01)

7385 Sukach, Jim. *Clever Quicksolve Whodunit Puzzles* (4–7). Illus. by Lucy Corvino. Series: Mini-Mysteries for You to Solve. 1999, Sterling $14.95 (0-8069-6569-X). 96pp. Thirty-five mini-mysteries are presented with answers appended. (Rev: SLJ 1/00)

7386 Taylor, Theodore. *The Cay* (5–8). 1987, Doubleday $16.95 (0-385-07906-0); Avon paper $4.95 (0-380-00142-X). 160pp. A blind boy and an old black sailor are shipwrecked on a coral island. (Rev: BL 9/1/89)

7387 Taylor, Theodore. *Ice Drift* (4–7). 2005, Harcourt $16.00 (0-15-205081-7). 240pp. Inuit brothers Alika, 14, and Sulu, 10, struggle to survive over the months that they are trapped on an ice floe that is slowly floating south in the Greenland Strait. (Rev: BL 2/1/05; SLJ 1/05)

7388 Taylor, Theodore. *The Odyssey of Ben O'Neal* (6–8). Illus. by Richard Cuffari. 1991, Avon paper $3.99 (0-380-71026-9). 224pp. Action and humor are skillfully combined in this story of a trip by Ben and his friend Tee to England at the turn of the century. Two others in the series: *Teetoncey; Teetoncey and Ben O'Neal* (both 1981).

7389 Taylor, Theodore. *Timothy of the Cay: A Prequel-Sequel* (5–7). 1993, Harcourt $16.00 (0-15-288358-4). 160pp. This tells what happened to the two main characters from the author's *The Cay* before their shipwreck on the Caribbean island and what happened after they were saved. (Rev: BCCB 11/93; BL 9/15/93; SLJ 10/93)

7390 Taylor, William. *Numbskulls* (4–6). 1995, Scholastic $14.95 (0-590-22629-0). 144pp. To help his younger sister, Chas submits to the ordeal of being placed in evil Alice's learning machine. A sequel to *Knitwits* (1992). (Rev: BL 10/15/95; SLJ 10/95)

7391 Thomas, Jane Resh. *Courage at Indian Deep* (5–7). 1984, Houghton Mifflin paper $6.95 (0-395-55699-6). 128pp. A young boy must help save a ship caught in a sudden storm.

7392 Thomas, Jane Resh. *Fox in a Trap* (3–5). Illus. by Troy Howell. 1987, Houghton Mifflin paper $5.95 (0-395-54426-2). 96pp. Daniel changes his mind about trapping once he accompanies his Uncle Pete. (Rev: BCCB 4/87; BL 4/1/87; SLJ 6–7/87)

7393 Torrey, Michele. *The Case of the Gasping Garbage* (3–5). Illus. 2001, Dutton $14.99 (0-525-

46657-6). 112pp. Fourth-graders Drake and Nell use intuition, observation, and scientific investigation to solve mysteries and problems that involve a noisy garbage can, endangered frogs, a stuck truck, and a love letter. (Rev: BCCB 6/01; BL 8/01; HBG 3/02; SLJ 8/01)

7394 Torrey, Michele. *The Case of the Graveyard Ghost* (3–6). Illus. by Barbara Johansen Newman. Series: Doyle and Fossey: Science Detectives. 2002, Dutton $14.99 (0-525-46893-5). 80pp. In this third book about the junior detectives, Doyle and Fossey use their scientific skills and knowledge to solve four cases, and there are activities and experiments for readers to try themselves. (Rev: BL 10/15/02; HBG 10/03; SLJ 8/02)

7395 Torrey, Michele. *The Case of the Mossy Lake Monster and Other Super-Scientific Cases* (3–5). Illus. by Barbara Johansen Newman. Series: Doyle and Fossey: Science Detectives. 2002, Dutton $14.99 (0-525-46815-3). 112pp. Fifth-graders Drake Doyle and Nell Fossey solve a string of mysteries using scientific reasoning in this easy-to-read second book in the series. (Rev: BL 1/1–15/02; HBG 10/02; SLJ 2/02)

7396 Torrey, Michele. *Voyage of Ice* (4–7). Series: Chronicle of Courage. 2004, Knopf LB $17.99 (0-375-92381-0). 192pp. In 1851, 15-year-od Nick signs on as a hand aboard the whaler *Sea Hawk* and soon discovers unexpected hardships, including struggling to survive in the Arctic. (Rev: BL 5/15/04; SLJ 7/04)

7397 Tuitel, Johnnie, and Sharon Lamson. *The Barn at Gun Lake* (4–6). Series: The Gun Lake Adventure. 1999, Cedar Tree paper $5.99 (0-9658075-0-9). 103pp. Wheelchair-bound Johnnie, who has cerebral palsy, stumbles onto a CD-pirating ring and tries to find its leader. Also use *Mystery Explosion!* (1999). (Rev: SLJ 8/99)

7398 Twain, Mark. *The Stolen White Elephant* (4–8). Illus. 1882, Ayer $19.95 (0-8369-3486-5). The tale of the elephant's guardian who naively is impressed by a corrupt police detective. (Rev: BL 5/1/88; SLJ 2/88)

7399 Updike, David. *A Spring Story* (3–5). Illus. by Robert Andrew Parker. 1989, Pippin LB $15.95 (0-945912-06-4). 40pp. When spring comes, the ice breaks up and two adventurous boys are stranded on an ice floe. (Rev: BCCB 3/90; BL 1/15/90; SLJ 1/90)

7400 Valgardson, W. D. *Winter Rescue* (4–6). Illus. by Ange Zhang. 1995, Simon & Schuster paper $15.00 (0-689-80094-0). An adventure story that involves a young boy and the Icelandic-Canadian fishermen around Lake Winnipeg. (Rev: BCCB 12/95; SLJ 11/95)

7401 Vanasse, Deb. *Out of the Wilderness* (5–8). 1999, Clarion $15.00 (0-395-91421-3). 176pp. Fifteen-year-old Josh, his father, and his older half-brother move to Willow Creek, Alaska, where they build a cabin and try to live off the land. (Rev: BL 3/15/99; HBG 10/99; SLJ 4/99)

7402 Van Draanen, Wendelin. *Sammy Keyes and the Art of Deception* (5–8). Series: Sammy Keyes.

2003, Knopf $15.95 (0-375-81176-1). 272pp. Sammy (with some help from Grams) solves a mystery involving an art thief. (Rev: BL 2/1/03; HBG 10/03; SLJ 3/03)

7403 Van Draanen, Wendelin. *Sammy Keyes and the Hotel Thief* (4–6). 1998, Knopf LB $16.99 (0-679-98839-4). 163pp. Samantha Keyes witnesses a robbery, but the police won't believe her so she must catch the criminal herself. (Rev: BCCB 7–8/98; HBG 10/98; SLJ 7/98)

7404 Van Draanen, Wendelin. *Shredderman: Meet the Gecko* (3–5). 2005, Knopf LB $14.99 (0-375-92353-5). 176pp. Nerdy Nolan Byrd assumes his Shredderman superhero persona to help a young TV star chase off a pesky reporter. (Rev: BL 2/1/05; SLJ 1/05)

7405 Vazquez, Diana. *Lost in Sierra* (4–6). Illus. by German Jaramillo. 2002, Coteau paper $7.95 (1-55050-184-4). 173pp. On a visit to Spain, 13-year-old Ana discovers why her grandmother's brother never came back from Spain's civil war. (Rev: SLJ 8/02)

7406 Verne, Jules. *Around the World in Eighty Days* (5–8). Trans. by George Makepeace Towle. Illus. by Barry Moser. 1988, Morrow $24.99 (0-688-07508-8). 256pp. Endpapers showing an 1829 world map highlight this handsome edition of the classic. (Rev: BL 2/15/89)

7407 Wallace, Barbara Brooks. *Peppermints in the Parlor* (4–6). 1993, Macmillan paper $4.99 (0-689-71680-X). 208pp. Emily encounters mystery and terror when she goes to her aunt's home in San Francisco.

7408 Wallace, Bill. *Blackwater Swamp* (4–6). Illus. 1994, Holiday House $15.95 (0-8234-1120-6). 185pp. A woman, known by all to be a witch, helps Ted catch a group of crooks responsible for some local robberies. (Rev: BCCB 5/94; BL 6/1–15/94; SLJ 4/94)

7409 Wallace, Bill. *Danger in Quicksand Swamp* (4–7). 1989, Holiday House $16.95 (0-8234-0786-1). 181pp. While searching for buried treasure, Ben and Jake become stranded on an island near Quicksand Swamp. (Rev: BL 1/1/90; SLJ 10/89)

7410 Wallace, Bill. *Eye of the Great Bear* (4–6). 1999, Pocket $14.00 (0-671-02504-X). 162pp. A fearful 12-year-old boy who is growing up in pioneer Texas gains courage when he encounters a big grizzly. (Rev: BL 2/1/99; HBG 10/99; SLJ 5/99)

7411 Wallace, Bill. *Skinny-Dipping at Monster Lake* (5–8). 2003, Simon & Schuster $16.95 (0-689-85150-2). 224pp. Kent helps solve the mystery of the Cedar Lake monster while on a fun-filled camping trip with his friends and father. (Rev: BL 5/15/03; HBG 4/04; SLJ 8/03)

7412 Wallace, Bill. *Trapped in Death Cave* (5–8). 1984, Holiday House $16.95 (0-8234-0516-8). 176pp. Gary is convinced his grandpa was murdered to secure a map indicating where gold is buried.

7413 Weir, Joan. *The Mysterious Visitor* (5–7). Series: Lion and Bobbi. 2002, Raincoast paper $6.99 (1-55192-404-4). 176pp. Two Canadian youngsters, Lion and sister Bobbi, try to solve the mystery of strange events occurring on a friend's land. (Rev: BL 5/1/02)

7414 Weltman, June. *Mystery of the Missing Candlestick* (5–8). 2004, Mayhaven $23.95 (1-878044-98-2). 216pp. Miranda, 17, and her friends Leila and Rebecca join forces to solve the mystery of a valuable antique candlestick that has been stolen from Rebecca's grandfather. (Rev: BL 5/1/04)

7415 White, Ruth. *The Search for Belle Prater* (4–7). 2005, Farrar $16.00 (0-374-30853-5). 176pp. In this sequel to *Belle Prater's Boy,* 13-year-old Woodrow and his cousin Gypsy continue to search for Woodrow's missing mother against the backdrop of mid-1950s segregation. (Rev: BL 2/15/05; SLJ 4/05)

7416 Wilson, Barbara. *A Clear Spring* (4–6). 2002, Feminist Pr. paper $12.50 (1-55861-277-7). 176pp. While working at a nature center with her aunt's lesbian partner, Willa teams up with her cousins to track down polluters. (Rev: BL 7/02; HBG 10/02)

7417 Wilson, Eric. *Murder on the Canadian: A Tom Austen Mystery* (4–8). Illus. by Richard Row. 2000, Orca paper $4.99 (1-55143-151-3). 95pp. A fast-moving mystery starring an intrepid hero who is also featured in *Vancouver Nightmare: A Tom Austen Mystery* (2000). (Rev: SLJ 1/01)

7418 Wizowaty, Suzi. *A Tour of Evil* (5–8). 2005, Philomel $10.99 (0-399-24251-1). Evil lurks in a cathedral in northern France in this novel involving an 11-year-old orphan, Alma, who discovers a plot to kidnap children. (Rev: BL 5/15/05)

7419 Woodruff, Elvira. *Ghosts Don't Get Goose Bumps* (4–6). Illus. by Joel Iskowitz. 1993, Holiday House $15.95 (0-8234-1035-8). 96pp. On her visit to West Virginia, Jenna befriends an impish girl and is soon involved in a haunted marble factory and a mysterious disappearance. (Rev: BL 11/15/93; SLJ 10/93)

7420 Woodson, Marion. *My Brother's Keeper* (5–7). 2002, Raincoast paper $6.95 (1-55192-488-9). 160pp. On Vancouver Island, 13-year-old Sarah believes she is being haunted by a cult leader who founded a colony there in the 1930s. (Rev: BL 5/1/02)

7421 Wright, Betty R. *The Dollhouse Murders* (4–7). 1983, Holiday House $16.95 (0-8234-0497-8). 160pp. Dolls in a dollhouse come to life in this mystery about long-ago murders.

7422 Wright, Betty R. *A Ghost in the Family* (4–6). 1998, Scholastic $15.95 (0-590-02955-X). 176pp. Friends Chad and Jeannie are spending two weeks visiting Jeannie's aunt at her boardinghouse in Milwaukee where a psychic warns Chad that he is in danger. (Rev: BL 6/1–15/98; HBG 10/98; SLJ 9/98)

7423 Wright, Betty R. *Too Many Secrets* (3–5). 1997, Scholastic $14.95 (0-590-25235-6). 128pp. Chad and his friend Jeannie decide to investigate without telling others when they hear a prowler in a neighbor's house. (Rev: BL 10/1/97; HB 7–8/97; HBG 3/98; SLJ 8/97)

7424 Wright, Susan K. *Dead Letters* (4–6). Series: Dead-End Road Mysteries. 1996, Herald Pr. paper $6.99 (0-8361-9036-X). 176pp. Nellie and her

friends set out to catch the culprit who is stealing mail from the boxes outside the Lucky Clover trailer park. (Rev: SLJ 9/96)

7425 Wynne-Jones, Tim. *The Boy in the Burning House* (5–9). 2001, Farrar $16.00 (0-374-30930-2). 213pp. Disturbed Ruth Rose and 14-year-old Jim investigate the mystery of his father's disappearance — was he killed by Ruth Rose's pastor stepfather? (Rev: BCCB 11/01; BL 9/1/01; HB 11–12/01; HBG 3/02; SLJ 10/01)

7426 Wyss, Johann D. *Swiss Family Robinson* (4–6). Illus. by Lynd Ward. 1949, Penguin Putnam $16.99 (0-448-06022-1). 400pp. The classic story of a shipwrecked family is presented for a younger audience.

7427 Yep, Laurence. *The Case of the Firecrackers* (4–7). 1999, HarperCollins LB $15.89 (0-06-024452-6). 144pp. In this Chinatown mystery, Tiger Lil and her great-niece Lily are on the trail of the murderer who killed the star of the television show in which they were extras. (Rev: BL 9/15/99; HBG 3/00; SLJ 9/99)

7428 Yep, Laurence. *The Case of the Goblin Pearls* (5–7). 1997, HarperCollins LB $15.89 (0-06-024446-1). 192pp. Lily and her Aunt Tiger Lil, a former actress, solve the mystery of the stolen pearls. (Rev: BCCB 5/97; BL 1/1–15/97; BR 9–10/97; SLJ 3/97)

7429 Yep, Laurence. *The Case of the Lion Dance* (4–6). Series: Chinatown Mystery. 1998, Harper-Collins LB $14.89 (0-06-024448-8). 224pp. Lily and her great aunt Tiger Lil, a public relations expert, try to find out who is responsible for ruining the opening of a new restaurant and stealing money meant for a charity. (Rev: BL 10/15/98; HBG 3/99; SLJ 11/98)

7430 Yolen, Jane, and Heidi E. Y. Stemple. *An Unsolved Mystery from History: The Mary Celeste* (3–5). Illus. 1999, Simon & Schuster $16.00 (0-689-81079-2). 32pp. The young narrator of this novel tackles the baffling true mystery of the *Mary Celeste,* a ship that was found floating in 1872 without its captain, his family, or crew members. (Rev: BCCB 11/99; BL 10/15/99; HBG 3/00; SLJ 11/99)

7431 Zambreno, Mary F. *Journeyman Wizard* (4–7). 1994, Harcourt $16.95 (0-15-200022-4). 240pp. Student wizard Jeremy is studying the casting of spells with Lady Allons when an unfortunate death occurs and he is accused of murder. (Rev: BL 5/1/94; SLJ 6/94)

7432 Zindel, Paul. *The E-mail Murders* (5–8). Series: P.C. Hawke Mysteries. 2001, Hyperion paper $4.99 (0-7868-1579-5). 113pp. P.C. and Mackenzie team up with an inspector's daughter to investigate a murder in Monaco. (Rev: SLJ 1/02)

7433 Zindel, Paul. *The Lethal Gorilla* (5–8). Series: P.C. Hawke Mysteries. 2001, Hyperion paper $4.99 (0-7868-1587-6). 137pp. Amateur detective P.C. Hawke and his sidekick Mackenzie Riggs face hair-raising adventures as they solve the murder of a scientist at the Bronx Zoo. (Rev: BL 3/1/02)

7434 Zindel, Paul. *The Square Root of Murder* (5–7). 2002, Hyperion paper $4.99 (0-7868-1588-4). 131pp. Amateur detective P.C. Hawke and her sidekick Mackenzie Riggs try to solve the mystery of the murder of a calculus teacher. (Rev: BL 5/1/02; SLJ 4/02)

Animal Stories

7435 Adler, C. S. *More Than a Horse* (5–7). 1997, Clarion $15.00 (0-395-79769-1). 192pp. Leeann and her mother move to a dude ranch in Arizona, where the young girl develops a love of horses. (Rev: BCCB 3/97; BL 3/15/97; SLJ 4/97)

7436 Adler, C. S. *One Unhappy Horse* (5–7). 2001, Clarion $15.00 (0-618-04912-6). 155pp. Set on a small ranch near Tucson, this novel features 12-year-old Jan, her horse, Dove, an old lady in a retirement home, and Jan's new friend, Lisa. (Rev: BL 3/1/01; HBG 10/01; SLJ 4/01)

7437 Ahlberg, Allan. *Half a Pig* (3–5). Trans. by Allan Ahlberg and Jessica Ahlberg. Illus. by Jessica Ahlberg. 2004, Candlewick $16.99 (0-7636-2373-3). 40pp. An amusing story of a married couple's conflict over the fate of their jointly owned pig, Esmeralda, also serves as the basis for tips on language and use of words. (Rev: BL 8/04; HB 7–8/04; SLJ 8/04)

7438 Alter, Judith. *Callie Shaw, Stable Boy* (5–8). 1996, Eakin $16.95 (1-57168-092-6). During the Great Depression, Callie, disguised as a boy, works in a stable and uncovers a race-fixing racket. (Rev: BL 2/1/97; SLJ 8/97)

7439 Alter, Judith. *Maggie and a Horse Named Devildust* (5–7). 1989, Ellen C. Temple paper $5.95 (0-936650-08-7). 160pp. Maggie is determined to ride her spirited horse in the Wild West show in this historical horse story. (Rev: BL 4/15/89)

7440 Alter, Judith. *Maggie and the Search for Devildust* (5–7). 1989, Ellen C. Temple paper $5.95 (0-936650-09-5). 159pp. Maggie, a gorgeous girl of the Old West, sets out to find her horse, which has been stolen. (Rev: BL 10/1/89)

7441 Arnosky, Jim. *Long Spikes* (4–7). Illus. 1992, Houghton Mifflin $15.00 (0-395-58830-8). 90pp. As spring turns to summer, a yearling buck and his twin sister travel together after the death of their mother. (Rev: BCCB 4/92; BL 5/1/92; SLJ 5/92)

7442 Avi. *The Good Dog* (3–6). 2001, Simon & Schuster $16.00 (0-689-83824-7). 256pp. A malamute dog reconsiders his position as a pet when a wolf comes to town. (Rev: BL 9/1/01; HB 1–2/02; HBG 3/02; SLJ 12/01)

7443 Bagnold, Enid. *National Velvet* (5–8). Illus. by Ted Lewin. 1985, Avon paper $4.99 (0-380-71235-0). 272pp. The now-classic story of Heather Brown and her struggle to ride in the Grand National. A reissue. (Rev: BL 12/15/85)

7444 Bailey, Linda. *Stanley's Party* (PS–3). Illus. by Bill Slavin. 2003, Kids Can $14.95 (1-55337-382-0). Stanley the dog samples forbidden pleasures while his owners are out. (Rev: HBG 10/03; SLJ 7/03)

7445 Bastedo, Jamie. *Tracking Triple Seven* (5–7). 2001, Red Deer paper $9.95 (0-88995-238-8).

224pp. Benji, a teenage boy grieving his mother's death, becomes involved with biologists tracking grizzly bears near his father's mine in Canada. (Rev: BL 2/1/02)

7446 Bauer, Marion Dane. *Runt* (3–6). 2002, Clarion $15.00 (0-618-21261-2). 144pp. A tale of a wolf born the runt of the litter and his struggle to improve his position in the pack and earn his father's approval. (Rev: BL 10/15/02; SLJ 9/02)

7447 Baylor, Byrd. *Hawk, I'm Your Brother* (3–5). Illus. by Peter Parnall. 1976, Macmillan $16.00 (0-684-14571-5); paper $5.99 (0-689-71102-6). 48pp. A desert boy captures a young hawk, hoping it will teach him how to fly.

7448 Bechtold, Lisze. *Buster and Phoebe: The Great Bone Game* (1–4). Illus. by author. 2003, Houghton Mifflin $15.00 (0-618-20862-3). Phoebe, the resident dog, greets newcomer Buster with skepticism, but the two soon come to terms in this beginning chapter book. (Rev: HB 9–10/03; HBG 4/04; SLJ 7/03)

7449 Bennett, Kelly. *Not Norman: A Goldfish Story* (K–3). Illus. by Noah Z. Jones. 2005, Candlewick $15.99 (0-7636-2384-9). 32pp. A goldfish isn't the kind of pet the narrator initially wants in this entertaining and eye-catching story. (Rev: BL 2/15/05; SLJ 3/05)

7450 Berends, Polly. *The Case of the Elevator Duck* (3–5). Illus. by Diane Allison. 1989, Random paper $3.99 (0-394-82646-9). 64pp. In spite of the rule that no pets are allowed in his housing development, little Gilbert decides to keep a duck in an elevator.

7451 *The Birthday Girl* (3–5). Illus. by June Lawrason. 2004, Orca paper $4.99 (1-55143-292-7). 64pp. Nell's joyous celebration of her eighth birthday is followed a day later by a frantic search for her missing cat. (Rev: BL 12/15/04)

7452 Bograd, Larry, and Coleen Hubbard. *Colorado Summer* (3–6). Illus. by Sandy Rabinowitz. Series: Treasured Horses Collection. 1999, Gareth Stevens LB $14.95 (0-8368-2277-3). 128pp. Eleven-year-old Carrie is spending a summer on her aunt's ranch in Colorado when she becomes interested in competing in a rodeo because of her joy in riding Georgia, a fabulous horse. (Rev: SLJ 8/99)

7453 Brandenburg, Jim. *Scruffy: A Wolf Finds His Place in the Pack* (2–4). Illus. 1996, Walker LB $16.85 (0-8027-8446-1). 32pp. A photo-essay about an outcast wolf that gradually finds status in the pack. (Rev: BCCB 10/96; BL 9/1/96; SLJ 12/96)

7454 Breathed, Berkeley. *Flawed Dogs: The Year-End Leftovers at the Piddleton "Last Chance" Dog Pound* (2–5). Illus. by author. 2003, Little, Brown $18.95 (0-316-71359-7). A moving fictional gallery of dogs that have been rejected by their original owners. (Rev: HBG 4/04; SLJ 1/04)

7455 Briggs-Bunting, Jane. *Laddie of the Light* (4–6). Illus. 1997, Black River Trading $17.00 (0-9649083-1-X). 43pp. Jessie adjusts to her parents' approaching divorce with the help of two dogs, one real and the other a fictitious one that her grandfather tells her about. (Rev: BL 7/97)

7456 Brooke, Lauren. *Heartland: Coming Home* (4–7). 2000, Scholastic paper $4.50 (0-439-13020-4). 144pp. When her mother dies, Amy works through her grief by helping horses with behavioral problems in this novel set on a Virginia horse farm. (Rev: BL 9/15/00)

7457 Broome, Errol. *Magnus Maybe* (2–4). Illus. by Ann James. 2002, Simon & Schuster paper $4.99 (0-7434-3796-9). 144pp. A shy pet mouse learns a lesson in courage when he escapes his cage and meets up with a family of wild mice. (Rev: BL 8/02; SLJ 8/02)

7458 Brown, F. K. *Last Hurdle* (4–6). Illus. by Peter Spier. 1988, Shoe String LB $18.50 (0-208-02212-0). 202pp. Kathy spends her savings on a broken-down horse, but manages to restore him in this book originally published in 1953.

7459 Bryant, Bonnie. *Horse Crazy* (4–6). 1996, Bantam paper $4.50 (0-553-48402-8). 144pp. Three girls become friends at a riding stable. Also use: *Horse Shy* (1996). (Rev: BL 2/15/89)

7460 Burgess, Melvin. *The Cry of the Wolf* (5–8). 1994, Morrow $17.99 (0-397-30693-8). 128pp. Young Ben Tilley insists that wolves run past his farm in rural Surrey, even though they have supposedly been gone from England for 500 years. (Rev: BL 10/15/92; SLJ 9/92)

7461 Byars, Betsy. *The Midnight Fox* (4–6). Illus. by Ann Grifalconi. 1968, Puffin paper $4.99 (0-14-031450-4). 160pp. When Tom spends two months on a farm with his aunt and uncle, he never expects that a black fox will become the focus of his life.

7462 Byars, Betsy. *Tornado* (3–5). Illus. 1996, HarperCollins LB $14.89 (0-06-026452-7). 64pp. To pass the time during a tornado watch, Pete, a farmhand, tells about another Tornado, an unusual dog. (Rev: BCCB 11/96; BL 9/15/96; HB 11–12/96; SLJ 11/96)

7463 Byars, Betsy, et al. *My Dog, My Hero* (3–6). Illus. 2000, Holt $16.00 (0-8050-6327-7). 48pp. Author Byars and her two daughters collaborated on this collection of eight stories about heroic dogs. (Rev: BL 1/1–15/01; HBG 3/01; SLJ 1/01)

7464 Carlow, Emma, and Trevor Dickinson. *Kitty Princess and the Newspaper Dress* (PS–2). Illus. by authors. 2003, Candlewick $16.99 (0-7636-2077-7). This whimsical tale of a poorly behaved kitten princess offers young readers some valuable lessons about the importance of manners. (Rev: HBG 4/04; SLJ 11/03)

7465 Carlson, Nolan. *Summer and Shiner* (5–8). 1992, Hearth paper $6.95 (0-9627947-4-0). 160pp. In a small Kansas town in the 1940s, 12-year-old Carley adopts a raccoon called Shiner. (Rev: BL 9/15/92)

7466 Cleary, Beverly. *Strider* (5–9). Illus. 1991, Morrow LB $16.89 (0-688-09901-7). In this sequel to the 1984 Newbery winner *Dear Mr. Henshaw*, Leigh Botts is beginning high school and still writing in his diary, with his beloved dog, Strider, by his side. (Rev: BCCB 10/91; BL 7/91*; HB 9–10/91; SLJ 9/91)

7467 Cole, Joanna, and Stephanie Calmenson, eds. *Give a Dog a Bone: Stories, Poems, Jokes, and Riddles About Dogs* (2–3). Illus. 1996, Scholastic $16.95 (0-590-46374-8). 96pp. An anthology of writings, anecdotes, and jokes about dogs. (Rev: BL 2/1/96; SLJ 3/96)

7468 Cone, Molly. *Mishmash* (3–5). Illus. by Leonard Shortall. 1962, Houghton Mifflin $16.00 (0-395-06711-1). 128pp. A dog, Mishmash, moves in, takes over, and then helps his owner to adjust to a new home. Other series titles are: *Mishmash and the Sauerkraut Mystery* (1974); *Mishmash and the Robot* (1991).

7469 Crisp, Marty. *My Dog, Cat* (3–6). Illus. 2000, Holiday House $15.95 (0-8234-1537-6). 64pp. Even though he always wanted a big dog, Abbie finds that size doesn't matter when he takes care of a little Yorkie while its owner is away. (Rev: BCCB 12/00; BL 1/1–15/01; HBG 10/01; SLJ 1/01)

7470 Daniels, Lucy. *Keeping Faith* (4–6). 2002, Hyperion paper $4.99 (0-7868-1618-X). 135pp. When 12-year-old Josie must find a new home for her elderly mare, she and her mother interview many potential owners before finding just the right one. (Rev: SLJ 8/02)

7471 Daniels, Lucy. *Last Hope* (4–6). Series: The Horseshoe Trilogies. 2002, Hyperion paper $4.99 (0-7868-1619-8). 134pp. Josie's family looks for a home for a horse with skin problems when they must close their stables. (Rev: SLJ 12/02)

7472 D'Ath, Justin. *Infamous* (3–6). 2004, Allen & Unwin paper $6.95 (1-74114-128-1). 120pp. Young Tim succeeds in disguising his dog to look like an extinct Tasmanian tiger in hopes of drawing visitors to his small Tasmanian hometown; when it appears there may indeed be a real surviving tiger, Tim springs into action to find the animal before it can be taken into captivity. (Rev: BL 9/1/04)

7473 DeJong, Meindert. *Along Came a Dog* (4–7). Illus. by Maurice Sendak. 1958, HarperCollins paper $5.99 (0-06-440114-6). 192pp. The friendship of a timid, lonely dog and a toeless red hen is the basis for a very moving story, full of suspense.

7474 DeJong, Meindert. *Hurry Home, Candy* (4–6). Illus. by Maurice Sendak. 1953, HarperCollins LB $15.89 (0-06-021486-4); paper $6.95 (0-06-440025-5). 244pp. Candy is a little dog who, after many adventures, finds a home.

7475 Dennard, Deborah. *Lemur Landing: A Story of a Madagascan Tropical Dry Forest* (3–4). Illus. by Kristin Kest. 2001, Soundprints $15.95 (1-56899-978-X). 32pp. This beautifully illustrated, fictional story about lemurs includes much factual detail. (Rev: BL 3/1/02)

7476 Eckert, Allan W. *Incident at Hawk's Hill* (6–8). Illus. by John Schoenherr. 1995, Bantam paper $5.95 (0-316-20948-1). 173pp. A 6-year-old boy wanders away from home and is nurtured and protected by a badger.

7477 Edwards, Julie Andrews. *Little Bo in France: The Further Adventures of Bonnie Boadicea* (2–4). Illus. by Henry Cole. 2002, Hyperion LB $19.49 (0-7868-2540-5). 117pp. Little Bo the cat and her sailor owner travel through France having adventures and looking for work. (Rev: HBG 3/03; SLJ 10/02)

7478 Erickson, John R. *The Case of the Vanishing Fishhook* (3–6). Illus. by Gerald L. Holmes. Series: Hank the Cowdog. 1999, Viking $14.99 (0-670-88438-3); paper $4.99 (0-14-130356-5). 144pp. When Hank, a lovable dog, eats the liver that his young owner is using for fish bait, he realizes that he has also eaten a fish hook. (Rev: HBG 10/99; SLJ 4/99)

7479 Farley, Terri. *The Wild One* (4–6). 2002, Avon paper $4.99 (0-06-441085-4). 224pp. Sam is determined to find her stallion, Blackie, who ran away after she fell off and hit her head. (Rev: BL 9/1/02; SLJ 12/02)

7480 Feldman, Eve B. *That Cat!* (2–4). Illus. 1994, Morrow $14.00 (0-688-13310-X). 112pp. Molly is devastated when her cat disappears, and she tries many tactics to get him home. (Rev: BL 10/1/94; SLJ 9/94)

7481 Gallaz, Christophe. *The Wolf Who Loved Music* (3–6). Illus. by Marshall Arisman. 2003, Creative Editions $17.95 (1-56846-178-X). 32pp. In this bittersweet tale set in Switzerland, Anne is devastated when townspeople hunt down and kill a wolf that may have been attracted by the young's girl violin playing. (Rev: HBG 4/04; SLJ 12/03)

7482 George, Jean Craighead. *The Cry of the Crow* (5–7). 1980, HarperCollins paper $5.99 (0-06-440131-6). 160pp. Mandy finds a helpless baby crow in the woods and tames it.

7483 George, Jean Craighead. *Frightful's Mountain* (5–8). 1999, Dutton $15.99 (0-525-46166-3). 176pp. Frightful, the falcon in *My Side of the Mountain,* is the central character in this novel in which she has difficult and enjoyable adventures in the wild. (Rev: BL 9/1/99; HBG 3/00; SLJ 9/99)

7484 George, Jean Craighead. *There's an Owl in the Shower* (3–5). Illus. 1995, HarperCollins $14.95 (0-06-024891-2). 144pp. Borden hates the spotted owl because his father lost his logging job through conservation efforts to save it, but later he finds himself caring for a young owl he has rescued. (Rev: BL 9/1/95; SLJ 11/95)

7485 George, Twig C. *A Dolphin Named Bob* (2–5). Illus. 1996, HarperCollins LB $13.89 (0-06-025363-0). 64pp. Presents, in a fictional format, the life cycle of a dolphin at the Maryland State Aquarium. (Rev: BL 2/1/96; SLJ 5/96)

7486 Ghent, Natale. *No Small Thing* (5–8). 2005, Candlewick $15.00 (0-7636-2422-5). 256pp. Nathaniel and his siblings struggle to keep their horse while their single mother struggles to keep her family afloat. (Rev: BL 3/1/05; SLJ 4/05)

7487 Ghent, Natale. *Piper* (5–7). 2001, Orca paper $6.95 (1-55143-167-X). 176pp. The love and attention young Wesley showers on a tiny Australian shepherd puppy helps her recover from the death of her father. (Rev: BL 3/1/01)

7488 Gipson, Fred. *Old Yeller* (6–8). Illus. by Carl Burger. 1956, HarperCollins $23.00 (0-06-011545-9); paper $4.95 (0-06-440382-3). 176pp. A power-

ful story set in the Texas hill country about a 14-year-old boy and the ugly stray dog he comes to love. Also use: *Savage Sam* (1976).

7489 Gleitzman, Morris. *Toad Heaven* (3–6). 2005, Random LB $16.99 (0-375-92764-6). 193pp. Convinced that he is about to die, an Australian cane toad leads relatives to an area he believes is a protected safe haven. (Rev: SLJ 1/05)

7490 Graeber, Charlotte. *Fudge* (3–5). Illus. by Cheryl Harness. 1989, Pocket paper $3.99 (0-671-70288-2). 128pp. Chad Garcia's parents say he can have a puppy, but no one has time to train it, so Chad must prove himself responsible. (Rev: BCCB 7–8/87; BL 8/87)

7491 Griffith, Helen V. *Foxy* (4–6). 1984, Greenwillow $15.00 (0-688-02567-6). 144pp. Jeff believes his dog Foxy is dead, but his neighbor, Amber, knows this isn't true.

7492 Haas, Jessie. *A Blue for Beware* (2–4). Illus. 1995, Greenwillow $14.00 (0-688-13678-8). 64pp. Lily and her horse Beware compete in their first horse show. A sequel to *Beware the Mare* (1993). (Rev: BCCB 3/95; BL 5/15/95; HB 5–6/95; SLJ 5/95)

7493 Haas, Jessie. *Runaway Radish* (2–4). Illus. 2001, Greenwillow LB $15.89 (0-06-029159-1). 56pp. A beginning chapter book about a pony named Radish and how he is cared for, first by Judy and later by Nina. (Rev: BCCB 7–8/01; BL 4/15/01; HB 5–6/01; HBG 10/01; SLJ 5/01)

7494 Hall, Elizabeth. *Child of the Wolves* (4–7). 1996, Houghton Mifflin $16.00 (0-395-76502-1). 176pp. Granite, a Siberian husky pup, must survive in the wilderness when he is separated from his family. (Rev: BCCB 3/96; BL 4/1/96)

7495 Hall, Lynn. *The Soul of the Silver Dog* (5–8). 1992, Harcourt $16.95 (0-15-277196-4). A handicapped dog bonds with his new teenage owner living in a troubled family. (Rev: BL 4/15/92; SLJ 6/92)

7496 Hanel, Wolfram. *Mary and the Mystery Dog* (2–4). Trans. by J. Alison James. Illus. by Kirsten Hocker. 1999, North-South LB $13.88 (0-7358-1044-3). 48pp. Mary finds a dog on the beach, and though he belongs to a local fisherman, he becomes her close companion. (Rev: BL 4/15/99; HBG 10/99; SLJ 5/99)

7497 Hearne, Betsy. *The Canine Connection: Stories About Dogs and People* (5–8). 2003, Simon & Schuster $15.95 (0-689-85258-4). 160pp. Twelve moving and arresting stories underline the close relationship between dogs and their human friends. (Rev: BL 4/15/03; HB 5–6/03*; HBG 10/03; SLJ 4/03)

7498 Henkes, Kevin. *Protecting Marie* (5–7). 1995, Greenwillow $16.99 (0-688-13958-2). 208pp. Fanny is afraid that she will lose her pet dog if her temperamental father decides the dog must go. (Rev: BCCB 3/95; BL 3/15/95; HB 7–8/95; SLJ 5/95*)

7499 Henry, Marguerite. *King of the Wind* (5–8). Illus. by Wesley Dennis. 1990, Macmillan $17.95 (0-02-743629-2); Aladdin paper $4.99 (0-689-

71486-6). 176pp. The story of the famous stallion Godolphin Arabian, ancestor of Man O'War and founder of the Thoroughbred breed. Newbery Medal winner, 1949. Also use *Black Gold* and *Born to Trot* (both 1987).

7500 Henry, Marguerite. *Mustang, Wild Spirit of the West* (6–8). Illus. by Robert Lougheed. 1992, Macmillan paper $4.99 (0-689-71601-X). 224pp. An excellent horse story written by a master.

7501 Henry, Marguerite. *San Domingo: The Medicine Hat Stallion* (4–6). Illus. by Robert Lougheed. 1992, Macmillan paper $4.99 (0-689-71631-1). 240pp. Set in the West during the mid-19th century, this is the story of a young man who rights a wrong inflicted on his father. Also from the same author and publisher: *Brighty of the Grand Canyon; Justin Morgan Had a Horse* (both 1991).

7502 Hermes, Patricia. *Fly Away Home: The Novel and Story Behind the Film* (5–8). 1996, Newmarket paper $6.95 (1-55704-303-5). This is the true story of a girl and her father, who raise 16 geese and use an ultralight plane to teach them to migrate south. (Rev:)

7503 Herriot, James. *Only One Woof* (2–4). Illus. by Peter Barrett. 1985, St. Martin's $13.00 (0-312-58583-7); paper $6.95 (0-312-09129-X). 32pp. The sentimental story of two sheepdogs and the one and only time one of them barks. (Rev: BL 1/1/86; HB 3–4/86; SLJ 1/86)

7504 Hesse, Karen. *Sable* (2–4). Illus. by Marcia Sewall. 1994, Holt $15.95 (0-8050-2416-6). 60pp. Tate is sure that her dog, Sable, who has been given away for misbehaving, will return. (Rev: BCCB 5/94; BL 6/1–15/94; HB 7–8/94; SLJ 5/94*)

7505 High, Linda O. *Hound Heaven* (5–8). 1995, Holiday House $15.95 (0-8234-1195-8). More than anything in the world, Silver Iris wants a dog, but her grandfather won't allow it. (Rev: BCCB 12/95; SLJ 11/95)

7506 Hosler, Jay. *Clan Apis* (5–7). Illus. 2001, Active Synapse paper $15.00 (0-9677255-0-X). 158pp. Nyuki, a honeybee, describes his hive's history and migration to a new location in a text presented in graphic-novel style that includes information about bees and their environment. (Rev: BL 7/01)

7507 Howe, James. *Pinky and Rex and the Just-Right Pet* (2–3). Illus. 2001, Simon & Schuster $15.00 (0-689-82861-6). 48pp. Pinky gives the new family kitten to his little sister Amanda, but when he becomes attached to the cat he regrets his generosity in this beginning chapter book. (Rev: BL 3/1/01; HBG 10/01)

7508 Hurwitz, Johanna. *A Llama in the Family* (2–4). Illus. 1994, Morrow $16.00 (0-688-13388-6). 96pp. Instead of the bike he has been hoping for as a surprise from his parents, Adam receives a llama. (Rev: BCCB 9/94; BL 9/1/94; SLJ 9/94)

7509 Hurwitz, Johanna. *Llama in the Library* (3–6). Illus. 1999, Morrow $15.00 (0-688-16138-3). 144pp. Ten-year-old Adam continues to care for his pet llama while adjusting to first love and to a new

baby in the family. (Rev: BCCB 3/99; BL 5/1/99; HBG 10/99; SLJ 6/99)

7510 Hurwitz, Johanna. *One Small Dog* (3–5). 2000, HarperCollins LB $15.89 (0-06-029220-2). 128pp. Curtis has always wanted a dog and finally gets one, but the small cocker spaniel causes enormous problems. (Rev: BCCB 9/00; BL 10/15/00; HB 9–10/00; HBG 3/01; SLJ 11/00)

7511 Hutchins, Hazel. *T J and the Cats* (2–4). 2002, Orca paper $4.99 (1-55143-205-6). 112pp. A beginning chapter book about a boy who doesn't like cats, but agrees to care for his grandmother's four while she's on vacation and slowly changes his mind. (Rev: BL 12/15/02; SLJ 2/03)

7512 Intrater, Roberta G. *The Christmas Puppy* (3–6). Illus. 1999, Scholastic $10.95 (0-439-08285-4). 64pp. Zach's beloved dog Tina runs away, and when she is finally located weeks later, she has become the pet of a homeless man. (Rev: BL 12/1/99; HBG 3/00; SLJ 10/99)

7513 Jimenez, Juan Ramon. *Platero y Yo / Platero and I* (5–7). Trans. by Myra Cohn Livingston and Joseph F. Dominguez. Illus. by Antonio Frasconi. 1994, Clarion $15.00 (0-395-62365-0). 47pp. Using both Spanish and English texts, this book contains excerpts from the prose poem about a writer and his donkey. (Rev: BL 6/1–15/94) [863]

7514 Joyce, William. *Buddy* (4–6). Illus. 1997, HarperCollins LB $15.00 (0-06-027661-4). 96pp. Gertrude Lintz buys a gorilla and treats it like a human. (Rev: BL 8/97; SLJ 8/97)

7515 Keehn, Sally M. *The First Horse I See* (5–9). 1999, Philomel $17.99 (0-399-23351-2). In this story filled with personal and family problems, the central issue involves Willo and the horse she has purchased in spite of its wild nature. (Rev: BCCB 9/99; BL 9/1/99; HBG 10/99; SLJ 7/99)

7516 Kehret, Peg. *Frightmares: Bone Breath and the Vandals* (4–6). 1995, Pocket paper $3.50 (0-671-89189-8). 113pp. Rosie's dog, Bone Breath, is instrumental in capturing a gang of vandals who have been destroying school property. (Rev: BL 5/1/95; SLJ 5/95)

7517 Kehret, Peg. *Saving Lilly* (3–6). 2001, Pocket $16.00 (0-671-03422-7). 160pp. Two sixth-graders boycott a class trip to the circus because of animal cruelty and persuade the class to raise funds to send performer Lilly to an elephant sanctuary. (Rev: BL 12/1/01; HBG 10/02; SLJ 11/01)

7518 Keith, Harold. *Chico and Dan* (4–6). Illus. by Scott Arbuckle. 1998, Eakin $15.95 (1-57168-216-3). In 1915, eleven-year-old Dan gets a job working on his great-uncle's cattle ranch in Nevada, where he tames a wild colt and teaches him to be a cow horse. (Rev: HBG 3/99; SLJ 10/98)

7519 Kerr, M. E. *Snakes Don't Miss Their Mothers* (4–6). 2003, HarperCollins LB $16.89 (0-06-052625-4). 208pp. The varied animals at the Critters shelter and their comings and goings are the focus of this story with a challenging cast of characters. (Rev: BL 9/15/03; HBG 4/04; SLJ 10/03)

7520 King-Smith, Dick. *The Cuckoo Child* (3–6). Illus. by Leslie Bowman. 1995, Hyperion paper

$3.95 (0-7868-1001-7). 128pp. Jack oversees the hatching of an ostrich egg and tends the offspring, Oliver, for two years in this humorous story. (Rev: BL 4/15/93; SLJ 4/93*)

7521 King-Smith, Dick. *The Invisible Dog* (2–4). Illus. by Roger Roth. 1995, Random paper $4.99 (0-679-87041-5). Janie can't have a pet dog so she invents one. (Rev: BCCB 4/93; BL 3/1/93; HB 5–6/93; SLJ 5/93)

7522 Kipling, Rudyard. *The Jungle Book: Mowgli's Story* (2–4). Illus. by Nicola Bayley. 2005, Candlewick $19.99 (0-7636-2317-2). 160pp. An appealing presentation of unabridged Mowgli adventures. (Rev: BL 5/1/05; SLJ 6/05)

7523 Kipling, Rudyard. *The Jungle Book: The Mowgli Stories* (4–7). Illus. by Jerry Pinkney. 1995, Morrow $24.99 (0-688-09979-3). 272pp. Eight stories about Mowgli are reprinted with 18 handsome watercolors. (Rev: BCCB 6/96; BL 10/15/95; SLJ 11/95)

7524 Kipling, Rudyard. *Just So Stories* (3–5). Illus. by David Frampton. 1991, HarperCollins $19.95 (0-06-023294-3). 128pp. Woodcuts enhance the retelling of these old favorites. (Rev: BL 11/15/91; HB 1–2/92; SLJ 11/91)

7525 Kipling, Rudyard. *Just So Stories* (4–6). Illus. by Barry Moser. 1996, Morrow $21.95 (0-688-13957-4). 160pp. Twelve classic stories are featured in this well-illustrated edition of Kipling favorites. (Rev: BL 11/1/96)

7526 Kjelgaard, James A. *Big Red* (6–8). Illus. by Bob Kuhn. 1945, Holiday House $19.95 (0-8234-0007-7); Bantam paper $5.50 (0-553-15434-6). 254pp. Adventures of a champion Irish setter and a trapper's son. Also use: *Irish Red: Son of Big Red* (1951); *Outlaw Red* (1953).

7527 Lantz, Francess. *Mom, There's a Pig in My Bed!* (4–6). 1992, Avon paper $3.50 (0-380-76112-2). 144pp. Mr. Ewing, fired from his job, moves to rural Kansas to raise seeing-eye pigs for blind people who are allergic to dogs, not realizing that pigs have poor eyesight too. (Rev: BL 4/15/92; SLJ 1/93)

7528 Lattimore, Deborah N. *Frida María: A Story of the Old Southwest* (2–4). Illus. by author. 1994, Harcourt $14.95 (0-15-276636-7). In this horse story set in Old California, Frida tries to be a conventional girl to please her mother, but her adventurous spirit prevails. (Rev: SLJ 5/94)

7529 Lawson, Julie. *Cougar Cove* (4–6). Illus. by David Powell. 1996, Orca paper $6.95 (1-55143-072-X). 138pp. An animal adventure involving a girl who is visiting relatives on Vancouver Island, Canada. (Rev: SLJ 9/96)

7530 Levin, Betty. *Away to Me, Moss* (5–7). 1994, Greenwillow $15.99 (0-688-13439-4). 192pp. When his master has a stroke, Moss, a border collie, runs out of control. (Rev: BCCB 12/94; BL 10/1/94; SLJ 10/94)

7531 Levin, Betty. *Creature Crossing* (3–5). 1999, Greenwillow $15.00 (0-688-16220-7). 96pp. Ben finds a strange animal he thinks is a dinosaur. When he discovers it is a salamander — an endangered

species — Ben and his friends try to make their community more aware of their environment. (Rev: BL 3/1/99; HB 5–6/99; HBG 10/99; SLJ 6/99)

7532 Levin, Betty. *Look Back, Moss* (5–8). 1998, Greenwillow $15.00 (0-688-15696-7). Young Moss, disturbed by his mother's lack of attention and his own weight problems, welcomes an injured sheepdog into the family. (Rev: BCCB 10/98; BL 8/98; HB 1–2/99; HBG 3/99; SLJ 11/98)

7533 Levin, Betty. *That'll Do, Moss* (4–6). 2002, HarperCollins LB $15.89 (0-06-000532-7). 128pp. Moss the Border collie and a girl named Diane, who works at the farm where Moss lives, rescue one of the farmer's sons who has run away. (Rev: BL 8/02; HBG 10/02; SLJ 10/02)

7534 Little, Jean. *Different Dragons* (4–6). Illus. 1987, Puffin paper $4.99 (0-14-031998-0). 144pp. Ben, who fears everything, especially his aunt's dog, learns that everyone sometimes has something to fear. (Rev: BCCB 7–8/87; BL 6/1/87; SLJ 6–7/87)

7535 London, Jack. *White Fang* (5–8). 1964, Airmont paper $4.10 (0-8049-0036-1). The classic dog story in one of many editions available. A reissue of the 1935 edition.

7536 London, Jonathan. *The Eyes of Gray Wolf* (K–5). Illus. by Jon Van Zyle. 1993, Chronicle $14.95 (0-8118-0285-X). 32pp. After losing his mate to hunters, Grey Wolf is consoled when he encounters a wolf pack with a white wolf that will be his future mate. (Rev: BL 11/1/93*; SLJ 1/94)

7537 Lowry, Lois. *Stay! Keeper's Story* (5–8). Illus. 1997, Houghton Mifflin $15.00 (0-395-87048-8). 128pp. A dog named Keeper narrates this story about his puppyhood and the three different masters he has had. (Rev: BL 11/1/97; HBG 3/98; SLJ 10/97)

7538 Lubar, David. *Dog Days* (3–6). 2004, Darby Creek $15.95 (1-58196-013-1). 112pp. Larry Haskins passes his summer playing baseball and taking care of three stray dogs; his worries about the rising price of dog food are resolved when he finds the solution to a mysterious stain. (Rev: BL 4/1/04; SLJ 5/04)

7539 Malone, Geoffrey. *Torn Ear* (4–6). 2003, Hodder paper $8.95 (0-340-86057-X). 144pp. Readers follow Torn Ear, a fox, as he grows to adulthood, survives dangers, mates, and has his own cubs. (Rev: BL 3/1/03)

7540 Malterre, Elona. *The Last Wolf of Ireland* (5–7). 1990, Houghton Mifflin $15.00 (0-395-54381-9). 124pp. Devin and his friend Katey hide wolf pups when the pups are threatened. (Rev: BCCB 10/90; BL 9/15/90*; SLJ 10/90)

7541 Maynard, Meredy. *Dreamcatcher* (5–7). 1995, Polestar paper $7.95 (1-896095-01-1). 137pp. With the help of an American Indian girl, a 13-year-old boy secretly raises a baby raccoon that was abandoned in the woods. (Rev: SLJ 5/96)

7542 Michaels, Vaughn. *Dodi's Prince* (3–5). Illus. by Jacqueline Rogers. 2003, Dutton $15.99 (0-525-47034-4). 96pp. Life in a trailer park in a remote Texas town is lonely for 8-year-old Dodi until a stray dog appears. (Rev: BL 3/15/03; HBG 10/03; SLJ 3/03)

7543 Mitchard, Jacquelyn. *Rosalie, My Rosalie: The Tale of a Duckling* (2–4). Illus. by John Bendall-Brunello. 2005, HarperCollins LB $16.89 (0-06-072220-7). 118pp. Henry is very fond of the duckling she has named Rosalie, but as Rosalie grows up, the practical problems mount. (Rev: BCCB 6/05; BL 7/05; SLJ 6/05)

7544 Moeyaert, Bart. *Bare Hands* (3–7). Trans. by David Colmer. 1999, Front Street $14.95 (1-886910-32-4). 112pp. In this translation of a powerful novel from the Netherlands, Young Ward seeks revenge when the village loner, who is also his mother's suitor, kills his dog. (Rev: BL 12/15/98*; HBG 10/99; SLJ 2/99)

7545 Morehead, Debby. *A Special Place for Charlee: A Child's Companion Through Pet Loss* (3–6). Illus. by Karen Cannon. 1996, Partners in Publishing paper $6.95 (0-9654049-0-0). 36pp. Mark gets help and counseling when the dog he has grown up with dies. (Rev: BL 11/15/96)

7546 Morey, Walt. *Gentle Ben* (5–8). Illus. 1991, Puffin paper $5.99 (0-14-036035-2). A warm story of deep trust and friendship between a boy and an Alaskan bear.

7547 Morey, Walt. *Scrub Dog of Alaska* (4–8). 1989, Blue Heron paper $7.95 (0-936085-13-4). 160pp. A pup, abandoned because of his small size, turns out to be a winner. Also use *Kavik the Wolf Dog* (1977, Dutton).

7548 Morey, Walt. *Year of the Black Pony* (5–8). Illus. by Fredrika Spillman. 1989, Blue Heron paper $6.95 (0-936085-14-2). 160pp. A family story about a boy's love for his pony in rural Oregon at the turn of the 20th century.

7549 Morgan, Clay. *The Boy Who Spoke Dog* (5–8). 2003, Dutton $15.99 (0-525-47159-6). 166pp. Marooned on an island dominated by two warring dog packs, Jack, a young cabin boy, feels very much alone until he develops a friendship with a border collie named Moxie. (Rev: BL 1/1–15/04; SLJ 1/04)

7550 Mowat, Farley. *The Dog Who Wouldn't Be* (4–7). Illus. by Paul Galdone. 1957, Bantam paper $4.99 (0-553-27928-9). 208pp. The humorous story of Mutt, a dog of character and personality, and his boy.

7551 Mukerji, Dhan Gopal. *Gay-Neck: The Story of a Pigeon* (4–8). Illus. by Boris Artzybasheff. 1968, Dutton $15.99 (0-525-30400-2). 192pp. A boy from India's brave carrier pigeon is selected to perform dangerous missions during World War I. Newbery Medal winner, 1928.

7552 Myers, Anna. *Flying Blind* (4–8). 2003, Walker $16.95 (0-8027-8879-3). 192pp. In the early 20th century, Ben, 13, and an unusually talented pet macaw deplore the killing of egrets for their feathers but understand the economic needs of the deprived hunters. (Rev: BL 9/15/03; SLJ 11/03)

7553 Myers, Anna. *Red-Dirt Jessie* (4–7). 1992, Walker $13.95 (0-8027-8172-1). 120pp. In this tale of the Depression era in Oklahoma, 12-year-old

Jessie helps keep her family together. (Rev: BCCB 10/92; BL 1/15/93; HB 1–2/93; SLJ 11/92*)

7554 Myers, Christopher. *Black Cat* (3–8). Illus. 1999, Scholastic $15.95 (0-590-03375-1). 40pp. An intriguing picture book with rap rhythm that tells of a black cat's progress walking through a city's streets. (Rev: BCCB 2/99; BL 4/15/99; HB 3–4/99; HBG 10/99; SLJ 3/99)

7555 Naylor, Phyllis Reynolds. *Saving Shiloh* (4–7). 1997, Simon & Schuster $15.00 (0-689-81460-7). 144pp. In this sequel to the Newbery Medal–winning *Shiloh* and *Shiloh Season*, Marty again encounters the evil Judd Travers, who has been accused of murder. (Rev: BL 9/1/97*; HB 9–10/97; HBG 3/98; SLJ 9/97)

7556 Naylor, Phyllis Reynolds. *Shiloh Season* (4–8). 1996, Simon & Schuster $15.00 (0-689-80647-7). 120pp. The evil Judd Travers wants his dog back from the Prestons in this sequel to *Shiloh* (1991). (Rev: BCCB 12/96; BL 11/15/96*; BR 9–10/97; HB 11–12/96; SLJ 11/96)

7557 Newman, Leslea. *Hachiko Waits* (3–5). Illus. by Machiyo Kodaira. 2004, Holt $15.95 (0-8050-7336-1). 112pp. This is the fictionalized story of a Japanese Akita who continued — for ten years — to wait at the station for his master's return. (Rev: BL 1/1–15/05; SLJ 11/04)

7558 Nielsen, Virginia. *Batty Hattie* (4–6). 1999, Marshall Cavendish $14.95 (0-7614-5047-5). 142pp. When her mother goes on tour with a jazz band, Harriet is left alone with her uncle and feels extreme loneliness until she rescues a helpless baby bat she finds on the ground. (Rev: BCCB 4/99; BL 3/1/99; HBG 10/99; SLJ 4/99)

7559 North, Sterling. *Rascal: A Memoir of a Better Era* (6–8). Illus. by John Schoenherr. 1984, Puffin paper $4.99 (0-14-034445-4). 192pp. Autobiographical memoir of the beauties of nature as experienced by an 11-year-old and his pet raccoon.

7560 Orr, Wendy. *Ark in the Park* (2–3). Illus. 2000, Holt $15.95 (0-8050-6221-1). 78pp. Seven-year-old Sophie desperately wants a pet and is delighted when she gets a chance to help Mr. and Mrs. Noah in their pet shop. (Rev: BCCB 9/00; BL 9/15/00; HBG 10/00; SLJ 6/00)

7561 Parker, Cam. *A Horse in New York* (4–8). 1989, Avon paper $2.75 (0-380-75704-4). 135pp. To save Blue, the horse she rode at summer camp, from destruction, Tiffin has to convince her parents to board him for the winter. (Rev: BL 12/15/89)

7562 Parker, Marjorie Hodgson. *Assault: The Crippled Champion: The King Ranch Racehorse* (2–4). Illus. by Charles Shaw. 2004, Bright Sky $14.95 (1-931721-34-3). 80pp. A colt called Assault describes his triumphant winning of the Triple Crown in 1946 despite the lameness he suffers. (Rev: SLJ 11/04)

7563 Patent, Dorothy Hinshaw. *Return of the Wolf* (4–6). Illus. by Jared T. Williams. 1995, Clarion $15.95 (0-395-72100-8). 67pp. A female wolf banished from her pack finds a new mate and a territory where she can begin a new pack. (Rev: BCCB 7–8/95; SLJ 7/95)

7564 Pennac, Daniel. *Eye of the Wolf* (5–8). Illus. by Max Grafe. 2003, Candlewick $15.99 (0-7636-1896-9). 112pp. A boy and a captive wolf, who have both suffered at the hands of humans, form a close connection. (Rev: BCCB 3/03; BL 3/1/03; HBG 10/03; SLJ 2/03)

7565 Popp, Monika. *Farm Year* (2–4). Illus. by Monika Popp and Regine Frick von Schmuck. 2002, Groundwood $18.95 (0-88899-452-4). A young farm boy takes special interest in a Holstein heifer and shepherds her tenderly through her first year of life. (Rev: HBG 10/02; SLJ 6/02)

7566 Pringle, Laurence. *The Dog of Discovery: A Newfoundland's Adventures with Lewis and Clark* (4–6). Illus. by Meryl Henderson. 2002, Boyds Mills $17.95 (1-56397-028-0). 152pp. A Newfoundland dog named Seaman was a valued member of the Lewis and Clark expedition, and his lightly fictionalized story is told here, based on entries in the explorers' journals and illustrated with drawings and photographs. (Rev: BL 12/1/02)

7567 Rawlings, Marjorie Kinnan. *The Yearling* (6–8). Illus. by N. C. Wyeth. 1985, Macmillan $28.00 (0-684-18461-3). 416pp. The contemporary classic of a boy and a fawn growing up together in the backwoods of Florida. A reissue of the 1938 edition.

7568 Ray, Mary Lyn. *Welcome, Brown Bird* (K–3). Illus. by Peter Sylvada. 2004, Harcourt $16.00 (0-15-292863-4). 32pp. Seasons apart and thousands of miles away from each other, two boys hail the arrival of a wood thrush for its migratory stay. (Rev: BL 4/15/04; SLJ 6/04)

7569 Rodowsky, Colby. *Not My Dog* (2–4). Illus. 1999, Farrar $15.00 (0-374-35531-2). 80pp. In this beginning chapter book, Ellie, who has been promised a puppy, has to settle for Preston, an older dog that her grandmother has to give up. (Rev: BCCB 3/99; BL 2/1/99; HB 3–4/99; SLJ 4/99)

7570 Rounds, Glen. *The Blind Colt* (3–6). Illus. by author. 1989, Holiday House $16.95 (0-8234-0010-7); paper $5.95 (0-8234-0758-6). 84pp. The story of the colt that overcame his blindness and the boy who saved him. A reissue.

7571 Ruepp, Krista. *Horses in the Fog* (2–4). Trans. by Alison James. 1997, North-South $13.88 (1-55858-805-1). 58pp. A young girl living on an island gets to ride a neighbor's Arabian stallion and finds a new riding companion in Mona. A sequel to *Midnight Rider* (1995). (Rev: BL 2/1/98; HBG 3/98)

7572 Sabuda, Robert. *Uh-Oh Leonardo! The Adventures of Providence Traveler* (2–4). Illus. 2003, Simon & Schuster $16.95 (0-689-81160-8). 48pp. Providence Traveler, a young mouse who has patterned her life after that of Leonardo da Vinci, is transported back to 16th-century Florence and an encounter with her idol. (Rev: BL 6/1–15/03; HBG 10/03; SLJ 6/03)

7573 Sachar, Louis. *Marvin Redpost: Alone in His Teacher's House* (2–4). 1994, Random LB $11.99 (0-679-91949-X); paper $3.99 (0-679-81949-5).

83pp. Marvin is upset and confused when the dog he is taking care of dies. (Rev: BL 6/1–15/94)

7574 Sachs, Betsy. *The Boy Who Ate Dog Biscuits* (2–4). Illus. by Margot Apple. 1989, Random paper $3.99 (0-394-84778-4). 64pp. Billy, who helps out at the vet's office and likes dog biscuits, prefers dogs to his baby sister. (Rev: BL 1/15/90)

7575 Sachs, Marilyn. *The Four Ugly Cats in Apartment 3D* (3–5). Illus. by Rosanne Litzinger. 2002, Simon & Schuster $15.00 (0-689-84581-2). 80pp. When her neighbor dies, 10-year-old Lily tries to find homes for his four cats. (Rev: BCCB 7–8/02; BL 5/1/02; HB 3–4/02; HBG 10/02; SLJ 3/02)

7576 Salten, Felix. *Bambi: A Life in the Woods* (5–8). 1926, Pocket paper $4.99 (0-671-66607-X). The growing to maturity of an Austrian deer.

7577 Saunders, Susan. *Lucky Lady* (3–7). 2000, HarperCollins $14.95 (0-380-97784-2). 144pp. The lives of 12-year-old Jennie and her dispirited grandfather change for the better when the girl buys a wild buckskin filly named Lucky Lady. (Rev: BCCB 5/00; BL 8/00; HBG 10/00; SLJ 7/00)

7578 Schlein, Miriam. *The Year of the Panda* (3–5). Illus. by Kam Mak. 1990, HarperCollins LB $15.89 (0-690-04866-1). 96pp. A Chinese farm boy cares for an orphaned baby panda. (Rev: BCCB 11/90; BL 9/15/90; HB 11–12/90; SLJ 10/90)

7579 Seuling, Barbara. *Robert and the Great Pepperoni* (2–3). Illus. by Paul Brewer. 2001, Cricket $14.95 (0-8126-2825-X). 118pp. Second-grader Robert really wants a dog and he starts a pet-sitting service that eventually but temporarily gives him a chance to look after one. (Rev: HB 1–2/02; HBG 3/02; SLJ 10/01)

7580 Sherlock, Patti. *Four of a Kind* (5–9). 1991, Holiday House $13.95 (0-8234-0913-9). Andy's grandfather agrees to lend him money to buy a pair of horses, and he sets his sights on winning the horse-pulling contest at a state fair. (Rev: BL 12/1/91; SLJ 10/91)

7581 Silverstein, Shel. *Lafcadio, the Lion Who Shot Back* (3–6). Illus. by author. 1963, HarperCollins LB $15.89 (0-06-025676-1). 112pp. His marksmanship makes him a success, but Lafcadio discovers it's not to his liking.

7582 Smith, Susan M. *The Booford Summer* (3–6). Illus. 1994, Clarion $13.95 (0-395-66590-6). 144pp. A girl takes pity on Booford, a neighbor's dog, and begins taking him for walks. (Rev: BL 9/15/94; SLJ 11/94)

7583 Snelling, Lauraine. *The Winner's Circle* (5–8). Series: Golden Filly. 1995, Bethany House paper $5.99 (1-55661-533-7). In this horse story, Trish Evanston, a high school senior who is also a jockey and Triple Crown winner, is being stalked by a mystery man who sends her threatening notes. (Rev: SLJ 10/95)

7584 Springer, Nancy. *A Horse to Love* (4–8). 1987, HarperCollins $11.95 (0-06-025824-1). Erin's parents buy her a horse hoping that this will help cure her shyness. (Rev: BL 3/87; SLJ 3/87)

7585 Spurr, Elizabeth. *Surfer Dog* (3–6). 2002, Dutton $15.99 (0-525-46898-6). 128pp. Eleven-year-old Pete, who is adjusting to a new home and school, finds a companion to surf with when he is joined by Blackie, a stray black Labrador retriever. (Rev: BCCB 9/02; BL 6/1–15/02; HBG 10/02; SLJ 7/02)

7586 Strickland, Brad. *When Mack Came Back* (3–6). 2000, Dial $15.99 (0-8037-2498-5). 112pp. Set in World War II Georgia, this is the story of 10-year-old Maury and the injured black dog he finds in the woods. (Rev: BCCB 5/00; BL 10/15/00; HBG 10/00; SLJ 6/00)

7587 Taylor, Theodore. *The Trouble with Tuck* (5–8). 1989, Doubleday $16.95 (0-385-17774-7); Avon paper $4.95 (0-380-62711-6). The story of a golden Labrador retriever who becomes blind.

7588 Taylor, Theodore. *Tuck Triumphant* (4–7). 1991, Avon paper $5.99 (0-380-71323-3). 150pp. A 1950s novel about a blind dog in a loving family and the deaf Korean boy they adopt. (Rev: BL 2/1/91)

7589 Taylor, William. *Agnes the Sheep* (5–7). 1991, Scholastic paper $13.95 (0-590-43365-2). 132pp. A wild and woolly story about an ornery and ill-kempt sheep and the two middle-graders who must care for her. (Rev: BCCB 3/91*; BL 5/15/91*)

7590 Torrey, Michele. *The Case of the Barfy Birthday: And Other Super-Scientific Cases* (3–5). Illus. by Barbara Johansen Newman. Series: Doyle and Fossey, Science Detectives. 2003, Dutton $14.99 (0-525-47107-3). 88pp. Fifth-graders Drake Doyle and Nell Fossey draw on their scientific knowhow and detective skills to investigate mysterious cases of food poisoning, misplaced tern hatchlings, a pig in a pit, and a haunted treehouse. (Rev: HBG 4/04; SLJ 12/03)

7591 Updike, David. *The Sounds of Summer* (3–5). Illus. by Robert Andrew Parker. 1993, Pippin $15.95 (0-945912-20-X). 40pp. After Homer's dog, Sophocles, dies, the boy remembers the good times they had together. (Rev: BCCB 10/93; BL 9/1/93; SLJ 10/93)

7592 Ure, Jean. *Muddy Four Paws* (4–6). Series: We Love Animals. 1999, Barron's paper $3.95 (0-7641-0968-5). 128pp. In this English story, 11-year-old Clara is upset when her mother will not let her adopt a puppy she has found in a ditch. (Rev: SLJ 6/99)

7593 Van Laan, Nancy. *Busy, Busy Moose* (1–2). Illus. by Amy Rusch. 2003, Houghton Mifflin $15.00 (0-395-96091-6). 48pp. In this sequel to *Moose Tales* (2001), the title character and his friends experience the changing seasons. (Rev: BL 7/03; HB 9–10/03; HBG 4/04; SLJ 9/03)

7594 Vincent, Gabrielle. *A Day, a Dog* (PS–4). Illus. 2000, Front Street $16.95 (1-886910-51-0). 72pp. A wordless book that tells the story of a dog that is dumped by its owners and how it learns to survive. (Rev: BCCB 4/00; BL 7/00; HB 5–6/00; HBG 10/00; SLJ 6/00)

7595 Wallace, Bill. *Coyote Autumn* (4–6). 2000, Holiday House $16.95 (0-8234-1628-3). 201pp. During his first autumn in rural Oklahoma, Brad finds an orphan coyote pup that he raises. (Rev: BCCB 11/00; BL 12/15/00; HBG 10/01; SLJ 10/00)

7596 Wallace, Bill. *A Dog Called Kitty* (4–7). 1980, Holiday House $15.95 (0-8234-0376-9); Pocket paper $3.99 (0-671-77081-0). 160pp. A boy tries to overcome his fear of dogs so he can help a stray.

7597 Wallace, Bill. *Goosed!* (2–4). Illus. by Jacqueline Rogers. 2002, Holiday House $16.95 (0-8234-1757-3). 128pp. T.P. the dog does not welcome the arrival of a Labrador puppy in his life in this beginning chapter book. (Rev: HBG 3/03; SLJ 12/02)

7598 Wallace, Carol, and Bill Wallace. *The Meanest Hound Around* (2–4). Illus. by John Steven Gurney. 2003, Simon & Schuster $15.95 (0-7434-3785-3). 160pp. In this heartwarming story of canine friendship, Freddie, an abandoned dog, befriends a watchdog named Spike and helps him to escape from his abusive owner. (Rev: HBG 10/03; SLJ 4/03)

7599 Wells, Rosemary. *Lassie Come-Home: Eric Knight's Original 1938 Classic* (3–5). Illus. by Susan Jeffers. 1995, Holt $16.95 (0-8050-3794-2). 48pp. A simplified picture-book version of Eric Knight's classic dog story set in the Scottish countryside. (Rev: BCCB 2/96; BL 12/1/95; SLJ 11/95*)

7600 Whelan, Gloria. *Silver* (2–4). Illus. by Stephen Marchesi. 1988, Random paper $3.99 (0-394-89611-4). 64pp. Rachel wants to compete in the Alaska Iditarod sled race, and she thinks she can win with her lead dog, Silver. (Rev: BCCB 7–8/88; BL 7/88; SLJ 10/88)

7601 Wiebe, Trina. *Hamsters Don't Glow in the Dark* (2–4). Illus. by Marisol Sarrazin. 2000, Lobster paper $5.95 (1-894222-15-6). 32pp. Abby brings the class hamster home for spring break and discovers that Mr. Nibbles was misnamed because she has given birth to eight babies. (Rev: SLJ 2/01)

7602 Wilbur, Frances. *The Dog with Golden Eyes* (4–7). Illus. 1998, Milkweed $15.95 (1-57131-614-0); paper $6.95 (1-57131-615-9). 160pp. Cassie befriends a white dog that turns out to be an arctic wolf, and she must find his owners before he becomes a target for the police or hunters. (Rev: BCCB 9/98; BL 9/1/98; BR 9–10/98; HBG 3/99; SLJ 7/98)

7603 Wittbold, Maureen. *Mending Peter's Heart* (K–6). Illus. by Larry Salk. 1995, Portunus paper $8.95 (0-9641330-2-4). 32pp. Peter needs consolation when his pet husky, Mishka, dies. (Rev: SLJ 11/95)

7604 Woods, Shirley. *Jack: The Story of a Beaver* (3–5). Illus. by Celia Godkin. 2002, Fitzhenry & Whiteside $14.95 (1-55041-733-9). 96pp. Nature lovers will enjoy the story of the first two years of life for Jack the Beaver, who evades predators, learns to avoid traps, and finally finds a mate. (Rev: BL 1/1–15/03; SLJ 3/03)

7605 Woods, Shirley. *Tooga: The Story of a Polar Bear* (4–6). Illus. by Muriel Wood. 2004, Fitzhenry & Whiteside $14.95 (1-55041-898-X). 96pp. Facts are interwoven into this story of a polar bear cub who makes his long and dangerous way home after floating hundreds of miles on an ice flow. (Rev: SLJ 4/05)

7606 Wright, Lynn F. *Flick* (3–5). Illus. by Tony Waters. 1995, Worry Wart $13.95 (1-881519-02-3);

paper $7.95 (1-881519-03-1). 68pp. Jack nurses back to health a badly injured puppy he has found on the railroad tracks. (Rev: SLJ 2/96)

Ethnic Groups

7607 Abraham, Susan Gonzales, and Denise Gonzales Abraham. *Cecilia's Year* (4–7). 2004, Cinco Puntos $16.95 (0-938317-87-3). 216pp. Inspired by the real-life story of the authors' mother, this is the story of a 14-year-old Hispanic American girl's determination to defy cultural tradition and continue her schooling in Depression-era New Mexico. (Rev: BL 1/1–15/05; SLJ 4/05)

7608 Ada, Alma F. *My Name Is Maria Isabel* (3–5). Trans. by Ana M. Cerro. Illus. by K. Dyble Thompson. 1993, Macmillan $13.00 (0-689-31517-1). 64pp. A Puerto Rican girl in the United States resents the fact that her teacher calls her Mary instead of Maria. (Rev: BCCB 6/93; BL 6/1–15/93; SLJ 4/93)

7609 Balgassi, Haemi. *Tae's Sonata* (5–8). 1997, Clarion $15.00 (0-395-84314-6). 122pp. When Tae, a Korean American, is given a school assignment on Korea she must come to terms with her native culture and the memories she has of her homeland. (Rev: BL 10/15/97; BR 5–6/98; HBG 3/98; SLJ 9/97)

7610 Banks, Jacqueline Turner. *A Day for Vincent Chin and Me* (3–6). Series: Project Wheels. 2001, Houghton Mifflin $15.00 (0-618-13199-X). 112pp. When the letters KKK are sprayed on Tommy's house, the sixth-grade Japanese American learns about activism, fitting in, and being proud of who you are. (Rev: BCCB 3/02; BL 11/1/01; HBG 3/02; SLJ 12/01)

7611 Bernier-Grand, Carmen T. *In the Shade of the Nispero Tree* (4–7). 1999, Orchard LB $16.99 (0-531-33154-7). 192pp. Prejudice and racism separate two friends in this story set in Ponce, Puerto Rico, during 1961. (Rev: BCCB 3/99; BL 4/1/99; HBG 10/99; SLJ 3/99)

7612 Caraballo, Samuel. *Estrellita Says Good-bye to Her Island / Estrellita se despide de su isla* (3–5). Illus. by Pablo Torrecilla. 2002, Arte Publico $14.95 (1-55885-338-3). 32pp. In this bilingual book, a young girl bids good-bye to her island home and all the sights and sounds that are important to her. (Rev: BL 5/1/02)

7613 Carter, Dorothy. *Grandma's General Store: The Ark* (3–5). Illus. by Thomas B. Allen. 2005, Farrar $16.00 (0-374-32766-1). 144pp. While their parents look for work up north, Pearl and her younger brother Prince live with their grandmother in a small segregated Florida town. (Rev: BL 2/1/05)

7614 Cheng, Andrea. *Honeysuckle House* (4–7). 2004, Front Street $16.95 (1-886910-99-5). 136pp. The problems of immigration and adjustment to new cultures are shown in this story of two girls of Chinese heritage, told in the girls' alternating voices. (Rev: BL 4/1/04; HB 7–8/04; SLJ 6/04)

7615 Cruz, Maria Colleen. *Border Crossing* (4–8). 2003, Arte Publico paper $9.95 (1-55885-405-3). 128pp. Ceci, 12, can't understand why her Mexican father won't speak Spanish or talk about his home, so she decides to go and investigate. (Rev: BL 11/15/03; SLJ 2/04)

7616 Curtis, Christopher Paul. *The Watsons Go to Birmingham — 1963* (4–8). 1995, Delacorte $16.95 (0-385-32175-9); Dell paper $6.50 (0-440-41412-1). 210pp. An African American family returns to Alabama from Michigan to place their troubled son with his grandmother in this novel set in the 1960s. (Rev: BL 8/95; SLJ 10/95*)

7617 Danticat, Edwidge. *Behind the Mountains* (5–9). Series: First Person Fiction. 2002, Scholastic paper $16.95 (0-439-37299-2). 176pp. Danticat skillfully introduces background information on Haitian history and politics into the journal of young Celiane Esperance, who leaves the island and moves to Brooklyn to join her much-missed father, a reunion that isn't as easy as she expected. (Rev: BCCB 2/03; BL 10/1/02; HBG 3/03; SLJ 10/02)

7618 Dole, Mayra L. *Drum, Chavi, Drum ! / Toca, Chavi, Toca!* (2–3). Illus. by Tonel. 2003, Children's Book Pr. $16.95 (0-89239-186-3). 32pp. In this charming and rhythmic bilingual book, Chavi sets out to prove that being a girl doesn't mean she can't be a great drummer. (Rev: BL 8/03; HBG 4/04; SLJ 12/03)

7619 Edwardson, Debby Dahl. *Whale Snow* (PS–2). Illus. by Annie Patterson. 2003, Charlesbridge $15.95 (1-57091-393-5). Amiqaqq, a young Inupiat boy, attends the first whaling feast of the winter season and learns about the important role the whale plays in Inupiat culture and the welfare of his small Alaskan village. (Rev: BL 8/03; HBG 4/04; LMC 2/04; SLJ 12/03)

7620 English, Karen. *Francie* (5–8). 1999, Farrar $17.00 (0-374-32456-5). Francie, a black girl growing up in segregated Alabama, places her family in danger when she helps a friend who is escaping a racist employer. (Rev: BCCB 10/99; BL 10/15/99; HB 9–10/99; HBG 3/00; SLJ 10/99)

7621 Fleischman, Paul. *Seedfolks* (4–8). Illus. 1997, HarperCollins LB $15.89 (0-06-027472-7). Thirteen people from many cultures explain why they have planted gardens in a vacant lot in Cleveland, Ohio. (Rev: BCCB 7–8/97; BL 5/15/97; BR 11–12/97; HB 5–6/97; SLJ 5/97*)

7622 Fleming, Candace. *Lowji Discovers America* (3–5). 2005, Simon & Schuster $15.95 (0-689-86299-7). 160pp. Lowji, newly arrived in Illinois from his native India, convinces the landlady to keep animals at his apartment building and gets to know his new neighbors. (Rev: BL 3/15/05; SLJ 4/05)

7623 Flood, Pansie Hart. *It's Test Day, Tiger Turcotte* (2–3). Illus. by Amy Wummer. 2004, Carolrhoda LB $15.95 (1-57505-056-0); paper $6.95 (1-57505-670-4). 72pp. Tiger—a boy of multiracial heritage—is already nervous about taking a test, but when it comes to filling in his race, he's genuinely puzzled. (Rev: BCCB 4/04; SLJ 7/04)

7624 Fogelin, Adrian. *Crossing Jordan* (5–8). Illus. by Suzy Schultz. 2000, Peachtree $14.95 (1-56145-215-7). 140pp. Set in contemporary Florida, this novel tells how 12-year-old Cass must keep her friendship with African American Jemmie a secret from her racist father. (Rev: BCCB 4/00; HBG 10/00; SLJ 6/00)

7625 Gardiner, John Reynolds. *Stone Fox* (3–6). Illus. by Marcia Sewall. 1980, HarperCollins LB $15.89 (0-690-03984-0); paper $4.95 (0-06-440132-4). 96pp. Ten-year-old Willy competes against the Indian mountain man, Stone Fox, in the national dogsled races.

7626 Garland, Sherry. *The Lotus Seed* (K–5). Illus. by Tatsuro Kluchi. 1993, Harcourt $16.00 (0-15-249465-0). 32pp. A young narrator tells of fleeing her Vietnamese homeland to settle with her family in America. (Rev: BL 3/15/93*; HB 5–6/93; SLJ 7/93)

7627 Giff, Patricia Reilly. *Maggie's Door* (3–6). 2003, Random LB $17.99 (0-385-90095-3). 160pp. In this poignant sequel to *Nory Ryan's Song,* Nory and her friend Sean describe in alternating chapters the horrors of their voyages — and their enduring spirit and optimism — from their native Ireland to join relatives in America. (Rev: BL 9/15/03; HB 9–10/03; HBG 4/04; SLJ 9/03)

7628 Greenfield, Eloise. *Koya DeLaney and the Good Girl Blues* (4–6). 1995, Scholastic paper $4.50 (0-590-43299-0). 176pp. Sixth-grader Koya DeLaney, whose talent is a gift of laughter, has some growing up to do when family conflicts arise. (Rev: BCCB 3/92; BL 2/15/92; SLJ 3/92)

7629 Hall, Bruce Edward. *Henry and the Kite Dragon* (PS–2). Illus. by William Low. 2004, Penguin Putnam $15.99 (0-399-23727-5). 40pp. A cultural clash in 1920s New York City pits kite-flying 8-year-old Henry and his friends from Chinatown against pet pigeon-owning children from nearby Little Italy. (Rev: BL 5/15/04; SLJ 8/04)

7630 Haugaard, Kay. *No Place* (4–6). 1998, Milkweed $15.95 (1-57131-616-7); paper $6.95 (1-57131-617-5). 175pp. Based on fact, this is the story of a yearlong project in which Arturo and his friends turn a junk-filled barrio lot in Los Angeles into a park. (Rev: BL 11/15/98; HBG 3/99)

7631 Hodge, Merle. *For the Life of Laetitia* (5–9). 1993, Farrar paper $6.95 (0-374-42444-6). Rooted in Caribbean culture and language, this novel celebrates place and community as it confronts divisions of race, class, and gender. (Rev: BL 12/1/92; SLJ 1/93)

7632 Hooks, William H. *Circle of Fire* (5–8). 1982, Macmillan $15.00 (0-689-50241-9). 144pp. In rural North Carolina of 1936, three boys — one white and two African American — try to thwart an attack on Irish gypsies by the Ku Klux Klan. (Rev: BL 3/1/88)

7633 Hoyt-Goldsmith, Diane. *Day of the Dead: A Mexican-American Celebration* (4–6). Illus. 1994, Holiday House LB $16.95 (0-8234-1094-3). 32pp. The Hispanic Day of the Dead celebration as seen through the experiences of an American family living in a Mexican American community. (Rev: BL 7/94; SLJ 9/94)

7634 Johnson, Angela. *A Sweet Smell of Roses* (K–2). Illus. by Eric Velasquez. 2005, Simon & Schuster $16.95 (0-689-83252-4). 32pp. Two African American sisters sneak out of their house to hear a speech by Martin Luther King Jr. (Rev: BL 2/1/05; SLJ 3/05)

7635 Johnston, Tony. *Any Small Goodness: A Novel of the Barrio* (4–7). Illus. by Raul Colon. 2001, Scholastic paper $15.95 (0-439-18936-5). 128pp. Eleven-year-old Arturo Rodriguez, whose Mexican family is new to Los Angeles, describes family life, school, celebrations, and dangers. (Rev: BL 9/15/01; HBG 3/02; SLJ 9/01)

7636 Lee, Lauren. *Stella: On the Edge of Popularity* (5–7). 1994, Polychrome $10.95 (1-879965-08-9). 178pp. A Korean American girl has to choose between being popular and being loyal to her Korean culture. (Rev: BCCB 7–8/94; SLJ 9/94)

7637 Lester, Julius. *Long Journey Home* (6–8). 1998, Viking paper $4.99 (0-14-038981-4). 160pp. Six based-on-fact stories concerning slaves, ex-slaves, and their lives in a hostile America.

7638 Littlesugar, Amy. *A Portrait of Spotted Deer's Grandfather* (2–4). Illus. 1997, Whitman LB $15.95 (0-8075-6622-5). 32pp. Spotted Deer's grandfather, Moose Horn, is afraid that if he has his portrait painted he will lose his spirit. (Rev: BL 1/1–15/98; HBG 3/98; SLJ 9/97)

7639 Lord, Bette Bao. *In the Year of the Boar and Jackie Robinson* (4–6). Illus. by Marc Simont. 1984, HarperCollins paper $4.95 (0-06-440175-8). 176pp. The story of a Chinese girl who leaves China to join her father in New York in 1947.

7640 Mak, Kam. *My Chinatown* (2–6). Illus. by author. 2002, HarperCollins LB $16.89 (0-06-029191-5). 32pp. A young boy from Hong Kong describes his old life and his new life in New York's Chinatown, using simple free-verse poems and realistic paintings that focus on individual people rather than the wider setting. (Rev: BL 12/1/01; HBG 3/02; SLJ 5/02)

7641 Martin, Bill, Jr., and John Archambault. *Knots on a Counting Rope* (PS–5). Illus. by Ted Rand. 1987, Holt $16.95 (0-8050-0571-4). 32pp. Each time his grandson asks him to repeat the story of Boy-Strength of Blue-Horses, Grandfather adds another knot in the counting rope, a metaphor for the passage of time. (Rev: BCCB 11/87; BL 11/15/87; SLJ 12/87)

7642 Matthews, Mary. *Magid Fasts for Ramadan* (3–6). Illus. 1996, Clarion $15.95 (0-395-66589-2). 48pp. Eight-year-old Magid wants to fast as his family does during the holy month for Moslems, Ramadan. (Rev: BCCB 2/96; BL 3/1/96; HB 7–8/96; SLJ 7/96)

7643 Medearis, Michael, and Angela Shelf Medearis. *Daisy and the Doll* (2–4). Illus. 2000, Vermont Folklife Center $14.95 (0-916718-15-8). 32pp. Daisy, an African American girl, is embarrassed when her classroom teacher gives her a black doll to hold during a program on different countries and nationalities. (Rev: BL 9/15/00; SLJ 9/00)

7644 Mochizuki, Ken. *Heroes* (2–4). Illus. by Dom Lee. 1995, Lee & Low $15.95 (1-880000-16-4). 32pp. During the Vietnam War, a Japanese American child becomes the butt of other children's bullying. (Rev: BL 3/15/95; HB 5–6/95; SLJ 7/95)

7645 Montes, Marisa. *Get Ready for Gabi! A Crazy Mixed-Up Spanglish Day* (3–6). Illus. by Joe Cepeda. 2003, Scholastic $12.95 (0-439-51710-9); paper $3.99 (0-439-47519-8). 124pp. Third-grader Gabi speaks Spanish at home and English at school, but when a classmate starts causing problems, what comes out of her mouth is a mixture of the two. (Rev: BL 9/1/03; HBG 10/03; SLJ 11/03)

7646 Murphy, Rita. *Black Angels* (5–7). 2001, Random paper $4.99 (0-440-22934-0). 152pp. In this exciting novel set in Mystic, Georgia, in 1961, an 11-year-old girl is caught up in the struggle that pits the freedom riders and black leaders against racists including the Klan. (Rev: BCCB 3/01; BL 2/15/01)

7647 Myers, Walter Dean. *The Dream Bearer* (5–8). 2003, HarperCollins LB $16.89 (0-06-054277-2). 240pp. David, 12 and living in Harlem, gains valuable insights about his heritage and his ambitions when he gets to know an old man who calls himself a "dream bearer." (Rev: BL 7/03; HBG 4/04; SLJ 6/03)

7648 Myers, Walter Dean. *145th Street: Stories* (5–9). 2000, Delacorte $15.95 (0-385-32137-6). 150pp. A Harlem neighborhood is the setting for this collection of short stories dealing with a wide range of human emotions. (Rev: BL 12/15/99; HB 3–4/00; HBG 10/00; SLJ 4/00)

7649 Naidoo, Beverley. *Journey to Jo'burg: A South African Story* (4–6). Illus. by Eric Velasquez. 1986, HarperCollins LB $15.89 (0-397-32169-4); paper $4.95 (0-06-440237-1). 96pp. The story of Naledi, from a South African village, who travels to the city with her brother to seek their mother, who works in the home of whites, because their baby sister is dying. (Rev: BCCB 5/86; BL 3/25/86; SLJ 8/86)

7650 Namioka, Lensey. *Half and Half* (3–5). 2003, Random $15.95 (0-385-73038-1). 144pp. Eleven-year-old Fiona Cheng is half Chinese and half Scottish; this causes problems when she must choose between heritages at the folk festival. (Rev: BL 9/1/03; SLJ 6/03)

7651 Namioka, Lensey. *Yang the Third and Her Impossible Family* (4–7). Illus. by Kees de Kiefte. 1996, Bantam paper $4.50 (0-440-41231-5). 144pp. Mary, part of a Chinese family newly arrived in Seattle, is embarrassed by her parents' old-country ways in this humorous story. (Rev: BCCB 5/95; BL 4/15/95; SLJ 8/95)

7652 Nelson, Vaunda M. *Beyond Mayfield* (3–5). 1999, Penguin Putnam $15.99 (0-399-23355-5). 144pp. In this sequel to *Mayfield Crossing*, also set in a small Pennsylvania town in the 1960s, the children are still encountering problems being bused to school where African Americans are not accepted and their older friend Sam Wood is trying to register

black voters. (Rev: BCCB 11/99; HBG 3/00; SLJ 8/99)

7653 Perry, Michael. *Daniel's Ride* (2–4). Illus. by Lee Ballard. 2001, Free Will $16.00 (0-9701771-9-4). 32pp. In this colorful glimpse of Latino culture, Daniel enjoys a ride in his big brother Hector's convertible and makes an important promise. (Rev: BL 9/1/01; SLJ 1/02)

7654 Pinkney, Andrea D. *Hold Fast to Dreams* (5–8). 1995, Morrow $16.00 (0-688-12832-7). 112pp. A bright, resourceful African American girl faces problems when she finds she is the only black student in her new middle school. (Rev: BCCB 5/95; BL 2/15/95; HB 9–10/95; SLJ 4/95)

7655 Pitts, Paul. *Racing the Sun* (5–7). 1988, Avon paper $5.99 (0-380-75496-7). 160pp. Brandon begins to understand his Navajo heritage after his grandfather comes to live with him. (Rev: BL 9/15/88; SLJ 2/89)

7656 Robinet, Harriette G. *Walking to the Bus-Rider Blues* (3–6). 2000, Simon & Schuster $16.00 (0-689-83191-9). 147pp. In 1956 at the time of the bus boycotts, African American Alfa Merryfield is involved both in the civil rights movement and a mystery involving a thief who has been stealing the family's meager savings. (Rev: BL 5/1/00; HBG 10/00; SLJ 5/00)

7657 Rodriguez, Luis J. *It Doesn't Have to Be This Way: A Barrio Story / No tiene que ser asi: una historia del barrio* (3–7). Illus. by Daniel Galvez. 1999, Children's Book Pr. $15.95 (0-89239-161-8). 32pp. In this bilingual book, Monchi, a young resident of the barrio, gradually sinks into the violence and crime of gang life, until a sudden death brings him to his senses. (Rev: BL 8/99; HBG 3/00; SLJ 10/99)

7658 Roseman, Kenneth. *The Other Side of the Hudson: A Jewish Immigrant Adventure* (5–8). Illus. Series: Do-It-Yourself Adventure. 1993, UAHC paper $8.95 (0-8074-0506-X). 140pp. Using an interactive format, readers can choose various destinations for a young male Jewish immigrant after he arrives in New York City from Germany in 1851. (Rev: SLJ 6/94)

7659 Sebestyen, Ouida. *Words by Heart* (5–7). 1979, Little, Brown $15.95 (0-316-77931-8). 144pp. Race relations are explored when an African American family moves to an all-white community during the Reconstruction era. (Rev: BL 6/1/88)

7660 Shalant, Phyllis. *When Pirates Came to Brooklyn* (4–7). 2002, Dutton $16.99 (0-525-46920-6). 176pp. When Lee, who is Jewish, befriends Polly, who is Catholic, the two imaginative 11-year-olds learn a harsh lesson about prejudice in this tale set in 1960 Brooklyn. (Rev: BCCB 12/02; BL 10/15/02; HBG 3/03; SLJ 10/02)

7661 Sing, Rachel. *Chinese New Year's Dragon* (3–5). Illus. by Shao Wei Liu. 1994, Simon & Schuster paper $5.99 (0-671-88602-9). 23pp. A young girl works with her family to prepare for the Chinese New Year and then enjoys participating in the joyous festival. (Rev: BL 4/15/94)

7662 Skrypuch, Marsha Forchuk. *Silver Threads* (2–4). Illus. by Michael Martchenko. 2004, Fitzhenry & Whiteside $16.95 (1-55041-901-3). 32pp. This picture-book story of Ukrainian immigrants' bittersweet experiences in early-20th-century Canada is based on the lives of the author's grandparents. (Rev: BL 12/1/04; SLJ 1/05)

7663 Son, John. *Finding My Hat* (4–8). Series: First Person Fiction. 2003, Scholastic $16.95 (0-439-43538-2). 192pp. Autobiography plays a large part in this frank, often funny novel about the son of Korean immigrants growing up in America in the 1970s and 1980s. (Rev: BL 11/15/03; HBG 4/04; LMC 11–12/03; SLJ 10/03)

7664 Soto, Gary. *Local News* (4–7). 1993, Harcourt $14.00 (0-15-248117-6). 144pp. This collection of 13 short stories deals with a number of Mexican American youngsters at home, school, and play. (Rev: BL 4/15/93; HB 7–8/93*)

7665 Soto, Gary. *Petty Crimes* (5–8). 1998, Harcourt $17.00 (0-15-201658-9). Ten short stories about Mexican American teenagers in California's Central Valley deal with some humorous situations but more often with gangs, violence, and poverty. (Rev: BL 3/15/98; HBG 10/98; SLJ 5/98)

7666 Soto, Gary. *Taking Sides* (5–7). 1991, Harcourt $17.00 (0-15-284076-1). 160pp. An unhappy Hispanic American youngster, whose family has recently moved to a new neighborhood, meets problems on the basketball team. (Rev: SLJ 11/91)

7667 Spinelli, Jerry. *Maniac Magee* (5–7). 1990, Little, Brown $15.95 (0-316-80722-2). 192pp. This thought-provoking Newbery Medal winner (1991) tells the story of an amazing white boy who runs away from home and suddenly becomes aware of the racism in his town. (Rev: BL 6/1/90*; SLJ 6/90)

7668 Stanek, Muriel. *I Speak English for My Mom* (3–5). Illus. by Judith Friedman. 1989, Whitman LB $13.95 (0-8075-3659-8). 32pp. A young Mexican American translates for her mother, who can't read English. (Rev: BCCB 2/89; BL 3/1/89; SLJ 5/89)

7669 Talbert, Marc. *Star of Luis* (5–9). 1999, Houghton Mifflin $15.00 (0-395-91423-X). Racial prejudice is the theme of this story, set in New Mexico during World War II, about a Hispanic American boy who discovers he is Jewish. (Rev: BCCB 5/99; BL 3/1/99; HBG 10/99; SLJ 5/99)

7670 Tolliver, Ruby C. *Sarita, Be Brave* (3–6). 1999, Eakin $14.95 (1-57168-184-1). 144pp. After the deaths of her grandmother and mother, 12-year-old Sara leaves Honduras for an eventful truck trip to Texas where she encounters problems and hardships before making a good adjustment. (Rev: HBG 3/00; SLJ 8/99)

7671 Vogiel, Eva. *Invisible Chains* (5–8). 2000, Judaica $19.95 (1-880582-57-0). 280pp. In 1948, 14-year-old Frumie is sent with her crippled younger sister, Judy, to a boarding school for religiously observant Jewish girls. (Rev: BL 7/00; HBG 10/00)

7672 Wahl, Jan. *Candy Shop* (K–3). Illus. by Nicole Wong. 2004, Charlesbridge $15.95 (1-57091-508-3). 32pp. Daniel, a young African American boy,

not only dresses as a cowboy but also tries to act like one, and he takes action when hateful words are written in front of his favorite candy store. (Rev: BL 4/15/04; SLJ 3/04)

7673 Walter, Mildred Pitts. *Ray and the Best Family Reunion Ever* (3–5). 2002, HarperCollins LB $15.89 (0-06-623625-8). 128pp. Eleven-year-old Ray attends his family reunion in Natchitoches, Louisiana, where he meets his estranged grandfather who teaches him about his Creole roots. (Rev: BL 1/1–15/02; HBG 10/02; SLJ 1/02)

7674 Walters, Eric. *War of the Eagles* (5–7). 1998, Orca $14.00 (1-55143-118-1); paper $7.95 (1-55143-099-1). 224pp. During the opening months of the war against Japan, a West Coast Canadian boy witnesses the growing prejudice against Japanese Canadians and also becomes aware of his own Indian heritage. (Rev: BL 12/15/98; BR 5–6/99; HBG 3/99; SLJ 12/98)

7675 Wiseman, Eva. *No One Must Know* (4–7). 2004, Tundra paper $8.95 (0-88776-680-3). 208pp. Thirteen-year-old Alexandra, who's been raised as a Catholic in Canada, learns that her parents are really Jewish Holocaust survivors. (Rev: BL 1/1–15/05; SLJ 6/05)

7676 Yee, Paul. *A Song for Ba* (2–5). Illus. by Jan Peng Wang. 2004, Douglas & McIntyre $16.95 (0-88899-492-3). 32pp. Singing Chinese opera is the forte of three generations of an immigrant family, and even though his father doesn't want him to follow in these footsteps, young Wei Lim is secretly tutored by his grandfather. (Rev: BL 4/1/04; SLJ 6/04)

7677 Yep, Laurence. *Dream Soul* (5–8). 2000, HarperCollins LB $14.89 (0-06-028309-4). 256pp. In this sequel to *Star Fisher* (1991), the Lees, a family of Chinese immigrants who live in Clarksburg, West Virginia, in 1927, face conflicts when the children want to celebrate Christmas. (Rev: BCCB 12/00; BL 12/1/00)

7678 Yep, Laurence. *Thief of Hearts* (5–8). 1995, HarperCollins paper $6.99 (0-06-440591-5). Stacy, who is half Chinese, goes back to San Francisco's Chinatown to trace her family roots. (Rev: BCCB 9/95; BL 7/95; SLJ 8/95)

Family Stories

7679 Adler, C. S. *Ghost Brother* (5–8). 1990, Houghton Mifflin $15.00 (0-395-52592-6). 150pp. After his older brother dies in an accident, 11-year-old Wally finds comfort in his ghost. (Rev: BCCB 5/90; BL 5/15/90; SLJ 5/90)

7680 Adler, C. S. *The No Place Cat* (5–8). 2002, Clarion $15.00 (0-618-09644-2). 153pp. Twelve-year-old Tess runs away from home only to find that life with her father and new stepfamily had its good side after all. (Rev: BCCB 4/02; HBG 10/02; SLJ 3/02)

7681 Adler, C. S. *One Sister Too Many* (5–7). 1989, Macmillan paper $3.95 (0-689-71521-8). 176pp. Casey and her reunited family are being driven crazy by the newest addition — a colicky baby. (Rev: BCCB 3/89; BL 3/15/89; SLJ 4/89)

7682 Adler, David A. *Andy and Tamika* (2–4). Illus. 1999, Harcourt $14.00 (0-15-201735-6). 144pp. While befriending a stray kitten and preparing for the fourth-grade carnival, young Andy Russell, along with his sister, tries to trick his parents into revealing the gender of the baby that is soon to arrive. (Rev: BL 3/1/99; HBG 10/99; SLJ 5/99)

7683 Alcott, Louisa May. *Little Women* (5–9). 1947, Penguin Putnam $19.99 (0-448-06019-1). One of the many fine editions of this enduring story. Two sequels are *Little Men* and *Jo's Boys*.

7684 Aliki. *The Two of Them* (K–4). Illus. by author. 1987, Morrow paper $4.95 (0-688-07337-9). 32pp. A moving story of a tender relationship between a child and her grandfather and of the death of the old man.

7685 Alvarez, Julia. *How Tia Lola Came to Visit Stay* (4–7). 2001, Knopf $15.95 (0-375-80215-0). 160pp. Aunt Lola from the Dominican Republic comes to visit 10-year-old Miguel and his family in Vermont and everywhere she goes she spreads friendliness, enthusiasm, stories, and surprise parties. (Rev: BCCB 4/01; BL 2/15/01; HBG 10/01; SLJ 3/01)

7686 Armstrong, William H. *Sounder* (6–8). Illus. by James Barkley. 1969, HarperCollins LB $15.89 (0-06-020144-4); paper $5.95 (0-06-440020-4). 128pp. Harsh customs and hard circumstances cripple the bodies of both the dog Sounder and his master. Newbery Award winner, 1970. A sequel is: *Sour Land* (1971).

7687 Arrington, Aileen. *Camp of the Angel* (5–8). 2003, Penguin Putnam $16.99 (0-399-23882-4). 160pp. Despite the intervention of caring professionals, Jordan and her brother continue to suffer physical abuse from their alcoholic father until ultimately the care and love they give to a stray cat prompts Jordan to stand up to her father. (Rev: BL 3/1/03; HBG 10/03; SLJ 3/03)

7688 Avi, and Rachel Vail. *Never Mind! A Twin Novel* (5–7). 2004, HarperCollins $15.99 (0-06-054314-0). 208pp. Told in alternating voices, this is the well-written and entertaining story of twins Meg and Edward, who are as different as oil and water. (Rev: BL 4/1/04*; HB 5–6/04; SLJ 5/04)

7689 Banks, Lynne Reid. *Alice-by-Accident* (4–8). 2000, HarperCollins $14.95 (0-380-97865-2). 144pp. Through school compositions and diaries, 9-year-old Alice describes her life, her mother — a lawyer and single parent, and her paternal grandmother. (Rev: BCCB 9/00; BL 6/1–15/00; HB 5–6/00; HBG 10/00; SLJ 6/00)

7690 Barnes, Emma. *Jessica Haggerthwaite: Watch Dispatcher* (3–6). Illus. by Tim Archbold. 2001, Walker $15.95 (0-8027-8794-0). 168pp. Young Jessica and her brother are aghast when their mother decides to make her living at witchcraft and her laid-off husband leaves in protest, in this amusing story set in Britain. (Rev: BL 12/1/01; HBG 10/02; SLJ 3/02)

7691 Bauer, Joan. *Stand Tall* (5–7). 2002, Penguin Putnam $16.99 (0-399-23473-X). 192pp. Tree, a tall 7th grader, has a lot of challenges in this nonetheless humorous novel: his height, his lack of athletic ability, shuffling between his divorced parents' homes, and his veteran grandfather's ailments, to name just a few. (Rev: BCCB 10/02; BL 9/15/02; HB 11–12/02; HBG 3/03; SLJ 8/02)

7692 Bawden, Nina. *Granny the Pag* (5–8). 1996, Clarion $15.00 (0-395-77604-X). Catriona is embarrassed by her grandmother's eccentric ways, such as riding motorbikes and wearing leather jackets, but that doesn't mean she wants to live with her parents instead. (Rev: BCCB 3/96; BL 4/1/96; BR 11–12/96; HB 9–10/96; SLJ 4/96*)

7693 Bawden, Nina. *Humbug* (4–6). 1992, Houghton Mifflin $13.95 (0-395-62149-6). 136pp. First there was her parents' trip to Japan, then her grandmother's trip to the hospital; it's all humbug, which Cora likes to think of as a magic word. (Rev: BCCB 11/92*; BL 10/1/92*; HB 3–4/93; SLJ 10/92*)

7694 Becker, Bonnie. *My Brother, the Robot* (4–6). 2001, Dutton $15.99 (0-525-46792-0). 144pp. Underachiever Chip is faced with a new challenge — a "perfect" robot that his parents feel will be an example to him. (Rev: BL 12/15/01; HBG 3/02; SLJ 10/01)

7695 Beiton, Sandra. *Beauty, Her Basket* (1–4). Illus. by Cozbi A. Cabrera. 2004, Greenwillow $15.99 (0-688-17821-9). 32pp. As she learns from her grandmother how to weave baskets from the grasses of the Sea Islands off the coast of Georgia, a young girl also becomes more familiar with her African ancestry. (Rev: BL 3/1/04; SLJ 6/04)

7696 Bertrand, Diane Gonzales. *Alicia's Treasure* (4–6). 1996, Arte Publico paper $7.95 (1-55885-086-4). 125pp. Ten-year-old Alicia spends her first weekend at the beach, thanks to her brother's girlfriend. (Rev: BL 5/1/96; SLJ 7/96)

7697 Betancourt, Jeanne. *Puppy Love* (5–6). Illus. 1986, Avon paper $2.50 (0-380-89958-2). Aviva is having trouble dealing with her divorced parents' new lives and her own crush on Bob Hanley. (Rev: BL 8/86; SLJ 12/86)

7698 Birdsall, Jeanne. *The Penderwicks: A Summer Tale of Four Sisters, Two Rabbits, and a Very Interesting Boy* (3–6). 2005, Knopf LB $17.99 (0-375-93143-0). 192pp. Four sisters, ages 4 to 12, spend a wonderful summer in the Berkshires with their father. (Rev: BL 4/1/05)

7699 Birdseye, Tom. *Tucker* (5–8). 1990, Holiday House $15.95 (0-8234-0813-2). A story set in rural Kentucky of a young boy reunited with his younger sister after seven years of separation caused by divorce. (Rev: BL 7/90; SLJ 6/90)

7700 Bledsoe, Lucy Jane. *Cougar Canyon* (5–8). 2001, Holiday House $16.95 (0-8234-1599-6). 130pp. A family story and environmental tale about a 13-year-old girl named Izzy who fights to save a cougar in the local park. (Rev: BCCB 2/02; BL 2/1/02; HBG 3/02; SLJ 2/02)

7701 Blume, Judy. *Double Fudge* (4–6). Series: Fudge. 2002, Dutton $15.99 (0-525-46926-5).

160pp. Twelve-year-old Peter Hatcher suffers many trials in this novel, as his younger brother Fudge (Farley) becomes obsessed with money, and a family of long-lost relatives arrives for an extended stay in New York. (Rev: BCCB 11/02; BL 9/15/02; HB 11–12/02; HBG 3/03; SLJ 9/02)

7702 Bonners, Susan. *Making Music* (3–4). 2002, Farrar $15.00 (0-374-34732-8). 96pp. Annie's disappointment with her new home and sadness over the loss of her horse collection begin to fade when she befriends an elderly neighbor. (Rev: BL 11/1/02; HBG 3/03; SLJ 10/02)

7703 Borders, Christine. *Gram Makes a House Call* (2–4). Illus. by author. 1999, Greenhills paper $5.95 (0-9671160-0-7). 77pp. A simple chapter book about the good times a boy has with his unconventional grandmother. (Rev: SLJ 1/00)

7704 Boyd, Candy Dawson. *Charlie Pippin* (5–7). 1988, Puffin paper $5.99 (0-14-032587-5). 192pp. A daughter tries to find out why her father is so embittered about his war experiences in Vietnam. (Rev: BCCB 5/87; BL 4/15/87; SLJ 4/87)

7705 Brand, Christianna. *Nurse Matilda* (3–5). Illus. by Edward Ardizzone. 2005, Bloomsbury $16.95 (1-58234-670-4). 384pp. Nurse Matilda tries to bring order to a family with innumerable children in this inspiration for the movie "Nanny McPhee." (Rev: BL 3/1/05)

7706 Brokaw, Nancy Steele. *Leaving Emma* (4–7). 1999, Clarion $15.00 (0-395-90699-7). 144pp. When Emma's best friend moves away and her father is sent to work overseas, the young girl is left with a mother who suffers from bouts of depression. (Rev: BCCB 3/99; BL 3/1/99; HBG 10/99; SLJ 5/99)

7707 Bryant, Ann. *One Mom Too Many! Bk. #1* (4–7). Series: Step-Chain. 2003, Lobster paper $3.95 (1-894222-78-4). 190pp. Sarah, 12, is not pleased to discover that both her divorced parents have found new romantic interests. (Rev: SLJ 5/04)

7708 Bunting, Eve. *Is Anybody There?* (4–7). 1990, HarperCollins paper $5.99 (0-06-440347-5). 176pp. Marcus is both scared and angry after his latchkey disappears and things are stolen. (Rev: BCCB 10/88; BL 12/15/88; SLJ 12/88)

7709 Burch, Robert. *Ida Early Comes over the Mountain* (4–8). 1990, Puffin paper $4.99 (0-14-034534-5). 140pp. The four motherless Sutton children find a new and most unusual housekeeper in Ida.

7710 Burnett, Frances Hodgson. *A Little Princess* (4–6). Illus. by Tasha Tudor. 1987, HarperCollins paper $3.95 (0-064-40187-1). 240pp. Sad story of a penniless orphan whose fortune is finally restored.

7711 Butcher, Kristin. *The Gramma War* (4–6). 2001, Orca paper $6.95 (1-55143-183-1). 170pp. Annie's life isn't enhanced when her difficult grandmother moves in and takes Annie's room, but an interest in genealogy brings them closer. (Rev: BCCB 1/02; BL 10/1/01; SLJ 9/01)

7712 Byars, Betsy. *Beans on the Roof* (3–5). Illus. 1990, Dell paper $3.99 (0-440-40314-6). 80pp. George's sister and the whole family are writing

roof poems and George feels awful until he can write one too. (Rev: BCCB 11/88; BL 11/1/88; SLJ 11/88)

7713 Byars, Betsy. *Cracker Jackson* (5–6). 1986, Puffin paper $5.99 (0-14-031881-X). 168pp. Eleven-year-old Cracker proves a caring friend to his ex-baby-sitter when he suspects she is a victim of wife beating. (Rev: BL 4/1/85; HB 5–6/85; SLJ 5/85)

7714 Byars, Betsy. *The Glory Girl* (6–8). 1985, Puffin paper $4.99 (0-14-031785-6). 144pp. Anna is the nonsinging member of a family of gospel singers.

7715 Canfield, Dorothy. *Understood Betsy* (4–6). Illus. by Martha Alexander. 1981, Buccaneer LB $25.95 (0-89966-342-7). 219pp. A new edition of the old favorite about Elizabeth Ann and the fearful new way of life that awaits her when she goes to live in the wilds of Vermont.

7716 Carey, Janet Lee. *Wenny Has Wings* (5–7). 2002, Simon & Schuster $15.95 (0-689-84294-5). 240pp. After young Will narrowly escapes death in an accident that killed his sister Wenny, he and his parents must work through their grief. (Rev: BCCB 7–8/02; BL 7/02; HBG 3/03; SLJ 7/02)

7717 Carlson, Margaret. *The Canning Season* (4–6). Illus. 1999, Carolrhoda paper $7.95 (1-57505-283-0). Peggie's family's prejudice threatens her friendship with an African American girl in 1950s Minnesota. (Rev: BL 2/15; HBG 3/00; SLJ 3/99)

7718 Chambers, Veronica. *Marisol and Magdalena: The Sound of Our Sisterhood* (5–9). 1998, Hyperion LB $15.49 (0-7868-2385-8). 141pp. Hispanic American Marisol is sent to live with her grandmother in Panama for a year, and hopes to track down her absent father. (Rev: BL 10/1/98; SLJ 12/98)

7719 Chase, Diana. *The Lighthouse Kids* (4–6). 2004, Fremantle Arts Centre paper $13.50 (1-86368-346-1). 271pp. When their mother dies, Ellen and Davey are sent to live with the lighthouse keeper grandfather they have never met. (Rev: SLJ 11/04)

7720 Choldenko, Gennifer. *Notes from a Liar and Her Dog* (5–8). 2001, Penguin Putnam $16.99 (0-399-23591-4). 244pp. A teacher helps Ant, short for Antonia, get a job in a zoo with her friend Harrison, which boosts Ant's self-confidence somewhat, but she continues to find it difficult to relate to her mother. (Rev: BCCB 7–8/01; BL 4/15/01*; HBG 3/02; SLJ 4/01*)

7721 Clavel, Bernard. *Castle of Books* (3–5). Illus. by Yan Nascimbene. 2002, Chronicle $14.95 (0-8118-3501-4). 32pp. A whimsical tale of a boy who builds a castle in his apartment building's courtyard with his poet father's books. (Rev: BL 2/15/02; HBG 10/02; SLJ 4/02)

7722 Cleary, Beverly. *Ramona the Pest* (3–5). Illus. by Louis Darling. 1968, Morrow $15.89 (0-688-31721-9). 192pp. The fine addition to this popular series follows spirited Ramona Quimby, sister to Beezus and neighbor to Henry, through her kindergarten escapades. Also use: *Beezus and Ramona* (1955); *Ribsy* (1964).

7723 Cleary, Beverly. *Ramona's World* (3–6). Illus. 1999, Morrow LB $14.93 (0-688-16818-3). 192pp. Ramona, now in fourth grade, has a new baby sister, enjoys having a best friend, and feels twinges of love for her old buddy, Yard Ape. (Rev: BCCB 9/99; BL 6/1–15/99*; HB 9–10/99; HBG 3/00; SLJ 8/99)

7724 Cleary, Beverly. *Sister of the Bride* (6–8). Illus. by Beth Krush and Joe Krush. 1963, Morrow $16.89 (0-688-31742-1); Avon paper $4.95 (0-380-72807-9). 256pp. All the excitement and confusion an approaching wedding brings to a household.

7725 Cleary, Beverly. *Socks* (4–6). Illus. by Beatrice Darwin. 1973, Morrow $15.93 (0-688-30067-7); Avon paper $4.99 (0-380-70926-0). 160pp. What happens when the family cat Socks realizes that his position of importance is threatened by the arrival of a baby.

7726 Clifton, Lucille. *The Lucky Stone* (3–5). Illus. by Dale Payson. 1986, Dell paper $3.99 (0-440-45110-8). 64pp. Several stories in the life of a girl's great-grandmother linked by the power of a stone.

7727 Clough, B. W. *An Impossumble Summer* (4–6). 1992, Walker $14.95 (0-8027-8150-0). 146pp. Rianne and her siblings discover their grumpy opossum can speak and grant wishes. (Rev: BL 3/1/92; SLJ 4/92)

7728 Cohen, Barbara. *The Carp in the Bathtub* (3–4). Illus. by Joan Halpern. 1972, Kar-Ben paper $5.95 (0-930494-67-9). 48pp. Two Jewish children decide that the carp in the bathtub should be rescued before it becomes Passover gefilte fish.

7729 Cohen, Miriam. *Mimmy and Sophie All Around the Town* (2–3). Illus. by Thomas F. Yezerski. 2004, Farrar $16.00 (0-374-34989-4). 80pp. Two girls living in Brooklyn during the Depression experience all the joys and irritations of sisterhood. (Rev: BL 1/1–15/04; SLJ 5/04)

7730 Cohn, Rachel. *The Steps* (4–7). 2003, Simon & Schuster $16.95 (0-689-84549-9). 144pp. Annabel resents the complexity of her family life as she reluctantly sets out to visit her father and his new wife, baby, and stepchildren in Australia, but she gradually learns to accept the situation in this humorous portrayal. (Rev: BCCB 2/03; BL 1/1–15/03; HB 5–6/03; HBG 10/03; SLJ 2/03*)

7731 Coman, Carolyn. *What Jamie Saw* (5–8). 1995, Front Street $13.95 (1-886910-02-2). 128pp. In this novel seen through the eyes of a young boy, a mother and her family flee her physically abusive husband. (Rev: BCCB 12/95; BL 12/15/95*; SLJ 12/95*)

7732 Conford, Ellen. *And This Is Laura* (4–6). 1992, Little, Brown paper $4.95 (0-316-15354-0). 192pp. A very ordinary girl discovers that she possesses psychic powers.

7733 Corcoran, Barbara. *The Potato Kid* (5–8). 1993, Avon paper $3.50 (0-380-71213-X). 192pp. In spite of her protests, Ellis must look after an underprivileged girl her mother takes in for the summer. (Rev: BCCB 11/89; BL 11/15/89; HB 1–2/90; SLJ 10/89)

7734 Couloumbis, Audrey. *Getting Near to Baby* (5–9). 1999, Penguin Putnam $17.99 (0-399-23389-X). 224pp. When their baby sister dies and their mother sinks into a depression, 12-year-old Willa Jo and Little Sister go to live with a bossy aunt in this story set in North Carolina. (Rev: BCCB 11/99; BL 11/1/99; HB 11–12/99; HBG 3/00; SLJ 10/99)

7735 Creech, Sharon. *Heartbeat* (3–6). 2004, HarperCollins $15.99 (0-06-054022-2). 192pp. Thoughtful 12-year-old Annie, who enjoys running but not competing, faces numerous personal challenges in this story told in free verse. (Rev: BL 2/1/04; HB 5–6/04; SLJ 2/04)

7736 Creech, Sharon. *Ruby Holler* (4–7). 2002, HarperCollins LB $16.89 (0-06-027733-5). 320pp. An elderly couple, Tiller and Sairy, invite 13-year-old troublesome twins Dallas and Florida to stay with them. (Rev: BCCB 7–8/02; BL 4/1/02; HB 5–6/02; HBG 10/02; SLJ 4/02)

7737 Cutler, Jane. *Leap, Frog* (3–5). Illus. by Tracey Campbell Pearson. 2002, Farrar $16.00 (0-374-34362-4). 208pp. Third-grader Edward has a busy time participating in a variety of projects, particularly the frog-jumping contest that honors Mark Twain, and dealing with newcomer Charlie, a first-grader who regards Edward with awe. (Rev: BCCB 12/02; BL 11/1/02; HB 9–10/02; HBG 3/03; SLJ 10/02)

7738 Danziger, Paula. *Amber Brown Is Green with Envy* (2–4). Illus. by Tony Ross. 2003, Penguin Putnam $15.99 (0-399-23181-1). 160pp. Amber's divorced parents are moving in new directions and the fourth grader finds the tensions difficult to cope with. (Rev: BL 9/1/03; HBG 4/04; SLJ 9/03)

7739 de Anda, Diane. *The Ice Dove and Other Stories* (3–5). 1997, Arte Publico paper $7.95 (1-55885-189-5). 72pp. In these four stories, two involving Christmas and two the classroom, Hispanic American youngsters gain the strength to face problems through help from their loving extended families. (Rev: BL 10/1/97)

7740 Deans, Sis. *Racing the Past* (4–7). 2001, Holt $15.95 (0-8050-6635-7). 151pp. Eleven-year-old Ricky, son of a recently deceased alcoholic father, finds that running provides him with comfort and growing self-esteem. (Rev: BCCB 6/01; BL 6/1–15/01; HB 7–8/01; HBG 10/01; SLJ 6/01*)

7741 DeGross, Monalisa. *Donavan's Word Jar* (2–3). Illus. 1994, HarperCollins LB $14.89 (0-06-020191-6). 80pp. Whereas his friends collect coins or comics, Donavan collects interesting words and puts them in a jar. (Rev: BL 6/1–15/94; SLJ 8/94)

7742 de Guzman, Michael. *Melonhead* (4–7). 2002, Farrar $17.00 (0-374-34944-4). 224pp. Sidney T. Mellon hops a bus to the East Coast to escape the cruelty of his mother and stepfamily in Seattle and the emotional detachment of his father in Los Angeles in a story rich with characterization and an emotionally satisfying ending. (Rev: BL 10/15/02; HBG 10/03; SLJ 9/02)

7743 Delacre, Lulu. *Salsa Stories* (4–7). Illus. 2000, Scholastic paper $15.95 (0-590-63118-7). 112pp. After each of her relatives tells a childhood story about a favorite food, Carmen Teresa records them and supplies appropriate recipes. (Rev: BCCB 5/00; BL 5/1/00; HBG 10/00; SLJ 3/00)

7744 Delton, Judy. *Angel Bites the Bullet* (3–5). Illus. 2000, Houghton Mifflin $15.00 (0-618-04085-4). 144pp. Angel and her best friend try everything to get rid of the unwanted guest who's sharing Angel's room. (Rev: BL 11/1/00; HBG 3/01; SLJ 10/00)

7745 Delton, Judy. *Angel's Mother's Baby* (4–6). Illus. by Margot Apple. 1989, Houghton Mifflin $16.00 (0-395-50926-2). 112pp. Angel is content with her new stepfather in the family, but she had not counted on a new baby. (Rev: BL 9/15/89; HB 11–12/89; SLJ 10/89)

7746 Delton, Judy. *Angel's Mother's Boyfriend* (3–5). Illus. by Margot Apple. 1986, Houghton Mifflin $16.00 (0-395-39968-8). 176pp. Angel and brother Rags are dismayed to discover that their mother has a boyfriend, and doubly dismayed to discover that he is a clown — a real one! Also use: *Angel in Charge* (1985); *Angel's Mother's Wedding* (1987). (Rev: BL 4/1/86; HB 7–8/86; SLJ 8/86)

7747 Delton, Judy. *Back Yard Angel* (3–5). Illus. by Leslie Morrill. 1983, Houghton Mifflin $16.00 (0-395-33883-2). 112pp. Ten-year-old Angel O'Leary is saddled with taking care of her little brother.

7748 Deuker, Carl. *High Heat* (5–8). 2003, Houghton Mifflin $16.00 (0-618-31117-3). 288pp. Even his baseball prowess seems to desert Shane when his father commits suicide and he must move to a tough new neighborhood and school. (Rev: BL 8/03; HBG 10/03; SLJ 7/03)

7749 Dickinson, Peter. *Inside Grandad* (3–6). Illus. by David Johnson. 2004, Random LB $17.99 (0-385-90873-3). 128pp. Eleven-year-old Gavin seeks help from a selkie to reestablish communication with his comatose grandfather in this story with a touch of fantasy. (Rev: BL 1/1–15/04; SLJ 1/04)

7750 Doucet, Sharon Arms. *Fiddle Fever* (4–7). 2000, Clarion $15.00 (0-618-04324-1). 176pp. Felix disobeys his mother, who hates fiddle playing, and builds one out of a cigar box and practices in secret. (Rev: BL 9/1/00; HB 9–10/00; HBG 3/01; SLJ 10/00)

7751 Dowell, Frances O'Roark. *Dovey Coe* (4–7). 2000, Simon & Schuster $16.00 (0-689-83174-9). 192pp. The mountain country of North Carolina in 1928 is the setting of this story of a plucky girl who cares for her siblings and who gets involved in a murder trial. (Rev: BL 4/15/00; HBG 10/00; SLJ 5/00)

7752 Doyle, Eugenie. *Stray Voltage* (5–7). 2002, Front Street $16.95 (1-886910-86-3). 136pp. The electrical problems in Ian's family barn reflect the flickering, unpredictable relationships at home, but a wise teacher helps Ian to cope with his circumstances. (Rev: BCCB 1/03; BL 1/1–15/03*; HBG 3/03; SLJ 10/02*)

7753 Dreyer, Ann L. *After Elaine* (4–8). 2002, Cricket $16.95 (0-8126-2651-6). 136pp. When her difficult older sister Elaine is killed in a car accident, Gina's grief manifests itself in destructive

ways. (Rev: BCCB 5/02; BL 7/02; HBG 10/02; SLJ 7/02)

7754 Duncan, Jane. *Brave Janet Reachfar* (4–6). Illus. by Mairi Hedderwick. 1975, Houghton Mifflin $7.95 (0-8164-3130-2). 32pp. Scottish farm life is depicted through the adventures of young Janet and her relationship with her tyrannical grandmother.

7755 Dunlop, Eileen. *Finn's Island* (4–6). 1992, Holiday House $13.95 (0-8234-0910-4). 128pp. Bored and grieving, Finn takes a trip from Scotland to the Hebrides island of his grandfather's birth, where he learns to see the man more realistically. (Rev: BL 2/1/92; SLJ 6/92)

7756 Dunmore, Helen. *Brother Brother, Sister Sister* (5–8). 2000, Scholastic paper $4.50 (0-439-11322-9). 116pp. Written in diary format, this is the story of Tanya, once an only child and now surrounded by babies after her mother has quadruplets. (Rev: SLJ 8/00)

7757 Elliott, Laura Malone. *Flying South* (5–7). 2003, HarperCollins LB $16.89 (0-06-001215-3). 160pp. In the turbulent political year of 1968, 10-year-old Alice describes her distant mother (who has marital ambitions) and the housekeeper and gardener who give Alice love and valuable advice. (Rev: BL 8/03; HBG 10/03; SLJ 5/03)

7758 Ellis, Sarah. *Out of the Blue* (5–7). Illus. 1995, Simon & Schuster paper $15.00 (0-689-80025-8). 120pp. Twelve-year-old Megan discovers that she has a 24-year-old half-sister whom her mother gave up for adoption years ago. (Rev: BCCB 4/95; BL 5/1/95; HB 7–8/95; SLJ 5/95)

7759 Encinas, Carlos. *The New Engine / La Maquina Nueva* (1–5). Illus. by author. 2001, Kiva $15.95 (1-885772-24-6). A man worried that a computer may replace him remembers his family's fear that the arrival of a diesel locomotive would put his own father out of work. (Rev: SLJ 1/02)

7760 Engel, Diana. *Holding On* (4–6). 1997, Marshall Cavendish $14.95 (0-7614-5016-5). 96pp. Tommy is fearful about spending two weeks with his erratic great-uncle, but slowly they become friends. (Rev: BL 9/15/97; HBG 3/98; SLJ 11/97)

7761 English, Karen. *Strawberry Moon* (5–8). Illus. 2001, Farrar $16.00 (0-374-47122-3). 128pp. On the drive to Los Angeles to visit Auntie Dot, Junie tells her children about the time she herself spent as a child with Auntie Dot, a time made difficult by her parents' separation, and her daughter Imani wonders why Dad has stayed in Chicago. (Rev: BCCB 2/02; BL 12/15/01; HBG 3/02; SLJ 10/01)

7762 Enright, Elizabeth. *Thimble Summer* (4–6). Illus. by author. 1938, Holt $17.95 (0-8050-0306-1); Dell paper $4.99 (0-440-48681-5). 124pp. A small girl on a Wisconsin farm finds a magic thimble. Newbery Award winner, 1939.

7763 Fenner, Carol. *Yolonda's Genius* (4–6). 1995, Simon & Schuster paper $17.00 (0-689-80001-0). 153pp. African American Yolanda tries to prove that her young brother, who does poorly at school, is really a musical genius. (Rev: BL 6/1–15/95; SLJ 7/95)

7764 Fitzhugh, Louise. *Nobody's Family Is Going to Change* (5–8). Illus. by author. 1986, Farrar paper $5.95 (0-374-45523-6). 221pp. There is considerable misunderstanding within a middle-class African American family but also much humor and warmth.

7765 Fleischman, Sid. *Bo and Mzzz Mad* (5–7). 2001, Greenwillow LB $15.89 (0-06-029398-5). 112pp. When his father dies, 12-year-old Bo accepts an invitation from relatives despite a longstanding family feud. (Rev: BL 5/15/01*; HB 5–6/01; HBG 10/01; SLJ 5/01)

7766 Fletcher, Brian. *Uncle Daddy* (4–6). 2001, Holt $15.95 (0-8050-6663-2). 133pp. Nine-year-old Rivers's peaceful life is upset when his long-absent father turns up without warning. (Rev: BCCB 5/01; BL 8/01; HB 7–8/01; HBG 10/01; SLJ 5/01)

7767 Fletcher, Ralph. *Fig Pudding* (5–7). 1995, Clarion $15.00 (0-395-71125-8). 160pp. A year that brings both tragedy and hilarity in the life of a family of six children. (Rev: BCCB 5/95; BL 5/15/95; SLJ 7/95)

7768 Flood, Pansie Hart. *Secret Holes* (4–6). Illus. by Felicia Marshall. 2003, Carolrhoda LB $15.95 (0-87614-923-9). 122pp. After moving with her mother from Florida to a farm in rural South Carolina, 10-year-old Sylvia discovers that her new best friend — 100-year-old Lula Maye — is also her great-grandmother and that the father she'd long believed was dead is very much alive. (Rev: HBG 4/04; SLJ 1/04)

7769 Fogelin, Adrian. *My Brother's Hero* (5–8). 2002, Peachtree $14.95 (1-56145-274-2). 224pp. When Ben and his family travel to Florida for a vacation, Ben meets a girl named Mica, whose life he finds exciting and mysterious. (Rev: BL 2/1/03; HBG 10/03; SLJ 2/03)

7770 Foggo, Cheryl. *One Thing That's True* (5–8). 1998, Kids Can $16.95 (1-55074-411-9). 128pp. Roxanne is heartbroken when her older brother runs away after learning that he is adopted. (Rev: BCCB 5/98; BL 2/15/98; BR 11–12/98; HBG 10/98; SLJ 4/98)

7771 French, Simon. *Change the Locks* (5–7). 1993, Scholastic paper $13.95 (0-590-45593-1). 112pp. Steven wants to know about his past, but his single-parent mother remains silent on the topic. (Rev: BCCB 5–6/93; BL 5/1/93)

7772 French, Simon. *Where in the World* (5–8). 2003, Peachtree $14.95 (1-56145-292-0). 208pp. A move from Germany to Australia is difficult for Ari, a talented young violinist who spends time living in the past while trying to find ways to cope with the present. (Rev: BL 12/1/03; HBG 4/04; SLJ 12/03*)

7773 Friedman, Laurie. *Mallory vs. Max* (2–4). Illus. by Tamara Schmitz. 2005, Carolrhoda LB $15.95 (1-57505-795-6). 159pp. Eight-year-old Mallory is not pleased when her brother Max's new puppy gets all the attention. (Rev: SLJ 4/05)

7774 Fritz, April Young. *Praying at the Sweetwater Motel* (4–7). 2003, Hyperion $15.99 (0-7868-1864-6). 224pp. Sarah Jane, 12, describes her new life living in a motel with her mother and sister, and her hope that her parents will reunite despite her father's abusive behavior. (Rev: BCCB 11/03; BL 10/15/03; HB 11–12/03; HBG 4/04; SLJ 11/03)

7775 Gantos, Jack. *Jack Adrift: Fourth Grade Without a Clue* (4–7). 2003, Farrar $16.00 (0-374-39987-5). 208pp. In this prequel to the four previous books, Jack Henry is nine and has just moved to Cape Hatteras where he has comic experiences and more serious conversations with his dad. (Rev: BL 8/03; HB 11–12/03; HBG 4/04; SLJ 9/03)

7776 Gates, Doris. *Blue Willow* (5–8). 1940, Penguin Putnam paper $5.99 (0-14-030924-1). An easily read novel about a poor girl and the china plate that belonged to her mother. (Rev: BCCB 12/99)

7777 Giff, Patricia Reilly. *Pictures of Hollis Woods* (5–7). 2002, Random $15.95 (0-385-32655-6). 160pp. Twelve-year-old Hollis Woods has finally found a foster home where she feels safe, but when the artist who takes her in begins to suffer from dementia, Hollis finds herself in the position of caregiver. Newbery Honor Book, 2003. (Rev: BCCB 12/02; BL 10/15/02; HB 1–2/03; HBG 3/03; SLJ 9/02)

7778 Gilliland, Hap, and William Walters. *Flint's Rock* (5–7). 1996, Roberts Rinehart paper $8.95 (1-879373-82-3). 144pp. Flint, a young Cheyenne, faces problems when he moves with his parents from the reservation to Butte, Montana. (Rev: BCCB 5/96; BL 5/1/96)

7779 Gilmore, Rachna. *Mina's Spring of Colors* (4–7). 2000, Fitzhenry & Whiteside $14.95 (1-55041-549-2); paper $8.95 (1-55041-534-4). 150pp. Mina is happy when her grandfather comes from India, but with his arrival comes a culture clash that troubles the girl. (Rev: BL 6/1–15/00; SLJ 9/00)

7780 Golding, Theresa Martin. *The Secret Within* (5–8). 2002, Boyds Mills $16.95 (1-56397-995-0). 240pp. Eighth-grader Carly's secret is that her father is abusive and a criminal; the neighbors in the family's new town help her and her mother to finally escape his grip. (Rev: BL 9/15/02; HBG 3/03; SLJ 8/02)

7781 Goodman, Joan E. *Songs from Home* (5–7). Illus. 1994, Harcourt paper $4.95 (0-15-203591-5). 224pp. Anna discovers the truth about her father, who has become a drifter in Italy singing for tips in restaurants. (Rev: BCCB 12/94; BL 9/1/94; SLJ 10/94)

7782 Graff, Nancy Price. *A Long Way Home* (4–7). 2001, Clarion $15.00 (0-618-12042-4). 200pp. Twelve-year-old Riley's mother has recently moved them to a small town, where her interest in an old boyfriend who refused to fight in Vietnam causes mixed feelings for the boy about courage, honor, and heroism. (Rev: BCCB 12/01; BL 11/15/01; HBG 3/02; SLJ 10/01)

7783 Greenfield, Eloise. *Sister* (5–7). Illus. by Moneta Barnett. 1974, HarperCollins $15.99 (0-690-00497-4); paper $4.99 (0-06-440199-5). 96pp. Four years in an African American girl's life, as revealed through scattered diary entries, during which she shows maturation, particularly in her attitude toward her sister.

7784 Griffin, Peni R. *The Music Thief* (5–7). 2002, Holt $16.95 (0-8050-7055-9). 160pp. Alma must decide what to do when her brother and his friend burglarize a neighbor's house where she often trespasses to listen to music in this story set in San Antonio. (Rev: BCCB 1/03; BL 9/15/02; HBG 3/03; SLJ 12/02)

7785 Griffith, Helen V. *Grandaddy and Janetta Together: The Three Stories in One Book* (2–5). Illus. 2001, Greenwillow LB $15.89 (0-06-029238-5). 80pp. Three great picture books — *Grandaddy's Place* (1987), *Grandaddy and Janetta* (1993), and *Grandaddy's Stars* (1995) — are reprinted in one volume that tells the continuing story of the bond between a city girl and her country grandfather. (Rev: BL 12/15/00; HBG 10/01)

7786 Haas, Jessie. *Shaper* (5–7). 2002, HarperCollins LB $16.89 (0-06-000171-2). 192pp. After 14-year-old Chad's dog dies, Chad's new neighbor helps him to train a new dog and to reconnect with his family. (Rev: BCCB 9/02; BL 7/02; HB 5–6/02*; HBG 10/02; SLJ 5/02)

7787 Haddix, Margaret Peterson. *Takeoffs and Landings* (5–8). 2001, Simon & Schuster $16.00 (0-689-83299-0). 208pp. Popular 14-year-old Lori and her overweight older brother Chuck go on a lecture tour with their mother, and together the three finally start to talk about the guilt they feel over the death of the children's father. (Rev: BCCB 10/01; BL 11/15/01; HBG 3/02; SLJ 8/01)

7788 Hahn, Mary D. *As Ever, Gordy* (5–8). 1998, Houghton Mifflin $15.00 (0-395-83627-1). After his grandmother's death, 13-year-old Gordy must move back to his hometown to live with his older brother, and there he finds himself in a downward spiral. A sequel to *Stepping on Cracks* and *Following My Own Footsteps*. (Rev: BCCB 6/98; BL 5/1/98; BR 11–12/98; HBG 10/98; SLJ 7/98)

7789 Hahn, Mary D. *The Jellyfish Season* (5–7). 1992, Avon paper $4.99 (0-380-71635-6). 176pp. Kathleen must learn to cope with change: a move to Chesapeake Bay, a hostile cousin, her father's drinking, and her mother's pregnancy. (Rev: BCCB 2/86; BL 10/1/85; SLJ 10/85)

7790 Hahn, Mary D. *Tallahassee Higgins* (5–7). 1987, Avon paper $4.99 (0-380-70500-1). 192pp. With her mother gone to Hollywood with a boyfriend, 12-year-old Tallahassee is stuck in her mother's hometown, where she finds out a lot about her mother's childhood. (Rev: BCCB 4/87; BL 3/1/87; HB 5–6/87)

7791 Hall, Donald. *Old Home Day* (3–6). Illus. by Emily Arnold McCully. 1996, Harcourt $16.00 (0-15-276896-3). 48pp. The changes in Blackwater Pond in New Hampshire from the Ice Age to the present, with emphasis on the time after the first settlers arrived in 1799. (Rev: BCCB 10/96; BL 9/1/96*; HB 11–12/96; SLJ 10/96)

7792 Hamilton, Morse. *The Garden of Eden Motel* (4–6). 1999, Greenwillow $16.00 (0-688-16814-0). 160pp. Dal, an 11-year-old, spends the summer of 1952 with his new stepfather in the Garden of Eden Motel in Eden, Idaho. (Rev: BCCB 11/99; BL 12/1/99; HBG 3/00; SLJ 10/99)

7793 Hamilton, Virginia. *Bluish* (4–6). 1999, Scholastic $15.95 (0-590-28879-2). 128pp. Dreenie tries to become friends with a girl nicknamed Bluish, wheelchair-ridden and suffering from cancer, who is in Dreenie's fifth-grade class. (Rev: BCCB 10/99; BL 9/15/99; HBG 3/00; SLJ 11/99)

7794 Hamilton, Virginia. *Plain City* (5–7). 1993, Scholastic paper $13.95 (0-590-47364-6). 194pp. Buhlaire's life changes dramatically when the father she believed to be dead unexpectedly arrives in town. (Rev: BCCB 11/93; BL 9/15/93*; SLJ 11/93*)

7795 Hamilton, Virginia. *Second Cousins* (5–8). 1998, Scholastic paper $14.95 (0-590-47368-9). In this sequel to *Cousins,* 12-year-old Cammy learns a secret during a family reunion in her small Ohio town. (Rev: BCCB 11/98; BL 8/98; HB 1–2/99; HBG 3/99; SLJ 11/98)

7796 Hamilton, Virginia. *Time Pieces: The Book of Times* (5–8). 2002, Scholastic paper $16.95 (0-590-28881-4). 128pp. A young girl living in rural Ohio hears stories about her great-grandfather's escape via the Underground Railroad in this semi-autobiographical novel. (Rev: BL 12/15/02; HBG 10/03; SLJ 12/02)

7797 Hansen, Joyce. *One True Friend* (4–7). 2001, Clarion $14.00 (0-395-84983-7). 151pp. Amir's correspondence with his friend Doris comforts him as he tries to fulfill a deathbed promise to his mother to keep his family together. (Rev: BCCB 12/01; BL 12/15/01; HBG 3/02; SLJ 12/01)

7798 Harlen, Jonathan. *The Cockroach War* (5–7). 2004, Allen & Unwin paper $7.95 (1-74114-168-0). 204pp. When the Judges of their obnoxious neighbors, they consider moving, but young Toby and Emma Judge devise a plan to unleash an army of electronically controlled cockroaches to drive the unwanted neighbors away. (Rev: BL 8/04)

7799 Harrison, Mette Ivie. *The Monster in Me* (5–8). 2003, Holiday House $16.95 (0-8234-1713-1). 176pp. A caring foster family and her growing enjoyment in running make Natalie, 13, more optimistic about life. (Rev: BL 4/1/03; HBG 10/03; SLJ 6/03)

7800 Hausman, Gerald, and Uton Hinds. *The Jacob Ladder* (5–8). 2001, Orchard paper $15.95 (0-531-30331-4). 119pp. This story of a young Jamaican who struggles valiantly to cope with poverty, a charismatic but neglectful father, and the problems of growing up is based on the youth of coauthor Uton Hinds. (Rev: BL 5/1/01; HBG 3/02; SLJ 4/01)

7801 Henkes, Kevin. *The Birthday Room* (5–7). 1999, Greenwillow $15.99 (0-688-16733-0). 176pp. Ben travels to Oregon with his mother to visit Uncle Ian who was responsible for Ben's losing his little finger in an accident. (Rev: BCCB 9/99; BL 7/99; HB 9–10/99; HBG 3/00; SLJ 10/99)

7802 Hermes, Patricia. *You Shouldn't Have to Say Good-bye* (5–8). 1982, Scholastic paper $3.25 (0-590-43174-9). 117pp. A moving novel about a girl whose mother is dying of cancer.

7803 Herschler, Mildred Barger. *The Darkest Corner* (5–9). 2000, Front Street $16.95 (1-886910-54-5). 240pp. In this novel set in the Deep South of the 1960s, 10-year-old Teddy is shocked to discover that her beloved dad participated in the lynching of her best friend's father. (Rev: BL 1/1–15/01; HBG 3/01; SLJ 2/01)

7804 Hickman, Janet. *Jericho* (5–8). 1994, Greenwillow $15.00 (0-688-13398-3). 144pp. When Angela takes care of her grandmother during her last illness, she learns about the many disappointments the old lady faced during her life. (Rev: BCCB 11/94; BL 9/1/94; HB 11–12/94; SLJ 9/94)

7805 Hicks, Betty. *Animal House and Iz* (4–7). 2003, Millbrook LB $22.90 (0-7613-2746-0). 176pp. Elizabeth moves in with her father's new family and is surprised to find she enjoys her noisy stepbrothers and their lively life. (Rev: BL 4/15/03; HBG 10/03; SLJ 7/03)

7806 High, Linda O. *Maizie* (4–8). 1995, Holiday House $14.95 (0-8234-1161-3). 177pp. Maizie, a survivor, succeeds in spite of being abandoned by her mother and left with an alcoholic father. (Rev: BCCB 4/95; BL 4/15/95; HB 5–6/95; SLJ 4/95)

7807 Hobbs, Valerie. *Carolina Crow Girl* (5–8). 2000, Puffin paper $5.99 (0-14-130976-8). Carolina, who lives in a school bus with her mother and baby sister, longs for a home like other 6th-graders have, but when she gets it, she realizes that there are more important things in life. (Rev: BCCB 6/99; BL 2/15/99; SLJ 4/99)

7808 Hobbs, Valerie. *Charlie's Run* (4–7). 2000, Farrar $16.00 (0-374-34994-0). 176pp. To escape his parents' impending separation, 11-year-old Joey hits the road and finds there are worse things in life than divorce. (Rev: BCCB 3/00; HB 3–4/00; HBG 10/00; SLJ 3/00)

7809 Hogeweg, Margriet. *The God of Grandma Forever* (4–6). 2001, Front Street $14.95 (1-886910-69-3). 112pp. Maria has a difficult relationship with her religious grandmother in this story translated from Dutch. (Rev: BCCB 6/01; BL 9/15/01; HBG 10/01; SLJ 7/01)

7810 Holcomb, Jerry Kimble. *The Chinquapin Tree* (5–9). 1998, Marshall Cavendish $14.95 (0-7614-5028-9). 189pp. Faced with being sent back to their abusive mother, three youngsters head for the wilderness in this survival story set in Oregon. (Rev: BL 5/1/98; BR 1–2/99; HBG 10/98; SLJ 5/98)

7811 Holm, Jenni. *Our Only May Amelia* (4–6). 1999, HarperCollins LB $15.89 (0-06-028354-8). 160pp. Told in diary form, this is the story of 12-year-old May Amelia, who lives with her large family in Washington State in the late 1800s, and of her troubles when her grandmother comes to stay. (Rev: BCCB 9/99; BL 9/1/99; HBG 10/99; SLJ 6/99)

7812 Holt, Kimberly Willis. *Dancing in Cadillac Light* (5–7). 2001, Penguin Putnam $16.99 (0-399-23402-0). 176pp. A strong, tender story about 11-year-old Jaynell, a tomboy who is growing up in Moon, Texas, in 1968. (Rev: BCCB 3/01; BL 2/1/01; HB 3–4/01; HBG 10/01; SLJ 3/01)

7813 Honeycutt, Natalie. *Twilight in Grace Falls* (5–9). 1997, Orchard LB $17.99 (0-531-33007-9). A moving novel about the closing of a lumber mill that brings unemployment to 11-year-old Dasie Jenson's father. (Rev: BCCB 6/97; BL 3/15/97*; BR 11–12/97; HB 7–8/97; SLJ 5/97)

7814 Hunter, Evan. *Me and Mr. Stenner* (5–8). 1976, HarperCollins $11.95 (0-397-31689-5). 128pp. Abby's attitudes toward her new stepfather gradually change from resentment to love.

7815 Hurwitz, Johanna. *DeDe Takes Charge!* (5–7). Illus. by Diane De Groat. 1984, Morrow $15.95 (0-688-03853-0). 128pp. DeDe's life is not the same A.D. (after divorce).

7816 Hurwitz, Johanna. *"E" Is for Elisa* (2–4). Illus. by Lillian Hoban. 1991, Morrow $12.88 (0-688-10440-1). 80pp. Episodes of everyday life with 8-year-old Russell who loves to tease his 4-year-old sister. (Rev: BCCB 9/91; BL 9/1/91*; HB 9–10/91; SLJ 8/91)

7817 Hurwitz, Johanna. *School's Out* (2–4). Illus. by Sheila Hamanaka. 1991, Morrow $15.00 (0-688-09938-6). 128pp. Lucas looks forward to the arrival of the French girl who has been hired to take care of his younger twin brothers. (Rev: BCCB 4/91; BL 1/15/91; HB 7–8/91; SLJ 5/91)

7818 Jarrett, Clare. *Jamie* (PS–2). Illus. by author. 2002, HarperCollins $13.95 (0-00-198414-4). Jamie and his grandfather care for a needy bird in this quiet tale. (Rev: SLJ 9/02)

7819 Jarrow, Gail. *If Phyllis Were Here* (5–7). 1989, Avon paper $2.75 (0-380-70634-2). 144pp. Libby, age 11, has to learn to adjust to living without her best friend — her grandmother who moves to Florida. (Rev: BL 10/15/87; SLJ 9/87)

7820 Jennings, Patrick. *Putnam and Pennyroyal* (4–7). 1999, Scholastic $15.95 (0-439-07965-9). 176pp. Uncle Frank's colorful story about two birds serves as an allegory of the difficult relations in Cora's family. (Rev: BCCB 12/99; BL 11/15/99; HBG 3/00; SLJ 3/00)

7821 Jocelyn, Marthe. *Mayfly* (PS–2). 2004, Tundra $14.95 (0-88776-676-5). 32pp. Three young siblings' happy summer at a rustic lakeside cabin are captured in paper-and-fabric collages. (Rev: BL 8/04; SLJ 5/04)

7822 Johnson, Angela. *Songs of Faith* (5–8). 1998, Orchard LB $16.99 (0-531-33023-0). Doreen is a child of divorce who is particularly upset by her younger brother's problems adjusting after their father moves away. (Rev: BCCB 6/98; BL 2/15/98; HBG 10/98; SLJ 3/98)

7823 Johnston, Lindsay Lee. *Soul Moon Soup* (5–7). 2002, Front Street $15.95 (1-886910-87-1). 134pp. When homeless Phoebe and her mother hit bottom, Phoebe goes to live with her grandmother and slowly learns to value her own resources in this story told in verse. (Rev: BCCB 2/03; BL 11/15/02; HB 1–2/03; HBG 3/03; SLJ 11/02)

7824 Joosse, Barbara M. *Pieces of the Picture* (5–8). 1989, HarperCollins LB $12.89 (0-397-32343-3); paper $3.50 (0-06-440310-6). 144pp. Emily is not happy when she and her mother move to Wisconsin after her father's death to earn a livelihood running an inn. (Rev: BL 6/1/89; BR 11–12/89; SLJ 4/89)

7825 Karas, Phyllis. *Cry Baby* (5–9). 1996, Avon paper $4.50 (0-380-78513-7). Sam Sloan, 14, the youngest of four daughters, is horrified to learn that her 47-year-old mother is pregnant, begins failing tests at school, and secretly dates the boyfriend of her best friend, who is suffering from a severe eating disorder. (Rev:)

7826 Kehret, Peg. *Sisters Long Ago* (5–8). 1992, Pocket paper $3.99 (0-671-78433-4). 149pp. While surviving a near drowning, Willow has a glimpse of herself living another life in ancient Egypt. (Rev: SLJ 3/90)

7827 Killingsworth, Monte. *Equinox* (5–8). Illus. 2001, Holt $16.95 (0-8050-6153-3). 118pp. Fourteen-year-old Autumn has been happy living on her remote island, but changing relations between her parents threaten this idyll. (Rev: BL 8/01; HBG 3/02; SLJ 9/01)

7828 Kirby, Susan E. *Ida Lou's Story* (4–6). Series: American Quilts. 2001, Simon & Schuster paper $4.99 (0-689-80972-7). 170pp. Lacey likes to hear stories of times past and her great-great-aunt Ida Lou who dreamed of becoming a trapeze artist. (Rev: SLJ 12/01)

7829 Klein, Norma. *Mom, the Wolfman and Me* (5–8). 1972, Avon paper $3.50 (0-380-00791-6). 160pp. Brett's mother is single but the Wolfman is becoming more than a steady boyfriend.

7830 Klein, Robin. *The Sky in Silver Lace* (6–8). 1996, Viking $13.00 (0-670-86266-5). 184pp. The four Melling sisters and their mother move to a large city in Australia to find better times in this sequel to *All in the Blue Unclouded Weather* (1992). (Rev: BCCB 2/96; BL 2/15/96; HB 5–6/96; SLJ 2/96)

7831 Lafaye, A. *The Strength of Saints* (5–9). 2002, Simon & Schuster $16.95 (0-689-83200-1). 192pp. Racial tensions and family problems plague 14-year-old Nissa, who is trying to run the local library in Harper, Louisiana, in this sequel to two earlier novels. (Rev: BL 6/1–15/02; HBG 10/02; SLJ 6/02)

7832 Laguna, Sofie. *Surviving Aunt Marsha* (4–6). 2005, Scholastic $15.95 (0-439-64485-2). 208pp. Tina, 11, and her young brothers dread the arrival of Aunt Marsha, who will look after them while their parents are away. (Rev: BL 6/1–15/05)

7833 Laminack, Lester L. *Saturdays and Teacakes* (PS–2). Illus. by Chris Soentpiet. 2004, Peachtree $16.95 (1-56145-303-X). 32pp. In this nostalgic tale set in 1960s Alabama, a boy rides his bicycle to his grandmother's house, where he mows the lawn and enjoys her teacakes. (Rev: BL 4/1/04; SLJ 4/04)

7834 L'Engle, Madeleine. *Meet the Austins* (5–8). 1981, Dell paper $5.50 (0-440-95777-X). The Austin family — a tightly knit, loving group with four children — is disrupted when a young orphan girl comes to live with them.

7835 Levoy, Myron. *The Witch of Fourth Street and Other Stories* (4–7). Illus. 1991, Peter Smith $19.75 (0-8446-6450-2); HarperCollins paper $4.99 (0-06-

440059-X). 128pp. Eight stories about growing up poor on the Lower East Side of New York City.

7836 Levy, Elizabeth. *Big Trouble in Little Twinsville* (3–6). 2001, HarperCollins LB $14.89 (0-06-028591-5). 96pp. Ten-year-old Eve finds her twin younger sisters a source of great annoyance, but her attitude changes when the two do badly in a talent contest. (Rev: BCCB 7–8/01; BL 7/01; HBG 10/01; SLJ 5/01)

7837 Levy, Elizabeth. *Night of the Living Gerbil* (3–5). Illus. by Bill Basso. 2001, HarperCollins LB $14.89 (0-06-028589-3). 96pp. When Robert's hamster dies, he has it stuffed by a taxidermist who puts the hamster in such a frightful pose that Robert and his brother fear he has been turned into a Zombie. (Rev: BL 11/1/01; HBG 3/02; SLJ 11/01)

7838 Levy, Elizabeth. *Wolfman Sam* (3–5). Illus. 1996, HarperCollins paper $3.95 (0-06-442048-5). 128pp. Young Robert resents his older brother's entry into puberty. (Rev: BL 11/15/96; SLJ 4/97)

7839 Lewis, Beverly. *The Chicken Pox Panic* (2–4). Illus. Series: Cul-de-Sac Kids. 1995, Bethany House paper $3.99 (1-55661-626-0). 80pp. While recovering from chicken pox, Abby plans a birthday party for her Korean brother; but when he arrives, everyone has chicken pox. Also in the series: *The Double Dabble Surprise* (1995). (Rev: BL 9/1/95)

7840 Lewis, Beverly. *Whispers down the Lane* (5–8). Series: Summerhill Secrets. 1995, Bethany House paper $5.99 (1-55661-476-4). 144pp. An Amish girl agrees to hide Lissa, who has run away from her father's abusive treatment. (Rev: BL 9/1/95; SLJ 2/96)

7841 Lexau, Joan M. *Striped Ice Cream* (2–5). Illus. by John Wilson. 1968, HarperCollins LB $14.89 (0-397-31047-1). 96pp. The conquest of poverty is realistically portrayed in this warmly told story about a fatherless African American family as they work together.

7842 Lindbergh, Anne. *The Worry Week* (5–7). Illus. by Kathryn Hewitt. 1985, Harcourt $12.95 (0-15-299675-3); Avon paper $2.95 (0-380-70394-7). 144pp. Left alone with her sisters for a week in Maine, 11-year-old "Legs" spends most of her time tending to and worrying about her siblings. (Rev: BL 6/1/85; HB 9–10/85; SLJ 8/85)

7843 Lindquist, Jennie D. *The Little Silver House* (3–5). Illus. by Garth Williams. 1986, Peter Smith $16.00 (0-8446-6190-2). A 9-year-old girl is intrigued by a mysterious boarded-up house. A reissue of a 1959 title.

7844 Little, Jean. *Emma's Strange Pet* (1–2). Illus. by Jennifer Plecas. Series: I Can Read. 2003, HarperCollins $15.99 (0-06-028350-5); paper $16.89 (0-06-028351-3). 64pp. In a concession to his sister Emma's allergies, Max gives up his quest for a dog and accepts a lizard in this sweet but challenging book for beginning readers. (Rev: BL 7/03; SLJ 10/03)

7845 Little, Jean. *Willow and Twig* (5–8). 2003, Viking $15.99 (0-670-88856-7). 236pp. Two children who believe they are friendless as well as homeless are rescued by their grandmother and must remake their lives. (Rev: BCCB 3/03; BL 7/03; HBG 10/03; SLJ 8/03*)

7846 Loredo, Betsy. *Faraway Families* (2–4). Illus. by Monisha Raja. Series: Family Ties. 1995, Silver Moon LB $14.95 (1-881889-61-0). 56pp. Five short stories, each dealing with a different racial minority, explore the emotional problems that result after families are separated. (Rev: SLJ 8/95)

7847 Lowry, Lois. *Us and Uncle Fraud* (4–6). 1984, Houghton Mifflin $16.00 (0-395-36633-X). 192pp. Two children become disillusioned with their Uncle Claude.

7848 Lurie, April. *Dancing in the Streets of Brooklyn* (5–9). 2002, Delacorte LB $17.99 (0-385-90066-X). 192pp. Judy, from a Norwegian immigrant family, is devastated to learn that the man she knows as "Pa" is not her birth father in this novel set in 1944. (Rev: BCCB 12/02; BL 11/15/02; HBG 3/03; SLJ 9/02)

7849 Lyons, Kelly Starling. *Eddie's Ordeal* (5–8). Illus. 2004, Just Us paper $3.95 (0-940975-16-5). 85pp. When Eddie's grades slip, his father makes him quit baseball. (Rev: BL 2/1/05)

7850 McDonough, Alison. *Do the Hokey Pokey* (3–5). Illus. 2001, Front Street $14.95 (0-8126-2699-0). 120pp. Shy, friendless Brendan is afraid he will be embarrassed by his boisterous mother when she is chosen to be DJ for the all-school party. (Rev: BCCB 9/01; BL 4/1/01; HBG 10/01; SLJ 5/01)

7851 Machado, Ana Maria. *Me in the Middle* (4–6). Trans. from Portuguese by David Unger. Illus. by Caroline Merola. 2002, Groundwood $14.95 (0-88899-463-X); paper $5.95 (0-88899-467-2). 110pp. Young Bel feels close to her late great-grandmother and hears in her mind her accounts of life in Brazil at the turn of the 20th century, but finds her admonitions on behavior difficult to accept. (Rev: BCCB 7–8/02; HBG 10/02; SLJ 8/02)

7852 Mack, Tracy. *Drawing Lessons* (5–8). 2000, Scholastic paper $15.95 (0-439-11202-8). 176pp. Aurora, who adores her artist father, must adjust her expectations when she catches him in a compromising position with one of his models. (Rev: BCCB 3/00; BL 3/15/00; HBG 10/00; SLJ 3/00)

7853 McKay, Hilary. *Saffy's Angel* (4–7). 2002, Simon & Schuster $16.00 (0-689-84933-8). 160pp. Saffron learns she was adopted into her artistic family and travels to Italy in search of her roots. (Rev: BCCB 5/02; BL 5/15/02; HB 7–8/02*; HBG 10/02; SLJ 5/02)

7854 MacLachlan, Patricia. *All the Place to Love* (5–8). Illus. 1994, HarperCollins LB $17.89 (0-06-021099-0). This picture book celebrates the love found in an extended rural family and the joy that a new arrival brings. (Rev: BCCB 7–8/94; BL 6/1–15/94*; SLJ 6/94)

7855 MacLachlan, Patricia. *Seven Kisses in a Row* (2–4). Illus. by Maria Pia Marrella. 1983, Harper-Collins LB $14.89 (0-06-024084-9); paper $4.95 (0-06-440231-2). 64pp. Seven stories about two youngsters who are cared for by an aunt and uncle.

7856 MacLean, Christine Kole. *Mary Margaret and the Perfect Pet Plan* (3–5). 2004, Dutton $15.99 (0-525-47183-9). 168pp. Nearly 9 years old, Mary Margaret wants a pet and makes many efforts to get one, but it's a long time before her allergic father and pregnant mother can see reason. (Rev: BCCB 6/04; SLJ 7/04)

7857 Mansfield, Creina. *Cherokee* (5–8). 2001, O'Brien paper $7.95 (0-86278-368-2). 127pp. Gene's wonderful life with his jazz musician grandfather, Cherokee, comes to an end when his aunt decides he needs a home and an education. (Rev: SLJ 11/01)

7858 Marino, Jan. *For the Love of Pete* (5–8). 1994, Avon paper $3.50 (0-380-72281-X). 197pp. Three devoted servants take Phoebe on a journey to find the father she has never met. (Rev: BCCB 7–8/93; BL 6/1–15/93; SLJ 5/93*)

7859 Marsden, Carolyn. *Silk Umbrellas* (3–6). 2004, Candlewick $14.99 (0-7636-2257-5). 144pp. Eleven-year-old Noi hopes to be able to support her family by creating and selling painted silk umbrellas in this story set in a small Thai village. (Rev: BL 2/1/04*; SLJ 3/04)

7860 Martin, Ann M. *Ten Kids, No Pets* (4–7). 1988, Scholastic paper $3.50 (0-590-43620-1). 184pp. The Rosso family — 12 strong — moves to New Jersey and a 100-year-old farmhouse. (Rev: BL 6/15/88; SLJ 5/88)

7861 Martin, Patricia A. *Travels with Rainie Marie* (5–7). 1997, Hyperion LB $16.49 (0-7868-2212-0). 192pp. When there is no one to care for her and her five brothers and sisters, Rainie Marie is afraid that her bossy aunt will try to split up the family among various relatives. (Rev: BL 5/15/97; SLJ 7/97)

7862 Matas, Carol. *Sparks Fly Upward* (4–8). 2002, Clarion $15.00 (0-618-15964-9). 192pp. Set in Manitoba in the early 20th century, this is the story of 12-year-old Rebecca, a Jewish girl, and her life with a Ukrainian foster family. (Rev: BCCB 7–8/02; BL 4/1/02; HBG 10/02; SLJ 3/02)

7863 Mathis, Sharon Bell. *The Hundred Penny Box* (3–5). Illus. by Leo Dillon and Diane Dillon. 1975, Puffin paper $5.99 (0-14-032169-1). 48pp. Old and frail Aunt Dew tells Michael about her experiences through a box that contains a penny for each year of her life.

7864 Matthews, Kezi. *Flying Lessons* (5–7). 2002, Cricket $16.95 (0-8126-2671-0). 168pp. A girl in a small southern town bonds with an eclectic bunch of adults after the airplane in which her mother was traveling disappears. (Rev: BL 12/15/02; HB 1–2/03; HBG 3/03; SLJ 12/02)

7865 Mazer, Norma Fox. *Girlhearts* (5–9). 2001, HarperCollins LB $16.89 (0-688-06866-9). 224pp. Thirteen-year-old Sarabeth faces many challenges and difficult choices when her single mother dies suddenly. (Rev: BCCB 4/01; BL 7/01; HBG 10/01; SLJ 5/01)

7866 Mead, Alice. *Junebug* (4–7). 1995, Farrar $16.00 (0-374-33964-3). 112pp. Junebug, a young boy, realizes that the only hope for his family is to move from the city project where they live. (Rev: BCCB 12/95; BL 9/15/95; SLJ 11/95)

7867 Mead, Alice. *Junebug in Trouble* (5–8). 2002, Farrar $16.00 (0-374-33969-4). 144pp. Young Junebug and his mother move out of the housing projects, but Junebug continues to get into the trouble his mother was hoping to avoid. (Rev: BCCB 6/02; BL 4/15/02; HB 5–6/02; HBG 10/02; SLJ 3/02)

7868 Mead, Alice. *Walking the Edge* (5–8). 1995, Whitman LB $14.95 (0-8075-8649-8). 190pp. Scott escapes the abuse of his drunken father by throwing himself into his 4-H science project. (Rev: SLJ 12/95)

7869 Medearis, Angela Shelf. *What Did I Do to Deserve a Sister Like You?* (3–5). Illus. by Don Tate and Mark Galbreath. 2002, Eakin $12.95 (1-57168-471-9); paper $7.95 (1-57168-642-8). 123pp. Sharie, 10, juggles her dislike of her older sister, her problems with her piano teacher, and a longing to ride on a roller-coaster. (Rev: HBG 10/02; SLJ 5/02)

7870 Miles, Betty. *Just the Beginning* (4–7). 1978, Avon paper $2.50 (0-380-01913-2). 148pp. Being relatively poor in an upper-class neighborhood causes problems for 13-year-old Catherine Myers.

7871 Miller, Dorothy R. *Home Wars* (5–8). 1997, Simon & Schuster $16.00 (0-689-81411-9). 176pp. Halley has misgivings when her father brings home three rifles, one for himself and the others for her two brothers. (Rev: BL 9/1/97; HBG 3/98; SLJ 10/97)

7872 Modiano, Patrick. *Catherine Certitude* (4–7). Trans. by William Rodarmor. Illus. by Jean-Jacques Sempe. 2001, Godine $17.95 (0-87923-959-X). 64pp. An adult Catherine reminisces about her life as a youngster in Paris — living with her father, puzzling over his job, going to ballet classes, eating in restaurants — in this stylishly illustrated chapter book delivered in picture-book format. (Rev: BL 12/15/01; HBG 3/02; SLJ 2/02)

7873 Montgomery, L. M. *Christmas with Anne and Other Holiday Stories* (4–7). 1996, McClelland & Stewart Tundra Books $12.95 (0-7710-6204-4). 214pp. A collection of 16 short pieces and stories (two from the Anne of Green Gables books) that deal with Christmas. (Rev: BL 9/1/96)

7874 Morris, Jennifer. *Come, Llamas* (4–6). 2005, Delacorte LB $17.99 (0-385-90229-8). 208pp. Nine-year-old JT describes the summer he plays a growing role in his family's Alaska llama ranch and must deal with his grandfather's illness. (Rev: BL 2/1/05; SLJ 1/05)

7875 Muldrow, Diane. *Stirring It Up* (4–6). 2002, Grosset paper $4.99 (0-448-42815-6). 160pp. Eleven-year-old twins Molly and Amanda spend an amusing summer learning to cook, making friends and helping neighbors in this book that includes recipes, activities, and tips. (Rev: BL 7/02; SLJ 8/02)

7876 Mulford, Philippa Greene. *The Holly Sisters on Their Own* (4–6). 1998, Marshall Cavendish $14.95 (0-7614-5022-X). 158pp. Charmaine, age 11, is not happy at the prospect of her older half sister's arrival to spend the summer in New York City, but

time produces a friendship. (Rev: BCCB 7–8/98; BL 5/1/98; HBG 10/98; SLJ 4/98)

7877 Myers, Anna. *Rosie's Tiger* (5–8). 1994, Walker $14.95 (0-8027-8305-8). When Rosie's brother returns from the Korean War, he brings a wife and son with him and Rosie becomes consumed by jealousy. (Rev: BL 9/15/94; SLJ 11/94)

7878 Namioka, Lensey. *Yang the Eldest and His Odd Jobs* (3–7). Illus. 2000, Little, Brown $15.95 (0-316-59011-8). 128pp. In this story about the Yangs, a family of new Chinese Americans, First Brother, who wants to buy a violin, takes odd jobs — babysitting, waiting tables, and so forth — to make money. (Rev: BL 2/15/00; HBG 10/00; SLJ 4/00)

7879 Nelson, Rosemary. *Hubcaps and Puppies* (3–6). 2002, Napoleon paper $8.95 (0-929141-98-9). 184pp. Thirteen-year-old Nikki faces difficult choices, such as whether to allow herself to love a stray puppy so soon after the death of her dog. (Rev: BL 3/1/03)

7880 Nelson, Theresa. *Earthshine* (5–9). 1994, Orchard LB $17.99 (0-531-08717-4). "Slim" decides to live with her father and his lover, who is dying of AIDS. At a support group, she meets Isaiah, whose pregnant mother also has AIDS. (Rev: BL 9/1/94; SLJ 9/94*)

7881 Nelson, Theresa. *Ruby Electric* (5–8). 2003, Simon & Schuster $16.95 (0-689-83852-2). 272pp. The movie script she is writing brings 12-year-old Ruby needed relief from the realities of her life. (Rev: BL 7/03; HB 7–8/03; HBG 10/03; SLJ 6/03*)

7882 Nixon, Joan Lowery. *Maggie Forevermore* (5–8). 1987, Harcourt $13.95 (0-15-250345-5). In this sequel to *Maggie, Too* and *And Maggie Makes Three* (both o.p.), 13-year-old Maggie resents spending Christmas with her father and his new wife in California. (Rev: BCCB 4/87; BL 3/1/87; SLJ 3/87)

7883 O'Connor, Barbara. *Moonpie and Ivy* (5–8). 2001, Farrar $16.00 (0-374-35059-0). 160pp. Twelve-year-old Pearl is hurt and confused when her mother leaves her at Aunt Ivy's home and disappears. (Rev: BCCB 5/01; BL 5/1/01*; HB 5–6/01; HBG 10/01; SLJ 5/01)

7884 Park, Barbara. *The Graduation of Jake Moon* (5–8). 2000, Simon & Schuster $15.00 (0-689-83912-X). 115pp. Jake Moon finds it impossible to cope with his grandfather's gradual disintegration from Alzheimer's disease. (Rev: BCCB 12/00; BL 6/1–15/00; HB 9–10/00; HBG 3/01; SLJ 9/00)

7885 Paterson, Katherine. *Come Sing, Jimmy Jo* (5–7). 1985, Avon paper $3.99 (0-380-70052-2). 208pp. The family decides it's time to include James in their singing group. (Rev: BL 9/1/87)

7886 Paterson, Katherine. *Jacob Have I Loved* (6–8). 1980, HarperCollins LB $15.89 (0-690-04079-2); paper $5.95 (0-06-440368-8). 228pp. A story set in the Chesapeake Bay region about the rivalry between two sisters. Newbery Award winner, 1981.

7887 Paterson, Katherine. *Park's Quest* (4–7). 1989, Puffin paper $5.99 (0-14-034262-1). 160pp. A boy searches for the cause of his father's death in Vietnam. (Rev: BCCB 4/88; HB 7–8/88; SLJ 5/88)

7888 Paterson, Katherine. *The Same Stuff as Stars* (5–7). 2002, Clarion $15.00 (0-618-24744-0). 256pp. An unhappy 11-year-old Angel and her younger brother Bernie are sent to live with their father's grandmother, where Angel finds comfort in a mysterious man who introduces her to astronomy. (Rev: BCCB 10/02; BL 9/15/02; HB 9–10/02; HBG 3/03; SLJ 8/02*)

7889 Pearson, Kit. *A Handful of Time* (4–7). 1988, Puffin paper $5.99 (0-14-032268-X). 192pp. Patricia is ill at ease staying with her aunt and cousins while her parents work out a divorce. (Rev: HB 7–8/88)

7890 Pearson, Mary E. *Scribbler of Dreams* (5–8). 2001, Harcourt $17.00 (0-15-202320-8). 240pp. Bram, whose family feuds constantly with the Crutchfield clan, finds she has fallen in love with a Crutchfield boy and must keep her identity a secret from him. (Rev: BCCB 5/01; BL 4/15/01; HBG 10/01; SLJ 5/01)

7891 Peck, Richard. *A Year Down Yonder* (5–8). 2000, Dial $16.99 (0-8037-2518-3). 130pp. In this Newbery medal winner, 15-year-old Mary Alice visits her feisty, independent, but lovable Grandma Dowdel in rural Illinois during the Great Depression. A sequel to the honor book *A Long Way from Chicago* (1998). (Rev: BCCB 1/01; BL 10/15/00; HB 11–12/00; HBG 3/01; SLJ 9/00)

7892 Perez, Amada Irma. *My Diary from Here to There / Mi Diario de Aqui Hasta Alla* (2–4). Trans. by Consuelo Hernandez. Illus. by Maya Christina Gonzalez. 2002, Children's Book Pr. $16.95 (0-89239-175-8). 32pp. Amada tells her diary her worries about moving from Mexico to California in this bilingual book with appealing illustrations. (Rev: BL 11/1/02; HB 9–10/02; HBG 3/03)

7893 Pfeffer, Susan Beth. *Devil's Den* (4–7). 1998, Walker $15.95 (0-8027-8650-2). 128pp. Joey faces the pain of rejection when he seeks out his real father, discovers he is not wanted by him, and must accept living permanently with his mom and loving stepfather. (Rev: BCCB 5/98; BL 5/15/98; HBG 10/98; SLJ 6/98)

7894 Pfeffer, Susan Beth. *Kid Power* (4–6). Illus. by Leigh Grant. 1991, Scholastic paper $3.99 (0-590-42607-9). 121pp. A spunky young girl organizes an employment agency for herself and friends when her mother loses her job.

7895 Porte, Barbara Ann. *Fat Fanny, Beanpole Bertha and the Boys* (4–6). Illus. by Maxie Chambliss. 1991, Orchard LB $16.99 (0-531-08528-7). 112pp. Fanny and Bertha are best friends despite their differences. (Rev: BCCB 4/91*; BL 3/1/91; HB 7–8/91; SLJ 2/91*)

7896 Pryor, Bonnie. *Toenails, Tonsils, and Tornadoes* (3–5). Illus. 1997, Morrow $15.00 (0-688-14885-9). 160pp. Fourth-grader Martin is not too happy when his Aunt Henrietta visits, principally because he has to give up his room. (Rev: BCCB 6/97; BL 5/15/97; SLJ 5/97)

7897 Regan, Dian C. *The Friendship of Milly and Tug* (2–3). Illus. by Jennifer Danza. Series: A Redfeather Chapter Book. 1999, Holt $15.95 (0-8050-5935-0). 61pp. A beginning chapter book about two sisters and how the older one is put in her place after she starts to get bossy. (Rev: HBG 10/99; SLJ 7/99)

7898 Rinn, Miriam. *The Saturday Secret* (4–7). Illus. 1998, Alef Design Group paper $7.95 (1-881283-26-7). 144pp. Jason's resentment and anger at having to obey the strict rules imposed by his devout Orthodox Jewish stepfather are made more intense because of his grief at the death of his beloved father. (Rev: BL 10/1/98; SLJ 2/99)

7899 Roberts, Diane. *Made You Look* (4–6). 2003, Delacorte LB $17.99 (0-385-90119-4). 150pp. In this hilarious tale of a family camping trip to California, sixth grader Jason finds he must endure a seemingly endless string of indignities on his quest to reach the West Coast and appear on his favorite TV game show. (Rev: HBG 10/03; SLJ 9/03)

7900 Robinson, Nancy K. *Angela and the Broken Heart* (3–5). 1991, Scholastic $12.95 (0-590-43212-5). 144pp. A warm story of family problems with Angela, who, in the second grade, wonders whether she is engaged or not, and her suddenly stuck-up brother. (Rev: BL 4/1/91; SLJ 4/91)

7901 Rodowsky, Colby. *Clay* (4–7). 2001, Farrar $16.00 (0-374-31338-5). 176pp. Eleven-year-old Elsie and her autistic younger brother have been living a desperate life since her mother kidnapped them from their father four years before. (Rev: BCCB 3/01; BL 5/1/01; HBG 10/01; SLJ 4/01)

7902 Rodowsky, Colby. *Not Quite a Stranger* (5–9). 2003, Farrar $16.00 (0-374-35548-7). 192pp. In alternating chapters, 13-year-old Charlotte (Tottie) and 17-year-old Zach describe the upheaval in their lives when Zach's mother dies and he seeks a home with his and Tottie's father, who believed that Zach had been given up for adoption. (Rev: BCCB 8/03; BL 11/15/03; HBG 4/04; SLJ 9/03)

7903 Rodowsky, Colby. *Spindrift* (5–8). 2000, Farrar $16.00 (0-374-37155-5). 112pp. A realistic family story about 13-year-old Cassie who lives at Spindrift, a seaside bed-and-breakfast run by her grandmother, and who tries to reunite her sister and estranged husband. (Rev: BCCB 3/00; BL 2/15/00; HBG 10/00; SLJ 3/00)

7904 Rylant, Cynthia. *In Aunt Lucy's Kitchen* (2–4). Illus. Series: Cobble Street Cousins. 1998, Simon & Schuster $15.00 (0-689-81711-8). 54pp. Three cousins start their own cookie company and find a boyfriend for their wonderful Aunt Lucy. (Rev: BCCB 1/99; BL 1/1–15/99; HBG 3/99; SLJ 2/99)

7905 Rylant, Cynthia. *Special Gifts* (3–5). Illus. Series: Cobble Street Cousins. 1999, Simon & Schuster $14.00 (0-689-81714-2). 55pp. Three cousins, who are staying with their aunt, are out of school for the summer and take up sewing as a hobby. (Rev: BL 6/1–15/99; HBG 10/99; SLJ 6/99)

7906 Rylant, Cynthia. *Summer Party* (2–4). Illus. Series: Cobble Street Cousins. 2001, Simon & Schuster $15.00 (0-689-83241-9). 64pp. A story of anticipation and parties that will please fans of the series. (Rev: BL 6/1–15/01; HBG 3/02; SLJ 5/01)

7907 Rylant, Cynthia. *Wedding Flowers* (2–4). Illus. by Wendy A. Halperin. Series: Cobble Street Cousins. 2002, Simon & Schuster $15.00 (0-689-83242-7). 80pp. Rosie, Lily, and their cousin Tess are enlisted to help plan their Aunt Lucy's wedding. (Rev: BL 2/15/02; HBG 10/02; SLJ 8/02)

7908 Salisbury, Graham. *Lord of the Deep* (5–8). 2001, Delacorte $15.95 (0-385-72918-9). 182pp. During his time working on his stepfather's deep-sea fishing boat, Mikey, 13, learns about financial problems, lying, unpleasant characters, and romance. (Rev: BCCB 7–8/01; BL 8/01; HB 9–10/01*; HBG 3/02; SLJ 8/01*)

7909 Salmansohn, Karen. *One Puppy, Three Tales* (4–6). Illus. by author. Series: Alexandra Rambles On! 2001, Tricycle $12.95 (1-58246-044-2). Twelve-year-old Alexandra shares vivid details of her life and her relationships with her mother, father, and friends. (Rev: HBG 10/01; SLJ 6/01)

7910 Salmansohn, Karen. *Wherever I Go, There I Am* (4–7). Illus. by author. Series: Alexandra Rambles On! 2002, Tricycle $12.95 (1-58246-079-5). Alexandra's journal reveals her angst about issues such as scary movies and becoming a teenager. (Rev: HBG 3/03; SLJ 2/03)

7911 Seidler, Tor. *Brothers Below Zero* (5–8). 2002, HarperCollins LB $14.89 (0-06-029180-X). 137pp. Artistic Tim, overwhelmed by his athletic younger brother, eventually runs away to the place he has felt most valued. (Rev: BCCB 3/02; BL 1/1–15/02; HBG 10/02; SLJ 4/02)

7912 Shange, Ntozake. *Daddy Says* (5–9). 2003, Simon & Schuster $15.95 (0-689-83081-5). 192pp. Two sisters on a Texas ranch grapple with family problems at the same time that there is rodeo excitement. (Rev: BCCB 3/03; BL 3/15/03; HBG 10/03; SLJ 2/03)

7913 Shearer, Alex. *The Great Blue Yonder* (5–8). 2002, Clarion $15.00 (0-618-21257-4). 192pp. Twelve-year-old Harry, who has died in an accident, experiences afterlife on the Other Side and has the opportunity to review his relations with other family members. (Rev: BCCB 6/02; HBG 10/02; SLJ 4/02)

7914 Sidney, Margaret. *The Five Little Peppers and How They Grew* (4–6). 1981, Buccaneer LB $27.95 (0-89966-340-0). 302pp. The classic of five children growing up many decades ago.

7915 Simon, Norma. *How Do I Feel?* (4–6). Illus. by Joe Lasker. 1970, Whitman LB $14.95 (0-8075-3414-5). A small boy has tangled, emotional problems with his twin and his older brother.

7916 Slate, Joseph. *Crossing the Trestle* (5–8). 1999, Marshall Cavendish $14.95 (0-7614-5053-X). 144pp. Set in West Virginia in 1944, this novel centers on 11-year-old Petey and the problems he and his family face after their father is killed in an accident. (Rev: BCCB 12/99; BL 1/1–15/00; HBG 3/00; SLJ 10/99)

7917 Smith, Jane Denitz. *Fairy Dust* (4–6). 2002, HarperCollins LB $15.89 (0-06-029280-6). 160pp.

Nine-year-old Ruthie has a confusing time when her new baby-sitter blends talk of fairies with shoplifting and theft. (Rev: BCCB 4/02; BL 12/1/01; HBG 10/02; SLJ 1/02)

7918 Smith, Janice Lee. *The Monster in the Third Dresser Drawer and Other Stories About Adam Joshua* (3–5). Illus. by Dick Gackenbach. 1981, HarperCollins LB $15.89 (0-06-025739-3); paper $4.25 (0-06-440223-1). 96pp. Adam Joshua faces many everyday problems, including a new baby sister, in these six stories. A sequel is: *The Kid Next Door and Other Headaches: Stories about Adam Joshua* (1984).

7919 Smith, Robert K. *The War with Grandpa* (4–6). Illus. by Richard Lauter. 1984, Dell paper $4.99 (0-440-49276-9). 128pp. Peter resents giving up his bedroom to his grandfather.

7920 Smith, Roland. *Zach's Lie* (5–8). 2001, Hyperion $15.99 (0-7868-0617-6). 240pp. Young Jack and Joanne have trouble adapting to their new roles as Zach and Wanda when they are taken into the witness protection program. (Rev: BL 5/15/01; HBG 10/01; SLJ 6/01)

7921 Springer, Nancy. *Separate Sisters* (5–7). 2001, Holiday House $16.95 (0-8234-1544-9). 84pp. Two teenage girls deal with the divorce of their parents in different ways. (Rev: BCCB 2/02; BL 2/1/02; HB 3–4/02; HBG 10/02; SLJ 2/02)

7922 Stacey, Cherylyn. *How Do You Spell Abducted?* (4–8). 1996, Red Deer paper $7.95 (0-88995-148-9). When their divorced father abducts Deb, Paige, and Cory, the three youngsters must escape from his home in the U.S. and make their way back to their mother in Canada. (Rev: BR 3–4/97; SLJ 12/96)

7923 Stevenson, Laura C. *Happily After All* (4–7). 1990, Houghton Mifflin $16.00 (0-395-50216-0). 256pp. Becca goes to live with her mother, who she believes abandoned her when she was young. (Rev: BCCB 5/90; BL 4/15/90; HB 5–6/90; SLJ 6/90)

7924 Stewart, Sarah. *The Journey* (2–4). Illus. by David Small. 2001, Farrar $16.00 (0-374-33905-8). 40pp. A young Amish girl from the country keeps a diary about her exciting visit to Chicago with her mother. (Rev: BL 3/15/01; HB 3–4/01; HBG 10/01; SLJ 3/01)

7925 Stolz, Mary. *Go Fish* (3–5). Illus. by Pat Cummings. 1991, HarperCollins LB $14.89 (0-06-025822-5). 80pp. Thomas and his grandfather spend warm times together. (Rev: BCCB 5/91; BL 5/15/91; HB 7–8/91; SLJ 5/91*)

7926 Stone, Phoebe. *All the Blue Moons at the Wallace Hotel* (5–7). 2000, Little, Brown $15.95 (0-316-81645-0). 208pp. This story about family love and problems centers around 11-year-old Fiona, her lively younger sister, their withdrawn mother, and the memories of the wealth the family once had. (Rev: BCCB 12/00; BL 12/1/00; HBG 3/01; SLJ 12/00)

7927 Talbert, Marc. *The Purple Heart* (5–8). 1992, HarperCollins $14.95 (0-06-020428-1); Avon paper $3.50 (0-380-71985-1). Luke's father has returned from Vietnam an anguished, brooding war hero, and

Luke loses his father's Purple Heart, leading to confrontation and reconciliation. (Rev: BL 12/15/91*; SLJ 2/92)

7928 Taylor, Sydney. *All-of-a-Kind Family* (3–6). Illus. by Helen John. 1980, Peter Smith $19.50 (0-8446-6253-4); Dell paper $4.99 (0-440-40059-7). 192pp. Warm and moving stories of Jewish family life in New York City. Also use: *Ella of All-of-a-Kind Family* (1980, Dell paper).

7929 Thesman, Jean. *When the Road Ends* (5–8). 1992, Houghton Mifflin $16.00 (0-395-59507-X). 184pp. Mary tells how she and other foster children spend a summer in a remote cabin with a sick adult. (Rev: BCCB 4/92; HB 5–6/92; SLJ 4/92)

7930 Uhlberg, Myron. *The Printer* (2–4). Trans. and illus. by Henri Sorensen. 2003, Peachtree $16.95 (1-56145-221-1). 32pp. In 1940 New York City, a young boy describes how his deaf father, a printer, alerted his hearing co-workers to a deadly fire in the pressroom; an endnote supplies historical details. (Rev: BL 9/1/03; HBG 4/04; SLJ 12/03)

7931 Van Steenwyk, Elizabeth. *Three Dog Winter* (5–8). 1987, Walker $13.95 (0-8027-6718-4). A story of dog racing, this family tale tells of 12-year-old Scott and his Malamute, Kaylah. (Rev: BL 2/1/88; SLJ 12/87)

7932 Viglucci, Patricia C. *Sun Dance at Turtle Rock* (5–7). 1996, Patri paper $4.95 (0-9645914-9-9). 128pp. The child of a racially mixed marriage feels uncomfortable when he visits his white grandfather. (Rev: BL 4/15/96)

7933 Walker, Pamela. *Pray Hard* (5–8). 2001, Scholastic paper $15.95 (0-439-21586-2). 177pp. After Amelia Forest's father dies in an airplane accident for which she feels responsible, her life and that of her family fall apart. (Rev: BL 3/1/01; HBG 10/01; SLJ 7/01)

7934 Wallace, Bill. *Beauty* (5–7). 1988, Holiday House $16.95 (0-8234-0715-2). 192pp. Luke finds the adjustment difficult when he and his mother go to live on his grandfather's Oklahoma farm. (Rev: BCCB 11/88; BL 2/1/89; SLJ 10/88)

7935 Wallace, Bill. *True Friends* (4–7). 1994, Holiday House $15.95 (0-8234-1141-9). 160pp. Everything in Courtney's life becomes a shambles and she must rely on her new friend Judy to help her. (Rev: BCCB 11/94; BL 10/15/94; SLJ 10/94)

7936 Walsh, Melanie. *Minnie and Her Baby Brother* (PS). Illus. by author. 2003, Candlewick $7.99 (0-7636-2060-2). In a small lift-the-flap format, 3-year-old Minnie compares her own attributes and abilities with those of her baby brother. (Rev: HBG 4/04; SLJ 11/03)

7937 Warner, Sally. *A Long Time Ago Today* (4–7). 2003, Viking $15.99 (0-670-03604-8). 208pp. At the age of 12, Dilly wants to know what her mother, who died when Dilly was 6, was really like. (Rev: BL 11/1/03; HBG 4/04; SLJ 12/03)

7938 Weeks, Sarah. *My Guy* (4–7). 2001, HarperCollins LB $14.89 (0-06-028370-X). 192pp. Guy and Lana agree on only one thing — they don't want to become part of a blended family — and they set out to make sure it won't happen. (Rev:

BCCB 6/01; BL 8/01; HB 7–8/01; HBG 10/01; SLJ 5/01)

7939 Welch, Sheila K. *The Shadowed Unicorn* (4–6). 2000, Front Street $15.95 (0-8126-2895-0). 192pp. Identical twins Brendan and Nick join their older, bossy sister Arni on a hunt for a black unicorn in this family story that borders on fantasy. (Rev: BCCB 10/00; BL 4/15/00; HBG 10/00; SLJ 7/00)

7940 Wesley, Valerie Wilson. *Willimena and the Cookie Money* (2–4). 2001, Hyperion $15.99 (0-7868-0465-3). 128pp. Young Willimena has spent the Girl Scout cookie money on a good cause, which is revealed after she and her older sister fail to recoup her losses. (Rev: HBG 10/01; SLJ 8/01)

7941 White, Ruth. *Belle Prater's Boy* (5–9). 1996, Farrar $17.00 (0-374-30668-0). Set in Appalachia in the 1950s, this moving, often humorous story tells about Gypsy and her unusual cousin Woodrow, who hides a secret involving his mother's disappearance. (Rev: BL 4/15/96; BR 9–10/96; SLJ 4/96*)

7942 White, Ruth. *Tadpole* (5–8). 2003, Farrar $16.00 (0-374-31002-5). 208pp. In this novel set in 1950s Appalachia, uncertain 10-year-old Carolina finds her own strengths when her 13-year-old cousin Tadpole arrives, running away from an abusive uncle. (Rev: BL 5/1/03; HB 5–6/03; HBG 10/03; SLJ 3/03*)

7943 Wilder, Laura Ingalls. *Little House in the Big Woods* (4–7). Illus. by Garth Williams. 1953, HarperCollins LB $17.89 (0-06-026431-4); paper $6.99 (0-06-440001-8). 238pp. Outstanding story of a log-cabin family in Wisconsin in the late 1800s. Also use *By the Shores of Silver Lake; Farmer Boy; Little House on the Prairie; Long Winter; On the Banks of Plum Creek; These Happy Golden Years* (all 1953); *Little Town on the Prairie* (1961); *The First Four Years* (1971).

7944 Wilder, Laura Ingalls. *West from Home: Letters of Laura Ingalls Wilder, San Francisco, 1915* (6–8). 1974, HarperCollins paper $4.95 (0-06-440081-6). 176pp. Laura visited her daughter Rose in San Francisco in the year that the city was preparing a world's fair, and she wrote about her experiences to her husband.

7945 Wiles, Deborah. *Each Little Bird That Sings* (4–6). 2005, Harcourt $16.00 (0-15-205113-9). 264pp. Comfort Snowberger, the daughter of undertakers, faces death in her own family for the first time in this engaging and sometimes funny novel set in rural Mississippi. (Rev: BL 3/1/05; SLJ 3/05)

7946 Wiles, Deborah. *Love, Ruby Lavender* (4–6). 2001, Harcourt $16.00 (0-15-202314-3). 128pp. Ruby misses her grandmother terribly when she goes to Hawaii on vacation, but over the course of the summer she finds that life goes on and that diversions arise. (Rev: BCCB 9/01; BL 5/1/01; HBG 10/01; SLJ 4/01*)

7947 Williams, Vera B. *Amber Was Brave, Essie Was Smart* (3–5). Illus. 2001, Greenwillow LB $15.89 (0-06-029461-2). 72pp. Poetic text and black-and-white sketches tell the story of two sisters who cling to each other during hard times. (Rev:

BCCB 9/01; BL 9/15/01; HB 9–10/01; HBG 3/02; SLJ 9/01*)

7948 Willis, Patricia. *The Barn Burner* (5–8). 2000, Clarion $15.00 (0-395-98409-2). 208pp. In 1933, 14-year-old Ross, a runaway, becomes involved with the Warfield family whose father is away looking for work. (Rev: BCCB 5/00; BL 4/15/00; HBG 10/00; SLJ 7/00)

7949 Wilson, Nancy Hope. *Mountain Pose* (5–7). 2001, Farrar $17.00 (0-374-35078-7). 240pp. Ellie is surprised to inherit her grandmother's farm, but when she reads the diaries left for her she begins to understand more about her family. (Rev: BCCB 6/01; BL 8/01; HB 7–8/01; HBG 10/01; SLJ 4/01*)

7950 Wishinsky, Frieda. *Just Call Me Joe* (2–4). 2004, Orca paper $4.99 (1-55143-249-8). 101pp. Ten-year-old Joseph and his teenage sister have migrated to New York from Russia in 1910 and face many difficulties as they wait for their parents to join them. (Rev: SLJ 5/04)

7951 Woodbury, Mary. *Brad's Universe* (5–8). 1998, Orca paper $7.95 (1-55143-120-3). In this novel set in a small Canadian town, Brad, at 14, is looking forward to being reunited with his absent father, but slowly comes to realize that the man has been convicted of child molesting. (Rev: SLJ 2/99)

7952 Woodruff, Elvira. *"Dear Napoleon, I Know You're Dead, But . . ."* (3–5). Illus. 1992, Holiday House $15.95 (0-8234-0962-7). 220pp. Marty is astounded when he receives a reply to his letter to Napoleon, after Gramps tells him about a courier at his nursing home who can deliver messages to the dead. (Rev: BCCB 12/92; BL 12/15/92; SLJ 10/92)

7953 Woodson, Jacqueline. *Hush* (5–9). 2002, Penguin Putnam $15.99 (0-399-23144-5). 192pp. A girl and her family are relocated in the witness protection program after her father, a police officer, testifies against fellow cops in a case that involves racial prejudice. (Rev: BCCB 3/02; BL 1/1–15/02; HB 1–2/02; HBG 10/02; SLJ 2/02*)

7954 Yep, Laurence. *Skunk Scout* (3–6). 2003, Hyperion $15.99 (0-7868-0670-2). 192pp. Ten-year-old Teddy, from San Francisco's Chinatown, narrates this amusing story of a surprise-filled weekend camping trip with his Uncle Curtis and younger brother, Bobby. (Rev: BL 6/1–15/03; HBG 10/03; SLJ 8/03)

7955 Zinnen, Linda. *Holding at Third* (5–7). 2004, Dutton $15.99 (0-525-47163-4). 160pp. Matt, 13 and a baseball player, faces many problems when he and his mother move to a different town so that his brother can undergo cancer treatment. (Rev: BL 2/1/04; SLJ 2/04)

Fantasy and the Supernatural

7956 Adler, C. S. *Good-bye Pink Pig* (5–7). 1986, Avon paper $2.75 (0-380-70175-8). 176pp. Shy Amanda takes comfort in the make-believe world of her miniature pink pig — away from the elegant world of her mother and easygoing life of her brother — until trouble enters her real and imaginary

worlds and she learns to assert herself. (Rev: BCCB 2/86; BL 12/15/85)

7957 Adler, C. S. *Help, Pink Pig!* (5–7). 1991, Avon paper $2.95 (0-380-71156-7). 176pp. Unsure of herself with her mother, Amanda retreats into the world of her miniature pink pig. (Rev: BL 5/1/90; SLJ 5/90)

7958 Ahlberg, Allan. *The Improbable Cat* (4–6). Illus. by Peter Bailey. 2004, Delacorte $9.95 (0-385-73186-8). 128pp. The kitten that they adopt grows ever bigger and more powerful, taking over the household, and David and his dog, Billy, are the only ones that can stop it. (Rev: SLJ 8/04)

7959 Alcock, Vivien. *The Haunting of Cassie Palmer* (5–8). 1997, Houghton Mifflin paper $6.95 (0-395-81653-X). 160pp. Cassie finds she is blessed with second sight.

7960 Alcock, Vivien. *The Red-Eared Ghosts* (5–8). 1997, Houghton Mifflin $15.95 (0-395-81660-2). Mary Frewin travels through time to solve a mystery involving her great-great-grandmother. (Rev: BL 3/1/97; BR 11–12/97; SLJ 4/97)

7961 Alcock, Vivien. *The Stonewalkers* (5–8). 1998, Houghton Mifflin paper $4.95 (0-395-81652-1). 192pp. Statues come to life and begin stalking two girls.

7962 Alexander, Lloyd. *The Book of Three* (5–8). 1964, Dell paper $5.99 (0-440-40702-8). 224pp. Welsh legend and universal mythology are blended in the tale of an assistant pig keeper who becomes a hero. Newbery Medal winner, 1969. Others in the Prydain cycle are *The Black Cauldron, The Castle of Llyr, Taran Wanderer*, and *The High King*.

7963 Alexander, Lloyd. *The First Two Lives of Lukas-Kasha* (5–8). 1998, Puffin paper $6.99 (0-141-30057-4). 224pp. Lukas awakens to find himself in a strange land.

7964 Alexander, Lloyd. *The Rope Trick* (4–7). 2002, Dutton $16.99 (0-525-47020-4). 256pp. A young magician sets out on a challenging journey to master the difficult rope trick. (Rev: BCCB 1/03; BL 10/15/02; HB 11–12/02; HBG 3/03; SLJ 9/02)

7965 Alexander, Lloyd. *Time Cat: The Remarkable Journeys of Jason and Gareth* (4–6). Illus. by Bill Sokol. 1996, Puffin paper $3.99 (0-140-37827-8). Jason's cat takes him to various times and places.

7966 Alexander, Lloyd. *The Wizard in the Tree* (4–6). Illus. by Laszlo Kubinyi. 1998, Viking paper $4.50 (0-140-38801-X). 144pp. A delightful fantasy of a good-versus-evil struggle involving an orphan, Mallory, his wizard, and their battle against Mrs. Parsel and Squire Scrupnor.

7967 Allen, Will. *Swords for Hire: Two of the Most Unlikely Heroes You'll Ever Meet* (5–8). Illus. by David Michael Beck. 2003, CenterPunch paper $6.95 (0-9724882-0-0). 168pp. A spoof of a fantasy in which inexperienced warrior 16-year-old Sam Hatcher and his eccentric mentor Rigby Skeet set off to rescue King Olive, who has been unseated by his evil brother. (Rev: BCCB 6/03; SLJ 8/03)

7968 Almond, David. *Heaven Eyes* (5–8). 2001, Delacorte $15.95 (0-385-32770-6). 240pp. A very ambitious novel about three young escapees from a detention center in England and the life they live in a forgotten warehouse where the watchman is a deranged man known as Heaven Eyes. (Rev: BCCB 4/01; BL 1/1–15/01*; HB 3–4/01; HBG 10/01; SLJ 3/01)

7969 Almond, David. *Skellig* (5–8). 1999, Delacorte $16.95 (0-385-32653-X). Michael discovers a ragged man in his garage existing on dead flies in this novel that is part fantasy, part mystery, and part family story. (Rev: BL 2/1/99*; HB 5–6/99; HBG 10/99; SLJ 2/99)

7970 Alphin, Elaine M. *Ghost Soldier* (5–7). 2001, Holt $16.95 (0-8050-6158-4). 216pp. Alex, who has special powers, meets a Civil War ghost and helps him discover what happened to his family. (Rev: BCCB 7–8/01; BL 8/01; HBG 10/02; SLJ 8/01)

7971 Alphin, Elaine M. *Tournament of Time* (4–6). 1994, Bluegrass paper $3.95 (0-9643683-0-7). 125pp. A young American girl in York, England, solves a historic murder mystery with the help of ghosts. (Rev: BL 3/15/95)

7972 Alton, Steve. *The Malifex* (5–8). 2002, Carolrhoda LB $17.95 (0-8225-0959-8). 182pp. Sam's vacation in contemporary England is complicated by a Wiccan's daughter, the release of the ghost of Merlin's apprentice, and a battle between good and evil. (Rev: BL 9/1/02; HBG 10/03; SLJ 11/02)

7973 Amato, Mary. *The Word Eater* (4–6). Illus. 2000, Holiday House $15.95 (0-8234-1468-X). 146pp. Lerner's pet worm Fip likes eating paper, but when he eats paper with an object's name on it, the object itself disappears in this comic fantasy. (Rev: BCCB 9/00; BL 10/15/00; HBG 3/01; SLJ 10/00)

7974 Amoss, Berthe. *Lost Magic* (5–7). 1993, Hyperion $14.95 (1-56282-573-9). 192pp. Fantasy and history mingle in this story set in the Middle Ages about a young girl who knows how to use both healing herbs and magic. (Rev: BL 11/1/93)

7975 Anderson, M. T. *The Game of Sunken Places* (5–8). 2004, Scholastic $16.95 (0-439-41660-4). 272pp. Brian and Gregory, both 13, find themselves embroiled in a dangerous and suspenseful game during a stay at the spooky mansion of Gregory's eccentric Uncle Max. (Rev: BL 4/15/04*; SLJ 9/04)

7976 Anderson, M. T. *Whales on Stilts!* (5–7). 2005, Harcourt $15.00 (0-15-205340-9). 192pp. Twelve-year-old Lily Gefelty enlists the help of two friends to foil a plan to take over the world using an army of mind-controlled whales on stilts; a fast-paced adventure full of tongue-in-cheek fun. (Rev: BL 2/15/05; SLJ 5/05)

7977 Anzaldua, Gloria. *Prietita and the Ghost Woman* (3–6). Illus. by Christina Gonzalez. 1996, Children's Book Pr. $15.95 (0-89239-136-7). While looking for an herb to cure her mother, Prietita gets lost in the woods in this English-Spanish fantasy. (Rev: BCCB 4/96; SLJ 7/96)

7978 Arkin, Alan. *The Lemming Condition* (4–7). Illus. by Joan Sandin. 1989, HarperCollins paper $9.00 (0-062-50048-1). 64pp. Bubber opposes the mass suicide of his companions in this interesting fable.

7979 Arnold, Louise. *Golden and Grey (An Unremarkable Boy and a Rather Remarkable Ghost)* (4–6). 2005, Simon & Schuster $15.95 (0-689-87473-1). 272pp. Two misfits — a ghost and an 11-year-old boy — become friends and help each other in their respective communities. (Rev: BL 6/1–15/05)

7980 Asch, Frank. *Battle in a Bottle: Class Pets* (2–4). Illus. by John Kanzler. Series: Class Pets Ser. 2003, Simon & Schuster $14.95 (0-689-84655-X). 96pp. Mouse siblings Molly and Jake have an exciting time when they take refuge in the wall of a classroom. (Rev: BL 6/1–15/03; HBG 10/03; SLJ 6/03)

7981 Auch, Mary Jane. *I Was a Third Grade Spy* (2–4). Illus. 2001, Holiday House $15.95 (0-8234-1576-7). 96pp. Young Josh and Artful the dog who can now speak take turns narrating their entertaining efforts to win the talent show. (Rev: BCCB 7–8/01; BL 5/1/01; HBG 10/01; SLJ 7/01)

7982 Augarde, Steve. *The Various* (4–8). 2004, Random LB $17.99 (0-385-75037-4). 448pp. Midge, a 12-year-old girl on vacation in the countryside, discovers a tribe of little people known as the Various, who are not as helpless as they seem. (Rev: BL 12/15/03; SLJ 3/04)

7983 Avi. *The Book Without Words* (5–8). 2005, Hyperion $15.99 (0-7868-0829-2). 208pp. Young Sybil searches for a book that reveals the magic of alchemy in this spooky and complex story set in medieval England. (Rev: BL 3/15/05; SLJ 5/05)

7984 Avi. *Bright Shadow* (5–8). 1994, Simon & Schuster paper $4.99 (0-689-71783-0). At the death of the great wizard, Morenna finds she possesses the last five wishes in the world. (Rev: SLJ 12/85)

7985 Avi. *Ereth's Birthday: A Tale from Dimwood Forest* (3–5). 2000, HarperCollins $15.95 (0-380-97734-6). 192pp. Ereth, a cranky porcupine, gets more than he bargained for when he looks after three little foxes after their mother dies. (Rev: BCCB 7–8/00; BL 4/1/00; HB 5–6/00; HBG 10/00; SLJ 5/00)

7986 Avi. *The Mayor of Central Park* (3–6). Illus. by Brian Floca. 2003, HarperCollins LB $16.89 (0-06-051556-2). 208pp. In New York City's Central Park in 1900, Oscar the squirrel leads the fight against an invading rat pack led by Big Daddy Duds. (Rev: BL 8/03; HBG 4/04; SLJ 12/03)

7987 Avi. *Perloo the Bold* (4–7). 1998, Scholastic paper $16.95 (0-590-11002-0). 240pp. Perloo, a member of the jackrabbitlike Montmer tribe, is the unlikely hero of this fantasy about the rivalry between the Montmers and the Felbarts, a coyote-like tribe. (Rev: BCCB 11/98; BL 12/15/98; HB 1–2/99; HBG 3/99; SLJ 11/98)

7988 Avi. *Poppy* (4–6). Illus. 1995, Orchard LB $16.99 (0-531-08783-2). 160pp. Tragedy occurs when a young deer mouse named Poppy disobeys her father and ventures out into the night with her boyfriend. (Rev: BCCB 1/96; BL 10/15/95*; SLJ 12/95*)

7989 Avi. *Poppy and Rye* (4–6). Illus. 1998, Avon $14.00 (0-380-97638-2). 160pp. Fearless deer mouse Poppy travels to visit another mouse family, where she foils the plans of some beavers to build a dam and also falls in love with another mouse named Rye. (Rev: BL 5/15/98; HB 7–8/98; HBG 10/98; SLJ 6/98)

7990 Avi. *Ragweed* (4–6). Illus. 1999, Avon $15.00 (0-380-97690-0). 192pp. Ragweed, a brave young mouse, becomes friends with members of a hip band and leads the opposition against Silversides, an angry white cat. (Rev: BCCB 10/99; BL 5/15/99; HBG 10/99; SLJ 7/99)

7991 Avi. *Something Upstairs: A Tale of Ghosts* (5–7). 1988, Orchard LB $16.99 (0-531-08382-9); Avon paper $4.99 (0-380-70853-1). 128pp. Kenny moves into a house in Rhode Island that is haunted by the ghost of a slave who was murdered in 1800. (Rev: BCCB 9/88; BL 11/1/88; SLJ 10/88)

7992 Babbitt, Natalie. *The Devil's Other Storybook* (4–6). Illus. by author. 1987, Farrar paper $4.95 (0-374-41704-0). 112pp. The devil generally fouls up things in these humorous tales, but sometimes does an unintentional good deed. (Rev: BCCB 7–8/87; BL 8/87; SLJ 8/87)

7993 Babbitt, Natalie. *The Search for Delicious* (4–7). Illus. by author. 1969, Farrar $17.00 (0-374-36534-2). 176pp. The innocent task of polling the kingdom's subjects for personal food preferences provokes civil war in a zestful spoof of taste and society.

7994 Babbitt, Natalie. *Tuck Everlasting* (4–6). 1975, Farrar $16.00 (0-374-37848-7); paper $4.95 (0-374-48009-5). 160pp. Violence erupts when the Tuck family members discover that their secret about a spring that brings immortality has been discovered.

7995 Bailey, Carolyn Sherwin. *Miss Hickory* (4–6). Illus. by Ruth Gannett. 1946, Puffin paper $4.99 (0-14-030956-X). 128pp. The adventures of a doll made from an apple branch with a hickory nut head. Newbery Award winner, 1947.

7996 Bailey, Len. *Clabbernappers* (4–6). 2005, TOR/Starscape $17.95 (0-765-30981-5). 240pp. An exciting land of pirates and chess characters awaits junior rodeo champ Danny Ray when he ventures through a mysterious door at an amusement park. (Rev: BL 1/1–15/05; SLJ 6/05)

7997 Bailey, Linda. *Adventures in Ancient China* (3–5). Illus. by Bill Slavin. Series: Good Times Travel Agency. 2003, Kids Can $14.95 (1-55337-453-3). 48pp. A fictional story about three children whisked magically to ancient China runs in cartoon fashion across the tops of the pages, while a guidebook below looks at everything from farming and transportation to family life and writing. (Rev: HBG 4/04; SLJ 1/04) [931]

7998 Bailey, Linda. *Adventures in the Middle Ages* (3–6). Illus. by Bill Slavin. 2000, Kids Can $14.95 (1-55074-538-7); paper $7.95 (1-55074-540-9). 48pp. A slapstick story about twins Josh and Emma and their trip to the Middle Ages via a yellowing guidebook that gives basic information about the period. (Rev: BL 9/15/03; HBG 3/01; SLJ 12/00)

7999 Bailey, Linda. *Adventures with the Vikings* (3–5). Illus. by Bill Slavin. Series: Good Times Travel Agency. 2001, Kids Can $14.95 (1-55074-

542-5); paper $7.95 (1-55074-544-1). 48pp. The Binkerton children travel back in time to the age of the Vikings in this comic-book-style story that interweaves fiction and nonfiction. (Rev: BL 10/15/01; HBG 3/02; SLJ 11/01)

8000 Baker, E. D. *Dragon's Breath* (4–7). 2003, Bloomsbury $15.95 (1-58234-858-8). In this humorous sequel to *The Frog Princess* (2002), Princess Esmeralda needs to find the ingredients for a magic potion. (Rev: BL 4/15/04; HBG 4/04; SLJ 12/03)

8001 Baker, E. D. *The Frog Princess* (5–8). 2002, Bloomsbury $15.95 (1-58234-799-9). 220pp. When Princess Esmeralda kisses the frog, she turns into one herself in this humorous twist on the traditional saga. (Rev: BCCB 2/03; BL 11/15/02; SLJ 1/03)

8002 Baker, Jeannie. *The Hidden Forest* (2–4). Illus. 2000, Greenwillow LB $16.89 (0-688-15761-0). 32pp. In this fantasy, Ben is led by his friend Sophie into the underwater world of a kelp forest where they encounter a whale. (Rev: BL 9/1/00; HB 7–8/00; HBG 10/00; SLJ 5/00)

8003 Baker, Jeannie. *Where the Forest Meets the Sea* (K–4). Illus. by author. 1988, Greenwillow $15.93 (0-688-06364-0). 32pp. A young boy travels through a reef and arrives in the rain forest in Australia and pretends he has gone back in time. (Rev: BCCB 5/88; BL 6/15/88; SLJ 7/88)

8004 Banks, Lynne Reid. *Angela and Diabola* (5–8). 1997, Avon $15.95 (0-380-97562-9). A wicked romp that chronicles the lives of twins, the angelic Angela and the truly horrible and destructive Diabola. (Rev: BR 9–10/97; SLJ 7/97)

8005 Banks, Lynne Reid. *Harry the Poisonous Centipede's Big Adventure* (3–5). Illus. 2001, HarperCollins LB $14.89 (0-06-029394-2). 192pp. Young centipede Harry finds himself trapped with many of his friends, and they have great adventures finding their way home after escaping. (Rev: BL 6/1–15/01; HBG 10/01; SLJ 5/01)

8006 Banks, Lynne Reid. *The Indian in the Cupboard* (3–5). Illus. by Brock Cole. 1985, Doubleday $16.95 (0-385-17051-3); Avon paper $4.99 (0-380-60012-9). 192pp. A magical cupboard turns toys into living things.

8007 Banks, Lynne Reid. *The Key to the Indian* (4–8). Illus. Series: Indian in the Cupboard. 1998, Avon $16.00 (0-380-97717-6). 240pp. In the fifth book of the Indian in the Cupboard series, Omri and Dad return to the time of Little Bear to help the Iroquois deal with European meddlers. (Rev: BL 11/15/98; HBG 3/99; SLJ 12/98)

8008 Banks, Lynne Reid. *The Mystery of the Cupboard* (4–8). Illus. Series: Indian in the Cupboard. 1993, HarperCollins paper $5.99 (0-380-72013-2). In this, the fourth book in the series, the young hero Omri uncovers a diary that reveals secrets about his magical cupboard. (Rev: BCCB 6/93; BL 4/1/93; HB 7–8/93; SLJ 6/93)

8009 Banks, Lynne Reid. *The Return of the Indian* (5–7). Illus. by William Geldart. Series: Indian in the Cupboard. 1986, Doubleday $16.95 (0-385-23497-X); Avon paper $5.99 (0-380-70284-3).

192pp. Omri brings his plastic Indian figures to life and discovers that his friend Little Bear has been wounded and needs his help. (Rev: BL 9/15/86; HB 11–12/86; SLJ 11/86)

8010 Banks, Lynne Reid. *The Secret of the Indian* (4–6). Illus. by Ted Lewin. 1989, Doubleday $15.95 (0-385-26292-2). 160pp. Once again, Omri's magic cupboard brings toy figures to life, and in this novel, friend Patrick travels back in time to the Old West. (Rev: BCCB 1/90; BL 9/15/89; HB 3–4/90; SLJ 10/89)

8011 Barlow, Steve, and Steve Skidmore. *Whizzard!* (4–6). Illus. by Fiona Land. Series: Tales of the Dark Forest. 2003, Collins paper $8.95 (0-00-710864-8). 252pp. In this fast-paced comic fantasy, Tym, the bumbling apprentice to the local wizard, cooks up a magical potion that endows him with the power to travel at super-fast speed. (Rev: SLJ 2/04)

8012 Barrett, Tracy. *Cold in Summer* (4–7). 2003, Holt $16.95 (0-8050-7052-4). 208pp. An enjoyable story about a lonely girl who slowly comes to realize that her new friend is a ghost. (Rev: BL 4/1/03; HB 5–6/03; HBG 10/03; SLJ 7/03)

8013 Barrett, Tracy. *On Etruscan Time* (5–8). 2005, Holt $16.95 (0-8050-7569-0). 176pp. Hector, 11, finds himself struggling to rescue an Etruscan boy from execution, in this time-travel fantasy set on an archaeological dig in Italy. (Rev: BL 6/1–15/05)

8014 Barrie, J. M. *Peter Pan* (5–7). Illus. 2000, Chronicle $19.95 (0-8118-2297-4). 173pp. Using illustrations from 15 different artists, this is an unusual, unabridged edition of Barrie's classic fantasy. (Rev: BL 11/1/00; HBG 3/01; SLJ 12/00)

8015 Barron, T. A. *Tree Girl* (4–8). 2001, Penguin Putnam $14.99 (0-399-23457-8). 128pp. Rowanna, 9, discovers she is descended from tree spirits after she is lured into the woods by a shape-shifting bear cub in this book for middle-graders. (Rev: BCCB 10/01; BL 11/1/01; HBG 3/02; SLJ 10/01)

8016 Base, Graeme. *TruckDogs* (4–6). Illus. 2004, Abrams $16.95 (0-8109-5031-6). 192pp. Creatures that are part animal, part vehicle — such as Truck-Sheep and TruckDogs — star in this story about an assault on their town by the RottWheeler gang. (Rev: BL 2/15/04; SLJ 3/04)

8017 Bateman, Colin. *Running with the Reservoir Pups* (4–7). 2005, Delacorte LB $17.99 (0-385-90268-9). 272pp. Eddie becomes involved with a gang of tough Belfast kids and ends up rescuing kidnapped babies from a horrible fate in this action-packed fantasy, the first installment in a trilogy. (Rev: BL 3/1/05; SLJ 1/05)

8018 Bauer, Marion Dane. *Ghost Eye* (3–6). Illus. by Trina S. Hyman. 1992, Scholastic $13.95 (0-590-45298-3). 64pp. Popcorn, a Cornish rex show cat who sees ghosts, leads a tantalizing cast of characters. (Rev: BL 9/15/92; SLJ 10/92)

8019 Bauer, Marion Dane. *Touch the Moon* (5–7). Illus. by Alix Berenzy. 1987, Houghton Mifflin $15.00 (0-89919-526-1). 96pp. Angry when she doesn't get a real horse, Jennifer throws away her toy horse gift and learns a lesson in responsibility. (Rev: BCCB 9/87; BL 9/15/87; HB 9–10/87)

8020 Baum, L. Frank. *The Marvelous Land of Oz* (4–6). Illus. by John R. Neill. 1985, Morrow $22.95 (0-688-05439-0). 288pp. This is a facsimile of the original 1904 edition with the illustrations in both color and black and white. Other titles in this series are published by Peter Smith and Amereon in hard cover and Dover and Puffin in paperback.

8021 Baum, L. Frank. *The Wizard of Oz* (PS–4). Illus. by Charles Santore. 1986, Ballantine paper $5.99 (0-345-33590-2). 96pp. For a younger audience than the original, this is an abridged, heavily illustrated version of the Baum classic. (Rev: SLJ 12/91)

8022 Baum, L. Frank. *The Wizard of Oz* (4–8). Illus. by Michael Hague. 2000, Holt $34.95 (0-8050-6430-3). 220pp. A gorgeous edition of the classic fantasy that is a reissue of the 1982 version with a few new illustrations. (Rev: BL 12/1/00; HBG 10/00)

8023 Baum, L. Frank. *The Wonderful Wizard of Oz* (4–8). Illus. by W. W. Denslow. 1987, Morrow $21.95 (0-688-06944-4). 316pp. A reissue of the 1900 classic with original colorplates. (Rev: BL 11/1/87)

8024 Baum, L. Frank. *The Wonderful Wizard of Oz* (4–8). Illus. by W. W. Denslow. 2000, Harper-Collins $24.99 (0-06-029323-3). 267pp. A handsome facsimile of the 1900 publication on high-quality paper and featuring 24 original color plates and 130 two-color drawings. (Rev: BL 12/1/00)

8025 Baum, L. Frank. *The Wonderful Wizard of Oz: A Commemorative Pop-Up* (4–8). Illus. by Robert Sabuda. 2001, Simon & Schuster $24.95 (0-689-81751-7). An extraordinary pop-up version of the classic fantasy told in a condensed text. (Rev: BL 12/1/00; HB 9–10/00; HBG 3/01; SLJ 11/00)

8026 Baum, Roger S. *Dorothy of Oz* (4–6). Illus. by Elizabeth Miles. 1989, Morrow $17.00 (0-688-07848-6). 176pp. A story true to the original in which Dorothy is called back to Oz because the Tin Woodman, the Scarecrow, and the Cowardly Lion need help. (Rev: BL 1/1/90; SLJ 10/89)

8027 Bell, Hilari. *The Wizard Test* (5–8). 2005, HarperCollins LB $16.89 (0-06-059941-3). 176pp. Fourteen-year-old Dayven is not thrilled when he learns he has magical abilities until he undergoes wizard training. (Rev: BL 2/1/05; SLJ 3/05)

8028 Bellairs, John. *The Ghost in the Mirror* (5–8). 1994, Puffin paper $5.99 (0-140-34934-0). 176pp. Fourteen-year-old Rose and white witch Mrs. Zimmerman are transported in time to 1828 on a secret mission. (Rev: SLJ 3/93)

8029 Bellairs, John. *The Mansion in the Mist* (5–7). 1992, Puffin paper $5.99 (0-140-34933-2). 176pp. Anthony Monday finds mystery and adventure on a remote island in northern Canada. (Rev: BL 8/92; SLJ 6/92)

8030 Bender, Robert, comp. *Lima Beans Would Be Illegal: Children's Ideas of a Perfect World* (2–5). Illus. by Robert Bender. 2000, Dial $12.00 (0-8037-2532-9). An appealing fantasy in which children describe what a perfect world would be like. (Rev: HBG 10/00; SLJ 7/00)

8031 Berger, Barbara Helen. *Gwinna* (4–8). Illus. 1990, Penguin Putnam $24.99 (0-399-21738-X). 126pp. A mystic coming-of-age fable when a couple's wish for a child is granted in the form of a daughter who grows wings. (Rev: BL 10/15/90; SLJ 12/90)

8032 Bial, Raymond. *The Fresh Grave: And Other Ghostly Stories* (5–7). 1997, Midwest Traditions paper $13.95 (1-883953-22-7). 162pp. A series of ten short, humorous ghost stories featuring two teenage heroes and their escapades in a small midwestern town. (Rev: SLJ 12/97)

8033 Billingsley, Franny. *The Folk Keeper* (5–8). 1999, Simon & Schuster $16.00 (0-689-82876-4); Aladdin paper $4.99 (0-689-84461-1). 162pp. Orphaned Corinna disguises herself as a boy to become a Folk Keeper, one who guards the fierce Folk who live underground. (Rev: BCCB 10/99; BL 9/1/99; HB 11–12/99; HBG 3/00; SLJ 10/99)

8034 Birdseye, Tom. *The Eye of the Stone* (4–6). 2000, Holiday House $15.95 (0-8234-1564-3). 165pp. Jackson, a fearful 13-year-old boy, is transported to a primitive society where he must find the courage to fight a monster and bring peace to his people. (Rev: BL 2/15/01; HBG 10/01; SLJ 12/00)

8035 Black, Holly. *The Ironwood Tree* (3–6). Illus. by Tony Diterlizzi. Series: The Spiderwick Chronicles. 2004, Simon & Schuster $9.95 (0-689-85939-2). 128pp. In the fourth installment in the series, Jared and Simon must rescue Mallory from evil dwarves. (Rev: SLJ 6/04)

8036 Black, Holly. *Lucinda's Secret* (3–6). Illus. by Tony Diterlizzi. Series: Spiderwick Chronicles. 2003, Simon & Schuster $9.95 (0-689-85938-4). 128pp. The Grace siblings visit their Aunt Lucinda to learn more about Arthur Spiderwick's *Field Guide to the Fantastical World Around You*. (Rev: HBG 4/04; SLJ 11/03)

8037 Blair, Margaret Whitman. *Brothers at War* (4–7). 1997, White Mane paper $7.95 (1-57249-049-7). 145pp. Two brothers and their friend Sarah find themselves transported back in time to the Battle of Antietam in 1862. (Rev: BL 8/97)

8038 Bode, N. E. *The Nobodies* (5–8). 2005, HarperCollins LB $16.89 (0-06-055739-7). 304pp. In this sequel to *The Anybodies* (2004), Fern and Howard are at a sinister camp for shape-shifting Anybodies. (Rev: BL 6/1–15/05)

8039 *The Book of Fairies* (3–6). Ed. by Michael Hague. Illus. 2000, HarperCollins $19.95 (0-688-10881-4). 128pp. Eight stories, songs, and poems celebrate this unworldly creature in a beautiful book illustrated by Michael Hague. (Rev: BL 12/15/00; HBG 3/01) [808.8]

8040 Borsky, Mary. *Benny Bensky and the Perogy Palace* (2–4). Illus. by Linda Hendry. 2001, Tundra paper $7.95 (0-88776-523-8). 120pp. Benny the dog plays an important role in solving the mystery of the downturn in the perogy business. (Rev: SLJ 8/01)

8041 Bradman, Tony. *Voodoo Child* (4–7). Illus. by Martin Chatterton. Series: Tales of Terror. 2005, Egmont paper $7.50 (1-4052-1126-1). 88pp. Megan hopes a voodoo doll will get rid of her father's girl-friend. Other scary titles in this series are *Deadly Game* and *Final Cut* (both 2005). (Rev: SLJ 6/05)

8042 Breathed, Berkeley. *The Last Basselope: One Ferocious Story* (4–7). Illus. 2001, Little, Brown paper $5.95 (0-3161-2664-0). 32pp. In this imaginative picture book for older readers, Opus and his reluctant adventurers are after the nearly extinct basselope. (Rev: BCCB 1/93; BL 12/15/92; SLJ 1/93)

8043 Briggs, Anita. *Hobart* (2–4). Illus. by Mary Rayner. 2002, Simon & Schuster $14.00 (0-689-84129-9). 64pp. Four little pigs practice their artistic pursuits and put on a show to help their farmer-owner with his finances. (Rev: BCCB 6/02; BL 5/1/02; HBG 10/02; SLJ 6/02)

8044 Brittain, Bill. *All the Money in the World* (4–6). Illus. by Charles Robinson. 1992, HarperCollins paper $4.95 (0-06-440128-6). 160pp. A leprechaun grants Quentin Stowe his wish for all the money in the world.

8045 Brittain, Bill. *Wings* (5–7). 1995, HarperCollins paper $4.95 (0-064-40612-1). 144pp. Troubles really begin for 12-year-old Ian when he sprouts wings. (Rev: BCCB 11/91; BL 1/1/91; SLJ 10/91)

8046 Britton, Susan McGee. *The Treekeepers* (4–7). 2003, Dutton $16.99 (0-525-46944-3). 256pp. Bird, a plucky orphan, discovers she is the ordained opener of a locket containing a sacred seed and is plunged into a dangerous journey. (Rev: BL 4/15/03; HBG 10/03; SLJ 7/03)

8047 Brown, Calef. *Polkabats and Octopus Slacks: 14 Stories* (3–5). Illus. 1998, Houghton Mifflin $15.00 (0-395-85403-2). 32pp. Nonsense verses introduce some wacky characters, including Kansas City Octopus, who goes out on the town in four-legged bell bottoms. (Rev: BL 3/15/98; HBG 10/98; SLJ 5/98)

8048 Brown, Jeff. *Stanley, Flat Again!* (2–4). Illus. by Scott Nash. Series: Flat Stanley. 2003, HarperCollins LB $15.89 (0-06-029826-X). 87pp. Stanley, first seen in *Flat Stanley* (1964), is flat once more and has a series of adventures in this entertaining early chapter book. (Rev: HBG 10/03; SLJ 3/03)

8049 Buffie, Margaret. *The Seeker* (5–8). 2002, Kids Can $16.95 (1-55337-358-8). 384pp. Emma is involved in a quest to reunite her family and becomes embroiled in interplanetary intrigue and gaming in this sequel to *The Watcher* (2000). (Rev: BL 10/1/02; HBG 10/03; SLJ 11/02)

8050 Buffie, Margaret. *The Watcher* (5–8). 2000, Kids Can $16.95 (1-55074-829-7). 264pp. Sixteen-year-old Emma discovers that she is really a changeling, a Watcher, whose mission is to protect her younger sister from warring factions. (Rev: BL 11/1/00; HBG 3/01; SLJ 10/00)

8051 Burgess, Melvin. *The Ghost Behind the Wall* (5–7). 2003, Holt $16.95 (0-8050-7149-0). 176pp. David finds more than he expects when he ventures into his building's ventilation system. (Rev: BCCB 2/03; BL 4/15/03; HBG 10/03; SLJ 7/03)

8052 Bush, Lawrence. *Emma Ansky-Levine and Her Mitzvah Machine* (4–6). Illus. by Joel Iskowitz.

1991, UAHC paper $7.95 (0-8074-0458-6). 115pp. Emma receives a machine from her uncle in Jerusalem that gives her personal guidance. (Rev: SLJ 7/91)

8053 Byars, Betsy. *Little Horse* (2–4). Illus. by David McPhail. 2002, Holt $15.95 (0-8050-6413-3). 64pp. A tiny horse gets lost in a land where the flowers are as big as trees in this beginning chapter book. (Rev: BCCB 6/02; BL 3/15/02; HB 5–6/02; HBG 10/02; SLJ 4/02)

8054 Byars, Betsy. *The Winged Colt of Casa Mia* (4–6). Illus. by Richard Cuffari. 1981, Avon paper $2.95 (0-380-00201-9). 132pp. In this fantasy, a young boy visits the Texas ranch of his uncle, an ex-stuntman, and encounters a colt with supernatural powers.

8055 Byng, Georgia. *Molly Moon Stops the World* (5–8). 2004, HarperCollins LB $17.89 (0-06-051413-2). 384pp. Molly Moon, a girl of unusual hypnotic powers, is dispatched to California to foil a power-mad hypnotist called Primo Cell. (Rev: BL 5/1/04; SLJ 5/04)

8056 Byng, Georgia. *Molly Moon's Incredible Book of Hypnotism* (4–6). 2003, HarperCollins LB $17.89 (0-06-051407-8). 371pp. A book about hypnotism proves to be unhappy Molly Moon's passport out of her orphanage and to stardom in New York City. (Rev: HBG 10/03; SLJ 6/03)

8057 Cameron, Eleanor. *The Court of the Stone Children* (5–7). 1990, Puffin paper $5.99 (0-14-034289-3). 192pp. Nina's move with her family to San Francisco is a disaster until she encounters a young ghost in a small museum.

8058 Cardo, Horacio. *The Story of Chess* (3–5). Illus. 1998, Abbeville $16.95 (0-7892-0250-6). 45pp. After their countries destroyed each other in a war, two kings listen to a war historian who uses the first chess set to explain every participant and every move. (Rev: BL 11/15/98; HBG 3/99; SLJ 4/99)

8059 Carman, Patrick. *The Dark Hills Divide* (4–6). Series: Land of Elyon. 2005, Scholastic $11.95 (0-439-70093-0). 272pp. Alexa, 12, discovers the secrets of her walled city and a plan to destroy it in this fantasy, the first volume in a trilogy. (Rev: BL 3/1/05; SLJ 4/05)

8060 Carmody, Isobelle. *Night Gate* (5–8). Series: Gateway Trilogy. 2005, Random LB $18.99 (0-375-93016-7). 272pp. On her way to visit her comatose mother, 12-year-old Rage is transported to another world. (Rev: BL 1/1–15/05; SLJ 1/05)

8061 Carroll, Lewis. *Alice in Wonderland* (3–6). Illus. by Lisbeth Zwerger. 1999, North-South $19.95 (0-7358-1166-0). 103pp. A newly illustrated edition of this beloved fantasy. (Rev: BL 11/1/99; SLJ 10/99)

8062 Carroll, Lewis. *Alice's Adventures in Wonderland* (3–6). Illus. by Helen Oxenbury. 1999, Candlewick $24.99 (0-7636-0804-1). 208pp. A fine edition of the Carroll classic illustrated by well-known British artist Helen Oxenbury. (Rev: BL 1/1–15/00; HBG 3/00; SLJ 1/00)

8063 Carroll, Lewis. *Alice's Adventures in Wonderland* (5–7). Illus. 2000, Chronicle $19.95 (0-8118-2274-5). 140pp. This oversize edition of the complete text of Carroll's classic features illustrations from 29 artists. (Rev: BL 11/1/00; HBG 3/01; SLJ 11/00)

8064 Carroll, Lewis. *Alice's Adventures in Wonderland* (5–12). Illus. by Iassen Ghiuselev. 2003, Simply Read $29.95 (1-894965-00-0). 136pp. Interesting illustrations by Ghiuselev that interpret incidents and characters in a different way highlight this new edition of an old classic. (Rev: BL 2/1/04; SLJ 6/04)

8065 Carroll, Lewis. *Alice's Adventures in Wonderland and Through the Looking Glass* (4–7). Illus. by John Tenniel. 1963, Penguin Putnam $16.99 (0-448-06004-3). One of many recommended editions of these enduring fantasies.

8066 Carroll, Lewis. *Through the Looking Glass, and What Alice Found There* (4–7). Illus. by John Tenniel. 1977, St. Martin's $14.95 (0-312-80374-5). 224pp. The sequel to *Alice's Adventures in Wonderland.* One of many editions.

8067 Carroll, Thomas. *The Colony* (4–7). 2000, Sunstone $18.95 (0-86534-295-4). 152pp. Fifth-grader Tony and his bullying arch-enemy Lawrence are shrunk to the size of ants by a Navajo charm and in their new environment join opposing forces. (Rev: HBG 3/01; SLJ 7/00)

8068 Carter, Angela. *Sea-Cat and Dragon King* (2–4). Illus. by Eva Tatcheva. 2002, Bloomsbury $12.95 (1-58234-768-9). 96pp. Dragon King, ruler of the sea, envies Sea-Cat's spectacular outfit of seaweed and jewels. (Rev: BL 8/02; SLJ 11/02)

8069 Carus, Marianne, ed. *That's Ghosts for You: 13 Scary Stories* (4–7). Illus. by YongSheng Xuan. 2000, Front Street $15.95 (0-8126-2675-3). 131pp. A fine collection of 13 chilling stories set in locations around the world, each with a supernatural twist. (Rev: BL 12/1/00; HBG 3/01; SLJ 12/00)

8070 Cazet, Denys. *Minnie and Moo and the Seven Wonders of the World* (2–4). Illus. by author. 2003, Simon & Schuster $16.95 (0-689-85330-0). 134pp. A chapter book in which bovine friends Minnie and Moo seek to save the farm by conducting tours of the "Seven Wonders of the World." (Rev: HBG 4/04; SLJ 11/03)

8071 Chabon, Michael. *Summerland* (5–9). 2002, Hyperion $22.95 (0-7868-0877-2). 512pp. Little Leaguer Ethan Feld is recruited to save the world from an old enemy in this fantasy adventure. (Rev: BCCB 1/03; BL 8/02; HB 11–12/02; HBG 3/03; SLJ 11/02*)

8072 Chamberlain, Penny. *The Olden Days Locket* (4–7). 2003, Sono Nis paper $6.95 (1-55039-128-3). 198pp. Past and present collide in this well-researched and absorbing story of two girls — one living in the late 19th century and the other in the late 20th century — with connections to the same house in British Columbia. (Rev: SLJ 8/03)

8073 Chan, Gillian. *The Carved Box* (5–8). 2001, Kids Can $16.95 (1-55074-895-5). 232pp. The acquisition of a dog and a carved box ease the transition for orphaned Callum, 15, who has moved from Scotland to Canada to live with his uncle, in this novel which has an element of fantasy that comes to the fore in the dramatic ending. (Rev: BL 10/01; HBG 3/02; SLJ 10/01)

8074 Chocolate, Debbi. *Pigs Can Fly* (2–4). Illus. by Leslie Tryon. 2004, Cricket $15.95 (0-8126-2706-7). 64pp. In this engaging collection of four stories, Harriet the potbellied pig realizes her dream of flying, helps a friend overcome her fear of heights, competes in a swimming contest, and nearly kills Homer Mouse with kindness. (Rev: BL 5/1/04; SLJ 5/04)

8075 Christian, Peggy. *The Bookstore Mouse* (4–6). Illus. by Gary Lippincott. 1995, Harcourt $16.00 (0-15-200203-0). 126pp. Cervantes, a bookstore mouse, is transported by a book to a medieval English monastery, where he meets Sigfried, a young scribe. (Rev: SLJ 11/95)

8076 Clark, Margaret, comp. *A Treasury of Dragon Stories* (2–5). Illus. by Mark Robertson. Series: Treasury. 1997, Kingfisher paper $6.95 (0-7534-5114-X). 156pp. A collection of 15 previously published stories or excerpts from books that deal with dragons. (Rev: SLJ 1/98)

8077 Clarke, Judith. *Starry Nights* (5–9). 2003, Front Street $15.95 (1-886910-82-0). 152pp. When Jess's family moves to a new house, a ghost seems to be involved in the family's emotional upheavals. (Rev: BL 6/1–15/03; HB 9–10/03; HBG 4/04)

8078 Clifford, Eth. *Flatfoot Fox and the Case of the Bashful Beaver* (2–4). Illus. by Brian Lies. 1995, Houghton Mifflin $16.00 (0-395-70560-6). 47pp. Flatfoot Fox and Secretary Bird solve the mystery of strange thefts involving forest animals. (Rev: BL 3/1/95; SLJ 4/95)

8079 Cole, Joanna. *Doctor Change* (2–4). Illus. by Donald Carrick. 1986, Morrow LB $12.88 (0-688-06136-2). 32pp. Young Tom discovers that Doctor Change can turn himself into a variety of objects; he learns the man's secrets and confronts the evil magic. (Rev: BCCB 10/86; BL 9/15/86; SLJ 10/86)

8080 Coleman, Alice Scovell. *Engraved in Stone* (4–7). Illus. by Anjal Ren e Armand. 2003, Tiara Bks. $14.95 (0-9729846-0-7). 147pp. A prince and princess who will do anything to avoid their planned marriage set off on a quest to get their fate changed in this humorous fantasy. (Rev: SLJ 12/03)

8081 Coleman, Janet W. *Fast Eddie* (3–4). Illus. by Alec Gillman. 1993, Macmillan LB $13.95 (0-02-722815-0). 144pp. Eddie the raccoon faces danger when he plays tricks on humans. (Rev: SLJ 6/93)

8082 Colfer, Eoin. *Artemis Fowl: The Arctic Incident* (5–8). 2002, Hyperion $16.95 (0-7868-0855-1). 277pp. Artemis and Captain Holly band together to free Artemis's father from the Russian Mafiya in this amusing, lively sequel to *Artemis Fowl* (2001). (Rev: BCCB 7–8/01; HBG 10/02; SLJ 7/02)

8083 Collins, Suzanne. *Gregor the Overlander* (4–7). 2003, Scholastic $16.95 (0-439-43536-6). 320pp. When his baby sister disappears into an air vent, 11-year-old Gregor doesn't hesitate to follow and finds himself in a whole new world, an Underland where an unexpected role awaits him. (Rev: BCCB 1/04; BL 11/15/03*; HB 9–10/03; HBG 9–10/03; LMC 11–12/03; SLJ 11/03)

8084 Collodi, Carlo. *Pinocchio* (3–5). Illus. by Ed Young. 1996, Penguin Putnam $18.95 (0-399-22941-8). 48pp. An abridged version of this classic that nevertheless captures its flavor and excitement. (Rev: BL 11/15/96; SLJ 10/96)

8085 Conly, Jane L. *R-T, Margaret, and the Rats of NIMH* (4–6). Illus. by Leonard Lubin. 1990, HarperCollins LB $14.89 (0-06-021364-7); paper $4.95 (0-06-440387-4). 288pp. The third installment of the brilliant rodents, in which two human children star. (Rev: BCCB 6/90; BL 5/15/90; SLJ 6/90)

8086 Conly, Jane L. *Racso and the Rats of NIMH* (5–7). Illus. by Leonard Lubin. 1986, HarperCollins LB $17.89 (0-06-021362-0). 288pp. This sequel to the Newbery Medal winner involves once again the smart rodents who wish to live in peace in Thorn Valley. (Rev: BCCB 6/86; BL 6/1/86; SLJ 4/86)

8087 Cooper, Susan. *The Boggart* (4–6). 1993, Macmillan $15.00 (0-689-50576-0). 200pp. An old desk unleashes the Boggart, a mischievous spirit who has lived in a Scottish castle for centuries. (Rev: BCCB 3/93; BL 1/15/93; HB 5–6/93*; SLJ 1/93)

8088 Cooper, Susan. *The Boggart and the Monster* (4–6). 1997, Simon & Schuster paper $16.00 (0-689-81330-9). 192pp. The Boggart, a Scottish spirit-creature, wants to accompany young Jessup and Emily when they go to Loch Ness to find the monster. (Rev: BCCB 5/97; BL 3/1/97; HB 5–6/97; SLJ 5/97)

8089 Cooper, Susan. *Green Boy* (4–8). 2002, Simon & Schuster $16.00 (0-689-84751-3). 208pp. Two young boys discover a futuristic world in which natural resources are depleted and a war to save the environment is being waged. (Rev: BCCB 5/02; BL 3/1/02; HB 5–6/02; HBG 10/02; SLJ 2/02)

8090 Cooper, Susan. *King of Shadows* (5–8). Illus. by John Clapp. 1999, Simon & Schuster $16.00 (0-689-82817-9). 192pp. Nat Field time-travels to 1599 London and assumes the child-actor role of Puck in *A Midsummer Night's Dream.* (Rev: BL 10/15/99*; HB 11–12/99; HBG 3/00; SLJ 11/99)

8091 Cooper, Susan. *Silver on the Tree* (5–7). 1980, Macmillan $18.00 (0-689-50088-2); paper $4.99 (0-689-71152-2). 256pp. In this fifth and last volume of a series, Will Stanton and his friends wage a final battle against the Dark, the powers of evil. The first four volumes are *Over Sea, Under Stone* (1966),*The Dark Is Rising* (1973), *The Grey King* (1975), and *Greenwitch* (1985). *The Grey King* won the 1976 Newbery Medal.

8092 Corbett, Sue. *12 Again* (5–8). 2002, Dutton $16.99 (0-525-46899-4). 160pp. Patrick's mother becomes 12 again after drinking a magic potion, and it's up to Patrick to save her. (Rev: BCCB 10/02; BL 9/1/02; HBG 3/03; SLJ 7/02)

8093 Corlett, William. *The Steps up the Chimney* (5–8). 2000, Pocket paper $4.99 (0-7434-1001-7). 272pp. Children stuck in a remote mansion in Wales with an uncle and his pregnant, vegetarian girlfriend discover a secret room that houses a magician. (Rev: SLJ 5/01)

8094 Coville, Bruce. *The Dragon of Doom* (2–4). Illus. by Katherine Coville. Series: Moongobble and Me. 2003, Simon & Schuster $14.95 (0-689-85754-3). 69pp. Young Edward finds life in his hometown of Pigbone terribly boring until a magician named Moongobble arrives and asks the boy to be his assistant. (Rev: HBG 4/04; SLJ 1/04)

8095 Coville, Bruce. *The Ghost in the Big Brass Bed* (4–6). 1991, Bantam paper $4.50 (0-553-15827-9). 184pp. Two ghosts appeal for help to Chris and Nina, who try to solve the mystery surrounding them. (Rev: SLJ 1/92)

8096 Coville, Bruce. *The Ghost Wore Gray* (5–8). 1988, Bantam paper $4.99 (0-553-15610-1). Nina and friend Chris investigate a haunted inn in the Catskill Mountains. (Rev: BL 9/15/88; SLJ 9/88)

8097 Coville, Bruce, ed. *A Glory of Unicorns* (5–8). Illus. 1998, Scholastic paper $16.95 (0-590-95943-3). A collection of stories by fantasy authors, including the editor and his wife, that deal with unicorns. (Rev: BL 6/1–15/98; BR 5–6/98; HBG 10/98; SLJ 5/98)

8098 Coville, Bruce. *Goblins in the Castle* (5–7). Illus. 1992, Pocket paper $4.99 (0-671-72711-7). 166pp. William, now 11, has grown up in Toad-in-a-Cage Castle and knows many of its secret passages. (Rev: BL 2/1/93)

8099 Coville, Bruce. *Juliet Dove, Queen of Love: A Magic Shop Book* (4–8). 2003, Harcourt $17.00 (0-15-204561-9). 190pp. Life changes for shy Juliet, 12, when she is given an amulet and the boys suddenly come flocking to her side. (Rev: BL 1/1–15/04; HBG 4/04; SLJ 12/03)

8100 Coville, Bruce. *The Monsters of Morley Manor: A Madcap Adventure* (4–6). 2001, Harcourt $16.00 (0-15-216382-4). 224pp. Supernatural events that threaten the world result when sixth-grader Anthony and his younger sister Sarah release a family of monsters from a spell. (Rev: BL 9/1/01; HBG 3/02; SLJ 1/02)

8101 Coville, Bruce. *The Prince of Butterflies* (3–5). Illus. by John Clapp. 2002, Harcourt $16.00 (0-15-201454-3). 40pp. Migrating monarchs turn a boy into a butterfly so he can help them on their journey in this socially conscious story. (Rev: BL 3/15/02; HBG 10/02; SLJ 5/02)

8102 Coville, Bruce. *Song of the Wanderer* (5–8). Series: Unicorn Chronicles. 1999, Scholastic paper $16.95 (0-590-45953-8). 336pp. Cara and her friends undertake a dangerous mission — returning to Earth to bring her grandmother, the Wanderer, back to Luster. This is a sequel to *Into the Land of the Unicorn.* (Rev: BL 3/1/00; HBG 3/00; SLJ 12/99)

8103 Cowell, Cressida. *How to Train Your Dragon: By Hiccup Horrendous Haddock III: Translated from an Old Norse Legend by Cressida Cowell* (4–8). Illus. 2004, Little, Brown paper $10.95 (0-316-73737-2). 224pp. The hilarious account of the fumbling efforts of nerdy Hiccup to capture and train a dragon and to take his rightful place as the next Warrior Chief. Also use *How to Be a Pirate: By Hiccup Horrendous Haddock III* (2005). (Rev: BL 4/15/04; SLJ 7/04)

8104 Creech, Sharon. *Pleasing the Ghost* (3–6). 1996, HarperCollins LB $14.89 (0-06-026986-3). 128pp. Dennis, who is visited by ghosts, has difficulty understanding the garbled language of the newest visitor, Uncle Arvie. (Rev: BCCB 10/96; BL 9/1/96; SLJ 11/96)

8105 Cresswell, Helen. *Time Out* (3–6). Illus. by Peter Elwell. 1997, Parkwest $12.95 (0-718-82658-2). 80pp. In 1887, a family is transported to 1987 for an unnerving vacation. (Rev: BL 2/1/90; SLJ 6/90)

8106 Crew, Gary. *The Viewer* (5–9). Illus. by Shaun Tan. 2003, Lothian $16.95 (0-85091-828-6). A well-illustrated dark fantasy linked to world catastrophes caused by mankind, from religious persecution to atomic war. (Rev: SLJ 3/04)

8107 Crilley, Mark. *Akiko and the Journey to Toog* (3–5). Illus. by author. 2003, Delacorte $9.95 (0-385-73042-X). 164pp. In this comic-style intergalactic fantasy, fifth grader Akiko and a number of her friends journey to the planet Toog on a rescue mission. (Rev: HBG 4/04; SLJ 12/03)

8108 Crilley, Mark. *Akiko in the Castle of Alia Rellapor* (3–5). Illus. 2001, Delacorte $9.95 (0-385-32728-5). 172pp. Fourth-grader Akiko and her celestial friends finally reach the castle and Prince Frogtoppit in this fourth — and mostly text-based — book in a series with graphic-novel roots. (Rev: BL 1/1–15/02; HBG 3/02; SLJ 11/01)

8109 Crilley, Mark. *Billy Clikk: Creatch Battler* (3–5). Illus. 2004, Delacorte $10.95 (0-385-73111-6). 240pp. Twelve-year-old Billy Clikk discovers that his parent's pest extermination business is really a front for a monster-disposal operation in this comic-book-style novel full of gross humor. (Rev: BL 4/15/04; SLJ 7/04)

8110 Crocker, Carter. *The Tale of the Swamp Rat* (4–8). Illus. 2003, Penguin Putnam $16.99 (0-399-23964-2). 240pp. Ossie the swamp rat, orphaned by a snake but rescued by an alligator, finds himself accused of causing the drought that is affecting his swamp. (Rev: BCCB 12/03; BL 11/15/03; HBG 4/04; SLJ 10/03)

8111 Cross, Gillian. *Pictures in the Dark* (5–8). 1996, Holiday House $16.95 (0-8234-1267-9). A boy whose life is miserable uses supernatural means to escape the pressures. (Rev: BCCB 1/97; BL 1/1–15/97; BR 3–4/97)

8112 Crosse, Joanna. *A Child's Book of Angels* (3–5). Illus. by Olwyn Whelan. 2000, Barefoot LB $19.99 (1-84148-082-7). 64pp. A young boy's guardian angel takes him on a tour of heaven where he meets different kinds of angels and learns about their responsibilities — looking after the seasons, for example, or healing. (Rev: HBG 10/01; SLJ 2/01)

8113 Crossley-Holland, Kevin. *At the Crossing Places* (5–8). 2002, Scholastic $17.95 (0-439-26598-3). 416pp. The story started in *The Seeing Stone* (2001) continues, with Arthur now on a quest to find his mother and trying to make peace with his discoveries about his father and his own relationship with Arthur-in-the-stone. (Rev: BL 11/1/02; HB 11–12/02; HBG 3/03; SLJ 11/02)

8114 Crossley-Holland, Kevin. *The Seeing Stone* (4–8). 2001, Scholastic $17.95 (0-439-26326-3). 340pp. In the time of Richard the Lion-Hearted, a 13-year-old boy named Arthur finds that his life mirrors that of the legendary King Arthur. (Rev: BL 10/1/01; HB 11–12/01*; HBG 3/02; SLJ 10/01)

8115 Crowley, Bridget. *Step into the Dark* (5–7). 2003, Hodder paper $8.95 (0-340-84416-7). 172pp. This ghost story is set in a theater and conveys the attraction of the stage. (Rev: BL 12/1/03)

8116 Curry, Jane Louise. *The Black Canary* (5–8). 2005, Simon & Schuster $16.95 (0-689-86478-7). 288pp. Twelve-year-old James, from a biracial family of musicians, resists pressure to develop his own musical abilities until he travels back in time to Elizabethan London and discovers he is also talented. (Rev: BL 2/15/05; SLJ 3/05)

8117 Curry, Jane Louise. *The Egyptian Box* (4–7). 2002, Simon & Schuster $16.00 (0-689-84273-2). 192pp. A suspenseful mystery about a middle-schooler who discovers a magical servant, an Egyptian statue come to life, who will obey her wishes. (Rev: BCCB 5/02; BL 6/1–15/02; HBG 10/02; SLJ 3/02)

8118 Cuyler, Margery. *The Battlefield Ghost* (2–4). Illus. 1999, Scholastic $15.95 (0-590-10848-4). 112pp. In this easy chapter book, a family moves to a Princeton house that is haunted by the ghost of a Revolutionary War soldier. (Rev: BL 11/15/99; HBG 3/00; SLJ 12/99)

8119 Cuyler, Margery. *Weird Wolf* (3–6). Illus. by Dirk Zimmer. 1991, Holt paper $6.95 (0-8050-1643-0). 72pp. Nine-year-old Harry Walpole has to find out how to rid himself of being a werewolf, just like his grandfather. (Rev: BCCB 1/90; BL 12/1/89; SLJ 4/90)

8120 Dadey, Debbie, and Marcia T. Jones. *Leprechauns Don't Play Basketball* (5–8). Illus. by John S. Gurney. 1992, Scholastic paper $3.99 (0-590-44822-6). 70pp. The Bailey Elementary 3rd grade thinks the gym teacher is a leprechaun. (Rev: BL 9/15/92)

8121 Dahl, Roald. *George's Marvelous Medicine* (4–6). Illus. by Quentin Blake. 1998, Puffin paper $4.99 (0-14-130111-2). 96pp. George concocts medicine that shrinks his mean grandmother.

8122 Dahl, Roald. *James and the Giant Peach* (3–5). Illus. by Lane Smith. 1996, Knopf LB $17.99 (0-679-98090-3). 144pp. James is unhappy living with his mean aunts until a magic potion produces an enormous peach, which becomes a home for him. (Rev: BL 5/1/96)

8123 Dahl, Roald. *The Witches* (3–6). Illus. by Quentin Blake. 1983, Farrar $16.00 (0-374-38457-6); Puffin paper $3.95 (0-14-031730-9). 208pp. A boy and his grandmamma save English children from being turned into mice by witches.

8124 Dale, Anna. *Whispering to Witches* (4–6). 2004, Bloomsbury $16.95 (1-58234-890-1). 304pp. Twelve-year-old Joe Binks's Christmas-time encounter with a novice witch named Twiggy sweeps him into a mission to retrieve a book of potions and spells before it can be put to evil use. (Rev: BL 11/15/04; SLJ 11/04)

8125 Dalton, Annie. *Losing the Plot* (4–7). Series: Angels Unlimited. 2002, HarperCollins paper $4.99 (0-06-008816-8). 154pp. In this sequel to *Winging It* (2002), Mel, the carefree 13-year-old girl killed in an accident and now an angel, is on a mission to rescue three wayward teenagers in Elizabethan England. (Rev: SLJ 4/03)

8126 Defelice, Cynthia. *Cold Feet* (2–4). Illus. by Robert Andrew Parker. 2000, DK $15.95 (0-7894-2636-6). 32pp. A poor Scottish bagpiper with great holes in his shoes stumbles on a dead body with a nice pair of boots in this ghost story told in a picture book for older readers. (Rev: BCCB 11/00; BL 9/1/00; HB 9–10/00; HBG 3/01; SLJ 9/00)

8127 Defelice, Cynthia. *The Ghost and Mrs. Hobbs* (4–6). 2001, Farrar $16.00 (0-374-38046-5). 192pp. A ghost asks 11-year-old Allie for help, but scary and mysterious happenings hamper her efforts. (Rev: BL 9/1/01; HB 11–12/01; HBG 3/02; SLJ 8/01)

8128 Defelice, Cynthia. *The Ghost of Fossil Glen* (4–6). 1998, Farrar $16.00 (0-374-31787-9). 176pp. Allie has been chosen by the ghost of a young girl to avenge her death in this tense thriller. (Rev: BCCB 3/98; BL 3/15/98; HB 9–10/98; HBG 10/98; SLJ 7/98)

8129 Denney, Jim. *Battle Before Time* (3–6). Series: Timebenders. 2002, Thomas Nelson paper $5.99 (1-4003-0039-8). 163pp. A young inventor's time machine transports him and three friends into prehistory and an adventure that involves a fierce battle between good and evil. (Rev: BL 10/1/02)

8130 Denney, Jim. *Doorway to Doom* (3–6). 2002, Thomas Nelson paper $5.99 (1-4003-0040-1). 163pp. This sequel to *Battle Before Time* (2002) takes the four time-travelers to the Middle Ages to face another band of villains. (Rev: BL 10/1/02)

8131 Derby, Sally. *Jacob and the Stranger* (3–5). Illus. 1994, Ticknor $11.95 (0-395-66897-2). 32pp. Jacob takes care of a plant that sprouts miniature animals that become his companions. (Rev: BL 9/1/94; HB 9–10/94; SLJ 9/94)

8132 Derby, Sally. *Two Fools and a Horse: An Original Tale* (1–4). Illus. by Robert Rayevsky. 2003, Marshall Cavendish $15.95 (0-7614-5119-6). Janski and Wilhelm, two simple-minded peasants, track a suspicious-looking peddler, convinced that he has concealed a stolen horse in a sack on his back. (Rev: HBG 10/03; SLJ 5/03)

8133 DiCamillo, Kate. *The Tale of Despereaux: Being the Story of a Mouse, a Princess, Some Soup, and a Spool of Thread* (3–7). Illus. 2003, Candlewick $17.99 (0-7636-1722-9). 272pp. The diminutive mouse named Despereaux inspires confidence despite his odd appearance in this multilayered story involving Princess Pea, peasant girl Miggery Sow, and a rat named Roscuro. Newbery Medal winner, 2004. (Rev: BL 7/03; HB 5–6/04; SLJ 8/03)

8134 Downer, Ann. *Hatching Magic* (4–7). Illus. by Omar Rayyan. 2003, Simon & Schuster $16.95 (0-689-83400-4). 242pp. A procession of a pet dragon, a wizard, and his archenemy travel through time from the 13th century to the 21st century, where an 11-year-old Bostonian becomes involved in their disputes. (Rev: BL 4/15/03; HB 7–8/03; HBG 10/03; SLJ 8/03)

8135 Doyle, Roddy. *The Giggler Treatment* (2–5). Illus. by Brian Ajhar. 2000, Scholastic $14.95 (0-439-16299-8). 112pp. A nonsense story about several well-wishers who rush to warn Mister Mack that there is "dog poo" in the path where he is walking that has been placed there by furry little creatures named Gigglers. (Rev: HBG 3/01; SLJ 11/00)

8136 Doyle, Roddy. *Rover Saves Christmas* (2–5). Illus. by Brian Ajhar. 2001, Scholastic $14.95 (0-439-30530-6). 160pp. The lively crew from *The Giggler Treatment* (2000) return in an irreverent romp that takes Rover to the North Pole to sub for Rudolph. (Rev: HBG 3/02; SLJ 10/01)

8137 *Dr. Ernest Drake's Dragonology: The Complete Book of Dragons* (5–12). Illus. 2003, Candlewick $18.99 (0-7636-2329-6). Presented as the recently discovered research of a 19th-cenutry scientist, this richly illustrated volume presents a very realistic encyclopedia of dragon facts and figures. (Rev: BL 4/15/04; SLJ 4/04)

8138 Drexler, Sam, and Fay Shelby. *Lost in Spillville* (5–9). Series: Erika and Oz Adventures in American History. 2000, Aunt Strawberry paper $6.99 (0-9669988-1-2). 150pp. Two teenagers accidentally are transported to the 1930s and must locate an important clock maker to be returned to the 1990s. (Rev: SLJ 11/00)

8139 Duane, Diane. *Deep Wizardry* (5–8). Series: Young Wizards. 2001, Magic Carpet Books LB $15.25 (0-613-36059-1); Harcourt paper $6.95 (0-15-216257-7). 288pp. Nita and Kit, the two young wizards of *So You Want to Be a Wizard,* again use their powers to prevent a great catastrophe. (Rev: HB 5–6/85)

8140 Duane, Diane. *So You Want to Be a Wizard* (5–8). Series: Young Wizards. 2003, Harcourt $16.95 (0-15-204738-7); paper $6.95 (0-15-216250-X). 288pp. Nita and friends embark on a journey to retrieve the Book of Night with Moon.

8141 Duel, John. *Wide Awake in Dreamland* (5–8). Illus. 1992, Stargaze Publg. $15.95 (0-9630923-0-8). An evil warlock threatens to steal a 9-year-old's imagination unless the young boy can find a friendly wizard first. (Rev: BL 3/1/92; SLJ 5/92)

8142 Duey, Kathleen. *The Silver Thread: The Unicorn's Secret #2* (2–4). 2001, Simon & Schuster paper $3.99 (0-689-84270-8). 80pp. A young girl must rescue a unicorn child who has been shot by a hunter's arrow in this second volume of a four-part fantasy. (Rev: BL 3/1/02)

8143 Dunkle, Clare B. *The Hollow Kingdom* (5–8). 2003, Holt $16.95 (0-8050-7390-6). 230pp. A beauty-and-the-beast story with a twist, in which Kate is persuaded to marry a goblin king and move to his underground world. (Rev: BL 11/15/03; HBG 4/04; SLJ 12/03)

8144 Dunlop, Eileen. *The Ghost by the Sea* (4–6). 1996, Holiday House $15.95 (0-8234-1264-4). 192pp. Robin uncovers details of a death that occurred 80 years ago and is haunted by a restless ghost. (Rev: BCCB 3/97; BL 1/1–15/97; SLJ 3/97)

8145 Dunlop, Eileen. *Websters' Leap* (4–7). 1995, Holiday House $15.95 (0-8234-1193-1). 160pp. In this time-slip fantasy, Jill gets involved with people who owned a Scottish castle 400 years before. (Rev: BL 10/1/95; SLJ 10/95)

8146 DuPrau, Jeanne. *The People of Sparks* (5–7). 2004, Random $15.95 (0-375-82824-9). 352pp. In this sequel to *The City of Ember,* Doon and Lina, plus the 400 people they have led from Ember to the surface of the Earth, seek aid from the people of Sparks. (Rev: BL 4/15/04; HB 7–8/04; SLJ 5/04)

8147 Easton, Patricia Harrison. *Davey's Blue-Eyed Frog* (2–4). Illus. by Mike Wohnoutka. 2003, Clarion $14.00 (0-618-18185-7). 104pp. Davey catches a blue-eyed frog that turns out to be a princess in this illustrated chapter book. (Rev: BL 3/1/03; HBG 10/03; SLJ 7/03)

8148 Einhorn, Edward. *Paradox in Oz* (4–6). Illus. 2000, Hungry Tiger $24.95 (1-929527-01-2). 240pp. This new Oz adventure is true to the famous series and contains familiar characters including Ozma and Glinda, the Good Witch of the South. (Rev: BL 4/15/00; SLJ 8/00)

8149 Ephron, Delia. *The Girl Who Changed the World* (3–6). 1993, Ticknor $13.95 (0-395-66139-0). 160pp. Tired of being bullied by her older brother, Violet rebels and organizes other sibling victims to do the same. (Rev: BCCB 10/93; BL 11/15/93; SLJ 11/93)

8150 Etchemendy, Nancy. *The Power of Un* (4–7). 2000, Front Street $14.95 (0-8126-2850-0). 160pp. Gib, a young boy, meets a strange old man who gives him an "unner," which can send him back in time in this thought-provoking fantasy. (Rev: BCCB 7–8/00; BL 5/1/00; HBG 10/00; SLJ 6/00)

8151 Falcone, L. M. *Walking with the Dead* (5–8). 2005, Kids Can $16.95 (1-55337-708-7). 196pp. Alex finds himself entangled in the world of Greek mythology when a mummy in his father's museum awakens to take care of some unfinished business in the underworld. (Rev: BL 3/15/05; SLJ 6/05)

8152 Favole, Robert J. *Through the Wormhole* (5–8). 2001, Flywheel $17.95 (1-930826-00-1). 192pp. Detailed endnotes add historical weight to this story of Michael and Kate, who travel through time to 1778 to aid the Marquis de Lafayette and rescue one of Michael's ancestors. (Rev: BL 3/1/01; SLJ 4/01)

8153 Fawcett, Melissa Jayne, and Joseph Bruchac. *Makiawisug: The Gift of the Little People* (3–5). Illus. by David Wagner. 1997, Little People $19.95 (0-9656933-2-5). 28pp. The story of the antics of the American Indian "little people," the Makiawisug. (Rev: BL 9/15/97)

8154 Fienberg, Anna. *The Witch in the Lake* (5–8). 2002, Annick LB $18.95 (1-55037-723-X); paper

$7.95 (1-55037-722-1). 216pp. This story of magic and suspense in 16th-century Italy interweaves fantasy with facts about the time. (Rev: HBG 3/03; SLJ 8/02)

8155 Findon, Joanne. *When Night Eats the Moon* (4–7). 2000, Red Deer paper $7.95 (0-88995-212-4). 176pp. Her flute music and some magic take Holly, a Canadian girl visiting England, back to prehistoric times at Stonehenge when the locals are being threatened with a Celtic invasion. (Rev: BL 8/00)

8156 Fisher, Catherine. *The Oracle Betrayed* (5–8). 2004, Greenwillow $16.99 (0-06-057157-8). 352pp. This suspenseful story set in an imaginary country that combines aspects of ancient Greece and ancient Egypt involves a young heroine, Mirany, on a dangerous quest. (Rev: BL 2/15/04; HB 3–4/04; SLJ 3/04)

8157 Fisher, Catherine. *The Sphere of Secrets* (5–8). Series: Oracle Prophecies Trilogy. 2005, Greenwillow LB $17.89 (0-06-057162-4). 384pp. Alexos, introduced in *The Oracle Betrayed* (2004), embarks on a journey to the Well of Songs while his friend Mirany serves the Oracle. (Rev: BL 3/15/05; SLJ 3/05)

8158 Fisk, Pauline. *Midnight Blue* (5–7). 2003, Bloomsbury $16.95 (1-58234-829-4). 218pp. Bonnie happens upon a magical balloon that takes her to a parallel world that is very familiar yet very different, where she finds the happy family she has always dreamed of. (Rev: BL 10/1/03; HBG 4/04; SLJ 11/03)

8159 Flanagan, John. *The Ruins of Gorlan* (5–8). 2005, Philomel $15.99 (0-399-24454-9). 256pp. Will becomes an apprentice ranger and plays a key role in protecting his kingdom in this memorable first installment in a new fantasy series. (Rev: BL 6/1–15/05; SLJ 6/05)

8160 Fleischman, Sid. *The 13th Floor: A Ghost Story* (4–6). Illus. 1995, Greenwillow $15.00 (0-688-14216-8). 144pp. When a ghost who lived in the 17th century asks for his help, Bud obligingly travels back in time. (Rev: BL 10/1/95; HB 11–12/95; SLJ 10/95)

8161 Fleischman, Sid. *The Midnight Horse* (3–6). Illus. by Peter Sis. 1990, Greenwillow $16.00 (0-688-09441-4). 84pp. An orphan boy named Touch, accompanied by a friendly ghost, is the center of this 19th-century tale. (Rev: BCCB 12/90; BL 8/90; HB 11–12/90; SLJ 9/90)

8162 Fleming, Candace. *Gator Gumbo* (K–3). Illus. by Sally Anne Lambert. 2004, Farrar $16.00 (0-374-38050-3). 32pp. Aging Monsieur Gator, taunted by his animal neighbors in the swamp, turns the table on them when he decides to cook up a pot of gumbo "just like Maman used to make." (Rev: BL 4/1/04; HB 3–4/04; SLJ 2/04)

8163 Fleming, Ian. *Chitty Chitty Bang Bang* (4–6). Illus. by John Burningham. 1964, Amereon LB $22.72 (0-88411-983-1). 159pp. Chitty Chitty Bang Bang, a magical racing car, flies, floats, and has a real talent for getting the Pott family in and out of trouble.

8164 Foon, Dennis. *The Dirt Eaters* (5–10). Series: Longlight Legacy Trilogy. 2003, Annick $19.95 (1-55037-807-4); paper $9.95 (1-55037-806-6). 320pp. In this well-written first installment of a trilogy, 15-year-old Roan finds himself torn between the peaceful ways of his upbringing and a desire to avenge a murderous attack on his village. (Rev: SLJ 1/04)

8165 Forrester, Sandra. *The Everyday Witch* (5–7). 2002, Barron's paper $4.95 (0-7641-2220-7). 192pp. To establish her magic rating, 11-year-old witch Beatrice is assigned to rescue a famous sorcerer and his daughters from an evil villain. (Rev: SLJ 10/02)

8166 Forrester, Sandra. *The Witches of Friar's Lantern* (4–6). Illus. 2003, Barron's paper $4.95 (0-7641-2436-6). 225pp. Twelve-year-old novice witch Beatrice, introduced in *The Everyday Witch* (2002), seeks the downfall of the villain called the Dally Rumpe in this tale reminiscent of Harry Potter. (Rev: SLJ 7/03)

8167 Forrester, Sandra. *The Witches of Sea-Dragon Bay: The Adventures of Beatrice Bailey* (5–8). 2003, Barron's paper $4.95 (0-7641-2633-4). 228pp. Another in the series starring 12-year-old apprentice witch Beatrice Bailey, likely to appeal to Harry Potter fans. (Rev: SLJ 3/04)

8168 Foster, Evelyn, and Olwyn Whelan. *The Mermaid of Cafur* (1–5). 1999, Barefoot LB $15.95 (1-902283-40-6). Through the courage of Meaghan, the evil power of the mermaid queen of Cafur is broken and her captive children are set free. (Rev: SLJ 3/99)

8169 Freeman, Martha. *The Spy Wore Shades* (4–6). 2001, HarperCollins LB $15.89 (0-06-029270-9). 235pp. Eleven-year-old Dougie helps a girl from an underground civilization to save her family's home from land developers. (Rev: BL 10/1/01; HBG 3/02; SLJ 8/01)

8170 Fromental, Jean-Luc. *Broadway Chicken* (5–8). Trans. by Suzi Baker. Illus. 1995, Hyperion LB $15.49 (0-7868-2048-9). A tale of success and failure with, yes, a dancing chicken as the protagonist. (Rev: BL 12/15/95; SLJ 2/96)

8171 Froud, Wendy, and Terri Windling. *A Midsummer Night's Faery Tale* (4–6). Illus. 1999, Simon & Schuster $18.00 (0-684-85559-3). 52pp. A young fairy named Sneezle sets out on a dangerous quest to save the life of his queen, Titania. (Rev: BL 2/1/00)

8172 Furlong, Monica. *Colman* (4–8). 2004, Random LB $17.99 (0-375-91514-1). 288pp. In this complex, posthumous sequel to *Wise Child* (1987) and *Juniper* (1990), Juniper and her companions must battle the evil Meroot and the Gray Knight and restore harmony in the land. (Rev: BL 1/1–15/04; SLJ 2/04)

8173 Gaiman, Neil. *Coraline* (5–8). Illus. by Dave McKean. 2002, HarperCollins LB $17.89 (0-06-623744-0). 176pp. An Alice-in-Wonderland type of tale for older readers in which a girl finds an alternate world in the empty apartment next door. (Rev: BCCB 11/02; BL 8/02; HB 11–12/02; HBG 3/03; SLJ 8/02*)

393

8174 Gaiman, Neil. *The Wolves in the Walls* (3–6). Illus. by Dave McKean. 2003, HarperCollins $16.00 (0-380-97827-X). Lucy says there are wolves in the walls of her house, but her family doesn't believe her — until the wolves come out — in this imaginatively illustrated story. (Rev: BL 2/1/04; HBG 4/04; SLJ 9/03)

8175 Gardner, Sally. *Boolar's Big Day Out* (2–4). Illus. by author. Series: Tales from the Box. 2003, Bloomsbury $14.95 (1-58234-833-2); paper $6.95 (1-58234-857-X). 120pp. Boolar, a starstruck doll, initially turns his back on his doll family and close mouse friends, but is accepted back when he realizes that family and friends far outshine the rewards of fame. (Rev: HBG 4/04; SLJ 1/04)

8176 Garland, Michael. *Miss Smith's Incredible Storybook* (1–4). Illus. by author. 2003, Dutton $16.99 (0-525-47133-2). A magic story book that brings the characters to life proves too much for the substitute teacher. (Rev: HBG 4/04; SLJ 10/03)

8177 Garretson, Jerri. *The Secret of Whispering Springs* (5–8). 2002, Ravenstone paper $6.99 (0-9659712-4-4). 206pp. A ghost and a threatening squatter vie for Cassie's attention in this suspenseful adventure. (Rev: BL 8/02; SLJ 8/02)

8178 Gerstein, Mordicai. *The Giant* (3–5). Illus. 1995, Hyperion LB $14.49 (0-7868-2104-3). 40pp. When three children rebuff a giant's attempts to become friends with them, later that night they hear him sobbing. (Rev: BL 10/15/95; SLJ 11/95)

8179 Gibbons, Faye. *Hook Moon Night: Spooky Stories from the Georgia Mountains* (3–6). Illus. 1997, Morrow $15.00 (0-688-14504-3). 128pp. In his Georgia home, Grandpa tells ghost stories, including one in which a sick woman is buried alive by her son-in-law. (Rev: BL 11/1/97; HBG 3/98; SLJ 10/97)

8180 Gideon, Melanie. *The Map That Breathed* (5–8). 2003, Holt $16.95 (0-8050-7142-3). 256pp. Dangerous and exciting adventures await Nora and Billy when they look into the alternate world of Sasarea. (Rev: BCCB 2/04; BL 11/15/03; HBG 4/04; SLJ 12/03)

8181 Gliori, Debi. *Pure Dead Brilliant* (4–8). 2003, Knopf LB $17.99 (0-375-91412-9). 224pp. The fun continues at the Strega-Borgia castle as Titus anticipates a large windfall, Pandora finds a time-travel clock, and there are some strange house guests. (Rev: BL 11/1/03; HBG 3/02; SLJ 10/03)

8182 Gliori, Debi. *Pure Dead Wicked* (5–8). 2002, Knopf $15.95 (0-375-81411-6). 224pp. Siblings Titus, Pandora, and Damp must leave their castle and move with their creepy extended family into the Auchenlochtermuchy Arms with disastrous but humorous consequences in this sequel to *Pure Dead Magic* (2001). (Rev: BL 9/15/02; HBG 10/03; SLJ 8/02)

8183 Gogol, Nikolai. *The Nose* (3–8). Illus. by Gennady Spirin. 1993, Godine $17.95 (0-87923-963-8). In this novel of the absurd set in St. Petersburg, Kovaliov finds that his nose has disappeared. (Rev: SLJ 8/93)

8184 Goldsmith, Howard. *The Twiddle Twins' Haunted House* (2–3). Illus. 1997, Mondo paper $4.50 (1-57255-222-0). 40pp. Hippo twins suspect a ghost when they are awakened one night by a tapping sound. Also use *Twiddle Twins' Music Box Mystery* (1997). (Rev: BL 2/1/98)

8185 Gonick, Larry. *Attack of the Smart Pies* (4–7). Illus. by author. 2005, Cricket $15.95 (0-8126-2740-7). 185pp. This complex novel with graphic elements blends fantasy, horror, mystery, and humor in the story of Emma, a 12-year-old orphan who flees from her threatening foster father and finds herself in Kokonino County, land of the New Muses. (Rev: SLJ 6/05)

8186 Gormley, Beatrice. *Best Friend Insurance* (5–7). Illus. by Emily Arnold McCully. 1988, Avon paper $2.50 (0-380-69854-4). 160pp. Maureen finds that her mother has been transformed into a new friend named Kitty. (Rev: SLJ 8/04)

8187 Gormley, Beatrice. *Fifth Grade Magic* (4–6). Illus. by Emily Arnold McCully. 1982, Avon paper $3.50 (0-380-67439-4). 128pp. Gretchen uses the help of an inept fairy godmother to get the lead in the school play.

8188 Gormley, Beatrice. *Mail-Order Wings* (3–5). Illus. by Emily Arnold McCully. 1984, Avon paper $2.95 (0-380-67421-1). 164pp. Andrea finds her Wonda-Wings are gradually transforming her into a bird.

8189 Gormley, Beatrice. *More Fifth Grade Magic* (3–5). Illus. by Emily Arnold McCully. 1990, Avon paper $3.50 (0-380-70883-3). 128pp. Amy uses the magical powers she finds in a calendar to grant her wishes. (Rev: BL 8/89)

8190 Goto, Hiromi. *The Water of Possibility* (5–7). Illus. by Aries Cheung. Series: In the Same Boat. 2002, Coteau paper $8.95 (1-55050-183-6). 319pp. Sayuri, 12, and her younger brother discover a magical world full of danger in this fantasy that includes many elements of Japanese folklore. (Rev: SLJ 8/02)

8191 Graff, Serena. *Blackwell's Island* (4–7). 2005, Delacorte LB $16.99 (0-385-90901-2). 192pp. In early-20th-century New York, Alex and his younger sister Anna face lunatics, criminals, and ghouls. (Rev: BL 6/1–15/05)

8192 Grahame, Kenneth. *The Wind in the Willows* (4–6). Illus. by Patrick Benson. 1995, St. Martin's $19.95 (0-312-13624-2). 272pp. A brilliantly illustrated edition of this classic, with pictures that rival the work of Ernest H. Shepard. (Rev: BL 2/1/96)

8193 Grahame, Kenneth. *The Wind in the Willows* (3–5). Illus. by Michael Foreman. 2002, Harcourt $24.00 (0-15-216807-9). 240pp. Lively illustrations ranging from endpaper maps to action-packed two-page watercolors accompany this version of the beloved British animal story. (Rev: BL 12/1/02; HBG 3/03; SLJ 1/03)

8194 Grahame, Kenneth. *The Wind in the Willows* (4–7). Illus. by E. H. Shepard. 1983, Macmillan $19.95 (0-684-17957-1). 256pp. The classic that introduced Mole, Ratty, and Mr. Toad. Two of many other editions are: illus. by Michael Hague

(1980, Henry Holt); illus. by John Burningham (1983, Viking).

8195 Grahame, Kenneth. *The Wind in the Willows: The Gates of Dawn. Vol. 3* (2–5). Trans. from French by Joe Johnson. Adapted by Michel Plessix. Illus. by author. 2000, NBM $15.95 (1-56163-245-7). 31pp. A graphic novel that retells key episodes from Chapters 7, 8, and 9 of *The Wind in the Willows*. (Rev: HBG 3/01; SLJ 7/00)

8196 Grambling, Lois G. *Abigail Muchmore: An Original Tale* (K–3). Illus. by Susan Havice. 2003, Marshall Cavendish $16.95 (0-7614-5116-1). Fed up with the constant buffeting of her property by Mr. West Wind, Abigail Muchmore comes up with a clever scheme to bring him around to her way of thinking. (Rev: BL 5/15/03; HBG 10/03; SLJ 5/03)

8197 Graves, Keith. *Three Nasty Gnarlies* (K–3). Illus. by author. 2003, Scholastic $16.95 (0-439-24090-5). Although inspired by a beautiful butterfly to improve their appearance, three nasty gnarlies — Grubby Gurgle, Stanky Stoo, and Ooga-Mooga — have little success. (Rev: BCCB 1/04; BL 11/15/03; HBG 4/04; SLJ 12/03)

8198 Gray, Luli. *Falcon and the Carousel of Time* (4–7). 2005, Houghton Mifflin $15.00 (0-618-44895-0). 128pp. Falcon, 13, and her Aunt Emily travel back to 1903 New York City in this novel that blends elements of *Timespinners* (2003) and the two previous Falcon novels. (Rev: BL 6/1–15/05)

8199 Gray, Luli. *Falcon and the Charles Street Witch* (4–7). 2002, Houghton Mifflin $15.00 (0-618-16410-3). 144pp. In this fantasy follow-up to 1995's *Falcon's Egg,* a 12-year-old girl becomes reacquainted with a dragon she released over New York City and befriends a witch who lives in Greenwich Village. (Rev: BL 3/15/02*; HBG 10/02; SLJ 4/02)

8200 Gray, Luli. *Falcon's Egg* (3–5). 1995, Houghton Mifflin $13.95 (0-395-71128-2). 144pp. A young girl hatches an egg she finds in Central Park and, as a result, is transported to a world of magical creatures. (Rev: BCCB 10/95; BL 9/15/95; SLJ 9/95*)

8201 Gray, Luli. *Timespinners* (4–6). 2003, Houghton Mifflin $15.00 (0-618-16412-X). 160pp. While visiting the dioramas in the American Museum of Natural History, twins Allie and Fig Newton are transported backward in time to 1913 France and then to 35,000 B.C. (Rev: BL 3/1/03; HBG 10/03; SLJ 4/03)

8202 Greenburg, Dan. *A Ghost Named Wanda* (3–5). Illus. by Jack E. Davis. Series: Zack Files. 1996, Grosset paper $3.99 (0-448-41261-6). 59pp. The story of Zack, a 10-year-old with the knack of getting into unusual situations. Also use *Zap! I'm a Mind Reader* (1996). (Rev: SLJ 2/97)

8203 Greenburg, Dan. *Great-Grandpa's in the Litter Box* (3–5). Illus. 1996, Penguin Putnam paper $3.95 (0-448-41260-8). 61pp. Zack adopts a cat that not only talks but also claims to be a relative. Zack has further adventures in *Through the Medicine Cabinet* (1996). (Rev: BL 1/1–15/97; SLJ 2/97)

8204 Greer, Gery, and Bob Ruddick. *Max and Me and the Time Machine* (5–8). 1983, HarperCollins paper $4.99 (0-06-440222-3). 140pp. Steve and Max travel back in time to England during the Middle Ages.

8205 Gregory, Valiska. *When Stories Fell Like Shooting Stars* (3–6). Illus. by Stefano Vitale. 1996, Simon & Schuster paper $16.00 (0-689-80012-6). 32pp. Two allegorical tales involving animals with supernatural powers. (Rev: BCCB 2/97; BL 1/1–15/97; SLJ 10/96)

8206 Griffin, Adele. *Witch Twins* (3–5). 2001, Hyperion $14.99 (0-7868-0739-3). 144pp. Fifth-grade twins Claire and Luna are given many opportunities both at home and at school to use their hidden powers as witches. (Rev: BL 4/15/01; HB 9–10/01; HBG 3/02; SLJ 7/01)

8207 Griffin, Adele. *Witch Twins and Melody Malady* (3–6). 2003, Hyperion $14.99 (0-7868-1940-5). 128pp. Jealousy rears its ugly head and a little magic becomes necessary when sixth-grade witch twins Claire and Luna get an opportunity to meet Melody Malady, a young star of film and television. (Rev: BL 9/15/03; HBG 4/04; SLJ 7/03)

8208 Griffin, Peni R. *The Ghost Sitter* (4–6). 2001, Dutton $14.99 (0-525-46676-2). 128pp. A gentle ghost story in which Charlotte tries to help a girl who died 50 years ago to find peace. (Rev: BL 8/01; HB 5–6/01; HBG 10/01; SLJ 6/01)

8209 Griffin, Peni R. *Margo's House* (3–6). 1996, Simon & Schuster $16.00 (0-689-80944-1). 122pp. A girl and her father project themselves into the bodies of two dolls. (Rev: BCCB 11/96; BL 9/1/96; SLJ 10/96)

8210 Griffith, Helen V. *Cougar* (4–6). 1999, Greenwillow $15.00 (0-688-16337-8). 112pp. In this engaging fantasy, Nickel, a neglected youngster, gets help from a ghost horse to cope with bully Robbo. (Rev: BCCB 3/99; BL 4/1/99; HB 5–6/99; HBG 10/99; SLJ 5/99)

8211 Grindley, Sally. *Breaking the Spell: Tales of Enchantment* (3–5). Illus. 1997, Kingfisher $17.95 (0-7534-5002-X). 80pp. Seven original folk and fairy tales set in exotic locales and written by both established and new writers. (Rev: BL 1/1–15/98; HBG 3/98; SLJ 12/97)

8212 Guiberson, Brenda Z. *Tales of the Haunted Deep* (3–6). Illus. 2000, Holt $15.95 (0-8050-6057-X). 70pp. This collection of ghost stories of the sea contains tales of monsters, pirates, lighthouses, and ships, many of them from folklore. (Rev: BCCB 9/00; BL 6/1–15/00; HBG 10/00; SLJ 11/00)

8213 Gutman, Dan. *Abner and Me* (5–8). Series: Baseball Card Adventure. 2005, HarperCollins LB $16.89 (0-06-053444-3). 176pp. Stosh and his mother travel back to visit the Battle of Gettysburg in an effort to learn more about baseball's origins. (Rev: BL 1/1–15/05)

8214 Gutman, Dan. *Babe and Me* (4–7). Illus. 2000, Avon $15.99 (0-380-97739-7). 160pp. Joe and his dad time-travel to the 1932 World Series to witness a historic moment with hitter Babe Ruth. (Rev: BL 2/1/00; HBG 10/00; SLJ 2/00)

8215 Gutman, Dan. *Honus and Me: A Baseball Card Adventure* (4–7). 1997, Avon paper $5.99 (0-380-78878-0). 160pp. Young Joe Stoshack finds a magical baseball card that allows him to travel through time and participate in the 1909 World Series. (Rev: BL 4/15/97; SLJ 6/97)

8216 Gutman, Dan. *Jackie and Me: A Baseball Card Adventure* (4–7). Illus. 1999, Avon $15.99 (0-380-97685-4). 144pp. While time-traveling to research a paper on Jackie Robinson, Joe Stoshack becomes an African American and experiences prejudice first hand. (Rev: BL 2/1/99; HBG 10/99; SLJ 3/99)

8217 Gutman, Dan. *Mickey and Me: A Baseball Card Adventure* (4–6). Series: Baseball Card Adventure. 2003, HarperCollins LB $16.89 (0-06-029248-2). 160pp. In this adventure, Joe is supposed to be heading back to 1951 to warn Mickey Mantle about a forthcoming accident, but instead ends up in 1944 with Girls Professional league player Mickey Maguire. (Rev: BL 1/1–15/03; HBG 10/03; SLJ 6/03)

8218 Gutman, Dan. *Qwerty Stevens Back in Time with Benjamin Franklin* (4–7). 2002, Simon & Schuster $16.95 (0-689-84553-7). 192pp. Benjamin Franklin is transported through time into Robert "Qwerty" Stevens's bedroom, and Qwerty and a friend accompany Franklin to 1776 to sign the Declaration of Independence. (Rev: BL 9/15/02; HBG 3/03; SLJ 8/02)

8219 Haber, Melissa Glenn. *Hercules Amsterdam* (4–6). 2003, Dutton $16.99 (0-525-47119-7). 224pp. Only 3 inches tall, Hercules Amsterdam is terrified of going to school with normal-size children, so he ducks into a mouse hole and initially finds himself totally at home. (Rev: HBG 10/03; SLJ 6/03)

8220 Haddix, Margaret. *Among the Brave* (4–7). Series: Shadow Children. 2004, Simon & Schuster $15.95 (0-689-85794-2). 240pp. This sequel to *Among the Barons* (2003) features Trey's efforts to rescue Luke and other third-born children. (Rev: BL 5/15/04; SLJ 6/04)

8221 Haddix, Margaret. *Running Out of Time* (4–7). 1995, Simon & Schuster $16.95 (0-689-80084-3). 185pp. Living in a historical site where the time is the 1840s, Jessie escapes into the present in this fantasy. (Rev: BCCB 11/95; BL 10/1/95; SLJ 10/95*)

8222 Hague, Michael, ed. *The Book of Dragons* (4–7). Illus. by Michael Hague. 1995, Morrow $21.99 (0-688-10879-2). 160pp. Seventeen classic tales about dragons by such authors as Tolkien and Kenneth Grahame are included in this interesting anthology. (Rev: BL 10/1/95; SLJ 10/95)

8223 Hahn, Mary D. *The Doll in the Garden: A Ghost Story* (4–6). Illus. 1989, Houghton Mifflin $15.00 (0-89919-848-1). 160pp. Ten-year-old Ashley and her mother try to start a new life in a house owned by a grouchy octogenarian. (Rev: BCCB 3/89; BL 3/15/89; SLJ 5/89)

8224 Hahn, Mary D. *Time for Andrew: A Ghost Story* (4–6). 1994, Clarion $14.95 (0-395-66556-6). 167pp. Drew changes places with his look-alike dis-

tant relative and travels back to 1910. (Rev: BCCB 4/94; BL 4/1/94; SLJ 5/94)

8225 Hahn, Mary D. *Wait Till Helen Comes: A Ghost Story* (5–7). 1986, Houghton Mifflin $15.00 (0-89919-453-2); Avon paper $5.99 (0-380-70442-0). 192pp. Things go from bad to worse for Molly and Michael and their stepsister Heather when Heather becomes involved in a frightening relationship with the ghost of a dead child. (Rev: BCCB 10/86; BL 9/1/86; SLJ 10/86)

8226 Halam, Ann. *Siberia* (5–8). 2005, Random LB $18.99 (0-385-90885-7). 272pp. In this richly layered novel set in a future ice-covered wilderness, 13-year-old Sloe must risk her life to deliver her arrested mother's genetically engineered animal life to a safe place. (Rev: BL 6/1–15/05; SLJ 6/05)

8227 Hale, Bruce. *The Big Nap* (2–6). Illus. Series: Chet Gecko Mystery. 2001, Harcourt $14.00 (0-15-202521-9). 112pp. Lizard detective Chet Gecko investigates why his classmates are turning into mindless model fourth-graders. (Rev: BL 12/1/01; HBG 3/02; SLJ 10/01)

8228 Hale, Bruce. *The Chameleon Wore Chartreuse* (3–6). Illus. Series: Chet Gecko Mystery. 2000, Harcourt $14.00 (0-15-202281-3). 112pp. Using a private-eye style of writing, this humorous mystery involves Chet Gecko, a fourth-grade lizard/investigator, who uncovers a plot to steal the team mascot. (Rev: BCCB 6/00; BL 5/15/00; HBG 3/01; SLJ 8/00)

8229 Hale, Bruce. *Farewell, My Lunchbag* (2–5). Illus. Series: Chet Gecko Mystery. 2001, Harcourt $14.00 (0-15-202275-9). 128pp. Detective Chet Gecko investigates the problem of the mystery food snatcher who is operating in his elementary school. (Rev: BL 3/15/01; HBG 10/01)

8230 Hale, Bruce. *Give My Regrets to Broadway* (3–5). Illus. Series: Chet Gecko Mystery. 2004, Harcourt $14.00 (0-15-216700-5). 112pp. Chet Gecko and sidekick Natalie look for Scott Freeh, who was supposed to play the lead in the school play, *Omlet: The Prince of Denver*. (Rev: BL 5/1/04)

8231 Hale, Bruce. *The Hamster of the Baskervilles* (3–5). Illus. Series: Chet Gecko Mystery. 2002, Harcourt $14.00 (0-15-202503-0). 132pp. Fourth-grader gecko detective Chet and his sidekick Natalie set out to find out who is trashing the classrooms at their school. (Rev: BL 5/1/02; HBG 10/02; SLJ 5/02)

8232 Hale, Bruce. *The Mystery of Mr. Nice* (4–6). Series: Chet Gecko Mystery. 2000, Harcourt $14.00 (0-15-202271-6). 112pp. Chet Gecko, the lizard detective, sets out to discover why his school principal is suddenly acting very nicely toward everyone. (Rev: BL 11/1/00; HBG 3/01; SLJ 12/00)

8233 Hale, Bruce. *This Gum for Hire* (3–5). Illus. Series: Chet Gecko Mystery. 2002, Harcourt $14.00 (0-15-202491-3). 132pp. Lizard detective Chet Gecko investigates mysterious goings-on on the school football team. (Rev: BL 10/1/02; HBG 3/03; SLJ 9/02)

8234 Hale, Bruce. *Trouble Is My Beeswax: From the Tattered Casebook of Chet Gecko, Private Eye* (3–6). Illus. by author. Series: Chet Gecko Mystery. 2003, Harcourt $14.00 (0-15-216718-8). 111pp. Chet Gecko, junior detective, enlists the help of mockingbird sidekick Natalie Attired to investigate cheating at Emerson Hicky Elementary. (Rev: HBG 4/04; SLJ 11/03)

8235 Hamilton, Virginia. *Jaguarundi* (2–5). Illus. by Floyd Cooper. 1994, Scholastic $14.95 (0-590-47366-2). 40pp. A wildcat (jaguarundi) persuades a coati to flee across the river to find a new home. (Rev: BCCB 2/95; BL 12/15/94; SLJ 12/94)

8236 Haptie, Charlotte. *Otto and the Flying Twins* (4–7). 2004, Holiday House $17.95 (0-8234-1826-X). 304pp. In the City of Trees, Otto is shocked to discover his father is king of the magical Karmidee. The sequel is *Otto and the Bird Charmers* (2005). (Rev: BL 4/15/04; SLJ 6/04)

8237 Haseley, Dennis. *Ghost Catcher* (3–5). Illus. by Lloyd Bloom. 1991, HarperCollins $15.95 (0-06-022244-1). 40pp. A man who can get close to ghosts without turning into one needs the help of his friends when he visits the shadow village. (Rev: BL 10/1/91; SLJ 11/91)

8238 Hatrick, Gloria. *Masks* (4–6). 1996, Orchard LB $16.99 (0-531-08864-2). 128pp. In this fantasy, Pete uses animal masks to communicate with his paralyzed older brother. (Rev: BCCB 3/96; BL 4/15/96; SLJ 5/96)

8239 Hearne, Betsy. *Wishes, Kisses, and Pigs* (4–6). 2001, Simon & Schuster $16.00 (0-689-84122-1). 133pp. In this fantasy, Louise's pesky older brother disappears and suddenly there is a new white pig on the farm. (Rev: BL 3/1/01; HB 5–6/01; HBG 10/01)

8240 Heneghan, James. *Flood* (5–8). 2002, Farrar $16.00 (0-374-35057-4). 192pp. The Little People save a boy from the flood that kills his parents, and save him from the neglectful father he never knew in this poignant story about loss and acceptance. (Rev: BCCB 4/02; BL 3/15/02; HB 7–8/02; HBG 10/02; SLJ 4/02)

8241 Hickman, Janet. *Ravine* (4–6). 2002, Harper-Collins LB $15.89 (0-06-029367-5). 192pp. Jeremy enters a dangerous world of fantasy and adventure through a "time slip" in a ravine. (Rev: BCCB 9/02; BL 7/02; HB 5–6/02; HBG 10/02; SLJ 10/02)

8242 Highwater, Jamake. *Rama: A Legend* (5–9). 1997, Replica LB $24.95 (0-7351-0001-2). When he's wrongfully banished from his father's kingdom and his wife, Sita, is kidnapped, valiant Prince Rama charges back to avenge the evil that's befallen his world. (Rev: BL 11/15/94; SLJ 12/94)

8243 Hill, Margaret Bateson. *Masha and the Firebird* (PS–3). Illus. by Anne Wilson. 2000, Zero to Ten $17.95 (1-84089-134-3). 32pp. In this original folk tale set in Russia, a brave girl confronts witch Baba Yaga to save the stolen egg of the Firebird. (Rev: BL 1/1–15/01)

8244 Hirsch, Odo. *Bartlett and the City of Flames* (3–6). Illus. by Andrew McLean. 2003, Bloomsbury $15.95 (1-58234-831-6). 201pp. In this gripping sequel to *Bartlett and the Ice Voyage,* the title char-

acter and Jacques le Grand try to free Darian, the son of the Pasha of the City of the Sun, from his captors in the underground City of Flames. (Rev: HBG 4/04; SLJ 12/03)

8245 Hiser, Constance. *Night of the Werepoodle* (2–4). Illus. 1994, Holiday House $14.95 (0-8234-1116-8). 122pp. After being bitten by a poodle, Jonathan turns into a "werepoodle" and must find some wolfbane to become a boy again. (Rev: BL 6/1–15/94; SLJ 6/94)

8246 Hoban, Russell. *The Mouse and His Child* (4–8). Illus. by David Small. 2001, Scholastic paper $16.95 (0-439-09826-2). 246pp. A toy mouse and his child embark on a quest to become "self-winding" and have sometimes scary, sometimes humorous adventures in this enchanting fantasy first published in 1967 and now updated with new illustrations. (Rev: BL 12/1/01; HBG 3/02)

8247 Hoban, Russell. *Trouble on Thunder Mountain* (2–4). Illus. 2000, Orchard $14.95 (0-531-30206-7). 40pp. When a family of dinosaurs are evicted from Thunder Mountain to make room for an amusement park, they vow to fight back. (Rev: BCCB 9/00; BL 6/1–15/00; HBG 10/00; SLJ 7/00)

8248 Hodges, Margaret, ed. *Comus* (4–6). Illus. by Trina S. Hyman. 1996, Holiday House $16.95 (0-8234-1146-X). 32pp. In this retelling of a work by John Milton, Alice resists the enchantment of the evil magician Comus. (Rev: BCCB 10/94; BL 3/1/96; SLJ 3/96)

8249 Hodges, Margaret. *Gulliver in Lilliput: From Gulliver's Travels by Jonathan Swift* (4–7). Illus. by Kimberly B. Root. 1995, Holiday House $16.95 (0-8234-1147-8). 32pp. The story of Gulliver in the land of the little people is retold with bright, detailed illustrations. (Rev: BCCB 6/95; BL 4/15/95; HB 7–8/95; SLJ 6/95*)

8250 Hodges, Margaret, ed. *Hauntings: Ghosts and Ghouls from Around the World* (5–8). Illus. by David Wenzel. 1991, Little, Brown $16.95 (0-316-36796-6). 144pp. A diverse collection of 16 familiar and lesser-known tales about the supernatural. (Rev: BL 11/15/91; HB 11–12/91; SLJ 11/91) [398.2]

8251 Hoeye, Michael. *No Time Like Show Time* (5–8). Series: A Hermux Tantamoq Adventure. 2004, Penguin Putnam $14.99 (0-399-23880-8). 277pp. Hermux the mouse investigates who is responsible for sending threatening letters to famous director Fluster Varmint. (Rev: SLJ 11/04)

8252 Hoeye, Michael. *The Sands of Time* (5–8). Series: A Hermux Tantamoq Adventure. 2002, Penguin Putnam $14.99 (0-399-23879-4). 277pp. In this sequel to *Time Stops for No Mouse* (2002), the mouse watchmaker and a chipmunk friend believe that mice were once the slaves of cats. (Rev: HBG 3/03; SLJ 10/02)

8253 Hoeye, Michael. *Time Stops for No Mouse* (5–9). Series: A Hermux Tantamoq Adventure. 2002, Penguin Putnam $14.99 (0-399-23878-6). 279pp. Hermux Tantamoq, a mouse, leads a quiet life as a watchmaker until Linka Perflinger turns up and Hermux becomes entangled in mystery and suspense. (Rev: BL 3/15/02*; HB 7–8/02; HBG 10/02; SLJ 5/02)

8254 Hoffman, Alice. *Aquamarine* (4–7). 2001, Scholastic paper $16.95 (0-439-09863-7). 112pp. Twelve-year-old friends Hailey and Claire find a lonely mermaid named Aquamarine, and they try to give her love and adventure. (Rev: BCCB 2/01; BL 3/1/01; HBG 10/01; SLJ 3/01)

8255 Hoffman, Alice. *Indigo* (4–7). Illus. 2002, Scholastic paper $16.95 (0-439-25635-6). 112pp. Three outcasts save their town from a terrible flood in this aquatic fantasy. (Rev: BCCB 6/02; BL 8/02; HBG 10/02; SLJ 8/02)

8256 Holch, Gregory. *The Things with Wings* (5–8). 1998, Scholastic paper $15.95 (0-590-93501-1). In this mystery fantasy, Newton and his classmate Vanessa learn about the Emerald Rainbow butterflies, become involved in the disappearance of a friend, and discover the magic of flying. (Rev: BL 8/98; HB 7–8/98; HBG 9/98; SLJ 5/98)

8257 Holm, Jennifer, and Jonathan Hamel. *The Stink Files, Dossier 001: The Postman Always Brings Mice* (3–5). Illus. by Brad Weinman. 2004, HarperCollins LB $15.89 (0-06-052980-6). 144pp. While trying to find out who murdered his owner, Sir Archibald, feline London-based sleuth James Edward Bristlefur is whisked away to New Jersey and a confusing new life amid middle-class children. (Rev: BL 5/1/04; SLJ 6/04)

8258 Howe, James. *Invasion of the Mind Swappers from Asteroid 6!* (3–6). Illus. by Brett Helquist. 2002, Simon & Schuster $9.95 (0-689-83949-9). 96pp. Lessons about writing are hidden in the tale of a delightful dachshund named Howie, who keeps a journal detailing his writing experiences as he pens a story about an alien invasion. Also use *It Came from Beneath the Bed!* (2002). (Rev: BL 8/02; HBG 3/03; SLJ 11/02)

8259 Hughes, Shirley. *Enchantment in the Garden* (3–5). Illus. 1997, Lothrop $18.00 (0-688-14597-3). 64pp. In this fantasy, a rich little girl in Italy during the 1920s brings to life the statue of a sea god's son. (Rev: BCCB 7–8/97; BL 5/15/97; HB 3–4/97; SLJ 5/97)

8260 Hunter, Mollie. *The Mermaid Summer* (5–8). 1988, HarperCollins $15.89 (0-06-022628-5); paper $5.99 (0-06-440344-0). 160pp. Eric Anderson refuses to recognize the power of the mermaid and leaves his Scottish fishing village after his boat is dashed to pieces on the rocks. (Rev: BCCB 5/88; BL 6/1/88; BR 1–2/89; SLJ 6–7/88)

8261 Hurmence, Belinda. *A Girl Called Boy* (5–8). 1982, Houghton Mifflin paper $5.95 (0-395-55698-8). 180pp. A contemporary African American girl travels back to the time of slavery.

8262 Hurst, Carol Otis. *The Wrong One* (3–6). 2003, Houghton Mifflin $15.00 (0-618-27599-1). 160pp. The Spencer children and their recently widowed mother move to a run-down farmhouse where strange things are happening. (Rev: BL 3/1/03; HBG 10/03; SLJ 5/03)

8263 Hurwitz, Johanna. *PeeWee and Plush* (2–4). Illus. by Patience Brewster. Series: Park Pals Adventure. 2002, North-South $14.95 (1-58717-191-0). 134pp. PeeWee, the talented guinea pig of Central Park, finds a mate and they produce four little ones in this story for beginning chapter-book readers. (Rev: HBG 3/03; SLJ 12/02)

8264 Hurwitz, Johanna. *PeeWee's Tale* (2–5). Illus. 2000, North-South $13.95 (1-58717-027-2). 96pp. PeeWee is a little guinea pig whose intelligence and ability to read help him escape danger when he is left in a park. (Rev: BL 10/1/00; HBG 3/01; SLJ 10/00)

8265 Hussey, Charmain. *The Valley of Secrets* (4–7). Illus. by Christopher Crump. 2005, Simon & Schuster $16.95 (0-689-87862-1). 400pp. A detailed, multifaceted novel about an orphan who inherits his great-uncle's estate and, through his uncle's journal, learns about the plight of the Amazon Indians. (Rev: BL 3/1/05; SLJ 2/05)

8266 Hutchins, Hazel. *The Prince of Tarn* (3–5). Illus. 1997, Annick $14.95 (1-55037-439-7). 143pp. The spoiled prince created by his author mother in one of her fantasies comes to life and takes Fred to his kingdom. (Rev: BL 2/15/98; SLJ 2/98)

8267 Ibbotson, Eva. *The Great Ghost Rescue* (3–6). Illus. by Kevin Hawkes. 2002, Dutton $15.99 (0-525-46769-6). 144pp. A homeless ghost family moves into a boys' school and meets young Rick, who tries to establish a "sanctuary" for displaced ghosts in this humorous, scary, and sometimes gruesome book. (Rev: BCCB 11/02; BL 7/02; HB 9–10/02; HBG 3/03; SLJ 8/02)

8268 Ibbotson, Eva. *The Haunting of Granite Falls* (3–7). Illus. by Kevin Hawkes. 2004, Dutton $15.99 (0-525-47192-8). 176pp. A Scottish castle imported to Texas brings many unexpected problems for the new owner and his daughter Helen. (Rev: BL 5/1/04; HB 7–8/04)

8269 Ibbotson, Eva. *The Secret of Platform 13* (4–7). Illus. 1998, Dutton $15.99 (0-525-45929-4). 224pp. In this fantasy, three unusual creatures — a wizard, an ogre, and a hag — set out to rescue from their enchanted kingdom a prince who has been kidnapped. (Rev: BL 2/15/98; HBG 10/98; SLJ 3/98*)

8270 Ibbotson, Eva. *Which Witch?* (5–8). 1999, Dutton $15.99 (0-525-46164-7). 224pp. This British fantasy involves a wizard who holds a competition to find a wife, a sweet witch who wants to win the wizard's heart. (Rev: BCCB 9/99; BL 8/99; HBG 3/00; SLJ 8/99)

8271 Icanberry, Mark. *Picnic on a Cloud* (3–5). Illus. by Mark Icanberry and Arthur Mount. Series: Look, Learn and Do. 2000, Tricycle $14.95 (1-893327-00-0); paper $7.95 (1-893327-02-7). 47pp. David, his dog Newton, and friend Jessica construct a blimp using 289 balloons and take a ride during which they picnic on a cloud. The trio build a greenhouse in *Super Salads* (2000). (Rev: SLJ 1/01)

8272 Irving, Washington. *The Legend of Sleepy Hollow: Found Among the Papers of the Late Diedrich Knickerbocker* (4–6). Illus. 1999, Ideals $16.95 (0-8249-4160-8). 64pp. A well-illustrated edition of this perennial favorite about Ichabod Crane, the

Headless Horseman, and the heiress Katrina Van Tassel. (Rev: BL 10/1/99)

8273 Irving, Washington. *Rip Van Winkle and the Legend of Sleepy Hollow* (5–7). Illus. by Felix O. Darley. 1980, Sleepy Hollow $19.95 (0-912882-42-5). 152pp. A handsome edition of these two classics.

8274 Jacques, Brian. *The Angel's Command: A Tale from the Castaways of the Flying Dutchman* (5–9). 2003, Penguin Putnam $23.99 (0-399-23999-5). 448pp. This action-packed fantasy, set in the 17th century, is the sequel to *Castaways of the Flying Dutchman*. (Rev: BL 2/1/03; HB 3–4/03; HBG 10/03; SLJ 3/03)

8275 Jacques, Brian. *The Bellmaker* (5–7). Illus. 1995, Penguin Putnam $23.99 (0-399-22805-5). 352pp. This seventh tale in the Redwall series of animal fantasies features Mariel, a courageous, outspoken mouse. (Rev: BCCB 4/95; BL 4/1/95; HB 5–6/95; SLJ 8/95)

8276 Jacques, Brian. *Castaways of the Flying Dutchman* (5–9). 2001, Penguin Putnam $22.95 (0-399-23601-5). 318pp. A mute boy stows away on the *Flying Dutchman*, a ship that is condemned to sail the seas forever, and there he meets the ghostly crew and the crazed captain in this story in which the boy has many adventures and eventually gains the power of speech and the gift of staying young forever. (Rev: BCCB 3/01; BL 3/1/01; HB 3–4/01; HBG 10/01; SLJ 3/01)

8277 Jacques, Brian. *The Great Redwall Feast* (4–6). Illus. by Christopher Denise. 1996, Penguin Putnam $18.99 (0-399-22707-5). 64pp. In this illustrated storybook, the creatures of Redwall prepare a magnificent feast. (Rev: BL 10/15/96; SLJ 12/96)

8278 Jacques, Brian. *The Legend of Luke: A Tale from Redwall* (5–8). Illus. 2000, Penguin Putnam $22.95 (0-399-23490-X). 384pp. This Redwall book focuses on the building of the abbey, Martin's search for his father Luke, and Luke's heroic career. (Rev: BL 12/15/99; HBG 10/00; SLJ 2/00)

8279 Jacques, Brian. *Loamhedge* (5–8). Series: Redwall. 2003, Penguin Putnam $23.99 (0-399-23724-0). 432pp. As Redwall stalwarts including Bragoon and Sarobando seek a cure for a haremaid's ills at Loamhedge Abbey, Redwall itself comes under attack. (Rev: BL 9/15/03; HB 11–12/03; HBG 4/04; SLJ 10/03)

8280 Jacques, Brian. *The Long Patrol* (5–8). Illus. 1998, Penguin Putnam $22.99 (0-399-23165-X). In this tenth Redwall adventure, the villainous Rapscallions decide to attack the peaceful Abbey of Redwall. (Rev: BCCB 4/98; BL 12/15/97; BR 3–4/98; HB 3–4/98; HBG 10/98; SLJ 1/98)

8281 Jacques, Brian. *Lord Brocktree* (5–8). 2000, Penguin Putnam $22.95 (0-399-23590-6). 320pp. In this installment of the Redwall saga, the villainous Ungatt Trunn and his Blue Hordes invade and capture the mountain fortress Salamandastron. (Rev: BCCB 9/00; BL 9/1/00; HB 9–10/00; HBG 3/01; SLJ 9/00)

8282 Jacques, Brian. *Mariel of Redwall* (5–7). Illus. by Gary Chalk. 1992, Penguin Putnam $23.99 (0-399-22144-1). 400pp. Fourth in the saga of the animals of Redwall Abbey, this story tells how the great Joseph Bell is brought to the abbey. (Rev: BCCB 3/92; BL 1/15/92*; HB 9–10/92; SLJ 3/92)

8283 Jacques, Brian. *Marlfox* (5–8). Illus. 1999, Penguin Putnam $22.99 (0-399-23307-5). 400pp. The famous tapestry depicting Martin and Warrior has been stolen from Redwall Abbey, and four young would-be heroes set out to recover it. (Rev: BL 12/15/98; BR 9–10/99; HB 1–2/99; HBG 10/99; SLJ 4/99)

8284 Jacques, Brian. *Martin the Warrior* (5–7). Illus. by Gary Chalk. 1994, Penguin Putnam $23.99 (0-399-22670-2). 375pp. This Redwall book tells how the mouse Martin the Warrior became the bold, courageous fighter that he is. (Rev: BCCB 1/94; BL 3/1/94; HB 9–10/94; SLJ 1/94)

8285 Jacques, Brian. *Mattimeo* (5–8). 1990, Penguin Putnam $23.99 (0-399-21741-X). The evil fox kidnaps the animal children of Redwall Abbey in this continuation of *Mossflower* (1988) and *Redwall* (1987). (Rev: BL 4/15/90; SLJ 9/90)

8286 Jacques, Brian. *Mossflower* (5–7). Illus. by Gary Chalk. 1988, Penguin Putnam $23.99 (0-399-21549-2); Avon paper $5.99 (0-380-70828-0). 432pp. How a brave and resourceful mouse took power from the evil wildcat. (Rev: BCCB 12/88; BL 11/1/88; SLJ 11/88)

8287 Jacques, Brian. *Outcast of Redwall* (5–8). Illus. Series: Redwall. 1996, Philomel $23.99 (0-399-22914-0). This episode in the Redwall saga involves the badger Sunflash, his buddy Skarlath the kestrel, and their enemy the ferret Swartt Sixclaw. (Rev: BCCB 3/96; BL 3/1/96; BR 3–4/96; SLJ 5/96)

8288 Jacques, Brian. *The Pearls of Lutra* (5–8). 1997, Penguin Putnam $23.99 (0-399-22946-9). 408pp. The evil marten Mad Eyes threatens the peaceful Redwall Abbey in this ninth book in the series. (Rev: BCCB 4/97; BL 2/15/97; SLJ 3/97*)

8289 Jacques, Brian. *Rakkety Tam* (5–8). Illus. by David Elliot. Series: Redwall. 2004, Penguin Putnam $23.99 (0-399-23725-9). 384pp. When Redwall is threatened by a murderous wolverine called Gulo the Savage, two warrior squirrels — Rakkety Tam McBurl and Wild Doogy Plumm — take action. (Rev: BL 9/15/04; SLJ 9/04)

8290 Jacques, Brian. *A Redwall Winter's Tale* (2–5). Illus. by Christopher Denise. 2001, Penguin Putnam $18.99 (0-399-23346-6). 80pp. The animals of Redwall Abbey gather once again to enjoy an end-of-autumn festival in this colorful picture book. (Rev: BL 9/1/01; HBG 3/02; SLJ 9/01)

8291 Jacques, Brian. *Salamandastron* (5–7). Illus. by Gary Chalk. 1993, Penguin Putnam $23.99 (0-399-21992-7). 400pp. These tales are centered on the badgers and hares of the castle of Salamandastron near the sea. (Rev: BCCB 7–8/93; BL 3/15/93; HB 5–6/93; SLJ 3/93)

8292 Jacques, Brian. *Seven Strange and Ghostly Tales* (4–7). 1991, Avon paper $3.99 (0-380-71906-1). 137pp. Seven genuinely scary stories with touches of humor. (Rev: BCCB 12/91; BL 1/1/91*; HB 5–6/92; SLJ 12/91)

8293 Jacques, Brian. *Taggerung* (5–8). Illus. 2001, Penguin Putnam $23.99 (0-399-23720-8). 448pp. The 14th book in the Redwall series features an otter named Taggerung who was kidnapped from the abbey as a baby and raised by an outlaw ferret. (Rev: BL 8/01; HB 11–12/01; HBG 3/02; SLJ 10/01)

8294 Jacques, Brian. *The Tale of Urso Brunov* (2–4). Illus. by Alexi Natchev. 2003, Penguin Putnam $16.99 (0-399-23762-3). 48pp. When four little bears go astray, Urso Brunov embarks on an adventure-filled rescue journey. (Rev: BL 9/1/03; HBG 4/04; SLJ 9/03)

8295 Jacques, Brian. *Triss* (5–8). 2002, Penguin Putnam $23.99 (0-399-23723-2). 432pp. An action-packed installment in the Redwall series in which squirrel Triss, an escaped slave, meets up with the badger Sagax and his friend Scarum. (Rev: BL 9/1/02; HB 1–2/03; HBG 3/03; SLJ 10/02)

8296 James, Mary. *Frankenlouse* (5–8). 1994, Scholastic paper $13.95 (0-590-46528-7). Nick, 14, is enrolled at Blister Military Academy, which is run by his father. He escapes into his own comic book creations featuring an insect named Frankenlouse. (Rev: BCCB 11/94; BL 10/15/94; SLJ 11/94)

8297 James, Mary. *Shoebag* (3–7). 1990, Scholastic $13.95 (0-590-43029-7); paper $3.99 (0-590-43030-0). 144pp. Shoebag, a cockroach named after his place of birth, turns into a boy. (Rev: BCCB 3/90; BL 4/15/90; SLJ 6/90*)

8298 James, Mary. *The Shuteyes* (4–7). 1994, Scholastic paper $3.25 (0-590-45070-0). 176pp. Chester has some unusual experiences when he journeys to Alert, a land where no one sleeps. (Rev: SLJ 4/93)

8299 Jarrell, Randall. *The Bat-Poet* (3–6). Illus. by Maurice Sendak. 1997, HarperCollins $13.95 (0-06-205084-2); paper $6.95 (0-06-205905-X). 44pp. A little-known bat makes up poems during the day to recite to his fellows.

8300 Jarvis, Robin. *The Crystal Prison: Book Two of the Deptford Mice Trilogy* (5–8). 2001, North-South $17.95 (1-58717-107-4). 240pp. In this sequel to *The Dark Portal*, city mouse Audrey is adapting to country life when she is accused of committing murder. (Rev: BL 8/01; HBG 3/02; SLJ 11/01)

8301 Jarvis, Robin. *The Dark Portal: Book One of The Deptford Mice* (5–8). 2000, North-South $17.95 (1-58717-021-3). 240pp. In this tale of horror, valor, and adventure, Albert, one of the mice living in an old, empty house in Deptford, London, must leave his household and enter the slimy sewers inhabited by deadly rats. (Rev: BL 10/15/00; HBG 3/01; SLJ 12/00)

8302 Jarvis, Robin. *The Final Reckoning: Book Three of the Deptford Mice Trilogy* (5–8). 2002, North-South $17.95 (1-58717-192-9). 304pp. Jupiter returns to wreak havoc on the Deptford mice in this thrilling conclusion to the trilogy. (Rev: BL 8/02; HBG 3/03; SLJ 9/02)

8303 Jarvis, Robin. *Thorn Ogres of Hagwood* (5–8). 2002, Harcourt $16.00 (0-15-216752-8). 256pp. Trouble is spreading through Hagwood, and a young, not-too-confident shape-shifting werling will play a role in a gripping battle between good and evil. (Rev: BCCB 12/02; BL 11/1/02; HBG 3/03; SLJ 11/02)

8304 Jenkins, Martin. *Jonathan Swift's Gulliver* (5–8). Illus. by Chris Riddell. 2005, Candlewick $19.99 (0-7636-2409-8). 144pp. A retelling of the classic tale using contemporary language and striking artwork. (Rev: BL 3/15/05; SLJ 3/05)

8305 Jennings, Patrick. *Faith and the Electric Dogs* (3–6). Illus. 1996, Scholastic $15.95 (0-590-69768-4). 128pp. Unhappy in Mexico and longing for the United States, Faith gets some comfort from a very unusual dog. (Rev: BCCB 1/97; BL 12/1/96*; SLJ 12/96)

8306 Jennings, Patrick. *Faith and the Rocket Cat* (4–6). 1998, Scholastic $15.95 (0-590-11004-7). 232pp. Faith and her dog Eddie, who can read and write in several languages, move from Mexico to San Francisco where they take an exciting rocket trip. (Rev: BL 9/15/98; HBG 3/99; SLJ 9/98)

8307 Jennings, Richard W. *Orwell's Luck* (4–7). 2000, Houghton Mifflin $15.00 (0-618-03628-8). 146pp. After a 12-year-old girl saves a rabbit's life, she begins receiving coded messages from him that change her life. (Rev: BCCB 11/00; BL 10/15/00*; HB 9–10/00; HBG 3/01; SLJ 10/00)

8308 Jensen, Dorothea. *The Riddle of Penncroft Farm* (5–7). 1989, Harcourt $16.00 (0-15-200574-9). 192pp. Lars finds a ghost from the American Revolution when his family moves to rural Pennsylvania near Valley Forge. (Rev: BCCB 11/89; BL 10/1/89; SLJ 10/89)

8309 Johansen, Hanna. *Dinosaur with an Attitude* (4–6). Trans. by Elisabetta Maccari. Illus. 1994, RDR $12.95 (1-57143-018-0). 144pp. In this fantasy, a boy faces problems caused by a dinosaur that hatched from one of his Easter eggs. (Rev: BL 8/94; SLJ 8/94)

8310 Johnson, Annabel. *I Am Leaper* (3–5). Illus. by Stella Ormai. 1992, Scholastic paper $2.99 (0-590-43399-7). 128pp. A talking kangaroo mouse leaves her burrow to warn humans that a monster is destroying the desert. (Rev: BL 11/15/90; SLJ 1/91)

8311 Johnson, Charles. *Pieces of Eight* (5–7). Illus. by Jennie Anne Nelson. 1989, Discovery $9.95 (0-944770-00-2). 110pp. David and Mitchell rouse a sea captain's ghost and get to meet Blackbeard the pirate. (Rev: BL 3/15/89)

8312 Johnston, Tony. *The Spoon in the Bathroom Wall* (3–4). 2005, Harcourt $16.00 (0-15-205292-5). 134pp. An Arthurian spoof in which fourth grader Martha Snapdragon discovers a jeweled spoon in the wall of the boys' bathroom. (Rev: SLJ 6/05)

8313 Jones, Diana Wynne. *Charmed Life* (4–6). 1998, Morrow paper $5.95 (0-688-15546-4). 224pp. Gwendole tries to obtain supernatural powers from her mysterious guardian. A sequel is: *Witch Week* (1988).

8314 Jones, Diana Wynne. *The Lives of Christopher Chant* (5–9). 1998, Morrow paper $5.99 (0-688-16365-3). At night Christopher can leave his body and travel from London to other worlds. (Rev: BR 5–6/88; SLJ 5/88)

8315 Jones, Diana Wynne. *Mixed Magics* (5–8). 2001, Greenwillow $15.89 (0-06-029706-9). 138pp. This fantasy contains four short stories each involving an enchanter named Chrestomanci, who has nine lives and oversees the use of magic in his world. (Rev: BL 4/15/01; HB 5–6/01; HBG 10/01; SLJ 7/01)

8316 Jones, Diana Wynne. *Wild Robert* (3–5). Illus. by Mark Zug. 2003, HarperCollins LB $16.89 (0-06-055531-9). 112pp. Bored with life in the castle where her parents are curators, Heather accidentally — and with humorous results — brings back to life a mischievous magician who lived there more than three centuries ago. (Rev: BL 9/15/03; HBG 4/04; SLJ 10/03)

8317 Jones, Miranda. *Make a Wish!* (2–4). Illus. by David Calver. Series: Little Genie. 2004, Delacorte LB $10.99 (0-385-90168-2). 128pp. The three wishes granted by the genie who emerges from her 1960s Lava lamp cause Ali as many problems as pleasures in this first installment in an easy chapter-book series. In the sequel *Double Trouble* (2004), Ali foolishly allows Little Genie to substitute for her at school. (Rev: BL 1/1–15/04; SLJ 2/04)

8318 Jordan, Sherryl. *The Hunting of the Last Dragon* (5–7). 2002, HarperCollins LB $15.89 (0-06-028903-1). 128pp. In 14th-century England a monk records young peasant Jude's story of his quest, accompanied by a young Chinese woman, to kill a dragon. (Rev: BCCB 9/02; BL 4/15/02; HBG 10/02; SLJ 7/02)

8319 Juster, Norton. *The Phantom Tollbooth* (4–6). Illus. by Jules Feiffer. 1972, Knopf $19.95 (0-394-81500-9); paper $5.50 (0-394-82037-1). 256pp. When Milo receives a tollbooth as a gift, he finds that it admits him to a land where many adventures take place. A favorite fantasy.

8320 Kalman, Maira. *Smartypants (Pete in School)* (2–4). 2003, Penguin Putnam $15.99 (0-399-23478-0). 32pp. Pete the dog eats an encyclopedia and acquires superintelligence in this entertaining story. (Rev: BL 8/03*; HBG 4/04; SLJ 8/03)

8321 Kalman, Maira. *Swami on Rye: Max in India* (4–8). Illus. 1995, Viking $14.99 (0-670-84646-0). 40pp. A sophisticated comic novel about a dog who goes to India to find the meaning of life. (Rev: BL 10/15/95; SLJ 11/95)

8322 Karon, Jan. *Jeremy: The Tale of an Honest Bunny* (3–5). Illus. 2000, Viking $15.99 (0-670-88104-X). 82pp. A sweet tale about a toy bunny and his adventures traveling from a small English cottage to his new home in North Carolina. (Rev: BL 4/15/00; HBG 10/00; SLJ 9/00)

8323 Karr, Kathleen. *Playing with Fire* (5–7). 2001, Farrar $16.00 (0-374-23453-1). 192pp. This story about the occult takes place in New York during the 1920s and involves Greer and her spiritualist mother. (Rev: BCCB 5/01; BL 4/1/01; HBG 10/01; SLJ 5/01)

8324 Kassem, Lou. *A Summer for Secrets* (5–7). 1989, Avon paper $2.95 (0-380-75759-1). 105pp. Laura's ability to communicate with animals causes complications. (Rev: BL 10/1/89)

8325 Kay, Elizabeth. *The Divide* (5–9). 2003, Scholastic $15.95 (0-439-45696-7). 320pp. Felix, a 13-year-old with a heart problem, passes out while on a trip to Costa Rica and wakes up in a world full of mythical creatures. The sequel is *Back to the Divide* (2004). (Rev: BL 6/1–15/03; HBG 4/04; SLJ 9/03)

8326 Keehn, Sally M. *Gnat Stokes and the Foggy Bottom Swamp Queen* (5–8). 2005, Penguin Putnam $16.99 (0-399-24287-2). 160pp. This fantasy, set in the Appalachian mountains, features a 12-year-old girl named Gnat who faces swamp creatures and spells in her quest to rescue Goodlow Pryce. (Rev: BL 3/1/05; SLJ 4/05)

8327 Kehret, Peg. *Ghost's Grave* (5–8). 2005, Dutton $16.99 (0-525-46162-0). 192pp. Josh expects to be bored when he stays in his aunt's old house, but the ghost of a coal miner who died in 1903 livens things up. (Rev: BL 5/15/05)

8328 Kehret, Peg. *Spy Cat* (4–6). 2003, Dutton $15.99 (0-525-47046-8). 192pp. Clever cat Pete, who understands everything but is frustrated by his inability to speak, plays a lead role in tracking down the neighborhood burglars. (Rev: BL 1/1–15/03; HBG 10/03; SLJ 1/03)

8329 Kempton, Kate. *The World Beyond the Waves: An Environmental Adventure* (5–7). Illus. 1995, Portunus $14.95 (0-9641330-6-7); paper $8.95 (0-9641330-1-6). 88pp. After being washed overboard during a violent storm, Sam visits a land where she meets ocean animals that have been misused by humans. (Rev: BL 4/15/95; SLJ 3/95)

8330 Kendall, Carol. *The Gammage Cup* (4–7). Illus. by Erik Blegvad. 1990, Harcourt paper $6.00 (0-15-230575-0). 283pp. A fantasy of the Minnipins, a small people of the "land between the mountains."

8331 Kessler, Liz. *The Tail of Emily Windsnap* (4–7). Illus. by Sarah Gibb. 2004, Candlewick $15.99 (0-7636-2483-7). 224pp. Twelve-year-old Emily Windsnap, who turns into a mermaid when she gets into the water, learns the truth about her parents. (Rev: BL 5/1/04; SLJ 6/04)

8332 Kimmel, Elizabeth C. *The Ghost of the Stone Circle* (5–8). 1998, Scholastic paper $15.95 (0-590-21308-3). Fourteen-year-old Cristyn, who is spending the summer in Wales with her historian father, discovers a ghost in the house her father has rented. (Rev: BCCB 3/98; BL 4/15/98; HBG 10/98; SLJ 4/98)

8333 Kimmel, Eric A. *Don Quixote and the Windmills* (2–4). Illus. by Leonard Everett Fisher. 2004, Farrar $16.00 (0-374-31825-5). 32pp. Don Quixote is an appealing hero in this boldly illustrated adaptation in which he mistakes the windmills for giants. (Rev: BL 4/15/04; SLJ 4/04)

8334 Kindl, Patrice. *Owl in Love* (5–9). 1993, Houghton Mifflin $16.00 (0-395-66162-5). Owl, a shapeshifter, is an ordinary high school girl by day, and she falls in love with her science teacher. (Rev: BL 9/1/93)

8335 King, Stephen. *The Girl Who Loved Tom Gordon: A Pop-up Book* (4–6). Adapted by Peter Abrahams. Illus. by Alan Dingman. 2004, Simon & Schuster $24.95 (0-689-86272-5). An effectively scary pop-up version of King's 1999 novel about a 9-year-old lost in the woods of Maine. (Rev: SLJ 11/04)

8336 King-Smith, Dick. *Animal Stories* (3–5). Illus. 1998, Orchard $18.95 (0-531-30099-4). 128pp. A collection of animal stories, including an excerpt from *Babe: the Gallant Pig* and a story involving Max, the heroic hedgehog. (Rev: BL 9/1/98; HBG 3/99; SLJ 11/98)

8337 King-Smith, Dick. *Billy the Bird* (3–5). Illus. 2001, Hyperion $14.99 (0-7868-0586-2). 128pp. Mary Bird, 8, confides in her cat and her guinea pig, telling them about her younger brother's ability to fly when the moon is full. (Rev: BL 7/01; HBG 10/01; SLJ 6/01)

8338 King-Smith, Dick. *Clever Lollipop* (3–5). Illus. by Jill Barton. 2003, Candlewick $15.99 (0-7636-2174-9). 144pp. Lady Lollipop, the lovable pig, gets lessons along with Princess Penelope and Johnny Skinner. (Rev: BL 9/15/03; HBG 4/04; SLJ 10/03)

8339 King-Smith, Dick. *The Golden Goose* (2–5). Illus. by Ann Kronheimer. 2005, Knopf LB $17.99 (0-375-92984-3). 128pp. The fortunes of a farmer who's been down on his luck change dramatically after one of his geese lays a golden egg. (Rev: BL 2/1/05)

8340 King-Smith, Dick. *Hogsel and Gruntel and Other Animal Stories* (3–4). Illus. 1999, Orchard $18.95 (0-531-30208-3). 128pp. A collection of 15 amusing and exciting imaginary animal tales. (Rev: BL 11/1/99; HBG 3/00; SLJ 10/99)

8341 King-Smith, Dick. *Lady Lollipop* (2–4). 2001, Candlewick $14.99 (0-7636-1269-3). 124pp. Spoiled Princess Penelope chooses a pig named Lollipop as her pet, and Lollipop's poor owner moves to the palace as the pig's keeper. (Rev: BCCB 9/01; BL 4/15/01; HB 5–6/01; HBG 10/01; SLJ 6/01*)

8342 King-Smith, Dick. *Pigs Might Fly* (3–5). Illus. by Mary Rayner. 1990, Puffin paper $4.99 (0-14-034537-X). 168pp. A pig named Daggie Dogfoot saves the day because he can swim.

8343 King-Smith, Dick. *The Roundhill* (5–7). Illus. 2000, Random paper $4.99 (0-440-41844-5). 96pp. In the English countryside in 1936, 14-year-old Evan meets a mysterious girl who seems to be the Alice of *Alice in Wonderland*. (Rev: BL 1/1–15/01; HBG 3/01; SLJ 12/00)

8344 King-Smith, Dick. *The School Mouse* (3–5). Illus. 1995, Hyperion LB $14.49 (0-7868-2029-2). 124pp. Flora's ability to read saves her illiterate mouse parents from eating poison that has been placed around the school where they live. (Rev: BCCB 1/96; BL 10/15/95; SLJ 12/95*)

8345 Kipling, Rudyard. *Rikki-Tikki-Tavi* (3–5). Illus. by Jerry Pinkney. 1997, Morrow $15.93 (0-688-14321-0). 40pp. In this classic tale, a mongoose repays a debt of kindness after he has been saved from drowning. (Rev: BL 9/1/97*; HBG 3/98; SLJ 8/97*)

8346 Kline, Suzy. *Horrible Harry and the Purple People* (2–4). Illus. by Frank Remkiewicz. 1997, Viking $13.99 (0-670-87035-8). 64pp. Harry maintains that there are invisible purple people in the classroom and plans to invite one to a class tea party to prove it. (Rev: HBG 3/98; SLJ 9/97)

8347 Koller, Jackie F. *The Dragonling* (2–4). Illus. by Judith Mitchell. 1995, Pocket paper $3.99 (0-671-86790-3). 64pp. Darek befriends a young dragon that has been orphaned. (Rev: BL 1/1/91; SLJ 2/91)

8348 Koller, Jackie F. *If I Had One Wish . . .* (5–8). 1991, Little, Brown $14.95 (0-316-50150-6). 161pp. When 8th-grader Alec is granted his wish that his little brother had never been born, he learns a lesson about charity, kindness, and old-fashioned family values. (Rev: BCCB 12/91; BL 11/1/91; SLJ 11/91)

8349 Kortum, Jeanie. *Ghost Vision* (5–8). Illus. by Dugald Stermer. 1983, Scholastic paper $3.50 (0-614-19197-1). 160pp. A Greenland Inuit realizes that his son has special mystical powers.

8350 Kraan, Hanna. *Flowers for the Wicked Witch* (3–5). Trans. by Wanda Boeke. Illus. Series: Wicked Witch. 1998, Front Street $15.95 (1-886910-35-9). 128pp. A collection of charming stories about the relationship between a wicked witch and different forest animals, including a hare, a hedgehog, and an owl. (Rev: BL 11/15/98; HBG 10/99; SLJ 2/99)

8351 Kraan, Hanna. *Tales of the Wicked Witch* (3–5). Illus. by Annemarie van Haeringen. 1995, Front Street $14.95 (1-886910-04-9). 128pp. Fourteen short stories about several forest creatures who have problems with the resident witch. (Rev: BL 1/1–15/96; SLJ 1/96)

8352 Kraan, Hanna. *The Wicked Witch Is at It Again* (3–5). Trans. by Wanda Boeke. Illus. 1997, Front Street $14.95 (1-886910-18-9). 128pp. Fourteen brief stories about the relationship between a wicked witch and the forest animals that live nearby. (Rev: BL 9/15/97; SLJ 7/97*)

8353 Kraft, Jim. *The Vampire Hound* (4–6). 2002, Troll paper $4.95 (0-8167-7315-7). 192pp. Set in Victorian London, this is the story of a good vampire dog called Barksdale who is being tracked by a hunter. (Rev: SLJ 2/03)

8354 Krensky, Stephen. *Arthur and the Big Blow-Up* (2–4). Illus. 2000, Little, Brown $12.95 (0-316-12129-0); paper $3.95 (0-316-12203-3). 64pp. A quarrel between Francine and the Brain threatens the future of their soccer team, so Arthur intervenes to reconcile the two. (Rev: BL 6/1–15/00; HBG 10/00)

8355 Krulik, Nancy. *Girls Don't Have Cooties* (2–4). Illus. by John Wendy and Wendy. Series: Katie Kazoo, Switcheroo. 2002, Grosset paper $3.99 (0-448-42705-2). 76pp. Shape-changing Katie finds herself on both sides of the gender gap when the boys and girls at her school decide to hold competing sleep-over parties. (Rev: SLJ 4/03)

8356 Kurtz, Jane. *The Feverbird's Claw* (5–8). 2004, Greenwillow $15.99 (0-06-000820-2). 304pp. Secretly trained in the art of combat by her grandfather, Moralin is swept into a series of harrowing adventures when she is kidnapped by the Arkera, longtime enemies of Moralin's clan. (Rev: BL 4/15/04; SLJ 5/04)

8357 Labatt, Mary. *Aliens in Woodford* (2–4). Illus. by Troy Hill-Jackson. 2000, Kids Can $12.95 (1-55074-611-1); paper $4.95 (1-55074-607-3). 110pp. Sam, a sheepdog, and her master, Jennie, who can understand the dog's thoughts, solve the mystery of strange nighttime activities at an abandoned airfield. (Rev: BL 9/15/03; HBG 3/01; SLJ 12/00)

8358 Labatt, Mary. *The Mummy Lives!* (3–5). Illus. by Troy Hill-Jackson. Series: Sam, Dog Detective. 2002, Kids Can $12.95 (1-55337-023-6); paper $4.95 (1-55337-042-2). 116pp. Telepathic Sam becomes convinced that she is the dog that an Egyptian mummy is seeking, in this novel suitable for reluctant readers. (Rev: HBG 10/02; SLJ 5/02)

8359 Labatt, Mary. *One Terrible Halloween* (2–5). Illus. by Troy Hill-Jackson. Series: Sam, Dog Detective. 2002, Kids Can $12.95 (1-55337-138-0); paper $4.95 (1-55337-139-9). 107pp. Sam the telepathic dog, with the help of owner Jennie and her friend Beth, investigates the mystery of the missing neighbors. (Rev: HBG 3/03; SLJ 10/02)

8360 Labatt, Mary. *The Secret of Sagawa Lake* (2–5). Series: Sam, Dog Detective. 2001, Kids Can $12.95 (1-55074-887-4); paper $4.95 (1-55074-889-0). 118pp. Ten-year-old Jennie, her telepathic dog Sam, and friend Beth investigate a mystery and become convinced there is a monster in the lake. (Rev: HBG 3/02; SLJ 11/01)

8361 Labatt, Mary. *Strange Neighbors* (2–4). 2000, Kids Can $12.95 (1-55074-605-7); paper $4.95 (1-55074-603-0). 116pp. Sam, the talking sheepdog who can only be understood by Jennie, is convinced that the three old ladies who have moved to their neighborhood are witches. (Rev: BL 5/1/00; HBG 10/00; SLJ 9/00)

8362 Labatt, Mary. *A Weekend at the Grand Hotel* (3–5). Illus. by Troy Hill-Jackson. Series: Sam, Dog Detective. 2001, Kids Can $12.95 (1-55074-883-1); paper $4.95 (1-55074-885-8). 104pp. Sam, the sheepdog detective, who can put thoughts in young Jennie's head, discovers a mystery on a weekend trip to the Grand Hotel. (Rev: HBG 10/01; SLJ 4/01)

8363 Lally, Soinbhe. *A Hive for the Honeybee* (5–8). Illus. by Patience Brewster. 1999, Scholastic $16.95 (0-590-51038-X). 224pp. This clever, thought-provoking fantasy is set in a beehive and explores the life and roles of several workers and drones. (Rev: HB 3–4/99; HBG 10/99; SLJ 5/99*)

8364 Langrish, Katherine. *Troll Fell* (5–7). 2004, HarperCollins $15.99 (0-06-058304-5). 272pp. Sent to live with his evil twin uncles after his father's death, 12-year-old Peer Ulfsson seeks a way to foil their plan to sell children to the trolls. (Rev: BL 4/15/04*; SLJ 7/04)

8365 Langton, Jane. *The Fledgling* (5–7). 1980, HarperCollins LB $16.89 (0-06-023679-5); paper $5.99 (0-06-440121-9). 192pp. A young girl learns to fly with her Goose Prince. A sequel is *The Frag-*

ile Flag (1984). Also use *The Diamond in the Window* (1962).

8366 Langton, Jane. *The Mysterious Circus* (3–5). 2005, HarperCollins LB $16.89 (0-06-009487-7). 224pp. Near Walden Pond, the Hall children are visited by an Indian relative bringing a seed that produces elephants. (Rev: BL 5/1/05; SLJ 5/05)

8367 Langton, Jane. *The Time Bike* (4–6). 2000, HarperCollins LB $15.89 (0-06-028438-2). 176pp. Eddy Hall and his older sister Eleanor time-travel and experience great adventure on their magic bicycle. (Rev: BCCB 7–8/00; HBG 10/00; SLJ 6/00)

8368 Lansky, Bruce, ed. *Newfangled Fairy Tales, Book 1* (3–5). 1998, Meadowbrook LB $3.95 (0-671-57704-2). 110pp. These fractured fairy tales involve such characters as a backpacking Sleeping Beauty and King Midas as a workaholic banker. (Rev: BL 3/1/98)

8369 Lasky, Kathryn. *The Capture* (5–8). 2003, Scholastic paper $4.99 (0-439-40557-2). 240pp. Soren, a happy, well-adjusted young barn owl, falls from his nest and is stolen away by a group of owlet thieves bent on reeducation. (Rev: BL 9/15/03; SLJ 10/03)

8370 Lassig, Jurgen. *Spiny* (2–4). Trans. by J. Alison James. Illus. 1995, North-South LB $13.88 (1-55858-402-1). 58pp. A young dinosaur's baby-sitter saves him from being eaten by the dreaded tyrannosaurus. (Rev: BL 5/1/95; SLJ 6/95)

8371 Lauber, Patricia. *Purrfectly Purrfect: Life at the Acatemy* (3–6). Illus. by Betsy Lewin. 2000, HarperCollins LB $15.89 (0-06-029209-1). 78pp. A witty, well-illustrated story about cats who attend a school, the Acatemy, where they learn to be "purrfect" by studying the "purriculum." (Rev: BCCB 12/00; HBG 3/01; SLJ 12/00)

8372 Lawrence, Michael. *The Poppykettle Papers* (5–9). Illus. by Robert Ingpen. 2000, Pavilion $22.95 (1-86205-282-4). 120pp. Two boys discover an ancient manuscript that tells of an adventure-filled voyage taken by five tiny people in a poppykettle, a vessel used to make tea for the gods. (Rev: SLJ 3/00)

8373 Lawson, Robert. *The Fabulous Flight* (4–6). Illus. by author. 1984, Little, Brown paper $5.95 (0-316-51731-3). 152pp. Peter becomes so small he can take a trip via a pet seagull.

8374 Lawson, Robert. *Rabbit Hill* (4–7). Illus. by author. 1944, Puffin paper $5.99 (0-14-031010-X). 128pp. A warm and humorous story about the small creatures of a Connecticut countryside — each with a distinct personality. Newbery Medal winner, 1945.

8375 Layefsky, Virginia. *Impossible Things* (5–8). 1998, Marshall Cavendish $14.95 (0-7614-5038-6). 207pp. Twelve-year-old Brady has several personal and family problems to solve along with taking care of the dragonlike creature that he is hiding. (Rev: HBG 3/99; SLJ 11/98)

8376 Lee, Tanith. *Wolf Queen* (5–8). Series: Claidi Journals. 2002, Dutton $16.99 (0-525-46895-1). 240pp. After *Wolf Tower* and *Wolf Star*, this concluding volume of the Claidi Journals trilogy tells how the fearless Claidi faces the power of the Raven Tower. (Rev: BCCB 6/02; BL 4/15/02; HBG 10/02; SLJ 6/02)

8377 Lee, Tanith. *Wolf Wing* (5–8). Series: Claidi Journals. 2003, Dutton $16.99 (0-525-47162-6). 240pp. Claidi and Argul, now married, set off on an exciting voyage to his mother's magical land in this novel that revisits many sites from previous volumes in the series. (Rev: BL 9/1/03; HBG 4/04; SLJ 10/03)

8378 Le Guin, Ursula K. *Jane on Her Own* (2–4). Illus. Series: Catwings. 1999, Orchard LB $15.99 (0-531-33133-4). 48pp. This fourth installment of the Catwings series features Jane, one of the winged cats, and her experiences when she leaves home to find adventure and friends. (Rev: BCCB 7–8/99; BL 2/1/99; HBG 10/99; SLJ 4/99)

8379 Le Guin, Ursula K. *Wonderful Alexander and the Catwings* (2–4). Illus. Series: Catwings. 1994, Orchard LB $15.99 (0-531-08701-8). 48pp. Alexander the kitten helps Jane — one of the flying cats called Catwings — regain her power of speech. (Rev: BL 9/15/94; SLJ 9/94)

8380 Lennon, Joan. *There's a Kangaroo in My Soup!* (2–3). Illus. by Wendy Rasmussen. 2000, Front Street $15.95 (0-8126-2898-5). 128pp. Gloria, a runaway circus kangaroo, brings young Kevin out of his shell in this beginning chapter book fantasy. (Rev: SLJ 12/00)

8381 Leonard, Elmore. *A Coyote's in the House* (5–8). 2004, HarperCollins $22.00 (0-06-072882-5). 149pp. A coyote named Antwan strikes up a friendship with a couple of pampered dogs from Hollywood. (Rev: BL 5/15/04)

8382 Levin, Betty. *The Banished* (5–8). 1999, Greenwillow $16.00 (0-688-16602-4). An engaging prequel to *The Ice Bear* in which Siri must make a dangerous sea journey to deliver an ice bear to her people's king. (Rev: BL 8/99; HB 11–12/99; HBG 3/00; SLJ 10/99)

8383 Levine, Gail Carson. *The Two Princesses of Bamarre* (4–7). 2001, HarperCollins LB $16.89 (0-06-029316-0). 256pp. Princess Addie sets out on a quest to find a cure for the Grey Death, a sickness that is destroying her older sister. (Rev: BCCB 10/01; BL 4/15/01; HB 5–6/01; HBG 10/01; SLJ 5/01)

8384 Levine, Gail Carson. *The Wish* (4–7). 2000, HarperCollins LB $15.89 (0-06-027901-X). 208pp. When a kindly old lady grants Wilma's wish to become popular at school, the girl forgets that she is graduating in only three weeks. (Rev: BCCB 5/00; BL 4/1/00; HBG 10/00; SLJ 5/00)

8385 Levinson, Marilyn. *Rufus and Magic Run Amok* (3–5). 2001, Marshall Cavendish $14.95 (0-7614-5102-1). 96pp. Rufus Breckenridge, 10, just wants to be normal but instead inherits magical powers from his parents and grandparents and has to cope with a heap of new problems. (Rev: BCCB 1/02; HBG 3/02; SLJ 10/01)

8386 Levy, Elizabeth. *The Principal's on the Roof* (2–4). Illus. by Mordicai Gerstein. Series: Fletcher Mysteries. 2002, Simon & Schuster LB $11.89 (0-

689-84630-4); paper $3.99 (0-689-84627-4). 73pp. Fletcher the dog and Jasper the flea tackle the mystery of the sneezing principal. (Rev: HBG 3/03; SLJ 1/03)

8387 Levy, Robert. *Escape from Exile* (4–8). 1993, Houghton Mifflin $16.00 (0-395-64379-1). 176pp. Daniel, 13, is struck by lightning and transported to Lithia, where his new telepathic powers help him cope with a bitter civil war. (Rev: BL 3/15/93; SLJ 5/93)

8388 Lewis, C. S. *The Lion, the Witch and the Wardrobe* (5–8). Illus. Series: Narnia. 1988, Macmillan LB $22.95 (0-02-758200-0). Four children enter the kingdom of Narnia through the back of an old wardrobe. A special edition illustrated by Michael Hague. The other six volumes in this series are *Prince Caspian, The Voyage of the Dawn Treader, The Silver Chair, The Horse and His Boy, The Magician's Nephew,* and *The Last Battle.*

8389 Lewis, C. S. *The Lion, the Witch and the Wardrobe: A Story for Children* (4–7). Illus. by Pauline Baynes. 1988, Macmillan paper $7.95 (0-02-044490-7). 160pp. A beautifully written adventure featuring four children who go into the magical land of Narnia.

8390 Lewis, Paul Owen. *The Jupiter Stone* (PS–3). Illus. by author. 2003, Tricycle $15.95 (1-58246-107-4). When a boy discovers a strange rock of extraterrestrial origin that has laid undiscovered on the Earth's surface for millions of years, he enlists the help of NASA to see that the stone is returned to the vastness of outer space. (Rev: SLJ 9/03)

8391 Lichtenheld, Tom. *Everything I Know About Monsters: A Collection of Made-up Facts, Educated Guesses, and Silly Pictures About Creatures of Creepiness* (1–4). Illus. by author. 2002, Simon & Schuster $16.95 (0-689-84381-X). An appealingly silly guide to the kinds of monsters you find in various places (under the bed, in the closet), with practical tips on monster avoidance. (Rev: HBG 3/03; SLJ 9/02)

8392 Lindbergh, Anne. *The Hunky-Dory Dairy* (5–7). Illus. by Julie Brinckloe. 1986, Harcourt $14.95 (0-15-237449-3); Dell paper $2.75 (0-380-70320-3). 147pp. Zannah visits a community magically removed from the 20th century and enjoys introducing the people to bubble gum, tacos, and other "modern" things. (Rev: BCCB 9/86; BL 4/1/86; SLJ 8/86)

8393 Lindbergh, Anne. *The Prisoner of Pineapple Place* (5–7). 1988, Harcourt $13.95 (0-15-263559-9); Avon paper $2.95 (0-380-70765-9). 173pp. Pineapple Place is invisible to everyone except the inhabitants, and somehow finds itself landing in Connecticut. (Rev: BL 7/88; SLJ 8/88)

8394 Lindgren, Astrid. *Mirabelle* (PS–2). Trans. from Swedish by Elisabeth Kallick Dyssegaard. Illus. by Pija Lindenbaum. 2003, R&S $15.00 (91-29-65821-7). Translated into English, this charming Swedish tale tells how eight-year-old Britta plants a seed given to her by a stranger and is pleasantly surprised when the seed sprouts into a doll like the one she has long been wanting. (Rev: BL 5/15/03; HBG 10/03; SLJ 8/03) [839.7]

8395 Lindgren, Astrid. *Ronia, the Robber's Daughter* (4–7). 1985, Puffin paper $5.99 (0-14-031720-1). 176pp. Ronia becomes friendly with the son of her father's rival in this fantasy.

8396 Lisle, Janet T. *Afternoon of the Elves* (4–6). 1989, Orchard LB $16.99 (0-531-08437-X). 128pp. Hilary discovers that the strange girl named Sara-Kate has a garden inhabited by elves. (Rev: BCCB 10/89; BL 8/89*; HB 9–10/89; SLJ 9/89*)

8397 Lisle, Janet T. *The Gold Dust Letters* (4–6). 1994, Orchard LB $16.99 (0-531-08680-1). 128pp. Angela's father fools her into believing that she is receiving messages from a fairy in an effort to effect a reconciliation. (Rev: BCCB 7–8/94; BL 2/1/94; SLJ 4/94)

8398 Lisle, Janet T. *The Lampfish of Twill* (4–8). Illus. by Wendy A. Halperin. 1991, Orchard paper $16.95 (0-531-05963-4). 176pp. Orphaned Eric faces forces of danger as he lives in the mysterious country of Twill. (Rev: BCCB 10/91; HB 1–2/92; SLJ 9/91*)

8399 Lisle, Janet T. *Looking for Juliette* (4–6). 1994, Orchard LB $16.99 (0-531-08720-4). 128pp. Georgina and her friend Poco believe that the strange Miss Bone is responsible for running down their cat Juliette. (Rev: BCCB 12/94; BL 9/15/94; SLJ 8/94*)

8400 Lisle, Janet T. *The Lost Flower Children* (4–6). Illus. 1999, Penguin Putnam $16.99 (0-399-23393-8). 112pp. Youngsters Olivia and Nellie discover a storybook in which children are turned into flowers and must find a way to break the spell. (Rev: BCCB 7–8/99; BL 5/15/99; HB 5–6/99; HBG 10/99; SLJ 6/99)

8401 Lisle, Rebecca. *Copper* (3–6). 2004, Penguin Putnam $15.99 (0-399-24211-2). 208pp. A girl called Copper and her sarcastic but valiant teddy bear embark on a perilous search for her missing parents in this fast-moving fantasy. (Rev: BL 2/15/04; SLJ 1/04)

8402 Lithgow, John. *I'm a Manatee* (2–4). Illus. by Ard Hoyt. 2003, Simon & Schuster $17.95 (0-689-85427-7). In this delightful fantasy story and song, written by actor John Lithgow and packaged with an audio CD, a little boy dreams of what life would be like as a manatee. (Rev: HBG 4/04; SLJ 10/03)

8403 Lofting, Hugh. *The Story of Doctor Dolittle* (3–6). Illus. by author. 1996, Dover paper $1.00 (0-486-29350-5). 144pp. Reissue of the 1970 edition, reedited to remove racially offensive passages. Also use the similarly edited 1923 Newbery Medal winner *The Voyages of Doctor Dolittle* (1988, Dell). (Rev: BL 7/88)

8404 Loux, Lynn Crosbie. *The Day I Could Fly* (2–4). Illus. by Guy Porfirio. 2003, NorthWord $15.95 (1-55971-866-8). A young girl is transformed into a crow for a day. (Rev: SLJ 10/03)

8405 Love, D. Anne. *The Secret Prince* (4–6). 2005, Simon & Schuster $16.95 (0-689-84426-3). 240pp. Twelve-year-old Thorn, informed that he is the prince of Kelhadden, embarks on a quest for the secret amulet that he needs to regain control of the throne from the evil Ranulf. (Rev: BL 1/1–15/05; SLJ 6/05)

8406 Lowry, Lois. *Gathering Blue* (5–9). 2000, Houghton Mifflin $16.00 (0-618-05581-9). 224pp. In an inhospitable future world, young Kira must use her courage and her artistic talents. (Rev: BL 6/1–15/00*; HB 9–10/00; HBG 3/01; SLJ 8/00*)

8407 Lyons, Mary. *Knockabeg: A Famine Tale* (4–7). 2001, Houghton Mifflin $15.00 (0-618-09283-8). 128pp. In order to protect the people of Knockabeg, faeries battle with the creatures who are causing the blight during the great Irish potato famine. (Rev: BL 11/15/01; HBG 3/02; SLJ 9/01)

8408 Lytle, Robert A. *Three Rivers Crossing* (5–8). 2000, River Road $15.95 (0-938682-55-5). 208pp. After he suffers an accident while fishing, 7th-grader Walker wakes to find he is in the 1820s village of his ancestors. (Rev: BL 5/15/00; SLJ 6/00)

8409 Macaulay, David. *Baaa* (5–7). Illus. by author. 1985, Houghton Mifflin $13.95 (0-395-38948-8); paper $5.95 (0-395-39588-7). 64pp. A sophisticated fantasy about a world inhabited by humanlike sheep. (Rev: SLJ 10/85)

8410 McCaffrey, Laura Williams. *Alia Waking* (5–7). 2003, Clarion $15.00 (0-618-19461-4). 224pp. Alia, 12, and her best friend Kay long to become "keenten," or warrior women. (Rev: BL 3/1/03; HBG 10/03; SLJ 6/03)

8411 McCaughrean, Geraldine. *A Pack of Lies* (5–7). 1990, Macmillan $16.95 (0-7451-1154-8). 168pp. Stories told by mysterious M.C.C. Berkshire, who wanders into an antique store run by adolescent Ailsa and her mother. (Rev: BCCB 5/89)

8412 McCusker, Paul. *Arin's Judgment* (5–8). 1999, Tommy Nelson paper $6.99 (1-56179-774-X). 180pp. In 1945, while awaiting word about his father who is missing in action, Wade is transported to another world where his knowledge of World War II places him at risk. (Rev: SLJ 4/00)

8413 MacDonald, Betty. *Hello, Mrs. Piggle-Wiggle* (3–5). Illus. by Hilary Knight. 1957, HarperCollins $15.95 (0-397-31715-8); paper $4.95 (0-06-440149-9). 132pp. Introducing the lady who loves all children, good or bad. Further adventures are: *Mrs. Piggle-Wiggle's Farm* (1954); *Mrs. Piggle-Wiggle* (1957); *Mrs. Piggle-Wiggle's Magic* (1957).

8414 McFarland, Lyn Rossiter. *The Pirate's Parrot* (2–4). Illus. 2000, Tricycle $14.95 (1-58246-014-0). 40pp. Near-blind pirate Captain Cur mistakes a bear for his new parrot in this farcical sea story. (Rev: BL 5/15/00; HBG 10/00; SLJ 5/00)

8415 McGraw, Eloise. *The Moorchild* (4–6). 1996, Simon & Schuster LB $17.00 (0-689-80654-X). 242pp. Set in the Middle Ages, this fantasy tells of Moql, who is born half human and half fairy, and her difficulties fitting into either world. (Rev: BCCB 6/96; BL 3/1/96*; HB 9–10/96; SLJ 4/96*)

8416 MacHale, D. J. *The Lost City of Faar* (5–8). Series: Pendragon. 2003, Simon & Schuster paper $5.99 (0-7434-3732-2). 385pp. After saving Denduron from Saint Dane in *The Merchant of Death* (2002), 14-year-old Bobby must confront the shape-changer again in Cloral, a world covered by water. (Rev: SLJ 5/03)

8417 MacHale, D. J. *The Never War* (5–8). Series: Pendragon. 2003, Simon & Schuster paper $5.99 (0-7434-3733-0). 336pp. In this third installment of a fast-paced quartet, Bobby Pendragon and his side-kick Spader travel through time to help foil the evil, shape-changing Saint Dane's campaign to win control of the universe. (Rev: SLJ 7/03)

8418 McMullan, Kate. *Pearl and Wagner: Two Good Friends* (K–2). Illus. by R. W. Alley. Series: Dial Easy-to-Read. 2003, Dial $13.99 (0-8037-2573-6). 48pp. Pearl the rabbit and Wagner the mouse join forces in three episodes about friendship — two involving a science fair — in this easy-reader. (Rev: HBG 4/04; SLJ 9/03)

8419 Maguire, Gregory. *Four Stupid Cupids* (4–6). Series: Hamlet Chronicles. 2000, Clarion $15.00 (0-395-83895-9). 184pp. A far-fetched comedy about four cupids who are freed when the magical vase that Fawn Petros brings to her Vermont school breaks. (Rev: BL 12/1/00; HBG 3/01; SLJ 10/00)

8420 Maguire, Gregory. *Seven Spiders Spinning* (4–6). Illus. by Dirk Zimmer. 1994, Clarion $15.00 (0-395-68965-1). 144pp. In this farce, seven tarantulas invade a classroom and go on their separate quests. (Rev: BCCB 10/94; BL 9/15/94; SLJ 10/94)

8421 Mahy, Margaret. *The Blood-and-Thunder Adventure on Hurricane Peak* (4–6). Illus. by Wendy Smith. 1989, Macmillan $13.95 (0-689-50488-8). 132pp. Huxley and Zaza find fantastic adventures at Unexpected School on Hurricane Peak. (Rev: BCCB 10/89; BL 10/15/89; HB 11–12/89*; SLJ 10/89)

8422 Mahy, Margaret. *The Five Sisters* (3–5). Illus. 1997, Viking $14.99 (0-670-87042-0). 80pp. Five paper dolls have a series of adventures that reveal their different personalities. (Rev: BCCB 5/97; BL 2/1/97; HB 3–4/97; SLJ 3/97*)

8423 Mahy, Margaret. *A Tall Story and Other Tales* (3–5). Illus. by Jan Nesbitt. 1992, Macmillan $15.95 (0-689-50547-7). 96pp. Eleven stories combine witches and monsters and such with everyday life. (Rev: BL 2/1/92; SLJ 3/92)

8424 Marsden, John. *The Rabbits* (2–8). Illus. by Shaun Tan. 2003, Simply Read $16.95 (0-9688768-8-9). In this allegory, native creatures welcome the newcomer rabbits, but the rabbits take over, devastate the landscape, and there is no happy ending. (Rev: SLJ 4/04)

8425 Martin, Ann M., and Laura Godwin. *The Doll People* (3–6). Illus. 2000, Hyperion $15.99 (0-7868-0361-4). 272pp. In this fantasy about dolls that are alive, Annabelle Doll tries to solve the mystery of the disappearance of Aunt Sarah Doll in 1955. (Rev: BCCB 1/01; BL 8/00; HBG 3/01; SLJ 11/00)

8426 Martin, Ann M., and Laura Godwin. *The Meanest Doll in the World* (5–8). Illus. by Brian Selznick. 2003, Hyperion $15.99 (0-7868-0878-0). 288pp. Through a series of mishaps, dolls Annabelle Doll and Tiffany Funcraft end up in the home of Mean Mimi, a doll with tyrannical tendencies, in

this sequel to *The Doll People* (2000). (Rev: BL 10/15/03; HB 11–12/03; HBG 4/04; SLJ 10/03*)

8427 Martini, Clem. *The Mob* (5–8). Series: Feather and Bone: The Crow Chronicles. 2004, Kids Can $16.95 (1-55337-574-2). 240pp. As hundreds of crows of the Kinaar clan come together for their annual socialization at the Gathering Tree, internal conflicts threaten to tear the avian family apart in this first volume in a trilogy. (Rev: BL 10/1/04; SLJ 12/04)

8428 Masson, Sophie. *Serafin* (5–8). 2000, Saint Mary's paper $5.50 (0-88489-567-X). 140pp. After he saves Calou from being lynched as a witch, Frederick is forced to flee his 17th-century French village with Calou and soon afterward realizes that the girl is a matagot, a half-angel half-human creature. (Rev: SLJ 8/00)

8429 Matas, Carol, and Perry Nodelman. *Out of Their Minds* (5–8). Illus. Series: Minds. 1998, Simon & Schuster $16.00 (0-689-81946-3). In this fantasy (the third in the series), Princess Lenora and Prince Coren journey to Andilla to marry but find that some force is upsetting The Balance. (Rev: HBG 3/99; SLJ 9/98)

8430 Mather, Karen Trella. *Silas: The Bookstore Cat* (2–4). Illus. by Chris Van Dusen. 1994, Down East $14.95 (0-89272-352-2). 32pp. Silas, the bookstore cat, helps his master find books about his favorite subject, soccer. (Rev: BL 2/1/95; SLJ 3/95)

8431 Meddaugh, Susan. *Lulu's Hat* (3–5). Illus. 2002, Houghton Mifflin $15.00 (0-618-15277-6). 64pp. Lulu's deep interest in magic leads her to follow a dog that has jumped into a top hat that has unusual powers. (Rev: BCCB 5/02; BL 5/1/02; HBG 10/02; SLJ 5/02)

8432 Medearis, Angela Shelf. *Haunts: Five Hair-Raising Tales* (4–7). Illus. by Trina S. Hyman. 1996, Holiday House $15.95 (0-8234-1280-6). 37pp. Five stories that contain elements of horror and the supernatural. (Rev: BL 2/1/97; SLJ 4/97)

8433 Meeks, Arone R. *Enora and the Black Crane* (4–6). 1993, Scholastic $14.95 (0-590-46375-6). 32pp. Enora, growing up in a rain forest, spoils the mystical experiences he has had in the wilds by killing a crane. (Rev: BL 10/1/93)

8434 Milne, A. A. *The World of Pooh: The Complete Winnie-the-Pooh; and the House at Pooh Corner* (1–4). Illus. by E. H. Shepard. 1988, Dutton $21.99 (0-525-44447-5). 320pp. A pleasing combination volume.

8435 Molloy, Michael. *The House on Falling Star Hill* (4–8). 2004, Scholastic $16.95 (0-439-57740-3). 384pp. While spending a vacation with his grandparents in a peaceful English village, Tim discovers an alternate world called Tallis and becomes involved in the turmoil taking place there. (Rev: BL 4/15/04; SLJ 4/04)

8436 Molloy, Michael. *The Time Witches* (5–8). 2002, Scholastic paper $4.99 (0-439-42090-3). 272pp. The characters from *The Witch Trade* (2002) return in this sequel in which Abby, a Light Witch, and her friends must travel into the past to foil a plot hatched by the nefarious Wolfbane. (Rev: BL 1/1–15/03; SLJ 8/03)

8437 Monsell, Mary Elise. *Toohy and Wood* (3–5). Illus. 1992, Macmillan $12.95 (0-689-31721-2). 80pp. Toohy the lizard is devastated by the death of Pearl, a musical dove, in this story of a world inhabited by affectionate animals. (Rev: BCCB 12/92; BL 10/1/92; SLJ 10/92)

8438 Montes, Marisa. *Something Wicked's in Those Woods* (4–7). 2000, Harcourt $17.00 (0-15-202391-7). 224pp. Javier is lonely after leaving Puerto Rico and relocating in northern California until he meets the ghost of a boy killed decades ago in an unsolved crime. (Rev: BCCB 10/00; BL 10/15/00; HBG 10/01; SLJ 12/00)

8439 Moranville, Sharelle Byars. *The Purple Ribbon* (2–5). Illus. by Anna Alter. 2003, Holt $17.95 (0-8050-6659-4). 80pp. A field mouse called Spring is raising her babies in an old car, dreaming of returning to live with Gran Dora, who gave her the purple ribbon she treasures. (Rev: BL 3/15/03; HBG 10/03; SLJ 5/03)

8440 Moredun, P. R. *The Dragon Conspiracy* (5–8). Series: World of Eldaterra. 2005, HarperCollins LB $17.89 (0-06-076664-6). 304pp. A complex first installment in which a British schoolboy in 1910 must battle female dragons to save both our world and the magical parallel world of Eldaterra. (Rev: BL 6/1–15/05)

8441 Moroney, Lynn. *Moontellers: Myths of the Moon from Around the World* (3–5). Illus. by Greg Shed. 1995, Northland LB $14.95 (0-87358-601-8). A collection of stories that reflect the attitudes of various cultures — such as the Aztecs and the Chinese — toward the moon, with a final section on modern astronomers. (Rev: SLJ 9/95)

8442 Morris, Gerald. *Parsifal's Page* (5–8). 2001, Houghton Mifflin $15.00 (0-618-05509-6). 240pp. Piers becomes a page to Parsifal and accompanies the innocent young man on his quest to become a knight. (Rev: BCCB 4/01; BL 4/15/01; HB 5–6/01; HBG 10/01; SLJ 4/01)

8443 Morris, Gerald. *The Savage Damsel and the Dwarf* (5–8). 2000, Houghton Mifflin $16.00 (0-395-97126-8). 224pp. Sixteen-year-old Lady Lynet travels to Camelot, in the company of a dwarf, to ask King Arthur's aid in defeating her sister's suitor. (Rev: BL 3/1/00; HB 5–6/00; HBG 10/00; SLJ 5/00)

8444 Morris, Jackie. *The Seal Children* (2–5). Illus. by author. 2004, Frances Lincoln $16.95 (1-84507-040-2). The son of a Welsh fisherman and a selkie woman travels to his mother's world beneath the sea and returns with a box of pearls that the people in his village can use to finance a trip to the New World. (Rev: SLJ 7/04)

8445 Moses, Will. *The Legend of Sleepy Hollow* (3–5). Illus. 1995, Penguin Putnam $18.99 (0-399-22687-7). 48pp. A simple retelling of this classic tale, with paintings of various sizes and shapes. (Rev: BL 10/1/95; SLJ 10/95)

8446 Moses, Will. *Rip Van Winkle* (3–5). Illus. 1999, Penguin Putnam $16.99 (0-399-23152-8).

48pp. This large-format book is a handsome, somewhat simplified version of the classic fantasy by Washington Irving. (Rev: BCCB 12/99; BL 11/1/99; HBG 3/00; SLJ 10/99)

8447 Mullin, Caryl Cude. *A Riddle of Roses* (4–7). 2000, Second Story paper $6.95 (1-896764-28-2). 180pp. Meryl, who has been expelled from school for a year, goes on a quest to Avalon to find her own wisdom. (Rev: BL 2/15/01)

8448 Murphy, Jill. *The Worst Witch* (4–6). 1982, Avon paper $2.50 (0-380-60665-8). 72pp. Mildred's first year at Miss Cackle's Academy for Witches is a disaster. A sequel is: *The Worst Witch Strikes Again* (1987).

8449 Myers, Walter Dean. *Three Swords for Granada* (3–6). Illus. by John Spiers. 2002, Holiday House $15.95 (0-8234-1676-3). 80pp. Sword-wielding Spanish cats stand up to the dogs of the Fidorean Guard in this exciting fantasy set in 1420. (Rev: BL 7/02; HBG 10/03; SLJ 9/02)

8450 Napoli, Donna Jo. *Gracie, the Pixie of the Puddle* (3–6). 2004, Dutton $16.99 (0-525-47264-9). 160pp. Gracie the frog goes to great lengths to prove her love for Jimmy, a frog with magical abilities. (Rev: BL 4/15/04; SLJ 6/04)

8451 Napoli, Donna Jo. *The Prince of the Pond: Otherwise Known as De Fawg Pin* (3–6). Illus. by Judith Byron Schachner. 1992, Dutton $15.99 (0-525-44976-0). 112pp. In this "different" telling of the frog prince tale, Jade, a female frog, meets the prince under his enchantment and never quite catches on that he really isn't a frog. (Rev: BCCB 1/93; BL 1/15/93; SLJ 10/92)

8452 Naylor, Phyllis Reynolds. *Carlotta's Kittens and the Club of Mysteries* (3–6). Illus. Series: Cat Pack. 2000, Simon & Schuster $16.00 (0-689-83269-9). 144pp. The male members of the Club of Mysteries share many adventures when they take care of five kittens until the young ones can be delivered to their new home. (Rev: BL 11/15/00; HBG 3/01; SLJ 1/01)

8453 Naylor, Phyllis Reynolds. *The Grand Escape* (5–7). Illus. Series: Cat Pack. 1993, Macmillan $16.95 (0-689-31722-0). 144pp. Two adventurous cats must solve three mysteries before they can join the Cats' Club of Mysteries. (Rev: BL 7/93; SLJ 8/93)

8454 Naylor, Phyllis Reynolds. *The Healing of Texas Jake* (3–6). Illus. 1997, Simon & Schuster $15.00 (0-689-81124-1). 128pp. Each of the cats who are members of the Club of Mystery rally around their leader, Texas Jake, when he is injured in a brawl. (Rev: BL 5/1/97; SLJ 4/97)

8455 Naylor, Phyllis Reynolds. *Jade Green: A Ghost Story* (5–8). 2000, Simon & Schuster $16.00 (0-689-82005-4). 176pp. Set in South Carolina about 100 years ago, this ghost story involves Judith Sparrow, age 15, and the mystery surrounding the gruesome death of a girl named Jade Green. (Rev: BL 12/15/99; HBG 10/00; SLJ 2/00)

8456 Naylor, Phyllis Reynolds. *Polo's Mother* (4–6). Illus. by Alan Daniel. Series: Cat Pack. 2005, Simon & Schuster $15.95 (0-689-86555-4). 176pp. Polo's mother finally turns up at the Club of Mysteries, but she is not what Polo expected. (Rev: BL 6/1–15/05; SLJ 5/05)

8457 Nesbit, Edith. *The Enchanted Castle* (4–6). Illus. by Paul O. Zelinsky. 1992, Morrow $22.95 (0-688-05435-8). 304pp. A handsome volume that showcases Nesbit's fantasy about four English children and their adventures with a magic ring, first published in 1907. (Rev: BL 12/15/92)

8458 Nesbit, Edith. *Five Children and It* (4–6). Illus. by H. R. Miller. 1981, Buccaneer LB $25.95 (0-89966-362-1). 188pp. An enchanting story about a group of children who discover a Psammead, a sand fairy, who both enlivens and confuses their lives. Two more stories about the children: *The Phoenix and the Carpet* (1985); *The Story of the Amulet* (1986).

8459 Newman, Robert. *Merlin's Mistake* (4–6). Illus. by Richard Lebenson. 1986, Peter Smith $16.25 (0-8446-6187-2). Sixteen-year-old Brian and his friend Tertius set out to find Merlin in this fantasy originally published in 1970. Followed by: *The Testing of Tertius* (1986).

8460 Nicholson, William. *The Wind Singer* (5–7). Illus. 2000, Hyperion $17.99 (0-7868-0569-2). 384pp. In the structured community of Amaranth, ruled by a caste system, twin brother and sister Kestrel and Bowman rebel and try to get help from the Wind Singer. (Rev: BL 10/15/00; HBG 10/01; SLJ 12/00)

8461 Nimmo, Jenny. *Charlie Bone and the Time Twister* (5–7). 2003, Scholastic $9.95 (0-439-49687-X). 416pp. In 1916 Henry Yewbeam finds a strange marble and is transported to the present-day Bloor's Academy, where Charlie Bone tests his magical abilities in an effort to send him home. A sequel to *Midnight for Charlie Bone* (2003). (Rev: BL 9/15/03; HBG 4/04; SLJ 10/03)

8462 Nimmo, Jenny. *Griffin's Castle* (5–8). 1997, Orchard LB $17.99 (0-531-33006-0). When Dinah and her young mother, Rosalie, move into the run-down mansion owned by Rosalie's boyfriend, Dinah brings to life several carved animals for protection. (Rev: SLJ 6/97)

8463 Nimmo, Jenny. *Midnight for Charlie Bone* (4–6). 2003, Scholastic paper $9.95 (0-439-47429-9). 416pp. Charlie Bone, who can look at photographs and hear the conversations and thoughts of the subjects, is sent to Bloor's Academy to enhance his skills and is drawn into a magical battle, makes friends, and becomes immersed in a mystery. (Rev: BL 1/1–15/03; HBG 10/03; SLJ 2/03)

8464 Nimmo, Jenny. *Orchard of the Crescent Moon* (5–7). 1990, Troll paper $2.95 (0-8167-2265-X). 170pp. Nia has begun to believe it when her family says "Nia-can't-do-nothing." (Rev: BL 8/89)

8465 Nix, Garth. *Above the Veil* (5–7). Series: The Seventh Tower. 2001, Scholastic paper $4.99 (0-439-17685-9). 248pp. In episode four in this series, Tal and Milla continue their otherworldly adventures full of action, secrets, and surprising twists and turns. (Rev: SLJ 9/01)

8466 Nix, Garth. *Grim Tuesday* (5–8). Series: Keys to the Kingdom. 2004, Scholastic paper $5.99 (0-439-43655-9). 321pp. Arthur Penhaligon returns in this second installment in the series to the house that holds an alternate universe and there must challenge the evil Grim Tuesday, who threatens to destroy everything. (Rev: SLJ 8/04)

8467 Nix, Garth. *Mister Monday* (5–8). Series: The Keys to the Kingdom. 2003, Scholastic paper $5.99 (0-439-55123-4). 361pp. When seventh-grader Arthur Penhaligon receives a healing key from a mysterious stranger, the gift turns out to be a mixed blessing that brings illness and strange creatures seeking to reclaim the key. (Rev: BCCB 1/04; SLJ 12/03)

8468 Nixon, Joan Lowery. *Gus and Gertie and the Missing Pearl* (2–4). Illus. 2000, North-South LB $15.88 (1-58717-023-X). 48pp. When penguins Gertie and Gus enter a seedy hotel on a tropical island, Gertie's necklace is stolen and they must solve the mystery and catch the thief. (Rev: BL 11/1/00; HBG 3/01; SLJ 10/00)

8469 Norton, Andre, and Phyllis Miller. *House of Shadows* (5–7). 1985, Tor paper $2.95 (0-8125-4743-8). 256pp. While staying with a great-aunt, three children learn about the family curse.

8470 O'Brien, Robert C. *Mrs. Frisby and the Rats of NIMH* (5–7). Illus. by Zena Bernstein. 1971, Macmillan $18.00 (0-689-20651-8); paper $5.50 (0-689-71068-2). 240pp. Saga of a group of rats made literate and given human intelligence by a series of experiments, who escape from their laboratory to found their own community. Newbery Medal winner, 1972.

8471 O'Connor, George. *Ker-splash!* (PS–2). Illus. 2005, Simon & Schuster $14.95 (0-689-87682-3). 40pp. The superhero-switching duo who appeared in *Kapow!* (2004) return in this tale about bullying at the beach. (Rev: BL 6/1–15/05; SLJ 6/05)

8472 Olson, Arielle North, and Howard Schwartz, eds. *Ask the Bones: Scary Stories from Around the World* (5–9). 1999, Viking $15.99 (0-670-87581-3). A collection of 22 scary stories about subjects ranging from ghosts to witches and voodoo spells, accompanied by spooky illustrations. (Rev: BCCB 4/99; BL 5/1/99; BR 9–10/99; HB 5–6/99; HBG 10/99; SLJ 4/99)

8473 Oppel, Kenneth. *Sunwing* (5–8). 2000, Simon & Schuster $17.00 (0-689-82674-5). 272pp. In this sequel to *Silverwing*, Shade, the Silverwing bat, sets out to find his father and has a series of adventures including confronting the forces of evil. (Rev: BCCB 5/00; BL 1/1–15/00; HB 3–4/00; HBG 10/00; SLJ 2/00)

8474 O'Rourke, Frank. *Burton and Stanley* (4–6). Illus. by Jonathan Allen. 1993, Godine $15.95 (0-87923-824-0). 56pp. Two talking birds from Africa are transported by a tornado to a small town in the Midwest. (Rev: BL 5/15/93; SLJ 5/93)

8475 O'Shea, Pat. *The Hounds of the Morrigan* (5–8). 1986, HarperCollins paper $7.99 (0-06-447205-1). 469pp. The forces of good and evil in Irish mythology battle over two children who are on a quest for a magic pebble. (Rev: BCCB 7–8/86; BL 4/1/86; HB 7–8/86; SLJ 3/86)

8476 Osterweil, Adam. *The Amulet of Komondor* (5–7). 2003, Front Street $15.95 (1-886910-81-2). 184pp. Finding themselves in a parallel world of "Japanimations," Joe and Katie face a mighty challenge, worry about how to get home, and continue their real-world romance in this lighthearted fantasy with *anime*-style illustrations. (Rev: BL 11/15/03; HBG 4/04; SLJ 12/03)

8477 Osterweil, Adam. *The Comic Book Kid* (4–6). Illus. 2001, Front Street $15.95 (1-886910-62-6). 152pp. Brian tries to travel back to 1939 and replace his father's prized Superman #1 comic book. (Rev: BL 5/15/01; HBG 10/01; SLJ 8/01)

8478 Palatini, Margie. *Lab Coat Girl in My Triple-Decker Hero* (3–5). Illus. by author. 2000, Hyperion $14.49 (0-7868-2442-5); paper $4.99 (0-7868-1348-2). 100pp. Fifth-graders Trudie and Ben are suspected of having a romance when they are really trying to keep secret their experiments with Ben's extraordinary powers. (Rev: SLJ 4/01)

8479 Paterson, Katherine. *The Field of the Dogs* (3–5). Illus. by Emily Arnold McCully. 2001, HarperCollins LB $14.89 (0-06-029475-2). 96pp. Josh, beset by bullies in the Vermont town where he has moved with his mother, discovers that he can understand the language of dogs. (Rev: BCCB 2/01; BL 10/15/01; HBG 10/01; SLJ 2/01)

8480 Pattison, Darcy. *The Wayfinder* (4–6). 2000, Greenwillow LB $15.89 (0-06-029157-5). 208pp. An adventure-fantasy in which a young boy is sent on a quest to find the Well of Life, whose waters can help stop a deadly plague. (Rev: BCCB 1/01; BL 12/15/00; HBG 3/01; SLJ 1/01)

8481 Paul, Donita K. *Dragonspell* (4–8). 2004, WaterBrook paper $12.99 (1-57856-823-4). 339pp. Fourteen-year-old Kale is the protagonist of this classic quest tale, set in the world of Amara, with Christian overtones reminiscent of C. S. Lewis. (Rev: SLJ 11/04)

8482 Paulsen, Gary. *The Time Hackers* (5–8). 2005, Random LB $17.99 (0-385-90896-2). 160pp. Twelve-year-old Dorso Clayman and best friend Frank team up to find out who's been tampering with time. (Rev: BL 1/1–15/05; SLJ 1/05)

8483 Pearce, Philippa. *Tom's Midnight Garden* (4–7). Illus. by Susan Einzig. 1959, HarperCollins $15.89 (0-397-30477-3); Dell paper $5.95 (0-06-440445-5). 240pp. When the clock strikes 13, Tom visits his garden and meets Hatty, a strange mid-Victorian girl.

8484 Peck, Richard. *The Ghost Belonged to Me* (5–8). 1997, Viking paper $5.99 (0-14-038671-8). 184pp. Richard unwillingly receives the aid of his nemesis, Blossom Culp, in trying to solve the mystery behind the ghost of a young girl. Two sequels are *Ghosts I Have Been* (1977); *The Dreadful Future of Blossom Culp* (1983).

8485 Peel, John. *Suddenly Twins!* (4–6). Series: The Magical States of America. 2001, Pocket paper $4.99 (0-7434-1762-3). 162pp. Chrissie Scott finds a magical twin in the mirror and the two work together to fight evil. (Rev: SLJ 12/01)

8486 Pennypacker, Sara. *Stuart Goes to School* (2–4). Illus. by Martin Matje. 2003, Scholastic $15.95 (0-439-30182-3). 64pp. In this humorous sequel to *Stuart's Cape,* the title character enters the third grade at a new school and finds that having a magical cape can sometimes cause embarrassing problems. (Rev: BL 7/03; SLJ 9/03)

8487 Pennypacker, Sara. *Stuart's Cape* (2–4). Illus. by Martin Matje. 2002, Scholastic $15.95 (0-439-30180-7). 64pp. When Stuart wears his superhero cape, magical things happen — he flies, his cat drives — and he can handle his misgivings about moving to a new town. (Rev: BL 9/1/02; HBG 3/03; SLJ 11/02)

8488 Perez, L. King. *Ghoststalking* (3–6). Illus. 1995, Carolrhoda LB $19.95 (0-87614-821-6). 56pp. Chuy and Emilio camp outdoors to find the ghost of La Llorona, a woman who has drowned her children in this Latino tale of the supernatural. (Rev: BL 9/15/95; SLJ 12/95)

8489 Perrin, Randy, et al. *Time Like a River* (5–7). 1997, RDR $14.95 (1-57143-061-X). 139pp. Margie travels back in time to find a cure for her mother's mysterious illness. (Rev: HBG 3/98; SLJ 3/98)

8490 Petti, Ken, et al. *Zenda and the Gazing Ball* (4–7). Illus. 2004, Grosset paper $5.99 (0-448-43223-4). 128pp. On the planet of Azureblue, 12-year-old Zenda can't resist a sneak peek at the crystal gazing ball that holds her destiny, and in the process drops and breaks the ball. In the sequel, *Zenda: A New Dimension,* she travels to a parallel dimension in search of shards. (Rev: BL 5/15/04; SLJ 9/04)

8491 Pierce, Tamora. *Briar's Book* (5–9). Series: Circle of Magic. 1999, Scholastic paper $15.95 (0-590-55359-3). In this fantasy, Briar, a former street urchin and petty thief, and his teacher, Rosethorn, search for the cause of a deadly plague that is sweeping through their land. (Rev: BL 2/15/99; HBG 10/99; SLJ 3/99)

8492 Pierce, Tamora. *The Circle Opens: Magic Steps* (5–9). Series: Circle Opens. 2000, Scholastic paper $16.95 (0-590-39588-2). 272pp. Fourteen-year-old Sandry and her friend Pasco use their magic to stop the murders of local merchants. (Rev: BCCB 3/00; BL 3/1/00; HB 5–6/00; HBG 10/00; SLJ 4/00)

8493 Pierce, Tamora. *First Test* (4–7). 1999, Random LB $17.99 (0-679-98914-5). 224pp. Keladry uses her wits and intelligence to conquer the many obstacles she encounters during her first year in knight training. (Rev: BCCB 7–8/99; BL 6/1–15/99; HBG 10/99; SLJ 7/99)

8494 Pierce, Tamora. *Page: Protector of the Small* (5–8). 2000, Random $16.00 (0-679-88915-9). 240pp. After successfully passing her first year of knight's training, Keladry moves on to the next three years as a page. (Rev: BCCB 9/00; BL 8/00; HBG 10/00; SLJ 8/00)

8495 Pierce, Tamora. *Tris's Book* (5–9). Series: Circle of Magic. 1998, Scholastic paper $15.95 (0-590-55357-7). 251pp. Tris and her three fellow mages combine forces to fight the pirates who are threatening to destroy their home in this sequel to *Sandry's Book*. (Rev: BCCB 4/98; BL 8/98; HBG 10/98; SLJ 4/98)

8496 Pilkey, Dav. *Captain Underpants and the Big, Bad Battle of the Bionic Booger Boy: Part 1: The Night of the Nasty Nostril Nuggets* (2–4). Illus. by author. 2003, Scholastic $16.95 (0-439-37609-2); paper $4.99 (0-439-37610-6). 173pp. The superhero and sidekicks George and Harold face off against Melvin Sneedley, who's transformed himself into the Bionic Booger Boy. A sequel is *Captain Underpants and the Big, Bad Battle of the Bionic Booger Boy, Part 2: The Revenge of the Ridiculous Robo-Boogers* (2003). (Rev: HBG 4/04; SLJ 1/04)

8497 Pilkey, Dav. *Ricky Ricotta's Giant Robot vs. the Voodoo Vultures from Venus* (2–4). Illus. by Martin Ontiveros. 2001, Scholastic $16.95 (0-439-23624-X). 125pp. Ricky the mouse and his giant robot friend tackle villains from Venus with dastardly plans. (Rev: HBG 10/01; SLJ 5/01)

8498 Pilkey, Dav. *Ricky Ricotta's Mighty Robot vs. the Jurassic Jackrabbits from Jupiter* (2–4). Illus. by Martin Ontiveros. 2002, Scholastic paper $3.99 (0-439-37643-2). 127pp. Ricky, his Mighty Robot, and cousin Lucy defeat General Jackrabbit, an invader from Jupiter with nefarious intent. (Rev: SLJ 12/02)

8499 Pilkey, Dav. *Ricky Ricotta's Mighty Robot vs. the Mecha-Monkeys from Mars* (2–4). Illus. by Martin Ontiveros. 2002, Scholastic paper $3.99 (0-439-25296-2). 143pp. Ricky and his robot friend battle the fiendish forces of an evil Martian monkey. (Rev: HBG 10/02; SLJ 4/02)

8500 Pipe, Jim. *The Werewolf* (4–7). Illus. Series: In the Footsteps Of. 1996, Millbrook LB $24.90 (0-7613-0450-9). 40pp. A horror story in which Bernard, a werewolf, commits terrible acts under the influence of a full moon. (Rev: SLJ 7/96)

8501 Place, Francois. *The Last Giants* (4–6). Trans. from French by William Rodarmor. Illus. by author. 1993, Godine $15.95 (0-87923-990-5). 74pp. This novel tells of the fearless explorer Archibald Ruthmore and his journey into the Land of the Giants. It is part fable, part fantasy, and part exciting adventure story. (Rev: HB 11–12/93; SLJ 12/93)

8502 Polacco, Patricia. *I Can Hear the Sun* (2–4). Illus. by author. 1996, Penguin Putnam $16.99 (0-399-22520-X). A fantasy in which a misunderstood, troubled boy accepts an invitation from the geese and flies away with them. (Rev: BL 11/1/96; SLJ 11/96)

8503 Porte, Barbara Ann. *Hearsay: Tales from the Middle Kingdom* (5–8). Illus. 1998, Greenwillow $15.00 (0-688-15381-X). Each of these 15 entertaining fantasies contains elements of Chinese folklore and culture. (Rev: BCCB 5/98; BR 11–12/98; HBG 10/98; SLJ 6/98)

8504 Potter, Ellen. *Olivia Kidney* (4–6). Illus. by Peter Reynolds. 2003, Penguin Putnam $15.99 (0-399-23850-6). 160pp. When Olivia's father lands a job as superintendent of a New York City apartment block, the 12-year-old finds the building is full of strange and wonderful characters. (Rev: BL 6/1–15/03; HB 9–10/03; HBG 4/04; SLJ 6/03)

8505 Potter, Ellen. *Olivia Kidney and the Exit Academy* (4–7). Illus. by Peter H. Reynolds. Series: Olivia Kidney. 2005, Penguin Putnam $15.99 (0-399-24162-0). 256pp. After her brother's death, Olivia and her father move into a creepy apartment building where, she discovers, people go to rehearse their deaths. (Rev: BL 3/15/05; SLJ 5/05)

8506 Pratchett, Terry. *Only You Can Save Mankind* (5–8). 2005, HarperCollins LB $16.89 (0-06-054186-5). 224pp. It's up to Johnny to save the aliens in a new computer game, and the situation forces him to do some thinking about the very nature of war. (Rev: BL 4/15/05)

8507 Preussler, Otfried. *The Satanic Mill* (5–8). 1987, Peter Smith $19.50 (0-8446-6196-1). 256pp. A young apprentice outwits a strange magician in this fantasy first published in 1972. (Rev: BL 6/1–15/98)

8508 Price, Reynolds. *A Perfect Friend* (5–8). 2000, Simon & Schuster $16.00 (0-689-83029-7). 128pp. Set in the early part of the 20th century, this story tells how Ben, whose mother has died, communes with a young circus elephant who has also just lost a loved one. (Rev: BCCB 10/00; BL 11/15/00; HB 9–10/00; HBG 3/01; SLJ 2/01)

8509 Priest, Robert. *The Town That Got Out of Town* (2–5). Illus. 1989, Godine $14.95 (0-87923-786-4). 48pp. One Labor Day, the city of Boston decides to pay a visit to Portland, Maine. (Rev: BL 1/1/90; SLJ 5/90)

8510 Prior, Natalie Jane. *Lily Quench and the Lighthouse of Skellig Mor* (3–5). Illus. by Janine Dawson. 2004, Puffin paper $4.99 (0-14-240059-9). 160pp. Lily Quench and Dragon Queen continue to face danger and challenges in their efforts to save the land of Ashby in this fourth volume in the series. (Rev: SLJ 11/04)

8511 Proysen, Alf. *Little Old Mrs. Pepperpot and Other Stories* (3–5). 1960, Astor-Honor $14.95 (0-8392-3021-4). The story of a woman who can shrink to the size of a pepper pot.

8512 Prue, Sally. *Cold Tom* (4–8). 2003, Scholastic $15.95 (0-439-48268-2). 192pp. Tom has disabilities that make him an outcast, and he flees from his elfin tribe to the city inhabited by demons (humans), where he is confronted with his human side. (Rev: BL 9/15/03; HB 7–8/03*; HBG 10/03; SLJ 9/03*)

8513 Pullman, Philip. *Clockwork* (4–7). Illus. by Leonid Gore. 1998, Scholastic paper $14.95 (0-590-12999-6). 128pp. Reality and fantasy interact when characters in a storyteller's tale come to life in this story set in a bygone German inn. (Rev: BCCB 12/98; BL 9/15/98*; BR 1–2/99; HB 11–12/98; HBG 3/99; SLJ 10/98)

8514 Pullman, Philip. *The Firework-Maker's Daughter* (3–6). Illus. 1999, Scholastic $15.95 (0-590-18719-8). 112pp. In a fanciful historical land, Lila sets out on a dangerous quest to find royal sulfur, a substance that will enable her to become a true fireworks maker. (Rev: BCCB 1/00; BL 9/15/99*; HBG 3/00; SLJ 11/99)

8515 Pullman, Philip. *I Was a Rat!* (4–6). 2000, Knopf LB $17.99 (0-375-90176-0). 192pp. A humorous spinoff on the Cinderella story in which a young foundling finds a home with an elderly couple, in spite of the fact that he keeps insisting he is a rat. (Rev: BCCB 2/00; BL 2/1/00; HBG 10/00; SLJ 3/00)

8516 Pullman, Philip. *Lyra's Oxford* (5–8). Illus. by John Lawrence. 2003, Knopf $10.95 (0-375-82819-2). 64pp. This slim volume takes readers back to the world of Pullman's His Dark Materials trilogy, with maps, postcards, and other ephemera. (Rev: BL 2/1/04; HBG 4/04; SLJ 1/04)

8517 Pyle, Howard. *The Garden Behind the Moon: A Real Story of the Moon Angel* (4–6). Illus. by author. 1988, Parabola paper $10.95 (0-930407-22-9). 180pp. A boy follows the path of the moonlight and visits the Moon-Angel and the Man-in-the-Moon in this fantasy. A reissue of the 1895 edition.

8518 Raham, Gary. *The Deep Time Diaries: As Recorded by Neesha and Jon Olifee* (4–6). Illus. by author. 2000, Fulcrum paper $17.95 (1-55591-415-2). 82pp. The author supplements the fictional diaries of a 22nd-century family of time travelers with notes, maps, interesting sites, and related activities. (Rev: SLJ 4/01)

8519 Raschka, Chris. *Elizabeth Imagined an Iceberg* (K–6). Illus. by author. Series: Richard Jackson Books. 1994, Orchard LB $15.99 (0-531-08667-4). Elizabeth meets an unusual, frightening woman and is able to repulse her advances in this unsettling picture book. (Rev: BCCB 5/94; SLJ 4/94)

8520 Ratnett, Michael. *Dracula Steps Out* (3–5). Illus. by June Goulding. 1998, Orchard $19.95 (0-531-30100-1). Dracula riddles and jokes are included in this interactive book where Dracula pops up in different places. (Rev: BL 1/1–15/99)

8521 Redmond, Shirley-Raye. *Grampa and the Ghost* (3–5). 1994, Avon paper $3.50 (0-380-77382-1). 82pp. When Mark and Sibyl advertise for a ghost writer, they get an assistant from beyond the grave named Tallulah. (Rev: SLJ 7/94)

8522 Rees, Celia. *The Soul Taker* (5–8). 2004, Hodder paper $7.95 (0-340-87817-7). 152pp. Lewis, overweight and lacking confidence, finds himself in thrall to a sinister toy maker. (Rev: BL 1/1–15/04)

8523 Reiche, Dietlof. *Freddy in Peril* (2–5). Trans. by John Brownjohn. Illus. by Joe Cepeda. 2004, Scholastic $16.95 (0-439-53155-1). 208pp. When an evil professor threatens to kidnap Freddy, the golden hamster prodigy, an odd assortment of friends and strangers comes to the hamster's aid. (Rev: BL 4/1/04; SLJ 5/04)

8524 Reiss, Kathryn. *Paint by Magic* (4–6). 2002, Harcourt $17.00 (0-15-216361-1). 288pp. A time-travel mystery about a boy who must be transported back to 1926 to help save his mother from the clutches of an evil 15th-century painter. (Rev: BCCB 9/02; BL 4/15/02; HBG 3/03; SLJ 5/02)

8525 Reiss, Kathryn. *Sweet Miss Honeywell's Revenge* (4–7). 2004, Harcourt $17.00 (0-15-216574-6). 288pp. A haunted dollhouse, a parallel story about the original owner of the antique, and the problems of blended family life are intertwined in this story about 12-year-old Zibby Thorne. (Rev: BL 5/1/04; SLJ 8/04)

8526 Richardson, Bill. *After Hamelin* (4–8). 2000, Annick $19.95 (1-55037-629-2). 144pp. In this entertaining fantasy that is a follow-up to the Pied Piper of Hamelin story, Penelope gets the gift of Deep Dreaming and is able to enter the Piper's secret world in the hope of rescuing the children. (Rev: BL 2/15/01; SLJ 4/01)

8527 Richemont, Enid. *The Time Tree* (4–6). 1990, Little, Brown $12.95 (0-316-74452-2). 96pp. A girl from the 16th century visits the 20th and takes back the skills she has learned. (Rev: BCCB 5/90; BL 8/90; SLJ 6/90)

8528 Roach, Marilynne K. *Encounters with the Invisible World* (5–9). Illus. by author. 1977, Amereon $18.95 (0-89190-874-9). Spooky stories about witches, demons, spells, and ghosts in New England.

8529 Roberts, Katherine. *Crystal Mask* (5–8). Series: The Echorium Sequence. 2002, Scholastic paper $15.95 (0-439-33864-6). 256pp. The Singers, a group of people who maintain peace in the world through their unusual powers, are confronted by evildoers known as the Frazhin. Also use *Dark Quetzal* (2003). (Rev: BL 4/15/02; HBG 10/02; SLJ 3/02)

8530 Roberts, Katherine. *Dark Quetzal* (5–8). Series: Echorium Sequence. 2003, Scholastic $15.95 (0-439-45697-5). 256pp. In this concluding volume, evil sorcerer Frazhin kidnaps Singer Rialle of the Isle of Echoes, but Frazhin's daughter Kyarra teams up with Shaiala and the Dark Quetzal to escape from the sorcerer's control and take Rialle with them. (Rev: HBG 10/03; SLJ 8/03)

8531 Roberts, Katherine. *Spellfall* (4–6). 2001, Scholastic $15.95 (0-439-29653-6). 250pp. In this fast-moving fantasy, 12-year-old Natalie learns she has inherited magic powers from her long-dead mother, and must use them to save a magical universe from an evil Spell Lord. (Rev: BCCB 2/02; BL 11/15/01; HBG 3/02; SLJ 10/01)

8532 Robertson, Barbara. *Rosemary and the Island Treasure: Back to 1947* (3–6). Illus. Series: The Hourglass Adventures. 2001, Winslow paper $4.95 (1-890817-58-9). 113pp. Rosemary travels back in time to meet her grandmother — another Rosemary — on an island in the Bahamas, where together they search for treasure. Also use *Rosemary at Sea: Back to 1919*, which takes place on the *Mauretania*. (Rev: SLJ 2/02)

8533 Robertson, Barbara. *Rosemary Meets Rosemarie: Berlin in 1870* (4–6). Illus. 2001, Winslow paper $4.95 (1-890817-55-4). 125pp. For her tenth birthday, Rosemary Rita receives a magical hourglass that whisks her back in time to 1870 Berlin where she meets her 10-year-old great-great-great-grandmother and the two solve a mystery. Also use

Rosemary in Paris: Back to 1889 (2001). (Rev: SLJ 10/01)

8534 Rodda, Emily. *The Charm Bracelet* (2–5). Illus. by Raoul Vitale. Series: Fairy Realm. 2003, HarperCollins LB $14.89 (0-06-009584-9). 128pp. Queen Jessica must return from the mortal world to renew the magical powers of the realm; when the wicked Valda tries to stop her, Jessica's grand-daughter Jessie uses her cleverness, a few helping hands, and some magic to save the day. (Rev: BL 1/1–15/03; HBG 10/03; SLJ 8/03)

8535 Rodda, Emily. *The Pigs Are Flying* (4–6). Illus. by Noela Young. 1988, Greenwillow paper $2.95 (0-380-70555-9). 160pp. Rachel's friend Burt, who has come to cheer her when she has a cold, makes her believe in the impossible. (Rev: BL 10/1/88; HB 11–12/88)

8536 Rodda, Emily. *Rowan and the Keeper of the Crystal* (3–6). Series: Rowan of Rin. 2002, Harper-Collins LB $15.89 (0-06-029777-8). 208pp. Rowan must take on his mother's duties to choose the next Keeper of the Crystal after she is poisoned in this third book in the series. (Rev: BCCB 4/02; BL 1/1–15/02; HB 3–4/02; HBG 10/02; SLJ 5/02)

8537 Rodda, Emily. *Rowan and the Travelers* (3–6). 2001, HarperCollins LB $14.89 (0-06-029774-3). 176pp. This enthralling, stand-alone sequel to *Rowan of Rin* (2001) follows the diminutive herder on a journey to save his village from a mysterious sleeping sickness. (Rev: BCCB 10/01; BL 11/15/01; HB 9–10/01; HBG 3/02; SLJ 1/02)

8538 Rodda, Emily. *Rowan and the Zebak* (3–6). Series: Rowan of Rin. 2002, HarperCollins LB $15.89 (0-06-029779-4). 208pp. Rowan embarks on a quest to rescue his kidnapped sister in this magical fantasy adventure, the fourth in the series. (Rev: BCCB 7–8/02; BL 3/1/02; HBG 10/02; SLJ 7/02)

8539 Rodda, Emily. *Rowan of Rin* (3–6). 2001, Greenwillow LB $14.89 (0-06-029708-5). 160pp. Young Rowan, who is a little timid, nonetheless joins a daring expedition to investigate why the peo-ple of Rin are without water and ends up being the bravest of them all. (Rev: BCCB 6/01; BL 5/1/01*; HB 7–8/01; HBG 10/01; SLJ 6/01)

8540 Roden, Katie. *The Mummy* (3–6). Illus. Series: In the Footsteps Of. 1996, Millbrook LB $21.90 (0-7613-0451-7). 40pp. Fiction and fact mix in this account of mummification and a horror story about King Tut's tomb. (Rev: SLJ 5/96)

8541 Ross, Gaby. *Damien the Dragon* (3–5). Illus. by Carla Daly. 1990, Poolbeg paper $6.95 (1-85371-078-4). 92pp. Alan and the residents of Gravellonia construct a companion for Lady Silk Dragon. (Rev: BL 12/15/90)

8542 Rowling, J. K. *Fantastic Beasts: And Where to Find Them* (4–7). 2001, Scholastic paper $3.99 (0-439-29501-7). 42pp. This guide to 75 magical beasts and their whereabouts is one of the texts that Harry Potter has studied, complete with his jottings in the margins. Similarly, *Quidditch Through the Ages* (2001) contains the game's history, rules, and league details. (Rev: BL 5/1/01; SLJ 6/01)

8543 Rowling, J. K. *Harry Potter and the Chamber of Secrets* (4–8). 1999, Scholastic $19.95 (0-439-06486-4). 352pp. During his second year at Hog-warts School of Witchcraft and Wizardry, Harry is baffled when he hears noises no one else can. (Rev: BCCB 9/99; BL 5/15/99*; BR 9–10/99; HB 7–8/99; HBG 10/99; SLJ 7/99)

8544 Rowling, J. K. *Harry Potter and the Goblet of Fire* (4–9). 2000, Scholastic $25.95 (0-439-13959-7). 734pp. This, the fourth installment of Harry Pot-ter's adventures, begins when Voldemort tries to regain the power he lost in his failed attempt to kill Harry. (Rev: BL 8/00*; HB 11–12/00; HBG 3/01; SLJ 8/00)

8545 Rowling, J. K. *Harry Potter and the Order of the Phoenix* (4–12). 2003, Scholastic LB $34.99 (0-439-56761-0). 870pp. Adolescence, adult hypocrisy, and the deadly threat of Voldemort and his evil sup-porters combine to make Harry's fifth year at Hog-warts as eventful as ever. (Rev: BL 7/03; HB 9–10/03; HBG 10/03; SLJ 8/03)

8546 Rowling, J. K. *Harry Potter and the Prisoner of Azkaban* (4–8). Illus. by Mary GrandPré. 1999, Scholastic $19.95 (0-439-13635-0). 448pp. In this third thrilling adventure, a murderer has escaped from prison and is after our young hero. (Rev: BCCB 10/99; BL 9/1/99*; HB 11–12/99; HBG 3/00; SLJ 10/99)

8547 Rowling, J. K. *Harry Potter and the Sorcerer's Stone* (4–8). Illus. 1998, Scholastic $19.95 (0-590-35340-3). In this humorous and suspenseful story, 11-year-old Harry Potter attends the Hogwarts School for Witchcraft and Wizardry, where he dis-covers that he is a wizard just as his parents had been and that someone at the school is trying to steal a valuable stone with the power to make peo-ple immortal. (Rev: BCCB 11/98; BL 9/15/98; HB 1–2/99; HBG 3/99; SLJ 10/98)

8548 Ruby, Laura. *Lily's Ghosts* (5–8). 2003, HarperCollins LB $17.89 (0-06-051830-8). 272pp. Thirteen-year-old Lily and her mother move into a Victorian house in Cape May, New Jersey, only to find it harbors both secrets and ghosts. (Rev: BCCB 9/03; HBG 4/04; SLJ 12/03)

8549 Ruiz, Joseph J. *The Little Ghost Who Wouldn't Go Away / El pequeño fantasma que no queria irse* (2–4). Trans. by Juan S. Lucero. Illus. by Kris Hotvedt. 2000, Sunstone paper $10.95 (0-86534-303-9). 95pp. The ghost of a young boy gets the help of Rebecca Garcia to locate his missing tomb-stone so he can rest in peace in this story in both Spanish and English. (Rev: SLJ 1/01)

8550 Runton, Andy. *Owly: The Way Home and the Bittersweet Summer* (3–5). Illus. 2004, Top Shelf paper $10.00 (1-891830-62-7). 160pp. Two sweet and simple graphic novellas feature lonely Owly the Owl and her new friend Wormy. (Rev: BL 2/1/05)

8551 Rupp, Rebecca. *The Dragon of Lonely Island* (4–6). 1998, Candlewick $16.99 (0-7636-0408-9). 160pp. Three children, ages 12, 10, and 8, are new arrivals on Lonely Island where they befriend a three-headed dragon who tells them a story from each of its heads. (Rev: BCCB 12/98; BL 2/1/99; HBG 3/99; SLJ 11/98)

8552 Ruskin, John. *King of the Golden River or the Black Brother* (5–8). Illus. by Richard Doyle. 1974, Dover paper $3.95 (0-486-20066-3). 56pp. Two mean brothers incur the wrath of the South-West Wind.

8553 Russell, Barbara T. *Blue Lightning* (4–8). 1997, Viking $14.99 (0-670-87023-4). Calvin dies but returns to life, only to find that the ghost of another boy, Rory, who "died" at the same time, has followed him and won't leave him alone. (Rev: BCCB 2/97; BL 2/15/97; HB 5–6/97; SLJ 2/97)

8554 Rylant, Cynthia. *The Bird House* (2–4). Illus. by Barry Moser. 1998, Scholastic $15.95 (0-590-47345-X). 32pp. In this charming fantasy, a young girl gradually forms a friendship with an old lady because of birds' intervention. (Rev: BL 10/15/98; HBG 3/99; SLJ 9/98)

8555 Rylant, Cynthia. *The Case of the Fidgety Fox* (1–3). Illus. by G. Brian Karas. 2003, Greenwillow LB $15.89 (0-06-009102-9). 56pp. Bunny and Jack, two animal detectives, are on the case when a bus-driving skunk reports that his lucky dice have been stolen. (Rev: HBG 10/03; SLJ 5/03)

8556 Rylant, Cynthia. *The Heavenly Village* (4–7). 1999, Scholastic paper $15.95 (0-439-04096-5). 96pp. A special book about the Heavenly Village — a place where some people stay who are not sure about going to heaven — and about some of the people who live in this in-between world. (Rev: BL 12/1/99*; HBG 3/00; SLJ 3/00)

8557 Rylant, Cynthia. *The High-Rise Private Eyes: The Case of the Puzzling Possum* (2–4). Illus. by G. Brian Karas. 2001, Greenwillow $14.95 (0-688-16308-4). 48pp. In this beginning chapter book, the mystery of why a trombone is continually stolen and returned is solved by detective Bunny Brown and her bumbling sidekick, the raccoon named Jack. (Rev: BL 12/1/00; HB 3–4/01; HBG 10/01)

8558 Rylant, Cynthia. *The Van Gogh Cafe* (4–6). 1995, Harcourt $14.00 (0-15-200843-8). 64pp. Seven vignettes about the people who frequent the Van Gogh Cafe situated off Highway 70 in Flowers, Kansas. (Rev: BCCB 9/95; BL 6/1–15/95; SLJ 7/95)

8559 Rylant, Cynthia. *The Whale* (2–4). Illus. by Preston McDaniels. Series: The Lighthouse Family. 2003, Simon & Schuster $14.95 (0-689-84881-1). 64pp. In this sequel to *The Lighthouse Family: The Storm*, mouse children Lila and Whistler, with the help of a grumpy cormorant, seek to reunite a lost baby whale with his mother. (Rev: BL 9/1/03; HBG 4/04; SLJ 11/03)

8560 Sage, Angie. *Book One: Magyk* (5–8). Illus. by Mark Zug. 2005, HarperCollins LB $18.89 (0-06-057732-0). 576pp. A fantasy of magic, spells, and evil forces, focusing on young Jenna, who was raised by Septimus Heap's family and who now must flee the evil Supreme Custodian. (Rev: BL 3/15/05; SLJ 4/05)

8561 Said, SF. *Varjak Paw* (4–7). Illus. by Dave McKean. 2003, Random LB $17.99 (0-385-75030-

7). 256pp. Varjak Paw, a purebred Mesopotamian Blue cat, leaves a life of luxury, learns martial arts, and has many adventures while seeking to defend his family. (Rev: HB 7–8/03; HBG 10/03; SLJ 6/03)

8562 Sampson, Fay. *Pangur Ban: The White Cat* (5–8). Series: Pangur Ban. 2003, Lion paper $7.95 (0-7459-4763-8). 160pp. A Welsh cat and an Irish monk encounter princesses and mermaids in this fantasy set in the Middle Ages. (Rev: BL 5/15/03; SLJ 11/03)

8563 Sampson, Fay. *Shape-Shifter: The Naming of Pangur Ban* (5–8). Series: Pangur Ban. 2003, Lion paper $7.95 (0-7459-4762-X). 160pp. A Welsh cat pursued by witches befriends an Irish monk in this first book in the series. (Rev: BL 5/15/03)

8564 San Souci, Robert D. *Dare to Be Scared: Thirteen Stories to Chill and Thrill* (4–8). Illus. by David Ouimet. 2003, Cricket $15.95 (0-8126-2688-5). 168pp. A baker's dozen of spooky stories suitable for this age group that feature diverse characters. (Rev: BL 10/1/03; HBG 10/03; SLJ 9/03)

8565 Sanvoisin, Eric. *A Straw for Two* (2–4). Illus. 1999, Delacorte $9.95 (0-385-32702-1). 48pp. Odilon, a vampire who drinks ink, meets Carmilla, who is a fellow follower of Draculink. (Rev: BL 12/1/99; HBG 3/00)

8566 Say, Allen. *Stranger in the Mirror* (3–6). Illus. 1995, Houghton Mifflin $16.95 (0-395-61590-9). 32pp. In this fantasy, Sam one morning discovers that he has the face of an old, wrinkled man. (Rev: BCCB 11/95; BL 10/1/95; SLJ 10/95*)

8567 Schaeffer, Susan F. *The Dragons of North Chittendon* (5–7). Illus. by Darcy May. 1986, Simon & Schuster paper $2.95 (0-685-14462-3). The story of Arthur, an unruly dragon, and his ESP relationship with the boy Patrick in a story of humans and dragons in and above North Chittendon, Vermont. (Rev: BL 8/86; SLJ 9/86)

8568 Schmidt, Gary D. *Pilgrim's Progress* (4–7). Illus. by Barry Moser. 1994, Eerdmans $20.00 (0-8028-5080-4). 88pp. A simple retelling of the classic in which Christian leaves his home to find the Celestial City. (Rev: BL 11/1/94; SLJ 12/94)

8569 Schmidt, Gary D. *Straw into Gold* (5–8). 2001, Clarion $15.00 (0-618-05601-7). 172pp. Two boys set off to find the answer to the king's riddle and thereby save the lives of rebels, only to discover much more than they had expected. (Rev: BCCB 9/01; HBG 10/01; SLJ 8/01)

8570 Schnur, Steven. *The Shadow Children* (4–7). Illus. by Herbert Tauss. 1994, Morrow $16.99 (0-688-13281-2). 86pp. The experiences of the Holocaust are relived by a boy when he visits an area in France where Jewish refugees lived before being sent to the death camps. (Rev: BCCB 12/94; BL 11/15/94; SLJ 10/94)

8571 Schwartz, Alvin. *Scary Stories 3: More Tales to Chill Your Bones* (4–7). Illus. by Stephen Gammell. 1991, HarperCollins LB $16.89 (0-06-021795-2); paper $5.99 (0-06-440418-8). 128pp. A modernized version of spooky tales handed down through the years. (Rev: BL 8/91; HB 11–12/91; SLJ 11/91)

8572 Scieszka, Jon. *Hey Kid, Want to Buy a Bridge?* (3–6). Illus. by Adam McCauley. 2002, Viking $14.99 (0-670-89916-X). 80pp. The Time Warp Trio is transported back to 1877 in their hometown of Brooklyn and gets to meet Thomas Edison and watch the building of the Brooklyn Bridge. (Rev: BL 2/1/02; HBG 10/02; SLJ 3/02)

8573 Scieszka, Jon. *It's All Greek to Me* (4–6). 1999, Viking $13.99 (0-670-88596-7). 80pp. The Time Warp Trio discover they are in ancient Greece where they must contend with the three-headed dog, Cerberus, and meet the gods of Mount Olympus. (Rev: BL 11/15/99; HBG 3/00; SLJ 10/99)

8574 Scieszka, Jon. *Me Oh Maya* (2–6). Illus. by Adam McCauley. Series: Time Warp Trio. 2003, Penguin Putnam $14.99 (0-670-03629-3). 80pp. The Time Warp Trio turn up in Chichen Itza and must derail an evil high priest's plans to sacrifice them to please the harvest gods. (Rev: BL 9/15/03; HBG 4/04; SLJ 12/03)

8575 Scieszka, Jon. *Sam Samurai* (4–6). Illus. by Adam McCauley. Series: Time Warp Trio. 2001, Viking $14.99 (0-670-89915-1). 80pp. While working on an assignment to write a haiku, the Time Warp Trio is accidentally transported back to 17th-century Japan in this wacky time-travel adventure. (Rev: BL 11/1/01; HBG 3/02; SLJ 11/01)

8576 Scieszka, Jon. *Summer Reading Is Killing Me* (3–6). Illus. by Lane Smith. 1998, Viking $13.99 (0-670-88041-8). 80pp. In this hilarious adventure, the Time Warp Trio get mixed up with characters from books on a summer reading list, such as Dracula, Winnie the Pooh, Long John Silver, and Frankenstein. (Rev: BL 6/1–15/98; HBG 3/99; SLJ 8/98)

8577 Scieszka, Jon. *Tut, Tut* (4–6). Illus. by Lane Smith. 1996, Viking $13.99 (0-670-84832-8). 80pp. The Time Warp Trio find themselves in ancient Egypt in the clutches of the pharaoh's evil priest. (Rev: BL 10/1/96; SLJ 9/04)

8578 Scieszka, Jon. *Viking It and Liking It* (2–4). Illus. by Adam McCauley. 2002, Viking $14.99 (0-670-89918-6). 80pp. The Time Warp Trio is thrown into the world of the Vikings and meets challenges including a feisty Leif Ericksson and meals of whale blubber. (Rev: BL 12/1/02; HBG 3/03; SLJ 1/03)

8579 Scott, Deborah. *The Kid Who Got Zapped Through Time* (4–7). 1997, Avon $14.00 (0-380-97356-1). 160pp. In this humorous time-travel fantasy, Flattop Kincaid is transported to England during the Middle Ages, where he becomes a serf. (Rev: BL 11/1/97; SLJ 9/97)

8580 Seabrooke, Brenda. *The Haunting at Stratton Falls* (5–8). 2000, Dutton $15.99 (0-525-46389-5). 150pp. Eleven-year-old Abby, who has recently moved to Stratton Falls, New York, while her father is fighting in Germany during World War II, sees wet footprints in the hall and wonders if the stories about the house being haunted are true. (Rev: BCCB 9/00; BL 7/00; HBG 3/01; SLJ 8/00)

8581 Seabrooke, Brenda. *The Haunting of Swain's Fancy* (4–6). 2003, Dutton $16.99 (0-525-46938-9). 154pp. Ghosts appear to be haunting the 18th-century house in which 11-year-old Taylor and her step-

sister Nicole are spending the summer; investigating this brings the two girls together. (Rev: BL 5/15/03; SLJ 8/03)

8582 Seabrooke, Brenda. *Stonewolf* (5–8). 2005, Holiday House $16.95 (0-8234-1848-0). 231pp. Young orphan Nicholas is taken captive by a group called the Synod but manages to escape, taking with him a sought-after secret formula. (Rev: BL 3/15/05; SLJ 3/05)

8583 Seabrooke, Brenda. *The Vampire in My Bathtub* (4–7). 1999, Holiday House $15.95 (0-8234-1505-8). 150pp. After 13-year-old Jeff moves to a new home with his mother, he finds a friendly vampire hidden inside an old trunk. (Rev: BL 1/1–15/00; HBG 3/00; SLJ 12/99)

8584 Sedgwick, Marcus. *The Dark Horse* (5–8). 2003, Random $15.95 (0-385-73054-3). 160pp. A fantasy in which young Sigurd, part of the ancient Storn tribe, helps his people fight the invading Dark Horse. (Rev: BL 2/1/03; HB 3–4/03; HBG 10/03; SLJ 3/03*)

8585 Seidler, Tor. *Mean Margaret* (4–6). Illus. by Jon Agee. 1997, HarperCollins LB $14.00 (0-06-205091-5). 176pp. Two newly married woodchucks decide to adopt a human child who has made her parents' life miserable. (Rev: BL 12/1/97; SLJ 11/97*)

8586 Seidler, Tor. *The Revenge of Randal Reese-Rat* (4–6). Illus. by Brett Helquist. 2001, Farrar $16.00 (0-374-36257-2). 240pp. Soon after Montague and Isabel are married, a fire destroys their home and the prime suspect is Isabel's old flame Randal in this enjoyable sequel to *A Rat's Tale* (1999). (Rev: BCCB 2/02; BL 11/1/01; HBG 3/02; SLJ 10/01)

8587 Seidler, Tor. *The Wainscott Weasel* (4–6). Illus. by Fred Marcellino. 1993, HarperCollins LB $19.89 (0-06-205033-8). 200pp. Although his girl friend, a fish, spurns him, a weasel named Bagley Brown, Jr. is determined to help when her pond is threatened. (Rev: BCCB 11/93; BL 11/1/93*; HB 11–12/93; SLJ 12/93)

8588 Selden, George. *The Cricket in Times Square* (3–6). Illus. by Garth Williams. 1960, Farrar $16.00 (0-374-31650-3); Dell paper $5.50 (0-440-41563-2). 160pp. A Connecticut cricket is transported in a picnic basket to New York's Times Square. Two sequels are: *Tucker's Countryside* (1969); *Harry Cat's Pet Puppy* (1974).

8589 Selden, George. *The Genie of Sutton Place* (5–6). 1985, Farrar paper $7.95 (0-374-42530-2). The summer Tim lives with his Aunt Lucy on Sutton Place in New York City, he evokes his own magical genie who works not only miracles but mishaps.

8590 Sepulveda, Luis. *The Story of a Seagull and the Cat Who Taught Her to Fly* (3–6). Trans. by Margaret Sayers Peden. Illus. by Chris Sheban. 2003, Scholastic $15.95 (0-439-40186-0). 128pp. Zorba the cat finds himself charged with the responsibilities of raising a seagull chick and teaching it to fly. (Rev: BL 9/1/03; HBG 4/04; SLJ 12/03)

8591 Service, Pamela F. *Storm at the Edge of Time* (4–6). 1994, Walker $16.95 (0-8027-8306-6).

192pp. Three children from different time periods are summoned to help Urkar, a Neolithic wise man. (Rev: BL 10/15/94; SLJ 12/94)

8592 Shalant, Phyllis. *Bartleby of the Mighty Mississippi* (4–6). 2000, Dutton $15.99 (0-525-46033-0). 160pp. The story of a brave, loyal, small turtle named Bartleby who begins an adventure-filled journey down the Mississippi. (Rev: BL 5/15/00; HBG 10/00; SLJ 8/00)

8593 Shan, Darren. *A Living Nightmare* (5–8). Series: Cirque Du Freak. 2001, Little, Brown $15.95 (0-316-60340-6). 272pp. A supernatural story about a young boy who visits the Cirque Du Freak and is turned into a vampire. (Rev: BL 4/15/01; HBG 10/01; SLJ 5/01)

8594 Shan, Darren. *Tunnels of Blood* (5–8). Series: Cirque Du Freak. 2002, Little, Brown $15.95 (0-316-60763-0). 240pp. Darren Shan, teenage half-vampire, sets out to investigate a spate of recent killings for which he believes his vampire master might be responsible. (Rev: BL 8/02; HBG 10/02; SLJ 5/02)

8595 Shan, Darren. *Vampire Mountain* (5–8). Series: Cirque Du Freak. 2002, Little, Brown $15.95 (0-316-60806-8). 208pp. Darren Shan, teenage half-vampire, and his mentor travel to Vampire Mountain. The fifth, sixth and seventh installments in the series are *Trials of Death, The Vampire Prince* (both 2003), and *Hunters of the Dusk* (2004). (Rev: BL 8/02; HBG 3/03; SLJ 9/02)

8596 Shan, Darren. *The Vampire's Assistant* (5–8). Series: Cirque Du Freak. 2001, Little, Brown $15.95 (0-316-60610-3). 256pp. The creepy, suspenseful second installment about a boy who is "half vampire" and his efforts to adjust to the world of a traveling freak show. (Rev: BL 10/15/01; HBG 3/02; SLJ 8/01)

8597 Shearer, Alex. *Professor Sniff and the Lost Spring Breezes* (4–6). Illus. 1998, Orchard $14.95 (0-531-30079-X). 112pp. Sam and Lorna discover that the wind cannot blow and seek the help of Professor Sniff who owns a hurricane he brought back from Florida. (Rev: BL 4/1/98; HBG 10/98; SLJ 4/98)

8598 Shearer, Alex. *The Summer Sisters and the Dance Disaster* (3–5). Illus. 1998, Orchard LB $15.99 (0-531-33080-X). 112pp. The three summer sisters decide to use magic to create different kinds of weather but unfortunately get their spells mixed up. (Rev: BL 4/15/98; HBG 10/98; SLJ 5/98)

8599 Shipton, Paul. *The Mighty Skink* (4–6). 2000, HarperCollins $15.95 (0-688-17420-5). 192pp. Kaz, a fearful rhesus monkey, joins up with fast-talking newcomer Skink and together they escape from their zoo to explore the outside world. (Rev: BCCB 5/00; BL 8/00; HBG 10/00; SLJ 6/00)

8600 Shreve, Susan. *Ghost Cats* (4–7). 1999, Scholastic paper $14.95 (0-590-37131-2). 128pp. A boy, who is trying to adjust to a new family home and the loss of his five cats, is helped when the cats return as ghosts. (Rev: BCCB 12/99; BL 9/1/99; HBG 3/00; SLJ 11/99)

8601 Sims, J. Michael. *Young Claus: Legend of the Boy Who Became Santa* (2–4). 1995, Cygnet Trumpeter $12.95 (0-9645976-6-7). 112pp. A fantasy about a young orphan who encounters many adventures in his mission to be Santa. (Rev: BL 11/15/95)

8602 Sincic, Alan. *Edward Is Only a Fish* (3–5). Illus. 1996, Holt paper $4.95 (0-8050-4906-1). 56pp. When the Billingsly home is flooded because of running bathwater, Edward the goldfish has a field day and a free tour of the house. (Rev: BL 1/15/95; SLJ 2/95)

8603 Singer, Marilyn. *The Circus Lunicus* (3–6). 2000, Holt $17.00 (0-8050-6268-8). 168pp. When Solly disobeys his mean stepmother and sneaks off to the circus, he encounters a mystery involving a sinister ringmaster, a weeping girl, and some singing alligators. (Rev: BL 12/1/00; SLJ 12/00)

8604 Sinykin, Sheri C. *A Matter of Time* (4–6). 1998, Marshall Cavendish $14.95 (0-7614-5019-X). 207pp. Jody, wanting to spend more time with his dad to understand him better, gets his wish when he time-travels back to 1958 and meets his father as a youngster. (Rev: BL 5/15/98; HBG 10/98; SLJ 5/98)

8605 Slepian, Jan. *Back to Before* (5–7). 1994, Scholastic paper $3.25 (0-590-48459-1). 144pp. Cousins Linny and Hilary travel back to a time before Linny's mother's death and Hilary's parents' separation. (Rev: BCCB 9/93; BL 9/1/93*; SLJ 10/93)

8606 Small, David. *George Washington's Cows* (3–4). Illus. 1994, Farrar $15.00 (0-374-32535-9). 32pp. Humorous rhymes that depict daily life of the animals at George Washington's Mount Vernon. (Rev: BL 11/1/94; SLJ 1/95*)

8607 Smith, Dodie. *The Hundred and One Dalmatians* (3–5). 1981, Avon paper $2.95 (0-380-00895-5). 208pp. Pongo and Missis must save the Dalmatian puppies captured by Cruella de Vil.

8608 Smith, Sherwood. *Crown Duel* (5–8). 1997, Harcourt $17.00 (0-15-201608-2). 272 pp. Young Meliara and her brother Bran lead a small band of friends against the wicked King Galdran. (Rev: BCCB 7–8/97; BL 4/15/97; SLJ 8/97)

8609 Smith, Sherwood. *Wren's Quest* (5–8). 1993, Harcourt $16.95 (0-15-200976-0). Wren takes time out from magician school to search for clues to her parentage. Sequel to *Wren to the Rescue* (1990). (Rev: BL 4/1/93*; SLJ 6/93)

8610 Smith, Sherwood. *Wren's War* (5–8). 1995, Harcourt $17.00 (0-15-200977-9). In this sequel to *Wren to the Rescue* and *Wren's Quest,* Princess Teressa struggles to control herself and her destiny when she finds her parents murdered. (Rev: BL 3/1/95*; SLJ 5/95)

8611 Sneve, Virginia Driving Hawk. *The Trickster and the Troll* (4–8). 1997, Univ. of Nebraska Pr. $25.00 (0-8032-4261-1). In this fantasy, two folktale characters, the Sioux trickster Iktomi and a troll who has followed a Norwegian family to this country, develop a friendship as they see the country grow and change. (Rev: BL 9/15/97; BR 1–2/98; HBG 3/98; SLJ 12/97)

8612 Snyder, Zilpha Keatley. *The Ghosts of Rathburn Park* (5–8). 2002, Delacorte LB $17.99 (0-385-90064-3). 192pp. Eleven-year-old Matthew explores Rathburn Park and comes across a mysterious girl dressed in clothes from a bygone era in this suspenseful, well-crafted tale. (Rev: BCCB 2/03; HBG 3/03; SLJ 9/02)

8613 Snyder, Zilpha Keatley. *The Unseen* (5–8). 2004, Delacorte $15.95 (0-385-73084-5). 208pp. The discovery of a magic feather, and the experiences it brings, help 12-year-old Xandra to feel less isolated and to appreciate her family more. (Rev: BL 3/1/04; SLJ 4/04)

8614 Somary, Wolfgang. *Night and the Candlemaker* (4–8). Illus. 2000, Barefoot $16.99 (1-84148-137-8). 32pp. In this allegory, a candle maker continues with his trade in spite of threats he receives from Night. (Rev: BL 9/15/00; HBG 10/01; SLJ 1/01)

8615 Soto, Gary. *The Cat's Meow* (2–5). Illus. 1995, Scholastic $13.95 (0-590-47001-9). 80pp. Graciela's cat, Pip, astounds everyone by suddenly speaking in Spanish. (Rev: BL 12/1/95; SLJ 10/95)

8616 Spalding, Andrea. *The Keeper and the Crows* (3–6). Illus. 2000, Orca paper $4.50 (1-55143-141-6). 119pp. Misha sets out to retrieve a key to a magic box that contains Hope, in this fantasy that is a spinoff on the Greek myth about Pandora's Box. (Rev: BL 11/15/00)

8617 Spalding, Andrea. *The White Horse Talisman* (4–7). 2002, Orca $12.95 (1-55143-187-4). 160pp. Two Canadian children vacationing in England help the magical White Horse fight the forces of the honey-tongued dragon. (Rev: BL 4/15/02; HBG 10/02; SLJ 11/02)

8618 Spires, Elizabeth. *The Mouse of Amherst* (2–5). Illus. 1999, Farrar $15.00 (0-374-35083-3). 64pp. A tiny mouse, Emmaline, who lives in Emily Dickinson's house, is so impressed with the poetry she reads that she begins writing her own. (Rev: BL 3/15/99; HBG 10/99; SLJ 5/99)

8619 Springer, Nancy, ed. *Ribbiting Tales* (5–7). Illus. 2002, Penguin Putnam paper $5.99 (0-698-11952-5). 128pp. This is an anthology of eight stories about frogs by such authors as Janet Taylor Lisle, Robert J. Harris, and Bruce Coville. (Rev: BL 11/1/00; SLJ 1/01)

8620 Springer, Nancy. *Sky Rider* (5–8). 2000, HarperCollins paper $4.95 (0-380-79565-5). In this contemporary supernatural mystery, Dusty's beloved horse Tazz is cured by a visitor who turns out to be the angry ghost of a teenage boy recently killed on her father's property. (Rev: BCCB 10/99; HBG 3/00; SLJ 8/99)

8621 Stahler, David. *Truesight* (5–7). 2004, HarperCollins LB $16.89 (0-06-052286-0). 168pp. A race of blind people living in a colony on a distant planet includes one teenager who discovers he can see, and he sees all sorts of flaws in the people of his community. (Rev: SLJ 3/04)

8622 Stanley, Diane. *The Mysterious Matter of I. M. Fine* (4–6). 2001, HarperCollins LB $15.89 (0-06-029619-4). 208pp. Fran and her friend Beamer must

find the woman who writes the fiendish Chiller series of books, which are affecting the health of young readers. (Rev: BCCB 10/01; BL 7/01; HBG 3/02; SLJ 8/01)

8623 Starkey, Dinah, ed. *Ghosts and Bogles* (5–10). Illus. 1987, David & Charles $17.95 (0-434-96440-9). A collection of 16 British ghost stories, each nicely presented with illustrations. (Rev: SLJ 9/87)

8624 Steele, Mary Q. *Journey Outside* (5–8). Illus. by Rocco Negri. 1984, Peter Smith $20.25 (0-8446-6169-4); Puffin paper $4.99 (0-14-030588-2). 144pp. Young Dilar, believing that his Raft People have been circling endlessly in their quest for a "Better Place," sets out to discover the origin and fate of his kind.

8625 Steig, William. *Abel's Island* (4–6). Illus. by author. 1976, Farrar $15.00 (0-374-30010-0); paper $4.95 (0-374-40016-4). 128pp. A tale of a pampered mouse who must fend for himself after being marooned on an isolated island.

8626 Steig, William. *Dominic* (4–6). Illus. by author. 1984, Farrar paper $4.95 (0-374-41826-8). 160pp. A resourceful and engaging hound dog helps a group of animals overcome the wicked Doomsday Gang.

8627 Steig, William. *The Real Thief* (4–5). Illus. by author. 1976, Farrar paper $3.95 (0-374-46208-9). 64pp. Gawain, a goose, is disgraced when gold and jewels begin disappearing from the Royal Treasury where he is the guard.

8628 Stewart, Jennifer J. *If That Breathes Fire, We're Toast!* (4–6). 1999, Holiday House $15.95 (0-8234-1430-2). 117pp. Mrs. Yang, a dragon, takes Rick and friend Natalie on several trips through time and imagination. (Rev: BCCB 9/99; BL 8/99; HBG 10/99; SLJ 12/99)

8629 Stine, R. L. *The Haunting Hour: Chill in the Dead of Night* (5–8). Illus. 2001, HarperCollins $14.89 (0-06-623605-3). 160pp. Ten chilling short stories, each with an introduction by the author. (Rev: BCCB 11/01; BL 1/1–15/02; HBG 3/02)

8630 Stine, R. L. *Nightmare Hour* (4–7). Illus. 1999, HarperCollins $15.99 (0-06-028688-1). 148pp. Ten scary stories by a master of mystery, with characters that include aliens, sorcerers, werewolves, witches, and ghosts. (Rev: BL 10/15/99; HBG 3/00; SLJ 12/99)

8631 Strasser, Todd. *Help! I'm Trapped in Obedience School* (5–8). 1995, Scholastic paper $4.50 (0-590-54209-5). Andy, trapped in a dog's body, must adjust to eating dog food and engaging in other typical canine activities. (Rev: BL 2/1/96; SLJ 2/96)

8632 Strasser, Todd. *Hey Dad, Get a Life!* (5–8). 1996, Holiday House $15.95 (0-8234-1278-4). Twelve-year-old Kelly and her younger sister use the ghost of their dead father to accomplish their everyday chores and finally let their mother know about their secret helper. (Rev: BCCB 3/97; BL 2/15/97; SLJ 3/97)

8633 Strauss, Linda Leopold. *A Fairy Called Hilary* (2–4). Illus. 1999, Holiday House $15.95 (0-8234-1418-3). 113pp. Nine related stories about Caroline, her family, and their adopted fairy, Hilary. (Rev: BL 3/1/99; HBG 10/99; SLJ 3/99)

8634 Strickland, Brad. *The Whistle, the Grave, and the Ghost* (5–8). 2003, Dial $16.99 (0-8037-2622-8). 160pp. A silver whistle frees a woman vampire, drawing Lewis Barnevalt and his friends into suspenseful adventures battling an ancient threat. (Rev: BL 8/03; HBG 4/04; SLJ 8/03)

8635 Swope, Sam. *Jack and the Seven Deadly Giants* (1–4). Illus. by Carll Cneut. 2004, Farrar $16.00 (0-374-33670-9). 112pp. Abandoned as an infant and long considered the village bad boy, Jack decides to leave town when he's unfairly blamed for the misdeeds of a band of giants. (Rev: BL 5/15/04; HB 5–6/04; SLJ 5/04)

8636 Tagg, Christine. *Metal Mutz!* (1–3). Illus. by David Ellwand. 2003, Candlewick $17.99 (0-7636-2083-1). When Tinribs the robot alien tires of traveling alone, he decides to build himself a canine friend out of castoffs from the scrap heap; all his efforts end in failure, but then his rejected creations come to the rescue, fashioning a pup that suits Tinribs just fine. (Rev: SLJ 8/03)

8637 Taylor, Theodore. *The Boy Who Could Fly Without a Motor* (3–6). 2002, Harcourt $15.00 (0-15-216529-0). 144pp. After Jon learns how to fly from a green-eyed magician, he becomes the center of attraction and even meets the President. (Rev: BL 6/1–15/02; HBG 10/02; SLJ 5/02)

8638 Tebbetts, Christopher. *Viking Pride* (4–6). Series: The Viking. 2003, Penguin Putnam paper $5.99 (0-14-250029-1). 192pp. Fourteen-year-old Zack stumbles into a battle between 9th-century Vikings who bear an uncanny resemblance to his Dad and Dad's friends back at the Minnesota Vikings tailgate party he just left. (Rev: BL 9/1/03; SLJ 12/03)

8639 Thomas, Jane Resh. *The Princess in the Pigpen* (4–6). 1989, Houghton Mifflin $15.00 (0-395-51587-4). 124pp. In a reverse time travel story, a girl is transported from 17th-century England to present-day America. (Rev: BL 9/15/89; SLJ 11/89)

8640 Thomas, Joyce C. *The Bowlegged Rooster and Other Tales That Signify* (2–5). Illus. 2000, HarperCollins LB $15.89 (0-06-025378-9). 112pp. Five original folktales in which animals mirror the human condition but solve their problems in a whimsical fashion. (Rev: BCCB 12/00; BL 10/1/00; HBG 3/01; SLJ 11/00)

8641 Thomson, Sarah L. *Imagine a Day* (3–6). Illus. by Rob Gonsalves. 2005, Simon & Schuster $16.95 (0-689-85219-3). 40pp. Surrealist images are accompanied by brief text in this large-format volume that is a companion to *Imagine a Night* (2003). (Rev: BL 1/1–15/05; SLJ 4/05)

8642 Thornton, Duncan. *Kalifax* (5–9). Illus. by Yves Noblet. 2000, Coteau paper $8.95 (1-55050-152-6). 168pp. In this fantasy novel, young Tom, with the help of Grandfather Frost, saves the crew of his ship after it becomes trapped in ice. (Rev: SLJ 1/01)

8643 Thornton, Duncan. *The Star-Glass* (5–8). Illus. by Yves Noblet. 2004, Coteau paper $10.95 (1-55050-269-7). 402pp. Tom and Jenny face new challenges in this sequel to the fantasies *Kalifax* and

Captain Jenny and the Sea of Wonders. (Rev: SLJ 4/04)

8644 Tibo, Gilles. *The Cowboy Kid* (2–5). Illus. 2000, Tundra $16.95 (0-88776-511-4). 24pp. In this fantasy, a youngster named the Cowboy Kid finds a horse and together they ride through the sky rescuing other horses from statues and paintings. (Rev: BL 6/1–15/00)

8645 Titus, Eve. *Basil of Baker Street* (4–6). Illus. by Paul Galdone. 1958, Pocket paper $2.50 (0-318-37408-0). A clever mystery about a mouse who moves to 221 Baker Street out of admiration for Mr. Holmes. Another in the series: *Basil in the Wild West* (1990).

8646 Tolan, Stephanie S. *The Face in the Mirror* (5–8). 1998, Morrow $15.00 (0-688-15394-1). 208pp. When Jared goes to live with his actor father, he becomes interested in acting and in making friends with a ghost who haunts the theater. (Rev: BCCB 9/98; HBG 3/99; SLJ 11/98)

8647 Tolan, Stephanie S. *Flight of the Raven* (5–8). 2001, HarperCollins LB $17.89 (0-06-029620-8). 304pp. Amber, whose father is responsible for a terrorist attack, and Elijah, an African American boy who has mysterious powers, attempt to stop further violence in this novel that blends science fiction and suspense. (Rev: BCCB 12/01; BL 10/15/01; HBG 10/02; SLJ 10/01)

8648 Tolan, Stephanie S. *Who's There?* (5–8). 1994, Morrow $15.00 (0-688-04611-8); paper $4.95 (0-688-15289-9). 240pp. Fourteen-year-old Drew is convinced that there is a ghost in her crusty grandfather's house, where she and her brother Evan, who has been mute since their parents' deaths, are currently living. (Rev: BCCB 12/94; BL 9/1/94; SLJ 10/94)

8649 Tolkien, J. R. R. *The Hobbit* (5–7). Illus. by author. 1938, Houghton Mifflin $14.95 (0-395-07122-4); Ballantine paper $6.99 (0-345-33968-1). 320pp. A saga of dwarfs and elves, goblins and trolls in a far-off, long ago land. There is a special edition illustrated by Michael Hague (1984).

8650 Tolkien, J. R. R. *Roverandom* (4–9). 1998, Houghton Mifflin $17.00 (0-395-89871-4); paper $12.00 (0-395-95799-0). This fantasy deals with a dog named Roverandom who has the misfortune of insulting a wizard and having to pay the consequences. (Rev: BL 7/98; SLJ 6/98)

8651 Townley, Roderick. *Into the Labyrinth* (5–7). 2002, Simon & Schuster $16.95 (0-689-84615-0). 272pp. In this sequel to *The Great Good Thing* (2001), Princess Sylvie and the other characters in their novel become exhausted as their popularity grows and they must rush from chapter to chapter; when the book goes digital, things spiral out of control and Sylvie must defeat an evil "bot" that threatens to destroy them. (Rev: BL 11/1/02; HBG 10/03; SLJ 10/02)

8652 Townsend, Tom. *The Trouble with an Elf* (5–8). Series: Fairie Ring. 1999, Royal Fireworks paper $9.99 (0-88092-525-6). 158pp. The adopted daughter of the king of the elves, Elazandra, journeys through a ring of mushrooms to the world of humans to stop the evil that will destroy both worlds. (Rev: SLJ 4/00)

8653 Tunnell, Michael O. *School Spirits* (5–8). 1997, Holiday House $15.95 (0-8234-1310-1). Three students at creepy Craven Hill School, including the son of the new principal, discover a ghost and solve a decades-old murder mystery involving an 8-year-old boy. (Rev: BCCB 3/98; BL 2/15/98; BR 11–12/98; HBG 3/98; SLJ 3/98)

8654 Turner, Ann. *Elfsong* (3–7). 1995, Harcourt $16.00 (0-15-200826-8). 208pp. Maddy and Grandpa discover a forest where elves live and they can hear birds and other animals speak. (Rev: BCCB 12/95; BL 10/1/95; SLJ 10/95)

8655 Turner, Ann. *Rosemary's Witch* (5–8). 1991, HarperCollins paper $3.95 (0-06-440494-3). Rosemary discovers that her new home is haunted by the spirit of a girl named Mathilda, who's become a witch because of her pain and anger. (Rev: BL 4/1/91; SLJ 5/91*)

8656 Turner, Megan W. *The Queen of Attolia* (5–8). 2000, Greenwillow $15.95 (0-688-17423-X). 288pp. In this sequel to *The Thief*, Gen, a slippery rogue, once more gets involved in the rivalry between two city states. (Rev: BL 4/15/00; HB 7–8/00; HBG 10/00; SLJ 5/00)

8657 Turner, Megan W. *The Thief* (5–8). 1996, Greenwillow $16.99 (0-688-14627-9). To escape life imprisonment, Gen must steal a legendary stone in this first-person fantasy set in olden days. (Rev: BCCB 11/96; BL 1/1–15/97; BR 11–12/96; HB 11–12/96; SLJ 10/96)

8658 Twain, Mark. *A Connecticut Yankee in King Arthur's Court* (5–8). Illus. by Trina S. Hyman. 1988, Morrow $23.00 (0-688-06346-2). 384pp. A smooth talker finds himself time traveling to Arthurian England. A reissued edition.

8659 Uhlberg, Myron. *Flying over Brooklyn* (3–6). Illus. 1999, Peachtree $16.95 (1-56145-194-0). 32pp. Set in Brooklyn in 1947, this dreamlike fantasy tells of a boy who dons a new coat that gives him the power to fly over the city's buildings. (Rev: BL 12/1/99; HBG 3/00; SLJ 12/99)

8660 Ure, Jean. *The Children Next Door* (4–6). 1996, Scholastic $14.95 (0-590-22293-7). 144pp. In this time-travel fantasy, Laura discovers the truth about two mysterious children who play in the garden next door. (Rev: BCCB 5/96; BL 1/1–15/96; SLJ 3/96)

8661 Van Allsburg, Chris. *The Sweetest Fig* (3–6). Illus. 1993, Houghton Mifflin $17.95 (0-395-67346-1). 32pp. All of his wildest dreams come true when a cruel dentist eats the figs given him in payment by a poor woman. (Rev: BCCB 11/93; BL 10/1/93*; SLJ 11/93*)

8662 Van Allsburg, Chris. *The Wreck of the Zephyr* (2–5). Illus. by author. 1983, Houghton Mifflin $17.95 (0-395-33075-0). 32pp. The story behind the wreck of a sailboat.

8663 Vande Velde, Vivian. *A Coming Evil* (5–9). 1998, Houghton Mifflin $17.00 (0-395-90012-3). Through encounters with the ghost of a 14th-century knight at her aunt's home in Nazi-occupied France, Lizette gains the courage to help her aunt hide several Jewish and Gypsy children. (Rev: BCCB 9/98; BL 10/1/98; HBG 3/99; SLJ 11/98)

8664 Vande Velde, Vivian. *Ghost of a Hanged Man* (3–6). 1998, Marshall Cavendish $14.95 (0-7614-5015-7). 96pp. A town falls under the deathly curse placed on it by murderous Jake Barnett before he was hanged, and now 11-year-old Ben and his sister Annabelle believe they are next to be murdered by Jake's ghost. (Rev: BCCB 10/98; BL 11/15/98; HB 11–12/98; HBG 3/99; SLJ 10/98)

8665 Vande Velde, Vivian. *Now You See It . . .* (5–8). 2005, Harcourt $17.00 (0-15-205311-5). 288pp. Wendy, 15, puts on a pair of sunglasses and a whole new fantasy world is revealed. (Rev: BL 1/1–15/05; SLJ 1/05)

8666 Vande Velde, Vivian. *Smart Dog* (4–6). 1998, Harcourt $16.00 (0-15-201847-6). 144pp. When Amy tries to help a talking dog who is fleeing from lab experiments, her life becomes a confused muddle in this humorous fantasy. (Rev: BCCB 11/98; BL 9/1/98; HB 11–12/98; HBG 3/99; SLJ 11/98)

8667 Vande Velde, Vivian. *There's a Dead Person Following My Sister Around* (4–7). 1999, Harcourt $16.00 (0-15-202100-0). 160pp. In this historical ghost story, 11-year-old Ted discovers that his house in Rochester, New York, is haunted by the ghosts of two runaway slaves who drowned in the Erie Canal. (Rev: BCCB 10/99; BL 9/1/99; HBG 3/00; SLJ 9/99)

8668 Van Leeuwen, Jean. *The Great Googlestein Museum Mystery* (3–6). Illus. by R. W. Alley. 2003, Penguin Putnam $16.99 (0-8037-2765-8). 208pp. Three mice have adventures while spending a week at the Guggenheim Museum in New York City. (Rev: BL 2/1/03; HBG 10/03; SLJ 5/03)

8669 Van Leeuwen, Jean. *The Great Rescue Operation* (3–5). Illus. by Margot Apple. 1982, Dial LB $10.89 (0-685-01456-8). 144pp. Two mice try to locate their friend who has disappeared in Macy's department store.

8670 Vansickle, Lisa. *The Secret Little City* (5–8). 2000, Palmae $15.95 (1-930167-11-3). 230pp. When 11-year-old Mackenzie moves with her family to a small town in Oregon, she discovers a whole civilization of inch-high people living beneath the floorboards of her new room. (Rev: SLJ 8/00)

8671 Vaugelade, Anais. *The War* (3–5). Trans. by Marie-Christine Rouffiac and Tom Streissguth. Illus. 2001, Carolrhoda $15.95 (1-57505-562-7). 32pp. In this picture-book allegory about the futility of war, a young idealist tricks the kings of the two warring sides into believing they have a common enemy and, therefore, must declare peace. (Rev: BL 3/15/01; HB 3–4/01; HBG 10/01)

8672 Vornholt, John. *The Troll King* (4–6). 2002, Simon & Schuster paper $4.99 (0-7434-2412-3). 240pp. A troll named Rollo escapes enslavement and finds himself embroiled in a revolution in this exciting fantasy. (Rev: BCCB 11/02; BL 8/02; SLJ 8/02)

8673 Wallace, Bill. *Snot Stew* (4–6). Illus. by Lisa McCue. 1989, Holiday House $15.95 (0-8234-0745-

4); Pocket paper $3.99 (0-671-69335-2). 96pp. The amusing tale of how Mama Cat moves her kittens out into the world. (Rev: BL 5/15/89; SLJ 4/89)

8674 Wallace, Bill. *Totally Disgusting* (4–6). Illus. by Leslie Morrill. 1991, Holiday House $15.95 (0-8234-0873-6); Pocket paper $3.99 (0-671-75416-5). 120pp. Feline Mewkiss wants to be brave and strong but isn't at all sure that he'll make it. (Rev: BCCB 6/91; BL 4/1/91; SLJ 6/91)

8675 Wallace, Carol, and Bill Wallace. *The Flying Flea, Callie, and Me* (2–5). Illus. by David Slonim. 1999, Pocket $15.00 (0-671-02505-8). 86pp. A beginning chapter book about a kitten who takes care of an abandoned baby mockingbird that has a fear of flying. (Rev: HBG 10/99; SLJ 8/99)

8676 Walsh, Jill Paton. *Pepi and the Secret Names* (3–5). Illus. by Fiona French. 1995, Lothrop $15.00 (0-688-13428-9). 32pp. In this fantasy set in ancient Egypt, Pepi gets animals to pose for her artist father by guessing their secret names. (Rev: BL 4/15/95; SLJ 4/95)

8677 Warfel, Elizabeth Stuart. *The Blue Pearls* (2–4). Illus. by Veronique Giarrusso. 2001, Barefoot $16.99 (1-902283-78-3). 32pp. In this fantasy, a group of angels are preparing a beautiful blue gown for a young mother who is about to die and be welcomed in heaven. (Rev: BL 4/15/01; HBG 10/01; SLJ 7/01)

8678 Watson, Patrick. *Ahmek* (5–6). Illus. by Tracy Thomson. 1999, Stoddart $14.95 (0-7737-3145-8). 167pp. Ahmek, a beaver, is forced to leave his beloved pond and travel north to find a new home and a mate for life. (Rev: SLJ 4/00)

8679 Waugh, Sylvia. *Earthborn* (4–6). 2002, Delacorte $15.95 (0-385-72964-2). 240pp. Nesta, 12, runs away so she won't be forced to return to the planet Ormingat with her alien parents in this companion to *Space Race* (2000), set in England. (Rev: BL 9/1/02; HB 9–10/02*; HBG 3/03; SLJ 9/02*)

8680 Waugh, Sylvia. *The Mennyms* (4–8). 1994, Greenwillow $16.00 (0-688-13070-4). 212pp. When their owner dies, a family of rag dolls comes to life and takes over her house in this beginning volume of an extensive series. (Rev: BCCB 5/94; HB 7–8/94; SLJ 4/94)

8681 Waugh, Sylvia. *Mennyms Alive* (4–6). 1997, Greenwillow $16.00 (0-688-15201-5). 224pp. The last book about the Mennyms, rag dolls who have problems finding a permanent home. (Rev: BL 9/15/97; HB 11–12/97; HBG 3/98; SLJ 9/97)

8682 Waugh, Sylvia. *Who Goes Home?* (4–7). 2004, Delacorte $15.95 (0-385-72965-0). 224pp. On his 13th birthday Jacob receives the sobering news that his father is an alien from the planet Ormingat, and so is Jacob. (Rev: BL 4/15/04; HB 3–4/04; SLJ 6/04)

8683 Waxman, Sydell, reteller. *The Rooster Prince* (2–5). Illus. by Giora Carmi. 2000, Pitspopany $16.95 (0-943706-45-9); paper $9.95 (0-943706-49-1). 40pp. In 18th-century Russia, a village boy is given the task of curing a prince who is behaving like rooster. (Rev: SLJ 1/01)

8684 Weinberg, Karen. *Window of Time* (5–7). Illus. by Annelle W. Ratcliffe. 1991, White Mane paper $9.95 (0-942597-18-4). 166pp. Ben climbs through a window and finds himself 125 years back in time. (Rev: SLJ 7/91)

8685 Welch, R. C. *Scary Stories for Stormy Nights* (5–7). Illus. 1995, Lowell House paper $5.95 (1-56565-262-2). 128pp. Ten contemporary horror stories that involve such characters as a werewolf and some pirates. (Rev: BL 5/1/95)

8686 Wells, Rosemary. *Rachel Field's Hitty: Her First Hundred Years* (4–6). Illus. by Susan Jeffers. 1999, Simon & Schuster $21.95 (0-689-81716-9). Part abridgement, part extension of specific incidents with new material, this is an interesting and original look at Field's classic, now issued with bright illustrations. (Rev: BL 11/15/99; HBG 3/00; SLJ 1/00)

8687 Wesley, Mary. *Haphazard House* (5–7). 1993, Overlook $14.95 (0-87951-470-1). 150pp. An artist's magic hat enables him to make money betting on the Derby race during a visit to England. (Rev: BCCB 10/93; BL 1/1/94)

8688 West, Tracey. *Abracadanger* (4–6). Illus. by Brian W. Dow. Series: Scream Shop. 2003, Grosset paper $4.99 (0-448-43224-2). 138pp. In the first installment of a series that allows readers to make choices of plot, a 12-year-old boy named Ben buys a magic set that belonged to a magician who vanished. The second in the series is *Now You See Me, Now You Don't!* (2004). (Rev: SLJ 6/04)

8689 West, Tracey. *Voyage of the Half Moon* (3–5). Illus. Series: Stories of the States. 1993, Silver Moon LB $14.95 (1-881889-18-1). 55pp. When Gwen is sent to live with a new foster family, she is haunted by a ghost that no one else can see. (Rev: SLJ 9/93)

8690 Westall, Robert. *Ghost Abbey* (5–9). 1990, Scholastic paper $3.25 (0-590-41693-6). Maggi realizes that the abbey her father is restoring seems to have a life of its own. (Rev: BCCB 2/89; BL 2/1/89; SLJ 3/89)

8691 Westwood, Chris. *He Came from the Shadows* (5–8). 1991, HarperCollins LB $14.89 (0-06-021659-X). In a cautionary tale about the dangers of wishing for too much, odd things start to happen after a stranger comes to town. (Rev: BL 4/1/91; SLJ 6/91)

8692 Wheeler, Lisa. *Fitch and Chip: New Pig in Town* (2–3). Illus. by Frank Ansley. Series: Ready-to-Read. 2003, Simon & Schuster $14.95 (0-689-84950-8). 48pp. Chip the pig and Fitch the wolf become great buddies in a story that shows the values of diversity and friendship. (Rev: BL 7/03; HBG 4/04)

8693 Whelan, Gerard. *Dream Invader* (5–7). 2002, O'Brien paper $7.95 (0-86278-516-2). 176pp. Only Simon's grandmother can break the spell behind the bad dreams he's been having in this supernatural tale set in Ireland. (Rev: BL 9/1/02)

8694 White, E. B. *Charlotte's Web* (3–5). Illus. by Garth Williams. 1952, HarperCollins LB $16.89 (0-06-026386-5); paper $5.95 (0-06-440055-7). 184pp.

Classic, whimiscal barnyard fable about a spider who saves the life of Wilbur the pig. Read about the ever-engaging mouse in: *Stuart Little* (1945).

8695 White, E. B. *The Trumpet of the Swan* (3–6). Illus. by Edward Frascino. 1970, HarperCollins LB $16.89 (0-06-026398-9); paper $5.95 (0-06-440048-4). 222pp. Louis, a voiceless trumpeter swan, is befriended by Sam, learns to play a trumpet, and finds fame, fortune, and fatherhood.

8696 Whybrow, Ian. *Little Wolf's Diary of Daring Deeds* (2–4). Illus. by Tony Ross. 2000, Carolrhoda LB $12.95 (1-57505-411-6). 127pp. A beginning chapter book told in hilarious letters by Little Wolf, who is trying to found a school called Adventure Academy with his cousin Yeller. (Rev: HBG 10/00; SLJ 6/00)

8697 Whybrow, Ian. *Little Wolf's Haunted Hall for Small Horrors* (2–4). Illus. by Tony Ross. 2000, Carolrhoda $12.95 (1-57505-412-4). 128pp. Little Wolf, his friend Yeller, and younger brother Smellybreff encounter the ghost of Little Wolf's uncle Bigbad Wolf in this amusing animal fantasy told through letters. (Rev: HBG 3/01; SLJ 9/00)

8698 Wiesner, David, and Kim Kahng. *The Loathsome Dragon* (PS–2). Illus. by David Wiesner. 2005, Clarion $16.00 (0-618-54359-7). 32pp. A revised edition of the fairy tale about a beautiful princess who is turned into a dragon by her jealous stepmother, the queen, and must await the return of her wandering brother to free her from the evil spell. (Rev: BL 2/15/05; SLJ 4/05) [398.2]

8699 Willard, Nancy. *The High Rise Glorious Skittle Skat Roarious Sky Pie Angel Food Cake* (3–5). Illus. by Richard J. Watson. 1990, Harcourt $15.95 (0-15-234332-6). 64pp. Grandma's cake has mysterious ingredients — an odd spell and the special help of angels. (Rev: BCCB 12/90; BL 9/1/90; SLJ 11/90*)

8700 Williams, Maiya. *The Golden Hour* (4–8). 2004, Abrams $16.95 (0-8109-4823-0). 272pp. Thirteen-year-old Rowan and his 11-year-old sister Nina are sent to live with two great-aunts after the death of their mother and find themselves — with their new friends Xanthe and Xavier — transported through a time portal to 1789 Paris. (Rev: BL 3/15/04; SLJ 4/04)

8701 Williams, Margery. *The Velveteen Rabbit: Or, How Toys Become Real* (2–4). Illus. by Michael Hague. 1983, Holt $16.95 (0-8050-0209-X). 48pp. Love brings a toy rabbit to life. One of many fine editions.

8702 Winter, Laurel. *Growing Wings* (4–6). 2000, Houghton Mifflin $15.00 (0-618-07405-8). 224pp. When 11-year-old Linnet begins to grow wings, her mother abandons her and she is taken in by a colony of winged people. (Rev: BL 10/15/00; HBG 3/01; SLJ 10/00)

8703 Winthrop, Elizabeth. *The Battle for the Castle* (4–7). 1993, Holiday House $15.95 (0-8234-1010-2). 216pp. William and friend Jason time-travel to the Middle Ages, where they become involved in a struggle to prevent the return of evil as a ruling power. A sequel to *The Castle in the Attic* (1985). (Rev: BL 9/1/93; HB 7–8/93; SLJ 5/93)

8704 Winthrop, Elizabeth. *The Castle in the Attic* (5–7). 1985, Holiday House $16.95 (0-8234-0579-6). 192pp. In an effort to keep his sitter from returning to England, William miniaturizes her and then must find a way to undo the deed. (Rev: BCCB 10/85; BL 1/15/86; SLJ 2/86)

8705 Winthrop, Elizabeth. *The Red-Hot Rattoons* (4–6). Illus. by Betsy Lewin. 2003, Holt $16.95 (0-8050-7229-2). 212pp. Five orphaned rat siblings head for the big city in hopes of achieving fame and fortune on the strength of their dancing abilities. (Rev: HBG 4/04; SLJ 10/03)

8706 Wood, Beverly, and Chris Wood. *Dog Star* (5–8). 1998, Orca paper $6.95 (0-896095-37-2). On a cruise to Alaska with his family, 13-year-old Jeff Beacon encounters a magical pet bull terrier who transports him back in time to the Juneau of 1932. (Rev: BR 1–2/99)

8707 Wood, David. *The Phantom Cat of the Opera* (2–5). Illus. by Peters Day. 2001, Watson-Guptill $16.95 (0-8230-4018-6). The classic story is retold with cats as characters, with sumptuous illustrations. (Rev: HBG 10/01; SLJ 11/01)

8708 Woodruff, Elvira. *Awfully Short for the Fourth Grade* (3–6). Illus. by Will Hillenbrand. 1989, Holiday House $15.95 (0-8234-0785-3). 112pp. Noah's toy soldiers and superheroes come to life and he becomes their size when he uses a special dust from his magic kit. (Rev: BL 1/1/90; SLJ 11/89)

8709 Woodruff, Elvira. *Orphan of Ellis Island* (4–7). 1997, Scholastic paper $15.95 (0-590-48245-9). 192pp. Left alone on Ellis Island, Dominic finds himself transported in time to the village in Italy his family came from. (Rev: BCCB 3/97; BL 6/1–15/97; SLJ 5/97)

8710 Woolfe, Angela. *Avril Crump and Her Amazing Clones* (4–6). 2005, Scholastic $9.90 (0-439-65130-1). 224pp. A zany story of a scientist who accidentally creates three "clones" (one of them a talking dog) and who must escape from the evil Dr. Blut; the first installment of a trilogy. (Rev: BL 3/1/05; SLJ 4/05)

8711 Wrede, Patricia. *Dealing with Dragons* (5–8). Series: Enchanted Forest Chronicles. 1990, Harcourt $17.00 (0-15-222900-0). Princess Cimorene is bored and decides to abandon her life of privilege to be servant and companion to a cranky dragon named Kazul in this first volume of a quartet. (Rev: BL 4/15/04)

8712 Wright, Betty R. *Christina's Ghost* (4–6). 1985, Holiday House $15.95 (0-8234-0581-8). 128pp. Dismayed at having to spend the summer with grumpy Uncle Ralph in his Victorian mansion, Christina is even more dismayed to discover a ghost in the house. (Rev: BCCB 2/86; BL 2/1/86)

8713 Wright, Betty R. *Crandalls' Castle* (4–7). 2003, Holiday House $16.95 (0-8234-1726-3). 192pp. This gripping suspense story combines supernatural elements with a look at teen girls' yearning to belong. (Rev: BL 4/1/03; HBG 10/03; SLJ 5/03)

8714 Wright, Betty R. *The Ghost in Room 11* (2–4). 1997, Holiday House $15.95 (0-8234-1318-7).

112pp. Matt can't convince his classmates that he is being visited by the ghost of an old school teacher. (Rev: BCCB 4/98; BL 3/1/98; HBG 10/98; SLJ 3/98)

8715 Wright, Betty R. *A Ghost in the House* (5–7). 1991, Scholastic paper $13.95 (0-590-43606-6). 160pp. Bizarre happenings take place when Sarah's elderly aunt moves in. (Rev: BCCB 11/91; BL 1/1/91; SLJ 11/91)

8716 Wright, Betty R. *The Ghost of Popcorn Hill* (2–4). Illus. by Karen Ritz. 1993, Holiday House $15.95 (0-8234-1009-9). 96pp. Martin and Peter are frightened by the ghost who visits their bedroom each night in their rustic home on Popcorn Hill. (Rev: BCCB 6/93; BL 2/15/93; HB 7–8/93; SLJ 5/93)

8717 Wright, Betty R. *Haunted Summer* (4–6). 1996, Scholastic $14.95 (0-590-47355-7). 128pp. Abby discovers that a wicked witch wants possession of a music box that Abby's aunt has sent as a gift. (Rev: BCCB 4/96; BL 4/1/96; HB 7–8/96; SLJ 5/96)

8718 Wright, Betty R. *The Moonlight Man* (4–6). 2000, Scholastic $15.95 (0-590-25237-2). 176pp. Jenny Joslin, 15, has moved to a new house with her father and younger sister, which they discover is haunted by a vindictive ghost. (Rev: BL 2/15/00; HBG 10/00; SLJ 2/00)

8719 Wright, Betty R. *Out of the Dark* (4–6). 1995, Scholastic $14.95 (0-590-43598-1). 128pp. Jessica's stay in her grandmother's home in the country becomes unexpectedly horrifying when she encounters a ghost. (Rev: BCCB 2/95; BL 12/1/94; SLJ 1/95)

8720 Wynne-Jones, Tim. *Some of the Kinder Planets* (5–8). 1995, Orchard LB $16.99 (0-531-08751-4). Nine imaginative stories about ordinary boys and girls in offbeat situations. (Rev: BCCB 5/95; BL 3/1/95*; HB 1–2/95, 5–6/95, 9–10/95; SLJ 4/95*)

8721 Yee, Paul. *Ghost Train* (3–5). Illus. by Harvey Chan. 1996, Douglas & McIntyre $15.95 (0-88899-257-2). 32pp. In this historical fantasy, a Chinese girl comes to the United States and discovers that her father has been killed while working as a railroad construction laborer. (Rev: BCCB 2/97; BL 11/1/96)

8722 Yep, Laurence. *Dragon of the Lost Sea* (5–8). 1982, HarperCollins paper $5.99 (0-06-440227-4). 224pp. Shimmer, a dragon, in the company of a boy, Thorn, sets out to destroy the villain Civet. (Rev: BL 4/15/04)

8723 Yep, Laurence. *The Tiger's Apprentice* (5–7). 2003, HarperCollins LB $16.89 (0-06-001014-2). 192pp. A scary, magical world envelops Tom Lee when his grandmother dies in this novel set in San Francisco that includes elements of Chinese legend and tradition. (Rev: BL 7/03; HBG 10/03; SLJ 4/03)

8724 Yep, Laurence. *Tiger's Blood* (4–7). Series: Tiger's Apprentice. 2005, HarperCollins LB $16.89 (0-06-001017-7). 240pp. Tom Lee, the Chinese American boy introduced in *The Tiger's Apprentice*, enlists the aid of three friends to keep the precious phoenix egg from falling into the hands of evildoers. (Rev: BL 1/1–15/05; SLJ 2/05)

8725 Yolen, Jane. *The Bagpiper's Ghost* (3–5). Series: Tartan Magic. 2002, Harcourt $16.00 (0-15-202310-0). 144pp. Twins Jennifer and Peter find adventure and mystery in a graveyard haunted by the ghost of a young woman. (Rev: BL 4/15/02; HBG 10/02; SLJ 3/02)

8726 Yolen, Jane. *Boots and the Seven Leaguers: A Rock-and-Troll Novel* (5–9). 2000, Harcourt $17.00 (0-15-202557-X). 192pp. In this lighthearted fantasy with a contemporary twist, adolescent troll Gog and his sidekick set out on a quest to rescue Gog's kidnapped little brother, Magog. (Rev: BL 11/1/00; HBG 3/01; SLJ 10/00)

8727 Yolen, Jane. *Here There Be Dragons* (3–8). Illus. by David Wilgus. Series: Jane Yolen Books. 1993, Harcourt $16.95 (0-15-209888-7); paper $10.00 (0-15-201705-4). 160pp. This original collection of pieces about dragons contains eight stories and five poems. (Rev: SLJ 12/93)

8728 Yolen, Jane. *Hobby: The Young Merlin Trilogy Book Two* (5–8). Illus. Series: Young Merlin Trilogy. 1996, Harcourt $16.00 (0-15-200815-2). The story of Merlin's youth, when he sets out alone into the medieval world, is held captive by a villain named Fowler, and eventually joins a traveling magic show, where he is known as Hobby and where the performers take advantage of his ability to look into the future. Book one is *The Passager* (1996). (Rev: BL 1/1–15/97; SLJ 9/96)

8729 Yolen, Jane. *Merlin* (5–8). Series: Young Merlin Trilogy. 1997, Harcourt $16.00 (0-15-200814-4); Scholastic paper $3.50 (0-590-37119-3). In this concluding volume of a trilogy, Hawk-Hobby (Merlin) escapes from his enemies with a young friend who will later become King Arthur. (Rev: BL 4/15/97; SLJ 5/97)

8730 Yolen, Jane. *Passager: The Young Merlin Trilogy, Book One* (4–7). 1996, Harcourt $16.00 (0-15-200391-6). 96pp. In medieval England, an abandoned 8-year-old boy named Merlin is taken in by a friendly man who becomes his master. Book two of the trilogy is *Hobby* (1996). (Rev: BL 5/1/96; HB 7–8/96; SLJ 5/96*)

8731 Yolen, Jane. *The Pictish Child* (3–6). Series: Tartan Magic. 1999, Harcourt $15.00 (0-15-202261-9). 144pp. Molly receives a talisman that begins a series of events involving Jennifer, a young Pict girl, who has time-traveled to modern times from ninth-century Britain. (Rev: BL 11/15/99; HBG 3/00; SLJ 12/99)

8732 Yolen, Jane. *Wizard's Hall* (4–6). 1991, Harcourt $13.95 (0-15-298132-2). 144pp. Henry, an 11-year-old novice wizard, can't seem to get anything right. (Rev: BCCB 7–8/91; BL 3/15/91; SLJ 7/91)

8733 Yolen, Jane. *The Wizard's Map* (3–6). Series: Tartan Magic. 1999, Harcourt $15.00 (0-15-202067-5). 144pp. Thirteen-year-old twins, Jennifer and Peter, and younger sister Molly are in Scotland visiting relatives when they encounter an evil sorcerer. (Rev: BL 5/15/99; HBG 10/99; SLJ 5/99)

8734 Yoshi. *The Butterfly Hunt* (5–8). Illus. 1991, Picture Book paper $14.95 (0-88708-137-1). In this fantasy, a young boy releases a butterfly and forevermore it becomes his own. (Rev: SLJ 6/91)

8735 Youmans, Marly. *The Curse of the Raven Mocker* (5–8). 2003, Farrar $18.00 (0-374-31667-8). 288pp. In pursuit of her parents, Adanta heads into the mountains of the Blue Ridge and finds a land of magic and sorcery in this novel based on Cherokee legend and local lore. (Rev: BL 9/1/03; HBG 4/04; SLJ 12/03)

8736 Zadrzynska, Ewa. *The Peaceable Kingdom* (4–6). Illus. by Tomek Olbinski. 1994, M.M. Art Bks. $14.95 (0-9638904-0-9). 32pp. In this fantasy, visitors to Brooklyn find that the three animals pictured in Hicks's painting "The Peaceable Kingdom," hanging in the Brooklyn Museum, are sitting in the park. (Rev: BL 7/94; SLJ 9/94)

Friendship Stories

8737 Appelbaum, Diana. *Cocoa Ice* (2–5). Illus. by Holly Meade. 1997, Orchard LB $17.99 (0-531-33040-0). 56pp. Two girls, one in Santo Domingo and the other in Maine, are linked by world trade, which brings chocolate to one and ice to the other. (Rev: BCCB 3/98; BL 11/1/97*; HBG 3/98; SLJ 1/98*)

8738 Bedard, Michael. *Emily* (3–5). Illus. by Barbara Cooney. 1992, Doubleday $16.95 (0-385-30697-0). A young girl visits her neighbor, the reclusive Emily Dickinson. (Rev: BCCB 1/93; BL 2/1/93; HB 1–2/93; SLJ 11/92)

8739 Bellingham, Brenda. *Lilly's Good Deed* (3–4). Illus. by Kathy Kaulbach. Series: First Novels. 1999, Formac paper $3.99 (0-88780-460-8). 64pp. A beginning chapter book from Canada in which Lilly discovers that first impressions can be wrong when she realizes the value of the friendship of a clumsy classmate. (Rev: SLJ 8/99)

8740 Bonners, Susan. *The Silver Balloon* (3–5). Illus. 1997, Farrar $14.00 (0-374-36913-5). 80pp. Two pen pals reveal facts about each other through a series of mystery gifts they exchange. (Rev: BL 9/15/97; SLJ 10/97)

8741 Bunting, Eve. *Summer Wheels* (3–5). Illus. by Thomas B. Allen. 1992, Harcourt $14.95 (0-15-207000-1). 48pp. Lawrence and Brady are annoyed by the new kid, who signs out a bike from the Bicycle Man with the clear intention of not returning it. (Rev: BCCB 3/92; BL 4/15/92; HB 7–8/92; SLJ 8/92)

8742 Burnett, Frances Hodgson. *The Secret Garden* (4–6). Illus. by Tasha Tudor. 1987, HarperCollins paper $4.95 (0-06-440188-X). 256pp. Three children find a secret garden and make it bloom again; the garden, in turn, changes the children. One of many fine editions.

8743 Burnett, Frances Hodgson. *The Secret Garden* (5–8). 1999, Scholastic paper $3.99 (0-439-09939-0). An easily read classic about a spoiled girl relocated to England and the unusual friendship she finds there.

8744 Buscaglia, Leo. *A Memory for Tino* (4–6). Illus. by Carol Newsom. 1988, Slack $12.95 (1-556-42020-X). 50pp. Tino becomes friends with elderly Mrs. Sunday, and gives her his family's TV set. (Rev: BL 4/1/88; SLJ 5/88)

8745 Butler, Dori Hillestad. *Trading Places with Tank Talbott* (4–6). 2003, Whitman LB $14.95 (0-8075-1708-9). 139pp. Tank and Jason — who have similar looks but dissimilar interests — become unlikely friends when they decide to switch unwanted assignments; Jason takes Tank's dancing lessons and Tank takes Jason's swimming lessons. (Rev: HBG 4/04; SLJ 6/03)

8746 Carlson, Natalie Savage. *The Family Under the Bridge* (3–5). Illus. by Garth Williams. 1958, HarperCollins LB $15.89 (0-06-020991-7); paper $5.95 (0-06-440250-9). 112pp. Old Armand, a Paris hobo, finds three children huddled in his hideaway under the bridge and befriends them.

8747 Choyce, Lesley. *Carrie's Crowd* (3–4). Illus. by Mark Thurman. Series: First Novels. 1999, Formac paper $3.99 (0-88780-464-0). 64pp. A beginning chapter book in which Carrie realizes that making a friend of Giselle, a member of the "in" crowd, was a mistake because Giselle is rude and lacks respect for others. (Rev: SLJ 8/99)

8748 Cooper, Susan. *Dawn of Fear* (5–6). Illus. by Margery Gill. 1989, Simon & Schuster paper $4.99 (0-689-71327-4). 157pp. Reality must be faced by a group of English boys when one of their friends is killed in an air raid during World War II.

8749 Cosby, Bill. *The Best Way to Play* (2–4). Illus. 1997, Scholastic $13.95 (0-590-13756-5); paper $3.99 (0-590-95617-5). 40pp. Little Bill wants a $50 video game but finds that he can have more fun making up a game with his friends. Also use *The Meanest Thing To Say* and *The Treasure Hunt* (both 1997). (Rev: BL 2/15/98; HBG 3/98; SLJ 12/97)

8750 Cox, Judy. *Butterfly Buddies* (2–4). Illus. by Blanche Sims. 2001, Holiday House $15.95 (0-8234-1654-2). 80pp. Third-grader Robin learns about being herself — and about butterflies — from a new friend and a new teacher. (Rev: BCCB 1/02; BL 9/1/01; HBG 3/02; SLJ 10/01)

8751 Cox, Judy. *That Crazy Eddie and the Science Project of Doom* (2–4). Illus. by Blanche Sims. 2005, Holiday House $15.95 (0-8234-1931-2). 88pp. Matt and Eddie's friendship is severely strained, threatening the success of their volcano science fair project. (Rev: BL 6/1–15/05)

8752 Danziger, Paula, and Ann M. Martin. *P.S. Longer Letter Later* (5–7). 1998, Scholastic $15.95 (0-590-21310-5). 240pp. This epistolary novel consists of letters between two recently separated girlfriends — one who is adjusting well and the other who is facing family problems after her father loses his job and the family must change their lifestyle. (Rev: BL 6/1–15/98; HBG 10/98; SLJ 5/98)

8753 Dower, Laura. *Only the Lonely: From the Files of Madison Finn* (4–6). Illus. 2001, Hyperion paper $4.99 (0-7868-1553-1). 144pp. Madison Finn spends an unexpectedly lonely summer before entering seventh grade and confides her concerns to her laptop computer. (Rev: BL 6/1–15/01; SLJ 8/01)

8754 Dutton, Sandra. *Capp Street Carnival* (4–6). 2003, Farrar $16.00 (0-374-31065-3). 144pp. Eleven-year-old Mary Mae, a bluegrass fan, organizes a neighborhood carnival featuring country music to raise money for a boy with a heart problem. (Rev: BL 3/15/03; HBG 10/03; SLJ 3/03)

8755 Farrell, Mame. *And Sometimes Why* (5–8). 2001, Farrar $16.00 (0-374-32289-9). 165pp. Thirteen-year-old Jack develops romantic feelings for long-time friend Chris, but his efforts to get together with her are stymied by misunderstandings and interference by others. (Rev: BCCB 4/01; BL 5/1/01; HB 5–6/01; HBG 10/01; SLJ 7/01)

8756 Freeman, Martha. *The Trouble with Babies* (2–4). Illus. by Cat B. Smith. 2002, Holiday House $15.95 (0-8234-1698-4). 80pp. Holly must learn to adapt — to her new life in San Francisco with her mother and stepfather, to her new friends, and to the fact that she is going to have a new sibling. (Rev: BCCB 11/02; BL 7/02; HBG 3/03; SLJ 8/02)

8757 Friedman, Laurie. *Mallory on the Move* (2–4). Illus. by Tamara Schmitz. 2004, Carolrhoda $15.95 (1-57505-538-4). 160pp. Mallory, 8, is nervous when her best friend Mary Ann comes to visit her new home and will no doubt meet Mallory's new friend Joey; told in the first person, this book will appeal to new chapter-book readers. (Rev: BL 4/15/04; SLJ 4/04)

8758 Gabhart, Ann. *Two of a Kind* (3–6). 1992, Avon paper $3.50 (0-380-76153-X). 170pp. Birdie decides it's better to be aloof, even with her likable aunt and uncle, so she won't feel so bad when she's sent to another foster home. (Rev: BL 8/92)

8759 Gilbert, Sheri. *The Legacy of Gloria Russell* (4–7). 2004, Knopf LB $17.99 (0-375-92823-5). 224pp. After his friend Gloria dies, Billy James, 12, ignores adult warnings and approaches the hermit called Satan. (Rev: BL 5/1/04; SLJ 4/04)

8760 Gonzalez, Rigoberto. *Soledad Sigh-Sighs / Soledad Suspiros* (1–3). Trans. by Jorge Argueta. Illus. by Rosa Ibarra. 2003, Children's Book Pr. $16.95 (0-89239-180-4). 32pp. Latchkey child Soledad lives a lonely life with an imaginary companion until two neighboring sisters befriend her and even envy her solitude, in this bilingual novel set in Brooklyn. (Rev: BL 5/15/03; HBG 10/03; SLJ 3/03)

8761 Greene, Bette. *I've Already Forgotten Your Name, Philip Hall!* (4–7). Illus. by Leonard Jenkins. 2004, HarperCollins $15.99 (0-06-051835-9). 176pp. A little white lie that strains her relationship with her best friend, Philip Hall, is only one of the dramas Beth Lambert must deal with in this story set in small-town Arkansas. (Rev: BL 5/1/04; HB 3–4/04; SLJ 3/04)

8762 Greene, Carol. *The Jenny Summer* (2–4). Illus. by Ellen Eagle. 1988, HarperCollins $11.95 (0-06-022208-5). 80pp. Robin learns a lot about friendship during one summer. (Rev: BL 6/15/88; SLJ 8/88)

8763 Hahn, Mary D. *Daphne's Book* (6–8). 1983, Houghton Mifflin $15.00 (0-89919-183-5); Avon

paper $4.50 (0-380-72355-7). 192pp. The story of a friendship between two very different girls. (Rev: BL 10/15/04)

8764 Hansen, Joyce. *Yellow Bird and Me* (4–6). 1986, Houghton Mifflin paper $6.95 (0-395-55388-1). 128pp. The continuing story of the growing up of Doris, an African American girl in the Bronx, New York, and her friendship with Yellow Bird, who suffers from dyslexia. (Rev: BCCB 4/86; BL 4/1/86; SLJ 5/86)

8765 Herman, Charlotte. *Max Malone Makes a Million* (3–5). Illus. 1991, Holt paper $6.95 (0-8050-2328-3). 77pp. Max wants to make a fortune, but learns a lesson in generosity instead. Also use: *Max Malone and the Great Cereal Rip-Off* (1990). (Rev: BCCB 6/91; BL 3/1/91; SLJ 6/91)

8766 Hoffman, Mary. *Starring Grace* (2–4). Illus. by Caroline Binch. 2000, Penguin Putnam $13.99 (0-8037-2559-0). 96pp. A lively chapter book about young Grace and her many summer adventures with friends, culminating in walk-on roles in a theatrical production. (Rev: BCCB 9/00; BL 2/15/00; HB 3–4/00; HBG 10/00; SLJ 7/00)

8767 Hossack, Sylvie A. *The Flying Chickens of Paradise Lane* (3–6). 1994, Avon paper $3.50 (0-380-72201-1). 144pp. Ten-year-old Brenda, who desperately wants to learn to fly, forms a secret club with friends and practices jumping from ever-increasing heights. (Rev: BL 3/1/93; SLJ 3/93)

8768 Hurwitz, Johanna. *The Cold and Hot Winter* (4–6). Illus. by Carolyn Ewing. 1988, Morrow $14.95 (0-688-07839-7). 144pp. The relationship of three children is strained because one may be a thief. (Rev: BCCB 11/88; BL 10/15/88; SLJ 9/88)

8769 Hurwitz, Johanna. *Spring Break* (3–5). Illus. 1997, Morrow $15.00 (0-688-14937-5). 144pp. An appealing novel about Cricket and her adventures when she is unable to go with her class to Washington, D.C., during spring break because of a broken ankle. (Rev: BCCB 4/97; BL 4/15/97; SLJ 5/97)

8770 Jacobson, Jennifer. *Truly Winnie* (2–4). Illus. by Alissa Imre Geis. 2003, Houghton Mifflin $15.00 (0-618-28008-1). 112pp. One lie leads to another as Winnie tries to hide the truth about her mother from her friends at camp in this sequel to *Winnie Dancing on Her Own* (2001). (Rev: BL 9/1/03; HBG 4/04; SLJ 11/03)

8771 Kaye, Marilyn. *Cabin Six Plays Cupid* (4–6). 1989, Avon paper $2.95 (0-380-75701-X). 116pp. Five friends in Cabin 6 at Camp Sunnyside try to help their counselor's love life. Also use: *No Boys Allowed* (1989). (Rev: BL 7/89; SLJ 9/89)

8772 Kaye, Marilyn. *A Friend Like Phoebe* (4–6). 1989, Harcourt $13.95 (0-15-200450-5). 144pp. Phoebe's best friend is chosen for an honor that Phoebe wanted, which causes a crisis in their friendship. A sequel to *Phoebe* (1987). (Rev: BL 8/89; SLJ 11/89)

8773 Kinsey-Warnock, Natalie. *Lumber Camp Library* (3–6). Illus. by James Bernardin. 2002, HarperCollins LB $14.89 (0-06-029322-5). 96pp. Young Ruby Sawyer is devastated when her father dies, but finds comfort in a friendship with a blind woman who has a house full of books. (Rev: BL 4/15/02; HBG 10/02; SLJ 5/02)

8774 Kline, Suzy. *Herbie Jones Moves On* (3–5). 2003, Penguin Putnam $14.99 (0-399-23635-X). 78pp. Herbie Jones, the title character from eight previous children's books, is back, and this time he's lamenting the imminent departure of his best friend, Raymond. (Rev: HBG 10/03; SLJ 6/03)

8775 Koller, Jackie F. *Impy for Always* (2–4). Illus. by Carol Newsom. 1989, Little, Brown $9.95 (0-316-50147-6); paper $3.95 (0-316-50149-2). 64pp. Eight-year-old Imogene's thoughts of another fun summer are dashed when 12-year-old cousin Christina arrives all grown up. (Rev: BL 6/15/59)

8776 Kornblatt, Marc. *Understanding Buddy* (3–5). 2001, Simon & Schuster $16.00 (0-689-83215-X). 115pp. A novel about friendship that involves two fifth-grade boys: Sam, a sensitive Jewish boy, and Buddy who, except for playing soccer, has retreated into isolation after his mother's death. (Rev: BCCB 3/01; BL 2/1/01; HB 3–4/01; HBG 10/01)

8777 Kvasnosky, Laura McGee. *One Lucky Summer* (3–6). 2002, Dutton $15.99 (0-525-46455-7). 112pp. Ten-year-old Steven, just recently moved to Sacramento, discovers that he and the girl next door have more in common than they thought when they rescue a baby squirrel. (Rev: BCCB 5/02; BL 3/1/02; HBG 10/02; SLJ 4/02)

8778 Lamb, Nancy. *The Great Mosquito, Bull, and Coffin Caper* (3–5). Illus. by Frank Remkiewicz. 1994, Morrow paper $4.95 (0-688-12944-7). 120pp. To make sure they will not forget each other when one moves away, two friends face three dares, each tougher than the last. (Rev: BL 10/15/92; SLJ 11/92)

8779 Lewis, Beverly. *Holly's First Love* (4–6). Series: Holly's Heart. 1993, Zondervan paper $6.99 (0-310-38051-0). 160pp. Holly and Andie's friendship is strained when they both find they are attracted to the new boy in town. Also use *Secret Summer Dreams* (1993). (Rev: SLJ 12/93)

8780 McGhee, Alison. *Snap* (4–6). 2004, Candlewick $15.99 (0-7636-2002-5). 132pp. Edwina Beckey, 11, who uses rubber bands to remember things, worries about her friend Sally, whose grandmother is dying. (Rev: BL 5/15/04; SLJ 4/04)

8781 Maguire, Gregory. *Six Haunted Hairdos* (4–6). Illus. 1997, Clarion $15.00 (0-395-78626-6). 148pp. A funny story about two rival school groups, the boys' Copycats and the girls' Tattletales, and how they amuse themselves by telling ghost stories. The sequel to *Seven Spiders Spinning* (1994). (Rev: BL 11/1/97; HBG 3/98; SLJ 9/97)

8782 Makris, Kathryn. *The Five Cat Club* (4–6). Series: Eco-Kids. 1994, Avon paper $3.50 (0-380-77049-0). 156pp. Three junior high girls find homes for five abandoned kittens and become interested in animal rights and environmental issues. Also use *The Green Team* and *The Clean-up Crew* (both 1994). (Rev: SLJ 9/94)

8783 Marsden, Carolyn. *Moon Runner* (3–5). 2005, Candlewick $15.99 (0-7636-2117-X). 112pp. Mina's new friendship with Ruth is tested when

Mina loses a race in a misguided attempt to let Ruth remain "the athletic one" in their group. (Rev: BL 3/1/05; SLJ 6/05)

8784 Matlin, Marlee. *Deaf Child Crossing* (4–6). 2002, Simon & Schuster $15.95 (0-689-82208-1). 208pp. Two 9-year-olds, one deaf and one hearing, become firm friends but face the usual — and some additional — childhood tensions and jealousies. (Rev: BCCB 11/02; BL 11/15/02; HBG 3/03; SLJ 12/02)

8785 Mazer, Norma Fox. *Mrs. Fish, Ape and Me, the Dump Queen* (5–7). 1981, Avon paper $3.50 (0-380-69153-1). 144pp. Three misfits band together in friendship.

8786 Medearis, Angela Shelf. *The Adventures of Sugar and Junior* (2–3). Illus. by Nancy Poydar. 1995, Holiday House LB $15.95 (0-8234-1182-6). 32pp. A simple story of a friendship between a Hispanic American and an African American youngster and their happy times together. (Rev: BL 10/15/95; SLJ 12/95)

8787 Moss, Marissa. *The All-New Amelia* (3–5). Illus. 1999, Pleasant Co. $12.95 (1-56247-784-0); paper $5.95 (1-56247-822-2). 32pp. Using diary entries and letters to tell the story, this novel's central character, Amelia, falls under the spell of a new girl in class and tries for a time to copy her in every way. (Rev: BL 11/1/99; HBG 3/00; SLJ 10/99)

8788 Moss, Marissa. *Luv, Amelia Luv, Nadia* (3–5). Illus. Series: Amelia. 1999, Pleasant Co. $14.95 (1-56247-839-7); paper $7.95 (1-56247-823-0). 32pp. Two girls exchange letters about their families and mutual problems. Some of the letters are pull-outs inside envelopes. (Rev: BL 11/1/99; HBG 3/00; SLJ 10/99)

8789 Myers, Christopher. *Fly!* (K–4). Illus. by author. 2001, Hyperion $15.99 (0-7868-0652-4). A lonely boy makes friends with a man who teaches him about the sparrows and pigeons they see from the roof of his building. (Rev: BCCB 1/02; HB 3–4/02; HBG 10/02; SLJ 12/01)

8790 Myers, Laurie. *Surviving Brick Johnson* (3–5). Illus. 2000, Clarion $15.00 (0-395-98031-3). 80pp. Fifth-grader Alex believes that newcomer Brick is a big bully, but when they both sign up for karate classes, he finds that he is wrong. (Rev: BCCB 11/00; BL 9/15/00; HBG 3/01; SLJ 10/00)

8791 Nagda, Ann Whitehead. *Dear Whiskers* (2–4). Illus. 2000, Holiday House $15.95 (0-8234-1495-7). 64pp. For a school assignment, Jenny writes to a younger Saudi Arabian girl in her school and gradually forms a friendship with this reclusive girl who knows little English. (Rev: BCCB 2/01; BL 11/15/00; HB 3–4/01; HBG 10/01; SLJ 1/01)

8792 Nicholson, Peggy, and John F. Warner. *The Case of the Furtive Firebug* (3–5). 1994, Lerner LB $14.95 (0-8225-0709-9). 120pp. Halley and her little brother Jason try to help a Vietnamese American girl who is falsely accused of arson. (Rev: BL 3/1/95)

8793 Nielsen-Fernlund, Susin. *Hank and Fergus* (PS–2). 2003, Orca $19.95 (1-55143-245-5). Hank, always conscious of his birthmark, conjures up an imaginary dog called Fergus, who keeps him company until he finds a real friend. (Rev: HBG 4/04; SLJ 2/04)

8794 O'Connor, Barbara. *Fame and Glory in Freedom, Georgia* (4–6). 2003, Farrar $16.00 (0-374-32258-9). 112pp. Sixth-grader Bird finds difficulties and rewards in her campaign to befriend new-boy-at-school Harlem. (Rev: BL 7/03*; HB 7–8/03; HBG 10/03; SLJ 6/03)

8795 O'Dell, Kathleen. *Agnes Parker . . . Happy Camper?* (4–6). 2005, Dial $16.99 (0-8037-2962-6). 160pp. When Agnes and her best friend, Prejean, are assigned to different cabins at science camp, Agnes rightly worries that the two will grow apart. (Rev: BL 1/1–15/05; SLJ 3/05)

8796 O'Dell, Kathleen. *Ophie Out of Oz* (3–5). Illus. by Rosie Winstead. 2004, Dial $15.99 (0-8037-2930-8). 192pp. Fourth-grader Ophie moves to Oregon and learns a lot about popularity and friendship. (Rev: HB 7–8/04; SLJ 7/04)

8797 Park, Linda Sue. *Project Mulberry* (5–8). 2005, Clarion $16.00 (0-618-47786-1). 232pp. Julia Song, a Korean American seventh-grader, and her new friend Patrick, raise silkworms for a state fair project in this interesting novel that raises many issues including ecology and race relations. (Rev: BL 2/15/05; SLJ 5/05)

8798 Paterson, Katherine. *Bridge to Terabithia* (6–8). Illus. by Donna Diamond. 1977, HarperCollins LB $15.89 (0-690-04635-9); paper $5.95 (0-06-440184-7). 144pp. Jess becomes a close friend of Leslie, a new girl in his school, and suffers agony after her accidental death. Newbery Award winner, 1978. (Rev: SLJ 1/00)

8799 Petersen, P. J. *My Worst Friend* (2–4). Illus. 1998, Dutton $14.99 (0-525-46028-4). 80pp. The friendship of Jenny and Sara is based on rivalry and playing tricks on each other — until Sara becomes seriously ill with a brain tumor. (Rev: BCCB 10/98; BL 10/15/98; HBG 3/99; SLJ 10/98)

8800 Radin, Ruth Yaffe. *Tac's Island* (3–6). Illus. by Gail Owens. 1989, Troll paper $2.95 (0-8167-1320-0). 80pp. The growing friendship between Tac, a year-round island boy, and Steve, vacationing on the coastal Virginia island. (Rev: BL 5/1/86; SLJ 8/86)

8801 Sachar, Louis. *Sixth Grade Secrets* (4–6). 1987, Scholastic paper $4.50 (0-590-46075-7). 208pp. Laura starts a club called Pig City, which eventually ends up by telling everyone's secrets. (Rev: BL 11/1/87; SLJ 9/87)

8802 Salmansohn, Karen. *Oh, and Another Thing* (4–6). Illus. by author. Series: Alexandra Rambles On! 2001, Tricycle $12.95 (1-58246-045-0). Twelve-year-old Alexandra gets advice on how to handle boys. (Rev: SLJ 2/02)

8803 Stauffacher, Sue. *Donuthead* (3–6). 2003, Knopf LB $17.99 (0-375-92468-X). 160pp. The amusing story of an unlikely friendship between timid and compulsive Franklin Delano Donuthead and assertive, self-neglecting Sarah Kervick. (Rev: BL 9/1/03; HBG 4/04; SLJ 11/03)

8804 Staunton, Ted. *Two False Moves* (3–5). 2000, Red Deer paper $4.95 (0-88995-205-1). 64pp. Relations between classmates Nick and Lindsey deteriorate when Lindsey's parents become prospective buyers of the rented home where Nick and his family live. (Rev: BL 2/15/01)

8805 Steele, Mary. *Featherbys* (4–6). 1996, Peachtree paper $6.95 (1-56145-135-5). 180pp. Sixth-graders Jess and Vicky befriend two elderly sisters and help them fight a menacing relative. (Rev: BL 12/15/96)

8806 Stolz, Mary. *The Noonday Friends* (4–6). Illus. by Louis Glanzman. 1965, HarperCollins LB $15.89 (0-06-025946-9); paper $4.95 (0-06-440009-3). 192pp. Eleven-year-old Franny's unskilled father is out of work, and the demanded family teamwork leaves her free from chores only during lunch periods.

8807 Walsh, Jill Paton. *Gaffer Samson's Luck* (4–6). Illus. by Brock Cole. 1984, Farrar paper $4.95 (0-374-42513-2). 112pp. Out to retrieve a good luck stone for his elderly friend Gaffer, James runs into the school bully and learns about different kinds of friendship.

8808 Warner, Sally. *Only Emma* (2–4). Illus. by Jamie Harper. Series: Emma. 2005, Viking $14.99 (0-670-05979-X). 128pp. In this first book of a series, Emma must deal with a new school, a new apartment, and a week-long visit from 4-year-old Anthony Scarpetto. (Rev: BL 3/1/05; SLJ 4/05)

8809 Willner-Pardo, Gina. *Figuring Out Frances* (4–6). 1999, Clarion $14.00 (0-395-91510-4). 144pp. In middle school, Abigail, who is coping with personal problems such as her grandmother's Alzheimer's disease, is dismayed when her longtime friend Travis drifts away and prefers the company of boys. (Rev: BCCB 10/99; BL 9/15/99; HBG 3/00; SLJ 9/99)

8810 Willner-Pardo, Gina. *When Jane-Marie Told My Secret* (3–4). Illus. 1995, Clarion $14.95 (0-395-66382-2). 40pp. Carolyn can't forgive her dear friend Jane-Marie after she has given away one of their secrets. (Rev: BL 8/95; SLJ 9/95)

8811 Yee, Lisa. *Millicent Min, Girl Genius* (4–6). 2003, Scholastic $16.95 (0-439-42519-0). 256pp. Eleven-year-old Millicent Min, a child prodigy frustrated by her inability to find friends who are her intellectual equal, decides to hide her genius in order to win Emily as a friend. (Rev: BL 9/1/03; HB 9–10/03; HBG 4/04; SLJ 3/04)

8812 York, Carol B. *The Key to the Playhouse* (2–4). Illus. by John Speirs. 1994, Scholastic $13.95 (0-590-46258-X). 69pp. Cousins Alice Ann and Megan behave cruelly toward their neighbor Cissie and later regret their actions. (Rev: BCCB 4/94; HB 9–10/94; SLJ 6/94)

Graphic Novels

8813 Brennan, Michael. *Electric Girl*, Vol. 2 (5–8). Illus. 2002, Mighty Gremlin paper $13.95 (0-970355-51-3). 160pp. In this graphic novel, Virginia, who can release bursts of electricity at will, locks horns with evil gremlin Oogleeoog. (Rev: BL 5/1/02; SLJ 5/02)

8814 Denton, Terry. *Storymaze 1: The Ultimate Wave* (3–6). Illus. 2003, Allen & Unwin paper $5.95 (1-86508-378-X). 144pp. An imaginative visit to a parallel universe, very similar to ours, where there is an ongoing battle between good and evil; a decoder glossary allows translation of digital speech. A recommended sequel is *Storymaze 2: The Eye of Ulam* (2003). (Rev: BL 5/15/03)

8815 *Fairy Tales of Oscar Wilde* (5–8). Illus. by P. Craig Russell. 1992, Nantier $15.95 (1-56163-056-X). 46pp. Cartoon art enlivens the retelling of two of Wilde's short stories. (Rev: BL 1/15/93) [741.5973]

8816 Fisher, Jane Smith. *WJHC: On the Air!* (4–8). Illus. 2003, Wilson Place paper $11.95 (0-9744235-0-5). 96pp. Six episodes catalog the entertaining misadventures of a diverse band of teens who launch a high school radio station. (Rev: BL 2/1/04)

8817 Gownley, Jimmy. *Amelia Rules! The Whole World's Crazy* (3–5). Illus. 2003, ibooks paper $14.95 (0-7434-7503-8). 160pp. This is a compilation of previously self-published comic-book episodes about the entertaining exploits, triumphs, and disappointments of fourth-grade Amelia. (Rev: BL 2/1/04)

8818 Hartman, Rachel. *Amy Unbounded: Belondweg Blossoming* (4–8). 2002, Pug House paper $16.95 (0-9717900-0-0). A collection of Hartman's self-published comic books set in the Middle Ages about a thoughtful 9-year-old girl who observes the life around her. (Rev: BL 2/1/04)

8819 Irwin, Jane, and Jeff Berndt. *Vogelein: Clockwork Faerie* (5–12). Illus. 2003, Fiery Studios paper $12.95 (0-9743110-0-6). 168pp. A beautiful 17th-century mechanical fairy who is immortal but depends on others to wind her up stars in this graphic novel. (Rev: BL 11/1/03)

8820 Lobdell, Scott. *The Ocean of Osyria* (4–6). Illus. by Lea Hernandez. 2005, Papercutz paper $7.95 (1-59707-001-7). 96pp. Joe and Frank Hardy appear in a fast-paced graphic novel full of high-tech features — the first in a new series — and attempt to rescue their best friend, who has been implicated in an important theft. (Rev: BL 5/15/05)

8821 London, Jack. *Graphic Classics: Jack London* (5–8). Illus. 2003, Eureka paper $9.95 (0-9712464-5-9). 144pp. Short stories by London are illustrated by diverse artists, some using a comic-book style, others with more traditional graphics. (Rev: BL 7/03; SLJ 10/03)

8822 Medley, Linda. *Castle Waiting: The Curse of the Brambly Hedge* (4–8). 1991, Olio paper $9.00 (0-9651852-1-4). A graphic novel retelling a story closely similar to "Sleeping Beauty" or "Briar Rose," with an elaborate appendix that includes help for those inexperienced with the form. (Rev: BL 2/1/04)

8823 Robbins, Trina. *The Time Team* (3–6). Illus. by Anne Timmons. Series: Go Girl! 2004, Dark Horse paper $5.95 (1-59307-230-9). 96pp. Three high

school girls find themselves stuck in the days of the dinosaurs. (Rev: BL 1/1–15/05)

8824 Rodi, Rob. *Crossovers* (5–12). Illus. 2003, CrossGeneration paper $15.95 (1-931484-85-6). 160pp. This graphic novel is an entertaining look at a suburban family whose members possess a unique power. (Rev: BL 2/1/04)

8825 Roman, Dave, and John Green. *Jax Epoch and the Quicken Forbidden* (4–8). 2002, Ait/Planet Lar paper $14.95 (1-932051-11-2). Jacqueline "Jax" Epoch, the teenage heroine of this graphic novel, accidentally becomes a traveler to another dimension, with unexpected results. (Rev: BL 2/1/04)

8826 Russell, P. Craig. *Fairy Tales of Oscar Wilde, Vol. 3: The Birthday of the Infanta* (5–8). Illus. 1998, NBM $15.95 (1-56163-213-9). A graphic-novel version of Wilde's fairy tale about the misshapen dwarf who dies of a broken heart. (Rev: BL 4/1/99)

8827 Saito, Chiho, et al. *Revolutionary Girl Utena, Vol. 1: To Till* (4–8). 2001, Viz $15.95 (1-56931-713-5). 200pp. Utena will only wear a boys' uniform to school in this entry in the popular manga series. (Rev: BL 2/1/04)

8828 Sewell, Anna. *Anna Sewell's Black Beauty: The Graphic Novel* (4–6). Ed. and illus. by June Brigman and Roy Richardson. Series: Puffin Graphics. 2005, Puffin $9.99 (0-14-240408-X). 176pp. A graphic-novel version of the classic Victorian story about an impressive horse's complex life. (Rev: BL 5/1/05) [741.5]

8829 Sfar, Joann. *Little Vampire Does Kung Fu!* (4–7). Illus. 2003, Simon & Schuster $12.95 (0-689-85769-1). 40pp. An oversize comic book combining humor and fantasy in which Little Vampire rescues Michael from a bully and Michael learns martial arts. (Rev: BL 9/15/03; HBG 4/04; SLJ 12/03)

8830 Slott, Dan, et al. *Justice League Adventures* (5–8). Illus. 2003, DC Comics paper $9.95 (1-56389-954-X). 160pp. Seven stories that each stand alone come from the comic book series of the same name and feature such familiar names as Superman, Batman, and Wonder Woman, battling the usual villains. (Rev: BL 8/03; SLJ 7/04)

8831 Smith, Jeff. *Bone: Out from Boneville* (4–8). 1991, Cartoon Books paper $12.95 (0-9636609-4-2). The adventures of the three Bone cousins — Fone Bone, Phoney Bone, and Smiley Bone — begin when they are expelled from Boneville and become lost in a desert. (Rev: BL 2/1/04)

8832 Taniguchi, Tomoko. *Call Me Princess* (5–8). Trans. from Japanese by Mutsumi Masuda and C. B. Cebulski. Illus. by author. 2003, CPM Manga paper $9.99 (1-58664-898-5). This graphic novel, set in Japan, centers on the young heroine's romantic attachments but gets a "G" rating. (Rev: SLJ 3/04)

8833 Templeton, Ty. *Batman Gotham Adventures* (5–10). 2000, DC Comics paper $9.95 (1-56389-616-8). 144pp. This graphic novel offers six short stories about Batman, Catwoman, Robin, and the usual villains, drawn by Rick Burkett and others. (Rev: BL 12/1/00)

8834 Tolkien, J. R. R. *The Hobbit; or, There and Back Again* (5–10). Adapted by Charles Dixon and Sean Deming. Illus. 1990, Eclipse paper $12.95 (0-345-36858-4). The classic story of Bilbo Baggins and his companions is introduced to reluctant readers in this full-color graphic novel. (Rev: BL 9/1/91)

8835 Trondheim, Lewis. *Mister O* (4–8). Illus. by author. 2004, NBM $12.95 (1-56163-382-8). 32pp. Mister O, portrayed in wordless rectangular cartoons, is a round caricature who — à la Wile E. Coyote — can't seem conquer a chasm, no matter how many successful crossings he views. (Rev: SLJ 9/04) [741.5]

8836 Watase, Yu. *Alice 19th: Lotis Master* (4–8). 2002, Viz paper $9.95 (1-59116-215-7). Alice and some new friends continue the battle to save Alice's sister Mayura from evil forces. (Rev: BL 2/1/04)

Growing into Maturity

Family Problems

8837 Adler, C. S. *The Silver Coach* (4–6). 1988, Avon paper $2.50 (0-380-75498-3). 112pp. Chris and her sister adjust to their parents' imminent divorce during a summer with their grandmother. A reissue.

8838 Amato, Mary. *The Naked Mole Rat Letters* (4–7). 2005, Holiday House $16.95 (0-8234-1927-4). 266pp. Through emails and diary entries, readers learn about Frankie's fear that her father is becoming involved in a new romance. (Rev: BL 6/1–15/05)

8839 Banks, Kate. *Dillon Dillon* (3–7). 2002, Farrar $16.00 (0-374-31786-0). 160pp. When 10-year-old Dillon learns that he was adopted as a baby, he finds comfort in observing a family of loons. (Rev: BCCB 10/02; BL 9/15/02; HB 11–12/02; HBG 3/03; SLJ 10/02)

8840 Baptiste, Tracey. *Angel's Grace* (5–8). Illus. 2005, Simon & Schuster $15.95 (0-689-86773-5). 176pp. Thirteen-year-old Grace, who has always felt different, embarks on a search for the man she believes is her biological father. (Rev: BL 2/1/05; SLJ 3/05)

8841 Birdseye, Tom. *Just Call Me Stupid* (4–6). 1993, Holiday House $15.95 (0-8234-1045-5). 128pp. Patrick's reading problems are complicated by an unfortunate home situation and his feelings of unworthiness. (Rev: BL 1/15/94; SLJ 10/93)

8842 Bryant, Ann. *You Can't Fall for Your Stepsister* (4–7). Series: Step-Chain. 2003, Lobster paper $3.95 (1-894222-77-6). 190pp. Ollie, 13, thinks he may be falling in love with his stepsister Frankie, but she ends up becoming his new best friend. (Rev: SLJ 5/04)

8843 Bunting, Eve. *The Summer of Riley* (4–6). 2001, HarperCollins LB $15.89 (0-06-029142-7). 176pp. The acquisition of a dog helps William to overcome his distress over his parents' separation and grandfather's death, but then the dog gets in trouble with the law. (Rev: BL 7/01; HBG 10/01; SLJ 6/01)

8844 Calhoun, Mary. *Katie John* (4–6). Illus. by Paul Frame. 1960, HarperCollins LB $14.89 (0-06-020951-8). 128pp. In spite of her worst fears, Katie John has a pleasant time and makes new friends during a summer in a small Southern town. Two sequels are: *Depend on Katie John; Katie John and Heathcliff* (both 1981).

8845 Campbell, Bebe Moore. *Sometimes My Mommy Gets Angry* (PS–2). Illus. by E. B. Lewis. 2003, Penguin Putnam $16.99 (0-399-23972-3). Young Annie worries constantly about her mother's state of mind but knows to call for her grandmother's help when things get out of hand. (Rev: HBG 4/04; SLJ 9/03)

8846 Clifford, Eth. *The Remembering Box* (4–6). Illus. 1985, Houghton Mifflin $16.00 (0-395-38476-1); Morrow paper $4.95 (0-688-11777-5). 64pp. Joshua enjoys a special relationship with his grandmother, who shortly before her death gives him a "remembering box" in which she places a girlhood picture of herself. (Rev: BCCB 12/85; BL 12/1/85; HB 3–4/86)

8847 Crist-Evans, Craig. *North of Everything* (4–6). 2004, Candlewick $14.99 (0-7636-2098-X). 80pp. Told from the viewpoint of a young boy, this spare — but moving — novel tells of the joys and tragedies that a family experiences after its move from Miami to a farm in Vermont. (Rev: BL 1/1–15/05; SLJ 11/04)

8848 Danziger, Paula. *Amber Brown Wants Extra Credit* (3–5). Illus. 1996, Penguin Putnam $14.99 (0-399-22900-0). 112pp. Troubled by her parents' divorce, Amber begins having problems with her schoolwork. (Rev: BCCB 10/96; BL 6/1–15/96; SLJ 8/96)

8849 Danziger, Paula. *Forever Amber Brown* (2–4). Illus. 1996, Penguin Putnam $14.99 (0-399-22932-9). 101pp. Amber's divorced mother is being courted by Max, and the young girl is concerned. (Rev: BL 11/15/96; SLJ 2/97)

8850 Doren, Marion. *Nell of Blue Harbor* (4–6). 1990, Harcourt $15.95 (0-15-256889-1). 160pp. From a commune in Vermont, 11-year-old Nell finds it difficult to adjust to life in Maine. (Rev: BCCB 1/91; BL 9/1/90; SLJ 11/90)

8851 Dowell, Frances O'Roark. *Chicken Boy* (4–7). 2005, Simon & Schuster $15.95 (0-689-85816-7). 208pp. A new friend called Henry brings some comfort into Tobin's sad life. (Rev: BL 5/15/05)

8852 Fletcher, Susan. *The Stuttgart Nanny Mafia* (4–6). 1991, Macmillan LB $14.95 (0-689-31709-3). 160pp. When her mother marries a dentist, Aurora realizes that her life is about to be "taken over." (Rev: BCCB 9/91; BL 12/15/91; SLJ 10/91)

8853 Fogelin, Adrian. *Anna Casey's Place in the World* (4–6). 2001, Peachtree $14.95 (1-56145-249-1). 207pp. Twelve-year-old orphan Anna must adjust to her new foster home and begin to make friends. (Rev: BL 10/15/01; HBG 3/02; SLJ 12/01)

8854 Geisert, Bonnie. *Lessons* (4–6). 2005, Houghton Mifflin $15.00 (0-618-47899-X). 192pp. In 1950s South Dakota, 10-year-old Rachel realizes that her new baby brother is making her father sad;

eventually she finds out about the baby who died and did not receive a Christian burial. (Rev: BL 5/15/05; SLJ 5/05)

8855 Greene, Stephanie. *Falling into Place* (3–5). 2002, Clarion $15.00 (0-618-17744-2). 128pp. Eleven-year-old Margaret has a lot to deal with now that her father has remarried, her stepmother is expecting a baby, and her grandmother's beloved husband has died. (Rev: BCCB 1/03; BL 10/15/02; HBG 3/03; SLJ 9/02)

8856 Henkes, Kevin. *Two Under Par* (4–6). Illus. by author. 1987, Greenwillow $15.95 (0-688-06708-5). 128pp. Wedge doesn't like his new stepfather — the miniature golf king! — and he's doubly unhappy with the prospect of a new baby. (Rev: BL 6/1/87; HB 7–8/87; SLJ 6–7/87)

8857 Holt, Kimberly Willis. *Mister and Me* (3–6). Illus. 1998, Penguin Putnam $13.99 (0-399-23215-X). 80pp. Jolene resents the fact that her widowed mother plans to remarry, but as she gets to know her mother's boyfriend, she gradually changes her attitude. (Rev: BL 11/15/98; HB 11–12/98; HBG 3/99; SLJ 11/98)

8858 Kaye, Marilyn. *Happily Ever After* (4–6). 1992, Avon paper $3.50 (0-380-76555-1). 116pp. When two friends become stepsisters, adjustment problems begin. (Rev: SLJ 4/92)

8859 Kinsey-Warnock, Natalie. *Gifts from the Sea* (2–5). 2003, Random $14.95 (0-375-82257-7). 128pp. In this historical novel set in Maine, 12-year-old Aquila finds comfort after her mother's death in caring for a baby she rescues from a shipwreck. (Rev: BL 6/1–15/03; HBG 10/03; SLJ 6/03)

8860 Klise, Kate. *Deliver Us from Normal* (5–8). 2005, Scholastic $16.95 (0-439-52322-2). 240pp. Charles Harrisong, 11, is embarrassed by his abnormal family life in Normal, Illinois, and horrified when his parents decide to move them all to a houseboat off the Alabama coast. (Rev: BL 3/1/05; SLJ 5/05)

8861 Koss, Amy Goldman. *Stranger in Dadland* (4–6). 2001, Dial $16.99 (0-8037-2563-9). 128pp. Twelve-year-old John is not optimistic when he goes to L.A. for his annual visit to his dad but a crisis brings the two closer. (Rev: BCCB 2/01; BL 3/1/01; HB 3–4/01; HBG 10/01; SLJ 3/01)

8862 Krishnaswami, Uma. *Naming Maya* (5–8). 2004, Farrar $16.00 (0-374-35485-5). 192pp. On a trip to India with her mother, 12-year-old Maya learns some important lessons about herself and the real reasons for the breakup of her parents' marriage. (Rev: BL 4/1/04; HB 7–8/04; SLJ 6/04)

8863 Lindbergh, Anne. *Nobody's Orphan* (4–6). 1983, Avon paper $2.95 (0-380-70395-5). Martha believes that she is adopted, though she has no proof.

8864 Lisle, Janet Taylor. *How I Became a Writer and Oggie Learned to Drive* (4–6). 2002, Penguin Putnam $15.99 (0-399-23394-6). 160pp. Eleven-year-old Archie creates wild stories to assuage his younger brother's fears as they shuttle between the homes of their divorced parents. (Rev: BL 2/1/02; HB 3–4/02; HBG 10/02; SLJ 3/02)

8865 Loftis, Chris. *The Boy Who Sat by the Window* (3–6). Illus. by Catharine Gallagher. 1997, New Horizon paper $12.95 (0-88282-147-4). 52pp. Using free verse, the author tells the story of a boy who has been randomly shot while riding his bike to school. (Rev: BL 6/1–15/97; SLJ 8/97)

8866 Lowery, Linda. *Laurie Tells* (4–6). 1994, Carolrhoda LB $19.93 (0-87614-790-2). 40pp. Eleven-year-old Laurie is ignored by her mother when she tells her of being sexually abused by her father. (Rev: BL 6/1–15/94; SLJ 7/94)

8867 Madden, Kerry. *Gentle's Holler* (5–8). 2005, Viking $15.99 (0-670-05998-6). 144pp. Livy Two, part of a large, poor family living in the North Carolina mountains, learns a lesson when her father is injured. (Rev: BL 3/1/05; SLJ 6/05)

8868 Mead, Alice. *Junebug and the Reverend* (4–6). 1998, Farrar $16.00 (0-374-33965-1). 192pp. Junebug, now out of the projects with his family, faces new problems like coping with his mother's new boyfriend and bullies at school, while accepting the responsibility of walking an old emphysema patient, nicknamed the Reverend. (Rev: BL 9/1/98; HB 9–10/98; HBG 3/99; SLJ 9/98)

8869 Mead, Alice. *Madame Squidley and Beanie* (4–7). 2004, Farrar $16.00 (0-374-34688-7). 144pp. Ten-year-old Beanie's mother has chronic fatigue syndrome and her illness is affecting the fifth-grader's life. (Rev: BL 4/15/04; SLJ 6/04)

8870 Mead, Alice. *Swimming to America* (5–8). 2005, Farrar $16.00 (0-374-38047-3). 160pp. Eighth grader Linda comes from an immigrant family determined to forget the past in this book about fitting in and telling the truth. (Rev: BL 3/1/05; SLJ 3/05)

8871 Monthei, Betty. *Looking for Normal* (5–8). 2005, HarperCollins LB $16.89 (0-06-072506-0). 192pp. Annie, 12, and her younger brother are sent to live with their grandparents after their father kills their mother and then himself; unfortunately, life does not improve as they must cope with Grandma's drinking and abuse and Grandpa's indifference. (Rev: BL 6/1–15/05; SLJ 4/05)

8872 Moss, Marissa. *Amelia's Family Ties* (3–5). Illus. Series: Amelia's Notebook. 2000, Pleasant Co. $12.95 (1-58485-079-5); paper $5.95 (1-58485-078-7). 40pp. After years of silence, Amelia receives a letter from her divorced father and goes to visit him and her stepmother in Chicago. (Rev: BL 2/15/00; HBG 10/00; SLJ 6/00)

8873 Park, Barbara. *Don't Make Me Smile* (4–6). 1981, Avon paper $2.95 (0-380-61994-6). Charles refuses to face the fact of his parents' divorce.

8874 Porter, Pamela. *Sky* (3–5). Illus. by Mary Jane Gerber. 2004, Groundwood $15.95 (0-88899-566-6). 83pp. Georgia, an 11-year-old Native American girl, finds comfort in a foal named Sky after a series of traumas including the deaths of her parents, a narrow escape from a burst dam, and an uncomfortable stay in a shelter where she and her grandparents experience prejudice. (Rev: BCCB 12/04; HB 1–2/05; SLJ 4/05)

8875 Sachs, Marilyn. *Fran Ellen's House* (4–6). 1989, Avon paper $2.75 (0-380-70583-4). Although her family is back together, Fran Ellen's baby sister won't talk to her and their house is in a shambles. A sequel to: *The Bears' House* (1987). (Rev: BCCB 11/87; BL 11/1/87; SLJ 10/87)

8876 Shawver, Margaret. *What's Wrong with Grandma? A Family's Experience with Alzheimer's* (3–6). Illus. 1996, Prometheus $14.95 (1-57392-107-6). 63pp. Ellen is confused and sometimes terrified when her grandmother begins to exhibit the erratic behavior associated with Alzheimer's disease. (Rev: BL 4/15/97)

8877 Shreve, Susan. *Blister* (4–6). 2001, Scholastic $15.95 (0-439-19313-3). 154pp. A girl who calls herself Blister tries to fit in at a new school after her mother has a stillborn baby and her father moves out. (Rev: BCCB 11/01; BL 9/15/01; HBG 10/02; SLJ 11/01)

8878 Shyer, Marlene Fanta. *Fleabiscuit Sings!* (3–6). 2005, Marshall Cavendish $15.95 (0-7614-5213-3). 150pp. Twelve-year-old Nicky discovers that Fleabiscuit, the dog he walks for Mr. Muffin, can sing and adds the pooch to his family's subway performances. (Rev: BCCB 5/05; HB 8–9/05; SLJ 5/05)

8879 Siebold, Jan. *Rope Burn* (4–6). Illus. 1998, Whitman $12.95 (0-8075-7109-1). 82pp. To fulfill a school writing assignment, 11-year-old Richard writes about the terrible effects his parents' divorce has had on him, his difficulties making new friends, and his problems communicating with his mother. (Rev: BCCB 6/98; BL 6/1–15/98; SLJ 6/98)

8880 Strauss, Linda Leopold. *Really, Truly, Everything's Fine* (5–8). 2004, Marshall Cavendish $15.95 (0-7614-5163-3). 160pp. Life changes dramatically for 14-year-old Jill Rider when her father is arrested for jewelry theft. (Rev: BL 5/15/04; SLJ 7/04)

8881 Van Leeuwen, Jean. *Dear Mom, You're Ruining My Life* (4–6). Illus. 1989, Puffin paper $4.99 (0-14-034386-5). 160pp. Samantha's sixth-grade year is filled with ups and downs. (Rev: BCCB 5/89; BL 5/1/89; HB 5–6/89)

8882 Ware, Cheryl. *Catty-Cornered* (4–6). Illus. by Paul Yalowitz. 1998, Orchard LB $16.99 (0-531-33067-2). 106pp. A smart, curious, and funny girl keeps a journal of the two months she had to spend with her grandmother in a trailer park. (Rev: BL 4/1/98; HBG 10/98; SLJ 3/98)

8883 Williams, Laura E. *Up a Creek* (5–8). 2001, Holt $17.00 (0-8050-6453-2). 135pp. Thirteen-year-old Starshine Bott, daughter of a young, single-mother activist, wonders if her mother cares more for her social causes than she does for her. (Rev: BCCB 2/01; BL 1/1–15/01; HBG 10/01; SLJ 1/01)

8884 Willner-Pardo, Gina. *Spider Storch's Carpool Catastrophe* (2–4). Illus. by Nick Sharratt. 1997, Whitman LB $11.95 (0-8075-7575-5); paper $3.95 (0-8075-7576-3). 60pp. Joey, nicknamed Spider, is afraid that his mother's friendship with Mrs. Brennerman will mean that he will have to get involved with her unpopular daughter. (Rev: HBG 3/98; SLJ 11/97)

8885 Wilson, Jacqueline. *The Illustrated Mum* (5–7). 2005, Delacorte LB $17.99 (0-385-90263-8). 224pp. Nine-year-old Dolphin and teenager Star struggle to deal with their manic-depressive mother. (Rev: BL 1/1–15/05; SLJ 3/05)

Personal Problems

8886 Adler, C. S. *Daddy's Climbing Tree* (5–7). 1993, Houghton Mifflin $15.00 (0-395-63032-0). 134pp. Jessica cannot adjust to the death of her father in a hit-and-run accident. (Rev: BCCB 7–8/93; BL 6/1–15/93; HB 7–8/93; SLJ 5/93)

8887 Adler, C. S. *The Lump in the Middle* (5–7). 1991, Avon paper $3.50 (0-380-71176-1). 160pp. Kelsey, the middle child, struggles for her identity after dad loses his job. (Rev: BL 10/1/89; SLJ 10/89)

8888 Adler, C. S. *Willie, the Frog Prince* (4–7). 1994, Clarion $15.00 (0-395-65615-X). 163pp. Willie's inability to accept responsibility almost causes the loss of his dog, Booboo. (Rev: BL 4/15/94; SLJ 6/94)

8889 Adler, David A. *The Many Troubles of Andy Russell* (2–5). Illus. 1998, Harcourt $14.00 (0-15-201295-8). 144pp. The story, in a simple chapter book format, of fourth-grader Andy Russell who faces many problems including a pregnant mother, a pet gerbil that escapes, and a friend who needs a new foster family. (Rev: BL 8/98; HBG 3/99; SLJ 12/98)

8890 Auch, Mary Jane. *Seven Long Years Until College* (4–7). 1991, Holiday House $13.95 (0-8234-0901-5). 160pp. Unhappy at home, Natalie runs away to join her older sister at college. (Rev: BCCB 1/92; SLJ 10/91)

8891 Bartek, Mary. *Funerals and Fly Fishing* (4–7). 2004, Holt $16.95 (0-8050-7409-0). 160pp. A visit to the grandfather he has never met gives Brad Stanislawski new confidence to deal with the classmates at his new school. (Rev: SLJ 8/04)

8892 Benjamin, Carol Lea. *The Wicked Stepdog* (4–7). Illus. by author. 1982, Avon paper $2.50 (0-380-70089-1). Louise is in the midst of puberty problems and her father's remarriage.

8893 Betancourt, Jeanne. *Kate's Turn* (5–8). 1992, Scholastic $13.95 (0-590-43103-X). This story of the young ballerina Kate, who decides the price of fame is too high, shows the grueling, often painful life of a dancer. (Rev: BL 1/1/92; SLJ 2/92)

8894 Birdseye, Tom. *Tarantula Shoes* (3–6). 1995, Holiday House $15.95 (0-8234-1179-6); Puffin paper $4.99 (0-14-037955-X). 96pp. With the help of a new friend and his pet tarantula, Ryan is able to buy the basketball shoes of his dreams. (Rev: BL 4/15/95; SLJ 5/95)

8895 Blume, Judy. *Then Again, Maybe I Won't* (5–8). 1971, Dell paper $4.99 (0-440-48659-9). Thirteen-year-old Tony faces many problems when his family relocates to suburban Long Island.

429

8896 Blume, Judy. *Tiger Eyes: A Novel* (6–8). 1981, Dell paper $4.99 (0-440-98469-6). 256pp. Davey must deal with reactions to her father's murder.

8897 Bohlmeijer, Arno. *Something Very Sorry* (5–8). 1996, Houghton Mifflin $15.00 (0-395-74679-5). A terrible automobile accident in which Rose and her family are involved brings death into the family and changes her life forever. (Rev: BL 4/1/96; SLJ 7/96*)

8898 Bonners, Susan. *Edwina Victorious* (3–5). Illus. by author. 2000, Farrar $16.00 (0-374-31968-5). 131pp. A charming story about a girl who forges her great-grandaunt's signature on letters to the mayor to try to win much-needed reforms. (Rev: BCCB 10/00; BL 9/1/03; HBG 3/01; SLJ 10/00)

8899 Bowdish, Lynea. *Brooklyn, Bugsy, and Me* (3–5). Illus. 2000, Farrar $15.00 (0-374-30993-0). 96pp. In 1953, 9-year-old Sam has problems adjusting to the move from his beloved West Virginia to Brooklyn. (Rev: BCCB 4/00; BL 2/15/00; HB 5–6/00; HBG 10/00; SLJ 6/00)

8900 Bradby, Marie. *Some Friend* (4–8). 2004, Simon & Schuster $15.95 (0-689-85615-6). 240pp. Pearl, an 11-year-old African American, relates her social problems in this moving story set against the backdrop of the civil rights movement. (Rev: BL 2/15/04; HB 3–4/04; SLJ 3/04)

8901 Buck, Pearl. *The Big Wave* (4–6). 1973, HarperCollins LB $16.89 (0-381-99923-8); paper $4.95 (0-06-440171-5). 88pp. The loss of family and home in a tidal wave reveals the courage of a little Japanese boy.

8902 Bulla, Clyde Robert. *The Paint Brush Kid* (2–4). Illus. by Ellen Beier. 1999, Random LB $11.99 (0-679-99282-0); paper $3.99 (0-679-89282-6). 64pp. In this beginning chapter book, the pictures Gregory has painted on a house depicting his uncle's life in Mexico are going to be destroyed because the house is slated for demolition. (Rev: HBG 10/99; SLJ 8/99)

8903 Bulla, Clyde Robert. *Shoeshine Girl* (3–5). Illus. by Leigh Grant. 1975, HarperCollins LB $15.89 (0-690-04830-0); paper $4.50 (0-06-440228-2). 80pp. A somewhat indolent 10-year-old girl matures during a summer working for Al at his shoeshine stand.

8904 Bunting, Eve. *Blackwater* (5–8). 1999, HarperCollins LB $15.89 (0-06-027843-9). 160pp. Brodie feels responsible for the drowning deaths of two young teenagers, but is unable to tell the truth and admit his guilt. (Rev: HBG 3/00; SLJ 8/99)

8905 Bunting, Eve. *Your Move* (2–5). Illus. by James E. Ransome. 1998, Harcourt $16.00 (0-15-200181-6). 32pp. A 10-year-old boy and his young brother are caught up in the violence that accompanies the rivalry between street gangs. (Rev: BCCB 6/98; BL 2/15/98; HBG 10/98; SLJ 5/98)

8906 Burch, Robert. *Queenie Peavy* (5–7). 1987, Penguin Putnam paper $5.99 (0-14-032305-8). Queenie, whose father is in prison, is growing up a defiant, disobedient girl in rural Georgia in the 1930s.

8907 Byars, Betsy. *The Cartoonist* (4–6). Illus. by Richard Cuffari. 1978, Puffin paper $3.99 (0-14-032309-0). 128pp. Alfie's refuge in his attic room with his cartoons is disrupted by his brother's return.

8908 Byars, Betsy. *The House of Wings* (4–6). Illus. by Daniel Schwartz. 1972, Puffin paper $4.99 (0-14-031523-3). 148pp. Sammy is distraught when he is left alone with his grandfather, but things get better when a wounded crane is found and must be taken care of.

8909 Cameron, Ann. *Colibri* (5–8). 2003, Farrar $17.00 (0-374-31519-1). 240pp. Twelve-year-old Rosa, who was kidnapped from her Mayan village when she was four, seeks to escape from the abusive "uncle" who is exploiting her. (Rev: BCCB 10/03; BL 10/1/03*; BR 9–10/03; HB 9–10/03; HBG 4/04; SLJ 10/03*)

8910 Cameron, Ann. *Gloria's Way* (2–4). 2000, Farrar $15.00 (0-374-32670-3). 112pp. In this easy chapter book, readers meet African American Gloria and, in six short episodes, learn about her problems with friendships and family. (Rev: BCCB 2/00; BL 2/15/00; HB 3–4/00; HBG 10/00; SLJ 3/00)

8911 Caseley, Judith. *Praying to A. L.* (5–8). 2000, Greenwillow $15.95 (0-688-15934-6). 192pp. After her father dies, 12-year-old Sierra transfers all her love to a portrait of Abraham Lincoln given to her by her father. (Rev: BL 5/15/00; HBG 10/00; SLJ 6/00)

8912 Cleaver, Vera, and Bill Cleaver. *Grover* (4–7). Illus. by Fred Marvin. 1970, HarperCollins $13.95 (0-397-31118-4). 128pp. After his mother's suicide and his father's resultant breakdown, 10-year-old Grover must face the hard reality of death and trouble.

8913 Clements, Andrew. *The Jacket* (3–6). Illus. by Dan Gonzalez. 2002, Simon & Schuster $12.95 (0-689-82595-1). 80pp. This story about a sixth-grade boy examining race relations and facing his own prejudices is sure to prompt discussion. (Rev: BCCB 3/02; BL 3/1/02; HBG 10/02; SLJ 3/02)

8914 Conford, Ellen. *Hail, Hail Camp Timberwood* (5–7). Illus. by Gail Owens. 1978, Little, Brown $14.95 (0-316-15291-9). Thirteen-year-old Melanie's first summer at camp.

8915 Conly, Jane L. *Crazy Lady!* (5–8). 1993, HarperCollins LB $16.89 (0-06-021360-4). 196pp. In a city slum, Vernon forms a friendship with an eccentric woman and helps her care for her disabled teenage son. (Rev: BCCB 7–8/93; BL 5/15/93*; SLJ 4/93*)

8916 Conly, Jane L. *What Happened on Planet Kid* (4–8). 2000, Holt $16.95 (0-8050-6065-0). 216pp. Twelve-year-old Dawn learns a lot about life, herself, and her dreams of becoming a major league pitcher during the summer she spends on a farm with her aunt and uncle. (Rev: BCCB 4/00; BL 5/15/00; HB 5–6/00; HBG 10/00; SLJ 5/00)

8917 Conrad, Pam. *Staying Nine* (4–6). Illus. by Mike Wimmer. 1988, HarperCollins paper $4.25 (0-06-440377-7). 80pp. A private few days in the life of a young girl who doesn't want to be ten. (Rev: BCCB 10/88; BL 11/15/88; SLJ 12/88)

8918 Coolidge, Susan. *What Katy Did* (4–6). 1988, Buccaneer LB $19.95 (0-899-66585-3). Tomboy Katy Carr overcomes a tragic accident in this classic story.

8919 Cooper, Ilene. *Absolutely Lucy* (2–4). Illus. Series: Read to Reading. 2000, Golden Books LB $10.99 (0-307-48502-0); paper $3.99 (0-307-26502-1). 76pp. An easy chapter book about a boy whose beagle puppy helps him conquer his shyness. (Rev: BCCB 5/00; BL 3/15/00; SLJ 3/01)

8920 Cooper, Ilene. *The Annoying Team* (2–4). Illus. by Colin Paine. Series: Road to Reading. 2002, Random LB $11.99 (0-307-46512-8); paper $3.99 (0-307-26512-9). 80pp. In this beginning chapter book, Tim tries a new approach to combat the bullying of Big Jon Ferguson. (Rev: BL 6/1–15/02; HBG 10/02)

8921 Cosby, Bill. *My Big Lie* (2–4). Illus. 1999, Scholastic $15.95 (0-590-52160-8); paper $3.99 (0-590-52161-6). 40pp. Late for dinner because of a baseball game, Little Bill tells a lie to protect himself and only gets into worse trouble. (Rev: BL 10/15/99; HBG 10/99; SLJ 8/99)

8922 Cottonwood, Joe. *Danny Ain't* (5–8). 1992, Scholastic $13.95 (0-590-45067-0). 240pp. When Danny's father, a Vietnam War vet, is taken to a VA hospital, the boy tries to survive on his own. (Rev: SLJ 10/92)

8923 Cox, Judy. *Mean, Mean Maureen Green* (2–5). Illus. 1999, Holiday House $15.95 (0-8234-1502-3). 88pp. Lilley is a fearful person who dreads going to school because of a mean neighborhood dog, a school bully, and her new bike without training wheels. (Rev: BCCB 2/00; BL 12/1/99; HBG 10/00; SLJ 3/00)

8924 Crowe, Carole. *Groover's Heart* (4–6). 2001, Boyds Mills $15.95 (1-56397-953-5). 144pp. Orphan Charlotte, age 11, has trouble adjusting to the ways of her guardian, wealthy Aunt Viola. (Rev: BL 4/15/01; HBG 10/01; SLJ 4/01)

8925 Cruise, Robin. *The Top-Secret Journal of Fiona Claire Jardin* (4–7). 1998, Harcourt $13.00 (0-15-201383-0). 160pp. At the advice of her therapist, Fiona, age 11, keeps a journal about her problems, chiefly coping with her parents' divorce and living under a joint-custody agreement. (Rev: BL 4/15/98; HBG 10/98; SLJ 4/98)

8926 Cummings, Priscilla. *A Face First* (5–8). 2001, Dutton $16.99 (0-525-46522-7). 224pp. After being severely burned in a car accident, Kelly sinks into a terrible depression particularly after she is told that she will have to wear a plastic face mask for two years. (Rev: BCCB 2/01; BL 2/1/01; HBG 10/01; SLJ 2/01)

8927 Curtis, Christopher Paul. *Bud, Not Buddy* (4–6). 1999, Delacorte $15.95 (0-385-32306-9). 272pp. In this Newbery Medal winner set in Michigan during the Great Depression, 10-year-old Bud, on the run from his orphanage and his latest foster parents, is determined to find his father. (Rev:

BCCB 11/99; BL 9/1/99; HB 11–12/99; HBG 3/00; SLJ 9/99)

8928 Curtis, Sandra R. *Gabriel's Ark* (2–5). Illus. 1998, Alef Design Group paper $7.95 (1-881283-22-4). 64pp. Gabe, who was born disabled, celebrates his bar mitzvah in his own way, thanks to a supportive family and an understanding rabbi. (Rev: BL 10/1/98; SLJ 1/99)

8929 Danziger, Paula. *United Tates of America* (4–6). 2002, Scholastic $15.95 (0-590-69221-6). 144pp. Skate Tate, an 11-year-old with problems adjusting to sixth grade, experiences additional stress when her favorite great-uncle dies. (Rev: BCCB 9/02; BL 4/15/02; HB 3–4/02; HBG 10/02)

8930 Deak, Erzsi, and Kristin Embry Litchman, eds. *Period Pieces: Stories for Girls* (4–8). 2003, HarperCollins LB $16.89 (0-06-623797-1). 160pp. A collection of 13 stories about girls' experiences with their first periods, featuring a variety of characters and settings. (Rev: BCCB 3/03; BL 3/15/03; HBG 10/03; SLJ 3/03)

8931 DiCamillo, Kate. *Because of Winn-Dixie* (4–6). 2000, Candlewick $15.99 (0-7636-0776-2). 184pp. In this Newbery Honor book, lonely 10-year-old India Opal Buloni adopts a stray dog, named Winn-Dixie, who changes her life. (Rev: BCCB 6/00; BL 5/1/00; HB 7–8/00; HBG 10/00; SLJ 6/00)

8932 DiCamillo, Kate. *The Tiger Rising* (4–6). 2001, Candlewick $12.99 (0-7636-0911-0). 128pp. This novel of grieving, friendship, and animal love involves Rob whose mother has just died, an outsider named Sistine with whom he becomes friends, and a caged tiger. (Rev: HB 5–6/01; HBG 10/01; SLJ 3/01)

8933 Dorman, N. B. *Petey and Miss Magic* (3–5). 1993, Shoe String LB $16.00 (0-208-02345-3). 99pp. A lonely boy who longs for a pet finds a worm that he begins to care for. (Rev: SLJ 3/93)

8934 Dreyer, Ellen. *Speechless in New York: Going to New York* (5–8). Series: Going To. 2000, Four Corners paper $7.95 (1-893577-01-5). 96pp. Jessie is beset with personal problems when she flies to New York from Minnesota with the Prairie Youth Chorale. (Rev: SLJ 3/00)

8935 Duffey, Betsy. *Fur-Ever Yours, Booker Jones* (4–6). 2001, Viking $14.99 (0-670-89287-4). 128pp. Long-suffering Booker must deal with lightweight and serious problems when his parents leave him and his sister alone with their grandfather. (Rev: BL 6/1–15/01; HBG 10/01; SLJ 7/01)

8936 Duffey, Betsy. *Spotlight on Cody* (2–4). Illus. 1998, Viking $14.99 (0-670-88077-9). 96pp. A beginning chapter book in which Cody Michaels, who has to perform in his third -grade talent show, is convinced he has nothing to offer. (Rev: BL 10/1/98; HB 11–12/98; HBG 3/99; SLJ 11/98)

8937 Dunnion, Kristyn. *Missing Matthew* (4–6). 2004, Red Deer paper $7.95 (0-88995-278-7). 112pp. The three girls in the Rebel Rescue Squad decide to investigate the disappearance of 10-year-old Matthew, and instead of a kidnapping they find a sad boy who has run away from home. (Rev: BL 3/1/04; SLJ 5/04)

431

8938 Easton, Kelly. *Trouble at Betts Pets* (3–6). 2002, Candlewick $14.99 (0-7636-1580-3). 144pp. Fifth-grader Aaron faces problems at his family's pet store, at school, and in his neighborhood — until he takes action. (Rev: BCCB 6/02; BL 9/1/02; HBG 10/02; SLJ 4/02)

8939 Eige, Lillian. *Dangling* (4–6). 2001, Simon & Schuster $16.00 (0-689-83581-7). 176pp. Eleven-year-old Ben describes how he learns that his best friend, Ring, was in foster care and wonders whether his supposed drowning was real or staged. (Rev: BCCB 3/01; BL 2/1/01; HBG 10/01)

8940 Ellis, Sarah. *Pick-Up Sticks* (5–8). 1992, Macmillan LB $15.00 (0-689-50550-7). A disgruntled teen learns a lesson in life after being sent to live with relatives. (Rev: BL 1/15/92; SLJ 3/92*)

8941 Emery, Joanna. *Brothers of the Falls* (4–6). Illus. by Dave Erickson. 2004, Silver Moon LB $14.95 (1-893110-37-0). 92pp. Irish orphan James, 13, arrives in America alone and must find shelter and money to help him search for the brother who was left behind. (Rev: SLJ 8/04)

8942 Evans, Douglas. *So What Do You Do?* (5–8). 1997, Front Street $14.95 (1-886910-20-0). Two middle-schoolers help their beloved former teacher who has become a homeless drunk. (Rev: BCCB 3/98; BL 11/1/97; BR 3–4/98; HBG 3/98; SLJ 1/98)

8943 Evans, Mari. *Dear Corinne, Tell Somebody! A Book About Secrets* (3–7). 1999, Just Us $12.95 (0-940975-81-5). 48pp. A book of letters in which Corinne's friends try to get her to seek help for her problem, which is later revealed as child abuse. (Rev: HBG 3/00; SLJ 12/99)

8944 Fagan, Cary. *The Market Wedding* (2–5). Illus. by Regolo Ricci. 2000, Tundra $16.95 (0-88776-492-4). The guests that Minnie and Morris invite to their wedding are so in awe of the luxurious trappings that they are afraid to attend. (Rev: BCCB 10/00; BL 12/1/00; HBG 3/01)

8945 Fenner, Carol. *The King of Dragons* (4–6). 1998, Simon & Schuster $17.00 (0-689-82217-0). 224pp. A group of people arrive to convert an empty courthouse into a gallery to house a kite exhibition, threatening homeless Ian, who thinks he is about 11, with the loss of his shelter. (Rev: BCCB 1/99; BL 11/15/98*; HB 1–2/99; HBG 3/99; SLJ 12/98)

8946 Flake, Sharon G. *A Freak Like Me* (5–9). 1999, Hyperion paper $5.99 (0-7868-1307-5). In her inner-city middle school, Maleeka Madison is picked on by classmates because she is poorly dressed, darker than the others, and gets good grades. (Rev: BL 9/1/98; SLJ 11/98)

8947 Fletcher, Ralph. *Tommy Trouble and the Magic Marble* (3–4). Illus. 2000, Holt $16.00 (0-8050-6387-0). 47pp. A beginning chapter book about a boy who tries to collect ten dollars to buy a ring that is supposed to protect him from nightmares. (Rev: BL 8/00; HBG 10/01; SLJ 9/00)

8948 Fletcher, Ralph J. *Spider Boy* (5–8). 1997, Houghton Mifflin $15.00 (0-395-77606-6). Bobby — nicknamed Spider Boy because he knows so much about spiders — has trouble adjusting to his new life in the town of New Paltz, New York. (Rev: BCCB 4/97; BL 6/1–15/97; HB 7–8/97; SLJ 7/97)

8949 Fox, Paula. *Monkey Island* (5–8). 1991, Watts LB $16.99 (0-531-08562-7). 160pp. A homeless, abandoned 11-year-old boy in New York City contracts pneumonia and is cared for by a homeless African American teenager and retired teacher, who share their place in the park with him. (Rev: BCCB 10/91*; BL 9/1/91*; HB 9–10/91*; SLJ 8/91)

8950 Fox, Paula. *Western Wind* (5–9). 1993, Orchard LB $17.99 (0-531-08652-6). At first resentful of being sent to spend a summer with her grandmother on a Maine island, Elizabeth gradually adjusts and learns a great deal about herself. (Rev: BCCB 9/93; BL 10/15/93; SLJ 12/93*)

8951 Frasier, Debra. *Miss Alaineus: A Vocabulary Disaster* (3–5). Illus. 2000, Harcourt $16.00 (0-15-202163-9). 32pp. Fifth-grader Sage mistakes the word *miscellaneous* for *Miss Alaineus* but turns this embarrassment into a triumph. (Rev: BL 9/15/00; HBG 3/01; SLJ 9/00)

8952 Freeman, Martha. *The Trouble with Cats* (2–4). 2000, Holiday House $15.95 (0-8234-1479-5). 76pp. A beginning chapter book about Holly, who is adjusting to a new life in San Francisco with a new stepfather and a new school situation. (Rev: BCCB 4/00; BL 3/15/00; HBG 10/00; SLJ 7/00)

8953 Friedman, Aileen. *A Cloak for the Dreamer* (3–5). Illus. by Kim Howard. 1995, Scholastic $15.95 (0-590-48987-9). 15pp. Misha sets out to find his fortune in an amazing cloak designed by his father and brothers. (Rev: BL 2/1/95; SLJ 4/95)

8954 Friesen, Gayle. *Men of Stone* (5–8). 2000, Kids Can $16.95 (1-55074-781-9). 216pp. While Ben Conrad traces his own family roots, he confronts a local bully in this story of a boy's journey to maturity. (Rev: HBG 3/01; SLJ 10/00)

8955 Fromm, Pete. *Monkey Tag* (4–7). 1994, Scholastic paper $14.95 (0-590-46525-2). 352pp. When his twin is paralyzed from an accident, Eli feels partly responsible. (Rev: BCCB 12/94; BL 10/15/94; SLJ 10/94)

8956 Garden, Nancy. *Holly's Secret* (5–8). 2000, Farrar $16.00 (0-374-33273-8). 144pp. When Holly and her family move to western Massachusetts, she decides to hide from her new classmates the fact that her parents are lesbians. (Rev: BCCB 9/00; BL 10/15/00; HB 9–10/00; HBG 3/01; SLJ 9/00)

8957 Gardner, Graham. *Inventing Elliot* (5–9). 2004, Dial $16.99 (0-8037-2964-2). 192pp. Despite efforts to avoid bullies at his new high school, 14-year-old Elliot Sutton finds himself embroiled with the Guardians, a group that metes out punishment to those it deems "losers." (Rev: BL 5/15/04; SLJ 3/04)

8958 Gifaldi, David. *Toby Scudder, Ultimate Warrior* (4–6). 1993, Clarion $15.00 (0-395-66400-4). 201pp. A new teacher helps overweight Toby find the self-esteem he lacks. (Rev: BCCB 11/93; BL 10/15/93; SLJ 10/93*)

8959 Giff, Patricia Reilly. *The Gift of the Pirate Queen* (4–6). Illus. by Jenny Rutherford. 1983, Dell paper $4.50 (0-440-43046-1). 160pp. Grace is looking forward to the arrival of Fiona from Ireland to take care of her family.

8960 Gilbert, Barbara Snow. *Stone Water* (5–9). 1996, Front Street $15.95 (1-886910-11-1). Fourteen-year-old Grant must decide if he will honor his ailing grandfather's wish to help him commit suicide. (Rev: BL 12/15/96; SLJ 12/96*)

8961 Golding, Theresa Martin. *Kat's Surrender* (5–8). 1999, Boyds Mills $16.95 (1-56397-755-9). 179pp. Thirteen-year-old Kat misses her deceased mother terribly, but she tries to hide it in her friendships for an old man and a wacky girl. (Rev: BL 10/15/99; HBG 3/00; SLJ 11/99)

8962 Gordon, Amy. *The Gorillas of Gill Park* (4–7). Illus. 2003, Holiday House $16.95 (0-8234-1751-4). 256pp. Shy, lonely Willie comes into his own when he spends the summer with his eccentric Aunt Bridget and meets her zany neighbors. (Rev: BL 6/1–15/03; HBG 10/03; SLJ 5/03)

8963 Gordon, Amy. *The Secret Life of a Boarding School Brat* (5–7). 2004, Holiday House $16.95 (0-8234-1779-4). 252pp. Lydia, already unhappy about her parents' divorce and her grandmother's death, becomes even more miserable at her new boarding school and chronicles her woes in her diary. (Rev: HB 7–8/04; SLJ 8/04)

8964 Gordon, Amy. *When JFK Was My Father* (5–9). 1999, Houghton Mifflin $15.00 (0-395-91364-0). 208pp. Georgia, who often imagines that President Kennedy is her caring father, has several problems including divorcing parents and adjustment to a Connecticut boarding school. (Rev: BL 6/1–15/99; HB 7–8/99; HBG 10/99; SLJ 4/99)

8965 Gosselin, Kim. *Smoking Stinks!!* (2–4). Illus. by Thom Buttner. 1997, JayJo $16.95 (0-9639449-5-9). When Maddie's grandfather comes to school to tell her class why he smokes, he agrees that smoking stinks. (Rev: BL 4/1/98; SLJ 1/98)

8966 Gray, Dianne E. *Holding Up the Earth* (5–8). 2000, Houghton Mifflin $15.00 (0-618-00703-2). 224pp. Sarah, a foster child now living on a Nebraska farm, does some research and uncovers stories of the many generations of women who preceded her on the farm and their struggles and problems. (Rev: BL 1/1–15/01; HB 9–10/00; HBG 3/01; SLJ 10/00)

8967 Groth, B. L., and Thomas Wray, eds. *Home Is Where We Live* (3–5). Illus. 1995, Cornerstone paper $7.95 (0-940895-34-X). 32pp. A simple story told in photos and narrative of a homeless child in a Chicago shelter. (Rev: BL 10/15/95; SLJ 12/95)

8968 Grove, Vicki. *Reaching Dustin* (5–8). 1998, Penguin Putnam paper $5.99 (0-698-11839-1). As part of a 6th-grade assignment, Carly must get to know Dustin Groat, the class outcast, and as she learns more about him and his family, she realizes that her attitudes toward him in the past have helped create his problems. (Rev: BCCB 3/98; BL 5/1/98; BR 11–12/98; SLJ 5/98)

8969 Grover, Lorie Ann. *Hold Me Tight* (5–8). 2005, Simon & Schuster $16.95 (0-689-85248-7). 336pp. In this moving novel written in free verse, 10-year-old Essie faces — and deals with — her father's departure from the family, her mother's depression,

a classmate's kidnapping, and sexual advances from a family friend. (Rev: BCCB 5/05; SLJ 3/05)

8970 Guest, Elissa Haden. *Iris and Walter* (1–3). Illus. 2000, Harcourt $14.00 (0-15-202122-1). 44pp. It takes time, but gradually Iris comes to enjoy living in the country far from the city activities she loved, in this beginning chapter book. (Rev: BCCB 12/00*; BL 10/15/00; HBG 3/01; SLJ 11/00)

8971 Haas, Jessie. *Will You, Won't You?* (5–8). 2000, Greenwillow LB $15.89 (0-06-029197-4). 192pp. Mad (short for Madison) is a shy middleschooler who comes out of her shell during a summer she spends with her wise grandmother in the country. (Rev: BCCB 10/00; BL 2/1/01; HBG 3/01; SLJ 10/00)

8972 Hahn, Mary D. *Anna on the Farm* (3–5). Illus. 2001, Clarion $15.00 (0-618-03605-9). 152pp. When 9-year-old Anna arrives at her aunt and uncle's farm for a week, she finds they have taken in an orphan named Theodore, and a hearty rivalry begins. (Rev: BL 2/15/01; HB 5–6/01; HBG 10/01; SLJ 3/01)

8973 Hahn, Mary D. *Following My Own Footsteps* (5–8). 1996, Clarion $15.00 (0-395-76477-7). Living with a grandmother to escape a drunken, abusive father, Gordy has problems adjusting and becomes friends with the boy next door, who has polio and is wheelchair bound. (Rev: BCCB 10/96; BL 9/15/96*; HB 9–10/96; SLJ 11/96)

8974 Hamilton, Virginia. *Cousins* (5–8). 1990, Penguin Putnam $17.99 (0-399-22164-6). 125pp. Cammy faces both guilt and grief when her cousin Patty Ann drowns. (Rev: BCCB 11/90*; HB 3–4/91; SLJ 12/90)

8975 Hamilton, Virginia. *Drylongso* (3–5). Illus. by Jerry Pinkney. 1992, Harcourt $18.95 (0-15-224241-4). 64pp. During a great duststorm on the prairie in 1975, a tall boy appears who helps Lindy and her family find water. (Rev: BCCB 10/92*; BL 7/92*; HB 9–10/92; SLJ 1/93)

8976 Hamilton, Virginia. *Zeely* (4–6). Illus. by Symeon Shimin. 1967, Macmillan $17.00 (0-02-742470-7); paper $4.99 (0-689-71695-8). 128pp. An 11-year-old African American city girl is lightly guided from her daydreams to reality by Zeely, who is as kind as she is tall and beautiful.

8977 Harrah, Madge. *The Nobody Club* (4–6). 1989, Avon paper $2.50 (0-380-75631-5). 166pp. Three misunderstood girls form a club to help solve one another's problems. (Rev: SLJ 8/89)

8978 Hartling, Peter. *Ben Loves Anna* (4–6). Trans. by J. H. Auerbach. Illus. by Ellen Weinstein. 1990, Overlook $12.95 (0-87951-401-9). 96pp. The feelings of a lovestruck 10-year-old boy are captured by one of Germany's most distinguished children's writers. (Rev: BCCB 4/91; BL 6/15/91; SLJ 5/91)

8979 Hatton, Caroline. *Vero and Philippe* (3–5). Illus. by Preston McDaniels. 2001, Front Street $14.95 (0-8126-2940-X). 120pp. Nine-year-old Vero and her family, Vietnamese immigrants to France, move from the country into the city, an adjustment made more difficult for Vero when her beloved nanny is fired. (Rev: BCCB 3/02; HBG 3/02; SLJ 12/01)

8980 Henkes, Kevin. *Sun and Spoon* (3–5). 1997, Greenwillow $15.00 (0-688-15232-5). 144pp. Spoon takes his dead grandmother's solitaire cards as a memento, but later he regrets his action. (Rev: BL 8/97; HB 9–10/97; HBG 3/98; SLJ 7/97*)

8981 Hershey, Mary. *My Big Sister Is So Bossy She Says You Can't Read This Book* (4–6). 2005, Random LB $17.99 (0-385-90917-9). 176pp. A realistic story about the various problems 10-year-old Effie faces at school and at home: her grandfather has died, her father is in prison, her best friend has moved away, and her older sister has stolen the Angel Scout funds. (Rev: BL 6/1–15/05; SLJ 6/05)

8982 Hesse, Karen. *Just Juice* (3–5). Illus. 1998, Scholastic $14.95 (0-590-03382-4). 144pp. Nine-year-old Juice, the middle child of five sisters growing up in a poor rural family, would rather stay home and help Pa in his machine shop and her diabetic mother instead of attending school where she has problems learning to read. (Rev: BCCB 12/98; BL 11/1/98; HB 11–12/98; HBG 3/99; SLJ 10/98)

8983 Hest, Amy. *The Great Green Notebook of Katie Roberts: Who Just Turned 12 on Monday* (3–5). Illus. 1998, Candlewick $14.99 (0-7636-0464-X). 112pp. Katie, now 12 and entering seventh grade, confides in her journal that she is suffering many of the problems of early adolescence. (Rev: BL 11/15/98; HB 1–2/99; HBG 3/99; SLJ 9/98)

8984 High, Linda O. *The Summer of the Great Divide* (5–8). 1996, Holiday House $15.95 (0-8234-1228-8). With the political events of 1969 as a backdrop, 13-year-old Wheezie sorts herself out at her relatives' farm. (Rev: BCCB 7–8/96; BL 6/1–15/96; BR 11–12/96; SLJ 4/96)

8985 Holden, Dwight. *Grand-Gran's Best Trick* (3–5). Illus. by Michael Chesworth. 1989, Brunner paper $8.95 (0-945354-16-9). 48pp. A young girl faces the sad experience of her beloved grandfather's death. (Rev: BL 12/1/89)

8986 Horvath, Penny. *Everything on a Waffle* (5–7). 2001, Farrar $16.00 (0-374-32236-8). 160pp. Eleven-year-old Primrose Squarp does not believe her parents drowned during a storm. In the meantime she is moved from pillar to post, ending up as a foster child to an elderly couple. (Rev: BCCB 3/01*; BL 2/15/01; HB 5–6/01*; HBG 10/01; SLJ 4/01)

8987 Hunt, Irene. *No Promises in the Wind* (5–8). 1987, Berkley paper $4.99 (0-425-09969-5). 100pp. During the Great Depression, Josh Grondowski is forced to make his own way in life.

8988 Hurwitz, Johanna. *Even Stephen* (5–9). Illus. 1996, Morrow $15.00 (0-688-14197-8). Allison's older brother, Stephen, who excels in both sports and school work, is considered both confident and independent until his basketball coach dies and he sinks into a deep depression. (Rev: BL 4/1/96; BR 9–10/96; SLJ 3/96)

8989 Hurwitz, Johanna. *Summer with Elisa* (2–4). Illus. 2000, HarperCollins $15.95 (0-688-17095-1). 96pp. Using a separate chapter for each incident, this book tells about a series of crises that a young girl faces during her summer vacation. (Rev: BL 9/15/00; HBG 3/01; SLJ 9/00)

8990 Hurwitz, Johanna. *Yellow Blue Jay* (3–5). Illus. by Donald Carrick. 1986, Morrow paper $4.95 (0-688-12278-7). 128pp. Shy city-boy Jay finds that two weeks at a Vermont cabin is not as bad as he feared. (Rev: BCCB 6/86; BL 6/15/86; SLJ 8/86)

8991 Huser, Glen. *Touch of the Clown* (5–9). 1999, Groundwood $15.95 (0-88899-343-9). 223pp. Since her mother's death, Barbara and her younger sister have been living with her abusive father and grandmother, both alcoholics, but her life seems to turn around when she secretly attends a clown workshop for teens and becomes friendly with the teacher. (Rev: SLJ 11/99)

8992 Irwin, Hadley. *The Lilith Summer* (6–8). 1979, Feminist Pr. $8.95 (0-912670-52-5). 126pp. Twelve-year-old Ellen learns about old age when she "lady sits" with 77-year-old Lilith Adams.

8993 Jarrow, Gail. *Beyond the Magic Sphere* (4–6). 1994, Harcourt $15.95 (0-15-200193-X). 192pp. S. B.'s only ray of hope during the summer she is spending with her unsympathetic cousin is meeting Cally, who plays a strange fantasy game. (Rev: BL 10/15/94; SLJ 11/94)

8994 Jiminez, Francisco. *Breaking Through* (5–8). 2001, Houghton Mifflin $15.00 (0-618-01173-0). 208pp. In this sequel to *The Circuit: Stories from the Life of a Migrant Child* (2001), 14-year-old Francisco recounts his efforts to improve his life and get a good education, as well as describing his school and romantic experiences. (Rev: BCCB 1/02; BL 9/1/01; HB 11–12/01; HBG 3/02; SLJ 9/01)

8995 Johnson, Emily Rhoads. *Write Me If You Dare!* (4–6). 2000, Front Street $15.95 (0-8126-2944-2). 208pp. While coping with her mother's death and her father's new girlfriend, 11-year-old Maddie decides that her pen pal is really a ghost. (Rev: BCCB 12/00; BL 11/1/00; HB 1–2/01; HBG 3/01; SLJ 11/00)

8996 Johnson, Spencer. *Who Moved My Cheese? for Kids: An A-Mazing Way to Change and Win!* (2–5). Illus. by Steve Pileggi. 2003, Penguin Putnam $19.99 (0-399-24016-0). 61pp. In this children's adaptation of the adult bestseller, the author recounts the adventures of four little friends as they learn to cope with the inevitable changes in their lives. (Rev: HBG 10/03; SLJ 10/03)

8997 Joosse, Barbara M. *Anna and the Cat Lady* (3–6). Illus. by Gretchen Will Mayo. 1992, HarperCollins LB $13.89 (0-06-020243-2). 176pp. Two third-graders rescue a kitten and meet an elderly eccentric woman who they later realize needs their help to survive. (Rev: BCCB 2/92; BL 1/1/92; SLJ 3/92)

8998 Kaye, Marilyn. *Real Heroes* (5–7). 1993, Avon paper $3.50 (0-380-72283-6). 144pp. Kevin finds he is in the middle of a situation involving quarrels between parents and between best friends, and a controversy about a teacher who is HIV positive. (Rev: BCCB 5/93; BL 4/1/93)

8999 Keene, Carolyn. *Love Times Three* (5–8). Series: River Heights. 1991, Pocket paper $3.50 (0-671-96703-7). 156pp. Nikki has a crush on Tim, but Brittany wants him too. (Rev: BL 12/15/89)

9000 Kehret, Peg. *My Brother Made Me Do It* (4–6). 2000, Pocket $16.00 (0-671-03418-9). 132pp. Written as a series of letters from 11-year-old Julie to a nursing home resident, this novel tells of Julie's problems with rheumatoid arthritis. (Rev: BL 6/1–15/00; HBG 10/00; SLJ 9/00)

9001 Kerr, Dan. *Candy on the Edge* (5–8). 2002, Coteau paper $8.95 (1-55050-189-5). 137pp. Candy, an 8th grader, finds herself drawn into a world of crime as she makes new friends and falls for Ramon. (Rev: SLJ 5/02)

9002 Killien, Christi. *Artie's Brief: The Whole Truth, and Nothing But* (5–7). 1989, Avon paper $2.95 (0-380-71108-7). 112pp. Sixth-grader Artie deals with the suicide of his older brother. (Rev: BL 5/15/89)

9003 Kinsey-Warnock, Natalie. *The Canada Geese Quilt* (4–6). Illus. by Leslie Bowman. 1989, Dutton $14.99 (0-525-65004-0). 64pp. Ariel and her grandmother adjust to the elderly woman's stroke and to a new baby in the family. (Rev: BCCB 1/90; BL 10/1/89*; SLJ 11/89*)

9004 Klass, Sheila S. *Kool Ada* (5–7). 1991, Scholastic paper $13.95 (0-590-43902-2). 176pp. Ada reacts only with her fists when she is sent to live in inner-city Chicago. (Rev: BL 10/15/91; SLJ 8/91*)

9005 Klass, Sheila S. *Little Women Next Door* (3–6). 2000, Holiday House $15.95 (0-8234-1472-8). 144pp. Lonely 11-year-old Susan Wilson's life changes when a group experimenting with communal life moves into the neighborhood. (Rev: HBG 3/01; SLJ 11/00)

9006 Klass, Sheila S. *The Uncivil War* (4–6). 1998, Holiday House $15.95 (0-8234-1329-2). 162pp. After she is taunted by the class bully, middle schooler Asa decides to mend her ways and, among other things, lose weight. (Rev: HBG 10/98; SLJ 4/98)

9007 Kline, Suzy. *Mary Marony and the Chocolate Surprise* (2–4). Illus. 1995, Penguin Putnam $14.99 (0-399-22829-2). 86pp. Mary Marony cheats to become a contest winner and later wonders if it was worth it. (Rev: BL 12/1/95; SLJ 12/95)

9008 Konigsburg, E. L. *Altogether, One at a Time* (4–6). Illus. by Gail E. Haley. 1971, Macmillan paper $4.99 (0-689-71290-1). 88pp. Four short stories by the Newbery Medal-winning writer, each of which explores the theme that compromise is often necessary to appreciate life fully.

9009 Konigsburg, E. L. *T-Backs, T-Shirts, Coat, and Suit* (5–8). 1993, Atheneum $16.95 (0-689-31855-3). When Chloe goes to visit her former flower-child aunt, she becomes part of a struggle for individual rights in the workplace. (Rev: BCCB 11/93; BL 11/1/93; SLJ 10/93*)

9010 Korman, Gordon. *Liar, Liar, Pants on Fire* (2–4). Illus. by JoAnn Adinolfi. 1997, Scholastic $14.95 (0-590-27142-3). 84pp. Third-grader Zoe lies so much that no one believes her when she tells the truth. (Rev: HBG 3/98; SLJ 9/97)

9011 Kornblatt, Marc. *Izzy's Place* (4–7). 2003, Simon & Schuster $16.95 (0-689-84639-8). 28pp. Summer with his grandmother proves more rewarding than 10-year-old Henry anticipated as he makes friends and gains a new outlook on life. (Rev: BL 6/1–15/03; HBG 10/03; SLJ 7/03)

9012 Koss, Amy Goldman. *The Girls* (5–9). 2000, Dial $16.99 (0-8037-2494-2). 128pp. In chapters narrated by different protagonists, this book tells of Maya who has been dropped for no apparent reason from a clique of five popular girls in the middle school she attends. (Rev: BCCB 6/00; BL 8/00; HB 7–8/00; HBG 10/00; SLJ 6/00)

9013 Krumgold, Joseph. *Onion John* (5–8). Illus. by Symeon Shimin. 1959, HarperCollins LB $16.89 (0-690-04698-7); paper $5.99 (0-06-440144-8). 248pp. A Newbery Medal winner (1960) about a boy's friendship with an old man. Also use the Newbery winner . . . *And Now Miguel* (1954).

9014 Lachtman, Ofelia Dumas. *The Summer of El Pintor* (5–8). 2001, Piñata paper $9.95 (1-55885-327-8). 234pp. Sixteen-year-old Monica's father loses his job and the two move from their wealthy neighborhood to the barrio house in which her dead mother grew up, where Monica searches for a missing neighbor and discovers the truth of her past. (Rev: BL 8/01; SLJ 7/01)

9015 Laser, Michael. *6-321* (4–7). 2001, Simon & Schuster $15.00 (0-689-83372-5). 115pp. In this autobiographical novel set in 1963, 6th-grader Marc Chaikin falls in love, experiences his parents' divorce, and reacts to the assassination of John F. Kennedy. (Rev: BCCB 2/01; BL 1/1–15/01; HBG 10/01; SLJ 5/01)

9016 Lawson, Julie. *Turns on a Dime* (5–8). 1999, Stoddart paper $7.95 (0-7737-5942-5). In this sequel to *Goldstone* (1998), set in British Columbia, 11-year-old Jo faces many new situations, including finding a boyfriend, discovering that she is adopted, and learning that her beloved babysitter is pregnant. (Rev: SLJ 6/99)

9017 Lemieux, Michele. *Stormy Night* (4–8). Illus. by author. 1999, Kids Can $15.95 (1-55074-692-8). 240pp. A long picture book in which a young girl who can't sleep ponders questions that are common to preteen girls. (Rev: BL 12/1/99; HBG 3/00; SLJ 12/99)

9018 Lester, Alison. *The Quicksand Pony* (5–8). 1998, Houghton Mifflin $15.00 (0-395-93749-3). In this novel set in Australia, 17-year-old Joycie fakes a drowning and seeks a new life in the bush with her infant son, but two young girls stumble on the truth nine years later. (Rev: BCCB 10/98; BL 12/15/98; HB 1–2/99; HBG 3/99; SLJ 10/98)

9019 Leverich, Kathleen. *Daisy* (2–4). Illus. 1997, HarperCollins paper $4.25 (0-06-442019-1). 96pp. Daisy is unhappy when she discovers she will be only one of several flower girls at an upcoming wedding. Other stories about flower girls are *Violet, Rose,* and *Heather* (all 1997). (Rev: BL 7/97; HB 5–6/97; SLJ 4/97)

9020 Leverich, Kathleen. *The New You* (5–8). 1998, Greenwillow $15.00 (0-688-16076-X). 128pp. Abby, who recently moved to New York City and entered a new school, is unhappy and friendless until she begins to share her experiences with others. (Rev: BL 11/1/98; HBG 3/99; SLJ 11/98)

9021 Levy, Elizabeth. *Cheater, Cheater* (5–8). 1994, Scholastic paper $3.50 (0-590-45866-3). Lucy Lovello has been labeled a cheater and even her teachers don't trust her. When she finds her best friend cheating, she faces a moral dilemma. (Rev: BL 10/1/93; SLJ 10/93)

9022 Levy, Elizabeth. *My Life as a Fifth-Grade Comedian* (4–6). Illus. 1997, HarperCollins $15.95 (0-06-026602-3). 128pp. Jimmy, a born joker, has problems at home and finds that his grades are slipping at school. (Rev: BL 8/97; HBG 3/98; SLJ 9/97)

9023 Lewis, Beverly. *Catch a Falling Star* (5–8). Series: Summerhill Secrets. 1995, Bethany House paper $5.99 (1-55661-478-0). 144pp. An Amish boy faces excommunication when he begins paying too much attention to a non-Amish girl. (Rev: BL 3/15/96)

9024 Lewis, Beverly. *Night of the Fireflies* (5–8). Series: Summerhill Secrets. 1995, Bethany House paper $5.99 (1-55661-479-9). In this sequel to *Catch a Falling Star* (1995), Levi, an Amish boy, tries to save his young sister, who has been struck by a car. (Rev: BL 3/15/96)

9025 Lewis, Maggie. *Morgy Makes His Move* (3–5). Illus. 1999, Houghton Mifflin $15.00 (0-395-92284-4). 80pp. A pleasant novel that tells of third-grader Morgan and his adjustment to his new home in Massachusetts, which involves coping with a bully named Ferguson. (Rev: BCCB 10/99; BL 12/15/99; HBG 3/00; SLJ 11/99)

9026 Little, Jean. *Birdie for Now* (3–5). Illus. 2002, Orca paper $4.99 (1-55143-203-X). 160pp. Troubled, hyperactive Dickon moves to a new home and finds joy and self-knowledge when he gets the opportunity to train an abused dog. (Rev: BL 11/1/02; SLJ 12/02)

9027 Love, D. Anne. *My Lone Star Summer* (4–6). 1996, Holiday House $15.95 (0-8234-1235-0). 192pp. Jill experiences the first problems of adolescence when she spends her 12th summer visiting her grandmother's ranch. (Rev: BCCB 7–8/96; BL 5/1/96; SLJ 3/96)

9028 McKay, Hilary. *Indigo's Star* (5–8). 2004, Simon & Schuster $15.95 (0-689-86563-5). 272pp. In this sequel to *Saffy's Angel* (2002), Saffy's younger siblings — 12-year-old Indigo and 8-year-old Rose — take a stand against school bullies with the help of a lonely young American called Tom. (Rev: BL 9/15/04; SLJ 9/04*)

9029 McKenna, Colleen O'Shaughnessy. *Fifth Grade: Here Comes Trouble* (4–6). 1991, Scholastic paper $3.25 (0-590-41734-7). 128pp. Collette feels insecure when her rich friend invites her to her first boy-girl party. (Rev: BCCB 10/89; SLJ 9/89)

9030 MacLachlan, Patricia. *The Facts and Fictions of Minna Pratt* (5–7). 1988, HarperCollins LB $15.89 (0-06-024117-9); paper $5.99 (0-06-440265-

7). 144pp. A budding young cellist on the verge of adolescence experiences her first boyfriend. (Rev: BCCB 4/88; BL 6/15/88; SLJ 6–7/88)

9031 MacLachlan, Patricia. *Unclaimed Treasures* (5–8). 1984, HarperCollins paper $4.95 (0-06-440189-8). 128pp. A romantic story of a young girl finding herself.

9032 Masterman-Smith, Virginia. *First Mate Tate* (5–9). 2000, Marshall Cavendish $14.95 (0-7614-5075-0). 204pp. The story of a young girl in Atlantic City and her parents who are addicted to gambling. (Rev: BL 10/15/00; HBG 3/01; SLJ 9/00)

9033 Miles, Miska. *Annie and the Old One* (2–5). Illus. by Peter Parnall. 1972, Little, Brown $16.95 (0-316-57117-2); paper $7.95 (0-316-57120-2). Annie, a young Navajo girl, realizes her wonderful grandmother is dying and tries to put off the inevitable.

9034 Miles, Miska. *Gertrude's Pocket* (3–5). Illus. by Emily Arnold McCully. 1984, Peter Smith $15.75 (0-8446-6164-3). A reissue of a 1970 title in which Gertrude's tormentor gets his comeuppance in a story about poor folk in Appalachia.

9035 Mills, Claudia. *Cally's Enterprise* (4–6). 1989, Avon paper $2.75 (0-380-70693-8). 128pp. Cally, the daughter of overachievers, breaks her foot and can't go to ballet and gym, and to her surprise learns that she likes being a businesswoman when her friend Chuck gets her to sell magazines. (Rev: BCCB 4/88; BL 6/1/88; SLJ 5/88)

9036 Mills, Claudia. *Gus and Grandpa and the Two-Wheeled Bike* (1–3). Illus. 1999, Farrar $13.00 (0-374-32821-8). 48pp. An easy chapter book about Gus who doesn't feel confident in trying to ride his new bike without, at least, training wheels. (Rev: BL 2/1/99; HB 3–4/99; HBG 10/99; SLJ 4/99)

9037 Mills, Claudia. *Makeovers by Marcia* (4–7). Series: West Creek Middle School. 2005, Farrar $16.00 (0-374-34654-2). 160pp. Marcia learns that beauty is more than skin deep — and that there are more important things than the school dance — when she gives makeovers to the women in a nursing home. (Rev: BL 3/1/05; SLJ 2/05)

9038 Mills, Claudia. *Perfectly Chelsea* (3–5). Illus. by Jacqueline Rogers. 2004, Farrar $16.00 (0-374-31244-3). 128pp. Perfectionist fourth-grader Chelsea must question her own behavior in this story in which religion plays a large role. (Rev: BL 2/1/04; HB 5–6/04; SLJ 5/04)

9039 Mills, Lauren. *The Rag Coat* (3–5). Illus. 1991, Little, Brown $16.95 (0-316-57407-4). 32pp. A picture book that celebrates Appalachia. (Rev: BCCB 1/92; BL 10/15/91; HB 11–12/91; SLJ 11/91*)

9040 Mohr, Nicholasa. *The Magic Shell* (2–4). Illus. 1995, Scholastic $13.95 (0-590-47110-4). 112pp. A young boy is not happy in his new home in New York City and misses his native land, the Dominican Republic. (Rev: BCCB 12/95; BL 8/95; SLJ 10/95)

9041 Montgomery, L. M. *Anne of Green Gables* (5–8). Illus. by Jody Lee. 1983, Penguin Putnam $15.99 (0-448-06030-2). 384pp. The old-fashioned story of an orphan girl and her adventures. Others in this series are available in paperback from Bantam.

9042 Moore, Emily. *Whose Side Are You On?* (5–7). 1988, Farrar paper $5.95 (0-374-48373-6). 128pp. Barbra is dismayed to find out that her math tutor is none other than T.J., the class pest. (Rev: BCCB 10/88; BL 1/15/89; SLJ 10/88)

9043 Morgan, Nicola. *Chicken Friend* (5–7). 2005, Candlewick $15.99 (0-7636-2735-6). 160pp. When her family moves to the country, Becca tries too hard to be cool and winds up in trouble in this story told from a believable pre-teen point of view. (Rev: BL 3/1/05; SLJ 4/05)

9044 Moss, Marissa. *Amelia Works It Out* (3–5). Illus. Series: Amelia's Notebook. 2000, Pleasant Co. $12.95 (1-58485-081-7). 44pp. In this novel in journal form, Amelia tries different jobs in an effort to make enough money to buy an expensive pair of shoes that her mother refuses to get for her. (Rev: BL 9/1/00; HBG 3/01; SLJ 9/00)

9045 Moss, Marissa. *Oh Boy, Amelia!* (2–5). Illus. by author. 2001, Pleasant Co. $12.95 (1-58485-344-1); paper $5.95 (1-58485-330-1). 38pp. Amelia's notebook is filled with humorous entries about her sister's crush on a boy and her own aversion to "feminine" activities such as cooking and sewing. (Rev: BL 1/1–15/02; HBG 3/02; SLJ 10/01)

9046 Murray, Martine. *The Slightly True Story of Cedar B. Hartley (Who Planned to Live an Unusual Life)* (5–8). Illus. 2003, Scholastic $15.95 (0-439-48622-X). 240pp. Cedar, 13, is indeed unusual in her questioning nature, her outlook on life, her advanced vocabulary, and her ability to connect with people of all sorts. (Rev: BCCB 9/03; BL 11/15/03*; HB 9–10/03; HBG 9–10/03; SLJ 10/03*)

9047 Myracle, Lauren. *Eleven* (4–7). 2004, Dutton $16.99 (0-525-47165-0). 208pp. Covering Winnie's life from her 11th birthday to her 12th, this novel reveals typical friendship and family tensions. (Rev: BL 4/15/04; SLJ 2/04)

9048 Olsson, Soren, and Anders Jacobsson. *In Ned's Head* (4–6). Trans. by Kevin Read. Illus. 2001, Simon & Schuster $16.00 (0-689-83870-0). 144pp. In diary format, this book describes the trials and tribulations of growing up as experienced by 11-year-old Ned Floyd, who uses the code name Treb Vladinsky. (Rev: BCCB 3/01; BL 4/1/01; HBG 10/01; SLJ 6/01)

9049 Paterson, Katherine. *The Great Gilly Hopkins* (4–6). 1978, HarperCollins LB $15.89 (0-690-03838-0); paper $5.95 (0-06-440201-0). 192pp. Precocious Gilly bounces from one foster home to another.

9050 Paulsen, Gary. *Brian's Return* (5–8). 1999, Delacorte $15.95 (0-385-32500-2). 117pp. Brian, the hero of *Brian's Winter,* becomes so disheartened with life at school away from the wilderness that he decides to leave society behind forever. (Rev: BL 2/1/99; HB 1–2/99; HBG 10/99; SLJ 2/99)

9051 Paulsen, Gary. *The Cookcamp* (5–7). 1991, Orchard paper $15.95 (0-531-05927-8). 128pp. After a 5-year-old boy discovers his mother is having an affair, he is sent off to northern Minnesota in this World War II story. (Rev: BCCB 3/91; BL 3/1/91; HB 3–4/91; SLJ 2/91*)

9052 Peterseil, Tehila. *The Safe Place* (5–8). 1996, Pitspopany $16.95 (0-943706-71-8); paper $12.95 (0-943706-72-6). 136pp. A moving story of an Israeli girl and the problems she faces at school because of a learning disability. (Rev: SLJ 12/96)

9053 Pevsner, Stella. *Is Everyone Moonburned But Me?* (4–7). 2000, Clarion $15.00 (0-395-95770-2). 208pp. In this lighthearted look at adolescent problems, 13-year-old Hannah shoulders many household responsibilities when her parents divorce. (Rev: BCCB 6/00; BL 5/1/00; HBG 10/00; SLJ 7/00)

9054 Philbrick, Rodman. *The Fire Pony* (5–8). 1996, Scholastic paper $14.95 (0-590-55251-1). Rescued from a foster home by his half-brother Joe, Roy hopes that life will be better on the ranch where Joe finds work. (Rev: BCCB 7–8/96; BL 5/1/96; HB 7–8/96; SLJ 9/96)

9055 Polikoff, Barbara Garland. *Why Does the Coqui Sing?* (5–8). 2004, Holiday House $16.95 (0-8234-1817-0). 213pp. Thirteen-year-old Luz and her brother Rome have trouble adjusting when they move from Chicago to Puerto Rico with their mother and stepfather. (Rev: BL 5/15/04; SLJ 6/04)

9056 Porter, Tracey. *A Dance of Sisters* (5–8). 2002, HarperCollins LB $17.89 (0-06-029239-3). 288pp. When a young ballet dancer's dreams are dashed, she is comforted by her sister. (Rev: BCCB 1/03; BL 2/15/03; HBG 3/03; SLJ 1/03)

9057 Prinz, Yvonne. *Still There, Clare* (5–8). 2005, Raincoast paper $6.95 (1-55192-644-X). 176pp. Clare's 13th summer is a time of change: a friend moves away, her aunt begins dating her gym teacher, and she realizes it is time to give up her imaginary friend. (Rev: BL 3/1/05; SLJ 4/05)

9058 Richardson, Judith B. *David's Landing* (4–6). Illus. by Molly Bang. 1984, Woods Hole $10.95 (0-9611374-1-X). 150pp. A boy troubled by his parents' divorce is healed in this old-fashioned story of life in a small town. (Rev: BL 8/85; HB 9–10/85)

9059 Robinson, Nancy K. *Countess Veronica* (4–6). 1994, Scholastic $13.95 (0-590-44485-9). 176pp. Pesky Veronica Schmidt tries to marry off her father to the local librarian. (Rev: BL 2/1/94; SLJ 4/94)

9060 Rodowsky, Colby. *Jason Rat-a-tat* (2–4). Illus. by Beth Peck. 2002, Farrar $15.00 (0-374-33671-7). 80pp. In Jason's family everyone else is engaged in a sport, but Jason's grandfather discovers the boy's true talent in this beginning chapter book. (Rev: BCCB 5/02; BL 6/1–15/02; HBG 10/02; SLJ 4/02)

9061 Rodowsky, Colby. *The Next-Door Dogs* (2–4). Illus. by Amy June Bates. 2005, Farrar $15.00 (0-374-36410-9). 112pp. Sara overcomes her fear of dogs in order to help her new next-door neighbor. (Rev: BL 3/1/05; SLJ 6/05)

9062 Rosen, Michael. *Michael Rosen's Sad Book* (2–4). Illus. by Quentin Blake. 2005, Candlewick $16.99 (0-7636-2597-3). 32pp. An honest and very moving look at the author's grief over the death of his son. (Rev: BL 5/15/05; SLJ 3/05)

9063 Rosen, Michael J. *The Blessing of the Animals* (3–6). 2000, Farrar $15.00 (0-374-30838-1). 96pp. A Jewish boy wants to take his dog to be blessed at the St. Francis Festival and consults a number of people about whether this is a proper thing for him to do. (Rev: BL 11/1/00; HBG 3/01; SLJ 11/00)

9064 Rottman, S. L. *Hero* (5–8). 1997, Peachtree $14.95 (1-56145-159-2). When his home life becomes unbearable, Sean is sent to Carbondale Ranch, where his sense of self-worth gradually grows. (Rev: BL 12/1/97; HBG 3/98; SLJ 12/97)

9065 Ryan, Mary C. *The Voice from the Mendelsohns' Maple* (5–7). Illus. by Irena Roman. 1990, Little, Brown $13.95 (0-316-76360-8). 132pp. Penny tries to cope with many problems, including finding out the identity of the woman who is hiding in the neighbor's maple tree. (Rev: SLJ 12/89)

9066 Sachar, Louis. *Marvin Redpost: Why Pick on Me?* (2–4). Illus. by Barbara Sullivan. 1993, Random LB $11.99 (0-679-91947-3); paper $3.99 (0-679-81947-9). 40pp. Marvin becomes a social outcast after he is wrongfully accused of picking his nose. (Rev: BCCB 2/93; BL 5/1/93)

9067 Sachar, Louis. *Stanley Yelnats' Survival Guide to Camp Green Lake* (5–7). Illus. by Jeff Newman. 2003, Dell paper $4.99 (0-440-41947-6). 90pp. In this companion book to *Holes* (1998), Stanley Yelnats provides additional information about the detention camp's idiosyncrasies and his fellow diggers, as well as survival tips such as how to identify rattlesnakes. (Rev: SLJ 9/03)

9068 Santucci, Barbara. *Loon Summer* (1–4). Illus. by Andrea Shine. 2001, Eerdmans $16.00 (0-8028-5182-7). Rainie has fun at the lake with her newly separated father and, although she wishes her mother were there, she learns to accept that things have changed. (Rev: SLJ 8/01)

9069 Say, Allen. *The Sign Painter* (5–9). Illus. 2000, Houghton Mifflin $17.00 (0-395-97974-9). 32pp. An Asian American youth who wants to be a serious artist gets a job painting signboards scattered through the desert. (Rev: BL 10/1/00; HB 9–10/00; HBG 3/01; SLJ 9/00)

9070 Schumacher, Julie. *The Chain Letter* (5–7). 2005, Delacorte LB $17.99 (0-385-90205-0). 195pp. Livvie, 12, throws away a chain letter, which seems to spawn a series of calamities. (Rev: LMC 3/05; SLJ 3/05)

9071 Shreve, Susan. *Jonah, the Whale* (4–6). 1998, Scholastic $14.95 (0-590-37133-9). 128pp. After his family moves to New Haven, Connecticut, overweight 11-year-old Jonah finds friendship with another outsider, the sassy Blister, and achieves fulfillment by fantasizing that he is a famous TV personality. (Rev: BCCB 4/98; BL 5/1/98; HBG 10/98; SLJ 4/98)

9072 Shura, Mary Francis. *The Search for Grissi* (4–6). Illus. by Ted Lewin. 1987, Avon paper $3.50 (0-380-70305-X). Eleven-year-old Peter has difficulty adjusting to life in Peoria until his little sister involves him in a search for her lost cat. (Rev: BCCB 7/85; BL 3/15/85; SLJ 5/85)

9073 Shura, Mary Francis. *The Sunday Doll* (5–7). 1988, Avon paper $2.95 (0-380-70618-0). 112pp. Thirteen-year-old Emmy is miffed when the family won't tell her what has happened to upset her older sister Jayne, until she learns that Jayne's boyfriend has committed suicide. (Rev: BCCB 7–8/88; BL 7/88; SLJ 8/88)

9074 Siebold, Jan. *Doing Time Online* (3–5). 2002, Whitman $13.95 (0-8075-5959-8). 96pp. Young Mitch learns an important lesson through his community-service e-mail correspondence with the elderly Wootie. (Rev: BL 5/15/02; HBG 10/02; SLJ 3/02)

9075 Silverman. *Mirror Mirror: Twisted Tales* (5–8). 2002, Scholastic paper $15.95 (0-439-29593-9). 192pp. Disturbing stories serve as metaphors for the problems of drug use, divorce, homelessness, and other ills. (Rev: BL 9/1/02; HBG 10/02; SLJ 8/02)

9076 Skinner, Daphne. *Almost Invisible Irene* (1–3). Illus. by Jerry Smath. Series: Science Solves It! 2003, Kane paper $4.99 (1-57565-129-7). 32pp. Little Irene is very, very shy, so she applies the lessons she's learned about animal camouflage to avoid unwanted attention by blending in with her surroundings. (Rev: SLJ 1/04)

9077 Slepian, Jan. *The Broccoli Tapes* (5–8). 1989, Penguin Putnam $15.99 (0-399-21712-6); Scholastic paper $3.50 (0-590-43473-X). Sara uses tapes during her stay in Hawaii to keep up with her class oral history project. (Rev: BCCB 4/89; BL 4/15/89; SLJ 4/89)

9078 Smith, Cynthia Leitich. *Rain Is Not My Indian Name* (5–9). 2001, HarperCollins LB $15.89 (0-06-029504-X). 144pp. Native American girl Rain's love of photography helps her to overcome her terrible grief at the death of a friend. (Rev: BCCB 9/01; HBG 3/02; SLJ 6/01)

9079 Smith, Doris Buchanan. *A Taste of Blackberries* (4–6). Illus. by Charles Robinson. 1973, HarperCollins LB $14.89 (0-690-80512-8); paper $4.95 (0-06-440238-X). 64pp. Young Jamie dies unexpectedly of a bee sting, and his friends adjust to this loss.

9080 Smith, Robert K. *Jelly Belly* (4–6). Illus. by Bob Jones. 1982, Dell paper $4.50 (0-440-44207-9). 160pp. A boy is sent to a weight-loss camp by his parents.

9081 Sonenklar, Carol. *Mighty Boy* (3–6). 1999, Orchard LB $16.99 (0-531-33203-9). 128pp. Transplanted to New York City, lonely 9-year-old Howard Weinstein retreats into a fantasy world when the class bully harasses him. (Rev: BCCB 1/00; BL 10/15/99; HBG 3/00; SLJ 10/99)

9082 Sonenklar, Carol. *My Own Worst Enemy* (5–8). 1999, Holiday House $15.95 (0-8234-1456-6). In this first-person narrative, Eve Belkin finds there is a price to pay when she outdoes herself to be popular in her new school. (Rev: BL 5/15/99; HBG 9/99; SLJ 8/99)

9083 Soto, Gary. *The Pool Party* (4–7). Illus. by Robert Casilla. 1992, Delacorte $13.95 (0-385-30890-6). 112pp. Rudy, part of a Mexican American family, has growing-up problems. (Rev: SLJ 6/93)

9084 Spinelli, Jerry. *Wringer* (4–7). 1997, Harper-Collins LB $16.89 (0-06-024914-5). 192pp. A sensitive boy must participate in the massacre of thousands of pigeons released at an annual fair. (Rev: BL 9/1/97*; HB 9–10/97; HBG 3/98; SLJ 9/97*)

9085 Spurr, Elizabeth. *Lupe and Me* (3–4). Illus. by Enrique O. Sanchez. 1995, Harcourt $13.00 (0-15-200522-6). 40pp. Susan is upset when her mother's housekeeper, 16-year-old Lupe, has to return to Mexico because she is an illegal alien. (Rev: BL 6/1–15/95; SLJ 6/95)

9086 Stewart, Jennifer J. *The Bean King's Daughter* (5–7). 2002, Holiday House $16.95 (0-8234-1644-5). 138pp. Phoebe, a 12-year-old heiress, reluctantly learns about herself and her young stepmother while at an Arizona ranch. (Rev: BL 9/1/02; HBG 10/02; SLJ 7/02)

9087 Stiles, Martha Bennett. *Sarah the Dragon Lady* (4–6). 1986, Avon paper $2.75 (0-380-70471-4). 96pp. Sarah tries to adjust to life in a small Kentucky town and face the fact of trouble in her parents' marriage. (Rev: BCCB 2/87; BL 1/1/87; SLJ 12/86)

9088 Stinson, Kathy. *King of the Castle* (3–4). Illus. by Kasia Charko. 2001, Second Story paper $5.95 (1-896764-35-5). 61pp. Watching his grandson at his studies inspires school custodian Mr. Elliott to learn to read himself. (Rev: SLJ 8/01)

9089 Stone, Phoebe. *Sonata #1 for Riley Red* (5–8). 2003, Little, Brown $15.95 (0-316-99041-8). 194pp. Thirteen-year-old Rachel and three friends share their deepest secrets with one another while they are in hiding after liberating a neglected elephant in this appealing novel set in 1960s Boston. (Rev: BL 1/1–15/04; HBG 4/04; SLJ 1/04)

9090 Strasser, Todd. *CON-fidence* (5–8). 2002, Holiday House $16.95 (0-8234-1394-2). 176pp. Shy Lauren falls under the spell of the dazzling Celeste, failing to perceive Celeste's underlying motives. (Rev: BCCB 2/03; BL 4/15/03; HBG 10/03; SLJ 1/03)

9091 Tabor, Nancy María Grande. *Bottles Break* (1–4). Illus. by author. 1999, Charlesbridge LB $15.95 (0-88106-317-7); paper $6.95 (0-88106-318-5). A young narrator, the child of an alcoholic mother, tells about his fears, confusion, and low self-esteem and about the help he receives from an understanding teacher. (Rev: HBG 10/99; SLJ 5/99)

9092 Tamar, Erika. *Katherine's Story* (4–6). Series: The Girls of Lighthouse Lane. 2004, HarperCollins LB $13.89 (0-06-054342-6). 165pp. Twelve-year-old Kat's artistic ambitions are stymied in this novel set in the early 20th century and the first in a series based on Thomas Kinkade's paintings. (Rev: SLJ 4/04)

9093 Testa, Maria. *Nine Candles* (3–5). Illus. 1996, Carolrhoda LB $19.93 (0-87614-940-9). 32pp. Raymond is looking forward to visiting his mother, who is in prison. (Rev: BCCB 9/96; BL 7/96; SLJ 9/96)

9094 Testa, Maria. *Someplace to Go* (3–5). Illus. 1996, Whitman LB $14.95 (0-8075-7524-0). 32pp. Unlike his classmates, Davey has no home to return to after school. (Rev: BCCB 3/96; BL 4/15/96; SLJ 5/96)

9095 Tolliver, Ruby C. *I Love You, Daisy Phew* (4–6). 1994, Hendrick-Long LB $14.95 (0-937460-86-9). 168pp. Blake finds an unusual pet in a goat named Daisy Phew when the troubled boy goes to live with his grandfather in Texas. (Rev: BL 1/15/95)

9096 Toten, Teresa. *The Onlyhouse* (5–8). 1996, Red Deer paper $7.95 (0-88995-137-3). Eleven-year-old Lucija, whose family was originally from Croatia, relocates to a new house in suburban Toronto after several years in a dense downtown neighborhood with a large immigrant population, and must adjust to a new school, peer pressures, and bullies. (Rev: SLJ 7/96)

9097 Trueman, Terry. *Stuck in Neutral* (5–9). 2000, HarperCollins LB $14.89 (0-06-028518-4). 114pp. Shawn McDaniel, a 14-year-old who appears to be retarded because of cerebral palsy, narrates this novel in a way that shows the reader he is really a near-genius. (Rev: BL 7/00; HB 5–6/00; HBG 10/00; SLJ 7/00)

9098 Ure, Jean. *Skinny Melon and Me* (5–7). Illus. 2001, Holt $16.00 (0-8050-6359-5). 202pp. An interesting British novel about a young Cherry Waterton, who keeps a diary; her mother's boyfriend who sends Cherry rebus letters to win her over; and Cherry's teacher, who writes to a friend about the girl's problem behavior. (Rev: BCCB 3/01; BL 1/1–15/01; HBG 10/01; SLJ 1/01)

9099 Vail, Rachel. *Daring to Be Abigail* (4–6). 1996, Orchard LB $16.99 (0-531-08867-7). 144pp. At summer camp, Abigail deliberately misbehaves so she won't be considered an outsider by the in-crowd. (Rev: BCCB 2/96; BL 3/1/96; HB 5–6/96; SLJ 3/96*)

9100 Vail, Rachel. *Do-Over* (5–9). 1992, Avon paper $3.99 (0-380-72180-5). The story of 13-year-old Whitman Levy's first crush, first kiss, first heartbreak, and first real boy-girl relationship, as well as assorted family problems. (Rev: BL 8/92*; SLJ 9/92)

9101 Vail, Rachel. *Ever After* (5–9). 1994, Orchard LB $16.99 (0-531-08688-7); Avon paper $3.99 (0-380-72465-0). Fourteen-year-old Molly is trying to act maturely but always seems to mess things up. (Rev: BCCB 4/94; BL 3/1/94; HB 5–6/94, 7–8/94; SLJ 5/94*)

9102 Wagner, Jane. *J.T.* (4–6). Photos by Gordon Parks. 1972, Dell paper $4.99 (0-440-44275-3). 128pp. J. T. Gamble lives in Harlem, and his most prized possessions are a tiny portable radio and a stray cat, for whom he has made a home.

9103 Wainwright, Richard M. *Mountains to Climb* (3–5). Illus. by Jack Crompton. 1991, Family Life $18.00 (0-9619566-3-1). 56pp. During his two-year stay in the United States, a young Ecuadoran boy gradually wins his classmates' acceptance. (Rev: BL 12/15/91; SLJ 1/92)

9104 Walker, Alice. *To Hell with Dying* (4–7). Illus. 1988, Harcourt paper $8.00 (0-15-289074-2). The Walker family won't let old Mr. Sweet die. (Rev: BCCB 4/88; BL 4/15/88; HB 7–8/88)

9105 Walpole, Peter. *The Healer of Harrow Point* (4–7). 2000, Hampton Roads paper $11.95 (1-57174-167-4). 131pp. A novel of love and compassion about a boy who is promised a hunting trip for his twelfth birthday but wonders if he can kill a deer, particularly after seeing one killed by poachers and after meeting Emma, who can heal animals with her touch. (Rev: SLJ 10/00)

9106 Walter, Mildred P. *Justin and the Best Biscuits in the World* (3–5). Illus. by Catherine Stock. 1986, Lothrop $16.00 (0-688-06645-3); Knopf paper $3.25 (0-679-80346-7). 128pp. Justin thinks some things are "women's work" until his grandfather shows him differently. (Rev: BCCB 12/86; BL 10/15/86; SLJ 11/86)

9107 Wetter, Bruce. *The Boy with the Lampshade on His Head* (5–8). 2004, Simon & Schuster $16.95 (0-689-85032-8). 304pp. Painfully shy, 11-year-old Stanley Krakow maintains a low profile but a rich inner life until he makes friends with an abused girl and finds the inner strength to be a real hero. (Rev: BL 5/1/04; SLJ 8/04)

9108 White Deer of Autumn. *The Great Change* (3–5). Illus. by Carol Grigg. 1992, Beyond Words $14.95 (0-941831-79-5). After Grandfather's death, a Native American woman explains the circle of life to her granddaughter. (Rev: SLJ 12/92)

9109 Williams, Karen L. *One Thing I'm Good At* (3–5). 1999, Lothrop $15.00 (0-688-16846-9). 144pp. Julie is developing an inferiority complex, but her ability to shoot marbles helps her gain a feeling of self-worth. (Rev: BCCB 12/99; BL 10/15/99; HBG 3/00; SLJ 12/99)

9110 Willner-Pardo, Gina. *Jumping into Nothing* (3–5). Illus. 1999, Clarion $14.00 (0-395-84130-5). 64pp. Sophie is afraid to jump off the high board at the local pool, but gradually she overcomes her fear. (Rev: BCCB 4/99; BL 3/15/99; HB 5–6/99; HBG 10/99; SLJ 5/99)

9111 Wilson, Jacqueline. *The Worry Web Site* (3–6). 2003, Delacorte LB $16.99 (0-385-90105-4). 105pp. To give his students an outlet for their fears and concerns, Mr. Speed creates a Web site where they can anonymously post stories about their personal problems. (Rev: BL 1/1–15/04; HBG 4/04; SLJ 12/03)

9112 Wilson, Johnniece M. *Poor Girl* (5–7). 1992, Scholastic $13.95 (0-590-44732-7). 176pp. A first-person story about Miranda, who spends the summer trying to earn money for contact lenses before the fall. (Rev: BCCB 4/92; BL 8/92; SLJ 4/92)

9113 Wilson, Johnniece M. *Robin on His Own* (4–6). 1992, Scholastic paper $2.95 (0-590-41809-2). 144pp. Watusi the cat comforts a young black boy when his mother dies. (Rev: BL 10/15/90; SLJ 1/91)

9114 Wojciechowska, Maia. *Shadow of a Bull* (5–8). Illus. by Alvin Smith. 1964, Macmillan $16.95 (0-689-30042-5); paper $4.99 (0-689-71567-6). 160pp.

Manolo, surviving son of a great bullfighter, has his own "moment of truth" when he faces his first bull. Newbery Medal winner, 1965.

9115 Wojciechowski, Susan. *Beany and the Dreaded Wedding* (3–5). Illus. 2000, Candlewick $15.99 (0-7636-0924-2). 128pp. Beany is worried about everything involving her role as flower girl at her cousin's wedding. (Rev: BCCB 12/00; BL 11/15/00; HBG 3/01; SLJ 10/00)

9116 Wood, June R. *Turtle on a Fence Post* (5–8). 1997, Penguin Putnam paper $6.99 (0-698-11783-2). 260pp. After the deaths of her parents and an uncle, Delrita, now living with an aunt and her husband, is so emotionally upset that it seems she will never love anyone again. A sequel to *The Man Who Loved Clowns* (1992). (Rev: BL 11/15/97; HBG 3/98; SLJ 9/97)

9117 Woodruff, Elvira. *The Secret Funeral of Slim Jim the Snake* (4–5). 1993, Holiday House $15.95 (0-8234-1014-5). 144pp. Nick lives over a funeral home and faces some problems with humorous solutions. (Rev: SLJ 3/93)

9118 Wright, Betty R. *The Summer of Mrs. MacGregor* (5–8). 1986, Holiday House $15.95 (0-8234-0628-8). 160pp. Meeting an exotic teenager who calls herself Mrs. Lillina MacGregor helps Linda solve her problem of jealousy toward her older sister. (Rev: BCCB 12/86; BL 11/1/86; SLJ 11/86)

9119 Wright, Betty R. *The Wish Master* (3–6). 2000, Holiday House $15.95 (0-8234-1611-9). 112pp. Transported to his grandparents' home in Wisconsin for the summer, unhappy Corby wishes on a pile of rocks known as the Wish Master for a way to go home. (Rev: BCCB 1/01; BL 11/1/00; HBG 10/01; SLJ 12/00)

9120 Young, Ronder T. *Moving Mama to Town* (5–8). 1997, Orchard LB $18.99 (0-531-33025-7). Although his father is a gambler and a failure, Fred never loses faith in him in this story of a boy who must help support his family although he's only 13. (Rev: BL 6/1–15/97; BR 9–10/97; HB 7–8/97; SLJ 6/97)

Physical and Emotional Problems

9121 Abbott, Deborah, and Henry Kisor. *One TV Blasting and a Pig Outdoors* (3–5). Illus. 1994, Whitman LB $14.95 (0-8075-6075-8). 40pp. A book that describes what it's like to live in a household where the father is deaf. (Rev: BL 9/15/94; SLJ 12/94)

9122 Bang, Molly. *Tiger's Fall* (3–6). 2001, Holt $15.95 (0-8050-6689-6). 110pp. After a fall leaves 11-year-old Lupe paralyzed from the waist down, she is sent to the village center for disabled people where she learns to cope with her challenges and finds hope for the future. (Rev: BCCB 12/01; BL 11/1/01; HBG 3/02; SLJ 12/01)

9123 Baskin, Nora Raleigh. *Almost Home* (5–8). 2003, Little, Brown $16.95 (0-316-09313-0). 173pp. Her friendship with Will helps 6th-grader Leah to gain confidence both at school and at her new home with her father and stepmother. (Rev: BL 5/1/03; HBG 10/03; SLJ 7/03)

9124 Bauer, Marion Dane. *An Early Winter* (4–7). 1999, Clarion $15.00 (0-395-90372-6). 128pp. When he convinces him to go on a camping trip, Tim doesn't realize that his Grandad is suffering from Alzheimer's disease. (Rev: BCCB 10/99; BL 12/1/99; HBG 3/00; SLJ 10/99)

9125 Betancourt, Jeanne. *My Name Is Brain/Brian* (4–6). 1993, Scholastic $14.95 (0-590-44921-4). 176pp. Brian, a sixth-grader who is dyslexic, matures and changes his attitudes toward his friends and teachers. (Rev: BCCB 4/93; BL 4/1/93; SLJ 4/93)

9126 Blue, Rose. *Me and Einstein: Breaking Through the Reading Barrier* (4–6). Illus. by Peggy Luks. 1984, Human Sciences $16.95 (0-87705-388-X); paper $10.95 (0-89885-185-8). Bobby, a dyslexic youngster, tries to hide the fact that he can't read.

9127 Brooks, Bruce. *Vanishing* (5–8). 1999, Harper-Collins LB $14.89 (0-06-028237-1). A challenging novel about a hospitalized girl who gives up eating so she can't be sent home to her dysfunctional family, and the boy she meets who is in remission from a fatal disease. (Rev: BL 5/15/99; HB 5–6/99; HBG 10/99; SLJ 6/99)

9128 Butts, Nancy. *Cheshire Moon* (5–7). 1996, Front Street $14.95 (1-886910-08-1). A friendless deaf girl grieves for a cousin who has drowned at sea in this novel in an island setting. (Rev: BL 10/15/96; SLJ 11/96)

9129 Byars, Betsy. *The Summer of the Swans* (5–7). Illus. by Ted Coconis. 1970, Puffin paper $5.99 (0-14-031420-2). 144pp. The story of a 14-year-old named Sara — moody, unpredictable, and on the brink of womanhood — and how her life changes when her younger, mentally retarded brother disappears. Newbery Medal winner, 1971.

9130 Carter, Anne Laurel. *In the Clear* (4–7). 2001, Orca paper $6.95 (1-55143-192-0). 133pp. A 12-year-old Canadian polio survivor in the 1950s works through her fears and struggles to recapture her lost childhood. (Rev: BL 11/15/01; SLJ 1/02)

9131 Cunningham, Julia. *Burnish Me Bright* (4–6). 1980, Peter Smith $18.75 (0-8446-6252-6). An imaginative mute boy named Auguste is scorned by the inhabitants of the French village where he lives.

9132 Denenberg, Barry. *Mirror, Mirror on the Wall: The Diary of Bess Brennan* (4–8). Series: Dear America. 2002, Scholastic paper $10.95 (0-439-19446-6). 144pp. When she comes home at weekends, 12-year-old Bess, who has lost her sight, shares her new life and school experiences with her twin sister, in this novel set in the Depression that includes many details of how the blind cope. (Rev: BL 10/1/02; HBG 3/03; SLJ 10/02)

9133 Farnes, Catherine. *Snow* (5–9). 1999, Bob Jones Univ. $6.49 (1-57924-199-9). 158pp. A thoughtful novel about an albino girl's problems being accepted, even among students who profess to have Christian charity. (Rev: BL 7/99)

9134 Fassler, Joan. *Howie Helps Himself* (2–4). Illus. by Joe Lasker. 1975, Whitman LB $14.95 (0-8075-3422-6). 32pp. Howie adjusts to cerebral palsy and the use of his wheelchair.

9135 Gantos, Jack. *Joey Pigza Loses Control* (4–7). 2000, Farrar $16.00 (0-374-39989-1). 208pp. Joey, a hyperactive kid, tries to please his father but goes haywire when his father destroys his medication in this Newbery Honor Book. (Rev: BCCB 9/00*; BL 9/1/00*; HB 9–10/00; HBG 3/01; SLJ 9/00)

9136 Gantos, Jack. *Joey Pigza Swallowed the Key* (4–8). 1998, Farrar $16.00 (0-374-33664-4). Joey, who suffers from attention deficit disorder, causes so much trouble that he is sent to a special education center, where he learns to cope with his problem. (Rev: BCCB 11/98; BL 12/15/98; HB 11–12/98; HBG 3/99; SLJ 12/98*)

9137 Gantos, Jack. *What Would Joey Do?* (5–8). 2002, Farrar $16.00 (0-374-39986-7). 240pp. Hyperactive Joey is nearly overwhelmed by the antics of his parents, his dying grandmother, and the needs of his blind homeschool partner, but manages to cope in his own unusual way in this final installment in the Joey Pigza trilogy. (Rev: BCCB 11/02; BL 10/1/02*; HB 11–12/02; HBG 3/03; SLJ 9/02*)

9138 Garfield, James B. *Follow My Leader* (4–6). Illus. 1994, Puffin paper $4.99 (0-140-36485-4). 192pp. With the aid of friends and a guide dog, an 11-year-old boy resumes his life.

9139 Gavalda, Anna. *95 Pounds of Hope* (5–8). 2003, Viking $14.99 (0-670-03672-2). 112pp. Grandpa encourages Gregory, 13 and still in 6th grade, to pursue his ambition of attending technical school and working with his hands. (Rev: BCCB 11/03; BL 11/15/03; HBG 4/04; SLJ 11/03)

9140 Gould, Marilyn. *Golden Daffodils* (5–7). 1991, Allied Crafts paper $10.95 (0-9632305-1-4). 17pp. Janis adjusts to her handicap resulting from cerebral palsy.

9141 Gould, Marilyn. *The Twelfth of June* (5–8). 1994, Allied Crafts LB $12.95 (0-9632305-4-9). Janis, who suffers from cerebral palsy, is suffering the first pangs of adolescence and is still fighting the battle to be treated like other girls her age, in this sequel to *Golden Daffodils* (1982). (Rev: SLJ 11/86)

9142 Griffin, Adele. *Hannah, Divided* (4–7). 2002, Hyperion $15.99 (0-7868-0879-9). 208pp. Hannah's amazing mathematic ability and obsessive-compulsive disorder make her different from everyone else, but with the help of her grandfather, a philanthropist, and a new friend, she perseveres in this novel set during the Depression. (Rev: BCCB 12/02; BL 10/1/02*; HB 11–12/02; HBG 3/03; SLJ 12/02)

9143 Haddix, Margaret Peterson. *Because of Anya* (3–6). 2002, Simon & Schuster $15.95 (0-689-38298-2). 128pp. Anya's friend Keely rallies round when Anya must wear a wig because of her alopecia. (Rev: SLJ 11/02)

9144 Hoopmann, Kathy. *Blue Bottle Mystery: An Asperger Adventure* (3–5). 2001, Jessica Kingsley paper $11.95 (1-85302-978-5). 93pp. Ben is diagnosed as having Asperger Syndrome, a kind of autism that explains his behavior problems, in this novel in which a blue bottle plays a leading role. (Rev: SLJ 8/01)

9145 Janover, Caroline. *Zipper: The Kid with ADHD* (4–7). Illus. 1997, Woodbine paper $11.95 (0-933149-95-6). 164pp. Zipper Wilson suffers from attention deficit hyperactivity disorder and gradually learns to cope with it. (Rev: BL 2/1/98; SLJ 3/98)

9146 Jung, Reinhardt. *Dreaming in Black and White* (5–8). Trans. from German by Anthea Bell. 2003, Penguin Putnam $15.99 (0-8037-2811-5). 112pp. A boy with disabilities has waking dreams in which he travels back to Nazi Germany and suffers at the hands of his classmates, teachers, and eventually his father, in this compelling novel translated from German. (Rev: BCCB 9/03; BL 5/15/03; HB 9–10/03*; HBG 4/04; SLJ 8/03)

9147 Kachur, Wanda G. *The Nautilus* (5–7). 1997, Peytral paper $7.95 (0-9644271-5-X). 171pp. A compassionate novel about a girl's rehabilitation after receiving spinal cord injuries in an automobile accident. (Rev: SLJ 9/97)

9148 Lachtman, Ofelia Dumas. *Leticia's Secret* (5–8). 1997, Arte Publico $14.95 (1-55885-205-5); paper $7.95 (1-55885-209-3). Rosario, from a Mexican American family, shares many adventures with her cousin, the pretty Leticia, and is devastated to learn that she has a fatal disease. (Rev: SLJ 1/98)

9149 Lasker, Joe. *He's My Brother* (2–4). Illus. by author. 1974, Whitman LB $14.95 (0-8075-3218-5). 40pp. A family's attitudes and their wonderful treatment of their retarded family member, Jamie, are told by his older brother.

9150 Levine, Edna S. *Lisa and Her Soundless World* (3–5). Illus. by Gloria Kamen. 1984, Human Sciences $14.95 (0-87705-104-6); paper $10.95 (0-89885-204-8). The plight of a deaf girl is explored in this gripping, realistic story of Lisa and her problems.

9151 Little, Jean. *From Anna* (4–6). Illus. by Joan Sandin. 1972, HarperCollins paper $4.95 (0-06-440044-1). 208pp. Anna's family emigrates to Canada to escape Nazi persecution, and this opens up a new world and a wonderful change for the partially sighted girl.

9152 McDaniel, Lurlene. *To Live Again* (5–9). 2001, Bantam paper $4.99 (0-553-57151-6). 152pp. After three years of remission from leukemia, 16-year-old Dawn suffers a stroke that produces a terrible bout of depression. (Rev: BL 3/1/01)

9153 McDonald, Megan. *Judy Moody Gets Famous* (2–4). Illus. by Peter Reynolds. 2001, Candlewick $15.99 (0-7636-0849-1). 126pp. In this beginning chapter book, Judy Moody is plagued by jealousy until she manages to become famous anonymously and finds she enjoys it. (Rev: HB 9–10/01; HBG 3/02; SLJ 10/01)

9154 McMahon, Patricia. *Summer Tunes: A Martha's Vineyard Vacation* (3–6). Photos by Peter Simon. 1996, Boyds Mills $16.95 (1-56397-572-6). 47pp. A photo-essay about Conor, a 10-year-old physically handicapped boy, and his family, who go to Martha's Vineyard for a vacation. (Rev: SLJ 10/96)

9155 Marino, Jan. *Eighty-Eight Steps to September* (5–7). 1989, Avon paper $2.95 (0-380-71001-3). 162pp. Amy and Robbie have the usual sibling rivalry, until Robbie develops leukemia. (Rev: BCCB 5/89; BL 8/89)

9156 Riskind, Mary. *Apple Is My Sign* (5–6). 1995, Houghton Mifflin paper $5.95 (0-395-65747-4). 160pp. A deaf and mute boy is sent to a special school in the early 1900s.

9157 Roos, Stephen. *The Gypsies Never Came* (4–7). 2001, Simon & Schuster $15.00 (0-689-83147-1). 128pp. Augie Knapp, who was born without a left hand, slowly develops confidence with the help of Lydie Rose, an eccentric outsider. (Rev: BCCB 5/01; BL 3/1/01; HB 5–6/01; HBG 10/01; SLJ 2/01)

9158 Seidler, Tor. *The Silent Spillbills* (5–8). 1998, HarperCollins LB $14.89 (0-06-205181-4). 224pp. Katrina faces problems trying to overcome her stuttering but stands up to her tyrannical grandfather to help save from extinction a rare bird known as the silent spillbill. (Rev: BCCB 1/99; BL 12/15/98; HBG 3/99; SLJ 4/99)

9159 Shyer, Marlene Fanta. *Welcome Home, Jellybean* (5–8). 1978, Macmillan paper $4.99 (0-689-71213-8). 160pp. Twelve-year-old Neil encounters a near-tragic situation when his older retarded sister comes home to stay.

9160 Slote, Alfred. *Hang Tough, Paul Mather* (4–7). 1973, HarperCollins paper $5.99 (0-06-440153-7). 160pp. Paul recollects from his hospital bed the details of his struggle with leukemia. Told candidly and without sentimentality.

9161 Strachan, Ian. *The Flawed Glass* (5–8). 1990, Little, Brown $14.95 (0-316-81813-5). 208pp. Physically disabled Shona makes friends with an American boy on an island off the Scottish coast. (Rev: BCCB 11/90; BL 12/1/90; SLJ 1/91)

9162 Striegel, Jana. *Homeroom Exercise* (4–7). 2002, Holiday House $16.95 (0-8234-1579-1). 192pp. A 12-year-old who dreams of becoming a professional dancer is diagnosed with juvenile rheumatoid arthritis. (Rev: BL 3/1/02; HBG 10/02; SLJ 6/02)

9163 Tashjian, Janet. *Multiple Choice* (5–9). 1999, Holt $16.95 (0-8050-6086-3). Fourteen-year-old Monica realizes she needs outside help when her attempts to cope with her obsessive drive for perfection spin out of control with almost tragic consequences. (Rev: BL 6/1–15/99; HB 7–8/99; HBG 10/99; SLJ 9/99)

9164 Tashjian, Janet. *Tru Confessions* (4–7). 1997, Holt $15.95 (0-8050-5254-2). 160pp. Young Tru, an amateur filmmaker, begins a documentary about her developmentally delayed twin brother, Eddie, in this novel made up of Tru's diary entries, Internet conversations, and Eddie's computer graphics. (Rev: BL 1/1–15/98; HBG 3/98; SLJ 12/97)

9165 Testa, Maria. *Thumbs Up, Rico!* (3–4). Illus. 1994, Whitman LB $14.95 (0-8075-7906-8). 40pp. Rico, a boy with Down's syndrome, tells about his trials and triumphs in this simple chapter book. (Rev: BL 4/15/94; SLJ 7/94)

9166 Wanous, Suzanne. *Sara's Secret* (2–4). Illus. by Shelly O. Haas. 1995, Carolrhoda LB $19.93 (0-87614-856-9). 40pp. Sara's secret is that she has a brother who is a victim of cerebral palsy and is mentally retarded. (Rev: BL 7/95; SLJ 8/95)

9167 Warner, Sally. *This Isn't About the Money* (4–6). 2002, Viking $15.99 (0-670-03574-2). 224pp. Twelve-year-old Janey, disfigured in the car crash that killed her parents, tries to adjust to her new life in Arizona with her grandfather and great-aunt. (Rev: BCCB 12/02; BL 9/1/02; HBG 3/03; SLJ 9/02)

9168 Welch, Sheila K. *Don't Call Me Marda* (4–6). Illus. 1991, Our Child Pr. $16.95 (0-9611872-3-9); paper $12.95 (0-9611872-4-7). 138pp. Marsha is disappointed when the girl her parents adopt is mentally handicapped. (Rev: SLJ 3/91)

9169 Whelan, Gloria. *Hannah* (3–5). Illus. by Leslie Bowman. 1991, Knopf LB $11.99 (0-679-91397-1). 42pp. In northern Michigan in 1887, 9-year-old Hannah is encouraged by the new teacher to attend school despite her blindness. (Rev: BCCB 6/91; BL 3/1/91; HB 5–6/91; SLJ 6/91)

9170 Wilson, Jacqueline. *Vicky Angel* (4–7). Illus. by Nick Sharratt. 2001, Delacorte $15.95 (0-385-72920-0). 172pp. A girl conjures up the angel of her dead best friend in this book that examines loss, guilt, suicidal thoughts, and life after death. (Rev: BCCB 10/01; BL 11/15/01; HBG 3/02; SLJ 10/01)

9171 Wright, Betty R. *Rosie and the Dance of the Dinosaurs* (4–6). 1989, Holiday House $15.95 (0-8234-0782-9). 112pp. Rosie, who has only nine fingers, is worried about the piano recital in which she must perform. (Rev: BCCB 2/90; BL 11/15/89; HB 3–4/90)

Historical Fiction and Foreign Lands

General and Miscellaneous

9172 Bell, Helen. *Idjhil: And the Land Cried for Its Lost Soul* (3–6). Illus. by author. 2003, Cygnet paper $11.95 (1-876268-90-5). 40pp. The life of Idjhil, a happy Aboriginal boy in Western Australia, is turned upside down when he is forcibly removed from his family and relocated by the government. (Rev: SLJ 10/03)

9173 Belpre, Pura. *Firefly Summer* (5–8). 1996, Piñata paper $9.95 (1-55885-180-1). This gentle novel depicts family and community life in rural Puerto Rico at the turn of the 20th century as experienced by young Teresa Rodrigo, who has just completed 7th grade. (Rev: BR 3–4/97; SLJ 2/97)

9174 Bruchac, Joseph. *The Winter People* (5–9). 2002, Dial $16.99 (0-8037-2694-5). 176pp. A 14-year-old Abenaki boy searches for his mother and sisters after they are kidnapped by English soldiers in the French and Indian War. (Rev: BL 10/1/02*; HBG 3/03; SLJ 11/02)

9175 Carmi, Daniella. *Samir and Yonatan* (4–8). Trans. from Hebrew by Yael Lotan. 2000, Scholastic paper $15.95 (0-439-13504-4). 192pp. Samir, a young Palestinian, is sent to a Jewish hospital for surgery and there he meets some Jewish contemporaries. (Rev: BCCB 4/00; BL 2/1/00; HBG 10/00; SLJ 3/00)

9176 Caswell, Maryanne. *Pioneer Girl* (5–8). Illus. by Lindsay Grater. 2001, Tundra $16.95 (0-88776-550-5). 82pp. In letters to her grandmother, a 14-year-old girl describes the hardships and interesting experiences of her journey from Ontario to the prairies in the late 1880s. (Rev: HBG 10/01; SLJ 10/01)

9177 Clinton, Cathryn. *A Stone in My Hand* (5–8). 2002, Candlewick $15.99 (0-7636-1388-6). 191pp. Eleven-year-old Maalak's father is killed in the violence of 1988 Gaza, and she must worry about her brother's future. (Rev: BL 9/15/02; HBG 3/03; SLJ 11/02*)

9178 Crook, Connie Brummel. *The Hungry Year* (5–8). 2001, Stoddart paper $7.95 (0-7737-6206-X). 190pp. Twelve-year-old Kate must care for her brothers and handle the household chores during a severe Canadian winter in the late 1700s. (Rev: BL 1/1–15/02; SLJ 11/01)

9179 Crook, Connie Brummel. *The Perilous Year* (5–7). 2003, Fitzhenry & Whiteside paper $7.95 (1-55041-818-1). 197pp. In this fast-paced sequel to *The Hungry Year* (2001), 11-year-old twins Alex and Ryan face constant challenges and adventures — including more encounters with pirates — in 18th-century Canada. (Rev: SLJ 3/04)

9180 Curtis, Chara M. *No One Walks on My Father's Moon* (4–8). Illus. 1996, Voyage LB $16.95 (0-9649454-1-X). A Turkish boy is accused of blasphemy when he states that a man has walked on the moon. (Rev: BL 11/15/96)

9181 D'Adamo, Francesco. *Iqbal: A Novel* (4–7). 2003, Simon & Schuster $15.95 (0-689-85445-5). 128pp. The sad story of the death of Iqbal, the young child labor activist, is brought to life through the fictional narrative of a young Pakistani girl who worked with him in the carpet factories. (Rev: BL 11/1/03; HB 11–12/03; HBG 4/04; SLJ 11/03)

9182 Danticat, Edwidge. *Anacaona, Golden Flower: Haiti, 1490* (5–8). Series: Royal Diaries. 2005, Scholastic $10.95 (0-439-49906-2). 208pp. In 15th-century Haiti, Anacaona, a girl of royal heritage, records her people's struggles against the Spanish explorers. (Rev: BL 5/15/05)

9183 Defelice, Cynthia. *Under the Same Sky* (5–9). 2003, Farrar $16.00 (0-374-38032-5). 215pp. Joe, the spoiled 14-year-old son of a New York state farmer, learns about a different kind of life when he starts working with the migrant laborers from Mexico. (Rev: BCCB 5/03; BL 6/03; HBG 10/03; LMC 8–9/03; SLJ 3/03)

9184 Downie, Mary Alice, and John Downie. *Danger in Disguise* (5–8). Series: On Time's Wing. 2001, Roussan paper $6.95 (1-896184-72-3). 170pp. Young Jamie, a Scot raised in Normandy in secrecy, is scooped up to serve in the British navy and sent to Quebec to fight the French in this complex tale of adventure and intrigue set in the mid-18th century. (Rev: SLJ 5/01)

9185 Doyle, Brian. *Mary Ann Alice* (4–7). 2002, Groundwood $15.95 (0-88899-453-2). 166pp. It's 1926 and a new dam brings many changes to the Canadian community that is home to Mary Ann Alice, a 7th grader with a love of rocks. (Rev: BCCB 6/02; HB 5–6/02*; HBG 10/02; SLJ 6/02)

9186 Eboch, Chris. *The Well of Sacrifice* (5–8). Illus. 1999, Houghton Mifflin $16.00 (0-395-90374-2). In this novel set during Mayan times, Evening-star Macaw sets out to avenge the death of her older brother, Smoke Shell. (Rev: BL 4/1/99; HBG 10/99; SLJ 5/99)

9187 Ellis, Deborah. *Mud City* (4–7). Series: Breadwinner Trilogy. 2003, Douglas & McIntyre $15.95 (0-88899-518-0). 164pp. Feisty Afghan refugee Shauzia sets off on her own, dreaming of a life of freedom in France and prepared to dress as a boy and beg, but circumstances force her back to the camp on the Pakistan border in this final novel in the trilogy. (Rev: BL 11/15/03; HBG 4/04; SLJ 11/03)

9188 Fitz-Gibbon, Sally. *Lizzie's Storm* (3–5). Illus. by Muriel Wood. Series: New Beginnings. 2004, Fitzhenry & Whiteside $14.95 (1-55041-793-2); paper $7.95 (1-55041-795-9). 67pp. Orphaned in 1931 at the age of 10, Lizzie leaves London to live with relatives on the challenging Canadian prairie and shows her mettle when a dangerous dust storm hits the farm. (Rev: BL 9/1/04; SLJ 10/04)

9189 French, Jackie. *Hitler's Daughter* (4–7). 2003, HarperCollins LB $16.89 (0-06-008653-X). 128pp. A story about a fictional daughter of Hitler inspires Mark, a young Australian, to wonder about evil and genocide. (Rev: BCCB 7–8/03; BL 9/15/03; HBG 10/03; SLJ 5/03)

9190 Gantos, Jack. *Jack's New Power: Stories from a Caribbean Year* (5–8). 1995, Farrar $16.00 (0-374-33657-1); paper $5.95 (0-374-43715-7). 214pp. Eight stories about the interesting people Jack meets when his family moves to the Caribbean. A sequel to *Heads or Tails* (1994). (Rev: BCCB 12/95; BL 12/1/95; SLJ 11/95*)

9191 Goldring, Ann. *Spitfire* (4–6). 2002, Raincoast paper $6.95 (1-55192-490-0). 160pp. A Canadian girl is determined to compete in a boys-only soapbox derby in this novel set in 1943. (Rev: BL 5/15/02; SLJ 4/02)

9192 Gray, Elizabeth Janet. *Adam of the Road* (5–8). Illus. by Robert Lawson. 1942, Puffin paper $5.99 (0-14-032464-X). 320pp. Adventures of a 13th-century minstrel boy. Newbery Medal winner, 1943.

9193 Hammer, Loretta J., and Gail L. Karwoski. *The Tree That Owns Itself: And Other Adventure Tales from Out of the Past* (3–6). Illus. by James Watling. 1996, Peachtree paper $8.95 (1-56145-120-7). 149pp. In these 12 stories, famous characters associated with the history of Georgia come to life and interact with fictitious young heroes and heroines. (Rev: SLJ 7/96)

9194 Harrison, Troon. *A Bushel of Light* (5–8). 2001, Stoddart paper $7.95 (0-7737-6140-3). 244pp. Fourteen-year-old orphan Maggie juggles her need to search for her twin sister and her responsibilities

for 4-year-old Lizzy, in this novel set in Canada in the early 1900s. (Rev: SLJ 10/01)

9195 Haworth-Attard, Barbara. *Home Child* (5–8). 1996, Roussan paper $6.95 (1-896184-18-9). Set in Canada during the early 1900s, this is the story of 13-year-old Arthur Fellowes, a London orphan who is treated like an outcast when he joins the Wilson family as a home child (that is, a cheap farm laborer). (Rev:)

9196 Holeman, Linda. *Promise Song* (5–8). 1997, Tundra paper $6.95 (0-88776-387-1). In 1900, Rosetta, an English orphan who has been sent to Canada, becomes an indentured servant. (Rev: BL 6/1–15/97; SLJ 10/97)

9197 Ibbotson, Eva. *Journey to the River Sea* (5–8). 2002, Dutton $17.99 (0-525-46739-4). 336pp. Orphaned Maia journeys from 1910 London to live with relatives in Brazil in this complex story that involves an unwelcoming family, a beloved governess, a child actor, a runaway, and the wonders of Brazil, all presented with a mix of drama and humor. (Rev: BCCB 4/02; BL 12/15/01; HB 1–2/02; HBG 10/02; SLJ 1/02*)

9198 Jocelyn, Marthe. *Mable Riley: A Reliable Record of Humdrum, Peril, and Romance* (5–10). Illus. 2004, Candlewick $15.99 (0-7636-2120-X). 288pp. This is a charming, humorous diary set in 1901 by a 14-year-old girl who accompanies her sister when she becomes a teacher in Stratford, Ontario. (Rev: BL 3/1/04; HB 5–6/04; SLJ 3/04)

9199 Kirkpatrick, Katherine. *Escape Across the Wide Sea* (4–6). 2004, Holiday House $16.95 (0-8234-1854-5). 210pp. This gripping novel follows 9-year-old Daniel and his Huguenot family as they flee religious persecution in their native France and find themselves on a slave ship to the New World. (Rev: BL 1/1–15/05; SLJ 11/04)

9200 Lawson, Julie. *Goldstone* (5–8). 1998, Stoddart paper $7.95 (0-7737-5891-7). Karin, a 13-year-old Swedish Canadian girl, lives with her family in a mountainous town in British Columbia in 1910 when heavy winter snows bring avalanches that cause death and destruction. (Rev: BL 7/97; SLJ 5/98)

9201 Lawson, Sue. *Ferret Boy* (4–6). Illus. by Annie Mertzlin. Series: Takeaways. 2003, Lothian paper $8.95 (0-7344-0465-4). 256pp. Josh Trimble faces unexpected challenges when, in a hasty moment, he agrees to race his beloved pet ferret in a derby. (Rev: SLJ 8/03)

9202 Levine, Anna. *Running on Eggs* (5–9). 1999, Front Street $15.95 (0-8126-2875-6). 136pp. The story of two girls — one Jewish and the other Palestinian — and a friendship that withstands cultural and political differences. (Rev: BCCB 11/99; BL 1/1–15/00; HBG 3/00; SLJ 12/99)

9203 Logan, Claudia. *The 5,000-Year-Old Puzzle: Solving a Mystery of Ancient Egypt* (3–5). Illus. by Melissa Sweet. 2002, Farrar $17.00 (0-374-32335-6). 48pp. Part fact and part fiction, this picture book for older children takes readers along on an actual 1924 expedition to uncover tombs from the days of ancient Egypt. (Rev: BL 4/15/02; HBG 10/02; SLJ 6/02)

9204 Lottridge, Celia B. *Ticket to Canada* (4–6). Illus. 1995, Silver Burdett LB $17.95 (0-382-39145-4). 144pp. In 1915, Sam and his family relocate from Iowa to rural Alberta and must build their own house. (Rev: BL 2/1/96; SLJ 2/96)

9205 Major, Kevin. *Ann and Seamus* (5–9). Illus. by David Blackwood. 2003, Groundwood $16.95 (0-88899-561-X). 128pp. Based on an early-19th-century shipwreck off the coast of Newfoundland, this historical novel in verse chronicles the romance that develops between 17-year-old Ann Harvey and the Irish teenager she rescues from the ship. (Rev: BL 3/1/04; HB 3–4/04; SLJ 2/04)

9206 Miklowitz, Gloria D. *Masada: The Last Fortress* (5–8). 1998, Eerdmans $16.00 (0-8028-5165-7). 188pp. The siege of Masada comes alive as seen through the eyes of 19-year-old Simon. (Rev: HBG 3/99; SLJ 12/98)

9207 Naidoo, Beverly. *The Other Side of Truth* (5–9). 2001, HarperCollins LB $17.89 (0-06-029629-1). 272pp. Two Nigerian children face a frightening sequence of events as they find themselves abandoned in London, afraid to trust anyone. Carnegie Medal winner, 2000. (Rev: BCCB 9/01; BL 9/1/01; HB 11–12/01*; HBG 3/02; SLJ 9/01*)

9208 Nunes, Susan. *To Find the Way* (4–6). Illus. by Cissy Gray. 1992, Univ. of Hawaii Pr. $12.95 (0-8248-1376-6). 48pp. A picture story of the amazing voyage by the ancient Polynesians from Tahiti to Hawaii, seen through a child's eyes. (Rev: BL 1/15/93)

9209 O'Dell, Scott. *My Name Is Not Angelica* (5–8). 1989, Houghton Mifflin $18.00 (0-395-51061-9). 144pp. A fictionalized account of the slave revolt in the Virgin Islands in 1733–1734. (Rev: BL 11/15/89*; BR 3–4/90; SLJ 10/89)

9210 Reekie, Jocelyn. *Tess* (5–8). 2003, Raincoast paper $7.95 (1-55192-471-4). 296pp. Thirteen-year-old Tess is a plucky, strong-willed girl who must leave her Scottish home and move to British Columbia in 1857. (Rev: BL 3/1/03)

9211 Riordan, James. *Escape from War* (4–6). 2005, Kingfisher paper $6.95 (0-7534-5794-6). 192pp. Parallel, intersecting stories present an English boy called Frank and a German Jewish refugee called Hannah and their experiences in the English countryside during World War II. (Rev: BL 5/15/05)

9212 Schwartz, Virginia Frances. *Messenger* (5–9). 2002, Holiday House $17.95 (0-8234-1716-6). 277pp. This story of the hardships and joys of a Croatian family living in Ontario's mining towns in the 1920s and 1930s is based on the lives of the author's mother and grandmother. (Rev: HBG 3/03; SLJ 11/02)

9213 Shulevitz, Uri. *The Travels of Benjamin of Tudela: Through Three Continents in the Twelfth Century* (4–7). Illus. 2005, Farrar $17.00 (0-374-37754-5). 48pp. Based on Benjamin's diaries, this picture book, which is incredibly detailed in both illustrations and text, tells of his perilous journey

through parts of Europe, the Mediterranean, and the Middle East. (Rev: BL 3/15/05; SLJ 4/05)

9214 Southern, Randy. *Ruled Out* (3–5). 2000, Bethany House paper $5.99 (1-56179-884-3). 112pp. In this story with a biblical basis, Ethan and his family remain faithful to the god of Moses when others have begun to worship the golden calf. (Rev: SLJ 2/01)

9215 Strasser, Todd. *The Diving Bell* (4–7). Illus. 1992, Scholastic paper $13.95 (0-590-44620-7). 192pp. When Spanish ships ladened with gold sink close to their island, some natives try to salvage them in this story set in the New World during the Spanish conquest. (Rev: SLJ 6/92)

9216 Taylor, Joanne. *There You Are: A Novel* (4–7). 2004, Tundra paper $8.95 (0-88776-658-7). 199pp. On post-World War II Cape Breton Island, 12-year-old Jeannie lives in a remote community and longs for a friend. (Rev: SLJ 11/04)

9217 Trottier, Maxine. *A Circle of Silver* (5–8). 2000, Stoddart paper $7.95 (0-7737-6055-5). 216pp. Set in the 1760s, this is the story of 13-year-old John MacNeil who is sent to Canada by his father to toughen him up. (Rev: SLJ 9/00)

9218 Valgardson, W. D. *Sarah and the People of Sand River* (3–5). Illus. by Ian Wallace. 1996, Douglas & McIntyre $16.95 (0-88899-255-6). 56pp. An Icelandic family, now relocated in Manitoba, Canada, is helped by Cree Indians. (Rev: BCCB 12/96; BL 11/1/96*; SLJ 12/96) [398.2]

9219 Ware, Jim. *Crazy Jacob* (3–5). Series: KidWitness Tales. 2000, Bethany House paper $5.99 (1-56179-885-1). 115pp. Based on a Bible story, this novel features Crazy Jacob whose demons are cast out by Jesus and turned into swine. (Rev: SLJ 2/01)

9220 Weir, Joan. *The Witcher* (5–7). 1998, Polestar paper $6.95 (1-896095-44-5). 157pp. In Canada's Gold Rush country, 12-year-old Lion and his older sister help their father solve the custody issues surrounding a young girl who possesses divining powers. (Rev: SLJ 3/99)

Prehistory

9221 Caselli, Giovanni. *An Ice Age Hunter* (3–5). 1992, Bedrick LB $12.95 (0-87226-103-4). 30pp. The story of a year in the life of an ice-age family as experienced by a young girl. (Rev: SLJ 7/92)

9222 Cowley, Marjorie. *Dar and the Spear-Thrower* (5–7). 1994, Clarion $15.00 (0-395-68132-4). 118pp. This is the story of Dar, a boy growing up in the Cro-Magnon period, and the problems he faces when beginning to accept adult responsibilities. (Rev: BL 8/94; SLJ 9/94)

9223 Craig, Ruth. *Malu's Wolf* (4–6). 1995, Orchard LB $16.99 (0-531-08784-0). 192pp. Set in Stone Age Europe, this novel tells how Malu domesticated a wolf cub named Kono. (Rev: BL 12/15/95; SLJ 10/95)

9224 Denzel, Justin. *Boy of the Painted Cave* (5–7). 1988, Penguin Putnam $17.99 (0-399-21559-X). 160pp. The story of a boy who longs to be a cave artist, set in Cro Magnon times. (Rev: BL 11/1/88; SLJ 11/88)

9225 Turnbull, Ann. *Maroo of the Winter Caves* (4–7). 1984, Houghton Mifflin paper $6.95 (0-395-54795-4). 144pp. A story centered on semi-nomadic people who lived in southern Europe during the last Ice Age.

Africa

9226 Asare, Meshack. *Sosu's Call* (1–4). Illus. by author. 2002, Kane $15.95 (1-929132-21-2). 37pp. Sosu, an African boy who is rejected by the villagers because he cannot walk, saves them from a terrible storm with the help of his dog. (Rev: BCCB 5/02; HBG 10/02; SLJ 6/02)

9227 Bunting, Eve. *I Am the Mummy Heb-Nefert* (3–6). Illus. by David Christiana. 1997, Harcourt $15.00 (0-15-200479-3). 32pp. A touching picture book in which a female mummy tells of her life as the wife of the pharaoh's brother and of her death and how her body was preserved. (Rev: BCCB 5/97; BL 5/15/97; SLJ 8/97)

9228 Burns, Khephra. *Mansa Musa: The Lion of Mali* (4–7). Illus. by Diane Dillon and Leo Dillon. 2001, Harcourt $18.00 (0-15-200375-4). 56pp. Lavish illustrations complement this handsome, challenging book about Mansa Musa's journey from a rural village boyhood to becoming the king of Mali. (Rev: BL 12/1/01; HB 11–12/01; HBG 3/02; SLJ 10/01)

9229 Ellis, Deborah. *The Heaven Shop* (5–8). 2004, Fitzhenry & Whiteside $16.95 (1-55041-908-0). 192pp. The AIDS epidemic has a devastating impact on the family of Binti, a 13-year-old Malawi girl. (Rev: BL 9/1/04; SLJ 10/04)

9230 Ellis, Veronica F. *Afro-Bets First Book About Africa* (2–5). Illus. by George Ford. 1990, Just Us LB $13.95 (0-940975-12-2); paper $6.95 (0-940975-03-3). 32pp. A classroom of African Americans learns about the history and culture of Africa. (Rev: BL 3/1/90*; SLJ 5/90)

9231 Farmer, Nancy. *Do You Know Me?* (4–6). Illus. by Shelley Jackson. 1993, Orchard LB $16.99 (0-531-08624-0). 112pp. There are culture clashes (many amusing) when 9-year-old Tapiwa's uncle comes from rural Mozambique to live with her family in the city. (Rev: BL 4/1/93; SLJ 4/93)

9232 Ferreira, Anton. *Zulu Dog* (5–8). 2002, Farrar $16.00 (0-374-39223-4). 208pp. Modern South Africa is the setting for this story, in which a racist white man has a change of heart when his daughter Shirley is rescued by a black boy's puppy. (Rev: BCCB 1/03; BL 9/15/02; HB 11–12/02; HBG 3/03; SLJ 9/02)

9233 Gormley, Beatrice. *Miriam* (4–6). 1999, Eerdmans paper $6.00 (0-8028-5156-8). 192pp. The story of 11-year-old Miriam, Moses' elder sister, who manages to get her baby brother into an Egyptian princess's house and her mother hired to care for him. (Rev: SLJ 5/99)

9234 Gregory, Kristiana. *Cleopatra VII: Daughter of the Nile* (5–8). Series: Royal Diaries. 1999, Scholas-

tic paper $10.95 (0-590-81975-5). 224pp. This mock-diary recounts various events in the life of 12-year-old Cleopatra who, even at that age, was involved in palace intrigue. (Rev: BL 1/1–15/00; HBG 3/00; SLJ 10/99)

9235 Grifalconi, Ann. *The Village That Vanished* (2–5). Illus. by Kadir Nelson. 2002, Dial $16.99 (0-8037-2623-6). 40pp. African villagers escape slavers by dismantling their village piece by piece. (Rev: BCCB 11/02; BL 9/15/02; HB 9–10/02; HBG 3/03; SLJ 12/02)

9236 Havill, Juanita. *Sato and the Elephants* (2–4). Illus. by Jean Tseng and Mou-Sien Tseng. 1993, Lothrop LB $14.93 (0-688-11156-4). 32pp. A young ivory carver realizes that animals must be killed to supply him with material and therefore decides to try working in stone the next time. (Rev: BL 10/15/93; SLJ 4/94)

9237 Kehret, Peg. *The Secret Journey* (4–7). 1999, Pocket $16.00 (0-671-03416-2). 138pp. In 1834, 12-year-old stowaway Emma is washed ashore on the coast of Liberia and must survive by learning from the chimps she observes. (Rev: BL 1/1–15/00; HBG 10/00; SLJ 3/00)

9238 Kurtz, Jane. *Saba: Under the Hyena's Foot* (5–8). Illus. by Jean-Paul Tibbles. Series: Girls of Many Lands. 2003, Pleasant Co. $15.95 (1-58485-829-X); paper $7.95 (1-58485-747-1). 207pp. Although she has been living a simple country life, 12-year-old Saba discovers she is in fact a member of the ruling family in this novel set in 19th-century Ethiopia and full of cultural and historical detail. (Rev: BL 10/1/03; HBG 4/04; SLJ 10/03)

9239 Kurtz, Jane. *The Storyteller's Beads* (5–8). Illus. 1998, Harcourt $15.00 (0-15-201074-2). Two Ethiopian refugees, one a girl from a traditional Ethiopian culture and the other a blind Jewish girl, overcome generations of prejudice against Jews when they face common danger as they flee war and famine during the 1980s. (Rev: BCCB 9/98; BL 5/1/98; HBG 10/98; SLJ 7/98)

9240 Laird, Elizabeth. *The Garbage King* (5–8). 2003, Barron's $14.95 (0-7641-5679-9); paper $5.95 (0-7641-2626-1). 336pp. Two Ethiopian boys find themselves homeless and join a gang that begs and scavenges for a livelihood. (Rev: BL 12/1/03; SLJ 12/03)

9241 Lattimore, Deborah N. *The Winged Cat: A Tale of Ancient Egypt* (3–6). Illus. 1992, HarperCollins $15.00 (0-06-023635-3). 32pp. A serving girl witnesses the killing of the sacred cat Bast in this handsomely illustrated tale of ancient Egypt. (Rev: BL 9/1/92; SLJ 4/92)

9242 Levitin, Sonia. *Dream Freedom* (5–9). 2000, Harcourt $17.00 (0-15-202404-2). 288pp. A novel that graphically portrays the plight of Sudanese slaves, juxtaposed with the story of an American 5th-grade class that joins the fight to free them. (Rev: BL 11/1/00; HBG 3/01; SLJ 10/00)

9243 McCaughrean, Geraldine. *Casting the Gods Adrift: A Tale of Ancient Egypt* (5–8). Illus. by Patricia D. Ludlow. 2003, Cricket $15.95 (0-8126-2684-2). 112pp. History and fiction are intertwined in this well-illustrated, suspenseful novel about two boys who are content to be taken in by the Pharoah Akhenaten, and a father enraged by the Pharaoh's refusal to worship the traditional Egyptian gods. (Rev: BCCB 10/03; BL 10/15/03; HBG 4/04; SLJ 8/03)

9244 McKissack, Patricia. *Nzingha: Warrior Queen of Matamba* (5–8). Illus. Series: Royal Diaries. 2000, Scholastic paper $10.95 (0-439-11210-9). 144pp. Based on fact, this is the story of 17th-century African queen Nzingha who, in present-day Angola, resisted the Portuguese colonizers and slave traders. (Rev: BL 11/1/00; HBG 3/01; SLJ 12/00)

9245 Mankell, Henning. *Secrets in the Fire* (4–8). 2003, Annick $14.95 (1-55037-801-5); paper $7.95 (1-55037-800-7). 176pp. This is the true story of Sofia, a courageous Mozambican girl who lost both legs — and her sister — when a landmine exploded. (Rev: BL 12/15/03*; SLJ 5/04)

9246 Marie, D. *Tears for Ashan* (3–6). Illus. by Norman Childers. 1989, Creative $12.95 (0-9621681-0-6). 32pp. Set in Africa years ago. Kumasi sees his best friend taken captive by slave traders. (Rev: BL 12/1/89)

9247 Marston, Elsa. *The Ugly Goddess* (5–8). 2002, Cricket $16.95 (0-8126-2667-2). 224pp. In 523 B.C. Egypt, a 14-year-old Egyptian princess, a young Greek soldier who is in love with her, and an Egyptian boy become embroiled in a mystery adventure that blends fact, fiction, and fantasy. (Rev: BL 1/1–15/03; HBG 3/03; SLJ 12/02)

9248 Mead, Alice. *Year of No Rain* (5–7). 2003, Farrar $16.00 (0-374-37288-8). 144pp. Torn from today's headlines, this moving story chronicles the wanderings of 11-year-old Stephen, who must flee when his village in southern Sudan is raided by government forces. (Rev: BL 8/03; HBG 4/04; SLJ 5/03)

9249 Mollel, Tololwa M. *Shadow Dance* (PS–3). Illus. by Donna Perrone. 1998, Clarion $15.00 (0-395-82909-7). 32pp. In this African folktale, Salome must outwit an ungrateful crocodile who threatens to eat her after she has saved him from a deep gully. (Rev: BCCB 1/99; BL 11/15/98; HBG 3/99; SLJ 12/98) [398.2]

9250 Naidoo, Beverley. *No Turning Back* (5–9). 1997, HarperCollins $15.89 (0-06-027506-5). Jaabu, a homeless African boy, looks for shelter in contemporary Johannesburg. (Rev: BCCB 2/97; BL 12/15/96*; BR 9–10/97; SLJ 2/97)

9251 Rubalcaba, Jill. *A Place in the Sun* (3–6). 1997, Clarion $13.95 (0-395-82645-4). 96pp. Set in 13th-century-B.C. Egypt, this fast-moving novel describes the fate of a boy who is exiled to the gold mines of Nubia. (Rev: BL 4/1/97; SLJ 4/97)

9252 Turner, Ann. *Maïa of Thebes: 1463 B.C.* (4–6). Series: Life and Times. 2005, Scholastic $10.95 (0-439-65223-5). 160pp. In the time of Queen Hatshepsut, 13-year-old Maïa finds her life in danger. (Rev: BL 6/1–15/05)

9253 Welch, Leona N. *Kai: The Lost Statue* (3–6). Illus. Series: Girlhood Journeys. 1997, Simon & Schuster paper $5.99 (0-689-81571-9). 72pp. In this

historical novel set in southwestern Nigeria, Kai encounters problems when she becomes an apprentice to a sculptor. (Rev: BL 4/1/98; SLJ 4/98)

9254 Williams, Mary. *Brothers in Hope: The Story of the Lost Boys of Sudan* (3–5). Illus. by R. Gregory Christie. 2005, Lee & Low $17.95 (1-58430-232-1). 40pp. Garang, a Sudanese boy, flees to Ethiopia and then Kenya, where he finds a home in a refugee camp and hopes to find a way to get to America; this first-person account includes evocative paintings. (Rev: BL 5/1/05; SLJ 6/05)

9255 Williams-Garcia, Rita. *No Laughter Here* (4–8). 2003, HarperCollins LB $16.89 (0-688-16248-7). 144pp. Akilah is shocked when her friend Victoria reveals she has undergone female circumcision while on vacation in Nigeria. (Rev: BL 12/1/03*; SLJ 2/04)

9256 Zemser, Amy Bronwen. *Beyond the Mango Tree* (4–8). 1998, Greenwillow $15.00 (0-688-16005-0). 176pp. Sarina, a white American living with her mother in Liberia, feels trapped between her erratic mother's behavior and an alien outside world. (Rev: HB 11–12/98; HBG 3/99; SLJ 10/98)

Asia

9257 Atkins, Jeannine. *Aani and the Tree Huggers* (2–5). Illus. by Venantius J. Pinto. 1995, Lee & Low $14.95 (1-880000-24-5). In this tale set in India, a village woman tries to save a tree from big-city developers by throwing her arms around it. (Rev: SLJ 12/95)

9258 Balgassi, Haemi. *Peacebound Trains* (3–5). Illus. by Chris K. Soentpiet. 1996, Clarion $14.95 (0-395-72093-1). 47pp. Sumi's grandmother tells about the perilous journey she took to escape the Communists during the Korean War. (Rev: BCCB 10/96; BL 9/15/96; SLJ 1/97)

9259 Bouchard, David. *Buddha in the Garden* (4–6). Illus. by Shong-Yang Huang. 2001, Raincoast $14.95 (1-55192-452-8). 32pp. An abandoned baby raised in a monastery learns to tend the garden in this quiet introduction to Buddhism illustrated with evocative water colors. (Rev: BL 1/1–15/02; SLJ 12/01)

9260 Choi, Sook N. *Echoes of the White Giraffe* (5–8). 1993, Houghton Mifflin $14.95 (0-395-64721-5). 144pp. In this sequel to *Year of Impossible Goodbyes* (1991), Sookan and her family once again are separated, this time by the Korean War. (Rev: SLJ 5/93)

9261 Chrisman, Arthur B. *Shen of the Sea* (4–6). Illus. by Else Hasselriis. 1968, Dutton $16.99 (0-525-39244-0). 224pp. These engaging short stories of Chinese life received the Newbery Award, 1926.

9262 Disher, Garry. *The Bamboo Flute* (5–8). 1993, Ticknor $15.00 (0-395-66595-7). In this brief, quiet novel of self-discovery, an Australian boy, age 12, brings music back into the life of his impoverished family. (Rev: BL 9/1/93)

9263 Divakaruni, Chitra Banerjee. *Neela: Victory Song* (5–8). Series: Girls of Many Lands. 2002, Pleasant Co. $12.95 (1-58485-597-5); paper $7.95

(1-58485-521-5). 196pp. Plucky Neela, 12, plunges into the frightening political fray of India in 1939, determined to help her father and a freedom fighter who are protesting British rule. (Rev: BL 11/15/02; HBG 3/03; SLJ 12/02)

9264 Ellis, Deborah. *The Breadwinner* (5–7). 2001, Groundwood $15.95 (0-88899-419-2). 170pp. In Kabul under the strict rule of the Taliban, Parvana dresses as a boy so she can work to feed the remaining women in her family. (Rev: BL 3/1/01; HBG 10/01; SLJ 7/01)

9265 Ellis, Deborah. *Parvana's Journey* (5–8). 2002, Douglas & McIntyre $15.95 (0-88899-514-8). 199pp. This sequel to *The Breadwinner* (2001) shows 13-year-old Parvana, whose father has recently died, making a difficult journey across Taliban-ruled Afghanistan disguised as a boy. (Rev: BL 12/1/02; HBG 3/03; SLJ 12/02*)

9266 Fletcher, Susan. *Shadow Spinner* (5–9). 1998, Simon & Schuster $17.00 (0-689-81852-1). 221pp. Marjan leaves the harem in search of someone who can tell her the ending of a story that Shahrazad is telling the Sultan as part of her 1,001-night cycle. (Rev: BCCB 7–8/98; HB 7–8/98; HBG 10/98; SLJ 6/98)

9267 Giles, Gail. *Breath of the Dragon* (4–7). Illus. 1997, Clarion $14.95 (0-395-76476-9). 112pp. In this story set in Thailand, Malila faces rejection and loneliness because her father was a thief. (Rev: BCCB 4/97; BL 4/1/97; SLJ 6/97)

9268 Glass, Tom. *Even a Little Is Something: Stories of Nong* (4–6). Illus. by Elena Gerard. 1997, Linnet LB $16.95 (0-208-02457-3). 119pp. Accurately depicts the daily struggle of peasants living hand-to-mouth in northeastern Thailand. (Rev: HBG 3/98; SLJ 2/98)

9269 Hill, Elizabeth Starr. *Chang and the Bamboo Flute* (2–5). Illus. by Lesley Hiu. 2002, Farrar $15.00 (0-374-31238-9). 64pp. Chang, a mute boy who lives with his family on a boat on the Li River, decides to sell his beloved flute — his only means of communication — to replace the wok his mother lost in a flood. (Rev: BL 10/15/02; HBG 3/03)

9270 Ho, Minfong. *The Clay Marble* (5–9). 1991, Houghton Mifflin $12.00 (0-395-77155-2). After fleeing from her Cambodian home in the early 1980s, 12-year-old Dara is separated from her family during an attack on a refugee camp on the Thailand border. (Rev: BL 11/15/91; SLJ 10/91)

9271 Holman, Sheri. *Sondok: Princess of the Moon and Stars, Korea, A.D. 595* (3–6). Series: The Royal Diaries. 2002, Scholastic $10.95 (0-439-16586-5). 187pp. In notes placed in an ancestral jar, the young princess and future ruler relates her confusion about religion and her love of astronomy. (Rev: HBG 3/03; SLJ 8/02)

9272 Hoobler, Dorothy, and Thomas Hoobler. *The Demon in the Teahouse* (5–8). 2001, Philomel $17.99 (0-399-23499-3). 208pp. Fourteen-year-old Seikei, who plans to become a samurai, investigates a series of fires and murders that appear to be connected to a popular geisha in this story set in 18th-

century Japan. (Rev: BCCB 6/01; BL 5/1/01; HB 7–8/01; HBG 10/01; SLJ 6/01)

9273 Hoobler, Dorothy, and Thomas Hoobler. *The Sword That Cut the Burning Grass* (5–8). 2005, Philomel $10.99 (0-399-24272-4). 224pp. In this fourth book about the aspiring young samurai, Seikei tackles a challenging task involving the teenage emperor. (Rev: BL 5/1/05)

9274 Huynh, Quang Nhuong. *The Land I Lost: Adventures of a Boy in Vietnam* (5–8). Illus. by Mai Vo-Dinh. 1990, HarperCollins $15.89 (0-397-32448-0); paper $4.99 (0-06-440183-9). 128pp. The story of a boy's growing up in rural Vietnam before the war.

9275 Kamal, Aleph. *The Bird Who Was an Elephant* (3–5). Illus. by Frane Lessac. 1990, HarperCollins LB $14.89 (0-397-32446-4). 32pp. The story of what a bird sees as it flies over an Indian village. (Rev: BCCB 7–8/90; BL 4/15/90; SLJ 8/90)

9276 Keido, Ippo, retel. *The Butterfly's Dream: Children's Stories from China* (3–6). Illus. by Kazuko G. Stone. 2003, Tuttle $15.95 (0-8048-3480-6). This richly illustrated collection features a number of stories, linked by the flight of a butterfly, based on the ancient Chinese Chuang-Tzu, which was written roughly 23 centuries ago during the Chou Dynasty. (Rev: HBG 4/04; SLJ 1/04)

9277 Lasky, Kathryn. *Jahanara: Princess of Princesses* (4–8). Series: Royal Diaries. 2002, Scholastic paper $10.95 (0-439-22350-4). 192pp. Princess Jaharana, the daughter of Shah Jahan (who built the Taj Mahal) writes detailed diary accounts of her 17th-century life, with rich descriptions of her surroundings, palace intrigues, and dealing with her family. (Rev: BL 1/1–15/03; HBG 3/03; SLJ 1/03)

9278 Lattimore, Deborah N. *Fool and the Phoenix: A Tale of Ancient Japan* (3–6). Illus. 1997, HarperCollins LB $14.89 (0-06-026211-7). 40pp. Hideo, a mute, falls in love with the phoenix bird of Japan and catches her in a net. (Rev: BL 8/97; HBG 3/98; SLJ 9/97)

9279 Mah, Adeline Yen. *Chinese Cinderella and the Secret Dragon Society* (5–8). 2005, HarperCollins LB $16.89 (0-06-056735-X). 242pp. During the Japanese occupation of Shanghai in World War II, 12-year-old Ye Xian is expelled from her home after an argument with her stepmother, joins a kung fu group, and seeks to help the American side. (Rev: SLJ 1/05)

9280 Neuberger, Anne E. *The Girl-Son* (3–6). Illus. 1994, Carolrhoda LB $21.27 (0-87614-846-1). 132pp. Based on fact, this is the story of a Korean girl born in 1896 and her fight for women's rights. (Rev: BCCB 2/95; BL 1/1/95; SLJ 2/95)

9281 Neville, Emily C. *The China Year* (5–8). 1991, HarperCollins $15.95 (0-06-024383-X). Henri, 14, has left his New York City home, school, and friends to go to Peking University for a year with his father. (Rev: BL 5/1/91; SLJ 5/91)

9282 Park, Linda Sue. *The Kite Fighters* (4–6). 2000, Clarion $15.00 (0-395-94041-9). 144pp. Contests involving kite flying are the subject of this exciting novel set in 15th-century Korea. (Rev:

BCCB 6/00; BL 4/1/00; HB 5–6/00; HBG 10/00; SLJ 6/00)

9283 Park, Linda Sue. *Seesaw Girl* (4–7). Illus. 1999, Clarion $14.00 (0-395-91514-7). 90pp. In 17th-century Korea, 12-year-old Jade Blossom wanders away from her aristocratic palace and discovers the reality and poverty of the world outside. (Rev: BCCB 12/99; BL 9/1/99; HBG 3/00; SLJ 9/99)

9284 Park, Linda Sue. *A Single Shard* (4–8). 2001, Clarion $15.00 (0-395-97827-0). 152pp. This Newbery Medal winner describes a Korean boy's journey through unknown territory to deliver two valuable pots. (Rev: BCCB 3/01; BL 4/1/01*; HBG 10/01; SLJ 5/01*)

9285 Park, Linda Sue. *When My Name Was Keoko* (5–9). 2002, Clarion $16.00 (0-618-13335-6). 208pp. A young brother and sister tell, in first-person accounts, what life was like during the Japanese occupation of Korea. (Rev: BCCB 5/02; BL 3/1/02; HB 5–6/02; HBG 10/02; SLJ 4/02)

9286 Paterson, Katherine. *The Master Puppeteer* (4–7). Illus. by Haru Wells. 1989, HarperCollins paper $5.99 (0-06-440281-9). 192pp. Feudal Japan is the setting for this story about a young apprentice puppeteer and his search for a mysterious bandit.

9287 Paterson, Katherine. *The Sign of the Chrysanthemum* (5–7). Illus. by Peter Landa. 1973, HarperCollins LB $14.89 (0-690-04913-7); paper $5.99 (0-06-440232-0). 128pp. At the death of his mother, a young boy sets out to find his samurai father in 12th-century Japan.

9288 Place, Francois. *The Old Man Mad About Drawing* (5–8). Trans. by William Rodarmor. Illus. 2003, Godine $19.95 (1-56792-260-0). 128pp. In 19th-century Edo (now Tokyo), Tojiro, a 9-year-old orphan who sells rice cakes, becomes the assistant to a famous old artist. (Rev: BL 3/15/04*; HB 3–4/04; SLJ 5/04)

9289 Russell, Ching Yeung. *Child Bride* (4–7). Illus. 1999, Boyds Mills $15.95 (1-56397-748-6). 133pp. Set in China in the early 1940s, this is the story of 11-year-old Ying, her arranged marriage, and an understanding bridegroom who allows her to go home to her ailing grandmother. (Rev: BL 3/1/99; HBG 10/99; SLJ 4/99)

9290 Russell, Ching Yeung. *Lichee Tree* (4–7). 1997, Boyds Mills $15.95 (1-56397-629-3). 182pp. Growing up in China during the 1940s, Ying dreams of selling lichee nuts and visiting Canton. (Rev: BCCB 4/97; BL 3/15/97; SLJ 6/97)

9291 Shea, Pegi Deitz. *The Carpet Boy's Gift* (2–5). Illus. by Leane Morin. 2003, Tilbury House $16.95 (0-88448-248-0). 40pp. This beautifully illustrated fictional picture-book tale of a young Pakistani boy working under dreadful conditions was inspired by the murder of 12-year-old activist Iqbal Masih. (Rev: BL 1/1–15/04; SLJ 2/04)

9292 Spivak, Dawnine. *Grass Sandals: The Travels of Basho* (3–5). Illus. by Demi. 1997, Simon & Schuster $16.00 (0-689-80776-7). 40pp. An outstanding picture book about the 17th-century poet and his travels around Japan. (Rev: BCCB 7–8/97; BL 5/1/97*; HBG 3/98; SLJ 4/97) [895.6]

9293 Sreenivasan, Jyotsna. *Aruna's Journeys* (4–7). Illus. 1997, Smooth Stone paper $6.95 (0-9619401-7-4). 136pp. Aruna denies her Indian heritage until she spends a summer in Bangalore, India. (Rev: BL 7/97)

9294 Tenzing, Norbu. *Himalaya* (3–5). Trans. from French by Shelley Tanaka. Illus. by author. 2002, Groundwood $16.95 (0-88899-480-X). A gripping saga, beautifully illustrated, about the Dolpo people of Nepal, their grueling treks through the mountains, and the transfer of leadership. (Rev: HBG 3/03; SLJ 1/03)

9295 Tenzing, Norbu, and Stephane Frattini. *Secret of the Snow Leopard* (3–5). Trans. from French by Shelley Tanaka. Illus. by Tenzing Norbu. 2004, Groundwood $16.95 (0-88899-544-X). In beautifully illustrated Nepal, young Tsering defies his stepfather and travels a dangerous pass where his father lost his life; there he encounters a snow leopard and must draw on his inner strength. (Rev: SLJ 8/04)

9296 Wartski, Maureen C. *A Boat to Nowhere* (4–5). 1981, NAL paper $4.99 (0-451-16285-4). 160pp. An adventure story about the Vietnamese "boat people."

9297 Whelan, Gloria. *Homeless Bird* (5–8). 2000, HarperCollins LB $16.89 (0-06-028452-8). 192pp. A novel set in contemporary India about a young girl and her arranged marriage to a young man who is dying of tuberculosis. (Rev: BL 3/1/00; HBG 10/00; SLJ 2/00)

9298 Whitesel, Cheryl Aylward. *Blue Fingers: A Ninja's Tale* (5–8). 2004, Clarion $15.00 (0-618-38139-2). 256pp. In 16th-century Japan, 12-year-old Koji is trained to become a ninja warrior. (Rev: BL 3/15/04; SLJ 3/04)

9299 Whitesel, Cheryl Aylward. *Rebel: A Tibetan Odyssey* (5–8). 2000, HarperCollins $15.95 (0-688-16735-7). 190pp. In Tibet about a century ago, a young boy named Thunder is sent to live with his uncle, an important lama in a Buddhist monastery. (Rev: BCCB 5/00; BL 4/15/00; HBG 3/01; SLJ 7/00)

9300 Wu, Priscilla. *The Abacus Contest: Stories from Taiwan and China* (5–8). Illus. 1996, Fulcrum $15.95 (1-55591-243-5). Six simple short stories explore life in a Taiwanese city. (Rev: BL 7/96; SLJ 6/96)

9301 Yep, Laurence. *Lady of Ch'iao Kuo: Warrior of the South* (5–8). Illus. Series: Royal Diaries. 2001, Scholastic $10.95 (0-439-16483-6). 300pp. In this volume of the Royal Diaries series, the teenage Princess Redbird of the Hsien tribe must use her diplomatic skills to save the lives of both her own people and Chinese colonists in the 6th century A.D. Historical notes add background information. (Rev: BL 11/1/01)

9302 Yep, Laurence. *Spring Pearl: The Last Flower* (4–7). Series: Girls of Many Lands. 2002, Pleasant Co. $12.95 (1-58485-595-9); paper $7.95 (1-58485-519-3). 224pp. An adventurous, intelligent orphan faces a difficult time when she goes to live with her artist father's patron in this novel set in the turmoil of 1857 China. (Rev: BL 12/15/02; HBG 3/03; SLJ 10/02)

Europe

9303 Anholt, Laurence. *Leonardo and the Flying Boy* (2–4). Illus. 2000, Barron's $13.95 (0-7641-5225-4). 32pp. A fictionalized account of da Vinci's life and accomplishments as reflected in anecdotes about his young apprentices. (Rev: BL 1/1–15/01; SLJ 2/01)

9304 Attema, Martha. *Daughter of Light* (3–5). Illus. 2001, Orca paper $4.99 (1-55143-179-3). 138pp. In this affecting novel, which takes place in the Nazi-occupied Netherlands during World War II, a 9-year-old girl braves German soldiers and risks her freedom to help her pregnant mother. (Rev: BL 2/1/02; SLJ 12/01)

9305 Balit, Christina. *Escape from Pompeii* (1–4). Illus. by author. 2003, Holt $17.95 (0-8050-7324-8). This fictionalized account of the fall of the Italian city of Pompeii tells of a young boy and girl who manage to flee to the sea before the eruption of Mount Vesuvius totally destroys the city. (Rev: HBG 4/04; SLJ 11/03) [823.9]

9306 Banks, Lynne Reid. *Tiger, Tiger* (5–8). 2005, Delacorte LB $17.99 (0-385-90264-6). 256pp. Two tiger cubs arrive in Rome destined for different fates; Brute is trained to be a killer of men in the Colosseum while Boots becomes a pet for the caesar's daughter, a decision with dangerous consequences. (Rev: BL 5/15/05; SLJ 6/05)

9307 Bawden, Nina. *The Real Plato Jones* (5–8). 1993, Clarion $15.00 (0-395-66972-3). British teen Plato Jones and his mother return to Greece for his grandfather's funeral, where Plato discovers that his grandfather may have been a coward and traitor while serving in the Greek Resistance. (Rev: BCCB 11/93; BL 10/15/93; SLJ 11/93*)

9308 Casanova, Mary. *Cecile: Gates of Gold* (4–7). Illus. Series: Girls of Many Lands. 2002, Pleasant Co. $12.95 (1-58485-594-0); paper $7.95 (1-58485-518-5). 191pp. For 12-year-old Cecile, a peasant in 18th-century France, the chance to work at the Palace of Versailles seems like a dream come true until she faces some of the harsh realities of court life. (Rev: BL 10/15/02; HBG 3/03; SLJ 9/02)

9309 Casanova, Mary. *Curse of a Winter Moon* (5–8). 2000, Hyperion $15.99 (0-7868-0547-1). 144pp. Set in 16th-century France, this novel tells of the conflict between the Huguenots and the Roman Catholics as seen from the point of view of young Marius. (Rev: BL 10/15/00; HBG 3/01; SLJ 10/00)

9310 Celenza, Anna Harwell. *The Farewell Symphony* (2–4). Illus. by JoAnn E. Kitchel. 2000, Charlesbridge LB $19.95 (1-57091-406-0). A fictional version of the story behind Haydn's "Farewell Symphony" and the effect it had on Prince Nicholas, the composer's sponsor. (Rev: HBG 3/01; SLJ 7/00)

9311 Clements, Bruce. *A Chapel of Thieves* (4–6). 2002, Farrar $16.00 (0-374-37701-4). 224pp. In this sequel to *I Tell a Lie Every So Often* (1974), Henry, an adventurous 15-year-old, journeys across the Atlantic to Paris in 1849 to rescue his older brother from a gang of thieves. (Rev: BCCB 4/02; BL 3/15/02; HBG 10/02; SLJ 5/02)

9312 Debon, Nicolas. *A Brave Soldier* (2–5). Illus. 2002, Groundwood $15.95 (0-88899-481-8). 32pp. This picture book for older children, narrated by a young Canadian soldier, introduces readers to the trenches of World War I. (Rev: BL 11/1/02; HBG 3/03; SLJ 2/03)

9313 DeJong, Meindert. *Wheel on the School* (4–7). Illus. by Maurice Sendak. 1954, HarperCollins LB $16.89 (0-06-021586-0); paper $5.99 (0-06-440021-2). 256pp. The storks are brought back to their island by the schoolchildren in a Dutch village. Newbery Medal winner, 1955.

9314 Delton, Judy. *Angel Spreads Her Wings* (3–5). Illus. 1999, Houghton Mifflin $15.00 (0-395-91006-4). 160pp. Angel flourishes when her stepdad takes the family to visit his hometown in Greece and live in a house without electricity. (Rev: BL 5/1/99; HB 7–8/99; HBG 10/99; SLJ 4/99)

9315 de Trevino, Elizabeth. *I, Juan de Pareja* (5–8). 1965, Farrar $13.95 (0-374-33531-1); paper $4.95 (0-374-43525-1). 192pp. Through the eyes of his devoted black slave, Juan de Pareja, the character of the artist Velasquez is revealed. Newbery Medal winner, 1966.

9316 Deverell, Catherine. *Stradivari's Singing Violin* (3–5). Illus. by Andrea Shine. 1992, Carolrhoda LB $21.27 (0-87614-732-5). 48pp. A fictional account of the historical figure behind what is perhaps the world's best-known musical instrument. (Rev: BL 2/15/93)

9317 Eisner, Will. *The Last Knight: An Introduction to Don Quixote by Miguel de Cervantes* (4–8). Illus. 2000, NBM $15.95 (1-56163-251-1). 32pp. Using an engaging text and a comic book format, this is a fine retelling of Cervantes' classic. (Rev: BL 6/1–15/00; HBG 10/00; SLJ 7/00)

9318 Ellis, Deborah. *A Company of Fools* (5–8). 2002, Fitzhenry & Whiteside $15.95 (1-55041-719-3). 180pp. Quiet Henri and free-spirited Micah try to cheer the people of a France devastated by the Black Death of 1348 by singing. (Rev: BCCB 1/03; BL 1/1–15/03; HB 1–2/03; HBG 3/03)

9319 Fagan, Cary. *Daughter of the Great Zandini* (3–5). Illus. by Cybele Young. 2001, Tundra LB $16.95 (0-88776-534-3). 57pp. The Great Zandini's son has been groomed to follow in his father's magician footsteps, but it is Fanny, the neglected daughter, who is the success in this story set in 19th-century Paris. (Rev: HBG 3/02; SLJ 4/02)

9320 Gordon, Sharon. *Greece* (2–4). Illus. Series: Discovering Cultures. 2003, Benchmark LB $17.95 (0-7614-1718-4). 48pp. This well-illustrated overview of Greece and its people includes the usual information offered for this age group, plus some less well-known details. (Rev: SLJ 4/04) [949.5]

9321 Greene, Jacqueline D. *Marie: Summer in the Country* (3–6). Illus. Series: Girlhood Journeys. 1997, Simon & Schuster paper $5.99 (0-689-81562-X). 72pp. In this historical novel set in France,

Marie plots to save her country cousin from being sent away to work as a servant. (Rev: BL 4/1/98; SLJ 4/98)

9322 Greene, Jacqueline D. *One Foot Ashore* (4–6). 1994, Walker $16.95 (0-8027-8281-7). 208pp. To escape servitude in Brazil, Maria stows away on a boat bound for Amsterdam, where she finds work in the home of Rembrandt. (Rev: BCCB 6/94; BL 4/1/94; HB 7–8/94; SLJ 6/94)

9323 Gregory, Kristiana. *Eleanor: Crown Jewel of Aquitaine* (3–6). Series: Royal Diaries. 2002, Scholastic $10.95 (0-439-16484-2). 192pp. Eleanor's fictional diary details her daily life in the 12th century — as a child and later as a queen — giving readers a good sense of her times. (Rev: BL 2/1/03; HBG 3/03; SLJ 1/03)

9324 Hautzig, Esther. *A Picture of Grandmother* (3–5). Illus. by Beth Peck. 2002, Farrar $15.00 (0-374-35920-2). 96pp. The lifestyle of a wealthy Jewish family in prewar Poland, portrayed in detail, plays an important role in this story of a girl discovering a family secret. (Rev: BCCB 12/02; BL 10/1/02; HBG 3/03; SLJ 10/02)

9325 Havill, Juanita. *Eyes Like Willy's* (6–9). Illus. by David Johnson. 2004, HarperCollins LB $16.89 (0-688-13673-7). 135pp. Guy, who lives in Paris, and Willy, an Austrian, have been friends since they met in the summer of 1906; now they may face each other across the trenches of World War I. (Rev: BL 3/1/04*; SLJ 7/04)

9326 Hest, Amy. *When Jessie Came Across the Sea* (2–4). Illus. by P. J. Lynch. 1997, Candlewick $16.99 (0-7636-0094-6). 40pp. A Jewish girl living in an Eastern European shtetl gets an opportunity to come to the United States, but she will have to leave her wonderful grandmother behind. (Rev: BCCB 3/98; BL 2/1/98; HBG 3/98; SLJ 11/97)

9327 Holub, Joseph. *The Robber and Me* (5–8). Trans. from German by Elizabeth D. Crawford. 1997, Holt $16.95 (0-8050-5591-1). On his way to live with his uncle, an orphan is helped by a mysterious stranger and he must later make a decision about whether to stand up to his uncle and the town authorities to clear the name of this man in this novel set in 19th-century Germany. (Rev: SLJ 12/97*)

9328 Hugo, Victor. *The Hunchback of Notre Dame* (4–6). Retold by Tim Wynne-Jones. Illus. by Bill Slavin. 1997, Orchard $15.95 (0-531-30055-2). This abridgement of the Hugo classic captures the spirit of Paris in the Middle Ages and Quasimodo's love for Esmeralda. (Rev: HBG 3/98; SLJ 4/98)

9329 Ibbotson, Eva. *The Star of Kazan* (4–8). Illus. by Kevin Hawkes. 2004, Dutton $16.99 (0-525-47347-5). 336pp. Set in the Austro-Hungarian empire, this richly detailed and very readable novel tells the story of 12-year-old Annika, who gets a rude awakening when her aristocratic mother whisks her away from her adoptive family. (Rev: BL 10/15/04*; SLJ 10/04*)

9330 Johnston, Tony. *The Harmonica* (3–6). Illus. by Ron Mazellan. 2004, Charlesbridge $15.95 (1-57091-547-4). 32pp. This moving tale of a young Jewish boy who plays his harmonica for the concentration camp commandant is based on truth. (Rev: BL 1/1–15/04; SLJ 5/04)

9331 Jones, Terry. *The Lady and the Squire* (5–7). Illus. 2001, Pavilion $22.95 (1-86205-417-7). 304pp. A beautiful aristocrat joins Tom and Ann as they make their way through a war-torn countryside to the papal court at Avignon. (Rev: BL 2/15/01; SLJ 3/01)

9332 Juster, Norton. *Alberic the Wise* (4–8). Illus. by Leonard Baskin. 1992, Picture Book $16.95 (0-88708-243-2). 32pp. In this picture book set in the Renaissance, Alberic becomes an apprentice to a stained-glass maker. (Rev: BCCB 2/93; BL 1/15/93; SLJ 3/93)

9333 Kacer, Kathy. *The Night Spies* (4–7). 2003, Second Story paper $5.95 (1-896764-70-3). 197pp. Hiding from the Nazis, Gabi and her family can leave their cramped quarters only at night, but Gabi and her cousin Max manage to help the partisans. (Rev: BL 1/1–15/04; SLJ 3/04)

9334 Kanefield, Teri. *Rivka's Way* (4–8). 2001, Front Street $15.95 (0-8126-2870-5). 144pp. Daily life inside and outside the Prague ghetto in 1778 is explored in this novel about an unconventional Jewish girl, 15-year-old Rivka Liebermann. (Rev: BCCB 3/02; BL 4/1/01; HBG 10/01; SLJ 3/01)

9335 Kelly, Eric P. *The Trumpeter of Krakow* (5–9). Illus. by Janina Domanska. 1966, Macmillan $17.95 (0-02-750140-X); paper $4.99 (0-689-71571-4). 224pp. Mystery surrounds a precious jewel and the youthful patriot who stands watch over it in a church tower in this novel of 15th-century Poland. Newbery Medal winner, 1929.

9336 Kimmel, Elizabeth Cody. *Before Columbus: The Leif Eriksson Expedition: A True Adventure* (3–6). Series: Landmark Books. 2003, Random $14.95 (0-375-81347-0). 112pp. Kimmel extrapolates from the little that is known about Eriksson's life and adventures to create a portrait of a bold Viking explorer. (Rev: BL 7/03; HBG 4/04; SLJ 10/03) [970.01]

9337 Kimmel, Eric A. *Count Silvernose: A Story from Italy* (3–6). Illus. by Omar Rayyan. 1996, Holiday House $15.95 (0-8234-1216-4). 30pp. Set in the late Renaissance, this adventure story tells how Assunta sets out to find her sisters, who have been abducted by Count Silvernose. (Rev: BCCB 7–8/96; BL 3/15/96*; HB 7–8/96; SLJ 3/96)

9338 Knight, Joan MacPhail. *Charlotte in Giverny* (4–6). Illus. 2000, Chronicle $15.95 (0-8118-2383-0). 64pp. In this novel set in France in the 1890s a young American girl gets to know many of the American artists who are studying with Monet at Giverny and even meets the reclusive painter himself. (Rev: BL 7/00; HBG 10/00; SLJ 6/00)

9339 Knight, Joan MacPhail. *Charlotte in Paris* (3–6). Illus. by Melissa Sweet. 2003, Chronicle $16.95 (0-8118-3766-1). It's 1893, and Charlotte — of *Charlotte in Giverny* (2000) — is now living in Paris and details in her journal all the places she goes and the people she meets. (Rev: HBG 4/04; SLJ 1/04)

9340 Lasky, Kathryn. *Broken Song* (5–8). 2005, Viking $15.99 (0-670-05931-5). 160pp. Reuven Bloom, a 15-year-old Jew and promising violinist, escapes from late-19th-century Russia with his baby sister, the only surviving member of his family. (Rev: BL 1/1–15/05; SLJ 3/05)

9341 Lasky, Kathryn. *Marie Antoinette: Princess of Versailles* (5–8). Series: Royal Diaries. 2000, Scholastic paper $10.95 (0-439-07666-8). 240pp. This fictional diary covers two years in the life of Marie Antoinette, beginning in 1769 when the 13-year-old was preparing for her fateful marriage. (Rev: BL 4/15/00; HBG 10/00; SLJ 5/00)

9342 Lasky, Kathryn. *Mary, Queen of Scots: Queen Without a Country* (5–8). Illus. Series: Royal Diaries. 2002, Scholastic paper $10.95 (0-439-19404-0). 224pp. Part of the Royal Diary series, this is a fictional diary of the year 1553, when Mary was betrothed to the son of King Henry II of France. (Rev: BL 5/15/02; HBG 10/02; SLJ 6/02)

9343 Lasky, Kathryn. *The Night Journey* (4–7). Illus. by Trina S. Hyman. 1986, Puffin paper $4.99 (0-14-032048-2). 152pp. Nana tells her great-granddaughter about her escape from Czarist Russia.

9344 Lewis, J. Patrick. *The Stolen Smile* (3–6). Illus. by Gary Kelley. 2004, Creative Editions $17.95 (1-56846-192-5). 40pp. Vincenzo Peruggia tells the story, based on real events, of his theft of the Mona Lisa from the Louvre in 1911. (Rev: SLJ 1/05)

9345 Littlesugar, Amy. *Marie in Fourth Position: The Story of Degas' "The Little Dancer"* (1–3). Illus. by Ian Schoenherr. 1996, Philomel $16.99 (0-399-22794-6). The story of a young ballet student who modeled for Degas to get money for her poor parents. (Rev: SLJ 10/96*)

9346 Macaulay, David. *Rome Antics* (4–8). Illus. 1997, Houghton Mifflin $17.00 (0-395-82289-3). 80pp. The reader gets a pigeon-eye view of vistas and building as the bird flies over Rome. (Rev: BL 9/15/97; SLJ 11/97*)

9347 Masini, Beatrice. *The Wedding Dress Mess* (K–4). Adapted by Lenny Hort. Illus. by Anna Laura Cantone. 2003, Watson-Guptill $15.95 (0-8230-1738-9). Filomena has long planned the perfect dress for her wedding, but things don't turn out quite the way she'd pictured in this rambunctious story with lively illustrations. (Rev: HBG 10/03; SLJ 5/03)

9348 Mead, Alice. *Girl of Kosovo* (5–10). 2001, Farrar $16.00 (0-374-32620-7). 128pp. A moving novel about the ethnic wars in Kosovo as seen through the eyes of an 11-year-old Albanian girl who has witnessed the death of her father and two brothers and whose foot is smashed during the fighting. (Rev: BCCB 6/01; BL 3/15/01*; HBG 10/01; SLJ 3/01)

9349 Meyer, Carolyn. *Anastasia: The Last Grand Duchess, Russia, 1914* (4–8). Series: Royal Diaries. 2000, Scholastic paper $10.95 (0-439-12908-7). 224pp. Anastasia's fictional diary begins when she is 12 in 1914 and ends with her captivity in 1918. (Rev: HBG 10/01; SLJ 10/00)

9350 Morpurgo, Michael. *Toro! Toro!* (4–6). Illus. by Michael Foreman. 2004, Collins paper $7.95 (0-

00-710718-8). 128pp. During the Spanish Civil War, young Antonio bonds with a bull calf born on the family farm but must let it go when the Nationalists attack their village. (Rev: BL 2/15/04; SLJ 5/04)

9351 Morrison, Taylor. *The Neptune Fountain: The Apprenticeship of a Renaissance Sculptor* (3–6). Illus. 1997, Holiday House LB $15.95 (0-8234-1293-8). 32pp. The creation of a marble sculpture is described in this novel about an apprentice to a famous sculptor in 17th-century Rome. (Rev: BL 6/1–15/97; SLJ 6/97)

9352 Moss, Marissa. *Galen: My Life in Imperial Rome* (3–6). Illus. 2002, Harcourt $15.00 (0-15-216535-5). 48pp. Historically accurate details about life in the house of Roman Emperor Augustus are revealed through the eyes of a fictitious Greek slave in a gripping text accompanied by maps, glossary, and captioned illustrations. (Rev: BL 12/15/02; HBG 3/03; SLJ 10/02)

9353 Nichol, Barbara. *Beethoven Lives Upstairs* (3–6). Illus. by Scott Cameron. 1994, Orchard $15.95 (0-531-06828-5). 48pp. When Beethoven moves into his house, young Christoph gradually learns to sympathize with the agonies suffered by Beethoven because of his deafness. (Rev: BCCB 2/94; BL 1/1/94*; HB 7–8/94; SLJ 4/94)

9354 Pernoud, Regine. *A Day with a Miller* (4–7). Trans. by Dominique Clift. Illus. by Giorgio Bacchin. 1997, Runestone LB $22.60 (0-8225-1914-3). 48pp. A description of the life of a miller and his family in the 12th century and how hydraulic energy was being introduced at that time. (Rev: HBG 3/98; SLJ 3/98)

9355 Pyle, Howard. *Otto of the Silver Hand* (6–8). Illus. by author. 1967, Dover paper $8.95 (0-486-21784-1). 173pp. Life in feudal Germany, the turbulence and cruelty of robber barons, and the peaceful, scholarly pursuits of the monks are presented in the story of the kidnapped son of a robber baron.

9356 Rappaport, Doreen. *The Secret Seder* (2–4). Illus. by Emily Arnold McCully. 2005, Hyperion $16.99 (0-7868-0777-6). 40pp. Young Jacques attends a secret seder in Nazi-occupied France. (Rev: BL 1/1–15/05; SLJ 2/05)

9357 Robertson, Bruce. *Marguerite Makes a Book* (3–6). 1999, Getty Museum $18.95 (0-89236-372-X). 48pp. A stunning picture book for older readers, set in 15th-century Paris, in which young Marguerite takes over her father's book-painting craft when the old man become too infirm to work. (Rev: BL 11/15/99; HBG 3/00; SLJ 1/00)

9358 Rosen, Sidney, and Dorothy S. Rosen. *The Magician's Apprentice* (5–8). 1994, Carolrhoda LB $19.95 (0-87614-809-7). An orphan in a French abbey in the Middle Ages is accused of having a heretical document in his possession and is sent to spy on Roger Bacon, the English scientist. (Rev: BL 5/1/94; SLJ 6/94)

9359 Rubalcaba, Jill. *The Wadjet Eye* (5–8). 2000, Clarion $15.00 (0-395-68942-2). 128pp. After mummifying his dead mother, Damon sets off to find his father and is later hired by Cleopatra as a spy in this action-filled novel set in the Roman Empire of 45 B.C. (Rev: BL 5/15/00; HBG 10/00; SLJ 6/00)

9360 Schwartz, Ellen. *Jesse's Star* (2–5). Illus. 2000, Orca paper $4.50 (1-55143-143-2). 108pp. Jesse travels back in time and becomes his great-great-grandfather, a Jewish boy growing up in Russia, reliving his part in helping villagers and himself escape the pogroms and make their way to Canada. (Rev: BL 7/00; SLJ 11/00)

9361 Seredy, Kate. *The Good Master* (4–6). Illus. by author. 1986, Puffin paper $4.99 (0-14-030133-X). 196pp. Warm and humorous story of a city girl on her uncle's farm in prewar Hungary.

9362 Skurzynski, Gloria. *The Minstrel in the Tower* (3–4). Illus. by Julek Heller. 1988, Random paper $3.99 (0-394-89598-3). 64pp. Alice and Roger search for their uncle after their father has been killed in the Crusades, in this story of life in the Middle Ages. (Rev: BCCB 7–8/88; BL 7/88)

9363 Trottier, Maxine. *The Paint Box* (2–4). Illus. by Stella East. 2003, Fitzhenry & Whiteside $16.95 (1-55041-804-1). A compelling fictional story about Marietta, daughter of Tintoretto and a talented artist herself, with beautiful illustrations and background information on the era. (Rev: BL 5/15/2003; SLJ 5/03)

9364 Visconti, Guido. *The Genius of Leonardo* (3–6). Trans. by Mark Roberts. Illus. 2000, Barefoot $16.99 (1-84148-301-X). 40pp. Using many quotes from the writings of Leonardo da Vinci, this novel tries to re-create this great man's in the eyes of his servant, Giacomo. (Rev: BCCB 10/00; BL 9/15/00; HBG 10/01; SLJ 9/00)

9365 Weston, Carol. *Melanie Martin Goes Dutch* (3–6). 2002, Knopf LB $17.99 (0-375-92195-8). 224pp. Melanie's diary of her trip to the Netherlands with her family and friend Cecily reveals a gradual growth to maturity. (Rev: BL 6/1–15/02; HBG 10/02; SLJ 5/02)

9366 Weston, Carol. *With Love from Spain, Melanie Martin* (4–6). 2004, Knopf LB $17.99 (0-375-92646-1). 256pp. Melanie and her family are off to Spain, where she worries about her mother, finds an attractive 12-year-old boy, whines about her brother, and confides many details of Spanish life and culture to her diary. (Rev: BL 1/1–15/04; SLJ 3/04)

9367 Wild, Margaret. *Let the Celebrations Begin!* (3–6). Illus. by Julie Vivas. 1991, Watts LB $14.99 (0-531-08537-6). 32pp. A picture book for older children about a group of Polish women in the Belsen death camp who organized a party for the surviving children after liberation. (Rev: BCCB 9/91; BL 8/91; SLJ 7/91)

9368 Williams, Laura E. *The Spider's Web* (5–7). Illus. 1999, Milkweed $15.95 (1-57131-621-3); paper $6.95 (1-57131-622-1). 134pp. Lexi, a modern German girl, joins a racist skinhead organization and discovers the consequences of irrational hatred — from her own actions and from speaking with an older woman who was once a member of Hitler's Youth. (Rev: BL 6/1–15/99; HBG 10/99)

9369 Wilson, John. *Flames of the Tiger* (5–8). 2003, Kids Can $16.95 (1-55337-618-8). 176pp. The horrors of World War II are seen through the eyes of 17-year-old Dieter, who with his younger sister is fleeing his native Germany as the war nears an end. (Rev: HBG 4/04; SLJ 1/04) [813]

9370 Zucker, N. F. *Benno's Bear* (4–7). 2001, Dutton $16.99 (0-525-46521-9). 256pp. Benno, a young pickpocket in Central Europe, is taken in by a kind family who help him discover the joys of reading. (Rev: BCCB 12/01; BL 11/15/01; HB 11–12/01; HBG 3/02; SLJ 10/01)

Great Britain and Ireland

9371 Avi. *Crispin: The Cross of Lead* (5–9). 2002, Hyperion $16.49 (0-7868-2647-9). 261pp. Thirteen-year-old orphan Crispin seeks protection from a juggler named Bear in this complex novel set in medieval England. Newbery Medal winner, 2003. (Rev: BL 5/15/02; HB 9–10/02; HBG 3/03; SLJ 6/02*)

9372 Blackwood, Gary. *Shakespeare's Spy* (5–8). 2003, Dutton $16.99 (0-525-47145-6). 280pp. Romance and intrigue are at hand as Widge continues his career at the Globe Theatre in this sequel to *The Shakespeare Stealer* (1998) and *Shakespeare's Scribe* (2000). (Rev: BL 9/1/03; HB 11–12/03; HBG 4/04; SLJ 10/03)

9373 Blackwood, Gary L. *Shakespeare Stealer* (5–8). 1998, NAL $15.99 (0-525-45863-8). A 14-year-old apprentice at the Globe Theater is sent by a rival theater company to steal Shakespeare's plays. (Rev: BL 6/1–15/98; HB 7–8/98; HBG 10/98; SLJ 6/98)

9374 Blackwood, Gary L. *Shakespeare's Scribe* (5–8). 2000, Dutton $15.99 (0-525-46444-1). 224pp. Set in Elizabethan England, this is the story of how young Widge discovers his true identity while traveling outside London with a theatrical troupe. (Rev: BL 9/1/00; HB 11–12/00; HBG 3/01; SLJ 9/00)

9375 Branford, Henrietta. *Fire, Bed, and Bone* (5–9). 1998, Candlewick $16.99 (0-7636-0338-4). This unusual novel, narrated from a dog's point of view, describes the oppression of the peasants in late 14th-century England and the revolt led by Wat Tyler and the preacher John Ball. (Rev: BCCB 5/98; BL 3/15/98; BR 9–10/98; HBG 10/98; SLJ 5/98)

9376 Burgess, Melvin. *The Copper Treasure* (3–6). Illus. 2000, Holt $15.95 (0-8050-6381-1). 104pp. Set in 19th-century London, this is an adventure story involving 11-year-old Jeremy and two friends who try to salvage a roll of copper that has sunk to the bottom of the Thames. (Rev: BCCB 7–8/00; BL 6/1–15/00; HB 7–8/00; HBG 10/00; SLJ 7/00)

9377 Chaucer, Geoffrey. *Canterbury Tales* (4–8). Adapted by Barbara Cohen. Illus. by Trina S. Hyman. 1988, Lothrop $21.99 (0-688-06201-6). 96pp. Several of the popular stories are retold with handsome illustrations by Trina Schart Hyman. (Rev: BL 9/1/88; SLJ 8/88)

9378 Chaucer, Geoffrey. *The Canterbury Tales* (5–9). Adapted by Geraldine McCaughrean. Illus. 1985, Checkerboard $14.95 (1-56288-259-7). An adaptation for young readers of 13 tales that still keep the flavor and spirit of the originals. (Rev: SLJ 2/86) [826]

9379 Conlon-McKenna, Marita. *Fields of Home* (5–7). Illus. by Donald Teskey. 1997, Holiday House paper $15.95 (0-8234-1295-4). 189pp. The story of the effects of the 19th-century potato famine in Ireland and the grinding poverty it produced on the young daughter of one of the survivers. (Rev: BCCB 7–8/97; SLJ 6/97)

9380 Cushman, Karen. *Matilda Bone* (4–8). 2000, Clarion $15.00 (0-395-88156-0). 176pp. Set in the 14th century, this novel describes the development of Matilda, 13, who serves as an assistant to the local bone setter in exchange for food and shelter. (Rev: BCCB 12/00; BL 8/00; HB 11–12/00; HBG 3/01; SLJ 9/00*)

9381 Dalton, Annie. *Isabel: Taking Wing* (3–7). Series: Girls of Many Lands. 2002, Pleasant Co. $12.95 (1-58485-593-2); paper $7.95 (1-58485-517-7). 178pp. A rebellious Isabel, 12, is sent from London to the country to live with an aunt who turns out to be really interesting, with the result that a more mature and capable Isabel returns home to deal with problems there in this novel set in the late 16th century, with lots of details about life at that time. (Rev: BL 11/1/02; HBG 3/03; SLJ 10/02)

9382 De Angeli, Marguerite. *The Door in the Wall* (5–7). Illus. by author. 1990, Dell paper $5.50 (0-440-40283-2). Crippled Robin proves his courage in plague-ridden 19th-century London. Newbery Medal winner, 1950.

9383 Dhami, Narinder. *Bindi Babes* (5–8). 2004, Delacorte LB $16.99 (0-385-90214-X). 69pp. The three Bindi sisters, aged 10 to 13, still trying to cope with their mother's death when an aunt arrives from India, look for ways to get the unwelcome visitor out of their lives. (Rev: BL 9/15/04; SLJ 8/04)

9384 Dickens, Charles. *A Christmas Carol* (5–8). Illus. by Carter Goodrich. 1996, Morrow $18.00 (0-688-13606-0). 64pp. An abridged version of Dickens's performance text, with excellent illustrations by Carter Goodrich. (Rev: BL 9/1/96; HB 1–2/96)

9385 Doherty, Berlie. *Street Child* (5–7). 1994, Orchard LB $18.99 (0-531-08714-X). 160pp. The story of a street urchin in Victorian London who is forced to work on a river barge until he escapes. (Rev: BCCB 11/94; BL 9/1/94; SLJ 10/94)

9386 Duey, Kathleen. *Lara and the Gray Mare* (4–6). Series: Hoofbeats. 2005, Dutton $15.99 (0-525-47332-7); paper $4.99 (0-14-240230-3). 128pp. In medieval Ireland, 9-year-old Lara cares for her beloved gray mare as the animal suffers through a difficult pregnancy. (Rev: BL 2/1/05)

9387 Flegg, Aubrey. *Katie's War* (5–8). 2000, O'Brien paper $7.95 (0-86278-525-1). 192pp. Set during Ireland's fight for independence from England, this story shows a girl torn between two sides when her father wants peace and her brother is preparing to use force. (Rev: BL 12/1/00)

9388 Giff, Patricia Reilly. *Nory Ryan's Song* (4–7). 2000, Delacorte $15.95 (0-385-32141-4). 176pp. Set in Ireland at the time of the great famine, 12-year-old Nory must fight starvation as well as care for her younger brother. (Rev: BL 9/15/00*; HB 1–2/01; HBG 3/01; SLJ 8/00)

9389 Goodman, Joan E. *The Winter Hare* (4–8). Illus. 1996, Houghton Mifflin $17.00 (0-395-78569-3). 240pp. In 12th-century England, Will becomes a page to the wicked Earl Aubrey. (Rev: BCCB 2/97; BL 11/15/96; BR 9–10/97; SLJ 11/96)

9390 Graves, Robert. *An Ancient Castle* (4–6). Illus. by Elizabeth Graves. 1991, Michael Kesend paper $8.95 (0-935576-33-9). 72pp. A novel of heroes, villains, and buried treasures set in pre-World War I Britain.

9391 Griffin, Margot. *Dancing for Danger: A Meggy Tale* (4–6). Illus. 2001, Stoddart $6.95 (0-7737-6136-5). 112pp. Meggy shows real bravery when her forbidden "hedge school" is under threat in 19th-century Ireland. (Rev: BL 6/1–15/01; SLJ 2/02)

9392 Harrison, Cora. *The Famine Secret* (5–7). Illus. by Orla Roche. Series: Drumshee Timeline. 1998, Irish American paper $6.95 (0-86327-649-0). 128pp. In 1847 the four McMahon children are orphaned and sent to an Irish workhouse, but their determination prevails and they are soon plotting to regain their home. (Rev: SLJ 12/98)

9393 Harrison, Cora. *The Secret of Drumshee Castle* (5–7). Illus. by Orla Roche. Series: Drumshee Timeline. 1998, Irish American paper $6.95 (0-86327-632-6). 128pp. Grace Barry, the orphaned heiress to a castle in Ireland during Elizabethan times, flees to England to escape threats by her acquisitive guardians. (Rev: SLJ 12/98)

9394 Harrison, Cora. *The Secret of the Seven Crosses* (4–7). Illus. 1998, Wolfhound paper $6.95 (0-86327-616-4). 128pp. In medieval Ireland, three youngsters hope to find hidden treasure by examining sources in their monastery library. Preceded by *Nauala and Her Secret Wolf* and followed by *The Secret of Drumshee Castle*. (Rev: BL 12/15/98)

9395 Holmes, Victoria. *The Horse from the Sea* (5–8). 2005, HarperCollins LB $16.89 (0-06-052029-9). 320pp. In 1588, Nora, an Irish girl, defies the English and helps a young Spanish sailor and a beautiful stallion, survivors of a shipwreck. (Rev: BL 5/15/05)

9396 Hooper, Mary. *At the Sign of the Sugared Plum* (5–8). 2003, Bloomsbury $16.95 (1-58234-849-9). 167pp. The horrors of the bubonic plague and the squalor of 17th-century London are brought to life in this story of Hannah and her sister Sarah, owner of a sweetmeats shop. (Rev: BL 9/15/03; HBG 4/04; SLJ 8/03)

9397 Horowitz, Anthony. *The Devil and His Boy* (5–8). 2000, Penguin Putnam $16.99 (0-399-23432-2). 128pp. In Elizabethan England, young Tom Falconer, a boy of the streets, ends up saving his queen. (Rev: BCCB 3/00; BL 1/1–15/00; HBG 10/00; SLJ 4/00)

9398 Howard, Ellen. *The Gate in the Wall* (5–7). 1999, Simon & Schuster $16.00 (0-689-82295-2). 160pp. In Victorian England, 10-year-old orphan Emma escapes the drudgery of factory work and gets a job on a canal boat where she helps load the cargo. (Rev: BCCB 5/99; BL 2/15/99; HB 3–4/99; HBG 10/99; SLJ 3/99)

9399 Kirwan, Anna. *Victoria: May Blossom of Britannia* (5–8). Series: Royal Diaries. 2001, Scholastic paper $10.95 (0-439-21598-6). 224pp. Young Victoria's fictional diary describes her over-regimented life at the ages of 10 and 11; background material adds some historical context to this account of the girl who grew up to rule England. (Rev: BL 12/1/01; HBG 10/02; SLJ 1/02)

9400 Lasky, Kathryn. *Elizabeth I: Red Rose of the House of Tudor* (4–7). Series: Royal Diaries. 1999, Scholastic paper $10.95 (0-590-68484-1). 192pp. Told in diary form, this is a fictionalized account of Elizabeth I's childhood after her mother was killed and she lived with her father, Henry VIII, and Catherine Parr. (Rev: BCCB 12/99; BL 9/15/99; HBG 3/00; SLJ 10/99)

9401 Lawrence, Iain. *The Buccaneers* (5–8). 2001, Delacorte $15.95 (0-385-32736-6). 232pp. In this final volume in the trilogy that began with *The Wreckers* and *The Smugglers*, 16-year-old John Spencer and his captain rescue a castaway and appear headed for disaster. (Rev: BCCB 7–8/01; BL 5/15/01; HBG 3/02)

9402 Lawrence, Iain. *The Smugglers* (5–8). 1999, Delacorte $15.95 (0-385-32663-7). 178pp. In this continuation of *The Wreckers*, 16-year-old John Spencer faces more adventures aboard the *Dragon,* where he faces powerful enemies and must bring the ship safely to port. (Rev: BCCB 7–8/99; BL 4/1/99*; HB 5–6/99; HBG 10/99; SLJ 6/99)

9403 Lawrence, Iain. *The Wreckers* (5–8). 1998, Delacorte $15.95 (0-385-32535-5); Bantam paper $5.50 (0-440-41545-4). In this historical novel, young John Spencer narrowly escapes with his life after the ship on which he is traveling is wrecked off the Cornish coast, lured to its destruction by a gang seeking to plunder its cargo. (Rev: BCCB 6/98; BL 6/1–15/98; BR 11–12/98; HB 7–8/98*; HBG 10/98; SLJ 6/98)

9404 Love, Anne D. *The Puppeteer's Apprentice* (3–6). 2003, Simon & Schuster $16.95 (0-689-84424-7). 192pp. In medieval England, an orphan girl called Mouse runs away to become a puppeteer's apprentice. (Rev: BL 3/15/03; HBG 10/03; SLJ 5/03)

9405 MacDonald, George. *Sir Gibbie* (4–6). 1987, Sunrise $27.50 (0-940652-55-2). The story of a Scottish waif and the triumph of love over hardship.

9406 Masefield, John. *Jim Davis: A High-Sea Adventure* (5–8). 2002, Scholastic paper $15.95 (0-439-40436-3). 224pp. This story about 12-year-old Jim and his adventures with smugglers is set in early-19th-century England and was originally published in 1911. (Rev: BL 11/15/02; HBG 3/03)

9407 Mayer, Marianna. *Sir Walter Scott's Ivanhoe* (4–6). Illus. by John Rush. 2004, Chronicle $17.95

(1-58717-248-8). 56pp. An attractive, large-format adaptation of the classic romantic adventure, with rich illustrations. (Rev: BL 2/1/05; SLJ 1/05)

9408 Merrill, Linda, and Sarah Ridley. *The Princess and the Peacocks: Or, The Story of the Room* (4–6). Illus. by Tennessee Dixon. 1993, Hyperion LB $15.49 (1-56282-328-0). 32pp. For older readers, this fictionalized account tells how the painter Whistler decorated his famous Peacock Room. (Rev: BL 6/1–15/93; SLJ 8/93)

9409 Meyer, Carolyn. *Beware, Princess Elizabeth* (5–8). Series: Young Royals. 2001, Harcourt $17.00 (0-15-202659-2). 224pp. A first-person account of the youth of Elizabeth I, whose mother was murdered by her father, Henry VIII, and whose life is surrounded with intrigue after Henry's death. (Rev: BL 3/1/01; HBG 10/01; SLJ 5/01)

9410 Morris, Gerald. *The Ballad of Sir Dinadan* (5–9). 2003, Houghton Mifflin $15.00 (0-618-19099-6). 256pp. An amusing retelling from Arthurian legend that features the younger brother of Sir Tristram as a music lover and reluctant knight. (Rev: BL 5/1/03; HB 5–6/03; HBG 10/03; SLJ 4/03*)

9411 Morris, Gerald. *The Squire, His Knight, and His Lady* (5–9). 1999, Houghton Mifflin $15.00 (0-395-91211-3). 240pp. This is a retelling, from the perspective of a knight's squire, of the classic story of Sir Gawain and the Green Knight. (Rev: BL 5/1/99; HBG 10/99; SLJ 5/99)

9412 Morris, Gerald. *The Squire's Tale* (5–9). 1998, Houghton Mifflin $15.00 (0-395-86959-5). The peaceful existence of 14-year-old Terence is shattered when he becomes the squire of Sir Gawain and becomes involved in a series of quests. (Rev: BL 4/15/98; BR 11–12/98; HB 7–8/98; SLJ 7/98)

9413 O'Brien, Patrick. *The Making of a Knight: How Sir James Earned His Armor* (3–6). Illus. 1998, Charlesbridge $15.95 (0-88106-354-1); paper $6.95 (0-88106-355-X). 32pp. This novel traces the studies, training, and experiences of young James and his journey from page to squire and finally to knight in medieval England. (Rev: BL 8/98; HBG 3/99; SLJ 9/98)

9414 Osborne, Mary Pope. *Kate and the Beanstalk* (PS–3). Illus. by Giselle Potter. 2000, Atheneum $16.00 (0-689-82550-1). 40pp. Kate, the daughter of a knight killed by the giant, is the heroine of this delightful version of Jack and the Beanstalk. (Rev: BCCB 1/01; BL 11/15/00*; HBG 3/01; SLJ 10/00) [398.2]

9415 Platt, Richard. *Castle Diary: The Journal of Tobias Burgess, Page* (3–5). Illus. 1999, Candlewick $21.99 (0-7636-0489-5). 64pp. In 1285 Tobias, an 11-year-old who is spending a year as a page at his uncle's castle, keeps a diary of the events he witnesses and his general impressions. (Rev: BCCB 12/99; BL 11/15/99; HBG 3/00; SLJ 12/99*)

9416 Pyle, Howard. *Men of Iron* (5–8). Adapted by Earle Hitchner. Illus. 1930, Troll paper $5.95 (0-8167-1872-5). 48pp. Brave deeds and knightly adventure in England — an old favorite.

9417 Rinaldi, Ann. *Mutiny's Daughter* (5–7). 2004, HarperCollins $15.99 (0-06-029638-0). 224pp. Fletcher Christian, who led the mutiny on *H.M.S. Bounty,* covertly returns to England with his young half-Tahitian daughter and leaves her to live with relatives, hiding the truth about her parentage. (Rev: BL 2/15/04; SLJ 3/04)

9418 Rogers, Gregory. *The Boy, the Bear, the Baron, the Bard* (K–2). Illus. by author. 2004, Roaring Brook $15.95 (1-59643-009-5). 32pp. A young boy finds himself transported to Elizabethan England and has many adventures, including encounters with Shakespeare and the Queen, in this wordless picture book. (Rev: BL 10/1/04; LMC 3/05; SLJ 12/04*)

9419 Schmidt, Gary D. *Anson's Way* (5–9). 1999, Houghton Mifflin $15.00 (0-395-91529-5). During the reign of George II, Anson begins his proud career in the British army as part of the forces occupying Ireland, then becomes disillusioned as he develops a growing respect and concern for the Irish. (Rev: BL 4/1/99*; HBG 10/99; SLJ 4/99)

9420 Snicket, Lemony. *The Austere Academy* (4–6). Illus. Series: Unfortunate Events. 2000, HarperCollins LB $14.89 (0-06-028884-0). 240pp. The Baudelaire orphans endure horrible hardships when they enroll as students at Prufrock Academy, where their only friends — the Quagmire orphans — are kidnapped by wicked Count Olaf. (Rev: BL 10/15/00)

9421 Sturtevant, Katherine. *At the Sign of the Star* (4–8). 2000, Farrar $16.00 (0-374-30449-1). 144pp. Growing up with her bookseller father in London during 1677, high-spirited Meg finds it difficult to adjust when her father remarries. (Rev: BCCB 1/01; BL 10/15/00*; HB 9–10/00; HBG 3/01; SLJ 9/00)

9422 Thomas, Dylan. *A Child's Christmas in Wales* (5–8). Illus. by Trina S. Hyman. 1985, Holiday House $16.95 (0-8234-0565-6). 48pp. A prose poem about the poet's childhood in a small Welsh village. [821.912]

9423 Vogiel, Eva. *Friend or Foe?* (5–8). 2001, Judaica $19.95 (1-880582-66-X). 269pp. In this novel set in London during 1948, the girls of the Migdal Binoh School for Orthodox Jewish girls notice strange happenings when the Campbell family moves next door. (Rev: BL 4/1/01)

9424 Wiley, Melissa. *Beyond the Heather Hills* (3–5). Illus. by Renee Graef. Series: Martha Years. 2003, HarperCollins $16.99 (0-06-027986-9); paper $5.99 (0-06-440715-2). 208pp. Set in 18th-century Scotland, this fourth volume continues the series on Laura Ingalls Wilder's great-grandmother. Here, she leaves home at age 10 to live with her married older sister. (Rev: BL 5/15/03; HBG 10/03)

9425 Williams, Laura. *The Executioner's Daughter* (5–8). 2000, Holt $16.95 (0-8050-6234-3). 136pp. Set in England during the Middle Ages, this is the story of poor Lily who, after her mother dies, must assume the position of helping her father, an official executioner. (Rev: BCCB 5/00; BL 4/1/00; HBG 10/00; SLJ 6/00)

9426 Woodruff, Elvira. *The Ravenmaster's Secret* (4–7). 2003, Scholastic $15.95 (0-439-28133-4).

225pp. Eleven-year-old Forrest becomes embroiled in dangerous intrigue in this story set inside the Tower of London in the early 18th century, with a glossary and historical notes appended. (Rev: BL 1/1–15/04; HBG 4/04; SLJ 1/04)

Latin America

9427 Cohn, Diana. *Dream Carver* (3–6). Illus. by Amy Cordova. 2002, Chronicle $15.95 (0-8118-1244-8). 32pp. A simple story based on the career of the artist Manuel Jimenez, about a young sculptor who carves small wooden animals but dreams of creating big, colorful animals. (Rev: BCCB 10/02; BL 6/1–15/02; HBG 10/02; SLJ 7/02)

9428 Lattimore, Deborah N. *The Flame of Peace: A Tale of the Aztecs* (4–6). Illus. 1987, HarperCollins paper $7.95 (0-06-443272-6). 48pp. Details about Aztec life are compiled in this folklorelike story. (Rev: BL 11/15/87; SLJ 11/87)

9429 Ramírez, Antonio. *Napí* (PS–2). Illus. by Domi. 2004, Groundwood $15.95 (0-88899-610-1). 32pp. This is a very visual portrayal of the importance of nature and colors in the life and dreams of a young Indian girl living in a Mexican village. (Rev: BL 11/15/04; SLJ 9/04)

9430 Rohmer, Harriet. *Uncle Nacho's Hat* (3–6). Illus. by Mira Reisberg. 1993, Children's Book Pr. $15.95 (0-89239-043-3); paper $7.95 (0-89239-112-X). 32pp. This bilingual book tells a Nicaraguan tale about how hard it is to break habits. A reissue.

9431 Skarmeta, Antonio. *The Composition* (3–5). Trans. by Elisa Amado. Illus. 2000, Douglas & McIntyre $14.95 (0-88899-390-0). 32pp. Set in a police state in Latin America, this picture book tells of a young boy who is under pressure from the police to betray his parents. (Rev: BL 5/1/00; HB 9–10/00; HBG 10/00; SLJ 8/00)

9432 Stanley, Diane. *Elena* (3–5). Illus. 1996, Hyperion LB $14.49 (0-7868-2211-2). 56pp. A daughter recalls the life of her Mexican mother, who defied authority and took her family on a dangerous journey to the United States. (Rev: BCCB 3/96; BL 4/1/96; SLJ 6/96)

9433 Yolen, Jane. *Encounter* (2–5). Illus. by David Shannon. 1992, Harcourt $16.00 (0-15-225962-7). 32pp. From the viewpoint of a Taino Indian boy, this picture book tells of the first meeting between Native Americans and Columbus. (Rev: BCCB 5/92; BL 3/1/92; SLJ 5/92)

United States

NATIVE AMERICANS

9434 Ackerman, Ned. *Spirit Horse* (5–8). 1998, Scholastic paper $15.95 (0-590-39650-1). Set in Blackfoot territory in the 1700s, this novel traces the adventures of young Running Crane, his struggle for survival alone in the wilderness, and his taming of the magnificent wild horse named Spirit Horse. (Rev: BCCB 3/98; BL 6/1–15/98; BR 5–6/98; HBG 9/98; SLJ 4/98)

9435 Armstrong, Nancy M. *Navajo Long Walk* (4–7). Illus. 1994, Roberts Rinehart $8.95 (1-879373-56-4). 120pp. The story of the Long Walk of the Navajo in 1864 and their confinement in an internment camp are vividly told. (Rev: BL 10/1/94; SLJ 1/95)

9436 Bird, E. J. *The Rainmakers* (4–6). Illus. 1993, Carolrhoda LB $21.27 (0-87614-748-1). 120pp. This novel about a young Indian boy and his pet bear is centered around the life of the Anasazi Indians, who disappeared from the Southwest around A.D. 1300. (Rev: BL 6/1–15/93)

9437 Bruchac, Joseph. *A Boy Called Slow: The True Story of Sitting Bull* (5–8). Illus. by Rocco Baviera. 1995, Penguin Putnam $16.99 (0-399-22692-3). 32pp. The story of the boyhood of Sitting Bull, who, because of his sluggishness, had been called Slow. (Rev: BCCB 4/95; BL 3/15/95; HB 9–10/95; SLJ 10/95)

9438 Bruchac, Joseph. *Crazy Horse's Vision* (2–4). Illus. by S. D. Nelson. 2000, Lee & Low $16.95 (1-880000-94-6). 40pp. This is the story of how a young Native American boy, nicknamed Curly, gained the name Crazy Horse and became a leader of the Lakota. (Rev: BCCB 9/00; BL 5/15/00; HB 7–8/00; HBG 10/00; SLJ 7/00)

9439 Bruchac, Joseph. *The Journal of Jesse Smoke: The Trail of Tears, 1838* (5–8). Illus. Series: My Name Is America. 2001, Scholastic paper $10.95 (0-439-12197-3). 206pp. Jesse, a 16-year-old Cherokee, chronicles in his diary the tribe's forced journey to Oklahoma and tries to understand the reasons behind this cruel action. (Rev: BL 7/01; HBG 10/01; SLJ 7/01)

9440 Bunting, Eve. *Cheyenne Again* (3–5). Illus. by Irving Toddy. 1995, Clarion $14.95 (0-395-70364-6). 32pp. In the 1880s, a young Cheyenne boy is taken from the reservation and sent to a white boarding school. (Rev: BCCB 9/95; BL 8/95; SLJ 12/95)

9441 Cooper, James Fenimore. *Last of the Mohicans* (3–5). Adapted by Les Martin. Illus. by Shannon Stirnweis. Series: Step-Up Classics. 1993, Random paper $3.99 (0-679-84706-5). 96pp. A simplified version of the Cooper classic that illuminates details and abridges the plot for young readers. (Rev: SLJ 10/93)

9442 Cooper, James Fenimore. *The Last of the Mohicans* (3–5). Illus. by N. C. Wyeth. 2002, Simon & Schuster $18.95 (0-689-84068-3). 54pp. The classic novel is reissued here in abridged form with the Wyeth illustrations from the 1919 edition newly photographed and reproduced. (Rev: BL 11/1/02; HBG 3/03)

9443 Erdrich, Louise. *The Game of Silence* (5–8). 2005, HarperCollins LB $16.89 (0-06-029790-5). 272pp. In 1850, as Omakayas, 9, is coming of age, the intrusion of the European settlers increasingly impacts the Ojibwe lifestyle in this sequel to *The Birchbark House* (1999). (Rev: BL 5/15/05)

9444 Grutman, Jewel H., and Gay Matthaei. *The Ledgerbook of Thomas Blue Eagle* (4–8). Illus. by Adam Cvijanovic. 1994, Thomasson-Grant $17.95 (1-56566-063-3). 72pp. A young Native American boy attends a white man's school but tries to retain his own identity and culture in this story that takes place in the West 100 years ago. (Rev: SLJ 12/94)

9445 Hudson, Jan. *Sweetgrass* (5–8). 1989, Scholastic paper $3.99 (0-590-43486-1). 160pp. A description of the culture of the Dakota Indians in the 1830s. (Rev: BCCB 4/89; BL 4/1/89; SLJ 4/89)

9446 Hunter, Sara H. *The Unbreakable Code* (2–4). Illus. by Julia Miner. 1996, Northland LB $15.95 (0-87358-638-7). A Navajo man reassures his grandson that he will adjust successfully to a move off the reservation with his mother and new stepfather. (Rev: SLJ 8/96)

9447 Keehn, Sally M. *I Am Regina* (5–8). 1991, Penguin Putnam $16.99 (0-399-21797-5). 219pp. Set in the mid-18th century, this is the story of a young girl's years of captivity by Indians. (Rev: SLJ 6/91)

9448 Kittredge, Frances. *Neeluk: An Eskimo Boy in the Days of the Whaling Ships* (3–5). Illus. by Howard Rock. 2001, Alaska Northwest paper $18.95 (0-88240-545-4). 88pp. Illustrations by an Inupiat artist combine with simple stories to present the Inupiat way of life in the late 1800s. (Rev: BL 8/01; HBG 3/02; SLJ 1/02)

9449 Lunge-Larsen, Lise, and Margi Preus. *The Legend of the Lady Slipper: An Ojibwe Tale* (PS–3). Illus. by Andrea Arroyo. 1999, Houghton Mifflin $15.00 (0-395-90512-5). 32pp. An Ojibwa tale about how a young girl's moccasins are turned into the plant known as lady slippers, as a reward for her saving her village from a plague. (Rev: BCCB 7–8/99; BL 4/15/99; HBG 10/99; SLJ 5/99) [398.2]

9450 Maher, Ramona. *Alice Yazzie's Year* (3–6). Illus. by Shonto Begay. 2004, Tricycle $15.95 (1-58246-080-9). 40pp. Reissued with new illustrations, this picture book written in verse chronicles a year in the life of an 11-year-old Navajo girl. (Rev: BL 8/03; HBG 4/04; SLJ 11/03)

9451 Marchand, Peter. *What Good Is a Cactus?* (3–5). Illus. by Craig Brown. 1994, Roberts Rinehart paper $7.95 (1-879373-83-1). Through talking to a wise Native American and observing nature, a scientist realizes the importance of all living things and the role each plays. (Rev: SLJ 11/94)

9452 Matthaei, Gay, and Jewel Grutman. *The Sketchbook of Thomas Blue Eagle* (4–7). Illus. 2001, Chronicle $16.95 (0-8818-2908-1). 64pp. Through drawings and narration, the Lakota artist Thomas Blue Eagle tells how he joined Buffalo Bill's show, traveled to Europe, and made enough money to marry. (Rev: BCCB 5/01; BL 4/1/01)

9453 O'Dell, Scott, and Elizabeth Hall. *Thunder Rolling in the Mountains* (5–9). 1992, Houghton Mifflin $17.00 (0-395-59966-0); Dell paper $5.50 (0-440-40879-2). From the viewpoint of Chief Joseph's daughter, this historical novel concerns the forced removal of the Nez Perce from their homeland in 1877. (Rev: BL 6/15/92*; SLJ 8/92)

9454 Osborne, Mary Pope. *Standing in the Light: The Captive Diary of Catharine Carey Logan* (3–6). Illus. Series: Dear America. 1998, Scholastic $9.95 (0-590-13462-0). 192pp. After 13-year-old Caty and her younger brother are captured by Lenape Indians in rural Pennsylvania in 1763, they gradually learn to appreciate the values in this foreign culture. (Rev: BL 10/15/98; HBG 3/99; SLJ 1/99)

9455 Raczek, Linda Theresa. *Rainy's Powwow* (3–5). Illus. by Gary Bennett. 1999, Northland $15.95 (0-87358-686-7). 32pp. Lorraine is seeking to develop her own special dance at the powwow, when an eagle feather changes her hopes. (Rev: BL 4/1/99; HBG 10/99; SLJ 6/99)

9456 Roop, Peter. *The Buffalo Jump* (2–4). Illus. by Bill Farnsworth. 1996, Northland LB $14.95 (0-87358-616-6). Little Blaze, a Native American boy, saves his older brother's life during a buffalo hunt. (Rev: SLJ 2/97)

9457 Schwartz, Virginia Frances. *Initiation* (5–8). Illus. 2003, Fitzhenry & Whiteside $16.95 (1-55005-053-2). 268pp. Kwakiuti indian twins Nana and Nanolatch prepare to face the responsibilities of adulthood in this story set on the West Coast of North America in the 15th century. (Rev: SLJ 3/04) [813]

9458 Shaw, Janet. *Meet Kaya: An American Girl* (3–5). Illus. by Bill Farnsworth. 2002, Pleasant Co. $12.95 (1-58485-424-3); paper $5.95 (1-58485-423-5). 70pp. Nine-year-old Kaya is distracted from babysitting by a riding challenge and the other children of the Nez Perce tribe won't let her forget it, in this tale that includes many historical details. Also use *Kaya's Escape! A Survival Story* (2002). (Rev: BL 1/1–15/03; HBG 3/03)

9459 Smith, Cynthia Leitich. *Indian Shoes* (3–6). Illus. by Jim Madsen. 2002, HarperCollins LB $15.89 (0-06-029532-5). 80pp. In six inter-related stories, Native Americans Ray and Grandpa Halfmoon recall their lives in Oklahoma and reflect on their present-day situation in Chicago. (Rev: BCCB 9/02; BL 6/1–15/02; HBG 10/02; SLJ 5/02)

9460 Smith, Patricia Clark. *Weetamoo: Heart of the Pocassets, Massachusetts — Rhode Island, 1653* (5–8). Illus. Series: Royal Diaries. 2003, Scholastic $10.95 (0-439-12910-9). 208pp. Weetamoo prepares to succeed her father as leader of the tribe and describes relationships with the European settlers and how daily life changes with the seasons. (Rev: BL 12/15/03; HBG 4/04; SLJ 1/04)

9461 Spalding, Andrea. *Solomon's Tree* (2–4). Illus. by Janet Wilson. 2002, Orca $16.95 (1-55143-217-X). 32pp. A Pacific Northwest Native American boy mourns when his beloved maple tree falls in a storm, and his uncle comforts him by teaching him to make a traditional wooden mask that celebrates the tree. (Rev: BL 1/1–15/03; HBG 3/03; SLJ 2/03)

9462 Stewart, Elisabeth J. *On the Long Trail Home* (5–7). 1994, Clarion $15.00 (0-395-68361-0). 106pp. A Cherokee girl escapes from the Trail of Tears and makes her way back to the Appalachian Mountains during the 1830s. (Rev: BCCB 12/94; BL 10/15/94; SLJ 12/94)

9463 Tapahonso, Luci. *Songs of Shiprock Fair* (2–4). Illus. by Anthony Chee Emerson. 1999, Kiva $15.95 (1-885772-11-4). This is the story of the oldest fair in the Navajo Nation at Shiprock, New Mex-

ico, as seen through the eyes of a little girl who experiences it from the early preparations to the ceremonial dances on the last night. (Rev: HBG 3/00; SLJ 4/00)

9464 Turner, Ann. *The Girl Who Chased Away Sorrow: The Diary of Sarah Nita, a Navajo Girl* (5–8). Illus. Series: Dear America. 1999, Scholastic $10.95 (0-590-97216-2). 208pp. A Navajo woman describes to her granddaughter the Long Walk from Arizona to New Mexico that she survived as a child. (Rev: BL 11/15/99; HBG 3/00; SLJ 2/00)

9465 Vick, Helen H. *Shadow* (5–7). Series: Courage of the Stone. 1998, Roberts Rinehart $15.95 (1-57098-218-X); paper $9.95 (1-57098-195-7). 122pp. Shadow, an independent Pueblo Indian girl in pre-Columbian Arizona, leaves her home to rescue her father. (Rev: SLJ 10/98)

9466 Von Ahnen, Katherine. *Heart of Naosaqua* (4–6). Illus. 1996, Roberts Rinehart paper $9.95 (1-57098-010-1). 160pp. In 1823, Naosaqua and her people, the Mesquakie Indians, must find a new home. (Rev: BL 7/96)

COLONIAL PERIOD

9467 Borden, Louise. *Sleds on Boston Common: A Story of the American Revolution* (3–5). Illus. 2000, Simon & Schuster $17.00 (0-689-82812-8). 40pp. Just before the Revolution, 9-year-old Henry Price and his brothers confront British soldiers on Boston Common and ask them to move so they can use the sled runs. (Rev: BCCB 7–8/00; BL 7/00; HB 11–12/00; HBG 3/01; SLJ 12/00)

9468 Buckey, Sarah Masters. *Enemy in the Fort* (4–7). Series: History Mystery. 2001, Pleasant Co. paper $5.95 (1-58485-306-9). 163pp. Ten-year-old Rebecca, whose family has been separated by Abenaki Indians, solves a mystery at her New Hampshire fort. (Rev: BL 10/1/01; HBG 3/02; SLJ 12/01)

9469 Bulla, Clyde Robert. *A Lion to Guard Us* (3–6). Illus. by Michele Chessare. 1981, HarperCollins LB $14.89 (0-690-04097-0); paper $4.95 (0-06-440333-5). 128pp. Three motherless children sail for America to be united with their father in the Jamestown, Virginia, colony.

9470 Butler, Amy. *Virginia Bound* (4–7). 2003, Clarion $15.00 (0-618-24752-1). 192pp. Thirteen-year-old Rob is kidnapped in London and shipped to Virginia as an indentured servant to work on a tobacco farm in 1627. (Rev: BL 3/1/03; HBG 10/03; SLJ 6/03)

9471 Collier, James Lincoln. *The Corn Raid: A Story of the Jamestown Settlement* (5–9). 2000, Jamestown paper $5.95 (0-8092-0619-6). 142pp. History and fiction mix in this adventure tale set in the Jamestown settlement and featuring a 12-year-old indentured servant and his cruel master. (Rev: SLJ 4/00)

9472 Couvillon, Alice, and Elizabeth Moore. *Evangeline for Children* (3–5). Illus. by Alison Davis Lyne. 2002, Pelican $14.95 (1-56554-709-8). 32pp. In this picture book for older children, the story of Evangeline and her love for Gabriel in colonial

Louisiana is retold. (Rev: BL 6/1–15/02; HBG 10/02; SLJ 7/02)

9473 Dalgliesh, Alice. *Courage of Sarah Noble* (3–5). Illus. by Leonard Weisgard. 1954, Macmillan $15.99 (0-684-18830-9); paper $4.99 (0-689-71540-4). 64pp. The true story of a brave little girl who in 1707 went with her father into the wilds of Connecticut.

9474 Dell, Pamela. *Giles and Metacom: A Story of Plimoth and the Wampanoag* (4–6). Series: Scrapbooks of America. 2002, Tradition LB $27.07 (1-59187-012-7). 47pp. Eleven-year-old Giles becomes friends with an Indian boy whom he suspects of stealing. (Rev: SLJ 5/03)

9475 Duey, Kathleen. *Sarah Anne Hartford* (4–7). Series: American Diaries. 1996, Simon & Schuster paper $4.99 (0-689-80384-2). 137pp. A story set in Puritan New England about two girls who are placed in a pillory for playing on the Sabbath. (Rev: BCCB 5/96; BL 5/15/96; HB 9–10/96; SLJ 6/96)

9476 Durrant, Lynda. *The Beaded Moccasins: The Story of Mary Campbell* (5–9). 1998, Clarion $15.00 (0-395-85398-2). Told in the first person, this is a fictionalized account of the true story of 12-year-old Mary Campbell who was captured by the Delaware Indians in 1759. (Rev: BCCB 5/98; BL 3/15/98; HBG 10/98; SLJ 6/98)

9477 Durrant, Lynda. *Echohawk* (5–9). 1996, Clarion $16.00 (0-395-74430-X). Raised by Mohican Indians after the death of his family in 1738, Jonathan Starr, renamed Echohawk, is eventually sent to a white teacher to learn English and becomes reacquainted with his true heritage. (Rev: BL 9/1/96; BR 3–4/97; SLJ 9/96)

9478 Durrant, Lynda. *Turtle Clan Journey* (5–9). 1999, Clarion $15.00 (0-395-90369-6). 192pp. In this sequel to *Echohawk,* Jonathan is forced to leave the Indians who raised him and is sent to live in Albany with an aunt he doesn't know. (Rev: BL 5/1/99; HBG 10/99; SLJ 6/99)

9479 Edmonds, Walter. *The Matchlock Gun* (5–7). Illus. by Paul Lantz. 1941, Penguin Putnam $16.99 (0-399-21911-0). 64pp. Exciting, true story of a courageous boy who protected his mother and sister from the Indians of the Hudson Valley. Newbery Medal winner, 1942.

9480 Grote, JoAnn A. *Queen Anne's War* (5–8). Series: The American Adventure. 1998, Chelsea LB $15.95 (0-7910-5045-9). During Queen Anne's War in 1710, Will Smith's family becomes involved in the attempt to drive the French out of New England, but 11-year-old Will is preoccupied with a jealous classmate. (Rev: HBG 3/99; SLJ 1/99)

9481 Hermes, Patricia. *Season of Promise* (3–6). Series: My America, Elizabeth's Jamestown Colony Diary. 2002, Scholastic $10.95 (0-439-38898-8); paper $4.95 (0-439-27206-8). 108pp. In 1611, ten-year-old Elizabeth continues to describe life in Jamestown as her twin brother Caleb returns, her father plans to remarry, and there is food to eat, although the colonial leaders are strict. (Rev: HBG 3/03; SLJ 2/03)

9482 Hoobler, Dorothy, and Thomas Hoobler. *Priscilla Foster: The Story of a Salem Girl* (3–6). Illus. 1997, Silver Burdett LB $17.95 (0-382-39640-5); paper $4.95 (0-382-39641-3). 128pp. A grandmother takes her granddaughter to Salem, Massachusetts, and tells her about the witch trials of 1692. (Rev: BL 8/97; SLJ 8/97)

9483 Howard, Ginger. *William's House* (K–3). Illus. by Larry Day. 2001, Millbrook LB $22.90 (0-7613-1674-4). 32pp. An informative story that describes how a colonist built a house like the one he left behind in England and gradually had to change and modify it to adjust to a new climate and environment. (Rev: BL 3/15/01*; HBG 10/01; SLJ 3/01)

9484 Hurst, Carol Otis, and Rebecca Otis. *A Killing in Plymouth Colony* (5–7). 2003, Houghton Mifflin $15.00 (0-618-27597-5). 160pp. John Bradford, the son of the governor of Plymouth Colony, has always struggled to gain his father's approval and feels an affinity toward an outcast who is accused of murder. (Rev: BL 12/1/03; HBG 4/04; SLJ 10/03)

9485 Jacobs, Paul S. *James Printer: A Novel of Rebellion* (5–8). 1997, Scholastic paper $15.95 (0-590-16381-7). 224pp. Though he has been raised as an Englishman in colonial Cambridge, Massachusetts, an Indian boy feels he must choose sides when the English and Indians go to war. (Rev: BCCB 3/97; BL 4/15/97; SLJ 6/97)

9486 Jaspersohn, William. *The Scrimshaw Ring* (2–4). Illus. by Vernon Thornblad. 2002, Vermont Folklife Center $15.95 (0-916718-19-0). 32pp. In this book set in 1710 New England and based on reality, an amazing thing happens to young William Bateman — one of the pirates plundering his home gives the boy a ring that is then passed down the generations. (Rev: BL 11/15/02; SLJ 12/02)

9487 Karr, Kathleen. *Worlds Apart* (4–7). 2005, Marshall Cavendish $15.95 (0-7614-5195-1). 196pp. In 1670 South Carolina, Christopher — a teenage settler — and Sewee Indian Asha-po become friends. (Rev: BCCB 5/05; LMC 10/05; SLJ 5/05)

9488 Karwoski, Gail Langer. *Surviving Jamestown: The Adventures of Young Sam Collier* (5–7). Illus. by Paul Casale. 2001, Peachtree $14.95 (1-56145-239-4); paper $8.95 (1-56145-245-9). 198pp. Full of facts, this novel tells the story of a 12-year-old English boy who sails in 1606 for the colony of Virginia, with details of the struggles the colonists faced. (Rev: HBG 10/01; SLJ 8/01)

9489 Lasky, Kathryn. *A Journey to the New World: The Diary of Remember Patience Whipple* (4–7). Series: Dear America. 1996, Scholastic paper $10.95 (0-590-50214-X). 144pp. Using diary entries as a format, this is the story of 12-year-old Mem Whipple, her journey on the *Mayflower,* and her first year in the New World. (Rev: BCCB 10/96; HB 9–10/96; SLJ 8/96)

9490 Littlesugar, Amy. *The Spinner's Daughter* (3–5). Illus. 1994, Pippin LB $14.95 (0-945912-22-6). 32pp. In her strict Puritan community in Connecticut, Elspeth is considered sinful because she has a cornhusk doll. (Rev: BL 9/1/94; SLJ 9/94)

9491 Martin, Jacqueline B. *Grandmother Bryant's Pocket* (2–4). Illus. by Petra Mathers. 1996, Houghton Mifflin $14.95 (0-395-68984-8). 48pp. Set in Maine during 1787, this is the story of how a young girl's grandmother helps her adjust to the death of her dog. (Rev: BCCB 7–8/96; BL 5/15/96; HB 7–8/96; SLJ 6/96*)

9492 Ovecka, Janice. *Cave of Falling Water* (4–8). Illus. by David K. Fadden. 1992, New England Pr. paper $10.95 (0-933050-98-4). 116pp. A cave in the hills of Vermont plays a part in the lives of three girls, one an Indian and one white, both from colonial times, and the last, a contemporary adolescent. (Rev: BL 5/1/93)

9493 Petry, Ann. *Tituba of Salem Village* (6–8). 1988, HarperCollins paper $5.95 (0-06-440403-X). 254pp. The story of the slave Tituba and her husband, John Indian, from the day they were sold in the Barbados until the tragic Salem witchcraft trials.

9494 Platt, Richard. *Pirate Diary: The Journal of Jake Carpenter* (3–6). Illus. by Chris Riddell. 2001, Candlewick $17.99 (0-7636-0848-3). 64pp. Readers of the entries in 9-year-old Jake's journal for 1716 learn all about his exciting adventures fighting pirates, and will also find good historical information about conditions aboard 18th-century ships and about famous pirates. (Rev: BL 12/15/01; HBG 10/02; SLJ 12/01*)

9495 Pryor, Bonnie. *Thomas in Danger* (4–6). 1999, Morrow $15.00 (0-688-16518-4). 160pp. After discovering a Tory plot, Thomas is kidnapped and left, desperately ill, with Iroquois who nurse him back to health. (Rev: BL 10/1/99; HBG 3/00; SLJ 12/99)

9496 Rees, Celia. *Witch Child* (5–9). 2001, Candlewick $15.99 (0-7636-1421-1). 261pp. Young Mary Newbury keeps a journal of her voyage to the New World and the way in which the Puritan community rejects her when they mistrust her ability to heal. (Rev: BCCB 7–8/01; BL 10/15/01; HB 9–10/01; HBG 3/02; SLJ 8/01)

9497 Rinaldi, Ann. *The Journal of Jasper Jonathan Pierce: A Pilgrim Boy, Plymouth, 1620* (4–8). 2000, Scholastic paper $10.95 (0-590-51078-9). 155pp. This fictionalized account of the Pilgrims in journal format follows the adventures of a 14-year-old indentured servant aboard the *Mayflower* and during his first year in the New World. (Rev: BL 2/15/00; HBG 10/00; SLJ 7/00)

9498 Sheely, Robert. *In the Hands of the Enemy* (4–6). Illus. by John Martin. Series: Adventures in America. 2003, Silver Moon LB $14.95 (1-893110-31-1). 75pp. In this suspenseful tale, 14-year-old John becomes lost after wandering away from Plymouth Colony only months after arriving from England on the *Mayflower*; he is rescued by a Nauset Indian boy, who resists his initial impulse to kill John in revenge for his father's murder by the English. (Rev: HBG 10/03; SLJ 9/03)

9499 Stainer, M. L. *The Lyon's Cub* (5–9). Illus. 1998, Chicken Soup Pr. LB $9.95 (0-9646904-5-4); paper $6.95 (0-9646904-6-2). This novel, a continuation of *The Lyon's Roar* (1997), tells what happened to the settlers of the lost colony of Roanoke

and their life with peaceful Indian tribes. Continued in *The Lyon's Pride* (1998). (Rev: SLJ 8/98)

9500 Strickland, Brad. *The Guns of Tortuga* (5–8). 2003, Simon & Schuster paper $4.99 (0-689-85297-5). 160pp. Young Davy helps the crew of the *Aurora* defeat a band of pirates in this sequel to *Mutiny!* (Rev: BL 2/1/03; SLJ 3/03)

9501 Strickland, Brad, and Thomas E. Fuller. *Heart of Steele* (5–8). 2003, Simon & Schuster paper $4.99 (0-689-85298-3). 208pp. Davy, his uncle, and Captain Hunter continue their hunt for the evil Jack Steele, who has been falsely implicating Captain Hunter in his murderous piracy. (Rev: BL 9/1/03; SLJ 10/03)

9502 Strickland, Brad, and Thomas E. Fuller. *Mutiny!* (5–8). 2002, Simon & Schuster paper $4.99 (0-689-85296-7). 208pp. Fourteen-year-old orphan Davy arrives in Jamaica to live with his Uncle Patch, only to find himself embroiled in a daring and complex effort to capture Caribbean pirates in a story embellished with interesting facts about the 1680s. (Rev: BL 12/1/02; SLJ 11/02)

9503 Strohmeier, Lenice. *Mingo* (2–4). Illus. by Bill Farnsworth. 2003, Marshall Cavendish $16.95 (0-7614-5111-0). 32pp. The importance of freedom is the main theme in this poignant story of the close relationship between young Olivia and the elderly Robin Mingo, a family slave; historical details about 18th-century Massachusetts are interwoven throughout the picture book. (Rev: BL 6/1–15/03; HBG 10/03; SLJ 6/03)

9504 Tripp, Valerie. *Changes for Felicity: A Winter Story* (2–5). Illus. by Dan Andreasen. Series: American Girl. 1992, Pleasant Co. $12.95 (1-56247-038-8); paper $5.95 (1-56247-037-X). 34pp. In this story of a girl who lives in colonial Williamsburg, the father of her best friend is jailed as a Loyalist. Also use: *Felicity Saves the Day: A Summer Story;* and *Happy Birthday, Felicity* (both 1992). (Rev: BL 5/1/92)

9505 Tripp, Valerie. *Felicity Learns a Lesson: A School Story* (3–5). Illus. by Dan Andreasen. Series: American Girl. 1991, Pleasant Co. paper $5.95 (1-56247-007-8). 69pp. Felicity learns to control her temper in this story set in colonial Williamsburg. (Rev: BL 1/1/91; SLJ 1/92)

9506 Tripp, Valerie. *Felicity's Surprise: A Christmas Story* (3–5). Illus. by Dan Andreasen. Series: American Girl. 1991, Pleasant Co. paper $5.95 (1-56247-010-8). 69pp. The family must depend more on Felicity when her mother is ill, in this story of colonial Williamsburg. (Rev: BL 1/1/91; SLJ 1/92)

9507 Troeger, Virginia B. *Secret Along the St. Mary's* (3–5). Illus. by Michael-Che Swisher. Series: Mysteries in Time. 2003, Silver Moon LB $14.95 (1-893110-35-4). 92pp. Motherless 12-year-old Susannah, who must keep house for her father and brother in 17th-century Maryland, faces tough choices — some involving indentured servitude — in this story that interweaves historical fact. (Rev: SLJ 3/04)

9508 Waters, Kate. *Mary Geddy's Day: A Colonial Girl in Williamsburg* (3–5). Illus. 1999, Scholastic

$16.95 (0-590-92925-9). 40pp. Set in Williamsburg on May 15, 1776, young Mary Geddy is the central character in this description of a day in colonial America. (Rev: BL 10/15/99; HBG 3/00; SLJ 9/99)

9509 Wisler, G. Clifton. *This New Land* (5–9). 1987, Walker LB $14.85 (0-8027-6727-3). Twelve-year-old Richard and his family begin a new life in Plymouth, Massachusetts, in 1620. (Rev: BL 3/15/88; BR 5–6/88; SLJ 11/87)

THE REVOLUTION

9510 Alsheimer, Jeanette E., and Patricia J. Friedle. *The Trouble with Tea* (5–8). 2002, Pentland $15.95 (1-57197-299-4). 208pp. When Patience visits her friend Anne in Boston in 1773, she witnesses many of the events that led to the American Revolution. (Rev: BL 6/1–15/02)

9511 Armstrong, Jennifer. *Thomas Jefferson: Letters from a Philadelphia Bookworm* (5–8). Illus. Series: Dear Mr. President. 2001, Winslow $8.95 (1-890817-30-9). 128pp. Twelve-year-old Amelia and President Jefferson discuss the events of the times in a continuing exchange of letters. (Rev: BL 5/15/01; HBG 10/01; SLJ 6/01)

9512 Avi. *The Fighting Ground* (5–9). Illus. by Ellen Thompson. 1984, HarperCollins LB $16.89 (0-397-32074-4); paper $5.99 (0-06-440185-5). 160pp. Thirteen-year-old Jonathan marches off to fight the British. (Rev: BL 4/87)

9513 Banim, Lisa. *Drums at Saratoga* (3–5). Series: Stories of the States. 1993, Silver Moon LB $14.95 (1-881889-20-3). 58pp. Young Nathaniel Phillips and a black servant are captured by the American forces during the Revolutionary War. (Rev: SLJ 10/93)

9514 Banim, Lisa. *The Hessian's Secret Diary* (3–5). Illus. 1997, Silver Moon LB $14.95 (1-881889-86-6). 80pp. In 1776, a young Brooklyn resident helps a wounded Hessian soldier, even though this endangers her family's safety. (Rev: BL 5/1/97; SLJ 4/97)

9515 Banim, Lisa. *A Spy in the King's Colony* (3–5). Illus. by Tatyana Yuditskaya. Series: Mysteries in Time. 1994, Silver Moon $14.95 (1-881889-54-8). 76pp. In 1775, 11-year-old Emily Parker is living in British-occupied Boston, where spies for both sides abound. (Rev: SLJ 7/94)

9516 Bartoletti, Susan Campbell. *The Flag Maker* (1–4). Illus. by Claire A. Nivola. 2004, Houghton Mifflin $16.00 (0-618-26757-3). 32pp. In this story of the British attack on Fort McHenry, Bartoletti focuses on the 13-year-old girl who helped her mother sew the garrison's huge American flag. (Rev: BL 3/1/04*; HB 5–6/04; SLJ 4/04)

9517 Berleth, Richard. *Samuel's Choice* (4–6). Illus. by James Watling. 1990, Whitman LB $14.95 (0-8075-7218-7). 40pp. Samuel, 14, is a young black slave in Brooklyn who plays a heroic role in the Battle of Long Island during the American Revolution. (Rev: BCCB 1/91; BL 1/1/91; SLJ 4/91)

9518 Bradley, Kimberly Brubaker. *Weaver's Daughter* (5–7). 2000, Delacorte $14.95 (0-385-32769-2). 166pp. Set in the South in the 1790s, this is the story of 10-year-old Lizzy Baker who suffers from asthma that is so severe that she is sent to live with a family in Charleston, to be near the sea air. (Rev: BCCB 11/00; BL 8/00; HBG 3/01; SLJ 10/00)

9519 Bruchac, Joseph. *The Arrow over the Door* (4–7). Illus. 1998, Dial $15.99 (0-8037-2078-5). 96pp. Two boys, one a Quaker and the other a Native American, share the narration of this story that takes place immediately before the Battle of Saratoga in 1777. (Rev: BCCB 4/98; BL 2/15/98; HBG 10/98; SLJ 4/98)

9520 Collier, James Lincoln, and Christopher Collier. *My Brother Sam Is Dead* (6–8). 1984, Simon & Schuster LB $17.00 (0-02-722980-7); Scholastic paper $4.50 (0-590-42792-X). 224pp. The story, based partially on fact, of a Connecticut family divided in loyalties during the Revolutionary War.

9521 Dell, Pamela. *Freedom's Light: A Story About Paul Revere's Midnight Ride* (4–6). Series: Scrapbooks of America. 2002, Tradition LB $27.07 (1-59187-016-X). 47pp. Fact and fiction are interwoven in this story of 12-year-old Mary Cates, a polisher in Revere's silver shop who becomes a spy when she discovers that a coworker is plotting against Revere. (Rev: SLJ 5/03)

9522 Denenberg, Barry. *The Journal of William Thomas Emerson: A Revolutionary War Patriot* (4–8). Series: My Name Is America. 1998, Scholastic paper $10.95 (0-590-31350-9). This historical novel consists of journal entries kept in 1774 by 12-year-old orphan Will, who becomes involved in political intrigue while working in a tavern. (Rev: BCCB 11/98; BL 11/1/98; HBG 3/99; SLJ 5/99)

9523 Durrant, Lynda. *Betsy Zane, the Rose of Fort Henry* (5–8). 2000, Clarion $15.00 (0-395-97899-8). 176pp. Toward the end of the Revolutionary War, Betsy sets out alone from Philadelphia to rejoin her five brothers in western Virginia. (Rev: BCCB 10/00; BL 9/15/00; HBG 3/01; SLJ 4/01)

9524 Ernst, Kathleen. *Betrayal at Cross Creek* (5–10). 2004, Pleasant Co. $10.95 (1-58485-879-6). 178pp. During the Revolutionary War, a young Scottish refugee and her grandparents are torn by conflicting loyalties. (Rev: BL 3/1/04; SLJ 5/04)

9525 Fleming, Candace. *The Hatmaker's Sign: A Story by Benjamin Franklin* (3–5). Illus. by Robert Andrew Parker. 1998, Orchard $16.95 (0-531-30075-7). 40pp. When Jefferson complains to Dr. Franklin about the mutilation of his Declaration of Independence by Congress, the good doctor tells him a comforting parable. (Rev: BL 2/15/98; HB 3–4/98; HBG 10/98; SLJ 4/98)

9526 Forbes, Esther. *Johnny Tremain: A Novel for Old and Young* (6–8). Illus. by Lynd Ward. 1943, Houghton Mifflin $15.00 (0-395-06766-9); Dell paper $6.50 (0-440-94250-0). 272pp. Story of a young silversmith's apprentice, who plays an important part in the American Revolution. Newbery Medal winner, 1944.

9527 Fritz, Jean. *George Washington's Breakfast* (3–5). Illus. by Paul Galdone. 1998, Penguin Putnam paper $5.99 (0-698-11611-9). 43pp. George W.

Allen knows all there is to know about our first president — except what he had for breakfast.

9528 Goodman, Joan E. *Hope's Crossing* (5–8). 1998, Houghton Mifflin $16.00 (0-395-86195-0). 160pp. Kidnapped by British loyalists during the Revolution, Hope must try to escape and find her way home. (Rev: BCCB 7–8/98; BL 6/1–15/98; HBG 10/98; SLJ 5/98)

9529 Gregory, Kristiana. *Five Smooth Stones: Hope's Diary* (3–5). Series: My America. 2001, Scholastic $8.95 (0-439-14827-8). 112pp. Set in 1776 Philadelphia and told in diary format, this novel tells of a 9-year-old girl and her family's problems at the beginning of the Revolutionary War. (Rev: BL 1/1–15/01; HBG 10/01)

9530 Gregory, Kristiana. *We Are Patriots: Hope's Revolutionary War Diary, Book Two* (2–4). Series: My America. 2002, Scholastic $8.95 (0-439-21039-9); paper $4.99 (0-439-36906-1). 108pp. Ten-year-old Hope tells her diary the details of the war raging around Philadelphia in 1777. (Rev: HBG 10/02; SLJ 8/02)

9531 Hansen, Joyce. *The Captive* (5–8). 1994, Scholastic paper $13.95 (0-590-41625-1). 195pp. The exciting story based on fact of a young African boy sold into slavery in Massachusetts and how he eventually escaped. (Rev: BCCB 3/94; HB 1–2/94, 5–6/94; SLJ 1/94)

9532 Kirkpatrick, Katherine. *Redcoats and Petticoats* (3–5). Illus. by Ronald Himler. 1999, Holiday House $15.95 (0-8234-1416-7). 32pp. When 13-year-old Thomas Strong is sent on some unusual errands, he is unaware at first that he is part of a spy network conveying messages to the forces of George Washington during the Revolutionary War. (Rev: BL 3/1/99; HBG 10/99; SLJ 4/99)

9533 Moore, Ruth Nulton. *Distant Thunder* (5–8). Illus. by Allan Eitzen. 1991, Herald Pr. paper $6.99 (0-8361-3557-1). 160pp. During the Revolution, when wounded Americans are sent to Pennsylvania to recover, young Kate experiences the horrors of war. (Rev: BCCB 1/92; SLJ 1/92)

9534 Moss, Marissa. *Emma's Journal* (3–5). Illus. Series: Young America Voices. 1999, Harcourt $15.00 (0-15-202025-X). 56pp. Set in journal format, this novel tells the story of 10-year-old Emma who helps the patriots in revolutionary Boston. (Rev: BL 9/15/99; HBG 3/00; SLJ 12/99)

9535 Noble, Trinka Hakes. *The Scarlet Stockings Spy* (2–4). Illus. by Robert Papp. 2004, Sleeping Bear $16.95 (1-58536-230-1). 48pp. Maddy Rose, a young seamstress in revolutionary-era Philadelphia, devises a clever signaling system to keep patriot forces informed about what ships are docked in the city's harbor. (Rev: BL 2/1/05)

9536 Nordan, Robert. *The Secret Road* (5–9). 2001, Holiday House $16.95 (0-8234-1543-0). 144pp. Young Laura helps an escaped slave on a long and suspenseful journey to freedom by posing as her sister. (Rev: BL 9/15/01; HBG 3/02; SLJ 10/01)

9537 O'Dell, Scott. *Sarah Bishop* (5–8). 1980, Houghton Mifflin $16.00 (0-395-29185-2); Scholastic paper $4.99 (0-590-44651-7). 240pp. A first-per-

son narrative of a girl who lived through the American Revolution and its toll of suffering and misery.

9538 Roop, Peter, and Connie Roop. *An Eye for an Eye: A Story of the Revolutionary War* (5–9). 2000, Jamestown paper $5.95 (0-8092-0628-5). 168pp. During the Revolutionary War, Samantha, disguised as boy, sets out to save her brother who is being held prisoner on a British ship. (Rev: BCCB 7–8/00; SLJ 4/00)

9539 Schurfranz, Vivian. *A Message for General Washington* (3–4). Illus. by John F. Martin. Series: Stories of the States. 1998, Silver Moon LB $13.95 (1-881889-89-0). 92pp. Hannah, age 12, undertakes a perilous journey from Yorktown to Williamsburg, where she delivers a message to General Washington. (Rev: HBG 10/98; SLJ 11/98)

9540 Sweetzer, Anna Leah. *Treason Stops at Oyster Bay* (4–6). Illus. 1999, Silver Moon LB $13.95 (1-893110-03-6). 96pp. Sally is attracted to Colonel Simcoe, a British officer billeted in her family's house on Long Island, and must decide if she should pass on vital information she has overheard to her brother who is a Patriot spy. (Rev: BL 8/99; HBG 3/00)

9541 Turner, Ann. *Love Thy Neighbor: The Tory Diary of Prudence Emerson* (4–7). Series: Dear America. 2003, Scholastic $10.95 (0-439-15308-5). 192pp. Prudence, a teenager in 1774 Massachusetts, describes the conflicts between Tories and Patriots and the effects on families and friends. (Rev: BL 7/03; HBG 10/03; SLJ 8/03)

9542 Van Leeuwen, Jean. *Hannah's Winter of Hope* (4–8). Illus. Series: Pioneer Daughters. 2000, Penguin Putnam $14.99 (0-8037-2492-6). 96pp. After the British burn down their home, the Perley family suffers even more privations in this story told from the viewpoint of 11-year-old Hannah Perley. (Rev: BL 8/00; HBG 10/00; SLJ 7/00)

9543 Walker, Sally M. *The 18 Penny Goose* (2–4). Illus. by Ellen Beier. Series: I Can Read. 1998, HarperCollins LB $14.89 (0-06-027557-X). 64pp. In this easy reader based on fact, a little girl is afraid that the British army raiders will eat her pet goose during the Revolutionary War. (Rev: BL 2/1/98; HB 5–6/98; HBG 10/98; SLJ 3/98)

9544 Waters, John F. *Night Raiders Along the Cape* (3–5). Illus. 1998, Silver Moon LB $14.95 (1-881889-85-8). 96pp. Asa rows from his island home to warn the mainlanders of a British plot in this novel set in Massachusetts during the American Revolution. (Rev: BL 2/15/98; HBG 10/98; SLJ 7/98)

9545 Wisler, G. Clifton. *Kings Mountain* (5–7). 2002, HarperCollins LB $15.89 (0-06-623793-9). 160pp. Fourteen-year-old Francis gets caught up in the intrigue and danger of the Revolutionary War when he is sent to South Carolina to help his grandmother run her tavern. Maps and a chronology add context. (Rev: BL 3/15/02; HBG 10/02; SLJ 7/02)

THE YOUNG NATION, 1789–1861

9546 Arbuckle, Scott. *Zeb, the Cow's on the Roof Again! And Other Tales of Early Texas Dwellings*

(3–7). Illus. by author. 1996, Eakin $17.75 (1-57168-102-7). 128pp. Four youngsters tell about their dwellings in stories that take place at various times in Texas history. (Rev: SLJ 4/97)

9547 Armstrong, Jennifer. *Steal Away* (5–8). 1992, Scholastic paper $3.99 (0-590-46921-5). 224pp. Susannah, who hates slavery, is given a slave when she moves to Virginia to live with her uncle and his family. (Rev: SLJ 2/92)

9548 Atkins, Jeannine. *Becoming Little Women: Louisa May at Fruitlands* (4–6). Illus. 2001, Penguin Putnam $16.99 (0-399-23619-8). 176pp. Based on factual sources such as letters and diaries, this novel explores the life of Louisa May Alcott as an 11-year-old, when her father moved the family to an experimental farm called Fruitlands. (Rev: BL 11/15/01; HB 9–10/01; HBG 3/02; SLJ 10/01)

9549 Auch, Mary Jane. *Frozen Summer* (4–8). 1998, Holt $16.95 (0-8050-4923-1). In this sequel to *Journey to Nowhere*, set in 1816 in upstate New York, 12-year-old Mem struggles to hold her family together in spite of her mother's bouts of severe depression. (Rev: BCCB 1/99; BL 1/1–15/99; BR 5–6/99; HB 1–2/99; HBG 3/99; SLJ 12/98)

9550 Berleth, Richard. *Mary Patten's Voyage* (4–6). Illus. by Ben Otero. 1994, Whitman LB $14.95 (0-8075-4987-8). 40pp. Based on facts involving an 1856 clipper ship race, this is the story of Mary Patten, who took command when her captain husband became ill. (Rev: BCCB 12/94; BL 1/1/95; SLJ 12/94)

9551 Blos, Joan W. *A Gathering of Days: A New England Girl's Journal, 1830–32* (6–8). 1979, Macmillan $15.00 (0-684-16340-3); paper $4.99 (0-689-71419-X). 144pp. A fictional diary kept by 13-year-old Catherine Cabot, who is growing up in the town of Meredith, New Hampshire. Newbery Medal winner, 1980.

9552 Bryant, Louella. *The Black Bonnet* (5–7). 1996, New England Pr. paper $12.95 (1-881535-22-3). 160pp. Two sisters are smuggled out of the South via the Underground Railroad to Burlington, Vermont. (Rev: BL 2/1/97; SLJ 2/97)

9553 Carrick, Carol. *Stay Away from Simon!* (4–6). Illus. by Donald Carrick. 1985, Houghton Mifflin paper $5.95 (0-89919-849-X). 64pp. Mentally handicapped Simon has a reputation of being dangerous, but Lucy discovers he also has a generous heart in this story set in Martha's Vineyard in the 1830s. (Rev: BCCB 11/85; BL 8/85; SLJ 4/85)

9554 Collier, James Lincoln, and Christopher Collier. *The Clock* (5–7). Illus. by Maddox Kelly. 1995, Dell paper $4.99 (0-440-40999-3). 176pp. Fifteen-year-old Annie Steele contends with the harsh life of mill work in Connecticut in 1810. (Rev: BCCB 4/92; BL 2/1/92; HB 3–4/92)

9555 Crook, Connie Brummel. *Laura Secord's Brave Walk* (2–5). Illus. by June Lawrason. 2001, Second Story $14.95 (1-896764-34-7). During the War of 1812, Laura Secord hears American soldiers' plans to attack at Beavers Dam, and sets off on a dangerous journey to warn the British in this

novel with realistic battlefield illustrations. (Rev: SLJ 7/01)

9556 Dahlberg, Maurine F. *The Spirit and Gilly Bucket* (5–8). 2002, Farrar $18.00 (0-374-31677-5). 192pp. Eleven-year-old Gilly longs to join her father in his search for gold, but must stay in Virginia on a plantation, where she befriends a young slave and helps her escape via the Underground Railroad in this novel full of suspense and surprises. (Rev: BL 1/1–15/03; HBG 3/03; SLJ 12/02)

9557 Defelice, Cynthia. *The Apprenticeship of Lucas Whitaker* (5–8). 1996, Farrar $16.00 (0-374-34669-0). In the mid-1800s, orphan Lucas becomes an apprentice to the local dentist/barber/undertaker. (Rev: BCCB 10/96; BL 10/1/96; BR 3–4/97; SLJ 8/96*)

9558 Denenberg, Barry. *So Far from Home: The Diary of Mary Driscoll, an Irish Mill Girl* (4–8). Series: Dear America. 1997, Scholastic paper $10.95 (0-590-92667-5). Using a diary format, this novel tells the story of Mary Driscoll's journey to the United States from Ireland and her ordeals as a worker in a Massachusetts textile mill in the 1800s. (Rev: BL 12/15/97; HBG 3/98; SLJ 10/97)

9559 Donaldson, Joan. *A Pebble and a Pen* (5–8). 2000, Holiday House $15.95 (0-8234-1500-7). 176pp. In 1853, to avoid an arranged marriage, 14-year-old Matty runs away to study penmanship at Mr. Spencer's famous Ohio school. (Rev: BCCB 12/00; BL 1/1–15/01; HBG 10/01; SLJ 12/00)

9560 Duey, Kathleen. *Zellie Blake: Lowell, Massachusetts, 1834* (4–6). Series: American Diaries. 2002, Simon & Schuster paper $4.99 (0-689-84405-0). 133pp. Twelve-year-old Zellie is an African American orphan who relates through her diary her dislike of her job at a boarding house in the mill town of Lowell and her pleasure when she finds a better situation. (Rev: SLJ 10/02)

9561 Duey, Kathleen, and Karen A. Bale. *Cave-In: St. Claire, Pennsylvania, 1859* (4–6). Series: Survival! 1998, Simon & Schuster paper $3.99 (0-689-82350-9). 158pp. In this survival story set in the coal mines of Pennsylvania during 1859, two boys and their landlady's daughter are trapped underground in a mine after a cave-in. (Rev: SLJ 2/99)

9562 Duey, Kathleen, and Karen A. Bale. *Hurricane: Open Seas, 1844* (5–7). Series: Survival! 1999, Simon & Schuster paper $4.50 (0-689-82544-7). 169pp. This exciting sea story, set in 1844, tells of two youngsters who are on a whaler when a killer hurricane strikes. (Rev: SLJ 8/99)

9563 Forrester, Sandra. *Dust from Old Bones* (5–7). 1999, Morrow $16.00 (0-688-16202-9). 144pp. In this novel set in New Orleans before the Civil War, young Simone resents her mother's strict discipline and instead likes to hang out with an aunt from Paris, who persuades her to help two slaves escape. (Rev: BCCB 10/99; BL 8/99; HBG 3/00; SLJ 10/99)

9564 Frederick, Heather Vogel. *The Voyage of Patience Goodspeed* (4–6). 2002, Simon & Schuster $16.00 (0-689-84851-X). 224pp. Patience, a 12-year-old girl, and her younger brother experience a number of amazing adventures when they join their widower father on a whaling voyage. (Rev: BL 6/1–15/02; HB 9–10/02; HBG 3/03; SLJ 7/02)

9565 Garland, Sherry. *In the Shadow of the Alamo* (5–8). Series: Great Episodes. 2001, Harcourt $17.00 (0-15-201744-5). 282pp. Fifteen-year-old Lorenzo Bonifacio, a conscript in the Mexican army of Santa Ana, describes the harsh life of the soldiers and the family members who follow them on the trek to Texas and the battle of the Alamo. (Rev: BCCB 1/02; BL 10/15/01; HB 11–12/01; HBG 3/02; SLJ 12/01)

9566 Garland, Sherry. *A Line in the Sand: The Alamo Diary of Lucinda Lawrence* (4–8). Illus. Series: Dear America. 1998, Scholastic paper $10.95 (0-590-39466-5). 208pp. Lucinda relates events in Gonzales, Texas, in 1835 that lead to the Texas War of Independence and to the massacre at the Alamo. (Rev: BL 3/1/99; HBG 3/99; SLJ 1/99)

9567 Givens, Steven J. *Levi Dust: A Tale from the Kerry Patch* (2–4). 1997, New Canaan paper $4.95 (1-889658-07-3). 56pp. Ten-year-old twins get lost on the streets of St. Louis in the 1850s and are brought home by a kindly bell ringer. (Rev: BL 2/1/98)

9568 Greenwood, Barbara. *The Last Safe House: A Story of the Underground Railroad* (3–6). Illus. by Heather Collins. 1998, Kids Can $16.95 (1-55074-507-7); paper $9.95 (1-55074-509-3). 119pp. Using a Canadian family's participation in the Underground Railroad in 1856 as a framework, this book supplies good background on the railroad's organization, accomplishments, and the fight against slavery. (Rev: HBG 3/99; SLJ 1/99)

9569 Gregory, Kristiana. *The Stowaway: A Tale of California Pirates* (4–6). 1995, Scholastic $3.99 (0-590-48822-8). 144pp. Carlito must endure the squalid life of being a pirate's captive in this tale set on the California coast during the early 1800s. (Rev: BCCB 10/95; BL 9/15/95; SLJ 9/95)

9570 Guccione, Leslie D. *Come Morning* (4–7). 1995, Carolrhoda LB $19.15 (0-87614-892-5). 120pp. A young boy takes over his father's duties as a conductor on the Underground Railroad. (Rev: BCCB 1/96; HB 11–12/95; SLJ 11/95)

9571 Hausman, Gerald. *Tom Cringle: Battle on the High Seas* (4–8). Illus. by Tad Hills. 2000, Simon & Schuster $16.95 (0-689-82810-1). 185pp. Set during the War of 1812, this novel tells of a young midshipman who is rescued by a pirate ship when his vessel sinks. (Rev: BCCB 7–8/00; HBG 3/01; SLJ 11/00)

9572 Hermann, Spring. *Seeing Lessons* (4–6). 1998, Holt $15.95 (0-8050-5706-4). 164pp. In this first person narrative, 10-year-old Abigail Carter leaves her farm near Boston in 1832 to attend Perkins School, the first school for the blind in America. (Rev: BL 12/1/98; HBG 3/99; SLJ 11/98)

9573 Hill, Donna. *Shipwreck Season* (5–8). 1998, Clarion $15.00 (0-395-86614-6). 215pp. In the 1800s, 16-year-old Daniel joins a crew of seamen who patrol America's eastern coastline, rescuing

people and cargo from shipwrecks. (Rev: BCCB 7–8/98; BL 6/1–15/98; HBG 3/99; SLJ 6/98)

9574 Hilts, Len. *Timmy O'Dowd and the Big Ditch: A Story of the Glory Days on the Old Erie Canal* (5–7). 1988, Harcourt $13.95 (0-15-200606-0). 91pp. Timmy and his cousin Dennis don't get along, but when the canals threaten to flood, they realize each other's strengths and stamina. (Rev: BCCB 12/88; BL 10/1/88; SLJ 12/88)

9575 Hopkinson, Deborah. *Sweet Clara and the Freedom Quilt* (3–5). Illus. by James E. Ransome. 1993, Knopf LB $16.99 (0-679-92311-X). 36pp. In this picture book for older readers, a slave girl maps out her escape to Canada on a brightly colored quilt. (Rev: BCCB 7–8/93; BL 4/15/93; HB 5–6/93*; HBG 10/03; SLJ 6/93)

9576 Houston, Gloria. *Bright Freedom's Song: A Story of the Underground Railroad* (4–7). 1998, Harcourt $16.00 (0-15-201812-3). 145pp. A tense, dramatic story about a girl who helps her parents operate a North Carolina station on the Underground Railroad. (Rev: BCCB 1/99; BL 11/1/98; BR 5–6/99; HBG 3/99; SLJ 12/98)

9577 Hurst, Carol Otis. *Through the Lock* (5–8). 2001, Houghton Mifflin $15.00 (0-618-03036-0). 172pp. In this novel set in Connecticut in the first half of the 19th century, a young orphan named Etta shares many adventures with a boy who lives in an abandoned cabin by a canal. (Rev: BCCB 3/01; BL 4/1/01; HB 3–4/01; HBG 10/01; SLJ 3/01)

9578 Jackson, Dave, and Neta Jackson. *The Runaway's Revenge* (4–6). Series: Trailblazer. 1995, Bethany House paper $5.99 (1-55661-471-3). 144pp. A novel about the life of John Newton, a slave trader who later became a minister and wrote such hymns as "Amazing Grace." (Rev: BL 1/1–15/96)

9579 Jackson, Dave, and Neta Jackson. *The Thieves of Tyburn Square* (3–6). Series: Trailblazer. 1995, Bethany House paper $5.99 (1-55661-470-5). 144pp. In this fictionalized account set in the early 1800s, the Quaker Elizabeth Fry helps two youngsters caught picking pockets. (Rev: BL 3/15/96)

9580 Jakes, John. *Susanna of the Alamo: A True Story* (3–5). Illus. by Paul Bacon. 1986, Harcourt $13.95 (0-15-200592-7); paper $7.00 (0-15-200595-1). 32pp. Only women, children, and slaves were spared by the Mexicans at the battle of the Alamo in 1836, and one, Susanna Dickinson, was spared to inform Sam Houston of the outcome. (Rev: BCCB 6/86; BL 6/15/86; SLJ 8/86)

9581 Johnson, Lois W. *Midnight Rescue* (4–6). 1996, Bethany House paper $5.99 (1-55661-353-9). 160pp. Twelve-year-old Libby, a riverboat captain's daughter, becomes involved with the Underground Railroad and an escaped slave. (Rev: BL 1/1–15/97)

9582 Karr, Kathleen. *The Great Turkey Walk* (4–8). 1998, Farrar $17.00 (0-374-32773-4). 199pp. In 1860, 15-year-old Simon decides to make his fortune by walking 1,000 turkeys from Missouri to Denver, where meat is scarce. (Rev: BCCB 5/98; BL 6/1–15/98; BR 1–2/99; HBG 10/98; SLJ 3/98*)

9583 Ketchum, Liza. *Orphan Journey Home* (5–7). Illus. 2000, Avon $15.99 (0-380-97811-3). 162pp. When their parents die in southern Illinois in 1828, Jesse and her three siblings must find their way to their grandmother in eastern Kentucky. (Rev: BCCB 6/00; BL 6/1–15/00; HBG 10/00; SLJ 8/00)

9584 Killcoyne, Hope Lourie. *The Lost Village of Central Park* (3–5). Illus. by Mary Lee Majno. Series: Mysteries in Time. 1999, Silver Moon LB $13.95 (1-893110-02-8). 89pp. An exciting story about life in Seneca Village, an African American settlement in 19th-century New York City, and the slave catchers that terrorized its people. (Rev: HBG 10/00; SLJ 2/00)

9585 Kohl, Susan. *The Ghost of Gracie Mansion* (3–5). Illus. by Ned Butterfield. Series: Mysteries in Time. 1999, Silver Moon LB $13.95 (1-893110-04-4). 96pp. When the Gracie family move to their new mansion in northern Manhattan in 1803, they encounter a mystery concerning disappearing objects. (Rev: SLJ 2/00)

9586 Kroll, Steven. *John Quincy Adams: Letters from a Southern Planter's Son* (4–6). Illus. Series: Dear Mr. President. 2001, Winslow $9.95 (1-890817-93-7). 122pp. A fictional correspondence between a young boy and President John Quincy Adams details historical events and gives insight into Adams's character and concerns. (Rev: BL 1/1–15/02; HBG 3/02; SLJ 12/01)

9587 LeSourd, Nancy. *The Personal Correspondence of Hannah Brown and Sarah Smith: The Underground Railroad, 1858* (4–7). 2003, Zondervan $9.99 (0-310-70350-6). 192pp. In letters to each other, two Quaker girls discuss their abolitionist ideals and become involved in helping a runaway slave. (Rev: BL 1/1–15/04)

9588 Lottridge, Celia B. *The Wind Wagon* (2–4). Illus. by Daniel Clifford. 1995, Silver Burdett LB $12.95 (0-382-24927-5); paper $4.95 (0-382-24929-1). 56pp. A fictionalized account of Sam Peppard and his invention of a wagon powered by the wind in Kansas in 1860. (Rev: SLJ 8/95)

9589 Lunn, Janet. *Laura Secord: A Story of Courage* (3–6). Illus. by Maxwell Newhouse. 2002, Tundra $16.95 (0-88776-538-6). Lunn's text and the accompanying illustrations give drama to the story of Secord's trek to warn the British during the War of 1812. (Rev: HB 3–4/02; HBG 10/02; SLJ 4/02)

9590 McKissack, Patricia. *A Picture of Freedom: The Diary of Clotee, a Slave Girl* (4–6). 1997, Scholastic $9.95 (0-614-25386-1). 208pp. Using a diary format, this novel describes the life of slaves on a Southern plantation as seen through the eyes of a young slave girl. (Rev: BL 4/15/97; SLJ 9/97)

9591 McKissack, Patricia, and Fredrick McKissack. *Let My People Go* (5–8). Illus. 1998, Simon & Schuster $20.00 (0-689-80856-9). This novel set in the early 19th century combines Bible stories and the hardships endured by slaves as told by Price Jefferson, a former slave who is now an abolitionist living in South Carolina. (Rev: BCCB 12/98; BL 10/1/98; HBG 3/99; SLJ 11/98)

9592 Minahan, John A. *Abigail's Drum* (2–5). Illus. 1995, Pippin $15.95 (0-945912-25-0). 64pp. During the War of 1812, Rebecca and Abigail try to save their father, who has been captured by the British. (Rev: BCCB 2/96; BL 2/15/96; SLJ 2/96)

9593 Monjo, F. N. *The Drinking Gourd* (2–4). Illus. by Fred Brenner. 1970, HarperCollins LB $15.89 (0-06-024330-9); paper $3.95 (0-06-444042-7). 64pp. A New England white boy helps a black family escape on the Underground Railroad.

9594 Paterson, Katherine. *Jip: His Story* (5–9). 1998, Puffin paper $5.99 (0-14-038674-2). Jip, a foundling boy in Vermont of the 1850s, wonders about his origins, particularly after he finds he is being watched by a mysterious stranger. (Rev: BCCB 12/96; BL 9/1/96*; BR 3–4/97; HB 11–12/96; SLJ 10/96*)

9595 Patrick, Denise Lewis. *The Adventures of Midnight Son* (5–8). 1997, Holt $16.00 (0-8050-4714-X). Fleeing slavery on a horse given to him by his parents, Midnight rides to Mexico and freedom. (Rev: BL 12/15/97; BR 3–4/98; HBG 3/98; SLJ 12/97)

9596 Rappaport, Doreen. *Freedom River* (3–5). Illus. 2000, Hyperion $14.99 (0-7868-0350-9). 32pp. Based on fact, this is a picture book for older readers that tells how John Parker, an ex-slave, helped a family to escape from Kentucky via the Underground Railroad. (Rev: BL 10/1/00; HBG 3/01; SLJ 10/00)

9597 Rinaldi, Ann. *The Blue Door* (5–8). Series: Quilt. 1996, Scholastic paper $15.95 (0-590-46051-X). In this final volume of the Quilt trilogy — following *A Stitch in Time* (1994) and *Broken Days* — Amanda is forced to take a mill job in Lowell, Massachusetts, after an adventurous trip north from her South Carolina home. (Rev: BL 11/1/96; BR 3–4/97)

9598 Robinet, Harriette G. *Twelve Travelers, Twenty Horses* (4–7). 2003, Simon & Schuster $16.95 (0-689-84561-8). 208pp. Ten slaves band together to foil their master's plan to prevent the delivery of a crucial message as they travel to California in 1860. (Rev: BL 2/15/03; HBG 10/03; SLJ 2/03)

9599 Rosen, Michael J. *A School for Pompey Walker* (4–6). Illus. 1995, Harcourt $16.00 (0-15-200114-X). 48pp. This story, based on fact, tells about a slave who sold himself several times into slavery to get the money to open a school for black children. (Rev: BCCB 1/96; BL 10/15/95; SLJ 11/95)

9600 Schneider, Mical. *Annie Quinn in America* (5–9). 2001, Carolrhoda LB $19.15 (1-57505-510-4). 252pp. In 1847, young Annie and her brother travel from Ireland, a land ravaged by the potato famine, to America, a land fraught with dangers of its own. (Rev: BL 11/15/01; HBG 3/02; SLJ 9/01)

9601 Schwartz, Virginia Frances. *Send One Angel Down* (5–8). 2000, Holiday House $15.95 (0-8234-1484-1). 163pp. This is the story of a young slave girl, Eliza, the skills she learns on the plantation, and how this knowledge helps her when she gains freedom. (Rev: BL 6/1–15/00; HB 7–8/00; HBG 10/00; SLJ 8/00)

9602 Shefelman, Janice. *Comanche Song* (5–8). Illus. by Tom Shefelman. 2000, Eakin $17.95 (1-57168-397-6). 255pp. The story of 16-year-old Tsena, son of a Comanche peace chief, and events that lead to the Battle of Plum Creek during the 1840s in Texas. (Rev: BL 2/15/01; HBG 10/01; SLJ 10/00)

9603 Siegelson, Kim L. *Escape South* (2–4). Illus. by Shelley Jackson. Series: Road to Reading. 2000, Golden Books $10.99 (0-307-46504-7). This easy chapter book tells, in fictionalized form, how some runaway slaves were given shelter and land by the Seminole Indians in Florida and later left for land out west. (Rev: BL 2/15/01; HBG 3/01)

9604 Siegelson, Kim L. *In the Time of the Drums* (2–5). Illus. by Brian Pinkney. 1999, Hyperion LB $16.49 (0-7686-2386-0). 32pp. Told from the standpoint of a young African American, this is the legend of the slave rebellion at Ibo's Landing in South Carolina's Sea Islands. (Rev: BL 4/1/99)

9605 Smucker, Barbara. *Runaway to Freedom* (3–5). Illus. by Charles Lilly. 1978, HarperCollins paper $4.95 (0-06-440106-5). 160pp. Two slave girls try to reach Canada and freedom.

9606 Stowe, Cynthia M. *The Second Escape of Arthur Cooper* (5–7). 2000, Marshall Cavendish LB $14.95 (0-7614-5069-6). 112pp. Based on a true story, this novel tells of Arthur Cooper, an escaped slave, and the Quakers on Nantucket Island who saved him from slave catchers in 1822. (Rev: BL 8/00; HBG 3/01; SLJ 10/00)

9607 Thomas, Velma M. *Lest We Forget: The Passage from Africa to Slavery and Emancipation* (5–8). Illus. 1997, Crown $29.95 (0-609-60030-3). An interactive book about slavery based on material from the Black Holocaust Museum. (Rev: BL 12/15/97) [973.6]

9608 Trottier, Maxine. *Under a Shooting Star* (5–8). Series: The Circle of Silver Chronicles. 2002, Stoddart paper $7.95 (0-7737-6228-0). 212pp. During the War of 1812, a 15-year-old boy who is half English and half Oneida Indian struggles with conflicting loyalties as he tries to protect the two American girls he is escorting. (Rev: SLJ 5/02)

9609 Turner, Glennette Tilley. *Running for Our Lives* (5–7). Illus. 1994, Holiday House $16.95 (0-8234-1121-4). 198pp. A thoroughly researched novel about a boy and his family who escape slavery in the 1850s and traveled on the Underground Railroad to Canada. (Rev: BCCB 6/94; BL 6/1–15/94; SLJ 4/94)

9610 Wait, Lea. *Seaward Born* (4–7). 2003, Simon & Schuster $16.95 (0-689-84719-X). 160pp. Michael, a young slave, makes a dangerous journey to Canada and freedom in this dramatic historical novel. (Rev: BL 2/15/03; HBG 10/03; SLJ 1/03)

9611 Wait, Lea. *Stopping to Home* (4–7). 2001, Simon & Schuster $16.00 (0-689-83832-8). 160pp. When 11-year-old Abbie's mother dies of smallpox and her father disappears, Abbie takes a job as a housemaid to provide for herself and her young brother in this story set in early-19th-century Maine.

(Rev: BCCB 12/01; BL 11/15/01; HB 1–2/02; HBG 3/02; SLJ 10/01)

9612 Wall, Bill. *The Cove of Cork* (5–9). 1999, Irish American paper $7.95 (0-85635-225-0). In this novel, the third in a trilogy revolving around the War of 1812, an Irish lad, the first mate of the American schooner *Shenandoah*, sees action in a battle against a British vessel and eventually wins the hand of the granddaughter of a shipbuilding magnate. (Rev: SLJ 7/99)

9613 Wanttaja, Ronald. *The Key to Honor* (5–9). 1996, Royal Fireworks paper $9.99 (0-88092-270-2). During the War of 1812, midshipman Nate Lawton has doubts about his courage in battle and worries about his father, who has been taken prisoner by the British. (Rev:)

9614 West, Tracey. *Mr. Peale's Bones* (4–6). Series: Stories of the States. 1994, Silver Moon LB $14.95 (1-881889-50-5). 63pp. In this novel, set in upstate New York in 1801, Will and his estranged father find a new bond when they help Charles Willson Peale and his excavation of mammoth bones. (Rev: SLJ 7/94)

9615 Whelan, Gloria. *Farewell to the Island* (5–8). 1998, HarperCollins $16.95 (0-06-027751-3). In this sequel to *Once on This Island,* Mary leaves her Michigan home after the War of 1812 and travels to England where she falls in love with Lord Lindsay. (Rev: BL 12/1/98; HBG 3/99; SLJ 1/99)

9616 Whelan, Gloria. *Friend on Freedom River* (3–5). Illus. by Gijsbert van Frankenhuyzen. 2005, Sleeping Bear $16.95 (1-58536-222-0). In 1850, on a cold December night on the Detroit River, young Louis is asked to ferry runaway slaves to Canada. (Rev: BL 5/15/04; SLJ 6/05)

9617 Whelan, Gloria. *Once on This Island* (4–7). 1995, HarperCollins LB $14.89 (0-06-026249-4). 224pp. In 1812, Mary and her older brother and sister must tend the family farm on Mackinac Island when their father goes off to war. (Rev: BCCB 11/95; BL 10/1/95; BR 3–4/96; SLJ 11/95)

9618 Wiley, Melissa. *On Tide Mill Lane* (4–8). Illus. 2001, HarperCollins $16.95 (0-06-027013-6). 208pp. Charlotte experiences a number of household crises in Roxbury, Massachusetts, where she lives with her blacksmith father at the time of the War of 1812. (Rev: BL 2/15/01; HBG 10/01)

9619 Wright, Courtni C. *Journey to Freedom: A Story of the Underground Railroad* (3–5). Illus. by Griffith Gershom. 1994, Holiday House LB $16.95 (0-8234-1096-X). 28pp. A picture book that tells of 8-year-old Joshua and his flight to freedom on the Underground Railroad. (Rev: BL 11/15/94; SLJ 1/95)

9620 Wyeth, Sharon Dennis. *Flying Free: Corey's Underground Railroad Diary* (2–4). Illus. Series: My America. 2002, Scholastic $8.95 (0-439-24443-9); paper $4.99 (0-439-36908-8). 112pp. In diary form, this novel traces the travels of Corey, a black boy, and his family to freedom in Canada via the Underground Railroad. (Rev: BL 6/1–15/02; HBG 10/02; SLJ 8/02)

PIONEERS AND WESTWARD EXPANSION

9621 Altman, Linda Jacobs. *The Legend of Freedom Hill* (2–4). Illus. by Cornelius Van Wright and Ying-hwa Hu. 2000, Lee & Low $15.95 (1-58430-003-5). 32pp. Set in Gold Rush California, this novel tells how Rosabel, the daughter of a runaway slave, and her Jewish friend Sophia pan enough gold to buy the freedom of Rosabel's mother. (Rev: BL 11/1/00; HBG 3/01; SLJ 8/00)

9622 Anderson, Joan. *Pioneer Children of Appalachia* (4–6). Illus. 1986, Houghton Mifflin paper $7.95 (0-395-54792-X). The Davis family is shown in everyday life in Appalachia of the early 1800s. (Rev: BCCB 12/86; BL 11/1/86; SLJ 10/86)

9623 Applegate, Stan. *The Devil's Highway* (5–8). Illus. by James Watling. 1998, Peachtree paper $8.95 (1-56145-184-3). 148pp. In this adventure novel set in the early 1800s, 14-year-old Zeb and his horse, Christmas, set out on the bandit-infested Natchez Trail to search for the boy's grandfather. (Rev: SLJ 2/99)

9624 Arrington, Frances. *Bluestem* (4–6). 2000, Penguin Putnam $16.99 (0-399-23564-7). 140pp. Eleven-year-old Polly and her younger sister must fend for themselves on the American frontier after their mother wanders away. (Rev: BCCB 9/00; BL 4/1/00; HB 5–6/00; HBG 10/00; SLJ 6/00)

9625 Arrington, Frances. *Prairie Whispers* (5–8). 2003, Philomel $17.99 (0-399-23975-8). 176pp. Promising to look after a dying woman's baby, Colleen, 12, substitutes the child for her own stillborn sister, but there's trouble when the baby's father arrives in this story set in South Dakota in the 1860s. (Rev: BL 5/15/03*; HB 7–8/03; HBG 10/03; SLJ 5/03)

9626 Avi. *The Barn* (5–8). 1994, Orchard paper $15.99 (0-531-08711-5). In this story set in 1850s Oregon, Ben and his siblings must run their farm alone after their father becomes paralyzed, and Ben decides they must fulfill their father's dream and build a barn. (Rev: BL 9/1/94*; SLJ 10/94)

9627 Avi. *Prairie School* (2–4). Illus. by Bill Farnsworth. Series: An I Can Read Chapter Book. 2001, HarperCollins LB $14.89 (0-06-027665-7). 48pp. In Colorado during the 1880s, young Noah learns the value of learning how to read in this easy chapter book. (Rev: BCCB 5/01; BL 4/15/01; HBG 10/01; SLJ 5/01)

9628 Ayres, Katherine. *Silver Dollar Girl* (4–8). 2000, Random paper $4.99 (0-440-41705-8). 195pp. Set in the silver rush days of the 1880s, this story tells how Valentine Harper disguises herself as a boy and sets out from Pittsburgh to find her father in Colorado. (Rev: BL 11/15/00; SLJ 11/00)

9629 Bailer, Darice. *The Last Rail* (3–5). Illus. by Bill Farnsworth. Series: Odyssey. 1996, Smithsonian Institution $14.95 (1-56899-362-5); paper $5.95 (1-56899-363-3). 32pp. Using a fictional format, this book tells about a young girl who witnesses the building of the first transcontinental railroad. (Rev: BL 10/15/96)

9630 Bauer, Marion Dane. *Land of the Buffalo Bones: The Diary of Mary Elizabeth Rodgers, an English Girl in Minnesota* (4–8). Series: Dear America. 2003, Scholastic $12.95 (0-439-22027-0). 224pp. Based on real-life events, Polly Rodgers's diary reveals the hardships endured by a group of English settlers who arrived in Minnesota in 1873. (Rev: BL 5/15/03; HBG 10/03; SLJ 9/01)

9631 Benner, J. A. *Uncle Comanche* (5–8). 1996, Texas Christian Univ. paper $12.95 (0-87565-152-6). Based on fact, this is the story of the adventures of 12-year-old Sul Ross, who runs away from home in pre-Civil War Texas and is pursued by a family friend nicknamed Uncle Comanche. (Rev:)

9632 Blakeslee, Ann R. *A Different Kind of Hero* (5–7). 1997, Marshall Cavendish $14.95 (0-7614-5000-9). 144pp. In 1881 Colorado, Renny is criticized for befriending and helping a Chinese boy new to town. (Rev: BL 9/1/97; HBG 3/98; SLJ 1/98)

9633 Bunting, Eve. *Dandelions* (2–4). Illus. by Greg Shed. 1995, Harcourt $16.00 (0-15-200050-X). 48pp. Zoe compares the dandelions she sees growing wild in a meadow to her family, which has just traveled west to the Nebraska Territory by covered wagon. (Rev: BCCB 9/95; BL 9/15/95; SLJ 11/95*)

9634 Bunting, Eve. *Train to Somewhere* (2–5). Illus. by Ronald Himler. 1996, Clarion $16.00 (0-395-71325-0). 32pp. The story of the Orphan Train as seen from the point of view of Marianne, a homeless girl who travels west in 1878 to find an adoptive family. (Rev: BCCB 3/96; BL 2/1/96*; SLJ 3/96*)

9635 Burks, Brian. *Wrango* (5–8). 1999, Harcourt $16.00 (0-15-201815-8). 128pp. In this historical novel, George, an African American boy, is forced out of town by the Klan and turns to the adventurous life of a cowboy. (Rev: BL 9/1/99; HBG 3/00; SLJ 12/99)

9636 Byars, Betsy. *Trouble River* (3–6). Illus. by Rocco Negri. 1989, Puffin paper $4.99 (0-14-034243-5). 160pp. Dewey uses his canoe to escape Indians.

9637 Calvert, Patricia. *Betrayed!* (5–8). 2002, Simon & Schuster $16.00 (0-689-83472-1). 224pp. Tyler Bohannon of *Bigger* (1994) and *Sooner* (1998) is back, this time traveling west, where he is taken captive by Sioux Indians. (Rev: BL 7/02; HBG 10/02; SLJ 6/02)

9638 Chrismer, Melanie. *Phoebe Clappsaddle for Sheriff* (1–3). Illus. by Virginia Marsh Roeder. 2003, Pelican $14.95 (1-58980-127-X). In this rollicking tale set in the early years of Texas's statehood, diminutive Phoebe Clappsaddle fills in as sheriff when she's selected by the governor to meet the stagecoach carrying the town's new schoolteacher. (Rev: HBG 4/04; SLJ 1/04)

9639 Collier, James Lincoln. *Wild Boy* (5–8). 2002, Marshall Cavendish $15.95 (0-7614-5126-9). 160pp. After knocking his father out during an argument, 12-year-old Jesse runs away from his frontier home to live in the mountains, where he has many adventures, learns many skills, and reflects on his own characteristics before finally deciding to return home in this story that appears to be set in the 19th century. (Rev: BL 11/1/02; HBG 10/03; SLJ 11/02)

9640 Cushman, Karen. *The Ballad of Lucy Whipple* (5–8). 1996, Clarion $15.00 (0-395-72806-1). 208pp. Lucy hates being stuck in the California wilderness with an overbearing mother who runs a boarding house. (Rev: BCCB 9/96; BL 8/96*; HB 9–10/96; SLJ 8/96*)

9641 Duey, Kathleen. *Anisett Lundberg: California, 1851* (4–7). Series: American Diaries. 1996, Simon & Schuster paper $4.99 (0-689-80386-9). 139pp. An adventure story featuring Anisett and her family, who live in the gold-mining region of California in 1851. (Rev: HB 9–10/96; SLJ 12/96)

9642 Durbin, William. *The Journal of Sean Sullivan: A Transcontinental Railroad Worker, Nebraska and Points West, 1867* (5–8). Series: My Name Is America. 1999, Scholastic paper $10.95 (0-439-04994-6). 188pp. This novel describes the early days of railroad construction in America as seen through the eyes of young Sean, who works his way up from a "water carrier" to "spiker." (Rev: BL 10/15/99; HBG 3/00; SLJ 11/99)

9643 Durrant, Lynda. *The Sun, the Rain, and the Apple Seed: A Novel of Johnny Appleseed's Life* (5–8). 2003, Clarion $15.00 (0-618-23487-X). 200pp. This fictionalized biography of John Chapman's life focuses on his eccentricities. (Rev: BL 5/15/03; HBG 10/03; SLJ 5/03)

9644 Ellsworth, Loretta. *The Shrouding Woman* (4–8). 2002, Holt $16.95 (0-8050-6651-9). 160pp. in this novel set in 19th-century Minnesota, 11-year-old Evie resists the efforts of her Aunt Flo ("the shrouding woman") to take care of her after Evie's mother dies. (Rev: BCCB 9/02; BL 5/15/02; HBG 10/02; SLJ 4/02)

9645 Ernst, Kathleen. *Trouble at Fort La Pointe* (4–8). 2000, Pleasant Co. $9.95 (1-58485-087-6). 165pp. In a fur trading post near Lake Superior in the early 18th century, 12-year-old Suzette sets out to investigate who is plotting against her father. (Rev: BL 10/1/00; HBG 10/01; SLJ 12/00)

9646 Finley, Mary Peace. *Meadow Lark* (5–8). Series: Santa Fe Trail trilogy. 2003, Filter $15.95 (0-86541-070-4). 208pp. In this sequel to *Soaring Eagle* (1993) and *White Grizzly* (2000) set in 1845, Teresita Montoya, 13, has various adventures on the Santa Fe Trail as she searches for her older brother and for a new life for herself. (Rev: BL 12/1/03; HBG 4/04; SLJ 2/04)

9647 Finley, Mary Peace. *White Grizzly* (5–9). 2000, Filter $15.95 (0-86541-053-4); paper $8.95 (0-86541-058-5). 215pp. Fifteen-year-old Julio sets out on an arduous journey along the Santa Fe Trail to discover his true identity. (Rev: BL 12/1/00; HBG 10/01; SLJ 1/01)

9648 Fleischman, Paul. *The Borning Room* (5–8). 1991, HarperCollins paper $4.99 (0-06-447099-7). 80pp. Georgina remembers important turning points in her life and the role played by the room set aside for giving birth and dying in her grandfather's house in 19th-century rural Ohio. (Rev: BCCB 9/91; BL 10/1/91*; HB 11–12/91*; SLJ 9/91*)

9649 Fleischman, Sid. *Bandit's Moon* (3–6). Illus. 1998, Greenwillow $15.00 (0-688-15830-7). 144pp. Based partly on fact, this is a humorous adventure story about Annyrose, a young girl who, disguised as a boy, joins a band of Mexican bandits led by Wakeen, the notorious robber. (Rev: BCCB 11/98; BL 10/1/98*; HB 11–12/98; HBG 3/99; SLJ 9/98)

9650 Fleischman, Sid. *Jim Ugly* (4–6). Illus. by Joseph A. Smith. 1992, Greenwillow $16.00 (0-688-10886-5). 144pp. In the time of the Old West, Jake — accompanied by his dad's mongrel dog — sets off in search of his missing father. (Rev: BCCB 3/92*; BL 5/15/92; SLJ 4/92)

9651 Garland, Sherry. *Valley of the Moon: The Diary of Rosalia de Milagros* (5–8). Illus. 2001, Scholastic paper $10.95 (0-439-08820-8). 224pp. Rosalia, a 13-year-old orphan, keeps a diary about working on a California ranch in 1846. (Rev: BL 4/1/01; HBG 3/02; SLJ 4/01)

9652 Glass, Andrew. *A Right Fine Life: Kit Carson on the Santa Fe Trail* (3–5). Illus. 1997, Holiday House LB $16.95 (0-8234-1326-8). 48pp. This tall tale tells about 16-year-old Kit Carson's first journey west and his many adventures along the way. (Rev: BL 2/1/98; HBG 3/98; SLJ 2/98)

9653 Glaze, Lynn. *Seasons of the Trail* (4–6). Illus. by Matthew Archambault. 2000, Silver Moon LB $14.95 (1-893110-20-6). 92pp. To avoid the oncoming Civil War, 14-year-old Lucy Scott and her family leave their home in Missouri and journey to California by covered wagon. (Rev: HBG 3/01; SLJ 1/01)

9654 Gregory, Kristiana. *Across the Wide and Lonesome Prairie: The Oregon Trail Diary of Hattie Campbell* (4–7). Illus. Series: Dear America. 1997, Scholastic paper $10.95 (0-590-22651-7). 149pp. In a diary format, this novel chronicles the hardships that pioneers endured during a trip west on the Oregon Trail. (Rev: SLJ 3/97)

9655 Gregory, Kristiana. *The Great Railroad Race: The Transcontinental Railroad Diary of Libby West* (4–8). Series: Dear America. 1999, Scholastic paper $10.95 (0-590-10991-X). The story of the building of the transcontinental railroad as seen through the eyes of a 14-year-old girl whose father is a reporter following the progress of the massive undertaking. (Rev: BL 4/1/99; HBG 10/99; SLJ 8/99)

9656 Gregory, Kristiana. *A Journey of Faith* (4–6). Series: Prairie River. 2003, Scholastic paper $4.99 (0-439-43991-4). 213pp. Thirteen-year-old Nessa, an orphan, relies on her faith to support her when she sets off by stagecoach for Prairie River, Kansas, in 1865. (Rev: SLJ 11/03)

9657 Gregory, Kristiana. *Seeds of Hope: The Gold Rush Diary of Susanna Fairchild* (4–8). 2001, Scholastic paper $10.95 (0-590-51157-2). 182pp. After Susanna's mother dies in 1849, the 14-year-old takes over her journal and describes the hardships she and her sisters face when their father decides to move the family to California in search of gold. (Rev: BL 9/1/01; HBG 10/01; SLJ 7/01)

9658 Hahn, Mary D. *The Gentleman Outlaw and Me — Eli: A Story of the Old West* (5–8). 1996, Clarion

$15.00 (0-395-73083-X). 224pp. In frontier days, Eliza, masquerading as a boy, travels west in search of her father. (Rev: BCCB 4/96; BL 4/1/96; BR 11–12/96; HB 9–10/96; SLJ 5/96)

9659 Heisel, Sharon E. *Precious Gold, Precious Jade* (5–8). 2000, Holiday House $16.95 (0-8234-1432-9). 185pp. At the end of the Gold Rush in southern Oregon, two sisters create hostilities when they befriend a Chinese family that has moved to town. (Rev: BCCB 4/00; HBG 10/00; SLJ 4/00)

9660 Helldorfer, M. C. *Hog Music* (K–4). Illus. by S. D. Schindler. 2000, Viking $15.99 (0-670-87182-6). Set in the first half of the 19th century, this book chronicles the routes and vehicles involved in transporting a hat from the east to Illinois. (Rev: BCCB 9/00; HBG 10/00; SLJ 5/00)

9661 Henry, Joanne L. *A Clearing in the Forest: A Story About a Real Settler Boy* (3–5). Illus. by Charles Robinson. 1992, Macmillan $14.95 (0-02-743671-3). 44pp. Action highlights this historical novel about growing up in Indianapolis in the 1830s. (Rev: BCCB 6/92; BL 3/1/92; SLJ 3/92)

9662 Hermes, Patricia. *Calling Me Home* (4–7). 1998, Avon $15.00 (0-380-97451-7). 144pp. In the late 1850s, Abbie and her family are living in their sod house in Missouri when a cholera epidemic strikes and her brother dies. (Rev: BL 1/1–15/99; HBG 3/99; SLJ 12/98)

9663 Hermes, Patricia. *A Perfect Place: Joshua's Oregon Trail Diary* (3–5). Series: My America. 2002, Scholastic $10.95 (0-439-19999-9); paper $4.99 (0-439-38900-3). 112pp. In this sequel to *Westward to Home* (2000), 9-year-old Joshua records the difficult conditions in the Willamette Valley as winter closes in. (Rev: BL 1/1–15/03; HBG 3/03; SLJ 11/02)

9664 Hermes, Patricia. *Westward to Home: Joshua's Diary* (3–5). 2001, Scholastic $8.95 (0-439-11209-5). 112pp. The hardships of pioneers are revealed in this novel in journal form about a 9-year-old boy on a wagon train from Missouri to the Oregon Territory. (Rev: BL 2/1/01; HBG 10/01)

9665 Hite, Sid. *Stick and Whittle* (5–8). 2000, Scholastic paper $16.95 (0-439-09828-9). 208pp. At the end of the Civil War, two young men, who adopt the nicknames Stick and Whittle, travel together in Comanche Territory and encounter kidnapping, romance, Indians, and a tornado. (Rev: BCCB 10/00; BL 11/1/00; HB 1–2/01; HBG 3/01; SLJ 9/00)

9666 Hoff, Carol. *Johnny Texas* (4–6). Illus. by Bob Meyers. 1992, Hendrick-Long paper $13.95 (0-937460-81-8). 160pp. Texas history is interwoven into this story of a pioneer German family. A reissue.

9667 Holland, Isabelle. *The Journey Home* (4–6). 1990, Scholastic $13.95 (0-590-43110-2). 192pp. Two orphaned girls start life anew in the second half of the 19th century when they are adopted by a couple in Kansas. (Rev: BCCB 12/90; SLJ 12/90)

9668 Holland, Isabelle. *The Promised Land* (5–8). 1996, Scholastic paper $15.95 (0-590-47176-7). Orphaned Maggie and Annie, who have been happi-

ly living with the Russell family on the Kansas frontier for three years, are visited by an uncle who wants them to come home with him to Catholicism and their Irish heritage in New York City. A sequel to *The Journey Home*. (Rev: BL 4/15/96; SLJ 8/96)

9669 Holling, Holling C. *Tree in the Trail* (4–7). Illus. by author. 1942, Houghton Mifflin $20.00 (0-395-18228-X); paper $11.95 (0-395-54534-X). 64pp. The history of the Santa Fe Trail, described through the life of a cottonwood tree, a 200-year-old landmark to travelers and a symbol of peace to the Indians.

9670 Holm, Jennifer L. *Boston Jane: An Adventure* (5–8). 2001, HarperCollins LB $17.89 (0-06-028739-X). 288pp. A well-bred young woman faces hardships as she searches the 19th-century Washington Territory for her lost fiancé. (Rev: BL 9/1/01; HB 9–10/01; HBG 3/02; SLJ 8/01)

9671 Holm, Jennifer L. *Boston Jane: The Claim* (5–8). 2004, HarperCollins $15.99 (0-06-029045-5). 240pp. In the third installment in Jane's story, an old rival named Sally and a former suitor cause difficulties for Jane. (Rev: BL 3/1/04; SLJ 5/04)

9672 Hooks, William H. *Pioneer Cat* (2–4). Illus. by Charles Robinson. 1988, Random paper $3.99 (0-394-82038-X). 64pp. Kate smuggles a cat aboard the prairie schooner as the family heads west on the Oregon Trail. (Rev: BCCB 12/88; BL 1/15/89; SLJ 3/89)

9673 Hopkinson, Deborah. *Adventure in Gold Town* (3–5). Illus. by Bill Farnsworth. 2004, Simon & Schuster LB $11.89 (0-689-86036-6); paper $3.99 (0-689-86035-8). 84pp. The final installment in the trilogy portraying life during the Alaska Gold Rush, in which 11-year-old Davey continues to search for his uncle, sells sourdough pancakes, and starts a dog pound. (Rev: SLJ 4/05)

9674 Hopkinson, Deborah. *Cabin in the Snow* (2–4). Series: Prairie Skies. 2002, Simon & Schuster LB $11.89 (0-689-84352-6); paper $3.99 (0-689-84351-8). 80pp. Charlie must care for his pregnant mother while his father is away in this story set in Kansas during the free-state movement. (Rev: BL 12/15/02; HBG 3/03; SLJ 1/03)

9675 Hopkinson, Deborah. *Our Kansas Home* (3–5). Illus. by Patrick Faricy. Series: Prairie Skies. 2003, Simon & Schuster paper $3.99 (0-689-84353-4). 80pp. In this final volume in the trilogy, Charlie and his father tangle with pro-slavery ruffians and Charlie helps a runaway slave. (Rev: BL 3/1/03; HBG 10/03; SLJ 3/03)

9676 Hopkinson, Deborah. *A Packet of Seeds* (PS–2). Illus. by Bethanne Andersen. 2004, Greenwillow LB $16.89 (0-06-009090-1). 32pp. Life on the prairie has been especially hard on Annie's mother, who desperately misses her home back east; to lift her mother's spirits, Annie plants a flower garden. (Rev: BL 5/15/04; SLJ 4/04)

9677 Hopkinson, Deborah. *Pioneer Summer* (2–4). Illus. by Patrick Faricy. Series: Prairie Skies. 2002, Simon & Schuster LB $15.00 (0-689-84350-X); paper $3.99 (0-689-84349-6). 64pp. Charlie Keller, his family, and other abolitionists travel to Kansas to prevent it from becoming a slave-holding state in this rich historical novel. (Rev: BL 5/1/02; HBG 10/02; SLJ 10/02)

9678 Hopkinson, Deborah. *Sailing for Gold* (2–4). Illus. by Bill Farnsworth. Series: Ready-for-Chapters. 2004, Simon & Schuster LB $11.89 (0-689-86032-3); paper $3.99 (0-689-86031-5). 64pp. The first installment in an exciting and information-packed trilogy about orphan David Hill, 11, who sets off from Seattle for the Klondike in search of his uncle. (Rev: BL 1/1–15/04; SLJ 7/04)

9679 Hurst, Carol Otis. *In Plain Sight* (4–6). 2002, Houghton Mifflin $15.00 (0-618-19699-4). 160pp. Sarah's father leaves the family in Massachusetts as he sets off to find gold in the West, and Sarah must take on many responsibilities to help her mother. (Rev: BCCB 3/02; BL 3/1/02; HB 5–6/02; HBG 10/02; SLJ 3/02)

9680 Karr, Katherine. *Exiled: Memoirs of a Camel* (4–8). 2004, Marshall Cavendish $15.95 (0-7614-5164-1). 240pp. This fascinating story of the U.S. Camel Corps is told from the viewpoint of Ali, an Egyptian camel drafted for service in this shortlived branch of the United States Army. (Rev: BL 5/1/04; SLJ 5/04)

9681 Karr, Kathleen. *Oregon Sweet Oregon* (5–8). Series: Petticoat Party. 1997, HarperCollins LB $14.89 (0-06-027234-1). This novel, set in Oregon City, Oregon, from 1846 through 1848, recounts the adventures of 13-year-old Phoebe Brown and her family when they stake a land claim along the Willamette River. (Rev: BL 7/97; SLJ 7/98)

9682 Karwoski, Gail L. *Seaman: The Dog Who Explored the West with Lewis and Clark* (4–8). 1999, Peachtree paper $8.95 (1-56145-190-8). This historical novel dramatizes the story of Seaman, the Newfoundland dog that accompanied Lewis and Clark on their expedition. (Rev: BL 8/99; BR 9–10/99; HBG 10/03; SLJ 10/99)

9683 Kent, Peter. *Quest for the West: In Search of Gold* (3–6). Illus. 1997, Millbrook LB $21.40 (0-7613-0302-2). 32pp. The Hornik family leave their Czech homeland in 1849 to find a new life in the United States in this novel with excellent pen-and-ink and watercolor illustrations. (Rev: BL 12/1/97; SLJ 6/98)

9684 Kerr, Rita. *Texas Footprints* (4–7). Illus. 1988, Eakin $13.95 (0-89015-676-X). 80pp. A tale of the author's great-great-grandparents who went to Texas in 1823. (Rev: BL 3/1/89)

9685 Kimmel, E. Cody. *The Adventures of Young Buffalo Bill: In the Eye of the Storm* (3–7). Series: Adventures of Young Buffalo Bill. 2003, Harper-Collins LB $16.89 (0-06-029116-8). 144pp. At the age of nine, young Bill must look after the Kansas homestead in his father's absence and feels resentment against these heavy duties. (Rev: BL 1/1–15/03; HBG 10/03; SLJ 2/03)

9686 Kimmel, E. Cody. *West on the Wagon Train* (3–7). Illus. by Scott Snow. Series: Adventures of Young Buffalo Bill. 2003, HarperCollins LB $16.89 (0-06-029114-1). 148pp. After the death of his father, a young Bill Cody is hired to help on a wagon train headed west and begins a friendship with the legendary Wild Bill Hickock. (Rev: HBG 10/03; SLJ 9/03)

9687 Kirkpatrick, Katherine. *The Voyage of the Continental* (5–8). 2002, Holiday House $16.95 (0-8234-1580-5). 297pp. A 17-year-old girl relates in her diary the events of her journey by ship from New England to Seattle in 1866, which involve her in adventure, mystery, and romance. (Rev: BL 12/15/02; HBG 3/03; SLJ 11/02)

9688 Kramer, Sydelle. *Wagon Train* (2–4). Illus. by Deborah Kogan Ray. Series: All Aboard Reading. 1997, Penguin Putnam paper $3.99 (0-448-41334-5). 48pp. This easy-to-read book follows a family as it crosses the United States wagon in 1848. (Rev: BL 2/1/98)

9689 Kurtz, Jane. *I'm Sorry, Almira Ann* (3–5). Illus. 1999, Holt $15.95 (0-8050-6094-4). 119pp. Eight-year-old Sarah and her friend Almira Ann find adventure when their families go west on the Oregon Trail. (Rev: BCCB 12/99; BL 11/15/99; HB 3–4/00; HBG 3/00; SLJ 11/99)

9690 Laurgaard, Rachel K. *Patty Reed's Doll: The Story of the Donner Party* (3–6). Illus. by Elizabeth Michaels. 1989, Tomato Enterprises paper $7.95 (0-9617357-2-4). 144pp. A fantasy seen through the eyes of a doll about a survivor of the Donner Party. A reissue. (Rev: SLJ 11/89)

9691 Lawlor, Laurie. *Addie Across the Prairie* (3–5). Illus. 1986, Whitman LB $13.95 (0-8075-0165-4); Pocket paper $3.99 (0-671-70147-9). 128pp. Nine-year-old Addie learns about sod houses and curious Indians as her family travels cross-country to the Dakota Territory. (Rev: BL 8/86; SLJ 10/86)

9692 Lawlor, Laurie. *Gold in the Hills* (4–6). 1995, Walker $15.95 (0-8027-8371-6). 152pp. When their father sets out to find gold, Hattie and her brother must stay with bitter, tyrannical cousin Tirzah in this novel set in Colorado during frontier days. (Rev: BCCB 7–8/95; BL 6/1–15/95; SLJ 8/95)

9693 Lawlor, Laurie. *The School at Crooked Creek* (2–5). Illus. by Ronald Himler. 2004, Holiday House $15.95 (0-8234-1812-X). 83pp. Lawlor paints an engaging portrait of life on the frontier in this story of 6-year-old Beansie, who lives with his family in a one-room cabin in 1820s Indiana and hates the idea of going to school. (Rev: BL 4/15/04)

9694 Lawlor, Laurie. *West Along the Wagon Road, 1852* (4–6). Series: American Sisters. 1998, Pocket $9.00 (0-671-01551-6). 183pp. Eleven-year-old Harriet Scott, along with her parents and her eight siblings, endures hardships, hunger, and threats of attack in this story about a family on the Oregon Trail. (Rev: BL 12/1/98; HBG 10/99; SLJ 12/98)

9695 Lawson, Julie. *Destination Gold!* (5–8). 2001, Orca $16.95 (1-55143-155-6). 210pp. Ned, Catherine, and Sarah are all on their way to the Klondike in 1897, spurred by different motivations, but their stories all come together in an exciting climax, made more realistic by the background information and maps provided. (Rev: BCCB 4/01; BL 2/15/01; HBG 10/01; SLJ 7/01)

9696 Leland, Dorothy K. *Sallie Fox: The Story of a Pioneer Girl* (4–6). 1995, Tomato Enterprises paper $8.95 (0-9617357-6-7). 115pp. A fictionalized account of the trek of 12-year-old Sallie Fox by wagon train with her family from Iowa to California in the mid 1800s. (Rev: SLJ 2/96)

9697 Levine, Ellen. *The Journal of Jedediah Barstow: An Emigrant on the Oregon Trail* (4–7). Series: My Name Is America. 2002, Scholastic $10.95 (0-439-06310-8). 176pp. Jedediah continues his mother's journal about their experiences on the Oregon Trail after she and the rest of his family are drowned while crossing a river. (Rev: BL 2/15/03; HBG 10/03; SLJ 11/02)

9698 Levitin, Sonia. *Clem's Chances* (4–7). 2001, Scholastic paper $17.95 (0-439-29314-6). 200pp. Fourteen-year-old Clem becomes acquainted with the hardships and rewards of frontier life when he travels to California to find his father in 1860. (Rev: BL 9/15/01; HB 11–12/01; HBG 3/02; SLJ 10/01)

9699 Love, D. Anne. *Bess's Log Cabin Quilt* (2–5). Illus. by Ronald Himler. 1995, Holiday House $15.95 (0-8234-1178-8). 72pp. In frontier Oregon, Bess hopes that by winning a quilt contest she can help ease her family's financial problems. (Rev: BCCB 6/95; BL 2/15/95; SLJ 6/95)

9700 Luger, Harriett M. *The Last Stronghold: A Story of the Modoc Indian War, 1872–1873* (5–8). 1995, Linnet paper $17.50 (0-208-02403-4). The Modoc Indian War of 1872–73 is re-created in this story involving three young people: Charka, a Modoc youth; Ned, a frontier boy; and Yankel, a Russian Jew who has been tricked into joining the army. (Rev:)

9701 MacBride, Roger L. *In the Land of the Big Red Apple* (3–7). Illus. by David Gilleece. 1995, HarperCollins LB $15.89 (0-06-024964-1). 352pp. In the mid-1890s, the farm at Rocky Ridge, where Rose Wilder Lane is growing up, gradually prospers. (Rev: BL 5/15/95; SLJ 9/95)

9702 MacBride, Roger L. *Little Farm in the Ozarks* (3–6). Illus. 1994, HarperCollins paper $5.95 (0-06-440510-9). 304pp. Based on the journals of Rose Wilder Lane, this novel tells about the Wilder family's first spring and summer in Mansfield, Missouri. (Rev: BL 5/1/94)

9703 MacBride, Roger L. *Little House on Rocky Edge* (3–7). Illus. by David Gilleece. 1993, HarperCollins paper $4.95 (0-06-440478-1). 304pp. This reworking of Laura Ingalls Wilder's material tells the story from Rose's perspective of the Wilder family's move from South Dakota to Missouri. This is the first part of a projected five-part series. (Rev: BL 6/1–15/93)

9704 MacBride, Roger L. *New Dawn on Rocky Ridge* (4–7). Illus. Series: Rocky Ridge. 1997, HarperCollins $15.95 (0-06-024971-4); paper $6.99 (0-06-440581-8). 320pp. This part of the Wilder family story covers 1900–1903 and focuses on Rose's difficult early teen years. (Rev: BL 11/1/97; HBG 3/98; SLJ 2/98)

9705 McCaughrean, Geraldine. *Stop the Train!* (5–8). 2003, HarperCollins LB $16.89 (0-06-

050750-0). 304pp. The challenges facing early homesteaders are brought to life in this story of a family that boards a train to nowhere in 1893. (Rev: BL 8/03*; HB 7–8/03; HBG 10/03; SLJ 8/03*)

9706 McDonald, Brix. *Riding on the Wind* (5–10). 1998, Avenue paper $5.95 (0-9661306-0-X). 243pp. In frontier Wyoming during the early 1860s, 15-year-old Carrie Sutton is determined to become a rider in the Pony Express after her family's ranch has been chosen as a relay station. (Rev: SLJ 1/99)

9707 McDonald, Megan. *All the Stars in the Sky: The Santa Fe Trail Diary of Florrie Mack Ryder* (4–7). Series: Dear America. 2003, Scholastic $10.95 (0-439-16963-1). 188pp. Florrie and her family make a long and difficult journey from Missouri to Santa Fe in 1848. (Rev: HBG 4/04; SLJ 11/03)

9708 McKissack, Patricia. *Run Away Home* (4–7). 1997, Scholastic paper $14.95 (0-590-46751-4). 176pp. In 1888 rural Alabama, a young African American girl helps shelter a fugitive Apache boy. (Rev: BL 10/1/97; HB 11–12/97; HBG 3/98; SLJ 11/97)

9709 MacLachlan, Patricia. *Sarah, Plain and Tall* (3–5). Illus. by Marcia Sewall. 1985, HarperCollins LB $14.89 (0-06-024102-0); paper $4.95 (0-06-440205-3). 64pp. Two children wait on the prairie for the arrival of their new stepmother, who has answered their father's ad for a wife. Newbery Medal winner, 1986. (Rev: BCCB 5/85; BL 5/1/89; SLJ 5/85)

9710 McMullan, Kate. *As Far as I Can See: Meg's Prairie Diary* (2–4). Series: My America. 2002, Scholastic $10.95 (0-439-42517-4); paper $4.99 (0-439-40321-9). 112pp. City girl Meg describes her new life in Kansas, where she and her brother have been sent to avoid a cholera epidemic in 1856, and writes about the help she gives to a runaway slave. (Rev: BL 10/1/02; HBG 3/03; SLJ 8/02)

9711 McMullan, Kate. *A Fine Start: Meg's Prairie Diary* (4–6). Series: My America. 2003, Scholastic LB $12.95 (0-439-37061-2); paper $4.99 (0-439-37062-0). 106pp. In this fictional diary, 9-year-old Meg recounts the hardships her family endures on the prairies of the Kansas Territory. (Rev: HBG 4/04; SLJ 1/04)

9712 McMullan, Kate. *My Travels with Capts. Lewis and Clark by George Shannon* (5–9). Illus. by Adrienne Yorinks. 2004, HarperCollins LB $16.89 (0-06-008100-7). 272pp. This well-researched fictional diary of a teenager traveling on the great expedition gives readers a good sense of life at the time and an insight into the key characters. (Rev: BCCB 10/04; BL 10/15/04; HB 11–12/04; SLJ 9/04)

9713 Mercati, Cynthia. *Wagons Ho! A Diary of the Oregon Trail* (3–5). Illus. 2000, Perfection Learning $13.95 (0-7807-9011-1). 56pp. A simple read in diary form about young Lisa and her adventures in a Conestoga wagon heading west with her family in 1849. (Rev: BL 10/15/00)

9714 Miller, Robert H. *A Pony for Jeremiah* (3–6). Illus. by Nneka Bennett. 1996, Silver Burdett LB $22.00 (0-382-39459-3); paper $4.95 (0-382-39460-

7). 64pp. A historial novel about a runaway slave and his family who settle in Nebraska. (Rev: BL 2/15/97; SLJ 3/97)

9715 Milligan, Bryce. *With the Wind, Kevin Dolan: A Novel of Ireland and Texas* (5–7). Illus. 1987, Corona paper $7.95 (0-931722-45-4). 194pp. The story of Kevin and Tom, brothers who leave the famine in Ireland in the 1830s and head for America. (Rev: BL 8/87; SLJ 9/87)

9716 Moeri, Louise. *Save Queen of Sheba* (5–7). 1990, Avon paper $3.50 (0-380-71154-0). 112pp. Young David survives a wagon train massacre and must take care of his young sister.

9717 Moss, Marissa. *Rachel's Journal* (3–6). Illus. 1998, Harcourt $15.00 (0-15-201806-9). 48pp. In journal format, this is the record of Rachel's travels west to California in 1850, with descriptions of crossing the Missouri River, tramping through deserts, and the birth of a sister en route. (Rev: BL 10/1/98; HBG 3/99; SLJ 9/98)

9718 Moss, Marissa. *True Heart* (2–4). Illus. 1999, Harcourt $16.00 (0-15-201344-X). 32pp. When the train's engineer is wounded by bandits, Bee gets her chance to take over in this tale set in the Wild West during the 1890s. (Rev: BCCB 4/99; BL 4/1/99; HBG 10/99; SLJ 4/99)

9719 Murphy, Jim. *My Face to the Wind: The Diary of Sarah Jane Price, a Prairie Teacher* (5–8). Series: Dear America. 2001, Scholastic paper $10.95 (0-590-43810-7). 192pp. To avoid being sent to an orphanage, 12-year-old Jessica pretends to be 16 and takes over her father's job as teacher in a 19th-century Nebraska town. (Rev: BL 12/1/01; HBG 3/02; SLJ 12/01)

9720 Murphy, Jim. *West to a Land of Plenty: The Diary of Teresa Angelino Viscardi, New York to Idaho Territory, 1883* (4–8). Series: Dear America. 1998, Scholastic paper $10.95 (0-590-73888-7). Written in diary format, this historical novel tells about Italian American Teresa Viscardi and her family as they travel west to relocate in the Idaho Territory. (Rev: BCCB 3/98; BL 4/1/98; BR 9–10/98; HBG 9/98; SLJ 4/98)

9721 Myers, Laurie. *Lewis and Clark and Me: A Dog's Tale* (3–6). Illus. by Michael Dooling. 2002, Holt $16.95 (0-8050-6368-4). 64pp. The Lewis and Clark expedition told from the point of view of Seaman, Lewis's Newfoundland dog, with excerpts from Lewis's journal, illustrations and a map of the route. (Rev: BL 9/1/02; HB 9–10/02; HBG 3/03; SLJ 9/02)

9722 Myers, Walter Dean. *The Journal of Joshua Loper: A Black Cowboy* (5–8). 1999, Scholastic paper $10.95 (0-590-02691-7). In this fictionalized biography, set in 1871, 16-year-old Joshua Loper learns that age, race, and background are unimportant when you are on a cattle drive on the Chisholm Trail. (Rev: BL 2/15/99; HBG 9/99; SLJ 4/99)

9723 Nixon, Joan Lowery. *In the Face of Danger* (5–8). 1996, Bantam paper $4.99 (0-440-22705-4). Megan fears she will bring bad luck to her adoptive family in this story set in the prairies of Kansas.

This is the third part of the Orphan Train Quartet. (Rev: BR 11–12/88; SLJ 12/88)

9724 Oatman, Eric. *Cowboys on the Western Trail: The Cattle Drive Adventures of Josh McNabb and Davy Bartlett* (4–7). Illus. Series: I Am America. 2004, National Geographic paper $6.99 (0-7922-6553-X). 40pp. The excitement of a cattle drive is shown in the journals and letters of two young teen boys in this blend of fact and fiction set in 1887 and presented in an appealing magazine format. (Rev: BL 5/15/04)

9725 O'Dell, Scott. *Streams to the River, River to the Sea: A Novel of Sacagawea* (5–9). 1986, Houghton Mifflin $16.00 (0-395-40430-4); Fawcett paper $5.99 (0-449-70244-8). 191pp. A fictionalized portrait of the real-life Indian woman who traveled west with Lewis and Clark on their famous journey. (Rev: BL 3/15/86; BR 9–10/86; HB 9–10/86; SLJ 5/86)

9726 Pearsall, Shelley. *Crooked River* (4–6). 2005, Knopf LB $17.99 (0-375-92389-6). 256pp. In early-19th-century Ohio, 13-year-old Rebecca learns about truth and justice as she watches the plight of a Native American accused of killing a trapper. (Rev: BL 5/15/05)

9727 Philbrick, Rodman. *The Journal of Douglas Allen Deeds: The Donner Party Expedition* (5–7). Series: My Name Is America. 2001, Scholastic paper $10.95 (0-439-21600-1). 160pp. A fictional account of the Donner Party's hardships as written in a 15-year-old orphaned boy's journal. (Rev: BL 1/1–15/02; HBG 3/02; SLJ 12/01)

9728 Pryor, Bonnie. *Luke: 1849 — On the Golden Trail* (3–6). Illus. 1999, Morrow $15.00 (0-688-15670-3). 160pp. Luke's pioneer family has such misfortune farming that the boy decides to leave and accompany his wealthy uncle to Boston. (Rev: BL 8/99; HBG 10/99; SLJ 8/99)

9729 Reichart, George. *A Bag of Lucky Rice* (4–6). Illus. by Mark Mitchell. 2002, Godine $17.95 (1-56792-166-3). 158pp. This humorous Old West mystery about treasure buried in the desert skillfully entwines facts about the times. (Rev: BL 10/15/02; HBG 10/03; SLJ 2/03)

9730 Reiss, Kathryn. *Riddle of the Prairie Bride* (5–7). Series: History Mystery. 2001, Pleasant Co. paper $5.95 (1-584-85308-5). 170pp. Ida Kate discovers that her father's mail-order bride is actually an impostor. (Rev: BL 4/1/01; HBG 3/02; SLJ 5/01)

9731 Rinaldi, Ann. *The Second Bend in the River* (5–9). 1997, Scholastic paper $15.95 (0-590-74258-2). In Ohio in 1798, 7-year-old Rebecca begins a long-lasting friendship with the Shawnee chief Tecumseh that eventually leads to a marriage proposal. (Rev: BCCB 3/97; BL 2/15/97; BR 5–6/97; HBG 3/98; SLJ 6/97)

9732 Ryan, Pam M. *Riding Freedom* (3–6). Illus. 1998, Scholastic $15.95 (0-590-95766-X). 144pp. Based on fact, this is the story of a girl who lived her life as a man in mid-19th-century America. (Rev: BCCB 5/98; BL 1/1–15/98; HBG 10/98; SLJ 3/98)

9733 Rylant, Cynthia. *Old Town in the Green Groves: Laura Ingalls Wilder's Last Little House Years* (3–7). Illus. by Jim LaMarche. 2002, Harper-Collins $15.95 (0-06-029562-7). 176pp. Using notes left by Wilder, Cynthia Rylant has created a novel that fills the gaps found in the Little House series. (Rev: BL 5/1/02; HBG 10/02; SLJ 4/02)

9734 Schultz, Jan Neubert. *Horse Sense* (5–7). 2001, Carolrhoda LB $19.15 (1-57505-998-3); paper $6.95 (1-57505-999-1). 180pp. Fourteen-year-old Will and his father do not get along, but they join a posse tracking dangerous outlaws in this adventure based on a true story. (Rev: BL 8/01; HBG 3/02)

9735 Seeley, Debra. *Grasslands* (5–8). 2002, Holiday House $16.95 (0-8234-1731-X). 128pp. The hard life on the prairie disappoints a 13-year-old newcomer from Virginia until he has the chance to ride as a cowboy in this novel set in the late 19th century. (Rev: BL 11/1/02; HBG 3/03; SLJ 1/03*)

9736 Shaw, Janet. *Happy Birthday Kirsten!* (3–5). Illus. 1987, Pleasant Co. $12.95 (0-937295-88-4); paper $5.95 (0-937295-33-7). 72pp. It is 1854 in Minnesota and Kirsten looks forward to the gift of a day off from household chores. Also use: *Changes for Kirsten; Kirsten Saves the Day* (both 1988). (Rev: BL 4/1/88)

9737 Shaw, Janet. *Kirsten Learns a Lesson: A School Story* (3–5). Illus. 1986, Pleasant Co. LB $12.95 (0-937295-82-5); paper $5.95 (0-937295-10-8). 72pp. Kirsten, a young immigrant girl, lives with her Swedish family in 1854 Minnesota. Others in this series are: *Kirsten's Surprise: A Christmas Story; Meet Kirsten: An American Girl* (both 1986). (Rev: BL 12/1/86)

9738 Smith, Roland. *The Captain's Dog: My Journey with the Lewis and Clark Tribe* (5–8). 1999, Harcourt $17.00 (0-15-201989-8). 208pp. This is the story of the Lewis and Clark expedition as experienced by the Newfoundland dog that accompanied the two explorers. (Rev: BL 10/15/99; HBG 3/00; SLJ 11/99)

9739 Stevens, Carla. *Trouble for Lucy* (4–6). Illus. by Ronald Himler. 1979, Houghton Mifflin paper $5.95 (0-89919-523-7). 80pp. Lucy's pup Finn causes trouble during a wagon trip to the Oregon Territory.

9740 Thomas, Joyce C. *I Have Heard of a Land* (3–6). Illus. by Floyd Cooper. 1998, HarperCollins LB $14.89 (0-06-023478-4). 32pp. This tribute to the pioneer spirit tells, through the eyes of a black woman, what it was like to come to the untamed frontier, build a home, and put down roots. (Rev: BCCB 6/98; BL 2/15/98*; HBG 10/98; SLJ 7/98)

9741 Tripp, Valerie. *Happy Birthday, Josefina! A Springtime Story* (3–5). Series: American Girls. 1998, Pleasant Co. $12.99 (1-56247-588-6); paper $5.95 (1-56247-587-8). 68pp. In the New Mexico of 1824, Josefina discovers she can become a healer after she cures a friend bitten by a rattlesnake. (Rev: BL 8/98; HBG 3/99)

9742 Tripp, Valerie. *Josefina Saves the Day: A Summer Story* (3–5). Illus. Series: American Girls. 1998, Pleasant Co. $12.95 (1-56247-590-8); paper $5.95

(1-56247-589-4). 68pp. A heavily illustrated novel, set in the New Mexico of 1824, in which young Josefina's father must decide whether or not to trust an American trader. (Rev: BL 8/98; HBG 3/99)

9743 Tripp, Valerie. *Meet Josefina: An American Girl* (3–5). Illus. Series: American Girls. 1997, Pleasant Co. paper $5.95 (1-56247-515-0). 85pp. In this story set in 1824 on a Mexican ranch in what is now New Mexico, the young heroine helps manage the ranch after her mother's death. Also use *Josefina Learns a Lesson: A School Story* (1997). (Rev: BL 10/1/97; HBG 3/98; SLJ 12/97)

9744 Welch, Catherine A. *Clouds of Terror* (2–4). Illus. by Laurie K. Johnson. 1994, Carolrhoda LB $21.27 (0-87614-771-6). 48pp. The harm caused by hordes of grasshoppers is depicted in this story set on a Minnesota farm during the 1870s. (Rev: BL 9/15/94; SLJ 8/94)

9745 Whelan, Gloria. *Miranda's Last Stand* (4–7). 1999, HarperCollins LB $14.89 (0-06-028252-5). 128pp. After her husband was killed at Little Big Horn, Miranda's mother can't bear to be around Indians, including Sitting Bull, who works with her at Buffalo Bill's Wild West Show. (Rev: BL 11/1/99; HBG 3/00; SLJ 11/99)

9746 Whelan, Gloria. *Next Spring an Oriole* (2–4). Illus. 1987, Random LB $6.99 (0-394-99125-7); paper $3.99 (0-394-89125-2). 64pp. The story of 10-year-old Libby who journeys to Michigan from Virginia in a covered wagon with her family in 1837. (Rev: BCCB 10/87; BL 10/1/87)

9747 Whelan, Gloria. *Return to the Island* (4–7). 2000, HarperCollins LB $15.89 (0-06-028254-1). 192pp. In the early 19th century on Mackinac Island, Mary must decide between two men who love her: White Hawk, an orphan raised by a white family, and James, an English painter. (Rev: BL 1/1–15/01; HBG 3/01; SLJ 12/00)

9748 Wilder, Laura Ingalls. *The Long Winter* (5–8). Illus. 1953, HarperCollins LB $17.89 (0-06-026461-6). Number six in the Little House books. In this one, the Ingalls face a terrible winter with only seed grain for food.

9749 Wilkes, Maria D. *Little Clearing in the Woods* (3–6). Illus. by Dan Andreasen. Series: The Caroline Years. 1998, HarperCollins LB $15.89 (0-06-026998-7). 315pp. Caroline Quiner (the mother of Laura Ingalls Wilder) and her family move to a small cabin in the woods, where her widowed mother takes a job cooking for neighborhood laborers. (Rev: HBG 10/98; SLJ 10/98)

9750 Wilkes, Maria D. *Little House in Brookfield* (3–6). Illus. by Dan Andreasen. Series: The Brookfield Years. 1996, HarperCollins paper $4.95 (0-06-440610-5). 298pp. This spinoff from the *Little House* books tells of the childhood in Brookfield, Wisconsin, of Caroline Quiner, who much later would become the mother of Laura Ingalls Wilder. (Rev: SLJ 8/96)

9751 Wills, Patricia. *Danger Along the Ohio* (4–7). 1997, Clarion $15.00 (0-395-77044-0). 192pp. This action-packed historical novel set in Ohio in 1795 tells how Amos and his younger brother and sister are captured by Indians. (Rev: BCCB 5/97; BL 5/1/97; SLJ 5/97)

9752 Wilson, Laura. *How I Survived the Oregon Trail: The Journal of Jesse Adams* (3–6). Series: Time Travelers. 1999, Morrow paper $9.95 (0-688-17276-8). 38pp. Beginning on April 29, 1852, this fictionalized diary account of a 10-year-old's journey with his family from Iowa to Oregon contains excellent illustrations and a fold-out map. (Rev: SLJ 2/00)

9753 Wisler, G. Clifton. *All for Texas: A Story of Texas Liberation* (4–8). 2000, Jamestown paper $5.95 (0-8092-0629-3). 140pp. A thirteen-year-old boy tells about moving west with his family in 1838 to Texas, where his father has been promised land if he will fight against Mexico. (Rev: BCCB 7–8/00; SLJ 8/00)

9754 Yep, Laurence. *The Journal of Wong Ming-Chung* (4–7). Illus. 2000, Scholastic paper $10.95 (0-590-38607-7). 224pp. Told in diary format beginning in October 1851, this is the story of a Chinese boy nicknamed Runt who travels from his native country to join an uncle in the gold mining fields of America. (Rev: BL 4/1/00; HBG 10/00; SLJ 4/00)

9755 Yep, Laurence. *When the Circus Came to Town* (3–5). Illus. by Suling Wang. 2001, HarperCollins LB $14.89 (0-06-029326-8). 128pp. After her face is scarred by smallpox, 10-year-old Ursula refuses to leave her home at a Montana stagecoach station and intervention by a circus arranged by the family's Chinese cook is required to bring her out of her shell. (Rev: BCCB 2/02; BL 12/15/01; HBG 10/02; SLJ 12/01)

THE CIVIL WAR

9756 Bearden, Romare. *Li'l Dan, the Drummer Boy: A Civil War Story* (K–3). Illus. by author. 2003, Simon & Schuster $18.95 (0-689-86237-7). This recently discovered book by the respected African American artist tells the story of a slave boy who uses his skill with his drum to save a group of black Union soldiers from an impending attack. (Rev: HB 9–10/03; HBG 4/04; SLJ 10/03)

9757 Beatty, Patricia. *Who Comes with Cannons?* (5–7). 1992, Morrow $15.99 (0-688-11028-2). 192pp. The Civil War brings danger to Truth Hopkins and her Quaker family because they are pacifists. (Rev: BCCB 10/92; BL 1/1/93; HB 1–2/93; SLJ 10/92)

9758 Brill, Marlene T. *Diary of a Drummer Boy* (4–7). 1998, Millbrook LB $23.90 (0-7613-0118-6). 48pp. Using a diary format, this novel tells of a 12-year-old's experiences as a drummer in the Union Army during the Civil War. (Rev: BL 3/1/98; HBG 10/98; SLJ 5/98)

9759 Bunting, Eve. *The Blue and the Gray* (3–5). Illus. by Ned Bittinger. 1996, Scholastic $14.95 (0-590-60197-0). 32pp. Using free verse, the author recreates a Civil War battle and points out what we have learned from this terrible conflict. (Rev: BCCB 2/97; BL 11/15/96; SLJ 12/96)

9760 Crist-Evans, Craig. *Moon over Tennessee: A Boy's Civil War Journal* (4–7). 1999, Houghton Mifflin $15.00 (0-395-91208-3). 64pp. In free-verse diary entries, 13-year-old Crist-Evans reports on the Civil War from his vantage point in a camp behind the front lines. (Rev: BCCB 6/99; BL 5/15/99; HBG 10/99; SLJ 8/99)

9761 Denslow, Sharon Phillips. *All Their Names Were Courage* (4–6). 2003, HarperCollins LB $16.89 (0-06-623810-2). 144pp. Eleven-year-old Sallie Burd writes to her soldier brother about her quest to learn about the horses of Union and Confederate generals. (Rev: BL 8/03; HBG 4/04; SLJ 10/03)

9762 Donahue, John. *An Island Far from Home* (4–7). 1994, Carolrhoda LB $19.15 (0-87614-859-3). 180pp. Joshua, a Union supporter, forms an unusual friendship through corresponding with a young Southern soldier who is a prisoner of war. (Rev: BCCB 2/95; BL 2/15/95; SLJ 2/95)

9763 Ernst, Kathleen. *Retreat from Gettysburg* (5–8). Illus. 2000, White Mane LB $17.95 (1-57249-187-6). 142pp. When a doctor orders 14-year-old Chig and his mother to care for a wounded Confederate soldier, the boy finds it hard to be kind to a man who belongs to the side that killed his father and brothers. (Rev: BL 9/15/00; HBG 10/01; SLJ 12/00)

9764 Garrity, Jennifer Johnson. *The Bushwhacker: A Civil War Adventure* (5–8). Illus. by Paul Bachem. 1999, Peachtree paper $8.95 (1-56145-201-7). 196pp. The clash of divided loyalties is the main conflict in this story of a boy torn between his Unionist feelings and the friendship he feels towards his protector, a Confederate sympathizer. (Rev: SLJ 4/00)

9765 Goodman, Susan E. *Robert Henry Hendershot* (1–4). Illus. by Doris Ettlinger. Series: Brave Kids. 2003, Simon & Schuster LB $11.89 (0-689-84981-8); paper $3.99 (0-689-84980-X). 56pp. A 12-year-old drummer boy becomes a hero after capturing a Confederate soldier in this historical novel based on a true story and suitable for beginning chapter-book readers. (Rev: BL 5/15/03; HBG 10/03; SLJ 10/03) [973.7]

9766 Hahn, Mary D. *Promises to the Dead* (4–6). 2000, Clarion $15.00 (0-395-96394-X). 202pp. When 12-year-old Jesse sets out to travel north to Baltimore to take the son of a dead slave to relatives, he doesn't anticipate the outbreak of the Civil War. (Rev: BCCB 5/00; BL 4/1/00; HBG 10/00; SLJ 6/00)

9767 Harness, Cheryl. *Ghosts of the Civil War* (3–5). Illus. by author. 2002, Simon & Schuster $17.00 (0-689-83135-8). 48pp. Lindsey attends a reenactment with her parents and is transported back in time by the ghost of Willie Lincoln in this excellent and attractive introduction to the Civil War. (Rev: BL 1/1–15/02; HBG 10/02; SLJ 1/02)

9768 Hart, Alison. *Fires of Jubilee* (5–7). 2003, Simon & Schuster paper $4.99 (0-689-85528-1). 192pp. Abby, 13, is suddenly a free person when the Civil War ends and finally able to search for her mother, who left long before. (Rev: BL 11/1/03; SLJ 3/04)

9769 Hawk, Fran. *The Story of the H. L. Hunley and Queenie's Coin* (3–5). Illus. by Dan Nance. 2004, Sleeping Bear $16.95 (1-58536-218-2). 40pp. This story of the ill-fated Confederate submarine *H. L. Hunley* focuses on the lucky coin given to its developer by his fiancee. (Rev; BL 1/1–15/05; SLJ 5/05)

9770 Hesse, Karen. *A Light in the Storm: The Civil War Diary of Amelia Martin* (4–7). Series: Dear America. 1999, Scholastic paper $10.95 (0-590-56733-0). 176pp. The story of Amelia Martin, the 15-year-old daughter of a lighthouse keeper in Delaware, and how her family became involved in the oncoming Civil War. (Rev: BL 10/15/99; HBG 3/00; SLJ 11/99)

9771 Hite, Sid. *The Journal of Rufus Rowe: A Witness to the Battle of Fredericksburg* (5–7). Series: My Name Is America. 2003, Scholastic $10.95 (0-439-35364-5). 132pp. The Battle of Fredericksburg takes place under the watchful eye of 16-year-old Rufus, who records moments of compassion as well as horror. (Rev: HBG 4/04; SLJ 11/03)

9772 Hoobler, Thomas, and Dorothy Hoobler. *Sally Bradford: The Story of a Rebel Girl* (4–7). Illus. 1997, Silver Burdett LB $14.95 (0-382-39258-2); paper $4.95 (0-382-39259-0). 128pp. The Civil War changes the lives of Sally Bradford and her family, who operate a farm without slaves in Norfolk, Virginia. (Rev: BL 6/1–15/97; SLJ 8/97)

9773 Hopkinson, Deborah. *Billy and the Rebel* (1–3). Illus. by Brian Floca. Series: Ready-to-Read. 2005, Simon & Schuster $14.95 (0-689-83964-2). 48pp. A young boy and his mother give sanctuary to a Confederate deserter at their farm near Gettysburg in this story based on a real incident. (Rev: BL 2/1/05; SLJ 4/05)

9774 Hunt, Irene. *Across Five Aprils* (6–8). 1993, Silver Burdett paper $5.00 (0-8136-7202-3). 100pp. A young boy's experiences during the Civil War in the backwoods of southern Illinois. One brother joins the Union forces, the other the Confederacy, and the family is divided.

9775 Jones, Elizabeth McDavid. *Watcher in the Piney Woods* (5–7). Illus. by Jean-Paul Tibbles and Greg Dearth. Series: History Mystery. 2000, Pleasant Co. $9.95 (1-58485-091-4); paper $5.95 (1-58485-090-6). 144pp. In southern Virginia during the last year of the Civil War, 12-year-old Cassie sets out to solve the mystery of objects disappearing from her home and farm. (Rev: HBG 10/01; SLJ 1/01)

9776 Kay, Alan N. *Nowhere to Turn* (5–8). Series: Young Heroes of History. 2003, White Mane paper $6.95 (1-57249-297-X). 149pp. In 1862, 12-year-old orphan Thomas — with his dog named Blue — experiences the horrors of war and faces personal challenges. (Rev: SLJ 11/03)

9777 Keehn, Sally M. *Anna Sunday* (4–8). 2002, Penguin Putnam $18.99 (0-399-23875-1). 272pp. In 1863, 12-year-old Anna travels with her younger brother from Pennsylvania to Virginia to find her

wounded father. (Rev: BCCB 9/02; BL 6/1–15/02; HBG 10/02; SLJ 6/02)

9778 Keith, Harold. *Rifles for Watie* (6–8). 1991, HarperCollins LB $15.89 (0-690-04907-2); paper $5.95 (0-06-447030-X). 332pp. Life of a Union soldier and spy fighting the Civil War in the West. Newbery Medal winner, 1958.

9779 Love, D. Anne. *Three Against the Tide* (5–8). 1998, Holiday House $15.95 (0-8234-1400-0). 162pp. In this Civil War novel, 12-year-old Confederate Susanna Simons must care for her two younger brothers when Yankee troops invade South Carolina. (Rev: BL 12/1/98; HBG 10/99; SLJ 1/99)

9780 Lyons, Mary E., and Muriel M. Branch. *Dear Ellen Bee: A Civil War Scrapbook of Two Union Spies* (5–8). Illus. 2000, Atheneum $17.00 (0-689-82379-7). 161pp. Set in Richmond, Virginia, before and during the Civil War, this novel, based on fact, tells how a strong-willed lady and her emancipated slave get involved in a spying adventure. (Rev: BCCB 10/00; BL 11/1/00; HBG 3/01; SLJ 10/00)

9781 McMullan, Margaret. *How I Found the Strong: A Civil War Story* (5–9). 2004, Houghton Mifflin $16.00 (0-618-35008-X). The Civil War changes the way a boy looks at life when it takes away his father and brother and comes close to his Mississippi home. (Rev: BL 2/15/04; SLJ 4/04)

9782 Matas, Carol. *The War Within* (5–8). 2001, Simon & Schuster $16.00 (0-689-82935-3). 151pp. The story of a 13-year-old Jewish southern girl and her family during the Civil War is told through diary entries. (Rev: BL 4/1/01; HBG 10/01; SLJ 6/01)

9783 Murphy, Jim. *The Journal of James Edmond Pease: A Civil War Union Soldier, Virginia, 1863* (5–8). Series: My Name Is America. 1998, Scholastic $9.95 (0-590-43814-X). 173pp. This novel takes the form of a journal kept by a 16-year-old private in the New York Volunteers during the Civil War and tells of his experiences, including the time he was lost behind enemy lines. (Rev: BCCB 11/98; HBG 3/99; SLJ 7/99)

9784 Nixon, Joan Lowery. *Keeping Secrets* (5–8). Series: Orphan Train Adventures. 1996, Demco $11.04 (0-606-08789-3). In Missouri during the Civil War, Peg, 11, unwittingly becomes involved with a Union spy. (Rev: BL 3/1/95; SLJ 3/95)

9785 O'Dell, Scott. *Sing Down the Moon* (5–8). 1970, Houghton Mifflin $17.00 (0-395-10919-1); Dell paper $5.50 (0-440-97975-7). 138pp. The tragic forced march of the Indians to Fort Sumter in 1864, told by a young Navajo girl.

9786 Owens, L. L. *The Code of the Drum* (3–6). Illus. by Margaret Sanfilippo. Series: Cover-to-Cover Books. 2000, Perfection Learning $13.95 (0-7807-9654-3); paper $8.95 (0-7891-5310-6). 54pp. When his father is killed in the Civil War, 12-year-old Jacob McCoy joins his dad's Union regiment as a drummer boy. (Rev: SLJ 12/00)

9787 Patrick, Denise Lewis. *The Longest Ride* (5–7). 1999, Holt $15.95 (0-8050-4715-8). 164pp. This sequel to *The Adventures of Midnight Son* explores slavery and Indian-black relations when a teenaged runaway slave is helped by a band of Arapaho Indians at the time of the Civil War. (Rev: HBG 3/00; SLJ 12/99)

9788 Paulsen, Gary. *Soldier's Heart* (5–8). 1998, Delacorte $15.95 (0-385-32498-7). 144pp. A powerful novel about the agony of the Civil War, based on the real-life experiences of a Union soldier who was only 15 when he went to war. (Rev: BCCB 9/98; BL 6/1–15/98*; HB 11–12/98; HBG 3/99; SLJ 9/98)

9789 Pinkney, Andrea Davis. *Abraham Lincoln: Letters from a Slave Girl* (4–7). Illus. Series: Dear Mr. President. 2001, Winslow $8.95 (1-890817-60-0). 136pp. Twelve-year-old Lettie Tucker, a slave, exchanges thought-provoking letters with President Abraham Lincoln in this story set in the 1860s packed with interesting illustrations. (Rev: BCCB 2/02; BL 9/1/01; HBG 3/02; SLJ 9/01)

9790 Polacco, Patricia. *Pink and Say* (K–5). Illus. 1994, Penguin Putnam $16.99 (0-399-22671-0). 32pp. Based on a true incident during the Civil War, this book tells of the friendship of two Union soldiers: Say, a white man who is rescued by a black man, Pinkus, known as Pink. (Rev: BCCB 9/94; BL 9/1/94; HB 11–12/94; SLJ 10/94*)

9791 Porter, Connie. *Addy Learns a Lesson* (3–6). Illus. by Melodye Rosales. Series: American Girls. 1993, Pleasant Co. $12.95 (1-56247-078-7); paper $5.95 (1-56247-077-9). 70pp. In the year 1864, young Addy and her mother try to escape slavery by fleeing to the North after her father is sold again and they are separated. (Rev: BL 8/93; SLJ 1/94)

9792 Porter, Connie. *Addy Saves the Day: A Summer Story* (2–4). Illus. by Bradford Brown. 1994, Pleasant Co. paper $5.95 (1-56247-083-3). 59pp. In this novel set in Philadelphia in 1864, Addy, a former slave, and her family try to make money to search for relatives lost in the Civil War. Also use *Happy Birthday, Addy!* (1994). (Rev: BL 11/1/94; SLJ 11/94)

9793 Pryor, Bonnie. *Joseph: 1861 — A Rumble of War* (3–7). Illus. 1999, Morrow $15.00 (0-688-15671-1). 160pp. Growing up in Kentucky in 1861, Joseph decides to join the abolitionist cause when he sees how inhumanely slaves are treated. (Rev: BL 7/99; HBG 10/99; SLJ 8/99)

9794 Pryor, Bonnie. *Joseph's Choice — 1861* (3–5). Illus. Series: American Adventures. 2000, HarperCollins LB $14.89 (0-06-029226-1). 176pp. At the beginning of the Civil War in a small Kentucky town, young Joseph realizes that he must take sides. (Rev: BL 12/15/00; HBG 10/01; SLJ 10/00)

9795 Reeder, Carolyn. *Captain Kate* (4–7). 1999, Avon $15.00 (0-380-97628-5). 192pp. Set during the Civil War, this novel tells how 12-year-old Kate and her stepbrother navigate the 184 miles of the Cumberland and Ohio Canal on the family's canal boat. (Rev: HBG 10/99; SLJ 1/99)

9796 Rinaldi, Ann. *Amelia's War* (5–9). 1999, Scholastic paper $15.95 (0-590-11744-0). 272pp. During the Civil War, young Amelia Grafton secretly finds a way to prevent the Confederate forces from destroying her Maryland town. (Rev: BL 11/15/99; HBG 3/00; SLJ 2/00)

9797 Rinaldi, Ann. *Girl in Blue* (5–8). 2001, Scholastic paper $15.95 (0-439-07336-7). 320pp. A first-person novel about Sarah, who disguises herself as a boy and joins the Union Army. (Rev: BCCB 6/01; BL 4/1/01; HBG 10/01; SLJ 3/01)

9798 Stolz, Mary. *A Ballad of the Civil War* (4–6). Illus. 1997, HarperCollins LB $13.89 (0-06-027363-1). 64pp. Based on a Civil War ballad, this is the story of two Southern brothers who enlist on opposite sides. (Rev: BL 10/1/97; SLJ 2/98)

9799 Thomas, Carroll. *Blue Creek Farm* (4–8). 2001, Smith & Kraus paper $9.95 (1-57525-243-0). 185pp. In Kansas of the 1860s, Matty Trescott and her father manage a farm and feel the effects of the Civil War. (Rev: BL 4/1/01)

9800 Turner, Ann. *Drummer Boy: Marching to the Civil War* (3–5). Illus. by Mark Hess. 1998, HarperCollins LB $14.89 (0-06-027697-5). 32pp. In this first-person account, a 13-year-old runs away from home to become a drummer boy during the Civil War and later encounters the reality of war and death. (Rev: BCCB 11/98; BL 9/15/98; HBG 3/99; SLJ 11/98)

9801 Winnick, Karen B. *Cassie's Sweet Berry Pie* (1–3). Illus. 2005, Boyds Mills $16.95 (1-56397-984-5). 32pp. When Yankee soldiers are approaching, Cassie must think quickly to protect her younger siblings in this story of the Civil War. (Rev: BL 2/15/05; SLJ 3/05)

RECONSTRUCTION TO WORLD WAR II, 1865–1941

9802 Adler, Susan S. *Meet Samantha: An American Girl* (3–5). Illus. 1986, Pleasant Co. LB $12.95 (0-937295-80-9); paper $5.95 (0-937295-04-3). 72pp. Samantha is an orphan living with her wealthy grandmother in the America of 1904. Two others in the series are: *Samantha Learns a Lesson; Samantha's Surprise* (both 1986). (Rev: BL 12/1/86)

9803 Alexander, Lloyd. *The Gawgon and the Boy* (5–7). 2001, Dutton $17.99 (0-525-46677-0). 256pp. Set in 1920s Philadelphia, this is the story of a young boy who is encouraged in his love of art by a fierce aunt, nicknamed "the Gawgon." (Rev: BCCB 6/01; BL 5/15/01; HB 7–8/01; HBG 10/01; SLJ 4/01*)

9804 Alter, Judith. *Luke and the Van Zandt County War* (5–9). Illus. 1984, Texas Christian Univ. $14.95 (0-912646-88-8). 132pp. Life in Reconstruction Texas as seen through the eyes of two 14-year-olds. (Rev: SLJ 3/85)

9805 Armstrong, Jennifer. *Theodore Roosevelt: Letters from a Young Coal Miner* (3–6). Illus. Series: Dear Mr. President. 2000, Winslow $8.95 (1-890817-27-9). 128pp. Using fictional letters between a 13-year-old Pennsylvania coal miner and Teddy Roosevelt, this book introduces the hardships of a miner's life as well as the character and administration of President Roosevelt. (Rev: BL 3/1/01; HBG 10/01)

9806 Atwell, Debby. *Pearl* (K–3). Illus. 2001, Houghton Mifflin $16.00 (0-395-88416-0). 32pp. Pearl, a woman in her 90s, covers a substantial part of American history in her reminiscences, which stretch from her grandfather's encounter with George Washington through World Wars I and II and her hope that her great-granddaughter might someday go to the moon. (Rev: BCCB 4/01; BL 5/1/01; HBG 10/01; SLJ 6/01)

9807 Avi. *Abigail Takes the Wheel* (2–4). Illus. by Don Bolognese. Series: I Can Read. 1999, Harper-Collins LB $14.89 (0-06-027663-0). 64pp. In this easily read story set in the 1880s, young Abigail steers a freight boat up the Hudson after the mate gets sick. (Rev: BCCB 6/99; BL 4/1/99; HB 3–4/99; HBG 10/99; SLJ 5/99)

9808 Avi. *The Secret School* (3–6). 2001, Harcourt $16.00 (0-15-216375-1). 153pp. Rather than risking her future education, 14-year-old Ida Bidson takes over as teacher and runs a secret school when the one-room schoolhouse in their mountain district is suddenly closed in 1925. (Rev: BCCB 10/01; HB 11–12/01; HBG 3/02; SLJ 9/01)

9809 Avi. *Silent Movie* (K–3). Illus. by C. B. Mordan. 2003, Simon & Schuster $16.95 (0-689-84145-0). 48pp. In black-and-white silent-movie format, this is the story of an immigrant mother and son arriving in America in the early 20th century, the difficulties they have finding Papa, and the near-miraculous reunion. (Rev: BL 3/1/03*; HB 3–4/03; HBG 10/03; SLJ 3/03)

9810 Ayres, Katherine. *Macaroni Boy* (5–8). 2003, Delacorte $15.95 (0-385-73016-0). 176pp. Sixth-grader Mike is living in Pittsburgh during the Depression and has many worries: lack of money, a bully who calls him "Macaroni Boy," and the possible connection between dying rats and his grandfather's illness. (Rev: BCCB 3/03; BL 1/1–15/03; HBG 10/03; SLJ 2/03)

9811 Ayres, Katherine. *Under Copp's Hill* (4–6). Illus. by Troy Howell and Laszlo Kubinyi. Series: History Mysteries. 2000, Pleasant Co. $9.95 (1-58485-089-2); paper $5.95 (1-58485-088-4). 163pp. In 1908 Boston, Innie and her cousin Teresa are alarmed when books begin disappearing from their settlement house library. (Rev: HBG 10/01; SLJ 3/01)

9812 Bader, Bonnie. *East Side Story* (3–5). Series: Stories of the States. 1993, Silver Moon LB $14.95 (1-881889-22-X). 72pp. The story of an 11-year-old Jewish immigrant girl and her sister, both of whom work in the Triangle Shirtwaist Factory in New York City during the early 1900s. (Rev: SLJ 2/94)

9813 Baier, Joan Foley. *Luvella's Promise* (3–5). 1999, Writers Club paper $9.95 (1-893652-04-1). 83pp. Luvella is growing up with her family in a logging town in Pennsylvania in 1905 when typhoid fever strikes. (Rev: SLJ 11/99)

9814 Barasch, Lynne. *Radio Rescue* (2–5). Illus. 2000, Farrar $16.00 (0-374-36166-5). 40pp. Based on fact, this novel set in New York in 1923 tells how a young amateur radio operator saved Florida hurricane victims by picking up their distress sig-nals. (Rev: BCCB 7–8/00; BL 9/15/00; HB 9–10/00; HBG 3/01; SLJ 10/00)

9815 Bartoletti, Susan Campbell. *A Coal Miner's Bride: The Diary of Anetka Kaminska* (5–9). Illus. 2000, Scholastic paper $10.95 (0-439-05386-2). 224pp. Based on a series of true events, this gripping historical novel tells the story of a young Polish immigrant girl and her struggle to survive in a coal mining town in Pennsylvania in the late 1890s. (Rev: BL 4/1/00; HBG 10/00; SLJ 8/00)

9816 Bartoletti, Susan Campbell. *The Journal of Finn Reardon, a Newsie* (4–6). Series: My Name Is America. 2003, Scholastic $10.95 (0-439-18894-6). 156pp. In this compelling fictional journal, 13-year-old Finn Reardon, an Irish American living in New York City in 1899, records his experiences working as a sidewalk newspaper vendor. (Rev: HBG 10/03; SLJ 10/03)

9817 Beard, Darleen Bailey. *The Babbs Switch Story* (5–8). 2002, Farrar $16.00 (0-374-30475-0). 176pp. A young girl saves her sister from a fire on Christmas Eve in 1924 in this fictional account of a real event. (Rev: BL 3/15/02; HBG 10/02; SLJ 3/02)

9818 Blackwood, Gary L. *Moonshine* (5–8). 1999, Marshall Cavendish $14.95 (0-7614-5056-4). 158pp. Thirteen-year-old Thad, growing up with his mother in rural Mississippi during the Depression, makes a little extra money by running an illegal still that produces moonshine for the locals. (Rev: BCCB 11/99; BL 9/1/99; HBG 3/00; SLJ 10/99)

9819 Blakeslee, Ann R. *Summer Battles* (5–8). 2000, Marshall Cavendish $14.95 (0-7614-5064-5). 127pp. The story of Kath, age 11, growing up in a small town in Indiana in 1926 and of her father, a preacher, who is attacked for opposing the Ku Klux Klan. (Rev: BCCB 3/00; BL 4/1/00; HBG 10/00; SLJ 4/00)

9820 Boling, Katharine. *January 1905* (4–7). 2004, Harcourt $16.00 (0-15-205119-8). 160pp. In alternating voices, 11-year-old mill worker Pauline and her deformed, stay-at-home twin sister Arlene describe the harsh circumstances of their early-20th-century life. (Rev: BL 5/15/04; HB 7–8/04; SLJ 7/04)

9821 Bornstein, Ruth Lercher. *Butterflies and Lizards, Beryl and Me* (5–7). 2002, Marshall Cavendish LB $14.95 (0-7614-5118-8). 160pp. Eleven-year-old Charley befriends an odd woman named Beryl while her mother works hard to make it through the Great Depression. (Rev: BL 5/15/02; HBG 10/02; SLJ 5/02)

9822 Bradley, Kimberley Brubaker. *The President's Daughter* (3–5). 2004, Delacorte LB $17.99 (0-385-90179-8). 176pp. This appealing blend of fact and fiction looks at the dramatic changes in 10-year-old Ethel Roosevelt's life when her father, Theodore, becomes president. (Rev: BL 2/15/05; SLJ 11/04)

9823 Bryant, Jen. *The Trial* (5–9). 2004, Knopf LB $16.99 (0-375-92752-2). 192pp. In this engaging historical novel told in poems, 12-year-old Katie recounts what happens to her quiet hometown when the sensational Lindbergh kidnapping trial is held in the county courthouse. (Rev: BL 5/1/04; HB 3–4/04; SLJ 6/04)

9824 Burleigh, Robert. *Into the Air: The Story of the Wright Brothers' First Flight* (5–8). Illus. by Bill Wylie. Series: American Heroes. 2002, Harcourt paper $6.00 (0-15-216803-6). A high-interest, comic-book presentation of the first flight with fictionalized dialogue. (Rev: HBG 3/03; SLJ 9/02)

9825 Byars, Betsy. *Keeper of the Doves* (5–8). 2002, Viking $14.99 (0-670-03576-9). 112pp. Young Amie McBee is a thoughtful child who loves to write and — unlike her older twin sisters — has the sensitivity to see the softer side of the mysterious Polish immigrant who lives on their estate and keeps doves in this story set at the turn of the 20th century and presented in 26 short, alphabetical chapters. (Rev: BCCB 1/03; BL 10/1/02*; HB 9–10/02*; HBG 3/03; SLJ 10/02)

9826 Carbone, Elisa. *Storm Warriors* (4–8). 2001, Knopf LB $18.99 (0-375-90664-9). 176pp. An exciting adventure story set on the Outer Banks of North Carolina in 1895, about a boy who wants to become part of the nearby rescue station that is manned by an African American crew. (Rev: BL 1/1–15/01; HB 5–6/01; HBG 10/01; SLJ 2/01)

9827 Carter, Alden R. *Crescent Moon* (5–8). 1999, Holiday House $16.95 (0-8234-1521-X). 153pp. In the early part of the 20th century, Jeremy joins Great-Uncle Mac on a log drive where they become friends with a Native American and his daughter and, through them, experience the shame of racial prejudice. (Rev: BCCB 1/00; BL 2/15/00; HB 3–4/00; HBG 10/00; SLJ 3/00)

9828 Clark, Clara Gillow. *Hattie on Her Way* (4–7). Series: Hattie. 2005, Candlewick $15.99 (0-7636-2286-9). 208pp. The sequel to *Hill Hawk Hattie* (2003) finds Hattie living with her grandmother after her mother's death and seeking to solve a family mystery. (Rev: BL 3/1/05; SLJ 3/05)

9829 Clark, Clara Gillow. *Hill Hawk Hattie* (4–7). 2003, Candlewick $15.99 (0-7636-1963-9). 176pp. After her mother's death in the late 1880s, 11-year-old Hattie dresses as a boy and joins her father on a dangerous logging trip down the Delaware. (Rev: BL 7/03*; HBG 10/03; SLJ 8/03)

9830 Crisp, Marty. *White Star: A Dog on the Titanic* (4–6). 2004, Holiday House $16.95 (0-8234-1598-8). 150pp. Sam Harris, a 12-year-old passenger on the *Titanic,* offers to help care for the dogs in the ship's kennel and develops a strong relationship with an Irish setter named Star; back matter gives historical detail on the disaster. (Rev: BL 5/15/04; SLJ 6/04)

9831 Cross, Gillian. *The Great American Elephant Chase* (5–8). 1993, Holiday House $16.95 (0-8234-1016-1). In 1881, Tad, 15, and young friend Cissie attempt to get to Nebraska with her showman father's elephant, pursued by two unsavory characters who claim they have bought the animal. (Rev: BCCB 6/93; BL 3/15/93*; SLJ 5/93*)

9832 Cummings, Priscilla. *Saving Grace* (4–7). 2003, Dutton $16.99 (0-525-47123-5). 192pp. Eleven-year-old Grace faces a tough dilemma when a wealthy family offers to adopt her while her own family is suffering grinding poverty and illness during the Depression. (Rev: BCCB 9/03; BL 5/15/03; HBG 10/03; SLJ 6/03)

9833 Currier, Katrina Saltonstall. *Kai's Journey to Gold Mountain* (4–7). Illus. by Gabhor Utomo. 2005, Angel Island $16.95 (0-9667352-7-7); paper $10.95 (0-9667352-4-2). 44pp. Based on the experiences of a Chinese immigrant to the United States in the 1930s, this troubling tale describes the internment of 12-year-old Kai on Angel Island in San Francisco Bay. (Rev: BL 2/15/05)

9834 Cushman, Karen. *Rodzina* (5–9). 2003, Clarion $16.00 (0-618-13351-8). 224pp. On an orphan train going from Chicago to California in 1881, plucky Rodzina worries about her fate and aims to find a better life than some of the other children on the train. (Rev: BCCB 3/03; BL 3/1/03*; HB 5–6/03; HBG 10/03; SLJ 4/03*)

9835 Cutler, Jane. *The Song of the Molimo* (5–8). Illus. 1998, Farrar $16.00 (0-374-37141-5). During the St. Louis World's Fair of 1904, 12-year-old Harry gets to know a group of pygmies who are on exhibit and encounters questions of race, intelligence, and fair play. (Rev: BCCB 10/98; BL 10/15/98; HBG 3/99; SLJ 11/98)

9836 Dadey, Debbie. *Whistler's Hollow* (4–6). 2002, Bloomsbury $14.95 (1-58234-789-1). 104pp. Eleven-year-old Lillie Mae goes to live with a great-aunt and uncle on a Kentucky farm in 1920 and learns the truth about her father's fate. (Rev: SLJ 7/02)

9837 De Angeli, Marguerite. *Copper-Toed Boots* (3–6). Illus. by author. 1996, Wayne State Univ. Pr. paper $15.95 (0-814-32654-4). 96pp. American family life in the early 20th century.

9838 DeClements, Barthe. *The Bite of the Gold Bug: A Story of the Alaskan Gold Rush* (3–6). Illus. by Dan Andreasen. Series: Once upon America. 1994, Puffin paper $4.99 (0-140-36081-6). 64pp. The story of 12-year-old Bucky who spends six months in the gold fields with his father and uncle. (Rev: BCCB 5/92; BL 5/15/92; SLJ 8/92)

9839 Dell, Pamela. *Liam's Watch: A Strange Story of the Great Chicago Fire* (4–6). Series: Scrapbooks of America. 2002, Tradition LB $27.07 (1-59187-014-3). 47pp. Twelve-year-old Liam and his family must flee their home during the Great Chicago Fire of 1871; background historical information is provided in boxed notes and a timeline. (Rev: SLJ 5/03)

9840 Drummond, Allan. *The Flyers* (PS–2). Illus. by author. 2003, Farrar $16.00 (0-374-32410-7). Five children watch as Wilbur and Orville Wright make their historic flight, each imagining future flying achievements. (Rev: HB 9–10/03; HBG 4/04; SLJ 10/03)

9841 Duey, Kathleen, and Karen A. Bale. *Shipwreck: The Titanic, 1912* (4–7). Series: Survival! 1998, Simon & Schuster paper $4.99 (0-689-81311-2). 175pp. The voyage of the *Titanic,* as experienced by Gavin Reilly, who is working his way to America, and by Karolina Green, who is returning to the United States after the death of her parents in England. (Rev: SLJ 9/98)

9842 Durbin, William. *Blackwater Ben* (5–8). 2003, Wendy Lamb Books LB $17.99 (0-385-90149-6). 208pp. At the end of the 19th century, 13-year-old Ben learns about lumberjacks from a distance as he works as a cook's helper in a logging camp. (Rev: BL 10/15/03; SLJ 12/03)

9843 Durbin, William. *Song of Sampo Lake* (4–7). 2002, Random LB $17.99 (0-385-90055-4). 217pp. This portrayal of a young Finnish immigrant's life in Minnesota in 1900 interweaves typical adolescent problems and joys with information on customs, culture, and geography. (Rev: BL 10/15/02; HBG 3/03; SLJ 11/02)

9844 Easton, Richard. *A Real American* (4–7). 2002, Clarion $15.00 (0-618-03339-9). 160pp. Against his father's wishes, 11-year-old Nathan befriends Arturo, the son of Italian immigrants newly arrived in a Pennsylvania coal-mining town. (Rev: BCCB 9/02; BL 5/15/02; SLJ 3/02)

9845 Erickson, John R. *Moonshiner's Gold* (5–9). 2001, Viking $15.99 (0-670-03502-5). 176pp. Fourteen-year-old Riley becomes embroiled in exciting intrigue involving moonshiners and corruption in this novel set in Texas in the 1920s. (Rev: HBG 3/02; SLJ 8/01)

9846 Fisher, Leonard E. *The Jetty Chronicles* (5–9). Illus. 1997, Marshall Cavendish $15.95 (0-7614-5017-3). A series of vignettes based on fact about the unusual people the author met while growing up in Sea Gate, New York, at a time when the United States was drifting into World War II. (Rev: BL 10/15/97; BR 3–4/98; HBG 3/98; SLJ 12/97)

9847 Fletcher, Susan. *Walk Across the Sea* (5–9). 2001, Simon & Schuster $16.00 (0-689-84133-7). 214pp. In spite of her father's dislike of immigrants, 15-year-old Eliza Jane helps a Chinese boy who rescued her and her goat in this story set in California in the late 19th century. (Rev: BCCB 12/01; BL 11/1/01; HBG 3/02; SLJ 11/01)

9848 Franklin, Kristine L. *Grape Thief* (5–9). 2003, Candlewick $16.99 (0-7636-1325-8). 304pp. In 1925 Washington State, a boy of Croatian heritage tries to find a way to stay in school even though his family is in financial difficulty. (Rev: BL 10/1/03; SLJ 9/03)

9849 Fuqua, Jonathon. *Darby* (4–7). 2002, Candlewick $15.99 (0-7636-1417-3). 256pp. A 9-year-old white girl, Darby, and her family become the target of KKK violence after she protests the killing of a black sharecropper's son in 1926 South Carolina. (Rev: BCCB 7–8/02; BL 3/15/02; HB 3–4/02; HBG 10/02; SLJ 3/02)

9850 Goodman, Susan. *Hazelle Boxberg* (2–4). Illus. by Doris Ettlinger. 2004, Simon & Schuster LB $11.89 (0-689-84983-4). 64pp. The moving story, based on truth, of 11-year-old Hazelle's trip to Texas by orphan train and her escape from the family that chooses her from a lineup at the Masonic Hall. (Rev: BL 3/1/04)

9851 Granfield, Linda. *97 Orchard Street, New York: Stories of Immigrant Life* (3–6). Photos by Arlene Alda. 2001, Tundra paper $15.00 (0-88776-580-7). 55pp. A detailed and appealing look at the immigrant experience through the stories of families who lived in the building that is now the Lower East Side Tenement Museum, with black-and-white photographs. (Rev: SLJ 12/01) [305.9]

9852 Gray, Dianne E. *Together Apart* (5–9). 2002, Houghton Mifflin $16.00 (0-618-18721-9). 208pp. After surviving the blizzard of 1888, Isaac and Hannah discover their love for each other while working for feminist publisher Eliza Moore. (Rev: BCCB 11/02; BL 9/15/02; HB 11–12/02; HBG 3/03; SLJ 12/02)

9853 Gregory, Kristiana. *Orphan Runaways* (5–7). 1998, Scholastic paper $15.95 (0-590-60366-3). 160pp. Two brothers run away from a San Francisco orphanage in 1879 to look for an uncle in the gold fields. (Rev: BCCB 3/98; BL 2/15/98; HBG 10/98; SLJ 3/98)

9854 Gundisch, Karin. *How I Became an American* (4–8). Trans. by James Skofield. 2001, Cricket $15.95 (0-8126-4875-7). 128pp. This is the story of Johann, a young German immigrant, who arrives in an Ohio steel town in the early 20th century. (Rev: BL 11/15/01; HBG 3/02; SLJ 12/01)

9855 Gutman, Dan. *Race for the Sky: The Kitty Hawk Diaries of Johnny Moore* (4–7). 2003, Simon & Schuster $15.95 (0-689-84554-5). 178pp. Fact and fiction are interwoven in this diary by 14-year-old John Moore, recording his firsthand observations of the Wright brothers' progress. (Rev: BL 1/1–15/04; HBG 4/04; SLJ 1/04)

9856 Hahn, Mary D. *Anna All Year Round* (3–5). Illus. 1999, Clarion $15.00 (0-395-86975-7). 144pp. Using an early 1900s urban setting, this warm family story tells about German immigrants and their children adjusting to America. (Rev: BCCB 6/99; BL 3/15/99; HB 7–8/99; HBG 10/99; SLJ 5/99)

9857 Hall, Donald. *The Milkman's Boy* (3–5). Illus. 1997, Walker LB $16.85 (0-8027-8465-8). 32pp. Around the time of World War I, Paul's father, a milkman, does not believe in the necessity of pasteurization. (Rev: BL 9/1/97; HBG 3/98; SLJ 9/97)

9858 Hansen, Joyce. *I Thought My Soul Would Rise and Fly: The Diary of Patsy, a Freed Girl* (4–8). Series: Dear America. 1997, Scholastic paper $10.95 (0-590-84913-1). 208pp. In this novel in the form of a diary, a freed slave girl wonders what to do with her life after leaving the plantation. (Rev: BL 12/15/97; HBG 3/98; SLJ 11/97)

9859 Harlow, Joan Hiatt. *Joshua's Song* (5–8). 2001, Simon & Schuster $16.00 (0-689-84119-1). 192pp. Thirteen-year-old Joshua has to adjust to many changes in this story that interweaves history and fiction: his father has died in the 1918 flu epidemic, his mother is taking in boarders, and Joshua has left school and is working as a newsboy and learning a different kind of life. (Rev: BL 12/15/01; HBG 3/02; SLJ 11/01)

9860 Harrar, George. *The Trouble with Jeremy Chance* (4–7). 2003, Milkweed $16.95 (1-57131-647-7); paper $6.95 (1-57131-646-9). 176pp. Tired of friction with his father, 12-year-old Jeremy travels from New Hampshire to Boston to meet his brother's troop ship in this novel set in 1919 and full of historical detail. (Rev: BL 10/1/03; HBG 4/04; SLJ 3/04)

9861 Harris, Carol Flynn. *A Place for Joey* (4–8). 2001, Boyds Mills $16.95 (1-56397-108-9). 90pp. Twelve-year-old Joey, an Italian immigrant living in Boston in the early 20th century, learns an important lesson through a heroic act. (Rev: BL 9/1/01; HBG 3/02; SLJ 9/01)

9862 Haseley, Dennis. *The Amazing Thinking Machine* (5–7). 2002, Dial $16.99 (0-8037-2609-0). 128pp. Brothers Patrick and Roy invent an "amazing thinking machine" to amuse themselves while they wait for their father's return from his search for work in this novel set in the Great Depression. (Rev: BCCB 5/02; BL 5/15/02; HB 7–8/02; HBG 10/02; SLJ 5/02)

9863 Henderson, Aileen Kilgore. *Hard Times for Jake Smith* (5–9). 2004, Milkweed $16.95 (1-57131-648-5). 192pp. Abandoned by her parents in the depths of the Great Depression, 12-year-old MaryJake diguises herself as a boy. (Rev: BL 4/15/04; SLJ 9/04)

9864 Hesse, Karen. *Letters from Rifka* (4–8). 1992, Holt $16.95 (0-8050-1964-2); Penguin Putnam paper $5.99 (0-14-036391-2). In letters back to Russia, Rifka, 12, recounts her long journey to the United States in 1919, starting with the dangerous escape over the border. (Rev: BCCB 10/92; BL 7/92; HB 9–10/92*; SLJ 8/92*)

9865 Hesse, Karen. *A Time of Angels* (5–8). 1995, Hyperion LB $16.49 (0-7868-2072-1). As influenza sweeps her city in 1918, killing thousands, Hannah tries to escape its ravages by moving to Vermont, where an old farmer helps her. (Rev: BCCB 1/96; BL 12/1/95; SLJ 12/95)

9866 Hesse, Karen. *Witness* (5–9). 2001, Scholastic $16.95 (0-439-27199-1). 176pp. Hesse uses fictional first-person accounts in free verse to tell about Ku Klux Klan activity in a 1924 Vermont town. (Rev: BCCB 11/01; BL 9/1/01; HB 11–12/01; HBG 3/02; SLJ 9/01*)

9867 Hill, Kirkpatrick. *Minuk: Ashes in the Pathway* (4–6). Series: Girls of Many Lands. 2002, Pleasant Co. $12.95 (1-58485-596-7); paper $7.95 (1-58485-520-7). 198pp. As a young Yup'ik Indian girl grows more mature in the late 19th century, she assesses her life, the culture of the Yup'iks, and the contrasting customs and influence of the missionaries, in an account that includes information on epidemics and historical photographs. (Rev: BL 10/1/02; HB 1–2/03*; HBG 3/03; SLJ 10/02)

9868 Holland, Isabelle. *Paperboy* (4–6). 1999, Holiday House $15.95 (0-8234-1422-1). 137pp. Growing up in a New York City slum in 1881, 12-year-old Kevin O'Donnell helps out his family by getting a job as a messenger for the owner of the *New York Chronicle*. (Rev: BCCB 10/99; HBG 3/00; SLJ 9/99)

9869 Hoobler, Dorothy, and Thomas Hoobler. *The First Decade: Curtain Going Up* (4–6). Illus. Series: Century Kids. 2000, Millbrook LB $21.90

(0-7613-1600-0). 160pp. Presents the first decade of the 20th century in the life of the Aldriches, a theatrical family living in Maine. (Rev: BCCB 7–8/00; BL 5/1/00; HBG 10/00; SLJ 7/00)

9870 Hoobler, Dorothy, and Thomas Hoobler. *Florence Robinson: The Story of a Jazz Age Girl* (3–6). Illus. by Robert Sauber. Series: Her Story. 1997, Silver Burdett LB $17.95 (0-382-39644-8); paper $4.95 (0-382-39645-6). 123pp. In the 1920s, an African American family moves north to Chicago in pursuit of freedom and a better life. (Rev: SLJ 8/97)

9871 Hoobler, Dorothy, and Tom Hoobler. *The Second Decade: Voyages* (4–6). Illus. Series: Century Kids. 2000, Millbrook LB $21.90 (0-7613-1601-9). 160pp. In the second decade of the 20th century, Peggy Aldrich and her sister photograph the factory workers in Lowell, Massachusetts, explore issues involving child labor and women's suffrage, and feel the effects of the sinking of the *Titanic*. (Rev: BCCB 7–8/00; BL 5/1/00; HBG 10/00; SLJ 7/00)

9872 Houston, Gloria. *Littlejim's Dreams* (5–8). Illus. by Thomas B. Allen. 1997, Harcourt $16.00 (0-15-201509-4). 231pp. Littlejim wants to become a writer, but his father thinks he should be a farmer and logger like himself, in this novel set in Appalachia in 1920. A sequel to *Littlejim* (1990). (Rev: SLJ 7/97)

9873 Hulme, Joy N. *Climbing the Rainbow* (4–6). 2004, HarperCollins LB $16.89 (0-06-054304-3). 224pp. In 1911, 10-year-old Dora's large family moves to New Mexico; there Dora faces various challenges, including starting school and the death of a friend. (Rev: BL 1/1–15/04; SLJ 2/04)

9874 Hulme, Joy N. *Through the Open Door* (4–6). 2000, HarperCollins $14.95 (0-380-97870-9). 162pp. Told by 9-year-old Dora Cookson, this is an appealing story of a Mormon family and their move from Utah to homestead in New Mexico in 1910. (Rev: BCCB 6/00; HBG 3/01; SLJ 8/00)

9875 Hurwitz, Johanna. *Faraway Summer* (5–7). Illus. by Mary Azarian. 1998, Morrow $14.95 (0-688-15334-8). 112pp. In 1910, a Jewish orphan who lives in a tenement in New York City is thrilled at the thought of spending two weeks on a farm in Vermont, thanks to the Fresh Air Fund. (Rev: BL 3/1/98; HB 7–8/98; HBG 10/98; SLJ 5/98)

9876 Hyatt, Patricia Rusch. *Coast to Coast with Alice* (3–6). Illus. 1995, Carolrhoda LB $21.27 (0-87614-789-9). 72pp. A fictionalized account of the first automobile cross-country trip by a woman in 1909. (Rev: BCCB 9/95; BL 7/95; HB 11–12/95; SLJ 8/95)

9877 Jackson, Alison. *Rainmaker* (5–8). 2005, Boyds Mills $16.95 (1-59078-309-3). 192pp. The farmers in Pidge Martin's town hire a rainmaker in the hopes that she will save their crops in this story set in 1939 Florida. (Rev: BL 3/15/05; SLJ 4/05)

9878 Janke, Katelan. *Survival in the Storm: The Dust Bowl Diary of Grace Edwards* (4–8). Series: Dear America. 2002, Scholastic paper $10.95 (0-439-21599-4). 192pp. The fictional diary of a girl living in the Texas panhandle during the Dust Bowl years. (Rev: BL 2/15/03; HBG 10/03; SLJ 12/02)

9879 Jaspersohn, William. *The Two Brothers* (2–4). Illus. Series: Family Heritage. 2000, Vermont Folklife Center $14.95 (0-916718-16-6). 32pp. Based on a true story, this novel tells of two German brothers who immigrated separately to the United States in the 1880s and were miraculously reunited. (Rev: BL 11/1/00; SLJ 9/00)

9880 Jocelyn, Marthe. *Earthly Astonishments* (4–8). 2000, Tundra paper $7.95 (0-88776-628-5). 179pp. The setting is New York City in the 1880s and the novel involves a girl who is only 22 inches tall and her career in a glorified freak show. (Rev: BCCB 2/00; HBG 10/00; SLJ 4/00)

9881 Jones, Elizabeth McDavid. *Secrets on 26th Street* (3–6). Illus. by Greg Dearth. 1999, Pleasant Co. $9.95 (1-56247-816-8); paper $5.95 (1-56247-760-9). 144pp. This novel affords an interesting behind-the-scenes look at the suffragette movement in New York during 1914 when the heroine's mother is arrested during a demonstration. (Rev: HBG 3/00; SLJ 4/00)

9882 Jorgensen, Norman. *In Flanders Fields* (4–7). Illus. by Brian Harrison-Lever. 2002, Fremantle Arts Centre $22.95 (1-86368-369-0). During a Christmas Day ceasefire in the World War I trenches, a soldier rescues a trapped robin. (Rev: SLJ 2/03)

9883 Kalman, Esther. *Tchaikovsky Discovers America* (3–5). Illus. by Laura Fernandez and Rick Jacobson. 1995, Orchard $16.95 (0-531-06894-3). 32pp. Through a diary kept by 11-year-old Eugenia, the reader learns about Tchaikovsky's trip to the United States in 1891. (Rev: BL 3/15/95; HB 1–2/95, 5–6/95; SLJ 4/95)

9884 Karwoski, Gail. *Quake! Disaster in San Francisco, 1906* (4–6). Illus. by Robert Papp. 2004, Peachtree $14.95 (1-56145-310-2). 192pp. A Jewish boy and a Chinese boy help each other in the aftermath of the 1906 San Francisco earthquake; historical notes round out the book. (Rev: BL 5/15/04; SLJ 6/04)

9885 Kimball, K. M. *The Secret of the Red Flame* (4–7). Illus. by Mark Elliot. 2002, Simon & Schuster paper $4.99 (0-689-85174-X). 224pp. In this complex novel, Jozef, a Polish American boy living in Chicago in 1871, joins a gang in an effort to thwart some local criminals. (Rev: BL 7/02; SLJ 8/02)

9886 Kinsey-Warnock, Natalie. *A Doctor Like Papa* (2–4). Illus. by James Bernardin. 2002, Harper-Collins LB $14.89 (0-06-029320-9). 80pp. During World War I in Vermont, Margaret puts her doctor-father's practices to work to protect herself and brother when a deadly flu epidemic strikes. (Rev: BL 4/1/02; HBG 10/02; SLJ 7/02)

9887 Klass, Sheila S. *A Shooting Star: A Novel About Annie Oakley* (4–8). 1996, Holiday House $15.95 (0-8234-1279-2). A fictionalized biography of the woman who rose from poverty to become a famous show-business sharpshooter. (Rev: BL 12/15/96; SLJ 5/97)

9888 Koller, Jackie F. *Nothing to Fear* (5–7). 1991, Harcourt $14.95 (0-15-200544-7); paper $8.00 (0-

15-257582-0). 288pp. Danny Garvey is a first-generation Catholic Irish American growing up in New York City in the 1930s. (Rev: BCCB 3/91; BL 3/1/91; SLJ 5/91)

9889 Koller, Jackie French. *Someday* (5–8). 2002, Scholastic paper $16.95 (0-439-29317-0). 224pp. Celie's allegiances are divided when her town is flooded to create a reservoir in Massachusetts during the 1930s. (Rev: BCCB 10/02; BL 6/1–15/02; HBG 10/02; SLJ 7/02)

9890 Kroll, Steven. *When I Dream of Heaven: Angelina's Story* (5–8). Series: Jamestown's American Portraits. 2000, Jamestown paper $5.95 (0-8092-0623-4). 155pp. Set at the beginning of the 20th century in New York City, this novel tells the story of a young Italian American girl who works in a sweatshop but longs for an education. (Rev: SLJ 9/00)

9891 Kudlinski, Kathleen V. *Shannon: The Schoolmarm Mysteries, San Francisco, 1880* (3–5). Illus. by Bill Farnsworth. Series: Girlhood Journeys. 1997, Simon & Schuster paper $5.99 (0-689-81561-1). 71pp. This mystery features Shannon O'Brien, a recent Irish immigrant living in San Francisco in 1880. (Rev: SLJ 4/98)

9892 Kudlinski, Kathleen V. *Shannon, Lost and Found: San Francisco, 1880* (4–6). Illus. 1997, Simon & Schuster paper $5.99 (0-689-80988-3). 72pp. In 1880, Shannon and her friend Mi Ling become involved in collecting books for the new San Francisco Public Library. (Rev: BCCB 11/96; BL 5/1/97)

9893 Kurtz, Jane. *Bicycle Madness* (5–7). Illus. by Beth Peck. 2003, Holt $15.95 (0-8050-6981-X). 128pp. Twelve-year-old Lillie is fascinated by the woman who is struggling to learn to ride a bicycle in this novel set in the late 1800s and based on the life of the feminist Frances Willard. (Rev: BCCB 11/03; BL 10/15/03; HB 9–10/03; HBG 4/04; SLJ 10/03)

9894 Lasky, Kathryn. *Dreams in the Golden Country: The Diary of Zipporah Feldman, a Jewish Immigrant Girl* (4–8). 1998, Scholastic paper $10.95 (0-590-02973-8). Twelve-year-old Zipporah Feldman, a Jewish immigrant from Russia, keeps a diary about her life with her family on New York's Lower East Side around 1910. (Rev: BL 4/1/98; HBG 9/98; SLJ 5/98)

9895 Lasky, Kathryn. *A Time for Courage: The Suffragette Diary of Kathleen Bowen, Washington, DC, 1917* (4–6). Series: Dear America. 2002, Scholastic $10.95 (0-590-51141-6). 217pp. Thirteen-year-old Kat records her increasing interest in politics and her activities supporting the women's suffrage movement. (Rev: HBG 10/02; SLJ 8/02)

9896 Lawrence, Iain. *Lord of the Nutcracker Men* (5–9). 2001, Delacorte $15.95 (0-385-72924-3). 196pp. Ten-year-old Johnny experiences World War I through the letters and carved soldiers his father sends to him from the front lines. (Rev: BCCB 10/01; BL 11/1/01; HB 11–12/01; HBG 3/02; SLJ 11/01*)

9897 Lenski, Lois. *Strawberry Girl* (4–6). Illus. by author. 1945, HarperCollins LB $17.89 (0-397-30110-3); paper $5.95 (0-06-440585-0). 192pp. Lively adventures of a little girl, full of the flavor of the Florida lake country. Newbery Medal winner, 1946.

9898 Lewis, Zoe. *Keisha Discovers Harlem* (3–5). Illus. by Dan Burr and Rich Grot. Series: Magic Attic Club. 1999, Magic Attic LB $17.40 (1-57513-144-7). 74pp. Keisha puts on a flapper costume and finds herself transported to New York City during the Harlem Renaissance. (Rev: SLJ 4/99)

9899 Littlefield, Holly. *Fire at the Triangle Factory* (4–6). Illus. 1996, Carolrhoda LB $21.27 (0-87614-868-2); paper $5.95 (0-87614-970-0). 48pp. Two young workers — Jewish Minnie and Catholic Tessa — work at the Triangle Shirtwaist Company at the time of the fire of 1911. (Rev: BL 8/96; SLJ 10/96)

9900 Love, D. Anne. *I Remember the Alamo* (4–6). 2000, Holiday House $15.95 (0-8234-1426-4). 156pp. The McCann family moves to San Antonio and becomes embroiled in the battle of the Alamo and its aftermath in this historical novel. (Rev: BL 1/1–15/00; HB 3–4/00; HBG 3/00; SLJ 1/00)

9901 Love, D. Anne. *A Year Without Rain* (4–6). 2000, Holiday House $15.95 (0-8234-1488-4). 118pp. Set in the late 19th century, this novel tells how Rachel, who lives on the Dakota prairie, tries to thwart her father's plans to remarry. (Rev: BCCB 7–8/00; BL 4/1/00; HB 7–8/00; HBG 10/00; SLJ 9/00)

9902 McDonough, Yona Z. *The Dollhouse Magic* (3–5). Illus. 2000, Holt $15.00 (0-8050-6464-8). 86pp. Set in the 1930s during the Great Depression, this beginning chapter book, tells how two sisters, Lila and Jane, inherit a dollhouse when their elderly friend dies. (Rev: BCCB 12/00; BL 11/15/00; HBG 3/01; SLJ 2/01)

9903 McKay, Sharon E. *Charlie Wilcox* (5–8). 2000, Stoddart paper $7.95 (0-7737-6093-8). 221pp. This is the story of a 14-year-old Canadian boy who becomes involved in the trench warfare in France during World War I. (Rev: SLJ 11/00)

9904 McKissack, Patricia. *Color Me Dark: The Diary of Nellie Lee Love, the Great Migration North* (4–6). Series: Dear America. 2000, Scholastic $10.95 (0-590-51159-9). 224pp. Told in diary form, this is the fictional story of African American Nellie Lee Love, whose family moves from Tennessee to Chicago in 1919 and encounters prejudice, corruption, and race riots. (Rev: BL 2/15/00; HBG 10/00; SLJ 7/00)

9905 Martin, Nora. *Flight of the Fisherbird* (5–7). 2003, Bloomsbury $15.95 (1-58234-814-6). 200pp. Life on an isolated island on the Washington coast in 1889 is dull until 13-year-old Clem becomes involved in the rescue of a Chinese immigrant. (Rev: BL 4/1/03; HBG 10/03; SLJ 5/03)

9906 Matas, Carol. *Rosie in New York City: Gotcha!* (3–6). 2003, Simon & Schuster paper $4.99 (0-689-85714-4). 124pp. In early-20th-century New York City, 11-year-old Rosie takes a factory job when her mother falls ill. (Rev: BL 5/15/03; SLJ 8/03)

9907 Mattern, Joanne. *Coming to America: The Story of Immigration* (4–8). Illus. by Margaret Sanfilippo. 2000, Perfection Learning $14.95 (0-7807-9715-9); paper $8.95 (0-7891-2851-9). 64pp. A fictional presentation centering on the Martini family and their journey from Italy at the turn of the 20th century to find a new home in America. (Rev: HBG 3/01; SLJ 2/01)

9908 Mills, Judith C. *The Stonehook Schooner* (2–4). Illus. by author. 1997, Firefly $14.95 (1-55013-653-4); paper $4.95 (1-55013-719-0). In this story, set on a ship in Lake Ontario in the early 1900s, young Matthew ties himself to the mast to help sight land during a violent storm. (Rev: SLJ 8/97)

9909 Mitchell, Margaree King. *Uncle Jed's Barber Shop* (2–5). Illus. by James E. Ransome. 1993, Simon & Schuster $16.00 (0-671-76969-3); paper $6.99 (0-689-81913-7). 40pp. Uncle Jed, an African American barber in the 1920s, hopes to open his own shop, but his generosity always prevents him from saving enough money. (Rev: BCCB 9/93; BL 9/1/93; HB 11–12/93; SLJ 10/93)

9910 Moss, Marissa. *Hannah's Journal: The Story of an Immigrant Girl* (3–5). Illus. 2000, Harcourt $15.00 (0-15-202155-8). 56pp. This novel in diary form tells about a 10-year-old Jewish girl who leaves her home in Lithuania in 1901, voyages to New York, is processed at Ellis Island, and begins work in the big city. (Rev: BL 10/1/00; HBG 3/01; SLJ 11/00)

9911 Moss, Marissa. *Rose's Journal: The Story of a Girl in the Great Depression* (3–5). Illus. by author. Series: Young American Voices. 2001, Harcourt $15.00 (0-15-202423-9). 56pp. In her pink-lined journal, young Rose records the hardships her family faces during the dust storms of 1935 Kansas and details outside events such as the Hauptmann trial. (Rev: HBG 3/02; SLJ 12/01)

9912 Myers, Anna. *Graveyard Girl* (5–8). 1995, Walker $14.95 (0-8027-8260-4). 125pp. During the yellow-fever epidemic in Memphis in 1878, young Eli, whose family has been decimated, forms a friendship with Grace, who rings the bell for the dead at the graveyard. (Rev: SLJ 10/95)

9913 Myers, Anna. *Hoggee* (5–7). 2004, Walker $16.95 (0-8027-8926-9). 182pp. Despite all his own problems, 14-year-old mule driver Howard decides to do what he can to help a deaf mute girl in this novel set in 19th-century New York State. (Rev: SLJ 11/04)

9914 Myers, Anna. *Tulsa Burning* (5–8). 2002, Walker $16.95 (0-8027-8829-7). 184pp. In 1921 Oklahoma, a 15-year-old boy helps a black man who is injured during race riots. (Rev: BCCB 12/02; BL 10/1/02*; HBG 3/03; SLJ 9/02)

9915 Oneal, Zibby. *A Long Way to Go* (3–5). Illus. by Michael Dooling. 1992, Puffin paper $4.99 (0-14-032950-1). 64pp. Lila's life changes when her grandmother is jailed for fighting for women's rights in 1917 America. (Rev: BCCB 9/90; BL 3/1/90; HB 7–8/90; SLJ 9/90)

9916 Paterson, Katherine. *Preacher's Boy* (5–8). 1999, Clarion $15.00 (0-395-83897-5). In small-town Vermont in 1899, a time of new ideas and technological change, Robbie, the restless, imaginative, questioning son of a preacher, causes unforeseen trouble when he plans his own kidnapping for profit. (Rev: BCCB 10/99; BL 8/99; HB 9–10/99; HBG 3/00; SLJ 8/99)

9917 Peck, Richard. *Fair Weather* (4–6). 2001, Dial $16.99 (0-8037-2516-7). 160pp. A 13-year-old Illinois farm girl and her family take an exciting trip to the 1893 World's Columbian Exposition in Chicago. (Rev: BCCB 10/01; BL 9/1/01; HB 11–12/01*; HBG 3/02; SLJ 9/01*)

9918 Peck, Richard. *A Long Way from Chicago: A Novel in Stories* (4–8). 1998, Dial $15.99 (0-8037-2290-7). 148pp. In the 1930s Joe and Mary Alice Dowdel spend part of their summers with an eccentric, high-spirited grandmother in this fast-paced, humorous novel set in rural Illinois. (Rev: BCCB 10/98; HB 11–12/98; HBG 3/99; SLJ 10/98*)

9919 Peck, Robert Newton. *Arly* (5–8). 1989, Walker $16.95 (0-8027-6856-3). A teacher changes the life of a young boy in a migrant camp in Florida in 1927. (Rev: BL 7/89; BR 9–10/89)

9920 Peck, Robert Newton. *A Day No Pigs Would Die* (6–8). 1972, Knopf $24.00 (0-394-48235-2). 144pp. A gentle story about a 12-year-old Vermont farm boy.

9921 Pfitsch, Patricia Curtis. *Riding the Flume* (5–8). 2002, Simon & Schuster $16.95 (0-689-83823-9). 240pp. This adventure story set in the late 19th century in California features a plucky and environmentally conscious 15-year-old called Francie who faces a dangerous ride on the log flume in her quest to solve a mystery. (Rev: BL 11/15/02; HBG 3/03; SLJ 11/02)

9922 Porter, Tracey. *Treasures in the Dust* (5–7). 1997, HarperCollins LB $14.89 (0-06-027564-2). 160pp. With alternating points of view, two girls from poor families in Oklahoma's Dust Bowl tell their stories. (Rev: BL 8/97; HB 9–10/97; HBG 3/98; SLJ 12/97*)

9923 Rabe, Berniece. *Hiding Mr. McMulty* (5–8). 1997, Harcourt $18.00 (0-15-201330-X). This novel, set in southeast Missouri in 1937, tells a story of race and class conflicts as experienced by 11-year-old Rass. (Rev: BL 10/15/97; HBG 3/98; SLJ 12/97)

9924 Ransom, Candice. *Fire in the Sky* (3–5). Illus. 1997, Carolrhoda LB $19.93 (0-87614-867-4). 72pp. In the late 1930s in New Jersey, Stenny becomes involved in the flight of the dirigible *Hindenburg* and the rescue operation after it burns. (Rev: BL 5/1/97; SLJ 8/97)

9925 Ransom, Candice. *Jimmy Crack Corn* (3–5). Illus. 1994, Carolrhoda LB $19.93 (0-87614-786-4). 56pp. The beginning of the Great Depression as seen through the experiences of a farm family sinking into poverty with no hope for the future. (Rev: BCCB 6/94; BL 7/94; SLJ 6/94)

9926 Raven, Margot T. *Angels in the Dust* (3–6). Illus. by Roger Essley. 1997, Troll $15.95 (0-8167-3806-8). 32pp. Based on a true story, this picture book describes the hardships of an Oklahoma family living in the 1930s Dust Bowl. (Rev: BL 4/15/97; SLJ 6/97)

9927 Ray, Delia. *Ghost Girl: A Blue Ridge Mountain Story* (5–8). 2003, Clarion $15.00 (0-618-33377-0). 224pp. In rural Virginia during the Depression, young April longs to go to the new school built by President Hoover and learn to read, but her family circumstances do not make this easy. (Rev: BCCB 11/03; BL 11/15/03; HB 1–2/04*; HBG 4/04; SLJ 11/03*)

9928 Reiss, Kathryn. *The Strange Case of Baby H* (4–7). Series: History Mystery. 2002, Pleasant Co. $10.95 (1-58485-534-7); paper $6.95 (1-58485-533-9). 163pp. Twelve-year-old Clara and her family survive the San Francisco earthquake of 1906 only to find an abandoned baby whose identity must be discovered. (Rev: BL 12/1/02; HBG 3/03; SLJ 11/02)

9929 Rinaldi, Ann. *The Staircase* (5–7). 2000, Harcourt $16.00 (0-15-202430-1). 256pp. The exciting story of a 19th-century teenager named Lizzy, who rooms with conniving Elinora at their Catholic girls' school. (Rev: BL 11/1/00; HBG 3/01)

9930 Robinet, Harriette G. *Forty Acres and Maybe a Mule* (4–7). 1998, Simon & Schuster $16.00 (0-689-82078-X). 144pp. After the Civil War, Gideon and other freed slaves begin working the 40 acres of land each has been promised in spite of the opposition of white settlers. (Rev: BL 1/1–15/99; HBG 3/99; SLJ 11/98)

9931 Robinet, Harriette G. *Missing from Haymarket Square* (4–6). 2001, Simon & Schuster $15.00 (0-689-83895-6). 160pp. An African American girl named Dinah Bell faces hardships as a child laborer in 1880s Chicago. (Rev: BCCB 10/01; BL 10/1/01; HBG 10/02; SLJ 7/01)

9932 Rogers, Lisa Waller. *Get Along, Little Dogies: The Chisholm Trail Diary of Hallie Lou Wells: South Texas, 1878* (4–7). 2001, Texas Tech $14.50 (0-89672-446-8); paper $8.95 (0-89672-448-4). 174pp. Feisty 14-year-old Hallie Lou records in her diary the details and dangers of a cattle drive from Texas to Kansas. (Rev: HBG 10/01; SLJ 7/01)

9933 Ryan, Pam M. *Esperanza Rising* (5–8). 2000, Scholastic paper $15.95 (0-439-12041-1). 272pp. During the Great Depression, poverty forces Esperanza and her mother to leave Mexico and seek work in an agricultural labor camp in California. (Rev: BCCB 12/00; BL 12/1/00; HB 1–2/01; HBG 3/01; SLJ 10/00)

9934 Sandin, Joan. *The Long Way Westward* (2–4). Illus. 1989, HarperCollins paper $3.95 (0-06-444198-9). 64pp. In this continuation of *A Long Way to a New Land* (1981), the immigrant Swedish family continues its journey to Minnesota. (Rev: BCCB 11/89; BL 9/15/89; HB 9–10/89; SLJ 9/89)

9935 Sherman, Eileen B. *Independence Avenue* (5–9). 1990, Jewish Publication Soc. $14.95 (0-8276-0367-3). This story of Russian Jews who immigrate to Texas in 1907 has a resourceful, engaging hero, an unusual setting, and plenty of action. (Rev: BL 2/15/91; SLJ 1/91)

9936 Steiner, Barbara. *Mystery at Chilkoot Pass* (5–8). Series: History Mystery. 2002, Pleasant Co. $10.95 (1-58485-488-X); paper $6.95 (1-58485-487-1). 164pp. Twelve-year-old Hetty and her father, uncle, and friends join the Klondike Gold Rush, encountering danger, physical hardships, and mysterious happenings along the way. (Rev: BL 9/1/02; HBG 10/02; SLJ 6/02)

9937 Stroud, Bettye. *Dance Y'All* (2–4). Illus. by Cornelius Van Wright and Ying-hwa Hu. 2001, Marshall Cavendish $15.95 (0-7614-5065-3). With some help, Jack Henry overcomes his fear of the snake in the barn in this novel set at the beginning of the 20th century. (Rev: HBG 3/02; SLJ 11/01)

9938 Tate, Eleanora E. *The Minstrel's Melody* (5–7). Series: History Mystery. 2001, Pleasant Co. paper $5.95 (1-58485-310-7). 156pp. In Missouri of 1904, Orphelia, an African American girl, runs away from home to begin a stage career during the St. Louis World's Fair. (Rev: BL 4/1/01; HBG 3/02; SLJ 8/01)

9939 Taylor, Theodore. *A Sailor Returns* (4–6). 2001, Scholastic $16.95 (0-439-24879-5). 160pp. Evan is thrilled to meet his long-lost sailor grandfather, who has a secret that is finally revealed in this novel set in 1914. (Rev: BCCB 3/01; BL 5/1/01; HBG 10/01; SLJ 4/01)

9940 Thesman, Jean. *A Sea So Far* (5–8). 2001, Viking $15.99 (0-670-89278-5). 224pp. Fourteen-year-old orphan Kate befriends dying Jolie in a story set during and after the 1906 San Francisco earthquake. (Rev: BCCB 11/01; BL 10/15/01; HBG 3/02; SLJ 10/01)

9941 Tolliver, Ruby C. *Boomer's Kids* (4–6). Illus. by Lyle Miller. 1992, Hendrick-Long paper $10.95 (0-885777-22-1). 128pp. Teenagers Andy and Ellie are tired of moving, as the family follows their father, a "boomer" in the oil fields in 1901. (Rev: BL 8/92)

9942 Tripp, Valerie. *Changes for Kit: A Winter Story* (3–5). Illus. by Walter Rane. Series: American Girl. 2001, Pleasant Co. $12.95 (1-58485-027-2); paper $5.95 (1-58485-026-4). 70pp. A section of historical facts and photographs follows the story of Kit seeking clothing donations for children at the local soup kitchen and learning to cope with her grumpy uncle during the Depression. (Rev: BL 12/1/01; HBG 3/02)

9943 Tripp, Valerie. *Changes for Samantha: A Winter Story* (3–5). Illus. by Robert Grace and Nancy Niles. 1988, Pleasant Co. LB $12.95 (0-937295-95-7); paper $5.95 (0-937295-47-7). 72pp. Wealthy New Yorker Samantha now lives with her aunt and uncle in a series that takes place in 1904 and includes: *Happy Birthday Samantha* (1987); *Samantha Saves the Day* (1988). (Rev: BL 1/1/89; SLJ 2/89)

9944 Tripp, Valerie. *Happy Birthday, Kit! A Springtime Story, 1934* (3–5). Illus. Series: American Girl. 2001, Pleasant Co. $12.95 (1-58485-023-X); paper $5.95 (1-58485-022-1). 70pp. Kit greets her Aunt Millie's arrival with mixed emotions. (Rev: BL 8/01; HBG 3/02)

9945 Tripp, Valerie. *Kit Learns a Lesson: A School Story* (3–5). Illus. 2000, Pleasant Co. $12.99 (1-58485-121-X). 67pp. As the Great Depression grows more serious, it affects all facets of Kit Kittredge's life including her family and school. (Rev: BL 9/1/00; HBG 3/01; SLJ 12/00)

9946 Tripp, Valerie. *Kit Saves the Day: A Summer Story, 1934* (3–5). Illus. Series: American Girl. 2001, Pleasant Co. $12.95 (1-58485-025-6); paper $5.95 (1-58485-024-8). 68pp. Kit discovers that a hobo's life isn't as much fun as she first thought. (Rev: BL 8/01; HBG 3/02)

9947 Tripp, Valerie. *Meet Kit: An American Girl* (3–5). Illus. by Walter Rane. Series: American Girls. 2000, Pleasant Co. $12.99 (1-58485-017-5). 70pp. In 1934, Kit Kittredge and her family feel the effects of the Great Depression when her father loses his job and her mother takes in boarders. (Rev: BL 9/1/00; HBG 3/01; SLJ 12/00)

9948 Tucker, Terry Ward. *Moonlight and Mill Whistles* (5–7). 1998, Summerhouse $15.00 (1-887714-32-4). 120pp. Thirteen-year-old Tommy is unaware how his life will change after he meets a gypsy girl named Rhona in this novel set in an early 1900s South Carolina cotton mill town. (Rev: BL 3/1/99; SLJ 5/99)

9949 Uchida, Yoshiko. *Samurai of Gold Hill* (5–8). Illus. by Ati Forberg. 1984, Creative Arts paper $8.95 (0-916870-86-3). 128pp. In this reissue of a 1972 title, a group of Japanese colonists try to farm an arid stretch of California in 1869.

9950 Vander Zee, Ruth. *Mississippi Morning* (3–6). Illus. by Floyd Cooper. 2004, Eerdmans $16.00 (0-8028-5211-4). A picture-book story of a 12-year-old boy in 1933 Mississippi who must come to terms with the racism that is all around him, even in his father. (Rev: BL 10/15/04*; SLJ 9/04)

9951 Waldman, Neil. *They Came from the Bronx: How the Buffalo Were Saved from Extinction* (2–5). Illus. by author. 2001, Boyds Mills $16.95 (1-56397-891-1). A Comanche grandmother and grandson await a small herd of buffalo in a story based on efforts to return bison to the plains in 1907. (Rev: HBG 10/02; SLJ 9/01)

9952 Warner, Sally. *Finding Hattie* (5–8). 2001, HarperCollins $15.95 (0-06-028464-1). 234pp. Hattie Knowlton's 1882 journal describes Miss Bulkey's school in Tarrytown, New York, and the people she meets there, including her sophisticated, shallow but popular cousin Sophie. (Rev: BCCB 6/01; BL 2/1/01; HB 5–6/01; HBG 10/01; SLJ 2/01)

9953 Wax, Wendy. *Empire Dreams* (3–6). Illus. by Todd Doney. Series: Adventures in America. 2000, Silver Moon LB $14.95 (1-893110-19-2). 91pp. Eleven-year-old Julie, growing up in New York during the construction of the Empire State Building, secretly takes a job to help out her family after her father becomes unemployed. (Rev: HBG 3/01; SLJ 3/01)

9954 Wells, Rosemary. *Wingwalker* (3–5). Illus. by Brian Selznick. 2002, Hyperion LB $16.49 (0-7868-2347-X). 64pp. A young boy's father takes a carnival job as a wing-walker during the Great Depression in this book with illustrations that evoke the atmosphere of the time. (Rev: BCCB 5/02; BL 3/15/02*; HB 7–8/02; HBG 10/02; SLJ 5/02*)

9955 Wells, Rosemary, and Tom Wells. *The House in the Mail* (2–5). Illus. by Dan Andreasen. 2002, Viking $16.99 (0-670-03545-9). 32pp. A scrapbook-style accounting by a 12-year-old girl of her family's mail-order home in 1927 Kentucky. (Rev: BCCB 2/02; BL 3/1/02; HBG 10/02; SLJ 3/02)

9956 West, Tracey. *Fire in the Valley* (3–5). Illus. Series: Stories of the States. 1993, Silver Moon LB $14.95 (1-881889-32-7). 80pp. Eleven-year-old Sarah becomes involved in mob violence concerning water rights in this novel set in 1905 California. (Rev: SLJ 12/93)

9957 White, Ellen E. *Voyage on the Great Titanic: The Diary of Margaret Ann Brady* (4–8). Series: Dear America. 1998, Scholastic paper $10.95 (0-590-96273-6). A moving, powerful novel about a young girl who earns her passage to America to be with her brother by serving as a companion to a wealthy woman aboard the *Titanic*. (Rev: BL 10/15/98; HBG 3/99; SLJ 12/98)

9958 White, Ellen Emerson. *Kaiulani: The People's Princess* (5–8). Series: Royal Diaries. 2001, Scholastic paper $10.95 (0-439-12909-5). 240pp. This story, told in diary form, begins in 1889, when 13-year-old Princess Kaiulani of Hawaii heads to England to finish her studies. (Rev: BL 4/1/01; HBG 10/01; SLJ 6/01)

9959 Whitmore, Arvella. *The Bread Winner* (4–6). 1990, Houghton Mifflin $16.00 (0-395-53705-3). 144pp. In this Depression-era story, the Pucketts are forced to sell their farm. (Rev: BCCB 1/91; BL 11/1/90; SLJ 10/90)

9960 Winthrop, Elizabeth. *Franklin Delano Roosevelt: Letters from a Mill Town Girl* (5–7). Illus. Series: Dear Mr. President. 2001, Winslow $9.95 (1-890817-61-9). 128pp. Fictional letters between Franklin Delano Roosevelt and a 12-year-old girl illustrate living conditions and government policy during the Depression. (Rev: BL 2/1/02; HBG 3/02; SLJ 12/01)

9961 Wolfert, Adrienne. *Making Tracks* (5–7). Illus. Series: Adventures in America. 2000, Silver Moon LB $14.95 (1-893110-16-8). 96pp. In this novel set in the Depression, young Henry leaves his foster home to ride the rails to Chicago to find his father. (Rev: BL 7/00; HBG 3/01; SLJ 11/00)

9962 Wyatt, Leslie J. *Poor Is Just a Starting Place* (5–8). 2005, Holiday House $16.95 (0-8234-1884-7). 196pp. In rural Kentucky during the Great Depression, 12-year-old Artie longs for a different life. (Rev: BL 6/1–15/05)

9963 Yolen, Jane. *Tea with an Old Dragon: A Story of Sophia Smith, Founder of Smith College* (2–4). Illus. by Monica Vachula. 1998, Boyds Mills $15.95 (1-56397-657-9). In this historical story set in a 19th-century New England town, a little girl becomes friends with Miss Sophy Smith, the founder of Smith College. (Rev: HBG 3/99; SLJ 10/98)

World War II and After

9964 Avi. *Don't You Know There's a War On?* (4–7). 2001, HarperCollins LB $16.89 (0-06-029214-8). 208pp. It's 1943 Brooklyn, and 11-year-old Howie Crispers sees war, intrigue, and potential romance on every corner. (Rev: BCCB 5/01; BL 6/1–15/01; HB 5–6/01; HBG 10/01; SLJ 6/01)

9965 Avi. *Who Was That Masked Man, Anyway?* (5–7). 1992, Orchard LB $17.99 (0-531-08607-0). 176pp. In a story told through dialogue, sixth-grader Frankie lives through World War II by immersing himself in his beloved radio serials. (Rev: BCCB 10/92*; BL 8/92*; HB 3–4/93; SLJ 10/92*)

9966 Ayres, Katherine. *Voices at Whisper Bend* (3–6). Illus. by Greg Dearth and Dahl Taylor. Series: History Mysteries. 1999, Pleasant Co. $9.95 (1-56247-817-6); paper $5.95 (1-56247-761-7). 162pp. During World War II in Pennsylvania, young Charlotte leads a drive to collect scrap metal and, later, must solve a mystery when it is stolen. (Rev: HBG 3/00; SLJ 2/00)

9967 Bishop, Claire Huchet. *Twenty and Ten* (4–6). Illus. by William Pene du Bois. 1984, Peter Smith $17.75 (0-8446-6168-6); Puffin paper $4.99 (0-14-031076-2). A nun and 20 French children hide ten young refugees from the Nazis.

9968 Buckvar, Felice. *Dangerous Dream* (4–6). Ed. by Myrna Kemnitz. 1998, Royal Fireworks paper $6.99 (0-88092-277-X). 123pp. A 13-year-old Holocaust survivor is suspicious of the man who claims to be her father. (Rev: SLJ 4/99)

9969 Cheaney, J. B. *My Friend the Enemy* (5–8). 2005, Knopf LB $17.99 (0-375-91432-3). 256pp. A friendship with a Japanese American boy tests the resolve of 11-year-old Hazel during World War II. (Rev: BL 5/15/05)

9970 Coerr, Eleanor. *Mieko and the Fifth Treasure* (4–7). 2003, Puffin paper $5.99 (0-698-11990-8). 78pp. A Japanese girl believes that she will never draw again after she is injured during the atomic bomb attack on Nagasaki. (Rev: BCCB 4/93; BL 4/1/93*; SLJ 7/93)

9971 Copeland, Cynthia. *Elin's Island* (5–7). 2003, Millbrook LB $22.90 (0-7613-2522-0). 144pp. Raised since infancy by lighthouse keepers, 13-year-old Elin is left on her own to tend the house and light on an eventful night in 1941. (Rev: BL 3/15/03; HBG 10/03; SLJ 7/03)

9972 Crum, Shutta. *Spitting Image* (5–8). 2003, Clarion $15.00 (0-618-23477-2). 224pp. Jessie has a busy summer in 1967 in her Kentucky hometown, tackling family problems and dealing with well-meaning volunteers and reporters who view them as "rural poor." (Rev: BL 3/1/03; HBG 10/03; SLJ 4/03*)

9973 Dahlberg, Maurine F. *Play to the Angel* (5–9). 2000, Farrar $16.00 (0-374-35994-6). 192pp. When Hitler invades Austria in 1938, Greta must help her

Jewish music teacher escape. (Rev: BL 7/00; HBG 3/01; SLJ 9/00)

9974 Davies, Jacqueline. *Where the Ground Meets the Sky* (5–8). 2002, Marshall Cavendish $15.95 (0-7614-5105-6). 224pp. During World War II, 12-year-old Hazel lives a lonely life in a compound in the New Mexico desert while her father works on a top secret project, until she makes a friend and uncovers a secret. (Rev: BL 9/1/02; HBG 10/02; SLJ 4/02)

9975 Deedy, Carmen A. *The Yellow Star: The Legend of King Christian X of Denmark* (3–5). 2000, Peachtree $16.95 (1-56145-208-4). Although in real life it did not happen, this picture book tells how the King of Denmark wore a Jewish star in World War II to show Hitler that in his country there are only Danes. (Rev: BCCB 11/00; BL 7/00; HBG 3/01; SLJ 9/00)

9976 DeJong, Meindert. *The House of Sixty Fathers* (6–8). Illus. by Maurice Sendak. 1956, Harper-Collins LB $15.89 (0-06-021481-3); paper $5.95 (0-06-440200-2). 192pp. Tien Pao and his pig, Glory-of-the-Republic, journey to find his parents in Japanese-occupied China.

9977 Denenberg, Barry. *One Eye Laughing, The Other Weeping* (5–7). Series: Dear America. 2000, Scholastic paper $12.95 (0-439-09518-2). 256pp. Thirteen-year-old Julie Weiss is able to flee Austria when the Nazis invade and travel to America to stay with her aunt, a famous stage star. (Rev: BL 7/00; HBG 3/01; SLJ 12/00)

9978 Elmer, Robert. *Into the Flames* (5–7). Series: Young Underground. 1995, Bethany House paper $5.99 (1-55661-376-8). 144pp. Danish twins are captured by the Gestapo while trying to rescue their uncle during World War II. (Rev: BL 5/15/95; SLJ 8/95)

9979 Evans, Freddi Williams. *A Bus of Our Own* (K–4). Illus. by Shawn Costello. 2001, Whitman $15.95 (0-8075-0970-1). 32pp. Based on a real event in segregated Mississippi, this is the story of an African American community that banded together to get a bus to carry their children to school. (Rev: BL 8/01; HBG 3/02; SLJ 9/01)

9980 Flood, Pansie Hart. *Sylvia and Miz Lula Maye* (3–5). Illus. by Felicia Marshall. 2002, Carolrhoda $15.95 (0-87614-204-8). 120pp. A 10-year-old African American girl and her 100-year-old neighbor form an unlikely friendship in this novel set in 1970s South Carolina. (Rev: BL 2/15/02; HBG 10/02; SLJ 4/02)

9981 Garrigue, Sheila. *The Eternal Spring of Mr. Ito* (4–6). 1994, Simon & Schuster paper $4.99 (0-689-71809-8). 176pp. This sequel to *All the Children Were Sent Away* (o.p.) continues the story of a young girl evacuated from London to Vancouver, British Columbia, during World War II. (Rev: BCCB 12/85; HB 1–2/86; SLJ 11/85)

9982 Geisert, Bonnie. *Prairie Summer* (4–6). Illus. by Arthur Geisert. 2002, Houghton Mifflin $15.00 (0-618-21293-0). 128pp. The story of a fifth-grade farm girl in rural South Dakota in the mid-1950s who shows courage and ingenuity when her mother

goes into early labor. (Rev: BL 3/1/02; HBG 10/02; SLJ 5/02)

9983 Giff, Patricia Reilly. *Lily's Crossing* (5–8). 1997, Delacorte $15.95 (0-385-32142-2). During World War II, motherless Lily loses her father when he is sent to fight in France but becomes friendly with Albert, an orphaned Hungarian refugee. (Rev: BCCB 4/97; BL 2/1/97; HB 3–4/97; SLJ 2/97)

9984 Going, K. L. *The Liberation of Gabriel King* (4–6). 2005, Penguin Putnam $15.99 (0-399-23991-X). 160pp. Ten-year-old Gabriel, a small and fearful white boy in 1976 Georgia, and his assertive African American friend Frita agree to tackle Gabe's (and her) fears and find themselves strong enough to withstand racist attacks. (Rev: BL 5/15/05; SLJ 6/05)

9985 Graff, Nancy Price. *Taking Wing* (5–8). 2005, Clarion $15.00 (0-618-53591-8). 224pp. A multilayered story set in 1942 Vermont and featuring 13-year-old Gus, who, over the course of the book, learns about prejudice, and about killing and death. (Rev: BL 5/15/05; SLJ 5/05)

9986 Griffis, Molly Levite. *The Feester Filibuster* (4–8). 2002, Eakin $16.95 (1-57168-541-3); paper $8.95 (1-57168-694-0). 224pp. John Allen Feester is determined to show he's not a spy in this sequel to *The Rachel Resistance* (2001). (Rev: BL 11/1/02; HBG 10/01)

9987 Hahn, Mary D. *Stepping on the Cracks* (5–8). 1991, Houghton Mifflin $16.00 (0-395-58507-4); Avon paper $5.99 (0-380-71900-2). 218pp. The compelling story of a sixth-grade girl during World War II and her difficult decision whether to help a pacifist deserter. (Rev: BCCB 12/91*; BL 10/15/91*; HB 11–12/91; SLJ 12/91*)

9988 Harrison, Barbara. *Theo* (5–9). 1999, Clarion $15.00 (0-395-19959-3). 176pp. A realistic war novel that tells of an orphan boy wandering alone in Greece during World War II, after his older brother has been executed. (Rev: SLJ 9/99)

9989 Hoestlandt, Jo. *Star of Fear, Star of Hope* (2–4). Trans. by Mark Polizzotti. Illus. by Johanna Kang. 1995, Walker LB $16.85 (0-8027-8374-0). 32pp. In World War II–occupied France, Helen witnesses the growing persecution of her Jewish friend Lydia. (Rev: BCCB 6/95; BL 5/1/95; HB 9–10/95; SLJ 8/95)

9990 Hoobler, Dorothy, and Tom Hoobler. *The 1940s: Secrets* (3–6). Illus. Series: Century Kids. 2001, Millbrook LB $21.90 (0-7613-1604-3). 176pp. The story of various branches of the Aldrich family and their contributions to the home front during World War II. (Rev: BL 4/1/01; HBG 10/01; SLJ 5/01)

9991 Kochenderfer, Lee. *The Victory Garden* (4–6). 2002, Delacorte $14.95 (0-385-32788-9). 166pp. Eleven-year-old Teresa writes to her pilot brother and helps her father tend a victory garden in this tale set in Kansas in 1943. (Rev: BCCB 3/02; BL 3/1/02; HBG 10/02; SLJ 1/02)

9992 Kudlinski, Kathleen V. *Pearl Harbor Is Burning! The Story of World War II* (4–6). Illus. by Ronald Himler. 1993, Puffin paper $4.99 (0-14-

034509-4). 64pp. Historical events are brought into perspective in a fictional framework as Frank, a newcomer to Hawaii, must learn to adjust to island living. (Rev: BCCB 10/91; BL 11/15/91; SLJ 2/92)

9993 Levine, Ellen. *Catch a Tiger by the Toe* (5–8). 2005, Viking $15.99 (0-670-88461-8). 208pp. Jamie's world is turned upside-down when her father is put in jail for refusing to reveal the names of other Communists to the House Un-American Activities Committee. (Rev: BL 3/15/05; SLJ 6/05)

9994 Lisle, Janet T. *The Art of Keeping Cool* (5–8). 2000, Simon & Schuster $17.00 (0-689-83787-9). 216pp. Robert is staying with his grandparents in New England during World War II and forms a friendship with his cousin, Eliot, who is helping an outcast German painter whom Robert thinks might be a spy. (Rev: BL 9/15/00*; HB 11–12/00; HBG 3/01; SLJ 10/00)

9995 Lowry, Lois. *Number the Stars* (5–7). 1989, Houghton Mifflin $16.00 (0-395-51060-0); Dell paper $5.99 (0-440-40327-8). 160pp. The story of war-torn Denmark and best friends Annemarie Johansen and Ellen Rosen. Newbery Medal winner, 1990. (Rev: BCCB 3/89; BL 3/1/89; SLJ 3/89)

9996 McGill, Alice. *Here We Go Round* (2–5). Illus. by Shane Evans. 2002, Houghton Mifflin $15.00 (0-618-16064-7). 128pp. A young African American girl named Roberta is sent to stay with her grandparents on their farm until the impending birth of her sibling in this thoughtful story set in 1946 North Carolina. (Rev: BCCB 7–8/02; BL 2/15/02; HBG 10/02; SLJ 4/02)

9997 McKissack, Patricia. *Abby Takes a Stand* (2–4). Illus. by Gordon C. James. Series: Scraps of Time. 2005, Viking $14.99 (0-670-06011-9). 112pp. Grandma Gee, an African American, tells her granddaughters about her humiliation when refused entry to a department store restaurant in 1960 and about her efforts to support the civil rights movement. (Rev: BL 5/15/05)

9998 McSwigan, Marie. *Snow Treasure* (4–7). Illus. by Andre Le Blanc. 1986, Scholastic paper $3.99 (0-590-42537-4). 156pp. Children smuggle gold out of occupied Norway on their sleds.

9999 Maguire, Gregory. *The Good Liar* (4–6). 1999, Clarion $15.00 (0-395-90697-0). 129pp. A first-person novel about a boy growing up in occupied France during World War II and the deception involved when his parents hide a Jewish woman and her daughter. (Rev: BCCB 3/99; BL 4/15/99*; HB 7–8/99; HBG 10/99; SLJ 5/99)

10000 Martin, Ann M. *A Corner of the Universe* (5–8). 2002, Scholastic $15.95 (0-439-38880-5). 208pp. Hattie recalls the summer she became 12, when a mentally disabled uncle came to stay with her family. Newbery Honor Book, 2003. (Rev: BCCB 2/03; BL 12/1/02; HB 1–2/03*; HBG 3/03; SLJ 9/02)

10001 Mazer, Harry. *A Boy at War: A Novel of Pearl Harbor* (5–9). 2001, Simon & Schuster $15.00 (0-689-84161-2). 112pp. Young Adam Pelko, new to Honolulu, is pressed into action on the morning of the attack on Pearl Harbor while trying to find his father, in this absorbing novel that also looks at relations with Japanese Americans. (Rev: BL 4/1/01; HB 5–6/01; HBG 10/01; SLJ 5/01)

10002 Mazer, Norma Fox. *Good Night, Maman* (5–9). 1999, Harcourt $16.00 (0-15-201468-3). A first-person account of a young Jewish girl's experiences in Europe during the Holocaust and later in a refugee camp in Oswego, New York. (Rev: BCCB 12/99; BL 8/99*; HB 11–12/99; HBG 3/00; SLJ 12/99)

10003 Moranville, Sharelle Byars. *Over the River* (5–7). 2002, Holt $16.95 (0-8050-7049-4). 240pp. Willa Mae's father finally returns from World War II, and although the 11-year-old is happy to have him home, family tensions and secrets persist. (Rev: BCCB 1/03; BL 11/15/02; HBG 3/03; SLJ 11/02)

10004 Mori, Hana. *Jirohattan* (3–6). Trans. from Japanese by Tamiko Kurosaki and Elizabeth Crowe. Illus. by Elizabeth Crowe. 1993, Bess Pr. paper $6.95 (1-880188-69-4). 76pp. In this tale set in World War II Japan, a slow-witted boy named Jirohattan helps others but is unable to comprehend death. (Rev: BCCB 2/94; SLJ 5/94)

10005 Myers, Walter Dean. *The Journal of Scott Pendleton Collins: A World War II Soldier* (5–9). Illus. Series: My Name Is America. 1999, Scholastic paper $10.95 (0-439-05013-8). Through a series of letters, readers get to know 17-year-old Collins, an American soldier who participates in the D-Day invasion of Europe. (Rev: BL 6/1–15/99; HBG 10/99; SLJ 7/99)

10006 Myers, Walter Dean. *Patrol: An American Soldier in Vietnam* (4–8). Illus. by Ann Grifalconi. 2002, HarperCollins LB $17.89 (0-06-028364-5). 40pp. A penetrating picture book for older readers told in narrative verse from the perspective of a teenage soldier in Vietnam. (Rev: BL 3/15/02; HB 7–8/02; HBG 10/02; SLJ 5/02)

10007 Orlev, Uri. *The Island on Bird Street* (5–7). 1984, Houghton Mifflin $16.00 (0-395-33887-5); paper $5.95 (0-395-61623-9). 176pp. A young Jewish boy inside the Warsaw ghetto during World War II.

10008 Osborne, Mary Pope. *My Secret War: The World War II Diary of Madeline Beck* (5–9). Illus. Series: Dear America. 2000, Scholastic paper $10.95 (0-590-68715-8). 192pp. Using a diary format, this novel set on Long Island during World War II tells of an 8th-grade girl who forms a club to help in the war effort. (Rev: BL 10/1/00; HBG 3/01; SLJ 10/00)

10009 Parkhurst, Liz. *Under One Flag: A Year at Rohwer* (3–5). Illus. by Tom Clifton. 2005, August House $16.95 (0-87483-759-6). 32pp. A young Japanese American intern and the son of the camp administrator become friends during World War II. (Rev: BL 5/15/05; SLJ 4/05)

10010 Paulsen, Gary. *The Quilt* (5–8). 2004, Random LB $17.99 (0-385-90886-5). 96pp. Based on events from the author's life, this gentle story, set against the backdrop of World War II, chronicles a young boy's extended stay with his grandmother in

Minnesota while his father is fighting in Europe. (Rev: BL 5/15/04; SLJ 5/04)

10011 Propp, Vera W. *When the Soldiers Were Gone* (4–9). 1999, Penguin Putnam $14.99 (0-399-23325-3). 101pp. The heartrending story of a young Jewish boy who, after World War II, must return to his own people and leave behind the loving farm family in Holland who had protected him and saved his life. (Rev: BCCB 2/99; BL 1/1–15/99; HB 7–8/99; HBG 10/99; SLJ 2/99)

10012 Radin, Ruth Yaffe. *Escape to the Forest: Based on a True Story of the Holocaust* (4–6). Illus. by Janet Hamlin. 2000, HarperCollins LB $13.89 (0-06-028521-4). 80pp. A realistic story of a Jewish girl named Sarah and her part in resistance against the Nazis during World War II. (Rev: BCCB 3/00; HBG 10/00; SLJ 3/00)

10013 Recorvits, Helen. *Where Heroes Hide* (4–6). 2002, Farrar $16.00 (0-374-33057-3). 144pp. Junior slowly comes to understand his gruff father, a World War II veteran, in this novel set in 1956 that deals with issues including polio and bullies. (Rev: BL 5/15/02; HBG 10/02; SLJ 5/02)

10014 Reiss, Johanna. *The Upstairs Room* (5–8). 1972, HarperCollins $15.95 (0-690-85127-8); paper $5.95 (0-06-440370-X). 196pp. Two young Jewish girls are hidden for over two years in the home of a simple Dutch peasant during the German occupation. A sequel is: *The Journey Back* (1976).

10015 Rodman, Mary Ann. *Yankee Girl* (4–8). 2004, Farrar $17.00 (0-374-38661-7). 224pp. In 1964, Alice's family moves from Chicago to Mississippi and sixth grader Alice must cope not only with the stress of a new school but also with her ambivalence about the only black girl in her class; newspaper headlines introducing each chapter keep the racial violence of the time in the reader's mind. (Rev: BL 3/1/04; SLJ 4/04)

10016 Rogers, Kenny, and Donald Davenport. *Christmas in Canaan* (5–8). 2002, HarperCollins $15.99 (0-06-000746-X). 336pp. In 1960s Texas, after a black boy and a white boy fight on the school bus, the adults decree that the two boys must spend time together, and a difficult start ends in the boys becoming fast friends when they help a wounded dog. (Rev: BL 11/1/02; HBG 3/03; SLJ 10/02)

10017 Ross, Stewart. *The Star Houses: A Story from the Holocaust* (5–7). Illus. Series: Survivors. 2002, Barron's $12.95 (0-7641-5528-8); paper $4.95 (0-7641-2204-5). 86pp. A 14-year-old Jewish boy describes his family's plight when the Nazis occupy Budapest. (Rev: BL 5/15/04)

10018 Say, Allen. *Music for Alice* (4–7). Illus. 2004, Houghton Mifflin $17.00 (0-618-31118-1). 32pp. Based on a real story, this is the moving portrait of a Japanese American couple who make the best of the challenges forced upon them during World War II. (Rev: BL 2/1/04; HB 5–6/04; SLJ 4/04)

10019 Serraillier, Ian. *The Silver Sword* (6–8). Illus. by C. Walter Hodges. 1959, Phillips $18.00 (0-87599-104-1). A World War II story of Polish children who are separated from their parents and finally reunited.

10020 Shemin, Margaretha. *The Little Riders* (4–6). Illus. by Peter Spier. 1988, Morrow paper $4.95 (0-688-12499-2). 80pp. An 11-year-old girl is trapped in German-occupied Netherlands during World War II. A reissue.

10021 Smith, D. James. *The Boys of San Joaquin* (5–8). 2005, Simon & Schuster $15.95 (0-689-87606-8). 240pp. An episodic tale set in the 1950s, in which 12-year-old Paolo describes events of his life and a mystery involving a half-eaten $20 bill. (Rev: BL 3/1/05; SLJ 1/05)

10022 Taylor, Marilyn. *Faraway Home* (5–8). 2000, O'Brien paper $7.95 (0-86278-643-6). 221pp. Taken from his Austrian homeland by the Kinder-transport, 13-year-old Karl is sent to County Down in Ireland where he endures the hardship of country life and the hostility of the locals. (Rev: BL 3/1/01)

10023 Testa, Maria. *Almost Forever* (2–5). 2003, Candlewick $14.99 (0-7636-1996-5). 80pp. In free verse, a first grader describes her feelings during the year her father spends as a doctor in the Vietnam War. (Rev: BL 9/1/03; SLJ 10/03)

10024 Tripp, Valerie. *Meet Molly: An American Girl* (3–5). Illus. by C. F. Payne. 1986, Pleasant Co. LB $12.95 (0-937295-81-7); paper $5.95 (0-937295-07-8). 72pp. Molly is growing up without a father during World War II in America. Others in the series are: *Molly Learns a Lesson* (1986); *Molly's Surprise* (1986); *Molly Saves the Day* (1988); *Happy Birthday, Molly!* (1987); *Changes for Molly* (1988). (Rev: BL 12/1/86)

10025 Uchida, Yoshiko. *The Bracelet* (1–5). Illus. by Joanna Yardley. 1993, Penguin Putnam $16.99 (0-399-22503-X). 32pp. Emi, a Japanese American girl, is confused and frightened when she is interned in a prison camp during World War II. (Rev: BCCB 9/93; BL 9/15/93; HB 11–12/93; SLJ 12/93)

10026 Vander Els, Betty. *The Bombers' Moon* (5–7). 1992, Farrar paper $4.50 (0-374-30877-7). 168pp. Missionary children Ruth and Simeon are evacuated to escape the Japanese invasion of China; they will not see their parents for four years. A sequel is *Leaving Point* (1987). (Rev: BCCB 9/85; BL 11/1/85; HB 9–10/85)

10027 Van Steenwyk, Elizabeth. *Maggie in the Morning* (4–6). 2001, Eerdmans $16.00 (0-8028-5222-X). 144pp. An 11-year-old girl who is staying with her aunt and uncle in the early 1940s discovers she is at the center of a family secret. (Rev: BL 1/1–15/02; HBG 3/02; SLJ 12/01)

10028 Vos, Ida. *Dancing on the Bridge at Avignon* (5–8). Trans. by Terese Edelstein and Inez Smidt. 1995, Houghton Mifflin $14.95 (0-395-72039-7). Rosa, a Jewish girl in the Netherlands during World War II, lives in constant fear that the Nazis will deport her and her family in this novel translated from Dutch. (Rev: BCCB 2/96; BL 10/15/95; SLJ 10/95)

10029 Watts, Irene. *Good-bye Marianne: A Story of Growing Up in Nazi Germany* (5–8). 1998, Tundra paper $7.95 (0-88776-445-2). In this autobiographical novel, 11-year-old Marianne Kohn is Jewish and experiencing Nazi persecution in 1938 Berlin when her parents decide to sent her to Britain as part of the Kindertransport rescue operation. (Rev: BCCB 7–8/98; BL 8/98; SLJ 8/98)

10030 Watts, Irene N. *Finding Sophie: A Search for Belonging in Postwar Britain* (5–8). 2002, Tundra paper $6.95 (0-88776-613-7). 144pp. In this sequel to *Remember Me* (2000), World War II has ended and 13-year-old Sophie waits anxiously to hear news of her Jewish family in Germany, at the same time hoping she will not have to leave her happy life in London. (Rev: BL 1/1–15/03; SLJ 3/03)

10031 Watts, Irene N. *Remember Me: A Search for Refuge in Wartime Britain* (5–8). 2000, Tundra paper $7.95 (0-88776-519-X). 176pp. A heart-tugging story of an 11-year-old Jewish girl who, at the beginning of World War II, is transported from her home in Berlin to live in a Welsh mining town where she knows no one and speaks no English. (Rev: BL 12/1/00; SLJ 1/01)

10032 Weatherford, Carole Boston. *Freedom on the Menu: The Greensboro Sit-ins* (1–3). Illus. by Jerome Lararrigue. 2005, Dial $16.99 (0-8037-2860-3). 32pp. Seen through the eyes of a young African American girl, this is the story of the 1960 lunch counter sit-ins in North Carolina. (Rev: BL 2/1/05; SLJ 4/05)

10033 Winkler, Allan M. *Cassie's War* (4–6). 1994, Royal Fireworks paper $9.99 (0-88092-106-4). 94pp. Cassie is growing up in California during World War II, which brings internment to her Japanese American friend and death to her soldier father. (Rev: BL 2/1/95)

10034 Woods, Brenda. *The Red Rose Box* (5–8). 2002, Penguin Putnam $16.99 (0-399-23702-X). 144pp. In 1953, Leah, a southern black girl, and her family travel to Los Angeles where they find a different culture and more progressive attitudes. (Rev: BCCB 7–8/02; BL 6/1–15/02; HBG 10/02; SLJ 6/02)

10035 Yep, Laurence. *Hiroshima* (4–7). 1995, Scholastic paper $9.95 (0-590-20832-2). 64pp. A powerful work of fiction that explores the bombing of Hiroshima in 1945 and its aftermath. (Rev: BCCB 6/95; BL 3/15/95*; HB 9–10/95; SLJ 5/95)

10036 Ylvisaker, Anne. *Dear Papa* (4–6). 2002, Candlewick $15.99 (0-7636-1618-4). 192pp. A nine-year-old girl, Isabelle, writes letters to her dead father in this touching novel set in Minnesota in 1943. (Rev: BL 8/02; HBG 3/03; SLJ 8/02)

10037 Yolen, Jane. *The Devil's Arithmetic* (4–8). 1988, Puffin paper $4.99 (0-14-034535-3). 160pp. This time-warp story transports a young Jewish girl back to Poland in the 1940s, conveying the horrors of the Holocaust. (Rev: SLJ 8/88)

10038 Zeinert, Karen. *To Touch the Stars: A Story of World War II* (5–8). Series: Jamestown's American Portraits. 2000, Jamestown paper $5.95 (0-8092-0630-7). 126pp. Eighteen-year-old Liz Erickson, who loves to fly airplanes, longs for independence while she investigates possible sabotage in the Women's Airforce Service pilots program. (Rev: SLJ 9/00)

Holidays and Holy Days

10039 Alcott, Louisa May. *An Old Fashioned Thanksgiving* (4–5). Illus. by Jody Wheeler. 1990, Applewood paper $5.95 (1-55709-135-8). 40pp. The happenings in a New Hampshire farm family in the 1820s, first published in 1881. (Rev: BL 10/1/89; SLJ 10/89)

10040 Axelrod, Amy. *Pigs Go to Market: Halloween Fun with Math and Shopping* (2–4). Illus. by Sharon McGinley-Nally. 1997, Simon & Schuster paper $14.00 (0-689-81069-5). At Halloween, the Pig family eats all the candy before the guests arrive. (Rev: HBG 3/98; SLJ 9/97)

10041 Bauer, Caroline Feller, ed. *Halloween: Stories and Poems* (3–6). Illus. by Peter Sis. 1989, HarperCollins LB $14.89 (0-397-32301-8). 96pp. An anthology with spooky happenings for reading on Halloween, although not directly related to the holiday. (Rev: BL 9/1/89; SLJ 10/89)

10042 Baum, L. Frank. *The Life and Adventures of Santa Claus* (3–5). Illus. by Michael Hague. 2003, Holt $19.95 (0-8050-3822-1). 175pp. Written by *Wizard of Oz* author Frank L. Baum and first published in 1902, this charming fantasy tale portrays Santa Claus as an ordinary human — adopted and raised by a host of magical creatures — who decides as an adult to devote his life to bringing joy to children around the world. (Rev: HBG 4/04; SLJ 10/03)

10043 Buck, Pearl S. *Christmas Day in the Morning* (3–6). Illus. by Mark Buehner. 2002, HarperCollins LB $18.89 (0-688-16268-1). 40pp. Oil paintings illustrate this reissue of the classic story, originally published in 1955, of a young boy who decides to do his father's farm chores on Christmas Day. (Rev: BL 10/15/02; HBG 3/03; SLJ 10/02)

10044 Burton, Tim. *The Nightmare Before Christmas* (3–5). Illus. 1993, Hyperion $15.95 (1-56282-411-2). 40pp. Based on the movie of the same name, this book tells of Jack Skellington's diabolical decision to trade places with Santa. (Rev: BL 10/1/93)

10045 Capote, Truman. *A Christmas Memory* (3–6). Illus. by Beth Peck. 1989, Knopf $19.00 (0-679-80040-9). A tender story about Christmas preparations in a parentless, poor household. (Rev: HB 3–4/90; SLJ 12/89)

10046 Caudill, Rebecca. *A Certain Small Shepherd* (3–6). Illus. by William Pene du Bois. 1997, Holt paper $6.95 (0-805-05392-1). A mute boy gets an opportunity to play one of the shepherds in a Christmas pageant.

10047 Chaikin, Miriam. *Alexandra's Scroll: The Story of the First Hanukkah* (4–6). Illus. by Stephen Fieser. 2002, Holt $18.95 (0-8050-6384-6). 113pp. Alexandra and her family are caught up in the tumultuous events that lead to the first Hanukkah in this brightly illustrated historical novel. (Rev: BL 9/1/02; HB 9–10/02; HBG 3/03; SLJ 10/02)

10048 *A Christmas Treasury: Very Merry Stories and Poems* (2–5). Illus. by Kevin Hawkes. 2001,

HarperCollins LB $16.89 (0-688-12040-7). 48pp. This combination of Christmas stories, carols, and poems is enhanced by Hawkes's detailed, full-color art. (Rev: BL 9/1/01; HBG 3/02; SLJ 10/01)

10049 Collington, Peter. *A Small Miracle* (2–5). Illus. 1997, Knopf $18.00 (0-679-88725-3). 32pp. An old woman who has rescued Nativity scene figures from the hands of a thief is in turn helped by them when she collapses in the snow. (Rev: BL 10/15/97*; HB 11–12/97; HBG 3/98; SLJ 10/97)

10050 Davis, C. L. *The Christmas Barn* (4–6). 2001, Pleasant Co. $12.95 (1-58485-414-6). 184pp. Twelve-year-old Roxie tells how her rural family struggles to celebrate Christmas during the Great Depression. (Rev: BL 9/1/01; HBG 3/02; SLJ 10/01)

10051 Dickens, Charles. *A Christmas Carol* (6–8). Illus. by Trina S. Hyman. 1983, Holiday House $18.95 (0-8234-0486-2). 128pp. A handsome edition of this classic.

10052 Grahame, Kenneth. *A Wind in the Willows Christmas* (3–5). Illus. 2000, North-South LB $15.88 (1-58717-007-8). 48pp. This is the Christmas chapter from *A Wind in the Willows*, abridged and turned into a charming Christmas book illustrated by Michael Hague. (Rev: BL 9/15/00; HBG 3/01)

10053 Hague, Michael. *Michael Hague's Family Christmas Treasury* (4–6). Illus. 1995, Holt $19.95 (0-8050-1011-4). 32pp. A selection of the author's favorite stories, poems, and carols about Christmas. (Rev: BL 11/1/95) [394]

10054 Hall, Lynn. *Here Comes Zelda Claus and Other Holiday Disasters* (4–6). 1989, Harcourt $16.00 (0-15-233790-3). 144pp. Each of the five stories about Zelda Claus in this collection deals with a different holiday. (Rev: BL 10/1/89; HB 3–4/90; SLJ 10/89)

10055 Hamilton, Virginia. *The Bells of Christmas* (3–5). Illus. by Lambert Davis. 1989, Harcourt $19.00 (0-15-206450-8). 60pp. A century ago a young boy celebrates the holiday with his family in Ohio. (Rev: BCCB 11/89; BL 10/1/89*; HB 11–12/89)

10056 Henry, O. *The Gift of the Magi* (5–8). Illus. by Carol Heyer. 1994, Ideals $14.95 (1-57102-003-9). 32pp. The classic story of unselfish love at Christmas gets some handsome illustrations. Another fine edition is illus. by Kevin King (1988, Simon & Schuster). (Rev: BL 8/94)

10057 Kertes, Joseph. *The Gift* (3–5). Illus. 1996, Douglas & McIntyre $12.95 (0-88899-235-1). 48pp. An immigrant Jewish boy gives an inappropriate Christmas gift to a friend. (Rev: BL 11/1/96)

10058 Kimmel, Eric A. *The Spotted Pony: A Collection of Hanukkah Stories* (3–6). Illus. by Leonard Everett Fisher. 1992, Holiday House $15.95 (0-8234-0936-8). 70pp. A collection of wonderfully earthy and joyous Jewish folktales. (Rev: BL 11/15/92)

10059 Kline, Suzy. *Horrible Harry and the Holidaze* (2–3). Illus. by Frank Remkiewicz. 2003, Penguin Putnam $13.99 (0-670-03642-0). 64pp. Horrible Harry's third grade class learns about five winter holidays — Three Kings' Day, Korean New Year, Kwanzaa, Hanukkah, and Christmas — while Harry worries about his grandfather's move to a nursing home. (Rev: BL 9/1/03; HBG 4/04; SLJ 10/03)

10060 Koller, Jackie F. *The Promise* (3–6). Illus. 1999, Knopf LB $17.99 (0-679-98484-X). 80pp. When Matt goes out with his dog one Christmas to feed suet to the birds, they are chased by a bear. (Rev: BL 9/1/99)

10061 Kraft, Eric P. *Lenny and Mel* (2–4). Illus. by author. 2002, Simon & Schuster $15.00 (0-689-84173-6). 64pp. Twins Lenny and Mel suffer through a school-year of holidays in this hilarious chapter book. (Rev: BL 3/1/02; HB 5–6/02; HBG 10/02; SLJ 2/02)

10062 Krensky, Stephen. *How Santa Got His Job* (2–4). Illus. by S. D. Schindler. 1998, Simon & Schuster $15.00 (0-689-80697-3). 32pp. A humorous picture book that traces Santa's career from chimney sweep to becoming a fixture at Christmas. (Rev: BL 9/1/98*; HBG 3/99; SLJ 10/98)

10063 Krosoczka, Jarrett J. *Annie Was Warned* (PS–3). Illus. by author. 2003, Knopf LB $17.99 (0-375-91567-2). By turns suspenseful and amusing, this engaging story tells what happens when Annie, acting on a dare, disregards her parents' warnings and visits a creepy neighborhood mansion on Halloween night. (Rev: HBG 4/04; SLJ 9/03)

10064 Lewis, Beverly. *The Crazy Christmas Angel Mystery* (2–4). Series: Cul-de-Sac Kids. 1995, Bethany House paper $3.99 (1-55661-627-9). 62pp. Eric is convinced that his strange new neighbor is dancing with angels in this holiday mystery story. (Rev: BL 9/15/95)

10065 Lovelace, Maud H. *The Trees Kneel at Christmas* (4–6). Illus. by Marie-Claude Monchaux. 1994, ABDO LB $16.98 (1-56239-999-3). 110pp. Afify and her young brother go to a Brooklyn park to see if trees really bow down on Christmas Eve, as the legend says. (Rev: BL 8/94)

10066 Low, Alice. *The Witch Who Was Afraid of Witches* (2–4). Illus. Series: I Can Read. 1999, HarperCollins LB $14.89 (0-06-028306-8). 48pp. In this easy chapter book, Wendy, a witch who doubts her own powers, gains confidence one Halloween night. (Rev: BL 9/1/99; HBG 3/00; SLJ 12/99)

10067 Maguire, Gregory. *Five Alien Elves* (3–5). Illus. by Elaine Clayton. 1998, Clarion $15.00 (0-395-83894-0). 176pp. On Christmas Eve, five space aliens kidnap the town mayor, and two rival clubs — the Copycats and the Tattletales — join forces to rescue him. (Rev: HBG 3/99; SLJ 10/98)

10068 Marsden, Carolyn. *Mama Had to Work on Christmas* (2–5). Illus. by Robert Casilla. 2003, Penguin Putnam $14.99 (0-670-03635-8). 96pp. Upset about having to spend Christmas Day at the hotel where her mother works, 9-year-old Gloria cheers up when she gets back to her Mexican border-town home and receives loving gifts. (Rev: BL 9/1/03; HBG 4/04; SLJ 10/03)

10069 Matthews, Caitlin. *While the Bear Sleeps: Winter Tales and Traditions* (4–6). Illus. 1999,

Barefoot $19.95 (1-902283-81-3). 80pp. A satisfying anthology of tales about winter holidays and customs, including Hanukkah, Kwanzaa, Christmas, and Twelfth Night, tied together by a story involving a little girl and her guide, a bear. (Rev: BL 11/15/99; SLJ 10/99)

10070 Osborne, Mary Pope. *Christmas in Camelot* (2–5). Series: Magic Tree House. 2001, Random LB $13.99 (0-375-91373.4). 116pp. Stalwart Jack and Annie time-travel to Camelot and must solve riddles to break the spell of the evil Mordred and save the knights of the Round Table. (Rev: BL 12/15/01; HBG 3/02; SLJ 10/01)

10071 Penn, Malka. *The Hanukkah Ghosts* (3–5). 1995, Holiday House $14.95 (0-8234-1145-1). 88pp. Susan — who is living with an elderly aunt on an English moor during Hanukkah — is visited by children who lived there during World War II. (Rev: BL 9/15/95)

10072 Pirotta, Saviour, reteller. *Joy to the World: Christmas Stories from Around the World* (3–4). Illus. by Sheila Moxley. 1998, HarperCollins $15.95 (0-06-027902-8). 44pp. This book retells five Christmas stories, one each from Syria, Malta, Mexico, Ghana, and Russia. (Rev: HBG 10/99; SLJ 10/98) [398.2]

10073 Polacco, Patricia. *Christmas Tapestry* (3–6). Illus. 2002, Penguin Putnam $16.99 (0-399-23955-3). 160pp. In this heartwarming Christmas story, a boy and his father use a tapestry to cover a hole in a church wall, only to find that the fabric has special meaning to a Jewish couple. (Rev: BCCB 10/02; BL 9/1/02; HBG 3/03; SLJ 10/02)

10074 Robinson, Barbara. *The Best Christmas Pageant Ever* (4–6). Illus. by Judith G. Brown. 1972, HarperCollins LB $15.89 (0-06-025044-5); paper $4.95 (0-06-440275-4). 96pp. When a family of unrestrained children takes over the church Christmas pageant, the results are hilarious.

10075 Russell, Ching Yeung. *Moon Festival* (3–5). Illus. by Christopher Zhong-Yuan. 1997, Boyds Mills $15.95 (1-56397-596-3). 32pp. Ying and her friends celebrate the summer Moon Festival in many ways, including making paper lanterns. (Rev: BL 9/15/97; HBG 3/98)

10076 Rylant, Cynthia. *Children of Christmas: Stories for the Season* (4–6). Illus. by S. D. Schindler. 1987, Orchard paper $6.95 (0-531-07042-5). 48pp. Six quiet stories about the emotions of Christmas. (Rev: BCCB 10/87; BL 9/1/87)

10077 Singer, Isaac Bashevis. *The Power of Light* (4–7). Illus. by Irene Lieblich. 1980, Avon paper $2.50 (0-380-60103-6). 80pp. A collection of eight charming, original stories celebrating Hanukkah, the Festival of Lights.

10078 Snow, Alan. *How Santa Really Works* (2–4). 2004, Simon & Schuster $15.95 (0-689-85817-5). 48pp. Is there a Santa? The answers in this picture book may be implausible but they will keep young readers highly entertained. (Rev: BL 11/15/04; SLJ 10/04)

10079 Spinelli, Eileen. *The Perfect Thanksgiving* (PS–2). Illus. by JoAnn Adinolfi. 2003, Holt $15.95

(0-8050-6531-8). Rhyming text and lively illustrations enhance this amusing comparison of the very different Thanksgiving experiences of two families. (Rev: HBG 4/04; SLJ 9/03)

10080 Thompson, Lauren. *A Christmas Gift for Mama* (3–5). Illus. by Jim Burke. 2003, Scholastic $16.95 (0-590-30725-8). 48pp. Inspired by O. Henry's "The Gift of the Magi," this holiday tale tells how Grace trades a treasured belonging to buy a matching figurine for her mother's collection, only to find that her mother disposed of the figurine to buy Grace a gift. (Rev: BL 9/1/03; HBG 4/04; SLJ 10/03)

10081 Thury, Fredrick H. *The Last Straw* (2–3). Illus. 1999, Charlesbridge $15.95 (0-88106-152-2). 32pp. An ailing, aged camel is too proud to refuse to carry any of the gifts, regardless of their weight, to the child in Bethlehem. (Rev: BL 9/1/99; HBG 3/00; SLJ 10/99)

10082 Trondheim, Lewis. *Happy Halloween, Li'l Santa* (1–3). Illus. by Thierry Robin. 2003, N B M Publishing $14.95 (1-56163-361-5). 48pp. In his second graphic novel, Li'l Santa is pitted against loggers who seem determined to cut down his forest of Christmas trees. (Rev: BL 11/15/03; HBG 4/04)

10083 Van Leeuwen, Jean. *The Great Christmas Kidnapping Caper* (3–5). Illus. by Steven Kellogg. 1975, Dial $12.95 (0-685-01454-1). 144pp. A group of mice who live in a dollhouse at Macy's solve the mystery of the disappearance of Santa Claus.

10084 Wallace, Ian. *The Man Who Walked the Earth* (3–5). Illus. by author. 2003, Groundwood $16.95 (0-88899-545-8). On a prairie farm in the 1930s, a mother, daughter, and son wait for the return of their long-absent husband and father — and on Christmas Day a mysterious stranger arrives. (Rev: HBG 4/04; SLJ 10/03)

10085 Walter, Mildred P. *Have a Happy . . .* (3–5). Illus. by Carole Byard. 1989, Avon paper $3.99 (0-380-71314-4). 144pp. In this story set during Kwanzaa, a week after Christmas, the fortunes of a struggling African American family are told. (Rev: BCCB 12/89; BL 9/1/89; HB 11–12/89)

10086 Weatherford, Carole Boston. *Juneteenth Jamboree* (2–4). Illus. by Yvonne Buchanan. 1995, Lee & Low $15.95 (1-880000-18-0). Two youngsters, new to Texas, celebrate Juneteenth, which commemorates the day Texas slaves learned that the Emancipation Proclamation freed them. (Rev: SLJ 1/96)

10087 Wiggin, Kate Douglas. *The Birds' Christmas Carol* (3–5). Illus. by Jessie Gillespie. 1941, Houghton Mifflin $9.95 (0-395-07205-0). A beautiful edition of a story first published in 1888. (Rev: HBG 3/98)

10088 Zalben, Jane Breskin. *The Magic Menorah: A Modern Chanukah Tale* (3–5). Illus. by Donna Diamond. 2001, Simon & Schuster $15.00 (0-689-82606-0). 56pp. Twelve-year-old Stanley dreads Hanukkah — lots of annoying relatives arrive and his grandfather always looks sad — but this year a strange man appears from a menorah Stanley finds in the attic and grants him three wishes. (Rev: HBG 3/02; SLJ 10/01)

Humorous Stories

10089 Ahlberg, Allan. *The Cat Who Got Carried Away* (1–3). Illus. by Katharine McEwen. 2003, Candlewick $15.99 (0-7636-2073-4). 96pp. This third installment in the entertaining Gaskitt saga includes the disappearance of two family pets while Dad handles the household chores and Mom spends most of her time in bed. (Rev: BL 6/1–15/03; HBG 10/03; SLJ 9/03)

10090 Ardagh, Philip. *Dreadful Acts* (4–7). Illus. by David Roberts. Series: Eddie Dickens. 2003, Holt $14.95 (0-8050-7155-5). 144pp. This zany sequel to *A House Called Awful End* (2002) throws more wild adventures at 12-year-old Eddie Dickens. (Rev: BL 4/15/03; HBG 10/03; SLJ 5/03)

10091 Ardagh, Philip. *The Fall of Fergal: Or, Not So Dingly in the Dell* (4–6). Illus. by David Roberts. Series: Unlikely Exploits. 2004, Holt paper $9.95 (0-8050-7476-7). 123pp. Fans of Lemony Snicket and of British wit will enjoy this introduction to the five children of the McNally family and their dilapidated father; the youngest brother falls to his death at the opening of the book. Also use *Heir of Mystery: The Second Unlikely Exploit* (2004). (Rev: BCCB 6/04; SLJ 7/04)

10092 Ardagh, Philip. *A House Called Awful End* (4–7). Illus. by David Roberts. 2002, Holt $14.95 (0-8050-6828-7). 144pp. Lemony Snicket fans will enjoy this complex story of 11-year-old Eddie, who winds up in a series of bizarre adventures when he has to leave his sick parents and live with eccentric relatives. (Rev: BCCB 12/02; BL 11/15/02; HBG 3/03; SLJ 9/02)

10093 Ardagh, Philip. *Terrible Times* (4–7). Illus. by David Roberts. 2003, Holt $12.95 (0-8050-7156-3). 160pp. Young Eddie Dickens sails for America and encounters all sorts of zany situations in this last installment in the trilogy set in Victorian England. (Rev: BL 2/1/04; HBG 4/04; SLJ 12/03)

10094 Atwater, Richard, and Florence Atwater. *Mr. Popper's Penguins* (4–6). Illus. by Robert Lawson. 1938, Little, Brown $16.95 (0-316-05842-4). 144pp. Mr. Popper has to get a penguin from the zoo to keep his homesick penguin company; soon there are 12.

10095 Auch, Mary Jane. *I Was a Third Grade Bodyguard* (1–3). Illus. by Herm Auch. 2003, Holiday House $15.95 (0-8234-1775-1). 73pp. When third grader Brian volunteers to look after the class chicken during Christmas vacation, the responsibility for watching the bird falls mainly on Arful, Brian's dog. (Rev: HBG 4/04; SLJ 12/03)

10096 Auch, Mary Jane. *I Was a Third Grade Science Project* (2–4). Illus. by Herm Auch. 1998, Holiday House $15.95 (0-8234-1357-8). 94pp. Brian tries to hypnotize his dog into believing he's a cat, but the spell works on one of Brian's classmates instead. (Rev: BL 3/15/98; HBG 10/98; SLJ 5/98)

10097 Banks, Kate. *Howie Bowles and Uncle Sam* (2–4). Illus. 2000, Farrar $15.00 (0-374-35116-3). 96pp. A delightful story in which third-grader Howie believes that he owes the IRS more than a hundred dollars and will soon be sent to jail because he can't produce the cash. (Rev: BCCB 1/01; BL 10/15/00; HBG 3/01; SLJ 12/00)

10098 Base, Graeme. *The Discovery of Dragons* (5–8). Illus. 1996, Abrams $16.95 (0-8109-3237-7). 32pp. A humorous account of the three pioneers in dragon research. (Rev: BL 11/15/96; SLJ 11/96)

10099 Bateman, Teresa. *The Ring of Truth* (3–6). Illus. by Omar Rayyan. 1997, Holiday House $16.95 (0-8234-1255-5). 32pp. In this picture book with an Irish flavor, a famous fibber, who is also a car salesman, is denied the right to lie. (Rev: BCCB 5/97; BL 7/97; SLJ 5/97)

10100 Beard, Darleen Bailey. *The Flimflam Man* (2–4). Illus. 1998, Farrar $15.00 (0-374-32346-1). 96pp. On a hot day in 1950, an advance man for a circus begins selling tickets for future performances, but some townspeople think that he is a fraud. (Rev: BCCB 5/98; BL 2/15/98; HB 3–4/98; HBG 10/98; SLJ 3/98)

10101 Benton, Jim. *Attack of the 50-Foot Cupid* (2–4). Illus. Series: Franny K. Stein, Mad Scientist. 2004, Simon & Schuster $14.95 (0-689-86292-X). 112pp. Franny's new lab assistant turns out to be a fairly inept mongrel who succeeds in unleashing a giant, arrow-shooting Cupid in this humorous beginning chapter book. Also use *The Invisible Fran* (2004). (Rev: BL 3/1/04; SLJ 5/04)

10102 Birdseye, Tom. *I'm Going to Be Famous* (4–6). 1986, Holiday House $15.95 (0-8234-0630-X). 144pp. Fifth-grader Arlo Moore is going to break the Guinness Book of World Records' time for eating bananas. (Rev: BCCB 1/87; BL 12/1/86)

10103 Birney, Betty G. *The World According to Humphrey* (2–5). 2004, Penguin Putnam $14.99 (0-399-24198-1). 144pp. Humphrey the hamster has a very varied and mostly enjoyable life as the class pet, but he worries about his future at the hands of Mrs. Brisbane. (Rev: BL 3/1/04; SLJ 4/04)

10104 Bliss, Corinne D. *Electra and the Charlotte Russe* (2–4). Illus. by Michael Garland. 1997, Boyds Mills $14.95 (1-56397-436-3). When she trips and upsets the cream on the pastries she is taking home, Electra tries to reshape them with her tongue. (Rev: HBG 3/98; SLJ 10/97)

10105 Blume, Judy. *Freckle Juice* (2–5). Illus. by Sonia O. Lisker. 1971, Macmillan $15.00 (0-02-711690-5); Dell paper $4.50 (0-440-42813-0). 40pp. A gullible second-grader pays 50 cents for a recipe to grow freckles.

10106 Bond, Michael. *Paddington Takes the Test* (3–5). Illus. 2002, Houghton Mifflin $15.00 (0-618-18384-1). 144pp. This new edition of a 1980 release about the ever-popular bear sports a new jacket illustration and a larger typeface. (Rev: BL 3/15/02; HBG 10/02)

10107 Brennan, Herbie. *Fairy Nuff* (3–5). Illus. by Ross Collins. 2002, Bloomsbury $13.95 (1-58234-770-0). 128pp. In this beginning chapter book, bungling Fairy Nuff burns down his cottage, launching a grenade into the grounds of Widow Buhiss, and the over-the-top antics begin. (Rev: BL 8/02; SLJ 8/02)

10108 Brisson, Pat. *Bertie's Picture Day* (2–3). Illus. 2000, Holt $16.00 (0-8050-6281-5). 70pp. In this easy chapter book, Bertie looks awful in his school picture after he loses a front tooth, gets a black eye, and is given a terrible haircut by his young sister. (Rev: BCCB 2/01; BL 12/1/00; HBG 10/01; SLJ 9/00)

10109 Brooke, William J. *A Is for AARRGH!* (5–8). 1999, HarperCollins LB $14.89 (0-06-023394-X). 160pp. A humorous story about a prehistoric boy, Mog, and his amazing discoveries about language and communication. (Rev: BCCB 11/99; BL 10/15/99; HB 9–10/99; HBG 3/00; SLJ 9/99)

10110 Bunting, Eve. *Nasty, Stinky Sneakers* (4–6). Illus. 1994, HarperCollins LB $14.89 (0-06-024237-X). 128pp. Colin thinks his sneakers are so smelly that they will win a prize, and then they suddenly disappear. (Rev: BL 5/1/94; SLJ 6/94)

10111 Butterworth, Oliver. *The Enormous Egg* (3–6). Illus. by Louis Darling. 1995, Houghton Mifflin $9.00 (0-395-73249-2). The story of a boy whose hen lays a large egg, which hatches a triceratops!

10112 Byars, Betsy. *Bingo Brown's Guide to Romance* (5–8). 2000, Puffin paper $5.99 (0-14-036080-8). Romance, confusion, and comedy occur when Bingo Brown meets his true love in the produce section of the grocery store. (Rev: BL 4/1/92; SLJ 4/92)

10113 Byars, Betsy. *The Cybil War* (4–6). Illus. by Gail Owens. 1981, Puffin paper $4.99 (0-14-034356-3). 144pp. A humorous story about the relationship between two boys and a girl, Cybil.

10114 Byars, Betsy. *Me Tarzan* (3–5). 2000, HarperCollins LB $14.89 (0-06-028707-1). 96pp. Dorothy's Tarzan yell is so effective that she wins the part of Tarzan in the school play, and also finds that animals respond to her call. (Rev: BCCB 6/00; BL 3/15/00; HB 5–6/00; HBG 10/00; SLJ 7/00)

10115 Byars, Betsy. *The Seven Treasure Hunts* (3–5). Illus. by Jennifer Barrett. 1992, HarperCollins paper $4.25 (0-06-440435-8). 80pp. Readers giggle and guess their way through the story of Jackson and friend Goat who are into treasure hunts. (Rev: BCCB 4/91; BL 3/15/91; HB 7–8/91; SLJ 6/91)

10116 Cabot, Meg. *Princess in Waiting* (5–7). Series: Princess Diaries. 2003, HarperCollins $15.99 (0-06-009607-1). 240pp. Princess Mia gets in a royal mess when her duties interfere with her love life. (Rev: BL 5/15/03; HBG 10/03; SLJ 5/03)

10117 Callen, Larry. *Who Kidnapped the Sheriff? Tales from Tickfaw* (4–6). Illus. by Stephen Gammell. 1985, Little, Brown $14.95 (0-316-12499-0). 176pp. The small town of Tickfaw has lots of characters, who are introduced in these related short stories. (Rev: BL 6/1/85; HB 5–6/85; SLJ 8/85)

10118 Calmenson, Stephanie, and Joanna Cole. *Gator Halloween* (2–4). Illus. 1999, Morrow LB $14.93 (0-688-14785-2). 64pp. Amy and Allie's plan to win the best Halloween costume prize gets sidetracked when they try to find a lost pet. (Rev: BL 9/1/99; HBG 3/00; SLJ 9/99)

10119 Calmenson, Stephanie, and Joanna Cole. *Get Well, Gators!* (2–4). Illus. Series: Gator Girls. 1998, Morrow LB $15.93 (0-688-14787-9). 64pp. When Allie, who was to sing a duet with Amy at the Swamp Town fair, comes down with swamp flu, Amy is afraid to sing solo in this simple, humorous story. (Rev: BL 11/15/98; HBG 3/99; SLJ 10/98)

10120 Cameron, Ann. *More Stories Huey Tells* (2–4). Illus. 1997, Farrar $13.00 (0-374-35065-5). 128pp. Some humorous everyday adventures experienced by a bright, eager 7-year-old named Huey. (Rev: BCCB 7–8/97; BL 4/15/97; HB 7–8/97; SLJ 6/97)

10121 Child, Lauren. *Utterly Me, Clarice Bean* (2–5). 2003, Orchard $15.99 (0-7636-2186-2). 160pp. Inspired by stories she's read, Clarice decides to exercise her own sleuthing abilities. (Rev: BL 9/15/03; HBG 4/04; SLJ 11/03)

10122 Cleary, Beverly. *Ellen Tebbits* (3–5). Illus. by Louis Darling. 1951, Morrow $15.89 (0-688-31264-0); Avon paper $4.99 (0-380-70913-9). 160pp. Eight-year-old Ellen has braces on her teeth, takes ballet lessons, and, worst of all, wears long woolen underwear.

10123 Cleary, Beverly. *Emily's Runaway Imagination* (3–6). Illus. by Beth Krush and Joe Krush. 1961, Morrow $15.89 (0-688-31267-5); Avon paper $4.95 (0-380-70923-6). 224pp. Emily's imagination helps get a library for Pitchfork, Oregon, in the 1920s.

10124 Cleary, Beverly. *Henry Huggins* (3–5). Illus. by Louis Darling. 1950, Morrow $14.89 (0-688-31385-X); Avon paper $4.99 (0-380-70912-0). 160pp. Henry is a small boy with a knack for creating hilarious situations. Others in the series: *Henry and Beezus* (1952); *Henry and Ribsy* (1954); *Henry and the Paper Route* (1957); *Henry and the Clubhouse* (1962). (Rev: HBG 10/01)

10125 Cleary, Beverly. *Otis Spofford* (3–6). Illus. by Louis Darling. 1953, Avon paper $4.99 (0-380-70919-8). 192pp. This story of Otis stirring up a little excitement at school is full of humor.

10126 Cleary, Beverly. *Runaway Ralph* (3–5). Illus. by Louis Darling. 1970, Morrow $15.93 (0-688-31701-4). 176pp. A motorcyclist mouse finds family life too stifling so he takes to his wheels, only to find that freedom is an evasive thing. Two others in the series: *The Mouse and the Motorcycle* (1965); *Ralph S. Mouse* (1982).

10127 Clifford, Eth. *Harvey's Horrible Snake Disaster* (3–5). 1984, Houghton Mifflin $15.00 (0-395-35378-5). 128pp. Harvey tries to disguise the fact that he is petrified of snakes.

10128 Conford, Ellen. *Jenny Archer to the Rescue* (3–5). Illus. by Diane Palmisciano. 1992, Little, Brown paper $4.95 (0-316-15369-9). 64pp. Jenny wants to be a hero, so she hunts for someone to save. Also use: *Can Do, Jenny Archer* (1991). (Rev: BL 11/1/90; SLJ 12/90)

10129 Conford, Ellen. *A Job for Jenny Archer* (2–4). Illus. by Diane Palmisciano. 1990, Little, Brown paper $4.50 (0-316-15349-4). Jenny's plans for an expensive present for her mother's birthday backfire, but she learns that small gifts can be precious, too. (Rev: BL 4/1/88; HB 7–8/88; SLJ 4/88)

10130 Conford, Ellen. *What's Cooking, Jenny Archer?* (2–4). Illus. by Diane Palmisciano. 1991, Little, Brown paper $4.95 (0-316-15357-5). 80pp. Jenny is inspired to make her own lunches after watching a cooking show. (Rev: BL 1/15/90; SLJ 1/90)

10131 Cooney, Doug. *The Beloved Dearly* (4–6). Illus. by Tony Diterlizzi. 2002, Simon & Schuster LB $16.00 (0-689-83127-7). 192pp. A 12-year-old goes into the pet funeral business in this humorous and inventive novel aimed at a middle-grade audience. (Rev: BCCB 5/02; BL 1/1–15/02; HBG 10/02; SLJ 1/02)

10132 Cooney, Doug. *I Know Who Likes You* (4–6). 2004, Simon & Schuster $15.95 (0-689-85419-6). 208pp. Little League and charm school are among the preoccupations of the well-drawn characters: Ernie, Dusty, and Swimming Pool. (Rev: BL 5/15/04; SLJ 2/04)

10133 Corbett, Scott. *The Lemonade Trick* (3–5). Illus. by Paul Galdone. 1988, Scholastic paper $4.50 (0-590-32197-8). 96pp. Kirby and his wonderful chemistry change good boys into bad boys and vice versa.

10134 Cowley, Joy. *Agapanthus Hum and the Eyeglasses* (K–3). Illus. by Jennifer Plecas. 1999, Penguin Putnam $13.99 (0-399-23211-7). 48pp. The young heroine of this easy chapter book is always rushing around and dropping her glasses. (Rev: BCCB 4/99; HBG 10/99; SLJ 4/99)

10135 Cox, Judy. *Third Grade Pet* (2–3). Illus. 1998, Holiday House $15.95 (0-8234-1379-9). 93pp. In this easy chapter book, Rosemary takes her class's pet rat home to save him from the class bully and has problems keeping him hidden and safe. (Rev: BCCB 2/99; BL 12/15/98; HBG 3/99; SLJ 2/99)

10136 Cox, Judy. *Weird Stories from the Lonesome Cafe* (2–5). Illus. 2000, Harcourt $15.00 (0-15-202134-5). 80pp. An easy chapter book in which Sam and his uncle open a roadside cafe to which celebrities come incognito. (Rev: BCCB 4/00; BL 4/15/00; HBG 10/00; SLJ 6/00)

10137 Crebbin, June. *Cows in the Kitchen* (PS). Illus. by Katharine McEwen. 1998, Candlewick $15.99 (0-7636-0645-6). 32pp. While a farmer sleeps in the haystack, his farm animals invade his house causing chaos and great fun. (Rev: BCCB 10/98; BL 9/1/98; HBG 3/99; SLJ 9/98)

10138 Creech, Sharon. *Absolutely Normal Chaos* (5–8). 1995, HarperCollins LB $16.89 (0-06-026992-8). Mary Lou, 13, keeps a journal during summer vacation, chronicling the roller-coaster process of adolescence — evolving friendships, her first kiss, and the gradual appreciation of people different from her. (Rev: BCCB 11/95; BL 10/1/95; SLJ 11/95)

10139 Cutler, Jane. *'Gator Aid* (3–5). Illus. 1999, Farrar $16.00 (0-374-32502-2). 144pp. Second-grader Edward, who has a vivid imagination, claims he has seen a baby alligator in a local lake, and soon the rumor gets out of hand. (Rev: BCCB 9/99; BL 8/99; HB 9–10/99; HBG 3/00; SLJ 9/99)

10140 Danko, Dan, and Tom Mason. *Operation Squish!* (5–8). Illus. by Barry Gott. Series: Sidekicks. 2003, Little, Brown $10.95 (0-316-16847-5); paper $4.99 (0-316-16846-7). 106pp. A parody of the comic book superhero genre, featuring superheroes with odd attributes such as Pumpkin Pete, who has the powers of a pumpkin. The book is illustrated, but is not a graphic novel. (Rev: HBG 4/04; SLJ 3/04)

10141 Danziger, Paula. *Amber Brown Goes Fourth* (2–4). Illus. 1995, Penguin Putnam $14.99 (0-399-22849-7). 112pp. Amber Brown, a fourth-grader unsure of herself, doesn't know how to react to her divorced mother's new boyfriend. (Rev: BCCB 11/95; BL 10/15/95; HB 11–12/95; SLJ 10/95*)

10142 Danziger, Paula. *Amber Brown Is Feeling Blue* (3–5). Illus. 1998, Penguin Putnam $14.99 (0-399-23179-X). 32pp. Amber's humorous adventures continue when her divorced mother takes a new boyfriend, her father returns from Paris, and a new girl in her class also has a color-name, Kelly Green. (Rev: BL 12/1/98; SLJ 11/98)

10143 Danziger, Paula. *Amber Brown Is Not a Crayon* (2–4). Illus. by Tony Ross. 1994, Penguin Putnam $13.99 (0-399-22509-9). 80pp. Amber Brown's close friendship with Justin Daniels will end soon because Justin's family is moving. (Rev: BCCB 6/94; BL 4/15/94; HB 7–8/94; SLJ 5/94*)

10144 Danziger, Paula. *Amber Brown Sees Red* (2–4). Illus. 1997, Penguin Putnam $14.99 (0-399-22901-9). 120pp. Amber Brown is now in the fourth grade and is increasingly upset with her parents' custody battles involving her. (Rev: BL 5/15/97; SLJ 7/97)

10145 Danziger, Paula. *I, Amber Brown* (3–6). Illus. by Tony Ross. 1999, Penguin Putnam $14.99 (0-399-23180-3). 140pp. Amber Brown, daughter of divorced parents, gets her ears pierced when she is with her father, in spite of her mother's objections. (Rev: BL 10/15/99; HBG 3/00; SLJ 11/99)

10146 Danziger, Paula. *You Can't Eat Your Chicken Pox, Amber Brown* (2–4). Illus. by Tony Ross. 1995, Penguin Putnam $14.99 (0-399-22702-4). 112pp. Amber visits London with her aunt while her parents are getting a divorce. A sequel to *Amber Brown Is Not a Crayon* (1994). (Rev: BCCB 4/95; BL 3/15/95; SLJ 6/95*)

10147 Derby, Kenneth. *The Top 10 Ways to Ruin the First Day of 5th Grade* (4–6). 2004, Holiday House $16.95 (0-8234-1851-0). 164pp. Fifth-grader Tony Madison, a big fan of David Letterman's late-night TV show, indulges in increasingly outrageous stunts in an effort to appear on the show. (Rev: BL 2/1/05; SLJ 1/05)

10148 Dhami, Narinder. *Bollywood Babes* (5–8). 2005, Delacorte LB $16.99 (0-385-90215-8). 176pp. The Bindi sisters (introduced in *Bindi*

494

Babes) hatch a scheme involving a washed-up Bollywood star in the hopes of helping their school in this light novel set in England. (Rev: BL 3/1/05; SLJ 4/05)

10149 du Bois, William Pene. *Twenty-One Balloons* (4–6). Illus. by author. 1947, Puffin paper $5.99 (0-14-032097-0). 184pp. Truth and fiction are combined in the adventures of a professor who sails around the world in a balloon. Newbery Medal winner, 1948.

10150 Duffey, Betsy. *Cody's Secret Admirer* (2–3). Illus. 1998, Viking $13.99 (0-670-87400-0). 80pp. A humorous story about 9-year-old Cody, who regards getting a valentine from a secret admirer as "gross." (Rev: BCCB 5/98; BL 2/1/98; HBG 10/98; SLJ 10/98)

10151 Evans, Douglas. *Math Rashes and Other Classroom Tales* (2–4). Illus. 2000, Front Street $15.95 (1-886910-66-9). 112pp. Wacky third-grade experiences are the subject of this collection of original short stories. (Rev: BL 12/15/00; HBG 3/01; SLJ 11/00)

10152 Feiffer, Jules. *The Man in the Ceiling* (5–7). Illus. 1993, HarperCollins $15.95 (0-06-205035-4); paper $7.99 (0-06-205907-6). 192pp. Jimmy turns to cartooning in an effort to gain some recognition in a family that is intent on ignoring him. (Rev: BCCB 12/93; BL 11/15/93; SLJ 2/94*)

10153 Ferguson, Alane. *The Practical Joke War* (3–6). 1993, Avon paper $3.50 (0-380-71721-2). 160pp. All-out war is declared when the Dillon children — lovers of practical jokes — are left to themselves one summer. (Rev: BCCB 7–8/91; BL 4/1/91; SLJ 6/91)

10154 Fienberg, Anna, and Barbara Fienberg. *Tashi and the Big Stinker* (2–4). Illus. by Kim Gamble. 2001, Allen & Unwin paper $5.95 (1-86508-350-X). 63pp. Line drawings illustrate two tall tales from Australia, one full of raucous humor, the other a variation on the Pied Piper of Hamelin. (Rev: SLJ 7/01)

10155 Fine, Anne. *The True Story of Christmas* (5–7). 2003, Delacorte LB $17.99 (0-385-90156-9). 144pp. Ralph's horrendous relatives all arrive on Christmas Day, with disastrous consequences, in this hilarious novel. (Rev: BCCB 10/03; BL 9/1/03; HB 11–12/03; HBG 4/04; SLJ 10/03*)

10156 Fleischman, Sid. *A Carnival of Animals* (3–6). Illus. 2000, Greenwillow $15.95 (0-688-16948-1). 48pp. A tall tale about a tornado that causes weird changes in the farm animals. (Rev: BCCB 1/01; BL 9/1/00; HBG 3/01; SLJ 10/00)

10157 Fleischman, Sid. *Chancy and the Grand Rascal* (5–7). Illus. by Eric Von Schmidt. 1966, Little, Brown $14.95 (0-316-28575-7); paper $4.95 (0-316-26012-6). 190pp. The boy and his uncle, the grand rascal, combine hard work and quick wits to outsmart a scoundrel, hoodwink a miser, and capture a band of outlaws.

10158 Fleischman, Sid. *The Ghost on Saturday Night* (3–5). Illus. by Eric Von Schmidt. 1974, Little, Brown $14.95 (0-316-28583-8). 64pp. Ten-year-old Opie's efforts to raise money for a saddle involve

him in a ghost-raising session and the recovery of money stolen from a bank.

10159 Fleischman, Sid. *McBroom Tells the Truth* (3–5). Illus. by Walter Lorraine. 1981, Little, Brown $12.45 (0-316-28550-1). 48pp. A tall tale about a New England farmer named McBroom. Also use: *McBroom and the Great Race* (1980). (Rev: SLJ 1/05)

10160 Fleischman, Sid. *Mr. Mysterious and Company* (3–5). Illus. by Eric Von Schmidt. 1997, Greenwillow $15.00 (0-688-14921-9); paper $4.95 (0-688-14922-7). A traveling magic show during the 1880s makes for an entertaining family story that is also an excellent historical novel.

10161 Foley, June. *Susanna Siegelbaum Gives Up Guys* (5–8). 1992, Scholastic paper $3.25 (0-590-43700-3). 160pp. Susanna, a flirt, makes a bet that she can give up guys for three months. (Rev: SLJ 8/91)

10162 Fowler, Susi G. *Albertina, the Animals, and Me* (3–5). Illus. 2000, Greenwillow LB $14.89 (0-06-029160-5). 96pp. A humorous story of two friends, Molly and Albertina, who try various schemes to get their parents to allow them to have pets. (Rev: BL 12/15/00; HBG 3/01; SLJ 12/00)

10163 Frank, Lucy. *The Annoyance Bureau* (5–8). 2002, Simon & Schuster $16.95 (0-689-84903-6). 176pp. Lucas, 12, is already having a very annoying Christmas holiday in New York when he meets a Santa who says he works for the Annoyance Bureau, and the irritations begin to multiply. (Rev: BCCB 12/02; BL 11/1/02; HBG 3/03; SLJ 10/02)

10164 Freeman, Martha. *The Polyester Grandpa* (4–5). 1998, Holiday House $15.95 (0-8234-1398-5). 145pp. Grandma turns up with a new husband — brash, uncouth Jimmy Barkenfalt — and 10-year-old Morgan Knight's family has a fit. (Rev: BCCB 1/99; BL 12/1/98; HBG 3/99; SLJ 12/98)

10165 Friedman, Robin. *How I Survived My Summer Vacation: And Lived to Write the Story* (5–9). 2000, Front Street $15.95 (0-8126-2738-5). 160pp. A humorous story about 13-year-old Jackie Monterey, his friends, family, and the vow he has made to write the great American novel. (Rev: BL 8/00; HBG 10/00; SLJ 6/00)

10166 Gannett, Ruth. *My Father's Dragon* (4–6). Illus. by author. 1986, Knopf paper $4.99 (0-394-89048-5). 88pp. Hilarious adventures of Elmer Elevator. Also use: *The Dragons of Blueland* (1963); *Elmer and the Dragon* (1987).

10167 Gardiner, John Reynolds. *Top Secret* (4–6). Illus. by Marc Simont. 1995, Little, Brown paper $4.95 (0-316-30363-1). 129pp. Allen is convinced he can solve the world's hunger problem, and when no one believes him he goes to the president of the United States. (Rev: BCCB 11/85; BL 1/15/86; SLJ 11/85)

10168 Geras, Adele. *The Fabulous Fantoras: Book One: Family Files* (4–6). 1998, Avon $14.00 (0-380-97547-5). 144pp. The antics of an eccentric English family, in which each member has a special zany talent, are recorded by the family cat, Ozymandias, or Ozzy for short. (Rev: BL 11/1/98; HBG 3/99; SLJ 1/99)

10169 Getz, David. *Almost Famous* (3–5). Illus. 1994, Holt paper $5.95 (0-805-03464-1). 182pp. Overbearing Maxine knows she's destined to be an inventor, but for now, she has to team up with Toni the troublemaker for an invention contest partner. (Rev: BL 12/15/92*; SLJ 2/93)

10170 Gleitzman, Morris. *Toad Rage* (3–6). 2004, Random $14.95 (0-375-82762-5). 176pp. A plucky Australian cane toad sets out to stop the carnage of his fellow amphibians on the roads. (Rev: BL 3/1/04; SLJ 4/04)

10171 Gondosch, Linda. *The Monsters of Marble Avenue* (2–4). Illus. by Cat B. Smith. 1988, Little, Brown $10.95 (0-316-31991-0). 64pp. Luke learns the meaning of "the show must go on" when the puppets for his upcoming show are given away by mistake. (Rev: BL 4/1/87; SLJ 8/88)

10172 Gorman, Carol. *Dork on the Run* (4–7). 2002, HarperCollins LB $16.89 (0-06-029410-8). 176pp. Flack, a 6th grader, doesn't foresee the unusual and often funny situations that will arise when he runs for class president. (Rev: BCCB 9/02; BL 6/1–15/02; HB 9–10/02; HBG 10/02; SLJ 6/02)

10173 Gorman, Carol. *Lizard Flanagan, Supermodel?? (4–7)*. 1998, HarperCollins $14.95 (0-06-024868-8). 160pp. Sixth-grader Lizard Flanagan will do anything to make enough money to go by bus from her home in Iowa to a game in Wrigley Field, but is entering a local fashion show for teens going too far? (Rev: BL 11/15/98; HBG 3/99; SLJ 10/98)

10174 Gormley, Beatrice. *The Magic Mean Machine* (4–6). Illus. by Emily Arnold McCully. 1989, Avon paper $2.95 (0-380-75519-X). 128pp. Marvin invents a special machine to ensure that friend Alison will beat bully Spencer at chess. (Rev: BL 7/89)

10175 Gray, Margaret. *The Lovesick Salesman* (4–6). Illus. by Randy Cecil. 2004, Holt $16.95 (0-8050-7558-5). 184pp. Misunderstandings and misalliances abound in this satirical sequel to *The Ugly Princess and the Wise Fool* before happy endings arrive for Irwin, Seymour, and the beautiful Julia. (Rev: BL 1/1–15/05; SLJ 12/04)

10176 Greenburg, Dan. *Tell a Lie and Your Butt Will Grow* (2–4). Illus. by Jack E. Davis. Series: Zack Files. 2002, Grosset paper $4.99 (0-448-42682-X). 58pp. Andrew, Zack's less-than-truthful partner on a science fair project, discovers to his dismay that his backside is getting bigger with every fib he tells. (Rev: SLJ 4/03)

10177 Greene, Stephanie. *Owen Foote, Money Man* (2–4). Illus. by Martha Weston. 2000, Clarion $14.00 (0-618-02369-0). 96pp. In this beginning chapter book, young Owen helps his neighbor, Mr. White, build a backyard goldfish pond so he can earn enough money to buy a whoopee cushion and some plastic vomit. (Rev: BCCB 10/00; BL 9/1/00; HB 9–10/00; HBG 3/01; SLJ 9/00)

10178 Greer, Gery, and Bob Ruddick. *This Island Isn't Big Enough for the Four of Us!* (4–6). 1987, HarperCollins paper $4.95 (0-06-440203-7). 160pp.

It's boys against girls in this tale of too many camping out on Turtle Island. (Rev: BCCB 9/87; BL 7/87; SLJ 8/87)

10179 Haas, Jessie. *Clean House* (2–4). 1996, Greenwillow $15.00 (0-688-14079-3). 56pp. When relatives visit Tess's newly cleaned house, she makes them feel at home by returning it to its usual state. (Rev: BCCB 3/96; BL 4/15/96; HB 5–6/96; SLJ 5/96)

10180 Hayes, Daniel. *Eye of the Beholder* (5–8). 1992, Fawcett paper $6.99 (0-449-00235-7). Tyler and Lymie are in trouble again when they fake some works of a famous sculptor. (Rev: BL 2/1/93; SLJ 12/92)

10181 Heide, Florence Parry. *The Shrinking of Treehorn* (2–5). Illus. by Edward Gorey. 1971, Holiday House LB $16.95 (0-8234-0189-8); paper $6.95 (0-8234-0975-9). 64pp. Treehorn has a special talent — he can become smaller by the moment — but nobody notices. A sequel is: *The Adventures of Treehorn* (1983).

10182 Hermes, Patricia. *Kevin Corbett Eats Flies* (4–6). Illus. 1986, Harcourt $13.95 (0-15-242290-0); Pocket paper $3.99 (0-671-69183-X). 160pp. Kevin and his father move around whenever the mood strikes; now Kevin doesn't want to move anymore and thinks that if his father fell in love, he wouldn't want to either. (Rev: BCCB 9/86; BL 8/86; SLJ 5/86)

10183 Horvath, Polly. *The Happy Yellow Car* (5–7). 2004, Farrar paper $5.95 (0-374-42879-4). 150pp. In a small Missouri town, where this humorous story takes place, 12-year-old Betty Grunt must find a dollar if she wants to be elected Pork-Fry Queen. (Rev: BCCB 11/94; BL 8/94; SLJ 9/94)

10184 Horvath, Polly. *An Occasional Cow* (4–6). Illus. by Gioia Fiammenghi. 1989, Farrar paper $4.95 (0-374-45573-2). 112pp. Imogene's camp burns down, so she is shipped off to Iowa to stay with relatives. (Rev: BCCB 5/89; BL 5/15/89; HB 5–6/89)

10185 Horvath, Polly. *The Trolls* (3–6). Illus. by Wendy A. Halperin. 1999, Farrar $16.00 (0-364-37787-1). 144pp. Aunt Sally spins some fanciful tales when she entertains two nieces and a nephew left in her care. (Rev: BL 3/1/99*; SLJ 4/99)

10186 Horvath, Polly. *When the Circus Came to Town* (5–8). 1996, Farrar paper $5.95 (0-374-48367-1). 144pp. Opinion is sharply divided in Ivy's town when a circus troupe decides to relocate there. (Rev: BCCB 12/96; BL 11/15/96; SLJ 12/96*)

10187 Howe, Deborah, and James Howe. *Bunnicula: A Rabbit Tale of Mystery* (4–6). Illus. by Alan Daniel. 1979, Macmillan LB $16.00 (0-689-30700-4); Avon paper $3.99 (0-380-51094-4). 112pp. A dog named Harold tells the story of a rabbit many believe to be a vampire. Two sequels by James Howe are: *Howliday Inn* (1982); *The Celery Stalks at Midnight* (1983).

10188 Howe, James. *Bunnicula Strikes Again!* (3–6). 1999, Simon & Schuster $15.00 (0-689-81463-1). 128pp. In this sequel to *Bunnicula*, the fanged rabbit, who needs a diet of carrot juice, is again pursued by Chester, who is afraid other vegetables might be endangered. (Rev: BL 10/1/99; HBG 3/00; SLJ 12/99)

10189 Howe, James. *Howie Monroe and the Doghouse of Doom* (3–5). Illus. by Brett Helquist. 2002, Simon & Schuster $9.95 (0-689-83951-0). 96pp. Puppy Howie is self-congratulatory about his literary creation, a funny parody of Harry Potter. (Rev: BL 10/1/02; HBG 3/03)

10190 Howe, James. *The New Nick Kramer or My Life as a Baby-Sitter* (5–9). 1995, Hyperion LB $14.49 (0-7868-2053-5). Nick and rival Mitch make an unusual bet on who will win the affections of newcomer Jennifer. (Rev: BL 12/15/95; SLJ 1/96)

10191 Howe, James. *Nighty-Nightmare* (3–6). Illus. by Leslie Morrill. 1987, Macmillan $15.00 (0-689-31207-5); Avon paper $3.99 (0-380-70490-0). 128pp. Harold the canine and friends set out on a camping trip. (Rev: BCCB 4/87; BL 3/1/87; SLJ 4/87)

10192 Howe, James. *Return to Howliday Inn* (3–6). Illus. by Alan Daniel. 1992, Macmillan $15.00 (0-689-31661-5). 174pp. With the vampire bunny off with friends, the focus is on the Chateau Bow-Wow where the family boards their cat and dogs. (Rev: BL 5/1/92; HB 7–8/92; SLJ 5/92)

10193 Hurwitz, Johanna. *Elisa in the Middle* (2–4). Illus. by Lillian Hoban. Series: Russell and Elisa. 1995, Morrow $15.00 (0-688-14050-5). 64pp. In her efforts to help members of her family, Elisa often causes mayhem and catastrophe in this humorous beginning chapter book. (Rev: BCCB 10/95; BL 9/1/95; HB 11–12/95; SLJ 10/95)

10194 Ives, David. *Monsieur Eek* (4–7). 2001, HarperCollins LB $15.89 (0-06-029530-9). 192pp. Thirteen-year-old Emmaline defends a monkey against criminal charges in the not-quite-right town of MacOongafoondsen, population 21. (Rev: BL 6/1–15/01; HBG 3/02; SLJ 6/01)

10195 Jennings, Richard W. *My Life of Crime* (4–8). 2002, Houghton Mifflin $15.00 (0-618-21433-X). 160pp. Nothing goes right when 6th-grader Fowler decides to "rescue" a caged parrot. (Rev: BL 1/1–15/03; HBG 3/03)

10196 Keller, Beverly. *Desdemona: Twelve Going on Desperate* (5–7). 1986, HarperCollins paper $5.99 (0-06-440226-6). 160pp. Mishap after mishap befalls Desdemona, including running into the handsomest boy in school. A sequel is *Fowl Play, Desdemona* (1989). (Rev: BCCB 12/86; BL 10/1/86; SLJ 11/86)

10197 Kerr, M. E. *Dinky Hocker Shoots Smack!* (6–8). 1972, HarperCollins paper $4.95 (0-06-447006-7). 204pp. Dinky, a compulsive eater, tries many ways to gain her parents' attention.

10198 Kidd, Ronald. *Sammy Carducci's Guide to Women* (5–7). 1995, Dramatic Publg. $5.60 (0-87129-522-9). 112pp. A somewhat sexist 6th grader discovers that, where women are concerned, perhaps he is not as irresistible as he thinks he is. (Rev: BCCB 1/92; BL 1/1/92; SLJ 1/92)

10199 King-Smith, Dick. *Titus Rules!* (2–5). Illus. by John Eastwood. 2003, Knopf $15.95 (0-375-81461-2). 128pp. Life among British royalty is described from the point of view of Titus, a palace corgi. (Rev: BL 2/1/03; HBG 10/03; SLJ 3/03)

10200 Kitamura, Satoshi. *Comic Adventures of Boots* (2–4). Illus. 2002, Farrar $16.00 (0-374-31455-1). 32pp. Boots the cat has three funny adventures presented in comic-book style. (Rev: BL 10/1/02; HBG 10/03; SLJ 8/02)

10201 Kline, Suzy. *Molly's in a Mess* (2–3). Illus. 1999, Penguin Putnam $13.99 (0-399-23131-5). 80pp. Molly is out to get the girl who tattles on her about accidentally knocking off the principal's hairpiece. (Rev: BL 8/99; HBG 3/00; SLJ 8/99)

10202 Kline, Suzy. *Orp Goes to the Hoop* (5–7). 1993, Avon paper $3.50 (0-380-71829-4). 109pp. Seventh-grader Orp gets a chance to play a big part in the basketball team's big game. (Rev: BCCB 7–8/91; BL 7/91; SLJ 7/91)

10203 Klise, Kate. *Regarding the Fountain: A Tale, in Letters, of Liars and Leaks* (4–6). Illus. 1998, Avon $14.00 (0-380-97538-6). 144pp. Dry Creek's school needs a new water fountain, causing a flurry of letters, memos, and other communications involving the school and fountain designer, Florence Waters. (Rev: BL 8/98; HB 5–6/98; HBG 10/98; SLJ 6/98)

10204 Korman, Gordon. *Maxx Comedy: The Funniest Kid in America* (4–6). 2003, Hyperion $15.99 (0-7868-0746-6). 160pp. The joke-filled story of Max Carmody's quest to be the funniest kind in America also resonates with themes of friendship and loyalty. (Rev: BL 6/1–15/03; HBG 10/03; SLJ 9/03)

10205 Laden, Nina. *Romeow and Drooliet* (2–6). Illus. by author. 2005, Chronicle $16.95 (0-8118-3973-7). Romance is surely doomed when cat Romeow and dog Drooliet fall for each other. (Rev: SLJ 6/05)

10206 Lawson, Robert. *Captain Kidd's Cat* (3–5). Illus. by author. 1984, Little, Brown paper $7.95 (0-316-51735-6). A narrative recount by McDermot, faithful cat of Captain William Kidd.

10207 Lawson, Robert. *Mr. Revere and I* (5–8). Illus. by author. 1953, Little, Brown paper $6.99 (0-316-51729-1). 152pp. A delightful account of certain episodes in Revere's life, as revealed by his horse Scheherazade. (Rev: SLJ 1/05)

10208 Levoy, Myron. *The Magic Hat of Mortimer Wintergreen* (4–6). 1988, HarperCollins $11.95 (0-06-023841-0). 224pp. Joshua and Amy escape from creepy Aunt Vootch with a magician and search for their grandparents. (Rev: BL 2/15/88; SLJ 3/88)

10209 Lewis, Cynthia C. *Dilly's Summer Camp Diary* (3–5). Illus. by Cynthia Copeland Lewis. 1999, Millbrook LB $19.90 (0-7613-1416-4). Told in diary form, this is the humorous story of Dilly's three weeks at summer camp with all its delights and trials. (Rev: HBG 10/99; SLJ 6/99)

10210 Lewis, J. Patrick. *The Shoe Tree of Chagrin Falls* (3–5). Illus. by Chris Sheban. 2001, Creative Editions $17.95 (1-56846-173-9). 32pp. Old cobbler

Susannah, tall as a barn, braves ice and snow to deliver a load of handmade shoes to Chagrin Falls by Christmas. (Rev: BL 12/15/01; HBG 3/02; SLJ 2/02)

10211 Lindgren, Astrid. *Pippi Longstocking* (4–6). Trans. by Florence Lamborn. Illus. by Louis Glanzman. 1950, Puffin paper $4.99 (0-14-030957-8). 158pp. A little Swedish tomboy who has a monkey and a horse for companions. Also use: *Pippi Goes on Board* (1957); *Pippi in the South Seas* (1959).

10212 Lindgren, Astrid. *Pippi's Extraordinary Ordinary Day* (2–3). Illus. by Michael Chesworth. Series: Pippi Longstocking Storybooks. 1999, Viking $13.99 (0-670-88073-6). 32pp. Chapters from the original *Pippi Longstocking* are included in this newly illustrated edition for younger readers. (Rev: BL 10/15/99; HBG 3/00)

10213 Lowry, Lois. *Anastasia, Absolutely* (4–6). Series: Anastasia Krupnik. 1995, Houghton Mifflin $16.00 (0-395-74521-7); Bantam paper $3.99 (0-440-41222-6). 176pp. Anastasia absentmindedly throws a bag filled with her dog's poop into a mailbox and incurs an investigation by the police. (Rev: BCCB 9/95; BL 10/1/95; HB 11–12/95; SLJ 10/95)

10214 Lowry, Lois. *Anastasia at This Address* (5–9). 1991, Houghton Mifflin $16.00 (0-395-56263-5); Dell paper $4.50 (0-440-40652-8). The irrepressible Anastasia answers a personal ad, using her mother's picture instead of her own, with typically hilarious results. (Rev: BCCB 3/91; BL 4/1/91; SLJ 8/91)

10215 Lowry, Lois. *Anastasia on Her Own* (5–7). Illus. 1985, Houghton Mifflin $16.00 (0-395-38133-9); Dell paper $4.50 (0-440-40291-3). 131pp. Seventh-grader Anastasia Krupnik must face both domestic crisis and romance. Another chapter in Anastasia's busy life is recounted in *Anastasia Has the Answers* (1986). (Rev: BL 5/15/85; HB 9–10/85; SLJ 8/85)

10216 Lowry, Lois. *Anastasia's Chosen Career* (5–7). 1987, Houghton Mifflin $16.00 (0-395-42506-9); Bantam paper $4.50 (0-440-40100-3). Thirteen-year-old Anastasia gets some surprises when she begs to go to charm school to change her freaky looks. Anastasia's baby brother is featured in *All About Sam* (1988). (Rev: BCCB 9/87; BL 9/1/87; SLJ 9/87)

10217 Lowry, Lois. *Attaboy, Sam!* (2–5). Illus. by Diane De Groat. 1992, Houghton Mifflin $16.00 (0-395-61588-7). 116pp. Anastasia Krupnik's little brother, Sam, decides to make perfume for his mother's birthday. (Rev: BCCB 4/92; BL 2/15/92*; HB 7–8/92*; SLJ 5/92*)

10218 Lowry, Lois. *See You Around, Sam!* (3–6). Illus. by Diane De Groat. 1996, Houghton Mifflin $15.00 (0-395-81664-5). 144pp. Sam decides to run away to Alaska because his mother won't let him wear his plastic fangs. (Rev: BCCB 11/96; BL 10/1/96*; HB 9–10/96; SLJ 10/96*)

10219 Lowry, Lois. *Zooman Sam* (3–5). Illus. 1999, Houghton Mifflin $15.00 (0-395-97393-7). 160pp. Sam Krupnick is in seventh heaven when he learns to read in his nursery school. (Rev: BCCB 9/99; BL 7/99; HB 9–10/99; HBG 3/00; SLJ 9/99)

10220 McCloskey, Robert. *Homer Price* (3–6). Illus. by author. 1943, Puffin paper $4.99 (0-14-030927-6). 160pp. Popular and preposterous adventures of a Midwestern boy. Continued in: *Centerburg Tales* (1951).

10221 MacDonald, Amy. *No More Nice* (4–7). Illus. 1996, Orchard LB $15.99 (0-531-08892-8). 128pp. A humorous story about a spring vacation spent by a boy with his eccentric great-aunt and -uncle. (Rev: BCCB 10/96; BL 9/1/96; SLJ 9/96)

10222 McDonald, Megan. *Judy Moody Predicts the Future* (2–4). Illus. by Peter H. Reynolds. Series: Judy Moody. 2003, Candlewick $15.99 (0-7636-1792-X). 160pp. Eight-year-old Judy Moody is convinced that she has newfound psychic abilities when she slips on the mood ring from the cereal box. (Rev: BL 9/15/03; HBG 4/04; SLJ 11/03)

10223 McDonald, Megan. *The Sisters Club* (4–7). 2003, Pleasant Co. $12.95 (1-58485-782-X). 196pp. A funny novel about three sisters ages 8 to 12, who each contribute in different ways to their theater-absorbed family. (Rev: BL 12/1/03; HBG 4/04; SLJ 11/03)

10224 Mackay, Claire, sel. *Laughs* (5–8). 1997, Tundra paper $6.95 (0-88776-393-6). An anthology of humorous stories (and some poems) by several well-known Canadian writers. (Rev: SLJ 9/97)

10225 McKenna, Colleen O'Shaughnessy. *Mother Murphy* (5–7). 1993, Scholastic paper $2.95 (0-590-44856-0). 160pp. With her mother confined to bed, 12-year-old Collette volunteers as mother-for-a-day with disasterous and funny results. (Rev: BCCB 2/92; BL 2/1/92; SLJ 2/92)

10226 MacLachlan, Patricia. *Arthur, for the Very First Time* (4–6). Illus. by Lloyd Bloom. 1980, HarperCollins LB $15.89 (0-06-024047-4); paper $4.95 (0-06-440288-6). 128pp. Arthur spends a summer on the farm of his aunt and uncle.

10227 Manes, Stephen. *Chocolate-Covered Ants* (4–6). 1993, Scholastic paper $2.95 (0-590-40961-1). 128pp. Max bets his brother that people do eat chocolate-covered ants. (Rev: BCCB 12/92; BL 9/1/90; SLJ 12/90)

10228 Manes, Stephen. *Make Four Million Dollars by Next Thursday!* (3–6). Illus. by George Ulrich. 1996, Bantam paper $4.50 (0-440-41370-2). 112pp. Would-be millionaire Jazon Nozzle finds a book that tells him how to do it. (Rev: BCCB 2/91; BL 2/15/91; SLJ 6/91)

10229 Mason, Simon. *The Quigleys* (2–4). Illus. by Helen Stephens. 2002, Knopf $14.95 (0-385-75006-4). 160pp. Each of the four members of the eccentric British Quigley family has his or her own chapter in this amusing book. (Rev: BCCB 9/02; BL 7/02; HB 7–8/02; HBG 10/02; SLJ 6/02)

10230 Merrill, Jean. *The Pushcart War* (5–7). Illus. by Ronni Solbert. 1987, Dell paper $4.99 (0-440-47147-8). 224pp. Mack, driving a Mighty Mammoth, runs down a pushcart belonging to Morris the Florist, and a most unusual war is on!

10231 Merrill, Jean. *The Toothpaste Millionaire* (4–6). Illus. by Jan Palmer. 1974, Houghton Mifflin $16.00 (0-395-18511-4). 96pp. Kate tells the delightful story of an African American boy, Rufus, who challenges the entire business community by marketing a product called simply "toothpaste."

10232 Mills, Claudia. *Alex Ryan, Stop That!* (4–7). Series: West Creek Middle School. 2003, Farrar $16.00 (0-374-34655-0). 160pp. All Alex's efforts to attract classmate Marcia go awry in this humorous account of 7th-grade and son-father relations. (Rev: BL 4/1/03; HBG 10/03; SLJ 4/03)

10233 Morgenstern, Susie. *Secret Letters from 0 to 10* (4–8). Trans. by Gill Rosner. Illus. 1998, Viking $16.99 (0-670-88007-8). 208pp. Ten-year-old Ernest Morlaisse, whose mother is dead and father gone, is living a bleak existence with a grim grandfather until he meets Victoria and her 13 outgoing brothers. (Rev: BCCB 10/98; BL 10/1/98*; HB 11–12/98; HBG 3/99; SLJ 10/98)

10234 Mulford, Philippa Greene. *Making Room for Katherine* (5–9). 1994, Macmillan $14.95 (0-02-767652-8). A 16-year-old is recovering from her father's death when a 13-year-old cousin arrives from Paris to visit for the summer. (Rev: BL 4/15/94; SLJ 5/94)

10235 Myers, Bill. *The Case of the Giggling Geeks* (2–4). Illus. 2002, Thomas Nelson paper $4.99 (1-4003-0094-0). 88pp. Secret Agent Dingledorf (really elementary school student Bernie) tries to stop the giggles virus that is infecting only intelligent people in this humorous adventure full of action. Also use *The Case of the Chewable Worms* (2002). (Rev: BL 11/15/02)

10236 Naylor, Phyllis Reynolds. *The Agony of Alice* (5–7). 1985, Macmillan $17.00 (0-689-31143-5); Dell paper $4.99 (0-689-81672-3). 144pp. Motherless 6th-grader Alice is longing for a female role model, and finally finds one in her teacher, Mrs. Plotkin. (Rev: BL 10/1/85; SLJ 1/86)

10237 Naylor, Phyllis Reynolds. *Alice in April* (5–8). 1993, Atheneum $16.00 (0-689-31805-7); Dell paper $4.50 (0-440-91032-3). Alice is back, this time caught between her desire to be a perfect housekeeper and her fascination with her developing body. (Rev: BL 3/1/93; SLJ 6/93)

10238 Naylor, Phyllis Reynolds. *Alice In-Between* (5–7). 1994, Atheneum $16.95 (0-689-31890-1). 160pp. Alice, now 13, along with her friends, is becoming very aware of her changing body and of boys in this humorous look at early adolescence. (Rev: BCCB 5/94; BL 5/1/94; HB 7–8/94; SLJ 6/94)

10239 Naylor, Phyllis Reynolds. *Alice the Brave* (5–7). 1995, Simon & Schuster $15.95 (0-689-80095-9); paper $4.99 (0-689-80598-5). 131pp. Alice conquers her fear of deep water and also feels the pangs of growing up in this amusing continuation of a popular series. (Rev: BCCB 4/95; BL 5/1/95; HB 7–8/95; SLJ 5/95)

10240 Naylor, Phyllis Reynolds. *All But Alice* (5–8). 1992, Macmillan $15.95 (0-689-31773-5). 128pp. Alice, now a 7th grader and still motherless, deals with the challenges of friendship and popularity. (Rev: BCCB 5/92; BL 3/1/92; HB 7–8/92; SLJ 5/92*)

10241 Naylor, Phyllis Reynolds. *Boys Against Girls* (4–6). 1994, Delacorte $14.95 (0-385-32081-7). 147pp. Boys and girls try to trick each other into believing that a strange monster exists, and maybe they are right. (Rev: BCCB 11/94; BL 9/1/94; SLJ 11/94)

10242 Naylor, Phyllis Reynolds. *Boys in Control* (3–5). 2003, Random LB $17.99 (0-385-90154-2). 160pp. The Hatford brothers and Malloy sisters square off once again as a baseball conflict and the girls' discovery of embarrassing photos of the boys offer opportunities for oneupmanship. (Rev: BL 9/15/03; HBG 4/04; SLJ 10/03)

10243 Naylor, Phyllis Reynolds. *The Girls Take Over* (4–6). 2002, Delacorte $15.95 (0-385-32738-2). 160pp. The latest entertaining competitions between the Malloy girls and the Hatford boys involve a river race, a spelling bee, and baseball. (Rev: BL 9/15/02; HBG 3/03; SLJ 9/02)

10244 Naylor, Phyllis Reynolds. *Outrageously Alice* (5–8). 1997, Simon & Schuster $15.00 (0-689-80354-0). 133pp. Thirteen-year-old Alice, now in the eighth grade, decides that she is too ordinary and wants to do something about it. (Rev: BCCB 7–8/97; HB 7–8/98; SLJ 6/97)

10245 Naylor, Phyllis Reynolds. *Reluctantly Alice* (5–8). 1991, Macmillan $16.00 (0-689-31681-X). 192pp. Alice's life in the 7th grade seems full of embarrassment. (Rev: BCCB 4/91*; BL 2/1/91; HB 7–8/91; SLJ 3/91*)

10246 O'Malley, Kevin. *Captain Raptor and the Moon Mystery* (K–4). Illus. by Patrick O'Brien. 2005, Walker $16.95 (0-8027-8935-8). Captain Raptor and his dinosaur crew blast into space to investigate the landing of a UFO — carrying alien humans — on one of Jurassica's moons. (Rev: BCCB 4/05; SLJ 4/05)

10247 O'Neal, Katherine Pebley. *The Malodorous Mess. Bk. #1* (2–3). Illus. by Daryll Collins. Series: Stink Squad. 2003, Simon & Schuster LB $11.89 (0-689-85698-9); paper $3.99 (0-689-85697-0). 80pp. After a break-in at the Olfactory and the theft of an important scent, the Stink Squad — Dr. Sniffton Shroeder, his nephew Gilbreath, and Whiff the dog — springs into action to track down the culprit. (Rev: SLJ 10/03)

10248 O'Neal, Katherine Pebley. *The Reek from Outer Space* (2–3). Illus. by Daryll Collins. Series: Stink Squad. 2003, Simon & Schuster LB $11.89 (0-689-85700-4); paper $3.99 (0-689-85699-7). 78pp. When strange smells threaten to ruin the town's annual Toot 'n' Nanny smellabration — and its centerpiece bean banquet — the Stink Squad is called in by NASA to investigate. (Rev: SLJ 10/03)

10249 Park, Barbara. *Buddies* (5–8). 1986, Avon paper $2.95 (0-380-69992-3). 144pp. Dinah's dreams of being popular at camp are dashed in this humorous novel because she is forever being accompanied by Fern, the camp nerd. (Rev: BCCB 5/85; BL 4/15/85; SLJ 5/85)

10250 Park, Barbara. *Junie B. Jones and a Little Monkey Business* (2–3). Illus. by Denise Brunkus. 1993, Random paper $3.99 (0-679-83886-4). 46pp.

Junie is amazed to learn that her new brother is a monkey after grandmother declares, "He's the cutest monkey I've ever seen!" (Rev: BL 3/1/93)

10251 Park, Barbara. *Junie B. Jones and the Stupid Smelly Bus* (2–3). Illus. by Denise Brunkus. 1992, Random $11.99 (0-679-92642-9); paper $3.99 (0-679-82642-4). 70pp. Junie B. is a cross between Lily Tomlin's Edith Ann and Eloise in this funny story of a youngster on her way to kindergarten. (Rev: BL 12/1/92; SLJ 11/92)

10252 Park, Barbara. *Junie B. Jones Is a Beauty Shop Guy* (2–3). 1998, Random LB $11.99 (0-679-98939-5); paper $3.99 (0-679-88931-0). 67pp. Junie B. Jones believes she has a calling to become a barber and, after practicing on various stuffed animals, decides to move on to a human subject — herself. (Rev: BL 11/15/98; SLJ 12/98)

10253 Park, Barbara. *Junie B. Jones Smells Something Fishy* (2–4). Illus. 1998, Random paper $3.99 (0-679-89130-7). 67pp. When all her plans to take a pet to school fail, a disappointed Junie brings a fish stick instead and wins a prize for the most well-behaved pet. (Rev: BL 3/15/99)

10254 Park, Barbara. *The Kid in the Red Jacket* (4–6). 1988, Knopf paper $3.99 (0-394-80571-2). 128pp. Ten-year-old Howard is having some trouble adjusting to life in Massachusetts when his family moves from Arizona. (Rev: BCCB 3/87; BL 2/15/87; SLJ 3/87)

10255 Park, Barbara. *Operation: Dump the Chump* (3–6). Illus. by Robert Sauber. 1989, Knopf paper $4.99 (0-394-82592-6). 128pp. Oscar Winkle devises a plan to get rid of his young brother.

10256 Paulsen, Gary. *Harris and Me: A Summer Remembered* (5–8). 1993, Harcourt $13.95 (0-15-292877-4); paper $4.99 (0-440-40994-2). A humorous story in which the narrator often gets the blame for mischief caused by troublemaker Harris. (Rev: SLJ 2/00)

10257 Peck, Robert Newton. *Higbee's Halloween* (5–7). 1990, Walker LB $14.85 (0-8027-6969-1). 101pp. Higbee decides something must be done about the unruly Striker children. (Rev: SLJ 10/90)

10258 Petty, J. T. *Clemency Pogue: Fairy Killer* (3–6). Illus. by Will Davis. 2005, Simon & Schuster $9.95 (0-689-87236-4). 125pp. A satirical tale in which Clemency is inadvertently responsible for killing six innocent fairies and must set things right. (Rev: SLJ 4/05)

10259 Pilkey, Dav. *The Adventures of Captain Underpants* (2–4). Illus. 1997, Scholastic $16.95 (0-590-84627-2). 128pp. A superhero spoof in which two boys capture their principal and turn him into Captain Underpants. (Rev: BL 7/97; HBG 3/98; SLJ 12/97)

10260 Pilkey, Dav. *The Adventures of Super Diaper Baby* (2–5). Illus. by author. 2002, Scholastic paper $4.99 (0-439-37606-8). 125pp. As a penance for bad behavior, Harold and George are ordered to tackle the topic of good citizenship and instead invent a diaper-clad superhero. (Rev: HBG 10/02; SLJ 6/02)

10261 Pilkey, Dav. *Captain Underpants and the Attack of the Talking Toilets* (3–5). Illus. 1999, Scholastic $16.95 (0-590-63136-5). 144pp. George, Harold, and their school principal, who is also Captain Underpants, get involved in an army of teacher-eating toilets led by supercommode Turbo Toilet 2000. (Rev: BCCB 5/99; BL 5/1/99; HBG 10/99; SLJ 6/99)

10262 Pilkey, Dav. *Captain Underpants and the Invasion of the Incredibly Naughty Cafeteria Ladies from Outer Space (and the Subsequent Assault of the Equally Evil Lunchroom Zombie Nerds)* (4–6). Illus. 1999, Scholastic $16.95 (0-439-04995-4). 144pp. Another wacky adventure featuring fourth-graders George and Harold, their principal who becomes Captain Underpants, and a threat from outer space. (Rev: BL 9/15/99; HBG 3/00; SLJ 11/99)

10263 Pilkey, Dav. *Captain Underpants and the Perilous Plot of Professor Poopypants* (3–5). Illus. 2000, Scholastic $16.95 (0-439-04997-0). 160pp. Captain Underpants, aka Mr. Krupp, an elementary school principal, and students George and Harold combat a mad scientific genius, Pippy Pee-pee Poopypants. (Rev: BL 2/15/00; HBG 10/00; SLJ 5/00)

10264 Pilkey, Dav. *Captain Underpants and the Wrath of the Wicked Wedgie Woman* (3–6). Illus. 2001, Scholastic $16.95 (0-439-04999-7); paper $4.99 (0-439-05000-6). 176pp. George and Harold of Captain Underpants fame create a comic book about their teacher, Mrs. Ribble, whom they dub Wicked Wedgie Woman. (Rev: BL 1/1–15/02; HBG 3/02)

10265 Pinkwater, Daniel. *The Artsy Smartsy Club* (4–6). Illus. by Jill Pinkwater. 2005, HarperCollins LB $16.89 (0-06-053558-X). 176pp. Chalk sidewalk portraits of Henrietta (the giant chicken of *The Hoboken Chicken Emergency* [1977]) prompt a group of friends to investigate, leading them to an exploration of art in general and entertaining efforts to start up a new art festival. (Rev: BL 5/1/05; SLJ 5/05)

10266 Pinkwater, Daniel. *Fat Camp Commandos* (2–4). Illus. 2001, Scholastic $14.95 (0-439-15527-4). 96pp. A very funny chapter book about three children who escape from a "fat camp" and return secretly to their hometown to campaign for the rights of fat people. (Rev: BCCB 6/01; BL 4/15/01; HB 5–6/01; HBG 10/01; SLJ 5/01)

10267 Pinkwater, Daniel. *Fat Camp Commandos Go West* (3–5). Illus. by Andy Rash. 2002, Scholastic $14.95 (0-439-29772-9). 96pp. Sylvia and Ralph, who are attending a fat camp, join forces with friend Mavis to bring two warring groups of locals to a truce. (Rev: BCCB 7–8/02; BL 6/1–15/02; HBG 10/02; SLJ 6/02)

10268 Pinkwater, Daniel. *Fat Men from Space* (3–6). Illus. by author. 1977, Dell paper $3.99 (0-440-44542-6). 64pp. Among other adventures, William encounters raiders of junk food from outer space in this nutrition-conscious farce.

10269 Poploff, Michelle. *Busy O'Brien and the Great Bubble Gum Blowout* (3–5). Illus. by Abby Carter. 1990, Walker LB $13.85 (0-8027-6984-5). 80pp. Ten-year-old Busy O'Brien wishes she had more time to spend with her mom so she devises a plan. (Rev: BL 12/15/90; SLJ 10/90)

10270 Pryor, Bonnie. *Vinegar Pancakes and Vanishing Cream* (2–4). Illus. by Gail Owens. 1987, Morrow $16.00 (0-688-06728-X). 128pp. The ups and downs of life for Martin Elwood Snodgrass, who has too-successful older siblings and a too-cute baby brother. (Rev: BL 6/15/87; SLJ 6–7/87)

10271 Raskin, Ellen. *The Mysterious Disappearance of Leon (I Mean Noel)* (4–6). Illus. by author. 1989, Puffin paper $5.99 (0-14-032945-5). 160pp. Humorous saga of Mrs. Carillon's search for her husband Leon (or Noel), who is the joint heir to a soup fortune.

10272 Robertson, Keith. *Henry Reed, Inc.* (5–7). Illus. by Robert McCloskey. 1989, Puffin paper $5.99 (0-14-034144-7). 240pp. Told deadpan in diary form, this story of Henry's enterprising summer in New Jersey presents one of the most amusing boys since Tom and Huck. Others in the series *Henry Reed's Journey* (1963); *Henry Reed's Baby-Sitting Service* (1966); *Henry Reed's Big Show* (1970).

10273 Robinson, Barbara. *The Best School Year Ever* (3–5). 1994, HarperCollins LB $14.89 (0-06-023043-6). 128pp. Beth has to write a complimentary composition about a classmate who appears to have no redeeming qualities. (Rev: BL 10/15/94; HB 11–12/94; SLJ 10/94)

10274 Robinson, Barbara. *My Brother Louis Measures Worms and Other Louis Stories* (3–6). 1988, HarperCollins LB $15.89 (0-06-025083-6); paper $4.95 (0-06-440362-9). 160pp. Events in ten stories of the wild Lawson family. (Rev: BCCB 12/88; BL 11/1/88; SLJ 12/88)

10275 Rockwell, Thomas. *How to Eat Fried Worms* (4–6). Illus. by Emily Arnold McCully. 1973, Watts LB $25.00 (0-531-02631-0); Dell paper $4.99 (0-440-44545-0). 128pp. In this very humorous story, Billy takes on a bet — he will eat 15 worms in 15 days. His family and friends help devise ways to cook them.

10276 Rodgers, Mary. *Freaky Friday* (4–7). 1972, HarperCollins LB $16.89 (0-06-025049-6); paper $5.99 (0-06-440046-8). 156pp. Thirteen-year-old Annabel learns some valuable lessons during the day she becomes her mother. Two sequels are *A Billion for Boris* (1974) and *Summer Switch* (1982). (Rev: BL 4/15/89)

10277 Ryan, Mary C. *My Friend, O'Connell* (3–5). Illus. by Patrick Chapin. 1991, Avon paper $2.95 (0-380-76145-9). 104pp. In this humorous story, Bradley and friend O'Connell get involved in such situations as running a golf tournament and organizing a school cafeteria boycott. (Rev: BL 6/15/91)

10278 Rylant, Cynthia. *Mr. Putter and Tabby Paint the Porch* (2–3). Illus. by Arthur Howard. 2000, Harcourt $13.00 (0-15-201787-9). 44pp. An easy chapter book in which Mr. Putter's project to paint the porch is almost ruined when different animals walk across the wet paint. (Rev: BL 4/15/00; HBG 10/00; SLJ 7/00)

10279 Sachar, Louis. *Marvin Redpost: Is He a Girl?* (2–4). Illus. by Barbara Sullivan. 1993, Random LB $11.99 (0-679-91948-1); paper $3.99 (0-679-81948-7). 74pp. Marvin wonders if he is turning into a girl because he seems to be developing feminine interests. (Rev: BCCB 6/94; BL 11/15/93)

10280 Sachar, Louis. *Sideways Arithmetic from Wayside School* (4–8). Series: Wayside School. 1992, Scholastic paper $4.50 (0-590-45726-8). 89pp. Sue learns a new kind of math and encounters some humorous brainteasers when she transfers to Wayside School. (Rev: BL 12/15/89)

10281 Scieszka, Jon. *Squids Will Be Squids: Fresh Morals, Beastly Fables* (2–6). Illus. by Lane Smith. 1998, Viking $17.99 (0-670-88135-X). 48pp. This book by the author of the *Stinky Cheese Man* presents 18 contemporary, goofy fables, each with a silly moral attached. (Rev: BCCB 11/98; BL 9/15/98; HB 11–12/98; HBG 3/99; SLJ 10/98)

10282 Scrimger, Richard. *The Way to Schenectady* (4–6). Illus. 1999, Tundra paper $5.95 (0-88776-427-4). 168pp. A girl who is traveling from Ontario to Massachusetts with her family takes pity on a homeless man and hides him in the back of the van. (Rev: BL 5/1/99; SLJ 6/99)

10283 Seuling, Barbara. *Oh No, It's Robert* (2–4). Illus. 1999, Front Street $14.95 (0-8126-2934-5). 128pp. Robert is anxious to excel at something, but things always go wrong, especially when he lets the class hamster loose in his living room. (Rev: BL 7/99; HBG 10/99; SLJ 7/99)

10284 Seuling, Barbara. *Robert and the Weird and Wacky Facts* (2–4). Illus. by Paul Brewer. 2002, Cricket $15.95 (0-8126-2653-2). 120pp. Robert believes that he has developed magical powers and can make his wishes come true in this humorous addition to an appealing series. (Rev: BL 4/1/02; HB 7–8/02; HBG 10/02; SLJ 7/02)

10285 Singer, Marilyn. *Josie to the Rescue* (3–4). Illus. 1999, Scholastic $14.95 (0-590-76339-3). 96pp. Second-grader Josie tries several schemes to help supplement the family income, but they all fail in a comical fashion. (Rev: BL 5/1/99; HBG 10/99; SLJ 6/99)

10286 Smallcomb, Pam. *The Last Burp of Mac McGerp* (3–5). Illus. by Lizzy Bromley. 2003, Bloomsbury $15.95 (1-58234-856-1). 120pp. No one can belch quite like fifth-grader Mac, but his hopes of entering the National Burping Competition are threatened by a strict new school principal. (Rev: BL 2/15/04; HBG 4/04; SLJ 9/03)

10287 Smith, Greg Leitich. *Ninjas, Piranhas, and Galileo* (5–8). 2003, Little, Brown $15.95 (0-316-77854-0). 192pp. Romance, a science fair, and dubious ethics are in the air as Elias, Shohei, and Honoria try to navigate the shoals of 7th grade. (Rev: BL 12/1/03; HBG 4/04; SLJ 1/04)

10288 Smith, Lane. *Glasses: Who Needs 'Em?* (3–4). Illus. 1991, Viking $15.99 (0-670-84160-9). 32pp. A nutty optometrist uses extreme measures to get a young boy to wear his glasses. (Rev: BL 9/1/91; HB 11–12/91; SLJ 10/91)

10289 Smith, Robert K. *Chocolate Fever* (4–6). Illus. by Gioia Fiammenghi. 1989, Penguin Putnam $11.99 (0-399-61224-6); Dell paper $4.50 (0-440-41369-9). 96pp. Henry Green develops the first recorded case of chocolate fever in this reissued story.

10290 Snicket, Lemony. *The Bad Beginning* (4–7). Illus. Series: A Series of Unfortunate Events. 1999, HarperCollins $10.99 (0-06-440766-7). 192pp. A humorous story about the ill-fated Beaudelaire orphans and the creepy, wicked villains they never seem to avoid. (Rev: BL 12/1/99; HBG 3/00; SLJ 11/99)

10291 Snicket, Lemony. *The Carnivorous Carnival* (4–8). Illus. by Brett Helquist. Series: A Series of Unfortunate Events. 2002, HarperCollins LB $14.89 (0-06-029640-2). 304pp. The Baudelaire orphans pose as carnival freaks in the ninth volume of this unhappily-ever-after series. (Rev: BL 12/15/02; HBG 3/03; SLJ 1/03)

10292 Snicket, Lemony. *The Wide Window* (4–7). Illus. Series: A Series of Unfortunate Events. 2000, HarperCollins LB $14.89 (0-06-028314-9). 128pp. The three Baudelaire children have a new guardian, timid cousin Josephine, but they are pursued by former keeper Count Olaf. (Rev: BL 2/1/00; HBG 10/00; SLJ 1/00)

10293 Soto, Gary. *Summer on Wheels* (5–8). 1995, Scholastic paper $13.95 (0-590-48365-X). 144pp. In this sequel to *Crazy Weekend* (1994), Hector and Mando take a bike ride from their barrio home in Los Angeles to Santa Monica. (Rev: BL 1/15/95; SLJ 4/95)

10294 Spiegelman, Art, and Fran oise Mouly, eds. *Little Lit: It Was a Dark and Silly Night* (2–5). Illus. Series: Little Lit. 2003, HarperCollins $19.99 (0-06-028628-8). 48pp. Fifteen authors and artists each offer a cartoon story that begins with the line "It was a dark and silly night. . . . " (Rev: HBG 4/04; SLJ 9/03)

10295 Spinelli, Jerry. *The Bathwater Gang* (2–4). Illus. by Meredith Johnson. 1990, Little, Brown $10.95 (0-316-80720-6). 59pp. Bertie is bored, so she forms a Girls Only gang, and the boys retaliate. (Rev: BCCB 9/90; BL 6/15/90; SLJ 5/90)

10296 Spinelli, Jerry. *The Library Card* (4–8). 1997, Scholastic paper $15.95 (0-590-46731-X). Four humorous, poignant stories about how books changed the lives of several youngsters. (Rev: BCCB 3/97; BL 2/1/97; BR 3–4/97; HB 3–4/97; SLJ 3/97)

10297 Spinelli, Jerry. *Tooter Pepperday* (3–5). Illus. 1995, Random LB $11.99 (0-679-94702-7); paper $3.99 (0-679-84702-2). 85pp. Tooter has some hilarious adventures while adjusting to life on a farm far from her beloved city. (Rev: BCCB 6/95; BL 5/1/95; HB 9–10/95; SLJ 7/95)

10298 Stanley, George E. *Hershell Cobwell and the Miraculous Tattoo* (4–8). 1991, Avon paper $2.95 (0-380-75897-0). 128pp. A junior high boy decides to gain popularity by getting a tattoo. (Rev: BL 3/15/91)

10299 Steig, Jeanne. *Tales from Gizzard's Grill* (3–6). Illus. by Sandy Turner. 2004, HarperCollins LB $17.89 (0-06-000960-8). 72pp. Arresting verses with a tall-tale flair portray the many different characters found in the Old West town of Fiasco. (Rev: HB 5–6/04; SLJ 6/04)

10300 Steiner, Barbara. *Oliver Dibbs to the Rescue!* (4–6). Illus. 1985, Avon paper $2.50 (0-380-70465-X). 96pp. To save threatened wildlife, Oliver paints his dog Dolby as a tiger and exhibits him in a shopping mall. When Dolby "escapes," Oliver lands in the police station. Also use: *Oliver Dibbs and the Dinosaur Cause* (1986). (Rev: BL 12/1/85; SLJ 3/86)

10301 Strasser, Todd. *Kidnap Kids* (5–7). 1998, Penguin Putnam paper $5.99 (0-698-11801-4). 208pp. Because two brothers rarely see their busy parents, they hatch a plan to kidnap them. (Rev: BCCB 3/98; BL 1/1–15/98; HBG 10/98; SLJ 3/98)

10302 Thompson, Jill. *Scary Godmother* (4–8). 2001, Sirius Entertainment paper $19.95 (1-57989-015-6). Lively illustrations spark this humorous story about trick-or-treating with supernatural help. (Rev: BL 2/1/04)

10303 Timberlake, Amy. *The Dirty Cowboy* (K–4). Illus. by Adam Rex. 2003, Farrar $16.00 (0-374-37191-7). A filthy cowboy is so transformed by his annual bath that his dog, assigned to guard his clothes while he bathed, doesn't recognize him and refuses to surrender the cowpoke's duds. (Rev: SLJ 9/03)

10304 Tolan, Stephanie S. *Surviving the Applewhites* (5–9). 2002, HarperCollins LB $17.89 (0-06-623603-7). 216pp. The convention-flouting Applewhite family's Creative Academy helps a 13-year-old troublemaker to discover hidden talents. Newbery Honor Book, 2003. (Rev: BCCB 10/02; BL 11/1/02; HBG 3/03; SLJ 9/02*)

10305 Trahey, Jane. *The Clovis Caper* (5–8). 1990, Avon paper $2.95 (0-380-75914-4). 138pp. Martin is so upset at leaving his dog, Clovis, when going to England that Aunt Hortense plots to smuggle the dog out of the country. (Rev: BL 7/90)

10306 Twain, Mark. *Adventures of Huckleberry Finn* (6–8). 1993, Random $16.50 (0-679-42470-9). One of many editions.

10307 Uderzo, Albert. *Asterix and Son* (4–8). Trans. by Anthea Bell and Derek Hockridge. Illus. 2002, Orion paper $9.95 (0-75284-775-9). 48pp. In comic-book format, this is the entertaining story of French heroes Asterix and Obelix and how they became guardians of a kidnapped baby. Also use *Asterix and the Black Gold* (2002) and *Asterix and the Great Divide* (2002). (Rev: BL 4/15/02)

10308 Uderzo, Albert. *Asterix and the Actress* (4–7). Trans. by Anthea Bell and Derek Hockridge. Illus. 2001, Sterling $12.95 (0-75284-657-4). 48pp. These pun-filled, graphic-novel exploits of Asterix the Gaul include a boisterous shared birthday with the rotund Obelix and a daring rescue of prisoners in a Roman jail. (Rev: BL 8/01)

10309 Van Draanen, Wendelin. *Shredderman: Secret Identity* (3–5). Illus. by Brian Biggs. 2004, Knopf $12.95 (0-375-82351-4). 144pp. To get the best of a school bully called Bubba, brainy but somewhat nerdy fifth-grader Nolan makes Bubba the "star" of a Web site. (Rev: BL 2/1/04*; SLJ 5/04)

10310 Voigt, Cynthia. *Bad, Badder, Baddest* (5–8). 1997, Scholastic paper $16.95 (0-590-60136-9). 272pp. A hilarious mix of funny situations and outrageous dialogue feature two 6th-grade outsiders who deserve their reputation for being bad. A sequel to *Bad Girls*. (Rev: BL 11/1/97; HBG 3/98; SLJ 11/97)

10311 Voigt, Cynthia. *Bad Girls* (4–6). 1996, Scholastic $16.95 (0-590-60134-2). 256pp. Mikey and Margalo, two fifth-graders with reputations for causing trouble, test their limits. (Rev: BCCB 4/96; BL 4/1/96; HB 7–8/96; SLJ 5/96)

10312 Wallace, Bill. *Ferret in the Bedroom, Lizards in the Fridge* (4–6). 1986, Holiday House $15.95 (0-8234-0600-8). 144pp. Liz would certainly win the sixth-grade presidency if it weren't that her zoology teacher-father keeps so many unusual animals around the house and scares away her friends. (Rev: BCCB 7–8/86; BL 6/15/86)

10313 Wardlaw, Lee. *101 Ways to Bug Your Parents* (3–6). 1996, Dial $15.99 (0-8037-1901-9). 208pp. Sneeze Wyatt uses a summer session at school to compile a book on how to annoy parents. (Rev: BCCB 11/96; BL 10/1/96; SLJ 10/96)

10314 Ware, Cheryl. *Venola in Love* (4–7). Illus. by Kristin Sorra. 2000, Orchard LB $16.99 (0-531-33306-X). 160pp. Told through diary entries, e-mail messages, and class notes, this humorous novel tells how 7th-grader Venola discovers the problems of falling in love. (Rev: BCCB 10/00; HBG 10/01; SLJ 10/00)

10315 Weeks, Sarah. *Regular Guy* (4–6). 1999, HarperCollins LB $14.89 (0-06-028368-8). 128pp. In this humorous book, Guy is so unhappy with the wild behavior of his hippy parents that he tries to switch them for another pair. (Rev: BCCB 7–8/99; BL 9/1/99; HB 5–6/99; HBG 10/99; SLJ 6/99)

10316 Weston, Martha. *Act I, Act II, Act Normal* (4–7). 2003, Millbrook LB $22.90 (0-7613-2859-9). 160pp. Topher wins the lead in the 8th-grade play but the glory is tempered by the realities of school life in this humorous novel. (Rev: BL 6/1–15/03; HBG 10/03; SLJ 6/03)

10317 Wisniewski, David. *The Secret Knowledge of Grown-ups* (3–5). Illus. 1998, Lothrop LB $16.89 (0-688-15340-2). 48pp. A zany book that explores the truth behind such parental directives as "Drink your milk" and "Don't bite your fingernails." (Rev: BCCB 7–8/98; BL 3/1/98; HBG 10/98; SLJ 3/98)

10318 Wynne-Jones, Tim. *Ned Mouse Breaks Away* (2–4). Illus. by Dusan Petricic. 2003, Groundwood $14.95 (0-88899-474-5). 68pp. Ned Mouse attempts an ingenious escape from prison in this surreally funny story. (Rev: SLJ 4/03)

10319 Yaccarino, Dan. *The Big Science Fair!* (2–5). Illus. by author. Series: Blast Off Boy and Blorp. 2002, Hyperion $15.99 (0-7868-0580-3); paper $4.99 (0-7868-1430-6). Science fairs test the wit of Blast Off Boy and Blorp in their respective exchange schools, with humorous and unexpected results. (Rev: HBG 3/03; SLJ 12/02)

10320 Young, Steve. *Winchell Mink: The Misadventure Begins* (4–6). 2004, HarperCollins LB $16.89 (0-06-053500-8). 135pp. Changes in font, musical notes, and asides and commentary add to the humor and liveliness of this fast-paced story involving bullies, time travel, and an 11-year-old boy exchanging bodies with his pet turtle, Hannibal. (Rev: BCCB 9/04; SLJ 6/04)

School Stories

10321 Adler, David A. *School Trouble for Andy Russell* (2–4). Illus. 1999, Harcourt $14.00 (0-15-202190-6). 144pp. In this third installment of the Andy Russell series, Andy has problems at school, first with his math teacher, Ms. Roman, and then with her replacement, Ms. Salmon, who seems to be out to get him. (Rev: BL 1/1–15/00; HBG 3/00; SLJ 11/99)

10322 Asch, Frank. *Hands Around Lincoln School* (4–6). 1994, Scholastic $13.95 (0-590-44149-3). 217pp. Amy, a sixth-grader, decides to start a Save the Earth Club in her school to fight pollution and help save the environment. (Rev: BL 1/15/94; SLJ 3/94)

10323 Bartlett, Susan. *Seal Island School* (2–4). Illus. 1999, Viking $13.99 (0-670-88349-2). 80pp. A beginning chapter book about a little girl attending school on Maine's Seal Island, where the school population is six. (Rev: BCCB 3/99; BL 3/15/99; HBG 10/99; SLJ 5/99)

10324 Bauer, Marion Dane. *The Double-Digit Club* (3–5). 2004, Holiday House $15.95 (0-8234-1805-7). 118pp. Nine-year-old Sarah is devastated when her best friend Paige, now 10, abandons her to join the exclusive Double-Digit Club. (Rev: BL 3/15/04; SLJ 4/04)

10325 Benjamin, Saragail Katzman. *My Dog Ate It* (4–6). 1994, Holiday House $14.95 (0-8234-1047-1). 166pp. Danny dislikes homework so much that he decides to go on strike, but his teacher comes up with a novel solution. (Rev: SLJ 5/94)

10326 Birdseye, Tom. *Attack of the Mutant Underwear* (3–6). 2003, Holiday House $16.95 (0-8234-1689-5). 199pp. Dreams of past underwear-related humiliation haunt Cody Lee Carson as he prepares to begin fifth grade in a new town; his entertaining diary recounts his progress. (Rev: BL 1/1–15/04; HBG 4/04; SLJ 1/04)

10327 Borden, Louise. *The Day Eddie Met the Author* (2–4). Illus. 2001, Simon & Schuster $15.00 (0-689-83405-5). 40pp. Third-grader Eddie gets his wish to ask a question of his favorite author when she visits his school. (Rev: BL 3/1/01; HBG 10/01)

10328 Byars, Betsy. *The 18th Emergency* (4–6). Illus. by Robert Grossman. 1981, Puffin paper $4.99 (0-14-031451-2). 128pp. A young boy, nicknamed

Mousi, incurs the wrath of the school bully and awaits his inevitable punishment with fear.

10329 Byars, Betsy. *The Burning Questions of Bingo Brown* (6–8). 1990, Puffin paper $4.99 (0-14-032479-8). 160pp. During Bingo's sixth-grade year, he falls in love three times for starters. (Rev: BCCB 4/88; BL 4/15/88; SLJ 5/88)

10330 Cameron, Ann. *Gloria Rising* (2–4). Illus. by Lis Toft. 2002, Farrar $15.00 (0-374-32675-4). 112pp. A young African American girl named Gloria stars in this easy chapter book involving an inspiring woman astronaut and an intimidating fourth-grade teacher. (Rev: BCCB 4/02; BL 2/15/02; HBG 10/02; SLJ 3/02)

10331 Cleary, Beverly. *Mitch and Amy* (3–5). Illus. by Bob Marstall. 1991, Morrow $15.00 (0-688-10806-7); Avon paper $4.99 (0-380-70925-2). 224pp. Twins Mitch and Amy squabble their way through fourth grade.

10332 Clements, Andrew. *Frindle* (3–6). Illus. 1996, Simon & Schuster $15.00 (0-689-80669-8). 105pp. Nick's desire to get even with a teacher gets out of hand. (Rev: BL 9/1/96; HB 11–12/96; SLJ 9/96)

10333 Clements, Andrew. *Jake Drake, Bully Buster* (2–4). Illus. by Amanda Harvey. 2001, Simon & Schuster paper $3.99 (0-689-83880-8). 73pp. Fourth-grader Jake helps out the bully who has been taunting him mercilessly when the bully turns out to be scared of public speaking. (Rev: SLJ 5/01)

10334 Clements, Andrew. *Jake Drake, Class Clown* (2–5). Illus. by Dolores Avendano. 2002, Simon & Schuster $15.00 (0-689-83921-9). 72pp. Jake is determined to make the new student teacher crack a smile. (Rev: HBG 10/02; SLJ 7/02)

10335 Clements, Andrew. *Jake Drake, Know-It-All* (3–5). Illus. by Dolores Avendano. 2001, Simon & Schuster $15.00 (0-689-83918-9). 96pp. In this beginning chapter book, fourth-grader Jake finds himself turning into a person he doesn't like when he must compete with the class know-it-alls in the school science fair. (Rev: BCCB 2/02; BL 11/1/01; HBG 3/02; SLJ 11/01)

10336 Clements, Andrew. *Jake Drake, Teacher's Pet* (3–5). Illus. by Dolores Avendano. 2001, Simon & Schuster $15.00 (0-689-83919-7). 80pp. In this beginning chapter book, Jake Drake faces the worst day of his life — the day he becomes the teacher's pet. (Rev: BL 1/1–15/02; HBG 10/02; SLJ 4/02)

10337 Clements, Andrew. *The Janitor's Boy* (3–7). 2000, Simon & Schuster $15.00 (0-689-81818-1). 144pp. Jack Rankin is ashamed that his father is the janitor in the middle school that he is attending. Once his classmates find out about his father, the teasing begins. (Rev: BCCB 9/00; BL 3/1/00; HB 7–8/00; HBG 10/00; SLJ 5/00)

10338 Clements, Andrew. *The Landry News* (3–7). Illus. 1999, Simon & Schuster $15.00 (0-689-81817-3). 128pp. When Cara's editorial about a lazy teacher causes him to lose his job, issues of responsibility and freedom of the press emerge. (Rev: BCCB 6/99; BL 6/1–15/99; HB 7–8/99; HBG 10/99; SLJ 7/99)

10339 Clements, Andrew. *The Report Card* (4–7). 2004, Simon & Schuster $15.95 (0-689-84515-4). 176pp. Nora, a bright fifth-grader, deliberately gets low grades in a bid to boost her friend Stephen's self-esteem, but her plans backfire. (Rev: BL 2/15/04; SLJ 3/04)

10340 Cohen, Barbara. *Two Hundred Thirteen Valentines* (3–5). Illus. by Wil Clay. 1993, Holt paper $4.95 (0-805-02627-4). 55pp. Two African American children who transfer to a school for the gifted must rethink their attitudes. (Rev: BCCB 1/92; BL 9/1/91; HB 3–4/92; SLJ 11/91)

10341 Conford, Ellen. *Dear Lovey Hart, I Am Desperate* (6–7). 1975, Little, Brown $14.95 (0-316-15306-0). 224pp. Freshman reporter Carrie Wasserman gets into trouble with her advice column in the school newspaper.

10342 Cox, Judy. *Cool Cat, School Cat* (2–4). Illus. by Blanche Sims. 2002, Holiday House $15.95 (0-8234-1714-X). 96pp. Young Gus is extremely forgetful and puts a stray cat in danger of being fumigated. (Rev: BCCB 2/03; HBG 3/03; SLJ 9/02)

10343 Creech, Sharon. *Love That Dog* (3–6). 2001, HarperCollins LB $14.89 (0-06-029289-X). 112pp. Despite himself, Jack finds he is drawn to poetry and even starts to write poems of his own. (Rev: BL 8/01; HB 11–12/01; HBG 3/02; SLJ 8/01*)

10344 Crew, Gary. *Troy Thompson's Excellent Peotry Book* (4–7). Illus. by Craig Smith. 2003, Kane/Miller $14.95 (1-929132-52-2). Troy Thompson, an 11-year-old Australian boy, uses different forms of poetry to express his feelings about various elements of his life, participating in a yearlong literature assignment and, we learn at the end, winning the grand prize. (Rev: HBG 4/04; SLJ 1/04)

10345 Cullen, Lynn. *Stink Bomb* (4–6). 1998, Avon $14.00 (0-380-97647-1). 120pp. When Kenny breaks wind during gym class, he blames it on the class nerd, Alice Glowers, who becomes known as "Stink Bomb." (Rev: HBG 10/98; SLJ 3/98)

10346 DeClements, Barthe. *Liar, Liar* (4–6). 1998, Marshall Cavendish $14.95 (0-7614-5021-1). 144pp. Sixth-grader Gretchen finds her secure and happy social and school life ends when newcomer Marybelle begins her scheming ways. (Rev: BCCB 7–8/98; BL 8/98; HB 7–8/98; HBG 10/98)

10347 DeClements, Barthe. *Nothing's Fair in Fifth Grade* (4–6). 1981, Puffin paper $4.99 (0-14-034443-8). 144pp. Overweight Elsie steals lunch money to feed her habits. A sequel is: *Seventeen and In-Between* (1984).

10348 DeClements, Barthe. *Sixth Grade Can Really Kill You* (4–6). 1995, Puffin paper $3.99 (0-140-37130-3). 146pp. "Bad Helen" acts up to cover her embarrassment about her reading problem in this portrayal of life for a learning-disabled child. (Rev: BCCB 12/85; BL 11/1/85; SLJ 11/85)

10349 DeLaCroix, Alice. *The Hero of the Third Grade* (2–4). Illus. by Cynthia Fisher. 2002, Holiday House $15.95 (0-8234-1745-X). 96pp. Randall, a third-grader, is miserable — his parents have split up, he's moved with his mom to a new town, the kids don't like him — until he remembers the example of the Scarlet Pimpernel and decides to devote himself to helping others. (Rev: BL 1/1–15/03; HBG 3/03; SLJ 12/02)

10350 Delton, Judy. *Kitty from the Start* (4–6). 1987, Houghton Mifflin $16.00 (0-395-42847-5). 141pp. The story of Kitty, a Catholic girl growing up in the 1940s, and her life in third grade. (Rev: BL 4/1/87; HB 5–6/87; SLJ 5/87)

10351 Dugan, Barbara. *Good-bye, Hello* (4–6). 1994, Greenwillow $13.00 (0-688-12447-X). 160pp. Bobbie thinks she has more than her share of problems at school until she discovers that her grandmother is dying. (Rev: BL 4/1/94; HB 7–8/94; SLJ 5/94)

10352 Edwards, Michelle. *The Talent Show* (2–4). Illus. Series: Jackson Friends. 2002, Harcourt $14.00 (0-15-216403-0). 64pp. Second-grader Howardina "Howie" Smith suffers a case of stagefright when she's slated to perform at her school's talent show. (Rev: BL 8/02; HBG 3/03; SLJ 10/02)

10353 Edwards, Michelle. *Zero Grandparents* (2–4). Illus. 2001, Harcourt $14.00 (0-15-202083-7). 64pp. Calliope has no grandparents to bring to school on Grandparents Day but she thinks of a clever way out of her problem. (Rev: BCCB 4/01; BL 4/1/01; HBG 10/01; SLJ 7/01)

10354 Floca, Brian. *The Frightful Story of Harry Walfish* (2–4). Illus. 1997, Orchard LB $16.99 (0-531-33008-7). 32pp. When Ms. Leonard-Brakhurst's class misbehaves at the natural-history museum, she tells them a cautionary tale that quiets them down. (Rev: BL 4/1/97; SLJ 3/97)

10355 Freeman, Martha. *Fourth Grade Weirdo* (3–5). 1999, Holiday House $16.95 (0-8234-1460-4). 147pp. Even though Dexter thinks he is the weirdest kid in Mr. Dizwinkle's fourth-grade class, he is able to catch the thief whose robberies have cast suspicions on his teacher. (Rev: HBG 3/00; SLJ 1/00)

10356 Friedman, Laurie. *Back to School, Mallory* (2–4). Illus. by Tamara Schmitz. 2004, Carolrhoda LB $15.95 (1-57505-658-5). 176pp. Mallory, 8, is at a new school and, if that isn't bad enough, her mother is the music teacher in this beginning chapter book with appealing illustrations. (Rev: SLJ 8/04)

10357 Gauthier, Gail. *The Hero of Ticonderoga* (4–6). 2001, Penguin Putnam $16.99 (0-399-23559-0). 240pp. Therese, an outcast in the sixth grade, delivers a stunning oral report on Ethan Allen, part of which is spoken during a class trip to Fort Ticonderoga. (Rev: BCCB 3/01; BL 4/1/01; HBG 10/01; SLJ 2/01)

10358 German, Carol. *A Midsummer Night's Dork* (4–7). 2004, HarperCollins $15.99 (0-06-050718-7). 224pp. In this sequel to *Dork on the Run* (2002), sixth-grader Jerry's class puts on an Elizabethan fair and Jerry has to stand up to another bully, even if it means making a fool of himself. (Rev: BL 2/1/04; SLJ 3/04)

10359 Giff, Patricia Reilly. *Fourth Grade Celebrity* (3–5). Illus. by Leslie Morrill. 1989, Bantam paper $4.50 (0-440-42676-6). 128pp. Casey decides that she wants to become famous, and she does, in a

most surprising way. Two sequels are: *The Girl Who Knew It All* (1979); *The Winter Worm Business* (1981).

10360 Giff, Patricia Reilly. *Look Out, Washington, D.C.!* (2–4). Illus. 1995, Dell paper $3.99 (0-440-40934-9). 118pp. A series of setbacks dull Emily's enthusiasm for the field trip the Polk Street School class is taking to Washington, D.C. (Rev: BCCB 7–8/95; BL 6/1–15/95; SLJ 10/95)

10361 Gilson, Jamie. *Bug in a Rug* (2–4). Illus. 1998, Clarion $15.00 (0-395-86616-2). 69pp. In this easily read chapter book, the reader follows Richard through a day in the second grade, including the embarrassment of having to wear purple pants — a gift from his visiting Aunt Nannie. (Rev: BL 4/15/98; HBG 10/98; SLJ 6/98)

10362 Gilson, Jamie. *It Goes Eeeeeeeeeeeee!* (2–4). Illus. by Diane De Groat. 1994, Clarion $15.00 (0-395-67063-2). 68pp. Patrick, a conceited new boy in school, is put in his place when he spreads misinformation about bats in class and is corrected by Dawn Marie. (Rev: BCCB 5/94; BL 4/1/94; SLJ 6/94)

10363 Greene, Stephanie. *Owen Foote, Second Grade Strongman* (2–3). Illus. 1996, Clarion $15.00 (0-395-72098-2). 96pp. When Owen openly criticizes the school nurse, Mrs. Jackson, he gets into trouble with the principal and his parents. (Rev: BCCB 3/96; BL 4/15/96; HB 5–6/96; SLJ 4/96)

10364 Greene, Stephanie. *Show and Tell* (2–3). Illus. 1998, Clarion $15.00 (0-395-88898-0). 96pp. Substitute teacher Miss Plunkett is not amused when Woody brings a dead fish to a show-and-tell session in his second-grade classroom. (Rev: BL 11/1/98; HBG 3/99; SLJ 10/98)

10365 Haddix, Margaret P. *The Girl with 500 Middle Names* (2–4). Illus. by Janet Hamlin. 2001, Simon & Schuster $15.00 (0-689-84135-3). 81pp. Third-grader Janie moves to a new school and is dismayed to find the girls there are richer and better dressed. (Rev: BCCB 5/01; HBG 10/01; SLJ 6/01)

10366 Herrera, Juan Felipe. *The Upside Down Boy / El niño de cabeza* (2–5). Illus. by Elizabeth Gomez. 2000, Children's Book Pr. $15.95 (0-89239-162-6). 31pp. Juanito, a young Hispanic American, is afraid that he won't fit into his new Anglo school, but he is pleasantly surprised. (Rev: BCCB 4/00; HB 9–10/00; HBG 10/00; SLJ 3/00)

10367 Hill, Kirkpatrick. *The Year of Miss Agnes* (4–6). 2000, Simon & Schuster $16.00 (0-689-82933-7). 128pp. Set in northern Canada, this is a gentle story about a schoolteacher named Miss Agnes and the changes she makes in her pupils during the year she teaches in a one-room schoolhouse. (Rev: BCCB 11/00; BL 10/15/00; HB 11–12/00; HBG 3/01; SLJ 9/00)

10368 Hoffman, Mary. *Encore, Grace!* (2–5). Illus. by June Allen. 2003, Penguin Putnam $14.99 (0-8037-2951-0). 112pp. Grace deals with a class play and difficult friends and family in this chapter book with occasional illustrations. (Rev: BL 12/1/03; HBG 4/04; SLJ 12/03)

10369 Holmes, Barbara W. *Charlotte Shakespeare and Annie the Great* (4–6). Illus. by John Himmelman. 1989, HarperCollins $12.95 (0-06-022614-5); paper $3.95 (0-06-440385-8). 126pp. Charlotte writes a Halloween school play and gets jealous because of all the attention the leading lady receives. (Rev: BCCB 11/89; BL 11/15/89; SLJ 11/89)

10370 Honeycutt, Natalie. *The All New Jonah Twist* (4–6). Illus. 1987, Avon paper $3.50 (0-380-70317-3). 128pp. Jonah is determined to change his image at the start of third grade — he'll no longer be inattentive in class, and he'll prove himself responsible enough for a pet. A sequel is: *The Best-Laid Plans of Jonah Twist* (1988). (Rev: BL 5/15/86; SLJ 8/86)

10371 Honeycutt, Natalie. *Invisible Lissa* (4–6). Illus. 1986, Avon paper $2.75 (0-380-70120-0). 192pp. Lissa challenges the student power structure in her fifth-grade class. (Rev: BCCB 7/85; BL 4/1/85; SLJ 8/85)

10372 Hornik, Laurie Miller. *The Secrets of Ms. Snickle's Class* (2–4). Illus. by Debbie Tilley. 2001, Clarion $15.00 (0-618-03435-8). 135pp. Lacey's zeal to find out everyone's secrets endangers her teacher's job. (Rev: HBG 10/01; SLJ 7/01)

10373 Hughes, Dean. *Re-Elect Nutty!* (4–6). 1995, Simon & Schuster $14.00 (0-671-31862-6). 122pp. In this humorous novel, Nutty decides to run for reelection even though he was considered the worst student council president his school has ever had. (Rev: BL 5/1/95; SLJ 6/95)

10374 Hurwitz, Johanna. *Class President* (3–5). Illus. by Sheila Hamanaka. 1990, Morrow $15.95 (0-688-09114-8); Scholastic paper $4.50 (0-590-44064-0). 160pp. Julio works to get his friend elected class president, but discovers that he's the one with leadership qualities. (Rev: BCCB 5/90; BL 4/1/90; HB 7–8/90; SLJ 5/90)

10375 Hurwitz, Johanna. *Ever-Clever Elisa* (2–4). Illus. by Lillian Hoban. 1997, Morrow $15.00 (0-688-15189-2). 64pp. Six short episodes about Elisa in first grade, including one in which she gives her mother's engagement ring to her teacher as a sign of love. (Rev: BL 7/97; HB 9–10/97; HBG 3/98; SLJ 11/97)

10376 Hurwitz, Johanna. *Starting School* (2–4). Illus. 1998, Morrow $15.00 (0-688-15685-1). 144pp. Twins Marcus and Marius decide to switch kindergarten classes to test the quality of each other's teacher, little knowing their teachers have also decided to do the same thing. (Rev: BL 8/98; HB 9–10/98; HBG 3/99; SLJ 9/98)

10377 Hurwitz, Johanna. *Tough-Luck Karen* (4–6). Illus. by Diane De Groat. 1982, Morrow $15.95 (0-688-01485-2). 160pp. Karen prefers housework to homework.

10378 Kline, Suzy. *Horrible Harry at Halloween* (2–3). Illus. 2000, Viking $13.99 (0-670-88864-8). 38pp. At Halloween, Harry must solve the mystery of a stolen party costume in this story about Class 3B. (Rev: BL 9/15/00; HBG 3/01; SLJ 9/00)

10379 Kline, Suzy. *Horrible Harry Moves Up to Third Grade* (2–3). Illus. 1998, Viking $13.99 (0-670-87873-1). 128pp. During a third-grade field trip to an underground mine, Harry has to conquer his fears and also find his nemesis, Sidney, who sud-

denly disappears. (Rev: BL 10/15/98; HBG 3/99; SLJ 9/98)

10380 Kline, Suzy. *Song Lee and the "I Hate You" Notes* (2–4). Illus. 1999, Viking $13.99 (0-670-87887-1). 64pp. Song Lee, the nicest girl in Doug's third-grade class, is hurt when she receives hate notes, but she learns how to strike back. (Rev: BL 5/1/99; HBG 10/99; SLJ 6/99)

10381 Knudsen, Michelle. *The Case of Vampire Vivian* (1–3). Illus. by Amy Wummer. 2003, Kane paper $4.99 (1-57565-127-0). 32pp. When Vivian, a new girl at Molly's school, seems obsessed with bats, her classmates begin to call her "Vampire Vivian"; after Molly gets to know the new girl a little better, she discovers that Vivian has built a bat house in her yard to provide shelter for homeless bats. (Rev: SLJ 1/04)

10382 Koehler-Pentacoff, Elizabeth. *Louise the One and Only* (3–5). Illus. 1996, Troll paper $2.95 (0-8167-3757-6). 64pp. In kindergarten, Louise longs to be the best at something. (Rev: BL 7/96; SLJ 8/96)

10383 Korman, Gordon. *The 6th Grade Nickname Game* (4–6). 1998, Hyperion LB $15.49 (0-7868-2382-7). 160pp. Typical problems encountered in the sixth grade are faced by Wiley and Jeff along with the anxiety of mounting a campaign to save the substitute teacher, Mr. Hughes. (Rev: BL 10/15/98)

10384 Korman, Gordon. *Something Fishy at Macdonald Hall* (4–6). 1995, Scholastic $14.95 (0-590-25521-5). 198pp. At Macdonald Hall School, Boots and Bruno are accused of pranks they didn't commit and so they set out to find the real culprit. (Rev: BL 8/95; SLJ 9/95)

10385 Korman, Gordon. *The Zucchini Warriors* (4–6). 1991, Scholastic paper $4.50 (0-590-44174-4). 208pp. The boys at a Canadian boarding school have a wild and woolly adventure. (Rev: BL 1/1/89; SLJ 9/88)

10386 Lauture, Denizé. *Running the Road to ABC* (1–5). Illus. by Reynold Ruffins. 1996, Simon & Schuster paper $16.00 (0-689-80507-1). A joyous picture book about a group of Haitian children happily going to school, where they hope to learn to read. (Rev: BCCB 3/96; HB 5–6/96; SLJ 6/96)

10387 Levy, Elizabeth. *Keep Ms. Sugarman in the Fourth Grade* (3–5). 1991, HarperCollins LB $14.89 (0-06-020427-3). 96pp. Smart-alecky and disruptive Jackie meets her match in Ms. Sugarman, a gifted teacher. (Rev: BL 12/1/91; SLJ 1/92)

10388 Lewis, Beverly. *Frog Power* (2–5). Illus. 1995, Bethany House paper $3.99 (1-55661-645-7). 80pp. Stacy, who is afraid of frogs, is dismayed when she learns that Jason has brought his pet frog to school. (Rev: BL 10/1/95)

10389 Lindberg, Becky T. *Thomas Tuttle, Just in Time* (2–4). Illus. 1994, Whitman LB $13.95 (0-8075-7898-3). 112pp. Thomas, a third-grader, might do a little better if he would only get organized. (Rev: BL 11/15/94; SLJ 10/94)

10390 Lovelace, Maud H. *Betsy-Tacy* (3–4). Illus. by Lois Lenski. 1940, HarperCollins paper $5.95 (0-06-440096-4). 113pp. Two 5-year-olds are inseparable at school and at play. One of a popular series. Five sequels are: *Betsy-Tacy and Tib* (1941); *Betsy and Tacy Go over the Big Hill* (1942); *Betsy and Tacy Go Downtown* (1943); *Heaven to Betsy* (1945); *Betsy in Spite of Herself* (1946).

10391 Lowry, Lois. *Gooney Bird and the Room Mother* (2–4). Illus. by Middy Thomas. Series: Gooney Bird. 2005, Houghton Mifflin $15.00 (0-618-53230-7). 80pp. Gooney Bird brings in a secret room mother and saves the class Thanksgiving pageant in this sequel to *Gooney Bird Greene*. (Rev: BL 3/1/05; SLJ 5/05)

10392 Lowry, Lois. *Gooney Bird Greene* (2–5). Illus. by Middy Thomas. 2002, Houghton Mifflin $15.00 (0-618-23848-4). 96pp. Gooney Bird is a colorful character: a new second-grader who has a fondness for dressing outrageously and telling fanciful stories. (Rev: BCCB 10/02; BL 9/1/02; HB 9–10/02; HBG 3/03; SLJ 11/02)

10393 Lurie, Jon. *Allison's Story: A Book About Homeschooling* (2–4). Illus. by Rebecca Dallinger. 1996, Lerner $21.27 (0-8225-2579-8). 40pp. A photo-essay about an 8-year-old's experiences with home schooling. (Rev: BL 11/1/96; SLJ 12/96) [649]

10394 MacDonald, Amy. *No More Nasty* (3–6). Illus. by Cat B. Smith. 2001, Farrar $16.00 (0-374-35529-0). 176pp. Eleven-year-old Simon is put in a difficult situation when his great-aunt becomes his substitute teacher. (Rev: BL 9/1/01; HB 11–12/01; HBG 3/02; SLJ 9/01)

10395 MacDonald, Maryann. *Secondhand Star* (2–5). Illus. by Eileen Christelow. 1994, Hyperion $11.95 (1-56282-616-6). 64pp. Francie, who is cast as Toto in the school production of "The Wizard of Oz," becomes a last-minute replacement for an ill Dorothy. (Rev: BL 7/94; SLJ 7/94)

10396 McDonald, Megan. *Judy Moody* (2–4). Illus. 2000, Candlewick $15.99 (0-7636-0685-5). 196pp. A beginning chapter book about Judy Moody, a third-grader, and her everyday trials and tribulations. (Rev: BCCB 5/00; BL 7/00; HBG 10/00; SLJ 7/00)

10397 McDonald, Megan. *Judy Moody Saves the World!* (2–5). Illus. by Peter Reynolds. 2002, Candlewick $15.99 (0-7636-1446-7). 160pp. Third-grader Judy is busy saving the world with a recycling project in this third installment in the series in which she stars. (Rev: BL 9/1/02; HBG 3/03)

10398 McKenna, Colleen O'Shaughnessy. *Live from the Fifth Grade* (4–6). Illus. 1994, Scholastic $13.95 (0-590-46684-4). 145pp. Practical joker Roger Friday becomes serious when a friendly custodian at his school is accused of theft. (Rev: BL 11/15/94; SLJ 10/94)

10399 McKenna, Colleen O'Shaughnessy. *Third Grade Stinks!* (2–4). Illus. by Stephanie Roth. 2001, Holiday House $15.95 (0-8234-1595-3). 99pp. Gordie is really disappointed when he learns he has to share his third-grade locker with show-off Lucy and concocts a plan to stink her out. (Rev: BCCB 11/01; BL 12/15/01; HBG 10/02; SLJ 11/01)

10400 Maguire, Gregory. *One Final Firecracker* (4–7). Illus. by Elaine Clayton. Series: The Hamlet Chronicles. 2005, Clarion $17.00 (0-618-27480-4). 226pp. In the final pun-filled installment in the series, the rival Tattletales and Copycats must cooperate to defend the class and the soon-to-be-wed Miss Earth from myriad threats. (Rev: SLJ 5/05)

10401 Maguire, Gregory. *Three Rotten Eggs* (3–7). Illus. by Elaine Clayton. Series: Hamlet Chronicles. 2002, Clarion $16.00 (0-618-09655-8). 192pp. The boys are in competition with the girls in Miss Earth's annual spring egg hunt until a swaggering bully named Thud Tweed joins their class. (Rev: BL 4/1/02; HBG 10/02; SLJ 3/02)

10402 Marsden, Carolyn. *The Gold-Threaded Dress* (3–5). 2002, Candlewick $13.99 (0-7636-1569-2). 73pp. Fourth-grader Oy is torn between her desire to make friends and her classmates' interest in her precious Thai dress. (Rev: BCCB 6/02; BL 5/1/02*; HBG 3/03; SLJ 4/02)

10403 Martin, Ann M. *Belle Teal* (4–6). 2001, Scholastic $15.95 (0-439-09823-8). 224pp. Fifth-grader Belle befriends the only black student in her class in this story about the early days of desegregation. (Rev: BCCB 2/02; BL 10/1/01; HB 1–2/02; HBG 3/02; SLJ 9/01)

10404 Matson, Nancy. *The Boy Trap* (4–6). Illus. 1999, Front Street $14.95 (0-8126-2663-X). 112pp. Emma decides that by entering the best project in her fifth-grade class's science fair, she will be able to prove that girls are better than boys. (Rev: BL 1/1–15/00; HBG 10/00; SLJ 11/99)

10405 Mills, Claudia. *Lizzie at Last* (4–6). 2000, Farrar $16.00 (0-374-34659-3). 160pp. Lizzie compromises her individuality to become popular with her classmates, but she comes to regret it. (Rev: BCCB 10/00; BL 11/1/00; HB 11–12/00; HBG 3/01; SLJ 11/00)

10406 Mills, Claudia. *7 x 9 = Trouble!* (2–4). Illus. by G. Brian Karas. 2002, Farrar $15.00 (0-374-36746-9). 112pp. Third-grader Wilson loves the class pet, a hamster, and his best friend, Josh, but he has terrible problems with math, particularly the 12 times tables. (Rev: BL 4/1/02; HB 3–4/02; HBG 10/02; SLJ 4/02)

10407 Morgenstern, Susie. *A Book of Coupons* (4–6). Illus. 2001, Viking $12.99 (0-670-89970-4). 64pp. An elderly teacher rewards his fifth-grade class with books of coupons that are redeemable for such treats as dancing in class, and not going to the blackboard when summoned. (Rev: BL 4/1/01; HB 5–6/01; HBG 10/01; SLJ 5/01)

10408 Morgenstern, Susie. *Sixth Grade* (5–6). Trans. from French by Gill Rosner. 2004, Viking $15.99 (0-670-03680-3). 144pp. This translation of a French novel follows young Margo through her entire sixth-grade year, which includes a class trip to Rome and a teacher strike. (Rev: SLJ 4/04)

10409 Murphy, Stuart J. *More or Less* (1–3). Illus. by David T. Wenzel. Series: MathStart. 2005, HarperCollins $15.99 (0-06-053165-7); paper $4.99 (0-06-053167-3). 40pp. Young Eddie, operating a booth at the school carnival, has to guess a person's age within six tries or get dunked. (Rev: BL 2/15/05)

10410 Naylor, Phyllis Reynolds. *Alice in Blunderland* (3–7). 2003, Simon & Schuster $15.95 (0-689-84397-6). 200pp. Fourth-grader Alice is well-intentioned but blunder-prone in this second of three prequels to the Alice books. (Rev: HBG 4/04; SLJ 9/03)

10411 Naylor, Phyllis Reynolds. *Starting with Alice* (3–8). 2002, Simon & Schuster $15.95 (0-689-84395-X). 192pp. In this prequel, Alice (first seen in *The Agony of Alice* in 1985) is in third grade in a new school in Maryland, initially has trouble finding friends, and still misses her dead mother. (Rev: BCCB 11/02; BL 11/15/02; HB 9–10/02; HBG 3/03; SLJ 9/02)

10412 O'Dell, Kathleen. *Agnes Parker . . . Girl in Progress* (4–6). Illus. by Charise Mericle Harper. 2003, Dial $16.99 (0-8037-2648-1). 160pp. Sixth-grader Agnes learns a lot about life and herself during sixth grade. (Rev: HB 3–4/03; HBG 10/03; SLJ 2/03)

10413 Papademetriou, Lisa. *Sixth-Grade: Glommers, Norks, and Me* (4–6). 2005, Hyperion $14.99 (0-7868-5169-4). 224pp. Allie must contend with squabbling friends and likes to invent new words to do so in this enjoyable look at life in middle school. (Rev: BL 3/15/05; SLJ 5/05)

10414 Park, Barbara. *Junie B., First Grader: Boss of Lunch* (2–3). Illus. by Denise Brunkus. Series: Junie B. Jones. 2002, Random $11.95 (0-375-81517-1). 80pp. There's a strong focus on food, as Junie B. gets a new lunchbox and debates the merits of brown-bagging it versus bought lunches. (Rev: BL 7/02; HBG 10/02; SLJ 8/02)

10415 Park, Barbara. *Junie B., First Grader: Cheater Pants* (1–2). 2003, Random LB $13.99 (0-375-92301-2). 96pp. Junie B. is back again, and she's learning some tough lessons about cheating at school. (Rev: BL 9/15/03; HBG 4/04; SLJ 9/03)

10416 Park, Barbara. *Junie B., First Grader: Toothless Wonder* (2–4). Illus. by Denise Brunkus. 2002, Random LB $13.99 (0-375-90295-3). 96pp. Junie B. is losing her first tooth and decides to look into the existence of the tooth fairy, which she rather doubts. (Rev: BL 11/1/02; HBG 3/03; SLJ 12/02)

10417 Park, Barbara. *Junie B. Jones and her Big Fat Mouth* (2–4). Illus. by Denise Brunkus. 1993, Random $11.99 (0-679-94407-9); paper $3.99 (0-679-84407-4). 72pp. In this hilarious story of kindergartner Junie B. Jones, the little girl has trouble with the Pledge of Allegiance, keeping quiet in class, and deciding what to be on Job Day. (Rev: BL 11/15/93)

10418 Park, Barbara. *Junie B. Jones and the Yucky Blucky Fruitcake* (2–4). Illus. by Denise Brunkus. Series: Junie B. Jones. 1995, Random paper $3.99 (0-679-86694-9). 71pp. A young kindergartner tells about her many troubles at school, where she is always a loser. (Rev: BL 12/15/95)

10419 Proimos, James. *Cowboy Boy* (3–6). Illus. 2003, Scholastic $14.95 (0-439-41681-7). 96pp. Cartoon art adds to the fun as sixth grader Ricky Smootz transforms himself into Cowboy Boy to foil a persistent bully. (Rev: BL 9/1/03; HBG 4/04; SLJ 11/03)

10420 Pryor, Bonnie. *Poison Ivy and Eyebrow Wigs* (3–5). Illus. by Gail Owens. 1993, Morrow $15.00 (0-688-11200-5). 156pp. Martin's problems in the fourth grade include wanting to be popular and having a crush on his teacher. (Rev: BL 4/15/93; SLJ 6/93)

10421 Rocklin, Joanne. *For Your Eyes Only* (4–6). 1997, Scholastic $14.95 (0-590-67447-1). 144pp. Sixth-grader Lucy blossoms under the attention of Mr. Moffat, a substitute teacher. (Rev: BCCB 4/97; BL 3/1/97; HBG 3/98; SLJ 3/97*)

10422 Sachar, Louis. *Marvin Redpost: Class President* (2–4). Illus. 1999, Random LB $11.99 (0-679-98999-4); paper $3.99 (0-679-88999-X). 80pp. In this beginning chapter book, Marvin's third-grade class has a surprise visit from the president of the United States. (Rev: BCCB 4/99; BL 4/15/99; HBG 10/99; SLJ 6/99)

10423 Sachar, Louis. *Wayside School Is Falling Down* (3–6). Illus. by Joel Schick. 1989, Lothrop $15.95 (0-688-07868-0); Avon paper $4.99 (0-380-75484-3). 192pp. Episodes with the children who inhabit the world's wackiest elementary school. (Rev: BL 5/1/89; SLJ 5/89)

10424 Seuling, Barbara. *Robert and the Back-to-School Special* (2–4). Illus. by Paul Brewer. 2002, Cricket $15.95 (0-8126-2662-1). 112pp. Insecure third-grader Robert thinks his classmates are mocking him because of the length of his hair, but his brother's efforts to fix it don't make things any better. (Rev: BL 1/1–15/03; HB 1–2/03; HBG 3/03; SLJ 1/03)

10425 Seuling, Barbara. *Robert Takes a Stand* (2–4). Illus. by Paul Brewer. 2004, Cricket $15.95 (0-8126-2712-1). 176pp. Third-grader Robert tackles a variety of topics — class politics, animal rights, and caring for a new puppy — in this appealing book for beginning readers. Also use *Robert Finds a Way* (2005). (Rev: BL 4/1/04; HB 7–8/04; SLJ 4/04)

10426 Sharmat, Marjorie W. *Getting Something on Maggie Marmelstein* (3–5). Illus. by Ben Shecter. 1971, HarperCollins LB $14.89 (0-06-025552-8). 110pp. When Thad's mortal enemy, Maggie, sees him cooking and begins teasing him, Thad must find some way of blackmailing her into silence. Two sequels are: *Maggie Marmelstein for President* (1975); *Mysteriously Yours, Maggie Marmelstein* (1982).

10427 Spinelli, Jerry. *Loser* (3–6). 2002, HarperCollins LB $15.89 (0-06-000483-5). 224pp. Donald Zinkoff, labeled a "loser" by his classmates, is nonetheless happy and secure, unconcerned about what others think of him. (Rev: BCCB 5/02; BL 5/15/02; HB 7–8/02; HBG 10/02; SLJ 5/02)

10428 Vega, Denise. *Click Here: (To Find Out How I Survived the Seventh Grade)* (5–7). 2005, Little, Brown $15.99 (0-316-98560-0). 211pp. Middle school is challenging enough for Erin before her private Web page, containing her diary, is posted on the school Intranet. (Rev: SLJ 5/05)

10429 Wesley, Valerie Wilson. *How to Lose Your Class Pet* (2–4). Illus. by Maryn Roos. Series: Willimena Rules! 2003, Hyperion $3.99 (0-7868-1322-9). 96pp. In an attempt to endear herself to her ill-tempered third-grade teacher, Willimena offers to look after the class pet — a guinea pig named Lester — over the weekend; when Lester slips away, Willimena faces the daunting prospect of disclosing the loss of the pet to her teacher and classmates. (Rev: SLJ 1/04)

10430 Willner-Pardo, Gina. *Spider Storch's Music Mess* (2–3). Illus. by Nick Sharratt. 1998, Whitman LB $11.95 (0-8075-7583-6); paper $3.95 (0-8075-7584-4). 76pp. In this easy chapter book, Spider tries to get out of music class, but when he succeeds in getting bounced, he finds he misses it. (Rev: HBG 3/99; SLJ 3/99)

10431 Willner-Pardo, Gina. *Spider Storch's Teacher Torture* (2–4). Illus. 1997, Whitman LB $11.95 (0-8075-7577-1); paper $3.95 (0-8075-7578-X). 60pp. Spider Storch thinks up some wild schemes to prevent his beloved teacher from retiring. (Rev: BL 1/1–15/98; HBG 3/98; SLJ 11/97)

10432 Winerip, Michael. *Adam Canfield of the Slash* (4–7). 2005, Candlewick $15.99 (0-7636-2340-7). 336pp. As editors of the *Slash*, the Harris Elementary/Middle School student newspaper, Adam and Jennifer chase scoops and tackle ethical questions. (Rev: BL 5/1/05; SLJ 3/05)

10433 Zollman, Pam. *Don't Bug Me!* (4–6). 2001, Holiday House $15.95 (0-8234-1584-8). 134pp. Megan, a sixth-grader, aims to complete her bug project despite her pesky, interfering brother and her annoying classmate Charlie. (Rev: BL 7/01; HBG 3/02; SLJ 10/01)

Science Fiction

10434 Anderson, Kevin J., and Ralph McQuarrie. *Stars Wars: Jabba's Palace Pop-Up Book* (2–4). Illus. 1996, Little, Brown $19.45 (0-316-53513-3). 14pp. A pop-up book using sound and pictures to illustrate parts of the *Star Wars* films. (Rev: BL 12/15/96)

10435 Applegate, K. A. *Animorphs #1: The Invasion* (5–8). 1996, Scholastic paper $4.99 (0-590-62977-8). Jake, an average suburban kid, is confronted one night by a creature from space who teaches him how to morph into the forms of other creatures. (Rev:)

10436 Asimov, Janet. *Norby and the Terrified Taxi* (4–8). 1997, Walker $15.95 (0-8027-8642-1). Norby, the bungling robot, is kidnapped, and while trying to find him, Jeff and his friends stumble on a plot by Garc the Great to take over the Federation. This is one of a large series of Norby books suitable for middle school readers. (Rev: BL 1/1–15/98; SLJ 12/97)

10437 Asimov, Janet. *The Package in Hyperspace* (5–7). Illus. 1988, Walker LB $14.85 (0-8027-6823-7). 84pp. Two space-wrecked children must fend for themselves as they try to reach Merkina. (Rev: BL 1/1/89; SLJ 11/88)

10438 Asimov, Janet, and Isaac Asimov. *Norby and the Invaders* (5–8). 1985, Walker LB $10.85 (0-8027-6607-2). Jeff and his unusual robot Norby travel to a planet to help one of Norby's ancestors. Part of a series that includes *Norby's Other Secret*. (Rev: BL 3/1/86; SLJ 2/86)

10439 Asimov, Janet, and Isaac Asimov. *Norby and the Oldest Dragon* (3–5). 1990, Walker LB $15.85 (0-8027-6910-1). 110pp. When Jeff visits the planet Jamyn, he finds that a mysterious vapor surrounds him and other residents. (Rev: SLJ 7/90)

10440 Asimov, Janet, and Isaac Asimov. *Norby and Yobo's Great Adventure* (5–8). 1989, Walker LB $13.85 (0-8027-6894-6). Norby the robot time-travels to help Admiral Yobo of Mars to trace his family roots. Part of a series that also includes *Norby Down to Earth*. (Rev: BL 10/15/89)

10441 Asimov, Janet, and Isaac Asimov. *Norby Finds a Villain* (4–8). 1987, Walker LB $13.85 (0-8027-6711-7). 102pp. Norby the robot and his human friends set out to free Pera, who has been robot-napped by the traitor Ing, in this sixth book of the Norby series. Also use *Norby and the Queen's Necklace* (1986). (Rev: BL 1/1/88; SLJ 11/87)

10442 Asimov, Janet, and Isaac Asimov. *Norby, the Mixed-up Robot* (4–6). 1984, Walker LB $10.85 (0-8027-6496-7). 96pp. Jeff, his brother Fargo, and a robot named Norby combat Ing the Ingrate. A sequel is: *Norby's Other Secret* (1984).

10443 Bawden, Nina. *Off the Road* (5–9). 1998, Clarion $16.00 (0-395-91321-7). In this science fiction novel set in a time when the elderly are exterminated, 11-year-old Tom follows his grandfather to the "savage jungle" Outside the Wall, where the old man hopes to escape his fate, and discovers a different kind of society. (Rev: BCCB 10/98; BL 9/15/98; BR 5–6/99; HBG 10/99; SLJ 11/98)

10444 Brennan, Herbie. *Zartog's Remote* (3–5). Illus. by Neal Layton. 2001, Carolrhoda LB $14.95 (1-57505-507-4). 96pp. A fearful 8-year-old alien named Zartog and a feisty 8-year-old girl named Rachel band together when Zartog loses the remote control for his spaceship. (Rev: HBG 10/01; SLJ 4/01)

10445 Butts, Nancy. *The Door in the Lake* (5–8). 1997, Front Street $15.95 (1-886910-27-8). Twenty-seven months after being abducted by aliens, Joey returns home to find that everything has changed while he has remained the same. (Rev: BCCB 7–8/98; BL 5/15/98; HBG 10/98; SLJ 6/98)

10446 Byars, Betsy. *The Computer Nut* (4–6). 1984, Puffin paper $4.99 (0-14-032086-5). 144pp. Through her computer, Kate encounters an extraterrestrial being.

10447 Cameron, Eleanor. *Mr. Bass's Planetoid* (4–6). Illus. by Louis Darling. 1958, Little, Brown $14.95 (0-316-12525-3). A further story about the Mushroom Planet, Mr. Bass, and two young heroes. Also use: *Stowaway to the Mushroom Planet* (1956).

10448 Cameron, Eleanor. *The Wonderful Flight to the Mushroom Planet* (4–6). Illus. by Robert Henneberger. 1988, Little, Brown paper $7.95 (0-316-12540-7). Science fiction combined with magic in the story of two boys who take off on a spaceship with a magical man named Tyco Bass.

10449 Cooper, Clare. *Ashar of Qarius* (5–8). 1990, Harcourt $14.95 (0-15-200409-2). A teenage girl, two children, and their pets are left alone in a space dome and must find a way to survive. (Rev: BL 5/15/90; SLJ 7/90)

10450 Cousins, Steven. *Frankenbug* (4–6). 2000, Holiday House $15.95 (0-8234-1496-5). 151pp. Adam gets revenge on the bully, Jeb, by creating a super bug by sewing together parts of insects he has bought through a mail-order catalog and, then, frightening his tormentor. (Rev: HBG 10/01; SLJ 3/01)

10451 Coville, Bruce. *The Attack of the Two-Inch Teacher* (3–6). Illus. by Tony Sansevero. Series: I Was a Sixth Grade Alien. 1999, Pocket paper $3.99 (0-671-02651-8). 165pp. Pleskit, a visiting alien, accidentally shrinks his sixth-grade teacher and best friend to matchbox size. (Rev: SLJ 2/00)

10452 Coville, Bruce, ed. *Bruce Coville's Alien Visitors* (4–7). 1999, Avon paper $4.99 (0-380-80254-6). 209pp. A collection of 14 short stories about aliens and alien encounters by such writers as Ray Bradbury. (Rev: BL 11/15/99)

10453 Coville, Bruce. *My Teacher Fried My Brains* (3–6). Illus. by John Pierard. 1991, Pocket paper $4.50 (0-671-72710-9). 136pp. Duncan is convinced his teacher is an alien when he finds a fake hand in a dumpster. (Rev: BL 9/15/91)

10454 Cowley, Joy. *Starbright and the Dream Eater* (5–8). 2000, HarperCollins LB $14.89 (0-06-028420-X). 144pp. A child born to a mentally disabled teenage mother and named Starbright is destined to save the earth from the Dream Eater. (Rev: BCCB 7–8/00; BL 4/15/00; HBG 10/00; SLJ 6/00)

10455 Craig, Joe. *Jimmy Coates: Assassin?* (4–7). 2005, HarperCollins LB $16.89 (0-06-077264-6). 224pp. Thirty-five percent human and 65 percent technologically engineered assassin, 11-year-old Jimmy Coates faces external dangers and internal struggles, all with action, suspense, and humor. (Rev: BL 5/1/05; SLJ 6/05)

10456 Crilley, Mark. *Akiko and the Alpha Centauri 5000* (3–5). Illus. by author. 2003, Delacorte $9.95 (0-385-72969-3). 153pp. Akiko joins three old friends for a cross-galaxy race that involves sabotage and a user's manual in a language called Jabblenese. (Rev: BL 5/15/03; HBG 10/03; SLJ 9/03)

10457 Crilley, Mark. *Akiko and the Great Wall of Trudd* (3–5). Illus. by author. 2001, Delacorte $9.95 (0-385-32727-7). Readers of the earlier volumes in this series (*Akiko on the Planet Smoo* and *Akiko in the Sprubly Islands*) will enjoy this continuation of the fantasy. (Rev: HBG 10/01; SLJ 4/01)

10458 Crilley, Mark. *Akiko in the Sprubly Islands* (3–5). 2000, Delacorte $9.95 (0-385-32726-9). 176pp. A fourth-grader leads her crew across the Moonguzzit Sea to rescue Prince Froptoppit in this far-fetched science fiction fantasy. (Rev: BL 1/1–15/01; HBG 3/01; SLJ 11/00)

10459 Crilley, Mark. *Akiko on the Planet Smoo* (4–7). Illus. 2000, Delacorte $9.95 (0-385-32724-2). 176pp. A fast-paced science fiction novel about Akiko, a 4th grader, and her flight into space to find the kidnapped son of King Froptoppit. (Rev: BL 3/1/00; HBG 10/00; SLJ 2/00)

10460 DeVita, James. *Blue* (4–7). 2001, Harper-Collins LB $15.89 (0-06-029546-5). 288pp. Morgan follows a marlin that has entered his living room and soon finds he is turning into a fish. (Rev: BCCB 5/01; BL 4/15/01; HBG 10/01; SLJ 5/01)

10461 Dong, Claxton. *Save Our Star: Luke* (4–7). Series: Save Our Star. 2002, Brown Swan paper $5.99 (0-9717993-0-X). 137pp. To save the Earth from a threatening black hole, 12-year-old Luke is sent back 200 years in time to the 21st century where he must figure out a way to convince space scientists to increase their research into this potentially devastating problem. (Rev: SLJ 6/03)

10462 Doyle, Debra, and James D. MacDonald. *Groogleman* (5–8). 1996, Harcourt $15.00 (0-15-200235-9). In this novel set in the future, 13-year-old Dan is immune to the plague that is devastating the countryside and sets out with friend Leesie to help tend the sick. (Rev: BCCB 12/96; BR 3–4/97; SLJ 12/96)

10463 DuPrau, Jeanne. *The City of Ember* (5–7). 2003, Random LB $17.99 (0-375-92274-1). 288pp. Lina and Doon work to find a way out of their isolated and decaying city, where the population is beginning to panic. (Rev: BL 4/15/03; HB 5–6/03; HBG 10/03; SLJ 5/03)

10464 Etra, Jonathan, and Stephanie Spinner. *Aliens for Breakfast* (3–5). Illus. 1988, Random $11.99 (0-394-92093-7); paper $3.99 (0-394-82093-2). 64pp. Richard meets an alien who needs help to find a secret weapon. (Rev: BCCB 12/88; BL 1/15/89; SLJ 3/89)

10465 Evans, Douglas. *The Classroom at the End of the Hall* (2–4). Illus. 1996, Front Street $14.95 (1-886910-07-3). 128pp. Typical third-graders have some atypical adventures in these 11 stories. (Rev: BCCB 9/96; BL 8/96; SLJ 10/96)

10466 Follett, Ken. *The Power Twins* (4–8). 1991, Scholastic paper $2.75 (0-590-42507-2). 90pp. Three youngsters travel to a planet where large, gentle worms live. (Rev: SLJ 1/91)

10467 Gilden, Mel. *Outer Space and All That Junk* (5–7). Illus. 1989, HarperCollins LB $12.89 (0-397-32307-7). 176pp. Myron's uncle is collecting junk, which he believes will help aliens return to their home in outer space. (Rev: BL 12/1/89; SLJ 12/89)

10468 Gormley, Beatrice. *Paul's Volcano* (4–6). Illus. 1988, Avon paper $2.50 (0-380-70562-1). 143pp. Adam and new kid Paul tangle over a science-fair volcano model that seems to have a mind of its own. (Rev: BL 5/15/87; SLJ 3/87)

10469 Gormley, Beatrice. *Wanted: UFO* (3–6). Illus. by Emily Arnold McCully. 1992, Avon paper $2.99 (0-380-71313-6). 128pp. Elise and Nick discover two aliens in the backyard. (Rev: BCCB 6/90; BL 7/90; SLJ 7/90)

10470 Greer, Gery, and Bob Ruddick. *Max and Me and the Wild West* (4–6). 1988, Harcourt $12.95 (0-15-253136-X). 138pp. Professor Flybender's time machine once more lands Steve and Max in the middle of an adventure — this time in 1882 Arizona Territory. (Rev: BL 2/15/88)

10471 Griffith, Helen V. *Journal of a Teenage Genius* (5–8). 1987, Troll paper $2.50 (0-8167-1325-1). In diary form, a young hero tells of his encounter with a time machine. (Rev: BR 11–12/87; SLJ 10/87)

10472 Gutman, Dan. *The Edison Mystery* (4–8). Series: Qwerty Stevens, Back in Time. 2001, Simon & Schuster $16.00 (0-689-84124-8). 201pp. The time machine he finds in his backyard sends 13-year-old Robert "Qwerty" Stevens to 1879 to Thomas Edison's workshop. (Rev: HBG 3/02; SLJ 8/01)

10473 Haddix, Margaret P. *Among the Barons* (5–8). 2003, Simon & Schuster $16.95 (0-689-83906-5). 182pp. Luke, a third child who has been living underground in this two-child society, comes close to exposure in this exciting installment in the series that began with *Among the Hidden* (1998). (Rev: BL 5/15/03; HBG 10/03; SLJ 6/03)

10474 Haddix, Margaret P. *Among the Betrayed* (5–9). 2002, Simon & Schuster $16.95 (0-689-83905-7). 160pp. In this third novel in the series that started with *Among the Hidden* (1998), illegal third child Nina faces danger and difficult decisions. (Rev: BCCB 10/02; HBG 10/02; SLJ 6/02)

10475 Haddix, Margaret P. *Among the Enemy* (5–8). Series: Shadow Children. 2005, Simon & Schuster $15.95 (0-689-85796-9). 224pp. Matthias, one of the third children illegal in his society, is mistakenly welcomed into the Population Police; there he is confused by divided loyalties. (Rev: BL 6/1–15/05; SLJ 6/05)

10476 Haddix, Margaret P. *Among the Hidden* (5–8). 1998, Simon & Schuster $16.95 (0-689-81700-2). 154pp. In a society where only two children are allowed per family, Luke, the third, endures a secret life hidden from authorities. (Rev: BR 5–6/99; HBG 3/99; SLJ 9/98)

10477 Haddix, Margaret P. *Among the Imposters* (5–7). 2001, Simon & Schuster $16.00 (0-689-83904-9). 172pp. As a third child in a society that allows only two per family, Luke has assumed a new identity and at age 12 enrolls in a nightmarish boarding school. (Rev: BCCB 9/01; BL 4/15/01; HBG 10/01; SLJ 7/01)

10478 Heintze, Ty. *Valley of the Eels* (5–8). 1993, Eakin $15.95 (0-89015-904-1). A dolphin leads two boys to an underwater station where friendly aliens are cultivating trees to replant on their own planet. (Rev: BL 3/1/94)

10479 Hill, William. *The Magic Bicycle* (5–8). 1998, Otter Creek paper $13.95 (1-890611-00-X). 326pp. For helping an alien escape, Danny receives a magical bicycle that is capable of transporting him

through time and space. (Rev: BL 1/1–15/98; SLJ 3/98)

10480 Hooks, William H. *The Girl Who Could Fly* (3–4). Illus. by Kees de Kiefte. 1995, Macmillan paper $14.00 (0-02-744433-3). 53pp. Tom, a girl, is actually an alien from outer space who can perform amazing feats like stopping a ball in midair. (Rev: BCCB 7–8/95; BL 8/95; SLJ 7/95)

10481 Kahn, Sharon. *Kacy and the Space Shuttle Secret: A Space Adventure for Young Readers* (4–6). Illus. by Mark Mitchell. 1996, Eakin $17.75 (1-57168-025-X). 128pp. An exciting science fiction adventure in which a young would-be scientist helps launch a space shuttle. (Rev: SLJ 4/96)

10482 Key, Alexander. *The Forgotten Door* (5–7). 1986, Scholastic paper $4.50 (0-590-43130-7). 144pp. When little Jon falls to earth from another planet, he encounters suspicion and hostility as well as sympathy. A reissue.

10483 L'Engle, Madeleine. *A Wrinkle in Time* (6–8). 1962, Farrar $17.00 (0-374-38613-7); Dell paper $6.50 (0-440-49805-8). 224pp. A provocative fantasy-science fiction tale of a brother and sister in search of their father, who is lost in the fifth dimension. Newbery Medal winner, 1963. Also use: *Wind in the Door* (1973); *A Swiftly Tilting Planet* (1978); *A Ring of Endless Light* (1981).

10484 Lisle, Janet T. *Angela's Aliens* (4–6). Series: Unknown. 1996, Orchard LB $15.99 (0-531-08891-X). 128pp. Angela is abducted by mysterious aliens in the fourth and final volume of the Unknown series. (Rev: BL 11/1/96; SLJ 11/96)

10485 Lowenstein, Sallie. *Evan's Voice* (5–8). Illus. 1998, Lion Stone paper $15.00 (0-9658486-1-2). 187pp. Teenager Jake cares for his catatonic younger brother while seeking civilization's last chance for survival in an area known as the Dead Zone. (Rev: BL 3/1/99)

10486 Lowenstein, Sallie. *Focus* (5–9). Illus. 2001, Lion Stone paper $15.00 (0-9658486-3-9). 284pp. The Haldrans leave their planet and relocate to Miners World, where humans live, in order to save their son from discrimination because of his creative intelligence. (Rev: BL 4/15/01; SLJ 8/01)

10487 Lubar, David. *Flip* (5–8). 2003, Tor $17.95 (0-765-30149-0). 300pp. A humorous science fiction novel in which 13-year-old underachiever Ryan, whose twin sister is overachiever Taylor, becomes entranced by a set of disks dropped by passing aliens that introduces him to the achievements of such earthly successes as Babe Ruth, Einstein, Elvis, and Queen Victoria. (Rev: BCCB 10/03; HBG 4/04; SLJ 8/03)

10488 MacGrory, Yvonne. *Emma and the Ruby Ring* (4–6). Illus. by Terry Myler. 2002, Milkweed $17.95 (1-57131-635-3); paper $6.95 (1-57131-634-5). 137pp. In this sequel to *The Secret of the Ruby Ring* (1994), 11-year-old Emma is transported to 19th-century Ireland and becomes involved in fulfilling a dying woman's last request. (Rev: HBG 10/02; SLJ 5/02)

10489 MacGrory, Yvonne. *The Secret of the Ruby Ring* (4–6). Illus. by Terry Myler. 1994, Milkweed paper $6.95 (0-915943-92-1). 192pp. A fantasy about a young Irish girl who time-travels to live in a nearby castle over a century ago. (Rev: BCCB 5/94; BL 3/1/94; SLJ 3/94)

10490 Mackel, Kathy. *Alien in a Bottle* (4–8). 2004, HarperCollins LB $16.89 (0-06-029282-2). 208pp. An entertaining and action-packed novel in which eighth-grader Sean Winger, an aspiring glassblower, mistakes an alien space ship for an ornate glass bottle and becomes swept up in intergalactic intrigue. (Rev: BL 5/1/04; SLJ 4/04)

10491 Mackel, Kathy. *From the Horse's Mouth* (5–7). 2002, HarperCollins LB $15.89 (0-06-029415-9). 224pp. Nick Thorpe is on another science fiction adventure involving a time warp and evil aliens that plan to destroy his town. (Rev: BL 5/1/02; HBG 10/02; SLJ 7/02)

10492 Mahy, Margaret. *Raging Robots and Unruly Uncles* (4–6). Illus. by Peter Stevenson. 1993, Overlook $13.95 (0-87951-469-8). 94pp. Twin uncles — one bad, one good — are saddled with children they regard as unsatisfactory. (Rev: BL 3/1/93; SLJ 3/93)

10493 Meacham, Margaret. *Quiet! You're Invisible* (3–5). 2001, Holiday House $15.95 (0-8234-1651-8). 80pp. Fifth-grader Hoby is visited by a boy from the future and must outsmart the middle-school bully to retrieve a stolen part from his new friend's space cruiser. (Rev: BL 1/1–15/02; HBG 3/02; SLJ 11/01)

10494 Philbrick, Rodman. *REM World* (4–6). 2000, Scholastic $16.95 (0-439-08362-1). 192pp. Ten-year-old Arthur gets stuck in the REM world when he tries to use a REM sleep machine to lose weight. (Rev: BCCB 6/00; BL 5/1/00; HBG 10/00; SLJ 5/00)

10495 Pierce, Tamora. *Street Magic* (5–9). Series: Circle Opens. 2001, Scholastic paper $16.95 (0-590-39628-5). 304pp. Briar, a 14-year-old former gang member, finds he is again caught between warring gangs when he helps a female street urchin in this futuristic novel. (Rev: BL 4/15/01; HB 3–4/01; HBG 10/01; SLJ 7/01)

10496 Regan, Dian C. *Princess Nevermore* (5–7). 1995, Scholastic $14.95 (0-590-47582-6). 232pp. A princess from another world gets her wish to visit Earth, where she is befriended by two teenagers, Sarah and Adam. (Rev: BCCB 11/95; SLJ 9/95)

10497 Rodda, Emily. *Finders Keepers* (4–7). Illus. by Noela Young. 1991, Greenwillow $12.95 (0-688-10516-5). 192pp. Patrick is transported onto the set of a quiz show in a parallel world beyond the "great barrier." (Rev: BCCB 12/91; BL 11/15/91; SLJ 8/91)

10498 Scieszka, Jon. *See You Later, Gladiator* (4–6). Illus. 2000, Viking $13.99 (0-670-89340-4). 80pp. The three members of the Time Warp Trio travel back to ancient Rome, where they attend gladiator school and fight in the Colosseum in this hilarious spoof. (Rev: BL 1/1–15/01; HBG 3/01; SLJ 11/00)

10499 Scrimger, Richard. *A Nose for Adventure* (3–6). 2001, Tundra paper $6.95 (0-88776-499-1). 184pp. After meeting on a plane to New York City, 13-year-old Alan and sassy, wheelchair-bound Frieda get involved in a smuggling plot at the airport and encounter Norbert, a small alien from Jupiter. (Rev: BL 2/15/01)

10500 Scrimger, Richard. *The Nose from Jupiter* (5–8). 1998, Tundra paper $5.95 (0-88776-428-2). Alan doesn't mind that Norbert, an alien from Jupiter, is living in his nose, but Norbert's outspoken remarks often get Alan into trouble. Also use *The Boy from Earth* (2004). (Rev: BL 7/98; BR 11–12/98)

10501 Service, Pamela F. *Stinker from Space* (3–6). 1988, Macmillan $12.95 (0-684-18910-1); Fawcett paper $5.50 (0-449-70330-4). 96pp. When his spaceship crashes to earth, Tsyng Tyr from the Sylon Confederacy takes over the body of a skunk. (Rev: BL 3/1/88; HB 9–10/88)

10502 Simons, Jamie, and E. W. Scollon. *Goners: The Hunt Is On* (4–7). Illus. 1998, Avon paper $3.99 (0-380-79730-5). 150pp. Four alien teens from the planet Roma time-travel to Monticello to fetch Thomas Jefferson. (Rev: BL 5/15/98)

10503 Slote, Alfred. *My Robot Buddy* (5–8). Illus. 1986, HarperCollins $12.95 (0-397-31641-0); paper $4.95 (0-06-440165-0). An easily read novel about Danny and the robot that is created for him. (Rev: BL 11/1/87)

10504 Spinner, Stephanie, and Terry Bisson. *Be First in the Universe* (4–6). 2000, Delacorte $14.95 (0-385-32687-4). 135pp. While staying with their hippie grandparents, twins Tod and Tessa explore a mall and encounter two young aliens who are trying to save their planet. (Rev: BCCB 2/00; BL 1/1–15/00; HBG 10/00; SLJ 2/00)

10505 Stevenson, Robert Louis. *The Strange Case of Dr. Jekyll and Mr. Hyde* (5–8). Illus. Series: Whole Story. 2003, Barnes & Noble paper $3.95 (1-593-08054-9). 112pp. Using lively ink-and-watercolor illustrations, this book offers the complete text of the classic in an attractive format. (Rev: BL 5/1/00; HBG 10/00)

10506 Thompson, Kate. *Fourth World* (5–8). Series: Missing Link. 2005, Bloomsbury $16.95 (1-58234-650-X). 320pp. Christie and his older stepbrother Danny go from Ireland to Scotland, where they discover strange developments at Fourth World, the compound where Danny's scientist mother lives and works, in this first volume of a trilogy. (Rev: BL 5/15/05)

10507 Walsh, Jill Paton. *The Green Book* (4–7). Illus. by Lloyd Bloom. 1982, Farrar paper $4.95 (0-374-42802-6). 80pp. The exodus of a group of Britons from dying Earth to another planet.

10508 Wells, H. G. *The Time Machine* (3–5). Adapted by Les Martin. Illus. by John Edens. 1990, Random paper $3.99 (0-679-80371-8). 93pp. A clever adaptation of a classic science fiction story about a time traveler and his friends. (Rev: SLJ 4/91)

10509 Whitman, John. *Star Wars: The Death Star* (2–5). Illus. by Barbara Gibson. 1997, Little, Brown $15.95 (0-316-93592-1). 12pp. Action-packed science fiction is featured in this pop-up book. Also use *Millennium Falcon* (1997). (Rev: BL 12/15/97)

10510 Wismer, Donald. *Starluck* (6–8). 1982, Ultramarine $20.00 (0-89366-255-0). 186pp. Paul becomes a threat to the Emperor of the Three Hundred Suns.

10511 Yolen, Jane, et al., eds. *Spaceships and Spells* (5–9). 1987, HarperCollins $12.95 (0-06-026796-8). A collection of 13 original tales, mostly science fiction but also some fantasy. (Rev: BL 1/15/88; BR 3–4/88; SLJ 11/87)

Short Stories and Anthologies

10512 Baylor, Byrd. *I'm in Charge of Celebrations* (4–6). Illus. 1986, Macmillan $17.00 (0-684-18579-2). 32pp. Poetic prose about rainbows, cactus greens, and desert browns. (Rev: BL 11/1/86; HB 1–2/87)

10513 Bennett, William J., ed. *The Book of Virtues for Young People: A Treasury of Great Moral Stories* (4–6). 1995, Silver Burdett LB $16.95 (0-382-24923-2). 384pp. A book of readings organized under such themes as friendship, self-discipline, work, and honesty. (Rev: BL 8/95; SLJ 8/95) [808.8]

10514 Canfield, Jack, et al., eds. *Chicken Soup for the Kid's Soul: 101 Stories of Courage, Hope and Laughter* (4–7). 1998, Health Communications paper $12.95 (1-55874-609-9). 396pp. A collection of inspiring true stories, some by well-known people, but mostly by children who sent them to the editors. (Rev: BL 9/1/98; HBG 3/99) [158.1]

10515 Canfield, Jack, et al., eds. *Chicken Soup for the Preteen Soul: 101 Stories of Changes, Choices and Growing Up for Kids Ages 9–13* (5–7). Illus. 2000, Health Communications $24.00 (1-55874-801-6); paper $12.95 (1-55874-800-8). 386pp. The usual mix of verse and prose written by and for preteens, with the aim of offering inspiration, comfort, and practical advice. (Rev: HBG 10/01; SLJ 4/01) [158.1]

10516 Carus, Marianne, ed. *Fire and Wings: Dragon Tales from East and West* (3–6). Illus. by Nilesh Mistry. 2002, Cricket $17.95 (0-8126-2664-8). 146pp. A collection of 15 stories, most of which have appeared in *Cricket* magazine, about all kinds of dragons, by authors including Jane Yolen, Patricia MacLachlan, Eric A. Kimmel, Vida Chu, and E. Nesbit. (Rev: HBG 3/03; SLJ 12/02)

10517 Dahl, Roald. *The Roald Dahl Treasury* (4–6). Illus. 1997, Viking $35.00 (0-670-87769-7). 448pp. An omnibus volume that features a generous selection of excerpts from Dahl's novels, autobiographies, and poetry, all handsomely illustrated by well-known artists. (Rev: BL 12/1/97; HBG 3/98) [820]

10518 Gac-Artigas, Alejandro. *Off to Catch the Sun* (5–8). 2001, Ediciones Nuevo Espacio paper $11.95 (1-930879-28-8). 148pp. Thirteen-year-old author Gac-Artigas explores serious issues through poetry, essays, and short stories. (Rev: BL 1/1–15/02)

10519 *Great Girl Stories: A Treasury of Classics from Children's Literature* (4–6). Ed. by Rosemary Sandberg. Illus. 1999, Kingfisher $18.95 (0-7534-5207-3). 160pp. A lavish gift book containing excerpts from 16 stories with central girl characters, including *Heidi, Anne of Green Gables,* and *The Great Gilly Hopkins.* (Rev: BL 10/15/99; HBG 3/00; SLJ 12/99)

10520 Highlights for Children, eds. *Ashanti Festival* (3–5). 1996, Boyds Mills paper $3.95 (1-56397-608-0). 96pp. Sixteen excellent short stories taken from the pages of *Highlights for Children.* (Rev: SLJ 1/97)

10521 Hurwitz, Johanna, ed. *Birthday Surprises: Ten Great Stories to Unwrap* (4–6). 1995, Morrow $16.00 (0-688-13194-8). 128pp. Ten short stories by such writers as Richard Peck and Ellen Conford deal with presents in containers that are empty. (Rev: BCCB 5/95; BL 4/15/95; SLJ 4/95*)

10522 Kantor, Susan, ed. *One-Hundred-and-One African-American Read-Aloud Stories* (3–8). 1998, Black Dog & Leventhal $12.98 (1-57912-039-3). 416pp. This book includes folktales, excerpts from novels, biographies, and history books, plus a sampling of songs, poetry, and chants all about African Americans and their heritage. (Rev: SLJ 6/99)

10523 Kurtz, Jane, ed. *Memories of Sun: Stories of Africa and America* (5–9). 2004, Greenwillow LB $16.89 (0-06-051051-X). 256pp. Fascinating stories and poems, by both well-known and less familiar writers, explore similarities and differences in the lives of Africans and Americans, including those who move and must adapt to very different cultures. (Rev: BL 1/1–15/04; SLJ 1/04)

10524 Maccaulay, David. *Black and White* (2–6). Illus. 1990, Houghton Mifflin $17.00 (0-395-52151-3). 32pp. With thought-provoking illustrations, four short stories are presented. Caldecott Medal winner, 1991. (Rev: BCCB 5/90; BL 4/1/90*; HB 9–10/90)

10525 Mazer, Anne, ed. *America Street: A Multicultural Anthology of Stories* (5–8). 1993, Persea paper $7.95 (0-89255-191-7). Fourteen short stories about growing up in America's diverse society by Robert Cormier, Langston Hughes, Grace Paley, Gary Soto, and others. (Rev: BCCB 11/93; BL 9/1/93; SLJ 11/93)

10526 Morpurgo, Michael, comp. *The Kingfisher Book of Great Boy Stories: A Treasury of Classics from Children's Literature* (4–8). Illus. 2000, Kingfisher $19.95 (0-7534-5320-7). 160pp. An attractively illustrated collection of stories from authors including Carlo Collodi, Roald Dahl, Ted Hughes, C. S. Lewis, A. A. Milne, Donald Sobol, and Mark Twain. (Rev: HBG 10/01; SLJ 4/01)

10527 *My Wish for Tomorrow: Words and Pictures from Children Around the World* (K–5). Illus. 1995, Morrow LB $15.93 (0-688-14456-X). 48pp. To celebrate the 50th birthday of the United Nations, this is a collection of writing and art by children ages 4 to 14 from around the world. (Rev: BL 10/15/95; SLJ 10/95)

10528 Paulsen, Gary, ed. *Shelf Life: Stories by the Book* (4–7). 2003, Simon & Schuster $16.95 (0-689-84180-9). 192pp. Books are the stars of these 10 stories by well-known authors that show that reading can change lives. (Rev: BL 8/03; HBG 4/04; SLJ 8/03)

10529 Pearce, Philippa. *Familiar and Haunting: Collected Stories* (5–8). 2002, HarperCollins LB $16.89 (0-06-623965-6). 368pp. Thirty-seven short stories, many of them about ghosts and the supernatural, are included in this intriguing collection. (Rev: BL 5/1/02; HB 5–6/02*; HBG 10/02; SLJ 7/02)

10530 Peck, Richard. *Past Perfect, Present Tense* (5–12). 2004, Dial $16.99 (0-8037-2998-7). 192pp. This anthology includes 11 previously published stories and two new ones, with comments on each story's inspiration and tips on writing fiction. (Rev: BL 4/1/04; HB 3–4/04; SLJ 4/04)

10531 Schulman, Janet, sel. *You Read to Me and I'll Read to You: 20th-Century Stories to Share* (K–3). 2001, Knopf $34.95 (0-375-81083-8). 250pp. A selection of stories for beginning readers by authors including Judy Blume, Roald Dahl, Astrid Lindgren, Louis Sachar, and Wiliam Steig. (Rev: HBG 3/02; SLJ 12/01)

10532 Spiegelman, Art, and Francoise Mouly, eds. *Little Lit: Strange Stories for Strange Kids* (4–9). Illus. 2001, HarperCollins paper $19.95 (0-06-028626-1). 64pp. This collection of offbeat, imaginative, graphic stories includes something for everyone, from humor to fantasy to horror, from Maurice Sendak to David Sedaris. (Rev: BL 12/15/01; HB 1–2/02; HBG 3/02; SLJ 3/02) [741.5]

Sports Stories

10533 Adler, C. S. *Winning* (5–8). 1999, Clarion $14.00 (0-395-65017-8). Eighth-grader Vicky lacks the courage and self-confidence to challenge her tennis partner when she catches her cheating. (Rev: BCCB 10/99; BL 10/1/99; HBG 3/00; SLJ 9/99)

10534 Adler, David A. *Mama Played Baseball* (K–3). Illus. by Chris O'Leary. 2003, Harcourt $16.00 (0-15-202196-5). Amy and her mother grow closer when Mama starts playing in the first women's pro baseball league during the early 1940s. (Rev: HBG 10/03; SLJ 4/03)

10535 Alvord, Douglas. *Sarah's Boat: A Young Girl Learns the Art of Sailing* (3–6). Illus. 1994, Tilbury House $16.95 (0-88448-117-4). 44pp. Sarah learns how to sail from her grandfather and enters her *Bluejay* sloop in the Labor Day race. (Rev: BL 7/94)

10536 Armstrong, Robb. *Runnin' with the Big Dawgs* (3–5). Illus. 1998, HarperCollins paper $3.99 (0-06-107067-X). 64pp. Twelve-year-old Patrick faces some ethical problems when he tries to join the coolest basketball team in town, the great Sky Walkers, led by their star, Dwayne "Dawg" Brewerton. (Rev: BL 9/1/98)

10537 Auch, Mary Jane. *Angel and Me and the Bayside Bombers* (2–4). Illus. by Cat B. Smith. 1989, Little, Brown $9.95 (0-316-05914-5); paper $2.95 (0-316-05915-3). 60pp. A poor soccer player, Brian bribes his way onto the team. (Rev: BL 1/15/90; HB 3–4/90; SLJ 3/90)

10538 Barwin, Steven, and Gabriel David Tick. *Slam Dunk* (5–7). Series: Sports Stories. 1999, Orca paper $5.50 (1-55028-598-X). 88pp. An easy read about a junior high basketball team in Canada that goes coed and the problems that result. (Rev: SLJ 1/00)

10539 Bates, Cynthia. *Shooting Star* (4–6). Series: Sports Stories. 2001, Lorimer paper $5.50 (1-55028-726-5). 102pp. Eight-grader Quyen Ha, who was a basketball star at her middle school, has some reservations about her decision to join a bantam team in this novel set in Canada that has information on Vietnamese family life. (Rev: SLJ 1/02)

10540 Bledsoe, Lucy Jane. *The Big Bike Race* (2–4). 1995, Holiday House $15.95 (0-8234-1206-7). 80pp. Though disappointed that he did not receive the bike of his dreams for his birthday, Ernie trains for the Citywide Cup race. (Rev: BCCB 12/95; BL 10/1/95; SLJ 11/95)

10541 Bledsoe, Lucy Jane. *Hoop Girlz* (5–7). 2002, Holiday House $16.95 (0-8234-1691-7). 128pp. When 11-year-old River is denied a place on the girls' basketball team, she forms her own team, with her brother as the coach. (Rev: BL 9/1/02; HBG 10/03; SLJ 12/02)

10542 Bo, Ben. *The Edge* (5–8). 1999, Lerner LB $17.95 (0-8225-3307-3). 139pp. Conflicted Declan is sent to a rehabilitation program in Canada's Glacier National Park, where he learns to snowboard and is drawn into a duel with the local champion. (Rev: BCCB 1/00; BL 10/15/99; HBG 3/00; SLJ 1/00)

10543 Bowen, Fred. *The Final Cut* (4–7). Illus. by Ann Barrow. Series: AllStar Sport Story. 1999, Peachtree paper $4.95 (1-56145-192-4). 102pp. A fast-paced novel about four friends and their efforts to make the junior high school basketball team. (Rev: SLJ 7/99)

10544 Bowen, Fred. *Full Court Fever* (3–6). Illus. by Ann Barrow. Series: AllStar Sport Story. 1998, Peachtree paper $4.95 (1-56145-160-6). 103pp. Michael and the rest of the seventh-grade basketball team are fearful about the coming match against the eighth graders. (Rev: SLJ 12/98)

10545 Bowen, Fred. *On the Line* (4–7). Illus. by Ann Barrow. 1999, Peachtree paper $4.95 (1-56145-199-1). 103pp. A young boy learns about self-image and open-mindedness while trying to improve his foul shots in this novel about an 8th grader and his basketball skills. (Rev: SLJ 4/00)

10546 Bowen, Fred. *Playoff Dreams* (3–5). Illus. 1997, Peachtree paper $4.95 (1-56145-155-X). 112pp. When Brendan begins to feel that he is the only salvation open to his baseball team, Uncle Jack steps in with some good advice. (Rev: BL 11/1/97; SLJ 3/98)

10547 Bowen, Fred. *T.J.'s Secret Pitch* (3–5). Illus. by Jim Thorpe. Series: AllStar Sport Story. 1996, Peachtree paper $4.95 (1-56145-119-3). 104pp. A young Little Leaguer copies the famous pitch of the legendary Truett "Rip" Sewell and achieves fame. (Rev: SLJ 7/96)

10548 Bowen, Fred. *Winners Take All* (3–7). Illus. by Paul Casale. 2000, Peachtree paper $4.95 (1-56145-229-7). 104pp. Twelve-year-old Kyle eventually confesses to faking a catch in this story that includes discussion of Christy Mathewson, a pro pitcher in the early 1900s who was admired for his sportsmanship. (Rev: SLJ 4/01)

10549 Brooks, Bruce. *Dooby* (5–8). Series: Wolfbay Wings. 1998, HarperCollins LB $14.89 (0-06-027898-6); paper $4.50 (0-06-440708-X). Dooby sulks when he is not made captain of his Peewee hockey team, but is completely humiliated to learn he has lost out to a girl. Also recommended in this series is *Reed* (1998). (Rev: HBG 3/99; SLJ 2/99)

10550 Brooks, Bruce. *Shark* (5–8). Series: Wolfbay Wings. 1998, HarperCollins LB $14.89 (0-06-027570-7); paper $4.50 (0-06-440681-4). In spite of being fat, slow, and confused, Shark becomes a valuable player on the Wolfbay Wings hockey team. (Rev: HBG 10/98; SLJ 6/98)

10551 Bruchac, Joseph. *The Warriors* (5–8). 2003, Darby Creek $15.95 (1-58196-002-6). 192pp. Jake Forrest, a Native American teenager and lacrosse whiz, leaves the reservation to attend a private school and encounters many new situations, including a different attitude toward sports. (Rev: BL 12/1/03; HBG 10/01; SLJ 10/03)

10552 Bunting, Eve. *Snowboarding on Monster Mountain* (4–6). Illus. by Karen Ritz. 2003, Cricket $15.95 (0-8126-2704-0). 80pp. Facing her fear of heights and her worries about new girl Izzy, 11-year-old Callie agrees to go snowboarding with her best friend Jen. (Rev: BL 1/1–15/04; HBG 4/04; SLJ 1/04)

10553 Butcher, Kristin. *Cairo Kelly and the Man* (4–8). 2002, Orca paper $6.95 (1-55143-211-0). 176pp. When Midge discovers that his baseball team's umpire, Hal Mann, is illiterate, Midge and his friend Kelly set out to solve the problem. (Rev: BL 9/1/02)

10554 Butler, Dori Hillestad. *Sliding into Home* (5–8). 2003, Peachtree $14.95 (1-56145-222-X). 192pp. Joelle, 13, refuses to accept a ban on girls playing baseball when she moves to a small town in Iowa. (Rev: BL 5/1/03; HBG 10/03; SLJ 1/04)

10555 Christopher, Matt. *Baseball Turnaround* (4–6). 1977, Little, Brown paper $4.50 (0-316-14264-6). 160pp. After Sandy has had a brush with the law, he tries to keep this part of his past a secret from his teammates. (Rev: BL 6/1–15/97; SLJ 8/97)

10556 Christopher, Matt. *The Comeback Challenge* (4–6). Illus. 1996, Little, Brown paper $4.50 (0-316-14152-6). 160pp. Twelve-year-old Mark has problems with Vince, the captain of his soccer team. (Rev: BL 1/1–15/96; SLJ 1/96)

10557 Christopher, Matt. *Dirt Bike Racer* (3–5). Illus. by Barry Bomzer. 1986, Little, Brown paper $4.50 (0-316-14053-8). Ron finds a bike at the bottom of a lake and begins dirt bike racing. Another sports story from the same author is: *Dirt Bike Runaway* (1989).

10558 Christopher, Matt. *The Dog That Called the Pitch* (1–3). Illus. 1998, Little, Brown $14.95 (0-316-14207-7). 48pp. An easily read story about baseball, young Mike, his telepathic dog Harry, and

the discovery that an umpire can also read minds. (Rev: BL 5/15/98; HBG 10/98; SLJ 9/98)

10559 Christopher, Matt. *The Dog That Pitched a No-Hitter* (2–4). Illus. by Daniel Vasconcellos. 1993, Little, Brown paper $3.95 (0-316-14103-8). 42pp. Mike's dog Harry has powers of ESP and helps Mike with his pitching game. (Rev: BL 5/15/88; SLJ 8/88)

10560 Christopher, Matt. *The Hit-Away Kid* (2–5). Illus. 1988, Little, Brown paper $4.50 (0-316-14007-4). 55pp. Barry McGee, left fielder for the Peach Street Mudders, learns a lesson in sportsmanship and telling the truth. Two other baseball stories are: *Supercharged Infield* (1985); *The Spy on Third Base* (1988). (Rev: BCCB 5/88; BL 4/1/88; SLJ 5/88)

10561 Christopher, Matt. *Mountain Bike Mania* (5–7). 1998, Little, Brown paper $4.50 (0-316-14292-1). 160pp. Will is at loose ends with no after-school activities until he becomes involved in a mountain bike club. (Rev: BL 2/1/99; HBG 10/99; SLJ 3/99)

10562 Christopher, Matt. *Penalty Shot* (3–5). Illus. 1997, Little, Brown paper $3.95 (0-316-14190-9). 134pp. Kevin is thrown off the hockey team for bad grades but is determined to get back on. (Rev: BL 1/1–15/97; SLJ 2/97)

10563 Christopher, Matt. *Prime-Time Pitcher* (4–7). 1998, Little, Brown paper $4.50 (0-316-14213-1). 138pp. Koby Caplin becomes arrogant about his winning streak on the baseball team and soon loses games because of his lack of teamwork. (Rev: HBG 3/99; SLJ 12/98)

10564 Christopher, Matt. *Red-Hot Hightops* (4–6). Illus. 1992, Little, Brown paper $4.50 (0-316-14089-9). 128pp. Shyness prevents Kelly from showing off her basketball skills or speaking to a boy she likes until she finds a pair of red sneakers in her locker. (Rev: BL 1/15/88)

10565 Christopher, Matt. *Return of the Home Run Kid* (4–7). Illus. by Paul Casale. 1994, Little, Brown paper $4.50 (0-316-14273-5). 176pp. In this sequel to *The Kid Who Only Hit Homers* (1972), Sylvester learns to be more aggressive on the field but gets criticism from his friends. (Rev: BL 4/15/92; SLJ 5/92)

10566 Christopher, Matt. *Roller Hockey Radicals* (3–7). 1998, Little, Brown paper $3.95 (0-316-13675-1). 153pp. Kirby wants to play roller hockey with a gang of street kids but his parents object. (Rev: HBG 10/98; SLJ 10/98)

10567 Christopher, Matt. *Shortstop from Tokyo* (3–5). Illus. by Harvey Kidder. 1988, Little, Brown paper $3.95 (0-316-13992-0). Stogie feels resentment when a Japanese boy takes his place on the baseball team. Also from the same author and publisher: *The Kid Who Only Hit Homers* (1972); *The Fox Steals Home* (1985); *The Year Mom Won the Pennant* (1986); *No Arm in Left Field* (1987).

10568 Christopher, Matt. *Snowboard Maverick* (4–7). 1997, Little, Brown paper $4.50 (0-316-14203-4). 152pp. Dennis overcomes his fears and begins snowboarding. (Rev: BL 4/1/98; HBG 3/98; SLJ 3/98)

10569 Christopher, Matt. *Soccer Halfback* (4–6). Illus. by Larry Johnson. 1985, Little, Brown paper $4.50 (0-316-13981-5). Everyone wants Jabber to play football, but his favorite sport is soccer.

10570 Cohen, Barbara. *Thank You, Jackie Robinson* (4–6). Illus. by Richard Cuffari. 1989, Scholastic paper $3.50 (0-590-42378-9). A memoir written by Sam about his friendship with an old man and his devotion as a boy to the Brooklyn Dodgers and Ebbets Field.

10571 Cooper, Ilene. *Choosing Sides* (4–6). 1990, Morrow $15.00 (0-688-07934-2). 224pp. Jonathan wants to quit the basketball team but does not want to disappoint his dad. (Rev: BCCB 9/90; BL 2/15/90; SLJ 5/90)

10572 Coy, John. *Strong to the Hoop* (2–5). Illus. 1999, Lee & Low $16.95 (1-880000-80-6). 32pp. In this basketball story, 10-year-old James is drafted to play with the older kids when one of their teammates hurts his ankle. (Rev: BL 12/15/99; HBG 10/00; SLJ 10/99)

10573 Curtis, Gavin. *The Bat Boy and His Violin* (3–5). Illus. by E. B. Lewis. 1998, Simon & Schuster $16.00 (0-689-80099-1). 32pp. In 1948 young Reginald heeds his father's orders and becomes batboy for the Dukes, a team in the Negro League, where he beguiles the players with his violin playing. (Rev: BL 6/1–15/98; HBG 10/98; SLJ 7/98)

10574 Drumtra, Stacy. *Face-Off* (4–8). 1992, Avon paper $3.50 (0-380-76863-1). 118pp. T.J. and his twin Brad become rivals for friends and for status on the hockey team. (Rev: BL 4/1/93; SLJ 1/05)

10575 Durant, Alan, sel. *Sports Stories* (5–9). Illus. by David Kearney. Series: Story Library. 2000, Kingfisher $14.95 (0-7534-5322-3). 221pp. A collection of 21 previously published short stories by well-known authors dealing with a variety of sports. (Rev: HBG 10/01; SLJ 11/00)

10576 Dygard, Thomas J. *Second Stringer* (5–8). 1998, Morrow $15.00 (0-688-15981-8). 174pp. Kevin, a second stringer, must learn confidence and earn the respect of his teammates when he takes over the school's football team after the star quarterback is injured. (Rev: HBG 3/99; SLJ 12/98)

10577 Fitzgerald, Dawn. *Getting in the Game* (4–7). 2005, Roaring Brook $15.95 (0-59643-044-3). 144pp. Being the only girl on the school ice-hockey team is only one of the issues Joanna must deal with in this story of sports and relationships. (Rev: BL 3/1/05)

10578 Forsyth, C. A. *Power Hitter* (4–6). Series: Sports Stories. 2001, Lorimer paper $5.50 (1-55028-732-X). 86pp. A 13-year-old boy goes to visit relatives in Winnipeg for a summer full of baseball, unaware that his parents are divorcing and his mother is ill. (Rev: SLJ 1/02)

10579 Greene, Stephanie. *Owen Foote, Soccer Star* (2–4). Illus. 1998, Clarion $14.00 (0-395-86143-8). 88pp. When Owen joins a local soccer team, he is not prepared for the powerhouse players he meets. A sequel to *Owen Foote, Second Grade Strongman*

(1996). (Rev: BL 3/15/98; HB 5–6/98; HBG 10/98; SLJ 7/98)

10580 Hale, Daniel J., and Matthew LaBrot. *Red Card* (4–7). Series: Zeke Armstrong Mystery. 2002, Top paper $7.95 (1-929976-15-1). 170pp. Someone is trying to kill the soccer coach, and young Zeke sets out to discover who and why. (Rev: SLJ 12/02)

10581 Hall, Donald. *When Willard Met Babe Ruth* (4–6). Illus. by Barry Moser. 1996, Harcourt $16.00 (0-15-200273-1). 48pp. A young New Hampshire farm boy and his father have a chance meeting with Babe Ruth. (Rev: BCCB 6/96; BL 3/15/96*; HB 9–10/96; SLJ 5/96)

10582 Heymsfeld, Carla. *Coaching Ms. Parker* (3–5). Illus. by Jane O'Connor. 1992, Macmillan LB $13.00 (0-02-743715-9). 96pp. Fourth-graders face the challenge of teaching Ms. Parker baseball in time for the faculty versus sixth-grade game. (Rev: BCCB 6/92; BL 6/15/92; SLJ 7/92)

10583 Hirschfeld, Robert. *Goalkeeper in Charge* (5–7). Series: Christopher Sports. 2002, Little, Brown $15.95 (0-316-07552-3); paper $4.50 (0-316-07548-5). 144pp. Seventh-grader Tina works to overcome her shyness on and off the soccer field. (Rev: BL 9/1/02; HBG 3/03)

10584 Holohan, Maureen. *Catch Shorty by Rosie* (4–8). Series: The Broadway Ballplayers. 1999, Broadway Ballplayers paper $6.95 (0-9659091-6-6). 160pp. Sixth-grader Rosie Jones devotes her time to organizing an all-girls football league while coping with a series of minor personal problems at home and school. (Rev: SLJ 3/00)

10585 Holohan, Maureen. *Everybody's Favorite* (4–6). Series: The Broadway Ballplayers. 1998, Broadway Ballplayers paper $6.95 (0-9659091-2-3). 107pp. Capable young Penny finds she is thrust into a position of responsibility when she and the Broadway Ballplayers (sports-loving neighborhood girls) try to earn money for a soccer camp. (Rev: BL 4/15/98)

10586 Holohan, Maureen. *Left Out* (4–6). Series: The Broadway Ballplayers. 1998, Broadway Ballplayers paper $6.95 (0-9659091-1-5). 160pp. The narrator, shy and nonacademic Rosie, tells about the summer she joined the All Star baseball team and encountered a coach who didn't want to give her a chance. (Rev: BL 4/15/98)

10587 Hurwitz, Johanna. *Baseball Fever* (3–6). Illus. by Ray Cruz. 1981, Morrow paper $3.95 (0-688-10495-9). 128pp. Mr. Feldman loathes baseball, but his son Ezra loves it.

10588 Isadora, Rachel. *Luke Goes to Bat* (PS–2). Illus. 2005, Penguin Putnam $15.99 (0-399-23604-X). 32pp. In this appealing tale set in 1950s Brooklyn, Luke, a young African-American boy who idolizes Jackie Robinson, longs for a chance to play stickball with the older boys in his neighborhood; when he finally gets his chance at bat, he strikes out but realizes that the keys to success are determination and persistence. (Rev: BL 2/1/05; SLJ 2/05)

10589 Jennings, Patrick. *Out Standing in My Field* (3–5). 2005, Scholastic $16.95 (0-439-46581-8). 176pp. Ty, a not-so-talented baseball player, has a revealing conversation with his sister while Ty's team loses yet another game. (Rev: BL 3/15/05; SLJ 4/05)

10590 Joosse, Barbara M. *The Losers Fight Back* (3–6). Illus. 1994, Clarion $15.00 (0-395-62335-9). 128pp. When the Bruisers, a losing soccer team, bribe Chuckie to join them, they find that he takes over their games. (Rev: BL 9/15/94; SLJ 11/94)

10591 Kline, Suzy. *Molly Gets Mad* (2–4). Illus. by Diana C. Bluthenthal. Series: Molly. 2001, Penguin Putnam $14.99 (0-399-23408-X). 72pp. Third-grader Molly's friend Morty is a good sport, even when Molly is a little too competitive on and off the ice. (Rev: BL 9/1/01; HBG 10/01; SLJ 8/01)

10592 Knudson, R. R. *Rinehart Lifts* (4–6). 1982, Avon paper $1.95 (0-380-57059-9). 88pp. A failure at all sports, Rinehart finds he can excel in weight lifting.

10593 Kroll, Steven. *New Kid in Town* (2–4). Illus. 1992, Avon paper $3.50 (0-380-76407-5). 80pp. Phil finally makes the Raymondtown Rockets baseball team, only to find his happiness threatened because his father may be transferred. (Rev: BL 3/15/92)

10594 Lynch, Chris. *Gold Dust* (5–8). 2000, HarperCollins LB $16.89 (0-06-028175-8). 208pp. Richard comes from a Boston working-class family and Napoleon is the son of a visiting professor from the Dominican Republic in this novel about friendship, baseball, and racial tensions. (Rev: BCCB 11/00; BL 9/1/00; HBG 3/01; SLJ 10/00)

10595 Maifair, Linda Lee. *Batter Up, Bailey Benson!* (3–5). 1997, Zondervan paper $3.99 (0-310-20705-3). 64pp. Bailey faces jealousy problems when she finds that she is on a different baseball team than her friend Nicole. (Rev: BL 3/15/97)

10596 Maifair, Linda Lee. *Go Figure, Gabriella Grant!* (3–5). 1997, Zondervan paper $3.99 (0-310-20702-9). 64pp. Gabriella has problems budgeting her time when she takes up figure skating. (Rev: BL 3/15/97)

10597 Manes, Stephen. *An Almost Perfect Game* (4–7). 1995, Scholastic paper $14.95 (0-590-44432-8). 163pp. Jake and Randy enjoy visiting their grandparents each summer because all of them are avid baseball fans. (Rev: BL 6/1–15/95; SLJ 6/95)

10598 Mantell, Paul. *Stealing Home* (3–6). Series: Matt Christopher. 2004, Little, Brown $15.95 (0-316-60739-8); paper $4.50 (0-316-60742-8). 135pp. Seventh grader Joey Gallagher enjoys being a baseball star and is not pleased at first to discover the exchange student visiting from Nicaragua, Jesus, also has real talent. (Rev: SLJ 11/04)

10599 Mazer, Abby. *The Amazing Days of Abby Hayes* (3–6). 2000, Scholastic paper $4.95 (0-439-14977-0). 144pp. Told in prose, journal entries, and drawings, this is the story of Abby Hayes, who tries without much success to shine at soccer. (Rev: BL 8/00)

10600 Mills, Claudia. *Gus and Grandpa at Basketball* (2–4). Illus. by Catherine Stock. 2001, Farrar $14.00 (0-374-32818-8). 48pp. In this seventh book in the series, Grandpa helps Gus overcome his anxi-

ety about playing basketball in front of a crowd. (Rev: BL 11/15/01; HB 11–12/01; HBG 3/02; SLJ 9/01)

10601 Myers, Walter Dean. *The Journal of Biddy Owens* (5–7). Series: My Name Is America. 2001, Scholastic paper $10.95 (0-439-09503-4). 142pp. A fictional journal that tells of the last year of the Negro Leagues, and of 17-year-old Biddy Owens and his involvement with the Birmingham Black Barons. (Rev: BL 2/15/01; HBG 10/01; SLJ 4/01)

10602 Myers, Walter Dean. *Me, Mop, and the Moondance Kid* (5–7). Illus. 1988, Dell paper $4.99 (0-440-40396-0). 128pp. The efforts of T.J. and Moondance to get their friend Mop adopted. (Rev: BCCB 12/88; BL 2/1/89; SLJ 1/88)

10603 Nishiyama, Yuriko. *Rebound: Volume 1* (5–8). Illus. 2004, Tokyopop paper $9.99 (1-931514-02-X). 192pp. The first volume in a manga sequel to the Harlem Beat series takes the Johnan High School basketball team to Sapporo, Japan. (Rev: BL 5/15/04)

10604 Nitz, Kristin Wolden. *Defending Irene* (5–7). 2004, Peachtree $14.95 (1-56145-309-9). 185pp. When her family moves to Italy for a year, 13-year-old Irene is determined to continue playing soccer, even if it's on the boys' team. (Rev: SLJ 9/04)

10605 Patneaude, David. *Haunting at Home Plate* (4–7). 2000, Whitman LB $14.95 (0-8075-3181-2). Twelve-year-old Nelson is amazed when mysterious instructions are left on the playing field in this baseball novel about a losing team that suddenly seems to be getting help from a ghost. (Rev: BCCB 11/00; BL 9/1/00; HBG 3/01; SLJ 9/00)

10606 Peers, Judi. *Shark Attack* (5–7). Series: Sports Stories. 1999, Orca paper $6.50 (1-55028-620-X). 74pp. An easily read story set in Canada, in which a young baseball player wants to impress his father but doesn't think he can ever reach his older brother's record. (Rev: SLJ 1/00)

10607 Ritter, John H. *The Boy Who Saved Baseball* (5–7). 2003, Penguin Putnam $17.99 (0-399-23622-8). 224pp. A small town depends on its baseball team to rescue it from big developers. (Rev: BL 5/1/03*; HBG 4/04; SLJ 6/03)

10608 Ritter, John H. *Choosing Up Sides* (5–9). 1998, Penguin Putnam $17.99 (0-399-23185-4). 176pp. Jake is a great southpaw in baseball, but his preacher father forbids the boy to use his left hand for pitching as it is the instrument of Satan. (Rev: BCCB 6/98; BL 5/1/98; HBG 10/98; SLJ 6/98)

10609 Rivers, Karen. *Waiting to Dive* (4–6). 2001, Orca paper $6.95 (1-55143-159-9). 106pp. When her best friend breaks her back in a diving accident, Carly, 10, loses her desire to become a diving champion and sinks into grief and depression. (Rev: BL 3/1/01)

10610 Roberts, Kristi. *My Thirteenth Season* (5–8). 2005, Holt $15.95 (0-8050-7495-3). 144pp. When Fran, whose mother has recently died, tries to play baseball for the boys' team in her new town, she is in for a world of trouble. (Rev: BL 3/15/05; SLJ 3/05)

517

10611 Schnur, Steven. *The Koufax Dilemma* (4–6). Illus. 1997, Morrow $15.00 (0-688-14221-4). 192pp. Danny faces problems because of his parents' divorce and the fact that his mother won't let him play baseball in the big game on Passover. (Rev: BCCB 5/97; BL 3/15/97; SLJ 5/97)

10612 Scholz, Jackson. *The Football Rebels* (5–7). 1993, Morrow paper $4.95 (0-688-12643-X). 256pp. Clint does his best on the intramural football team when he doesn't make the varsity. Also use *Rookie Quarterback* (1993). Both are reissues.

10613 Shannon, David. *How Georgie Radbourn Saved Baseball* (1–5). Illus. 1994, Scholastic $14.95 (0-590-47410-3). 32pp. A rich and powerful wheeler-dealer decides to ban baseball, and it's up to young Georgie Radbourn to save it. (Rev: BL 1/15/94; SLJ 4/94*)

10614 Sloan, Holly Goldberg. *Keeper* (5–8). 2003, Scobre paper $9.95 (0-9708992-3-8). 146pp. Afraid of almost everything, eighth-grader Sasha Lewis is dragged kicking and shouting into sports by her best friend, Courtney. (Rev: SLJ 10/03)

10615 Slote, Alfred. *Finding Buck McHenry* (4–6). 1991, HarperCollins LB $15.89 (0-06-021653-0). 256pp. Is Jason's baseball coach really the former great player he sees on a baseball card? (Rev: BCCB 5/91; BL 3/15/91; SLJ 5/91)

10616 Smith, Charles R. *Tall Tales: Six Amazing Basketball Dreams* (5–8). Illus. 2000, Dutton $17.99 (0-525-46172-8). 40pp. This book consists of six fantasy short stories about basketball. In one, for example, people find out that the best player in the neighborhood is blind. (Rev: BCCB 5/00; BL 3/1/00; HBG 10/00; SLJ 9/00)

10617 Sullivan, Ann. *Molly Maguire: Wide Receiver* (4–6). 1992, Avon paper $2.99 (0-380-76114-9). 104pp. Molly wants to show a certain bully that she can play football, with the help of her next-door neighbor, who played for Notre Dame. (Rev: BL 10/1/92)

10618 Telander, Rick. *String Music* (4–6). 2002, Cricket $15.95 (0-8126-2647-5). 144pp. Robbie, a fifth-grader with plenty of problems, runs away to the big city, sneaks into a basketball game, and meets basketball's greatest player. (Rev: BCCB 7–8/02; BL 5/1/02)

10619 Trembath, Don. *Frog Face and the Three Boys* (4–7). Series: Black Belt. 2001, Orca paper $6.95 (1-55143-165-3). 157pp. Three very different 7th-graders are enrolled in a karate class to teach them discipline. (Rev: BL 3/1/01; SLJ 9/01)

10620 Tunis, John R. *The Kid from Tomkinsville* (5–8). 1990, Harcourt $14.95 (0-15-242568-3); paper $6.00 (0-15-242567-5). "Kid" Tucker's rookie year with the 1940 Brooklyn Dodgers. Other Tunis classics are: *Rookie of the Year; Keystone Kids* (both 1990). (Rev: BL 8/87)

10621 Wallace, Bill. *Never Say Quit* (5–7). 1993, Holiday House $16.95 (0-8234-1013-7). 212pp. A group of misfits who don't make the soccer team decide to form one of their own. (Rev: BL 4/15/93)

10622 Walter, Mildren P. *Suitcase* (3–6). 1999, Lothrop $15.00 (0-688-16547-8). 112pp. Xander, a tall African American boy with great artistic talent, disappoints his father when he proves to be inept at basketball, but regains his affection as a star pitcher on the baseball team. (Rev: BCCB 10/99; BL 9/15/99; HB 11–12/99; HBG 3/00; SLJ 9/99)

10623 Walters, Eric. *Full Court Press* (3–5). 2001, Orca paper $4.50 (1-55143-169-6). 152pp. Though only in the third grade, Nick and Kia decide to try out for the fifth-grade basketball team. (Rev: BL 4/1/01)

10624 Walters, Eric. *Long Shot* (2–5). Illus. by John Mantha. 2002, Orca paper $4.99 (1-55143-216-1). 140pp. The new coach of Nick and Kia's basketball team is so unpleasant that all the players walk out. (Rev: SLJ 7/02)

10625 Walters, Eric. *Three on Three* (3–5). Illus. 2000, Orca paper $4.50 (1-55143-170-X). 122pp. Third-graders Nick and Kia, excellent basketball players, get the best player in school to join them for a 3-on-3 tournament, but unforeseen problems arise. (Rev: BCCB 6/00; BL 6/1–15/00)

10626 Webster-Doyle, Terrence. *Breaking the Chains of the Ancient Warrior: Tests of Wisdom for Young Martial Artists* (5–8). Illus. 1995, Martial Arts for Peace paper $14.95 (0-942941-32-2). A collection of inspirational stories, karate parables, and tests that promote ethical behavior, with accompanying follow-up questions and a message for adult readers. (Rev: SLJ 1/96)

10627 Wolff, Virginia E. *Bat 6* (5–9). 1998, Scholastic paper $16.95 (0-590-89799-3). 240pp. In this novel narrated by the members of the opposing teams, a Japanese American girl just out of an internment camp meets a bitter girl whose father was killed at Pearl Harbor, and the two become rivals in baseball. (Rev: BCCB 6/98; BL 5/1/98*; HBG 10/98; SLJ 5/98)

10628 Wooldridge, Frosty. *Strike Three! Take Your Base* (5–9). Illus. by Pietri Freeman. 2001, Brookfield Reader $16.95 (1-930093-01-2); paper $6.95 (1-930093-07-1). 160pp. Baseball provides the setting as two brothers deal individually with the sudden death of their umpire father. (Rev: SLJ 3/02)

10629 Zirpoli, Jane. *Roots in the Outfield* (5–7). 1988, Houghton Mifflin $16.00 (0-395-45184-1). 133pp. Josh spends a summer with his newly married father in Wisconsin and discovers some baseball memorabilia that help him overcome his own fears and ineptness in right field. (Rev: BL 4/1/88; SLJ 5/88)

Fairy Tales

10630 Allen, Debbie. *Brothers of the Knight* (K–3). Illus. by Kadir Nelson. 1999, Dial $15.99 (0-8037-2488-8). 40pp. Set in Harlem, this variation on *The Twelve Dancing Princesses* involves a clergyman's 12 sons who sneak out every night to dance. (Rev: BL 11/15/99; HBG 3/00; SLJ 10/99) [398.2]

10631 Andersen, Hans Christian. *For Sure! For Sure!* (1–4). Trans. from German by Mus White. Illus. by Stefan Czernecki. 2004, August House $16.95 (0-87483-742-1). Andersen's tale about a chicken who views herself as more beautiful with one less feather and how the story is amplified as it spreads across the town. (Rev: SLJ 11/04) [398.2]

10632 Andersen, Hans Christian. *The Little Match Girl* (4–6). Illus. by Blair Lent. 1975, Houghton Mifflin paper $1.95 (0-685-02294-3). The touching story of the lonely, shivering little match girl who sees visions in the flames of the matches she cannot sell. [398.2]

10633 Andersen, Hans Christian. *Little Mermaids and Ugly Ducklings: Favorite Fairy Tales by Hans Christian Andersen* (4–6). Illus. by Gennady Spirin. 2001, Chronicle $15.95 (0-8118-3320-8). 59pp. Handsome, imaginative illustrations of differing styles and sizes enhance six well-known tales. (Rev: BL 12/1/01; HBG 3/02) [839.8]

10634 Andersen, Hans Christian. *The Steadfast Tin Soldier* (K–4). Retold by Tor Seidler. Illus. by Fred Marcellino. 1997, HarperCollins paper $5.95 (0-062-05900-9). 32pp. This version of the popular tale sticks to the traditional story and acknowledges the author. (Rev: BL 12/1/92*; HB 3–4/93; SLJ 2/93) [398.2]

10635 Andersen, Hans Christian. *Stories from Hans Christian Andersen* (2–4). Retold by Andrew Matthews. Illus. by Alan Snow. 1993, Orchard $18.95 (0-531-05463-2). 96pp. Eleven popular Andersen fairy tales, like *The Steadfast Tin Soldier* and *The Little Mermaid*, are retold in a simplified, conversational manner. (Rev: SLJ 12/93) [398.2]

10636 Andersen, Hans Christian. *Tales of Hans Christian Andersen* (4–6). Trans. by Naomi Lewis.

Illus. by Joel Stewart. 2004, Candlewick $22.99 (0-7636-2515-9). 208pp. Thirteen of Andersen's best-known stories are included in this handsome, large-format volume. (Rev: BL 1/1–15/05) [839.8]

10637 Andersen, Hans Christian. *Thumbelina* (PS–2). Retold by Brian Pinkney. Illus. by retel. 2003, Greenwillow LB $17.89 (0-688-17477-9). Pinkney's picture-book retelling is faithful to the original and features interesting artwork that differs from his usual style. (Rev: HBG 4/04; SLJ 9/03)

10638 Andersen, Hans Christian. *Thumbelina* (1–5). Illus. by reteller. 2005, Little, Brown $16.99 (0-316-57359-0). Thumbelina's story is retold with a few changes that enhance readability, plus new, appealing illustrations. (Rev: SLJ 5/05) [398.2]

10639 Andersen, Hans Christian. *The Top and the Ball* (K–2). Illus. by Elisabeth Nyman. 1992, Ideals LB $15.00 (0-8249-8583-4). 32pp. In the 19th century, a wooden top loves a ball in a boy's toy box. (Rev: BL 10/15/92)

10640 Andersen, Hans Christian. *The Ugly Duckling* (PS–3). Illus. by Bernadette Watts. 2000, North-South LB $15.88 (0-7358-1389-2). The double-page illustrations are outstanding in this retelling of the Andersen classic. (Rev: BL 5/15/00; HBG 10/01)

10641 Anholt, Laurence. *Little Red Riding Wolf* (2–4). Illus. by Arthur Robins. Series: Seriously Silly Stories. 2004, Compass Point LB $13.26 (0-7565-0632-8). 64pp. Black-and-white cartoons illustrate this story in which the poor little wolf on his way to visit granny is terrorized by a big bad girl. Also use *Shampoozel*, a Rapunzel variation (2004). (Rev: SLJ 7/04)

10642 Balcells, Jacqueline. *The Enchanted Raisin* (3–6). Trans. by Elizabeth G. Miller. Illus. 1989, Latin American Literary Review Pr. paper $11.00 (0-935480-38-2). 103pp. Ten contemporary fairy stories by a noted Chilean writer for children. (Rev: BL 12/1/89)

10643 Batt, Tanya. *The Princess and the White Bear King* (1–3). Illus. by Nicoletta Ceccoli. 2004, Bare-foot $16.99 (1-84148-339-7). 40pp. Borrowing from three traditional folktales, Batt has created a charming story about a beautiful young princess who is kidnapped by a white bear and taken to his stately palace. (Rev: BL 11/1/04; SLJ 1/05) [398.2]

10644 Batt, Tanya Robyn. *The Faerie's Gift* (K–3). Illus. by Nicoletta Ceccoli. 2003, Barefoot $16.99 (1-84148-998-0). 32pp. A fairy offers a woodcutter one wish, and the wish he makes pleases everyone in his family. (Rev: BL 2/15/03; HBG 10/03; SLJ 6/03) [398.221]

10645 Bazilian, Barbara. *The Red Shoes* (K–2). Illus. 1997, Whispering Coyote $15.95 (1-879085-56-9). 40pp. This attractive retelling of Andersen's story has been changed to make it less preachy and gory. (Rev: BL 11/1/97; HBG 3/98; SLJ 10/97)

10646 Birdseye, Tom. *Look Out, Jack! The Giant Is Back!* (K–3). Illus. by Will Hillenbrand. 2001, Holiday House $16.95 (0-8234-1450-7). 32pp. The giant of "Jack and the Beanstalk" fame has a big brother who wants revenge — and Jack narrowly escapes him in this colorful picture book. (Rev: BCCB 10/01; BL 9/1/01; HBG 3/02; SLJ 10/01)

10647 Blackaby, Susan, retel. *The Little Mermaid* (K–2). Illus. by Charlene DeLage. Series: Read-It! Readers Fairy Tales. 2004, Picture Window LB $13.95 (1-4048-0221-5). 32pp. In this attractive retelling of Hans Christian Andersen's classic story, a beautiful mermaid longs to become human so that she can win the heart of a handsome prince. (Rev: SLJ 1/04)

10648 Blackaby, Susan, retel. *The Princess and the Pea* (K–2). Illus. by Charlene DeLage. Series: Read-It! Readers Fairy Tales. 2004, Picture Window LB $13.95 (1-4048-0223-1). 32pp. In this beautifully illustrated adaptation of Hans Christian Andersen's classic fairy tale, an unlikely looking young woman claims to be a princess and proves she is when a tiny pea under a pile of 20 mattresses keeps her from a good night's sleep. (Rev: SLJ 1/04)

10649 Boada, Francesc. *Cinderella / Cenicienta* (PS–1). Illus. by Monse Fransoy. Series: Bilingual Editions. 2001, Chronicle paper $6.95 (0-8118-3090-X). 32pp. A bilingual version full of humor that stays close to the original tale. (Rev: BL 7/01; HBG 10/01) [398.2]

10650 Brown, Marc. *Arthur's Really Helpful Bedtime Book* (PS–2). Adapted by Stephen Krensky. Illus. by author. 1998, Random LB $15.99 (0-679-88468-2). 44pp. The characters from the Arthur books are featured in these retellings of ten classic stories including "The Princess and the Pea," "The Three Little Pigs," and "The Frog Prince." (Rev: SLJ 3/99)

10651 Campbell, Ann. *Once Upon a Princess and a Pea* (PS–3). Illus. by Kathy O. Young. 1993, Stewart, Tabori & Chang $14.95 (1-55670-289-2). 32pp. In a modern version of this fairy tale, a runaway princess must prove her sensitivity. (Rev: BL 8/93)

10652 Charles, Veronika M. *The Crane Girl* (K–2). Illus. 1995, Orchard paper $6.95 (0-773-75718-X). 32pp. After she feels rejected by her parents, Yoshiko begs the cranes to transform her into one of

them so she can fly away. (Rev: BL 5/1/93; SLJ 7/93)

10653 Climo, Shirley. *The Persian Cinderella* (PS–4). Illus. by Robert Florczak. 1999, HarperCollins LB $15.89 (0-06-026765-8). 32pp. In this Persian variation on the Cinderella story, the heroine, Settareh, has a pari — a kind of fairy — who lives in a blue jar and turns Settareh into a turtledove. (Rev: BL 7/99; HBG 10/99; SLJ 6/99) [398.2]

10654 Climo, Shirley, comp. and reteller. *A Pride of Princesses: Princess Tales from Around the World* (3–5). Illus. by Angelo Tillery. 1999, HarperCollins paper $4.25 (0-06-442102-3). 96pp. Issued first as a picture book, these seven stories involving characters such as Psyche and a frog princess are now in a chapter-book format. Also use *A Serenade of Mermaids* (1999), which contains seven more stories from around the world. (Rev: SLJ 6/99)

10655 Coatsworth, Elizabeth. *The Cat Who Went to Heaven* (4–6). Illus. by Lynd Ward. 1990, Simon & Schuster LB $17.00 (0-02-719710-7); Macmillan paper $4.99 (0-689-71433-5). 72pp. A charming legend of a Japanese artist, his cat, and a Buddhist miracle. Newbery Medal winner, 1931.

10656 Cole, Brock. *The Giant's Toe* (K–2). Illus. by author. 1986, Farrar paper $5.95 (0-374-42557-4). 32pp. A "revisionist" version of Jack and the Beanstalk, with a grandfatherly giant and a teeny boy. (Rev: BCCB 7–8/86; BL 8/86; SLJ 10/86)

10657 Craft, K. Y. *Cinderella* (2–4). Illus. 2000, North-South LB $15.88 (1-58717-005-1). 32pp. An exquisite version of Cinderella based on the Lang and Rackham text and accompanied by wonderful oil-over-watercolor paintings. (Rev: BCCB 11/00; BL 11/1/00*; HBG 3/01; SLJ 11/00)

10658 Craft, Mahlon F. *Sleeping Beauty* (2–4). Illus. by Kinuko Craft. 2002, North-South LB $16.50 (1-58717-121-X). 32pp. A beautifully illustrated retelling of the traditional fairy tale. (Rev: BCCB 1/03; BL 9/15/02; HBG 3/03; SLJ 10/02) [398.2]

10659 Datlow, Ellen, and Terri Windling, eds. *Swan Sister: Fairy Tales Retold* (5–10). 2003, Simon & Schuster $16.95 (0-689-84613-4). 176pp. Retellings by well-known authors of traditional stories are inventive and entertaining. (Rev: BCCB 11/03; BL 9/15/03; HB 9–10/01; HBG 4/04; SLJ 12/03)

10660 Datlow, Ellen, and Terri Windling, eds. *A Wolf at the Door: And Other Retold Fairy Tales* (5–8). 2000, Simon & Schuster $16.00 (0-689-82138-7). 166pp. These are interesting variations on standard fairy tales that have been written in imaginative ways by well-known authors. (Rev: BL 9/1/00; HBG 3/01; SLJ 8/00)

10661 de Hann, Linda, and Stern Nijland. *King and King* (PS–2). Illus. 2002, Tricycle $14.95 (1-58246-061-2). 32pp. When his mother the queen wants him to marry, a prince falls in love with another prince, and they marry and live happily ever after in this alternative fairy tale. (Rev: BL 7/02; HB 7–8/02; HBG 10/02; SLJ 3/02)

10662 de la Paz, Myrna J. *Abadeha: The Philippine Cinderella* (K–3). Illus. by Youshan Tang. 2001, Shens $16.95 (1-885008-17-1). 32pp. A Philippine version of the Cinderella story in which Abadeha is helped by kindly spirits and wins the prince by removing a ring that is stuck on his finger. (Rev: BL 7/01; HBG 3/02; SLJ 12/01) [398.2]

10663 Delessert, Etienne. *The Seven Dwarfs* (3–4). Illus. 2001, Creative Editions LB $17.95 (1-56846-139-9). 32pp. One of Snow White's dwarfs, Stephane, recounts the princess's story in this imaginative take on the fairy tale. (Rev: BL 1/1–15/02; HB 1–2/02; HBG 3/02) [398.2]

10664 Demi. *The Emperor's New Clothes* (PS–3). Illus. 2000, Simon & Schuster $19.95 (0-689-83068-8). 42pp. Employing a Chinese motif in the illustrations, this is a new, interesting, multicultural retelling of the Andersen tale. (Rev: BL 6/1–15/00; HB 5–6/00; HBG 10/00; SLJ 6/00)

10665 dePaola, Tomie. *Adelita: A Mexican Cinderella Story* (PS–2). Illus. 2002, Penguin Putnam $16.99 (0-399-23866-2). 32pp. This Cinderella story features a young Mexican girl named Adelita who wins the heart of her prince through her own resources. (Rev: BL 8/02; HBG 3/03; SLJ 9/02) [398.2]

10666 Doherty, Berlie. *Fairy Tales* (3–6). Illus. 2000, Candlewick $19.99 (0-7636-0997-8). 224pp. This retelling of 12 favorite tales, like those about Sleeping Beauty and Aladdin, is modern in language but true to the original stories. (Rev: BL 11/15/00; HBG 3/01; SLJ 10/00)

10667 Donnelly, Jennifer. *Humble Pie* (PS–2). Illus. by Stephen Gammell. 2002, Simon & Schuster $16.95 (0-689-84435-2). 32pp. Stuffed into a "humble pie" by his grandmother, selfish Theo narrowly escapes being eaten and mends his ways in this colorful picture book set in the past with lively illustrations that enhance the story. (Rev: BCCB 11/02; BL 7/02; HBG 3/03; SLJ 9/02)

10668 Edens, Cooper, ed. *Princess Stories: A Classic Illustrated Edition* (2–4). Series: Classics Illustrated Editions. 2004, Chronicle $19.95 (0-8118-4032-8). 136pp. Familiar stories — by Hans Christian Andersen, the Grimm brothers, and Charles Perrault, among others — of princesses pursuing romantic aspirations are paired with vintage images. (Rev: BL 10/15/04; SLJ 1/05) [398.22]

10669 Ernst, Lisa Campbell. *Goldilocks Returns* (K–2). Illus. 2000, Simon & Schuster $16.00 (0-689-82537-4). 40pp. Middle-aged Goldilocks tries to make up for the harm she did to the bears 50 years before, giving them a new lock for the door and some healthy food and redecorating for them. (Rev: BCCB 5/00; BL 4/1/00; HBG 10/00; SLJ 5/00)

10670 Ernst, Lisa Campbell. *The Three Spinning Fairies: A Tale from the Brothers Grimm* (PS–3). Illus. by author. 2002, Dutton $16.99 (0-525-46826-9). 40pp. The Royal Baker's lazy daughter Zelda gets what is coming to her in this stylishly illustrated version of a Grimm fairy tale. (Rev: BL 1/1–15/02; HBG 10/02; SLJ 2/02) [398.2]

10671 Ferris, Jean. *Once Upon a Marigold* (5–8). 2002, Harcourt $17.00 (0-15-216791-9). 272pp. Christian falls in love with Princess Marigold and wins her heart through his bravery in this fairy tale

full of fun. (Rev: BCCB 2/03; BL 9/15/02; HB 9–10/02; HBG 3/03; SLJ 11/02)

10672 French, Vivian. *The Kingfisher Book of Fairy Tales* (4–6). Illus. 2000, Kingfisher $19.95 (0-7534-5223-5). 96pp. Seven standard fairy tales like "Jack and the Beanstalk," "Cinderella," and "Beauty and the Beast" are retold and accompanied by elegant illustrations. (Rev: BL 11/15/00; HBG 10/01; SLJ 1/01)

10673 French, Vivian, retel. *The Kingfisher Book of Nursery Tales* (PS–2). Illus. by Stephen Lambert. 2003, Kingfisher $15.00 (0-7534-5482-3). 91pp. Author Vivan French offers up whimsical retellings of eight popular fairy tales, including "Little Red Riding Hood" and "The Three Little Pigs." (Rev: HBG 4/04; SLJ 1/04) [823.9]

10674 Geras, Adele. *Sleeping Beauty* (2–4). Illus. by Christian Birmingham. 2004, Scholastic $18.95 (0-439-58180-X). 64pp. Black-and-white illustrations and a number of beautiful pastels enhance this retelling. (Rev: BL 5/1/04; SLJ 8/04) [398.2]

10675 Goode, Diane. *Cinderella: The Dog and Her Little Glass Slipper* (K–3). Illus. 2000, Scholastic $15.95 (0-439-07166-6). 40pp. A tongue-in-cheek version of Cinderella in which all the characters are dogs. (Rev: BL 11/1/00; HBG 3/01; SLJ 9/00)

10676 Goode, Diane. *The Dinosaur's New Clothes* (PS–1). Illus. 1999, Scholastic $15.95 (0-590-38360-4). 40pp. This variation on the Andersen tale is set in the Palace of Versailles and features dinosaurs as characters. (Rev: BCCB 12/99; BL 11/15/99; HBG 3/00; SLJ 9/99)

10677 Goodhart, Pippa. *Arthur's Tractor: A Fairy Tale with Mechanical Parts* (PS–2). Illus. by Colin Paine. 2003, Bloomsbury $15.95 (1-58234-847-2). 32pp. While Arthur is busy working on his tractor, he stumbles into a funny fairy tale. (Rev: BL 2/15/03; HBG 10/03; SLJ 3/03)

10678 Grahame, Kenneth. *The Reluctant Dragon* (2–4). Illus. by E. H. Shepard. 1938, Holiday House $14.95 (0-8234-0093-X); paper $6.95 (0-8234-0755-1). 58pp. Tongue-in-cheek story of a boy who makes friends with a peace-loving dragon. Another fine edition is: Illus. by Michael Hague (1983, Holt).

10679 Gray, Margaret. *The Ugly Princess and the Wise Fool* (3–6). Illus. by Randy Cecil. 2002, Holt $15.95 (0-8050-6847-3). 176pp. There's a happy ending to this tale despite the fact that the princess is ugly and wisdom has been banned from the land. (Rev: BCCB 12/02; BL 11/15/02; HBG 3/03; SLJ 10/02)

10680 Grimm Brothers. *The Frog Prince* (1–2). Adapted by Sindy McKay. Illus. by George Ulrich. Series: We Both Read. 1998, Treasure Bay $7.99 (1-891327-02-X). This fairy tale is retold twice — with an adult's and a child's vocabulary. (Rev: SLJ 12/98)

10681 Gustafson, Scott, sel. *Classic Fairy Tales* (PS–6). Illus. by Scott Gustafson. 2003, Greenwich Workshop $19.95 (0-86713-089-X). 144pp. Scott Gustafson's breathtaking artwork highlights these retellings of 10 classic fairy tales, including "Snow

White," "Puss in Boots," and "Hansel and Gretel." (Rev: BL 1/1–15/04; SLJ 12/03) [398.2]

10682 Haylesworth, Jim, retel. *Goldilocks and the Three Bears* (PS–2). Illus. by Barbara McClintock. 2003, Scholastic $15.95 (0-439-39545-3). A handsome retelling with traditional illustrations and language that will appeal nonetheless to today's readers. (Rev: HB 11–12/03; HBG 4/04; SLJ 10/03) [398.2]

10683 Hoberman, Mary Ann. *You Read to Me, I'll Read to You: Very Short Fairy Tales to Read Together* (2–4). Illus. by Michael Emberly. 2004, Little, Brown $16.95 (0-316-14611-0). 32pp. Designed for two voices, this pcture book features retellings of eight popular fairy tales. (Rev: BL 7/04; HB 5–6/04; SLJ 5/04) [428.6]

10684 Hoffman, Mary. *The Barefoot Book of Brother and Sister Tales* (2–5). Illus. 2000, Barefoot $19.99 (1-84148-029-0). 63pp. An anthology of uplifting original stories about children who suffer hardships resulting from such problems as cruel queens, witches, and stepmothers. (Rev: BL 11/15/00; HBG 3/01; SLJ 1/01)

10685 Hopkins, Jackie Mims. *The Horned Toad Prince* (PS–2). Illus. by Michael Austin. 2000, Peachtree $15.95 (1-56145-195-9). 32pp. This breezy update of the fairy tale is set in the Southwest and features a frog who demands that the heroine feed him chili. (Rev: BCCB 7–8/00; BL 5/15/00; HBG 10/00; SLJ 4/00)

10686 Impey, Rose. *Read Me a Fairy Tale: A Child's Book of Classic Fairy Tales* (3–6). Illus. by Ian Beck. 1993, Scholastic $16.95 (0-590-49431-7). 128pp. A collection of 14 favorite fairy tales told in an informal style. (Rev: BL 1/15/94; SLJ 2/94)

10687 Jackson, Ellen. *Cinder Edna* (PS–3). Illus. by Kevin O'Malley. 1994, Lothrop $16.00 (0-688-12322-8). 32pp. Whereas Cinderella is a passive wimp, Cinder Edna is a spirited girl who mows lawns to make money so she can attend the ball. In this book, the two stories are told side by side. (Rev: BL 3/15/94; SLJ 4/94)

10688 Kroll, Steven. *Queen of the May* (PS–3). Illus. by Patience Brewster. 1993, Holiday House LB $15.95 (0-8234-1004-8). 32pp. Sylvie becomes Queen of the May in spite of her meddling stepmother and stepsister. (Rev: BL 4/1/93; SLJ 7/93)

10689 Lach, William, ed. *Fairyland: In Art and Poetry* (3–7). Illus. by Richard Doyle. 2002, Holt $17.95 (0-8050-7006-0). 40pp. Illustrations from Richard Doyle's classic *In Fairyland* (1870) are paired with selections from writers including Shakespeare, de la Mare, Langston Hughes, and Laura Ingalls Wilder in a handsome volume suited to browsing. (Rev: HBG 10/02; SLJ 7/02) [398.2]

10690 Lamm, C. Drew. *The Prog Frince: A Mixed-Up Tale* (2–4). Illus. 1999, Orchard LB $17.99 (0-531-33135-0). 32pp. This is a humorous version of the fairy tale in which a prince is turned into a frog for loving a stable girl. (Rev: BCCB 2/99; BL 2/1/99; HB 3–4/99; HBG 10/99; SLJ 3/99)

10691 Lang, Andrew, ed. *Blue Fairy Book* (4–6). 1965, Dover paper $8.95 (0-486-21437-0). 390pp.

A fine edition of this classic collection. There are 11 other "color" Fairy Books. Some are: *Green Fairy Book* (1965); *Yellow Fairy Book* (1966); *Grey Fairy Book; Orange Fairy Book; Red Fairy Book* (all 1968).

10692 Langton, Jane. *The Queen's Necklace: A Swedish Folktale* (3–5). Illus. by Ilse Plume. 1994, Hyperion LB $16.49 (0-7868-2007-1). 40pp. When a queen gives away pearls to help the poor, her cruel king demands her life. (Rev: BL 10/1/94; SLJ 10/94)

10693 Levine, Gail C. *Cinderellis and the Glass Hill* (4–6). Illus. 2000, HarperCollins LB $8.89 (0-06-028337-8). 96pp. This humorous variation on the Cinderella story has as its central character a boy named Ellis who is ignored by his older brothers but eventually wins the princess Marigold. (Rev: BL 1/1–15/00; HBG 10/00)

10694 Levine, Gail C. *Ella Enchanted* (5–8). 1997, HarperCollins LB $16.89 (0-06-027511-1). 240pp. A spirited, cleverly plotted retelling of the Cinderella story in which Ella is finally paired with the Prince Charmant. (Rev: BCCB 5/97; BL 4/15/97*; BR 1–2/98; HB 5–6/97; SLJ 4/97*)

10695 Levine, Gail C. *The Fairy's Mistake* (3–6). Illus. 1999, HarperCollins LB $8.89 (0-06-028061-1). 80pp. This is a reworking of a traditional fairy tale from France in which a fairy is disappointed in her evaluation of two sisters. (Rev: BCCB 5/99; BL 4/15/99; HB 5–6/99; HBG 10/99; SLJ 5/99)

10696 Levine, Gail C. *The Fairy's Return* (3–5). Series: Princess Tales. 2002, HarperCollins LB $14.89 (0-06-623801-3). 112pp. Using bits and pieces of fairy tales and folklore, this book tells the story of a princess who falls in love with a baker's son. Another entry in the series is *For Biddle's Sake* (2002). (Rev: BL 8/02; HBG 3/03; SLJ 9/02)

10697 Levine, Gail C. *Princess Sonora and the Long Sleep* (4–6). Illus. Series: Princess Tales. 1999, HarperCollins LB $8.89 (0-06-028065-4). 96pp. This retelling of the *Sleeping Beauty* story involves Princess Sonora, who is so brilliant she reads books while having her diaper changed. (Rev: BCCB 10/99; BL 11/15/99; HBG 3/00; SLJ 10/99)

10698 Levine, Gail C. *The Princess Test* (3–6). Illus. 1999, HarperCollins LB $8.89 (0-06-028063-0). 80pp. In this variation on *The Princess and the Pea,* a blacksmith's daughter turns out to be more sensitive than a princess. (Rev: BL 4/15/99)

10699 Lewis, Naomi, reteller. *Elf Hill: Tales from Hans Christian Andersen* (K–3). Illus. by Emma C. Clark. 1999, Star Bright $17.95 (1-887734-70-8). 68pp. A straightforward retelling of nine tales from the familiar "The Princess and the Pea" to the unfamiliar "The Money-Box Pig." (Rev: SLJ 1/00)

10700 Ljungkvist, Laura. *Snow White and the Seven Dwarfs* (PS–2). Illus. 2003, Abrams $14.95 (0-8109-4241-0). 38pp. Snow White gets a contemporary look in this beautifully illustrated simple retelling. (Rev: BL 4/15/03; HBG 10/03; SLJ 7/03) [398.2]

10701 Long, Laurel, and Jacqueline K. Ogburn, retels. *The Lady and the Lion: A Brothers Grimm*

Tale (2–4). Illus. by Laurel Long. 2003, Dial $16.99 (0-8037-2651-1). Lush oil paintings decorate this romantic adaptation of a Grimm story about a lion who turns into a prince at night. (Rev: BL 1/1/04; HBG 4/04; SLJ 2/04) [398.2]

10702 Lorenz, Albert. *Jack and the Beanstalk: How a Small Fellow Solved a Big Problem* (PS–3). Illus. 2002, Abrams $16.95 (0-8109-1160-4). 40pp. Realistic, highly detailed illustrations emphasize the importance of size and Jack's inventiveness. (Rev: BL 10/1/02; HBG 3/03; SLJ 10/02) [398.2]

10703 Lowell, Susan. *Cindy Ellen: A Wild Western Cinderella* (K–3). Illus. by Jane Manning. 2000, HarperCollins LB $16.99 (0-06-027447-6). 40pp. This version of the Cinderella story features a mean stepmother, a godmother with a six-gun, and a cowboy hero named Joe Prince. (Rev: BCCB 9/00; BL 5/15/00; HBG 10/00)

10704 MacDonald, George. *The Golden Key* (2–6). Illus. by Maurice Sendak. 1993, Farrar paper $6.95 (0-374-42590-6). 96pp. In this classic fairy tale, two young people search for a keyhole where their golden key will fit.

10705 MacDonald, George. *The Light Princess* (1–6). Adapted by Robin McKinley. Illus. by Katie T. Treherne. 1988, Harcourt $13.95 (0-15-245300-8). 44pp. A prince breaks the spell of a princess who has been deprived of gravity. (Rev: BL 7/88)

10706 MacDonald, George. *The Princess and the Goblin* (4–7). Illus. by Jessie Willcox Smith. 1986, Morrow $24.99 (0-688-06604-6). 208pp. A full-color edition of the 1920 classic about the princess who is protected by the goblins beneath the castle. (Rev: BL 10/15/86)

10707 MacDonald, Margaret Read. *The Old Woman Who Lived in a Vinegar Bottle: A British Fairy Tale* (PS–2). Illus. by Nancy D. Fowlkes. 1995, August House $15.95 (0-87483-415-5). 32pp. In this English folktale, a fairy discovers that there is no pleasing some people when she supplies better housing for an old woman who had been living in a vinegar bottle. (Rev: BL 10/1/95; SLJ 1/96) [398.2]

10708 Mahy, Margaret. *The Chewing-Gum Rescue* (3–4). Illus. by Jan Ormerod. 1992, Overlook $19.95 (0-87951-424-8). 141pp. A collection of 11 short stories, most of which are fairy tales or contain elements of fantasy. (Rev: SLJ 2/92)

10709 Marcantonio, Patricia Santos. *Red Ridin' in the Hood, and Other Cuentos* (3–5). Illus. by Renato Alarcão. 2005, Farrar $16.00 (0-374-36241-6). 208pp. Traditional fairy tales, turned inside-out and given Latino flair and meaningful morals. (Rev: BL 3/15/05; SLJ 4/05) [398.2]

10710 Martin, Rafe. *The Storytelling Princess* (PS–3). Illus. by Kimberly B. Root. 2001, Penguin Putnam $15.99 (0-399-22924-8). 32pp. A prince and princess who have both refused arranged marriages find their respective criteria are met in each other. (Rev: BCCB 7–8/01; BL 7/01; HBG 3/02; SLJ 9/01)

10711 Matthews, Caitlin. *The Barefoot Book of Princesses* (4–6). Illus. 1998, Barefoot $17.95 (1-901223-74-4). 64pp. In a collection of fairy tales

from around the world, the reader meets a number of princesses (some familiar, such as Sleeping Beauty, others not) and their challenging situations. (Rev: BL 11/15/98; SLJ 11/98) [398.2]

10712 Mayer, Marianna. *The Adventures of Tom Thumb* (K–4). Illus. by Kinuko Craft. 2001, North-South LB $15.88 (1-58717-065-5). 32pp. Little Tom cleverly survives being eaten by a cow, a fish, and a giant, and is knighted by King Arthur in this illustrated retelling. (Rev: BL 10/15/01; HB 9–10/01; HBG 3/02; SLJ 12/01) [398.2]

10713 Melmed, Laura K. *The Rainbabies* (PS–2). Illus. by Jim LaMarche. 1992, Lothrop LB $15.93 (0-688-10756-7). 32pp. An elderly couple care for 12 teeny babies they find in the grass. (Rev: BL 11/1/92; HB 3–4/93; SLJ 12/92)

10714 Minters, Frances. *Cinder-Elly* (K–3). Illus. by G. Brian Karas. 1994, Viking $15.99 (0-670-84417-9). 32pp. A present-day version of Cinderella, with the heroine living in New York City and her godmother changing a garbage can into a bicycle so that Elly can go to an important basketball game. (Rev: BCCB 4/94; BL 1/15/94; SLJ 6/94) [398.2]

10715 Minters, Frances. *Princess Fishtail* (PS–2). Illus. by G. Brian Karas. 2002, Viking $15.99 (0-670-03529-7). 32pp. This modern version of Hans Christian Andersen's mermaid tale has the underwater princess rescuing a surfer and shopping in Los Angeles. (Rev: BCCB 12/02; BL 10/15/02; HBG 3/03; SLJ 9/02)

10716 Mitchell, Marianne. *Joe Cinders* (PS–3). Illus. by Bryan Langdo. 2002, Holt $16.95 (0-8050-6529-6). 32pp. A hilarious, twisted retelling of the classic Cinderella, in which a put-upon young cowpoke and his cantankerous stepbrothers are invited to Miss Rosalinda's fiesta. (Rev: BL 10/15/02; HBG 3/03; SLJ 12/02) [398.2]

10717 Mitchell, Stephen. *The Nightingale* (2–4). Illus. by Bagram Ibatoulline. 2002, Candlewick $17.99 (0-7636-1521-8). 48pp. Artwork with an Asian influence and a lively contemporary text are used in this version of Andersen's tale. (Rev: BCCB 11/02; BL 11/1/02; HBG 3/03; SLJ 11/02) [398.2]

10718 Morpurgo, Michael. *Gentle Giant* (K–3). Illus. by Michael Foreman. 2004, Collins $16.95 (0-00-711064-2). 32pp. A lonely giant finds acceptance when he saves the village of Ballyloch from ecological disaster. (Rev: BL 4/15/04; SLJ 5/04)

10719 Murphy, Shirley Rousseau. *Wind Child* (K–4). Illus. by the Dillons. 1999, HarperCollins LB $15.89 (0-06-024904-8). 40pp. A romantic fairy tale about a lonely girl whose extraordinary weaving skills attract a prince who falls in love with her. (Rev: BL 6/1–15/99; HBG 10/99; SLJ 4/99)

10720 Nesbit, Edith. *Melisande* (K–3). Illus. by P. J. Lynch. 1989, Harcourt $13.95 (0-15-253164-5). 48pp. The fairies take their revenge when a royal family excludes them from the daughter's christening party. (Rev: BL 10/1/89*; HB 11–12/89; SLJ 1/90)

10721 Nikly, Michelle. *The Perfume of Memory* (3–7). Illus. by Jean Claverie. 1999, Scholastic $16.95 (0-439-08206-4). In this fairy tale, a young child uses various perfumes to restore the memory of the queen. (Rev: HBG 3/00; SLJ 11/99)

10722 Ogburn, Jacqueline K. *The Magic Nesting Doll* (PS–3). Illus. by Laurel Long. 2000, Dial $16.99 (0-8037-2414-4). 32pp. An original fairy tale set in Russia about a girl who inherits a set of nesting dolls with magical powers. (Rev: BL 9/15/00; HBG 3/01; SLJ 12/00)

10723 O'Neal, Shaquille. *Shaq and the Beanstalk: And Other Very Tall Tales* (K–4). Illus. by Shane W. Evans. 1999, Scholastic $15.95 (0-590-91823-0). 80pp. A collection of fractured fairy tales that feature Shaq O'Neal and such characters as the Big Bad Wolf, the three bears, and a hen that lays golden basketballs. (Rev: HBG 10/00; SLJ 2/00)

10724 Orgel, Doris. *The Bremen Town Musicians and Other Animal Tales from Grimm* (PS–2). Illus. by Bert Kitchen. 2004, Roaring Brook $18.95 (1-59643-040-9). 48pp. Six animal-themed fairy tales from the brothers Grimm are accompanied by arresting illustrations. (Rev: BL 1/1–15/05) [398.2]

10725 Palatini, Margie. *The Three Silly Billies* (PS–2). Illus. by Barry Moser. 2005, Simon & Schuster $15.95 (0-689-85862-0). 32pp. A troll stops characters from different fairy tales from crossing his bridge in this rollicking takeoff on the Billy Goats Gruff story. (Rev: BL 3/1/05)

10726 Paterson, Katherine. *The Wide-Awake Princess* (2–5). Illus. 2000, Clarion $15.00 (0-395-53777-0). 48pp. The story of a princess who leaves her castle to find out about the common people in her kingdom and how they live. (Rev: BL 3/15/00; HBG 10/00; SLJ 7/00)

10727 Pinkney, Jerry. *The Little Match Girl* (3–5). Illus. 1999, Penguin Putnam $16.99 (0-8037-2314-8). 32pp. A beautifully illustrated version of the tragic tale by Han Christian Andersen about the little girl who is sent out to sell artificial flowers and matches on New Year's Eve. (Rev: BL 10/15/99*; HBG 3/00; SLJ 10/99)

10728 Pinkney, Jerry. *The Nightingale* (K–4). Illus. 2002, Penguin Putnam $16.99 (0-8037-2426-0). 40pp. The familiar fairy tale of a king and a nightingale with a magical voice is transplanted to Morocco and accompanied by beautiful illustrations. (Rev: BCCB 11/02; BL 9/1/02)

10729 Pinkney, Jerry. *The Ugly Duckling* (PS–3). 1999, Morrow LB $15.93 (0-688-15933-8). 40pp. Gorgeous double-page spreads are used in this handsome retelling of Hans Christian Andersen's classic story. (Rev: BCCB 3/99; BL 3/1/99*; HB 5–6/99; HBG 10/99; SLJ 5/99)

10730 Poole, Amy Lowry. *The Pea Blossom* (K–2). Illus. 2005, Holiday House $16.95 (0-8234-1864-2). 32pp. A watercolor picture book, set in China, retelling the Hans Christian Andersen tale of a pea that helps a sick little girl. (Rev: BL 3/1/05; SLJ 3/05)

10731 Prokofiev, Sergei. *Peter and the Wolf* (1–4). Illus. by Barbara Cooney. 1986, Viking $19.99 (0-670-80849-0). 10pp. A three-dimensional celebration of the famous tale. (Rev: BL 6/1/86; SLJ 5/86)

10732 Pyle, Howard. *The Swan Maiden* (K–3). Illus. by Robert Sauber. 1994, Holiday House LB $15.95 (0-8234-1088-9). 28pp. In this fairy tale, one of the king's sons discovers that a swan maiden is stealing pears from his father's pear tree. (Rev: BL 10/15/94; SLJ 1/95)

10733 Pyle, Howard. *The Wonder Clock: Or Four and Twenty Marvelous Tales* (4–6). Illus. by author. 1915, Dover paper $8.95 (0-486-21446-X). 319pp. Tales for each hour in the day, told by figures on a clock.

10734 Rae, Jennifer. *Dog Tales* (1–3). Illus. by Rose Cowles. 1999, Tricycle $14.95 (1-58246-011-6). 28pp. Six fractured fairy tales are told using dogs as characters. One example is "The Doberman's New Clothes." (Rev: HBG 10/00; SLJ 12/99)

10735 Roberts, Lynn, retel. *Rapunzel: A Groovy Fairy Tale* (PS–2). Illus. by David Roberts. 2003, Abrams $16.95 (0-8109-4242-9). In this retelling set in the 1970s, Rapunzel is locked away in an apartment building by her evil aunt, who chops off Rapunzel's long hair when she discovers the girl is sneaking time with a rock singer. (Rev: HBG 4/04; SLJ 11/03) [398.2]

10736 Russell, P. Craig. *The Fairy Tales of Oscar Wilde: The Devoted Friend, The Nightengale, and the Rose* (5–8). Illus. by author. 2004, N B M Publishing $15.95 (1-56163-391-7). 32pp. Two of Oscar Wilde's fairy tales — "The Devoted Friend" and "The Nightingale and the Rose" — are presented in a rich, picture-book-size graphic novel format. (Rev: BL 8/04; SLJ 11/04) [741.5]

10737 Sanderson, Ruth. *Cinderella* (PS–3). Illus. 2002, Little, Brown $15.95 (0-316-77965-2). 32pp. An exquisitely produced version of the Cinderella story with detailed illustrations and an elegant text. (Rev: BL 4/15/02*; HBG 10/02; SLJ 6/02)

10738 San Jose, Christine. *The Emperor's New Clothes* (PS–3). Illus. by Anastassija Archipowa. 1998, Boyds Mills $15.95 (1-56397-699-4). 32pp. A new version of Andersen's familiar story in a large-format picture book with graceful watercolor pictures. (Rev: BL 4/1/98; HBG 10/98; SLJ 4/98)

10739 San Jose, Christine. *The Little Match Girl* (PS–3). Illus. by Kestutis Kasparavicius. 2002, Boyds Mills $15.95 (1-59078-000-0). 32pp. Lovely illustrations accompany this retelling of the sad story in which the little girl dies. (Rev: BL 10/1/02; HBG 3/03; SLJ 10/02) [398.2]

10740 San Jose, Christine. *Sleeping Beauty* (K–3). Illus. by Dominic Catalano. 1997, Boyds Mills $14.95 (1-56397-636-6). 32pp. Dormouse characters are used in this successful retelling of the traditional fairy tale. (Rev: BL 10/15/97; HBG 3/98; SLJ 9/97) [398]

10741 San Souci, Robert D. *Cendrillon: A Caribbean Cinderella* (PS–3). Illus. by Brian Pinkney. 1998, Simon & Schuster $16.00 (0-689-80668-X). 40pp. An enchanting new version of the Cinderella story that is based on a French Creole tale and uses Martinique as its setting. (Rev: BCCB 1/99; BL 10/15/98; HB 11–12/98; HBG 3/99; SLJ 9/98) [398.2]

10742 San Souci, Robert D. *Cinderella Skeleton* (3–5). Illus. by David Catrow. 2000, Harcourt $16.00 (0-15-202003-9). 32pp. A macabre variation on the Cinderella story in which the heroine is a stick-figure skeleton who lives in Boneyard Acres and falls in love with Prince Charnel. (Rev: BCCB 10/00; BL 9/1/00; HB 9–10/00; HBG 3/01; SLJ 9/00)

10743 San Souci, Robert D. *Little Gold Star: A Spanish American Cinderella Tale* (2–4). Illus. 2000, HarperCollins LB $15.89 (0-688-14781-X). 32pp. Using a Southwestern setting, this Cinderella retelling involves Teresa, who tends the Holy Infant for Mary and is rewarded with the help she needs to marry her Prince Charming, Don Miguel. (Rev: BCCB 12/00; BL 10/1/00; HBG 3/01; SLJ 10/00)

10744 San Souci, Robert D., reteller. *The White Cat: An Old French Fairy Tale* (3–4). Illus. by Gennady Spirin. 1990, Orchard LB $17.99 (0-531-08409-4). 32pp. The retelling of the story of three princes who vie for their father's kingdom. (Rev: BCCB 11/90; BL 9/1/90; HB 11–12/90; SLJ 10/90)

10745 Scieszka, Jon. *The Frog Prince Continued* (1–4). Illus. by Steve Johnson. 1991, Viking $14.95 (0-670-83421-1). 32pp. After the princess and the former frog are married, he still keeps hopping about and wonders if he should change back into a frog. (Rev: BCCB 5/91; BL 6/1/91; HB 7–8/91; SLJ 5/91)

10746 Scott-Mitchell, Clare. *Cinderella* (PS–2). Illus. by Gordon Fitchett. 2001, Penguin Putnam $16.99 (0-8037-2577-8). 32pp. In this fresh version of Cinderella all the characters are animals, including the heroine, who is a black-and white cat. (Rev: BL 1/1–15/01; SLJ 2/01)

10747 Setterington, Ken. *Hans Christian Andersen's The Snow Queen* (3–5). Illus. by Nelly Hofer and Ernst Hofer. 2000, Tundra $16.95 (0-88776-497-5). 48pp. A secular retelling of the Andersen story illustrated with old-fashioned black-and-white silhouettes. (Rev: BL 12/15/00; HBG 10/01; SLJ 3/01)

10748 Sierra, Judy. *The Gift of the Crocodile* (PS–3). Illus. by Reynold Ruffins. 2000, Simon & Schuster $17.00 (0-689-82188-3). 40pp. This is an exotic version of Cinderella, set in the Spice Islands, with a river crocodile serving as Grandmother Crocodile, the fairy godmother. (Rev: BCCB 12/00; BL 1/1–15/01; HB 1–2/01; HBG 3/01; SLJ 11/00)

10749 Stanley, Diane. *Goldie and the Three Bears* (PS–1). Illus. by author. 2003, HarperCollins LB $16.89 (0-06-000009-0). Goldie has been looking high and low for a friend "to love with all her heart;" her quest ends when she goes snooping around in the home of the Three Bears. (Rev: HB 9–10/03; HBG 4/04; SLJ 11/03) [398.2]

10750 Steig, Jeanne. *A Handful of Beans* (PS–3). Illus. by William Steig. 1998, HarperCollins $17.95 (0-06-205162-8). 144pp. Six favorite fairy tales, including *Rumpelstiltskin, Hansel and Gretel,* and *Jack and the Beanstalk,* are informally retold with cartoon-style drawings. (Rev: BL 11/15/98*; HB 1–2/99; HBG 3/99; SLJ 12/98)

10751 Stewig, John Warren. *Whuppity Stoorie* (2–4). Illus. by Preston McDaniels. 2004, Holiday House $16.95 (0-8234-1749-2). 32pp. This picture-book story of a young widow who foils a fairy's attempts to steal her son is set in Scotland, with suitable dialect and illustrations. (Rev: BL 2/15/04; SLJ 3/04) [398.2]

10752 Thomas, Joyce Carol. *The Gospel Cinderella* (PS–2). Illus. by David Diaz. 2004, HarperCollins $15.99 (0-06-025387-8). 40pp. In this retelling, the daughter of Queen Mother Rhythm falls into the clutches of Cruel Crooked Foster Mother and can only be saved by her talent as a gospel singer. (Rev: BL 2/15/04; SLJ 5/04) [398.2]

10753 Thompson, Lauren. *One Riddle, One Answer* (K–3). Illus. by Linda S. Wingerter. 2001, Scholastic $15.95 (0-590-31333-5). 32pp. In this original fairy tale, a sultan's daughter gets permission from her father to a pose a riddle to each of her prospective husbands. (Rev: BL 2/1/01)

10754 Thurber, James. *Many Moons* (2–4). Illus. by Marc Simont. 1990, Harcourt $14.95 (0-15-251872-X). 48pp. A sick princess asks her father for the moon to help her get better. The original edition, illustrated by Louis Slobodkin, was the 1944 Caldecott Medal winner. (Rev: BL 9/15/90; HB 1–2/90*; SLJ 1/91)

10755 Townley, Roderick. *The Great Good Thing* (4–6). 2001, Simon & Schuster $17.00 (0-689-84324-0). 216pp. In this fairy tale, all the characters, including heroine Princess Sophie, live in a book and only come to life when a Reader opens it. (Rev: BL 3/15/01; HBG 10/01)

10756 Treherne, Katie T., reteller. *The Little Mermaid* (1–5). Illus. by Katie T. Treherne. 1989, Harcourt $15.95 (0-15-246320-8). 48pp. A retelling of Andersen's familiar story of the mermaid who falls in love with a prince. (Rev: BL 1/1/90; SLJ 11/89)

10757 Vande Velde, Vivian. *The Rumpelstiltskin Problem* (4–6). 2000, Houghton Mifflin $15.00 (0-618-05523-1). 116pp. After a criticism of the logic behind this famous fairy tale, the author presents six new versions of the tale that, supposedly, make more sense. (Rev: BCCB 2/01; HBG 3/01; SLJ 11/00)

10758 Waters, Fiona. *The Emperor and the Nightingale* (PS–3). Illus. by Paul Birkbeck. 2000, Bloomsbury $19.95 (0-7475-3559-0). 32pp. A fine retelling of this classic fairy tale with lavish illustrations and sensitive language. (Rev: BL 11/15/00; SLJ 1/01)

10759 Wegman, William. *Cinderella* (PS–2). Illus. 1993, Hyperion $16.95 (1-56282-348-5). 38pp. The characters in this reworking of the Cinderella story are all dogs, but the story remains the same. (Rev: BCCB 7–8/93; BL 5/15/93; SLJ 4/93)

10760 Wenzel, David, and Doug Wheeler. *Fairy Tales of the Brothers Grimm* (4–6). Illus. 1995, NBM $15.95 (1-56163-130-2). 48pp. Using a comic book format, some of the best-known tales of the Grimm Brothers are retold, with an emphasis on story-telling pictures. (Rev: BL 4/15/96) [398.2]

10761 Whipple, Laura. *If the Shoe Fits* (5–8). Illus. by Laura Beingessner. 2002, Simon & Schuster

$17.95 (0-689-84070-5). 80pp. A handsome retelling of the Cinderella story using blank verse. (Rev: BCCB 3/02; BL 5/1/02; HBG 10/02; SLJ 8/02) [398.2]

10762 Wilcox, Leah. *Falling for Rapunzel* (PS–2). Illus. by Lydia Monks. 2003, Penguin Putnam $14.99 (0-399-23794-1). In this hilarious variation, Rapunzel misinterprets the prince's pleas, throwing down socks instead of lock, her maid instead of her braid. (Rev: BL 12/1/03; HB 11–12/03; HBG 4/04; SLJ 12/03)

10763 *The Wild Swans* (4–6). Retold by Ken Setterington. Illus. by Ernst Hofer and Nelly Hofer. 2003, Tundra $17.95 (0-88776-615-3). 40pp. The story of how Elise saves her brothers from being turned into swans is presented in clear, flowing text and intricate cut-paper art. (Rev: BL 11/15/03; HBG 4/04; SLJ 12/03)

10764 Wilde, Oscar. *The Happy Prince* (3–5). Illus. by Robin Muller. 2002, Stoddart $15.95 (0-7737-3218-3). 24pp. Wilde's unusual fairy tale in which a swallow and a statue make sacrifices for each other is retold with effective illustrations. (Rev: BL 3/15/02)

10765 Willard, Nancy. *Cinderella's Dress* (K–2). Illus. by Jane Dyer. 2003, Scholastic $16.95 (0-590-56927-9). With the help of two magpies, a ring hammered from fairy gold, and her fairy godmother,

Cinderella finally makes it to the ball despite the best efforts of the horrible stepsisters. (Rev: HBG 4/04; SLJ 11/03) [398.2]

10766 Wisniewski, David. *The Warrior and the Wise Man* (3–5). Illus. by author. 1989, Lothrop LB $15.93 (0-688-07890-7). 32pp. Twin sons of the emperor of Japan search for five magical elements of the world. (Rev: BL 5/1/89; HB 7–8/89; SLJ 4/89)

10767 Wood, Audrey. *Heckedy Peg* (PS–2). Illus. by Don Wood. 1987, Harcourt $16.00 (0-15-233678-8); paper $7.00 (0-15-233679-6). 32pp. Mother promises gifts to her seven children, all named for days of the week, taken from a 16th-century game still played in England. (Rev: BCCB 12/87; BL 9/15/87; SLJ 11/87)

10768 Yep, Laurence. *The Ghost Fox* (3–5). Illus. by Jean Tseng and Mou-Sien Tseng. 1994, Scholastic $13.95 (0-590-47204-6). 70pp. In this Chinese fairy tale, Little Lee must save his mother from a dangerous ghost fox that is stealing her soul. (Rev: BCCB 3/94; BL 11/15/93; SLJ 5/94)

10769 Zalben, Jane Breskin. *Hey, Mama Goose* (PS–K). Illus. by Emilie Chollat. 2005, Dutton $15.99 (0-525-47097-2). 32pp. Mama Goose, real estate agent, brokers deals in which familiar fairy-tale characters exchange dwellings with one another. (Rev: BL 2/15/05; SLJ 2/05) [398.2]

Folklore

General

10770 Adler, Naomi. *The Barefoot Book of Animal Tales* (2–4). Illus. by Amanda Hall. 2002, Barefoot $19.99 (1-84148-941-7). 80pp. Lovely, vivid illustrations brighten retellings of nine animal tales, including a Native American story and the German classic about the Bremen musicians. (Rev: BL 1/1–15/03; HBG 3/03; SLJ 6/03) [398.2]

10771 Adler, Naomi. *Play Me a Story: Nine Tales About Musical Instruments* (3–6). Illus. 1998, Millbrook LB $23.40 (0-7613-0401-0). 80pp. Beginning with the tale of the Pied Piper of Hamelin, this book contains nine stories about musical instruments from different countries, including a Native American story and a myth from ancient Greece. (Rev: BL 7/98; HBG 10/98; SLJ 4/98) [398]

10772 Andrews, Jan. *Out of the Everywhere: Tales for a New World* (2–6). Illus. by Simon Ng. 2001, Groundwood $19.95 (0-88899-402-8). 95pp. Andrews retells stories, setting them in the New World and showing their relevance to immigrants or people seeking new situations. (Rev: HB 9–10/01; HBG 3/02; SLJ 9/01) [813]

10773 Batt, Tanya. *The Fabrics of Fairytale: Stories Spun from Far and Wide* (4–6). Illus. 2000, Barefoot $19.99 (1-84148-061-4). 80pp. This book contains seven retold folktales, each related to a different kind of fabric or an article of clothing, like silk brocade, a patchwork coat, or a feather cloak. Patchwork illustrations are reminiscent of a story quilt. (Rev: BL 11/15/00; HBG 10/01; SLJ 11/00) [398.23]

10774 Batt, Tanya Robyn. *A Child's Book of Faeries* (3–5). Illus. by Gail Newey. 2002, Barefoot $19.99 (1-84148-954-9). 64pp. Four stories, with snippets of poetry and folklore, introduce the magical world of fairies and leprechauns. (Rev: BL 12/15/02; HBG 3/03; SLJ 1/03) [398.21]

10775 *Bear Tales: Three Treasured Stories* (PS–1). Ed. by Vlasta van Kampen. Illus. 2000, Annick LB $18.95 (1-55037-619-5); paper $6.95 (1-55037-618-7). 40pp. Three bear stories are retold here, one from Czech sources, one from Russian, and one from Native American folklore. (Rev: BL 6/1–15/00; HBG 10/00; SLJ 10/00) [398.2]

10776 Beeler, Selby B. *Throw Your Tooth on the Roof: Tooth Traditions from Around the World* (PS–3). Illus. by G. Brian Karas. 1998, Houghton Mifflin $16.00 (0-395-89108-6). 32pp. As well as some basic facts about teeth, this book outlines lost-tooth traditions from around the world, each of which makes placing the tooth under a pillow to get money from the tooth fairy seem very tame. (Rev: BCCB 11/98; BL 7/98; HBG 3/99; SLJ 9/98) [398]

10777 Bini, Renata, reteller. *A World Treasury of Myths, Legends, and Folktales: Stories from Six Continents* (3–6). Trans. from Italian by Alexandra Bonfante-Warren. Illus. by Mikhail Fiodorov. 2000, Abrams $24.95 (0-8109-4554-1). 126pp. These brief retellings of tales from around the world cover many cultures and times; about one-quarter are from Native American sources. (Rev: BL 1/1–15/01; HBG 3/01; SLJ 12/00) [398.2]

10778 Borlenghi, Patricia. *Chaucer the Cat and the Animal Pilgrims* (3–6). Illus. by Giles Greenfield. 2000, Bloomsbury $22.95 (0-7475-4491-3). 77pp. A group of animal pilgrims from around the world led by Chaucer the Cat from London tell folk tales on their way to honor Saint Francis at Assisi. (Rev: SLJ 1/01) [398.2]

10779 Brill, Marlene T. *Tooth Tales from Around the World* (K–2). Illus. by Katya Krenina. 1998, Charlesbridge LB $15.95 (0-88106-398-3); paper $6.95 (0-88106-399-1). 32pp. An outline of the many traditions and beliefs from around the world concerning lost teeth. For example, ancient Egyptians threw their teeth to the sun in the belief that the sun made teeth strong. (Rev: BL 7/98; HBG 10/98) [398]

10780 Caduto, Michael J. *Earth Tales from Around the World* (5–8). Illus. 1997, Fulcrum paper $17.95 (1-55591-968-5). 192pp. This collection of 48 folktales from around the world emphasizes respect for the natural world. (Rev: BL 4/1/98; SLJ 5/98) [398.27]

10781 Carle, Eric. *Eric Carle's Treasury of Classic Stories for Children by Aesop, Hans Christian Andersen, and the Brothers Grimm* (2–4). Illus. by author. 1988, Orchard $24.95 (0-531-05742-9). 160pp. Familiar stories with Carle's distinctive mark. (Rev: BCCB 6/88; BL 3/1/88; SLJ 4/88) [398.2]

10782 Cecil, Laura. *Cunning Cat Stories* (K–2). Illus. by Emma Chichester Clark. 2003, Pavilion $19.95 (1-86205-376-6); paper $.00 (1-84365-023-1). 80pp. Three feline-themed folk tales — "Puss in Boots," "Sir Pussycat," and "The White Cat" — are retold in this attractively illustrated collection. (Rev: BL 6/1–15/04; SLJ 5/04)

10783 Climo, Shirley. *King of the Birds* (PS–3). Illus. by Ruth Heller. 1991, HarperCollins paper $5.95 (0-06-443273-4). 32pp. The long-ago legend of how the birds chose a king. (Rev: BL 2/15/88; SLJ 8/88) [398.2]

10784 Climo, Shirley. *A Treasury of Mermaids: Mermaid Tales from Around the World* (4–8). Illus. by Jean Tseng and Mou-Sien Tseng. 1997, HarperCollins $17.95 (0-06-023876-3). 80pp. A fine retelling of eight folktales from around the world about mermaids and other enchanted sea creatures. (Rev: BL 11/15/97; HBG 3/98; SLJ 10/97) [398.2]

10785 Cooling, Wendy. *Farmyard Tales from Far and Wide* (PS–2). Illus. by Rosslyn Moran. 1998, Barefoot $15.95 (1-901223-38-8). 48pp. Each of these seven folktales deals with common farmyard animals and comes from the folklore of a different country. (Rev: BL 11/1/98; SLJ 11/98) [398.2]

10786 Craig, Helen. *The Random House Book of Nursery Stories* (PS–2). Illus. 2000, Random $19.95 (0-375-80586-9). 96pp. Ten favorite folktales, among them "Little Red Riding Hood," "The Three Little Pigs," and "The Gingerbread Man," are retold with bright line drawings. (Rev: BL 12/1/00; HBG 3/01; SLJ 12/00) [398.2]

10787 Crum, Shutta. *Who Took My Hairy Toe?* (PS–3). Illus. by Katya Krenina. 2001, Whitman $15.95 (0-8075-5972-5). 40pp. A light-fingered old man soon regrets picking up that hairy toe, as its owner was quite attached to it. (Rev: BL 8/01; HBG 3/02; SLJ 10/01) [398.2]

10788 Czarnota, Lorna MacDonald. *Medieval Tales That Kids Can Read and Tell* (3–6). Series: World Folktale Collections. 2000, August House $21.95 (0-87483-589-5); paper $12.95 (0-87483-588-7). 96pp. This collection of folk tales suitable for children to tell features such characters as Robin Hood, William Tell, Robert Bruce, Joan of Arc, and Beowulf. (Rev: HBG 10/00; SLJ 2/01) [398.2]

10789 dePaola, Tomie, ed. *Tomie dePaola's Favorite Nursery Tales* (PS–3). Illus. by Tomie dePaola. 1986, Penguin Putnam $24.95 (0-399-21319-8). 128pp. The artist's favorite childhood remembrances in an attractive package. (Rev: BCCB 2/87; BL 11/1/86; SLJ 1/87) [398.2]

10790 Despain, Pleasant. *Tales of Cats* (3–5). Illus. by Don Bell. Series: The Books of Nine Lives. 2003, August House $14.95 (0-87483-713-8). 80pp. Nine folktales about cats from diverse cultures may appeal in particular to reluctant readers. (Rev: HBG 4/04; SLJ 1/04) [398.2]

10791 Despain, Pleasant. *Tales of Enchantment* (3–5). Illus. by Don Bell. Series: The Books of Nine Lives. 2003, August House $14.95 (0-87483-711-1). 80pp. This collection of nine folk tales offers stories of fantasy and the supernatural from cultures around the world. (Rev: HBG 4/04; SLJ 1/04) [398.2]

10792 Despain, Pleasant. *Tales of Nonsense and Tomfoolery* (3–5). Illus. Series: Books of Nine Lives. 2001, August House paper $3.99 (0-87483-645-X). 80pp. A collection of tales from around the world that specialize in nonsense. (Rev: BL 7/01) [398.2]

10793 Despain, Pleasant. *Tales of Tricksters* (3–5). Illus. Series: Books of Nine Lives. 2001, August House paper $3.99 (0-87483-644-1). 80pp. A collection of tales from around the world that specialize in tricksters. (Rev: BL 7/01) [398.2]

10794 Despain, Pleasant. *Tales of Wisdom and Justice* (3–5). Illus. Series: Books of Nine Lives. 2001, August House paper $3.99 (0-87483-646-8). 80pp. A collection of tales from around the world that specialize in wise decisions. (Rev: BL 7/01) [398.2]

10795 Despain, Pleasant. *Tales to Frighten and Delight* (3–5). Illus. by Don Bell. Series: The Books of Nine Lives. 2003, August House $14.95 (0-87483-712-X). 80pp. Nine spine-chilling folktales are collected from cultures around the world. (Rev: HBG 4/04; SLJ 1/04) [398.27]

10796 Despain, Pleasant, reteller. *Thirty-Three Multicultural Tales to Tell* (3–7). Illus. by Joe Shlichta. Series: American Folklore and Storytelling. 1993, August House paper $15.00 (0-87483-266-7). 126pp. An interesting international collection of folktales that span a number of subjects and moods. (Rev: SLJ 6/94) [398.2]

10797 Dijkstra, Lida. *Little Mouse* (PS–K). Illus. by Lida Grobler. 2004, Front Street $15.95 (1-932425-06-3). 32pp. A retelling of a traditional tale in which a little mouse, accompanied by her adoptive hermit father, searches for "the strongest being on earth" to be her mate. (Rev: BL 1/1–15/05; SLJ 2/05) [398.2]

10798 Downard, Barry. *The Little Red Hen* (K–2). Illus. 2004, Simon & Schuster $14.95 (0-689-85962-7). 32pp. Eye-catching photo-collages bring new humor to the traditional folktale. (Rev: BL 3/1/04; SLJ 4/04) [398.24]

10799 Evetts-Secker, Josephine. *The Barefoot Book of Father and Son Tales* (3–6). Illus. 1999, Barefoot $19.95 (1-902283-32-5). 80pp. Father-son relationships are explored in this collection of folktales that includes the Daedalus-Icarus myth. (Rev: BL 4/1/99; SLJ 6/99) [398.27]

10800 Evetts-Secker, Josephine. *The Barefoot Book of Mother and Son Tales* (3–6). 1999, Barefoot $19.95 (1-902283-05-8). 80pp. Using colorful illustrations and a choice of tales from the world's folklore, this collection explores mother-son relationships. (Rev: BL 4/1/99; SLJ 6/99) [398.27]

10801 Forest, Heather. *Wisdom Tales from Around the World* (4–7). 1996, August House $27.95 (0-87483-478-3); paper $19.95 (0-87483-479-1). 160pp. Fifty fables, folktales, and myths from around the world. (Rev: BCCB 2/97; BL 3/1/97) [398.2]

10802 Forest, Heather. *Wonder Tales from Around the World* (4–6). Illus. 1995, August House paper $16.95 (0-87483-422-8). 160pp. A collection of 27 traditional stories, some familiar and others never anthologized before. (Rev: BL 11/15/95; SLJ 4/96) [398.2]

10803 Gibbons, Gail. *Behold . . . the Dragons!* (K–3). Illus. 1999, Morrow LB $15.93 (0-688-15527-8). 32pp. Drawing on the world's folklore, this book follows dragons through different cultures and times. (Rev: BL 5/1/99; HBG 10/99; SLJ 4/99) [398]

10804 Gilchrist, Cherry. *A Calendar of Festivals* (3–7). Illus. 1998, Barefoot $18.95 (1-901223-68-X). 80pp. This anthology includes folktales and stories for many of the major holidays celebrated annually around the world. (Rev: BL 9/15/98; SLJ 12/98) [394.2]

10805 Gilchrist, Cherry. *Stories from the Silk Road* (3–7). Illus. 1999, Barefoot $19.95 (1-902283-25-2). 80pp. Seven exotic folktales represent the culture and history of the countries along the fabled Silk Road that stretched from China to Persia. (Rev: BL 9/15/99; SLJ 11/99) [398.27]

10806 Gilchrist, Cherry. *Sun-Day, Moon-Day: How the Week Was Made* (3–5). Illus. by Amanda Hall. 1998, Barefoot $18.95 (1-901223-63-9). 80pp. Each day of the week is highlighted, with background information and a tale from Greek, Norse, Roman, Babylonian, and other folklore traditions. (Rev: SLJ 9/98) [398.2]

10807 Hamilton, Martha, and Mitch Weiss. *How and Why Stories: World Tales Kids Can Read and Tell* (5–10). Illus. 1999, August House $21.95 (0-87483-562-3); paper $12.95 (0-87483-561-5). 96pp. This excellent collection of 25 pourquoi (how and why) stories from around the world also contains a useful introduction on folklore, plus tips on delivering each of the tales. (Rev: BL 5/15/00; HBG 3/00; SLJ 1/00) [398.2]

10808 Hamilton, Martha, and Mitch Weiss. *Noodlehead Stories: World Tales Kids Can Read and Tell* (3–5). Illus. 2000, August House $21.95 (0-87483-584-4); paper $12.95 (0-87483-585-2). 96pp. Includes 23 humorous stories from around the world, with tips on effective delivery and general storytelling advice. (Rev: BL 2/15/01; HBG 10/01; SLJ 1/01) [389.2]

10809 Hamilton, Virginia. *A Ring of Tricksters: Animal Tales from North America, the West Indies, and Africa* (3–6). Illus. by Barry Moser. 1997, Scholastic $19.95 (0-590-47374-3). 112pp. This is a stunning collection of trickster tales, many from Africa and others that were adapted by slaves to reflect

conditions in the West Indies and the United States. (Rev: BL 1/1–15/98; HBG 3/98; SLJ 11/97) [398.2]

10810 Hartman, Bob. *The Lion Storyteller Book of Animal Tales* (K–3). Illus. by Susie Poole. 2004, Lion paper $13.95 (0-7459-4838-3). 116pp. A diverse and entertaining collection of more than 30 tales to do with animals. (Rev: SLJ 8/04) [398.2]

10811 Helmer, Marilyn. *Three Teeny Tiny Tales* (K–2). Illus. by Veselina Tomova. Series: Once-Upon-a-Time. 2001, Kids Can $10.95 (1-55074-841-6). 32pp. "The Elves and the Shoemaker," "The Gingerbread Man," and "Thumbelina" are retold in picture-book format. (Rev: BL 7/01; HBG 3/02; SLJ 6/01) [398.2]

10812 Hirsch, Odo. *Bartlett and the Ice Voyage* (4–7). Illus. by Andrew McLean. 2003, Bloomsbury $14.95 (1-58234-797-2). 175pp. When a queen demands a far-off fruit, the intrepid explorer Bartlett is ready to oblige. (Rev: BL 2/1/03; HBG 10/03; SLJ 1/03*)

10813 Hoffman, Mary. *A Twist in the Tail: Animal Stories from Around the World* (K–3). Illus. by Jan Ormerod. 1998, Holt $18.95 (0-8050-5945-6). 68pp. Ten lively folktales about animals from such places as India, China, Malaysia, and Nigeria are included in this anthology. (Rev: BL 11/15/98; SLJ 11/98) [398.245]

10814 Holt, David, and Bill Mooney, eds. *More Ready-to-Tell Tales from Around the World* (4–10). 2000, August House $24.95 (0-87483-592-5); paper $14.95 (0-87483-583-6). 256pp. Well-known storytellers have chosen a total of 45 pieces that are certain crowd-pleasers. (Rev: BL 12/15/00; HBG 10/01; SLJ 11/00) [398.2]

10815 Hutchinson, Duane. *The Gunny Wolf and Other Fairy Tales* (4–6). Illus. 1993, Foundation paper $6.95 (0-934988-29-3). 88pp. A total of seven folktales, including Tom Thumb and The Six Swans, are included in this collection. (Rev: BL 5/15/93) [398.2]

10816 Jaffe, Nina, and Steve Zeitlin. *The Cow of No Color: Riddle Stories and Justice Tales from Around the World* (5–8). Illus. 1998, Holt $17.00 (0-8050-3736-5). 160pp. A collection of folktales from around the world that deal with the theme of justice. (Rev: BCCB 12/98; BL 11/1/98; HBG 3/99; SLJ 12/98) [398.2]

10817 Ketteman, Helen. *Armadilly Chili* (K–3). Trans. and illus. by Will Terry. 2004, Whitman $16.95 (0-8075-0457-2). 32pp. This charming retelling of the Little Red Hen story is transposed to the American Southwest. (Rev: BL 6/1–15/04; SLJ 5/04) [398.2]

10818 Krishnaswami, Uma. *Stories of the Flood* (4–6). Illus. 1994, Roberts Rinehart $15.95 (1-57098-007-1). 41pp. In a picture-book format, nine flood myths from such places as ancient Sumeria and Hawaii are retold. (Rev: BL 2/1/95; SLJ 2/95) [291.13]

10819 Laird, Elizabeth. *Beautiful Bananas* (PS–2). Illus. by Liz Pichon. 2004, Peachtree $15.95 (1-56145-305-6). 32pp. In this charming circular folktale, young Beatrice sets off for her grandfather's house with a bunch of bananas balanced on her head; various encounters with animals along the way cause substitutions for the bananas. (Rev: BL 5/1/04; SLJ 4/04) [398.2]

10820 Lansky, Bruce, sel. *Girls to the Rescue: Tales of Clever, Courageous Girls from Around the World* (3–6). 1995, Meadowbrook paper $3.95 (0-88166-215-1). 100pp. A collection of stories about resourceful young women, many of which originated in the world's folklore. (Rev: SLJ 12/95) [398.2]

10821 Lansky, Bruce, ed. *Girls to the Rescue Book 2: Tales of Clever, Courageous Girls from Around the World* (3–6). 1996, Meadowbrook LB $3.95 (0-671-57375-6). 103pp. In each of the folktales gathered from around the world, young women must rely on their ingenuity to overcome obstacles. (Rev: SLJ 2/97) [398.2]

10822 Lunge-Larsen, Lise. *The Hidden Folk: Stories of Fairies, Gnomes, Selkies, and Other Secret Beings* (3–5). Illus. by Beth Krommes. 2004, Houghton Mifflin $18.00 (0-618-17495-8). 80pp. Drawing on the folkloric traditions of northern Europe, Lunge-Larsen offers up eight tales about magical beings. (Rev: BL 9/1/04) [398.2]

10823 Lupton, Hugh, ed. *The Songs of Birds: Stories and Poems from Many Cultures* (4–7). Illus. 2000, Barefoot $19.95 (1-84148-045-2). 80pp. A beautifully illustrated collection of stories (mostly creation myths) and poems about birds culled from a wide range of cultures. (Rev: BL 3/15/00; SLJ 9/00) [808.819]

10824 Lupton, Hugh. *The Story Tree: Tales to Read About* (PS–2). Illus. by Sophie Fatus. 2001, Barefoot $18.99 (1-84148-312-5). 64pp. This volume includes seven folktales from around the world, including favorites such as "The Three Billy Goats Gruff" and "The Magic Porridge Pot." (Rev: BL 10/1/01; HBG 3/02; SLJ 11/01) [398.2]

10825 Lupton, Hugh, reteller. *Tales of Wisdom and Wonder* (2–6). Illus. by Niamh Sharkey. 1998, Barefoot $18.95 (1-901223-09-4). 64pp. Seven traditional stories from different cultures, such as Haitian, Cree, West African, Russian, and Irish, are retold in this anthology. (Rev: SLJ 10/98) [398.2]

10826 MacDonald, Margaret Read, comp. *Earth Care: World Folktales to Talk About* (3–7). 1999, Linnet LB $26.50 (0-208-02416-6); paper $17.50 (0-208-02426-3). 161pp. These 41 folk stories from 30 countries deal with humans and their relationship to nature. (Rev: BL 1/1–15/00; HBG 3/00; SLJ 4/00) [398.2]

10827 MacDonald, Margaret Read. *Peace Tales: World Folktales to Talk About* (5–7). Illus. 1992, Shoe String LB $25.00 (0-208-02328-3); paper $17.50 (0-208-02329-1). 114pp. Stories and proverbs directed toward achieving world peace. (Rev: BL 6/15/92; SLJ 10/92) [398.2]

10828 Mama, Raouf. *The Barefoot Book of Tropical Tales* (3–5). Illus. 2000, Barefoot $19.95 (1-902283-21-X). 64pp. Backed up by extensive source notes, this book contains eight folktales that come from either African or Afro-Caribbean traditions. (Rev: BL 4/1/00; SLJ 9/00) [398.2]

10829 Matthews, Andrew. *Marduk the Mighty and Other Stories of Creation* (4–6). Illus. by Sheila Moxley. 1997, Millbrook LB $22.40 (0-7613-0204-2). 96pp. A collection of 24 creation stories, beginning with Genesis and ending with a Norse myth about the fall of the gods. (Rev: BCCB 6/97; BL 6/1–15/97; SLJ 7/97) [291.1]

10830 Matthews, John. *The Barefoot Book of Knights* (4–7). Illus. by Giovanni Manna. 2002, Barefoot $19.99 (1-84148-064-9). 80pp. This book contains retellings of seven tales of knights and chivalry from countries around the world. (Rev: BCCB 9/02; BL 4/15/02; HBG 10/02; SLJ 6/02) [398.2]

10831 Matthews, John. *Giants, Ghosts and Goblins* (4–6). Illus. 1999, Barefoot $19.95 (1-902283-27-9). 80pp. Nine stories of ghosts, some of them friendly, from such faraway places as Australia. (Rev: BL 10/15/99; SLJ 10/99) [398.2]

10832 Matthews, John, and Caitlin Matthews. *The Wizard King and Other Spellbinding Tales* (3–6). Illus. 1998, Barefoot $18.95 (1-901223-84-1). 80pp. An interesting collection of nine folk and fairy stories from around the world that feature dragons, monsters, spells, and wizards. (Rev: BL 10/15/98; SLJ 12/98) [398.2]

10833 Mayer, Marianna. *Iron John* (K–3). Illus. by Winslow Pels. 1999, Morrow LB $14.93 (0-688-11555-1). 40pp. Elements from traditional folk and fairy tales are used in this story of a young boy, Hans, who frees a wild man named Iron John and follows him like a son into an enchanted forest. (Rev: BL 9/1/99; HBG 3/00; SLJ 9/99) [398.2]

10834 Milord, Susan. *Bird Tales from Near and Far* (1–5). Illus. 1999, Williamson $14.95 (1-885593-18-X). 96pp. From many cultures, this collection of folktales about a variety of birds also contains factual information, projects, and crafts. (Rev: BL 2/15/99; SLJ 11/98) [398.2]

10835 Milord, Susan. *Tales Alive! Ten Multicultural Folktales with Activities* (4–6). Illus. 1995, Williamson paper $15.95 (0-913589-79-9). 128pp. This book contains 19 folktales plus such related material as riddles, puzzles, and craft projects. (Rev: BL 4/15/95; SLJ 3/95) [398.2]

10836 Milord, Susan, reteller. *Tales of the Shimmering Sky: Ten Global Folktales with Activities* (3–6). Illus. by JoAnn E. Kitchel. Series: A Williamson Tales Alive! Book. 1996, Williamson paper $15.95 (1-885593-01-5). 128pp. Ten folktales from different cultures explore such topics as the sky, wind, seasons, colors, and the weather, with additional background material and many suggested projects. (Rev: SLJ 2/97) [398.2]

10837 Minard, Rosemary, ed. *Womenfolk and Fairy Tales* (4–6). Illus. by Suzanna Klein. 1975, Houghton Mifflin $18.00 (0-395-20276-0). 176pp. In each of these 18 stories, the female characters triumph because of wit, spunk, and courage. [398.2]

10838 Mutén, Burleigh. *Grandfather Mountain: Stories of Gods and Heroes from Many Cultures* (4–7). Retold by Burleigh Muten. Illus. by Siân Bailey. 2004, Barefoot $19.99 (1-84148-789-9). 80pp. Strong male protagonists are featured in folktales from England, Greece, Ireland, Japan, Mexico, New Zealand, Nigeria, and the Seneca Indians. (Rev: BL 11/15/04; SLJ 1/05) [398.2]

10839 Mutén, Burleigh. *Grandmothers' Stories: Wise Woman Tales from Many Cultures* (3–5). Illus. 1999, Barefoot $19.95 (1-902283-24-4). 80pp. An anthology of folktales from around the world that portray older women in a favorable light. (Rev: BL 11/15/99; SLJ 3/00) [398.27]

10840 Norman, Howard. *Between Heaven and Earth: Bird Tales from Around the World* (3–7). Illus. by Leo Dillon and Diane Dillon. 2004, Harcourt $22.00 (0-15-201982-0). 96pp. Five beautifully illustrated bird-themed folktales hail from Africa, Australia, China, Norway, and Sri Lanka. (Rev: BL 11/1/04) [398.2]

10841 *Not One Damsel in Distress: World Folktales for Strong Girls* (3–6). Ed. by Jane Yolen. Illus. 2000, Harcourt $17.00 (0-15-202047-0). 112pp. A collection of folktales from such different locales as Argentina, Romania, and Germany in which girls face obstacles difficult to surmount. (Rev: BCCB 4/00; BL 3/1/00; HBG 10/00; SLJ 7/00) [398.22]

10842 Oliver, Narelle. *Mermaids Most Amazing* (2–4). Illus. 2005, Penguin Putnam $15.99 (0-399-24288-0). 32pp. The origins of folklore and mythology about mermaids are briefly explored in this attractive import from Australia. (Rev: BL 2/1/05; SLJ 2/05) [398.21]

10843 *Once Upon a Fairy Tale: Four Favorite Stories* (K–5). 2001, Viking $30.00 (0-670-03500-9). 61pp. Celebrities are portrayed as characters in these retellings of four classic folktales with modern twists, with accompanying CD read by the stars. (Rev: HBG 3/02; SLJ 1/02) [398.2]

10844 Opie, Iona, and Peter Opie, eds. *The Classic Fairy Tales* (4–8). Illus. 1992, Oxford paper $17.95 (0-19-520219-8). 256pp. Contains the earliest published text of these tales.

10845 Oram, Hiawyn. *Not-So-Grizzly Bear Stories* (3–4). 1998, Little Tiger $16.95 (1-888444-41-X). 96pp. An exciting retelling of ten folktales about bears from around the world. (Rev: BL 3/1/99; HBG 3/99; SLJ 4/99) [398.24]

10846 Osborne, Mary P. *Favorite Medieval Tales* (4–9). Illus. 1997, Scholastic paper $17.95 (0-590-60042-7). This collection of tales about medieval heroes such as Beowulf, King Arthur, Roland, Robin Hood, and Gawain is also a good introduction to the art and literature of the Middle Ages and the development of the English language. (Rev: BL 5/1/98; HBG 9/98; SLJ 8/98) [398.2]

10847 Osborne, Mary Pope, ed. *Mermaid Tales from Around the World* (3–6). Illus. by Troy Howell. 1993, Scholastic $16.95 (0-590-44377-1). 96pp. Twelve stories about mermaids collected from the world's folklore. (Rev: BCCB 2/94; BL 10/15/93; SLJ 11/93) [398.21]

10848 Pearson, Maggie. *The Fox and the Rooster and Other Tales* (K–3). Illus. by Joanne Moss. 1997, Little Tiger $14.95 (1-888444-17-7). 77pp. Fourteen countries — e.g., Norway, Japan, and Ireland — are represented in this collection of folk-

tales. (Rev: BCCB 3/98; BL 2/15/98; HBG 10/98) [398.2]

10849 Pearson, Maggie. *The Headless Horseman and Other Ghoulish Tales* (4–7). Illus. 2001, Interlink $18.95 (1-56656-377-1). 96pp. From Bluebeard to Baba Yaga and Ichabod Crane, this is a collection of 14 tales about eerie beings. (Rev: BL 3/1/01; HBG 10/01; SLJ 1/01) [398.2]

10850 Peters, Andrew F. *Strange and Spooky Stories* (3–6). Illus. 1997, Millbrook LB $23.90 (0-7613-0321-9). 80pp. Nine unusual but appealing tales from North America, the British Isles, Central Europe, and the Czech Republic. (Rev: BL 2/1/98; HBG 3/98) [398.2]

10851 Phelps, Ethel Johnston. *Tatterhood and Other Tales* (3–6). Illus. by Pamela Baldwin-Ford. 1978, Feminist Pr. paper $9.95 (0-912670-50-9). 192pp. Tales in which women play a vital and decisive role. [398.2]

10852 Philip, Neil. *The Little People: Stories of Fairies, Pixies, and Other Small Folk* (4–8). Illus. 2002, Abrams $24.95 (0-8109-0570-1). 128pp. Beautiful illustrations accompany stories about fairies and other "magical beings" from Europe. (Rev: BL 2/15/03; HBG 3/03; SLJ 12/02) [398.21]

10853 Polacco, Patricia. *Babushka's Mother Goose* (PS–1). Illus. 1995, Penguin Putnam $18.99 (0-399-22747-4). 64pp. A retelling of the stories and legends told by a babushka (grandmother) to her granddaughter. (Rev: BL 10/15/95; SLJ 10/95) [398.8]

10854 Powell, Patricia Hurby. *Blossom Tales: Flower Stories of Many Folk* (1–3). Illus. by Sarah Dillard. 2002, Moon Mountain $15.95 (0-9677929-8-3). 32pp. A charming collection of short folktales about flowers from around the world. (Rev: BL 4/1/02; HBG 10/02; SLJ 7/02) [398.24]

10855 Riordan, James. *The Storytelling Star: Tales of the Sun, Moon and Stars* (K–6). Illus. by Amanda Hall. 2000, Pavilion $19.95 (1-86205-202-6). 60pp. A collection of nine folktales each from a different culture including Norse, Inca, Greek, Chinese, Chippewa, Aztec, and Seneca. (Rev: SLJ 11/00) [398.2]

10856 Root, Phyllis. *Big Momma Makes the World* (PS–2). Illus. by Helen Oxenbury. 2003, Candlewick $16.99 (0-7636-1132-8). 48pp. Glowing illustrations depict the take-charge Big Momma, baby on hip, as she creates the world and admires her work, though she does have to keep an eye on the humans to make sure they "straighten up." (Rev: BCCB 2/03; BL 1/1–15/03*; HB 3–4/03*; HBG 10/03; SLJ 3/03) [398.2]

10857 Rosen, Michael J. *How the Animals Got Their Colors* (5–8). Illus. by John Clemenston. 1992, Harcourt $14.95 (0-15-236783-7). 48pp. Tales from around the world that explain such things as a leopard's spots and the green on a frog's back. (Rev: BCCB 7–8/92; BL 6/15/92; SLJ 9/91) [398.2]

10858 Rossel, Seymour. *Sefer Ha-Aggadah: The Book of Legends for Young Readers* (4–7). Illus. by Judy Dick. 1996, UAHC paper $14.00 (0-8074-0603-1). 67pp. A collection of legends based on stories about the Jewish people from the Old Testament. (Rev: SLJ 3/97) [398.2]

10859 Schmidt, Gary. *Mara's Stories: Glimmers in the Darkness* (4–8). 2001, Holt $16.95 (0-8050-6794-9). 150pp. Mara tells stories from Jewish folklore to comfort the women and children in her concentration camp. (Rev: BL 10/1/01; HB 1–2/02*; HBG 3/02; SLJ 12/01) [398.2]

10860 Shannon, George. *Stories to Solve: Folktales from Around the World* (4–6). Illus. by Peter Sis. 1985, Morrow paper $4.95 (0-688-10496-7). 56pp. Fourteen stories combine puzzles and folklore asking readers how the problem was figured out or the mystery solved. (Rev: BL 12/1/85; HB 9–10/85; SLJ 9/85) [398.2]

10861 Sherman, Josepha. *Magic Hoofbeats: Horse Tales from Many Lands* (2–4). Illus. by Linda Wingerter. 2004, Barefoot $19.99 (1-84148-091-6). 80pp. Horses with magical abilities are the focus of these brief folktales. (Rev: BL 11/1/04; SLJ 2/05) [398.2]

10862 Sherman, Josepha. *Merlin's Kin: World Tales of the Heroic Magician* (5–8). 1998, August House paper $11.95 (0-87483-519-4). A splendid international collection of folktales that feature magicians, sorcerers, shamans, healers, and wizards. (Rev: BL 4/15/99; BR 1–2/99; SLJ 3/99) [398.21]

10863 Sherman, Josepha. *Told Tales: Nine Folktales from Around the World* (4–6). Illus. 1995, Silver Moon LB $14.95 (1-881889-64-5). 80pp. A general introduction for beginning storytellers that uses a question-and-answer technique and supplies nine folktales from around the world. (Rev: BL 2/1/96; SLJ 1/96) [398.2]

10864 Sierra, Judy. *Can You Guess My Name? Traditional Tales Around the World* (3–5). Illus. by Stefano Vitale. 2002, Clarion $20.00 (0-618-13328-3). 128pp. In this handsome volume with lengthy endnotes, Sierra has collected 15 folktales from all corners of the world that are variants of five favorite stories. (Rev: BL 11/15/02; HB 1–2/03*; HBG 3/03; SLJ 11/02*) [398.2]

10865 Sierra, Judy, ed. *Nursery Tales Around the World* (4–6). Illus. by Stefano Vitale. 1996, Clarion $20.00 (0-395-67894-3). 114pp. This fascinating work retells folktales with similar themes as they exist in different cultures. (Rev: BCCB 2/96; BL 3/1/96; HB 5–6/96; SLJ 4/96) [398.2]

10866 Sierra, Judy. *Silly and Sillier: Read-Aloud Tales from Around the World* (PS–2). Illus. by Valeri Gorbachev. 2002, Knopf $19.95 (0-375-80609-1). 96pp. These 20 folktales from around the world and the wonderful illustrations that accompany them are sure to bring smiles to young readers' faces. (Rev: BL 12/15/02; HBG 3/03; SLJ 11/02) [398.2]

10867 Singh, Rina, and Debbie Lush. *Moon Tales: Myths of the Moon from Around the World* (3–6). 2000, Bloomsbury $22.95 (0-7475-4112-4). 77pp. A stylish retelling of folk tales from around the world dealing with the moon and its powers. (Rev: SLJ 3/01) [398.2]

10868 Spencer, Ann. *And Round Me Rings: Bell Tales and Folklore* (4–7). Illus. by Lindsay Grater. 2003, Tundra paper $11.95 (0-88776-597-1). 240pp. A collection of folklore, poetry, fact, and fiction about bells that includes entries from Europe, the Far East, and North Amreica. (Rev: BL 12/1/03; SLJ 1/04) [398.27]

10869 Spencer, Ann. *Song of the Sea: Myths, Tales, and Folklore* (4–6). Illus. 2001, Tundra paper $17.95 (0-88776-487-8). 208pp. A handsome and varied collection of sea-related lore from around the world. (Rev: BL 8/01; SLJ 7/01) [398.23]

10870 Spiegelman, Art. *Little Lit: Folklore and Fairy Tale Funnies* (4–9). Illus. 2000, Harper-Collins $19.95 (0-06-028624-5). 64pp. In this presentation in graphic format, 15 different artists create brilliant variations on standard fairy and folk tales. (Rev: BL 1/1–15/01*; HB 9–10/00; HBG 3/01; SLJ 12/00) [398.2]

10871 Thompson, Stith, ed. *One Hundred Favorite Folktales* (5–8). Illus. by Franz Altschuler. 1968, Indiana Univ. Pr. $39.95 (0-253-15940-7); paper $19.95 (0-253-20172-1). 456pp. A selection from an international store of folktales. [398.2]

10872 Van Kampen, Vlasta. *A Drop of Gold* (PS–2). Illus. 2001, Annick LB $18.95 (1-55037-677-2); paper $7.95 (1-55037-676-4). 32pp. Spirited artwork illustrates this pourquoi tale of how Mother Nature and her helpers colored the world's birds. (Rev: BL 2/1/02; HBG 3/02; SLJ 1/02) [813]

10873 Vogel, Carole G. *Legends of Landforms: Native American Lore and the Geology of the Land* (4–6). Illus. 1999, Millbrook LB $27.90 (0-7613-0272-7). 96pp. This book contains 14 legends about such geological formations as the Grand Canyon and Martha's Vineyard, with scientific background material on each. (Rev: BL 11/15/99; HBG 10/00; SLJ 1/00) [398.2]

10874 Waldherr, Kris. *Sacred Animals* (3–6). Illus. 2001, HarperCollins LB $16.89 (0-688-16380-7). 48pp. Animal folklore and legends from around the world are organized in four sections — earth, water, fire, and air animals — and surrounded with wonderful illustrations and borders. (Rev: BL 10/1/01; HBG 3/02; SLJ 11/01) [398.2]

10875 Walker, Barbara K., ed. *A Treasury of Turkish Folktales for Children* (4–7). 1988, Shoe String LB $25.00 (0-208-02206-6). 155pp. A witty collection interspersed with riddles. (Rev: BL 10/15/88; SLJ 10/88) [398.2]

10876 Walker, Paul R. *Giants! Stories from Around the World* (3–6). Illus. 1995, Harcourt $17.00 (0-15-200883-7). 80pp. A collection of seven stories about giants, some obscure and others as familiar as "Jack and the Beanstalk." (Rev: BL 11/1/95; SLJ 2/96) [398.2]

10877 Walker, Paul R. *Little Folk: Stories from Around the World* (K–4). Illus. by James Bernardin. 1997, Harcourt $17.00 (0-15-200327-4). 80pp. The retelling of eight tales about pixies, including *Rumpelstiltskin* and a story about a leprechaun. (Rev: BCCB 7–8/97; BL 3/15/97; HBG 3/98; SLJ 4/97) [398.2]

10878 Walker, Richard. *The Barefoot Book of Pirates* (4–6). Illus. 1998, Barefoot $17.95 (1-901223-79-5). 64pp. Pirates and robbers from folklore, including Robin Hood and Pirate Grace, are included in this entertaining collection of folktales from around the world. (Rev: BL 11/15/98; SLJ 9/98) [398.2]

10879 Walker, Richard. *The Barefoot Book of Trickster Tales* (3–6). Illus. 1998, Barefoot $18.95 (1-902283-08-2). 80pp. A collection of trickster tales from around the world, including an Anansi story, a Jack tale, a Brer Rabbit adventure, and a Red Riding Hood story from Bengal. (Rev: BL 1/1–15/99; SLJ 11/98) [398]

10880 *Wicked Wolf Stories* (K–2). Retold by Laura Cecil. Illus. by Emma Chichester Clark. 2003, Pavilion $19.95 (1-86205-460-6); paper $10.95 (1-84365-018-5). 80pp. Three popular children's stories featuring wolves are featured in this attractive volume. (Rev: BL 6/1–15/04)

10881 Willey, Margaret. *Clever Beatrice and the Best Little Pony* (K–2). Illus. by Heather Solomon. 2004, Simon & Schuster $16.95 (0-689-85339-4). 40pp. Beatrice triumphs over the lutin, a leprechaun-like being, who seems to be riding her pony at night. (Rev: BL 2/1/05; SLJ 11/04) [398.2]

10882 Williams, Rose. *The Book of Fairies: Nature Spirits from Around the World* (5–7). Illus. 1997, Beyond Words $18.95 (1-885223-56-0). 80pp. Fairies play a major role in these eight stories from such countries as France, Ireland, and India. (Rev: BL 1/1–15/98; HBG 3/98; SLJ 1/98) [398.2]

10883 Yolen, Jane, ed. *Mightier than the Sword: World Folktales for Strong Boys* (4–8). Illus. by Raul Colon. 2003, Harcourt $19.00 (0-15-216391-3). 128pp. Yolen has collected stories from countries including Afghanistan, Angola, and China that portray intelligence as an invaluable asset. (Rev: BL 4/1/03; HB 5–6/03; HBG 10/03; SLJ 5/03) [398.2]

10884 Yolen, Jane. *Once Upon a Bedtime Story* (K–3). Illus. by Ruth T. Councell. 1997, Boyds Mills $17.95 (1-57397-484-3). 96pp. This is a charming collection of 16 folktales, fairy tales, and fables, chiefly from Europe. (Rev: BL 11/15/97; SLJ 9/97) [398.2]

10885 Young, Richard A., and Judy Dockery Young, eds. *Stories from the Days of Christopher Columbus: A Multicultural Collection for Young Readers* (5–9). 1992, August House paper $8.95 (0-87483-198-9). An anthology of stories translated from a variety of languages, including Italian, Spanish, Portuguese, and Aztec. (Rev: BL 9/15/92; SLJ 7/92) [398.2]

10886 Zeitlin, Steve. *The Four Corners of the Sky: Creation Stories and Cosmologies from Around the World* (5–10). Illus. by Chris Raschka. 2000, Holt $17.00 (0-8050-4816-2). 135pp. Theories and beliefs about the creation of the world from 16 ancient cultures, with a folktale illustrating each one. (Rev: BL 11/15/00; HB 1–2/01; HBG 3/01; SLJ 12/00) [398.2]

Africa

10887 Aardema, Verna, reteller. *Bringing the Rain to Kapiti Plain: A Nandi Tale* (PS–2). Illus. by Beatriz Vidal. 1981, Puffin paper $5.99 (0-14-054616-2). 32pp. A rhyming book on how the rain was brought to an African plain. [398.2]

10888 Aardema, Verna. *The Lonely Lioness and the Ostrich Chicks* (PS–2). Illus. by Yumi Heo. 1996, Knopf LB $18.99 (0-679-96934-0). 32pp. In this Masai story, a lonely lioness is determined to raise an ostrich's four chicks. (Rev: BCCB 2/97; BL 11/15/96; SLJ 12/96*) [398.2]

10889 Aardema, Verna. *Rabbit Makes a Monkey of Lion* (K–1). Illus. by Jerry Pinkney. 1989, Puffin paper $5.99 (0-14-054593-X). 32pp. A Swahili tale of a wily little rabbit outwitting the big brawny lion. (Rev: BL 3/1/89; HB 5–6/89; SLJ 6/89) [398.2]

10890 Aardema, Verna. *Sebgugugu the Glutton: A Bantu Tale from Rwanda, Africa* (4–6). Illus. by Nancy L. Clouse. 1993, Africa World $14.95 (0-86543-377-1). 32pp. In this Rwandian folktale, a foolish man loses everything because of his greed. (Rev: BL 4/1/93; SLJ 6/93) [398.2]

10891 Aardema, Verna, ed. *Why Mosquitoes Buzz in People's Ears: A West African Tale* (K–3). Illus. by Leo Dillon and Diane Dillon. 1992, Puffin paper $6.99 (0-14-054905-6). 32pp. Bold, stylized paintings illustrate this tale of a mosquito who tells a whopping lie, thus setting off a chain of events. Caldecott Medal winner, 1976. [398.2]

10892 Anderson, David A. *The Origin of Life on Earth: An African Creation Myth* (2–6). Illus. by Kathleen A. Wilson. 1991, Sights LB $18.95 (0-9629978-5-4). This African myth tells how earthly creatures were formed and how the world began spinning. (Rev: SLJ 7/92) [398.2]

10893 Appiah, Peggy. *Tales of an Ashanti Father* (2–7). Illus. by Mora Dickson. 1989, Beacon paper $7.95 (0-8070-8313-5). 160pp. Twenty-two stories about trickster Ananse. [398.2]

10894 Araujo, Frank P. *The Perfect Orange: A Tale from Ethiopia* (K–3). Illus. by Xiao Jun Li. Series: Toucan Tales. 1994, Rayve $16.95 (1-877810-94-0). In this Ethiopian folktale, a simple girl impresses a king with her generosity, and he rewards her with gold and jewels. (Rev: SLJ 3/95) [398.2]

10895 Arkhurst, Joyce Cooper. *The Adventures of Spider: West African Folktales* (4–7). Illus. by Jerry Pinkney. 1992, Little, Brown paper $8.99 (0-316-05107-1). Six humorous stories featuring the crafty spider. [398.2]

10896 Ashabranner, Brent, and Russell Davis. *The Lion's Whiskers and Other Ethiopian Tales* (4–7). Illus. 1997, Linnet LB $19.95 (0-208-02429-8). 96pp. A classic collection of 16 Ethiopian folktales originally published in 1995. (Rev: BL 10/1/97; SLJ 5/97*) [398.2]

10897 Barbosa, Rogerio Andrade. *African Animal Tales* (4–6). Trans. by Feliz Guthrie. Illus. by Cica Fittipaldi. 1993, Volcano $17.95 (0-912078-96-0). 63pp. Weak, small animals outwit stronger animals in this collection of ten African folktales. (Rev: BL 2/15/94) [398.2]

10898 Bryan, Ashley. *Beat the Story-Drum, Pum-Pum* (K–4). Illus. by author. 1987, Macmillan paper $8.95 (0-689-71107-7). 80pp. A retelling of five Nigerian folktales. [398.2]

10899 Bryan, Ashley. *Beautiful Blackbird* (K–2). Illus. 2003, Simon & Schuster $16.95 (0-689-84731-9). 40pp. Bold collages illustrate the Zambian tale of Blackbird, who is the envy of all the brightly colored birds in Africa and generously agrees to share his blackening potion, so that all the birds can be black and beautiful. (Rev: BCCB 2/03; BL 1/1–15/03; HB 3–4/03*; HBG 10/03; SLJ 1/03) [398.2]

10900 Bryan, Ashley. *The Night Has Ears: African Proverbs* (K–3). Illus. 1999, Simon & Schuster $16.00 (0-689-82427-0). 32pp. Presenting one proverb per page, this is a collection of 26 aphorisms from various African tribes. (Rev: BL 9/15/99; HBG 3/00; SLJ 1/00) [398.9]

10901 Chocolate, Deborah M. *Imani in the Belly* (PS–3). Illus. by Alex Boies. 1994, Troll $14.95 (0-8167-3466-6). 32pp. Imani sets out to catch Simba the lion, who has taken her children. (Rev: BL 10/15/94; SLJ 12/94) [398.2]

10902 Courlander, Harold, and George Herzog. *The Cow-Tail Switch: And Other West African Stories* (4–6). Illus. by Madye Lee Chastain. 1988, Holt paper $9.95 (0-8050-0298-7). 160pp. Originally published in 1947, this is a fine collection of folktales about foolish and wise men and animals. [398.2]

10903 Cummings, Pat. *Ananse and the Lizard* (PS–3). Illus. 2002, Holt $16.95 (0-8050-6476-1). 40pp. The trickster spider meets his match when a cunning lizard wins the competition for the hand of the chief's daughter. (Rev: BL 11/1/02; HBG 3/03; SLJ 10/02) [398.2]

10904 Day, Nancy Raines. *The Lion's Whiskers: An Ethiopian Folktale* (PS–2). Illus. by Ann Grifalconi. 1995, Scholastic $14.95 (0-590-45803-5). 32pp. A stepmother seeks the aid of a medicine man in her efforts to win the affection of the stepson who rejects her. (Rev: BCCB 3/95; BL 2/15/95; SLJ 4/95*) [398.2]

10905 Dee, Ruby. *Two Ways to Count to Ten: A Liberian Folktale* (PS–1). Illus. by Susan Meddaugh. 1990, Holt paper $6.95 (0-8050-1314-8). 32pp. The antelope outsmarts them all when the king advertises for a successor. (Rev: BL 7/88; SLJ 6–7/88) [398.2]

10906 Diakite, Baba Wague, reteller. *The Hatseller and the Monkeys* (K–3). Illus. by Baba Wague Diakite. 1999, Scholastic $15.95 (0-590-96069-5). This is an interesting West African version of the traditional tale about a peddler whose hats are stolen by a group of monkeys. (Rev: BCCB 2/99; HB 5–6/99; HBG 10/99; SLJ 2/99) [398.2]

10907 Diakite, Baba Wague. *The Hunterman and the Crocodile: A West African Folktale* (K–3). Illus. 1997, Scholastic $15.95 (0-590-89828-0). 32pp. A West African folktale about the Hunterman who runs afoul of Bamba the Crocodile and is helped by Rabbit. (Rev: BCCB 2/97; BL 3/15/97; SLJ 3/97) [398.2]

10908 Diakite, Baba Wague. *The Magic Gourd* (2–4). Illus. 2003, Scholastic $16.95 (0-439-43960-4). 32pp. A retelling of a folktale from Mali about a rabbit who, when his magic gourd is stolen, receives a magic rock to help recover it. (Rev: BCCB 3/03; BL 2/15/03; HBG 10/03; SLJ 2/03) [398.2]

10909 Echewa, T. Obinkaram. *The Magic Tree: A Folktale from Nigeria* (PS–3). Illus. by E. B. Lewis. 1999, Morrow LB $15.93 (0-688-16232-0). 32pp. In this Nigerian folktale, a young outsider gains power and prestige when a magic udara tree gives him fruit and obeys his commands. (Rev: BCCB 4/99; BL 6/1–15/99*; HBG 10/99; SLJ 8/99) [398.2]

10910 Eisner, Will. *Sundiata: A Legend of Africa* (5–8). Illus. 2003, NBM $15.95 (1-56163-332-1). 32pp. A retelling, in comic book style, of an African folktale about a lame prince who conquers an evil king. (Rev: BL 2/1/03; HBG 10/03; SLJ 2/03) [398.2]

10911 Gershator, Phillis. *Only One Cowry* (K–3). Illus. by David Soman. 2000, Orchard LB $17.99 (0-531-33288-8). 32pp. This African folktale in picture-book format tells about tricksters, weddings, and dowries and employs collages made of cut and torn paper to illustrate its events. (Rev: BCCB 1/01; BL 10/15/00; HBG 3/01; SLJ 9/00) [398.2]

10912 Gershator, Phillis. *Zzzng! Zzzng! Zzzng! A Yoruba Tale* (PS–1). Illus. by Theresa Smith. 1998, Orchard LB $16.99 (0-531-08873-1). 32pp. In this Yoruba folktale from Nigeria, Mosquito faces rejection when he tries to marry above his station and takes out his anger by buzzing and biting. (Rev: BCCB 10/98; BL 8/98; HBG 3/99; SLJ 10/98) [398.2]

10913 Greaves, Nick. *When Hippo Was Hairy: And Other Tales from Africa* (4–8). Illus. 1988, Barron's paper $11.95 (0-8120-4548-3). 144pp. Thirty-one traditional African tales, a combination of folklore and fact. (Rev: BL 2/15/89; SLJ 2/89) [398.2]

10914 Green, Roger L. *Tales of Ancient Egypt* (5–9). 1972, Penguin Putnam paper $4.99 (0-14-036716-0). A collection of folktales from ancient Egypt including one about the source of the Nile. [398]

10915 Gregorowski, Christopher. *Fly, Eagle, Fly!* (K–4). Illus. by Niki Daly. 2000, Simon & Schuster $16.00 (0-689-82398-3). 32pp. This Ghanaian folktale tells how an eagle is raised as a chicken but eventually finds its native environment and freedom. (Rev: BL 1/1–15/00; HBG 10/00; SLJ 3/00) [398.2]

10916 Grifalconi, Ann. *The Village of Round and Square Houses* (PS–2). Illus. by author. 1986, Little, Brown $16.95 (0-316-32862-6). 32pp. This blend of fiction, anthropology, and folklore centers around the central African remote village of Tos. (Rev: BCCB 6/86; BL 6/15/86; SLJ 8/86) [398.2]

10917 Haley, Gail E. *A Story, a Story* (1–4). Illus. by author. 1970, Macmillan LB $17.00 (0-689-20511-2); paper $5.99 (0-689-71201-4). 36pp. How African "spider stories" began is traced back to the time when Ananse, the Spider Man, made a bargain with the Sky God. Caldecott Medal winner, 1971. [398.2]

10918 Hull, Robert, reteller. *Egyptian Stories* (4–6). Illus. by Noel Bateman and Barbara Loftus. Series: Tales from Around the World. 1994, Thomson Learning LB $24.26 (1-56847-155-6). 48pp. Introduces seven traditional tales, including a creation story, as well as life in ancient Egypt. (Rev: SLJ 8/94) [398.2]

10919 Janisch, Heinz. *The Fire: An Ethiopian Folk Tale* (PS–2). Trans. by Shelley Tanaka. Illus. by Fabricio Vandenbroeck. 2002, Groundwood $15.95 (0-88899-450-8). 32pp. A slave must spend the night on a snow-capped mountain peak with no clothes or shelter to win his freedom in this Ethiopian folktale with evocative double-page paintings. (Rev: BL 12/15/02; HBG 3/03; SLJ 2/03) [398.2]

10920 Kimmel, Eric A. *Anansi and the Magic Stick* (PS–2). Illus. by Janet Stevens. 2001, Holiday House $16.95 (0-8234-1443-4). 32pp. Things don't go as Anansi the tricky spider plans when he steals a magic stick to do his work for him. (Rev: BCCB 12/01; BL 9/15/01; HBG 3/02; SLJ 9/01) [398.2]

10921 Kimmel, Eric A. *Anansi and the Moss-Covered Rock* (PS–3). Illus. by Janet Stevens. 1988, Holiday House LB $16.95 (0-8234-0689-X); paper $6.95 (0-8234-0798-5). 32pp. Anansi the trickster discovers a magic rock that knocks animals out, and then he steals their food. (Rev: BCCB 10/88; BL 10/1/88; SLJ 11/88) [398.2]

10922 Kimmel, Eric A. *Anansi and the Talking Melon* (PS–3). Illus. by Janet Stevens. 1994, Holiday House LB $16.95 (0-8234-1104-4). 32pp. Hiding inside a melon, Anansi the Spider tricks all the animals into believing that the melon can speak in this African folktale. (Rev: BCCB 6/94; BL 2/15/94; SLJ 3/94*) [398.2]

10923 Kimmel, Eric A. *Anansi Goes Fishing* (K–3). Illus. by Janet Stevens. 1992, Holiday House LB $16.95 (0-8234-0918-X). 32pp. Lazy but lovable trickster Anansi is outwitted by the clever turtle in this contemporary rendition of an old tale. (Rev: BL 3/15/92; SLJ 5/92) [398.2]

10924 Kimmel, Eric A. *Rimonah of the Flashing Sword: A North African Tale* (K–3). Illus. by Omar Rayyan. 1995, Holiday House LB $15.95 (0-8234-1093-5). 32pp. An Egyptian folktale that is a variation on the Snow White story about a princess fleeing the wrath of a wicked stepmother. (Rev: BL 3/1/95; SLJ 3/95) [398.2]

10925 Knutson, Barbara. *How the Guinea Fowl Got Her Spots: A Swahili Tale of Friendship* (PS–2). Illus. 1990, Carolrhoda LB $19.95 (0-87614-416-4). 24pp. Cow returns a favor given by Nganga the Guinea Fowl by giving her spots that can help her hide from enemies. (Rev: BCCB 7–8/90*; BL 6/15/90; HB 9–10/90; SLJ 9/90) [398.2]

10926 Kurtz, Jane. *Trouble* (4–7). Illus. by Durga Bernhard. 1997, Harcourt $16.00 (0-15-200219-7). 40pp. An Eritrean story about a young goatherd who has a knack for getting into trouble. (Rev: BL 3/15/97; SLJ 4/97) [398.2]

10927 Lake, Mary D., reteller. *The Royal Drum: An Ashanti Tale* (K–2). Illus. by Carol O'Malia. 1996, Mondo $14.95 (1-57255-140-2). Using a rebus approach, this tale from Ghana tells how Anansi the spider gets all of the animals to participate in making a drum for Lion the king. (Rev: SLJ 11/96) [398.2]

10928 Lester, Julius. *How Many Spots Does a Leopard Have?* (K–5). Illus. by David Shannon. 1994, Scholastic paper $5.95 (0-590-41972-2). 72pp. This is a splendid retelling of 12 folktales, ten of which are African and the other two Jewish. (Rev: BCCB 9/89; BL 11/15/89; HB 1–2/90; SLJ 11/89) [398.2]

10929 Lester, Julius. *What a Truly Cool World* (PS–3). Illus. by Joe Cepeda. 1999, Scholastic $15.95 (0-590-86468-8). 40pp. In this African creation myth, God, with the help of the angel Shaniqua, adds the finishing touches to the world he has made. (Rev: BCCB 2/99; BL 2/15/99; HBG 10/99; SLJ 4/99) [398.2]

10930 Lester, Julius. *Why Heaven Is Far Away* (K–3). Illus. by Joe Cepeda. 2002, Scholastic $16.95 (0-439-17871-1). 40pp. In this delightfully illustrated sequel to *What a Truly Cool World* (1999), God gives snakes their venom but the snakes are too quick to use this gift and problems ensue. (Rev: BCCB 12/02; BL 10/1/02; HB 11–12/02; HBG 3/03; SLJ 10/02) [398.2]

10931 Lexau, Joan M. *Crocodile and Hen: A Bakongo Folktale* (K). Illus. by Doug Cushman. 2001, HarperCollins LB $14.89 (0-06-028487-0). 48pp. In this easy-to-read tale from the Congo, Crocodile spares the life of Hen because he is persuaded that she is his relative. (Rev: BL 4/15/01; HBG 10/01; SLJ 6/01) [398.2]

10932 Lilly, Melinda. *Kwian and the Lazy Sun: African Tales and Myths* (K–3). Series: African Tales and Myths. 1998, Rourke LB $19.95 (1-57103-243-6). In this South African tale, a young girl figures out how to get the sun and the moon into the sky. Also use from the same series and author *Tamba and the Chief: A Tenne Tale* and *Warrior Son of a Warrior Son: A Masai Tale* (both 1998). (Rev: SLJ 4/99) [398.2]

10933 Lilly, Melinda, reteller. *Spider and His Son Find Wisdom: An Akan Tale* (2–4). Illus. by Charles Reasoner. Series: African Tales and Myths. 1998, Rourke LB $16.95 (1-57103-244-4). 31pp. The spider, Anansi, tries to retrieve all the good advice he has given to unappreciative villagers in this Akan tale told in a picture-book format. (Rev: SLJ 3/99) [398.2]

10934 Lilly, Melinda, reteller. *Wanyana and Matchmaker Frog: A Bagandan Tale* (2–4). Illus. by Charles Reasoner. Series: African Tales and Myths. 1998, Rourke LB $16.95 (1-57103-247-9). 31pp. To repay a kindness he received when in distress, a frog gives a young girl good advice in choosing a husband in this African folk tale. (Rev: SLJ 3/99) [398.2]

10935 Lilly, Melinda, reteller. *Zimani's Drum: A Malawian Tale* (2–4). Illus. by Charles Reasoner. Series: African Tales and Myths. 1998, Rourke LB

$16.95 (1-57103-248-7). 31pp. Blind Zimani rescues his brother and two sisters from the clutches of Mkango the Lion. (Rev: SLJ 3/99) [398.2]

10936 Linn, Dennis, et al. *What Is My Song?* (2–4). Illus. by Francisco Miranda. 2005, Paulist Press $16.95 (0-8091-6722-0). 32pp. In this adaptation of an African folktale, a boy strives to live up to what he believes to be his God-given purpose in life. (Rev: BL 12/1/04)

10937 Lottridge, Celia B., reteller. *The Name of the Tree* (K–5). Illus. by Ian Wallace. 1990, Macmillan $16.00 (0-689-50490-X). This Bantu tale begins with hungry animals finding a tree laden with every fruit imaginable. (Rev: BCCB 4/90; SLJ 3/90) [398.2]

10938 McDermott, Gerald. *Anansi, the Spider: A Tale from the Ashanti* (K–3). Illus. by author. 1972, Holt LB $16.95 (0-8050-0310-X); paper $6.95 (0-8050-0311-8). 48pp. Because Anansi and his sons quarrel, the moon remains in the sky. [398.2]

10939 McDermott, Gerald. *Zomo the Rabbit: A Trickster Tale from West Africa* (PS–3). Illus. 1992, Harcourt $14.95 (0-15-299967-1). 32pp. An enduring Nigerian tale of a trickster who is cunning but not always wise. (Rev: BCCB 9/92*; BL 9/15/92*; SLJ 11/92*) [398.2]

10940 MacDonald, Margaret Read. *Mabela the Clever* (PS–3). Illus. by Tim Coffey. 2001, Whitman $15.95 (0-8075-4902-9). 32pp. A clever mouse outwits a crafty cat in this West African tale. (Rev: BCCB 5/01; BL 7/01; HB 9–10/01; HBG 3/02; SLJ 6/01*) [398.2]

10941 McIntosh, Gavin. *Hausaland Tales from the Nigerian Marketplace* (4–9). Illus. 2002, Linnet $22.50 (0-208-02523-5). 98pp. This collection of 12 Nigerian folktales skillfully interweaves details of contemporary Hausa society. (Rev: HBG 3/03; SLJ 11/02) [398.2]

10942 Mama, Raouf, retel. *Why Goats Smell Bad and Other Stories from Benin* (4–8). Illus. 1998, Linnet LB $21.50 (0-208-02469-7). A delightful collection of 20 folktales from the Fon culture of Benin, handsomely illustrated with woodcuts. (Rev: BCCB 5/98; BL 2/15/98; HBG 9/98; SLJ 4/98) [398.2]

10943 Martin, Francesca. *Clever Tortoise* (2–3). Illus. 2000, Candlewick $14.99 (0-7636-0506-9). 32pp. In this East African folktale, Tortoise outsmarts the bullies Hippopotamus and Elephant. (Rev: BL 5/15/00; HBG 10/01; SLJ 9/00) [398.2]

10944 Medearis, Angela Shelf. *The Singing Man* (PS–3). Illus. by Terea D. Shaffer. 1994, Holiday House LB $16.95 (0-8234-1103-6). 36pp. Banzar is scorned in his Nigerian village because he wants to become a musician, but eventually he returns to his home in triumph. (Rev: BL 7/94; SLJ 9/94) [398.2]

10945 Mollel, Tololwa M. *Ananse's Feast: An Ashanti Tale* (K–3). Illus. by Andrew Glass. 1997, Clarion $14.95 (0-395-67402-6). 32pp. Akye the turtle gets revenge on Ananse the spider in this gentle Ashanti tale. (Rev: BL 4/15/97; SLJ 5/97) [398.2]

10946 Mollel, Tololwa M. *Kitoto the Mighty* (K–3). Illus. by Kristi Frost. 1998, Stoddart $14.95 (0-7737-3019-2). An African folktale about Kitoto, a mouse who sets out to find a force strong enough to protect him from a hawk. (Rev: BCCB 11/98; SLJ 2/99) [398.2]

10947 Mollel, Tololwa M. *Subira Subira* (PS–2). Illus. by Linda Saport. 2000, Clarion $15.00 (0-395-91809-X). 32pp. A Tanzanian folktale in which a brave young girl named Tatu is given advice by a spirit woman on how to control her difficult younger brother. (Rev: BCCB 5/00; BL 2/15/00; HBG 10/00; SLJ 4/00) [398.22]

10948 Mollel, Tololwa M. *To Dinner, for Dinner* (PS–3). Illus. by Synthia Saint James. 2000, Holiday House $16.95 (0-8234-1527-9). 32pp. Based on a Tanzanian story, this tale tells of a rabbit, Juhudi, and his tricks to keep from becoming Leopard's dinner. (Rev: BL 9/1/00; HBG 10/01; SLJ 8/00) [398.2]

10949 Musgrove, Margaret. *The Spider Weaver: A Legend of Kente Cloth* (PS–3). Illus. by Julia Cairns. 2001, Scholastic $16.95 (0-590-98787-9). 40pp. In this Ghanaian folk tale, two weavers learn from a spider complicated patterns that they use in their kente cloth. (Rev: BCCB 3/01; BL 2/15/01; HBG 10/01; SLJ 2/01) [398.2]

10950 Olaleye, Isaac. *In the Rainfield: Who Is the Greatest?* (K–3). Illus. by Ann Grifalconi. 2000, Scholastic $16.95 (0-590-48363-3). 32pp. In this folktale from Nigeria, three elements — Wind, Fire, and Rain — compete to see which is greatest. (Rev: BCCB 2/00; BL 2/15/00; HBG 10/00; SLJ 4/00) [398.2]

10951 Oram, Hiawyn, reteller. *Counting Leopard's Spots: Animal Stories from Africa* (K–4). Illus. by Tim Warnes. 1998, Little Tiger $16.95 (1-888444-31-2). 96pp. A handsome book that contains a variety of tales from Africa, including cautionary, pourquoi, and trickster stories. (Rev: BL 8/98; HBG 10/98; SLJ 12/98) [398.2]

10952 Paye, Won-Ldy, and Margaret H. Lippert. *Head, Body, Legs: A Story from Liberia* (PS–2). Illus. by Julie Paschkis. 2002, Holt $16.95 (0-8050-6570-9). 32pp. This amusing tale from Liberia about disjointed body parts teaches the value of cooperation. (Rev: BL 8/02; HB 5–6/02; HBG 10/02; SLJ 4/02) [398.2]

10953 Paye, Won-Ldy, and Margaret H. Lippert, retels. *Mrs. Chicken and the Hungry Crocodile* (PS–3). Illus. by Julie Paschkis. 2003, Holt $16.95 (0-8050-7047-8). Mrs. Chicken manages to survive a difficult encounter with a crocodile in this newly illustrated folktale from the Dan people of Liberia that appeared in *Why Leopard Has Spots* (Fulcrum, 1998). (Rev: HB 5–6/03; HBG 10/03; SLJ 7/03) [398.2]

10954 Rodanas, Kristina. *The Blind Hunter* (K–2). Illus. by author. 2003, Marshall Cavendish $16.95 (0-7614-5132-3). Blind Chirobo accompanies Muteye on a hunting trip and proves that there is much that he can "see" with his other senses in this picture

536

book based on a Shona folktale. (Rev: HBG 4/04; SLJ 1/04) [398.2]

10955 Savory, Phyllis. *Zulu Fireside Tales* (4–6). Illus. by Sylvia Baxter. 1993, Carol Publishing paper $9.95 (0-8065-1380-2). 240pp. This is an authentic collection of ten Zulu tales that originated in the area now known as Kwazulu. (Rev: BL 5/1/93) [398.2]

10956 Seeger, Pete, adapt. *Abiyoyo: Based on a South African Lullaby and Folk Story* (PS–1). Illus. by Michael Hays. 1986, Macmillan LB $16.00 (0-02-781490-4). 48pp. An ostracized father and little boy who plays the ukelele find a way to best the giant Abiyoyo. (Rev: BCCB 6/86; BL 5/1/86; SLJ 8/86) [398.2]

10957 Seeger, Pete, and Paul Dubois Jacobs. *Abiyoyo Returns* (1–3). Illus. by Michael Hays. 2001, Simon & Schuster $17.00 (0-689-83271-0). 40pp. The giant Abiyoyo returns to help the villagers build a dam in this sequel to Seeger's 1986 retelling of a South African folktale. (Rev: BCCB 11/01; BL 11/15/01; HB 11–12/01; HBG 3/02; SLJ 11/01) [398.2]

10958 Steptoe, John. *Mufaro's Beautiful Daughters: An African Tale* (PS–2). Illus. by author. 1987, Lothrop LB $15.89 (0-688-04046-2). 32pp. Two sisters of opposite natures vie for the hand of the king. (Rev: BCCB 4/87; BL 4/15/87; SLJ 6–7/87) [398.2]

10959 *Tales from Africa* (2–5). Ed. by Mary Medlicott. Illus. 2000, Kingfisher paper $11.95 (0-7534-5290-1). 96pp. Writers from 12 different African nations contributed a variety of folktales to this volume, including trickster stories and animal fables. (Rev: BL 5/15/00) [398.2]

10960 Tchana, Katrin. *Sense Pass King: A Story from Cameroon* (PS–2). Illus. by Trina S. Hyman. 2002, Holiday House $16.95 (0-8234-1577-5). 32pp. Sense Pass King is the name that a child prodigy acquires when she succeeds in discrediting the stupid king and becomes leader of her people. (Rev: BL 11/1/02; HB 11–12/02; HBG 3/03; SLJ 9/02) [398.2]

10961 Tchana, Katrin. *The Serpent Slayer and Other Stories of Strong Women* (4–7). Illus. 2000, Little, Brown $21.95 (0-316-38701-0). 128pp. A collection of 18 folktales from around the world featuring brave, creative, and strong women and girls. (Rev: BCCB 11/00*; BL 12/15/00; HB 11–12/00; HBG 3/01; SLJ 11/00) [398.2]

10962 Washington, Donna L. *A Pride of African Tales* (2–5). Illus. by lames Ransome. 2004, Harper-Collins $16.99 (0-06-024929-3). 80pp. These effective retellings introduce African trickster, pourquoi, and other tales from varied cultures. (Rev: BL 3/15/04; SLJ 8/04) [398.2]

10963 Williams, Sheron. *Imani's Music* (PS–4). Illus. by Jude Daly. 2002, Simon & Schuster $17.00 (0-689-82254-5). 32pp. A grasshopper brings music to the people of Africa, and then to America when he is captured and transported with slaves. (Rev: BL 2/15/02; HBG 10/02; SLJ 1/02)

10964 Wisniewski, David. *Sundiata: Lion King of Mali* (K–5). Illus. 1992, Houghton Mifflin $17.00 (0-395-61302-7). 32pp. The dying king gives his kingdom to a sickly prince who cannot walk or speak, but in time, he becomes a great and brave leader. (Rev: BL 12/1/92*; HB 3–4/93; SLJ 10/92*) [398.2]

10965 Wolkstein, Diane. *The Day Ocean Came to Visit* (PS–3). Illus. by Steve Johnson and Lou Fancher. 2001, Harcourt $16.00 (0-15-201774-7). 40pp. Sun and Moon are married and live on Earth until Sun invites Ocean home for dinner in this pourquoi tale based on an African creation myth. (Rev: BL 7/01; HBG 3/02; SLJ 8/01) [398.8]

10966 Yohannes, Gebregeorgis. *Silly Mammo: An Ethiopian Tale* (PS). Illus. by Bogale Belachew. 2002, African Sun paper $10.00 (1-883701-04-X). 32pp. A contemporary Ethiopian village is the setting for this traditional tale in which a hapless lad gets everything wrong until he kisses a fair lady. (Rev: BL 10/1/02; SLJ 2/03) [398.2]

Asia

General and Miscellaneous

10967 Berger, Barbara Helen. *All the Way to Lhasa: A Tale from Tibet* (PS–2). Illus. 2002, Penguin Putnam $15.99 (0-399-23387-3). 32pp. Courage and perseverance win over headlong speed in this tale of two young men journeying to the holy city of Lhasa, with illustrations that contain many Tibetan Buddhist touches. (Rev: BL 10/1/02; HBG 3/03; SLJ 9/02) [398.2]

10968 Chodzin, Sherab, and Alexandra Kohn. *The Wisdom of the Crows and Other Buddhist Tales* (3–5). Illus. 1998, Tricycle $16.95 (1-883672-68-6). 80pp. This collection of Asian folktales illustrated with clear watercolors represents various facets of Buddhist thought and beliefs. (Rev: BL 6/1–15/98; SLJ 04/98) [294]

10969 Climo, Shirley. *The Korean Cinderella* (K–3). Illus. by Ruth Heller. 1993, HarperCollins $15.95 (0-06-020432-X). 48pp. After Pear Blossom's mother dies and her father remarries, she is mistreated by her stepmother and stepsister. (Rev: BCCB 6/93; BL 5/1/93; SLJ 8/93) [398.2]

10970 Davison, Katherine. *Moon Magic: Stories from Asia* (3–5). Illus. 1994, Carolrhoda LB $19.95 (0-87614-751-1). 56pp. A retelling of four Asian myths that deal with the moon and its phases. (Rev: BL 5/15/94; SLJ 6/94) [398.2]

10971 Demi. *The Donkey and the Rock* (PS–3). Illus. 1999, Holt $16.95 (0-8050-5959-8). 32pp. An Asian folktale — probably Buddhist in origin — of the consequences that result when one man's donkey accidentally shatters another man's jar of oil. (Rev: BL 6/1–15/99; HBG 10/99; SLJ 3/99) [398.2]

10972 Froese, Deborah. *The Wise Washerman: A Folktale from Burma* (K–3). Illus. by Wang Kui. 1996, Hyperion LB $15.49 (0-7868-2232-5). A jealous neighbor tries to get an industrious washerwoman into trouble in this Burmese folktale. (Rev: BCCB 12/96; SLJ 1/97) [398.2]

10973 Garland, Sherry. *Children of the Dragon: Selected Tales from Vietnam* (3–5). Illus. 2001, Harcourt $18.00 (0-15-224200-7). 64pp. Six tales from Vietnam are introduced by material on the land, its history, and folk traditions. (Rev: BL 7/01; HBG 3/02; SLJ 10/01*) [398.2]

10974 Ginsburg, Mirra. *The Chinese Mirror* (1–3). Illus. by Margot Zemach. 1991, Harcourt paper $6.00 (0-15-217508-3). 26pp. An old folktale from Korea tells of a man who brings home a mirror — unknown to his fellow villagers — from a trip to China. (Rev: BCCB 5/88; BL 4/15/88; SLJ 4/88) [398.2]

10975 Han, Suzanne C. *The Rabbit's Tail: A Story from Korea* (K–3). Illus. by Richard Wehrman. 1999, Holt $15.95 (0-8050-4580-5). 32pp. A charming folktale in which Tiger, through a series of misunderstandings, becomes involved with a rabbit that loses its tail. (Rev: BCCB 6/99; BL 2/15/99; HBG 10/99; SLJ 3/99) [398.2]

10976 Heo, Yumi. *The Green Frogs* (K–3). Illus. 1996, Houghton Mifflin $14.95 (0-395-68378-5). 32pp. Two disobedient frogs decide to honor their mother's last wish in this Korean folktale. (Rev: BCCB 10/96; BL 7/96; HB 11–12/96) [398.2]

10977 Holt, Daniel D., sel. *Tigers, Frogs, and Rice Cakes: A Book of Korean Proverbs* (2–4). Illus. by Soma Han Stickler. 1999, Shen's $15.95 (1-885008-10-4). Each of the 20 Korean proverbs included are given in both English and Korean, with explanations. (Rev: BCCB 5/99; HBG 10/99; SLJ 6/99) [398.2]

10978 O'Brien, Anne S. *The Princess and the Beggar: A Korean Folktale* (K–3). Illus. 1993, Scholastic $14.95 (0-590-46092-7). 32pp. In this Korean folktale, a princess is banished from her father's castle because she refuses to marry a man she doesn't love. (Rev: BCCB 6/93; BL 4/15/93; SLJ 5/93) [398.2]

10979 Park, Janie Jaehyun. *The Tiger and the Dried Persimmon* (K–3). Illus. 2002, Groundwood $15.95 (0-88899-485-0). 32pp. Vibrant artwork accompanies this version of a comic Korean folktale about a tiger who misinterprets a woman's words to her child and ends up terrified of persimmons. (Rev: BL 12/15/02; HBG 3/03) [398.2]

10980 Rose, Naomi. *Tibetan Tales for Little Buddhas* (PS–2). Trans. by Pasang Tenzin. Illus. by author. 2003, Clear Light $16.95 (1-57416-081-8). 63pp. Three traditional folktales are retold In this charming bilingual (English and Tibetan) picture book. (Rev: BL 12/15/04; SLJ 3/05) [398.2]

10981 San Souci, Daniel. *In the Moonlight Mist: A Korean Tale* (PS–3). Illus. by Eujin Kim Neilan. 1999, Boyds Mills $15.95 (1-56397-754-0). 32pp. In this Korean tale, a poor woodcutter saves a deer and, as a reward, is granted his wish to have a wife who loves him. (Rev: BCCB 4/99; BL 3/1/99; HBG 10/99; SLJ 4/99) [398.2]

10982 San Souci, Daniel, retel. *The Rabbit and the Dragon King: Based on a Korean Folk Tale* (1–4).

Illus. by Eujin Kim Neilan. 2002, Boyds Mills $15.95 (1-56397-880-6). San Souci retells with humor and drama the story of the king who rules the ocean, who in this case is convinced that eating a rabbit's heart will cure his ills. (Rev: SLJ 11/02) [398.2]

10983 Seros, Kathleen, adapt. *Sun and Moon: Fairy Tales from Korea* (2–5). Illus. by Norman Sibley and Robert Krause. 1983, Hollym $18.50 (0-930878-25-6). 61pp. A collection of seven stories from Korea. [398.2]

10984 Shah, Idries. *The Man with Bad Manners* (K–3). Illus. by Rose Mary Santiago. 2003, Hoopoe $18.00 (1-883536-30-8). Colorful and simple illustrations lighten this retelling of an Afghani folktale about conflict resolution, now set in the present. (Rev: SLJ 4/04) [398.2]

10985 Yep, Laurence. *The Khan's Daughter* (K–3). Illus. by Jean Tseng and Mou-Sien Tseng. 1997, Scholastic $16.95 (0-590-48389-7). 32pp. A Mongolian folktale in which the hero's most formidable opponent is the khan's daughter. (Rev: BCCB 3/97; BL 2/1/97*; HB 3–4/97; SLJ 2/97*) [398.2]

China

10986 Bouchard, David. *The Great Race* (3–6). Illus. by Zhong-Yang Huang. 1997, Millbrook LB $21.40 (0-7613-0305-7). 32pp. This folktale tells that the order of the animals in the Chinese zodiac was determined by a great race. (Rev: BL 2/1/98; HBG 3/98; SLJ 1/98) [398.2]

10987 Carpenter, F. R. *Tales of a Chinese Grandmother* (5–7). Illus. by Malthe Hasselriis. 1973, Amereon LB $24.95 (0-89190-481-6); Tuttle paper $8.95 (0-8048-1042-7). 293pp. A boy and a girl listen to 30 classic Chinese tales. [398.2]

10988 Casanova, Mary. *The Hunter* (PS–3). Illus. by Ed Young. 2000, Simon & Schuster $16.95 (0-689-82906-X). 32pp. This is a Chinese tale of a simple hunter who is granted the ability to understand the language of animals. He bravely tells his people that a great flood is coming and that he has learned of it from the animals, but he is turned to stone for divulging his secret ability. (Rev: BCCB 11/00*; BL 5/15/00; HBG 10/01; SLJ 8/00) [398.2]

10989 Chen, Debby. *Monkey King Wreaks Havoc in Heaven* (4–6). Illus. by Wenhai Ma. 2001, Pan Asian $16.95 (1-57227-068-3). 36pp. A retelling of a Chinese tale about the sly Monkey King. (Rev: BL 10/15/01) [398.2]

10990 Chin, Yin-lien C., ed. *Traditional Chinese Folktales* (5–8). Illus. by Lu Wang. 1989, East Gate $44.95 (0-87332-507-9). 180pp. This is a collection of 12 Chinese folktales that express a variety of themes and genres from faithful lovers to trickster tales. (Rev: SLJ 8/89) [398.2]

10991 Demi. *The Dragon's Tale and Other Animal Fables of the Chinese Zodiac* (3–6). Illus. 1996, Holt $18.95 (0-8050-3446-3). 26pp. A collection of 12 fables that involve the animals in the Chinese zodiac. (Rev: BCCB 1/97; BL 9/15/96; SLJ 10/96) [398.2]

10992 Demi. *The Empty Pot* (K–2). Illus. by author. 1990, Holt $16.95 (0-8050-1217-6). 32pp. Young Ping finds out that honesty pays when the emperor gives seeds to each child in the kingdom to produce the best flower. (Rev: BL 4/1/90; HB 5–6/90 & 1–2/91; SLJ 7/90) [398.2]

10993 Demi. *The Greatest Treasure* (PS–3). Illus. 1998, Scholastic $16.95 (0-590-31339-8). 32pp. In this retelling of a traditional Chinese folktale, poor peasant Li receives a gift of money from his rich neighbor and his lifestyle changes as he begins to worry about how to care for his newfound wealth. (Rev: BL 8/98*; HBG 3/99; SLJ 9/98) [398.2]

10994 Fu, Shelley, retel. *Ho Yi the Archer and Other Classic Chinese Tales* (4–8). Illus. by Joseph F. Abboreno. 2001, Linnet LB $22.50 (0-208-02487-5). 145pp. This collection of folktales and myths, some of which may be familiar, includes notes, a pronunciation guide, and list of characters. (Rev: BL 7/01; HB 9–10/01; HBG 3/02; SLJ 7/01) [398.2]

10995 Han, Carolyn. *Why Snails Have Shells: Minority and Han Folktales from China* (4–6). Trans. by Jay Han. Illus. 1994, Univ. of Hawaii Pr. $14.95 (0-8248-1505-X). 73pp. Attractive paintings accompany this splendid collection of 20 folktales from China. (Rev: BL 8/94; SLJ 2/05) [398.2]

10996 Heyer, Marilee. *The Weaving of a Dream: A Chinese Folktale* (3–5). Illus. by author. 1989, Puffin paper $5.99 (0-14-050528-8). 32pp. The third of an old widow's sons retrieves her precious brocade, from whence steps the Red Fairy, and all three live happily ever after. (Rev: BL 4/15/86; SLJ 4/86) [398.2]

10997 Hong, Lily T. *Two of Everything: A Chinese Folktale* (K–3). Illus. 1993, Whitman LB $15.95 (0-8075-8157-7). 32pp. Elderly Mr. Haktak finds a magical brass pot in his garden. (Rev: BL 3/15/93*; HB 7–8/93*; SLJ 6/93*) [398.2]

10998 Kendall, Carol, and Li Yao-wen. *Sweet and Sour: Tales from China* (5–7). Illus. 1990, Houghton Mifflin paper $7.95 (0-395-54798-9). 112pp. A choice collection of some enchanting Chinese folktales. [398.2]

10999 Kimmel, Eric A. *The Rooster's Antlers: A Story of the Chinese Zodiac* (PS–3). Illus. by Yong-Sheng Xuan. 1999, Holiday House $16.95 (0-8234-1385-3). This Chinese folktale tells how Rooster gets his revenge when he isn't chosen by the emperor to be part of the Chinese calendar. (Rev: BCCB 10/99; BL 12/15/99; HBG 3/00; SLJ 10/99) [398.2]

11000 Kimmel, Eric A. *Ten Suns: A Chinese Legend* (K–3). Illus. by YongSheng Xuan. 1998, Holiday House $15.95 (0-8234-1317-9). 32pp. When the ten sons (suns) of Di Jun decide that they will no longer make their solitary journeys across the sky each day but instead walk together, their father is afraid the combined heat will destroy the earth. (Rev: BCCB 6/98; BL 5/1/98; HBG 10/98; SLJ 5/98) [398.2]

11001 Krasno, Rena, and Yeng-Fong Chiang. *Cloud Weavers: Ancient Chinese Legends* (2–6). 2003, Pacific View $22.95 (1-881896-26-9). 96pp. Nearly two dozen Chinese stories — legends, tales from Chinese history, and stories from Chinese literature — are introduced with background information and accompanied by Chinese posters from the early 20th century. (Rev: BL 7/03; SLJ 8/03) [398.2]

11002 Lee, Jeanne M. *The Song of Mu Lan* (5–8). Illus. 1995, Front Street $15.95 (1-886910-00-6). 32pp. Mu Lan disguises herself as a boy and joins the emperor's army in this traditional Chinese tale. (Rev: BL 11/15/95; SLJ 12/95) [398.2]

11003 Louie, Ai-Ling, reteller. *Yeh-Shen: A Cinderella Story from China* (2–6). Illus. by Ed Young. 1982, Penguin Putnam $16.99 (0-399-20900-X). 32pp. A Chinese story about a poor girl living with her cruel stepmother and stepsisters. [398.2]

11004 Mahy, Margaret. *The Seven Chinese Brothers* (K–3). Illus. by Jean Tseng. 1992, Scholastic paper $5.99 (0-590-42057-7). 40pp. Each of seven Chinese brothers has an amazing gift, used to help one another. (Rev: BCCB 7–8/90; BL 4/1/90; HB 7–8/90; SLJ 3/90*) [398.2]

11005 Mosel, Arlene. *Tikki Tikki Tembo* (K–2). Illus. by Blair Lent. 1968, Holt $16.95 (0-8050-0662-1); paper $6.95 (0-8050-1166-8). 32pp. Explains why the Chinese no longer honor their firstborn with an unusually long name. [398.2]

11006 *The Painted Wall and Other Strange Tales* (4–7). Ed. by Michael Bedard. 2003, Tundra $16.95 (0-88776-652-8). 120pp. Chinese folktales collected centuries ago are full of action and the supernatural. (Rev: BL 1/1–15/04; HBG 4/04; SLJ 1/04) [398.2]

11007 Poole, Amy Lowry. *How the Rooster Got His Crown* (K–3). Illus. 1999, Holiday House $15.95 (0-8234-1389-6). 32pp. A little rooster persuades a sun to leave its cave and is rewarded with a crown in this Chinese pourquoi tale. (Rev: BL 4/15/99; HB 5–6/99; HBG 10/99; SLJ 5/99) [398.2]

11008 Sanfield, Steve. *Just Rewards, or Who Is That Man in the Moon and What's He Doing Up There Anyway?* (PS–3). Illus. by Emily Lisker. 1996, Orchard LB $15.99 (0-531-08885-5). 32pp. The origin of the belief that there is a man in the moon is retold in this Chinese folktale. (Rev: BL 10/1/96; HB 11–12/96; SLJ 9/96*) [398.2]

11009 Shepard, Aaron. *Lady White Snake: A Tale from Chinese Opera* (4–6). Illus. by Song Nan Zhang. 2001, Pan Asian $16.95 (1-57227-072-1). 30pp. A lavishly illustrated story from Chinese opera about a snake that turns into a beautiful woman. (Rev: BL 10/15/01; SLJ 3/02) [398.2]

11010 Te Loo, Sanne. *Ping-Li's Kite* (PS–1). Illus. 2002, Front Street $15.95 (1-886910-75-8). 32pp. A young Chinese boy angers the Emperor of the Sky when he flies an undecorated kite in this book based on a Chinese folktale. (Rev: BL 8/02; HBG 10/02; SLJ 5/02) [398.2]

11011 Tseng, Grace. *White Tiger, Blue Serpent* (K–3). Illus. by Jean Tseng and Mou-Sien Tseng. 1999, Lothrop $16.00 (0-688-12515-8). 32pp. A Chinese folktale in which a young peasant, Kai, faces many dangers while journeying to the palace of the goddess Qin to retrieve a silk brocade. (Rev: BL 8/99; HBG 10/99; SLJ 7/99) [398.2]

11012 Wang, Rosalind C. *The Magical Starfruit Tree: A Chinese Folktale* (K–2). Illus. by Shao Wei

Liu. 1994, Beyond Words $14.95 (0-941831-89-2). 30pp. In this Chinese tale, a stranger rewards a young acrobat for his kindness and punishes a miser for his nastiness. (Rev: BL 7/94; HB 1–2/05; SLJ 2/05) [398.2]

11013 Wang, Rosalind C. *The Treasure Chest: A Chinese Tale* (PS–3). Illus. by Will Hillenbrand. 1995, Holiday House LB $15.95 (0-8234-1114-1). 32pp. In this Chinese tale, a humble peasant gets help from the Ocean King to fight an evil despot. (Rev: BL 6/1–15/95; SLJ 6/95) [398.2]

11014 Xuan, Yong-Sheng. *The Dragon Lover and Other Chinese Proverbs* (K–3). 1999, Shen's $16.95 (1-885008-11-2). 32pp. Illustrated with Chinese paper cuts, this lovely book contains the stories behind five well-known Chinese proverbs. (Rev: BCCB 7–8/99; BL 5/15/99; HBG 10/99; SLJ 8/99) [398.2]

11015 Ye, Ting-xing. *Three Monks, No Water* (K–3). Illus. by Harvey Chan. 1997, Annick LB $16.95 (1-55037-443-5); paper $6.95 (1-55037-442-7). 32pp. This story supposedly explains the origin of the Chinese expression "Three monks, no water," which is used when children try to avoid chores. (Rev: BL 2/1/98; SLJ 12/97) [398.2]

11016 Yep, Laurence. *The Junior Thunder Lord* (K–3). Illus. by Robert Van Nutt. 1994, Troll $15.95 (0-8167-3454-2). 32pp. Yue's chance kindness toward a stranger helps saves his village from drought in this Chinese folktale. (Rev: BCCB 12/94; BL 11/1/94; SLJ 10/94) [398.2]

11017 Yep, Laurence. *The Man Who Tricked a Ghost* (K–3). Illus. by Isadore Seltzer. 1993, Troll $15.95 (0-8167-3030-X). 32pp. In ancient China, a fearless boy encounters a ghost. (Rev: BL 6/1–15/93*) [398.2]

11018 Yep, Laurence. *Tiger Woman* (PS–4). Illus. by Robert Roth. 1995, BridgeWater $15.95 (0-8167-3464-X). In this version of a Shantung folk song, a selfish old woman won't share her food with a beggar. (Rev: SLJ 2/96) [398.2]

11019 Yip, Mingmei. *Chinese Children's Favorite Stories* (3–5). Illus. 2004, Tuttle $16.95 (0-8048-3589-6). 96pp. Thirteen varied stories introduce readers to traditional Chinese characters — dragons, emperors, scholars, and so forth. (Rev: BL 2/1/05; SLJ 3/05) [398.2]

11020 Yolen, Jane. *The Emperor and the Kite* (K–3). Illus. by Ed Young. 1988, Penguin Putnam $16.99 (0-399-21499-2). 32pp. Oriental-like paper cuts illustrate this Chinese legend about the unshakable loyalty of the emperor's smallest daughter. First published in 1967. [398.2]

11021 Young, Ed. *Lon Po Po: A Red-Riding-Hood Story from China* (2–4). Illus. 1989, Penguin Putnam $16.99 (0-399-21619-7). 32pp. In this variation of the Red Riding Hood story, Mother visits Grandmother, leaving her three children in danger from a marauding wolf. Caldecott Medal winner, 1990. (Rev: BCCB 11/89*; BL 11/15/89; HB 1–2/90*; SLJ 12/89*) [398.2]

11022 Young, Ed. *The Sons of the Dragon King: A Chinese Legend* (3–5). Illus. 2004, Simon & Schus-

ter $16.95 (0-689-85184-7). 32pp. This beautifully illustrated Chinese folktale about the Dragon King and his nine sons recounts how the king comes to accept and take advantage of his sons' unique talents and abilities. (Rev: BL 5/15/04; SLJ 6/04) [398.2]

11023 Zhang, Song Nan. *A Time of Golden Dragons* (3–6). Illus. 2000, Tundra LB $16.95 (0-88776-506-8). 24pp. This is a collection of dragon lore from China that includes material and stories about the dragon's origin, dragon homes, dragon boat races, and other bits of dragon information. (Rev: BL 11/1/00; HBG 10/01; SLJ 10/00) [398.2]

India

11024 Arenson, Roberta. *Manu and the Talking Fish* (PS–3). Illus. 2000, Barefoot $15.95 (1-84148-032-0). 32pp. This Indian variation on the Noah story tells of Manu, a prince, who rescues a fish. When the fish grows up, he warns Manu of an impending flood that will destroy the world. (Rev: BL 4/1/00; SLJ 6/00) [398.2]

11025 Bateson-Hill, Margaret. *Chanda and the Mirror of Moonlight* (3–4). Illus. by Karin Littlewood. 2001, Zero to Ten $17.95 (1-84089-217-X). An evil stepmother tries to trick the prince into marrying her daughter instead of Chanda, but the mirror reveals the truth. (Rev: SLJ 5/02) [398.2]

11026 Beach, Milo Cleveland. *The Adventures of Rama* (4–6). Illus. 1983, Smithsonian Institution $15.00 (0-934686-51-3). 64pp. Tales from the Hindu epic Ramayana. (Rev: SLJ 2/05) [398.2]

11027 Birch, David. *The King's Chessboard* (3–5). Illus. by Devis Grebu. 1988, Puffin paper $6.99 (0-14-054880-7). 32pp. A wise man outsmarts a vain king when he is offered a reward. (Rev: BL 5/15/88; SLJ 4/88) [398.2]

11028 Conover, Sarah, ed. *Kindness: A Treasury of Buddhist Wisdom for Children and Parents* (4–7). Illus. 2001, Eastern Washington Univ. paper $19.95 (0-910055-67-X). 164pp. Thirty-one stories related to Buddhism, including Jataka tales about the Buddha's incarnations, have been effectively translated and adapted for this anthology. (Rev: BL 2/15/01; SLJ 3/01) [294.3]

11029 Demi. *One Grain of Rice* (3–6). Illus. 1997, Scholastic $19.95 (0-590-93998-X). 40pp. Rani outwits the rajah to gain food for her people in this Indian folktale. (Rev: BCCB 2/97; BL 3/1/97*; SLJ 3/97*) [398.2]

11030 Ernst, Judith, reteller. *The Golden Goose King: A Tale Told by the Buddha* (3–6). Illus. by Judith Ernst. 1995, Parvardigar $19.95 (0-9644362-0-5). A Jataka tale about a queen who captures the Golden Goose King, who is actually Buddha. (Rev: BL 9/1/95; SLJ 9/95) [398.2]

11031 French, Fiona, reteller. *Jamil's Clever Cat: A Folk Tale from Bengal* (PS–2). Illus. by Fiona French and Dick Newby. 1999, Star Bright $13.95 (1-887734-72-4). In this tale from Bengal, a cat helps his master gain riches and a bride. (Rev: SLJ 3/00) [398.2]

11032 Galdone, Paul. *The Monkey and the Crocodile: A Jataka Tale from India* (K–3). Illus. by author. 1969, Houghton Mifflin paper $6.95 (0-89919-524-5). 32pp. A crocodile decides he will catch a monkey. [398.2]

11033 *Heart of Gold* (2–4). Illus. by Rosalyn White. 1989, Dharma paper $7.95 (0-89800-193-5). In this retelling of a Jataka story, a wealthy man gives away all his possessions. Another Jataka story is *The Rabbit in the Moon* (1989). (Rev: BL 8/89) [294.3]

11034 Jacobs, Joseph. *Indian Fairy Tales* (3–6). Illus. by John D. Batten. 1969, Dover paper $9.95 (0-486-21828-7). 255pp. A standard collection by the well-known authority. [398.2]

11035 Jaffrey, Madhur. *Seasons of Splendor: Tales, Myths, and Legends from India* (5–8). Illus. by Michael Foreman. 1985, Puffin paper $7.95 (0-317-62172-6). 128pp. Folktales and family stories as well as accounts of Rama and Krishna. (Rev: BCCB 1/86; BL 1/15/86) [398.2]

11036 Jendresen, Erik, and Joshua M. Greene, retellers. *Hanuman: Based on Valmiki's Ramayana* (3–6). Illus. by Li Ming. 1998, Tricycle $15.95 (1-883672-78-3). A retelling of the section of the Ramayana in which the monkey clan under Hanuman helps Rama rescue his wife Sita. (Rev: BCCB 3/99; HBG 10/99; SLJ 11/98) [398.2]

11037 Krishnaswami, Uma, reteller. *Shower of Gold: Girls and Women in the Stories of India* (5–9). Illus. by Maniam Selven. 1999, Linnet LB $19.95 (0-208-02484-0). 125pp. All of the enchanting tales in this fine collection of Indian folklore feature wise and powerful women. (Rev: BCCB 5/99; HBG 3/00; SLJ 8/99) [398.2]

11038 Lee, Jeanne M. *I Once Was a Monkey: Stories Buddha Told* (2–4). Illus. 1999, Farrar $16.00 (0-374-33548-6). 40pp. This handsome volume contains six *Jatakas* or birth stories from the Buddhist faith. (Rev: BCCB 4/99; BL 3/15/99; HBG 10/99; SLJ 3/99) [294.3]

11039 Martin, Rafe. *The Brave Little Parrot* (K–3). Illus. by Susan Gaber. 1998, Penguin Putnam $15.99 (0-399-22825-X). 32pp. As a reward for trying to put out a forest fire, a little parrot is given colored plumage in this Indian jataka tale. (Rev: BCCB 3/98; BL 2/15/98; SLJ 5/98) [298.2]

11040 Martin, Rafe. *Foolish Rabbit's Big Mistake* (PS–2). Illus. by Ed Young. 1985, Penguin Putnam $16.99 (0-399-21178-0). 32pp. A tale from India reminiscent of Chicken Little, about a little rabbit who fears the end of the world and tells everyone that the earth is breaking up. A Jataka tale. (Rev: BCCB 12/85; BL 12/15/85; HB 3–4/86; SLJ 2/05) [398.2]

11041 Moseley, James. *The Ninth Jewel of the Mughal Crown: The Birbal Tales from the Oral Traditions of India* (3–6). Illus. 2001, Summerwind $24.95 (0-9704447-1-0). 154pp. A collection of stories from India that involve the 14th-century Emperor Akbar and his clever and amusing adviser Birbal. (Rev: BL 7/01; SLJ 10/01) [398.2]

11042 Ness, Caroline. *The Ocean of Story: Fairy Tales from India* (4–6). Illus. 1996, Lothrop $17.00 (0-688-13584-6). 128pp. Eighteen fairy tales from India that have been collected from unusual and often obscure source materials. (Rev: BCCB 5/96; BL 4/15/96; SLJ 4/96) [398.2]

11043 Rao, Sandhya, reteller. *And Land Was Born* (1–4). Illus. by Uma Krishnaswamy. Series: Visual Expressions. 1999, Banyan Tree $19.99 (81-86895-13-2). A delightful creation story from central India that tells how a tortoise helps produce land in a world where only water existed. (Rev: SLJ 7/99) [398.2]

11044 Shepard, Aaron, reteller. *Savitri: A Tale of Ancient India* (3–6). Illus. by Vera Rosenberry. 1992, Whitman LB $16.95 (0-8075-7251-9). 40pp. In picture-book format, the retelling of India's epic poem, the Mahabharata. (Rev: BCCB 3/92; BL 3/15/92; SLJ 5/92) [398.2]

11045 So, Meilo. *Gobble, Gobble, Slip, Slop: A Tale of a Very Greedy Cat* (K–2). Illus. 2004, Knopf $15.95 (0-375-82504-5). 32pp. An Indian tale in which a hungry cat swallows everything in its path until two crabs make a hole in its stomach and let all the people and animals out. (Rev: BL 3/15/04; SLJ 2/04) [398.2]

11046 Thornhill, Jan. *The Rumor: A Jataka Tale from India* (PS–2). Illus. 2002, Maple Tree $17.95 (1-894379-39-X). 32pp. Lush illustrations accompany this tale from India of an anxious hare who believes the world is breaking apart when she hears a mango fall to the ground. (Rev: BL 12/15/02; SLJ 11/02) [398.254]

11047 Young, Ed. *Seven Blind Mice* (PS–3). Illus. 1992, Penguin Putnam $17.99 (0-399-22261-8). 44pp. A stunning picture book illustrating a version of the old Indian folktale about seven blind men and one elephant. (Rev: BCCB 3/92*; BL 4/1/92*; HB 3–4/92; SLJ 4/92) [398.2]

Japan

11048 Bodkin, Odds. *The Crane Wife* (K–4). Illus. by Gennady Spirin. 1998, Harcourt $16.00 (0-15-201407-1). 32pp. This well-known Japanese folktale tells how a poor sail maker saves a crane who returns as a beautiful maiden whom he marries but later loses when she sacrifices herself to save him. (Rev: BCCB 10/98; BL 11/15/98*; HB 11–12/98; HBG 3/99; SLJ 10/98) [398.2]

11049 Edmonds, I. G. *Ooka the Wise: Tales of Old Japan* (3–6). Illus. by Sanae Yamazaki. 1994, Linnet LB $16.00 (0-208-02379-8). 96pp. A collection of 17 Japanese folktales featuring the legendary judge Ooka Tadasuke, who is devoted to the cause of justice. (Rev: BL 5/15/94) [398.2]

11050 Hamilton, Morse. *Belching Hill* (1–3). Illus. by Forest Rogers. 1997, Greenwillow $15.00 (0-688-14561-2). 32pp. A variation on the Japanese folktale about a little old woman who outsmarts some disgusting monsters. (Rev: BL 4/15/97; SLJ 4/97) [398.2]

11051 Hedlund, Irene. *Mighty Mountain and the Three Strong Women* (PS–3). Trans. by Judith Elkin. Illus. 1990, Volcano $14.95 (0-912078-86-3). 32pp. A sumo wrestler meets three women who surpass him in strength. (Rev: BL 6/1/90; SLJ 10/90) [398.2]

11052 Hodges, Margaret, adapt. *The Boy Who Drew Cats* (K–3). Illus. by Aki Sogabe. 2002, Holiday House $16.95 (0-8234-1594-5). 32pp. A young boy's obsession with drawing cats everywhere he goes eventually changes his life in this tale of the supernatural. (Rev: BCCB 4/02; BL 6/1–15/02; HB 5–6/02; HBG 10/02; SLJ 3/02) [398.2]

11053 Kimmel, Eric A. *The Greatest of All: A Japanese Folktale* (PS–3). Illus. by Giora Carmi. 1991, Holiday House LB $16.95 (0-8234-0885-X). 32pp. The father of Chuko Mouse is not happy when she tells him she wants to marry a humble, but handsome, field mouse. (Rev: BL 10/15/91; SLJ 10/91) [398.2]

11054 Kimmel, Eric A. *Three Samurai Cats: A Story from Japan* (PS–2). Illus. by Mordicai Gerstein. 2003, Holiday House $16.95 (0-8234-1742-5). 32pp. In this colorful adaptation of a Japanese folktale, a feudal lord seeks help from a trio of samurai cats to rid his castle of a bothersome rat. (Rev: BL 4/15/03; HB 7–8/03; HBG 10/03; SLJ 6/03) [398.2]

11055 McCarthy, Ralph F. *The Inch-High Samurai* (K–3). Illus. by Shiro Kasamatsu. 1993, Kodansha $19.95 (4-7700-1758-8). 48pp. Pint-sized Inchy Bo performs some mighty deeds, including fighting an ogre, in this Japanese folktale. (Rev: BL 12/15/93; SLJ 2/94) [398.2]

11056 McCarthy, Ralph F. *The Moon Princess* (3–6). Illus. by Kancho Oda. Series: Children's Classics. 1993, Kodansha $19.95 (4-7700-1756-1). 48pp. Retellings in verse of three Japanese folktales, one about a virtuous old man and his dog, another a Tom Thumb–like character, and another, the title story, about a couple who find a tiny girl inside a bamboo. (Rev: SLJ 2/94) [398.2]

11057 McDermott, Gerald. *The Stonecutter: A Japanese Folk Tale* (K–3). Illus. by author. 1975, Puffin paper $5.99 (0-14-050289-0). 32pp. The familiar tale of the stonecutter who kept demanding greater power is brilliantly illustrated with colorful, stylized collage paintings. [398.2]

11058 Merrill, Jean. *The Girl Who Loved Caterpillars: A Twelfth-Century Tale from Japan* (5–8). Illus. by Floyd Cooper. 1992, Penguin Putnam $16.99 (0-399-21871-8). 32pp. The story of a young Izumi who has no interest in lute playing or writing poetry but is fascinated with "creepy crawlies" instead. (Rev: BCCB 11/92; BL 9/1/92*; SLJ 9/92) [398.2]

11059 Myers, Tim. *Tanuki's Gift: A Japanese Tale* (K–3). Illus. by Robert Roth. 2003, Marshall Cavendish $16.95 (0-7614-5101-3). 32pp. A Japanese folktale of a fond relationship between a Buddhist priest and a magical creature called a tanuki. (Rev: BL 3/15/03; HBG 10/03; SLJ 7/03) [398.2]

11060 Sakade, Florence, ed. *Japanese Children's Favorite Stories* (2–4). Illus. by Yoshio Kurosaki.

1958, Tuttle $16.95 (0-8048-0284-X). 120pp. Twenty folktales traditionally told to Japanese children. [398.2]

11061 Schroeder, Alan. *The Tale of Willie Monroe* (1–3). Illus. by Andrew Glass. 1999, Clarion $15.00 (0-395-69852-9). 32pp. An adaptation of the Japanese folktale that uses a hillbilly hero instead of a Japanese wrestler. (Rev: BCCB 6/99; BL 4/15/99; HB 3–4/99; HBG 10/99; SLJ 6/99) [398.2]

11062 Snyder, Dianne. *The Boy of the Three-Year Nap* (K–3). Illus. by Allen Say. 1988, Houghton Mifflin $16.95 (0-395-44090-4). 32pp. In this Japanese folktale adaptation, Taro, who does nothing but eat and sleep, schemes to marry his rich neighbor's daughter. (Rev: BCCB 4/88; BL 4/1/88; HB 5–6/88) [398.2]

11063 Uchida, Yoshiko. *Magic Listening Cap* (4–6). Illus. by author. 1987, Creative Arts paper $8.95 (0-88739-016-1). 160pp. Japanese folktales retold with charm and simplicity. [398.2]

11064 Wada, Stephanie. *Momotaro and the Island of Ogres* (2–4). Illus. by Kano Naganobu. 2005, George Braziller $21.95 (0-8076-1552-8). 398pp. Silk handscrolls from the 19th century illustrate this retelling of the Japanese legend about a child, born from a peach, who succeeds in defeating threatening ogres. (Rev: BL 5/15/05) [398.2]

11065 Williams, Carol Ann. *Tsubu the Little Snail* (K–3). Illus. by Tatsuro Kiuchi. 1995, Simon & Schuster $15.00 (0-671-87167-6). 24pp. Love transforms a snail into a handsome young man in this Japanese folktale. (Rev: BL 6/1–15/95) [398.2]

Southeast Asia

11066 Coburn, Jewell Reinhart, and Tzexa Cherta Lee, adapt. *Jouanah: A Hmong Cinderella* (K–3). Illus. by Anne S. O'Brien. 1996, Shen's $15.95 (1-885008-01-5). This version of the Cinderella story from the Hmong of Southeast Asia takes place in a peasant village. (Rev: BCCB 12/96; SLJ 3/97) [398.2]

11067 Day, Nancy Raines. *Piecing Earth and Sky Together* (2–4). Illus. by Genna Panzarella. 2001, Shens $17.95 (1-885008-19-8). 32pp. In this creation story from Laos with beautiful illustrations, two heavenly brothers set out to create the sky and the earth. (Rev: BL 4/1/02; HBG 10/02; SLJ 7/02) [398.2]

11068 Lee, Jeanne M., reteller. *Toad Is the Uncle of Heaven: A Vietnamese Folk Tale* (4–7). Illus. by Jeanne M. Lee. 1985, Holt paper $6.95 (0-8050-1147-1). 32pp. This book tells the story of Toad who collects companions on his way to see the King of Heaven, who makes rain. (Rev: BL 11/1/85; HB 3–4/86) [398.2]

11069 MacDonald, Margaret Read, reteller. *The Girl Who Wore Too Much: A Folktale from Thailand* (PS–3). Illus. by Yvonne Davis. 1998, August House $15.95 (0-87483-503-8). In this updated folktale from Thailand, a young girl learns the value of simplicity when she wears all her beautiful dresses to a dance and is so weighted down she can't keep up with her friends. (Rev: HBG 10/98; SLJ 6/98) [398.2]

11070 Mason, Victor, and Gillian Beal, retels. *Balinese Children's Favorite Stories* (1–4). Illus. by Trina Bohan-Tyrie. 2001, Tuttle $16.95 (962-593-440-5). 96pp. Eleven tales from Bali, many of which are about animals, are paired with varied illustrations including detailed Balinese costumes. (Rev: SLJ 5/02) [398.2]

11071 Meeker, Clare Hodgson. *A Tale of Two Rice Birds: A Folktale from Thailand* (4–8). Illus. by Christine Lamb. 1994, Sasquatch $14.95 (1-57061-008-8). 32pp. Two rice birds are reincarnated as a princess and a farmer's son in this Thai folktale. (Rev: BL 1/15/95; SLJ 11/94) [398.2]

11072 Shepard, Aaron. *The Crystal Heart: A Vietnamese Legend* (K–3). Illus. by Joseph Daniel Fiedler. 1998, Simon & Schuster $16.00 (0-689-81551-4). 32pp. In this Vietnamese folktale, Mi Nuong's rejection of a suitor causes his death; however, her tears set his spirit free. (Rev: BCCB 7–8/98; BL 10/1/98; HBG 3/99; SLJ 11/98) [398.2]

11073 Souhami, Jessica. *No Dinner! The Story of the Old Woman and the Pumpkin* (PS–1). Illus. 2000, Marshall Cavendish $15.95 (0-7614-5059-9). 32pp. In this South Asian folktale, Grandma outwits a wolf, a tiger, and a bear on her way to and from visiting her granddaughter in the forest. (Rev: BCCB 3/00; BL 3/1/00; HBG 10/00; SLJ 4/00) [823.914]

11074 Vuong, Lynette Dyer. *The Brocaded Slipper and Other Vietnamese Tales* (5–7). Illus. by Vo-Dinh Mai. 1982, HarperCollins paper $4.95 (0-06-440440-4). 96pp. Five Vietnamese fairy tales, some of which are similar to our own. [398.2]

11075 Weitzman, David. *Rama and Sita: A Tale from Ancient Java* (1–3). Illus. 2002, Godine $19.95 (1-56792-151-5). 32pp. A retelling of the story *The Ramayana*, in the style of Javanese shadow puppetry. (Rev: BL 2/15/03; HBG 10/03; SLJ 6/03) [398.2]

11076 Xiong, Blia. *Nine-in-One, Grr! Grr!* (3–6). Adapted by Cathy Spagnoli. Illus. by Nancy Hom. 1993, Children's Book Pr. $14.95 (0-89239-048-4); paper $7.95 (0-89239-110-3). 32pp. In this folktale from Laos, Bird comes up with a trick to prevent the earth from being overpopulated with tigers. A reissue. [398.2]

Australia and the Pacific Islands

11077 Galdone, Paul. *The Turtle and the Monkey: A Philippine Tale* (K–2). Illus. by author. 1990, Houghton Mifflin paper $6.95 (0-395-54425-4). 32pp. Turtle asks monkey to help him save a banana tree. [398.2]

11078 Gittins, Anne. *Tales from the South Pacific Islands* (4–6). Illus. by Frank Rocca. 1977, Stemmer $12.95 (0-916144-02-X). 96pp. Twenty-two folktales from such places as Fiji and Samoa in which the sea and its creatures play prominent roles. [398.3]

11079 Morin, Paul. *Animal Dreaming: An Aboriginal Dreamtime Story* (3–6). Illus. by author. 1998, Harcourt $16.00 (0-15-200054-2). A folktale from Australia that tells how three animals — a kangaroo, a turtle, and an emu — try to bring peace to a warring world. (Rev: HBG 10/98; SLJ 3/98) [398.2]

11080 Romulo, Liana. *Filipino Children's Favorite Stories* (3–6). Illus. 2001, Periplus $16.95 (962-593-765-X). 96pp. This is an engaging collection of 14 traditional myths and folktales from the Philippines. (Rev: BL 4/1/01; HBG 3/02; SLJ 11/01) [398.2]

11081 Wolfson, Margaret O. *Turtle Songs: A Tale for Mothers and Daughters* (K–3). Illus. by Karla Sachi. 1999, Beyond Words $15.95 (1-885223-95-1). 32pp. Set on a Fijian island, this folktale tells how an island princess and her daughter were turned into sea turtles. (Rev: BL 8/99; HBG 3/00; SLJ 7/99) [398.2]

11082 Wolkstein, Diane. *Sun Mother Wakes the World: An Australian Creation Story* (PS–2). Illus. by Bronwyn Bancroft. 2004, HarperCollins $15.99 (0-688-13915-9). 32pp. This colorfully illustrated retelling of an aboriginal folktale offers an appealing explanation of the Earth's creation. (Rev: BL 4/15/04; SLJ 4/04) [398.2]

Europe

Central and Eastern Europe

11083 Bodnar, Judit Z. *A Wagonload of Fish* (PS–2). Illus. by Alexi Natchev. 1996, Lothrop LB $14.93 (0-688-12173-X). 32pp. In this Hungarian folktale, a nagging wife demands that her husband bring her some fish to eat. (Rev: BL 4/1/96; SLJ 5/96) [398.21]

11084 Brett, Jan. *The Mitten* (PS–2). Illus. 1990, Penguin Putnam $16.99 (0-399-21920-X). In this Ukrainian folktale, Nicki loses in the snow one of the mittens that his grandmother knit him. (Rev: BCCB 12/89; BL 9/15/89*; HB 11–12/89; SLJ 11/89) [398.2]

11085 Gorbachev, Valeri. *Fool of the World and the Flying Ship* (1–3). Illus. by author. 1998, Star Bright $15.95 (1-887734-19-8). 40pp. A new adaptation of the Ukrainian tale about a tsar who promises his daughter in marriage to the man who brings him a flying ship. (Rev: SLJ 4/99) [398.2]

11086 Hogrogian, Nonny. *One Fine Day* (K–3). Illus. by author. 1971, Macmillan $16.00 (0-02-744000-1); paper $5.99 (0-02-043620-3). 32pp. Based on an Armenian folktale, this cumulative story is ideal for reading aloud. Caldecott Medal winner, 1972. [398.2]

11087 Kimmel, Eric A. *The Castle of Cats: A Story from Ukraine* (PS–2). Retold by Eric A. Kimmel. Illus. by Katya Krenina. 2004, Holiday House $16.95 (0-8234-1565-1). 32pp. A farmer tests the mettle of his three sons by sending them on a mission in this story based on a Latvian folktale. (Rev: BL 10/15/04; SLJ 11/04)

11088 Kimmel, Eric A. *Sirko and the Wolf* (K–3). Illus. by Robert Sauber. 1997, Holiday House LB

$15.95 (0-8234-1257-1). 32pp. When a dog grows too old to be useful, he strikes a bargain with a wolf in this Ukrainian folktale. (Rev: BL 9/15/97; HBG 3/98; SLJ 11/97) [398.2]

11089 Kushner, Tony. *Brundibar* (1–4). Illus. by Maurice Sendak. 2003, Hyperion $19.95 (0-7868-0904-3). 56pp. This poignant story, based on a Czech opera originally performed by children at a concentration camp, tells how two children, Pepecik and Anniku, struggle to get milk for their sick mother. (Rev: BL 11/15/03; HBG 4/04; SLJ 12/03)

11090 Larson, Jean Russell. *The Fish Bride and Other Gypsy Tales* (4–6). Illus. 2000, Linnet $22.50 (0-208-02474-3). 90pp. Sixteen tales of romance, adventure, and humor from the rich traditions of Rom or Gypsies are attractively retold in this entertaining collection. (Rev: BL 11/1/00; HB 11–12/00; HBG 3/01; SLJ 9/00) [398.2]

11091 Lottridge, Celia Barker. *The Little Rooster and the Diamond Button* (K–3). Illus. by Joanne Fitzgerald. 2001, Douglas & McIntyre $16.95 (0-88899-443-5). 32pp. A retelling of a traditional Hungarian folktale about a rooster whose tenacity earns him a reward. (Rev: BL 9/1/01; HBG 3/02; SLJ 1/02) [398.2]

11092 Marshall, Bonnie C., retel. *Tales from the Heart of the Balkans* (3–5). Illus. Series: World Folklore. 2001, Libraries Unlimited $29.00 (1-56308-870-3). 166pp. Marshall retells folk and fairy tales from the region, preceded by historical and cultural information. (Rev: SLJ 2/02) [398.2]

11093 Molnar, Irma. *One-Time Dog Market at Buda and Other Hungarian Folktales* (5–8). Illus. by Georgeta-Elena Enesel. 2001, Linnet $25.00 (0-208-02505-7). 160pp. A collection of 23 clever, thought-provoking Hungarian folktales for older readers. (Rev: BL 1/1–15/02; HBG 3/02; SLJ 2/02) [398.2]

11094 Philip, Neil. *Noah and the Devil* (PS–3). Illus. by Isabelle Brent. 2001, Clarion $16.00 (0-618-11754-7). 32pp. The devil makes trouble aboard the ark in this retelling of the Bible story. (Rev: BL 10/1/01; HBG 3/02; SLJ 8/01) [398.2]

11095 Rascol, Sabina I. *The Impudent Rooster* (PS–2). Illus. by Holly Berry. 2004, Dutton $17.99 (0-525-47179-0). 32pp. A rooster foils the attempts of a greedy nobleman to steal a coin-filled purse intended for the rooster's master in this adaptation of a Romanian folktale. (Rev: BL 2/15/04; HB 5–6/04; SLJ 4/04) [398.2]

11096 San Souci, Robert D., reteller. *A Weave of Words* (2–5). Illus. by Raul Colon. 1998, Orchard LB $17.99 (0-531-33053-2). In this Armenian tale, an imprisoned king uses his weaving skills to communicate with his wife. (Rev: BCCB 4/98; HBG 10/98; SLJ 3/98) [398.2]

11097 Tresselt, Alvin, ed. *The Mitten* (K–2). Illus. by Yaroslava Mills. 1964, Lothrop LB $14.93 (0-688-51053-1); paper $5.95 (0-688-09238-1). 30pp. An old Ukrainian folktale about a little boy and his lost mitten. [398.2]

11098 Weber, Ilse. *Mendel Rosenbusch: Tales for Jewish Children* (3–6). Trans. from German by Ruth Fisher and Hans Fisher. 2001, Herodias $14.00

(1-928746-19-5). 102pp. A collection of Czech tales about a poor but wise man who lives behind a synagogue and is visited one night by an angel who gives him a gift — the ability to become invisible. (Rev: HBG 3/02; SLJ 11/01) [398.2]

France

11099 Brett, Jan, reteller. *Beauty and the Beast* (PS–3). Illus. 1989, Houghton Mifflin $16.00 (0-89919-497-4). 32pp. A smooth, brief retelling of the old classic. (Rev: BCCB 12/89; BL 10/1/89; SLJ 11/89) [398.2]

11100 Brown, Marcia. *Stone Soup* (1–4). Illus. by author. 1979, Macmillan $16.00 (0-684-92296-7); paper $5.99 (0-689-71103-4). 48pp. An old French tale about three soldiers who make soup from stones. [398.2]

11101 Defelice, Cynthia, and Mary DeMarsh. *Three Perfect Peaches* (K–2). Illus. by Irene Trivas. 1995, Orchard LB $16.99 (0-531-08722-0). 32pp. In this French folktale, a young farmboy claims the hand of a princess he helped save from death. (Rev: BCCB 4/95; BL 1/15/95; SLJ 4/95) [398.2]

11102 Forest, Heather. *Stone Soup* (PS–3). Illus. by Susan Gaber. 1998, August House $15.95 (0-87483-498-8). 32pp. Using a contemporary village as its setting, this is a handsome retelling of the ancient tale that originated in France and, in a different version, Sweden. (Rev: BL 9/1/98; HBG 10/98; SLJ 5/98) [398.2]

11103 Gershator, David, and Phyllis Gershator. *Kallaloo! A Caribbean Tale* (PS–3). Illus. by Diane Greenseid. 2005, Marshall Cavendish $16.95 (0-7614-5110-2). A hungry grandmother decides to make soup from a shell, and the curious neighbors contribute various ingredients in this West Indian version of "Stone Soup." (Rev: SLJ 6/05) [398.2]

11104 Huck, Charlotte. *Toads and Diamonds* (K–3). Illus. by Anita Lobel. 1996, Greenwillow $15.89 (0-688-13681-8). 32pp. A downtrodden girl is rewarded for her kindness in this retelling of a folktale. (Rev: BCCB 1/97; BL 11/1/96*; HB 11–12/96; SLJ 9/96) [398.2]

11105 Huling, Jan. *Puss in Cowboy Boots* (PS–2). Illus. by Phil Huling. 2002, Simon & Schuster $16.00 (0-689-83119-6). 40pp. The classic cat tale with a Texas twist. (Rev: BCCB 10/02; BL 8/02; HB 7–8/02; HBG 10/02; SLJ 6/02) [398.2]

11106 Kimmel, Eric A. *Three Sacks of Truth: A Story from France* (PS–3). Illus. by Robert Rayevsky. 1993, Holiday House LB $15.95 (0-8234-0921-X). 32pp. In this French folktale, a king promises his daughter to the man who can bring him the perfect peach. (Rev: BCCB 7–8/93; BL 4/15/93; SLJ 7/93) [398.2]

11107 McGovern, Ann, adapt. *Stone Soup* (PS–1). Illus. by Winslow Pels. 1986, Scholastic paper $3.25 (0-590-41602-2). 32pp. The old story of the young man who asks for food and is refused by the old woman, then he asks her for a stone. (Rev: BCCB 2/87; BL 10/15/86; SLJ 11/86) [398.2]

11108 Mayer, Marianna. *Beauty and the Beast* (3–5). Illus. by author. 1987, Simon & Schuster paper $6.95 (0-689-71151-4). 48pp. A fine retelling made memorable by dazzling pictures. Another version is: *Beauty and the Beast* by Deborah Apy, illus. by Michael Hague (1995, Henry Holt). [398.2]

11109 Muth, Jon J. *Stone Soup* (K–2). Illus. 2003, Scholastic $16.95 (0-439-33909-X). 32pp. In this version of the traditional tale, Buddhist monks want Chinese villagers to learn the joy of sharing, and as contributions come into the soup pot and the mix richens, so do the colors of the lush illustrations. (Rev: BCCB 3/03; BL 1/1–15/03; HB 3–4/03; HBG 10/03; SLJ 3/03) [398.2]

11110 Perrault, Charles. *The Complete Fairy Tales of Charles Perrault* (4–6). Trans. by Neil Philip and Nicoletta Simborowski. Illus. by Sally Holmes. 1993, Clarion $24.00 (0-395-57002-6). 156pp. Eleven tales by Perrault, newly translated and illustrated with watercolors and printed with fine historical notes. (Rev: BL 11/1/93; SLJ 9/93) [398]

11111 Perrault, Charles. *Perrault's Fairy Tales* (4–6). Illus. by Gustave Dore. 1969, Dover paper $7.95 (0-486-22311-6). 117pp. A classic edition with illustrations by the French master. [398.2]

11112 Perrault, Charles. *Puss in Boots* (K–3). Illus. by Paul Galdone. 1983, Houghton Mifflin paper $6.95 (0-89919-192-4). 32pp. A favorite French folktale. [398.2]

11113 Perrault, Charles. *Puss in Boots* (K–4). Illus. by Fred Marcellino. 1990, Farrar $16.00 (0-374-36160-6). 32pp. A handsomely illustrated version of this classic tale. (Rev: BCCB 12/90; BL 12/1/90*; HB 3–4/91*; SLJ 1/91) [398.2]

11114 Perrault, Charles. *Puss in Boots* (K–2). Trans. by Anthea Bell. Illus. by Giuliano Lunelli. 1999, North-South LB $15.88 (0-7358-1159-8). 25pp. A lively retelling of Perrault's tale of a son who inherits a mere cat, not realizing how resourceful that feline will be. (Rev: BL 11/1/99; HBG 3/00; SLJ 12/99) [398.2]

11115 Pullman, Philip. *Puss in Boots: The Adventures of That Most Enterprising Feline* (PS–3). Illus. by Ian Beck. 2001, Knopf $16.95 (0-375-81354-3). 32pp. Pullman's version adds a few new characters and a couple of mysteries to be solved. (Rev: BCCB 5/02; BL 7/01; HBG 3/02; SLJ 8/01) [398.2]

11116 Watts, Bernadette. *The Rich Man and the Shoemaker: A Fable by La Fontaine* (2–4). Illus. 2002, North-South LB $16.50 (0-7358-4676-X). 32pp. A Renaissance setting graces this tale of the shoemaker who returns a bribe when the gold causes him anxiety. (Rev: BL 10/1/02; HBG 3/03) [398.2]

Germany

11117 Aiken, Joan. *Snow White and the Seven Dwarfs* (PS–2). Illus. by Belinda Downes. 2002, DK $15.99 (0-7894-8799-3). 48pp. The magic mirror, the dark forest, and the lovely but evil queen are beautifully depicted in embroidered artwork, and the sly, fluid text adds new enjoyment to the classic

fairy tale. (Rev: BCCB 1/03; BL 1/1–15/03; HBG 3/03) [398.2]

11118 Andreasen, Dan. *Rose Red and the Bear Prince* (PS–1). Illus. 2000, HarperCollins LB $16.89 (0-06-027967-2). 40pp. In this version of the Brothers Grimm tale, Rose Red helps a wandering bear to break the enchantment that has turned him from a prince to this animal. (Rev: BL 1/1–15/00; HBG 10/00; SLJ 2/00) [398.2]

11119 Artell, Mike. *Petite Rouge: A Cajun Red Riding Hood* (PS–2). Illus. by Jim Harris. 2001, Dial $15.99 (0-8037-2514-0). 32pp. The wolf becomes an alligator and the little girl a duck in this Louisiana version of the classic tale. (Rev: BL 7/01; HBG 10/01; SLJ 6/01) [398.2]

11120 Babbitt, Natalie. *Ouch!* (2–4). Illus. by Fred Marcellino. 1998, HarperCollins $14.95 (0-06-205066-4). 32pp. In this retelling of a Grimm Brothers story, a king sets a baby boy afloat in a river after he hears a prediction that the baby will eventually marry his daughter. (Rev: BL 11/15/98; HB 1–2/99; HBG 3/99; SLJ 12/98) [398.2]

11121 Bateman, Teresa. *The Princesses Have a Ball* (K–3). Illus. by Lynne W. Cravath. 2002, Whitman $15.95 (0-8075-6626-8). 32pp. A suspicious king asks detectives to find out what his girls are up to, but a cobbler finds the answer first and advises the young ladies to reveal their athletic skills in this basketball version of "The Twelve Dancing Princesses." (Rev: BL 11/1/02; HB 1–2/03; HBG 3/03; SLJ 12/02) [398.2]

11122 Carter, David, and Noelle Carter. *The Nutcracker* (4–6). Illus. 2000, Simon & Schuster $19.95 (0-689-83285-0). A pop-up version of the E. T. A. Hoffman classic story. (Rev: BL 12/1/00) [398.2]

11123 de la Mare, Walter. *The Turnip* (1–4). Illus. by Kevin Hawkes. 1992, Godine $18.95 (0-87923-934-4). 32pp. Based on a Grimm brothers tale, the story of a good but poor man with an enormous turnip and his greedy, rich half-brother. (Rev: BL 11/15/92; HB 1–2/93; SLJ 12/92) [398.2]

11124 Dugina, Olga, and Andrej Dugin. *The Brave Little Tailor* (PS–3). Illus. 2000, Abrams $15.95 (0-8109-4113-9). 32pp. The classic tale from the Brothers Grimm about the little tailor that kills seven flies with one blow and, as a result, becomes king, is handsomely retold. (Rev: BL 12/1/00; HBG 3/01; SLJ 11/00) [398.2]

11125 Eisner, Will. *The Princess and the Frog: By the Grimm Brothers* (4–7). Illus. 1999, NBM $15.95 (1-56163-244-9). 32pp. A retelling of the familiar fairy tale in graphic-novel style. (Rev: BL 12/15/99; HBG 3/00) [398.2]

11126 Evetts-Secker, Josephine. *Little Red Riding Hood* (PS–2). Illus. by Nicoletta Ceccoli. 2004, Barefoot $16.99 (1-84148-621-3). 32pp. Nicoletta Ceccoli's stunning artwork enlivens this child-friendly retelling. (Rev: BL 3/15/04; SLJ 8/04) [389.2]

11127 Foreman, Michael. *Rock-A-Doodle-Do!* (K–2). Illus. 2000, Andersen $16.95 (0-86264-951-X). 32pp. This entertaining version of *The Bremen*

Town Musicians takes place in the American Southwest in the 1950s. (Rev: BL 3/1/01)

11128 Grimm Brothers. *The Complete Grimm's Fairy Tales* (4–6). Illus. by Josef Scharl. 1974, Pantheon paper $18.00 (0-394-70930-6). Based on Margaret Hunt's translation, this has become the standard edition of these perennial favorites. [398.2]

11129 Grimm Brothers. *The Elves and the Shoemaker* (PS–K). Retold and illus. by Paul Galdone. 1984, Houghton Mifflin paper $6.95 (0-89919-422-2). 32pp. A poor shoemaker is visited by elves at night. [398.2]

11130 Grimm Brothers. *Household Stories of the Brothers Grimm* (4–7). Illus. by Walter Crane. 1963, Dover paper $8.95 (0-486-21080-4). 269pp. First published in the United States in 1883. [398.2]

11131 Grimm Brothers. *Little Red Riding Hood / Caperucita roja: A Bilingual Book* (K–2). Trans. by James Surges. Illus. by Pau Estrada. 1999, Chronicle $12.95 (0-8118-2561-2); paper $6.95 (0-8118-2562-0). A bilingual version of the favorite folktale with charming yet scary illustrations. (Rev: SLJ 2/00) [398.2]

11132 Grimm Brothers. *Rumpelstiltskin* (PS–1). Illus. by Paul Galdone. 1985, Houghton Mifflin $16.00 (0-89919-266-1); paper $6.95 (0-395-52599-3). 32pp. Bold drawings highlight this straightfoward version of the little man who spins straw into gold. Another fine edition is: Illus. by John Wallner (1984, Prentice). (Rev: BL 6/1/ 5; SLJ 8/85) [398.2]

11133 Grimm Brothers. *Rumpelstiltskin* (PS–2). Retold and illus. by Paul O. Zelinsky. 1986, Dutton $16.99 (0-525-44265-0). 40pp. Closeups and much detail in the illustrations highlight the retelling of this old favorite. (Rev: BCCB 10/86; BL 9/1/86; SLJ 10/86) [398.2]

11134 Grimm Brothers. *The Shoemaker and the Elves* (K–2). Illus. by Adrienne Adams. 1982, Evanescent $60.00 (0-945303-04-1). 16pp. A favorite German tale illustrated with soft watercolors. [398.2]

11135 Grimm Brothers. *The Shoemaker and the Elves* (K–2). Retold and illus. by Ilse Plume. 1991, Harcourt $14.95 (0-15-274050-3). This folktale is relocated to Renaissance Italy, but the plot is the same except that the elves now number four. (Rev: SLJ 1/92) [398.2]

11136 Grimm Brothers. *The Three Feathers* (5–8). Illus. by Eleonore Schmid. 1984, Creative Editions LB $13.95 (0-87191-941-9). 32pp. A version for older readers that is faithful to the original. [398.2]

11137 Grimm Brothers. *The Three Languages* (3–5). Illus. by Ivan Chermayeff. 1984, Creative Ed. LB $13.95 (0-87191-940-0). 32pp. The tale of the seemingly foolish son who ends up as Pope of Rome. [398.2]

11138 Grimm Brothers. *The Water of Life: A Tale from the Brothers Grimm* (PS–3). Retold by Barbara Rogasky. Illus. by Trina S. Hyman. 1986, Holiday House LB $15.95 (0-8234-0552-4). 40pp. Three brothers journey to find the water of life for their

ailing father. (Rev: BCCB 11/86; BL 9/15/86; HB 3–4/87) [398.2]

11139 Hamilton, Virginia. *The Girl Who Spun Gold* (PS–3). Illus. by Leo Dillon and Diane Dillon. 2000, Scholastic $16.95 (0-590-47378-6). 40pp. Stunning illustrations and stirring prose mark this outstanding retelling of the Rumpelstiltskin folktale using a West Indian setting. (Rev: BCCB 12/00; BL 8/00*; HB 9–10/00; HBG 3/01; SLJ 9/00) [398.2]

11140 Hoberman, Mary Ann. *The Marvelous Mouse Man* (1–4). Illus. by Laura Forman. 2002, Harcourt $16.00 (0-15-201715-1). 40pp. The pied piper gets a fresh, American update in entertaining rhyming verse with a new twist at the end. (Rev: BL 3/15/02; HBG 10/02; SLJ 5/02)

11141 Hodges, Margaret. *The Hero of Bremen* (3–6). Illus. by Charles Mikolaycak. 1993, Holiday House LB $16.95 (0-8234-0934-1). 32pp. In this German folktale, a disabled cobbler is helped by the ghost of Roland, the legendary knight who saved the city of Bremen centuries before. (Rev: BCCB 10/93; BL 10/15/93; HB 11–12/93; SLJ 10/93) [398.2]

11142 Hoffmann, E. T. A. *The Nutcracker* (1–5). Illus. by Julie Paschkis. 2001, Chronicle $19.95 (0-8118-2962-6). Selections on CD, played by the London Symphony Orchestra, accompany this handsome adaptation of the famous tale that includes the "Story of the Hard Nut." (Rev: HBG 3/02; SLJ 10/01) [398.2]

11143 Jackson, Bobby L., reteller. *Little Red Ronnika* (1–4). Illus. by Rhonda Mitchell. 1998, Multicultural Publns. LB $16.95 (1-884242-80-4). 32pp. In this version of Little Red Riding Hood, the characters are all African Americans. Granny is a hip senior and the wolf is a rapper. (Rev: SLJ 1/99) [398.2]

11144 Kimmel, Eric A. *The Goose Girl: A Story from the Brothers Grimm* (4–6). Illus. by Robert Sauber. 1995, Holiday House LB $15.95 (0-8234-1074-9). 32pp. A retelling of the Brothers Grimm tale of the young princess who is cheated out of her birthright by a greedy serving girl. (Rev: BL 10/15/95; SLJ 10/95) [398.2]

11145 Kimmel, Eric A. *Iron John* (K–4). Illus. by Trina S. Hyman. 1994, Holiday House LB $16.95 (0-8234-1073-0). 32pp. An adaptation of a Grimm tale about Prince Walter, who meets Iron John in the forest and breaks a spell that has been cast over him. (Rev: BCCB 12/94; BL 11/1/94; SLJ 12/94) [398.2]

11146 Kimmel, Eric A. *Seven at One Blow: A Tale from the Brothers Grimm* (PS–1). Illus. by Megan Lloyd. 1998, Holiday House $16.95 (0-8234-1383-7). 32pp. After amazing himself by killing seven flies on his jelly sandwich with one blow, a little tailor sets out to seek his fortune in this tale from the Brothers Grimm. (Rev: BL 11/15/98; HB 1–2/99; HBG 3/99; SLJ 12/98) [398.2]

11147 McDermott, Denis. *The Golden Goose* (PS–2). Illus. 2000, HarperCollins LB $15.89 (0-688-11403-2). 32pp. In this version of the Grimm Brothers tale, young Hans is rewarded for helping a troll by the gift of a talking golden goose. (Rev: BL 5/15/00; HBG 10/00; SLJ 7/00) [398.2]

11148 Marshall, James, reteller. *Hansel and Gretel* (K–3). Illus. 1990, Puffin paper $5.99 (0-14-050836-8). A retelling of the famous story with innovative, often humorous, illustrations. (Rev: SLJ 12/90*) [398.2]

11149 Norling, Beth. *Sister Night and Sister Day* (PS–2). Illus. 2001, Allen & Unwin $14.95 (1-86448-863-8). 32pp. There are quite different outcomes when twin sisters Ruby and Rose go to work for Mother Earth, in this retelling of a Grimm tale. (Rev: BL 8/01; SLJ 6/01) [398.2]

11150 Osborne, Mary Pope. *The Brave Little Seamstress* (K–3). Illus. by Giselle Potter. 2002, Atheneum $16.00 (0-689-84486-7). 40pp. A clever retelling of "The Brave Little Tailor" folktale using a saucy young girl as its heroine. (Rev: BCCB 5/02; BL 4/1/02; HBG 10/02; SLJ 4/02) [398.2]

11151 Price, Kathy. *The Bourbon Street Musicians* (4–6). Illus. by Andrew Glass. 2002, Clarion $16.00 (0-618-04076-5). 40pp. A retelling of "The Bremen Town Musicians" moved to New Orleans and with a Cajun beat. (Rev: BL 6/1–15/02; HBG 10/02; SLJ 5/02) [398.2]

11152 Shulman, Janet. *The Nutcracker* (K–5). Illus. by Renee Graef. 1999, HarperCollins $19.95 (0-06-027814-5). 48pp. An adaptation of Hoffman's story *The Nutcracker and the Mouse King,* with a CD consisting of the narration and some excerpts from the Tchaikovsky ballet. (Rev: BL 9/1/99; HBG 3/00; SLJ 10/99)

11153 Stewig, John W. *Mother Holly* (K–3). Illus. by Johanna Westerman. 2001, North-South LB $15.88 (1-55858-925-2). 40pp. A retelling of a Grimm tale of two sisters, one good and the other the typical evil stepsister, that ends with the stepsister reforming. (Rev: BCCB 10/01; BL 7/01; HBG 3/02) [398.2]

11154 Vande Velde, Vivian. *Tales from the Brothers Grimm and the Sisters Weird* (4–8). Illus. Series: Jane Yolen Books. 1995, Harcourt $17.00 (0-15-200220-0). Using a role-reversal technique, the author examines the nature of good and evil in some of the standard tales from the Brothers Grimm. (Rev: BCCB 10/95; SLJ 1/96) [398.2]

11155 Wallace, Ian. *Hansel and Gretel* (2–4). Illus. 1996, Douglas & McIntyre $14.95 (0-88899-212-2). 32pp. A scary retelling in a contemporary setting of the famous Grimms folktale. (Rev: BL 6/1–15/96; SLJ 5/96) [398.2]

11156 Wallis, Diz. *Battle of the Beasts* (2–5). Illus. 2000, Ragged Bear $16.95 (1-929927-15-0). 32pp. An oversize, elegant book that retells the folk tale from the Brothers Grimm about the problems in the animals kingdom when a bear insults the King of Birds, the wren. (Rev: BL 12/1/00; HBG 10/01; SLJ 1/01) [398.2]

11157 Wolkstein, Diane, reteller. *The Glass Mountain* (K–4). Illus. by Louisa Bauer. 1999, Morrow LB $15.93 (0-688-14848-4). A lesser-known Grimm Brothers tale in which a young girl is held prisoner in an underground cave by an unpleasant old man named Old Rinkrank. (Rev: BCCB 3/99; HBG 10/99; SLJ 7/99) [398.2]

11158 Zelinsky, Paul O. *Rapunzel* (3–5). Illus. 1997, Dutton $16.99 (0-525-45607-4). 48pp. Rich oil paintings illustrate this tale of the enduring power of love. Caldecott Medal winner, 1998. (Rev: BL 11/15/97*; HBG 3/98; SLJ 11/97*) [398.2]

Great Britain and Ireland

11159 Asch, Frank. *Ziggy Piggy and the Three Little Pigs* (PS–1). Illus. 1998, Kids Can $14.95 (1-55074-515-8). 32pp. A variation on the story of the three little pigs in which a fourth little pig, Ziggy, rescues his brothers from the wolf and takes them to a raft he made from driftwood. (Rev: BL 11/15/98; HB 11–12/98; HBG 3/99) [398.2]

11160 Aylesworth, Jim. *The Gingerbread Man* (PS–2). Illus. by Barbara McClintock. 1998, Scholastic $15.95 (0-590-97219-7). 32pp. A traditional retelling of the old folktale about the cheerful elderly couple who created a gingerbread man who comes to life and leads them a merry chase. (Rev: BL 4/1/98; HBG 10/98; SLJ 4/98) [398.21]

11161 Barton, Byron. *The Little Red Hen* (PS–2). Illus. 1993, HarperCollins LB $15.89 (0-06-021676-X). 32pp. A new interpretation of this favorite story of the industrious hen, with appealing illustrations. (Rev: BL 5/1/93; SLJ 7/93) [398.2]

11162 Barton, Byron. *The Three Bears* (PS). Illus. 1991, HarperCollins LB $15.89 (0-06-020424-9). 32pp. For the very young, this is a retelling of the story of Goldilocks and the Three Bears. (Rev: BL 1/1/91; SLJ 11/91) [398.2]

11163 Behan, Brendan. *The King of Ireland's Son* (3–5). Illus. by P. J. Lynch. 1997, Orchard $16.95 (0-531-09549-5). 32pp. A rich retelling of the Irish folktale about three princes who set out to find the origin of the heavenly music that is heard in their land. (Rev: BCCB 4/97; BL 4/15/97; SLJ 6/97) [398.2]

11164 Beneduce, Ann Keay. *Jack and the Beanstalk* (1–3). Illus. by Gennady Spirin. 1999, Penguin Putnam $15.99 (0-399-23118-8). 32pp. An expanded version of the classic tale, based on a Victorian retelling, in which a fairy figures prominently as Jack's helper. (Rev: BCCB 12/99; BL 11/1/99; HBG 3/00; SLJ 11/99) [398.2]

11165 Bofill, Francesc. *Jack and the Beanstalk / Juan y los frijoles magicos* (2–4). 1998, Chronicle $13.95 (0-8118-2062-9). 32pp. Using an easy English/Spanish text, this is an attractive retelling of the classic folktale. (Rev: BL 11/15/98; SLJ 8/98) [398.2]

11166 Brett, Jan. *Gingerbread Baby* (PS–3). Illus. 1999, Penguin Putnam $16.99 (0-399-23444-6). 32pp. In this updated version of the old tale, Gingerbread Baby escapes and wreaks havoc in the Swiss village where he had been baked. (Rev: BL 11/15/99; HBG 3/00; SLJ 11/99)

11167 Brown, Marcia. *Dick Whittington and His Cat* (K–3). Illus. by author. 1988, Macmillan $16.00 (0-684-18998-4). 32pp. A reissue of a Caldecott Honor Book published in 1950 about the boy who went to London to seek his fortune. [398.2]

11168 Byrd, Robert. *Finn MacCoul and His Fearless Wife: A Giant of a Tale from Ireland* (K–3). Illus. 1999, Dutton $16.99 (0-525-45971-5). 40pp. A traditional tale from Ireland about the giant Finn Mac-Coul, his wife Oonagh, and the bully and outsider, Cucullin. (Rev: BL 1/1–15/99; HBG 10/99; SLJ 2/99) [398.2]

11169 Calmenson, Stephanie. *The Teeny Tiny Teacher* (PS–K). Illus. by Denis Roche. 1998, Scholastic $15.95 (0-590-37123-1). 32pp. In this English folktale, a teeny tiny teacher takes her teeny tiny class for a walk in a teeny tiny park and finds a teeny tiny bone that belongs to a ghost that is not teeny tiny. (Rev: BCCB 10/98; BL 8/98; HB 9–10/98; HBG 3/99; SLJ 11/98) [398.2]

11170 Carpenter, Stephen. *The Three Billy Goats Gruff* (PS). Illus. Series: Harper Growing Tree. 1998, HarperCollins $9.95 (0-694-01033-2). 24pp. For the very young, this is a simple but accurate retelling of the old English folktale using double-page pictures. (Rev: BL 5/15/98; HBG 10/98; SLJ 7/98) [398.2]

11171 Christelow, Eileen. *Where's the Big Bad Wolf?* (PS–1). Illus. 2002, Clarion $15.00 (0-618-18194-6). 32pp. This humorous retelling of the classic tale — featuring cartoon illustrations and dialogue balloons — is written as a mystery, featuring Detective Doggedly in search of BBW (Big Bad Wolf). (Rev: BL 10/15/02; HBG 3/03; SLJ 9/02) [398.2]

11172 Climo, Shirley. *Magic and Mischief: Tales from Cornwall* (3–7). Illus. 1999, Clarion $17.00 (0-395-86968-4). 127pp. A brilliant retelling of ten Cornish folktales about enchantment, the sea, and supernatural beings. (Rev: BCCB 10/99; BL 8/99; HBG 3/00; SLJ 8/99) [398.2]

11173 Collins, Sheila Hebert. *Jolie Blonde and the Three Heberts: A Cajun Twist to an Old Tale* (K–4). Illus. by Patrick Soper. 1999, Pelican $14.95 (1-56554-324-6). In this Cajun version of Goldilocks, the heroine is Jolie Blonde and the bears are three humans named Hebert whose gumbo is eaten while they are away. (Rev: HBG 10/99; SLJ 6/99) [398.2]

11174 Collins, Sheila Hebert, reteller. *Les Trois Cochons* (2–5). Illus. by Patrick Soper. 1999, Pelican $14.95 (1-56554-325-4). A Cajun rendering of the "Three Little Pigs" that contains a number of Cajun phases that are fun but can be confusing. (Rev: SLJ 4/00) [398.2]

11175 Cooper, Susan, reteller. *The Silver Cow: A Welsh Tale* (K–4). Illus. by Warwick Hutton. 1991, Simon & Schuster paper $5.99 (0-689-71512-9). 32pp. A greedy farmer inherits a silver cow from his son, who received it for his harp playing. [398.2]

11176 Creswick, Paul. *Robin Hood* (6–8). Illus. by N. C. Wyeth. 1984, Macmillan $28.00 (0-684-18162-2). 362pp. A classic edition now reissued. [398.2]

11177 Davis, Donald. *The Pig Who Went Home on Sunday: An Appalachian Folktale* (K–4). Illus. by Jennifer Mazzucco. 2004, August House $16.95 (0-87483-571-2). In this Appalachian variation of "The Three Little Pigs," only one youngster heeds his

mother's advice and survives to come home at the weekend. (Rev: SLJ 8/04) [398.2]

11178 dePaola, Tomie, reteller. *Fin M'Coul: The Giant of Knockmany Hill* (PS–3). Illus. by Tomie dePaola. 1981, Holiday House LB $16.95 (0-8234-0384-X); paper $6.95 (0-8234-0385-8). 32pp. Fin's wife saves him from the most feared giant in Ireland. [398.2]

11179 dePaola, Tomie. *Jamie O'Rourke and the Big Potato: An Irish Folktale* (PS–3). Illus. 1992, Penguin Putnam $16.99 (0-399-22257-X). 32pp. Lazy Jamie gets a seed from a leprechaun and produces an enormous potato. (Rev: BL 2/15/92; SLJ 4/92) [398.2]

11180 Doyle, Malachy. *Tales from Old Ireland* (3–6). Illus. 2000, Barefoot $19.99 (1-902283-97-X). 96pp. A heady collection of traditional Irish tales that includes the familiar "Children of Lir" and "The Soul Cages." (Rev: BL 11/15/00; HB 3–4/01; HBG 10/01; SLJ 11/00) [398.2]

11181 Early, Margaret. *Robin Hood* (3–5). Illus. 1996, Abrams $17.95 (0-8109-4428-6). 32pp. A lavishly illustrated edition of 14 of the most popular stories about Robin Hood and his Merry Men. (Rev: BL 6/1–15/96; SLJ 8/96) [398.22]

11182 Escott, John, retel. *The Little Red Hen* (PS–K). Illus. by Annie West. 2003, Gingham Dog $15.95 (1-57768-492-3). 32pp. A retelling of the story of the Little Red Hen and her unhelpful friends. (Rev: HBG 4/04; SLJ 4/04) [398.2]

11183 Fearnley, Jan. *Mr. Wolf and the Three Bears* (PS–2). Illus. by author. 2002, Harcourt $16.00 (0-15-216423-5). Goldilocks arrives uninvited at Baby Bear's birthday party, but Grandma Wolf knows how to deal with her. (Rev: HBG 10/02; SLJ 6/02) [398.2]

11184 Finch, Mary. *The Little Red Hen and the Ear of Wheat* (PS–K). Illus. by Elisabeth Bell. Series: A Barefoot Beginner Book. 1999, Barefoot $15.95 (1-902283-47-3). A retelling of the famous folktale about the little red hen who can't find helpers to prepare a loaf of bread. (Rev: SLJ 5/99) [398.2]

11185 Forest, Heather. *The Woman Who Flummoxed the Fairies: An Old Tale from Scotland* (K–3). Illus. by Susan Gaber. 1990, Harcourt $14.95 (0-15-299150-6). In this retelling of a tale from Scotland, the fairies kidnap a baker so she will make cakes only for them. (Rev: BL 4/1/90; SLJ 6/90) [398.2]

11186 Galdone, Paul. *The Gingerbread Boy* (PS–1). Illus. by author. 1983, Houghton Mifflin $16.00 (0-395-28799-5); paper $6.95 (0-89919-163-0). 40pp. Humorous and vigorous illustrations enhance this favorite folktale of the adventures of a runaway gingerbread boy. [398.2]

11187 Galdone, Paul. *Henny Penny* (K–2). Illus. by author. 1979, Houghton Mifflin $16.00 (0-395-28800-2); paper $6.95 (0-89919-225-4). 32pp. A retelling of the favorite cumulative folktale of the hen who thought the sky was falling. [398.2]

11188 Galdone, Paul. *The Little Red Hen* (K–2). Illus. by author. 1979, Houghton Mifflin $15.00 (0-395-28803-7); paper $5.95 (0-89919-349-8). A little hen works for her lazy housemates in this reworking of the old tale. Another fine edition is: *The Little Red Hen: An Old Story,* illus. by Margot Zemach (1983, Farrar). [398.2]

11189 Galdone, Paul. *The Three Bears* (K–2). Illus. by author. 1979, Houghton Mifflin $15.00 (0-395-28811-8); paper $6.95 (0-89919-401-X). 32pp. The illustrations for this familiar story are large, colorful, and humorous; excellent to use with a group. [398.2]

11190 Galdone, Paul. *The Three Little Pigs* (PS–1). Illus. by author. 1979, Houghton Mifflin $15.00 (0-395-28813-4). The old folktale told in verse. Another recommended edition is: Illus. by Erik Blegvad (1980, Macmillan). [398.2]

11191 *Goldilocks and the Three Bears: A Tale Moderne* (PS–3). Illus. by Steven Guarnaccia. 2000, Abrams $15.95 (0-8109-4139-2). 32pp. Goldilocks is a con artist in this hip version of an old favorite. (Rev: BL 5/15/00; HBG 10/00; SLJ 4/00) [398.2]

11192 Green, Roger L. *Adventures of Robin Hood* (5–9). 1994, Knopf $15.00 (0-679-43636-7); Puffin paper $4.99 (0-14-036700-4). The exploits of this folk hero are retold in this reissue of a classic version. [398]

11193 Greene, Ellin. *The Little Golden Lamb* (PS–2). Illus. by Rosanne Litzinger. 2000, Clarion $15.00 (0-395-71526-1). 32pp. Anyone who touches the lamb with a golden fleece becomes stuck to it in this amusing folktale. (Rev: BCCB 5/00; BL 3/15/00; HB 5–6/00; HBG 10/00; SLJ 6/00) [398.22]

11194 Gross, Gwen, ed. *Knights of the Round Table* (2–5). Illus. by Norman Green. 1992, Random paper $3.99 (0-394-87579-6). 112pp. A retelling of many of the most popular Arthurian legends. (Rev: BCCB 9/85; SLJ 2/86) [398.2]

11195 Hague, Michael. *Kate Culhane: A Ghost Story* (1–3). Illus. 2001, North-South LB $15.88 (1-58717-059-0). 40pp. A retelling of a spooky Irish ghost story about a young woman who cunningly outsmarts a ghoul. (Rev: BL 9/15/01; HBG 3/02; SLJ 9/01) [398.2]

11196 Harris, Jim, reteller. *The Three Little Dinosaurs* (K–3). Illus. by Jim Harris. 1999, Pelican $14.95 (1-56554-371-8). In this version the three little pigs folktale, three young brachiosaurs build different homes to withstand the big bad Tyrannosaurus rex. (Rev: HBG 3/00; SLJ 2/00) [398.2]

11197 Hastings, Selina, reteller. *Sir Gawain and the Loathly Lady* (5–8). Illus. by Juan Wijngaard. 1987, Lothrop paper $4.95 (0-688-07046-9). 32pp. Noble Sir Gawain agrees to honor a pledge for a husband to a deformed old hag and discovers that he has broken an old spell and released a beautiful woman. (Rev: BCCB 11/85; BL 11/15/85) [398.2]

11198 Heaney, Marie, reteller. *The Names Upon the Harp: Irish Myth and Legend* (4–9). Illus. by P. J. Lynch. 2000, Scholastic $19.95 (0-590-68052-8). 95pp. These stories from Ireland are filled with magic, conflict, and creatures and deal with such themes as overcoming obstacles, searching for identity, and finding true love. (Rev: BCCB 3/01; BL 1/1–15/01; HBG 3/01; SLJ 1/01) [398.2]

11199 Hewitt, Kathryn, adapt. *The Three Sillies* (K–3). Illus. by Kathryn Hewitt. 1989, Harcourt paper $3.95 (0-15-286856-9). A suitor sets out to find three sillier people than his betrothed's family. (Rev: BCCB 5/86; BL 4/1/86; SLJ 5/86) [398.2]

11200 Heyer, Carol, reteller. *Robin Hood* (2–4). Illus. by Carol Heyer. 1993, Ideals LB $15.00 (0-8249-8648-2). This handsome book retells the most famous of Robin Hood's exploits, culminating in the King's pardon. (Rev: SLJ 11/93) [398.2]

11201 Hodges, Margaret, reteller. *The Kitchen Knight: A Tale of King Arthur* (3–6). Illus. by Trina S. Hyman. 1990, Holiday House LB $15.95 (0-8234-0787-X). A lavishly illustrated version of the story of the king who hides his identity to work in the kitchen at King Arthur's court. (Rev: BCCB 11/90*; HB 3–4/91; SLJ 1/91) [398.2]

11202 Hodges, Margaret. *St. George and the Dragon: A Golden Legend* (2–5). Illus. by Trina S. Hyman. 1984, Little, Brown $16.95 (0-316-36789-3). A reworking of the English tale as it appeared in Edmund Spenser's Fairie Queen. Caldecott Medal winner, 1985. [398.2]

11203 Hodges, Margaret. *Up the Chimney* (K–2). Illus. by Amanda Harvey. 1998, Holiday House $15.95 (0-8234-1354-3). 32pp. When a girl goes out to seek her fortune, she is helped by all the objects and animals she has helped in the past, but when her uncharitable, cruel sister goes out, her fate is different. (Rev: BCCB 12/98; BL 11/15/98; HBG 3/99; SLJ 1/99) [398.2]

11204 Huck, Charlotte. *The Black Bull of Norroway* (2–4). Illus. by Anita Lobel. 2001, Greenwillow LB $15.89 (0-688-16901-5). 40pp. A Scottish beauty-and-the-beast tale, richly illustrated and accompanied by a discussion of the story's origins and variants. (Rev: BCCB 5/01; BL 9/15/01; HB 5–6/01; HBG 10/01; SLJ 6/01) [398.2]

11205 Hunter, Mollie. *Gilly Martin the Fox* (PS–1). Illus. by Dennis McDermott. 1994, Hyperion $15.95 (1-56282-517-8). 40pp. A Scottish folktale about a fox that helps a young prince win the hand of a beautiful princess. (Rev: BL 4/1/94; SLJ 6/94) [398.2]

11206 Jacobs, Joseph. *Celtic Fairy Tales* (3–6). Illus. by John D. Batten. 1968, Peter Smith $22.25 (0-8446-2302-4); Dover paper $6.95 (0-486-21826-0). 267pp. A classic collection. Followed by: *More Celtic Fairy Tales* (1969, Dover paper). [398.2]

11207 Jacobs, Joseph. *English Fairy Tales* (3–6). Illus. by John D. Batten. 1969, Peter Smith $21.75 (0-8446-2303-2); Dover paper $7.95 (0-486-21818-X). A standard collection by a master storyteller. [398.2]

11208 Johnson, Paul Brett. *Jack Outwits the Giants* (PS–3). Illus. 2002, Simon & Schuster $16.00 (0-689-83902-2). 32pp. "Jack the Giant Killer" set in Appalachia and with a few hilarious new twists. (Rev: BCCB 7–8/02; BL 6/1–15/02; HB 7–8/02; HBG 10/02; SLJ 11/02) [398.2]

11209 Jones, Carol. *The Gingerbread Man* (PS–K). Illus. 2002, Houghton Mifflin $15.00 (0-618-18822-3). 32pp. In this spirited retelling, it is nursery rhyme characters who chase the gingerbread boy. (Rev: BL 2/15/02; HBG 10/02; SLJ 4/02) [398.2]

11210 Kellogg, Steven. *The Three Little Pigs* (K–3). Illus. 1997, Morrow $15.93 (0-688-08732-9). 32pp. A humorous retelling of the old story, with inventive new details sure to please. (Rev: BL 8/97*; HBG 3/98; SLJ 9/97) [398.2]

11211 Kilgannon, Eily. *Folktales of the Yeats Country* (5–8). Illus. 1990, Mercier paper $10.95 (0-85342-861-1). Seventeen folktales that originate in County Sligo in Ireland. (Rev: BL 8/90; SLJ 2/91) [398.2]

11212 Kimmel, Eric A. *The Gingerbread Man* (PS–K). Illus. by Megan Lloyd. 1993, Holiday House LB $16.95 (0-8234-0824-8). 32pp. This is a modern version of a classic tale about the cookie that says he can't be caught. (Rev: BL 3/15/93; SLJ 6/93*) [398.2]

11213 Kimmel, Eric A. *The Old Woman and Her Pig* (PS–3). Illus. by Giora Carmi. 1992, Holiday House LB $16.95 (0-8234-0970-8). 32pp. An excellent retelling of the classic British folktale. (Rev: BL 1/1/93; SLJ 10/92) [398.2]

11214 Leavy, Una. *Irish Fairy Tales and Legends* (4–8). Illus. 1997, Roberts Rinehart $18.95 (1-57098-177-9). An attractive book that contains 10 Irish legends, some going back 2,000 years. (Rev: BL 2/1/98; HBG 10/98; SLJ 2/98) [398.2]

11215 Light, Steve. *Puss in Boots* (PS–2). Illus. 2002, Abrams $14.95 (0-8109-4368-9). 24pp. Collages illustrate this faithful version of a favorite folktale. (Rev: BCCB 5/02; BL 4/15/02; HBG 10/02; SLJ 4/02) [398.2]

11216 Lowell, Susan. *Dusty Locks and the Three Bears* (PS–1). Illus. by Randy Cecil. 2001, Holt $15.95 (0-8050-5862-1). 32pp. A western version of Goldilocks starring a bad-tempered, ill-mannered runaway. (Rev: BCCB 7–8/01; BL 7/01; HB 7–8/01; HBG 10/01; SLJ 7/01) [398.2]

11217 Lupton, Hugh. *Pirican Pic and Pirican Mor* (2–4). Illus. by Yumi Heo. 2003, Barefoot $16.99 (1-84148-070-3). 40pp. A humorous cumulative Celtic folktale recounts the conflict between Pirican Pic and Pirican Mor over the latter's theft of the former's hard-won walnuts. (Rev: BL 4/1/03; HB 7–8/03; HBG 10/03; SLJ 5/03) [398.2]

11218 MacDonald, Margaret Read. *Slop! A Welsh Folktale* (K–2). Illus. by Yvonne Davis. 1997, Fulcrum $15.95 (1-55591-352-0). 24pp. In this Welsh folktale, fairies become annoyed when their neighbor continually empties his slop bucket on top of their cottage. (Rev: BL 11/1/97; HBG 3/98; SLJ 11/97) [398.2]

11219 McGovern, Ann. *Too Much Noise* (K–3). Illus. by Simms Taback. 1967, Houghton Mifflin $16.00 (0-395-18110-0); paper $6.95 (0-395-62985-3). 48pp. An old man follows the advice of the village wise man when he complains that his house is too noisy. [398.2]

11220 McKay, Sindy, adapt. *Jack and the Beanstalk* (1–2). Illus. by Lydia Halverson. Series: We Both Read. 1998, Treasure Bay $7.99 (1-891327-00-3). This traditional English folktale is told twice —

with an adult's and a child's vocabulary. (Rev: SLJ 12/98) [398.2]

11221 Malory, Thomas. *Merlin and Making of the King* (4–6). Retold by Margaret Hodges. Illus. by Trina Schart Hyman. 2004, Holiday House $16.95 (0-8234-1647-X). 40pp. The Arthurian tales of the "Sword in the Stone," "Excalibur," and "The Lady of the Lake" are simply told and beautifully illustrated with rich medieval effects. (Rev: BL 9/15/04; SLJ 9/04*) [398.2]

11222 Mata, Marta. *Goldilocks and the Three Bears / Ricitos de Oro y los tres osos* (2–4). Trans. by Alis Alejandro. 1988, Chronicle $12.95 (0-8118-2075-0). 32pp. Using a bilingual format in English and Spanish, and bold, contemporary illustrations, this is an easy retelling of the English folktale. (Rev: BL 11/15/98; SLJ 8/98) [398.2]

11223 Matthews, Caitl'n, retel. *Celtic Memories* (1–6). Illus. by Olwyn Whelan. 2003, Barefoot $19.99 (1-84148-097-5). 80pp. The Celts of Ireland, Wales, Scotland, and Brittany are the source of this well-illustrated collection of folktales, songs, blessings, and poems, which includes informative notes and pronunciation guides. (Rev: BL 1/1–15/04; HBG 4/04; SLJ 3/04) [398.2]

11224 Milligan, Bryce. *Brigid's Cloak: An Ancient Irish Story* (1–3). Illus. by Helen Cann. 2002, Eerdmans $16.00 (0-8028-5224-6). 32pp. This book with Celtic and early Christian undertones tells the story of Saint Brigid, who is transported to Jerusalem in a vision and helps care for the baby Jesus. (Rev: BL 10/15/02; HBG 3/03; SLJ 2/03) [398.2]

11225 Milligan, Bryce. *The Prince of Ireland and the Three Magic Stallions* (1–3). Illus. by Preston McDaniels. 2003, Holiday House $16.95 (0-8234-1573-2). 32pp. An Irish folktale in which a story saves the lives of the storyteller and his friends. (Rev: BL 3/15/03*; HBG 10/03; SLJ 6/03) [398.2]

11226 Moser, Barry. *The Three Little Pigs* (PS–1). Illus. 2001, Little, Brown $14.95 (0-316-58544-0). 32pp. A humorous retelling that retains much of the original, with delightful illustrations. (Rev: BCCB 3/01; BL 6/1–15/01; HB 5–6/01; HBG 10/01; SLJ 5/01) [398.24]

11227 Philip, Neil. *Celtic Fairy Tales* (4–8). Illus. 1999, Viking $21.99 (0-670-88387-5). 144pp. The 20 stories in this fine anthology originated in Ireland, Scotland, Brittany, Wales, Cornwall, and the Isle of Man. (Rev: BL 11/15/99; HBG 10/00) [398.2]

11228 *A Pot o' Gold: A Treasury of Irish Stories, Poetry, Folklore and (of Course) Blarney* (4–8). Ed. by Kathleen Krull. Illus. by David McPhail. 2004, Hyperion $16.99 (0-7868-0625-7). 192pp. This is a comprehensive collection — including riddles, blessing, and battle cries — with attractive and appropriate illustrations. (Rev: BL 2/15/04; SLJ 3/04) [820.8]

11229 Pyle, Howard. *The Merry Adventures of Robin Hood* (5–8). Illus. by author. 1968, Dover paper $9.95 (0-486-22043-5). 296pp. Stories about Robin Hood and the inhabitants of Sherwood Forest. [398.2]

11230 Pyle, Howard. *The Story of King Arthur and His Knights* (6–8). Illus. by author. 1966, Dover paper $8.95 (0-486-21445-1). One of the most famous editions of these classic stories. A sequel is: *The Story of the Champions of the Round Table* (1968). [398.2]

11231 Pyle, Howard. *The Story of the Grail and the Passing of Arthur* (5–8). Illus. by author. 1985, Macmillan paper $10.95 (0-486-27361-X). 340pp. The last title of a four-volume King Arthur series, first published in 1910. (Rev: BL 12/15/85) [398.2]

11232 Rosales, Melodye Benson. *Leola and the Honeybears: An African-American Retelling of Goldilocks and the Three Bears* (PS–1). Illus. 1999, Scholastic $15.95 (0-590-38358-2). 38pp. The changes in the text of this classic tale are minor, but the paintings are outstanding in this version of Goldilocks in which the heroine is an African American. (Rev: BCCB 10/99; BL 11/1/99; HBG 3/00; SLJ 11/99) [398.22]

11233 Ross, Tony, reteller. *Goldilocks and the Three Bears* (K–3). Illus. 1992, Viking $13.95 (0-87951-453-1). 28pp. An enjoyable retelling of the old classic with modern updating. (Rev: BL 2/15/93) [398.2]

11234 Ryan, Patrick. *Shakespeare's Storybook: Folk Tales That Inspired the Bard* (3–5). Illus. by James Mayhew. 2001, Barefoot $19.99 (1-84148-307-9). 80pp. A retelling of seven folk tales that may have served as the inspiration for works by Shakespeare. (Rev: BL 11/15/01; HBG 3/02; SLJ 1/02) [822.3]

11235 San Souci, Robert D. *Brave Margaret: An Irish Adventure* (1–4). Illus. by Sally Wern Comport. 1999, Simon & Schuster $17.00 (0-689-81072-5). 40pp. An intrepid girl survives a shipwreck, challenges a giant, and saves her boyfriend in this adaptation of an Irish folktale. (Rev: BCCB 5/99; BL 3/1/99; HBG 10/99; SLJ 9/99) [398.2]

11236 Schmidt, Gary. *The Wonders of Donal O'Donnell: A Folktale of Ireland* (4–6). Illus. by Loren Long. 2002, Holt $17.95 (0-8050-6516-4). 40pp. Donal and his wife have permitted no visitors since their son's death, but when three peddlers consecutively appeal for help, they let them in and draw comfort from their traditional Irish tales. (Rev: BL 1/1–15/03; HBG 3/03; SLJ 12/02) [398.2]

11237 Scieszka, Jon. *The True Story of the Three Little Pigs: By A. Wolf* (PS–2). Illus. 1989, Viking $16.99 (0-670-82759-2). 32pp. A hip and funny version, from the wolf's point of view. (Rev: BCCB 9/89*; BL 9/1/89; HB 1–2/90; SLJ 10/89) [398.2]

11238 Shepard, Aaron. *King o' the Cats* (1–3). Illus. by Kristin Sorra. 2004, Simon & Schuster $16.95 (0-689-82082-8). 32pp. Newly hired church sexton Peter Black, burdened by a reputation for telling tall tales, has difficulty getting anyone to believe accounts of his encounters with a strange group of cats. (Rev: BL 10/15/04; SLJ 8/04) [398.2]

11239 Shulman, Lisa. *The Matzo Ball Boy* (PS–1). Illus. by Rosanne Litzinger. 2005, Dutton $15.99 (0-525-47169-3). 32pp. A grandmother preparing chicken soup for the Passover Seder creates a matzo ball boy who jumps from the soup and takes off to

see the world in this appealing variation of the Gingerbread Boy. (Rev: BL 2/1/05; SLJ 3/05) [398.2]

11240 Singer, Marilyn. *The Maiden on the Moor* (1–3). Illus. by Troy Howell. 1995, Morrow LB $14.93 (0-688-08765-6). 40pp. In this English ballad, two shepherd brothers discover a young woman lying unconscious and must decide if they should care for her. (Rev: BL 4/15/95; SLJ 4/95) [398.2]

11241 *Sir Gawain and the Green Knight* (4–7). Retold by Michael Morpurgo. Illus. by Michael Foreman. 2005, Candlewick $18.99 (0-7636-2519-1). 112pp. Morpurgo retells in contemporary prose the story of the Green Knight's challenge to the court of King Arthur. (Rev: BL 11/1/04*; SLJ 10/04) [398.2]

11242 Souhami, Jessica. *Mrs. McCool and the Giant Cuhullin: An Irish Tale* (K–3). Illus. 2002, Holt $16.95 (0-8050-6852-X). 32pp. A giant of Irish lore, Cuhullin, goes in search of another, Finn McCool, to see who is strongest, but Finn's wife turns out to be strongest of all. (Rev: BL 2/15/02; HB 5–6/02*; HBG 10/02; SLJ 3/02) [398.2]

11243 Sturges, Philemon. *The Little Red Hen (Makes a Pizza)* (PS–2). Illus. by Amy Ward. 1999, Dutton $15.99 (0-525-45953-7). 32pp. In this variation on the classic folktale, the industrious Little Red Hen makes pizza instead of bread. (Rev: BCCB 2/00; BL 11/15/99; HBG 3/00; SLJ 12/99*) [398.2]

11244 Sutcliff, Rosemary, reteller. *Beowulf* (5–8). Illus. by Charles Keeping. 1984, Smith $20.75 (0-8446-6165-1). This is a reissue of the Anglo-Saxon tale published originally in 1962. Also use the King Arthur story, *The Sword and the Circle* (1981, Dutton). [398.2]

11245 Talbott, Hudson, reteller. *King Arthur and the Round Table* (2–4). Illus. by Hudson Talbott. Series: Tales of King Arthur. 1995, Morrow $15.89 (0-688-11341-9). Three stories about King Arthur in which he forms the Round Table and marries Guinevere. (Rev: SLJ 12/95) [398.2]

11246 Talbott, Hudson. *Lancelot* (5–7). Illus. 1999, Morrow LB $15.89 (0-688-14833-6). 40pp. A retelling of the life of Lancelot, from his rescue as a child by the Lady of the Lake to his love for Guinevere, marriage to Elaine, and fathering of Galahad. (Rev: BL 9/1/99; HBG 3/00; SLJ 10/99) [398.2]

11247 Vivian, E. Charles. *Robin Hood: A Classic Illustrated Edition* (4–7). Illus. 2002, Chronicle $19.95 (0-8118-3399-2). 174pp. Illustrations ranging from medieval tapestries to comic book drawings by artists including Howard Pyle and N. C. Wyeth give visual interest to this retelling of the beloved Robin Hood tale. (Rev: BL 12/1/02; HBG 3/03; SLJ 3/03) [398.2]

11248 Wahl, Jan. *Little Johnny Buttermilk* (PS–1). Illus. by Jennifer Mazzucco. 1999, August House $15.95 (0-87483-559-3). 32pp. An English tale about Little Johnny and how he escapes from a witch after being captured on his way to market. (Rev: BL 12/15/99; HBG 3/00; SLJ 2/00) [398.2]

11249 Whatley, Bruce. *Wait! No Paint!* (K–2). Illus. 2001, HarperCollins LB $15.89 (0-06-028271-1). 32pp. It's the illustrator himself who threatens the fate of the three little pigs and the big bad wolf in this colorful and inventive retelling. (Rev: BL 8/01; HB 9–10/01; HBG 3/02; SLJ 7/01) [398.2]

11250 Wiesner, David. *The Three Pigs* (K–6). Illus. by author. 2001, Clarion $16.00 (0-618-00701-6). This is a fresh twist on the familiar tale, with excellent and inventive illustrations, that has a bewildered wolf searching for pigs that have been blown into a fantasy universe until they return and set the world to rights. Caldecott Medal winner, 2002. (Rev: BCCB 5/01; BL 5/15/01*; HB 5–6/01*; HBG 10/01; SLJ 4/01*) [398.2]

11251 Zemach, Harve. *Duffy and the Devil: A Cornish Tale Retold* (1–3). Illus. by Margot Zemach. 1973, Farrar $17.00 (0-374-31887-5); paper $6.95 (0-374-41897-7). 40pp. A variant of "Rumpelstiltskin," this folktale is told with humor and verve and boldly illustrated. Caldecott Medal winner, 1974. [398.2]

Greece and Italy

11252 Aesop. *The Aesop for Children* (3–5). Illus. by Milo Winter. 1984, Checkerboard $12.95 (1-56288-039-X); paper $5.99 (0-590-47977-6). This edition, reissued with the original artwork, includes 126 tales. [398.2]

11253 Aesop. *Aesop's Fables* (3–5). Illus. by Fulvio Testa. 1989, Barron's $14.95 (0-8120-5958-1). 48pp. Twenty familiar tales illustrated with paintings that use a Middle East oasis as a setting. (Rev: BCCB 5/89; HB 7–8/89; SLJ 3/05) [398.2]

11254 Aesop. *Fables of Aesop* (4–6). Illus. by David Levine. 1984, Harvard Common $13.95 (0-87645-074-5); paper $8.95 (0-87645-116-4). 108pp. One of many recommended editions of this classic. [398.2]

11255 Aesop. *The Tortoise and the Hare: An Aesop Fable* (PS–K). Illus. by Janet Stevens. 1984, Holiday House LB $15.95 (0-8234-0510-9); paper $6.95 (0-8234-0564-8). 32pp. An updated, charming retelling of the classic fable. [398.2]

11256 Aesop. *The Town Mouse and the Country Mouse* (PS–1). Illus. by T. R. Garcia. 1979, Troll LB $15.95 (0-89375-131-6); paper $3.95 (0-89375-109-X). 32pp. The classic story faithfully and entertainingly retold. [398.2]

11257 Ash, Russell, and Bernard A. Higton, eds. *Aesop's Fables* (3–6). Illus. 1991, Chronicle $17.95 (0-87701-780-8). 95pp. More than 50 fables reprinted and illustrated with artists from the past. (Rev: SLJ 3/91) [398.2]

11258 Barnes-Murphy, Frances. *The Fables of Aesop* (3–5). Illus. 1994, Lothrop $19.95 (0-688-07051-5). 96pp. An extensive collection of more than 100 fables with lively illustrations. (Rev: BL 12/1/94; SLJ 10/94) [398.2]

11259 Brown, Stephanie Gwyn. *Professor Aesop's the Crow and the Pitcher* (K–4). Illus. by author. 2003, Tricycle $15.95 (1-58246-087-6). A clever crow, temporarily foiled in his attempts to drink from a pitcher, comes up with an ingenious solution. (Rev: HBG 10/03; SLJ 9/03) [398.2]

11260 Collodi, Carlo. *The Adventures of Pinocchio* (5–7). Illus. by Iassen Ghiuselev. 2002, Simply Read $29.95 (0-9688768-0-3). 160pp. The full text of the original is used here with effective black-and-white illustrations and several full-page watercolors. (Rev: BL 4/1/02)

11261 Corwin, Oliver J. *Hare and Tortoise Race to the Moon* (K–3). Illus. 2002, Abrams $14.95 (0-8109-0566-3). 40pp. In this modern twist on Aesop's classic, Tortoise and Hare race to the moon in rocket ships. (Rev: BL 10/15/02; HBG 3/03; SLJ 11/02) [398.2]

11262 dePaola, Tomie. *Days of the Blackbird: A Tale of Northern Italy* (K–3). Illus. 1997, Penguin Putnam $15.99 (0-399-22929-9). 32pp. An Italian tale about a faithful bird that stays through the winter to sing for an ailing duke. (Rev: BL 3/15/97; HB 3–4/97; SLJ 3/97*)

11263 dePaola, Tomie. *The Mysterious Giant of Barletta: An Italian Folktale* (K–3). Illus. by author. 1988, Harcourt paper $6.00 (0-15-256349-0). 32pp. A statue of an old lady saves the town from marauders. [398.2]

11264 dePaola, Tomie. *Strega Nona* (PS–2). Illus. by author. 1979, Simon & Schuster paper $6.95 (0-671-66606-1). 32pp. The old Italian folktale retold. Also use: *Big Anthony and the Magic Ring* (1979) and *Strega Nona's Magic Lessons* (1982). [398.2]

11265 dePaola, Tomie. *Strega Nona: Her Story* (PS–3). Illus. 1996, Penguin Putnam $16.99 (0-399-22818-7). 32pp. This book supplies background information on the birth and youth of Nona and how she became the village strega. (Rev: BL 9/15/96; HB 11–12/96; SLJ 10/96) [398.2]

11266 Fox, Paula. *Amzat and His Brothers: Three Italian Tales* (3–5). Illus. by Emily Arnold McCully. 1993, Orchard $16.95 (0-531-05462-4). 80pp. Tales retold from a grandfather who lived in a small Italian village. (Rev: BCCB 3/93*; BL 3/15/93; HB 7–8/93; SLJ 7/93) [398.2]

11267 Gal, Laszlo, and Raffaella Gal. *The Parrot* (K–3). Illus. 1997, Douglas & McIntyre $16.95 (0-88899-287-4). 32pp. In this Italian folktale, a prince assumes the identity of a parrot to help a princess. (Rev: BL 9/15/97; SLJ 10/97) [398.2]

11268 Herman, Gail, reteller. *The Lion and the Mouse* (1). Illus. by Lisa McCue. Series: Early Step into Reading. 1998, Random paper $3.99 (0-679-88674-5). 32pp. The classic Aesop fable is retold dramatically in a simple text suitable for beginning readers. (Rev: BL 11/1/98; SLJ 2/99) [398.2]

11269 Hovey, Kate. *Ancient Voices* (5–8). Illus. by Murray Kimber. 2004, Simon & Schuster $18.95 (0-689-83342-3). The life of the Greek gods on Mount Olympus and elsewhere is described in poetic form in this imaginatively illustrated volume. (Rev: BL 1/1–15/04; SLJ 3/04) [811]

11270 Jones, Carol. *The Hare and the Tortoise* (K–3). Illus. 1996, Houghton Mifflin $13.95 (0-395-81368-9). 32pp. Peepholes and detailed illustrations are used in this retelling of the famous Aesop fable. (Rev: BL 9/1/96; SLJ 9/96) [398.24]

11271 Lowell, Susan. *The Tortoise and the Jackrabbit* (PS–2). Illus. by Jim Harris. 1994, Northland LB $15.95 (0-87358-586-0). 32pp. This favorite Aesop fable is retold with the tortoise an aged grandmother and the hare a conceited egocentric. (Rev: BL 1/15/95; HB 3–4/05; SLJ 2/95)

11272 Lynch, Tom, adapt. *Fables from Aesop* (3–5). Illus. by Tom Lynch. 2000, Viking $15.99 (0-670-88948-2). A striking presentation of 13 of the most famous fables from Aesop. (Rev: HBG 10/01; SLJ 10/00) [398.2]

11273 McClintock, Barbara. *Animal Fables from Aesop* (4–6). Illus. 1991, Godine $18.95 (0-87923-913-1). 48pp. The text is an expansion of nine fables complete with dialogue and dramatic situations. (Rev: BCCB 1/92; BL 1/1/92; HB 1–2/92; SLJ 1/92) [398.2]

11274 Morpurgo, Michael. *The McElderry Book of Aesop's Fables* (PS–2). Illus. by Emma Clark. 2005, Simon & Schuster $19.95 (1-4169-0290-2). 96pp. Twenty-one classic fables are retold in conversational style with humorous watercolors. (Rev: BL 5/1/05; SLJ 6/05) [398.2]

11275 Morrison, Toni, and Slade Morrison. *The Ant or the Grasshopper?* (K–5). Illus. by Pascal Lemaitre. Series: Who's Got Game? 2003, Scribner $16.95 (0-7432-2247-4). Kid A, an ant, and his close grasshopper buddy Foxy G decide the time for summer fun has passed and begin to prepare for the coming of winter. (Rev: BL 5/15/03; HBG 10/03; SLJ 9/03) [741.5]

11276 Morrison, Toni, and Slade Morrison. *The Lion or the Mouse?* (2–5). Illus. by Pascal Lema tre. Series: Who's Got Game? 2003, Scribner $16.95 (0-7432-2248-2). Mouse comes to Lion's rescue when Lion is brought low by a thorn in his paw in this contemporary adaptation of the Aesop fable. (Rev: HBG 4/04; SLJ 12/03) [398.2]

11277 Morrison, Toni, and Slade Morrison. *Who's Got Game? Poppy or the Snake?* (1–4). Illus. by Pascal Lemaitre. 2004, Scribner $17.95 (0-7432-2249-0). 40pp. In this adaptation of the Aesop fable, Poppy, an African American grandfather, tells a small boy about an encounter with a snake. (Rev: BL 2/15/04) [813.54]

11278 Pinkney, Jerry. *Aesop's Fables* (2–4). Illus. 2000, North-South $19.95 (1-58717-000-0). 96pp. A first-rate collection of 60 of Aesop's tales retold and illustrated by this acclaimed artist. (Rev: BCCB 12/00; BL 12/15/00*; HB 1–2/01; HBG 3/01; SLJ 10/00) [398.24]

11279 Poole, Amy Lowry. *The Ant and the Grasshopper* (PS–1). Illus. 2000, Holiday House $16.95 (0-8234-1477-9). 32pp. This version of Aesop's fable is transported to China, and the ink and gouache illustrations on rice paper impart a quaint Oriental look. (Rev: BCCB 12/00; BL 8/00; HBG 3/01; SLJ 9/00) [398.24]

11280 Repchuk, Caroline. *The Race* (K–3). Illus. by Alison Jay. 2002, Chronicle $15.95 (0-8118-3500-6). 24pp. This update has the hare and the tortoise racing around the world. (Rev: BL 4/15/02; HBG 10/02; SLJ 7/02) [398.24]

11281 Santangelo, Colony Elliot. *Brother Wolf of Gubbio: A Legend of Saint Francis* (K–3). Illus. 2000, Handprint $15.95 (1-929766-07-6). 32pp. In this old Italian tale, Saint Francis tames a wolf that has been terrorizing a village. (Rev: BCCB 1/01; BL 1/1–15/01; HBG 3/01; SLJ 2/01) [398.2]

11282 Sneed, Brad, retel. *Aesop's Fables* (2–5). Illus. by Brad Sneed. 2003, Dial $16.99 (0-8037-2751-8). Contemporary language is used in these lighthearted retellings of 15 tales, with eye-catching illustrations. (Rev: HBG 4/04; SLJ 11/03) [398.2]

11283 Sogabe, Aki, reteller. *Aesop's Fox* (K–3). Illus. by Aki Sogabe. 1999, Harcourt $16.00 (0-15-201671-6). Several of Aesop's fables involving the fox are interwoven into a single narrative with striking pictures. (Rev: BCCB 11/99; HBG 3/00; SLJ 12/99) [398.2]

11284 Ward, Helen. *The Hare and the Tortoise* (PS–3). Illus. 1999, Millbrook LB $23.90 (0-7613-1318-4). 40pp. A witty, straightforward retelling of the fable, illustrated with outstanding watercolor paintings. (Rev: BCCB 6/99; BL 5/15/99*; HBG 10/99; SLJ 7/99) [398.24]

11285 Ward, Helen. *Unwitting Wisdom: An Anthology of Aesop's Fables* (2–5). Illus. 2004, Chronicle $18.95 (0-8118-4450-1). 64pp. Arresting ink-and-watercolor illustrations accompany well-worded retellings of a dozen Aesop tales. (Rev: BL 9/15/04; SLJ 10/04) [398.2]

11286 Watts, Bernadette, reteller. *The Lion and the Mouse: An Aesop Fable* (PS–2). Illus. by Bernadette Watts. 2000, North-South LB $15.88 (0-7358-1221-7). An expansion of the traditional Aesop fable that is illustrated with paintings of jungle scenes. (Rev: HBG 10/00; SLJ 8/00) [398.2]

11287 Watts, Bernadette. *The Town Mouse and the Country Mouse: An Aesop Fable* (PS–2). Illus. 1998, North-South LB $15.88 (1-55858-988-0). 28pp. A delightful version of the old Aesop fable about two mice that visit each other and discover that home is best. (Rev: BL 11/15/98; HBG 3/99; SLJ 3/99) [398.2]

Russia

11288 Afanasyev, Alexander, ed. *Russian Fairy Tales* (4–7). Illus. by Alexander Alexeieff. 1976, Pantheon paper $18.00 (0-394-73090-9). The definitive collection of folktales reissued in the 1945 edition. [398.2]

11289 Arnold, Katya, reteller. *That Apple Is Mine!* (PS–1). Illus. by Katya Arnold. 2000, Holiday House $15.95 (0-8234-1629-1). In this Russian folktale, Bear teaches the animals to share when they all want the same apple. (Rev: HB 1–2/01; HBG 3/01; SLJ 12/00) [398.2]

11290 Davis, Aubrey. *The Enormous Potato* (PS–1). Illus. by Dusan Petricic. 1998, Kids Can $14.95 (1-55074-386-4). 32pp. This variation on the Russian tale about a turnip uses a gigantic potato that again requires the help of everyone, including a tiny mouse, to get it out of the ground. (Rev: BCCB 10/98; BL 11/1/98; HBG 3/99; SLJ 11/98) [398.2]

11291 De Regniers, Beatrice S. *Little Sister and the Month Brothers* (K–3). Illus. by Margot Tomes. 1976, Houghton Mifflin $8.95 (0-8164-3147-7). 48pp. A delightful retelling of an old Slavic tale reminiscent of the Cinderella theme. [398.2]

11292 Ginsburg, Mirra. *Clay Boy* (PS–3). Illus. by Joseph A. Smith. 1997, Greenwillow $15.89 (0-688-14410-1). 32pp. In this Russian folktale, a grandpa makes a clay boy who comes to life and has a voracious appetite. (Rev: BL 4/15/97*; HB 3–4/97; SLJ 5/97) [398.2]

11293 Ginsburg, Mirra. *Good Morning, Chick* (PS–K). Illus. by Byron Barton. 1980, Greenwillow $15.89 (0-688-84284-4); Morrow paper $5.95 (0-688-08741-8). 32pp. A Russian folktale about a chick who must learn his identity. [398.2]

11294 Hester, Denia Lewis. *Grandma Lena's Big Ol' Turnip* (K–2). Illus. by Jackie Urbanovic. 2005, Whitman $15.95 (0-8075-3027-1). 32pp. It takes a whole family to pull up the giant turnip in Grandma Lena's garden, but the reward afterward is home-cooked soul food in this story based on Alexei Tolstoy's "The Turnip." (Rev: BL 3/15/05; SLJ 5/05)

11295 Hoffman, Mary. *Clever Katya: A Fairy Tale from Old Russia* (K–3). Illus. by Marie Cameron. 1998, Barefoot $15.95 (1-901223-64-7). 32pp. In this Russian folktale, 7-year-old Katya so impresses the czar with her intelligence that he asks her to visit him in his palace. (Rev: BL 10/1/98; SLJ 10/98) [398.2]

11296 Hogrogian, Nonny. *The Contest* (3–5). Illus. by author. 1976, Greenwillow $15.89 (0-688-84042-6). 32pp. Adaptation of the folktale about two robbers who discover that they are engaged to the same girl. [398.2]

11297 Jackson, Ellen. *The Impossible Riddle* (K–3). Illus. by Alison Winfield. 1995, Whispering Coyote $14.95 (1-879085-93-3). 32pp. In this Russian folktale, a czar hopes to prevent his daughter's marriage by demanding that prospective suitors answer an impossible riddle. (Rev: BL 1/1–15/96) [398.2]

11298 Kimmel, Eric A. *Baba Yaga: A Russian Folktale* (K–3). Illus. by Megan Lloyd. 1991, Holiday House LB $16.95 (0-8234-0854-X). 32pp. A traditional Russian folktale about Marina, whose wicked stepmother sends her to the forest witch. (Rev: BL 5/1/91; SLJ 6/91) [398.2]

11299 Kimmel, Eric A. *Bearhead: A Russian Folktale* (K–3). Illus. by Charles Mikolaycak. 1991, Holiday House LB $16.95 (0-8234-0902-3). 32pp. A peasant woman finds an odd-looking foundling with the body of a human and the head of a bear. (Rev: BCCB 12/91; BL 9/1/91; SLJ 10/91) [398.2]

11300 Kimmel, Eric A. *The Birds' Gift: A Ukrainian Easter Story* (PS–3). Illus. by Katya Krenina. 1999, Holiday House $16.95 (0-8234-1384-5). 34pp. After saving a group of birds, on Easter morning townspeople find beautifully decorated eggs left behind as gifts. (Rev: BL 4/15/99; HBG 10/99; SLJ 6/99) [398.2]

11301 Kimmel, Eric A. *I Know Not What, I Know Not Where: A Russian Tale* (4–6). Illus. by Robert Sauber. 1994, Holiday House LB $16.95 (0-8234-1020-X). 64pp. In this Russian fairy tale, a hunter is rewarded for saving an enchanted dove's life by getting help to perform tasks demanded by the czar. (Rev: BCCB 7–8/94; BL 3/1/94; SLJ 6/94) [398.2]

11302 Kimmel, Eric A. *One Eye, Two Eyes, Three Eyes: A Hutzul Tale* (PS–3). Illus. by Dirk Zimmer. 1996, Holiday House LB $15.95 (0-8234-1183-4). 32pp. A traveler unwittingly bargains away his daughter in this Ukrainian tale. (Rev: BL 11/1/96; SLJ 1/97) [398.2]

11303 Langton, Jane. *Salt: From a Russian Folktale* (K–3). Trans. by Alice Plume. Illus. by Ilse Plume. 1992, Hyperion $14.95 (1-56282-178-4). 48pp. A Russian folktale about three brothers who go to sea to seek their fortunes. (Rev: BCCB 1/93; BL 10/15/92; SLJ 12/92) [398.2]

11304 Lottridge, Celia B. *Music for the Tsar of the Sea* (K–3). Illus. by Harvey Chan. 1998, Douglas & McIntyre $16.95 (0-88899-328-5). 32pp. A lengthy retelling of the Russian folktale about musician Sadko and the Tsar of the Sea, who takes an unwilling Sadko to his underwater kingdom to play for him forever. (Rev: BL 1/1–15/99; SLJ 1/99) [398.2]

11305 McCaughrean, Geraldine. *Grandma Chickenlegs* (K–3). Illus. by Moira Kemp. 1999, Carolrhoda $15.95 (1-57505-415-9). 32pp. In this classic Russian folktale, young Tatia is sent to the witch's house to borrow a needle and is soon a prisoner of the horrible Baba Yaga. (Rev: BL 10/15/99; HBG 3/00; SLJ 1/00) [398.2]

11306 Marshak, Samuel, reteller. *The Month-Brothers: A Slavic Tale* (K–4). Illus. by Diane Stanley. 1983, Morrow $15.93 (0-688-01510-7). 32pp. A folktale involving such familiar elements as a girl and a mean stepmother. [398.2]

11307 Martin, Rafe. *The Language of Birds* (1–4). Illus. by Susan Gaber. 2000, Penguin Putnam $15.99 (0-399-22925-6). 32pp. In this Russian folktale, young Vasilii saves his brothers at sea when he learns the language of the birds. (Rev: BCCB 10/00; BL 5/15/00; HB 7–8/00; HBG 3/01; SLJ 7/00) [398.2]

11308 Martin, Rafe. *The Twelve Months* (2–4). Illus. by Vladyana Langer Krykorka. 2001, Stoddart $15.95 (0-7737-3249-7). 32pp. In this Russian variation on the Cinderella story, 12 men, representing the 12 months, help the poor young heroine supply the exotic gifts that her mean aunt and cousin demand. (Rev: BL 4/15/01; SLJ 11/01) [398.2]

11309 Mayer, Marianna. *Baba Yaga and Vasilisa the Brave* (PS–3). Illus. by Kinuko Craft. 1994, Morrow $16.95 (0-688-08500-8). 40pp. Vasilisa survives both the schemes of her wicked stepmother and a visit to the witch Baba Yaga and finally marries the czar. (Rev: BL 6/1–15/94; SLJ 7/94*) [398.2]

11310 Pogorelsky, Antony, and Elizabeth James. *The Little Black Hen* (1–3). Retold by Elizabeth James. Illus. by Gennady Spirin. 2003, Simply Read $16.95 (1-894965-03-5). 32pp. This fable, written for Alexei Tolstoi by his uncle, recounts the story of Alyosha, a Russian boy who is granted one wish but is almost undone by his greed and arrogance. (Rev: BL 9/15/03; SLJ 12/03) [398.2]

11311 Polacco, Patricia. *Luba and the Wren* (1–3). Illus. 1999, Penguin Putnam $16.99 (0-399-23168-4). 32pp. In this Russian folktale, Luba wants none of the wishes given her after saving an enchanted wren, but her parents want wealth and power. (Rev: BL 5/15/99; HBG 10/99; SLJ 6/99) [398.2]

11312 Prokofiev, Sergei. *Peter and the Wolf* (4–8). Adapted by Miguelanxo Prado. Illus. by author. 1998, NBM $15.95 (1-56163-200-7). 22pp. A somber version of the Russian folktale filled with menacing situations and scary settings. (Rev: HBG 10/98; SLJ 6/98) [398.2]

11313 Radunsky, Vladimir. *The Mighty Asparagus* (4–7). Illus. 2004, Harcourt $16.00 (0-15-216743-9). 34pp. In this entertaining version of the Russian folktale "The Enormous Turnip" with eye-catching illustrations full of artistic allusions, a gigantic stalk of asparagus sprouts in the courtyard of an Italian king. (Rev: BL 5/15/04; SLJ 7/04) [398.2]

11314 Ransome, Arthur. *The Fool of the World and the Flying Ship* (1–4). Illus. by Uri Shulevitz. 1968, Farrar $16.00 (0-374-32442-5); paper $6.95 (0-374-42438-1). 48pp. Colorful, panoramic scenes extend this retelling of a popular Russian folktale about a simple peasant boy who acquires a flying ship. Caldecott Medal winner, 1969. [398.2]

11315 Reyher, Becky. *My Mother Is the Most Beautiful Woman in the World* (2–5). Illus. by Ruth Gannett. 1945, Lothrop LB $16.93 (0-688-51251-8). 40pp. A girl tries to find her mother in this Russian setting. [398.2]

11316 Robbins, Ruth. *Baboushka and the Three Kings* (2–4). Illus. by Nicholas Sidjakov. 1960, Houghton Mifflin $16.00 (0-395-27673-X); paper $6.95 (0-395-42647-2). 32pp. The Russian legend of the old woman who refused to follow the three kings in search of the Holy Child. Caldecott Medal winner, 1961. [398.2]

11317 Sanderson, Ruth. *The Golden Mare, the Firebird, and the Magic Ring* (3–5). Illus. 2001, Little, Brown $15.95 (0-316-76906-1). 32pp. This picture book for older readers includes elements from several Russian tales in a story of adventure and romance. (Rev: BL 4/1/01; HBG 10/01; SLJ 4/01) [398.2]

11318 Shepard, Aaron. *The Sea King's Daughter: A Russian Legend* (4–6). Illus. by Gennady Spirin. 1997, Simon & Schuster $17.00 (0-689-80759-7). 40pp. In this Russian folktale Sadko, a talented musician, must decide whether he loves the daughter of the King of the Sea enough to remain in the underwater kingdom for the rest of his life. (Rev: BL 11/15/97; HBG 3/98; SLJ 12/97) [398.2]

11319 Spirin, Gennady. *The Tale of the Firebird* (K–3). Trans. by Tatiana Popova. Illus. 2002, Penguin Putnam $16.99 (0-399-23584-1). 32pp. The tsar's youngest son survives a number of tests before finding the firebird and winning the love of the beautiful Yelena in this lush picture book that melds three traditional Russian tales. (Rev: BCCB 11/02; BL 11/15/02; HBG 3/03; SLJ 9/02) [398.2]

11320 Stihler, Cherie B. *The Giant Cabbage: An Alaska Folktale* (PS–2). Illus. by Jeremiah Tram-

mell. 2003, Sasquatch paper $9.95 (1-57061-357-5). In this Alaskan variation on a traditional Russian folktale, Moose enlists the help of a band of animals to get his giant cabbage to the fair for judging. (Rev: SLJ 8/03) [398.2]

11321 Tolstoy, Aleksei. *The Gigantic Turnip* (PS–2). Illus. by Niamh Sharkey. Series: Barefoot Beginner. 2000, Barefoot $15.95 (1-902283-12-0). 40pp. A rather complicated retelling of the popular Russian folktale about a husband and wife who need help to uproot a huge turnip. (Rev: BCCB 7–8/99; SLJ 4/99) [398.2]

11322 Vagin, Vladimir. *Peter and the Wolf* (PS–3). Illus. 2000, Scholastic $15.95 (0-590-38608-5). 32pp. This retelling of the musical fairy tale makes a few changes, for example, the duck is saved and the wolf ends up in a zoo. (Rev: BL 11/15/00; HBG 10/01; SLJ 11/00) [398.2]

11323 Yolen, Jane. *The Firebird* (PS–3). Illus. by Vladimir Vagin. 2002, HarperCollins LB $15.89 (0-06-028539-7). 32pp. An effective retelling of the Russian story that combines elements from the original story with the ballet version. (Rev: BCCB 7–8/02; BL 6/1–15/02; HBG 10/02; SLJ 6/02) [398.2]

11324 Yolen, Jane. *The Flying Witch* (K–3). Illus. by Vladimir Vagin. 2003, HarperCollins LB $16.89 (0-06-028537-0). 32pp. Baba Yaga comes up against a clever young heroine determined to foil the child-eating witch in this richly illustrated adaptation of the Russian folktale. (Rev: HBG 4/04; SLJ 9/03) [398.2]

11325 Zunshine, Tatiana, retel. *A Little Story About a Big Turnip* (PS–1). Illus. by Evgeny Antonenkov. 2004, Pumpkin House $15.95 (0-9646010-0-1). A simple retelling of the Russian folktale, in which it takes the combined strength of grandfather, grandmother, granddaughter, dog, cat, and mouse to pull the turnip out of the ground. (Rev: SLJ 11/04) [398.2]

Scandinavia

11326 Asbjornsen, Peter C. *The Three Billy Goats Gruff* (PS–2). Retold by Glen Rounds. Illus. 1993, Holiday House LB $16.95 (0-8234-1015-3). 32pp. This veteran illustrator noted for animal drawings illustrates and retells this famous Norweigan folktale. (Rev: BL 4/15/93; HB 7–8/93; SLJ 6/93*) [398.2]

11327 Asbjornsen, Peter C., and Jorgen Moe. *Norwegian Folk Tales* (3–6). Illus. by Erik Werenskiold and Theodor Kittelsen. 1978, Pantheon paper $14.00 (0-394-71054-1). This edition retains the original illustrations from the 1845 edition. [398.2]

11328 Brett, Jan. *Who's That Knocking on Christmas Eve?* (K–2). Illus. 2002, Penguin Putnam $16.99 (0-399-23873-5). 32pp. A beautifully illustrated folktale of a Christmas Eve feast nearly ruined by hungry trolls. (Rev: BCCB 10/02; BL 9/1/02; HBG 3/03; SLJ 10/02)

11329 Finch, Mary, retel. *The Three Billy Goats Gruff* (PS). Illus. by Roberta Arenson. 2001, Barefoot LB $15.99 (1-84148-349-4). A gentler version of the tale for this young age group, with colorful goats and a singing troll. (Rev: HBG 3/02; SLJ 11/01) [398.2]

11330 Galdone, Paul. *The Three Billy Goats Gruff* (PS–3). Illus. by author. 1973, Houghton Mifflin $16.00 (0-395-28812-6). 32pp. A troll meets his match. (Rev: SLJ 3/05) [398.2]

11331 Hassett, John, and Ann Hassett. *The Three Silly Girls Grubb* (PS–1). Illus. 2002, Houghton Mifflin $16.00 (0-618-14183-9). 32pp. The three Grubb girls must get past Ugly-Boy Bobby in this goofy version of "The Three Billy Goats Gruff." (Rev: BCCB 11/02; BL 9/15/02; HB 9–10/02; HBG 3/03; SLJ 11/02*) [398.2]

11332 Kimmel, Eric A. *Boots and His Brothers: A Norwegian Tale* (PS–3). Illus. by Kimberly B. Root. 1992, Holiday House LB $14.95 (0-8234-0886-8). 32pp. In this Norwegian folktale, three brothers set out to seek their fortunes, but only the youngest, Boots, succeeds. (Rev: BCCB 3/92; BL 3/1/92) [398.2]

11333 Kimmel, Eric A. *Easy Work! An Old Tale* (PS–3). Illus. by Andrew Glass. 1998, Holiday House $15.95 (0-8234-1349-7). 32pp. In this variation on the classic Norwegian folktale, farmer McTeague and his wife decide to exchange roles for a day, with disastrous results. (Rev: BL 4/15/98; HBG 10/98; SLJ 6/98) [398.2]

11334 Lunge-Larsen, Lise. *The Race of the Birkebeiners* (1–3). Illus. by Mary Azarian. 2001, Houghton Mifflin $16.00 (0-618-10313-9). 32pp. A tale based on a real event in the early 13th century in which an infant prince is rescued from danger in a dramatic ski journey through a blizzard. (Rev: BCCB 10/01; BL 7/01; HBG 3/02; SLJ 9/01) [398.2]

11335 Lunge-Larsen, Lise. *The Troll with No Heart in His Body* (2–4). Illus. 1999, Houghton Mifflin $18.00 (0-395-91371-3). 96pp. A collection of nine Norwegian folktales, including "Three Billy Goats Gruff." (Rev: BCCB 1/00; BL 9/1/99; HB 11–12/99; HBG 3/00; SLJ 11/99) [398.2]

11336 MacDonald, Margaret Read. *Fat Cat* (PS–3). Illus. by Julie Paschkis. 2001, August House $15.95 (0-87483-616-6). 32pp. Brilliant illustrations and rhythmic prose are featured in this Danish folktale about a cat that gobbles up anyone who calls him fat, and the cunning mouse that saves them all. (Rev: BL 11/15/01; HBG 3/02; SLJ 1/02) [398.2]

11337 Salley, Coleen. *Who's That Tripping over My Bridge?* (K–2). Illus. by Amy Jackson Dixon. 2002, Pelican $14.95 (1-56554-890-6). In this retelling of the Norwegian tale, the three Gruff goats live north of Baton Rouge and must cross a bridge guarded by a troll in order to reach the green grasses on the other side. (Rev: HBG 10/02; SLJ 5/02) [398.2]

11338 Shepard, Aaron. *The Princess Mouse: A Tale of Finland* (K–3). Illus. by Leonid Gore. 2003, Simon & Schuster $16.95 (0-689-82912-4). 32pp. A mouse turns out to be a princess and a bride for a worthy brother in this entertaining folktale. (Rev: BL 2/1/03; HBG 10/03; SLJ 2/03) [398.2]

11339 Wisniewski, David. *Elfwyn's Saga* (4–5). Illus. 1990, Viking LB $13.89 (0-688-09590-9). 32pp. Boldly colored dramatic artwork provides the scene for these Icelandic sagas. (Rev: BL 11/1/90; HB 11–12/90; SLJ 10/90*) [398.2]

11340 Youngquist, Catherine Valente. *The Three Billygoats Gruff and Mean Calypso Joe* (K–3). Illus. by Kristin Sorra. 2002, Simon & Schuster $16.00 (0-689-82824-1). 32pp. The classic story of the three billy goats gets a Caribbean twist, complete with a troll named Calypso Joe. (Rev: BL 8/02; HBG 10/02; SLJ 11/02) [398.2]

Spain and Portugal

11341 Ada, Alma F. *The Three Golden Oranges* (K–3). Illus. by Reg Cartwright. 1999, Simon & Schuster $16.00 (0-689-80775-9). 32pp. A retelling of the Spanish folktale about the three princes who want wives, and to get them must bring three oranges to a wise old woman. (Rev: BCCB 7–8/99; BL 5/15/99; HBG 10/99; SLJ 7/99) [398.2]

11342 Araujo, Frank P. *Nekane, the Lamina and the Bear: A Tale of the Basque Pyrenees* (K–2). Illus. by Xiao Jun Li. 1993, Rayve $20.25 (1-877810-01-0). 32pp. In this Basque version of the standard fairy tale, Red Riding Hood becomes Nekane, who is stopped by a forest spirit on her way to her uncle's home. (Rev: BCCB 3/94; BL 2/1/94; SLJ 5/94) [398.2]

11343 Campoy, F. Isabel. *Rosa Raposa* (K–3). Illus. by Jose Aruego and Ariane Dewey. 2002, Harcourt $16.00 (0-15-202161-2). 32pp. Rosa, a wily fox, outwits a jaguar in these three traditional Spanish tales set in the Amazon rain forest. (Rev: BCCB 11/02; BL 9/1/02; HB 1–2/03; HBG 3/03; SLJ 9/02) [398.2]

11344 Hall, Amanda. *Prince of the Birds* (PS–2). Illus. 2005, Frances Lincoln $15.95 (1-84507-102-6). 32pp. A classic love story, set in southern Spain, in which a prince and a princess, each imprisoned in a tower, find each other with the aid of birds. (Rev: BL 5/1/05) [398.2]

11345 Kimmel, Eric A. *Bernal and Florinda: A Spanish Tale* (K–3). Illus. by Robert Rayevsky. 1994, Holiday House LB $15.95 (0-8234-1089-7). 32pp. A comic fairy tale about two Spanish lovers who are united in marriage despite the objections of the bride's father. (Rev: BCCB 9/94; BL 9/15/94; SLJ 11/94) [398.2]

11346 Kimmel, Eric A. *Squash It! A True and Ridiculous Tale* (3–5). Illus. by Robert Rayevsky. 1997, Holiday House LB $15.95 (0-8234-1299-7). 32pp. The Spanish tale of the king who adopted a louse as his favorite pet. (Rev: BL 6/1–15/97; HB 7–8/97; SLJ 7/97) [398.2]

11347 Robbins, Sandra. *The Firefly Star: A Hispanic Folk Tale* (PS–3). Illus. by Iku Oseki. 1995, SeeMore's Workshop paper $6.95 (1-882601-23-8). 32pp. In this Spanish folktale, the important holiday Three Kings' Day almost doesn't take place until a mouse and a ladybug intervene. (Rev: BL 12/1/95; SLJ 2/96) [398.2]

11348 Sierra, Judy. *The Beautiful Butterfly: A Folktale from Spain* (K–3). Illus. by Victoria Chess. 2000, Clarion $15.00 (0-395-90015-8). 32pp. This popular Spanish folktale ends happily when the fish that had swallowed Butterfly's new husband — a mouse — spits him out, thus reuniting the happy pair. (Rev: BCCB 5/00; BL 3/15/00; HBG 10/00; SLJ 8/00) [398.2]

Jewish Folklore

11349 Aroner, Miriam. *The Kingdom of Singing Birds* (K–5). Illus. by Shelly O. Haas. 1993, KarBen $13.95 (0-929371-43-7); paper $5.95 (0-929371-44-5). In this Jewish folktale, a rabbi tells a king that the only way to get his birds to sing is to set them free. (Rev: SLJ 9/93) [398.2]

11350 Blades, Ann. *Too Small* (K–2). Illus. by author. 2000, Groundwood $15.95 (0-88899-400-1). A variation on the traditional Yiddish tale about a house that becomes crowded when a lot of friends and animals are invited in. (Rev: HBG 3/01; SLJ 10/00) [398.2]

11351 Clement, Gary. *Just Stay Put: A Chelm Story* (K–4). Illus. 1996, Douglas & McIntyre $14.95 (0-88899-239-4). 32pp. A resident of Chelm, Poland, mistakes his hometown for Warsaw. (Rev: BL 9/15/96; SLJ 6/96) [398.2]

11352 Davis, Aubrey. *Bone Button Borscht* (K–3). Illus. by Dusan Petricic. 1997, Kids Can $15.95 (1-55074-224-8). 32pp. An Eastern European version of *Stone Soup*, in which a beggar persuades the synagogue caretaker to let him make borscht from his coat buttons. (Rev: BL 11/1/97; SLJ 11/97) [398.2]

11353 Fowles, Shelley. *The Bachelor and the Bean* (PS–2). Illus. 2003, Farrar $16.00 (0-374-30478-5). 32pp. In this Jewish folktale, an old bachelor drops a bean down a well, setting off a series of magical events. (Rev: BL 3/15/03; HBG 10/03; SLJ 3/03) [398.2]

11354 Freedman, Florence B. *It Happened in Chelm: A Story of the Legendary Town of Fools* (K–4). Illus. by Nik Krevitsky. 1990, Shapolsky paper $9.95 (0-933503-22-9). A retelling of one of the Jewish folktales about the fools who live in Chelm. (Rev: SLJ 3/91) [398.2]

11355 Geras, Adele. *My Grandmother's Stories: A Collection of Jewish Folk Tales* (1–5). Illus. by Anita Lobel. 2003, Knopf LB $21.99 (0-375-92285-7). 96pp. In this beautifully illustrated collection, each of 10 stories is introduced by a young girl's question to her grandmother. (Rev: HBG 4/04; SLJ 8/03) [398.2]

11356 Gerstein, Mordicai. *The Shadow of a Flying Bird: A Legend from the Kurdistani Jews* (1–5). Illus. 1994, Hyperion LB $16.49 (0-7868-2012-8). 32pp. God comes to earth to claim the life of his faithful servant Moses in this Jewish folktale. (Rev: BL 10/1/94; SLJ 9/94) [398.2]

11357 *Ghosts and Golems: Haunting Tales of the Supernatural* (4–6). Ed. by Malka Penn. Illus. by Theodor Black. 2001, Jewish Publication Soc.

$14.95 (0-8276-0733-4). 110pp. Ten supernatural short stories with Jewish themes will send chills down the spines of middle-graders and prompt discussions about values. (Rev: BL 11/1/01; HBG 3/02; SLJ 2/02) [398.2]

11358 Gilman, Phoebe. *Something from Nothing* (PS–3). Illus. 1993, Scholastic $15.95 (0-590-47280-1). 32pp. This folktale tells how a frugal grandfather recycles the material from a jacket to ever smaller objects, ending with the covering for a button. (Rev: BCCB 2/94; BL 9/1/93; HB 11–12/93; SLJ 1/94) [398.2]

11359 Icenoggle, Jodi. `Til the Cows Come Home* (K–4). Illus. by Normand Chartier. 2004, Boyds Mills $15.95 (1-56397-987-X). The Jewish folktale "The Button Story," newly set in the American West, follows a piece of leather over the years as it becomes a pair of chaps, then a pair of gloves, and finally a button. (Rev: SLJ 3/04)

11360 Jaffe, Nina. *Tales for the Seventh Day: A Collection of Sabbath Stories* (3–7). Illus. by Kelly Stribling Sutherland. 2000, Scholastic $15.95 (0-590-12054-9). 73pp. A collection of Jewish tales that honor the traditions and the celebration of the Sabbath. (Rev: BL 12/15/00; HBG 3/01; SLJ 11/00) [398.2]

11361 Jaffe, Nina. *The Way Meat Loves Salt: A Cinderella Tale from the Jewish Tradition* (PS–2). Illus. by Louise August. 1998, Holt $15.95 (0-8050-4384-5). A Yiddish folktale that combines King Lear with Cinderella and casts Elijah the Prophet in the role of fairy godmother. (Rev: BCCB 11/98; BL 10/1/98; HB 9–10/98; HBG 3/99; SLJ 9/98) [398.2]

11362 *A Journey to Paradise: And Other Jewish Tales* (1–4). Ed. by Howard Schwartz. Illus. by Giora Carmi. 2000, Pitspopany $16.95 (0-943706-21-1); paper $9.95 (0-943706-16-5). 48pp. A collection of eight Jewish folktales that revolve around mystery, magic, and life after death. (Rev: BL 4/15/00; HBG 10/00; SLJ 6/00) [296.1]

11363 Kimmel, Eric A. *The Adventures of Hershel of Ostropol* (K–4). Illus. by Trina S. Hyman. 1995, Holiday House $15.95 (0-8234-1210-5). 64pp. Ten Jewish folktales that use as a locale a village community in the Ukraine during the 19th century. (Rev: BL 10/15/95; SLJ 11/95) [398.2]

11364 Kimmel, Eric A. *Gershon's Monster* (2–4). Illus. by Jon J. Muth. 2000, Scholastic $16.95 (0-439-10839-X). 32pp. Based on an early Hasidic legend, this is the story of Gershon and how his sins catch up with him. (Rev: BCCB 10/00; BL 10/1/00; HB 9–10/00; HBG 3/01; SLJ 9/00) [398.2]

11365 Kimmel, Eric A. *The Jar of Fools: Eight Hanukkah Stories from Chelm* (PS–3). Illus. by Mordicai Gerstein. 2000, Holiday House $18.95 (0-8234-1463-9). 56pp. This collection of eight stories — some original plus some traditional Fools of Chelm tales — is filled with silliness and slapstick. (Rev: BL 9/1/00; HB 9–10/00; HBG 3/01)

11366 Kimmel, Eric A. *Onions and Garlic* (PS–3). Illus. by Katya Arnold. 1996, Holiday House $15.95 (0-8234-1222-9). 32pp. In this Hebrew folktale, young Getzel is able to use a sackful of onions to obtain a fortune in diamonds. (Rev: BCCB 6/96; BL 4/1/96; SLJ 7/96) [398.2]

11367 Patterson, Jose. *Angels, Prophets, Rabbis and Kings: From the Stories of the Jewish People* (3–6). Illus. by Claire Bushe. 1991, Bedrick LB $24.95 (0-87226-912-4). 144pp. A treasure chest of stories and parables. (Rev: BL 9/15/91; SLJ 8/91) [398.2]

11368 Podwal, Mark. *Golem: A Giant Made of Mud* (K–4). Illus. 1995, Greenwillow LB $14.93 (0-688-13812-X). 32pp. A collection of stories about the mysterious shape-changing creature that is associated with Prague. (Rev: BL 10/1/95; SLJ 11/95) [398.2]

11369 Prose, Francine. *The Angel's Mistake: Stories of Chelm* (PS–4). Illus. by Mark Podwal. 1997, Greenwillow $14.89 (0-688-14906-5). 24pp. A series of anecdotes about the city of Chelm — where fools reside — its creation and eventual destruction. (Rev: BCCB 7–8/97; BL 3/1/97; HB 7–8/97; SLJ 4/97) [398.2]

11370 Prose, Francine. *You Never Know: A Legend of the Lamed-vavniks* (K–4). Illus. by Mark Podwal. 1998, Greenwillow LB $14.93 (0-688-15807-2). 24pp. Gradually the town of Plotchnik realizes that poor Schmuel the Shoemaker is one of God's holy Lamed-vavniks — 36 righteous people living in secret throughout the world. (Rev: BCCB 7–8/98; BL 6/1–15/98; HBG 10/98; SLJ 8/98) [398.2]

11371 Rogasky, Barbara. *The Golem* (4–6). Illus. by Trina S. Hyman. 1996, Holiday House $18.95 (0-8234-0964-3). 96pp. The story of the giant monster of the 16th century and its use to help protect the Jewish people in Prague from persecution. (Rev: BCCB 9/96; BL 10/1/96*; HB 1–2/96; SLJ 10/96) [398.2]

11372 Rothenberg, Joan. *Yettele's Feathers* (PS–3). Illus. 1995, Hyperion LB $15.49 (0-7868-2081-0). 40pp. A rabbi makes Yettele realize how harmful her gossiping can be. (Rev: BL 5/1/95; SLJ 4/95) [398.2]

11373 Schram, Peninnah. *Ten Classic Jewish Children's Stories* (3–6). Illus. 1998, Pitspopany $16.95 (0-943706-96-3). 48pp. A volume that contains the retelling of ten traditional Jewish tales — many that illustrate situations in the Torah — with questions to reflect on the lessons taught. (Rev: BL 11/15/98; SLJ 3/99) [296.1]

11374 Schwartz, Howard. *Before You Were Born* (PS–2). Illus. by Kristina Swarner. 2005, Roaring Brook $16.95 (1-59643-028-1). 32pp. From Jewish legend, this is the story of the angel Lailah, who guides the human soul. (Rev: BL 5/15/05; SLJ 4/05) [398.2089]

11375 Schwartz, Howard, and Barbara Rush, sels. and retellers. *A Coat for the Moon and Other Jewish Tales* (2–5). Illus. by Michael Iofin. 1999, Jewish Publication Soc. $14.95 (0-8276-0596-X). 81pp. An engaging collection of 15 folktales from Europe and the Middle East, many from the Israel Folktale Archive. (Rev: HB 11–12/99; HBG 3/00; SLJ 10/99) [398.2]

11376 Sherman, Josepha. *Rachel the Clever and Other Jewish Folktales* (4–6). Illus. 1993, August

House paper $10.95 (0-87483-307-8). 176pp. Jewish tales gathered from many lands. (Rev: BL 3/15/93) [398.2]

11377 Shollar, Leah. *A Thread of Kindness: A Tzedaka Story* (2–4). Illus. by Shoshana Mekibel. 2000, Hachai $9.95 (1-929628-01-3). 32pp. This traditional tale tells of a poor but virtuous farmer who gains wealth through his kindness to others. (Rev: BL 10/1/00; HBG 10/01; SLJ 1/01) [398.2]

11378 Silverman, Erica. *Raisel's Riddle* (K–4). Illus. by Susan Gaber. 1999, Farrar $16.00 (0-374-36168-1). 40pp. This variation on the Cinderella story tells of a poor Jewish girl in Poland who helps an old woman and, as a reward, is granted three wishes. (Rev: BCCB 2/99; BL 5/1/99*; HB 3–4/99; HBG 10/99; SLJ 3/99) [398.2]

11379 Singer, Isaac Bashevis. *Stories for Children* (4–7). 1984, Farrar paper $14.00 (0-374-46489-8). 338pp. A collection of stories that draw on Yiddish folklore. [398.2]

11380 Stampler, Ann Redisch. *Something for Nothing* (1–3). Illus. by Jacqueline M. Cohen. 2003, Clarion $15.00 (0-618-15982-7). 32pp. A clever dog devises a scheme to free his life of three pesky cats in this Jewish folktale. (Rev: BL 5/15/03 ; HBG 10/03; SLJ 4/03) [398.2]

11381 Taback, Simms. *Joseph Had a Little Overcoat* (PS–2). Illus. 1999, Viking $15.99 (0-670-87855-3). 40pp. The many uses of a piece of cloth — from an overcoat to only enough material to cover a button — is the subject of this picture book based on an old Yiddish song. The mixed-media and collage illustrations are warm and lively. (Rev: BCCB 3/00; BL 1/1–15/00; HBG 3/00; SLJ 1/00) [398.2]

11382 Tarbescu, Edith. *The Boy Who Stuck Out His Tongue: A Yiddish Folktale* (PS–1). Illus. by Judith C. Mills. 2000, Barefoot $16.99 (1-84148-067-3). 32pp. A disobedient son sticks out his tongue and it freezes to a cold iron fence. All the villagers try to free him in this Jewish folktale. (Rev: BCCB 11/00; BL 5/15/00; HBG 3/01; SLJ 9/00) [398.2]

11383 Uhlberg, Myron. *Lemuel the Fool* (PS–3). Illus. by Sonja Lamut. 2001, Peachtree $15.95 (1-56145-220-3). 32pp. In this Yiddish folktale, a dreamer sets out to see the world but, because he is walking in a circle, finds himself back home. (Rev: BL 4/15/01; HBG 10/01; SLJ 8/01) [398.2]

11384 Wisniewski, David. *Golem* (3–6). Illus. 1996, Clarion $15.95 (0-395-72618-2). 30pp. The terrifying story of the golem, who was created by Rabbi Loew in the 16th century to help protect his people in the Prague ghetto. Caldecott Medal winner, 1997. (Rev: BCCB 9/96; BL 10/1/96*; SLJ 10/96) [398.2]

11385 Zemach, Margot. *It Could Always Be Worse: A Yiddish Folktale* (K–3). Illus. by author. 1976, Scholastic paper $4.95 (0-374-43636-3). 32pp. A Yiddish version of an old tale with colorful, humorous illustrations. [398.2]

Middle East

11386 dePaola, Tomie. *The Legend of the Persian Carpet* (K–3). Illus. by Claire Ewart. 1993, Penguin Putnam $15.99 (0-399-22415-7). 32pp. When his prize diamond is stolen and shattered, a Persian king finds solace in a beautiful new carpet woven for him. (Rev: BL 10/1/93; SLJ 1/94) [398.2]

11387 Hickox, Rebecca. *The Golden Sandal: A Middle Eastern Cinderella Story* (K–3). Illus. by Will Hillenbrand. 1998, Holiday House $15.95 (0-8234-1331-4). 32pp. A vivid retelling with atmospheric illustrations of an Iraqi folktale that is a variation of the Cinderella story. (Rev: BCCB 6/98; BL 4/1/98; HB 3–4/98; HBG 10/98; SLJ 4/98) [398.2]

11388 Hofmeyr, Dianne. *The Star-Bearer: A Creation Myth from Ancient Egypt* (3–5). Illus. by Judy Daly. 2001, Farrar $16.00 (0-374-37481-4). 32pp. In this picture book for older readers, a creation myth from Egypt is retold in which the god of rain and dew and the god of air emerge from a lotus bud. (Rev: BCCB 3/01; BL 2/15/01) [299]

11389 Johnson-Davies, Denys. *Goha the Wise Fool* (2–4). Illus. by Hany El Saed Ahmed and Hag Hamdy Mohamed Fattouh. 2005, Philomel $16.99 (0-399-24222-8). 40pp. Traditional tapestries illustrate a collection of memorable tales about a Middle Eastern trickster-fool called Goha. (Rev: BL 6/1–15/05; HB 9–10/05) [398.2]

11390 Kherdian, David. *The Golden Bracelet* (K–4). Illus. by Nonny Hogrogian. 1998, Holiday House $16.95 (0-8234-1362-4). 32pp. An Armenian story about a prince who uses his skill as a weaver to send a message to his wife when he is held prisoner by an evil sorcerer. (Rev: BL 6/1–15/98; HBG 10/98; SLJ 8/98) [398.2]

11391 Kimmel, Eric A. *The Tale of Aladdin and the Wonderful Lamp: A Story from the Arabian Nights* (PS–3). Illus. by Ju-Hong Chen. 1992, Holiday House LB $14.95 (0-8234-0938-4). 32pp. A humorous retelling of the famous story. (Rev: BL 11/1/92; SLJ 12/92) [398.2]

11392 Kimmel, Eric A. *The Three Princes* (K–3). Illus. by Leonard Everett Fisher. 1994, Holiday House LB $16.95 (0-8234-1115-X). 30pp. A beautiful princess shows great wisdom in choosing her husband from the three noble cousins who are her suitors in this Middle Eastern folktale. (Rev: BCCB 4/94; BL 3/1/94*; SLJ 3/94) [398.2]

11393 Lang, Andrew. *The Arabian Nights Entertainments* (5–9). Illus. 1969, Dover paper $9.95 (0-486-22289-6). Aladdin and Sinbad are only two of the characters in these 26 tales of Arabia and the East. (Rev: BL 9/1/89) [398.2]

11394 McVilly, Walter, reteller. *Ali Baba and the Forty Thieves* (K–4). Illus. by Margaret Early. 1989, Abrams $17.95 (0-8109-1888-9). 32pp. Vivid recreation of the most famous story of the Thousand and One Nights. (Rev: BL 5/15/89; HB 7–8/89) [398.2]

11395 Oppenheim, Shulamith Levey. *Iblis* (1–4). Illus. by Ed Young. 1994, Harcourt $15.95 (0-15-238016-7). 32pp. In this Islamic version of Adam and Eve's expulsion from Eden, the devil is called Iblis. (Rev: BCCB 4/94; BL 3/15/94; SLJ 4/94) [297]

11396 Philip, Neil. *The Arabian Nights* (4–6). Illus. by Sheila Moxley. 1994, Orchard $19.95 (0-531-06868-4). 160pp. With lovely paintings and colorful prose, this is an excellent retelling of 16 of the Arabian Nights stories, including Ali Baba, Scheherazade, and Aladdin. (Rev: BL 12/15/94; HB 5–6/94; SLJ 12/94*) [398.2]

11397 Pullman, Philip. *Aladdin and the Enchanted Lamp* (3–5). Illus. by Sophy Williams. 2005, Scholastic $16.95 (0-439-69255-5). 64pp. An exotic presentation, full of wit and dramatic art. (Rev: BL 5/1/05) [398.22]

11398 Shah, Idries. *The Boy Without a Name* (PS–2). Illus. by Mona Caron. 2000, Hoopoe $17.00 (1-883536-20-0). 32pp. Based on an Islamic story, this folktale tells of a boy who visits a wise man to get a name. (Rev: BL 12/1/00; SLJ 2/01) [398.22]

11399 Shah, Idries. *The Clever Boy and the Terrible, Dangerous Animal* (1–4). Illus. by Rose Mary Santiago. 2000, Hoopoe $17.00 (1-883536-18-9). In this Middle Eastern folktale, a young boy quiets some villagers by explaining that the animal they fear is really just a melon. (Rev: SLJ 12/00) [398.2]

11400 Shah, Idries. *The Lion Who Saw Himself in the Water* (PS–2). Illus. by Ingrid Rodriguez. 1998, Hoopoe $17.00 (1-883536-12-X). 32pp. In this Sufi tale from Islam, a lion is so frightened by his reflection in the water that he can't drink from the pool until a friendly butterfly helps him conquer his fear. (Rev: BL 10/1/98; SLJ 12/98) [398.24]

11401 Shah, Idries. *The Magic Horse* (3–5). Illus. by Julie Freeman. 1998, Hoopoe $17.00 (1-883536-11-1). 34pp. This picture-book version of a Muslim Sufi tale involves two brothers and their separate quests. (Rev: SLJ 2/99) [398.2]

11402 Shah, Idries. *Neem the Half-Boy* (PS–2). Illus. by Midori Mori and Robert Revels. 1998, Hoopoe $17.00 (1-883536-10-3). 32pp. In this story based on an ancient Sufi tale from Islam, Neem remains a half-boy until he successfully confronts a dragon in his lair. (Rev: BL 10/1/98; SLJ 1/99) [398.22]

11403 Wolfson, Margaret Olivia. *The Patient Stone: A Persian Love Story* (3–7). Illus. by Juan Caneba Clavero. 2001, Barefoot $16.99 (1-84148-085-1). 32pp. This retelling of the story of Fatima, who after many trials earns the love of a prince thanks to a magic stone, is accompanied by beautiful watercolors and handsome borders, as well as an author's note that explains some of the symbolism. (Rev: BL 9/15/01; HBG 3/02; SLJ 2/02) [398.2]

11404 Young, Ed. *What About Me?* (K–3). Illus. 2002, Penguin Putnam $16.99 (0-399-23624-4). 40pp. A colorful cumulative tale of Sufi origin about a boy who must provide the grand master with a carpet before he will give the youngster the gift of knowledge. (Rev: BCCB 7–8/02; BL 5/1/02*; HB 7–8/02; HBG 10/02; SLJ 6/02) [398.2]

11405 Zeman, Ludmila. *Sindbad: From the Tales of the Thousand and One Nights* (3–5). Illus. 1999,

Tundra $17.95 (0-88776-460-6). 32pp. Using extraordinary illustrations, the author-artist tells the stories of two of the famous voyages of Sinbad, one involving a giant whale and the other featuring a huge bird. (Rev: BL 1/1–15/00*; SLJ 1/00) [813.54]

11406 Zeman, Ludmila. *Sindbad in the Land of Giants* (PS–3). Illus. 2001, Tundra $17.95 (0-88776-461-4). 32pp. Sindbad's cunning and courage are tested in this beautifully illustrated adventure. (Rev: BL 8/01; HBG 10/01; SLJ 8/01) [398.2]

11407 Zeman, Ludmila, retel. *Sindbad's Secret: From The Tales of the Thousand and One Nights* (2–5). Illus. by Ludmila Zeman. 2003, Tundra $17.95 (0-88776-462-2). Sindbad recounts two wondrous escapes and his discovery of the ultimate treasure is this last volume of Zeman's trilogy. (Rev: HBG 10/03; SLJ 3/03) [813.54]

North America

Canada

11408 Carrier, Roch, retel. *The Flying Canoe* (3–6). Trans. from French by Sheila Fischman. Illus. by Sheldon Cohen. 2004, Tundra $15.95 (0-88776-636-6). On a New Year's Eve in the mid-19th century, 11-year-old Baptiste and his homesick lumberjack friends are transported home by magical canoe; a French Canadian folktale. (Rev: SLJ 4/05) [398.2]

11409 Johnson, Emily Pauline. *The Lost Island* (2–4). Illus. by Atanas Matsoureff. 2005, Simply Read $16.95 (1-894965-07-8). 40pp. In this retelling of an Indian folktale, an elderly man tells of his search for a mysterious lost island said to hold the bravery of a once-powerful leader of the Squamish. (Rev: BL 1/1–15/05) [398.2]

11410 Jorisch, Stephane, adapt. *As for the Princess? A Folktale from Quebec* (K–3). Illus. by Stephane Jorisch. 2001, Annick LB $19.95 (1-55037-695-0); paper $7.95 (1-55037-694-2). A not-very-bright young man finally gets his revenge against a beautiful but light-fingered princess. (Rev: HBG 3/02; SLJ 3/02) [398.2]

Inuit

11411 Bierhorst, John, ed. *The Dancing Fox: Arctic Folktales* (4–6). Illus. 1997, Morrow $15.00 (0-688-14406-3). 192pp. After an introduction to the land and people of the American Arctic, the author presents 18 Inuit folktales. (Rev: BCCB 7–8/97; BL 4/15/97; HB 5–6/97; SLJ 6/97) [398.2]

11412 Dabcovich, Lydia, reteller. *The Polar Bear Son: An Inuit Tale* (K–2). Illus. by Lydia Dabcovich. 1997, Clarion $16.00 (0-395-72766-9). 37pp. In this Inuit tale, the men of a village want to kill the polar bear that one of their women had adopted when it was an orphaned cub. (Rev: SLJ 6/97) [398.2]

11413 Hall, Amanda. *The Stolen Sun: A Story of Native Alaska* (PS–3). Illus. 2002, Eerdmans $17.00 (0-8028-5225-4). 32pp. A Native Alaskan tale with folkloric flavor about the creation of the world and

its inhabitants. (Rev: BL 2/15/02; HBG 10/02; SLJ 9/02) [398.2]

11414 Houston, James. *Tikta'liktak: An Eskimo Legend* (4–6). Illus. by author. 1990, Harcourt paper $10.00 (0-15-287748-7). 63pp. Legend of a young Inuit hunter who is carried out to sea on a drifting ice floe with only his bow and arrows and a harpoon. Also use: *The White Archer: An Eskimo Legend* (1990). [398.2]

11415 Murphy, Claire R. *Caribou Girl* (K–3). Illus. by Linda Russell. 1998, Roberts Rinehart $16.95 (1-57098-145-0). A young Inuit changes into a caribou to bring the herd to her starving people. (Rev: HBG 10/98; SLJ 7/98) [398.2]

Native Americans

11416 Ata, Te. *Baby Rattlesnake* (PS–K). Adapted by Lynn Moroney. Illus. by Veg Reisberg. 1990, Children's Book Pr. $14.95 (0-89239-049-2); paper $7.95 (0-89239-111-1). 32pp. A baby rattlesnake doesn't know how to behave when he is given a rattle before reaching maturity. (Rev: BL 3/1/90; SLJ 4/90) [398.2]

11417 Bierhorst, John. *Is My Friend at Home? Pueblo Fireside Tales* (2–4). Illus. by Wendy Watson. 2001, Farrar $16.00 (0-374-33550-8). 32pp. Seven Hopi pourquoi tales involve trickster inclinations among the animals. (Rev: BL 7/01; HB 9–10/01; HBG 3/02; SLJ 9/01) [398.2]

11418 Bierhorst, John. *The Woman Who Fell from the Sky: The Iroquois Story of Creation* (K–4). Illus. by Robert Andrew Parker. 1993, Morrow LB $14.93 (0-688-10681-1). 32pp. Sky Woman, with the help of her two sons, creates the earth. (Rev: BCCB 5/93; BL 3/15/93; HB 5–6/93; SLJ 4/93) [398.2]

11419 Bouchard, David. *Qu'Appelle* (3–6). Illus. by Michael Lonechild. 2002, Raincoast $15.95 (1-55192-475-7). A young Cree woman, heartbroken when her betrothed must go to war, calls out to him while dying. (Rev: SLJ 10/02) [398.2]

11420 Bruchac, Joseph. *Between Earth and Sky: Legends of Native American Sacred Places* (2–5). Illus. by Thomas Locker. 1996, Harcourt $16.00 (0-15-200042-9). 32pp. A retelling of ten legends dealing with sacred places from various Native American tribes. (Rev: BL 4/1/96; HB 5–6/96; SLJ 7/96) [398.2]

11421 Bruchac, Joseph. *Dog People: Native Dog Stories* (3–6). Illus. by Murv Jacob. 1995, Fulcrum $14.95 (1-55591-228-1). 63pp. This book contains five very readable stories about the Abenaki Indian children and their dogs. (Rev: SLJ 1/96) [398.2]

11422 Bruchac, Joseph. *Flying with the Eagle, Racing the Great Bear: Stories from Native North America* (5–8). Illus. 1993, Troll paper $13.95 (0-8167-3026-1). 144pp. Sixteen stories, arranged geographically, introduce coming-of-age rites for males in Native American cultures. (Rev: BL 12/15/93; SLJ 9/93) [398.2]

11423 Bruchac, Joseph. *Native American Animal Stories* (5–8). Illus. 1992, Fulcrum paper $12.95 (1-

55591-127-7). Animal stories from various Native American tribes, for reading aloud and storytelling. (Rev: BL 9/1/92; SLJ 11/92) [398.2]

11424 Bruchac, Joseph. *Native Plant Stories* (4–8). Illus. 1995, Fulcrum paper $12.95 (1-55591-212-5). 128pp. A collection of stories about plants that come from various Native American cultures in North and Central America. (Rev: BL 9/1/95) [398.24]

11425 Bruchac, Joseph, and James Bruchac. *How Chipmunk Got His Stripes: A Tale of Bragging and Teasing* (1–3). Illus. by Ariane Dewey and Jose Aruego. 2001, Dial $15.99 (0-8037-2404-7). 32pp. In this Native American story, squirrel is punished for teasing Big Bear by having the now-familiar chipmunk stripe placed on his back. (Rev: BCCB 3/01; BL 2/1/01; HBG 10/01; SLJ 2/01) [398.24]

11426 Bruchac, Joseph, and James Bruchac. *When the Chenoo Howls* (3–6). Illus. 1998, Walker $15.95 (0-8027-8638-3). 128pp. This anthology consists of 12 scary stories from the Northeast woodland Native Americans — most of them traditional folktales together with a few original stories that incorporate legendary characters. (Rev: BCCB 9/98; BL 8/98; HBG 3/99; SLJ 12/98) [398.2]

11427 Bushyhead, Robert H. *Yonder Mountain: A Cherokee Legend* (PS–3). Illus. by Kristina Rodanas. 2002, Marshall Cavendish $16.95 (0-7614-5113-7). 32pp. In this Cherokee folktale, an old chief tests three young men to determine who will be his successor. (Rev: BL 2/15/03; HBG 10/03; SLJ 12/02) [398.2]

11428 Charles, Veronika M., retel. *Maiden of the Mist: A Legend of Niagara Falls* (1–3). Illus. by Veronika M. Charles. 2001, Stoddart $13.95 (0-7737-3297-7); paper $6.95 (0-7737-6207-8). A beautifully illustrated story of the maiden who sacrifices herself to the Thunder God in order to save her people from illness. (Rev: SLJ 1/02) [398.2]

11429 Cohen, Caron L. *The Mud Pony: A Traditional Skidi Pawnee Tale* (K–3). Illus. by Shonto Begay. 1988, Scholastic $15.95 (0-590-41525-5). 32pp. The moving story of a boy too poor to have a pony of his own who grows up to become chief of his people. (Rev: BCCB 12/88; BL 12/1/88; SLJ 1/89) [398.2]

11430 Connolly, James E. *Why the Possum's Tail Is Bare: And Other North American Indian Nature Tales* (4–7). Illus. 1992, Stemmer $15.95 (0-88045-069-X); paper $7.95 (0-88045-107-6). 64pp. Nature and folklore are combined in 13 Native American animal tales. (Rev: BL 9/1/85; SLJ 10/85) [398.2]

11431 Crook, Connie Brummel. *Maple Moon* (K–4). Illus. by Scott Cameron. 1998, Stoddart $15.95 (0-7737-3017-6). 32pp. A crippled young Mississauga boy accidentally discovers tree sap as a source of food for his people in this adaptation of two Native American folktales. (Rev: BL 4/15/98; SLJ 4/98) [398.2]

11432 Curry, Jane Louise. *Hold Up the Sky and Other Native American Tales from Texas and the Southern Plains* (3–7). Illus. 2003, Simon & Schuster $17.95 (0-689-85287-8). 176pp. These varied folktales offer a mix of adventure, pourquoi stories,

and humor and are accompanied by brief supplementary information about the 14 tribes from which they originated. (Rev: BL 4/1/03; HBG 10/03; SLJ 10/03) [398.2]

11433 Curry, Jane Louise. *The Wonderful Sky Boat* (3–7). Illus. 2001, Simon & Schuster $17.00 (0-689-83595-7). 160pp. A collection of nearly 30 Native American creation, pourquoi, and trickster stories. (Rev: BL 5/15/01; HB 9–10/01; HBG 3/02) [398.2]

11434 De Montano, Marty Kreipe. *Coyote in Love with a Star* (PS–3). Illus. by Tom Coffin. 1998, Abbeville $14.95 (0-7892-0162-3). 31pp. In this updated pourquoi tale that explains why coyotes howl at the moon, Coyote travels to New York City and there falls in love with a star. (Rev: BL 12/1/98; HB 3–4/99; HBG 3/99; SLJ 2/99) [398.2]

11435 Dengler, Marianna. *The Worry Stone* (3–5). Illus. by Sibyl G. Gerig. 1996, Northland LB $15.95 (0-87358-642-5). 34pp. When her grandfather dies, Amanda finds that she gets comfort from rubbing a stone that the old man had given to her. (Rev: BL 12/15/96; SLJ 1/97) [398.2]

11436 dePaola, Tomie, reteller. *The Legend of the Bluebonnet: An Old Tale of Texas* (K–3). Illus. by Tomie dePaola. 1983, Penguin Putnam $16.99 (0-399-20937-9). 32pp. This book retells the Comanche Indian story of the origin of the Texas bluebonnet flower. [398.2]

11437 Dominic, Gloria, adapt. *Brave Bear and the Ghosts: A Sioux Legend* (2–4). Illus. by Charles Reasoner. Series: Native American Lore and Legends. 1996, Rourke LB $16.95 (0-86593-429-0). 47pp. A charming trickster tale with a surprise ending from the Sioux. Also use *Coyote and the Grasshoppers: A Pomo Legend* and *Song of the Hermit Thrush: An Iroquois Legend* (both 1996). (Rev: SLJ 3/97) [398.2]

11438 Drucker, Malka. *The Sea Monster's Secret* (PS–3). Illus. by Christopher Aja. 1999, Harcourt $16.00 (0-15-200619-2). 32pp. A folktale from Alaska that tells how an unassuming hero secretly supplies his village with food. (Rev: BL 10/15/99; HBG 10/99; SLJ 6/99) [398.24]

11439 Dwyer, Mindy, reteller. *Coyote in Love* (PS–3). Illus. by Mindy Dwyer. 1997, Alaska Northwest $15.95 (0-88240-485-7). This Native American tale of how Crater Lake was formed tells of Coyote's unrequited love for a star. (Rev: SLJ 7/97) [398.2]

11440 Esbensen, Barbara J. *Ladder to the Sky: How the Gift of Healing Came to the Ojibway Nation* (K–3). Illus. by Helen K. Davie. 1989, Little, Brown $15.95 (0-316-24952-1). 32pp. Although the Ojibwa (Chippewa) lost their direct connection to the Great Spirit, they were granted healing powers. (Rev: BCCB 2/90; BL 11/1/89; SLJ 10/89) [398.2]

11441 Esbensen, Barbara J. *The Star Maiden: An Ojibway Tale* (3–5). Illus. by Helen K. Davie. 1991, Little, Brown paper $5.95 (0-316-24955-6). 32pp. A star appears in a dream to a young brave, falls to earth, and becomes a water lily. (Rev: BCCB 4/88; BL 4/1/88; SLJ 6–7/88) [398.2]

561

11442 Goble, Paul. *Crow Chief: A Plains Indian Story* (K–3). Illus. by author. 1992, Orchard LB $17.99 (0-531-08547-3). 32pp. This Plains Indian legend explains why crows have black feathers. (Rev: BCCB 4/92; BL 2/15/92; HB 3–4/92; SLJ 3/92) [398.2]

11443 Goble, Paul. *The Great Race: Of the Birds and Animals* (K–3). Illus. by author. 1991, Simon & Schuster paper $5.99 (0-689-71452-1). 32pp. The story of the great race between the animals and humans in which the people won and now have responsibility to care for animals. (Rev: BCCB 9/85; BL 9/15/85; SLJ 9/85) [398.2]

11444 Goble, Paul. *Iktomi and the Berries: A Plains Indian Story* (K–2). Illus. by author. 1992, Orchard paper $6.95 (0-531-07029-8). 32pp. A witty folktale about a disreputable hero. (Rev: BCCB 12/89*; BL 9/15/89; HB 11–12/89; SLJ 9/89*) [398.2]

11445 Goble, Paul. *Iktomi and the Boulder: A Plains Indian Story* (3–5). Illus. by author. 1988, Orchard $16.95 (0-531-05760-7); paper $6.95 (0-531-07023-9). 32pp. Iktomi, a trickster, is the hero of many humorous adventures in these Sioux tales. (Rev: BCCB 7–8/88; BL 8/88; HB 9–10/88) [398.2]

11446 Goble, Paul. *Iktomi and the Buffalo Skull: A Plains Indian Story* (K–3). Illus. by author. 1996, Orchard paper $5.95 (0-531-07077-8). 32pp. Iktomi the trickster tries to impress girls but ends up with his head stuck in a buffalo skull. (Rev: BL 2/1/91; HB 5–6/91; SLJ 3/91) [398.2]

11447 Goble, Paul. *Iktomi and the Coyote: A Plains Indian Story* (3–5). Illus. by author. 1998, Orchard LB $17.99 (0-531-33108-3). Iktomi, a trickster, thinks he has found himself a meal of prairie dog, but he is outwitted by a clever coyote. (Rev: BCCB 1/99; HBG 3/99; SLJ 11/98) [398.2]

11448 Goble, Paul. *The Legend of the White Buffalo Woman* (4–8). Illus. 1998, National Geographic $16.95 (0-7922-7074-6). In this picture book for older readers recounting a Lakata Indian tale, an earth woman and an eagle mate after a great flood to produce a new people. (Rev: BL 3/15/98; HBG 10/98; SLJ 5/98) [398.2]

11449 Goble, Paul. *Mystic Horse* (2–3). 2003, HarperCollins $16.99 (0-06-029813-8); paper $17.89 (0-06-029814-6). 40pp. Inspired by a Pawnee folktale, this is a mystical story of a boy and a magical horse. (Rev: BL 7/03; HB 5–6/03; HBG 10/03; SLJ 5/03) [398.2]

11450 Goble, Paul. *Remaking the Earth: A Creation Story from the Great Plains of North America* (3–6). Illus. 1996, Orchard LB $16.99 (0-531-08874-X). 32pp. In this creation myth, Earth Maker re-creates the land after a destructive flood. (Rev: BL 9/15/96; SLJ 10/96) [398.2]

11451 Goble, Paul, reteller. *Star Boy* (2–4). 1991, Simon & Schuster paper $5.99 (0-689-71499-8). 32pp. A legend on how Star Boy was able to rid himself of a disfiguring scar. [398.2]

11452 Goble, Paul. *Storm Maker's Tipi* (2–5). Illus. 2001, Atheneum $18.00 (0-689-84137-X). 40pp. A retelling of a Blackfoot legend about the origin of tipis (tepees), with drawings, photographs, and instructions for making a paper tipi. (Rev: BCCB 1/02; BL 10/1/01; HBG 3/02; SLJ 10/01) [398.2]

11453 Hausman, Gerald. *The Story of Blue Elk* (K–4). Illus. by Kristina Rodanas. 1998, Clarion $15.00 (0-395-84512-2). 32pp. In this Pueblo Indian legend, a voiceless boy is able to communicate by using a flute fashioned from a cedar tree that grew from the antlers of Blue Elk. (Rev: BL 5/15/98; HBG 10/98; SLJ 8/98) [398.2]

11454 Highwater, Jamake. *Anpao: An American Indian Odyssey* (5–8). Illus. by Fritz Scholder. 1993, HarperCollins paper $7.95 (0-06-440437-4). 256pp. A young hero encounters great danger on his way to meet his father, the Sun, in this dramatic American Indian folktale. [398.2]

11455 Hillerman, Tony, ed. *The Boy Who Made Dragonfly: A Zuni Myth* (5–7). Illus. by Laszlo Kubinyi. 1986, Univ. of New Mexico Pr. paper $8.95 (0-8263-0910-0). 85pp. A Zuni boy and his little sister are left behind by their tribe and survive hunger and deprivation through the intervention of the Cornstalk Being. [398.2]

11456 Jones, Jennifer B. *Heetunka's Harvest: A Tale of the Plains Indians* (K–3). Illus. by Shannon Keegan. 1995, Roberts Rinehart $15.95 (1-879373-17-3). 32pp. Nature takes revenge on a thieving Dakota Indian woman who steals from Heetunka the bean mouse. (Rev: BL 1/1/95; SLJ 4/95) [398.2]

11457 *Kokopelli, Drum in Belly* (3–5). Trans. and illus. by Gail E. Haley. 2003, Filter $18.95 (0-86541-069-0). Rich illustrations enhance this telling of the Native American legend of Kokopelli the Cicada. (Rev: BL 10/15/03; HBG 4/04; SLJ 2/04)

11458 Larrabee, Lisa. *Grandmother Five Baskets* (2–4). Illus. by Lori Sawyer. 1993, Harbinger paper $9.95 (0-943173-90-6). 60pp. Using five baskets that have been made by a Poarch Creek Indian woman as a metaphor, different stages of life are explained. (Rev: SLJ 3/94)

11459 Lavitt, Edward, and Robert E. McDowell. *Nihancan's Feast of Beaver: Animal Tales of the North American Indians* (2–6). Illus. by Bunny P. Huffman. 1990, Museum of New Mexico paper $12.95 (0-89013-211-9). 120pp. This handsome book contains 36 tales from nine different cultural areas in North America. (Rev: BL 3/1/91) [398.2]

11460 Lind, Michael. *Bluebonnet Girl* (K–3). Illus. by Kate Kiesler. 2003, Holt $16.95 (0-8050-6573-3). 40pp. A Comanche legend telling why bluebonnets bloom in Texas. (Rev: BL 3/15/03; HBG 4/04; SLJ 4/03) [398.2]

11461 Luenn, Nancy. *The Miser on the Mountain: A Nisqually Legend of Mount Rainier* (3–6). Illus. by Pierre Morgan. 1997, Sasquatch $15.95 (1-57061-082-7). 32pp. An Indian legend set on Ta-co-bet, or Mount Rainier, in which greed leads to a man's downfall. (Rev: BL 9/15/97; HBG 3/98; SLJ 1/98) [398.2]

11462 McDermott, Gerald. *Coyote: A Trickster Tale from the American Southwest* (PS–K). Illus. 1994, Harcourt $15.00 (0-15-220724-4). 32pp. Obnoxious Coyote has a comedown when he tries to fly with the crows. (Rev: BCCB 11/94; BL 8/94*; SLJ 11/94) [398.2]

11463 McDermott, Gerald. *Raven: A Trickster Tale from the Pacific Northwest* (K–4). Illus. by author. 1993, Harcourt $16.00 (0-15-265661-8). 32pp. A traditional tale told by the tribes of the area and illustrated by a Caldecott Medal winner. (Rev: BCCB 6/93*; BL 3/1/93*; HB 7–8/93*; SLJ 5/93*) [398]

11464 Malotki, Ekkehart, comp. *The Magic Hummingbird: A Hopi Folktale* (2–4). Illus. by Michael Lacapa. 1996, Kiva $15.95 (1-885772-04-1). In this Hopi tale, a boy makes a toy hummingbird that comes to life and helps end a drought by taking the boy and his sister to the fertility god. (Rev: SLJ 11/96) [398.2]

11465 Martin, Rafe. *The Rough-Face Girl* (1–4). Illus. by David Shannon. 1992, Penguin Putnam LB $16.99 (0-399-21859-9). 32pp. This variation on the Cinderella tale takes place in an Algonquin village on the shores of Lake Ontario. (Rev: BL 4/15/92; HB 7–8/92; SLJ 5/92) [398.2]

11466 Martin, Rafe. *The World Before This One* (5–8). Illus. by Calvin Nichols. 2002, Scholastic paper $16.95 (0-590-37976-3). 208pp. Crow, a Seneca Indian, comes upon a storytelling stone that tells him about the origins of the earth in this series of stories. (Rev: BL 2/15/03; HBG 3/03; SLJ 12/02) [398.2]

11467 Max, Jill, ed. *Spider Spins a Story: Fourteen Legends from Native America* (3–6). Illus. 1997, Northland $16.95 (0-87358-611-5). 72pp. Spider plays a prominent role in these folktales, illustrated by six Native American artists. (Rev: BL 12/15/97; HBG 10/98; SLJ 1/98) [398.2]

11468 Mayo, Gretchen Will, reteller. *Big Trouble for Tricky Rabbit!* (2–4). Illus. by Gretchen Will Mayo. Series: Native American Trickster Tales. 1994, Walker LB $13.85 (0-8027-8276-0). 38pp. Using simple vocabulary and short sentences, the author retells five trickster tales from Native American folklore, all involving Rabbit. (Rev: BCCB 6/94; SLJ 7/94) [398.2]

11469 Mayo, Gretchen Will. *Earthmaker's Tales: North American Indian Stories About Earth Happenings* (4–6). Illus. 1989, Walker LB $13.85 (0-8027-6840-7). 96pp. Legends that center on the earth itself. (Rev: BL 3/1/89) [398.2]

11470 Mayo, Gretchen Will. *Here Comes Tricky Rabbit!* (2–4). Illus. Series: Native American Trickster Tales. 1994, Walker LB $13.85 (0-8027-8274-4). 48pp. These five folktales reveal Rabbit to be a wily trickster. (Rev: BCCB 6/94; BL 8/94; SLJ 7/94) [398.2]

11471 Mayo, Gretchen Will, reteller. *Meet Tricky Coyote!* (2–5). Illus. by Gretchen Will Mayo. Series: Native American Trickster Tales. 1993, Walker LB $13.85 (0-8027-8199-3). 36pp. A retelling of some short, humorous Native American stories about the clever trickster coyote. Companion volumes are *That Tricky Coyote!* and *Magical Tales from Many Lands* (both 1993). (Rev: SLJ 9/93) [398.2]

11472 Mayo, Gretchen Will. *Star Tales: North American Indian Stories About the Stars* (4–7). Illus. by author. 1987, Walker LB $13.85 (0-8027-6673-0). 96pp. Fourteen tales, each introduced by a one-page commentary on a constellation. (Rev: BL 6/15/87; SLJ 5/87) [398.2]

11473 Mayo, Gretchen Will. *That Tricky Coyote!* (PS–3). Illus. 1993, Walker LB $13.85 (0-8027-8201-9). 32pp. Five short stories from different tribes that deal with the escapades of the trickster Coyote. (Rev: BL 9/1/93; SLJ 9/93) [398.2]

11474 Medicine Crow, Joe. *Brave Wolf and the Thunderbird* (PS–3). Illus. by Linda R. Martin. 1998, Abbeville $14.95 (0-7892-0160-7). 31pp. Written and illustrated by Native Americans, this is the traditional tale of the kidnapping of Brave Wolf by Thunderbird to assist in the rescue of Thunderbird's chicks from a sea monster. (Rev: BL 12/1/98; HBG 3/99; SLJ 4/99) [398.2]

11475 Monroe, Jean Guard, and Ray A. Williamson. *They Dance in the Sky: Native American Star Myths* (4–8). Illus. 1987, Houghton Mifflin $16.00 (0-395-39970-X). 130pp. Numerous Native American legends about stars. (Rev: BL 9/1/87; SLJ 9/87) [398.2]

11476 Nelson, S. D. *Gift Horse: A Lakota Story* (PS–3). Illus. 1999, Abrams $14.95 (0-8109-4127-9). 40pp. Flying Cloud earns his status as a Lakota warrior when he joins a raiding party to return horses stolen by Crow enemies. (Rev: BL 12/1/99; HBG 3/00; SLJ 11/99) [978]

11477 Norman, Howard. *The Girl Who Dreamed Only Geese and Other Stories of the Far North* (4–8). Illus. 1997, Harcourt $22.00 (0-15-230979-9). A fine collection of Inuit tales, enhanced by illustrations resembling stone carvings. (Rev: BL 9/15/97*; SLJ 11/97*) [398.2]

11478 *The People with Five Fingers: A Native Californian Creation Tale* (K–3). Ed. by John Bierhorst. Illus. by Robert Andrew Parker. 2000, Marshall Cavendish $15.95 (0-7614-5058-0). 32pp. A Native American creation tale about how Coyote put the animals to work to prepare for the arrival of humans in the world. (Rev: BCCB 3/00; BL 4/1/00; HBG 10/00; SLJ 6/00) [398.2]

11479 Pollock, Penny. *The Turkey Girl: A Zuni Cinderella Story* (4–6). Illus. by Ed Young. 1996, Little, Brown $16.95 (0-316-71314-7). 32pp. In this Zuni folktale, Turkey Girl's magical transformation ends in disaster when she forgets her promise to return to her flock of birds. (Rev: BCCB 4/96; BL 4/15/96; HB 5–6/96; SLJ 5/96) [398.2]

11480 Powell, Patricia Hruby. *Zinnia: How the Corn Was Saved* (1–5). Trans. by Peter A. Thomas. Illus. by Kendrick Benally. 2004, Salina Bookshelf $17.95 (1-893354-38-5). This authentic retelling, in both Navajo and English, of a folktale about a knowledgeable Spider Woman is notable for its illustrations. (Rev: SLJ 6/04) [398.2]

11481 Raczek, Linda. *Stories from Native North America* (2–4). Illus. by Richard Hook. Series: Multicultural Stories. 2000, Raintree LB $27.12 (0-7398-1336-6). 48pp. A fine collection of Native

American folktales that represents many geographical locations. (Rev: HBG 10/00; SLJ 11/00) [398.2]

11482 Riordan, James. *The Songs My Paddle Sings* (2–5). Illus. 1998, Pavilion paper $16.95 (1-86205-076-7). 128pp. An anthology of 20 legends from various Native American peoples, including creation stories, hero legends, and cautionary tales. (Rev: BL 3/15/98; SLJ 5/98) [398.2]

11483 Rodanas, Kristina, adapt. *The Dragonfly's Tale* (PS–3). Illus. 1992, Houghton Mifflin $14.95 (0-395-57003-4). 28pp. The Ashiwi's waste of food causes the Corn Maiden to bring famine to the village, but a boy and his sister find a way to harvest a successful crop. (Rev: BCCB 6/92; BL 4/1/92; SLJ 7/92) [398.2]

11484 Runningwolf, Michael, and Patrick Clark Smith. *On the Trail of Elder Brother* (3–6). Illus. 2000, Persea $16.95 (0-89255-248-4). 128pp. Sixteen tales including creation myths and pourquoi stories are included in this collection of Micmac folktales about Glous'gap, called Elder Brother, the embodiment of the Great Spirit. (Rev: BCCB 6/00; BL 7/00; HBG 10/00) [398.2]

11485 San Souci, Robert D. *Two Bear Cubs* (K–4). Illus. by Daniel San Souci. 1997, Yosemite $14.95 (0-939666-87-1). Two bear cubs fall asleep on a rock that grows into a mountain in this Native American folktale that explains the rock formation known as El Capitan in Yosemite National Park. (Rev: BCCB 3/98; BL 1/1–15/98; SLJ 4/98) [398.2]

11486 Shenandoah, Joanne, and Douglas M. George-Kanentiio. *Skywoman: Legends of the Iroquois* (4–8). Illus. 1998, Clear Light $14.95 (0-940666-99-5). Good writing and effective artwork are combined in this retelling of nine traditional Iroquois tales, including a series of creation stories. (Rev: HBG 10/99; SLJ 2/99) [398.2]

11487 Steptoe, John, reteller. *The Story of Jumping Mouse: A Native American Legend* (1–4). 1984, Morrow paper $5.95 (0-688-08740-X). 40pp. The legend of the mouse who, because of good acts, is transformed into an eagle. [398.2]

11488 Stevens, Janet. *Coyote Steals the Blanket: A Ute Tale* (4–6). Illus. 1993, Holiday House LB $16.95 (0-8234-0996-1). 32pp. In this amusing legend, a rock chases a coyote after the animal steals a blanket that had covered it. (Rev: BCCB 5/93*; BL 4/1/93; SLJ 6/93) [398.2]

11489 Stevens, Janet. *Old Bag of Bones: A Coyote Tale* (K–4). Illus. 1996, Holiday House LB $16.95 (0-8234-1215-6). 32pp. Coyote, who resents growing old, persuades Young Buffalo to share his youth with him in this Shoshone tale. (Rev: BCCB 5/96; BL 5/1/96; HB 7–8/96; SLJ 5/96*) [398.24]

11490 Strauss, Susan. *Coyote Stories for Children* (2–7). Illus. by Gary Lund. 1992, Beyond Words paper $7.95 (0-941831-62-0). A collection of four stories from Native American cultures that tell about the trickster coyote. (Rev: SLJ 4/92) [398.2]

11491 Swamp, Chief Jake. *Giving Thanks: A Native American Good Morning Message* (PS–1). Illus. by Erwin Printup. 1995, Lee & Low $15.95 (1-880000-15-6). 24pp. A Mohawk chieftain gives thanks for Mother Earth and the universe that surrounds her. (Rev: BL 10/15/95; SLJ 11/95) [299]

11492 Taylor, C. J. *How We Saw the World: Nine Native Stories of the Way Things Began* (4–6). Illus. 1993, Tundra $17.99 (0-88776-302-2). 32pp. These nine stories from various tribes explain the origin of several animals, like horses, and geographical landmarks, like Niagara Falls. (Rev: BL 11/1/93; SLJ 2/94) [398.3]

11493 Taylor, C. J. *The Secret of the White Buffalo* (K–3). Illus. 1993, Tundra paper $13.95 (0-88776-321-9). 24pp. Two Native American scouts encounter a beautiful woman when they set out to track buffalo in this Oglala Indian folktale. (Rev: BL 1/1/94) [398.2]

11494 Van Laan, Nancy. *In a Circle Long Ago: A Treasury of Native Lore from North America* (3–5). Illus. 1995, Knopf LB $21.99 (0-679-95807-5). 128pp. Nature is explored in 25 geographically arranged tales, with an introduction to their cultural origins. (Rev: BL 11/15/95; SLJ 11/95) [392.2]

11495 Van Laan, Nancy. *Shingebiss: An Ojibwe Legend* (3–4). Illus. by Betsy Bowen. 1997, Houghton Mifflin $16.00 (0-395-82745-0). 32pp. In this Ojibwa (Chippewa) legend, it appears that Shingebiss, a duck, will freeze during the winter because he has only four logs to heat his lodge. (Rev: BL 7/97; HB 11–12/97; SLJ 10/97) [398.2]

11496 Waboose, Jan B. *SkySisters* (PS–2). Illus. by Brian Deines. 2000, Kids Can $15.95 (1-55074-697-9). 32pp. Two Ojibwaa sisters encounter three guardian spirits — a rabbit, a deer, and a coyote — as they venture out one night to see the Northern Lights. (Rev: BL 11/15/00; HBG 3/01; SLJ 1/01) [398.2]

11497 Webster, M. L., retel. *On the Trail Made of Dawn: Native American Creation Stories* (4–9). 2001, Linnet LB $19.50 (0-208-02497-2). 69pp. The author retells 13 creation stories and places them in cultural context. (Rev: HBG 3/02; SLJ 12/01) [398.2]

11498 Wisniewski, David. *The Wave of the Sea-Wolf* (3–6). Illus. by author. 1994, Clarion $17.00 (0-395-66478-0). This Tlingit Indian legend tells how Princess Kchokeen saves her people by luring destructive white traders to their death. (Rev: BCCB 11/94; SLJ 10/94) [398.2]

11499 Wolfson, Evelyn. *Inuit Mythology* (5–9). Illus. by William Sauts Bock. Series: Mythology. 2001, Enslow LB $20.95 (0-7660-1559-9). 128pp. Seven tales from Inuit folklore are accompanied by information on the history and culture of the Inuit peoples. (Rev: BL 4/15/02; HBG 3/02; SLJ 3/02) [398.2]

11500 Wood, Audrey. *The Rainbow Bridge: Inspired by a Chumash Tale* (1–4). Illus. by Robert Florczak. 1995, Harcourt $16.00 (0-15-265475-5). 32pp. In this Chumash tale, earth goddess Hutash turns some of her people into dolphins to save them from drowning. (Rev: BCCB 12/95; BL 12/1/95; SLJ 10/95) [398.24]

11501 Wood, Nancy. *The Girl Who Loved Coyotes: Stories of the Southwest* (K–4). Illus. by Diana

Bryer. 1995, Morrow $16.00 (0-688-13981-7). 48pp. Twelve stories about the coyote who manages to survive in its native habitat in spite of the invasions of strangers of many cultures. (Rev: BL 9/15/95; SLJ 12/95) [398.2]

11502 Young, Richard, and Judy D. Young, eds. *Race with Buffalo: And Other Native American Stories for Young Readers* (3–7). Illus. by Wendell E. Hall. 1994, August House $19.95 (0-87483-343-4); paper $9.95 (0-87483-342-6). 175pp. This collection of 32 American Indian folktales includes such genres as creation and trickster stories. (Rev: SLJ 8/94) [398.2]

United States

11503 Anaya, Rudolfo A. *My Land Sings: Stories from the Rio Grande* (5–9). 1999, Morrow $17.00 (0-688-15078-0). A magical collection of 10 stories, set mostly in New Mexico, that deal with Mexican and Native American folklore. (Rev: BL 8/99; HBG 10/00; SLJ 9/99) [398.2]

11504 Birdseye, Tom. *Soap! Soap! Don't Forget the Soap! An Appalachian Folktale* (3–6). Illus. by Andrew Glass. 1993, Holiday House LB $16.95 (0-8234-1005-6). 32pp. An adaptation of a familiar story about a forgetful hero sent to the store by his mother. (Rev: BCCB 6/93; BL 3/15/93; HB 5–6/93) [398.2]

11505 Brimner, Larry Dane, retel. *Captain Stormalong* (PS–2). Illus. by Chi Chung. Series: Imagination Series: Tall Tales. 2004, Compass Point LB $22.60 (0-7565-0601-8). 32pp. Captain Stormalong, a larger-than-life character who first appeared in an old sea chantey, springs to life again in this spirited retelling of some of his most audacious adventures. (Rev: SLJ 7/04) [398.2]

11506 Brown, Marcia. *Backbone of the King: The Story of Paka'a and His Son Ku* (5–7). Illus. by author. 1984, Univ. of Hawaii Pr. $9.95 (0-8248-0963-7). 180pp. A reissue of the book based on a Hawaiian legend of a boy who wants to help his exiled father. [398.2]

11507 Cohen, Daniel. *Railway Ghosts and Highway Horrors* (3–5). Illus. by Stephen Marchesi. 1993, Scholastic paper $2.95 (0-590-45423-4). 112pp. Phantom hitchhikers and accident victims fill this anthology of American and British travelers' lore. (Rev: BL 11/15/91) [133.1]

11508 Cohen, Daniel. *Southern Fried Rat and Other Gruesome Tales* (6–8). Illus. by Peggy Brier. 1989, Avon paper $3.50 (0-380-70655-5). 128pp. Grisly folktales — some funny, some gruesome. [398.2]

11509 Davis, Aubrey. *Sody Salleratus* (PS–2). Illus. by Alan Daniel and Lea Daniel. 1998, Kids Can $14.95 (1-55074-281-7). 32pp. In this American folktale, a wise squirrel solves the problem of having a bear in town that delights in eating everyone. (Rev: BL 3/15/98; HBG 10/98; SLJ 4/98) [398.2]

11510 Davis, Donald. *Jack and the Animals* (PS–2). Illus. by Kitty Harvill. 1995, August House $15.95 (0-87483-413-9). 32pp. Jack and a group of unhap-py animals outwit a gang of robbers in this Appalachian tale. (Rev: BL 10/1/95; SLJ 1/96)

11511 Despain, Pleasant. *Sweet Land of Story: Thirty-Six American Tales to Tell* (4–6). Illus. 2000, August House $19.95 (0-87483-569-0). 176pp. This anthology of 36 American folktales ranges from tall tales and Native American stories to Jack tales and traditional ghost stories. (Rev: BL 12/15/00; HBG 10/01; SLJ 12/00) [398.2]

11512 Doucet, Sharon Arms. *Lapin Plays Possum: Trickster Tales from the Louisiana Bayou* (4–6). Illus. by Scott Cook. 2002, Farrar $18.10 (0-374-34328-4). 64pp. This is a well-illustrated collection of three tales about the trickster rabbit from Cajun country told with many humorous bayou phrases. (Rev: BL 4/15/02; HB 5–6/02; HBG 10/02; SLJ 4/02) [398.2]

11513 Doucet, Sharon Arms. *Why Lapin's Ears Are Long and Other Tales from the Louisiana Bayou* (4–6). Illus. by David Catrow. 1997, Orchard LB $19.99 (0-531-33041-9). 64pp. Three entertaining folktales from Cajun country that feature the trickster rabbit. (Rev: BL 8/97; HB 9–10/97; HBG 3/98; SLJ 9/97) [398.2]

11514 Farmer, Nancy. *Casey Jones's Fireman: The Story of Sim Webb* (PS–3). Illus. by James Bernardin. 1999, Penguin Putnam $15.99 (0-8037-1929-9). 40pp. A retelling of the story of the legendary train wreck as experienced by Sim Webb, the black fireman on Casey Jones's Cannonball Express. (Rev: BCCB 1/00; BL 9/15/99*; HBG 3/00; SLJ 10/99) [398.2]

11515 Forest, Heather. *The Baker's Dozen: A Colonial American Tale* (PS–2). Illus. by Susan Gaber. 1993, Harcourt paper $5.00 (0-152-05687-4). 28pp. A baker in colonial New York State cuts back on his cookie recipe, and when a woman demands 13 cookies for the dozen and he refuses, his baking is cursed. (Rev: BCCB 10/88; BL 9/15/88; SLJ 4/89) [398.2]

11516 Galdone, Joanna. *The Tailypo: A Ghost Story* (1–3). Illus. by Paul Galdone. 1984, Houghton Mifflin paper $6.95 (0-395-30084-3). In this ghostly story, a mysterious creature returns to retrieve his tail, cut off by an old man. [398.2]

11517 Hamilton, Virginia. *Bruh Rabbit and the Tar Baby Girl* (K–4). Illus. by James E. Ransome. 2003, Scholastic $16.95 (0-590-47376-X). Rich watercolors and the Gullah dialect make this an appealing retelling of the familiar story. (Rev: HBG 4/04; SLJ 11/03) [398.2]

11518 Hamilton, Virginia. *Her Stories: African American Folktales, Fairy Tales, and True Tales* (5–8). Illus. 1995, Scholastic paper $19.95 (0-590-47370-0). Nineteen tales about African American females are retold in the wonderful style of Virginia Hamilton. (Rev: BL 11/1/95*; SLJ 11/95*) [398.2]

11519 Hamilton, Virginia. *The People Could Fly: American Black Folk Tales* (4–9). Illus. by Leo Dillon and Diane Dillon. 1985, Knopf LB $18.99 (0-394-96925-1); paper $13.00 (0-679-84336-1). 192pp. A retelling of 24 folktales — some little known, others familiar, such as Tar Baby. (Rev: BCCB 7/85; BL 7/85; SLJ 11/85) [398.2]

11520 Hamilton, Virginia. *The People Could Fly: The Picture Book* (3–9). Illus. by Leo Dillon and Diane Dillon. 2004, Knopf LB $18.99 (0-375-92405-1). 40pp. A beautifully illustrated picture-book version of the folktale about slaves' dreams in the face of diversity. (Rev: BL 9/15/04; SLJ 4/05*) [398.2]

11521 Hamilton, Virginia. *When Birds Could Talk and Bats Could Sing: The Adventures of Bruh Sparrow, Sis Wren, and Their Friends* (4–6). Illus. by Barry Moser. 1996, Scholastic $17.95 (0-590-47372-7). 72pp. Each of these eight tales from the American South deals with unpleasant, often foolish birds, and each ends with an important moral. (Rev: BCCB 6/96; BL 4/15/96*; HB 9–10/96; SLJ 5/96*) [398.2]

11522 Harper, Wilhelmina, retel. *The Gunniwolf* (PS–1). Illus. by Barbara Upton. 2003, Dutton $15.99 (0-525-46785-8). Harper's classic tale of the Little Girl who disregards warnings and encounters the not-so-fearsome Gunniwolf appears with new illustrations and a woodland setting. (Rev: HBG 10/03; SLJ 9/03) [398.2]

11523 Harris, Jim. *Jack and the Giant: A Story Full of Beans* (K–4). Illus. 1997, Northland LB $15.95 (0-87358-680-8). 32pp. This version of "Jack and the Beanstalk" had Jack living on a ranch in Arizona with his mother, Annie Okey-Dokey. (Rev: BL 2/1/98; HBG 3/98; SLJ 2/98) [398.2]

11524 Harris, Joel Chandler. *Jump! The Adventures of Brer Rabbit* (3–5). Adapted by Van Dyke Parks and Malcolm Jones. Illus. by Barry Moser. 1986, Harcourt $15.95 (0-15-241350-2); paper $7.00 (0-15-201493-4). 40pp. An edition with tracings of the stories' roots in oral tradition. (Rev: BCCB 11/86; BL 1/1/87; SLJ 11/86) [398.2]

11525 Hayes, Joe. *El Cucuy! A Bogeyman Cuento in English and Spanish* (K–4). Illus. by Honorio Robledo. 2001, Cinco Puntos $15.95 (0-938317-54-7). 32pp. A southwestern bogeyman comes down from his mountain to carry off bad children. (Rev: BL 7/01; HBG 10/01; SLJ 7/01) [398.2]

11526 Hayes, Joe. *Juan Verdades: The Man Who Couldn't Tell a Lie* (2–4). Illus. by Joseph Daniel Fiedler. 2001, Scholastic $16.95 (0-439-29311-1). 32pp. The honesty of Juan Valdez (known as Juan Verdades for his amazing truthfulness) is tested in this romantic and richly illustrated tale set in the early American Southwest. (Rev: BL 12/1/01; HBG 3/02; SLJ 12/01) [398.2]

11527 Hayes, Joe. *Little Gold Star / Estrellita de oro: A Cinderella Cuento* (PS–3). Illus. by Gloria Osuna Perez and Lucia Angela Perez. 2000, Cinco Puntos $15.95 (0-938317-49-0). 32pp. Told in English and Spanish, this is an interesting version of the Cinderella story that is popular in the mountain communities of New Mexico. (Rev: BCCB 7–8/00; BL 5/15/00; HBG 10/00; SLJ 6/00) [398.2]

11528 Hayes, Joe. *Pajaro Verde / The Green Bird* (2–4). Illus. by Antonio Castro L. 2002, Cinco Puntos $16.95 (0-938317-65-2). 40pp. A young woman marries a bird to save him from evil in this New Mexican folktale, told in both Spanish and English, filled with magic and monsters. (Rev: BL 10/15/02; HBG 3/03) [398.2]

11529 Hayward, Linda. *All Stuck Up* (1–3). Illus. by Normand Chartier. 1990, Random paper $3.99 (0-679-80216-9). 32pp. The tar baby story featuring Brer Rabbit is retold. (Rev: BCCB 7–8/92; BL 6/1/90; SLJ 8/90) [398.2]

11530 Hayward, Linda. *Hello, House!* (1–2). Illus. by Lynn Munsinger. 1988, Random paper $3.99 (0-394-88864-2). 32pp. The Uncle Remus tale in which Brer Rabbit outsmarts sly Brer Wolf. (Rev: BL 10/1/88) [398.2]

11531 Hicks, Ray, and Lynn Salsi. *The Jack Tales* (3–5). Illus. 2000, Callaway $24.95 (0-935112-58-8). 40pp. Two different versions of each of three plucky Jack tales are effectively presented in print and on a CD. (Rev: BL 11/15/00*; HBG 3/01; SLJ 11/00) [398.2]

11532 Hoberman, Mary Ann. *Miss Mary Mack: A Hand-Clapping Rhyme* (K–3). Illus. by Nadine Bernard Westcott. 1998, Little, Brown $14.95 (0-316-93118-7). 32pp. A catchy hand-clapping rhyme that uses appropriate cartoon illustrations. (Rev: BCCB 5/98; BL 3/15/98; HBG 10/98; SLJ 5/98) [398.2]

11533 Hooks, William H. *The Three Little Pigs and the Fox* (PS–2). Illus. by S. D. Schindler. 1997, Simon & Schuster paper $5.99 (0-689-80962-X). 32pp. A refreshing version drawn from Appalachian sources. (Rev: BCCB 1/90*; BL 9/1/89; HB 3–4/90; SLJ 10/89) [398.2]

11534 Hunt, Angela E. *The Tale of Three Trees: A Traditional Folktale* (K–2). Illus. by Tim Jonke. 1989, Lion $14.99 (0-7459-1743-7). 32pp. A folktale about three trees — a manger for the Christ child, a fishing boat that carries Jesus, and timbers that become the cross. (Rev: BL 11/1/89) [398.2]

11535 Jacobs, Jimmy. *Moonlight Through the Pines: Tales from Georgia Evenings* (5–7). Illus. 2000, Franklin-Sarrett paper $11.95 (0-9637477-3-8). 115pp. A collection of humorous reminiscences, family stories, tall tales, and other examples of folklore, all from the South. (Rev: BL 8/00) [398.2]

11536 Johnson, Paul Brett. *Fearless Jack* (K–3). Illus. 2001, Simon & Schuster $16.00 (0-689-83296-6). 32pp. An Appalachian tale in which Jack amazes people with his prowess, overwhelming "varmints" left and right. (Rev: BCCB 9/01; BL 7/01; HB 9–10/01; HBG 3/02; SLJ 7/01) [398.8]

11537 Keats, Ezra Jack. *John Henry: An American Legend* (1–3). Illus. by author. 1965, Knopf paper $5.99 (0-394-89052-3). 32pp. Large, bold figures capture the spirit of the hero who died with a hammer in his hand. [398.2]

11538 Kellogg, Steven. *Paul Bunyan* (K–4). Illus. by author. 1984, Morrow $16.89 (0-688-03850-6); paper $5.95 (0-688-05800-0). 40pp. Several stories about Paul and the blue ox Babe, all wittily illustrated. (Rev: BL 2/1/04) [398.2]

11539 Kellogg, Steven, reteller. *Pecos Bill* (K–3). Illus. by Steven Kellogg. 1986, Scholastic paper

$5.95 (0-688-09924-6). 32pp. Humor permeates these tall tales of the American folk hero. (Rev: BCCB 11/86; BL 9/1/86; SLJ 9/86) [398.2]

11540 Kellogg, Steven. *Sally Ann Thunder Ann Whirlwind Crockett* (PS–3). Illus. 1995, Morrow $16.89 (0-688-14043-2). 48pp. A humorous look at the life of Davy Crockett's wife and her equally amazing exploits. (Rev: BCCB 9/95; BL 8/95; SLJ 10/95) [398.2]

11541 Kidd, Ronald, ed. *On Top of Old Smoky: A Collection of Songs and Stories from Appalachia* (4–6). Illus. by Linda Anderson. 1992, Ideals $13.95 (0-8249-8569-9). 38pp. A handsome collection of songs and stories from Appalachia with distinctive illustrations. (Rev: BL 12/1/92; SLJ 4/05) [782]

11542 Kimmel, Eric A. *The Runaway Tortilla* (K–2). Illus. by Randy Cecil. 2000, Winslow $16.95 (1-890817-18-X). A silly tortilla runs away but is finally caught and eaten by Señor Coyote. (Rev: BCCB 12/00; HBG 10/01; SLJ 10/00) [398.2]

11543 Liddell, Janice. *Imani and the Flying Africans* (2–5). Illus. by Linda Nickens. 1994, Africa World $14.95 (0-86543-365-8); paper $6.95 (0-86543-366-6). After hearing about the Flying Africans, who could rise into the air and escape slavery, young Imani dreams that he is captured by kidnappers and uses the same method to achieve freedom. (Rev: SLJ 11/94) [398.2]

11544 Lyons, Mary. *Roy Makes a Car* (PS–2). Illus. by Terry Widener. 2005, Simon & Schuster $16.95 (0-689-84640-1). 32pp. A tall tale about auto mechanic Roy's designn for an accident-proof car, based on a folktale collected by Zora Neale Hurston in the 1930s. (Rev: BL 2/1/05; SLJ 2/05) [398.2]

11545 McCormick, Dell J. *Paul Bunyan Swings His Axe* (4–6). Illus. by author. 1936, Caxton $15.95 (0-87004-093-6). The stories of the giant woodsman and his great blue ox named Babe are favorites among American folktales. [398.2]

11546 McGill, Alice. *Sure as Sunrise: Stories of Bruh Rabbit and His Walkin' Talkin' Friends* (PS–3). Illus. by Don Tate. 2004, Houghton Mifflin $17.00 (0-618-21196-9). 48pp. Characterful illustrations accompany these five trickster tales that McGill learned when she was growing up in an African American community in North Carolina. (Rev: BL 4/15/04*; SLJ 6/04) [398.2]

11547 Martin, Rafe. *The Shark God* (PS–3). Illus. by David Shannon. 2001, Scholastic $15.95 (0-590-39500-9). 32pp. Younger readers will thrill to the dynamic illustrations and this ancient Hawaiian tale of two children who are condemned to death by their king. (Rev: BCCB 1/02; BL 11/1/01; HB 11–12/01; HBG 3/02; SLJ 9/01) [398.2]

11548 Medearis, Angela Shelf. *Tailypo: A Newfangled Tall Tale* (K–3). Illus. by Sterling Brown. 1996, Holiday House LB $15.95 (0-8234-1249-0). 32pp. A variation on the folktale about a monster that leaves its tail behind in the cabin of an African American boy. (Rev: BL 11/1/96; SLJ 1/97) [398.2]

11549 Nordenstrom, Michael. *Pele and the Rivers of Fire* (2–4). Illus. 2002, Bess Pr. $9.95 (1-57306-079-8). 32pp. The power of Pele, the Hawaiian vol-cano goddess, is brought to life by spectacular, vivid paintings accompanied by a simple retelling of Pele's move to Hawaii from Tahiti and her battles with her sister. (Rev: BL 12/1/02; HBG 3/03; SLJ 1/03) [299]

11550 Osborne, Mary Pope. *American Tall Tales* (4–7). Illus. by Michael McCurdy. 1991, Knopf LB $23.99 (0-679-90089-6). 115pp. Nine tall tales perfect for telling to all ages. (Rev: BCCB 1/92; BL 3/15/92; SLJ 12/91*) [398.2]

11551 Reneaux, J. J. *Haunted Bayou: And Other Cajun Ghost Stories* (4–8). 1994, August House paper $9.95 (0-87483-385-X). 158pp. Thirteen scary, entertaining folktales from Cajun country are retold effectively. (Rev: SLJ 12/94) [398.2]

11552 Reneaux, J. J. *Why Alligator Hates Dog* (1–3). Illus. by Donnie Lee Green. 1995, August House $15.95 (0-87483-412-0). 32pp. Dog loves to torment Alligator, but the wily reptile plots his revenge. (Rev: BL 10/15/95; SLJ 1/96) [398.3]

11553 Rounds, Glen. *Ol' Paul, the Mighty Logger* (3–6). Illus. by author. 1976, Holiday House paper $5.95 (0-8234-0713-6). 96pp. An account of the incredible exploits of one of our national folk heroes. [398.2]

11554 San Souci, Robert D. *Cut from the Same Cloth: American Women of Myth, Legend and Tall Tale* (4–6). Illus. by Brian Pinkney. 1993, Penguin Putnam $19.99 (0-399-21987-0). 142pp. This is a lively collection of folktales retold by the author, each of which features a female central character. (Rev: BCCB 6/93*; BL 4/15/93; SLJ 6/93) [398.2]

11555 San Souci, Robert D. *Little Pierre: A Cajun Story from Louisiana* (1–4). Illus. by David Catrow. 2003, Harcourt $16.00 (0-15-202482-4). Drawn from Cajun folklore, this variation on the Tom Thumb theme tells how Pierre, dwarfed by his four older brothers, saves the day and rescues his fumbling brothers and the comely Marie-Louise from the Swamp Ogre. (Rev: HBG 4/04; SLJ 1/04) [398.2]

11556 San Souci, Robert D. *The Secret of the Stones* (2–4). Illus. by James E. Ransome. 1999, Penguin Putnam $16.99 (0-8037-1640-0). 40pp. In this folktale with roots in both Arkansas and Zaire, a childless couple tries to rescue two orphans who have been turned into pebbles. (Rev: BCCB 1/00; BL 1/1–15/00; HBG 3/00; SLJ 2/00) [398.2]

11557 San Souci, Robert D. *Six Foolish Fishermen* (PS–3). Illus. by Doug Kennedy. 2000, Hyperion LB $15.49 (0-7868-2335-6). 32pp. The author has combined and expanded several "noodle" stories from around the world and presented them in a goofy tale set in Cajun country. (Rev: BL 5/15/00; HBG 10/00; SLJ 7/00) [398.2]

11558 Schwartz, Alvin. *More Scary Stories to Tell in the Dark* (4–7). Illus. by Stephen Gammell. 1984, HarperCollins LB $16.89 (0-397-32082-5); paper $5.99 (0-06-440177-4). 128pp. Brief tales from folk stories and hearsay with a scary bent. [398.2]

11559 Schwartz, Alvin, ed. *Scary Stories to Tell in the Dark* (3–8). Illus. by Stephen Gammell. 1981, HarperCollins LB $15.89 (0-397-31927-4); paper

$4.95 (0-06-440170-7). 128pp. Ghost stories collected from American folklore. [398.2]

11560 Stevens, Janet. *Tops and Bottoms* (PS–2). Illus. 1995, Harcourt $16.00 (0-15-292851-0). 32pp. An African American folktale about how Hare takes unfair advantage of Bear in a garden project. (Rev: BCCB 4/95; BL 3/15/95*; HB 5–6/95; SLJ 5/95) [398.2]

11561 *Stockings of Buttermilk: American Folktales* (4–5). Ed. by Neil Philip. Illus. 1999, Clarion $20.00 (0-395-84980-2). 124pp. A collection of 18 folktales that had their roots in Europe (e.g., "Jack and the Beanstalk") but were changed when imported into America — often by African American storytellers. (Rev: BL 9/1/99; HB 11–12/99; HBG 3/00; SLJ 10/99) [398.2]

11562 Thomas, Joyce Carol. *What's the Hurry, Fox? And Other Animal Stories* (PS–3). Illus. by Bryan Collier. 2004, HarperCollins LB $16.89 (0-06-000644-7). 32pp. Originally collected by Zora Neale Hurston in the 1930s, these folktales from the rural South are skillfully adapted in this richly illustrated book. (Rev: BL 5/15/04; SLJ 4/04) [398.2]

11563 Vagin, Vladimir. *The Enormous Carrot* (K–2). Illus. 1998, Scholastic $15.95 (0-590-45491-9). 32pp. A reworking of the old folktale "The Enormous Turnip," with an engaging cast of animal characters. (Rev: BCCB 6/98; BL 3/1/98; HBG 10/98; SLJ 3/98) [398.2]

11564 Walker, Paul R. *Big Men, Big Country: A Collection of American Tall Tales* (4–6). Illus. by James Bernardin. 1993, Harcourt $16.95 (0-15-207136-9). 80pp. After an introduction on the origins of American tales, there is a rollicking, retelling of the exploits of such characters as Davy Crockett, Paul Bunyan, and lesser-known figures like Gib Morgan and Big Mose. (Rev: BCCB 6/93; BL 4/1/93; SLJ 5/93) [398.2]

11565 Washington, Donna. *A Big, Spooky House* (1–5). Illus. by Jacqueline Rogers. 2000, Hyperion $15.99 (0-7868-0349-5). A traditional African American folktale in which a strong man who has taken refuge in a spooky house is warned by cats of the arrival of big bad John. (Rev: BCCB 1/01; BL 9/15/00; HBG 3/01; SLJ 9/00) [398.2]

11566 Willey, Margaret. *Clever Beatrice* (PS–3). Illus. by Heather Solomon. 2001, Simon & Schuster $16.00 (0-689-83254-0). 40pp. A tall tale from the wilds of Michigan in which a little girl named Beatrice outwits a rich giant. (Rev: BL 7/01; HB 11–12/01*; HBG 3/02; SLJ 10/01) [398.2]

11567 Wooldridge, Connie N. *Wicked Jack* (K–3). Illus. by Will Hillenbrand. 1995, Holiday House LB $16.95 (0-8234-1101-X). 32pp. A retelling of the Southern tale about a mean blacksmith who outwits the Devil and his young sons. (Rev: BCCB 12/95; BL 11/1/95; SLJ 12/95*) [398.2]

South and Central America

Mexico and Other Central American Lands

11568 Bierhorst, John. *Doctor Coyote: A Native American Aesop's Fables* (3–5). Illus. by Wendy Watson. 1987, Macmillan LB $15.95 (0-02-709780-3). 48pp. Aesop's fables as they were translated into Spanish in the New World. (Rev: BCCB 3/87; BL 3/15/87; SLJ 5/87) [398.2]

11569 Bierhorst, John, ed. *The Monkey's Haircut: And Other Stories Told by the Maya* (4–6). Illus. by Robert Andrew Parker. 1986, Morrow $16.00 (0-688-04269-4). 160pp. Forms of folklore in a collection of Maya legends, most from the early 1900s. (Rev: BCCB 5/86; BL 7/86; SLJ 8/86) [398.2]

11570 Climo, Shirley, reteller. *The Little Red Ant and the Great Big Crumb* (PS–2). Illus. by Francisco Mora. 1995, Clarion $16.00 (0-395-70732-3). 39pp. A tiny ant seeks help in vain from other animals to move a heavy crumb in this Mexican tale. (Rev: SLJ 11/95) [398.2]

11571 Coburn, Jewell Reinhart. *Domitila: A Cinderella Tale from the Mexican Tradition* (3–5). Illus. 2000, Shen's $16.95 (1-885008-13-9). 32pp. This variation on the story of Cinderella comes from the folklore of Hidalgo, Mexico. (Rev: BL 5/15/00; HBG 10/00; SLJ 7/00) [398.2]

11572 Czernecki, Stefan, and Timothy Rhodes. *The Sleeping Bread* (1–3). Illus. by Stefan Czernecki. 1992, Hyperion $14.95 (1-562-82183-0). 40pp. In this Central American folktale, the tears of a beggar who is driven out of town change the village's bread when they are added to the dough. (Rev: BCCB 9/92; BL 4/15/92; SLJ 8/92) [398.2]

11573 dePaola, Tomie. *The Legend of the Poinsettia* (K–4). Illus. 1994, Penguin Putnam LB $16.99 (0-399-21692-8). 32pp. Lucinda is unhappy because she has ruined the blanket that was intended for use in a Christmas procession. (Rev: BL 8/94; HB 11–12/94; SLJ 4/05) [398.2]

11574 de Sauza, James. *Brother Anansi and the Cattle Ranch / El Hermano Anansi y el Rancho de Ganada* (3–6). Adapted by Harriet Rohmer. Illus. by Stephen Von Mason. 1989, Children's Book Pr. $14.95 (0-89239-044-1). 32pp. A bilingual retelling of the ancient folktale about the trickster spider, now transplanted to Nicaragua. Two others in this dual-language series are: *Mr. Sugar Came to Town/La Visita del Señor Azucar* (1989); *Uncle Nacho's Hat/El Sombrero de Tio Nacho* (1989). (Rev: BL 11/15/89) [398.2]

11575 Ehlert, Lois. *Cuckoo / Cucu* (PS–2). Trans. by Gloria de Aragon Andujar. Illus. 1997, Harcourt $16.00 (0-15-200274-X). 40pp. In this Mayan tale, Cuckoo saves the annual harvest of seeds on which the other birds live during the winter. (Rev: BCCB 6/97; BL 4/1/97*; HBG 3/98; SLJ 3/97) [398.2]

11576 Endredy, James. *The Journey of Tunuri and the Blue Deer: A Huichol Indian Story* (1–4). 2003, Bear & Company $15.95 (1-59143-016-X). 32pp. Based on a traditional folk tale, this gentle story highlighted by traditional yarn art tells how an enchanted deer leads a young Huichol boy on a magical journey to meet the spirits of nature. (Rev: BL 12/1/03; SLJ 1/04)

11577 Gerson, Mary-Joan. *Fiesta Feminina: Celebrating Women in Mexican Folktales* (4–8). Illus. 2001, Barefoot $19.99 (1-84148-365-6). 64pp. This volume includes eight tales from Mexican folklore about strong and magical women, presented with bold illustrations, a pronunciation guide, and a glossary. (Rev: BL 9/15/01; HBG 3/02; SLJ 10/01) [398.2]

11578 Harper, Jo. *The Legend of Mexicatl* (K–3). Illus. by Robert Casilla. 1998, Turtle $15.95 (1-890515-05-1). 32pp. A handsome retelling of the Mexican legend about the teenage boy who is destined to lead his people out of the desert. (Rev: BL 4/15/98) [398.2]

11579 Kimmel, Eric A. *Cactus Soup* (1–3). Trans. and illus. by Phil Huling. 2004, Marshall Cavendish $16.95 (0-7614-5155-2). 32pp. "Stone Soup" meets chiles and beans in this Mexico-based variant involving hungry revolutionary forces. (Rev: BL 9/15/04*; SLJ 10/04) [398.2]

11580 Kimmel, Eric A. *Montezuma and the Fall of the Aztecs* (2–5). Illus. by Daniel San Souci. 2000, Holiday House $16.95 (0-8234-1452-3). 32pp. After introducing the history and culture of the Aztecs, this picture book covers the reign of Montezuma, the coming of Cortes, and the Aztec leader's defeat. (Rev: BL 1/1–15/00; HBG 10/00; SLJ 3/00) [972]

11581 Kimmel, Eric A. *The Two Mountains: An Aztec Legend* (3–5). Illus. 2000, Holiday House $16.95 (0-8234-1504-X). 32pp. This Aztec legend tells how two young lovers are transformed into the two mountains that overlook the Valley of Mexico. (Rev: BL 5/15/00; HBG 10/00; SLJ 4/00) [398.2]

11582 Love, Hallie N., and Bonni Larson, retellers. *Watakame's Journey: The Story of the Great Flood and the New World: A Huichol Indian Tale* (2–6). Illus. 1999, Clear Light $14.95 (1-56416-029-X). 84pp. This is a Mexican version of the Noah story featuring a young boy who is selected by the goddess of all growing things to build a boat to withstand the coming flood. (Rev: SLJ 12/99) [398.2]

11583 Madrigal, Antonio H. *The Eagle and the Rainbow: Timeless Tales from México* (4–7). Illus. by Tomie dePaola. 1997, Fulcrum $15.95 (1-55591-317-2). 56pp. A collection of wise, wonderful, but little-known folktales from Mexico. (Rev: BL 7/97; HBG 4/04) [398.2]

11584 Marcos, Subcomandante. *The Story of Colors / La Historia de los Colores: A Folktale from the Jungles of Chiapas* (K–4). Trans. by Anne Bar Din. Illus. by Domitila Domínguez. 1999, Cinco Puntos $15.95 (0-938317-45-8). This folktale told in both Spanish and English explains the origins of the colors in the world and how the macaw got its bright plumage. (Rev: HBG 10/99; SLJ 5/99) [398.2]

11585 Montejo, Victor, reteller. *Popol Vuh: A Sacred Book of the Maya* (5–8). Trans. by David Under. Illus. by Luis Garay. 1999, Groundwood $19.95 (0-88899-334-X). 85pp. A creation story from the Mayans in a beautifully designed book that

features gods, giants, mortals, and animals. (Rev: HBG 3/00; SLJ 12/99) [398.2]

11586 Mora, Pat. *The Night the Moon Fell* (PS–K). Illus. by Domi. 2000, Douglas & McIntyre $16.95 (0-88899-398-6). 32pp. A Mayan myth about how Luna, the moon, is shattered when she falls from the sky and how she gathers strength to repair herself and return to her home. (Rev: BL 9/1/00; HBG 3/01; SLJ 11/00) [398.2]

11587 Mora, Pat. *The Race of Toad and Deer* (PS–1). Illus. by Domi. 2001, Groundwood $15.95 (0-88899-434-6). 32pp. This is a newly illustrated and rewritten version of the Mayan take on the tortoise and the hare, first published in 1995. (Rev: BCCB 12/01; BL 12/15/01; HBG 3/02) [398.2]

11588 Ober, Hal. *How Music Came to the World: An Ancient Mexican Myth* (1–4). Illus. by Carol Ober. 1994, Houghton Mifflin $17.00 (0-395-67523-5). 32pp. How music came to the world is the subject of this folktale dating to pre-Columbian times. (Rev: BL 3/15/94; SLJ 10/94) [398.2]

11589 Philip, Neil, ed. *Horse Hooves and Chicken Feet: Mexican Folktales* (4–8). Illus. by Jacqueline Main. 2003, Clarion $19.00 (0-618-19463-0). 83pp. Bright folk-art illustrations accompany 14 stories that feature humor and the importance of the Catholic church. (Rev: BL 10/15/03; HBG 4/04; SLJ 9/03) [398.2]

11590 Rockwell, Anne. *The Boy Who Wouldn't Obey* (2–4). Illus. 2000, Greenwillow $15.95 (0-688-14881-6). 24pp. In this Mayan legend a young boy steals the tools of Chac, the god of the sky, but doesn't know how to control them. (Rev: BCCB 7–8/00; BL 5/15/00; HBG 10/00; SLJ 6/00) [398.2]

11591 Strauss, Susan. *When Woman Became the Sea: A Costa Rican Creation Myth* (K–3). Illus. by Cristina Acosta. 1998, Beyond Words $14.95 (1-885223-85-4). 32pp. A retelling of the Costa Rican folktale that tells how Thunder's pregnant wife, Sea, is killed by a snake and how her body splits and produces all the waters of the world. (Rev: BL 10/15/98; HBG 3/99; SLJ 11/98) [398.2]

Puerto Rico and Other Caribbean Islands

11592 Alvarez, Julia. *The Secret Footprints* (1–4). Illus. by Fabian Negrin. 2000, Knopf $16.95 (0-679-89309-1). 32pp. A folktale from the Taino Indians of the Dominican Republic about the ciguapas, beautiful humanlike creatures whose feet are on backwards and who have a great fear of humans. (Rev: BCCB 10/00; BL 8/00; HBG 3/01; SLJ 9/00) [398.2]

11593 Breinburg, Petronella. *Stories from the Caribbean* (2–4). Illus. by Syrah Arnold and Tina Barber. Series: Multicultural Stories. 2000, Raintree LB $27.12 (0-7398-1334-X). 48pp. Ghost stories, creation fables, and animal stories are included in this interesting anthology. (Rev: HBG 10/00; SLJ 11/00) [398.2]

11594 Gershator, Phillis. *Tukama Tootles the Flute* (PS–3). Illus. by Synthia Saint James. 1994, Orchard LB $16.99 (0-531-08661-5). 32pp. A flute-playing youngster uses his music to escape the clutches of a giant in this folktale from the Virgin Islands. (Rev: BCCB 4/94; BL 5/1/94; HB 5–6/94; SLJ 4/94) [398.2]

11595 Gonzalez, Lucia M. *The Bossy Gallito* (K–3). Illus. by Lulu Delacre. 1994, Scholastic $15.95 (0-590-46843-X). 32pp. In this cumulative tale from Cuba, a rooster must involve a great number of animals in order to get his beak cleaned. (Rev: BCCB 7–8/94; BL 5/15/94; HB 9–10/94; SLJ 4/94) [398.2]

11596 Hallworth, Grace. *Sing Me a Story: Song and Dance Stories from the Caribbean* (K–3). Illus. by John Clementson. 2002, August House $19.95 (0-87483-672-7). 48pp. Caribbean folktales that involve song are accompanied by music and lyrics as well as lively and evocative collage borders. (Rev: BL 11/1/02; HBG 3/03; SLJ 9/02) [398.2]

11597 Izcoa, Carmen Rivera, adapt. *Mediopollito / Half-a-Chick* (K–3). Illus. by Nívea O. Montáñez. 1996, Ediciones Huracan $10.50 (0-929157-43-5). A Puerto Rican folktale about a bird that punishes the king for being mean and selfish. (Rev: BL 2/1/04; SLJ 11/97) [398.2]

11598 Jaffe, Nina. *The Golden Flower: A Taino Myth from Puerto Rico* (K–3). Illus. by Enrique O. Sanchez. 1996, Simon & Schuster $16.95 (0-689-80469-5). 32pp. The creation of the island of Puerto Rico is told in this Taino myth about a magical pumpkin. (Rev: BCCB 6/96; BL 6/1–15/96; SLJ 7/96) [398.2]

11599 Keens-Douglas, Richard. *Mama God, Papa God: A Caribbean Tale* (K–2). Illus. by Stefan Czernecki. 1999, Crocodile LB $15.95 (1-56656-307-0). A Caribbean Island folktale attractively illustrated that tells a creation story centering around Mama God and Papa God and how they created diversity in the people that they made. (Rev: HBG 10/99; SLJ 7/99) [398.2]

11600 Linzer, Lila. *Once Upon an Island* (2–5). 1999, Front Street $15.95 (1-886910-10-3). 76pp. Four tales about animals (including bees, goats, and doves) from the island of St. Croix are retold in a dialect that captures the lilting rhythms of West Indian English. (Rev: HBG 10/99; SLJ 4/99) [398.2]

11601 MacDonald, Amy. *Please, Malese!* (K–3). Illus. by Emily Lisker. 2002, Farrar $16.00 (0-374-36000-6). 32pp. This variation of a Haitian folktale tells the story of wily Malese, a trickster who can convince the villagers of anything. (Rev: BL 8/02; HB 9–10/02; HBG 3/03; SLJ 9/02) [398.2]

11602 Moreton, Daniel. *La Cucaracha Martina: A Caribbean Folktale* (PS–2). Illus. 1997, Turtle $14.95 (1-890515-03-5). 32pp. A refined cockroach finally finds her mate, a handsome cricket, in this Caribbean folktale. (Rev: BL 1/1–15/98; SLJ 11/97) [398.2]

11603 San Souci, Robert D. *The Faithful Friend* (K–4). Illus. by Brian Pinkney. 1995, Simon & Schuster paper $16.00 (0-02-786131-7). 40pp. On the island of Martinique, Hippolyte tries to save his friend's wedding from destruction by the bride's

evil uncle. (Rev: BCCB 9/95; BL 4/15/95*; HB 9–10/95; SLJ 6/95) [398.2]

11604 San Souci, Robert D. *The Twins and the Bird of Darkness: A Hero Tale from the Caribbean* (K–4). Illus. by Terry Widener. 2002, Simon & Schuster $16.95 (0-689-83343-1). 40pp. Twin brothers — one nasty, one nice — vie to rescue a princess in this Caribbean tale. (Rev: BL 8/02; SLJ 9/02) [398.297]

11605 Wolkstein, Diane. *Bouki Dances the Kokioko: A Comical Tale from Haiti* (K–3). Illus. by Jesse Sweetwater. 1997, Harcourt $15.00 (0-15-200034-8). 32pp. In this Haitian trickster tale, a king invents a dance and offers a large reward for anyone who can master it. (Rev: BL 9/15/97; HBG 3/98; SLJ 11/97) [398.2]

South America

11606 Aldana, Patricia, ed. *Jade and Iron: Latin American Tales from Two Cultures* (5–8). Trans. by Hugh Hazelton. Illus. 1996, Douglas & McIntyre $18.95 (0-88899-256-4). 64pp. Fourteen folktales on a variety of subjects and from many regions in Latin America are retold in this large-format picture book. (Rev: BCCB 1/97; BL 12/1/96) [398.2]

11607 Delacre, Lulu, retel. *Golden Tales: Myths, Legends, and Folktales from Latin America* (4–8). Illus. 1996, Scholastic paper $18.95 (0-590-48186-X). Twelve important Latin American folktales from before and after the time of Columbus are featured. (Rev: BL 12/15/96; SLJ 9/96) [398.2]

11608 Despain, Pleasant. *The Dancing Turtle: A Folktale from Brazil* (K–3). Illus. by David Boston. 1998, August House $15.95 (0-87483-502-X). 32pp. Through trickery, wily Turtle escapes from her human captors in this Brazilian folktale set in a tropical rain forest. (Rev: BL 5/1/98; HBG 10/98; SLJ 5/98) [398.2]

11609 Dorson, Mercedes, and Jeanne Wilmot. *Tales from the Rain Forest: Myths and Legends from the Amazonian Indians of Brazil* (5–8). Illus. 1997, Ecco $18.00 (0-88001-567-5). 133pp. Ten entertaining folktales from the Amazonian Indians of Brazil. (Rev: BL 2/15/98; HB 3–4/98; HBG 10/98) [398.2]

11610 Ehlert, Lois. *Moon Rope: A Peruvian Folktale* (4–8). Illus. 1992, Harcourt $17.00 (0-15-255343-6). 40pp. In both English and Spanish, this is the story of Fox, who wants to go to the moon and persuades his friend Mole to go along. (Rev: BCCB 12/92; BL 10/15/92*; HB 11–12/92; SLJ 10/92*) [398.2]

11611 Gonzalez, Lucia M. *Señor Cat's Romance and Other Favorite Stories from Latin America* (1–3). Illus. by Lulu Delacre. 1997, Scholastic $17.95 (0-590-48537-7). 48pp. Six enchanting folktales popular in Latin America. (Rev: BCCB 4/97; BL 2/1/97; HB 3–4/97; SLJ 2/97) [398.2]

11612 Knutson, Barbara. *Love and Roast Chicken: A Trickster Tale from the Andes Mountains* (PS–2). Illus. Series: Carolrhoda Picture Books Ser. 2004, Carolrhoda $16.95 (1-57505-657-7). 32pp. A tiny guinea pig outwits both a fox and a farmer in this trickster tale set in the Andes. (Rev: BL 9/15/04; SLJ 11/04) [398.2]

11613 McDermott, Gerald. *Jabuti the Tortoise: A Trickster Tale from the Amazon* (K–2). Illus. 2001, Harcourt $16.00 (0-15-200496-3). 32pp. A brilliantly colorful retelling of the story of Jabuti, a tortoise who is tricked by a jealous vulture, who in turn is punished as the other birds gain colors and songs. (Rev: BL 9/15/01; HBG 3/02; SLJ 9/01) [398.2]

11614 MacDonald, Margaret Read, retel. *A Hen, a Chick and a String Guitar* (PS). Illus. by Sophie Fatus. 2005, Barefoot $17.99 (1-84148-796-1). An entertaining, musical, and instructive cumulative tale with Chilean origins in which a child's collection of animals grows until he has 16, plus a string guitar; a CD is included. (Rev: BCCB 5/05; SLJ 5/05) [398.2]

11615 Maggi, Maria Elena. *The Great Canoe: A Karina Legend* (PS–3). Illus. by Gloria Calderon. 2001, Douglas & McIntyre $15.95 (0-88899-444-3). 32pp. In a tale similar to that of Noah and his ark, four couples must build a canoe and rescue animals and plants from a great flood. (Rev: BL 11/15/01; HB 1–2/02; HBG 3/02; SLJ 10/01*) [398.2]

11616 Munduruku, Daniel. *Tales of the Amazon: How the Munduruku Indians Live* (5–8). Trans. by Jane Springer. Illus. by Laurabeatriz. 2000, Groundwood $18.95 (0-88899-392-7). 56pp. This is an interesting view of the life of the human inhabitants of the Amazon rain forest with material on lifestyles,

houses, languages, myths, and marriage. (Rev: BL 9/1/03; HBG 3/01; SLJ 9/00) [981]

11617 Olaondo, Susana. *Julieta, ?Que Plantaste? / Julieta, What Did You Plant?* (K–2). Illus. 2001, Montevideo: Alfaguara/Santillana paper $9.95 (9974-671-00-0). 32pp. This folktale about industrious Julieta the armadillo and the indolent but clever fox who tries to outwit her is sprinkled with Uruguayan phrases and accompanied by cartoonlike illustrations. (Rev: BL 12/15/01) [398.2]

11618 Pitcher, Caroline. *Mariana and the Merchild: A Folk Tale from Chile* (PS–3). Illus. by Jackie Morris. 2000, Eerdmans $17.00 (0-8028-5204-1). 32pp. In this Chilean folktale, Mariana, who lives alone on the beach, raises an infant mermaid until she is old enough to survive in the sea. (Rev: BL 3/1/00; HBG 10/00; SLJ 5/00) [398.2]

11619 Van Laan, Nancy. *The Magic Bean Tree: A Legend from Argentina* (PS–3). Illus. by Beatriz Vidal. 1998, Houghton Mifflin $15.00 (0-395-82746-9). 32pp. In this Argentinian folktale, young Topec must frighten away the evil Bird of the Underworld so that rain will return to the pampas and save his beloved carob tree. (Rev: BCCB 7–8/98; BL 4/1/98; HBG 10/98; SLJ 6/98) [398.2]

11620 Weiss, Jacqueline Shachter. *Young Brer Rabbit: And Other Trickster Tales from the Americas* (4–6). Illus. 1985, Stemmer $14.95 (0-88045-037-1); paper $9.95 (0-88045-138-6). 80pp. Fifteen stories translated from Spanish, French, and Portuguese. (Rev: BCCB 1/86; BL 3/1/86; SLJ 1/86) [398.2]

Mythology

General and Miscellaneous

11621 Dalal, Anita. *Myths of Oceania* (5–8). Series: Mythic World. 2002, Raintree LB $27.12 (0-7398-4978-6). 48pp. Information about Oceania and its people is included as well as 10 myths about the sea, fishing, and other unique aspects of island living. (Rev: BL 7/02; HBG 10/02) [398.3]

11622 Dalal, Anita. *Myths of Russia and the Slavs* (5–8). Series: Mythic World. 2002, Raintree LB $27.12 (0-7398-4979-4). 48pp. This lavishly illustrated, oversize volume contains 10 myths from Eastern Europe as well as material on the society that created them. (Rev: BL 7/02; HBG 10/02; SLJ 5/02) [398.2]

11623 Edwards, Katie. *Myths and Monsters: Secrets Revealed* (K–5). Illus. by Simon Mendez. 2004, Charlesbridge LB $16.95 (1-57091-581-4); paper $6.95 (1-57091-582-2). 29pp. Introduces 10 mythical creatures and shows the real animals on which these "monsters" may have been based. (Rev: SLJ 2/05) [398.24]

11624 Fisher, Leonard Everett. *The Gods and Goddesses of Ancient China* (2–5). 2003, Holiday House $16.95 (0-8234-1694-1). 36pp. This colorful picture book introduces 17 deities found in the myths of ancient China and includes a pronunciation guide, glossary, and map. (Rev: BL 7/03; HBG 4/04; SLJ 10/03) [299]

11625 Fisher, Leonard Everett. *Gods and Goddesses of the Ancient Maya* (4–7). Illus. 1999, Holiday House $16.95 (0-8234-1427-2). 36pp. This book provides a fascinating introduction to Mayan mythology by describing 10 gods and two goddesses. (Rev: BL 2/1/00; HBG 3/00; SLJ 12/99) [299]

11626 Gibbons, Gail. *Behold . . . the Unicorns!* (2–4). Illus. 2001, HarperCollins LB $15.89 (0-688-17958-4). 32pp. This handsomely designed book introduces the unicorn and all the myths and symbolism that surround one-horned beasts. (Rev:

BCCB 12/01; BL 12/1/01; HBG 3/02; SLJ 12/01) [398.24]

11627 Green, Jen. *Myths of China and Japan* (5–8). Series: Mythic World. 2002, Raintree LB $27.12 (0-7398-4977-8). 48pp. This handsome, oversize book explores the ancient mythology of China and Japan and, in addition to the retelling of 10 myths, contains information on the societies that created them. (Rev: BL 7/02; HBG 10/02) [398.2]

11628 Harris, Geraldine. *Gods and Pharaohs from Egyptian Mythology* (5–8). Illus. by David O'Connor and John Sibbick. 1992, Bedrick LB $24.95 (0-87226-907-8). 132pp. A collection of myths and legends from ancient Egypt. [398.2]

11629 January, Brendan. *The New York Public Library Amazing Mythology: A Book of Answers for Kids* (5–8). Illus. 2000, Wiley paper $12.95 (0-471-33205-4). 169pp. This compendium of information covers Middle Eastern, African, Mediterranean, Asian, Pacific, Northern European, and North and Central American mythology. (Rev: BL 11/1/00; SLJ 9/00) [291.1]

11630 Koenig, Viviane. *A Family Treasury of Myths from Around the World* (PS–3). Trans. by Anthony Zielonka. Illus. 1998, Abrams $29.95 (0-8109-4380-8). 160pp. This attractive retelling of ten myths from around the world includes stories from ancient Egypt, the legend of Romulus and Remus, Ulysses's adventure with the Sirens, and the epic of Moses in Egypt. (Rev: BL 1/1–15/99; HBG 3/99) [398.2]

11631 Leeming, David A., ed. *The Children's Dictionary of Mythology* (4–7). 1999, Watts LB $33.00 (0-531-11708-1). 128pp. A basic introduction to world mythology through alphabetically arranged characters, stories, and motifs from a wide variety of cultures. (Rev: BL 12/15/99; SLJ 11/99) [291.1]

11632 Martell, Hazel M. *Myths and Civilization of the Celts* (3–6). Illus. 2000, Bedrick $16.95 (0-87226-591-9). 48pp. Using double-page spreads, Celtic myths are retold and followed by historical and cultural background material. (Rev: BL 3/1/00) [299]

11633 Morley, Jacqueline. *Egyptian Myths* (4–6). 2000, Bedrick $22.50 (0-87226-589-7). 64pp. With illustrations that take their cues from ancient Egyptian art, this handsome volume contains several Egyptian myths involving such characters as Osiris and Isis. (Rev: BL 4/1/00; HBG 10/00; SLJ 3/00) [299]

11634 Mutén, Burleigh, retel. *The Lady of Ten Thousand Names: Goddess Stories from Many Cultures* (4–7). Illus. by Helen Cann. 2001, Barefoot $19.99 (1-84148-048-7). 79pp. Eight myths that feature goddesses from cultures around the world are retold in this appealing volume. (Rev: HBG 3/02; SLJ 11/01) [291.2]

11635 Penner, Lucille Recht. *Dragons* (3–5). Trans. and illus. by Peter David Scott. 2004, Random LB $11.99 (0-307-46417-2); paper $3.99 (0-307-26417-3). 48pp. The dragon's role in the mythologies and cultures of many nations and peoples are explored here. (Rev: BL 8/04) [398.24]

11636 Philip, Neil. *The Illustrated Book of Myths: Tales and Legends of the World* (5–8). Illus. by Nilesh Mistry. 1995, DK paper $19.99 (0-7894-0202-5). 192pp. Ancient myths from both the Old World and the New World have been collected under such headings as creation, destruction, and fertility. (Rev: BL 12/1/95; SLJ 12/95) [291.1]

11637 Sherman, Pat. *The Sun's Daughter* (2–4). Illus. by R. Gregory Christie. 2005, Clarion $16.00 (0-618-32430-5). 32pp. The harvest is explained through a story based on Iroquois myths. (Rev: BL 3/15/05; SLJ 6/05) [398.2]

Classical

11638 Balit, Christina. *Atlantis* (3–5). Illus. 2000, Holt $16.95 (0-8050-6334-X). 32pp. Adapted from ancient sources, this is the story of how Poseidon built the city of Atlantis and later destroyed it by sinking it to the ocean floor. (Rev: BCCB 9/00; BL 5/15/00*; HBG 10/00; SLJ 5/00) [398.23]

11639 Barber, Antonia, reteller. *Apollo and Daphne: Masterpieces of Greek Mythology* (5–9). 1998, Getty Museum $16.95 (0-89236-504-8). 45pp. A stunning book that retells famous Greek myths, including stories of the Trojan War and the return of Odysseus, with full-page reproductions of 19 splendid paintings. (Rev: BL 10/15/98; HBG 3/99; SLJ 9/98) [398.2]

11640 Burleigh, Robert. *Pandora* (3–6). Illus. by Raul Colon. 2002, Harcourt $16.00 (0-15-202178-7). 32pp. A handsome retelling of the Greek myth about Pandora, her longings to open the box, and the terror it produced when she did. (Rev: BCCB 5/02; BL 6/1–15/02; HBG 10/02; SLJ 5/02) [398.2]

11641 Catran, Ken. *Voyage with Jason* (5–8). 2003, Lothian paper $10.95 (0-7344-0151-5). 208pp. A new twist on the story of Jason and the Argonauts, narrated by a youth who is part of the eventful three-year quest for the Golden Fleece and concen-

trating on character as well as adventure. (Rev: SLJ 4/04) [398.2]

11642 Claybourne, Anna, and Kamini Khanduri, retellers. *Greek Myths: Ulysses and the Trojan War* (5–10). Illus. 1999, EDC $24.95 (0-7460-3361-3). A chatty retelling of the adventures of Ulysses on his way home from Troy, with illustrations that resemble comic-book drawings. (Rev: HBG 3/00; SLJ 6/99) [398.2]

11643 Climo, Shirley. *Atalanta's Race: A Greek Myth* (3–5). Illus. by Alexander Koshkin. 1995, Clarion $16.00 (0-395-67322-4). 32pp. A retelling of the Greek myth about Atalanta, who, abandoned at birth, becomes the world's fastest runner. (Rev: BCCB 6/95; BL 4/15/95; SLJ 4/95*) [398.21]

11644 Craft, Charlotte. *King Midas and the Golden Touch* (1–3). Illus. by Kinuko Craft. 1999, Morrow LB $15.93 (0-688-13166-2). 32pp. A traditional retelling of the story of King Midas, using the Middle Ages as a setting. (Rev: BCCB 3/99; BL 4/15/99; HBG 10/99; SLJ 3/99) [398.2]

11645 Cuyler, Margery. *Roadsigns: A Harey Race with a Tortoise* (PS–1). Illus. by Steve Haskamp. 2000, Winslow $15.95 (1-890817-23-6). 40pp. The Aesop fable of the race between the tortoise and the hare is cleverly retold using road signs and bright, cartoonlike illustrations. (Rev: BL 12/1/00; HBG 3/01; SLJ 9/00) [398.2]

11646 D'Aulaire, Ingri, and Edgar D'Aulaire. *D'Aulaire's Book of Greek Myths* (3–6). Illus. by authors. 1962, Dell paper $18.95 (0-440-40694-3). Full-color pictures highlight these brief stories, which are excellent for first readers in mythology. [398.2]

11647 Demi. *King Midas* (2–4). Illus. 2002, Simon & Schuster $19.95 (0-689-83297-4). 48pp. Rich illustrations accompany this retelling of the King Midas tale for younger readers. (Rev: BL 3/15/02; HB 5–6/02; HBG 10/02; SLJ 5/02) [398.2]

11648 Fisher, Leonard Everett. *Cyclops* (1–6). Illus. 1991, Holiday House paper $5.95 (0-8234-1062-5). 32pp. The retelling of this classical tale inspires pity and terror in the reader. (Rev: BCCB 12/91; BL 1/1/91*; SLJ 1/92) [398.2]

11649 Fisher, Leonard Everett. *Theseus and the Minotaur* (3–6). Illus. by author. 1988, Holiday House paper $5.95 (0-8234-0954-6). 32pp. The story of the birth of Theseus, his adventures, and his killing of the Minotaur. (Rev: BCCB 10/88; BL 10/15/88; SLJ 10/88) [398.2]

11650 Green, Jen. *Myths of Ancient Greece* (5–8). Illus. Series: Mythic World. 2001, Raintree LB $27.12 (0-7398-3191-7). 48pp. This volume for older readers separates myth from reality about ancient Greece. (Rev: BL 3/1/02; HBG 3/02; SLJ 12/01) [398.2]

11651 Hawthorne, Nathaniel. *Wonder Book and Tanglewood Tales* (5–7). 1972, Ohio State Univ. Pr. $72.95 (0-8142-0158-X). 476pp. This is a highly original retelling of the Greek myths, originally published in 1853. (Rev: BL 2/15/04; SLJ 4/04) [398.2]

11652 Homer. *The Odyssey* (3–5). Adapted by Adrian Mitchell. Illus. by Stuart Robertson. 2000, DK $14.95 (0-7894-5455-6). 64pp. A handsomely illustrated version of the Odyssey that covers all the major plot developments and the journeys of Odysseus. (Rev: BL 9/1/03; HBG 4/04; SLJ 9/00) [398.2]

11653 Low, Alice. *The Macmillan Book of Greek Gods and Heroes* (4–6). Illus. by Arvis Stewart. 1985, Macmillan LB $18.00 (0-02-761390-9). 192pp. Well-known myths and legends from ancient Greece in a large-format edition. (Rev: BCCB 11/85; BL 11/15/85; SLJ 1/86) [398.2]

11654 McCarty, Nick, reteller. *The Iliad* (4–8). Illus. by Victor G. Ambrus. 2000, Kingfisher $22.95 (0-7534-5330-4); paper $15.95 (0-7534-5321-5). 95pp. This account of the Trojan War uses an exciting text and action-packed illustrations. (Rev: SLJ 1/01) [398.2]

11655 McCaughrean, Geraldine. *Greek Gods and Goddesses* (4–7). Illus. 1998, Simon & Schuster $20.00 (0-689-82084-4). 112pp. This book, illustrated in ancient Greek style, contains a lively retelling of a number of Greek myths, including the story of Hermes. (Rev: BL 11/15/98; HBG 3/99; SLJ 10/98) [292.13]

11656 Malam, John. *Myths and Civilization of the Ancient Romans* (3–6). Illus. Series: Myths and Civilization. 2000, Bedrick $16.95 (0-87226-590-0). 45pp. After each of the myths that are covered here in double-page spreads, there is material on the history and culture of ancient Rome. (Rev: BL 3/1/00; HBG 10/00; SLJ 12/00) [292]

11657 Mayer, Marianna. *Pegasus* (3–6). Illus. by Kinuko Craft. 1998, Morrow $16.00 (0-688-13382-7). 40pp. A retelling of the Greek myth about the winged horse Pegasus and how it helped Bellerophon kill Chimera the monster. (Rev: BL 3/15/98; HBG 10/98; SLJ 4/98) [398.2]

11658 Morley, Jacqueline, reteller. *Greek Myths* (3–6). Illus. by Giovanni Caselli. 1998, Bedrick $22.50 (0-87226-560-9). 96pp. Beginning with the rise of the Titans and ending with Odysseus's wanderings, the myths in this book include those involving Prometheus, Arachne, Psyche, the Minotaur, and Apollo. (Rev: HBG 10/98; SLJ 7/98) [398.2]

11659 Myers, Christopher. *Wings* (PS–4). Illus. 2000, Scholastic $16.95 (0-590-03377-8). 40pp. In this modern retelling of the Icarus myth, a young boy who can fly nearly crashes, not because he flies too close to the sun but because repressive adults and bullying kids in the schoolyard try to break his spirit. (Rev: BCCB 12/00; BL 5/15/00; HBG 3/01; SLJ 10/00)

11660 Nardo, Don. *Greek and Roman Mythology* (5–8). Series: World History. 1997, Lucent LB $27.45 (1-56006-308-4). 112pp. The author provides a background on classical mythology — where the myths came from and why they were an important part of each country's culture — and relates the most famous stories from ancient Greek and Roman times. (Rev: SLJ 5/98) [398.2]

11661 *Odysseus* (4–8). Retold by Geraldine McCaughrean. 2004, Cricket $15.95 (0-8126-2721-0). 128pp. Homer's dramatic story is retold in rhythmic prose. (Rev: BL 12/15/04; SLJ 12/04)

11662 Osborne, Mary Pope. *Favorite Greek Myths* (3–6). Illus. by Troy Howell. 1989, Scholastic paper $18.95 (0-590-41338-4). 96pp. This large-format book contains 13 of the best-known stories from classical mythology. (Rev: BL 8/89) [398.2]

11663 Osborne, Mary Pope. *The One-Eyed Giant* (4–8). Series: Tales from the Odyssey. 2002, Hyperion $9.99 (0-7868-0770-9). 112pp. Osborne recounts the return from the Trojan War and Odysseus's encounter with the Cyclops, followed by guides to the Greek gods and to pronunciation and information on Homer. Also use *The Land of the Dead* (2002). (Rev: BL 11/15/02; HBG 3/03; SLJ 1/03) [883]

11664 Osborne, Mary Pope. *Sirens and Sea Monsters* (3–6). Illus. by Troy Howell. Series: Tales from the Odyssey. 2003, Hyperion $9.99 (0-7868-0772-5). 106pp. This third volume in the series follows the continuing adventures of Odysseus and his hardy band as they confront dangers including a deadly whirlpool and a sea monster. (Rev: BL 8/03; HBG 10/03; SLJ 7/03) [883]

11665 Oyibo, Papa. *Big Brother, Little Sister* (PS–3). Illus. by John Clementson. 2000, Barefoot $15.95 (1-84148-117-3). 40pp. The Aesop fable about the lion and the mouse is retold using an elephant instead of a lion. (Rev: BL 4/1/00; SLJ 8/00)

11666 Philip, Neil, reteller. *The Adventures of Odysseus* (3–6). Illus. by Peter Malone. 1997, Orchard $17.95 (0-531-30000-5). 72pp. A fine retelling of the epic journey home by Odysseus and his encounters with such creatures as Cyclops, Circe, and the Sirens. (Rev: SLJ 5/97*) [292.1]

11667 Pickels, Dwayne E. *Roman Myths, Heroes, and Legends* (5–8). Series: Costume, Tradition, and Culture: Reflecting on the Past. 1998, Chelsea $19.75 (0-7910-5164-1). Using double-page spreads and old collectors' cards as illustrations, this work retells the major Roman myths and introduces their important characters. (Rev: BL 3/15/99; HBG 10/99) [398.2]

11668 Richards, Jean. *The First Olympic Games: A Gruesome Greek Myth with a Happy Ending* (2–4). Illus. 2000, Millbrook LB $22.90 (0-7613-1311-7). 32pp. The story of Pelops, who was killed and eaten by his father, Tantalus, restored to life by the gods, and later created the first Olympic Games. (Rev: BCCB 11/00; BL 10/15/00; HBG 10/01; SLJ 11/00) [398.2]

11669 Richardson, I. M. *The Adventures of Eros and Psyche* (3–6). Illus. by Robert Baxter. 1983, Troll paper $3.95 (0-89375-862-0). 32pp. How Psyche is able to prove her love for Eros in this retelling of the Greek myth. Others by this author and publisher are: *The Adventures of Hercules; Demeter and Persephone: The Seasons of Time; Prometheus and the Story of Fire* (all 1983). [398.2]

11670 Spires, Elizabeth. *I Am Arachne* (4–7). Illus. 2001, Farrar $15.00 (0-374-33525-7). 160pp. Spires takes a fresh look at some ancient stories, breathing new life and humor into first-person tales of Midas, Pan, Narcissus, and Eurydice. (Rev: BL 6/1–15/01; HB 9–10/01; HBG 3/02; SLJ 5/01) [813]

11671 Stewig, John W. *King Midas* (K–3). Illus. by Omar Rayyan. 1999, Holiday House $15.95 (0-8234-1423-X). 32pp. Filled with illustrations containing comic details, this is a fine retelling of the tale about the greedy king who turned his daughter into gold. (Rev: BCCB 3/99; BL 2/15/99; HBG 10/99; SLJ 3/99) [398.2]

11672 Usher, Kerry. *Heroes, Gods and Emperors from Roman Mythology* (5–8). Illus. by John Sibbick. 1992, Bedrick LB $24.95 (0-87226-909-4). 132pp. The story of the Aeneid plus those of the Tarquino and Romulus and Remus are three of the legends retold here. [398.2]

11673 Woff, Richard. *Bright-Eyed Athena: Stories from Ancient Greece* (5–8). Illus. 1999, Getty Museum paper $12.95 (0-89236-558-7). 48pp. Using full-color illustrations from Greek sculpture and vase paintings, this book retells the important Greek myths involving Athena. (Rev: BL 11/15/99; HBG 3/00; SLJ 2/00) [398.2]

11674 Woff, Richard. *A Pocket Dictionary of Greek and Roman Gods and Goddesses* (4–8). 2003, Getty $9.95 (0-89236-706-7). 48pp. Varied reproductions from the British Museum add visual appeal to this brief who's who. (Rev: HBG 4/04; SLJ 2/04) [292.2]

11675 Yolen, Jane. *Jason and the Gorgon's Blood* (4–6). Series: Young Heroes. 2004, HarperCollins $15.99 (0-06-029452-3). 256pp. The story of Jason (of Greek mythology) as a youth, already leading a group of followers on adventures complete with harpies, centaurs, and goddesses. (Rev: BL 2/15/04; SLJ 2/04) [398.2]

11676 Yolen, Jane, and Robert J. Harris. *Atalanta and the Arcadian Beast* (4–6). Series: Young Heroes. 2003, HarperCollins LB $16.89 (0-06-029455-8). 256pp. The ancient Greek myth of Atalanta, a girl who, accompanied by a bear, searches for her father's killer and discovers her true heritage. (Rev: BL 2/1/03; HBG 10/03; SLJ 2/03) [398.2]

Scandinavian

11677 Fisher, Leonard Everett. *Gods and Goddesses of the Ancient Norse* (K–4). Illus. 2002, Holiday House $16.95 (0-8234-1569-4). 40pp. An introduction to 15 ancient Norse gods and goddesses, with a pronunciation guide and a family tree. (Rev: BCCB 6/02; BL 3/1/02; HBG 10/02; SLJ 3/02) [293]

11678 Osborne, Mary Pope. *Favorite Norse Myths* (4–6). Illus. by Troy Howell. 1996, Scholastic $17.95 (0-590-48046-4). 96pp. A masterful retelling of Norse myths, with a thorough glossary of names, places, events, and symbols connected with these tales. (Rev: BL 3/1/96; SLJ 4/96*) [293]

11679 Philip, Neil, reteller. *Odin's Family: Myths of the Vikings* (3–6). Illus. by Maryclare Foa. 1996, Orchard $19.95 (0-531-09531-2). 124pp. Fifteen Viking myths — including "Thor's Hammer" and "The Death of Balder" — are retold with vivid illustrations. (Rev: BCCB 10/96; SLJ 11/96*) [398.2]

Poetry

11680 *The 20th Century Children's Poetry Treasury* (3–5). Ed. by Jack Prelutsky. Illus. 1999, Random $19.95 (0-679-89314-8). 96pp. On each of the illustrated two-page spreads, there are four to six poems on a single theme, for a total of more than 200 poems by 137 poets. (Rev: BL 12/15/99; HBG 3/00; SLJ 12/99*) [811]

11681 *Absolutely Angels: Poems for Children and Other Believers* (PS–3). Ed. by Mary Lou Carney. Illus. by Viqui Maggio. 1998, Boyds Mills $14.95 (1-56397-708-7). A collection of poems, mostly by contemporary poets, about the role of angels as protectors and helpers. (Rev: BL 11/1/98; HBG 3/99; SLJ 11/98) [808.81]

11682 Adoff, Arnold. *All the Colors of the Race* (4–7). Illus. by John Steptoe. 1982, Lothrop LB $15.93 (0-688-00880-1). 56pp. Poems that deal with the many races of mankind.

11683 Adoff, Arnold. *Love Letters* (1–4). Illus. by Lisa Desimini. 1997, Scholastic $15.95 (0-590-48478-8). 32pp. All sorts and conditions of love are the subjects of this delightful work with outstanding illustrations. (Rev: BCCB 3/97; BL 1/1–15/97; SLJ 3/97*) [811]

11684 Adoff, Arnold. *Touch the Poem* (PS–3). Illus. by Lisa Desimini. 2000, Scholastic $16.95 (0-590-47970-9). 32pp. Common childhood experiences like walking on a beach or feeling the fuzz on a peach are explored in this collection of original poems illustrated with photographs. (Rev: BCCB 2/00; BL 3/15/00; HBG 10/00; SLJ 6/00) [811]

11685 Alarcon, Francisco X. *From the Bellybutton of the Moon and Other Summer Poems: Del Ombligo de la Luna y otros poemas de verano* (K–5). Illus. by Maya Christina Gonzalez. 1998, Children's Book Pr. $15.95 (0-89239-153-7). 32pp. A collection of 22 bilingual poems that celebrates the author's childhood in Mexico. (Rev: BL 10/15/98; HBG 3/99; SLJ 12/98) [811]

11686 Alarcon, Francisco X. *Laughing Tomatoes and Other Spring Poems / Jitomates Risueños y Otros Poemas de Primavera* (K–3). Illus. by Maya Christina Gonzalez. 1997, Children's Book Pr. $15.95 (0-89239-139-1). 32pp. A bilingual collection of short poems, many about California, by the Chicano poet Alarcón. (Rev: BCCB 6/97; BL 6/1–15/97; SLJ 5/97) [811]

11687 *Alfred, Lord Tennyson* (5–8). Ed. by John Maynard. Illus. by Allen Garns. Series: Poetry for Young People. 2004, Sterling $14.95 (0-8069-6612-2). 48pp. This large-format introduction to Tennyson's works includes an informative profile of the poet, selections accompanied by notes, and rich illustrations. (Rev: BL 2/15/04) [821]

11688 Anaya, Rudolfo A. *Elegy on the Death of Cesar Chavez* (4–7). Illus. 2000, Cinco Puntos $16.95 (0-938317-51-2). 32pp. This is an elegiac poem that celebrates the life, work, and struggle of the respected labor leader. (Rev: BL 12/15/00; HBG 3/01; SLJ 1/01) [811]

11689 Andrews, Sylvia. *Dancing in My Bones* (PS). Illus. by Ellen Mueller. 2001, HarperCollins $9.95 (0-694-01316-1). 24pp. A multicultural cast of kids dance their way through a park, adding lines to a rhyme along the way. (Rev: BL 11/1/01; HBG 3/02; SLJ 12/01) [811]

11690 Argueta, Jorge. *A Movie in My Pillow / Una Pelicula en Mi Almohada* (4–8). Illus. by Elizabeth Gomez. 2001, Children's Book Pr. $15.95 (0-89239-165-0). 32pp. The author remembers in poetry his family's immigration to the United States from El Salvador, with each poem accompanied by the translation and rich illustrations. (Rev: BL 10/1/01; HBG 10/01; SLJ 5/01*) [861]

11691 *Around the World in Eighty Poems* (3–5). Ed. by James Berry. Illus. by Katherine Lucas. 2002, Chronicle $19.95 (0-8118-3506-5). 96pp. A collection of poems from countries around the world, illustrated with paintings. (Rev: BCCB 1/03; BL 7/02; HBG 3/03; SLJ 4/03) [808.81]

11692 Ashman, Linda. *The Essential Worldwide Monster Guide* (1–3). Illus. by David Small. 2003, Simon & Schuster $16.95 (0-689-82640-0). 40pp. Monsters and ogres from 13 different world cultures are introduced in amusing and cautionary rhyming verse. (Rev: BL 11/1/03; HBG 4/04; SLJ 9/03)

11693 Bauer, Caroline Feller, ed. *Rainy Day: Stories and Poems* (3–5). Illus. by Michele Chessare. 1986, HarperCollins LB $15.89 (0-397-32105-8). 96pp. Poems and stories from mostly well-known children's poets such as John Ciardi and Langston Hughes. Also use: *Snowy Day: Stories and Poems* (1986). (Rev: BCCB 9/86; BL 7/86; SLJ 9/86)

11694 Bauer, Marion Dane. *If Frogs Made Weather* (PS–2). Illus. by Dorothy Donohue. 2005, Holiday House $16.95 (0-8234-1622-4). A boy speculates about how the weather would be if the animals had their way. (Rev: SLJ 5/05) [811]

11695 Bauer, Marion Dane. *Love Song for a Baby* (PS–K). Illus. by Dan Andreasen. 2002, Simon & Schuster $15.95 (0-689-82268-5). 40pp. A tender poem about parents' love for their growing baby, with excellent oil paintings and rhyming text. (Rev: BL 9/1/02; HBG 3/03; SLJ 8/02) [811]

11696 Baylor, Byrd. *The Way to Start a Day* (3–5). Illus. by Peter Parnall. 1978, Macmillan $16.00 (0-684-15651-2); paper $5.99 (0-689-71054-2). 32pp. A poetic tribute to the many ways people have greeted a new day.

11697 Becker, Helaine. *Mama Likes to Mambo* (K–2). Illus. by John Beder. 2002, Stoddart $15.95 (0-7737-3316-7). 32pp. A collection of amusing, attractively illustrated poems of differing lengths on varied subjects. (Rev: BL 9/15/02; HBG 10/02; SLJ 5/02) [811]

11698 Benet, Rosemary, and Stephen Vincent Benet. *Johnny Appleseed* (PS–2). Illus. by S. D. Schindler. 2001, Simon & Schuster $16.00 (0-689-82975-2). 40pp. Colored-pencil illustrations accompany the verses of this poem that was first published in 1933. (Rev: BL 6/1–15/01; HBG 3/02; SLJ 8/01) [811]

11699 Bennett, Jill, ed. *A Cup of Starshine: Poems and Pictures for Young Children* (PS–1). Illus. by Graham Percy. 1991, Harcourt $16.95 (0-15-220982-4). 64pp. These include the traditional rhymes with modern verse and full-color drawings. (Rev: BL 10/15/91; SLJ 12/91) [811]

11700 Bennett, Jill, ed. *Spooky Poems* (1–5). Illus. by Mary Rees. 1990, General Dist. Services $14.95 (0-7737-2350-1). 32pp. From a variety of poets comes a collection of scary poems about ghosts, monsters, and other supernatural beings. (Rev: BL 12/1/89; HB 1–2/90; SLJ 1/90) [811]

11701 Bernier-Grand, Carmen T. *Cesar: ¡Sí, Se Puede! Yes, We Can!* (3–6). Illus. by David Diaz. 2004, Marshall Cavendish $16.95 (0-7614-5172-2). 48pp. A series of 19 free-verse poems chronicles the life of Cesar Chavez, from his migrant worker childhood to his leadership in the struggle for farm workers' rights. (Rev: BL 10/15/04; SLJ 10/04) [811]

11702 Berry, James. *A Nest Full of Stars* (2–5). Illus. by Ashley Bryan. 2004, Greenwillow $15.99 (0-06-052747-1). 104pp. The Jamaican-born poet showcases the charm and musicality of his native Caribbean patois in this collection of 60 poems accompanied by striking illustrations. (Rev: BL 3/1/04; HB 3–4/04; SLJ 3/04) [811]

11703 Blake, Quentin. *All Join In* (PS–2). Illus. 1991, Little, Brown $14.95 (0-316-09934-1). 32pp. The theme of cooperation is explored in six bright poems. (Rev: BCCB 5/91; BL 4/15/91; SLJ 7/91) [821]

11704 Borden, Louise. *America Is . . .* (2–4). Illus. by Stacey Schuett. 2002, Simon & Schuster $16.95 (0-689-83900-6). 40pp. This patriotic poem for younger readers examines life in America through many prisms. (Rev: BL 8/02; HBG 10/02; SLJ 6/02) [811]

11705 Brewton, Sara, et al., eds. *Of Quarks, Quasars and Other Quirks: Quizzical Poems for the Supersonic Age* (5–8). Illus. by Quentin Blake. 1977, HarperCollins LB $13.89 (0-690-04885-8). 128pp. Contemporary poems that poke fun at such modern innovations as transplants and water beds.

11706 Brown, Margaret Wise. *Give Yourself to the Rain: Poems for the Very Young* (PS–1). Illus. by Teri L. Weidner. 2002, Simon & Schuster $16.95 (0-689-83344-X). 32pp. A collection of 24 previously unpublished poems for young readers, illustrated in beautiful warm pastels. (Rev: BL 2/15/02; HBG 10/02; SLJ 3/02) [811]

11707 Brown, Margaret Wise. *Love Songs of the Little Bear* (PS–1). Illus. by Susan Jeffers. 2001, Hyperion LB $16.95 (0-7868-2445-X). 32pp. A collection of previously unpublished poetry by Brown that uses as a connective device illustrations of a plump young bear. (Rev: BL 3/15/01; HBG 10/01; SLJ 3/01) [811]

11708 Bryan, Ashley. *Sing to the Sun: Poems and Pictures* (K–8). Illus. 1996, HarperCollins paper $4.95 (0-064-43437-0). Short poems with a Caribbean lilt. (Rev: BCCB 10/92; BL 10/15/92; HB 3–4/93; SLJ 10/92) [811.54]

11709 Bunting, Eve. *Sing a Song of Piglets: A Calendar in Verse* (PS–1). Illus. by Emily Arnold McCully. 2002, Clarion $16.00 (0-618-01137-4). 32pp. Readers follow a pair of piglets through the year, with lively watercolors that match the bounciness of the simple rhymes. (Rev: BL 11/15/02; HBG 3/03; SLJ 8/02) [811]

11710 Burkholder, Kelly. *Poetry* (2–5). Series: Artistic Adventures. 2001, Rourke LB $21.27 (1-57103-354-8). 24pp. This book explains the basic elements of poetry like rhythm, rhyme, and repetition, introduces different types of poems, and gives advice on how to write your own poetry. (Rev: SLJ 2/01) [811]

11711 Calmenson, Stephanie. *Good for You! Toddler Rhymes for Toddler Times* (PS). Illus. by Melissa Sweet. 2001, HarperCollins LB $16.89 (0-06-029811-1). 64pp. These poems and riddles feature everyday items, activities, and new experiences in a toddler's life: playing, learning, making friends, and so forth. (Rev: BCCB 11/01; BL 10/15/01; HBG 3/02; SLJ 10/01) [811]

11712 Calmenson, Stephanie. *Welcome, Baby! Baby Rhymes for Baby Times* (PS). Illus. by Melissa Sweet. 2002, HarperCollins LB $18.89 (0-06-000492-4). 64pp. Charmingly illustrated peppy poems about and for toddlers bouncily describe events in a baby's life from birth to about 18 months, finishing up with educational poems about the alphabet and colors. (Rev: BCCB 12/02; BL 12/1/02; HBG 3/03; SLJ 9/02) [811]

11713 Carlson, Lori M. *Sol a Sol* (2–5). Illus. by Emily Lisker. 1998, Holt $17.00 (0-8050-4373-X). A bilingual anthology of poems that describe the daily activities of a Hispanic family. (Rev: BCCB 5/98; BL 4/1/98; HB 5–6/98; HBG 10/98; SLJ 3/98) [808]

11714 Carroll, Lewis. *Jabberwocky* (K–2). Illus. by Joel Stewart. 2003, Candlewick $15.99 (0-7636-2018-1). 32pp. An imaginatively illustrated version of the classic nonsense poem. (Rev: BL 3/15/03*; HBG 10/03; SLJ 7/03) [811]

11715 Cleary, Brian P. *Rainbow Soup: Adventures in Poetry* (3–6). Illus. by Neal Layton. 2004, Carolrhoda $16.95 (1-57505-597-X). 96pp. In multiple poetry forms, Cleary celebrates various aspects of children's everyday lives, including school, sports, and food. (Rev: BL 4/1/04; SLJ 6/04) [808.1]

11716 Cooling, Wendy. *Come to the Great World: Poems from Around the Globe* (PS–3). Illus. by Shelia Moxley. 2004, Holiday House $16.95 (0-8234-1822-7). 32pp. Diverse poems about children and the issues that affect them are illustrated with colorful paintings. (Rev: BL 3/15/04; SLJ 4/04) [811]

11717 Cooney, Barbara, reteller. *Chanticleer and the Fox* (1–4). Illus. by Barbara Cooney. 1958, Harper-Collins LB $16.89 (0-690-18562-6); paper $3.95 (0-690-04318-X). 36pp. Chaucer's Nun's Priest Tale retold by the illustrator. Caldecott Medal winner, 1959.

11718 *Daddy Poems* (3–5). Ed. by John Micklos. Illus. 2000, Boyds Mills $15.95 (1-56397-735-4). 32pp. This anthology of poems about dads and how they interact with their children contains the work of both well-known and less-well-known poets. (Rev: BL 8/00; HBG 10/00; SLJ 10/00) [811]

11719 Dakos, Kalli. *Mrs. Cole on an Onion Roll and Other School Poems* (1–3). Illus. by JoAnn Adinolfi. 1995, Simon & Schuster paper $14.00 (0-02-725583-2). 40pp. A collection of 32 poems about the behavior and concerns of elementary school children. (Rev: BL 6/1–15/95; SLJ 8/95) [811]

11720 Dakos, Kalli. *Put Your Eyes up Here: And Other School Poems* (2–5). Illus. by G. Brian Karas. 2003, Simon & Schuster $16.95 (0-689-81117-9). 64pp. An unusual teacher, Ms. Roys, inspires her students to write poems about their experiences with her. (Rev: BL 8/03; HBG 4/04; SLJ 7/03) [811]

11721 Dawes, Kwame Senu Neville. *I Saw Your Face* (3–5). Illus. by Tom Feelings. 2005, Dial $16.99 (0-8037-1894-2). 32pp. Sketches of black faces around the world are paired with evocative poetry celebrating their global reach. (Rev: BL 2/1/05; SLJ 3/05) [811]

11722 *Days Like This: A Collection of Small Poems* (PS–1). Ed. by Simon James. Illus. 2000, Candlewick $17.99 (0-7636-0812-2). 48pp. This anthology of 19 simple poems, accompanied by line-and-watercolor illustrations, explores the everyday life and experiences of children. (Rev: BCCB 7–8/00; BL 3/15/00; HB 5–6/00; HBG 10/00; SLJ 4/00) [811.008]

11723 *Days to Celebrate: A Full Year of Poetry, People, Holidays, History, Fascinating Facts, and More* (4–7). Ed. by Lee Bennett Hopkins. Illus. by Stephen Alcorn. 2005, Greenwillow LB $18.89 (0-06-000766-4). 112pp. A wide-ranging collection organized by month, each introduced by a calendar page that highlights important dates. (Rev: BL 1/1–15/05; SLJ 1/05) [811]

11724 De Regniers, Beatrice S., ed. *Sing a Song of Popcorn: Every Child's Book of Poems* (PS–6). Illus. by Marcia Brown. 1988, Scholastic $18.95 (0-590-43974-X). 160pp. A treasure from highly regarded poets, with exciting artwork. (Rev: BCCB 10/88; BL 8/88; SLJ 8/88)

11725 Di Pasquale, Emanuel. *Cartwheel to the Moon: My Sicilian Childhood* (3–6). Illus. by K. Dyble Thompson. 2003, Cricket $16.95 (0-8126-2679-6). 64pp. Di Pasquale's poems paint a vivid word picture of his chidhood in Sicily during the 1940s and 1950s. (Rev: BL 4/1/03; HBG 10/03; SLJ 7/03) [811]

11726 *Dirty Laundry Pile* (3–6). Ed. by Paul B. Janeczko. 2001, HarperCollins LB $15.89 (0-688-16252-5). 40pp. An anthology of 27 poems told from the standpoint of an object or an animal such as a seashell, a cat, and a tree. (Rev: BL 4/15/01*; HB 7–8/01*; HBG 10/01; SLJ 8/01) [811]

11727 Dotlich, Rebecca. *Lemonade Sun and Other Summer Poems* (PS–3). Illus. by Jan S. Gilchrist. 1998, Boyds Mills paper $15.95 (1-56397-660-9). 32pp. This book of poems shows children in everyday situations and depicts their sense of wonder. (Rev: BL 2/15/98; HBG 10/98; SLJ 3/98) [811]

11728 Dotlich, Rebecca Kai. *In the Spin of Things: Poetry of Motion* (2–5). Illus. by Karen M. Dugan. 2003, Boyds Mills $16.95 (1-56397-145-3). 32pp. Everyday items whirl into motion in this collection of free-form poems. (Rev: BL 4/1/03; HBG 10/03; SLJ 3/03) [811]

11729 Dotlich, Rebecca Kai. *Over in the Pink House* (PS–2). Illus. by Melanie Hall. 2004, Boyds Mills $15.95 (1-59078-027-2). 32pp. Rhythm and sound trump meaning in this collection of rhyming verses. (Rev: BL 5/1/04; SLJ 4/04) [796.2]

11730 Dotlich, Rebecca Kai. *When Riddles Come Rumbling: Poems to Ponder* (2–5). Illus. 2001, Boyds Mills $15.95 (1-56397-846-6). 32pp. Short, rhythmic poems along with picture clues form riddles about everyday objects. (Rev: BL 11/1/01; HBG 3/02; SLJ 10/01) [811]

11731 *Dream Makers: Young People Share Their Hopes and Aspirations* (3–6). Illus. by Neil Waldman. 2003, Boyds Mills $15.95 (1-59078-178-3). 32pp. The dreams and aspirations of 42 American boys and girls are collected in this attractive large-format volume of rhyming and free verse marking the 150th anniversary of the Children's Aid Society. (Rev: BL 9/1/03; HBG 4/04; SLJ 12/03) [811]

11732 *Drift Upon a Dream: Poems for Sleepy Babies* (PS–1). Illus. by Melanie Williamson. 2004, Charlesbridge paper $6.95 (1-57091-578-4). 32pp. This anthology of 21 bedtime poems includes selections by Tennyson, Lee Bennett Hopkins, Eve Merriam, Eleanor Farjeon, and by Foster himself. (Rev: BL 9/1/04) [811]

11733 *The Drowsy Hours: Poems for Bedtime* (PS–1). Ed. by Susan Pearson. Illus. by Peter Malone. 2002, HarperCollins LB $16.89 (0-06-029421-3). 40pp. This thoughtful anthology captures the bedtime mood perfectly, but will be appreciated any time of the day. (Rev: BL 10/15/02; HBG 10/02; SLJ 6/02) [811.008]

11734 Dunning, Stephen, et al., eds. *Reflections on a Gift of Watermelon Pickle and Other Modern Verse* (6–8). Illus. 1967, Lothrop $20.00 (0-688-41231-9). 144pp. An attractive volume of 114 expressive poems by recognized modern poets, illustrated with striking photographs. (Rev: SLJ 5/05)

11735 Eastwick, Ivy O. *I Asked a Tiger to Tea* (2–6). Illus. by Melanie Hall. 2002, Boyds Mills $15.95 (1-56397-515-7). 32pp. This is a richly illustrated, lyrical collection of poems about nature and childhood. (Rev: BL 12/15/02; HBG 3/03; SLJ 11/02) [811.54]

11736 Eastwick, Ivy O. *Some Folks Like Cats and Other Poems* (1–3). Ed. by Walter B. Barbe. Illus. by Mary Kurnich Maass. 2002, Boyds Mills $15.95 (1-56397-450-9). 28pp. A collection of 20 of the author's poems that deal with such subjects as sunflowers, leaves, rain, and small animals. (Rev: BL 4/15/02; HBG 10/02; SLJ 7/02) [811.54]

11737 Eccleshare, Julia, ed. *First Poems* (PS–3). Illus. by Selina Young. 1994, Bedrick $16.95 (0-87226-373-8). 64pp. A collection of happy, often humorous poems, including a number of old favorites and several by contemporary poets. (Rev: BL 7/94; SLJ 8/94) [821]

11738 *Edna St. Vincent Millay* (3–7). Ed. by Frances Schoonmaker. Illus. Series: Poetry for Young People. 2000, Sterling $14.95 (0-8069-5928-2). 48pp. A representative collection of Millay's poetry illustrated with evocative watercolors. (Rev: BL 3/15/00; HBG 10/00; SLJ 2/00) [811]

11739 Esbensen, Barbara J. *Who Shrank My Grandmother's House? Poems of Discovery* (1–3). Illus. by Eric Beddows. 1992, HarperCollins $15.00 (0-060-21827-4). 48pp. This book presents a celebration of everything in a collection of 23 poems. (Rev: BCCB 4/92; BL 6/1/92; HB 5–6/92; SLJ 4/92*) [811]

11740 Evans, Dilys, ed. *Monster Soup and Other Spooky Poems* (PS–1). Illus. by Jacqueline Rogers. 1992, Scholastic $14.95 (0-590-45208-8). 40pp. Watercolor paintings illustrate 16 poems that monster fans are sure to love. (Rev: BL 8/92; SLJ 10/92) [811]

11741 Ferris, Helen, ed. *Favorite Poems Old and New* (4–6). Illus. by Leonard Weisgard. 1957, Dou-

bleday $24.95 (0-385-07696-7). 598pp. A book brimming with all kinds of poetry — lyrics, rhymes, doggerel, songs.

11742 *The Fish Is Me: Bathtime Rhymes* (PS). Ed. by Neil Philip. Illus. by Claire Henley. 2002, Clarion $16.00 (0-618-15939-8). 28pp. These 18 rhymes are drawn from poets from several countries, and will immediately appeal to children, whether they enjoy baths or not. (Rev: BL 11/1/02; HBG 3/03; SLJ 8/02) [811.008]

11743 Fisher, Aileen. *I Heard a Bluebird Sing* (2–5). Illus. by Jennifer Emery. 2002, Boyds Mills $18.95 (1-56397-191-7). 64pp. The 41 poems included in this anthology were selected by children around the United States; they are preceded by excerpts from an article by Fisher and by introductions to the thematically organized sections. (Rev: BL 11/15/02; HBG 3/03; SLJ 10/02) [811.54]

11744 Fisher, Aileen. *Sing of the Earth and Sky: Poems About Our Planet and the Wonders Beyond* (2–4). Illus. 2001, Boyds Mills $15.95 (1-56397-802-4). 48pp. A collection of short original poems that are divided into four subjects: earth, sun, moon, and stars. (Rev: BL 3/15/01; HBG 10/01) [811]

11745 Fleischman, Paul. *Big Talk: Poems for Four Voices* (4–7). Illus. 2000, Candlewick $17.99 (0-7636-0636-7). 48pp. This collection of spirited, evocative poems for four voices to read aloud covers a variety of topics. (Rev: BCCB 4/00; BL 6/1–15/00; HB 5–6/00; HBG 10/00; SLJ 6/00) [811]

11746 Fletcher, Ralph. *Buried Alive: The Elements of Love* (5–8). 1996, Simon & Schuster $14.00 (0-689-80593-4). A series of free-verse poems that explore various aspects of love — puppy and otherwise. (Rev: BCCB 6/96; BL 5/1/96; SLJ 5/96) [811]

11747 Fletcher, Ralph. *Have You Been to the Beach Lately? Poems* (4–7). Photos by Andrea Sperling. 2001, Scholastic paper $15.95 (0-531-30330-6). 48pp. More than 30 chatty poems, illustrated with black-and-white photographs, are written from the perspective of a smart and funny 11-year-old. (Rev: HBG 10/01; SLJ 8/01) [811]

11748 Fletcher, Ralph. *Relatively Speaking: Poems About Family* (5–7). Illus. 1999, Orchard LB $15.99 (0-531-33141-5). 48pp. From an 11-year-old boy's point of view, these original poems explore relationships as family members go through periods of change. (Rev: BCCB 5/99; BL 7/99; HBG 10/99; SLJ 4/99) [811]

11749 Fletcher, Ralph. *A Writing Kind of Day* (3–5). Illus. by April Ward. 2005, Boyds Mills $17.95 (1-59078-276-3); paper $9.95 (1-59078-353-0). 32pp. A collection of 27 poems by a young author who isn't afraid to write about the everyday and even the silly. (Rev: BL 3/15/05; SLJ 4/05) [811]

11750 Franco, Betsy. *Counting Our Way to the 100th Day! 100 Poems and 100 Pictures to Celebrate the 100th Day of School* (K–2). Illus. by Steven Salerno. 2004, Simon & Schuster $15.95 (0-689-84793-9). 48pp. Many of the 100 poems in this stylishly illustrated collection focus on the number "100" and will help students count down the first 100 days of school. (Rev: BL 8/04; SLJ 7/04) [811]

11751 Frost, Helen. *Spinning Through the Universe: A Novel in Poems from Room 214* (5–7). 2004, Farrar $16.00 (0-374-37159-8). 112pp. A variety of poetic forms — including haiku, tercelle, sonnet, pantoun, and tanka — are used in these diverse and compelling poems about the lives of a fifth-grade teacher and her students. (Rev: BL 4/1/04; SLJ 4/04) [811]

11752 Frost, Robert. *A Swinger of Birches: Poems of Robert Frost for Young People* (4–7). Illus. by Peter Koeppen. 1982, Stemmer $21.95 (0-916144-92-5); paper $14.95 (0-916144-93-3). 80pp. A collection of 38 poems suitable for young people.

11753 George, Kristine O'Connell. *Fold Me a Poem* (1–3). Illus. by Lauren Stringer. 2005, Harcourt $16.00 (0-15-202501-4). 56pp. A boy creates origami animals and then uses them for imaginative play in this book of 32 poems. (Rev: BL 3/15/05; SLJ 3/05) [811]

11754 George, Kristine O'Connell. *Swimming Upstream: Middle School Poems* (5–8). Illus. by Debbie Tilley. 2002, Clarion $14.00 (0-618-15250-4). 80pp. Brief poems describe how one girl navigates the rapids of middle school, discussing everything from school lunches and lockers to making friends and relationships with boys. (Rev: BL 1/1–15/03; HB 1–2/03; HBG 3/03; SLJ 9/02) [811]

11755 George, Kristine O'Connell. *Toasting Marshmallows: Camping Poems* (K–4). Illus. by Kate Kiesler. 2001, Clarion $15.00 (0-618-04597-X). 48pp. Thirty simple poems clearly depict a family camping trip, from the details of pitching a tent to the wonders of the natural world, with attractive and varied artwork. (Rev: HBG 10/01; SLJ 7/01*) [811]

11756 Gillooly, Eileen, ed. *Rudyard Kipling* (4–8). Illus. by Jim Sharpe. 2000, Sterling $14.95 (0-8069-4484-6). 48pp. This book contains complete poems or excerpts from 28 poems by this well-liked writer including "If" and "The Ballad of East and West." (Rev: HBG 3/01; SLJ 5/00) [821]

11757 *Good Night, Sleep Tight: A Poem for Every Night of the Year* (PS–3). Ed. by Ivan Jones and Mal Jones. Illus. 2000, Scholastic $22.95 (0-439-18813-X). 256pp. A fine anthology of 366 (one for Leap Year) poems chiefly by English poets that cover different kinds of rhymes, situations, and moods. (Rev: BL 1/1–15/01; HBG 10/01) [811.08]

11758 Graham, Joan B. *Flicker Flash* (3–6). Illus. 1999, Houghton Mifflin $15.95 (0-395-90501-X). 32pp. A collection of verses in geometric forms associated with light, among them a camera, a firefly, a lightbulb, and fireworks. (Rev: BL 1/1–15/00; HBG 3/00; SLJ 12/99*) [811]

11759 *A Grand Celebration: Grandparents in Poetry* (3–7). Ed. by Carol G. Hittleman and Daniel R. Hittleman. Illus. by Kay Life. 2002, Boyds Mills $16.95 (1-56397-901-2). 32pp. This anthology of 26 poems about grandparents represents a variety of cultures, levels of activity, and ages. (Rev: BL 4/1/02; HBG 10/02; SLJ 6/02) [808.819]

11760 *Grandad's Tree: Poems About Families* (2–4). Illus. by Julia Cairns. 2003, Barefoot $16.99 (1-84148-541-1). 32pp. Twenty poems comple-

mented by watercolor illustrations explore various aspects of family life; poets featured include Eloise Greenfield, Judith Viorst, Christina Rossetti, and Carl Sandburg. (Rev: BL 4/1/03; HBG 10/03) [811.008]

11761 Greenberg, David T. *The Book of Boys (for Girls) and The Book of Girls (for Boys)* (K–3). Illus. by Joy Allen. 2005, Little, Brown $15.99 (0-316-36210-7). 32pp. Rhyming text presents opposing points of view from the two genders on a variety of everyday issues. (Rev: BL 5/15/05) [811]

11762 Greenberg, Jan, ed. *Heart to Heart: New Poems Inspired by Twentieth-Century American Art* (5–10). Illus. 2001, Abrams $19.95 (0-8109-4386-7). 80pp. This book contains specially commissioned poems from well-known writers to accompany some of the finest artworks of the 20th century. (Rev: BL 3/15/01*; HBG 10/01; SLJ 4/01*) [811]

11763 Greenfield, Eloise. *Under the Sunday Tree* (2–5). Illus. by Amos Ferguson. 1988, HarperCollins paper $10.95 (0-06-443257-2). 48pp. Poems of life in the Bahamas. (Rev: BCCB 12/88; HB 11–12/88)

11764 Grimes, Nikki. *Aneesa Lee and the Weaver's Gift* (3–6). Illus. by Ashley Bryan. 1999, Lothrop $16.00 (0-688-15997-4). A collection of 14 interrelated poems that deal with various aspects of the art and craft of weaving. (Rev: HBG 3/00; SLJ 12/99) [811]

11765 Grimes, Nikki. *A Dime a Dozen* (5–8). Illus. 1998, Dial $17.99 (0-8037-2227-3). 56pp. Through a series of original poems, the writer explores her childhood: its happy moments, its painful memories — including divorce, foster homes, and parents with drinking and gambling problems — and her search for herself as a teenager. (Rev: BL 12/1/98; HBG 3/99; SLJ 11/98) [811]

11766 Grimes, Nikki. *A Pocketful of Poems* (K–3). Illus. by Javaka Steptoe. 2001, Clarion $15.00 (0-618-93868-6). 32pp. Poems by a young African American girl named Tiana about urban topics — pigeons, baseball, the moon — are presented in double-page spreads, each traditional poem facing a haiku. (Rev: BL 2/15/01*) [811]

11767 Grimes, Nikki. *Shoe Magic* (2–5). Illus. by Terry Widener. 2000, Orchard LB $17.99 (0-531-33286-1). 32pp. In this collection of poems about different kinds of shoes, each shoe embodies a young person's pride in accomplishment and hope for the future. (Rev: BL 9/15/00; HBG 3/01; SLJ 10/00) [811]

11768 Grimes, Nikki. *Tai Chi Morning: Snapshots of China* (4–8). Illus. by Ed Young. 2004, Cricket $15.95 (0-8126-2707-5). 64pp. Grimes's journal in verse describes her impressions on a tour of China. (Rev: BL 3/1/04; SLJ 5/04) [811]

11769 Grimes, Nikki. *What Is Goodbye?* (4–8). Illus. by Raul Colon. 2004, Hyperion $15.99 (0-7868-0778-4). 64pp. A brother and sister mourn the death of their older brother in poems in alternating voices. (Rev: BL 5/1/04; SLJ 6/04) [811]

11770 Gunning, Monica. *America, My New Home* (2–5). Illus. by Ken Condon. 2004, Boyds Mills $15.95 (1-59078-057-4). 32pp. Simple poems and bright illustrations paint a vivid portrait of a Jamaican child's bittersweet immigrant experience. (Rev: BL 11/15/04) [811]

11771 Gunning, Monica. *Under the Breadfruit Tree* (3–6). Illus. 1998, Boyds Mills $15.95 (1-56397-539-4). 48pp. These 38 poems describe the Caribbean peoples and their culture from the standpoint of a young Jamaican girl. (Rev: BL 2/15/98; HB 7–8/04; HBG 10/98; SLJ 4/98) [811]

11772 Hague, Michael, sel. *The Book of Fairy Poetry* (K–5). Illus. by Michael Hague. 2004, Harper-Collins $19.99 (0-688-14004-1). 156pp. An oversize collection of varied works by poets including Walter de la Mare, Sir Walter Scott, Annie R. Rentoul, and Shakespeare. (Rev: SLJ 5/05) [811]

11773 Hale, Glorya, ed. *An Illustrated Treasury of Read-Aloud Poems for Young People: More Than 100 of the World's Best-Loved Poems for Parent and Child to Share* (2–6). Illus. 2003, Black Dog & Leventhal $14.95 (1-57912-289-2). 192pp. This thematically organized anthology of poetry — perfect for reading aloud — contains more than 100 poems from such well-known American and English poets as Maya Angelou, Robert Frost, Rudyard Kipling, Henry Wadsworth Longfellow, and William Wordsworth. (Rev: HBG 4/04; SLJ 11/03) [821.008]

11774 Hall, Donald. *The Man Who Lived Alone* (4–7). Illus. 1998, Godine paper $11.95 (1-56792-050-0). 36pp. A narrative poem concerning a man who ran away from abuse to see the world and returns in later life.

11775 Harley, Avis. *Fly with Poetry: An ABC of Poetry* (3–5). Illus. by author. 2000, Boyds Mills $13.95 (1-56397-798-2). 48pp. A collection of 27 original short poems, generally one for each letter of the alphabet (Y leaves space to write one's own poem). (Rev: SLJ 9/00) [811]

11776 Harrison, David L. *The Alligator in the Closet: And Other Poems Around the House* (2–4). Illus. by Jane Kendall. 2003, Boyds Mills $16.95 (1-56397-944-2). 48pp. Common childhood experiences in the home are the focus of these short and accessible poems. (Rev: BL 4/1/03) [811]

11777 Harrison, David L. *The Alligator in the Closet: And Other Poems Around the House* (1–5). Illus. by Jane Kendall. 2003, Boyds Mills $16.95 (1-56397-994-2). 48pp. Everyday items are the focus of this collection of lighthearted poems. (Rev: HBG 10/03; SLJ 3/03) [811]

11778 Harrison, David L. *The Purchase of Small Secrets* (3–5). Illus. by Meryl Henderson. 1998, Boyds Mills $14.95 (1-56397-054-6). 48pp. This introspective collection of poems touches upon some of the landmark occasions in a boy's journey to maturity, such as fistfights, flirting, and shooting a gun. (Rev: HBG 3/99; SLJ 11/98) [811]

11779 Harrison, Michael, and Christopher Stuart-Clark, eds. *One Hundred Years of Poetry for Children* (5–7). Illus. 1999, Oxford $25.00 (0-19-276190-0). 195pp. Arranged by theme, this

collection of 20th-century verse contains one poem from each of approximately 150 poets. (Rev: BL 9/1/99; HBG 3/00; SLJ 7/99) [821.9]

11780 Harrison, Michael, and Christopher Stuart-Clark, comps. *The Oxford Treasury of Time Poems* (4–9). 1999, Oxford LB $25.00 (1-19-276175-7). 155pp. From John Milton and William Blake to W. H. Auden and Sylvia Plath, this anthology contains poetry and thoughts about time. (Rev: SLJ 7/99) [811]

11781 Harrison, Michael, and Christopher Stuart-Clark, eds. *The Young Oxford Book of Christmas Poems* (5–8). Illus. 2001, Oxford $19.95 (0-19-276247-8). 160pp. A richly illustrated collection of poems with Christmas themes by poets including Ted Hughes, Sylvia Plath, and Seamus Heaney. (Rev: BCCB 2/02; BL 12/1/01; HBG 3/02) [821]

11782 Hegley, John. *My Dog Is a Carrot* (3–6). Illus. by author. 2003, Candlewick $12.99 (0-7636-1932-9). 64pp. Nonsense verse about everyday items, family, and nature will please lovers of wordplay. (Rev: BL 5/15/03; HBG 10/03; SLJ 3/03) [811]

11783 *Hello Sunshine, Good Night Moonlight* (K–3). Illus. by John Wallace. 2004, Abrams $14.95 (0-8109-4834-6). 32pp. The mundane routine of a child's daily life is the focus of this collection of poems by diverse poets, many of them British. (Rev: BL 4/1/04; SLJ 7/04) [811.008]

11784 High, Linda Oatman. *A Humble Life: Plain Poems* (2–4). Illus. by Bill Farnsworth. 2001, Eerdmans $17.00 (0-8028-5207-6). 40pp. Graceful poems and evocative paintings depict a year in a Mennonite and Amish county in Pennsylvania. (Rev: BL 12/15/01; HBG 3/02; SLJ 10/01) [811]

11785 Hirsch, Robin. *FEG: Stupid (Ridiculous) Poems for Intelligent Children* (5–8). Illus. by Ha. 2002, Little, Brown $15.95 (0-316-36344-8). 48pp. A collection of amusing, sometimes hilarious, original poems that rely on playing with words and their meanings. (Rev: BL 6/1–15/02; HBG 10/02; SLJ 4/02) [821.914]

11786 Hoberman, Mary Ann. *You Read to Me, I'll Read to You: Very Short Stories to Read Together* (2–3). Illus. by Michael Emberley. 2001, Little, Brown $15.95 (0-316-36350-2). 32pp. A collection of short poems designed to be spoken aloud by two readers. (Rev: BL 8/01; HB 11–12/01; HBG 3/02; SLJ 8/01*) [811.54]

11787 Hollander, John, ed. *American Poetry* (4–10). Illus. by Sally Wern Comport. Series: Poetry for Young People. 2004, Sterling $14.95 (1-4027-0517-4). 48pp. A colorful celebration of American life, containing 26 poems by well-known poets including Robert Frost, Walt Whitman, Maya Angelou, and Langston Hughes. (Rev: SLJ 8/04) [811]

11788 *Home to Me: Poems Across America* (2–5). Ed. by Lee Bennett Hopkins. Illus. by Stephen Alcorn. 2002, Scholastic $17.95 (0-439-34096-9). 48pp. From trailer parks to Indian reservations, from cities to prairies, this expansive anthology features poems about Americans and America. (Rev: BL 10/15/02; HB 1–2/03; HBG 3/03; SLJ 10/02) [811.008]

11789 Hooper, Patricia. *Where Do You Sleep, Little One?* (PS–K). Illus. by John Winch. 2001, Holiday House $16.95 (0-8234-1668-2). 32pp. Animals answer the title's question in verse, and gather around a manger to see a sleeping child in this book that features beautiful collage illustrations. (Rev: BL 9/1/01; HBG 3/02; SLJ 9/01) [811]

11790 Hopkins, Lee Bennett, ed. *Good Books, Good Times* (K–3). Illus. by Harvey Stevenson. 1990, HarperCollins LB $16.89 (0-06-022528-9). 32pp. Fourteen short poems celebrate book reading. (Rev: BL 11/15/90; HB 1–2/91; SLJ 10/90*) [811]

11791 Hopkins, Lee Bennett, ed. *Hand in Hand* (5–8). 1994, Simon & Schuster $21.95 (0-671-73315-X). An overview of the history of American poetry, with an interesting selection of poems arranged chronologically. (Rev: BCCB 1/95; BL 1/1/95; SLJ 12/94) [811]

11792 Hopkins, Lee Bennett, sel. *Lives: Poems About Famous Americans* (4–8). Illus. 1999, HarperCollins LB $16.89 (0-06-027768-8). Poetry brings to life 16 important Americans, among them Paul Revere, Eleanor Roosevelt, Babe Ruth, and Langston Hughes. (Rev: BCCB 5/99; HBG 9/99; SLJ 6/99) [811]

11793 Hopkins, Lee Bennett, sel. *My America: A Poetry Atlas of the United States* (3–8). Illus. by Stephen Alcorn. 2000, Simon & Schuster $19.95 (0-689-81247-7). 83pp. Seven regions of the United states including Washington, D.C., are explored in this anthology of 51 poems by 40 different poets. (Rev: BCCB 10/00; BL 9/1/03; HBG 3/01; SLJ 9/00) [811]

11794 Hopkins, Lee Bennett, ed. *Surprises* (K–4). Illus. by Megan Lloyd. 1984, HarperCollins paper $3.95 (0-06-444105-9). 64pp. A collection of simple poems for beginning readers.

11795 *Hot Potato: Mealtime Rhymes* (PS–1). Ed. by Neil Philip. Illus. by Claire Henley. 2004, Clarion $16.00 (0-618-31554-3). 32pp. The bouncy rhyming poems in this vividly illustrated picture-book collection focus on the sounds and rhythms of eating. (Rev: BL 4/15/04; SLJ 5/04) [811]

11796 Hubbell, Patricia. *City Kids* (PS–1). Illus. by Teresa Flavin. 2001, Marshall Cavendish $15.95 (0-7614-5079-3). 32pp. Simple poems and cheery pictures show kids engaged in such big-city activities as playing stickball, skipping rope, and stretching up like a skyscraper. (Rev: BL 3/1/01; HBG 10/01) [811]

11797 Hughes, Shirley. *Olly and Me* (PS–2). 2004, Candlewick $15.99 (0-7636-2374-1). 32pp. This collection of poetry and prose explores a variety of everyday experiences as seen through the eyes of a young girl. (Rev: BL 6/1–15/04; SLJ 5/04) [811]

11798 Janeczko, Paul B. *The Place My Words Are Looking For: What Poets Say About and Through Their Work* (4–9). Illus. 1990, Macmillan $17.95 (0-02-747671-5). 128pp. A collection of works by some of the best contemporary poets. (Rev: BCCB 7–8/90; BL 5/1/90; HB 5–6/90*; SLJ 5/90) [811]

11799 Janeczko, Paul B. *Worlds Afire* (4–8). 2004, Candlewick $15.99 (0-7636-2235-4). 112pp. This moving book written in verse tells, from many points of view, the story of a tragic circus fire in 1944 that killed 167 people. (Rev: BL 1/1–15/04; HB 5–6/04; SLJ 4/04) [811]

11800 Johnson, Angela. *Running Back to Ludie* (5–8). 2001, Scholastic paper $15.95 (0-439-29316-2). 64pp. A teenage girl's friends and family, including her wayward mother, are introduced through a series of free-verse poems. (Rev: BCCB 1/02; BL 1/1–15/02; HB 11–12/01; HBG 3/02; SLJ 12/01)

11801 Johnson, Dave, ed. *Movin': Teen Poets Take Voice* (5–10). Illus. by Chris Raschka. 2000, Orchard $15.95 (0-531-30258-X); paper $6.95 (0-531-07171-5). 52pp. An anthology of poems by teens who participated in New York Public Library workshops or submitted their work via the Web. (Rev: BL 3/15/00; HBG 10/00; SLJ 5/00) [811]

11802 Johnston, Tony. *The Ancestors Are Singing* (4–8). Illus. by Karen Barbour. 2003, Farrar $16.00 (0-374-30347-9). 64pp. Mexico's geography, history, and culture are portrayed in poems full of vivid images. (Rev: BL 4/1/03; HBG 10/03; SLJ 4/03) [811]

11803 Johnston, Tony. *My Mexico / México Mío* (K–3). Illus. by F. John Sierra. 1996, Penguin Putnam $15.99 (0-399-22275-8). 36pp. Mexican scenes are presented in double-page spreads with 18 poems in both English and Spanish. (Rev: BCCB 7–8/96; HB 5–6/96; SLJ 4/96) [811]

11804 Joseph, Lynn. *Coconut Kind of Day: Island Poems* (K–2). Illus. by Sandra Speidel. 1990, Lothrop LB $13.88 (0-688-09120-2). 32pp. A portrait of a young black girl in the West Indies. (Rev: BCCB 1/91; BL 9/15/90; SLJ 11/90) [811]

11805 Katz, Susan. *Mrs. Brown on Exhibit and Other Museum Poems* (2–4). Illus. by R. W. Alley. 2002, Simon & Schuster $16.95 (0-689-82970-1). 40pp. A collection of poems about Mrs. Brown's class field trips to museums and the many discoveries they find there. (Rev: BL 6/1–15/02; HBG 3/03; SLJ 8/02) [811]

11806 Katz, Susan. *A Revolutionary Field Trip: Poems of Colonial America* (1–4). Illus. by R. W. Alley. 2004, Simon & Schuster $16.95 (0-689-84004-7). 37pp. Poems about life in colonial America are presented through the eyes of a class trip to historic sites. (Rev: SLJ 9/04) [811]

11807 Kennedy, X. J., and Dorothy M. Kennedy, eds. *Talking Like the Rain: A First Book of Poems* (PS–3). Illus. by Jane Dyer. 1992, Little, Brown $19.95 (0-316-48889-5). 96pp. This is a cheerful collection of 100 well-illustrated poems in a variety of subjects and moods. (Rev: BCCB 7–8/92; BL 3/15/92; HB 7–8/92; SLJ 6/92) [821]

11808 *A Kick in the Head: An Everyday Guide to Poetic Forms* (4–6). Ed. by Paul B. Janeczko. Illus. by Chris Raschka. 2005, Candlewick $17.99 (0-7636-0662-6). 64pp. Twenty-nine different types of poems (sonnets, ballads, haiku, etc.) are introduced; some funny, some sad, some silly, but all engaging and accompanied by beautiful collages. (Rev: BL 3/15/05; SLJ 3/05) [811.008]

11809 *The Kingfisher Book of Family Poems* (3–5). Ed. by Belinda Hollyer. Illus. by Holly Swain. 2003, Kingfisher $18.95 (0-7534-5557-9). 224pp. Poems in this large and varied anthology touch on all aspects of family life and emotions. (Rev: BL 5/1/03; HBG 10/03; SLJ 7/03) [821.008]

11810 Koch, Kenneth, and Kate Farrell. *Talking to the Sun: An Illustrated Anthology of Poems for Young People* (5–9). Illus. 1985, Holt $35.00 (0-8050-0144-1). A collection of poems on many subjects, illustrated with reproductions from the Metropolitan Museum of Art. (Rev: BL 1/1/86; BR 9–10/86; SLJ 1/87) [808.81]

11811 Kuskin, Karla. *Moon, Have You Met My Mother? The Collected Poems of Karla Kuskin* (2–4). Illus. by Sergio Ruzzier. 2003, HarperCollins LB $17.89 (0-06-027174-4). 336pp. Poems written over a period of more than 40 years are collected here and arranged according to themes such as animals, seasons, and human personality. (Rev: BL 4/1/03; HBG 10/03; SLJ 2/03) [811]

11812 Kuskin, Karla. *The Sky Is Always in the Sky* (PS–3). Illus. by Isabelle Dervaux. 1998, Harper-Collins LB $14.89 (0-06-027084-5). 48pp. A brilliant collection of poems culled from the author's many collections and illustrated in a folk-art style. (Rev: BL 5/15/98; HBG 10/98; SLJ 7/98) [811]

11813 Lansky, Bruce, ed. *No More Homework! No More Tests! Kids' Favorite Funny School Poems* (2–6). Illus. 1997, Meadowbrook LB $8.00 (0-671-57702-6). 80pp. Humorous, often outrageous, poems that deal with real and fantastic school situations. (Rev: BL 9/15/97) [811]

11814 Lee, Claudia M., ed. *Messengers of Rain and Other Poems from Latin America* (2–6). Illus. by Rafael Yockteng. 2002, Groundwood $18.95 (0-88899-470-2). 80pp. An anthology of more than 60 poems on a wide range of topics, translated from Spanish, by well-known and less-familiar writers. (Rev: SLJ 1/03) [811]

11815 Lesynski, Loris. *Dirty Dog Boogie* (2–5). Illus. by author. 1999, Annick LB $16.95 (1-55037-572-5); paper $6.95 (1-55037-573-3). 32pp. A joyous collection of poems that are filled with musical rhythms and quirky language. (Rev: HBG 10/99; SLJ 7/99) [811]

11816 Lesynski, Loris. *Zigzag: Zoems for Zindergarten* (PS–K). Illus. by author. 2004, Annick LB $19.95 (1-55037-875-9); paper $8.95 (1-55037-882-1). 32pp. Great for reading aloud, thse poems feature nonsense verse and bouncy rhythms. (Rev: BL 12/1/04; SLJ 1/05) [811]

11817 Levin, Jonathan, ed. *Walt Whitman: Poetry for Young People* (5–9). Illus. 1997, Sterling $14.95 (0-8069-9530-0). After a brief biographical sketch, this volume contains 26 poems and excerpts from longer poems, each introduced with an analysis. (Rev: HBG 3/98; SLJ 11/97) [811]

11818 Levy, Constance. *When Whales Exhale and Other Poems* (3–5). Illus. 1996, Simon & Schuster $15.00 (0-689-80946-8). 42pp. A group of poems about the wonders of small things that are part of larger objects or events. (Rev: BL 12/15/96; SLJ 12/96) [811]

11819 Lewis, Claudia. *Long Ago in Oregon* (3–7). Illus. by Joel Fontaine. 1987, HarperCollins $11.95 (0-06-023839-9). 64pp. Short poems that recall the nostalgia of childhood in Oregon in the early 1900s. (Rev: BCCB 5/87; BL 7/87; SLJ 9/87)

11820 Lewis, J. Patrick. *A Burst of Firsts: Doers, Shakers, and Record Breakers* (2–4). Illus. by Brian Ajhar. 2001, Dial $15.99 (0-8037-2108-0). 40pp. This collection of imaginative original poems celebrates famous firsts, such as the first African American to win the Nobel prize. (Rev: BL 3/15/01; HBG 10/01) [811]

11821 Lewis, J. Patrick. *Doodle Dandies: Poems That Take Shape* (3–5). Illus. by Lisa Desimini. 1998, Simon & Schuster $16.00 (0-689-81075-X). 32pp. A collection of delightful, original poems that make a physical shape on the page. For example, a poem named "Dachshund" fills a dog-shaped illustration. (Rev: BCCB 9/98; BL 7/98; HBG 3/99; SLJ 8/98) [811]

11822 Lewis, J. Patrick. *Heroes and She-roes: Poems of Amazing and Everyday Heroes* (4–7). Illus. by Jim Cooke. 2005, Dial $16.99 (0-8037-2925-1). 40pp. Helen Keller, Rosa Parks, and Gandhi are among the courageous individuals featured in this collection of poems. (Rev: BL 1/1–15/05; SLJ 3/05) [811]

11823 Lewis, J. Patrick. *Please Bury Me in the Library* (2–4). Illus. by Kyle M. Stone. 2005, Harcourt $16.00 (0-15-216387-5). 32pp. Sixteen original poems celebrate the joys of reading. (Rev: BL 2/15/05; SLJ 6/05) [811]

11824 Lewis, J. Patrick. *A World of Wonders: Geographic Travels in Verse and Rhyme* (3–5). Illus. by Alison Jay. 2002, Dial $16.99 (0-8037-2579-5). 40pp. Geographic terminology and facts are skillfully woven into verse in this attractive volume that touches on topics including seas, deserts, the poles, and the equator. (Rev: BL 3/15/02; HB 3–4/02; HBG 10/02; SLJ 4/02) [811]

11825 Lillegard, Dee. *Hello School! A Classroom Full of Poems* (PS–1). Illus. by Don Carter. 2001, Knopf $14.95 (0-375-81020-X). 32pp. Short poems introduce many simple aspects of school. (Rev: BCCB 6/01; BL 8/01; HBG 3/02; SLJ 7/01) [811.54]

11826 Lindbergh, Reeve. *On Morning Wings* (PS–1). Illus. by Holly Meade. 2002, Candlewick $15.99 (0-7636-1106-9). 32pp. A poem, based on Psalm 139 and illustrated in watercolors, thanking God for His loving care. (Rev: BL 9/15/02; HBG 3/03; SLJ 12/02)

11827 Little, Jean. *I Gave My Mom a Castle* (4–7). Illus. by Kady MacDonald Denton. 2004, Orca paper $7.95 (1-55143-253-6). 80pp. Gifts — expected and unexpected, rewarding and trying — are the theme of this diverse collection of prose poems. (Rev: BL 3/1/04; SLJ 4/04) [811]

11828 Liu, Siyu, and Orel Protopopescu. *A Thousand Peaks: Poems from China* (5–10). Illus. by Siyu Liu. 2002, Pacific View $19.95 (1-881896-24-2). 52pp. Thirty-five translations of Chinese poems are accompanied by information giving historical and cultural context, the original in Chinese characters and pinyin transliteration, a literal translation, and black-and-white drawings. (Rev: BL 3/15/02; SLJ 2/02*) [811]

11829 *Lives: Poems About Famous Americans* (3–6). Ed. by Lee Bennett Hopkins. Illus. 1999, Harper-Collins $15.95 (0-06-027767-X). 40pp. Fourteen poems — 12 new to this collection — celebrate the lives of such famous Americans as Sacagawea, Thomas Edison, Eleanor Roosevelt, and Rosa Parks. (Rev: BL 3/15/99; HBG 10/99; SLJ 6/99) [811.008]

11830 Longfellow, Henry Wadsworth. *The Children's Hour* (K–2). Illus. by Glenna Lang. 1993, Godine $17.95 (0-87923-971-9). 32pp. The classic poem is illustrated with paintings depicting Longfellow spending time with his children. (Rev: BL 11/15/93) [811]

11831 Longfellow, Henry Wadsworth. *The Children's Own Longfellow* (5–8). Illus. 1908, Houghton Mifflin $20.00 (0-395-06889-4). 109pp. Eight selections from the best-known and best-loved of Longfellow's poems. (Rev: BL 2/15/04*; SLJ 3/04)

11832 Longfellow, Henry Wadsworth. *Hiawatha and Megissogwon* (4–7). Illus. by Jeffrey Thompson. 2001, National Geographic $16.95 (0-7922-6676-5). 32pp. Artwork with an authentic Native American feel illustrates Hiawatha's exciting adventures in the "Pearl-Feather" section of Longfellow's epic poem. (Rev: BCCB 3/02; BL 11/15/01; HBG 3/02; SLJ 9/01) [811]

11833 Longfellow, Henry Wadsworth. *The Midnight Ride of Paul Revere* (2–4). Illus. by Christopher Bing. 2001, Handprint $17.95 (1-929766-13-0). 40pp. Bing's design juxtaposes historical objects, watercolors, and scratchboard work to great effect in this rendering of Longfellow's famous poem that also includes maps and notes. (Rev: BCCB 2/02; BL 12/15/01; HB 3–4/02; HBG 10/02; SLJ 12/01*) [811]

11834 Longfellow, Henry Wadsworth. *Paul Revere's Ride* (2–4). Illus. by Nancy Winslow Parker. 1985, Morrow paper $4.95 (0-688-12387-2). 48pp. Soft illustrations relieve the suspense of this famous ride. (Rev: BCCB 5/85; BL 3/1/85; HB 5–6/85)

11835 Longfellow, Henry Wadsworth. *Paul Revere's Ride* (2–5). Illus. by Monica Vachula. 2003, Boyds Mills $16.95 (1-56397-799-0). 32pp. Longfellow's famous poem, with attractive illustrations that show background scenery. (Rev: BL 2/1/03; HBG 10/03; SLJ 5/03) [811]

11836 Longfellow, Henry Wadsworth. *Paul Revere's Ride: The Landlord's Tale* (2–5). Illus. by Charles Santore. 2003, HarperCollins LB $17.89 (0-06-623747-5). 40pp. The poem about Revere's famous ride is accompanied here by dramatic illustrations that convey a sense of urgency. (Rev: BL 2/1/03; HBG 10/03; SLJ 3/03) [811]

11837 *Love to Mama: A Tribute to Mothers* (PS–4). Ed. by Pat Mora. Illus. by Paula S. Barragan M. 2001, Lee & Low $16.95 (1-58430-019-1). 32pp. A celebration of Latina mothers and grandmothers that ends with a glossary and notes about the poets.

(Rev: BL 5/1/01; HB 7–8/01; HBG 10/01; SLJ 4/01*) [811]

11838 McCord, David. *All Day Long: Fifty Rhymes of the Never Was and Always Is* (4–7). Illus. by Henry B. Kane. 1975, Little, Brown paper $6.95 (0-316-55532-0). A collection of poems on a variety of subjects, chiefly times that are important in childhood.

11839 McCord, David. *One at a Time: His Collected Poems for the Young* (3–8). Illus. by Henry B. Kane. 1986, Little, Brown $18.95 (0-316-55516-9). All seven of the poet's anthologies in one handsome volume.

11840 McDonald, Megan. *Baya, Baya, Lulla-by-a* (PS–1). Illus. by Vera Rosenberry. 2003, Simon & Schuster $16.95 (0-689-84932-X). In this haunting poem, a Hindu mother sings a lullaby to her little girl as nearby a weaver bird, or baya, makes a nest of grasses and flowers; the bright yellow bird later saves the infant from a venomous snake. (Rev: HBG 4/04; SLJ 8/03)

11841 McGough, Roger, sel. *The Kingfisher Book of Funny Poems* (4–7). Illus. by Caroline Holden. 2002, Kingfisher $19.00 (0-7534-5480-7). 256pp. An anthology of poems arranged by theme that includes many by familiar names such as Ogden Nash, Lewis Carroll, and Shel Silverstein. (Rev: SLJ 6/02) [811]

11842 Marzollo, Jean. *I Love You: A Rebus Poem* (PS). Illus. by Suse MacDonald. 2000, Scholastic paper $7.95 (0-590-37656-X). 40pp. A rebus puzzle book is used to present a series of simple poems about loving one another. (Rev: BL 12/15/99; HBG 10/00; SLJ 2/00) [811.54]

11843 Mavor, Salley, ed. *You and Me: Poems of Friendship* (PS–3). Illus. 1997, Orchard LB $17.99 (0-531-33045-1). 32pp. An anthology of 19 enjoyable poems that celebrate the joys and problems that come with friendships. (Rev: BL 7/97; HBG 3/98; SLJ 9/97) [811]

11844 Medina, Jane. *The Dream on Blanca's Wall / El sueño pegado en la pared de Blanca: Poems in English and Spanish / Poemas en ingles y espanol* (4–6). Illus. by Robert Casilla. 2004, Boyds Mills $16.95 (1-56397-740-0); paper $9.95 (1-59078-264-X). 48pp. Sixth-grader Blanca has wanted to be a teacher since the second grade; poems in English and Spanish describe her dreams and the looming personal and economic challenges. (Rev: SLJ 4/04) [811]

11845 Medina, Jane. *My Name Is Jorge: On Both Sides of the River* (3–7). Illus. by Fabricio Vandenbroeck. 1999, Boyds Mills $14.95 (1-56397-811-3). 48pp. An immigrant boy from Mexico describes his experiences in a series of 27 poems in English and Spanish. (Rev: HBG 3/00; SLJ 2/00) [811]

11846 Medina, Tony. *Love to Langston* (3–6). Illus. by R. Gregory Christie. 2002, Lee & Low $16.95 (1-58430-041-8). A celebration in poetry of the life and work of poet Langston Hughes, with biographical notes appended. (Rev: BCCB 3/02; BL 2/15/02; HBG 10/02; SLJ 3/02) [811]

11847 Micklos, John, comp. *Grandparent Poems* (K–4). Illus. by Layne Johnson. 2004, Boyds Mills $15.95 (1-56397-900-4). 32pp. A collection of more than 20 poems by contemporary poets about grandparents and the special relationships between generations. (Rev: SLJ 3/04) [811]

11848 Mitchell, Stephen. *The Wishing Bone and Other Poems* (3–6). Illus. by Tom Pohrt. 2003, Candlewick $16.99 (0-7636-1118-2). 56pp. Whimsical illustrations accompany these humorous and thought-provoking poems. (Rev: BL 4/1/03; HB 7–8/03; HBG 10/03; SLJ 5/03) [811]

11849 *Mommy Poems* (K–3). Ed. by John Micklos. Illus. by Lori McElrath-Eslick. 2001, Boyds Mills $15.95 (1-56397-849-0); paper $8.95 (1-56397-908-X). 32pp. An anthology of 18 poems about mothers by such writers as Gary Soto and Nikki Giovanni. (Rev: BL 3/15/01; HBG 10/01) [811]

11850 Moore, Lilian. *I'm Small and Other Verses* (PS–2). Illus. by Jill McElmurry. 2001, Candlewick $13.99 (0-7636-1169-7). The delights and trials of childhood are the focus of these friendly poems. (Rev: HB 5–6/01; HBG 10/01; SLJ 5/01) [811]

11851 Mora, Pat. *Confetti* (1–4). Illus. by Enrique O. Sanchez. 1996, Lee & Low $15.95 (1-880000-25-3). 32pp. A series of poems that mingle Spanish expressions with basic English. (Rev: BL 11/15/96; SLJ 11/96) [811]

11852 Morninghouse, Sundaira. *Nightfeathers* (PS–K). Illus. by Jody Kim. 1990, Open Hand $9.95 (0-940880-27-X); paper $4.95 (0-940880-28-8). 32pp. In 24 short poems, a typical day in the life of an African American child is portrayed. (Rev: BL 6/1/90) [811]

11853 Morrison, Lillian, ed. *More Spice than Sugar: Poems About Feisty Females* (4–7). Illus. 2001, Houghton Mifflin $15.00 (0-618-06892-9). 80pp. This anthology of poems by many famous writers deals with women in three sections: women's identity, women in sports, and women's rights. (Rev: BL 3/15/01; HBG 10/01; SLJ 3/01) [811]

11854 Morrison, Lillian. *Way to Go! Sports Poems* (4–8). Illus. by Susan Spellman. 2001, Boyds Mills $16.95 (1-56397-961-6). 48pp. Sport lovers will appreciate this collection of poems full of rhythm and life, with vibrant illustrations. (Rev: HBG 3/02; SLJ 10/01) [811]

11855 Moss, Jeff. *Bone Poems* (3–5). Illus. by Tom Leigh. 1997, Workman $14.95 (0-7611-0884-X). 78pp. A group of rhymes that explore facts about dinosaurs and make paleontology fun. (Rev: HBG 3/98; SLJ 12/97*) [811]

11856 Moss, Jeff. *The Butterfly Jar* (2–5). Illus. by Chris L. Demarest. 1989, Bantam $17.95 (0-553-05704-9). 128pp. Upbeat poetry, including the silly and the serious. (Rev: BL 2/1/90; SLJ 7/90) [811]

11857 Mullins, Tom, ed. *Running Lightly . . .: Poems for Young People* (4–9). 1998, Mercier paper $12.95 (1-85342-193-9). A charming collection of old songs and ballads, nonsense rhymes, and lyrics. (Rev: BL 5/15/98; SLJ 7/98) [811]

11858 *My First Oxford Book of Poems* (PS–4). Ed. by John Foster. Illus. 2000, Oxford $22.95 (0-19-276201-X). 96pp. About 100 poems are illustrated by different artists in this fine anthology that includes some old favorites by writers like Stevenson and Lear as well as a good selection of more contemporary works. (Rev: BL 9/15/00; HBG 10/00; SLJ 8/00) [811]

11859 Myers, Walter Dean. *Blues Journey* (5–8). Illus. by Christopher Myers. 2003, Holiday House $18.95 (0-8234-1613-5). 48pp. Poems reflecting the soulfulness of blues music, accompanied by illustrations. (Rev: BL 2/15/03; HB 5–6/03; HBG 10/03; SLJ 4/03*) [811]

11860 Noda, Takayo. *Dear World* (K–3). Illus. by author. 2003, Dial $16.99 (0-8037-2644-9). Wonderful illustrations enhance this series of brief poems framed as letters from a child. (Rev: BL 4/15/03; HBG 10/03; SLJ 3/03) [811]

11861 Nye, Naomi S. *Come with Me: Poems for a Journey* (K–3). Illus. by Dan Yaccarino. 2000, Greenwillow LB $15.89 (0-688-15947-8). 40pp. From real trips to travels of the imagination, this collection of 16 original free-verse poems celebrates different kinds of journeys. (Rev: BCCB 10/00; BL 10/15/00; HB 9–10/00; HBG 3/01; SLJ 9/00) [811]

11862 Nye, Naomi S. *19 Varieties of Gazelle: Poems of the Middle East* (5–10). 2002, Greenwillow LB $16.89 (0-06-009766-3). 142pp. Poems by Palestinian American Nye confide details of her life and the impact of war and terrorism on the peoples of Middle Eastern heritage. (Rev: BL 4/1/02; HB 9–10/02*; HBG 10/02; SLJ 5/02*) [811]

11863 *Oh, No! Where Are My Pants?* (PS–2). Ed. by Lee Bennett Hopkins. Illus. by Wolf Erlbruch. 2005, HarperCollins LB $16.89 (0-688-17861-8). 32pp. Simple works by well-known poets about the impact of everyday disasters are paired with lovely illustrations. (Rev: BL 2/15/05; SLJ 2/05) [811]

11864 O'Huigin, Sean. *Ghost Horse of the Mounties* (5–7). Illus. by Barry Moser. 1991, Godine $14.95 (0-87923-721-X). 72pp. A long poem about a black midsummer night in 1874 on the empty plains of the Northwest Territories in Canada. (Rev: BCCB 7–8/91; BL 5/1/91) [811]

11865 *On Her Way: Stories and Poems About Growing Up Girl* (4–8). Ed. by Sandy Asher. 2004, Dutton $17.99 (0-525-47170-7). 224pp. Poems and stories about the difficulties of adolescence will strike a chord for many readers. (Rev: BL 2/15/04; SLJ 3/04) [810.8]

11866 *Once Upon a Poem: Favorite Poems That Tell Stories* (4–7). Illus. 2004, Scholastic $18.95 (0-439-65108-5). 128pp. This appealing collection of 15 narrative poems includes offerings from Lewis Carroll, Longfellow, C. S. Lewis, Roald Dahl, Edward Lear, and Robert Service. (Rev: BL 1/1–15/05; SLJ 1/05) [811]

11867 O'Neill, Mary. *Hailstones and Halibut Bones* (PS–3). Illus. by Leonard Weisgard. 1973, Doubleday paper $8.95 (0-385-41078-6). Imaginative poems about color. (Rev: BL 3/1/04)

11868 O'Neill, Mary. *The Sound of Day, the Sound of Night* (PS–2). Illus. by Cynthia Jabar. 2003, Farrar $16.50 (0-374-37135-0). Two poems highlight the importance of sound as a family goes through a day of anticipation and night of peace with the arrival of the new baby. (Rev: HBG 4/04; SLJ 12/03) [811]

11869 *The Oxford Illustrated Book of American Children's Poems* (PS–4). Ed. by Donald Hall. Illus. 1999, Oxford $19.95 (0-19-512373-5). 93pp. From classics like *A Visit from St. Nicholas* to works by Robert Frost, Shel Silverstein, Nikki Giovanni, Karla Kuskin, and others, this is an attractive anthology, perfect for reading aloud. (Rev: BL 1/1–15/00; HBG 3/00; SLJ 1/00) [811]

11870 Paraskevas, Betty. *Junior Kroll* (2–4). Illus. by Michael Paraskevas. 1993, Harcourt $13.95 (0-15-241497-5). Fifteen poems about a mischievous boy and his adventures. (Rev: BCCB 5/93; BL 3/1/04; SLJ 6/93) [822]

11871 Paul, Ann W. *All by Herself* (3–5). Illus. 1999, Harcourt $17.00 (0-15-201477-2). 32pp. A collection of 14 original poems celebrates the lives of such women as Rachel Carson, Pocahontas, Sacajawea, and Amelia Earhart. (Rev: BL 12/1/99; HBG 3/00; SLJ 1/00) [811]

11872 Perdomo, Willie. *Visiting Langston* (2–4). Illus. by Bryan Collier. 2002, Holt $15.95 (0-8050-6744-2). A young girl anticipates in poetry a visit to poet Langston Hughes's house in Harlem. (Rev: BCCB 3/02; BL 2/15/02; HBG 10/02; SLJ 4/02) [811]

11873 Philip, Neil, ed. *Songs Are Thoughts: Poems of the Inuit* (K–4). Illus. by Maryclare Foa. 1995, Orchard $15.95 (0-531-06893-5). 32pp. Short Inuit poems are featured in double-page spreads, each containing a poem and an illustration. (Rev: BCCB 5/95; BL 4/15/95; SLJ 4/95) [897]

11874 Philip, Neil, ed. *War and the Pity of War* (5–9). Illus. by Michael McCurdy. 1998, Clarion LB $20.00 (0-395-84982-9). 96pp. An anthology of antiwar poems by well-known and obscure poets, with striking illustrations. (Rev: HBG 10/99; SLJ 9/98) [811]

11875 *Pocket Poems* (PS–1). Ed. by Bobbi Katz. Illus. by Marilyn Hafner. 2004, Dutton $15.99 (0-525-47172-3). 32pp. This collection of playful short poems is organized into chronological periods throughout the day. (Rev: BL 2/1/04; SLJ 2/04) [811]

11876 *Poetry by Heart: A Child's Book of Poems to Remember* (3–5). Ed. by Liz Attenborough. Illus. 2001, Scholastic $17.95 (0-439-29657-9). 128pp. An eclectic, enchanting collection of poetry for younger readers. (Rev: BL 1/1–15/02; HBG 10/02; SLJ 2/02) [811.54]

11877 Pomerantz, Charlotte. *If I Had a Paka: Poems in Eleven Languages* (PS–3). Illus. by Nancy Tafuri. 1993, Morrow paper $4.95 (0-688-12510-7). 32pp. In each of these poems, English is interspersed with one of 11 languages. A reissue. [811]

11878 Prelutsky, Jack. *The Frogs Wore Red Suspenders* (PS–3). Illus. by Petra Mathers. 2002, Greenwillow LB $16.89 (0-688-16720-9). 64pp. Splendid illustrations accompany whimsical rhymes in this charming book for preschoolers and young

readers. (Rev: BCCB 3/02; BL 3/15/02; HB 3–4/02; HBG 10/02; SLJ 2/02*) [811]

11879 Prelutsky, Jack. *The Gargoyle on the Roof* (2–6). Illus. by Peter Sis. 1999, Greenwillow LB $15.93 (0-688-16553-2). 40pp. A picture book for older children that contains imaginative poems about werewolves, goblins, vampires, trolls, and so on, with illustrations that catch the sinister mood of the poems. (Rev: BCCB 10/99; BL 10/1/99*; HBG 10/00; SLJ 10/99) [811]

11880 Prelutsky, Jack. *Monday's Troll* (4–6). Illus. by Peter Sis. 1996, Greenwillow $15.89 (0-688-14373-3). 40pp. Seventeen original poems that deal with supernatural beings like witches, trolls, wizards, and ogres. (Rev: BCCB 3/96; BL 4/15/96; HB 5–6/96; SLJ 4/96*) [811]

11881 Prelutsky, Jack. *Nightmares: Poems to Trouble Your Sleep* (5–8). Illus. by Arnold Lobel. 1976, Greenwillow LB $16.89 (0-688-84053-1). 38pp. Shuddery, macabre poems that will frighten but amuse a young audience. A sequel is *The Headless Horseman Rides Tonight: More Poems to Trouble Your Sleep* (1980).

11882 Prelutsky, Jack. *A Pizza the Size of the Sun* (3–6). Illus. by James Stevenson. 1996, Greenwillow $17.93 (0-688-13236-7). 160pp. Humorous, imaginative light verses explore a variety of subjects. (Rev: BCCB 9/96; BL 9/15/96*; HB 9–10/96; SLJ 9/96*) [811]

11883 Prelutsky, Jack, ed. *The Random House Book of Poetry for Children* (2–6). Illus. by Arnold Lobel. 1983, Random LB $21.99 (0-394-95010-0). 248pp. Old standbys and new gems are included in this fine anthology of 572 poems.

11884 Prelutsky, Jack. *Scranimals* (2–4). Illus. by Peter Sis. 2002, HarperCollins LB $18.89 (0-688-17820-0). 48pp. The imaginary animals that inhabit Scranimal Island (the "Bananconda" and the "Orangutangerine," for example) are described in fanciful verse and art. (Rev: BCCB 10/02; BL 9/15/02; HB 1–2/03; HBG 3/03; SLJ 9/02*) [811]

11885 Quattlebaum, Mary. *Family Reunion* (2–3). Illus. by Andrea Shine. 2004, Eerdmans $16.00 (0-8028-5237-8). 32pp. Ten-year-old Jodie's summer trip to a family reunion is engagingly portrayed in this collection of varied short poems. (Rev: BL 4/1/04; SLJ 6/04) [811]

11886 Rogasky, Barbara, ed. *Leaf by Leaf: Autumn Poems* (5–8). Illus. by Marc Tauss. 2001, Scholastic paper $15.95 (0-590-25347-6). 40pp. Verses by poets including Shelley, Yeats, and Whitman accompany stunning autumnal photographs. (Rev: BL 7/01; HBG 3/02; SLJ 9/01*) [811.008]

11887 Rosen, Michael. *The Best of Michael Rosen* (3–5). Illus. by Quentin Blake. 1995, Wetlands paper $16.95 (1-57143-046-6). 136pp. Sixty-five insightful, often lighthearted poems by the popular English poet. (Rev: BL 2/1/96; SLJ 5/05) [808.81]

11888 Rosen, Michael, sel. *Classic Poetry: An Illustrated Collection* (5–10). Illus. by Paul Howard. 1998, Candlewick $21.99 (1-56402-890-9). 159pp. A handsome chronological collection of representative poems from 38 poets including Shakespeare,

Byron, Shelley, and Yeats, plus a generous selection of contemporary writers. (Rev: HBG 3/99; SLJ 5/99) [808.81]

11889 Rosen, Michael, ed. *Poems for the Very Young* (PS–2). Illus. by Bob Graham. 1993, Kingfisher $17.95 (1-85697-908-3). 80pp. A delightful collection of rhymes for young children, chiefly from American and British sources and illustrated with charming cartoonlike drawings. (Rev: BL 1/1/94*; SLJ 1/94) [821]

11890 Rosenthal, Betsy R. *My House Is Singing* (PS–3). Illus. by Margaret Chodos-Irvine. 2004, Harcourt $16.00 (0-15-216293-3). 40pp. Rosenthal's poems describe a little girl's reactions to all the weird and wonderful sounds her house produces. (Rev: BL 4/1/04; HB 3–4/04; SLJ 7/04) [811]

11891 Rossetti, Christina. *Sing Song: A Nursery Rhyme Book* (K–3). Illus. by Arthur Hughes. 1969, Dover paper $4.95 (0-486-22107-5). 130pp. Many of the poems are about small creatures and familiar objects and have a singing quality that young children enjoy.

11892 Rosten, Norman. *A City Is* (PS–2). Illus. by Melanie Hope Greenberg. 2004, Holt $16.95 (0-8050-6793-0). 32pp. Varied short poems in free verse evoke both the hustle and bustle and the quiet moments of life in a city, many of them specifically about New York. (Rev: BL 3/1/04; SLJ 4/04) [811]

11893 *Salting the Ocean: 100 Poems by Young Poets* (4–12). Ed. by Naomi Shihab Nye. Illus. 2000, Greenwillow $16.95 (0-688-16193-6). 128pp. This anthology of poetry by young people from grades one through 12 has been culled by the editor from her 25 years of teaching poetry in schools. (Rev: BL 3/15/00; HB 7–8/00; HBG 10/00; SLJ 7/00) [811]

11894 Schertle, Alice. *Keepers* (1–4). Illus. by Ted Rand. 1996, Lothrop LB $15.93 (0-688-11635-3). 32pp. A collection of original poems in which everyday objects become transformed through one's imagination. (Rev: BL 10/15/96; SLJ 12/96) [811]

11895 Schertle, Alice. *Teddy Bear, Teddy Bear* (PS–2). Illus. by Linda Hill Griffith. 2003, HarperCollins LB $16.89 (0-688-16871-X). Subjects dear to children are presented in bouncy poems. (Rev: HBG 10/03; SLJ 7/03) [811]

11896 Schertle, Alice. *When the Moon Is High* (PS). Illus. by Julia Noonan. 2003, HarperCollins LB $16.89 (0-688-15144-2). When baby can't fall asleep, Daddy decides to take a moonlight stroll with the child in his arms and on their way they encounter a number of nighttime creatures. (Rev: HBG 10/03; SLJ 7/03)

11897 Schmidt, Gary D., ed. *Robert Frost* (5–7). Illus. by Henri Sorensen. Series: Poetry for Young People. 1994, Sterling $14.95 (0-8069-0633-2). 48pp. An anthology of 25 poems suitable for young people, with watercolor illustrations that picture the New England landscape that Frost loved. (Rev: BL 12/1/94; SLJ 2/95) [811]

11898 Schoonmaker, Frances, ed. *Henry Wadsworth Longfellow* (4–8). Illus. Series: Poetry for Young People. 1999, Sterling $14.95 (0-8069-9417-7). A generous, carefully selected presentation of Long-

fellow's poetry illustrated by full-color paintings and accompanied by biographical notes. (Rev: BL 3/15/99; HBG 9/99; SLJ 3/99) [811]

11899 Shakespeare, William. *To Sleep, Perchance to Dream: A Child's Book of Rhymes* (PS–1). Illus. by James Mayhew. 2001, Scholastic $16.95 (0-439-29655-2). 32pp. This handsome, large-format picture book introduces young readers to extracts from Shakespeare's works. (Rev: BL 12/1/01; HBG 3/02; SLJ 11/01) [822.3]

11900 Shields, Carol D. *Lunch Money and Other Poems About School* (1–3). Illus. by Paul Meisel. 1995, Dutton $15.99 (0-525-45345-8). 48pp. Daily events at school are celebrated in this charming group of poems. (Rev: BL 11/15/95; HB 3–4/04; SLJ 1/96) [811]

11901 Shields, Carol Diggory. *Brain Juice: American History Fresh Squeezed!* (4–8). Illus. by Richard Thompson. 2002, Handprint $14.95 (1-929766-62-9). 80pp. A timeline runs across the tops of these pages of poems about events in American history. (Rev: HBG 3/03; SLJ 1/03) [811]

11902 Sidman, Joyce. *Eureka! Poems About Inventors* (4–6). Illus. by K. Bennett Chavez. 2002, Millbrook LB $24.90 (0-7613-1665-5). 48pp. Sidman celebrates the lives and inventions of people throughout history in a chronological collection of free-verse poetry. (Rev: BL 10/15/02; HBG 3/03; SLJ 1/03) [811.54]

11903 Siebert, Diane. *Heartland* (K–4). Illus. by Wendell Minor. 1989, HarperCollins paper $6.95 (0-06-443287-4). 32pp. A lyrical celebration of the Midwest. (Rev: BL 3/1/89; SLJ 5/89)

11904 Siebert, Diane. *Motorcycle Song* (K–4). Illus. 2002, HarperCollins LB $16.89 (0-06-028733-0). 32pp. Invigorating poetry and energetic artwork capture the thrill of a motorcycle ride. (Rev: BL 2/1/02; HBG 10/02; SLJ 4/02) [793.73]

11905 Silverstein, Shel. *Falling Up* (3–6). Illus. 1996, HarperCollins LB $17.89 (0-06-024803-3). 176pp. More than 150 delightful original poems that amuse and amaze. (Rev: BCCB 6/96; BL 7/96*; HB 9–10/96; SLJ 7/96) [811]

11906 Silverstein, Shel. *Where the Sidewalk Ends* (3–6). Illus. by author. 1974, HarperCollins LB $17.89 (0-06-025668-0). 176pp. The author explores various facets and interests of children, with appropriate cartoonlike drawings. Also use: *A Light in the Attic* (1981).

11907 Simon, Francesca. *Toddler Time* (PS–K). Illus. by Susan Winter. 2000, Orchard $15.95 (0-531-30251-2). 40pp. The 17 poems in this original collection celebrate toddlers' accomplishments — everything from walking to riding bicycles. (Rev: BL 5/1/00; HBG 10/00; SLJ 5/00) [821]

11908 Simon, Seymour, ed. *Star Walk* (4–8). Illus. 1995, Morrow LB $14.93 (0-688-11887-7). 32pp. Simple poems and outstanding photographs create an impressive introduction to stars and outer space. (Rev: BL 3/1/95; SLJ 4/95) [811]

11909 Singer, Marilyn. *All We Needed to Say: Poems About School from Tanya and Sophie* (PS–3). Illus. by Lorna Clark. 1996, Simon &

587

Schuster $15.00 (0-689-80667-1). 28pp. Two girls compare their school experiences in a series of short monologues. (Rev: BCCB 9/96; BL 8/96; SLJ 9/96) [811]

11910 Singer, Marilyn. *Central Heating: Poems About Fire and Warmth* (3–5). Illus. by Meilo So. 2005, Knopf LB $17.99 (0-375-82912-1). 48pp. From the warmth of chili peppers and roasted marshmallows to the heat of electricity and bombs, Singer explores the properties of fire. (Rev: BL 12/1/04; SLJ 1/05*) [811]

11911 Singer, Marilyn. *Monster Museum* (1–5). Illus. by Gris Grimly. 2001, Hyperion $14.99 (0-7868-0520-X). 40pp. A humorous, poetic tour through a museum of monsters. (Rev: BCCB 10/01; HBG 3/02; SLJ 11/01) [811]

11912 *A Small Child's Book of Cozy Poems* (PS). Ed. by Cyndy Szekeres. Illus. 1999, Scholastic $6.95 (0-590-38364-7). 32pp. From Mother Goose to nonsense verse, this is a sweet collection of rhymes for the very young. (Rev: BL 2/1/99; HBG 10/99; SLJ 4/99) [811.008]

11913 Smith, Charles R. *Perfect Harmony: A Musical Journey with the Boys Choir of Harlem* (4–7). Illus. 2002, Hyperion $15.99 (0-7868-0758-X). 32pp. Photographs of the Boys Choir of Harlem provide a dynamic backdrop for these upbeat poems about songs and singing. (Rev: BL 8/02; HBG 3/03; SLJ 8/02) [811]

11914 Smith, Charles R. *Short Takes: Fast-Break Basketball Poetry* (4–7). Illus. 2001, Dutton $17.99 (0-525-46454-9). 32pp. Young fans of basketball will enjoy this collection of original poems that capture the sights, sounds, and excitement of the game. (Rev: BCCB 2/01; BL 2/15/01; HBG 10/01; SLJ 3/01) [811]

11915 Smith, William Jay, comp. *Up the Hill and Down: Poems for the Very Young* (PS–2). Illus. by Allan Eitzen. 2003, Boyds Mills $16.95 (1-56397-028-7). 32pp. Robert Louis Stevenson, Aileen Fisher, and Marchette Chute are among the writers represented in this collection of nearly 30 poems. (Rev: HBG 4/04; SLJ 11/03) [811]

11916 *Soft Hay Will Catch You* (3–8). Ed. by Sandford Lyne. Illus. by Julie Monks. 2004, Simon & Schuster $17.95 (0-689-83460-8). 128pp. Poems by students are grouped by theme and reveal new perspectives on age-old worries and delights. (Rev: BL 3/15/04; SLJ 4/04) [811]

11917 *Someone I Like: Poems About People* (3–5). Ed. by Judith Nicholls. Illus. 2000, Barefoot $16.95 (1-84148-004-5). 40pp. This anthology of 26 poems explores children's feelings for family members and friends. (Rev: BL 4/1/00; SLJ 7/00) [808.819]

11918 *Songs, Seas, and Green Peas: Poems for Anywhere* (K–4). Series: Poetry Parade. 2000, Heinemann LB $21.36 (1-57572-400-6). 32pp. A collection of poems by both well-known and obscure poets that contains no particular theme or subjects. Also use *Wishes, Wings, and Other Things: Poems for Anytime* (2000). (Rev: HBG 3/01; SLJ 2/01) [811]

11919 Soto, Gary. *Canto Familiar* (4–6). Illus. 1995, Harcourt $18.00 (0-15-200067-4). 88pp. Simple poems, many involving Mexican Americans, celebrate experiences at school, home, and in the street. A companion to *Neighborhood Odes* (1992). (Rev: BL 10/1/95; SLJ 12/95*) [811]

11920 Soto, Gary. *Fearless Fernie: Hanging Out with Fernie and Me* (4–6). Illus. by Regan Dunnick. 2002, Penguin Putnam $14.99 (0-399-23615-5). 64pp. Older readers are invited into the mind and life of an unnamed middle-school boy in this exceptional collection of poems. (Rev: BL 3/15/02; HB 7–8/02; HBG 10/02; SLJ 3/02*) [811]

11921 Soto, Gary. *Neighborhood Odes* (4–6). Illus. by David Diaz. 1992, Harcourt $15.95 (0-15-256879-4). 80pp. Unrhymed verses celebrate such items in a Mexican-American neighborhood as pinatas, weddings, libraries, and tennis shoes. (Rev: BL 6/15/92; HB 5–6/92*; SLJ 5/92) [811]

11922 Spinelli, Eileen. *In Our Backyard Garden* (2–5). Illus. by Marcy Ramsey. 2004, Simon & Schuster $15.95 (0-689-82666-4). 40pp. The ups and downs of family life are keenly observed in this collection of poems revolving around a garden. (Rev: BL 3/1/04; SLJ 4/04) [811]

11923 Spinelli, Eileen. *Tea Party Today: Poems to Sip and Savor* (1–3). Illus. by Karen M. Dugan. 1999, Boyds Mills $15.95 (1-56397-662-5). 32pp. Tea and teatime inspired this group of poems about the ceremony and the emotions it evokes. (Rev: BL 4/1/99; HBG 10/99; SLJ 4/99) [811.54]

11924 Stavans, Ilan, ed. *Wachale! Poetry and Prose About Growing Up Latino in America* (5–8). 2001, Cricket $16.95 (0-8126-4750-5). 160pp. A bilingual anthology about Latino experiences, both in the past and in the present. (Rev: BCCB 2/02; BL 2/1/02; HBG 10/02; SLJ 2/02) [810.8]

11925 Steig, Jeanne. *Alpha Beta Chowder* (5–8). Illus. 1992, HarperCollins LB $14.89 (0-06-205007-9). A collection of nonsense verses celebrating the joy of words — their sound and meaning — with each verse playing with a letter of the alphabet. (Rev: BL 11/15/92; SLJ 12/92) [811]

11926 Stevenson, James. *Candy Corn* (2–5). Illus. 1999, Greenwillow $15.00 (0-688-15837-4). 56pp. Humorous recollections and details of ordinary life are the subjects of this delightful book of poems illustrated with ink-and-watercolor pictures. (Rev: BCCB 5/99; BL 3/15/99*; HB 7–8/99; HBG 10/99; SLJ 5/99) [811]

11927 Stevenson, James. *Corn Chowder* (2–5). Illus. 2003, HarperCollins LB $16.89 (0-06-053060-X). 48pp. Stevenson's eighth volume of simple poems and ink-and-watercolor illustrations continues his fascinating — and humorous — look at the stuff of everyday life. (Rev: BL 6/1–15/03*; HB 5–6/03; HBG 10/03; SLJ 5/03) [811]

11928 Stevenson, James. *Corn-Fed* (K–4). Illus. 2002, Greenwillow LB $15.89 (0-06-000598-X). 48pp. Lovely watercolor sketches pair with thought-provoking verses to challenge readers' perceptions of everyday scenes. (Rev: BCCB 4/02; BL 3/1/02; HBG 10/02; SLJ 3/02) [811]

11929 Stevenson, James. *Cornflakes: Poems* (3–5). Illus. 2000, Greenwillow $15.95 (0-688-16718-7). 48pp. An eclectic collection of short verses on many subjects, illustrated with bright, clear, ink-and-watercolor pictures. (Rev: BL 3/15/00; HB 7–8/00; HBG 10/00; SLJ 6/00) [811]

11930 Stevenson, Robert. *Block City* (PS). Illus. by Daniel Kirk. 2005, Simon & Schuster $14.95 (0-689-86964-9). 32pp. Stevenson's 1883 poem gets new life in a picture book that shows the joys of building — and then destroying — towers of building blocks. (Rev: BL 6/1–15/05) [811]

11931 Stevenson, Robert Louis. *A Child's Garden of Verses* (PS). Illus. by Joanna Isles. 1994, Abrams $17.95 (0-8109-3196-6). 87pp. A freshly illustrated edition of this classic, published to commemorate the centenary of the author's death. (Rev: SLJ 10/94) [821]

11932 Stevenson, Robert Louis. *A Child's Garden of Verses* (K–4). Illus. 1989, Chronicle $17.95 (0-87701-608-9). 121pp. A handsome edition of the old favorite, using some 100 19th-century illustrations. (Rev: BL 11/1/89*; SLJ 2/90) [821]

11933 Stevenson, Robert Louis. *Poetry for Young People: Robert Louis Stevenson* (3–5). Illus. Series: Poetry for Young People. 2000, Sterling $14.95 (0-8069-4956-2). 48pp. Chosen mainly from *A Child's Garden of Verses,* this is a representative collection of Stevenson's work for children preceded by a biographical note. (Rev: BL 3/15/00; HBG 10/00; SLJ 7/00) [821]

11934 Stockland, Patricia M., comp. *Cobwebs, Chatters, and Chills: A Collection of Scary Poems* (3–6). Illus. by Sara Rojo Perez. Series: The Poet's Toolbox. 2004, Compass Point LB $22.60 (0-7565-0565-8). 32pp. An illustrated anthology of poems by well-known writers that demonstrate poetic forms and concepts. (Rev: SLJ 6/04) [811]

11935 Stockland, Patricia M., comp. *The Free and the Brave: A Collection of Poems About the United States* (3–6). Illus. by Sara Rojo Perez. Series: The Poet's Toolbox. 2004, Compass Point LB $22.60 (0-7565-0563-1). 32pp. Patriotic poetry by authors ranging from Carl Sandburg to Ogden Nash is illustrated with cartoon art and used to demonstrate poetic concepts. (Rev: SLJ 6/04) [811]

11936 Sturges, Philemon. *Down to the Sea in Ships* (3–5). Illus. by Giles Laroche. 2005, Penguin Putnam $16.99 (0-399-23464-0). 32pp. Birch canoes, Viking ships, cod schooners, and modern ferries are among the vessels depicted in stunning illustrations and varied verses. (Rev: BL 5/15/05; SLJ 6/05) [811]

11937 Swados, Elizabeth. *Hey You! C'mere: A Poetry Slam* (2–5). Illus. by Joe Cepeda. 2002, Scholastic $15.95 (0-439-09257-4). 47pp. A collection of poems, presented by a group of urban children, that reflect their everyday concerns. (Rev: BL 4/15/02; HBG 10/02; SLJ 4/02) [811]

11938 Swenson, May. *The Complete Poems to Solve* (5–8). Illus. by Christy Hale. 1993, Macmillan $13.95 (0-02-788725-1). 128pp. From simple riddles to more complex questions, each of these

poems contains a puzzle. (Rev: HB 3–4/93; SLJ 5/93) [811]

11939 Taberski, Sharon, ed. *Morning, Noon, and Night: Poems to Fill Your Day* (PS–3). Illus. by Nancy Doniger. 1996, Mondo $14.95 (1-57255-128-3). 32pp. The day's activities are traced in 29 poems by well-known writers. (Rev: BL 12/15/96; SLJ 5/96) [811]

11940 *Talking Drums: A Selection of Poems from Africa South of the Sahara* (4–8). Ed. and illus. by Veronique Tadjo. 2004, Bloomsbury $15.95 (1-58234-813-8). 96pp. Arranged by theme, these 75 poems — traditional and contemporary — cover a broad range of topics. (Rev: BL 3/1/04; SLJ 4/04) [811]

11941 Temperley, Howard. *In the Days of Dinosaurs: A Rhyming Romp Through Dino History* (3–5). Illus. by Michael Kline. 2004, Williamson paper $12.95 (0-8249-8662-8). 61pp. Nearly 40 humorous and fact-filled poems describe specific dinosaurs and reflect on dinosaur-related issues. (Rev: SLJ 3/05) [811]

11942 Testa, Maria. *Becoming Joe DiMaggio* (5–8). Illus. by Scott Hunt. 2002, Candlewick $14.99 (0-7636-1537-4). 64pp. The story of an Italian American boy and his family, told through a series of poems set against a backdrop of radio-broadcast baseball games. (Rev: BCCB 5/02; BL 2/15/02; HBG 3/03; SLJ 5/02) [811]

11943 Thayer, Ernest Lawrence. *Casey at the Bat: A Ballad of the Republic Sung in the Year 1888* (4–8). Illus. by C. F. Payne. 2003, Simon & Schuster $16.95 (0-689-85494-3). 40pp. An impossibly muscular Casey is the star of this version of the classic baseball poem. (Rev: BCCB 1/01*; BL 2/1/03; HBG 10/03; SLJ 3/03*) [811]

11944 *This Place I Know: Poems of Comfort* (3–5). Ed. by Georgia Heard. Illus. 2002, Candlewick $16.99 (0-7636-1924-8). 48pp. In a bid to offer comfort to children traumatized by the terrorist attacks of September 11, Heard compiled this collection of 18 works dealing with fear and loss by poets including Langston Hughes, Emily Dickinson, and Walt Whitman, and illustrated by such artists as William Steig, Chris Raschka, and G. Brian Karas. (Rev: BL 7/02; HBG 3/03; SLJ 9/02) [811.008]

11945 Viorst, Judith. *If I Were in Charge of the World and Other Worries: Poems for Children and Their Parents* (5–8). Illus. 1984, Macmillan paper $5.99 (0-689-70770-3). Easily read poems focus on topics familiar to young people. [811]

11946 Wallace, Daisy, ed. *Ghost Poems* (4–7). Illus. by Tomie dePaola. 1979, Holiday House paper $4.95 (0-8234-0849-3). 32pp. New and old poems to delight and frighten young readers.

11947 Wallace, Daisy, ed. *Witch Poems* (3–6). Illus. by Trina S. Hyman. 1976, Holiday House LB $14.95 (0-8234-0281-9); paper $4.95 (0-8234-0850-7). 32pp. Eighteen poems chosen from several different sources on a wide variety of witches.

11948 Wallace, Nancy Elizabeth, comp. *The Sun, the Moon, and the Stars* (PS–2). Illus. by Nancy Elizabeth Wallace. 2003, Houghton Mifflin $12.00 (0-

618-26353-5). Attractive illustrations accompany poems celebrating the sun, moon, and stars by the compiler and by writers including Christina Rossetti and Walter de la Mare. (Rev: BL 1/1–15/04; HBG 4/04; SLJ 12/03) [811]

11949 Waters, Fiona, comp. *Dark as a Midnight Dream: Poetry Collection 2* (5–8). Illus. by Zara Slattery. 1999, Evans Brothers $24.95 (0-237-51845-7). 286pp. An extensive anthology of poetry arranged by subjects such as "Mythical Creatures" and "City Life" that features such writers as Robert Browning, William Shakespeare, William Butler Yeats, William Wordsworth, Langston Hughes, and Carl Sandburg. (Rev: SLJ 11/99) [811]

11950 Weatherford, Carole Boston. *Sidewalk Chalk: Poems of the City* (3–6). Illus. by Dimitrea Tokunbo. 2001, Boyds Mills $15.95 (1-56397-084-8). 32pp. Poems about the pleasures of urban life are accompanied by colorful full-page illustrations. (Rev: BL 9/15/01; HBG 3/02; SLJ 1/02) [811]

11951 Whipple, Laura. *Eric Carle's Dragons Dragons and Other Creatures That Never Were* (2–6). Illus. by Eric Carle. 1991, Penguin Putnam $19.99 (0-399-22105-0). 69pp. This is a collection of poems about dragons and other mythological creatures illustrated by Eric Carle. (Rev: BCCB 12/91; BL 11/1/91; HB 11–12/91; SLJ 10/91) [811]

11952 *Whisper and Shout: Poems to Memorize* (4–6). Ed. by Patrice Vecchione. 2002, Cricket $16.95 (0-8126-2656-7). 144pp. An anthology of 55 accessible poems (many by contemporaries) with a lengthy introduction on poetry and a closing section on resources and biographies. (Rev: BL 4/15/02; HBG 10/02; SLJ 5/02) [811]

11953 Whitman, Walt. *Nothing but Miracles* (K–2). Illus. by Susan L. Roth. 2003, National Geographic $15.95 (0-7922-6143-7). A joyful cat family, shown in naive collages, illustrates the words to Whitman's poem from *Leaves of Grass*. (Rev: HBG 4/04; SLJ 1/04) [811.3]

11954 Whitman, Walt. *When I Heard the Learn'd Astronomer* (K–3). Illus. by Loren Long. 2004, Simon & Schuster $16.95 (0-689-86397-7). 32pp. A young boy's growing appreciation of the universe around him is shown in vivid acrylic artwork and the Whitman verse. (Rev: BL 11/15/04*) [811]

11955 Wilbur, Richard. *Runaway Opposites* (4–6). Illus. by Henrik Drescher. 1995, Harcourt $15.00 (0-15-258722-5). 32pp. An intriguing, involved book of poems that deal with synonyms and antonyms. (Rev: BCCB 4/95; BL 4/15/95; SLJ 5/95) [811]

11956 Willard, Nancy. *A Visit to William Blake's Inn: Poems for Innocent and Experienced Travelers* (2–5). Illus. by Alice Provensen and Martin Provensen. 1981, Harcourt $16.00 (0-15-293822-2); paper $7.00 (0-15-293823-0). 44pp. A collection of poems that won the Newbery Award, 1982.

11957 Winnick, Karen B. *A Year Goes Round: Poems for the Months* (K–2). Illus. by author. 2001, Boyds Mills $15.95 (1-56397-898-9). A look at the months of the year in short, simple poems about

children's activities. (Rev: HBG 3/02; SLJ 11/01) [811]

11958 Winter, Jeanette. *Emily Dickinson's Letters to the World* (4–7). Illus. 2002, Farrar $16.00 (0-374-32147-7). 40pp. Brief biographical information is paired with 21 of Emily Dickinson's poems in this small-format picture book told from her sister's point of view. (Rev: BL 3/1/02; HBG 10/02; SLJ 3/02) [811]

11959 Winters, Kay. *Voices of Ancient Egypt* (3–6). Illus. by Barry Moser. 2003, National Geographic $16.95 (0-7922-7560-8). 32pp. Two-page spreads introduce ancient Egyptian workers — among them a scribe, a pyramid builder, and a herdsman — who describe their lives in first-person free verse. (Rev: BL 9/15/03; HBG 4/04; SLJ 9/03) [932]

11960 *Wonderful Words: Poems About Reading, Writing, Speaking, and Listening* (3–6). Ed. by Lee Bennett Hopkins. Illus. by Karen Barbour. 2004, Simon & Schuster $16.95 (0-689-83588-4). 32pp. This colorfully illustrated collection of poems celebrates the wonders of language. (Rev: BL 2/1/04; SLJ 3/04) [811]

11961 Wong, Janet S. *Knock on Wood: Poems About Superstitions* (2–5). Illus. by Julie Paschkis. 2003, Simon & Schuster $17.95 (0-689-85512-5). 40pp. Vampires, ghosts, broken mirrors, and black cats are just some of the topics of these aptly illustrated poems about potential bad luck. (Rev: BL 11/15/03; HB 9–10/03; HBG 4/04; SLJ 12/03)

11962 Wong, Janet S. *Night Garden* (3–6). Illus. 2000, Simon & Schuster $16.00 (0-689-82617-6). 32pp. This collection of 15 original poems explores the world of dreams and is illustrated with suitably near-surreal gouaches. (Rev: BCCB 1/00; BL 1/1–15/00; HBG 10/00; SLJ 3/00) [811.54]

11963 Wong, Janet S. *The Rainbow Hand: Poems About Mothers and Children* (5–8). Illus. 1999, Simon & Schuster $15.00 (0-689-82148-4). This collection of 18 poems deals with maternal love, from the mother's point of view and from the child's. (Rev: BL 4/1/99; HBG 10/99; SLJ 4/99) [811]

11964 Wong, Janet S. *A Suitcase of Seaweed and Other Poems* (4–7). 1996, Simon & Schuster $15.95 (0-689-80788-0). 42pp. A group of personal poems that deal with the author's cultural backgrounds — Korean, Chinese, and American. (Rev: BCCB 4/96; BL 4/1/96; HB 7–8/96; SLJ 9/96) [811]

11965 Worth, Valerie. *Peacock and Other Poems* (3–6). Illus. by Natalie Babbitt. 2002, Farrar $15.00 (0-374-35766-8). 48pp. A posthumously published collection of 26 poems in the author's signature style, beautifully illustrated with detailed pencil drawings. (Rev: BCCB 6/02; BL 8/02; HB 7–8/02*; HBG 10/02; SLJ 5/02) [811]

11966 Worthen, Tom, ed. *Broken Hearts . . . Healing: Young Poets Speak Out on Divorce* (5–9). Illus. by Kyle Hernandez. Series: Young Poets Speak Out. 2001, Poet Tree $26.95 (1-58876-150-9); paper $14.95 (1-58876-151-7). 234pp. This large selection of poems written by their peers about divorce, family breakups, and blended families will resonate with young readers. (Rev: SLJ 9/01) [811]

11967 Yolen, Jane. *O Jerusalem* (4–6). Illus. by John Thompson. 1996, Scholastic $15.95 (0-590-48426-5). A group of original poems that explore the importance of Jerusalem in Judaism, Christianity, and Islam. (Rev: BL 2/1/96*; SLJ 3/96*) [811]

11968 Yolen, Jane. *Sacred Places* (5–9). Illus. 1996, Harcourt $16.00 (0-15-269953-8). An international collection of informational poems about the places sacred to various faiths. (Rev: BCCB 12/00; BL 10/1/96; SLJ 3/96) [811]

11969 Yolen, Jane, and Heidi E. Y. Stemple. *Dear Mother, Dear Daughter* (3–5). Illus. 2001, Boyds Mills $15.95 (1-56397-886-5). 32pp. Using simple verses this book consists of double-page spreads; on one side is a letter from a daughter to her mother, on the other the reply. (Rev: BL 3/15/01; HBG 10/01) [811]

11970 Zemach, Kaethe. *The Question Song* (PS–1). Illus. by author. 2003, Little, Brown $16.95 (0-316-66601-7). A reassuring adult calms a child upset by various problems and accidents. (Rev: HBG 4/04; SLJ 8/03) [398.8]

African American Poetry

11971 Adedjouma, Davida, ed. *The Palm of My Heart: Poetry by African American Children* (1–4). Illus. by Gregory Christie. 1996, Lee & Low $15.95 (1-880000-41-5). 32pp. Twenty poems by African American children about the beauty and joy of being black. (Rev: BCCB 12/96; BL 2/15/97; SLJ 1/97) [811]

11972 Boling, Katharine. *New Year Be Coming! A Gullah Year* (K–3). Illus. by Daniel Minter. 2002, Whitman $15.95 (0-8075-5590-8). 32pp. These twelve poems — one for each month of the year — are written in the unique Gullah dialect of a group of African Americans living on the coast of South Carolina and Georgia. (Rev: BCCB 1/03; BL 11/15/02; HB 11–12/02; HBG 3/03; SLJ 9/02) [811]

11973 Brooks, Gwendolyn. *Bronzeville Boys and Girls* (2–5). Illus. by Ronni Solbert. 1956, HarperCollins LB $15.89 (0-06-020651-9). 48pp. Everyday experiences of African American children growing up in Chicago are revealed in these simple poems.

11974 Bryan, Ashley. *Ashley Bryan's ABC of African American Poetry* (PS–4). Illus. 1997, Simon & Schuster $16.00 (0-689-81209-4). 32pp. A collection of charming African American poetry using the alphabet as a framework. (Rev: BL 9/1/97; HBG 3/98; SLJ 9/97) [811]

11975 Burleigh, Robert. *Langston's Train Ride* (3–6). Trans. and illus. by Leonard Jenkins. 2004, Scholastic LB $16.95 (0-439-35239-8). 32pp. Langston Hughes's well-known poem "The Negro Speaks of Rivers," written when he was only 18, is beautifully complemented by the collage artwork. (Rev: BL 9/15/04) [811]

11976 Clifton, Lucille. *Everett Anderson's Goodbye* (K–2). Illus. by Ann Grifalconi. 1983, Holt $16.95 (0-8050-0235-9); paper $5.95 (0-8050-0800-4). 32pp. Poems about a young African American boy. (Rev: BL 3/1/04)

11977 Clinton, Catherine. *I, Too, Sing America: Three Centuries of African American Poetry* (5–10). Illus. by Stephen Alcorn. 1998, Houghton Mifflin $20.00 (0-395-89599-5). 128pp. An excellent, beautifully designed anthology of African American poetry from the 1700s to the present. (Rev: HBG 3/99; SLJ 11/98) [811]

11978 Giovanni, Nikki. *Knoxville, Tennessee* (PS–3). Illus. by Larry Johnson. 1994, Scholastic $14.95 (0-590-47074-4). 32pp. Nikki Giovanni re-creates the summers she spent growing up in Knoxville and the simple pleasures she enjoyed. (Rev: BCCB 7–8/94; BL 2/15/94; HB 9–10/94; SLJ 4/94) [811]

11979 Giovanni, Nikki. *The Sun Is So Quiet* (K–2). Illus. by Ashley Bryan. 1996, Holt $14.95 (0-8050-4119-2). 32pp. Thirteen poems that depict everyday occurrences, with illustrations that feature African American children in many cultures. (Rev: BL 10/15/96; SLJ 1/97) [811]

11980 Greenfield, Eloise. *Honey, I Love* (PS–2). Illus. by Jan S. Gilchrist. 2003, HarperCollins LB $16.89 (0-06-009124-X). 32pp. An illustrated collection of poems about the loves of a young African American girl (such as her mother, car rides, swimming), first published in 1978. (Rev: BL 2/15/03; HBG 10/03; SLJ 2/03) [811.54]

11981 Greenfield, Eloise. *Honey, I Love, and Other Love Poems* (2–4). Illus. by Diane Dillon and Leo Dillon. 1978, HarperCollins $14.95 (0-690-01334-5); paper $5.95 (0-06-443097-9). 48pp. Sixteen poems on family love and friendship as experienced by an African American girl.

11982 Greenfield, Eloise. *Nathaniel Talking* (2–5). Illus. by Jan S. Gilchrist. 1988, Writers & Readers $12.95 (0-86316-200-2). 32pp. Simple poems on an African American's recollection of childhood. (Rev: BL 12/15/89; HB 9–10/90; SLJ 8/89) [811]

11983 Grimes, Nikki. *Danitra Brown Leaves Town* (PS–3). Illus. by Floyd Cooper. 2002, HarperCollins LB $15.89 (0-688-13156-5). 32pp. Best friends Danitra and Zuri describe their very different summer experiences through letters in this book of free-verse poems. (Rev: BCCB 4/02; BL 2/15/02; HBG 10/02; SLJ 2/02) [811]

11984 Grimes, Nikki. *Hopscotch Love: A Family Treasury of Love Poems* (4–8). Illus. 1999, Lothrop $15.95 (0-688-15667-3). This collection of poems celebrates all kinds of love as experienced by African Americans, including sibling love, teenage crushes, parental love, and love of a husband and wife and a graying couple. (Rev: BL 2/15/99; HBG 9/99; SLJ 1/99) [811]

11985 Grimes, Nikki. *My Man Blue* (2–5). Illus. by Jerome Lagarrigue. 1999, Dial $15.99 (0-8037-2326-1). 32pp. In a series of lyrical poems, Damon describes being a child in Harlem and his friendship for an older man, Blue, whose son was killed on the streets. (Rev: BL 10/15/99; HBG 10/99; SLJ 5/99) [811]

11986 Grimes, Nikki. *A Pocketful of Poems* (K–4). Illus. by Javaka Steptoe. 2001, Clarion $15.00 (0-395-93868-6). 30pp. A lively collection of verses and haikus that look at city life through the year. (Rev: HBG 10/01; SLJ 5/01) [811]

11987 Grimes, Nikki. *Stepping Out with Grandma Mac* (4–7). Illus. 2001, Orchard paper $16.95 (0-531-30320-9). 48pp. A loving 10-year-old girl describes a very independent grandmother. (Rev: BL 5/15/01*; HBG 10/01; SLJ 7/01) [811.54]

11988 Grimes, Nikki. *When Daddy Prays* (PS–K). Illus. by Tim Ladwig. 2002, Eerdmans $16.00 (0-8028-5152-5). 32pp. An African American child's impressions of his father's reliance on faith during everyday activities such as gardening, attending a baseball game, and celebrating the New Year. (Rev: BL 3/1/02; HBG 10/02; SLJ 4/02) [811.54]

11989 Hudson, Wade, ed. *Pass It On: African-American Poetry for Children* (PS–3). Illus. by Floyd Cooper. 1993, Scholastic $15.95 (0-590-45770-5). 32pp. A fine anthology with contributions by such writers as Langston Hughes and Gwendolyn Brooks. (Rev: BL 1/15/93*) [811]

11990 *In Daddy's Arms I Am Tall: African Americans Celebrating Fathers* (3–5). Illus. by Javaka Steptoe. 1997, Lee & Low $15.95 (1-880000-31-8). 32pp. An impressively illustrated book of poems about African American fathers and their many roles. (Rev: BL 2/15/98*; HB 5–6/05; HBG 3/98; SLJ 2/98) [811]

11991 Johnson, Angela. *The Other Side: Shorter Poems* (5–7). 1998, Orchard LB $16.99 (0-531-33114-8). 64pp. This African American poet gives us glimpses of her childhood in Alabama, her family life, and her views on such issues as Vietnam, racism, and the Black Panthers. (Rev: HB 11–12/98; HBG 3/99; SLJ 9/98) [811]

11992 Lewis, J. Patrick. *Freedom Like Sunlight: Praisesongs for Black Americans* (5–12). Illus. 2000, Creative $17.95 (1-56846-163-1). 40pp. This collection of original poems pays tribute to such important African Americans as Sojourner Truth, Arthur Ashe, Rosa Parks, Marian Anderson, Malcolm X, and Langston Hughes. (Rev: BL 9/15/00*; HBG 3/01; SLJ 12/00) [811]

11993 Medina, Tony. *DeShawn Days* (2–5). Illus. by R. Gregory Christie. 2001, Lee & Low $16.95 (1-58430-022-1). DeShawn is a young African American boy who describes in verse his home in the projects, the constant sound of sirens, the grim news on TV, his friends, and the music they enjoy. (Rev: HBG 10/01; SLJ 7/01*) [811]

11994 Myers, Walter Dean. *Angel to Angel: A Mother's Gift of Love* (4–8). Illus. 1998, HarperCollins LB $15.89 (0-06-027722-X). 40pp. A photo/poetry montage with 10 distinctly styled poems and photographs focusing on African American mothers and children, and reflecting the relationship between words and pictures. (Rev: BL 2/15/98; HBG 10/98; SLJ 6/98) [811]

11995 Nikola-Lisa, W. *Bein' with You This Way* (PS–2). Illus. by Michael Bryant. 1994, Lee & Low $15.95 (1-880000-05-9). 32pp. A rap poem led by an African American girl talks about racial tolerance. (Rev: BL 7/94; SLJ 7/94) [811]

11996 Shange, Ntozake. *Ellington Was Not a Street* (3–5). Illus. by Kadir Nelson. 2004, Simon & Schuster $15.95 (0-689-82884-5). 40pp. Adapted from Shange's poem "Mood Indigo," this richly illustrated picture book for older readers celebrates his childhoold home and the many African American intellectuals and artists who visited. (Rev: BL 2/15/04; SLJ 1/04) [811]

11997 Shine, Deborah S., ed. *Make a Joyful Sound: Poems for Children by African-American Poets* (2–7). Illus. by Cornelius Van Wright and Ying-hwa Hu. 1996, Scholastic $13.95 (0-590-67432-3). 107pp. More than 60 well-illustrated poems by 23 poets are found in this collection celebrating life in general and African American life in particular. (Rev: BL 6/1/91; SLJ 10/96) [811]

11998 Smith, Hope Anita. *The Way a Door Closes* (5–8). Illus. by Shane W. Evans. 2003, Holt $18.95 (0-8050-6477-X). 64pp. A series of poems convey the feelings of a 13-year-old African American boy whose warm, loving home is destroyed when his father loses his job. (Rev: BL 5/1/03; HBG 10/03; SLJ 5/03*) [811]

11999 Thomas, Joyce Carol. *Crowning Glory* (PS–3). Illus. by Brenda Joysmith. 2002, HarperCollins LB $15.89 (0-06-023474-1). 32pp. A collection of free-verse poems that lovingly describe African American hair and hairstyles, accompanied by illustrations. (Rev: BCCB 10/02; BL 9/15/02; HBG 10/02; SLJ 6/02) [811]

12000 Troupe, Quincy. *Little Stevie Wonder* (2–4). Illus. by Lisa Cohen. 2005, Houghton Mifflin $18.00 (0-618-34060-2). 32pp. Vibrant illustrations highlight this free-verse account of Stevie Wonder's childhood and early success. (Rev: BL 2/1/05; SLJ 6/05) [811]

12001 Woodson, Jacqueline. *Locomotion* (3–6). 2003, Penguin Putnam $15.99 (0-399-23115-3). 128pp. A young boy whose parents have died and whose sister is in a different foster home expresses his grief through poetry. (Rev: BCCB 3/03; BL 2/15/03; HB 3–4/03*; HBG 10/03; SLJ 1/03) [811]

12002 *Words with Wings: A Treasury of African-American Poetry and Art* (4–10). Ed. by Belinda Rochelle. Illus. 2001, HarperCollins LB $16.89 (0-06-029363-2). 48pp. An outstanding collection of 20 poems by such African American writers as Langston Hughes and Alice Walker with accompanying paintings by artists like Elizabeth Catlett and Romare Bearden. (Rev: BCCB 3/01; BL 12/15/00*; HBG 10/01; SLJ 2/01) [811.008]

Animals

12003 Ackerman, Diane. *Animal Sense* (3–7). Illus. by Peter Sis. 2003, Knopf $14.95 (0-375-82384-0). 40pp. Arresting, thoughtful, and sometimes humorous poems about animals, with accompanying artwork. (Rev: BCCB 3/03; BL 2/15/03*; HB 1–2/03; HBG 10/03; SLJ 2/03) [811]

12004 Andreae, Giles. *Rumble in the Jungle* (PS). Illus. by David Wojtowycz. 1997, Little Tiger $14.95 (1-888444-08-8). A collection of poems about the animals that a small group of ants encounter as they march through the jungle. (Rev: HBG 3/98; SLJ 11/97) [811]

12005 *Animal Poems* (5–7). Ed. by John Hollander. Illus. by Simona Mulazzani. Series: Poetry for Young People. 2005, Sterling $14.95 (1-4027-0926-9). 48pp. A collection of classic poems (by such poets as Blake, Frost, Melville, and Yeats) accompanied by artwork and explanatory notes. (Rev: BL 4/1/05; SLJ 3/05) [808.81]

12006 Belle, Jennifer. *Animal Stackers* (1–3). Illus. by David McPhail. 2005, Hyperion $15.99 (0-7868-1834-4). 40pp. The names of different animals (in alphabetical order) inspire vertical poems in this entertaining collection. (Rev: BL 4/1/05; SLJ 4/05) [811]

12007 *Big, Bad and a Little Bit Scary: Poems That Bite Back* (K–3). Illus. by Wade Zahares. 2001, Viking $16.99 (0-670-03513-0). 32pp. Animals that bite are the subject of this collection of poems by authors including Eve Merriam and Dick King-Smith, with illustrations that focus on the scary parts. (Rev: BL 10/15/01; HBG 3/02; SLJ 10/01) [811.008]

12008 Carryl, Charles Edward. *The Camel's Lament* (K–3). Illus. by Charles Santore. 2004, Random LB $18.99 (0-375-91426-9). 32pp. Stunning watercolors breathe new life into Edward Carryl Charles's poem about the lowly camel. (Rev: BL 7/04; SLJ 10/04*) [811]

12009 Chorao, Kay. *The Baby's Book of Baby Animals* (PS–K). Illus. by author. 2004, Dutton $16.99 (0-525-47199-5). 40pp. Old-fashioned illustrations accompany this collection of animal-themed poems and nursery rhymes that includes excerpts from Wordsworth, Blake, and Tennyson. (Rev: BL 1/1–15/04; SLJ 1/04) [811]

12010 Cole, William, ed. *An Arkful of Animals: Poems for the Very Young* (3–5). Illus. by Lynn Munsinger. 1992, Houghton Mifflin paper $4.95 (0-395-61618-2). 128pp. A fine collection of humorous poems about animals.

12011 De Vos, Philip. *Carnival of the Animals* (1–4). Illus. by Piet Grobler. 2000, Front Street $16.95 (1-886910-47-2). 38pp. Surreal paintings accompany clever verses to bring to life the Saint-Saens musical fantasy. (Rev: BL 8/00; HBG 10/00; SLJ 7/00) [821]

12012 Emmett, Jonathan. *Through the Heart of the Jungle* (K–3). Illus. by Elena Gomez. 2003, Tiger Tales $15.95 (1-58925-029-X); paper $5.95 (1-58925-380-9). In this lushly illustrated cumulative rhyme, young readers are introduced to the food chain of the jungle, in which smaller creatures become meals for their larger neighbors, right on up to Lion, the king of the jungle. (Rev: SLJ 9/03)

12013 Fleischman, Paul. *I Am Phoenix: Poems for Two Voices* (4–9). Illus. 1985, HarperCollins paper $5.99 (0-06-446092-4). A group of love poems about birds that are designed to be read by two voices or groups of voices. (Rev: BL 12/1/85; BR 3–4/86) [811]

12014 Fleischman, Paul. *Joyful Noise: Poems for Two Voices* (3–6). Illus. by Eric Beddows. 1988, HarperCollins LB $14.89 (0-06-021853-3); paper $5.95 (0-06-446093-2). 64pp. Poems for reading aloud that explore the lives of insects. Newbery Medal winner, 1989. (Rev: BL 2/15/88; HB 5–6/88; SLJ 2/88)

12015 Florian, Douglas. *Bow Wow Meow Meow* (PS–2). Illus. 2003, Harcourt $17.00 (0-15-216395-6). 56pp. A collection of offbeat poems about cats and dogs, accompanied by watercolor illustrations. (Rev: BL 2/1/03*; HB 5–6/03; HBG 10/03; SLJ 5/03) [811]

12016 Florian, Douglas. *In the Swim* (1–4). Illus. 1997, Harcourt $16.00 (0-15-201307-5). 48pp. A collection of 21 original poems about freshwater and saltwater creatures. (Rev: BCCB 5/97; BL 3/15/97; HB 7–8/97; SLJ 5/97*) [811]

12017 Florian, Douglas. *Insectlopedia* (3–5). Illus. 1998, Harcourt $16.00 (0-15-201306-7). 56pp. A well-designed book of poems about insects and spiders. (Rev: BCCB 7–8/98; BL 3/15/98; SLJ 4/98) [811]

12018 Florian, Douglas. *Lizards, Frogs, and Polliwogs* (3–5). Illus. 2001, Harcourt $16.00 (0-15-202591-X). 48pp. Playful poetry and imaginative artwork are combined in this book of short original poems about a variety of reptiles and amphibians. (Rev: BL 3/15/01*; HB 5–6/01; HBG 10/01) [811]

12019 Florian, Douglas. *Mammalabilia* (2–4). Illus. 2000, Harcourt $16.00 (0-15-202167-1). 48pp. Twenty-one short, clever rhymes and inventive illustrations examine various members of the animal kingdom. (Rev: BCCB 3/00; BL 3/15/00; HB 3–4/00; HBG 10/00; SLJ 4/00) [811]

12020 Florian, Douglas. *Omnibeasts: Animal Poems and Paintings* (1–4). 2004, Harcourt $18.00 (0-15-205038-8). 96pp. Entertaining wordplay and inventive shapes add to this inviting collection of poems and art about animals. (Rev: BL 10/15/04; SLJ 10/04) [811]

12021 Florian, Douglas. *On the Wing* (3–5). Illus. 1996, Harcourt $16.00 (0-15-200497-1). 48pp. Twenty-one poems celebrate a wide variety of birds, from hummingbirds to vultures. (Rev: BCCB 4/96; BL 3/15/96; SLJ 6/96) [811]

12022 Florian, Douglas. *Zoo's Who: Poems and Paintings* (K–3). Illus. 2005, Harcourt $17.00 (0-15-204639-9). 56pp. Clever, brief verses about all sorts of animals (not just the ones found in zoos) are accompanied by unusual art. (Rev: BL 3/15/05; SLJ 4/05) [811]

12023 Foster, John, comp. *My First Oxford Book of Animal Poems* (K–4). Illus. 2002, Oxford LB $19.95 (0-19-276269-9). 94pp. An anthology of classic and new poems about wild and domestic animals that includes much humor and arresting illustrations. (Rev: HBG 3/03; SLJ 9/02) [811]

12024 Frost, Robert. *The Runaway* (PS–2). Illus. by Glenna Lang. 1998, Godine $17.95 (1-56792-006-3). 32pp. Lovely illustrations accompany this poem about a colt's reaction to the first snowfall. (Rev: BL 3/1/99; HBG 3/99; SLJ 3/99) [811]

12025 *Fur, Fangs, and Footprints: A Collection of Animal Poems* (3–6). Ed. by Patricia M. Stockland. Illus. by Sara Rojo Perez. Series: Poet's Toolbox. 2004, Compass Point LB $22.60 (0-7565-0562-3). 32pp. Poems about animals by a selection of writers introduce various poetry concepts. (Rev: BL 4/1/04) [808.81]

12026 George, Kristine O'Connell. *Little Dog and Duncan* (PS–2). Illus. by June Otani. 2002, Clarion $12.00 (0-618-11758-X). 38pp. Preschoolers and beginning readers alike will enjoy the gentle poetry and charming watercolors in this story of two dogs having a sleepover. (Rev: BL 3/1/02; HB 7–8/02*; HBG 10/02; SLJ 3/02*) [811]

12027 George, Kristine O'Connell. *Little Dog Poems* (PS–K). Illus. by June Otani. 1999, Clarion $12.00 (0-395-82266-1). 40pp. Charming watercolors illustrate these simple, original poems about a little girl and her beloved dog. (Rev: BL 3/15/99; HB 3–4/99; HBG 10/99; SLJ 5/99) [811]

12028 Ghigna, Charles. *Animal Tracks: Wild Poems to Read Aloud* (K–3). Illus. by John Speirs. 2004, Abrams $14.95 (0-8109-4841-9). 38pp. Animals occupy center stage in this collection of 32 brief, illustrated poems, many of which will generate a laugh. (Rev: BL 5/1/04; SLJ 4/04) [811]

12029 Gottfried, Maya. *Good Dog* (K–3). Illus. by Robert Rahway Zakanitch. 2005, Knopf LB $17.99 (0-375-93049-3). Free-verse poems express the thoughts of a variety of canine personalities and their views of their human companions. (Rev: SLJ 4/05) [811]

12030 Greenberg, David T. *Bugs!* (K–3). Illus. by Lynn Munsinger. 1997, Little, Brown $14.95 (0-316-32574-0). 32pp. In humorous verses, a number of insects and their distinctive characteristics are introduced. (Rev: BL 9/1/97; HBG 3/98; SLJ 9/97) [811]

12031 Hoberman, Mary Ann. *A Fine Fat Pig* (K–5). Illus. by Malcah Zeldis. 1991, HarperCollins $14.95 (0-06-022425-8). These 14 poems deal with animals, their characteristics, and habits. (Rev: HB 5–6/91; SLJ 4/91) [811]

12032 *Hoofbeats, Claws and Rippled Fins: Creature Poems* (3–7). Ed. by Lee Bennett Hopkins. Illus. by Stephen Alcorn. 2002, HarperCollins LB $15.89 (0-688-17943-6). 32pp. Fourteen poets each contribute a single poem inspired by the outstanding woodcuts by Stephen Alcorn that picture animals including the camel and the iguana. (Rev: BL 5/1/02*; HB 3–4/02; HBG 10/02; SLJ 4/02) [811.008]

12033 Hopkins, Lee Bennett. *A Pet for Me: Poems* (1–3). Illus. by Jane Manning. Series: An I Can Read Book. 2003, HarperCollins LB $16.89 (0-06-029112-5). 48pp. Brief poems by recognized authors, combined with watercolor illustrations fea-

turing happy children, celebrate the joy of pets and will appeal to beginning readers. (Rev: BL 1/1–15/03; HBG 10/03; SLJ 3/03) [811.008]

12034 Howitt, Mary. *The Spider and the Fly* (2–5). Illus. by Tony Diterlizzi. 2002, Simon & Schuster $16.95 (0-689-85289-4). 40pp. Outstanding monochrome artwork brings new life to the classic poem. Caldecott Honor Book, 2003. (Rev: BCCB 11/02; BL 10/1/02; HBG 3/03; SLJ 9/02*) [811]

12035 Hubbell, Patricia. *Earthmates* (K–4). Illus. by Jean Cassels. 2000, Marshall Cavendish $15.95 (0-7614-5062-9). 32pp. A collection of impressive poems about such animals as a lion, rat, frog, bat, and deer. (Rev: BL 3/15/00; HBG 10/00; SLJ 3/00) [811]

12036 Hughes, Ted. *The Cat and the Cuckoo* (3–6). Illus. by Flora McDonnell. 2003, Millbrook LB $22.90 (0-7613-2572-7). 64pp. Vivid poems bring to life the sounds and behavior of the animals that are the leading characters in this collection. (Rev: BL 4/1/03; HB 7–8/03; HBG 10/03; SLJ 5/03) [821]

12037 Johnston, Tony. *Cat, What Is That?* (1–4). Illus. by Wendell Minor. 2001, HarperCollins LB $15.89 (0-06-027743-2). 32pp. Abstract verses and detailed, realistic illustrations bring to life cats of all kinds in a variety of typical feline activities. (Rev: BL 10/1/01; HBG 3/02; SLJ 9/01)

12038 Johnston, Tony. *Gopher Up Your Sleeve* (PS–3). Illus. by Trip Park. 2002, Rising Moon $15.95 (0-87358-794-4). Humorous poems about animals are accompanied by fanciful illustrations. (Rev: HBG 10/02; SLJ 11/02) [811]

12039 Johnston, Tony. *It's About Dogs* (2–4). 2000, Harcourt $16.00 (0-15-202022-5). 48pp. Many short, mostly free-verse poems typify the moods and behavior of various canines, domesticated and not. (Rev: BL 3/15/00; HBG 10/00; SLJ 6/00) [811]

12040 Kiesler, Kate. *Wings on the Wind: Bird Poems* (PS–2). Illus. 2002, Clarion $14.00 (0-618-13333-X). 32pp. Vivid oil paintings are used to illustrate this collection of poems about birds by such writers as Edward Lear, Carl Sandburg, and Margaret Wise Brown. (Rev: BL 4/15/02; HBG 10/02; SLJ 4/02) [811.008]

12041 Levy, Constance. *I'm Going to Pet a Worm Today and Other Poems* (3–5). Illus. by Ronald Himler. 1991, Macmillan $14.00 (0-689-50535-3). 48pp. This book of original poems celebrates such creatures of nature as spiders, worms, and beetles. (Rev: BCCB 2/92*; BL 11/15/92; SLJ 10/91) [811]

12042 Livingston, Myra Cohn, ed. *If You Ever Meet a Whale* (1–4). Illus. by Leonard Everett Fisher. 1992, Holiday House LB $14.95 (0-8234-0940-6). 32pp. Seventeen whale poems with full-color paintings. (Rev: BL 11/15/92) [811]

12043 Lujan, Jorge. *Rooster / Gallo* (PS–1). Illus. by Manuel Monroy. 2004, Groundwood $14.95 (0-88899-558-X). 24pp. Brief poetic text celebrates the rooster and its relationship to the cycle of day and night. (Rev: BL 5/15/04; HB 3–4/04; SLJ 9/04) [811]

12044 Nichol, Barbara. *Biscuits in the Cupboard* (K–4). Illus. by Philippe Beha. 1998, Stoddart

$12.95 (0-7737-3025-7). 32pp. A delightful collection of poems about dogs, written entirely from their point of view. (Rev: BL 3/1/04; SLJ 3/98) [808]

12045 Pearson, Susan. *Squeal and Squawk: Barnyard Talk* (K–3). Illus. by David Slonim. 2004, Marshall Cavendish $16.95 (0-7614-5160-9). 31pp. Humorous illustrations enhance poems about barnyard animals, from a lovelorn rooster to flying pigs. (Rev: SLJ 6/04) [811]

12046 Pearson, Susan. *Who Swallowed Harold?* (K–4). Illus. by David Slonim. 2005, Marshall Cavendish $16.95 (0-7614-5193-5). 31pp. Eighteen humorous poems look at children's relationships with their pets. (Rev: BL 2/1/04*; SLJ 4/05) [811]

12047 Polisar, Barry L. *Insect Soup: Bug Poems* (K–4). Illus. by David Clark. 1999, Rainbow $14.95 (0-938663-22-4). Fifteen original poems about insects that are sometimes humorous, sometimes gross, and sometimes amazing. (Rev: SLJ 8/99) [811]

12048 Prelutsky, Jack, ed. *The Beauty of the Beast: Poems from the Animal Kingdom* (3–7). Illus. by Meilo So. 1997, Knopf $25.00 (0-679-87058-X). 101pp. A wonderful, beautifully illustrated collection of more than 200 animal poems by 20th-century writers whose works are arranged by animal genus. (Rev: BL 9/15/97; HBG 3/98; SLJ 1/98*) [811]

12049 Prelutsky, Jack. *The Dragons Are Singing Tonight* (K–4). Illus. by Peter Sis. 1993, Greenwillow $15.89 (0-688-12511-5). 40pp. These 17 poems all deal with the pastimes and problems that dragons face in their everyday life. (Rev: BL 9/1/93*; HB 9–10/93; SLJ 10/93*) [811]

12050 Prelutsky, Jack. *If Not for the Cat* (PS–3). Illus. by Ted Rand. 2004, Greenwillow LB $17.89 (0-06-059678-3). 40pp. Seventeen haiku poems explore life from the vantage point of various animals. (Rev: BL 10/1/04; SLJ 10/04) [811]

12051 Prelutsky, Jack. *Tyrannosaurus Was a Beast* (2–5). Illus. by Arnold Lobel. 1988, Morrow paper $4.95 (0-688-11569-1). 32pp. Poems and watercolor portraits bring dinosaurs to life. (Rev: BCCB 9/88; BL 8/88; HB 9–10/88)

12052 Ryder, Joanne. *Mouse Tail Moon* (2–4). Illus. by Maggie Kneen. 2002, Holt $16.95 (0-8050-6404-4). 32pp. A white-tail mouse describes his night in brief poems, from praising darkness for its safe haven from predators to dealing with fleas and rain to celebrating the morning sun. (Rev: BL 1/1–15/03; HBG 3/03; SLJ 2/03) [811]

12053 Schwartz, Betty Ann, ed. *My Kingdom for a Horse: An Anthology of Poems About Horses* (1–4). Illus. by Alix Berenzy. 2001, Holt $17.95 (0-8050-6212-2). Impressionistic illustrations enhance this collection of poems about horses of all kinds and in all places by poets including Shakespeare, Walt Whitman, Robert Frost, and Jack Prelutsky. (Rev: HBG 3/02; SLJ 11/01) [811]

12054 Sierra, Judy. *Antarctic Antics: A Book of Penguin Poems* (PS–2). Illus. by Jose Aruego and Ariane Dewey. 1998, Harcourt $16.00 (0-15-201006-8). 32pp. Thirteen poems of varying length and accompanying pictures describe the behavior and play of baby penguins in their Antarctic home. (Rev: BL 5/1/98; HBG 10/98; SLJ 5/98) [811]

12055 Singer, Marilyn. *The Company of Crows: A Book of Poems* (2–4). Illus. by Linda Saport. 2002, Clarion $16.00 (0-618-08340-5). 48pp. The intelligent crow is presented in poems written from the viewpoint of onlookers, including children, a farmer, and other animals. (Rev: BL 11/15/02; HBG 3/03; SLJ 11/02) [811]

12056 Singer, Marilyn. *Creature Carnival* (2–4). Illus. by Gris Grimly. 2004, Hyperion $15.99 (0-7868-1877-8). 40pp. This poetic excursion introduces young readers to such fantastical beasts as a mermaid and a dragon. (Rev: BL 4/1/04; SLJ 4/04) [811]

12057 Singer, Marilyn. *Fireflies at Midnight* (2–4). Illus. by Ken Robbins. 2003, Simon & Schuster $16.95 (0-689-82492-0). 32pp. Computer-enhanced photograph collages illustrate verses about animals and their behavior on a summer day. (Rev: BL 4/1/03; HBG 10/03; SLJ 5/03) [811]

12058 Sklansky, Amy E. *From the Doghouse: Poems to Chew On* (1–4). Illus. 2002, Holt $17.95 (0-8050-6673-X). 44pp. A delightful collection of poems from the canine perspective about things dogs like — walks in the park and car rides, for example — and things dogs don't like — such as fleas and baths. (Rev: HBG 3/03; SLJ 8/02) [811]

12059 Spinelli, Eileen. *Feathers: Poems About Birds* (1–3). Illus. by Lisa McCue. 2004, Holt $16.95 (0-8050-6713-2). 40pp. Each of the 27 poems in this brightly illustrated collection focuses on a different species of bird. (Rev: BL 3/15/04; SLJ 4/04) [811]

12060 Spinelli, Eileen. *Song for the Whooping Crane* (PS–3). Illus. by Elsa Warnick. 2000, Eerdmans $16.00 (0-8028-5172-X). 32pp. A poem that celebrates the endangered whooping crane, its beauty, and its life cycle. (Rev: BL 10/1/00; HBG 3/01; SLJ 3/01) [811]

12061 Tiller, Ruth. *Cats Vanish Slowly* (K–3). Illus. by Laura L. Seeley. 1995, Peachtree $16.95 (1-56145-106-1). 32pp. Twelve poems about the cats (including B.P., for "bad penny") that are found on the farm of the author's grandmother. (Rev: BL 1/1–15/96; SLJ 1/96) [811]

12062 Whipple, Laura, ed. *Eric Carle's Animals Animals* (PS–3). Illus. by Eric Carle. 1989, Penguin Putnam $21.99 (0-399-21744-4). Eric Carle's collages illustrate various writers' poems, each dealing with an animal. (Rev: BCCB 10/89*; BL 9/1/89*; HB 11–12/89; SLJ 11/89) [811]

12063 Yolen, Jane. *Fine Feathered Friends: Poems for Young People to Perform* (3–6). Illus. by Jason Stemple. 2004, Boyds Mills $17.95 (1-59078-193-7). 32pp. Poetry and photographs combine to convey striking images of individual species of birds. (Rev: BL 11/1/04; SLJ 12/04) [811]

12064 Yolen, Jane. *Wild Wings: Poems for Young People* (3–6). Illus. by Jason Stemple. 2002, Boyds Mills $17.95 (1-56397-904-7). 32pp. Unusual photographs accompany beautiful poems about birds. (Rev: BL 5/15/02; HBG 10/02; SLJ 6/02) [811.54]

Haiku

12065 Chaikin, Miriam. *Don't Step on the Sky: A Handful of Haiku* (K–4). Illus. by Hiroe Nakata. 2002, Holt $16.95 (0-8050-6474-5). 28pp. A delightful book of haiku for younger readers. (Rev: BL 3/15/02; HBG 10/02; SLJ 5/02) [811]

12066 Donegan, Patricia. *Haiku: Asian Arts and Crafts for Creative Kids* (4–8). Illus. 2004, Tuttle $9.95 (0-8048-3501-2). 64pp. Haiku advice and exercises follow an introduction to the verse form. (Rev: BL 3/15/04; SLJ 8/04) [372.6]

12067 *In the Eyes of the Cat: Japanese Poetry for All Seasons* (PS–3). Trans. by Tze-si Huang. Illus. by Demi. 1994, Holt paper $6.95 (0-8050-3383-1). 80pp. These short Japanese poems, known as haiku, use words and images appreciated by young readers. (Rev: BCCB 5/92; BL 4/15/92; SLJ 5/92) [895.6]

12068 Janeczko, Paul B., ed. *Stone Bench in an Empty Park* (5–12). Illus. 2000, Orchard LB $16.99 (0-531-33259-4). 40pp. An inspired collection of haiku from a variety of poets, illustrated with stunning black-and-white photographs. (Rev: BCCB 6/00; BL 3/15/00*; HB 3–4/00; HBG 10/00; SLJ 3/00) [811]

12069 Yolen, Jane. *Least Things: Poems About Small Natures* (K–5). Photos by Jason Stemple. 2003, Boyds Mills $17.95 (1-59078-098-1). 32pp. The wonders of nature are celebrated in this appealing blend of haikus by Jane Yolen and vibrant color photographs by her son, Jason Stemple. (Rev: HBG 4/04; SLJ 10/03) [811]

Holidays

12070 Bailey, Mary Bryant. *Jeoffry's Halloween* (K–3). Illus. by Elizabeth Sayles. 2003, Farrar $16.00 (0-374-33677-6). As daylight fades on Halloween, Jeoffry the cat and his faithful canine companion hurry toward home; although a bit frightened themselves, they come to the aid of a pair of trick-or-treaters who've lost their way. (Rev: HBG 4/04; SLJ 9/03) [811]

12071 *Bright Star Shining: Poems for Christmas* (3–8). Ed. by Michael Harrison and Christopher Stuart-Clark. Illus. 1998, Eerdmans $15.00 (0-8028-5177-0). 48pp. Illustrated by three different artists, this is a fine collection of 32 Christmas poems. (Rev: BL 9/1/98; HBG 3/99) [808.81]

12072 Bronson, Linda, comp. *Sleigh Bells and Snowflakes: A Celebration of Christmas* (1–3). Illus. by Linda Bronson. 2002, Holt $17.95 (0-8050-6755-8). 45pp. A nicely illustrated anthology of poetry and song lyrics that includes many well-known favorites. (Rev: HBG 3/03; SLJ 10/02) [811.008]

12073 Cummings, E. E. *Little Tree* (K–4). Illus. by Chris Raschka. 2001, Hyperion $16.99 (0-7868-0795-4). 32pp. A young evergreen travels a long way as it fulfills its dream of becoming a Christmas

tree in this appealing and visually satisfying story inspired by an e. e. cummings poem. (Rev: BCCB 11/01; BL 12/1/01; HBG 3/02; SLJ 10/01*) [811]

12074 Cunningham, Julia. *The Stable Rat and Other Christmas Poems* (3–6). Illus. by Anita Lobel. 2001, Greenwillow LB $15.89 (0-688-17800-6). 24pp. These interconnected poems portray Christmas from the viewpoint of the animal and other observers, with vivid artwork. (Rev: BCCB 11/01; BL 9/15/01; HB 11–12/01; HBG 3/02; SLJ 10/01) [811]

12075 Ghigna, Charles, and Debra Ghigna. *Christmas Is Coming* (PS–3). Illus. by Mary O'Keefe. 2000, Charlesbridge $15.95 (0-88106-113-1). 32pp. A number of Christmas preparations, like selecting a tree and baking cookies, are depicted in these 27 original poems with expressive illustrations. (Rev: BL 9/1/00; HBG 3/01) [811]

12076 Grimes, Nikki. *At Jerusalem's Gate: Poems of Easter* (5–8). Illus. by David Frampton. 2005, Eerdmans $20.00 (0-8028-5183-5). 48pp. More than 20 poems are introduced by thoughtful paragraphs and enhanced by handsome illustrations. (Rev: BL 2/15/05; SLJ 3/05) [232.96]

12077 Grimes, Nikki. *Under the Christmas Tree* (PS–2). Illus. by Kadir Nelson. 2002, HarperCollins LB $17.89 (0-688-16000-X). 32pp. An African American family celebrates an urban Christmas in this picture book of 23 poems presented from a child's point of view. (Rev: BL 9/1/02; HBG 3/03; SLJ 10/02*) [811]

12078 Hopkins, Lee Bennett, ed. *Christmas Presents: Holiday Poetry* (K–3). Illus. by Melanie W. Hall. Series: An I Can Read. 2004, HarperCollins LB $16.89 (0-06-008055-8); paper $3.99 (0-06-008056-6). 32pp. Twelve Christmas poems explore all aspects of the holiday and demonstrate different styles and devices. (Rev: BL 8/04; SLJ 10/04) [811]

12079 Horton, Joan. *Halloween Hoots and Howls* (2–5). Illus. 1999, Holt $15.95 (0-8050-5805-2). 32pp. A collection of amusing — sometimes wacky — poems about Halloween. (Rev: BCCB 9/99; BL 9/1/99; HBG 3/00; SLJ 10/99) [811]

12080 Koontz, Dean. *Every Day's a Holiday: Amusing Rhymes for Happy Times* (3–6). Illus. by Phil Parks. 2003, HarperCollins LB $18.89 (0-06-008585-1). 144pp. Each of the 64 poems in this collection celebrates a special day on the calendar — holidays and other landmark days, such as the beginning of autumn and the shortest day of the year. (Rev: HBG 4/04; SLJ 10/03) [811]

12081 Lansky, Bruce, et al. *Happy Birthday to Me! Kids Pick the Funniest Birthday Poems* (2–5). Illus. by Jack Lindstrom. 1998, Meadowbrook $8.95 (0-671-57703-4). 27pp. Nine poets are represented in this joyous collection of 21 poems that celebrate birthdays. (Rev: SLJ 5/98) [811]

12082 Livingston, Myra Cohn, ed. *Celebrations* (1–4). Illus. by Leonard Everett Fisher. 1985, Holiday House LB $16.95 (0-8234-0550-8); paper $6.95 (0-8234-0654-7). 32pp. A handsome book of verse illustrating 16 celebrations, such as Valentine's Day, birthdays, and Easter. (Rev: BCCB 4/85; BL 4/1/85; HB 5–6/85)

12083 Livingston, Myra Cohn, ed. *Christmas Poems* (PS–3). Illus. by Trina S. Hyman. 1984, Holiday House LB $15.95 (0-8234-0508-7). 32pp. A collection of 18 poems, half of which were commissioned for the volume.

12084 Livingston, Myra Cohn, ed. *Poems for Jewish Holidays* (K–6). Illus. by Lloyd Bloom. 1986, Holiday House LB $15.95 (0-8234-0606-7). 32pp. Poems that contain the essence of major Jewish holidays. (Rev: BCCB 2/87; BL 11/1/86; HB 1–2/87)

12085 Livingston, Myra Cohn, ed. *Valentine Poems* (3–6). Illus. 1987, Holiday House LB $15.95 (0-8234-0587-7). 32pp. Sprightly poems from established names and modern ones, too. (Rev: BL 1/15/87; SLJ 12/86)

12086 Merriam, Eve. *Spooky ABC* (3–6). Illus. by Lane Smith. 2002, Simon & Schuster $16.95 (0-689-85356-4). 32pp. A redesigned and renamed version of the blood-curdling *Halloween ABC* (1987) that includes information on the creation of the original book. (Rev: BL 10/1/02; HBG 3/03) [811]

12087 Moore, Clement Clarke. *The Night Before Christmas* (PS–1). Illus. by Cheryl Harness. 1990, Random $8.99 (0-394-82698-1). 40pp. A traditional treatment of the classic holiday poem. (Rev: BL 11/1/90; HB 11–12/90) [811]

12088 Moore, Clement Clarke. *The Night Before Christmas* (PS–3). Illus. by Ted Rand. 1995, North-South LB $16.88 (1-55858-466-8). 32pp. A large-format picture book with new illustrations for the classic poem, each using a double-page spread. (Rev: BL 10/15/95) [871]

12089 Moore, Clement Clarke. *The Night Before Christmas* (PS–3). Illus. by Ruth Sanderson. 1997, Little, Brown $13.95 (0-316-57963-7). 32pp. An old-fashioned version of this classic poem. (Rev: BL 9/15/97; HBG 3/98; SLJ 10/97) [811]

12090 Moore, Clement Clarke. *The Night Before Christmas* (PS–2). Illus. by Jan Brett. 1998, Penguin Putnam LB $16.99 (0-399-23190-0). This version of the classic Christmas poem contains illustrations of a Victorian house, an old-world Santa, and two stowaway elves. (Rev: HBG 3/99; SLJ 10/98) [811]

12091 Moore, Clement Clarke. *The Night Before Christmas* (PS–1). Ed. by Cooper Edens and Harold Darling. Illus. 1998, Chronicle $16.95 (0-8118-1712-1). 44pp. This new edition of the classic poem uses illustrations that originally appeared between 1890 and 1928. (Rev: BL 10/1/98; HBG 3/99; SLJ 10/98) [811]

12092 Moore, Clement Clarke. *The Night Before Christmas* (PS–2). Illus. by Tasha Tudor. 1999, Little, Brown $14.95 (0-316-85579-0). Wild and domestic animals on a Vermont farm form an important part of the illustrations in this version of the classic poem. (Rev: HBG 3/00; SLJ 10/99) [811]

12093 Moore, Clement Clarke. *The Night Before Christmas* (PS–3). Illus. by Bruce Whatley. 1999, HarperCollins LB $16.89 (0-06-028380-7). 40pp. The pictures in this attractive edition of the favorite poem depict events from the father's point of view. (Rev: BL 9/1/99*; HBG 3/00; SLJ 10/99) [811]

12094 Moore, Clement Clarke. *The Night Before Christmas* (PS–3). Illus. by Tomie dePaola. 1980, Holiday House LB $16.95 (0-8234-0414-5); paper $6.95 (0-8234-0417-X). 32pp. A lovely edition of this popular and loved Christmas poem. Another edition is: Illus. by Anita Lobel (Knopf 1996).

12095 Moore, Clement Clarke. *The Night Before Christmas: A Visit from St. Nicholas* (PS–1). Illus. by Max Grover. 1999, Harcourt $16.00 (0-15-201713-5). 32pp. In this version of the famous poem, the pictures are all of the present day, with automobiles on the streets and Christmas lights in the houses. (Rev: BL 9/1/99; HBG 3/00; SLJ 10/99) [811]

12096 Moore, Clement Clarke. *The Night Before Christmas: Or, a Visit of St. Nicholas* (PS–3). Illus. 1989, Penguin Putnam $17.95 (0-399-21614-6). 32pp. This handsomely produced edition of the famous poem was illustrated years ago by a now-forgotten artist. (Rev: BL 9/15/89) [811]

12097 Moore, Clement Clarke. *The Teddy Bears' Night Before Christmas* (PS–K). Illus. by Monica Stevenson. 1999, Scholastic $12.95 (0-590-03243-7). 40pp. Photographs of stuffed animals in snowy scenes illustrate this version of the classic rhyme. (Rev: BL 9/1/99; HBG 3/00; SLJ 10/99) [811]

12098 Prelutsky, Jack. *It's Thanksgiving* (PS–4). Illus. by Marylin Hafner. 1982, Greenwillow $15.89 (0-688-00442-3). 48pp. Twelve poems covering various aspects of Thanksgiving.

12099 Prelutsky, Jack. *It's Valentine's Day* (1–4). Illus. by Yossi Abolafia. 1985, Scholastic paper $2.50 (0-590-40979-4). 48pp. Bright, humorous poems in celebration of love and Valentine's Day.

12100 *A Small Treasury of Easter: Poems and Prayers* (K–4). Illus. by Susan Spellman. 1997, Boyds Mills $8.95 (1-56397-647-1). 32pp. An illustrated collection of secular and religious Easter poems, divided into two parts: "A Time to Play" and "A Time to Pray." (Rev: SLJ 7/97) [811]

12101 Snell, Gordon. *'Twas the Day After Christmas* (PS–2). Illus. by Sean Delonas. 2003, HarperCollins LB $16.89 (0-06-028953-8). This amusing variation on Clement C. Moore's holiday poem paints a portrait of the somewhat messy day after Christmas from the viewpoint of a tiny mouse. (Rev: HBG 4/04; SLJ 10/03) [811]

12102 *'Twas the Night Before Christmas; or, Account of a Visit from St. Nicholas* (PS–2). Illus. by Matt Tavares. 2002, Candlewick $16.00 (0-7636-1585-4). 32pp. The classic, original version of the poem, accompanied by old-fashioned artwork. (Rev: BL 9/1/02; HBG 3/03) [811]

12103 *Valentine Hearts: Holiday Poetry* (1–3). Ed. by Lee Bennett Hopkins. Illus. by JoAnn Adinolfi. Series: An I Can Read Book. 2004, HarperCollins LB $16.89 (0-06-008058-2). 32pp. Romance and humor are features of these poems by various authors that are accompanied by bright illustrations. (Rev: BL 1/1–15/05; SLJ 1/05) [811]

12104 Yolen, Jane. *The Three Bears Holiday Rhyme Book* (PS–2). Illus. by Jane Dyer. 1995, Harcourt $15.00 (0-15-200932-9). 32pp. Fifteen poems featuring Goldilocks and the Three Bears are used to introduce such holidays as Valentine's Day, Arbor Day, and Groundhog Day. (Rev: BL 3/15/95; SLJ 6/95) [811.54]

Humorous Poetry

12105 Aylesworth, Jim. *The Burger and the Hot Dog* (K–3). Illus. by Stephen Gammell. 2001, Simon & Schuster $16.95 (0-689-83897-2). 32pp. A collection of funny poems about anthropomorphic foods with effective, messy illustrations. (Rev: BCCB 12/01; BL 10/1/01; HBG 3/02; SLJ 1/02) [811]

12106 Bagert, Brod. *Giant Children* (K–3). Illus. by Tedd Arnold. 2002, Dial $15.99 (0-8037-2556-6). 32pp. Side-splitting artwork is the perfect accompaniment to this eclectic collection of poems for young readers. (Rev: BL 8/02; HBG 3/03; SLJ 8/02) [811]

12107 Base, Graeme. *Lewis Carroll's Jabberwocky: A Book of Brillig Dioramas* (3–5). Illus. 1996, Abrams $19.95 (0-8109-3520-1). 14pp. Three-dimensional dinosaurs are used to illustrate Lewis Carroll's *Jabberwocky*. (Rev: BL 12/15/96; SLJ 4/04) [811]

12108 Billings, John. *My Pet Crocodile and Other Slightly Outrageous Verse* (PS–3). Illus. by Janette Todd. 1993, Chokecherry $16.95 (1-884035-55-8). 128pp. Humorous poems on such subjects as bungee jumping, nose picking, and bubble gum. (Rev: BL 1/1/94) [811]

12109 Brown, Calef. *Dutch Sneakers and Flea Keepers: 14 More Stories* (3–5). Illus. 2000, Houghton Mifflin $15.00 (0-618-05183-X). 32pp. A collection of original poems that introduce the reader to several odd and eccentric characters, such as the Flea Keepers, who train fleas for cash. (Rev: BCCB 7–8/00; BL 4/1/00; HBG 10/00; SLJ 4/00) [811.54]

12110 Bush, Timothy. *Ferocious Girls, Steamroller Boys, and Other Poems in Between* (1–4). Illus. by author. 2000, Orchard LB $17.99 (0-531-33250-0). A funny book that uses seven poems to explore unusual boys and girls and their strange behavior. (Rev: HBG 10/00; SLJ 7/00) [811]

12111 Carroll, Lewis. *Jabberwocky* (1–4). Illus. by Graeme Base. 1989, Abrams $16.95 (0-8109-1150-7). 32pp. Carroll's nonsense poem is given a fresh treatment with illustrations picturing a medieval locale. (Rev: SLJ 8/89) [821]

12112 Ciardi, John. *The Hopeful Trout and Other Limericks* (2–6). Illus. by Susan Meddaugh. 1992, Houghton Mifflin paper $5.95 (0-395-61616-6). 52pp. Forty-one humorous limericks with wacky drawings. (Rev: BL 3/15/89; SLJ 3/89) [811]

12113 Ciardi, John. *You Read to Me, I'll Read to You* (4–6). Illus. by Edward Gorey. 1987, HarperCollins paper $7.95 (0-06-446060-6). 64pp. A collection of original verse for both adults and children.

12114 Cole, William, ed. *Poem Stew* (2–6). Illus. by Karen Ann Weinhaus. 1981, HarperCollins $7.66 (0-397-31963-0); paper $4.95 (0-06-440136-7). 96pp. A collection of 57 witty poems about food.

12115 Cuetara, Mittie. *Baby Business* (PS–2). Illus. by author. 2003, Dutton $15.99 (0-525-47026-3). 29pp. Twenty-four short funny poems about babies are complemented by colorful illustrations. (Rev: HBG 10/03; SLJ 6/03) [811]

12116 Dakos, Kalli. *The Bug in Teacher's Coffee: And Other School Poems* (K–2). Illus. by Mike Reed. Series: An I Can Read Book. 1999, HarperCollins LB $14.89 (0-06-027940-0). 38pp. For beginning readers, a book of humorous poetry with zany illustrations that use everyday objects found in a school. (Rev: HBG 3/00; SLJ 12/99) [811]

12117 Florian, Douglas. *Bing Bang Boing* (4–6). Illus. 1994, Harcourt $16.00 (0-15-233770-9). 144pp. A lighthearted, imaginative collection of short, humorous verses. (Rev: BCCB 11/94; BL 12/1/94; SLJ 11/94) [811]

12118 Florian, Douglas. *Laugh-Eteria* (3–5). Illus. 1999, Harcourt $17.00 (0-15-202084-5). 158pp. A collection of 150 original, humorous poems that will appeal to a child's sometimes gross sense of humor. (Rev: BCCB 4/99; BL 3/15/99; HBG 10/99; SLJ 6/99) [811]

12119 Grandits, John. *Technically, It's Not My Fault: Concrete Poems* (4–6). Illus. by author. 2004, Clarion paper $5.95 (0-618-50361-7). Eleven-year-old Robert's unique — and sometimes gross — vision of the world around him is expressed in arresting poetry with an inventive presentation. (Rev: BL 12/15/04; SLJ 4/05) [811]

12120 Greenberg, David T. *Whatever Happened to Humpty Dumpty? And Other Surprising Sequels to Mother Goose Rhymes* (3–6). Illus. by S. D. Schindler. 1999, Little, Brown $14.95 (0-316-32767-0). An outrageous book of sequels to 20 Mother Goose rhymes in which, for example, Jack and Jill accidentally flush themselves down a toilet. (Rev: HBG 10/99; SLJ 8/99) [811]

12121 Greenfield, Eloise. *I Can Draw a Weeposaur and Other Dinosaurs* (K–3). Illus. by Jan S. Gilchrist. 2001, Greenwillow LB $14.89 (0-688-17635-6). 31pp. A group of poems about fanciful, imaginary dinosaurs along with drawings of them by the girl who dreamed them up. (Rev: HBG 10/01; SLJ 3/01) [811]

12122 Grimes, Nikki. *Is It Far to Zanzibar? Poems About Tanzania* (PS–3). Illus. by Betsy Lewin. 2000, Lothrop LB $15.89 (0-688-13158-1). 32pp. A series of rhyming, singsong verses that fancifully describe life in Tanzania. (Rev: BL 3/15/00; HBG 10/00; SLJ 5/00) [811]

12123 Horton, Joan. *I Brought My Rat for Show-and-Tell* (1–3). Trans. and illus. by Melanie Siegel. Series: All Aboard Poetry Reader Ser. 2004, Penguin Putnam LB $13.89 (0-448-43364-8). 48pp. The eye-catching cartoon illustrations and nonsensical rhyming poems in this collection will appeal to beginning readers. (Rev: BL 8/04; SLJ 10/04) [811]

12124 *I Invited a Dragon to Dinner: And Other Poems to Make You Laugh Out Loud* (PS–1). Illus. by Chris L. Demarest. 2002, Penguin Putnam $16.99 (0-399-23567-1). 40pp. A collection of silly poetry for preschoolers and young readers. (Rev: BL 3/15/02; HBG 10/02; SLJ 2/02) [811]

12125 Katz, Bobbi. *A Rumpus of Rhymes: A Book of Noisy Poems* (1–3). Illus. by Susan Estelle Kwas. 2001, Dutton $15.99 (0-525-46718-1). 32pp. Alliteration and onomatopoeia make for noisy, humorous poems of varying length and subject matter. (Rev: BL 9/1/01; HBG 3/02; SLJ 11/01) [811]

12126 Kennedy, X. J. *Uncle Switch: Loony Limericks* (1–3). Illus. by John O'Brien. 1997, Simon & Schuster $15.00 (0-689-80967-0). 32pp. Twenty-two funny limericks involving the dimwitted Uncle Switch. (Rev: BCCB 4/97; BL 5/1/97; SLJ 4/97) [811]

12127 Korman, Gordon, and Bernice Korman. *The D-Poems of Jeremy Bloom: A Collection of Poems About School, Homework, and Life (Sort of)* (4–6). 1992, Scholastic paper $3.50 (0-590-44819-6). 98pp. The engaging and funny poems of rambunctious sixth-grader Jeremy Bloom. (Rev: BL 1/15/93; SLJ 2/93) [811]

12128 Krensky, Stephen. *There Once Was a Very Odd School* (2–5). Illus. by Tamara Petrosino. 2004, Penguin Putnam $10.99 (0-525-46974-5). 40pp. Twenty-four limericks chronicle activities at a very unusual school, where there are no classes and food with a mind of its own. (Rev: BL 9/1/04; SLJ 8/04) [821]

12129 Lansky, Bruce, ed. *A Bad Case of the Giggles: Kids' Favorite Funny Poems* (2–5). Illus. by Stephen Carpenter. 1994, Meadowbrook $14.00 (0-88166-213-5). 132pp. A great collection of humorous poems that includes puns, tongue twisters, and parodies, many by well-known writers. (Rev: BL 11/15/94; SLJ 2/95) [811]

12130 Lansky, Bruce, ed. *Miles of Smiles: Kids Pick the Funniest Poems, Book 3* (2–6). Illus. by Stephen Carpenter. 1998, Meadowbrook $16.00 (0-88166-313-1). 115pp. A collection of 72 humorous poems some of them earthy in content and dealing with subjects such as underwear and bathroom humor. (Rev: HBG 3/99; SLJ 11/98) [811]

12131 Lansky, Bruce, ed. *Rolling in the Aisles: A Collection of Laugh-Out-Loud Poems* (3–6). Illus. by Stephen Carpenter. 2004, Meadowbrook $17.00 (0-88166-473-1). 115pp. Organized by kid-friendly topics, these poems — many by familiar authors and selected by young readers — are accompanied by large cartoons. (Rev: SLJ 1/05) [811]

12132 Lear, Edward. *Complete Nonsense Book of Edward Lear* (4–6). Illus. by author. 1951, Dover paper $7.95 (0-486-20167-8). 287pp. Verse, prose, drawings, alphabets, and other amusing absurdities.

12133 Lear, Edward. *Hilary Knight's "The Owl and the Pussy-Cat"* (PS–3). Illus. by Hilary Knight. 2001, Simon & Schuster $17.00 (0-689-83927-8). 40pp. Otto and Polly become the owl and the pussycat during a reading of the poem, in this reissue of a 1984 title. (Rev: BL 8/01; HBG 10/01) [821.914]

12134 Lear, Edward. *Nonsense!* (1–5). Illus. by Valorie Fisher. 2004, Simon & Schuster $16.95 (0-689-86380-2). Fifteen limericks are accompanied by

elaborate photographic illustrations full of humor. (Rev: SLJ 11/04) [821]

12135 Lear, Edward. *The Owl and the Pussycat* (PS–1). Illus. by Anne Wilson. 2003, Chronicle $15.95 (0-8118-3903-6). This appealing new edition of Lear's familiar poem has eye-catching illustrations in mixed media. (Rev: BL 5/15/03; HBG 10/03; SLJ 6/03) [811]

12136 Lear, Edward. *The Owl and the Pussycat* (PS–1). Illus. by Jan Brett. 1991, Penguin Putnam $15.95 (0-399-21925-0). 32pp. Beautiful double-page spreads enhance the enchantment of this retelling. (Rev: BL 3/1/91*; SLJ 2/91*) [821]

12137 Lear, Edward. *The Owl and the Pussycat* (PS–1). Illus. by James Marshall. 1998, Harper-Collins LB $15.89 (0-06-205011-7). 32pp. Fresh and funny artwork from James Marshall highlight this edition of the classic nonsense poem. (Rev: BL 2/1/99; HB 3–4/99; HBG 10/99; SLJ 12/98) [821]

12138 Lear, Edward. *Poetry for Young People* (3–5). Ed. by Edward Mendelson. Illus. by Huliska-Beit Laura. 2002, Sterling $14.95 (0-8069-3077-2). 48pp. An introduction to the limericks and poetry of Edward Lear. (Rev: BL 3/1/02; HBG 10/02) [821]

12139 Lear, Edward. *The Quangle Wangle's Hat* (PS–2). Illus. by Louise Voce. 2005, Candlewick $15.99 (0-7636-1289-8). 32pp. The Quangle Wangle, all alone in his tree, is glad when his giant hat becomes home to other animals as fanciful as he. (Rev: BL 3/1/05; SLJ 1/05) [811]

12140 Lee, Dennis. *The Ice Cream Store* (PS–3). Illus. by David McPhail. 1992, Scholastic $14.95 (0-590-45861-2). 64pp. A collection of sassy and bright poems, with occasional flashes of schoolyard humor. (Rev: BCCB 12/92; BL 11/15/92; SLJ 9/92*) [811]

12141 Lesynski, Loris. *Nothing Beats a Pizza* (3–6). Illus. by author. 2001, Annick LB $18.95 (1-55037-701-9); paper $7.95 (1-55037-700-0). 32pp. Lesynski's verses take a humorous approach to the serious topic of pizza. (Rev: HBG 3/02; SLJ 2/02) [811]

12142 McGough, Roger, ed. *Wicked Poems* (4–8). Illus. by Neal Layton. 2005, Bloomsbury paper $15.00 (0-7475-6195-8). 198pp. Misbehavior of varying degrees is displayed in this varied collection of poems accompanied by cartoons. (Rev: SLJ 1/05) [811]

12143 Morrison, Lillian. *I Scream, You Scream: A Feast of Food Rhymes* (3–5). Illus. 1997, August House $12.95 (0-87483-495-3). 96pp. Food is the subject of this humorous collection of rhymes, autograph-book verses, tongue twisters, and jokes. (Rev: BL 11/15/97; HBG 3/98; SLJ 11/97) [811]

12144 Mozz. *The Pearls of Wisdumb* (3–6). 2003, Goofy Guru $17.95 (0-9726130-0-5). 168pp. In this delightful collection of original nonsense poems, readers will find a bizarre assortment of characters and situations; titles include "Boomerang Bill and Boomerang Betty," "Lucky Escape," and "A Strange Spectacle." (Rev: SLJ 8/03)

12145 Opie, Iona, and Peter Opie, eds. *I Saw Esau: The Schoolchild's Pocket Book* (2–5). Illus. by Maurice Sendak. 1992, Candlewick $19.99 (1-

56402-046-0). 160pp. Schoolyard folk rhymes that are absurd, fierce, vulgar, and compelling. (Rev: BCCB 5/92*; BL 4/15/92*; SLJ 6/92*) [811]

12146 Paraskevas, Betty. *Junior Kroll and Company* (K–3). Illus. by Michael Paraskevas. 1994, Harcourt $13.95 (0-15-292855-3). 40pp. A mischievous, shrewd toddler has a series of adventures, like learning to waltz with Cousin Blanche. (Rev: BL 4/15/94; SLJ 5/94) [811]

12147 Perry, Andrea. *Here's What You Do When You Can't Find Your Shoe: Ingenious Inventions for Pesky Problems* (3–5). Illus. by Alan Snow. 2003, Simon & Schuster $16.95 (0-689-83067-X). 40pp. Humorous poems imagine the invention of such child-friendly innovations as a spray that will empty the family shopping cart of offensive vegetables and a leaf-eater to help with raking. (Rev: BL 4/1/03; HBG 10/03; SLJ 5/03) [811]

12148 Phinn, Gervase. *What I Like! Poems for the Very Young* (PS–K). Illus. by Jane Eccles. 2005, Child's Play paper $7.99 (1-904550-12-6). 32pp. A lively collection of amusing rhymes and illustrations about subjects close to young children's hearts. (Rev: BL 5/1/05) [811]

12149 *Poetry for Young People: Lewis Carroll* (3–5). Ed. by Edward Mendelson. Illus. 2001, Sterling $14.95 (0-8069-5541-4). 48pp. The poetry that is scattered throughout Lewis Carroll's books is collected here, including some of his nonsense creations like *Jabberwocky*. (Rev: BL 3/1/01; HBG 10/01; SLJ 3/01) [821]

12150 *A Poke in the I: A Collection of Concrete Poems* (3–8). Ed. by Paul B. Janeczko. Illus. by Chris Raschka. 2001, Candlewick $15.99 (0-7636-0661-8). 36pp. A collection of original humorous poems each of which takes a different shape on the page, for example, the poem about a popsicle is on a stick. (Rev: BL 3/15/01*; HB 7–8/01*; HBG 10/01) [811.008]

12151 Prelutsky, Jack. *Awful Ogre's Awful Day* (PS–3). Illus. by Paul O. Zelinsky. 2001, Greenwillow LB $15.89 (0-688-07779-X). 40pp. Humorous poems look at an ogre's daily routine — from breakfast to bedtime — with amusing illustrations. (Rev: BCCB 9/01; BL 10/15/01; HB 9–10/01; HBG 3/02; SLJ 9/01*) [811.54]

12152 Prelutsky, Jack. *It's Raining Pigs and Noodles* (PS–3). Illus. by James Stevenson. 2000, Greenwillow LB $17.89 (0-06-029195-8). 160pp. There are more than 100 nonsense rhymes in this delightful collection; scribbly drawings carry on the humor. (Rev: BCCB 10/00; BL 11/1/00; HBG 3/01; SLJ 11/00) [811]

12153 Prelutsky, Jack. *The New Kid on the Block: Poems* (3–6). Illus. by James Stevenson. 1984, Greenwillow $17.89 (0-688-02272-3). 160pp. A collection of over 100 humorous poems by this prolific master.

12154 Prelutsky, Jack. *Ride a Purple Pelican* (PS–2). Illus. by Garth Williams. 1986, Greenwillow $17.95 (0-688-04031-4). 64pp. New verses that sound like old favorites. (Rev: BL 10/1/86; HB 1–2/87; SLJ 11/86)

12155 Prelutsky, Jack. *The Sheriff of Rottenshot* (2–4). Illus. by Victoria Chess. 1982, Greenwillow $14.93 (0-688-00198-X). 32pp. A collection of the author's humorous poetry, with many a well-turned rhyme.

12156 Prelutsky, Jack. *Something Big Has Been Here* (4–6). Illus. by James Stevenson. 1990, Greenwillow $17.95 (0-688-06434-5). 160pp. A bountiful collection of witty poems. (Rev: BCCB 12/90; BL 9/1/90*; HB 11–12/90*; SLJ 10/90*) [811]

12157 Proimos, James. *If I Were in Charge the Rules Would Be Different* (3–5). Illus. 2002, Scholastic $16.95 (0-439-20864-5). 80pp. Playful poems about childhood, with humorous illustrations. (Rev: BL 5/15/02; HBG 10/02; SLJ 3/02) [811]

12158 Rash, Andy. *The Robots Are Coming* (2–5). Illus. 2000, Scholastic $15.95 (0-439-06306-X). 40pp. This collection of 16 original poems includes as subjects an abominable snowman, a werewolf, and the Loch Ness Monster. (Rev: BCCB 12/00; BL 11/15/00; HBG 3/01; SLJ 11/00) [811]

12159 *Recess, Rhyme, and Reason: A Collection of Poems About School* (3–6). Ed. by Patricia M. Stockland. Illus. by Sara Rojo Perez. 2004, Compass Point LB $22.60 (0-7565-0564-X). 32pp. This lighthearted anthology of poems about school is designed to entertain and to educate young readers about different poetry concepts. (Rev: BL 4/1/04; SLJ 6/04) [808.81]

12160 Shapiro, Karen Jo. *Because I Could Not Stop My Bike—and Other Poems* (3–6). Illus. by Matt Faulkner. 2003, Charlesbridge LB $15.95 (1-58089-035-0). 32pp. With apologies to the authors, Shapiro borrows rhymes and meters from 26 classic poems and transforms them for today's young readers. (Rev: HBG 4/04; SLJ 8/03) [811]

12161 Shields, Carol Diggory. *Almost Late to School and More School Poems* (1–3). Illus. by Paul Meisel. 2003, Penguin Putnam $15.99 (0-525-45743-7). 32pp. Humorous poems and vivid cartoon illustrations highlight a variety of elementary-school experiences. (Rev: BL 8/03; HBG 4/04; SLJ 8/03) [811]

12162 Silverstein, Shel. *Runny Babbit: A Billy Sook* (2–4). Illus. 2005, HarperCollins LB $18.89 (0-06-028404-8). 96pp. Runny Babbit and friends including Toe Jurtle and Goctor Doose feature in clever spoonerist poems. (Rev: BL 5/1/05; SLJ 4/05) [811]

12163 Smith, William J. *Around My Room* (PS–K). Illus. by Erik Blegvad. 2000, Farrar $16.00 (0-374-30406-8). 32pp. A collection of original humorous poems, many of which are delightful nonsense rhymes. (Rev: BL 2/1/00; HB 3–4/00; HBG 10/00; SLJ 4/00) [811]

12164 Smith, William J. *Laughing Time: Collected Nonsense* (3–5). Illus. by Fernando Krahn. 1990, Farrar paper $3.50 (0-374-44315-7). 176pp. New poems have been added to this satisfyingly silly collection. Revision of the 1980 edition. (Rev: BL 2/15/90; SLJ 3/91) [811]

12165 Soto, Gary. *Worlds Apart: Traveling with Fernie and Me* (4–6). Illus. by Greg Clarke. 2005, Penguin Putnam $14.99 (0-399-24218-X). 64pp.

Fernie and his best friend go on a globe-trotting adventure in this book composed of poems illustrated in black and white. (Rev: BL 3/15/05; SLJ 3/05) [811]

12166 Steinberg, David. *Grasshopper Pie and Other Poems* (K–2). Illus. by Adrian C. Sinnott. Series: All Aboard Poetry Reader Ser. 2004, Grosset LB $13.89 (0-448-43491-1); paper $3.99 (0-448-43347-8). 48pp. Nonsense poetry with bouncy illustrations is full of arresting rhymes. (Rev: BL 7/04; SLJ 10/04) [811]

12167 Tripp, Wallace, ed. *A Great Big Ugly Man Came Up and Tied His Horse to Me: A Book of Nonsense Verse* (K–3). Illus. by Wallace Tripp. 1974, Little, Brown LB $14.95 (0-316-85280-5). 48pp. The hilarious drawings that accompany this selection of nonsense verses make this an especially entertaining book.

12168 Turner, Steve. *Dad, You're Not Funny and Other Poems* (3–5). Illus. by David Mostyn. 2000, Lion $16.95 (0-7459-4024-2). 96pp. A collection of humorous light verse from this well-known English writer. (Rev: BL 9/15/03; HBG 4/04; SLJ 11/00) [821]

12169 Westcott, Nadine Bernard. *The Lady with the Alligator Purse* (PS–1). Illus. by author. 1988, Little, Brown paper $4.95 (0-316-93136-5). The lady with the alligator purse chooses pizza instead of penicillin in this jump-rope rhyme. (Rev: BL 3/15/88; HB 5–6/88; HBG 4/04)

12170 Westcott, Nadine Bernard, ed. *Never Take a Pig to Lunch and Other Poems About the Fun of Eating* (PS–3). Illus. 1994, Orchard $18.95 (0-531-06834-X). 64pp. A collection of poems — mostly humorous, many nonsensical — about the joy and crises caused by eating. (Rev: BCCB 6/94; BL 2/1/94; HB 5–6/94; SLJ 3/94*) [811]

12171 Wheeler, Lisa. *Wool Gathering: A Sheep Family Reunion* (PS–3). Illus. by Frank Ansley. 2001, Simon & Schuster $16.00 (0-689-84369-0). 32pp. A fuzzy family reunion provides plenty of characters for this collection of hilarious poems about sheep. (Rev: BL 11/1/01; HBG 3/02; SLJ 10/01) [811]

12172 Whitehead, Jenny. *Lunch Box Mail and Other Poems* (2–4). Illus. 2001, Holt $16.95 (0-8050-6259-9). 48pp. Everyday life and experiences are captured in this collection of poems that emphasizes the humorous side of life. (Rev: BL 4/1/01; HBG 3/02; SLJ 10/01) [811]

Native Americans

12173 Bruchac, Joseph, and Jonathan London. *Thirteen Moons on Turtle's Back: A Native American Year of Moons* (1–5). Illus. by Thomas Locker. 1992, Penguin Putnam $16.99 (0-399-22141-7). 32pp. For each of the 13 moon cycles in a year, this book contains a poem and an oil painting illustrating it. (Rev: BL 3/1/92; SLJ 7/92) [811.54]

12174 Longfellow, Henry Wadsworth. *The Song of Hiawatha* (3–10). Illus. by Margaret Early. 2003,

Handprint $16.95 (1-59354-002-7). A beautifully illustrated edition of the epic poem that traces the eventful life of the Native American leader. (Rev: HBG 4/04; SLJ 1/04) [811]

12175 Pollock, Penny. *When the Moon Is Full: A Lunar Year* (K–3). Illus. by Mary Azarian. 2001, Little, Brown $15.95 (0-316-71317-1). 32pp. Native American names for the moon are the subject of this book of graceful poems illustrated by Caldecott winner Mary Azarian. (Rev: BL 11/1/01; HBG 3/02; SLJ 9/01) [811]

12176 Sneve, Virginia Driving Hawk, ed. *Dancing Teepees: Poems of American Indian Youth* (3–8). Illus. by Stephen Gammell. 1989, Holiday House LB $16.95 (0-8234-0724-1); paper $8.95 (0-8234-0879-5). 32pp. A collection of traditional tribal prayers, songs, and short poems. (Rev: BCCB 5/89; BL 5/15/89; SLJ 6/89)

Nature and the Seasons

12177 Alarcon, Francisco X. *Angels Ride Bikes and Other Fall Poems: Los Angeles Andan en Bicicleta y Otros Poems de Otono* (K–3). Illus. by Maya Christina Gonzalez. 1999, Children's Book Pr. $15.95 (0-89239-160-X). 32pp. Twenty poems written in English and Spanish tell about the fall season in Los Angeles. (Rev: BL 12/1/99; HBG 3/00; SLJ 10/99) [811.54]

12178 Alarcon, Francisco X. *Iguanas in the Snow and Other Winter Poems / Iguanas en la Nieve y Otros Poemas de Invierno* (1–3). Illus. by Maya Christina Gonzalez. 2001, Children's Book Pr. $15.95 (0-89239-168-5). 32pp. A collection of poems about the beauty of winter in northern California, in Spanish and English. (Rev: BL 10/1/01; HBG 3/02; SLJ 8/01) [811]

12179 Asch, Frank. *Cactus Poems* (3–6). Illus. by Ted Levin. 1998, Harcourt $18.00 (0-15-200676-1). 48pp. A poet and a nature photographer combine talents to explore the desert and the animals and plants that live there. (Rev: BL 3/15/98; HBG 10/98; SLJ 6/98) [811]

12180 Baird, Audrey B. *A Cold Snap! Frosty Poems* (2–5). Illus. by Patrick O'Brien. 2002, Boyds Mills $15.95 (1-56397-633-1). 32pp. Effective poems and illustrations capture winter's chill. (Rev: BL 9/15/02; HBG 3/03; SLJ 12/02) [811.54]

12181 Baird, Audrey B. *Storm Coming!* (2–4). Illus. by Patrick O'Brien. 2001, Boyds Mills $15.95 (1-56397-887-3). 32pp. Twenty-two original poems explore the nature and effects of storms from many points of view. (Rev: BL 3/15/01; HBG 10/01) [811]

12182 Bishop, Rudine Sims, comp. *Wonders: The Best Children's Poems of Effie Lee Newsome* (K–3). Illus. by Lois Mailou Jones. 1999, Boyds Mills paper $8.95 (1-56397-825-3). 40pp. A collection of original nature poems by Effie Lee Newsome that were published 60 years ago and were long out of print. (Rev: BCCB 2/00; HBG 3/00; SLJ 4/00) [811]

12183 Brenner, Barbara, ed. *The Earth Is Painted Green: A Garden of Poems About Our Planet* (3–5). Illus. by S. D. Schindler. 1994, Scholastic $16.95 (0-590-45134-0). 96pp. An excellent collection of poetry about nature and the environment that includes many by contemporary poets but also old favorites like "Daffodils." (Rev: BL 1/15/94; SLJ 4/94) [808.81]

12184 Buchanan, Ken, and Debby Buchanan. *It Rained on the Desert Today* (2–4). Illus. by Libba Tracy. 1994, Northland LB $14.95 (0-87358-575-5). 32pp. A rainstorm in the desert is evoked in free verse and evocative watercolors. (Rev: BL 10/15/94; SLJ 8/94) [811]

12185 Cameron, Eileen. *Canyon* (3–5). Illus. by Michael Collier. 2002, Mikaya $16.95 (1-931414-03-3). 32pp. Water flows from mountains to rivers to a canyon in this poetic book illustrated with striking photographs of nature. (Rev: BL 5/15/02; HBG 10/02; SLJ 5/02) [811]

12186 Cyrus, Kurt. *Oddhopper Opera: A Bug's Garden of Verses* (3–5). Illus. 2001, Harcourt $16.00 (0-15-202205-8). 32pp. A variety of garden creatures are featured in both the art and the poems in this original collection. (Rev: BL 3/15/01; HBG 10/01) [811]

12187 Esbensen, Barbara J. *Swing Around the Sun* (K–3). Illus. 2003, Carolrhoda LB $16.95 (0-87614-143-2). 48pp. The seasons are the focus of this collection that is illustrated by four well-known artists. (Rev: HBG 10/03; SLJ 3/03) [811]

12188 Florian, Douglas. *Autumnblings: Poems and Paintings* (2–5). Illus. by author. 2003, Greenwillow LB $16.89 (0-06-009279-3). 48pp. Rhyming verse, creative word play, and lovely illustrations bring autumn to life. (Rev: HB 11–12/03; HBG 4/04; SLJ 10/03) [811]

12189 Florian, Douglas. *Summersaults* (K–4). Illus. 2002, HarperCollins LB $15.89 (0-06-029268-7). 48pp. The freedom and beauty of summer are evoked in this collection of short, rhymed poems with playful pictures. (Rev: BCCB 5/02; BL 4/1/02; HB 7–8/02; HBG 10/02; SLJ 5/02*) [811]

12190 Florian, Douglas. *Winter Eyes* (K–4). Illus. 1999, Greenwillow $16.00 (0-688-16458-7). 48pp. A series of short, quiet poems that show the effects of winter on a small child. (Rev: BCCB 11/99; BL 11/1/99; HB 11–12/99; HBG 3/00; SLJ 9/99) [811.54]

12191 Franco, Betsy. *Mathematickles!* (2–5). Illus. by Steven Salerno. 2003, Simon & Schuster $17.95 (0-689-84357-7). Word- and math-play results in such delightful equations as "feet - shoes + grass = barefoot!" (Rev: BL 5/15/03; HB 7–8/03; HBG 10/03; SLJ 6/03) [811]

12192 Frank, John. *A Chill in the Air: Nature Poems for Fall and Winter* (K–3). Illus. by Mike Reed. 2003, Simon & Schuster $15.95 (0-689-83923-5). Poems celebrate the chills and wonders of the fall and winter seasons. (Rev: HBG 4/04; SLJ 9/03) [811]

12193 Geis, Jacqueline. *Where the Buffalo Roam* (PS–3). Illus. 1992, Ideals LB $14.00 (0-8249-8584-

2). 32pp. With illustrations and verses to the familiar cowboy tune, the American Southwest is celebrated. (Rev: BL 11/15/92; SLJ 1/93) [811]

12194 George, Kristine O'Connell. *The Great Frog Race and Other Poems* (4–6). Illus. by Kate Kiesler. 1997, Clarion $15.00 (0-395-77607-4). 40pp. A richly atmospheric picture book that captures some of the outdoor activities of children, including watching captured frogs race. (Rev: BCCB 6/97; BL 3/15/97*; SLJ 4/97*) [811]

12195 George, Kristine O'Connell. *Old Elm Speaks: Tree Poems* (2–6). Illus. by Kate Kiesler. 1998, Clarion $15.00 (0-395-87611-7). 48pp. A collection of original poems that celebrates every wonderful aspect of trees. (Rev: BL 9/1/98*; HBG 3/99; SLJ 9/98) [811]

12196 George, Kristine O'Connell. *Toasting Marshmallows: Camping Poems* (2–6). Illus. 2001, Clarion $15.00 (0-395-04597-X). 32pp. A family's camping trip is the subject of this collection of original poems that express different moods and celebrate the wonders of the wilderness. (Rev: BL 3/15/01*) [811]

12197 Harrison, David L. *Wild Country* (4–6). Illus. 1999, Boyds Mills $14.95 (1-56397-784-2). 48pp. A collection of original nature poems that celebrates such natural wonders as butterflies, mountains, and forests. (Rev: BL 11/15/99; HBG 3/00; SLJ 12/99) [811]

12198 Hazeltine, Alice I., and Elva Smith, eds. *The Year Around: Poems for Children* (4–6). Illus. by Paula Hutchison. 1973, Ayer $18.95 (0-8369-6403-9). A collection of seasonal poems.

12199 Highwater, Jamake. *Songs for the Seasons* (PS–4). Illus. by Sandra Speidel. 1995, Lothrop LB $14.93 (0-688-10659-0). 32pp. A gentle look at the changes that occur with plants and animals during the cycle of the four seasons. (Rev: BL 4/15/95; SLJ 4/95) [811]

12200 Hines, Anna Grossnickle. *Pieces: A Year in Poems and Quilts* (K–4). Illus. 2001, Greenwillow LB $15.89 (0-688-16964-3). 32pp. Intricate quilting squares illustrate these poems that deal with each of the seasons. (Rev: BCCB 2/01; BL 1/1–15/01*; HBG 10/01; SLJ 3/01) [811]

12201 Hopkins, Lee Bennett, ed. *Small Talk: A Book of Short Poems* (2–4). Illus. by Susan Gaber. 1995, Harcourt $14.00 (0-15-276577-8). 48pp. Short poems by distinguished authors are arranged according to seasonal changes. (Rev: BCCB 5/95; BL 8/95; HB 5–6/95; SLJ 5/95*) [811]

12202 Hubbell, Patricia. *Black Earth, Gold Sun* (2–6). 2001, Marshall Cavendish $15.95 (0-7614-5090-4). 32pp. Watercolor illustrations echo the sentiments of these poems about the delights of a garden. (Rev: BL 9/15/01; HBG 3/02; SLJ 11/01) [811.54]

12203 Hundal, Nancy. *Prairie Summer* (3–5). Illus. 1999, Fitzhenry & Whiteside $16.95 (1-55041-403-8). 32pp. A poem, illustrated with impressionistic paintings, that depicts life on the prairie. (Rev: BL 11/1/99) [813.54]

12204 *Imaginary Gardens: American Poetry and Art for Young People* (3–7). Illus. by Charles Sullivan. 1989, Abrams $19.95 (0-8109-1130-2). 111pp. A number of garden poems are matched with beautiful color reproductions of famous paintings. (Rev: HB 1–2/90; SLJ 2/90) [811]

12205 Johnston, Tony. *An Old Shell: Poems of the Galapagos* (3–6). Illus. 1999, Farrar $15.00 (0-374-35648-3). 64pp. The 34 original poems in this collection chronicle the author's trip to the Galapagos Islands. (Rev: BCCB 10/99; BL 12/1/99; SLJ 10/99) [811]

12206 Katz, Susan. *Looking for Jaguar: And Other Rain Forest Poems* (2–4). Illus. by Lee Christiansen. 2005, Greenwillow LB $16.89 (0-06-029793-X). 40pp. Nineteen poems introduce the flora and fauna of the world's rain forests; supplementary features include an essay about the importance of these habitats and a compilation of relevant facts and figures. (Rev: BL 2/15/05; SLJ 3/05) [811]

12207 Levy, Constance. *Splash! Poems of Our Watery World* (3–6). Illus. by David Soman. 2002, Scholastic $16.95 (0-439-29318-9). 48pp. A charming collection of 34 poems about water, its characteristics, and its uses. (Rev: BCCB 6/02; BL 4/1/02; HB 7–8/02; HBG 10/02; SLJ 5/02) [811]

12208 Lewis, J. Patrick. *Earth and Us — Continuous: Nature's Past and Future* (K–3). Illus. by Christopher Canyon. Series: Sharing Nature with Children. 2001, Dawn $16.95 (1-58469-024-0); paper $7.95 (1-58469-023-2). 32pp. A book of attractively illustrated poems about the wonders of the earth and our responsibility to care for it. (Rev: BL 9/1/01; HBG 3/02) [550]

12209 Livingston, Myra Cohn. *A Circle of Seasons* (3–5). Illus. by Leonard Everett Fisher. 1982, Holiday House paper $5.95 (0-8234-0656-3). 32pp. A group of poems that brings the seasons to life.

12210 Livingston, Myra Cohn. *Up in the Air* (3–5). Illus. by Leonard Everett Fisher. 1989, Holiday House LB $14.95 (0-8234-0736-5). 32pp. A celebration of flight begins as an airliner takes off. (Rev: BCCB 5/89; BL 5/15/89)

12211 Merriam, Eve. *The Singing Green: New and Selected Poems for All Seasons* (3–7). Illus. by Kathleen C. Howell. 1992, Morrow $14.00 (0-688-11025-8). 112pp. The wordplay romps and frolics in this celebration of sun, trees, and the child in us all. (Rev: BCCB 2/93; BL 12/1/92; HB 1–2/93; SLJ 12/92) [811]

12212 Moore, Lillian. *Adam Mouse's Book of Poems* (2–5). Illus. by Kathleen G. McCord. 1992, Macmillan $12.95 (0-689-31765-4). 48pp. Poems from the natural world, written by a country mouse. (Rev: BCCB 3/93; BL 9/15/92; SLJ 10/92) [811]

12213 Mora, Pat. *The Desert Is My Mother / El Desierto Es Mi Madre* (PS–3). Illus. by Daniel Lechon. 1994, Arte Publico $14.95 (1-55885-121-6). 32pp. In this bilingual book of poems, everyday life in the desert is seen through the eyes of a child. (Rev: BL 1/15/95) [811]

12214 Mora, Pat. *This Big Sky* (K–2). Illus. by Steve Jenkins. 1998, Scholastic $15.95 (0-590-37120-7).

32pp. Through poems and dynamic illustrations, the spirit and beauty of the American Southwest are captured. (Rev: BCCB 4/98; BL 2/15/98; HBG 10/98; SLJ 7/98) [811]

12215 Nicholls, Judith, comp. *The Sun in Me: Poems About the Planet* (1–4). Illus. by Beth Krommes. 2003, Barefoot $16.99 (1-84148-058-4). 40pp. An anthology of poems from different places and times that celebrate nature. (Rev: HBG 10/03; SLJ 3/03) [811]

12216 Paolilli, Paul, and Dan Brewer. *Silver Seeds* (K–2). Illus. by Lou Fancher and Steve Johnson. 2001, Viking $15.99 (0-670-88941-5). 32pp. In each of these 15 nature poems the first letters of each line spell out the name of the poem. (Rev: BL 12/15/00; HBG 10/01) [811.6]

12217 Peters, Lisa Westberg. *Earthshake: Poems from the Ground Up* (2–4). Illus. by Cathie Felstead. 2003, HarperCollins LB $17.89 (0-06-029266-0). 32pp. Twenty-two poems exploring various aspects of earth science — including fossils, tectonic plates, lava, and strata — are accompanied by relevant collages in this large-format book. (Rev: BL 11/15/03; HBG 4/04; SLJ 9/03) [811]

12218 Powell, Consie. *Amazing Apples* (PS–4). Illus. by author. 2003, Whitman LB $14.95 (0-8075-0399-1). Simple acrostic poems follow an apple orchard through the seasons. (Rev: HBG 4/04; SLJ 10/03) [811]

12219 Prelutsky, Jack. *Dog Days: Rhymes Around the Year* (PS–K). Illus. by Dyanna Wolcott. 1999, Knopf LB $16.00 (0-375-80104-3). 32pp. In these 12 original poems, one for each month, a dog reveals his favorite activities in each season. (Rev: BL 11/1/99) [811]

12220 Rickey, Ann Heiskell. *Bugs and Critters I Have Known* (3–6). Illus. by Ardeane Heiskell Smith. 1998, Old Canyon $12.95 (0-9667834-1-7). 93pp. Illustrated with pen-and-ink drawings, this humorous collection of original poems deals mainly with insects. (Rev: SLJ 6/99) [811]

12221 Roemer, Heidi. *Come to My Party: And Other Shape Poems* (PS–3). Trans. and illus. by Hideko Takahashi. 2004, Holt $17.95 (0-8050-6620-9). 32pp. Organized by season, this collection of brief poems explores common experiences and introduces interesting sounds and shapes. (Rev: BL 6/1–15/04; HB 5–6/04; SLJ 5/04) [811]

12222 Rogasky, Barbara. *Winter Poems* (3–6). Illus. by Trina S. Hyman. 1994, Scholastic $15.95 (0-590-42872-1). 40pp. An anthology of poems that deal with winter around the world and activities associated with it. (Rev: BCCB 1/95; BL 9/15/94; HB 11–12/94; SLJ 10/94*) [811]

12223 *Sea Dream: Poems from Under the Waves* (2–5). Ed. by Nikki Siegen-Smith. Illus. by Joel Stewart. 2002, Barefoot $16.99 (1-84148-905-0). 40pp. An absorbing anthology of 26 poems about sea creatures both real and imagined. (Rev: BL 10/15/02; HBG 3/03; SLJ 12/02) [808.81]

12224 Sidman, Joyce. *Just Us Two: Poems About Animal Dads* (1–4). Illus. by Susan Swan. 2000, Millbrook LB $22.90 (0-7613-1563-2). Using double-page illustrations, this book of 11 original poems is about different fathers in the animal world. (Rev: HBG 3/01; SLJ 12/00) [811]

12225 Sidman, Joyce. *Song of the Waterboatman and Other Pond Poems* (3–5). Illus. by Becky Prange. 2005, Houghton Mifflin $16.00 (0-618-13547-2). 32pp. Poems that teach about the ecology of a pond are accompanied by woodcut illustrations. (Rev: BL 3/15/05) [811]

12226 Singer, Marilyn. *How to Cross a Pond: Poems About Water* (3–5). Illus. by Meilo So. 2003, Knopf LB $16.99 (0-375-82376-X). 48pp. Water — in all its many forms — is the common theme running through the varied poems in this appealing collection. (Rev: BL 8/03; HBG 4/04; SLJ 8/03) [811]

12227 Updike, John. *A Child's Calendar* (3–5). Illus. by Trina S. Hyman. 1999, Holiday House $16.95 (0-8234-1445-0). 32pp. Updike has written a poem for each month, depicting seasonal activities of a multiracial family in rural New Hampshire. (Rev: BCCB 3/00; BL 9/1/99; HBG 3/00; SLJ 9/99) [811]

12228 Whipple, Laura, comp. *A Snowflake Fell: Poems About Winter* (PS–3). Illus. by Hatsuki Hori. 2003, Barefoot $16.99 (1-84148-033-9). 40pp. Beautifully illustrated, this anthology includes diverse poems about winter by poets including Douglas Florian, Nancy Wood, James Whitcomb Riley, and Marilyn Singer. (Rev: HBG 4/04; SLJ 11/03) [811]

12229 Windham, Sophie. *The Mermaid and Other Sea Poems* (3–5). Illus. 1996, Scholastic $16.95 (0-590-20898-5). 32pp. Sea creatures from mermaids to fish are featured in 18 poems by well-known writers. (Rev: BL 2/1/96; SLJ 5/96) [821]

12230 Yolen, Jane. *Color Me a Rhyme: Nature Poems for Young People* (4–6). Illus. 2000, Boyds Mills $15.95 (1-56397-892-X). 32pp. Using related photos as illustrations, these poems each evoke a particular color in nature. (Rev: BL 10/15/00*; HBG 3/01; SLJ 12/00) [811.54]

12231 Yolen, Jane, sel. *Once Upon Ice: And Other Frozen Poems* (4–8). 1997, Boyds Mills $17.95 (1-56397-408-8). A collection of 17 poems inspired by photographs of ice formations, which are also included. (Rev: BL 2/1/97; SLJ 3/97) [811]

12232 Yolen, Jane. *Snow, Snow: Winter Poems for Children* (2–5). Illus. by Jason Stemple. 1998, Boyds Mills $16.95 (1-56397-721-4). 32pp. Inspired by photographs of snow scenes, these original poems depict occurrences and express various moods involving winter landscapes and activities. (Rev: BCCB 10/98; BL 11/15/98; HBG 3/99; SLJ 12/98) [811.5]

12233 Zolotow, Charlotte. *Seasons* (1–3). Illus. by Erik Blegvad. 2002, HarperCollins LB $14.89 (0-06-026699-6). 64pp. A collection of poems that take children through the four seasons in this alluring book for beginning readers. (Rev: BL 2/1/02; HBG 10/02; SLJ 6/02) [811]

Sports

12234 Burg, Brad. *Outside the Lines: Poetry at Play* (PS–4). Illus. by Rebecca Gibbon. 2002, Penguin Putnam $15.99 (0-399-23446-2). 32pp. The words work with the illustrations to create visual movement in this book of verse about children's activities. (Rev: BL 3/15/02; HBG 10/02; SLJ 3/02) [811]

12235 Burleigh, Robert. *Hoops* (4–8). Illus. 1997, Harcourt $16.00 (0-15-201450-0). A poem that expresses the joy, exhilaration, and excitement of basketball, as seen from the players' point of view. (Rev: BL 11/15/97*; HBG 3/98; SLJ 11/97*) [811]

12236 Greenfield, Eloise. *For the Love of the Game: Michael Jordan and Me* (PS–4). Illus. by Jan S. Gilchrist. 1997, HarperCollins LB $15.89 (0-06-027299-6). 32pp. The basketball moves made by Michael Jordan are used as a metaphor for the game of life in this inspiring poem. (Rev: BCCB 3/97; BL 2/15/97; HB 3–4/97; SLJ 3/97) [811]

12237 Hopkins, Lee Bennett, ed. *Extra Innings: Baseball Poems* (4–6). Illus. by Scott Medlock. 1993, Harcourt $16.00 (0-15-226833-2). 48pp. Nineteen poems about baseball. (Rev: BL 3/15/93; SLJ 4/93) [811]

12238 Hopkins, Lee Bennett, ed. *Opening Days: Sports Poems* (3–6). Illus. by Scott Medlock. 1996, Harcourt $16.00 (0-15-200270-7). 48pp. There are 18 poems in this collection dealing with a variety of sports, each accompanied by a full-page painting. (Rev: BL 2/15/96; HB 5–6/96; SLJ 5/96) [811]

12239 Korman, Gordon, and Bernice Korman. *The Last-Place Sports Poems of Jeremy Bloom: A Collection of Poems About Winning, Losing, and Being a Good Sport (Sometimes)* (3–6). 1996, Scholastic paper $3.99 (0-590-25516-9). 92pp. A book that explores the world of sports by using different kinds of poetry, from haiku to narrative verse. (Rev: SLJ 4/97) [811]

12240 Morrison, Lillian, ed. *At the Crack of the Bat* (4–6). Illus. by Steve Cieslawski. 1992, Little, Brown LB $15.49 (1-56282-177-6). 64pp. Full-color paintings add to the hero-loving glory of this all-American sport. (Rev: BCCB 5/92; BL 8/92; SLJ 6/92) [811]

12241 Smith, Charles R. *Diamond Life: Baseball Sights, Sounds, and Swings* (1–4). Illus. 2004, Scholastic $14.95 (0-439-43180-8). 32pp. Brightly illustrated, the poems — some of them cleverly shaped — in this collection celebrate baseball and its players. (Rev: BL 3/1/04; SLJ 3/04) [796.357]

12242 Smith, Charles R. *Hoop Kings* (4–7). Illus. 2004, Candlewick $14.99 (0-7636-1423-8). 40pp. This celebration of basketball, presented in a blend of rap-style poetry with eye-catching photographs, focuses on 12 of the biggest stars. (Rev: BL 2/15/04; SLJ 3/04) [811]

12243 Smith, Charles R. *Hoop Queens* (3–6). Illus. 2003, Candlewick $14.99 (0-7636-1422-X). 40pp. Lively rap-style tributes honor 12 of basketball's

WNBA stars. (Rev: BL 8/03; HBG 4/04; SLJ 9/03) [811]

12244 *Sports! Sports! Sports! A Poetry Collection* (1–3). Ed. by Lee Bennett Hopkins. Illus. by Brian Floca. 1999, HarperCollins LB $14.89 (0-06-027801-3). 48pp. The thrills and excitement of sports activities are captured in this collection of poems by several authors, including the editor. (Rev: BCCB 2/99; BL 4/1/99; HB 1–2/99; HBG 10/99; SLJ 3/99) [811]

12245 Thayer, Ernest Lawrence. *Casey at the Bat* (2–6). Illus. by LeRoy Neiman. 2002, HarperCollins $19.95 (0-06-009068-5). 96pp. The famous baseball poem, illustrated in a bold, striking manner; with an introduction by Jose Torre. (Rev: BCCB 1/01*; BL 9/1/02) [811]

12246 Thayer, Ernest Lawrence. *Ernest L. Thayer's Casey at the Bat: A Ballad of the Republic Sung in the Year 1888* (K–3). Illus. by Christopher Bing. 2000, Handprint $17.95 (1-929766-00-9). 32pp. Fictional clippings and scratchboard engravings are used as illustrations to give an actual-event atmosphere to this poem about Casey's terrible defeat at bat. (Rev: BCCB 1/01*; BL 2/15/01; HB 3–4/01; HBG 10/01; SLJ 1/01) [811.5]

Plays

General

12247 Birch, Beverley. *Shakespeare's Stories: Histories* (5–8). Illus. 1988, Bedrick paper $6.95 (0-87226-226-X). 126pp. Retelling the classic stories of Shakespeare. (Rev: BL 2/15/89; SLJ 2/89) [813.54]

12248 Birch, Beverley. *Shakespeare's Stories: Tragedies* (5–8). Illus. 1988, Bedrick paper $6.95 (0-87226-227-8). 126pp. Retelling the great tragedies. (Rev: BL 2/15/89; SLJ 2/89) [813.54]

12249 Birch, Beverley. *Shakespeare's Tales* (5–8). Illus. by Stephen Lambert. 2002, Hodder $22.95 (0-340-79725-8). 126pp. This appealing and accessible large-format book introduces modern teens to the plots and language of four Shakespeare plays — *Hamlet, Othello, Antony and Cleopatra,* and *The Tempest.* (Rev: BL 1/1–15/03; SLJ 4/03) [823.914]

12250 Bruchac, Joseph. *Pushing Up the Sky: Seven Native American Plays for Children* (2–6). Illus. 2000, Dial $17.99 (0-8037-2168-4). 96pp. Several folktales from Native American cultures are adapted into simple plays that are easily produced. (Rev: BCCB 2/00; BL 3/1/00; HBG 10/00; SLJ 3/00) [812]

12251 Burkholder, Kelly. *Plays* (2–5). Series: Artistic Adventures. 2001, Rourke LB $21.27 (1-57103-357-2). 24pp. Details on putting on a play are given including material on writing scripts, costumes, props, characters, and using voice and movement. (Rev: SLJ 2/01) [792]

12252 Butterfield, Moira. *Hansel and Gretel* (2–4). Photos by Trever Clifford. Illus. by Frances Cony. Series: Playtales. 1997, Heinemann $19.92 (1-57572-648-3). 24pp. Contains the script of a play based on this folktale plus direction on how to stage it, from casting and making props to the actual performance. Also use *Sleeping Beauty* (1997). (Rev: BL 4/1/04; HB 3–4/04; HBG 3/98; SLJ 2/98) [809]

12253 Butterfield, Moira. *Little Red Riding Hood* (2–4). Photos by Trever Clifford. Illus. by Frances Cony. Series: Playtales. 1997, Heinemann $19.92 (1-57572-650-5). 24pp. Provides a script based on this fairy tale, as well as a list of parts, directions for production of the play, and instructions for making costumes and sets. Also use *Puss-in-Boots* (1997). (Rev: HBG 3/98; SLJ 3/98) [809]

12254 Carlson, Lori Marie, ed. *You're On! Seven Plays in English and Spanish* (3–7). Illus. 1999, Morrow $17.00 (0-688-16237-1). 144pp. These plays by authors including Federico Garcia Lorca, Pura Belpre, and Gary Soto offer a range of styles suitable for young cast members. (Rev: BCCB 9/99; BL 10/1/99; HBG 4/04; SLJ 10/99) [812.008]

12255 Dahl, Roald. *James and the Giant Peach: A Play* (3–5). 1983, Puffin paper $4.99 (0-14-031464-4). 128pp. A condensed version of the story about James, who has fantastic adventures.

12256 Early, Margaret, and William Shakespeare. *Romeo and Juliet* (4–8). Illus. 1998, Abrams $18.95 (0-8109-3799-9). A retelling in prose, illustrated with paintings in the style of Italian Renaissance art. (Rev: BL 5/1/98; BR 11–12/98; HBG 9/98; SLJ 6/98) [822]

12257 Fredericks, Anthony D. *Tadpole Tales and Other Totally Terrific Treats for Readers Theatre* (4–8). 1997, Libraries Unlimited paper $23.00 (1-56308-547-X). 139pp. A delightful collection of scripts for young performers that are spin-offs from folktales, fables, and nursery rhymes. (Rev: BL 3/1/98) [372.67]

12258 Garfield, Leon. *Shakespeare Stories* (5–9). Illus. 1991, Houghton Mifflin $26.00 (0-395-56397-6). Modern retellings of 12 of Shakespeare's most popular plays. (Rev: BL 1/1/86) [822.3]

12259 Gerke, Pamela. *Multicultural Plays for Children Grades K–3* (K–3). 1996, Smith & Kraus paper $19.95 (1-57525-005-5). 159pp. Ten entertaining plays, each of which deals with a different racial group. Also use volume 2 (1996), which contains ten plays for grades four to six. (Rev: BL 12/1/96; SLJ 9/96) [812]

12260 Jennings, Coleman A., and Aurand Harris, eds. *Plays Children Love, Volume II: A Treasury of Contemporary and Classic Plays for Children* (5–8). Illus. by Susan Swan. 1988, St. Martin's $19.95 (0-312-01490-2). 512pp. A group of 20 plays requiring royalties based on such stories as Charlotte's Web, The Wizard of Oz, and The Wind in the Willows. [812.00809282]

12261 Kahle, Peter V. T. *Shakespeare's The Tempest: A Prose Narrative* (5–8). Illus. by Barbara Nickerson. 1999, Seventy Fourth Street $22.95 (0-9655702-2-3). 96pp. An illustrated retelling of Shakespeare's play that uses much of its dialogue. (Rev: SLJ 1/00) [822.3]

12262 Kamerman, Sylvia, ed. *The Big Book of Large-Cast Plays: 27 One-Act Plays for Young Actors* (5–10). 1994, Plays $12.95 (0-8238-0302-3). Thirty short plays on varied subjects, arranged according to audience appeal. (Rev: BL 3/15/95) [812]

12263 Kamerman, Sylvia, ed. *Great American Events on Stage: 15 Plays to Celebrate America's Past* (5–8). 1996, Plays paper $15.95 (0-8238-0305-8). A collection of short plays, each of which revolves around a single incident or individual important in U.S. history. (Rev: BR 5–6/97; SLJ 5/97) [812]

12264 Kamerman, Sylvia E., ed. *Thirty Plays from Favorite Stories: Royalty-Free Dramatizations of Myths, Folktales, and Legends from Around the World* (2–4). 1997, Plays paper $15.95 (0-8238-0306-6). 291pp. Thirty short plays based loosely on folktales from around the world. (Rev: SLJ 12/97) [809]

12265 Kohl, MaryAnn F. *Making Make-Believe: Fun Props, Costumes, and Creative Play Ideas* (PS–4). 1999, Gryphon paper $14.95 (0-87659-198-5). 191pp. Using simple materials, this book supplies ideas for creating 138 different make-believe situations or plays. (Rev: SLJ 10/99) [809]

12266 McCullough, L. E. *"Now I Get It!" Vol. I: 12 Ten-Minute Classroom Drama Skits for Science, Math, Language, and Social Studies* (4–6). Series: Now I Get It! 2001, Smith & Kraus $11.95 (1-57525-161-2). 136pp. In addition to these 12 curriculum-related skits, there are before and after activities, discussion questions, and staging suggestions. Also use *"Now Get It Right!" Volume II* (2001). (Rev: BL 2/1/01) [812]

12267 McCullough, L. E. *Plays from Fairy Tales: Grades K–3* (1–3). 1998, Smith & Kraus $14.95 (1-57525-109-4). 192pp. Using well-known fairy tales as a basis, this collection of original plays includes recommendations for casting, costumes, sets, and related material. (Rev: BL 9/15/98; SLJ 8/98) [812]

12268 McCullough, L. E. *Plays from Mythology: Grades 4–6* (4–6). 1998, Smith & Kraus $14.95 (1-57525-110-8). 192pp. This is a collection of original plays based on important world myths such as the stories of Midas and Gilgamesh, with accompanying detailed notes and production tips. (Rev: BL 9/15/98; SLJ 7/98) [812]

12269 McCullough, L. E. *Plays of America from American Folklore for Children Grades K–6* (3–6). Series: Young Actors. 1996, Smith & Kraus paper $14.95 (1-57525-038-1). 161pp. A collection of 15 plays from American folklore and history that represent many cultural backgrounds. (Rev: SLJ 8/96) [808.82]

12270 McCullough, L. E. *Plays of the Wild West* (3–7). 1997, Smith & Kraus paper $19.95 (1-57525-105-1). 224pp. Both serious and slapstick views of the Wild West are reflected in these 12 plays, mostly musicals. A companion volume is *Plays of the Wild West: Grades K–3* (1997). (Rev: BL 11/1/97; SLJ 1/98) [812]

12271 MacDonald, Margaret Read. *The Skit Book: 101 Skits from Kids* (3–6). Illus. by Marie-Louise Scull. 1990, Shoe String LB $25.00 (0-208-02258-9); paper $18.00 (0-208-02283-X). 160pp. Funny, silly skits from kids that kids will like. (Rev: BL 6/1/90; SLJ 6/90) [812]

12272 Miller, Helen L. *First Plays for Children* (3–7). 1985, Plays paper $12.95 (0-8238-0268-X). 295pp. A useful collection of nonroyalty plays.

12273 Nolan, Paul T. *Folk Tale Plays Round the World: A Collection of Royalty-Free, One-Act Plays About Lands Far and Near* (4–7). 1982, Plays paper $15.00 (0-8238-0253-1). Johnny Appleseed and Robin Hood are heroes featured in two of the 17 plays in this collection.

12274 Shakespeare, William. *William Shakespeare* (5–7). Ed. by David Scott Kastan and Marina Kastan. Illus. Series: Poetry for Young People. 2000, Sterling $14.95 (0-8069-4344-0). 48pp. In a large format illustrated by paintings, this volume contains three sonnets and 23 short excerpts from the plays of William Shakespeare. (Rev: BL 1/1–15/01; HBG 3/01; SLJ 1/01) [821]

12275 Slaight, Craig, and Jack Sharrar, eds. *Great Scenes and Monologues for Children* (5–8). Series: Young Actors. 1993, Smith & Kraus paper $12.95 (1-880399-15-6). Includes selections from children's novels and fairy tales, as well as adult drama and short stories. (Rev: BL 10/1/93; SLJ 11/93) [808.82]

12276 Smith, Marisa, ed. *The Seattle Children's Theatre: Six Plays for Young Audiences* (5–8). Series: Young Actors. 1997, Smith & Kraus $16.95 (1-57525-008-X). 308pp. Six plays that contain young adolescents as characters, adapted from books like *Afternoon of the Elves* and *Anne of Green Gables*. (Rev: SLJ 6/97) [809]

12277 Soto, Gary. *Novio Boy: A Play* (5–8). 1997, Harcourt paper $7.00 (0-15-201531-0). 96pp. A lighthearted play about Rudy, a 9th-grade Hispanic American boy, and his date with an older girl. (Rev: BL 4/15/97; SLJ 6/97) [812]

12278 Stevens, Chambers. *Magnificent Monologues for Kids* (4–8). Ed. by Renee Rolle-Whatley. 1999, Sandcastle Publg. paper $13.95 (1-883995-08-6). A collection of 51 monologues — some best for girls, others for boys — representing different situations and emotions. (Rev: BL 4/1/99; SLJ 8/99) [808.82]

12279 Stevenson, Robert Louis. *Treasure Island* (5–9). Illus. by N. C. Wyeth. Series: Scribner Storybook Classic. 2003, Simon & Schuster $18.95 (0-689-85468-4). 64pp. This picture-book adaptation of the classic story features beautiful paintings by N. C. Wyeth. (Rev: BL 8/03; HBG 4/04)

12280 Trimble, Marcia. *Malinda Martha Meets Mariposa: A Star Is Born* (2–4). Illus. by John Lund. 1999, Images LB $15.95 (1-891577-57-3). 32pp. Malinda Martha conjures an unusual play presenting the four stages in the development of the Monarch butterfly with costumed children as cast members. (Rev: SLJ 9/99) [812]

12281 Van Steenwyk, Elizabeth. *One Fine Day: A Radio Play* (3–5). Illus. by Bill Farnsworth. 2003, Eerdmans $16.00 (0-8028-5234-3). 32pp. A fictional conversation between Orville and Wilbur Wright during their first flight is presented in the form of a radio play. (Rev: BL 1/1–15/03; HBG 10/03; SLJ 4/03)

12282 Vigil, Angel. *¡Teatro! Hispanic Plays for Young People* (4–8). Illus. 1996, Teacher Ideas paper $25.00 (1-56308-371-X). 220pp. This collection contains 14 English-language scripts that integrate elements of the Hispanic traditions of the Southwest. (Rev: BL 3/1/97; BR 3–4/97) [812]

Shakespeare

12283 Burdett, Lois. *Hamlet for Kids* (2–4). Series: Shakespeare Can Be Fun! 2000, Firefly LB $19.95 (1-55209-522-3); paper $8.95 (1-55209-530-4). 64pp. A retelling of *Hamlet* in rhymed couplets with illustrations by the author's students, ages seven to 12. (Rev: HBG 3/01; SLJ 8/00) [822]

12284 Coville, Bruce. *William Shakespeare's Hamlet* (4–8). Illus. by Leonid Gore. 2004, Dial $16.99 (0-8037-2708-9). 40pp. This masterful prose retelling makes the famous play accessible to young people. (Rev: BL 5/15/04; SLJ 2/04) [822.3]

12285 Coville, Bruce. *William Shakespeare's Romeo and Juliet* (4–6). 1999, Dial $16.99 (0-8037-2462-4). 40pp. A successful retelling of the Shakespearean tragedy with lushly romantic illustrations. (Rev: BL 12/1/99; HBG 3/00; SLJ 1/00) [822.3]

12286 Coville, Bruce. *William Shakespeare's Twelfth Night* (3–6). Illus. by Tim Raglin. 2003, Dial $16.99 (0-8037-2318-0). 40pp. Coville provides an easy-reading version of the humorous play, accompanied by appealing ink drawings. (Rev: BL 1/1–15/03; HBG 10/03; SLJ 3/03) [822]

12287 Davidson, Rebecca Piatt. *All the World's a Stage* (K–3). Illus. by Anita Lobel. 2003, Greenwillow LB $16.89 (0-06-029627-5). This introduction to Shakespeare and nine of his best-known plays takes the form of an extended rhyming poem and action-packed illustrations. (Rev: HBG 10/03; SLJ 5/03) [822.3]

12288 McKeown, Adam, retel. *Hamlet* (5–8). Illus. by Sally Wern Comport. Series: The Young Reader's Shakespeare. 2003, Sterling $14.95 (1-4027-0003-2). 80pp. In this appealing retelling, McKeown remains true to Shakespeare's plot line and incorporates many of the best-known lines. (Rev: HBG 4/04; SLJ 2/04) [822.3]

12289 McKeown, Adam, retel. *Macbeth* (5–10). Illus. by Lynne Cannoy. Series: The Young Reader's Shakespeare. 2005, Sterling $14.95 (1-4027-1116-6). 96pp. This conversational prose retelling includes an introduction to the play and incorporates many of the important poetic passages. (Rev: SLJ 5/05) [822.3]

12290 McKeown, Adam. *Macbeth* (5–8). Illus. by Lynne Cannoy. 2005, Sterling $7.95 (1-4027-2476-4). 96pp. The Shakespeare tragedy, illustrated and rewritten to be accessible to students in the middle grades. (Rev: BL 3/1/05) [813]

12291 McKeown, Adam, and William Shakespeare. *Romeo and Juliet: Young Reader's Shakespeare* (5–10). Illus. by Peter Fiore. 2004, Sterling $14.95 (1-4027-0004-0). 96pp. Faithful to the original, this retelling uses finely crafted prose and interweaves many of the best-known poetic stanzas. (Rev: BL 8/04; SLJ 10/04) [822.3]

12292 Packer, Tina. *Tales from Shakespeare* (5–8). Illus. 2004, Scholastic $24.95 (0-439-32107-7). 192pp. Ten of Shakespeare's most popular plays are retold in prose in this attractively illustrated, large-format volume. (Rev: BL 3/15/04; SLJ 4/04) [822.3]

Biography

Adventurers and Explorers

Collective

12293 Atkins, Jeannine. *Wings and Rockets: The Story of Women in Air and Space* (4–8). Illus. by Dusan Petricic. 2003, Farrar $17.00 (0-374-38450-9). Katherine Wright, Bessie Coleman, Blanche Stuart Scott, and Amelia Earhart are among those profiled in this book about women who overcame challenges in a male world. (Rev: BL 3/1/04; HBG 10/03) [920]

12294 Currie, Stephen. *Polar Explorers* (5–9). Series: History Makers. 2002, Gale LB $27.45 (1-56006-957-0). 112pp. The polar explorers profiled here are Roald Amundsen, John Franklin, Matthew Henson, Robert Peary, and Robert Scott. (Rev: SLJ 7/02) [919.804]

12295 Fritz, Jean. *Around the World in a Hundred Years: From Henry the Navigator to Magellan* (4–6). Illus. 1994, Penguin Putnam $18.99 (0-399-22527-7); paper $6.99 (0-698-11638-0). 128pp. A history of exploration and explorers, from 1421 to 1522, in a series of short biographies. (Rev: BCCB 6/94; BL 5/15/94; HB 7–8/94; SLJ 8/94) [920]

12296 Gueldenpfennig, Sonia. *Spectacular Women in Space* (4–6). Series: The Women's Hall of Fame. 2005, Second Story paper $7.95 (1-896764-88-6). 111pp. After a history of women's achievements in the field of space exploration, this volume profiles 10 women who made significant contributions. (Rev: SLJ 4/05) [920]

12297 Hacker, Carlotta. *Explorers* (3–6). Series: Women in Profile. 1998, Crabtree LB $21.28 (0-7787-0004-6); paper $8.95 (0-7787-0026-7). 48pp. Six famous female explorers are featured, with profiles on about a dozen more. (Rev: SLJ 9/98) [920]

12298 Haskins, Jim. *Against All Opposition: Black Explorers in America* (5–9). 1992, Walker LB $14.85 (0-8027-8138-1). A collective biography of African and African American explorers. (Rev: BL 2/15/92; SLJ 6/92) [910]

12299 Jones, Charlotte Foltz. *Westward Ho! Explorers of the American West* (5–8). Illus. 2005, Holiday House $22.95 (0-8234-1586-4). 233pp. Intriguing narrative describes the lives and adventures of 11 explorers, including Zebulon Pike and John Wesley Powell. (Rev: BL 5/1/05) [920]

12300 Kimmel, Elizabeth Cody. *The Look-It-Up Book of Explorers* (5–9). Illus. 2004, Random LB $17.99 (0-375-92478-7); paper $10.99 (0-375-82478-2). 128pp. Chronologically arranged spreads introduce explorers from Leif Eriksson to Robert Ballard, with maps, illustrations, and historical context. (Rev: SLJ 1/05) [920]

12301 MacDonald, Fiona. *Exploring the World* (3–6). Illus. by Gerald Wood. Series: Voyages of Discovery. 1996, Bedrick $18.95 (0-87226-487-4). 48pp. With superb illustrations and many maps, this book tells of the voyages of Magellan and Drake. (Rev: SLJ 1/97) [920]

12302 McLean, Jacqueline. *Women of Adventure* (5–9). Series: Profiles. 2003, Oliver LB $19.95 (1-881508-73-0). 160pp. Seven 19th- and 20th-century women with diverse interests who broke social barriers by exploring far from home are profiled here, with biographical information, photographs, and maps. (Rev: BCCB 5/03; HBG 10/03; SLJ 7/03) [910]

12303 McLoone, Margo. *Women Explorers of the Air: Harriet Quimby, Bessie Coleman, Amelia Earhart, Beryl Markham, Jacqueline Cochran* (3–6). Series: Capstone Short Biographies. 1999, Capstone $19.93 (0-7368-0310-6). 48pp. In a series of brief chapters with full-color illustrations, the achievements of five pioneering women aviators are highlighted. (Rev: BL 3/15/00) [920]

12304 McLoone, Margo. *Women Explorers of the Mountains: Nina Mazuchelli, Fanny Bullock Workman, Mary Vaux Walcott, Gertrude Benham, Junko Tabei* (3–6). Illus. Series: Capstone Short Biographies. 1999, Capstone LB $19.93 (0-7368-0311-4). 48pp. This book profiles five adventurous female mountaineers and includes information on their achievements as well as maps and photos. (Rev: BL 3/1/00) [920]

12305 McLoone, Margo. *Women Explorers of the World: Isabella Bird Bishop, Florence Dixie, Nellie Bly, Gertrude Bel, Margaret Bourke-White* (3–6). Illus. Series: Capstone Short Biographies. 1999, Capstone LB $19.93 (0-7368-0313-0). 48pp. Brief biographies of five female explorers, including material on their accomplishments, influences, and family life, plus photos and maps. (Rev: BL 3/1/00) [920]

12306 Maynard, Christopher. *Pirates! Raiders of the High Seas* (2–4). Illus. Series: Eyewitness Reader. 1998, DK $12.95 (0-7894-3768-6); paper $3.95 (0-7894-3443-1). 48pp. Double-page spreads are used to outline the lives and ways of a number of pirates, such as Henry Morgan, Billy the Kidd, and Blackbeard. (Rev: BL 3/1/99; HBG 10/99) [920]

12307 Rozakis, Laurie. *Dick Rutan and Jena Yeager: Flying Non-Stop Around the World* (3–4). Illus. by Jerry Harston. Series: Partners. 1994, Blackbirch LB $9.95 (1-56711-087-8). 47pp. The story of this pair of adventurers and their nonstop flight around the world. (Rev: SLJ 1/95) [920]

12308 Schraff, Anne. *American Heroes of Exploration and Flight* (5–9). Illus. Series: Collective Biographies. 1996, Enslow LB $20.95 (0-89490-619-4). 112pp. From the Wright Brothers, Lindbergh, and Earhart to Neil Armstrong and Sally Ride, this is a history of 12 Americans who dared the unknown. (Rev: BL 4/15/96; BR 9–10/96; SLJ 5/96) [920]

12309 Sharp, Anne Wallace. *Daring Pirate Women* (5–8). Series: Biography. 2002, Lerner LB $25.26 (0-8225-0031-0). 112pp. Profiles are given of notorious and ruthless female pirates such as Anne Bonny, Mary Read, and Grace O'Malley. (Rev: BL 6/1–15/02; HBG 10/02; SLJ 8/02) [920]

12310 *Talking with Adventurers* (3–6). Ed. by Pat Cummings and Linda Cummings. Illus. 1998, National Geographic $19.95 (0-7922-7068-1). 96pp. In this book of profiles with accompanying photos, 12 adventurous scientists including an anthropologist and an ecologist answer questions about their lives and careers. (Rev: BL 11/15/98; HB 11–12/98; HBG 3/99; SLJ 11/98) [920]

12311 Twist, Clint. *Magellan and da Gama: To the Far East and Beyond* (4–7). Illus. Series: Beyond the Horizons. 1994, Raintree LB $24.26 (0-8114-7254-X). 48pp. Describes the period in which these two explorers lived, as well as their voyages and accomplishments. (Rev: BL 8/94) [920]

12312 Weatherly, Myra. *Women Pirates: Eight Stories of Adventure* (4–7). Illus. 1998, Morgan Reynolds LB $21.95 (1-883846-24-2). 112pp. These stories of eight women pirates from the 17th and 18th centuries — including Grace O'Malley, Maria Cobham, and Rachel Wall — are enlivened by period prints and portraits and good maps. (Rev: BCCB 4/98; BL 4/15/98; HBG 3/99; SLJ 7/98) [920]

Individual

ANZA, JUAN BAUTISTA DE

12313 Bankston, John. *Juan Bautista de Anza* (5–7). Series: Latinos in American History. 2003, Mitchell Lane LB $19.95 (1-58415-196-X). 48pp. The biography of the Spanish explorer of the American Southwest who was a governor of New Mexico in the late 18th century. (Rev: BL 1/1–15/04) [921]

ARMSTRONG, NEIL

12314 Bredeson, Carmen. *Neil Armstrong: A Space Biography* (4–6). Series: Countdown to Space. 1998, Enslow LB $17.95 (0-89490-973-8). 48pp. A well-illustrated biography of the first human to walk on the moon. (Rev: BL 8/98; HBG 10/98; SLJ 7/98) [921]

12315 Brown, Don. *One Giant Leap: The Story of Neil Armstrong* (PS–2). Illus. 1998, Houghton Mifflin $16.00 (0-395-88401-2). 32pp. A picture biography of Neil Armstrong in which the first half describes his childhood and the second his flight to the moon. (Rev: BL 8/98; HBG 3/99; SLJ 9/98) [921]

12316 Byers, Ann. *Neil Armstrong: The First Man on the Moon* (4–7). Illus. Series: The Library of Astronaut Biographies. 2004, Rosen LB $29.25 (0-8239-4461-1). 112pp. A lively overview focusing mainly on Armstrong's education and training. (Rev: SLJ 1/05) [921]

12317 Kramer, Barbara. *Neil Armstrong: The First Man on the Moon* (5–7). Illus. Series: People to Know. 1997, Enslow LB $20.95 (0-89490-828-6). 112pp. This biography covers Armstrong's public and private life, with details on his specialized training and many space missions. (Rev: HBG 3/98; SLJ 12/97) [921]

12318 Zemlicka, Shannon. *Neil Armstrong* (2–5). Illus. Series: History Maker Bios. 2002, Lerner LB $23.93 (0-8225-0395-6). 48pp. A simple, absorbing account of the life of the first man to reach the moon, with helpful sidebars that amplify material in the text. (Rev: HBG 3/03; SLJ 12/02) [921]

ARNER, LOUISE

12319 Anema, Durlynn. *Louise Arner Boyd: Arctic Explorer* (4–6). Illus. 2000, Morgan Reynolds $11.95 (1-883546-42-0). Louise Arner became fascinated with the far north in the early 20th century and financed several scientific expeditions to the Arctic in which she and her crews mapped previously uncharted regions and collected plant specimens. (Rev: BL 5/1/00) [921]

BALBOA, VASCO NUNEZ DE

12320 Otfinoski, Steven. *Vasco Nunez de Balboa: Explorer of the Pacific* (5–8). Series: Great Explorations. 2004, Benchmark LB $20.95 (0-7614-1609-9). 79pp. After material on Balboa's early life,

Otfinoski looks at the Spanish explorer's trip to the Pacific. (Rev: SLJ 3/05) [921]

BALLARD, ROBERT

12321 Hill, Christine M. *Robert Ballard* (4–6). Series: People to Know. 1999, Enslow LB $19.95 (0-7660-1147-X). 128pp. An exciting, well-illustrated biography of the oceanographer who discovered the *Titanic.* (Rev: BL 1/1–15/00; HBG 3/00; SLJ 3/00) [921]

BLANCHARD, JEAN-PIERRE

12322 Wallner, Alexandra. *The First Air Voyage in the United States: The Story of Jean-Pierre Blanchard* (K–4). Illus. 1996, Holiday House $15.95 (0-8234-1224-5). 32pp. The story of the man who participated in 1793 in the first air flight in the United States. (Rev: BCCB 5/96; BL 5/15/96; SLJ 6/96) [921]

BLUFORD, GUION

12323 Haskins, Jim, and Kathleen Benson. *Space Challenger: The Story of Guion Bluford* (4–7). Illus. 1984, Carolrhoda LB $30.35 (0-87614-259-5). 64pp. The story of the first African American man in space. [629.4540924]

12324 Jeffrey, Laura S. *Guion Bluford: A Space Biography* (4–6). Illus. Series: Countdown to Space. 1998, Enslow LB $17.95 (0-89490-977-0). 48pp. A concise biography that tells about Bluford, the first African American to travel in space, his childhood, his training, and his personal qualities. (Rev: BL 8/98; HBG 10/98) [921]

BOONE, DANIEL

12325 Armentrout, David, and Patricia Armentrout. *Daniel Boone* (2–4). Series: Discover Someone Who Made a Difference. 2001, Rourke LB $18.60 (1-58952-052-1). As well as a life of this famous outdoorsman, this biography explains how he has influenced our lives today. (Rev: BCCB 3/02; BL 1/1–15/02; SLJ 3/02) [921]

12326 Calvert, Patricia. *Daniel Boone: Beyond the Mountains* (5–8). Series: Great Explorations. 2001, Marshall Cavendish LB $28.50 (0-7614-1243-3). An attractive biography of the American pioneer who explored the Cumberland Gap region and helped settlers in the Kentucky region. (Rev: BCCB 3/02; BL 4/1/02; HBG 3/02; SLJ 3/02) [921]

12327 Kozar, Richard. *Daniel Boone and the Exploration of the Frontier* (4–6). Series: Explorers of New Worlds. 2000, Chelsea LB $16.95 (0-7910-5510-8). 63pp. Using a variety of illustrations and a crisp text, this book gives good information about Daniel Boone and the forces that inspired him to explore the frontier. (Rev: HBG 10/00; SLJ 7/00) [921]

12328 McCarthy, Pat. *Daniel Boone* (5–8). Series: Historical American Biographies. 2000, Enslow LB $20.95 (0-7660-1256-5). A well-organized and thoroughly documented biography of the legendary pioneer and hero of the American Revolution who died in 1820. (Rev: BL 1/1–15/00; HBG 10/00; SLJ 5/00) [921]

12329 Raphael, Elaine, and Don Bolognese. *Daniel Boone: Frontier Hero* (3–5). Series: Drawing America. 1996, Scholastic $14.95 (0-590-47900-8). An attractive book that presents the salient events in this frontiersman's life. (Rev: SLJ 3/96) [921]

12330 Riehecky, Janet. *Daniel Boone* (3–6). Series: Raintree Biographies. 2003, Raintree LB $25.69 (0-7398-5672-3). 32pp. A simple biography of the pioneer's life and achievements, with sidebar features containing primary and background material. (Rev: BCCB 3/02; HBG 3/03; SLJ 3/03) [921]

12331 Sanford, William R., and Carl R. Green. *Daniel Boone: Wilderness Pioneer* (4–6). Illus. Series: Legendary Heroes of the Wild West. 1997, Enslow LB $16.95 (0-89490-674-7). 48pp. This short biography of the colorful frontiersman who promoted the settlement of Kentucky tries to separate fact from legend. (Rev: BL 3/15/97; SLJ 4/97) [921]

BOYD, LOUISE ARNER

12332 Anema, Durlynn. *Louise Arner Boyd: Arctic Explorer* (4–6). Series: Notable Americans. 2000, Morgan Reynolds $19.95 (1-883846-42-0). 112pp. A wealthy woman, Boyd financed and led polar expeditions in the 1920s but received little recognition for her achievements and her photographs, maps, and specimens. (Rev: BCCB 11/00; HBG 9/00; SLJ 4/00) [910.92]

BROADWICK, GEORGIA "TINY"

12333 Roberson, Elizabeth Whitley. *Tiny Broadwick: The First Lady of Parachuting* (4–8). Illus. 2001, Pelican paper $9.95 (1-56554-780-2). 112pp. Less than 5 feet tall, "Tiny" Broadwick joined a hot-air balloon act as a teenager and became the first woman to jump with a parachute. (Rev: BL 7/01) [797.5]

BYRD, ADMIRAL RICHARD EVELYN

12334 Burleigh, Robert. *Black Whiteness: Admiral Byrd Alone in the Antarctic* (4–8). Illus. by Walter L. Krudop. 1998, Simon & Schuster $16.95 (0-689-81299-X). 40pp. An outstanding picture biography, with generous quotations from Byrd's diary that describe his great endurance and his lonely vigil in a small underground structure in the Antarctic. (Rev: BL 1/1–15/98*; HB 3–4/98; HBG 10/98; SLJ 3/98) [921]

CABEZA DE VACA, ALVAR NUNEZ

12335 Menard, Valerie. *Alvar Nunez Cabeza de Vaca* (5–7). Series: Latinos in American History. 2002, Mitchell Lane LB $19.95 (1-58415-153-6). 48pp. A biography of the 16th-century Spanish nobleman who lived with Native Americans for eight years and who claimed Florida, Louisiana, and

Texas for Spain. (Rev: BL 2/15/03; HBG 10/03) [921]

12336 Waldman, Stuart. *We Asked for Nothing: The Remarkable Journey of Cabeza de Vaca* (5–8). Illus. by Tom McNeely. Series: A Great Explorers Book. 2003, Mikaya $19.95 (1-931414-07-6). 46pp. Drawing on the writings of Cabeza de Vaca, Waldman tells the riveting story of the Spaniard's eight years in 16th-century Texas and Mexico. (Rev: SLJ 2/04) [921]

CABOT, JOHN

12337 Doak, Robin S. *Cabot: John Cabot and the Journey to North America* (4–6). Series: Exploring the World. 2003, Compass Point LB $21.26 (0-7565-0420-1). 48pp. Chronicles his 1497 voyage, with material on his early life and with rich historical context, including the impact of these foreigners' arrival on the native inhabitants. (Rev: SLJ 12/03) [921]

12338 Shields, Charles J. *John Cabot and the Rediscovery of North America* (4–8). Series: Explorers of New Worlds. 2001, Chelsea $19.75 (0-7910-6438-7); paper $8.95 (0-7910-6439-5). 63pp. An absorbing biography that focuses on Cabot's expeditions at the end of the 15th century in search of a passage to Asia. (Rev: SLJ 3/02) [921]

CARSON, KIT

12339 Boraas, Tracey. *Kit Carson: Mountain Man* (4–6). Series: Let Freedom Ring. 2002, Capstone LB $22.60 (0-7368-1349-7). 48pp. An absorbing account of the life and exploits of the legendary trapper and scout. (Rev: HBG 3/03; SLJ 2/03) [921]

12340 Sanford, William R., and Carl R. Green. *Kit Carson: Frontier Scout* (4–6). Illus. Series: Legendary Heroes of the Wild West. 1996, Enslow LB $16.95 (0-89490-650-X). 48pp. A lively biography of the frontier scout and mountain man, with details on how he survived in the wilderness. (Rev: SLJ 7/96) [921]

CARTIER, JACQUES

12341 Blashfield, Jean F. *Cartier: Jacques Cartier in Search of the Northwest Passage* (4–6). Series: Exploring the World. 2001, Compass Point LB $21.26 (0-7565-0122-9). 48pp. The story of Cartier's efforts to find a route to China, with color reproductions of maps, paintings, and prints, and information on his contemporaries. (Rev: SLJ 1/02) [921]

CHAMPLAIN, SAMUEL DE

12342 Faber, Harold. *Samuel de Champlain: Explorer of Canada* (5–8). Series: Great Explorations. 2004, Benchmark LB $20.95 (0-7614-1608-0). 80pp. Drawing on Champlain's own accounts, this well-illustrated volume examines his voyages to Canada and achievements as governor of New France. (Rev: SLJ 3/05) [921]

12343 Moore, Christopher. *Champlain* (4–6). Illus. by Francis Back. 2004, Tundra $18.95 (0-88776-657-9). 56pp. This attractive, revised edition chronicles the French explorer's early-17th-century journeys in eastern Canada and places his importance in historical context. (Rev: BL 10/15/04; SLJ 11/04) [921]

12344 Sherman, Josepha. *Samuel de Champlain: Explorer of the Great Lakes Region and Founder of Quebec* (4–7). Series: The Library of Explorers and Exploration. 2003, Rosen LB $32.00 (0-8239-3629-5). 112pp. In addition to covering Champlain's life, this volume places his explorations in historical context and gives interesting information on the fur trade and relations with Native Americans. (Rev: SLJ 9/03) [971.01]

CID, EL

12345 Koslow, Philip. *El Cid* (5–8). Illus. Series: Hispanics of Achievement. 1993, Chelsea LB $21.95 (0-7910-1239-5). 112pp. The story of Spain's national hero, who gained fame fighting the Moors. (Rev: BL 9/15/93) [921]

COCHRAN, JACQUELINE

12346 Smith, Elizabeth Simpson. *Coming Out Right: The Story of Jacqueline Cochran, the First Woman Aviator to Break the Sound Barrier* (5–8). Illus. 1991, Walker LB $15.85 (0-8027-6989-6). 114pp. From her impoverished childhood to her triumphs in the air and later, this is the story of a female aviation pioneer. (Rev: BL 4/15/91; SLJ 5/91) [921]

COLEMAN, BESSIE

12347 Borden, Louise, and Mary Kay Kroeger. *Fly High! The Story of Bessie Coleman* (1–4). Illus. by Teresa Flavin. 2001, Simon & Schuster $16.00 (0-689-82457-2). 40pp. A highly illustrated, short biography of airplane pilot Bessie Coleman, who in 1921 became the first African American to get a pilot's license. (Rev: BCCB 2/01; BL 2/15/01; HBG 10/01; SLJ 1/01) [921]

12348 Fisher, Lillian M. *Brave Bessie: Flying Free* (4–7). Illus. 1995, Hendrick-Long $16.95 (0-937460-94-X). 88pp. This biography tells of the struggles of Bessie Coleman, who became the first African American aviatrix in the United States. (Rev: BL 2/15/96; SLJ 2/96) [921]

12349 Grimes, Nikki. *Talkin' About Bessie: The Story of Aviator Elizabeth Coleman* (2–5). Illus. by E. B. Lewis. 2002, Scholastic $16.95 (0-439-35243-6). 48pp. In this unusual biography, Grimes uses the voices of friends and relatives at Coleman's funeral to tell the story of her love of flying and her achievements as the first African American woman flyer. (Rev: BL 11/15/02; HB 1–2/03*; HBG 3/03; SLJ 10/02) [629.13]

12350 Hart, Philip S. *Up In the Air: The Story of Bessie Coleman* (5–8). 1996, Carolrhoda LB $16.95 (0-87614-949-2). Forced by restrictions in the United States to get her training in France in the 1920s,

Coleman became the first African American female airplane pilot. (Rev: BL 8/96; SLJ 8/96) [921]

12351 Plantz, Connie. *Bessie Coleman: First Black Woman Pilot* (4–8). 2001, Enslow LB $20.95 (0-7660-1545-9). 128pp. This is a readable biography that breathes life into Coleman's childhood, training as a pilot, and tragic death. (Rev: HBG 3/02; SLJ 1/02) [921]

COLUMBUS, CHRISTOPHER

12352 Adler, David A. *A Picture Book of Christopher Columbus* (K–3). Illus. by John Wallner. Series: Picture Book Biographies. 1991, Holiday House LB $16.95 (0-8234-0857-4); paper $6.95 (0-8234-0949-X). 32pp. The life of this famous explorer is described in simple text and many illustrations. (Rev: BL 6/1/91; SLJ 5/91) [921]

12353 Clare, John D., ed. *The Voyages of Christopher Columbus* (5–8). Illus. Series: Living History. 1992, Harcourt $16.95 (0-15-200507-2). 64pp. Using actors and backdrops of the period, this account reconstructs each of Columbus's New World voyages. (Rev: SLJ 11/92) [921]

12354 Columbus, Christopher. *The Log of Christopher Columbus' First Voyage to America in the Year 1492 as Copied Out in Brief by Bartholomew Las Casas* (4–6). Illus. by John O'Hara Cosgrove. 1989, Shoe String LB $17.00 (0-208-02247-3). 84pp. An abridged log giving day-to-day events of Columbus's sea journey. A reissue. [921]

12355 Fritz, Jean. *Where Do You Think You're Going, Christopher Columbus?* (3–5). Illus. by Margot Tomes. 1980, Penguin Putnam $13.95 (0-399-20723-6); paper $5.99 (0-698-11580-5). 80pp. A fresh, interesting account of Columbus and his voyages. [921]

12356 Molzahn, Arlene Bourgeois. *Christopher Columbus: Famous Explorer* (3–5). Illus. Series: Explorers! 2003, Enslow LB $18.95 (0-7660-2066-5). 48pp. Arresting illustrations and well-written text make this an appealing volume. (Rev: HBG 10/03; SLJ 8/03) [921]

12357 Pelta, Kathy. *Discovering Christopher Columbus: How History Is Invented* (5–7). Illus. 1991, Lerner LB $23.93 (0-8225-4899-2). 112pp. After telling what we know about Columbus, the author examines how myths and legends about him have grown over the years. (Rev: BL 10/1/91) [921]

COOK, CAPTAIN JAMES

12358 Meltzer, Milton. *Captain James Cook: Three Times Around the World* (5–8). Series: Great Explorations. 2001, Marshall Cavendish LB $28.50 (0-7614-1240-9). Using both text and illustrations, this is a fine biography of the English mariner and explorer who, among other feats, explored the west coast of North America. (Rev: BL 4/1/02; HBG 3/02) [921]

CORONADO, FRANCISCO VASQUEZ DE

12359 Doak, Robin S. *Coronado: Francisco Vásquez de Coronado Explores the Southwest* (4–6). Series: Exploring the World. 2001, Compass Point LB $21.26 (0-7565-0123-7). 48pp. The story of Coronado's quest for gold in the Southwest, with color reproductions of maps, paintings, and prints, and information on his contemporaries. (Rev: SLJ 1/02) [921]

CORTES, HERNAN

12360 West, David, and Jackie Gaff. *Hernan Cortes: The Life of a Spanish Conquistador* (4–6). Illus. by Jim Eldridge. Series: Rosen's Graphic Nonfiction. 2005, Rosen LB $26.50 (1-4042-0244-7). 48pp. The story of the explorer's life in a comic-book format. (Rev: BL 3/15/05) [921]

COUSTEAU, JACQUES

12361 Bankston, John. *Jacques-Yves Cousteau: His Story Under the Sea* (4–5). Series: Unlocking the Secrets of Science. 2002, Mitchell Lane LB $17.95 (1-58415-112-9). 48pp. A concise look at the pioneering undersea explorer and inventor of the aqualung that opened up exploration of the ocean. (Rev: BL 8/02; HBG 3/03; SLJ 9/02) [921]

12362 DuTemple, Lesley A. *Jacques Cousteau* (4–6). Series: A&E Biography. 2000, Lerner LB $25.26 (0-8225-4979-4). 112pp. This is the story of the pioneering underwater adventurer and filmmaker who spent most of his life exploring the silent world beneath the sea. (Rev: BL 6/1–15/00; HBG 3/01; SLJ 9/00) [921]

12363 King, Roger. *Jacques Cousteau and the Undersea World* (4–6). Illus. Series: Explorers of New Worlds. 2000, Chelsea LB $17.95 (0-7910-5956-1); paper $8.95 (0-7910-6166-3). 63pp. This account of Cousteau's life starts with his childhood, and covers his creativity in designing equipment for underwater exploration as well as his other important contributions. (Rev: SLJ 4/01) [921]

CROCKETT, DAVY

12364 Adler, David A. *A Picture Book of Davy Crockett* (K–3). Illus. by John Wallner. Series: Picture Book Biographies. 1996, Holiday House $15.95 (0-8234-1212-1). 32pp. With simple, brief text and many illustrations, this is a beginning biography of a frontier hero. (Rev: BL 4/15/96; SLJ 5/96) [921]

12365 Alphin, Elaine Marie. *Davy Crockett* (2–4). Illus. Series: History Maker Bios. 2002, Lerner LB $23.93 (0-8225-0393-X). 48pp. Legend and fact are clearly separated in this biography that looks mainly at Crockett's career. (Rev: HBG 3/03; SLJ 12/02)

12366 Feeney, Kathy. *Davy Crockett* (2–4). Series: Photo-Illustrated Biographies. 2002, Capstone LB $13.95 (0-7368-1110-9). 24pp. Crockett's life and contributions to the exploration of the West are presented, with care to distinguish between fact and legend. (Rev: SLJ 7/02) [921]

615

12367 Krensky, Stephen. *Davy Crockett: A Life on the Frontier* (1–3). Illus. by Debra Bandelin and Bob Dacey. Series: Ready-to-Read Stories of Famous Americans. 2004, Simon & Schuster LB $11.89 (0-689-85945-7); paper $3.99 (0-689-85944-9). 48pp. Krensky provides both legend and fact in this engaging biography of the frontiersman. (Rev: BL 12/1/04; SLJ 3/05) [921]

12368 Sanford, William R., and Carl R. Green. *Davy Crockett: Defender of the Alamo* (4–6). Illus. Series: Legendary Heroes of the Wild West. 1996, Enslow LB $16.95 (0-89490-648-8). 48pp. A brief action-filled biography of Davy Crockett that tries to sort out fact from fiction. (Rev: BL 7/96; SLJ 7/96) [921]

12369 Santrey, Laurence. *Davy Crockett: Young Pioneer* (4–6). Illus. 1983, Troll paper $3.95 (0-89375-848-5). 48pp. All sorts of stories about Davy Crockett, one of the most interesting frontier scouts. [921]

DA GAMA, VASCO

12370 Calvert, Patricia. *Vasco da Gama: So Strong a Spirit* (5–8). Series: Great Explorations. 2004, Benchmark LB $20.95 (0-7614-1611-0). 96pp. After material on da Gama's early life, Calvert looks at the 15th-century Portuguese explorer's voyages. (Rev: SLJ 3/05) [921]

12371 Draper, Allison Stark. *Vasco da Gama: The Portuguese Quest for a Sea Route from Europe to India* (5–8). Illus. Series: Library of Explorers and Exploration. 2003, Rosen LB $31.95 (0-8239-3632-5). 112pp. Da Gama's achievements and brutal behavior are given equal exposure in this well-illustrated volume. (Rev: BL 6/1–15/03) [910]

12372 Kratoville, Betty Lou. *Vasco da Gama* (4–7). Series: Trade Route Explorers. 2000, High Noon paper $17.00 (1-57128-168-1). 44pp. The story of the famous explorer who rounded the Cape of Good Hope and visited India, told in a simple, interesting account. (Rev: SLJ 3/01) [921]

DAVIS, JAN

12373 Greenberg, Keith E. *Stunt Woman: Daredevil Specialist* (4–7). Illus. Series: Risky Business. 1996, Blackbirch LB $24.94 (1-56711-159-9). 32pp. The story of Jan Davis, who, for fun and profit, engages in such activities as jumping from airplanes. (Rev: BL 2/1/97; SLJ 1/97) [921]

DE SOTO, HERNANDO

12374 Gibbons, Faye. *Hernando de Soto: A Search for Gold and Glory* (4–6). Illus. by Bruce Dupree. Series: American Stories. 2002, Crane Hill paper $9.95 (1-57587-198-X). 112pp. A balanced introduction to the Spanish explorer's travels. (Rev: BL 2/1/03) [970.1]

12375 Stein, R. Conrad. *Hernando De Soto: A Life of Adventure* (4–6). Illus. Series: A Proud Heritage: The Hispanic Library. 2005, Child's World LB $28.50 (1-59296-385-4). 40pp. The story of the

Spaniard's life and explorations in the New World. [921]

12376 Whiting, Jim. *Hernando de Soto* (5–7). Series: Latinos in American History. 2002, Mitchell Lane LB $19.95 (1-58415-147-1). 48pp. A simple biography of the Spanish explorer who discovered the Mississippi River in the 16th century while traveling through what is now the southern United States. (Rev: BL 2/15/03; HBG 10/03; SLJ 6/03) [921]

DRAKE, SIR FRANCIS

12377 Gallagher, Jim. *Sir Francis Drake and the Foundation of a World Empire* (4–8). Series: Explorers of New Worlds. 2000, Chelsea $19.75 (0-7910-5950-2); paper $8.95 (0-7910-6160-4). 63pp. This appealing and readable biography of Sir Francis Drake presents his life from childhood and details his major accomplishments, with photographs, sidebar features, documents, and maps. (Rev: HBG 10/01; SLJ 4/01) [921]

12378 Rice, Earle, Jr. *Sir Francis Drake: Navigator and Pirate* (5–8). Series: Great Explorations. 2002, Benchmark LB $19.95 (0-7614-1483-5). 76pp. A profile of the 16th-century British explorer who circumnavigated the globe and fought the Spanish Armada, with maps, timeline, and reproductions. (Rev: HBG 10/03; SLJ 6/03) [942.05]

EARHART, AMELIA

12379 Adler, David A. *A Picture Book of Amelia Earhart* (1–3). Illus. by Jeff Fisher. Series: Picture Book Biographies. 1998, Holiday House $15.95 (0-8234-1315-2). 32pp. Single- and double-page illustrations are used in this interesting biography that highlights Amelia Earhart's unusual childhood. (Rev: BL 4/15/98; HBG 10/98; SLJ 4/98) [921]

12380 Brown, Jonatha A. *Amelia Earhart* (2–4). Illus. Series: People We Should Know. 2005, Gareth Stevens LB $14.50 (0-8368-4465-3). 24pp. An easy-to-read basic biography of the famous pilot, with photographs. (Rev: BL 3/1/05) [629.13]

12381 Bull, Angela. *Flying Ace: The Story of Amelia Earhart* (2–4). Illus. by Chris Forsey. Series: Eyewitness Reader. 2000, DK $12.95 (0-7894-5436-X); paper $3.95 (0-7894-5435-1). 48pp. An interesting biography for beginning readers that reveals many details of Earhart's life and speculates on the cause of her disappearance. (Rev: HBG 10/00; SLJ 7/00) [921]

12382 Burleigh, Robert. *Amelia Earhart: Free in the Skies* (2–4). Series: American Heroes. 2003, Silver Whistle $16.00 (0-15-202498-0). 48pp. A full-color comic-book format effectively introduces Earhart's character and exploits. (Rev: BL 9/1/03; HBG 4/04; SLJ 12/03) [921]

12383 Davies, Kath. *Amelia Earhart Flies Around the World* (3–6). Illus. Series: Great 20th Century Expeditions. 1994, Dillon LB $16.95 (0-87518-531-2). 32pp. This is a lively biography that clearly summarizes Amelia Earhart's exciting and rebellious life. (Rev: SLJ 11/94) [921]

12384 Lakin, Patricia. *Amelia Earhart: More Than a Flier* (2–3). Illus. by Alan Daniel and Lea Daniel. Series: Childhood of Famous Americans. 2003, Simon & Schuster LB $11.89 (0-689-85576-1); paper $3.99 (0-689-85575-3). 46pp. A simple, colorful account of Earhart's childhood, love for adventure, and achievements as a woman aviator. (Rev: HBG 10/03; SLJ 10/03) [921]

12385 Landsman, Susan. *What Happened to Amelia Earhart?* (3–5). Illus. 1991, Avon paper $3.50 (0-380-76221-8). 96pp. While giving background information on Amelia Earhart, this book focuses on her disappearance. (Rev: BL 9/15/91) [921]

12386 Langley, Andrew. *Amelia Earhart: The Pioneering Pilot* (2–4). Illus. Series: What's Their Story? 1998, Oxford LB $12.95 (0-19-521403-X). 32pp. Dramatic moments and heroic deeds in the life of Amelia Earhart are highlighted as well as details of her youthful adventures and independent spirit. (Rev: BL 8/98; HBG 10/98; SLJ 10/98) [921]

12387 Lauber, Patricia. *Lost Star: The Story of Amelia Earhart* (5–7). Illus. 1988, Scholastic paper $4.50 (0-590-41159-4). 96pp. A candid biography of the famed lost aviator. (Rev: BL 10/1/88; SLJ 12/88) [921]

12388 Mara, Wil. *Amelia Earhart* (K–2). Series: Rookie Biographies. 2002, Children's Book Pr. LB $19.00 (0-516-22522-7); paper $4.95 (0-516-27338-8). 32pp. For beginning readers, this is a simple introduction to the famed aviatrix. (Rev: SLJ 12/02) [921]

12389 Parr, Jan. *Amelia Earhart: First Lady of Flight* (5–8). Illus. Series: Book Report Biographies. 1997, Watts LB $22.00 (0-531-11407-4). 112pp. A short, useful biography that relates the public and private life of this adventurer who broke many records and helped open up the world of flight for women. (Rev: BL 11/15/97; HBG 3/98; SLJ 11/97) [921]

12390 Sabin, Francene. *Amelia Earhart: Adventure in the Sky* (3–5). Illus. by Karen Milone. 1983, Troll LB $17.25 (0-89375-839-6); paper $3.95 (0-89375-840-X). 48pp. A biography that shows this amazing woman's courage and endurance. [921]

12391 Sloate, Susan. *Amelia Earhart: Challenging the Skies* (5–8). Illus. 1990, Fawcett paper $6.99 (0-449-90396-6). The aviator's life story is told along with an examination of all the theories concerning her disappearance. (Rev: SLJ 6/90) [921]

12392 Szabo, Corinne. *Sky Pioneer: A Photobiography of Amelia Earhart* (4–8). Illus. 1997, National Geographic $16.00 (0-7922-3737-4). 64pp. A lavishly illustrated biography of Earhart that concentrates more on her accomplishments than her disappearance. (Rev: BL 2/15/97; SLJ 4/97) [921]

ERIKSSON, LEIF

12393 Klingel, Cynthia, and Robert B. Noyed. *Leif Eriksson: Norwegian Explorer* (3–5). Series: Spirit of America: Our People. 2002, Child's World LB $27.07 (1-56766-163-7). 32pp. Eriksson's story is placed in the context of Viking exploration, settlement, society, and family life. (Rev: SLJ 12/02)

EXQUEMELIN

12394 Exquemelin, A. O. *Exquemelin and the Pirates of the Caribbean* (5–8). Ed. by Jane Shuter. Illus. Series: History Eyewitness. 1995, Raintree LB $24.26 (0-8114-8282-0). 48pp. An edited version of the exciting journal of the 17th-century Frenchman who joined a pirate gang as a barber-surgeon. (Rev: BL 4/15/95) [921]

FREMONT, JOHN C.

12395 Faber, Harold. *John Charles Fremont: Pathfinder to the West* (5–8). Series: Great Explorations. 2002, Benchmark LB $19.95 (0-7614-1481-9). 79pp. A profile of the 19th-century explorer who helped open the American West to settlers, with maps, timeline, and reproductions. (Rev: HBG 10/03; SLJ 6/03) [979]

12396 Sanford, William R., and Carl R. Green. *John C. Fremont: Soldier and Pathfinder* (4–6). Illus. Series: Legendary Heroes of the Wild West. 1996, Enslow LB $16.95 (0-89490-649-6). 48pp. A biography of the soldier and politician who also participated in many explorations that opened up the West, including California. (Rev: BL 7/96; SLJ 7/96) [921]

GRISSOM, GUS

12397 Bredeson, Carmen. *Gus Grissom: A Space Biography* (3–7). Illus. Series: Space Biography. 1998, Enslow LB $17.95 (0-89490-974-6). 48pp. Using large color pictures and a simple text, this book traces the exciting career of this space pioneer and his many contributions to the NASA space program. (Rev: BL 4/1/98; HBG 10/98; SLJ 5/98) [629.45]

HENRY THE NAVIGATOR

12398 Gallagher, Aileen. *Prince Henry the Navigator: Pioneer of Modern Exploration* (5–8). Illus. Series: Library of Explorers and Exploration. 2003, Rosen LB $31.95 (0-8239-3621-X). 112pp. During the 15th century, Prince Henry of Portugal spurred others to seek a route to India, claim new territory, and spread Christianity. (Rev: BL 6/1–15/03) [946.9]

HENSON, MATTHEW

12399 Armentrout, David, and Patricia Armentrout. *Matthew Henson* (1–3). Illus. Series: Discover a Life of an American Legend. 2003, Rourke LB $20.64 (1-58952-658-9). 24pp. An introduction to the life and achievements of the African American polar explorer. (Rev: BL 2/1/04; SLJ 3/04) [919.8]

12400 Ferris, Jeri. *Arctic Explorer: The Story of Matthew Henson* (3–6). Illus. 1989, Carolrhoda LB $24.50 (0-87614-370-2). 80pp. Robert Peary described his African American assistant as "a most nearly indispensable man." (Rev: BL 6/1/89; HB 7–8/89)

12401 Gaines, Ann Graham. *Matthew Henson and the North Pole Expedition* (4–6). Series: Journey to Freedom. 2000, Child's World LB $25.64 (1-56766-743-0). 40pp. The gripping story of the African American Arctic explorer and his role in the famous North Pole expedition. (Rev: BL 11/15/00; HBG 3/01; SLJ 3/01) [921]

12402 Weidt, Maryann N. *Matthew Henson* (2–4). Illus. Series: History Maker Bios. 2002, Lerner LB $23.93 (0-8225-0397-2). 48pp. Henson's explorations are the main focus of this biography that touches on his youth. (Rev: SLJ 12/02) [921]

HEYERDAHL, THOR

12403 Malam, John. *Thor Heyerdahl* (1–4). Series: Tell Me About. 1999, Carolrhoda LB $19.93 (1-57505-364-0). 24pp. A lively biography of the fearless voyager who set out in a balsa-wood raft, the *Kon Tiki*, to explore the Pacific Ocean. (Rev: HBG 10/99; SLJ 8/99) [921]

HILLARY, SIR EDMUND

12404 Brennan, Kristine. *Sir Edmund Hillary: Modern-Day Explorer* (4–8). Series: Explorers of New Worlds. 2000, Chelsea $19.75 (0-7910-5953-7); paper $8.95 (0-7910-6163-9). 63pp. An appealing overview of the life and accomplishments of the mountaineer and explorer, with photographs and maps. (Rev: SLJ 4/01) [796.52]

12405 Coburn, Broughton. *Triumph on Everest: A Photobiography of Sir Edmund Hillary* (5–8). 2000, National Geographic $17.95 (0-7922-7114-9). 64pp. Using many quotations and excellent photographs, this work records the lifetime accomplishments of one of the first men to reach the top of Mount Everest. (Rev: BCCB 9/00; HBG 3/01; SLJ 10/00) [921]

12406 Stewart, Whitney. *Sir Edmund Hillary: To Everest and Beyond* (5–8). Photos by Anne B. Keiser. Illus. Series: Newsmakers. 1996, Lerner LB $30.35 (0-8225-4927-1). 128pp. The life of this famous mountain climber is presented with interesting details about his other interests, including bee keeping, conservation, and helping the Sherpa people. (Rev: SLJ 9/96) [921]

HUDSON, HENRY

12407 Doak, Robin S. *Hudson: Henry Hudson Searches for a Passage to Asia* (4–6). Series: Exploring the World. 2003, Compass Point LB $21.26 (0-7565-0422-8). 48pp. Traces the four voyages of English-born explorer Henry Hudson in search of a short navigable route from Europe to the Far East. (Rev: LMC 11-12/03; SLJ 12/03) [921]

12408 Goodman, Joan E. *Beyond the Sea of Ice: The Voyages of Henry Hudson* (3–6). Illus. Series: Great Explorers Books. 1999, Mikaya $19.95 (0-9650493-8-8). 48pp. This biography focuses on Hudson's four voyages of exploration. (Rev: BL 11/1/99; HBG 3/00; SLJ 3/00) [921]

12409 Saffer, Barbara. *Henry Hudson: Ill-Fated Explorer of North America's Coast* (4–8). Series: Explorers of New Worlds. 2001, Chelsea $19.95 (0-7910-6436-0); paper $8.95 (0-7910-6437-9). 63pp. This absorbing biography focuses on Hudson's early 17th-century expeditions from England in search of a sea route to the Far East. (Rev: HBG 10/02; SLJ 3/02) [921]

JEMISON, MAE

12410 Burby, Liza N. *Mae Jemison: The First African American Woman Astronaut* (1–3). Series: Making Their Mark: Women in Science and Medicine. 1997, Rosen LB $13.95 (0-8239-5027-1). 24pp. A short, clearly written biography of this space pioneer for beginning readers. (Rev: SLJ 7/98) [921]

12411 Naden, Corinne J., and Rose Blue. *Mae Jemison: Out of This World* (2–5). Illus. Series: Gateway. 2003, Millbrook LB $23.90 (0-7613-2570-0). 48pp. The life story of the first African American woman in space. (Rev: BL 2/15/03; HBG 10/03) [629.45]

12412 Streissguth, Thomas. *Mae Jemison* (2–4). Illus. Series: Explore Space! 2003, Capstone LB $18.60 (0-7368-1626-7). 24pp. A slim, basic biography of the first African American woman to travel in space. (Rev: HBG 10/03; SLJ 3/04) [921]

12413 Yannuzzi, Della A. *Mae Jemison: A Space Biography* (4–6). Illus. Series: Countdown to Space. 1998, Enslow LB $17.95 (0-89490-813-8). 48pp. As well as information about her youth, training, and personality, this book covers Mae Jemison's flight on the *Endeavor* in 1992, when she became the first African American woman to travel in space. (Rev: BL 8/98; HBG 10/98) [921]

KINGSLEY, MARY

12414 Brown, Don. *Uncommon Traveler: Mary Kingsley in Africa* (PS–3). Illus. 2000, Houghton Mifflin $16.00 (0-618-00273-1). 32pp. A picture-book biography of the intrepid Englishwoman who twice journeyed alone to West Africa in the 19th century and later wrote and lectured about her experiences. (Rev: BCCB 7–8/00; BL 7/00*; HB 9–10/00; HBG 3/01; SLJ 9/00) [921]

LA SALLE, CAVELIER DE

12415 Faber, Harold. *La Salle: Down the Mississippi* (5–8). Series: Great Explorations. 2001, Marshall Cavendish LB $28.50 (0-7614-1239-5). The exciting story of the French explorer who traveled down the Mississippi River to the Gulf of Mexico and named the region Louisiana. (Rev: BL 4/1/02; HBG 3/02; SLJ 3/02) [921]

12416 Goodman, Joan Elizabeth. *Despite All Obstacles: La Salle and the Conquest of the Mississippi* (3–6). Illus. by Tom McNeely. Series: Great Explorers. 2001, Mikaya $19.95 (1-931414-01-7). 48pp. Journal entries, excerpts from letters, a map, and attractive illustrations enhance this life of explorer Rene-Robert Cavalier, Sieur de La Salle. (Rev: BL 1/1–15/02; HBG 10/02; SLJ 4/02) [973.2]

LAW, RUTH

12417 Brown, Don. *Ruth Law Thrills a Nation* (1–3). Illus. 1993, Ticknor $15.00 (0-395-66404-7). 32pp. A simple biography about the woman flier who broke a nonstop cross-country record. (Rev: BL 8/93) [921]

LEWIS AND CLARK

12418 Adler, David A. *A Picture Book of Lewis and Clark* (2–4). Illus. by Ronald Himler. Series: Picture Book Biographies. 2003, Holiday House $16.95 (0-8234-1735-2). 32pp. Biographical information about the two explorers and information on the expedition itself are found in this accessible book. (Rev: BL 2/15/03; HBG 10/03; SLJ 3/03) [917.804]

12419 Kroll, Steven. *Lewis and Clark: Explorers of the American West* (1–5). Illus. by Richard Williams. 1994, Holiday House LB $16.95 (0-8234-1034-X). 32pp. An appealing picture book that dramatically describes the famous journey of Lewis and Clark. (Rev: BCCB 11/94; BL 11/1/94; SLJ 9/94) [921]

12420 Stein, R. Conrad. *Lewis and Clark* (3–5). Series: Cornerstones of Freedom. 1997, Children's Book Pr. LB $20.50 (0-516-20461-0). 32pp. A well-illustrated, attractive introduction to the famous Western expedition and the men who carried it out. (Rev: BL 12/15/97; HBG 3/98) [921]

12421 Streissguth, Thomas. *Lewis and Clark: Explorers of the Northwest* (4–9). Series: Historical American Biographies. 1998, Enslow LB $20.95 (0-7660-1016-3). The story of the two intrepid explorers who made their way overland to the Pacific Ocean. (Rev: BL 8/98) [921]

LINDBERGH, CHARLES

12422 Burleigh, Robert. *Flight: The Journey of Charles Lindbergh* (2–4). Illus. by Mike Wimmer. 1991, Penguin Putnam $16.99 (0-399-22272-3). 32pp. A picture book that uses Lindbergh's autobiography as a basis for the text. (Rev: BCCB 11/91; BL 9/1/91*; HB 11–12/91*; SLJ 10/91) [921]

LUCID, SHANNON

12423 Bredeson, Carmen. *Shannon Lucid* (4–6). Illus. 1998, Millbrook LB $20.90 (0-7613-0406-1). 48pp. A biography of America's most experienced astronaut who spent 188 days on *Mir* and later joked that she hadn't showered for six months. (Rev: BL 1/1–15/99; HBG 3/99; SLJ 1/99) [921]

MCAULIFFE, CHRISTA

12424 Jeffrey, Laura S. *Christa McAuliffe: A Space Biography* (4–6). Series: Countdown to Space. 1998, Enslow LB $17.95 (0-89490-976-2). The biography of the teacher who was to have been the first civilian in space. (Rev: BL 8/98; HBG 10/98; SLJ 9/98) [921]

12425 Naden, Corinne J., and Rose Blue. *Christa McAuliffe: Teacher in Space* (3–5). Illus. Series: Gateway Biographies. 1991, Millbrook LB $20.90

(1-56294-046-5). 48pp. Personal anecdotes about America's "first private citizen in space" are crisscrossed with space program information. (Rev: BL 1/1/92; SLJ 1/92) [921]

12426 Streissguth, Thomas. *Christa McAuliffe* (2–4). Illus. Series: Explore Space! 2003, Capstone LB $18.60 (0-7368-1624-0). 24pp. This slim volume offers basic information on the life and work of one of the teacher who perished in the *Challenger* disaster in 1986. (Rev: HBG 10/03; SLJ 3/04) [921]

MACCREADY, PAUL B.

12427 Taylor, Richard L. *The First Human-Powered Flight: The Story of Paul B. MacCready and His Airplane, the Gossamer Condor* (4–8). Illus. Series: First Books. 1995, Watts LB $23.00 (0-531-20185-6). 63pp. After an introduction to the history of human-powered flight, this account focuses on MacCready's amazing flight in 1977. (Rev: SLJ 11/95) [921]

MCNAIR, RONALD

12428 Naden, Corinne J. *Ronald McNair* (5–8). Illus. Series: Black Americans of Achievement. 1991, Chelsea LB $21.95 (0-7910-1133-X). 109pp. An inspirational biography of the second African American astronaut, a victim of the *Challenger* disaster. (Rev: BL 4/1/91; SLJ 3/91) [921]

MAGELLAN, FERDINAND

12429 Burgan, Michael. *Magellan: Ferdinand Magellan and the First Trip Around the World* (4–6). Series: Exploring the World. 2001, Compass Point LB $21.26 (0-7565-0125-3). 48pp. An encompassing look at Magellan's achievements with excellent illustrations, a timeline, and Web site information. (Rev: SLJ 1/02) [921]

12430 Burnett, Betty. *Ferdinand Magellan: The First Voyage Around the World* (4–7). Series: The Library of Explorers and Exploration. 2003, Rosen LB $32.00 (0-8239-3617-1). 112pp. In addition to covering Magellan's life, this volume places his 16th-century voyage in historical context and gives interesting information on the funding of such expeditions and life at sea. (Rev: SLJ 9/03) [910]

12431 Gallagher, Jim. *Ferdinand Magellan and the First Voyage Around the World* (4–6). Series: Explorers of New Worlds. 2000, Chelsea LB $16.95 (0-7910-5508-6). 63pp. With well-chosen illustrations and a lively text, this book re-creates the historic voyages of Magellan, the first man to circle the globe. (Rev: HBG 10/00; SLJ 7/00) [921]

12432 Levinson, Nancy Smiler. *Magellan and the First Voyage Around the World* (5–8). Illus. 2001, Clarion $19.00 (0-395-98773-3). 144pp. A straightforward biography of Magellan, with information on his times and insightful analysis of his character. (Rev: BCCB 2/02; BL 2/1/02; HB 1–2/02; HBG 3/02; SLJ 1/02) [910.92]

12433 Meltzer, Milton. *Ferdinand Magellan: First to Sail Around the World* (5–8). Illus. Series: Great

Explorations. 2001, Benchmark LB $28.50 (0-7614-1238-7). 80pp. An encompassing look at Magellan's achievements is complemented by excellent illustrations, a timeline, and Web site information. (Rev: BL 1/1–15/02; HBG 3/02; SLJ 3/02) [910]

12434 Molzahn, Arlene Bourgeois. *Ferdinand Magellan: First Explorer Around the World* (3–5). Series: Explorers! 2003, Enslow LB $18.95 (0-7660-2068-1). 48pp. Illustrations and maps enhance this account of Magellan's life and travels. (Rev: HBG 10/03; SLJ 9/03) [921]

MALLORY, GEORGE

12435 Salkeld, Audrey. *Mystery on Everest: A Photobiography of George Mallory* (5–8). Illus. Series: Photobiography. 2000, National Geographic $17.95 (0-7922-7222-6). 64pp. The life of the famous English mountain climber George Mallory, who died in 1924 in a climbing accident on Mount Everest, written by a member of the team that discovered his body in 1999. (Rev: BCCB 9/00; BL 11/1/00; HBG 3/01; SLJ 11/00) [921]

MARKHAM, BERYL

12436 Bowen, Andy Russell. *Flying Against the Wind: A Story About Beryl Markham* (3–6). Illus. 1998, Carolrhoda LB $14.95 (1-57505-081-1). 64pp. From her childhood in East Africa to her solo transatlantic flight in 1936, this is a thrilling biography of the English aviator. (Rev: BL 10/15/98; HBG 10/98; SLJ 8/98) [921]

OCHOA, ELLEN

12437 Paige, Joy. *Ellen Ochoa: The First Hispanic Woman in Space* (4–7). Illus. Series: The Library of Astronaut Biographies. 2004, Rosen LB $29.25 (0-8239-4457-3). 112pp. A lively overview focusing mainly on Ochoa's education and training. (Rev: SLJ 1/05) [921]

PEARY, ROBERT E.

12438 Calvert, Patricia. *Robert E. Peary: To the Top of the World* (5–8). Series: Great Explorations. 2001, Marshall Cavendish LB $28.50 (0-7614-1242-5). The exciting story of the Arctic explorer who, after several attempts, reached the North Pole in 1909. (Rev: BL 4/1/02; HBG 3/02; SLJ 3/02) [921]

12439 Charleston, Gordon. *Peary Reaches the North Pole* (4–6). Illus. Series: Great 20th Century Expeditions. 1993, Dillon LB $16.95 (0-87518-535-5). 32pp. Focuses on Peary's last expedition in 1910, in which he reached the North Pole. (Rev: BL 9/15/93; SLJ 9/93) [921]

PIKE, ZEBULON

12440 Calvert, Patricia. *Zebulon Pike: Lost in the Rockies* (5–8). Series: Great Explorations. 2004, Benchmark LB $20.95 (0-7614-1612-9). 96pp. Presents the life and career of the army officer who

explored the West and Southwest. (Rev: SLJ 3/05) [921]

12441 Sanford, William R., and Carl R. Green. *Zebulon Pike: Explorer of the Southwest* (4–6). Illus. Series: Legendary Heroes of the Wild West. 1996, Enslow LB $16.95 (0-89490-671-2). 48pp. The story of the Western explorer who, on one of his expeditions, traveled up the Arkansas River and sighted a peak later named after him. (Rev: BL 10/15/96; SLJ 9/96) [921]

12442 Witteman, Barbara. *Zebulon Pike: Soldier and Explorer* (4–6). Series: Let Freedom Ring. 2002, Capstone LB $22.60 (0-7368-1351-9). 48pp. An absorbing account of the life and exploits of the explorer who discovered Pikes Peak. (Rev: HBG 3/03; SLJ 2/03) [921]

POLO, MARCO

12443 Otfinoski, Steven. *Marco Polo: To China and Back* (4–8). Series: Great Explorations. 2002, Benchmark LB $19.95 (0-7614-1480-0). 77pp. Readable text accompanied by many illustrations and sidebar features traces Polo's life and adventures. (Rev: HBG 10/03; SLJ 5/03) [915.04]

12444 Smalley, Roger. *The Adventures of Marco Polo* (4–6). Illus. by Brian Bascle. Series: Graphic Library. 2005, Capstone LB $16.95 (0-7368-3830-9). 32pp. This story of the explorer's life is presented in comic-book format. (Rev: BL 3/15/05) [921]

PONCE DE LEON, JUAN

12445 Dolan, Sean. *Juan Ponce de León* (5–9). Series: Hispanics of Achievement. 1995, Chelsea LB $21.95 (0-7910-2023-1). The story of the Spanish explorer who after accompanying Columbus on his second voyage set out on his own and eventually became the discoverer of Florida. (Rev: BL 10/15/95) [921]

12446 Harmon, Dan. *Juan Ponce de León and the Search for the Fountain of Youth* (4–6). Series: Explorers of New Worlds. 2000, Chelsea LB $16.95 (0-7910-5517-5). 63pp. As well as the life of Ponce de Leon and his exploits, this book gives good background information on the social and political forces that inspired him. (Rev: HBG 10/00; SLJ 7/00) [921]

12447 Otfinoski, Steven. *Juan Ponce de Leon: Discoverer of Florida* (5–8). Series: Great Explorations. 2004, Benchmark LB $20.95 (0-7614-1610-2). 76pp. A well-illustrated account of the explorer's life and discoveries, dismissing the idea that he was really searching for the fountain of youth. (Rev: SLJ 3/05) [921]

12448 Whiting, Jim. *Juan Ponce de Leon* (5–7). Series: Latinos in American History. 2002, Mitchell Lane LB $19.95 (1-58415-149-8). 48pp. This is the story of the man who is credited with discovering Florida in 1513 while searching for the fountain of youth. (Rev: BL 2/15/03; HBG 10/03; SLJ 6/03) [921]

12449 Worth, Richard. *Ponce de Leon and the Age of Spanish Exploration in World History* (5–9).

Series: In World History. 2003, Enslow LB $20.95 (0-7660-1940-3). 112pp. As well as a biography of this great adventurer from Spain, this book describes the work of other Spanish explorers in the Americas. (Rev: BL 11/15/03; HBG 4/04) [921]

POWELL, JOHN WESLEY

12450 Bruns, Roger A. *John Wesley Powell: Explorer of the Grand Canyon* (5–8). Illus. Series: Historical American Biographies. 1997, Enslow LB $20.95 (0-89490-783-2). 128pp. This biography tells about Powell's youth, education, and Civil War days, as well as his many expeditions and research activities. (Rev: SLJ 10/97) [921]

12451 Ross, Michael E. *Exploring the Earth with John Wesley Powell* (3–5). Series: Naturalist's Apprentice. 2000, Carolrhoda $19.93 (1-57505-254-7). 48pp. This biography of the noted explorer, geologist, and naturalist covers his important expeditions into the Grand Canyon and the Colorado plateau region. (Rev: BL 4/15/00; SLJ 8/00) [921]

QUIMBY, HARRIET

12452 Moss, Marissa. *Brave Harriet* (2–4). Illus. by C. F. Payne. 2001, Harcourt $16.00 (0-15-202380-1). 32pp. A picture book for older readers telling in first person the story of Harriet Quimby, the first woman to fly solo across the English Channel. (Rev: BL 7/01; HBG 3/02; SLJ 9/01) [629.1]

RALEIGH, SIR WALTER

12453 Korman, Susan. *Sir Walter Raleigh: English Explorer and Author* (4–6). Series: Colonial Leaders. 2001, Chelsea LB $16.95 (0-7910-5969-3); paper $8.95 (0-7910-6126-4). 80pp. Korman gives readers a good overview of the many sides of Raleigh, covering his roles as soldier, scientist, and courtier as well as his efforts to colonize Virginia. (Rev: SLJ 7/01) [942.05]

RAMON, ILAN

12454 Sofer, Barbara. *Ilan Ramon: Israel's Space Hero* (4–8). 2004, Lerner LB $16.95 (1-58013-115-8); paper $6.95 (1-58013-116-6). 63pp. The story of the first Israeli astronaut, from his early life and schooling to his selection for the crew of the ill-fated Columbia space shuttle that broke apart on re-entry in 2003. (Rev: SLJ 6/04) [921]

RIDE, SALLY

12455 Hurwitz, Jane, and Sue Hurwitz. *Sally Ride: Shooting for the Stars* (5–8). 1989, Ballantine paper $6.99 (0-449-90394-X). An interestingly written account in paperback format of the female space pioneer. (Rev: BL 12/15/89; BR 3–4/90; SLJ 2/90) [921]

12456 Kramer, Barbara. *Sally Ride: A Space Biography* (4–8). Illus. Series: Countdown to Space. 1998, Enslow LB $18.95 (0-89490-975-4). A brief, well-written biography of Sally Ride that describes her training, experience, and space flights. (Rev: BL 4/1/98; BR 9–10/98; HBG 9/98; SLJ 5/98) [921]

12457 Wade, Linda R. *Sally Ride: The Story of the First American Female in Space* (4–5). Series: Unlocking the Secrets of Science. 2002, Mitchell Lane LB $17.95 (1-58415-139-0). 56pp. Profiles the first American woman to travel in space. (Rev: HBG 10/03)

SCOTT, BLANCHE STUART

12458 Cummins, Julie. *Tomboy of the Air: Daredevil Pilot Blanche Stuart Scott* (3–6). Illus. 2001, HarperCollins LB $16.89 (0-06-029243-1). 80pp. Scott was a daredevil from childhood, graduating from driving cars to stunt-flying, and was the first American woman flyer. (Rev: BL 5/15/01; HB 5–6/01; HBG 3/02; SLJ 6/01*) [629.13]

SHACKLETON, SIR ERNEST

12459 Calvert, Patricia. *Sir Ernest Shackleton: By Endurance We Conquer* (4–8). Series: Great Explorations. 2002, Benchmark LB $19.95 (0-7614-1485-1). 80pp. Readable text accompanied by many illustrations and sidebar features traces Shackleton's life and adventures. (Rev: HBG 10/03; SLJ 5/03) [919.8904]

12460 Kostyal, K. M. *Trial by Ice: A Photobiography of Sir Ernest Shackleton* (4–8). Illus. 1999, National Geographic $17.95 (0-7922-7393-1). 64pp. A biography that details the life of Sir Ernest Shackleton, his 1915 Antarctic expedition, and the survival of the explorers aboard the *Endurance*. (Rev: BCCB 12/99; BL 12/1/99; HBG 3/00; SLJ 3/00) [921]

12461 Marcovitz, Hal. *Sir Ernest Shackleton and the Struggle Against Antarctica* (4–6). Illus. Series: Explorers of New Worlds. 2001, Chelsea LB $19.75 (0-7910-6424-7). 63pp. Photographs from Shackleton's last expedition and quotations from his own writings add interest to this exploration of his motivations and his voyages. (Rev: HBG 10/02; SLJ 4/02)

SHEPARD, ALAN

12462 Orr, Tamra B. *Alan Shepard: The First American in Space* (4–7). Illus. Series: The Library of Astronaut Biographies. 2004, Rosen LB $29.25 (0-8239-4455-7). 112pp. A lively overview focusing mainly on Shepard's education and training. (Rev: SLJ 1/05) [921]

SLOCUM, JOSHUA

12463 Lasky, Kathryn. *Born in the Breezes: The Seafaring Life of Joshua Slocum* (3–5). Illus. by Walter L. Krudop. 2001, Scholastic $16.95 (0-439-29305-7). 48pp. Joshua Slocum went to sea at 14, married and raised his children on a ship, and eventually became the first man, in 1898, to sail around the world alone. (Rev: BL 11/1/01; HBG 3/02; SLJ 11/01) [387.5]

SMITH, JEDEDIAH

12464 Nelson, Sharlene, and Ted Nelson. *Jedediah Smith* (3–6). Series: Watts Library. 2004, Scholastic LB $24.50 (0-531-12287-5); paper $8.95 (0-531-16676-7). 64pp. Jedediah Smith's explorations of the American West are covered here with many illustrations, maps, a timeline, and other helpful features. (Rev: BL 6/1–15/04) [921]

SMITH, JOHN

12465 Doak, Robin S. *Smith: John Smith and the Settlement of Jamestown* (4–6). Series: Exploring the World. 2003, Compass Point LB $21.26 (0-

7565-0423-6). 48pp. Examines the important role played by John Smith in opening North America to European settlement. (Rev: SLJ 12/03) [921]

TERESHKOVA, VALENTINA

12466 Feldman, Heather. *Valentina Tereshkova: The First Woman in Space* (2–3). Series: Space Firsts. 2003, Rosen LB $19.50 (0-8239-6246-6). 24pp. A good choice for young readers who know little of the early U.S.-Soviet race for space, this brief biography of Valentina Tereshkova chronicles the life and career of the first woman in space. (Rev: SLJ 11/03) [629.45]

Artists, Composers, Entertainers, and Writers

12467 Benedict, Kitty, and Karen Covington. *The Literary Crowd: Writers, Critics, Scholars, Wits* (5–9). Series: Remarkable Women. 2000, Raintree LB $32.82 (0-8172-5732-2). 80pp. Profiles of 150 women writers and others associated with the literary world, including Virginia Woolf, Jane Austen, and Maya Angelou. (Rev: SLJ 8/00) [920]

12468 Bostrom, Kathleen Long. *Winning Authors: Profiles of the Newbery Medalists* (5–10). Series: Popular Authors. 2003, Libraries Unlimited $52.00 (1-56308-877-0). 338pp. Report writers will find useful information on the authors who won this prestigious award, including quotations and material on experiences that relate to the winning books. (Rev: SLJ 6/04) [920]

12469 Bredeson, Carmen. *American Writers of the 20th Century* (5–8). Illus. 1996, Enslow LB $20.95 (0-89490-704-2). 104pp. Ten writers for adults, including Toni Morrison and F. Scott Fitzgerald, are introduced in brief profiles. (Rev: BL 6/1–15/96; BR 9–10/96; SLJ 9/96) [920]

12470 Covington, Karen. *Creators: Artists, Designers, Craftswomen* (5–9). Series: Remarkable Women. 2000, Raintree LB $32.85 (0-8172-5725-X). 80pp. Mary Cassatt, Georgia O'Keefe, Frido Kahlo, and Beatrix Potter are four of the 150 female artists celebrated in this collective biography. (Rev: BL 6/1–15/00; SLJ 8/00) [920]

12471 Curry, Barbara K., and James Michael Brodie. *Sweet Words So Brave: The Story of African American Literature* (5–8). Illus. 1996, Zino $24.95 (1-55933-179-8). An outline of African American literature, from slave narratives to the great writers of today, such as Nikki Giovanni and Toni Morrison. (Rev: BL 2/15/97*; SLJ 4/97) [810.9]

12472 Datnow, Claire. *American Science Fiction and Fantasy Writers* (5–8). Illus. Series: Collective Biographies. 1999, Enslow LB $20.95 (0-7660-1090-2). 128pp. Science fiction and fantasy writers

profiled in this book include Asimov, Heinlein, Bradbury, Anderson, Norton, L'Engle, and Le Guin. (Rev: BL 4/15/99) [920]

12473 Ford, Carin T. *Legends of American Dance and Choreography* (5–7). Series: Collective Biographies. 2000, Enslow LB $20.95 (0-7660-1378-2). 128pp. This collective work presents 10 short biographies of such dance luminaries as George Balanchine and Martha Graham. (Rev: BL 6/1–15/00; HBG 10/00; SLJ 7/00) [920]

12474 Gaines, Ann Graham. *American Photographers: Capturing the Image* (4–7). Series: Collective Biographies. 2002, Enslow LB $20.95 (0-7660-1833-4). 112pp. The lives and contributions of 10 well-known photographers are presented with photographs and a brief history of photography. (Rev: HBG 10/02; SLJ 10/02) [921]

12475 Hacker, Carlotta. *Great African Americans in Jazz* (3–5). Series: Outstanding African Americans. 1997, Crabtree LB $22.60 (0-86505-804-0); paper $8.95 (0-86505-818-0). 64pp. Seven portraits of great African American jazz musicians are given, among them Louis Armstrong, Duke Ellington, Billie Holiday, and Bessie Smith, plus seven other brief profiles. (Rev: BL 9/15/97) [920]

12476 Hacker, Carlotta. *Great African Americans in the Arts* (3–5). Series: Outstanding African Americans. 1997, Crabtree LB $22.60 (0-86505-807-5); paper $8.95 (0-86505-821-0). 64pp. Seven African Americans — e.g., Gordon Parks, Alvin Ailey, and Marion Anderson — are given lengthy coverage, with seven others introduced in shorter profiles. (Rev: BL 9/15/97; SLJ 12/97) [920]

12477 Hardy, P. Stephen, and Sheila Jackson Hardy. *Extraordinary People of the Harlem Renaissance* (5–9). Series: Extraordinary People. 2000, Children's Book Pr. LB $39.00 (0-516-21201-X); paper $16.95 (0-516-27170-9). 288pp. Black-and-white photographs, reproductions of sheet music, and interesting artwork enhance the extensive information on the artists, photographers, musicians, writers, and poets of Harlem in the 1920s and 1930s. (Rev: BL 11/15/00; SLJ 6/01) [700]

12478 Hasday, Judy L. *Extraordinary People in the Movies* (5–9). Series: Extraordinary People. 2003, Children's Book Pr. LB $39.00 (0-516-22348-8); paper $16.95 (0-516-27857-6). 288pp. Brief biographies of individuals associated with the movie business are arranged chronologically by date of birth and interspersed with short essays on related topics. (Rev: SLJ 7/03) [791.43]

12479 Hill, Christine M. *Ten Terrific Authors for Teens* (5–7). Series: Collective Biographies. 2000, Enslow LB $20.95 (0-7660-1380-4). 112pp. Among the authors profiled are Judy Blume, Virginia Hamilton, Julius Lester, Lois Lowry, Katherine Paterson, Gary Soto, and Lawrence Yep. (Rev: BL 9/15/00; HBG 10/01; SLJ 12/00) [920]

12480 Holme, Merilyn, and Bridget McKenzie. *Expressionists* (5–9). Series: Artists in Profile. 2002, Heinemann LB $28.50 (1-58810-647-0). 64pp. Introduces the movement and gives biographical information on the major artists and their key works, with reproductions and photographs. Also use *Impressionists* and *Pop Artists* (both 2002). (Rev: HBG 3/03; SLJ 3/03) [759.06]

12481 Hudson, Wade, and Cheryl W. Hudson, comps. *In Praise of Our Fathers and Our Mothers: A Black Family Treasury by Outstanding Authors and Artists* (4–7). Illus. 1997, Just Us $29.95 (0-940975-59-9). 131pp. A collection of reminiscences of family life told by 40 African American writers and illustrators, e.g., Virginia Hamilton and Walter Dean Myers. (Rev: BL 4/15/0; HB 3–4/97; SLJ 6/97) [920]

12482 Hunter, Shaun. *Visual and Performing Artists* (3–6). Series: Women in Profile. 1999, Crabtree LB $15.96 (0-7787-0035-6); paper $8.06 (0-7787-0013-5). 48pp. This salute to women in show business features six profiles of important performing artists and brief entries for 15 more. (Rev: BL 9/15/99; SLJ 8/99) [920]

12483 Ishizuka, Kathy. *Asian American Authors* (5–9). Series: Collective Biographies. 2000, Enslow LB $20.95 (0-7660-1376-6). 128pp. Writers for children (including Laurence Yep) and for adults (such as Amy Tan) are included in this collective biography of 10 Asian American writers. (Rev: HBG 10/01; SLJ 3/01) [920]

12484 Krull, Kathleen. *Lives of the Artists: Masterpieces, Messes (and What the Neighbors Thought)* (4–6). Illus. by Kathryn Hewitt. 1995, Harcourt $20.00 (0-15-200103-4). 96pp. Nineteen thumbnail sketches on such artists as van Gogh, O'Keeffe, and Warhol. (Rev: BCCB 11/95; BL 11/1/95; SLJ 10/95) [920]

12485 Krull, Kathleen. *Lives of the Musicians: Good Times, Bad Times (And What the Neighbors Thought)* (5–8). Illus. 1993, Harcourt $20.00 (0-15-248010-2). Biographies of 16 musical giants, from Vivaldi, Mozart, and Beethoven to Gershwin, Joplin, and Woody Guthrie. (Rev: BL 4/1/93*; SLJ 5/93*) [920]

12486 Krull, Kathleen. *Lives of the Writers: Comedies, Tragedies (and What the Neighbors Thought)* (3–6). Illus. by Kathryn Hewitt. 1994, Harcourt $20.00 (0-15-248009-9). 96pp. Twenty profiles of authors, some well known, like E. B. White and Shakespeare, and others more obscure. (Rev: BCCB 10/94; BL 9/15/94; SLJ 10/94*) [920]

12487 Krull, Kathleen, and Stephen Alcorn. *The Book of Rock Stars: 24 Musical Icons That Shine Through History* (4–6). 2003, Hyperion $16.99 (0-7868-1950-2). 48pp. Twenty-four icons of American popular music are profiled in this boldly illustrated book, which also includes a list of suggested resources for further research. (Rev: BL 10/15/03; HBG 4/04; SLJ 2/04)

12488 Krystal, Barbara. *100 Artists Who Changed the World* (4–6). Illus. Series: People Who Changed the World. 2003, World Almanac $26.60 (0-8368-5469-1). 112pp. From Washington Allston to James Whistler, this volume briefly profiles 100 important artists of the last 2,500 years. (Rev: SLJ 11/03) [920]

12489 Lester, Julius. *The Blues Singers: Ten Who Rocked the World* (5–8). Illus. by Lisa Cohen. 2001, Hyperion $15.99 (0-7868-0463-7). 48pp. Profiles of 10 African Americans who sang the blues or were influenced by the blues are accompanied by attention-grabbing illustrations and a good discography. (Rev: BL 6/1–15/01; HBG 10/01; SLJ 6/01*) [781.643]

12490 Marcus, Leonard S. *A Caldecott Celebration: Six Artists and Their Paths to the Caldecott Medal* (4–6). Illus. 1998, Walker LB $19.95 (0-8027-8658-8). 48pp. Six Caldecott-winning artists (one for each decade of the prize) introduce their prize-winning books and supply background information on each. The artists are Sendak, McCloskey, Marcia Brown, Steig, Van Allsburg, and Wiesner. (Rev: BL 11/15/98; HB 11–12/98; HBG 3/99; SLJ 12/98) [920]

12491 Marquez, Heron. *Latin Sensations* (5–9). 2001, Lerner LB $25.26 (0-8225-4993-X); paper $12.75 (0-8225-9695-4). 112pp. A collective biography that features profiles of Selena, Ricky Martin, Jennifer Lopez, Marc Anthony, and Enrique Iglesias. (Rev: HBG 10/01; SLJ 3/01) [920]

12492 Martin, Marvin. *Extraordinary People in Jazz* (5–9). Series: Extraordinary People. 2004, Children's Pr. LB $39.00 (0-516-22275-9). 288pp. Duke Ellington, Billie Holiday, and John Coltrane are among the jazz musicians included in this chronologically arranged volume. (Rev: SLJ 1/05) [781.65]

12493 Orgill, Roxane. *Shout, Sister, Shout! Ten Girl Singers Who Shaped a Century* (5–8). 2001, Simon & Schuster $19.95 (0-689-81991-9). 148pp. Orgill has chosen one female singer to represent each decade of the 20th century, revealing much about social mores and technological innovations as well as musical styles. (Rev: BL 1/1–15/01*; HBG 10/01; SLJ 5/01) [970]

12494 Parker, Janice. *Great African Americans in Film* (3–5). Illus. Series: Outstanding African Americans. 1997, Crabtree LB $22.60 (0-86505-

808-3); paper $8.95 (0-86505-822-9). 64pp. Among the 13 important African Americans highlighted here are Dorothy Dandridge, Richard Pryor, and Denzel Washington. (Rev: BL 9/15/97; SLJ 12/97) [920]

12495 Press, Skip. *Candice and Edgar Bergen* (4–8). Illus. Series: Star Families. 1995, Silver Burdett paper $7.95 (0-382-24940-2). 48pp. The story of a father and daughter who had vastly different talents, yet each became a star. (Rev: SLJ 9/95) [920]

12496 Press, Skip. *Natalie and Nat King Cole* (4–8). Illus. Series: Star Families. 1995, Silver Burdett LB $15.95 (0-89686-879-6); paper $4.95 (0-382-24942-9). 48pp. A short book that describes the upbringing and home life of Natalie Cole and her father's influence on her career. (Rev: SLJ 9/95) [920]

12497 Rediger, Pat. *Great African Americans in Entertainment* (4–6). Illus. Series: Outstanding African Americans. 1996, Crabtree LB $22.60 (0-86505-799-0); paper $8.95 (0-86505-813-X). 64pp. Bill Cosby, Spike Lee, and Whoopi Goldberg are three of the 13 African Americans profiled. (Rev: BL 9/15/96) [920]

12498 Rediger, Pat. *Great African Americans in Literature* (4–6). Illus. Series: Outstanding African Americans. 1996, Crabtree LB $22.60 (0-86505-802-4); paper $8.95 (0-86505-816-4). 64pp. Some of the 13 African Americans profiled are Maya Angelou, Toni Morrison, James Baldwin, and Alex Haley. (Rev: BL 9/15/96; SLJ 8/96) [920]

12499 Rediger, Pat. *Great African Americans in Music* (4–6). Illus. Series: Outstanding African Americans. 1996, Crabtree LB $22.60 (0-86505-800-8); paper $8.95 (0-86505-814-8). 64pp. Ray Charles, Nat King Cole, Ella Fitzgerald, and the rapper Hammer are profiled, along with nine others. (Rev: BL 9/15/96) [920]

12500 Rubin, Susan Goldman. *The Yellow House: Vincent van Gogh and Paul Gauguin Side by Side* (K–3). Illus. by Joseph A. Smith. 2001, Abrams $17.95 (0-8109-4588-6). 40pp. Juxtaposed illustrations introduce the works of Vincent van Gogh and Paul Gauguin who, for a short time in 1888, lived and worked together in a studio in the south of France. (Rev: BL 11/15/01; HBG 3/02; SLJ 1/02) [759.4]

12501 Stewart, Gail B. *Great Women Comedians* (5–8). Series: History Makers. 2002, Gale LB $27.45 (1-56006-953-8). 96pp. The comedians Gracie Allen, Lucille Ball, Whoopi Goldberg, Roseanne Barr, and Ellen DeGeneres are profiled in this account that focuses on their groundbreaking achievements. (Rev: SLJ 8/02) [921]

12502 Strickland, Michael R. *African-American Poets* (5–10). Illus. Series: Collective Biographies. 1996, Enslow LB $20.95 (0-89490-774-3). The lives and works of 10 prominent African American poets from Phillis Wheatley to Rita Dove are covered, with quotations from their works and a single full-length poem from each. (Rev: BL 2/15/97; SLJ 1/97) [920]

12503 Tate, Eleanora E. *African American Musicians* (4–7). Series: Black Stars. 2000, Wiley $24.95 (0-

471-25356-1). 170pp. This collective biography highlights both past and present contributions to different kinds of music by several African Americans. (Rev: BL 7/00; HBG 3/01; SLJ 7/00) [920]

12504 Wilkinson, Brenda. *African American Women Writers* (4–7). Illus. Series: Black Stars. 1999, Wiley $22.95 (0-471-17580-3). 166pp. Arranged chronologically, this collective biography contains short profiles of more than 20 important female African American writers. (Rev: BL 2/15/00; HBG 10/00; SLJ 2/00) [910]

Artists

ADAMS, ANSEL

12505 Dunlap, Julie. *Eye on the Wild: A Story About Ansel Adams* (3–6). Illus. Series: Creative Minds. 1995, Carolrhoda LB $21.27 (0-87614-944-1). 64pp. A brief biography about the great nature photographer Ansel Adams. (Rev: BL 10/15/95; SLJ 12/95) [921]

ARCIMBOLDO, GIUSEPPE

12506 Strand, Claudia. *Hello, Fruit Face! The Paintings of Giuseppe Arcimboldo* (3–5). Trans. by Michele A. Schons. Illus. 1999, Prestel $14.95 (3-7913-2084-X). 30pp. This is a well-illustrated biography of Arcimboldo, a 16th-century Italian artist who was noted for using everyday objects such as fruits and flowers and arranging them to present a human portrait. (Rev: BL 9/15/99; SLJ 1/00) [921]

AUDUBON, JOHN JAMES

12507 Armstrong, Jennifer. *Audubon: Painter of Birds in the Wild Frontier* (2–4). Illus. by Jos. A. Smith. 2003, Abrams $17.95 (0-8109-4238-0). 38pp. An excellent introduction to the early life of naturalist-painter John James Audubon, this large-format picture book recounts many of the artist's experiences on the American frontier, including his meeting with the legendary Daniel Boone. (Rev: BL 4/1/03; HBG 10/03; SLJ 5/03) [598]

12508 Burleigh, Robert. *Into the Woods: John James Audubon Lives His Dream* (2–5). Illus. by Wendell Minor. 2003, Simon & Schuster $16.95 (0-689-83040-8). 40pp. Charming watercolors and selections of Audubon's own detailed drawings combine with simple, poetic text and quotes from Audubon's journals to give a good picture of the bird-lover who rejected urban life. (Rev: BL 1/1–15/03; HBG 10/03; SLJ 2/03) [921]

12509 Davies, Jacqueline. *The Boy Who Drew Birds: A Story of John James Audubon* (2–4). Illus. by Melissa Sweet. 2004, Houghton Mifflin $15.00 (0-618-24343-7). 32pp. This engaging biography focuses on Audubon's early enthusiasm for birds and his decision to band them to trace their movements. (Rev: BL 11/1/04) [598]

12510 Kastner, Joseph. *John James Audubon* (5–8). Illus. Series: First Impressions. 1992, Abrams $19.95 (0-8109-1918-4). 92pp. A lively account of the adventurous life of Audubon, with many fine art reproductions. (Rev: HB 3–4/93; SLJ 12/92) [921]

12511 Roop, Peter, and Connie Roop, eds. *Capturing Nature* (5–7). Illus. by Rick Farley. 1993, Walker LB $17.85 (0-8027-8205-1). 48pp. Audubon's prints and original paintings and excerpts from his journals are combined to produce a stunning biography. (Rev: BCCB 12/93; BL 12/15/93; SLJ 1/94) [921]

BEARDEN, ROMARE

12512 Greenberg, Jan. *Romare Bearden: Collage of Memories* (3–9). Illus. 2003, Abrams $17.95 (0-8109-4589-4). 48pp. Text and Bearden's own collages recount this African American artist's life — his youth in North Carolina, his years in Harlem, his love of jazz — in a handsome oversize volume. (Rev: BL 9/15/03*; HB 11–12/03; HBG 4/04; SLJ 9/03) [709.]

BENTLEY, SNOWFLAKE

12513 Martin, Jacqueline B. *Snowflake Bentley* (K–3). Illus. by Mary Azarian. 1998, Houghton Mifflin $16.00 (0-395-86162-4). 32pp. As a child Bentley was so obsessed with snow that he devoted his attention to photographing snow crystals and, now nicknamed Snowflake, gained a reputation as a nature photographer. (Rev: BCCB 12/98; BL 10/1/98*; HB 9–10/98; HBG 3/99; SLJ 9/98) [921]

BERENSTAIN, JAN AND BERENSTAIN, STAN

12514 Berenstain, Stan, and Jan Berenstain. *Down a Sunny Dirt Road: An Autobiography* (5–8). Illus. 2002, Random $20.00 (0-375-81403-5). 208pp. This engrossing joint biography of the co-creators of the Berenstain Bears is filled with photographs, early cartoons, and other fascinating artwork. (Rev: BL 12/15/02; HB 1–2/03; HBG 3/03; SLJ 12/02) [813]

BOTTICELLI, SANDRO

12515 Connolly, Sean. *Botticelli* (4–8). Illus. Series: Lives of the Artists. 2005, World Almanac LB $22.50 (0-8368-5648-1). 48pp. A tall, slender volume full of facts about Botticelli's life and times, with many color reproductions. (Rev: SLJ 3/05) [921]

BOURKE-WHITE, MARGARET

12516 Welch, Catherine A. *Margaret Bourke-White* (2–4). Illus. 1997, Carolrhoda LB $19.93 (0-87614-890-9). 56pp. The life of this outstanding photographer reveals the excitement and danger involved in her work. (Rev: BL 9/1/97; HBG 3/98; SLJ 8/97) [921]

12517 Welch, Catherine A. *Margaret Bourke-White: Racing with a Dream* (4–8). Illus. 1998, Carolrhoda LB $30.35 (1-57505-049-8). 104pp. A fine biography of the important photographer whose subjects

included skyscrapers, the Depression, Buchenwald, and South African miners. (Rev: BL 10/1/98; HBG 3/99; SLJ 7/98) [921]

BRADY, MATHEW

12518 Pflueger, Lynda. *Mathew Brady* (5–8). Series: Historical American Biographies. 2001, Enslow LB $20.95 (0-7660-1444-4). A biography of the photographer known primarily for his coverage of the Civil War, illustrated with many of his works. (Rev: BL 1/1–15/02; HBG 10/01; SLJ 9/01) [921]

BRUEGEL, PIETER

12519 Malam, John. *Pieter Bruegel* (2–4). Series: Tell Me About. 1999, Carolrhoda LB $19.93 (1-57505-366-7). 24pp. The author explores Bruegel's life and times as well as his ideas and masterpieces. (Rev: HBG 10/99; SLJ 7/99) [921]

12520 Woodhouse, Jane. *Pieter Bruegel* (3–4). Series: The Life and Work Of. 2000, Heinemann LB $19.92 (1-57572-344-1). 32pp. This biography of the Flemish painter includes many examples of his paintings of earthy peasants and their surroundings. (Rev: BL 10/15/00; HBG 10/01; SLJ 2/01) [921]

CALDECOTT, RANDOLPH

12521 Hegel, Claudette. *Randolph Caldecott: An Illustrated Life* (5–9). Series: Avisson Young Adult. 2004, Avisson $27.50 (1-888105-60-7). Many of Caldecott's drawings are included in this account of the artist's life and work, with coverage of the children's award named in his honor. (Rev: BL 10/1/04; SLJ 11/04) [741.6]

CALDER, ALEXANDER

12522 Lipman, Jean, and Margaret Aspenwall. *Alexander Calder and His Magical Mobiles* (5–8). Illus. 1981, Hudson Hills $19.95 (0-933920-17-2). 96pp. An exciting biography of this controversial sculptor.

CARLE, ERIC

12523 Carle, Eric. *Flora and Tiger: 19 Very Short Stories from My Life* (4–8). Illus. 1997, Penguin Putnam $17.99 (0-399-23203-6). An autobiography of the famous picture-book artist who was born in Germany but who has lived in the United States since 1952. (Rev: BL 12/15/97; HBG 3/98; SLJ 2/98) [921]

CARR, EMILY

12524 Bogart, Jo Ellen. *Emily Carr: At the Edge of the World* (4–8). Illus. by Maxwell Newhouse. 2003, Tundra $18.95 (0-88776-640-4). 40pp. This picture book for older readers presents the life and work of the Canadian artist and writer who became famous for her depictions of the native peoples of the Pacific Coast. (Rev: BL 11/1/03; HBG 4/04; SLJ 12/03) [759.11]

12525 Debon, Nicolas. *Four Pictures by Emily Carr* (5–9). Illus. 2003, Douglas & McIntyre $15.95 (0-88899-532-6). 32pp. This small comic-book biography uses four of Carr's paintings to introduce chapters that trace the Canadian artist's life and interest in Native Americans. (Rev: BL 12/1/03; HB 1–2/04; HBG 3/02; SLJ 11/03) [759.11]

12526 Griek, Susan Vande. *The Art Room* (PS–3). Illus. by Pascal Milelli. 2002, Groundwood $15.95 (0-88899-449-4). 24pp. This biography of the West Coast Canadian artist concentrates on her teaching of young students and the inspiration she gave them. (Rev: BL 4/1/02; HBG 10/02; SLJ 6/02) [921]

CASSATT, MARY

12527 Ferrara, Cos. *Mary Cassatt: The Life and Art of a Genteel Rebel* (5–8). Illus. Series: Girls Explore, Reach for the Stars. 2005, Girls Explore $20.00 (0-9749456-3-3). 101pp. Cassatt's art, shown in small full-color reproductions, is introduced in this biography that also discusses her independence and feminist views. (Rev: BL 2/15/05) [921]

12528 Giesecke, Ernestine. *Mary Cassatt* (3–5). Illus. Series: Life and Work Of. 1999, Heinemann LB $13.95 (1-57572-955-5). 32pp. This biography of the famous American artist who lived and worked in Paris is complemented by many examples of her work. (Rev: BL 2/1/00; SLJ 1/00) [921]

12529 Hoena, Blake A. *Mary Cassatt* (2–4). Series: Masterpieces: Artists and Their Works. 2003, Capstone LB $19.93 (0-7368-2229-1). 24pp. A small-format introductory biography of the artist featuring simple text and color reproductions, with emphasis on Cassatt's association with the Impressionists and how she faced prejudice because of her gender. (Rev: SLJ 3/04) [921]

12530 Meyer, Susan E. *Mary Cassatt* (4–8). Illus. Series: First Impressions. 1991, Abrams $19.95 (0-8109-3154-0). 92pp. The story of the American artist who spent her most productive painting years in France. (Rev: SLJ 5/91) [921]

12531 O'Connor, Jane. *Mary Cassatt: Family Pictures* (3–4). Illus. by Jennifer Kalis. Series: Smart and Art. 2003, Grosset LB $14.89 (0-448-43153-X); paper $5.99 (0-448-43152-1). 32pp. Presented as a school report, this is a simple but appealing overview of the artist's life. (Rev: HBG 10/03; SLJ 7/03) [921]

12532 Streissguth, Thomas. *Mary Cassatt* (4–8). Series: Trailblazers. 1999, Lerner LB $30.35 (1-57505-291-1). Full-color illustrations enhance this biography of the American painter who was associated with the Impressionists and spent most of her adult life in France. (Rev: BL 5/1/99; HBG 10/99; SLJ 9/99) [921]

CATLIN, GEORGE

12533 Plain, Nancy. *The Man Who Painted Indians: George Catlin* (3–6). Series: Biographies. 1996,

Benchmark LB $21.36 (0-7614-0486-4). 48pp. The story of the artist, born in 1796, who left his law career to live in the American wilderness and paint its people and places. (Rev: SLJ 2/97) [921]

CÉZANNE, PAUL

12534 Connolly, Sean. *Paul Cézanne* (3–4). Series: The Life and Work Of. 1999, Heinemann LB $13.95 (1-57572-957-1). 32pp. Covers the life and work of this famous Impressionist painter. (Rev: BL 2/15/00; SLJ 1/00) [921]

12535 harris, Nathaniel. *Paul Cezanne* (5–8). Illus. Series: Artists in Their Time. 2003, Watts LB $22.00 (0-531-12242-5); paper $6.95 (0-531-16646-5). 48pp. An interesting life of Cezanne, with reproductions of his works and of those of fellow painters, and a timeline that adds historical context. [921]

12536 Sellier, Marie. *Cézanne from A to Z* (4–8). Trans. from French by Claudia Zoe Bedrick. Illus. Series: Artists from A to Z. 1996, Bedrick LB $14.95 (0-87226-476-9). 59pp. An imaginative, well-executed account of the life and works of Cézanne, enhanced by reproductions of many of his paintings. (Rev: SLJ 5/96) [921]

12537 Venezia, Mike. *Paul Cézanne* (4–6). Series: Getting to Know. 1998, Children's Book Pr. LB $21.00 (0-516-20762-8). Along with an easy-to-read text and full-color reproductions, this introduction to the life and art of Cézanne includes many amusing cartoon illustrations. (Rev: BL 8/98; HBG 10/98) [921]

CHAGALL, MARC

12538 Hopler, Brigitta. *Marc Chagall: Life Is a Dream* (4–7). Trans. by Catherine McCreadie. Illus. Series: Adventures in Art. 1999, Prestel $14.95 (3-7913-1986-8). 30pp. This biography of the surrealist painter not only relates the artist's life story but also encourages the reader to discover the meanings behind the images. (Rev: BL 2/1/99; SLJ 2/99) [921]

12539 Lemke, Elisabeth, and Thomas David. *Marc Chagall: What Colour Is Paradise?* (4–8). Illus. Series: Adventures in Art. 2001, Prestel $14.95 (3-7913-2393-8). 28pp. Using Chagall's biographical paintings as a focus, this innovative biography tells of his life, career, and work. (Rev: BL 1/1–15/01; SLJ 4/01) [921]

12540 Mason, Antony. *Marc Chagall* (4–8). Illus. Series: Lives of the Artists. 2005, World Almanac LB $22.50 (0-8368-5649-X). 48pp. A tall, slender volume full of facts about Chagall's life and times, with many color reproductions. (Rev: SLJ 3/05) [921]

12541 Venezia, Mike. *Marc Chagall* (2–4). Series: Getting to Know. 2000, Children's Book Pr. LB $22.00 (0-516-21055-6). 32pp. A biography of the innovative 20th-century painter told with an easy-to-read text, full-color reproductions, and amusing cartoons. (Rev: BL 5/15/00) [921]

12542 Welton, Jude. *Marc Chagall* (5–8). Illus. Series: Artists in Their Time. 2003, Watts LB $22.00 (0-531-12235-2); paper $6.95 (0-531-16645-7). 48pp. An interesting life of Chagall, with reproductions of his works and of those of fellow painters, and a timeline that adds historical context. [921]

CHANG, WAH MING

12543 Riley, Gail B. *Wah Ming Chang: Artist and Master of Special Effects* (4–8). Illus. Series: Multicultural Junior Biographies. 1995, Enslow LB $20.95 (0-89490-639-9). A thorough, well-documented biography of this Chinese American who has gained prominence in the field of special effects. (Rev: BL 2/15/96; SLJ 2/96) [921]

COROT, JEAN CAMILLE

12544 Larroche, Caroline. *Corot from A to Z* (5–8). Trans. from French by Claudia Zoe Bedrick. Series: Artists from A to Z. 1996, Bedrick LB $14.95 (0-87226-477-7). Although the text is somewhat confusing, the strength of this account of Corot's life and work is the full-color reproductions of his work. (Rev: SLJ 1/97) [921]

DA VINCI, LEONARDO

12545 Byrd, Robert. *Leonardo, Beautiful Dreamer* (4–6). Illus. by author. 2003, Penguin Putnam $17.99 (0-525-47033-6). 40pp. This large-format overview of da Vinci's life and work is beautifully illustrated and packed with information that is presented in varied and appropriate styles. (Rev: BL 8/03; HB 9–10/03; HBG 4/04; SLJ 9/03) [921]

12546 Connolly, Sean. *Leonardo da Vinci* (3–4). Series: The Life and Work Of. 1999, Heinemann LB $13.95 (1-57572-954-7). 32pp. This book explores the life and accomplishments of Leonardo da Vinci and tells how events influenced his masterpieces. (Rev: BL 2/15/00; SLJ 1/00) [921]

12547 Hart, Tony. *Leonardo da Vinci* (3–5). Illus. by Susan Hellard. Series: Famous Children. 1994, Barron's paper $6.95 (0-8120-1828-1). This biography focuses on the childhood of Leonardo and how his genius was shown at an early age. (Rev: SLJ 8/94) [921]

12548 Herbert, Janis. *Leonardo da Vinci for Kids: His Life and Ideas* (4–8). Illus. 1998, Chicago Review paper $16.95 (1-55652-298-3). 101pp. This biography of Leonardo da Vinci contains background information on history, art techniques, science, and philosophy. (Rev: BL 3/1/99; SLJ 4/99) [921]

12549 Kuhne, Heinz. *Leonardo da Vinci: Dreams, Schemes, and Flying Machines* (4–8). Illus. Series: Adventures in Art. 2000, Prestel $14.95 (3-7913-2166-8). 32pp. This well-illustrated biography covers da Vinci's accomplishments as a scientist, engineer, inventor, and artist. (Rev: BL 7/00) [921]

12550 *Leonardo da Vinci* (5–8). Series: Lives of the Artists. 2004, World Almanac LB $29.26 (0-8368-

5599-X). 48pp. Lots of facts and illustrations are included in this tall-format volume covering da Vinci's life and work. (Rev: SLJ 8/04) [921]

12551 Malam, John. *Leonardo da Vinci* (2–4). Series: Tell Me About. 1999, Carolrhoda LB $19.93 (1-57505-367-5). 24pp. A biography that gives details on da Vinci's life and accomplishments as well as material on the period in which he lived. (Rev: HBG 10/99; SLJ 7/99) [921]

12552 Mason, Antony. *Leonardo da Vinci* (4–8). Illus. 1994, Barron's paper $7.95 (0-8120-1997-0). 32pp. A brief biography that chronicles the achievements of this multifaceted genius and supplies pictures of some of his great triumphs. (Rev: BL 12/1/94) [921]

12553 O'Connor, Barbara. *Leonardo da Vinci: Renaissance Genius* (5–8). Series: Trailblazer Biographies. 2002, Carolrhoda LB $30.35 (0-87614-467-9). 112pp. An excellent biography that details Leonardo's life from childhood, discusses some of his famous paintings, and looks at his inventions and experiments. (Rev: BL 3/15/03; HBG 3/03; SLJ 11/02) [921]

12554 Reed, Jennifer. *Leonardo da Vinci: Genius of Art and Science* (4–7). Illus. Series: Great Minds of Science. 2005, Enslow LB $26.60 (0-7660-2500-4). 128pp. Reed describes da Vinci's wide-ranging achievements — showing, for example, his urban planning ideas, his design for a flying machine, and his anatomical drawings — and emphasizes his originality and creativity. (Rev: SLJ 6/05) [921]

12555 Venezia, Mike. *Da Vinci* (2–5). Illus. by author. Series: Getting to Know. 1989, Children's Book Pr. LB $22.00 (0-516-02275-X). 32pp. Using text, cartoons, and the artist's paintings, this is an introduction to the life and work of Leonardo da Vinci. (Rev: SLJ 3/90) [921]

DALI, SALVADOR

12556 Anderson, Robert. *Salvador Dali* (5–8). Illus. Series: Artists in Their Time. 2002, Watts LB $22.00 (0-531-12231-X); paper $6.95 (0-531-16624-4). 48pp. This volume presents Dali's life and influence with many illustrations, news clippings, and useful information. (Rev: BL 10/15/02) [709]

DEGAS, EDGAR

12557 Venezia, Mike. *Edgar Degas* (2–4). Illus. Series: Getting to Know. 2000, Children's Book Pr. LB $22.50 (0-516-21593-0); paper $6.95 (0-516-27172-5). 32pp. An easy-to-read text, several reproductions, and humorous cartoons are used to introduce the life and works of this French master. (Rev: BL 9/15/00) [921]

DE KOONING, WILLEM

12558 Hawes, Louise. *Willem de Kooning: The Life of an Artist* (4–6). Series: Artist Biographies. 2002, Enslow LB $18.95 (0-7660-1884-9). 48pp. Covers de Kooning's life from youth, his artistic techniques and work habits, and the impact of his lifestyle. (Rev: HBG 10/03; SLJ 3/03) [921]

DELACROIX, EUGENE

12559 Venezia, Mike. *Eugene Delacroix* (1–3). Illus. Series: Getting to Know the World's Greatest Artists. 2003, Children's Pr. LB $24.00 (0-516-22576-6); paper $6.95 (0-516-26976-3). 32pp. An easy-to-read text and humorous cartoons are used to introduce this famous French artist and his work. [921]

DESJARLAIT, PATRICK

12560 Williams, Neva. *Patrick DesJarlait: Conversations with a Native American Artist* (5–7). Illus. 1994, Lerner LB $27.15 (0-8225-3151-8). 56pp. A beautifully illustrated biography of the Native American artist who worked at the Red Lake Indian Reservation in Minnesota. (Rev: BL 1/1/95; SLJ 1/95) [921]

DISNEY, WALT

12561 Cole, Michael D. *Walt Disney: Creator of Mickey Mouse* (4–7). Illus. Series: People to Know. 1996, Enslow LB $20.95 (0-89490-694-1). 112pp. A thoughtful biography of the great animator, perfectionist, and founder of an entertainment empire. (Rev: BL 6/1–15/96; SLJ 8/96) [921]

12562 Ford, Barbara. *Walt Disney* (4–8). Illus. 1989, Walker LB $17.00 (0-8027-6865-2). 160pp. The story of Disney's youth and his struggle to fulfill his dreams. (Rev: BL 5/15/89) [791.430924]

12563 Nardo, Don. *Walt Disney* (4–8). Series: The Importance Of. 2000, Lucent LB $27.45 (1-56006-605-9). A well-researched biography of Walt Disney that quotes from many original and secondary sources, documents facts, and gives an honest appraisal of his work. (Rev: BL 1/1–15/00; HBG 10/00) [921]

12564 Selden, Bernice. *The Story of Walt Disney, Maker of Magical Worlds* (4–6). Illus. Series: Yearling Biographies. 1989, Dell paper $4.50 (0-440-40240-9). 92pp. A balanced account of the genius who established the art of animation in Hollywood. (Rev: BL 3/15/90; SLJ 4/90) [921]

EL GRECO

12565 Venezia, Mike. *El Greco* (2–4). Series: Getting to Know. 1997, Children's Book Pr. LB $22.00 (0-516-20586-2). 32pp. This appealing introduction to El Greco and his works contains several color reproductions plus the author's playful cartoons. (Rev: BL 10/15/97; HBG 3/98) [921]

GAUGUIN, PAUL

12566 Anderson, Robert. *Paul Gauguin* (4–8). Series: Artists in Their Time. 2003, Watts LB $22.00 (0-531-12239-5); paper $6.95 (0-531-16647-3). 46pp. An interesting life of Gauguin, with reproductions of his works and of those of fellow painters, with a timeline that adds historical context. (Rev: SLJ 6/03) [759.4]

GEHRY, FRANK O.

12567 Greenberg, Jan, and Sandra Jordan. *Frank O. Gehry: Outside In* (4–7). 2000, DK paper $19.95 (0-7894-2677-3). 47pp. A stunning profile of this innovative architect who was responsible for the Guggenheim Museum in Bilbao, Spain, and the Experience Music Project in Seattle. (Rev: BCCB 10/00; BL 10/1/00; HB 9–10/00; HBG 3/01; SLJ 9/00) [921]

GIACOMETTI, ALBERTO

12568 Gaff, Jackie. *Alberto Giacometti* (5–8). Series: Artists in Their Time. 2002, Watts LB $22.00 (0-531-12224-7); paper $6.95 (0-531-16617-1). 48pp. The life of this Italian artist noted for his elongated sculptures is re-created with comments on his social period and reproductions of his work. (Rev: BL 10/15/02) [921]

GIOTTO

12569 Venezia, Mike. *Giotto* (2–4). Series: Getting to Know. 2000, Children's Book Pr. LB $22.00 (0-516-21592-9). 32pp. The story of the Florentine Renaissance artist and architect who influenced all of European painting is told in text, reproductions, and witty cartoons. (Rev: BL 5/15/00) [921]

GORMAN, R. C.

12570 Hermann, Spring. *R. C. Gorman: Navajo Artist* (4–8). Illus. Series: Multicultural Junior Biographies. 1995, Enslow LB $20.95 (0-89490-638-0). 104pp. The story of this contemporary Native American artist, who reflects his heritage in his work. (Rev: BL 2/15/96; SLJ 3/96) [921]

GOYA, FRANCISCO

12571 Schiaffino, Mariarosa. *Goya* (4–8). Illus. by Thomas Trojer and Claudia Saraceni. Series: Masters of Art. 2000, Bedrick $22.50 (0-87226-529-3). 64pp. Each of the double-page spreads in this attractive book is devoted to an aspect of Goya's life or work; for example, his contemporaries and his drawings of the bullfight. (Rev: HBG 10/00; SLJ 3/00) [921]

12572 Venezia, Mike. *Francisco Goya* (2–5). Illus. Series: Getting to Know. 1991, Children's Book Pr. LB $22.00 (0-516-02292-X). 32pp. This is an introduction to the life and work of the great Spanish portrait artist who was also a bitter social satirist. (Rev: BL 8/91; SLJ 12/91) [921]

12573 Waldron, Ann. *Francisco Goya* (5–8). Illus. Series: First Impressions. 1992, Abrams $19.95 (0-8109-3368-3). 92pp. Covers the stormy life of Goya and the many intrigues at court, and includes many reproductions. (Rev: SLJ 12/92) [921]

629

HOKUSAI, KATSUSHIKA

12574 Ray, Deborah Kogan. *Hokusai* (2–4). Illus. 2001, Farrar $18.00 (0-374-33263-0). 40pp. Covers the life of Japanese artist Hokusai from birth, with excellent descriptions of life in late 18th- and 19th-century Japan. (Rev: BL 11/1/01; HBG 3/02; SLJ 12/01*) [796.92]

HOMER, WINSLOW

12575 *Winslow Homer* (1–3). Illus. by Mike Venezia. Series: Getting to Know the World's Greatest Artists. 2004, Scholastic LB $26.00 (0-516-26979-8). 32pp. This beautifully illustrated biography chronicles the life and work of the late-19th-century American artist. (Rev: BL 6/1–15/04) [921]

HOPPER, EDWARD

12576 Foa, Emma. *Edward Hopper* (4–8). Series: Artists in Their Time. 2003, Watts LB $22.00 (0-531-12240-9); paper $6.95 (0-531-16641-4). 46pp. An interesting life of Hopper, with reproductions of his works and of those of fellow painters, and a timeline that adds historical context. (Rev: SLJ 6/03) [759.13]

12577 Lyons, Deborah. *Edward Hopper: Summer at the Seaside* (4–8). Series: Adventures in Art. 2003, Prestel $14.95 (3-7913-2737-2). 30pp. The story of the American painter who died in 1967, with a good analysis of many of his important works. (Rev: BL 11/15/03; SLJ 9/03) [921]

12578 Spangenburg, Ray, and Kit Moser. *Edward Hopper: The Life of an Artist* (3–5). Series: Artist Biographies. 2002, Enslow LB $18.95 (0-7660-1881-4). 48pp. A look at the life and work of the artist and his realistic paintings. (Rev: HBG 10/03; SLJ 4/03) [921]

HOUSTON, JAMES

12579 Houston, James. *Fire into Ice: Adventures in Glass Making* (5–9). Illus. 1998, Tundra $15.95 (0-88776-459-2). The author, who lived with and wrote about the Inuit, tells how he left the Arctic in the early 1960s and became a Steuben glass designer, incorporating his Inuit-influenced drawings into a new medium. (Rev: BL 4/15/99; HBG 3/99; SLJ 1/99) [921]

HUNTER, CLEMENTINE

12580 Lyons, Mary E., ed. *Talking with Tebe: Clementine Hunter, Memory Artist* (4–9). 1998, Houghton Mifflin $16.00 (0-395-72031-1). 48pp. Using her own words from recorded interviews, this biography tells the story of the African American primitive painter who lived to be 101. (Rev: BCCB 1/99; HB 9–10/98; HBG 3/99; SLJ 9/98) [921]

JACKSON, WILLIAM HENRY

12581 Lawlor, Laurie. *Window on the West: The Frontier Photography of William Henry Jackson* (5–8). 1999, Holiday House $18.95 (0-8234-1380-

2). 132pp. In addition to tracing the life of this famous photographer who captured the life and spirit of frontier America, this account covers the history and development of the West and pioneer life. (Rev: BL 2/15/00; HB 3–4/00; HBG 10/00; SLJ 3/00) [921]

KAHLO, FRIDA

12582 Frazier, Nancy. *Frida Kahlo: Mysterious Painter* (5–7). Illus. Series: Library of Famous Women. 1993, Rosen $26.19 (1-56711-012-6). 64pp. A biography of this enigmatic artist with examples of her work. (Rev: BL 2/15/93) [921]

12583 Frith, Margaret. *Frida Kahlo: The Artist Who Painted Herself* (3–5). Illus. by Tomie dePaola. Series: Smart About Art. 2003, Grosset LB $14.89 (0-448-43239-0); paper $5.99 (0-448-42677-3). This picture-book biography presents the life of the Mexican artist as seen through the eyes of a young girl who is researching her for a school report. (Rev: HB 11–12/03; HBG 4/04; SLJ 11/03) [921]

12584 Garza, Hedda. *Frida Kahlo* (5–9). Series: Hispanics of Achievement. 1994, Chelsea LB $21.95 (0-7910-1698-6); paper $9.95 (0-7910-1699-4). Known once only as the wife of Diego Rivera, this painter, who lived most of her life in Mexico, is now considered a great artist. (Rev: BL 3/1/94) [921]

12585 Holzhey, Magdalena. *Frida Kahlo: The Artist in the Blue House* (4–8). Series: Adventures in Art. 2003, Prestel $14.95 (3-7913-2863-8). 30pp. A colorful introduction to this Mexican painter with an interesting analysis of individual paintings. (Rev: BL 11/15/03; SLJ 9/03) [921]

12586 Laidlaw, Jill A. *Frida Kahlo* (5–8). Series: Artists in Their Time. 2003, Watts LB $22.00 (0-531-12236-0); paper $6.95 (0-531-16642-2). 46pp. An interesting life of Kahlo, with reproductions of her works and a timeline and informative sidebars that add historical context. (Rev: SLJ 6/03) [759]

12587 Venezia, Mike. *Frida Kahlo* (2–4). Series: Getting to Know. 1999, Children's Book Pr. LB $22.00 (0-516-20975-2). 32pp. A brief biography of Kahlo that includes many reproductions of her works and some humorous cartoons about her by the author. (Rev: BL 9/15/99) [921]

12588 Winter, Jonah. *Frida* (PS–3). Illus. by Ana Juan. 2002, Scholastic $16.95 (0-590-20320-7). 32pp. An inspirational biography of Mexican artist Frida Kahlo. (Rev: BCCB 2/02; BL 3/1/02; HB 3–4/02; HBG 10/02; SLJ 3/02) [759.9]

12589 Woronoff, Kristen. *Frida Kahlo: Mexican Painter* (3–5). Series: Famous Women Juniors. 2002, Gale LB $21.54 (1-56711-594-2). 32pp. This account focuses on Kahlo's youth and the events that led to her life as an artist. (Rev: SLJ 9/02) [921]

KEATS, EZRA JACK

12590 Engel, Dean, and Florence B. Freedman. *Ezra Jack Keats: A Biography with Illustrations* (3–6). Illus. 1995, Silver Moon $24.95 (1-881889-65-3). 96pp. Using first-hand sources, including interviews, this is the story of the artist/author best known for *The Snowy Day*. (Rev: BCCB 9/95; BL 4/15/95; HB 5–6/95, 9–10/95; SLJ 6/95) [921]

KLEE, PAUL

12591 Connolly, Sean. *Paul Klee* (3–4). Series: The Life and Work Of. 1999, Heinemann LB $13.95 (1-57572-952-0). 32pp. An illustrated introduction to the life and work of the Swiss abstract painter. (Rev: BL 2/15/00) [921]

12592 Laidlaw, Jill A. *Paul Klee* (5–8). Series: Artists in Their Time. 2002, Watts LB $22.00 (0-531-12230-1); paper $6.95 (0-531-16623-6). 46pp. Photographs, reproductions, maps, and a timeline that links world events with events in the artist's life make this suitable both for browsing and report writing. (Rev: BL 10/15/02; SLJ 1/03) [921]

12593 Venezia, Mike. *Paul Klee* (2–5). Illus. Series: Getting to Know. 1991, Children's Book Pr. LB $22.00 (0-516-02294-6). 32pp. An informal, simple biography of this Swiss artist, as well as many examples of his work and comments on his style. (Rev: BL 1/15/92) [921]

KLIMT, GUSTAV

12594 Wenzel, Angela. *Gustav Klimt: Silver, Gold, and Precious Stones* (4–8). Illus. Series: Adventures in Art. 2000, Prestel $14.95 (3-7913-2328-8). 32pp. The life of this Austrian artist is presented along with analysis of many of his paintings, including the famous *The Kiss*. (Rev: BL 7/00) [921]

KURELEK, WILLIAM

12595 Kurelek, William. *A Prairie Boy's Summer* (3–5). Illus. by author. 1975, Tundra paper $10.99 (0-88776-116-X). 48pp. Each of this Canadian artist's paintings depicts a farm activity, which the accompanying text describes in this companion piece to the author's earlier *A Prairie Boy's Winter* (1984).

LANGE, DOROTHEA

12596 Venezia, Mike. *Dorothea Lange* (2–4). Illus. Series: Getting to Know. 2000, Children's Book Pr. LB $22.50 (0-516-22026-8); paper $6.95 (0-516-27171-7). 32pp. A biography — enriched with amusing cartoons — of the famous American photographer noted mainly for her haunting pictures of migrant workers and victims of the Great Depression. (Rev: BL 9/15/00) [921]

LAWRENCE, JACOB

12597 Duggleby, John. *Story Painter: The Life of Jacob Lawrence* (5–8). Illus. 1998, Chronicle $16.95 (0-8118-2082-3). 64pp. Using 50 color reproductions, this biography of the great African American illustrator and painter tells how he moved to Harlem in the 1930s and developed his own techniques and style. (Rev: BCCB 1/99; BL 10/15/98; HB 3–4/99; HBG 3/99; SLJ 12/98) [921]

12598 Leach, Deba Foxley. *I See You I See Myself: The Young Life of Jacob Lawrence* (5–9). Illus. by Jacob Lawrence. 2002, Phillips Collection $20.00 (0-943044-26-X). 64pp. A look at the early life and work of the African American artist, with information on his paintings as a teen. (Rev: SLJ 12/02) [759.13]

12599 Venezia, Mike. *Jacob Lawrence* (2–4). Illus. by author. Series: Getting to Know. 1999, Children's Book Pr. LB $22.00 (0-516-21012-2). 32pp. A fine introduction to the life and work of this contemporary African American artist that focuses on the aspects of his life that affected his art. (Rev: SLJ 5/00) [921]

LEWIN, TED

12600 Lewin, Ted. *Touch and Go: Travels of a Children's Book Illustrator* (4–6). Illus. 1999, Lothrop $15.00 (0-688-14109-9). 80pp. The famous children's book illustrator tells how he has gathered material for his work from around the world and describes his adventures along the way. (Rev: BL 4/15/99; SLJ 7/99) [921]

LEWIS, MAUD

12601 Bogart, Jo Ellen. *Capturing Joy: The Story of Maud Lewis* (3–6). Illus. by Mark Lang. 2002, Tundra $16.95 (0-88776-568-8). 32pp. The story of the life and work of the Canadian artist who used a folk-art style. (Rev: BL 6/1–15/02; HBG 10/02; SLJ 7/02) [921]

LIN, MAYA

12602 Ling, Bettina. *Maya Lin* (5–7). Illus. Series: Contemporary Asian Americans. 1997, Raintree LB $17.98 (0-8172-3992-8). 48pp. A profile of the Asian American architect and an introduction to many of her projects, including the Vietnam War Memorial in Washington, D.C. (Rev: BL 5/1/97) [921]

12603 Malone, Mary. *Maya Lin: Architect and Artist* (4–6). Illus. Series: People to Know. 1995, Enslow LB $20.95 (0-89490-499-X). 112pp. The life story of the renowned architect best known for her Vietnam Veterans Memorial. (Rev: BL 4/15/95; SLJ 5/95) [921]

MARTINEZ, MARIA

12604 Morris, Juddi. *Tending the Fire: The Story of Maria Martinez* (5–8). 1997, Northland paper $6.95 (0-87358-654-9). The life story of New Mexico's most famous potter, who was born in an Indian pueblo in 1887. (Rev: BL 12/1/97; BR 11–12/97; HBG 3/98; SLJ 12/97) [921]

MATISSE, HENRI

12605 Hollein, Max, and Nina Hollein. *Matisse: Cut-Out Fun with Matisse* (4–8). Series: Adventures in Art. 2003, Prestel $14.95 (3-7913-2858-1). 30pp. This large-formatted book that originated in Germany, successfully introduces the life and work of the great French master. (Rev: BL 11/15/03; HBG 3/02; SLJ 8/01) [921]

12606 Sturm, Ellen. *Matisse* (2–4). Series: Masterpieces: Artists and Their Works. 2003, Capstone LB $19.93 (0-7368-2227-5). 24pp. A small-format introductory biography of the artist featuring simple text and color reproductions and including material on his early life, training, and influences. (Rev: SLJ 3/04) [921]

12607 Venezia, Mike. *Henri Matisse* (2–4). Illus. Series: Getting to Know. 1997, Children's Book Pr. LB $22.00 (0-516-20311-8). 32pp. A light but realistic overview of Matisse and his work, with many color reproductions, clever cartoon illustrations, and an interesting story line. (Rev: BL 7/97) [921]

12608 Welton, Jude. *Henri Matisse* (5–8). Series: Artists in Their Time. 2002, Watts LB $22.00 (0-531-12228-X); paper $6.95 (0-531-16621-X). 48pp. The artistic and social periods during which Matisse worked are re-created along with a biography and several color examples of his work. (Rev: BL 10/15/02; SLJ 1/03) [921]

MICHELANGELO

12609 Hart, Tony. *Michelangelo* (3–5). Illus. by Susan Hellard. Series: Famous Children. 1994, Barron's paper $6.95 (0-8120-1827-3). An attractive biography that focuses on the boyhood of Michelangelo and how he revealed his genius as a young apprentice. (Rev: SLJ 8/94) [921]

12610 *Michelangelo* (5–8). Series: The Lives of the Artists. 2004, World Almanac LB $29.26 (0-8368-5600-7). 48pp. A tall, slender volume full of facts about Michelangelo's life and times, with many color reproductions. (Rev: SLJ 8/04) [921]

12611 Stanley, Diane. *Michelangelo* (5–8). Illus. 2000, HarperCollins LB $17.89 (0-688-15086-1). 48pp. An intriguing biography of Michelangelo that also gives extensive coverage on the history of the Italian Renaissance. (Rev: BCCB 10/00; BL 8/00*; HBG 3/01; SLJ 8/00) [921]

12612 Tames, Richard. *Michelangelo Buonarroti* (3–4). Series: The Life and Work Of. 2000, Heinemann LB $19.92 (1-57572-343-3). 32pp. A brief biography of Michelangelo that gives examples of some of his finest works, including the Sistine Chapel. (Rev: BL 10/15/00; HBG 10/01; SLJ 2/01) [921]

MILLER, TOM

12613 Miller, Tom, and Camay C. Murphy. *Can a Coal Scuttle Fly?* (2–5). Illus. 1996, Maryland Historical Soc. $14.00 (0-938420-55-0). 32pp. Baltimore artist Tom Miller tells about his life and the great joy that can be found in art. (Rev: BL 10/15/96) [921]

MONET, CLAUDE

12614 Connolly, Sean. *Claude Monet* (4–8). Illus. Series: Lives of the Artists. 2005, World Almanac

LB $22.50 (0-8368-5650-3). 48pp. A tall, slender volume full of facts about Monet's life and times, with many color reproductions. (Rev: SLJ 3/05) [921]

12615 Connolly, Sean. *Claude Monet* (3–4). Series: The Life and Work Of. 1999, Heinemann LB $13.95 (1-57572-956-3). 32pp. This is a simple introduction to the life and works of Monet, with photos showing him at different stages in his career. (Rev: BL 2/15/00; SLJ 1/00) [921]

12616 Hodge, Susie. *Claude Monet* (5–8). Illus. Series: Artists in Their Time. 2002, Watts LB $22.00 (0-531-12226-3); paper $6.95 (0-531-16619-8). 46pp. Photographs, reproductions, maps, and a timeline that links world events with events in the artist's life make this suitable both for browsing and report writing. (Rev: SLJ 1/03) [921]

12617 Kelley, True. *Claude Monet: Sunshine and Waterlilies* (2–4). Illus. Series: Smart About Art. 2001, Penguin Putnam $14.89 (0-448-42613-7); paper $7.50 (0-448-42522-X). 32pp. An interesting overview of Claude Monet's life and work, presented in the Smart About Art school-report format with cartoon drawings. (Rev: BL 11/1/01; HBG 3/02; SLJ 11/01) [759.4]

12618 Koja, Stephan, and Katja Miksovsky. *Claude Monet: The Magician of Color* (3–7). Trans. by Andrea Belloli. Illus. Series: Adventures in Art. 1997, Prestel $14.95 (3-7913-1812-8). A straightforward biography of Monet that is enlivened by drawings, paintings, and photos. (Rev: SLJ 1/98) [921]

12619 Malam, John. *Claude Monet* (2–4). Series: Tell Me About. 1998, Carolrhoda LB $19.93 (1-57505-250-4). 24pp. Numerous color reproductions and a simple text are used to bring to life the artist Monet and his career. (Rev: HBG 3/99; SLJ 1/99) [921]

12620 Venezia, Mike. *Monet* (2–5). Illus. Series: Getting to Know. 1990, Children's Book Pr. LB $22.00 (0-516-02276-8). 32pp. Using many paintings by Monet, this book introduces the reader to Impressionism. (Rev: SLJ 11/90) [921]

MOORE, HENRY

12621 Connolly, Sean. *Henry Moore* (3–5). Illus. Series: Life and Work Of. 1999, Heinemann LB $13.95 (1-57572-953-9). 32pp. Color photos show examples of Moore's work while black-and-white photos document his life in this biography of the famous English sculptor. (Rev: BL 2/1/00; SLJ 1/00) [921]

12622 Gardner, Jane M. *Henry Moore: From Bones and Stones to Sketches and Sculptures* (2–4). Illus. 1993, Macmillan $15.95 (0-02-735812-7). 32pp. A simple biography told mainly through photographs of the great British 20th-century sculptor, Henry Moore. (Rev: BCCB 4/93; BL 4/15/93; HB 7–8/93; SLJ 6/93) [921]

12623 O'Reilly, Sally. *Henry Moore* (5–8). Illus. Series: Artists in Their Time. 2003, Watts LB $22.00 (0-531-12241-7); paper $6.95 (0-531-16643-0). 48pp. An interesting life of Moore, with reproductions of his works and of those of fellow artists, and a timeline that adds historical context. [921]

MOSES, GRANDMA

12624 Oneal, Zibby. *Grandma Moses: Painter of Rural America* (5–7). Illus. by Donna Ruff. 1987, Puffin paper $4.99 (0-14-032220-5). 64pp. The story of Anna Mary Robertson, who became famous as Grandma Moses. (Rev: BCCB 10/86; BL 11/1/86; SLJ 10/86) [921]

12625 Wallner, Alexandra. *Grandma Moses* (PS–3). Illus. 2004, Holiday House $16.95 (0-8234-1538-4). 32pp. Moses did not become an active artist until late in life; this picture book illustrated in a style reminiscent of the artist's primitives also describes her early years. (Rev: BL 3/1/04; HB 7–8/04; SLJ 5/04) [759.13]

MOUNT, WILLIAM SIDNEY

12626 Howard, Nancy S. *William Sidney Mount: Painter of Rural America* (4–7). Illus. 1994, Sterling $14.95 (1-87192-275-4). 48pp. An interactive book that explores the work and paintings of the 19th-century American painter William Sidney Mount. (Rev: BL 1/15/95) [921]

NAST, THOMAS

12627 Pflueger, Lynda. *Thomas Nast: Political Cartoonist* (5–8). Series: Historical American Biographies. 2000, Enslow LB $20.95 (0-7660-1251-4). 128pp. An informative, entertaining, and well-written biography of this influential political cartoonist and critic. (Rev: BL 9/15/00; HBG 10/01; SLJ 11/00) [921]

OBATA, CHIURA

12628 Ross, Michael E. *Nature Art with Chiura Obata* (3–6). Series: Naturalist's Apprentice. 2000, Lerner $19.95 (1-57505-378-0). 48pp. From his childhood in Japan to his move to the U.S. in 1903 to his death in 1975, this is the story of the great painter who used Japanese painting techniques to depict the American landscape. (Rev: BCCB 3/00; BL 2/1/00; HBG 10/00; SLJ 4/00) [921]

O'KEEFFE, GEORGIA

12629 Bryant, Jen. *Georgia's Bones* (2–4). Illus. by Bethanne Andersen. 2005, Eerdmans $16.00 (0-8028-5217-3). 32pp. This beautifully illustrated book introduces readers to Georgia O'Keeffe's life and preoccupation with shapes and structures. (Rev: BL 2/15/05; SLJ 4/05) [921]

12630 Kucharczyk, Emily Rose. *Georgia O'Keeffe: Desert Painter* (3–5). Series: Famous Women Juniors. 2002, Gale LB $21.54 (1-56711-592-6). 32pp. This account focuses on the artist's youth and the events that led to her life as an artist. (Rev: SLJ 9/02) [921]

12631 Lowery, Linda. *Georgia O'Keeffe* (2–4). Illus. 1996, Carolrhoda LB $19.93 (0-87614-860-7);

paper $5.95 (0-87614-898-4). 48pp. A simple account of the life and work of this amazing painter of the Southwest. (Rev: BL 9/1/96; SLJ 8/96) [921]

12632 Spangenburg, Ray, and Kit Moser. *Georgia O'Keeffe: The Life of an Artist* (2–4). Illus. Series: Artist Biographies. 2002, Enslow LB $18.95 (0-7660-1882-2). 48pp. This informative profile of American painter Georgia O'Keeffe includes a timeline, glossary, list of Web sites, and full-color reproductions of selected O'Keeffe paintings. (Rev: BL 4/1/03; HBG 10/03) [759.13]

12633 Winter, Jeanette. *My Name Is Georgia* (2–4). Illus. 1998, Harcourt $16.00 (0-15-201649-X). 48pp. Told from the artist's point of view, this is a quiet but intense look at the life and work of Georgia O'Keeffe. (Rev: BCCB 11/98; BL 10/15/98*; HB 9–10/98; HBG 3/99; SLJ 12/98) [921]

PEET, BILL

12634 Peet, Bill. *Bill Peet: An Autobiography* (2–5). Illus. 1989, Houghton Mifflin $20.00 (0-395-50932-7). 192pp. The autobiography of the author/illustrator who worked at the Disney Studio for many years. (Rev: BL 7/89; HB 7–8/89*; SLJ 7/89) [921]

PICASSO, PABLO

12635 Gogerly, Liz. *Pablo Picasso: Master of Modern Art* (3–5). 2004, Raintree LB $29.93 (0-7398-6628-1). 48pp. Picasso's youth, education, and artistic evolution are strong features of this biography that includes photographs, quotations, and a timeline. (Rev: SLJ 1/05) [921]

12636 Hodge, Susie, and Pablo Picasso. *Pablo Picasso* (4–8). Series: Lives of the Artists. 2004, Gareth Stevens LB $29.26 (0-8368-5606-6). 48pp. Works by the young Picasso are a feature of this well illustrated profile. (Rev: BL 6/1–15/04) [921]

12637 Holland, Gini. *Pablo Picasso* (5–8). Series: Trailblazers of the Modern World. 2003, World Almanac LB $26.60 (0-8368-5084-X). 48pp. A clear portrayal of Picasso's life and work that places him in historical and social context. (Rev: SLJ 7/03) [921]

12638 Lowery, Linda. *Pablo Picasso* (2–3). Illus. by Janice L. Porter. Series: On My Own Biography. 1999, Lerner $19.93 (1-57505-331-4); paper $5.95 (1-57505-370-5). 48pp. An easy-to-read biography that touches on Picasso's different painting periods, his personal life, and his great originality. (Rev: BL 2/1/00; HBG 3/00; SLJ 2/00) [921]

12639 Meadows, Matthew. *Pablo Picasso* (5–7). Illus. Series: Art for Young People. 1996, Sterling $14.95 (0-8069-6160-0). 32pp. In double-page spreads, presents the life and work of this multitalented Spanish artist. (Rev: BL 2/1/97; HB 5–6/96; SLJ 3/97) [921]

12640 Pfleger, Susanne. *A Day with Picasso* (4–7). Series: Adventures in Art. 2000, Prestel $14.95 (3-7913-2165-X). 30pp. An introduction to the life and work of Picasso, including many full-color reproductions. (Rev: BL 2/15/00; SLJ 2/00) [921]

12641 *Picasso: Soul on Fire* (4–7). Trans. by Rick Jacobson. Illus. by Rick Jacobson and Laura Fernandez. 2004, Tundra $15.95 (0-88776-599-8). 32pp. Oil paintings of the Spanish-born artist, along with reproductions of some of his best-known pieces, introduce his work and brief facts about his life. (Rev: BL 11/1/04) [921]

12642 Scarborough, Kate. *Pablo Picasso* (5–8). Series: Artists in Their Time. 2002, Watts LB $22.00 (0-531-12229-8); paper $6.95 (0-531-16622-8). 48pp. This biography of the 20th century's most famous artist is accompanied by material on the social conditions of his time. (Rev: BL 10/15/02; SLJ 1/03) [921]

12643 Selfridge, John W. *Pablo Picasso* (5–9). Series: Hispanics of Achievement. 1993, Chelsea LB $21.95 (0-7910-1777-X). A colorful biography of this great Spanish painter, who lived most of his life as a political exile in France, with some examples of his enormous output. (Rev: BL 3/1/94) [9212]

12644 Venezia, Mike. *Picasso* (PS–4). Illus. 1988, Children's Book Pr. LB $22.00 (0-516-02271-7); paper $6.95 (0-516-42271-5). 32pp. Amusing facts are tucked in with information about the artist and his work. (Rev: BL 10/1/88; SLJ 9/88)

12645 Wallis, Jeremy. *Pablo Picasso* (5–8). Series: Creative Lives. 2001, Heinemann LB $27.07 (1-58810-206-8). 64pp. Picasso's eccentricities are highlighted in this volume that covers his life, his family, and his work. (Rev: HBG 10/02; SLJ 3/02) [921]

POLITI, LEO

12646 Stalcup, Ann. *Leo Politi: Artist of the Angels* (4–9). Illus. by Leo Politi. 2004, Silver Moon $24.95 (1-893110-38-9). 104pp. The life of the American-born man who spent his formative years in Italy and returned as an adult to make his home in Los Angeles and protray the ethnic communities there in his books for children. (Rev: SLJ 4/05) [921]

POLLOCK, JACKSON

12647 Bennett, Leonie. *Jackson Pollock* (1–3). Illus. Series: Life and Work. 2005, Heinemann LB $16.95 (1-4034-5073-0). 32pp. The life and work of the artist, with photographs of both. (Rev: BL 3/15/05) [921]

12648 Greenberg, Jan, and Sandra Jordan. *Action Jackson* (2–5). Illus. by Robert Andrew Parker. 2002, Millbrook LB $22.90 (0-7613-2770-3). 32pp. An informative, thought-provoking biography that focuses on Pollock's famous painting *Lavender Mist*. (Rev: BCCB 11/02; BL 9/15/02; HB 11–12/02*; HBG 3/03; SLJ 10/02) [759.13]

12649 Oliver, Clare. *Jackson Pollock* (5–8). Series: Artists in Their Time. 2003, Watts LB $22.00 (0-531-12237-9); paper $6.95 (0-531-16644-9). 46pp. An interesting life of Pollock, with reproductions of his works and of those of fellow painters, and a timeline that adds historical context. (Rev: SLJ 5/03) [759]

RECTOR, ANNE ELIZABETH

12650 Rector, Anne Elizabeth. *Anne Elizabeth's Diary: A Young Artist's True Story* (3–7). Ed. by Kathleen Krull. Illus. 2004, Little, Brown $16.95 (0-316-07204-4). 64pp. Krull's sidebars add context to this fascinating diary, started when Rector was 12 years old, that reflects the young artist's life in both text and illustrations. (Rev: BL 6/1–15/04; SLJ 9/04) [974.7]

REMBERT, WINFRED

12651 Rembert, Winfred. *Don't Hold Me Back: My Life and Art* (4–7). Illus. 2003, Cricket $19.95 (0-8126-2703-2). 40pp. Rembert reflects on his life in the South as a sharecropper's son — picking cotton, dealing with racism, the civil rights movement — and displays his evocative works of art with comments on their creation. (Rev: BL 11/1/03*; HBG 4/04; SLJ 12/03*) [759.1]

REMBRANDT VAN RIJN

12652 De Bie, Ceciel, and Martijn Leenen. *Rembrandt: See and Do Children's Book* (3–7). Illus. 2001, Getty $19.95 (0-89236-621-4). 64pp. An effectively organized biography is combined with activities that encourage children to look closely at the art. (Rev: HBG 3/02; SLJ 4/02) [921]

12653 Mason, Antony. *Rembrandt* (4–8). Illus. Series: Lives of the Artists. 2005, World Almanac LB $22.50 (0-8368-5651-1). 48pp. A tall, slender volume full of facts about Rembrandt's life and times, with many color reproductions. (Rev: SLJ 3/05) [921]

12654 Niz, Xavier. *Rembrandt* (2–4). Series: Masterpieces: Artists and Their Works. 2003, Capstone LB $19.93 (0-7368-2230-5). 24pp. An introductory biography of the 17th-century artist, including material on his childhood and early training plus discussion of his techniques. (Rev: SLJ 3/04) [921]

12655 Venezia, Mike. *Rembrandt* (PS–4). Illus. 1988, Children's Book Pr. LB $22.00 (0-516-02272-5); paper $6.95 (0-516-42272-3). 32pp. Learning about art and great artists can be fun. (Rev: BL 10/1/88; SLJ 9/88)

REMINGTON, FREDERIC

12656 Giesecke, Ernestine. *Frederic Remington* (3–4). Series: The Life and Work Of. 1999, Heinemann LB $13.95 (1-57572-951-2). 32pp. This account of Remington's life and career as a painter, illustrator, and sculptor of the American West includes many illustrations of his works and photos of the artist and his world. (Rev: BL 2/15/00; SLJ 1/00) [921]

RENOIR, AUGUSTE

12657 Parsons, Tom. *Pierre Auguste Renoir* (5–7). Illus. Series: Art for Young People. 1996, Sterling $14.95 (0-8069-6162-7). 32pp. The life and work of this prolific French artist are examined in a series of double-page spreads. (Rev: BL 2/1/97; SLJ 3/97) [921]

12658 Venezia, Mike. *Pierre Auguste Renoir* (2–4). Illus. Series: Getting to Know. 1996, Children's Book Pr. LB $22.00 (0-516-02225-3). 32pp. This biography includes examples of Renoir's paintings and an introduction to Impressionism. (Rev: BL 9/15/96; SLJ 12/96) [921]

RIVERA, DIEGO

12659 Bankston, John. *Diego Rivera* (5–7). Series: Latinos in American History. 2003, Mitchell Lane LB $19.95 (1-58415-208-7). 48pp. A biography of the famous 20th-century Mexican artist who is best known for his murals with political overtones. (Rev: BL 1/1–15/04; HBG 4/04; SLJ 2/04) [921]

12660 Cockcroft, James D. *Diego Rivera* (5–9). Series: Hispanics of Achievement. 1991, Chelsea LB $21.95 (0-7910-1252-2). The life of this Mexican artist and activist, with several illustrations. (Rev: BL 11/1/91; SLJ 1/92) [921]

12661 Kent, Deborah. *Diego Rivera: Painting Mexico* (3–6). Series: A Proud Heritage. 2005, Child's World LB $28.50 (1-59296-384-6). 40pp. Covers Rivera's childhood and education, discussing in age-appropriate language his four marriages and how his communist leanings are reflected in his paintings. (Rev: SLJ 6/05) [921]

ROCKWELL, NORMAN

12662 Cohen, Joel H. *Norman Rockwell: America's Best-Loved Illustrator* (4–6). Illus. 1997, Watts LB $22.50 (0-531-20266-6). 64pp. Using 16 full-color reproductions, this book introduces the life of this all-American artist who lived in small towns in New England and painted their inhabitants. (Rev: BL 11/1/97; SLJ 8/97) [921]

12663 Gherman, Beverly. *Norman Rockwell: Storyteller with a Brush* (4–7). Illus. 2000, Simon & Schuster $19.95 (0-689-82001-1). 58pp. An appealing biography of this New England artist who reflected mid-20th-century American life and values in his many paintings. (Rev: BCCB 7–8/00; BL 2/15/00; HB 3–4/00; HBG 10/00; SLJ 2/00) [921]

12664 Roy, Jennifer Rozines, and Gregory Roy. *Norman Rockwell: The Life of an Artist* (4–6). Series: Artist Biographies. 2002, Enslow LB $18.95 (0-7660-1883-0). 48pp. Rockwell's early interest in art and his popularity are highlighted in this account of his life and work. (Rev: HBG 10/03; SLJ 3/03) [921]

12665 Venezia, Mike. *Norman Rockwell* (2–4). Series: Getting to Know. 2000, Children's Book Pr. LB $22.50 (0-516-21594-9). 32pp. The popular American artist is introduced with many full color reproductions, a lively text, and some amusing cartoons. (Rev: BL 1/1–15/01) [921]

RODIN, AUGUSTE

12666 Tames, Richard. *Auguste Rodin* (3–4). Series: The Life and Work Of. 2000, Heinemann LB $19.92 (1-57572-342-5). 32pp. This book chronicles the life and work of Rodin and includes material on the events that influenced his growth and development as an artist. (Rev: BL 10/15/00; HBG 10/01) [921]

ROUSSEAU, HENRI

12667 Pfleger, Susanne. *Henri Rousseau: A Jungle Expedition* (4–7). Trans. by Catherine McCreadie. Illus. Series: Adventures in Art. 1999, Prestel $14.95 (3-7913-1987-6). 28pp. The story of Henri Rousseau and the art that evolved from his visits to a botanical garden. (Rev: BL 2/1/99; SLJ 2/99) [921]

12668 Venezia, Mike. *Henri Rousseau* (2–4). Series: Getting to Know the World's Greatest Artists. 2002, Children's Book Pr. LB $23.00 (0-516-22495-6); paper $6.95 (0-516-26998-4). An easy-to-read text and humorous cartoons are used to introduce this famous French artist and his work. (Rev: BL 4/1/02) [921]

SARGENT, JOHN SINGER

12669 Kreiter, Eshel, and Marc Zabludoff. *John Singer Sargent: The Life of an Artist* (2–4). Illus. Series: Artist Biographies. 2002, Enslow LB $18.95 (0-7660-1879-2). 48pp. This concise, well-illustrated introduction to the life and work of the American painter includes a glossary, timeline, and list of Web sites. (Rev: BL 4/1/03; HBG 10/03) [759.13]

SCHULZ, CHARLES

12670 Marvis, Barbara. *Charles Schulz: The Story of the Peanuts Gang* (4–8). Illus. Series: Robbie Reader. 2004, Mitchell Lane LB $16.95 (1-58415-289-3). 32pp. This photo-filled biography traces Schulz's life and his love of cartoons; it is especially suitable for reluctant readers.

12671 Whiting, Jim. *Charles Schulz* (3–4). Series: Real-Life Reader Biographies. 2002, Mitchell Lane LB $15.95 (1-58415-131-5). 32pp. A simple retelling of the life of the talented storyteller and cartoonist who created the comic strip "Peanuts." (Rev: BL 9/15/02; SLJ 4/03) [921]

12672 Woods, Mae. *Charles Schulz* (2–4). Series: Children's Authors. 2000, ABDO LB $13.95 (1-57765-425-0). 24pp. An attractive, brief biography of the creator of Peanuts and the gang. (Rev: HBG 3/01; SLJ 1/01) [921]

SEURAT, GEORGES

12673 Burleigh, Robert. *Seurat and la Grande Jatte: Connecting the Dots* (3–6). 2004, Abrams $17.95 (0-8109-4811-7). 32pp. The well-known painting of "La Grande Jatte" serves as an introduction to Seurat's work and time in this oversized picture book for older readers. (Rev: BL 6/1–15/04; SLJ 6/04) [759.4]

SIMMONS, PHILIP

12674 Lyons, Mary E. *Catching the Fire: Philip Simmons, Blacksmith* (4–8). 1997, Houghton Mifflin $17.00 (0-395-72033-8). A biography of the contemporary African American craftsman and artist from Charleston, South Carolina, with extensive quotations from personal interviews. (Rev: BL 9/1/97; HBG 3/98; SLJ 9/97) [921]

TITIAN

12675 Venezia, Mike. *Titian* (1–3). Illus. Series: Getting to Know the World's Greatest Artists. 2003, Children's Pr. LB $24.00 (0-516-22575-8); paper $6.95 (0-516-26975-5). 32pp. An easy-to-read text and humorous cartoons are used to introduce this famous Italian artist and his work. [921]

TOULOUSE-LAUTREC, HENRI

12676 Burleigh, Robert. *Toulouse-Lautrec: The Moulin Rouge and the City of Light* (3–5). Illus. 2005, Abrams $17.95 (0-8109-5867-8). 32pp. A biography of the French artist, with plenty of colorful reproductions of his work and information about the Paris of his day. (Rev: BL 3/1/05; SLJ 5/05) [921]

TURNER, JOSEPH

12677 Woodhouse, Jane. *Joseph Turner* (3–4). Series: The Life and Work Of. 2000, Heinemann LB $19.92 (1-57572-345-X). 32pp. The life and works of this English painter noted chiefly for his luminous seascapes are covered in this brief, well-illustrated biography. (Rev: BL 10/15/00; HBG 10/01) [921]

VAN GOGH, VINCENT

12678 Bucks, Brad, and Joan Holub. *Vincent van Gogh: Sunflowers and Swirly Stars* (2–4). Series: Smart About Art. 2001, Grosset $5.99 (0-448-42521-1). Using lively cartoon drawings and reproductions of the artist's works, the life and output of van Gogh are introduced through the eyes of a young student. (Rev: BL 1/1–15/02; HBG 3/02) [921]

12679 Connolly, Sean. *Vincent van Gogh* (3–4). Series: The Life and Work Of. 1999, Heinemann LB $13.95 (1-57572-958-X). 32pp. A biography of Vincent van Gogh, encompassing his work as well as the people and events that influenced him most. (Rev: BL 2/15/00) [921]

12680 Green, Jen. *Vincent van Gogh* (5–8). Series: Artists in Their Time. 2002, Watts LB $22.00 (0-531-12238-7); paper $6.95 (0-531-16648-1). 48pp. The life and times of this 20th-century artistic genius are covered, with a number of reproductions of his paintings. (Rev: BL 10/15/02) [921]

12681 Lucas, Eileen. *Vincent van Gogh* (2–4). Illus. 1997, Carolrhoda LB $21.27 (1-57505-038-2). 56pp. A simple biography that captures the life and anxieties of the artist, with a good commentary on his work. (Rev: BCCB 9/96; BL 9/1/97; HBG 3/98; SLJ 9/97) [921]

12682 Malam, John. *Vincent van Gogh* (K–3). Series: Tell Me About. 1998, Carolrhoda LB $19.93 (1-57505-249-0). 24pp. This brief account that describes van Gogh's troubled life is illustrated with photographs and reproductions of his paintings. (Rev: HBG 3/99; SLJ 3/99) [921]

VELAZQUEZ, DIEGO

12683 *Diego Velazquez* (1–3). Illus. by Mike Venezia. Series: Getting to Know the World's Greatest Artists. 2004, Scholastic LB $26.00 (0-516-26980-1). 32pp. Full-color reproductions and cartoons add to the basic information about the life of the17th-century Spanish painter. (Rev: BL 6/1–15/04) [921]

VERMEER, JOHANNES

12684 Venezia, Mike. *Johannes Vermeer* (2–4). Series: Getting to Know the World's Greatest Artists. 2002, Children's Book Pr. LB $23.00 (0-516-22282-1); paper $6.95 (0-516-26999-2). The life and work of this Dutch master are presented with a simple text and many cartoons. (Rev: BL 4/1/02) [921]

WANG YANI

12685 Zhensun, Zheng, and Alice Low. *A Young Painter: The Life and Paintings of Wang Yani — China's Extraordinary Young Artist* (5–8). 1991, Scholastic paper $17.95 (0-590-44906-0). The story of a self-taught prodigy whose paintings are highly regarded in China. Includes many examples of her unique work, based on the traditional Chinese style. (Rev: BCCB 9/91; BL 10/1/91*; SLJ 8/91) [921]

WARHOL, ANDY

12686 Bolton, Linda. *Andy Warhol* (5–8). Series: Artists in Their Time. 2002, Watts LB $22.00 (0-531-12225-5); paper $6.95 (0-531-16618-X). 48pp. This biography includes material on the social period in which Warhol worked. (Rev: BL 10/15/02) [921]

12687 Ford, Carin T. *Andy Warhol: The Life of an Artist* (3–5). Series: Artist Biographies. 2002, Enslow LB $18.95 (0-7660-1880-6). 48pp. Warhol's personal life is covered in this brief biography that also introduces his famous works. (Rev: HBG 10/03; SLJ 4/03) [921]

12688 Venezia, Mike. *Andy Warhol* (2–4). Illus. Series: Getting to Know. 1996, Children's Book Pr. LB $22.00 (0-516-20053-4); paper $6.95 (0-516-26075-8). 32pp. An appealing introduction to this pop artist's life and work, with many fine art reproductions. (Rev: BL 12/15/96; HB 5–6/96) [921]

WEST, BENJAMIN

12689 Brenner, Barbara. *The Boy Who Loved to Draw: Benjamin West* (1–3). Illus. by Olivier Dunrea. 1999, Houghton Mifflin $15.00 (0-395-85080-0). 48pp. A portrait of the colonial painter whose talent was so great that his parents sent him to Philadelphia to study with an artist at age nine. (Rev: BL 9/15/99; HB 9–10/99; HBG 3/00; SLJ 10/99) [921]

WOOD, GRANT

12690 Duggleby, John. *Artist in Overalls: The Life of Grant Wood* (4–8). 1996, Chronicle $15.95 (0-8118-1242-1). The life of this American artist tells of his difficult struggle with poverty and his great attachment to the Midwest. (Rev: BCCB 6/96; BL 4/15/96; HB 7–8/96; SLJ 5/96) [921]

WOOD, MICHELE

12691 Igus, Toyomi. *Going Back Home: An Artist Returns to the South* (4–8). Illus. 1996, Children's Book Pr. $16.95 (0-89239-137-5). The author recreates the family history and life of the African American illustrator Michele Wood. (Rev: BCCB 12/96; BL 9/15/96; SLJ 7/97) [921]

WRIGHT, FRANK LLOYD

12692 Davis, Frances A. *Frank Lloyd Wright: Maverick Architect* (5–9). Illus. 1996, Lerner LB $30.35 (0-8225-4953-0). A well-documented life of this influential 20th-century architect, with many black-and-white photographs of his most important buildings. (Rev: BL 1/1–15/97; SLJ 1/97) [921]

12693 Mayo, Gretchen Will. *Frank Lloyd Wright* (5–8). Series: Trailblazers of the Modern World. 2004, World Almanac LB $29.27 (0-8368-5101-3). 48pp. Report writers will find useful information on Wright's life, achievements, and lasting contributions. (Rev: SLJ 7/04) [921]

12694 Middleton, Haydn. *Frank Lloyd Wright* (5–8). Series: Creative Lives. 2001, Heinemann LB $27.07 (1-58810-203-3). 64pp. An attractive look at the architect's life and career with illustrations and a useful timeline. (Rev: HBG 10/02; SLJ 3/02) [921]

12695 Thorne-Thomsen, Kathleen. *Frank Lloyd Wright for Kids* (4–6). Illus. 1994, Chicago Review paper $14.95 (1-55652-207-X). 144pp. In addition to providing a life of this famous architect, this book contains many projects related to his work and a recipe for his favorite breakfast. (Rev: BL 4/15/94; SLJ 7/94) [921]

ZHANG, ANGE

12696 Zhang, Ange. *Red Land, Yellow River: A Story from the Cultural Revolution* (5–8). 2004, Groundwood $16.95 (0-88899-489-3). 56pp. In this compelling autobiography, artist Ange Zhang tells how he came of age during one of the most turbulent periods in modern Chinese history — the Cultural Revolution of the late 1960s. (Rev: BL 12/1/04*; SLJ 12/04) [921]

Composers

BACH, JOHANN SEBASTIAN

12697 Lynch, Wendy. *Bach* (K–3). Series: Lives and Times. 2000, Heinemann LB $13.95 (1-57572-214-3). 24pp. A brief account of the highlights of Bach's life illustrated with drawings and photographs. (Rev: SLJ 9/00) [921]

12698 Venezia, Mike. *Johann Sebastian Bach* (2–4). Series: Getting to Know. 1998, Children's Book Pr. LB $21.00 (0-516-20760-1). 32pp. A mix of historic prints and clever cartoon drawings help bring this prolific composer to life. (Rev: BL 5/15/98; HBG 10/98) [921]

12699 Winter, Jeanette. *Sebastian: A Book About Bach* (2–4). Illus. 1999, Harcourt $16.00 (0-15-200629-X). 40pp. A simple picture book that explores Bach's life, music, and times. (Rev: BCCB 5/99; BL 4/1/99*; HB 7–8/99; HBG 10/99; SLJ 4/99) [921]

BEETHOVEN, LUDWIG VAN

12700 Balcavage, Dynise. *Ludwig Van Beethoven: Composer* (4–8). Series: Great Achievers: Lives of the Physically Challenged. 1997, Chelsea LB $21.95 (0-7910-2082-7). This is an information-rich account of the composer's public and private life, with good coverage of his compositions. (Rev: SLJ 7/97) [921]

12701 Venezia, Mike. *Ludwig Van Beethoven* (2–4). Illus. Series: Getting to Know. 1996, Children's Book Pr. LB $22.00 (0-516-04542-3). 32pp. An informal portrait of Beethoven and an introduction to his music. (Rev: BL 9/15/96) [921]

BERLIN, IRVING

12702 Furstinger, Nancy. *Say It with Music: The Story of Irving Berlin* (5–9). Illus. Series: Masters of Music. 2003, Morgan Reynolds LB $21.95 (1-931798-12-5). 128pp. Well-researched and very readable, this account traces Berlin's life from Russia to the United States and his popular and lasting success as a songwriter. (Rev: BL 6/1–15/03; HBG 4/04; SLJ 10/03) [780.92]

12703 Streissguth, Thomas. *Say It with Music: A Story About Irving Berlin* (3–5). Illus. 1994, Carolrhoda LB $14.95 (0-87614-810-0). 64pp. This biography of the great American songwriter concentrates on his first 30 years, from childhood in Russia to success on Broadway. (Rev: BL 5/1/94; SLJ 8/94) [921]

BERLIOZ, HECTOR

12704 Whiting, Jim. *The Life and Times of Hector Berlioz* (5–7). Series: Masters of Music: The World's Greatest Composers. 2004, Mitchell Lane LB $19.95 (1-58415-259-1). 48pp. A brief biography of the talented and troubled creator of the *Symphonie fantastique*. (Rev: SLJ 2/05) [921]

BERNSTEIN, LEONARD

12705 Blashfield, Jean F. *Leonard Bernstein: Composer and Conductor* (4–7). Series: Ferguson Career Biographies. 2001, Ferguson LB $16.95 (0-89434-337-8). 127pp. Numerous black-and-white photographs accompany the easily read text in this interesting account of Bernstein's life and career. (Rev: SLJ 7/01) [780]

12706 Hurwitz, Johanna. *Leonard Bernstein: A Passion for Music* (4–8). Illus. by Sonia O. Lisker. 1993, Jewish Publication Soc. $14.95 (0-8276-0501-3). 80pp. The career of this amazing conductor and composer who was also a gifted pianist and teacher. (Rev: BL 2/15/94; SLJ 12/93) [921]

12707 Venezia, Mike. *Leonard Bernstein* (2–4). Series: Getting to Know. 1997, Children's Book Pr. LB $22.00 (0-516-20492-0). 32pp. A brief profile of this great American composer, who also excelled as a conductor and pianist. (Rev: BL 10/15/97; HBG 3/98) [921]

CHOPIN, FREDERIC

12708 Dineen, Jacqueline. *Frederic Chopin* (K–3). Series: Tell Me About. 1998, Carolrhoda LB $19.93 (1-57505-248-2). 24pp. A short chapterless book on the life and accomplishments of the Polish pianist and composer who died prematurely of tuberculosis. (Rev: HBG 3/99; SLJ 3/99) [921]

GERSHWIN, GEORGE

12709 Mitchell, Barbara. *America, I Hear You: A Story About George Gershwin* (3–5). Illus. 1987, Carolrhoda LB $19.93 (0-87614-309-5). 64pp. The life, times, and career of one of America's great musicians. (Rev: BCCB 11/87; BL 10/1/87; SLJ 12/87)

12710 Reef, Catherine. *George Gershwin: American Composer* (5–8). Illus. Series: Masters of Music. 2000, Morgan Reynolds LB $21.95 (1-883846-58-7). 112pp. This biography traces the life one of America's great composers, giving insight into his personality, family, and times. (Rev: BL 2/15/00; HBG 10/00; SLJ 3/00) [921]

12711 Venezia, Mike. *George Gershwin* (2–4). Illus. by author. Series: Getting to Know. 1994, Children's Book Pr. LB $22.00 (0-516-04536-9). 32pp. A breezy retelling of the life and times of this multi-talented American composer of both classical and popular music. (Rev: SLJ 4/95) [921]

12712 Vernon, Roland. *Introducing Gershwin* (5–7). Illus. 1996, Silver Burdett LB $14.95 (0-382-39161-6); paper $8.95 (0-382-39160-8). 32pp. This oversize volume with copious illustrations re-creates the life and times of George Gershwin. (Rev: BL 5/1/96; SLJ 9/96) [921]

12713 Whiting, Jim. *The Life and Times of George Gershwin* (4–6). Series: Masters of Music: The World's Greatest Composers. 2004, Mitchell Lane

LB $19.95 (1-58415-279-6). 48pp. The challenges that Gershwin faced in both his personal and professional lives are discussed and placed in historical perspective. (Rev: SLJ 5/05) [921]

GUTHRIE, WOODY

12714 Christensen, Bonnie. *Woody Guthrie: Poet of the People* (3–5). Illus. 2001, Knopf LB $18.99 (0-375-91113-8). 32pp. This book for younger readers uses words and woodcut illustrations to tell the story of singer Woody Guthrie, best known for his song "This Land Is Your Land." (Rev: BL 9/1/01; HB 1–2/02*; HBG 3/02; SLJ 10/01) [782.42162]

12715 Coombs, Karen Mueller. *Woody Guthrie: America's Folksinger* (4–6). Series: Trailblazer Biographies. 2002, Carolrhoda LB $25.95 (1-57505-464-7). 120pp. A balanced look at the life of the singer/songwriter who died in 1967. (Rev: HBG 10/02; SLJ 7/02) [921]

HANDEL, GEORGE FRIDERIC

12716 Anderson, M. T. *Handel, Who Knew What He Liked* (3–6). Illus. by Kevin Hawkes. 2001, Candlewick $16.99 (0-7636-1046-1). 48pp. Here's an irreverent large-format account of the interesting life of composer Handel, including lively anecdotes and detailed, dramatic illustrations that give a flavor of the time with a dollop of humor. (Rev: BCCB 1/02; BL 12/15/01; HB 11–12/01*; HBG 3/02; SLJ 12/01*)

HANDY, W. C.

12717 Summer, L. S. *W. C. Handy: Founder of the Blues* (4–6). Series: Journey to Freedom: The African American Library. 2001, Child's World LB $17.95 (1-56766-927-1). 40pp. The life of this African American jazz pioneer is told in a concise text with many sepia-toned illustrations. (Rev: BL 12/15/01; HBG 3/02) [921]

IVES, CHARLES

12718 Gerstein, Mordicai. *What Charlie Heard* (3–5). Illus. 2002, Farrar $17.00 (0-374-38292-1). 40pp. This picture-book biography focuses on the American composer Charles Ives and his childhood influences. (Rev: BCCB 4/02; BL 4/1/02; HB 5–6/02*; HBG 10/02; SLJ 3/02) [921]

JONES, QUINCY

12719 Kavanaugh, Lee H. *Quincy Jones: Musician, Composer, Producer* (5–8). 1998, Enslow LB $20.95 (0-89490-814-6). This biography describes Quincy Jones's 50-year career in music and how he overcame poverty, racism, and health problems to become a musical director, composer, producer, arranger, and driving force behind many award-winning recordings. (Rev:) [921]

JOPLIN, SCOTT

12720 Bankston, John. *The Life and Times of Scott Joplin* (5–7). Series: Masters of Music: The World's Greatest Composers. 2004, Mitchell Lane LB $19.95 (1-58415-270-2). 48pp. Joplin's career as a ragtime piano player and composer is documented, with coverage of his African American heritage. (Rev: SLJ 2/05) [921]

12721 Mitchell, Barbara. *Raggin': A Story About Scott Joplin* (3–5). Illus. 1987, Carolrhoda LB $21.27 (0-87614-310-9); paper $5.95 (0-87614-589-6). 64pp. The story of a great American musician whose genius was not recognized until after his death. (Rev: BL 10/1/87; SLJ 12/87)

12722 Sabir, C. Ogbu. *Scott Joplin: The King of Ragtime* (4–6). Series: Journey to Freedom. 2000, Child's World LB $25.64 (1-56766-746-5). 40pp. The story of the jazz pianist and composer known as the King of Ragtime. (Rev: BL 11/15/00; HBG 3/01; SLJ 1/01) [921]

MENDELSSOHN, FANNY

12723 Kamen, Gloria. *Hidden Music: The Life of Fanny Mendelssohn* (4–6). Illus. 1996, Simon & Schuster $15.00 (0-689-31714-X). 82pp. Fanny Mendelssohn, the sister of Felix, was also a talented musician and composer, but being a woman, she was denied the same opportunities as her brother. (Rev: BCCB 5/96; BL 3/15/96; HB 9–10/96) [921]

MOZART, WOLFGANG AMADEUS

12724 Allman, Barbara. *Musical Genius: A Story About Wolfgang Amadeus Mozart* (3–5). Illus. by Janet Hamlin. Series: Creative Minds Biographies. 2004, Carolrhoda LB $21.27 (1-57505-604-6); paper $6.95 (1-57505-637-2). 64pp. An accessible introduction to Mozart that starts with his childhood. (Rev: SLJ 8/04) [921]

12725 Lynch, Wendy. *Mozart* (K–3). Series: Lives and Times. 2000, Heinemann LB $13.95 (1-57572-219-4). 24pp. After a brief biography of Mozart, there is a section on how young readers can learn more about him. (Rev: SLJ 9/00) [921]

12726 Malam, John. *Wolfgang Amadeus Mozart* (2–4). Series: Tell Me About. 1998, Carolrhoda LB $19.93 (1-57505-247-4). 24pp. Illustrations include period paintings of Mozart's family, musical scores, and outdoor scenes of Salzburg and Vienna, in this life of Mozart told simply for young readers. (Rev: HBG 3/99; SLJ 1/99) [921]

12727 Ross, Stewart. *Wolfgang Amadeus Mozart: Musical Genius* (3–5). Series: Famous Lives. 2004, Raintree LB $29.93 (0-7398-6627-3). 48pp. A simple, lively, and well-illustrated biography that chronicles Mozart's major works. (Rev: SLJ 1/05) [921]

12728 Vernon, Roland. *Introducing Mozart* (5–7). Illus. 1996, Silver Burdett LB $14.95 (0-382-39159-4); paper $8.95 (0-382-39158-6). 32pp. The life and times of Mozart are covered in the oversize, heavily illustrated volume. (Rev: BL 5/1/96; SLJ 1/97) [921]

SATIE, ERIK

12729 Anderson, M. T. *Strange Mr. Satie* (1–3). Illus. by Petra Mathers. 2003, Penguin Putnam $16.99 (0-670-03637-4). 32pp. The offbeat life and unusual music of French composer Erik Satie are explored in this engaging picture-book biography. (Rev: BL 11/1/03; HB 9–10/03; HBG 4/04; SLJ 10/03)

SCHUBERT, FRANZ PETER

12730 Bankston, John. *The Life and Times of Franz Peter Schubert* (4–6). Series: Masters of Music. 2003, Mitchell Lane LB $19.95 (1-58415-177-3). 48pp. Bankston examines the short but prolific life and career of the 19th-century Austrian composer and includes interesting sidebars that add context. (Rev: SLJ 2/04) [921]

STRAVINSKY, IGOR

12731 Venezia, Mike. *Igor Stravinsky* (2–4). Illus. Series: Getting to Know. 1996, Children's Book Pr. LB $22.00 (0-516-20054-2). 32pp. The life of this great 20th-century composer and his work are briefly presented, with many illustrations. (Rev: BCCB 7–8/96; BL 12/15/96) [921]

TCHAIKOVSKY, PETER

12732 Venezia, Mike. *Peter Tchaikovsky* (2–4). Illus. by author. Series: Getting to Know. 1994, Children's Book Pr. LB $22.00 (0-516-04537-7). 32pp. An introduction to the life, times, and music of this Russian composer, in a visually pleasing format. (Rev: SLJ 4/95) [921]

VERDI, GIUSEPPE

12733 Whiting, Jim. *The Life and Times of Giuseppe Verdi* (4–6). Series: Masters of Music: The World's Greatest Composers. 2004, Mitchell Lane LB $19.95 (1-58415-281-8). 48pp. The challenges that Verdi faced in both his personal and professional lives are discussed and placed in historical perspective. (Rev: SLJ 5/05) [921]

Entertainers

ABDUL, PAULA

12734 Ford, M. Thomas. *Paula Abdul: Straight Up* (3–6). Illus. Series: Taking Part. 1992, Macmillan LB $18.95 (0-87518-508-8). 72pp. The life story of the pop entertainer, who takes special interest in a young audience. (Rev: BL 11/15/92; SLJ 7/92) [921]

12735 Zannos, Susan. *Paula Abdul* (4–8). Series: Real-Life Reader Biographies. 1999, Mitchell Lane LB $15.95 (1-883845-74-2). A brief biography of this choreographer and recording artist that recounts her many problems, including a struggle with bulimia and a series of failed marriages. (Rev: BL 6/1–15/99) [921]

639

AGUILERA, CHRISTINA

12736 Granados, Christine. *Christina Aguilera* (3–4). Series: Real-Life Reader Biographies. 2000, Mitchell Lane LB $15.95 (1-58415-044-0). 32pp. The story of the little girl with the big voice who started out as a member of the *New Mickey Mouse Club.* (Rev: BL 11/15/00) [921]

AILEY, ALVIN

12737 Cruz, Barbara C. *Alvin Ailey: Celebrating African-American Culture in Dance* (5–9). Series: African-American Biographies. 2004, Enslow LB $26.60 (0-7660-2293-5). 112pp. Ailey's life and contributions to dance are detailed, including a chapter on the classic "Revelations" and information on his contemporaries. (Rev: SLJ 1/05) [921]

ANDERSON, MARIAN

12738 Ferris, Jeri. *What I Had Was Singing: The Story of Marian Anderson* (3–6). Illus. 1994, Carolrhoda LB $23.93 (0-87614-818-6); paper $6.95 (0-87614-634-5). 96pp. The story of this African American contralto's struggles and triumphs, including her appearances at the Lincoln Memorial in 1939 and the Metropolitan Opera in the 1950s. (Rev: BL 7/94) [921]

12739 Freedman, Russell. *The Voice That Challenged a Nation: Marian Anderson and the Struggle for Equal Rights* (4–8). 2004, Houghton Mifflin $18.00 (0-618-15976-2). 128pp. Beautifully illustrated with period photographs, this picture-book biography of the African American vocalist describes her life and the events leading up to her historic concert at the Lincoln Memorial. (Rev: BL 6/1–15/04; HB 5–6/04; SLJ 7/04) [782.1]

12740 Livingston, Myra Cohn. *Keep on Singing: A Ballad of Marian Anderson* (K–3). Illus. by Samuel Byrd. 1994, Holiday House LB $15.95 (0-8234-1098-6). 32pp. In a narrative poem, the life and career of Marian Anderson is celebrated. (Rev: BL 11/1/94; SLJ 3/95) [921]

12741 McKissack, Patricia, and Fredrick McKissack. *Marian Anderson: A Great Singer* (2–4). Illus. Series: Great African Americans. 1991, Enslow LB $14.95 (0-89490-303-9). 32pp. A biography of the great American concert singer, the first African American to sing with the Metropolitan Opera in New York City. (Rev: SLJ 11/91) [921]

12742 Meadows, James. *Marian Anderson: 1897–1993* (4–6). Series: Journey to Freedom: The African American Library. 2001, Child's World LB $17.95 (1-56766-921-2). 40pp. Lavishly illustrated with color and sepia-toned illustrations, this is an attractive biography of the great black singer who broke the color barrier at the Metropolitan Opera. (Rev: BL 12/15/01; SLJ 1/02) [921]

12743 Ryan, Pam Munoz. *When Marian Sang: The True Recital of Marian Anderson* (K–3). Illus. by Brian Selznick. 2002, Scholastic $16.95 (0-439-26967-9). 40pp. This large-format picture-book biography presents Anderson's life in glowing words and pictures and interweaves the spirituals

that Anderson sang. (Rev: BL 11/15/02; HB 11–12/02; HBG 3/03; SLJ 11/02*) [782.1]

ARMSTRONG, LOUIS

12744 Fahlenkamp-Merrell, Kindle. *Louis Armstrong: 1901–1971* (4–6). Series: Journey to Freedom: The African American Library. 2001, Child's World LB $17.95 (1-56766-919-0). 40pp. Color and sepia-toned illustrations are used on every page in this attractive, well-organized biography of the jazz great. (Rev: BL 12/15/01) [921]

12745 McKissack, Patricia, and Fredrick McKissack. *Louis Armstrong: Jazz Musician* (2–4). Illus. Series: Great African Americans. 1991, Enslow LB $14.95 (0-89490-307-1). 32pp. A simple biography of this well-loved American musician. (Rev: BL 1/1/92; SLJ 2/92) [921]

12746 Old, Wendie C. *Louis Armstrong: King of Jazz* (5–9). Series: African-American Biographies. 1998, Enslow LB $20.95 (0-89490-997-5). The life and accomplishments of the legendary jazz trumpeter know as Satchmo who lived from 1900 to 1971. (Rev: BL 11/15/98; SLJ 11/98) [921]

12747 Orgill, Roxane. *If I Only Had a Horn* (PS–3). Illus. by Leonard Jenkins. 1997, Houghton Mifflin $16.00 (0-395-75919-6); paper $5.95 (0-618-25076-X). A biography of jazz musician Louis Armstrong, with colorful illustrations. (Rev: BL 2/15/03) [921]

BALANCHINE, GEORGE

12748 Kristy, Davida. *George Balanchine: American Ballet Master* (5–9). Illus. Series: Biographies. 1996, Lerner LB $30.35 (0-8225-4951-4). 128pp. The story of the Russian émigré choreographer and how he changed the world of American ballet. (Rev: BL 9/1/96; SLJ 8/96) [921]

BALL, LUCILLE

12749 Krohn, Katherine E. *Lucille Ball: Pioneer of Comedy* (4–6). Illus. Series: Achievers. 1992, Lerner LB $21.27 (0-8225-0543-6). 64pp. A biography that tries to capture the hilarity that was the "I Love Lucy" show. (Rev: BL 6/15/92; SLJ 7/92) [921]

BANKS, TYRA

12750 Levin, Pam. *Tyra Banks* (5–8). Illus. Series: Black Americans of Achievement. 1999, Chelsea $21.95 (0-7910-5195-1); paper $9.95 (0-7910-4964-7). 104pp. This is the story of an "ugly duckling" who was awkward and uncoordinated as a child but who later became a supermodel. (Rev: BL 2/15/00; HBG 3/00) [921]

BARNUM, P. T.

12751 Fleming, Alice. *P. T. Barnum: The World's Greatest Showman* (5–8). 1993, Walker LB $15.85 (0-8027-8235-3). A look at the circus owner's childhood and various successful entrepreneurial ventures. (Rev: BL 1/15/94; SLJ 12/93) [921]

12752 Tompert, Ann. *The Greatest Showman on Earth: A Biography of P.T. Barnum* (5–8). Illus. 1987, Dillon LB $13.95 (0-87518-370-0). An entertaining profile of the flamboyant showman and a discussion of his many money-making schemes. (Rev: BL 2/15/88; SLJ 3/88) [921]

12753 Warrick, Karen Clemens. *P. T. Barnum: Genius of the Three-Ring Circus* (5–8). Series: Historical American Biographies. 2001, Enslow LB $20.95 (0-7660-1447-9). 112pp. The story of the showman and creator of "The Greatest Show on Earth" who presented such attractions as General Tom Thumb and Jenny Lind. (Rev: BL 4/15/01; HBG 10/01; SLJ 7/01) [921]

BARR, ROSEANNE

12754 Gaines, Ann. *Roseanne: Entertainer* (5–8). Series: Overcoming Adversity. 1999, Chelsea LB $21.95 (0-7910-4706-7); paper $8.95 (0-7910-4707-5). The story of how this overweight housewife made difficult decisions and many sacrifices to achieve her goal of becoming successful not just in show business, but also in the difficult field of comedy, and later as a TV personality. (Rev:) [921]

BARRYMORE, DREW

12755 Zannos, Susan. *Drew Barrymore* (3–4). Series: Real-Life Reader Biographies. 2000, Mitchell Lane LB $15.95 (1-58415-035-1). 32pp. The ups and downs in the career and life of the actress who starred in such films as *E. T.* as a child are touched on in this brief biography. (Rev: BL 11/15/00) [921]

BEATLES (MUSICAL GROUP)

12756 Roberts, Jeremy. *The Beatles* (5–8). Series: Biography. 2001, Lerner LB $25.26 (0-8225-4998-0). This is the story of the Beatles, from Liverpool to international stardom and eventual separation. (Rev: BL 4/1/02; HBG 10/02) [921]

12757 Venezia, Mike. *The Beatles* (2–4). Illus. Series: Getting to Know. 1997, Children's Book Pr. LB $22.00 (0-516-20310-X). 32pp. Color photos, humorous cartoons, and a clever text are used to re-create the fabulous careers of these boys from Liverpool. (Rev: BL 5/15/97) [920]

12758 Woog, Adam. *The Beatles* (4–8). Series: Importance Of. 1997, Lucent LB $27.45 (1-56006-088-3). 128pp. Outlines the lives and careers of these four Liverpool natives and their many achievements. (Rev: BL 10/15/97; SLJ 12/97) [921]

BLACK, SHIRLEY TEMPLE

12759 Bankston, John. *Shirley Temple: Child Star* (4–6). Series: A Blue Banner Biography. 2003, Mitchell Lane LB $16.95 (1-58415-172-2). 32pp. This brief biography of Shirley Temple Black focuses primarily on her years as one of America's most popular child stars but also touches on key events in her adult life, including her involvement in Republican politics and her appointment as U.S. ambassador to Ghana. (Rev: SLJ 11/03) [791.43]

BLADES, RUBEN

12760 Cruz, Barbara C. *Ruben Blades: Salsa Singer and Social Activist* (4–9). Series: Hispanic Biographies. 1997, Enslow LB $20.95 (0-89490-893-6). The inspiring story of the Panama-born musician and his involvement in social activism and politics. (Rev: BR 5–6/98; HBG 3/98; SLJ 1/98) [921]

12761 Marton, Betty A. *Rubén Blades* (5–9). Series: Hispanics of Achievement. 1992, Chelsea LB $21.95 (0-7910-1235-2). The story of the Panamanian salsa singer who is also a poet and activist. (Rev: BL 10/1/92; SLJ 11/92) [921]

BOONE, JOHN WILLIAM

12762 Harrah, Madge. *Blind Boone* (5–8). Illus. 2003, Carolrhoda LB $25.26 (1-57505-057-9). 112pp. The son of a runaway slave, Boone became blind as an infant but soon revealed a musical talent and went on to become a composer and concert pianist. (Rev: BL 12/1/03; HBG 3/02; SLJ 10/01) [781.64]

BRANDY (SINGER)

12763 Hayes, Donna. *Brandy* (3–4). Series: Real-Life Reader Biographies. 1999, Mitchell Lane LB $15.95 (1-883845-93-9). 32pp. A simple biography of this successful African American singer. (Rev: BL 10/15/99) [921]

12764 Newman, Michael. *Brandy* (5–8). Series: Galaxy of Superstars. 2000, Chelsea $19.75 (0-7910-5781-X). 64pp. A biography of the famous singer and star of *Moesha*. (Rev: BL 12/15/00; HBG 10/01) [921]

BROOKS, GARTH

12765 Powell, Phelan. *Garth Brooks: Award-Winning Country Music Star* (4–7). Series: Real-Life Reader Biographies. 1999, Mitchell Lane LB $15.95 (1-58415-004-1). 32pp. A biography of the award-winning country music star and how he got there. (Rev: SLJ 1/00)

12766 Tallman, Edward. *Garth Brooks* (3–6). Illus. Series: Taking Part. 1993, Dillon LB $13.95 (0-87518-595-9). 64pp. The story of the country music superstar. (Rev: BL 10/15/93; SLJ 2/94) [921]

BULLOCK, SANDRA

12767 Hill, Anne E. *Sandra Bullock* (5–8). Series: People in the News. 2000, Lucent LB $27.45 (1-56006-711-X). 96pp. Quotations from Bullock and others expand this biography and explain how and why she has gained prominence as a Hollywood actress. (Rev: BL 9/15/00) [921]

12768 Zannos, Susan. *Sandra Bullock* (3–4). Series: Real-Life Reader Biographies. 2000, Mitchell Lane LB $15.95 (1-58415-027-0). 32pp. A simple biography of the movie actress that stresses her hard work and determination. (Rev: BL 11/15/00; SLJ 1/01) [921]

641

BURKE, CHRIS

12769 Geraghty, Helen M. *Chris Burke* (5–9). Series: Great Achievers: Lives of the Physically Challenged. 1994, Chelsea LB $19.95 (0-7910-2081-9). This biography of the star of TV's *Life Goes On* looks at Burke's family life and career success despite Down's syndrome. (Rev: BL 10/15/94) [921]

CAREY, MARIAH

12770 Cole, Melanie. *Mariah Carey* (5–10). Series: A Real-Life Reader Biography. 1997, Mitchell Lane LB $15.95 (1-883845-51-3). For high-low collections, this biography of the popular singer tells of her difficulties in reaching the top and of her career since then. (Rev: BL 6/1–15/98; HBG 3/98; SLJ 2/98) [921]

12771 Parker, Judy. *Mariah Carey* (5–8). Illus. Series: Celebrity Bios. 2001, Children's Book Pr. LB $20.00 (0-516-23425-0); paper $6.95 (0-516-29600-0). 48pp. An attractive simple introduction that looks at the popular singer's childhood and first breaks. (Rev: BL 12/15/01) [782.42164]

CASALS, PABLO

12772 Garza, Hedda. *Pablo Casals* (5–9). Series: Hispanics of Achievement. 1993, Chelsea LB $21.95 (0-7910-1237-9). The story of the legendary Spanish cellist and his exile from his homeland during Franco's regime. (Rev: BL 4/1/93; SLJ 7/93) [921]

CHAPLIN, CHARLIE

12773 Turk, Ruth. *Charlie Chaplin: Genius of the Silent Screen* (5–9). 2000, Lerner LB $30.35 (0-8225-4957-3). 112pp. A competent overview of this great movie maker's life from his childhood in England to his exile in Switzerland. (Rev: BL 2/15/00; HBG 10/00; SLJ 4/00) [921]

CHARLES, RAY

12774 Turk, Ruth. *Ray Charles: Soul Man* (5–8). Illus. Series: Newsmakers. 1996, Lerner LB $30.35 (0-8225-4928-X). 112pp. A candid biography of the great blind entertainer that includes compelling details about his childhood. (Rev: SLJ 8/96) [921]

CHRISTENSEN, HAYDEN

12775 Friedman, Katherine. *Hayden Christensen* (5–8). Series: Celebrity Bios. 2002, Children's Book Pr. LB $20.00 (0-516-23907-4); paper $6.95 (0-516-23481-1). 48pp. A high-interest, simple biography of the young Canadian actor who plays Anakin Skywalker in the *Star Wars* prequels. (Rev: BL 6/1–15/02) [921]

COOK, RACHEL LEIGH

12776 Rivera, Ursula. *Rachel Leigh Cook* (5–8). Series: Celebrity Bios. 2002, Children's Book Pr.

LB $20.00 (0-516-23908-2); paper $6.95 (0-516-23484-6). 48pp. Ms. Cook, a Minnesota native, starred in such movies as *Get Carter* and *Josie and the Pussycats*. (Rev: BL 6/1–15/02) [921]

COSBY, BILL

12777 Conord, Bruce W. *Bill Cosby: Family Man* (3–5). Series: Junior World Biographies. 1993, Chelsea LB $16.95 (0-7910-1761-3). 76pp. A biography of this famous actor and comedian. (Rev: SLJ 6/93) [921]

12778 Haskins, Jim. *Bill Cosby: America's Most Famous Father* (5–7). Illus. 1988, Walker LB $17.00 (0-8027-6786-9). 128pp. The childhood and career of this famous entertainer. (Rev: BL 6/1/88) [921]

12779 Schuman, Michael A. *Bill Cosby: Actor and Comedian* (4–6). Illus. Series: People to Know. 1995, Enslow LB $20.95 (0-89490-548-1). 128pp. The life of this multitalented African American entertainer is told in a highly readable style. (Rev: BL 9/15/95; SLJ 2/96) [921]

12780 Woods, Harold, and Geraldine Woods. *Bill Cosby: Making America Laugh and Learn* (4–7). Illus. 1988, Macmillan LB $13.95 (0-87518-240-2). 48pp. A biography of the outstanding African American comedian, educator, and humanitarian. [921]

CRUZ, CELIA

12781 Chambers, Veronica. *Celia Cruz, Queen of Salsa* (2–4). Illus. by Julie Maren. 2005, Dial $15.99 (0-8037-2970-7). 40pp. From her childhood in Cuba to her status as a global superstar, this is the story of the salsa singer, with a discography and glossary of Spanish words. (Rev: BL 5/15/05) [921]

DAMON, MATT

12782 Greene, Meg. *Matt Damon* (5–8). Series: Galaxy of Superstars. 2000, Chelsea $19.75 (0-7910-5779-8). 64pp. An entertaining biography of the actor who gained star status as the cowriter and lead actor in *Good Will Hunting*. (Rev: BL 12/15/00; HBG 10/01) [921]

DICAPRIO, LEONARDO

12783 Stauffer, Stacey. *Leonardo DiCaprio* (5–8). Illus. Series: Galaxy of Superstars. 1999, Chelsea $19.75 (0-7910-5151-X); paper $8.95 (0-7910-5326-1). 63pp. The story of this young actor's life, with special attention to his role in *Titanic*. (Rev: BL 4/15/99; BR 9–10/99; HBG 10/99; SLJ 5/99) [921]

DION, CELINE

12784 Cole, Melanie. *Celine Dion* (3–6). Series: Real-Life Reader Biographies. 1998, Mitchell Lane LB $15.95 (1-883845-76-9). 32pp. This overview of the life of singer Celine Dion uses many quotes and sidebar facts. (Rev: SLJ 2/99) [921]

12785 Lutz, Norma Jean. *Celine Dion* (5–8). Series: Galaxy of Superstars. 2000, Chelsea $19.75 (0-7910-5777-1). 64pp. The story of the amazing career of this French Canadian singer and how she gained worldwide popularity. (Rev: BL 10/15/00; HBG 10/01) [921]

DOMINGO, PLÁCIDO

12786 Stefoff, Rebecca. *Plácido Domingo* (5–9). Series: Hispanics of Achievement. 1992, Chelsea LB $21.95 (0-7910-1563-7). The story of the amazing Spanish-born tenor and his sensational international career, with some information on his private life. (Rev: BL 12/1/92; SLJ 1/93) [921]

DUFF, HILARY

12787 Kjelle, Marylou Morano. *Hilary Duff: Actress and Singer* (2–4). Illus. Series: Robbie Reader. 2004, Mitchell Lane LB $19.95 (1-58415-295-8). 32pp. This photo-filled biography traces the life of Hilary Duff and is especially suitable for reluctant readers. [921]

DUNCAN, ISADORA

12788 O'Connor, Barbara. *Barefoot Dancer: The Story of Isadora Duncan* (5–7). Illus. 1994, Carolrhoda LB $30.35 (0-87614-807-0). 96pp. The story of this eccentric individualist who influenced and liberated a generation of dancers. (Rev: BCCB 10/94; BL 7/94) [921]

DUNHAM, KATHERINE

12789 O'Connor, Barbara. *Katherine Dunham: Pioneer of Black Dance* (5–8). Illus. 2000, Carolrhoda LB $30.35 (1-57505-353-5). 104pp. A fine biography of the African American choreographer who used her study of anthropology to create works for her own dance company and for stage and screen productions. (Rev: BL 5/15/00; HBG 10/00; SLJ 7/00) [921]

ELLINGTON, DUKE

12790 Pinkney, Andrea Davis. *Duke Ellington: The Piano Prince and His Orchestra* (K–3). Illus. by Brian Pinkney. 1998, Hyperion $15.95 (0-7868-0178-6). The story of the jazz great and his wonderful music, with vivid illustrations. (Rev: BL 2/15/03; HBG 9/98; SLJ 5/98) [781.65]

ESTEFAN, GLORIA

12791 Benson, Michael. *Gloria Estefan* (4–6). Series: A&E Biography. 2000, Lerner LB $25.26 (0-8225-4982-4). 112pp. A candid look at a singer who is also a devoted wife and mother, a humanitarian, and an outstanding performer. (Rev: BL 6/1–15/00; HBG 10/00) [921]

12792 Boulais, Sue. *Gloria Estefan* (3–4). Series: Real-Life Reader Biographies. 1998, Mitchell Lane LB $15.95 (1-883845-62-9). 32pp. The story of this

music star, born in Cuba, and the accident in 1990 that almost ended her career. (Rev: BL 10/15/98; HBG 10/98) [921]

12793 Gonzales, Doreen. *Gloria Estefan: Singer and Entertainer* (5–9). Series: Hispanic Biographies. 1998, Enslow LB $20.95 (0-89490-890-1). This story of the singer who started with the Miami Sound Machine and then branched out as a soloist also reveals her devotion to her family and many social causes. (Rev: BR 9–10/98; HBG 3/99; SLJ 10/98) [921]

12794 Rodriguez, Janel. *Gloria Estefan* (4–8). Illus. Series: Contemporary Hispanic Americans. 1995, Raintree LB $24.26 (0-8172-3982-0). A fine biography of this Cuban American entertainer who, at the height of her career, overcame severe medical problems and remained a star singer. (Rev: BL 3/15/96; SLJ 1/96) [921]

12795 Shirley, David. *Gloria Estefan* (4–7). Illus. Series: Hispanics of Achievement. 1994, Chelsea LB $15.95 (0-7910-2114-4); paper $7.65 (0-7910-2117-3). 80pp. A nicely illustrated biography of the Cuban-born rock star. (Rev: BL 11/15/94; SLJ 10/94) [921]

12796 Stefoff, Rebecca. *Gloria Estefan* (5–9). Series: Hispanics of Achievement. 1991, Chelsea LB $21.95 (0-7910-1244-1). The story of the singer who broke her back in a 1990 accident but bounced back to success. (Rev: BL 8/91; SLJ 12/91) [782.42164]

12797 Strazzabosco, Jeanne M. *Learning About Determination from the Life of Gloria Estefan* (2–5). Illus. Series: A Character Building Book. 1996, Rosen LB $15.93 (0-8239-2416-5). 24pp. The life story of this important entertainer, emphasizing that her success came from the determination to overcome obstacles. (Rev: BL 10/15/96; SLJ 12/96) [921]

FITZGERALD, ELLA

12798 Pinkney, Andrea Davis. *Ella Fitzgerald: The Tale of a Vocal Virtuosa* (3–5). Illus. by Brian Pinkney. 2002, Hyperion $16.99 (0-7868-0568-4). 32pp. A picture-book biography told by Scat Cat Monroe with a lengthy text about the singer's life and the thrill of witnessing one of her performances. (Rev: BL 4/1/02; HBG 10/02; SLJ 5/02) [921]

FONDA, JANE

12799 Shorto, Russell. *Jane Fonda: Political Activist* (4–6). Series: New Directions. 1991, Houghton Mifflin paper $5.70 (0-395-63564-0). 101pp. Covers Jane Fonda's public and private life, her acting career, and her devotion to a number of causes. (Rev: SLJ 10/91) [921]

GELLAR, SARAH MICHELLE

12800 Powell, Phelan. *Sarah Michelle Gellar* (3–4). Series: Real-Life Reader Biographies. 2000, Mitchell Lane LB $15.95 (1-58415-034-3). 32pp. This short biography tells the story of the popular

star of *Buffy the Vampire Slayer,* who began acting
at age 4. (Rev: BL 11/15/00) [921]

GOLDBERG, WHOOPI

12801 Adams, Mary A. *Whoopi Goldberg: From
Street to Stardom* (4–6). Illus. Series: Taking Part.
1993, Macmillan LB $18.95 (0-87518-562-2). 64pp.
An easily read biography of this talented comedian,
actress, and talk-show hostess. (Rev: BL 5/1/93;
SLJ 7/93) [921]

12802 Katz, Sandor. *Whoopi Goldberg: Performer
with a Heart* (5–8). Series: Junior Black Americans
of Achievement. 1996, Chelsea $18.65 (0-7910-
2396-6). A look at Whoopi Goldberg's life and
career, focusing on how she feels about her profession and the causes she believes in. (Rev: BL
10/15/96; SLJ 1/97) [921]

GOULD, GLENN

12803 Konieczny, Vladimir. *Struggling for Perfec-
tion: The Story of Glen Gould* (3–5). Illus. by
Chrissie Wysotski. Series: Stories of Canada. 2004,
Napoleon $16.95 (0-929141-13-X). 96pp. The
Canadian-born pianist's talents and eccentricities
are all discussed in this entertaining volume. (Rev:
BL 7/04; SLJ 9/04) [786.2]

GRAHAM, MARTHA

12804 Freedman, Russell. *Martha Graham: A Dancer's Life* (4–8). 1998, Clarion $18.00 (0-395-74655-
8). Martha Graham's amazing talents, driving force,
and complex personality are well depicted in this
handsomely illustrated biography. (Rev: BCCB
6/98; BL 4/1/98; SLJ 5/98) [921]

12805 Pratt, Paula B. *Martha Graham* (4–8). Illus.
Series: The Importance Of. 1995, Lucent LB $27.45
(1-56006-056-5). 112pp. The life of this amazing
dancer, choreographer, and dance company founder.
(Rev: BL 1/15/95; SLJ 1/95) [921]

12806 Probosz, Kathilyn S. *Martha Graham* (5–8).
Illus. Series: People in Focus. 1995, Dillon paper
$7.95 (0-382-24961-5). 184pp. A biography that
tells of this dancer's many accomplishments while
also giving details of her youth and the influences
on her work. (Rev: SLJ 10/95) [921]

GRANT, AMY

12807 Italia, Bob. *Amy Grant: From Gospel to Pop*
(4–6). Illus. Series: Leading Lady. 1992, ABDO LB
$12.94 (1-56239-145-3). 32pp. An engaging biogra-
phy with high-low interest. (Rev: BL 2/1/93; SLJ
4/93) [921]

HAMMER, M. C.

12808 Saylor-Marchant, Linda. *Hammer: 2 Legit 2
Quit* (3–6). Illus. Series: Taking Part. 1992, Macmillan LB $18.95 (0-87518-522-3). 64pp. The life
of the popular African American rap musician and
his struggle to succeed. (Rev: BL 1/15/93; SLJ
2/93) [921]

HANSON (MUSICAL GROUP)

12809 Powell, Phelan. *Hanson* (5–8). Series: Galaxy
of Superstars. 1999, Chelsea $19.75 (0-7910-5148-
X); paper $8.95 (0-7910-5325-3). 63pp. An attrac-
tive volume with information on the three-brother
singing group that hails from Tulsa, Oklahoma.
(Rev: BL 4/15/98; BR 9–10/99; HBG 10/99) [921]

HART, MELISSA JOAN

12810 Ciacobello, John. *Melissa Joan Hart* (5–8).
Series: Celebrity Bios. 2002, Children's Book Pr.
LB $20.00 (0-516-23906-6); paper $6.95 (0-516-
23483-8). 48pp. An easily read, heavily illustrated
biography of the young actress who gained stardom
as *Sabrina, the Teenage Witch.* (Rev: BL 6/1–15/02;
SLJ 8/02) [921]

12811 Gaines, Ann Graham. *Melissa Joan Hart*
(3–4). Series: Real-Life Reader Biographies. 2000,
Mitchell Lane LB $15.95 (1-58415-036-X). 32pp. A
simple profile of the TV actress best known for her
roles as Clarissa and Sabrina. (Rev: BL 11/15/00)
[921]

HENDRIX, JIMI

12812 Markel, Rita J. *Jimi Hendrix* (5–9). 2001,
Lerner LB $25.26 (0-8225-4990-5); paper $7.95 (0-
8225-9697-0). 112pp. A better-than-average account
of the short life of this guitarist of the 1960s. (Rev:
BL 2/15/01; HBG 10/01; SLJ 3/01) [921]

HENSON, JIM

12813 Durrett, Deanne. *Jim Henson* (2–5). Illus.
Series: Inventors and Creators. 2002, Gale LB
$23.70 (0-7377-0996-0). 48pp. This look at the life
of the Muppets creator includes lots of details on the
popular characters. (Rev: BL 11/1/02) [791.5]

HEWITT, JENNIFER LOVE

12814 Severs, Vesta-Nadine. *Jennifer Love Hewitt*
(3–4). Series: Real-Life Reader Biographies. 2000,
Mitchell Lane LB $15.95 (1-58415-032-7). 32pp.
The story of the popular actress who has been a professional since doing Barbie commercials for Mattel
as a preteen. (Rev: BL 11/15/00) [921]

HILL, FAITH

12815 Hinman, Bonnie. *Faith Hill* (5–9). 2001,
Chelsea $19.75 (0-7910-6471-9). 64pp. A look at
the life and career of the country music star, with
information on Nashville's Grand Ole Opry. (Rev:
HBG 10/02; SLJ 4/02) [921]

HILL, LAURYN

12816 Greene, Meg. *Lauryn Hill* (5–8). Series:
Galaxy of Superstars. 1999, Chelsea $19.75 (0-
7910-5495-0). 64pp. A biography of the music
superstar who won five Grammy Awards for her
breakout solo album. (Rev: BL 3/15/00; HBG
10/00) [921]

HINES, GREGORY

12817 DeAngelis, Gina. *Gregory Hines* (4–7). Illus. Series: Black Americans of Achievement. 1999, Chelsea $21.95 (0-7910-5197-8); paper $9.95 (0-7910-5198-6). 99pp. Though he is known primarily as a dancer, this biography of Gregory Hines points out his many other talents, including acting. (Rev: BL 2/15/00; HBG 3/00) [921]

HOLMES, KATIE

12818 Boulais, Sue. *Katie Holmes* (3–4). Series: Real-Life Reader Biographies. 2000, Mitchell Lane LB $15.95 (1-58415-038-6). 32pp. A brief biography of the young actress who wisely completed high school before accepting the role in *Dawson's Creek* that made her famous. (Rev: BL 11/15/00) [921]

HOUDINI, HARRY

12819 Cox, Clinton. *Houdini: Master of Illusion* (5–9). Illus. 2001, Scholastic paper $16.95 (0-590-94960-8). 208pp. A fast-paced account of the life of the world-famous magician from childhood on, with eight pages of photographs and reproductions. (Rev: BL 11/15/01; HB 1–2/02; HBG 3/02; SLJ 12/01) [793.8]

12820 Krull, Kathleen. *Houdini: The World's Greatest Mystery Man and Escape King* (1–3). Illus. by Eric Velasquez. 2005, Walker $16.95 (0-8027-8953-6). 32pp. A picture-book biography of the famous magician, illustrated with oil paintings. (Rev: BL 3/1/05; SLJ 4/05) [793.8]

12821 Lalicki, Tom. *Spellbinder: The Life of Harry Houdini* (5–8). Illus. 2000, Holiday House $18.95 (0-8234-1499-X). 88pp. A biography of Elrich Weiss, aka Harry Houdini, and his career as a magician and escape artist. (Rev: BCCB 3/01; BL 9/1/00; HBG 3/01; SLJ 9/00) [921]

HOUSTON, WHITNEY

12822 Cox, Ted. *Whitney Houston: Singer Actress* (5–8). Illus. Series: Black Americans of Achievement. 1997, Chelsea LB $21.95 (0-7910-4455-6); paper $8.95 (0-7910-4456-4). A readable biography that shows Whitney Houston growing up in New Jersey, the major influences in her life, her rise to fame, marriage, and philanthropic endeavors. (Rev: BL 8/98; HBG 10/98) [921]

HOWARD, RON

12823 Kramer, Barbara. *Ron Howard: Child Star and Hollywood Director* (5–9). Series: People to Know. 1998, Enslow LB $19.95 (0-89490-981-9). 112pp. From his days on *The Andy Griffith Show* when he was only six to his present work as a movie director, this is a workmanlike overview of the career of Ron Howard. (Rev: HBG 3/99; SLJ 3/99) [921]

IGLESIAS, ENRIQUE

12824 Granados, Christine. *Enrique Iglesias* (3–4). Series: Real-Life Reader Biographies. 2000, Mitchell Lane LB $15.95 (1-58415-045-9). 32pp. A profile of the son of singer Julio Iglesias and how he started out in show business as Enrique Martinez because he wanted to gain recognition based not his father's name but on his own ability. (Rev: BL 11/15/00) [921]

JACKSON, JANET

12825 Dyson, Cindy. *Janet Jackson* (4–7). Series: Black Americans of Achievement. 2000, Chelsea $21.95 (0-7910-5283-4). 109pp. The life story of the popular singer and the ups and downs of her career. (Rev: BL 6/1–15/00; HBG 10/00) [921]

JACKSON, MAHALIA

12826 Orgill, Roxane. *Mahalia: A Life in Gospel Music* (5–9). Illus. 2002, Candlewick $19.99 (0-7636-1011-9). 144pp. An impassioned biography about the life of gospel singer Mahalia Jackson set against the backdrop of social and political events of the times. (Rev: BL 2/15/02; HBG 10/02; SLJ 1/02) [782.25]

JACKSON, MICHAEL

12827 Graves, Karen Marie. *Michael Jackson* (5–8). Series: People in the News. 2001, Lucent LB $35.15 (1-56006-707-1). The unusual life of this show business legend is outlined in text and photographs. (Rev: BL 4/1/02) [921]

12828 Nicholson, Lois. *Michael Jackson* (4–8). Illus. Series: Black Americans of Achievement. 1994, Chelsea LB $21.95 (0-7910-1929-2); paper $8.95 (0-7910-1930-6). 104pp. A biography of the pop star that examines his loneliness and his family ties, and touches on the allegations against him of sexual abuse. (Rev: BL 10/15/94; SLJ 10/94) [921]

JACKSON, SAMUEL L.

12829 Dils, Tracey E. *Samuel L. Jackson* (4–7). Series: Black Americans of Achievement. 2000, Chelsea $21.95 (0-7910-5281-8). 104pp. The life story of the African American actor who has portrayed diverse characters in films including *Pulp Fiction* and *A Time to Kill*. (Rev: BL 6/1–15/00; HBG 10/00) [921]

JULIA, RAUL

12830 Perez, Frank, and Ann Well. *Raul Julia* (4–8). Illus. Series: Contemporary Hispanic Americans. 1995, Raintree LB $28.80 (0-8172-3984-7). 48pp. The story of the brilliant stage and film actor who gained fame in *The Addams Family* and on *Sesame Street*. This biography was written before his untimely death. (Rev: BL 3/15/96; SLJ 1/96) [921]

LATIFAH, QUEEN

12831 Bloom, Sara R. *Queen Latifah* (4–7). Series: Black Americans of Achievement. 2001, Chelsea $21.95 (0-7910-6287-2). Numerous photographs add interest to this biography of the amazing singer-actress and her rise to fame. (Rev: BL 4/1/02; HBG 10/02; SLJ 6/02) [921]

12832 Ruth, Amy. *Queen Latifah* (5–8). Series: A&E Biography. 2000, Lerner LB $25.26 (0-8225-4988-3). 112pp. The story of the female rap singer who used her positive attitudes, hard work, and determination to get ahead. (Rev: BL 3/1/01; HBG 10/01) [921]

LEE, BRUCE

12833 Tagliaferro, Linda. *Bruce Lee* (5–10). Series: A&E Biography. 2000, Lerner LB $25.26 (0-8225-4948-4); paper $7.95 (0-8225-9688-1). 112pp. This colorful biography of the famous action star is filled with information about him, his films, and his family. (Rev: HBG 10/00; SLJ 5/00) [921]

LEE, SPIKE

12834 Shields, Charles J. *Spike Lee* (5–7). Illus. 2002, Chelsea $22.95 (0-7910-6715-7). 112pp. This look at Spike Lee's career, working methods, and importance includes both strengths and weaknesses and includes many photographs and quotations. (Rev: BL 11/1/02; HBG 3/03) [791.43]

LENNON, JOHN

12835 Gogerly, Liz. *John Lennon* (4–6). Series: Famous Lives. 2003, Raintree LB $27.12 (0-7398-5522-0). 48pp. The story of the legendary member of the Beatles and how he influenced young people to cherish peace and love. (Rev: BL 2/15/03; HBG 10/03) [921]

12836 Wright, David K. *John Lennon: The Beatles and Beyond* (4–6). Illus. Series: People to Know. 1996, Enslow LB $20.95 (0-89490-702-6). 112pp. The story of the famous Beatle, his rise to fame, his activities outside music, and his tragic death. (Rev: BL 10/15/96; SLJ 12/96) [921]

LOPEZ, JENNIFER

12837 Hill, Anne E. *Jennifer Lopez* (5–8). Series: Galaxy of Superstars. 2000, Chelsea $19.75 (0-7910-5775-5). 64pp. This book chronicles the career of the young Latina star who is a fine singer and actress. (Rev: BL 10/15/00; HBG 10/01) [921]

12838 Menard, Valerie. *Jennifer Lopez* (3–4). Series: Real-Life Reader Biographies. 2000, Mitchell Lane LB $15.95 (1-58415-025-4). 32pp. This popular singer-actress got her big break when she played another young singer, Selena. (Rev: BL 11/15/00) [921]

LUCAS, GEORGE

12839 Shields, Charles J. *George Lucas* (5–7). Illus. Series: Behind the Camera. 2002, Chelsea $22.95 (0-7910-6712-2). 112pp. A profile of the famous filmmaker, with information on his strengths and weaknesses, his working methods, and his importance to the American film industry, backed up by many photographs and quotations. (Rev: BL 11/1/02; HBG 3/03) [791.43]

12840 White, Dana. *George Lucas* (5–8). Series: A&E Biography. 1999, Lerner LB $30.35 (0-8225-4975-1); paper $7.95 (0-8225-9684-9). 128pp. This book covers the childhood and early career of this filmmaker but concentrates on his masterpiece, the creation of the *Star Wars* saga. (Rev: HBG 3/00; SLJ 3/00) [921]

MCGREGOR, EWAN

12841 Jones, Veda Boyd. *Ewan McGregor* (5–8). Series: Galaxy of Superstars. 1999, Chelsea $19.75 (0-7910-5501-9). 64pp. A well-illustrated biography of the Scottish-born actor in the *Star Wars* prequels. (Rev: BL 3/15/00; HBG 10/00) [921]

MARSALIS, WYNTON

12842 Ellis, Veronica F. *Wynton Marsalis* (4–6). Illus. Series: Contemporary African Americans. 1997, Raintree LB $24.26 (0-8172-3998-X). 48pp. A fine biography of this Grammy award–winning musician who is equally at home with jazz and classical music. (Rev: BL 5/15/97; SLJ 2/98) [921]

12843 Gourse, Leslie. *Wynton Marsalis* (4–6). Series: Book Report Biographies. 1999, Watts LB $22.00 (0-531-11673-5). 112pp. Extensively illustrated with black-and-white photographs, this is an attractive biography of the black trumpeter whose versatility extends to both jazz and classical music. (Rev: BL 11/15/99; SLJ 4/00) [921]

MARTIN, RICKY

12844 Menard, Valerie. *Ricky Martin* (3–4). Series: Real-Life Reader Biographies. 1999, Mitchell Lane LB $15.95 (1-58415-059-9). 32pp. Black-and-white photos illustrate this easily read biography of the Puerto Rican singing sensation. (Rev: BL 11/15/99) [921]

MILANO, ALYSSA

12845 Bankston, John. *Alyssa Milano* (3–4). Series: Real-Life Reader Biographies. 2000, Mitchell Lane LB $15.95 (1-58415-040-8). 32pp. The life story of the young actress who grew up on TV's *Who's the Boss* and went on to star in *Charmed*. (Rev: BL 11/15/00) [921]

MONK, THELONIOUS

12846 Raschka, Chris. *Mysterious Thelonious* (3–7). Illus. 1997, Orchard LB $14.99 (0-531-33057-5). 32pp. In a lively mixture of color and motion, this book presents an unusual handling of an unusual subject, a tribute to jazz musician Thelonious Monk. (Rev: BL 11/1/97; HBG 3/98; SLJ 9/97*) [921]

MORENO, RITA

12847 Suntree, Susan. *Rita Moreno* (5–9). Series: Hispanics of Achievement. 1992, Chelsea LB $21.95 (0-7910-1247-6). A biography of the Puerto Rican entertainer and her successes on stage and screen. (Rev: BL 2/1/93) [921]

MUNIZ, FRANKIE

12848 Beyer, Mark. *Frankie Muniz* (5–8). Series: Celebrity Bios. 2002, Children's Book Pr. LB $20.00 (0-516-23910-4); paper $6.95 (0-516-23480-3). 48pp. Using simple sentences and many color photographs, this is a brief biography of the young actor who scored a big hit in "Malcolm in the Middle." (Rev: BL 6/1–15/02; SLJ 8/02) [921]

NEW KIDS ON THE BLOCK (MUSICAL GROUP)

12849 McGibbon, Robin. *New Kids on the Block: The Whole Story* (5–8). Illus. 1990, Avon paper $6.95 (0-380-76344-3). 120pp. Stories about members of this band have been collected from a variety of sources, including the members themselves. (Rev: BL 10/1/90) [921]

NIMOY, LEONARD

12850 Micklos, John. *Leonard Nimoy: A Star's Trek* (3–6). Illus. 1988, Macmillan LB $13.95 (0-87518-376-X). 64pp. A simple biography of the man best known as Mr. Spock on "Star Trek." (Rev: BL 7/88; SLJ 10/88)

NORRIS, CHUCK

12851 Cole, Melanie. *Chuck Norris* (3–6). Series: Real-Life Reader Biographies. 1998, Mitchell Lane LB $15.95 (1-883845-91-2). 32pp. This action star of movies and television is a martial arts guru and claims Native American ancestry. (Rev: SLJ 2/99) [921]

NUREYEV, RUDOLF

12852 Maybarduk, Linda. *The Dancer Who Flew: A Memoir of Rudolf Nureyev* (5–9). Illus. 1999, Tundra $18.95 (0-88776-415-0). 188pp. The author, a friend and colleague of Nureyev, not only gives a straightforward biography of the dancer but also tells many backstage stories and introduces his most important roles. (Rev: BL 1/1–15/00; HBG 3/00; SLJ 2/00) [921]

OAKLEY, ANNIE

12853 Dadey, Debbie. *Shooting Star: Annie Oakley, the Legend* (K–3). Illus. by Scott Goto. 1997, Walker LB $16.85 (0-8027-8485-2). 32pp. Fact and fiction mingle in this tall tale about the famous Western sharp shooter. (Rev: BCCB 6/97; BL 3/15/97; HB 5–6/97; SLJ 4/97*) [921]

12854 Flynn, Jean. *Annie Oakley: Legendary Sharpshooter* (4–9). Series: Historical American Biogra-

phies. 1998, Enslow LB $20.95 (0-7660-1012-0). Using a concise text, fact boxes, and a chronology, this is the story of the star attraction of Buffalo Bill's Wild West Show. (Rev: BL 8/98; SLJ 8/98) [921]

12855 Krensky, Stephen. *Shooting for the Moon: The Amazing Life and Times of Annie Oakley* (1–4). Illus. by Bernie Fuchs. 2001, Farrar $17.00 (0-374-36843-0). 32pp. A combination of simple, concise text and skillful oil paintings convey the life of Annie Oakley, from her childhood to her fame for her shooting skills. (Rev: BL 9/15/01; HBG 3/02; SLJ 9/01) [799.3]

12856 Landau, Elaine. *Annie Oakley: Wild West Sharpshooter* (3–6). Series: Best of the West Biographies. 2004, Enslow LB $18.95 (0-7660-2205-6). 48pp. Period photographs add to this engaging account of Oakley's personal and professional life that will appeal to reluctant readers. (Rev: SLJ 8/04) [921]

12857 Macy, Sue. *Bull's-Eye: A Photobiography of Annie Oakley* (5–8). Illus. 2001, National Geographic $17.95 (0-7922-7008-8). 64pp. This book separates fact from fiction in the life of Phoebe Ann Moses Butler, who came to be known as Annie Oakley. (Rev: BL 11/15/01; HBG 3/02; SLJ 10/01) [799.3]

12858 Porterfield, Jason. *Annie Oakley: Wild West Sharpshooter* (2–4). Illus. Series: Primary Sources of Famous People in American History. 2004, Rosen LB $15.95 (0-8239-4102-7). 32pp. A simple biography of Annie Oakley, which traces the sharpshooter's life and career from her birth in Ohio to her 16-year tour as a featured attraction with "Buffalo Bill" Cody's Wild West Show. (Rev: BL 9/15/04) [921]

12859 Wukovits, John. *Annie Oakley* (4–8). Series: Legends of the West. 1997, Chelsea LB $18.65 (0-7910-3906-4). A profile of the famous sharpshooter and her career with Buffalo Bill's Wide West Show. (Rev: SLJ 10/97) [921]

O'DONNELL, ROSIE

12860 Granados, Christine. *Rosie O'Donnell* (3–4). Series: Real-Life Reader Biographies. 1999, Mitchell Lane LB $15.95 (1-883845-98-X). 32pp. The story of the comedienne, actress, and talk-show host who has used her success to give to others. (Rev: BL 10/15/99) [921]

12861 Kallen, Stuart A. *Rosie O'Donnell* (4–8). Series: People in the News. 1999, Lucent LB $27.45 (1-56006-546-X). An interesting, well-researched biography of this popular actress, comedienne, and talk-show host, covering her personal and professional life. (Rev: BL 8/99; HBG 3/00) [921]

12862 Krohn, Katherine E. *Rosie O'Donnell* (4–8). Series: A&E Biography. 1998, Lerner LB $25.26 (0-8225-4939-5). A breezy look at O'Donnell's rise from stand-up comic to TV fame with glimpses into her personal life, her mother's death when she was a child, and her fulfilling adoption of two children. (Rev: HBG 3/99; SLJ 2/99) [921]

12863 Meachum, Virginia. *Rosie O'Donnell* (4–6). Series: People to Know. 2000, Enslow LB $19.95 (0-7660-1148-8). 128pp. The life story of the comedian and talk-show host who is noted both for her show business career and for championing worthy causes. (Rev: BL 1/1–15/00; HBG 10/00) [921]

12864 Stone, Tanya L. *Rosie O'Donnell: America's Favorite Grown-Up Kid* (4–7). Illus. 2000, Millbrook LB $23.90 (0-7613-1724-4). 48pp. A well-designed, chatty biography of the popular talk-show host and comedienne. (Rev: BL 12/15/00; HBG 3/01) [792.7]

OLMOS, EDWARD JAMES

12865 Carrillo, Louis. *Edward James Olmos* (4–8). Illus. Series: Contemporary Hispanic Americans. 1997, Raintree LB $17.98 (0-8172-3989-8). 48pp. Along with a timeline and glossary, this account traces the life of this contemporary human rights activist and actor. (Rev: BL 4/15/97) [921]

OZAWA, SEIJI

12866 Tan, Sheri. *Seiji Ozawa* (5–7). Illus. Series: Contemporary Asian Americans. 1997, Raintree LB $17.98 (0-8172-3993-6). 48pp. A profile of the Asian American musician who has been the chief conductor of the Boston Symphony for more than 20 years. (Rev: BL 5/1/97; SLJ 9/97) [921]

PAVLOVA, ANNA

12867 Allman, Barbara. *Dance of the Swan: A Story About Anna Pavlova* (3–6). Illus. by Shelly O. Haas. Series: Creative Minds Biographies. 2001, Carolrhoda LB $21.27 (1-57505-463-9). 64pp. Allman presents Pavlova's life from childhood and discusses her love of nature and of children as well as her commitment to ballet. (Rev: HBG 10/01; SLJ 7/01) [792.8]

12868 Levine, Ellen. *Anna Pavlova: Genius of the Dance* (5–7). 1995, Scholastic paper $14.95 (0-590-44304-6). 128pp. The life and career of this legendary ballerina, with coverage of the famous ballets in which she danced. (Rev: BCCB 5/95; BL 1/1/95; SLJ 4/95*) [921]

PICKETT, BILL

12869 Pinkney, Andrea D. *Bill Pickett: Rodeo-Ridin' Cowboy* (PS–3). Illus. by Brian Pinkney. 1996, Harcourt $16.00 (0-15-200100-X). 32pp. The story of Bill Pickett, African American rodeo superstar and superb horseman. (Rev: BCCB 11/96; BL 11/1/96; HB 11–12/96; SLJ 10/96) [921]

12870 Sanford, William R., and Carl R. Green. *Bill Pickett: African-American Rodeo Star* (4–6). Illus. Series: Legendary Heroes of the Wild West. 1997, Enslow LB $16.95 (0-89490-676-3). 48pp. This is a short biography of the colorful rodeo star who is considered one of the legends of the Wild West. (Rev: BL 3/15/97) [921]

PRESLEY, ELVIS

12871 Krohn, Katherine E. *Elvis Presley: The King* (5–7). Illus. 1994, Lerner LB $18.60 (0-8225-2877-0). 64pp. A somewhat sanitized biography of Elvis Presley that highlights important events in his career. (Rev: BL 7/94; SLJ 7/94) [921]

PRICE, LEONTYNE

12872 McNair, Joseph. *Leontyne Price* (4–6). Series: Journey to Freedom. 2000, Child's World LB $25.64 (1-56766-720-1). 40pp. The life story of the famous opera star who rose from poverty to sing in all the major opera houses of the world. (Rev: BL 11/15/00; HBG 3/01) [921]

12873 Steins, Richard. *Leontyne Price: Opera Star* (4–6). Illus. Series: The Library of Famous Women. 1993, Blackbirch LB $17.95 (1-56711-009-6). 64pp. A candid view of the singer who, while thrilling millions, broke color barriers in the world of opera. (Rev: BL 6/1–15/93; SLJ 8/93) [921]

PRINZE, FREDDIE, JR.

12874 Wilson, Wayne. *Freddie Prinze, Jr.* (3–4). Series: Real-Life Reader Biographies. 2000, Mitchell Lane LB $15.95 (1-58415-063-7). 32pp. The story of the talented performer and actor whose famous father died before he could get to know him. (Rev: BL 11/15/00) [921]

PUENTE, TITO

12875 Olmstead, Mary. *Tito Puente* (4–7). Illus. Series: Hispanic-American Biographies. 2004, Raintree LB $31.36 (1-4109-0713-9). 64pp. A concise account of the life and career of Tito Puente, the popular American bandleader and percussionist who in the 1950s was nicknamed the Mambo King. (Rev: BL 2/1/05) [784.4]

QUINN, ANTHONY

12876 Amdur, Melissa. *Anthony Quinn* (5–9). Series: Hispanics of Achievement. 1993, Chelsea LB $19.95 (0-7910-1251-4). The life of this Mexican American actor is told with many interesting asides concerning his career and black-and-white stills from his movies. (Rev: BL 9/15/93) [921]

REESE, DELLA

12877 Dean, Tanya. *Della Reese* (4–7). Series: Black Americans of Achievement. 2001, Chelsea $21.95 (0-7910-6291-0). The life and career of this show business giant are outlined with special coverage on her recent successes in television. (Rev: BL 4/1/02) [921]

RIMES, LEANN

12878 Zymet, Cathy Alter. *LeAnn Rimes* (5–8). Series: Galaxy of Superstars. 1999, Chelsea $19.75 (0-7910-5152-8); paper $8.95 (0-7910-5327-X). 63pp. This book covers the rise to stardom and the career of this country-western singer who hails from Jackson, Mississippi. (Rev: BL 4/15/98; BR 9–10/99; HBG 10/99) [921]

ROBERTS, JULIA

12879 Wilson, Wayne. *Julia Roberts* (3–4). Series: Real-Life Reader Biographies. 2000, Mitchell Lane LB $15.95 (1-58415-028-9). 32pp. A simple biography with plenty of pictures of the actress whose career took off after her performance in *Pretty Woman*. (Rev: BL 11/15/00; SLJ 1/01) [921]

ROBESON, PAUL

12880 McKissack, Patricia, and Fredrick McKissack. *Paul Robeson: A Voice to Remember*. Rev. ed. (2–5). Series: Great African Americans. 2001, Enslow LB $14.95 (0-7660-1674-9). 32pp. Presents Robeson's personal and professional life and the hardships he faced because of his race and beliefs. (Rev: HBG 10/01; SLJ 8/01) [921]

12881 Wright, David K. *Paul Robeson: Actor, Singer, Political Activist* (5–9). Illus. Series: African-American Biographies. 1998, Enslow LB $20.95 (0-89490-944-4). 128pp. This book details Robeson's personal and professional life and the hardships he faced because of his race and beliefs. (Rev: BL 11/15/98; SLJ 11/98) [921]

ROBINSON, BILL "BOJANGLES"

12882 Dillon, Leo, and Diane Dillon. *Rap a Tap Tap: Here's Bojangles — Think of That!* (PS–2). Illus. 2002, Scholastic $15.95 (0-590-47883-4). 32pp. A brilliantly illustrated picture book about legendary tap artist Bill "Bojangles" Robinson. (Rev: BL 10/15/02; HBG 3/03; SLJ 9/02) [792.7]

ROCK, CHRIS

12883 Blue, Rose, and Corinne J. Naden. *Chris Rock* (4–7). Series: Black Americans of Achievement. 2000, Chelsea $21.95 (0-7910-5277-X). 104pp. The story of the comedian and actor who began his career on *Saturday Night Live* and is noted for his acerbic wit. (Rev: BL 6/1–15/00; HBG 10/00) [921]

RODRIGUEZ, ROBERT

12884 Marvis, Barbara. *Robert Rodriguez* (5–10). Series: A Real-Life Reader Biography. 1997, Mitchell Lane LB $15.95 (1-883845-48-3). This simple, attractive biography of the successful movie maker focuses on his problems growing up in a large family and clinging to his career dreams. (Rev: BL 6/1–15/98; HBG 3/98; SLJ 2/98) [921]

ROGERS, WILL

12885 Bennett, Cathereen L. *Will Rogers: Quotable Cowboy* (4–6). Illus. 1995, Lerner LB $19.93 (0-8225-3155-0). 96pp. The exciting life of Will Rogers — noted actor, writer, humorist, and humanitarian. (Rev: BL 3/1/96; SLJ 12/95) [921]

12886 Dadey, Debbie. *Will Rogers: Larger than Life* (K–3). Illus. by Scott Goto. 1999, Walker LB $16.85 (0-8027-8682-0). 32pp. A picture-book introduction to the laconic, humble entertainer who displayed a unique sense of humor. (Rev: BL 4/1/99; HBG 10/99; SLJ 9/99)

12887 Keating, Frank. *Will Rogers* (K–3). Illus. by Mike Wimmer. 2002, Harcourt $16.00 (0-15-202405-0). 32pp. A beautifully illustrated profile of the humorist and newspaper columnist who lived from 1879 to 1935, written by Oklahoma governor Frank Keating. (Rev: BL 9/15/02; HBG 3/03; SLJ 11/02) [792.7]

12888 Malone, Mary. *Will Rogers: Cowboy Philosopher* (4–7). Illus. Series: People to Know. 1996, Enslow LB $20.95 (0-89490-695-X). 128pp. A lively look at the life and accomplishments of this cowboy and show business idol. (Rev: BL 5/15/96; SLJ 6/96) [921]

RONSTADT, LINDA

12889 Amdur, Melissa. *Linda Ronstadt* (5–9). Series: Hispanics of Achievement. 1993, Chelsea LB $21.95 (0-7910-1781-8). This biography of the popular Mexican American singer describes her roots and pride in her Hispanic heritage. (Rev: BL 9/15/93; SLJ 10/93) [921]

RUSSELL, KERI

12890 Hasday, Judy. *Keri Russell* (3–4). Series: Real-Life Reader Biographies. 2000, Mitchell Lane LB $15.95 (1-58415-033-5). 32pp. An easily read biography of the young actress who plays Felicity. (Rev: BL 11/15/00) [921]

RYDER, WINONA

12891 Menard, Valerie. *Winona Ryder* (3–4). Series: Real-Life Reader Biographies. 2000, Mitchell Lane LB $15.95 (1-58415-039-4). 32pp. A simple biography of the talented actress who appeared in 23 movies before her 30th birthday. (Rev: BL 11/15/00) [921]

SANDLER, ADAM

12892 Seldman, David. *Adam Sandler* (5–8). Series: Galaxy of Superstars. 2000, Chelsea $19.75 (0-7910-5773-9). 64pp. An entertaining biography of the actor and comedian who gained notoriety from his roles in *The Waterboy* and *Big Daddy*. (Rev: BL 12/15/00; HBG 10/01) [921]

SARALEGUI, CRISTINA

12893 Menard, Valerie. *Cristina Saralegui* (3–4). Illus. Series: Real-Life Reader Biographies. 1998, Mitchell Lane LB $15.95 (1-883845-60-2). 32pp. A Cuban refugee, Cristina is an Emmy Award-winning talk show host who is known as the Spanish-language Oprah Winfrey. (Rev: BL 10/15/98; HBG 10/98) [921]

SAVION

12894 Glover, Savion, and Bruce Weber. *Savion! My Life in Tap* (5–10). 2000, Morrow $19.95 (0-688-15629-0). 79pp. A fascinating autobiography of the young dancer and choreographer whose tap dancing includes rap and hip-hop in a wonderful combination that has entranced audiences. (Rev: BCCB 2/00; BL 1/1–15/00; HBG 10/00; SLJ 3/00) [921]

SCHUMANN, CLARA

12895 Allman, Barbara. *Her Piano Sang: A Story About Clara Schumann* (4–7). Illus. 1996, Carolrhoda LB $25.55 (1-57505-012-9). 64pp. The story of this groundbreaking composer and pianist who also championed her husband's music. (Rev: BL 1/1–15/97; SLJ 1/97) [921]

12896 Reich, Susanna. *Clara Schumann: Piano Virtuoso* (5–8). 1999, Houghton Mifflin $18.00 (0-395-89119-1). 128pp. A thorough, well-researched biography of this amazing pianist and composer that describes her life as a child prodigy, her marriage to Robert Schumann, and her life promoting his music after his death. (Rev: BL 8/99; HB 3–4/99; HBG 10/99; SLJ 4/99*) [921]

SELENA (SINGER)

12897 Marvis, Barbara. *Selena* (5–10). Series: A Real-Life Reader Biography. 1997, Mitchell Lane LB $15.95 (1-883845-47-5). A simple, attractive biography of the singer, her supportive family, and her tragic death. (Rev: BL 6/1–15/98; HBG 3/98; SLJ 2/98) [921]

12898 Romero, Maritza. *Selena Perez: Queen of Tejano Music* (2–3). Series: Great Hispanics of Our Time. 1998, Rosen LB $13.95 (0-8239-5086-7). 24pp. Double-page spreads are used to tell the story of this popular Tejano singer and her tragic, premature death. (Rev: SLJ 9/98) [921]

SILVERSTONE, ALICIA

12899 Powell, Phelan. *Alicia Silverstone* (3–4). Series: Real-Life Reader Biographies. 2000, Mitchell Lane LB $15.95 (1-58415-037-8). 32pp. The life story of this popular young actress who began modeling at age 6 and had been in several movies by the time she turned 20. (Rev: BL 11/15/00) [921]

SMITH, BESSIE

12900 Manera, Alexandria. *Bessie Smith* (2–5). Series: African-American Biographies. 2003, Raintree LB $28.56 (0-7398-6875-6). 64pp. A simple profile of the singer, with interesting sidebars and good archival photographs that convey a sense of the time in which she lived. (Rev: HBG 4/04; SLJ 11/03) [921]

SMITS, JIMMY

12901 Cole, Melanie. *Jimmy Smits* (3–4). Illus. Series: Real-Life Reader Biographies. 1998, Mitchell Lane LB $15.95 (1-883845-59-9). 32pp. The story of the Latin American actor from New York who starred in such TV shows as *L.A. Law* and *NYPD Blue*. (Rev: BL 10/15/98; HBG 10/98) [921]

SPEARS, BRITNEY

12902 Gaines, Ann Graham. *Britney Spears* (3–4). Series: Real-Life Reader Biographies. 1999, Mitchell Lane LB $15.95 (1-58415-060-2). 32pp. This is a simple biography of the singer who is a former Mouseketeer and who once shared the stage with 'N Sync. (Rev: BL 11/15/99) [921]

12903 Lutz, Norma Jean. *Britney Spears* (5–8). Series: Galaxy of Superstars. 1999, Chelsea $19.75 (0-7910-5499-3). 64pp. A profile of the popular entertainer, telling how her childhood influenced her career path. (Rev: BL 3/15/00; HBG 10/00) [921]

SPICE GIRLS (MUSICAL GROUP)

12904 Shore, Nancy. *Spice Girls* (5–8). Series: Galaxy of Superstars. 1999, Chelsea $19.75 (0-7910-5149-8); paper $8.95 (0-7910-5328-8). 63pp. Biographies of members of the popular singing group that took first Britain and then the world by storm. (Rev: BL 4/15/98; BR 9–10/99; HBG 10/99; SLJ 5/99) [921]

SPIELBERG, STEVEN

12905 Meachum, Virginia. *Steven Spielberg: Hollywood Filmmaker* (4–6). Illus. Series: People to Know. 1996, Enslow LB $20.95 (0-89490-697-6). 112pp. The creator of such movie hits as *ET, Jaws,* and *Schindler's List,* is profiled in this easily read biography. (Rev: BL 8/96; SLJ 10/96) [921]

12906 Rubin, Susan Goldman. *Steven Spielberg: Crazy for Movies* (5–8). Illus. 2001, Abrams $19.95 (0-8109-4492-8). 94pp. Director Steven Spielberg's love of photography from his youth, his fascination with storytelling, and his successful movie career are presented in lively text and large photographs. (Rev: BL 12/1/01; HBG 3/02; SLJ 12/01) [791.43]

12907 Schoell, William. *Magic Man: The Life and Films of Steven Spielberg* (4–7). Illus. 1998, Tudor $18.95 (0-936389-57-5). 128pp. This biography of Spielberg concentrates on how he produces the astonishing special effects for his movies. (Rev: BL 5/15/98; SLJ 2/99) [921]

SUPREMES (MUSICAL GROUP)

12908 Rivera, Ursula. *The Supremes* (4–8). Illus. Series: Rock and Roll Hall of Famers. 2002, Rosen LB $29.25 (0-8239-3527-2). 112pp. The Supremes' rise to stardom — and eventual fall from fame without leader Diana Ross — is chronicled here with photographs, glossary, discography, and bibliography. (Rev: BL 10/1/02; SLJ 5/02) [782.421644]

TALLCHIEF, MARIA

12909 Tallchief, Maria, and Rosemary Wells. *Tallchief: America's Prima Ballerina* (3–5). 1999, Viking $15.99 (0-670-88756-0). 32pp. An autobiography of New York City Ballet's former star who began taking dance lessons while growing up on an Osage Indian reservation in Oklahoma. (Rev: BL 11/1/99*; HBG 3/00; SLJ 11/99) [921]

TWAIN, SHANIA

12910 Gallagher, Jim. *Shania Twain: Grammy Award-Winning Singer* (4–7). Series: Real-Life Reader Biographies. 1999, Mitchell Lane LB $15.95 (1-58415-000-9). 32pp. The story of the entertainer who was adopted into the Ojibwa tribe, began singing in bars at age eight, and went on to marry producer Mutt Lange. (Rev: SLJ 1/00) [921]

TYLER, LIV

12911 Boulais, Sue. *Liv Tyler* (3–4). Series: Real-Life Reader Biographies. 2000, Mitchell Lane LB $15.95 (1-58415-041-6). 32pp. This is the story of the talented model and actress who didn't learn until her teens that her father was Aerosmith's Steven Tyler. (Rev: BL 11/15/00) [921]

VAN DER BEEK, JAMES

12912 McCracken, Kristin. *James Van Der Beek* (5–8). Illus. Series: Celebrity Bios. 2001, Children's Book Pr. LB $20.00 (0-516-23429-3); paper $6.95 (0-516-29604-3). 48pp. The combination of easy text, photographs, gossip, and details of Van Der Beek's youth will appeal especially to reluctant readers. (Rev: BL 12/15/01) [791.45]

VON TRAPP, MARIA

12913 Ransom, Candice F. *Maria von Trapp: Beyond the Sound of Music* (4–6). Illus. Series: Trailblazer Biographies. 2002, Carolrhoda LB $25.26 (1-57505-444-2). 112pp. A portrait of Maria von Trapp, based on her own writings, that describes her life in war-torn Austria and move to a ski lodge in Vermont. (Rev: BL 3/1/02; HBG 10/02; SLJ 5/02) [782.42]

WALTERS, BARBARA

12914 Remstein, Henna. *Barbara Walters* (5–8). 1998, Chelsea $21.95 (0-7910-4716-4); paper $9.95 (0-7910-4717-2). The life story of Barbara Walters, who broke many barriers for women in the communications field and has become an icon in the field of journalism. (Rev: HBG 3/99) [921]

WASHINGTON, DENZEL

12915 Simmons, Alex. *Denzel Washington* (4–6). Illus. Series: Contemporary African Americans. 1997, Raintree LB $25.69 (0-8172-3986-3). 48pp. In this biography of actor Denzel Washington, he claims that his mother and the Boys Club saved him from a life of crime. (Rev: BL 5/15/97; SLJ 2/98) [921]

WHITE, DIANA

12916 White, Diana. *Ballerina Dreams* (1–3). Illus. by Jacqueline Rogers. Series: Hello Reader! 1998, Scholastic paper $3.99 (0-590-37233-5). This easy chapter book is the autobiography of a ballerina with the New York City Ballet that contains a description of how she overcame many problems to achieve her goals. (Rev: SLJ 3/99) [921]

WILLIAMS, ROBIN

12917 Zannos, Susan. *Robin Williams* (3–4). Series: Real-Life Reader Biographies. 2000, Mitchell Lane LB $15.95 (1-58415-029-7). 32pp. From playing Mork the alien on TV to winning an Oscar for his film work, this is a brief biography of the famous comedian and actor. (Rev: BL 11/15/00) [921]

WILLIAMS, VANESSA

12918 Boulais, Sue. *Vanessa Williams* (4–8). Series: Real-Life Reader Biographies. 1999, Mitchell Lane LB $15.95 (1-883845-75-0). The life story of the African American who lost her title of Miss America in 1983 but rebounded with a brilliant career in show business. (Rev: BL 6/1–15/99) [921]

WINFREY, OPRAH

12919 Krohn, Katherine. *Oprah Winfrey* (5–8). Series: Biography. 2001, Lerner LB $25.26 (0-8225-4999-9). The media genius and talk-show hostess is profiled in an interesting text with many photographs. (Rev: BL 4/1/02; HBG 10/02) [921]

12920 Nicholson, Lois. *Oprah Winfrey: Talking with America* (5–8). Series: Junior Black Americans of Achievement. 1997, Chelsea LB $18.65 (0-7910-2390-7); paper $4.95 (0-7910-4460-2). A biography that skims the life of this personality, with material on her difficult childhood, sexual abuse, college experiences, early career, weight problems, and success on television. (Rev: SLJ 8/97) [921]

12921 Stone, Tanya Lee. *Oprah Winfrey: Success with an Open Heart* (4–7). Illus. Series: Gateway Biographies. 2001, Millbrook LB $23.90 (0-7613-1814-3). 48pp. Oprah's story, with concise text and excellent photographs, will attract and inspire young readers. (Rev: BL 6/1–15/01; HBG 10/01) [791.45]

12922 Woods, Geraldine. *The Oprah Winfrey Story: Speaking Her Mind* (3–6). Series: Taking Part. 1991, Macmillan LB $13.95 (0-87518-463-4). 79pp. From dire poverty and abuse to talk show stardom, this is the story of Oprah Winfrey. (Rev: SLJ 3/92) [921]

Writers

AARDEMA, VERNA

12923 Aardema, Verna. *A Bookworm Who Hatched* (2–5). Illus. by Dede Smith. Series: Meet the Author. 1993, Richard C. Owen $14.95 (1-878450-39-5). 32pp. In this autobiographical account, the noted author reveals stories about her life, writing techniques, and how she interacts with her reading audience. (Rev: BL 9/1/93; HB 9–10/93) [921]

ADLER, DAVID A.

12924 Adler, David A. *My Writing Day* (3–5). Series: Meet the Author. 1999, Richard C. Owen LB $14.95 (1-57274-326-3). 32pp. The creator of the Cam Jansen mysteries tells a little about his life, writing career, and workday. (Rev: BL 9/15/99; HBG 3/00; SLJ 11/99) [921]

ALCOTT, LOUISA MAY

12925 Aller, Susan Bivin. *Beyond Little Women: A Story About Louisa May Alcott* (3–5). Illus. by Qi Z. Wang. Series: Creative Minds Biographies. 2004, Carolrhoda LB $21.27 (1-57505-602-X); paper $6.95 (1-57505-636-4). 64pp. An engaging account of Alcott's life from childhood and of the responsibilities she bore as the principal money earner in the family. (Rev: SLJ 8/04) [921]

12926 Ruth, Amy. *Louisa May Alcott* (4–7). Series: A&E Biography. 1999, Lerner LB $25.26 (0-8225-4938-7). 128pp. A clear, readable life of the author who wrote from personal experience about family life at the time of the Civil War and later. (Rev: BL 3/15/00; HBG 3/99; SLJ 1/99) [921]

12927 Silverthorne, Elizabeth. *Louisa May Alcott* (4–7). Illus. Series: Who Wrote That? 2002, Chelsea $22.95 (0-7910-6721-1). 112pp. A look at the life and works of author Louisa May Alcott, with particular emphasis on how her family influenced her work. (Rev: BL 10/15/02; HBG 3/03; SLJ 10/02) [813]

12928 Warrick, Karen Clemens. *Louisa May Alcott: Author of Little Women* (5–8). Series: Historical American Biographies. 2000, Enslow LB $20.95 (0-7660-1254-9). 128pp. Using many direct quotations from Alcott, along with fact boxes, maps, a chronology, and chapter notes, this is an interesting biography of the prolific writer from Pennsylvania. (Rev: BL 3/15/00; HBG 10/00) [921]

ALEICHEM, SHOLOM

12929 Silverman, Erica. *Sholom's Treasure: How Sholom Aleichem Became a Writer* (K–3). Illus. by Mordicai Gerstein. 2005, Farrar $16.00 (0-374-38055-4). 40pp. A child-friendly biography of the Yiddish author, emphasizing his difficult youth in a Russian shtetl and his enduring love of stories and fun. (Rev: BL 2/1/05; SLJ 4/05) [921]

ALLENDE, ISABEL

12930 Benatar, Raquel. *Isabel Allende: Recuerdos para un cento / Memories for a Story* (3–5). Trans. by Patricia Petersen. Illus. by Fernando Molinari. 2004, Piñata $14.95 (1-55885-379-0). A bilingual picture-book biography that emphasizes the importance of Allende's unusual childhood. (Rev: SLJ 9/04) [921]

ANDERSEN, HANS CHRISTIAN

12931 Brust, Beth Wagner. *The Amazing Paper Cuttings of Hans Christian Andersen* (3–6). Illus. 1994, Ticknor $17.00 (0-395-66787-9). 80pp. The story of Hans Christian Andersen's life is told and illustrated with many examples of his famous paper cuttings. (Rev: BCCB 3/94; BL 3/1/94; HB 7–8/94; SLJ 3/94) [921]

12932 Burch, Joann J. *A Fairy-Tale Life: A Story About Hans Christian Andersen* (3–5). Illus. 1994, Carolrhoda LB $21.27 (0-87614-829-1). 64pp. A biography that concentrates on Andersen's childhood and his development as a writer. (Rev: BL 9/1/94) [921]

12933 Langley, Andrew. *Hans Christian Andersen: The Dreamer of Fairy Tales* (3–5). Series: What's Their Story? 1998, Oxford $12.95 (0-19-521435-8). 32pp. Vivid watercolors illustrate this simple, entertaining biography of the Danish fairy-tale writer. (Rev: BL 2/15/99; HBG 3/99; SLJ 1/99) [921]

12934 Yolen, Jane. *The Perfect Wizard: Hans Christian Andersen* (1–3). Illus. by Dennis Nolan. 2005, Dutton $16.99 (0-525-46955-9). 40pp. This biography focuses on Andersen's youth, looking in particular at incidents from his childhood that were later incorporated into his fairy tales. (Rev: BL 2/1/05; SLJ 3/05) [921]

ANGELOU, MAYA

12935 Cuffie, Terrasita A. *Maya Angelou* (4–8). Series: The Importance Of. 1999, Lucent LB $27.45 (1-56006-532-X). 80pp. A biography that traces Maya Angelou's life from her childhood exposure to poverty and bigotry in the rural South to her eventual fame as a writer. (Rev: BL 9/15/99; SLJ 11/99) [921]

12936 Harper, Judith E. *Maya Angelou* (4–6). Series: Journey to Freedom. 1999, Child's World LB $16.95 (1-56766-570-5). 40pp. Stresses the important achievements and contributions of this contemporary African American writer. (Rev: BL 7/99; HBG 10/99; SLJ 7/99) [921]

12937 King, Sarah E. *Maya Angelou Greeting the Morning* (3–5). Illus. Series: Gateway Biographies. 1994, Millbrook LB $22.90 (1-56294-431-2). 48pp. The inspiring story of the great African American writer and the terrible difficulties she has overcome. (Rev: BL 8/94; SLJ 4/94) [921]

12938 Kirkpatrick, Patricia. *Maya Angelou* (5–9). Illus. by John Thompson. Series: Voices in Poetry. 2003, Creative LB $19.95 (1-58341-281-6). 48pp. This picture-book biography introduces readers to

Angelou's poetry and life from childhood. (Rev: BL 12/1/03; SLJ 12/03) [811]

12939 Kite, L. Patricia. *Maya Angelou* (4–7). Series: A&E Biography. 1999, Lerner $25.26 (0-8225-4944-1). 112pp. Black-and-white photographs illustrate this biography of the woman who overcame great obstacles to become a leading African American author. (Rev: BL 3/15/00; SLJ 7/99) [921]

12940 Raatma, Lucia. *Maya Angelou: Author and Documentary Filmmaker* (4–8). Series: Ferguson Career Biographies. 2001, Ferguson LB $16.95 (0-89434-336-X). 127pp. As well as a life of Maya Angelou, this book includes information on how to become a writer, filmmaker, and director. (Rev: SLJ 2/01) [921]

ASCH, FRANK

12941 Asch, Frank. *One Man Show* (1–4). Photos by Jan Asch. Illus. Series: Meet the Author. 1997, Richard C. Owen $14.95 (1-57274-095-7). 32pp. In this autobiography, author Asch introduces himself and his family, interests, and writing techniques. (Rev: HBG 3/98; SLJ 9/97) [921]

ASIMOV, ISAAC

12942 Boerst, William J. *Isaac Asimov: Writer of the Future* (5–9). Illus. 1998, Morgan Reynolds LB $21.95 (1-883846-32-3). 112pp. An engaging biography of the amazingly prolific author and scientist who was considered a misfit in his youth. (Rev: BL 12/1/98; BR 9–10/99; SLJ 1/99) [921]

12943 Judson, Karen. *Isaac Asimov: Master of Science Fiction* (5–9). Illus. 1998, Enslow LB $20.95 (0-7660-1031-7). 112pp. A biography of Asimov that includes two chapters particularly helpful to researchers: on his importance as a writer of science fiction and on his work in other genres. (Rev: BL 12/1/98; HBG 3/99; SLJ 2/99) [921]

AUSTEN, JANE

12944 Ruth, Amy. *Jane Austen* (5–8). Series: A&E Biography. 2001, Lerner LB $25.26 (0-8225-4992-1). This is the intriguing story of Jane Austen, who lived a quiet, obscure life yet produced some of the world's greatest novels. (Rev: BL 6/1–15/01; HBG 10/01; SLJ 11/01) [921]

AVI

12945 Markham, Lois. *Avi* (5–8). 1996, Learning Works paper $7.99 (0-88160-280-9). This profile of the gifted writer recounts his triumph over dysgraphia, a learning disability that makes writing difficult, and explores his creative process and the major themes of his work. (Rev: BL 4/1/96; SLJ 8/96) [921]

12946 Sommers, Michael A. *Avi* (5–8). Series: The Library of Author Biographies. 2004, Rosen LB $26.50 (0-8239-4522-7). 112pp. Covers Avi's life and career as a YA author, with analysis of his work, an interview, and lists of works and awards. (Rev: SLJ 1/05) [921]

BLUME, JUDY

12947 Nault, Jennifer. *Judy Blume* (2–4). Series: My Favorite Writer. 2004, Weigl LB $18.20 (1-59036-025-7). 32pp. This attractively illustrated biography of Judy Blume is particularly suitable for report writers. (Rev: BL 4/1/04; SLJ 10/04) [813]

12948 Wheeler, Jill C. *Judy Blume* (2–4). Series: Children's Authors. 2005, ABDO LB $14.95 (1-59197-604-9). 24pp. After introducing some of Blume's works, Wheeler discusses the author's childhood, influences on her work, and her determination to write about topics of real concern to children. (Rev: SLJ 4/05) [921]

BORGES, JORGE LUÍS

12949 Lennon, Adrian. *Jorge Luís Borges* (5–9). Series: Hispanics of Achievement. 1991, Chelsea LB $19.95 (0-7910-1236-0). A simple account that describes the life and work of one of South America's great contemporary writers. (Rev: BL 3/15/92; SLJ 7/92) [921]

BRIDWELL, NORMAN

12950 Wheeler, Jill C. *Norman Bridwell* (2–4). Series: Children's Authors. 2005, ABDO LB $14.95 (1-59197-605-7). 24pp. After introducing some of Bridwell's works, Wheeler discusses the author's childhood, influences on his work, and his recognition of the limitations of Clifford the Big Red Dog. (Rev: SLJ 4/05) [921]

BRONTË FAMILY

12951 Kenyon, Karen Smith. *The Brontë Family: Passionate Literary Geniuses* (5–9). Series: Lerner Biographies. 2002, Lerner LB $30.35 (0-8225-0071-X). 128pp. An absorbing introduction to the individual members of this literary family, with many illustrations and quotations from letters. (Rev: HBG 3/03; SLJ 1/03) [921]

BRUCHAC, JOSEPH

12952 Bruchac, Joseph. *Seeing the Circle* (3–5). Series: Meet the Author. 1999, Richard C. Owen LB $14.95 (1-57274-327-1). 32pp. Bruchac's account of his life includes his work as a children's author, focusing on Native American fiction and outstanding retellings of folklore and history. (Rev: BL 9/15/99; HBG 3/00; SLJ 11/99) [921]

BUCK, PEARL S.

12953 Mitchell, Barbara. *Between Two Worlds: A Story About Pearl Buck* (3–6). Illus. by Karen Ritz. 1988, Carolrhoda LB $21.27 (0-87614-332-X). 56pp. The life of this child of American missionaries in China, who grew up to become a famous novelist. (Rev: BL 3/1/89; SLJ 2/89) [921]

BUNTING, EVE

12954 Bunting, Eve. *Once Upon a Time* (2–5). Illus. 1995, Richard C. Owen $14.95 (1-878450-59-X). 32pp. An autobiography of the prolific writer of children's books, who spent her childhood in Ireland. (Rev: BCCB 7–8/95; BL 8/95; HB 7–8/95) [921]

12955 McGinty, Alice B. *Meet Eve Bunting* (2–4). Illus. Series: About the Author. 2003, Rosen LB $18.75 (0-8239-6411-6). 24pp. Readers learn about Bunting's youth and later life and how and why she started writing for children, with excerpts from her books, reprints from covers, photographs, and other illustrations. (Rev: BL 6/1–15/03; SLJ 3/03) [921]

BURNETT, FRANCES HODGSON

12956 Carpenter, Angelica S., and Jean Shirley. *Frances Hodgson Burnett: Beyond the Secret Garden* (4–8). Illus. 1990, Lerner LB $30.35 (0-8225-4905-0). 128pp. A glimpse into the private life of the woman who wrote *The Secret Garden*. (Rev: BCCB 12/90; BL 1/1/91; SLJ 3/91*) [921]

BURROUGHS, EDGAR RICE

12957 Boerst, William J. *Edgar Rice Burroughs: Creator of Tarzan* (5–8). Illus. Series: World Writers. 2000, Morgan Reynolds LB $21.95 (1-883846-56-0). 112pp. A concise biography of the prolific author who created Tarzan and was a pioneer of the science fiction genre. (Rev: BL 7/00; HBG 3/01; SLJ 1/01) [921]

BYARS, BETSY

12958 Byars, Betsy. *The Moon and I* (4–7). Illus. 1996, Morrow paper $4.99 (0-688-13704-0). 96pp. A memoir from this well-known children's author, which gives her the opportunity to tell how she likes both writing and snakes. (Rev: BCCB 3/92*; BL 5/15/92; SLJ 4/92) [921]

12959 Cammarano, Rita. *Betsy Byars* (4–7). Series: Who Wrote That? 2002, Chelsea $22.95 (0-7910-6720-3). 106pp. A profile in text and pictures of one of America's best-loved authors and winner of the Newbery and other prizes. (Rev: BL 10/15/02; HBG 3/03) [921]

CATHER, WILLA

12960 Streissguth, Thomas. *Writer of the Plains: A Story About Willa Cather* (4–7). Illus. 1997, Carolrhoda LB $25.55 (1-57505-015-3). 64pp. A simple introduction to the works of Willa Cather and the places where she lived and wrote. (Rev: BL 6/1–15/97; SLJ 10/97) [921]

CERVANTES, MIGUEL DE

12961 Goldberg, Jake. *Miguel de Cervantes* (5–9). Series: Hispanics of Achievement. 1993, Chelsea LB $21.95 (0-7910-1238-7). The absorbing story of the Spanish writer whose life rivaled that of his

adventurous hero, Don Quixote. (Rev: BL 9/15/93) [921]

CHERRY, LYNNE

12962 Cherry, Lynne. *Making a Difference in the World* (3–5). Series: Meet the Author. 2000, Richard C. Owen $14.95 (1-57274-373-5). 32pp. This noted author and illustrator of children's picture books talks about her life and how, when, and why she works. (Rev: BL 7/00; HBG 3/01; SLJ 12/00) [921]

CHRISTIE, AGATHA

12963 Dommermuth-Costa, Carol. *Agatha Christie: Writer of Mystery* (5–9). Series: Biographies. 1997, Lerner LB $30.35 (0-8225-4954-9). A biography of the "First Lady of Crime," with material on her personal life, including her two marriages. (Rev: SLJ 8/97)

CISNEROS, SANDRA

12964 Mirriam-Goldberg, Caryn. *Sandra Cisneros: Latina Writer and Activist* (5–8). Illus. Series: Hispanic Biographies. 1998, Enslow LB $19.95 (0-7760-1045-7). A biography, enlivened with many quotations, of the woman who received Cs and Ds in school and later became a first-rate author and leading Hispanic American activist. (Rev: BL 1/1–15/99) [921]

CLEARY, BEVERLY

12965 Ring, Susan. *Beverly Cleary* (2–4). Series: My Favorite Writer. 2003, Weigl LB $18.20 (1-59036-030-3). 32pp. This attractively illustrated biography is particularly suitable for report writers. (Rev: HBG 3/03)

COLE, JOANNA

12966 Cole, Joanna, and Wendy Saul. *On the Bus with Joanna Cole* (2–6). Illus. Series: Creative Sparks. 1996, Heinemann $16.95 (0-435-08131-4). 61pp. The creator of the Magic School Bus series talks about her life and writing. (Rev: HB 9–10/96; SLJ 6/96*) [921]

CORMIER, ROBERT

12967 Thomson, Sarah L. *Robert Cormier* (5–9). Series: Library of Author Biographies. 2003, Rosen LB $26.50 (0-8239-3776-3). 112pp. The late Robert Cormier, author of such young adult favorites as *The Chocolate War, I Am the Cheese,* and *Frenchtown Summer,* is profiled here. (Rev: SLJ 8/03) [921]

CRANE, STEPHEN

12968 Kepnes, Caroline. *Stephen Crane* (5–8). Series: Classic Storytellers. 2004, Mitchell Lane LB $19.95 (1-58415-272-9). 48pp. An introduction to Crane's life, work, and legacy, with background information on relevant historical, cultural, and economic factors. (Rev: SLJ 1/05) [921]

CURTIS, CHRISTOPHER PAUL

12969 Gaines, Ann. *Christopher Paul Curtis* (3–6). Series: Real-Life Reader Biographies. 2001, Mitchell Lane LB $15.95 (1-58415-076-9). 32pp. The fascinating story of the determination that took African American Curtis from writing in a journal during breaks on a car assembly line to winning notable awards. (Rev: SLJ 9/01) [813]

DAHL, ROALD

12970 Craats, Rennay. *Roald Dahl* (2–4). Series: My Favorite Writer. 2003, Weigl LB $18.20 (1-59036-029-X). 32pp. This attractively illustrated biography of Roald Dahl is particularly suitable for report writers. (Rev: SLJ 10/04)

12971 Powling, Chris. *Roald Dahl* (2–3). Series: Tell Me About. 1998, Carolrhoda $19.93 (1-57505-274-1). 24pp. Using many full-color photographs, this book traces the important events in Dahl's professional life, with emphasis on the use of imagination in writing. (Rev: BCCB 1/99; HBG 3/99; SLJ 1/99) [921]

12972 Shields, Charles J. *Roald Dahl* (4–7). Series: Who Wrote That? 2002, Chelsea $22.95 (0-7910-6722-X). 106pp. A brief biography of the master of whimsical stories that involve such strange elements as secretive chocolate factories and giant peaches. (Rev: BL 10/15/02; HBG 3/03) [921]

D'ANGELO, PASCAL

12973 Murphy, Jim. *Pick and Shovel Poet: The Journeys of Pascal D'Angelo* (5–10). 2000, Clarion $20.00 (0-395-77610-4). 162pp. The story of the Italian American poet who also wrote an important autobiography about coming to the New World. (Rev: BCCB 12/00; BL 3/1/01; HB 1–2/01; HBG 3/01; SLJ 1/01) [921]

DEPAOLA, TOMIE

12974 dePaola, Tomie. *Here We All Are: A 26 Fairmount Avenue Book* (2–5). Illus. 2000, Penguin Putnam $13.99 (0-399-23496-9). 80pp. A short chapter book that continues Tomie dePaola's *26 Fairmount Avenue* memoir when, as a 5-year-old, he gets a new baby sister. (Rev: BCCB 9/00; BL 5/1/00; HB 5–6/00; HBG 10/00; SLJ 6/00) [921]

12975 dePaola, Tomie. *On My Way* (2–4). Illus. 2001, Penguin Putnam $13.99 (0-399-23583-3). 32pp. A continuation of dePaola's remembrances of his childhood that includes a visit to the 1940 World's Fair. (Rev: BCCB 3/01; BL 12/15/00; HB 3–4/01; HBG 10/01; SLJ 2/01)

12976 dePaola, Tomie. *Things Will Never Be the Same* (2–4). Illus. 2003, Penguin Putnam $13.99 (0-399-23982-0). 80pp. DePaola's autobiography, with his own drawings, continues through 1941, when he turned seven, and details his everyday life until the morning of December 7, when everything changed.

(Rev: BCCB 3/03; BL 3/1/03; HBG 10/03; SLJ 5/03) [813.54]

12977 dePaola, Tomie. *26 Fairmount Avenue* (3–5). Illus. 1999, Penguin Putnam paper $13.99 (0-399-23246-X). 64pp. A charming memoir of his childhood by the famous children's writer. (Rev: BCCB 6/99; BL 8/99; HB 5–6/99; HBG 10/99; SLJ 6/99) [813]

12978 dePaola, Tomie. *What a Year!* (2–4). Illus. 2002, Penguin Putnam $13.99 (0-399-23797-6). 80pp. DePaola's memoirs continues here, taking readers into the life of 6-year-old Tomie from the beginning of first grade to New Year's Eve in 1940. (Rev: BCCB 3/02; BL 3/1/02; HB 3–4/02; HBG 10/02; SLJ 3/02) [813.54]

DICKENS, CHARLES

12979 Collins, David R. *Tales for Hard Times: A Story About Charles Dickens* (4–8). Illus. by David Mataya. Series: Creative Minds. 1991, Carolrhoda LB $25.55 (0-87614-433-4). 64pp. The life of Charles Dickens, including his poverty-ridden childhood. (Rev: SLJ 3/91) [921]

12980 Stanley, Diane, and Peter Vennema. *Charles Dickens: The Man Who Had Great Expectations* (3–8). Illus. by Diane Stanley. 1993, Morrow $14.93 (0-688-09111-3). 48pp. A candid retelling of the author's life, which was often as dramatic as his novels. (Rev: BCCB 11/93; BL 9/1/93; HB 11–12/93; SLJ 8/93) [921]

DORRIS, MICHAEL

12981 Weil, Ann. *Michael Dorris* (4–7). Illus. Series: Contemporary Native Americans. 1997, Raintree LB $17.98 (0-8172-3994-4). 48pp. The life story of the late Native American writer and teacher and his crusade to fight alcohol abuse. (Rev: BL 6/1–15/97) [921]

DOYLE, SIR ARTHUR CONAN

12982 Adams, Cynthia. *The Mysterious Case of Sir Arthur Conan Doyle* (5–8). Illus. Series: World Writers. 1999, Morgan Reynolds LB $21.95 (1-883846-34-X). This book traces the life of Sir Arthur Conan Doyle from his Scottish boyhood and failed medical practice to success as a writer and creator of Sherlock Holmes. (Rev: BL 3/1/99; BR 9–10/99; SLJ 9/99) [921]

EHLERT, LOIS

12983 Ehlert, Lois. *Under My Nose* (3–5). Illus. 1996, Richard C. Owen $13.95 (1-57274-027-2). 32pp. A simple autobiography of this artist whose children's books are widely read. (Rev: BL 9/1/96; HB 9–10/96; SLJ 12/96) [921]

FITZGERALD, F. SCOTT

12984 Bankston, John. *F. Scott Fitzgerald* (5–8). Series: Classic Storytellers. 2004, Mitchell Lane LB $19.95 (1-58415-249-4). 48pp. An introduction to

Fitzgerald's life, work, and legacy, with background information on relevant historical, cultural, and economic factors. (Rev: SLJ 1/05) [921]

12985 Stewart, Gail B. *F. Scott Fitzgerald* (4–8). Series: The Importance Of. 1999, Lucent LB $27.45 (1-56006-541-9). 112pp. The story of the famous Jazz Age author whose enduring works reflect American life in his era. (Rev: BL 9/15/99) [921]

FLEISCHMAN, SID

12986 Freedman, Jeri. *Sid Fleischman* (5–9). Series: The Library of Author Biographies. 2004, Rosen LB $26.50 (0-8239-4019-5). 112pp. Traces the popular, Newbery-winning author's life and looks at his works, writing process, and inspirations, concluding with an interview and reference material. (Rev: SLJ 9/04) [921]

FOX, PAULA

12987 Daniel, Susanna. *Paula Fox* (5–8). Series: The Library of Author Biographies. 2004, Rosen LB $26.50 (0-8239-4525-1). 112pp. Covers Fox's life and career, with analysis of her work and its themes, an interview, and lists of works and awards. (Rev: SLJ 1/05) [921]

FRITZ, JEAN

12988 Fritz, Jean. *Surprising Myself* (2–5). Illus. by Andrea F. Pfleger. Series: Meet the Author. 1993, Richard C. Owen $12.95 (1-878450-37-9). 32pp. As well as telling the reader about her life, Fritz explains how she does research for her many historical biographies. (Rev: BL 9/1/93; HB 9–10/93) [921]

GEISEL, THEODOR

12989 Dean, Tanya. *Theodor Geisel (Dr. Seuss)* (4–7). Illus. Series: Who Wrote That? 2002, Chelsea $22.95 (0-7910-6724-6). 112pp. A look at the life and works of the author and illustrator known as Dr. Seuss. (Rev: BL 10/15/02; HBG 3/03) [813]

12990 Foran, Jill. *Dr. Seuss* (2–4). Series: My Favorite Writer. 2003, Weigl LB $18.20 (1-59036-028-1). 32pp. This attractively illustrated biography of Theodor Geisel is particularly suitable for report writers. (Rev: SLJ 10/04)

12991 Ford, Carin T. *Dr. Seuss: Best-Loved Author* (4–8). Series: People to Know. 2003, Enslow LB $20.95 (0-7660-2106-8). 112pp. This readable biography covers the life of the author from his childhood in Springfield, Massachusetts, to his emergence as creator of some of America's most beloved children's books. (Rev: HBG 4/04; SLJ 11/03) [921]

12992 Krull, Kathleen. *The Boy on Fairfield Street: How Ted Geisel Grew Up to Become Dr. Seuss* (3–5). Illus. by Steve Johnson and Lou Fancher. 2004, Random $16.95 (0-375-82298-4). 42pp. Concentrating on Geisel's youth, this picture-book biography includes examples of his work. (Rev: BL 2/1/04; SLJ 1/04) [813]

12993 Lynch, Wendy. *Dr. Seuss* (1–4). Series: Lives and Times. 2000, Heinemann LB $13.95 (1-57572-216-X). 24pp. A simple biography of Theodor Geisel's alter ego with original drafts of artwork and many photographs. (Rev: HBG 3/01; SLJ 8/00) [921]

12994 Weidt, Maryann N. *Oh, the Places He Went: A Story About Dr. Seuss* (3–6). Illus. by Kerry Maguire. Series: Creative Minds Biographies. 1994, Carolrhoda LB $21.27 (0-87614-823-2); paper $5.95 (0-87614-627-2). 64pp. The life story of the famous children's author that tells of his many hardships and of some of his most important books. (Rev: BCCB 2/95; SLJ 1/95) [921]

12995 Woods, Mae. *Dr. Seuss* (2–4). Illus. Series: Children's Authors. 2000, ABDO $13.95 (1-57765-110-3). This book discusses the life and career on Theodor Geisel, better known as Dr. Seuss. (Rev: HBG 3/01; SLJ 1/01) [921]

GEORGE, JEAN CRAIGHEAD

12996 Cary, Alice. *Jean Craighead George* (4–6). Illus. 1996, Learning Works paper $6.95 (0-88160-283-3). 136pp. A lively re-creation of the life of this renowned nature writer and Newbery Award winner. (Rev: BL 11/15/96; SLJ 9/96) [921]

GOBLE, PAUL

12997 Goble, Paul. *Hau Kola Hello Friend* (2–4). Illus. by Gerry Perrin. Series: Meet the Author. 1994, Richard C. Owen $13.95 (1-878450-44-1). 32pp. This dedicated author, who has specialized in Native American folk material, tells about his life and writing. (Rev: BL 8/94; SLJ 8/94) [921]

GRIMM BROTHERS

12998 Hettinga, Donald R. *The Brothers Grimm: Two Lives, One Legacy* (5–8). Illus. 2001, Clarion $22.00 (0-618-05599-1). 192pp. An interesting biography that places the brothers' lives in the context of their time and discusses their skills as lexicographers and scholars. (Rev: BL 7/01; HB 1–2/02; HBG 3/02; SLJ 10/01) [430]

GRISHAM, JOHN

12999 Weaver, Robyn M. *John Grisham* (5–8). Illus. Series: People in the News. 1999, Lucent LB $27.45 (1-56006-530-3). 80pp. An accessible, laudatory biography of the lawyer and politician turned best-selling author. (Rev: BL 10/1/99; HBG 3/00; SLJ 11/99) [921]

HANSBERRY, LORRAINE

13000 Scheader, Catherine. *Lorraine Hansberry: Playwright and Voice of Justice* (5–10). Series: African American Biographies. 1998, Enslow LB $19.95 (0-89490-945-2). 128pp. The story of the gifted playwright who was also a civil rights activist and a fighter for justice. (Rev: HBG 3/99; SLJ 11/98) [921]

HELLER, RUTH

13001 Heller, Ruth. *Fine Lines* (3–5). Illus. 1996, Richard C. Owen $14.95 (1-878450-76-X). 32pp. In this autobiography, the author tells about her childhood, training, writing, and artwork. (Rev: BL 9/1/96; HB 9–10/96; SLJ 1/97) [921]

HENRY, MARGUERITE

13002 Collins, David R. *Write a Book for Me: The Story of Marguerite Henry* (4–6). Illus. 1999, Morgan Reynolds $18.95 (1-883846-39-0). 112pp. A straightforward biography of Marguerite Henry, the great writer of horse stories. (Rev: BL 3/15/99; SLJ 9/99) [921]

HINTON, S. E.

13003 Wilson, Antoine. *S. E. Hinton* (5–9). 2003, Rosen LB $26.50 (0-8239-3778-X). 112pp. S. E. Hinton, author of such popular young adult novels as *The Outsiders* and *That Was Then, This Is Now*, is profiled here. (Rev: SLJ 8/03) [921]

HOMER

13004 Tracy, Kathleen. *The Life and Times of Homer* (5–8). Series: Biography of Ancient Civilizations. 2004, Mitchell Lane LB $.00 (1-58415-260-5). 48pp. Drawing on ancient legends, this is a profile of ancient Greek poet and storyteller Homer. (Rev: BL 10/15/04; SLJ 12/04)

HOPKINS, LEE BENNETT

13005 Hopkins, Lee Bennett. *The Writing Bug* (2–5). Illus. by Diane Rubinger. Series: Meet the Author. 1993, Richard C. Owen $14.95 (1-878450-38-7). 32pp. The acclaimed poet, author, and anthologist tells about his life and the experiences that inspire him to write. (Rev: BL 9/1/93; HB 9–10/93) [921]

13006 Strong, Amy. *Lee Bennett Hopkins: A Children's Poet* (5–8). Series: Great Life Stories. 2003, Watts LB $29.50 (0-531-12315-4). 111pp. An inspiring biography that chronicles Hopkins's early struggles and his love for his work. (Rev: SLJ 2/04) [921]

HOWE, JAMES

13007 Howe, James. *Playing with Words* (1–4). Photos by Michael Craine. Series: Meet the Author. 1994, Richard C. Owen $12.95 (1-878450-40-9). 32pp. People who love this author's zany mysteries will enjoy reading about how he writes, gets his inspiration, and spends a typical day. (Rev: BL 8/94; SLJ 8/94) [921]

HUGHES, LANGSTON

13008 Bryant, Philip S. *Langston Hughes* (2–5). Series: African-American Biographies. 2003, Raintree LB $28.56 (0-7398-6871-3). 64pp. This basic biography profiles Hughes's life and achievements

and places them in historical context. (Rev: SLJ 11/03) [921]

13009 Cooper, Floyd. *Coming Home: From the Life of Langston Hughes* (3–6). Illus. 1994, Penguin Putnam $16.99 (0-399-22682-6). 32pp. A sensitive retelling of Langston Hughes's unhappy childhood and his search for a permanent home. (Rev: BCCB 1/95; BL 10/1/94; HB 9–10/94; SLJ 11/94) [921]

13010 McKissack, Patricia, and Fredrick McKissack. *Langston Hughes: Great American Poet* (2–4). Series: Great African Americans. 2002, Enslow LB $14.95 (0-7660-1695-1). 32pp. An interesting biography of the African American author noted for both his poetry and fiction and for his role in the Harlem Renaissance. (Rev: BL 7/02; HBG 10/02) [921]

13011 Walker, Alice. *Langston Hughes: American Poet* (2–5). Illus. by Catherine Deeter. 2002, HarperCollins LB $16.89 (0-06-021519-4). 37pp. This revised, larger-format edition of a 1974 publication gives young readers a look at the difficulties of Langston's boyhood. (Rev: HBG 10/02; SLJ 2/02) [921]

HURSTON, ZORA NEALE

13012 Bryant, Philip S. *Zora Neale Hurston* (2–5). Series: African-American Biographies. 2003, Raintree LB $28.56 (0-7398-6872-1). 64pp. A simple profile of the author, with interesting sidebars and good archival photographs that convey a sense of the time in which she lived. (Rev: HBG 4/04; SLJ 11/03) [921]

13013 Calvert, Roz. *Zora Neale Hurston* (5–8). Illus. Series: Black Americans of Achievement. 1993, Chelsea LB $15.95 (0-7910-1766-4). 80pp. A lively account of the life of the famous writer and folklorist. (Rev: BL 5/1/93; SLJ 6/93) [921]

13014 McKissack, Patricia, and Fredrick McKissack. *Zora Neale Hurston: Writer and Storyteller* (2–4). Series: Great African Americans. 2002, Enslow LB $14.95 (0-7660-1694-3). 32pp. A simple biography of the African American writer who is currently enjoying a revival of interest because of her excellent novels. (Rev: BL 7/02; HBG 3/03) [921]

IRVING, WASHINGTON

13015 Collins, David R. *Washington Irving: Storyteller for a New Nation* (4–8). Illus. Series: World Writers. 2000, Morgan Reynolds LB $21.95 (1-883846-50-1). 112pp. This biography introduces the globetrotting American writer and gives details of his work and personality. (Rev: BL 4/1/00; HBG 3/00; SLJ 5/00) [921]

ISSA

13016 Gollub, Matthew. *Cool Melons Turn to Frogs! The Life and Poems of Issa* (3–5). Illus. by Kazuko Stone. 1998, Lee & Low $16.95 (1-880000-71-7). 32pp. Using lovely Japanese-like paintings and fine calligraphy, the life of Issa, the famous haiku poet is traced with many examples of his work. (Rev:

BCCB 2/99; BL 12/1/98; HB 11–12/98; HBG 3/99; SLJ 11/98) [921]

JUANA INES DE LA CRUZ, SISTER

13017 Martinez, Elizabeth C. *Sor Juana: A Trailblazing Thinker* (3–6). Illus. Series: Hispanic Heritage. 1994, Millbrook LB $19.90 (1-56294-406-1). 32pp. The story of the 17th-century Mexican-born poet who is considered the finest writer of Mexico's colonial period. (Rev: BL 6/1–15/94; SLJ 4/94) [921]

13018 Mora, Pat. *A Library for Juana: The World of Sor Juana Ines* (1–3). Illus. by Beatriz Vidal. 2002, Knopf $15.95 (0-375-80643-1). 40pp. This is an absorbing account of the inspiring life of Sor Juana Ines, a child prodigy born in Mexico in the 17th century who became a nun and internationally known scholar and poet. (Rev: BL 11/15/02; HB 11–12/02; HBG 3/03; SLJ 11/02) [861]

KEHRET, PEG

13019 Kehret, Peg. *Five Pages a Day: A Writer's Journey* (4–7). 2002, Whitman LB $14.95 (0-8075-8650-1). 192pp. Aspiring young writers will particularly enjoy Kehret's account of her writing life, from starting a newspaper about the neighborhood dogs to entering writing contests to her career as an author of children's books. (Rev: BL 12/15/02; HBG 3/03; SLJ 9/02) [813]

KING, STEPHEN

13020 Wilson, Suzan. *Stephen King* (4–6). Series: People to Know. 2000, Enslow LB $19.95 (0-7660-1233-6). 128pp. A well-documented, thorough account of the life of this former high-school teacher who became a best-selling writer of suspense and horror novels. (Rev: BL 1/1–15/00; HBG 10/00; SLJ 5/00) [921]

KUSKIN, KARLA

13021 Kuskin, Karla. *Thoughts, Pictures, and Words* (2–5). Illus. Series: Meet the Author. 1995, Richard C. Owen $14.95 (1-878450-41-7). 32pp. This renowned writer discusses her prose, poetry, and illustrations, and discusses how she approaches writing. (Rev: BCCB 7–8/95; BL 8/95; HB 7–8/95; SLJ 9/95) [921]

L'ENGLE, MADELEINE

13022 Gonzales, Doreen. *Madeleine L'Engle: Author of "A Wrinkle in Time"* (5–8). Series: People in Focus. 1991, Dillon LB $13.95 (0-87518-485-5). A short biography of the beloved writer of such juvenile favorites as *A Wrinkle in Time* and the many books about the Austin family. (Rev: BL 2/15/92; SLJ 3/92) [921]

LESTER, HELEN

13023 Lester, Helen. *Author: A True Story* (2–4). Illus. 1997, Houghton Mifflin $11.00 (0-395-82744-2). 32pp. A delightful autobiography illustrated with her own cartoons. (Rev: BCCB 4/97; BL 3/15/97; HB 5–6/97; SLJ 5/97*) [921]

LEVINE, GAIL CARSON

13024 McGinty, Alice B. *Meet Gail Carson Levine* (2–4). Series: About the Author. 2003, Rosen LB $18.75 (0-8239-6409-4). 24pp. Sample passages, book covers, childhood photographs, and an interview make this an appealing, easy-to-read profile of Levine and her writing career. (Rev: BL 6/1–15/03; SLJ 5/03) [921]

LOCKER, THOMAS

13025 Locker, Thomas. *The Man Who Paints* (3–5). Series: Meet the Author. 1999, Richard C. Owen LB $14.95 (1-57274-328-X). 32pp. An autobiography of the artist and author of children's books noted for such nature stories as *Where the River Begins* and *The Land of Grey Wolf*. (Rev: BL 9/15/99; HBG 3/00; SLJ 11/99) [921]

LONDON, JACK

13026 Bankston, John. *Jack London* (4–7). Illus. Series: Classic Storytellers. 2005, Mitchell Lane LB $19.95 (1-58415-263-X). 48pp. An introduction to London's life, work, and legacy, with background information on relevant historical, cultural, and economic factors. [921]

13027 Lisandrelli, Elaine S. *Jack London* (4–6). Series: People to Know. 1999, Enslow LB $19.95 (0-7660-1144-5). 128pp. Part author and part adventurer, Jack London lived an action-packed but short life. This biography relates his story in an honest and balanced way. (Rev: BL 1/1–15/00; HBG 3/00; SLJ 1/00) [921]

13028 Streissguth, Tom. *Jack London* (4–7). Series: A&E Biography. 2000, Lucent LB $25.26 (0-8225-4987-5). 112pp. The story of an adventurer and author who battled personal hardships and wrote eloquently about nature and survival. (Rev: BL 12/15/00; HBG 3/01; SLJ 3/01) [921]

LOVECRAFT, H. P.

13029 Schoell, William. *H. P. Lovecraft: Master of Weird Fiction* (5–8). Illus. 2003, Morgan Reynolds LB $21.95 (1-931798-15-X). 128pp. Lovecraft, known for his stories of horror and the supernatural, was born into privilege that ended with his parents' early deaths; his works only received real acclaim after his death. (Rev: BL 9/15/03; HBG 4/04; SLJ 12/03) [813]

LOWRY, LOIS

13030 Lowry, Lois. *Looking Back: A Book of Memories* (4–8). Illus. 1998, Houghton Mifflin $16.00 (0-395-89543-X). 192pp. This autobiographical work centers around a series of photographs and the author's comments on each. (Rev: BL 11/1/98; BR 5–6/99; HB 1–2/99; HBG 3/99; SLJ 9/98) [921]

13031 Markham, Lois. *Lois Lowry* (5–8). Series: Meet the Author. 1995, Learning Works paper $7.99 (0-88160-278-7). This biography of the Newbery Medal–winning author tells how she became a writer and looks at the personal experiences that are reflected in her books. (Rev: SLJ 1/96) [921]

LYON, GEORGE ELLA

13032 Lyon, George E. *A Wordful Child* (3–5). Illus. 1996, Richard C. Owen $14.95 (1-57274-016-7). 32pp. The author tells about her life and the stories she heard as a child that influenced her work. (Rev: BL 9/1/96; HB 9–10/96; SLJ 1/97) [921]

MCKISSACK, PATRICIA

13033 McKissack, Patricia. *Can You Imagine?* (2–5). Illus. Series: Meet the Author. 1997, Richard C. Owen $14.95 (1-878450-61-1). 32pp. An autobiographical account of this fantasy writer in which she tells of the importance of imagination in her life. (Rev: BL 6/1–15/97; HBG 3/98; SLJ 9/97) [921]

MCPHAIL, DAVID

13034 McPhail, David. *In Flight with David McPhail* (2–6). Illus. by author. Series: Creative Sparks. 1996, Heinemann $15.95 (0-435-08132-2). 45pp. This famous artist talks about his life and the processes involved in illustrating a book. (Rev: HB 9–10/96; SLJ 6/96*) [921]

MAGEE, JOHN

13035 Granfield, Linda. *High Flight: A Story of World War II* (5–7). Illus. 1999, Tundra $15.95 (0-88776-469-X). 32pp. The moving story of John Magee, a young Canadian Air Force pilot who was killed in World War II and who is best known for writing the poem "High Flight." (Rev: BCCB 12/99; BL 1/1–15/00; HBG 3/00; SLJ 2/00) [921]

MAHY, MARGARET

13036 Mahy, Margaret. *My Mysterious World* (2–5). Illus. Series: Meet the Author. 1995, Richard C. Owen $13.95 (1-878450-58-1). 32pp. The New Zealand writer describes her many interests and how she approaches writing. (Rev: BCCB 7–8/95; BL 8/95; HB 7–8/95; SLJ 9/95) [921]

MARTÍ, JOSÉ J.

13037 West, Alan. *José Martí: Man of Poetry, Soldier of Freedom* (5–8). Illus. Series: Hispanic Heritage. 1994, Millbrook LB $23.90 (1-56294-408-8). 32pp. The life story of the famous 19th-century Cuban poet, with excerpts from his work in both Spanish and English. (Rev: SLJ 1/95) [921]

MARTIN, RAFE

13038 Martin, Rafe. *A Storyteller's Story* (3–6). Illus. by Jill Krementz. Series: Meet the Author. 1992, Owen $14.95 (0-913461-03-2). 32pp. The author takes readers to his home to meet family and friends. (Rev: BCCB 9/92; BL 8/92; SLJ 8/92) [921]

MONTGOMERY, LUCY MAUD

13039 MacLeod, Elizabeth. *Lucy Maud Montgomery: A Writer's Life* (3–5). Illus. 2001, Kids Can LB $14.95 (1-55074-487-9). 32pp. Both black-and-white and color illustrations are used to enhance this biography of one of Canada's most famous writers. (Rev: BL 4/1/01; HBG 10/01; SLJ 4/01) [921]

MORRISON, TONI

13040 Haskins, Jim. *Toni Morrison: The Magic of Words* (4–6). Illus. Series: Gateway Biographies. 2001, Millbrook $21.90 (0-7613-1806-2). 48pp. Young readers may not be familiar with Morrison's work, but will still enjoy this clearly presented photo-essay introducing her life from childhood, her work, and her support for other writers. (Rev: BL 6/1–15/01; HBG 10/01; SLJ 5/01) [813.5]

13041 Jones, Amy Robin. *Toni Morrison: 1931–* (4–6). Series: Journey to Freedom: The African American Library. 2001, Child's World LB $17.95 (1-56766-925-5). 40pp. An oversize, attractive volume that presents the life, accomplishments, and importance of this towering figure in contemporary literature. (Rev: BL 12/15/01) [921]

13042 Patrick-Wexler, Diane. *Toni Morrison* (4–6). Illus. Series: Contemporary African Americans. 1997, Raintree LB $25.69 (0-8172-3987-1). 48pp. A fine biography of this influential writer, who has won both the Nobel and Pulitzer prizes. (Rev: BL 5/15/97; SLJ 2/98) [921]

NAYLOR, PHYLLIS REYNOLDS

13043 Naylor, Phyllis Reynolds. *How I Came to Be a Writer*. Rev. ed. (4–9). 2001, Simon & Schuster paper $4.99 (0-689-83887-5). 139pp. Naylor describes the joys and difficulties of life as a writer and includes excerpts of her work in this autobiographical account. (Rev: SLJ 5/01) [921]

NIXON, JOAN LOWERY

13044 Wade, Mary Dodson. *Joan Lowery Nixon: Masterful Mystery Writer* (5–8). Series: Authors Teens Love. 2004, Enslow LB $26.60 (0-7660-2194-7). 128pp. Examines Nixon's life, writings, and her focus on girls of character and strength. (Rev: SLJ 11/04) [921]

PAREDES, AMERICO

13045 Murcia, Rebecca Thatcher. *Americo Paredes* (5–7). Series: Latinos in American History. 2003, Mitchell Lane LB $19.95 (1-58415-207-9). 48pp. The story of the Mexican American author, folklorist, and professor at the University of Texas in Austin who is also famous for establishing a center for intercultural studies. (Rev: BL 1/1–15/04) [921]

PATERSON, KATHERINE

13046 Cary, Alice. *Katherine Paterson* (5–8). Illus. Series: Meet the Author. 1997, Learning Works paper $7.99 (0-88160-281-7). 136pp. A biography of the two-time Newbery winner, with many quotations from interviews and autobiographical essays. (Rev: BL 5/1/97; SLJ 7/97) [921]

13047 Kjelle, Marylou Morano. *Katherine Paterson* (4–7). Illus. Series: Classic StoryTellers. 2004, Mitchell Lane LB $15.95 (1-58415-268-0). 48pp. Examines the life and times of the award-winning children's author, including her work as a missionary in Japan and how religious faith informs her writing. (Rev: BL 1/1–15/05; SLJ 3/05) [921]

PAULSEN, GARY

13048 Fine, Edith Hope. *Gary Paulsen: Author and Wilderness Adventurer* (5–8). Series: People to Know. 2000, Enslow LB $20.95 (0-7660-1146-1). 128pp. The story of an outdoorsman who turned many of his exciting adventures into stories for children and young adults. (Rev: BL 9/15/00; HBG 10/00; SLJ 9/00) [921]

13049 Gaines, Ann. *Gary Paulsen* (3–6). Series: Real-Life Reader Biographies. 2001, Mitchell Lane LB $15.95 (1-58415-077-7). 32pp. Gaines presents Paulsen's difficult childhood, his love of reading, and his fascination with sled dogs and adventure. (Rev: SLJ 9/01) [813]

13050 Paterra, Elizabeth. *Gary Paulsen* (4–7). Series: Who Wrote That? 2002, Chelsea $22.95 (0-7910-6723-8). 106pp. A profile of the prolific author (of almost 200 books) who is best known for his young adult outdoor survival stories. (Rev: BL 10/15/02; HBG 3/03) [921]

13051 Paulsen, Gary. *Caught by the Sea* (5–8). 2001, Delacorte $15.95 (0-385-32645-9). 104pp. The author describes his ongoing love of the sea and the adventures he's had, some funny, some scary. (Rev: BL 9/15/01; HBG 3/02; SLJ 10/01) [818]

13052 Paulsen, Gary. *Guts: The True Stories Behind Hatchet and the Brian Books* (5–10). 2001, Delacorte $16.95 (0-385-32650-5). 150pp. These six exciting stories re-create childhood experiences of the author, who was born to alcoholic parents in 1939 and who developed a love of hunting and fishing in the woods of Minnesota. (Rev: BL 2/15/01; HB 3–4/01; HBG 10/01; SLJ 2/01) [813]

13053 Peters, Stephanie True. *Gary Paulsen* (4–8). Illus. 1999, Learning Works paper $7.99 (0-88160-324-4). 111pp. A straightforward biography of the outdoorsman and author that tells about his books, his interests, his alcoholism, and his continuing health problems. (Rev: BL 6/1–15/99; SLJ 6/99) [921]

13054 Thomson, Sarah L. *Gary Paulsen* (5–9). Series: Library of Author Biographies. 2003, Rosen LB $26.50 (0-8239-3773-9). 112pp. Examines the

life and writings of the popular author of books for young adults. (Rev: SLJ 8/03)

PINKWATER, DANIEL

13055 McGinty, Alice B. *Meet Daniel Pinkwater* (2–4). Illus. Series: About the Author. 2003, Rosen LB $18.75 (0-8239-6406-X). 24pp. Readers learn about Pinkwater's youth and later life, his varied interests, how and why he started writing for children, and how he uses his own childhood experiences in his books. (Rev: SLJ 3/03) [921]

POE, EDGAR ALLAN

13056 Kent, Zachary. *Edgar Allan Poe* (5–8). Series: Historical American Biographies. 2001, Enslow LB $20.95 (0-7660-1600-5). An informative, well-presented biography of this writer whose unique stories changed the history of American literature. (Rev: BL 1/1–15/02; HBG 3/02; SLJ 9/01) [921]

13057 Streissguth, Tom. *Edgar Allan Poe* (5–8). Series: A&E Biography. 2001, Lerner LB $25.26 (0-8225-4991-3). The tortured life of this early master of the short story is brought to life in an interesting text and many black-and-white illustrations. (Rev: BL 6/1–15/01; HBG 10/01; SLJ 8/01) [921]

POTTER, BEATRIX

13058 Collins, David R. *The Country Artist: A Story About Beatrix Potter* (3–5). Illus. by Karen Ritz. 1989, Carolrhoda LB $21.27 (0-87614-344-3); paper $5.95 (0-87614-509-8). 56pp. The story of the creator of Peter Rabbit and other famous creatures. (Rev: BL 5/1/89) [921]

13059 Malam, John. *Beatrix Potter* (1–4). Series: Tell Me About. 1998, Carolrhoda LB $19.93 (1-57505-275-X). 24pp. A brief biography of this writer and artist that covers the basics of her life and gives examples of her enchanting work. (Rev: BCCB 1/99; HBG 3/99; SLJ 2/99) [921]

13060 Wallner, Alexandra. *Beatrix Potter* (K–3). Illus. 1995, Holiday House LB $16.95 (0-8234-1181-8). 32pp. A fascinating account of the life of this children's book author who was also an expert on mushrooms and an early conservationist. (Rev: BL 9/1/95; SLJ 10/95) [921]

13061 Winter, Jeanette. *Beatrix: Various Episodes from the Life of Beatrix Potter* (PS–2). Illus. 2003, Farrar $15.00 (0-374-30655-9). 64pp. Excerpts from Potter's writings are incorporated in this small-format biography that looks mainly at her life as a child and young woman. (Rev: BL 3/1/03; HB 5–6/03; HBG 10/03; SLJ 3/03) [823]

PRINGLE, LAURENCE

13062 Pringle, Laurence. *Nature! Wild and Wonderful* (2–5). Illus. Series: Meet the Author. 1997, Richard C. Owen $14.95 (1-57274-071-X). 32pp. An autobiographical account of this writer of more than 80 books that tells how he became interested in nature study and in writing about it. (Rev: BL 6/1–15/97; HBG 3/98; SLJ 9/97) [921]

PYLE, ERNIE

13063 O'Connor, Barbara. *The Soldiers' Voice: The Story of Ernie Pyle* (4–7). Illus. 1996, Carolrhoda LB $30.35 (0-87614-942-5). 80pp. The story of the renowned World War II correspondent who died in the South Pacific while covering the war. (Rev: BCCB 10/96; BL 9/1/96; SLJ 8/96) [921]

RAWLINGS, MARJORIE KINNAN

13064 Cook, Judy, and Laura Lee Smith. *Natural Writer: A Story About Marjorie Kinnan Rawlings* (4–6). Illus. by Laurie Harden. Series: Creative Minds Biographies. 2001, Carolrhoda LB $21.27 (1-57505-468-X). 64pp. This easily read biography with full-page illustrations tells the life story of the author of *The Yearling*. (Rev: HBG 10/01; SLJ 8/01) [921]

RIVERA, TOMAS

13065 Medina, Jane. *Tomas Rivera* (1–2). Illus. by Edward Martinez. Series: Green Light Reader, Level 2. 2004, Harcourt LB $12.95 (0-15-205145-7). 24pp. Medina recounts a life-changing experience from the childhood of Mexican American writer/educator Tomas Rivera. (Rev: BL 7/04) [921]

RODRIGUEZ, LUIS

13066 Schwartz, Michael. *Luis Rodriguez* (4–8). Illus. Series: Contemporary Hispanic Americans. 1997, Raintree LB $17.98 (0-8172-3990-1). 48pp. The life of this contemporary Hispanic American who went from gang leader and drug addict to writer, journalist, publisher, speaker, and youth activist. (Rev: BL 4/15/97; SLJ 6/97) [921]

ROWLING, J. K.

13067 Gaines, Ann. *J. K. Rowling* (3–6). 2001, Mitchell Lane LB $15.95 (1-58415-078-5). 32pp. Gaines chronicles Rowling's struggles as a single mother seeking a publisher before *Harry*'s success. (Rev: BCCB 2/02; SLJ 9/01) [813]

13068 Shapiro, Marc. *J. K. Rowling: The Wizard Behind Harry Potter* (5–8). 2000, St. Martin's paper $4.99 (0-312-27224-3). The creator of Harry Potter is profiled, with material on university life, her year in Paris, and her struggle to keep writing. (Rev: BL 11/15/00; SLJ 12/00) [921]

13069 Steffens, Bradley. *J. K. Rowling* (5–7). Series: People in the News. 2002, Gale LB $27.45 (1-56006-776-4). 112pp. Rowling's early life and education figure prominently in this account of her life that also looks at the plot and setting of her novels and wonders what she will do when the series is finished. (Rev: BCCB 2/02; SLJ 10/02) [921]

RYLANT, CYNTHIA

13070 Rylant, Cynthia. *Best Wishes* (3–6). Illus. by Carlo Ontal. 1992, Owen $14.95 (1-878450-20-4). 32pp. The author takes her readers to her home in Ohio, then travels back to her childhood in West Virginia. (Rev: BCCB 9/92; BL 8/92; SLJ 8/92) [921]

SACHAR, LOUIS

13071 Greene, Meg. *Louis Sachar* (5–9). Series: The Library of Author Biographies. 2004, Rosen LB $26.50 (0-8239-4017-9). 112pp. Traces the popular, Newbery-winning author's life and looks at his works, writing process, and inspirations, concluding with an interview and reference material. (Rev: SLJ 9/04) [921]

SANDBURG, CARL

13072 Meltzer, Milton. *Carl Sandburg: A Biography* (5–10). Illus. 1999, Millbrook LB $31.90 (0-7613-1364-8). 144pp. The story of a literary giant who, in addition to his poetry, is noted for nonfiction works including a biography of Abraham Lincoln. (Rev: BL 12/15/99; HBG 10/00) [921]

13073 Mitchell, Barbara. *"Good Morning Mr. President": A Story About Carl Sandburg* (3–6). 1988, Carolrhoda LB $21.27 (0-87614-329-X). 56pp. The story of Sandburg's growing up and the experiences that were later reflected in his poetry. (Rev: BL 3/1/89; SLJ 2/89) [921]

13074 Niven, Penelope, and Carl Sandburg. *Carl Sandburg: Adventures of a Poet* (2–5). Illus. by Marc Nadel. 2003, Harcourt $17.00 (0-15-204686-0). 32pp. Niven's informative text on Sandburg's life is paired with selections of his writings and pen-and-watercolor images in this appealing picture book. (Rev: BL 9/1/03*; HBG 4/04; SLJ 9/03) [921]

SANDOZ, MARI

13075 Wilkerson, J. L. *Scribe of the Great Plains: Mari Sandoz* (3–5). Illus. 1999, Acorn $8.95 (0-9664470-0-X). 144pp. This biography of the author who wrote about the history of the Great Plains describes in detail her childhood struggle to survive the hardships of pioneer life. (Rev: BL 2/1/99; SLJ 3/99) [921]

SHAKESPEARE, WILLIAM

13076 Aliki. *William Shakespeare and the Globe* (4–7). Illus. 1999, HarperCollins LB $15.89 (0-06-027821-8). 48pp. Shakespeare and Elizabethan England come to life in this detailed picture book that uses many quotations from his plays and also tells of the recent rebuilding of the Globe theater. (Rev: BCCB 4/99; BL 6/1–15/99*; HB 5–6/99; HBG 10/99; SLJ 5/99) [921]

13077 Dommermuth-Costa, Carol. *William Shakespeare* (5–8). Series: Biography. 2001, Lerner LB $25.26 (0-8225-4996-4). A readable, well-illustrated biography of the Bard of Avon with material on many of his plays. (Rev: BL 4/1/02; HBG 10/02; SLJ 3/02) [921]

13078 Fandel, Jennifer. *William Shakespeare* (5–9). Photos by Marcel Imsand. Series: Voices in Poetry. 2003, Creative Editions LB $19.95 (1-58341-283-

2). 45pp. A brief and appealing introduction to Shakespeare's life and work, with examples of his poems, excerpts from his plays, and illustrations. (Rev: SLJ 12/03) [822.3]

13079 Middleton, Haydn. *William Shakespeare: The Master Playwright* (3–5). Series: What's Their Story? 1998, Oxford $12.95 (0-19-521430-7). 32pp. Large type and color illustrations are used to tell the story of Shakespeare, who left his home in Stratford at 19 to journey to London where he became an actor, theater owner, and the greatest English playwright in history. (Rev: BL 2/15/99; HBG 3/99; SLJ 3/99) [921]

13080 Nettleton, Pamela Hill. *William Shakespeare: Playwright and Poet* (5–9). Series: Signature Lives. 2005, Compass Point $30.60 (0-7565-0816-9). 112pp. Nettleton places facts about Shakespeare's life within the context of everyday life of the time, with details about the theater and publishing. (Rev: SLJ 6/05) [921]

13081 Rosen, Michael. *Shakespeare: His Work and His World* (5–9). Illus. by Robert Ingpen. 2001, Candlewick $19.99 (0-7636-1568-4). 104pp. An insightful look at Elizabethan culture and the life of William Shakespeare, as well as several of his plays. (Rev: BL 11/1/01; HBG 3/02; SLJ 11/01*) [822.3]

13082 Stanley, Diane, and Peter Vennema. *Bard of Avon: The Story of William Shakespeare* (3–8). Illus. by Diane Stanley. 1992, Morrow $16.95 (0-688-09108-3). 48pp. A handsome volume on the life of Shakespeare. (Rev: BCCB 12/92; BL 9/1/92*; HB 11–12/92*; SLJ 11/92) [921]

13083 Thrasher, Thomas. *The Importance of William Shakespeare* (4–8). Series: The Importance Of. 1998, Lucent LB $27.45 (1-56006-374-2). This work discusses Shakespeare and his contribution to world culture. (Rev: BL 12/15/98) [921]

SHARMAT, MARJORIE WEINMAN

13084 Wheeler, Jill C. *Marjorie Weinman Sharmat* (2–4). Series: Children's Authors. 2005, ABDO LB $14.95 (1-59197-608-1). 24pp. After introducing some of Sharmat's works, Wheeler discusses the author's childhood and influences on her work. (Rev: SLJ 4/05) [921]

SHELLEY, MARY WOLLSTONECRAFT

13085 Darrow, Sharon. *Through the Tempests Dark and Wild: A Story of Mary Shelley, Creator of Frankenstein* (4–7). Illus. by Angela Barren. 2003, Candlewick $16.99 (0-7636-0835-1). 40pp. The dramatic story of Mary Shelley's troubled youth is told in this beautifully illustrated, fictionalized picture-book biography. (Rev: BL 6/1–15/03; HBG 10/03; SLJ 6/03) [823]

SILVERSTEIN, SHEL

13086 Ward, S. *Meet Shel Silverstein* (2–3). Series: About the Author. 2001, Rosen LB $18.75 (0-8239-5709-8). 24pp. This introduction to the author of "The Giving Tree" describes his life and work. (Rev: SLJ 6/01) [921]

SIMON, SEYMOUR

13087 Simon, Seymour. *From Paper Airplanes to Outer Space* (3–5). Series: Meet the Author. 2000, Richard C. Owen $14.95 (1-57274-374-3). 32pp. A noted writer of science books for young people talks about his life and how he writes. (Rev: BL 7/00; HBG 3/01; SLJ 12/00) [921]

SINGER, ISAAC BASHEVIS

13088 Singer, Isaac Bashevis. *A Day of Pleasure: Stories of a Boy Growing Up in Warsaw* (6–8). Illus. by Roman Vishniac. 1969, Farrar paper $7.95 (0-374-41696-6). 160pp. A Hasidic Jew's fond remembrances of the world in which he grew up. [921]

SPINELLI, JERRY

13089 McGinty, Alice B. *Meet Jerry Spinelli* (2–4). Illus. Series: About the Author. 2003, Rosen LB $18.75 (0-8239-6408-6). 24pp. Readers learn about Spinelli's youth and later life, his varied interests, how and why he started writing for children, and how he uses his own childhood experiences in his books. (Rev: SLJ 3/03) [921]

13090 Seidman, David. *Jerry Spinelli* (5–9). Series: The Library of Author Biographies. 2004, Rosen LB $26.50 (0-8239-4016-0). 112pp. Traces the popular, Newbery-winning author's life and looks at his works, writing process, and inspirations, concluding with an interview and reference material. (Rev: SLJ 9/04) [921]

13091 Spinelli, Jerry. *Knots in My Yo-Yo String: The Autobiography of a Kid* (5–8). 1998, Knopf LB $16.99 (0-679-98791-6); paper $10.95 (0-679-88791-1). A frank, delightful memoir of growing up in Norristown, Pennsylvania, during the 1950s by the renowned Newbery Medal–winning writer of fiction for young people. (Rev: BCCB 7–8/98; BL 5/1/98; HBG 10/98; SLJ 6/98) [921]

STEINBECK, JOHN

13092 Tracy, Kathleen. *John Steinbeck* (5–8). Series: Classic Storytellers. 2004, Mitchell Lane LB $19.95 (1-58415-271-0). 48pp. An introduction to Steinbeck's life, work, and legacy, with background information on relevant historical, cultural, and economic factors. (Rev: SLJ 1/05) [921]

STEVENSON, ROBERT LOUIS

13093 Carpenter, Angelica S., and Jean Shirley. *Robert Louis Stevenson: Finding Treasure Island* (5–8). Illus. 1997, Lerner LB $30.35 (0-8225-4955-7). A lively biography of this great writer, who was a disappointment to his family because he did not become a minister. (Rev: BL 11/15/97; HBG 3/98; SLJ 12/97) [921]

STINE, R. L.

13094 Cohen, Joel H. *R. L. Stine* (5–8). Series: People in the News. 2000, Lucent LB $27.45 (1-56006-608-3). 96pp. This well-documented biography, illustrated with several black-and-white photographs, tells the story of an author who enjoys scaring his readers. (Rev: BL 6/1–15/00; HBG 10/00; SLJ 8/00) [921]

13095 Stine, R. L., and Joe Arthur. *It Came From Ohio! My Life as a Writer* (4–6). Illus. 1997, Scholastic $9.95 (0-590-36674-2). 144pp. An autobiography of the creator of the hugely successful Fear Street and Goosebumps series. (Rev: BCCB 6/97; BL 8/97; HB 7–8/97; SLJ 7/97) [921]

STOWE, HARRIET BEECHER

13096 Adler, David A. *A Picture Book of Harriet Beecher Stowe* (2–4). Illus. by Colin Bootman. Series: Picture Book Biographies. 2003, Holiday House $16.95 (0-8234-1646-1). 32pp. This picture-book biography uses realistic oil paintings to reinforce the information about this inspiring woman and the injustices of slavery. (Rev: BL 6/1–15/03; HBG 10/03; SLJ 5/03) [921]

13097 Bland, Celia. *Harriet Beecher Stowe: Antislavery Author* (3–5). Illus. Series: Junior World Biographies. 1993, Chelsea LB $16.95 (0-7910-1773-7). 79pp. The story of the renowned writer and her courageous stand against slavery. (Rev: SLJ 10/93) [921]

13098 Fritz, Jean. *Harriet Beecher Stowe and the Beecher Preachers* (5–9). 1994, Penguin Putnam $15.99 (0-399-22666-4). In addition to covering *Uncle Tom's Cabin*, this biography gives a full account of Harriet Beecher's private life, marriage, and extended family. (Rev: BCCB 10/94; BL 8/94; HB 9–10/94; SLJ 9/94*) [921]

13099 Gelletly, LeeAnne. *Harriet Beecher Stowe: Author of Uncle Tom's Cabin* (3–6). 2001, Chelsea LB $18.95 (0-7910-6009-8). 80pp. Easy-to-read information on Stowe's life and work is accompanied by illustrations and sidebars that profile some of her contemporaries, including Harriet Tubman and William Lloyd Garrison. (Rev: SLJ 10/01) [921]

THOMAS, DYLAN

13100 Thomas, Dylan. *A Child's Christmas in Wales* (3–6). Illus. by Chris Raschka. 2004, Candlewick $17.99 (0-7636-2161-7). 32pp. This new edition of Thomas's memoir of childhood Christmases in Wales features striking artwork in ink and gouache. (Rev: BL 10/1/04; SLJ 10/04) [821]

THOREAU, HENRY DAVID

13101 Burleigh, Robert. *A Man Named Thoreau* (4–6). Illus. 1985, Macmillan $15.00 (0-689-31122-2). 48pp. A profile of the 19th-century thinker in prose that makes him available to the younger grades. (Rev: BCCB 12/85; BL 3/15/86; SLJ 1/86) [921]

13102 Thoreau, Henry David. *Henry David's House* (2–4). Ed. by Steven Schnur. Illus. by Peter M. Fiore. 2002, Charlesbridge $16.95 (0-88106-116-6). 32pp. Using Thoreau's words, this picture book describes the construction of his cottage in the woods near Walden Pond. (Rev: BL 4/1/02; HBG 10/02; SLJ 5/02) [921]

TOLKIEN, J. R. R.

13103 Lynch, Doris. *J. R. R. Tolkien* (5–8). Illus. 2003, Watts LB $29.50 (0-531-12253-0). 128pp. An attractive biography that reveals how much the author of *The Lord of the Rings* was influenced by his surroundings and experiences. (Rev: BL 12/15/03; SLJ 7/04) [828]

TWAIN, MARK

13104 Aller, Susan Bivin. *Mark Twain* (5–8). Series: A&E Biography. 2001, Lerner LB $25.26 (0-8225-4994-8). The colorful life of one of America's favorite authors is re-created in accessible text, black-and-white photographs, and such additions as interesting sidebars and extensive reading lists. (Rev: BL 6/1–15/01; HBG 10/01) [921]

13105 Anderson, William. *River Boy: The Story of Mark Twain* (1–4). Illus. by Dan Andreasen. 2003, HarperCollins LB $16.89 (0-06-028401-3). The importance of the Mississippi in Twain's youth is highlighted in this account that includes coverage of his leaving school at the age of 12, working on a steamboat, searching for gold, and his career as a writer and humorist. (Rev: BL 4/15/03; HBG 10/03; SLJ 3/03) [921]

13106 Armentrout, David, and Patricia Armentrout. *Mark Twain* (1–3). Series: Discover the Life of an American Legend. 2004, Rourke LB $20.64 (1-58952-660-0). 24pp. An introductory biography that includes period photographs and other illustrations plus a glossary and pronunciation guide. (Rev: SLJ 3/04) [818]

13107 Brown, Don. *American Boy: The Adventures of Mark Twain* (2–6). Illus. by author. 2003, Houghton Mifflin $16.00 (0-618-17997-6). Presented with wit and visual appeal, this biography focuses on Samuel Clemens's youth. (Rev: HBG 4/04; SLJ 9/03) [921]

13108 Collins, David R. *Mark T-W-A-I-N! A Story About Samuel Clemens* (3–5). Illus. by Vicky Carey. 1994, Carolrhoda LB $21.27 (0-87614-801-1). 64pp. Beginning with his boyhood in Hannibal, Missouri, through his many jobs as a youth, to his distinguished career as a writer, this is a lively biography of Clemens. (Rev: BL 3/1/94; SLJ 3/94) [921]

13109 Cox, Clinton. *Mark Twain: America's Humorist, Dreamer, Prophet* (5–9). 1995, Scholastic paper $14.95 (0-590-45642-3). A biography that includes a discussion of Twain's views on race and how they changed. (Rev: BL 9/15/95; SLJ 9/95) [921]

13110 Goldsmith, Howard. *Mark Twain at Work!* (PS–2). Illus. by Frank Habbas. Series: Childhood of Famous Americans. 2003, Simon & Schuster LB

$11.89 (0-689-85400-5); paper $3.99 (0-689-85399-8). 31pp. A blend of fact and fiction, this profile of Mark Twain's childhood focuses on a real-life fence-painting scam from Twain's youth that was later incorporated into *Tom Sawyer,* one of his most popular novels. (Rev: HBG 10/03; SLJ 8/03)

13111 Lasky, Kathryn. *A Brilliant Streak: The Making of Mark Twain* (4–7). Illus. by Barry Moser. 1998, Harcourt $18.00 (0-15-252110-0). 48pp. Using many quotations and anecdotes from the author's work, this nicely illustrated biography of Mark Twain concentrates on his first 30 years when he was a steamboat pilot, prospector, reporter, and budding writer. (Rev: BCCB 7–8/98; BL 4/1/98; HB 5–6/98; HBG 10/98; SLJ 4/98) [921]

13112 Pflueger, Lynda. *Mark Twain* (5–8). Series: Historical American Biographies. 1999, Enslow LB $20.95 (0-7660-1093-7). A balanced, well-documented biography that includes chapter notes, a bibliography, glossary, and some period black-and-white illustrations. (Rev: BL 1/1–15/00; HBG 3/00; SLJ 1/00) [921]

13113 Rasmussen, R. Kent. *Mark Twain for Kids: His Life and Times, 21 Activities* (4–7). Illus. Series: For Kids. 2004, Chicago Review paper $14.95 (1-55652-527-3). 160pp. An engaging biography that reveals interesting details of Twain's life and shows how many of the episodes in his books were based on his own experiences. (Rev: BL 9/15/04; SLJ 9/04) [921]

VERNE, JULES

13114 Schoell, William. *Remarkable Journeys: The Story of Jules Verne* (4–8). Series: World Writers. 2002, Morgan Reynolds LB $21.95 (1-883846-92-7). 112pp. Writing was not Verne's first love, as Schoell explains in this accessible biography. (Rev: BL 6/1–15/02; HBG 10/02; SLJ 9/02) [843.8]

13115 Streissguth, Thomas. *Science Fiction Pioneer: A Story About Jules Verne* (3–6). Illus. by Ralph L. Ramstad. 2000, Carolrhoda LB $21.27 (1-57505-440-X). 64pp. This biography traces the life and career of this novelist and how he used his interest and knowledge of science in his works. (Rev: HBG 3/01; SLJ 10/00) [921]

13116 Teeters, Peggy. *Jules Verne: The Man Who Invented Tomorrow* (5–7). Illus. 1993, Walker LB $14.85 (0-8027-8191-8). 128pp. The life of the famous writer of science fiction, including his childhood in France. (Rev: BL 3/15/93; SLJ 5/93) [921]

WALKER, ALICE

13117 Kramer, Barbara. *Alice Walker: Author of the Color Purple* (4–6). Illus. Series: People to Know. 1995, Enslow LB $20.95 (0-89490-620-8). 128pp. The life, struggles, and work of this celebrated African American writer are covered concisely in a conversational style. (Rev: BL 9/15/95; SLJ 11/95) [921]

WARNER, GERTRUDE CHANDLER

13118 Ellsworth, Mary Ellen. *Gertrude Chandler Warner and the Boxcar Children* (3–5). Illus. 1997, Whitman LB $14.95 (0-8075-2837-4). 61pp. The life story of the author who created the Boxcar Children and lived her entire life in Connecticut. (Rev: BL 8/97; HB 7–8/97; SLJ 7/97) [921]

13119 Wheeler, Jill C. *Gertrude Chandler Warner* (2–4). Series: Children's Authors. 2005, ABDO LB $14.95 (1-59197-609-X). 24pp. After introducing some of Warner's works, Wheeler discusses the author's childhood and influences on her work. (Rev: SLJ 4/05) [921]

WELLS, H. G.

13120 Boerst, William J. *Time Machine: The Story of H. G. Wells* (5–8). Illus. Series: World Writers. 1999, Morgan Reynolds LB $21.95 (1-883846-40-4). 112pp. The story of the intriguing English author, including material on his childhood, romances, political views, and literary works. (Rev: BL 1/1–15/00; HBG 3/00) [921]

WHEATLEY, PHILLIS

13121 Gregson, Susan R. *Phillis Wheatley* (4–6). Illus. Series: Let Freedom Ring. 2001, Capstone LB $22.60 (0-7368-1033-1). 48pp. Wheatley's early life, education, marriage, and writing career are placed in historical context and accompanied by excerpts of her poems. (Rev: HBG 3/02; SLJ 7/02)

13122 Kent, Deborah. *Phillis Wheatley: First Published African-American Poet* (4–7). Series: Our People. 2003, Child's World LB $27.07 (1-59296-009-X). 32pp. The life of the 18th-century poet is outlined in this well-illustrated work that features large type and includes historical background. (Rev: SLJ 4/04) [921]

13123 Lasky, Kathryn. *A Voice of Her Own: The Story of Phillis Wheatley, Slave Poet* (2–4). Illus. by Paul Lee. 2003, Candlewick $16.99 (0-7636-0252-3). 40pp. A biography of the slave and poet, focusing on her childhood. (Rev: BL 2/15/03; HBG 10/03; SLJ 1/03) [921]

13124 McLendon, Jacquelyn. *Phillis Wheatley: A Revolutionary Poet* (4–7). Series: Library of American Lives and Times. 2003, Rosen LB $31.95 (0-8239-5750-0). 112pp. Kidnapped into slavery from Senegal, Phillis Wheatley became a major voice in the American literary scene. (Rev: BL 6/1–15/03; SLJ 5/03) [921]

13125 Salisbury, Cynthia. *Phillis Wheatley: Legendary African-American Poet* (5–8). Series: Historical American Biographies. 2001, Enslow LB $20.95 (0-7660-1394-4). The life story of the first important African American poet, who was brought to America as a slave and bought by a Quaker family who allowed her to develop her talents. (Rev: BL 3/1/01; HBG 10/01; SLJ 7/01) [921]

13126 Sherrow, Victoria. *Phillis Wheatley: Poet* (4–7). Illus. Series: Junior World Biography. 1992,

Chelsea LB $15.95 (0-7910-1753-2). 80pp. The biography of the poet who is considered to be the first important African American writer. (Rev: BL 8/92; SLJ 8/92) [921]

13127 Weidt, Maryann N. *Revolutionary Poet: A Story About Phillis Wheatley* (3–6). Illus. Series: Creative Minds. 1997, Carolrhoda LB $21.27 (1-57505-037-4); paper $5.95 (1-57505-059-5). 64pp. The story of the poetry-writing slave girl who was the first African American to have a book published. (Rev: BL 2/15/98; HBG 3/98) [921]

WHITE, E. B.

13128 Collins, David R. *To the Point: A Story About E. B. White* (3–5). Illus. by Amy Johnson. 1989, Carolrhoda LB $21.27 (0-87614-345-1); paper $5.95 (0-87614-508-X). 56pp. The story of a writer who made a great impact on children's reading. (Rev: BL 5/1/89) [921]

13129 Craats, Rennay. *E. B. White* (2–4). Series: My Favorite Writer. 2004, Weigl LB $18.20 (1-59036-026-5). 32pp. This attractively illustrated profile of the life and career of the author of classics including *Stuart Little* is particularly suitable for report writers. (Rev: BL 4/1/04; HBG 3/03) [818]

13130 Litwin, Laura Baskes. *E. B. White: Beyond Charlotte's Web and Stuart Little* (4–8). Series: People to Know. 2003, Enslow LB $20.95 (0-7660-2107-6). 112pp. This readable biography traces the life and career of the essayist and poet who made his start in children's literature at the age of 54. (Rev: HBG 4/04; SLJ 11/03) [921]

13131 Murcia, Rebecca Thatcher. *E. B. White* (5–8). Series: Classic Storytellers. 2004, Mitchell Lane LB $19.95 (1-58415-273-7). 48pp. An introduction to White's life, work, and legacy, with background information on relevant historical, cultural, and economic factors. (Rev: SLJ 1/05) [921]

WHITMAN, WALT

13132 Kerley, Barbara. *Walt Whitman: Words for America* (4–8). Illus. by Brian Selznick. 2004, Scholastic $16.95 (0-439-35791-8). 56pp. Whitman's experiences during the Civil War, including his service as a nurse to injured and dying soldiers, are highlighted in this picture-book biography. (Rev: BL 11/15/04; SLJ 11/04) [811]

13133 Loewen, Nancy, ed. *Walt Whitman* (5–8). Illus. by Rob Day. 1994, Creative Ed. LB $23.95 (0-88682-608-X). 45pp. With generous quotes from *Leaves of Grass* and color photos, various vignettes from Whitman's life are retold. (Rev: SLJ 7/94*) [921]

WIESEL, ELIE

13134 Lazo, Caroline. *Elie Wiesel* (4–7). Illus. 1994, Dillon paper $7.95 (0-382-24715-9). 64pp. The story of the distinguished writer and spokesman on

the Holocaust who won the Nobel Peace Prize in 1986. (Rev: BL 2/15/95; SLJ 7/95) [921]

13135 Pariser, Michael. *Elie Wiesel: Bearing Witness* (4–6). Illus. Series: Gateway Biographies. 1994, Millbrook LB $20.90 (1-56294-419-3). 48pp. A slim biography of the Nobel Prize winner, who at age 15 was sent to Auschwitz. (Rev: SLJ 4/95) [921]

WILDER, LAURA INGALLS

13136 Anderson, William. *Laura's Album: A Remembrance Scrapbook of Laura Ingalls Wilder* (3–6). Illus. 1998, HarperCollins $19.95 (0-06-027842-0). 80pp. This is a loving scrapbook of photos, early writings, letters, and drawings by the author of the Little House series. (Rev: BL 1/1–15/99; HBG 10/99) [921]

13137 Anderson, William. *Pioneer Girl: The Story of Laura Ingalls Wilder* (2–4). Illus. by Dan Andreasen. 1998, HarperCollins LB $15.89 (0-06-027244-9). This biography of the author covers the significant events in her life. (Rev: HBG 10/98; SLJ 3/98) [921]

13138 Anderson, William. *Prairie Girl: The Life of Laura Ingalls Wilder* (2–5). Illus. by Ren e Graef. 2004, HarperCollins LB $13.89 (0-06-028974-0). 74pp. A well-written introductory biography of the author of the Little House on the Prairie series, starting with her childhood on the American frontier. (Rev: SLJ 4/04) [921]

13139 Armentrout, David, and Patricia Armentrout. *Laura Ingalls Wilder* (1–3). Illus. Series: Discover a Life of an American Legend. 2003, Rourke LB $20.64 (1-58952-663-5). 24pp. Young fans of Wilder will enjoy this brief, photo-filled profile. (Rev: BL 2/1/04) [921]

13140 Giff, Patricia Reilly. *Laura Ingalls Wilder: Growing Up in the Little House* (3–6). Illus. by Eileen McKeating. 1988, Puffin paper $4.99 (0-14-032074-1). 64pp. Stories of growing up in the Big Woods of Wisconsin, long, long ago. (Rev: BCCB 9/87; BL 8/87; SLJ 4/87) [921]

13141 Strudwick, Leslie. *Laura Ingalls Wilder* (2–4). Series: My Favorite Writer. 2003, Weigl LB $18.20 (1-59036-027-3). 32pp. This attractively illustrated biography is particularly suitable for report writers. (Rev: SLJ 10/04)

13142 Wadsworth, Ginger. *Laura Ingalls Wilder: Storyteller of the Prairie* (5–8). Series: Biography. 1997, Lerner LB $30.35 (0-8225-4950-6). A solid, readable biography of this author that clarifies the chronology in the Little House books. (Rev: BL 3/1/97; SLJ 4/97) [921]

13143 Wallner, Alexandra. *Laura Ingalls Wilder* (K–3). Illus. 1997, Holiday House LB $16.95 (0-8234-1314-4). 32pp. A concise biography that traces Wilder's life from childhoood to her emergence as a juvenile book author. (Rev: BL 10/1/97; HBG 3/98; SLJ 11/97) [921]

13144 Woods, Mae. *Laura Ingalls Wilder* (2–3). Series: Children's Authors. 2000, ABDO LB $13.95

(1-57765-113-8). 24pp. Eight double-page chapters cover Wilder's life from her birth in 1867 to her death in 1957. (Rev: HBG 3/01; SLJ 3/01) [921]

WILLIAMS, WILLIAM CARLOS

13145 Berry, S. L. *William Carlos Williams* (5–9). Illus. by Yan Nascimbene. Series: Voices in Poetry. 2003, Creative LB $19.95 (1-58341-284-0). 48pp. This picture-book biography introduces readers to Williams's poetry and life from childhood. (Rev: BL 12/1/03; HBG 4/04) [808]

YEP, LAURENCE

13146 McGinty, Alice B. *Meet Laurence Yep* (2–3). Series: About the Author. 2003, Rosen LB $18.75 (0-8239-6410-8). 24pp. Sample passages, book covers, childhood photographs, and an interview make this an appealing, easy-to-read profile of the Asian American writer and his career. (Rev: SLJ 5/03) [921]

YOLEN, JANE

13147 McGinty, Alice B. *Meet Jane Yolen* (2–4). Illus. Series: About the Author. 2003, Rosen LB $18.75 (0-8239-6407-8). 24pp. Readers learn about Yolen's youth and later life and how and why she started writing for children, with excerpts from her books and reprints of covers. (Rev: SLJ 3/03) [921]

13148 Yolen, Jane. *A Letter from Phoenix Farm* (3–6). Illus. by Jason Stemple. 1992, Owen $14.95 (1-878450-36-0). 32pp. Spending a day with this writer of children's books. (Rev: BCCB 9/92; BL 8/92; SLJ 8/92) [921]

ZINDEL, PAUL

13149 Daniel, Susanna. *Paul Zindel* (5–8). Series: The Library of Author Biographies. 2004, Rosen LB $26.50 (0-8239-4524-3). 112pp. Covers Zindel's career as a YA author, with analysis of his work, an interview, and lists of works and awards. (Rev: SLJ 1/05) [921]

Contemporary and Historical Americans

Collective

13150 Adams, Simon. *The Presidents of the United States* (3–7). 2001, Two-Can $16.95 (1-58728-093-0); paper $9.95 (1-58728-092-2). 96pp. Double-page spreads give basic information on each president, with interesting anecdotes, timelines, full-color portraits, reproductions, and a carefully chosen quotation. (Rev: SLJ 7/01) [973.0099]

13151 Adler, David A. *Enemies of Slavery* (3–6). Illus. by Donald A. Smith. 2004, Holiday House $16.95 (0-8234-1596-1). 32pp. Fourteen Americans who played important roles in the fight against slavery are briefly introduced, with relevant quotations, in this picture book for older children. (Rev: BL 10/1/04; SLJ 3/05) [326.8]

13152 Adler, David A. *Heroes of the Revolution* (1–4). Illus. by Donald A. Smith. 2003, Holiday House $16.95 (0-8234-1471-X). 32pp. Among the 12 men and women profiled here are Crispus Attucks, Deborah Sampson, Molly Pitcher, Ethan Allen, and Thomas Jefferson; each entry includes an illustration, birth and death dates, and the person's contributions to the Revolutionary War. (Rev: HBG 4/04; SLJ 11/03) [920]

13153 Allen, Paula Gunn, and Patricia C. Smith. *As Long As the Rivers Flow: The Stories of Nine Native Americans* (5–8). Illus. 1996, Scholastic paper $15.95 (0-590-47869-9). Nine notable Native Americans are profiled, including Geronimo, Will Rogers, and Maria Tallchief. (Rev: BL 12/1/96; BR 1–2/97; SLJ 1/97) [920]

13154 Altman, Susan. *Extraordinary African-Americans: From Colonial to Contemporary Times*. Rev. ed. (5–8). Series: Extraordinary People. 2001, Children's Book Pr. LB $39.00 (0-516-22549-9). 288pp. This revision of a 1989 title adds 36 new profiles and offers a good starting point for research into important African Americans throughout history. (Rev: SLJ 3/02) [921]

13155 Ashby, Ruth. *Extraordinary People* (5–8). Series: Civil War Chronicles. 2002, Smart Apple LB $28.50 (1-58340-182-2). 48pp. Key military and civilian figures from both North and South are profiled. (Rev: HBG 3/03; SLJ 2/03) [973.7]

13156 Barber, James, and Amy Pastan. *Presidents and First Ladies* (4–8). Illus. 2002, DK LB $19.99 (0-7894-8454-4); paper $12.99 (0-7894-8453-6). 96pp. For each president and his First Lady, there are biographies, a list of key events, and a box highlighting an important event during that administration, plus plenty of color illustrations. (Rev: BL 4/1/02; HBG 10/02; SLJ 5/02) [920]

13157 Beiden, Tonya. *Portraits of African-American Heroes* (3–5). Illus. by Ansel Pitcairn. 2004, Dutton $18.99 (0-525-47043-3). 96pp. Profiles of figures including Dizzy Gillespie and Gwendolyn Brooks use personal memoirs to draw the reader in. (Rev: BL 3/15/04; SLJ 1/04) [920]

13158 Bowdish, Lynea. *With Courage: Seven Women Who Changed America* (4–6). Illus. 2004, Mondo paper $6.95 (1-59336-280-3). 48pp. Rachel Carson, Condoleezza Rice, and Maya Lin are among the seven women profiled for their achievements in mainly male-dominated fields. (Rev: BL 3/1/04; SLJ 7/04) [920]

13159 Brooks, Philip. *Extraordinary Jewish Americans* (5–9). Series: Extraordinary People. 1998, Children's Book Pr. LB $39.00 (0-516-20609-5); paper $16.95 (0-516-26350-1). 288pp. In chronological order, this book presents brief biographical sketches of 60 prominent Jews from a wide variety of fields including science, business, sports, the arts, entertainment, and politics. (Rev: HBG 3/99; SLJ 10/98) [920]

13160 Bruning, John Robert. *Elusive Glory: African-American Heroes of World War II* (5–8). Illus. Series: Avisson Young Adult. 2001, Avisson paper $19.95 (1-888105-48-8). 144pp. The true stories of African American servicemen, including six Tuskegee Airmen, who served the United States during

World War II. (Rev: BL 1/1–15/02; SLJ 4/02) [940.54]

13161 Buller, Jon, et al. *Smart About the Presidents* (4–7). Illus. by authors. Series: Smart About History. 2004, Penguin Putnam paper $5.99 (0-448-43372-9). 64pp. Pertinent facts about each president are conveyed in an informative, accessible style. (Rev: BL 9/1/04; SLJ 4/05) [920]

13162 Burgan, Michael. *Great Women of the American Revolution* (4–6). Series: We the People. 2005, Compass Point LB $22.60 (0-7565-0838-X). 48pp. Women's exploits and achievements during the Revolutionary War are placed in historical context. (Rev: SLJ 6/05) [920]

13163 Burleigh, Robert. *Who Said That? Famous Americans Speak* (5–8). Illus. 1997, Holt $16.95 (0-8050-4394-2). Brief, insightful profiles use quotations in presenting 33 famous personalities including Benjamin Franklin, Sojourner Truth, Marilyn Monroe, and Louis Armstrong. (Rev: BL 3/1/97*; SLJ 5/97) [920]

13164 Caravantes, Peggy. *Petticoat Spies: Six Women Spies of the Civil War* (5–8). Illus. 2002, Morgan Reynolds LB $21.95 (1-883846-88-9). 112pp. An exciting volume about six women who spied for the Union and Confederacy during the Civil War, with photographs, source notes, a glossary, and a bibliography. (Rev: BL 3/15/02; HBG 10/02; SLJ 8/02) [973.7]

13165 Cheney, Lynne. *A Is for Abigail: An Almanac of Amazing American Women* (2–4). Illus. by Robin Glasser. 2003, Simon & Schuster $16.95 (0-689-85819-1). 48pp. Cheney celebrates the contributions of American women in all walks of life, from athletes and performers to inventors and scientists. (Rev: BL 2/1/04; HBG 4/04; SLJ 9/03) [973]

13166 Cox, Clinton. *African American Teachers* (4–7). Series: Black Stars. 2000, Wiley $22.95 (0-471-24649-2). 172pp. A collection of short profiles of important African American teachers who have inspired their students and championed the cause of education. (Rev: BL 7/00; HBG 3/01; SLJ 7/00) [920]

13167 Davidson, Sue. *Getting the Real Story: Nellie Bly and Ida B. Wells* (4–6). 1992, Seal Pr. paper $8.95 (1-878067-16-8). 152pp. The story of two gallant women news reporters, both of whom fought for justice and against corruption. (Rev: SLJ 7/92) [920]

13168 Davis, Burke. *Black Heroes of the American Revolution* (4–6). Illus. 1992, Harcourt paper $5.00 (0-15-208561-0). 80pp. A look at American blacks who performed key roles in the American Revolution. [920]

13169 Davis, Kenneth C. *Don't Know Much About the Presidents* (4–6). Illus. by Pedro Martin. Series: Don't Know Much About. 2002, HarperCollins LB $15.89 (0-06-028616-4). 64pp. A question-and-answer format is used to introduce basic facts and trivia about the presidents, with bright cartoons, portraits, quotations, and timelines. (Rev: HBG 10/02; SLJ 1/02) [973.099]

13170 Delisle, Jim. *Kidstories: Biographies of 20 Young People You'd Like to Know* (PS–3). Illus. 1991, Free Spirit paper $9.95 (0-915793-34-2). 168pp. This collection of short biographies tells about young people from different life-styles and locales. (Rev: BCCB 1/92; BL 12/15/91; SLJ 1/92) [920]

13171 Doherty, Kieran. *Explorers, Missionaries, and Trappers: Trailblazers of the West* (5–8). Series: Shaping America. 2000, Oliver LB $22.95 (1-881508-52-8). 176pp. Nine important pioneers of the American West are profiled including a Spanish conquistador, two Spanish priests, John Sutter, Marcus and Narcissa Whitman, and Brigham Young. (Rev: HBG 10/00; SLJ 5/00) [920]

13172 Doherty, Kieran. *Voyageurs, Lumberjacks, and Farmers: Pioneers of the Midwest* (5–8). Series: Shaping America. 2004, Oliver LB $22.95 (1-881508-54-4). 176pp. The lives and accomplishments of eight individuals — including Antoine Cadillac, Jean du Sable, and Josiah and Abigail Snelling — who played key roles in the settlement of the Midwest are placed in historical context, with discussion of the plight of Native Americans in the region. (Rev: SLJ 9/04) [920]

13173 Dudley, Karen. *Great African Americans in Government* (3–5). Series: Outstanding African Americans. 1997, Crabtree LB $21.28 (0-86505-806-7); paper $8.95 (0-86505-820-2). 64pp. In-depth profiles of seven African Americans in government — e.g., Adam Clayton Powell, Colin Powell, and Shirley Chisholm — with seven shorter sketches that include Julian Bond and David Dinkins. (Rev: BL 9/15/97; SLJ 1/98) [920]

13174 Furbee, Mary R. *Outrageous Women of Colonial America* (3–6). Illus. Series: Outrageous Women. 2001, Wiley paper $12.95 (0-471-38299-X). 120pp. Fourteen women are profiled here, in sections on New England, the middle colonies, and the South. (Rev: BL 5/15/01) [920]

13175 Furbee, Mary Rodd. *Outrageous Women of Civil War Times* (3–6). 2003, Jossey-Bass paper $12.95 (0-471-22926-1). 124pp. This fascinating collective biography profiles a number of women — some outrageous, others not — who played important roles during the Civil War era; sidebars, photographs, prints, and paintings add appeal. (Rev: BL 10/1/03) [920]

13176 Gormley, Beatrice. *First Ladies: Women Who Called the White House Home* (4–6). Illus. 1997, Scholastic paper $6.99 (0-590-25518-5). 96pp. A collection of short profiles of U.S. presidents' wives, from Martha Washington to Hillary Clinton. (Rev: BL 3/15/97) [920]

13177 Green, Carl R. *The Younger Brothers* (4–6). Illus. Series: Outlaws and Lawmen. 1995, Enslow LB $16.95 (0-89490-592-9). 48pp. The story of the interesting characters who were involved with Jesse James in the old West. (Rev: SLJ 9/95) [920]

13178 Green, Carl R., and William R. Sanford. *Confederate Generals of the Civil War* (5–8). Illus. Series: Collective Biographies. 1998, Enslow LB $20.95 (0-7660-1029-5). 112pp. After a brief introduction to the Civil War, this book highlights the careers of 10 Southern generals and their contributions to the Confederate cause. (Rev: BL 8/98) [920]

13179 Green, Carl R., and William R. Sanford. *Union Generals of the Civil War* (5–8). Illus. 1998, Enslow LB $20.95 (0-7660-1028-7). 112pp. Using period photographs and prints plus a concise text, this book outlines the careers of 10 Union generals and supplies background material on the Civil War, including charts and maps. (Rev: BL 8/98) [920]

13180 Greenfield, Eloise. *How They Got Over: African Americans and the Call of the Sea* (4–6). Illus. by Jan S. Gilchrist. 2003, HarperCollins LB $17.89 (0-06-028992-9). 128pp. The biographies of seven African Americans who sailed on, dove in, or studied the sea, with illustrations and a bibliography. (Rev: BL 2/15/03; HB 3–4/03; HBG 10/03; SLJ 1/03) [920]

13181 Hacker, Carlotta. *Great African Americans in History* (5–8). Series: Outstanding African Americans. 1997, Crabtree LB $22.60 (0-86505-805-9); paper $8.95 (0-86505-819-9). There are profiles of 13 great African Americans in American history, including Frederick Douglass, Harriet Tubman, W. E. B. Du Bois, Mary McLeod Bethune, and George Washington Carver. (Rev: BL 9/15/97; SLJ 1/98) [920]

13182 Hansen, Joyce. *Women of Hope: African Americans Who Made a Difference* (5–12). Illus. 1998, Scholastic $16.95 (0-590-93973-4). 32pp. A large-size volume that celebrates the lives and accomplishments of 13 female African American leaders from various walks of life, including civil rights activists such as Fannie Lou Hamer and writers such as Maya Angelou. (Rev: BL 12/1/98; HBG 3/99; SLJ 10/98) [920]

13183 Harmon, Rod. *American Civil Rights Leaders* (5–7). Series: Collective Biographies. 2000, Enslow LB $20.95 (0-7660-1381-2). 104pp. This collective biography profiles 10 individuals who are currently or once were active in the civil rights movement in the United States. (Rev: BL 12/15/00; HBG 10/01) [920]

13184 Harness, Cheryl. *Rabble Rousers: 20 Women Who Made a Difference* (3–6). Illus. 2003, Dutton $17.99 (0-525-47035-2). 64pp. Girls especially will be drawn to these inspiring two-page accounts of feminists ranging from the famous, such as Susan B. Anthony, to less-known figures, including Ann Lee, founder of the Shaker movement, all presented with handsome sepia portraits, timelines, and addresses of relevant organizations. (Rev: BL 1/1–15/03; HBG 10/03; SLJ 1/03) [305.42]

13185 Harness, Cheryl. *Remember the Ladies* (4–7). Illus. 2001, HarperCollins $16.99 (0-688-17017-X). 64pp. Brief profiles of 100 important American women are each accompanied by a portrait. (Rev: BL 4/15/01; HBG 10/01; SLJ 2/01) [920]

13186 Harris, Laurie L., ed. *Biography for Beginners: Presidents of the United States* (3–6). Series: Biography for Beginners. 1998, Omnigraphics LB $50.00 (0-7808-0262-4). 467pp. A fine introduction

to the lives and accomplishments of each of our presidents, ending with Clinton. (Rev: SLJ 11/98) [920]

13187 Haskins, Jim. *One More River to Cross: The Stories of Twelve Black Americans* (4–8). Illus. 1992, Scholastic $13.95 (0-590-42896-9). 160pp. Eight men and four women who defied the odds to achieve prominence in their fields are introduced, including Ralph Bunche, Shirley Chisholm, and Ron McNair. (Rev: BCCB 4/92; BL 2/1/92; SLJ 4/92) [920]

13188 Hoose, Phillip. *We Were There, Too! Young People in U.S. History* (5–8). Illus. 2001, Farrar $28.00 (0-374-38252-2). 276pp. Hoose tells the stories of dozens of young people who contributed to the making of America — some famous but many who will be new to readers. (Rev: BCCB 10/01; BL 8/01; HB 9–10/01*; HBG 3/02; SLJ 8/01*) [973]

13189 Hudson, Wade, and Valerie Wesley Wilson. *Afro-Bets Book of Black Heroes from A to Z: An Introduction to Important Black Achievers* (4–7). Illus. 1988, Just Us paper $7.95 (0-940975-02-5). 64pp. Forty-nine African American men and women of outstanding accomplishment. (Rev: BL 1/1/89; SLJ 12/88) [920]

13190 Hughes, Chris. *The Constitutional Convention* (5–9). Series: People at the Center Of. 2005, Gale/Blackbirch LB $23.70 (1-56711-918-2). 48pp. After an overview of the convention, this volume provides biographical information on key figures including George Washington, Benjamin Franklin, James Madison, and Alexander Hamilton. (Rev: SLJ 6/05) [920]

13191 Igus, Toyomi, ed. *Great Women in the Struggle* (3–6). Illus. Series: Book of Black Heroes. 1992, Just Us LB $17.95 (0-940975-27-0); paper $10.95 (0-940975-26-2). 107pp. More than 80 contemporary African American women are profiled. (Rev: SLJ 8/92) [920]

13192 Katz, William L. *Black People Who Made the Old West* (6–8). Illus. 1992, Africa World $35.00 (0-86543-363-1); paper $14.95 (0-86543-364-X). Sketches of 35 black explorers, pioneers, etc., who helped open up the West.

13193 Keenan, Sheila. *Scholastic Encyclopedia of Women in United States History* (4–9). 1996, Scholastic paper $17.95 (0-590-22792-0). More than 200 brief biographies of American women representing a variety of professions and accomplishments, organized into six chronologically arranged chapters. (Rev: BR 3–4/97; SLJ 2/97) [920]

13194 King, David C. *First Facts About American Heroes* (3–6). Illus. 1995, Blackbirch LB $25.95 (1-56711-165-3). 112pp. The lives and accomplishments of 42 famous Americans are presented, each with a full-page photograph or painting and a single page of facts. (Rev: SLJ 2/96) [920]

13195 Knapp, Ron. *American Generals of World War II* (5–8). Series: Collective Biographies. 1998, Enslow LB $20.95 (0-7660-1024-4). 128pp. The 10 U.S. generals profiled here are Henry Arnold, Omar Bradley, Dwight Eisenhower, Curtis LeMay, Douglas MacArthur, George Marshall, George Patton,

Matthew Ridgway, Holland Smith, and Joseph Stilwell. (Rev: SLJ 9/98) [920]

13196 Kramer, Barbara. *Trailblazing American Women* (5–7). Series: Collective Biographies. 2000, Enslow LB $20.95 (0-7660-1377-4). 112pp. This collection of biographies profiles women who dared to branch out into new fields and break new ground. (Rev: BL 9/15/00; HBG 10/01; SLJ 12/00) [920]

13197 Krohn, Katherine. *Women of the Wild West* (4–6). Series: A&E Biography. 2000, Lerner LB $25.26 (0-8225-4980-8). 112pp. Among its several profiles, this book examines the lives of some infamous women of the Wild West: Calamity Jane, Belle Starr, Pearl Hart, and Annie Oakley. (Rev: BL 6/1–15/00; HBG 3/01; SLJ 9/00) [920]

13198 Krull, Kathleen. *Lives of the Presidents: Fame, Shame (and What the Neighbors Thought)* (4–8). Illus. by Kathryn Hewitt. 1998, Harcourt $20.00 (0-15-200808-X). 96pp. An entertaining collective biography that stresses the human side of U.S. presidents, with interesting, insightful tidbits and details that bring the presidents to life. (Rev: BL 8/98; HB 11–12/98; HBG 3/99; SLJ 9/98) [920]

13199 Lindop, Edmund. *Dwight D. Eisenhower, John F. Kennedy, Lyndon B. Johnson* (4–7). Illus. Series: Presidents Who Dared. 1996, Twenty-First Century LB $23.90 (0-8050-3404-8). 64pp. The highlights of these three administrations are presented, preceded by an introduction to the American presidency. (Rev: BL 4/15/96; SLJ 6/96) [920]

13200 Lindop, Edmund. *George Washington, Thomas Jefferson, Andrew Jackson* (4–7). Illus. Series: Presidents Who Dared. 1995, Twenty-First Century LB $23.90 (0-8050-3401-3). 64pp. After a general introduction on the duties of the president, brief biographies of three are given, with emphasis on their accomplishments in office. (Rev: BL 1/1–15/96; SLJ 11/95) [920]

13201 Lindop, Edmund. *James K. Polk, Abraham Lincoln, Theodore Roosevelt* (4–7). Illus. Series: Presidents Who Dared. 1995, Twenty-First Century LB $23.90 (0-8050-3402-1). 64pp. Highlights and evaluations of the presidencies of Polk, Lincoln, and Theodore Roosevelt. (Rev: BL 1/1–15/96; SLJ 11/95) [920]

13202 Lindop, Edmund. *Richard M. Nixon, Jimmy Carter, Ronald Reagan* (4–8). Series: Presidents Who Dared. 1996, Twenty-First Century LB $23.90 (0-8050-3405-6). This account traces salient events in each of these presidents' terms, for example: Nixon and Watergate and relations with China; Carter and ending the war between Egypt and Israel; and Reagan and his arms agreement with the Soviet Union. (Rev: BL 4/15/96; SLJ 6/96) [920]

13203 Lindop, Edmund. *Woodrow Wilson, Franklin D. Roosevelt, Harry S. Truman* (5–8). Illus. Series: Presidents Who Dared. 1995, Twenty-First Century LB $23.90 (0-8050-3403-X). 64pp. After an overview of the presidency and brief profiles of these men, this account looks at daring decisions they made as presidents. (Rev: BL 1/1–15/96; BR 3–4/96; SLJ 11/95) [920]

13204 Lutz, Norma Jean. *Business and Industry* (5–8). Series: Female Firsts in Their Fields. 1999, Chelsea LB $16.95 (0-7910-5142-0). 64pp. The six women who are profiled in this book are Madam C. J. Walker, Katharine Graham, Mary Kay Ash, Martha Stewart, Oprah Winfrey, and Sherry Lansing. (Rev: HBG 10/99; SLJ 9/99) [920]

13205 McDonough, Yona Z. *Sisters in Strength: American Women Who Made a Difference* (3–5). 2000, Holt $17.95 (0-8050-6102-9). 48pp. A colorful, oversize volume that highlights the lives of such important American women as Pocahontas, Harriet Tubman, Susan B. Anthony, Amelia Earhart, and Eleanor Roosevelt. (Rev: BL 3/1/00; HBG 10/00; SLJ 4/00) [920]

13206 McLean, Jacqueline. *Women with Wings* (4–7). Illus. Series: Profiles. 2001, Oliver $19.95 (1-881508-70-6). 160pp. An absorbing account of the achievements of women pilots, including Bessie Coleman, Amelia Earhart, and Anne Morrow Lindbergh. (Rev: BL 5/15/01; HBG 10/01; SLJ 10/01) [629.13]

13207 Marvis, Barbara. *Famous People of Asian Ancestry*, Vol. 4 (4–7). Illus. Series: Contemporary American Success Stories. 1994, Mitchell Lane paper $10.95 (1-883845-09-2). 96pp. A collective biography of Asian Americans, including actor Dustin Nguyen, novelist Amy Tan, and businessman Rocky Aoki. Also use volumes 1 through 3 (2nd ed., 1997). (Rev: BL 10/1/94; SLJ 11/94) [920]

13208 Marvis, Barbara. *Famous People of Hispanic Heritage*, Vol. 1 (4–7). Illus. Series: Contemporary American Success Stories. 1995, Mitchell Lane LB $21.95 (1-883845-21-1); paper $12.95 (1-883845-20-3). 96pp. This is the first of three volumes that give brief biographies of Hispanic Americans from all walks of life who have made significant contributions to our country. (Rev: BL 11/15/95; SLJ 1/96) [920]

13209 Marvis, Barbara. *Famous People of Hispanic Heritage*, Vol. 4 (5–9). Illus. 1996, Mitchell Lane paper $12.95 (1-883845-29-7). The lives of two Hispanic men and two women who have succeeded in their careers are presented in an easy-to-read style. Other volumes in this series by the same author are available. (Rev: BL 12/15/96; SLJ 1/97) [920]

13210 Meisner, James, and Amy Ruth. *American Revolutionaries and Founders of the Nation* (5–7). Series: Collective Biographies. 1999, Enslow LB $20.95 (0-7660-1115-1). 112pp. Ten brief biographies of prominent leaders of the American Revolution, each with a black-and-white portrait. (Rev: BL 9/15/99) [920]

13211 Morin, Isobel V. *Women Chosen for Public Office* (5–7). Illus. 1995, Oliver LB $19.95 (1-881508-20-X). 160pp. Nine biographies of women who are involved in the federal government from the superintendent of army nurses to Supreme Court Justice Ruth Bader Ginsburg. (Rev: BL 5/1/95; SLJ 6/95) [920]

13212 Morris, Juddi. *At Home with the Presidents* (4–8). 1999, Wiley paper $12.95 (0-471-25300-6).

172pp. In three to five pages each, this account profiles the presidents of the United States from Washington through Clinton. (Rev: SLJ 3/00) [920]

13213 Munson, Sammye. *Today's Tejano Heroes* (5–8). Illus. 2000, Eakin $13.95 (1-57168-328-3). 80pp. In alphabetical order, this volume introduces 16 important 20th-century Mexican Americans who have contributed to the history and culture of Texas, including Vikki Carr, Attorney General Dan Morales, and federal judge Hilda Tagle. (Rev: BL 2/1/01) [920]

13214 O'Connor, Jane. *If the Walls Could Talk: Family Life at the White House* (4–7). Illus. by Gary Hovland. 2004, Simon & Schuster $16.95 (0-689-86863-4). 48pp. This inside view of family life within the White House — with caricatures and interesting trivia — is similar to Judith St. George's *So You Want to Be President* (Putnam, 2000). (Rev: BL 8/04; SLJ 9/04)

13215 Orr, Tamara. *The Salem Witch Trials* (5–8). Illus. Series: People at the Center. 2004, Gale/ Blackbirch LB $18.96 (1-56711-770-8). 48pp. This collective biography introduces some of the men and women who played key roles in the Salem Witch Trials. (Rev: BL 5/15/04; SLJ 9/04) [133.4]

13216 Pascoe, Elaine. *First Facts About the Presidents* (4–8). Illus. Series: First Facts About. 1996, Blackbirch $34.94 (1-56711-167-X). 112pp. Divided into four historical periods, this book introduces each of the presidents, briefly describes his presidency, and looks at the major historical events of the time. (Rev: SLJ 5/96) [920]

13217 Pelz, Ruth. *Black Heroes of the Wild West* (3–5). Illus. by Leandro Della Piana. 1989, Open Hand $12.95 (0-940880-25-3); paper $6.95 (0-940880-26-1). 56pp. The stories of five black men and four black women who contributed to the history of the Old West. (Rev: BL 6/1/90) [920]

13218 Pelz, Ruth. *Women of the Wild West: Biographies from Many Cultures* (3–5). Illus. 1995, Open Hand paper $6.95 (0-940880-50-4). 64pp. The biographies of eight women — e.g., Sacajawea and exslave Biddy Mason — who played important roles in the history of the American West. (Rev: BL 3/1/95) [921]

13219 Pinkney, Andrea D. *Let It Shine: Stories of Black Women Freedom Fighters* (5–8). Illus. 2000, Harcourt $20.00 (0-15-201005-X). 120pp. This work contains chatty profiles of 10 important African American women, including Sojourner Truth, Rosa Parks, and Shirley Chisholm. (Rev: BCCB 11/00; BL 11/15/00; HB 11–12/00; HBG 3/01; SLJ 10/00) [921]

13220 Raatma, Lucia. *Great Women of the Civil War* (4–6). Series: We the People. 2005, Compass Point LB $22.60 (0-7565-0839-8). 48pp. Women's exploits and achievements during the Civil War are placed in historical context. (Rev: BL 5/15/04; HBG 3/98; SLJ 6/05) [920]

13221 Rappaport, Doreen. *In the Promised Land: Lives of Jewish Americans* (4–7). Illus. by Cornelius Van Wright. 2005, HarperCollins LB $16.89 (0-06-059395-4). 32pp. A look at the lives and diverse

accomplishments of 13 notable Jewish Americans, including Asser Levy, Harry Houdini, Jonas Salk, and Steven Spielberg. (Rev: BL 1/1–15/05; SLJ 5/05) [920]

13222 Rappaport, Doreen. *We Are the Many: A Picture Book of American Indians* (K–3). Illus. by Cornelius Van Wright and Ying-hwa Hu. 2002, HarperCollins LB $17.89 (0-06-001139-4). 32pp. A collection of 13 brief biographies of Native Americans from different tribes, including Tisquantum (Squanto), Jim Thorpe, and Maria Tallchief. (Rev: BL 10/15/02; HBG 3/03; SLJ 9/02) [970.004]

13223 Rediger, Pat. *Great African Americans in Business* (4–6). Illus. Series: Outstanding African Americans. 1996, Crabtree LB $22.60 (0-86505-803-2); paper $8.95 (0-86505-817-2). 64pp. Such people as John H. Johnson and Oprah Winfrey are profiled. (Rev: BL 9/15/96; SLJ 8/96) [920]

13224 Rediger, Pat. *Great African Americans in Civil Rights* (4–6). Illus. Series: Outstanding African Americans. 1996, Crabtree LB $22.60 (0-86505-798-2); paper $8.95 (0-86505-812-1). 64pp. In short chapters, such civil rights leaders as Thurgood Marshall, Rosa Parks, and Jesse Jackson are introduced. (Rev: BL 9/15/96; SLJ 8/96) [920]

13225 Redmond, Shirley Raye. *Patriots in Petticoats: Heroines of the American Revolution* (3–5). Illus. Series: Landmark Books. 2004, Random $14.95 (0-375-82357-3). 144pp. Spotlighting the contributions of 24 women patriots, this volume includes reproductions and photographs. (Rev: BL 3/1/04; SLJ 4/04) [973.3]

13226 St. George, Judith. *Dear Dr. Bell . . . Your Friend, Helen Keller* (5–7). Illus. 1992, Morrow paper $4.95 (0-688-12814-9). 172pp. A joint biography about the friendship between Alexander Graham Bell and Helen Keller. (Rev: BCCB 11–12/92 & 2/93; SLJ 12/92) [920]

13227 Sullivan, Otha Richard. *African American Millionaires* (5–10). Series: Black Stars. 2004, Wiley $24.95 (0-471-46928-9). 158pp. Tyra Banks and Oprah Winfrey are included here, but so are many names that may be unfamiliar to readers, such as William Alexander Leidesdorff and Annie Turnbo Malone. (Rev: SLJ 5/05) [920]

13228 Thomson, Sarah L. *What Presidents Are Made Of* (2–4). Illus. by Hanoch Piven. 2004, Simon & Schuster $15.95 (0-689-86880-4). 40pp. Collage caricatures and brief text give wry and unusual portraits of 17 of America's presidents and their outstanding characteristics or interests. (Rev: BL 8/04; SLJ 8/04) [973]

13229 Wheeler, Jill C. *America's Leaders* (4–7). Series: War on Terrorism. 2002, ABDO LB $25.65 (1-57765-661-X). 48pp. This book contains brief profiles of important American figures in the war against terrorism such as President Bush, Colin Powell, John Ashcroft, and Rudy Giuliani. (Rev: BL 5/15/02; HBG 10/02) [920]

African Americans

ABERNATHY, DAVID

13230 Reef, Catherine. *Ralph David Abernathy* (5–8). Illus. Series: People in Focus. 1995, Dillon $18.95 (0-87518-653-X); paper $7.95 (0-382-24965-8). 167pp. A biography that describes this civil rights leader's youth and many accomplishments. (Rev: SLJ 10/95) [921]

ALLEN, RICHARD

13231 Klots, Steve. *Richard Allen* (5–8). Illus. Series: Black Americans of Achievement. 1990, Chelsea LB $19.95 (1-55546-570-6). 112pp. Born a slave in 1780, this convert to Christianity founded the first African American Methodist Church. (Rev: SLJ 2/91) [921]

BALL, CHARLES

13232 Shuter, Jane, ed. *Charles Ball and American Slavery* (5–8). Illus. Series: History Eyewitness. 1995, Raintree LB $24.26 (0-8114-8281-2). 48pp. This autobiographical account in simple language brings the horrors of slavery to life, with period prints and maps. (Rev: BL 4/15/95; SLJ 5/95) [975]

BATES, CLAYTON "PEG LEG"

13233 Barasch, Lynne. *Knockin' on Wood: Starring Peg Leg Bates* (2–3). 2004, Lee & Low $16.95 (1-58430-170-8). 32pp. In the early 20th century, African American Clayton "Peg Leg" Bates found fame as a dancer despite losing a leg in a childhood accident and despite his race. (Rev: BL 6/1–15/04; SLJ 6/04) [792.7]

BETHUNE, MARY MCLEOD

13234 Greenfield, Eloise. *Mary McLeod Bethune* (2–4). Illus. by Jerry Pinkney. 1994, HarperCollins paper $6.95 (0-06-446168-8). 40pp. Bethune was the only one of 17 children in her family to go to school. Through courage and hard work, she became an educator of national importance. [921]

13235 Kelso, Richard. *Building a Dream: Mary Bethune's School* (2–4). Illus. by Debbe Heller. Series: Stories of America. 1993, Raintree LB $27.12 (0-8114-7217-5). 46pp. The story of Mary Bethune and how she realized her dream of building a school for poor African American children. (Rev: SLJ 7/93) [921]

13236 McKissack, Patricia, and Fredrick McKissack. *Mary McLeod Bethune: A Great Teacher*. Rev. ed. (2–4). Series: Great African Americans. 2001, Enslow LB $14.95 (0-7660-1680-3). 32pp. An updated biography of the former slave who dedicated her life to the education of African Americans, with new illustrations. (Rev: HBG 3/02; SLJ 5/02) [921]

13237 Meltzer, Milton. *Mary McLeod Bethune: Voice of Black Hope* (4–7). Illus. 1988, Puffin paper $4.99 (0-14-032219-1). 64pp. An effective profile of the African American educator. (Rev: BCCB 5/87; BL 3/15/87; SLJ 3/87) [370.0924]

13238 Somervill, Barbara A. *Mary McLeod Bethune: African-American Educator* (4–7). Series: Our People. 2003, Child's World LB $27.07 (1-59296-008-1). 32pp. A profile of the African American educator and leader, with sidebars that add historical context. (Rev: SLJ 4/04) [921]

BROWN, AUNT CLARA

13239 Lowery, Linda. *Aunt Clara Brown: Official Pioneer* (2–4). Illus. by Janice L. Porter. Series: On My Own Biography. 1999, Carolrhoda LB $14.95 (1-57505-045-5). 48pp. The inspiring story of a freed slave who used the wealth she accumulated in Colorado to help other freed blacks after the Civil War. (Rev: BCCB 12/99; HBG 3/00; SLJ 11/99*) [921]

BUNCHE, RALPH J.

13240 McKissack, Patricia, and Fredrick McKissack. *Ralph J. Bunche: Peacemaker* (2–4). Series: Great African Americans. 2002, Enslow LB $14.95 (0-7660-1701-X). 32pp. The inspiring story of the African American diplomat who was active in UN affairs and won the Nobel Peace Prize in 1950. (Rev: BL 7/02; HBG 10/02) [921]

CARMICHAEL, STOKELY

13241 Cwiklik, Robert. *Stokely Carmichael and Black Power* (4–6). Illus. Series: Gateway Civil Rights. 1993, Millbrook LB $20.90 (1-56294-276-X). 32pp. The life of the controversial civil rights leader who coined the term "black power." (Rev: BCCB 5/93; BL 8/93) [921]

CARY, MARY ANN SHADD

13242 Ferris, Jeri Chase. *Demanding Justice: A Story About Mary Ann Shadd Cary* (2–4). Illus. by Kimanne Smith. Series: Creative Minds Biographies. 2003, Carolrhoda LB $21.27 (1-57505-177-X); paper $5.95 (0-87614-928-X). 64pp. Cary was a free black woman who worked as a teacher and lawyer during the 18th century and sought to improve the lives of other African Americans. (Rev: HBG 10/03; SLJ 8/03) [921]

CHISHOLM, SHIRLEY

13243 Pollack, Jill S. *Shirley Chisholm* (3–5). Illus. Series: First Books. 1994, Watts LB $22.00 (0-531-20168-6). 64pp. An interesting biography of this African American, with emphasis on her political career in Washington, D.C. (Rev: BL 1/15/95) [921]

DOUGLASS, FREDERICK

13244 Adler, David A. *A Picture Book of Frederick Douglass* (K–3). Illus. by Samuel Byrd. Series: Headliners. 1993, Holiday House LB $16.95 (0-

8234-1002-1). 32pp. A simple life story of the famous African American abolitionist who died in 1895. (Rev: BL 4/1/93; SLJ 8/93) [921]

13245 Becker, Helaine. *Frederick Douglass* (4–7). Series: The Civil War. 2001, Gale LB $27.44 (1-56711-557-8). 104pp. Readers of this biography that covers Douglass's life and work as an abolitionist will be particularly interested in the account of his youth as a slave in Maryland and his escape to freedom. (Rev: HBG 3/02; SLJ 4/02) [921]

13246 Lutz, Norma Jean. *Frederick Douglass: Abolitionist and Author* (3–5). Illus. 2001, Chelsea $18.95 (0-7910-6003-9); paper $8.95 (0-7910-6141-8). This brief introduction to the life of the abolitionist includes material on his youth and education. (Rev: BL 5/1/01) [972.81]

13247 McKissack, Patricia, and Fredrick McKissack. *Frederick Douglass: Leader Against Slavery*. Rev. ed. (2–4). Illus. Series: Great African Americans. 2002, Enslow LB $14.95 (0-7660-1696-X). 32pp. An updated version of a previously released biography about the slave-turned-abolitionist, which includes archival photographs and Web site information. (Rev: BL 2/15/02; SLJ 5/02) [973.8]

13248 Marlowe, Sam. *Learning About Dedication from the Life of Frederick Douglass* (2–5). Illus. Series: Character Building Book. 1996, Rosen LB $15.93 (0-8239-2425-4). 24pp. Both slavery and the life of the man who fought against it are covered in this short book. (Rev: BL 10/15/96; SLJ 1/97) [921]

13249 Miller, William. *Frederick Douglass: The Last Day of Slavery* (2–4). Illus. by Cedric Lucas. 1995, Lee & Low $14.95 (1-880000-17-2). 32pp. A picture-book biography of this freedom fighter who suffered the cruelty of slavery. (Rev: BL 3/15/95; SLJ 6/95) [921]

13250 Passaro, John. *Frederick Douglass* (4–6). Series: Journey to Freedom. 1999, Child's World LB $16.95 (1-56766-621-3). 32pp. The inspiring biography of the gifted African American who managed to escape slavery and become one of the earliest fighters for civil rights and freedom. (Rev: BL 10/15/99; HBG 3/00) [921]

13251 Schomp, Virginia. *He Fought for Freedom: Frederick Douglass* (3–6). Illus. Series: Biographies. 1996, Benchmark LB $21.36 (0-7614-0488-0). 48pp. A brief but thorough account of the former slave who led the antislavery movement, with quotes from his autobiography. (Rev: HB 11–12/96; SLJ 2/97) [921]

DU BOIS, W. E. B.

13252 Cavan, Seamus. *W. E. B. Du Bois and Racial Relations* (3–5). Illus. Series: Gateway Civil Rights. 1993, Millbrook LB $20.90 (1-56294-288-3). 32pp. The story of the life and contributions of this great African American civil rights leader and author who died in 1963. (Rev: BL 10/1/93; SLJ 10/93) [921]

13253 Moss, Nathaniel. *W. E. B. Du Bois: Civil Rights Leader* (5–8). Series: Junior World Biography. 1996, Chelsea LB $15.95 (0-7910-2382-6). A brief, somewhat superficial overview of this great

pioneer in the civil rights movement and his accomplishments. (Rev: SLJ 7/96) [921]

13254 Troy, Don. *W. E. B. Du Bois* (3–6). Series: Journey to Freedom. 1999, Child's World LB $16.95 (1-56766-555-1). 39pp. An attractive and clearly written biography of Du Bois that contains photos on each page, a timeline, and sources for further information. (Rev: BL 7/99; HBG 10/99; SLJ 7/99) [921]

EVERS, MEDGAR

13255 St. Lawrence, Genevieve. *Medgar Evers* (3–5). Illus. Series: African-American Biographies. 2003, Raintree LB $28.56 (0-7398-7028-9). 64pp. An account of the short life of the civil rights leader who was assassinated at the age of 37. (Rev: BL 1/1–15/04; HBG 4/04) [921]

FARMER, JAMES

13256 Jakoubek, Robert E. *James Farmer and the Freedom Rides* (3–5). Illus. Series: Gateway Civil Rights. 1994, Millbrook LB $20.90 (1-56294-381-2). 32pp. The story of the Freedom Riders and their leader, James Farmer, who dedicated his life to the struggle for civil rights. (Rev: BL 4/15/94; SLJ 6/94) [921]

FIELDS, MARY

13257 Miller, Robert H. *The Story of Stagecoach Mary Fields* (1–4). Illus. by Cheryl Hanna. 1995, Silver Burdett LB $14.95 (0-382-24390-0); paper $5.95 (0-382-24394-3). 32pp. In the late 1800s, Mary Fields, a freed slave, was the first African American woman letter carrier. (Rev: BL 4/15/95; SLJ 5/95) [921]

FORTEN, JAMES

13258 Krebs, Laurie. *A Day in the Life of a Colonial Sailmaker* (2–3). Series: The Library of Living and Working in Colonial Times. 2004, Rosen LB $18.75 (0-8239-6231-8). 24pp. Fact and fiction are interwoven as James Forten, an African American living in Philadelphia who became a wealthy man through his innovative sails, goes about his daily business. (Rev: BL 9/1/04) [921]

FORTUNE, AMOS

13259 Yates, Elizabeth. *Amos Fortune, Free Man* (6–8). Illus. by Nora S. Unwin. 1950, Puffin paper $4.99 (0-14-034158-7). 181pp. The simplicity and dignity of the human spirit and its triumph over degradation are movingly portrayed in this portrait of a slave who bought his freedom. Newbery Medal winner, 1951.

HAMER, FANNIE LOU

13260 Donovan, Sandy. *Fannie Lou Hamer* (3–5). Illus. Series: African-American Biographies. 2003, Raintree LB $28.56 (0-7398-7030-0). 64pp. The life of the woman, the youngest of 20 children of a Mississippi sharecropper, who become a civil rights activist. (Rev: BL 1/1–15/04) [921]

HILL, ANITA

13261 Italia, Bob. *Anita Hill: Speaking Out Against Harassment* (4–6). Illus. Series: Everyone Contributes. 1993, ABDO LB $12.94 (1-56239-259-X). 32pp. This biography concentrates on the Clarence Thomas hearings and Anita Hill's role in them. (Rev: BL 12/1/93; SLJ 1/94) [921]

JACKSON, JESSE

13262 Meadows, James. *Jesse Jackson* (4–6). Series: Journey to Freedom. 2000, Child's World LB $25.64 (1-56766-742-2). 40pp. The story of a religious leader who has also become one of the most powerful civil rights activists in the country. (Rev: BL 11/15/00; HBG 3/01) [921]

13263 Steffens, Bradley, and Dan Wood. *Jesse Jackson* (5–8). Series: People in the News. 2000, Lucent LB $27.45 (1-56006-631-8). 126pp. This well-documented look at the life of the religious and civil rights leader gives interesting information on the events and people who influenced him. (Rev: BL 6/1–15/00; HBG 10/00) [921]

JACOBS, HARRIET A.

13264 Fleischner, Jennifer. *I Was Born a Slave: The Story of Harriet Jacobs* (4–8). Illus. 1997, Millbrook LB $26.90 (0-7613-0111-9). The turbulent life of Harriet Jacobs, who was born into slavery and lived for many years as a fugitive before winning her freedom and becoming an abolitionist. (Rev: BL 9/15/97; BR 1–2/98; HBG 3/98; SLJ 1/98) [921]

JORDAN, BARBARA

13265 McNair, Joseph. *Barbara Jordan: African American Politician* (4–6). Series: Journey to Freedom. 2000, Child's World LB $25.64 (1-56766-741-4). 40pp. A biography of the noted politician who was Texas's first African American female senator and later served in Congress for six years. (Rev: BL 11/15/00; HBG 3/01) [921]

13266 Patrick-Wexler, Diane. *Barbara Jordan* (4–6). Illus. Series: Contemporary African Americans. 1995, Raintree LB $25.69 (0-8172-3976-6). 48pp. The story of the famous African American congresswoman from childhood through her later career as an educator. (Rev: BL 2/15/96; SLJ 4/96) [921]

KING, CORETTA SCOTT

13267 Bankston, John. *Coretta Scott King and the Story Behind the Coretta Scott King Award* (4–8). Series: Great Achievement Awards. 2003, Mitchell Lane LB $19.95 (1-58415-202-8). 48pp. The story of the widow of Martin Luther King, Jr., her continuing fight for civil rights, and the children's book

prize named after her are covered in this biography. (Rev: BL 10/15/03; SLJ 10/03) [921]

13268 Klingel, Cynthia. *Coretta Scott King* (4–6). Illus. Series: Journey to Freedom. 1999, Child's World LB $16.95 (1-56766-567-5). 40pp. A life of Coretta Scott King, who gave up her singing career to follow in her husband's footsteps as a civil rights leader. (Rev: BL 5/1/99; HBG 10/99) [921]

13269 Mattern, Joanne. *Coretta Scott King: Civil Rights Activist* (1–3). Illus. Series: Women Who Shaped History. 2003, Rosen LB $17.25 (0-8239-6504-X). 24pp. The life of Coretta Scott King, for new readers. (Rev: BL 2/15/03) [323]

13270 Rhodes, Lisa R. *Coretta Scott King* (5–8). Illus. Series: Black Americans of Achievement. 1999, Chelsea $21.95 (0-7910-4690-7); paper $9.95 (0-7910-4691-5). This biography of Coretta Scott King describes her childhood, education, marriage, participation in the civil rights movement, and her work since her husband's assassination. (Rev: BL 8/98; HBG 10/98; SLJ 8/98) [323.092]

KING, DR. MARTIN LUTHER

13271 Myers, Walter Dean. *I've Seen the Promised Land: The Life of Dr. Martin Luther King, Jr.* (1–4). Illus. by Leonard Jenkins. 2004, HarperCollins $15.99 (0-06-027703-3). A moving and well-illustrated picture-book biography that covers King's political and private lives. (Rev: SLJ 4/04) [921]

KING, HORACE

13272 Gibbons, Faye. *Horace King: Bridges to Freedom* (5–8). Illus. 2002, Crane Hill paper $9.95 (1-57587-199-8). 112pp. The story of a slave who went on to become a builder and later a public servant in the post-Civil War South. (Rev: BL 2/15/03) [328.761]

KING, MARTIN LUTHER, JR.

13273 Adler, David A. *Dr. Martin Luther King, Jr.* (1–3). Illus. by Colin Bootman. Series: Holiday House Reader. 2001, Holiday House $14.95 (0-8234-1572-4). 48pp. A brief account of King's life, achievements, and legacy that will also appeal to older children who are having difficulties reading. (Rev: BL 7/01; SLJ 6/01) [323]

13274 Adler, David A. *A Picture Book of Martin Luther King, Jr.* (PS–2). Illus. by Robert Casilla. Series: Picture Book Biographies. 1989, Holiday House LB $16.95 (0-8234-0770-5); paper $6.95 (0-8234-0847-7). 32pp. The life of the civil rights leader is presented in picture book format. (Rev: BCCB 2/90; BL 11/1/89; SLJ 9/89) [921]

13275 Bray, Rosemary L. *Martin Luther King* (2–4). Illus. by Malcah Zeldis. 1995, Greenwillow paper $5.95 (0-688-15219-8). 48pp. A large-format biography that supplies basic information with dramatic paintings on each page. (Rev: BL 2/15/95; HB 5–6/95; SLJ 2/95*) [921]

13276 Brown, Jonatha A. *Martin Luther King Jr.* (2–4). Illus. Series: People We Should Know. 2005,

Gareth Stevens LB $14.50 (0-8368-4467-X). 24pp. For beginning readers, a simple explanation of King's importance with attractive layout and historical and contemporary photographs. [921]

13277 Darby, Jean. *Martin Luther King, Jr.* (4–8). Illus. Series: Lerner Biographies. 1990, Lerner LB $30.35 (0-8225-4902-6). 144pp. An in-depth look at King's life and the civil rights movement. (Rev: BL 7/90; SLJ 11/90) [921]

13278 Farris, Christine King. *My Brother Martin* (K–3). Illus. by Chris Soentpiet. 2003, Simon & Schuster $17.95 (0-689-84387-9). 40pp. A fond biography of Dr. Martin Luther King, Jr., by his older sister. (Rev: BL 2/15/03; HB 3–4/03; HBG 10/03; SLJ 2/03) [323]

13279 Haskins, Jim. *I Have a Dream* (4–6). Illus. 1992, Millbrook LB $27.40 (1-56294-087-2). 112p. A well-researched biography, supported by excerpts from King's writings and speeches. (Rev: BL 2/15/93) [921]

13280 Haskins, Jim. *The Life and Death of Martin Luther King, Jr.* (5–7). Illus. 1992, Morrow paper $6.95 (0-688-11690-6). 176pp. Covering the life and career of the African American leader, with focus on the civil rights movement. [921]

13281 January, Brendan. *Martin Luther King Jr.: Minister and Civil Rights Activist* (4–8). Series: Ferguson Career Biographies. 2001, Ferguson LB $16.95 (0-89434-342-4). 127pp. This concise account focuses on King's career as a minister as well as his work as an advocate of civil rights and includes a section on training for the ministry. (Rev: SLJ 4/01) [921]

13282 Lambert, Kathy K. *Martin Luther King, Jr.* (4–7). Illus. Series: Junior World Biography. 1992, Chelsea LB $18.65 (0-7910-1759-1). 82pp. A well-designed biography using many photographs to re-create the life of the great civil rights leader. (Rev: BL 11/1/92) [921]

13283 Lowery, Linda. *Martin Luther King Day* (2–4). Illus. by Hetty Mitchell. 1987, Carolrhoda LB $21.27 (0-87614-299-4); Lerner paper $5.95 (0-87614-468-7). 56pp. Origins of the holiday and high points of Dr. King's life. (Rev: BL 4/1/87; SLJ 6–7/87) [921]

13284 McKissack, Patricia, and Fredrick McKissack. *Martin Luther King, Jr.: Man of Peace.* Rev. ed. (2–4). Series: Great African Americans. 2001, Enslow LB $14.95 (0-7660-1678-1). 32pp. A newly illustrated edition of this title that includes information on King's early life. (Rev: HBG 3/02; SLJ 5/02) [921]

13285 McLeese, Don. *Martin Luther King, Jr.* (2–5). Series: Equal Rights Leaders. 2002, Rourke LB $19.27 (1-58952-286-9). 24pp. Simple text and well-chosen illustrations tell the story of King's life, with good coverage of his youth and education. (Rev: SLJ 1/03) [323]

13286 Marzollo, Jean. *Happy Birthday, Martin Luther King* (PS–3). Illus. by Brian Pinkney. 1992, Scholastic $15.95 (0-590-44065-9). 32pp. The focus is on King's ability to bring people together in this simple biography. (Rev: BL 12/15/92; SLJ 3/93) [921]

13287 Pastan, Amy. *Martin Luther King Jr.* (5–10). Illus. Series: DK Biography. 2004, DK LB $14.99 (0-7566-0491-5); paper $4.99 (0-7566-0342-0). 128pp. A heavily illustrated, attractive biography of King that offers broad historical background. [921]

13288 Patrick, Denise Lewis. *A Lesson for Martin Luther King Jr.* (K–2). Illus. by Rodney S. Pate. Series: Childhood of Famous Americans. 2003, Simon & Schuster LB $11.89 (0-689-85398-X); paper $3.99 (0-689-85397-1). 32pp. A childhood event that helped Martin Luther King Jr. to define his mission in life is the focus of this slim volume. (Rev: HBG 4/04; SLJ 2/04) [921]

13289 Patrick, Diane. *Martin Luther King, Jr.* (4–8). Illus. 1990, Watts paper $21.00 (0-531-10892-9). 144pp. A colorful format helps to make this look at King's life accessible to middle-grade readers. (Rev: BL 7/90; SLJ 9/90) [921]

13290 Roop, Peter, and Connie Roop. *Martin Luther King, Jr.* (2–3). Series: Lives and Times. 1997, Heinemann $19.92 (1-57572-560-6). 24pp. A simple picture-book biography that gives a very brief introduction to the life and contributions of Martin Luther King, Jr. (Rev: BL 3/15/98; HB 5–6/97; SLJ 6/98) [921]

13291 Schloredt, Valerie, and Pam Brown. *Martin Luther King Jr.* (5–10). Illus. Series: World Peacemakers. 2004, Gale LB $27.44 (1-56711-977-8). 64pp. A readable account of this civil rights leader and the times in which he lived. (Rev: BL 2/15/04; SLJ 2/94) [921]

13292 Schuman, Michael A. *Martin Luther King, Jr.: Leader for Civil Rights* (5–8). Series: African-American Biographies. 1996, Enslow LB $20.95 (0-89490-687-9). A straightforward biography that covers the important events in King's life. (Rev: SLJ 12/96) [921]

13293 Strazzabosco, Jeanne M. *Learning About Dignity from the Life of Martin Luther King, Jr.* (2–5). Illus. Series: A Character Building Book. 1996, Rosen $13.95 (0-8239-2415-7). 24pp. This brief biography describes King's many virtues, above all his innate dignity. (Rev: BL 10/15/96; SLJ 12/96) [921]

LOVE, NAT

13294 Miller, Robert, and Michael Bryant. *The Story of Nat Love* (K–3). Illus. 1994, Silver Burdett LB $14.95 (0-382-24389-7); paper $5.95 (0-382-24393-5). 32pp. A picture-book biography of the cowboy of the Old West, Nat Love, who began his life as a slave. (Rev: BL 1/1/95; SLJ 1/95) [921]

13295 Penn, Sarah. *Nat Love: African American Cowboy* (2–4). Illus. Series: Primary Sources of Famous People in American History. 2004, Rosen LB $21.25 (0-8239-4116-7). 32pp. Primary sources — including maps and paintings — add to the simple narrative telling the story of the African American cowboy. [921]

13296 Penn, Sarah. *Nat Love: African American Cowboy / Vaquero afroamericano* (4–6). Trans. by

Eida de la Vega. Series: Primary Sources of Famous People in American History. 2004, Rosen LB $21.25 (0-8239-4164-7). 32pp. A brief, solid, bilingual introduction to the cowboy who was known for his riding and roping skills. (Rev: SLJ 9/04) [921]

LYON, MARITCHA REYMOND

13297 Bolden, Tanya. *Maritcha: A Nineteenth-Century American Girl* (4–7). Illus. 2005, Abrams $17.95 (0-8109-5045-6). 48pp. Drawing on primary sources, Bolden tells the story of Maritcha Remond Lyon, a free black girl who succeeded in her fight to attend an all-white high school in Rhode Island in the mid-19th century. (Rev: BL 2/1/05; SLJ 2/05) [921]

MCCARTY, OSEOLA

13298 Coleman, Evelyn. *The Riches of Oseola McCarty* (3–7). Illus. 1998, Whitman $14.95 (0-8075-6961-5). 48pp. This is the heartwarming story of the modest washerwoman who, at her death, gave her hard-earned fortune to the University of Mississippi for scholarships. (Rev: BCCB 3/99; BL 12/15/98; HB 1–2/99; HBG 3/99; SLJ 1/99) [921]

MALCOLM X

13299 Adoff, Arnold. *Malcolm X*. Rev. ed. (3–6). Illus. 2000, HarperCollins paper $4.25 (0-06-442118-X). 64pp. This clearly written biography reflects the intense drama of the African American leader's life and death. (Rev: BL 2/15/00) [921]

13300 Benson, Michael. *Malcolm X* (5–8). Series: Biography. 2001, Lerner LB $25.26 (0-8225-5025-3). An accessible text and many photographs are used to enliven this biography of the African American civil rights leader who was assassinated in 1965. (Rev: BL 4/1/02; HBG 3/02; SLJ 3/02) [921]

13301 Collins, David R. *Malcolm X: Black Rage* (5–9). 1992, Dillon LB $13.95 (0-87518-498-7). A short biography of the influential African American activist, tracing the early events that led to his belief that whites were the enemy. (Rev: BL 10/15/92; SLJ 1/93) [921]

13302 Graves, Renee. *Malcolm X* (3–5). Series: Cornerstones of Freedom. 2003, Children's Pr. LB $24.00 (0-516-24224-5). 48pp. A vivid, well-written life of the African American leader. (Rev: SLJ 2/04) [921]

13303 Myers, Walter Dean. *Malcolm X: A Fire Burning Brightly* (3–6). Illus. 2000, HarperCollins LB $15.89 (0-06-027708-4). 32pp. Using many quotes from Malcolm X, this biography focuses on the inner conflicts that plagued this amazing leader. (Rev: BCCB 4/00; BL 2/15/00; HB 5–6/00; HBG 10/00; SLJ 2/00) [921]

13304 Myers, Walter Dean. *Malcolm X: By Any Means Necessary* (5–8). Illus. 1993, Scholastic $13.95 (0-590-46484-1). 210pp. Malcolm X's life dealt with in four parts. (Rev: BCCB 3/93; SLJ 2/93) [921]

MARSHALL, THURGOOD

13305 Adler, David A. *A Picture Book of Thurgood Marshall* (3–4). Illus. by Robert Casilla. Series: Picture Book Biographies. 1997, Holiday House LB $16.95 (0-8234-1308-X). 32pp. The life of this Supreme Court justice is well re-created in simple language that chronicles his battles against segregation and discrimination. (Rev: BL 11/15/97; HBG 3/98; SLJ 1/98) [921]

13306 Carpenter, Eric. *Young Thurgood Marshall: Fighter for Equality* (2–4). Illus. Series: Troll First Start. 1996, Troll paper $3.50 (0-8167-3771-1). 32pp. A beginning biography that stresses the childhood and early influences as well as the adult accomplishments of this Supreme Court justice. (Rev: BL 2/15/96) [921]

13307 Frost, Helen. *Thurgood Marshall* (K–2). Illus. Series: Famous Americans. 2003, Capstone LB $14.60 (0-7368-1643-7). 24pp. This brief biography of Thurgood Marshall introduces young readers to the life and career of the African American attorney who helped bring an end to school segregation and was later appointed to the U.S. Supreme Court. (Rev: HBG 10/03; SLJ 11/03) [347.73]

13308 Kallen, Stuart A. *Thurgood Marshall: A Dream of Justice for All* (3–5). Illus. Series: I Have a Dream. 1993, ABDO LB $15.98 (1-56239-258-1). 40pp. The story of the first African American to serve on the Supreme Court and his contributions to the struggle for civil rights. (Rev: BL 2/1/94) [921]

13309 Prentzas, G. S. *Thurgood Marshall: Champion of Justice* (4–8). Illus. Series: Junior World Biography. 1993, Chelsea LB $15.95 (0-7910-1769-9); paper $4.95 (0-7910-1969-1). 79pp. An interesting biography of Thurgood Marshall that touches on his civil rights work but focuses on his years as a Supreme Court justice. (Rev: SLJ 11/93) [921]

13310 Williams, Carla. *Thurgood Marshall: 1908–1993* (4–6). Series: Journey to Freedom: The African American Library. 2001, Child's World LB $17.95 (1-56766-924-7). 40pp. The story of the noted liberal black Supreme Court justice who was a civil rights advocate particularly in the fight to end school segregation. (Rev: BL 12/15/01; HBG 3/02; SLJ 1/02) [921]

MASON, BIDDY

13311 Ferris, Jeri Chase. *With Open Hands: A Story About Biddy Mason* (4–6). Illus. by Ralph L. Ramstad. 1999, Carolrhoda LB $21.27 (1-57505-330-6). 64pp. The inspiring story of the woman, born a slave, who accompanied her Mormon master and his family to Utah where she later became a midwife, a wealthy landowner, and a philanthropist. (Rev: BL 2/1/99; HBG 10/99; SLJ 5/99) [921]

MATZELIGER, JAN

13312 Mitchell, Barbara. *Shoes for Everyone: A Story About Jan Matzeliger* (3–5). Illus. 1986, Carolrhoda LB $21.27 (0-87614-290-0); Lerner paper $5.95 (0-87614-473-3). 64pp. The life of the African American inventor who changed the industry with his shoe-lasting machine. (Rev: BCCB 7–8/86; BL 8/86; SLJ 9/86) [921]

MEREDITH, JAMES

13313 Elish, Dan. *James Meredith and School Desegregation* (3–5). Illus. Series: Gateway Civil Rights. 1994, Millbrook LB $20.90 (1-56294-379-0). 32pp. The biography of the young African American man who was a pioneer in integrating institutions of higher education in Mississippi. (Rev: BL 4/15/94; SLJ 5/94) [921]

PARKS, ROSA

13314 Adler, David A. *A Picture Book of Rosa Parks* (2–4). Illus. by Robert Casilla. Series: Picture Book Biographies. 1993, Holiday House LB $16.95 (0-8234-1041-2). 30pp. The life story of the civil rights leader who refused to give up her bus seat to a white passenger. (Rev: BL 10/15/93; SLJ 12/93) [921]

13315 Benjamin, Anne. *Young Rosa Parks: Civil Rights Heroine* (2–4). Illus. Series: First Start Biography. 1996, Troll paper $3.50 (0-8167-3775-4). 32pp. Attractive color illustrations are included in this account of the life of a civil rights activist that emphasizes her childhood. (Rev: BL 2/15/96) [921]

13316 Davis, Kenneth C. *Don't Know Much About Rosa Parks* (4–7). Illus. by Sergio Martinez. Series: Don't Know Much About. 2005, HarperCollins LB $15.89 (0-06-028819-1); paper $4.99 (0-06-442126-0). 128pp. A question-and-answer format, interesting sidebars, and news photographs enliven this profile of Parks, which emphasizes her long-term commitment to civil rights. (Rev: BL 2/1/05) [323]

13317 Dubois, Murel L. *Rosa Parks* (2–4). Illus. Series: Photo-Illustrated Biographies. 2003, Capstone LB $18.60 (0-7368-1607-0). 24pp. A useful introduction to Rosa Parks and her pivotal role in the American civil rights movement. (Rev: HBG 10/03; SLJ 1/04)

13318 Fine, Edith Hope. *Rosa Parks: Meet a Civil Rights Hero* (3–4). Illus. Series: Meeting Famous People. 2004, Enslow LB $17.95 (0-7660-2099-1). 32pp. The story of Rosa Parks and her role in the struggle for civil rights is recounted in this brief but effective biography. (Rev: BL 2/15/04) [323]

13319 Giovanni, Nikki. *Rosa* (3–5). Illus. by Bryan Collier. 2005, Holt $16.95 (0-8050-7106-7). 40pp. This compelling picture-book biography brings Rosa and her reluctance to accept the status quo into new focus. (Rev: BL 6/1–15/05) [323]

13320 Greenfield, Eloise. *Rosa Parks* (2–4). Illus. by Eric Marlow. 1996, HarperCollins LB $14.89 (0-06-027110-8); paper $4.25 (0-06-442025-6). 40pp. A convincing sketch of the woman whose brave stand precipitated the Montgomery bus strike and her ensuing involvement with the civil rights struggle. [921]

13321 Holland, Gini. *Rosa Parks* (2–4). Illus. by David Price. Series: First Biographies. 1997, Raintree LB $24.26 (0-8172-4451-4). 32pp. A simple account of Rosa Parks's life, covering her child-

hood, civil rights work, imprisonment, and release. (Rev: SLJ 2/98) [921]

13322 Klingel, Cynthia, and Robert B. Noyed. *Rosa Parks* (K–2). Series: Wonder Books. 2001, Child's World LB $21.36 (1-56766-951-4). 24pp. A basic introduction for beginning readers that explains complex concepts in simple vocabulary. (Rev: HBG 3/02; SLJ 2/02) [921]

13323 McLeese, Don. *Rosa Parks* (2–5). Series: Equal Rights Leaders. 2002, Rourke LB $19.27 (1-58952-287-7). 24pp. Simple text and well-chosen illustrations tell the story of Parks's life, with good coverage of her youth and education. (Rev: SLJ 1/03) [323]

13324 Parks, Rosa, and Jim Haskins. *I Am Rosa Parks* (2–4). Illus. Series: Dial Easy-to-Read. 1997, Dial $13.99 (0-8037-1206-5). 48pp. An easy-to-read version of the civil rights leader's autobiography that retains its message and honesty. (Rev: BCCB 6/97; BL 5/1/97; HB 5–6/97; SLJ 5/97) [921]

13325 Ringgold, Faith. *If a Bus Could Talk: The Story of Rosa Parks* (K–4). Illus. 1999, Simon & Schuster $16.00 (0-689-81892-0). 32pp. A picture-book biography that combines elements of fantasy with the true story of Rosa Parks, often called the mother of the Civil Rights movement. (Rev: BCCB 1/00; BL 1/1–15/00; HBG 3/00; SLJ 1/00) [921]

13326 Summer, L. S. *Rosa Parks* (4–6). Series: Journey to Freedom. 1999, Child's World LB $16.95 (1-56766-622-1). 32pp. A biography that pays tribute to the gallant African American who started an amazing chain of events in 1955 when she refused to give up her bus seat to a white person in Montgomery, Alabama. (Rev: BL 10/15/99; HBG 3/00) [921]

RANDOLPH, A. PHILIP

13327 Cwiklik, Robert. *A. Philip Randolph and the Labor Movement* (3–5). Series: Gateway Civil Rights. 1993, Millbrook LB $20.90 (1-56294-326-X). 32pp. The story of the African American who organized the sleeping-car porters into a union and later directed a march on Washington, D.C., in 1941, to protest unfair labor practices. (Rev: BL 10/1/93; SLJ 10/93) [921]

13328 Hanley, Sally. *A. Philip Randolph* (5–9). 1988, Chelsea LB $19.95 (1-55546-607-9); paper $8.95 (0-7910-0222-5). 112pp. A life of the African American labor leader who founded the Brotherhood of Sleeping Car Porters. (Rev: BL 10/1/88; BR 1–2/89) [921]

TAYLOR, MARSHALL B.

13329 Cline-Ransome, Lesa. *Major Taylor, Champion Cyclist* (2–4). Illus. by James E. Ransome. 2004, Simon & Schuster $16.95 (0-689-83159-5). 40pp. Prejudice is a theme throughout this biography of the African American cyclist who won the world championship in 1899. (Rev: BL 2/15/04; SLJ 2/04) [796.2]

13330 Scioscia, Mary. *Bicycle Rider* (2–5). Illus. by Ed Young. 1983, HarperCollins paper $5.95 (0-06-

443295-5). 48pp. The fictionalized biography of the African American man who at one time was the fastest bicyclist in the world.

TAYLOR, SUSIE KING

13331 Jordan, Denise. *Susie King Taylor: Destined to Be Free* (3–5). Illus. by Higgins Bond. 1994, Just Us paper $5.00 (0-940975-50-5). 42pp. The story of the freed slave who, after the Civil War, became a teacher of African American children and adults and wrote an account of her life. (Rev: SLJ 7/95) [921]

TERRELL, MARY CHURCH

13332 Fradin, Dennis Brindell, and Judith Bloom Fradin. *Fight On! Mary Church Terrell's Battle for Integration* (5–9). Illus. 2003, Clarion $17.00 (0-618-13349-6). 192pp. Terrell's efforts to end discrimination are detailed in a readable, large-format biography that includes primary sources and lots of illustrations. (Rev: BL 6/1–15/03; HB 7–8/03; HBG 10/03; SLJ 5/03*) [323]

13333 Lommel, Cookie. *Mary Church Terrell: Speaking Out for Civil Rights* (4–7). Series: African-American Biographies. 2003, Enslow LB $20.95 (0-7660-2116-5). 112pp. This interesting account of Terrell's life and her passion for education and activism contains many black-and-white photographs. (Rev: HBG 4/04; SLJ 10/03) [323]

13334 McKissack, Patricia, and Fredrick McKissack. *Mary Church Terrell: Leader for Equality*. Rev. ed. (2–4). Illus. Series: Great African Americans. 2002, Enslow LB $14.95 (0-7660-1697-8). 32pp. An updated version of a previously released biography about the 19th-century activist, including archival photographs and Web site information. (Rev: BL 2/15/02; HBG 10/02; SLJ 5/02) [323]

13335 Swain, Gwenyth. *Civil Rights Pioneer: A Story About Mary Church Terrell* (3–6). Illus. 1999, Lerner $21.27 (1-57505-355-1). 64pp. A straightforward biography of the well-educated African American woman who devoted her life to fighting for civil rights. (Rev: BL 1/1–15/00; HBG 3/00; SLJ 2/00) [921]

TILLAGE, LEON

13336 Tillage, Leon W. *Leon's Story* (4–9). Illus. 1997, Farrar $15.00 (0-374-34379-9). An autobiographical account of growing up African American and poor in the segregated South and of participating in the civil rights movement. (Rev: BL 10/1/97*; BR 5–6/98; HB 11–12/97; HBG 3/98; SLJ 12/97) [975.6]

TRUTH, SOJOURNER

13337 Adler, David A. *A Picture Book of Sojourner Truth* (2–4). Illus. by Gershom Griffith. Series: Picture Book Biographies. 1994, Holiday House LB $16.95 (0-8234-1072-2). In an easily read format, the life and works of Sojourner Truth are introduced. (Rev: SLJ 6/94) [921]

13338 Bernard, Catherine. *Sojourner Truth: Abolitionist and Women's Rights Activist* (5–8). Series: Historical American Biographies. 2001, Enslow LB $20.95 (0-7660-1257-3). 112pp. The life story of the freed slave who traveled throughout the North preaching emancipation and women's rights before the Civil War. (Rev: BL 4/15/01; HBG 10/01) [921]

13339 Butler, Mary G. *Sojourner Truth: From Slave to Activist for Freedom* (4–8). Series: Library of American Lives and Times. 2003, Rosen LB $31.95 (0-8239-5736-5). 112pp. A forerunner of the modern civil rights movement, Sojourner Truth rose from slavery to become a crusader for good race relations and women's rights. (Rev: BL 6/1–15/03; SLJ 5/03) [921]

13340 Collins, Kathleen. *Sojourner Truth: Equal Rights Advocate* (2–4). Illus. Series: Primary Sources of Famous People in American History. 2004, Rosen LB $21.25 (0-8239-4121-3). 32pp. Primary sources — including maps and paintings — add to this simple account of Truth's life. [921]

13341 Ferris, Jeri. *Walking the Road to Freedom: A Story About Sojourner Truth* (3–6). Illus. 1988, Carolrhoda LB $21.27 (0-87614-318-4); Lerner paper $5.95 (0-87614-505-5). 64pp. The story of the woman born into slavery who vowed to travel the land singing of its evils. (Rev: BL 3/1/88; SLJ 3/88)

13342 Leebrick, Kristal. *Sojourner Truth* (4–6). Illus. Series: Let Freedom Ring. 2002, Capstone LB $16.95 (0-7368-1090-0). 48pp. An accessible account of Truth's life and influence on others, with sidebar features, maps, reproductions, quotations from primary sources, and a timeline. (Rev: HBG 3/03; SLJ 8/02) [921]

13343 Macht, Norman L. *Sojourner Truth* (4–7). Illus. Series: Junior World Biography. 1992, Chelsea LB $18.65 (0-7910-1754-0). 80pp. The story of the freed slave who traveled through the North preaching emancipation and women's rights. (Rev: BL 10/1/92; SLJ 12/92) [921]

13344 McKissack, Patricia, and Fredrick McKissack. *Sojourner Truth: A Voice for Freedom* (2–4). Series: Great African Americans. 2002, Enslow LB $14.95 (0-7660-1693-5). 32pp. A simple biography of the black American evangelist and reformer who gained fame as a preacher and fighter for women's suffrage. (Rev: BL 7/02) [921]

13345 McKissack, Patricia, and Fredrick McKissack. *Sojourner Truth: Ain't I a Woman?* (5–8). 1992, Scholastic paper $13.95 (0-590-44690-8). Drawing on the 1850 autobiography *Narrative of Sojourner Truth: A Northern Slave,* the authors integrate her personal story with a history of slavery, resistance, and abolitionism. (Rev: BL 11/15/92; SLJ 2/93) [921]

13346 Mattern, Joanne. *Sojourner Truth: Early Abolitionist* (1–3). Illus. Series: Women Who Shaped History. 2003, Rosen LB $17.25 (0-8239-6502-3). 24pp. The life of Sojourner Truth, for new readers. (Rev: BL 2/15/03) [305.5]

13347 Rockwell, Anne. *Only Passing Through* (4–8). Illus. 2000, Knopf $16.95 (0-679-89186-2). 32pp. A moving picture-book biography of Sojourner Truth, who was a pioneer in the struggle for racial equality and devoted her life to the abolitionist movement. (Rev: BCCB 1/01; BL 11/15/00; HB 11–12/00; HBG 3/01; SLJ 12/00) [921]

13348 Roop, Peter, and Connie Roop. *Sojourner Truth* (3–5). Illus. Series: In Their Own Words. 2003, Scholastic paper $4.50 (0-439-26323-9). 128pp. A simply written account of the former slave who became an abolitionist, drawing from Truth's own words. (Rev: BL 2/15/03; SLJ 7/03) [305.5]

13349 Soinale, Laura. *Sojourner Truth* (4–6). Series: Journey to Freedom. 1999, Child's World LB $16.95 (1-56766-623-X). 32pp. The story of the African American woman, born a slave in New York State and freed in 1827, who became an early abolitionist and inspiring orator. (Rev: BL 10/15/99; HBG 3/00) [921]

TUBMAN, HARRIET

13350 Adler, David A. *A Picture Book of Harriet Tubman* (2–4). Illus. by Samuel Byrd. Series: Picture Book Biographies. 1992, Holiday House LB $16.95 (0-8234-0926-0). 32pp. Easy-to-read text describes the life of this famous American who helped slaves gain freedom. (Rev: BCCB 7–8/92; BL 6/15/92; SLJ 6/92) [921]

13351 Burns, Bree. *Harriet Tubman* (4–7). Illus. Series: Junior World Biography. 1992, Chelsea LB $18.65 (0-7910-1751-6). 80pp. This is a straightforward account of the escaped slave who helped free more than 300 slaves via the Underground Railroad. (Rev: BL 10/1/92; SLJ 12/92) [921]

13352 Carlson, Judy. *Harriet Tubman: Call to Freedom* (5–8). 1989, Ballantine paper $5.99 (0-449-90376-1). A biography that is a lively account of the early fighter against slavery. (Rev: BL 12/15/89; BR 3–4/90; SLJ 2/90) [921]

13353 Ferris, Jeri. *Go Free or Die: A Story About Harriet Tubman* (3–6). Illus. 1988, Carolrhoda LB $21.27 (0-87614-317-6); Lerner paper $5.95 (0-87614-504-7). 64pp. The story of the former slave and her fight to rid the country of slavery. (Rev: BL 3/1/88; SLJ 3/88) [921]

13354 Gayle, Sharon. *Harriet Tubman and the Freedom Train* (1–3). Illus. by Felicia Marshall. Series: Ready-to-Read Stories of Famous Americans. 2003, Simon & Schuster LB $11.89 (0-689-85481-1); paper $3.99 (0-689-85480-3). 32pp. A fictionalized account of the former slave's efforts to free others. (Rev: BL 2/15/03; HBG 10/03; SLJ 3/03) [973.7]

13355 Klingel, Cynthia. *Harriet Tubman: Abolitionist and Underground Railroad Conductor* (3–6). Series: Our People. 2003, Child's World LB $27.07 (1-59296-004-9). 32pp. An interesting profile of Tubman and her anti-slavery activities. (Rev: BL 1/1–15/04; SLJ 4/04)

13356 Kulling, Monica. *Escape North! The Story of Harriet Tubman* (2–4). Illus. by Teresa Flavin. Series: Step into Reading. 2000, Random $11.99 (0-375-90154-X). A book for beginning readers that tells the life story of Harriet Tubman and re-creates one of her journeys on the Underground Railroad. (Rev: BL 2/15/01; HBG 10/01) [921]

13357 Mosher, Kiki. *Learning About Bravery from the Life of Harriet Tubman* (2–5). Illus. Series: A Character Building Book. 1996, Rosen LB $15.93 (0-8239-2424-6). 24pp. This short biography shows how the element of courage was paramount in the life of this leader of the Underground Railroad. (Rev: BL 10/15/96; SLJ 1/97) [921]

13358 Nielsen, Nancy L. *Harriet Tubman* (4–6). Illus. Series: Let Freedom Ring. 2002, Capstone LB $16.95 (0-7368-1087-0). 48pp. An accessible account of Tubman's life and influence on others, with sidebar features, maps, reproductions, quotations from primary sources, and a timeline. (Rev: HBG 3/03; SLJ 8/02) [921]

13359 Rowley, John. *Harriet Tubman* (2–3). Illus. Series: Lives and Times. 1997, Heinemann $19.92 (1-57572-558-4). 24pp. A simple picture-book biography that talks about slavery and tells of the life, courage, and endurance of this leader on the Underground Railroad. (Rev: BL 3/15/98; SLJ 6/98) [921]

13360 Schraff, Anne. *Harriet Tubman: Moses of the Underground Railroad* (4–8). Series: African-American Biographies. 2001, Enslow LB $20.95 (0-7660-1548-3). 128pp. This is an absorbing account of the life of the Underground Railroad leader that covers her work as a nurse, a scout, and a spy. (Rev: HBG 3/02; SLJ 10/01) [921]

13361 Sullivan, George. *Harriet Tubman* (3–5). Series: In Their Own Words. 2002, Scholastic $12.95 (0-439-32667-2); paper $4.50 (0-439-16584-9). 128pp. Using original sources including letters and autobiographical writings, the life of Harriet Tubman and her role in the Underground Railroad are re-created. (Rev: BL 8/02; HBG 10/02; SLJ 11/02) [921]

13362 Taylor, M. W. *Harriet Tubman* (5–8). Illus. Series: Black Americans of Achievement. 1990, Chelsea LB $21.95 (1-55546-612-5). 111pp. The story of the famous conductor on the Underground Railroad. (Rev: SLJ 1/91) [921]

13363 Troy, Don. *Harriet Ross Tubman* (4–6). Series: Journey to Freedom. 1999, Child's World LB $16.95 (1-56766-568-3). 40pp. The life of a gallant, energetic former slave and abolitionist who is best remembered for her work with the Underground Railroad. (Rev: BL 7/99; HBG 10/99; SLJ 7/99) [921]

TURNER, NAT

13364 Bagley, Katie. *Nat Turner: Rebellious Slave* (3–5). Illus. Series: Let Freedom Ring. 2003, Capstone LB $18.60 (0-7368-1555-4). 48pp. This absorbing biography tells how the slave, convinced that God wanted him to free himself and others in bondage, led a bloody but ultimately unsuccessful slave revolt in 1830s Virginia. (Rev: HBG 10/03; SLJ 9/03)

13365 Hendrickson, Ann-Marie. *Nat Turner: Rebel Slave* (4–7). Illus. Series: Junior World Biography. 1995, Chelsea LB $18.65 (0-7910-2386-9). 77pp. An attractive biography of this slave who led a revolution and became a symbol of heroism for his people. (Rev: BL 10/15/95) [921]

13366 Neshama, Rivvy. *Nat Turner and the Virginia Slave Revolt* (4–6). Series: Journey to Freedom. 2000, Child's World LB $25.64 (1-56766-744-9). 40pp. The story of the charismatic slave preacher who was hanged for his part in the slave revolt of 1831. (Rev: BL 11/15/00; HBG 3/01; SLJ 3/01) [921]

WALKER, MAGGIE

13367 Branch, Muriel M., and Dorothy M. Rice. *Pennies to Dollars: The Story of Maggie Lena Walker* (4–8). 1997, Linnet LB $19.50 (0-208-02453-0); paper $13.95 (0-208-02455-7). Maggie Walker, the daughter of a former slave, helped African Americans through her financial schemes, including the founding of the Penny Savings Bank. (Rev: BL 11/1/97; SLJ 10/97) [921]

WASHINGTON, BOOKER T.

13368 Amper, Thomas. *Booker T. Washington* (2–5). Illus. 1998, Carolrhoda $18.60 (1-57505-094-3). 48pp. The inspiring story of the young Booker T. Washington and his determination to receive an education in spite of his race and his extreme poverty. (Rev: BL 11/15/98; HBG 3/99; SLJ 11/98) [921]

13369 McKissack, Patricia, and Fredrick McKissack. *Booker T. Washington: Leader and Educator* (2–4). Illus. Series: Great African Americans. 2001, Enslow LB $14.95 (0-7660-1679-X). 32pp. Updated artwork gives this previously published biography of former slave and educator Booker T. Washington a new look. (Rev: BL 1/1–15/02; HBG 3/02) [370]

13370 Troy, Don. *Booker T. Washington* (4–6). Illus. Series: Journey to Freedom. 1999, Child's World LB $16.95 (1-56766-556-X). 40pp. The story of the famous African American leader who was born a slave in Virginia and became a prominent educational and political leader. (Rev: BL 5/1/99; HBG 10/99) [921]

WATTS, J. C.

13371 Lutz, Norma Jean. *J. C. Watts* (4–7). Series: Black Americans of Achievement. 2000, Chelsea $21.95 (0-7910-5338-5). 110pp. The story of a former Oklahoma University football player who entered politics and was first elected to the House of Representatives in 1994. (Rev: BL 6/1–15/00; HBG 10/00) [921]

WELLS-BARNETT, IDA B.

13372 Freedman, Suzanne. *Ida B. Wells-Barnett and the Anti-Lynching Crusade* (3–5). Illus. Series: Gateway Civil Rights. 1994, Millbrook LB $20.90 (1-56294-377-4). 32pp. The biography of the African American journalist who fought for civil rights and justice in the South. (Rev: BL 4/15/94; SLJ 5/94) [921]

13373 McKissack, Patricia, and Fredrick McKissack. *Ida B. Wells-Barnett: A Voice Against Violence* (2–4). Illus. Series: Great African Americans. 1991, Enslow LB $14.95 (0-89490-301-2). 32pp. A sim-

ple biography of the founder of the NAACP. (Rev: SLJ 11/91) [921]

WELLS, IDA B.

13374 Fradin, Dennis B., and Judith B. Fradin. *Ida B. Wells: Mother of the Civil Rights Movement* (5–10). 2000, Clarion $18.00 (0-395-89898-6). 178pp. An inspiring biography of the African American who was born a slave and went on to become a school teacher, journalist, and an activist who fought for black women's right to vote and helped found the NAACP. (Rev: BL 2/15/00; HB 5–6/00; HBG 10/00; SLJ 4/00*) [921]

13375 Welch, Catherine A. *Ida B. Wells-Barnett: Powerhouse with a Pen* (5–8). Illus. Series: Trailblazer Biographies. 2000, Carolrhoda LB $30.35 (1-57505-352-7). 104pp. This book introduces Wells-Barnett, who was born a slave and became a powerful journalist and activist as well as a spokesperson for all African Americans. (Rev: BL 6/1–15/00; HBG 10/00; SLJ 7/00) [921]

WHITE, WALTER

13376 Jakoubek, Robert E. *Walter White and the Power of Organized Protest* (3–5). Illus. Series: Gateway Civil Rights. 1994, Millbrook LB $20.90 (1-56294-378-2). 32pp. Background material on the NAACP is given through the life story of one of its leaders, Walter White. (Rev: BL 4/15/94; SLJ 6/94) [921]

WOODSON, CARTER G.

13377 Haskins, Jim, and Kathleen Benson. *Carter G. Woodson: The Man Who Put "Black" in American History* (4–6). Illus. 2000, Millbrook LB $24.90 (0-7613-1264-1). 48pp. This biography examines the obstacles and triumphs experienced by the man who created the Association for the Study of Negro Life and History in 1915 and Negro History Week in 1926. (Rev: BL 4/1/00; HBG 10/00; SLJ 7/00) [921]

13378 McKissack, Patricia, and Fredrick McKissack. *Carter G. Woodson: The Father of Black History* (2–4). Series: Great African Americans. 2002, Enslow LB $14.95 (0-7660-1698-6). 32pp. A beginning chapter book that covers the life of the black historian who founded the Association for the Study of Negro Life and History in 1915 and began its *Journal of Negro History*. (Rev: BL 7/02) [921]

Hispanic Americans

ANTONNETTY, EVELINA LOPEZ

13379 Mohr, Nicholasa. *All for the Better: A Story of El Barrio* (2–5). Illus. by Rudy Gutierrez. 1993, Raintree LB $27.12 (0-8114-7220-5). 56pp. The story of Evelina Lopez Antonnetty and the difference she made in Spanish Harlem, New York. (Rev: BCCB 7–8/93; SLJ 5/93) [921]

CHAVEZ, CESAR

13380 Brown, Jonatha A. *Cesar Chavez* (5–8). Series: Trailblazers of the Modern World. 2004, World Almanac LB $29.27 (0-8368-5097-1). 48pp. Report writers will find lots of suitable information in this work that covers Chavez's life and accomplishments. (Rev: SLJ 7/04) [921]

13381 Collins, David R. *Farmworker's Friend: The Story of Cesar Chavez* (3–5). Illus. 1996, Carolrhoda LB $23.93 (0-87614-982-4). 80pp. The story of this champion of poor farm workers is retold from a variety of original sources. (Rev: BL 12/15/96) [921]

13382 Griswold del Castillo, Richard. *César Chávez: The Struggle for Justice / La lucha por la justicia* (2–4). Illus. by Anthony Accardo. 2002, Arte Publico $14.95 (1-55885-324-3). 32pp. Bilingual text and full-page paintings bring Mexican American labor leader César Chávez to life. (Rev: BL 12/15/02) [331.88]

13383 Krull, Kathleen. *Harvesting Hope: The Story of Cesar Chavez* (2–4). Illus. by Yuyi Morales. 2003, Harcourt $17.00 (0-15-201437-3). 48pp. This inspiring picture-book biography chronicles Chavez's rise from the ranks of migrant workers to a leadership position in the American labor movement. (Rev: BL 6/1–15/03; HB 7–8/03; HBG 10/03; SLJ 6/03) [921]

13384 McLeese, Don. *Cesar E. Chavez* (2–5). 2002, Rourke LB $19.27 (1-58952-285-0). 24pp. Simple text and well-chosen illustrations tell the story of Chavez's life, with good coverage of his youth, education, and early years working in the fields. (Rev: SLJ 1/03) [331.88]

13385 Tracy, Kathleen. *Cesar Chavez* (5–7). Series: Latinos in American History. 2003, Mitchell Lane LB $19.95 (1-58415-224-9). 48pp. This biography covers the life and accomplishments of the Mexican American labor leader who founded the United Farm Workers. (Rev: BL 1/1–15/04) [921]

13386 Wadsworth, Ginger. *Cesar Chavez* (2–4). Illus. by Mark Schroeder. Series: On My Own Biography. 2005, Lerner LB $23.93 (1-57505-652-6); paper $5.95 (1-57505-764-6). 48pp. Chavez's own story and the plight of migrant farm workers are intertwined in this picture-book biography. (Rev: BL 5/1/05) [921]

13387 Zannos, Susan. *Cesar Chavez* (3–6). Series: Real-Life Reader Biographies. 1998, Mitchell Lane LB $15.95 (1-883845-71-8). 32pp. A life of this inspired Latino labor leader whose hard work and accomplishments are still influential. (Rev: SLJ 2/99) [921]

CISNEROS, HENRY

13388 Martinez, Elizabeth Coonrod. *Henry Cisneros: Mexican-American Leader* (3–6). Illus. Series: Hispanic Heritage. 1993, Millbrook LB $19.90 (1-56294-368-5). 32pp. A biography of the Mexican American who was once a mayor and is still an important politician. (Rev: BL 11/15/93) [921]

DE ZAVALA, LORENZO

13389 Tracy, Kathleen. *Lorenzo de Zavala* (5–7). Series: Latinos in American History. 2002, Mitchell Lane LB $19.95 (1-58415-154-4). 48pp. The biography of the 19th-century Mexican who became vice president of the Republic of Texas and was one of the signers of its constitution. (Rev: BL 2/15/03; HBG 10/03) [921]

GAC-ARTIGAS, ALEJANDRO

13390 Gac-Artigas, Alejandro. *Yo, Alejandro* (5–7). 2000, Ediciones Nuevo Espacio paper $11.95 (1-930879-21-0). 106pp. This is a collection of personal essays written by the author before his 12th birthday about his life in Puerto Rico, the state of Georgia, and later New York City. (Rev: BL 3/1/01) [921]

GALAN, NELY

13391 Rodriguez, Janel. *Nely Galan* (4–8). Illus. Series: Contemporary Hispanic Americans. 1997, Raintree LB $17.98 (0-8172-3991-X). 48pp. The life of this contemporary Hispanic American who, as a Hollywood producer, is responsible for developing TV and video projects for other Hispanic Americans. (Rev: BL 4/15/97) [921]

HUERTA, DOLORES

13392 Murcia, Rebecca Thatcher. *Dolores Huerta* (5–7). Series: Latinos in American History. 2002, Mitchell Lane LB $19.95 (1-58415-155-2). 48pp. The story of the gallant woman who worked along with Cesar Chavez to protect the rights of farm workers. (Rev: BL 2/15/03; HBG 10/03) [921]

13393 Perez, Frank. *Dolores Huerta* (4–8). Illus. Series: Contemporary Hispanic Americans. 1995, Raintree LB $28.80 (0-8172-3981-2). The accomplishments of Dolores Huerta, a Hispanic American who cofounded the United Farm Workers, are described in this informative biography. (Rev: BL 3/15/96) [921]

IDAR, JOVITA

13394 Gibson, Karen Bush. *Jovita Idar* (5–7). Series: Latinos in American History. 2002, Mitchell Lane LB $19.95 (1-58415-151-X). 48pp. The inspiring story of the Latin American woman who started San Antonio's first free kindergarten and who founded the League of Mexican American women in 1911 to educate poor children. (Rev: BL 2/15/03; HBG 10/03) [921]

MARIN, LUIS MUNOZ

13395 Bernier-Grand, Carmen T. *Poet and Politician of Puerto Rico: Don Luis Muñoz Marín* (5–8). 1995, Orchard LB $16.99 (0-531-08737-9). This story of the life of the man who helped make Puerto Rico a commonwealth also includes a history of the island. (Rev: BL 5/15/95; SLJ 4/95) [921]

13396 George, Linda, and Charles George. *Luis Munoz Marin: Father of Modern Puerto Rico* (3–5). Series: Community Builders. 1999, Children's Book Pr. LB $23.00 (0-516-21586-8). 48pp. An appealing and well-illustrated biography of the man who shaped the future of modern Puerto Rico. (Rev: BL 11/15/99) [921]

QUINTANILLA, GUADALUPE

13397 Wade, Mary D. *Guadalupe Quintanilla: Leader of the Hispanic Community* (4–8). Illus. Series: Multicultural Junior Biographies. 1995, Enslow LB $20.95 (0-89490-637-2). An inspiring story of a woman who once was considered mentally disabled and now is a leader in her Spanish American community. (Rev: BL 3/1/96; SLJ 2/96) [921]

SERRA, JUNÍPERO

13398 Dolan, Sean. *Junípero Serra* (5–9). Series: Hispanics of Achievement. 1991, Chelsea LB $21.95 (0-7910-1255-7). The story of the devoted Spanish Franciscan missionary who was responsible for founding the famous missions on the coast of California. (Rev: BL 11/1/91; SLJ 2/92) [921]

13399 Whiting, Jim. *Junípero José Serra* (5–7). Series: Latinos in American History. 2003, Mitchell Lane LB $19.95 (1-58415-187-0). 48pp. Profiles the monk who was responsible for founding nine California missions and converting thousands of Native Americans to Christianity. (Rev: BL 1/1–15/04; SLJ 3/00) [921]

VALLEJO, MARIANO GUADALUPE

13400 Tracy, Kathleen. *Mariano Guadalupe Vallejo* (5–7). Series: Latinos in American History. 2002, Mitchell Lane LB $19.95 (1-58415-152-8). 48pp. The story of the 19th-century military man who supported the U.S. annexation of California and later served in the state's first Senate. (Rev: BL 2/15/03; HBG 10/03) [921]

Historical Figures and Important Contemporary Americans

ADAMS, SAMUEL

13401 Adler, David A., and Michael S. Adler. *A Picture Book of Samuel Adams* (1–3). Illus. by Ronald Himler. Series: A Picture Book of. 2005, Holiday House $16.95 (0-8234-1846-4). 32pp. Historical details are woven into the succinct information on Adams's youth and achievements as an adult. (Rev: BL 6/1–15/05; SLJ 6/05) [973.3]

13402 Burgan, Michael. *Samuel Adams: Patriot and Statesman* (4–7). Illus. Series: Signature Lives (Revolutionary War Era). 2005, Compass Point LB $22.95 (0-7565-0823-1). 48pp. Profiles the man who played a key role in the tax rebellion and Boston Tea Party. [921]

13403 Fradin, Dennis B. *Samuel Adams: The Father of American Independence* (5–9). Illus. 1998, Houghton Mifflin $18.00 (0-395-82510-5). An attractive biography of the amazing Sam Adams, whom Jefferson called "the Man of the Revolution." (Rev: BCCB 7–8/98; BL 7/98; BR 11–12/98; SLJ 7/98) [921]

13404 Fritz, Jean. *Why Don't You Get a Horse, Sam Adams?* (3–5). Illus. by Trina S. Hyman. 1974, Penguin Putnam paper $5.99 (0-698-11416-7). 48pp. How Sam Adams was finally persuaded to ride a horse is told in this humorous re-creation of Revolutionary times.

ALBRIGHT, MADELEINE

13405 Blue, Rose, and Corinne J. Naden. *Madeleine Albright: U.S. Secretary of State* (3–5). Illus. 1998, Blackbirch LB $16.95 (1-56711-253-6). 64pp. The rise of this secretary of state is traced, along with a description of the job, the responsibilities, and its history. (Rev: BL 12/1/98; HBG 3/99) [921]

13406 Byman, Jeremy. *Madam Secretary: The Story of Madeleine Albright* (5–9). Series: Notable Americans. 1997, Morgan Reynolds LB $21.95 (1-883846-23-4). 96pp. The emphasis in this biography is on Albright's public life, first as adviser to various political figures, then as ambassador to the United Nations, and finally as secretary of state. (Rev: BL 12/15/97; SLJ 4/98) [921]

13407 Maass, Robert. *UN Ambassador: A Behind-the-Scenes Look at Madeleine Albright's World* (3–5). Illus. 1995, Walker LB $17.85 (0-8027-8356-2). 48pp. A biography of Madeleine Albright, who, at the time of writing, was U.S. ambassador to the United Nations. (Rev: BL 11/15/95; SLJ 11/95) [921]

ALLEN, ETHAN

13408 Aronson, Virginia. *Ethan Allen: Revolutionary Hero* (4–6). 2000, Chelsea LB $18.95 (0-7910-5974-X); paper $8.95 (0-7910-6132-9). 80pp. This introduction to the life of Ethan Allen presents both his triumphs and his failings. (Rev: SLJ 7/01) [973.3]

13409 Haugen, Brenda. *Ethan Allen: Green Mountain Rebel* (4–7). Illus. Series: Signature Lives (Revolutionary War Era). 2005, Compass Point LB $22.95 (0-7565-0824-X). 48pp. Traces the life of the man who, along with Benedict Arnold, led the Green Mountain Boys in capturing Fort Ticonderoga from the British. [921]

13410 Raabe, Emily. *Ethan Allen: The Green Mountain Boys and Vermont's Path to Statehood* (4–7). Series: Library of American Lives and Times. 2001, Rosen LB $23.95 (0-8239-5722-5). 112pp. Extraordinary illustrations and fine text tell the story of the controversial founder of Vermont who led the Green Mountain Boys in the capture of Fort Ticonderoga and Crown Point. (Rev: BL 10/15/01) [921]

ARNOLD, BENEDICT

13411 Dell, Pamela. *Benedict Arnold: From Patriot to Traitor* (4–7). Illus. Series: Signature Lives (Revolutionary War Era). 2005, Compass Point LB $22.95 (0-7565-0825-8). 48pp. A well-designed and informative profile of the man who betrayed his country. [921]

13412 Gaines, Ann Graham. *Benedict Arnold: Patriot or Traitor?* (5–8). Series: Historical American Biographies. 2001, Enslow LB $20.95 (0-7660-1393-6). 112pp. Many facets of the character of this controversial American are examined in this well-illustrated volume. (Rev: BL 4/15/01; HBG 10/01; SLJ 6/01) [921]

13413 Gregson, Susan R. *Benedict Arnold* (5–6). Series: Let Freedom Ring. 2001, Capstone LB $22.60 (0-7368-1032-3). 48pp. An introduction to Arnold's life and contributions, with discussion of the reasons why he became a traitor. (Rev: HBG 3/02; SLJ 4/02) [921]

13414 King, David C. *Benedict Arnold and the American Revolution* (5–9). Series: Notorious Americans and Their Times. 1998, Blackbirch LB $27.44 (1-56711-221-8). Benedict Arnold's life and military accomplishments are placed in the context of the period in which he lived and the conflicts he faced. (Rev: BL 12/15/98; HBG 3/99; SLJ 12/98) [921]

13415 Powell, Walter L. *Benedict Arnold: Revolutionary War Hero and Traitor* (5–8). Series: Library of American Lives and Times. 2004, Rosen LB $31.95 (0-8239-6627-5). 112pp. The life of Benedict Arnold, the American patriot who switched his allegiance to the British cause. (Rev: SLJ 7/04) [921]

ATTUCKS, CRISPUS

13416 Beier, Anne. *Crispus Attucks: Hero of the Boston Massacre* (2–4). Illus. Series: Primary Sources of Famous People in American History. 2004, Rosen LB $21.25 (0-8239-4106-X). 32pp. Primary sources — including maps and paintings — add to the simple narrative telling the story of the Boston Massacre and the controversial killing of Crispus Attucks. [921]

13417 Beier, Anne. *Crispus Attucks: Hero of the Boston Massacre / Heroe de la Masacre de Boston* (4–6). Trans. by Tomas Gonzalez. Series: Primary Sources of Famous People in American History. 2004, Rosen LB $21.25 (0-8239-4154-X). 32pp. A brief, solid, bilingual introduction to the former slave who died in the pre-Revolutionary Boston Massacre. (Rev: SLJ 9/04) [921]

AUSTIN, STEPHEN F.

13418 Haley, James L. *Stephen F. Austin and the Founding of Texas* (5–8). Series: The Library of American Lives and Times. 2003, Rosen LB $31.95 (0-8239-5738-1). 112pp. A concise biography of the pioneer who became one of the founders of Texas. (Rev: SLJ 5/03) [976.4]

BEAN, JUDGE ROY

13419 Green, Carl R., and William R. Sanford. *Judge Roy Bean* (4–6). Illus. Series: Outlaws and Lawmen. 1995, Enslow LB $16.95 (0-89490-591-0). 48pp. A biography of this colorful, many-sided character from the old Wild West. (Rev: SLJ 9/95) [921]

BILLY THE KID

13420 Bruns, Roger A. *Billy the Kid* (5–8). Series: Historical American Biographies. 2000, Enslow LB $20.95 (0-7660-1091-0). A well-researched and thoroughly documented biography of America's famous outlaw. (Rev: BL 1/1–15/00; HBG 10/00; SLJ 5/00) [921]

13421 Green, Carl R., and William R. Sanford. *Billy the Kid* (4–8). Illus. Series: Outlaws and Lawmen of the Wild West. 1992, Enslow LB $16.95 (0-89490-364-0). 48pp. The life story of the outlaw William H. Bonney, who lived from 1859 to 1881. (Rev: BL 7/92; SLJ 8/92) [921]

BLY, NELLIE

13422 Butcher, Nancy. *It Can't Be Done, Nellie Bly! A Reporter's Race Around the World* (2–5). Illus. by Jen L. Singh. 2003, Peachtree $12.95 (1-56145-289-0). The story of reporter Nellie Bly's attempt to beat the round-the-world journey of Jules Verne's fictional Phineas Fogg. (Rev: BL 3/1/04; HBG 4/04; SLJ 6/04) [921]

13423 Emerson, Kathy L. *Making Headlines: A Biography of Nellie Bly* (4–6). Illus. 1989, Macmillan LB $18.95 (0-87518-406-5). 112pp. The life of this journalist and outspoken reformer is presented. (Rev: BCCB 12/89; BL 7/89; SLJ 9/89) [921]

13424 Fredeen, Charles. *Nellie Bly: Daredevil Reporter* (5–9). Series: Lerner Biographies. 2000, Lerner LB $25.26 (0-8225-4956-5). 112pp. The story of the daring reporter who traveled around the world in 72 days and was a champion of the women's suffrage movement. (Rev: HBG 10/00; SLJ 3/00) [921]

13425 Kendall, Martha E. *Nellie Bly: Reporter for the World* (3–5). Illus. Series: Gateway Biographies. 1992, Millbrook LB $21.90 (1-56294-061-9); paper $8.95 (0-395-64538-7). 48pp. The life story of the famous woman journalist whose real name was Elizabeth Seaman. (Rev: BL 8/92; SLJ 11/92) [921]

13426 Krensky, Stephen. *Nellie Bly: A Name to Be Reckoned With* (3–4). Illus. by Rebecca Guay. Series: Milestone. 2003, Simon & Schuster paper $3.99 (0-689-85573-7). 80pp. This is an appealing biography of the pioneering woman journalist who made a 72-day trip around the world, with lots of vivid illustrations. (Rev: BL 6/1–15/03; HBG 4/04) [921]

13427 Peck, Ira, and Nellie Bly. *Nellie Bly's Book: Around the World in 72 Days* (5–10). 1998, Twenty-First Century $26.90 (0-7613-0971-3). 128pp. An abridged version of *New York World* reporter Nellie Bly's entertaining account of her trip around the world during the 1880s and her many interesting observations of the world at that time. (Rev: HBG 10/99; SLJ 4/99) [921]

BOOTH, EDWIN AND JOHN WILKES

13428 Giblin, James Cross. *Good Brother, Bad Brother: The Story of Edwin Booth and John Wilkes Booth* (5–8). Illus. 2005, Clarion $22.00 (0-618-09642-6). 256pp. In a compelling and highly readable narrative, Giblin reveals the alcoholism and depression that plagued the theatrical Booth family, the disagreement between the two brothers over the Civil War, and the effects of the assassination on Edwin's later life. (Rev: BL 5/1/05; SLJ 5/05) [792.02]

BOOTH, JOHN WILKES

13429 Otfinoski, Steven. *John Wilkes Booth and the Civil War* (5–9). Series: Notorious Americans and Their Times. 1998, Blackbirch LB $27.44 (1-56711-222-6). The colorful life and death of John Wilkes Booth, born into a theatrical family, who turned political over the slavery issue and plotted to kill President Lincoln. (Rev: BL 12/15/98; HBG 3/99; SLJ 12/98) [921]

BOWIE, JIM

13430 Edmondson, J. R. *Jim Bowie: Frontier Legend, Alamo Hero* (4–7). Series: Library of American Lives and Times. 2003, Rosen LB $31.95 (0-8239-5734-9). 112pp. As well as being a rogue, slave trader, and murderer, Jim Bowie was also a hero of the famous battle of the Alamo. (Rev: BL 6/1–15/03; SLJ 7/03) [921]

13431 Gaines, Ann Graham. *Jim Bowie* (5–8). Series: Historical American Biographies. 2000, Enslow LB $20.95 (0-7660-1253-0). A well-documented biography of Jim Bowie, a hero of the revolution in Texas who was best known for fighting in the battle of the Alamo. (Rev: BL 1/1–15/00; HBG 10/00; SLJ 5/00) [921]

BRADFORD, WILLIAM

13432 Doherty, Kieran. *William Bradford: Rock of Plymouth* (5–9). 1999, Twenty-First Century LB $24.90 (0-7613-1304-4). 192pp. Using Bradford's own writings and other contemporary accounts as sources, this is an objective biography of the man who was the governor of the Plymouth Plantation. (Rev: BL 12/1/99; HBG 3/00; SLJ 1/00) [921]

BRADLEY, BILL

13433 Andryszewski, Tricia. *Bill Bradley: Scholar, Athlete, Statesman* (4–6). Illus. Series: Gateway Biographies. 1999, Millbrook LB $21.90 (0-7613-1669-8). 48pp. Using material from Bill Bradley's autobiography, this account describes the life and struggles of the famous basketball star turned successful politician. (Rev: BL 11/15/99; HBG 3/00) [921]

13434 Buckley, James, Jr. *Bill Bradley* (5–8). Illus. Series: Basketball Hall of Famers. 2002, Rosen LB $29.25 (0-8239-3479-9). 112pp. An easy-to-read, detailed biography of the former athlete, with plenty of photographs. (Rev: BL 9/1/02) [921]

BRANDEIS, LOUIS

13435 Freedman, Suzanne. *Louis Brandeis* (4–9). Illus. Series: Justices of the Supreme Court. 1996, Enslow LB $20.95 (0-89490-678-X). A biography of the great justice who advocated many public causes and was known as the "people's attorney." (Rev: BL 8/96; SLJ 11/96) [921]

BROWN, JOHN

13436 Becker, Helaine. *John Brown* (4–7). Series: The Civil War. 2001, Gale LB $27.44 (1-56711-558-6). 104pp. Brown's life is detailed from childhood through his adult achievements, and is carefully placed in the context of the time and his family background. (Rev: HBG 3/02; SLJ 4/02) [921]

13437 Brackett, Virginia. *John Brown: Abolitionist* (3–5). Series: Famous Figures of the Civil War Era. 2001, Chelsea LB $20.85 (0-7910-6408-5). Told with many color illustrations and a vivid text, this is the story of the obsessive abolitionist who was hanged for treason in 1859. (Rev: BL 4/1/02; HBG 10/02; SLJ 5/02) [921]

13438 Streissguth, Thomas. *John Brown* (2–4). Illus. by Ralph L. Ramstad. Series: On My Own Biography. 1999, Carolrhoda LB $14.95 (1-57505-334-9). 48pp. This is a fine life story of the abolitionist, his beliefs and actions, plus a good look at the dispute over slavery before the Civil War. (Rev: HBG 3/00; SLJ 11/99) [921]

BURR, AARON

13439 Ingram, W. Scott. *Aaron Burr and the Young Nation* (5–8). Series: Major World Leaders. 2002, Chelsea $27.44 (1-56711-250-1). 112pp. The story of the controversial political leader who killed Alexander Hamilton in a duel and later was tried and found guilty of treason. (Rev: BL 1/1–15/03; SLJ 10/02) [921]

13440 Melton, Buckner F. *Aaron Burr: The Rise and Fall of an American Politician* (5–8). Series: Library of American Lives and Times. 2004, Rosen LB $31.95 (0-8239-6626-7). 112pp. This engaging biography chronicles the rise and fall of the Revolutionary War hero who was later branded a traitor. (Rev: SLJ 7/04) [921]

CALAMITY JANE

13441 Faber, Doris. *Calamity Jane: Her Life and Her Legend* (5–9). 1992, Houghton Mifflin $16.00 (0-395-56396-8). The author carefully distinguishes what is certain, what is possible, and what is blatantly untrue in the legend of Calamity Jane and her later show business career. (Rev: BL 8/92; SLJ 10/92) [921]

13442 Sanford, William R., and Carl R. Green. *Calamity Jane* (4–6). Illus. Series: Legendary Heroes of the Wild West. 1996, Enslow LB $16.95 (0-89490-647-X). 48pp. The life of the legendary Western belle is presented with historical photos. (Rev: BL 7/96; SLJ 7/96) [921]

CAMPBELL, BEN NIGHTHORSE

13443 Henry, Christopher. *Ben Nighthorse Campbell: Cheyenne Chief and U.S. Senator* (5–8). Illus. Series: North American Indians of Achievement. 1994, Chelsea $19.95 (0-7919-2046-0). The story of the Cheyenne leader who gained prominence not only among his own people but also in the U.S. Congress. (Rev: BL 6/1–15/93) [921]

CAPONE, AL

13444 King, David C. *Al Capone and the Roaring Twenties* (5–9). Illus. Series: Notorious Americans and Their Times. 1998, Blackbirch LB $27.44 (1-56711-218-8). 80pp. In this biography of the gangster, the reader also gets information on the Jazz Age, the Ku Klux Klan, and other personalities of the time, such as Earhart and Lindbergh. (Rev: BL 12/15/98; HBG 3/99; SLJ 12/98) [921]

CASSIDY, BUTCH

13445 Green, Carl R., and William R. Sanford. *Butch Cassidy* (4–8). Series: Outlaws and Lawmen of the Wild West. 1995, Enslow LB $16.95 (0-89490-587-2). 48pp. The Wild West is re-created in this brief account of the life of this colorful outlaw, whose death remains a mystery. (Rev: BL 6/1–15/95; SLJ 7/95) [921]

13446 Wukovits, John F. *Butch Cassidy* (4–7). Series: Legends of the West. 1997, Chelsea $18.65 (0-7910-3857-2). 64pp. This biography of Robert Leroy Parker, who is better known as Butch Cassidy, emphasizes the fact that he was a ruthless criminal and not the idealized character of the movies. (Rev: HBG 3/98; SLJ 4/98) [921]

CHAPMAN, JOHN

13447 Aliki. *The Story of Johnny Appleseed* (K–3). Illus. by author. 1971, Simon & Schuster paper $5.95 (0-671-66746-7). A picture story of the man who wandered through the Midwest spreading love and apple seeds.

13448 Hodges, Margaret. *The True Tale of Johnny Appleseed* (K–3). Illus. by Kimberly B. Root. 1997, Holiday House LB $16.95 (0-8234-1282-2). 32pp. A biography that tells about John Chapman's childhood in Massachusetts and his relocation in the West, where he was noted for planting and caring for apple trees. (Rev: BL 7/97; SLJ 9/97) [921]

13449 Kellogg, Steven. *Johnny Appleseed* (2–4). Illus. by author. 1988, Morrow $16.89 (0-688-06418-3). 48pp. The story of the famed John Chapman, who traveled the country in the 1700s spreading good cheer and apple seeds. (Rev: BCCB 11/88; BL 9/1/88; SLJ 10/88)

13450 Moses, Will. *Johnny Appleseed: The Story of a Legend* (4–6). Illus. 2001, Penguin Putnam $16.99 (0-399-23153-6). 32pp. This account of the life of Johnny Appleseed is enhanced by the author's folk-art paintings. (Rev: BL 9/1/01; HBG 3/02; SLJ 9/01) [634]

13451 Warrick, Karen Clemens. *John Chapman: The Legendary Johnny Appleseed* (5–8). Series: Historical American Biographies. 2001, Enslow LB $20.95 (0-7660-1443-6). 112pp. An engrossing, nicely illustrated portrait of the man who wandered the Midwest promoting apple cultivation. (Rev: BL 4/15/01; HBG 10/01; SLJ 4/01) [921]

CODY, BUFFALO BILL

13452 Sanford, William R., and Carl R. Green. *Buffalo Bill Cody: Showman of the Wild West* (4–6). Illus. Series: Legendary Heroes of the Wild West. 1996, Enslow LB $16.95 (0-89490-646-1). 48pp. The life of the Wild West hero in brief text and many black-and-white photos. (Rev: BL 7/96; SLJ 7/96) [921]

13453 Shields, Charles J. *Buffalo Bill Cody* (3–6). Series: Famous Figures of the American Frontier. 2001, Chelsea LB $19.75 (0-7910-6497-2); paper $8.95 (0-7910-6498-0). 64pp. An appealing account of Cody's life with black-and-white and full-color illustrations and handy fact boxes. (Rev: SLJ 3/02) [921]

13454 Spies, Karen B. *Buffalo Bill Cody: Western Legend* (5–8). Series: Historical American Biographies. 1998, Enslow LB $20.95 (0-7660-1015-5). An in-depth look at this legendary frontiersman and the Wild West show he founded. (Rev: BL 3/15/98; SLJ 5/98) [921]

COFFIN, LEVI

13455 Swain, Gwenyth. *President of the Underground Railroad: A Story About Levi Coffin* (3–6). Illus. by Ralph L. Ramstad. Series: Creative Minds Biographies. 2001, Carolrhoda LB $21.27 (1-57505-551-1); paper $5.95 (1-57505-552-X). 64pp. This is a readable account of the life of Levi Coffin, a Quaker from North Carolina who devoted time and money to helping slaves escape to freedom. (Rev: HBG 10/01; SLJ 7/01) [973.7]

CUSTER, GEORGE ARMSTRONG

13456 Anderson, Paul Christopher. *George Armstrong Custer: The Indian Wars and the Battle of the Little Big Horn* (4–8). Series: The Library of American Lives and Times. 2004, Rosen LB $31.95 (0-8239-6631-3). 112pp. The importance of understanding history is emphasized in this balanced and well-illustrated look at Custer's life and stance at Little Big Horn. (Rev: SLJ 7/04) [920]

13457 Kent, Zachary. *George Armstrong Custer* (5–8). Series: Historical American Biographies. 2000, Enslow LB $20.95 (0-7660-1255-7). Using extensive chapter notes, a glossary, bibliography, and index, this is a well-documented and objective assessment of Custer's life and deeds. (Rev: BL 1/1–15/00; HBG 10/00) [921]

13458 Link, Theodore. *George Armstrong Custer: General of the U. S. Calvary* (2–4). Illus. Series: Primary Sources of Famous People in American History. 2004, Rosen LB $21.25 (0-8239-4110-8). 32pp. Primary sources — including maps and paintings — add to the simple narrative telling the story of the general who lost to Sitting Bull at the Battle of Little Bighorn. [921]

DAVIS, JEFFERSON

13459 Burch, Joann J. *Jefferson Davis: President of the Confederacy* (5–8). Series: Historical American Biographies. 1998, Enslow LB $20.95 (0-7660-1064-3). Using personal documents and well-chosen illustrations, this lively biography describes Jefferson Davis's life as well as the causes and major events of the Civil War. (Rev: BL 10/15/98; SLJ 1/99) [921]

13460 Frazier, Joey. *Jefferson Davis: Confederate President* (3–5). Illus. 2001, Chelsea $18.95 (0-7910-6006-3); paper $8.95 (0-7910-6144-2). 80pp. A brief biography that covers Davis's life, with information on his education, his rise to become president of the Confederacy, and the problems of his administration. (Rev: BL 5/1/01; SLJ 9/01) [973.7]

13461 Ingram, W. Scott. *Jefferson Davis* (5–8). Series: Triangle Histories of the Civil War. 2002, Gale LB $27.44 (1-56711-565-9). 104pp. A useful account of Davis's life and career with a sidebar feature on the servant who perhaps was a spy. (Rev: SLJ 1/03) [921]

DOLE, BOB

13462 Lisandrelli, Elaine S. *Bob Dole, Legendary Senator* (4–6). Series: People to Know. 1997, Enslow LB $20.95 (0-89490-825-1). 128pp. An illustrated biography of this senator and unsuccessful presidential candidate. (Rev: BL 10/15/97; HBG 3/98) [921]

DOUGLAS, STEPHEN

13463 Bonner, Mike. *Stephen Douglas: Champion of the Union* (3–5). Series: Famous Figures of the Civil War Era. 2001, Chelsea LB $20.85 (0-7910-6402-6). The story of the American politician named the "Little Giant" who engaged in a famous series of debates with Lincoln but later became his staunch supporter. (Rev: BL 4/1/02; HBG 10/02; SLJ 5/02) [921]

EARP, WYATT

13464 Alagana, Magdalena. *Wyatt Earp: Lawman of the American West* (2–4). Illus. Series: Primary Sources of Famous People in American History. 2004, Rosen LB $21.25 (0-8239-4123-X). 32pp. Period photographs are used to illustrate this brief biography of the famous marshall. [921]

13465 Green, Carl R., and William R. Sanford. *Wyatt Earp* (4–8). Illus. Series: Outlaws and Lawmen of the Wild West. 1992, Enslow LB $16.95 (0-89490-367-5). 48pp. With maps and authentic illustrations, this biography tells the story of the deputy marshal who tried to clean up Tombstone, Arizona. (Rev: BL 10/1/92; SLJ 11/92) [921]

13466 Staeger, Rob. *Wyatt Earp* (3–6). Series: Famous Figures of the American Frontier. 2001, Chelsea LB $19.75 (0-7910-6485-9); paper $8.95 (0-7910-6486-7). 64pp. An appealing biography of the famous gunfighter, with black-and-white and full-color illustrations and handy fact boxes. (Rev: HBG 10/02; SLJ 3/02) [921]

13467 Urban, William. *Wyatt Earp: The O. K. Corral and the Law of the American West* (4–7). Illus. Series: Library of American Lives and Times. 2003, Rosen LB $31.95 (0-8239-5740-3). 112pp. The importance of understanding history is emphasized in this balanced and inviting look at Earp's life. [921]

EDWARDS, JONATHAN

13468 Lutz, Norma Jean. *Jonathan Edwards: Colonial Religious Leader* (5–7). Series: Colonial Leaders. 2001, Chelsea $20.85 (0-7910-5961-8); paper $8.95 (0-7910-6118-3). 80pp. The life of Edwards, a leader in the Great Awakening spiritual movement and preacher among Native American tribes, is presented here with discussion of his contributions and his failings. (Rev: SLJ 5/01) [921]

FARRAGUT, DAVID

13469 Adelson, Bruce. *David Farragut: Union Admiral* (3–5). Series: Famous Figures of the Civil War Era. 2001, Chelsea LB $20.85 (0-7910-6416-6). The story of the American admiral who served in the War of 1812 and the Mexican War, and gained fame as a blockade runner during the Civil War. (Rev: BL 4/1/02) [921]

13470 Roop, Peter, and Connie Roop. *Take Command, Captain Farragut!* (3–5). Illus. by Michael McCurdy. 2002, Simon & Schuster $16.00 (0-689-83022-X). 48pp. Part fact and part fiction, this is the story of the early life of the great naval hero as revealed in a series of fictitious letters written by him at age 13. (Rev: BCCB 4/02; BL 4/15/02; HBG 10/02; SLJ 4/02) [921]

13471 Shorto, Russell. *David Farragut and the Great Naval Blockade* (4–7). Illus. Series: The Story of the Civil War. 1991, Silver Burdett paper $7.95 (0-382-24050-2). 135pp. The story of the outstanding naval commander who closed the Gulf ports to Confederate blockade-running during the Civil War. (Rev: BL 9/1/91) [921]

13472 Stein, R. Conrad. *David Farragut: First Admiral of the U.S. Navy* (3–6). Series: A Proud Heritage. 2005, Child's World LB $28.50 (1-59296-383-8). 40pp. Covers Farragut joining the navy at the age of 10 and his rise to become an admiral. (Rev: SLJ 6/05) [921]

FRANKLIN, BENJAMIN

13473 Adler, David A. *B. Franklin, Printer* (4–8). Illus. 2001, Holiday House $19.95 (0-8234-1675-5). 128pp. Quotations, anecdotes, and wonderful illustrations round out this excellent volume about the life and accomplishments of Benjamin Franklin. (Rev: BCCB 2/02; BL 1/1–15/02; HBG 10/02; SLJ 2/02*) [973.3]

13474 Adler, David A. *A Picture Book of Benjamin Franklin* (K–3). Illus. by John Wallner and Alexandra Wallner. Series: Picture Book Biographies. 1990, Holiday House LB $16.95 (0-8234-0792-6); paper $6.95 (0-8234-0882-5). 32pp. Glimpses of personality and family are interwoven in this simple biography. (Rev: BL 4/15/90; HB 5–6/90; SLJ 5/90) [921]

13475 Ashby, Ruth. *The Amazing Mr. Franklin: Or the Boy Who Read Everything* (3–5). Illus. by Michael Montgomery. 2004, Peachtree $12.95 (1-56145-306-4). 144pp. Readers will learn about Franklin's youth as well as his later accomplishments in this attractive, small-format volume. (Rev: BL 7/04; SLJ 11/04) [973.3]

13476 Cousins, Margaret. *Ben Franklin of Old Philadelphia* (6–8). 1981, Random paper $5.99 (0-394-84928-0). 160pp. A well-rounded portrait of this major figure in American history.

13477 Ford, Carin T. *Benjamin Franklin: Inventor and Patriot* (1–3). Illus. Series: Famous Inventors. 2003, Enslow LB $17.95 (0-7660-1859-8). 32pp. For young report writers, this volume presents the salient facts about Franklin in an attractive and accessible manner. (Rev: HBG 10/03; SLJ 1/04) [921]

13478 Foster, Leila M. *Benjamin Franklin: Founding Father and Inventor* (5–8). Series: Historical American Biographies. 1997, Enslow LB $20.95 (0-89490-784-0). An admiring biography that describes Franklin's many talents — as a printer, businessman, scientist, inventor, and statesman. (Rev: SLJ 11/97) [921]

13479 Fradin, Dennis Brindell. *Who Was Ben Franklin?* (3–5). Illus. by John O'Brien. 2002, Penguin Putnam paper $4.99 (0-448-42495-9). 112pp. This book traces the fascinating, eclectic life and varied careers of Benjamin Franklin. (Rev: BL 3/1/02; HBG 10/02; SLJ 3/02) [973.3]

13480 Glass, Maya. *Benjamin Franklin: Early American Genius* (2–4). Illus. Series: Primary Sources of Famous People in American History. 2004, Rosen LB $21.25 (0-8239-4103-5). 32pp. Primary sources — including maps and paintings — add to the simple narrative describing Franklin's life and importance. [921]

13481 Greene, Carol. *Benjamin Franklin: A Man with Many Jobs* (2–3). Illus. 1988, Children's Book Pr. paper $4.95 (0-516-44202-3). 48pp. Introducing the important points in the life of this multitalented, multifaceted American. (Rev: BL 2/15/89; SLJ 4/89)

13482 Krensky, Stephen. *Ben Franklin and His First Kite* (1–3). Illus. by Bert Dodson. Series: Childhood of Famous Americans. 2002, Simon & Schuster LB

$11.89 (0-689-84985-0); paper $3.99 (0-689-84984-2). 31pp. The story of young Franklin's first experiment with a kite is told for beginning readers. (Rev: HBG 3/03; SLJ 10/02) [921]

13483 Nettleton, Pamela Hill. *Benjamin Franklin: Writer, Inventor, Statesman* (K–3). Illus. by Jeff Yesh. Series: Biographies. 2003, Picture Window LB $21.26 (1-4048-0186-3). 24pp. A brightly illustrated profile that is suitable for beginning readers. (Rev: SLJ 4/04) [921]

13484 Quackenbush, Robert. *Benjamin Franklin and His Friends* (2–3). Illus. 1991, Pippin $14.95 (0-945912-14-5). 40pp. A friend is described in each chapter, emphasizing the influence on Franklin's life. (Rev: BL 12/1/91; SLJ 11/91) [921]

13485 Randolph, Ryan P. *Benjamin Franklin: Inventor, Writer, and Patriot* (4–7). Illus. Series: Library of American Lives and Times. 2003, Rosen LB $31.95 (0-8239-5751-9). 112pp. The importance of understanding history is emphasized in this balanced and well-illustrated look at Franklin's life and contributions. [921]

13486 Riley, John. *Benjamin Franklin: A Photo Biography* (1–3). Series: First Biographies. 2000, Morgan Reynolds LB $15.95 (1-883846-64-1). 24pp. A very simple biography of Franklin for beginning readers that has a full-page illustration opposite each page of text. (Rev: HBG 10/00; SLJ 8/00) [921]

13487 Schanzer, Rosalyn. *How Ben Franklin Stole the Lightning* (2–4). Illus. by author. 2003, HarperCollins LB $17.89 (0-688-16994-5). A lively account of Franklin's role as an inventor, with a focus on his flying a kite during a rainstorm. (Rev: BCCB 3/03; HBG 10/03; SLJ 1/03) [530]

13488 Sherrow, Victoria. *Benjamin Franklin* (3–4). Series: History Maker Bios. 2002, Lerner LB $23.93 (0-8225-0198-8). 48pp. The life of this multitalented genius of the colonial period is presented in a simple text with many illustrations. (Rev: BL 6/1–15/02; HBG 3/03) [921]

13489 Streissguth, Tom. *Benjamin Franklin* (4–6). Series: Just the Facts Biographies. 2005, Lerner LB $27.93 (0-8225-2210-1). 112pp. This attractive and informative biography covers Franklin's youth and education as well as his later life, with interesting factboxes. (Rev: SLJ 2/05) [921]

13490 Streissguth, Tom. *Benjamin Franklin* (5–8). Series: Biography. 2001, Lerner LB $25.26 (0-8225-4997-2). A readable biography of the many-faceted genius of the newly formed United States. (Rev: BL 4/1/02; HBG 10/02) [921]

GALLAUDET, THOMAS

13491 Bowen, Andy Russell. *A World of Knowing: A Story About Thomas Hopkins Gallaudet* (3–5). Illus. Series: Creative Minds Biographies. 1995, Carolrhoda LB $21.27 (0-87614-871-2). 64pp. The story of the man who empathized with deaf persons and developed sign language to enable them to communicate with others. (Rev: BL 1/1–15/96; SLJ 1/96) [921]

GANCI, PETER J.

13492 Ganci, Chris. *Chief: The Life of Peter J. Ganci, a New York Firefighter* (3–5). Illus. 2003, Scholastic $16.95 (0-439-44386-5). 40pp. This loving portrait of a New York City firefighter who lost his life on September 11, 2001, was written by his son and is dedicated to firefighters around the world. (Rev: BL 4/15/03; HBG 10/03; SLJ 4/03) [921]

GINSBURG, RUTH BADER

13493 Ayer, Eleanor. *Ruth Bader Ginsburg: Fire and Steel on the Supreme Court* (5–8). 1995, Dillon LB $22.00 (0-87518-651-3); paper $7.95 (0-382-24721-3). A biography of the second woman Supreme Court justice, with emphasis on the many obstacles she had to overcome. (Rev: BL 5/15/95; SLJ 4/95) [921]

GIULIANI, RUDOLPH W.

13494 Freemont, Eleanor. *Rudolph W. Giuliani* (4–8). 2002, Simon & Schuster paper $4.99 (0-689-85423-4). 96pp. The story of the man *Time* magazine called "the mayor of the world" including material on his personal life and his rise to prominence with the attacks on September 11, 2001. (Rev: BL 9/1/02; SLJ 9/02) [974.7]

GLENN, JOHN

13495 Cole, Michael D. *John Glenn: Astronaut and Senator* (5–8). Series: People to Know. 2000, Enslow LB $20.95 (0-7660-1532-7). 128pp. A biography of the astronaut and politician with coverage of his two trips into space. (Rev: BL 9/15/00; HBG 3/01) [921]

13496 Holden, Henry M. *Trailblazing Astronaut John Glenn* (4–6). Illus. Series: Space Flight Adventures and Disasters. 2004, Enslow LB $18.95 (0-7660-5166-8). 48pp. Supported by Web sites, this is an account of the life of the astronaut who went into space twice, decades apart. [921]

13497 Kramer, Barbara. *John Glenn: A Space Biography* (4–6). Series: Countdown to Space. 1998, Lerner LB $17.95 (0-89490-964-9). 48pp. The story of the Marine Corps pilot who was the first American to orbit the earth and later became a distinguished statesman. (Rev: BL 8/98; HBG 10/98; SLJ 7/98) [921]

13498 Streissguth, Thomas. *John Glenn* (2–4). Illus. Series: Explore Space! 2003, Capstone LB $18.60 (0-7368-1625-9). 24pp. A slim, basic profile of the first American to orbit the earth, who went on to be a United States Senator. (Rev: HBG 10/03; SLJ 3/04) [921]

13499 Streissguth, Thomas. *John Glenn* (5–8). Series: A&E Biography. 1999, Lerner LB $25.26 (0-8225-4947-6); paper $7.95 (0-8225-9685-7). 112pp. This account of John Glenn's life includes childhood influences, his career with NASA, and his political life as a senator. (Rev: HBG 3/00; SLJ 3/00) [921]

13500 Vogt, Gregory L. *John Glenn's Return to Space* (4–7). Illus. 2000, Twenty-First Century LB $24.90 (0-7613-1614-0). 72pp. As well as describing John Glenn's two space flights on the *Mercury* capsule and later the *Discovery,* this biography gives information on astronauts' training and equipment. (Rev: BL 9/15/00; HBG 10/01; SLJ 1/01) [921]

GORE, AL

13501 Italia, Bob. *Al Gore: The Vice President of the United States* (4–6). Illus. Series: All the President's Men and Women. 1993, ABDO LB $14.98 (1-56239-253-0). 32pp. This biography of Gore covers his personality and interests, as well as his public life. (Rev: SLJ 3/94) [921]

13502 Jeffrey, Laura S. *Al Gore* (4–6). Series: People to Know. 1999, Enslow LB $19.95 (0-7660-1232-8). 112pp. Black-and-white photos accompany a well-documented text that tells of Al Gore's life up to, but not including, the 2000 election. (Rev: BL 1/1–15/00; HBG 10/00) [921]

13503 Stefoff, Rebecca. *Al Gore: Vice President* (3–5). Illus. Series: Gateway Biographies. 1994, Millbrook LB $20.90 (1-56294-433-9). 48pp. The life story of the vice president and his climb to high political office. (Rev: BL 8/94; SLJ 4/94) [921]

HALE, NATHAN

13504 Krizner, L. J., and Lisa Sita. *Nathan Hale: Patriot and Martyr of the American Revolution* (4–7). Series: Library of American Lives and Times. 2001, Rosen $23.95 (0-8239-5724-1). 112pp. Nathan Hale, executed by the British in 1776, represented the life-and-death issues fought for in the Revolution and became a symbol of courage and patriotism. (Rev: BL 10/15/01) [921]

13505 Libertson, Jody. *Nathan Hale: Hero of the American Revolution* (2–4). Illus. Series: Primary Sources of Famous People in American History. 2004, Rosen LB $21.25 (0-8239-4117-5). 32pp. Primary sources — including maps and paintings — tell the story of Nathan Hale and his execution as a spy. [921]

13506 Zemlicka, Shannon. *Nathan Hale: Patriot Spy* (2–4). Illus. by Craig Orback. Series: On My Own Biography. 2002, Carolrhoda LB $22.60 (0-87614-597-7); paper $6.95 (0-87614-905-0). 48pp. For beginning readers, this is an absorbing life of the Revolutionary War hero who was executed for spying. (Rev: HBG 3/03; SLJ 12/02) [973.3]

HAMILTON, ALEXANDER

13507 DeCarolis, Lisa. *Alexander Hamilton: Federalist and Founding Father* (4–7). Series: Library of American Lives and Times. 2003, Rosen LB $31.95 (0-8239-5736-7). 112pp. The story of the military hero of the American Revolution who was the first secretary of the treasury and helped write the Federalist Papers. (Rev: BL 6/1–15/03) [921]

13508 Degraw, Aleine. *Alexander Hamilton: American Statesman* (2–4). Illus. Series: Primary Sources of Famous People in American History. 2004, Rosen LB $21.25 (0-8239-4101-9). 32pp. Primary sources — including maps and paintings — add to the simple account of Hamilton's achievements. [921]

13509 Haugen, Brenda. *Alexander Hamilton: Founding Father and Statesman* (4–7). Illus. Series: Signature Lives (Revolutionary War Era). 2005, Compass Point LB $22.95 (0-7565-0827-4). 48pp. Traces the life of the man who became the first secretary of the treasury. [921]

13510 Kallen, Stuart A. *Alexander Hamilton* (4–6). Series: Founding Fathers. 2001, ABDO LB $16.95 (1-57765-006-9). 64pp. A lively biography of the first secretary of the U.S. Treasury that covers his underprivileged early life and details his importance in the creation of the United States. (Rev: HBG 3/02; SLJ 1/02) [921]

HANCOCK, JOHN

13511 Fritz, Jean. *Will You Sign Here, John Hancock?* (3–5). Illus. by Trina S. Hyman. 1997, Penguin Putnam paper $5.99 (0-698-11440-X). 48pp. Under the sprightly title is a delightful, well-researched biography of this signer of the Declaration of Independence.

13512 Ransom, Candice. *John Hancock* (3–4). Illus. Series: History Maker Bios. 2004, Lerner LB $25.26 (0-8225-1547-4). 48pp. A simple biography, useful for report writers, with information about Hancock's youth and good photographs and illustrations. (Rev: SLJ 1/05) [921]

HENRY, PATRICK

13513 Adler, David A. *A Picture Book of Patrick Henry* (K–3). Illus. by John Wallner and Alexandra Wallner. Series: Picture Book Biographies. 1995, Holiday House LB $16.95 (0-8234-1187-7). 32pp. The story of the famous patriot who served five terms as governor of Virginia. (Rev: BL 9/15/95; SLJ 12/95) [921]

13514 Kukla, Amy, and Jon Kukla. *Patrick Henry: Voice of the Revolution* (4–7). Illus. Series: Library of American Lives and Times. 2001, Rosen $23.95 (0-8239-5725-X). 112pp. Detailed text, a variety of illustrations, and a timeline give readers a good understanding of Henry's importance. (Rev: BL 10/15/01) [973.3]

HERSHEY, MILTON S.

13515 Burford, Betty. *Chocolate by Hershey: A Story About Milton S. Hershey* (3–6). Illus. by Loren Chantland. Series: Creative Minds. 1994, Carolrhoda LB $21.27 (0-87614-830-5); paper $5.95 (0-87614-641-8). 64pp. An engrossing biography of the candy-making entrepreneur and his many philanthropies. (Rev: SLJ 1/95) [921]

HESCHEL, ABRAHAM JOSHUA

13516 Rose, Or. *Abraham Joshua Heschel* (4–8). Illus. 2003, Jewish Publication Soc. paper $9.95 (0-8276-0758-X). 72pp. A portrait of the rabbi and teacher who was born in Poland, emigrated to the United States, and became a leader in the civil rights movement. (Rev: BL 6/1–15/03) [921]

HICKOK, WILD BILL

13517 Green, Carl R., and William R. Sanford. *Wild Bill Hickok* (4–8). Illus. Series: Outlaws and Lawmen of the Wild West. 1992, Enslow LB $16.95 (0-89490-366-7). 48pp. The life story of the famous frontier marshal in Kansas is retold in text and pictures. (Rev: BL 7/92; SLJ 8/92) [921]

13518 Phillips, Larissa. *Wild Bill Hickok: Legend of the Wild West* (2–4). Illus. Series: Primary Sources of Famous People in American History. 2004, Rosen LB $21.25 (0-8239-4122-1). 32pp. Primary sources — including maps and paintings — add to the simple narrative telling the story of the frontier marshall. [921]

13519 Rosa, Joseph G. *Wild Bill Hickok: Sharpshooter and U.S. Marshal of the Wild West* (4–8). Series: The Library of American Lives and Times. 2004, Rosen LB $31.95 (0-8239-6632-1). 112pp. The importance of understanding history is emphasized in this balanced and well-illustrated look at Hickok's life. (Rev: SLJ 7/04) [921]

HOLLIDAY, DOC

13520 Green, Carl R., and William R. Sanford. *Doc Holliday* (5–8). Series: Outlaws and Lawmen of the Wild West. 1995, Enslow LB $16.95 (0-89490-589-9). The life and exploits of this colorful western hero are reproduced with the help of photographs and maps. (Rev: BL 6/1–15/95) [921]

HOOVER, J. EDGAR

13521 Streissguth, Tom. *J. Edgar Hoover: Powerful FBI Director* (5–8). Series: Historical American Biographies. 2002, Enslow LB $20.95 (0-7660-1623-4). 128pp. Streissguth looks at Hoover's life from youth, his personality, and his work as head of the FBI, and explores the areas in which his influence was felt, including civil rights and politics. (Rev: HBG 10/02; SLJ 8/02) [363.25092]

HOUSTON, SAM

13522 Boraas, Tracey. *Sam Houston: Soldier and Statesman* (3–5). Illus. Series: Let Freedom Ring. 2002, Capstone LB $22.60 (0-7368-1350-0). 48pp. A thorough look at the life and multiple careers of Sam Houston, who led the fight to wrest Texas from Mexican control. (Rev: HBG 3/03; SLJ 4/03)

13523 Caravantes, Peggy. *An American in Texas: The Story of Sam Houston* (5–8). Series: Founders of the Republic. 2003, Morgan Reynolds LB $21.95 (1-931798-19-2). 144pp. A portrait of the colorful general who became the first president of the

Republic of Texas. (Rev: HBG 4/04; SLJ 5/04) [921]

13524 Wade, Mary D. *I Am Houston* (3–5). Illus. 1993, Colophon $14.95 (1-882539-05-2); paper $6.95 (1-882539-06-0). 64pp. The biography of the soldier and politician who has become one of Texas's favorite heroes. (Rev: BL 4/15/93) [921]

13525 Woodward, Walter M. *Sam Houston: For Texas and the Union* (5–8). Series: The Library of American Lives and Times. 2003, Rosen LB $31.95 (0-8239-5739-X). 112pp. A concise biography of the man credited with gaining Texas's independence. (Rev: SLJ 5/03) [976.4]

JACKSON, STONEWALL

13526 Bennett, Barbara J. *Stonewall Jackson: Lee's Greatest Lieutenant* (4–7). Illus. Series: The History of the Civil War. 1990, Silver Burdett paper $7.95 (0-382-24048-0). 135pp. The story of the Confederate general who gained his nickname beause he stood "like a stone wall." (Rev: BL 9/1/91) [921]

13527 Pflueger, Lynda. *Stonewall Jackson: Confederate General* (5–8). Illus. Series: Historical American Biographies. 1997, Enslow LB $20.95 (0-89490-781-6). This sympathetic biography of Jackson, who favored neither slavery nor secession but became a Confederate general in the Civil War, provides good material on his personal life and beliefs, quoting generously from firsthand sources. (Rev: BL 10/1/97) [921]

13528 Robertson, James I. *Standing like a Stone Wall: The Life of General Thomas J. Jackson* (5–8). Illus. 2001, Simon & Schuster $22.00 (0-689-82419-X). 192pp. Readers will gain a good understanding of Jackson's early life and career before the Civil War as well as his leadership during the war years. (Rev: BL 5/1/01; HBG 10/01; SLJ 6/01) [973.7]

JAMES, JESSE

13529 Bruns, Roger. *Jesse James: Legendary Outlaw* (5–8). Series: Historical American Biographies. 1998, Enslow LB $20.95 (0-7660-1055-4). Using fact boxes, maps, a chronology, and chapter notes as well as an interesting text and black-and-white photographs, this book gives a fine biography of Jesse James and his exploits. (Rev: BL 10/15/98; SLJ 8/98) [921]

13530 Collins, Kathleen. *Jesse James: Western Bank Robber* (2–4). Illus. Series: Primary Sources of Famous People in American History. 2004, Rosen LB $15.95 (0-8239-4112-4). 32pp. Period photographs are used to illustrate this brief biography of Jesse James, who became one of the Wild West's most notorious outlaws during the second half of the 19th century. (Rev: BL 9/15/04) [921]

13531 Green, Carl R., and William R. Sanford. *Jesse James* (4–8). Illus. Series: Outlaws and Lawmen of the Wild West. 1992, Enslow LB $16.95 (0-89490-365-9). 48pp. This easy-to-read text portrays the legendary gunman as both outlaw and hero. (Rev: BL 3/1/92; SLJ 5/92) [921]

13532 Wukovits, John F. *Jesse James* (5–8). Illus. Series: Legends of the West. 1996, Chelsea $18.65 (0-7910-3876-9). 60pp. An action-packed biography that tries to probe the complex nature of the famous Western outlaw. (Rev: BR 5–6/97; SLJ 4/97) [921]

JAY, JOHN

13533 Kallen, Stuart A. *John Jay* (4–6). Series: Founding Fathers. 2001, ABDO LB $16.95 (1-57765-013-1). 64pp. A lively biography of the first chief justice of the Supreme Court that covers his life and details his importance in the creation of the United States. (Rev: SLJ 1/02) [921]

JOHNSTON, JOSEPH E.

13534 Ditchfield, Christin. *Joseph E. Johnston: Confederate General* (3–5). Series: Famous Figures of the Civil War Era. 2001, Chelsea LB $20.85 (0-7910-6412-3). The story of the Confederate general who commanded forces during the Civil War and later served a term in the U.S. House of Representatives. (Rev: BL 4/1/02) [921]

JONES, JOHN PAUL

13535 Bradford, James C. *John Paul Jones and the American Navy* (4–7). Series: Library of American Lives and Times. 2001, Rosen $23.95 (0-8239-5726-8). 112pp. This attractively designed volume combines the life story of the naval hero of the American Revolution with a history of the birth and growth of the American navy. (Rev: BL 10/15/01) [921]

13536 Egan, Tracie. *John Paul Jones* (2–4). Illus. Series: Primary Sources of Famous People in American History. 2004, Rosen LB $21.25 (0-8239-4113-2). 32pp. Primary sources — including maps and paintings — add to the simple narrative telling the story of John Paul Jones. [921]

13537 Lutz, Norma Jean. *John Paul Jones: Father of the U.S. Navy* (3–6). Series: Revolutionary War Leaders. 2000, Chelsea LB $16.95 (0-7910-5359-8). 80pp. From his boyhood in Scotland to his death at age 45, this is the biography of a hero of the Revolutionary War. (Rev: HBG 10/00; SLJ 5/00) [921]

13538 Riley, John. *John Paul Jones: A Photo Biography* (1–3). Series: First Biographies. 2000, Morgan Reynolds LB $15.95 (1-883846-63-3). 24pp. A heavily illustrated simple biography for beginning readers of the Revolutionary War hero. (Rev: HBG 10/00; SLJ 8/00) [921]

13539 Tibbitts, Alison Davis. *John Paul Jones: Father of the American Navy* (5–8). Series: Historical American Biographies. 2002, Enslow LB $20.95 (0-7660-1448-7). The life of the American naval officer noted for his role in the Revolution and for the statement, "I have not yet begun to fight." (Rev: BL 4/1/02; HBG 10/02; SLJ 5/02) [921]

KENNEDY, JOHN F., JR.

13540 Landau, Elaine. *John F. Kennedy Jr.* (5–9). 2000, Twenty-First Century LB $26.90 (0-7613-

1857-7). 128pp. Beginning with the tragic plane crash that ended his life, and moving back in time, this biography of JFK Jr. captures his personality and the aura that surrounded him. (Rev: BL 12/15/00; HBG 3/01; SLJ 3/01) [921]

KEY, FRANCIS SCOTT

13541 Gregson, Susan R. *Francis Scott Key: Patriotic Poet* (3–5). Illus. Series: Let Freedom Ring. 2003, Capstone LB $18.60 (0-7368-1554-6). 48pp. Chronicles the life of the lawyer and poet who wrote the words that were eventually to become the lyrics of America's national anthem. (Rev: HBG 10/03; SLJ 9/03)

KING, RICHARD

13542 Sanford, William R., and Carl R. Green. *Richard King: Texas Cattle Rancher* (4–6). Illus. Series: Legendary Heroes of the Wild West. 1997, Enslow LB $16.95 (0-89490-673-9). 48pp. This short biography of the colorful Texan tells how he was able to amass the land that became one of the largest ranches in the world. (Rev: BL 3/15/97; SLJ 4/97) [921]

KOREMATSU, FRED

13543 Chin, Steven A. *When Justice Failed: The Fred Korematsu Story* (3–6). Illus. by David Tamura. 1993, Raintree LB $28.55 (0-8114-7236-1). 105pp. The biography of the Japanese American whose rights were continually violated during World War II. (Rev: SLJ 7/93) [921]

LEE, ROBERT E.

13544 Adler, David A. *A Picture Book of Robert E. Lee* (3–4). Illus. by Alexandra Wallner and John Wallner. Series: Picture Book Biographies. 1994, Holiday House LB $16.95 (0-8234-1111-7). Using a story format, this simple account covers the highlights of Lee's life and military career. (Rev: SLJ 5/94) [921]

13545 Anderson, Paul Christopher. *Robert E. Lee: Legendary Commander of the Confederacy* (4–7). Series: Library of American Lives and Times. 2003, Rosen LB $31.95 (0-8239-5748-9). 112pp. Extensive original sources are used to re-create the life of this Confederate general and the times in which he lived. (Rev: BL 6/1–15/03) [921]

13546 Dubowski, Cathy E. *Robert E. Lee: The Rise of the South* (4–7). Illus. Series: The History of the Civil War. 1990, Silver Burdett paper $7.95 (0-382-24051-0). 135pp. The life of the Confederate general who was a stirring commander and a man of great character. (Rev: BL 9/1/91) [921]

13547 Kerby, Mona. *Robert E. Lee: Southern Hero of the Civil War* (5–8). Illus. Series: Historical American Biographies. 1997, Enslow LB $20.95 (0-89490-782-4). 128pp. This thorough, sympathetic biography of Lee points out that he did not approve of slavery or the South's secession from the Union. (Rev: BL 10/1/97; SLJ 9/97) [921]

LIEBERMAN, JOSEPH

13548 Feinberg, Barbara Silberdick. *Joseph Lieberman: Keeping the Faith* (4–6). Illus. 2001, Millbrook LB $22.90 (0-7613-2303-1). 48pp. This profile of the first Jewish candidate for the vice presidency of the United States includes photographs, a timeline, and a bibliography. (Rev: BL 9/15/01; HBG 3/02) [973.929]

MACARTHUR, DOUGLAS

13549 Darby, Jean. *Douglas MacArthur* (4–7). Illus. Series: Lerner Biographies. 1989, Lerner LB $25.26 (0-8225-4901-8). 112pp. This biography highlights the general's leadership during World War II and his later dismissal by Truman. (Rev: BL 11/15/89) [921]

13550 Finkelstein, Norman H. *The Emperor General: A Biography of Douglas MacArthur* (5–9). Illus. 1989, Dillon LB $13.95 (0-87518-396-4). The high points in the life of General MacArthur are covered in this attractive biography. (Rev: BL 3/1/89; SLJ 4/89) [921]

13551 Fox, Mary V. *Douglas MacArthur* (4–8). Series: The Importance Of. 1999, Lucent LB $27.45 (1-56006-545-1). 96pp. The story of one of the nation's most prominent generals, whose unorthodox actions made him a controversial figure. (Rev: BL 9/15/99) [921]

13552 Gaines, Ann Graham. *Douglas MacArthur: Brilliant General, Controversial Leader* (5–8). Series: Historical American Biographies. 2001, Enslow LB $20.95 (0-7660-1445-2). 112pp. Using many black-and-white photographs as illustrations, this account gives a well-rounded, unbiased picture of this controversial general. (Rev: BL 4/15/01; HBG 10/01; SLJ 6/01) [921]

MCCAIN, JOHN

13553 Feinberg, Barbara S. *John McCain: Serving His Country* (4–7). Illus. Series: Gateway. 2000, Millbrook LB $23.90 (0-7613-1974-3). 48pp. A biography of the senator that tells about his youth and later political career but concentrates on his stint in the navy and his imprisonment during the Vietnam War. (Rev: BL 3/1/01; HBG 10/01) [921]

MCCARTHY, JOSEPH

13554 Sherrow, Victoria. *Joseph McCarthy and the Cold War* (5–9). Illus. Series: Notorious Americans and Their Times. 1998, Blackbirch LB $27.44 (1-56711-219-6). 80pp. The story of Washington's witch hunting under Joseph McCarthy includes good background information on the Cold War. (Rev: BL 12/15/98; HBG 3/99; SLJ 1/99) [973.921]

MCCLELLAN, GEORGE

13555 Kelley, Brent. *George McClellan: Union General* (3–5). Series: Famous Figures of the Civil War Era. 2001, Chelsea LB $20.85 (0-7910-6404-2). The life of this important Union army leader, who was removed from his command by Lincoln, is re-created in pictures and text. (Rev: BL 4/1/02; SLJ 5/02) [921]

MANJIRO

13556 Blumberg, Rhoda. *Shipwrecked! The True Adventures of a Japanese Boy* (5–9). Illus. 2001, HarperCollins $16.95 (0-688-17484-1). 80pp. The story of a shipwrecked Japanese boy who was adopted by an American sea captain, brought to Massachusetts for an education, and became the first Japanese person to live in the United States. (Rev: BCCB 3/01; BL 2/1/01*; HB 3–4/01; HBG 10/01; SLJ 2/01) [921]

MARION, FRANCIS

13557 Towles, Louis P. *Francis Marion: The Swamp Fox of the American Revolution* (4–7). Series: Library of American Lives and Times. 2001, Rosen LB $23.95 (0-8239-5728-4). The life of the Revolutionary War hero known as the Swamp Fox because of his stealthy retreats into the swamp lands. (Rev: BL 1/1–15/02) [921]

MEADE, GEORGE GORDON

13558 Adelson, Bruce. *George Gordon Meade: Union General* (3–5). Series: Famous Figures of the Civil War Era. 2001, Chelsea LB $20.85 (0-7910-6410-7). The story of the Civil War general who fought in battles including Bull Run, Antietam, Chancellorsville, and Gettysburg. (Rev: BL 4/1/02; HBG 10/02) [921]

MORRIS, GOUVERNEUR

13559 Crompton, Samuel Willard. *Gouverneur Morris: Creating a Nation* (5–8). Series: America's Founding Fathers. 2004, Enslow LB $20.95 (0-7660-2213-7). 128pp. An introduction to the life and legacy of Gouverneur Morris, who helped to edit the final draft of the Declaration of Independence. (Rev: SLJ 7/04) [973.4]

NEWTON, JOHN

13560 Granfield, Linda. *Amazing Grace: The Story of the Hymn* (4–8). Illus. 1997, Tundra $15.95 (0-88776-389-8). The life story of John Newton, a sea captain in the slave trade who later rejected slavery, became a minister, and wrote several hymns, including "Amazing Grace." (Rev: SLJ 8/97) [921]

O'CONNOR, SANDRA DAY

13561 Deegan, Paul J. *Sandra Day O'Connor* (4–6). Illus. Series: Supreme Court Justices. 1992, ABDO LB $19.99 (1-56239-089-9). 40pp. This biography includes material on Judge O'Connor's position on various issues and quotes from her written opinions. (Rev: BL 6/1–15/93) [921]

13562 McElroy, Lisa. *Sandra Day O'Connor: Supreme Court Justice* (4–6). Series: Gateway Biogra-

phies. 2003, Millbrook LB $23.90 (0-7613-2502-6). 48pp. Published before O'Connor announced her plans to retire, this biography chronicles her life and legal career in concise, lively text with many photographs and quotations. (Rev: HBG 4/04; SLJ 1/04) [921]

13563 McElroy, Lisa Tucker. *Meet My Grandmother: She's a Supreme Court Justice* (2–4). Illus. Series: Grandmothers at Work. 1999, Millbrook LB $17.18 (0-7613-1566-7). 32pp. An affectionate portrait of a woman who is both a Supreme Court justice and a beloved grandmother. (Rev: BL 1/1–15/00; HBG 3/00; SLJ 12/99) [921]

13564 Macht, Norman L. *Sandra Day O'Connor: Supreme Court Justice* (4–7). Illus. Series: Junior World Biography. 1992, Chelsea paper $8.95 (0-7910-0448-1). 80pp. In clear text with many photographs, this is a simple account of the first female Supreme Court Justice. (Rev: BL 8/92; SLJ 8/92) [921]

13565 Williams, Jean Kinney. *Sandra Day O'Connor: Lawyer and Supreme Court Justice* (4–6). Series: Ferguson Career Biographies. 2001, Ferguson LB $16.95 (0-89434-355-6). 127pp. The story of O'Connor's life from childhood plus information on the confirmation process for Supreme Court appointees and on how to become a lawyer or judge. (Rev: SLJ 5/01) [921]

OGLETHORPE, JAMES

13566 Lommel, Cookie. *James Oglethorpe: Humanitarian and Soldier* (4–6). Series: Colonial Leaders. 2001, Chelsea LB $16.95 (0-7910-5963-4); paper $8.95 (0-7910-6120-5). 80pp. Oglethorpe, the English founder and first governor of the colony of Georgia, was active in a number of areas including prison reform, the guarantee of religious freedom, and relations with Native Americans. (Rev: HBG 10/01; SLJ 7/01) [975.8]

OLMSTED, FREDERICK LAW

13567 Dunlap, Julie. *Parks for the People: A Story About Frederick Law Olmsted* (3–6). Illus. by Susan F. Lieber. Series: Creative Minds Biographies. 1994, Carolrhoda LB $21.27 (0-87614-824-0). 63pp. The life story of America's first landscape architect, his masterpiece — Central Park in New York City — and how he tried to save Yosemite from commercial exploitation. (Rev: SLJ 2/95) [921]

13568 Wishinsky, Frieda. *The Man Who Made Parks: The Story of Parkbuilder Frederick Law Olmsted* (2–4). Illus. by Song Nan Zhang. 1999, Tundra $15.95 (0-88776-435-5). A short, illustrated biography of the man who created and designed some of the most beautiful parks in America, including Central Park in New York City. (Rev: BL 8/99; HBG 10/99; SLJ 10/99) [921]

PAINE, THOMAS

13569 Burgan, Michael. *Thomas Paine: Great Writer of the Revolution* (4–7). Illus. Series: Signature Lives (Revolutionary War Era). 2005, Compass Point LB $22.95 (0-7565-0830-4). 48pp. A well-designed profile of the revolutionary thinker. [921]

13570 McCarthy, Pat. *Thomas Paine: Revolutionary Patriot and Writer* (5–8). Series: Historical American Biographies. 2001, Enslow LB $20.95 (0-7660-1446-0). 112pp. A balanced, well-researched biography of the American political theorist and writer who created controversy throughout his lifetime. (Rev: BL 4/15/01; HBG 10/01) [921]

13571 McCartin, Brian. *Thomas Paine: Common Sense and Revolutionary Pamphleteering* (4–7). Series: Library of American Lives and Times. 2001, Rosen $23.95 (0-8239-5729-2). 112pp. The story of the British-born colonialist who heard the cries for liberty around him and whose writings set the stage for the Declaration of Independence. (Rev: BL 10/15/01) [921]

13572 Waxman, Laura Hamilton. *Uncommon Revolutionary: A Story About Thomas Paine* (3–5). Illus. by Craig Orback. Series: Creative Minds Biographies. 2003, Carolrhoda LB $21.27 (1-57505-180-X). 64pp. An illustrated biography of the Revolutionary War pamphleteer who supported the cause of American independence. (Rev: HBG 4/04; SLJ 5/04) [921]

PARKER, CYNTHIA ANN

13573 Egan, Tracie. *Cynthia Ann Parker: Comanche Captive* (2–4). Illus. Series: Primary Sources of Famous People in American History. 2004, Rosen LB $21.25 (0-8239-4107-8). 32pp. Primary sources — including maps and paintings — tell the story of the girl who was kidnapped and raised by Comanches, and became mother of the warrior Quanah. [921]

PATTON, GEORGE

13574 Peifer, Charles. *Soldier of Destiny: A Biography of George Patton* (5–8). Illus. 1988, Macmillan LB $13.95 (0-87518-395-6). 128pp. The life and times of the colorful general who commanded the Third Army in Europe during World War II. (Rev: BL 3/1/89; SLJ 4/89) [921]

PENN, WILLIAM

13575 Kroll, Steven. *William Penn: Founder of Pennsylvania* (3–5). Illus. 2000, Holiday House $16.95 (0-8234-1439-6). 29pp. This picture book on the life of William Penn discusses his conversion to the Quaker faith and the land grant that was given him in the New World. (Rev: BL 2/15/00; HBG 10/00; SLJ 4/00) [974.8]

PEROT, ROSS

13576 Italia, Bob. *Ross Perot: The Man Who Woke Up America* (4–6). Illus. Series: Everyone Contributes. 1993, ABDO LB $18.49 (1-56239-236-0).

40pp. The story of Perot's childhood and business success, with emphasis on his run for the presidency. (Rev: BL 12/1/93; SLJ 1/94) [921]

PINKERTON, ALLAN

13577 Green, Carl R., and William R. Sanford. *Allan Pinkerton* (4–8). Illus. Series: Outlaws and Lawmen of the Wild West. 1995, Enslow LB $16.95 (0-89490-590-2). 48pp. A profile of the Scottish immigrant who organized Pinkerton's National Detective Agency, whose specialty was antiunion actions. (Rev: BL 11/15/95) [921]

13578 Josephson, Judith P. *Allan Pinkerton: The Original Private Eye* (5–8). Illus. 1996, Lerner LB $17.21 (0-8225-2923-9). 128pp. The story of the famed criminal-catcher who founded the world-famous detective agency. (Rev: BL 10/15/96; SLJ 10/96) [921]

POWELL, COLIN

13579 Blue, Rose, and Corinne J. Naden. *Colin Powell: Straight to the Top*. Rev. ed. (4–8). Series: Gateway Biographies. 1997, Millbrook LB $23.90 (0-7613-0256-5); paper $9.95 (0-7613-0242-5). A balanced biography of Colin Powell that focuses on his adult life and his stint as chairman of the Joint Chiefs of Staff. (Rev: BL 9/15/97; SLJ 1/98) [921]

13580 Finlayson, Reggie. *Colin Powell* (5–8). Series: A&E Biography. 2003, Lerner LB $25.26 (0-8225-4966-2); paper $7.95 (0-8225-9698-9). 112pp. Documents Powell's rise through the military and transition into the political and diplomatic world. (Rev: BL 1/1–15/04; HBG 4/04) [921]

13581 Finlayson, Reggie. *Colin Powell: People's Hero* (5–8). Series: Achievers Biographies. 1997, Lerner LB $25.55 (0-8225-2891-6). From his birth in Harlem to his distinguished military career, this is a fine biography of Colin Powell. (Rev: SLJ 4/97) [921]

13582 Passaro, John. *Colin Powell* (4–6). Series: Journey to Freedom. 1999, Child's World LB $16.95 (1-56766-619-1). 32pp. The life story of the African American army officer who gained prominence during the Gulf War. (Rev: BL 10/15/99; HBG 3/00; SLJ 4/00) [921]

13583 Patrick-Wexler, Diane. *Colin Powell* (4–6). Illus. Series: Contemporary African Americans. 1995, Raintree LB $25.69 (0-8172-3977-4). 48pp. A simple biography of the man who grew up in the Bronx and rose to be a four-star general and chairman of the Joint Chiefs of Staff. (Rev: BL 2/15/96; SLJ 1/96) [921]

13584 Senna, Carl. *Colin Powell: A Man of War and Peace* (4–8). Illus. 1992, Walker LB $16.85 (0-8027-8181-0). 192pp. The life of the general who became the first African American chairman of the Joint Chiefs of Staff. (Rev: BL 3/15/93) [921]

13585 Strazzabosco, Jeanne M. *Learning About Responsibility from the Life of Colin Powell* (2–4). Illus. Series: Character Building Book. 1996, Rosen LB $15.93 (0-8239-2414-9). 24pp. This biography emphasizes the many important responsibilities that

Colin Powell faced in his various positions in the U.S. government. (Rev: SLJ 5/97) [921]

13586 Wukovits, John F. *Colin Powell* (5–8). Series: People in the News. 2000, Lucent LB $27.45 (1-56006-632-6). 112pp. This account of the African American military leader ends before he became part in the Bush administration, but it gives good coverage of his formative years and his early accomplishments. (Rev: BL 6/1–15/00; HBG 10/00) [921]

PRINTZ, MICHAEL

13587 Bankston, John. *Michael L. Printz and the Story of the Michael L. Printz Award* (4–8). Illus. Series: Great Achievement Awards. 2003, Mitchell Lane LB $19.95 (1-58415-182-X). 48pp. Printz's career as a high school librarian is highlighted in this account of his establishment of the well-known award for YA literature, which includes a list of prize winners. (Rev: BL 10/15/03; SLJ 10/03) [020]

REVERE, PAUL

13588 Adler, David A. *A Picture Book of Paul Revere* (K–3). Illus. Series: Picture Book Biographies. 1995, Holiday House LB $16.95 (0-8234-1144-3). 42pp. A simple biography of this Revolutionary War hero, with an emphasis on colorful illustrations. (Rev: BL 3/15/95; SLJ 4/95) [921]

13589 Ford, Carin T. *Paul Revere: Patriot* (2–4). Series: Heroes of American History. 2003, Enslow LB $17.95 (0-7660-2001-0). 32pp. A concise introduction to Revere and his midnight ride, with full-color reproductions. (Rev: HBG 10/03; SLJ 6/03) [921]

13590 Klingel, Cynthia, and Robert B. Noyed. *Paul Revere's Ride* (1–3). Series: Wonder Books. 2001, Child's World LB $21.36 (1-56766-960-3). 32pp. Paul Revere's life and importance are presented here with color illustrations and a map. (Rev: HBG 3/02; SLJ 11/01) [921]

13591 McCarthy, Rose. *Paul Revere: Freedom Rider* (2–4). Illus. Series: Primary Sources of Famous People in American History. 2004, Rosen LB $21.25 (0-8239-4118-3). 32pp. Primary sources — including maps and paintings — tell the story of Revere's famous ride. [921]

13592 Randolph, Ryan P. *Paul Revere and the Minutemen of the American Revolution* (4–7). Series: Library of American Lives and Times. 2001, Rosen $23.95 (0-8239-5727-6). 112pp. Fairly large type and many illustrations bring to life Paul Revere, a businessman and family man but also a soldier and spy, and the group of patriots known as the Minutemen. (Rev: BL 10/15/01) [921]

13593 Sutcliffe, Jane. *Paul Revere* (3–4). Series: History Maker Bios. 2002, Lerner LB $23.93 (0-8225-0195-3). 48pp. This basic biography describes the life of this patriot who fought in the Revolutionary War and also worked as a silversmith, dentist, coppersmith, and printer. (Rev: BL 6/1–15/02; HBG 3/03) [921]

13594 Winter, Jonah. *Paul Revere and the Bell Ringers* (K–2). Illus. by Bert Dodson. 2003, Simon & Schuster LB $11.89 (0-689-85636-9); paper $3.99 (0-689-85635-0). 32pp. This brief profile focuses on a childhood experience that helped to instill a sense of responsibility. (Rev: HBG 4/04; SLJ 2/04) [921]

RICE, CONDOLEEZZA

13595 Cunningham, Kevin. *Condoleezza Rice: U. S. Secretary of State* (5–8). Illus. Series: Journey to Freedom: The African American Library. 2005, Child's World LB $28.50 (1-59296-231-9). 40pp. A lavishly illustrated account of Rice's life, describing her many successes. [921]

13596 Ditchfield, Christin. *Condoleezza Rice* (5–8). Illus. Series: Great Life Stories. 2003, Watts LB $29.50 (0-531-12307-3). 112pp. This attractive biography details Rice's life from her childhood in Alabama to becoming the first woman to hold the post of national security adviser. (Rev: BL 12/15/03) [355]

13597 Ryan, Bernard. *Condoleezza Rice: National Security Advisor and Musician* (5–8). 2003, Ferguson LB $21.95 (0-8160-5480-0). 155pp. Rice's life and career are detailed, up to the invasion of Iraq. (Rev: SLJ 5/04) [921]

13598 Wade, Mary Dodson. *Condoleezza Rice: Being the Best* (4–7). Illus. 2003, Millbrook LB $23.90 (0-7613-2619-7). 48pp. An interesting profile with a focus on Rice's talented youth and southern upbringing. (Rev: BL 3/1/03; HBG 10/03; SLJ 4/03) [355]

RICHARDS, ANN

13599 Siegel, Dorothy S. *Ann Richards: Politician, Feminist, Survivor* (4–7). Illus. Series: People to Know. 1996, Enslow LB $20.95 (0-89490-497-3). 112pp. In a conversational style, this biography covers the important events in the life of this Texas politician. (Rev: BL 5/15/96; SLJ 10/96) [921]

ROGERS, ROBERT

13600 Quasha, Jennifer. *Robert Rogers: Rogers' Rangers and the French and Indian War* (4–7). Series: Library of American Lives and Times. 2001, Rosen $23.95 (0-8239-5731-4). 112pp. A beautifully illustrated biography of Major Robert Rogers, who recruited companies of soldiers known as Rogers' Rangers to fight for the British in the French and Indian War. (Rev: BL 10/15/01) [921]

ROSS, BETSY

13601 Duden, Jane. *Betsy Ross* (4–6). Illus. Series: Let Freedom Ring. 2001, Capstone LB $22.60 (0-7368-1036-6). 48pp. Ross's early life, her work as an upholsterer, and the famous sewing of the flag are placed in historical context. (Rev: HBG 3/02; SLJ 7/02) [921]

13602 Franchino, Vicky. *Betsy Ross: Patriot* (2–4). Illus. Series: Spirit of America: Our People. 2002,

Child's World LB $27.07 (1-56766-169-6). 32pp. A solid introduction to the life of Betsy Ross and her work as a seamstress. (Rev: SLJ 1/03) [921]

13603 Miller, Susan Martins. *Betsy Ross: American Patriot* (3–6). Series: Revolutionary War Leaders. 2000, Chelsea LB $16.95 (0-7910-5360-1). 80pp. The story of the Quaker seamstress who went on to create the most recognized symbol of the United States. (Rev: HBG 10/00; SLJ 5/00) [921]

13604 Randolph, Ryan P. *Betsy Ross: The American Flag and Life in a Young America* (4–7). Series: Library of American Lives and Times. 2001, Rosen $23.95 (0-8239-5730-6). This contemporary of George Washington was supposedly the creator of the American flag. (Rev: BL 1/1–15/02) [921]

13605 St. George, Judith. *Betsy Ross: Patriot of Philadelphia* (3–6). Illus. 1997, Holt $15.95 (0-8050-5439-1). 118pp. A biography of Betsy Ross that tells of her childhood as a Quaker in Philadelphia as well as the meeting with George Washington that led to making our first flag. (Rev: BL 1/1–15/98; SLJ 2/98) [921]

13606 Silate, Jennifer. *Betsy Ross: Creator of the American Flag* (2–4). Illus. Series: Primary Sources of Famous People in American History. 2004, Rosen LB $21.25 (0-8239-4104-3). 32pp. Primary sources — including maps and paintings — add to the simple narrative telling the story of Betsy Ross and the American flag. [921]

13607 Wallner, Alexandra. *Betsy Ross* (K–3). Illus. 1994, Holiday House LB $16.95 (0-8234-1071-4). 32pp. A biography of the famous seamstress who advised General Washington on the nature of the nation's first flag and ran the family business until her death in 1836. (Rev: BCCB 3/94; BL 2/15/94; SLJ 4/94) [921]

SCHWARZENEGGER, ARNOLD

13608 Brandon, Karen. *Arnold Schwarzenegger* (5–8). Series: People in the News. 2004, Gale LB $28.70 (1-59018-539-0). 112pp. A thorough and appealing overview of actor-turned-governor Schwarzenegger's life and career. (Rev: BL 11/1/04; SLJ 11/04) [921]

13609 Sexton, Colleen A. *Arnold Schwarzenegger* (5–8). Series: A&E Biography. 2004, Lerner LB $27.93 (0-8225-1634-9). 112pp. This evenhanded profile, with many photographs and quotations, covers Schwarzenegger's life from his childhood in Austria to his election as governor of California and appends a list of his films. (Rev: BL 11/1/04) [921]

SEWARD, WILLIAM

13610 Burgan, Michael. *William Henry Seward: Senator and Statesman* (3–5). Series: Famous Figures of the Civil War Era. 2001, Chelsea LB $20.85 (0-7910-6418-2). A clear and concise biography of the man who was secretary of state during the Civil War and who later negotiated the purchase of Alaska from Russia. (Rev: BL 4/1/02; HBG 10/02) [921]

13611 Kent, Zachary. *William Seward: The Mastermind of the Alaska Purchase* (5–8). Series: Histori-

cal American Biographies. 2001, Enslow LB $20.95 (0-7660-1391-X). The story of the man who was appointed secretary of state by Lincoln and who engineered the purchase of Alaska, an act that many called "Seward's folly." (Rev: BL 3/1/01; HBG 10/01; SLJ 5/01) [921]

SHERBURNE, ANDREW

13612 Sherburne, Andrew. *The Memoirs of Andrew Sherburne: Patriot and Privateer of the American Revolution* (5–8). Ed. by Karen Zeinert. Illus. 1993, Linnet LB $17.50 (0-208-02354-2). This excerpt from Sherburne's autobiography of the war years describes his early life at sea and his capture and imprisonment by the British. (Rev: BL 5/15/93; SLJ 7/93) [921]

SHERIDAN, PHILIP

13613 Balcavage, Dynise. *Philip Sheridan: Union General* (3–5). Series: Famous Figures of the Civil War Era. 2001, Chelsea LB $20.85 (0-7910-6406-9). About 20 full-color illustrations are used with a simple text to tell the story of the Civil War army commander who forced Lee's surrender at Appomattox. (Rev: BL 4/1/02) [921]

SHERMAN, WILLIAM T.

13614 King, David C. *William T. Sherman* (5–8). Series: Triangle Histories of the Civil War. 2002, Gale LB $27.44 (1-56711-563-2). 104pp. Sherman's march to the sea and relationship with Joseph Johnston, the confederate general, are among the topics covered in this solid introduction. (Rev: SLJ 1/03) [921]

SHREVE, HENRY MILLER

13615 McCall, Edith. *Mississippi Steamboatman: The Story of Henry Miller Shreve* (5–8). Illus. 1986, Walker $11.95 (0-8027-6597-1). The story of Henry Shreve, whose freight and passenger boats helped open up the Midwest. (Rev: BR 5–6/86; SLJ 3/86) [921]

SIEGEL, BUGSY

13616 Otfinoski, Steven. *Bugsy Siegel and the Postwar Boom* (5–9). Series: Notorious Americans and Their Times. 2000, Blackbirch LB $19.95 (1-56711-224-2). 112pp. The story of the gangster who began a life of crime while a boy in New York, continued in California, and helped create Las Vegas casinos in the 1940s. (Rev: BL 12/1/00; HBG 3/01; SLJ 1/01) [921]

STANTON, EDWIN

13617 Allison, Amy. *Edwin Stanton: Union War Secretary* (3–5). Series: Famous Figures of the Civil War Era. 2001, Chelsea LB $20.85 (0-7910-6420-4). The fascinating story of the lawyer and public official who was secretary of war during the

Civil War and whose feud with President Johnson was legendary. (Rev: BL 4/1/02) [921]

STUART, JEB

13618 Greene, Meg. *James Ewell Brown Stuart: Confederate General* (3–5). Series: Famous Figures of the Civil War Era. 2001, Chelsea LB $20.85 (0-7910-6414-X). Known as Jeb Stuart, this distinguished Confederate army leader was killed in 1864 at Spotsylvania Courthouse. (Rev: BL 4/1/02; HBG 10/02) [921]

13619 Pflueger, Lynda. *Jeb Stuart: Confederate Cavalry General* (5–8). Series: Historical American Biographies. 1998, Enslow LB $20.95 (0-7660-1013-9). The life of the brilliant general who had successes at the battles of Bull Run, Antietam, and Fredericksburg, but who committed a tactical error at Gettysburg. (Rev: BL 8/98; SLJ 8/98) [921]

STUYVESANT, PETER

13620 Krizner, L. J., and Lisa Sita. *Peter Stuyvesant: New Amsterdam, and the Origins of New York* (4–7). Series: Library of American Lives and Times. 2001, Rosen LB $38.35 (0-8239-5732-2). 112pp. The story of New Amsterdam's best-known leader and how the Dutch presence in America influenced our culture for years to come. (Rev: BL 10/15/01; SLJ 7/01*) [921]

SUTTER, JOHN

13621 Engstrand, Iris, and Ken Owens. *John Sutter: Sutter's Fort and the California Gold Rush* (4–8). Series: The Library of American Lives and Times. 2004, Rosen LB $31.95 (0-8239-6630-5). 112pp. The importance of understanding history is emphasized in this balanced and well-illustrated look at Sutter's life. (Rev: SLJ 7/04) [921]

13622 Hayhurst, Chris. *John Sutter: California Pioneer* (2–4). Illus. Series: Primary Sources of Famous People in American History. 2004, Rosen LB $21.25 (0-8239-4114-0). 32pp. Primary sources — including maps and paintings — add to the simple narrative telling the story of Sutter and his short-lived colony in California. [921]

THOMAS, DAVE

13623 Kramer, Barbara. *Dave Thomas: Honesty Pays* (3–5). Illus. 2005, Enslow LB $17.95 (0-7660-2375-3). 48pp. An interesting profile of Thomas, the founder of Wendy's, who was adopted at birth and has worked to improve the lives of others. (Rev: BL 4/1/05) [338.7]

TWEED, WILLIAM "BOSS"

13624 Johnson, Suzan. *Boss Tweed and Tammany Hall* (5–8). Series: Major World Leaders. 2002, Chelsea LB $27.44 (1-56711-224-4). 112pp. The amazing life of the corrupt New York politician who defrauded the city of more than $30 million

and whose life ended in prison. (Rev: BL 1/1–15/03) [921]

WEBSTER, DANIEL

13625 Harvey, Bonnie Carman. *Daniel Webster* (5–8). Series: Historical American Biographies. 2001, Enslow LB $20.95 (0-7660-1392-8). An engrossing biography of the American statesman, lawyer, and orator who fought to save the Union. (Rev: BL 1/1–15/02; HBG 3/02; SLJ 12/01) [921]

WILSON, BILL

13626 White, Tom. *Bill W., a Different Kind of Hero* (4–7). Illus. 2003, Boyds Mills $16.95 (1-59078-067-1). 64pp. The founder of Alcoholics Anonymous is the subject of this biography that describes his long battle with addiction. (Rev: BL 4/15/03; HBG 10/03; SLJ 2/03) [362.292]

WINTHROP, JOHN

13627 Pell, Ed. *John Winthrop: Governor of the Massachusetts Bay Colony* (4–6). Series: Let Freedom Ring. 2004, Capstone LB $23.93 (0-7368-2455-3). 48pp. The life of the Massachusetts Bay Colony's first governor is documented in large type and many illustrations. (Rev: SLJ 8/04) [921]

YOUNG, BRIGHAM

13628 Gunderson, Cory Gideon. *Brigham Young: Pioneer and Prophet* (3–5). Illus. Series: Let Freedom Ring. 2002, Capstone LB $22.60 (0-7368-1346-2). 48pp. With good illustrations, this profile of Young's controversial life includes solid information and historical context. (Rev: HBG 3/03; SLJ 4/03) [921]

13629 Sanford, William R., and Carl R. Green. *Brigham Young: Pioneer and Mormon Leader* (4–6). Illus. Series: Legendary Heroes of the Wild West. 1996, Enslow LB $16.95 (0-89490-672-0). 48pp. A simple account that chronicles the life and career of the great Mormon leader Brigham Young. (Rev: BL 10/15/96; SLJ 9/96) [921]

13630 Simon, Charnan. *Brigham Young: Mormon and Pioneer* (3–5). Illus. 1998, Children's Book Pr. LB $23.00 (0-516-20392-4). 48pp. The story of the great Mormon leader and the founding of the LDS church in Utah. (Rev: BL 1/1–15/99; HBG 3/99; SLJ 2/99) [921]

Native Americans

BLACK ELK

13631 Shaw, Maura D. *Black Elk: Native American Man of Spirit* (4–6). Series: Spiritual Biographies for Young Readers. 2004, Skylight Paths $12.99 (1-59473-043-1). 32pp. The violent aspects of the life of the thoughtful Lakota Sioux warrior named Black Elk are in contrast to his conviction that humans must learn to love and respect the earth and all living things. (Rev: BL 12/15/04)

CHIPETA

13632 Krudwig, Vickie Leigh. *Searching for Chipeta: The Story of a Ute and Her People* (4–7). 2004, Fulcrum paper $12.95 (1-55591-466-7). 128pp. In the second half of the 19th century, Chipeta and her Ute husband worked tirelessly — but ultimately unsuccessfully — to forge an agreement with the U.S. government that would allow the tribe to remain in its traditional homeland. (Rev: BL 9/1/04) [921]

COCHISE (APACHE CHIEF)

13633 Phillips, Larissa. *Cochise: Apache Chief* (2–4). Illus. Series: Primary Sources of Famous People in American History. 2004, Rosen LB $21.25 (0-8239-4105-1). 32pp. Primary sources — including maps and paintings — tell the story of the Apache chief. [921]

CRAZY HORSE, CHIEF

13634 Birchfield, D. L. *Crazy Horse* (3–6). Series: Raintree Biographies. 2003, Raintree LB $25.69 (0-7398-5673-1). 32pp. A simple biography of the Sioux chief's life and achievements, with sidebar features containing primary and background material. (Rev: HBG 3/03; SLJ 3/03) [978]

13635 Brennan, Kristine. *Crazy Horse* (4–7). Series: Famous Figures of the American Frontier. 2001, Chelsea $19.75 (0-7910-6493-X); paper $8.95 (0-7910-6494-8). 64pp. Report writers will find this a useful source of information on this Native American leader's adult life and achievements in battle. (Rev: HBG 10/02; SLJ 4/02) [921]

13636 Cunningham, Chet. *Chief Crazy Horse* (4–6). Series: A&E Biography. 2000, Lerner LB $25.26 (0-8225-4978-6). 112pp. This biography relates the life of the military leader of the Lakota Indians and tells how he became known for his bravery and ferocity in battle. (Rev: BL 6/1–15/00; HBG 3/01; SLJ 9/00) [921]

GERONIMO

13637 Hermann, Spring. *Geronimo: Apache Freedom Fighter* (4–6). Illus. Series: Native American Biographies. 1997, Enslow LB $20.95 (0-89490-864-2). 128pp. The story of the great Apache chieftain who led his people first against the Mexicans and then against the Americans. (Rev: BL 4/15/97; SLJ 6/97) [921]

13638 Thompson, Bill, and Dorcas Thompson. *Geronimo* (4–7). Series: Famous Figures of the American Frontier. 2001, Chelsea $19.75 (0-7910-6491-3); paper $8.95 (0-7910-6492-1). 64pp. A balanced biography of the Apache leader that report writers will find a useful resource. (Rev: HBG 10/02; SLJ 4/02) [921]

13639 Welch, Catherine A. *Geronimo* (3–5). Illus. Series: History Maker Bios. 2004, Lerner LB $23.93 (0-8225-0698-X). 47pp. A well-illustrated

profile of the Apache chief who fought strongly against attempts to confine his people to reservations. (Rev: SLJ 4/04) [921]

HARRIS, LA DONNA

13640 Schwartz, Michael. *La Donna Harris* (4–7). Illus. Series: Contemporary Native Americans. 1997, Raintree LB $17.98 (0-8172-3995-2). 48pp. The life story and accomplishments of this Native American, who has openly championed her people's rights before the Senate. (Rev: BL 6/1–15/97) [921]

ISHI

13641 Kroeber, Theodora. *Ishi, Last of the Tribe* (5–7). Illus. by Ruth Robbins. 1973, Bantam paper $5.99 (0-553-24898-7). 224pp. A California Yahi, the last of his tribe, leaves his primitive life and enters the modern world. [979.4]

JOSEPH, CHIEF

13642 Klingel, Cynthia, and Robert B. Noyed. *Chief Joseph: Chief of the Nez Perce* (3–6). Illus. Series: Our People. 2002, Child's World LB $27.07 (1-56766-165-3). 32pp. This is an attractive, brief introduction to the leader of the Nez Perce Indians. (Rev: BL 1/1–15/03; SLJ 2/03) [979.004]

13643 Sutcliffe, Jane. *Chief Joseph* (3–5). Illus. Series: History Maker Bios. 2004, Lerner LB $23.93 (0-8225-0696-3). 48pp. Focuses on the famed Nez Perce chief who fought fiercely against European settlers' encroachment on his people's land. (Rev: SLJ 4/04) [921]

KA'IULANI, PRINCESS

13644 Linnea, Sharon. *Princess Ka'iulani: Hope of a Nation, Heart of a People* (5–8). 1999, Eerdmans $18.00 (0-8028-5145-2). The story of the Hawaiian princess who tried to prevent the annexation of her country by the United States and of her untimely death at age 22. (Rev: BL 7/99; SLJ 6/99) [921]

13645 Stanley, Fay. *The Last Princess: The Story of Princess Ka'iulani of Hawaii* (4–6). Illus. by Diane Stanley. 1991, Macmillan LB $18.00 (0-02-786785-4). 40pp. The ill-fated princess who never achieved her goal of being queen of Hawaii. (Rev: BL 3/15/91*) [921]

LADUKE, WINONA

13646 Silverstone, Michael. *Winona LaDuke: Restoring Land and Culture in Native America* (5–8). Series: Women Changing the World. 2001, Feminist Pr. $19.95 (1-55861-260-2). 112pp. A candidate for the vice presidency under Ralph Nader in 2000, this author and environmental and Native American rights activist lives on a reservation in Minnesota, where she is dedicated to restoring the land and the culture. (Rev: BL 12/15/01; HBG 10/02) [921]

LILIUOKALANI, QUEEN

13647 Guzzetti, Paula. *The Last Hawaiian Queen: Liliuokalani* (3–5). Illus. Series: Biographies. 1996, Benchmark LB $21.36 (0-7614-0490-2). 48pp. A history of Hawaii with special emphasis on the life of its last queen, the fascinating Liliuokalani. (Rev: SLJ 3/97) [921]

LOYIE, LARRY

13648 Loyie, Larry, and Constance Brissenden. *As Long as the Rivers Flow* (3–6). Illus. by Heather D. Holmlund. 2003, Douglas & McIntyre $16.95 (0-88899-473-7). 40pp. Loyie describes the summer he was 10, living happily among his extended Cree family in the wilds of Alberta but dreading the impending threat of government-enforced boarding school. (Rev: BL 4/15/03; SLJ 10/03) [971.23]

MANKILLER, WILMA

13649 Glassman, Bruce. *Wilma Mankiller: Chief of the Cherokee Nation* (5–7). Illus. Series: Library of Famous Women. 1992, Blackbirch $17.95 (1-56711-032-0). 64pp. This is an inspiring biography of the amazing woman who led her Cherokee Indians through difficult crises. (Rev: BL 6/1/92; SLJ 4/92) [921]

13650 Lazo, Caroline. *Wilma Mankiller* (4–7). Illus. Series: Peacemakers. 1995, Silver Burdett paper $7.95 (0-382-24716-7). 64pp. The dramatic story of the woman who contributed to peace within the Native American community. (Rev: BL 7/95; SLJ 7/95) [921]

13651 Lowery, Linda. *Wilma Mankiller* (2–4). Illus. 1996, Carolrhoda LB $19.93 (0-87614-880-1); paper $5.95 (0-87614-953-0). 56pp. The great hardships that were faced by the Native American woman are the focus of this inspiring, simple biography. (Rev: BCCB 9/96; BL 9/1/96; SLJ 9/96) [921]

OSCEOLA

13652 Bland, Celia. *Osceola, Seminole Rebel* (5–8). Illus. Series: North American Indians of Achievement. 1994, Chelsea LB $21.95 (0-7910-1716-8). The story of the Seminole leader who resisted the removal of his people from Florida in the 1830s and died under mysterious circumstances in 1838. (Rev: BL 6/1–15/94) [921]

13653 Koestler-Grack, Rachel A. *Osceola: 1804–1838* (3–6). Illus. Series: American Indian Biographies. 2003, Capstone LB $22.60 (0-7368-1211-3). 32pp. In addition to covering Osceola's leadership against American forces, this concise volume looks at his childhood and the Seminole culture. (Rev: HBG 3/03; SLJ 4/03) [921]

PARKER, CHIEF QUANAH

13654 Zemlicka, Shannon. *Quanah Parker* (3–5). Illus. Series: History Maker Bios. 2004, Lerner LB $23.93 (0-8225-0724-2). 48pp. Quanah Parker, the

last chief of the Comanche, is profiled in this well-illustrated entry that highlights the losses suffered by the Native Americans. (Rev: SLJ 4/04) [921]

PARKER, ELY

13655 Van Steenwyk, Elizabeth. *Seneca Chief, Army General: A Story About Ely Parker* (4–6). Illus. by Karen Ritz. Series: Creative Minds Biographies. 2000, Carolrhoda LB $21.27 (1-57505-431-0). 64pp. The story of the Native American who was appointed by Ulysses Grant as Commissioner of Indian Affairs, the first Native American to hold that post. (Rev: HBG 3/01; SLJ 2/01) [921]

PHILIP (SACHEM OF THE WAMPANOAGS)

13656 Averill, Esther. *King Philip: The Indian Chief* (5–8). Illus. by Vera Belsky. 1993, Shoe String LB $20.00 (0-208-02357-7). 148pp. The story of the Wampanoag chief who befriended the Pilgrims and later waged war against the settlers. (Rev: BL 7/93) [921]

13657 Cwiklik, Robert. *King Philip and the War with the Colonists* (4–7). Illus. Series: Biography Series of American Indians. 1989, Silver Burdett LB $12.95 (0-382-09573-1); paper $7.95 (0-382-09762-9). 144pp. A biography of the Wampanoag Indian chief who led his people in the most important Indian War in New England. (Rev: BL 1/1/90) [921]

PICOTTE, SUSAN LAFLESCHE

13658 Ferris, Jeri. *Native American Doctor: The Story of Susan LaFlesche Picotte* (4–6). Illus. 1991, Carolrhoda LB $23.93 (0-87614-443-1). The story of the first Native American woman to earn a medical degree. (Rev: BCCB 12/91; BL 1/1/91; HB 1–2/92) [921]

13659 Wilkerson, J. L. *A Doctor to Her People: Dr. Susan LaFlesche Picotte* (4–6). Illus. 1999, Acorn paper $8.95 (0-9664470-2-6). 100pp. Many maps, drawings, and photographs enhance this biography of Susan LaFlesche Picotte, the first female Native American doctor. (Rev: BL 6/1–15/99; SLJ 12/99) [921]

POCAHONTAS

13660 Holler, Anne. *Pocahontas: Powhatan Peacemaker* (5–8). Illus. Series: North American Indians of Achievement. 1993, Chelsea $21.95 (0-7910-1705-2); paper $9.95 (0-7910-1952-7). 103pp. A brief biography of the woman who helped the English settlers survive at Jamestown. (Rev: SLJ 4/93) [921]

13661 Iannone, Catherine. *Pocahontas* (4–7). Illus. Series: Junior World Biography. 1995, Chelsea LB $18.65 (0-7910-2496-2); paper $18.65 (0-7910-2497-0). 80pp. The fascinating story of the Native American who married a white man and was received by English royalty. (Rev: BL 10/15/95; SLJ 10/95) [921]

13662 Nettleton, Pamela Hill. *Pocahontas: Peacemaker and Friend to the Colonists* (K–3). Illus. by Jeff Yesh. 2003, Picture Window LB $21.26 (1-4048-0187-1). 24pp. A brightly illustrated profile that is suitable for beginning readers. (Rev: SLJ 4/04) [921]

13663 Raatma, Lucia. *Pocahontas* (1–5). 2001, Compass Point LB $19.93 (0-7565-0115-6). 32pp. An accessible and attractive book that is careful to distinguish facts from legends. (Rev: SLJ 1/02) [921]

13664 Raphael, Elaine, and Don Bolognese. *Pocahontas: Princess of the River Tribes* (1–3). Illus. by authors. Series: Drawing America. 1993, Scholastic $12.95 (0-590-44371-2). Important episodes in the life of Pocahontas are retold in this brief picture-book biography. (Rev: SLJ 10/93) [921]

13665 Sullivan, George. *Pocahontas* (3–5). Series: In Their Own Words. 2002, Scholastic $12.95 (0-439-32668-0); paper $4.50 (0-439-16585-7). 128pp. After explaining the difference between primary and secondary sources, the author re-creates the life of Pocahontas by quoting from original documents. (Rev: BL 8/02; HBG 10/02; SLJ 11/02) [921]

13666 Zemlicka, Shannon. *Pocahontas* (2–3). Illus. by Jeni Reeves. Series: On My Own Biography. 2002, Carolrhoda LB $22.60 (0-87614-598-5); paper $6.95 (0-87614-906-9). 48pp. This biography for beginning readers covers the Powhatan Indian's birth, contacts with English settlers, family life, and death, and points out what information is reliable and where exaggeration may occur. (Rev: SLJ 1/03) [921]

SACAGAWEA

13667 Adler, David A. *A Picture Book of Sacagawea* (1–4). Illus. by Dan Brown. Series: Picture Book. 2000, Holiday House $16.95 (0-8234-1485-X). 32pp. The important known facts about Sacagawea, from her birth to the silver dollar in her image, are recounted in this competent biography. (Rev: BL 6/1–15/00; HBG 10/00; SLJ 6/00) [921]

13668 Dekeyser, Stacy. *Sacagawea* (3–6). Series: Watts Library. 2004, Scholastic LB $24.50 (0-531-12290-5); paper $8.95 (0-531-16385-7). 64pp. The story of Sacagawea and her journeys with Lewis and Clark's Corps of Discovery is recounted with many illustrations, maps, a timeline, and other helpful features. (Rev: BL 6/1–15/04) [978.004]

13669 Erdrich, Lise. *Sacagawea* (2–6). 2003, Carolrhoda $16.95 (0-87614-646-9). 40pp. This large-format biography of Sacagawea, which features full-page oil paintings, stays close to historical facts as it traces the story of the Shoshone woman who traveled with Lewis and Clark. (Rev: BL 9/1/03; HBG 4/04; SLJ 10/03) [921]

13670 Marcovitz, Hal. *Sacagawea: Guide for the Lewis and Clark Expedition* (4–6). Illus. Series: Explorers of New Worlds. 2000, Chelsea LB $17.95 (0-7910-5959-6); paper $8.95 (0-7910-6169-8). 63pp. In addition to the usual information on Sacagawea's life, this biography discusses why she has remained such an inspiration. (Rev: SLJ 4/01) [921]

13671 Rowland, Della. *The Story of Sacajawea: Guide to Lewis and Clark* (4–6). Illus. by Richard Leonard. 1989, Dell paper $3.99 (0-440-40215-8). 96pp. In brief text, this account tells of the courage and daring of the Shoshone woman who guided Lewis and Clark. (Rev: BCCB 9/89; BL 12/15/89; SLJ 12/89) [921]

13672 St. George, Judith. *Sacagawea* (4–6). 1997, Penguin Putnam $16.99 (0-399-23161-7). 128pp. A sympathetic account of the life of this Shoshone Indian woman and her exciting adventures while helping in the Lewis and Clark expedition. (Rev: BL 8/97; HBG 3/98; SLJ 3/98) [921]

13673 Sanford, William R., and Carl R. Green. *Sacagawea: Native American Hero* (4–6). Illus. Series: Legendary Heroes of the Wild West. 1997, Enslow LB $16.95 (0-89490-675-5). 48pp. A short biography of the gallant Shoshone Indian woman who accompanied Lewis and Clark west during 1805–1806. (Rev: BL 3/15/97; SLJ 3/97) [921]

13674 White, Alana J. *Sacagawea: Westward with Lewis and Clark* (4–8). Series: Native American Biographies. 1997, Enslow LB $20.95 (0-89490-867-7). A well-written account of this gallant woman's life, accompanied by a reading list, chapter notes, and a chronology. (Rev: BL 4/15/97; SLJ 8/97) [921]

13675 Witteman, Barbara. *Sacagawea* (2–4). Series: Photo-Illustrated Biographies. 2002, Capstone LB $13.95 (0-7368-1112-5). 24pp. A concise exploration of the little that is known about Sacagawea's life and of her contribution to the Lewis and Clark Expedition. (Rev: SLJ 7/02) [921]

SEQUOYAH

13676 Cwiklik, Robert. *Sequoyah and the Cherokee Alphabet* (4–7). Illus. Series: Biography Series of American Indians. 1989, Silver Burdett LB $12.95 (0-382-09570-7). 144pp. The story of the great Cherokee leader who was able to translate the language of his people to written form. (Rev: BL 1/1/90; SLJ 4/90) [921]

13677 Fitterer, C. Ann. *Sequoyah: Native American Scholar* (2–4). Series: Spirit of America: Our People. 2002, Child's World LB $27.07 (1-56766-167-X). 32pp. A concise introduction to the life of the Cherokee Indian who invented an alphabet for their language. (Rev: SLJ 12/02) [921]

13678 Klausner, Janet. *Sequoyah's Gift: A Portrait of the Cherokee Leader* (4–7). Illus. 1993, HarperCollins LB $16.89 (0-06-021236-5). 128pp. The life of this Cherokee leader is retold, with material on his invention of a written alphabet and his behavior during the Trail of Tears journey. (Rev: BL 9/1/93; HB 9–10/93; SLJ 11/93) [921]

13679 Rumford, James. *Sequoyah: The Cherokee Man Who Gave His People Writing* (1–3). Trans. by Anna Sixkiller Huckaby. Illus. 2004, Houghton Mifflin $16.00 (0-618-36947-3). 32pp. Cherokee translations appear below the English text in this tall slim volume on Sequoyah. (Rev: BL 10/15/04; SLJ 8/04) [921]

SITTING BULL (SIOUX CHIEF)

13680 Aller, Susan Bivin. *Sitting Bull* (3–5). Illus. Series: History Maker Bios. 2004, Lerner LB $23.93 (0-8225-0700-5). 47pp. The valiant Sioux chief's life is detailed in this well-illustrated biography that highlights the losses suffered by the Native Americans. (Rev: SLJ 4/04) [921]

13681 Black, Sheila. *Sitting Bull and the Battle of the Little Bighorn* (4–7). Illus. Series: Biography Series of American Indians. 1989, Silver Burdett LB $12.95 (0-382-09572-3); paper $7.95 (0-382-09761-0). 144pp. A biography of the Sioux leader who defeated Custer at the Little Bighorn. (Rev: BL 1/1/90; SLJ 4/90) [921]

13682 Hayhurst, Chris. *Sitting Bull: Sioux War Chief* (2–4). Illus. Series: Primary Sources of Famous People in American History. 2004, Rosen LB $21.25 (0-8239-4120-5). 32pp. Period photographs illustrate this brief biography of the warrior who struggled to maintain the lifestyle of the Sioux. [921]

13683 Marcovitz, Hal. *Sitting Bull* (3–6). Series: Famous Figures of the American Frontier. 2001, Chelsea LB $19.75 (0-7910-6487-5); paper $8.95 (0-7910-6488-3). 64pp. The Sioux chief's efforts to improve relations between the Native Americans and the European newcomers are emphasized in this appealing biography. (Rev: SLJ 3/02) [921]

13684 Schleichert, Elizabeth. *Sitting Bull: Sioux Leader* (4–6). Illus. Series: Native American Biographies. 1997, Enslow LB $20.95 (0-89490-868-5). 112pp. As well as describing the life of this great leader who fought to save the lands occupied by the Sioux, there is information on the life and culture of the Sioux. (Rev: BL 4/15/97; SLJ 6/97) [921]

SQUANTO

13685 Bulla, Clyde Robert. *Squanto, Friend of the Pilgrims* (3–6). Illus. by Peter Burchard. 1990, Scholastic paper $4.50 (0-590-44055-1). 112pp. The story of the first Native American to reach Europe.

13686 Kessel, Joyce K. *Squanto and the First Thanksgiving* (2–3). Illus. by Lisa Donze. 1983, Carolrhoda LB $21.27 (0-87614-199-8); paper $5.95 (0-87614-452-0). 48pp. An easily read story of a Native American sold into slavery but eventually freed close to the Plymouth Colony.

TECUMSEH

13687 Koestler-Grack, Rachel A. *Tecumseh: 1768–1813* (3–6). Illus. Series: American Indian Biographies. 2003, Capstone LB $22.60 (0-7368-1212-1). 32pp. In addition to covering Tecumseh's efforts to bring together the Native American tribes, this concise volume looks at his childhood and the Shawnee culture. (Rev: HBG 3/03; SLJ 4/03) [921]

WEBER, EDNAH NEW RIDER

13688 Weber, EdNah New Ryder. *Rattlesnake Mesa: Stories from a Native American Childhood* (4–8). 2004, Lee & Low $18.95 (1-58430-231-3). In this poignant memoir, Weber tells of her life as a student at a government-run boarding school for Native Americans during the 1920s. (Rev: BL 12/15/04; SLJ 12/04) [921]

WINNEMUCCA, SARAH

13689 Morrow, Mary Frances. *Sarah Winnemucca* (3–5). Illus. by Ken Bronikowski. Series: American Indian Stories. 1990, Raintree paper $4.95 (0-8114-4095-8). 32pp. The life story of the Paiute woman who stood for Native American rights and education. (Rev: SLJ 10/90) [921]

Presidents

ADAMS, JOHN

13690 Behrman, Carol H. *John Adams* (5–8). Illus. Series: Presidential Leaders. 2003, Lerner LB $26.60 (0-8225-0820-6). 112pp. This biography provides lots of details and illustrations, covering Adams's life and career. (Rev: BL 1/1–15/04; HBG 4/04) [973.4]

13691 Feinberg, Barbara Silberdick. *John Adams* (5–8). Illus. Series: Encyclopedia of Presidents. 2003, Children's Pr. LB $33.00 (0-516-22680-0). 128pp. An informative and appealing account of Adams's life and achievements, with glossary, timeline, and lists of books and Web sites. (Rev: BL 1/1–15/04) [973.4]

13692 Feinstein, Stephen. *John Adams* (5–9). 2002, Enslow/MyReportLinks.com LB $19.95 (0-7660-5001-7). 48pp. A well-written and accessible overview of Adams's life and contributions that is extended by a number of recommended Web sites. (Rev: SLJ 6/02) [921]

13693 Harness, Cheryl. *The Revolutionary John Adams* (3–6). Illus. 2002, National Geographic $17.95 (0-7922-6970-5). 48pp. Ample quotes, appealing illustrations, and a timeline enhance this biography of America's somewhat neglected second president. (Rev: BL 12/1/02; HBG 3/03; SLJ 2/03) [973.3]

13694 Welsbacher, Anne. *John Adams* (K–2). Series: United States Presidents. 1999, ABDO LB $13.95 (1-56239-738-9). 32pp. For beginning readers, this simple biography of John Adams gives an overview of his life and administration with a section on important facts and statistics. (Rev: HBG 10/99; SLJ 7/99) [921]

ADAMS, JOHN AND ABIGAIL

13695 Ashby, Ruth. *John and Abigail Adams* (5–8). Illus. Series: Presidents and First Ladies. 2005, Gareth Stevens LB $22.50 (0-8368-5755-0). 48pp. An accessible, balanced, and attractive discussion of the Adamses and the contributions each made to their joint lives. [921]

ADAMS, JOHN QUINCY

13696 Feinstein, Stephen. *John Quincy Adams* (5–9). 2002, Enslow/MyReportLinks.com LB $19.95 (0-7660-5002-5). 48pp. Adams's early and later life are covered in this concise biography that includes several pages of annotated Web site recommendations. (Rev: HBG 10/02; SLJ 10/02) [921]

13697 McCollum, Sean. *John Quincy Adams* (4–6). Illus. Series: Encyclopedia of Presidents. 2003, Children's Pr. LB $33.00 (0-516-22867-6). 110pp. An updated profile that looks at Adams's life and contributions, providing many illustrations and sidebars. (Rev: SLJ 1/04) [921]

13698 Venezia, Mike. *John Quincy Adams: Sixth President* (1–3). Illus. by author. Series: Getting to Know the U.S. Presidents. 2004, Children's Pr. LB $26.00 (0-516-22611-8); paper $7.95 (0-516-27480-5). 32pp. This unusual biography takes a light-hearted approach to the key details of the president's life, adding comic-book-style graphics and dialogue bubbles to the large type. (Rev: HBG 4/04; SLJ 4/05) [921]

13699 Walker, Jane C. *John Quincy Adams* (4–6). Series: United States Presidents. 2000, Enslow LB $19.95 (0-7660-1161-5). 128pp. A well-organized profile of the man who was a Revolutionary War leader, vice president, and was elected president in 1824. (Rev: BL 10/15/00; HBG 3/01) [921]

ARTHUR, CHESTER A.

13700 Young, Jeff C. *Chester A. Arthur* (4–7). Series: Presidents. 2002, Enslow/MyReportLinks. com LB $19.95 (0-7660-5077-7). 48pp. As well as an overview of the life and accomplishments of Chester A. Arthur, this book gives a pre-evaluated listing of Web sites where more material can be found. (Rev: BL 12/15/02) [921]

BUCHANAN, JAMES

13701 Young, Jeff C. *James Buchanan* (4–7). Series: Presidents. 2003, Enslow/MyReportLinks.com LB $19.95 (0-7660-5101-3). 48pp. The story of the fifteenth president who had an extensive political career before becoming president. (Rev: BL 6/1–15/03; HBG 10/03) [921]

BUSH, GEORGE

13702 Spies, Karen B. *George Bush: Power of the President* (3–6). Illus. Series: Taking Part. 1991, Macmillan LB $18.95 (0-87518-487-1). 64pp. A profile of the former president, with references to Gorbachev and Iran-Contra. (Rev: BL 3/15/92; SLJ 3/92) [921]

BUSH, GEORGE W.

13703 Burgan, Michael. *George W. Bush: Our Forty-Third President* (3–5). Illus. Series: Our Presidents. 2005, Child's World LB $19.95 (1-59296-494-X). 48pp. With much material on the war on terrorism, this volume covers Bush's life from childhood through the 2004 elections. [921]

13704 Cohen, Daniel. *George W. Bush: The Family Business* (4–6). Illus. 2000, Millbrook $21.90 (0-7613-1851-8). 48pp. This slim biography ends before the 2000 election that resulted in Bush winning the presidency, but gives valuable information about his youth and family. (Rev: BL 5/1/00; HBG 10/00) [921]

13705 Gormley, Beatrice. *President George W. Bush* (4–7). Illus. 2001, Simon & Schuster paper $4.99 (0-689-84123-X). 176pp. An appealing, chronological account of Bush's life that shows him against his family background and looks at his uneven record of achievement. (Rev: BL 5/15/01; SLJ 6/01) [973.931]

13706 Jones, Veda Boyd. *George W. Bush* (5–8). Series: Major World Leaders. 2002, Chelsea $23.95 (0-7910-6940-0). 124pp. Using both color and sepia photographs, this account introduces George W. Bush and his family with coverage through the early part of his presidency. (Rev: BL 1/1–15/03; HBG 3/03) [921]

13707 Kachurek, Sandra J. *George W. Bush* (4–7). Series: United States Presidents. 2004, Enslow LB $26.60 (0-7660-2040-1). 128pp. A balanced and well-documented profile with plenty of photographs plus lists of Web sites and places to visit. (Rev: BL 9/15/04) [921]

13708 Marquez, Heron. *George W. Bush* (5–8). Series: Biography. 2001, Lerner LB $25.26 (0-8225-4995-6). The life story of our president from birth through the turmoil of his presidential election. (Rev: BL 4/1/02; HBG 10/02) [921]

13709 Ryan, Patrick. *George W. Bush* (1–3). Illus. Series: United States Presidents. 2001, ABDO LB $14.95 (1-57765-302-5). 32pp. Report writers will find the basic information they need on Bush's life, with many clear photographs in both color and black and white. (Rev: HBG 10/01; SLJ 9/01) [921]

13710 Thompson, Bill, and Dorcas Thompson. *George W. Bush* (4–8). Illus. Series: Childhoods of the Presidents. 2003, Mason Crest $17.95 (1-59084-281-2). 48pp. Bush's privileged childhood and education, his role as eldest son, and the death of his sister from leukemia are covered in an interesting narrative that highlights his character. (Rev: BL 6/1–15/03; SLJ 2/03) [973.931]

13711 Wheeler, Jill C. *George W. Bush* (4–7). Series: War on Terrorism. 2002, ABDO LB $25.65 (1-57765-662-8). 48pp. A brief profile of President Bush with particular emphasis on his war on terrorism. (Rev: BL 5/15/02; HBG 10/02) [921]

13712 Wukovits, John F. *George W. Bush* (5–8). Series: People in the News. 2000, Lucent LB $27.45 (1-56006-693-8). 96pp. Published before the 2000 election, this biography uses extensive quotations from Mr. Bush, his friends, and critics. (Rev: BL 9/15/00; HBG 3/01; SLJ 10/00) [921]

CARTER, JIMMY

13713 Kent, Deborah. *Jimmy Carter* (4–7). Illus. Series: Encyclopedia of Presidents-Second. 2005,

Children's Pr. LB $33.00 (0-516-22975-3). 112pp. Updated from the 1989 volume, this new, redesigned edition covers the former president's life and career and adds information about his recent work. (Rev: BL 6/1–15/05) [973.926]

13714 Lazo, Caroline. *Jimmy Carter: On the Road to Peace* (4–7). Series: People in Focus. 1996, Silver Burdett LB $13.95 (0-382-39262-0); paper $7.95 (0-382-39263-9). Jimmy Carter's written words are used effectively in this biography that covers both his political career and his post-presidential humanitarian efforts. (Rev: BL 8/96; SLJ 8/96) [921]

13715 O'Shei, Tim. *Jimmy Carter* (5–9). 2002, Enslow/MyReportLinks.com LB $19.95 (0-7660-5051-3). 48pp. This introduction to Carter's life, including his childhood, and his contributions contains a long list of recommended Web sites that extend the printed material. (Rev: HBG 10/02; SLJ 6/02) [921]

13716 Richman, Daniel A. *James E. Carter* (5–8). Series: Presidents of the United States. 1989, GEC LB $21.27 (0-944483-24-0). 121pp. The story of this former U.S. president, his political career, family, and present charitable activities. (Rev: SLJ 9/89) [921]

13717 Santella, Andrew. *James Earl Carter Jr.* (4–7). Series: Profiles of the Presidents. 2002, Compass Point LB $23.93 (0-7565-0283-7). 64pp. A straightforward profile that touches on Carter's southern roots, his successes and failures as president, and his subsequent work in the fields of human rights and democracy. (Rev: SLJ 1/03) [921]

13718 Slavin, Ed. *Jimmy Carter* (4–8). Illus. 1989, Chelsea LB $19.95 (1-55546-828-4). 112pp. Introducing the 39th president of the United States. (Rev: BL 7/89) [921]

13719 Smith, Betsy. *Jimmy Carter, President* (5–7). Illus. 1986, Walker LB $13.85 (0-8027-6652-8). 128pp. A profile of Jimmy Carter and his one-term presidency. (Rev: BL 2/15/87; SLJ 12/86) [921]

CLINTON, BILL

13720 Cwiklik, Robert. *Bill Clinton: President of the 90's*. Rev. ed. (4–8). Series: Gateway Biographies. 1997, Millbrook $22.90 (0-7613-0129-1); paper $8.95 (0-7613-0146-1). A readable biography that concentrates on Clinton's career as governor of Arkansas and his early years as president. (Rev: BL 9/15/97; SLJ 7/97) [921]

13721 Greenberg, Keith E. *Bill and Hillary: Working Together in the White House* (2–6). Illus. by Jerry Harston. Series: Partners. 1994, Blackbirch LB $9.95 (1-56711-067-3). 47pp. Deals with the cooperative and joint creative efforts that have made the Clintons the successful couple they are. (Rev: SLJ 7/94) [921]

13722 Heinrichs, Ann. *William Jefferson Clinton* (4–8). Series: Profiles of the Presidents. 2002, Compass Point LB $28.75 (0-7565-0207-1). 64pp. This absorbing account of Clinton's life and career covers both the good and bad sides of his presidency and includes a discussion of Hillary's role. (Rev: SLJ 6/02) [921]

13723 Landau, Elaine. *Bill Clinton and His Presidency* (4–8). Series: First Books: Biographies. 1997, Watts LB $22.00 (0-531-20295-X). Traces the life and career of Bill Clinton through his first term as president. (Rev: BL 9/15/97; SLJ 9/97) [921]

13724 Marcovitz, Hal. *Bill Clinton* (4–8). Illus. Series: Childhoods of the Presidents. 2003, Mason Crest LB $17.95 (1-59084-273-1). 48pp. This brief, well-illustrated overview of Clinton's childhood and adolescence looks in particular at his relationships with family members, his support for civil rights, and his popularity. (Rev: BL 6/1–15/03; SLJ 2/03) [973.929]

13725 Sherrow, Victoria. *Bill Clinton* (3–6). Illus. Series: Taking Part. 1993, Dillon LB $13.95 (0-87518-620-3). 72pp. A biography of the president that ends shortly after his first national election. (Rev: BL 10/15/93; SLJ 12/93) [921]

CLINTON, BILL AND HILLARY

13726 Ashby, Ruth. *Bill and Hillary Rodham Clinton* (5–8). Illus. Series: Presidents and First Ladies. 2005, Gareth Stevens LB $22.50 (0-8368-5756-9). 48pp. The story of the Clintons before, during, and after Mr. Clinton's presidency; with photographs and a bibliography. (Rev: BL 3/1/05) [921]

COOLIDGE, CALVIN

13727 Joseph, Paul. *Calvin Coolidge* (2–5). Illus. Series: United States Presidents. 1999, ABDO LB $13.95 (1-57765-237-1). 32pp. In this biography of Coolidge, there are chapters on youth, marriage, early career, presidential issues, and final years. (Rev: HBG 3/00; SLJ 12/99) [921]

EISENHOWER, DWIGHT D.

13728 Adler, David A. *A Picture Book of Dwight David Eisenhower* (1–3). Illus. Series: Picture Book Biographies. 2002, Holiday House $16.95 (0-8234-1702-6). 32pp. Traces the life of the 34th president, Dwight D. Eisenhower, from his childhood in Kansas to his death in 1969. (Rev: BL 10/15/02; HBG 3/03; SLJ 10/02) [921]

13729 Alphin, Elaine Marie, and Arthur B. Alphin. *Dwight D. Eisenhower* (3–4). Illus. Series: History Maker Bios. 2004, Lerner LB $25.26 (0-8225-1544-X). 48pp. A simple biography, useful for report writers, with information about Eisenhower's youth and good photographs and illustrations. (Rev: SLJ 1/05) [921]

13730 Darby, Jean. *Dwight D. Eisenhower: A Man Called Ike* (4–7). Illus. Series: Lerner Biographies. 1989, Lerner LB $25.26 (0-8225-4900-X). 112pp. The story of the World War II general who later became president of the United States. (Rev: BL 11/15/89) [921]

13731 Deitch, Kenneth, and Joanne B. Weisman. *Dwight D. Eisenhower: Man of Many Hats* (5–7). Illus. by Jay Connolly. 1990, Discovery LB $14.95 (1-878668-02-1). 48pp. Each stage of Eisenhower's

702

multifaceted career is represented. (Rev: SLJ 2/91) [921]

13732 Raatma, Lucia. *Dwight D. Eisenhower* (4–7). Series: Profiles of the Presidents. 2002, Compass Point LB $23.93 (0-7565-0279-9). 64pp. A straightforward account that focuses on Eisenhower's military career and successes in World War II. (Rev: SLJ 1/03) [921]

13733 Van Steenwyk, Elizabeth. *Dwight David Eisenhower, President* (5–8). Illus. 1987, Walker LB $13.85 (0-8027-6671-4). 128pp. The focus is on the career of this war-hero president. (Rev: BL 5/15/87) [921]

FORD, GERALD R.

13734 Francis, Sandra. *Gerald R. Ford: Our Thirty-Eighth President* (3–5). Illus. Series: Spirit of America: Our Presidents. 2001, Child's World LB $27.07 (1-56766-872-0). 48pp. This brief biography of Ford includes photographs, sidebars, a timeline, and lists of additional resources. (Rev: BL 10/15/01) [973.925]

GARFIELD, JAMES A.

13735 Young, Jeff C. *James A. Garfield* (4–7). Series: Presidents. 2003, Enslow/MyReportLinks. com LB $19.95 (0-7660-5100-5). 48pp. The story of the twentieth president of the U.S. who served as a major general during the Civil War and was assassinated while he was still in office. (Rev: BL 6/1–15/03) [921]

GRANT, ULYSSES S.

13736 Alter, Judy. *Ulysses S. Grant* (5–9). 2002, Enslow/MyReportLinks.com LB $19.95 (0-7660-5014-9). 48pp. Grant's early and later life are covered in this concise and balanced biography that includes several pages of annotated Web site recommendations. (Rev: SLJ 10/02) [921]

13737 Rickarby, Laura A. *Ulysses S. Grant and the Strategy of Victory* (4–7). Illus. Series: The Story of the Civil War. 1991, Silver Burdett paper $7.95 (0-382-24053-7). 160pp. This book focuses mainly on Grant's role in the winning of the Civil War for the North. (Rev: BL 9/1/91) [921]

HARDING, WARREN G.

13738 Joseph, Paul. *Warren G. Harding* (2–5). Illus. Series: United States Presidents. 1999, ABDO LB $13.95 (1-57765-234-7). 32pp. In addition to Harding's life story, this account includes a section on little-known facts and two pages of vital statistics. (Rev: HBG 3/00; SLJ 12/99) [921]

HARRISON, WILLIAM HENRY

13739 Gaines, Ann Graham. *William Henry Harrison: Our Ninth President* (4–6). Series: Spirit of America: Our Presidents. 2001, Child's World LB $27.07 (1-56766-848-8). 48pp. A well-illustrated and appealing biography that discusses influences

that shaped Harrison's policies and looks at his legacy. (Rev: SLJ 12/01) [920]

13740 Venezia, Mike. *William Henry Harrison* (3–4). Illus. Series: Getting to Know the U.S. Presidents. 2005, Children's Pr. LB $26.00 (0-516-22614-2); paper $7.95 (0-516-27483-X). 32pp. A light-hearted approach to the key details of Harrison's life, adding comic-book-style graphics and dialogue bubbles to the large-type text. [921]

HOOVER, HERBERT

13741 Hilton, Suzanne. *The World of Young Herbert Hoover* (4–8). Illus. 1987, Walker LB $13.85 (0-8027-6709-5). This brief biography takes Hoover through his college years and gives some indication of events to follow. (Rev: SLJ 1/88) [921]

13742 Holford, David M. *Herbert Hoover* (5–8). Series: United States Presidents. 1999, Enslow LB $20.95 (0-7660-1035-X). 128pp. An insightful look at the president who was orphaned as a child and gained a reputation for being rigid and insensitive. (Rev: SLJ 1/00) [921]

13743 Ruth, Amy. *Herbert Hoover* (5–8). Series: Presidential Leaders. 2004, Lerner LB $26.60 (0-8225-0821-4). 112pp. Quotations, photographs, and informative sidebars add to the engaging text about Hoover's life and times. (Rev: SLJ 1/05) [921]

JACKSON, ANDREW

13744 Behrman, Carol H. *Andrew Jackson* (5–8). Series: Presidential Leaders. 2002, Lerner LB $31.95 (0-8225-0093-0). 111pp. Jackson's life and character are brought to life in this narrative that points out his failings as well as his achievements. (Rev: HBG 3/03; SLJ 1/03) [921]

13745 Feinstein, Stephen. *Andrew Jackson* (5–9). 2002, Enslow/MyReportLinks.com LB $19.95 (0-7660-5003-3). 48pp. A well-written and accessible overview of Jackson's life and contributions that is extended by a number of recommended Web sites. (Rev: SLJ 6/02) [921]

13746 Venezia, Mike. *Andrew Jackson: Seventh President, 1829–1837* (3–4). Illus. Series: Getting to Know the U.S. Presidents. 2005, Children's Pr. LB $26.00 (0-516-22612-6); paper $7.95 (0-516-27481-3). 32pp. A light-hearted approach to the key details of Jackson's life, adding comic-book-style graphics and dialogue bubbles to the large-type text. [921]

JEFFERSON, THOMAS

13747 Adler, David A. *A Picture Book of Thomas Jefferson* (K–3). Illus. by John Wallner and Alexandra Wallner. Series: Picture Book Biographies. 1990, Holiday House LB $16.95 (0-8234-0791-8); paper $6.95 (0-8234-0881-7). 32pp. Basic facts and personal glimpses make up this simple biography of the third U.S. president. (Rev: BL 4/15/90; SLJ 5/90) [921]

13748 Aldridge, Rebecca. *Thomas Jefferson* (5–6). Series: Let Freedom Ring. 2001, Capstone LB $22.60 (0-7368-1035-8). 48pp. An introduction to the life and work of Jefferson that touches on his attachment to Sally Hemmings. (Rev: HBG 3/02; SLJ 4/02) [921]

13749 Davis, Kenneth C. *Don't Know Much About Thomas Jefferson* (4–7). Illus. by Rob Shepperson. Series: Don't Know Much About. 2005, Harper-Collins LB $15.89 (0-06-028821-3); paper $4.99 (0-06-442128-7). 128pp. Jefferson's many accomplishments and contributions are presented in a question-and-answer format amplified by sidebar features, maps, and quotations that add context. (Rev: SLJ 5/05) [921]

13750 Ferris, Jeri. *Thomas Jefferson: Father of Liberty* (5–8). 1998, Lerner LB $30.35 (1-57505-009-9). This readable biography covers both the public and the private sides of Jefferson's life, with details on his personality and his family. (Rev: BL 3/1/99; HBG 3/99; SLJ 12/98) [921]

13751 Ford, Carin T. *Thomas Jefferson: The Third President* (2–4). Illus. Series: Heroes of American History. 2003, Enslow LB $17.95 (0-7660-1861-X). 32pp. Jefferson's life and achievements are covered here, as are questions about his ownership of slaves. (Rev: HBG 10/03; SLJ 9/03) [921]

13752 Giblin, James Cross. *Thomas Jefferson: A Picture Book Biography* (4–6). Illus. by Michael Dooling. 1994, Scholastic $16.95 (0-590-44838-2). 48pp. This handsome, historically accurate biography of Thomas Jefferson covers his presidency and his accomplishments. (Rev: BCCB 10/94; BL 10/15/94; SLJ 9/94) [921]

13753 Gomez, Rebecca. *Thomas Jefferson* (2–3). Illus. Series: First Biographies. 2003, ABDO LB $14.95 (1-57765-947-3). 32pp. For young report writers, this is a simple account of Jefferson's major accomplishments. (Rev: HBG 4/04; SLJ 9/03) [921]

13754 Harness, Cheryl. *Thomas Jefferson* (4–7). Illus. 2004, National Geographic $17.95 (0-7922-6496-7). 48pp. Harness paints a personal portrait of Jefferson and his various roles in this picture book, enhanced by maps and eye-catching illustrations. (Rev: BL 2/1/04; SLJ 2/04) [973.4]

13755 Nardo, Don. *Thomas Jefferson* (3–6). Series: Encyclopedia of Presidents. 2003, Children's Pr. LB $33.00 (0-516-22768-8). 110pp. A well-designed biography with maps, drawings, facts, a timeline, and other features that will be useful for report writers. (Rev: SLJ 4/04) [921]

13756 Old, Wendie C. *Thomas Jefferson* (5–8). Series: United States Presidents. 1997, Enslow LB $20.95 (0-89490-837-5). An account of the life and career of the multifaceted Jefferson. (Rev: BL 2/1/98; HBG 3/98; SLJ 3/98) [921]

13757 Reiter, Chris. *Thomas Jefferson* (4–7). Illus. Series: MyReportLinks.com. 2002, Enslow/MyReportLinks.com LB $19.95 (0-7660-5071-8). 48pp. A concise biography suitable for students doing reports that provides extensive Web links for further research and uses Web site images among the many illustrations. (Rev: BL 9/1/02; HBG 3/03) [973.4]

13758 Sherrow, Victoria. *Thomas Jefferson* (3–4). Illus. Series: History Maker Bios. 2002, Lerner LB $23.93 (0-8225-0197-X). 48pp. A heavily illustrated story of the multitalented man who was also an important president. (Rev: BL 6/1–15/02) [973.4]

13759 Venezia, Mike. *Thomas Jefferson* (3–4). Illus. Series: Getting to Know the U.S. Presidents. 2004, Children's Pr. LB $26.00 (0-516-22608-8); paper $7.95 (0-516-27477-5). 32pp. A light-hearted approach to the key details of Jefferson's life, adding comic-book-style graphics and dialogue bubbles to the large-type text. [921]

JOHNSON, ANDREW

13760 Alter, Judy. *Andrew Johnson* (5–8). 2002, Enslow/MyReportLinks.com LB $19.95 (0-7660-5007-6). 48pp. This overview of Johnson's life and career contains a listing of about 30 Web sites that will extend the information contained in the book. (Rev: SLJ 6/02) [921]

13761 Stevens, Rita. *Andrew Johnson: 17th President of the United States* (5–7). Illus. 1989, Garrett LB $21.27 (0-944483-16-X). 122pp. Story of the man who became president on Lincoln's assassination. (Rev: BL 5/1/89) [973.810924]

JOHNSON, LYNDON B.

13762 Colbert, Nancy A. *Great Society: The Story of Lyndon Baines Johnson* (4–8). Illus. 2002, Morgan Reynolds LB $21.95 (1-883846-84-6). 144pp. A solid, readable life of the hardworking president that presents fairly both his virtues and defects. (Rev: BL 4/15/02; HBG 3/03; SLJ 8/02) [921]

13763 Falkof, Lucille. *Lyndon B. Johnson: 36th President of the United States* (5–8). Illus. 1989, Garrett LB $21.27 (0-944483-20-8). An informative biography that covers both the public and private life of this president. (Rev: BL 5/1/89; BR 9–10/89; SLJ 8/89) [921]

13764 Levy, Debbie. *Lyndon B. Johnson* (5–9). Series: Presidential Leaders. 2003, Lerner LB $31.95 (0-8225-0097-3). 112pp. A look at the fascinating personal and political life of the president known for his support for civil rights and for increasing the U.S. involvement in Vietnam. (Rev: HBG 10/03; SLJ 2/03) [921]

KENNEDY, JOHN F.

13765 Adler, David A. *A Picture Book of John F. Kennedy* (2–4). Illus. by Robert Casilla. Series: Picture Book Biographies. 1991, Holiday House LB $16.95 (0-8234-0884-1). A straightforward account in an attractive format that provides basic information about President John F. Kennedy. (Rev: SLJ 12/91) [921]

13766 Anderson, Catherine Corley. *John F. Kennedy* (5–8). Series: Presidential Leaders. 2004, Lerner LB $26.60 (0-8225-0812-5). 112pp. Quotations, photographs, and informative sidebars add to the engaging text about Kennedy's life and times. (Rev: SLJ 1/05) [921]

13767 Cole, Michael D. *John F. Kennedy: President of the New Frontier* (4–7). Illus. Series: People to Know. 1996, Enslow LB $20.95 (0-89490-693-3).

128pp. A profile of the life and accomplishments of this charismatic president. (Rev: BL 5/15/96; SLJ 6/96) [921]

13768 Heiligman, Deborah. *High Hopes: A Photobiography of John F. Kennedy* (4–6). Ed. by Nancy Feresten. 2003, National Geographic $17.95 (0-7922-6141-0). 64pp. This lavishly illustrated biography looks at Kennedy's achievements and his assassination. (Rev: BL 11/15/03; HBG 4/04; SLJ 4/04) [921]

13769 Kaplan, Howard S. *John F. Kennedy* (5–10). Illus. Series: DK Biography. 2004, DK paper $4.99 (0-7566-0340-4). 128pp. A heavily illustrated, attractive biography of Kennedy that offers broad historical background. [921]

13770 Schultz, Randy. *John F. Kennedy* (4–7). Illus. Series: MyReportLinks.com. 2002, Enslow/MyReportLinks.com LB $19.95 (0-7660-5012-2). 48pp. A basic, illustrated account of Kennedy's life and accomplishments that provides extensive Web links for students to do further research. (Rev: BL 9/1/02) [973.922]

13771 Sommer, Shelley. *John F. Kennedy: His Life and Legacy* (5–8). Illus. 2005, HarperCollins LB $17.89 (0-06-054136-9). 160pp. This engaging biography presents a favorable profile of the 35th president's private and public lives and assesses his legacy. (Rev: BL 1/1–15/05) [921]

13772 Time for kids eds., and Ritu Upadhyay. *John F. Kennedy: The Making of a Leader* (3–5). Series: Time for Kids Biographies. 2005, HarperCollins $14.99 (0-06-057603-0); paper $3.99 (0-06-057602-2). 44pp. Attractive photo-filled pages describe Kennedy's childhood, education, and later life, with interesting sidebar features on topics including Jackie's redecoration of the White House. (Rev: SLJ 2/05) [921]

LINCOLN, ABRAHAM

13773 Adler, David A. *A Picture Book of Abraham Lincoln* (PS–3). Illus. by John Wallner and Alexandra Wallner. 1989, Holiday House LB $16.95 (0-8234-0731-4); paper $6.95 (0-8234-0801-9). 32pp. The life of perhaps our most famous president told in a profusely illustrated format. (Rev: BL 6/1/89; SLJ 5/89)

13774 Bial, Raymond. *Where Lincoln Walked* (3–6). Illus. 1998, Walker $16.95 (0-8027-8630-8). 48pp. This unusual biography of Lincoln concentrates on the years before he became president and on the sight and people he knew at that time. (Rev: BL 3/1/98; HBG 10/98; SLJ 2/98) [921]

13775 Brenner, Martha. *Abe Lincoln's Hat* (1–3). Illus. by Donald Cook. 1994, Random paper $3.99 (0-679-84977-7). 48pp. A simple biography of Lincoln that makes him a believable person through the retelling of simple anecdotes. (Rev: BL 9/15/94; SLJ 11/94) [921]

13776 Burgan, Michael. *The Assassination of Abraham Lincoln* (3–6). Illus. Series: We the People. 2004, Compass Point LB $16.95 (0-7565-0678-6). 48pp. A well-illustrated, concise introduction to Lincoln's untimely death. [921]

13777 Burke, Rick. *Abraham Lincoln* (1–4). Series: American Lives. 2003, Heinemann LB $24.22 (1-4034-0155-1). 32pp. This easy-to-understand biography discusses Lincoln's youth and achievements, and includes plentiful, interesting illustrations. (Rev: HBG 10/03; SLJ 7/03) [921]

13778 Cohn, Amy L., and Suzy Schmidt. *Abraham Lincoln* (K–3). Illus. by David A. Johnson. 2002, Scholastic $16.95 (0-590-93566-6). 40pp. A large-format picture book that tells of the heroism and importance of Lincoln through a lively text and memorable illustrations. (Rev: BCCB 2/02; BL 4/1/02; HB 3–4/02; HBG 10/02; SLJ 2/02*) [921]

13779 Davis, Kenneth C. *Don't Know Much About Abraham Lincoln* (4–8). Illus. by Rob Shepperson. Series: Don't Know Much About. 2004, HarperCollins LB $15.89 (0-06-028820-5); paper $4.99 (0-06-442127-9). 142pp. A question-and-answer format gives easy access to key details about Lincoln's life. (Rev: SLJ 2/04) [921]

13780 Fontes, Justine, and Ron Fontes. *Abraham Lincoln: Lawyer, Leader, Legend* (2–4). Illus. Series: Dorling Kindersley Readers. 2001, DK $12.95 (0-7894-7376-3); paper $3.95 (0-7894-7375-5). 48pp. An accessible introduction to Lincoln's life with many facts, illustrations, and maps. (Rev: BCCB 2/02; HBG 10/01; SLJ 8/01) [921]

13781 Ford, Carin T. *Abraham Lincoln: The 16th President* (2–4). Illus. Series: Heroes of American History. 2003, Enslow LB $17.95 (0-7660-2000-2). 32pp. A well-illustrated and well-written biography that covers Lincoln's flaws as well as his great achievements. (Rev: HBG 10/03; SLJ 9/03) [921]

13782 Freedman, Russell. *Lincoln: A Photobiography* (4–8). Illus. 1987, Houghton Mifflin $18.00 (0-89919-380-3); paper $7.95 (0-395-51848-2). 160pp. A no-nonsense, unromanticized look at this beloved president. Newbery Medal winner, 1988. (Rev: BL 12/15/87; SLJ 12/87) [921]

13783 Gross, Ruth Belov. *True Stories About Abraham Lincoln* (2–5). Illus. by Jill Kastner. 1991, Scholastic paper $2.50 (0-590-43879-4). 48pp. This is a collection of anecdotes about Lincoln. Originally published in 1973. (Rev: BCCB 3/90; BL 3/1/90; SLJ 4/90) [921]

13784 Harness, Cheryl. *Abe Lincoln Goes to Washington, 1837–1865* (1–4). Illus. 1997, National Geographic $18.00 (0-7922-3736-6). 48pp. In this sequel to *Young Abe Lincoln* (1996), Lincoln's life from his arrival in Springfield, Illinois, to his assassination is covered. (Rev: BL 1/1–15/97; SLJ 3/97*) [921]

13785 Harness, Cheryl. *Young Abe Lincoln* (1–4). Illus. 1996, National Geographic $15.95 (0-7922-2713-1). 32pp. A picture book that traces Lincoln's early life until he leaves for Springfield, Illinois. (Rev: BL 9/1/96; SLJ 6/96) [921]

13786 Holzer, Harold. *The President Is Shot! The Assassination of Abraham Lincoln* (5–8). Illus. 2004, Boyds Mills $17.95 (1-56397-985-3). 144pp. A riveting account of Lincoln's assassination, with archival illustrations and historical context. (Rev: BL 3/1/04*; SLJ 2/04) [973.7]

13787 Ito, Tom. *Abraham Lincoln* (5–8). Illus. Series: Mysterious Deaths. 1996, Lucent LB $24.94 (1-56006-259-2). 96pp. A look at the various conspiracy theories that surround Lincoln's death. (Rev: BL 2/15/97; SLJ 5/97) [921]

13788 Judson, Karen. *Abraham Lincoln* (4–6). Series: United States Presidents. 1998, Enslow LB $19.95 (0-89490-939-8). 128pp. Original source documents and a chronology are included in this insightful biography of a great president. (Rev: BL 12/15/98; HBG 3/99) [921]

13789 Mara, Wil. *Abraham Lincoln* (1–2). Illus. Series: Rookie Biographies. 2002, Children's Book Pr. LB $19.00 (0-516-22518-9); paper $4.95 (0-516-27334-5). 31pp. A simple account of Lincoln's life for beginning readers. (Rev: BCCB 2/02; SLJ 1/03) [921]

13790 Mosher, Kiki. *Learning About Honesty from the Life of Abraham Lincoln* (2–5). Illus. Series: A Character Building Book. 1996, Rosen LB $13.95 (0-8239-2420-3). 24pp. A brief biography of Lincoln that emphasizes his belief in honesty and truth. (Rev: BL 10/15/96; SLJ 12/96) [921]

13791 Roberts, Jeremy. *Abraham Lincoln* (5–7). Series: Presidential Leaders. 2003, Lerner LB $26.60 (0-8225-0817-6). 112pp. From childhood through assassination, this is a thorough, well-illustrated, and well-organized account of Lincoln's life. (Rev: HBG 4/04; SLJ 2/04) [921]

13792 Sandburg, Carl. *Abe Lincoln Grows Up* (6–8). Illus. by James Daugherty. 1975, Harcourt paper $7.00 (0-15-602615-5). 222pp. The classic account of Lincoln's boyhood based on Volume I of *The Prairie Years.*

13793 Schott, Jane A. *Abraham Lincoln* (3–4). Series: History Maker Bios. 2002, Lerner LB $23.93 (0-8225-0196-1). 48pp. Using many true stories, historical photography, and other artwork, this lively biography describes Lincoln's journey from log cabin to the White House. (Rev: BCCB 2/02; BL 6/1–15/02) [921]

13794 Sloate, Susan. *Abraham Lincoln: The Freedom President* (5–8). 1989, Ballantine paper $15.00 (0-449-90375-3). An accessible account of the president who led his country through division back to unity. (Rev: BL 12/15/89; BR 3–4/90) [921]

13795 Stone, Tanya Lee. *Abraham Lincoln* (5–10). Illus. Series: DK Biography. 2005, DK $14.99 (0-7566-0833-3); paper $4.99 (0-7566-0834-1). 128pp. A heavily illustrated, attractive biography of Lincoln that offers broad historical background. [921]

13796 Sullivan, George. *Abraham Lincoln* (3–5). Illus. Series: In Their Own Words. 2001, Scholastic $12.95 (0-439-14750-6); paper $4.50 (0-439-09554-9). 128pp. Using speeches, letters, and other primary sources, this is an entertaining, appealing biography of Lincoln. (Rev: BCCB 2/02; BL 4/1/01; HBG 10/01; SLJ 4/01) [921]

13797 Sullivan, George. *Picturing Lincoln: Famous Photographs That Popularized the President* (5–8). Illus. 2000, Clarion $16.00 (0-395-91682-8). 88pp. Using five images of Lincoln taken between 1846 and 1864, this book gives historical and biographi-

cal information on each and tells how they have been used for posters, button, ribbons, postage stamps, and currency. (Rev: BL 2/1/01; HB 3–4/01; HBG 10/01; SLJ 3/01) [921]

13798 Van Steenwyk, Elizabeth. *When Abraham Talked to the Trees* (K–3). Illus. by Bill Farnsworth. 2000, Eerdmans $16.00 (0-8028-5191-6). 32pp. A picture book that tells of Lincoln's youth, his many outdoor activities, and the books he read. (Rev: BL 10/1/00; HBG 3/01; SLJ 12/00) [921]

13799 Winters, Kay. *Abe Lincoln: The Boy Who Loved Books* (K–2). Illus. by Nancy Carpenter. 2003, Simon & Schuster $16.95 (0-689-82554-4). 40pp. Simple language and detailed illustrations describe Lincoln's childhood and young adult years, with a focus on his love of reading. (Rev: BL 1/1–15/03; HBG 10/03; SLJ 1/03) [973.7]

MADISON, JAMES

13800 Fritz, Jean. *The Great Little Madison* (5–8). Illus. 1989, Penguin Putnam $16.99 (0-399-21768-1). With wit and imagination the author captures the life of the fourth president. (Rev: BCCB 10/89; BL 10/1/89; BR 3–4/90; HB 3–4/90*; SLJ 11/89) [921]

13801 Kent, Zachary. *James Madison: Creating a Nation* (5–8). Series: America's Founding Fathers. 2004, Enslow LB $26.60 (0-7660-2180-7). 128pp. This profile of Madison focuses largely on his public life from the period leading up to the American Revolution through his presidency. (Rev: BL 6/1–15/04) [921]

13802 Malone, Mary. *James Madison* (4–6). Illus. 1997, Enslow LB $20.95 (0-89490-834-0). 128pp. This interesting, well-researched biography of James Madison focuses on his presidency. (Rev: BL 9/15/97; HBG 3/98; SLJ 9/97) [921]

13803 Quackenbush, Robert. *James Madison and Dolley Madison and Their Times* (3–6). Illus. 1992, Pippin $14.95 (0-945912-18-8). 40pp. A fact-filled short biography of James and Dolley Madison with many interesting bits about their personal lives. (Rev: BL 1/15/93; SLJ 1/93) [921]

13804 Santella, Andrew. *James Madison* (3–5). Series: Profiles of the Presidents. 2002, Compass Point LB $23.93 (0-7565-0252-7). 64pp. Madison's adult years are the focus of this volume that includes a brief chapter on his youth. (Rev: SLJ 4/03) [921]

13805 Venezia, Mike. *James Madison* (3–4). Illus. Series: Getting to Know the U.S. Presidents. 2004, Children's Pr. LB $26.00 (0-516-22609-6); paper $7.95 (0-516-27478-3). 32pp. A light-hearted approach to the key details of Madison's life, adding comic-book-style graphics and dialogue bubbles to the large-type text. [921]

MADISON, JAMES AND DOLLEY

13806 Ashby, Ruth. *James and Dolley Madison* (5–8). Illus. Series: Presidents and First Ladies. 2005, Gareth Stevens LB $22.50 (0-8368-5757-7). 48pp. An accessible, balanced, and attractive discussion of the Madisons and the contributions each made to their joint lives. [921]

MONROE, JAMES

13807 Old, Wendie C. *James Monroe* (4–6). Series: United States Presidents. 1998, Enslow LB $19.95 (0-89490-941-X). 128pp. Profiles the fifth president, who is noted for drafting the doctrine that barred European intervention in the New World. (Rev: BL 12/15/98; HBG 3/99) [921]

13808 Teitelbaum, Michael. *James Monroe* (3–5). Series: Profiles of the Presidents. 2002, Compass Point LB $23.93 (0-7565-0253-5). 64pp. Monroe's adult years are the focus of this volume that includes a brief chapter on his youth. (Rev: SLJ 4/03) [921]

13809 Venezia, Mike. *James Monroe* (3–4). Illus. Series: Getting to Know the U.S. Presidents. 2004, Children's Pr. LB $26.00 (0-516-22610-X); paper $7.95 (0-516-27479-1). 32pp. A light-hearted approach to the key details of Monroe's life, adding comic-book-style graphics and dialogue bubbles to the large-type text. [921]

13810 Welsbacher, Anne. *James Monroe* (K–2). Series: United States Presidents. 1999, ABDO LB $13.95 (1-56239-810-5). 32pp. A biography for beginning readers that gives basic facts about Monroe and the meaning of the doctrine that bears his name. (Rev: HBG 10/99; SLJ 7/99) [921]

NIXON, RICHARD M.

13811 Joseph, Paul. *Richard Nixon* (K–2). Series: United States Presidents. 1999, ABDO LB $13.95 (1-56239-746-X). 32pp. For beginning readers, this is an overview of Nixon's life and accomplishments with a double-page spread of important facts and statistics. (Rev: HBG 10/99; SLJ 7/99) [921]

13812 Marquez, Heron. *Richard M. Nixon* (5–7). Series: Presidential Leaders. 2003, Lerner LB $31.95 (0-8225-0098-1). 112pp. The Vietnam War, relations with China, and Watergate all feature prominently in this look at Nixon's private and public life. (Rev: BL 4/15/03; HBG 10/03; SLJ 2/03) [921]

PIERCE, FRANKLIN

13813 Brown, Fern G. *Franklin Pierce* (5–8). Series: Presidents of the United States. 1989, GEC LB $21.27 (0-944483-25-9). 121pp. The story of Pierce, his political life and presidency, plus material on his personal life. (Rev: SLJ 9/89) [921]

POLK, JAMES K.

13814 Tibbitts, Alison Davis. *James K. Polk* (4–6). Series: United States Presidents. 1999, Enslow LB $19.95 (0-7660-1037-6). 128pp. The story of the 11th president of the United States, whose term encompassed the 1846–1848 war with Mexico, which brought California and New Mexico into the union. (Rev: BL 9/15/99; HBG 10/99) [921]

13815 Venezia, Mike. *James K. Polk: Eleventh President, 1845–1849* (3–4). Illus. Series: Getting to Know the U.S. Presidents. 2005, Children's Pr. LB $26.00 (0-516-22616-9); paper $7.95 (0-516-27485-6). 32pp. A light-hearted approach to the key details of Polk's life, adding comic-book-style graphics and dialogue bubbles to the large-type text. [921]

REAGAN, RONALD

13816 Hinkle, Donald Henry. *Ronald Reagan* (4–7). Series: Presidents. 2003, Enslow/MyReportLinks. com LB $19.95 (0-7660-5112-9). 48pp. The life story of the fortieth president with material on the successes and failures of his two terms. (Rev: BL 6/1–15/03; HBG 10/03) [921]

13817 Robbins, Neal. *Ronald W. Reagan: 40th President of the United States* (K–2). Illus. Series: Presidents of the United States. 1990, Garrett LB $21.27 (0-944483-66-6). 124pp. The life of Ronald Reagan is presented. (Rev: BL 8/90) [921]

13818 Sullivan, George. *Ronald Reagan* (5–8). Illus. 1991, Simon & Schuster $14.98 (0-671-74537-9). 142pp. This revised edition adds new material on Reagan's second term. (Rev: BL 1/15/92) [921]

ROOSEVELT, FRANKLIN AND ELEANOR

13819 Ashby, Ruth. *Franklin and Eleanor Roosevelt* (5–8). Illus. Series: Presidents and First Ladies. 2005, Gareth Stevens LB $22.50 (0-8368-5758-5). 48pp. An accessible, balanced, and attractive discussion of the Roosevelts and the contributions each made to their joint lives. [921]

13820 Harness, Cheryl. *Franklin and Eleanor* (3–5). 2004, Penguin Putnam $17.99 (0-525-47259-2). 48pp. This fascinating biography shows how the lives of distant cousins Franklin and Eleanor came together — as husband and wife — and looks at their leadership during a time of turmoil. (Rev: BL 11/1/04) [921]

ROOSEVELT, FRANKLIN D.

13821 Allport, Alan. *Franklin Delano Roosevelt* (5–7). Series: Great American Presidents. 2003, Chelsea House LB $21.85 (0-7910-7598-2). 102pp. A concise life of the longest-serving president in U.S. history, from his childhood through his years in the White House, with a foreword by Walter Cronkite. (Rev: SLJ 4/04) [921]

13822 Burgan, Michael. *Franklin D. Roosevelt* (4–8). Series: Profiles of the Presidents. 2002, Compass Point LB $28.75 (0-7565-0203-9). 64pp. An absorbing introduction to Roosevelt's life and career, with details of his youth and education and the role that his illness played in shaping his character. (Rev: SLJ 6/02) [973.917092]

13823 Freedman, Russell. *Franklin Delano Roosevelt* (5–8). Illus. 1990, Houghton Mifflin $20.00 (0-89919-379-X). 200pp. A carefully researched and well-illustrated account of the man and the times. (Rev: HB 3–4/90; SLJ 12/90*) [921]

13824 Greenblatt, Miriam. *Franklin D. Roosevelt: 32nd President of the United States* (5–8). Illus. 1989, Garrett LB $21.27 (0-944483-06-2). A clearly written, objective biography of the man who guided the country through World War II, with information on his family life. (Rev: BL 5/1/89; SLJ 8/89) [921]

13825 Knapp, Ron. *Franklin D. Roosevelt* (5–9). 2002, Enslow/MyReportLinks.com LB $19.95 (0-7660-5009-2). 48pp. A listing of recommended Web sites extends the contents of this introduction to Roosevelt's life and presidency. (Rev: HBG 10/02; SLJ 6/02) [921]

13826 Morris, Jeffrey. *The FDR Way* (5–8). Illus. Series: Great Presidential Decisions. 1996, Lerner LB $23.93 (0-8225-2929-7). A straightforward, incisive analysis of far-reaching, often painful decisions that FDR made, and an assessment of their consequences. (Rev: BL 3/15/96) [921]

13827 Schuman, Michael A. *Franklin D. Roosevelt: The Four-Term President* (4–7). Illus. Series: People to Know. 1996, Enslow LB $20.95 (0-89490-696-8). 128pp. A thoughtful, serious look at this great president, his important decisions, and his significance in history. (Rev: BL 6/1–15/96; SLJ 8/96) [921]

ROOSEVELT, THEODORE

13828 Fritz, Jean. *Bully for You, Teddy Roosevelt!* (5–8). Illus. by Mike Wimmer. 1991, Penguin Putnam $16.99 (0-399-21769-X). 103pp. An affectionate portrait of the president who considered himself a "true American." (Rev: BL 4/15/91; HB 7–8/91; SLJ 7/91*) [921]

13829 Harness, Cheryl. *Young Teddy Roosevelt* (3–5). Illus. 1998, National Geographic $17.95 (0-7922-7094-0). 48pp. Illustrated with lavish watercolors, this picture-book biography tells of Roosevelt's sickly childhood and ends with him becoming president of the United States. (Rev: BCCB 4/98; BL 3/15/98; HBG 10/98) [921]

13830 Kelley, Alison Turnbull. *Theodore Roosevelt* (5–7). Series: Great American Presidents. 2003, Chelsea House LB $21.85 (0-7910-7606-7). 102pp. An illustrated profile of the 26th president, from his childhood through his public life and legacy. (Rev: HBG 4/04; SLJ 4/04) [921]

13831 Kraft, Betsy Harvey. *Theodore Roosevelt: Champion of the American Spirit* (5–9). Illus. 2003, Clarion $19.00 (0-618-14264-9). 180pp. The determination that carried Roosevelt through a difficult childhood and drove his successful career is emphasized in this engrossing biography of his life and survey of his diverse accomplishments. (Rev: BL 10/15/03; HB 11–12/03; HBG 4/04; SLJ 12/03*) [973.9]

13832 Roosevelt, Theodore. *My Tour of Europe: By Teddy Roosevelt, Age 10* (1–3). Ed. by Ellen Jackson. Illus. by Catherine Brighton. 2003, Millbrook LB $23.90 (0-7613-2516-6). 32pp. This collection of excerpts from Teddy Roosevelt's boyhood journal describes the 10-year-old future president's experiences on a family trip to Europe. (Rev: BL 4/15/03; HBG 10/03; SLJ 6/03) [973.91]

13833 St. George, Judith. *You're on Your Way, Teddy Roosevelt!* (2–4). Illus. by Matt Faulkner. Series: Turning Point Book. 2004, Philomel $16.99 (0-399-23888-3). 48pp. Teddy Roosevelt's childhood is the focus of this picture-book biography that looks at his love for animals and his victory over asthma, which paved the way for his success as both an athlete and a student. (Rev: BL 11/1/04; SLJ 10/04) [921]

13834 Schuman, Michael A. *Theodore Roosevelt* (5–8). Series: United States Presidents. 1997, Enslow LB $20.95 (0-89490-836-7). An objective biography of the life of this active president whose life spanned both the Civil War and World War I, with good background information. (Rev: BL 2/1/98; HBG 3/98; SLJ 2/98) [921]

13835 Time for kids eds., and Lisa DeMauro. *Theodore Roosevelt: The Adventurous President* (3–5). Series: Time for Kids Biographies. 2005, HarperCollins $14.99 (0-06-057606-5); paper $3.99 (0-06-057604-9). 44pp. Attractive photo-filled pages describe Roosevelt's childhood, education, love for nature, and later life, with interesting sidebar features on topics ranging from the Teddy bear and Mount Rushmore to his "Big Stick" policy. (Rev: BL 3/15/04; SLJ 2/05) [921]

TAYLOR, ZACHARY

13836 Brunelli, Carol. *Zachary Taylor: Our Twelfth President* (4–6). Series: Spirit of America: Our Presidents. 2001, Child's World $27.07 (1-56766-836-4). 48pp. A well-illustrated and appealing biography that discusses influences that shaped Taylor's policies and looks at his legacy. (Rev: SLJ 12/01) [921]

13837 Collins, David R. *Zachary Taylor: 12th President of the United States* (5–7). Illus. 1989, Garrett LB $21.27 (0-944483-17-8). 121pp. Tells the life story of a military man elected president in 1848. (Rev: BL 5/1/89) [921]

13838 Venezia, Mike. *Zachary Taylor: Twelfth President, 1849–1850* (3–4). Illus. Series: Getting to Know the U.S. Presidents. 2005, Children's Pr. LB $26.00 (0-516-22617-7); paper $7.95 (0-516-27486-4). 32pp. A light-hearted approach to the key details of Taylor's life, adding comic-book-style graphics and dialogue bubbles to the large-type text. [921]

TRUMAN, HARRY S.

13839 Cannarella, Deborah. *Harry S. Truman* (3–5). Series: Profiles of the Presidents. 2002, Compass Point LB $23.93 (0-7565-0278-0). 64pp. Truman's adult years are the focus of this volume that includes a brief chapter on his youth. (Rev: SLJ 4/03) [921]

13840 Gaines, Ann Graham. *Harry S. Truman: Our Thirty-Third President* (3–5). Illus. Series: Spirit of America: Our Presidents. 2001, Child's World LB $27.07 (1-56766-867-4). 48pp. This brief biography of the president features photographs, sidebars, a timeline, and lists of additional print and Web resources. (Rev: BL 10/15/01; SLJ 12/01) [973.918]

13841 Greenberg, Morrie. *The Buck Stops Here: A Biography of Harry Truman* (5–9). Illus. 1989, Dillon LB $13.95 (0-87518-394-8). A competent retelling of the major events in Truman's life and of his importance as a U.S. president. (Rev: SLJ 4/89) [921]

13842 Joseph, Paul. *Harry S. Truman* (2–5). Illus. Series: United States Presidents. 1999, ABDO LB $13.95 (1-56239-743-5). 32pp. A good biography of Truman that also contains a section on trivia, a map, and two pages of vital statistics. (Rev: HBG 3/00; SLJ 12/99) [921]

13843 Lazo, Caroline Evensen. *Harry S Truman* (5–7). Illus. Series: Presidential Leaders. 2003, Lerner LB $26.60 (0-8225-0096-5). 112pp. Truman's youth, education, family life, and career are all covered in this concise biography full of photographs. (Rev: BL 4/15/03; HBG 10/03) [973.918]

TYLER, JOHN

13844 Ochester, Betsy. *John Tyler* (4–6). Illus. Series: Encyclopedia of Presidents. 2003, Children's Pr. LB $33.00 (0-516-22850-1). 110pp. An updated profile that looks at Tyler's life and contributions, providing many illustrations and sidebars. (Rev: SLJ 1/04) [921]

VAN BUREN, MARTIN

13845 Doak, Robin S. *Martin Van Buren* (4–7). 2003, Compass Point LB $17.95 (0-7565-0256-X). 64pp. Van Buren's strengths and weakness receive equal weight in this balanced and readable biography that covers his life from a young age. (Rev: SLJ 11/03) [973.5]

13846 Ellis, Rafaela. *Martin Van Buren: 8th President of the United States* (5–7). Illus. 1989, Garrett LB $21.27 (0-944483-12-7). 120pp. The story of a New York governor who became president. (Rev: BL 5/1/89) [921]

13847 Favor, Lesli J. *Martin Van Buren* (3–6). Series: Encyclopedia of Presidents. 2003, Children's Pr. LB $33.00 (0-516-22770-X). 110pp. A concise illustrated biography of the eighth president of the United States, with plenty of illustrations and sidebars. (Rev: SLJ 4/04) [921]

13848 Ferry, Steven. *Martin Van Buren: Our Eighth President* (4–6). Series: Spirit of America: Our Presidents. 2001, Child's World LB $27.07 (1-56766-837-2). 48pp. A well-illustrated and appealing biography that discusses influences that shaped Van Buren's policies and looks at his legacy. (Rev: SLJ 12/01) [921]

13849 Venezia, Mike. *Martin Van Buren: Eighth President 1837–1841* (3–4). Illus. Series: Getting to Know the U.S. Presidents. 2005, Children's Pr. LB $26.00 (0-516-22613-4); paper $7.95 (0-516-27482-7). 32pp. A light-hearted approach to the key details of Van Buren's life, adding comic-book-style graphics and dialogue bubbles to the large-type text. [921]

WASHINGTON, GEORGE

13850 Adler, David A. *George Washington: An Illustrated Biography* (5–7). 2004, Holiday House $24.95 (0-8234-1838-3). 288pp. Adler presents a balanced and well-researched biography of Washington, giving details of his character as well as information on key events of his time. (Rev: BL 9/15/04; SLJ 12/04) [973.4]

13851 Adler, David A. *A Picture Book of George Washington* (PS–3). Illus. by John Wallner and Alexandra Wallner. 1989, Holiday House LB $16.95 (0-8234-0732-2); paper $6.95 (0-8234-0800-0). 32pp. A picture biography of America's first president for young readers. (Rev: BL 6/1/89; SLJ 5/89)

13852 Armentrout, David, and Patricia Armentrout. *George Washington* (1–3). Series: Discover the Life of an American Legend. 2004, Rourke LB $20.64 (1-58952-662-7). 24pp. An introductory book about the first U.S. president, including a glossary and chronology. (Rev: SLJ 3/04) [973.4]

13853 Bial, Raymond. *Where Washington Walked* (3–6). 2004, Walker LB $17.95 (0-8027-8900-5). 48pp. This lavishly illustrated volume revisits many of the places in America that figured prominently in the life of George Washington. (Rev: BL 12/15/04; SLJ 2/05) [921]

13854 Burke, Rick. *George Washington* (1–4). Series: American Lives. 2003, Heinemann LB $24.22 (1-4034-0158-6). 32pp. Easy to read, this richly illustrated biography covers Washington's life from childhood. (Rev: HBG 10/03; SLJ 7/03) [921]

13855 Chandra, Deborah, and Madeleine Comora. *George Washington's Teeth* (K–3). Illus. by Brock Cole. 2003, Farrar $16.00 (0-374-32534-0). 40pp. George Washington's dental problems are examined in lively, witty verses perfectly paired with sprightly watercolors. (Rev: BCCB 2/03; BL 1/1–15/03; HB 3–4/03*; HBG 10/03; SLJ 1/03) [973.4]

13856 Collier, James Lincoln. *The George Washington You Never Knew* (4–6). Illus. by Greg Copeland. Series: You Never Knew. 2003, Children's Pr. LB $24.50 (0-516-24343-8). 80pp. In an accessible style, Collier reveals the inner man behind the legend, combining historical facts and debunking myths while providing a solid account of the early days of the United States. (Rev: SLJ 1/04) [921]

13857 Egan, Tracie. *George Washington: Father of the Nation* (2–4). Illus. Series: Primary Sources of Famous People in American History. 2004, Rosen LB $21.25 (0-8239-4111-6). 32pp. Primary sources — including maps and paintings — add to the simple narrative telling the story of George Washington. [921]

13858 Falkof, Lucille. *George Washington: 1st President of the United States* (5–8). Illus. 1989, Garrett LB $21.27 (0-944483-19-4). An objective, readable portrait of the life and times of our first president. (Rev: BL 5/1/89; BR 9–10/89; SLJ 8/89) [921]

13859 Ford, Carin T. *George Washington: The First President* (2–4). Series: Heroes of American History. 2003, Enslow LB $17.95 (0-7660-1999-3). 32pp.

A concise introduction to the military and political leader. (Rev: HBG 10/03; SLJ 6/03) [921]

13860 Harness, Cheryl. *George Washington* (3–5). Illus. 2000, National Geographic $17.95 (0-7922-7096-7). 48pp. A heavily illustrated, large-format biography that covers the important events in Washington's life and describes his personality. (Rev: BL 3/1/00; HBG 10/00; SLJ 4/00) [921]

13861 Hilton, Suzanne. *The World of Young George Washington* (5–8). 1987, Walker $12.95 (0-8027-6657-9). Washington as a youth plus detailed information on life in pre-Revolutionary America. (Rev: BR 5–6/87; SLJ 4/87) [921]

13862 Hort, Lenny. *George Washington* (5–10). Illus. Series: DK Biography. 2005, DK $14.99 (0-7566-0832-5); paper $4.99 (0-7566-0835-X). 128pp. A heavily illustrated, attractive biography of the man born in Virginia. [921]

13863 Mara, Wil. *George Washington* (K–4). Illus. 2002, Children's Book Pr. LB $19.00 (0-516-22519-7); paper $4.95 (0-516-27335-3). 32pp. A simple account of Washington's life for beginning readers. (Rev: SLJ 1/03) [921]

13864 Mosher, Kiki. *Learning About Leadership from the Life of George Washington* (2–5). Illus. Series: A Character Building Book. 1996, Rosen LB $13.95 (0-8239-2421-1). 24pp. A brief biography of Washington that emphasizes his leadership qualities. (Rev: BL 10/15/96; SLJ 12/96) [921]

13865 Nettleton, Pamela Hill. *George Washington: Farmer, Soldier, President* (K–3). Illus. by Jeff Yesh. Series: Biographies. 2003, Picture Window LB $21.26 (1-4048-0184-7). 24pp. A brightly illustrated profile that is suitable for beginning readers. (Rev: SLJ 4/04) [921]

13866 Old, Wendie C. *George Washington* (5–8). Illus. Series: United States Presidents. 1997, Enslow LB $20.95 (0-89490-832-4). Washington's personal life and political career are dealt with equally in this thoughtful biography. (Rev: BL 9/15/97; SLJ 12/97) [921]

13867 Ransom, Candice F. *George Washington* (3–4). Series: History Maker Bios. 2002, Lerner LB $23.93 (0-8225-0374-3). 48pp. An introductory biography of the man who was chosen to lead the army and then the country during and after the American Revolution. (Rev: BL 6/1–15/02) [921]

13868 Roberts, Jeremy. *George Washington* (5–7). Series: Presidential Leaders. 2003, Lerner LB $26.60 (0-8225-0818-4). 112pp. This engaging biography chronicles the life and achievements of America's first president and dispels some widely believed myths. (Rev: HBG 4/04; SLJ 2/04) [921]

13869 St. George, Judith. *Take The Lead George Washington* (2–4). Illus. by Daniel Powers. Series: Turning Points. 2005, Penguin Putnam $16.99 (0-399-23887-5). 48pp. Washington's first job — as a surveyor, at the age of 16 — is the turning point in this picture-book profile of his transition from childhood to adult. (Rev: BL 12/1/04; SLJ 1/05) [921]

WILSON, WOODROW

13870 Collins, David R. *Woodrow Wilson: 28th President of the United States* (5–8). Illus. 1989, Garrett LB $21.27 (0-944483-18-6). 121pp. A compact biography of a Nobel Peace Prize–winning president. (Rev: BL 5/1/89; SLJ 8/89) [921]

13871 Randolph, Sallie. *Woodrow Wilson, President* (5–9). Series: Presidential Biography. 1992, Walker LB $15.85 (0-8027-8144-6). Offers a concise overview of Wilson's tragic personal and political struggles, his achievements, and his place in history. (Rev: BL 12/15/91; SLJ 3/92) [921]

13872 Schraff, Anne. *Woodrow Wilson* (5–8). Series: United States Presidents. 1998, Enslow LB $20.95 (0-89490-936-3). 112pp. The story of the brilliant 28th president, his initial opposition to entering World War I, the defeat of his proposals concerning the League of Nations, and the stroke he suffered. (Rev: SLJ 9/98) [921]

WILSON, WOODROW AND EDITH

13873 Ashby, Ruth. *Woodrow and Edith Wilson* (5–8). Illus. Series: Presidents and First Ladies. 2005, Gareth Stevens LB $22.50 (0-8368-5759-3). 48pp. An accessible, balanced, and attractive discussion of the Wilsons and the contributions each made to their joint lives. [921]

First Ladies and Other Women

ADAMS, ABIGAIL

13874 Ching, Jacqueline. *Abigail Adams: A Revolutionary Woman* (4–7). Series: Library of American Lives and Times. 2001, Rosen $23.95 (0-8239-5723-3). 112pp. This biography of Abigail Adams stresses the fact that her husband, John Adams, relied heavily on her advice and that her vision of equality and justice inspired the early consideration of women's rights. (Rev: BCCB 4/01; BL 10/15/01) [921]

13875 Ferris, Jeri Chase. *Remember the Ladies: A Story About Abigail Adams* (3–5). Illus. by Ellen Beier. Series: Creative Minds Biographies. 2000, Carolrhoda LB $21.27 (1-57505-292-X). 64pp. A biography of this early first lady that relies heavily on original sources including the writings of Abigail Adams. (Rev: HBG 3/01; SLJ 1/01) [921]

13876 Glass, Maya. *Abigail Adams: Famous First Lady* (2–4). Illus. Series: Primary Sources of Famous People in American History. 2004, Rosen LB $21.25 (0-8239-4100-0). 32pp. Primary sources — including maps and paintings — add to the simple narrative describing the life of Abigail Adams. [921]

13877 McCarthy, Pat. *Abigail Adams: First Lady and Patriot* (5–8). Series: Historical American Biographies. 2002, Enslow LB $20.95 (0-7660-1618-8). The life story of the prolific letter-writer who was wife of the second president of the United

States, John Adams. (Rev: BCCB 4/01; BL 4/1/02; HBG 10/02; SLJ 7/02) [921]

13878 Wallner, Alexandra. *Abigail Adams* (K–3). Illus. 2001, Holiday House $16.95 (0-8234-1442-6). 32pp. A picture-book biography that examines the life of Abigail Adams, the wife of a president, the mother of another, and a champion of women's rights. (Rev: BL 3/15/01; HB 7–8/01; HBG 10/01) [921]

ADDAMS, JANE

13879 Armentrout, David, and Patricia Armentrout. *Jane Addams* (2–4). Series: Discover Someone Who Made a Difference. 2001, Rourke LB $18.60 (1-58952-054-8). A beginning biography of the famous American social worker who won a Nobel Peace Prize. (Rev: BL 1/1–15/02; SLJ 3/02) [921]

13880 Caravantes, Peggy. *Waging Peace: The Story of Jane Addams* (5–8). 2004, Morgan Reynolds LB $21.95 (1-931798-40-0). 144pp. Covers Addams's life and achievements, with good material on her youth and the lessons she learned from her Quaker father. (Rev: SLJ 2/05) [921]

13881 Harvey, Bonnie Carman. *Jane Addams: Nobel Prize Winner and Founder of Hull House* (5–8). Illus. Series: Historic American Biographies. 1999, Enslow LB $20.95 (0-7660-1094-5). 128pp. This biography of the Nobel Peace Prize winner and founder of Hull House traces her life and her outstanding achievements as a social worker. (Rev: BL 11/1/99; HBG 3/00; SLJ 11/99) [921]

13882 McPherson, Stephanie S. *Peace and Bread: The Story of Jane Addams* (5–8). 1993, Carolrhoda LB $30.35 (0-87614-792-9). An introduction to Jane Addams's work among the poor of Chicago and her leadership in international organizations on behalf of world peace. (Rev: BL 1/15/94; SLJ 2/94) [921]

13883 Wheeler, Leslie. *Jane Addams* (5–8). Illus. Series: Pioneers in Change. 1990, Silver Burdett LB $17.95 (0-382-09962-1); paper $6.95 (0-382-09968-0). 138pp. The story of the outspoken social activist who lived in turn-of-the-century Chicago. (Rev: BL 1/15/91; SLJ 4/91) [921]

ANTHONY, SUSAN B.

13884 Klingel, Cynthia, and Robert B. Noyed. *Susan B. Anthony: Reformer* (3–6). Illus. 2002, Child's World LB $27.07 (1-56766-171-8). 32pp. An attractive, brief introduction to the life of Susan B. Anthony. (Rev: BL 1/1–15/03) [305.42]

13885 Levin, Pamela. *Susan B. Anthony: Fighter for Women's Rights* (3–5). Illus. Series: Junior World Biographies. 1993, Chelsea LB $16.95 (0-7910-1762-1). 79pp. An informative, interesting biography of the great fighter for social causes, including women's right to vote. (Rev: SLJ 10/93) [921]

13886 McLeese, Don. *Susan B. Anthony* (2–5). Series: Equal Rights Leaders. 2002, Rourke LB $19.27 (1-58952-284-2). 24pp. Simple text and well-chosen illustrations tell the story of Anthony's

life, with good coverage of her youth and education. (Rev: SLJ 1/03) [324.6]

13887 Mosher, Kiki. *Learning About Fairness from the Life of Susan B. Anthony* (2–5). Illus. Series: A Character Building Book. 1996, Rosen LB $13.95 (0-8239-2422-X). 24pp. The spirit of fairness and justice is shown in the life of this leader for women's rights. (Rev: BL 10/15/96; SLJ 12/96) [921]

13888 Parker, Barbara Keevil. *Susan B. Anthony: Daring to Vote* (4–6). Illus. Series: Gateway Biographies. 1998, Millbrook LB $20.90 (0-7613-0358-8). 48pp. This interesting biography of this early abolitionist and fighter in the suffrage movement also contains brief biographies of other early feminists. (Rev: BL 6/1–15/98; HBG 10/98; SLJ 7/98) [921]

13889 Roop, Peter, and Connie Roop. *Susan B. Anthony* (2–3). Series: Lives and Times. 1997, Heinemann $21.36 (1-57572-563-0). 24pp. A simple picture-book biography that gives a short introduction to the life and times of this fighter for women's rights. (Rev: BL 3/15/98) [921]

13890 Weidt, Maryann N. *Fighting for Equal Rights: A Story About Susan B. Anthony* (3–5). Illus. by Amanda Sartor. Series: Creative Minds Biographies. 2003, Carolrhoda LB $21.27 (1-57505-181-8). 64pp. A straightforward account of the life of the women's rights campaigner, starting with her childhood and schooling, and of the time in which she lived. (Rev: HBG 4/04; SLJ 3/04) [921]

BAKER, S. JOSEPHINE

13891 Ptacek, Greg. *Champion for Children's Health: A Story About Dr. S. Josephine Baker* (3–5). Illus. by Lydia M. Anderson. 1994, Carolrhoda LB $21.27 (0-87614-806-2). 64pp. The story of the woman who pioneered public-health standards for children at the turn of the century. (Rev: BL 3/1/94; SLJ 3/94) [921]

BANNAKY, MOLLY

13892 McGill, Alice. *Molly Bannaky* (PS–4). Illus. by Chris K. Soentpiet. 1999, Houghton Mifflin $15.00 (0-395-72287-X). 32pp. This is the amazing story of white colonialist Molly Bannaky, who dared to buy and marry a slave and eventually became the grandmother of Benjamin Banneker, the famous African American astronomer and mathematician. (Rev: BCCB 10/99; BL 9/15/99; HBG 3/00; SLJ 10/99) [921]

BARTON, CLARA

13893 Deady, Kathleen W. *Clara Barton* (2–4). Illus. Series: Photo-Illustrated Biographies. 2003, Capstone LB $18.60 (0-7368-1604-6). 24pp. A simple profile suitable for beginning report writers, with large, easy-to-read text and full-page illustrations. (Rev: HBG 10/03; SLJ 1/04) [921]

13894 Francis, Dorothy. *Clara Barton: Founder of the American Red Cross* (4–6). Series: Gateway

Greens. 2002, Millbrook LB $23.90 (0-7613-2621-9). 48pp. The story of the Red Cross founder who obtained and distributed supplies for the wounded during the Civil War. (Rev: BL 7/02; HBG 3/03) [921]

13895 Hamilton, Leni. *Clara Barton* (5–10). Illus. 1987, Chelsea LB $19.95 (1-55546-641-9). The story of the Civil War nurse and how she prepared for the founding of the American Red Cross. (Rev: BL 11/1/87) [921]

13896 Koestler-Grack, Rachel A. *The Story of Clara Barton* (4–7). Illus. Series: Breakthrough Biographies. 2004, Chelsea House LB $14.95 (0-7910-7312-2). 32pp. From her childhood and early career to her founding of the American Red Cross, this profile gives personal details and historical context. (Rev: BL 3/1/04; HBG 4/04; SLJ 9/04) [361.763]

13897 Rose, Mary Catherine. *Clara Barton: Soldier of Mercy* (3–5). Illus. 1991, Chelsea LB $16.95 (0-7910-1403-7). A simply written account of this courageous nurse who founded the Red Cross.

13898 Whitelaw, Nancy. *Clara Barton: Civil War Nurse* (5–9). Series: Historical American Biographies. 1997, Enslow LB $20.95 (0-89490-778-6). Using material from her diaries and published books, this biography relates Barton's life story and amazing accomplishments. (Rev: BL 3/15/98; SLJ 2/98) [921]

BRIDGMAN, LAURA DEWEY

13899 Hunter, Edith Fisher. *Child of the Silent Night* (3–5). Illus. 1963, Houghton Mifflin $16.00 (0-395-06835-5). 128pp. The story of a blind-deaf child who paved the way for the successes of Helen Keller.

BUSH, BARBARA

13900 Spies, Karen B. *Barbara Bush: Helping America Read* (3–6). Illus. Series: Taking Part. 1991, Macmillan LB $18.95 (0-87518-488-X). 64pp. A look at the former First Lady, with some data on her interest in the literacy campaign. (Rev: BL 3/15/92; SLJ 3/92) [921]

BUSH, LAURA WELCH

13901 Gormley, Beatrice. *Laura Bush: America's First Lady* (5–8). Illus. 2003, Simon & Schuster LB $11.89 (0-689-85628-8); paper $4.99 (0-689-85366-1). 112pp. A chronological account of Laura Bush's life, with information on her childhood as well as her later public life. (Rev: BL 3/1/03; HBG 10/03; SLJ 5/03) [973.931]

13902 Stone, Tanya Lee. *Laura Welch Bush* (4–6). Illus. 2001, Millbrook LB $22.90 (0-7613-2304-X). 48pp. A biography of President George W. Bush's wife, with photographs and "fun facts." (Rev: BL 9/15/01; HBG 3/02; SLJ 9/01) [973.931]

CATT, CARRIE CHAPMAN

13903 Somervill, Barbara A. *Votes for Women! The Story of Carrie Chapman Catt* (5–8). Illus. 2002, Morgan Reynolds LB $21.95 (1-883846-96-X). 128pp. This is the story of Carrie Chapman Catt, who devoted her early life to the quest for women's right to vote and later turned her energies to helping Jewish refugees. (Rev: BL 11/15/02; HBG 3/03; SLJ 1/03) [324.6]

CHILD, LYDIA MARIA

13904 Stux, Erica. *Writing for Freedom: A Story About Lydia Maria Child* (3–5). Illus. Series: Creative Minds Biographies. 2000, Carolrhoda $21.27 (1-57505-439-6). A biography of the poet who was also an abolitionist and courageously fought against slavery. (Rev: HBG 10/01; SLJ 1/01) [921]

CLINTON, HILLARY RODHAM

13905 Guernsey, JoAnn Bren. *Hillary Rodham Clinton* (5–8). Illus. 2005, Lerner LB $27.93 (0-8225-2372-8); paper $7.95 (0-8225-9613-X). 112pp. Traces Clinton's life from childhood, and covers the trials of her husband's second term in office in some detail. (Rev: BL 6/1–15/05) [921]

13906 Levert, Suzanne. *Hillary Rodham Clinton: First Lady* (3–5). Illus. Series: Gateway Biographies. 1994, Millbrook paper $8.95 (1-56294-726-5). 48pp. A biography of the First Lady that ends in 1993. (Rev: BL 7/94) [921]

13907 Sherrow, Victoria. *Hillary Rodham Clinton* (3–6). Illus. Series: Taking Part. 1993, Dillon LB $13.95 (0-87518-621-1). 64pp. A biography of the First Lady that focuses on her schooling and law career. (Rev: BL 10/15/93; SLJ 12/93) [921]

CRANDALL, PRUDENCE

13908 Lucas, Eileen. *Prudence Crandall: Teacher for Equal Rights* (1–3). Illus. by Kimanne Smith. 2001, Carolrhoda LB $21.27 (1-57505-480-9). 48pp. A biography for beginning readers of Crandall, a Quaker teacher who struggled to run a school for African American students in the 1830s. (Rev: HBG 3/02; SLJ 1/02) [921]

DAY, DOROTHY

13909 Shaw, Maura D. *Dorothy Day: A Catholic Life of Action* (3–6). Illus. by Stephen Marchesi. Series: Spiritual Biographies for Young Readers. 2004, Skylight Paths $12.95 (1-59473-011-3). 32pp. Roman Catholic journalist/social activist Dorothy Day worked to help the homeless and hungry. (Rev: BL 10/1/04) [921]

DIX, DOROTHEA

13910 Herstek, Amy Paulson. *Dorothea Dix* (5–8). Series: Historical American Biographies. 2001, Enslow LB $20.95 (0-7660-1258-1). The life of this militant reformer who fought for more humane treatment of the insane. (Rev: BL 1/1–15/02; HBG 3/02; SLJ 1/02) [921]

DOLE, ELIZABETH

13911 Lucas, Eileen. *Elizabeth Dole: A Leader in Washington* (4–6). Illus. Series: Gateway Biographies. 1998, Millbrook LB $20.90 (0-7613-0203-4). 48pp. This book takes the reader from Elizabeth Dole's childhood in North Carolina through her recent career in government and public service. (Rev: BL 6/1–15/98; HBG 10/98; SLJ 6/98) [921]

EDELMAN, MARIAN WRIGHT

13912 Old, Wendie C. *Marian Wright Edelman: Fighting for Children's Rights* (4–6). Illus. Series: People to Know. 1995, Enslow LB $20.95 (0-89490-623-2). 112pp. The story of this 20th-century American and her fight for the rights of children. (Rev: BL 10/15/95; SLJ 12/95) [921]

EDMONDS, EMMA

13913 Reit, Seymour. *Behind Rebel Lines: The Incredible Story of Emma Edmonds, Civil War Spy* (5–8). 1988, Harcourt $12.95 (0-15-200416-5); paper $6.00 (0-15-200424-6). 144pp. The remarkable Canadian-born spy who helped to defend the Union in the Civil War. (Rev: BL 3/1/88; SLJ 3/88) [973.785]

FEINSTEIN, DIANNE

13914 McElroy, Lisa Tucker. *Meet My Grandmother: She's a United States Senator* (2–4). Series: Grandmothers at Work. 2000, Millbrook LB $22.90 (0-7613-1721-X). 32pp. Dianne Feinstein, once mayor of San Francisco and now a U.S. senator, as seen through the eyes of her 6-year-old granddaughter. (Rev: BL 3/15/00; HBG 10/00; SLJ 1/01) [921]

GORE, TIPPER

13915 Guernsey, JoAnn B. *Tipper Gore: Voice for the Voiceless* (4–6). Illus. 1994, Lerner LB $19.93 (0-8225-2876-2); paper $6.95 (0-8225-9651-2). 64pp. This biography of the vice president's wife reveals her to be an independent, determined woman who champions a number of worthy causes. (Rev: BL 9/15/94; SLJ 7/94) [921]

13916 Kramer, Barbara. *Tipper Gore* (4–7). Illus. Series: People to Know. 1999, Enslow LB $20.95 (0-7660-1142-9). 112pp. The story of the life of the former vice president's wife and her activities as a mother, professional photographer, and social issues advocate. (Rev: BL 8/99) [921]

GRAHAM, KATHARINE

13917 Mattern, Joanne. *Katharine Graham and 20th Century American Journalism* (1–4). Series: Women Who Shaped History. 2003, Rosen LB $17.25 (0-8239-6500-7). 24pp. The story of the woman who

ran the *Washington Post* after her husband's death and who helped uncover the Watergate scandal. (Rev: BL 2/15/03; SLJ 5/03) [921]

GRIMKE, SARAH AND ANGELINA

13918 McPherson, Stephanie S. *Sisters Against Slavery: A Story About Sarah and Angelina Grimke* (4–7). Illus. by Karen Ritz. Series: Creative Minds Biographies. 1999, Carolrhoda LB $25.55 (1-57505-361-6). 64pp. The story of the remarkable Grimke sisters from South Carolina who fought against slavery and later became suffragettes. (Rev: BCCB 1/00; HBG 3/00; SLJ 12/99) [921]

HOOVER, LOU

13919 Colbert, Nancy A. *Lou Hoover: The Duty to Serve* (5–8). Illus. 1997, Morgan Reynolds LB $21.95 (1-883846-22-6). President Hoover's wife was a most interesting person, who, among other accomplishments, was the first woman to get a degree in geology in this country, was the translator — with her husband — of a 16th-century Latin mining text, was an advocate of physical education for women, and was fluent in seven languages, including Chinese. (Rev: BL 2/15/98; HBG 3/98; SLJ 3/98) [973.91]

HUTCHINSON, ANNE

13920 Ilgenfritz, Elizabeth. *Anne Hutchinson* (5–8). Illus. Series: American Women of Achievement. 1990, Chelsea LB $19.95 (1-55546-660-5). 111pp. The story of the woman in pre-Revolutionary days who stood trial to defend religious liberty. (Rev: SLJ 4/91) [921]

13921 Mangal, Melina. *Anne Hutchinson: Religious Reformer* (4–6). Series: Let Freedom Ring. 2004, Capstone LB $23.93 (0-7368-2454-5). 48pp. Hutchinson was a religious liberal whose outspoken opinions resulted in her banishment from the Massachusetts Bay Colony; she later helped to found the colony of Rhode Island. (Rev: SLJ 8/04) [921]

INGLES, MARY DRAPER

13922 Furbee, Mary R. *Shawnee Captive: The Story of Mary Draper Ingles* (5–8). Illus. 2001, Morgan Reynolds LB $21.95 (1-883846-69-2). 112pp. The tragic and exciting story of a pioneer woman captured by Shawnee Indians, her daring escape, and her long and difficult journey home. (Rev: BL 5/15/01; HBG 10/01; SLJ 6/01) [975.5]

JOHNSON, LADY BIRD

13923 Appelt, Kathi. *Miss Lady Bird's Wildflowers: How a First Lady Changed America* (1–3). Illus. by Joy Fisher Hein. 2005, HarperCollins LB $17.89 (0-06-001108-4). 40pp. Lady Bird Johnson's lifelong passion for flowers and her campaign as First Lady to beautify the nation's highways and cities by planting wildflowers are at the center of this volume. (Rev: BL 2/15/05) [973.923]

KELLER, HELEN

13924 Adler, David A. *Helen Keller* (1–2). Illus. by John C. Wallner. Series: Holiday House Reader. 2003, Holiday House $14.95 (0-8234-1606-2). 32pp. Written in simple language that is well suited for early readers, this biography covers Keller's youth and her work as an adult. (Rev: BL 7/03; HBG 4/04; SLJ 11/03) [921]

13925 Adler, David A. *A Picture Book of Helen Keller* (2–4). Illus. by John Wallner and Alexandra Wallner. Series: Picture Book Biographies. 1990, Holiday House LB $16.95 (0-8234-0818-3); paper $6.95 (0-8234-0950-3). 32pp. This account focuses on Keller's personality, stamina, and accomplishments. (Rev: BL 12/15/90; SLJ 11/90) [921]

13926 Dash, Joan. *The World at Her Fingertips: The Story of Helen Keller* (4–7). Illus. 2001, Scholastic paper $15.95 (0-590-90715-8). 223pp. A straightforward account of the girl who was left blind and deaf at 19 months and of her determination to be independent. (Rev: BCCB 3/01; BL 2/15/01; HB 3–4/01; HBG 10/01; SLJ 4/01*) [921]

13927 Garrett, Leslie. *Helen Keller: Biography* (5–10). Series: DK Biography. 2004, DK paper $4.99 (0-7566-0339-0). 128pp. Keller's struggles to conquer her physical disabilities and her worldwide recognition as a political activist and public speaker are covered in the usual rich DK format. (Rev: BL 6/1–15/04) [921]

13928 Graff, Stewart, and Polly Graff. *Helen Keller: Toward the Light* (3–5). Illus. 1992, Chelsea LB $16.95 (0-7910-1412-6). 80pp. A simply written biography of the woman who overcame the handicaps of blindness and deafness.

13929 Kent, Deborah. *Helen Keller: Author and Advocate for the Disabled* (3–6). Series: Our People. 2003, Child's World LB $27.07 (1-59296-005-7). 32pp. Report writers will find solid material in this biography that includes "Interesting Facts" sidebars. (Rev: BL 1/1–15/04; SLJ 4/04) [921]

13930 Lakin, Patricia. *Helen Keller and the Big Storm* (1–2). Illus. by Diana Magnuson. Series: Childhood of Famous Americans. 2002, Simon & Schuster LB $11.89 (0-689-84025-X); paper $3.99 (0-689-84104-3). 30pp. An anecdote about her teacher rescuing Helen when she is caught in a tree during a storm serves to introduce beginning readers to Helen's character and problems. (Rev: HBG 10/02; SLJ 7/02) [921]

13931 Lawlor, Laurie. *Helen Keller: Rebellious Spirit* (4–8). Illus. 2001, Holiday House $22.95 (0-8234-1588-0). 161pp. This account puts Keller's life in the context of her time and looks at the opinions and beliefs that made her a "rebellious spirit," with photographs, quotations, a bibliography, and the manual alphabet. (Rev: BL 9/1/01; HB 9–10/01; HBG 3/02; SLJ 9/01*) [362.4]

13932 MacLeod, Elizabeth. *Helen Keller: A Determined Life* (3–5). Illus. Series: Snapshots: Images of People and Places in History. 2004, Kids Can $14.95 (1-55337-508-4). 32pp. Attractive double-page spreads with well-positioned and interesting text make this profile inviting for browsers. (Rev: BL 3/1/04; SLJ 5/04) [921]

13933 Shichtman, Sandra H. *Helen Keller: Out of a Dark and Silent World* (4–6). Series: Gateway Greens. 2002, Millbrook LB $23.90 (0-7613-2550-6). 48pp. The inspiring story of the woman who overcame multiple handicaps to become a role model for others. (Rev: BL 7/02; HBG 3/03) [921]

13934 Sullivan, George. *Helen Keller* (3–5). Illus. 2001, Scholastic $12.95 (0-439-14751-4); paper $4.50 (0-439-59555-7). 128pp. Using excerpts from her biographical works, the author presents an interesting picture of Keller, her problems, and her life. (Rev: BL 4/1/01; HBG 10/01) [921]

13935 Sutcliffe, Jane. *Helen Keller* (2–4). Illus. by Elaine Verstraete. Series: On My Own Biography. 2002, Carolrhoda LB $22.60 (0-87614-600-0); paper $5.95 (0-87614-903-4). 48pp. For beginning readers, this is an appealing introduction to Keller's life. (Rev: HBG 3/03; SLJ 12/02) [921]

KELLEY, FLORENCE

13936 Saller, Carol. *Florence Kelley* (2–4). Illus. by Ken Green. Series: On My Own Biography. 1997, Carolrhoda LB $19.93 (1-57505-016-1). 48pp. The story of the labor leader and her fight against child labor. (Rev: BCCB 7–8/97; BL 6/1–15/97; SLJ 11/97) [921]

LINCOLN, MARY TODD

13937 Hull, Mary E. *Mary Todd Lincoln* (5–8). Series: Historical American Biographies. 2000, Enslow LB $20.95 (0-7660-1252-2). This biography faithfully records the tragic life of Lincoln's widow, whose emotional health declined after the deaths of her son and her husband. (Rev: BL 1/1–15/00; HBG 10/00; SLJ 5/00) [921]

LYON, MARY

13938 Rosen, Dorothy S. *A Fire in Her Bones: The Story of Mary Lyon* (5–7). Illus. 1995, Carolrhoda LB $30.35 (0-87614-840-2). 88pp. A biography of the woman who defied social barriers and founded Mount Holyoke Female Seminary, now known as Mount Holyoke College. (Rev: BL 6/1–15/95; SLJ 4/95) [921]

MADISON, DOLLEY

13939 Klingel, Cynthia, and Robert B. Noyed. *Dolley Madison: First Lady* (2–4). Illus. Series: Spirit of America: Our People. 2002, Child's World LB $27.07 (1-56766-170-X). 32pp. A solid introduction to the life of Dolley Madison and her skill as a hostess. (Rev: SLJ 1/03) [921]

13940 Patrick, Jean L. S. *Dolley Madison* (3–4). Illus. Series: History Maker Bios. 2002, Lerner LB $23.93 (0-8225-0194-5). 48pp. Using both cartoons and regular illustrations, this is a biography of the brave and gracious first lady who became a famous hostess. (Rev: BL 6/1–15/02; HBG 3/03) [921]

13941 Pflueger, Lynda. *Dolley Madison: Courageous First Lady* (5–8). Series: Historical American Biographies. 1999, Enslow LB $20.95 (0-7660-1092-9). An interesting biography of the woman who defined the role of First Lady and who was known for her political acumen and diplomatic and social skills as well as her patriotism and her ability to inspire others. (Rev: BR 5–6/99; SLJ 1/99) [921]

13942 Shulman, Holly C., and David B. Mattern. *Dolley Madison: Her Life, Letters, and Legacy* (4–7). Illus. Series: Library of American Lives and Times. 2003, Rosen LB $31.95 (0-8239-5749-7). 112pp. An inviting life of the socially adept wife of the fourth president of the United States. [921]

13943 Weatherly, Myra. *Dolley Madison: America's First Lady* (5–8). Illus. Series: Founders of the Republic. 2002, Morgan Reynolds LB $21.95 (1-883846-95-1). 128pp. This portrait of Dolley Madison conveys her popularity and courage, with reproductions of period paintings, prints, and maps. (Rev: BL 11/1/02; HBG 3/03; SLJ 3/03) [973.5]

MARTINI, HELEN DELANEY

13944 Lyon, George Ella. *Mother to Tigers* (K–3). Illus. by Peter Catalanotto. 2003, Simon & Schuster $16.95 (0-689-84221-X). 32pp. A picture-book biography of the woman who looked after tiger cubs in her own home before she established a nursery at the Bronx Zoo. (Rev: BL 3/1/03; HB 5–6/03; HBG 10/03; SLJ 3/03) [590]

NATION, CARRY A.

13945 Harvey, Bonnie Carman. *Carry A. Nation: Saloon Smasher and Prohibitionist* (5–8). Series: Historical American Biographies. 2002, Enslow LB $20.95 (0-7660-1907-1). 128pp. A lively and balanced biography of the prohibitionist who fought alcohol with violence. (Rev: HBG 3/03; SLJ 1/03) [921]

ONASSIS, JACQUELINE KENNEDY

13946 Anderson, Catherine C. *Jackie Kennedy Onassis* (4–7). Illus. 1995, Lerner LB $21.27 (0-8225-2885-1). 88pp. An adoring biography of the former First Lady, who was a model of courage and dignity. (Rev: BL 2/1/96) [921]

PITCHER, MOLLY

13947 Rockwell, Anne. *They Called Her Molly Pitcher* (3–5). Illus. by Cynthia von Buhler. 2002, Knopf $15.95 (0-679-89187-0). 32pp. The story of the gallant Revolutionary War heroine who offered water to soldiers during the Battle of Monmouth and fired her husband's canon after he was shot. (Rev: BCCB 6/02; BL 4/15/02; HB 5–6/02; HBG 10/02; SLJ 6/02) [921]

ROOSEVELT, ELEANOR

13948 Adler, David A. *A Picture Book of Eleanor Roosevelt* (K–3). Illus. by Robert Casilla. Series: Picture Book Biographies. 1991, Holiday House LB $16.95 (0-8234-0856-6). 32pp. The life of this well-known First Lady is described in simple text and many illustrations. (Rev: BCCB 4/91; BL 6/1/91; SLJ 5/91) [921]

13949 Brown, Jonatha A. *Eleanor Roosevelt* (2–4). Illus. Series: People We Should Know. 2005, Gareth Stevens LB $14.50 (0-8368-4468-8). 24pp. For beginning readers, a simple explanation of Eleanor Roosevelt's importance with an attractive layout and historical and contemporary photographs. [921]

13950 Cooney, Barbara. *Eleanor* (K–3). Illus. 1996, Viking $15.99 (0-670-86159-6). 40pp. A picture-book biography that supplies details on Eleanor Roosevelt's life, particularly her lonely childhood. (Rev: BCCB 11/96; BL 9/15/96*; HB 9–10/96; SLJ 9/96*) [921]

13951 Faber, Doris. *Eleanor Roosevelt: First Lady to the World* (5–7). Illus. by Donna Ruff. 1986, Puffin paper $4.99 (0-14-032103-9). 64pp. Eleanor Roosevelt's life before and after FDR is discussed. (Rev: BL 9/1/85; HB 9–10/85; SLJ 8/85) [973.9170924]

13952 Feinberg, Barbara Silberdick. *Eleanor Roosevelt: A Very Special Lady* (3–5). Illus. Series: Gateway. 2003, Millbrook LB $23.90 (0-7613-2623-5). 48pp. A biography of the First Lady, with photographs, a timeline, and a list of relevant Web sites. (Rev: BL 2/1/03; HBG 10/03; SLJ 4/03) [973.917]

13953 Freedman, Russell. *Eleanor Roosevelt: A Life of Discovery* (5–9). 1993, Clarion $17.95 (0-89919-862-7). This admiring photobiography captures Roosevelt's public role and personal sadness. (Rev: BL 7/93*; SLJ 8/93*) [921]

13954 Koestler-Grack, Rachel A. *The Story of Eleanor Roosevelt* (4–7). Illus. Series: Breakthrough Biographies. 2004, Chelsea House LB $14.95 (0-7910-7313-0). 32pp. This brief biography covers Roosevelt's early years as well as her later contributions to her country and to the world. (Rev: BL 3/1/04; HBG 4/04) [973917]

13955 Lazo, Caroline. *Eleanor Roosevelt* (4–7). Illus. Series: Peacemakers. 1993, Dillon $13.95 (0-87518-594-0). 64pp. A biography of the famous First Lady that focuses on her many lasting contributions, particularly in promoting world peace. (Rev: BL 12/15/93; SLJ 1/94) [921]

13956 Mattern, Joanne. *Eleanor Roosevelt: More than a First Lady* (1–4). Series: Women Who Shaped History. 2003, Rosen LB $17.25 (0-8239-6501-5). 24pp. Through classic photographs and an accessible text, readers will learn about the amazing woman who changed the role of the first lady and had a great influence on world affairs. (Rev: BL 2/15/03) [921]

13957 Rosenberg, Pam. *Eleanor Roosevelt: First Lady, Humanitarian, and World Citizen* (3–6). Series: Our People. 2003, Child's World LB $27.07

(1-59296-001-4). 32pp. An accessible life of Roosevelt, emphasizing her contributions to society. (Rev: BL 1/1–15/04)

13958 Weidt, Maryann N. *Stateswoman to the World: A Story About Eleanor Roosevelt* (4–6). Illus. by Lydia M. Anderson. 1991, Carolrhoda LB $21.27 (0-87614-663-9). 64pp. A frank biography of the First Lady so admired and respected throughout the world. (Rev: BL 12/15/91; SLJ 12/91) [921]

13959 Westervelt, Virginia Veeder. *Here Comes Eleanor: A New Biography of Eleanor Roosevelt for Young People* (5–8). Series: Avisson Young Adult. 1999, Avisson paper $16.00 (1-888105-33-X). 142pp. A clear account of the life of Eleanor Roosevelt that gives a fine assessment of her many contributions to humankind. (Rev: BL 2/15/99; SLJ 7/99) [921]

13960 Winget, Mary. *Eleanor Roosevelt* (5–8). Series: A&E Biography. 2000, Lerner LB $25.26 (0-8225-4985-9). 112pp. Growing up in a troubled but loving family, Eleanor Roosevelt showed that an ordinary woman can achieve greatness. (Rev: BL 3/1/01; HBG 10/01) [921]

SAMPSON, DEBORAH

13961 McGovern, Ann. *The Secret Soldier: The Story of Deborah Sampson* (4–6). Illus. by Ann Grifalconi. 1987, Macmillan paper $4.50 (0-590-43052-1). 64pp. The story of the woman who disguised herself as a man and joined the Continental army. A reissue.

SHAW, ANNA HOWARD

13962 Brown, Don. *A Voice from the Wilderness: The Story of Anna Howard Shaw* (1–3). Illus. 2001, Houghton Mifflin $16.00 (0-618-08362-6). 32pp. This is the story of Anna Howard Shaw, who came to America in the mid-19th century and overcame adversity to become a teacher and champion of women's suffrage. (Rev: BL 9/15/01; HB 11–12/01; HBG 3/02; SLJ 9/01) [324.6]

STANTON, ELIZABETH CADY

13963 Fritz, Jean. *You Want Women to Vote, Lizzie Stanton?* (4–7). Illus. 1995, Penguin Putnam $17.99 (0-399-22786-5). 96pp. An exciting, witty re-creation of the life of Elizabeth Cady Stanton, fighter for women's rights, including suffrage. (Rev: BCCB 10/95; BL 8/95*; SLJ 9/95*) [921]

13964 Loos, Pamela. *Elizabeth Cady Stanton* (5–8). Illus. Series: Women of Achievement. 2000, Chelsea $19.95 (0-7910-5293-1). 120pp. Drawing largely on Stanton's autobiography, this is the life story of the well-known suffragist of the 19th century. (Rev: BL 2/15/01; HBG 10/01) [921]

13965 Salisbury, Cynthia. *Elizabeth Cady Stanton: Leader of the Fight for Women's Rights* (5–8). Series: Historical American Biographies. 2002, Enslow LB $20.95 (0-7660-1616-1). The life of the fighter for women's suffrage and the organizer of

the first women's rights convention. (Rev: BL 4/1/02; HBG 10/02; SLJ 5/02) [921]

13966 Swain, Gwenyth. *The Road to Seneca Falls* (3–6). Illus. Series: Creative Minds. 1996, Carolrhoda LB $21.27 (0-87614-947-6); paper $5.95 (1-57505-025-0). 64pp. This biography of Elizabeth Cady Stanton chronicles the birth of the women's rights movement. (Rev: BL 2/15/97; SLJ 3/97) [921]

STARR, BELLE

13967 Naden, Corinne J., and Rose Blue. *Belle Starr and the Wild West* (5–9). Series: Notorious Americans and Their Times. 2000, Blackbirch LB $27.44 (1-56711-223-4). 112pp. A fascinating biography of the legendary female outlaw who died a violent death at age 51. (Rev: HBG 3/01; SLJ 1/01) [921]

STEINEM, GLORIA

13968 Hoff, Mary. *Gloria Steinem: The Women's Movement* (4–6). Illus. Series: New Directions. 1991, Millbrook LB $21.90 (1-878841-19-X). 96pp. The life story of this journalist who questioned women's roles in modern society. (Rev: SLJ 4/91) [921]

13969 Lazo, Caroline. *Gloria Steinem: Feminist Extraordinaire* (5–7). Illus. Series: Lerner Biographies. 1998, Lerner LB $25.26 (0-8225-4934-4). 128pp. The story of Steinem, who overcame a troubled childhood to become a great humanitarian, writer, and leader of the feminist movement. (Rev: BL 7/98; SLJ 7/98) [921]

STINSON, KATHERINE

13970 Winegarten, Debra L. *Katherine Stinson: The Flying Schoolgirl* (4–7). 2001, Eakin $26.95 (1-57168-459-X). 115pp. An absorbing introduction to Stinson's accomplishments, which include a whole series of "firsts," that interweaves fiction and fact. (Rev: HBG 10/01; SLJ 6/01) [629.13092]

STONE, LUCY

13971 McPherson, Stephanie S. *I Speak for the Women: A Story About Lucy Stone* (4–6). Illus. by Brian Liedahl. Series: Creative Minds. 1992, Carolrhoda LB $19.93 (0-87614-740-6). 64pp. The life of a dedicated abolitionist and champion of women's rights in 19th-century America. (Rev: BCCB 3/93; BL 3/15/93; SLJ 2/93) [921]

WASHINGTON, MARTHA

13972 McPherson, Stephanie S. *Martha Washington: First Lady* (4–6). Illus. Series: Historical American Biographies. 1998, Enslow LB $19.95 (0-7660-1017-1). 128pp. Using many period paintings and contemporary photos, this book traces the life of Martha Washington, her two marriages, and her private and public lives. (Rev: BL 1/1–15/99; SLJ 1/99) [921]

WASHINGTON, MARY BALL

13973 Fritz, Jean. *George Washington's Mother* (2–3). Illus. by DyAnne DiSalvo-Ryan. 1992, Penguin Putnam paper $3.95 (0-448-40384-6). 48pp. A simple biography of Mary Ball Washington, the mother of the first president. (Rev: BL 10/1/92; SLJ 10/92) [921]

WOODHULL, VICTORIA

13974 Krull, Kathleen. *A Woman for President: The Story of Victoria Woodhull* (3–5). Illus. by Jane Dyer. 2004, Walker $16.95 (0-8027-8908-0). Woodhull's fascinating life included working as a spiritualist and financial adviser, amassing wealth, starting a newspaper, and running for president. (Rev: SLJ 9/04) [921]

Scientists, Inventors, Naturalists, and Business Figures

Collective

13975 Aaseng, Nathan. *Business Builders in Computers* (5–8). Series: Business Builders. 2000, Oliver LB $22.95 (1-881508-57-9). 160pp. Bill Gates, Steve Jobs of Apple, and Steve Case of AOL are among the individuals profiled in this interesting volume on the growth of the computer industry. (Rev: BL 2/1/01; HBG 10/01; SLJ 5/01) [338.4]

13976 Aaseng, Nathan. *Business Builders in Fast Food* (5–8). Series: Business Builders. 2001, Oliver $22.95 (1-881508-58-7). 160pp. An interesting look at the creators of fast food empires such as McDonald's and Wendy's. (Rev: BL 9/15/01; HBG 10/01; SLJ 9/01) [381]

13977 Aaseng, Nathan. *Business Builders in Oil* (5–8). Series: Business Builders. 2000, Oliver LB $22.95 (1-881508-56-0). 160pp. This lively introduction to the oil industry provides profiles of key individuals such as John D. Rockefeller, Andrew Mellon, and J. Paul Getty. (Rev: BL 2/1/01; HBG 10/01; SLJ 5/01) [338.2]

13978 Aaseng, Nathan. *Construction: Building the Impossible* (5–9). Illus. 2000, Oliver LB $21.95 (1-881508-59-5). 144pp. This book profiles eight famous builders — from Imhotep, who built the first stone pyramids in Egypt, to Frank Crowe, the visionary behind the Hoover Dam. (Rev: BL 5/1/00; HBG 10/00; SLJ 10/00) [920]

13979 Bankston, John. *Francis Crick and James Watson: Pioneers in DNA Research* (5–7). Series: Unlocking the Secrets of Science. 2002, Mitchell Lane LB $17.95 (1-58415-122-6). 56pp. An accessible account of the discovery of the structure of DNA and the lives of the two scientists involved. (Rev: HBG 10/03; SLJ 1/03) [576.5]

13980 Camp, Carole Ann. *American Astronomers: Searchers and Wonderers* (5–8). Series: Collective Biographies. 1996, Enslow LB $20.95 (0-89490-631-3). This volume presents brief profiles of important astronomers including Maria Mitchell, Edwin Hubble, and Carl Sagan. (Rev: BL 4/15/96; BR 9–10/96; SLJ 5/96) [920]

13981 Camp, Carole Ann. *American Women Inventors* (5–10). Illus. Series: Collective Biographies. 2004, Enslow LB $20.95 (0-7660-1913-6). 104pp. A collective biography of 10 important American female inventors, their lives, and their discoveries. (Rev: BL 3/1/04) [920]

13982 Cox, Clinton. *African American Healers* (4–7). Illus. Series: Black Stars. 1999, Wiley $24.95 (0-471-24650-6). 164pp. Using entries of two to three pages each, this work profiles more than 20 African Americans who have achieved prominence in medicine and related areas. (Rev: BL 2/15/00; HBG 10/00; SLJ 2/00) [910]

13983 Curtis, Robert H. *Great Lives: Medicine* (5–8). Series: Great Lives. 1992, Scribner $24.00 (0-684-19321-3). Biographies of doctors and other medical professionals who made major contributions and discoveries throughout history. (Rev: BL 12/15/92; SLJ 6/93) [920]

13984 DeAngelis, Gina. *Science and Medicine* (5–9). Series: Female Firsts in Their Fields. 1999, Chelsea $18.65 (0-7910-5143-9). 64pp. The six women profiled here are Elizabeth Blackwell, Clara Barton, Marie Curie, Margaret Mead, Rachel Carson, and Antonia Novello. (Rev: BL 5/15/99; HBG 10/99; SLJ 9/99) [920]

13985 French, Laura. *Internet Pioneers: The Cyber Elite* (5–9). Series: Collective Biographies. 2001, Enslow LB $20.95 (0-7660-1540-8). 112pp. French tells the stories of 10 Internet innovators — including Andrew Grove, Bill Gates, Larry Ellison, and Jeff Bezos — detailing their successes and revealing their very different backgrounds. (Rev: HBG 3/02; SLJ 9/01) [920]

13986 Greenberg, Lorna, and Margot F. Horwitz. *Digging into the Past: Pioneers of Archeology* (5–9). Series: Lives in Science. 2001, Watts LB $25.00 (0-531-11857-6). 127pp. Chronologically arranged biographies of important archaeologists including Howard Carter and Kathleen Kenyon give information on the individual's life and work and also on the state of scientific knowledge at the time. (Rev: BL 11/15/01; SLJ 11/01)

13987 Hacker, Carlotta. *Scientists* (3–6). Series: Women in Profile. 1998, Crabtree LB $21.28 (0-7787-0006-2); paper $8.95 (0-7787-0028-3). 48pp. This collection focuses on six female scientists, with about a dozen shorter sketches of others. (Rev: SLJ 9/98) [920]

13988 Hansen, Ole Steen. *The Wright Brothers and Other Pioneers of Flight* (4–7). Series: The Story of Flight. 2003, Crabtree $23.93 (0-7787-1200-1). 32pp. In text and pictures, this book introduces the pioneers of flight, with a concentration on the Wright brothers. (Rev: BL 10/15/03) [921]

13989 Harris, Laurie L., ed. *Biography Today: Profiles of People of Interest to Young Readers* (4–7). Illus. Series: Scientists and Inventors. 1996, Omnigraphics LB $39.00 (0-7808-0068-0). 194pp. Profiles of 14 important contemporaries including Carl Sagan and Jane Goodall are accompanied by those of some lesser-known figures, such as geneticist and AIDS fighter Mathilde Krim. (Rev: SLJ 2/97) [920]

13990 Hudson, Wade. *Book of Black Heroes: Scientists, Healers and Inventors* (5–8). Illus. 2002, Just Us $9.95 (0-940975-97-1). 70pp. One historic or present-day African American figure is presented on each page of this collective biography of doctors, engineers, and inventors. (Rev: BL 2/15/03) [925]

13991 Hunter, Shaun. *Leaders in Medicine* (3–6). Illus. Series: Women in Profile. 1999, Crabtree LB $15.96 (0-7787-0010-0); paper $8.06 (0-7787-0032-1). 48pp. Maria Montessori, Helen Taussig, and Elisabeth Kubler-Ross are among the women featured in this collective biography that contains six long profiles and 15 thumbnail sketches of famous women involved in medicine. (Rev: BL 9/15/99; SLJ 8/99) [920]

13992 Jeffrey, Laura S. *Great American Businesswomen* (4–7). Illus. 1996, Enslow LB $20.95 (0-89490-706-9). 112pp. Profiles of 10 successful American businesswomen, including Maggie L. Walker and Katharine Graham. (Rev: BL 9/1/96; SLJ 9/96) [920]

13993 Jones, Lynda. *Great Black Heroes: Five Brilliant Scientists* (2–3). Illus. by Ron Garnett. Series: Hello Reader! 2000, Scholastic paper $3.99 (0-590-48031-6). 48pp. This easy-to-read book profiles five African American scientists, among them Ernest Just, a marine biologist, and Percy Lavon Julian, a chemist. (Rev: BL 7/00; SLJ 8/00) [920]

13994 Keene, Ann T. *Earthkeepers: Observers and Protectors of Nature* (4–8). Illus. 1993, Oxford $50.00 (0-19-507867-5). 222pp. Profiles are given for more than 40 people throughout history who have worked to preserve the environment, beginning with the self-educated botanist John Bartram, who worked in the 1700s. (Rev: HB 11–12/93; SLJ 8/94*) [920]

13995 Kent, Jacqueline C. *Women in Medicine* (4–6). Series: Profiles. 1998, Oliver LB $16.95 (1-881508-46-3). 160pp. A collective biography of eight American women pioneers in medicine,

including Elizabeth Blackwell, May Edward Chinn, and Dorothy Lavinia Brown. (Rev: SLJ 10/98) [920]

13996 Kirsh, Shannon, and Florence Kirsh. *Fabulous Female Physicians* (4–8). 2002, Second Story paper $7.95 (1-896764-43-6). 100pp. Using short chapters and black-and-white photographs, this account profiles 10 mostly unknown female doctors and their accomplishments. (Rev: BL 6/1–15/02) [921]

13997 McClure, Judy. *Healers and Researchers: Physicians, Biologists, Social Scientists* (5–9). Series: Remarkable Women. 2000, Raintree LB $32.85 (0-8172-5734-9). 80pp. This book profiles 150 women from the scientific community including Barbara McClintock, Anna Freud, Jocelyn Elders, and Sushila Nyir. (Rev: SLJ 8/00) [920]

13998 McCutcheon, Marc. *The Kid Who Named Pluto and the Stories of Other Extraordinary Young People in Science* (3–6). Illus. by Jon Cannell. 2004, Chronicle $15.95 (0-8118-3770-X). 85pp. A collection of profiles of nine young people who made significant contributions to science while they still were young. (Rev: BL 4/1/04; SLJ 6/04) [920]

13999 Mayberry, Jodine. *Business Leaders Who Built Financial Empires* (5–8). Illus. Series: 20 Events. 1995, Raintree LB $27.12 (0-8114-4934-3). 48pp. The biographies of 19 financial wizards and entrepreneurs, beginning with Levi Strauss and Andrew Carnegie and ending with Steven Jobs and Anita Roddick. (Rev: SLJ 7/95) [920]

14000 Mulcahy, Robert. *Medical Technology: Inventing the Instruments* (5–8). Illus. Series: Innovators. 1997, Oliver LB $21.95 (1-881508-34-X). 144pp. Seven short biographies of scientists who were responsible for such inventions as the X-ray, stethoscope, thermometer, and electrocardiograph. (Rev: BCCB 7–8/97; BR 11–12/97; SLJ 7/97) [920]

14001 Platt, Richard. *Eureka! Great Inventions and How They Happened* (4–8). Illus. 2003, Kingfisher $18.95 (0-7534-5580-3). 95pp. Inventors and their inventions — including the cotton gin, the smallpox vaccination, the microwave, and the Internet — are profiled in two-page spreads with many illustrations. (Rev: HBG 4/04; SLJ 3/04) [920]

14002 Polking, Kirk. *Oceanographers and Explorers of the Sea* (5–9). Series: Collective Biographies. 1999, Enslow LB $20.95 (0-7660-1113-5). 128pp. Profiles 10 scientists and adventurers who have devoted their lives to the oceans, marine life, and ocean-related pursuits, including Maurice Ewing, who mapped the ocean floor, and Robert Ballard, discoverer of the *Titanic*. (Rev: BL 8/99; SLJ 9/99) [920]

14003 Richie, Jason. *Space Flight: Crossing the Last Frontier* (5–9). Illus. Series: Innovators. 2002, Oliver LB $21.95 (1-881508-77-3). 144pp. Biographies of seven men who were instrumental in the development of space flight — including Robert Goddard, Wernher von Braun, and Sergei Korolev — are arranged in chronological order. (Rev: HBG 3/03; LMC 4–5/03; SLJ 4/03) [629.4]

14004 Shell, Barry. *Great Canadian Scientists* (5–8). Illus. 1998, Polestar paper $14.95 (1-896095-36-4).

In profiles that average five or six pages, 19 important contemporary Canadian scientists and their work are introduced; an additional section gives short profiles of over 100 more. (Rev: SLJ 9/98) [920]

14005 Sherman, Josepha. *Jerry Yang and David Filo: Chief Yahoos of Yahoo* (5–8). Series: Techies. 2001, Millbrook LB $23.90 (0-7613-1961-1). This is the story of the creators of Yahoo!, the world's most heavily trafficked Web site. (Rev: BL 4/1/02; HBG 3/02; SLJ 12/01) [921]

14006 Stanley, Phyllis M. *American Environmental Heroes* (4–7). Illus. 1996, Enslow LB $20.95 (0-89490-630-5). 128pp. John Muir, Barry Commoner, Sylvia Earle, and seven other environmentalists are profiled. (Rev: BL 9/1/96; SLJ 7/96) [920]

14007 Sullivan, Otha R. *African American Inventors* (5–8). Ed. by Jim Haskins. Illus. Series: Black Stars. 1998, Wiley $24.95 (0-471-14804-0). Among the African American inventors profiled in two- and three-page spreads are Benjamin Banneker, Madam C. J. Walker, and Dr. Charles Drew, whose research laid the basis for blood donation. (Rev: BL 7/98; BR 11–12/98; SLJ 6/98) [920]

14008 Thimmesh, Catherine. *The Sky's the Limit: Stories of Discovery by Women and Girls* (5–7). Illus. by Melissa Sweet. 2002, Houghton Mifflin $16.00 (0-618-07698-0). 80pp. Details discoveries in the sciences, all made by women and girls. A sequel to *Girls Think of Everything* (2000). (Rev: BL 3/1/02; HB 5–6/02; HBG 10/02; SLJ 5/02) [500]

14009 VanCleave, Janice. *Janice VanCleave's Scientists Through the Ages* (4–7). Illus. 2003, Wiley paper $12.95 (0-471-25222-0). 128pp. A collective biography profiling 25 scientists, with explanations of each one's important work and a relevant experiment for the reader to perform. (Rev: BL 12/1/03) [509]

14010 Wilkinson, Philip, and Michael Pollard. *Scientists Who Changed the World* (3–5). Illus. by Robert Ingpen. Series: Turning Points. 1994, Chelsea LB $19.95 (0-7910-2763-5). 93pp. Twenty brief biographies of scientists, including Galileo, Marie Curie, DNA decoders, and the first men on the moon. (Rev: BL 12/1/94) [920]

Individual

ALVAREZ, LUIS

14011 Allison, Amy. *Luis Alvarez and the Development of the Bubble Chamber* (5–8). Series: Unlocking the Secrets of Science. 2002, Mitchell Lane LB $17.95 (1-58415-140-4). 48pp. Alvarez was a scientist of wide-ranging interests who won a Nobel Prize for developing a bubble chamber to track atomic particles. (Rev: HBG 3/03; SLJ 2/03) [921]

ANDREESSEN, MARC

14012 Ehrenhaft, Daniel. *Marc Andreessen: Web Warrior* (5–8). Illus. Series: The Techies. 2001, Twenty-First Century LB $23.90 (0-7613-1964-6).

80pp. This biography introduces Marc Andreessen, who coauthored the Web-browsing software Mosaic, cofounded the firm Netscape, and was a multimillionaire at age 24. (Rev: BL 3/15/01; HBG 10/01; SLJ 7/01) [921]

ANDREWS, ROY CHAPMAN

14013 Bausum, Ann. *Dragon Bones and Dinosaur Eggs: A Photobiography of Explorer Roy Chapman Andrews* (5–8). Illus. 2000, National Geographic $17.95 (0-7922-7123-8). 48pp. A biography of the famous paleontologist who made several important dinosaur discoveries in central Asia and later became director of the American Museum of Natural History in New York City. (Rev: BCCB 5/00*; BL 3/15/00; HBG 10/00; SLJ 3/00) [921]

14014 Marrin, Albert. *Secrets from the Rocks: Dinosaur Hunting with Roy Chapman Andrews* (4–8). Illus. 2002, Dutton $18.99 (0-525-46743-2). 80pp. This photo-biography of the famous paleontologist concentrates on his Mongolian expeditions in the 1920s and his great dinosaur discoveries. (Rev: BL 4/15/02; HB 7–8/02; HBG 10/02; SLJ 4/02) [921]

ANNING, MARY

14015 Anholt, Laurence. *Stone Girl, Bone Girl: The Story of Mary Anning* (K–3). Illus. by Sheila Moxley. 1999, Orchard $15.95 (0-531-30148-6). 32pp. The story of the 12-year-old British fossil hunter who discovered the skeleton of a huge sea creature, 165 million years old, in the limestone cliffs near Lyme Regis, Dorset. (Rev: BCCB 2/99; BL 2/1/99*; HBG 10/99; SLJ 5/99) [921]

14016 Atkins, Jeannine. *Mary Anning and the Sea Dragon* (K–4). Illus. by Michael Dooling. 1999, Farrar $16.00 (0-374-34840-5). 32pp. A picture book that tells of the exciting life of fossil hunter Mary Anning and her discoveries. (Rev: BL 9/1/99; HBG 3/00; SLJ 10/99) [560]

14017 Brighton, Catherine. *The Fossil Girl: Mary Anning's Dinosaur Discovery* (2–4). Illus. by author. 1999, Millbrook LB $21.40 (0-7613-1468-7). Born in 1799, Mary Anning was the amazing youngster who discovered and studied fossils, including an enormous creature embedded in rock that she found close to her English coastal home. (Rev: HBG 10/99; SLJ 5/99) [921]

14018 Brown, Don. *Rare Treasure: Mary Anning and Her Remarkable Discoveries* (K–3). Illus. 1999, Houghton Mifflin $15.00 (0-395-92286-0). 32pp. This picture-book biography of Mary Anning's life emphasizes her fossil discoveries in England at the beginning of the 18th century. (Rev: BCCB 1/00; BL 11/15/99; HBG 3/00; SLJ 10/99) [921]

14019 Goodhue, Thomas. *Curious Bones: Mary Anning and the Birth of Paleontology* (5–8). Illus. 2002, Morgan Reynolds LB $21.95 (1-883846-93-5). 112pp. A readable biography of the groundbreaking female paleontologist (1799–1847) that places her achievements in historical context, with a glossary, bibliography, and timeline. (Rev: BL 7/02; HBG 3/03; SLJ 9/02) [560.92]

14020 Walker, Sally M. *Mary Anning: Fossil Hunter* (2–3). Series: On My Own. 2000, Carolrhoda LB $19.93 (1-57505-425-6). 48pp. Using many original documents as sources, this simple biography tells the life story of Mary Anning, who hunted for fossils on the cliffs of Lyme Regis in England. (Rev: BL 8/00; HBG 3/01; SLJ 12/00) [921]

AVERY, OSWALD

14021 Severs, Vesta-Nadine, and Jim Whiting. *Oswald Avery and the Story of DNA* (4–7). Series: Unlocking the Secrets of Science. 2002, Mitchell Lane LB $17.95 (1-58415-110-2). 48pp. The importance of Avery's early research is reinforced by a description of DNA evidence being used to free wrongly accused prisoners. (Rev: HBG 10/02; SLJ 6/02) [579.3092]

BAIRD, JOHN LOGIE

14022 Reid, Struan. *John Logie Baird* (4–6). Series: Groundbreakers. 2000, Heinemann LB $25.64 (1-57572-372-7). 48pp. The ground-breaking inventor of television is featured in this biography that tells of his poor health and his many setbacks. (Rev: HBG 3/01; SLJ 3/01) [921]

BANNEKER, BENJAMIN

14023 Blue, Rose, and Corinne J. Naden. *Benjamin Banneker: Mathematician and Stargazer* (4–6). Illus. Series: Gateway Biographies. 2001, Millbrook LB $22.90 (0-7613-1805-4). 48pp. An informative introduction to Banneker's life and achievements as America's "first major black man of science." (Rev: HBG 3/02; SLJ 9/01) [921]

14024 Conley, Kevin. *Benjamin Banneker* (5–9). Illus. 1989, Chelsea LB $9.95 (1-55546-573-0). Banneker was a remarkable 18th-century African American who excelled in mathematics and science. (Rev: BL 1/1/90; SLJ 5/90) [921]

14025 Ferris, Jeri. *What Are You Figuring Now? A Story About Benjamin Banneker* (3–6). Illus. 1988, Lerner LB $21.27 (0-87614-331-1); Carolrhoda paper $5.95 (0-87614-521-7). 56pp. The life of this African American who was a math whiz. (Rev: BL 1/1/89; SLJ 2/89)

14026 Marupin, Melissa. *Benjamin Banneker* (4–6). Series: Journey to Freedom. 1999, Child's World LB $16.95 (1-56766-618-3). 32pp. The story of the famous 18th-century author and mathematician who produced the first scientific publication by an African American. (Rev: BL 10/15/99; HBG 3/00; SLJ 4/00) [921]

14027 Pinkney, Andrea D. *Dear Benjamin Banneker* (1–4). Illus. by Brian Pinkney. 1994, Harcourt $16.00 (0-15-200417-3). 32pp. Born into a family of freed slaves, Banneker became an important astronomer and corresponded with Thomas Jefferson. (Rev: BCCB 11/94; BL 9/15/94; SLJ 11/94) [921]

BARNARD, CHRISTIAAN

14028 Bankston, John. *Christiaan Barnard and the Story of the First Successful Heart Transplant* (4–5). Series: Unlocking the Secrets of Science. 2002, Mitchell Lane LB $17.95 (1-58415-120-X). 48pp. A concise but complete look with interesting anecdotal information at the life of the courageous doctor who performed the first successful heart transplant. (Rev: BL 8/02; SLJ 10/02) [921]

BARTRAM, WILLIAM

14029 Ray, Deborah Kogan. *The Flower Hunter: William Bartram, America's First Naturalist* (3–5). Illus. 2004, Farrar $17.00 (0-374-34589-9). 40pp. This brief but information-packed biography of Bartram tells how a childhood interest in his father's botanical studies grew into a full-time occupation as America's first naturalist. (Rev: BL 4/15/04; SLJ 5/04) [580]

BELL, ALEXANDER GRAHAM

14030 Bankston, John. *Alexander Graham Bell and the Story of the Telephone* (5–8). Illus. Series: Uncharted, Unexplored, and Unexplained. 2004, Mitchell Lane LB $19.95 (1-58415-243-5). 48pp. As a teacher of the deaf and son of a deaf mother, Bell had a special interest in finding new and better ways to communicate. [921]

14031 Gaines, Ann. *Alexander Graham Bell* (2–3). Series: Discover the Life of an Inventor. 2001, Rourke LB $18.60 (1-58952-117-X). 24pp. Besides a life of this great inventor, this book describes the science behind the telephone. (Rev: BL 10/15/01; SLJ 1/02) [921]

14032 Lewis, Cynthia C. *Hello, Alexander Graham Bell Speaking* (4–7). Illus. Series: Taking Part. 1991, Macmillan LB $13.95 (0-87518-461-8). 64pp. This inventor studied human speech and created one of the greatest means of communication, the telephone. (Rev: BL 9/1/91; SLJ 12/91) [921]

14033 MacLeod, Elizabeth. *Alexander Graham Bell: An Inventive Life* (4–6). Illus. 1999, Kids Can $12.95 (1-55074-456-9); paper $5.95 (1-55074-458-5). 32pp. A series of double-page spreads cover Bell's invention of the telephone, his experiments building airplanes, and summers spent with his family on Cape Breton Island. (Rev: BL 4/15/99; HBG 10/99; SLJ 5/99) [921]

14034 Matthews, Tom L. *Always Inventing: A Photobiography of Alexander Graham Bell* (3–6). Illus. 1999, National Geographic $16.99 (0-7922-7391-5). 64pp. A large-format book filled with period photographs tells about the inventor of the telephone and his many other interests and contributions. (Rev: BL 6/1–15/99; HB 7–8/99; HBG 10/99; SLJ 3/99) [921]

14035 Pollard, Michael. *Alexander Graham Bell: Father of Modern Communication* (5–7). Series: Giants of Science. 2000, Blackbirch LB $27.44 (1-56711-334-6). 64pp. Known primarily for the invention of the telephone, Bell also invented the first hydrofoil, an air-conditioning system, and an early fax machine. (Rev: BL 1/1–15/01; HBG 3/01) [921]

14036 Reid, Struan. *Alexander Graham Bell* (4–6). Series: Groundbreakers. 2000, Heinemann LB $25.64 (1-57572-366-2). 48pp. This biography of Bell covers the invention of the telephone plus other innovations he pioneered and his important work with the deaf. (Rev: SLJ 3/01) [921]

14037 Sherrow, Victoria. *Alexander Graham Bell* (1–3). Illus. by Elaine Verstraete. Series: On My Own Biography. 2001, Carolrhoda LB $21.27 (1-57505-460-4); paper $6.95 (1-57505-533-3). 48pp. Bell's early working years and growing interest in inventions are the focus of this biography that will suit reluctant and beginning readers, with an afterword that covers his personal life and later career. (Rev: HBG 3/02; SLJ 1/02) [921]

BENZ, KARL

14038 Bankston, John. *Karl Benz and the Single Cylinder Engine* (5–8). Illus. Series: Uncharted, Unexplored, and Unexplained. 2004, Mitchell Lane LB $19.95 (1-58415-244-3). 48pp. The first person to build a three-wheeled automobile, Benz went on to design many more-sophisticated cars. [921]

BERNERS-LEE, TIM

14039 Gaines, Ann. *Tim Berners-Lee and the Development of the World Wide Web* (4–7). Series: Unlocking the Secrets of Science. 2001, Mitchell Lane LB $17.95 (1-58415-096-3). 48pp. A profile of the man who created the user-friendly way of accessing much of the information on the Internet. (Rev: HBG 10/02; SLJ 2/02) [921]

14040 Stewart, Melissa. *Tim Berners-Lee: Inventor of the World Wide Web* (4–7). Series: Ferguson Career Biographies. 2001, Ferguson LB $16.95 (0-89434-367-X). 127pp. Young readers will be fascinated by the details of Berners-Lee's life and career and the accompanying information on the skills needed to become a computer programmer. (Rev: SLJ 10/01) [921]

BEZOS, JEFF

14041 Garty, Judy. *Jeff Bezos* (5–8). Illus. Series: Internet Biographies. 2003, Enslow LB $18.95 (0-7660-1972-1). 48pp. A reader-friendly biography of the creator of Amazon.com, with plenty of information on his youth. (Rev: BL 3/15/03; HBG 10/03) [380.1]

14042 Sherman, Josepha. *Jeff Bezos: King of Amazon* (5–8). Illus. 2001, Twenty-First Century LB $23.90 (0-7613-1963-8). 80pp. Jeff Bezos, the genius behind Amazon.com, is introduced along with information on his struggle to found a book company on the Web. (Rev: BL 3/15/01; HBG 10/01; SLJ 7/01) [921]

BLACKWELL, ELIZABETH

14043 Kent, Deborah. *Elizabeth Blackwell: Physician and Health* (3–6). Series: Our People. 2003, Child's World LB $27.07 (1-59296-002-2). 32pp. The life and career of Elizabeth Blackwell, the first woman to graduate from medical school and a pioneer in medical education for women. (Rev: SLJ 4/04) [610]

14044 Kline, Nancy. *Elizabeth Blackwell: A Doctor's Triumph* (5–9). Series: Barnard Biography. 1997, Conari paper $6.95 (1-57324-057-5). The story of the first woman doctor in America, with generous excerpts from her journal and letters. (Rev: BL 2/15/97; BR 9–10/97; SLJ 6/97) [921]

14045 Peck, Ira. *Elizabeth Blackwell: The First Woman Doctor* (4–5). Illus. 2000, Millbrook $21.90 (0-7613-1854-2). 48pp. This solid biography tells the story of the first woman to graduate from medical school in the United States and of her many accomplishments in her field. (Rev: BL 9/15/00; HBG 10/01) [921]

BRAILLE, LOUIS

14046 Adler, David A. *A Picture Book of Louis Braille* (2–4). Illus. by John Wallner and Alexandra Wallner. Series: Picture Book Biographies. 1997, Holiday House $16.95 (0-8234-1291-1). 34pp. For young readers, this is a simple, well-illustrated biography that also includes a page of the braille raised-dot alphabet and numbers. (Rev: BL 4/15/97; SLJ 6/97) [921]

14047 Bryant, Jennifer. *Louis Braille: Inventor* (5–7). Illus. 1994, Chelsea LB $21.95 (0-7910-2077-0). 112pp. This well-researched biography of Braille tells about the horror of his own blindness as well as the development of the alphabet that allows blind people to read. (Rev: BL 7/94; SLJ 8/94) [921]

14048 Fradin, Dennis B. *Louis Braille: The Blind Boy Who Wanted to Read* (2–4). Illus. 1997, Silver Burdett LB $15.95 (0-382-39468-2); paper $5.95 (0-382-39469-0). 32pp. A picture-book biography of the amazing blind Frenchman who invented his famous reading system when he was only 15. (Rev: BL 5/1/97; SLJ 7/97) [921]

14049 Freedman, Russell. *Out of Darkness: The Story of Louis Braille* (4–8). Illus. 1997, Clarion $16.00 (0-395-77516-7). The story of the blind Frenchman who, more than 170 years ago, invented a system of reading using raised dots. (Rev: BCCB 5/97; BL 3/1/97; BR 9–10/97; HB 5–6/97; SLJ 3/97*) [686.2]

14050 O'Connor, Barbara. *The World at His Fingertips: A Story About Louis Braille* (3–5). Illus. by Rochelle Draper. Series: Creative Minds Biographies. 1997, Carolrhoda LB $21.27 (1-57505-052-8). 64pp. A fast-paced biography that reveals many interesting facts about this inventor of a writing system for the blind. (Rev: HBG 3/98; SLJ 10/97) [921]

14051 Woodhouse, Jayne. *Louis Braille* (2–3). Series: Lives and Times. 1997, Heinemann $19.92 (1-57572-559-2). 24pp. The life and contributions of this famous French blind man are told in this simple picture-book biography with a brief text. (Rev: BL 3/15/98) [921]

BROWN, HELEN GURLEY

14052 Falkof, Lucille. *Helen Gurley Brown: The Queen of Cosmopolitan* (5–8). Series: Wizards of Business. 1992, Garrett LB $17.26 (1-56074-013-2). An interesting, accessible, and inspiring biography of the magazine magnate. (Rev: BL 6/15/92; SLJ 7/92) [921]

BURROUGHS, JOHN

14053 Wadsworth, Ginger. *John Burroughs: The Sage of Slabsides* (5–8). Illus. 1997, Clarion $16.95 (0-395-77830-1). A biography of the American naturalist and essayist who lived in a cabin in the Catskill Mountains and wrote about his observations. (Rev: BCCB 5/97; BL 3/15/97; BR 9–10/97; HB 7–8/97; SLJ 5/97) [508.73]

CARLSON, CHESTER

14054 Zannos, Susan. *Chester Carlson and the Development of Xerography* (4–5). Series: Unlocking the Secrets of Science. 2002, Mitchell Lane LB $17.95 (1-58415-117-X). 56pp. The story of the man whose determination to simplify the process of copying documents led to the invention of xerography. (Rev: BL 9/15/02; HBG 3/03; SLJ 11/02) [921]

CAROTHERS, WALLACE

14055 Gaines, Ann Graham. *Wallace Carothers and the Story of DuPont Nylon* (4–5). Series: Unlocking the Secrets of Science. 2001, Mitchell Lane LB $17.95 (1-58415-097-1). 56pp. This biography of the inventor of nylon includes information on his suicide. (Rev: BL 10/15/01; SLJ 11/01) [547]

CARSON, RACHEL

14056 Bruchac, Joseph. *Rachel Carson: Preserving a Sense of Wonder* (3–5). Illus. by Thomas Locker. 2004, Fulcrum $17.95 (1-55591-482-9). 32pp. Bruchac captures Carson's intense care for the environment and in particular her love of the sea, and includes details of her youth and of her writings. (Rev: BL 7/04; SLJ 6/04) [333.95]

14057 Ehrlich, Amy. *Rachel: The Story of Rachel Carson* (2–4). Illus. by Wendell Minor. 2003, Harcourt $16.00 (0-15-216227-5). 32pp. Fine illustrations enhance this picture-book biography that concentrates on Carson's environmental concerns. (Rev: BL 6/1–15/03; HBG 10/03; SLJ 5/03) [921]

14058 Harlan, Judith. *Sounding the Alarm: A Biography of Rachel Carson* (5–7). Illus. Series: People in Focus. 1989, Macmillan LB $13.95 (0-87518-407-3). 128pp. A good account of this founder of the modern ecology movement. (Rev: BL 10/1/89; SLJ 11/89) [921]

14059 Kudlinski, Kathleen V. *Rachel Carson: Pioneer of Ecology* (3–6). Illus. 1988, Puffin paper $4.99 (0-14-032242-6). 64pp. The life of the famous nature writer and environmentalist, born in 1907. (Rev: BL 3/15/88; SLJ 8/88) [921]

14060 Landau, Elaine. *Rachel Carson and the Environmental Movement* (4–6). Series: Cornerstones of Freedom. 2004, Children's Pr. LB $24.00 (0-516-24232-6). 48pp. Carson's life and accomplishments are laid out in clear prose, with photographs and covers of her books. (Rev: SLJ 7/04) [921]

14061 Presnall, Judith J. *Rachel Carson* (4–8). Illus. Series: The Importance Of. 1995, Lucent LB $27.45 (1-56006-052-2). 96pp. The life of this innovative scientist whose writings, including *Silent Spring*, made the world aware of conservation and the erosion of our environment. (Rev: BL 1/15/95; SLJ 1/95) [921]

14062 Ransom, Candice. *Listening to Crickets: A Story About Rachel Carson* (3–5). Illus. by Shelly O. Haas. 1993, Carolrhoda LB $21.27 (0-87614-727-9). 64pp. Beginning with her childhood, this account traces the life of the woman who helped make millions aware of the destruction of their environment. (Rev: BL 5/15/93; SLJ 7/93) [921]

14063 Ring, Elizabeth. *Rachel Carson: Caring for the Earth* (3–5). Illus. Series: Eyewitness Juniors. 1992, Millbrook LB $19.90 (1-56294-056-2). 48pp. The story of the pioneer conservationist whose book Silent Spring influenced a whole generation. (Rev: BL 8/92; SLJ 11/92) [921]

14064 Wadsworth, Ginger. *Rachel Carson: Voice for the Earth* (5–7). Illus. Series: Lerner Biographies. 1992, Lerner LB $30.35 (0-8225-4907-7). 128pp. The life and work of the conservationist and author, best known for *Silent Spring*. (Rev: BL 6/1/92; HB 7–8/92; SLJ 7/92) [921]

CARVER, GEORGE WASHINGTON

14065 Adler, David A. *A Picture Book of George Washington Carver* (2–4). Illus. by Dan Brown. Series: Picture Book Biographies. 1999, Holiday House $15.95 (0-8234-1429-9). A biography of this famous scientist with an emphasis on his private life and the racism he encountered. (Rev: BL 4/15/99; HBG 10/99; SLJ 5/99) [921]

14066 Benge, Janet, and Geoff Benge. *George Washington Carver, What Do You See?* (3–4). Illus. by Kennon James. Series: Another Great Achiever. 1997, Advance Publg. LB $14.95 (1-57537-102-2). 48pp. This biography stresses Carver's humanity, inventiveness, and deep religious faith. (Rev: SLJ 8/97) [921]

14067 Carey, Charles W. *George Washington Carver* (4–6). Series: Journey to Freedom. 1999, Child's World LB $16.95 (1-56766-569-1). 40pp. Using plenty of illustrations and interesting sidebars, this biography covers the life-shaping events of the great African American scientist. (Rev: BL 7/99; HBG 10/99; SLJ 7/99) [921]

14068 Carter, Andy, and Carol Saller. *George Washington Carver* (2–3). Series: On My Own. 2000, Carolrhoda LB $19.93 (1-57505-427-2); paper $5.95 (1-57505-458-2). 48pp. Born a slave near the end of the Civil War, Carver became famous for helping farmers grow better crops while sharing with them his love of nature. (Rev: BL 8/00; HBG 3/01) [921]

14069 McKissack, Patricia, and Fredrick McKissack. *George Washington Carver: The Peanut Scientist* (2–4). Series: Great African Americans. 2002, Enslow LB $14.95 (0-7660-1700-1). 32pp. Black-and-white photographs and a readable style are highlights of this biography about the famous African American botanist who was the son of slave parents. (Rev: BL 7/02) [921]

14070 Mitchell, Barbara. *A Pocketful of Goobers: A Story About George Washington Carver* (3–5). Illus. 1986, Carolrhoda LB $21.27 (0-87614-292-7); Lerner paper $5.95 (0-87614-474-1). 64pp. An introductory biography partly fictionalized, with much information on Carver's research with peanuts. (Rev: BL 8/86; SLJ 9/86)

14071 Riley, John. *George Washington Carver: A Photo Biography* (1–3). Series: First Biographies. 2000, Morgan Reynolds LB $15.95 (1-883846-62-5). 24pp. With full-page pictures and a simple text this is a biography of the great African American scientist for beginning readers. (Rev: HBG 10/00; SLJ 8/00) [921]

CASE, STEVE

14072 Ashby, Ruth. *Steve Case: America Online Pioneer* (5–8). Series: Techies. 2002, Millbrook LB $23.90 (0-7613-2655-3). The story of the Honolulu native who was a leader of AOL and the driving force behind its merger with Time-Warner. (Rev: BL 4/1/02; HBG 10/02) [921]

CHIEN-SHIUNG WU

14073 Cooperman, Stephanie H. *Chien-Shiung Wu: Pioneering Physicist and Atomic Researcher* (5–8). Illus. Series: Women Hall of Famers in Mathematics and Science. 2004, Rosen LB $29.95 (0-8239-3875-1). 112pp. This biography describes Wu's life and achievements, explaining how she found a flaw in a widely held assumption about atoms. (Rev: BL 3/1/04; SLJ 9/04) [921]

CLARK, EUGENIE

14074 Butts, Ellen R., and Joyce R. Schwartz. *Eugenie Clark: Adventures of a Shark Scientist* (5–8). Illus. 2000, Linnet $19.50 (0-208-02440-9). 107pp. An interesting biography of a contemporary American scientist — an ichthyologist who has produced some startling research on sharks. (Rev: BCCB 2/00; BL 2/15/00; HBG 10/00; SLJ 7/00) [921]

14075 Ross, Michael. *Fish Watching with Eugenie Clark* (3–5). Series: Naturalist's Apprentice. 2000, Lerner LB $19.93 (1-57505-384-5). 48pp. This American scientist of Japanese ancestry has been fascinated by fish since childhood and has turned her interest into a groundbreaking scientific career. (Rev: BL 8/00; HBG 10/00; SLJ 7/00) [921]

COPERNICUS

14076 Andronik, Catherine M. *Copernicus: Founder of Modern Astronomy* (4–8). Illus. Series: Great Minds of Science. 2002, Enslow LB $20.95 (0-7660-1755-9). 112pp. This absorbing biography that covers Copernicus's youth and succeeds in explaining necessary scientific concepts also includes activities that reinforce this understanding. (Rev: HBG 10/02; SLJ 6/02) [520.92]

14077 Fradin, Dennis Brindell. *Nicolaus Copernicus: The Earth Is a Planet* (3–6). Illus. by Cynthia von Buhler. 2004, Mondo $15.95 (1-59336-006-1). 32pp. This succinct, illustrated profile of Polish astronomer Copernicus recounts his life and explores how he developed his theory that the planets revolve around the sun. (Rev: BL 4/1/04; SLJ 6/04) [921]

14078 Ingram, Scott. *Nicolaus Copernicus: Father of Modern Astronomy* (5–9). Series: Giants of Science. 2004, Gale/Blackbirch LB $24.95 (1-56711-489-X). 64pp. Copernicus's life, the influences of the church, and his important contributions to science are presented in clear prose and historical context. (Rev: SLJ 6/05) [921]

CURIE, MARIE

14079 Birch, Beverley. *Marie Curie: Courageous Pioneer in the Study of Radioactivity* (5–7). Illus. Series: Giants of Science. 2000, Blackbirch LB $27.44 (1-56711-333-8). 64pp. This biography of Marie Curie covers her youth, her struggles to get an education, her marriage, and her scientific career and accomplishments. (Rev: BL 1/1–15/01; HBG 3/01) [921]

14080 Poynter, Margaret. *Marie Curie: Discoverer of Radium* (4–7). Illus. Series: Great Minds of Science. 1994, Enslow LB $20.95 (0-89490-477-9). 128pp. The life and significance of this discoverer of radium are covered, with a chapter of suggested activities. (Rev: BL 1/1/95; SLJ 10/94) [921]

14081 Santella, Andrew. *Marie Curie* (3–6). Series: Trailblazers of the Modern World. 2001, World Almanac LB $26.60 (0-8368-5061-0). 48pp. An attractive, chronological biography of Curie's life and devotion to scientific research. (Rev: SLJ 1/02) [921]

14082 Wishinsky, Frieda. *Manya's Dream: A Story of Marie Curie* (2–5). 2003, Maple Tree $19.95 (1-894379-53-5); paper $6.95 (1-894379-54-3). 32pp. This inspiring biography of Polish-born scientist Marie Curie focuses principally on the facts of her life, including her childhood in Poland, studies at the Sorbonne in Paris, and rescue work during World War I. (Rev: BL 12/15/03)

DAMADIAN, RAYMOND

14083 Kjelle, Marylou Morano. *Raymond Damadian and the Development of MRI* (5–7). Series: Unlocking the Secrets of Science. 2002, Mitchell Lane LB $17.95 (1-58415-141-2). 48pp. This account focuses on Damadian's scientific accomplishments. (Rev: HBG 10/03; SLJ 1/03) [921]

DARWIN, CHARLES

14084 Anderson, Margaret J. *Charles Darwin: Naturalist* (4–7). Illus. Series: Great Minds of Science.

1994, Enslow LB $20.95 (0-89490-476-0). 128pp. In addition to a biography of this controversial naturalist, there is a chapter on activities for the reader. (Rev: BL 1/1/95; SLJ 10/94) [921]

14085 Fullick, Ann. *Charles Darwin* (4–6). Series: Groundbreakers. 2000, Heinemann LB $25.64 (1-57572-368-9). 48pp. This biography of the scientist who formulated the theory of evolution concentrates on his five-year voyage on the *H.M.S. Beagle.* (Rev: SLJ 2/01) [921]

14086 Lawson, Kristan. *Darwin and Evolution for Kids: His Life and Ideas with 21 Activities* (5–9). Illus. 2003, Chicago Review paper $16.95 (1-55652-502-8). 146pp. The naturalist's life and work are examined in clear, interesting text, with thorough coverage of his five-year research voyage on *H.M.S. Beagle* and the continuing controversy over his theories. (Rev: SLJ 4/04) [921]

14087 Senker, Cath. *Charles Darwin* (4–8). Illus. Series: Scientists Who Made History. 2002, Raintree LB $27.12 (0-7398-4843-7). 48pp. Darwin's life and contributions are presented in clear text and ample illustrations, with historical detail that places the information in context. (Rev: HBG 10/02; SLJ 9/02) [576.8092]

14088 Sis, Peter. *The Tree of Life: Charles Darwin* (4–7). Illus. 2003, Farrar $18.00 (0-374-45628-3). 44pp. Highly illustrated, this imaginative and visual biography traces Darwin's life and development as a naturalist, with a focus on his voyages on the *Beagle.* (Rev: BL 10/15/03; HB 11–12/03*; HBG 4/04; SLJ 10/03*) [576.8]

14089 Sproule, Anna. *Charles Darwin: Visionary Behind the Theory of Evolution* (4–7). Illus. Series: Giants of Science. 2003, Gale $27.44 (1-56711-655-8). 64pp. Darwin's life and accomplishments are presented in concise text. (Rev: SLJ 1/03) [921]

DEERE, JOHN

14090 Hall, Margaret. *John Deere* (2–4). Series: Lives and Times. 2004, Heinemann LB $22.79 (1-4034-5327-6). 32pp. Profiles the life and achievements of John Deere, a blacksmith whose invention of an improved farm plow launched the farm equipment business that still bears his name. (Rev: BL 7/04; SLJ 9/04) [921]

DE LA RENTA, OSCAR

14091 Carrillo, Louis. *Oscar de la Renta* (4–8). Illus. Series: Contemporary Hispanic Americans. 1995, Raintree LB $28.80 (0-8172-3980-4). This account focuses on the professional life of the renowned Hispanic American fashion designer who was born in the Dominican Republic. (Rev: BL 3/15/96; SLJ 1/96) [921]

DE PASSE, SUZANNE

14092 Mussari, Mark. *Suzanne De Passe: Motown's Boss Lady* (5–8). Illus. Series: Wizards of Business. 1992, Garrett LB $17.26 (1-56074-026-4). 64pp. The story of the woman who helped make Motown

the great name in the music industry. (Rev: BL 6/15/92) [921]

DOMAGK, GERHARD

14093 Bankston, John. *Gerhard Domagk and the Discovery of Sulfa* (4–5). Series: Unlocking the Secrets of Science. 2002, Mitchell Lane LB $17.95 (1-58415-115-3). 56pp. The story of the man who discovered the antibiotic properties of sulfa but whose accomplishments were overshadowed by other advances in antibiotics. (Rev: BL 9/15/02; SLJ 11/02) [921]

DREW, CHARLES

14094 Whitehurst, Susan. *Dr. Charles Drew: Medical Pioneer* (4–6). Series: Journey to Freedom: The African American Library. 2001, Child's World LB $17.95 (1-56766-926-6). 40pp. An attractive biography of this pioneering American black scientist who was noted for his research in blood plasma and his work in developing the concept of the Blood Bank. (Rev: BL 12/15/01; HBG 3/02; SLJ 1/02) [921]

DYSON, ESTHER

14095 Jablonski, Carla. *Esther Dyson: Web Guru* (5–8). Series: Techies. 2002, Millbrook LB $23.90 (0-7613-2657-X). A leading light in the computer world, Dyson is the owner of EDventure Holdings, and is an active developer of emerging technologies and companies. (Rev: BL 4/1/02; HBG 10/02) [921]

14096 Morales, Leslie. *Esther Dyson: Internet Visionary* (5–8). Series: Internet Biographies. 2003, Enslow LB $18.95 (0-7660-1973-X). 48pp. Dyson, a skillful businesswoman, has played an influential role in the development of the Internet as a tool suitable for everyday use. (Rev: HBG 10/03; SLJ 10/03) [338.4]

EARLE, SYLVIA

14097 Baker, Beth. *Sylvia Earle: Guardian of the Sea* (4–7). Illus. Series: Lerner Biographies. 2000, Lerner LB $30.35 (0-8225-4961-1). 112pp. This is a thrilling biography of the famous underwater explorer and marine scientist who was one of the first humans to swim with whales. (Rev: BL 10/15/00; HBG 3/01; SLJ 11/00) [921]

EASTMAN, CHARLES

14098 Ross, Michael E. *Wildlife Watching with Charles Eastman* (4–6). Illus. by Laurie A. Caple. Series: Naturalist's Apprentice. 1997, Carolrhoda LB $14.95 (1-57505-004-8). 48pp. Charles Eastman, who was born in 1858 in the Dakota Nation, became a physician and later used his childhood experiences to teach children to love and respect nature. (Rev: BL 5/15/98; HBG 3/98; SLJ 3/98) [921]

EASTMAN, GEORGE

14099 Gillis, Jennifer Blizin. *George Eastman* (2–4). 2004, Heinemann LB $22.79 (1-4034-5326-8). 32pp. This concise biography profiles the life and work of George Eastman, whose late-19th-century introduction of the Kodak camera first made photography widely available to the public. (Rev: BL 7/04) [921]

EASTWOOD, ALICE

14100 Ross, Michael E. *Flower Watching with Alice Eastwood* (3–5). Illus. Series: Naturalist's Apprentice. 1997, Carolrhoda LB $19.93 (1-57505-005-6). 46pp. This account of the life of Alice Eastwood — an African American who became an expert on the wildflowers of the Rockies and the West Coast — also gives tips to the amateur flower watcher. (Rev: BL 3/1/98; HBG 3/98; SLJ 3/98) [921]

EDISON, THOMAS ALVA

14101 Dolan, Ellen M. *Thomas Alva Edison: Inventor* (5–8). Series: Historical American Biographies. 1998, Enslow LB $20.95 (0-7660-1014-7). Direct quotations, fact boxes, a chronology, and chapter notes make this an attractive life of the great inventor. (Rev: BL 8/98) [921]

14102 Gaines, Ann. *Thomas Edison* (2–3). Series: Discover the Life of an Inventor. 2001, Rourke LB $18.60 (1-58952-122-6). 24pp. A simple, introductory biography that describes Edison's life, contributions, and struggles. (Rev: BL 10/15/01; SLJ 1/02) [921]

14103 Gomez, Rebecca. *Thomas Edison* (2–3). Illus. Series: First Biographies. 2003, ABDO LB $14.95 (1-57765-945-7). 32pp. A brief easy-reader overview of the inventor's life and accomplishments. (Rev: HBG 4/04; SLJ 9/03) [921]

14104 Mason, Paul. *Thomas A. Edison* (4–6). Illus. Series: Scientists Who Made History. 2001, Raintree LB $18.98 (0-7398-4414-8). 48pp. This well-illustrated profile of Edison and his life and work will be useful for report writers. (Rev: HBG 10/02; SLJ 2/02) [921]

14105 Mitchell, Barbara. *The Wizard of Sound: A Story About Thomas Edison* (4–6). Illus. by Hetty Mitchell. Series: Creative Minds. 1991, Carolrhoda LB $21.27 (0-87614-445-8). 64pp. The story of how a shy, inept youngster became the inventor of wonders. (Rev: SLJ 1/92) [921]

14106 Sproule, Anna. *Thomas Edison: The World's Greatest Inventor* (5–7). Series: Giants of Science. 2000, Blackbirch paper $27.44 (1-56711-331-1). 64pp. A prolific inventor, Edison not only worked on the electric light bulb but also the phonograph, the movie projector, and an early answering machine. (Rev: BL 1/1–15/01; HBG 3/01; SLJ 1/01) [921]

EHRLICH, PAUL

14107 Zannos, Susan. *Paul Ehrlich and Modern Drug Development* (4–5). Series: Unlocking the Secrets of Science. 2002, Mitchell Lane LB $17.95 (1-58415-121-8). 56pp. The story of the man often called the "father of modern drug development" and his discovery of a "magic bullet." (Rev: BL 9/15/02; SLJ 3/03) [921]

EINSTEIN, ALBERT

14108 Bankston, John. *Albert Einstein and the Theory of Relativity* (5–8). Series: Unlocking the Secrets of Science. 2002, Mitchell Lane LB $17.95 (1-58415-137-4). 56pp. Einstein's accomplishments and the many challenges he faced are explored in concise text with many black-and-white photographs. (Rev: SLJ 2/03) [921]

14109 Brown, Don. *Odd Boy Out: Young Albert Einstein* (3–5). Illus. 2004, Houghton Mifflin $16.00 (0-618-49298-4). 32pp. Einstein's awkward and unpromising youth is described in this picture-book biography that also introduces his adult achievements. (Rev: BL 9/1/04; SLJ 10/04) [921]

14110 Delano, Marfé Ferguson. *Genius: A Photobiography of Albert Einstein* (5–8). Illus. 2005, National Geographic $17.95 (0-7922-9544-7). 64pp. Photographs of the scientist's life, as well as brief explanations of his work, help to make the man and his theories more accessible to young readers; an oversized and engaging volume. (Rev: BL 4/1/05; SLJ 5/05) [921]

14111 Heinrichs, Ann. *Albert Einstein* (4–7). Series: Trailblazers of the Modern World. 2002, World Almanac LB $29.26 (0-8368-5069-6). 48pp. The impact of Einstein's work on the scientists of the 20th century is highlighted in this biography describing his life and contributions. (Rev: SLJ 7/02) [530.092]

14112 MacDonald, Fiona. *Albert Einstein: The Genius Behind the Theory of Relativity* (5–7). Illus. Series: Giants of Science. 2000, Blackbirch LB $27.44 (1-56711-330-3). 64pp. As well as his childhood, education, theories, personal life, and international awards, this biography of Albert Einstein assesses his lasting contributions to physics and mathematics. (Rev: BL 1/1–15/01; HBG 3/01; SLJ 1/01) [921]

14113 MacLeod, Elizabeth. *Albert Einstein: A Life of Genius* (5–7). Illus. 2003, Kids Can $14.95 (1-55337-396-0); paper $6.95 (1-55337-397-9). 32pp. Small photographs and illustrations accompany this attractive chronological introduction to the life of Einstein that focuses on the man rather than his theories. (Rev: BL 3/1/03; HBG 10/03; SLJ 5/03) [530]

14114 McPherson, Stephanie S. *Ordinary Genius: The Story of Albert Einstein* (4–7). Illus. 1995, Carolrhoda LB $30.35 (0-87614-788-0). 96pp. Good historical background information is given on the life of Einstein plus a clear explanation of his discoveries. (Rev: BL 6/1–15/95; SLJ 9/95) [921]

14115 Reef, Catherine. *Albert Einstein: Scientist of the 20th Century* (4–7). Illus. Series: Taking Part. 1991, Macmillan LB $13.95 (0-87518-462-6). 64pp. Einstein gave the world a new way of looking at time, space, gravity, and the nature of light. (Rev: BL 9/1/91; SLJ 12/91) [921]

14116 Wyborny, Sheila. *Albert Einstein* (3–6). Series: Inventors and Creators. 2003, Gale/Kid-Haven LB $18.96 (0-7377-1278-3). 48pp. An interesting biography of the German-born physicist and his lasting contributions to scientific knowledge. (Rev: SLJ 6/03) [921]

ELION, GERTRUDE

14117 MacBain, Jennifer. *Gertrude Elion: Nobel Prize Winner in Physiology and Medicine* (5–8). Illus. Series: Women Hall of Famers in Mathematics and Science. 2004, Rosen LB $29.95 (0-8239-3876-X). 112pp. Elion, a biochemist and pharmacologist who never earned a doctorate, won a Nobel Prize for her advances in the field of chemotherapy. (Rev: BL 3/1/04; SLJ 9/04) [615]

ELLISON, LARRY

14118 Ehrenhaft, Daniel. *Larry Ellison: Sheer Nerve* (5–8). Series: Techies. 2001, Millbrook LB $23.90 (0-7613-1962-X). The life story of one of the world's richest men and co-founder of Oracle, the world's leading supplier of software for information management. (Rev: BL 4/1/02; HBG 3/02; SLJ 12/01) [921]
14119 Peters, Craig. *Larry Ellison: Database Genius of Oracle* (5–8). Series: Internet Biographies. 2003, Enslow LB $18.95 (0-7660-1974-8). 48pp. A look at the life and accomplishments of the cofounder of Oracle Corporation. (Rev: HBG 10/03; SLJ 10/03) [338.7]

ERICSSON, JOHN

14120 Brophy, Ann. *John Ericsson: The Inventions of War* (4–7). Illus. Series: The History of the Civil War. 1990, Silver Burdett paper $7.95 (0-382-24052-9). 135pp. In clear text, this is the life story of the Swedish engineer who designed and constructed the *Monitor*. (Rev: BL 9/1/91) [921]

FANNING, SHAWN

14121 Mitten, Christopher. *Shawn Fanning: Napster and the Music Revolution* (5–8). Series: Techies. 2002, Millbrook LB $23.90 (0-7613-2656-1). Using many photographs and an interesting text, this is the biography of the creator of Napster, a software package for downloading music from computers. (Rev: BL 4/1/02; HBG 10/02; SLJ 6/02) [921]

FARNSWORTH, PHILO

14122 McPherson, Stephanie S. *TV's Forgotten Hero: The Story of Philo Farnsworth* (4–7). Illus. 1996, Carolrhoda LB $30.35 (1-57505-017-X). 96pp. The biography of the genius who invented electronic television when he was only 14. (Rev: BL 2/1/97; SLJ 2/97) [921]
14123 Roberts, Russell. *Philo T. Farnsworth; the Life of Television's Forgotten Inventor* (4–5). Series: Unlocking the Secrets of Science. 2003, Mitchell Lane LB $17.95 (1-58415-176-5). 48pp. This brief biography recounts the bittersweet story of Philo T. Farnsworth, whose pioneering developments in the field of television were never fully acknowledged during his lifetime. (Rev: BL 11/15/03; SLJ 9/03)

FLEMING, ALEXANDER

14124 Bankston, John. *Alexander Fleming and the Story of Penicillin* (5–8). Series: Unlocking the Secrets of Science. 2001, Mitchell Lane LB $17.95 (1-58415-106-4). 56pp. This absorbing biography of the Scottish Nobel Prize winner covers his personal life as well as his scientific career. (Rev: HBG 3/02; SLJ 1/02) [616.014092]
14125 Birch, Beverley. *Alexander Fleming: Pioneer with Antibiotics* (4–7). Illus. Series: Giants of Science. 2003, Gale $27.44 (1-56711-656-6). 64pp. Fleming's life, education, research, and discovery of penicillin are presented in concise text. (Rev: SLJ 1/03) [921]
14126 Hantula, Richard. *Alexander Fleming* (5–8). Series: Trailblazers of the Modern World. 2003, World Almanac LB $26.60 (0-8368-5083-1). 48pp. An absorbing introduction to the Nobel Prize winner's life, achievements, and legacy, with quotations and plenty of illustrations. (Rev: BL 6/1–15/03; SLJ 9/03) [921]
14127 Tocci, Salvatore. *Alexander Fleming: The Man Who Discovered Penicillin* (5–8). Series: Great Minds of Science. 2002, Enslow LB $20.95 (0-7660-1998-5). 128pp. An absorbing account of Fleming's childhood and later life, with solid information on his contributions to medical science and his legacy. (Rev: HBG 10/02; SLJ 9/02) [921]

FORD, HENRY

14128 Bankston, John. *Henry Ford and the Assembly Line* (4–5). Series: Unlocking the Secrets of Science. 2003, Mitchell Lane LB $17.95 (1-58415-173-0). 48pp. This brief biography chronicles the life of Henry Ford and includes photographs and reproductions. (Rev: BL 11/15/03; SLJ 9/03)
14129 Gaines, Ann. *Henry Ford* (2–3). Illus. Series: Discover the Life of an Inventor. 2001, Rourke LB $18.60 (1-58952-120-X). 24pp. This biography of Ford concentrates on his influence on the automobile industry. (Rev: BL 10/15/01) [338.7]
14130 Kulling, Monica. *Eat My Dust! Henry Ford's First Race* (1–2). Series: Step into Reading. 2004, Random LB $11.99 (0-375-91510-9); Random paper $3.99 (0-375-81510-4). 48pp. Beginning readers, especially boys, will enjoy this dramatic account of Henry Ford's auto race victory against Alexander Winton. (Rev: BL 8/04) [338.7]
14131 McCarthy, Pat. *Henry Ford: Building Cars for Everyone* (5–8). Series: Historical American Biographies. 2002, Enslow LB $20.95 (0-7660-1620-X). 128pp. Ford is shown as an eccentric but successful father, engineer, and businessman, who made the automobile widely available but expected his workers to suffer difficult conditions. (Rev: HBG 3/03; SLJ 1/03) [338.76292092]

14132 Mitchell, Barbara. *We'll Race You, Henry: A Story About Henry Ford* (3–5). Illus. 1986, Carolrhoda LB $21.27 (0-87614-291-9); Lerner paper $5.95 (0-87614-471-7). 64pp. The focus is on race-car ventures in this partly fictionalized biography. (Rev: BL 8/86; SLJ 9/86) [921]

14133 Schaefer, Lola M. *Henry Ford* (K–2). Series: Famous People in Transportation. 2000, Capstone LB $13.25 (0-7368-0546-X). 24pp. For beginning readers, this is a biography of Henry Ford that uses double-page spreads to present important facts about his life and accomplishments. (Rev: HBG 10/00; SLJ 9/00) [921]

FOSSEY, DIAN

14134 Blue, Rose, and Corinne J. Naden. *Dian Fossey: At Home with the Giant Gorillas* (4–6). Series: Gateway Greens. 2002, Millbrook LB $23.90 (0-7613-2569-7). 48pp. A brief, nicely illustrated biography of the U.S.-born zoologist who studied the mountain gorilla in its natural habitat in Africa and was killed because of her efforts. (Rev: BL 7/02; HBG 3/03) [921]

14135 Gogerly, Liz. *Dian Fossey* (5–8). Series: Scientists Who Made History. 2003, Raintree LB $27.12 (0-7398-5225-6). 48pp. A riveting profile of the woman who became an expert on gorillas and the militant stance that may have led to her murder. (Rev: HBG 10/03; SLJ 4/03) [921]

14136 Matthews, Tom L. *Light Shining Through the Mist: A Photobiography of Dian Fossey* (4–6). Illus. 1998, National Geographic $17.95 (0-7922-7300-1). 64pp. An illustrated book relating the life and work of Dian Fossey, founder of the Karisoke Research Center in Rwanda, who studied mountain gorillas and worked to prevent poachers from killing off this endangered species. (Rev: BL 9/15/98; HB 9–10/98; HBG 3/99; SLJ 9/98) [921]

14137 Schott, Jane A. *Dian Fossey and the Mountain Gorillas* (2–3). Series: On My Own Biography. 2000, Carolrhoda LB $19.93 (1-57505-082-X). 48pp. The exciting story one of the foremost primate researchers of the 20th century, her groundbreaking work observing mountain gorillas in their native habitat, and her efforts to stop their poaching. (Rev: BL 6/1–15/00; HBG 10/00; SLJ 6/00) [921]

FRANKLIN, ROSALIND

14138 Senker, Cath. *Rosalind Franklin* (5–8). Illus. Series: Scientists Who Made History. 2003, Raintree $27.12 (0-7398-5226-4). 48pp. An interesting biography of the woman who never gained credit for her contributions to the discovery of the structure of DNA. (Rev: BL 3/1/03; HBG 10/03; SLJ 4/03) [572.8]

FULTON, ROBERT

14139 Bowen, Andy Russell. *A Head Full of Notions: A Story About Robert Fulton* (4–6). Illus. 1997, Carolrhoda LB $19.93 (0-87614-876-3); paper $5.95 (1-57505-026-9). 64pp. A brief biography of the life and times of the man who worked first on plans for a submarine and then on his famous steamboat. (Rev: BL 4/15/97; SLJ 3/97) [921]

14140 Flammang, James M. *Robert Fulton: Inventor and Steamboat Builder* (5–8). Illus. Series: Historical American Biographies. 1999, Enslow LB $20.95 (0-7660-1141-0). 128pp. Beginning with Fulton's 1807 demonstration of his steamboat, this biography moves back and forth in time to trace the complete career of this man who changed America's transportation history. (Rev: BL 11/1/99; HBG 3/00) [921]

14141 Gillis, Jennifer Blizin. *Robert Fulton* (1–4). Series: Lives and Times. 2004, Heinemann LB $22.79 (1-4034-5328-4). 32pp. Report writers will find useful information in this biography that has a timeline and "Fact File" boxes. (Rev: SLJ 9/04)

14142 Pierce, Morris A. *Robert Fulton and the Development of the Steamboat* (4–8). Series: Library of American Lives and Times. 2003, Rosen LB $31.95 (0-8239-5737-3). 112pp. The inventor of the steamboat was a man of determination and wide interests who also worked on naval weapons. (Rev: BL 6/1–15/03; SLJ 4/03) [921]

GALDIKAS, BIRUTE

14143 Gallardo, Evelyn. *Among the Orangutans: The Birute Galdikas Story* (4–7). Illus. Series: Great Naturalists. 1993, Chronicle paper $9.95 (0-8118-0408-9). 48pp. The story of this important primate specialist who began studying orangutans in 1971. (Rev: BL 4/1/93; SLJ 6/93) [921]

GALILEO

14144 Goldsmith, Mike. *Galileo Galilei* (4–6). Illus. Series: Scientists Who Made History. 2001, Raintree LB $18.98 (0-7398-4416-4). 48pp. This well-illustrated profile of Galileo and his life and work will be useful for report writers. (Rev: HBG 10/02; SLJ 2/02) [921]

14145 Hightower, Paul. *Galileo: Astronomer and Physicist* (4–7). Illus. Series: Great Minds of Science. 1997, Enslow LB $20.95 (0-89490-787-5). 128pp. This biography not only includes material on the life and accomplishments of this courageous scientist but also contains several activities that give an understanding of his work. (Rev: BL 6/1–15/97) [921]

14146 Sis, Peter. *Starry Messenger* (4–6). Illus. 1996, Farrar $16.00 (0-374-37191-1). 32pp. The world of Galileo and his amazing life and accomplishments are re-created in this unusual picture book. (Rev: BCCB 11/96; BL 10/15/96*; SLJ 10/96*) [921]

14147 White, Michael. *Galileo Galilei: Inventor, Astronomer, and Rebel* (5–8). Series: Giants of Science. 1999, Blackbirch LB $27.44 (1-56711-325-7). 64pp. The dramatic story of Galileo's life, his persecutions, accomplishments, and lasting contributions to science. (Rev: HBG 10/00; SLJ 2/00) [921]

GATES, BILL

14148 Barton-Wood, Sara. *Bill Gates: Computer Legend* (4–6). Illus. Series: Famous Lives. 2001, Raintree LB $18.98 (0-7398-4432-6). 48pp. An introduction to the life and career of Microsoft founder Bill Gates. (Rev: BL 1/1–15/02; HBG 10/02) [338.7]

14149 Dickinson, Joan D. *Bill Gates: Billionaire Computer Genius* (5–8). Series: People to Know. 1997, Enslow LB $20.95 (0-89490-824-3). This biography of the computer genius traces his life from his birth in 1955, showing how his personal drive made him into the richest man in America. (Rev: BL 10/15/97; BR 1–2/98; HBG 3/98; SLJ 12/97) [921]

14150 Lesinski, Jeanne. *Bill Gates* (4–6). Series: A&E Biography. 2000, Lerner LB $25.26 (0-8225-4949-2). 112pp. The story of the man whose name has become synonymous with computers, software, and wealth. (Rev: BL 6/1–15/00; HBG 3/01; SLJ 9/00) [921]

14151 Peters, Craig. *Bill Gates* (5–8). Illus. Series: Internet Biographies. 2003, Enslow LB $18.95 (0-7660-1969-1). 48pp. A reader-friendly biography of the creator of Microsoft, with information on his youth as well as his successful later life. (Rev: BL 3/15/03; HBG 10/03) [338.7]

14152 Sherman, Josepha. *Bill Gates: Computer King* (4–6). Series: Gateway Biographies. 2000, Millbrook LB $22.90 (0-7613-1771-6). 48pp. This book successfully tells the story of Bill Gates's life and gives a history of Microsoft. (Rev: HBG 3/01; SLJ 11/00) [921]

14153 Woog, Adam. *Bill Gates* (4–7). Illus. Series: Famous People. 2003, Gale $23.70 (0-7377-1400-X). 48pp. Woog covers Gates's childhood, education, interest in computers, and career, with photographs. (Rev: BL 6/1–15/03) [338.7]

GODDARD, ROBERT

14154 Bankston, John. *Robert Goddard and the Liquid Rocket Engine* (4–7). Series: Unlocking the Secrets of Science. 2001, Mitchell Lane LB $17.95 (1-58415-107-2). 56pp. Bankston combines an introduction to Goddard's commitment to rocketry and his difficulty finding funding with an understandable explanation of the scientific challenges. (Rev: HBG 3/02; SLJ 2/02) [621.43]

14155 Streissguth, Thomas. *Rocket Man: The Story of Robert Goddard* (5–7). Illus. Series: Trailblazers. 1995, Carolrhoda LB $30.35 (0-87614-863-1). 88pp. A history of rocketry, with emphasis on the life and accomplishments of Goddard. (Rev: BL 10/15/95; SLJ 9/95) [921]

GOODALL, JANE

14156 Goodall, Jane. *My Life with the Chimpanzees* (3–6). Illus. 1992, Houghton Mifflin paper $11.04 (0-395-61849-5). The famed zoologist talks about her life studying the chimps of Africa. (Rev: BCCB 5/88; BL 7/88; SLJ 4/88)

14157 January, Brendan. *Jane Goodall: Animal Behaviorist and Writer* (4–7). Series: Ferguson Career Biographies. 2001, Ferguson LB $16.95 (0-89434-370-X). 127pp. This easily read biography will appeal in particular to reluctant readers and students seeking quick information for a report. (Rev: SLJ 9/01) [921]

14158 Pratt, Paula B. *Jane Goodall* (4–8). Illus. Series: The Importance Of. 1997, Lucent LB $27.45 (1-56006-082-4). The story of the great naturalist who studied and protected the primates of Africa. (Rev: BL 1/1–15/97; BR 9–10/97; SLJ 2/97) [921]

14159 Sean, J. A. *Jane Goodall: Naturalist* (4–6). Illus. Series: Library of Famous Women. 1993, Blackbirch LB $17.95 (1-56711-010-X). 64pp. An accurate, engrossing account of the life of this great naturalist, who produced landmark studies on apes and their society. (Rev: BL 11/15/93; SLJ 2/94) [921]

GUTENBERG, JOHANN

14160 Burch, Joann J. *Fine Print: A Story About Johann Gutenberg* (3–6). Illus. by Kent A. Aldrich. 1991, Carolrhoda LB $21.27 (0-87614-682-5). 64pp. An account of the man who changed world history by inventing the process of printing books from movable type. (Rev: BL 1/1/92; SLJ 3/92) [686.2]

14161 Pollard, Michael. *Johann Gutenberg: Master of Modern Printing* (5–7). Series: Giants of Science. 2001, Blackbirch LB $27.44 (1-56711-335-4). 64pp. Good use of illustrations and an interesting text are highlights of this life of the German printer who first used movable type. (Rev: BL 8/1/01; HBG 3/02) [921]

HAMILTON, ALICE

14162 McPherson, Stephanie S. *The Workers' Detective: A Story About Dr. Alice Hamilton* (3–6). Illus. by Janet Schulz. Series: Creative Minds. 1992, Carolrhoda LB $21.27 (0-87614-699-X). 64pp. Introducing the woman who studied the effects of lead and other lethal materials on workers' health and changed industrial medicine. (Rev: BL 1/15/93; SLJ 10/92) [921]

HARRISON, JOHN

14163 Borden, Louise. *Sea Clocks: The Story of Longitude* (2–4). Illus. by Erik Blegvad. 2004, Simon & Schuster $18.95 (0-689-84216-3). 48pp. John Harrison's struggles to promote his chronomoter — and to gain credit for its invention — are recounted in an attractive picture-book biography. (Rev: BL 12/1/03; HB 3–4/04; SLJ 1/04)

14164 Lasky, Kathryn. *The Man Who Made Time Travel* (3–5). Illus. by Kevin Hawkes. 2003, Farrar $17.00 (0-374-37488-3). 48pp. This oversize book presents the story of John Harrison, who worked for 50 years to perfect a timepiece that would track longitude in shipboard navigation. (Rev: BL 3/1/03*; SLJ 4/03) [526]

HARVEY, WILLIAM

14165 Yount, Lisa. *William Harvey: Discoverer of How Blood Circulates* (4–8). Illus. Series: Great Minds of Science. 1994, Enslow LB $20.95 (0-89490-481-7). 128pp. A biography of the 17th-century scientist that describes early theories about the blood system and the importance of Harvey's discoveries. (Rev: SLJ 2/95) [921]

HEWLETT, WILLIAM

14166 Tracy, Kathleen. *William Hewlett: Pioneer of the Computer Age* (5–7). Series: Unlocking the Secrets of Science. 2002, Mitchell Lane LB $17.95 (1-58415-142-0). 48pp. This accessible account focuses on Hewlett's scientific accomplishments and career in business. (Rev: SLJ 1/03) [921]

HILL, JULIA BUTTERFLY

14167 Fitzgerald, Dawn. *Julia Butterfly Hill: Saving the Redwoods* (4–6). Series: Gateway Greens. 2002, Millbrook LB $23.90 (0-7613-2654-5). 48pp. This is a handsome biography of the environmental activist who lived in a 200-foot-tall redwood named Luna from December 1997 to December 1999. (Rev: BL 7/02; HBG 3/03) [921]

HOPPER, GRACE

14168 Mattern, Joanne. *Grace Hopper: Computer Pioneer* (1–4). Series: Women Who Shaped History. 2003, Rosen LB $17.25 (0-8239-6505-8). 24pp. The amazing story of the U.S. Navy rear admiral who was a pioneer software engineer and the inventor of the compiler that translates English to the language of the target computer. (Rev: BL 2/15/03; SLJ 5/03) [921]

14169 Murphy, Patricia J. *Grace Hopper: Computer Whiz* (2–4). Series: Famous Inventors. 2004, Enslow LB $22.60 (0-7660-2273-0). 32pp. Describes Hopper's trail-blazing achievements and pioneering work in computers. (Rev: SLJ 2/05) [921]

HOUNSFIELD, GODFREY

14170 Zannos, Susan. *Godfrey Hounsfield and the Invention of CAT Scans* (4–5). Series: Unlocking the Secrets of Science. 2002, Mitchell Lane LB $17.95 (1-58415-119-6). 56pp. The story of the man who realized that X-rays could be manipulated by computers and later invented the amazingly accurate diagnostic device known as the computerized axial tomography or CAT scanner. (Rev: BL 9/15/02; SLJ 1/03) [921]

HUBBLE, EDWIN

14171 Datnow, Claire. *Edwin Hubble: Discoverer of Galaxies* (4–8). Illus. Series: Great Minds of Science. 1997, Enslow LB $20.95 (0-89490-934-7). 128pp. A portrait of the great astronomer, noted for his amazing scientific abilities and quirky pretentions. (Rev: BL 12/1/97; HBG 3/98; SLJ 3/98) [921]

JARVIK, ROBERT

14172 Bankston, John. *Robert Jarvik and the First Artificial Heart* (4–5). Series: Unlocking the Secrets of Science. 2002, Mitchell Lane LB $17.95 (1-58415-116-1). 48pp. This readable biography with interesting, unexpected facts covers the life and work of the doctor who invented the first artificial heart. (Rev: BL 8/02; HBG 3/03; SLJ 10/02) [921]

JOBS, STEVE

14173 Brashares, Ann. *Steve Jobs: Thinks Different* (5–8). Series: Techies. 2001, Twenty-First Century LB $23.90 (0-7613-1959-X). 80pp. The life story of the amazing creator of Apple computers and his phenomenal success as a businessman and entrepreneur. (Rev: BL 3/15/01; HBG 10/01) [921]

14174 Gaines, Ann Graham. *Steve Jobs* (3–4). Series: Real-Life Reader Biographies. 2000, Mitchell Lane LB $15.95 (1-58415-026-2). 32pp. The story of the founder of Apple computers who, after leaving the company he built, was brought back to rescue it from mismanagement. (Rev: BL 11/15/00) [921]

14175 Wilson, Suzan. *Steve Jobs: Wizard of Apple Computer* (5–8). Series: People to Know. 2001, Enslow LB $20.95 (0-7660-1536-X). 128pp. An engrossing biography that will attract computer-lovers, in which Jobs's early passion for electronics is shown as paving the way for his success — and failures — at Apple and other companies. (Rev: HBG 3/02; SLJ 3/02) [921]

KARAN, DONNA

14176 Tippins, Sherill. *Donna Karan: Designing an American Dream* (5–8). Illus. Series: Wizards of Business. 1992, Garrett LB $17.26 (1-56074-019-1). 64pp. Along with the life story of one of America's top fashion designers is advice for those who wish to enter the field. (Rev: BL 6/15/92) [921]

KENNY, ELIZABETH

14177 Crofford, Emily. *Healing Warrior: A Story About Sister Elizabeth Kenny* (3–6). Illus. by Steve Michaels. Series: Creative Minds. 1989, Carolrhoda LB $21.27 (0-87614-382-6). 64pp. The story of the Australian nurse renowned for her revolutionary therapy and rehabilitation work with polio patients. (Rev: BL 2/15/90; SLJ 3/90) [921]

KNIGHT, MARGARET

14178 Brill, Marlene Targ. *Margaret Knight: Girl Inventor* (2–5). Illus. by Joanne Friar. 2001, Millbrook $22.90 (0-7613-1756-2). 32pp. Margaret Knight was driven to invent life- and labor-saving devices by her early experiences working in a textile mill. (Rev: BL 9/15/01; HBG 3/02; SLJ 12/01) [609.2]

KOLFF, WILLEM

14179 Tracy, Kathleen. *Willem Kolff and the Invention of the Dialysis Machine* (5–8). Illus. Series: Unlocking the Secrets of Science. 2002, Mitchell Lane LB $17.95 (1-58415-135-8). 48pp. Kolff invented the dialysis machine in 1942 in the Nazi-occupied Netherlands. (Rev: HBG 3/03; SLJ 12/02) [617.461059092]

LAMARR, HEDY

14180 Gaines, Ann. *Hedy Lamarr* (2–3). Illus. Series: Discover the Life of an Inventor. 2001, Rourke LB $18.60 (1-58952-119-6). 24pp. The little-known story of the actress Hedy Lamarr and the communications system she devised during World War II, for beginning readers. (Rev: BL 10/15/01; SLJ 1/02) [621.382]

LAVOISIER, ANTOINE

14181 Yount, Lisa. *Antoine Lavoisier: Founder of Modern Chemistry* (4–7). Illus. Series: Great Minds of Science. 1997, Enslow LB $20.95 (0-89490-785-9). 128pp. In addition to providing an assessment of the life and works of Lavoisier, called the Father of Chemistry, this book includes several hands-on activities that depend on an understanding of his work. (Rev: BL 6/1–15/97) [921]

LEAKEY, LOUIS AND MARY

14182 Poynter, Margaret. *The Leakeys: Uncovering the Origins of Humankind* (5–8). Illus. Series: Great Minds of Science. 1997, Enslow LB $20.95 (0-89490-788-3). 128pp. The story of the famous husband-and-wife team of scientists, Louis and Mary Leakey, and how they expanded our knowledge of evolution. (Rev: BL 12/1/97; HBG 3/98; SLJ 12/97) [921]

LEEUWENHOEK, ANTONI VAN

14183 Yount, Lisa. *Antoni van Leeuwenhoek: First to See Microscopic Life* (4–8). Series: Great Minds of Science. 1996, Enslow LB $20.95 (0-89490-680-1). A brief biography of the Dutch maker of microscopes, who was also the first to examine closely bacteria and blood cells. (Rev: BL 10/15/96; SLJ 12/96) [921]

LEOPOLD, ALDO

14184 Lorbiecki, Marybeth. *Of Things Natural, Wild, and Free: A Story About Aldo Leopold* (4–7). Illus. 1993, Carolrhoda LB $25.55 (0-87614-797-X). 64pp. The story of a man who was a great hunter until he realized the importance of the balance in nature, and then turned a tract of farmland into a nature refuge. (Rev: BL 11/1/93; SLJ 11/93) [921]

14185 Yannuzzi, Della. *Aldo Leopold: Protector of the Wild* (4–6). Series: Gateway Greens. 2002, Millbrook LB $23.90 (0-7613-2465-8). 48pp. An attractive biography of the U.S. environmentalist who

helped create the first national wildlife area in 1924 and founded the Wilderness Society in 1935. (Rev: BL 7/02; HBG 3/03) [921]

LINNAEUS, CARL

14186 Anderson, Margaret J. *Carl Linnaeus: Father of Classification* (4–8). Series: Great Minds of Science. 1997, Enslow LB $20.95 (0-89490-786-7). This biography discusses the personal life of Linnaeus, including his explorations in Lapland, but the focus is on the development of his important biological classification system. (Rev: BL 12/1/97; HBG 3/98; SLJ 9/97) [921]

LOVELACE, ADA

14187 Wade, Mary D. *Ada Byron Lovelace: The Lady and the Computer* (5–8). Illus. 1995, Silver Burdett LB $13.95 (0-87518-598-3); paper $7.95 (0-382-24717-5). 128pp. A biography of the poet Byron's amazing daughter, who was a distinguished mathematician and pioneer computer programmer. (Rev: BL 5/1/95) [921]

MCCLINTOCK, BARBARA

14188 Tracy, Kathleen. *Barbara McClintock: Pioneering Geneticist* (4–7). Series: Unlocking the Secrets of Science. 2001, Mitchell Lane LB $17.95 (1-58415-111-0). 48pp. An absorbing look at the life and research of this Nobel Prize winner. (Rev: HBG 3/02; SLJ 2/02) [921]

MALONE, ANNIE TURNBO

14189 Wilkerson, J. L. *Story of Pride, Power and Uplift: Annie T. Malone* (4–8). Illus. 2003, Acorn $9.95 (0-9664470-8-5). 96pp. Malone, a child of slaves, created beauty products for African American women at the turn of the 20th century and became a wealthy woman and philanthropist. (Rev: BL 3/1/03; SLJ 7/03) [646.7]

MARCONI, GUGLIELMO

14190 Birch, Beverley. *Guglielmo Marconi: Radio Pioneer* (5–8). Series: Giants of Science. 2001, Gale LB $27.44 (1-56711-337-0). 64pp. This account of Marconi and his accomplishments also looks at how his inventions have evolved. (Rev: HBG 3/02; SLJ 2/02) [921]

MAYO, WILLIAM AND CHARLES

14191 Crofford, Emily. *Frontier Surgeons: A Story About the Mayo Brothers* (3–6). Illus. by Karen Ritz. Series: Creative Minds Biographies. 1989, Carolrhoda LB $21.27 (0-87614-381-8); paper $5.95 (0-87614-553-5). 56pp. The fascinating story of the brothers, William and Charles, who started what became a world-class medical facility. (Rev: BL 2/15/90; SLJ 3/90) [921]

MEAD, MARGARET

14192 Horn, Geoffrey M. *Margaret Mead* (5–8). Series: Trailblazers of the Modern World. 2004, World Almanac LB $29.27 (0-8368-5099-8). 48pp. Report writers will find useful information on Mead's life, achievements, and lasting contributions. (Rev: SLJ 7/04) [921]

14193 Pollard, Michael. *Margaret Mead: Bringing World Cultures Together* (5–8). Series: Giants of Science. 1999, Blackbirch LB $27.44 (1-56711-327-3). 64pp. This biography stresses the contribution Margaret Mead made to anthropology through her work in the South Pacific. (Rev: HBG 10/00; SLJ 2/00) [921]

14194 Ziesk, Edra. *Margaret Mead* (5–8). Illus. Series: American Women of Achievement. 1990, Chelsea LB $19.95 (1-55546-667-2). 109pp. A useful volume covering the career and personal life of this unconventional anthropologist. (Rev: BL 2/15/90; SLJ 9/90) [921]

MENDEL, GREGOR

14195 Bankston, John. *Gregor Mendel and the Discovery of the Gene* (5–8). Illus. Series: Uncharted, Unexplored, and Unexplained. 2004, Mitchell Lane LB $19.95 (1-58415-266-4). 48pp. Profiles the 19th-century Austrian monk who discovered the laws of genetics. (Rev: SLJ 12/04) [921]

14196 Klare, Roger. *Gregor Mendel: Father of Genetics* (5–7). Illus. Series: Great Minds of Science. 1997, Enslow LB $20.95 (0-89490-789-1). 128pp. The science of genetics is introduced through the life of Mendel and his experimentation with peas. (Rev: BL 12/1/97; HBG 3/98; SLJ 12/97) [921]

MENDELEYEV, DMITRI

14197 Zannos, Susan. *Dmitri Mendeleev and the Periodic Table* (5–8). Series: Uncharted, Unexplored, and Unexplained. 2004, Mitchell Lane LB $.00 (1-58415-267-2). 48pp. This brief biography looks at the life of the inventor of the periodic table, focusing initially on his childhood and offering political context. (Rev: BL 10/15/04) [540]

MITCHELL, MARIA

14198 McPherson, Stephanie S. *Rooftop Astronomer: A Story About Maria Mitchell* (4–6). 1990, Carolrhoda LB $21.27 (0-87614-410-5). 64pp. The woman who became the first professional female astronomer in the United States. (Rev: BCCB 11/90; BL 11/15/90; SLJ 1/91) [921]

MORGAN, ANN

14199 Ross, Michael E. *Pond Watching with Ann Morgan* (3–5). Series: Naturalist's Apprentice. 2000, Carolrhoda $19.93 (1-57505-385-3). 48pp. A biography about the expert on ponds that also serves as a field guide to pond ecology. (Rev: BL 4/15/00; HBG 10/00; SLJ 7/00) [921]

MORSE, SAMUEL

14200 Hall, M. C. *Samuel Morse* (1–4). Series: Lives and Times. 2004, Heinemann LB $22.79 (1-4034-5329-2). 32pp. Report writers will find useful information in this biography that has a timeline and "Fact File" boxes. (Rev: SLJ 9/04) [921]

MORTON, J. STERLING

14201 Beaty, Sandy, and J. L. Wilkerson. *Champion of Arbor Day: J. Sterling Morton* (4–6). Series: The Great Heartlanders. 1999, Acorn paper $8.95 (0-9664470-1-8). 130pp. The story of the early conservationist who inspired Nebraskans to plant one million trees on the first Arbor Day in 1872. (Rev: SLJ 3/99) [921]

MUIR, JOHN

14202 Armentrout, David, and Patricia Armentrout. *John Muir* (2–4). Illus. 2002, Rourke LB $18.60 (1-58952-055-6). 24pp. A simple introduction for younger readers to the life of naturalist John Muir. (Rev: BL 1/1–15/02; SLJ 3/02) [333.7]

14203 Dunlap, Julie, and Marybeth Lorbiecki. *John Muir and the Stickeen: An Icy Adventure with a No Good Dog* (2–4). Illus. by Bill Farnsworth. 2004, T&N Children's Publishing $16.95 (1-55971-903-6). 32pp. Beautifully illustrated and drawing heavily on Muir's personal journals, this engaging book tells how a dog named Stickeen helped to guide the famed conservationist through a brush with death in Alaska. (Rev: BL 11/15/04) [921]

14204 Ito, Tom. *The Importance of John Muir* (4–8). Illus. Series: The Importance Of. 1996, Lucent $27.45 (1-56006-054-9). A short biography of the great naturalist and traveler who pioneered the U.S. conservation movement. (Rev: BL 5/15/96) [921]

14205 Locker, Thomas. *John Muir: America's Naturalist* (2–4). 2004, Fulcrum $17.95 (1-55591-393-8). 32pp. This brief picture-book biography of the Scottish-born naturalist is beautifully illustrated with paintings of his beloved Yosemite. (Rev: BL 6/1–15/03; HBG 4/04; SLJ 9/03) [921]

14206 Naden, Corinne J., and Rose Blue. *John Muir: Saving the Wilderness* (3–5). Illus. Series: Gateway Biographies. 1992, Millbrook LB $19.90 (1-56294-110-0). 48pp. The life and work of this well-known conservationist, especially his role in founding the national parks. (Rev: BL 5/1/92; SLJ 6/92)

14207 Wadsworth, Ginger. *John Muir: Wilderness Protector* (4–6). Illus. 1992, Lerner LB $23.93 (0-8225-4912-3). 144pp. From his childhood in Scotland to adulthood in California, this biography focuses on why Muir became a conservationist and his efforts in this area. (Rev: SLJ 9/92) [921]

MURRAY, JOSEPH E.

14208 Mattern, Joanne. *Joseph E. Murray and the Story of the First Human Kidney Transplant* (5–8). Illus. Series: Unlocking the Secrets of Science. 2002, Mitchell Lane LB $17.95 (1-58415-136-6). 48pp. A look at the work of the surgeon who performed the first successful kidney transplant. (Rev: SLJ 12/02) [617.95092]

MURRELL, MELVILLE

14209 Seymour, Tres. *Our Neighbor Is a Strange, Strange Man* (PS–3). Illus. by Walter L. Krudop. 1999, Orchard LB $16.99 (0-531-33107-5). 32pp. A picture-book story of Melville Murrell, who built the first human-powered airplane in 1876, years before the Wright brothers. (Rev: BCCB 2/99; BL 2/1/99; HBG 10/99; SLJ 3/99) [629.13]

NAVY, CARYN

14210 Verheyden-Hilliard, Mary Ellen. *Mathematician and Computer Scientist, Caryn Navy* (2–4). Illus. 1988, Equity paper $8.50 (0-932469-12-4). 32pp. Brief biography of a woman scientist who is blind. (Rev: BL 2/15/89; SLJ 1/89)

NEWTON, ISAAC

14211 Anderson, Margaret J. *Isaac Newton: The Greatest Scientist of All Time* (4–7). Illus. Series: Great Minds of Science. 1996, Enslow LB $20.95 (0-89490-681-X). 128pp. The life of the great English mathematician and physicist who formulated the laws of motion and gravity. (Rev: BL 10/15/96; SLJ 12/96) [921]

14212 Mason, Paul. *Isaac Newton* (4–8). Illus. Series: Scientists Who Made History. 2002, Raintree LB $27.12 (0-7398-4845-3). 48pp. Newton's life and contributions are presented in clear text and ample illustrations, with historical detail that places the information in context. (Rev: HBG 10/02; SLJ 9/02) [530.092]

14213 White, Michael. *Isaac Newton: Discovering Laws That Govern the Universe* (5–8). Series: Giants of Science. 1999, Blackbirch LB $27.44 (1-56711-326-5). 64pp. A visually appealing biography of the great English mathematician who was the first scientist to be knighted. (Rev: HBG 10/00; SLJ 2/00) [921]

NICE, MARGARET MORSE

14214 Dunlap, Julie. *Birds in the Bushes: A Story About Margaret Morse Nice* (3–5). Illus. by Ralph L. Ramstad. Series: Creative Minds. 1996, Carolrhoda LB $19.93 (1-57505-006-4). 63pp. A biography of the noted American ornithologist and conservationist who died in 1974. (Rev: SLJ 10/96) [921]

14215 Ross, Michael E. *Bird Watching with Margaret Morse Nice* (4–6). Illus. by Laurie A. Caple. Series: Naturalist's Apprentice. 1997, Carolrhoda LB $19.93 (1-57505-002-1). 48pp. At the turn of the century, Margaret Morse Nice raised her family while pursuing her hobby of bird watching. (Rev: HBG 3/98; SLJ 3/98) [921]

NOBEL, ALFRED

14216 Bankston, John. *Alfred Nobel and the Story of the Nobel Prize* (4–8). Series: Great Achievement Awards. 2003, Mitchell Lane LB $19.95 (1-58415-168-4). 48pp. An intriguing biography of the inventor of dynamite and the founder of the famous prizes. (Rev: BL 10/15/03; SLJ 9/03) [921]

PACHCIARZ, JUDITH

14217 Verheyden-Hilliard, Mary Ellen. *Scientist and Physician, Judith Pachciarz* (2–4). Illus. 1988, Equity paper $8.50 (0-932469-13-2). 32pp. The story of an M.D. and microbiologist who is deaf. (Rev: BL 2/15/89; SLJ 4/89) [921]

PASTEUR, LOUIS

14218 Alphin, Elaine Marie. *Germ Hunter: A Story About Louis Pasteur* (3–6). Illus. by Elaine Verstraete. 2003, Carolrhoda LB $21.27 (1-57505-179-6); paper $5.95 (0-87614-929-8). 64pp. Pasteur's early life is covered well in this simple biography that reads more like a novel and is more suitable for reluctant readers than for report writers. (Rev: HBG 10/03; SLJ 7/03) [921]

14219 Armentrout, David, and Patricia Armentrout. *Louis Pasteur* (2–4). Series: Discover Someone Who Made a Difference. 2001, Rourke LB $18.60 (1-58952-056-4). This basic biography describes the life and times of Pasteur and how his accomplishments affect our lives today. (Rev: BL 1/1–15/02; SLJ 3/02) [921]

14220 Birch, Beverley. *Louis Pasteur: Father of Modern Medicine* (5–7). Series: Giants of Science. 2001, Blackbirch LB $27.44 (1-56711-336-2). 64pp. A readable, well-organized biography of the French chemist whose varied accomplishments include discovery of the process known now as pasteurization. (Rev: BL 8/1/01; HBG 3/02) [921]

14221 Fullick, Ann. *Louis Pasteur* (4–6). 2000, Heinemann LB $25.64 (1-57572-373-5). 48pp. As well as covering Pasteur's life, this book tells of the impact of his discoveries on medicine and science. (Rev: SLJ 2/01) [921]

14222 Smith, Linda W. *Louis Pasteur: Disease Fighter* (4–8). Illus. Series: Great Minds of Science. 1997, Enslow LB $20.95 (0-89490-790-5). The story of the "father of microbiology," who discovered pasteurization while working on a wine problem for Napoleon. (Rev: BL 12/1/97; HBG 3/98; SLJ 12/97) [921]

PAULING, LINUS

14223 Zannos, Susan. *Linus Pauling and the Chemical Bond* (4–5). Series: Unlocking the Secrets of Science. 2003, Mitchell Lane LB $17.95 (1-58415-123-4). 48pp. This brief biography recounts the life and scientific achievements of American chemist Linus Pauling. (Rev: BL 11/15/03; SLJ 10/03) [921]

PINCHOT, GIFFORD

14224 Hines, Gary. *Midnight Forests* (3–5). Illus. by Robert Casilla. 2005, Boyds Mills $16.95 (1-56397-148-8). 32pp. Gifford Pinchot, an American who became secretary of agriculture in 1898 and who was responsible for saving large areas of forest in the West, is introduced in this large-format picture-book biography. (Rev: BL 5/15/05; SLJ 4/05) [333.75]

PLOTKIN, MARK

14225 Pascoe, Elaine, adapt. *Mysteries of the Rain Forest: 20th Century Medicine Man* (4–8). Series: The New Explorers. 1997, Blackbirch LB $18.95 (1-56711-229-3). An exploration of the life and discoveries of Mark Plotkin, an ethnobotanist fascinated by the plants and people of the Amazon. (Rev: HBG 3/98; SLJ 2/98) [921]

PULITZER, JOSEPH

14226 Zannos, Susan. *Joseph Pulitzer and the Story Behind the Pulitzer Prize* (4–8). Illus. Series: Great Achievement Awards. 2003, Mitchell Lane LB $19.95 (1-58415-179-X). 48pp. Pulitzer's difficulty personality and passion for journalism are highlighted in this account of his establishment of the well-known awards. (Rev: BL 10/15/03; SLJ 9/03) [070.9]

RICHARDS, ELLEN

14227 Vare, Ethlie A. *Adventurous Spirit: A Story About Ellen Swallow Richards* (3–6). Illus. by Jennifer Hagerman. Series: Creative Minds. 1992, Carolrhoda LB $14.95 (0-87614-733-3). 64pp. The life of the first woman accepted at M.I.T. (Rev: BL 1/15/93) [921]

RICHTER, CHARLES

14228 Zannos, Susan. *Charles Richter and the Story of the Richter Scale* (4–5). Series: Unlocking the Secrets of Science. 2003, Mitchell Lane LB $17.95 (1-58415-175-7). 48pp. This brief biography of Charles Richter chronicles the life and achievements of the American physicist and seismologist who is credited with developing the scale for measuring earthquake intensity. (Rev: BL 11/15/03; SLJ 10/03) [921]

ROBERTS, EDWARD

14229 Zannos, Susan. *Edward Roberts and the Story of the Personal Computer* (5–7). Series: Unlocking the Secrets of Science. 2002, Mitchell Lane LB $17.95 (1-58415-118-8). 48pp. This accessible account focuses on Roberts's accomplishments as an electronic engineer. (Rev: HBG 10/03; SLJ 1/03) [921]

ROCKEFELLER, JOHN D.

14230 Laughlin, Rosemary. *John D. Rockefeller: Oil Baron and Philanthropist* (5–8). Illus. Series: American Business Leaders. 2001, Morgan Reynolds LB $21.95 (1-883846-59-5). 128pp. A biography of the determined and skilled businessman who made Standard Oil the dominant company in the oil industry and who was later noted for his philanthropy. (Rev: BL 3/1/01; HBG 10/01; SLJ 7/01) [921]

ROENTGEN, WILHELM

14231 Garcia, Kimberly. *Wilhelm Roentgen and the Discovery of X Rays* (4–5). Series: Unlocking the Secrets of Science. 2002, Mitchell Lane LB $17.95 (1-58415-114-5). 48pp. The story of the German physical scientist who stumbled upon X-rays while working on experiments with electricity. (Rev: BL 8/02; HBG 3/03; SLJ 10/02) [921]

ROOKS, JUNE

14232 Verheyden-Hilliard, Mary Ellen. *Scientist and Strategist, June Rooks* (2–4). Illus. 1988, Equity paper $8.50 (0-932469-14-0). 32pp. The story of June Rooks, an African American who battled poverty and polio to gain a degree in physics and a research analysis job in the navy. (Rev: BL 2/15/89; SLJ 1/89)

SAGAN, CARL

14233 Butts, Ellen R., and Joyce R. Schwarts. *Carl Sagan* (5–8). Series: A&E Biography. 2000, Lerner LB $25.26 (0-8225-4986-7). 112pp. The story of the great astronomer who interested millions in the study of the stars and the question of whether there is life elsewhere in our universe. (Rev: BL 10/15/00; HBG 3/01; SLJ 10/00) [921]

14234 Byman, Jeremy. *Carl Sagan: In Contact with the Cosmos* (5–8). Illus. Series: Great Scientists. 2000, Morgan Reynolds LB $21.95 (1-883846-55-2). 112pp. An informative biography of the scientist who popularized astronomy while maintaining a highly productive scholarly life. (Rev: BL 11/1/00; HBG 10/00; SLJ 8/00) [921]

SALK, JONAS

14235 Bankston, John. *Jonas Salk and the Polio Vaccine* (4–5). Series: Unlocking the Secrets of Science. 2001, Mitchell Lane LB $17.95 (1-58415-093-9). 56pp. A biography of the famous scientist, with photographs, a glossary, and a list of additional resources. (Rev: BL 10/15/01; SLJ 11/01) [610]

14236 Durrett, Deanne. *Jonas Salk* (2–5). Illus. Series: Inventors and Creators. 2002, Gale LB $23.70 (0-7377-1277-5). 48pp. This brief biography presents Salk's life from childhood and his determination to persevere to find a cure for polio, with many photographs, a glossary, and a bibliography. (Rev: BL 11/1/02; SLJ 10/02) [610]

14237 McPherson, Stephanie Sammartino. *Jonas Salk: Conquering Polio* (5–8). Series: Lerner

Biographies. 2001, Lerner LB $30.35 (0-8225-4964-6). 128pp. An absorbing account of Salk's life and contributions to medicine that discusses his confrontation with Sabin and the early failures of Salk's vaccine. (Rev: HBG 3/02; SLJ 4/02) [921]

14238 Tocci, Salvatore. *Jonas Salk: Creator of the Polio Vaccine* (4–7). Illus. Series: Great Minds of Science. 2003, Enslow LB $20.95 (0-7660-2097-5). 128pp. This book covers the life of the scientist and the importance and impact of the vaccine he developed. (Rev: BL 5/15/03; HBG 10/03) [610]

STEARNER, PHYLLIS

14239 Verheyden-Hilliard, Mary Ellen. *Scientist and Activist, Phyllis Stearner* (2–4). Illus. 1988, Equity paper $8.50 (0-932469-15-9). 32pp. A biography of an expert in radiation biology who has cerebral palsy. (Rev: BL 2/15/89; SLJ 1/89) [921]

STRAUSS, LEVI

14240 Van Steenwyk, Elizabeth. *Levi Strauss: The Blue Jeans Man* (5–9). 1988, Walker LB $14.85 (0-8027-6796-6). A biography of the Bavarian immigrant, Levi Strauss, who became the blue jeans king of the western world. (Rev: BL 6/15/88; SLJ 10/88) [921]

14241 Weidt, Maryann N. *Mr. Blue Jeans: A Story About Levi Strauss* (3–5). Illus. 1990, Carolrhoda LB $21.27 (0-87614-421-0). 64pp. The story of the phenomenal blue jeans and of their phenomenal creator. (Rev: BL 12/1/90; SLJ 1/91) [921]

STRONG, MAURICE

14242 Westrup, Hugh. *Maurice Strong: Working for Planet Earth* (3–6). Illus. 1994, Millbrook LB $20.90 (1-56294-414-2). 48pp. A biography of the Canadian environmentalist who organized the Rio de Janeiro Earth Summit. (Rev: BL 12/1/94; SLJ 12/94) [921]

SWANSON, ANNE BARRETT

14243 Verheyden-Hilliard, Mary Ellen. *Scientist and Teacher, Anne Barrett Swanson* (2–4). Illus. 1988, Equity paper $8.50 (0-932469-16-7). 32pp. The story of a scientist who overcame a brittle bone condition that hampered her physical growth. (Rev: BL 2/15/89; SLJ 4/89) [921]

TELLER, EDWARD

14244 Bankston, John. *Edward Teller and the Development of the Hydrogen Bomb* (5–8). Series: Unlocking the Secrets of Science. 2001, Mitchell Lane LB $17.95 (1-58415-108-0). 56pp. The life of the scientist born in Hungary who played a key role in the development of the H-bomb. (Rev: HBG 3/02; SLJ 1/02) [539.7092]

TESLA, NIKOLA

14245 Dommermuth-Costa, Carol. *Nikola Tesla: A Spark of Genius* (5–9). 1994, Lerner LB $30.35 (0-8225-4920-4). Traces the life and career of this pioneer in the field of electricity. (Rev: BL 12/15/94; SLJ 2/95) [921]

TORVALDS, LINUS

14246 Brashares, Ann. *Linus Torvalds: Software Rebel* (5–8). Series: Techies. 2001, Millbrook LB $23.90 (0-7613-1960-3). The story of the computer genius who created the Linux operating system. (Rev: BL 4/1/02; HBG 3/02; SLJ 12/01) [921]

TURNER, HENRY

14247 Ross, Michael E. *Bug Watching with Charles Henry Turner* (3–5). Illus. Series: Naturalist's Apprentice. 1997, Carolrhoda $19.93 (1-57505-003-X). 48pp. As well as providing many hints on bug watching, this book is a biography of the important African American zoologist who studied insects for many years. (Rev: BL 3/1/98; HBG 3/98; SLJ 3/98) [921]

WAKSMAN, SELMAN

14248 Gordon, Karen. *Selman Waksman and the Discovery of Streptomycin* (4–5). Series: Unlocking the Secrets of Science. 2002, Mitchell Lane LB $17.95 (1-58415-138-5). 48pp. An interesting profile of the scientist who discovered streptomycin and coined the term "antibiotic." [921]

14249 Gordon, Karen. *Selman Waksman and the Discovery of Streptomycin* (5–7). Series: Unlocking the Secrets of Science. 2002, Mitchell Lane LB $17.95 (1-58415-138-2). 48pp. An accessible account of Waksman's life and scientific research. (Rev: HBG 10/03; SLJ 1/03) [921]

WALKER, MADAM C. J.

14250 Bundles, A'Lelia. *Madam C. J. Walker* (5–10). Series: Black Americans of Achievement. 1993, Chelsea LB $21.95 (1-55546-615-X); paper $9.95 (0-7910-0251-9). Written by Walker's great-great-granddaughter, this volume describes the developer of a line of hair-care products whose entrepreneurial ability made her into the "foremost colored businesswoman in America." (Rev: BL 3/1/94) [921]

14251 Colman, Penny. *Madam C. J. Walker: Building a Business Empire* (3–6). Illus. 1994, Millbrook LB $20.90 (1-56294-338-3). 48pp. The success story of the African American woman who rose from extreme poverty to found a beauty preparation empire. (Rev: BL 6/1–15/94; SLJ 9/94) [921]

14252 Hobkirk, Lori. *Madam C. J. Walker* (4–6). Series: Journey to Freedom. 2000, Child's World LB $25.64 (1-56766-721-X). 40pp. The story of the African American entrepreneur who made a fortune in cosmetics. (Rev: BL 11/15/00; HBG 3/01) [921]

14253 McKissack, Patricia, and Fredrick McKissack. *Madam C. J. Walker: Self-Made Millionaire* (2–4).

Illus. by Michael Bryant. Series: Great African Americans. 1992, Enslow LB $14.95 (0-89490-311-X). 32pp. The story of the woman who built a cosmetics empire and became the first self-made African American woman millionaire. (Rev: BL 10/15/92; SLJ 12/92) [921]

WATT, JAMES

14254 Sproule, Anna. *James Watt: Master of the Steam Engine* (5–8). Series: Giants of Science. 2001, Gale LB $27.44 (1-56711-338-9). 64pp. This exploration of Watt's life and accomplishments also looks at how his inventions have evolved. (Rev: HBG 3/02; SLJ 2/02) [921]

WEINBERG, ROBERT A.

14255 Gaines, Ann, and Jim Whiting. *Robert A. Weinberg and the Search for the Cause of Cancer* (4–7). Series: Unlocking the Secrets of Science. 2002, Mitchell Lane LB $17.95 (1-58415-095-5). 48pp. The life and achievements of the scientist who specializes in the genetic causes of disease. (Rev: HBG 10/02; SLJ 6/02) [616.9940092]

WELCH, THOMAS BRAMWELL

14256 Carney, Mary Lou. *Dr. Welch and the Great Grape Story* (1–3). Illus. by Sherry Meidell. 2005, Boyds Mills $16.95 (1-59078-039-6). 32pp. This picture-book biography traces Thomas Bramwell Welch's efforts to find a nonalcoholic drink based on grapes. (Rev: BL 5/1/05) [921]

WHITNEY, ELI

14257 Gaines, Ann. *Eli Whitney* (2–3). Series: Discover the Life of an Inventor. 2001, Rourke LB $18.60 (1-58952-118-8). 24pp. The life of the inventor of the cotton gin is presented simply with material on how this invention works. (Rev: BL 10/15/01) [921]

WILLIAMS, DANIEL HALE

14258 Kaye, Judith. *The Life of Daniel Hale Williams* (5–8). Illus. Series: Pioneers in Health and Medicine. 1993, Twenty-First Century LB $16.90 (0-8050-2302-X). 80pp. The life story of the famous doctor who pioneered heart surgery and also helped open up the medical profession to African Americans. (Rev: SLJ 1/94) [921]

WOZNIAK, STEPHEN

14259 Gold, Rebecca. *Steve Wozniak: A Wizard Called Woz* (3–5). Illus. Series: Achievers. 1994, Lerner LB $21.27 (0-8225-2881-9). 72pp. The biography of the math whiz and multimillionaire who founded the Apple Computer Company. (Rev: BL 12/1/94) [921]

14260 Riddle, John, and Jim Whiting. *Stephen Wozniak and the Story of Apple Computer* (4–7). Series: Unlocking the Secrets of Science. 2001, Mitchell

Lane LB $17.95 (1-58415-109-9). 48pp. A profile of the life and achievements of the co-founder of Apple, who is known for his philanthropy and teaching in elementary schools. (Rev: HBG 10/02; SLJ 2/02) [921]

WRIGHT, WILBUR AND ORVILLE

14261 Borden, Louise, and Trish Marx. *Touching the Sky: The Flying Adventures of Wilbur and Orville Wright* (2–4). Illus. by Peter M. Fiore. 2003, Simon & Schuster $18.95 (0-689-84876-5). 64pp. Wilbur and Orville are shown as celebrities in this picture book that recounts unusual appearances they made separately. (Rev: BL 9/15/03; HBG 4/04; SLJ 10/03) [921]

14262 Buller, Jon, and Susan Schade. *The Wright Brothers Take Off* (K–4). Illus. by authors. Series: Smart About History. 2003, Grosset LB $14.89 (0-448-43240-4); paper $5.99 (0-448-43899-7). 32pp. The story of heavier-than-air flight and the pioneering Wright brothers is imaginatively set in the format of a school report. (Rev: HBG 4/04; SLJ 6/04) [921]

14263 Busby, Peter. *First to Fly* (3–5). Illus. by David Craig. 2003, Crown $19.95 (0-375-81287-3). 32pp. The obstacles surmounted by the Wright brothers as they took to the sky are handsomely presented in this large, richly illustrated text. (Rev: BL 1/1–15/03; HBG 10/03; SLJ 3/03) [921]

14264 Collins, Mary. *Airborne: A Photobiography of Wilbur and Orville Wright* (4–8). Illus. 2003, National Geographic $18.95 (0-7922-6957-8). 64pp. Sixty photographs are only the beginning of this intriguing book packed with information about the brothers and their famous flight. (Rev: BL 2/1/03*; HB 3–4/03; HBG 10/03; SLJ 3/03) [629.13]

14265 Ford, Carin T. *The Wright Brothers: Heroes of Flight* (2–4). Illus. Series: Famous Inventors. 2003, Enslow LB $17.95 (0-7660-2002-9). 32pp. Photographs enhance this well-written account of the Wright brothers' inventive abilities. (Rev: HBG 10/03; SLJ 10/03) [921]

14266 Gaines, Ann. *Orville and Wilbur Wright* (2–3). Series: Discover the Life of an Inventor. 2001, Rourke LB $18.60 (1-58952-121-8). 24pp. A very simple biography of the Wright brothers with material on their struggles and an explanation of how the airplane works. (Rev: BL 10/15/01) [973]

14267 McCourt, Lisa. *A Dream to Fly: The Wright Brothers at Kitty Hawk* (2–4). Illus. by Robert F. Goetzl. 2003, Troll $15.95 (0-8167-7720-9). 32pp. A picture-book biography that looks at the Wright brothers' lives and achievements, this volume features informative text and complementary illustrations. (Rev: BL 9/1/03; HBG 4/04; SLJ 10/03) [629.13]

14268 MacLeod, Elizabeth. *The Wright Brothers: A Flying Start* (3–5). Illus. 2002, Kids Can $14.95 (1-55074-933-1). 32pp. Using double-page spreads, with pictures on one and text on the other, this attractive biography is a fine introduction to the Wright brothers and their work. (Rev: BL 4/1/02; HBG 10/02; SLJ 7/02) [921]

14269 McPherson, Stephanie Sammartino, and Joseph Sammartino Gardner. *Wilbur and Orville Wright: Taking Flight* (4–7). Illus. Series: Trailblazer Biographies. 2003, Carolrhoda LB $25.26 (1-57505-443-4). 120pp. A well-written, detailed account of the Wright brothers' landmark experiments, enlivened with period photographs and other illustrations. (Rev: HBG 4/04; SLJ 4/04) [921]

14270 Old, Wendie C. *The Wright Brothers* (5–8). Series: Historical American Biographies. 2000, Enslow LB $20.95 (0-7660-1095-3). An accurate and objective biography of the heroes of Kitty Hawk, containing chapter notes, a bibliography, and a glossary. (Rev: BL 1/1–15/00; HBG 10/00; SLJ 7/00) [921]

14271 Reynolds, Quentin. *The Wright Brothers* (5–8). 1963, Random paper $5.99 (0-394-84700-8). An easily read account of the two young men and their dream of flight. [921]

14272 Schaefer, Lola M. *The Wright Brothers* (K–2). 2000, Capstone LB $13.25 (0-7368-0549-4). 24pp. For beginning readers, this is an attractive biography of the Wright brothers, whose lives and accomplishments are presented in double-page spreads. (Rev: HBG 10/00; SLJ 9/00) [921]

14273 Sproule, Anna. *The Wright Brothers: The Birth of Modern Aviation* (5–8). Series: Giants of Science. 1999, Blackbirch LB $27.44 (1-56711-328-1). 64pp. This slim biography with an inviting format stresses the lasting contributions of the Wright brothers to world transportation. (Rev: HBG 10/00; SLJ 2/00) [921]

14274 Sullivan, George. *The Wright Brothers* (3–6). Series: In Their Own Words. 2003, Scholastic paper $4.50 (0-439-26320-4). 127pp. Suitable for report writers, this profile draws on the Wright siblings' correspondence, interviews, and notes. (Rev: SLJ 7/03) [921]

14275 Taylor, Richard L. *The First Flight: The Story of the Wright Brothers* (5–8). Illus. 1990, Watts paper $22.00 (0-531-10891-0). The story of the famous brothers and the drive and determination that finally led them to Kitty Hawk. (Rev: BL 4/15/90; SLJ 9/90) [921]

14276 Yolen, Jane. *My Brothers' Flying Machine: Wilbur, Orville, and Me* (3–5). Illus. by Jim Burke. 2003, Little, Brown $16.95 (0-316-97159-6). 32pp. The story of the Wright brothers is told in free verse by their sister Katherine, who looked after the brothers while they tended to their dream. (Rev: BL 3/1/03; HBG 10/03; SLJ 3/03) [629.13]

Sports Figures

Collective

14277 Aaseng, Nathan. *Top 10 Basketball Scoring Small Forwards* (4–7). Series: Sports Top 10. 1999, Enslow LB $18.95 (0-7660-1152-6). 48pp. Each of these 10 basketball forwards is covered by a two-page biography, a full-page picture, and a page of sports statistics. (Rev: BL 11/15/99; HBG 10/00) [920]

14278 Aaseng, Nathan. *True Champions* (5–9). 1993, Walker LB $15.85 (0-8027-8247-7). Tales of legendary athletes who have demonstrated heroism and self-sacrifice off the field. (Rev: BL 8/93; SLJ 6/93) [921]

14279 Aaseng, Nathan. *Women Olympic Champions* (5–9). Series: History Makers. 2000, Lucent LB $27.45 (1-56006-709-8). 112pp. This collective biography contains profiles of women athletes who have excelled at the Olympic Games. (Rev: BL 12/15/00; SLJ 4/01) [796.0820922]

14280 Bjarkman, Peter C. *Top 10 Baseball Base Stealers* (3–6). Illus. Series: Sports Top 10. 1995, Enslow LB $18.95 (0-89490-609-7). 48pp. Short biographies of ten famous baseball players, past and present, known statistically as the top base stealers. (Rev: BL 9/15/95) [920]

14281 Bjarkman, Peter C. *Top 10 Basketball Slam Dunkers* (3–6). Illus. Series: Sports Top 10. 1995, Enslow LB $18.95 (0-89490-608-9). 48pp. Full-page photos and a two-page biography are given for each of these ten basketball stars. (Rev: BL 9/15/95) [920]

14282 Bryant, Jill. *Amazing Women Athletes* (4–8). Illus. Series: Women's Hall of Fame. 2002, Second Story paper $7.95 (1-896764-44-4). 100pp. This book contains profiles of 10 distinguished women athletes including mountain climber Annie Smith Peck and tennis stars Venus and Serena Williams. (Rev: BL 6/1–15/02; SLJ 8/02) [920]

14283 Christopher, Andre. *Top 10 Men's Tennis Players* (4–7). Series: Sports Top 10. 1998, Enslow LB $17.95 (0-7600-1009-0). 48pp. Brief biographies of past and present tennis greats, with fact boxes, career statistics, and chapter notes. (Rev: BL 3/15/98) [920]

14284 Crisfield, Deborah. *Louisville Slugger Book of Great Hitters* (4–8). Series: Mountain Lion. 1998, Wiley paper $12.95 (0-471-19772-6). 186pp. One hundred brief profiles introduce baseball's outstanding hitters, past and present, with plenty of accompanying black-and-white portraits and action shots. (Rev: SLJ 4/98) [920]

14285 Deane, Bill. *Top 10 Baseball Home Run Hitters* (4–7). Illus. Series: Sports Top 10. 1997, Enslow LB $18.95 (0-89490-804-9). 48pp. Ten brief biographies of baseball hitters, e.g., Hank Aaron, Mickey Mantle, Jimmie Foxx, and Frank Thomas. (Rev: BL 9/15/97; HBG 3/98) [920]

14286 Deane, Bill. *Top 10 Men's Baseball Hitters* (4–7). Series: Sports Top 10. 1998, Enslow LB $17.95 (0-7600-1007-4). 48pp. Brief biographies of great past and present baseball hitters, with fact boxes, career statistics, and chapter notes. (Rev: BL 3/15/98) [920]

14287 Ditchfield, Christin. *Top 10 American Women's Olympic Gold Medalists* (4–7). Illus. Series: Sports Top 10. 2000, Enslow LB $18.95 (0-7660-1277-8). 48pp. Along with the profiles of 10 female athletes, this book contains fact boxes, career statistics, and chapter notes. (Rev: BL 9/15/00; HBG 10/01) [920]

14288 Dolin, Nick, et al. *Basketball Stars* (4–8). Illus. 1997, Black Dog & Leventhal $24.98 (1-884822-61-4). This oversize book contains 50 double-page profiles with statistics of contemporary basketball stars. (Rev: BL 8/97) [920]

14289 Donkin, Andrew. *Going for Gold!* (2–4). Series: Eyewitness Reader. 1999, DK $12.95 (0-7894-4765-7); paper $3.95 (0-7894-4764-9). 48pp. Tennis, swimming, and the shot put are three of the sports covered in this biography of six Olympians including Jesse Owen, Shelley Mann, Mamo

Wolde, and Kerri Strug. (Rev: HBG 3/00; SLJ 2/00) [920]

14290 Golenbock, Peter. *Teammates* (1–3). Illus. by Paul Bacon. 1990, Harcourt $16.00 (0-15-200603-6). 32pp. Segregated life in the United States of the 1940s introduces the reader to the Negro Leagues. (Rev: BCCB 4/90; BL 4/1/90; HB 5–6/90; SLJ 6/90) [796.357]

14291 Green, Septima. *Top 10 Women Gymnasts* (4–7). Series: Sports Top 10. 1999, Enslow LB $18.95 (0-89490-809-X). 48pp. Each of these star gymnasts from the past and present gets a two-page biography, a page of important statistics, and a black-and-white photograph. (Rev: BL 11/15/99; HBG 10/00) [920]

14292 Hall, Kirsten. *Kids in Sports: A Chapter Book* (3–6). Series: True Tales. 2004, Children's Pr. LB $21.50 (0-516-23733-0); paper $4.95 (0-516-24685-2). 48pp. True stories of young people who have excelled in the area of sports. (Rev: SLJ 1/05) [920]

14293 Harrington, Denis J. *Top 10 Women Tennis Players* (3–6). Illus. Series: Sports Top 10. 1995, Enslow LB $18.95 (0-89490-612-7). 48pp. Biographies of the top ten women tennis players of all time, with a photograph of each and accompanying statistics. (Rev: BL 7/95; SLJ 11/95) [921]

14294 Hunter, Shaun. *Great African Americans in the Olympics* (3–5). Series: Outstanding African Americans. 1997, Crabtree LB $22.60 (0-86505-809-1); paper $8.95 (0-86505-823-7). 64pp. In-depth profiles of seven African Americans — e.g., Gail Devers, George Foreman, Sugar Ray Leonard — and additional shorter profiles of six others. (Rev: BL 9/15/97) [920]

14295 Kaminsky, Marty. *Uncommon Champions: Fifteen Athletes Who Battled Back* (5–8). Illus. 2000, Boyds Mills $14.95 (1-56397-787-7). 147pp. Profiles of 15 athletes in several different sports who have conquered such mental and physical problems as blindness and drug addiction to achieve their goals. (Rev: BCCB 1/01; BL 11/1/00; HBG 3/01; SLJ 10/00) [921]

14296 Kelly, J. *Superstars of Women's Basketball* (4–6). Series: Female Sports Stars. 1997, Chelsea LB $15.95 (0-7910-4389-4). 64pp. Five outstanding female basketball stars are featured in this book, which tells about each one's rise to fame. (Rev: SLJ 4/98) [920]

14297 Knapp, Ron. *Top 10 American Men Sprinters* (4–7). Series: Sports Top 10. 1999, Enslow LB $18.95 (0-7660-1074-0). 48pp. Profiles and photographs are given of 10 important American male sprinters past and present. (Rev: BL 3/15/99; HBG 10/99) [920]

14298 Knapp, Ron. *Top 10 American Men's Olympic Gold Medalists* (4–7). Illus. Series: Sports Top 10. 2000, Enslow LB $18.95 (0-7660-1274-3). 48pp. This book of 10 American male Olympic stars covers a number of sports, including track and field and diving. (Rev: BL 9/15/00; HBG 10/00) [920]

14299 Knapp, Ron. *Top 10 Basketball Centers* (3–6). Illus. Series: Sports Top 10. 1994, Enslow LB $18.95 (0-89490-515-5). 48pp. For each basketball

star, there are about two pages of text and photographs. (Rev: BL 1/15/95; SLJ 6/95) [920]

14300 Knapp, Ron. *Top 10 Basketball Scorers* (3–6). Illus. Series: Sports Top 10. 1994, Enslow LB $18.95 (0-89490-516-3). 48pp. Ten short biographies of basketball's top scorers, past and present, with tables of comparative statistics. (Rev: BL 1/15/95; SLJ 6/95) [920]

14301 Knapp, Ron. *Top 10 Hockey Scorers* (3–6). Illus. Series: Sports Top 10. 1994, Enslow LB $18.95 (0-89490-517-1). 48pp. Statistics, a brief biography, and two photographs are given for each hockey player highlighted. (Rev: BL 1/15/95) [920]

14302 Knapp, Ron. *Top 10 NFL Super Bowl Most Valuable Players* (4–7). Series: Sports Top 10. 2000, Enslow LB $18.95 (0-7660-1273-5). 48pp. This book profiles 10 of the past and present most valuable players in the National Football League's Super Bowl. (Rev: BL 12/15/00; HBG 10/01) [920]

14303 Krull, Kathleen. *Lives of the Athletes* (4–7). Illus. by Kathryn Hewitt. 1997, Harcourt $20.00 (0-15-200806-3). 96pp. A collective biography that describes the public and private lives of 20 famous athletes, including Johnny Weissmuller, Red Grange, Babe Didrikson Zaharias, Sonja Henie, and Bruce Lee. (Rev: BCCB 6/97; BL 3/15/97; HB 5–6/97; SLJ 5/97) [920]

14304 Kuhn, Betsy. *Top 10 Jockeys* (4–7). Series: Sports Top 10. 1999, Enslow LB $18.95 (0-7660-1130-5). 48pp. Important jockeys, both past and present, are featured with a short biography, a portrait, and a page of pertinent statistics. (Rev: BL 11/15/99; HBG 10/00) [920]

14305 Lace, William W. *Top 10 Football Quarterbacks* (3–6). Illus. Series: Sports Top 10. 1994, Enslow LB $18.95 (0-89490-518-X). 48pp. Star quarterbacks both past and present are highlighted in ten brief biographies, each with a photograph and a record of achievements. (Rev: BL 1/15/95) [920]

14306 Lace, William W. *Top 10 Football Rushers* (3–6). Illus. Series: Sports Top 10. 1994, Enslow LB $18.95 (0-89490-519-8). 48pp. Each of the ten featured stars gets a two-page biography, a photograph, and coverage of important statistics. (Rev: BL 1/15/95) [920]

14307 McDaniel, Melissa. *Pushing the Limits: A Chapter Book* (3–6). Series: True Tales. 2004, Children's Pr. LB $21.50 (0-516-23734-9); paper $4.95 (0-516-24688-7). 48pp. A look at athletes in the areas of marathon running, triathlons, weight lifting, and sled dog racing. (Rev: SLJ 1/05) [920]

14308 Molzahn, Arlene Bourgeois. *Top 10 American Women Sprinters* (4–8). Series: Sports Top 10. 1998, Enslow LB $18.95 (0-7660-1011-2). An easily read survey of the lives and accomplishments of 10 important women runners in track and field. (Rev: BL 8/98; HBG 10/99; SLJ 1/99) [920]

14309 Nichols, Catherine. *Record Breakers: A Chapter Book* (3–6). Series: True Tales. 2004, Children's Pr. LB $21.50 (0-516-23732-2); paper $4.95 (0-516-24689-5). 48pp. Gertrude Ederle and Mark McGwire are two of the record-setting individuals featured in this volume. (Rev: SLJ 1/05) [921]

14310 Packard, Mary. *Beating the Odds: A Chapter Book* (3–6). Illus. Series: True Tales. 2004, Children's Pr. LB $21.50 (0-516-23731-4); paper $4.95 (0-516-24682-8). 48pp. Wilma Rudolph (polio) and Lance Armstrong (cancer) are two of the inspiring individuals featured in this volume of true tales about overcoming physical difficulties. (Rev: SLJ 1/05) [920]

14311 Pietrusza, David. *Top 10 Baseball Managers* (4–7). Series: Sports Top 10. 1999, Enslow LB $18.95 (0-7660-1076-7). 48pp. This work gives brief profiles of 10 famous past and present managers of American baseball teams. (Rev: BL 1/1–15/99; HBG 10/99) [920]

14312 Poynter, Margaret. *Top 10 American Women's Figure Skaters* (4–7). Series: Sports Top 10. 1998, Enslow LB $18.95 (0-7660-1075-9). This work offers brief profiles and photographs of 10 female figure skaters. (Rev: BL 11/15/98; HBG 10/99) [920]

14313 Rappoport, Ken. *Guts and Glory: Making It in the NBA* (4–8). 1997, Walker LB $16.85 (0-8027-8431-3). The 10 basketball players profiled in this book had to overcome obstacles to get to the top. (Rev: BL 8/97; BR 11–12/97; SLJ 7/97) [920]

14314 Rappoport, Ken. *Ladies First: Women Athletes Who Made a Difference* (5–8). Illus. 2005, Peachtree $14.95 (1-56145-338-2). 160pp. Gymnast Nadia Comaneci and dogsled racer Susan Butcher are only two of the many women in diverse sports featured in this collective biography that also gives a brief history of women's participation in sports. (Rev: BL 5/1/05; SLJ 6/05) [920]

14315 Rappoport, Ken. *Top 10 Basketball Legends* (3–6). Illus. Series: Sports Top 10. 1995, Enslow LB $18.95 (0-89490-610-0). 48pp. Biographies of the top ten basketball players of the past, with statistics to prove the unique contribution of each. (Rev: BL 7/95; SLJ 11/95) [920]

14316 Rediger, Pat. *Great African Americans in Sports* (4–6). Illus. Series: Outstanding African Americans. 1996, Crabtree LB $22.60 (0-86505-801-6); paper $8.95 (0-86505-815-6). 64pp. Three of the 13 sports heroes profiled are Michael Jordan, Jackie Joyner-Kersee, and Carl Lewis. (Rev: BL 9/15/96) [920]

14317 Rennert, Richard S., ed. *Book of Firsts: Sports Heroes* (5–8). Illus. Series: Profiles of Great Black Americans. 1993, Chelsea LB $15.95 (0-7910-2055-X); paper $7.65 (0-7910-2056-8). 63pp. Contains profiles of these great African American athletes: Arthur Ashe, Chuck Cooper, Althea Gibson, Jesse Owens, Jackie Robinson, Jack Johnson, Frank Robinson, and Bill Russell. (Rev: SLJ 12/93) [920]

14318 Riley, Gail B. *Top 10 NASCAR Drivers* (3–4). Illus. Series: Sports Top 10. 1995, Enslow LB $18.95 (0-89490-611-9). 48pp. Ten of the top race car drivers are highlighted in these short biographies. (Rev: BL 9/15/95) [796.7]

14319 Rutledge, Rachel. *The Best of the Best in Figure Skating* (4–7). Series: Women of Sports. 1998, Millbrook LB $24.90 (0-7613-1302-8). 64pp. After

a brief history of figure skating and mention of its women pioneers, this book devotes separate chapters to the sport's present-day female leaders. (Rev: BL 2/15/99; HBG 10/99) [920]

14320 Rutledge, Rachel. *The Best of the Best in Gymnastics* (5–8). Series: Women of Sports. 1999, Millbrook LB $24.90 (0-7613-1321-4); paper $7.95 (0-7613-0784-2). 64pp. After an overview of the sport and its history, the author profiles eight important contemporary female gymnasts, five of whom are American. (Rev: HBG 10/99; SLJ 7/99) [920]

14321 Rutledge, Rachel. *The Best of the Best in Soccer* (4–7). Series: Women of Sports. 1998, Millbrook LB $24.90 (0-7613-1315-X). 64pp. A revised edition of the 1998 title, containing a brief history of women's soccer and profiles of the top women players of yesterday, today, and tomorrow. (Rev: BL 2/15/99; HBG 10/99) [920]

14322 Rutledge, Rachel. *The Best of the Best in Track and Field* (5–8). Series: Women of Sports. 1999, Millbrook LB $24.90 (0-7613-1300-1); paper $7.95 (0-7613-0446-0). 64pp. A brief history of track and field is followed by profiles of eight female athletes from the United States and abroad, with material on their careers and off-the-field lives. (Rev: HBG 10/99; SLJ 7/99) [920]

14323 Savage, Jeff. *Home Run Kings* (4–6). Illus. 1999, Raintree $22.83 (0-7398-0216-X); paper $6.95 (0-7398-0215-1). 48pp. Brief profiles are given of such home-run record setters as Babe Ruth, Roger Maris, Mark McGwire, Sammy Sosa, Hank Aaron, Mickey Mantle, and Willie Mays plus lots of World Series action. (Rev: BL 5/15/99; HBG 10/99) [920]

14324 Savage, Jeff. *Top 10 Basketball Point Guards* (4–7). Series: Sports Top 10. 1997, Enslow LB $18.95 (0-89490-807-3). 48pp. Each of the athletes is presented in four pages containing a biography, statistics, and two photographs. Also use *Top 10 Basketball Power Forwards* (1997). (Rev: BL 9/15/97) [920]

14325 Savage, Jeff. *Top 10 Football Sackers* (4–7). Series: Sports Top 10. 1997, Enslow LB $18.95 (0-89490-805-7). 48pp. Each of the 10 football stars highlighted is covered in four pages that include a short biography, two photographs, and a statistics table. (Rev: BL 9/15/97) [920]

14326 Savage, Jeff. *Top 10 Heisman Trophy Winners* (4–7). Series: Sports Top 10. 1999, Enslow LB $18.95 (0-7660-1072-4). 48pp. This work profiles 10 winners of the trophy given each year to the most outstanding college football player in America. (Rev: BL 1/1–15/99; HBG 10/99) [920]

14327 Savage, Jeff. *Top 10 Physically Challenged Athletes* (4–7). Series: Sports Top 10. 2000, Enslow LB $18.95 (0-7660-1272-7). 48pp. Each of the 10 short biographies in this book on physically handicapped athletes has an accompanying photo (usually in color) and a page of statistics. (Rev: BL 2/15/00; HBG 10/00; SLJ 10/00) [920]

14328 Savage, Jeff. *Top 10 Professional Football Coaches* (4–7). Series: Sports Top 10. 1998, Enslow LB $17.95 (0-7660-1006-6). 48pp. From professional football Hall of Famers George Halas and Curly Lambeau to the Miami Dolphins' Jimmy Johnson, this book profiles ten super coaches, with each given a two-page biography, photographs, and a career summary. (Rev: HBG 10/98; SLJ 9/98) [920]

14329 Schnakenberg, Robert E. *Teammates: Karl Malone and John Stockton* (5–7). Illus. 1998, Millbrook LB $23.90 (0-7613-0300-6). 96pp. Despite very different backgrounds, these two leading players on the Utah Jazz basketball team have become close personal friends. (Rev: BL 8/98; HBG 10/98; SLJ 5/98) [920]

14330 Schwabacher, Martin. *Superstars of Women's Tennis* (4–6). Illus. Series: Female Sports Stars. 1997, Chelsea LB $16.95 (0-7910-4393-2). 64pp. Profiles tennis greats Billie Jean King, Chris Evert, Martina Navratilova, Steffi Graff, and Monica Seles. (Rev: SLJ 8/97) [920]

14331 Sehnert, Chris W. *Top 10 Sluggers* (5–8). Illus. Series: Top 10 Champions. 1997, ABDO LB $25.65 (1-56239-797-4). An overview of the careers of such notable hitters as Babe Ruth, Hank Aaron, and Roberto Clemente. (Rev: BL 1/1–15/98; HBG 3/98) [920]

14332 Smith, Pohla. *Superstars of Women's Figure Skating* (4–6). Illus. Series: Female Sports Stars. 1997, Chelsea LB $16.95 (0-7910-4392-4). 64pp. A clear easy reader that includes profiles of Sonja Henie, Peggy Fleming, Dorothy Hamill, Katarina Witt, Kristi Yamaguchi, and Oksana Baiul. (Rev: SLJ 8/97) [920]

14333 Spiros, Dean. *Top 10 Hockey Goalies* (4–6). Series: Sports Top 10. 1998, Enslow $18.95 (0-7660-1010-4). Past and present star goalies are featured in ten short profiles. (Rev: BL 8/98; HBG 10/99) [921]

14334 Strudwick, Leslie. *Athletes* (3–6). Series: Women in Profile. 1999, Crabtree LB $15.96 (0-7787-0015-1); paper $8.06 (0-7787-0037-2). 48pp. Color photos and interesting information are included in this book that profiles six internationally known female athletes and briefly sketches an additional 12. (Rev: BL 9/15/99) [920]

14335 Sullivan, George. *Power Football: The Greatest Running Backs* (4–9). 2001, Simon & Schuster $18.00 (0-689-82432-7). 60pp. Profiles eighteen 20th-century running backs, including O. J. Simpson, Terrell Davis, and Emmitt Smith. (Rev: HBG 3/02; SLJ 11/01) [920]

14336 Sullivan, Michael J. *Top 10 Baseball Pitchers* (3–6). Illus. Series: Sports Top 10. 1994, Enslow LB $18.95 (0-89490-520-1). 48pp. Star pitchers from both the past and present are featured, each receiving a two-page biography and color photograph. (Rev: BL 1/15/95) [920]

14337 Thornley, Stew. *Top 10 Football Receivers* (3–6). Illus. Series: Sports Top 10. 1995, Enslow LB $18.95 (0-89490-607-0). 48pp. The position of receiver is highlighted in the biographies of ten of the greatest, past and present. (Rev: BL 7/95; SLJ 11/95) [920]

14338 Torres, John A. *Top 10 Basketball Three-Point Shooters* (4–7). Series: Sports Top 10. 1999, Enslow LB $18.95 (0-7660-1071-6). 48pp. A profile and a photograph of 10 star basketball players make up this slender volume. (Rev: BL 1/1–15/99; HBG 10/99) [920]

14339 Torres, John A. *Top 10 NBA Finals Most Valuable Players* (4–7). Illus. Series: Sports Top 10. 2000, Enslow LB $18.95 (0-7660-1276-X). 48pp. Short profiles of these NBA players also include photographs and some sports statistics. (Rev: BL 9/15/00; HBG 10/00) [920]

14340 Ungs, Tim. *Superstars of Men's Soccer* (3–5). Series: Male Sports Stars. 1998, Chelsea LB $15.95 (0-7910-4588-9). 64pp. After an introduction to soccer, this collective biography profiles Pele, Franz Beckenbauer, Johann Cruyff, and Diego Maradona. (Rev: HBG 3/99; SLJ 12/98) [920]

14341 Wickham, Martha. *Superstars of Women's Track and Field* (4–6). Series: Female Sports Stars. 1997, Chelsea LB $15.95 (0-7910-4394-0). 64pp. This book profiles five important female track-and-field stars, with details on their careers and a good selection of action photos. (Rev: SLJ 4/98) [920]

14342 Winter, Jonah. *Beisbol! Latino Baseball Pioneers and Legends* (3–8). Illus. 2001, Lee & Low $16.95 (1-58430-012-4). 32pp. Sports fans will appreciate the format here, with statistics and other facts about 14 Latino baseball players presented in trading-card-style profiles. (Rev: BCCB 10/01; BL 10/1/01; HBG 10/01; SLJ 7/01) [796.357]

14343 Winter, Jonah. *Fair Ball! 14 Great Stars from Baseball's Negro Leagues* (3–5). Illus. 1999, Scholastic $15.95 (0-590-39464-9). 32pp. Using double-page spreads, this book profiles 14 great baseball players from the Negro Leagues, including Cool Papa Bell, Josh Gibson, and Satchel Paige. (Rev: BL 4/15/99; HBG 10/99; SLJ 3/99) [920]

14344 Young, Jeff C. *Top 10 Basketball Shot-Blockers* (4–7). Series: Sports Top 10. 2000, Enslow LB $18.95 (0-7660-1275-1). 48pp. For each of the basketball stars profiled, there is a full-page picture, a two-page biography, and a page of statistics. (Rev: BL 2/15/00; HBG 10/00) [920]

14345 Young, Ken. *Cy Young Award Winners* (4–6). Illus. 1994, Walker LB $15.85 (0-8027-8301-5). 160pp. Profiles of ten winners of the Cy Young Award for pitching, e.g., Whitey Ford, Sandy Koufax, Fernando Valenzuela, and Dwight Gooden. (Rev: BL 9/1/94; SLJ 8/94) [920]

Automobile Racing

EARNHARDT, DALE

14346 Steenkamer, Paul. *Dale Earnhardt: Star Race Car Driver* (4–6). Illus. Series: Sports Reports. 2000, Enslow LB $19.95 (0-7660-1335-9). 104pp. As well as a profile of Dale Earnhardt, this book has some action photos and gives a behind-the-scenes look at car racing. (Rev: BL 9/15/00; HBG 3/01) [921]

EARNHARDT, DALE, JR.

14347 Stewart, Mark. *Dale Earnhardt Jr.: Driven by Destiny* (5–8). Series: Auto Racing's New Wave. 2003, Millbrook LB $22.90 (0-7613-2908-0). 48pp. An exciting biography of the NASCAR driver who was voted the most popular driver of 2003. (Rev: BL 6/1–15/03; HBG 10/03; SLJ 10/03) [796.72]

GORDON, JEFF

14348 Powell, Phelan. *Jeff Gordon* (3–4). Series: Real-Life Reader Biographies. 1999, Mitchell Lane LB $15.95 (1-58415-005-X). 32pp. A simple biography of the race-car driving star and his climb to fame. (Rev: BL 10/15/99) [921]

PETTY FAMILY

14349 Stewart, Mark. *The Pettys: Triumphs and Tragedies of Auto Racing's First Family* (4–8). Illus. 2001, Millbrook LB $24.90 (0-7613-2273-6). 64pp. Photographs, quotations, anecdotes, and informative text introduce readers to the famous Petty family and their sometimes tragic involvement in automobile racing. (Rev: BL 9/1/01; HBG 3/02) [796.72]

STEWART, TONY

14350 Leebrick, Kristal. *Tony Stewart* (4–7). Illus. Series: NASCAR Racing. 2004, Capstone LB $22.60 (0-7368-2425-1). 32pp. This profile of auto racing star Tony Stewart chronicles his meteoric rise from go-karts and midget racers to the top ranks of NASCAR. (Rev: BL 4/1/04) [790.72]

Baseball

AARON, HANK

14351 Golenbock, Peter. *Hank Aaron: Brave in Every Way* (2–4). Illus. by Paul Lee. 2001, Harcourt $16.00 (0-15-202093-4). 32pp. Part of this stirring biography focuses on Hank Aaron's goal of breaking Babe Ruth's batting record and the controversy it caused because he was African American. (Rev: BL 2/15/01; HBG 10/01) [921]
14352 Spencer, Lauren. *Hank Aaron* (4–7). Series: Baseball Hall of Famers. 2003, Rosen LB $29.25 (0-8239-3600-7). 112pp. In 1974, Hank Aaron, an African American, was crowned home run king, taking the title away from Babe Ruth. This is his story. (Rev: BL 6/1–15/03; SLJ 6/03) [921]
14353 Tackach, James. *Hank Aaron* (4–6). Illus. Series: Baseball Legends. 1991, Chelsea LB $16.95 (0-7910-1165-8). 64pp. In addition to the life of baseball legend Aaron, this biography includes sections of statistics, a chronology, and numerous photographs. (Rev: BL 12/1/91) [921]

ABBOTT, JIM

14354 Johnson, Rick L. *Jim Abbott: Beating the Odds* (4–7). Illus. Series: Taking Part. 1991, Macmillan LB $13.95 (0-87518-459-6). 64pp. This account re-creates the life of the baseball pitcher who overcame a severe disability. (Rev: BL 9/1/91) [921]
14355 Savage, Jeff. *Jim Abbott* (5–8). Series: Sports Greats. 1993, Enslow LB $17.95 (0-89490-395-0). The amazing career of the one-handed pitcher who came up with the California Angels and threw a no-hitter for the New York Yankees. (Rev: BL 3/1/93) [921]
14356 White, Ellen E. *Jim Abbott: Against All Odds* (3–5). Illus. Series: Scholastic Biography. 1990, Scholastic paper $2.99 (0-590-43503-5). 86pp. The amazing pitcher for the California Angels, who once pitched a no-hitter for the New York Yankees, who has only one hand. (Rev: SLJ 10/90) [921]

ALEXANDER, GROVER CLEVELAND

14357 Kavanagh, Jack. *Grover Cleveland Alexander* (4–6). Illus. Series: Baseball Legends. 1990, Chelsea LB $16.95 (0-7910-1166-6). 63pp. A fine profile of one of the greats of the baseball game. (Rev: BL 6/1/90) [921]

ALOMAR, ROBERTO

14358 Macht, Norman L. *Roberto Alomar* (4–8). Series: Latinos in Baseball. 1999, Mitchell Lane LB $18.95 (1-883845-84-X). 64pp. Using extensive interviews with Alomar, his family, friends, and colleagues, this biography of the famous Puerto Rican baseball player shows his strong self-discipline, work ethic, and close family ties. (Rev: HBG 10/99; SLJ 5/99) [921]
14359 Thornley, Stew. *Roberto Alomar: Star Second Baseman* (4–6). Series: Sports Reports. 1999, Enslow LB $19.95 (0-7660-1079-1). 104pp. Career statistics, action photos, and behind-the-scenes coverage are included in this biography of the famous second baseman. (Rev: BL 2/15/99; HBG 10/99) [921]

BELL, COOL PAPA

14360 McCormack, Shaun. *Cool Papa Bell* (4–7). Series: Baseball Hall of Famers of the Negro Leagues. 2002, Rosen LB $29.25 (0-8239-3474-8). 112pp. A biography of James Thomas "Cool Papa" Bell of Negro League baseball, who is said to have stolen 175 bases in one season. (Rev: BL 7/02) [921]

BENCH, JOHNNY

14361 Shannon, Mike. *Johnny Bench* (4–6). Illus. Series: Baseball Legends. 1990, Chelsea LB $16.95 (0-7910-1168-2). 64pp. Biographical data plus background statistics, a chronology, and many photos. (Rev: BL 10/1/90; SLJ 1/91) [921]

BONDS, BARRY

14362 Savage, Jeff. *Barry Bonds: Mr. Excitement* (4–8). Series: Sports Achievers. 1996, Lerner paper

$5.95 (0-8225-9748-9). The story of this fantastic baseball player who has won the Most Valuable Player Award three times and who grew up in the shadow of a famous father. (Rev: BL 4/15/97; SLJ 2/97) [921]

BONILLA, BOBBY

14363 Knapp, Ron. *Bobby Bonilla* (5–8). Illus. Series: Sports Greats. 1993, Enslow LB $17.95 (0-89490-417-5). 64pp. Using easy-to-read prose and a number of action photographs, this is a lively introduction to baseball star Bobby Bonilla. (Rev: BL 9/15/93) [921]

14364 Rappoport, Ken. *Bobby Bonilla* (5–9). 1993, Walker LB $15.85 (0-8027-8256-6). A biography of the baseball player who rose from poverty in the South Bronx to superstardom and multimillionaire status. (Rev: BL 5/15/93; SLJ 5/93) [921]

CANSECO, JOSÉ

14365 Aaseng, Nathan. *Jose Canseco: Baseball's Forty-Forty Man* (4–7). Illus. 1989, Lerner paper $4.95 (0-8225-9586-9). 56pp. The ups and downs of this sometimes controversial baseball star of the Oakland A's. (Rev: BCCB 9/89; BL 7/89; SLJ 8/89) [921]

CLEMENTE, ROBERTO

14366 Bjarkman, Peter C. *Roberto Clemente* (4–6). Illus. Series: Baseball Legends. 1991, Chelsea LB $16.95 (0-7910-1171-2). 64pp. The inspiring career of the Puerto Rican baseball legend. (Rev: BL 3/1/91) [921]

14367 Gilbert, Tom. *Roberto Clemente* (5–8). Illus. 1991, Chelsea LB $21.95 (0-7910-1240-9). 112pp. The life of the first Hispanic in the Baseball Hall of Fame. (Rev: BL 8/91) [921]

14368 Kingsbury, Robert. *Roberto Clemente* (4–7). Series: Baseball Hall of Famers. 2003, Rosen LB $29.25 (0-8239-3602-3). 112pp. The story of the National League battling champion who faced racism and discrimination because of his Hispanic background. (Rev: BL 6/1–15/03; SLJ 6/03) [921]

14369 Marquez, Heron. *Roberto Clemente: Baseball's Humanitarian Hero* (4–7). Illus. 2005, Carolrhoda LB $27.93 (1-57505-767-0). 112pp. The story of the ballplayer, from his birth in Puerto Rico to his death in a plane crash, with photographs. (Rev: BL 3/15/05; SLJ 5/05) [796.357]

14370 Winter, Jonah. *Roberto Clemente: Pride of the Pittsburgh Pirates* (2–4). Illus. by Raul Colon. 2005, Simon & Schuster $16.95 (0-689-85643-1). 40pp. Clemente's character, career success, and tragic death are all covered in this engaging picture-book biography. (Rev: BL 2/15/05; SLJ 5/05) [921]

COBB, TY

14371 Macht, Norman L. *Ty Cobb* (4–6). Illus. Series: Baseball Legends. 1992, Chelsea LB $15.95 (0-685-48322-3). 64pp. The life of this baseball great is recalled in a text that gives coverage of piv-

otal games, plus statistics and a chronology. (Rev: BL 4/1/93) [921]

DEAN, DIZZY

14372 Kavanagh, Jack. *Dizzy Dean* (4–6). Illus. Series: Baseball Legends. 1991, Chelsea LB $16.95 (0-7910-1173-9). 64pp. The story of the famous pitcher for the St. Louis Cardinals. (Rev: BL 2/1/91) [921]

DIMAGGIO, JOE

14373 Appel, Marty. *Joe DiMaggio* (4–6). Illus. Series: Baseball Legends. 1990, Chelsea LB $16.95 (0-7910-1164-X). 63pp. A biography of the ultimate baseball hero. (Rev: BL 6/1/90; SLJ 10/90) [921]

14374 Sakany, Lois. *Joe DiMaggio* (4–6). Series: Baseball Hall of Famers. 2004, Rosen LB $29.25 (0-8239-3779-8). 112pp. Report writers will find solid information on the life and career of the Yankees star. (Rev: SLJ 6/04) [921]

14375 Sanford, William R., and Carl R. Green. *Joe DiMaggio* (4–6). Illus. Series: Sports Immortals. 1993, Macmillan LB $16.95 (0-89686-738-2). 48pp. The biography of Joe DiMaggio, alias "The Yankee Clipper," who was given the Greatest Living Player Award in the 1969 Summer Olympics. (Rev: BL 4/15/93; SLJ 8/93) [921]

DOUTY, SHEILA CORNELL

14376 Douty, Sheila Cornell, and Judith Cohen. *You Can Be a Woman Softball Player* (3–6). Illus. 2000, Cascade Pass $13.95 (1-880599-47-3); paper $7.00 (1-880599-46-5). 40pp. This is the story of Sheila Douty, from her youth, when she was considered a "problem" child, to the 1996 Olympics, where she helped her team win a gold medal. (Rev: BL 7/00) [921]

FELLER, BOB

14377 Eckhouse, Morris. *Bob Feller* (4–6). Illus. Series: Baseball Legends. 1990, Chelsea LB $16.95 (0-7910-1174-7). 64pp. The life and career of the legendary baseball pitcher are re-created. (Rev: BL 10/1/90) [921]

GAGNE, ERIC

14378 Gagné, Eric, and Greg Brown. *Eric Gagne: Break Barriers* (3–6). Series: Athletes. 2004, Positively for Kids $15.95 (0-9634650-6-6). 48pp. A lively and attractively designed first-person account of Gagne's life and career in baseball, with lots of personal details about his childhood, family life, and sporting successes. (Rev: BL 9/1/04) [921]

GALARRAGA, ANDRES

14379 Boulais, Sue. *Andres Galarraga* (3–4). Series: Real-Life Reader Biographies. 1998, Mitchell Lane LB $15.95 (1-883845-61-0). 32pp. The story of a baseball hero from Caracas, Venezuela, his career in

Atlanta, and his struggle with cancer. (Rev: BL 10/15/98; HBG 10/98; SLJ 12/98) [921]

GEHRIG, LOU

14380 Adler, David A. *Lou Gehrig: The Luckiest Man* (3–5). Illus. by Terry Widener. 1997, Harcourt $16.00 (0-15-200523-4). 32pp. An excellent biography of the "Iron Horse," the baseball legend who was a model of sportsmanship and courage. (Rev: BCCB 4/97; BL 5/15/97; HB 7–8/97, 9–10/97; SLJ 5/97) [921]

14381 Macht, Norman L. *Lou Gehrig* (4–6). Illus. Series: Baseball Legends. 1993, Chelsea LB $16.95 (0-7910-1176-3). 64pp. The story of this baseball great and gallant American is told with particular attention to his most important games. (Rev: BL 4/1/93) [921]

14382 Viola, Kevin. *Lou Gehrig* (4–7). Series: Sports Heroes and Legends. 2004, Lerner LB $26.60 (0-8225-5311-2). Starting with Gehrig's sad retirement and his "Luckiest Man" speech, this well-written and informative biography goes back to look at his life and successful career. (Rev: BL 9/1/04) [921]

GIBSON, JOSH

14383 Mellage, Nanette. *Coming Home: A Story of Josh Gibson, Baseball's Greatest Home Run Hitter* (PS–3). Illus. by Cornelius Van Wright and Ying-hwa Hu. 2001, Troll $15.95 (0-8167-7009-3). 32pp. An African American grandfather tells his grandson of the life of Josh Gibson, the star player of the Negro Leagues, and of the championship game he attended many years ago. (Rev: BL 3/1/01; HBG 10/01) [921]

14384 Twemlow, Nick. *Josh Gibson* (4–7). Series: Baseball Hall of Famers of the Negro Leagues. 2002, Rosen LB $29.25 (0-8239-3475-6). 112pp. In addition to racial prejudice in the world of baseball, Josh Gibson suffered many personal misfortunes as this life story recounts. (Rev: BL 7/02) [921]

GONZALEZ, JUAN

14385 Gutman, Bill. *Juan Gonzalez: Outstanding Outfielder* (4–6). Illus. Series: Sports World. 1995, Millbrook LB $19.90 (1-56294-567-X). 48pp. A brief, well-illustrated biography of this baseball star. (Rev: BL 9/15/95; SLJ 1/96) [921]

GRIFFEY, KEN, JR.

14386 Gutman, Bill. *Ken Griffey, Jr. Baseball's Best* (4–6). Series: Sports World. 1998, Millbrook LB $19.90 (0-7613-0415-0). 48pp. A lively biography that describes Griffey's life, character, and contributions to baseball. (Rev: BL 11/15/98; HBG 3/99) [921]

14387 Macnow, Glen. *Ken Griffey, Jr: Star Outfielder* (4–6). Series: Sports Reports. 1997, Enslow LB $20.95 (0-89490-802-2). 104pp. The life and career of this baseball star are covered, with action photos

and behind-the-scenes coverage. (Rev: BL 2/15/98; HBG 3/98) [921]

HERSHISER, OREL

14388 Knapp, Ron. *Orel Hershiser* (5–8). Series: Sports Greats. 1993, Enslow LB $17.95 (0-89490-389-6). An easily read sports biography that re-creates the great moments in this baseball star's career up to 1993. (Rev: BL 4/1/93) [921]

HORNSBY, ROGERS

14389 Kavanagh, Jack. *Rogers Hornsby* (4–6). Illus. Series: Baseball Legends. 1991, Chelsea LB $16.95 (0-7910-1178-X). 64pp. A well-illustrated biography of this baseball great. (Rev: BL 2/1/91) [921]

IRVIN, MONTE

14390 Haegele, Katie. *Monte Irvin* (4–7). Series: Baseball Hall of Famers of the Negro Leagues. 2002, Rosen LB $29.25 (0-8239-3477-2). 112pp. Though recruited into the Negro leagues when he was 17, Irvin, a very talented player, was past his prime when he finally became a major leaguer. (Rev: BL 7/02) [921]

JACKSON, REGGIE

14391 Woods, Andrew. *Young Reggie Jackson: Hall of Fame Champion* (2–4). Illus. Series: Troll First Start. 1996, Troll paper $3.50 (0-8167-3763-0). 32pp. With emphasis on his early life, this is an easily read biography of this baseball legend. (Rev: BL 2/15/96) [921]

JETER, DEREK

14392 Stewart, Mark. *Derek Jeter: Substance and Style* (4–6). Series: Baseball's New Wave. 1999, Millbrook LB $19.90 (0-7613-1516-0). 48pp. This biography that ends with the 1998 season gives a good close-up view of the star shortstop of the New York Yankees. (Rev: HBG 3/00; SLJ 2/00) [921]

14393 Thornley, Stew. *Derek Jeter* (3–6). Illus. Series: Sports Leaders. 2004, Enslow LB $20.95 (0-7660-2035-5). 104pp. An accessible profile of the shortstop's life and career. [921]

14394 Torres, John. *Derek Jeter* (3–4). Series: Real-Life Reader Biographies. 2000, Mitchell Lane LB $15.95 (1-58415-031-9). 32pp. A brief, attractive biography of the young star of the New York Yankees. (Rev: BL 11/15/00) [921]

JOHNSON, JUDY

14395 Billus, Kathleen. *Judy Johnson* (4–7). Illus. Series: Baseball Hall of Famers of the Negro Leagues. 2002, Rosen LB $29.25 (0-8239-3476-4). 112pp. A biography of Johnson covering his years as player, coach, manager, and scout, with black-and-white photographs, glossary, timeline, and lists of additional resources. (Rev: BL 7/02) [796.357]

JOHNSON, MAMIE "PEANUT"

14396 Green, Michelle Y. *A Strong Right Arm: The Story of Mamie "Peanut" Johnson* (4–7). 2002, Dial $15.99 (0-8037-2661-9). 128pp. The life story of the woman who was one of three to play professional baseball and of her career as pitcher with the Negro Leagues' Indianapolis Clowns. (Rev: BL 6/1–15/02*; HBG 3/03; SLJ 8/02) [921]

JOHNSON, WALTER

14397 Kavanagh, Jack. *Walter Johnson* (4–8). Illus. Series: Baseball Legends. 1991, Chelsea LB $18.65 (0-7910-1179-8). 144pp. A biography of a baseball giant, including coverage of important games and many black-and-white photographs. (Rev: BL 1/15/92) [921]

LEONARD, BUCK

14398 Payment, Simone. *Buck Leonard* (4–7). Series: Baseball Hall of Famers of the Negro Leagues. 2002, Rosen LB $29.25 (0-8239-3473-X). 112pp. The story of one of the greatest baseball players of all time, who missed worldwide fame because of his color. (Rev: BL 7/02) [921]

MCGWIRE, MARK

14399 Dougherty, Terri. *Mark McGwire* (2–4). Series: Jam Session. 1999, ABDO LB $14.95 (1-57765-349-1). 32pp. A heavily illustrated biography of the amazing batter that uses quotes from friends and family. (Rev: HBG 10/99; SLJ 8/99) [921]

14400 Thornley, Stew. *Mark McGwire: Star Home Run Hitter* (4–8). Series: Sports Reports. 1999, Enslow LB $20.95 (0-7660-1329-4). A look at the life and accomplishments of this exciting baseball player. (Rev: BL 3/15/99; HBG 9/99; SLJ 7/99) [921]

MADDUX, GREG

14401 Gutman, Bill. *Greg Maddux* (4–6). Series: Sports World. 1999, Millbrook LB $19.90 (0-7613-1454-7). 46pp. A simple biography that stresses Greg Maddux's many contributions to the Chicago Cubs and the Atlanta Braves. (Rev: BL 1/1–15/00; HBG 3/00) [921]

14402 Thornley, Stew. *Greg Maddux* (5–8). Illus. Series: Sports Greats. 1997, Enslow LB $17.95 (0-89490-873-1). 64pp. The life of this baseball great, supplemented by career statistics and many action photographs. (Rev: BL 2/15/97) [921]

MANTLE, MICKEY

14403 Marlin, John. *Mickey Mantle* (4–7). Series: Sports Heroes and Legends. 2004, Lerner LB $26.60 (0-8225-1796-5). A concise, well-written biography that focuses on Mantle's illustrious career. (Rev: BL 9/1/04; SLJ 11/04) [921]

14404 Weinstein, Howard. *Mickey Mantle* (4–6). Series: Baseball Hall of Famers. 2004, Rosen LB $29.25 (0-8239-3782-8). 112pp. Report writers will find solid information on the life and career of the Yankees star. (Rev: SLJ 6/04) [921]

MATHEWSON, CHRISTY

14405 Macht, Norman L. *Christy Mathewson* (4–6). Illus. Series: Baseball Legends. 1991, Chelsea LB $16.95 (0-7910-1182-8). 64pp. The life of the great pitcher, including important games in his career. (Rev: BL 9/15/91) [921]

MAYS, WILLIE

14406 Grabowski, John. *Willie Mays* (4–6). Illus. Series: Baseball Legends. 1990, Chelsea LB $16.95 (0-7910-1183-6). 63pp. A profile of one of baseball's greatest hitters. (Rev: BL 6/1/90) [921]

14407 Mandel, Peter. *Say Hey! A Song of Willie Mays* (K–3). Illus. by Don Tate. 2000, Hyperion LB $16.49 (0-7868-2417-4). 32pp. The basics of Willie Mays's life are covered in this picture book that uses a sing-along text and computer-generated art. (Rev: BL 2/15/00; HBG 10/00; SLJ 8/00) [921]

MITCHELL, JACKIE

14408 Moss, Marissa. *Mighty Jackie: The Strike-Out Queen* (K–3). Illus. by C. F. Payne. 2004, Simon & Schuster $16.95 (0-689-86329-2). Jackie's story opens with the day in 1931 when — at age 17 — she struck out both Lou Gehrig and Babe Ruth. (Rev: BL 1/1–15/04; SLJ 2/04) [921]

PAIGE, SATCHEL

14409 Cline-Ransome, Lesa. *Satchel Paige* (2–4). Illus. by James E. Ransome. 2000, Simon & Schuster $16.00 (0-689-81151-9). 40pp. The mythic hero of baseball comes to life, with all his swagger and accomplishments, in this biography. (Rev: BCCB 2/00; BL 12/15/99*; HB 3–4/00; HBG 10/00; SLJ 3/00) [921]

14410 McKissack, Patricia, and Fredrick McKissack. *Satchel Paige: The Best Arm in Baseball* (2–4). Illus. by Michael D. Blegel. Series: Great African Americans. 1992, Enslow LB $14.95 (0-89490-317-9). 32pp. The life story of the Hall of Famer who was the first African American pitcher in the American League. (Rev: BL 10/15/92; SLJ 1/93) [921]

14411 Schmidt, Julie. *Satchel Paige* (4–7). Illus. Series: Baseball Hall of Famers of the Negro Leagues. 2002, Rosen LB $29.25 (0-8239-3478-0). 112pp. A biography of the famous pitcher who became the oldest rookie ever, with black-and-white photographs, glossary, timeline, and lists of additional resources. (Rev: BL 7/02) [796.357]

PALMEIRO, RAFAEL

14412 Marvis, Barbara. *Rafael Palmeiro* (3–5). Series: Real-Life Reader Biographies. 1998, Mitchell Lane LB $15.95 (1-883845-49-1). 32pp. Using short chapters, black-and-white photos, and a simple vocabulary, this is the story of Rafael Palmeiro, the Cuban refugee who became first baseman for the Texas Rangers. (Rev: BL 6/1–15/98; HBG 3/98) [921]

PUCKETT, KIRBY

14413 Puckett, Kirby, and Greg Brown. *Kirby Puckett: Be the Best You Can Be* (2–4). Illus. by Tim Houle. 1993, Waldman $14.95 (0-931674-20-4). A picture-book autobiography of the star of the Minnesota Twins, filled with advice on how to achieve one's potential. (Rev: BL 8/93; SLJ 2/94) [921]

RIPKEN, CAL, JR.

14414 Macnow, Glen. *Cal Ripken, Jr.* (5–8). Series: Sports Greats. 1993, Enslow LB $17.95 (0-89490-387-X). The story of the baseball giant who gained fame as the star shortstop for the Baltimore Orioles. (Rev: BL 4/1/93) [921]

14415 Savage, Jeff. *Cal Ripken, Jr.: Star Shortstop* (4–6). Illus. Series: Sports Reports. 1994, Enslow LB $20.95 (0-89490-485-X). 104pp. A book about the star baseball player who gained fame as an all-star shortstop for the Baltimore Orioles. (Rev: SLJ 2/95) [921]

ROBINSON, BROOKS

14416 Wolff, Rick. *Brooks Robinson* (4–6). Illus. Series: Baseball Legends. 1990, Chelsea LB $16.95 (0-7910-1186-0). 64pp. This biography tells the life of Brooks Robinson and his most important games. (Rev: BL 10/1/90) [921]

ROBINSON, FRANK

14417 Macht, Norman L. *Frank Robinson* (4–6). Illus. Series: Baseball Legends. 1991, Chelsea LB $16.95 (0-7910-1187-9). 64pp. This account gives good coverage of Robinson's crucial games. (Rev: BL 2/1/91) [921]

ROBINSON, JACKIE

14418 Adler, David A. *Jackie Robinson: He Was the First* (3–5). Illus. by Robert Casilla. 1989, Holiday House LB $15.95 (0-8234-0734-9). 48pp. A profile of the first African American player in the major leagues. (Rev: BL 7/89) [921]

14419 Adler, David A. *A Picture Book of Jackie Robinson* (K–3). Illus. by Robert Casilla. Series: Picture Book Biographies. 1994, Holiday House LB $16.95 (0-8234-1122-2). 32pp. This simple biography of the baseball giant reads like a story for young children. (Rev: BL 11/15/94; SLJ 12/94) [921]

14420 Coombs, Karen Mueller. *Jackie Robinson: Baseball's Civil Rights Legend* (5–7). Illus. Series: African-American Biographies. 1997, Enslow LB $20.95 (0-89490-690-9). 128pp. The story of the baseball great who stood up to racism in athletics. (Rev: BL 6/1–15/97) [921]

14421 Davidson, Margaret. *The Story of Jackie Robinson: Bravest Man in Baseball* (3–7). Illus. 1988, Dell paper $3.99 (0-440-40019-8). 92pp. The

life of the man who broke the baseball color barrier. (Rev: BL 6/1/88; SLJ 5/88)

14422 DeAngelis, Gina. *Jackie Robinson: Overcoming Adversity* (5–8). Illus. Series: Overcoming Adversity. 2000, Chelsea $21.95 (0-7910-5897-2). 104pp. Using a highly readable text and black-and-white photographs, this book gives a real picture of Robinson that touches on the reasons he felt extreme anger and his great determination to make a difference. (Rev: BL 2/15/01; HBG 10/01) [921]

14423 De Marco, Tony. *Jackie Robinson: 1919–1972* (4–6). Series: Journey to Freedom: The African American Library. 2001, Child's World LB $17.95 (1-56766-918-2). 40pp. An attractive biography illustrated with sepia-toned photographs that presents the life of this trailblazing baseball great. (Rev: BL 12/15/01; HBG 3/02; SLJ 1/02) [921]

14424 Denenberg, Barry. *Stealing Home: The Story of Jackie Robinson* (4–6). Illus. 1997, Scholastic paper $4.50 (0-590-42560-9). 116pp. A biography that balances Robinson's life and significance on and off the baseball diamond. (Rev: SLJ 1/91) [921]

14425 Grabowski, John. *Jackie Robinson* (4–6). Illus. Series: Baseball Legends. 1990, Chelsea LB $16.95 (0-7910-1188-7). 64pp. The life story of the pro baseball player who broke the color line. (Rev: BL 11/15/90) [921]

14426 *Jackie Robinson: Strong Inside and Out* (2–4). Ed. by Time for Kids Editorial Staff with Denise Lewis Patrick. Illus. Series: Time for Kids Biographies. 2005, HarperCollins $14.99 (0-06-057601-4); paper $3.99 (0-06-057600-6). 48pp. A lively overview of Robinson's life drawing on the archives of Time-Life and ending with an interview with his daughter Sharon. (Rev: BL 2/1/05) [921]

14427 Mara, Wil. *Jackie Robinson* (K–2). Series: Rookie Biographies. 2002, Children's Book Pr. LB $19.00 (0-516-22520-0); paper $4.95 (0-516-27336-1). 32pp. For beginning readers, this is a simple introduction to the legendary baseball player. (Rev: SLJ 12/02) [821]

14428 O'Connor, Jim. *Jackie Robinson and the Story of All-Black Baseball* (3–5). Illus. by Jim Butcher. 1989, Random paper $3.99 (0-394-82456-3). 48pp. The story of Jackie Robinson and the Negro Leagues, preceding his entry into pro ball. (Rev: BCCB 9/89; BL 7/89) [921]

14429 Robinson, Sharon. *Promises to Keep: How Jackie Robinson Changed America* (3–7). Illus. 2004, Scholastic $16.95 (0-439-42592-1). 64pp. The inspiring story of Robinson's life and his struggle to break into major league baseball is told by his daughter. (Rev: BL 2/15/04*; SLJ 3/04) [796.357]

14430 Scott, Richard. *Jackie Robinson* (5–10). Illus. 1987, Chelsea LB $21.95 (1-55546-609-5). A well-researched biography giving good material on Robinson's life outside baseball. (Rev: BL 9/1/87; SLJ 9/87) [921]

RODRIGUEZ, ALEX

14431 Macnow, Glen. *Alex Rodriguez* (5–8). Series: Sports Greats. 2002, Enslow LB $17.95 (0-7660-1845-8). 64pp. An easy-to-read yet fairly detailed biography of the baseball player, with plenty of statistics and quotations. (Rev: BL 9/1/02; HBG 10/02) [796.357]

14432 Stewart, Mark. *Alex Rodriguez: Gunning for Greatness* (4–6). Series: Baseball's New Wave. 1999, Millbrook LB $19.90 (0-7613-1515-2). 48pp. An attractive biography with sidebars and plenty of photos on this superstar shortstop of the Seattle Mariners that ends with the 1998 season. (Rev: HBG 10/00; SLJ 2/00) [921]

RUTH, BABE

14433 Burleigh, Robert. *Home Run: The Story of Babe Ruth* (3–6). Illus. by Mike Wimmer. 1998, Harcourt $16.00 (0-15-200970-1). 32pp. A picture book for older readers that relates the life, career, character, and accomplishments of one of baseball's great heroes. (Rev: BCCB 9/98; BL 8/98; HBG 3/99; SLJ 8/98) [921]

14434 Macht, Norman L. *Babe Ruth* (4–6). Illus. Series: Baseball Legends. 1991, Chelsea LB $16.95 (0-7910-1189-5). 64pp. The life of the legendary left-handed pitcher, outfielder, and slugger is re-created. (Rev: BL 4/15/91) [921]

14435 Murphy, Frank. *Babe Ruth Saves Baseball!* (1–3). Illus. by Richard Walz. Series: Step into Reading. 2005, Random LB $11.99 (0-375-93048-5); paper $3.99 (0-375-83048-0). 48pp. Babe Ruth's character comes to the fore in this lively biography for beginning readers. (Rev: BL 6/1–15/05) [921]

14436 Nicholson, Lois. *Babe Ruth: Sultan of Swat* (5–8). Illus. 1995, Goodwood $17.95 (0-9625427-1-7). 119pp. This well-written account of the famous slugger explains his lasting influence on baseball. (Rev: SLJ 7/95) [921]

14437 Sanford, William R., and Carl R. Green. *Babe Ruth* (4–6). Illus. Series: Sports Immortals. 1992, Macmillan LB $16.95 (0-89686-741-2). 48pp. Numerous photos enhance this bio of the great Yankee star for middle-grade readers. (Rev: BL 2/1/93; SLJ 1/93) [921]

RYAN, NOLAN

14438 Lace, William W. *Nolan Ryan* (5–8). Series: Sports Greats. 1993, Enslow LB $17.95 (0-89490-394-2). The amazing story of this baseball phenomenon who became the baseball strike-out king. (Rev: BL 6/1–15/93) [921]

14439 Rappoport, Ken. *Nolan Ryan: The Ryan Express* (3–6). Illus. Series: Taking Part. 1992, Macmillan LB $18.95 (0-87518-524-X). 64pp. The life story of the amazing baseball player who has developed a large following. (Rev: BL 1/15/93) [921]

SNIDER, DUKE

14440 Bjarkman, Peter C. *Duke Snider* (4–6). Illus. Series: Baseball Legends. 1994, Chelsea LB $16.95 (0-7910-1190-9). 63pp. A biography of the superstar from the golden age of baseball. (Rev: BL 10/15/94) [921]

SOSA, SAMMY

14441 Dougherty, Terri. *Sammy Sosa* (2–4). Series: Jam Session. 1999, ABDO LB $14.95 (1-57765-348-3). 32pp. Using quotes from friends, family, and teammates, this simple, heavily illustrated biography presents the life and accomplishments of amazing batter Sammy Sosa. (Rev: HBG 10/99; SLJ 8/99) [921]

14442 Muskat, Carrie. *Sammy Sosa* (4–8). Series: Latinos in Baseball. 1999, Mitchell Lane LB $18.95 (1-883845-92-0). 64pp. This biography tells of Sosa's rise from extreme poverty, his ties to his homeland, the Dominican Republic, and his devotion to his game. (Rev: HBG 10/99; SLJ 5/99) [921]

STRAWBERRY, DARRYL

14443 Torres, John A., and Michael J. Sullivan. *Darryl Strawberry* (4–6). Illus. Series: Sports Great Books. 1990, Enslow LB $17.95 (0-89490-291-1). 64pp. The story of the fine but controversial baseball player, with good coverage of his childhood. (Rev: SLJ 11/90) [921]

SUZUKI, ICHIRO

14444 Leigh, David S. *Ichiro Suzuki* (4–6). 2004, Lerner LB $26.60 (0-8225-1792-2). 106pp. Suzuki's youth and career in Japan are covered in addition to his contributions in the U.S. major leagues. (Rev: SLJ 11/04) [921]

14445 Stewart, Mark. *Ichiro Suzuki: Best in the West* (4–7). Illus. Series: Sports New Wave. 2002, Millbrook LB $22.90 (0-7613-2616-2). 48pp. A well-constructed biography of the famous Japanese Seattle Mariners player that offers information on the game itself as well as statistics, color photographs, and quotations that illustrate his achievements. (Rev: BL 9/1/02; HBG 3/03) [796.357]

14446 Stout, Glenn. *At the Plate with . . . Ichiro* (4–8). Series: Matt Christopher Sports Bio Bookshelf. 2003, Little, Brown paper $4.99 (0-316-13679-4). 95pp. In this engaging biography of Ichiro Suzuki, part of the Matt Christopher Sports Bio Bookshelf series, author Glenn Stout tells how the Japanese baseball player rose to stardom in his native country and in 2001 became the first non-pitcher from Japan to play major league ball in America. (Rev: SLJ 6/03)

THOMAS, FRANK

14447 Gutman, Bill. *Frank Thomas: Power Hitter* (4–6). Illus. Series: Sports World. 1996, Millbrook LB $19.90 (1-56294-569-6). 48pp. This biography of the baseball superstar tells about his life and his talent. (Rev: BL 5/15/96; SLJ 6/96) [921]

14448 Spiros, Dean. *Frank Thomas: Star First Baseman* (4–6). Illus. Series: Sports Reports. 1996, Enslow LB $20.95 (0-89490-659-3). 104pp. The life of this baseball hero is covered, with emphasis on key games and important career decisions. (Rev: BL 11/15/96) [921]

WEISS, ALTA

14449 Hopkinson, Deborah. *Girl Wonder: A Baseball Story in Nine Innings* (2–4). Illus. by Terry Widener. 2003, Simon & Schuster $16.95 (0-689-83300-8). 40pp. Alta Weiss's inspiring story swings along in lyrical prose, relating her adventures as a teenage baseball phenomenon who pitched for a men's team in 1907 at the age of 17. (Rev: BL 1/1–15/03*; HB 3–4/03; HBG 10/03; SLJ 3/03)

WILLIAMS, TED

14450 McCormack, Shaun. *Ted Williams* (4–6). Series: Baseball Hall of Famers. 2004, Rosen LB $29.25 (0-8239-3783-6). 112pp. Report writers will find solid information on the life and career of the Boston Red Sox star. (Rev: SLJ 6/04) [921]

YOUNG, CY

14451 Macht, Norman L. *Cy Young* (4–6). Illus. Series: Baseball Legends. 1991, Chelsea LB $15.95 (0-7910-1196-8). 144pp. The story of this legendary pitcher, with interesting background and team information. (Rev: BL 1/15/92) [921]

Basketball

ABDUL-JABBAR, KAREEM

14452 Kneib, Martha. *Kareem Abdul-Jabbar* (5–8). Series: Basketball Hall of Famers. 2002, Rosen LB $29.25 (0-8239-3483-7). 112pp. An in-depth look at this basketball great's life, with highlights from his childhood through his NBA career. (Rev: BL 9/1/02) [921]

14453 Sanford, William R., and Carl R. Green. *Kareem Abdul-Jabbar* (4–6). Illus. Series: Sports Immortals. 1993, Macmillan LB $11.95 (0-89686-737-4). 48pp. The life and career of Lew Alcindor, better known as Kareem Abdul-Jabbar, who was named the NBA Most Valuable Player six times. (Rev: BL 4/15/93; SLJ 8/93) [921]

ANTHONY, CARMELO

14454 Anthony, Carmelo, and Greg Brown. *Carmelo Anthony: It's Just the Beginning* (3–6). Illus. Series: Athletes. 2004, Positively for Kids $15.95 (0-9634650-7-4). 48pp. A lively and attractively designed first-person account of Anthony's life and career in basketball, with lots of personal details about his childhood, family life, and sporting successes. [921]

BARKLEY, CHARLES

14455 Dolan, Sean. *Charles Barkley* (5–7). Illus. Series: Basketball Legends. 1996, Chelsea LB $18.65 (0-7910-2433-4). 62pp. The life of this basketball superstar, with details on his record on the court. (Rev: BL 7/96) [921]

14456 Knapp, Ron. *Charles Barkley: Star Forward* (4–6). Illus. Series: Sports Reports. 1996, Enslow LB $20.95 (0-89490-655-0). 104pp. A short biography of this basketball star, with career statistics and many action photos. (Rev: BL 8/96; SLJ 8/96) [921]

14457 Macnow, Glen. *Charles Barkley* (5–8). Series: Sports Greats. 1992, Enslow LB $17.95 (0-89490-386-1). A short biography of this basketball star, with career statistics and action photographs. (Rev: BL 10/15/92) [921]

BIRD, LARRY

14458 Kavanagh, Jack. *Larry Bird* (4–8). Illus. Series: Sports Greats. 1992, Enslow LB $17.95 (0-89490-368-3). 64pp. The extraordinary story of the basketball player who drove his team, the Boston Celtics, to five NBA finals. (Rev: BL 7/92; SLJ 10/92) [921]

BIRD, SUE

14459 Bird, Sue, and Greg Brown. *Sue Bird: Be Yourself* (3–6). Illus. Series: Athletes. 2004, Positively for Kids $15.95 (0-9634650-5-8). 48pp. A lively and attractively designed first-person account of Bird's life and career in basketball, with lots of personal details about her childhood, family life, and sporting successes. [921]

BRYANT, KOBE

14460 Kennedy, Nick. *Kobe Bryant: Star Guard* (4–8). Series: Sports Reports. 2002, Enslow LB $20.95 (0-7660-1828-8). 104pp. An accessible biography of the basketball player, with detailed descriptions of career highlights. (Rev: BL 9/1/02; HBG 3/03) [796.323]

14461 Savage, Jeff. *Kobe Bryant: Basketball Big Shot* (4–7). Illus. Series: Sports Biography. 2000, Lerner LB $27.15 (0-8225-3680-3). 64pp. A very readable, attractive biography of the new NBA sensation that ends with the 1999–2000 season. (Rev: BL 1/1–15/01; HBG 10/01) [921]

14462 Schnakenberg, Robert E. *Kobe Bryant* (4–6). Illus. Series: Basketball Legends. 1998, Chelsea $16.95 (0-7910-5005-X). 64pp. A detailed biography of the Lakers star who became the youngest man ever to play in an NBA game. (Rev: BL 3/1/99; HBG 10/99) [921]

14463 Stewart, Mark. *Kobe Bryant: Hard to the Hoop* (4–8). Series: Basketball's New Wave. 2000, Millbrook LB $20.90 (0-7613-1800-3). 48pp. The life story of this basketball star who was the son of an NBA player and who became the youngest player in league history to star in the All-Star Game. (Rev: HBG 10/00; SLJ 8/00) [921]

14464 Thornley, Stew. *Super Sports Star Kobe Bryant* (2–5). Illus. Series: Super Sports Stars. 2001, Enslow LB $18.95 (0-7660-1514-9). 48pp. Photographs and statistics accompany text about the famous basketball player, from his childhood to his professional career with the L.A. Lakers. (Rev: BL 10/15/01; HBG 3/02) [796.323]

14465 Torres, John. *Kobe Bryant* (3–4). Series: Real-Life Reader Biographies. 2000, Mitchell Lane LB

$15.95 (1-58415-030-0). 32pp. An easily read biography of the well-known basketball player who was a star before he graduated from high school. (Rev: BL 11/15/00) [921]

CARTER, VINCE

14466 Carter, Vince, and Greg Brown. *Vince Carter: Choose Your Course* (3–6). Series: Athletes. 2004, Positively for Kids $15.95 (0-9634650-2-3). 48pp. A first-person account of Carter's life and career in basketball, with lots of details about his childhood, family life, and sporting successes. (Rev: BL 9/1/04) [921]

14467 Savage, Jeff. *Vince Carter* (5–8). Series: Sports Greats. 2002, Enslow LB $17.95 (0-7660-1767-2). 64pp. An accessible biography of the Toronto Raptors basketball player that will be useful for students writing reports. (Rev: BL 9/1/02; HBG 10/02) [796.323]

14468 Thornley, Stew. *Super Sports Star Vince Carter* (2–5). Series: Super Sports Stars. 2002, Enslow LB $18.95 (0-7660-1805-9). 48pp. The life of the Toronto Raptors guard-forward is told in an account that features simple text, large type, and many color photographs. (Rev: BL 9/1/02; HBG 10/02) [921]

14469 Torres, John Albert. *Vince Carter: Slam Dunk Artist* (3–6). Illus. Series: Sports Leaders. 2004, Enslow LB $19.95 (0-7660-2173-4). 104pp. An accessible profile of the talented basketball player's life and career. [921]

COOPER, CYNTHIA

14470 Schnakenberg, Robert E. *Cynthia Cooper* (5–9). Series: Women Who Win. 2000, Chelsea $19.75 (0-7910-5796-8). 64pp. A biography of this basketball star that focuses on her career and game-related information. (Rev: HBG 3/01; SLJ 2/01) [921]

DUNCAN, TIM

14471 Adams, Sean. *Tim Duncan* (4–7). Illus. Series: Sports Heroes and Legends. 2004, Lerner LB $21.96 (0-8225-1793-0). 106pp. A balanced, well-crafted life of the basketball star. [921]

14472 Byman, Jeremy. *Tim Duncan* (4–8). Illus. Series: Great Athletes. 2000, Morgan Reynolds LB $18.95 (1-883846-43-9). 64pp. This biography about a basketball hero who has been playing professionally for only a short time focuses on his college years, his outstanding talent, and his determination. (Rev: BL 6/1–15/00; HBG 3/01) [921]

14473 Rappoport, Ken. *Tim Duncan: Star Forward* (5–8). Series: Sports Reports. 2000, Enslow LB $20.95 (0-7660-1334-0). 112pp. A look at one of basketball's star forwards, accompanied by statistics and action photographs. (Rev: BL 10/15/00; HBG 3/01) [921]

14474 Stewart, Mark. *Tim Duncan: Tower of Power* (4–8). Series: Basketball's New Wave. 1999, Millbrook LB $22.90 (0-7613-1513-6). 48pp. Although this biography of basketball's rising star is brief, the information is ample and important topics are all covered. (Rev: HBG 10/00; SLJ 7/00) [921]

14475 Torres, John Albert. *Tim Duncan* (5–8). Series: Sports Greats. 2002, Enslow LB $17.95 (0-7660-1766-4). 64pp. The life of this basketball star is re-created using an easy-reading text and many photographs. (Rev: BL 9/1/02; HBG 10/02) [921]

EWING, PATRICK

14476 Kavanagh, Jack. *Patrick Ewing* (5–8). Illus. Series: Sports Greats. 1992, Enslow LB $17.95 (0-89490-369-1). 64pp. An easily read, candid look at the basketball great from Jamaica. (Rev: BL 9/1/92) [921]

14477 Wiener, Paul. *Patrick Ewing* (4–6). Illus. Series: Basketball Legends. 1996, Chelsea LB $16.95 (0-7910-2434-2). 64pp. The story of this New York Knicks center and his quest for an NBA championship. (Rev: BL 7/96) [921]

GARNETT, KEVIN

14478 Bernstein, Ross. *Kevin Garnett: Star Forward* (4–8). Series: Sports Reports. 2002, Enslow LB $20.95 (0-7660-1829-6). 104pp. An in-depth look at the life of this basketball star in a simple account suitable for reluctant readers. (Rev: BL 9/1/02; HBG 3/03) [921]

14479 Stewart, Mark. *Kevin Garnett: Shake Up the Game* (4–7). Series: Sports New Wave. 2002, Millbrook LB $22.90 (0-7613-2615-4). 48pp. A short biography that chronicles the career of the new star of the Minnesota Timberwolves. (Rev: BL 9/1/02; HBG 10/02) [921]

14480 Thornley, Stew. *Super Sports Star Kevin Garnett* (2–5). Series: Super Sports Stars. 2001, Enslow LB $18.95 (0-7660-1515-7). 48pp. Garnett, a small forward for the Minnesota Timberwolves, gets an interesting profile complete with game details and statistics plus plenty of action photographs. (Rev: BL 10/15/01; HBG 3/02) [921]

HARDAWAY, ANFERNEE

14481 Rekela, George R. *Anfernee Hardaway* (5–8). Illus. Series: Sports Greats. 1996, Enslow LB $17.95 (0-89490-758-1). Career statistics and many black-and-white photographs enliven the biography of this famous basketball star. (Rev: BL 3/15/96) [921]

HARDAWAY, PENNY

14482 Rappoport, Ken. *Super Sports Star Penny Hardaway* (2–5). Illus. Series: Super Sports Stars. 2001, Enslow LB $18.95 (0-7660-1516-5). 48pp. Photographs and statistics accompany text about the famous basketball player, from his childhood to his professional career. (Rev: BL 10/15/01; HBG 3/02) [796.323]

HILL, GRANT

14483 Gutman, Bill. *Grant Hill: Basketball's High Flier* (3–6). Illus. Series: Sports World. 1996, Millbrook LB $19.90 (0-7613-0038-4). 48pp. A brief biography that concentrates on Hill's basketball career, particularly at Duke University and with the Detroit Pistons. (Rev: SLJ 2/97) [921]

14484 Lowenstein, Felicia. *Grant Hill* (2–5). Series: Super Sports Stars. 2001, Enslow LB $18.95 (0-7660-1517-3). Simple sentences and many color photographs are used in this beginning biography of the Orlando Magic forward. (Rev: BL 4/1/02; HBG 10/02) [921]

14485 Thornley, Stew. *Grant Hill: Star Forward* (4–6). Series: Sports Reports. 1999, Enslow LB $19.95 (0-7660-1078-3). 104pp. An in-depth look at the life and career of this basketball star, with many action photographs. (Rev: BL 2/15/99; HBG 10/99) [921]

HOWARD, JUWAN

14486 Savage, Jeff. *Juwan Howard* (5–8). Series: Sports Greats. 1998, Enslow LB $17.95 (0-7660-1065-1). 64pp. The Washington Wizards basketball star is profiled in this lively account, supplemented by many black-and-white photographs. (Rev: BL 2/15/99; HBG 10/99) [921]

14487 Sirak, Ron. *Juwan Howard* (5–8). 1998, Chelsea LB $18.65 (0-7910-4575-7). A biography of one of the great basketball players of the 1990s, with good material on his early years and the influence of his grandmother. (Rev: BR 11–12/98; HBG 3/99) [921]

JAMES, LEBRON

14488 Mattern, Joanne. *LeBron James* (2–5). Series: A Robbie Reader. 2004, Mitchell Lane LB $16.95 (1-58415-293-1). 32pp. This photo-filled biography that presents information on James's childhood and career is especially suitable for reluctant readers. (Rev: BL 11/15/04) [921]

JOHNSON, MAGIC

14489 Greenberg, Keith E. *Magic Johnson: Champion with a Cause* (4–7). Illus. Series: Achievers. 1992, Lerner LB $27.15 (0-8225-0546-0). 64pp. The story of the gifted athlete for the L.A. Lakers, whose career was cut short when he discovered he was HIV-positive. (Rev: BL 8/92; SLJ 7/92) [921]

14490 Haskins, Jim. *Magic Johnson*. Rev. ed. (5–8). Series: Sports Greats. 1992, Enslow LB $17.95 (0-89490-348-9). This revised and updated edition includes a discussion of the basketball star's HIV status, his 1991 retirement from the Lakers, and his role in the fight against AIDS. (Rev: BL 10/15/92) [921]

JORDAN, MICHAEL

14491 Aaseng, Nathan. *Michael Jordan* (5–8). Illus. Series: Sports Greats. 1992, Enslow LB $17.95 (0-

89490-370-5). 64pp. Michael Jordan's life, his successes as guard of the Chicago Bulls, and his commercials for TV are discussed in this easily read book. (Rev: BL 10/15/92) [921]

14492 Berger, Phil, and John Rolfe. *Michael Jordan* (4–7). Illus. 1990, Little, Brown paper $4.95 (0-316-09229-0). 124pp. This account covers Jordan's childhood and his career development. (Rev: BL 12/15/90; SLJ 4/91) [921]

14493 Christopher, Matt. *On the Court with . . . Michael Jordan* (3–7). Illus. Series: Matt Christopher Sports Biography. 1996, Little, Brown paper $4.95 (0-316-13792-8). 144pp. The life of this pro basketball legend whose self-determination and family support helped him rise to the top. (Rev: BL 2/15/97; SLJ 6/97) [921]

14494 Cooper, Floyd. *Jump! From the Life of Michael Jordan* (K–3). 2004, Penguin Putnam $15.99 (0-399-24230-9). 40pp. Eye-catching illustrations and conversational text reveal the successes and challenges of Jordan's childhood and adolescence. (Rev: BL 9/1/04) [921]

14495 Gutman, Bill. *Michael Jordan: Basketball Champ* (4–6). Illus. Series: Sports World. 1992, Houghton Mifflin paper $4.80 (0-395-64545-X). The life and dedication to hard work of one of basketball's greatest stars. (Rev: BL 11/1/91; SLJ 12/92) [921]

14496 Rambeck, Richard. *Michael Jordan* (3–6). Series: Sports Superstars. 1999, Child's World LB $14.95 (1-56766-520-9). 23pp. A simple biography of the basketball superstar, suitable for reluctant readers because of its format and colorful photos. (Rev: BL 5/15/99; HBG 10/99) [921]

KEMP, SHAWN

14497 Thornley, Stew. *Shawn Kemp: Star Forward* (4–6). Series: Sports Reports. 1998, Enslow LB $20.95 (0-89490-929-0). 104pp. An account that stresses this fine basketball player's good character traits and strong athletic abilities. (Rev: BL 2/15/98; HBG 10/98) [921]

KIDD, JASON

14498 Gray, Valerie A. *Jason Kidd: Star Guard* (5–8). Series: Sports Reports. 2000, Enslow LB $20.95 (0-7660-1333-2). 112pp. The story of the basketball superstar with behind-the-scenes reporting on his life and career. (Rev: BL 10/15/00; HBG 10/00) [921]

14499 Rappoport, Ken. *Jason Kidd: Leader on the Court* (3–6). Illus. Series: Sports Leaders. 2004, Enslow LB $19.95 (0-7660-2214-5). 104pp. An accessible profile of the basketball star's life and career. [921]

14500 Thornley, Stew. *Super Sports Star Jason Kidd* (2–5). Series: Super Sports Stars. 2002, Enslow LB $18.95 (0-7660-1806-7). 48pp. Complete with game statistics and sports action, this is a simple, attractive biography of the star guard of the New Jersey Nets. (Rev: BL 9/1/02; HBG 10/02) [921]

14501 Torres, John A. *Jason Kidd* (5–8). Series: Sports Greats. 1998, Enslow LB $17.95 (0-7660-1001-5). 64pp. An action-filled biography of this basketball star, complete with career statistics and black-and-white photographs of Kidd on the court. (Rev: BL 7/98; HBG 10/98) [921]

LESLIE, LISA

14502 Kelley, Brent. *Lisa Leslie* (5–9). Series: Women Who Win. 2000, Chelsea $19.75 (0-7910-5794-1). 64pp. This profile of a pioneer in the Women's National Basketball Association contains much game-related information. (Rev: HBG 3/01; SLJ 2/01) [921]

LIEBERMAN-CLINE, NANCY

14503 Greenberg, Doreen, and Michael Greenberg. *A Drive to Win: The Story of Nancy Lieberman-Cline* (4–8). Illus. by Phil Velikan. Series: Anything You Can Do — New Sports Heroes for Girls. 2000, Wish paper $9.95 (1-930546-40-8). 98pp. Based on personal interviews, this is an informative biography of the basketball star Lieberman-Cline. (Rev: SLJ 3/01) [921]

LUCAS, JOHN

14504 Simmons, Alex. *John Lucas* (4–6). Illus. Series: Contemporary African Americans. 1995, Raintree LB $25.69 (0-8172-3978-2). 48pp. An inspiring story of the man who conquered drug addiction and became the first African American coach of the San Antonio Spurs. (Rev: BL 2/15/96; SLJ 4/96) [921]

MALONE, KARL

14505 Rekela, George R. *Karl Malone: Star Forward* (4–6). Series: Sports Reports. 1998, Enslow LB $18.95 (0-89490-931-2). Plenty of action photographs and career statistics illustrate this biography of the Utah Jazz's great power forward. (Rev: BL 8/98; HBG 10/98) [921]

MARBURY, STEPHON

14506 Plum-Ucci, Carol. *Super Sports Star Stephon Marbury* (2–5). Series: Super Sports Stars. 2002, Enslow LB $18.95 (0-7660-1810-5). 48pp. An exciting life story of Marbury, the black basketball player who has established a reputation as point guard for the Phoenix Suns. (Rev: BL 2/15/03; HBG 3/03) [921]

MILLER, REGGIE

14507 Thornley, Stew. *Reggie Miller* (5–8). Series: Sports Greats. 1996, Enslow LB $17.95 (0-89490-874-X). The life of this basketball star is traced, with special emphasis on key games. (Rev: BL 9/15/96) [921]

MING, YAO

14508 Savage, Jeff. *Yao Ming* (2–4). Illus. Series: Amazing Athletes/LernerSports. 2005, Lerner LB $22.60 (0-8225-2432-5). 32pp. A well-illustrated introduction to the Chinese-born basketball player. [921]

14509 Young, Jeff C. *Yao Ming: Basketball's Big Man* (3–6). Illus. Series: Sports Leaders. 2005, Enslow LB $19.95 (0-7660-2422-9). 104pp. An accessible profile of the Chinese-born basketball player's life and career. [921]

MOURNING, ALONZO

14510 Fortunato, Frank. *Alonzo Mourning* (5–8). Illus. Series: Sports Greats. 1997, Enslow LB $17.95 (0-89490-875-8). 64pp. An easily read biography of this amazing basketball star. (Rev: BL 2/15/97) [921]

14511 Gutman, Bill. *Alonzo Mourning: Center of Attention* (4–6). Illus. Series: Sports World. 1997, Millbrook LB $19.90 (0-7613-0061-9). 48pp. This action-filled biography of the basketball star supplies good career statistics. (Rev: BL 4/15/97) [921]

MULLIN, CHRIS

14512 Morgan, Terri, and Shmuel Thaler. *Chris Mullin: Sure Shot* (4–8). Illus. Series: Sports Achievers. 1994, Lerner LB $10.13 (0-8225-2887-7). 64pp. The story of this amazing basketball star who overcame many obstacles, including alcoholism. (Rev: BL 1/1/95; SLJ 1/95) [921]

NUNEZ, TOMMY

14513 Boulais, Sue, and Barbara Marvis. *Tommy Nunez* (3–5). Illus. Series: Real-Life Reader Biographies. 1998, Mitchell Lane LB $15.95 (1-883845-52-1). 32pp. A simple biography that traces Nunez's life from the Phoenix barrio to a career as a referee in the National Basketball Association. (Rev: BL 6/1–15/98; HBG 3/98) [921]

OLAJUWON, HAKEEM

14514 Gutman, Bill. *Hakeem Olajuwon: Superstar Center* (4–6). Illus. Series: Sports World. 1995, Millbrook LB $19.90 (1-56294-568-8). 64pp. A fast-moving, well-illustrated biography of this basketball star. (Rev: BL 9/15/95; SLJ 1/96) [921]

14515 McMane, Fred. *Hakeem Olajuwon* (5–7). Series: Basketball Legends. 1997, Chelsea LB $18.65 (0-7910-4385-1). 64pp. The story of this basketball star of the Houston Rockets, his boyhood in Nigeria, and his role as part of the U.S. Olympic "Dream Team." (Rev: BL 9/15/97) [921]

14516 Torres, John A. *Hakeem Olajuwon: Star Center* (4–6). Series: Sports Reports. 1997, Enslow LB $20.95 (0-89490-803-0). 104pp. This biography of the star basketball player also contains career statistics, action photos, and chapter notes. (Rev: BL 11/15/97; HBG 3/98) [921]

O'NEAL, SHAQUILLE

14517 Macnow, Glen. *Shaquille O'Neal: Star Center* (4–6). Illus. Series: Sports Reports. 1996, Enslow LB $20.95 (0-89490-656-9). 104pp. An account of this pro basketball star, with career statistics and a behind-the-scenes look at his life and interests. (Rev: BL 11/15/96) [921]

14518 Sullivan, Michael J. *Shaquille O'Neal* (5–8). Series: Sports Greats. 1998, Enslow LB $17.95 (0-7660-1003-1). 64pp. The life and career of this well-known basketball star are covered in this easily read biography containing career statistics and many illustrations. (Rev: BL 2/15/99; HBG 10/99) [921]

14519 Tallman, Edward. *Shaquille O'Neal* (3–6). Illus. 1994, Silver Burdett $14.95 (0-87518-637-8). 72pp. The life of the NBA star who is also known as an actor and a rap artist. (Rev: BL 2/1/95) [921]

14520 Torres, John Albert. *Shaquille O'Neal: Gentle Giant* (3–6). Illus. Series: Sports Leaders. 2004, Enslow LB $20.95 (0-7660-2175-0). 104pp. Report writers and basketball fans will appreciate this overview of Shaq's life and career. (Rev: BL 4/1/04) [796.323]

14521 Townsend, Brad. *Shaquille O'Neal: Center of Attention* (3–5). Illus. Series: Sports Achievers. 1994, Lerner LB $22.60 (0-8225-2879-7); paper $5.95 (0-8225-9655-5). 56pp. This life story tells about O'Neal's childhood, his school basketball career, and his first year in the NBA. (Rev: BL 5/15/94; SLJ 9/94) [921]

14522 Ungs, Tim. *Shaquille O'Neal* (5–7). Illus. Series: Basketball Legends. 1996, Chelsea LB $18.65 (0-7910-2437-7). 64pp. An interesting portrait of the unstoppable Lakers basketball superstar. (Rev: BL 7/96) [921]

PAYTON, GARY

14523 Bernstein, Ross. *Gary Payton: Star Guard* (4–6). Illus. Series: Sports Reports. 2000, Enslow LB $19.95 (0-7660-1330-8). 104pp. An in-depth look at this star basketball player, including his career statistics and some action photographs. (Rev: BL 9/15/00; HBG 10/00) [921]

14524 Mandell, Judith. *Super Sports Star Gary Payton* (2–5). Series: Super Sports Stars. 2001, Enslow LB $1895.00 (0-7660-1519-X). 48pp. With large type and colorful photographs, this is an easily read biography of the black point guard of the Los Angeles Lakers. (Rev: BL 10/15/01; HBG 3/02) [921]

PIPPEN, SCOTTIE

14525 Bjarkman, Peter C. *Scottie Pippen* (5–8). Series: Sports Greats. 1996, Enslow LB $17.95 (0-89490-755-7). Action photographs, career statistics, and an account of important games are highlights of this basketball biography. (Rev: BL 9/15/96) [921]

14526 McMane, Fred. *Scottie Pippen* (5–7). Illus. Series: Basketball Legends. 1996, Chelsea LB $18.65 (0-7910-2498-9). 64pp. The life of this basketball star, highlighting his special abilities and his court record. (Rev: BL 7/96) [921]

14527 Pippen, Scottie, and Greg Brown. *Reach Higher* (4–7). 1997, Taylor $14.95 (0-87833-981-7). 40pp. The story of the famous Chicago Bulls basketball star, who came from a family of 12 and whose original sports were baseball and football. (Rev: BL 10/1/97) [921]

RICE, GLEN

14528 Rappoport, Ken. *Super Sports Star Glen Rice* (2–5). Series: Super Sports Stars. 2002, Enslow LB $18.95 (0-7660-1808-3). 48pp. Large type, colorful photographs, and an appealing format highlight this simple biography of the Houston Rockets star. (Rev: BL 9/1/02; HBG 10/02) [921]

RICHMOND, MITCH

14529 Grody, Carl W. *Mitch Richmond* (5–8). Series: Sports Greats. 1998, Enslow LB $17.95 (0-7660-1070-8). 64pp. Using many black-and-white photographs and a lively text, this book re-creates the life of the basketball great. (Rev: BL 2/15/99; HBG 10/99) [921]

ROBINSON, DAVID

14530 Aaseng, Nathan. *David Robinson* (5–8). Illus. Series: Sports Greats. 1992, Enslow LB $17.95 (0-89490-373-X). 64pp. This easily read biography highlights David Robinson of the San Antonio Spurs, the 1990 Rookie of the Year. (Rev: BL 10/15/92) [921]

14531 Bock, Hal. *David Robinson* (5–7). Series: Basketball Legends. 1997, Chelsea LB $18.65 (0-7910-4387-8). 64pp. The story of this star of the San Antonio Spurs, who was a brilliant student and an officer in the U.S. Navy before turning to professional sports. (Rev: BL 9/15/97) [921]

14532 Green, Carl R., and Roxanne Ford. *David Robinson* (4–8). Illus. Series: Sports Headliners. 1994, Silver Burdett LB $13.95 (0-89686-839-7); paper $7.95 (0-382-24808-2). 48pp. A slim biography of this basketball star, who gained fame during the 1987 Navy–Duke game. (Rev: BL 10/1/94) [921]

14533 Gutman, Bill. *David Robinson: NBA Super Center* (4–6). Illus. Series: Millbrook Sports World. 1993, Millbrook LB $19.90 (1-56294-228-X). 48pp. A brief biography about Robinson's contributions to basketball and his career with the San Antonio Spurs. (Rev: BL 3/15/93) [921]

14534 Macnow, Glen. *David Robinson: Star Center* (4–6). Illus. Series: Sports Reports. 1994, Enslow LB $20.95 (0-89490-483-3). 104pp. The life of this sports hero who gained fame as an all-pro center for the San Antonio Spurs. (Rev: SLJ 2/95) [921]

RODMAN, DENNIS

14535 Frank, Steven. *Dennis Rodman* (4–8). Series: Basketball Legends. 1997, Chelsea LB $18.65 (0-7910-4388-6). 64pp. A candid look at the bad boy of basketball, his troubled youth, and rebellious attitudes. (Rev: HBG 3/98; SLJ 4/98) [921]

752

14536 Thornley, Stew. *Dennis Rodman* (5–8). Illus. Series: Sports Greats. 1996, Enslow LB $17.95 (0-89490-759-X). The life of this controversial basketball star is told in a brisk text with many black-and-white photographs. (Rev: BL 3/15/96) [921]

SPREWELL, LATRELL

14537 Pellowski, Michael J. *Super Sports Star Latrell Sprewell* (2–5). Series: Super Sports Stars. 2002, Enslow LB $18.95 (0-7660-1811-3). 48pp. With color photographs on each page plus a simple text, this is an exciting biography of the NBA star who plays guard and forward for the New York Knicks. (Rev: BL 9/1/02; HBG 3/03) [921]

STILES, JACKIE

14538 Stewart, Mark. *Jackie Stiles: Gym Dandy* (4–7). Illus. Series: Sports New Wave. 2002, Millbrook LB $22.90 (0-7613-2614-6). 48pp. A biography of the WNBA star, with information on her childhood and family, statistics, color photographs, and general material on the game itself. (Rev: BL 9/1/02; HBG 3/03) [796.323]

STOCKTON, JOHN

14539 Aaseng, Nathan. *John Stockton* (5–8). Illus. Series: Sports Greats. 1995, Enslow LB $17.95 (0-89490-598-8). A short biography of the basketball great John Stockton, with sports action and lively photographs. (Rev: BL 9/15/95) [921]

THOMAS, ISIAH

14540 Knapp, Ron. *Isiah Thomas* (5–8). Illus. Series: Sports Greats. 1992, Enslow LB $17.95 (0-89490-374-8). 64pp. Using a standard chronological approach and many photographs, this is an accurate, appealing biography of this great African American basketball player. (Rev: BL 9/1/92) [921]

VAN HORN, KEITH

14541 Kelley, Brent. *Keith Van Horn* (4–6). Illus. Series: Basketball Legends. 1998, Chelsea $16.95 (0-7910-5009-2). 64pp. This biography stressing team spirit traces the life and career of the New Jersey Nets player who helped his team reach the playoffs for the first time in four years. (Rev: BL 3/1/99; HBG 10/99) [921]

WEBBER, CHRIS

14542 Knapp, Ron. *Chris Webber: Star Forward* (4–6). Illus. Series: Sports Reports. 1997, Enslow LB $20.95 (0-89490-799-9). 104pp. Complete with career statistics and action photos, this is the story of the star basketball player and his rise to the top. (Rev: BL 8/97) [921]

14543 Thornley, Stew. *Chris Webber* (2–5). Series: Super Sports Stars. 2002, Enslow LB $18.95 (0-7660-1807-5). A simple biography with many action photographs of Webber, the NBA power for-ward of the Sacramento Kings. (Rev: BL 4/1/02; HBG 10/02) [921]

WEST, JERRY

14544 Ramen, Fred. *Jerry West* (5–8). Series: Basketball Hall of Famers. 2002, Rosen LB $29.25 (0-8239-3482-9). 112pp. Facts, stories, and full-color photographs are used to bring alive the story of this basketball great, with material on his NBA career and beyond. (Rev: BL 9/1/02) [921]

WILKINS, DOMINIQUE

14545 Bjarkman, Peter C. *Dominique Wilkins* (5–8). Series: Sports Greats. 1996, Enslow LB $17.95 (0-89490-754-9). The story of this basketball star, with profiles of his most exciting games and career statistics. (Rev: BL 9/15/96) [921]

Boxing

ALI, MUHAMMAD

14546 Bolden, Tonya. *The Champ: The Story of Muhammad Ali* (2–5). Illus. by K. Gregory Christie. 2004, Knopf LB $19.99 (0-375-92401-9). 40pp. This engaging biography shows Ali as child, fighter, activist, and poet. (Rev: BL 11/15/04; SLJ 1/05*) [921]

14547 Garrett, Leslie. *The Story of Muhammad Ali* (2–4). Illus. 2002, DK $12.95 (0-7894-8516-8); paper $3.95 (0-7894-8517-6). 48pp. A chapter-book biography of Muhammad Ali, from childhood to his battle with Parkinson's disease. (Rev: BL 3/1/02; HBG 10/02; SLJ 4/02) [796.83]

14548 Haskins, Jim. *Champion: The Story of Muhammad Ali* (3–6). Illus. by Eric Velasquez. 2002, Walker $17.95 (0-8027-8784-3). Ali's boyhood, career as Cassius Clay, conversion to Islam, and battle with Parkinson's are among the topics covered in this easy-to-read picture-book biography. (Rev: HB 7–8/02; HBG 10/02; SLJ 7/02) [921]

14549 Latimer, Clay. *Muhammad Ali* (4–6). Series: Journey to Freedom. 2000, Child's World LB $25.64 (1-56766-723-6). 40pp. The story of the great boxer and civil rights activist who became an inspiration around the world. (Rev: BL 11/15/00; HBG 10/01) [921]

14550 Shange, Ntozake. *Float Like a Butterfly* (2–4). Illus. by Edel Rodriguez. 2002, Hyperion $15.99 (0-7868-0554-4). 40pp. An appealing picture-book portrait of Muhammad Ali, from his childhood to his heavyweight championships and including material on civil rights, religion, and Vietnam. (Rev: BL 9/1/02; HB 11–12/02; HBG 3/03; SLJ 10/02) [796.83]

CHAVEZ, JULIO CESAR

14551 Dolan, Terrance. *Julio Cesar Chavez* (5–8). Illus. Series: Hispanics of Achievement. 1994, Chelsea LB $21.95 (0-7910-2021-5). 128pp. A biography of the fighting boxer and his struggle to get to the top. (Rev: BL 9/15/94) [921]

DE LA HOYA, OSCAR

14552 Menard, Valerie. *Oscar De La Hoya* (3–4). Illus. Series: Real-Life Reader Biographies. 1998, Mitchell Lane LB $15.95 (1-883845-58-0). 24pp. The story of the amazing boxer whose father predicted he would be a champion after taking him to a gym at age six. (Rev: BL 10/15/98; HBG 10/98) [921]

14553 Torres, John A. *Oscar De La Hoya* (5–8). Series: Sports Greats. 1998, Enslow LB $17.95 (0-7660-1066-X). A brief biography of the boxing sensation, with action photographs and career statistics. (Rev: BL 2/15/98; HBG 10/99) [921]

Figure Skating

BOITANO, BRIAN

14554 Boitano, Brian, and Suzanne Harper. *Boitano's Edge: Inside the Real World of Figure Skating* (4–8). Illus. 1997, Simon & Schuster $25.00 (0-689-81915-3). In this autobiography, Boitano tells about his life, the 1988 Olympics, his training programs, touring, and preparing for competitions. (Rev: BCCB 3/98; BL 2/15/98; SLJ 4/98) [921]

COHEN, SASHA

14555 Cohen, Sasha, and Amanda Maciel. *Sasha Cohen: Fire on Ice: Autobiography of a Champion Figure Skater* (4–6). Illus. by Kathy Goedeken. 2005, HarperCollins $16.99 (0-06-072490-0). 192pp. The absorbing story of Cohen's climb to fame, with details of injuries, anxieties, and problems with coaches and even outfits. (Rev: BL 5/15/05) [796.91]

GORDEEVA, EKATERINA

14556 Shea, Pegi Deitz. *Ekatarina Gordeeva* (4–8). Series: Female Figure Skating Legends. 1999, Chelsea LB $18.65 (0-7910-5027-0). 64pp. Sports lovers will enjoy this look at the life of the famous skater before and after the death of her partner and husband, Sergei Grinkov. (Rev: SLJ 4/99) [921]

HAMILL, DOROTHY

14557 Sanford, William R., and Carl R. Green. *Dorothy Hamill* (4–6). Illus. Series: Sports Immortals. 1993, Macmillan LB $11.95 (0-89686-799-X). 48pp. The life and career of this remarkable ice skater is told in this slim volume filled with many black-and-white photos. (Rev: BL 10/1/93) [921]

HUGHES, SARAH

14558 Krawiec, Richard. *Sudden Champion: The Sarah Hughes Story* (4–6). Series: Avisson Young Adult. 2002, Avisson paper $19.95 (1-888105-53-4). 100pp. A profile of Sarah Hughes, the figure

skater who won the gold medal at the 2002 Winter Olympics in Salt Lake City. (Rev: SLJ 4/03) [921]

KERRIGAN, NANCY

14559 Edelson, Paula. *Nancy Kerrigan* (4–6). Illus. 1998, Chelsea LB $16.95 (0-7910-5028-9). 64pp. The triumphs and tragedies of an Olympic medal winner are outlined in this biography. (Rev: BL 3/1/99) [921]

KWAN, MICHELLE

14560 James, Laura. *Michelle Kwan: Heart of a Champion* (4–8). Illus. 1997, Scholastic paper $14.95 (0-590-76340-7). A highly personal account of this figure-skating champion, who describes how she succeeded in placing second at the World Championships in 1997 only one month after two falls cost her the position of U.S. women's champion, and who reveals a maturity beyond her years. (Rev: BL 11/15/97; HBG 3/98; SLJ 11/97) [921]

14561 Stewart, Mark, and Mike Kennedy. *Michelle Kwan: Quest for Gold* (4–6). Illus. 2002, Millbrook LB $24.90 (0-7613-2622-7). 64pp. A chronological biography of Chinese American figure skater Michelle Kwan with color photographs. (Rev: BL 3/1/02; HBG 10/02) [796.91]

LIPINSKI, TARA

14562 Gutman, Bill. *Tara Lipinski* (4–6). Series: Sports World. 1999, Millbrook LB $19.90 (0-7613-1456-3). 48pp. This biography of the prize-winning figure skater stresses her determination and talent as well as her accomplishments. (Rev: BL 1/1–15/00; HBG 3/00) [921]

14563 Rambeck, Richard. *Tara Lipinski* (3–6). Series: Sports Superstars. 1999, Child's World LB $14.95 (1-56766-525-5). 23pp. This biography of the diminutive American figure skater is suitable for reluctant readers because of the large number of photographs included and the brevity of the text. (Rev: BL 5/15/99) [921]

WITT, KATARINA

14564 Coffey, Wayne. *Katarina Witt* (4–7). Illus. 1992, Blackbirch $16.45 (1-56711-001-0). 64pp. This biography highlights the 1988 Olympic Games, where this figure skater became a star. (Rev: SLJ 11/92) [921]

14565 Kelly, Evelyn B. *Katarina Witt* (4–6). Illus. 1998, Chelsea LB $16.95 (0-7910-5026-2). 64pp. This biography of the Olympic ice skater describes her years growing up in East Germany and her determination, in spite of her age, to compete in the 1994 Olympics. (Rev: BL 3/1/99) [921]

YAMAGUCHI, KRISTI

14566 Savage, Jeff. *Kristi Yamaguchi* (3–6). Illus. Series: Taking Part. 1993, Dillon LB $18.95 (0-87518-583-5). 64pp. A biography of the Japanese

American ice skater and her triumph at the Olympic Games. (Rev: BL 10/15/93; SLJ 2/94) [921]

Football

AIKMAN, TROY

14567 Gutman, Bill. *Troy Aikman: Super Quarterback* (4–6). Illus. Series: Sports World. 1996, Millbrook LB $19.90 (1-56294-570-X). 48pp. A colorful biography that tells about the life, talent, and drive of this football hero. (Rev: BL 5/15/96; SLJ 6/96) [921]

14568 Macnow, Glen. *Troy Aikman* (5–8). Illus. Series: Sports Greats. 1995, Enslow LB $17.95 (0-89490-593-7). 64pp. The life story of the football great Troy Aikman, with good action photographs and sports statistics. (Rev: BL 9/15/95) [921]

14569 Spiros, Dean. *Troy Aikman: Star Quarterback* (4–6). Series: Sports Reports. 1997, Enslow LB $20.95 (0-89490-927-4). 104pp. An in-depth look at this star quarterback, with career statistics, action photos, and a behind-the-scenes look at this colorful player. (Rev: BL 12/15/97; HBG 3/98) [921]

BARBER, RONDE AND TIKI

14570 Barber, Tiki, and Ronde Barber. *By My Brother's Side* (1–3). Illus. by Barry Root. 2004, Simon & Schuster $16.95 (0-689-86559-7). 32pp. The NFL player twins describe their energetic youth. (Rev: BL 9/1/04; SLJ 11/05) [921]

BETTIS, JEROME

14571 Majewski, Stephen. *Jerome Bettis* (5–8). Illus. Series: Sports Greats. 1997, Enslow LB $17.95 (0-89490-872-3). The great football hero Jerome Bettis and his amazing career are highlighted in this easily read biography. (Rev: BL 2/15/97) [921]

BRADY, TOM

14572 Gatto, Kimberly. *Tom Brady: Never-Quit Quarterback* (3–6). Illus. Series: Sports Leaders. 2005, Enslow LB $19.95 (0-7660-2475-X). 104pp. An accessible profile of the quarterback's life and career. [921]

14573 Stewart, Mark. *Tom Brady: Heart of the Huddle* (4–7). Series: Sports New Wave. 2003, Millbrook LB $22.90 (0-7613-2907-2). 48pp. The story of the popular young football player who is quarterback for the New England Patriots. (Rev: BL 6/1–15/03; HBG 10/03) [921]

BRUNELL, MARK

14574 Steenkamer, Paul. *Mark Brunell: Star Quarterback* (4–8). Series: Sports Reports. 2002, Enslow LB $20.95 (0-7660-1830-X). 104pp. The life story of the Jacksonville Jaguars quarterback, told with detailed summaries of his greatest moments. (Rev: BL 9/1/02; HBG 3/03) [921]

BRYANT, PAUL W.

14575 Smith, E. S. *Bear Bryant: Football's Winning Coach* (6–8). Illus. 1984, Walker $11.95 (0-8027-6526-2). 128pp. The story of one of the most famous coaches in football history. [921]

CULPEPPER, DAUNTE

14576 Stewart, Mark. *Daunte Culpepper: Command and Control* (4–7). Series: Sports New Wave. 2002, Millbrook LB $22.90 (0-7613-2613-8). 48pp. This brief biography celebrates the career of the young African American footballer and his achievements as quarterback of the Minnesota Vikings. (Rev: BL 9/1/02; HBG 10/02) [921]

14577 Thornley, Stew. *Super Sports Star Daunte Culpepper* (2–5). Series: Super Sports Stars. 2002, Enslow LB $18.95 (0-7660-2051-7). 48pp. The life of Culpepper, the black quarterback of the Minnesota Vikings, is excitingly re-created with colorful photographs and interesting game statistics. (Rev: BL 2/15/03; HBG 10/03) [921]

DAVIS, TERRELL

14578 Majewski, Stephen. *Terrell Davis: Star Running Back* (4–6). Illus. Series: Sports Reports. 2000, Enslow LB $19.95 (0-7660-1331-6). 104pp. Employing action photos, career statistics, and a clear text, this is a fine biography of this football star. (Rev: BL 9/15/00; HBG 3/01) [921]

14579 Stewart, Mark. *Terrell Davis: Toughing It Out* (4–8). Series: Football's New Wave. 1999, Millbrook LB $22.90 (0-7613-1514-4). 48pp. A brief biography of this football hero that uses color photographs and many fact boxes. (Rev: HBG 10/00; SLJ 7/00) [921]

ESIASON, BOOMER

14580 Esiason, Boomer. *A Boy Named Boomer* (1–2). Illus. by Jacqueline Rogers. 1995, Scholastic paper $3.99 (0-590-52835-1). 46pp. Boomer Esiason, a former NFL quarterback, recalls several incidents from his childhood in this easy reader. (Rev: BL 1/1–15/96; SLJ 3/96) [921]

FAVRE, BRETT

14581 Gutman, Bill. *Brett Favre: Leader of the Pack* (3–6). Illus. Series: Sports World. 1998, Millbrook LB $19.90 (0-7613-0310-3); paper $6.95 (0-7613-0328-6). 48pp. A short, readable biography of Brett Favre, the Green Bay Packers' famous quarterback. (Rev: BL 8/98; HBG 10/98) [921]

14582 Mooney, Martin. *Brett Favre* (5–7). Illus. Series: Football Legends. 1997, Chelsea LB $18.65 (0-7910-4396-7). 64pp. The story of the famous quarterback who took the Green Bay Packers to victory in the 1997 Super Bowl. (Rev: BL 1/1–15/98; HBG 3/98) [921]

14583 Rekela, George R. *Brett Favre: Star Quarterback* (5–8). Series: Sports Reports. 2000, Enslow LB $20.95 (0-7660-1332-4). 112pp. A brief biography of one of football's star quarterbacks that provides good career statistics and behind-the-scenes reporting. (Rev: BL 10/15/00; HBG 10/00) [921]

14584 Savage, Jeff. *Brett Favre* (5–8). Series: Sports Greats. 1998, Enslow LB $17.95 (0-7660-1000-7). An exciting biography of the star quarterback of the Green Bay Packers. (Rev: BL 3/15/98; HBG 10/98) [921]

14585 Thornley, Stew. *Super Sports Star Brett Favre* (2–5). Series: Super Sports Stars. 2002, Enslow LB $18.95 (0-7660-2048-7). 48pp. Using colorful photographs and exciting game details, this is the story of Brett Favre, quarterback of the Green Bay Packers. (Rev: BL 2/15/03; HBG 10/03) [921]

GONZALEZ, TONY

14586 Gonzales, Tony, and Greg Brown. *Tony Gonzalez: Catch and Connect* (3–6). Illus. Series: Athletes. 2004, Positively for Kids $15.95 (0-9634650-8-2). 48pp. A lively and attractively designed first-person account of Gonzalez's life and career in football, with lots of personal details about her childhood, family life, and sporting successes. [921]

JACKSON, BO

14587 Devaney, John. *Bo Jackson: A Star for All Seasons* (5–7). Illus. 1992, Walker LB $15.85 (0-802-78179-9). 110pp. Biography of the Kansas City Royals baseball star, who also played pro football for the Los Angeles Raiders. (Rev: BL 2/15/89; SLJ 1/89) [921]

14588 Knapp, Ron. *Bo Jackson* (5–8). Illus. Series: Sports Greats. 1990, Enslow LB $17.95 (0-89490-281-4). 64pp. A standard biography that includes unexpected aspects of Jackson's personality. (Rev: BL 10/15/90; SLJ 3/91) [921]

JOHNSON, BRAD

14589 Johnson, Brad, and Greg Brown. *Brad Johnson: Play with Passion* (3–6). Illus. Series: Athletes. 2004, Positively for Kids $15.95 (0-9634650-4-X). 48pp. A lively and attractively designed first-person account of Johnson's life and career in football, with lots of personal details about her childhood, family life, and sporting successes. [921]

KELLY, JIM

14590 Harrington, Denis J. *Jim Kelly* (5–8). Illus. Series: Sports Greats. 1996, Enslow LB $17.95 (0-89490-670-4). A short, action-filled biography of this former star quarterback, complete with career statistics. (Rev: BL 3/15/96) [921]

LOMBARDI, VINCE

14591 Roensch, Greg. *Vince Lombardi* (4–7). Series: Football Hall of Famers. 2003, Rosen LB $29.25 (0-8239-3610-4). 112pp. A lively, detailed, and inspiring biography of the legendary coach for whom the Super Bowl trophy is named. (Rev: SLJ 4/03) [796.332]

MCNABB, DONOVAN

14592 Mattern, Joanne. *Donovan McNabb: Football Star* (2–4). Illus. Series: Robbie Reader. 2004, Mitchell Lane LB $19.95 (1-58415-294-X). 32pp. This photo-filled biography traces the life and career of Donovan McNabb and is especially suitable for reluctant readers. [921]

MANNING, PEYTON

14593 Savage, Jeff. *Peyton Manning: Precision Passer* (4–7). Series: Sports Achievers. 2001, Lerner LB $27.15 (0-8225-3683-8); paper $5.95 (0-8225-9865-5). Sports statistics, action photographs, and an accessible text highlight this biography of the Indianapolis Colts quarterback. (Rev: BL 4/1/02; HBG 10/02) [921]

14594 Stewart, Mark. *Peyton Manning: Rising Son* (4–8). Series: Football's New Wave. 2000, Millbrook LB $22.90 (0-7613-1517-9). 48pp. An easily read account of the professional football player's life and family, including a father who also played in the NFL. (Rev: HBG 10/00; SLJ 1/01) [921]

MARINO, DAN

14595 Kennedy, Nick. *Dan Marino: Star Quarterback* (4–6). Series: Sports Reports. 1998, Enslow LB $19.95 (0-89490-933-9). Career statistics and action photos supplement this simple biography of the football great. (Rev: BL 8/98; HBG 10/99) [921]

MONTANA, JOE

14596 Kavanagh, Jack. *Joe Montana* (4–8). Illus. Series: Sports Greats. 1992, Enslow LB $17.95 (0-89490-371-3). 64pp. In simple text, this is the story of the quarterback who led his San Francisco 49ers to four Super Bowl championships. (Rev: BL 7/92; SLJ 10/92) [921]

MOSS, RANDY

14597 Bernstein, Ross. *Randy Moss: Star Wide Receiver* (4–8). Series: Sports Reports. 2002, Enslow LB $20.95 (0-7660-1503-3). 104pp. A well-illustrated account of the life of this Minnesota Vikings star, told with plenty of sports action. (Rev: BL 9/1/02; HBG 10/02) [921]

14598 Stewart, Mark. *Randy Moss: First in Flight* (4–8). Illus. Series: Football's New Wave. 2000, Millbrook LB $22.90 (0-7613-1518-7). The story of the footballer who came from a poor, segregated West Virginia town, was arrested as a young man, but went on to attend college and play professional football. (Rev: HBG 10/00; SLJ 1/01) [921]

14599 Thornley, Stew. *Super Sports Star Randy Moss* (2–5). Series: Super Sports Stars. 2002, Enslow LB $18.95 (0-7660-2049-5). 48pp. An easily read biography of the black wide receiver of the Minnesota Vikings. (Rev: BL 2/15/03; HBG 10/03) [921]

RICE, JERRY

14600 Dickey, Glenn. *Jerry Rice* (5–8). Illus. Series: Sports Greats. 1993, Enslow LB $17.95 (0-89490-419-1). 64pp. A brief biography of the star football player who gained fame with the San Francisco 49ers. (Rev: BL 9/15/93) [921]

14601 Thornley, Stew. *Jerry Rice: Star Wide Receiver* (4–6). Series: Sports Reports. 1998, Enslow LB $20.95 (0-89490-928-2). 104pp. A biography of the football player for the San Francisco 49ers that tells about both his athletic abilities and his good character traits. (Rev: BL 2/15/98; HBG 10/98) [921]

SANDERS, BARRY

14602 Aaseng, Nathan. *Barry Sanders: Star Running Back* (4–7). Illus. Series: Sports Reports. 1994, Enslow LB $20.95 (0-89490-484-1). 104pp. This biography of the football star of the Detroit Lions contains many quotations about him from his associates. (Rev: SLJ 8/94) [921]

14603 Knapp, Ron. *Barry Sanders* (5–8). Illus. Series: Sports Greats. 1993, Enslow LB $17.95 (0-89490-418-3). 64pp. This brief biography of the star football player contains many action photographs and a separate section on his career statistics. (Rev: BL 9/15/93) [921]

14604 Knapp, Ron. *Sports Great Barry Sanders* (5–8). Series: Sports Great Books. 1998, Enslow LB $16.95 (0-7660-1067-8). 64pp. The life and career of the football great are covered in this account that includes sport statistics and action photographs. (Rev: BL 2/15/99; HBG 10/99) [921]

SANDERS, DEION

14605 Savage, Jeff. *Deion Sanders: Star Athlete* (4–6). Illus. Series: Sports Reports. 1996, Enslow LB $20.95 (0-89490-652-6). 104pp. An in-depth look at this football hero, with black-and-white photos. (Rev: BL 4/15/96) [921]

SEAU, JUNIOR

14606 Savage, Jeff. *Junior Seau: Star Linebacker* (4–6). Illus. Series: Sports Reports. 1997, Enslow LB $20.95 (0-89490-800-6). 104pp. A biography of this famous football player, complete with career statistics and action photos. (Rev: BL 8/97) [921]

SMITH, EMMITT

14607 Grabowski, John. *Emmitt Smith* (5–8). Series: Sports Greats. 1998, Enslow LB $17.95 (0-7660-1002-3). A high-interest biography of this football great that contains career statistics, action photographs, and exciting game action. (Rev: BL 7/98; HBG 10/98) [921]

14608 Savage, Jeff. *Emmitt Smith: Star Running Back* (4–6). Illus. Series: Sports Reports. 1996, Enslow LB $20.95 (0-89490-653-4). 104pp. The professional life of one of the stars of the Dallas Cowboys is highlighted in this biography, which

also covers Smith's childhood and character traits. (Rev: BL 4/15/96) [921]

14609 Thornley, Stew. *Emmitt Smith: Relentless Rusher* (4–8). Series: Sports Achievers. 1996, Lerner LB $27.15 (0-8225-2897-5). The professional life of one of the Dallas Cowboys is highlighted, supplemented by career statistics and action photographs. (Rev: BL 4/15/97; SLJ 8/97) [921]

TARKENTON, FRAN

14610 Hulm, David. *Fran Tarkenton* (4–7). Series: Football Hall of Famers. 2003, Rosen LB $29.25 (0-8239-3608-2). 112pp. A lively, detailed, and inspiring biography of the star of the Minnesota Vikings and the New York Giants who went on to become a successful businessman. (Rev: SLJ 4/03) [796.332]

THOMAS, THURMAN

14611 Savage, Jeff. *Thurman Thomas: Star Running Back* (4–7). Illus. Series: Sports Reports. 1994, Enslow LB $20.95 (0-89490-445-0). 104pp. This life story of the football hero also contains action photographs, fact boxes, and statistics. (Rev: SLJ 8/94) [921]

WALKER, HERSCHEL

14612 Benagh, Jim. *Herschel Walker* (5–8). Illus. Series: Sports Greats. 1990, Enslow LB $17.95 (0-89490-207-5). 64pp. This account tells how Walker grew up in Georgia and went on to a career in professional football. (Rev: BL 10/15/90; SLJ 3/91) [921]

YOUNG, STEVE

14613 Knapp, Ron. *Steve Young: Star Quarterback* (4–6). Illus. Series: Sports Reports. 1996, Enslow LB $20.95 (0-89490-654-2). 104pp. A profile of the San Francisco 49ers quarterback, his professional career, character traits, and outside interests. (Rev: BL 4/15/96) [921]

14614 Morgan, Terri, and Shmuel Thaler. *Steve Young: Complete Quarterback* (4–8). Illus. Series: Sports Achievers. 1995, Lerner paper $9.55 (0-8225-9716-0). 64pp. A profile of the San Francisco 49ers quarterback, with material on his professional career, his character, and outside interests. (Rev: BL 11/15/95) [921]

Tennis

AGASSI, ANDRE

14615 Knapp, Ron. *Andre Agassi: Star Tennis Player* (5–8). Series: Sports Reports. 1997, Enslow LB $20.95 (0-89490-798-0). An in-depth look at the life and career of this tennis star, with details of his childhood and his father's influence. (Rev: BL 8/97; SLJ 8/97) [921]

14616 Savage, Jeff. *Andre Agassi: Reaching the Top — Again* (4–8). Series: Sports Achievers. 1997,

Lerner paper $9.55 (0-8225-9750-0). 64pp. A short, easily read biography of this volatile tennis star. (Rev: BL 1/1–15/98; HBG 3/98) [921]

ASHE, ARTHUR

14617 Cunningham, Kevin. *Arthur Ashe: Athlete and Activist* (5–8). Illus. Series: Journey to Freedom: The African American Library. 2005, Child's World LB $19.95 (1-59296-228-9). 40pp. Chronicles the Virginia-born athlete's rise to tennis stardom and his involvement in the fight against apartheid. (Rev: BL 2/1/05) [921]

14618 Dexter, Robin. *Young Arthur Ashe: Brave Champion* (2–4). Illus. by R. W. Alley. Series: First Start Biography. 1996, Troll paper $3.50 (0-8167-3773-8). 32pp. The life and death of this courageous tennis champion are dealt with in simple text and numerous color illustrations. (Rev: BL 2/15/96) [921]

14619 Lazo, Caroline. *Arthur Ashe* (4–7). Series: A&E Biography. 1999, Lerner $25.26 (0-8225-1932-8). 128pp. The inspiring story of this great African American tennis star and humanitarian is told in a clear, well-organized text with several black-and-white photographs. (Rev: BL 3/15/00) [921]

14620 Wright, David K. *Arthur Ashe: Breaking the Color Barrier in Tennis* (4–7). Illus. Series: African American Biographies. 1996, Enslow LB $20.95 (0-89490-689-5). 128pp. The story of the groundbreaking tennis star and his battle with AIDS. (Rev: SLJ 10/96) [921]

CHANG, MICHAEL

14621 Ditchfield, Christin. *Michael Chang* (5–8). Series: Sports Greats. 1999, Enslow LB $17.95 (0-7660-1223-9). A biography of this tennis phenomenon, with career statistics and plenty of action photographs. (Rev: BL 3/15/99; HBG 10/99) [921]

FERNANDEZ, MARY JOE

14622 Cole, Melanie. *Mary Joe Fernandez* (3–4). Series: Real-Life Reader Biographies. 1998, Mitchell Lane LB $15.95 (1-883845-63-7). 32pp. The story of the talented and charitable tennis star who turned pro at age 14 but continued with her education. (Rev: BL 10/15/98; HBG 10/98; SLJ 12/98) [921]

HINGIS, MARTINA

14623 Rambeck, Richard. *Martina Hingis* (3–6). Series: Sports Superstars. 1999, Child's World LB $14.95 (1-56766-519-5). 23pp. A colorful, simple biography — that will appeal to reluctant readers — of the famous tennis star, with highlights from her career. (Rev: BL 5/15/99; HBG 10/99) [921]

KING, BILLIE JEAN

14624 Sanford, William R., and Carl R. Green. *Billie Jean King* (4–6). Illus. Series: Sports Immortals.

1993, Macmillan LB $16.95 (0-89686-781-1). 48pp. Illustrated with many black-and-white photos, this slim biography of tennis star Billie Jean King also contains several trivia questions. (Rev: BL 10/1/93) [921]

SAMPRAS, PETE

14625 Rambeck, Richard. *Pete Sampras* (2–5). Illus. 1996, Child's World LB $21.36 (1-56766-262-5). 23pp. A very brief biography, with more photos than text, about this tennis wonder. (Rev: SLJ 6/97) [921]

14626 Sherrow, Victoria. *Sports Great Pete Sampras* (5–8). Illus. Series: Sports Great Books. 1996, Enslow LB $17.95 (0-89490-756-5). 64pp. The story of this amazing tennis star, his accomplishments, and his career statistics, with a number of black-and-white photos. (Rev: BL 3/15/96) [921]

SELES, MONICA

14627 Murdico, Suzanne J. *Monica Seles* (5–8). Illus. Series: Overcoming the Odds. 1998, Raintree $28.80 (0-8172-4128-0). The story of the great tennis player and the courtside stabbing that resulted in a trauma difficult to overcome. (Rev: HBG 9/98) [921]

14628 Rambeck, Richard. *Monica Seles* (2–5). Illus. 1996, Child's World LB $21.36 (1-56766-312-5). 23pp. A short biography of the tennis star, with coverage on her tragic stabbing and her comeback. (Rev: SLJ 6/97) [921]

WILLIAMS, VENUS AND SERENA

14629 Aronson, Virginia. *Venus Williams* (5–8). Illus. Series: Galaxy of Superstars. 1999, Chelsea $19.75 (0-7910-5153-6); paper $8.95 (0-7910-5329-6). 63pp. The story of this superstar of tennis, how her father trained her, and how he made her education more important than her tennis. (Rev: BL 4/15/99; BR 9–10/99; HBG 10/99; SLJ 5/99) [921]

14630 Brown, Jonatha A. *Venus and Serena Williams* (2–4). Illus. Series: People We Should Know. 2005, Gareth Stevens LB $14.50 (0-8638-4470-X). 24pp. For beginning readers, a simple account of the Williams sisters' triumphs with an attractive layout and many photographs. [921]

14631 Fillon, Mike. *Young Superstars of Tennis: The Venus and Serena Williams Story* (4–8). Series: Avisson Young Adult. 1999, Avisson LB $19.95 (1-888105-43-7). 144pp. This biography of the Williams sisters tells about their childhood, the influence of their father, and their determination to get to the top in tennis. (Rev: BL 12/15/99; SLJ 3/00) [921]

14632 Morgan, Terri. *Venus and Serena Williams: Grand Slam Sisters* (4–7). Series: Sports Achievers. 2001, Lerner LB $27.15 (0-8225-3684-6); paper $5.95 (0-8225-9866-3). An action-packed biography of the amazing tennis duo that covers their careers and their family. (Rev: BL 4/1/02; HBG 10/02) [921]

14633 Stewart, Mark. *Venus and Serena Williams: Sisters in Arms* (4–7). Series: Tennis's New Wave. 2000, Millbrook LB $22.90 (0-7613-1803-8). 48pp. A simple biography of the amazing tennis-playing sisters with good coverage of their early lives. (Rev: HBG 3/01; SLJ 3/01) [921]

14634 Stout, Glenn. *On the Court with . . . Venus and Serena Williams* (4–6). Illus. Series: Matt Christopher Sports Bio Bookshelf. 2002, Little, Brown paper $4.95 (0-316-13814-2). 128pp. A biography of the tennis greats, with information on their childhoods and family (and the influential role of their father) and details of important matches. (Rev: BL 9/1/02) [796.342]

Track and Field

DEVERS, GAIL

14635 Gutman, Bill. *Gail Devers* (3–6). Illus. Series: Overcoming the Odds. 1996, Raintree LB $25.69 (0-8172-4122-1). 48pp. The story of this track star who was largely self-trained, her childhood in San Diego, and her participation in the 1993 World Championships. (Rev: SLJ 11/96) [921]

JONES, MARION

14636 Rutledge, Rachel. *Marion Jones: Fast and Fearless* (4–7). 2000, Millbrook LB $22.90 (0-7613-1870-4). 48pp. A biography of the track-and-field star of the 2000 Sydney Olympics that stresses her drive and tenacity. (Rev: HBG 3/01; SLJ 3/01) [921]

JOYNER-KERSEE, JACKIE

14637 Green, Carl R. *Jackie Joyner-Kersee* (4–8). Illus. Series: Sports Headliners. 1994, Macmillan LB $13.95 (0-89686-838-9). 48pp. A biography of the track star that uses quotations and photographs to highlight important events in her career. (Rev: BL 10/1/94) [921]

JOYNER, FLORENCE GRIFFITH

14638 Aaseng, Nathan. *Florence Griffith Joyner: Dazzling Olympian* (4–6). Illus. Series: Sports Achievers. 1989, Lerner LB $18.60 (0-8225-0495-2); paper $4.95 (0-8225-9587-7). 56pp. A profile of this gold medalist in the 1988 Summer Olympics. (Rev: BCCB 1/90; BL 12/15/89; SLJ 3/90) [921]

LEWIS, CARL

14639 Aaseng, Nathan. *Carl Lewis: Legend Chaser* (4–8). Illus. 1985, Lerner LB $18.60 (0-8225-0496-0). 56pp. Childhood, college, and Olympic performances are covered in this biography, including both praise and criticism about Lewis's attempt at the long-jump record. (Rev: BCCB 11/85; BL 7/85; SLJ 8/85) [796.420924]

LEWIS, RAY

14640 Cooper, John. *Rapid Ray: The Story of Ray Lewis* (5–9). 2002, Tundra paper $8.95 (0-88776-612-9). 144pp. An absorbing profile of the Canadian-born black athlete (and train porter) who won a bronze medal in the 1932 Olympics and the racial hurdles he had to overcome. (Rev: SLJ 6/03) [796.42]

O'BRIEN, DAN

14641 Gutman, Bill. *Dan O'Brien* (5–8). Series: Overcoming the Odds. 1998, Raintree $28.80 (0-8172-4129-9). A biography of this great decathlete that describes his struggles to overcome attention-deficit hyperactivity disorder as well as various injuries. (Rev: HBG 9/98) [921]

OWENS, JESSE

14642 Adler, David A. *A Picture Book of Jesse Owens* (K–3). Illus. by Robert Casilla. Series: Picture Book Biographies. 1992, Holiday House LB $16.95 (0-8234-0966-X); paper $6.95 (0-8234-1066-8). 32pp. Relying heavily on illustrations to supply details, this is an introduction to the famous track-and-field star. (Rev: BL 11/15/92; SLJ 12/92) [921]

14643 McKissack, Patricia, and Fredrick McKissack. *Jesse Owens: Olympic Star*. Rev. ed. (2–5). Series: Great African Americans. 2001, Enslow LB $14.95 (0-7660-1681-1). 32pp. This is an updated version of the 1992 book about the African American athlete whose four medals in the 1936 Olympics displeased Hitler, with factual updates, improved illustrations, and lists of print and Internet resources. (Rev: HBG 10/01; SLJ 8/01) [921]

14644 Rennert, Richard S. *Jesse Owens* (4–7). Illus. Series: Junior World Biography. 1991, Chelsea LB $16.95 (0-7910-1570-X). 80pp. An attractive, well-illustrated account of this famous track-and-field star who embarrassed Hitler by winning four gold medals at the 1936 Olympic Games. (Rev: BL 9/1/91; SLJ 9/91) [921]

14645 Streissguth, Thomas. *Jesse Owens* (4–6). Illus. Series: A&E Biography. 1999, Lerner $25.26 (0-8225-4940-9). 112pp. A biography of the remarkable African American athlete who won four gold medals at the 1936 Summer Olympics in Berlin. (Rev: BL 2/15/00; HBG 3/00) [921]

14646 Sutcliffe, Jane. *Jesse Owens* (2–3). Series: On My Own. 2000, Carolrhoda LB $19.93 (1-57505-451-5); paper $5.95 (1-57505-487-6). 48pp. A simple biography of the athlete who overcame sickness, poverty, and discrimination to become a gold medal winner in Berlin in 1936. (Rev: BL 8/00; HBG 10/01) [921]

RUDOLPH, WILMA

14647 Harper, Jo. *Wilma Rudolph: Olympic Runner* (3–6). Illus. by Meryl Henderson. Series: Childhood of Famous Americans. 2004, Simon & Schuster paper $4.99 (0-689-85873-6). 192pp. A moving, fictionalized account of Rudolph's triumph over polio, prejudice, and poverty. (Rev: BL 5/15/04)

14648 Krull, Kathleen. *Wilma Unlimited: How Wilma Rudolph Became the World's Fastest Woman* (2–5). Illus. by David Diaz. 1996, Harcourt $16.00 (0-15-201267-2). 48pp. A biography of the amazing Wilma Rudolph, who overcame incredible obstacles to become a track star. (Rev: BL 5/1/96*; HB 9–10/96; SLJ 6/96*) [921]

14649 Ruth, Amy. *Wilma Rudolph* (4–6). Series: A&E Biography. 2000, Lerner LB $25.26 (0-8225-4976-X). 112pp. The inspiring story of the African American athlete who overcame polio and won three gold medals in Olympic track-and-field events in 1960. (Rev: BL 6/1–15/00; HBG 10/00) [921]

14650 Sherrow, Victoria. *Wilma Rudolph* (2–3). Illus. by Larry Johnson. Series: On My Own Biography. 2000, Lerner LB $19.93 (1-57505-246-6); paper $5.95 (1-57505-442-6). 48pp. The story of how a young girl whose legs were thin and crooked from polio grew up to win Olympic gold medals for running is told with simplicity and dignity. (Rev: BL 2/15/00; HBG 10/00; SLJ 2/00) [921]

14651 Sherrow, Victoria. *Wilma Rudolph: Olympic Champion* (4–6). Illus. Series: Junior World Biographies. 1995, Chelsea LB $16.95 (0-7910-2290-0). 79pp. The life of this great track star and of the poverty, bad health, and emotional challenges she faced and overcame in her desire to succeed. (Rev: BCCB 4/96; SLJ 8/95) [921]

THORPE, JIM

14652 Bruchac, Joseph. *Jim Thorpe's Bright Path* (2–3). Trans. and illus. by S. D. Nelson. 2004, Lee & Low $17.95 (1-58430-166-X). 40pp. This inspiring profile of Jim Thorpe focuses on the future Olympic champion's childhood, tracing his life from birth in a log cabin to the start of his scholastic football career at Carlisle Indian School in Pennsylvania. (Rev: BL 8/04; SLJ 6/04) [921]

14653 Long, Barbara. *Jim Thorpe: Legendary Athlete* (5–7). Illus. Series: Native American Biographies. 1997, Enslow LB $20.95 (0-89490-865-0). 128pp. The story of the amazing Native American athlete whose career had tremendous highs and lows. (Rev: BL 6/1–15/97) [921]

Miscellaneous Sports

ARMSTRONG, LANCE

14654 Armstrong, Kristin. *Lance Armstrong: The Race of His Life* (2–3). Illus. Series: All Aboard Reading. 2000, Penguin Putnam $13.89 (0-448-42415-0); paper $3.90 (0-448-42407-X). 48pp. A book for beginning readers that tells about this famous cyclist, his many triumphs, and his battle with cancer — written by his wife. (Rev: BL 12/1/00; HBG 3/01) [921]

14655 Benson, Michael. *Lance Armstrong: Cyclist* (5–8). Series: Ferguson Career Biographies. 2003, Ferguson LB $21.95 (0-8160-5479-7). 139pp.

Traces the inspiring life of the great bicycle-racer through his fifth Tour de France win, with an emphasis on his perseverance and optimism. (Rev: SLJ 5/04) [796.6]

14656 Donovan, Sandy. *Lance Armstrong* (2–4). Illus. Series: Amazing Athletes. 2005, Lerner LB $22.60 (0-8225-3691-9). 32pp. Armstrong's cycling career is the focus of this easy-reading biography that also touches on his childhood. (Rev: BL 2/15/05; SLJ 3/05) [921]

14657 Garcia, Kimberly. *Lance Armstrong* (3–4). Series: Real-Life Reader Biographies. 2002, Mitchell Lane LB $15.95 (1-58415-125-0). 32pp. Using a conversational style and black-and-white photographs, this is a biography of the Tour de France-winning cyclist who overcame cancer. (Rev: BL 9/15/02; SLJ 12/02) [921]

14658 Stewart, Mark. *Sweet Victory: Lance Armstrong's Incredible Journey: The Amazing Story of the Greatest Comeback in Sports* (4–8). 2000, Millbrook LB $23.90 (0-7613-1861-5). 64pp. The inspiring story of the man who won the Tour de France bicycle race despite struggles with cancer. (Rev: BL 8/00; HBG 10/00; SLJ 8/00) [921]

BASS, TOM

14659 Wilkerson, J. L. *From Slave to World-Class Horseman: Tom Bass* (4–8). 2000, Acorn paper $9.95 (0-9664470-3-4). 135pp. A fast-paced narrative about the man who was born a slave and later became such a renowned horseman that he performed for Queen Victoria. (Rev: SLJ 4/00) [921]

BLAIR, BONNIE

14660 Blair, Bonnie, and Greg Brown. *A Winning Edge* (3–5). Illus. 1996, Taylor $14.95 (0-87833-931-0). 40pp. The autobiography of the Olympic medal-winning speed skater, with insights into her life off the ice. (Rev: BL 5/15/96) [921]

BUTCHER, SUSAN

14661 Wadsworth, Ginger. *Susan Butcher: Sled Dog Racer* (4–7). Illus. Series: Sports Achievers. 1994, Lerner LB $18.60 (0-8225-2878-9). 63pp. This exciting biography brings to life the four-time Iditarod winner and the rigors and courage each race involved. (Rev: SLJ 6/94) [921]

DIMAS, TRENT

14662 Menard, Valerie, and Sue Boulais. *Trent Dimas* (3–5). Series: Real-Life Reader Biographies. 1998, Mitchell Lane LB $15.95 (1-883845-50-5). 32pp. The story of a young gymnast who saw his dreams come true when he took the gold medal in the 1992 Olympics. (Rev: BL 6/1–15/98; HBG 3/98; SLJ 4/98) [921]

EDERLE, GERTRUDE

14663 Adler, David A. *America's Champion Swimmer: Gertrude Ederle* (2–4). Illus. by Terry Widener. 2000, Harcourt $16.00 (0-15-201969-3). 32pp. A simple biography of the amazing athlete who was the first woman to swim across the English Channel. (Rev: BCCB 4/00; BL 3/15/00*; HB 5–6/00; HBG 10/00; SLJ 6/00) [921]

EL CHINO

14664 Say, Allen. *El Chino* (3–6). Illus. 1990, Houghton Mifflin $16.00 (0-395-52023-1). 32pp. The first-person narrative of a Chinese American civil engineer who becomes a matador. (Rev: BCCB 9/90*; BL 9/1/90*; HB 1–2/91; SLJ 11/90) [921]

GRETZKY, WAYNE

14665 Fortunato, Frank. *Wayne Gretzky: Star Center* (4–6). Series: Sports Reports. 1998, Enslow LB $20.95 (0-89490-930-4). 104pp. An in-depth look at the life and career of this amazing hockey player. (Rev: BL 2/15/98; HBG 10/98) [921]
14666 Rappoport, Ken. *Wayne Gretzky* (5–8). Illus. Series: Sports Greats. 1996, Enslow LB $17.95 (0-89490-757-3). A brief biography of this hockey phenomenon, illustrated with black-and-white action photographs. (Rev: BL 3/15/96) [921]

HAMM, MIA

14667 Rutledge, Rachel. *Mia Hamm: Striking Superstar* (3–6). Series: Soccer's New Wave. 2000, Millbrook LB $20.90 (0-7613-1802-X). 48pp. A fully rounded biography of the soccer star who was a member of the 1991 and 1999 Gold Medal World Cup Soccer teams. (Rev: HBG 10/00; SLJ 7/00) [921]
14668 Torres, John. *Mia Hamm* (3–4). Series: Real-Life Reader Biographies. 1999, Mitchell Lane LB $15.95 (1-883845-94-7). 32pp. An inspiring biography of this great female soccer player and how she succeeded through spirit and determination. (Rev: BL 10/15/99) [921]
14669 Zarzycki, Daryl. *Mia Hamm* (2–5). Series: Robbie Reader. 2004, Mitchell Lane LB $16.95 (1-58415-286-9). 32pp. This photo-filled biography that presents information on Hamm's childhood and career is especially suitable for reluctant readers. (Rev: BL 11/15/04) [921]

HOGAN, HULK

14670 Zannos, Susan. *Hollywood Hulk Hogan: The Story of Terry Bollea* (3–4). Series: Real-Life Reader Biographies. 1999, Mitchell Lane LB $15.95 (1-58415-021-1). 32pp. A simple biography about this world-famous wrestler and how he devotes time and money to charities that help sick children. (Rev: BL 10/15/99) [921]

KRONE, JULIE

14671 Callahan, Dorothy. *Julie Krone: A Winning Jockey* (4–6). Illus. 1990, Macmillan LB $18.95 (0-87518-425-1). 64pp. A biography of the woman

who became the leading female jockey at the age of 25. (Rev: BCCB 9/90; BL 7/90; SLJ 9/90) [921]
14672 Gutman, Bill. *Julie Krone* (3–6). Illus. Series: Overcoming the Odds. 1996, Raintree LB $25.69 (0-8172-4121-3). 48pp. An absorbing biography of this female jockey, her participation in more than 16,000 races, and the 1993 accident that left her seriously injured. (Rev: SLJ 2/97) [921]

LEE, SAMMY

14673 Yoo, Paula. *Sixteen Years in Sixteen Seconds: The Sammy Lee Story* (2–4). Illus. by Dom Lee. 2005, Lee & Low $16.95 (1-58430-247-X). 32pp. All about the Korean American Olympic diver, who in 1948 defied prejudice and family expectations to become the first Asian American to win a gold medal. (Rev: BL 3/15/05; SLJ 4/05) [797.2]

LEMIEUX, MARIO

14674 Rossiter, Sean. *Mario Lemieux* (4–8). Illus. Series: Hockey Heroes. 2001, Sterling $12.95 (1-55054-870-0). 64pp. A detailed look at the career of Pittsburgh Penguin Mario Lemieux. (Rev: BL 2/15/02) [796.962]
14675 Stewart, Mark. *Mario Lemieux: Own the Ice* (5–8). Illus. 2002, Millbrook LB $24.90 (0-7613-2555-7); paper $8.95 (0-7613-1687-6). 64pp. A readable biography of the ice hockey star, with photographs, statistics, and information about the athlete's personal life and work ethic. (Rev: BL 9/15/02; HBG 3/03) [796.962]

LEMOND, GREG

14676 Porter, A. P. *Greg LeMond: Premier Cyclist* (4–7). Illus. Series: Sports Achievers. 1990, Lerner LB $18.60 (0-8225-0476-6). 64pp. Although he suffered severe injuries in a hunting accident, LeMond won the Tour de France bicycle race. (Rev: BL 6/15/90; SLJ 9/90) [921]

LINDROS, ERIC

14677 Rappoport, Ken. *Eric Lindros* (5–8). Series: Sports Greats. 1997, Enslow LB $17.95 (0-89490-871-5). A biography of the famous hockey star that includes career statistics and action photographs. (Rev: BL 10/15/97) [921]

MESSIER, MARK

14678 Sullivan, Michael J. *Mark Messier: Star Center* (4–6). Series: Sports Reports. 1997, Enslow LB $20.95 (0-89490-801-4). 104pp. This biography of Messier contains career statistics, action photos, and a behind-the-scenes look at this hockey star. (Rev: BL 12/15/97; HBG 3/98) [921]

MOCEANU, DOMINIQUE

14679 Durrett, Deanne. *Dominique Moceanu* (5–8). Series: People in the News. 1999, Lucent LB $27.45 (1-56006-099-9). 111pp. Drawing heavily on

Moceanu's autobiography, this is the life story of the phenomenal gymnast, with behind-the scenes glimpses of competitions, training, scoring, and routines. (Rev: HBG 3/00; SLJ 8/99) [921]

14680 Quiner, Krista. *Dominique Moceanu: A Gymnastics Sensation* (4–7). Illus. 1997, Bradford paper $12.95 (0-9643460-3-6). 191pp. The story of the United States' youngest gold medal winner in gymnastics, with a special 24-page insert of photographs. (Rev: SLJ 3/97) [921]

MONPLAISIR, SHARON

14681 Greenberg, Doreen, and Michael Greenberg. *Sword of a Champion: The Story of Sharon Monplaisir* (4–8). Illus. by Phil Velikan. Series: Anything You Can Do — New Sports Heroes for Girls. 2000, Wish paper $9.95 (1-930546-39-4). 81pp. The life story of the timid, shy high schooler who found her place in fencing via a coach who encouraged her to develop her natural talents. (Rev: SLJ 3/01) [796.8]

NASH, KEVIN

14682 Mudge, Jacqueline. *Kevin Nash* (4–7). Series: Pro Wrestling Legends. 2000, Chelsea paper $8.95 (0-7910-5828-X). 64pp. This is the biography of the wrestler known as "Diesel." (Rev: BL 10/15/00; HBG 3/01) [921]

PAK, SE RI

14683 Stewart, Mark. *Se Ri Pak: Driven to Win* (4–8). Series: Golf's New Wave. 2000, Millbrook LB $22.90 (0-7613-1519-5). 48pp. The story of the South Korean who won the Ladies Professional Golf Association Championship in 1998. (Rev: HBG 10/00; SLJ 8/00) [921]

PELE

14684 Arnold, Caroline. *Pele: The King of Soccer* (4–8). Illus. Series: First Books. 1992, Watts paper $22.00 (0-531-20077-9). 64pp. Traces Pele's soccer career from early promise to international superstardom. (Rev: BL 10/1/92) [921]

PHELPS, MICHAEL

14685 Zuehlke, Jeffrey. *Michael Phelps* (2–4). Illus. Series: Amazing Athletes/LernerSports. 2005, Lerner LB $22.60 (0-8225-2431-7). 32pp. A well-illustrated introduction to the Olympic swimmer. [921]

REECE, GABRIELLE

14686 Morgan, Terri. *Gabrielle Reece: Volleyball's Model Athlete* (4–7). Illus. Series: Sports Achievers. 1999, Lerner LB $22.60 (0-8225-3667-6). 64pp. An accessible biography of the woman who is not only a volleyball champ but also a fashion model and TV personality. (Rev: BL 10/15/99; HBG 3/00) [921]

RIDDLES, LIBBY

14687 Riddles, Libby. *Storm Run: The Story of the First Woman to Win the Iditarod Sled Dog Race* (2–5). Illus. by Shannon Cartwright. 2002, Sasquatch $16.95 (1-57061-298-6). 48pp. Initially published in 1986, this first-person account of training and racing in the Iditarod, written by the first woman ever to win it, is bolstered by fresh illustrations. (Rev: BL 3/1/02; HBG 10/02) [798.8]

ROSENFELD, FANNY BOBBIE

14688 Dublin, Anne. *Bobbie Rosenfeld: The Olympian Who Could Do Everything* (5–8). 2004, Second Story paper $11.95 (1-896764-82-7). 120pp. Fanny Bobbie Rosenfeld migrated from the Ukraine to Canada in 1905, became an outstanding athlete excelling in many sports, and led the Canadian women's relay team to an Olympic gold in 1928. (Rev: BL 9/1/04) [921]

THOMPSON, JENNY

14689 Greenberg, Doreen, and Michael Greenberg. *Fast Lane to Victory: The Story of Jenny Thompson* (3–6). Illus. by Phil Velikan. Series: Anything You Can Do — New Sports Heroes for Girls. 2001, Wish paper $9.95 (1-930546-38-6). 141pp. Swimmer Jenny Thompson's determination to excel and the highlights of her career are presented here. (Rev: SLJ 8/01) [797.21]

TREVINO, LEE

14690 Gilbert, Thomas. *Lee Trevino* (5–9). Series: Hispanics of Achievement. 1991, Chelsea LB $19.95 (0-7910-1256-5). The story of one of golf's all-time greats to 1990. (Rev: BL 3/15/92) [796.352]

VENTURA, JESSE

14691 Cohen, Daniel. *Jesse Ventura: The Body, the Mouth, the Mind* (5–8). 2001, Twenty-First Century LB $25.40 (0-7613-1905-0). 112pp. A comprehensive profile of Ventura's private life and his stints as Navy Seal, talk-show host, actor, wrestler, and politician. (Rev: BL 10/1/01; HBG 3/02; SLJ 12/01)

14692 Greenberg, Keith E. *Jesse Ventura* (5–8). Illus. Series: A&E Biography. 1999, Lerner LB $30.35 (0-8225-4977-8); paper $7.95 (0-8225-9680-6). 112pp. A look at this larger-than-life pop culture hero who has been an actor, a professional wrestler, a Navy SEAL, and the governor of Minnesota. (Rev: BL 3/1/00; HBG 3/00; SLJ 2/00) [921]

14693 Uschan, Michael V. *Jesse Ventura* (5–8). Series: People in the News. 2001, Lucent LB $35.15 (1-56006-777-2). From a career in wrestling to a state governorship, this is the story of the amazing Jesse Ventura. (Rev: BL 4/1/02) [921]

WOODS, TIGER

14694 Boyd, Aaron. *Tiger Woods* (5–7). Illus. 1997, Morgan Reynolds LB $18.95 (1-883846-19-6). 64pp. A brief, straightforward biography of this amazing golfer who was a young prodigy. (Rev: BL 5/1/97; HBG 3/98; SLJ 8/97) [921]

14695 Brown, Jonatha A. *Tiger Woods* (2–4). Illus. Series: People We Should Know. 2005, Gareth Stevens LB $14.50 (0-8368-4313-4). 24pp. For beginning readers, a simple account of Woods's life and triumphs, with an attractive layout and many photographs. [921]

14696 Christopher, Matt. *On the Course with . . . Tiger Woods* (3–5). Illus. 1998, Little, Brown paper $4.50 (0-316-13445-7). 128pp. A brief biography of Tiger Woods, including a short history of golf and its rules. (Rev: BL 7/98) [921]

14697 Collins, David R. *Tiger Woods: Golf Superstar* (K–3). Illus. by Larry Nolte. 1999, Pelican $14.95 (1-56554-321-1). This simple biography stresses the determination and hard work that made Tiger Woods the golf star that the world admires. (Rev: SLJ 6/99) [921]

14698 Collins, David R. *Tiger Woods, Golfing Champion* (5–8). Illus. by Larry Nolte. 1999, Pelican $14.95 (1-56554-322-X). 88pp. A chronologically arranged book ending in 1999 that reveals Tiger Woods's determination and love of the game. (Rev: SLJ 1/00) [921]

14699 Gutman, Bill. *Tiger Woods: Golf's Shining Young Star* (3–6). Illus. Series: Sports World. 1998, Millbrook LB $19.90 (0-7613-0309-X); paper $6.95 (0-7613-0329-4). 48pp. This biography of Tiger Woods stresses his family background, racial and age problems, and his career highlights. (Rev: BL 8/98; HBG 10/98) [921]

14700 Roberts, Jeremy. *Tiger Woods* (5–8). Series: Biography. 2002, Lerner LB $30.35 (0-8225-0030-2). The story of the likable wonder boy of golf is told in text and pictures. (Rev: BL 4/1/02; HBG 10/02) [921]

14701 Savage, Jeff. *Tiger Woods: King of the Course* (4–5). Illus. 1998, Lerner LB $14.95 (0-8225-3655-2). 64pp. Lavish color photographs illustrate this biography of Tiger Woods, which includes his fami-

ly background, his training, style, and tournament action. (Rev: BL 7/98; HBG 10/98; SLJ 6/98) [921]

14702 Sirimarco, Elizabeth. *Tiger Woods* (3–6). Series: Sports Heroes. 2000, Capstone LB $21.26 (0-7368-0581-8). 48pp. This brief biography focuses on Woods's athletic development from childhood and the key accomplishments in his career, with plenty of photographs and statistics. (Rev: SLJ 5/01) [921]

14703 Teague, Allison L. *Prince of the Fairway: The Tiger Woods Story* (4–7). Illus. 1997, Avisson LB $18.50 (1-888105-22-4). 106pp. A biography that emphasizes the wholesome behavioral traits of this golf phenomenon, the youngest professional player to win the Masters Tournament in Augusta, Georgia. (Rev: SLJ 10/97) [921]

ZAHARIAS, BABE DIDRIKSON

14704 Freedman, Russell. *Babe Didrikson Zaharias: The Making of a Champion* (5–12). Illus. 1999, Clarion $18.00 (0-395-63367-2). 192pp. Although this athlete was known to most for her golf career, this entertaining biography points out that Babe Didrikson Zaharias was also an Olympic athlete, a track star, leader of a woman's amateur basketball team, and entrepreneur. (Rev: BCCB 10/99; BL 7/99; HB 9–10/99; HBG 3/00; SLJ 7/99) [921]

14705 Sutcliffe, Jane. *Babe Didrikson Zaharias: All-Around Athlete* (2–3). Series: On My Own Biography. 2000, Carolrhoda LB $19.93 (1-57505-421-3). 48pp. A simple biography of one of the greatest athletes of the 20th century, winner of three medals in track and field at the 1932 Olympics. (Rev: BL 6/1–15/00; HBG 10/00; SLJ 6/00) [921]

14706 Wakeman, Nancy. *Babe Didrikson Zaharias: Driven to Win* (4–7). Illus. Series: Biography. 2000, Lerner LB $25.26 (0-8225-4917-4). 112pp. The account focuses on this sportswoman's professional career and her strong personality plus her accomplishments in track and field, basketball, and baseball. (Rev: BL 6/1–15/00; HBG 10/00; SLJ 7/00) [921]

World Figures

Collective

14707 Aaseng, Nathan. *The Peace Seekers: The Nobel Peace Prize* (5–8). Illus. 1987, Lerner LB $18.60 (0-8225-0654-8); paper $7.95 (0-8225-9604-0). 80pp. Martin Luther King, Jr., and Lech Walesa are among those whose lives and works are introduced. (Rev: BL 2/1/88) [327.1720922]

14708 Avakian, Monique. *Reformers: Activists, Educators, Religious Leaders* (5–9). Series: Remarkable Women. 2000, Raintree LB $32.85 (0-8172-5733-0). 80pp. This book contains 150 profiles of woman who, throughout history and from many cultures, have fought for human rights, including Harriet Tubman, Mother Teresa, and Dolores Huerta. (Rev: SLJ 8/00) [920]

14709 Bardhan-Quallen, Sudipta. *The Mexican-American War* (5–9). Series: People at the Center Of. 2005, Gale/Blackbirch LB $23.70 (1-56711-927-1). 48pp. After an overview of the war, this volume provides biographical information on key figures including James K. Polk, Abraham Lincoln, Santa Anna, and Zachary Taylor. (Rev: SLJ 6/05) [920]

14710 Billinghurst, Jane. *Growing Up Royal: Life in the Shadow of the British Throne* (4–7). Illus. 2001, Annick $22.95 (1-55037-623-3); paper $12.95 (1-55037-622-5). 176pp. A look at what it's like to be young and royal, with a focus on the lives of today's British royalty, with color photographs and interesting anecdotes. (Rev: BL 9/1/01; HBG 3/02; SLJ 11/01) [971.082]

14711 Blue, Rose, and Corinne J. Naden. *People of Peace* (4–7). Illus. 1994, Millbrook LB $26.90 (1-56294-409-6). 80pp. Brief biographies of 10 people in modern history who have made great sacrifices for world peace, including Mohandas Gandhi and Desmond Tutu. (Rev: BL 12/15/94; SLJ 2/95) [920]

14712 Chin-Lee, Cynthia. *Amelia to Zora: Twenty-Six Women Who Changed the World* (4–7). Illus. 2005, Charlesbridge $15.95 (1-57091-522-9). 32pp.

Brief information on 26 remarkable and varied women (scientists, artists, athletes, inventors) along with beautiful artwork and quotations from the subjects. (Rev: BL 4/1/05; SLJ 4/05) [920.72]

14713 Gulatta, Charles. *Extraordinary Women in Politics* (5–9). Series: Extraordinary People. 1998, Children's Book Pr. LB $37.50 (0-516-20610-9). 288pp. From Cleopatra, Queen Victoria, and Catherine the Great to Margaret Thatcher, Bella Abzug, Sandra Day O'Connor, and Hillary Rodham Clinton, this book profiles 55 women who have had a powerful influence in the world's political arena. (Rev: BL 1/1–15/99; HBG 3/99; SLJ 1/99) [920]

14714 Hacker, Carlotta. *Humanitarians* (3–6). Illus. Series: Women in Profile. 1999, Crabtree LB $15.96 (0-7787-0011-9); paper $8.06 (0-7787-0033-X). 48pp. Six major profiles and 15 brief biographies of female humanitarians, including Helen Keller and Mother Teresa, are included in this informative title. (Rev: BL 9/15/99; SLJ 8/99) [920]

14715 Hacker, Carlotta. *Nobel Prize Winners* (3–6). Illus. Series: Women in Profile. 1998, Crabtree LB $15.96 (0-7787-0007-0); paper $8.06 (0-7787-0029-1). 48pp. In addition to biographies of six female Nobel Prize winners, including Barbara McClintock, Toni Morrison, Marie Curie, and Nadine Gordimer, this collection contains short profiles of dozens of other notables, such as Mother Teresa and Jane Addams. (Rev: BL 9/1/98; SLJ 9/98) [920]

14716 Hacker, Carlotta. *Rebels* (3–6). Series: Women in Profile. 1999, Crabtree LB $15.96 (0-7787-0014-3); paper $8.06 (0-7787-0036-4). 48pp. This work provides six major profiles and 15 brief sketches about women who, throughout history, have challenged the status quo. (Rev: BL 9/15/99; SLJ 8/99) [920]

14717 Hansen, Joyce. *African Princess: The Amazing Lives of Africa's Royal Women* (4–8). Illus. by Laurie McGaw. 2004, Hyperion $16.99 (0-7868-5116-3). 48pp. Fom Hatshepsut of ancient Egypt to Princess Elizabeth of today's Togo, this volume profiles six African women of note. (Rev: BL 9/15/04; SLJ 11/04) [920]

14718 Hazell, Rebecca. *The Barefoot Book of Heroic Children* (4–7). Illus. 2000, Barefoot $19.95 (1-902283-23-6). 96pp. This book presents the lives of 12 heroic children from different times and places, among them Anne Frank, Fanny Mendelssohn, Annie Sullivan, and Iqbal Masih. (Rev: BL 4/15/00) [920]

14719 Hazell, Rebecca. *Heroes: Great Men Through the Ages* (5–8). Illus. 1997, Abbeville $19.95 (0-7892-0289-1). A collection of 12 biographies, from Socrates to Martin Luther King, Jr., and including Shakespeare, Mohandas Gandhi, Leonardo da Vinci, and Jorge Louis Borges. (Rev: SLJ 6/97) [920]

14720 Hazell, Rebecca. *Heroines: Great Women Through the Ages* (5–8). Illus. 1996, Abbeville $19.95 (0-7892-0210-7). This is a collective biography of 12 great women spanning the period from ancient Greece to modern times, including Sacagawea, Madame Sun Yat-Sen, Frido Kahlo, Joan of Arc, Harriet Tubman, and Marie Curie. (Rev: SLJ 12/96) [920]

14721 Humphrey, Sandra McLeod. *Dare to Dream! 25 Extraordinary Lives* (4–7). 2005, Prometheus paper $14.00 (1-59102-280-0). 115pp. Twenty-five individuals — including artists, athletes, politicians, and scientists — who overcame obstacles to achieve greatness are profiled, with information on childhood and adult life. (Rev: BL 3/1/05; SLJ 6/05) [920]

14722 Hunter, Ryan Ann. *In Disguise: Stories of Real Women Spies* (5–8). Illus. 2004, Beyond Words paper $9.95 (1-58270-095-8). 133pp. Profiles 26 women who risked their lives to spy for causes in which they believed, from 1640 to the Cold War. (Rev: SLJ 8/04) [920]

14723 Krull, Kathleen. *Lives of Extraordinary Women: Rulers, Rebels (and What the Neighbors Thought)* (5–8). Illus. Series: Extraordinary Lives. 2000, Harcourt $20.00 (0-15-200807-1). 96pp. Short biographies of women who affected the course of history, from Cleopatra to contemporary Burma's Aung San Suu Kyi. (Rev: BCCB 9/00; BL 9/1/00; HB 11–12/00; HBG 3/01; SLJ 9/00) [920]

14724 Kupferberg, Audrey. *The Spanish-American War* (5–9). Series: People at the Center Of. 2005, Gale/Blackbirch LB $23.70 (1-56711-924-7). 48pp. After an overview of the war, this volume provides biographical information on key figures including Grover Cleveland, William Randolph Hearst, and Theodore Roosevelt. (Rev: SLJ 6/05) [920]

14725 Lace, William W. *Leaders and Generals* (5–10). Series: American War. 2000, Lucent LB $27.45 (1-56006-664-4). 112pp. The following World War II leaders are profiled: Erwin Rommel, Georgi Zhukov, Erich von Manstein, Yamamoto Isoroku, Douglas MacArthur, Chester Nimitz, Dwight Eisenhower, and Bernard Law Montgomery. (Rev: BL 4/15/00; HBG 10/00; SLJ 6/00) [920]

14726 Leon, Vicki. *Outrageous Women of Ancient Times* (4–7). Illus. 1997, Wiley paper $12.95 (0-471-17006-2). 128pp. Fifteen unusual women from ancient civilizations in Asia, Europe, and Africa are profiled, among them warriors, philosophers, empresses, artists, and professional poisoners, and including Cleopatra and Sappho. (Rev: BL 11/1/97; SLJ 12/97) [920]

14727 Leon, Vicki. *Outrageous Women of the Middle Ages* (4–7). Illus. 1998, Wiley paper $12.95 (0-471-17004-6). 128pp. Using a witty writing style and modern comparisons, this fascinating book profiles a diverse group of amazing women who lived from the 6th through the 14th centuries in Europe, Asia, and Africa. (Rev: BL 4/15/98; SLJ 8/98) [920]

14728 McLuskey, Krista. *Entrepreneurs* (3–6). Series: Women in Profile. 1999, Crabtree LB $15.96 (0-7787-0012-7); paper $8.06 (0-7787-0034-8). 48pp. Six female entrepreneurs, including Oprah Winfrey, are profiled here, with brief sketches of 15 more. (Rev: BL 9/15/99) [920]

14729 Marzollo, Jean. *My First Book of Biographies: Great Men and Women Every Child Should Know* (2–4). Illus. by Irene Trivas. 1994, Scholastic $14.95 (0-590-45014-X). 80pp. Brief profiles of 45 famous people whom youngsters have heard about, from Cleopatra to Beatrix Potter. (Rev: BL 12/1/94; SLJ 9/94) [920]

14730 Meltzer, Milton. *Ten Kings and the Worlds They Ruled* (5–8). Illus. by Bethanne Andersen. 2002, Scholastic paper $21.95 (0-439-31293-0). 144pp. Ten kings from around the world and across the ages are discussed in this attractive book that includes impressive portraits and other illustrations. Also use *Ten Queens* (1998). (Rev: BCCB 9/02; BL 7/02; HBG 10/02; SLJ 10/02*) [920.02]

14731 Norris, Kathleen. *The Holy Twins: Benedict and Scholastica* (K–3). Illus. by Tomie dePaola. 2001, Penguin Putnam $16.99 (0-399-23424-1). 32pp. The abbot who became Saint Benedict and founded the Benedictine order is much better known than his twin sister Saint Scholastica, but the story of both siblings' lives is told here with illustrations that evoke Italy in the sixth century. (Rev: BCCB 7–8/01; BL 10/1/01; HBG 3/02; SLJ 9/01) [271]

14732 Parker, Janice. *Political Leaders* (3–6). Illus. 1998, Crabtree LB $15.96 (0-7787-0008-9); paper $8.95 (0-7787-0030-5). 48pp. As well as detailed sketches of Corazon Aquino, Benazir Bhutto, Indira Gandhi, Golda Meir, Margaret Thatcher, and Eva Peron, this book contains shorter profiles of other important female political leaders. (Rev: BL 9/1/98) [920]

14733 Pollard, Michael. *People Who Care* (4–6). Series: Pioneers in History. 1992, Garrett LB $19.93 (1-56074-035-3). 48pp. Nineteen individuals who devoted their lives to helping others are profiled in this book. People who participated in revolutions are covered in *Revolutionary Power* (1992) and great philosophers in *Thinkers* (1992). (Rev: SLJ 9/92) [920]

14734 Roehm, Michelle. *Girls Who Rocked the World 2: Heroines from Harriet Tubman to Mia*

Hamm (4–6). Illus. by Jerry McCann. 2000, Beyond Words paper $8.95 (1-58270-025-7). 160pp. Profiles 30 outstanding women who hailed from many different countries, lived in various time periods, and accomplished advances in a number of fields. (Rev: SLJ 12/00) [920]

14735 Sanderson, Ruth. *Saints: Lives and Illuminations* (4–6). Illus. 2003, Eerdmans $20.00 (0-8028-5220-3). 40pp. The lives and deaths of 40 saints, accompanied by painted portraits. (Rev: BL 2/1/03; HBG 10/03; SLJ 5/03) [270]

14736 Shaw, Maura D. *Ten Amazing People: And How They Changed the World* (4–7). Illus. 2002, Skylight Paths $17.95 (1-893361-47-0). 48pp. Shaw presents 10 well-illustrated biographies of 20th-century religious figures, each with timelines, a quotation, a glossary, and an emphasis on the individual's beliefs. (Rev: BL 10/1/02; HBG 3/03; SLJ 12/02) [200]

14737 Sinnott, Susan. *Extraordinary Asian Americans and Pacific Islanders*. Rev. ed. (5–9). Series: Extraordinary People. 2003, Children's Book Pr. LB $39.00 (0-516-22655-X); paper $16.95 (0-516-29355-9). 288pp. Brief biographies of Asian Americans and Pacific Islanders representing many walks of life are arranged chronologically by date of birth and interspersed with short essays on related topics. (Rev: SLJ 7/03) [920]

14738 Sullivan, George. *In the Line of Fire* (3–6). Illus. 1996, Scholastic paper $3.99 (0-590-48294-7). 118pp. From the American Revolution through World War II, the stories of eight female spies are retold. (Rev: BL 6/1–15/96) [920]

14739 Thimmesh, Catherine. *Madam President: The Extraordinary, True (and Evolving) Story of Women in Politics* (3–6). Illus. by Douglas B. Jones. 2004, Houghton Mifflin $17.00 (0-618-39666-7). 80pp. Profiles more than 20 women who have been influential in the political arena, including Margaret Chase Smith, Nancy Pelosi, Sirimavo Bandaranaike, and Margaret Thatcher. (Rev: BL 10/1/04*; SLJ 11/04) [920]

14740 Welden, Amelie. *Girls Who Rocked the World: Heroines from Sacagawea to Sheryl Swoopes* (4–8). Illus. 1998, Beyond Words paper $8.95 (1-885223-68-4). This collective biography contains short profiles of 33 women who achieved extraordinary things before age 20, arranged chronologically, starting with Cleopatra and ending with tennis star Martina Hingis. (Rev: BL 7/97; SLJ 7/98) [920]

14741 Wilkinson, Philip, and Jacqueline Dineen. *People Who Changed the World* (3–5). Illus. by Robert Ingpen. Series: Turning Points. 1994, Chelsea LB $19.95 (0-7910-2764-3). 93pp. Includes brief biographies of religious leaders, philosophers, and explorers like Pericles, Jesus Christ, Karl Marx, and Martin Luther King, Jr. Also use *Statesmen Who Changed the World* (1994). (Rev: BL 12/15/94) [920]

14742 Wilkinson, Philip, and Michael Pollard. *Generals Who Changed the World* (4–6). Illus. by Robert Ingpen. Series: Turning Points. 1994, Chelsea LB $19.95 (0-7910-2761-9). 93pp. A pro-

file of 20 important military men and how their accomplishments changed the course of history. (Rev: SLJ 11/94) [920]

Individual

ALEXANDER THE GREAT

14743 Greenblatt, Miriam. *Alexander the Great and Ancient Greece* (5–8). Illus. Series: Rulers and Their Times. 1999, Marshall Cavendish LB $28.50 (0-7614-0913-0). 80pp. The first part of this biography introduces Alexander the Great and his accomplishments and the second tells about daily life in ancient Greece. (Rev: BL 1/1–15/00; HBG 10/00; SLJ 2/00) [921]

ALVAREZ, FRANCISCA

14744 Egan, Tracie. *Francisca Alvarez: The Angel of Goliad / El angel de Goliad* (4–6). Trans. by Eida de la Vega. Series: Primary Sources of Famous People in American History. 2004, Rosen LB $21.25 (0-8239-4157-4). 32pp. A brief, solid, bilingual introduction to the Mexican woman who saved more than 20 Texan rebels from being shot during the Texas Revolution. (Rev: SLJ 9/04) [921]

ANIELEWICZ, MORDECHAI

14745 Callahan, Kerry P. *Mordechai Anielewicz: Hero of the Warsaw Uprising* (5–8). Series: Holocaust Biographies. 2001, Rosen LB $26.50 (0-8239-3377-6). 112pp. The story of Anielewicz and other members of the Jewish resistance in the Warsaw ghetto is told in gripping text accompanied by black-and-white photographs. (Rev: BL 10/15/01) [921]

ARAFAT, YASIR

14746 Headlam, George. *Yasser Arafat* (5–8). Series: A&E Biography. 2003, Lerner LB $25.26 (0-8225-5004-0); paper $7.95 (0-8225-9902-3). 112pp. The story of the Palestinian leader, his rise to power, and his current status. (Rev: BL 1/1–15/04; HBG 4/04; SLJ 2/04)

14747 Williams, Colleen Madonna Flood. *Yasir Arafat* (5–8). Illus. 2002, Chelsea $23.95 (0-7910-6941-9); paper $9.95 (0-7910-7186-3). 112pp. The controversial PLO leader is shown as a man of conviction who struggles to balance the desires of his people and of the rest of the world. (Rev: BL 1/1–15/03; HBG 3/03; SLJ 2/03) [956.9405]

ARISTOTLE

14748 Anderson, Margaret J., and Karen F. Stephenson. *Aristotle: Philosopher and Scientist* (5–8). Series: Great Minds of Science. 2004, Enslow LB $20.95 (0-7660-2096-7). 112pp. Aristotle's life, times, and contributions to philosophy and science are examined in concise text. (Rev: SLJ 7/04) [921]

BEGIN, MENACHEM

14749 Brackett, Virginia. *Menachem Begin* (5–8). Series: Major World Leaders. 2002, Chelsea $23.95 (0-7910-6946-X). 104pp. The life of the important Israeli prime minister who was in office when peace was declared between Israel and Egypt. (Rev: BL 1/1–15/03; SLJ 2/03) [921]

BHATT, ELA

14750 Sreenivasan, Jyotsna. *Ela Bhatt: Uniting Women in India* (5–8). Illus. Series: Women Changing the World. 2000, Feminist Pr. $19.95 (1-55861-229-7). 112pp. Inspired by Gandhi, this Indian lawyer founded an organization to help and protect the lives of her country's poorest women and organized a labor union for them. (Rev: BL 9/15/00; HBG 3/01; SLJ 12/00) [921]

BIN LADEN, OSAMA

14751 Loehfelm, Bill. *Osama bin Laden* (5–8). Series: Heroes and Villains. 2003, Gale/Lucent LB $27.45 (1-59018-294-4). 112pp. Examines bin Laden's early life and the factors contributing to the al-Qaeda leader's influence over a number of Islamic fundamentalists. (Rev: SLJ 7/03) [921]

14752 Louis, Nancy. *Osama bin Laden* (4–7). Series: War on Terrorism. 2002, ABDO LB $25.65 (1-57765-663-6). 48pp. A brief biography of the terrorist leader told through a matter-of-fact text and many color photographs. (Rev: BL 5/15/02; HBG 10/02) [921]

14753 Woolf, Alex. *Osama Bin Laden* (5–8). Series: A&E Biography. 2003, Lerner LB $25.26 (0-8225-5003-2); paper $7.95 (0-8225-9900-7). 112pp. The story of the leader of the Al Qaeda terrorist movement and his family background in Saudi Arabia. (Rev: BL 1/1–15/04; HBG 4/04; SLJ 2/04) [921]

BLAIR, TONY

14754 Hinman, Bonnie. *Tony Blair* (5–8). Series: Major World Leaders. 2002, Chelsea $23.95 (0-7910-6939-7). 110pp. A profile of the leader of the British Labour Party who in 1997 became the youngest prime minister in nearly 200 years. (Rev: BL 1/1–15/03) [921]

14755 Wilson, Wayne, and Jim Whiting. *Tony Blair* (3–6). 2002, Mitchell Lane LB $15.95 (1-58415-143-9). 32pp. Blair's colorful youth — as mild rebel and as aspiring rock singer — will draw readers into the story of his later achievements that puts an emphasis on his support of the United States. (Rev: SLJ 12/02) [921]

BONETTA, SARAH FORBES

14756 Myers, Walter Dean. *At Her Majesty's Request: An African Princess in Victorian England* (5–8). Illus. 1999, Scholastic paper $15.95 (0-590-48669-1). The intriguing story of the African princess who at age 7 was saved from becoming a sacrifice and sent her to England, where she became the ward of Queen Victoria. (Rev: BCCB 2/99; BL 4/1/99; HBG 10/99; SLJ 1/99) [921]

BRESNICK-PERRY, ROSLYN

14757 Bresnick-Perry, Roslyn. *Leaving for America* (K–3). Illus. by Mira Reisberg. 1992, Children's Book Pr. $14.95 (0-89239-105-7). 32pp. Remembrances by the author, who left Russia in 1929 as a young child. (Rev: BCCB 2/93; BL 1/15/93; SLJ 2/93) [947]

CAESAR, JULIUS

14758 Green, Robert. *Julius Caesar* (5–8). Series: First Books: Ancient Biographies. 1996, Watts LB $23.00 (0-531-20241-0). The story of Caesar's political and military careers, how he expanded the Roman Empire, and his lasting importance. (Rev: SLJ 2/97) [921]

CALLAHAN, STEVEN

14759 Cefrey, Holly. *Steven Callahan: Adrift at Sea* (4–7). Series: Survivor. 2003, Children's Pr. LB $20.00 (0-516-24330-6); paper $6.95 (0-516-27868-1). 48pp. The exciting story of Callahan's survival after capsizing off Africa, plus the vivd photographs, will appeal to reluctant readers. (Rev: SLJ 2/04) [921]

CAROLINE, PRINCESS OF MONACO

14760 Wheeler, Jill C. *Princess Caroline of Monaco* (4–6). Illus. Series: Leading Ladies. 1992, ABDO LB $13.98 (1-56239-117-8). 32pp. A simple biography of the princess who is the daughter of the late Grace Kelly. (Rev: BL 2/1/93; SLJ 3/93) [921]

CASTRO, FIDEL

14761 Platt, Richard. *Fidel Castro: From Guerrilla to World Statesman* (5–7). Series: Twentieth-Century History Makers. 2003, Raintree LB $32.85 (0-7398-6141-7). 112pp. Platt traces Castro's life from childhood through today, presenting opposing opinions of his achievements in a chapter called "Hero or Monster?" (Rev: HBG 4/04; SLJ 9/03) [973.9106]

14762 Press, Petra. *Fidel Castro: An Unauthorized Biography* (5–7). Series: Heinemann Profiles. 2000, Heinemann LB $24.22 (1-57572-497-9). 56pp. An interesting introduction to the life of Cuba's dictator, with photographs that show urban and rural Cuba. (Rev: SLJ 6/01) [972.91064092]

CHAMPOLLION, JEAN-FRANCOIS

14763 Rumford, James. *Seeker of Knowledge: The Man Who Deciphered Egyptian Hieroglyphs* (3–5). Illus. 2000, Houghton Mifflin $15.00 (0-395-97934-X). 32pp. The story of Jean-Francois Champollion, who studied the Rosetta Stone and found the key to understanding Egyptian hieroglyphs. (Rev: BCCB 4/00; BL 4/15/00; HBG 10/00; SLJ 5/00) [493]

CHRISTOPHER, SAINT

14764 dePaola, Tomie. *Christopher: The Holy Giant* (K–3). Illus. 1994, Holiday House LB $16.95 (0-8234-0862-0). 32pp. The story of Saint Christopher and how Jesus gave him that name for his good works. (Rev: BL 5/1/94; HB 5–6/94; SLJ 3/94*) [398.22]

CHURCHILL, SIR WINSTON

14765 Ashworth, Leon. *Winston Churchill* (5–8). Illus. Series: British History Makers. 2002, Cherry-tree $17.95 (1-84234-072-7). 32pp. A balanced look at the life and career of the British statesman, with a useful timeline and excellent illustrations. (Rev: SLJ 8/02) [941.082092]

14766 Binns, Tristan Boyer. *Winston Churchill* (5–8). Series: Great Life Stories. 2004, Watts LB $29.50 (0-531-12361-8). 127pp. The complex life of Churchill is well portrayed in this biography that covers his youth and career, triumphs and losses, and many and varied interests. (Rev: SLJ 3/05) [921]

14767 Driemen, J. E. *Winston Churchill: An Unbreakable Spirit* (5–8). Illus. Series: People in Focus. 1990, Macmillan LB $13.95 (0-87518-434-0). 128pp. A biography of this amazing statesman, leader, and writer. (Rev: SLJ 8/90) [921]

14768 MacDonald, Fiona. *Winston Churchill* (5–8). Series: Trailblazers of the Modern World. 2003, World Almanac LB $26.60 (0-8368-5082-3). 48pp. An appealing biography of Churchill, with plenty of black-and-white photographs, that reveals his youthful deficiencies as well as his adult accomplishments. (Rev: SLJ 8/03) [921]

14769 Severance, John B. *Winston Churchill: Soldier, Statesman, Artist* (5–8). Illus. 1996, Clarion $17.95 (0-395-69853-7). A well-organized, clearly written account of the life and works of Britain's great statesman. (Rev: BL 4/15/96; HB 7–8/96; SLJ 4/96*) [941.084]

CIARAN, SAINT

14770 Schmidt, Gary D. *Saint Ciaran: The Tale of a Saint of Ireland* (3–5). Illus. 2000, Eerdmans $18.00 (0-8028-5170-3). 40pp. The story of the gentle sixth-century Irish saint who, after journeying to Rome, went back to his home country to build a church. (Rev: BL 4/1/00; HBG 10/00; SLJ 8/00) [921]

CLEOPATRA

14771 Middleton, Haydn. *Cleopatra* (1–3). Series: What's Their Story? 1998, Oxford LB $12.95 (0-19-521404-8). In simple language with color illustrations, the author presents the story of Cleopatra, her dreams of restoring her country's glory, and the tragedy that ensued. (Rev: BL 5/15/98; HBG 10/98; SLJ 9/98) [921]

14772 Streissguth, Thomas. *Queen Cleopatra* (4–7). Series: A&E Biography. 2000, Lerner LB $25.26 (0-8225-4946-8). 112pp. The story of Cleopatra and

her impact on world history. (Rev: BL 3/15/00; HBG 10/00; SLJ 5/00) [921]

COLUMBA, SAINT

14773 Brown, Don. *Across a Dark and Wild Sea* (K–4). Illus. 2002, Millbrook LB $22.90 (0-7613-2415-1). 32pp. The story of the sixth-century Irish monk and scholar Columcille, or Saint Columba, who founded a monastery on the Scottish island of Iona. (Rev: BCCB 5/02; BL 4/1/02*; HB 5–6/02; HBG 10/02; SLJ 5/02) [921]

CONFUCIUS

14774 Freedman, Russell. *Confucius: The Golden Rule* (4–8). Illus. by Frederic Clement. 2002, Scholastic paper $15.95 (0-439-13957-0). 48pp. This absorbing account of the life and philosophy of Confucius gives new insight into the character of the man who had so much influence on China. (Rev: BL 10/1/02*; HB 1–2/03; HBG 3/03; SLJ 9/02*) [181]

DALAI LAMA

14775 Demi. *The Dalai Lama* (3–6). Illus. by author. 1998, Holt $17.95 (0-8050-5443-X). This biography of the contemporary, now-exiled, Dalai Lama also supplies details of his functions, mission, and responsibilities. (Rev: BCCB 4/98; HB 3–4/98; HBG 10/98; SLJ 3/98) [921]

14776 Gibb, Chris. *The Dalai Lama* (4–6). Series: Famous Lives. 2003, Raintree LB $27.12 (0-7398-5520-4). 48pp. The story of Tibet's exiled political and spiritual leader and of his teachings of peace and civil disobedience. (Rev: BL 2/15/03; HBG 10/03; SLJ 5/03) [921]

14777 Stewart, Whitney. *The 14th Dalai Lama: Spiritual Leader of Tibet* (5–8). Series: Newsmakers. 1996, Lerner LB $30.35 (0-8225-4926-3). As well as describing the life and spiritual beliefs of the 14th Dalai Lama, this account describes the political situation in Tibet at the time. (Rev: SLJ 6/96) [921]

DALOKAY, VEDAT

14778 Dalokay, Vedat. *Sister Shako and Kolo the Goat: Memories of My Childhood in Turkey* (5–7). Trans. by Guner Ener. 1994, Lothrop $14.00 (0-688-13271-5). 96pp. A memoir by the former mayor of Ankara about growing up Muslim in rural Turkey in the 1930s and his friendship with an indomitable widow named Sister Shako. (Rev: BCCB 4/94; BL 5/1/94; SLJ 6/94) [921]

DE GAULLE, CHARLES

14779 Whitelaw, Nancy. *Charles de Gaulle: "I Am France"* (5–8). 1991, Dillon LB $13.95 (0-87518-486-3). Details the life and accomplishments of France's controversial leader. (Rev: BL 2/15/92) [921]

DE PORTOLA, GASPAR

14780 Whiting, Jim. *Gaspar de Portola* (5–7). Series: Latinos in American History. 2002, Mitchell Lane LB $19.95 (1-58415-148-X). 48pp. The story of the Latino governor of "Las Californias" from 1768 to 1770 who was responsible for expelling Jesuits from the area. (Rev: BL 2/15/03; HBG 10/03) [921]

DIANA, PRINCESS OF WALES

14781 Brennan, Kristine. *Diana, Princess of Wales* (5–8). Series: Women of Achievement. 1998, Chelsea $21.95 (0-7910-4714-8); paper $9.95 (0-7910-4715-6). This book covers the facts about Diana's life, disappointing marriage, struggle for happiness, and untimely death. (Rev: HBG 3/99) [921]

14782 Licata, Renora. *Princess Diana: Royal Ambassador* (4–6). Illus. Series: The Library of Famous Women. 1993, Blackbirch LB $17.95 (1-56711-013-4). 64pp. Princess Diana comes alive in this account that covers her celebrity status and her public service work. (Rev: BL 6/1–15/93; SLJ 8/93) [921]

14783 Oleksy, Walter. *Princess Diana* (5–8). Series: People in the News. 2001, Lucent LB $27.45 (1-56006-579-6). A well-documented life of this tragic, troubled princess, with many quotations and black-and-white photographs. (Rev: BCCB 10/98; BL 4/1/02; HBG 3/01) [921]

14784 Wood, Richard. *Diana: The People's Princess* (4–7). Illus. 1998, Raintree paper $7.95 (0-8172-7849-4). 48pp. A biography that reveals some personal information about this multifaceted woman and details the many causes she supported. (Rev: BL 7/98; HBG 10/98; SLJ 8/98) [921]

ELIZABETH I, QUEEN OF ENGLAND

14785 Green, Robert. *Queen Elizabeth I* (4–7). Illus. Series: First Books. 1997, Watts LB $23.00 (0-531-20302-6). 64pp. This account of the life of Elizabeth I also includes material on the religious conflicts of the day, her suitors, and the war with Spain. (Rev: BL 2/1/98; HBG 3/98; SLJ 1/98) [921]

14786 Havelin, Kate. *Elizabeth I* (5–8). Series: Biography. 2002, Lerner LB $25.26 (0-8225-0029-9). 112pp. The story of one of the most powerful queens in history and how she learned, at an early age, the politics of survival. (Rev: BCCB 12/99; BL 6/1–15/02; HBG 10/02; SLJ 7/02) [921]

14787 Stanley, Diane, and Peter Vennema. *Good Queen Bess: The Story of Elizabeth of England* (4–6). Illus. 1990, Macmillan LB $16.95 (0-02-786810-9). 40pp. An excellent biography of Elizabeth I, with emphasis on understanding the reasons for her actions in the context of the time. (Rev: BCCB 10/90; BL 9/1/90*; HB 1–2/91*; SLJ 12/90) [921]

14788 Thomas, Jane Resh. *Behind the Mask: The Life of Queen Elizabeth I* (5–8). Illus. 1998, Clarion $20.00 (0-395-69120-6). 196pp. A behind-the-scenes look at the long-lived queen, discussing her childhood, how she overcame opposition to become queen, and her subsequent manipulation of people, the court, and foreigners to attain greatness. (Rev: BL 12/15/98; BR 5–6/99; HB 1–2/99; HBG 3/99; SLJ 12/98*) [921]

ELIZABETH II, QUEEN OF ENGLAND

14789 Barton-Wood, Sara. *Queen Elizabeth II: Monarch of Our Times* (4–6). Illus. Series: Famous Lives. 2001, Raintree LB $18.98 (0-7398-4430-X). 48pp. An affectionate look at the life of Queen Elizabeth II, from childhood through her Golden Jubilee. (Rev: BL 1/1–15/02; HBG 10/02; SLJ 3/02) [941.085]

14790 Green, Robert. *Queen Elizabeth II* (4–6). Illus. Series: First Books. 1997, Watts LB $32.50 (0-531-20303-4). 64pp. This account tells about Elizabeth's childhood during World War II, how she came to the throne, and changes that have occurred during her reign. (Rev: BL 12/1/97; HBG 3/98; SLJ 12/97) [921]

14791 Malam, John. *Queen Elizabeth II* (2–4). Series: Tell Me About: Kings and Queens. 2002, Evans Brothers LB $13.95 (0-237-52394-9). 22pp. This brief account of the queen's life and reign includes plenty of photographs. (Rev: SLJ 10/02) [921]

FOX, VICENTE

14792 Paprocki, Sherry Beck. *Vicente Fox* (5–8). Series: Major World Leaders. 2002, Chelsea $23.95 (0-7910-6944-3). 104pp. The story of the man who became president of Mexico in July 2000, the first opposition candidate to gain presidential office in more than 70 years. (Rev: BL 1/1–15/03) [921]

FRANCIS OF ASSISI, SAINT

14793 dePaola, Tomie. *Francis: The Poor Man of Assisi* (4–7). Illus. by author. 1982, Holiday House $18.95 (0-8234-0435-8); paper $9.95 (0-8234-0812-4). 48pp. A simple retelling of the life of St. Francis with fine pictures by dePaola. [921]

14794 Kennedy, Robert F., Jr. *Saint Francis of Assisi: A Life of Joy* (2–4). Illus. by Dennis Nolan. 2005, Hyperion $18.99 (0-7868-1875-1). 31pp. Environmental activist Robert F. Kennedy Jr. chronicles the life of Saint Francis of Assisi, his patron saint. (Rev: BL 2/15/05; SLJ 5/05) [921]

14795 Wildsmith, Brian. *Saint Francis* (1–3). Illus. 1996, Eerdmans $20.00 (0-8028-5123-1). 36pp. A large-size picture book that tells the story of St. Francis as a first-person narrative with a biographical note following the story. (Rev: BCCB 7–8/96; BL 1/1–15/96; SLJ 2/96) [921]

FRANK, ANNE

14796 Adler, David A. *A Picture Book of Anne Frank* (2–4). Illus. by Karen Ritz. 1993, Holiday House LB $16.95 (0-8234-1003-X). 32pp. A simple biography for young readers. (Rev: BCCB 3/93; BL 3/1/93; SLJ 5/93) [921]

14797 Alagna, Magdalena. *Anne Frank: Young Voice of the Holocaust* (5–8). Series: Holocaust Biographies. 2001, Rosen LB $26.50 (0-8239-3373-3). 112pp. This book describes Anne's childhood, her time spent in hiding, her diary, and her life in the concentration camps. (Rev: BL 10/15/01) [921]

14798 Frank, Anne. *Anne Frank: The Diary of a Young Girl* (5–8). 1967, Pocket paper $3.95 (0-685-05466-7). 312pp. The moving diary of a young Jewish girl hiding from the Nazis in World War II Amsterdam. [921]

14799 Gold, Alison L. *Memories of Anne Frank: Reflections of a Childhood Friend* (4–8). Illus. 1997, Scholastic paper $16.95 (0-590-90722-0). Anne Frank's story as told through recollections of her best friend in Amsterdam, Hannah Goslar, a survivor of the Holocaust. (Rev: BL 9/1/97; BR 11–12/97; HBG 3/98; SLJ 11/97) [921]

14800 Hurwitz, Johanna. *Anne Frank: Life in Hiding* (4–7). Illus. by Vera Rosenberry. 1989, Jewish Publication Soc. $13.95 (0-8276-0311-8). 64pp. This biography describes Anne's life in hiding. (Rev: BL 4/15/89) [921]

14801 Lee, Carol Ann. *Anne Frank's Story: Her Life Retold for Children* (4–6). 2002, Troll paper $4.95 (0-8167-7427-7). 105pp. Anne's brief life is chronicled here in clear text with black-and-white photographs, a letter to a pen pal, and information on memorials around the world. (Rev: SLJ 11/02) [921]

14802 Poole, Josephine. *Anne Frank* (4–7). Illus. by Angela Barrett. 2005, Knopf LB $19.99 (0-375-93242-9). 40pp. This picture-book biography for older readers presents Anne's story clear text and haunting illustrations. (Rev: BL 6/1–15/05) [921]

14803 Sawyer, Kem Knapp. *Anne Frank: A Photographic Story of a Life* (5–10). Illus. Series: DK Biography. 2004, DK LB $14.99 (0-7566-0341-2); paper $4.99 (0-7566-0490-7). 128pp. This richly illustrated biography draws on Anne's diary and accounts by her father and by Miep Gies. (Rev: BL 6/1–15/04) [921]

GANDHI, MAHATMA

14804 Barraclough, John. *Mohandas Gandhi* (2–3). Illus. Series: Lives and Times. 1997, Heinemann $19.92 (1-57572-561-4). 24pp. A simple picture-book biography that tells of Gandhi's work in South Africa and his struggle against British rule in India. (Rev: BL 3/15/98) [921]

14805 Claybourne, Anna. *Gandhi* (4–6). Series: Famous Lives. 2003, Raintree LB $27.12 (0-7398-5521-2). 48pp. A brief biography of the Indian leader, his triumphs and hardships, and the story of the nonviolent movement he led. (Rev: BCCB 12/01; BL 2/15/03; HBG 10/03; SLJ 5/03) [921]

14806 Demi. *Gandhi* (3–6). Illus. 2001, Simon & Schuster $19.95 (0-689-84149-3). 40pp. A moving look at a remarkable man that brings to life his character and the time in which he lived. (Rev: BCCB 12/01; BL 6/1–15/01; HB 9–10/01; HBG 3/02; SLJ 8/01) [954.03]

14807 Heinrichs, Ann. *Mahatma Gandhi* (4–7). Series: Trailblazers of the Modern World. 2001, World Almanac LB $29.26 (0-8368-5064-5). 48pp. A clear and concise biography that focuses on Gandhi's personal life as well as his struggles to free India and belief in nonviolence. (Rev: SLJ 1/02) [921]

14808 Martin, Christopher. *Mohandas Gandhi* (4–7). Series: A&E Biography. 2000, Lucent LB $25.26 (0-8225-4984-0). 112pp. The story of the man who sought to unite and free his people not through violence but by prayer, civil disobedience, and communication. (Rev: BL 12/15/00; HBG 3/01; SLJ 1/01) [921]

14809 Mitchell, Pratima. *Gandhi: The Father of Modern India* (3–5). Illus. Series: What's Their Story? 1998, Oxford LB $12.95 (0-19-521434-X). 32pp. A biography of Gandhi that stresses his peaceful efforts to persuade the British to leave India. (Rev: BL 2/15/99; HBG 3/99; SLJ 4/99) [921]

14810 Shaw, Maura D. *Gandhi: India's Great Soul* (3–6). Illus. by Stephen Marchesi. Series: Spiritual Biographies for Young Readers. 2004, Skylight Paths $12.95 (1-893361-91-8). 32pp. An overview of Gandhi's life and beliefs is followed by discussion of how his ideals remain relevant and achievable. (Rev: BL 2/15/04; SLJ 9/04) [921]

14811 Wilkinson, Philip. *Gandhi: The Young Protestor Who Founded a Nation* (4–7). Illus. Series: World History Biographies. 2005, National Geographic LB $27.90 (0-7922-3648-3). 64pp. Gandhi's character shines through the straightforward text and interesting anecdotes in this biography that gives historical context plus maps and photographs. (Rev: BL 6/1–15/05) [954.03]

GEORGE III, KING OF ENGLAND

14812 Green, Robert. *King George III* (4–6). Series: First Books. 1997, Watts LB $22.50 (0-531-20333-6). 64pp. An objective account of the life of the troubled monarch whose policies toward his colonies caused the American Revolution. (Rev: BL 12/15/97; HBG 3/98; SLJ 12/97) [921]

HANH, THICH NHAT

14813 Shaw, Maura D. *Thich Nhat Hanh: Buddhism in Action* (4–6). Illus. by Stephen Marchesi. Series: Spiritual Biographies for Young Readers. 2004, Skylight Paths $12.95 (1-893361-87-X). 32pp. This brief biography of the Vietnamese Buddhist monk touches lightly on his anti-war activism; it offers an introduction to the benefits of peace and tranquility. (Rev: BL 2/1/04; SLJ 9/04) [294.3]

HANNIBAL

14814 Green, Robert. *Hannibal* (5–8). Series: First Books: Ancient Biographies. 1996, Watts LB $22.00 (0-531-20240-2). An engrossing account of the military genius who trekked through the Alps with elephants and threatened to topple the might of the Roman Empire. (Rev: SLJ 2/97) [921]

HENRY VIII, KING OF ENGLAND

14815 Green, Robert. *King Henry VIII* (4–6). Illus. Series: First Books. 1998, Watts LB $21.00 (0-531-20305-0). 64pp. A biography of the much-married Tudor king, sketching his life, his wives, and the world in which he lived. (Rev: BL 6/1–15/98; HBG 10/98) [921]

HITLER, ADOLF

14816 Ayer, Eleanor. *Adolf Hitler* (4–8). Illus. Series: The Importance Of. 1996, Lucent LB $27.45 (1-56006-072-7). 128pp. This study of Hitler's rise and impact on Germany and the world includes analyses of the dictator's mental state, leadership qualities, and personality traits. (Rev: BL 3/15/96; SLJ 1/96) [921]

HUSSEIN, SADDAM

14817 Anderson, Dale. *Saddam Hussein* (5–8). Series: A&E Biography. 2003, Lerner LB $25.26 (0-8225-5005-9); paper $7.95 (0-8225-9901-5). 112pp. This biography of the Iraqi despot tells his story up to the decision that led to the American invasion. (Rev: BL 1/1–15/04; HBG 4/04; SLJ 2/04) [921]

14818 Shields, Charles J. *Saddam Hussein* (5–8). Illus. Series: Major World Leaders. 2002, Chelsea $22.95 (0-7910-6943-5). 112pp. An account of the Iraqi leader's regime, with information on the Iran-Iraq and Persian Gulf wars and on United Nations sanctions and weapons inspections. (Rev: BL 2/1/03; HBG 3/03; SLJ 4/03) [956.7044]

JOAN OF ARC

14819 Bunson, Margaret, and Matthew Bunson. *St. Joan of Arc* (4–6). Illus. Series: Saints You Should Know. 1992, Sunday Visitor paper $5.95 (0-87973-558-9). 56pp. A clear, unsentimental portrait of the saint who lost her life trying to save her country. (Rev: BL 1/1/93) [921]

14820 Corey, Shana. *Joan of Arc* (2–3). Illus. by Dan Andreasen. Series: Step into Reading. 2003, Random paper $3.99 (0-375-80620-2). 48pp. The dramatic story of Joan of Arc is presented in picture-book form for beginning readers. (Rev: BL 7/03; HBG 4/04) [921]

14821 Hodges, Margaret. *Joan of Arc: The Lily Maid* (2–4). Illus. by Robert Rayevsky. 1999, Holiday House $16.95 (0-8234-1424-8). A simple, understandable account of the life of Joan of Arc and her devotion and bravery. (Rev: BL 11/1/99*; HBG 3/00; SLJ 9/99) [921]

14822 Lee, William W. *Joan of Arc and the Hundred Years' War in World History* (5–9). Series: In World History. 2003, Enslow LB $20.95 (0-7660-1938-1). 128pp. This combination of biography and history tells the story of Joan of Arc and gives details on the long conflict between France and England. (Rev: BL 6/1–15/03; HBG 10/03; SLJ 9/03) [921]

14823 Poole, Josephine. *Joan of Arc* (K–3). Illus. by Angela Barrett. 1998, Knopf LB $19.99 (0-679-99041-0). 32pp. A lovely picture book that highlights the life of Joan of Arc, with emphasis on her courage and sense of purpose. (Rev: BCCB 9/98; BL 8/98*; HBG 3/99; SLJ 9/98) [921]

14824 Roberts, Jeremy. *Saint Joan of Arc* (4–6). Series: A&E Biography. 2000, Lerner LB $25.26 (0-8225-4981-6). 112pp. The story of a young woman whose honesty, devotion, and courage inspired an army, a king, and eventually a country to follow her. (Rev: BL 6/1–15/00; HBG 10/00) [921]

14825 Stanley, Diane. *Joan of Arc* (4–8). Illus. 1998, Morrow $16.89 (0-688-14330-X). Using glorious illustrations, this picture book for older readers gives a detailed history of the life and times of Joan of Arc. (Rev: BCCB 9/98; BL 8/98; HB 9–10/98*; HBG 3/99; SLJ 9/98) [921]

14826 Tompert, Ann. *Joan of Arc: Heroine of France* (1–4). Illus. by Michael Garland. 2003, Boyds Mills $15.95 (1-59078-009-4). 32pp. This solid account puts the events in Joan's life in clear historical context. (Rev: BL 3/1/03; HBG 10/03; SLJ 3/03) [944]

JOHN PAUL II, POPE

14827 Mohan, Claire J. *The Young Life of Pope John Paul II* (4–6). Illus. 1995, Young Sparrow $14.95 (0-943135-11-7); paper $7.95 (0-943135-12-5). 64pp. The story of Pope John Paul II when he was Karol Wojtyla growing up in Poland. (Rev: BL 9/1/95; SLJ 11/95) [921]

JUAREZ, BENITO

14828 Palacios, Argentina. *Viva Mexico! A Story of Benito Juarez and Cinco de Mayo* (2–4). Illus. by Howard Berelson. 1993, Raintree LB $25.69 (0-8114-7214-0). 32pp. For very young readers, this is a simple biography of the man often referred to as the architect of modern Mexico. (Rev: BL 5/15/93; SLJ 7/93) [921]

KELLY, EMMETT SR.

14829 Wilkerson, J. L. *Sad-Face Clown: Emmett Kelly* (5–8). Illus. Series: The Great Heartlanders. 2004, Acorn paper $9.95 (0-9664470-9-3). 118pp. The story of Emmett Kelly, Sr., who — as Weary Willie — became possibly the world's most famous circus clown. (Rev: SLJ 4/04) [791.3]

KHERDIAN, JERON

14830 Kherdian, Jeron. *The Road from Home: The Story of an Armenian Girl* (6–8). 1979, Greenwillow $15.89 (0-688-84205-4); Morrow paper $5.95 (0-688-14425-X). 256pp. A memoir of a survivor of the Turkish slaughter of Armenians. [921]

KOLBE, SAINT MAXIMILIAN

14831 Mohan, Claire J. *Saint Maximilian Kolbe: The Story of the Two Crowns* (4–8). Illus. 1999, Young Sparrow paper $8.95 (0-962-15003-7). 72pp. The story of a Polish Catholic monk who took the place of a fellow prisoner who was condemned to die at Auschwitz. (Rev: BL 2/1/00) [921]

KOLLEK, TEDDY

14832 Rabinovich, Abraham. *Teddy Kollek: Builder of Jerusalem* (5–8). Illus. 1996, Jewish Publication Soc. $14.95 (0-8276-0559-5); paper $9.95 (0-8276-0561-7). The story of the former mayor of Jerusalem, who supervised the city's unification after the Six Days War in 1967. (Rev: BL 5/15/96; BR 9–10/96) [921]

KORCZAK, JANUSZ

14833 Adler, David A. *A Hero and the Holocaust: The Story of Janusz Korczak and His Children* (3–5). Illus. by Bill Farnsworth. 2002, Holiday House $16.95 (0-8234-1548-1). 32pp. The story of Janusz Korczak's efforts to care for young Jewish children in the Warsaw ghetto and on the trip to the Treblinka death camp, presented in memorable illustrations and a simple text, accompanied by quotes from his diary. (Rev: BL 12/1/02; HBG 3/03; SLJ 3/03) [943.8]

KOSSMAN, NINA

14834 Kossman, Nina. *Behind the Border* (5–7). 1994, Lothrop $14.00 (0-688-13494-7). 128pp. This book contains 12 episodes about the author's childhood in Communist Russia before emigrating to the United States. (Rev: BCCB 10/94; BL 8/94; SLJ 10/94) [921]

LAFAYETTE, MARQUIS DE

14835 Collins, Kathleen. *Marquis De Lafayette: French Hero of the American Revolution* (2–4). Illus. Series: Primary Sources of Famous People in American History. 2004, Rosen LB $21.25 (0-8239-4115-9). 32pp. Primary sources — including maps and paintings — tell the story of Lafayette's contributions to the revolution. [921]

14836 Fritz, Jean. *Why Not, Lafayette?* (5–8). Illus. 1999, Penguin Putnam $16.99 (0-399-23411-X). Using plenty of quotations, interesting anecdotes, and dry humor, this is a fine biography of General Lafayette, the French-born hero of the American Revolution. (Rev: BCCB 12/99; BL 9/15/99; HB 11–12/99; HBG 3/00; SLJ 12/99) [921]

14837 Payan, Gregory. *Marquis de Lafayette: French Hero of the American Revolution* (4–7). Illus. Series: Library of American Lives and Times. 2001, Rosen $23.95 (0-8239-5733-0). 112pp. Payan introduces the French general who assisted the American cause, with illustrations, maps, and other aids to understanding his times. (Rev: BL 10/15/01) [944.04]

LEKUTON, JOSEPH LEMASOLAI

14838 Lekuton, Joseph Lemasolai. *Facing the Lion: Growing Up Maasai on the African Savanna* (5–12). 2003, National Geographic $15.95 (0-7922-5125-3). 144pp. Lekuton, a member of a nomadic Masai tribe and now a teacher in Virginia, remembers his youth in Kenya. (Rev: BL 9/15/03; HBG 4/04; SLJ 10/03*) [967.62]

MANDELA, NELSON

14839 Connolly, Sean. *Nelson Mandela: An Unauthorized Biography* (5–7). 2000, Heinemann LB $24.22 (1-57572-225-9). 56pp. An appealing biography that contains good background material on South Africa, past and present. (Rev: SLJ 1/01) [921]

14840 Cooper, Floyd. *Mandela: From the Life of the South African Statesman* (2–4). Illus. 1996, Penguin Putnam $15.99 (0-399-22942-6). 40pp. A picture-book biography that focuses on Mandela's childhood and youth. (Rev: BL 9/15/96; SLJ 11/96*) [921]

14841 Finlayson, Reggie. *Nelson Mandela* (4–8). Illus. Series: A&E Biography. 1999, Lerner LB $25.26 (0-8225-4936-0). 112pp. An overview that concentrates on Mandela's childhood, his training as a lawyer, and his rise through the ranks of the African National Congress, with only brief coverage of his imprisonment, release, and presidency. (Rev: BL 2/15/00; HBG 3/99; SLJ 2/99) [921]

14842 Holland, Gini. *Nelson Mandela* (2–4). Illus. by Mike White. Series: First Biographies. 1997, Raintree LB $24.26 (0-8172-4454-9). 32pp. A simple retelling of Nelson Mandela's life from his childhood as the son of a black chieftain to his release from prison in 1990 and resumption of his political career. (Rev: SLJ 2/98) [921]

14843 Pogrund, Benjamin. *Nelson Mandela* (5–10). Illus. Series: World Peacemakers. 2004, Gale LB $27.44 (1-56711-978-6). 64pp. As well as a fine biography of Mandela, this book gives a concise history of apartheid in South Africa. (Rev: BL 2/15/04; SLJ 5/04) [921]

14844 Roberts, Jack L. *Nelson Mandela: Determined to Be Free* (2–4). Illus. Series: Gateway Biographies. 1995, Millbrook LB $20.90 (1-56294-558-0). 48pp. A short, direct biography illustrated by numerous photographs. (Rev: BL 5/1/95) [921]

14845 Strazzabosco, Jeanne M. *Learning About Forgiveness from the Life of Nelson Mandela* (2–5). Illus. Series: Character Building Book. 1996, Rosen LB $16.95 (0-8239-2413-0). 24pp. Covers, in a small-format book, the life of this South African hero and politician who fought successfully against apartheid. (Rev: BL 10/15/96; SLJ 11/96) [921]

MARSHAL, WILLIAM

14846 Weatherly, Myra. *William Marshal: Medieval England's Greatest Knight* (5–8). Illus. 2001, Morgan Reynolds LB $21.95 (1-883846-48-X). 112pp. The story of the brave medieval English knight whose accomplishments numbered fighting in tournaments, traveling to the Holy Land, helping to draw up the Magna Carta, and serving as regent when Henry III was a child. (Rev: BCCB 3/01; BL 1/1–15/01; HBG 10/01; SLJ 3/01) [921]

MILLMAN, ISAAC

14847 Millman, Isaac. *Hidden Child* (4–7). Illus. 2005, Farrar $18.00 (0-374-33071-9). 80pp. The author relates his experiences as a child in World War II, when he was hidden in various homes in France to save him from the Nazis. (Rev: BL 6/1–15/05) [921]

MONTESSORI, MARIA

14848 O'Connor, Barbara. *Mammolina: A Story About Maria Montessori* (3–6). Illus. by Sara Campitelli. Series: Creative Minds. 1993, Carolrhoda LB $18.95 (0-87614-743-0). 64pp. Describes the life of the educational philosopher who developed revolutionary ideas on child development and their application in schools. (Rev: BCCB 4/93; BL 4/1/93; SLJ 4/93) [921]

14849 Shephard, Marie T. *Maria Montessori: Teacher of Teachers* (5–7). Illus. 1996, Lerner LB $30.35 (0-8225-4952-2). 128pp. A biography of the Italian educator and her unusual teaching methods for the young. (Rev: BL 8/96; SLJ 9/96) [921]

MORRIS, SAMUEL

14850 Jackson, Dave, and Neta Jackson. *Quest for the Lost Prince* (3–6). Illus. by Julian Jackson. Series: Trailblazer. 1996, Bethany House paper $5.99 (1-55661-472-1). 144pp. The true story of an African prince, born in 1872, who became a Christian and came to the United States. (Rev: BL 10/1/96) [921]

MUGABE, ROBERT

14851 Worth, Richard. *Robert Mugabe of Zimbabwe* (5–8). Illus. Series: In Focus Biographies. 1990, Silver Burdett LB $13.95 (0-671-68987-8); paper $7.95 (0-671-70684-5). 111pp. Tells the story of Zimbabwe's first prime minister, along with a history of this emerging country. (Rev: SLJ 2/91) [921]

MUHAMMAD

14852 Demi. *Muhammad* (4–7). Illus. 2003, Simon & Schuster $19.95 (0-689-85264-9). 48pp. This readable account of the life of the founding prophet of Islam is accompanied by quotations from the Koran and intricate illustrations. (Rev: BL 6/1–15/03*; HB 7–8/03; HBG 4/04; SLJ 8/03) [297.6]

14853 Marston, Elsa. *Muhammad of Mecca: Prophet of Islam* (4–6). Series: Book Report Biographies. 2001, Watts LB $22.00 (0-531-15554-4). 28pp. A concise, well-researched biography of the seventh-century prophet and founder of one of the world's great religions. (Rev: BL 8/1/01; SLJ 9/01) [921]

NIGHTINGALE, FLORENCE

14854 Adler, David A. *A Picture Book of Florence Nightingale* (K–3). Illus. by John Wallner. Series: Picture Book Biographies. 1992, Holiday House LB $16.95 (0-8234-0965-1). 32pp. Through simple text and illustrations that supply details of time and place, the life of this gallant nurse is introduced. (Rev: BL 11/15/92; SLJ 10/92) [921]

14855 Armentrout, David, and Patricia Armentrout. *Florence Nightingale* (2–4). Illus. Series: People Who Made a Difference. 2001, Rourke LB $18.60 (1-58952-053-X). 24pp. A simple introduction for younger readers to the life of nursing pioneer Florence Nightingale. (Rev: BL 1/1–15/02; SLJ 3/02) [610.73]

14856 Barnham, Kay. *Florence Nightingale* (4–6). Series: Famous Lives. 2003, Raintree LB $27.12 (0-7398-5523-9). 48pp. The inspirational story of the gallant nurse who treated the wounded soldiers on the front lines during the Crimean War. (Rev: BL 2/15/03; HBG 10/03; SLJ 7/03) [921]

14857 Gorrell, Gena K. *Heart and Soul: The Story of Florence Nightingale* (5–8). Illus. 2000, Tundra $18.95 (0-88776-494-0). 146pp. A readable biography of Florence Nightingale that details her drive and determination and how she became known as "the lady with the lamp." (Rev: BL 1/1–15/01; HB 1–2/01; HBG 3/01; SLJ 12/00) [921]

O'GRADY, SCOTT

14858 Somervill, Barbara A. *Scott O'Grady: Behind Enemy Lines* (4–7). Series: Survivor. 2003, Children's Pr. LB $20.00 (0-516-24332-2); paper $6.95 (0-516-27871-1). 48pp. The story of O'Grady's success in escaping detection for six days after being shot down over Bosnia. (Rev: SLJ 2/04) [949.703]

PAHLAVI, MOHAMMED REZA

14859 Barth, Linda. *Mohammed Reza Pahlavi* (5–8). Series: Major World Leaders. 2002, Chelsea $23.95 (0-7910-6948-6). 104pp. An engrossing biography of the last Shah of Iran, who ruled during a tumultuous time in the region. (Rev: BL 1/1–15/03) [921]

PATRICK, SAINT

14860 dePaola, Tomie. *Patrick: Patron Saint of Ireland* (PS–3). Illus. 1992, Holiday House LB $16.95 (0-8234-0924-4). 32pp. Simple text and glowing pictures portray the life of Ireland's saint. (Rev: BCCB 4/92; BL 3/15/92; HB 9–10/92; SLJ 5/92) [921]

PETER THE GREAT

14861 Greenblatt, Miriam. *Peter the Great and Tsarist Russia* (5–8). Illus. Series: Rulers and Their Times. 1999, Marshall Cavendish LB $28.50 (0-7614-0914-9). 80pp. A biography of the czar who westernized Russia is followed by a section on daily life during his reign. (Rev: BL 1/1–15/00; HBG 10/00; SLJ 2/00) [921]

PETIT, PHILIPPE

14862 Gerstein, Mordicai. *The Man Who Walked Between the Towers* (PS–3). Illus. by author. 2003, Millbrook LB $24.90 (0-7613-2868-8). This beautifully illustrated book vividly captures the day in 1974 when French aerialist Philippe Petit performed tricks on a high wire strung between the twin towers of New York City's World Trade Center. Caldecott Medal, 2004. (Rev: HB 11–12/03; HBG 4/04; SLJ 11/03) [921]

PULASKI, CASIMIR

14863 Collins, David R. *Casimir Pulaski: Soldier on Horsback* (4–8). Illus. 1995, Pelican $14.95 (1-56554-082-4). A smoothly written biography of the Polish patriot who, though he could scarcely speak English, became an important figure helping the colonists during the Revolutionary War. (Rev: BL 2/15/96) [921]

PUTIN, VLADIMIR

14864 Shields, Charles J. *Vladimir Putin* (5–8). Illus. Series: Major World Leaders. 2002, Chelsea $22.95 (0-7910-6945-1). 112pp. Putin's family life, ambitions to be a spy, and accession to power are all covered in this fine biography. (Rev: BL 2/1/03; HBG 3/03; SLJ 3/03) [947.086]

RAMPHELE, MAMPHELA

14865 Harlan, Judith. *Mamphela Ramphele: Challenging Apartheid in South Africa* (5–8). Illus. Series: Women Changing the World. 2000, Feminist Pr. $19.95 (1-55861-227-0). 112pp. This is the inspiring story of the black South African woman who fought racial segregation and injustice in her country and went on to be a doctor and educator. (Rev: BL 9/15/00; HBG 3/01; SLJ 12/00) [921]

RINGELBLUM, EMMANUEL

14866 Beyer, Mark. *Emmanuel Ringelblum: Historian of the Warsaw Ghetto* (5–8). Illus. Series: Holocaust Biographies. 2001, Rosen LB $26.50 (0-8239-3375-X). 112pp. This true story of a man who recorded events in the Warsaw Ghetto during the Holocaust includes black-and-white photographs. (Rev: BL 10/15/01) [940.53]

SADAT, ANWAR

14867 Kras, Sara Louise. *Anwar Sadat* (5–8). Series: Major World Leaders. 2002, Chelsea $23.95 (0-7910-6949-4). 112pp. An absorbing account of the life of the famous Egyptian leader who shared the 1978 Nobel Peace Prize with Israeli Prime Minister Menachem Begin. (Rev: BL 1/1–15/03; HBG 3/03) [921]

SALADIN

14868 Stanley, Diane. *Saladin: Noble Prince of Islam* (5–8). Illus. 2002, HarperCollins LB $18.89 (0-688-17136-2). 48pp. A lavish picture-book biography of a noted Muslim commander during the Crusades that includes good background information on history, geography, and religion. (Rev: BL 9/1/02; HB 1–2/03; HBG 3/03; SLJ 9/02) [956]

SANTA ANNA, ANTONIO LOPEZ DE

14869 Bankston, John. *Antonio López de Santa Anna* (5–7). Series: Latinos in American History. 2003, Mitchell Lane LB $19.95 (1-58415-209-5). 48pp. A biography of the Mexican general, president, and statesman who is best known for his part in the Battle of the Alamo. (Rev: BL 1/1–15/04; HBG 4/04; SLJ 2/04) [921]

SAUTUOLA, MARIA DE

14870 Fradin, Dennis B. *Maria de Sautuola: The Bulls in the Cave* (3–5). Illus. Series: Remarkable Children. 1997, Silver Burdett LB $18.95 (0-382-39470-4); paper $5.95 (0-382-39471-2). 32pp. The story of the young Spanish girl who discovered the first known prehistoric cave paintings in 1879. (Rev: BL 6/1–15/97; HBG 3/98; SLJ 7/97) [921]

SILVA, MARINA

14871 Hildebrant, Ziporah. *Marina Silva: Defending Rainforest Communities in Brazil* (5–8). Series: Women Changing the World. 2001, Feminist Pr. $19.95 (1-55861-292-9). 112pp. Though battling a serious illness, this gallant women, once a leader of the native Amazonians, has become a leading figure in protecting the forests of Brazil. (Rev: BL 12/15/01) [921]

SOYER, ALEXIS

14872 Arnold, Ann. *The Adventurous Chef: Alexis Soyer* (3–6). Illus. 2002, Farrar $17.00 (0-374-31665-1). 40pp. A fascinating, well-illustrated biography that introduces a famous 19th-century chef and innovator who cooked for the rich but also strove to improve nutrition for the poor, the hungry, and the military. (Rev: BL 12/15/02; HB 11–12/02; HBG 3/03; SLJ 10/02) [641.5]

SUGIHARA, CHIUNE

14873 Gold, Alison L. *A Special Fate: Chiune Sugihara: Hero of the Holocaust* (5–10). 2000, Scholastic paper $15.95 (0-590-39525-4). 176pp. The life story of the Japanese diplomat who saved thousands of Jewish lives during the Holocaust while he was stationed in Lithuania. (Rev: BCCB 5/00; BL 4/1/00; HB 5–6/00; HBG 10/00; SLJ 5/00) [921]

SUZUKI, SHINICHI

14874 Collins, David R. *Dr. Shinichi Suzuki: Teaching Music from the Heart* (4–8). 2001, Morgan Reynolds LB $21.95 (1-883846-49-8). 112pp. This account covers Suzuki's childhood, his interest in music, and his development of a successful method of teaching music, especially the violin, to young children. (Rev: BL 12/15/01; HBG 3/02; SLJ 4/02) [780]

TERESA, MOTHER

14875 Barraclough, John. *Mother Teresa* (2–3). Series: Lives and Times. 1997, Heinemann $19.92 (1-57572-562-2). 24pp. A simple picture-book biography that gives a very brief introduction to the life and contributions of Mother Teresa. (Rev: BL 3/15/98) [921]

14876 Demi. *Mother Teresa* (3–5). Illus. 2005, Simon & Schuster $19.95 (0-689-86407-8). 40pp. This informative picture-book biography looks at the nun's life, mission, and religious devotion. (Rev: BL 1/1–15/05; SLJ 2/05) [291]

14877 Dils, Tracey E. *Mother Teresa* (4–8). Series: Women of Achievement. 2001, Chelsea $21.95 (0-7910-5887-5). 112pp. An absorbing account of the humanitarian's life from her childhood in Albania through her early years in India and her international work with the Missionaries of Charity. (Rev: HBG 3/02; SLJ 11/01) [921]

14878 Giff, Patricia Reilly. *Mother Teresa: Sister to the Poor* (3–5). Illus. 1987, Puffin paper $4.99 (0-14-032225-6). 64pp. Beginning with her childhood in Macedonia, this is the story of the woman who has won the Nobel Peace Prize for her work to better thousands of lives. (Rev: BCCB 4/86; BL 8/86; SLJ 9/86) [921]

14879 Jacobs, William J. *Mother Teresa: Helping the Poor* (3–5). Illus. Series: Gateway Biographies. 1991, Millbrook LB $20.90 (1-56294-020-1). 48pp. An admiring portrait of this woman of compassion and peace, including an overview of her work with the poor. (Rev: BL 1/1/92; SLJ 1/92) [921]

14880 Mohan, Claire J. *The Young Life of Mother Teresa of Calcutta* (4–6). Illus. by Jane Robbins. 1996, Young Sparrow $14.95 (0-943135-26-5); paper $7.95 (0-943135-25-7). 64pp. This biography concentrates on Mother Teresa's life from when she was called to serve God at age 12 to her leaving the convent to go to Calcutta. (Rev: SLJ 1/97) [921]

14881 Morgan, Nina. *Mother Teresa: Saint of the Poor* (4–7). Illus. 1998, Raintree paper $7.95 (0-8172-7848-6). 48pp. A biography of the nun whose work with the poor of India made her an international celebrity and earned her a Nobel Peace Prize. (Rev: BL 7/98; HBG 10/98; SLJ 7/98) [921]

14882 Pond, Mildred. *Mother Teresa: A Life of Charity* (4–7). Illus. Series: Junior World Biography. 1992, Chelsea LB $15.95 (0-7910-1755-9). 80pp. The inspiring life story of the nun who gave her life to serve and help the poor, particularly in India. (Rev: BL 8/92; SLJ 7/92) [921]

14883 Ransom, Candice F. *Mother Teresa* (1–3). Illus. by Elaine Verstraete. Series: On My Own Biography. 2001, Carolrhoda LB $19.93 (1-57505-441-8). 48pp. Mother Teresa's life from childhood and devotion to charitable work are presented in easy-reading text and full-page, realistic art. (Rev: HBG 10/01; SLJ 7/01) [921]

14884 Rice, Tanya. *Mother Teresa* (5–8). Illus. Series: The Life and Times Of. 1999, Chelsea LB $18.65 (0-7910-4637-0). A straightforward account of the life of Mother Teresa, from her birth in Albania to devout Catholic parents and her religious calling as a child, to her work in India and her commitment to helping the poor, to the winning of the Nobel Peace Prize, and her death. (Rev: SLJ 8/98) [921]

14885 Tilton, Rafael. *Mother Teresa* (4–8). Series: The Importance Of. 2000, Lucent LB $18.96 (1-56006-565-6). This thoroughly researched account describes the life of Mother Teresa and gives an honest appraisal of her importance. (Rev: BL 1/1–15/00; HBG 9/00) [921]

THATCHER, MARGARET

14886 Hughes, Libby. *Madam Prime Minister: A Biography of Margaret Thatcher* (5–7). Illus. 1989, Macmillan LB $13.95 (0-87518-410-3). 144pp. This solid biography shows both the public and private sides of the former British prime minister. (Rev: BL 11/1/89*; SLJ 1/90) [921]

THERESE OF LISIEUX, SAINT

14887 Driscoll, Chris. *God's Little Flower: The Story of St. Therese of Lisieux* (PS–3). Illus. by Patrick Kelley. 2001, Ambassador $13.95 (1-929039-05-0). 32pp. A simple, illustrated story of the little girl who became a saint. (Rev: BL 10/1/01; HBG 10/01) [270]

TRYSZNKA, LUBA

14888 Tryszynska-Frederick, Luba. *Luba: The Angel of Bergen-Belsen* (3–6). Illus. by Ann Marshall. 2004, Tricycle $16.95 (1-58246-098-1). 48pp. The true story of Luba Trysznka, a Polish Jew who sheltered and fed more than 50 Dutch Jewish children she found abandoned near her Bergen-Belsen barracks, is recounted in simple, moving prose and accompanied by factual front and back matter. (Rev: BL 11/1/03; HBG 4/04; SLJ 12/03)

TUTANKHAMEN, KING

14889 Sabuda, Robert. *Tutankhamen's Gift* (K–4). Illus. 1994, Atheneum $17.00 (0-689-31818-9). 32pp. A fictionalized account of the boyhood of Tutankhamen and how he became pharaoh at an early age. (Rev: BL 4/15/94; SLJ 5/94) [921]

VICTORIA, QUEEN OF ENGLAND

14890 Green, Robert. *Queen Victoria* (4–6). Illus. Series: First Books. 1998, Watts LB $21.00 (0-531-20330-1). 64pp. This book on Queen Victoria discusses her childhood, education, and marriage and gives an assessment of her long reign and its significance. (Rev: BL 6/1–15/98; HBG 10/98; SLJ 6/98) [921]

VILLA, PANCHO

14891 O'Brien, Steven. *Pancho Villa* (5–9). Series: Hispanics of Achievement. 1994, Chelsea LB $21.95 (0-7910-1257-3). The life and accomplishments of this Mexican freedom fighter. (Rev: BL 9/15/94) [921]

WALESA, LECH

14892 Lazo, Caroline. *Lech Walesa* (4–7). Illus. Series: Peacemakers. 1993, Dillon LB $13.95 (0-87518-525-8). 64pp. The story of the Polish Solidarity labor movement leader is told with generous quotes from Walesa's autobiography and speeches. (Rev: BL 12/15/93; SLJ 1/94) [921]

WALLENBERG, RAOUL

14893 Linnea, Sharon. *Raoul Wallenberg: The Man Who Stopped Death* (5–7). Illus. 1993, Jewish Publication Soc. paper $9.95 (0-8276-0448-3). 120pp. This Swedish architect saved thousands of Jews in Hungary from the Nazi Holocaust. (Rev: BL 6/1–15/93) [940]

WARNER, ANDREA

14894 Warren, Andrea. *Escape from Saigon: How a Vietnam War Orphan Became an American Boy* (5–12). Illus. 2004, Farrar $17.00 (0-374-32224-4). 128pp. An inspiring account of a young Amerasian war orphan's long journey from Vietnam to a new and successful life in the United States. (Rev: BL 6/1–15/04*; SLJ 10/04) [959.704]

WILLIAM THE CONQUEROR

14895 Green, Robert. *William the Conqueror* (4–6). Series: First Books. 1998, Watts LB $21.00 (0-531-20353-0). 64pp. This lively account of the Norman king who conquered England contains many period illustrations and photographs of historical sites. (Rev: BL 6/1–15/98; HBG 10/98) [921]

WILLIAM, PRINCE

14896 Dougherty, Terry. *Prince William* (5–8). Series: People in the News. 2001, Lucent LB $27.45 (1-56006-982-1). Using many quotes, good photographs, and an interesting text, this is a biography of the royal Prince Charming. (Rev: BL 4/1/02) [921]

14897 Landau, Elaine. *Prince William: W.O.W., William of Wales* (4–6). Illus. Series: Gateway Biographies. 2002, Millbrook LB $22.90 (0-7613-2120-9). 48pp. A competent biography that explores the life of the very popular prince and his family through text and many color photographs. (Rev: BL 4/15/02; HBG 10/02) [921]

14898 Wyborny, Sheila. *Prince William* (4–7). Illus. Series: Famous People. 2003, Gale $23.70 (0-7377-1401-8). 48pp. An interesting biography of the young prince that covers his mother's death and the difficulties of living in the limelight, with lots of color photographs. (Rev: BL 6/1–15/03) [941.085]

XIAOPING, DENG

14899 Stewart, Whitney. *Deng Xiaoping: Leader in a Changing China* (4–7). Series: Lerner Biographies. 2001, Lerner LB $30.35 (0-8225-4962-X). 128pp. An accessible biography of the most powerful man in China from the 1970s until his death, with details of how his reputation was tarnished by the Tiananmen Square massacre. (Rev: BL 9/15/01; HBG 10/01; SLJ 7/01) [921]

The Arts and Language

Art and Architecture

General and Miscellaneous

14900 *A Is for Artist* (PS–1). Illus. 1997, Getty Museum $16.95 (0-89236-377-0). 60pp. Using an alphabetical approach, this book introduces 26 glorious paintings from the Getty Museum. (Rev: BL 10/15/97; HBG 3/98) [708.194]

14901 Ajmera, Maya, and John D. Ivanko. *To Be an Artist* (K–3). Illus. 2004, Charlesbridge $15.95 (1-57091-503-2). 32pp. This photo-filled excursion shows young people in countries around the world participating in various artistic activities; a map pinpoints their locations. (Rev: BL 3/1/04; SLJ 3/04) [700]

14902 Alcraft, Rob. *Zoom City* (3–6). Illus. by Jonathan Adams. 1998, Heinemann LB $17.95 (1-57572-717-X). 32pp. Using strange camera angles and perspectives, this view of city life includes full-page photos of a traffic jam, underground life, a harbor, a skyscraper, parks, and a stadium. (Rev: HBG 10/99; SLJ 3/99) [725]

14903 Ancona, George. *Murals: Walls That Sing* (5–8). Illus. 2003, Marshall Cavendish $17.95 (0-7614-5131-5). 48pp. A photoessay showing murals stretching back from today's urban frescos to the cave paintings of Lascaux. (Rev: BL 4/15/03; HBG 4/04; SLJ 5/03) [751.7]

14904 Andrews-Goebel, Nancy. *The Pot That Juan Built* (2–4). Illus. by David Diaz. 2002, Lee & Low $16.95 (1-58430-038-8). 32pp. This almost-multimedia introduction to the work of Mexican potter Juan Quezada allows the reader to choose between rhyme, prose, illustration, and photography that all describe facets of the artist's life and work. (Rev: BL 9/15/02; HBG 3/03; SLJ 9/02*) [738]

14905 Barber, Nicola. *Islamic Art and Culture* (5–8). Illus. Series: World Art and Culture. 2005, Raintree LB $21.95 (1-4109-1105-5). 56pp. High-quality color photographs document the architecture, sculpture, painting, pottery, music, dance, and other art forms found in the Islamic world from early times to the present.

14906 Baumbusch, Brigitte. *Animals Observed* (PS–3). Trans. from Italian by Erika Paoli. Series: Art for Children. 1999, Stewart, Tabori & Chang $9.95 (1-55670-970-6). 29pp. The works of artists both famous, like Picasso and Matisse, and unknown are used to show the animal world as reflected in art. Also use: *Looking at Nature* (1999). (Rev: HBG 10/00; SLJ 1/00) [701]

14907 Baumbusch, Brigitte. *Figuring Figures* (1–4). Trans. by Erika Paoli. Series: Art for Children. 1999, Stewart, Tabori & Chang $9.95 (1-55670-969-2). 29pp. From ancient to contemporary times and in a variety of media, this book focuses on how the human figure has been depicted in art. A companion volume is *The Many Faces of the Face* (1999). (Rev: HBG 10/00; SLJ 12/99) [709]

14908 Bigham, Julia. *The 60s: The Plastic Age* (5–7). Series: 20th Century Design. 2000, Gareth Stevens LB $25.26 (0-8368-2708-2). 32pp. A heavily illustrated title that looks at design and technology in the 1960s with coverage of fashion, art, household appliances, furniture, and architecture. (Rev: HBG 10/01; SLJ 3/01) [700]

14909 Bingham, Jane. *Indian Art and Culture* (5–8). Illus. Series: World Art and Culture. 2004, Raintree LB $29.99 (0-7398-6607-9). 56pp. High-quality color photographs document the architecture, sculpture, painting, pottery, music, dance, and other art forms found in India from early times to the present. Also use *Aboriginal Art and Culture* (2004). (Rev: HBG 4/04; SLJ 2/04) [709]

14910 Björk, Christina. *Linnea in Monet's Garden* (1–4). Trans. by Joan Sandin. Illus. by Lena Anderson. 1987, Farrar $13.00 (9-129-58314-4). 56pp. Linnea, a young French girl, learns about flowers, the painter Monet, and Impressionism from her friend Mr. Bloom. (Rev: BL 12/1/87)

14911 Blake, Quentin. *Tell Me a Picture* (K–6). Illus. by author. 2003, Millbrook LB $29.90 (0-7613-2748-7). 128pp. Adapted from an exhibit at

London's National Gallery, this book contains 26 pictures — some from picture books and others from British art galleries — and guidance for finding the story in each. (Rev: HB 7–8/03; HBG 10/03; SLJ 10/03)

14912 Blanquet, Claire-Helene. *Miró: Earth and Sky* (5–7). Trans. from French by John Goodman. Illus. Series: Art for Children. 1994, Chelsea LB $15.95 (0-7910-2813-5). 59pp. Using a conversational style and some fictitious characters, the life and works of the famous 20th-century French painter Miró are introduced. (Rev: SLJ 12/94) [709]

14913 Blizzard, Gladys S. *Come Look with Me: Enjoying Art with Children* (1–4). Illus. 1991, Thomasson-Grant $13.95 (0-934738-76-9). 32pp. Readers are urged to examine 12 paintings of children by famous artists. (Rev: BCCB 5/91; BL 6/1/91) [750.1]

14914 Blizzard, Gladys S. *Come Look with Me: Exploring Landscape Art with Children* (1–4). Illus. 1992, Thomasson-Grant $13.95 (0-934738-95-5). 32pp. For primary-grade youngsters, this is an introduction to different styles of landscape painting as seen through the work of 12 important artists. (Rev: BL 3/1/92; HB 9–10/92) [758.1]

14915 Blizzard, Gladys S. *Come Look with Me: World of Play* (1–4). Illus. 1993, Thomasson-Grant $13.95 (1-56566-031-5). 32pp. This art appreciation book reproduces 11 paintings and one sculpture that depict various ways in which children play. (Rev: BL 9/1/93) [701.1]

14916 Bolton, Linda. *Impressionism* (4–5). Series: Art Revolution. 2000, NTC $16.95 (0-87226-611-7). 32pp. After a brief overview of Impressionism in art, there are separate sections on ten leading artists and their works. Also use *Surrealism* (2000). (Rev: HBG 3/01; SLJ 11/00) [701]

14917 Browne, Anthony. *The Shape Game* (K–4). Illus. by author. 2003, Farrar $16.00 (0-374-36764-7). Browne's inventive account of a visit to an art museum offers plenty of humor and facts about art. (Rev: HB 9–10/03; HBG 4/04; SLJ 9/03) [708]

14918 Capek, Michael. *Artistic Trickery: The Tradition of Trompe l'Oeil Art* (5–8). Illus. 1995, Lerner LB $22.60 (0-8225-2064-8). 64pp. The art of creating images so perfect that the viewer thinks they are real is introduced, with many historical and contemporary examples. (Rev: BCCB 7–8/95; BL 6/1–15/95; SLJ 7/95) [758]

14919 Capek, Michael. *Murals: Cave, Cathedral, to Street* (5–8). Illus. 1996, Lerner LB $28.80 (0-8225-2065-6). A history of mural painting, from cave painting to such modern masters as Diego Rivera. (Rev: BL 6/1–15/96; SLJ 10/96) [751.7]

14920 Chaplik, Dorothy. *Latin American Arts and Cultures* (5–8). Illus. 2001, Davis $26.95 (0-87192-547-8). 128pp. An encompassing look at Latin American art, architecture, and culture, from pre-Columbian to present-day, complete with pronunciation guide and captioned reproductions or photographs on each page. (Rev: BL 11/1/01) [700.9]

14921 Corbishley, Mike. *The World of Architectural Wonders* (5–8). Illus. Series: The World Of. 1997,

Bedrick $19.95 (0-87226-279-0). The story of 14 architectural wonders worldwide, including Stonehenge, the pyramids of Egypt, Chartes Cathedral, the Taj Mahal, and Hoover Dam. (Rev: BL 6/1–15/97; SLJ 7/97) [720]

14922 Coyne, Jennifer Tarr. *Come Look with Me: Discovering Women Artists for Children* (4–7). Illus. Series: Come Look with Me. 2005, Lickle $15.95 (1-890674-08-7). 32pp. Beautifully reproduced examples of works by women artists' are paired with brief biographical information and questions that direct the reader's attention to different aspects of art. (Rev: BL 5/1/05; SLJ 6/05) [709]

14923 Cressy, Judith. *Can You Find It?* (2–5). Illus. 2002, Abrams $15.95 (0-8109-3279-2). 48pp. Readers are challenged to search for details (bows, cats, flowers, and other items) within artwork from New York City's Metropolitan Museum of Art. (Rev: BL 2/15/03; HBG 3/03; SLJ 1/03) [759]

14924 Cressy, Judith. *Can You Find It, Too? Search and Discover More Than 150 Details in 20 Works of Art* (2–5). 2004, Abrams $15.95 (0-8109-5046-4). 40pp. This sequel to *Can You Find It?* (2003) invites readers to search for features of 20 pieces of art. (Rev: BL 11/1/04) [750]

14925 Cummings, Pat. *Talking with Artists*, Vol. 3 (4–8). Series: Talking with Artists. 1999, Clarion $20.00 (0-395-89132-9). This is the third volume of interviews with children's artists and includes Peter Sis, Betsy Lewin, and Paul O. Zelinsky, with examples of their works. (Rev: BCCB 4/99; BL 3/15/99; HB 5–6/99; HBG 9/99; SLJ 4/99) [741.6]

14926 Delafosse, Claude. *Animals* (PS–2). Illus. by Tony Ross. Series: First Discovery Art. 1995, Scholastic $11.95 (0-590-55202-3). 26pp. Youngsters are introduced to art through a series of laminated pages that alternate with transparencies and give the impression of change and motion. (Rev: BL 1/1–15/96; SLJ 1/96) [701]

14927 Delafosse, Claude. *Landscapes* (4–7). Illus. Series: First Discovery Art. 1996, Scholastic $11.95 (0-590-50216-6). 24pp. The art and techniques of landscape painting are introduced, with many examples from the masters in various historical periods. (Rev: BL 6/1–15/96; SLJ 7/96) [750]

14928 Delafosse, Claude. *Paintings* (4–7). Illus. Series: First Discovery Art. 1996, Scholastic $11.95 (0-590-55201-5). 28pp. A general introduction to painting, with many reproductions and lessons in art appreciation. (Rev: BL 6/1–15/96; SLJ 7/96) [750]

14929 Delafosse, Claude. *Portraits* (PS–2). Illus. by Tony Ross. Series: First Discovery Art. 1995, Scholastic $11.95 (0-590-55200-7). 26pp. Objects gain new dimensions when seen through transparencies in this introduction to art appreciation. (Rev: BL 1/1–15/96; SLJ 1/96) [701]

14930 D'Harcourt, Claire. *Art Up Close: From Ancient to Modern* (3–5). 2003, Chronicle $19.95 (2-02-059694-6). 63pp. Readers are challenged to find details in 23 representative works that span the history of art; the second part of this oversize book with flaps provides information on the works and artists. (Rev: HBG 4/04; SLJ 12/03) [709]

14931 Finley, Carol. *Aboriginal Art of Australia: Exploring Cultural Traditions* (5–9). Series: Art Around the World. 1999, Lerner LB $23.93 (0-8225-2076-1). 56pp. The author covers aboriginal art, aboriginal beliefs, and the contemporary works that reflect the Australian natives' struggle for equality. (Rev: HBG 4/00; SLJ 11/99) [701]

14932 Forward, Toby. *Shakespeare's Globe: An Interactive Pop-up Theatre* (5–8). Illus. by Juan Wijngaard. 2005, Candlewick $19.99 (0-7636-2694-5). 14pp. A large-format pop-up model of the Globe Theatre, with narrative by a Shakespeare colleague and scenes from Shakespeare's plays. (Rev: BL 5/1/05) [792]

14933 Gaff, Jackie. *1900–20: The Birth of Modernism* (5–7). Series: 20th Century Design. 2000, Gareth Stevens LB $25.26 (0-8368-2705-8). 32pp. This account traces developments in the worlds of art, design, and technology for the first 20 years of the past century. (Rev: HBG 10/01; SLJ 3/01) [708]

14934 Gaff, Jackie. *1920–40: Realism and Surrealism* (4–8). Series: 20th Century Art. 2001, Gareth Stevens LB $25.26 (0-8368-2850-X). 32pp. This appealing overview of art movements — mainly in Europe — offers accessible text, high-quality color reproductions, and black-and-white photographs of important individuals. Also use *1900–10: New Ways of Seeing* and *1910–20: The Birth of Abstract Art* (both 2001). (Rev: HBG 10/01; SLJ 7/01) [708]

14935 Gibbons, Gail. *The Art Box* (PS–3). Illus. 1998, Holiday House $16.95 (0-8234-1386-1). 32pp. In a series of brightly colored illustrations, the author displays the various tools and supplies that an artist uses. (Rev: BL 9/15/98; HBG 3/99; SLJ 12/98) [702]

14936 Gonyea, Mark. *A Book About Design: Complicated Doesn't Make It Good* (3–5). Illus. 2005, Hyperion $18.95 (0-7868-7575-5). 144pp. A stylish but challenging introduction to the principles of graphic design, covering topics including shape, color, and contrast. (Rev: BL 5/1/05) [745.4]

14937 *Groom Your Room: Terrific Touches to Brighten Your Bedroom!* (3–8). Photos by Michael Walker and Fritz Geiger. Series: American Girl. 1997, Pleasant Co. paper $7.95 (1-56247-531-2). 48pp. A beginning decorating book that also gives tips on cleaning and organizing possessions. (Rev: SLJ 3/98) [745]

14938 Heslewood, Juliet. *The History of Western Painting: A Young Person's Guide* (5–9). Illus. 1995, Raintree LB $25.68 (0-8172-4000-4). Beginning with cave paintings, this large-format book gives a cursory overview of Western painting, with several pages devoted to contemporary artists and movements. (Rev: BL 1/1–15/96; SLJ 12/95) [759]

14939 Heslewood, Juliet. *The History of Western Sculpture* (5–9). Illus. 1995, Raintree LB $25.68 (0-8172-4001-2). This oversize, heavily illustrated book traces the history of Western sculpture from the ancient Greeks to contemporary masters. (Rev: BL 1/1–15/96; SLJ 12/95) [730]

14940 Hibbert, Clare. *Chinese Art and Culture* (5–8). Illus. Series: World Art and Culture. 2005, Raintree LB $21.95 (1-4109-1107-1). 56pp. High-quality color photographs document the architecture, sculpture, painting, pottery, music, dance, and other art forms found in China from early times to the present.

14941 *The History of Printmaking* (3–6). Illus. Series: Voyages of Discovery. 1996, Scholastic $19.95 (0-590-47649-1). 48pp. Overlays and foldouts are used to present a history of prints and print images, including computer images. (Rev: BL 12/15/97) [769]

14942 Hosack, Karen. *Animals* (2–4). Series: How Artists View. 2004, Heinemann LB $24.22 (1-4034-4850-7). Animals are the subject of this interesting volume in a series that looks at the ways in which artists view and depict various themes. Also in this series are *Nature, Families, Weather, Food,* and *Homes* (all 2004). (Rev: BL 12/1/04) [704.9]

14943 Jockel, Nils. *Bruegel's Tower of Babel: The Builder with the Red Hat* (4–7). Illus. Series: Adventures in Art. 1998, Prestel $14.95 (3-7913-1941-8). 30pp. A detailed analysis of Pieter Bruegel's surreal masterpiece, using one of the characters in the painting to supply a point of view and an examination of the meaning of its contents. (Rev: BL 8/98; SLJ 8/98) [759.9493]

14944 Johmann, Carol A. *Skyscrapers!* (3–6). Illus. by Michael Kline. Series: Kaleidoscope Kids. 2001, Williamson paper $10.95 (1-885593-50-3). 96pp. Cartoonlike drawings and black-and-white photographs are including in this appealing and informative look at skyscrapers, their history, and the structural and design challenges they pose, which also includes a a number of related activities. (Rev: BL 12/15/01; SLJ 3/02) [720]

14945 Jones, Helen. *40s and 50s: War and Postwar Years* (5–7). Series: 20th Century Design. 2000, Gareth Stevens LB $25.26 (0-8368-2707-4). 32pp. Developments in art, design, and technology during and after World War II are chronicled in this heavily illustrated book. (Rev: HBG 10/01; SLJ 3/01) [708]

14946 Kalman, Bobbie. *The Victorian Home* (3–5). Illus. by Barbara Bedell. Series: Historic Communities. 1997, Crabtree LB $20.60 (0-86505-431-2); paper $7.95 (0-86505-461-4). 32pp. Examines 19th-century homes, their exteriors, interior rooms, and furnishings. (Rev: SLJ 7/97) [690]

14947 Khanduri, Kamini. *Japanese Art and Culture* (5–8). Illus. Series: World Art and Culture. 2004, Raintree LB $29.99 (0-7398-6609-5). 56pp. High-quality color photographs document the architecture, sculpture, painting, pottery, music, dance, and other art forms found in Japan from early times to the present. (Rev: HBG 4/04)

14948 King, Penny, and Clare Roundhill. *Animals* (2–4). Illus. Series: Artists' Workshop. 1996, Crabtree LB $19.96 (0-86505-851-2); paper $8.95 (0-86505-861-X). 32pp. Readers learn how animals are depicted in art, examine six appropriate art works, and are given tips on how to create their own pictures. Also use *Landscapes, Portraits,* and *Stories* (all 1996). (Rev: SLJ 1/97) [709]

781

14949 King, Penny, and Clare Roundhill. *Myths and Legends* (3–6). Illus. by Lindy Norton. Series: Artists' Workshop. 1997, Crabtree LB $19.96 (0-86505-855-5); paper $8.95 (0-86505-865-2). 32pp. This book presents famous paintings from the 15th through the 20th century that depict mythological figures and scenes from around the world, as well as works on similar subjects by children. (Rev: HBG 3/98; SLJ 4/98) [750]

14950 King, Penny, and Clare Roundhill. *Sports and Games* (3–6). Illus. by Lindy Norton. Series: Artists' Workshop. 1997, Crabtree LB $19.96 (0-86505-854-7); paper $8.95 (0-86505-864-4). 32pp. Famous works of art from ancient times to the present are combined with children's art to show how various sports such as swimming, sailing, wrestling, and childhood games have been depicted. (Rev: HBG 3/98; SLJ 4/98) [750]

14951 Knapp, Ruthie, and Janice Lehmberg. *Impressionist Art* (5–9). Illus. Series: Off the Wall Museum Guides for Kids. 1999, Davis paper $9.95 (0-87192-385-8). 72pp. This pocket-size guide supplies an overview of Impressionism and brief introductions to major artists, including Sisley and Monet. (Rev: BL 1/1–15/99) [709.03]

14952 Knapp, Ruthie, and Janice Lehmberg. *Modern Art* (5–9). Series: Off the Wall Museum Guides for Kids. 2001, Davis paper $9.95 (0-87192-458-6). 72pp. A lively and colorful survey of 20th-century art including examples from expressionists, cubists, surrealists, and pop artists. (Rev: BL 8/1/01) [709]

14953 Kutschbach, Doris. *The Blue Rider: The Yellow Cow Sees the World in Blue* (3–7). Trans. by Andrea Belloli. Illus. Series: Adventures in Art. 1997, Prestel $14.95 (3-7913-1811-X). 35pp. This art appreciation volume explores a group of painters — including Klee and Kandinsky — who freed color and form from reality. (Rev: SLJ 1/98) [709]

14954 Loumaye, Jacqueline. *Chagall: My Sad and Joyous Village* (4–8). Trans. from French by John Goodman. Illus. by Veronique Boiry. Series: Art for Children. 1994, Chelsea LB $15.95 (0-7910-2807-0). 57pp. A youngster learns about Chagall and his paintings from a violinist who grew up in the artist's home town in Russia. (Rev: SLJ 8/94) [709]

14955 Loumaye, Jacqueline. *Degas: The Painted Gesture* (4–8). Trans. from French by John Goodman. Illus. by Nadine Massart. Series: Art for Children. 1994, Chelsea LB $15.95 (0-7910-2809-7). 57pp. Using a series of workshops for children at the Orsay Museum (Paris) as a focus, the life and works of Degas are introduced. (Rev: SLJ 8/94) [709]

14956 Loumaye, Jacqueline. *Van Gogh: The Touch of Yellow* (4–8). Trans. from French by John Goodman. Illus. by Claudine Roucha. Series: Art for Children. 1994, Chelsea LB $15.95 (0-7910-2817-8). 57pp. Two youngsters visit the museums in Amsterdam to learn about van Gogh, his tragic life, and his paintings. (Rev: SLJ 8/94) [709]

14957 MacDonald, Fiona. *Design* (3–5). Illus. Series: Culture Encyclopedia. 2002, Mason Crest LB $18.95 (1-59084-476-9). 40pp. The importance of design in such areas as fashion, food, technology, and architecture is discussed in this introduction to style around the world. (Rev: SLJ 3/03)

14958 Mallat, Kathy, and Bruce McMillan. *The Picture That Mom Drew* (2–4). Illus. 1997, Walker LB $15.85 (0-8027-8618-9). 24pp. Using "The House That Jack Built" as a framework, the materials and techniques used by an artist are introduced. (Rev: BL 1/1–15/97*; SLJ 4/97) [741.2]

14959 Mason, Antony. *Art* (3–5). Illus. Series: Culture Encyclopedia. 2002, Mason Crest LB $18.95 (1-59084-475-0). 40pp. An introduction to art over the centuries that looks at all kinds of drawing, painting, sculpture, photography, commercial art, and so forth. (Rev: SLJ 3/03)

14960 Merlo, Claudio. *The History of Art: From Ancient to Modern Times* (4–7). Trans. from Italian by Nathaniel Harris. Series: Masters of Art. 2000, Bedrick $29.95 (0-87226-531-5). 124pp. This ambitious volume, which tries to cover world art in all media in a single volume, is particularly valuable for its color illustrations. (Rev: HBG 10/00; SLJ 4/00) [750]

14961 Micklethwait, Lucy. *A Child's Book of Art: Great Pictures, First Words* (1–4). Illus. 1993, DK $16.95 (1-56458-203-5). 64pp. Combines a word book with art appreciation by showing how common concepts like work and numbers are shown in great works of art. (Rev: BL 1/15/94; SLJ 2/94) [701]

14962 Milo, Francesco. *The Story of Architecture* (4–8). Illus. 2000, Bedrick $22.50 (0-87226-528-5). 64pp. The wealth of information on building materials, cultures, and trends in this book lend a historical perspective to the discussion of world architecture. It is colorfully illustrated with drawings, photographs, and diagrams. (Rev: BL 6/1–15/00; HBG 10/00; SLJ 8/00) [720.9]

14963 Nilsen, Anna. *Art Fraud Detective* (4–6). Illus. 2000, Kingfisher $15.95 (0-7534-5308-8). 48pp. The reader becomes an art forgery detective in this oversize book that compares originals and forgeries of works by such artists as da Vinci, Picasso, and van Gogh. (Rev: BL 10/15/00; HBG 10/01; SLJ 12/00) [751.5]

14964 Nilsen, Anna. *The Great Art Scandal: Solve the Crime, Save the Show!* (4–9). Illus. 2003, Kingfisher $16.95 (0-7534-5587-0). 48pp. Readers must solve a mystery involving an art exhibition in this comic-book-format work that introduces many famous paintings and artists. (Rev: HBG 4/04; SLJ 3/04) [759.06]

14965 Norton, Mary Lynn. *Vernon Grant's Santa Claus* (3–7). Illus. by Vernon Grant. 2003, Abrams $14.95 (0-8109-4518-5). 58pp. The lustrous images of Santa Claus in this collection were painted by Vernon Grant, who is best known as the creator of Kellogg's elfin advertising icons, Snap! Crackle! and Pop!; accompanying the Santa paintings are a number of seasonal stories and poems. (Rev: HBG 4/04; SLJ 10/03)

14966 Presilla, Maricel E. *Mola: Cuna Life Stories and Art* (5–7). Illus. 1996, Holt $17.95 (0-8050-

3801-9). 32pp. An examination of the life and art of the Cuna Indians, who live on islands off the coast of Panama. (Rev: BCCB 1/97; BL 10/1/96; SLJ 10/96) [305.48]

14967 Raczka, Bob. *Art Is . . .* (K–5). 2003, Millbrook LB $22.90 (0-7613-2874-2). 32pp. An excellent introductory guide to art and its appreciation, this attractive title exposes readers to images of 26 famous works of art, each of which is accompanied by explanatory text discussing the art's significance and quality. (Rev: HBG 10/03; SLJ 10/03)

14968 Raczka, Bob. *No One Saw: Ordinary Things Through the Eyes of an Artist* (PS–3). Illus. 2002, Millbrook LB $23.90 (0-7613-2370-8). 32pp. Simple verse introduces young readers to the singular viewpoints of modern artists including Georgia O'Keefe and Vincent Van Gogh. (Rev: BL 1/1–15/02; HBG 10/02; SLJ 1/02) [759.06]

14969 Raimondo, Joyce. *Imagine That! Activities and Adventures in Surrealism* (4–6). Series: New Children's: Art Explorers. 2004, Watson-Guptill $12.95 (0-8230-2502-0). 48pp. This engaging volume encourages readers to try their hands at projects that incorporate elements of surrealism. (Rev: BL 12/1/04; SLJ 9/04) [709]

14970 Raimondo, Joyce. *Picture This! Activities and Adventures in Impressionism* (1–5). Illus. 2004, Watson-Guptill $12.95 (0-8230-2503-9). 48pp. Monet, Pissarro, and Degas are among the artists used to demonstrate the techniques of Impressionism in this volume faturing discussion and step-by-step activities. (Rev: SLJ 1/05) [701]

14971 Richards, Julie. *Stadiums and Domes* (4–6). Illus. Series: Smart Structures. 2003, Smart Apple Media LB $16.95 (1-58340-349-3). 32pp. An overview of the use of the dome in construction, from Roman times to the present, with helpful photographs and diagrams. (Rev: SLJ 3/04) [721]

14972 Richardson, Joy. *Looking at Faces in Art* (1–4). Series: How to Look at Art. 2000, Gareth Stevens LB $14.95 (0-8368-2624-8). 32pp. In a series of double-page spreads, famous paintings are examined with close-ups and questions and answers to promote art appreciation. Also use *Showing Distance in Art* and *Using Shadows in Art* (both 2000). (Rev: HBG 10/00; SLJ 8/00) [709]

14973 Richardson, Joy. *Looking at Pictures: An Introduction to Art for Young People* (5–8). Illus. 1997, Abrams $19.95 (0-8109-4252-6). A large-size volume that introduces art appreciation to middle-graders and describes different types of pictures and techniques. (Rev: BCCB 7–8/97; BL 4/15/97; SLJ 6/97*) [750]

14974 Richmond, Robin. *Children in Art: The Story in a Picture* (4–6). Illus. by author. 1992, Ideals LB $16.00 (0-8249-8588-5). 48pp. Children are introduced to art by the use of pictures with children as subjects. (Rev: BL 12/15/92; SLJ 2/93) [750]

14975 Roalf, Peggy. *Cats* (5–8). Illus. Series: Looking at Paintings. 1992, Hyperion paper $6.95 (1-56282-091-5). 48pp. This history of art shows how cats have been portrayed through the ages. Others in

this series are: *Dancers; Families;* and *Seascapes* (all 1992). (Rev: SLJ 8/92) [709]

14976 Roalf, Peggy. *Dogs* (5–8). Illus. Series: Looking at Paintings. 1993, Hyperion paper $6.95 (1-56282-530-5). 48pp. Various ways that dogs have been represented in paintings are reproduced, with explanations, in this attractive book on art appreciation. (Rev: BL 2/15/94; SLJ 2/94) [758.3]

14977 Rohmer, Harriet, ed. *Just Like Me: Stories and Self-Portraits by Fourteen Artists* (3–6). Illus. 1997, Children's Book Pr. $15.95 (0-89239-149-9). 32pp. In double-page spreads, 14 artists, all of whom have produced books for children, talk about themselves and their inspirations. (Rev: BL 9/1/97; HBG 3/98; SLJ 12/97) [704.9]

14978 Rolling, James Haywood, Jr. *Come Look with Me: Discovering African American Art for Children* (K–5). Series: Come Look with Me. 2005, Lickle $15.95 (1-890674-07-9). 32pp. Twelve examples of African American art, by artists including Romare Bearden and Jacob Lawrence, are paired with background information and questions that encourage young readers to examine the art. (Rev: SLJ 6/05)

14979 Rubin, Susan Goldman. *Art Against the Odds* (5–8). Illus. by Margeaux Lucas. 2004, Crown $19.95 (0-375-82406-5). 64pp. This inspiring book explores art created in the face of adversity, such as the quilts of slaves and the graffiti painted on city walls by underprivileged teens. (Rev: BL 2/15/04; SLJ 3/04) [700]

14980 Rubin, Susan Goldman. *Degas and the Dance: The Painter and the Petits Rats, Perfecting Their Art* (3–5). Illus. 2002, Abrams $17.95 (0-8109-0567-1). 32pp. This volume, with excellent reproductions of preliminary sketches as well as finished works, will attract budding artists and budding ballet dancers; the "petits rats" are young dancers who posed for the painter. (Rev: BL 12/1/02; HBG 3/03; SLJ 12/02) [759.4]

14981 Rubin, Susan Goldman. *There Goes the Neighborhood: Ten Buildings People Loved to Hate* (4–7). 2001, Holiday House $18.95 (0-8234-1435-3). 96pp. Many buildings create an uproar from their earliest design but later become nostalgic favorites, among them the Eiffel Tower and Guggenheim Museum, which are profiled here in an absorbing, colorful account that discusses materials and methods of construction. (Rev: BCCB 9/01; BL 8/01; HBG 3/02; SLJ 9/01) [720]

14982 Sayre, Henry M. *Cave Paintings to Picasso: The Inside Scoop on 50 Famous Masterpieces* (3–7). Illus. 2004, Chronicle $22.95 (0-8118-3767-X). 96pp. This short but impressive historical overview chronicles the evolution of the visual arts from prehistoric cave paintings to the 1960s, presenting 50 major works and including historical context and information on the artist. (Rev: BL 11/1/04; SLJ 10/04) [709]

14983 Scott, Elaine. *Funny Papers: Behind the Scenes of the Comics* (3–6). Photos by Margaret Miller. 1993, Morrow LB $14.93 (0-688-11576-4). 96pp. A richly illustrated history of comic strips, their different forms, and how they are created, sold, and distributed. (Rev: BCCB 1/94; BL 11/15/93; SLJ 11/93) [741.5]

14984 Sellier, Marie. *Matisse from A to Z* (3–7). Trans. from French by Claudia Zoe Bedrick. Illus. 1995, Bedrick LB $14.95 (0-87226-475-0). 59pp. The subjects used by Matisse in his paintings and events in his life feature in this unusual alphabet book containing many reproductions of his work. (Rev: SLJ 12/95) [759.4]

14985 Slaymaker, Melissa Eskridge. *Bottle Houses: The Creative World of Grandma Prisbrey* (1–3). Illus. by Julie Paschkis. 2004, Holt $16.95 (0-8050-7131-8). 32pp. Grandma Prisbrey's offbeat creations open young readers' eyes to artistic possibilities. (Rev: BL 3/1/04; HB 7–8/04; SLJ 9/04) [745]

14986 Teitelbaum, Michael. *The Story of Spider-Man* (3–4). Illus. Series: Dorling Kindersley Readers. 2001, DK LB $12.95 (0-7894-7920-6); paper $3.95 (0-7894-7921-4). 48pp. Teitelbaum tells the story of Spider-Man's creation, with sidebar features, photographs, drawings, and reproductions of the comic strips. (Rev: HBG 3/02; SLJ 2/02) [741.5]

14987 Terzian, Alexandra M. *The Kids' Multicultural Art Book: Art and Craft Experiences from Around the World* (3–6). Illus. 1993, Williamson paper $12.95 (0-913589-72-1). 160pp. Using a walking tour across the continents as a framework, this book introduces the cultures of many areas in Africa, Asia, and Central America, with a section on the Indians of North America. (Rev: BL 9/1/93; SLJ 8/93) [745]

14988 Thomson, Ruth. *Creatures* (2–5). Illus. Series: First Look at Art. 2004, Chelsea House LB $14.95 (0-7910-7945-7). 32pp. Readers are introduced to the elements of art through a variety of works depicting animals and imaginary creatures. Also use *Portraits* (2004). (Rev: BL 5/1/04; SLJ 9/04) [750]

14989 Thomson, Ruth. *Places* (3–6). Illus. Series: A First Look at Art. 2004, Chelsea Clubhouse LB $14.95 (0-7910-7947-3). 32pp. Using famous works representing various styles as examples, this book looks at the depiction of landscapes and other places and includes creative activities. Also use *Families* (2004) and *Celebrations* (2005). (Rev: SLJ 9/04) [704.9]

14990 Voss, Gisela. *Museum Colors* (PS–1). Illus. 1994, Museum of Fine Arts, Boston $14.00 (0-87846-369-0). 20pp. Works of art are used to point out different colors in this board book. Also use *Museum Numbers* and *Museum Shapes* (both 1994). (Rev: BL 5/1/94; SLJ 8/94) [701.8]

14991 Warhola, James. *Uncle Andy's: A Faabbulous Visit with Andy Warhol* (K–3). Illus. 2003, Penguin Putnam $16.99 (0-399-23869-7). 32pp. A young boy (the author as a child) enjoys visiting his eccentric artist uncle, Andy Warhol, and is inspired by his work. (Rev: BL 2/15/03; HB 3–4/03; HBG 10/03; SLJ 4/03) [700]

14992 Wellington, Monica. *Squeaking of Art: The Mice Go to the Museum* (PS–3). Illus. 2000, Dutton $15.99 (0-525-46165-5). 32pp. Seventy-seven of the world's greatest paintings are introduced in a delightful way as ten young mice visit an imaginary

art museum. (Rev: BL 2/15/00; HBG 10/00; SLJ 5/00) [701.1]

14993 Wenzel, Angela. *Edgar Degas: Dance Like a Butterfly* (4–6). Trans. from German by Rosie Jackson. Series: Adventures in Art. 2002, Prestel $14.95 (3-7913-2736-4). 28pp. Degas's ballet paintings are presented in a way that encourages readers to appreciate movement, light, and color. (Rev: HBG 3/03; SLJ 11/02)

14994 Wenzel, Angela. *Rene Magritte: Now You See It — Now You Don't* (4–7). Illus. Series: Adventures in Art. 1998, Prestel $14.95 (3-7913-1873-X). 30pp. An examination of some of the works of Belgian surrealist Rene Magritte. (Rev: BL 8/98; SLJ 8/98) [759.949]

14995 White, Matt. *Cameras on the Battlefield: Photos of War* (5–7). Series: High Five Reading. 2002, Capstone LB $22.60 (0-7368-4004-4). 64pp. For reluctant readers, this is an appealing look at photographs of war, both those that celebrate war and those that document its horrors. (Rev: SLJ 8/02) [779.9355]

14996 Wolfe, Gillian. *Look! Body Language in Art* (3–5). 2004, Lincoln $16.95 (1-84507-034-8). 40pp. In this excellent introduction to art appreciation, Wolfe asks readers — incorporating activity ideas and leading questions — to observe the body language depicted in paintings by artists including Vincent Van Gogh and Pablo Picasso. (Rev: BL 11/1/04) [758.9]

14997 Wolfe, Gillian. *Look! Zoom In on Art!* (2–5). Illus. 2002, Oxford $19.95 (0-19-521912-0). 40pp. Readers are encouraged to look at a number of paintings in a new way and to make art of their own. (Rev: BL 9/1/02; HBG 3/03; SLJ 5/03) [750]

14998 Wolfe, Gillian. *Oxford First Book of Art* (1–4). Illus. 1999, Oxford $18.95 (0-19-521556-7). 48pp. Excellent reproductions and a thoughtful text highlight this fine introduction to art for young people; paintings, drawings, sculpture, etc., are arranged by topic. (Rev: BCCB 1/00; BL 2/1/00; HBG 3/00; SLJ 12/99) [700]

14999 Zaunders, Bo. *Gargoyles, Girders, and Glass Houses* (3–6). Illus. by Roxie Munro. 2004, Penguin Putnam $17.99 (0-525-47284-3). 48pp. Among the architects profiled in this large-format overview of major design and engineering feats are Gustave Eiffel, Antoni Gaudi, and the Roeblings. (Rev: BL 11/1/04; SLJ 12/04) [720.9]

Africa

15000 Finley, Carol. *The Art of African Masks: Exploring Cultural Traditions* (5–9). Series: Art Around the World. 1999, Lerner LB $23.93 (0-8225-2078-8). 64pp. This account on African mask making past and present focuses on the western Sudan, the Guinea Coast, and Central Africa. (Rev: HBG 9/99; SLJ 11/99) [745.5]

15001 Stelzig, Christine. *Can You Spot the Leopard? African Masks* (3–6). Trans. from German by Fiona Elliot. Series: Adventures in Art. 1997, Prestel

$14.95 (3-7913-1874-8). 28pp. An appealing book that pictures over 30 masks from different African peoples and explains where each came from, how it was made, and its significance. (Rev: SLJ 6/98) [750]

The Ancient World

15002 Chrisp, Peter. *Ancient Rome* (4–8). Series: History in Art. 2004, Raintree LB $29.93 (1-4109-0520-9). 48pp. A look at what art can reveal about the culture and technology of a society. (Rev: SLJ 4/05) [709]

15003 Knapp, Ruthie, and Janice Lehmberg. *Egyptian Art* (5–9). Illus. Series: Off the Wall Museum Guides for Kids. 1999, Davis paper $9.95 (0-87192-384-X). 72pp. This pocket-size art appreciation book discusses mummies, sculpture, hieroglyphs, and other artifacts from Egyptian art. (Rev: BL 1/1–15/99) [709.32]

15004 Knapp, Ruthie, and Janice Lehmberg. *Greek and Roman Art* (5–9). Series: Off the Wall Museum Guides for Kids. 2001, Davis paper $9.95 (0-87192-549-4). 72pp. Using many photographs, this account highlights a number of art objects, explains relevant terms associated with them, describes their uses, and gives details on Greek and Roman culture. (Rev: BL 8/1/01) [936]

15005 Langley, Andrew. *Ancient Greece* (4–8). Series: History in Art. 2004, Raintree LB $29.93 (1-4109-0517-9). 48pp. A look at what art can reveal about the culture and technology of a society. (Rev: SLJ 4/05) [709]

15006 Shuter, Jane. *Ancient Chinese Art* (4–6). Illus. Series: Art in History. 2001, Heinemann LB $23.58 (1-58810-090-1). 32pp. Painting, calligraphy, bronzes, terracotta, and lacquer and jade are among the art forms featured. (Rev: HB 5–6/03; HBG 3/02; SLJ 12/01)

Native American Arts and Crafts

15007 Arnold, Caroline. *Stories in Stone: Rock Art Pictures by Early Americans* (4–6). Illus. by Richard Hewitt. 1996, Clarion $15.95 (0-395-72092-3). 48pp. Highlights of the rock art of Native Americans found in the Coso Range in California. (Rev: BL 12/15/96; SLJ 12/96) [709]

15008 Finley, Carol. *Art of the Far North: Inuit Sculpture, Drawing, and Printmaking* (4–6). Illus. Series: Art Around the World. 1998, Lerner LB $22.60 (0-8225-2075-3). 56pp. Inuit art from 1950 to the present is the focus of this heavily illustrated book containing a lengthy chapter on the influence of myths and legends. (Rev: BL 11/15/98; HBG 10/99; SLJ 1/99) [704.03]

15009 January, Brendan. *Native American Art and Culture* (5–8). Series: World Art and Culture. 2005, Raintree LB $31.36 (1-4109-1108-X). 56pp. Pottery, textiles, carving, painting, textiles, and architecture are all discussed, along with body art, ceremonies, songs, and dances; many color photographs are included and a list of museums is appended. (Rev: SLJ 6/05)

15010 Keams, Geri. *Snail Girl Brings Water: A Navajo Story* (2–4). Illus. by Richard Ziehler-Martin. 1998, Rising Moon $15.95 (0-87358-662-X). 32pp. A retelling of the Navajo myth that relates how slow-moving Snail Girl was able to bring water to the Earth's surface. (Rev: BL 11/15/98; HBG 10/99; SLJ 5/99) [398.2]

15011 Press, Petra. *Native American Art* (4–6). Illus. Series: Art in History. 2001, Heinemann LB $23.58 (1-58810-092-8). 32pp. Rock art, stone sculpture, sand painting, textiles, and basketry are among the kinds of art featured here. (Rev: HBG 3/02; SLJ 12/01)

Middle Ages and the Renaissance

15012 Barter, James. *A Renaissance Painter's Studio* (5–9). Series: The Working Life. 2003, Gale LB $21.96 (1-59018-178-6). 112pp. An exploration of daily life for a painter at a time when art was growing in social importance. (Rev: HBG 10/03; SLJ 5/03) [759.5]

15013 Bergin, Mark. *A Medieval Castle* (5–8). Illus. 2003, McGraw-Hill $20.95 (1-57768-980-1). 48pp. Cutaway illustrations and insets provide magnified views of castles and explain their design, construction, defense, and the nature of the people who inhabited them. (Rev: BL 9/15/03; HBG 4/04) [728.8]

15014 Fritz, Jean. *Leonardo's Horse* (4–7). Illus. by Hudson Talbott. 2001, Penguin Putnam $16.99 (0-399-23576-0). 40pp. The story of a Leonardo da Vinci sculpture that was begun in 1493 and finally completed — thanks to the efforts of Charles Dent — in 1999, along with biographical information about da Vinci and examples of his work. (Rev: BCCB 10/01; BL 10/15/01; HB 9–10/01; HBG 3/02; SLJ 9/01) [730]

15015 Macaulay, David. *Building the Book Cathedral* (5–9). 1999, Houghton Mifflin $29.95 (0-395-92147-3). The author retells the fascinating story behind the creation of the original *Cathedral* book 25 years ago and adds numerous changes as he leads a tour of the cathedral, such as alterations in scale and page placement. (Rev: BCCB 12/99; BL 11/15/99; HB 9–10/99; SLJ 9/99) [726]

15016 Macaulay, David. *Castle* (5–8). Illus. by author. 1977, Houghton Mifflin $18.00 (0-395-25784-0); paper $8.95 (0-395-32920-5). 80pp. Another of the author's brilliant, detailed works, this one on the planning and building of a Welsh castle. [940.1]

15017 Macaulay, David. *Cathedral: The Story of Its Construction* (6–8). Illus. by author. 1973, Houghton Mifflin $18.00 (0-395-17513-5). 80pp. Gothic architecture as seen through a detailed examination of the construction of an imaginary cathedral.

15018 Ross, Stewart. *Art and Architecture* (5–8). Series: Medieval Realms. 2004, Gale/Lucent LB $27.45 (1-59018-534-X). 48pp. Romanesque, Gothic, Moorish, and Islamic art and architecture are covered in this well-organized and well-illustrated volume that includes discussions of houses of the poor as well as castles, manors, monasteries, and cathedrals. (Rev: SLJ 3/05) [720]

United States

15019 Arbogast, Joan Marie. *Buildings in Disguise: Architecture That Looks Like Animals, Food, and Other Things* (4–7). 2004, Boyds Mills $16.95 (1-59078-099-X). 48pp. Buildings in the shapes of milk bottles, elephants, wigwams, and baskets are among the wonders shown in many period and contemporary photographs. (Rev: BL 11/1/04; SLJ 1/05) [720]

15020 Baverstock, Alison. *Joseph Cornell: Secrets in a Box* (3–6). Illus. Series: Prestel Adventures in Art. 2003, Prestel $14.95 (3-7913-2928-6). 30pp. The collage boxes of artist Joseph Cornell are explored in detail in this richly illustrated book, which also shows readers how they can make similar creations of their own. (Rev: BL 11/1/03) [709.2]

15021 Butler, Jerry. *A Drawing in the Sand: A Story of African American Art* (4–7). Illus. 1999, Zino $24.95 (1-55933-216-6). 64pp. This oversize book contains two narratives; the first is a history of African American art and artists, the second, an autobiography of Jerry Butler, the African American artist. (Rev: BL 2/15/99*) [704.03]

15022 Degezelle, Terri. *The U.S. Capitol* (K–2). Series: American Symbols. 2003, Capstone LB $19.93 (0-7368-2294-1). 24pp. A well-illustrated profile of the U.S. Capitol, from the initial design contest to the numerous changes and expansions made to the building over the years. (Rev: SLJ 4/04) [975.3]

15023 Esterman, M. M. *A Fish That's a Box: Folk Art from the National Museum of American Art, Smithsonian Institution* (4–6). Illus. 1990, Great Ocean $12.95 (0-915556-21-9). 32pp. An eye-pleasing introduction to American folk art. (Rev: BCCB 2/91; BL 12/15/90; SLJ 3/91) [745]

15024 Glenn, Patricia Brown. *Under Every Roof: A Kid's Style and Field Guide to the Architecture of American Houses* (5–8). 1993, Preservation $16.95 (0-89133-214-6). An introduction to the history and styles of architecture of American homes, with a look at more than 70 houses. (Rev: BL 7/94; SLJ 6/94) [728]

15025 Howard, Nancy S. *Jacob Lawrence: American Scenes, American Struggles* (4–7). Illus. 1996, Davis $14.95 (0-87192-302-5). 48pp. The narrative paintings of this contemporary African American

artist are featured, with several suggested follow-up activities. (Rev: BL 11/1/96) [759.13]

15026 Knapp, Ruthie, and Janice Lehmberg. *American Art* (5–9). Series: Off the Wall Museum Guides for Kids. 1999, Davis paper $9.95 (0-87192-386-6). An informal pocket-size art appreciation book that features portraits from several centuries of American art, plus various artifacts and furniture. (Rev: BL 1/1–15/99) [709.73]

15027 Macaulay, David. *Mill* (5–8). Illus. by author. 1983, Houghton Mifflin $18.00 (0-395-34830-7); paper $9.95 (0-395-52019-3). 128pp. Rhode Island textile mills of the 19th century are described in text and excellent drawings. [690]

15028 Morrison, Taylor. *The Buffalo Nickel* (2–4). Illus. 2002, Houghton Mifflin $16.00 (0-618-10855-6). 32pp. The story of the artist who designed the buffalo nickel, with information about coin production. (Rev: BL 5/15/02; HBG 10/02; SLJ 4/02) [730]

15029 Murray, Julie. *Gateway Arch* (2–3). Illus. Series: All Aboard America. 2003, ABDO LB $14.95 (1-57765-671-7). 24pp. This photo-filled book takes young readers on a tour of St. Louis's Gateway Arch, constructed to memorialize the Missouri city's role as a gateway to the West. (Rev: HBG 10/03; SLJ 11/03) [725]

15030 Murray, Julie. *Mount Rushmore* (2–3). Illus. Series: All Aboard America. 2003, ABDO LB $14.95 (1-57765-667-9). 24pp. A brief overview of the creation of the giant presidential profiles carved into the mountain. (Rev: HBG 10/03; SLJ 11/03) [978.3]

15031 Nikola-Lisa, W. *The Year with Grandma Moses* (2–5). Illus. 2000, Holt $20.00 (0-8050-6243-2). 32pp. The seasons as they are experienced in rural America are chronicled in 13 paintings by Grandma Moses; the narrative, some of it drawn from the artist's memoir, describes seasonal activities. (Rev: BCCB 11/00; BL 10/15/00; HBG 3/01; SLJ 10/00) [759.13]

15032 Pascoe, Elaine, ed. *The Pentagon* (4–7). Series: Super Structures of the World. 2003, Gale/Blackbirch LB $23.70 (1-56711-867-4). 48pp. An architectural tour of the Pentagon, headquarters of the U.S. Department of Defense. (Rev: SLJ 4/04) [355.6]

15033 Seltzer, Isadore. *The House I Live In: At Home in America* (2–5). Illus. by author. 1992, Macmillan $14.95 (0-02-781801-2). 32pp. Describes 12 American house designs, from log cabins to apartment buildings. (Rev: BCCB 4/92; BL 3/15/92; SLJ 5/92) [728]

15034 Weaver, Janice. *Building America* (5–8). Illus. by Bonnie Shemie. 2002, Tundra $17.95 (0-88776-606-4). 56pp. This brief history of architecture in America, from the 17th century to today, features detailed renderings, an illustrated timeline, and a useful glossary. (Rev: HBG 3/03; SLJ 5/03) [721]

Communication

General and Miscellaneous

15035 Platt, Richard. *Communication from Hieroglyphs to Hyperlinks* (4–6). Illus. Series: Kingfisher Knowledge. 2004, Kingfisher $11.95 (0-7534-5769-5). 64pp. Tracing the development of communication from early days to modern high-tech media, this colorful overview will attract browsers and reluctant older readers. (Rev: BL 9/1/04; SLJ 11/04) [302.2]

Codes and Ciphers

15036 Dickson, Louise. *Lu and Clancy's Secret Languages* (1–4). Illus. by Pat Cupples. 2001, Kids Can $14.95 (1-55337-025-2); paper $6.95 (1-55074-695-2). 40pp. Dog detectives Lu and Clancy hone their knowledge of language (Pig Latin, pictograms, invisible ink, and so forth). Also use *Lu and Clancy's Spy Stuff* (2001). (Rev: HBG 10/01; SLJ 8/01) [652.8]

15037 Janeczko, Paul B. *Top Secret: A Handbook of Codes, Ciphers, and Secret Writing* (4–7). Illus. by Jenna LaReau. 2004, Candlewick $16.99 (0-7636-0971-4). 144pp. Would-be cryptographers and secret agents will enjoy this collection of tips for developing codes and covertly passing information to others. (Rev: BL 5/15/04; SLJ 5/04) [652]

Flags

15038 Armbruster, Ann. *The American Flag* (4–6). Illus. 1991, Watts LB $22.00 (0-531-20045-0). 64pp. In addition to a history of the American flag, this illustrated account covers such subjects as the flag as a symbol, saluting, and modern flag manufacturing. (Rev: BL 1/1/92; SLJ 1/92) [929.9]

15039 Ayer, Eleanor. *Our Flag* (4–6). Illus. Series: I Know America. 1992, Millbrook paper $9.95 (1-878841-86-6). 48pp. This volume gives a colorfully illustrated introduction to the U.S. flag, its parts, and their meaning. (Rev: BL 5/15/92) [929.9]

15040 Ferry, Joseph. *The American Flag* (5–7). Series: American Symbols and Their Meanings. 2002, Mason Crest LB $18.95 (1-59084-026-7). 48pp. Designs that preceded the familiar flag accompany material on Betsy Ross and Francis Scott Key, illustrations of important flag raisings, and discussion of proper use and treatment of the flag, all in a package that will appeal to reluctant readers. (Rev: SLJ 4/02) [929.9]

15041 Prince, April Jones. *Meet Our Flag, Old Glory* (PS–2). Illus. by Joan Paley. 2004, Little, Brown $15.95 (0-316-73809-3). The flag's history and symbolism are described in rhyming text and bright illustrations. (Rev: SLJ 8/04) [929.9]

15042 Quiri, Patricia R. *The American Flag* (2–4). Illus. Series: True Books. 1998, Children's Book Pr. LB $21.00 (0-516-20617-6). 48pp. This story of the American flag includes material on Betsy Ross, the writing of "The Star-Spangled Banner," and how to honor the flag. (Rev: BL 8/98; HBG 10/98) [929.9]

15043 Radlauer, Ruth. *Honor the Flag: A Guide to Its Care and Display* (4–7). Illus. by J. J. Smith-Moore. 1992, Forest LB $14.95 (1-878363-61-1). 48pp. Lots of information about the American flag and its care. (Rev: BL 10/15/92) [929.92]

15044 Rollo, Vera F. *The American Flag* (3–6). Illus. by Alvin C. Jasper. 1990, Maryland $12.95 (0-917882-28-8). 78pp. The history of the U.S. flag plus myths that have grown up about its origins. (Rev: BL 6/1/90) [929.9]

15045 Ryan, Pam M. *The Flag We Love* (2–4). Illus. by Ralph Masiello. 1996, Charlesbridge $16.95 (0-88106-845-4). 32pp. The origins of the American flag, its history, and its uses are described in this colorful picture book. (Rev: BL 1/1–15/96; SLJ 5/96) [929.9]

15046 Smith, Whitney. *Flag Lore of All Nations* (4–6). Illus. 2001, Millbrook $29.90 (0-7613-1753-8). 112pp. One hundred and ninety-one flags are represented in this book. (Rev: BL 9/1/01; SLJ 9/01) [929.9]

15047 Spencer, Eve. *A Flag for Our Country* (K–3). Illus. by Mike Eagle. Series: Stories of America. 1993, Raintree LB $25.69 (0-8114-7211-6). The story of how Betsy Ross made the first American flag. (Rev: SLJ 5/93) [929.9]

15048 Thomson, Sarah L. *Stars and Stripes: The Story of the American Flag* (1–3). Illus. by Bob Dacey and Debra Bandelin. 2003, HarperCollins LB $16.89 (0-06-050417-X). 32pp. Double-page spreads pair brief text opposite full-page illustrations showing the evolution of the flag from its inception through its renewed visibility since September 11, 2001. (Rev: BL 9/15/03; HBG 10/03; SLJ 7/03) [929]

15049 Williams, Earl P. *What You Should Know About the American Flag* (4–8). Illus. 1989, Thomas Publns. paper $5.95 (0-939631-10-5). 68pp. A comprehensive guide to facts and legends, history and traditions concerning the U.S. flag. (Rev: BL 11/15/87) [929.9]

Language and Languages

15050 Baker, Rosalie. *In a Word: 750 Words and Their Fascinating Stories and Origins* (4–8). Illus. by Tom Lopes. 2003, Cobblestone $17.95 (0-8126-2710-5). 250pp. Useful for reference, this guide to the origins and meanings of words and phrases is drawn from a monthly column in *Cobblestone*. (Rev: BL 2/15/04; SLJ 4/04) [422]

15051 Burns, Peggy. *Writing* (3–5). Illus. Series: Stepping Through History. 1995, Raintree LB $5.00 (1-56847-341-9). 32pp. A history of writing from ancient forms like hieroglyphics to the many languages of today. (Rev: BL 7/95) [411]

15052 Cooper, Kay. *Why Do You Speak as You Do? A Guide to World Languages* (5–8). Illus. by Brandon Kruse. 1992, Children's Book Pr. LB $14.85 (0-8027-8165-9). 66pp. A simple yet lively presentation of linguistics. (Rev: BCCB 2/93; BL 1/15/93) [400]

15053 Elya, Susan Middleton. *Say Hola to Spanish* (PS–4). Illus. by Loretta Lopez. 1996, Lee & Low $15.95 (1-880000-29-6). 32pp. More than 70 common Spanish words are introduced in delightful rhymes with pencil illustrations. (Rev: BL 5/1/96; SLJ 6/96) [468.1]

15054 Fine, Edith Hope. *Cryptomania! Teleporting into Greek and Latin with the CryptoKids* (4–6). Illus. by Kim Doner. 2004, Tricycle $15.95 (1-58246-062-0). 44pp. Zander and his friends teleport to various places and times, amassing information on Greek and Latin words for a vocabulary assignment; with extensive index/glossary. (Rev: SLJ 11/04)

15055 Goldstein, Peggy. *Long Is a Dragon: Chinese Writing for Children* (2–5). Illus. 1991, China

Books $17.95 (1-881896-01-3). 32pp. This introduction to Chinese writing gives a brief history and 75 simple characters, including the numbers 1 to 12. (Rev: BCCB 5/91; BL 6/1/91; SLJ 7/91) [495.1]

15056 Johnson, Stephen T. *Alphabet City* (4–7). Illus. 1995, Viking $16.99 (0-670-85631-2). 32pp. A sophisticated alphabet book that consists of a series of paintings, each of which represents a letter. (Rev: BCCB 11/95; BL 1/1–15/96; HB 11–12/95; SLJ 1/96*) [421]

15057 Kenny, Chantal Lacourciere. *The Kids Can Press French and English Phrase Book* (1–4). Illus. by Linda Hendry. 1999, Kids Can $12.95 (1-55074-477-1). 40pp. The daily life of an 8-year-old girl is illustrated with drawings and the actions are described in both French and English phrases. A companion book is *The Kids Can Press Spanish and English Phrase Book* (1999). (Rev: SLJ 10/99) [407]

15058 Lee, Huy Voun. *In the Park* (PS–3). Illus. 1998, Holt $15.95 (0-8050-4128-1). 32pp. Using scenes from a park visit as an inspiration, Xiao Ming's mother draws Chinese characters that illustrate objects from nature. (Rev: BL 7/98; HBG 10/98; SLJ 5/98)

15059 Lee, Huy Voun. *At the Beach* (PS–3). Illus. 1994, Holt $16.95 (0-8050-2768-8). 32pp. Introduces ten Mandarin Chinese characters and the object each suggests. (Rev: BL 6/1–15/94; SLJ 7/94) [495.1]

15060 Roberts, Michael. *Mumbo Jumbo: The Creepy ABC* (4–8). Illus. by author. 2000, Callaway $24.95 (0-935112-49-9). A scary alphabet book that features such subjects as vampires, eyeball stew, quicksand, and bats. (Rev: HBG 3/01; SLJ 3/01) [428]

15061 Stojic, Manya. *Hello World! Greetings in 42 Languages Around the Globe!* (K–2). Illus. 2002, Scholastic $14.95 (0-439-36202-4). 40pp. Readers learn how to pronounce 42 words for hello, each introduced by a simple, bold painting of a child from the country and the name of the language concerned. (Rev: BL 12/1/02; HBG 3/03; SLJ 12/02) [413]

15062 Takahashi, Peter X. *Jimi's Book of Japanese: A Motivating Method to Learn Japanese* (3–6). Illus. by Yumie Toka. 2002, PB&J paper $16.95 (0-9723247-0-4). 72pp. A book featuring the Japanese characters (*kana*) and how to write them, for beginning speakers and writers of the language. (Rev: BL 2/15/03) [495.6]

15063 Vinton, Ken. *Alphabetic Antics: Hundreds of Activities to Challenge and Enrich Letter Learners of All Ages* (5–8). Illus. 1996, Free Spirit paper $19.95 (1-57542-008-2). For each letter of the alphabet, there is a history, how it appears in different alphabets, important words that begin with the letter, a quotation from someone whose name starts with it, and a number of interesting related projects. (Rev: SLJ 1/97) [411]

15064 Young, Ed. *Voices of the Heart* (4–8). Illus. 1997, Scholastic paper $17.95 (0-590-50199-2). In this sumptuous picture book, the author lists and explains 26 Chinese characters, each of which expresses a different emotion. (Rev: BCCB 4/97; BL 4/15/97; HB 5–6/97; SLJ 6/97) [179]

Reading, Speaking, and Writing

Books, Printing, Libraries, and Schools

15065 Armstrong, Thomas. *You're Smarter Than You Think: A Kid's Guide to Multiple Intelligences* (5–8). 2003, Free Spirit paper $15.95 (1-57542-113-5). 192pp. Eight different intelligences are defined in understandable terms, with quizzes that help readers investigate their own strengths. (Rev: BL 4/15/03; SLJ 6/03) [153.9]

15066 Asimov, Isaac. *Science Fiction: Vision of Tomorrow?* (3–5). Illus. Series: Isaac Asimov's 21st Century Library of the Universe. 2004, Gareth Stevens LB $24.67 (0-8368-3952-8). 32pp. A revised, well-illustrated edition of a previously published book, this discusses the major themes found in science fiction, looking also at real developments that were predicted in advance. (Rev: SLJ 3/05) [500]

15067 Brown, Don. *Kid Blink Beats the World* (2–5). Illus. by author. 2004, Roaring Brook $16.95 (1-59643-003-6). 32pp. Young newspaper vendors' 1899 rebellion against William Randolph Hearst and Joseph Pulitzer is described in this arresting picture book for older children. (Rev: BL 9/15/04) [331]

15068 Cummins, Julie. *The Inside-Outside Book of Libraries* (1–4). Illus. by Roxie Munro. 1996, Dutton $15.99 (0-525-45608-2). 40pp. All sorts of libraries — big and small; public, school, and special — are visited in this introduction. (Rev: BCCB 10/96; BL 10/15/96; HB 9–10/96; SLJ 8/96*) [027]

15069 Davidson, Tish. *School Conflict* (4–8). Series: Life Balance. 2003, Watts LB $19.50 (0-531-12251-4); paper $6.95 (0-531-15571-4). 80pp. This book examines the various conflicts, including violence, that exist in public education today and how these affect the lives and mental health of students. (Rev: BL 10/15/03; SLJ 3/04) [370]

15070 *Dear Author: Students Write About the Books That Changed Their Lives* (5–9). 1995, Conari paper $9.95 (1-57324-003-6). A collection of young adults' letters to authors, both dead and alive, expressing, with wit and honesty, how the authors' books have affected them. (Rev: BL 1/1–15/96; SLJ 11/95) [028.5]

15071 Farrell, Juliana, and Beth Mayall. *Middle School: The Real Deal* (5–7). Illus. 2001, HarperCollins paper $7.99 (0-380-81313-0). 144pp. Advice on coping with school work, teachers, and social life is presented in an appealing format. (Rev: BL 6/1–15/01) [373.18]

15072 Fowler, Allan. *The Dewey Decimal System* (3–5). Illus. 1996, Children's Book Pr. LB $22.00 (0-516-20132-8). 47pp. An explanation of the Dewey Decimal System, using clear text and many examples. (Rev: BL 2/1/97; SLJ 4/97) [025.4]

15073 Fowler, Allan. *The Library of Congress* (2–6). Illus. Series: True Books. 1996, Children's Book Pr. LB $22.00 (0-516-20137-9). 48pp. An information-packed account that describes the history, contents, and functions of the Library of Congress. (Rev: SLJ 2/97) [027]

15074 Fridell, Ron. *Education for All: Floating Schools, Cave Classrooms, and Backpacking Teachers* (5–9). Series: In a Perfect World. 2003, 21st Century Bks. LB $26.90 (0-7613-2624-3). 80pp. Report writers will find useful information on the obstacles facing educators in many parts of the world — insufficient funding, shortages of equipment and personal, discrimination, and so forth. (Rev: HBG 10/03; SLJ 8/03)

15075 Funk, Gary. *A Balancing Act: Sports and Education* (5–8). Illus. Series: Sports Issues. 1995, Lerner LB $28.75 (0-8225-3301-4). A frank, thorough discussion of the many issues involved in sports and their place in educational institutions. (Rev: BL 1/1–15/95; SLJ 9/95) [796.04]

15076 Gibbons, Gail. *Check It Out: The Book About Libraries* (K–3). Illus. 1985, Harcourt $16.00 (0-15-216400-6); paper $6.00 (0-15-216401-4). 32pp. An overview of what the library is and how it functions in picture-book format that is lively enough for older readers. (Rev: BCCB 9/85; BL 10/1/85; HB 11–12/85)

15077 Glassman, Peter, ed. *Oz: The Hundredth Anniversary Celebration* (4–8). 2000, HarperCollins $24.95 (0-688-15915-X). 64pp. In this tribute to the children's classic, authors and illustrators — fans of the Oz books — pay homage in words and pictures. (Rev: BL 12/1/00; HBG 3/01; SLJ 11/00) [807]

15078 Gorman, Jacqueline Laks. *The Library* (K–2). Illus. Series: I Like to Visit. 2005, Weekly Reader LB $14.50 (0-8368-4452-1). 24pp. A simple photoessay that shows what to expect on a visit to the library. Others in this series include *The Museum*, *The Aquarium*, and *The Playground* (all 2005). (Rev: BL 4/1/05) [027]

15079 Hauser, Jill Frankel. *Wow! I'm Reading! Fun Activities to Make Reading Happen* (PS–3). Illus. by Stan Jaskiel. Series: A Williamson Little Hands Book. 2000, Williamson paper $12.95 (1-885593-41-4). 141pp. A collection of activities designed to smooth the path to reading, with references to recommended picture books and bright black-and-white cartoons. (Rev: SLJ 4/01) [372.41]

15080 Heiligman, Deborah. *The New York Public Library Kid's Guide to Research* (5–8). Illus. by David Cain. 1998, Scholastic paper $14.95 (0-590-30715-0). 134pp. A fine introduction to research techniques including material on taking notes, using print and nonprint resources, conducting interviews and surveys, searching the Internet, and locating toll-free numbers. (Rev: HBG 3/99; SLJ 2/99) [808.023]

15081 Knowlton, Jack. *Books and Libraries* (2–5). Illus. by Harriett Barton. 1991, HarperCollins LB $14.89 (0-06-021610-7). 48pp. The history of books and libraries is traced from cave paintings to the present. (Rev: BCCB 3/91; BL 4/1/91; SLJ 4/91) [002]

15082 Koscielniak, Bruce. *Johann Gutenberg and the Amazing Printing Press* (2–5). 2003, Houghton Mifflin $16.00 (0-618-26351-9). 40pp. This history of early book making traces the evolution of the process from the Chinese development of paper up to Johann Gutenberg's 15th-century invention of the printing press. (Rev: BL 7/03; HBG 4/04; SLJ 9/03) [686.2]

15083 Leedy, Loreen. *Look at My Book: How Kids Can Write and Illustrate Terrific Books* (K–3). Illus. 2004, Holiday House $16.95 (0-8234-1590-2). 32pp. This picture book covers all aspects of publishing a work, from initial concept through writing, revision, and selecting design and binding. (Rev: BL 2/15/04; SLJ 4/04) [808]

15084 McElroy, Lisa Tucker, and Abigail Jane Cobb. *Meet My Grandmother: She's a Children's Book Author* (1–4). Photos by Joel Benjamin. 2001, Millbrook LB $22.90 (0-7613-1972-7). 31pp. Vicki Cobb's 9-year-old granddaughter describes her mother's work and how books are created and published. (Rev: HBG 3/02; SLJ 8/01) [509.2]

15085 Madama, John. *Desktop Publishing: The Art of Communication* (5–8). Illus. Series: Media Workshop. 1993, Lerner LB $21.27 (0-8225-2303-5). 64pp. The history of desktop publishing, the equipment used, and the production of a newsletter. (Rev: SLJ 6/93) [686.2]

15086 Marcus, Leonard S. *Side by Side: Five Favorite Picture-Book Teams Go to Work* (4–7). Illus. 2001, Walker LB $23.85 (0-8027-8779-7). 64pp. A look at how members of five well-known collaborative teams work together to create picture books, from concept to finished product. (Rev: BL 11/15/01; HB 1–2/02; HBG 3/02; SLJ 11/01) [070.5]

15087 Marshall, Pam. *From Idea to Book* (PS–2). Series: Start to Finish. 2004, Lerner LB $18.60 (0-8225-1385-4). The basics of book development are laid out in simple terms for young readers. (Rev: BL 6/1–15/04; SLJ 9/04) [002]

15088 Nathan, Amy. *Surviving Homework: Tips from Teens* (5–8). Illus. 1997, Millbrook LB $24.90 (1-56294-185-2). Using answers on questionnaires given to high school juniors and seniors, this book supplies many useful study tips and suggestions on how to organize one's time. (Rev: BL 6/1–15/97; BR 11–12/96; SLJ 7/97) [372.12]

15089 Pfeffer, Susan Beth. *Who Were They Really? The True Stories Behind Famous Characters* (3–6). Illus. 1999, Millbrook LB $22.40 (0-7613-0405-3). 72pp. This book explores the real people behind such fictional characters as Alice in Wonderland, the Lost Boys of Peter Pan, and Christopher Robin. (Rev: BL 12/15/99; HBG 10/00; SLJ 12/99) [820.9]

15090 Pickering, Marianne. *Lessons for Life: Education and Learning* (5–8). Series: Our Human Family. 1995, Blackbirch LB $31.19 (1-56711-127-0). A look at educational practices around the world that shows great similarities regardless of the culture. (Rev: SLJ 1/96) [370]

15091 Raatma, Lucia. *Libraries* (2–4). Series: True Books. 1998, Children's Book Pr. LB $21.00 (0-516-20672-9). 47pp. From the clay tablets of

Mesopotamia to the specialized multimedia centers of today, this account traces the history and functions of the world's libraries. (Rev: HBG 10/98; SLJ 9/98) [027]

15092 Radabaugh, Melinda. *Going to the Library* (PS–1). Series: First Time. 2003, Heinemann LB $18.50 (1-4034-0230-2). 24pp. A reassuring, simple introduction to a library and its contents. (Rev: HBG 10/03; SLJ 6/03) [027]

15093 Rhatigan, Joe. *In Print! 40 Cool Publishing Projects for Kids* (3–7). 2003, Sterling $19.95 (1-57990-359-2). 128pp. Layout and design are among the aspects discussed in this guide to writing and publishing. (Rev: BL 8/03; HBG 10/03; SLJ 10/03) [808.02]

15094 Schneider, Meg. *Help! My Teacher Hates Me* (5–8). 1994, Workman paper $7.95 (1-56305-492-2). Helpful hints for developing a positive attitude in school. (Rev: BL 3/15/95) [371.8]

15095 *Scholastic Explains Reading Homework: Everything Children (and Parents) Need to Survive 2nd and 3rd Grade* (2–3). Series: Scholastic Explains Homework. 1998, Scholastic $14.95 (0-590-39755-9); paper $6.95 (0-590-39758-3). 64pp. Using a variety of learning approaches, this book helps primary-grade students develop reading comprehension. (Rev: SLJ 12/98) [372.4]

15096 Schumm, Jeanne Shay. *School Power: Strategies for Succeeding in School* (5–8). Illus. 1992, Free Spirit paper $15.95 (0-915793-42-3). Sensible suggestions for improving study skills: organization, note taking, improving reading, and writing reports. (Rev: BL 3/1/93) [371.3]

15097 Senisi, Ellen B. *Reading Grows* (PS–K). Photos by author. 1999, Whitman LB $15.95 (0-8075-6898-8). Colorful photographs show children reacting to books, from babies looking at board books to older children reading alone or with others. (Rev: HBG 10/99; SLJ 8/99) [790.1]

15098 Stevens, Janet. *From Pictures to Words: A Book About Making a Book* (2–4). Illus. 1995, Holiday House LB $16.95 (0-8234-1154-0). 42pp. This manual for youngsters who want to create their own picture books deals with such topics as setting, plot, and characterization. (Rev: BCCB 6/95; BL 4/15/95; SLJ 7/95*) [741.6]

15099 Swain, Gwenyth. *Bookworks: Making Books by Hand* (4–7). Illus. 1995, Carolrhoda LB $22.60 (0-87614-858-5). 64pp. After a brief history of books and printing, this account gives directions for making paper and various kinds of books. (Rev: BL 7/95; SLJ 8/95*) [745.5]

15100 Wu, Dana Y. *Our Libraries* (2–4). Series: I Know America. 2001, Millbrook LB $22.90 (0-7613-1856-9). 48pp. The Dewey decimal system, the Library of Congress, Banned Books Week, and even MARC records are among the topics covered in this comprehensive overview of libraries. (Rev: HBG 10/01; SLJ 7/01) [027.073]

15101 Zeman, Anne, and Kate Kelly. *Everything You Need to Know About American History Homework: A Desk Reference for Students and Parents* (4–6). Illus. Series: Scholastic Homework Reference.

1994, Scholastic $18.95 (0-590-49362-0). 136pp. This book helps youngsters understand concepts in American history and how to apply them while doing homework assignments. Also use *Everything You Need to Know About Math Homework* and *Everything You Need to Know About Science Homework* (both 1994). (Rev: SLJ 1/95) [372.13]

Signs and Symbols

15102 Bateman, Teresa. *Red, White, Blue and Uncle Who? The Stories Behind Some of America's Patriotic Symbols* (3–6). Illus. by John O'Brien. 2001, Holiday House $15.95 (0-8234-1285-7). 64pp. The meaning of patriotic symbols such as Uncle Sam, war memorials, and Mount Rushmore is explained with surprising detail in simple, appealing, and often humorous terms, enhanced by sprightly line drawings. (Rev: BL 12/15/01; HBG 10/02; SLJ 11/01) [929.9]

15103 Gross, Ruth Belov. *You Don't Need Words! A Book About Ways People Talk Without Words* (1–4). Illus. by Susannah Ryan. 1991, Scholastic $14.95 (0-590-43897-2). 48pp. A demonstration of how people talk nonverbally. (Rev: BL 12/15/91; SLJ 1/92) [302]

15104 Gryski, Camilla. *Hands On, Thumbs Up: Secret Handshakes, Fingerprints, Sign Languages and More Handy Ways to Have Fun with Hands* (3–6). Illus. by Pat Cupples. 1991, Addison-Wesley paper $8.95 (0-201-56756-3). 112pp. All about the human hand — facts, trivia, superstitions, jokes, and more. (Rev: BL 12/15/91) [611.97]

15105 Heller, Lora. *Sign Language for Kids: A Fun and Easy Guide to American Sign Language* (4–6). 2004, Sterling $14.95 (1-4027-0672-3). 96pp. Color photographs and clear directions make this an excellent introduction to sign language. (Rev: BL 9/15/04) [419]

15106 Jango-Cohen, Judith. *The Bald Eagle* (K–2). Series: Pull Ahead Books. 2003, Lerner LB $22.60 (0-8225-3645-5); paper $5.95 (0-8225-4750-3). 32pp. For beginning report writers, this is a simple, well-illustrated look at the eagle and its choice as a national symbol. (Rev: SLJ 1/04) [929.9]

15107 Jeffrey, Laura S. *All About Braille: Reading by Touch* (2–4). Illus. Series: Transportation and Communication. 2004, Enslow LB $18.95 (0-7660-2184-X). 48pp. A simple, easy-to-read overview of the invention of the Braille system and how it changed the lives of blind people, with true stories. [411]

15108 Kramer, Jackie, and Tali Ovadia. *You Can Learn Sign Language! More Than 300 Words in Pictures* (3–7). Illus. by John Smith. 2000, Troll paper $4.95 (0-8167-6336-4). 48pp. An easy-to-understand introduction to American Sign Language that presents both letters and numbers. (Rev: SLJ 7/00) [419]

15109 Kubler, Annie. *My First Signs* (PS). Illus. 2005, Child's Play $6.99 (1-904550-39-8). 12pp. An introduction to American Sign Language, for both hearing and deaf children. (Rev: BL 5/15/05) [302.2]

15110 Lowenstein, Felicia. *All About Sign Language: Talking With Your Hands* (2–4). Illus. Series: Transportation and Communication. 2004, Enslow LB $17.95 (0-7660-2028-2). 48pp. A simple, easy-to-read overview of the history of sign language and how it changed the lives of deaf people, with true stories. (Rev: SLJ 12/04) [419]

15111 Mignon, Philippe. *Labyrinths: Can You Escape from the 26 Letters of the Alphabet?* (2–5). Illus. 2002, Firefly $14.95 (1-55297-559-2); paper $9.95 (1-55297-579-7). 64pp. A complex and attractive combination of alphabet book, mazes, poetry, and intriguing tidbits both ancient and modern. (Rev: BL 1/1–15/03; HBG 3/03; SLJ 12/02) [843]

15112 Milich, Zoran. *City Signs* (PS–K). Illus. 2002, Kids Can $15.95 (1-55337-003-1). 32pp. A photographic look at worded signs that will leave preschoolers proud of their "reading" skills. (Rev: BL 10/15/02; HB 1–2/03; HBG 3/03) [659.13]

15113 Rankin, Laura. *The Handmade Alphabet* (PS–6). Illus. 1991, Dial $16.99 (0-8037-0974-9). 32pp. Hands do the talking in this sign-language alphabet book. (Rev: BCCB 9/91; BL 8/91*; HB 11–12/91; SLJ 10/91*) [419]

15114 Votry, Kim, and Curt Waller. *Baby's First Signs* (PS–2). Illus. 2001, Gallaudet Univ. $6.95 (1-56368-114-5). Basic words are introduced in sign language, showing a child signing and clear directions for signing the word yourself. Also use *More Baby's First Signs* (2001). (Rev: SLJ 2/02) [419]

15115 Woods, Mary B., and Michael Woods. *Ancient Communication: From Grunts to Graffiti* (5–8). Series: Ancient Technologies. 2000, Runestone LB $25.26 (0-8225-2996-3). 88pp. Beginning with cave paintings and hieroglyphics and ending with modern alphabets and universal languages, this account of the history of communication emphasizes ancient cultures. (Rev: BL 9/15/00; HBG 3/01; SLJ 1/01) [652]

15116 Yanuck, Debbie L. *Uncle Sam* (K–2). Series: American Symbols. 2003, Capstone LB $19.93 (0-7368-2295-X). 24pp. An introduction to Uncle Sam, the bearded symbol of the United States who grew from a political cartoon to an image known around the world. (Rev: SLJ 4/04) [398.2]

Words and Grammar

15117 Agee, Jon. *Palindromania!* (3–7). Illus. 2002, Farrar $15.51 (0-374-35730-7). 112pp. Hundreds of clever and amusing palindromes are presented beside black-and-white drawings. (Rev: BL 10/15/02; HB 9–10/02; HBG 3/03; SLJ 11/02) [793.734]

15118 Agee, Jon. *Sit on a Potato Pan, Otis! More Palindromes* (4–8). Illus. 1999, Farrar $14.41 (0-374-31808-5). A whimsical book illustrated with black-and-white cartoons that contains 60 humorous palindromes. (Rev: BCCB 2/99; BL 3/1/99; HB 3–4/99; HBG 9/99; SLJ 3/99) [418]

15119 Agee, Jon. *Who Ordered the Jumbo Shrimp? And Other Oxymorons* (5–10). Illus. 1998, Harper-Collins $15.95 (0-06-205159-8). An amusing collection of oxymorons such as "permanent temp" and "Great Depression," cleverly illustrated with black-and-white cartoons. (Rev: BCCB 12/98; HBG 3/99; SLJ 11/98) [412]

15120 Bailey, LaWanda. *Miss Myrtle Frag, the Grammar Nag* (5–9). Illus. by Brian Strassburg. 2000, Absey paper $13.95 (1-888842-19-9). 84pp. A clever book that explains key grammar rules through a series of witty letters from Miss Myrtle Frag. (Rev: SLJ 2/01) [415]

15121 Beinstein, Phoebe. *Dora's Book of Words / Libro de Palabras de Dora* (PS–2). Trans. by Argentina Palacios Ziegler. Illus. by Thompson Bros. 2003, Simon & Schuster $10.95 (0-689-85626-1). Dora the Explorer looks at some everyday words loved by children in a format that allows the reader to switch from English to Spanish by pulling on a tab. (Rev: SLJ 3/03)

15122 Brennan-Nelson, Denise. *My Momma Likes to Say* (2–4). Illus. by Jane Monroe Donovan. 2003, Sleeping Bear $15.95 (1-58536-106-2). 32pp. Illustrations and rhymes expand on the meanings of such phrases as "money doesn't grow on trees" and "cat got your tongue?" (Rev: BL 7/03; SLJ 9/03) [398.9]

15123 Cleary, Brian P. *Dearly, Nearly, Insincerely: What Is an Adverb?* (2–4). Illus. by Brian Gable. Series: Words Are CATegorical. 2003, Carolrhoda LB $14.95 (0-87614-924-7). Energetic illustrations accompany a bouncy rhyming text that introduces adverbs of all kinds. (Rev: HBG 10/03; SLJ 3/03)

15124 Cleary, Brian P. *Hairy, Scary, Ordinary: What Is an Adjective?* (PS–3). Illus. by Jenya Prosmitsky. 2000, Lerner $12.95 (1-57505-401-9). 32pp. A playful rhyming text helps to explain what an adjective is and how it functions. (Rev: BL 6/1–15/00; HBG 10/00; SLJ 7/00) [428.2]

15125 Cleary, Brian P. *I and You and Don't Forget Who: What Is a Pronoun?* (2–4). Illus. by Brian Gable. Series: Words Are Categorical. 2004, Carolrhoda $14.95 (1-57505-596-1). 32pp. This clever blend of rhyming text and cartoon drawings makes its lessons about pronouns easy to digest. (Rev: BL 5/1/04; SLJ 7/04) [428.2]

15126 Cleary, Brian P. *A Mink, a Fink, a Skating Rink: What Is a Noun?* (2–4). Illus. by Jenya Prosmitsky. Series: Words Are Categorical. 1999, Carolrhoda LB $12.95 (1-57505-402-7). Humorous rhymes and illustrations are used to introduce various kinds of nouns. (Rev: HBG 3/00; SLJ 11/99) [415]

15127 Cleary, Brian P. *Pitch and Throw, Grasp and Know: What Is a Synonym?* (2–4). Illus. by Brian Gable. Series: Words Are Categorical. 2005, Carolrhoda $14.95 (1-57505-796-4). 32pp. Bright cartoon illustrations of humorous situations introduce synonyms. (Rev: BL 2/1/05; SLJ 3/05) [428.1]

15128 Cleary, Brian P. *To Root, to Toot, to Parachute: What Is a Verb?* (K–3). Illus. by Jenya Prosmitsky. 2001, Carolrhoda $14.95 (1-57505-403-5). 32pp. A delightful, lively introduction to verbs with

action-packed illustrations. (Rev: BL 4/15/01; HBG 10/01; SLJ 7/01) [428.2]

15129 Cleary, Brian P. *Under, Over, By the Clover: What Is a Preposition?* (2–4). Illus. by Brian Gable. 2002, Carolrhoda $14.95 (1-57505-524-4). 32pp. A pack of crazy-colored cartoonlike animals and rhyming text teach younger readers all about prepositions. (Rev: BL 3/1/02; HBG 10/02; SLJ 6/02) [428.2]

15130 Cooper, Barbara. *Alan Apostrophe* (2–4). Illus. by Maggie Raynor. Series: Meet the Puncs: A Remarkable Punctuation Family. 2005, Gareth Stevens LB $23.33 (0-8368-4223-5). 32pp. Alan Apostrophe, captain of a fishing boat, wears an eye patch in the shape of an apostrophe and his speech, with many dropped letters, involves much use of the punctuation for which he is named. Also in this series from Britain: *Christopher Comma* and *Emma Exclamation Point* (both 2005). (Rev: SLJ 4/05)

15131 Dobkin, Bonnie. *Go-With Words* (1–2). Illus. by Tom Dunnington. Series: Rookie Readers. 1993, Children's Book Pr. LB $17.00 (0-516-02016-1). 32pp. An easy-to-read book that explores the concept of vocabulary and the value of words. (Rev: BL 3/1/94) [428.1]

15132 Gonzalez, Ralfka, and Ana Ruiz. *My First Book of Proverbs / Mi Primer Libro de Dichos* (2–5). Illus. by authors. 1995, Children's Book Pr. $15.95 (0-89239-134-0). A bilingual book of 27 Mexican dichos (proverbs) illustrated in bright, glowing colors. (Rev: SLJ 2/96) [398.9]

15133 Heller, Ruth. *Behind the Mask: A Book About Prepositions* (2–4). Illus. 1995, Penguin Putnam $17.99 (0-448-41123-7). 48pp. Using rhymes, a variety of prepositions are introduced and used. (Rev: BL 12/15/95) [428.2]

15134 Heller, Ruth. *Fantastic! Wow! and Unreal! A Book About Interjections and Conjunctions* (1–3). Illus. 1998, Penguin Putnam $16.99 (0-448-41862-2). 32pp. This book explains interjections and conjunctions, using vivid images in glowing colors and helpful examples. (Rev: BL 2/15/99; HBG 10/99; SLJ 3/99) [425]

15135 Heller, Ruth. *Many Luscious Lollipops* (1–4). Illus. by author. 1989, Penguin Putnam $17.99 (0-448-03151-5). In a series of rhymes, a variety of adjectives are introduced and identified. (Rev: BCCB 11/89; SLJ 1/90) [415]

15136 Heller, Ruth. *Up, Up and Away: A Book About Adverbs* (2–5). Illus. 1991, Penguin Putnam $17.99 (0-448-40249-1); paper $6.99 (0-698-11663-1). 32pp. In color drawings and catchy rhymes, Heller explains how adverbs answer precisely the questions of how, how often, when, and where. Also use by Heller: *A Cache of Jewels and Other Collective Nouns* (on collective nouns) and *Kites Sail High* (on verbs) (both 1998). (Rev: BCCB 1/92; BL 1/15/92; SLJ 2/92) [418]

15137 Hepworth, Cathi. *Bug Off! A Swarm of Insect Words* (3–6). Illus. 1998, Penguin Putnam $15.99 (0-399-22640-0). 32pp. Words that contain insect names (e.g., encroach, frisbee) are acted out by several bugs in a series of witty illustrations. (Rev:

BCCB 9/98; BL 6/1–15/98*; HBG 10/98; SLJ 5/98) [428.1]

15138 Hill, Eric. *Spot's Big Book of Words* (PS). Illus. by author. 1988, Penguin Putnam $11.95 (0-399-21563-8). 28pp. Lovable Spot teaches young readers the words of their everyday world. (Rev: BL 10/1/88; SLJ 11/88)

15139 Juster, Norton. *As: A Surfeit of Similes* (2–5). Illus. by David Small. 1989, Morrow LB $15.93 (0-688-08140-1). 80pp. A long list of similes enter the conversation of two funny little men. (Rev: BCCB 5/89; BL 5/15/89; SLJ 4/89)

15140 Lederer, Richard. *The Circus of Words: Acrobatic Anagrams, Parading Palindromes, Wonderful Words on a Wire, and More Lively Letter Play* (5–8). Illus. by Dave Morice. 2001, Chicago Review paper $12.95 (1-55652-380-7). 143pp. Lovers of words will find lots of entertainment in this selection of challenging exercises. (Rev: SLJ 8/01) [428.1]

15141 Leedy, Loreen, and Pat Street. *There's a Frog in My Throat: 440 Animal Sayings a Little Bird Told Me* (2–5). Illus. by Loreen Leedy. 2003, Holiday House $16.95 (0-8234-1774-3). 32pp. An amusing romp through animal-related expressions such as "social butterfly" and "barrel of monkeys." (Rev: BL 3/15/03*; HB 5–6/03; HBG 10/03; SLJ 4/03) [428.1]

15142 McKerns, Dorothy, and Leslie Motchkavitz. *The Kid's Guide to Good Grammar* (3–7). 1998, Lowell House paper $8.95 (1-56565-697-0). 96pp. An entertaining guide that combines information on grammar, spelling, parts of speech, common errors, and vocabulary, with related craft projects, puzzles, and games. (Rev: SLJ 4/99) [425]

15143 *My First Spanish Farm Board Book / Mi primer libro de la granja: A Bilingual Word Book* (PS–1). Series: My First Word Books. 2003, DK $6.99 (0-7894-9522-8). English and Spanish words are given for a variety of farm-related images. (Rev: SLJ 12/03) [428.1]

15144 Riley, Jeni. *First Word Book* (PS). Illus. by Mandy Stanley. 2000, Kingfisher $12.95 (0-7534-5272-3). 47pp. This early vocabulary-building title uses simple drawings to introduce a number of common words. (Rev: HBG 3/01; SLJ 8/00) [423]

15145 Root, Betty. *My First Dictionary* (PS–2). Illus. by Jonathan Langley. Series: My First Reference. 1993, DK $17.95 (1-56458-277-9). 96pp. Definitions and illustrations are given for 1,000 words commonly used by children plus an appended collection of word games. (Rev: SLJ 1/94) [423]

15146 Rovetch, Lissa. *Ook the Book and Other Silly Rhymes* (PS–1). Illus. by Shannon McNeill. 2001, Chronicle $12.95 (0-8118-2660-0). A humorous introduction to vowel sounds and the appearance of letters that will appeal to beginning readers. (Rev: HBG 10/01; SLJ 8/01) [428.1]

15147 Scarry, Richard. *Richard Scarry's Best Word Book Ever* (PS–2). Illus. by author. 1963, Western $13.99 (0-307-15510-2). 72pp. A diverse, unorthodox picture dictionary for children who like lots of little pictures.

15148 Shields, Carol Diggory. *English, Fresh Squeezed! 40 Thirst-for-Knowledge-Quenching Poems* (4–7). Illus. by Tony Ross. Series: BrainJuice. 2005, Handprint $14.95 (1-59354-053-1). 80pp. A humorous, rhyming look at annoying grammatical and other rules of language, with appealing illustrations and useful mnemonic devices. (Rev: BL 2/15/04; HB 5–6/04; SLJ 5/05)

15149 Shiffman, Lena. *My First Book of Words: 1,000 Words Every Child Should Know* (PS). Illus. by author. 1992, Scholastic $13.95 (0-590-45142-1). 62pp. Through a series of illustrations, many objects, actions, and emotions are identified in this basic word book. (Rev: SLJ 3/92)

15150 Terban, Marvin. *Building Your Vocabulary* (4–8). Illus. Series: Scholastic Guides. 2002, Scholastic paper $12.95 (0-439-28561-5). 188pp. In addition to techniques for increasing vocabulary, Terban discusses etymology and how to use a dictionary and thesaurus, giving clear, often entertaining examples throughout. (Rev: SLJ 8/02) [428.1]

15151 Terban, Marvin. *Checking Your Grammar* (5–8). Series: Scholastic Guides. 1993, Scholastic paper $10.95 (0-590-49454-6). 144pp. An attractive, witty guide to effective writing of all sorts of letters, book reports, essays, and reviews. (Rev: BL 10/1/93; SLJ 2/94) [428.2]

15152 Terban, Marvin. *The Dove Dove: Funny Homograph Riddles* (4–7). Illus. by Tom Huffman. 1988, Houghton Mifflin paper $7.95 (0-89919-810-4). 64pp. Making homographs less puzzling. Also use *Mad As a Wet Hen! and Other Funny Idioms* (1987). (Rev: BL 1/1/89) [818.5402]

15153 Terban, Marvin. *Eight Ate: A Feast of Homonym Riddles* (2–3). Illus. by Giulio Maestro. 1982, Houghton Mifflin paper $7.95 (0-89919-086-3). 64pp. A question-and-answer approach to introducing a variety of homonyms.

15154 Terban, Marvin. *Guppies in Tuxedos: Funny Eponyms* (3–6). Illus. by Giulio Maestro. 1988, Houghton Mifflin paper $7.95 (0-89919-770-1). 64pp. Telling the story behind 100 eponyms arranged by categories. (Rev: BL 7/88; SLJ 8/88)

15155 Terban, Marvin. *In a Pickle and Other Funny Idioms* (3–6). Illus. by Giulio Maestro. 1983, Houghton Mifflin paper $6.95 (0-89919-164-9). 64pp. Common idioms are explained, and their origins are given.

15156 Terban, Marvin. *Punching the Clock: Funny Action Idioms* (3–6). Illus. by Tom Huffman. 1990, Houghton Mifflin paper $6.95 (0-89919-865-1). 64pp. Such expressions as "playing possum" and "batting a thousand" are among the nearly 100 explained and illustrated with amusing drawings. (Rev: BL 6/15/90; SLJ 7/90) [428.1]

15157 Terban, Marvin. *Too Hot to Hoot: Funny Palindrome Riddles* (3–6). Illus. by Giulio Maestro. 1985, Houghton Mifflin paper $7.95 (0-89919-320-X). 64pp. A wordplay book exploring palindromes: words, phrases, sentences, and numbers that are the same read forward and backward. (Rev: BCCB 6/85; BL 5/15/85; SLJ 9/85)

15158 Terban, Marvin. *Your Foot's on My Feet! And Other Tricky Nouns* (3–5). Illus. by Giulio Maestro. 1986, Houghton Mifflin paper $6.95 (0-89919-413-3). 64pp. A lively look at sometimes confusing singular and plural nouns. (Rev: BL 7/86; SLJ 9/86)

15159 Thomson, Ruth. *A First Thesaurus* (K–3). Illus. 2003, Thameside LB $24.25 (1-931983-08-9). 64pp. Pictures and words are combined to introduce youngsters to the thesaurus; children are encouraged to select alternative words from the illustrated choices provided. Also use *A First Word Bank* (2003). (Rev: BL 12/1/02) [423]

15160 *Tiny the Mouse Dictionary for 1-year-olds* (PS). Series: Tiny the Mouse. 1999, Sterling $4.95 (0-8069-5932-0). In this board book, a familiar object is pictured and on the verso four related items are also shown. There are also Tiny the Mouse Dictionaries for 2-, 3-, and 4-year-olds in this series. (Rev: SLJ 9/99)

15161 Treays, Rebecca, and Kate Needham, eds. *The Usborne Book of Everyday Words: A Picture Word Book* (PS–1). Photos by Howard Allman. Illus. by Jo Litchfield. Series: Everyday Words. 1999, EDC $12.95 (0-7460-2766-4). 47pp. This beginning word book with clever illustrations introduces more than 500 words. (Rev: HBG 3/00; SLJ 2/00) [422]

15162 Van Allsburg, Chris. *The Z Was Zapped: A Play in Twenty-Six Acts* (3–8). Illus. 1987, Houghton Mifflin $17.95 (0-395-44612-0). 56pp. The 26 acts turn out to be a new way to introduce the alphabet. (Rev: BL 11/1/87; SLJ 11/87)

15163 Verdick, Elizabeth. *Words Are Not for Hurting* (PS). Illus. by Marieka Heinlen. 2004, Free Spirit $7.95 (1-57542-156-9). 24pp. Verdick urges children to consider the power of the words they use and to assess their capacity to reassure or to wound. (Rev: BL 10/15/04; SLJ 11/04) [177]

15164 Wilbur, Richard. *Opposites* (5–7). Illus. by author. 1991, Harcourt $11.95 (0-15-258720-9). 39pp. Through verses and cartoonlike illustrations, antonyms are given for a series of words. [811.52]

15165 Wittels, Harriet, and Joan Greisman. *A First Thesaurus* (4–6). Illus. 1985, Western paper $8.99 (0-307-15835-7). 144pp. Simple entry words are in boldface with synonyms and antonyms for more than 2,000 words. (Rev: BL 11/1/85; SLJ 2/86)

15166 Ziefert, Harriet. *Baby Buggy, Buggy Baby* (PS–2). Illus. by Richard Brown. Series: Word Play Flap Book. 1997, Houghton Mifflin $10.95 (0-395-85161-0). Using flaps, this word book shows how phrases change meaning if one reverses the word order. Homonyms are introduced in *Night, Knight* (1997). (Rev: BCCB 4/97; SLJ 7/97)

Writing and Speaking

15167 Alagna, Magdalena. *War Correspondents: Life Under Fire* (5–10). Series: Extreme Careers. 2003, Rosen LB $26.50 (0-8239-3798-4). 64pp. The dangers of wartime assignments are emphasized in this volume that also stresses job requirements that include a good education and broad knowledge of world events. (Rev: BL 9/15/03; SLJ 11/03) [808]

15168 Asher, Sandy. *Where Do You Get Your Ideas? Helping Young Writers Begin* (5–7). Illus. 1987, Walker LB $13.85 (0-8027-6691-9). 96pp. Keeping a journal and other interesting ideas for would-be journalists. (Rev: BCCB 12/87; BL 9/15/87; SLJ 9/87) [808.02]

15169 *Author Talk* (4–6). Ed. by Leonard S. Marcus. Illus. 2000, Simon & Schuster $22.00 (0-689-81383-X). 112pp. After each brief biography there is a question-and-answer session with these 15 popular authors of children's books, including Judy Blume, Bruce Brooks, E. L. Konigsburg, Lois Lowry, Gary Paulsen, and Laurence Yep. (Rev: BL 6/1–15/00; HB 7–8/00; HBG 3/01; SLJ 8/00) [810.9]

15170 Bailly, Sharon. *Pass It On!* (3–5). Illus. 1995, Millbrook LB $23.40 (1-56294-588-2). 64pp. Hints on how to perk up the writing and sending of notes, including secret codes. (Rev: BL 2/1/96; SLJ 2/96) [652]

15171 Bauer, Marion Dane. *What's Your Story? A Young Person's Guide to Writing Fiction* (5–10). 1992, Clarion paper $7.95 (0-395-57780-2). An award-winning writer gives advice to young authors, including suggestions for planning, writing, and revising. (Rev: BL 4/15/92; SLJ 6/92*) [808.3]

15172 Bauer, Marion Dane. *A Writer's Story from Life to Fiction* (5–8). 1995, Clarion $14.95 (0-395-72094-X); paper $6.95 (0-395-75053-9). Readers and aspiring writers will enjoy this famous author's explanations of how she draws on her own experiences to develop her works. (Rev: BL 9/15/95; SLJ 10/95) [813]

15173 Bentley, Nancy, and Donna Guthrie. *Writing Mysteries, Movies, Monster Stories, and More* (5–8). Illus. 2001, Millbrook LB $24.90 (0-7613-1452-0). 80pp. This book gives solid information on all kinds of fictional writing, including novels, short stories, fantasy, science fiction, humor, and even movie scripts. (Rev: BL 3/15/01; HBG 10/01; SLJ 4/01) [808]

15174 Betz, Adrienne, comp. *Scholastic Treasury of Quotations for Children* (4–8). 1998, Scholastic paper $16.95 (0-590-27146-6). 254pp. From Socrates to Bill Clinton, this is a useful compendium of quotations arranged under 75 subjects. (Rev: SLJ 2/99) [080]

15175 Bruchac, Joseph. *Tell Me a Tale* (4–8). 1997, Harcourt $16.00 (0-15-201221-4). 144pp. A master storyteller reveals tricks of the trade, tells where to find stories, and explores their origins and effects, with many examples from various cultures. (Rev: BL 3/15/97; SLJ 8/97) [808.5]

15176 Burkholder, Kelly. *Pen Pals* (2–5). Series: Artistic Adventures. 2001, Rourke LB $21.27 (1-57103-353-X). 24pp. This title tells how and why one wants to communicate with others through regular mail and e-mail, with a section on safety tips involving the computer. (Rev: SLJ 2/01) [808]

15177 Burkholder, Kelly. *Stories* (2–5). Series: Artistic Adventures. 2001, Rourke LB $21.27 (1-57103-356-4). 24pp. This book introduces different types of writing — descriptive, persuasive, expository, and narrative — with ideas on expressing one-self through writing plus material on editing and revising. (Rev: SLJ 2/01) [808]

15178 Burns, Peggy. *News* (3–5). Illus. Series: Stepping Through History. 1995, Thomson Learning LB $5.00 (1-56847-342-7). 32pp. A history of journalism and the distribution of news from ancient times to the present. (Rev: BL 7/95) [070.4]

15179 Christelow, Eileen. *What Do Authors Do?* (3–5). Illus. 1995, Clarion $15.00 (0-395-71124-X). 32pp. Using cartoonlike drawings, the process of writing a book is traced using the experiences of two imaginary authors. (Rev: BCCB 11/95; BL 9/15/95; HB 11–12/95; SLJ 12/95*) [808.06]

15180 Cibula, Matt. *How to Be the Greatest Writer in the World* (4–8). Illus. by Brian Strassburg. 1999, Zino $11.95 (1-55933-276-X). 92pp. A spiral-bound book that presents 88 interesting and engaging exercises to help youngsters who feel they have nothing to write about. (Rev: SLJ 2/00) [808]

15181 Detz, Joan. *You Mean I Have to Stand Up and Say Something?* (4–8). Illus. 1986, Macmillan LB $13.95 (0-689-31221-0). 96pp. A chatty guide to effective speaking before an audience. (Rev: BCCB 2/87; BL 2/1/87)

15182 Dubrovin, Vivian. *Storytelling Adventures: Stories Kids Can Tell* (4–7). Illus. by Bobbi Shupe. 1997, Storycraft paper $14.95 (0-9638339-2-8). 64pp. This book not only includes a selection of stories to tell but also suggests appropriate props to use, with directions on how to make them. (Rev: SLJ 5/97) [808.5]

15183 Dubrovin, Vivian. *Storytelling for the Fun of It* (4–8). Illus. by Bobbi Shupe. 1994, Storycraft paper $16.95 (0-9638339-0-1). 160pp. This useful guide is divided into three parts that give general information, where and what kinds of stories to tell, and how to learn and perform them. (Rev: SLJ 4/94) [808.5]

15184 Edwards, Wallace. *Monkey Business* (4–8). Illus. 2004, Kids Can $16.95 (1-55337-462-2). 32pp. Whimsical artwork introduces such common idioms as "opening a can of worms" and "a bull in a china shop"; readers will also enjoy looking for hidden monkeys. (Rev: BL 11/1/04; SLJ 9/04*) [423]

15185 Englart, Mindi Rose. *Newspapers from Start to Finish* (3–5). Series: Made in the USA. 2001, Blackbirch LB $17.95 (1-56711-484-9). 32pp. The whole manufacturing process — from paper production to the finished edition — is covered in this concise, well-illustrated account. (Rev: BL 3/15/02; HBG 3/02) [070.1]

15186 Fletcher, Ralph. *How Writers Work: Finding a Process That Works for You* (4–8). 2000, HarperCollins paper $4.99 (0-380-79702-X). 114pp. Using a conversational style, the author explains the process of writing with material on brainstorming, rough drafts, revising, proofreading, and publishing. (Rev: SLJ 12/00) [808]

15187 Fletcher, Ralph. *Poetry Matters: Writing a Poem from the Inside Out* (4–7). 2002, HarperCollins paper $4.99 (0-380-79703-8). 128pp. A how-to book for young poets, with ideas on how to

make images and "music" with words. (Rev: BL 5/15/02; HBG 10/02; SLJ 2/02*) [808.1]

15188 Gibbons, Gail. *Deadline! From News to Newspaper* (K–3). 1987, HarperCollins LB $15.89 (0-690-04602-2). 32pp. With a small-town newspaper as a backdrop, readers can follow the workings of the press. (Rev: BL 6/15/87; HB 5–6/87; SLJ 6–7/87)

15189 Graham, Paula W. *Speaking of Journals: Children's Book Writers Talk About Their Diaries, Notebooks and Sketchbooks* (5–8). Illus. 1999, Boyds Mills paper $14.95 (1-56397-741-9). 226pp. A book that discusses the how-tos and the rewards of keeping a personal journal, and features interviews with 27 writers including Jim Arnosky, Pam Conrad, and Jean George. (Rev: BL 3/1/99; BR 9–10/99; SLJ 5/99) [818]

15190 Grant, Janet. *The Young Person's Guide to Becoming a Writer*. Rev. Ed. (5–8). 1995, Free Spirit paper $13.95 (0-915793-90-3). This comprehensive beginner's guide provides information young people interested in writing as a career should know, such as ways to explore writing, different writing genres in the publishing industry and how an individual might be drawn toward one or another, practical information about the writing industry, how to find a publisher, manuscript preparation, and marketing. (Rev: SLJ 12/95) [808]

15191 Guthrie, Donna, and Nancy Bentley. *The Young Journalist's Book: How to Write and Produce Your Own Newspaper* (4–7). Illus. 1998, Millbrook $24.40 (0-7613-0360-X). 64pp. The authors explain what a journalist does and, in addition to explaining the parts of a newspaper, tells how to start one. (Rev: BL 3/1/99; HBG 3/99; SLJ 12/98) [070.1]

15192 Hambleton, Vicki, and Cathleen Greenwood. *So, You Wanna Be a Writer? How to Write, Get Published, and Maybe Even Make It Big!* (5–9). Illus. by Laura Eldridge and Corey Mistretta. Series: So, You Wanna Be. 2001, Beyond Words paper $8.95 (1-58270-043-5). 160pp. Practical advice is offered in straightforward text with lots of examples, sample letters, interviews with published writers, details of writing contests, and lists of magazines that accept submissions from young writers. (Rev: SLJ 10/01) [808]

15193 Hamilton, Fran Santoro. *Hands-On English* (4–8). Illus. 1998, Portico paper $9.95 (0-9664867-0-6). A user-friendly volume that takes a visual approach to illustrate sentence patterns, such as using icons to represent the eight parts of speech, with clear, interesting explanations. Also included are irregular verbs, using modifiers, spelling rules, punctuation and capitalization, homonyms, and how to make outlines. (Rev: SLJ 2/99) [415]

15194 Hamilton, Martha, and Mitch Weiss. *Stories in My Pocket: Tales Kids Can Tell* (4–7). Illus. 1997, Fulcrum paper $15.95 (1-55591-957-X). 184pp. This handbook of storytelling for young storytellers includes 30 tales to begin with. (Rev: BL 1/1–15/97) [372.6]

15195 Harrison, David Lee. *Writing Stories* (4–8). Series: Scholastic Guides. 2004, Scholastic $16.95 (0-439-51914-4). 128pp. This straightforward guide to writing offers clear advice on plot, setting, character, and voice as well as the importance of revision and practice. (Rev: BL 11/1/04; SLJ 1/05) [808.3]

15196 Henderson, Kathy. *The Young Writer's Guide to Getting Published: Over 150 Listings of Opportunities for Young Writers*. Rev. ed. (5–12). Illus. 2001, Writer's Digest paper $18.99 (1-58297-057-2). 246pp. This guide provides useful tips on identifying the best opportunities for budding writers and relates some young writers' success stories. (Rev: BL 6/1–15/01; SLJ 11/01) [808]

15197 Holbrook, Sara. *Wham! It's a Poetry Jam: Discovering Performance Poetry* (2–5). 2002, Boyds Mills paper $9.95 (1-59078-011-6). 55pp. Holbrook includes some of her poems in this guide to performing poetry — how to move, project your voice, express emotion, and so forth. (Rev: HBG 10/02; SLJ 5/02)

15198 Hulme, Joy N., and Donna Guthrie. *How to Write, Recite, and Delight in All Kinds of Poetry* (3–6). 1996, Millbrook LB $24.90 (1-56294-576-9). 96pp. Using examples of poetry written by grade school children, this book introduces different types of poetry and gives help in writing and reciting poems. (Rev: SLJ 12/96) [811]

15199 James, Elizabeth, and Carol Barkin. *How to Write Super School Reports*. Rev. ed. (4–9). Series: A School Survival Guide Book. 1998, Lothrop $15.00 (0-688-16132-4). 90pp. This research guide takes readers through the steps involved in writing a research paper with material on choosing a topic, finding facts, using a library, organizing notes, and putting the report together. (Rev: HBG 3/99; SLJ 2/99) [808.023]

15200 James, Elizabeth, and Carol Barkin. *How to Write Terrific Book Reports*. Rev. ed. (3–5). Series: A School Survival Guide Book. 1998, Lothrop $15.00 (0-688-16131-6). 80pp. A step-by-step guide to writing good book reports that gives several examples of reports and makes suggestions on how to avoid common pitfalls. (Rev: HBG 3/99; SLJ 1/99) [808]

15201 James, Elizabeth, and Carol Barkin. *How to Write Your Best Book Report* (4–6). Illus. by Roy Doty. 1998, Lothrop paper $4.95 (0-688-16140-5). 80pp. A chatty account of dos and don'ts that can make book report writing seem almost painless. (Rev: BL 11/15/86)

15202 Janeczko, Paul B. *How to Write Poetry* (4–8). Series: Scholastic Guides. 1999, Scholastic paper $12.95 (0-590-10077-7). 128pp. An enthusiastic, clearly written how-to manual that uses many examples from well-known poems. (Rev: BL 3/15/99; HBG 10/99; SLJ 7/99) [808.1]

15203 Janeczko, Paul B., comp. *Poetry from A to Z: A Guide for Young Writers* (4–8). Illus. Series: Net-Guide. 1994, Simon & Schuster $16.95 (0-02-747672-3). This book of 72 poems, alphabetized by topic, gives examples to get young writers started,

and the 23 poets represented give advice on how to become a better poet. (Rev: BCCB 3/95; BL 12/15/94) [808.1]

15204 Janeczko, Paul B. *Writing Winning Reports and Essays* (5–8). Series: Scholastic Guides. 2003, Scholastic LB $16.95 (0-439-28717-0); paper $7.95 (0-439-28718-9). 224pp. Suggests useful strategies for researching and writing tasks including descriptive essays, book reports, persuasive and personal essays, and social studies reports. (Rev: HBG 4/04; SLJ 1/04) [808]

15205 *Kids' Letters to Harry Potter* (3–6). Ed. by Bill Adler. 2001, Carroll & Graf $18.00 (0-7867-0890-5). 200pp. Fans of the Harry Potter novels share thoughts on the books and characters through letters to the boy wizard. (Rev: BL 11/1/01; SLJ 11/01) [826]

15206 Leedy, Loreen. *Messages in the Mailbox: How to Write a Letter* (2–4). Illus. 1991, Holiday House LB $16.95 (0-8234-0889-2). 32pp. In this cheery guide, an alligator teacher shows the class of children and animals how to write a letter. (Rev: BCCB 12/91; BL 1/1/91; SLJ 9/91*) [295.4]

15207 McGuinness, Diane. *My First Phonics Book* (K–3). Series: My First. 1999, DK $16.95 (0-7894-4737-1). 48pp. Riddles and a whimsical text introduce 42 sounds including vowels, consonants, and blends. (Rev: HBG 3/00; SLJ 1/00) [410]

15208 O'Reilly, Gillina. *Slangalicious: Where We Got That Crazy Lingo* (4–6). Illus. by Krista Johnston. 2004, Annick $24.95 (1-55037-765-5); paper $12.95 (1-55037-764-7). 88pp. Two computer characters with their own Slangalicious Web site feature in the fictional story that serves as a framework for this entertaining overview of slang. (Rev: BL 12/15/04; SLJ 1/05)

15209 Otfinoski, Steven. *Speaking Up, Speaking Out: A Kid's Guide to Making Speeches, Oral Reports, and Conversation* (5–8). Illus. 1996, Millbrook LB $24.90 (1-56294-345-6). All kinds of public-speaking situations are introduced, with suggestions on how to be a success at each. (Rev: BL 1/1–15/97; SLJ 1/97) [808.5]

15210 Potter, Giselle. *The Year I Didn't Go to School* (1–3). Illus. 2002, Simon & Schuster $16.95 (0-689-84730-0). 40pp. The author remembers the year she was seven, when she toured Italy with her family's puppet theater, using excerpts from the journal she kept at the time and appealing illustrations of typical Italian scenes. (Rev: BCCB 10/02; BL 11/1/02; HBG 10/03; SLJ 11/02) [818]

15211 Rivera, Shelia. *The Media War* (5–8). Illus. Series: World in Conflict. 2004, ABDO LB $17.95 (1-59197-418-6). 48pp. A brief overview of American journalism's impact on war from the Civil War to the U.S. invasion of Afghanistan. (Rev: BL 4/1/04) [070.1]

15212 Roy, Jennifer Rozines. *You Can Write a Story or Narrative* (4–8). Illus. Series: You Can Write! 2003, Enslow LB $17.95 (0-7660-2085-1). 64pp. Sound advice for plotting and writing a wide array of different narratives, including adventure, history, fantasy, and folklore. (Rev: HBG 10/03; SLJ 1/04) [808]

15213 Ryan, Elizabeth A. *How to Build a Better Vocabulary* (5–9). 1991, Troll paper $3.95 (0-8167-2461-X). A traditional study of prefixes, suffixes, and roots, with sections on foreign words. (Rev: BL 4/1/92; SLJ 4/92) [372.6]

15214 *Scholastic Explains Writing Homework: Everything Children (and Parents) Need to Survive 2nd and 3rd Grade* (2–3). Series: Scholastic Explains Homework. 1998, Scholastic $14.95 (0-590-39756-7); paper $6.95 (0-590-39759-1). 64pp. This book helps children and parents understand such writing concepts as characters, reviews, and basic grammar. (Rev: SLJ 12/98) [808]

15215 Senn, Joyce. *The Young People's Book of Quotations* (5–10). 1999, Millbrook LB $39.90 (0-7613-0267-0). Beginning with "accomplishment" and ending with "zoos," this is a collection of 2,000 quotations of special interest to young people, arranged by topic. (Rev: BL 3/1/99*; SLJ 4/99) [082]

15216 Somervill, Barbara A. *Backstage at a Newscast* (5–8). Illus. Series: Backstage Pass. 2003, Children's Book Pr. LB $20.00 (0-516-24326-8); paper $6.95 (0-516-24388-8). 48pp. Somerville provides information on how a newscast is created, along with guidance on careers in journalism. (Rev: BL 5/1/03) [070.1]

15217 Terban, Marvin. *Punctuation Power: Punctuation and How to Use It* (4–9). Illus. by Eric Brace. 2000, Scholastic paper $12.95 (0-590-38673-5). 96pp. After a description of each punctuation mark and its uses, this account covers topics including bibliographies, quotations, play scripts, and sentences, and the kinds of punctuation they require. (Rev: SLJ 7/00) [410]

15218 *To Swim in Our Own Pond: A Book of Vietnamese Proverbs* (3–6). Trans. from Vietnamese by Ngoc-Dung Tran. Illus. by Xuan-Quang Dang. 1998, Shen's $15.95 (1-885008-08-2). This collection of 22 Vietnamese proverbs also contains the best Western equivalents plus a series of delightful paintings. (Rev: SLJ 3/99) [398]

15219 Trueit, Trudi Strain. *Keeping a Journal* (4–8). Illus. 2004, Watts LB $19.50 (0-531-12262-X). 80pp. Trueit encourages readers to keep journals, offering tips on getting started, writing prompts and exercises, a calendar of ideas, and alternatives for those who don't enjoy writing, such as scrapbooks and drawing. (Rev: SLJ 3/05) [808]

15220 Veljkovic, Peggy, and Arthur Schwartz, eds. *Writing from the Heart: Young People Share Their Wisdom* (5–9). 2001, Templeton Foundation paper $12.95 (1-890151-48-3). 189pp. A collection of the best essays by young people that have been submitted to the Laws of Life program since it began in 1987. (Rev: SLJ 6/01) [170]

15221 Vinton, Ken. *Alphabet Antics: Hundreds of Activities to Challenge and Enrich Letter Learners of All Ages* (5–8). Illus. by author. 1996, Free Spirit paper $19.95 (0-915793-98-9). 135pp. For each letter of the alphabet, there is a history, how it appears in different alphabets, important words that begin with that letter, a quotation from someone whose name starts with it, and a number of interesting related projects. (Rev: SLJ 1/97) [411]

15222 Wong, Janet S. *You Have to Write* (2–4). Illus. by Teresa Flavin. 2002, Simon & Schuster $17.00 (0-689-83409-8). 40pp. Wong uses poetic text and a photo album approach to spur young people to think about writing assignments in new ways. (Rev: BL 7/02; HBG 3/03; SLJ 7/02) [811]

15223 Young, Sue. *Writing with Style* (5–8). Series: Scholastic Guides. 1997, Scholastic $12.95 (0-590-50977-2). A guide for the novice writer, with chapters on planning, presenting, and publishing one's work. (Rev: BL 3/1/97; SLJ 5/97) [372.6]

Music

General

15224 Aliki. *Ah, Music!* (1–3). Illus. 2003, Harper-Collins LB $17.89 (0-06-028727-6). 48pp. Rhythm, harmony, melody, jazz, instruments, and a brief history are among the many aspects of music that Aliki manages to cover in this slim volume. (Rev: BL 6/1–15/03; HB 5–6/03; HBG 10/03; SLJ 5/03) [780]

15225 Amendola, Dana. *A Day at the New Amsterdam Theatre* (4–9). Photos by Gino Domenico. 2004, Disney $24.95 (0-7868-5438-3). 125pp. A behind-the-scenes look at a production of a musical in the renovated theater in New York City, introducing the wide variety of individuals involved. (Rev: SLJ 1/05) [792]

15226 Ayazi-Hashjin, Sherry. *Rap and Hip Hop: The Voice of a Generation* (4–7). Illus. Series: Library of African American Arts and Culture. 1999, Rosen LB $19.95 (0-8239-1855-6). 62pp. This account traces the history of rap and hip hop music from their origins in spirituals, jazz, blues, and storytelling traditions; it also gives some information on musicians. (Rev: BL 2/15/00; SLJ 1/00) [782.4]

15227 Barber, Nicola. *Music: An A–Z Guide* (4–8). Illus. 2001, Watts LB $33.00 (0-531-11898-3). 128pp. Basic information on everything from performers and instruments to various forms of music is presented with illustrations and sidebar features. (Rev: SLJ 9/01) [780]

15228 Cefrey, Holly. *Backstage at a Music Video* (5–8). Illus. Series: Backstage Pass. 2003, Children's Book Pr. LB $20.00 (0-516-24324-1); paper $6.95 (0-516-24386-1). 48pp. The history of music videos is coupled with information on how they are financed and produced, along with guidance on careers in the music business. (Rev: BL 5/1/03) [791.45]

15229 Celenza, Anna Harwell. *Pictures at an Exhibition* (K–4). Illus. by JoAnn E. Kitchel. 2003, Charlesbridge LB $19.95 (1-57091-492-3). Drawing on primary-source documents, Celenza has created an arresting account of the friendship that was the catalyst for Mussorgsky's famous piece. (Rev: HBG 4/04; SLJ 4/03)

15230 *Chatter with the Angels: An Illustrated Songbook for Children* (2–6). Ed. by Linda A. Richer and Anita Stoltzfus Breckbill. Illus. 2000, GIA $29.95 (1-57999-082-7). 90pp. An outstanding songbook containing 90 selections of Christian music from different countries and cultures that are printed with piano and guitar arrangements. (Rev: BL 10/1/00; HBG 3/01) [782.25]

15231 Elmer, Howard. *Blues: Its Birth and Growth* (4–7). Series: The Library of African American Arts and Culture. 1999, Rosen LB $17.95 (0-8239-1853-X). 64pp. This title traces the history of the blues, its origins, and its influence on American society as well as on the development of jazz and rock 'n' roll. (Rev: SLJ 8/99) [781]

15232 Ench, Rick, and Jay Cravath. *North American Indian Music* (5–7). Illus. Series: Watts Library: Indians of the Americas. 2002, Watts LB $24.00 (0-531-11772-3); paper $8.95 (0-531-16230-3). 64pp. This title looks at the importance of music in the rituals of North American Indian tribes and describes the forms of beat, rhythm, and melody, with illustrations, a glossary, bibliography, and timeline. (Rev: BL 7/02) [782.62]

15233 Englander, Roger. *Opera! What's All the Screaming About?* (6–8). Illus. 1983, Walker $12.95 (0-8027-6491-6). 192pp. A history of opera and an explanation of the different parts of an opera.

15234 Ganeri, Anita, and Nicola Barber. *The Young Person's Guide to the Opera: With Music from the Great Operas on CD* (4–8). 2001, Harcourt $25.00 (0-15-216498-7). 55pp. A bright and friendly introduction to opera that provides historical information and profiles some of the important singers and opera houses, with a companion CD of vocal and instrumental tracks. (Rev: HBG 3/02; SLJ 12/01) [792.1]

15235 Garty, Judy. *Techniques of Marching Bands* (5–8). Series: Let's Go Team. 2003, Mason Crest LB $19.95 (1-59084-538-2). 64pp. The slim volume

798

supplies a look at the functions of a marching band, how they operate, and the joys of playing in one. (Rev: BL 10/15/03; SLJ 11/03) [785.06]

15236 Gatti, Anne, reteller. *The Magic Flute* (4–8). Illus. by Peter Malone. 1997, Chronicle $17.95 (0-8118-1003-8). An elegant retelling of the Mozart opera, with each scene given a full-color painting and a page of text. The accompanying CD has 16 selections coded to each page. (Rev: SLJ 1/98*) [782.1]

15237 George-Warren, Holly. *Shake, Rattle and Roll: The Founders of Rock and Roll* (4–7). 2001, Houghton Mifflin $15.00 (0-618-05540-1). 32pp. After an informative introduction on the history of rock and roll, there is a series of one-page biographies of famous personalities. (Rev: BL 3/1/01; HBG 10/01; SLJ 5/01*) [781.66]

15238 Husain, Shahrukh. *The Barefoot Book of Stories from the Opera* (4–6). Illus. 1999, Barefoot $19.95 (1-902283-28-7). 80pp. The plots of seven operas that would appeal to children because of their familiar stories (e.g., *La Cenerentola, Hansel and Gretel, The Magic Flute*) are retold with many illustrations. (Rev: BL 11/1/99; SLJ 10/99) [782.1]

15239 Igus, Toyomi. *I See the Rhythm* (5–8). Illus. 1998, Children's Book Pr. $15.95 (0-89239-151-0). Using a timeline to set the social context, this title traces African American contributions to such musical forms as the blues, big band, jazz, bebop, gospel, and rock. (Rev: BCCB 7–8/98; BL 2/15/98; SLJ 6/98) [780]

15240 Kirk, Daniel. *Go!* (PS–3). Illus. 2001, Hyperion $18.99 (0-7868-0305-3). 48pp. This collection of fast-moving poems about motion combines the attraction of various kinds of transport, humor, lively illustration, and a tuneful CD. (Rev: BL 12/15/01; HBG 3/02; SLJ 12/01) [782.42]

15241 Lee, Jeanne. *Jam! The Story of Jazz Music* (4–7). Illus. Series: Library of African American Arts and Culture. 1999, Rosen LB $31.95 (0-8239-1852-1). 62pp. This book tells about the African American musicians who were responsible for the early development of jazz and blues. (Rev: BL 2/15/00; SLJ 1/00) [781.65]

15242 McMullan, Kate. *Rock-a-Baby Band* (PS). Illus. by Janie Bynum. 2003, Little, Brown $15.95 (0-316-60858-0). When ten racially diverse toddlers decide to make music, they rock the day care center in this appealing picture book, which is packaged with an audio CD. (Rev: HBG 10/03; SLJ 8/03)

15243 Morris, Neil. *Music and Dance* (5–8). Illus. by Antonella Pastorelli. Series: Discovering World Cultures. 2001, Crabtree paper $8.95 (0-7787-0249-9). 38pp. A heavily illustrated overview of musical instruments and forms of dance around the world. (Rev: SLJ 5/02) [780]

15244 Moss, Lloyd. *Music Is* (PS–3). Illus. by Philippe Petit-Roulet. 2003, Penguin Putnam $14.99 (0-399-23336-9). In rhyming text, author Lloyd Moss, who hosts a New York City classical music radio station, celebrates the joys of music in all its many forms. (Rev: HBG 10/03; SLJ 7/03)

15245 Price, Leontyne, reteller. *Aida* (4–8). Illus. by Leo Dillon and Diane Dillon. 1990, Harcourt $20.00 (0-15-200405-X). The story of one of the grandest of operas retold by one of opera's grandest divas. (Rev: BCCB 10/90; HB 3–4/91; SLJ 11/90*) [782.1]

15246 Rowe, Julian. *Music* (4–7). Illus. Series: Science Encounters. 1997, Rigby paper $25.55 (1-57572-091-4). 32pp. This book shows how scientific principles are used in music, musical instruments, hearing, and recording devices. (Rev: SLJ 10/97) [780]

15247 Saint-Saens, Camille. *Carnival of the Animals* (PS–2). Illus. by Sue Williams. 1999, Holt $19.95 (0-8050-6180-0). 45pp. This book gives a one-page explanation of each part of this piece by Saint-Saens; the accompanying CD contains the music. (Rev: SLJ 1/00) [780]

15248 Schaefer, A. R. *Forming a Band* (5–8). Illus. Series: Rock Music Library. 2003, Capstone LB $22.60 (0-7368-2146-5). 32pp. A hip and practical guide suitable for reluctant readers. Also use *Booking a First Gig* (2003). (Rev: BL 12/1/03) [784.100]

15249 *This Little Light of Mine* (PS–2). Illus. by E. B. Lewis. 2005, Simon & Schuster $16.95 (0-689-83179-X). 32pp. The words of this familiar African American spiritual spring to life in the vibrant illustrations as a boy moves through his community, sharing experiences. (Rev: BL 2/1/05; SLJ 3/05) [782.25]

Ballads and Folk Songs

15250 Arnold, Tedd. *Catalina Magdalena Hoopensteiner Wallendiner Hogan Logan Bogan Was Her Name* (PS–2). Illus. by author. 2004, Scholastic $10.95 (0-590-10994-4). A classic camp song serves as inspiration for an unlikely heroine. (Rev: SLJ 8/04) [782.421]

15251 Berger, Melvin. *The Story of Folk Music* (6–8). Illus. 1976, Phillips LB $29.95 (0-87599-215-3). How and why American folk music evolved, with biographical information on singers from Woody Guthrie to John Denver.

15252 Burke, Bobby, and Horace Gerlach. *Daddy's Little Girl* (PS–2). Illus. by Maggie Kneen. 2004, HarperCollins $14.99 (0-06-028722-5). The 1950s song "Daddy's Little Girl" becomes a book starring a family of rabbits. (Rev: SLJ 5/04) [782.4]

15253 Cabrera, Jane. *If You're Happy and You Know It!* (PS). Illus. 2005, Holiday House $16.95 (0-8234-1881-2). 32pp. Readers clap their hands and stamp their feet along with a cast of assorted animals. (Rev: BL 2/15/05; SLJ 3/05) [782.42]

15254 Catalano, Dominic. *Frog Went A-Courting: A Musical Play in Six Acts* (PS–1). Illus. 1998, Boyds Mills $14.95 (1-56397-637-4). 32pp. This charming adaptation of the folk song includes stunning paintings and charcoal drawings. (Rev: BL 10/15/98; HBG 3/99; SLJ 10/98) [782.42]

15255 Clarke, Gus. *E I E I O: The Story of Old MacDonald Who Had a Farm* (PS–K). Illus. 1993,

Lothrop $14.00 (0-688-12215-9). 32pp. With cartoonlike illustrations, this is an old favorite folk song with a surprise ending. (Rev: BL 5/1/93) [782.42]

15256 Cony, Frances, and Iain Smyth. *Old MacDonald Had a Farm* (PS–K). Illus. 1999, Orchard $9.95 (0-531-30129-X). A pop-up version of the familiar song, with chickens moving their heads in time to the music. (Rev: BL 12/15/99; SLJ 6/99) [784.4]

15257 Cooper, Floyd. *Cumbayah* (PS–3). Illus. 1998, Morrow $16.00 (0-688-13543-9). 32pp. The illustrations that accompany this folk song show a multiracial group enjoying themselves. (Rev: BL 2/15/98; HBG 10/98; SLJ 5/98) [782.42]

15258 *Fiddle-i-fee* (PS). Illus. by Santiago Cohen. 2003, Handprint $7.95 (1-59354-020-5). A boardbook version of the cumulative rhyme, featuring a parade of happy animals and their sounds. (Rev: SLJ 1/04) [782.42]

15259 Gammell, Stephen. *Once Upon MacDonald's Farm* (PS–3). Illus. 2000, Simon & Schuster $15.00 (0-689-82885-3). 32pp. This humorous version of the old song has MacDonald trying to farm with an elephant, a baboon, and a lion. (Rev: BL 5/15/00; HBG 10/00) [784.4]

15260 Goodman, Steve. *The Train They Call the City of New Orleans* (K–3). Illus. by Michael McCurdy. 2003, Penguin Putnam $16.99 (0-399-23853-0). 32pp. McCurdy's artful blend of scratchboard and watercolor illustrations depict the train ride and landscapes featured in the popular 1970s folk song. (Rev: BL 5/1/03; HBG 10/03; SLJ 10/03) [782.42164]

15261 Guthrie, Woody. *New Baby Train* (PS–1). Illus. by Marla Frazee. 2004, Little, Brown $15.99 (0-316-07203-6). 32pp. Frazee brings to life a Guthrie song about newborns making their arrival via baby train. (Rev: BL 10/15/04; SLJ 10/04) [782.42164]

15262 Guthrie, Woody. *This Land Is Your Land* (3–6). Illus. by Kathy Jakobsen. 1998, Little, Brown $14.95 (0-316-39215-4). 32pp. This beautiful picture book depicts a variety of people singing the folk song inspired by the Great Depression. (Rev: BCCB 11/98; BL 8/98*; HB 11–12/98; HBG 3/99; SLJ 8/98) [782.4216]

15263 Hillenbrand, Will. *Fiddle-I-Fee* (2–4). Illus. 2002, Harcourt $16.00 (0-15-201945-6). 40pp. Farm animals form a band to welcome a new baby in this colorful version of the folk song. (Rev: BL 7/02; HB 7–8/02; HBG 10/02; SLJ 3/02) [782.421642]

15264 Hoberman, Mary Ann. *The Eensy-Weensy Spider* (PS–1). Illus. by Nadine Bernard Westcott. 2000, Little, Brown $12.95 (0-316-36330-8). 32pp. The traditional song is expanded in a delightful way to include many adventures for Eensy-Weensy beyond the drainpipe. (Rev: BCCB 3/00; BL 3/1/00; HBG 10/00; SLJ 4/00) [782.4]

15265 *Hush, Little Baby: A Folk Song* (PS–K). Illus. by Marla Frazee. 1999, Harcourt $15.00 (0-15-201429-2). 40pp. The Appalachian folk song about a small girl who suggests that her father buy all sorts of gifts, including a mockingbird, to keep her

baby sibling quiet. (Rev: BCCB 12/99; BL 11/15/99; HB 11–12/99; HBG 3/00; SLJ 10/99) [792.42]

15266 Karas, G. Brian. *I Know an Old Lady* (PS–1). Illus. 1995, Scholastic $14.95 (0-590-46575-9). 32pp. An uproarious version of the traditional cumulative nonsense rhyme. (Rev: BCCB 2/95; BL 1/15/95*; SLJ 3/95) [782]

15267 Kovalski, Maryann. *Take Me Out to the Ballgame* (PS–2). Illus. 1993, Scholastic $14.95 (0-590-45638-5). 32pp. Jenny and Joanna go to the ball game with their wacky and fun-loving grandmother. (Rev: BL 1/15/93; SLJ 4/93) [811]

15268 Kroll, Steven. *By the Dawn's Early Light: The Story of the Star Spangled Banner* (2–4). Illus. by Dan Andreasen. 1994, Scholastic $15.95 (0-590-45054-9). 40pp. The circumstances of writing our national anthem are re-created, along with a history of the Battle of Baltimore, in this handsomely illustrated book. (Rev: BL 12/15/93; SLJ 3/94) [349.73]

15269 Langstaff, John. *Frog Went A-Courtin'* (K–3). Illus. by Feodor Rojankovsky. 1955, Harcourt $14.95 (0-15-230214-X); paper $7.00 (0-15-633900-5). 32pp. A rollicking folk song with matching illustrations. Caldecott Medal winner, 1956.

15270 Langstaff, Nancy, and John Langstaff. *Sally Go Round the Moon* (K–4). Illus. by Jan Pienkowski. 1986, Revels paper $14.95 (0-9640836-3-9). 127pp. A collection of folk songs and singing games originally published in 1970.

15271 McGill, Alice. *In the Hollow of Your Hand: Slave Lullabies* (5–7). Illus. 2000, Houghton Mifflin $18.00 (0-395-85755-4). 40pp. Family life in the days of slavery is revealed in this moving collection of 13 folk lullabies; a CD of the songs is also included. (Rev: BCCB 1/01; BL 11/15/00; HBG 3/01; SLJ 12/00) [811.008]

15272 McNeil, Keith, and Rusty McNeil. *Colonial and Revolution Songbook: With Historical Commentary* (4–7). 1996, WEM Records paper $11.95 (1-878360-08-6). 71pp. This songbook contains 39 traditional songs from the 17th century through the War of 1812, with brief historical comments for each. (Rev: SLJ 12/96) [973]

15273 Margolin, H. Ellen. *Goin' to Boston: An Exuberant Journey in Song* (PS–2). Illus. by Emily Bolam. 2002, Handprint $15.95 (1-929766-45-9). A girl on a bicycle leads a growing parade of people on their way to Boston Common in this new version of an Appalachian folk song. (Rev: HBG 10/02; SLJ 7/02) [782.42164]

15274 Mattox, Cheryl W., ed. *Shake It to the One That You Love the Best: Play Songs and Lullabies from Black Musical Traditions* (PS–6). Illus. by Varnette P. Honeywood. 1990, Warren-Mattox paper $9.95 (0-9623381-0-9). 56pp. Music and lyrics for 16 songs and ten lullabies. (Rev: BL 12/1/90*) [781.62]

15275 Nic Leodhas, Sorche. *Always Room for One More* (K–3). Illus. by Nonny Hogrogian. 1965, Holt $14.95 (0-8050-0331-2); paper $5.95 (0-8050-0330-4). 32pp. From the Scottish folk song about Machie MacLachlan, who had so many people into his house that it burst. Caldecott Medal winner, 1966.

15276 O'Neal, Debbie Trafton. *Twinkle, Twinkle, Little Star* (PS). Illus. by Benrei Huang. Series: Sing-It. 2003, Augsburg $8.99 (0-8066-4350-1). This beautifully illustrated book celebrates the familiar children's song and even adds a new verse written by the author. (Rev: HBG 10/03; SLJ 9/03)

15277 Presley, Elvis. *Elvis Presley's "Love Me Tender"* (K–2). Illus. by Tom Browning. 2003, Harper-Collins $15.99 (0-06-027797-1). This celebration of a father's love for his daughter uses the words of Presley's hit song and includes an Elvis CD. (Rev: HBG 10/03; SLJ 7/03) [782.42164]

15278 Raffi. *This Little Light of Mine* (PS–3). Illus. by Stacey Schuett. Series: Raffi Songs to Read. 2004, Knopf LB $17.99 (0-375-92871-5). This book-CD package uses the framework of children preparing for a performance of the song, and uses a variety of lights effectively. (Rev: SLJ 7/04) [782.42]

15279 *Rock-a-Bye Baby: Lullabies for Bedtime* (PS–2). Illus. by Margaret Walty. 1998, Barefoot $14.95 (1-902283-03-1). 40pp. This is a charming collection of 16 bedtime songs including "Twinkle, Twinkle, Little Star." (Rev: BL 12/15/98; SLJ 1/99) [781.5]

15280 Rounds, Glen, ed. *I Know an Old Lady Who Swallowed a Fly* (PS–3). Illus. by Glen Rounds. 1990, Holiday House LB $16.95 (0-8234-0814-0). 32pp. This humorous folk song is cleverly illustrated with mottled colors. (Rev: BCCB 9/90; BL 5/15/90; SLJ 8/90) [782]

15281 Schwartz, Amy. *Old MacDonald* (PS–1). Illus. 1999, Scholastic $15.95 (0-590-46189-3). 32pp. Double-page spreads and wonderful paintings breathe new life into this humorous traditional song. (Rev: BL 5/15/99; HB 3–4/99; HBG 10/99; SLJ 6/99) [782.42162]

15282 Seeger, Pete. *One Grain of Sand: A Lullaby* (PS–1). Illus. by Linda Wingerter. 2003, Little, Brown $15.95 (0-316-78140-1). Readers travel the world and recognize its diversity and vulnerability in this lullaby accompanied by beautiful illustrations. (Rev: HBG 4/04; SLJ 8/03) [782.42]

15283 Seeger, Pete, adapt. *Turn! Turn! Turn! Words from Ecclesiastes Circa 250 B.C.E., Translated into English in London in 1607* (3–5). Illus. by Wendy Anderson Halperin. 2003, Simon & Schuster $17.95 (0-689-85235-5). The words of Seeger's familiar folksong, taken from the Old Testament book of Ecclesiastes, are presented in imaginative circular art and accompanied by a CD with versions of the song by Seeger and the Byrds. (Rev: HBG 4/04; SLJ 10/03) [782.4]

15284 Shulman, Lisa. *Old MacDonald Had a Woodshop* (PS–2). Illus. by Ashley Wolff. 2002, Penguin Putnam $16.99 (0-399-23596-5). 32pp. Old Mac-Donald, a female sheep, shares her woodshop with the other farm animals in this entertaining version of the familiar song. (Rev: BL 9/15/02; HB 9–10/02; HBG 3/03; SLJ 9/02*) [784.4]

15285 Silverman, Jerry. *Children's Songs* (4–6). Illus. 1993, Chelsea paper $9.95 (0-7910-1847-4).

64pp. This collection of 31 African American songs includes church songs, slave songs, and folk songs. (Rev: BL 2/15/94; SLJ 12/93) [782]

15286 Silverman, Jerry. *Singing Our Way West: Songs and Stories of America's Westward Expansion* (4–6). Illus. 1998, Millbrook LB $27.40 (0-7613-0417-7). 96pp. Twelve stories and folk songs associated with specific events in the settling of the West, including the railroad, the Erie Canal, and the Chisholm and Oregon Trails. (Rev: BL 12/1/98; HBG 3/99; SLJ 6/99) [782.4]

15287 Siomades, Lorianne. *The Itsy Bitsy Spider* (PS). Illus. 1999, Boyds Mills $9.95 (1-56397-727-3). 24pp. The spider, in this version of the catchy rhyme and song, carries an umbrella and waves a flashlight. (Rev: BL 3/1/99; HBG 10/99; SLJ 4/99)

15288 Sloat, Teri. *There Was an Old Lady Who Swallowed a Trout!* (PS–1). Illus. by Reynold Ruffins. 1998, Holt $15.95 (0-8050-4294-6). 32pp. Set in the Pacific Northwest, this variation on the popular cumulative rhyme has the old lady swallowing a trout, salmon, otter, seal, porpoise, walrus, and even a whale. (Rev: BL 11/15/98*; HBG 3/99; SLJ 11/98) [782]

15289 Souhami, Jessica. *Old MacDonald* (PS–K). Illus. 1996, Orchard $11.95 (0-531-09493-6). 24pp. Old MacDonald uses a variety of vehicles to transport all of the animals he has on his farm. (Rev: BL 4/1/96; HB 5–6/96; SLJ 5/96) [784.4]

15290 *This Old Man* (PS–1). Illus. by Carol Jones. 1990, Houghton Mifflin $15.00 (0-395-54699-0). An attractively designed edition of this well-loved children's song. (Rev: SLJ 1/91) [784.7]

15291 Trapani, Iza. *Froggie Went A-Courtin'* (PS–3). Illus. by author. 2002, Charlesbridge LB $15.95 (1-58089-028-8). A new, humorous version of the song about Froggie's constant rejections. (Rev: HBG 3/03; SLJ 7/02) [784]

15292 Trapani, Iza. *The Itsy Bitsy Spider* (K–1). Illus. 1993, Whispering Coyote $16.95 (1-879085-77-1). 32pp. Building on the popular song, this book continues the adventures of the tiny spider. (Rev: BL 3/1/93)

15293 Trapani, Iza. *Row Row Row Your Boat* (PS–1). Illus. by author. 1999, Whispering Coyote $15.95 (1-58089-022-9). The traditional song is reprinted with additional verses and pictures that depict a bear family on a boat excursion. (Rev: HBG 3/00; SLJ 11/99) [782]

15294 Tyler, Gillian. *Froggy Went a-Courtin'* (PS–2). Illus. 2005, Candlewick $15.99 (0-7636-2306-7). 32pp. Eyecatching watercolor-and-ink artwork highlights this adaptation of the familiar folk song about the unlikely romantic relationship between a frog and a mouse. (Rev: BL 1/1–15/05; SLJ 1/05) [782.4]

15295 Wallner, Alexandra. *The Farmer in the Dell* (PS). Illus. 1998, Holiday House $15.95 (0-8234-1382-9). 32pp. An illustrated version of this favorite children's song, including the music and complete lyrics. (Rev: BL 9/1/98; HBG 3/99; SLJ 11/98) [782.4216]

15296 Wells, Rosemary. *Old MacDonald* (PS). Illus. by author. Series: Bunny Reads Back. 1998, Scholastic $4.95 (0-590-76985-5). A board-book version of the traditional song, featuring a rabbit in overalls as Old MacDonald. (Rev: HBG 10/98; SLJ 10/98) [782]

15297 Westcott, Nadine Bernard. *I Know an Old Lady Who Swallowed a Fly* (2–4). Illus. by author. 1980, Little, Brown paper $6.95 (0-316-93127-6). 32pp. A newly illustrated edition of this outrageously funny song.

15298 Westcott, Nadine Bernard. *I've Been Working on the Railroad* (PS–1). Illus. 1996, Hyperion LB $14.49 (0-7868-2041-1). 32pp. This familiar folk song is seen through the eyes of a small boy who, with his dog, have adventures on a train. (Rev: BL 4/1/96; SLJ 6/96) [782]

Holidays

15299 Boys Choir of Harlem Staff. *O Holy Night: Christmas with the Boys Choir of Harlem* (PS–3). Illus. by Faith Ringgold. 2004, HarperCollins LB $19.89 (0-06-051819-7). 40pp. Rich illustrations of an African American holy family and onlookers of all races accompany the words to five Christmas carols, which are featured on the CD. (Rev: BL 9/1/04; SLJ 10/04)

15300 Delacre, Lulu. *Las Navidades: Popular Christmas Songs from Latin America* (K–4). Illus. 1990, Scholastic $13.95 (0-590-43548-5). 32pp. Christmas traditions of Latin America through seasonal songs. (Rev: BL 11/15/90) [782.42]

15301 *Elvis Presley's the First Noel* (K–3). Illus. by Bruce Whatley. 1999, HarperCollins $12.95 (0-06-028126-X). A visual interpretation of the Christmas carol plus a CD of Elvis Presley singing it. (Rev: HBG 3/00; SLJ 10/99) [782]

15302 Feliciano, Jose. *Feliz Navidad: Two Stories Celebrating Christmas* (PS–K). Illus. by David Diaz. 2003, Scholastic $15.95 (0-439-51717-6). The lyrics of Feliciano's popular Christmas song are presented in Spanish and English, with beautiful illustrations of Puerto Rican and traditional American festivities. (Rev: HBG 4/04; SLJ 10/03) [782]

15303 Fine, Howard. *A Piggie Christmas* (K–3). Illus. 2000, Hyperion $15.99 (0-7868-0587-0). 32pp. A jolly book, illustrated with drawings of pigs in happy moods, that presents five Christmas carols, among them "Jingle Bells," "Deck the Halls," and "The Twelve Days of Christmas." (Rev: BL 9/1/00; HBG 3/01) [782.42]

15304 Freeman, Martha. *Who Is Stealing the 12 Days of Christmas?* (4–6). 2003, Holiday House $16.95 (0-8234-1788-3). 200pp. When Christmas displays at the 12 houses on Chickadee Court — each decorated for a different stanza of "The 12 Days of Christmas" — begin disappearing, Alex Parakeet and his best friend Yasmeen try to find out who — or what — is responsible. (Rev: HB 11–12/03; HBG 4/04; SLJ 10/03)

15305 *The Glorious Christmas Songbook* (3–7). Illus. 1999, Chronicle $18.95 (0-8118-2204-4). 77pp. A collection of traditional and modern Christmas carols and songs, with charming period illustrations and a few bars of the music. (Rev: BL 9/1/99; HBG 3/00; SLJ 10/99) [782.42172]

15306 Granfield, Linda. *Silent Night: The Song from Heaven* (2–4). Illus. by Nelly Hofer and Ernst Hofer. 1997, Tundra $15.95 (0-88776-395-2). The story of the writing and first performance of this hymn, as experienced by two children who are helping in the church in Obendorf, Austria, where it was written in 1818. (Rev: HBG 3/98; SLJ 10/97)

15307 *Had Gadya: A Passover Song* (K–3). Illus. by Seymour Chwast. 2005, Roaring Brook $16.95 (1-59643-033-8). 32pp. Introduces the song that is traditionally sung at the conclusion of the Jewish Passover Seder. (Rev: BL 2/15/05; SLJ 4/05) [296.4]

15308 Hills, Tad. *The 12 Days of Christmas: A Carol-and-Count Flap Book* (PS–2). Illus. by author. 2003, Simon & Schuster $9.99 (0-689-84976-1). In this lift-the-flap interpretation of the familiar Christmas song, Anita Pig is showered with the song's 12 gifts by an ardent suitor. (Rev: HBG 4/04; SLJ 10/03)

15309 Long, Sylvia. *Deck the Hall* (PS–1). Illus. 2000, Candlewick $12.95 (0-8118-2821-2). 32pp. An illustrated version of the lovely Christmas carol featuring a rabbit family engaging in holiday activities. (Rev: BL 9/1/00; HBG 3/01) [782.42]

15310 McCullough, L. E. *Stories of the Songs of Christmas* (3–5). Illus. by Irene Kelly. 1997, Smith & Kraus paper $8.95 (1-57525-116-7). 149pp. Background material on such Christmas carols and songs as "Silent Night," "Jingle Bells," and "The Twelve Days of Christmas." (Rev: SLJ 10/97) [782]

15311 McGinley, Sharon. *The Friendly Beasts* (PS–K). Illus. 2000, Greenwillow $15.95 (0-688-17421-3). 24pp. This joyful picture book illustrates the text of the carol "The Friendly Beasts," which describes the roles played by several different animals during the Nativity. (Rev: BCCB 11/00; BL 9/15/00; HBG 10/01) [782.28]

15312 Orozco, Jose-Luis. *Fiestas: A Year of Latin American Songs of Celebration* (2–4). Illus. by Elisa Kleven. 2002, Dutton $17.99 (0-525-45937-5). 56pp. Orozco presents 21 songs in Spanish and English, with music,. (Rev: BL 9/15/02; HBG 3/03) [782.42]

15313 Sabuda, Robert. *The Twelve Days of Christmas: A Pop-up Celebration* (K–4). Illus. 1996, Simon & Schuster paper $19.95 (0-689-80865-8). 12pp. A delightful pop-up version of the popular Christmas carol. (Rev: BCCB 9/96; BL 9/1/96*; HB 11–12/96) [782]

15314 Stevens, Jan R. *Twelve Lizards Leaping: A New Twelve Days of Christmas* (PS–3). Illus. by Christine Mau. 1999, Rising Moon $14.95 (0-87358-744-8). A southwestern version of the standard Christmas carol with music, lyrics, and vivid paintings. (Rev: HBG 3/00; SLJ 10/99) [782]

15315 *The Twelve Days of Christmas* (PS–3). Illus. by Vladimir Vagin. 1999, HarperCollins LB $15.89 (0-06-028399-8). 32pp. A finely illustrated version of this carol that evokes allusions to both Russian folklore and New England landscapes. (Rev: BL 1/1–15/00; HBG 3/00) [782.42]

15316 Tyrrell, Frances. *Woodland Christmas: Twelve Days of Christmas in the North Woods* (PS–2). Illus. 1996, Scholastic $15.95 (0-590-86367-3). 32pp. Woodland creatures portray the "true love's" gifts on each of the 12 days of Christmas. (Rev: BL 9/1/96) [782]

Musical Instruments

15317 Day, Eileen M. *I'm Good at Making Music* (PS–1). Series: I'm Good At. 2003, Heinemann LB $18.50 (1-4034-0900-5). 24pp. A beginning look at making music on such simple instruments as the triangle, kazoo, and drum. (Rev: HBG 4/04; SLJ 4/04) [780]

15318 Dunleavy, Deborah. *The Kids Can Press Jumbo Book of Music* (2–6). Illus. by Louise Phillips. Series: A Kids Can Press Jumbo Book. 2001, Kids Can paper $14.95 (1-55074-723-1). 208pp. Instructions for making a variety of musical instruments from everyday materials are accompanied by suggestions of appropriate music and groupings of instruments. (Rev: SLJ 4/01) [780]

15319 Ganeri, Anita. *The Young Person's Guide to the Orchestra: Benjamin Britten's Composition on CD* (4–6). Illus. 1996, Harcourt $25.00 (0-15-201304-0). 64pp. The text explains and illustrates the various instruments of the orchestra, with an accompanying CD of Britten's music. (Rev: BL 10/1/96; SLJ 10/96) [784.2]

15320 Grace, Kayla. *Percussion Instruments* (1–3). Series: Music Makers. 2002, Child's World LB $22.79 (1-56766-986-7). 24pp. A description of the instruments of the percussion family, the sounds they make, and their importance in music throughout history. Also use *Stringed Instruments* (2002). (Rev: SLJ 12/02) [784]

15321 Hayes, Ann. *Meet the Marching Smithereens* (K–3). Illus. by Karmen Thompson. 1995, Harcourt $15.00 (0-15-253158-0). 32pp. Several musical instruments are introduced through a description of an animal marching band called the Smithereens. (Rev: BCCB 6/95; BL 7/95; SLJ 5/95) [784.3]

15322 Hayes, Ann. *Meet the Orchestra* (4–7). Illus. by Karmen Thompson. 1991, Harcourt $16.00 (0-15-200526-9). 32pp. Animals in evening dress introduce young readers to the orchestra. (Rev: BCCB 3/91; BL 4/15/91; SLJ 5/91) [784.19]

15323 Hooper, Maureen Brett. *Highlights Fun to Play Recorder Book: Learn with Easy Steps and Familiar Songs* (2–6). Illus. by Judith Hunt. 2001, Boyds Mills $14.95 (1-56397-965-9). 49pp. Basic instructions for playing the recorder are accompanied by suitable songs that increase in difficulty as the reader progresses through the book. (Rev: SLJ 6/01) [784]

15324 Koscielniak, Bruce. *The Story of the Incredible Orchestra* (K–4). Illus. 2000, Houghton Mifflin $15.00 (0-395-96052-5). 40pp. This account traces the growth of the orchestra and the development of modern musical instruments and also comments on the work of several composers. (Rev: BCCB 6/00; BL 4/15/00; HBG 10/00; SLJ 6/00) [784.2]

15325 Levine, Robert. *The Story of the Orchestra* (5–7). Illus. by Meredith Hamilton. 2001, Black Dog & Leventhal $19.98 (1-57912-148-9). 96pp. Orchestra Bob introduces young readers to orchestra history, famous conductors and their eras, and instruments, in a guided tour that includes amusing cartoons, illustrations, and links to selections on the accompanying CD. (Rev: BL 12/15/01; SLJ 9/01) [784.2]

15326 Lynch, Wendy. *Brass* (2–4). Series: Musical Instruments. 2001, Heinemann LB $21.36 (1-58810-233-5). A look at the brass family of instruments in words and pictures, with material on the trumpet, tuba, and trombone. (Rev: BL 1/1–15/02; HBG 3/02) [788]

15327 Lynch, Wendy. *Keyboards* (2–4). Illus. Series: Musical Instruments. 2001, Heinemann LB $21.36 (1-58810-234-3). 32pp. Lynch introduces younger readers to keyboard instruments, how they work and how they sound, with back matter that includes a glossary and a bibliography. Also use *Percussion* (2001). (Rev: BL 1/1–15/02; HBG 3/02) [786]

15328 Lynch, Wendy. *Strings* (2–4). Series: Musical Instruments. 2001, Heinemann LB $21.36 (1-58810-236-X). All the stringed instruments of an orchestra are described in text and pictures with an activity based on creating the simulated sound of stringed instruments. (Rev: BL 1/1–15/02; HBG 3/02) [787]

15329 Lynch, Wendy. *Woodwind* (2–4). Series: Musical Instruments. 2001, Heinemann LB $21.36 (1-58810-237-8). All the woodwinds — including the clarinet, bassoon, and saxophone — are pictured and described, and common household objects are used to simulate their sounds. (Rev: BL 1/1–15/02; HBG 3/02) [788]

15330 Moss, Lloyd. *Zin! Zin! Zin! A Violin* (1–3). Illus. by Marjorie Priceman. 1995, Simon & Schuster $16.00 (0-671-88239-2). 28pp. Ten instruments of the orchestra are introduced in rhyming couplets. (Rev: BL 5/15/95; SLJ 5/95*)

15331 Rubin, Mark. *The Orchestra* (2–4). Illus. by Alan Daniel. 1992, Firefly paper $8.95 (0-920668-99-2). After a general introduction to music, this book introduces each of the instruments of the orchestra. (Rev: SLJ 6/92) [781.91]

15332 Sabbeth, Alex. *Rubber-Band Banjos and a Java Jive Bass: Projects and Activities on the Science of Music and Sound* (4–7). Illus. 1997, Wiley paper $12.95 (0-471-15675-2). 112pp. Describes the basic elements of music while giving directions for making a variety of homemade instruments. (Rev: BL 3/15/97; SLJ 6/97) [781]

15333 Thyacott, Louise. *Musical Instruments* (5–7). Illus. Series: Traditions Around the World. 1995, Thomson Learning LB $24.26 (1-56847-228-5).

48pp. A continent-by-continent survey of the many kinds of musical instruments found in various cultures. (Rev: BCCB 11/94; BL 9/15/95) [784.3]

15334 Wiseman, Ann Sayre, and John Langstaff. *Making Music: How to Create and Play 70 Homemade Musical Instruments* (3–5). Illus. by Ann Sayre Wiseman. 2003, Storey Kids $19.95 (1-58017-513-9); paper $9.95 (1-58017-512-0). 96pp. Spoons, forks, and flowerpots are among the household items that become musical instruments in this illustrated "how-to" book. (Rev: SLJ 3/04) [784.192]

15335 Woods, Samuel G. *Guitars: From Start to Finish* (3–5). Illus. Series: Made in the USA. 1999, Blackbirch LB $16.95 (1-56711-392-3). 32pp. This account focuses on the manufacture of guitars and supplies a guided tour of the Martin Guitar Company in Nazareth, Pennsylvania. (Rev: BL 12/1/99; HBG 3/00; SLJ 3/00) [787.87]

National Anthems and Patriotic Songs

15336 Bates, Katharine Lee. *America the Beautiful* (4–7). Illus. by Chris Gall. 2004, Little, Brown $16.95 (0-316-73743-7). 32pp. The lyrics of this patriotic song are accompanied by striking images that underline the sentiments expressed and give additional historical emphasis. (Rev: BL 5/1/04; SLJ 4/04) [811]

15337 Bates, Katharine Lee. *America the Beautiful* (K–3). Illus. by Wendell Minor. 2003, Penguin Putnam $16.99 (0-399-23885-9). Paintings on double-page spreads illustrate the verses of this poem, spanning events in the history of the country. (Rev: HBG 10/03; SLJ 7/03) [811]

15338 Berlin, Irving. *God Bless America* (PS). Illus. by Lynn Munsinger. 2002, HarperCollins $15.99 (0-06-009788-4). 32pp. The Irving Berlin classic song set to illustration, depicting a family of bears traveling across America. (Rev: BL 8/02; HBG 3/03) [782.421599]

15339 Bowdish, Lynea. *Francis Scott Key and "The Star Spangled Banner"* (K–3). Illus. by Harry Burman. 2002, Mondo $15.95 (1-59034-195-3). 32pp. A large-format book for younger readers about Francis Scott Key's penning of the national anthem in 1814. (Rev: BL 12/15/02; HBG 3/03) [973.5]

15340 Johnson, James W. *Lift Every Voice and Sing* (PS–8). Illus. by Elizabeth Catlett. 1993, Walker LB $15.85 (0-8027-8251-5). 36pp. Dramatic linecut prints highlight the song known as the African American national anthem. (Rev: BCCB 4/93; BL 2/15/93*; SLJ 3/93) [782.42]

15341 Johnson, James W. *Lift Ev'ry Voice and Sing* (PS–4). Illus. by Jan S. Gilchrist. 1995, Scholastic $14.95 (0-590-46982-7). 32pp. Using the lyrics of this beautiful anthem as a framework, the history and culture of African Americans are traced in touching illustrations. (Rev: BL 2/15/95*; SLJ 2/95) [782]

15342 Johnson, James Weldon. *Lift Every Voice and Sing: A Pictorial Tribute to the Negro National Anthem* (3–6). Illus. 2001, Hyperion $15.99 (0-7868-0626-5). The famous anthem, accompanied by photographs highlighting the history of African Americans. (Rev: BL 2/15/03; HBG 10/01; SLJ 1/01)

15343 Sonneborn, Liz. *The Star-Spangled Banner: The Story Behind Our National Anthem* (3–5). Illus. Series: America in Words and Song. 2004, Chelsea House LB $14.95 (0-7910-7337-8). 32pp. This slim volume covers the history of the national anthem and the changes it has undergone over the years. Also use *America the Beautiful: The Story Behind Our National Hymn* (2004). (Rev: BL 4/1/04; HBG 4/04) [929.9]

15344 Yanuck, Debbie L. *The Star-Spangled Banner* (K–2). Series: American Symbols. 2003, Capstone LB $19.93 (0-7368-2293-3). 24pp. An account of the events that inspired Francis Scott Key to write the poem that — more than 100 years later — became the lyrics to the national anthem of the United States. (Rev: SLJ 4/04) [782.42]

Singing Games and Songs

15345 Amery, Heather, comp. *The Usborne Children's Songbook* (PS–3). Illus. by Stephen Cartwright. 1998, Usborne paper $10.95 (0-7460-2981-0). 64pp. A collection of 35 traditional songs (e.g., "Twinkle, twinkle, little star") with musical arrangements and chords for a variety of different instruments. (Rev: SLJ 2/99) [782]

15346 Boynton, Sandra. *Philadelphia Chickens* (PS–5). Illus. by author. 2002, Workman $16.95 (0-7611-2636-8). 64pp. A cast of animal characters bounce through pages of lyrics and musical notations, while the songs are performed on the accompanying CD by celebrities including Meryl Streep and Natasha Richardson. (Rev: SLJ 3/03) [782.1]

15347 Browne, Anthony. *Animal Fair: A Spectacular Pop-Up* (PS–3). Illus. by author. 2002, Candlewick $14.99 (0-7636-1831-4). The big baboon and other animals of the title song star in an illustrated romp that involves many flaps. (Rev: SLJ 12/02)

15348 Bucchino, John. *Grateful: A Song of Giving Thanks* (PS–4). Illus. by Anna-Liisa Hakkarainen. 2003, HarperCollins LB $17.89 (0-06-051634-8). A song of faith, celebrating the many gifts of life; the well-illustrated book is packaged with a CD performed by Art Garfunkel. (Rev: HBG 4/04; SLJ 9/03) [782.4]

15349 Carle, Eric. *Today Is Monday* (PS–K). Illus. 1992, Penguin Putnam $15.95 (0-399-21966-8). 32pp. A picture book that bursts with food, animals, and energy, and also includes music and lyrics, so everyone can sing along. (Rev: BL 1/1/93*; SLJ 4/93) [782]

15350 Delacre, Lulu, ed. *Arroz con Leche: Popular Songs and Rhymes from Latin America* (PS–1). Trans. by Elena Paz. Illus. by Lulu Delacre. 1989,

Scholastic paper $4.99 (0-590-41886-6). A bilingual collection of folk rhymes, chants, and fingerplays. (Rev: BCCB 5/89)

15351 Emberley, Barbara. *Drummer Hoff* (K–3). Illus. by Ed Emberley. 1967, Simon & Schuster $16.00 (0-671-66248-1); paper $5.95 (0-671-66245-X). 32pp. The classic song about the assembling of a cannon. Caldecott Medal winner, 1968.

15352 Farjeon, Eleanor. *Morning Has Broken* (PS–3). Illus. by Tim Ladwig. 1996, Eerdmans $15.00 (0-8028-5127-4); paper $7.50 (0-8028-5132-0). 32pp. An illustrated version of the hymn that was once recorded by Cat Stevens. (Rev: BL 10/1/96; SLJ 12/96) [782]

15353 *The Farmer in the Dell* (PS). Illus. by Ilse Plume. 2004, Godine $17.95 (1-56792-270-8). 28pp. The familiar song is set in Pennsylvania Dutch countryside. (Rev: BL 9/15/04) [782.4]

15354 *For Our Children: A Book to Benefit the Pediatric AIDS Foundation* (PS–3). Illus. 1991, Disney LB $16.89 (1-56282-112-1). 72pp. An album of 20 songs by Carol King, Little Richard, and other artists. (Rev: BL 10/1/91; SLJ 10/91) [782.42]

15355 Garcia, Jerry, and David Grisman. *There Ain't No Bugs on Me* (PS). Illus. by Bruce Whatley. 1999, HarperCollins $15.95 (0-06-028142-1). 40pp. A cheerful rendition of the popular song, with a tape to accompany the words. (Rev: BL 8/99; SLJ 7/99) [782.4]

15356 Hart, Jane, ed. *Singing Bee! A Collection of Favorite Children's Songs* (PS–3). Illus. by Anita Lobel. 1989, Lothrop $22.95 (0-688-41975-5). 160pp. A collection of 125 simple songs with piano and guitar arrangements.

15357 Hinojosa, Tish. *Cada Nino / Every Child: A Bilingual Songbook for Kids* (3–6). Illus. by Lucia Angela Perez. 2002, Cinco Puntos $18.95 (0-938317-60-1). 56pp. This is a charming bilingual songbook, with music, presenting 11 traditional and original songs that celebrate the simple things in life. (Rev: BL 6/1–15/02; HBG 10/02) [782.42]

15358 Hoberman, Mary Ann, adapt. *Mary Had a Little Lamb* (PS–2). Illus. by Nadine Bernard Westcott. Series: Sing-Along Stories. 2003, Little, Brown $15.95 (0-316-60687-1). Young readers will enjoy this extended version of the popular children's song about Mary and her little lamb that recounts what happens after the lamb gets to school. (Rev: HBG 4/04; SLJ 12/03) [782.42164]

15359 Hort, Lenny. *The Seals on the Bus* (PS–1). Illus. by G. Brian Karas. 2000, Holt $15.95 (0-8050-5952-0). 32pp. This variation on the song "The Wheels on the Bus" tells of a series of wild animals who find their way onto a city bus. (Rev: BCCB 5/00; BL 4/1/00; HB 5–6/00; HBG 10/00; SLJ 5/00) [782.4]

15360 Hudson, Wade, and Cheryl W. Hudson. *How Sweet the Sound: African-American Songs for Children* (PS–3). Illus. by Floyd Cooper. 1995, Scholastic $15.95 (0-590-48030-8). 48pp. A collection of the words of African American songs, from spirituals and work songs to jazz and the works of Stevie Wonder. (Rev: BL 9/15/95; SLJ 11/95) [844]

15361 Johnson, Paul Brett. *Little Bunny Foo Foo* (PS–1). Illus. 2004, Scholastic $15.95 (0-439-37301-8). 32pp. In a lively adaptation full of eye-catching vehicles, the Good Fairy describes the transgressions of naughty bunny Foo Foo; music, lyrics, and suggested movements are included. (Rev: BL 1/1–15/04; SLJ 4/04)

15362 Kanzler, John. *The Big Rock Candy Mountain* (PS–2). Illus. by author. 2004, Mondo $15.95 (1-59336-062-2). 24pp. The folk song becomes a lively picture book as a family goes camping, boating, square dancing, and meets up with interesting creatures including some musical bears; lyrics and music are appended. (Rev: SLJ 5/04) [782.42]

15363 Katz, Alan. *Take Me out of the Bathtub and Other Silly Dilly Songs* (PS–1). Illus. by David Catrow. 2001, Simon & Schuster $15.00 (0-689-82903-5). 32pp. Amusing adaptations of a number of familiar songs are accompanied by equally silly illustrations. (Rev: BL 7/01; HBG 10/01; SLJ 4/01) [782.4216]

15364 Kennedy, Jimmy. *The Teddy Bears' Picnic* (PS–1). Illus. by Michael Hague. 1995, Holt paper $6.95 (0-8050-5349-2). 32pp. A large format and drawings complement this popular song about teddy bears gathering for a picnic. (Rev: BL 4/15/92; SLJ 6/92) [782]

15365 Lessac, Frane. *Camp Granada: Sing-Along Camp Songs* (2–5). Illus. 2003, Holt $18.95 (0-8050-6683-7). 48pp. Colorful, humorous illustrations and a brief story about camp activities form a backdrop for the lyrics to 34 camp songs. (Rev: BL 3/1/03; HBG 10/03; SLJ 6/03) [782.42164]

15366 Loesser, Frank. *I Love You! A Bushel and a Peck* (PS). Illus. by Rosemary Wells. 2004, HarperCollins LB $16.89 (0-06-028550-8). 32pp. Loesser's song from *Guys and Dolls* forms the framework for this charming story of a budding romance between two flirtatious ducklings. (Rev: BL 11/15/04; SLJ 2/05) [782.42]

15367 MacDonald, Margaret Read, and Winifred Jaeger. *The Round Book: Rounds Kids Love to Sing* (4–6). Illus. 1999, Linnet $22.50 (0-208-02441-7); paper $16.50 (0-208-02472-7). 124pp. A paperback containing 80 songs designed to be sung as rounds. (Rev: BL 9/1/99; HBG 10/99; SLJ 7/99) [782.42]

15368 Miller, J. Philip, and Sheppard M. Greene. *We All Sing with the Same Voice* (PS–K). Illus. by Paul Meisel. 2001, HarperCollins $15.95 (0-06-027475-1). This book-and-CD set features the Sesame Street song about understanding one another's cultures and the similarities of children all over the world. (Rev: HBG 10/01; SLJ 2/01) [784]

15369 Moreillon, Judi. *Sing Down the Rain* (2–5). Illus. by Michael Chiago. 1997, Kiva $14.95 (1-885772-07-6). This choral reading in eight parts celebrates the Saguaro Wine Ceremony of the Tohono O'odham tribe of the Sonoran desert. (Rev: SLJ 1/98) [811]

15370 Newcome, Zita. *Head, Shoulders, Knees, and Toes and Other Action Rhymes* (PS). Illus. 2002, Candlewick $15.99 (0-7636-1899-3). 64pp. Familiar songs and rhymes, with illustrations of children performing movements to accompany them. (Rev: BL 9/15/02; HBG 3/03; SLJ 10/02) [398.8]

15371 Schafer, Milton. *That Crazy Barb'ra* (PS–2). Illus. by G. Brian Karas. 2003, Dial $16.99 (0-8037-2584-1). A children's song made popular by Danny Kaye serves as the framework for this amusing story of Barbr'a who has fallen head over heels for Hubert Clumpty, who wishes his pesky admirer would simply disappear. (Rev: HBG 4/04; SLJ 9/03)

15372 *Senor Don Gato: A Traditional Song* (PS–2). Illus. by John Manders. 2003, Candlewick $15.99 (0-7636-1724-5). This English translation of a traditional Mexican rhyme about a charming cat tells the story of his terrible fall from a roof, the assumption that he is dead, and the happy circumstances of his revival. (Rev: HBG 4/04; SLJ 11/03) [782.4]

15373 Sherman, Allan, and Lou Busch. *Hello Muddah, Hello Faddah! A Letter from Camp* (K–4). Illus. by Jack E. Davis. 2004, Dutton $12.99 (0-525-46942-7). The song made famous in the 1960s by comedian Allan Sherman is the basis for this humorous picture book about a boy who is unhappy in summer camp. (Rev: SLJ 6/04) [782.4]

15374 Sturges, Philemon. *She'll Be Comin' 'Round the Mountain* (1–3). Illus. by Ashley Wolff. 2004, Little, Brown $15.95 (0-316-82256-6). 32pp. In bouncing verse, animals of the Southwest await the arrival of a special visitor. (Rev: BL 8/04; SLJ 7/04)

15375 Trapani, Iza, reteller. *How Much Is That Doggie in the Window?* (PS–3). Score and lyrics by Bob Merrill. Illus. by Iza Trapani. 1997, Whispering Coyote $15.95 (1-879085-74-7). This expanded version of the once-popular song tells about a little boy who wants a spotted puppy in a pet shop but can't afford to buy it. (Rev: HBG 3/98; SLJ 3/98) [782]

15376 Weiss, George D., and Bob Thiele. *What a Wonderful World* (PS–3). Illus. by Ashley Bryan. 1995, Simon & Schuster LB $16.00 (0-689-80087-8). 32pp. Children use a puppet stage to introduce this song. (Rev: BL 5/15/95; SLJ 5/95)

15377 Zelinsky, Paul O., adapt. *The Wheels on the Bus* (PS–1). Illus. 1990, Dutton paper $16.99 (0-525-44644-3). A pop-up edition with pull tabs of the familiar song. (Rev: BCCB 10/90; SLJ 10/90) [784]

Performing Arts

Circuses, Fairs, and Parades

15378 Alter, Judith. *Amusement Parks, Roller Coasters, Ferris Wheels, and Cotton Candy* (4–6). Illus. 1997, Watts $22.50 (0-531-20304-2). 64pp. The author traces the history of amusement parks, starting with the Columbian Exposition of 1893, and then describes some current favorites, like Coney Island and Disney World. (Rev: BL 12/15/97; HBG 3/98) [791.06]

Dance

15379 Augustyn, Frank, and Shelley Tanaka. *Footnotes: Dancing the World's Best-Loved Ballets* (5–8). Illus. 2001, Millbrook LB $24.90 (0-7613-2323-6). 96pp. A readable account that introduces ballet from a backstage perspective, with material on how it feels to be a dancer in a large ballet company. (Rev: BL 4/15/01; HBG 10/01; SLJ 6/01*) [792.8]

15380 Barber, Antonia. *Shoes of Satin, Ribbons of Silk: Tales from the Ballet* (4–6). Illus. 1995, Kingfisher $18.95 (1-85697-693-2). 96pp. In dramatic retellings, the stories of nine ballets (several less well known) are presented. (Rev: BL 11/15/95; SLJ 1/96) [792.8]

15381 Berger, Melvin. *The World of Dance* (6–8). Illus. 1978, Phillips $29.95 (0-87599-221-8). An overview of the subject that begins in prehistoric times and ends with today's social dancing and ballet.

15382 Bray-Moffat, Naia. *Ballet School* (K–3). Illus. 2003, DK $12.99 (0-7894-9228-8). 48pp. Ample illustrations grace this friendly, large-format introduction to ballet and its techniques, methods of instruction, costumes, and performances. (Rev: BL 4/15/03; HBG 10/03; SLJ 9/03) [792.8]

15383 Castle, Kate. *Ballet* (4–6). Illus. 1996, Kingfisher $16.95 (0-7534-5001-1). 64pp. A well-illustrated introduction to the world of ballet, with material on the composer, choreographer, designer, famous dancers, and stories of well-known ballets. (Rev: SLJ 12/96) [792.8]

15384 Cooper, Elisha. *Dance!* (2–4). Illus. 2001, Greenwillow $15.95 (0-06-029418-3). 32pp. This is a very visual introduction to the world of dance, with feathery watercolor illustrations and minimal text. (Rev: BL 9/15/01; HB 11–12/01; HBG 3/02; SLJ 9/01) [793.8]

15385 Elliott, Donald. *Frogs and Ballet* (4–6). Illus. by Clinton Arrowood. 1979, Harvard Common paper $8.95 (0-87645-119-9). Familiar ballet steps and how they are woven into the classical ballet.

15386 Friedman, Lise. *First Lessons in Ballet* (3–5). Illus. 1999, Workman $14.95 (0-7611-1804-7); paper $8.95 (0-7611-1352-5). 64pp. Illustrated with photographs, this book for beginning ballet students explains techniques, positions, exercises, and more. (Rev: BL 2/15/00; SLJ 4/00) [792.8]

15387 Frith, Margaret. *Hooray for Ballet!* (2–4). Illus. by Amanda Haley. Series: Smart About the Arts. 2003, Grosset LB $14.89 (0-448-43155-6); paper $5.99 (0-448-42884-9). With plenty of interesting detail, Elizabeth relates the story of her visit to Lincoln Center to see *Swan Lake*. (Rev: HBG 10/03; SLJ 9/03) [792.8]

15388 Geras, Adele. *Sleeping Beauty* (3–5). Illus. Series: The Magic of Ballet. 2001, David & Charles $10.95 (1-86233-246-0). 26pp. The story of Sleeping Beauty is told from the perspective of four characters. Also use *Swan Lake* (2001). (Rev: BCCB 1/03; BL 7/01; SLJ 11/01) [823.914]

15389 Geras, Adele. *Time for Ballet* (PS–2). Illus. by Shelagh McNicholas. 2004, Dial $16.99 (0-8037-2978-2). 32pp. Soft watercolors illustrate the tale of Tilly, an aspiring dancer, as she and the other members of her ballet class prepare for a recital. (Rev: BL 2/1/04*; SLJ 2/04)

15390 Hayden, Melissa, ed. *The Nutcracker Ballet* (K–4). Illus. by Stephen T. Johnson. 1992, Andrews & McMeel $14.95 (0-8362-4501-6). 32pp. This retelling is based on Balanchine's version of the ballet. (Rev: BL 2/1/93) [792]

15391 Hayward, Linda. *A Day in the Life of a Dancer* (PS–K). Series: Dorling Kindersley Readers: Jobs People Do. 2001, DK $12.95 (0-7894-7370-4); paper $3.95 (0-7894-7369-0). 32pp. Using a very limited vocabulary and simple sentences, this beginning reader explores the everyday life of a ballet dancer. (Rev: BL 8/1/01; HBG 10/01) [792.8]

15392 Hoffmann, E. T. A. *The Nutcracker* (PS). Illus. by Thea Kliros. 2003, HarperCollins $5.99 (0-06-052745-5). A simplified, attractively illustrated version of the story behind Tchaikovsky's world-famous ballet. (Rev: SLJ 10/03)

15393 Johnson, Anne E. *Jazz Tap: From African Drums to American Feet* (4–7). Series: The Library of African American Arts and Culture. 1999, Rosen LB $19.95 (0-8239-1856-4). 64pp. This book traces the history of jazz tap from a variety of African dances to its emergence in the 1920s and its later development in night clubs, on Broadway, and in movies. (Rev: SLJ 1/00) [793.3]

15394 Klingel, Cynthia, and Robert B. Noyed. *Dancers* (K–1). Series: Wonder Books. 2001, Child's World LB $21.36 (1-56766-939-5). 24pp. This book for beginning readers gives basic information about dancers and dancing. (Rev: HBG 3/02; SLJ 2/02)

15395 Pavlova, Anna. *I Dreamed I Was a Ballerina* (3–5). Illus. by Edgar Degas. 2001, Simon & Schuster $16.00 (0-689-84676-2). 32pp. Beautiful Degas illustrations accompany the true story, in her own words, of Pavlova's inspiring first visit to a ballet and her subsequent rise to fame. (Rev: BL 12/1/01; HBG 3/02; SLJ 11/01) [792.8]

15396 Riordan, James. *Favorite Stories of the Ballet* (4–6). Illus. by Victor G. Ambrus. 1993, Checkerboard $14.95 (1-56288-252-X). These ballet stories include *The Nutcracker, Swan Lake, Sleeping Beauty,* and *Cinderella.*

15397 *Step-by-Step Ballet Class: The Official Illustrated Guide* (4–6). Illus. 1994, Contemporary paper $14.95 (0-8092-3499-8). 144pp. This guide developed by the Royal Academy of Dancing in England gives material for various levels of development, including positions, movements, and advice on appearance. (Rev: BL 12/1/94) [792.8]

15398 Tchaikovsky, Pyotr I. *Swan Lake* (2–4). Trans. by Marianne Martens. Illus. by Lisbeth Zwerger. 2002, North-South LB $16.50 (0-7358-1703-0). 32pp. Hauntingly detailed paintings bring the characters to life in this attractive retelling of the familiar classic that has a happy ending, which is explained in an author's note. (Rev: BCCB 11/02; BL 1/1–15/03; HBG 3/03; SLJ 12/02) [792.8]

15399 Tythacott, Louise. *Dance* (5–7). Illus. Series: Traditions Around the World. 1995, Thomson Learning LB $24.26 (1-56847-275-7). 48pp. The ways people dance around the world and the reasons they do are presented with many color photographs. (Rev: BL 6/1–15/95; SLJ 9/95) [793.3]

15400 Vagin, Vladimir. *The Nutcracker Ballet* (K–3). Illus. 1995, Scholastic $14.95 (0-590-47220-8). 32pp. All the characters in the *Nutcracker,* including Clara and Herr Drosselmeier, come to life in this retelling of the ballet story with effective, detailed illustrations. (Rev: BL 9/15/95)

15401 Varriale, Jim. *Kids Dance: The Students of Ballet Tech* (4–6). Illus. 1999, Dutton $15.99 (0-525-45536-1). 32pp. The story of Ballet Tech — the first public school in America to train ballet dancers. (Rev: BCCB 1/00; BL 9/15/99; HB 11–12/99; HBG 3/00; SLJ 12/99) [792.8]

15402 Wilkes, Angela. *The Best Book of Ballet* (1–4). Series: The Best Book Of. 2000, Kingfisher $12.95 (0-7534-5275-8). 32pp. A fine introduction to ballet that includes material on history, famous ballets, a ballet class, basic positions and steps, and what professional dancers do. (Rev: HBG 3/01; SLJ 7/00) [792.8]

15403 Yolen, Jane, and Heidi Stemple. *The Barefoot Book of Ballet Stories* (5–7). Illus. by Rebecca Guay. 2004, Barefoot $19.99 (1-84148-229-3). 96pp. The stories behind seven of the world's classic ballets — including "Cinderella," "The Nutcracker," "Coppelia," and "Sleeping Beauty" — are introduced by a general discussion of ballet as an art form and accompanied by production notes on each work. (Rev: BL 11/1/04; SLJ 12/04) [792.8]

Marionettes and Puppets

15404 Bryant, Jill, and Catherine Heard. *Making Shadow Puppets* (4–6). Series: Kids Can Do It! 2002, Kids Can $12.95 (1-55337-028-7); paper $5.95 (1-55337-029-5). 40pp. Two-dimensional puppets that can be created with easily found materials are presented with good step-by-step instructions. (Rev: BL 9/15/02; HBG 3/03; SLJ 12/02) [745.5]

15405 Renfro, Nancy. *Puppet Show Made Easy!* (3–6). Illus. 1984, Renfro $18.95 (0-931044-13-8). 96pp. Creating puppets and how to stage a show.

Motion Pictures, Radio, and Television

15406 Beatty, Scott. *Batman, the Animated Series Guide* (3–5). Illus. Series: DC Animated Series Guides. 2003, DK $9.99 (0-7894-9580-5). 48pp. A companion guide to *Batman: The Animated Series,* which originally aired on TV between 1992 and 1995, providing a wealth of information about story lines, characters, and Batman-related trivia. (Rev: SLJ 1/04)

15407 Beatty, Scott. *Superman, the Animated Series Guide* (3–5). Illus. Series: DC Animated Series Guides. 2003, DK $9.99 (0-7894-9584-8). 48pp. A companion guide to *Superman: The Animated*

Series, which originally aired on TV between 1996 and 1999, providing a wealth of information about story lines, characters, and Superman-related trivia. (Rev: SLJ 1/04)

15408 Fingeroth, Danny. *Backstage at an Animated Series* (4–8). Series: Backstage Pass. 2003, Children's Book Pr. LB $20.00 (0-516-24323-3); paper $6.95 (0-516-24385-3). 48pp. Fingeroth explores the world of animated films, discussing their history, recent technological advances, and the mechanics of production, and suggesting ways to become involved. Also use *Backstage at a Movie Set* (2003). (Rev: SLJ 10/03) [791.43]

15409 Gleasner, Diana C. *The Movies (Inventions That Changed Our Lives)* (4–6). Illus. 1983, Walker LB $8.85 (0-8027-6483-5). A history of moviemaking.

15410 *The History of Moviemaking* (3–6). Illus. 1995, Scholastic $19.95 (0-590-47645-9). 47pp. A history of film is enlivened by transparencies, flaps, and other interactive devices. (Rev: BL 2/1/96; SLJ 5/96) [791]

15411 Krauss, Ronnie. *Take a Look, It's in a Book: How Television Is Made at Reading Rainbow* (2–4). Illus. by Christopher Hornsby. 1997, Walker LB $16.85 (0-8027-8489-5). 32pp. A behind-the-scenes look at the television program *Reading Rainbow* and how it is put together. (Rev: BL 3/1/97; SLJ 6/97*) [791.45]

15412 Krull, Kathleen. *The Night the Martians Landed: Just the Facts (Plus the Rumors) About Invaders from Mars* (4–7). Illus. by Christopher Santoro. 2003, HarperCollins LB $15.89 (0-688-17247-4); paper $4.25 (0-688-17246-6). 80pp. The fascinating story of the 1938 radio broadcast of H. G. Wells's "The War of the Worlds" is amplified by a discussion of hoaxes in general and our tendency to believe them. (Rev: BCCB 10/03; HBG 4/04; SLJ 10/03)

15413 Lund, Kristin. *Star Wars, Episode I: Incredible Locations* (3–6). Illus. 2000, DK $19.95 (0-7894-6692-9). 48pp. A visual treat that uses fold-out pages to present drawings and scenes from the movie *The Phantom Menace*. (Rev: BL 1/1–15/01; HBG 3/01) [791.43]

15414 Miller, Marilyn. *Behind the Scenes at the TV News Studio* (PS–3). Illus. Series: Behind the Scenes. 1996, Raintree LB $21.40 (0-8172-4089-6). 32pp. A fascinating inside look at the inner workings of a TV news studio. (Rev: BL 4/15/96; SLJ 12/96) [070.1]

15415 Reynolds, David West. *Star Wars: Incredible Cross-Sections* (4–8). 1998, DK $19.95 (1-7894-3480-6). This large-format book includes cross-sections of the TIE fighter, the X-wing fighter, the AT-AT, the Millennium Falcon, Jabba's sail barge, and the Death Star. (Rev: BL 12/15/98) [791.43]

15416 Reynolds, David West. *Star Wars: The Visual Dictionary* (4–8). 1998, DK $19.95 (0-7894-3481-4). Using a large-format dictionary approach, the people, creatures, and droids of the *Star Wars* saga are presented, with large photographs of the charac-

ters and many stills from the movies. (Rev: BL 12/15/98; HBG 3/99; SLJ 2/99) [791.43]

15417 Reynolds, David West. *Star Wars Episode I: Incredible Cross-Sections: The Definitive Guide to the Craft of Star Wars Episode I* (4–8). Illus. by Hans Jenssen and Richard Chasemore. 1999, DK $19.95 (0-7894-3962-X). 32pp. An excellent guidebook that features cross-sections of vehicles and spacecraft featured in *Star Wars: Episode I*. (Rev: HBG 3/00; SLJ 12/99) [791]

15418 Reynolds, David West. *Star Wars Episode I: The Visual Dictionary* (4–8). Illus. 1999, DK $19.95 (0-7894-4701-0). 64pp. In this large-format book, a follow-up to *Star Wars: The Visual Dictionary*, the author, an archaeologist, reports on creatures and events in *Episode 1*, using movie stills and posed photographs to explain the galaxy's history, technology, anthropology, and politics. (Rev: BL 8/99) [791.43]

Theater and Play Production

15419 Bany-Winters, Lisa. *Funny Bones: Comedy Games and Activities for Kids* (3–6). Illus. 2002, Chicago Review paper $14.95 (1-55652-444-7). 155pp. In addition to learning games, skits, and songs, readers will find some history of comedy and will gain insight on how to use props, music, makeup, and other techniques to be funny. (Rev: SLJ 12/02) [793]

15420 Bany-Winters, Lisa. *On Stage: Theater Games and Activities for Kids* (4–7). Illus. 1997, Chicago Review paper $14.95 (1-55652-324-6). 160pp. This book provides a number of theater games involving improvisation, creating characters, using and becoming objects, and ideas for pantomime and puppetry. (Rev: BL 2/1/98; SLJ 3/98) [327.12]

15421 Bany-Winters, Lisa. *Show Time! Music, Dance, and Drama Activities for Kids* (3–6). Illus. by Fran Lee. 2000, Chicago Review paper $14.95 (1-55652-361-0). 189pp. Using short chapters, this covers musical theater from Shakespeare to Sondheim with added activities like games, scenes for experimentation, and short scripts to stage. (Rev: BL 9/1/03; SLJ 8/00) [327.12]

15422 Caruso, Sandra, and Susan Kosoff. *The Young Actor's Book of Improvisation: Dramatic Situations Based on Literature: Ages 7–11* (2–6). 1998, Heinemann paper $19.95 (0-325-00048-4). 164pp. Describes hundreds of books, such as *Shiloh,* from which readers can create scenes and dramatic monologues. (Rev: BL 9/15/98) [792]

15423 Dunleavy, Deborah. *The Jumbo Book of Drama* (4–8). Illus. by Jane Kurisu. 2004, Kids Can paper $14.95 (1-55337-008-2). 208pp. Divided into Acts, this volume covers all aspects of drama and stagecraft, from body movement to lighting and props. (Rev: BL 5/1/04; SLJ 6/04) [372.66]

15424 McCullough, L. E. *Plays for Learning: Israel Reborn: Legends of the Diaspora and Israel's Modern Rebirth for Grades 4–6* (4–6). Series: Young Actors. 2001, Smith & Kraus paper $15.95 (1-

57525-253-8). 204pp. A collection of 12 plays drawn from a variety of sources that portray the Jewish experience from the expulsion from Israel to the creation of the modern state. (Rev: SLJ 6/02)

15425 Malam, John. *Theater: From First Rehearsal to Opening Night* (3–5). Illus. Series: Building Works. 2000, Bedrick $16.95 (0-87226-588-9). 32pp. This guided tour of a theater includes the box office, orchestra pit, and dressing rooms plus a brief history of theaters. (Rev: BL 7/00; HBG 10/00; SLJ 11/00) [792]

15426 Miller, Kimberly M. *Backstage at a Play* (4–8). Series: Backstage Pass. 2003, Children's Book Pr. LB $20.00 (0-516-24327-6); paper $6.95 (0-516-24389-6). 48pp. Miller explores the world of theater, discussing how they are produced and the degree of commitment necessary, and suggesting ways to become involved. (Rev: SLJ 10/03) [792]

15427 Morley, Jacqueline. *A Shakespearean Theater* (5–8). Illus. by John James. Series: Magnifications.

2003, McGraw-Hill $20.95 (1-57768-979-8). 48pp. Cutaway illustrations and insets provide magnified views of theaters in Shakespeare's days, with details on the history of drama, the actors, and the grimy state of 16th-century London. (Rev: BL 9/15/03; HBG 4/04) [792]

15428 Morley, Jacqueline. *Shakespeare's Theater* (4–6). Illus. Series: Inside Story. 1995, Bedrick LB $18.95 (0-87226-309-6). 48pp. Details on Shakespeare's Globe Theatre and performances that took place there are preceded by a brief history of European theater. (Rev: BL 4/15/95) [792]

15429 Siberell, Anne. *Bravo! Brava! A Night at the Opera: Behind the Scenes, with Composers, Cast, and Crew* (3–6). Illus. by author. 2001, Oxford $19.95 (0-19-513966-6). 64pp. An excellent introduction to the many facets of opera, from its history to behind-the-scenes tasks such as makeup and set design. (Rev: BL 2/15/02; HBG 3/02; SLJ 1/02*) [782.1]

History and Geography

History and Geography in General

Miscellaneous

15430 Aaseng, Nathan. *You Are the Explorer* (4–8). Illus. Series: Great Decisions. 2000, Oliver LB $19.95 (1-881508-55-2). 160pp. In this interactive book about famous explorers, the reader is asked to make decisions similar to those made by real explorers such as Columbus, Cortes, Champlain, and Robert Scott. (Rev: BL 5/1/00; HBG 10/00; SLJ 9/00) [910]

15431 Ajmera, Maya K., and John D. Ivanko. *Back to School* (PS–3). Series: It's a Kid's World. 2001, Charlesbridge LB $15.95 (1-57091-383-8); paper $6.95 (1-57091-384-6). This brief look at schooling around the world, with minimal text and color photographs, shows students studying in different situations, unusual methods of getting to school, and various kinds of clothing. (Rev: HBG 3/02; SLJ 6/02)

15432 Ajmera, Maya K., and John D. Ivanko. *To Be a Kid* (PS–1). Illus. 1999, Charlesbridge $15.95 (0-88106-841-1). 32pp. Children from around the world share a community of interests involving play, families, schools, animals, and friends. (Rev: BL 2/1/99; HBG 10/99; SLJ 4/99) [305.23]

15433 Ajmera, Maya K., and Anna R. Versola. *Children from Australia to Zimbabwe: A Photographic Journey Around the World* (3–6). Illus. 1997, Charlesbridge $18.95 (0-88106-999-X). 64pp. A photographic journey around the globe that introduces 25 countries and gives basic fact about each. (Rev: BL 1/1–15/98; HBG 3/98; SLJ 7/97) [305.23]

15434 Arnold, Caroline. *The Geography Book: Activities for Exploring, Mapping, and Enjoying Your World* (4–7). Illus. by Tina Cash-Walsh. 2001, Wiley paper $12.95 (0-471-41236-8). 112pp. An organized introduction to several geography concepts along with step-by-step instructions for projects and experiments. (Rev: BL 2/15/02; SLJ 3/02) [910]

15435 Bramwell, Martyn. *Central and South America* (4–6). Illus. Series: World in Maps. 2000, Carolrhoda $23.93 (0-8225-2912-2). 48pp. This collection of maps of all the countries in Central and South America also covers population, government, languages, currency, size, and capitals. (Rev: BL 10/15/00; HBG 10/01; SLJ 1/01) [917.28]

15436 Burger, Leslie, and Debra L. Rahm. *Sister Cities in a World of Difference* (4–8). Illus. 1996, Lerner LB $22.60 (0-8225-2697-2). The pairing of cities internationally is covered with material on the results, mostly positive. (Rev: BL 9/1/96; SLJ 9/96) [303.48]

15437 Burleigh, Robert. *Earth from Above for Young Readers* (4–9). Photos by Yann Arthus-Bertrand. Illus. by David Giraudon. 2002, Abrams $14.95 (0-8109-3486-8). 77pp. Large aerial views show landscapes around the world, from remote areas of natural beauty to New York's Yankee Stadium. (Rev: HBG 3/03; SLJ 1/03) [779]

15438 Collard, Sneed B. *1,000 Years Ago on Planet Earth* (3–6). Illus. 1999, Houghton Mifflin $15.00 (0-395-90866-3). 32pp. Double-page spreads describe what was happening in the year 1000 in various civilizations around the world. (Rev: BL 8/99; HBG 3/00; SLJ 9/99) [909]

15439 Dewey, Jennifer Owings. *Finding Your Way* (4–6). Illus. 2001, Millbrook LB $23.90 (0-7613-0956-X). 64pp. The author relates several tales that involve travel, using one's sense of direction, and becoming lost, in an absorbing text that conveys some basics of map reading. (Rev: BL 5/1/01; HBG 10/01; SLJ 7/01) [795.58]

15440 Gallimard Jeunesse, and Donald Grant. *Atlas of Islands* (PS–2). Series: First Discovery. 1999, Scholastic $12.95 (0-439-04402-2). 24pp. This simple book explains what islands are and covers other basic geographical terms. (Rev: BL 10/15/99; HBG 3/00) [551.4]

15441 Halley, Ned. *Disasters* (3–6). Illus. 1999, Kingfisher $15.95 (0-7534-5221-9). 64pp. Disasters in history such as earthquakes, tornadoes, famine, volcanoes, and the sinking of the *Titanic* are covered in this well-illustrated book. (Rev: BL 10/15/99; HBG 3/00; SLJ 12/99) [363.34]

15442 Hibbert, Clare. *Real Pirates* (3–6). Illus. by John James. 2003, Enchanted Lion $15.95 (1-59270-018-7). 48pp. Seagoing bandits of both sexes, from Blackbeard to Anne Bonny, and details of their ships, weapons, and tactics are presented in four geographical areas. (Rev: SLJ 5/04) [910.4]

15443 Hollyer, Beatrice. *Wake Up, World! A Day in the Life of Children Around the World* (K–3). Illus. 1999, Holt $16.95 (0-8050-6293-9). A boy in Siberia and a girl in northern Brazil are two of the eight children from around the world in this introductory book on different environments. (Rev: BL 9/15/99; HBG 3/00; SLJ 12/99) [306.09]

15444 Jackson, Ellen. *It's Back to School We Go! First Day Stories from Around the World* (1–3). Illus. by Jan Davey Ellis. 2003, Millbrook LB $23.90 (0-7613-2562-X). 32pp. A look at the first day of school in 11 countries, with facts about food, clothes, subjects studied, and games played. (Rev: BL 8/03; HBG 4/04) [371]

15445 Kindersley, Barnabas, and Anabel Kindersley. *Children Just Like Me: A Unique Celebration of Children Around the World* (3–6). Illus. 1995, DK $19.95 (0-7894-0201-7). 79pp. An attractive book that views children around the world, arranged by continents. (Rev: BCCB 2/95; SLJ 1/96) [305]

15446 Lewis, J. Patrick. *Earth and You: A Closer View: Nature's Features* (2–4). Illus. by Christopher Canyon. 2001, Dawn $16.95 (1-58469-016-X); paper $7.95 (1-58469-015-1). The author and illustrator present a vivid and lyrical close-up look at natural features of the earth and its plants and animals, urging children to treat their environment with care. (Rev: HBG 10/01; SLJ 4/01) [508]

15447 Llewellyn, Claire. *Great Discoveries and Amazing Adventures: The Stories of Hidden Marvels and Lost Treasures* (4–7). Illus. 2004, Kingfisher $18.95 (0-7534-5783-0). 76pp. Important discoveries — and hoaxes — are described in inviting text, plus many illustrations, factoids, and a foreword by Robert Ballard. (Rev: SLJ 1/05) [509]

15448 Llewellyn, Claire. *Our Planet Earth* (K–3). Illus. Series: Scholastic First Encyclopedia. 1997, Scholastic paper $14.95 (0-590-87929-4). 77pp. An introductory book on the Earth's origins, physical geography, and the life forms that inhabit our planet. (Rev: SLJ 2/98) [910]

15449 Mellett, Peter. *Pyramids* (3–6). Illus. Series: Young Scientist Concepts and Projects. 1999, Gareth Stevens LB $16.95 (0-8368-2267-6). 64pp. After a general introduction to pyramids, this book focuses on the pyramids of Egypt, with interesting related projects. (Rev: BL 4/15/99) [909]

15450 Parker, Steve, and Sally Morgan. *Ultimate Atlas of Almost Everything* (4–6). 1999, Sterling $24.95 (0-8069-7759-0). 117pp. An atlas that contains information on the earth, wildlife, people, and places. (Rev: HBG 3/00; SLJ 2/00) [900]

15451 Pascoe, Elaine, and Deborah Kops. *Scholastic Kid's Almanac for the 21st Century* (4–7). Illus. by

Bob Italiano and David C. Bell. 1999, Scholastic paper $12.95 (0-590-30724-X). 352pp. An almanac that covers subjects including aerospace, animals, chemistry, computers, energy, geography, plants, religion, and sports. (Rev: SLJ 2/00) [900]

15452 Petersen, David. *North America* (2–4). Illus. Series: True Books. 1998, Children's Book Pr. LB $21.00 (0-516-20768-7). 48pp. Excellent maps, satellite photos, and drawings are used to highlight the topographical features, animals and plants, and the native peoples of North America. (Rev: BL 1/1–15/99; HBG 3/99) [970]

15453 Rhatigan, Joe, and Heather Smith. *Geography Crafts for Kids: 50 Cool Projects and Activities for Exploring the World* (4–6). Illus. 2002, Sterling $24.95 (1-57990-196-4). 144pp. This collection of projects and activities related to geography is an excellent tool for hands-on learning. (Rev: BL 8/02; HBG 10/02; SLJ 7/02) [372.89]

15454 Sammis, Fran. *Measurements* (2–5). 1997, Marshall Cavendish LB $22.79 (0-7614-0539-9). 32pp. Explains how geographical distances are measured and how these systems began. (Rev: BL 2/15/98; HBG 3/98) [910]

15455 Scandiffio, Laura. *Escapes!* (5–9). Illus. by Stephen MacEachern. Series: True Stories from the Edge. 2004, Annick $18.95 (1-55037-823-6); paper $7.95 (1-55037-822-8). 170pp. Ten stories of great escapes and escape attempts, from the first century B.C. to the late 1970s, with a concentration on resourcefulness and bravery. (Rev: SLJ 6/04) [904]

15456 Siegel, Alice, and Margo McLoone. *The Blackbirch Kid's Almanac of Geography* (4–7). 2000, Blackbirch $49.94 (1-56711-300-1). 336pp. A good browsing book that contains information on such topics as natural and manmade wonders, countries, currencies, events, weather, languages, foods, and culture. (Rev: HBG 3/01; SLJ 2/01) [910]

15457 Wood, Robert W. *Easy Geography Activities* (3–6). Illus. by John D. Wood. 1991, TAB $16.95 (0-8306-2493-7); paper $9.95 (0-8306-2492-9). 141pp. Helping to understand the principles and vocabulary of geography through such activities as reading road maps, making a compass, and understanding continental drift. (Rev: BL 2/1/92) [910]

Maps and Globes

15458 Anderson, Scoular. *Space Pirates: A Map-Reading Adventure* (2–5). Illus. by author. 2004, Annick $19.95 (1-55037-881-3); paper $8.95 (1-55037-880-5). Basic map-reading skills are introduced within the framework of a space adventure. (Rev: SLJ 1/05) [793.73]

15459 *Atlas of Countries* (1–3). Illus. by Donald Grant. Series: First Discovery Atlases. 1996, Scholastic $12.95 (0-590-58282-8). This atlas explains maps and globes, landforms, the earth's evolution and rotation, while also supplying maps of the world's countries. (Rev: SLJ 9/96) [912]

15460 Berger, Melvin, and Gilda Berger. *The Whole World in Your Hands: Looking at Maps* (2–3). Illus.

by Robert Quackenbush. Series: Discovery Readers. 1993, Ideals paper $4.50 (0-8249-8609-1). 48pp. This book for beginning readers introduces maps from simple to complex. (Rev: BCCB 4/93; BL 7/93) [912]

15461 Bramwell, Martyn. *How Maps Are Made* (5–8). Illus. Series: Maps and Mapmakers. 1998, Lerner LB $22.60 (0-8225-2920-3). 48pp. The difficulties in representing the globe on a flat surface are explored, plus details on how maps are made — both by hand and by computer — and on the use of aerial photography in mapmaking. (Rev: BL 3/15/99; HBG 3/99; SLJ 2/99) [526]

15462 Bramwell, Martyn. *Mapping Our World* (4–8). Illus. Series: Maps and Mapmakers. 1998, Lerner LB $22.60 (0-8225-2924-6). This work shows how different kinds of maps can be used to illustrate topography, geology, climate, vegetation, population, geography, minerals, trade, pollution, and habitat. (Rev: BL 3/15/99; SLJ 2/99) [912]

15463 Bramwell, Martyn. *Mapping the Seas and Airways* (5–8). Series: Maps and Mapmakers. 1998, Lerner LB $22.60 (0-8225-2921-1). 48pp. This volume deals with special kinds of maps prepared and used by oceanographers and by airline cartographers. (Rev: BL 3/15/99; HBG 3/99) [912]

15464 Bramwell, Martyn. *Maps in Everyday Life* (5–8). Illus. Series: Maps and Mapmakers. 1998, Lerner LB $22.60 (0-8225-2923-8). 48pp. This book explains how different maps are used for different purposes, e.g., tourist maps and climate maps. (Rev: BL 3/15/99; HBG 3/99) [912]

15465 Bredeson, Carmen. *Looking at Maps and Globes* (1–2). Illus. Series: Rookie Read-About Geography. 2001, Children's Book Pr. LB $19.00 (0-516-22351-8). 32pp. An introduction to maps and globes, along with explanations about features such as legends, scale, and the equator. (Rev: BL 11/1/01) [912]

15466 Chancellor, Deborah. *Maps and Mapping* (K–3). Series: Kingfisher Young Knowledge. 2004, Houghton Mifflin $8.95 (0-7534-5759-8). 48pp. Attractive double-page spreads with many illustrations and diagrams present basic information on maps and mapmaking. (Rev: BL 9/1/04) [912]

15467 DiSpezio, Michael A. *Map Mania: Discovering Where You Are and Getting to Where You Aren't* (3–5). Illus. by Dave Garbot. 2002, Sterling $19.95 (0-8069-4407-2). 80pp. An entertaining introduction to the usefulness of floor plans, maps, and the ability to navigate, with quizzes, activities, and discussion of mysterious sites such as the Bermuda Triangle. (Rev: HBG 3/03; SLJ 9/02)

15468 Hennessy, B. G. *Once upon a Time Map Book* (1–4). Illus. by Peter Joyce. 2005, Candlewick

$11.99 (0-7636-2521-3). 16pp. Maps of Oz, Neverland, and Snow White's forest — among others — offer interesting features and the opportunity to develop map skills. (Rev: BL 10/1/04)

15469 Johnson, Sylvia A. *Mapping the World* (4–7). Illus. 1999, Simon & Schuster $16.95 (0-689-81813-0). 32pp. A history of maps and mapmaking from Ptolemy in ancient Greece to the satellite and computer images of today. (Rev: BCCB 11/99; BL 12/1/99; HBG 3/00; SLJ 12/99*) [912]

15470 Knowlton, Jack. *Maps and Globes* (2–4). Illus. 1985, HarperCollins paper $6.95 (0-06-446049-5). 48pp. This is a clear introduction to maps and globes and how to read them. (Rev: BCCB 3/86; BL 12/15/85)

15471 Oleksy, Walter. *Mapping the World* (5–7). Series: Watts Library: Geography. 2002, Watts LB $24.00 (0-531-12029-5); paper $8.95 (0-531-16636-8). 64pp. A history of how maps have been made, from the explorers, merchants, and mapmakers of old to the accurate modern products that use new technology. Also use *Mapping the Seas* and *Maps in History* (both 2002). (Rev: BL 10/15/02) [912]

15472 Robson, Pam. *Maps and Plans* (2–4). Illus. by Tony Kenyon. Series: Geography for Fun. 2001, Millbrook LB $22.90 (0-7613-2165-9). 32pp. This combination of maps, charts, games, and activities introduces some basic concepts in an entertaining way. (Rev: HBG 10/01; SLJ 9/01)

15473 Smith, A. G. *Where Am I? The Story of Maps and Navigation* (4–8). Illus. 1997, Stoddart paper $13.95 (0-7737-5836-4). Important discoveries and innovations in the history of mapmaking are explained. (Rev: BL 9/1/97) [910]

15474 Stienecker, David L. *Maps* (2–5). Series: Discovering Geography. 1997, Marshall Cavendish LB $22.79 (0-7614-0538-0). 32pp. The evolution of maps is traced, and basic map-reading skills are introduced. (Rev: BL 2/15/98; HBG 3/98; SLJ 4/98) [912]

15475 Wilkinson, Philip. *The Kingfisher Student Atlas* (5–8). 2003, Kingfisher $24.95 (0-7534-5589-7). 128pp. An atlas of the earth, with detail on each area's physical characteristics and political boundaries and material on such problems as pollution and deforestation. An accompanying CD offers printable maps. (Rev: HBG 4/04; SLJ 4/04)

15476 Wyse, Elizabeth, and Caroline Lucas, eds. *Dorling Kindersley Children's Atlas* (4–8). Illus. 2000, DK paper $24.99 (0-7894-5845-4). 176pp. An excellent all-purpose atlas that includes material on history, climate, vegetation, population, and more. (Rev: BL 10/15/00; HBG 10/01; SLJ 5/01) [912]

Paleontology and Dinosaurs

15477 Agenbroad, Larry D., and Lisa Nelson. *Mammoths: Ice-Age Giants* (5–8). Illus. Series: Discovery! 2002, Lerner LB $31.95 (0-8225-2862-2). 120pp. A detailed look at mammoths, theories on mammoth extinction, and mammoth discoveries, with sidebar features on topics such as human hunters in the Ice Age, and geologic timelines. (Rev: BL 6/1–15/02; HBG 10/02; SLJ 7/02) [569]

15478 Aliki. *Digging Up Dinosaurs* (2–4). Illus. by author. 1989, HarperCollins LB $15.89 (0-690-04716-9); paper $4.95 (0-06-445078-3). 32pp. This book answers the question "How do dinosaurs get into museums?"

15479 Aliki. *Dinosaur Bones* (PS–3). Illus. by author. 1988, HarperCollins paper $4.95 (0-06-445077-5). 32pp. In this book, her fourth on dinosaurs, Aliki discusses the discovery of fossils and the many theories that emerged about their meaning. (Rev: BCCB 1/88; BL 2/1/88; SLJ 4/88)

15480 Aliki. *My Visit to the Dinosaurs* (PS–3). Illus. by author. 1985, HarperCollins LB $15.89 (0-690-04423-2); paper $4.95 (0-06-445020-1). 32pp. Revision of the 1969 book, including new material. Also use: *Dinosaurs Are Different* (1985). (Rev: BCCB 10/85; BL 9/15/85; SLJ 1/86)

15481 Andreae, Giles. *Dinosaurs Galore!* (PS–3). Illus. by David Wojtowycz. 2005, Tiger Tales $16.95 (1-58925-044-3). A varied group of dinosaurs introduces themselves and their characteristcs in humorous rhyming verse. (Rev: SLJ 5/05) [567.9]

15482 Armentrout, David, and Patricia Armentrout. *Dinosaurs* (PS–2). 2002, Rourke LB $26.60 (1-58952-342-3). 32pp. Simple definitions are given for 50 words about dinosaurs, along with a sentence that includes the word. (Rev: SLJ 3/03)

15483 Arnold, Caroline. *Dinosaur Mountain: Graveyard of the Past* (4–7). Illus. 1990, Ticknor $16.00 (0-89919-693-4). A visit to the Dinosaur National Monument quarry in Utah. (Rev: BL 5/15/89) [567.910979221]

15484 Arnold, Caroline. *Dinosaurs All Around: An Artist's View of the Prehistoric World* (3–6). Photos by Richard Hewett. 1993, Houghton Mifflin $14.95 (0-395-62363-4). 48pp. This book concentrates on the art of creating dinosaur models from miniature and life-sized ones. (Rev: BCCB 4/93; BL 4/15/93; HB 7–8/93; SLJ 5/93) [567.9]

15485 Arnold, Caroline. *Dinosaurs with Feathers: The Ancestors of the Modern Birds* (4–5). Illus. by Laurie Caple. 2001, Clarion $15.00 (0-618-00398-3). 32pp. Arnold presents information on the links between dinosaurs (specifically, theropods) and the birds of today, with illustrations. (Rev: BL 10/1/01; HBG 10/02; SLJ 11/01) [568]

15486 Arnold, Caroline. *Giant Shark: Megalodon, Prehistoric Super Predator* (4–6). Illus. 2000, Clarion $15.00 (0-395-91419-1). 32pp. This book introduces the megalodon, an extinct giant shark, and explains how paleontologists have determined its characteristics and how it behaved. (Rev: BL 11/1/00; HBG 3/01; SLJ 11/00) [567]

15487 Arnold, Caroline. *Pterosaurs: Rulers of the Skies in the Dinosaur Age* (2–4). Illus. by Laurie A. Caple. 2004, Houghton Mifflin $16.00 (0-618-31354-0). 40pp. The pterosaurs — reptiles with a wing span of nearly 40 feet — are introduced here, with plenty of facts and clear illustrations. (Rev: BL 12/1/04) [567.918]

15488 Arnold, Caroline. *When Mammoths Walked the Earth* (3–5). Illus. by Laurie Caple. 2002, Clarion $16.00 (0-618-09633-7). 40pp. An informative, well-illustrated book about key fossil discoveries and the lives of mammoths. (Rev: BL 8/02; HB 11–12/02; HBG 3/03; SLJ 10/02) [569]

15489 Asimov, Isaac. *What Killed the Dinosaurs?* (3–5). Illus. Series: Isaac Asimov's 21st Century Library of the Universe. 2004, Gareth Stevens LB $24.67 (0-8368-3955-2). 32pp. A revised, well-illustrated edition of a previously published book, this discusses possible reasons for the extinction of the dinosaurs and looks at the gigantic Chicxulub crater. (Rev: SLJ 3/05) [567.9]

15490 Bailey, Jacqui. *The Day of the Dinosaurs* (3–5). Illus. by Matthew Lilly. Series: Cartoon History of the Earth. 2001, Kids Can $16.95 (1-55337-073-2); paper $7.95 (1-55337-082-1). 32pp. A comic-book-style presentation of the age of the dinosaurs. (Rev: BL 10/15/01; HBG 3/02; SLJ 1/02) [567.9]

15491 Bailey, Jacqui. *Monster Bones: The Story of a Dinosaur Fossil* (2–4). Illus. by Matthew Lilly. Series: Science Works. 2004, Picture Window LB $22.60 (1-4048-0565-6). 31pp. After a dramatic story that draws the reader in, Bailey explores the process of fossilization and the discovery, classification, reconstruction, and exhibit of fossils. (Rev: SLJ 8/04) [567.9]

15492 Barner, Bob. *Dinosaur Bones* (PS–2). Illus. 2001, Chronicle $15.95 (0-8118-3158-2). 36pp. The lively cut-paper collage illustrations are the highlight of this book about dinosaurs and their bones. (Rev: BCCB 9/01; BL 11/1/01; HBG 3/02; SLJ 9/01) [567.9]

15493 Barton, Byron. *Dinosaurs, Dinosaurs* (PS–1). Illus. 1989, HarperCollins LB $15.89 (0-690-04768-1); paper $5.95 (0-06-443298-X). 40pp. Dinosaur characteristics in splashy colors. (Rev: BL 3/15/89; HB 5–6/89; SLJ 4/89)

15494 Benton, Michael. *Dinosaur and Other Prehistoric Animal Factfinder* (3–6). Illus. 1992, Kingfisher paper $14.95 (1-85697-802-8). 256pp. A quick reference source about prehistoric life, including profiles of dinosaurs and other animals. (Rev: BL 12/15/92) [560]

15495 Benton, Michael. *Dinosaurs* (3–6). Illus. 1998, Kingfisher $15.95 (0-7534-5131-X). 64pp. An easy-to-read account of the rise and fall of the dinosaurs, explaining why they became extinct. (Rev: BL 11/15/98; HBG 3/99; SLJ 11/98) [567.9]

15496 Berger, Melvin. *Mighty Dinosaurs* (4–8). Illus. 1990, Avon paper $2.95 (0-380-76052-5). 128pp. Covers various kinds of dinosaurs and includes the latest research on their extinction. (Rev: BL 12/15/90) [567.9]

15497 Berger, Melvin, and Gilda Berger. *Did Dinosaurs Live in Your Backyard? Questions And Answers About Dinosaurs* (3–5). Series: Question and Answer. 1999, Scholastic $12.95 (0-590-13078-1); paper $5.95 (0-590-08568-3). 148pp. Using questions that children would ask about dinosaurs, this well-organized account supplies succinct answers and useful illustrations. (Rev: BL 11/15/99; HBG 3/00; SLJ 12/99) [567.9]

15498 Bilgrami, Shaheen. *Amazing Dinosaur Discovery* (PS–3). Illus. by Mike Phillips and Phil Garner. Series: Magic Skeleton. 2002, Sterling $9.95 (0-8069-8591-7). 24pp. A visit to a museum introduces younger readers to dinosaurs and their skeletons in this picture book with an appealing format. (Rev: BL 8/02)

15499 Bishop, Nic. *Digging for Bird-Dinosaurs: An Expedition to Madagascar* (4–6). Illus. Series: Scientists in the Field. 2000, Houghton Mifflin $16.00 (0-395-96056-8). 48pp. Shifting from Madagascar to a lab in New York, this account traces the work

of paleontologist Cathy Forster, who is investigating the link between birds and dinosaurs. (Rev: BCCB 5/00; BL 4/15/00*; HB 5–6/00; HBG 10/00; SLJ 5/00) [567.9]

15500 Bishop, Roma. *My First Pop-up Book of Prehistoric Animals* (K–3). Illus. 1994, Simon & Schuster $12.95 (0-671-86556-7). An engaging text and a series of pop-ups introduce the world of the dinosaur to primary graders. (Rev: BL 11/15/94) [560]

15501 Bonner, Hannah. *When Bugs Were Big, Plants Were Strange, and Terrapods Stalked the Earth: A Cartoon Prehistory of Life Before Dinosaurs* (2–5). Illus. 2004, National Geographic $16.95 (0-7922-6326-X). 48pp. This fascinating, cartoon-filled excursion into the end of the Paleozoic period more than 250 million years ago offers a blend of natural history and humor. (Rev: BL 2/15/04*; SLJ 2/04) [565]

15502 Branley, Franklyn M. *What Happened to the Dinosaurs?* (1–3). Illus. by Marc Simont. 1989, HarperCollins LB $15.89 (0-690-04749-5). 32pp. A good discussion of what might have happened to cause the end of the dinosaurs. (Rev: BL 9/1/89; HB 11–12/89; SLJ 10/89) [567.9]

15503 Brett-Surman, Michael, and Thomas R. Holtz, Jr. *James Gurney: The World of Dinosaurs* (5–8). Illus. by James Gurney. 1998, GWP paper $19.95 (0-86713-046-6). 48pp. This story of the 15 dinosaur stamps designed for the U.S. Postal Service includes a description of each of the beasts. (Rev: SLJ 9/98) [567.9]

15504 Burton, Jane, and Kim Taylor. *The Nature and Science of Fossils* (3–6). Series: Exploring the Science of Nature. 1999, Gareth Stevens LB $14.95 (0-8368-2183-1). 32pp. A well-illustrated introduction to paleontology that explains where and how fossils were formed. A section is devoted to projects and activities using simple materials. (Rev: BL 7/99; SLJ 1/00) [560]

15505 Camper, Cathy. *Bugs Before Time: Prehistoric Insects and Their Relatives* (3–5). Illus. by Steve Kirk. 2002, Simon & Schuster $16.95 (0-689-82092-5). 40pp. An eye-catching introduction to the world of prehistoric insects and arthropods. (Rev: BL 3/15/02; HBG 10/02; SLJ 5/02) [565]

15506 Carr, Karen. *Dinosaur Hunt: Texas — 115 Million Years Ago* (3–6). Illus. by author. 2002, HarperCollins LB $19.89 (0-06-029704-2). Dramatic illustrations are used in this reenactment of a prehistoric battle between two dinosaurs, based on fossil footprints found in Texas. (Rev: HBG 3/03; SLJ 10/02)

15507 Chin, Karen, and Thorn Holmes. *Dino Dung: The Scoop on Fossil Feces* (2–4). Illus. by Karen Carr. Series: Step into Reading. 2005, Random LB $11.99 (0-375-92702-6); paper $3.99 (0-375-82702-1). 48pp. The topic of dinosaur dung makes a fine introduction to the science of paleontology for beginning readers. (Rev: BL 6/1–15/05) [567.9]

15508 Chrisp, Peter. *Dinosaur Detectives* (2–4). Illus. Series: Dorling Kindersley Readers. 2001, DK $12.95 (0-7894-7384-4); paper $3.95 (0-7894-7383-

6). 48pp. Chrisp interweaves facts about dinosaurs with fictionalized first-person accounts by fossil hunters in a package that makes good browsing for beginning readers. (Rev: HBG 10/01; SLJ 9/01) [560]

15509 Christian, Spencer, and Antonia Felix. *Is There a Dinosaur in Your Backyard? The World's Most Fascinating Fossils, Rocks, and Minerals* (5–8). Series: Spencer Christian's World of Wonders. 1998, Wiley paper $12.95 (0-471-19616-9). In addition to discussing dinosaurs, this fascinating book introduces earth science, with interesting details about rocks, minerals, and fossils. (Rev: BL 9/1/98; SLJ 10/98) [552]

15510 Cohen, Daniel. *Allosaurus* (K–2). Illus. Series: Discovering Dinosaurs. 2003, Capstone LB $18.60 (0-7368-1618-6). 24pp. A slim, basic overview of the Allosaurus for the beginning reader, with suggested activities and experiments. Also use *Ankylosaurus* and *Brachiosaurus* (both 2003). (Rev: HBG 10/03; SLJ 3/04) [567.9]

15511 Cohen, Daniel. *Pteranodon* (3–4). Series: Discovering Dinosaurs. 2000, Bridgestone LB $17.26 (0-7368-0617-2). 24pp. A basic title that introduces this prehistoric animal. Also use *Stegosaurus* (2000). (Rev: HBG 3/01; SLJ 1/01) [567.9]

15512 Cole, Joanna. *The Magic School Bus in the Time of the Dinosaurs* (K–4). Illus. by Bruce Degen. 1994, Scholastic $15.95 (0-590-44688-6). 46pp. Through time travel, Ms. Frizzle takes her students to various geological periods when dinosaurs lived in this fact-filled book about prehistoric life. (Rev: BCCB 10/94; BL 8/94; HB 11–12/94; SLJ 9/94) [567.9]

15513 Currie, Philip J., and Colleayn O. Mastin. *The Newest and Coolest Dinosaurs* (4–8). Illus. 1998, Grasshopper $18.95 (1-895910-41-2). Using double-page spreads, this useful volume introduces 15 of the most recent finds in the world of dinosaurs. (Rev: SLJ 1/99) [560]

15514 Cutchins, Judy, and Ginny Johnston. *Giant Predators of the Ancient Seas* (4–7). Illus. Series: Southern Fossil Discoveries. 2001, Pineapple $14.95 (1-56164-237-1). 63pp. A look at the reptiles, fish, whales, sharks, and sea snakes that were found in the seas that once covered much of North America, as well as a discussion of the methods scientists used to reconstruct them. (Rev: HBG 3/02; SLJ 12/01) [566]

15515 Dal Sasso, Cristiano. *Animals: Origins and Evolution* (4–8). Illus. Series: Beginnings — Origins and Evolution. 1995, Raintree LB $24.26 (0-8114-3333-1). 48pp. This well-illustrated account traces the development of animals from bacteria to the invertebrates and then fish, amphibians, reptiles, birds, and mammals. (Rev: BL 5/1/95; SLJ 6/95) [591]

15516 Davis, Kenneth C. *Don't Know Much About Dinosaurs* (2–4). Illus. by Pedro Martin. Series: Don't Know Much About. 2004, HarperCollins LB $16.89 (0-06-028620-2). 48pp. A conversational question-and-answer format and colorful cartoons are used to introduce species of dinosaurs, with use-

ful pronunciation guidance; suitable for browsers. (Rev: SLJ 4/04) [567.9]

15517 De Magalhaes, Roberto Carvalho. *Prehistory* (4–6). Series: Art and Civilization. 2000, Bedrick $16.95 (0-87226-615-X). 36pp. Using illustrations of many artifacts, this book explains daily life and culture during prehistoric times. (Rev: HBG 3/01; SLJ 1/01) [930.1]

15518 Diffily, Deborah. *Jurassic Shark* (1–3). Illus. by Karen Carr. 2004, HarperCollins LB $18.89 (0-06-008250-x). 32pp. A pregnant Hybodus, an ancestor of the white shark, is the focus of this story of survival portrayed with drama but relatively little gore. (Rev: BL 5/15/04; SLJ 4/04) [567]

15519 *Dinosaur* (3–5). Ed. by Samantha Gray and Sarah Walker. Illus. Series: Eye Wonder. 2001, DK LB $17.95 (0-7894-8179-0); paper $9.95 (0-7894-7851-X). 48pp. Model dinosaurs show how the massive beasts moved, hunted, and lived; theories about their demise are also included. (Rev: BL 12/1/01; HBG 3/02) [567.9]

15520 *Dinosaurs* (1–3). Illus. by James Prunier and Henri Galeron. Series: First Discovery. 1993, Scholastic $12.95 (0-590-46358-6). With cutaway illustrations and transparencies, different dinosaurs and their anatomy are shown. (Rev: SLJ 8/93) [567.9]

15521 Dixon, Dougal. *Ankylosaurus and Other Mountain Dinosaurs* (K–3). Illus. by Steve Weston and James Field. Series: Dinosaur Find. 2004, Picture Window LB $22.60 (1-4048-0670-9). 24pp. Basic facts are presented in brief sentences, and include references to the dinosaur's habitat and comparisons to contemporary animals. Also use *Deltadromeus and Other Shoreline Dinosaurs* and *Triceratops and Other Forest Dinosaurs* (2004). (Rev: SLJ 2/05) [567.9]

15522 Dixon, Dougal. *Be a Dinosaur Detective* (1–4). Illus. 1988, Lerner paper $6.95 (0-8225-9538-9). 32pp. The author explains how all evidence for dinosaurs is deduced from fossils. (Rev: BL 5/1/88; SLJ 8/88)

15523 Dixon, Dougal. *Dinosaurs: The Good, the Bad, and the Ugly* (4–8). Series: Secret Worlds. 2001, DK $5.99 (0-7894-7972-9). 96pp. Dramatic color illustrations and a lively text are used to create interest in this introduction to dinosaurs and their world. (Rev: BL 10/15/01; HBG 3/02) [567.9]

15524 Dixon, Dougal. *Dougal Dixon's Amazing Dinosaurs* (3–6). Illus. 2000, Boyds Mills $17.95 (1-56397-773-7). 128pp. An attractive, informative field book that introduces groups of dinosaurs and offers solid information on their physical makeup, habits, and special characteristics. (Rev: BL 3/15/00; HBG 10/00; SLJ 5/00) [567.9]

15525 Dixon, Dougal. *Dougal Dixon's Dinosaurs* (4–8). Illus. 1998, Boyds Mills $19.95 (1-56397-722-2). This updated revision of the 1993 volume remains a good basic resource on dinosaurs. (Rev: HBG 10/98; SLJ 6/98) [567.9]

15526 Dixon, Dougal. *Herbivores* (4–6). Illus. Series: Dinosaurs. 2001, Gareth Stevens LB $23.93 (0-8368-2916-6). 36pp. This account explores the world of the herbivore dinosaurs during the Mesozoic Era and discusses related modern species. Also use *Carnivores* and *In the Sky* (2001). (Rev: HBG 3/02; SLJ 3/02) [567.9]

15527 Dixon, Dougal. *The Search for Dinosaurs* (4–7). Illus. Series: Digging Up the Past. 1995, Thomson Learning LB $24.26 (1-56847-396-6). 48pp. A history of the various discoveries that paleontologists have made about dinosaurs and other prehistoric beasts. (Rev: SLJ 2/96) [567.9]

15528 Dixon, Dougal. *Triceratops: And Other Forest Dinosaurs* (K–2). Series: Dinosaur Find. 2005, Picture Window $22.60 (1-4048-0668-7). 24pp. A profile of Triceratops, a large herbivorous dinosaur, and other giant reptiles that also favored forested habitats. (Rev: BL 10/15/04)

15529 Dodson, Peter. *An Alphabet of Dinosaurs* (2–4). Illus. by Wayne D. Barlowe. 1995, Scholastic $16.95 (0-590-46486-8). 64pp. Twenty-six kinds of dinosaurs are introduced in text and drawings in this unusual alphabet book. (Rev: BL 1/15/95; SLJ 3/95*) [567.9]

15530 Eastman, David. *Story of Dinosaurs* (K–2). Illus. by Joel Snyder. 1997, Troll paper $3.50 (0-89375-649-0). Simple material presented in short sentences with many illustrations.

15531 Farlow, James O. *Bringing Dinosaur Bones to Life: How Do We Know What Dinosaurs Were Like?* (4–7). Illus. 2001, Watts LB $25.00 (0-531-11403-1). 64pp. An interesting look at the life of dinosaurs and at the methods paleontologists use to learn about the beasts, pointing out that although scientists can reconstruct animals from skeletons and fossil evidence, they must always differentiate between fact and educated guesses. (Rev: BL 12/15/01; SLJ 12/01) [567.9]

15532 Fisher, Enid. *The Great Dinosaur Record Book* (3–5). Illus. by Richard Grant. Series: World of Dinosaurs. 1998, Gareth Stevens LB $14.95 (0-8368-2176-9). 32pp. Large colorful illustrations are used in this book that tells about the record holders (biggest, fastest, etc.) of the dinosaur world. (Rev: HBG 10/99; SLJ 2/99) [567.9]

15533 Fisher, Enid. *They Lived with the Dinosaurs* (4–6). Illus. by Richard Grant. Series: World of Dinosaurs. 1999, Gareth Stevens LB $14.95 (0-8368-2292-7). 32pp. This book covers a multitude of living creatures including insects, turtles, mammals, and plants that lived at the time of dinosaurs. Also use *True-Life Monsters of the Prehistoric Seas* (1999) and *True-Life Monsters of the Prehistoric Skies* (both 1999). (Rev: SLJ 8/99) [567.9]

15534 Fowler, Allan. *It Could Still Be a Dinosaur* (1–2). Illus. Series: Rookie Readers. 1993, Children's Book Pr. LB $19.00 (0-516-06002-3). 32pp. For beginning readers, this is a very simple book about dinosaurs. (Rev: BL 3/1/94) [567.9]

15535 French, Vivian. *T. Rex* (PS–2). Illus. by Alison Bartlett. 2005, Candlewick $15.99 (0-7636-2184-6). 32pp. During a visit to a T. rex exhibition, a boy and his grandfather discuss in engaging rhythmic rhyme what is known — and what science has

yet to discover — about the prehistoric creature. (Rev: BL 12/1/04) [567.912]

15536 Gallant, Jonathan R. *The Tales Fossils Tell* (5–9). Series: The Story of Science. 2000, Benchmark LB $28.50 (0-7614-1153-4). 80pp. A fascinating introduction to paleontology that explains how the importance of fossils was only clearly understood after the ideas of evolution and extinction were accepted. (Rev: BL 12/15/00; HBG 10/01; SLJ 2/01) [560]

15537 Gallant, Roy A. *Fossils* (3–5). Illus. Series: Kaleidoscope. 2000, Marshall Cavendish $15.95 (0-7614-1041-4). 48pp. Beginning with basic information on fossils that shows, for example, how a dying fish can become a fossil, this book goes on to more complex subjects related to paleontology. (Rev: BL 2/1/01; HBG 3/01; SLJ 3/01) [560]

15538 Geraghty, Paul. *Dinosaur in Danger* (3–4). Illus. by author. 2004, Barron's $13.95 (0-7641-5732-9). Talon, a young Deinonychus, searches for the rest of her pack after a fire; large illustrations accompany the text. (Rev: SLJ 11/04) [567.9]

15539 Gibbons, Gail. *Dinosaurs* (2–4). Illus. 1987, Holiday House LB $16.95 (0-8234-0657-1); paper $6.95 (0-8234-0708-X). 32pp. Giant reptiles explained in simple terms for the young set. (Rev: BL 12/15/87; SLJ 11/87)

15540 Gibbons, Gail. *Prehistoric Animals* (K–2). Illus. 1988, Holiday House LB $16.95 (0-8234-0707-1). 32pp. A brief overview of a subject that fascinates young readers. (Rev: BL 9/1/88; SLJ 10/88)

15541 Granger, Judith. *Amazing World of Dinosaurs* (1–3). Illus. by Pamela Baldwin Ford. 1982, Troll LB $17.25 (0-89375-562-1); paper $3.50 (0-89375-563-X). 32pp. This book describes many plant and meat-eating dinosaurs.

15542 Gray, Susan H. *Apatosaurus* (3–5). Illus. Series: Exploring Dinosaurs. 2004, Child's World LB $27.07 (1-59296-043-X). 32pp. Following a dramatic scene, information on physical characteristics, behavior, diet, and so forth is presented along with discussion of paleontology as a science. Also use *Oviraptor* and *Iguanodon* (both 2004). (Rev: SLJ 9/04) [567.9]

15543 Gray, Susan H. *Coelophysis* (3–6). Illus. Series: Exploring Dinosaurs. 2004, Child's World LB $27.07 (1-59296-185-1). 32pp. This volume in the Exploring Dinosaurs series looks at the world of the coelophysis, a small but swift carnivore of the late Triassic Period; dramatic scenes draw the reader in to facts and theories about the animals. Also use *Maiasaura* (2004). (Rev: BL 5/1/04; SLJ 9/04) [507.912]

15544 Gray, Susan H. *Megalosaurus* (3–5). Illus. Series: Exploring Dinosaurs. 2004, Child's World LB $27.07 (1-59296-236-X). 32pp. After a fictional opening chapter, there is information the animal's characteristics and behavior plus material on its discovery. Also use *Psittacosaurus* and *Spinosaurus* (both 2004). (Rev: SLJ 2/05) [567.9]

15545 Green, Tamara. *Cretaceous Dinosaur World* (3–5). Illus. by Richard Grant. Series: World of

Dinosaurs. 1998, Gareth Stevens LB $14.95 (0-8368-2173-4). 32pp. This colorful account of the last age of the dinosaurs also gives material on plants and other animals of the period. (Rev: HBG 10/99; SLJ 2/99) [567.9]

15546 Green, Tamara. *Dinosaur Babies* (4–6). Illus. by Richard Grant. Series: World of Dinosaurs. 1999, Gareth Stevens LB $14.95 (0-8368-2290-0). 32pp. This book introduces baby dinosaurs of various kinds and explains their care and feeding. Also use *Great Dinosaur Hunters* (1999). (Rev: SLJ 8/99) [567.9]

15547 Green, Tamara. *Jurassic Dinosaur World* (3–5). Illus. by Richard Grant. Series: World of Dinosaurs. 1998, Gareth Stevens LB $14.95 (0-8368-2174-2). 32pp. This review of the Jurassic period that was characterized by large dinosaurs also includes material on the first birds and mammals and the vegetation of the time. (Rev: HBG 10/99; SLJ 2/99) [567.9]

15548 Halls, Kelly Milner. *Dinosaur Mummies: Beyond Bare-Bone Fossils* (4–6). Illus. by Rick Spears. Series: A Junior Library Guild Selection. 2003, Darby Creek $17.95 (1-58196-000-X). 48pp. This fascinating book explains how the discovery of fossilized soft-tissue remains of dinosaurs has expanded scientific knowledge about these prehistoric creatures. (Rev: BL 11/1/03; SLJ 12/03)

15549 Harris, Nicholas. *The Incredible Journey Through the World of the Dinosaurs* (2–5). Illus. by Inklink Firenze. 2002, McGraw-Hill $18.95 (0-87226-671-0). 32pp. An oversize book that looks at the types, structure, and lifestyles of the dinosaurs that lived in what is now the western United States. (Rev: BL 6/1–15/02; HBG 3/02) [567.9]

15550 Harrison, Carol. *Dinosaurs Everywhere!* (PS–2). Illus. by Richard Courtney. 1998, Scholastic $12.95 (0-590-00089-6). 40pp. An introduction to various kinds of dinosaurs, their habits, appearance, size, and behavior — all in a big, beautiful picture book. (Rev: BL 11/15/98; HBG 3/99; SLJ 1/99) [567.9]

15551 Helm, Charles. *Daniel's Dinosaurs: A True Story of Discovery* (K–3). Photos by author. Illus. by Joan Zimmer. 2004, Maple Tree $16.95 (1-897066-06-6); paper $6.95 (1-897066-07-4). 32pp. This photoessay tells the story of 8-year-old Daniel Helm's discovery of dinosaur tracks in British Columbia. (Rev: LMC 4/05; SLJ 1/05)

15552 Hincks, Joseph. *Dinosaur Dictionary* (4–6). 1999, Rourke LB $24.95 (0-86593-586-6). 96pp. A highly readable, well-illustrated dictionary that presents two or three short paragraphs about each dinosaur. (Rev: SLJ 2/00) [567.9]

15553 Johnston, Marianne. *From the Dinosaurs of the Past to the Birds of the Present* (3–5). Illus. Series: Prehistoric Animals and Their Modern-Day Relatives. 2000, Rosen LB $18.60 (0-8239-5204-5). 24pp. This account points out the structural similarities between dinosaurs and birds and tells why scientists think they are related. (Rev: BL 12/1/00) [567]

15554 Keiran, Monique. *Ornithomimus: Pursuing the Bird-Mimic Dinosaur* (4–6). Illus. 2002, Raincoast $26.95 (1-55192-348-3). 64pp. A look at the discovery of a featherless beaked fossil in Canada with discussion of fossils and evolution in general, enhanced by color photographs and paintings. (Rev: BL 12/1/02; SLJ 11/02) [567.914]

15555 Kelsey, Elin. *Canadian Dinosaurs* (4–6). Illus. Series: Wow Canada. 2004, Maple Tree $29.95 (1-894379-55-1). 96pp. Canada's rich dinosaur heritage is the subject of this large-format book, which explores not only discoveries in Canada but also the research and exhibits that take place there. (Rev: BL 3/15/04; SLJ 7/04) [567.9]

15556 Kelsey, Elin. *Finding Out About Dinosaurs* (3–5). Illus. 2000, Owl $19.95 (1-895688-97-3); paper $9.95 (1-895688-98-1). 40pp. Questions about dinosaurs are asked on each double-page spread, and the answers reveal how paleontologists work and what they have learned about these prehistoric animals. (Rev: BL 12/1/00; HBG 3/01; SLJ 10/00) [567.9]

15557 Kerley, Barbara. *The Dinosaurs of Waterhouse Hawkins* (3–5). Illus. by Brian Selznick. 2001, Scholastic $16.95 (0-439-11494-2). 48pp. The true story of Waterhouse Hawkins, the 19th-century British artist who built life-sized dinosaur models, with detailed, dramatic illustrations. (Rev: BCCB 10/01; BL 9/1/01; HBG 3/02; SLJ 10/01) [567.9]

15558 Kittinger, Jo S. *Stories in Stone: The World of Animal Fossils* (4–6). Illus. Series: Earth and Sky Science. 1998, Watts LB $21.00 (0-531-20384-0). 64pp. About 500 million years are covered in this book that discusses all forms of animal fossils, including dinosaurs, from trilobites to mammals. (Rev: BL 2/1/99; HBG 3/99; SLJ 4/99) [560]

15559 Krueger, Richard. *The Dinosaurs* (5–8). Illus. Series: Prehistoric North America. 1996, Millbrook LB $22.90 (1-56294-548-3). With plenty of color illustrations, this chatty overview tells about North American dinosaurs. (Rev: BL 5/15/96; SLJ 4/96) [567.9]

15560 Lambert, David. *DK Guide to Dinosaurs: A Thrilling Journey Through Prehistoric Times* (2–7). 2000, DK $19.95 (0-7894-5237-5). 64pp. An appealing oversize volume that portrays a number of different dinosaurs in their natural habitats. (Rev: BCCB 9/00; HBG 10/00; SLJ 7/00) [567.9]

15561 Larson, Peter, and Kristin Donnan. *Bones Rock! Everything You Need to Know to Be a Paleontologist* (5–9). Illus. 2004, Invisible Cities paper $19.95 (1-931229-35-X). 204pp. A comprehensive, accessible guide to paleontology, describing how to dig for fossils, clean them, keep records, and develop and test theories, with interesting accounts of the authors' experiences. (Rev: SLJ 11/04) [560]

15562 Lauber, Patricia. *How Dinosaurs Came to Be* (4–6). Illus. 1996, Simon & Schuster $17.00 (0-689-80531-4). 48pp. The ancestors of dinosaurs are described in this account that traces the evolution of these giant reptiles. (Rev: BL 4/15/96; SLJ 5/96) [567.9]

15563 Lessem, Don. *Armored Dinosaurs* (2–4). Illus. by John Bindon. Series: Meet the Dinosaurs. 2004, Lerner LB $23.93 (0-8225-1374-9); paper $7.95 (0-8225-2570-4). 32pp. Facts about these dinosaurs are presented in a lively narrative that includes present-tense scenes. Also use *Giant Meat-Eating Dinosaurs* and *Horned Dinosaurs* (both 2004). (Rev: SLJ 2/05) [567.9]

15564 Lessem, Don. *The Dinosaur Atlas: A Complete Look at the World of Dinosaurs* (4–8). Illus. by John Bindon. 2003, Firefly $18.95 (1-55297-830-3). 64pp. Don Lessem, children's author and dinosaur expert, offers readers a sweeping overview of the Age of Dinosaurs and also looks at changes in the Earth since the demise of the giant reptiles. (Rev: SLJ 12/03) [567.9]

15565 Lessem, Don. *Dinosaur Worlds: New Dinosaurs, New Discoveries* (5–8). Illus. 1996, Boyds Mills $19.95 (1-56397-597-1). 192pp. The reader visits various dinosaur digs worldwide in a review of what we know about these amazing creatures. (Rev: BL 11/15/96; BR 5–6/97; SLJ 12/96*) [567.9]

15566 Lessem, Don. *Feathered Dinosaurs* (2–4). Illus. by John Bindon. Series: Meet the Dinosaurs. 2005, Lerner LB $23.95 (0-8225-1423-0); paper $7.95 (0-8225-2621-2). 32pp. Simple text and dramatic illustrations explore the link between dinosaurs and birds. (Rev: BL 6/1–15/05) [567.912]

15567 Lessem, Don. *Ornithomimids: The Fastest Dinosaur* (3–6). Illus. Series: Special Dinosaurs. 1996, Carolrhoda LB $19.95 (0-87614-813-5). 40pp. How the remains of these speedy dinosaurs were discovered and how our knowledge of them was collected highlight this well-illustrated volume. (Rev: BL 2/15/96; SLJ 4/96) [567.9]

15568 Lessem, Don. *Scholastic Dinosaurs A to Z: The Ultimate Dinosaur Encyclopedia* (4–8). Illus. by Jan Sovak. 2003, Scholastic $22.95 (0-439-16591-1). 224pp. Young dinosaur lovers will enjoy browsing through this compendium of facts and figures about the giant reptiles; in addition to more than 700 alphabetically organized entries, the book offers introductory essays that provide additional insights into the Age of Dinosaurs. (Rev: HBG 4/04; SLJ 12/03) [567.9]

15569 Lessem, Don. *Seismosaurus: The Longest Dinosaur* (3–5). Illus. by Donna Braginetz. Series: Special Dinosaurs. 1996, Carolrhoda LB $19.95 (0-87614-987-5). 40pp. This account introduces the seismosaurus and its characteristics and explains how we have determined these facts from fossils. (Rev: SLJ 9/96) [567.9]

15570 Lessem, Don. *Troodon: The Smartest Dinosaur* (3–6). Illus. Series: Special Dinosaurs. 1996, Carolrhoda LB $14.96 (0-87614-798-8). 40pp. The role of paleontologists in piecing together bits of information about this dinosaur is covered, along with information on its appearance, habits, and intelligence. (Rev: BL 2/15/96; SLJ 4/96) [567.9]

15571 Llamas, Andreu. *The Era of the Dinosaurs* (4–8). Illus. Series: Development of the Earth. 1996, Chelsea LB $17.55 (0-7910-3452-6). Various kinds of dinosaurs are introduced, with an emphasis on their evolution and on how geology and climate affected their development. (Rev: SLJ 7/96) [567.9]

15572 Llamas, Andreu. *The First Amphibians* (4–8). Illus. Series: Development of the Earth. 1996, Chelsea LB $17.55 (0-7910-3453-4). Using many color illustrations, this book begins with the earliest land vertebrates and gives clear explanations of their adaptations over time. (Rev: SLJ 7/96) [567.9]

15573 McMullan, Kate. *Dinosaur Hunters* (2–4). Illus. by John R. Jones. 1989, Random paper $3.99 (0-394-81150-X). 46pp. An easy reader on how fossils are found and studied, with coverage on new theories about dinosaurs. (Rev: BCCB 12/89; SLJ 9/89) [567.9]

15574 Manning, Mick, and Brita Granström. *Dinomania: Things to Do with Dinosaurs* (3–5). Illus. 2002, Holiday House $15.95 (0-8234-1641-0). 48pp. This book consists of a series of projects related to dinosaurs, such as creating a diorama of habitats and a mobile of flying creatures. (Rev: BL 6/1–15/02; HBG 10/02; SLJ 4/02) [745.5]

15575 Markle, Sandra. *Outside and Inside Dinosaurs* (3–5). Illus. 2000, Simon & Schuster $16.00 (0-689-82300-2). 40pp. This is a rundown of what scientists know about dinosaurs, their behavior, and their internal and external structures. (Rev: BL 12/1/00; HB 9–10/00; HBG 3/01; SLJ 11/00) [567.9]

15576 Maynard, Christopher. *The Best Book of Dinosaurs* (3–5). 1998, Kingfisher $10.95 (0-7534-5116-6). 33pp. A clearly written, lavishly illustrated introduction to several groups of dinosaurs, focusing on specific traits of about 20 of them. (Rev: HBG 10/98; SLJ 7/98) [567.9]

15577 Miller, Debbie S. *A Woolly Mammoth Journey* (2–3). Illus. by Jon Van Zyle. 2001, Little, Brown $15.95 (0-316-57212-8). 32pp. Readers follow a fictional woolly mammoth family through a spring, summer, and fall in what is now Alaska. (Rev: BL 5/1/01; HBG 10/01; SLJ 6/01) [569]

15578 Moody, Richard. *Over 65 Million Years Ago: Before the Dinosaurs Died* (4–6). Illus. Series: History Detective. 1992, Macmillan LB $16.95 (0-02-767270-0). 32pp. How paleontologists have found out about dinosaurs and a summary of how they lived. (Rev: SLJ 12/92) [567.92]

15579 Morrison, Taylor. *The Great Unknown* (3–5). Illus. 2001, Houghton Mifflin $16.00 (0-395-97494-1). 32pp. An account of Peale's discovery of mastodon bones in New York state in 1799 and their assembly into a skeleton. (Rev: BCCB 7–8/01; BL 5/1/01; HBG 10/01; SLJ 5/01) [569]

15580 Most, Bernard. *Dinosaur Cousins?* (1–3). Illus. by author. 1987, Harcourt paper $6.00 (0-15-223498-5). 40pp. Musing about whether a rhinoceros, for instance, could be a dinosaur's cousin leads to facts about prehistoric animals. (Rev: BL 2/15/87; SLJ 5/85)

15581 Most, Bernard. *How Big Were the Dinosaurs?* (PS–2). Illus. 1994, Harcourt $16.00 (0-15-236800-0). 32pp. The size of 20 different dinosaurs is shown by comparisons with everyday modern objects, like a school bus or a bowling alley. (Rev: BL 3/1/94; SLJ 4/94) [567.9]

15582 Most, Bernard. *Where to Look for a Dinosaur* (1–4). Illus. 1993, Harcourt $12.95 (0-15-295616-6). 32pp. An actual geographical guidebook pinpointing the remains of more than 25 beasts. (Rev: BL 2/15/93; SLJ 6/93) [567.9]

15583 Munro, Margaret. *The Story of Life on Earth* (3–5). Illus. 2000, Douglas & McIntyre $19.95 (0-88899-401-X). 32pp. This informative introduction to the evolution of life on Earth uses double-page spreads to illustrate the flora and fauna of different geological periods. (Rev: BL 11/1/00; HBG 3/01; SLJ 12/00) [560]

15584 Nye, Bill, and Ian G. Saunders. *Bill Nye the Science Guy's Great Big Dinosaur Dig* (5–6). Illus. by Michael Koelsch. 2002, Hyperion $17.49 (0-7868-2472-7). 48pp. The Science Guy fills us in on dinosaurs, what we learn from their fossils, and the animals' eventual evolution into birds. (Rev: HBG 3/03; SLJ 1/03) [567.9]

15585 O'Brien, Patrick. *Mammoth* (K–3). Illus. 2002, Holt $16.95 (0-8050-6596-2). 40pp. O'Brien interweaves historical information about mammoths with contemporary scenes of scientists excavating and identifying a skeleton, in a well-illustrated, large-format overview of these animals that touches on their modern elephant relatives. (Rev: BL 12/1/02; HBG 3/03; SLJ 11/02) [569]

15586 O'Brien, Patrick. *Megatooth* (PS–3). Illus. by author. 2001, Holt $16.95 (0-8050-6214-9). O'Brien presents the theories scientists have made about the giant beast also known as the megalodon. (Rev: HBG 10/01; SLJ 6/01)

15587 Olien, Becky. *Fossils* (2–4). Series: The Bridgestone Science Library. 2001, Capstone LB $13.95 (0-7368-0951-1). 24pp. Fossils, famous fossil finds, and fuels made from fossils are covered in this slim volume. (Rev: HBG 3/02; SLJ 2/02)

15588 Osborne, Will, and Mary Pope Osborne. *Dinosaurs: A Nonfiction Companion to Dinosaurs Before Dark* (2–4). Illus. by Sal Murdocca. Series: Magic Tree House Research Guide. 2000, Random LB $11.99 (0-375-90296-1); paper $4.99 (0-375-80296-7). 119pp. Using a time-travel format involving two children, this book discusses the kinds of dinosaurs, their characteristics, misconceptions about them, and the other creatures that lived at the same time. (Rev: HBG 3/01; SLJ 11/00) [567.9]

15589 Pascoe, Elaine, adapt. *New Dinosaurs: Skeletons in the Sand* (4–6). Illus. Series: New Explorers. 1997, Blackbirch LB $17.95 (1-56711-231-5). 48pp. An account of the hardships and eventual success of a group of paleontologists who went to the Sahara in 1993 to find evidence of new dinosaurs. (Rev: HBG 3/98; SLJ 2/98) [567.9]

15590 Patent, Dorothy Hinshaw. *In Search of Maiasaurs* (4–7). Series: Frozen in Time. 1998, Benchmark LB $27.07 (0-7614-0787-1). 64pp. This book on dinosaurs describes the recent find of a huge bed of bones and Jack Horner's work to retrieve the fossils and learn from them. (Rev: HBG 10/99; SLJ 3/99) [567.9]

15591 Pope, Joyce. *Fossil Detective* (3–6). Illus. by Chris Forsey. Series: Nature Club. 1993, Troll LB $17.25 (0-8167-2781-3); paper $4.95 (0-8167-2782-

1). 31pp. This introduction to paleontology as a hobby contains material on what fossils are, how they were formed, and how young people can collect them. (Rev: SLJ 3/94) [560]

15592 Press, Judy. *The Kids' Natural History Book: Making Dinos, Fossils, Mammoths and More* (3–5). Illus. Series: Kids Can! 2000, Williamson $12.95 (1-885593-24-4). 144pp. A discussion of the animal classification system and how scientists have discovered and organized information about animals, with many related craft projects. (Rev: BL 12/15/00; SLJ 1/01) [745.5]

15593 Relf, Patricia. *A Dinosaur Named Sue: The Story of the Colossal Fossil* (3–6). Illus. 2000, Scholastic $15.95 (0-439-09985-4). 64pp. This is the story of the largest and most complete Tyrannosaurus rex skeleton ever found, how it was transported from South Dakota to the Field Museum in Chicago, and what life was like when Sue was alive. (Rev: BL 12/1/00; HBG 3/01; SLJ 1/01) [567.912]

15594 Rey, Luis V. *Extreme Dinosaurs* (3–7). Illus. by author. 2001, Chronicle $16.95 (0-8118-3086-1). 62pp. Bright, lively illustrations accompany a friendly text that provides lots of information about dinosaur evolution, dinosaur species grouped by continent, and fossil discoveries. (Rev: HBG 3/02; SLJ 9/01)

15595 Royston, Angela. *Dinosaurs* (PS–2). Illus. by Jane Cradock-Watson and Dave Hopkins. Series: Eye Openers. 1991, Macmillan paper $8.99 (0-689-71518-8). 24pp. Many of the most important kinds of dinosaurs are introduced. (Rev: BL 9/15/91; SLJ 1/92) [567.9]

15596 Ryder, Joanne. *Tyrannosaurus Time* (K–4). Illus. by Michael Rothman. 1999, Morrow $16.00 (0-688-13682-6). 32pp. A vivid re-creation of a day in the life of a Tyrannosaurus rex and a memorable depiction of prehistoric life in a picture-book format. (Rev: BL 9/1/99; HBG 3/00; SLJ 9/99) [567.9]

15597 Schlein, Miriam. *Discovering Dinosaur Babies* (2–4). Illus. by Margaret Colbert. 1991, Macmillan LB $14.95 (0-02-778091-0). 40pp. Explaining what is known about dinosaur babies and how mothers cared for them. (Rev: BL 3/1/91; SLJ 7/91) [567.9]

15598 Simon, Seymour. *New Questions and Answers About Dinosaurs* (2–5). Illus. by Jennifer Dewey. 1990, Morrow $15.93 (0-688-08196-7). 48pp. Using a question-and-answer approach, covers interesting facts and figures about dinosaurs. (Rev: BCCB 5/90; BL 2/15/90; HB 7–8/90; SLJ 5/90) [567.9]

15599 Sloan, Christopher. *Feathered Dinosaurs* (3–6). Illus. 2000, National Geographic $17.95 (0-7922-7219-6). 64pp. Using recent paleontological discoveries as its starting point, this book explores what feathered dinosaurs, the distant ancestors of modern birds, might have looked like. (Rev: BL 11/1/00; HBG 3/01; SLJ 11/00) [567.9]

15600 Sloan, Christopher. *Supercroc and the Origin of Crocodiles* (5–8). Illus. 2002, National Geographic $18.95 (0-7922-6691-9). 64pp. A fascinating account of the discovery in Africa of the fossil *Sarcosuchus*, or Supercroc, with additional information on paleontology and crocodile evolution. (Rev: BCCB 5/02; BL 9/15/02; HBG 10/02; SLJ 7/02*) [567.9]

15601 Tanaka, Shelley. *New Dinos: The Latest Finds! The Coolest Dinosaur Discoveries!* (3–5). Illus. by Alan Barnard. 2003, Simon & Schuster $16.95 (0-689-85183-9). 48pp. Recent dinosaur finds are the topic of this lively book full of colorful illustrations and interesting sidebars and diagrams. (Rev: BL 6/1–15/03; HBG 10/03; SLJ 9/03) [567.9]

15602 Taylor, Barbara. *Oxford First Book of Dinosaurs* (K–3). Illus. 2002, Oxford $19.95 (0-19-521847-7). 48pp. An accessible, oversized introduction to dinosaurs that is full of colorful illustrations. (Rev: HBG 10/02; SLJ 5/02)

15603 Thompson, Sharon E. *Death Trap: The Story of the La Brea Tar Pits* (4–8). Illus. 1995, Lerner LB $28.75 (0-8225-2851-7). 72pp. A history of the 40,000-year-old tar pits in Los Angeles and of the many species of prehistoric animals that were trapped in them, with color photographs. (Rev: BL 6/1–15/95; SLJ 5/95) [560]

15604 Unwin, David. *The New Book of Dinosaurs* (3–6). Illus. 1997, Millbrook LB $23.90 (0-7613-0568-8); paper $9.95 (0-7613-0589-0). 32pp. Computer-generated illustrations bring different dinosaurs alive, with lucid accompanying text. (Rev: BL 9/15/97; SLJ 9/97) [567.9]

15605 VanCleave, Janice. *Dinosaurs for Every Kid: Easy Activities That Make Learning Science Fun* (4–7). Illus. Series: Science for Every Kid. 1994, Wiley paper $12.95 (0-471-30812-9). 224pp. With accompanying activities, this book explores the world of dinosaurs and how paleontology has discovered, through fossils, how they lived. (Rev: BL 4/1/94; SLJ 7/94) [567.9]

15606 Wenzel, Gregory. *Feathered Dinosaurs of China* (4–6). Illus. by author. 2004, Charlesbridge $16.95 (1-57091-561-X); paper $6.95 (1-57091-562-8). 32pp. A trip more than 100 million years back in time to study the dinosaurs of prehistoric China and their theoretical relationship to modern-day birds. (Rev: SLJ 4/04) [567.9]

15607 Wenzel, Gregory. *Giant Dinosaurs of the Jurassic* (2–5). Illus. by Gregory Wenzel. 2004, Charlesbridge $16.95 (1-57091-563-6); paper $6.95 (1-57091-564-4). 32pp. The lives of a variety of dinosaurs are shown during a typical day in the prehistoric American West. (Rev: BL 10/1/04; SLJ 7/04) [507.9]

15608 Westrup, Hugh. *The Mammals* (5–8). Illus. Series: Prehistoric North America. 1996, Millbrook LB $22.90 (1-56294-546-7). The woolly mammoth and saber-toothed tiger are two of the prehistoric mammals described in words and pictures. (Rev: BL 5/15/96; SLJ 4/96) [569]

15609 Whitfield, Philip. *Macmillan Children's Guide to Dinosaurs and Other Prehistoric Animals* (3–6). Illus. 1992, Macmillan LB $19.95 (0-02-762362-9). 96pp. A handsome guide to prehistoric animal life. (Rev: BL 10/15/92; SLJ 12/92) [567.9]

15610 Wilkes, Angela. *The Big Book of Dinosaurs: A First Book for Young Children* (PS–2). Illus. 1994, DK $14.95 (1-56458-718-5). 32pp. An over-size book that contains double-page spreads introducing a wide variety of dinosaurs, including some that are little known. (Rev: BL 11/15/94; SLJ 1/95) [567.9]

15611 Worth, Bonnie. *Oh Say Can You Say Di-nosaur? All About Dinosaurs* (K–3). Illus. by Steve Haefele. Series: The Cat in the Hat's Learning Library. 1999, Random LB $11.99 (0-679-99114-X). 45pp. Several of Dr. Seuss's characters introduce different dinosaurs and their physical traits using illustrations and rhyming couplets. (Rev: SLJ 9/99) [567.9]

15612 Zimmerman, Howard. *Beyond the Dinosaurs! Sky Dragons, Sea Monsters, Mega-Mammals, and Other Prehistoric Beasts* (4–6). Illus. 2001, Simon & Schuster $18.00 (0-689-84113-2). 64pp. A large-format and very appealing presentation full of dramatic illustrations and brief, up-to-date text. (Rev: BL 6/1–15/01; HBG 10/01; SLJ 7/01) [567.9]

15613 Zimmerman, Howard. *Dinosaurs! The Biggest Baddest Strangest Fastest* (2–5). Illus. 2000, Simon & Schuster $17.95 (0-689-83276-1). 64pp. An oversize volume that is particularly noteworthy for its excellent illustrations of all sorts of dinosaurs. (Rev: BL 9/1/00; HBG 10/00; SLJ 5/00) [567.9]

15614 Zoehfeld, Kathleen W. *Did Dinosaurs Have Feathers?* (K–4). Illus. by Lucia Washburn. Series: Let's-Read-and-Find-Out Science. 2004, HarperCollins LB $16.89 (0-06-029027-7); paper $4.99 (0-06-445218-2). 33pp. Dinosaur fossils and feathers are discussed, with mention of early discoveries and of the links between dinosaurs and birds. (Rev: BL 1/1–15/04; SLJ 2/04) [568]

15615 Zoehfeld, Kathleen W. *Dinosaur Babies* (K–3). Illus. by Lucia Washburn. Series: Let's-Read-and-Find-Out. 1999, HarperCollins LB $15.89 (0-06-027142-6); paper $4.95 (0-06-445162-3). 40pp. This simple science book explains the wonders of paleontology and how scientists use fossils to find out about dinosaurs. (Rev: BL 11/15/99; HBG 3/00; SLJ 9/99) [567.9]

15616 Zoehfeld, Kathleen W. *Dinosaur Parents, Dinosaur Young: Uncovering the Mystery of Dinosaur Families* (3–6). Illus. Series: Let's-Read-and-Find-Out Science. 2001, Clarion $17.00 (0-395-91338-2). 60pp. This book explains what we know about dinosaur parenting and how paleontologists have arrived at this information. (Rev: BL 4/15/01) [567.9]

15617 Zoehfeld, Kathleen W. *Dinosaurs Big and Small* (PS–1). Illus. by Lucia Washburn. Series: Let's-Read-and-Find-Out Science. 2002, HarperCollins LB $15.89 (0-06-027936-2); paper $4.95 (0-06-445182-8). 40pp. Dinosaurs are compared with buses, elephants, and other items to help children grasp their size. (Rev: BL 7/02; HBG 10/02; SLJ 7/02) [567.9]

15618 Zoehfeld, Kathleen W. *Terrible Tyrannosaurs* (PS–2). Illus. by Lucia Washburn. 2001, HarperCollins LB $15.89 (0-06-027934-6); paper $4.95 (0-06-445181-X). 40pp. This book highlights the most familiar and most feared dinosaur and tells what we know about it from science. (Rev: BL 2/1/01; HBG 10/01) [567.912]

Anthropology and Prehistoric Life

15619 Ackroyd, Peter. *The Beginning* (4–8). Illus. Series: Voyages Through Time. 2003, DK $19.99 (0-7894-9836-7). 144pp. An attractive and readable tour of the early years of our planet, through the emergence of Cro-Magnon man, with eye-catching and amazingly realistic images of dinosaurs as they are currently envisaged. (Rev: BL 12/15/03*; HBG 4/04; SLJ 1/04) [576.8]

15620 *Atlas of People* (PS–2). Illus. Series: First Discovery. 1996, Scholastic $12.95 (0-590-58281-X). 24pp. A basic introduction to the various races of humankind, with attractive visuals. (Rev: BL 10/15/96; SLJ 2/97) [305.8]

15621 Bailey, Jacqui. *The Dawn of Life* (3–5). Illus. by Matthew Lilly. Series: Cartoon History of the Earth. 2001, Kids Can $16.95 (1-55337-072-4); paper $7.95 (1-55337-081-3). 32pp. The beginnings of plant and animal life on Earth, presented in a comic-book format. Also use *The Birth of the Earth*, *The Day of the Dinosaurs*, and *The Stick and Stone Age* (all 2001). (Rev: BL 10/15/01; HBG 3/02; SLJ 1/02) [576.83]

15622 Bailey, Jacqui. *The Stick and Stone Age* (3–5). Illus. by Matthew Lilly. Series: Cartoon History of the Earth. 2001, Kids Can $16.95 (1-55337-074-0); paper $7.95 (1-55337-083-X). 32pp. A comic-book-style presentation of early prehistoric human culture. (Rev: BL 10/15/01; HBG 3/02; SLJ 1/02) [591.3]

15623 Batten, Mary. *Anthropologist: Scientist of the People* (4–7). Illus. Series: Scientists in the Field. 2001, Houghton Mifflin $16.00 (0-618-08368-5). 64pp. Striking photographs of a Paraguayan tribe of hunter-gatherers serve as a powerful backdrop to this explanation of the work of anthropologists. (Rev: BL 8/01; HB 1–2/02*; HBG 3/02; SLJ 9/01) [627]

15624 Briscoe, Diana C. *King Tut: Tales from the Tomb* (3–5). Illus. Series: High Five Reading. 2002, Capstone LB $22.60 (0-7368-9553-1). 48pp. For reluctant readers, this is a dramatic account of the discovery of the tomb, the life and death of the

young Tut, the process of mummification, and the so-called mummy's curse. (Rev: HBG 10/03; SLJ 8/03) [932]

15625 Childress, Diana. *Prehistoric People of North America* (3–5). Illus. Series: Junior Library of American Indians. 1996, Chelsea $16.95 (0-7910-2481-4); paper $9.95 (0-7910-2482-2). 80pp. The story of the people who inhabited America in prehistoric times, with material on how they survived. (Rev: BL 11/15/96; SLJ 12/96) [970.01]

15626 Corbishley, Mike. *What Do We Know About Prehistoric People?* (4–7). Illus. Series: What Do We Know About. 1996, Bedrick LB $18.95 (0-87226-383-5). 40pp. Using double-page spreads, this book explores the known facts about human prehistoric life around the world. (Rev: BL 6/1–15/96) [930.1]

15627 Facchini, Fiorenzo. *Humans: Origins and Evolution* (4–8). Illus. Series: Beginnings — Origins and Evolution. 1995, Raintree LB $24.26 (0-8114-3336-6). 48pp. Theories and facts explaining human evolution are presented in a straightforward way, with extensive artwork and diagrams. (Rev: BL 4/15/95; SLJ 6/95) [573.2]

15628 Gallant, Roy A. *Early Humans* (5–8). Series: The Story of Science. 1999, Benchmark LB $28.50 (0-7614-0960-2). 80pp. Neanderthals, Homo erectus, and early hominids are covered in this work on human evolution and important anthropological finds. (Rev: BL 2/15/00; HBG 3/00; SLJ 3/00) [573.2]

15629 Garassino, Alessandro. *Life, Origins and Evolution* (5–8). Series: Beginnings — Origins and Evolution. 1995, Raintree LB $24.26 (0-8114-3335-8). Using informative visuals, the author presents theories concerning the beginnings of life in the world. (Rev: BL 5/1/95) [575]

15630 Hodge, Susie. *Prehistoric Art* (3–6). Series: Art in History. 1997, Heinemann LB $13.95 (1-57572-553-3). 32pp. This book focuses on the materials and methods used by prehistoric people to create art objects in such areas as the Pacific,

Africa, and North and South America. (Rev: SLJ 4/98) [930]

15631 Jenkins, Steve. *Life on Earth: The Story of Evolution* (3–6). Illus. 2002, Houghton Mifflin $16.00 (0-618-16476-6). 40pp. Superb cut-paper illustrations depict the fundamentals of evolution, touching on Darwin, natural selection, and mutation, and ending with an extraordinary timeline. (Rev: BL 12/15/02; HB 9–10/02*; HBG 3/03; SLJ 12/02) [576.8]

15632 McCutcheon, Marc. *The Beast in You! Activities and Questions to Explore Evolution* (4–8). Illus. by Michael Kline. Series: A Kaleidoscope Kids Book. 1999, Williamson paper $10.95 (1-885593-36-8). 96pp. In a humorous, creative presentation, the author shows the similarities between humans and other animals and introduces the topic of evolution, our early ancestors, and their development. (Rev: SLJ 3/00) [575]

15633 McGowen, Tom. *Giant Stones and Earth Mounds* (4–8). Illus. 2000, Millbrook LB $25.90 (0-7613-1372-9). 80pp. A history of the New Stone Age of about 9,000 years ago and the constructions that still exist in the United States today from that period. (Rev: BL 10/1/00; HBG 10/01; SLJ 10/00) [930.1]

15634 Martell, Hazel M. *Over 6,000 Years Ago: In the Stone Age* (3–6). Illus. by Chris Rothero. 1992, Macmillan LB $20.00 (0-02-762429-3). 32pp. A look at life in the Stone Age, with watercolor drawings and photos. (Rev: BL 9/15/92; SLJ 12/92) [930.12]

15635 Patent, Dorothy Hinshaw. *Mystery of the Lascaux Cave* (4–7). Series: Frozen in Time. 1998, Benchmark LB $27.07 (0-7614-0784-7). 64pp. As well as displaying these remarkable cave paintings, this book covers what is known or surmised about the prehistoric people who produced these artistic wonders. (Rev: HBG 10/99; SLJ 3/99) [930.12]

15636 Patent, Dorothy Hinshaw. *Secrets of the Ice Man* (4–7). Series: Frozen in Time. 1998, Benchmark LB $27.07 (0-7614-0782-0). 72pp. The author discusses life during the Ice Age with material from recent discoveries. (Rev: HBG 10/99; SLJ 3/99) [937]

15637 Perham, Molly, and Julian Rowe. *People* (4–6). Illus. Series: Mapworlds. 1996, Watts LB $20.00 (0-531-14362-7). 32pp. The important races of the world and their homelands are identified in an atlaslike format with many illustrations. (Rev: BL 10/15/96; SLJ 1/97) [306]

15638 Pickering, Robert. *The People* (5–8). Illus. Series: Prehistoric North America. 1996, Millbrook LB $22.90 (1-56294-550-5). An account of the development of the prehistoric North American tribes that may have crossed the land bridge from Asia to the Americas. (Rev: SLJ 4/96) [973.01]

15639 Pye, Claire. *The Wild World of the Future* (4–8). Illus. 2003, Firefly $24.95 (1-55297-727-7); paper $14.95 (1-55297-725-0). 96pp. This lively, attractive volume speculates on the animals of the future, basing the projections on previous evolutionary development. (Rev: BL 7/03; SLJ 6/03) [576.8]

15640 Ruiz, Andres L. *Evolution* (3–5). Illus. Series: Cycles of Life. 1997, Sterling $13.95 (0-8069-9329-4). 32pp. A step-by-step explanation of evolution, beginning with single-cell organisms and ending with the appearance of humans. (Rev: SLJ 6/97) [575]

15641 Sloan, Christopher. *Bury the Dead: Tombs, Corpses, Mummies, Skeletons, and Rituals* (5–9). Illus. 2002, National Geographic $18.95 (0-7922-7192-0). 64pp. Young readers will be fascinated by this serious account of burial practices throughout the ages, with timelines, color photographs, diagrams, and clear descriptions of rites around the world. (Rev: BL 12/1/02; HBG 3/03; SLJ 10/02*) [393]

15642 Turner, Alan. *Prehistoric Mammals* (4–6). Illus. by Mauricio Antón. 2004, National Geographic $29.95 (0-7922-7134-3). 192pp. Dramatic illustrations and brief text introduce prehistoric mammals that roamed the earth after the time of the dinosaurs. (Rev: BL 11/1/04; SLJ 1/05*) [569]

15643 Wilkinson, Philip, and Jacqueline Dineen. *The Early Inventions* (5–8). Illus. 1995, Chelsea LB $21.95 (0-7910-2766-X). A look at the invention of early tools and processes, mostly for human survival purposes — eating and staying warm. (Rev: BR 5–6/96; SLJ 11/95) [930]

825

Archaeology

15644 Arnold, Caroline. *Stone Age Farmers Beside the Sea: Scotland's Prehistoric Village of Skara Brae* (5–8). 1997, Clarion $15.95 (0-395-77601-5). A stunning volume that tells the story of the Stone Age village of Skara Brae, dating to about 3000 B.C., that was unearthed in the Orkney Islands in 1850. (Rev: BCCB 4/97; BL 4/15/97; SLJ 7/97) [930]

15645 Avi-Yonah, Michael. *Dig This! How Archaeologists Uncover Our Past* (5–8). Series: Buried Worlds. 1993, Lerner LB $28.75 (0-8225-3200-X). A history of the discipline of archaeology, an examination of excavating methods, and a look at several ancient civilizations. (Rev: BL 1/15/94; SLJ 2/94) [930.1]

15646 Barber, Nicola. *The Search for Lost Cities* (4–6). Illus. Series: Treasure Hunters. 1997, Raintree LB $27.12 (0-8172-4840-4). 46pp. Using double-page spreads for each site, this account covers such places as Troy, Knossos, Pompeii, and Angkor Wat. (Rev: BL 11/15/97; HBG 3/98; SLJ 1/98) [909]

15647 Barber, Nicola, and Anita Ganeri. *The Search for Sunken Treasure* (4–6). Series: Treasure Hunters. 1997, Raintree LB $27.12 (0-8172-4838-2). 46pp. This overview covers such topics as the lost treasures in sunken ships and the sacred well of Chichén Itzá, with additional material on how ancient artifacts have been recovered and what they tell us about other times. (Rev: BL 11/15/97; HBG 3/98) [930]

15648 Barnes, Trevor. *Archaeology* (4–6). Series: Kingfisher Knowledge. 2004, Houghton Mifflin $11.95 (0-7534-5768-7). 64pp. This colorful overview of archaeological finds and techniques will attract browsers and reluctant older readers. (Rev: BL 9/1/04; SLJ 11/04) [930.1]

15649 Buell, Janet. *Greenland Mummies* (5–8). Series: Time Travelers. 1998, Twenty-First Century LB $25.90 (0-7613-3004-6). By examining mummified human corpses found in Greenland, archaeologists have been able to reconstruct the life and culture of Inuits who lived 500 years ago. (Rev: SLJ 10/98) [930]

15650 Buell, Janet. *Ice Maiden of the Andes* (5–8). Illus. Series: Time Travelers. 1997, Twenty-First Century paper $25.90 (0-8050-5185-6). The story of the discovery of the frozen body of a young Inca girl who died 500 years ago and of how forensic methods such as DNA testing have revealed insights into Inca society, its religion, and gender roles. (Rev: BL 2/1/98; SLJ 3/98) [985]

15651 Caselli, Giovanni. *In Search of Knossos: The Quest for the Minotaur's Labyrinth* (4–6). Illus. by author. Series: In Search Of. 2000, Bedrick $18.95 (0-87226-544-7). 44pp. This account explores the Minoan civilization on ancient Crete, tells the legend of the Minotaur, and covers the work of several archaeologists including Sir Arthur Evans. (Rev: HBG 10/00; SLJ 6/00) [931]

15652 Caselli, Giovanni. *In Search of Troy* (4–7). Illus. Series: In Search Of. 1999, Bedrick $18.95 (0-87226-542-0). 48pp. Each of the two-page spreads in this book focuses on different aspects of Heinrich Schliemann's quest to find the city of Troy and on the archaeological discoveries he made. (Rev: BL 10/15/99; HBG 3/00; SLJ 8/99) [939]

15653 *Dazzling! Jewelry of the Ancient World* (5–8). Illus. Series: Buried Worlds. 1995, Lerner LB $28.75 (0-8225-3203-4). 64pp. An exploration of the jewels that archaeologists have retrieved from various ancient sites. (Rev: BL 7/95; SLJ 4/95) [739.27]

15654 Donnelly, Judy. *True-Life Treasure Hunts* (2–4). Illus. by Thomas La Padula. 1993, Random paper $3.99 (0-679-83980-1). 48pp. True stories of finding hidden treasure in all sorts of places, like sunken ships. (Rev: BL 4/1/94) [930.1]

15655 Duke, Kate. *Archaeologists Dig for Clues* (1–4). Series: Let's-Read-and-Find-Out. 1997, HarperCollins LB $15.89 (0-06-027057-8). 32pp. Archaeologist Sophie describes how her colleagues collect information and analyze their findings. (Rev: BL 12/1/96; SLJ 2/97*) [930]

15656 Funston, Sylvia. *Mummies* (5–7). Illus. by Joe Weissmann. Series: Strange Science. 2000, Owl $19.95 (1-894379-03-9); paper $9.95 (1-894379-04-7). 40pp. All kinds of mummified human remains are discussed, from those in ancient Egypt to the 1999 discovery of George Mallory's body on Mount Everest. (Rev: HBG 3/01; SLJ 11/00) [909]

15657 Ganeri, Anita. *The Search for Tombs* (4–6). Illus. Series: Treasure Hunters. 1997, Raintree LB $27.12 (0-8172-4839-0). 46pp. This fascinating account covers such burial places as the Egyptian pyramids, the royal tombs of China, and the Roman catacombs. (Rev: BL 11/15/97; HBG 3/98; SLJ 2/98) [393]

15658 Goldenstern, Joyce. *Lost Cities* (3–6). Illus. Series: Weird and Wacky Science. 1996, Enslow LB $18.95 (0-89490-615-1). 48pp. The history and rediscovery of such lost cities as Troy, Machu Picchu, Mohenjo-daro, and Herculaneum are covered. (Rev: SLJ 6/96) [930]

15659 Greene, Meg. *Buttons, Bones, and the Organ-Grinder's Monkey: Tales of Historical Archaeology* (5–8). Illus. 2001, Linnet LB $25.00 (0-208-02498-0). 117pp. This introduction to historical archaeology looks at finds at five different sites in the United States. (Rev: BL 10/1/01; HBG 10/02; SLJ 1/02) [973]

15660 Guiberson, Brenda Z. *Mummy Mysteries: Tales from North America* (4–7). Illus. by author. Series: A Redfeather Chapter Book. 1998, Holt $15.95 (0-8050-5369-7). 74pp. Reading like a mystery story, this book focuses on mummies found in North America, how and where they were found, and the information they reveal. (Rev: BCCB 2/99; HBG 3/99; SLJ 12/98) [937]

15661 Hoobler, Dorothy. *Lost Civilizations* (5–7). Illus. by Thomas Hoobler. 1992, Walker LB $15.85 (0-8027-8153-5). 176pp. Interesting discussion of Stonehenge, the Mound Builders, and other lost ancient civilizations. (Rev: BL 5/1/92; SLJ 9/92) [930]

15662 Jameson, W. C. *Buried Treasures of the Atlantic Coast: Legends of Sunken Pirate Treasures, Mysterious Caches, and Jinxed Ships — From Maine to Florida* (4–8). Series: Buried Treasure. 1997, August House $11.95 (0-87483-484-8). An account of how buried treasures were acquired and lost and the modern efforts to locate and retrieve them. Also use *Buried Treasures of New England* (1997). (Rev: BR 5–6/99; SLJ 10/97) [910.4]

15663 Kallen, Stuart A. *Mummies* (4–7). Illus. Series: Wonders of the World. 2003, Gale LB $18.96 (0-7377-1031-7). 48pp. Coverage of various types of mummies, the mummification process, and mummies of note will be especially useful for report writers. (Rev: BL 5/1/03) [393]

15664 Knapp, Ron. *Mummies* (3–6). Illus. Series: Weird and Wacky Science. 1996, Enslow LB $18.95 (0-89490-618-6). 48pp. Describes how bodies have been preserved in different cultures and sit-

uations, ending with the recent discovery of the Ice Man in the Alps. (Rev: SLJ 6/96) [930]

15665 Knight, Margy B. *Talking Walls* (3–5). Illus. by Anne S. O'Brien. 1992, Tilbury House $17.95 (0-88448-102-6). 40pp. Prehistoric paintings on walls in Australia and notable walls from six continents introduce children to the world and its many cultures. (Rev: BL 8/92*; SLJ 9/92) [900]

15666 Lourie, Peter. *The Mystery of the Maya: Uncovering the Lost City of Palenque* (5–8). Illus. 2001, Boyds Mills $19.95 (1-56397-839-3). 48pp. The author relates his interesting and often exciting experiences at a dig in Mexico and describes the work of the archaeologists and the history of the site. (Rev: BL 9/15/01; HBG 3/02; SLJ 11/01) [972.75]

15667 Malam, John. *Mummies* (5–8). Illus. Series: Kingfisher Knowledge. 2003, Kingfisher $11.95 (0-7534-5623-0). 63pp. A highly illustrated, readable exploration of preserved bodies of all eras and areas of the world. (Rev: HBG 4/04; SLJ 12/03) [393]

15668 Orna-Ornstein, John. *Archaeology: Discovering the Past* (5–8). Illus. 2003, Oxford LB $18.95 (0-19-521909-0). 40pp. Methodology, digs and digging, past finds, and individual archaeologists are all included in this attractive profile. (Rev: HBG 10/03; SLJ 6/03) [930.1]

15669 Panchyk, Richard. *Archaeology for Kids: Uncovering the Mysteries of Our Past with 25 Activities* (5–8). Illus. 2001, Chicago Review paper $14.95 (1-55652-395-5). 160pp. An introduction for older readers to the history and scientific method of archaeology, full of illustrations and with interesting activities. (Rev: BL 1/1–15/02; SLJ 12/01) [930.1]

15670 Patent, Dorothy Hinshaw. *Treasures of the Spanish Main* (4–7). Series: Frozen in Time. 1999, Benchmark LB $18.95 (0-7614-0786-3). 64pp. This book describes the sinking of Spanish galleons near the Florida Keys in the 1600s and how their excavation has brought us amazing information about life and culture in the New World at that time. (Rev: BL 2/15/00; HBG 10/00; SLJ 3/00) [910.4]

15671 Place, Robin. *Bodies from the Past* (4–7). Illus. Series: Digging Up the Past. 1995, Thomson Learning LB $24.26 (1-56847-397-4). 48pp. Explores the preserved remains of people around the world from burial sites in China and mummies in peat bogs to the Ice Man recently discovered in the Alps. (Rev: SLJ 2/96) [567.9]

15672 Reid, Struan. *The Children's Atlas of Lost Treasures* (4–7). Illus. Series: Children's Atlases. 1997, Millbrook paper $14.95 (0-7613-0240-9). 96pp. Using a double-page spread for each site, this book supplies a survey of the world-famous discoveries of treasures that began as religious offerings, pirate booty, and items lost in war or by natural disasters. (Rev: HBG 3/98; SLJ 3/98) [930.1]

15673 Reinhard, Johan. *Discovering the Inca Ice Maiden: My Adventures on Ampato* (5–8). Illus. 1998, National Geographic $19.95 (0-7922-7142-4). In this oversize book featuring many photographs, the anthropologist who discovered the Inca girl buried in the Andes for more than 500 years reconstructs her life and death. (Rev: BCCB 5/98; BL 5/15/98; HBG 10/98; SLJ 5/98) [985]

15674 Smith, K. C. *Exploring for Shipwrecks* (5–7). Series: Shipwrecks. 2000, Watts LB $24.00 (0-531-20377-8). 64pp. This book explains and explores the world of underwater archaeology, the techniques and training involved, and gives many examples from specific shipwreck studies. (Rev: BL 10/15/00) [930.1]

15675 Smith, K. C. *Shipwrecks of the Explorers* (5–7). Illus. Series: Watts Library: Shipwrecks. 2000, Watts LB $24.00 (0-531-20378-6); paper $8.95 (0-531-16485-3). 64pp. A look at underwater archaeology tells how scientists locate shipwrecks and what the ships reveal about the explorers who sailed in them. There are also descriptions of famous voyages including those of Columbus and Amundsen. (Rev: BL 10/15/00) [910.4]

15676 Wilcox, Charlotte. *Mummies and Their Mysteries* (5–7). Illus. 1993, Carolrhoda LB $28.75 (0-87614-767-8). 64pp. An account of how throughout history many civilizations and religions have attempted to preserve bodies. (Rev: BCCB 7–8/93*; BL 6/1–15/93*) [393.3]

15677 Wilcox, Charlotte. *Mummies, Bones, and Body Parts* (4–7). Illus. 2000, Lerner paper $12.75 (1-57505-486-8). 64pp. The study of human remains is covered, including material on how death is treated in various cultures, embalming practices, and the work of archaeologists and anthropologists. (Rev: BCCB 9/00; BL 9/1/00; HBG 10/01; SLJ 10/00) [393]

World History

General

15678 Barber, Nicola. *The Search for Gold* (4–6). Series: Treasure Hunters. 1997, Raintree LB $27.12 (0-8172-4837-4). 46pp. This overview covers such topics as the Spanish destruction of the Aztec and Inca cultures, the African gold trade, and the California Gold Rush. (Rev: BL 11/15/97; HBG 3/98) [900]

15679 Barnard, Bryn. *Dangerous Planet: Natural Disasters That Changed History* (5–8). Illus. 2003, Crown LB $19.99 (0-375-92249-0). 48pp. A fascinating look at nine natural disasters that hit our planet, with maps, full-page illustrations, and speculation about the impact of global warming. (Rev: BCCB 11/03; BL 12/1/03*; HBG 3/02; SLJ 11/03) [363.34]

15680 Blackwood, Gary L. *Highwaymen* (5–8). Illus. Series: Bad Guys. 2001, Marshall Cavendish LB $28.50 (0-7614-1017-1). 72pp. Period artwork, photographs, and intriguing tales bring real highway robbers, and the times they lived in, to life. (Rev: BL 1/1–15/02; HBG 3/02; SLJ 1/02) [364.15]

15681 Blackwood, Gary L. *Swindlers* (5–8). Illus. Series: Bad Guys. 2001, Marshall Cavendish LB $28.50 (0-7614-1031-7). 72pp. The author presents famous swindlers and cheats throughout history, providing illustrations, source notes, and recommended Web sites and further reading. (Rev: BL 1/1–15/02; HBG 3/02) [364.16]

15682 Chambers, Catherine. *Africa* (4–7). Illus. Series: Origins. 1997, Watts LB $21.00 (0-531-14416-X). 32pp. The story of emigration from Africa, the slave trade, and the conditions that African Americans have faced through history on their arrival in the United States. (Rev: BL 4/15/97; SLJ 7/97) [960]

15683 *Children's History of the 20th Century* (5–9). Illus. Series: DK Millennium. 2001, DK paper $29.95 (0-7894-4722-3). 344pp. An attractive, col-orful presentation of the major world events of the past century. (Rev: BL 11/15/99; SLJ 2/00) [909.82]

15684 Chisholm, Jane. *The Usborne Book of World History Dates: The Key Events in History* (4–8). 1998, EDC paper $22.95 (0-7460-2318-9). 194pp. Timelines and double-page spreads with brief topical essays present a panorama of world history. (Rev: SLJ 5/99) [910]

15685 Claybourne, Anna, and Caroline Young. *The Usborne Book of Treasure Hunting* (4–7). Illus. 1999, Usborne paper $14.95 (0-7460-3445-8). 79pp. In a series of short chapters, this book covers famous treasures that were buried underground, lost at sea, or existed in ancient times — with coverage of such subjects as the clay soldiers in Huang Di's tomb and the restoration of the Tudor ship *Mary Rose*. (Rev: BL 4/1/99) [622.19]

15686 Cooper, Paul. *Going to War in the 18th Century* (4–7). Illus. Series: Armies of the Past. 2001, Watts LB $24.00 (0-531-14593-X). 32pp. All about the armies and navies involved in the American Revolution and major conflicts in Europe — forms of recruitment, artillery, cavalry, uniforms, strategies, camp life, and so forth. Also use *Going to War in the 19th Century* (2001). (Rev: SLJ 2/02) [355.009033]

15687 Dalal, Anita. *Myths of Pre-Columbian America* (5–8). Illus. Series: Mythic World. 2002, Raintree LB $27.12 (0-7398-3193-3). 48pp. This volume for older readers separates myth from reality about cultures present in America in pre-Columbian times. (Rev: BL 3/1/02; HBG 3/02; SLJ 12/01) [398.2]

15688 Davis, Kenneth C. *Don't Know Much About Mummies* (2–5). Illus. by S. D. Schindler. 2005, HarperCollins LB $16.89 (0-06-028782-9). 48pp. Mummies from around the world and the various processes of mummification are presented in an informative, conversational text and colorful illustrations. (Rev: BL 2/1/04; SLJ 4/05) [393]

15689 Fleischman, Paul, ed. *Cannibal in the Mirror* (5–10). Photos by John Whalen. 2000, Twenty-First Century LB $24.90 (0-7613-0968-3). 64pp. This thought-provoking book takes 27 quotations that describe barbarous behavior of primitive societies and pairs each with a telling photograph of similar behavior in modern American society. (Rev: BL 4/15/00; HBG 10/00; SLJ 4/00) [150]

15690 Gelber, Carol. *Masks Tell Stories* (5–7). Illus. Series: Beyond Museum Walls. 1993, Millbrook LB $24.90 (1-56294-224-7). 62pp. Explores the nature, meaning, and uses of masks in different cultures at various times. (Rev: BL 8/93) [391]

15691 Gold, Susan D. *Governments of the Western Hemisphere* (5–8). Illus. Series: Comparing Continents. 1997, Twenty-First Century LB $24.90 (0-8050-5602-5). This book examines the struggles for independence in the United States, Canada, Mexico, Central America, and South America and the different directions taken by each once independence was achieved, highlighting the diversity across the nations. (Rev: BL 2/1/98; SLJ 3/98) [320.3]

15692 Goodman, Susan E. *On This Spot: An Expedition Back Through Time* (2–4). Illus. by Lee Christiansen. 2004, Greenwillow $16.89 (0-688-16914-7). 32pp. Introduce young readers to the march of time and the impact of geologic change with this dramatically illustrated exploration of the history of the New York City area. (Rev: BL 6/1–15/04) [974.7]

15693 Harris, Nicholas. *The Incredible Journey to the Beginning of Time* (4–7). Illus. by Andrea Ricciardi di Gaudesi and Alessandro Rabatti. 1998, Bedrick $18.95 (0-87226-293-6). 32pp. Beginning with the present and working backward, this book recounts world history in various locations and times as far back as 10 billion years ago. (Rev: HBG 3/99; SLJ 3/99) [900]

15694 Hart, Avery, and Paul Mantell. *Who Really Discovered America? Unraveling the Mystery and Solving the Puzzle* (5–7). Illus. by Michael Kline. Series: A Kaleidoscope Kids Book. 2001, Williamson paper $10.95 (1-885593-46-5). 96pp. Several theories are presented about the discovery of America, and students are urged to examine them with open minds, using activities that help them to question and explore. (Rev: SLJ 10/01) [970.01]

15695 Harward, Barnaby. *The Best Book of Pirates* (3–5). Illus. Series: The Best Book Of. 2002, Kingfisher $12.95 (0-7534-5449-1). 31pp. Covers pirates through the ages with pirate flags, information on pirate ships and equipment, and a page on contemporary buccaneers. (Rev: HBG 3/03; SLJ 3/03) [910.4]

15696 Haskins, Jim, and Kathleen Benson. *Bound for America: The Forced Migration of Africans to the New World* (4–9). Illus. by Floyd Cooper. Series: From African Beginnings. 1999, Lothrop LB $17.89 (0-688-10259-X). 48pp. This stirring account traces the fate of African slaves from capture, imprisonment, and branding to the brutal conditions on slave ships and finally to the survivors' arrival in the New World. (Rev: BCCB 3/99; BL 12/15/98; BR 5–6/99; HBG 10/99; SLJ 1/99*) [382]

15697 Haslam, Andrew. *Living History: The Hands-On Approach to History* (3–6). Illus. Series: Make It Work! 2001, Two-Can $29.95 (1-58728-381-6).

256pp. This assemblage of volumes from the Make It Work! series features activities pertaining to daily life in Old Japan, ancient Egypt, ancient Rome, and Native American cultures, such as making togas. (Rev: BL 3/1/02; HBG 3/02) [900]

15698 Horrell, Sarah. *The History of Emigration from Eastern Europe* (4–8). Series: Origins. 1998, Watts LB $21.00 (0-531-14449-6). 32pp. Seven short chapters cover emigration from Eastern Europe from the 17th century to the present and its impact on such areas as North America, Western Europe, and Israel. (Rev: HBG 10/98; SLJ 9/98) [940]

15699 Jackson, Ellen. *Turn of the Century* (3–5). Illus. by Jan Davey Ellis. 1998, Charlesbridge LB $15.95 (0-88106-369-X). 32pp. This book outlines life at the turn of each century from A.D. 1000 to the present, as seen through the eyes of a child in Great Britain and later in America. (Rev: BL 7/98*; HBG 3/99; SLJ 9/98) [305.2]

15700 Jones, Charlotte F. *Yukon Gold: The Story of the Klondike Gold Rush* (4–8). 1999, Holiday House $18.95 (0-8234-1403-5). 99pp. A solid account of the Alaska/Yukon Gold Rush that is enlivened by black-and-white photographs and intriguing asides and anecdotes. (Rev: BCCB 6/99; HB 7–8/99; HBG 9/99; SLJ 5/99) [979.8]

15701 Kallen, Stuart A. *Mummies* (4–6). 2003, Gale/KidHaven LB $18.96 (0-7377-1031-4). 48pp. This overview of mummies and the mummification process ranges from ancient times to the role of the mummy in modern movies. (Rev: SLJ 4/03) [930]

15702 Knight, Margy B. *Talking Walls: The Stories Continue* (3–7). Illus. by Anne S. O'Brien. 1996, Tilbury House $17.95 (0-88448-164-6). Double-page spreads are used to introduce some famous walls, like the dikes in the Netherlands, Hadrian's Wall, the Belfast Peace Lines, and prayer-wheel walls in India and Tibet. (Rev: SLJ 10/96) [900]

15703 Lauber, Patricia. *What You Never Knew About Tubs, Toilets, and Showers* (2–4). Illus. 2001, Simon & Schuster $16.00 (0-689-82420-3). 40pp. An amusing and informative account of plumbing and personal hygiene through the ages that is bound to entertain young readers. (Rev: BCCB 7–8/01; BL 5/15/01; HB 5–6/01; HBG 10/01; SLJ 6/01*) [391.6]

15704 Lauber, Patricia. *Who Came First? New Clues to Prehistoric Americans* (5–10). Illus. 2003, National Geographic $18.95 (0-7922-8228-0). 64pp. An attractive, oversized volume that encompasses anthropology, archaeology, genetics, and linguistics in its discussion of the provenance of the peoples of the Americas. (Rev: BL 7/03*; HB 7–8/03; HBG 10/03; SLJ 8/03*) [970.01]

15705 Levy, Elizabeth. *Awesome Ancient Ancestors! Mound Builders, Maya, and More* (5–8). Illus. by Daniel McFeely. Series: America's Horrible Histories. 2001, Scholastic $12.95 (0-439-30349-4); paper $4.99 (0-590-10795-X). 156pp. A humorous and chatty cockroach introduces the early inhabitants of North America and Mesoamerica. (Rev: HBG 10/02; SLJ 5/02) [970.01]

15706 Lichtenheld, Tom. *Everything I Know About Pirates: A Collection of Made-up Facts, Educated Guesses and Silly Pictures About Bad Guys of the High Seas* (PS–2). Illus. 2000, Simon & Schuster $16.00 (0-689-82625-7). 40pp. Mixed in with factual material about pirates, this fanciful book also makes some guesses about their lifestyles. (Rev: BCCB 4/00; BL 5/15/00; HBG 10/00; SLJ 5/00) [910.4]

15707 MacDonald, Fiona. *Women in a Changing World: 1945–2000* (4–6). Series: The Other Half of History. 2001, Bedrick $17.95 (0-87226-572-2). 48pp. Traces the position of women in the United States and England from the 1950s to the present. This book is preceded by *Women in Peace and War: 1900–1950* (2001). (Rev: HBG 10/01; SLJ 3/01) [909]

15708 MacDonald, Fiona. *Women in 19th-Century Europe* (4–8). Series: The Other Half of History. 1999, Bedrick $17.95 (0-87226-565-X). 48pp. Describes women's progress and contributions in 19th-century Europe and gives biographies of famous women of the time. (Rev: HBG 3/00; SLJ 11/99) [940.2]

15709 McGowen, Tom. *Assault from the Sea: Amphibious Invasions in the Twentieth Century* (5–8). Series: Military Might. 2002, Twenty-First Century LB $26.90 (0-7613-1811-9). 64pp. Invasions launched from the sea during World Wars I and II and the Korean War are the subject of this introduction that includes black-and-white photographs and maps. Also use *Assault from the Sky: Airborne Infantry of World War II* (2002). (Rev: HBG 10/02; SLJ 6/02) [355.460904]

15710 Mason, Antony. *People Around the World* (5–7). Illus. 2002, Kingfisher $24.95 (0-7534-5497-1). 256pp. An oversize guide to people of different cultures around the world, organized by continent, featuring hundreds of full-color photographs and illustrations, and detailing such topics as diet, language, employment, and leisure of urban and rural dwellers. (Rev: BL 5/1/03; HBG 10/03; SLJ 4/03) [305.8]

15711 Maynard, Christopher. *The History News: Revolution* (4–7). Illus. 1999, Candlewick $16.99 (0-7636-0491-7). 32pp. Using a tabloid-newspaper format, this book covers four revolutions: the American, French, Russian, and Chinese. (Rev: BL 12/15/99; HBG 3/00; SLJ 10/99) [909]

15712 Meltzer, Milton. *Witches and Witch-Hunts: A History of Persecution* (5–9). 1999, Scholastic paper $16.95 (0-590-48517-2). 128pp. This is a record of scapegoating through history on the basis of gender, religion, or politics, beginning with witches in the Middle Ages and continuing through the 20th century to Hitler's Germany and Senator McCarthy's hearings. (Rev: BCCB 10/99; BL 11/1/99; HB 11–12/99; HBG 3/00; SLJ 11/99) [303]

15713 Millard, Anne. *A Street Through Time* (4–8). Illus. 1998, DK $17.99 (0-7894-3426-1). Western European history is traced in this oversize book that contains 14 views of the same riverside location at various times in history, including the Stone Age,

Viking times, the Roman period, the Middle Ages, and modern times. (Rev: BL 1/1–15/99; HB 1–2/99; HBG 3/99; SLJ 12/98) [936]

15714 Morgan, Kate. *The Story of Things* (3–5). Illus. by Joyce A. Zarins. 1991, Walker LB $15.85 (0-8027-6919-5). 32pp. A history of civilization in a slim volume that will attract a child's interest. (Rev: BL 6/15/91; SLJ 7/91) [523.4]

15715 Pirotta, Saviour. *Buried Treasure* (3–5). Series: Mysteries of the Past. 2001, Raintree LB $17.98 (0-7398-4336-2). 32pp. Egyptian tombs, burial mounds in England, pirate legends, and Nazi loot are among the topics addressed in this overview of underground lore. (Rev: HBG 3/02; SLJ 2/02)

15716 Pirotta, Saviour. *Pirates and Treasure* (4–5). Illus. Series: Remarkable World. 1995, Thomson Learning LB $24.26 (1-56847-366-4). 47pp. A history of piracy from the days of the Phoenicians onward, with full-color art reproductions, maps, and many sidebars. (Rev: SLJ 1/96) [910.4]

15717 Prior, Natalie Jane. *The Encyclopedia of Preserved People: Pickled, Frozen, and Mummified Corpses from Around the World* (5–8). Illus. 2003, Crown LB $16.99 (0-375-92287-3). 64pp. Egyptian mummies and bog bodies feature here, but so do Lenin and Einstein's brain as part of the discussion of what we can learn from preserved corpses as opposed to skeletons. (Rev: HBG 4/04; SLJ 4/03)

15718 Reid, Struan. *Cultures and Civilizations* (5–9). Illus. Series: The Silk and Spice Routes. 1994, Silver Burdett LB $15.95 (0-02-726315-0). An attractive, oversize introduction to the many historic cultures that thrived along the ancient trade route to the East, with stunning illustrations. (Rev: BL 12/15/94; SLJ 12/94) [909]

15719 Reid, Struan. *Inventions and Trade* (5–8). Illus. Series: Silk and Spice Routes. 1994, Silver Burdett LB $15.95 (0-02-726316-9). 48pp. A history of the trade between China and Europe along the Spice Route and of the technological advances that occurred because of this cultural exchange. (Rev: BL 12/15/94; SLJ 12/94) [382.09]

15720 Ross, Stewart. *Conquerors and Explorers* (5–7). Illus. Series: Fact or Fiction? 1996, Millbrook LB $26.90 (0-7613-0532-7). 48pp. The subtitle of this work is "The Greed, Cunning, and Bravery of the Travelers and Plunderers Who Opened Up the World." (Rev: BL 10/15/96; SLJ 4/97) [910]

15721 Ruggiero, Adriane. *The Ottoman Empire* (5–8). Series: Cultures of the Past. 2002, Marshall Cavendish $19.95 (0-7614-1494-0). 80pp. A handsome account that traces the rise and fall of the great Ottoman Empire from its beginning in the 15th century to its collapse and the formation of modern Turkey after World War I. (Rev: BL 1/1–15/03; HBG 3/03; SLJ 2/03) [956]

15722 Rumford, James. *Traveling Man: The Journey of Ibn Battuta, 1325–1354* (3–6). Illus. by author. 2001, Houghton Mifflin $16.00 (0-618-08366-9). Rumford retells the story of the epic travels across Asia and Africa of the 14th-century explorer and scholar Ibn Battuta, with lyric text that flows through the beautiful illustrations. (Rev: HB 1–2/02; HBG 3/02; SLJ 10/01) [910]

15723 Rutsala, David. *The Sea Route to Asia* (4–7). Series: Exploration and Discovery. 2002, Mason Crest LB $19.95 (1-59084-046-1). 64pp. Rutsala presents Portuguese explorers' efforts to find a route around Africa to Asia, with information on Prince Henry the Navigator, Bartholomeu Dias, and Vasco da Gama. (Rev: SLJ 12/02) [910]

15724 Seibert, Patricia. *We Were Here: A Short History of Time Capsules* (3–6). Illus. 2002, Millbrook LB $22.90 (0-7613-0423-1). 48pp. A history of time capsules, including the Century Safe that was assembled in 1876 and opened in 1976. (Rev: BL 4/1/02; HBG 10/02; SLJ 3/02) [151]

15725 Steele, Philip. *Pirates* (3–5). Illus. 1997, Kingfisher $16.95 (0-7534-5052-6). 64pp. A chronologically arranged history of piracy from Roman times through the Vikings to modern high-jackings. (Rev: HBG 3/98; SLJ 5/97) [910]

15726 Stienecker, David L. *Countries* (2–5). Series: Discovering Geography. 1997, Marshall Cavendish LB $22.79 (0-7614-0542-9). 32pp. Basic geographical concepts are explored in a question-and-answer format. (Rev: BL 2/15/98; HBG 3/98) [910]

15727 Swanson, Diane. *Tunnels!* (5–8). Series: True Stories from the Edge. 2003, Annick $18.95 (1-55037-781-7); paper $6.95 (1-55037-780-9). 144pp. Ten thrilling stories of tunnel escapes and escapades are accompanied by maps. (Rev: BL 4/15/03; SLJ 5/03) [624.1]

15728 Wells, Don. *The Spice Trade* (5–8). Illus. Series: Great Journeys. 2004, Weigl $26.00 (1-59036-208-X); paper $7.95 (1-59036-261-6). 32pp. Colorful illustrations and an attractive format will appeal to browsers seeking information about the spice trade; a useful timeline and links to Web sites are included.

15729 Williams, Brian. *The Modern World: From the French Revolution to the Computer Age* (5–8). Illus. by James Field. Series: Timelink. 1994, Bedrick LB $18.95 (0-87226-312-6). 64pp. An overview of the 200 years of world history that outlines major events, with useful timelines and maps. (Rev: SLJ 1/95) [909]

15730 Williams, Brian, and Brenda Williams. *The Age of Discovery: From the Renaissance to American Independence* (5–8). Illus. by James Field. Series: Timelink. 1994, Bedrick LB $18.95 (0-87226-311-8). 64pp. An overview of world history from the Renaissance through the American Revolution presented in 50-year segments. (Rev: SLJ 1/95) [909]

15731 Wilson, Janet. *Imagine That!* (4–8). Illus. by author. 2000, Stoddart $14.95 (0-7737-3221-7). In the form of a reminiscence by 100-year-old Auntie Violet, this is a brief history of the past century, with major events highlighted. (Rev: SLJ 11/00) [909]

15732 Worth, Richard. *The Great Empire of China and Marco Polo in World History* (5–8). Illus. Series: In World History. 2003, Enslow LB $20.95 (0-7660-1939-X). 112pp. Quotations from primary

documents and excerpts from Polo's own writings add context to this account of his 13th-century journeys to the Far East. (Rev: HBG 4/04; SLJ 3/04) [915.04]

Ancient History

General and Miscellaneous

15733 Altman, Susan, and Susan Lechner. *Ancient Africa* (2–5). Illus. by Donna Perrone. Series: Modern Rhymes About Ancient Times. 2001, Children's Book Pr. LB $28.00 (0-516-21151-X). 48pp. Rhyming text and colorful illustrations introduce young readers to a variety of facts about the cultures and peoples of ancient Africa. (Rev: SLJ 4/02)

15734 Ash, Russell. *Great Wonders of the World* (4–7). Illus. by Richard Bonson. Series: Eyewitness Books. 2000, DK paper $19.99 (0-7894-6505-1). 64pp. The seven wonders of the ancient world are presented with material comparing them to other ancient and modern technological marvels. (Rev: HBG 10/01; SLJ 9/00) [930]

15735 Avi-Yonah, Michael. *Piece by Piece! Mosaics of the Ancient World* (5–8). Illus. Series: Buried Worlds. 1993, Lerner LB $28.75 (0-8225-3204-2). This book shows how and where mosaics were made in the ancient world and how, through the wonders of archaeology, they are still being uncovered today. (Rev: BL 1/15/94; SLJ 3/94) [738.5]

15736 Bentley, Diana. *The Seven Wonders of the Ancient World* (4–6). Illus. 2002, Oxford LB $17.95 (0-19-521913-9). 32pp. Each of the wonders is covered in four concise, fact-filled pages that include watercolors, photographs, maps, diagrams, quotations, and comparisons with modern icons. (Rev: HBG 3/03; SLJ 1/03) [930]

15737 Broida, Marian. *Ancient Israelites and Their Neighbors: An Activity Guide* (4–7). Illus. 2003, Chicago Review paper $16.95 (1-55652-457-9). 160pp. Readers will find out what life was like for the ancient Israelis, Phoenicians, and Philistines through the information and activities in this attractive book. (Rev: BL 5/15/03; SLJ 8/03) [933]

15738 Burrell, Roy. *Oxford First Ancient History* (4–7). Illus. 1994, Oxford $37.95 (0-19-521058-1). 320pp. A survey of ancient civilizations, particularly those of the Mediterranean but also including the Chinese and Assyrians. (Rev: BL 7/94) [930]

15739 Carlson, Laurie. *Classical Kids: An Activity Guide to Life in Ancient Greece and Rome* (4–6). Illus. by Fran Lee. 1998, Chicago Review paper $14.95 (1-55652-290-8). 186pp. After background information on these two civilizations, there are many projects under such categories as eating, dressing up, and the arts. (Rev: SLJ 1/99) [930]

15740 Corbishley, Mike. *How Do We Know Where People Came From?* (5–8). Series: How Do We Know. 1995, Raintree LB $24.26 (0-8114-3880-5). Using double-page spreads, this book covers early cultures and touches on such subjects as early writing, Stonehenge, the Great Wall of China, the Easter

Island statues, and the pyramids. (Rev: SLJ 1/96) [930]

15741 Curlee, Lynn. *Parthenon* (5–8). Illus. by author. 2004, Simon & Schuster $17.95 (0-689-84490-5). 40pp. A beautifully composed overview of the construction and history of the temple built by the ancient Greeks to honor the goddess Athena. (Rev: BL 9/15/04*; HB 7–8/04; SLJ 6/04) [726]

15742 Curlee, Lynn. *Seven Wonders of the Ancient World* (3–6). Illus. 2002, Simon & Schuster $17.00 (0-689-83182-X). 40pp. An informative introduction for older readers to the wonders of the ancient world, with precise illustrations and thought-provoking text. (Rev: BCCB 3/02; BL 1/1–15/02; HBG 10/02; SLJ 9/02) [709]

15743 Deangelis, Therese. *Wonders of the Ancient World* (5–8). Illus. Series: Costume, Tradition, and Culture: Reflecting on the Past. 1998, Chelsea $19.75 (0-7910-5170-6). 64pp. This work features, in double-page spreads, such wonders as the Great Pyramids, Easter Island, and Stonehenge. (Rev: BL 3/15/99; HBG 10/99) [930]

15744 Gonen, Rivka. *Fired Up! Making Pottery in Ancient Times* (5–8). Illus. Series: Buried Worlds. 1993, Lerner LB $28.75 (0-8225-3202-6). This book explains how pottery was made in ancient times, showing examples from different cultures, and tells how archaeologists are uncovering more and more examples. (Rev: BL 1/15/94; SLJ 4/94) [738.3]

15745 Greene, Jacqueline D. *Slavery in Ancient Greece and Rome* (4–7). Series: Watts Library: History of Slavery. 2000, Watts LB $24.00 (0-531-11693-X). 64pp. Topics covered include the treatment of slaves in Greece and Rome, how they thrived in Greece's democracy, the slave fire brigades, battles of slave gladiators, and the attitudes toward slavery in the early Christian church. (Rev: BL 3/1/01; SLJ 3/01) [930]

15746 Hook, Jason. *Lost Cities* (3–5). Series: Mysteries of the Past. 2001, Raintree LB $17.98 (0-7398-4337-0). 32pp. Ur, Knossos, Babylon, and Troy are among the cities addressed in this introduction to the mysteries surrounding the sites and the efforts to uncover the truth. (Rev: HBG 3/02; SLJ 2/02)

15747 Hunter, Erica C. D., and Mike Corbishley. *First Civilizations.* Rev. ed. (5–8). Illus. Series: Cultural Atlas for Young People. 2003, Facts on File $35.00 (0-8160-5149-6). 96pp. Colorful topical spreads introduce readers to the culture, geography, history, and politics of Mesopotamia, Persia, and Assyria. (Rev: SLJ 1/04) [939]

15748 Jessop, Joanne. *The X-Ray Picture Book of Big Buildings of the Ancient World* (2–6). Illus. 1994, Watts LB $25.00 (0-531-14286-8). 48pp. This handsomely illustrated book shows cutaway views of such structures as the Great Pyramid, the Parthenon, the Coliseum, Notre Dame, Mont St. Michel, and the Taj Mahal. (Rev: BL 6/1–15/94; SLJ 7/94) [720]

15749 Jovinelly, Joann, and Jason Netelkos. *The Crafts and Culture of the Ancient Hebrews* (5–8).

Illus. Series: Crafts of the Ancient World. 2002, Rosen LB $29.25 (0-8239-3511-6). 48pp. The crafts of the ancient Hebrews and projects related to them are used to give basic information on their history and how they lived. (Rev: BL 4/1/02) [932]

15750 Nardo, Don. *Ancient Persia* (4–6). Illus. Series: Life During the Great Civilizations. 2004, Gale/Blackbirch LB $18.96 (1-56711-740-6). 48pp. Nardo explores day-to-day life in ancient Persia, looking at everything from clothes and jobs to social structures and religion. (Rev: BL 5/15/04; SLJ 8/04) [935]

15751 Nardo, Don. *Greek and Roman Sport* (5–10). Series: World History. 1999, Lucent LB $27.45 (1-56006-436-6). 112pp. A very detailed account, using many quotations from classical sources, that gives a realistic picture of the place of sports in both ancient Greece and Rome, the different events, and the rewards and hardships of participants. (Rev: BL 7/99; SLJ 8/99) [930]

15752 Nelson, Julie. *West African Kingdoms* (3–5). Series: Ancient Civilizations. 2001, Raintree LB $15.98 (0-7398-3581-5). 48pp. Readers will gain an understanding of the history and culture of the ancient civilizations of Ghana, Mali, and Songhai. (Rev: SLJ 2/02)

15753 Odijk, Pamela. *The Israelites* (4–7). Illus. Series: Ancient World. 1990, Silver Burdett LB $14.95 (0-382-09888-9). 48pp. Covers the early history of the Jewish people, from their origins in Canaan through the Diaspora. (Rev: BL 7/90; SLJ 8/90) [956.94]

15754 Odijk, Pamela. *The Phoenicians* (4–7). Illus. Series: Ancient World. 1989, Silver Burdett LB $14.95 (0-382-09891-9). 48pp. The ancient traders of the Mediterranean Sea are introduced. (Rev: BL 1/15/90; SLJ 5/90) [939.44]

15755 Service, Pamela F. *300 B.C.* (5–8). Series: Around the World In. 2002, Benchmark $19.95 (0-7614-1080-5). 96pp. The author explores what was going on in Europe, Africa, Asia, and the Americas in the year 300 B.C. Also use *1200* (2002). (Rev: HBG 3/03; SLJ 2/03) [930]

15756 Shuter, Jane. *Ancient West African Kingdoms* (3–5). Illus. Series: History Opens Windows. 2002, Heinemann LB $22.79 (1-4034-0255-8). 32pp. Readers will learn about government, trade, and everyday life in the kingdoms of Ghana, Mali, and Songhai. (Rev: HBG 3/03; SLJ 3/03)

15757 Shuter, Jane. *The Indus Valley* (3–5). Illus. Series: History Opens Windows. 2002, Heinemann LB $22.79 (1-4034-0253-1). 32pp. An overview of government, trade, and everyday life in ancient times in the Indus Valley that is now in Pakistan and western India. (Rev: HBG 3/03; SLJ 3/03)

15758 Smith, K. C. *Ancient Shipwrecks* (5–7). Series: Shipwrecks. 2000, Watts LB $24.00 (0-531-20381-6). 64pp. From the Bronze Age through the Roman Empire, this volume explores the fascinating stories behind ancient wrecks found in the Mediterranean and explored by archaeologists. (Rev: BL 10/15/00) [930]

15759 Stefoff, Rebecca. *The Ancient Mediterranean* (5–8). Series: World Historical Atlases. 2004, Benchmark LB $27.07 (0-7614-1641-2). 48pp. Maps, text, and illustrations give a broad overview of the cultures found in the ancient Mediterranean. Also use *The Ancient Near East* and *The Asian Empires* (both 2004). (Rev: SLJ 2/05) [930]

15760 Trumble, Kelly. *The Library of Alexandria* (5–7). Illus. by Robina MacIntyre Marshall. 2003, Clarion $17.00 (0-395-75832-7). 72pp. An introduction to the famous library, its collection, its scholars, and its destruction by fire. (Rev: BCCB 1/04; BL 11/15/03; HBG 4/04; SLJ 1/04) [027.032]

15761 Waldman, Neil. *Masada* (4–6). Illus. 1998, Morrow $16.00 (0-688-14481-0). 64pp. The story of the Masada fortress, built in the first century B.C. and captured by the Romans in 72–73 A.D. Rather than surrender, the Jewish defenders committed suicide. (Rev: BCCB 10/98; BL 10/1/98; HBG 3/99; SLJ 11/98) [933]

15762 Wells, Donald. *The Silk Road* (5–8). Series: Great Journeys. 2004, Weigl LB $.00 (1-59036-207-1). Colorful illustrations and an attractive format will appeal to browsers seeking information on this ancient trade route; a useful timeline and links to Web sites are included. (Rev: BL 11/1/04) [950]

15763 Wilkinson, Philip, and Jacqueline Dineen. *The Mediterranean* (4–7). Illus. by Robert Ingpen. Series: Mysterious Places. 1994, Chelsea LB $21.95 (0-7910-2751-1). 92pp. Ten sites around the Mediterranean are investigated, including Knossos, Rhodes, Delphi, Mistra, the Topkapi Palace, and Hagia Sophia. (Rev: BL 1/15/94; SLJ 5/94) [930.3]

15764 Woods, Michael, and Mary Woods. *Ancient Agriculture: From Foraging to Farming* (5–8). Series: Ancient Technologies. 2000, Runestone LB $25.26 (0-8225-2995-5). 88pp. Beginning with prehistoric food-gathering peoples, this book traces the history of plant cultivation and agriculture through each of the great ancient civilizations. (Rev: BL 8/00; HBG 10/00; SLJ 6/00) [630]

15765 Woods, Michael, and Mary Woods. *Ancient Machines from Wedges to Waterwheels* (5–8). Series: Ancient Technologies. 1999, Lerner LB $25.26 (0-8225-2994-7). 88pp. This heavily illustrated account describes the important machines that came into being from ancient history to the fall of the Western Roman Empire. (Rev: BL 1/1–15/00; HBG 10/00; SLJ 6/00) [936]

15766 Woods, Michael, and Mary B. Woods. *Ancient Medicine: From Sorcery to Surgery* (5–8). Illus. Series: Ancient Technologies. 2000, Lerner LB $25.26 (0-8225-2992-0). 88pp. Medical practices in ancient times and cultures — the Stone Age, ancient Egypt, and early Hindu cultures, for example — are discussed in this volume. (Rev: BL 1/1–15/00; HBG 10/00; SLJ 5/00) [610]

15767 Woods, Michael, and Mary B. Woods. *Ancient Transportation: From Camels to Canals* (5–8). Illus. Series: Ancient Technologies. 2000, Lerner LB $25.26 (0-8225-2993-9). 88pp. This book covers such topics related to early transportation as the first bridges and roads, early skis and sleds, primi-

tive wagons, and the beginnings of maps. (Rev: BL 1/1–15/00; HBG 10/00; SLJ 6/00) [629.04]

15768 Wyborny, Sheila. *The Celts* (4–6). Illus. Series: Life During the Great Civilizations. 2005, Gale/Blackbirch LB $18.96 (1-4103-0583-X). 48pp. Wyborny explores day-to-day life for the ancient Celts, looking at everything from clothes and jobs to social structures and religion.

Egypt and Mesopotamia

15769 Alcraft, Rob. *Valley of the Kings* (5–7). Series: Visiting the Past. 1999, Heinemann LB $24.22 (1-57572-860-5). 32pp. This account uses double-page spreads to cover topics including the history, landscape, beliefs, and daily life of the ancient Egyptians. (Rev: SLJ 3/00) [932]

15770 Aliki. *Mummies Made in Egypt* (3–5). Illus. by author. 1979, HarperCollins LB $15.89 (0-690-03859-3); paper $6.95 (0-06-446011-8). 32pp. The burial practices and beliefs of the ancient Egyptians are explored in text and handsome illustrations.

15771 Altman, Susan, and Susan Lechner. *Ancient Egypt* (2–5). Illus. by Sandy Appleoff. Series: Modern Rhymes About Ancient Times. 2001, Children's Book Pr. LB $28.00 (0-516-21149-8). 48pp. Rhyming text and colorful illustrations introduce young readers to the culture and peoples of ancient Egypt. (Rev: SLJ 4/02)

15772 Bailey, Linda. *Adventures in Ancient Egypt* (2–5). Illus. Series: Good Times Travel Agency. 2000, Kids Can $14.95 (1-55074-546-8); paper $7.95 (1-55074-548-4). 48pp. Using an old travel guide, three children are transported to Egypt in 2500 B.C. where they become acquainted with the sights and sites as well as becoming involved in a series of adventures. (Rev: BL 1/1–15/01; HBG 3/01; SLJ 12/00) [932]

15773 Balkwill, Richard. *Clothes and Crafts in Ancient Egypt* (4–6). Series: Clothing and Crafts in History. 2000, Gareth Stevens LB $21.27 (0-8368-2733-3). 32pp. As well as coverage on ancient Egyptian painting, pottery, carving, clothes, and jewelry, this book gives step-by-step instructions for several craft projects including making a snake game and fashioning a clay pot. (Rev: BL 1/1–15/01; HBG 10/01) [932]

15774 Berger, Melvin, and Gilda Berger. *Mummies of the Pharaohs: Exploring the Valley of the Kings* (4–7). Illus. 2001, National Geographic $17.95 (0-7922-7223-4). 64pp. Beginning with King Tut's tomb and continuing through other sites, this book uses stunning photographs and a clear text to describe workings of archaeological digs that are studying Egypt's past. (Rev: BL 2/1/01) [932]

15775 Bingham, Caroline. *Pyramid* (2–5). Series: Eye Wonder. 2004, DK LB $17.99 (0-7566-0286-6). 48pp. Pyramids around the world — in Mexico, Sudan, and India, for example — are featured in addition to the most famous ones in Giza. (Rev: BL 9/15/04) [726]

15776 Broida, Marian. *Ancient Egyptians and Their Neighbors: An Activity Guide* (4–8). Illus. 1999,

Chicago Review paper $16.95 (1-55652-360-2). 208pp. The lives and times of the ancient Egyptians, Nubians, Hittites, and Mesopotamians are examined using text and a series of 40 fascinating projects. (Rev: BL 3/15/00; SLJ 2/00) [939]

15777 Caselli, Giovanni. *In Search of Tutankhamun: The Discovery of a King's Tomb* (4–7). Series: In Search Of. 1999, Bedrick $18.95 (0-87226-543-9). 48pp. As well as supplying information on King Tut's tomb, this heavily illustrated book supplies good general material on the culture and history of the ancient Egyptian civilization. (Rev: BL 10/15/99; HBG 3/00; SLJ 8/99) [932]

15778 Chapman, Gillian. *The Egyptians* (4–8). Series: Crafts from the Past. 1997, Heinemann LB $25.64 (1-57572-556-8). A variety of craft projects related to the ancient Egyptians are introduced and placed within their cultural context. (Rev: SLJ 4/98) [932]

15779 Chrisp, Peter. *Ancient Egypt Revealed* (4–8). Illus. 2002, DK paper $12.99 (0-7894-8883-3). 38pp. This absorbing introduction to ancient Egypt uses a crisp text, a variety of beautiful photographs, computer graphics, and transparent cutaways to reveal the secrets of tombs and temples, and to inform readers about culture, writing methods, myths, and so forth. (Rev: BL 1/1–15/03; HBG 3/03; SLJ 3/03) [932]

15780 Clare, John D., ed. *Pyramids of Ancient Egypt* (4–6). Illus. Series: Living History. 1992, Harcourt $16.95 (0-15-200509-9). 64pp. Besides telling about the building of the Pyramids, this book uses human models to describe the daily life of the ancient Egyptians. (Rev: SLJ 10/92) [932]

15781 Clarke, Sue. *The Tombs of the Pharaohs: A Three-Dimensional Discovery* (2–5). Illus. 1994, Hyperion $16.95 (1-56282-485-6). 10pp. In this interactive book shaped like a pyramid, pop-ups and flaps are used to introduce topics involving ancient Egypt. (Rev: BL 11/15/94) [932]

15782 Cole, Joanna. *Ms. Frizzle's Adventures: Ancient Egypt* (3–6). Illus. by Bruce Degen. 2001, Scholastic $15.95 (0-590-44680-0). 48pp. Ms. Frizzle (of Magic School Bus fame) leads a tour group back in time to explore ancient Egypt with the usual bright mix of fiction, nonfiction, and humor. (Rev: BL 9/1/01; HB 11–12/01; HBG 3/02; SLJ 9/01*) [932]

15783 Cooper, Roscoe. *The Great Pyramid: An Interactive Book* (PS–K). Illus. by Carolyn Croll. 1998, Troll $18.95 (0-8167-4390-8). This pyramid-shaped book, with many pop-ups, traces the building of King Khufu's pyramid from the beginning to his mummification. (Rev: BL 1/1–15/99) [932]

15784 Crisp, Peter. *Mesopotamia: Iraq in Ancient Times* (4–7). Illus. Series: Picturing the Past. 2004, Enchanted Lion $15.95 (1-59270-024-1). 32pp. History and archaeology are the highlights of this nicely illustrated overview of Mesopotamian civilization. (Rev: BL 10/15/04; SLJ 11/04) [935]

15785 Crosher, Judith. *Technology in the Time of Ancient Egypt* (4–8). Series: Technology in the Time Of. 1998, Raintree LB $27.12 (0-8172-4875-

7). 48pp. Each double-page spread presents an aspect of technology in ancient Egypt in such areas as food production, transportation, and building. (Rev: HBG 10/98; SLJ 3/99) [932]

15786 David, Rosalie. *Growing Up in Ancient Egypt* (3–5). Illus. by Angus McBride. Series: Growing Up In. 1993, Troll paper $4.95 (0-8167-2718-X). 32pp. Everyday life in the different social classes of ancient Egypt is covered, with a focus on children and their upbringing. (Rev: BL 1/15/94) [932]

15787 Day, Nancy. *Your Travel Guide to Ancient Egypt* (4–8). Series: Passport to History. 2000, Runestone LB $26.60 (0-8225-3075-9). 96pp. Written in the style of a modern-day travel guide, this book on ancient Egypt covers such subjects as sites to see, food, clothing, religious beliefs, politics, and daily life. (Rev: BL 11/15/00; HBG 3/01; SLJ 5/01) [932]

15788 Delafosse, Claude, and Philippe Biard. *Pyramids* (PS–2). Illus. by authors. Series: First Discovery. 1995, Scholastic $12.95 (0-590-42786-5). Describes how the pyramids of Egypt were built, as well as mummification and the seven wonders of the ancient world. (Rev: SLJ 3/96) [932]

15789 Fisher, Leonard Everett. *The Gods and Goddesses of Ancient Egypt* (3–5). Illus. 1997, Holiday House LB $16.95 (0-8234-1286-5). 32pp. With accompanying stories, this book introduces 13 Egyptian deities, including Horus and Osiris. (Rev: BL 12/1/97; HBG 3/98; SLJ 11/97) [299]

15790 Frank, John. *The Tomb of the Boy King* (K–3). Illus. by Tom Pohrt. 2001, Farrar $16.00 (0-374-37674-3). 32pp. Using free verse, the author first tells about the boy king, Tutankhamen, and then describes the expedition that discovered his tomb and the wonders that were found inside. (Rev: BL 3/1/01; HB 3–4/01*; HBG 10/01) [932.014]

15791 Gibbons, Gail. *Mummies, Pyramids, and Pharaohs: A Book About Ancient Egypt* (PS–2). 2004, Little, Brown $16.95 (0-316-30928-1). 32pp. The history and mysteries of ancient Egypt — including mummies, pharaohs, and pyramids — are explored in an engaging blend of brief, simple narrative and ink-and-watercolor artwork. (Rev: BL 6/1–15/04; SLJ 6/04) [932]

15792 Grant, Neil, ed. *The Egyptians* (4–6). Illus. Series: Spotlights. 1996, Oxford paper $11.95 (0-19-521239-8). 46pp. Double-page spreads are used to introduce such topics about ancient Egypt as its history, culture, social life, religion, and political organization. (Rev: SLJ 9/96) [932]

15793 Greene, Jacqueline D. *Slavery in Ancient Egypt and Mesopotamia* (4–7). Series: Watts Library: History of Slavery. 2000, Watts LB $24.00 (0-531-11692-1). 64pp. This unusual book covers the earliest forms of slavery, how the pharaohs used slaves to construct the pyramids, and the place of slavery in Hebrew society. (Rev: BL 3/1/01; SLJ 3/01) [930]

15794 Harris, Geraldine. *Ancient Egypt*. Rev. ed. (5–8). Illus. Series: Cultural Atlas for Young People. 2003, Facts on File $35.00 (0-8160-5148-8). 96pp. Colorful topical spreads introduce readers to the culture, history, and politics of ancient Egypt. (Rev: SLJ 1/04) [932]

15795 Hart, Avery, and Paul Mantell. *Pyramids! 50 Hands-on Activities to Experience Ancient Egypt* (3–5). Illus. Series: Kaleidoscope Kids. 1997, Williamson paper $10.95 (1-885593-10-4). 96pp. Some of the craft projects that explore the culture of ancient Egypt are building model pyramids, writing messages in hieroglyphics, and preparing clothes, food, and games for an Egyptian costume party. (Rev: BL 11/15/97) [932]

15796 Hawass, Zahi. *Curse of the Pharaohs: My Adventures with Mummies* (4–6). 2004, National Geographic $19.95 (0-7922-6665-X). 160pp. Excellent photographs and detailed endmatter add to the interesting discussion of mysteries associated with the tombs of the pharaohs. (Rev: BL 6/1–15/04; SLJ 11/04)

15797 Hodge, Susie. *Ancient Egyptian Art* (3–6). Series: Art in History. 1997, Heinemann LB $13.95 (1-57572-550-9). 32pp. This book presents the art of ancient Egypt as a reflection of its culture in such areas as religion and science. (Rev: HBG 3/98; SLJ 4/98) [932]

15798 Honan, Linda. *Spend the Day in Ancient Egypt: Projects and Activities That Bring the Past to Life* (3–6). Illus. by Ellen Kosmer. 1999, Wiley paper $12.95 (0-471-29006-8). 116pp. Craft projects and other activities are used to introduce the culture and everyday of the ancient Egyptians. (Rev: SLJ 1/00) [932]

15799 James, Louise. *How We Know About the Egyptians* (3–6). Series: How We Know About. 1998, Bedrick $0.00 (0-87226-236-6). 32pp. Using double-page spreads, this work focuses on ancient Egypt and explains the detective-like work of archaeologists and others who have increased our knowledge of this civilization. (Rev: BL 5/15/98) [932]

15800 Jovinelly, Joann, and Jason Netelkos. *The Crafts and Culture of the Ancient Egyptians* (5–8). Series: Crafts of the Ancient World. 2002, Rosen LB $29.25 (0-8239-3509-4). 48pp. As well as learning about the mysteries of ancient Egypt, readers can engage in such craft projects as designing a pharaoh's headdress and necklace and re-creating an ancient marbles game. (Rev: BL 5/15/02; SLJ 6/02) [932]

15801 Kallen, Stuart A. *Pyramids* (5–8). Illus. Series: The Mystery Library. 2002, Gale LB $27.45 (1-56006-773-X). 112pp. Kallen uses many quotations from Egyptologists in this exploration of the reasons for building the pyramids and the construction techniques used. (Rev: BL 7/02; SLJ 7/02)

15802 Krensky, Stephen. *Egypt* (2–3). Series: Scholastic History Readers. 2002, Scholastic paper $3.99 (0-439-27195-9). 48pp. An appealing introduction to Egypt for beginning readers that emphasizes the importance of the Nile and covers such topics as daily life, the life of a ruler, the calendar, and the writing system. (Rev: SLJ 2/03)

15803 Landau, Elaine. *The Babylonians* (4–6). Illus. Series: Cradle of Civilization. 1997, Millbrook LB $21.40 (0-7613-0216-6). 64pp. The history, religion, and contributions of this early civilization that invented the wheel and was the first to establish laws and government. (Rev: BL 1/1–15/98; HBG 3/98; SLJ 3/98) [935]

15804 Landau, Elaine. *The Curse of Tutankhamen* (4–6). Illus. Series: Mysteries of Science. 1996, Millbrook LB $20.90 (0-7613-0014-7). 48pp. The story of the discovery of King Tut's tomb and of the curse that supposedly plagued the archaeologists that were involved. (Rev: BL 10/15/96; SLJ 11/96) [931]

15805 Landau, Elaine. *The Sumerians* (4–6). Illus. Series: Cradle of Civilization. 1997, Millbrook LB $21.40 (0-7613-0215-8). 64pp. An overview of the Sumerians, their rulers and gods, and their contributions to science, government, and the arts. (Rev: BL 1/1–15/98; HBG 3/98; SLJ 3/98) [935]

15806 Macaulay, David. *Pyramid* (5–8). Illus. by author. 1975, Houghton Mifflin $18.00 (0-395-21407-6). 80pp. The engineering and architectural feats of the Egyptians are explored with detailed drawings.

15807 McCall, Henrietta. *Egyptian Mummies* (3–5). Illus. by David Antram. Series: Fast Forward. 2000, Watts LB $26.50 (0-531-11877-0); paper $9.95 (0-531-16443-8). 32pp. A concise look at mummies and embalming that uses split spreads that can be opened to reveal additional information. (Rev: SLJ 6/01) [393.3]

15808 McCall, Henrietta. *Gods and Goddesses: In the Daily Life of the Ancient Egyptians* (4–7). Illus. 2002, McGraw-Hill $18.95 (0-87226-635-4). 48pp. A colorful overview of religion in ancient Egypt in a series of double-page spreads that cover particular gods, religious practices, and various pharaohs. (Rev: BL 5/1/02; HBG 10/02) [200]

15809 McNeill, Sarah. *Ancient Egyptian People* (4–8). Illus. Series: People and Places. 1997, Millbrook LB $21.90 (0-7613-0056-2). This basic introduction to the people of ancient Egypt and how they lived consists of several attractive double-page spreads and a brief text. (Rev: BL 2/15/97; SLJ 3/97) [932]

15810 McNeill, Sarah. *Ancient Egyptian Places* (4–8). Illus. Series: People and Places. 1997, Millbrook LB $21.90 (0-7613-0057-0). Some of the great constructions of ancient Egypt are pictured in a series of elegant double-page spreads with a simple text. (Rev: BL 2/15/97; SLJ 3/97) [932]

15811 Malam, John. *Ancient Egypt* (3–6). Illus. Series: Picturing the Past. 2004, Enchanted Lion $15.95 (1-59270-021-7). 32pp. Well-written two-page chapters cover geography, history, government, religion, the arts, and home life, with maps, photos and illustrations, and informative sidebars detailing sources. (Rev: SLJ 11/04) [932]

15812 Malam, John. *Ancient Egypt* (5–8). Series: Remains to Be Seen. 1998, Evans Brothers $19.95 (0-237-51839-2). 47pp. This introduction to ancient Egypt's culture and history is organized in double-page spreads and is noteworthy for its many sidebars, charts, and illustrations. (Rev: SLJ 9/98) [932]

15813 Malam, John. *Ancient Egyptian Jobs* (5–7). Illus. 2002, Heinemann LB $25.64 (1-4034-0311-2). 48pp. The daily activities of workers such as scribes, bakers, dancers, jewelers, pyramid builders, and embalmers are described in this slim volume that also offers a general introduction to ancient Egypt. (Rev: HBG 10/03; SLJ 4/03) [331.7]

15814 Malam, John. *Mesopotamia and the Fertile Crescent: 10,000 to 539 B.C.* (5–8). Series: Looking Back. 1999, Raintree $19.98 (0-8172-5434-X). 32pp. The story of the ancient civilizations that grew up in the rich area around the Tigris and Euphrates rivers. (Rev: BL 5/15/99; SLJ 7/99) [930]

15815 Mann, Elizabeth. *The Great Pyramid* (4–7). Illus. Series: Wonders of the World. 1996, Mikaya $19.95 (0-9650493-1-0). 48pp. The building of this architectural marvel is told graphically, with details on the society of ancient Egypt. (Rev: BL 2/1/97; SLJ 6/97*) [932]

15816 Manning, Ruth. *Ancient Egyptian Women* (5–8). Illus. Series: People in the Past. 2002, Heinemann LB $27.07 (1-40340-313-9). 48pp. A look at the life of, and options open to, women in ancient Egypt. (Rev: BL 3/1/03; SLJ 4/03) [305.42]

15817 Marston, Elsa. *The Ancient Egyptians* (5–8). Series: Cultures of the Past. 1995, Benchmark LB $28.50 (0-7614-0073-7). With photographs of artifacts, monuments, and historical scenes, this book tells of ancient Egyptian history and culture, the rise and fall of the dynasties, and the people's religious beliefs and practices. (Rev: BR 9–10/96; SLJ 6/96) [932]

15818 Millard, Anne. *Going to War in Ancient Egypt* (5–7). Illus. 2001, Watts LB $24.00 (0-531-14589-1). 32pp. Soldiers, weapons, and military strategies of ancient Egypt are presented with many illustrations and a timeline. (Rev: SLJ 10/01) [355.00932]

15819 Millard, Anne. *The World of the Pharaoh* (4–6). Illus. by Louis R. Galante. Series: The World Of. 1998, Bedrick $19.95 (0-87226-292-8). 48pp. This book describes how ancient Egypt was ruled, with material on the power of the pharaohs, priests, viziers, and members of the royal family. (Rev: HBG 3/99; SLJ 1/99) [932]

15820 Milton, Joyce. *Mummies* (2–3). Illus. by Susan Swan. 1996, Penguin Putnam paper $3.99 (0-448-41325-6). 48pp. The purpose and process of mummification are explained, with special reference to ancient Egypt. (Rev: BL 11/15/96; SLJ 6/97) [932]

15821 Minnis, Ivan. *You Are in Ancient Egypt* (3–6). Illus. Series: You Are There! 2004, Raintree LB $26.36 (1-4109-0616-7); paper $7.50 (1-4109-1008-3). 32pp. In present-tense narrative, Minnis introduces the sites, sounds, food, and varied living conditions of ancient Egypt. (Rev: SLJ 2/05) [932]

15822 Montavon, Jay. *The Curse of King Tut's Tomb* (3–5). Illus. 1991, Avon paper $3.50 (0-380-76220-X). 96pp. Tells about King Tut and the discovery of his tomb, but focuses on the supposed curse that was associated with its opening. (Rev: BL 9/15/91) [932]

15823 Morley, Jacqueline. *An Egyptian Pyramid* (4–6). Illus. by Mark Bergin and John James. Series: Inside Story. 1991, Bedrick $18.95 (0-87226-346-0). 32pp. This work explains how pyramids were built and their purposes and parts. (Rev: BL 11/15/91; SLJ 12/91) [932]

15824 Morley, Jacqueline. *The Living Tomb* (3–6). Illus. Series: Magnifications. 2000, Bedrick $18.95 (0-87226-651-6). 48pp. Information on early Egyptian temples, tombs, and mummification is presented on double-page spreads; enlargements of parts of illustrations are used effectively. (Rev: BL 10/15/00; HBG 3/01; SLJ 1/01) [932]

15825 Morris, Neil. *The Atlas of Ancient Egypt* (4–8). Series: Atlas. 2000, Bedrick $19.95 (0-87226-610-9). 59pp. Using many illustrations as well as maps, this is an attractive, colorful account of ancient Egypt that covers history, people, culture, lifestyles, and geography. (Rev: HBG 3/01; SLJ 3/01) [932]

15826 Moscovitch, Arlene. *Egypt, the Culture* (4–6). Series: Lands, Peoples, and Cultures. 2000, Crabtree LB $15.45 (0-86505-234-4); paper $7.16 (0-86505-314-6). 32pp. This book deals with the culture of ancient Egypt, the accomplishments of its people and their religious beliefs. (Rev: SLJ 7/00) [932]

15827 Nardo, Don. *Ancient Egypt* (3–6). Illus. 2002, Gale LB $23.70 (0-7377-0955-3). 48pp. A basic introduction to the people of ancient Egypt, nobility and peasants, and to the importance of their religious beliefs. (Rev: SLJ 9/02)

15828 Nardo, Don. *Ancient Egypt* (5–8). Illus. Series: History of the World. 2001, Gale LB $23.70 (0-7377-0774-7). 48pp. Topics covered in this basic introduction to ancient Egypt include customs of worship and burial, the role of the pharaoh, Egyptian history, and important artifacts. (Rev: BL 4/1/02) [932]

15829 Nardo, Don. *King Tut's Tomb* (3–6). Series: Wonders of the World. 2004, Gale/KidHaven LB $23.70 (0-7377-2352-1). 48pp. Nardo discusses what we know of King Tutankhamen's life and death, and describes the discovery of his tomb. (Rev: SLJ 6/05) [932]

15830 Odijk, Pamela. *The Egyptians* (4–7). Illus. Series: Ancient World. 1989, Silver Burdett LB $14.95 (0-382-09886-2). 48pp. An introduction to the history of ancient Egypt. (Rev: BL 1/15/90; SLJ 5/90) [932]

15831 Odijk, Pamela. *The Sumerians* (4–7). Illus. Series: Ancient World. 1990, Silver Burdett LB $14.95 (0-382-09892-7). 48pp. History and contributions of the Sumerians in the Fertile Crescent. (Rev: BL 11/1/90; SLJ 1/91) [935.01]

15832 Payne, Elizabeth. *The Pharaohs of Ancient Egypt* (6–8). Illus. 1981, Random paper $5.99 (0-394-84699-0). 42pp. A fascinating study of this important period in Egyptian history.

15833 Pemberton, Delia. *Egyptian Mummies: People from the Past* (3–6). Illus. 2001, Harcourt $18.00 (0-15-202600-2). 48pp. The author introduces seven ancient Egyptian mummies and discusses who they were during their lifetimes, as well as presenting readable information on archaeology, museums, and the study of mummies. (Rev: BL 9/15/01; HBG 3/02; SLJ 9/01) [932]

15834 Perl, Lila. *The Ancient Egyptians* (4–7). Series: People of the Ancient World. 2004, JULIE SEE THIS LB $29.50 (0-531-12345-6). 112pp. Pharaohs, mummy makers, farmers, and brewers are among the people presented in this overview of life in ancient Egypt. (Rev: SLJ 2/05) [930]

15835 Perl, Lila. *Mummies, Tombs, and Treasure: Secrets of Ancient Egypt* (5–7). Illus. 1987, Houghton Mifflin $16.00 (0-89919-407-9). 128pp. An inviting look at the fascinating preservation techniques of the early Egyptians. (Rev: BCCB 6/87; BL 6/15/87; SLJ 8/87) [932]

15836 Putnam, James. *The Ancient Egypt Pop-Up Book* (5–8). Illus. 2003, Universe $29.95 (0-7893-0985-8). Seven imaginatively designed pop-up spreads introduce ancient Egypt, including its pryamids, pharaohs, and mummies. (Rev: SLJ 3/04)

15837 Quie, Sarah. *The Myths and Civilization of the Ancient Egyptians* (4–8). Illus. Series: Myths and Civilization. 1999, Bedrick $16.95 (0-87226-282-0). Using the popular myths of the ancient Egyptians as a beginning, this book introduces the culture, history, and artifacts of this era. (Rev: HBG 10/99; SLJ 3/99) [932]

15838 Rees, Rosemary. *The Ancient Egyptians* (3–4). Illus. Series: Understanding People in the Past. 1997, Heinemann $22.79 (0-431-07789-4). 64pp. Photos of museum artifacts plus maps, diagrams, and drawings are used liberally to introduce such topics about the ancient Egyptians as their pharaohs, gods, history, pyramids, and mummies. (Rev: SLJ 9/97) [932]

15839 Schomp, Virginia. *Ancient Mesopotamia: The Sumerians, Babylonians, and Assyrians* (5–8). Series: People of the Ancient World. 2004, Watts LB $29.50 (0-531-11818-5). 112pp. This fascinating volume covers the history and culture of the Sumerians, Babylonians, and Assyrians, looking at writing, warfare, and the daily life of people ranging from farmers and traders to warriors and nobles. (Rev: SLJ 3/05) [935]

15840 Shuter, Jane. *Ancient Egypt* (4–6). Series: History Beneath Your Feet. 1999, Raintree LB $25.69 (0-8172-5751-9). 48pp. This work on ancient Egypt covers topics including burials, pyramids, mummies, hieroglyphs, temples, tombs, and towns plus coverage on how archaeologists have accumulated these facts. (Rev: HBG 10/00; SLJ 3/00) [932]

15841 Shuter, Jane. *The Ancient Egyptians* (3–5). Series: History Starts Here! 2000, Raintree LB $22.83 (0-7398-1351-X). 32pp. This overview of ancient Egypt includes material on history, culture, daily life, structures, and religion. (Rev: HBG 10/00; SLJ 7/00) [932]

15842 Shuter, Jane. *Egypt* (5–10). Series: Ancient World. 1998, Raintree LB $27.12 (0-8172-5058-1). Ancient Egypt's mysterious hieroglyphics, treasure-filled tombs, puzzling pyramid construction, and embalming techniques, as well as its history, politics, ideas, religion, art, architecture, science, and

everyday life are covered in this introductory volume. (Rev: BL 1/1–15/99; HBG 3/99; SLJ 3/99) [932]

15843 Smith, Carter. *The Pyramid Builders* (5–8). Series: Turning Points in World History. 1991, Silver Burdett LB $14.95 (0-382-24131-2); paper $7.95 (0-382-24137-1). A testimonial to a brilliant culture at its peak. (Rev: BL 3/15/92) [932]

15844 Steele, Philip. *The Best Book of Mummies* (3–6). Series: The Best Book Of. 1998, Kingfisher $10.95 (0-7534-5132-8). 33pp. This book of ancient Egypt gives a step-by-step glimpse at the process of mummification and also includes Egyptian tomb descriptions. (Rev: HBG 3/99; SLJ 10/98) [932]

15845 Steele, Philip. *The Egyptians and the Valley of the Kings* (4–6). Illus. Series: Hidden Worlds. 1994, Dillon $16.95 (0-87518-539-8). 32pp. Some of the topics covered are mummification, hieroglyphics, the Rosetta Stone, and archaeological findings. (Rev: SLJ 12/94) [932]

15846 Stewart, David. *You Wouldn't Want to Be an Egyptian Mummy! Disgusting Things You'd Rather Not Know* (4–6). Illus. by David Antram. 2001, Watts LB $25.00 (0-531-14597-2); paper $9.95 (0-531-16206-0). 32pp. The symbolism of elaborate Egyptian burials and the process of mummification are explained with many illustrations and cartoon art. (Rev: SLJ 9/01)

15847 Tagholm, Sally. *Ancient Egypt: A Guide to Egypt in the Time of the Pharaohs* (4–7). Series: Sightseers. 1999, Kingfisher $8.95 (0-7534-5182-4). 31pp. In the form of a tourist guide to ancient Egypt, this book tells the traveler what to wear, see, eat, and buy. (Rev: HBG 10/99; SLJ 8/99) [932]

15848 Trumble, Kelly. *Cat Mummies* (3–6). Illus. 1996, Clarion $15.95 (0-395-68707-1). 50pp. An introduction to the place of cats in ancient Egypt and to the process of mummification. (Rev: BCCB 10/96; BL 9/15/96; SLJ 8/96) [932]

15849 Walker, Jane. *Ancient Egypt* (3–6). Illus. Series: 100 Things You Should Know about. 2002, Mason Crest LB $18.95 (1-59084-445-9). 48pp. Organized topically, this collection of 100 facts covers history, government, religion, daily life, dress, and cuisine, and will appeal to reluctant readers. (Rev: SLJ 6/03) [932]

Greece

15850 Bailey, Linda. *Adventures in Ancient Greece* (3–5). Illus. by Bill Slavin. Series: Good Times Travel Agency. 2002, Kids Can $14.95 (1-55074-534-4); paper $7.95 (1-55074-536-0). 48pp. Readers take a trip to ancient Greece and learn about democracy, the Olympics, everyday life, and other aspects in an appealing layout that includes cartoon panels. (Rev: BL 11/1/02; HBG 3/03) [938]

15851 Blacklock, Dyan. *Olympia: Warrior Athletes of Ancient Greece* (5–8). Illus. by David Kennett. 2001, Walker $17.95 (0-8027-8790-8). 48pp. A lavishly illustrated introduction to the ancient Olympic Games. (Rev: BL 9/15/01; HBG 3/02; SLJ 10/01) [796.48]

15852 Chapman, Gillian. *The Greeks* (4–7). Series: Crafts from the Past. 1998, Heinemann LB $25.64 (1-57572-733-1). 39pp. Double-page spreads each outline a project inspired by an art object, i.e. a Greek vase yields pâpier-maché pottery. (Rev: SLJ 2/99) [938]

15853 Clare, John D., ed. *Ancient Greece* (3–6). Illus. Series: Living History. 1994, Harcourt $16.95 (0-15-200516-1). 64pp. An overview of the history of ancient Greece, with emphasis on its heritage and contributions to world civilization. (Rev: BL 4/15/94; SLJ 4/94) [938]

15854 Day, Nancy. *Your Travel Guide to Ancient Greece* (4–8). Illus. Series: Passport to History. 2000, Runestone LB $26.60 (0-8225-3076-7). 96pp. An outstanding introduction to ancient Greece arranged in the format of a guided tour and covering topics including geography, history, customs, and places to visit in an exciting, interesting way. (Rev: BL 10/15/00*; HBG 3/01; SLJ 2/01) [938]

15855 Freeman, Charles, ed. *The Ancient Greeks* (4–6). Illus. Series: Spotlights. 1996, Oxford $11.95 (0-19-521238-X). 46pp. Traces the history of ancient Greece, tells about its religion and the pantheon of gods, and supplies generous quotes from original sources. (Rev: SLJ 9/96) [938]

15856 Hart, Avery, and Paul Mantell. *Ancient Greece! 40 Hands-On Activities to Experience This Wonderous Age* (4–7). Illus. 1999, Williamson paper $10.95 (1-885593-25-2). 96pp. A concise text and several craft projects introduce us to the world of ancient Greece, its geography, history, people, culture, and lasting contributions. (Rev: BL 9/15/99; SLJ 8/99) [938]

15857 Hicks, Peter. *Ancient Greece* (4–6). Series: History Beneath Your Feet. 1999, Raintree LB $25.69 (0-8172-5750-0). 48pp. Using pictures of artifacts, buildings, and monuments, this account uses double-page spreads to describe the work of archaeologists and what we know, from them, about life in ancient Greece. (Rev: HBG 10/00; SLJ 3/00) [938]

15858 Hodge, Susie. *Ancient Greek Art* (4–8). Series: Art in History. 1998, Heinemann LB $24.22 (1-57572-551-7). A solid introduction to ancient Greek art, covering painting, mosaics, pottery, architecture, and sculpture. (Rev: HBG 3/98; SLJ 5/98) [938]

15859 Jovinelly, Joann, and Jason Netelkos. *The Crafts and Culture of the Ancient Greeks* (5–8). Series: Crafts of the Ancient World. 2002, Rosen LB $29.25 (0-8239-3510-8). 48pp. As well as basic information on ancient Greece, this book outlines many craft projects. (Rev: BL 5/15/02) [938]

15860 Little, Emily. *The Trojan Horse: How the Greeks Won the War* (2–4). Illus. by Mike Eagle. 1988, Random paper $3.99 (0-394-89674-2). 48pp. A lesson in ancient history in this account of the Trojan horse. (Rev: BCCB 1/89; BL 3/1/89; SLJ 2/89) [398.2]

15861 MacDonald, Fiona. *I Wonder Why Greeks Built Temples and Other Questions About Ancient Greece* (2–4). Illus. Series: I Wonder Why. 1997, Kingfisher $9.95 (0-7534-5056-9). 32pp. Each double-page spread in this book answers two or three basic questions about the ancient Greeks, how they lived, and their accomplishments. (Rev: HBG 3/98; SLJ 9/97) [938]

15862 MacDonald, Fiona. *You Wouldn't Want to Be a Slave in Ancient Greece! A Life You'd Rather Not Have* (4–6). Illus. by David Antram. Series: You Wouldn't Want To. 2001, Watts LB $25.00 (0-531-14600-6); paper $9.95 (0-531-16203-6). 32pp. The story of a woman who is kidnapped and taken to Greece as a slave serves as a good starting point to prove the premise of this book. (Rev: SLJ 9/01)

15863 Malam, John. *Ancient Greece* (4–7). Series: Picturing the Past. 2004, Enchanted Lion $15.95 (1-59270-022-5). 32pp. This photo-filled volume uses images of ancient Greek artifacts and structures to introduce the civilization's governmental organization, religion, mythology, recreation, and theater. (Rev: BL 10/15/04; SLJ 11/04) [938]

15864 Malam, John. *Exploring Ancient Greece* (5–8). Series: Remains to Be Seen. 1999, Evans Brothers $19.95 (0-237-51994-1). 47pp. Particularly noteworthy in this basic account of the history of ancient Greece are the stunning photographs of temples, theaters, artifacts, and landscapes. (Rev: SLJ 1/00) [938]

15865 Malam, John. *Gods and Goddesses* (4–7). Series: Ancient Greece. 2000, Bedrick $18.95 (0-87226-598-6). 48pp. This book identifies and describes each of the major gods and goddesses of ancient Greece and retells the myths in which they are characters. (Rev: BL 1/1–15/01; HBG 10/00; SLJ 8/00) [938]

15866 Martell, Hazel M. *The Myths and Civilization of the Ancient Greeks* (4–8). Illus. Series: Myths and Civilization. 1999, Bedrick $16.95 (0-87226-283-9). A handsome volume that combines Greek myths and legends with information about ancient Greek artifacts, culture, and history. (Rev: HBG 10/99; SLJ 3/99) [938]

15867 Middleton, Haydn. *Ancient Greek Jobs* (4–6). Series: People in the Past. 2002, Heinemann LB $25.64 (1-58810-638-1). 48pp. The tasks of the doctor, banker, farmer, merchant, and other professions are explained and placed in historical context. Also use *Ancient Greek Women* and *Ancient Greek Children*. (Rev: HBG 3/03; SLJ 12/02)

15868 Minnis, Ivan. *You Are in Ancient Greece* (3–6). Illus. Series: You Are There! 2004, Raintree LB $26.36 (1-4109-0617-5); paper $7.50 (1-4109-1009-1). 32pp. In present-tense narrative, Minnis introduces the sites, sounds, food, and varied living conditions of ancient Greece. (Rev: SLJ 2/05) [938]

15869 Nardo, Don. *Ancient Athens* (5–8). Illus. Series: A Travel Guide To. 2002, Gale $27.45 (1-59018-016-X). 112pp. This fact-filled "guidebook" introduces aspiring travelers to everyday life in ancient Athens, in addition to information on climate, geography, important sights, and so forth. (Rev: BL 1/1–15/03; SLJ 2/03) [914.75]

15870 Nardo, Don. *Ancient Greece* (4–6). Illus. Series: Life During the Great Civilizations. 2004,

Gale/Blackbirch LB $18.96 (1-56711-741-4). 48pp. Nardo explores day-to-day life in ancient Greece, looking at everything from clothes and jobs to social structures and religion.

15871 Nardo, Don. *Ancient Greece* (3–5). Illus. Series: Daily Life. 2002, Gale LB $21.54 (0-7377-0956-1). 48pp. Nardo presents material on everyday life in ancient Greece, covering everything from food and dress to politics and the rights of women and slaves in an easy-to-read style. (Rev: BL 12/1/02; SLJ 9/02) [938]

15872 Nardo, Don. *Greek Temples* (5–7). Illus. Series: Famous Structures. 2002, Watts LB $24.00 (0-531-12035-X); paper $8.95 (0-531-16225-7). 64pp. Nardo looks at the construction, elements, use, and importance of ancient Greek temples, with illustrations. (Rev: BL 9/1/02; SLJ 8/02) [726]

15873 Odijk, Pamela. *The Greeks* (4–7). Illus. Series: Ancient World. 1989, Silver Burdett LB $14.95 (0-382-09884-6). 48pp. An oversize book that covers history, art, architecture, clothing, and other aspects of ancient Greece. (Rev: BL 1/15/90; SLJ 5/90) [938]

15874 Pipe, Jim. *Trojan Horse* (3–5). Illus. by Roger Hutchins and Donald Hartley. Series: Mystery History. 1997, Millbrook LB $23.90 (0-7613-0614-5). 32pp. Using games, puzzles, and hidden pictures, this simple account introduces the causes of the Trojan War, the people involved, and the ruse that ended it. (Rev: HBG 3/98; SLJ 4/98) [938]

15875 Powell, Anton. *Ancient Greece*. Rev. ed. (5–8). Illus. Series: Cultural Atlas for Young People. 2003, Facts on File $35.00 (0-8160-5146-1). 96pp. Colorful topical spreads introduce readers to the culture, history, and politics of ancient Greece, with information on the Olympics, daily life, and women's role. (Rev: SLJ 1/04) [938]

15876 Rees, Rosemary. *The Ancient Greeks* (3–4). Illus. Series: Understanding People in the Past. 1997, Heinemann $24.22 (0-431-07790-8). 64pp. Photos of museum artifacts plus maps, diagrams, and drawings are used liberally to introduce such topics about the ancient Greeks as their history, accomplishments, buildings, Olympic games, theater, family life, and trade. (Rev: SLJ 9/97) [938]

15877 Ross, Stewart. *Daily Life* (4–7). Illus. Series: Ancient Greece. 2000, Bedrick $18.95 (0-87226-599-4). 48pp. An attractive volume that explores daily life in ancient Greece with coverage of topics including food, dress, eating habits, war, and religion. (Rev: BL 1/1–15/01; HBG 10/00) [938]

15878 Ross, Stewart. *Greek Theatre* (4–7). Series: Ancient Greece. 2000, Bedrick $18.95 (0-87226-597-8). 48pp. This book describes ancient Greek theaters and their parts and introduces the major playwrights and their works. (Rev: BL 1/1–15/01; HBG 10/00; SLJ 9/00) [938]

15879 Schomp, Virginia. *The Ancient Greeks* (5–8). Series: Cultures of the Past. 1995, Benchmark LB $28.50 (0-7614-0070-2). Using quotations from period literature and many photographs and drawings, this volume examines the history of ancient Greece, its culture, and the importance of the

numerous Greek gods and goddesses. (Rev: BR 9–10/96; SLJ 6/96) [938]

15880 Shuter, Jane. *The Acropolis* (5–7). Series: Visiting the Past. 1999, Heinemann LB $24.22 (1-57572-855-9). 32pp. As well as describing the main buildings found in ancient Greece, this account uses double-page spreads to introduce the daily life and culture of the Athenians. (Rev: SLJ 3/00) [938]

15881 Shuter, Jane. *Builders, Traders and Craftsmen* (4–5). Series: Ancient Greece. 1999, Heinemann LB $14.95 (1-57572-736-6). 32pp. This book covers the builders in ancient Greece who worked on the Parthenon, the craftsmen who made clothing, statues, and pottery, and the merchants who traded goods for grain. (Rev: HBG 10/99; SLJ 7/99) [938]

15882 Shuter, Jane. *Cities and Citizens* (4–5). Series: Ancient Greece. 1999, Heinemann LB $14.95 (1-57572-738-2). 32pp. This book on ancient Greece describes city-states and the interests and social life of citizens including theater, acting, and sports. (Rev: HBG 10/99; SLJ 7/99) [938]

15883 Shuter, Jane. *Discoveries, Inventions and Ideas* (2–5). Series: Ancient Greece. 1999, Heinemann LB $14.95 (1-57572-739-0). 32pp. Following a map and timeline, this book covers many Greek innovations such as the development of libraries, advances in medicine, and progress in mapmaking. (Rev: HBG 10/99; SLJ 7/99) [938]

15884 Shuter, Jane. *Farmers and Fighters* (2–5). Series: Ancient Greece. 1999, Heinemann LB $14.95 (1-57572-737-4). 32pp. A heavily illustrated book that describes various aspects of warfare and the weapons used plus an account of farming methods, tools, and food preparation. (Rev: HBG 10/99; SLJ 7/99) [938]

15885 Solway, Andrew. *Ancient Greece* (3–6). Illus. by Peter Connolly. Series: Ancient World. 2001, Oxford $18.95 (0-19-910810-2). 64pp. Exceptional artwork and detailed descriptions of life and institutions in ancient Greece. (Rev: BL 3/1/02; HBG 3/02; SLJ 2/02) [938.04]

15886 Steele, Philip. *Clothes and Crafts in Ancient Greece* (4–6). Series: Clothing and Crafts in History. 2000, Gareth Stevens LB $21.27 (0-8368-2734-1). 32pp. This book describes such crafts as pottery, metalwork, architecture, temple decorations, paintings, and textiles as well as outlining projects including creating a soldier's shield and making a painting for a palace wall. (Rev: BL 1/1–15/01; HBG 10/01) [938]

15887 Tyler, Deborah. *The Greeks and Troy* (4–7). Illus. Series: Hidden Worlds. 1993, Dillon $13.95 (0-87518-537-1). 32pp. The story of the Trojan War is retold, along with a tour of the ruins of Troy and a re-creation of what it once was. (Rev: BL 12/1/93) [938]

15888 Woodford, Susan. *The Parthenon* (6–8). Illus. 1981, Cambridge Univ. Pr. paper $13.95 (0-521-22629-5). 48pp. The history and structure of the Parthenon and a description of the religion of ancient Greece.

Rome

15889 Ash, Rhiannon. *Roman Colosseum* (3–5). Illus. by Mike Bell, et al. Series: Mystery History. 1997, Millbrook LB $23.90 (0-7613-0613-7). 32pp. Games, puzzles, hidden pictures, and a simple text are used to introduce the Colosseum in Rome and the activities it housed. (Rev: HBG 3/98; SLJ 4/98) [937]

15890 Blacklock, Dyan. *The Roman Army* (5–8). Illus. by David Kennett. 2004, Walker $17.95 (0-8027-8896-3). 48pp. The soldiers, weaponry, fighting techniques, and ingenuity of the Romans are detailed here in clear text and effective cartoon-style illustrations. (Rev: BL 3/1/04*; SLJ 4/04) [355]

15891 Butterfield, Moira. *Going to War in Roman Times* (5–7). Illus. Series: Armies of the Past. 2001, Watts LB $24.00 (0-531-14591-3); paper $6.95 (0-531-16352-0). 32pp. Soldiers, weapons, and military strategies of Roman times are presented with many illustrations and a timeline. (Rev: SLJ 10/01) [355.00937]

15892 Chapman, Gillian. *The Romans* (4–7). Series: Crafts from the Past. 1998, Heinemann LB $25.64 (1-57572-734-X). 39pp. Using double-page spreads, this work describes Roman culture while outlining several craft projects inspired by art objects, places, or people. (Rev: HBG 10/99; SLJ 2/99) [937]

15893 Clare, John D., ed. *Classical Rome* (3–6). Illus. Series: Living History. 1993, Harcourt $16.95 (0-15-200513-7). 64pp. With informative text and photos showing people in period costume, this is a good introduction to ancient Rome. (Rev: BL 2/15/93) [937.06]

15894 Corbishley, Mike. *Ancient Rome*. Rev. ed. (5–8). Illus. Series: Cultural Atlas for Young People. 2003, Facts on File $35.00 (0-8160-5147-X). 96pp. Colorful topical spreads introduce readers to the culture, history, and politics of ancient Rome, with information on architecture and major cities of the provinces. (Rev: SLJ 1/04) [937]

15895 Corbishley, Mike. *Growing Up in Ancient Rome* (3–5). Illus. by Christine Molan. Series: Growing Up In. 1993, Troll paper $4.95 (0-8167-2722-8). 32pp. The social life and customs of ancient Rome are covered, with a particular focus on the life-style of children. (Rev: BL 1/15/94) [937]

15896 Curry, Jane Louise. *Brave Cloelia: Retold from the Account in the History of Early Rome by the Roman Historian Titus Livius* (2–4). Illus. by Jeff Crosby. 2004, Getty Publications $16.95 (0-89236-763-6). 32pp. A brave Roman girl earns the respect of the Etruscan invader in this picture book based on the writing of Livy. (Rev: BL 11/15/04; SLJ 2/05) [937]

15897 Dargie, Richard. *Ancient Rome* (3–6). Illus. Series: Picturing the Past. 2004, Enchanted Lion $15.95 (1-59270-023-3). 32pp. Well-written two-page chapters cover geography, history, government, religion, the arts, and home life, with maps, photos and illustrations, and informative sidebars detailing sources. (Rev: SLJ 11/04) [937]

15898 DuTemple, Lesley A. *The Colosseum* (4–7). Series: Great Building Feats. 2003, Lerner LB $27.93 (0-8225-4693-0). Using many colorful diagrams and illustrations, this is the story of the construction of the famous colosseum in Rome. (Rev: BL 11/15/03; HBG 4/04) [937]

15899 Ganeri, Anita. *The Ancient Romans* (3–5). Series: History Starts Here! 2000, Raintree LB $22.83 (0-7398-1349-8). 32pp. A brief overview that introduces ancient Rome, its daily life, culture, social structure, history, and fall. (Rev: HBG 10/00; SLJ 7/00) [937]

15900 Guittard, Charles. *The Romans: Life in the Empire* (4–6). Trans. by Mary K. LaRose. Illus. by Annie-Claude Martin. Series: People of the Past. 1992, Millbrook LB $22.40 (1-56294-200-X). 64pp. This account presents an overview of how life was lived in the Roman Empire and gives information on such topics as history, culture, and religion. (Rev: BL 10/15/92) [937]

15901 Hart, Avery, and Sandra Gallagher. *Ancient Rome! Exploring the Culture, People and Ideas of This Powerful Empire* (4–6). Illus. by Michael Kline. Series: A Kaleidoscope Kids Book. 2002, Williamson paper $10.95 (1-885593-60-0). 96pp. A fact-filled overview that introduces readers to all aspects of ancient Rome — history, legends and myths, government, transportation, wars, key individuals, and so forth — and provides activities such as building a triumphal arch. (Rev: SLJ 3/03)

15902 Hodge, Susie. *Ancient Roman Art* (4–8). Series: Art in History. 1997, Heinemann LB $24.22 (1-57572-552-5). 32pp. This slim, well-illustrated volume outlines Roman contributions to architecture, sculpture, pottery, and mosaics. (Rev: SLJ 5/98) [937.6]

15903 Humphrey, Kathryn L. *Pompeii: Nightmare at Midday* (4–6). Illus. 1995, Houghton Mifflin $9.28 (0-395-73265-4). 64pp. The destruction caused by the eruption of Mount Vesuvius in A.D. 79. (Rev: BL 4/15/90) [937]

15904 Johnson, Stephen. *A Roman Fort* (3–6). Illus. Series: Magnifications. 2000, Bedrick $18.95 (0-87226-650-8). 48pp. This introduction to Roman forts uses close-up pictures to describe a fort's layout, barracks, lifestyle, amusements, religion, and hygiene. (Rev: BL 10/15/00; HBG 3/01; SLJ 1/01) [355.7]

15905 Jovinelly, Joann, and Jason Netelkos. *The Crafts and Culture of the Romans* (5–8). Series: Crafts of the Ancient World. 2002, Rosen LB $29.25 (0-8239-3513-2). 48pp. The daily life and contributions of the ancient Romans are covered, as well as such craft projects as designing a toga. (Rev: BL 5/15/02; SLJ 6/02) [937]

15906 Macaulay, David. *City: A Story of Roman Planning and Construction* (6–8). Illus. by author. 1983, Houghton Mifflin $18.00 (0-395-19492-X); paper $8.95 (0-395-34922-2). 112pp. The imaginary Roman city of Verbonia is constructed through accurate and finely detailed drawings.

15907 MacDonald, Fiona. *Ancient Rome* (3–6). Illus. Series: 100 Things You Should Know About. 2002,

Mason Crest LB $18.95 (1-59084-446-7). 48pp. Organized topically, this collection of 100 facts covers history, government, religion, daily life, dress, and cuisine, and will appeal to reluctant readers. (Rev: SLJ 6/03) [937]

15908 MacDonald, Fiona. *I Wonder Why Romans Wore Togas and Other Questions About Ancient Rome* (2–4). Illus. Series: I Wonder Why. 1997, Kingfisher $9.95 (0-7534-5057-7). 32pp. Each double-page spread in this book answers two or three basic questions about the ancient Romans, how they lived, their empire, and their accomplishments. (Rev: HBG 3/98; SLJ 9/97) [937]

15909 MacDonald, Fiona. *Women in Ancient Rome* (4–8). Series: The Other Half of History. 2000, NTC $17.95 (0-87226-570-6). 48pp. Topics about women in ancient Rome include their roles at home and at work, their health and beauty, and famous individuals. (Rev: HBG 3/01; SLJ 9/00) [937]

15910 Malam, John. *You Wouldn't Want to Be a Roman Gladiator! Gory Things You'd Rather Not Know* (4–6). Illus. by David Antram. Series: You Wouldn't Want To. 2001, Watts LB $25.00 (0-531-14598-0); paper $9.95 (0-531-16204-4). 32pp. Cartoon art belies the grimness of the content in this book in which readers will find plenty of hard information on how gladiators were acquired and trained, their rules of battle, and details of other savage forms of entertainment. (Rev: SLJ 9/01)

15911 Mann, Elizabeth. *The Roman Colosseum* (4–7). Illus. Series: Wonders of the World. 1998, Mikaya $19.95 (0-9650493-3-7). 48pp. An oversize book that is crammed with factual material on the Colosseum in Rome. (Rev: BL 12/15/98; SLJ 2/99) [937]

15912 Markel, Rita J. *Your Travel Guide to Ancient Rome* (4–6). Illus. Series: Passport to History. 2003, Lerner LB $26.60 (0-8225-3071-6). 96pp. Information about ancient Rome — everything from historical anecdotes to profiles of key indviduals to details of dress and behavior — is conveyed in the style of a travel guide complete with photographs and prints. (Rev: BL 2/15/04; HBG 4/04; SLJ 4/04) [937]

15913 Minnis. *Ancient Rome* (3–6). Series: Raintree Perspectives. 2004, Raintree LB $25.70 (1-4109-0618-3). 32pp. Double-page spreads with plenty of illustrations and a low readling level introduce readers to ancient Rome's culture and lifestyle. (Rev: BL 12/1/04; SLJ 2/05) [937]

15914 Morley, Jacqueline. *A Roman Villa* (4–6). Illus. by John James. Series: Inside Story. 1992, Bedrick LB $18.95 (0-87226-360-6). 48pp. Through many double-page spreads and cutaway drawings, the interiors and exteriors of Roman villas are explored. (Rev: BL 12/15/92; SLJ 1/93) [937]

15915 Nardo, Don. *Ancient Rome* (4–6). Illus. Series: Life During the Great Civilizations. 2004, Gale/Blackbirch LB $18.96 (1-56711-742-2). 48pp. Nardo explores day-to-day life in ancient Rome, looking at everything from clothes and jobs to social structures and religion.

15916 Nardo, Don. *Ancient Rome* (4–6). Series: Daily Life. 2002, Gale LB $21.54 (0-7377-0612-0).

48pp. In this look at daily life in Rome, Nardo covers home and family life, work and education, public baths, and religion, and looks at the roles of men and women, young and old, rich and poor, and free men and slaves. (Rev: SLJ 7/02)

15917 Nardo, Don. *Roman Amphitheaters* (5–7). Illus. Series: Famous Structures. 2002, Watts LB $24.00 (0-531-12036-8); paper $8.95 (0-531-16224-9). 64pp. A clear overview of the construction, elements, use, and importance of ancient Roman amphitheaters, with illustrations. (Rev: BL 9/1/02; SLJ 8/02) [725]

15918 Nardo, Don. *The Roman Empire* (4–6). Illus. Series: History of the World. 2002, Gale LB $23.70 (0-7377-0775-5). 48pp. A concise overview of the important events and figures of the Roman Empire, with discussion of how archaeological finds have contributed to our knowledge. (Rev: SLJ 5/02)

15919 Ochoa, George. *The Assassination of Julius Caesar* (5–8). Series: Turning Points in World History. 1991, Silver Burdett LB $14.95 (0-382-24130-4); paper $7.95 (0-382-24136-3). A study of the circumstances surrounding the murder of the Roman leader and its historical impact. (Rev: BL 3/15/92) [937]

15920 Odijk, Pamela. *The Romans* (4–7). Illus. Series: Ancient World. 1989, Silver Burdett LB $14.95 (0-382-09885-4). 48pp. An oversize book about the ancient Romans and their way of life. (Rev: BL 1/15/90; SLJ 5/90) [937]

15921 Patent, Dorothy Hinshaw. *Lost City of Pompeii* (4–7). Series: Frozen in Time. 1999, Benchmark LB $27.07 (0-7614-0785-5). 64pp. The story of the ancient city of Pompeii, its destruction, and how its excavation has given us a wealth of information about ancient Rome. (Rev: BL 2/1/00; HBG 10/00; SLJ 3/00) [937]

15922 Petrén, Birgitta, and Elisabetta Putini. *Why Are You Calling Me a Barbarian?* (2–5). Trans. from Italian by Mary Becker. Illus. by Lara Artone and Monica Barsotti. 1999, Getty Museum paper $17.95 (0-89236-559-5). 59pp. Set in the time of the Romans, a slave girl and the son of a Scandinavian merchant compare their lives and lifestyles in this colorful introduction to life in the ancient Roman Empire from a non-Roman point of view. (Rev: SLJ 4/00) [937]

15923 Rees, Rosemary. *The Ancient Romans* (3–6). Series: Understanding People in the Past. 1999, Heinemann LB $15.95 (1-57572-890-7). 64pp. Double-page spreads with illustrations of historical sites, artifacts, art, and maps help the reader envision the daily life and contributions of the ancient Romans. (Rev: BL 6/1–15/99) [937]

15924 Ridd, Stephen, ed. *Julius Caesar in Gaul and Britain* (5–8). Illus. Series: History Eyewitness. 1995, Raintree LB $24.26 (0-8114-8283-9). An edited version of Caesar's fascinating accounts of the Gallic Wars, with pictures and maps. (Rev: BL 4/15/95; SLJ 5/95) [937.05]

15925 Sheehan, Sean. *Ancient Rome* (4–6). Series: History Beneath Your Feet. 1999, Raintree LB $25.69 (0-8172-5752-7). 48pp. This account, which focuses on the ruins of Pompeii, re-creates the daily life of the Romans and describes how archaeologists have gathered this information. (Rev: HBG 10/00; SLJ 3/00) [937]

15926 Sheehan, Sean, and Pat Levy. *Rome* (5–10). Series: Ancient World. 1998, Raintree LB $27.12 (0-8172-5057-3). A brief history of Rome and the Roman Empire, including its culture, buildings, amusements, and emperors. (Rev: BL 1/1–15/99; HBG 3/99; SLJ 3/99) [937]

15927 Snedden, Robert. *Technology in the Time of Ancient Rome* (4–8). Series: Technology in the Time Of. 1998, Raintree LB $27.12 (0-8172-4876-5). 48pp. Weaving, food production, construction, transportation, and metalwork are covered in this discussion of Roman technology. (Rev: HBG 10/98; SLJ 3/99) [937]

15928 Solway, Andrew. *Ancient Rome* (3–6). Illus. by Peter Connolly. Series: Ancient World. 2001, Oxford $18.95 (0-19-910809-9). 64pp. Exceptional artwork and detailed descriptions of daily life, culture, religion, and sports in ancient Rome. (Rev: BL 3/1/02; HBG 3/02; SLJ 1/02) [937.6]

15929 Solway, Andrew. *Rome: In Spectacular Cross-Section* (4–7). Illus. by Stephen Biesty. 2003, Scholastic paper $18.95 (0-439-45546-4). 32pp. An inside look at life in ancient Rome, with views of a private home, the Colosseum, the docks, and a bustling festival. (Rev: BL 2/15/03; HBG 10/03; SLJ 7/03) [937]

15930 Steele, Philip. *Clothes and Crafts in Roman Times* (4–6). Illus. Series: Clothing and Crafts in History. 2000, Gareth Stevens $21.27 (0-8368-2737-6). 32pp. After a brief introduction to Roman history, this book introduces Roman artisans and gives directions for craft projects including making a dolphin brooch, a mosaic, an actor's mask, and small clay statues. (Rev: BL 1/1–15/01; HBG 3/02) [745]

15931 Steele, Philip. *Food and Feasts in Ancient Rome* (4–8). Illus. Series: Food and Feasts. 1994, New Discovery LB $14.95 (0-02-726321-5). 32pp. A description of food and food preparation in ancient Rome and how it differed among the classes, as well as a selection of tasty recipes. (Rev: BCCB 10/94; SLJ 12/94) [937]

15932 Stroud, Jonathan. *Ancient Rome: A Guide to the Glory of Imperial Rome* (4–7). Series: Sightseers. 2000, Kingfisher $8.95 (0-7534-5235-9). 30pp. This book on ancient Rome is presented like a handbook for tourists, with material on such topics as accommodations, shopping, key sites, etc. (Rev: HBG 3/01; SLJ 9/00) [937]

15933 Watkins, Richard. *Gladiator* (5–8). Illus. 1997, Houghton Mifflin $18.00 (0-395-82656-X). In 12 brief chapters, 700 years of Roman gladiator sports are described, including equipment, animals used, contests, and the architecture and construction of the great amphitheaters. (Rev: BL 11/1/97; BR 9–10/98; HBG 3/98; SLJ 10/97*) [937]

15934 Whittock, Martyn. *The Roman Empire* (4–6). Illus. Series: Biographical History. 1996, Bedrick $17.95 (0-87226-118-2). 64pp. A history of the Roman Empire, its expansion, and life in the republic are given, with many short biographies and excerpts from both primary and secondary sources. (Rev: SLJ 9/96) [937]

15935 Williams, Brian. *Ancient Roman Women* (5–8). Illus. Series: People in the Past. 2002, Heinemann LB $27.07 (1-58810-632-2). 48pp. A look at the life of, and options open to, women in ancient Rome. (Rev: BL 3/1/03; HBG 10/03; SLJ 4/03) [305.8]

Middle Ages

15936 *Castles* (PS–3). Illus. Series: First Discovery. 1993, Scholastic $12.95 (0-590-46377-2). 30pp. A highly visual introduction to castles that supplies basic information with an interactive approach. (Rev: BL 10/1/93; SLJ 8/93) [940.1]

15937 Child, John, et al. *The Crusades* (4–6). Illus. Series: Biographical History. 1996, Bedrick $17.77 (0-87226-119-0). 64pp. Describes the nature and the causes of the various Crusades and covers important events, battles, and people. (Rev: SLJ 9/96) [940.1]

15938 Clare, John D. *Fourteenth-Century Towns* (3–6). Illus. Series: Living History. 1993, Harcourt $16.95 (0-15-200515-3). 64pp. Life in a medieval town is portrayed with double-page spreads and informative text. (Rev: BL 2/15/923) [307]

15939 Clare, John D., ed. *Knights in Armor* (3–6). Illus. 1992, Harcourt $17.00 (0-15-200508-0). 64pp. Photos of people in period costume help bring to life this historical era. (Rev: BL 12/1/92; SLJ 11/92) [940]

15940 Corbishley, Mike. *The Medieval World* (5–7). Illus. Series: Timelink. 1993, Bedrick LB $18.95 (0-87226-362-2). 64pp. Using a chronological approach, this book covers the years 450 through 1500 in Europe, Asia, Africa, and the Americas. (Rev: SLJ 8/93) [940.1]

15941 Dawson, Imogen. *Clothes and Crafts in the Middle Ages* (4–6). Illus. Series: Clothing and Crafts in History. 2000, Gareth Stevens $21.27 (0-8368-2736-8). 32pp. After a brief history of the Middle Ages, craftsmen and their materials are introduced with projects including making medieval clothing, jewelry, a pilgrim's badge, and an illuminated manuscript. (Rev: BL 1/1–15/01; HBG 3/02) [745]

15942 Dawson, Imogen. *Food and Feasts in the Middle Ages* (4–8). Series: Food and Feasts. 1994, New Discovery LB $14.95 (0-02-726324-X). 32pp. This account re-creates the culinary aspects of the Middle Ages, with material on farming, dishes, and town and city fare plus several recipes and many attractive illustrations. (Rev: BCCB 10/94; SLJ 12/94) [940.1]

15943 Doherty, Katherine M., and Craig A. Doherty. *King Richard the Lionhearted and the Crusades in World History* (5–9). Series: In World History. 2002, Enslow LB $20.95 (0-7660-1459-2). 128pp. This introduction to Richard and his chivalrous yet cruel personality conveys the religious fervor and economic needs that inspired the Crusades. (Rev: BL 4/1/02; HBG 10/02; SLJ 6/02)

15944 Dunn, John M. *Life During the Black Death* (5–9). Series: The Way People Live. 2000, Lucent LB $27.45 (1-56006-542-7). 96pp. This account traces the spread of the Black Death from Mongolia in 1320 to Western Europe and its lasting effects on history, society, and culture. (Rev: HBG 10/00; SLJ 6/00) [940]

15945 Galloway, Priscilla. *Archers, Alchemists, and 98 Other Medieval Jobs You Might Have Loved or Loathed* (4–6). Illus. by Martha Newbigging. 2003, Annick LB $24.95 (1-55037-811-2); paper $14.95 (1-55037-810-4). 96pp. One hundred medieval occupations are described in conversational style, with cartoon illustrations and informative castle-shaped sidebars. (Rev: BL 1/1–15/04; SLJ 1/04) [909.07]

15946 George, Linda S. *800* (5–8). Illus. Series: Around the World. 2003, Marshall Cavendish LB $28.50 (0-7614-1085-6). 96pp. This absorbing look at civilizations around the world in the year 800 includes color reproductions, photographs, a timeline, a glossary, and lists of resources. (Rev: BL 6/1–15/03; HBG 3/03) [909.07]

15947 Hart, Avery, and Paul Mantell. *Knights and Castles: 50 Hands-On Activities to Experience the Middle Ages* (3–6). Illus. 1998, Williamson paper $10.95 (1-885593-17-1). 96pp. Directions for making a catapult, a castle, and a knight's helmet are three of the projects in this craft book that also supplies good information about life in the Middle Ages. (Rev: BL 11/15/98; SLJ 2/99) [940.1]

15948 Hinds, Kathryn. *The Castle* (5–8). Series: Life in the Middle Ages. 2000, Marshall Cavendish LB $28.50 (0-7614-1007-4). 80pp. A book that explores the construction and parts of the medieval castle as well as the lifestyles of those who lived in them, from kings and knights to humble servants. (Rev: BL 3/1/01; HBG 3/01; SLJ 3/01) [940]

15949 Hinds, Kathryn. *The Church* (5–8). Series: Life in the Middle Ages. 2000, Marshall Cavendish LB $28.50 (0-7614-1008-2). 80pp. Explains the role of the church and the clergy in medieval life as well as giving examples of church construction. (Rev: BL 3/1/01; HBG 3/01; SLJ 3/01) [940]

15950 Hinds, Kathryn. *The City* (5–8). Illus. Series: Life in the Middle Ages. 2000, Marshall Cavendish LB $28.50 (0-7614-1005-8). 80pp. A beautifully designed book that tells about daily life in medieval cities and their functions as centers of learning, commerce, worship, construction, and recreation as well as disease and disaster. (Rev: BL 2/15/01; HBG 3/01; SLJ 3/01) [940.1]

15951 Hinds, Kathryn. *The Countryside* (5–8). Illus. Series: Life in the Middle Ages. 2000, Marshall Cavendish LB $28.50 (0-7614-1006-6). 80pp. The author explains manorialism — a primary social structure in rural areas during the Middle Ages — and describes a medieval village, its residents, and their work and pastimes. (Rev: BL 2/15/01; HBG 3/01; SLJ 3/01) [940.1]

15952 Howe, John. *Knights* (3–6). Illus. 1995, Orchard $18.95 (0-531-09456-1). 16pp. Aspects of the Middle Ages — like castles, armor, and the Crusades — come alive in this pop-up book. (Rev: BL 2/1/96) [940]

15953 MacDonald, Fiona. *A Medieval Castle* (4–6). Illus. by Mark Bergin. Series: Inside Story. 1990, Bedrick LB $18.95 (0-87226-340-1). 48pp. An oversize volume that surveys the development of castles and highlights life in the Middle Ages. (Rev: BL 3/1/91; SLJ 6/91) [940.1]

15954 MacDonald, Fiona. *Medieval Cathedral* (3–6). Illus. by John James. Series: Inside Story. 1991, Bedrick $18.95 (0-87226-350-9). 48pp. This book explains in many pictures how cathedrals were built in the Middle Ages, their various parts and the roles they played in medieval civilization. (Rev: BL 12/1/91; SLJ 12/91) [726.6]

15955 MacDonald, Fiona. *Women in Medieval Times* (4–8). Series: The Other Half of History. 2000, NTC $17.95 (0-87226-569-2). 48pp. Using a topical arrangement this book discusses the role of women in medieval times in the castle, in the workplace, and at court. (Rev: HBG 3/01; SLJ 9/00) [940]

15956 McNeill, Sarah. *The Middle Ages* (3–6). Illus. Series: Spotlights. 1998, Oxford $10.95 (0-19-521394-7). 46pp. An eye-catching account of the Middle Ages, tracing important events, culture, and social conditions. (Rev: BL 12/1/98; SLJ 10/98) [909.07]

15957 Marston, Elsa. *The Byzantine Empire* (5–8). Series: Cultures of the Past. 2002, Marshall Cavendish $19.95 (0-7614-1495-9). 80pp. Well-written text and colorful graphics present the history and culture of the surviving eastern part of the Roman Empire. (Rev: BL 1/1–15/03; HBG 3/03; SLJ 2/03) [949.5]

15958 Martin, Alex. *Knights and Castles: Exploring History Through Art* (5–8). Illus. Series: Picture That! 2004, Two-Can $19.95 (1-58728-441-3). 64pp. Paintings serve as the vehicle to draw students into the discussion of life in Europe during the late medieval period. (Rev: BL 11/1/04; SLJ 2/05) [940.1]

15959 Morgan, Gwyneth. *Life in a Medieval Village* (5–7). Illus. by author. 1991, HarperCollins paper $14.00 (0-06-092046-7). A story of activities in a medieval village and of the church's importance in life in the Middle Ages. [306.094265]

15960 Osband, Gillian. *Castles* (4–6). Illus. by Robert Andrew. 1991, Orchard $18.95 (0-531-05949-9). 16pp. Impressive and informative pop-ups add to the appeal of this book. (Rev: BL 9/15/91) [728.8]

15961 Pernoud, Regine. *A Day with a Noblewoman* (5–8). Trans. by Dominique Clift. Illus. Series: A Day With. 1997, Runestone LB $27.15 (0-8225-1916-X). After a brief introduction to the Middle Ages, this book describes a busy day in the life of Blanche, the countess of Champagne, a French widow in the 13th century. (Rev: BL 1/1–15/98; HBG 3/98; SLJ 2/98) [940.1]

15962 Pernoud, Regine. *A Day with a Stonecutter* (3–6). Illus. 1997, Runestone LB $22.60 (0-8225-1913-5). 48pp. Includes both an introduction to medieval society and a case study of a stonecutter who is working on a project for an abbey. (Rev: BL 11/1/97; HBG 3/98; SLJ 1/98) [731.4]

15963 Ross, Stewart. *Monarchs* (5–8). Illus. Series: Medieval Realms. 2004, Gale $27.45 (1-59018-535-8). 48pp. This colorfully illustrated, oversize volume explores the structure of European governments during the Middle Ages and such topics as the birth of new nations, wars, and the Crusades. (Rev: BL 10/15/04) [940.1]

15964 Scarry, Huck. *Looking into the Middle Ages* (3–6). Illus. 1985, HarperCollins $12.50 (0-06-025224-3). 12pp. This 12-page pop-up book literally allows readers to look into the Middle Ages — into castles, cathedrals, jousting tournaments. (Rev: BCCB 6/85; BL 9/15/85)

15965 Sherrow, Victoria. *Life in a Medieval Monastery* (5–9). Series: The Way People Live. 2001, Lucent LB $27.45 (1-56006-791-8). 96pp. An absorbing account of religious life in the Middle Ages, with details of clothing, diet, and hairstyles as well as maps and black-and-white reproductions. (Rev: BL 6/1–15/01; SLJ 8/01) [271]

15966 Shuter, Jane. *The Middle Ages* (3–6). Series: History Opens Windows. 1999, Heinemann LB $14.95 (1-57572-886-9). 32pp. This useful account of the medieval period uses double-page spreads and many illustrations to bring the social forces and events of this period to life. (Rev: SLJ 2/00) [940.1]

15967 Steele, Philip. *Castles* (5–7). Illus. 1995, Kingfisher $16.95 (1-85697-547-9). 64pp. In this oversized, well-designed book, castles, jousting, armor, and feast days are described. (Rev: BL 8/95; SLJ 4/95) [940.1]

15968 Steele, Philip. *Knights* (3–6). Illus. 1998, Kingfisher $15.95 (0-7534-5154-9). 64pp. Chivalry, heraldry, tournaments, daily life, and famous knights of fiction are a few of the topics handled in a series of double-page spreads on knighthood in the Middle Ages. (Rev: BL 11/15/98; HBG 3/99) [940.1]

15969 Tanaka, Shelley. *In the Time of Knights: The Real-Life Story of History's Greatest Knight* (4–7). Illus. by Greg Ruhl. Series: I Was There. 2000, Hyperion $16.99 (0-7868-0651-6). 48pp. This fictionalized account of the life of William Marshal, who became a famous knight during the 12th century, also gives a great deal of information on life during the Middle Ages. (Rev: BCCB 2/01; HBG 10/01; SLJ 3/01) [921]

15970 Walker, Jane. *Knights and Castles* (3–6). Illus. Series: 100 Things You Should Know About. 2002, Mason Crest LB $18.95 (1-59084-450-5). 48pp. Information about daily life in the Middle Ages, tournaments, banquets, and battles will appeal to reluctant readers. (Rev: SLJ 6/03) [940.1]

15971 Woolf, Alex. *Education* (5–8). Series: Medieval Realms. 2004, Gale/Lucent LB $27.45 (1-59018-532-3). 48pp. Discusses the forms of education available during the Middle Ages — including apprenticeships, song schools, monastic schools, universities — and who was able to enjoy them and what they learned, ending with material on the rise of humanism. (Rev: SLJ 3/05) [370]

Renaissance

15972 Barter, James. *Renaissance Florence* (5–8). Illus. Series: A Travel Guide To. 2002, Gale $27.45 (1-59018-145-X). 112pp. Travel back in time to Renaissance Florence with this guidebook that gives period-appropriate historical and sight-seeing information as well as a flavor of everyday life in the city. (Rev: BL 1/1–15/03; SLJ 4/03) [914.4]

15973 Day, Nancy. *Your Travel Guide to Renaissance Europe* (4–8). Series: Passport to History. 2000, Lerner LB $26.60 (0-8225-3080-5). 96pp. This book uses a travel guide format to introduce the reader to the life and people of Europe from 1350 to 1550 with coverage of culture, style, inventions, religious beliefs, and scientific discoveries. (Rev: BL 3/1/01; HBG 10/01) [940.2]

15974 Halliwell, Sarah, ed. *The Renaissance: Artists and Writers* (5–8). Series: Who and When? 1997, Raintree LB $28.55 (0-8172-4725-4). 96pp. This introduction to 13 artists and three writers of the Renaissance relies heavily of Giorgi Vasari and his eyewitness book about Renaissance art. (Rev: SLJ 1/98) [940.2]

15975 Hinds, Kathryn. *The City* (5–8). Illus. Series: Life in the Renaissance. 2003, Marshall Cavendish LB $20.95 (0-7614-1678-1). 96pp. Using London, Paris, and Florence among the examples, this entry in a four-volume series explores most aspects of daily life within the walled cities of Western Europe during the 15th and 16th centuries. Also use *The Court* (2003). (Rev: BL 2/1/04; SLJ 4/04) [940.1]

15976 Morley, Jacqueline. *A Renaissance Town* (4–6). Illus. Series: Inside Story. 1997, Bedrick LB $18.95 (0-87226-276-6). 48pp. This richly illustrated book focuses on Florence during the Renaissance, with material on government, social life, customs, art, and the economy. (Rev: BL 2/15/97) [945]

15977 Prum, Deborah Mazzotta. *Rats, Bulls, and Flying Machines: A History of Renaissance and Reformation* (4–8). Illus. Series: Core Chronicles. 1999, Core Knowledge $21.95 (1-890517-19-4); paper $11.95 (1-890517-18-6). 106pp. A handsome volume that gives a basic history of the Renaissance and Reformation and highlights the accomplishments of people such as the Medici family, Machiavelli, Michelangelo, Cervantes, Shakespeare, and Gutenberg. (Rev: BL 12/15/99) [909.08]

15978 Schomp, Virginia. *1500* (5–8). Illus. Series: Around the World. 2003, Marshall Cavendish LB $28.50 (0-7614-1082-1). 96pp. This absorbing look at civilizations around the world in the year 1500 includes color reproductions, photographs, a timeline, a glossary, and lists of resources. (Rev: BL 6/1–15/03; HBG 3/03) [909]

15979 Schomp, Virginia. *The Italian Renaissance* (5–8). Series: Cultures of the Past. 2002, Marshall Cavendish $19.95 (0-7614-1492-4). 80pp. A handsome volume that gives a balanced, well-organized account of the Italian Renaissance, its history, personalities, art, and artifacts. (Rev: BL 1/1–15/03; HBG 3/03) [940.2]

15980 Shuter, Jane. *The Renaissance* (3–6). Series: History Opens Windows. 1999, Heinemann LB $14.95 (1-57572-887-7). 32pp. The people, events, and social forces that produced the Renaissance are described in text and pictures. (Rev: SLJ 2/00) [940.2]

15981 Waldman, Nomi J. *The Italian Renaissance* (5–7). Series: Daily Life. 2004, Gale/KidHaven LB $30.35 (0-7377-1398-4). 48pp. In simple language, this slim volume describes Italy's rebirth, the blossoming of commerce and culture, and daily life for people of different backgrounds. (Rev: SLJ 2/05) [945]

15982 Wood, Tim. *The Renaissance* (5–8). Series: See Through History. 1993, Viking $19.99 (0-670-85149-3). A series of double-page spreads explore the day-to-day lives of people during the Renaissance, including Far East trade, Italian city-states, women at court, art, and technology. (Rev: BL 12/15/93; SLJ 2/94) [940.2]

World War I

15983 Clare, John D., ed. *First World War* (5–8). Illus. Series: Living History. 1995, Gulliver $16.95 (0-15-200087-9). 64pp. Excellent visuals and a vivid text are used in this history of World War I. (Rev: SLJ 6/95) [940.53]

15984 Conway, John Richard. *World War I* (4–6). Illus. Series: U.S. Wars. 2003, Enslow LB $19.95 (0-7660-5142-0). 48pp. Supported by verified and updated Web links, this is a useful overview of the main events of World War I. (Rev: HBG 4/04)

15985 Gay, Kathlyn, and Martin Gay. *World War I* (5–8). Illus. Series: Voices from the Past. 1995, Twenty-First Century LB $25.90 (0-8050-2848-X). 64pp. The causes, major battles, and effects of World War I are covered, with many excerpts from personal accounts. (Rev: BL 12/15/95; SLJ 2/96) [940.3]

15986 George, Linda S. *World War I* (5–8). Series: Letters from the Homefront. 2001, Benchmark LB $28.50 (0-7614-1096-1). 96pp. Life at the front and at home during the First World War is depicted through letters and other firsthand accounts. (Rev: BL 10/15/01; HBG 3/02) [973.9]

15987 Gilbert, Adrian. *Going to War in World War I* (4–6). Illus. Series: Armies of the Past. 2001, Watts LB $23.00 (0-531-14595-6). 32pp. Examines World War I from many perspectives, including strategy, weapons, and its effect on society. (Rev: BL 3/1/02; SLJ 10/01) [355.109041]

15988 Granfield, Linda. *Where Poppies Grow: A World War I Companion* (4–7). 2002, Stoddart $16.95 (0-7737-3319-1). 48pp. The horrors of war

in the trenches are portrayed in this scrapbook full of photographs, propaganda, and ephemera that includes accounts of two Canadian soldiers. (Rev: BL 6/1–15/02; HBG 10/02; SLJ 7/02) [940.3]

15989 Grant, Reg. *World War I: Armistice 1918* (5–8). Series: The World Wars. 2001, Raintree LB $27.12 (0-7398-2753-7). 64pp. The negotiations that ended World War I are detailed here, with discussion of the failure of the League of Nations and the lead-up to World War II. (Rev: SLJ 6/01) [940.3]

15990 Hamilton, John. *Aircraft of World War I* (5–8). Illus. Series: World War I. 2003, ABDO LB $16.95 (1-57765-912-0). 32pp. How aircraft became a valuable military tool for the first time in World War I, and how some of the pilots became internationally famous. (Rev: SLJ 6/04) [940.4]

15991 Hamilton, John. *Battles of World War I* (5–8). Illus. Series: World War I. 2003, ABDO LB $16.95 (1-57765-913-9). 32pp. A review of key battles that took place during the three years before the United States entered the conflict in 1917, with information on key figures. (Rev: SLJ 6/04) [940.4]

15992 Hamilton, John. *Events Leading to World War I* (5–8). Illus. Series: World War I. 2003, ABDO LB $16.95 (1-57765-914-7). 32pp. An evenhanded description of events and circumstances during the years leading up to World War I in each of the countries that became involved in the conflict. (Rev: SLJ 6/04) [940.3]

15993 Hansen, Ole Steen. *Military Aircraft of WWI* (4–7). Series: The Story of Flight. 2003, Crabtree $23.93 (0-7787-1201-X). 32pp. This book introduces in text and pictures the aircraft used by the allies and enemies during World War I. (Rev: BL 10/15/03) [940.3]

15994 Hansen, Ole Steen. *World War I: War in the Trenches* (5–8). Series: The World Wars. 2001, Raintree LB $27.12 (0-7398-2752-9). 64pp. The causes of World War I are introduced, followed by information on the major battles and descriptions of the misery of life in the trenches, with plenty of photographs, reproductions, maps, sidebars, and excerpts from primary sources. (Rev: SLJ 6/01) [940.3]

15995 Marquette, Scott. *World War I* (4–7). Illus. Series: America at War. 2002, Rourke LB $27.93 (1-58952-392-X). 48pp. This book for middle graders studies the war itself and the events that led up to it. [940.3]

15996 Preston, Diana. *Remember the Lusitania!* (5–8). Illus. 2003, Walker LB $23.85 (0-8027-8847-5). 112pp. This gripping account of the sinking of the *Lusitania* includes many personal stories that will hold young readers' attention. (Rev: BL 4/15/03; HB 7–8/03; HBG 10/03; SLJ 7/03) [940.4]

15997 Ross, Stewart. *Assassination in Sarajevo: The Trigger for World War I* (4–9). Illus. by Stefan Chabluk. Series: Point of Impact. 2001, Heinemann LB $24.22 (1-58810-074-X). 32pp. The assassination of the Archduke of Austria, a precipitating factor in World War I, is put into context and the alliances among the world's nations at the time are clearly explained. (Rev: HBG 10/01; SLJ 7/01) [940.3]

15998 Ross, Stewart. *The Battle of the Somme* (5–8). Series: The World Wars. 2003, Raintree LB $28.56 (0-7398-5479-8). 64pp. An examination of the first Battle of the Somme in 1916, an all-out assault on entrenched German forces in northern France by British and French troops, and of the enormous carnage involved. (Rev: HBG 4/04; SLJ 5/04) [940.4]

15999 Ross, Stewart. *Leaders of World War I* (4–8). Illus. Series: World Wars. 2003, Raintree LB $28.56 (0-7398-5481-X). 64pp. Stewart presents concise details on the large cast of world and military leaders involved in this conflict. (Rev: BL 12/1/03; HBG 10/03) [023]

16000 Ross, Stewart. *The Technology of World War I* (4–8). Illus. Series: World Wars. 2003, Raintree LB $28.56 (0-7398-5482-8). 64pp. New technologies used during World War I included torpedoes, mines, submarines, tanks, planes with machine guns, and mustard gas; all are shown here with maps, diagrams, period reproductions, and posters. (Rev: BL 12/1/03; HBG 10/03; SLJ 7/03) [023]

World War II

16001 Adams, Simon. *World War II* (4–8). Illus. 2000, DK $15.95 (0-7894-3298-2). 64pp. Each double-page spread presents a different aspect of World War II, such as the Battle of Britain, military equipment, women at work, and conditions inside the Soviet Union. (Rev: BL 11/1/00) [940.53]

16002 Adler, David A. *Child of the Warsaw Ghetto* (3–6). Illus. by Karen Ritz. 1995, Holiday House LB $15.95 (0-8234-1160-5). 32pp. The story of the Warsaw Ghetto during World War II as seen through the eyes of a survivor. (Rev: BCCB 5/95; BL 4/1/95; SLJ 7/95) [943.8]

16003 Adler, David A. *Hiding from the Nazis* (3–5). Illus. by Karen Ritz. 1997, Holiday House LB $15.95 (0-8234-1288-1). 32pp. This picture book for older children tells how Lore, a young Jewish girl, is hidden and cared for by a Dutch family during World War II. (Rev: BL 11/1/97; HBG 3/98; SLJ 2/98) [940.53]

16004 Adler, David A. *Hilde and Eli: Children of the Holocaust* (3–5). Illus. by Karen Ritz. 1994, Holiday House $16.95 (0-8234-1091-9). 32pp. A picture book that tells the true stories of two Jewish children who were killed in the Holocaust. (Rev: BCCB 11/94; BL 9/15/94; SLJ 12/94) [940.54]

16005 Adler, David A. *We Remember the Holocaust* (4–7). 1995, Holt paper $14.95 (0-8050-3715-2). 147pp. Through interview excerpts, the terrible days of the Holocaust are remembered. (Rev: SLJ 12/89) [940.54]

16006 Allen, Thomas B. *Remember Pearl Harbor: American and Japanese Survivors Tell Their Stories* (5–9). Illus. 2001, National Geographic $17.95 (0-7922-6690-0). 64pp. First-person accounts by Japanese and American men and women give readers a close-up view of the 1941 Japanese attack on Pearl Harbor, with maps and photographs. (Rev: BL 9/1/01; HBG 3/02; SLJ 9/01*) [940.54]

16007 Altman, Linda J. *Crimes and Criminals of the Holocaust* (5–10). Illus. Series: Holocaust in History. 2004, Enslow LB $20.95 (0-7660-1995-0). 104pp. This book focuses on the end of World War II and the war crimes trials in Nuremberg as well as other cases such as that of Adolf Eichmann. (Rev: BL 5/1/04) [940.53]

16008 Altman, Linda J. *The Forgotten Victims of the Holocaust* (5–10). Illus. Series: Holocaust in History. 2003, Enslow LB $20.95 (0-7660-1993-4). 104pp. Altman looks at populations victimized by the Nazis that are often overlooked: Poles, Russians, gypsies, homosexuals, and the disabled. Also use *The Jewish Victims of the Holocaust* (2003), which describes Hitler's genocide of the Jews. (Rev: BL 7/03; HBG 4/04; SLJ 10/03) [940.53]

16009 Altman, Linda J. *Impact of the Holocaust* (5–10). Illus. Series: Holocaust in History. 2004, Enslow LB $20.95 (0-7660-1996-9). 104pp. This book discusses the Holocaust's influence in the creation of a homeland for the Jews and a Universal Declaration of Human Rights. (Rev: BL 5/1/04) [940.53]

16010 Altman, Linda Jacobs. *The Jewish Victims of the Holocaust* (5–10). Illus. Series: Holocaust in History. 2003, Enslow LB $20.95 (0-7660-1992-6). 104pp. A look at the horrors of the Holocaust. (Rev: BL 7/03; HBG 4/04; SLJ 10/03) [940.53]

16011 Anflick, Charles. *Resistance: Teen Partisan and Resisters Who Fought Nazi Tyranny* (5–9). Series: Teen Witnesses to the Holocaust. 1999, Rosen LB $26.50 (0-8239-2847-0). 64pp. This volume celebrates the teenagers who fought against the Nazis in ghettos, concentration camps, inside Germany, and in the lands that the Nazis conquered. (Rev: BL 4/15/98; BR 9–10/99) [940.54]

16012 Auerbacher, Inge. *I Am a Star: Child of the Holocaust* (5–7). Illus. 1993, Puffin paper $5.99 (0-14-036401-3). 80pp. The memoirs of a former child survivor of the Terezin concentration camp in Czechoslovakia. (Rev: BCCB 7–8/87; BL 6/1/87; SLJ 4/87) [940.5]

16013 Axelrod, Toby. *In the Camps: Teens Who Survived the Nazi Concentration Camps* (5–9). Series: Teen Witnesses to the Holocaust. 1999, Rosen LB $18.50 (0-8239-2844-6). These are the stories of teenagers who survived the death camps, their despair and sadness, and the hope they maintained despite the horror around them. (Rev: BL 7/99) [940.54]

16014 Axelrod, Toby. *Rescuers Defying the Nazis: Non-Jewish Teens Who Rescued Jews* (5–8). Series: Teen Witnesses to the Holocaust. 1999, Rosen LB $26.50 (0-8239-2848-9). Inspiring stories of teenage gentiles in Poland, Denmark, and Germany who risked their lives to rescue Jews from the Holocaust. (Rev: BL 7/99; SLJ 8/99) [940.54]

16015 Ayer, Eleanor. *In the Ghettos: Teens Who Survived the Ghettos of the Holocaust* (5–8). Series: Teens Witnesses to the Holocaust. 1999, Rosen LB $26.50 (0-8239-2845-4). The harrowing stories of courageous teenagers who survived life in the ghettos of Lodz, Theresienstadt, and Warsaw. (Rev: BL 7/99; SLJ 8/99) [940.54]

16016 Ballard, Robert D. *Exploring the Bismarck* (5–8). Illus. 1991, Scholastic $15.95 (0-590-44268-6). 64pp. This is an account of the history and rediscovery of the German battleship *Bismarck*, which was sunk more than 50 years ago. (Rev: BL 1/1/91; SLJ 8/91) [943]

16017 Black, Wallace B., and Jean F. Blashfield. *Bataan and Corregidor* (5–7). Illus. Series: World War II 50th Anniversary. 1991, Macmillan LB $12.95 (0-89686-557-6). 48pp. Using documentary photographs, this book examines the major events in the struggle over the Philippines in World War II. (Rev: BL 12/1/91; SLJ 2/92) [940.54]

16018 Black, Wallace B., and Jean F. Blashfield. *Battle of Britain* (5–7). Illus. Series: World War II 50th Anniversary. 1991, Macmillan LB $12.95 (0-89686-553-3). 48pp. The story of Britain's valiant stand against the German power. Also use *Blitzkrieg* (1991). (Rev: BL 6/15/91; SLJ 9/91) [940.53]

16019 Black, Wallace B., and Jean F. Blashfield. *Battle of the Atlantic* (5–7). Illus. Series: World War II 50th Anniversary. 1991, Macmillan LB $12.95 (0-89686-558-4). 48pp. The war in the Atlantic Ocean during World War II, when the Allies tried to keep the seas open for the movement of troops and supplies, is retold in text and pictures. (Rev: BL 12/1/91; SLJ 2/92) [940.54]

16020 Black, Wallace B., and Jean F. Blashfield. *Battle of the Bulge* (5–7). Illus. Series: World War II 50th Anniversary. 1993, Macmillan LB $12.95 (0-89686-568-1). 48pp. This account describes Hitler's desperate offensive and his gamble to split the Allied army in two. (Rev: BL 4/15/93) [940.54]

16021 Black, Wallace B., and Jean F. Blashfield. *Bombing Fortress Europe* (5–7). Illus. Series: World War II 50th Anniversary. 1992, Macmillan LB $12.95 (0-89686-562-2). 48pp. The thrilling, heroic exploits of British and American airmen and their war over the skies of Europe are retold in this illustrated account. (Rev: BL 8/92; SLJ 1/93) [940.54]

16022 Black, Wallace B., and Jean F. Blashfield. *D-Day* (5–7). Illus. Series: World War II 50th Anniversary. 1992, Macmillan LB $12.95 (0-89686-566-5). 48pp. The fateful day when the Allied forces invaded France during World War II. (Rev: BL 2/1/93; SLJ 4/93) [940.54]

16023 Black, Wallace B., and Jean F. Blashfield. *Desert Warfare* (5–7). Illus. Series: World War II 50th Anniversary. 1992, Macmillan LB $12.95 (0-89686-561-4). 48pp. This account chronicles the Allied campaigns in North Africa against the desert forces of the Germans and Italians. (Rev: BL 8/92; SLJ 1/93) [940.54]

16024 Black, Wallace B., and Jean F. Blashfield. *Flattops at War* (5–7). Illus. Series: World War II 50th Anniversary. 1991, Macmillan LB $12.95 (0-89686-559-2). 48pp. The use of aircraft carriers in the Pacific area of combat is described in this account. (Rev: BL 12/1/91) [940.54]

16025 Black, Wallace B., and Jean F. Blashfield. *Guadalcanal* (5–7). Illus. Series: World War II 50th Anniversary. 1992, Macmillan LB $12.95 (0-89686-560-6). 48pp. The war in the South Pacific, as revealed in the battle of Guadalcanal during 1942–1943, is retold in text and pictures. (Rev: BL 8/92; SLJ 1/93) [940.54]

16026 Black, Wallace B., and Jean F. Blashfield. *Hiroshima and the Atomic Bomb* (5–7). Illus. Series: World War II 50th Anniversary. 1993, Macmillan LB $12.95 (0-89686-571-1). 48pp. This is a chronicle of President Truman's decision to drop the atomic bomb on Hiroshima and Nagasaki and the results of that decision. (Rev: BL 4/15/93; SLJ 10/93) [940.54]

16027 Black, Wallace B., and Jean F. Blashfield. *Invasion of Italy* (5–7). Illus. Series: World War II 50th Anniversary. 1992, Macmillan LB $12.95 (0-89686-565-7). 48pp. This book describes the campaign by the Allied forces to liberate Italy from the Axis. (Rev: BL 2/1/93; SLJ 4/93) [940.54]

16028 Black, Wallace B., and Jean F. Blashfield. *Island Hopping in the Pacific* (5–7). Illus. Series: World War II 50th Anniversary. 1992, Macmillan LB $12.95 (0-89686-567-3). 48pp. The campaign to retake Pacific islands from the Japanese is described in brief text and many photographs. (Rev: BL 2/1/93; SLJ 4/93) [940.54]

16029 Black, Wallace B., and Jean F. Blashfield. *Iwo Jima and Okinawa* (5–7). Illus. Series: World War II 50th Anniversary. 1993, Macmillan LB $12.95 (0-89686-569-X). 48pp. The story of the savage battles that the Allies faced while taking these two islands from the Japanese during World War II. (Rev: BL 4/15/93; SLJ 10/93) [940.54]

16030 Black, Wallace B., and Jean F. Blashfield. *Jungle Warfare* (5–7). Illus. Series: World War II 50th Anniversary. 1992, Macmillan LB $12.95 (0-89686-563-0). 48pp. This generously illustrated account re-creates the World War II campaigns waged in the jungle of southeastern Asia. (Rev: BL 8/92; SLJ 1/93) [940.54]

16031 Black, Wallace B., and Jean F. Blashfield. *Pearl Harbor!* (5–7). Illus. Series: World War II 50th Anniversary. 1991, Macmillan LB $4.95 (0-89686-555-X). 48pp. The Japanese surprise attack that shocked the United States into World War II. (Rev: BL 6/15/91; SLJ 9/91) [940.53]

16032 Black, Wallace B., and Jean F. Blashfield. *Russia at War* (5–7). Illus. Series: World War II 50th Anniversary. 1991, Macmillan LB $12.95 (0-89686-556-8). 48pp. Describes the role played by Russia in World War II and how they stopped the Germans in spite of terrible losses, with many documentary photographs. (Rev: BL 12/1/91; SLJ 2/92) [940.54]

16033 Black, Wallace B., and Jean F. Blashfield. *Victory in Europe* (5–7). Illus. Series: World War II 50th Anniversary. 1993, Macmillan LB $12.95 (0-89686-570-3). 48pp. This account outlines the events that led to the Allied victory in Europe including the Russian advance and the fall of Berlin. (Rev: BL 4/15/93) [940.54]

16034 Black, Wallace B., and Jean F. Blashfield. *War Behind the Lines* (5–7). Illus. Series: World War II 50th Anniversary. 1992, Macmillan LB $12.95 (0-89686-564-9). 48pp. This book tells about the many gallant underground movements that tried to undermine the Fascist powers from within. (Rev: BL 2/1/93; SLJ 4/93) [940.54]

16035 Brooks, Philip. *The Tuskegee Airmen* (3–6). Illus. Series: We the People. 2004, Compass Point LB $16.95 (0-7565-0683-2). 48pp. A well-illustrated, concise account of the achievements of the African American pilots who flew during World War II.

16036 Butterfield, Moira. *Going to War in World War II* (5–7). Illus. 2001, Watts LB $24.00 (0-531-14596-4). 32pp. Soldiers, weapons, and military strategies of World War II are briefly presented with many illustrations and a timeline. (Rev: SLJ 10/01) [940.54]

16037 Chaikin, Miriam. *A Nightmare in History: The Holocaust 1933–1945* (4–6). Illus. 1992, Houghton Mifflin paper $10.00 (0-395-61580-1). 128pp. From the history of Judaism, the author traces the horror of the Holocaust. (Rev: BL 12/15/87)

16038 Coerr, Eleanor. *Sadako* (1–5). Illus. by Ed Young. 1993, Penguin Putnam $17.99 (0-399-21771-1). 40pp. A picture-book version of the story of a young Japanese girl dying of leukemia as a result of the bombing of Hiroshima. (Rev: BCCB 12/93; BL 11/1/93*; SLJ 12/93*) [362.1]

16039 Cretzmeyer, Stacy. *Your Name Is Renée: Ruth Kapp Hartz's Story as a Hidden Child in Nazi-Occupied France* (5–8). 2003, Bt. Bound $22.50 (0-613-56879-6). 240pp. The story of a German Jewish family living in France during the Holocaust, how they survived, and how young Ruth hid in an orphanage run by Catholic nuns. (Rev: BCCB 7–8/99; SLJ 8/99) [940.54]

16040 Crewe, Sabrina, and Dale Anderson. *The Atom Bomb Project* (3–5). Series: Events that Shaped America. 2005, Gareth Stevens LB $24.67 (0-8368-3404-6). 32pp. A simple, straightforward account of the Manhattan Project featuring direct quotations, editorial cartoons, photographs, reproductions, and newspaper clippings. (Rev: SLJ 3/05) [355.8]

16041 Cross, Robin. *Children and War* (4–7). Illus. Series: World War II. 1994, Thomson Learning LB $24.26 (1-56847-180-7). 48pp. True case histories of children in various circumstances during World War II, including in a gulag, the resistance movement, and a death camp. (Rev: BL 12/15/94; SLJ 2/95) [940.53]

16042 Daily, Robert. *The Code Talkers: American Indians in World War II* (4–8). Illus. Series: First Books. 1995, Watts LB $23.00 (0-531-20190-2). 63pp. Describes the roles that Native Americans played in World War II, both as soldiers and as translators. (Rev: SLJ 10/95) [940.54]

16043 Davis, Gary. *Submarine Wahoo* (3–5). Illus. Series: Those Daring Machines. 1995, Macmillan paper $5.95 (0-382-24753-1). 48pp. A brief account of the exploits of the World War II submarine that distinguished itself in the Pacific campaign. (Rev: BL 2/15/95) [940.54]

16044 Devaney, John. *America Goes to War: 1941* (5–8). 1991, Walker LB $17.85 (0-8027-6980-2). An illustrated, datelined, day-by-day account that covers personal and public events of America's first year of World War II. (Rev: BL 10/1/91; SLJ 8/91) [940.53]

16045 Drez, Ronald J. *Remember D-Day: The Plan, the Invasion, Survivor Stories* (4–8). 2004, National Geographic $17.95 (0-7922-6666-8). 64pp. Filled with period photographs and personal stories, this large-format survey of the Allied invasion of Normandy focuses on the military operation and on the strategic planning that preceded it. (Rev: BL 7/04; SLJ 7/04) [940.54]

16046 Drogues, Valerie. *Battleship Missouri* (3–5). Illus. Series: Those Daring Machines. 1995, Macmillan LB $17.95 (0-89686-825-7). 48pp. A short, well-illustrated description of the battleship *Missouri* and its amazing record during World War II. (Rev: BL 2/15/95) [359.3]

16047 Drucker, Olga L. *Kindertransport* (5–8). 1995, Holt paper $8.95 (0-8050-4251-2). 146pp. A true account of a Jewish girl sent from Germany to live in England until she could join her parents in New York City in 1945. (Rev: BCCB 1/93; SLJ 11/92) [940.54]

16048 Dvorson, Alexa. *The Hitler Youth: Marching Toward Madness* (5–9). Illus. Series: Teen Witnesses to the Holocaust. 1999, Rosen LB $26.50 (0-8239-2783-0). 64pp. This volume describes how thousands of German boys and girls joined the Hitler Youth, why they were seduced into obeying the Nazis, and how their dreams were eventually shattered. (Rev: BL 4/15/99; BR 9–10/99) [943.086]

16049 Fox, Anne L., and Eva Abraham-Podietz. *Ten Thousand Children: True Stories Told by Children Who Escaped the Holocaust on the Kindertransport* (5–8). Illus. 1998, Behrman paper $12.95 (0-87441-648-5). 128pp. The moving stories of 21 survivors who were part of the rescue operation known as the Kindertransport that took 10,000 Jewish children from Nazi-occupied Europe to freedom during late 1938 and 1939. (Rev: BL 1/1–15/99) [940.53]

16050 Giddens, Sandra. *Escape: Teens Who Escaped the Holocaust to Freedom* (5–9). Series: Teen Witnesses to the Holocaust. 1999, Rosen LB $26.50 (0-8239-2843-8). 64pp. This volume focuses on the ordeals of four Jewish teens who were able to elude the Nazis during the Holocaust. (Rev: BL 4/15/98; BR 9–10/99) [940.54]

16051 Gourley, Catherine. *Welcome to Molly's World, 1944: Growing Up in World War Two America* (3–6). Illus. Series: American Girls Collection. 1999, Pleasant Co. $14.95 (1-56247-773-0). 58pp. This book focuses on the human side of World War II, employing material on a USO canteen, blackouts in the U.S., rationing, air raids in England, and V-E Day. (Rev: BL 1/1–15/00; HBG 3/00) [940.53]

16052 Hopkinson, Deborah. *Pearl Harbor* (4–6). Illus. Series: Places in American History. 1991,

Macmillan LB $14.95 (0-87518-475-8). 72pp. A visual and narrative introduction to this well-known site of World War II. (Rev: BL 2/15/92; SLJ 4/92) [940.54]

16053 Jones, Steven L. *The Red Tails: World War II's Tuskegee Airmen* (4–8). Illus. Series: Cover-to-Cover. 2002, Perfection Learning $15.95 (0-7569-0251-7); paper $8.95 (0-7891-5487-0). 64pp. The story of the heroic African American squadron of World War II fighter pilots, their successful missions, and the prejudices they faced. (Rev: BL 5/1/02) [940.5404]

16054 Kacer, Kathy. *The Underground Reporters: A True Story* (5–8). Illus. 2005, Second Story $11.95 (1-896764-85-1). 156pp. Based on real events, this inspiring story tells how a newspaper, published by a group of Jewish teenagers in Budejovice, Czechoslovakia, helped to lift the spirits of the Jewish community during the years of Nazi occupation. (Rev: BL 2/15/05) [940.53]

16055 King, David C. *World War II Days: Discover the Past with Exciting Projects, Games, Activities, and Recipes* (4–6). Illus. by Cheryl K. Noll. Series: American Kids in History. 2000, Wiley paper $12.95 (0-471-37101-7). 100pp. Interspersed with material on the home front during World War II are easy-to-perform projects such as making a victory garden, a flashlight, a periscope, a crystal radio, and a wind vane. (Rev: SLJ 2/01) [940.54]

16056 Kodama, Tatsuharu. *Shin's Tricycle* (5–8). Trans. by Kazuko Hokumen-Jones. Illus. by Noriyuki Ando. 1995, Walker LB $16.85 (0-8027-8376-7). 32pp. A father recalls the life of his young son, who was killed in the bombing of Hiroshima. (Rev: BCCB 12/95; BL 9/1/95*; SLJ 12/95) [940.54]

16057 Kuhn, Betsy. *Angels of Mercy* (5–8). Illus. 1999, Simon & Schuster $18.00 (0-689-82044-5). 128pp. A series of narratives on courage and bravery gives us a fascinating look at the contributions of nurses in World War II. (Rev: BCCB 12/99; BL 10/15/99; HBG 3/00; SLJ 11/99) [940.54]

16058 Kustanowitz, Esther. *The Hidden Children of the Holocaust: Teens Who Hid from the Nazis* (5–9). Series: Teen Witnesses to the Holocaust. 1999, Rosen LB $26.50 (0-8239-2562-5). 64pp. Many first-person narratives are used in this account of teenage Jews who hid in homes, barns, and forests or disguised themselves as non-Jews to escape the Nazis. (Rev: BL 7/99; SLJ 8/99) [940.54]

16059 Landau, Elaine. *Holocaust Memories: Speaking the Truth* (4–6). Series: In Their Own Voices. 2001, Watts LB $22.50 (0-531-11742-1). 95pp. Landau combines survivors' stories of Kristallnacht, the Warsaw Ghetto rebellion, and concentration camps with background information and black-and-white photographs to present a moving whole that includes a story of her own grandfather. (Rev: BL 9/1/01; SLJ 9/01) [940.53]

16060 Langley, Wanda. *Flying Higher: The Women Airforce Service Pilots of World War II* (5–8). Illus. 2002, Linnet $25.00 (0-208-02506-5). 128pp. The women who flew in World War II gained little glory for performing many vital tasks; this arresting volume focuses on the director of the service, Jacqueline Cochran, and one of the pilots. (Rev: BL 11/1/02; HBG 3/03; SLJ 8/02) [940.54]

16061 Lawson, Don. *The French Resistance* (5–9). 1984, Messner LB $8.79 (0-671-50832-6). The story of the many gallant French men and women who defied death to oppose the German forces that occupied their country. [940.53]

16062 Lawton, Clive. *The Story of the Holocaust* (5–8). Illus. 2000, Watts LB $26.00 (0-531-14524-7). 48pp. A graphically illustrated account of the rise of anti-Semitism in Germany, a trend that culminated in the horror of the concentration camps. (Rev: BL 7/00) [940.53]

16063 Levine, Ellen. *Darkness Over Denmark: The Danish Resistance and the Rescue of the Jews* (5–8). 2000, Holiday House $18.95 (0-8234-1447-7). 164pp. This is a straightforward history that uses many first-person accounts to relate the remarkable efforts of the Danish people to save their Jewish citizens during World War II. (Rev: BL 7/00; HB 9–10/00; HBG 10/00; SLJ 8/00) [940.54]

16064 Levine, Karen. *Hana's Suitcase* (5–8). Illus. 2003, Whitman $15.95 (0-8075-3148-0). 112pp. A Japanese curator of a Holocaust exhibit traces the owner of a suitcase and learns the story of young Hana, who died in Auschwitz. (Rev: BL 3/15/03; HB 5–6/03; HBG 10/03) [940.53]

16065 Levy, Pat. *Causes* (5–9). Series: The Holocaust. 2001, Raintree LB $28.54 (0-7398-3257-3). 64pp. Levy discusses the causes of the Holocaust, looking at historical, religious, political, social, and economic factors. Also use *The Death Camps* (2002). (Rev: HBG 10/02; SLJ 2/02) [940.5318]

16066 Levy, Pat. *The Home Front in World War II* (5–8). Series: The World Wars. 2003, Raintree LB $28.56 (0-7398-6065-8). 64pp. A description of life on the home front in World War II, both in the Allied countries and the Axis countries, including the bombing, refugees, and various shortages. (Rev: HBG 4/04; SLJ 5/04) [940.53]

16067 McGowen, Tom. *Carrier War: Aircraft Carriers in World War II* (5–7). Series: Military Might. 2001, Twenty-First Century LB $26.90 (0-7613-1808-9). 64pp. An introduction to the importance of aircraft carriers in World War II, with coverage of Pearl Harbor and major battles in the Pacific. (Rev: HBG 10/01; SLJ 6/01) [940.54]

16068 McGowen, Tom. *Germany's Lightning War: Panzer Divisions of World War II* (5–8). Series: Military Might. 1999, Twenty-First Century LB $26.90 (0-7613-1511-X). 64pp. After a general history of tank warfare, this account focuses on the Germans' Panzer tank divisions and the part they played in World War II. (Rev: HBG 3/00; SLJ 9/99) [940.54]

16069 McGowen, Tom. *Sink the Bismarck: Germany's Super-Battleship of World War II* (5–8). Series: Military Might. 1999, Twenty-First Century LB $26.90 (0-7613-1510-1). 64pp. A history of German sea power during World War II and the many (eventually successful) British efforts to sink the *Bismarck*. (Rev: HBG 3/00; SLJ 9/99) [940.54]

16070 McNeese, Tim. *The Attack on Pearl Harbor* (5–8). Illus. Series: First Battles. 2001, Morgan Reynolds LB $21.95 (1-883846-78-1). 112pp. This book details the 1941 attack on Pearl Harbor and explains the conditions in Japan that led to the assault. (Rev: BL 10/1/01; HBG 3/02; SLJ 1/02) [940.54]

16071 Marquette, Scott. *World War II* (4–7). Illus. Series: America at War. 2002, Rourke LB $27.93 (1-58952-393-8). 48pp. This book for middle graders studies the war itself and the events that led up to it. [940.54]

16072 Maruki, Toshi. *Hiroshima No Pika* (3–6). Illus. by author. 1982, Lothrop $16.00 (0-688-01297-3). 48pp. The story of a seven-year-old girl and the bombing of Hiroshima in 1945.

16073 Marx, Trish. *Echoes of World War II* (5–8). Illus. 1994, Lerner LB $19.93 (0-8225-4898-4). 96pp. The true stories of six children around the world whose lives were changed dramatically by World War II. (Rev: BCCB 5/94; BL 9/15/94; SLJ 5/94) [940.53]

16074 Milman, Barbara. *Light in the Shadows* (5–9). Illus. 1997, Jonathan David paper $14.95 (0-8246-0401-6). Illustrated with powerful woodcut prints, this book tells the story of five Holocaust survivors. (Rev: BL 11/15/97) [940.53]

16075 Mochizuki, Ken. *Passage to Freedom: The Sugihara Story* (3–5). Illus. by Dom Lee. 1997, Lee & Low $15.95 (1-880000-49-0). 32pp. The story of Chiune Sugihara, the Japanese consul in Lithuania, and how he issued visas during the Holocaust that enabled Polish Jews to escape. (Rev: BL 5/15/97; HB 11–12/97; HBG 3/98; SLJ 7/97) [940.53]

16076 Panchyk, Richard. *World War II for Kids: A History with 21 Activities* (5–7). Illus. 2002, Chicago Review paper $14.95 (1-55652-455-2). 164pp. Features on such topics as living on rations for a day, growing a victory garden, and tracking a ship's movements depict conditions in America and Europe during the war. (Rev: SLJ 12/02) [940.53]

16077 Perl, Lila, and Marion B. Lazan. *Four Perfect Pebbles: A Holocaust Story* (5–9). Illus. 1996, Greenwillow $15.99 (0-688-14294-X). A memoir of the horror and incredible tribulations suffered by the author's family in the detention camps and later death camps during the Holocaust. (Rev: BL 4/1/96; BR 9–10/96; SLJ 5/96) [940.53]

16078 Pettit, Jayne. *A Time to Fight Back: True Stories of Wartime Resistance* (5–8). 1996, Houghton Mifflin $14.95 (0-395-76504-8). Eight true stories about courageous acts involving young people during World War II. (Rev: BCCB 3/96; BL 4/1/96; BR 11–12/96; SLJ 4/96) [940.53]

16079 Pfeifer, Kathryn B. *The 761st Tank Battalion* (5–8). Series: African American Soldiers. 1994, Twenty-First Century LB $24.90 (0-8050-3057-3). The history of an outfit of African American soldiers who served with distinction during World War II but were marginalized by racism. (Rev: BL 9/1/94; SLJ 11/94) [940.54]

16080 Pringle, Laurence. *One Room School* (1–4). Illus. by Barbara Garrison. 1998, Boyds Mills $15.95 (1-56397-583-1). This is a memoir by the noted author in which he remembers the year 1944, when he was attending a one-room school and collecting scrap metal for the war effort. (Rev: BCCB 4/98; BL 3/1/98; HBG 10/98; SLJ 4/98) [371]

16081 Raven, Margot Theis. *Mercedes and the Chocolate Pilot* (2–5). Illus. by Gijsbert van Frankenhuyzen. 2002, Sleeping Bear $17.95 (1-58536-069-4). 48pp. The true story of a friendship between a young German girl and an American pilot who dropped candy for the children during the Berlin Airlift. (Rev: BL 7/02; SLJ 8/02) [943]

16082 Reed, Nancy Amis. *The Orphans of Normandy: A True Story of World War II Told Through Drawings by Children* (3–6). 2003, Simon & Schuster $17.95 (0-689-84143-4). 48pp. Drawings and comments in French, with translations into English, chronicle the experiences of 100 girls who were forced to flee their Normandy orphanage in 1944. (Rev: BL 6/1–15/03; HBG 10/03; SLJ 11/03)

16083 Rogasky, Barbara. *Smoke and Ashes: The Story of the Holocaust*. Rev. ed. (5–10). 2002, Holiday House $27.50 (0-8234-1612-7); paper $14.95 (0-8234-1677-1). 256pp. In this new edition, Rogasky updates information where new facts have come to light and expands the details of resistance efforts. (Rev: BL 10/15/02; HBG 3/03; SLJ 10/02)

16084 Rogow, Sally M. *Faces of Courage: Young Heroes of World War II* (5–9). 2003, Granville Island $12.95 (1-894694-20-1). 144pp. Based on true stories, this volume presents 12 fictionalized accounts of heroic actions by teenagers under Nazi rule in Europe. (Rev: BL 10/15/03) [940.53]

16085 Rubin, Susan G. *Fireflies in the Dark: The Story of Friedl Dicker-Brandeis and the Children of Terezin* (5–10). Illus. 2000, Holiday House $18.95 (0-8234-1461-2). 48pp. A heartbreaking picture book that reproduces some of the artwork and writings of the children imprisoned at the Terezin concentration camp, where only 100 of 15,000 children survived. (Rev: BCCB 11/00; BL 7/00*; HB 9–10/00; HBG 9/00; SLJ 8/00) [940.53]

16086 Rubin, Susan Goldman. *The Flag with Fifty-Six Stars* (4–6). Illus. by Bill Farnsworth. 2005, Holiday House $16.95 (0-8234-1653-4). 40pp. A picture book for older readers about the prisoners at the Mauthausen concentration camp and the American flag they sewed — with six extra stars. (Rev: BL 3/15/05; SLJ 5/05) [940.53]

16087 Rubin, Susan Goldman. *Searching for Anne Frank: Letters from Amsterdam to Iowa* (5–12). 2003, Abrams $19.95 (0-8109-4514-2). 144pp. A brief penpal exchange between two sisters in Iowa and Anne Frank and her sister serves as the basis for a comparison between life in America and life for Jews in Europe. (Rev: BL 11/1/03; HB 11–12/03; HBG 4/04; SLJ 11/03) [940.5]

16088 Russo, Marisabina. *Always Remember Me: How One Family Survived World War II* (3–5). Illus. 2005, Simon & Schuster $16.95 (0-689-86920-7). 48pp. In this moving picture book for older readers, Oma shows her granddaughter family photographs and tells about her Jewish relatives' experiences in the Second World War. (Rev: BL 3/1/05; SLJ 4/05) [940.53]

16089 Santella, Andrew. *Navajo Code Talkers* (3–6). Illus. Series: We the People. 2004, Compass Point LB $22.60 (0-7565-0611-5). 48pp. This absorbing account of the work of the Navajo Code Talkers during World War II includes a chart of code words for the letters of the alphabet. (Rev: BL 5/1/04; SLJ 8/04) [940.54]

16090 Santella, Andrew. *Pearl Harbor* (4–6). Series: We the People. 2004, Compass Point LB $22.60 (0-7565-0680-8). 48pp. A well-illustrated brief discussion of the attack, the events leading up to it, and the building of the memorial. (Rev: SLJ 2/05) [940.54]

16091 Schroeder, Peter W., and Dagmar Schroeder-Hildebrand. *Six Million Paper Clips: The Making of a Children's Holocaust Memorial* (5–8). Illus. 2004, Kar-Ben $17.95 (1-58013-169-7); paper $7.95 (1-58013-176-X). 64pp. This is the story of a Tennessee school project in which students collected 11 million paper clips to help them grasp the magnitude of the Holocaust's human toll. (Rev: BL 1/1–15/05) [940.53]

16092 Shapiro, Stephen, and Tina Forrester. *Ultra Hush-Hush: Espionage and Special Missions* (5–8). Illus. by David Craig. Series: Outwitting the Enemy. 2003, Annick LB $29.95 (1-55037-779-5); paper $14.95 (1-55037-778-7). 96pp. Undercover activities during World War II are the focus of this volume that covers such groups and missions as the Navajo Code Talkers and Britain's double agents. (Rev: BL 8/03; SLJ 5/04) [940.54]

16093 Sheehan, Sean. *The Technology of World War II* (5–8). 2003, Raintree LB $28.56 (0-7398-6064-X). 64pp. New technologies introduced during World War II include radar, microwave transmissions, V-1 and V-2 rockets, the jet, codes, chemical and biological weapons, and the atom bomb. (Rev: HBG 10/03; SLJ 7/03) [940.54]

16094 Shuter, Jane, ed. *Christabel Bielenberg and Nazi Germany* (5–8). Illus. Series: History Eyewitness. 1996, Raintree LB $24.26 (0-8114-8285-5). Using a first-person narrative as a framework, this account traces the growth, flowering, and defeat of Nazism in Germany. (Rev: BL 5/15/96; SLJ 6/96) [943.086]

16095 Stalcup, Ann. *On the Home Front: Growing Up in Wartime England* (4–6). Illus. 1998, Linnet $19.50 (0-208-02482-4). 103pp. Important English children's writers, including Nina Bawden and Robert Westall, share their memories of growing up in wartime England. (Rev: BCCB 9/98; BL 10/15/98; HBG 10/98) [940.54]

16096 Stein, R. Conrad. *World War II in Europe: "America Goes to War"* (5–7). Illus. Series: American War. 1994, Enslow LB $20.95 (0-89490-525-2). 128pp. An unbiased account of the European theater of war during World War II, with emphasis on American participation. (Rev: BL 10/15/94; SLJ 1/95) [940.54]

16097 Stein, R. Conrad. *World War II in the Pacific* (4–6). Illus. Series: U.S. Wars. 2002, Enslow LB

$19.95 (0-7660-5093-9). 48pp. Supported by verified and updated Web links, this is a useful overview of the fighting in the Pacific during World War II. Also use *World War II in Europe* (2002). (Rev: HBG 3/03)

16098 Stein, R. Conrad. *World War II in the Pacific: Remember Pearl Harbor* (5–7). Illus. Series: American War. 1994, Enslow LB $20.95 (0-89490-524-4). 128pp. A well-organized, concise account of the Pacific war from the attack on Pearl Harbor to V-J Day that describes key battles and important personnel. (Rev: BL 7/94; SLJ 7/94) [940.54]

16099 Steins, Richard. *The Allies Against the Axis: World War II (1940–1950)* (5–8). Series: First Person America. 1994, Twenty-First Century LB $20.90 (0-8050-2586-3). An introduction to World War II and early postwar conditions, with generous use of primary sources. (Rev: BL 5/15/94; SLJ 12/94) [940.53]

16100 Talbott, Hudson. *Forging Freedom* (4–7). Illus. 2000, Penguin Putnam $15.99 (0-399-23434-9). 64pp. This is the story of Jaap Penraat, a young architectural student in Amsterdam during the Nazi occupation who saved hundreds of Jews from deportation by forging papers and smuggling them out of the city. (Rev: BCCB 11/00; BL 7/00; HB 1–2/01; HBG 3/01; SLJ 11/00) [940.53]

16101 Tanaka, Shelley. *Attack on Pearl Harbor: The True Story of the Day America Entered World War II* (5–8). Illus. Series: I Was There. 2001, Hyperion $19.99 (0-7868-0736-9). 64pp. An absorbing account of Pearl Harbor that presents the real-life, and very different, experiences of four young men who were there. (Rev: BL 8/01; HBG 10/01; SLJ 11/01) [940.54]

16102 Tanaka, Shelley. *D-Day: They Fought to Free Europe from Hitler's Tyranny* (4–6). Illus. by David Craig. Series: A Day That Changed America. 2004, Hyperion $16.99 (0-7868-1881-6). 48pp. The stories of four American servicemen who survived the invasion of Normandy help to bring home the massive scope of the D-Day operation. (Rev: BL 8/04; SLJ 8/04)

16103 Taylor, Theodore. *Air Raid — Pearl Harbor: The Story of December 7, 1941* (5–8). 1991, Harcourt paper $6.00 (0-15-201655-4). 179pp. A fine account of why the attack occurred and the effects that were felt around the world. A revised edition. (Rev: SLJ 12/91) [940.54]

16104 Tito, E. Tina. *Liberation: Teens in the Concentration Camps and the Teen Soldiers Who Liberated Them* (5–9). Illus. Series: Teen Witnesses to the Holocaust. 1999, Rosen LB $26.50 (0-8239-2846-2). 64pp. A harrowing account in which two teenage Nazi camp survivors and two American soldiers who were also teenagers during World War II tell their respective stories. (Rev: BL 4/15/99; BR 9–10/99) [940.53]

16105 Uschan, Michael V. *The Bombing of Pearl Harbor* (4–7). Series: Landmark Events in American History. 2003, World Almanac LB $26.60 (0-8368-5373-3). 48pp. An excellent, well-illustrated overview, this volume describes the attack itself and the tensions that led up to the bombing. (Rev: SLJ 9/03) [940.54]

16106 Vander Zee, Ruth. *Erika's Story* (3–6). Illus. by Roberto Innocenti. 2003, Creative $15.95 (1-56846-176-3). 24pp. A Jewish woman tells how an infant was thrown by her mother from a train headed for a concentration camp. (Rev: BL 11/1/03; HBG 4/04; SLJ 12/03)

16107 van Maarsen, Jacqueline, and Carol Ann Lee. *A Friend Called Anne: One Girl's Story of War, Peace, and a Unique Friendship with Anne Frank* (5–8). 2005, Viking $15.99 (0-670-05958-7). 176pp. Anne Frank's ordinary life before the war, and how things changed once the Nazis arrived, told by Anne's childhood friend. (Rev: BL 4/1/05; SLJ 4/05) [940.53]

16108 Warren, Andrea. *Surviving Hitler: A Boy in the Nazi Death Camps* (5–10). Illus. 2001, Harper-Collins LB $17.89 (0-06-029218-0). 160pp. The true story of Jack Mandelbaum, who as a teenager survived three years in Nazi death camps through a combination of luck, courage, and friendship. (Rev: BCCB 3/01; BL 1/1–15/01; HB 3–4/01; HBG 10/01; SLJ 3/01) [940.53]

16109 *Weapons of War* (5–9). Series: American War. 2000, Lucent LB $18.96 (1-56006-584-2). 112pp. This book covers the weaponry, tank combat, U-boat activities, fighter planes, aircraft carriers, and some of the better-known campaigns of World War II. (Rev: BL 9/15/00; HBG 10/00; SLJ 7/00) [940.54]

16110 Welch, Catherine A. *Children of the Relocation Camps* (3–6). Series: Picture the American Past. 2000, Carolrhoda $16.95 (1-57505-350-0). 48pp. The story of the relocation of thousands of Japanese Americans after Pearl Harbor, how the children reacted, and how they built new lives within the camps. (Rev: BL 6/1–15/00; HBG 10/00; SLJ 10/00) [940.54]

16111 Whitman, Sylvia. *Children of the World War II Home Front* (3–6). Series: Picture the American Past. 2001, Carolrhoda LB $22.60 (1-57505-484-1). 48pp. The lifestyle of children in America during World War II is presented through text and historic photographs. (Rev: BL 6/1–15/01; HBG 10/01; SLJ 7/01) [940.54]

16112 Whitman, Sylvia. *Uncle Sam Wants You!* (5–7). Illus. 1993, Lerner LB $30.35 (0-8225-1728-0). 80pp. This work describes the experiences of the many men and women who served in the various armed forces during World War II. (Rev: BL 5/1/93) [940.54]

16113 Wills, Charles A. *Pearl Harbor* (5–7). Illus. Series: Turning Points. 1991, Silver Burdett LB $14.95 (0-382-24125-8); paper $7.95 (0-382-24119-3). 64pp. The "Day of Infamy" that brought America into World War II is re-created through text and pictures. (Rev: BL 1/15/92) [940.54]

16114 Wukovits, John F. *Life as a POW* (5–9). Series: American War. 2000, Lucent LB $18.96 (1-56006-665-2). 112pp. This book describes the treatment of World War II prisoners of war by the Germans and Japanese, the emotional upheavals

involved, and the transition to freedom after release. (Rev: BL 9/15/00; HBG 10/00; SLJ 7/00) [940.54]

16115 Wukovits, John F. *Life of an American Soldier in Europe* (5–10). Series: American War. 2000, Lucent LB $18.96 (1-56006-666-0). 112pp. As well as giving a history of World War II and the major battles involving Americans, this account tells about U.S. army personnel, their training, daily life, and living conditions. (Rev: BL 4/15/00; HBG 10/00; SLJ 6/00) [940.54]

16116 Yancy, Diane. *The Internment of the Japanese* (5–8). Series: World History. 2002, Gale LB $27.45 (1-59018-013-5). 112pp. An accessible source of information on the internment during World War II and its aftermath. (Rev: BL 8/02; SLJ 8/02) [940.54]

16117 Younkin, Paula. *V-2 Rockets* (3–5). Illus. Series: Those Daring Machines. 1995, Silver Burdett paper $5.95 (0-614-09467-4). 48pp. The history of the development of the *V-2* rocket by Germany, its use against the British in World War II, and the career of its developer, Wernher von Braun. (Rev: BL 2/15/95) [940.54]

Modern History

16118 Bjornlund, Britta. *The Cold War* (5–9). Series: World History. 2002, Gale LB $27.45 (1-59018-003-8). 128pp. Bjornlund looks at the origins and development of the Cold War, and details the crises and periods of reduced tension that marked the length of the conflict. (Rev: BL 8/02; SLJ 10/02) [940.55]

16119 Chrisp, Peter. *The Cuban Missile Crisis* (5–8). Illus. Series: Cold War. 2002, World Almanac LB $31.93 (0-8368-5273-7). 4pp. This look at the Cold War crisis focuses on the events leading up to the standoff and the reasons for the deteriorating relationship between Moscow and Washington. Also use *The Causes of the Cold War*, *The Vietnam War*, and *The End of the Cold War* (all 2002). (Rev: BL 11/15/02; SLJ 7/02) [973.922]

16120 Gunderson, Cory. *The Need for Oil* (5–8). Illus. Series: World in Conflict. 2004, ABDO LB $17.95 (1-59197-417-8). 48pp. This history of conflicts over oil includes useful statistics and will be helpful to students seeking information for reports or background context before the recent Iraq war. (Rev: BL 4/1/04; SLJ 3/04) [338.2]

16121 Holden, Henry M. *The Persian Gulf War* (4–8). Series: U.S. Wars. 2003, Enslow/MyReportLinks.com LB $19.95 (0-7660-5109-9). 48pp. This concise, interesting account of the conflict in the early 1990s is enhanced by Internet access to a set of monitored Web links. (Rev: HBG 10/03; SLJ 8/03) [956.7]

16122 Kent, Zachary. *The Persian Gulf War: "The Mother of All Battles"* (5–7). Illus. 1994, Enslow LB $20.95 (0-89490-528-7). 128pp. The story of the 1991 Gulf War, its causes and effects, told with striking action photographs. (Rev: BL 4/15/95; SLJ 2/95) [956.7]

16123 Lomas, Clare. *The 80s and 90s: Power Dressing to Sportswear* (5–10). Series: 20th Century Fashion. 2000, Gareth Stevens LB $25.26 (0-8368-2603-5). 32pp. Power dressing, androgyny, sportswear, and grunge characterize the world of fashion during the 1980s and 1990s in this book that covers both design and social history. (Rev: HBG 9/00; SLJ 6/00) [973.9]

16124 Mee, Sue. *1900–20: Linen and Lace* (5–10). Series: 20th Century Fashion. 2000, Gareth Stevens LB $25.26 (0-8368-2598-5). 32pp. The fashion and design of the first two decades of the last century are pictured and described in this book that also contains a great deal of social history. (Rev: HBG 9/00; SLJ 6/00) [973.9]

16125 Powe-Temperley, Kitty. *The 60s: Mods and Hippies* (5–10). Series: 20th Century Fashion. 2000, Gareth Stevens LB $25.26 (0-8368-2601-9). 32pp. Mods, hippies, miniskirts, Eastern influences, and art as fashion are covered in this overview of clothing fads of the 1960s, along with background information. (Rev: HBG 9/00; SLJ 6/00) [973.9]

16126 Reynolds, Helen. *The 40s and 50s: Utility to New Look* (5–10). Series: 20th Century Fashion. 2000, Gareth Stevens LB $25.26 (0-8368-2600-0). 32pp. Using a lively style and many period illustrations, this book highlights the world of fashion and design during and after World War II and gives some background social history. (Rev: HBG 9/00; SLJ 6/00) [973.9]

16127 Schaffer, David. *The Iran-Iraq War* (5–8). Illus. Series: World History. 2002, Gale LB $27.45 (1-59018-184-0). 128pp. Schaffer traces the causes and progress of this long war, incorporating useful primary and secondary source material plus interesting sidebar features. (Rev: BL 5/1/03) [955.05]

16128 Schnapper, LaDena. *Teenage Refugees from Ethiopia Speak Out* (5–10). Series: Teenage Refugees Speak Out. 1997, Rosen LB $16.95 (0-8239-2438-6). Ethiopian teens now living in America tell of the violence, famine, and civil war that drove them from their country and of their reception in America. (Rev: SLJ 2/98) [963]

16129 Smith, Carter. *The Korean War* (4–7). Illus. Series: Turning Points. 1990, Silver Burdett LB $14.95 (0-382-09953-2); paper $7.95 (0-382-09949-4). 64pp. Covers the causes and events of the Korean War, as well as its significance in American history. (Rev: BL 3/1/91; SLJ 5/91) [951]

16130 Stanley, George E. *America and the Cold War (1949–1969)* (5–8). Illus. Series: A Primary Source History of the United States. 2005, World Almanac LB $22.50 (0-8368-5830-1). 48pp. A simple narrative links well-chosen primary sources documenting the key events of the Cold War. Also use *America in Today's World (1969–2004)* (2005).

16131 Stein, R. Conrad. *The Korean War: "The Forgotten War"* (5–7). Illus. 1994, Enslow LB $20.95 (0-89490-526-0). 128pp. This well-organized account of the Korean War presents a balanced picture of the war and includes personal observations. (Rev: BL 4/15/95; SLJ 2/95) [951]

16132 Stolley, Richard B., ed. *Life: Our Century in Pictures for Young People* (5–12). Illus. 2000, Little, Brown $25.45 (0-316-81577-2). 225pp. Adapted from an adult coffee-table book, this survey of the last century is divided into nine chronological, heavily illustrated chapters with contributions from many children's writers including Lois Lowry and Robert Cormier. (Rev: BL 12/15/00) [909.82]

16133 Taylor, David. *The Cold War* (5–9). Illus. Series: 20th Century Perspectives. 2001, Heinemann LB $25.64 (1-57572-434-0). 48pp. An easily understood account of the causes of tension between the Soviet Union and the West and the major crises of the "war." (Rev: HBG 3/02; SLJ 11/01) [909.825]

16134 Twagilimana, Aimable. *Teenage Refugees from Rwanda Speak Out* (5–10). Series: Teenage Refugees Speak Out. 1997, Rosen LB $16.95 (0-8239-2443-2). Teenage refugees from Rwanda describe the warfare between Tutsi and Hutu peoples, the terrible living conditions that forced them to leave their country, and the challenges and difficulties they have experienced in the United States. (Rev: SLJ 2/98) [967]

16135 Willoughby, Douglas. *The Vietnam War* (5–9). Series: 20th Century Perspectives. 2001, Heinemann LB $27.07 (1-57572-439-1). 48pp. An easily understood and attractive account of Vietnam's relations with China, and of French and U.S. involvement in the country's affairs. (Rev: SLJ 11/01) [959]

16136 Wright, David K. *War in Vietnam* (5–10). 1998, Children's Book Pr. paper $20.60 (0-516-02287-3). This is the first volume of an excellent four-volume set. The other volumes are *War in Vietnam, Book II: A Wider War; War in Vietnam, Book III: Vietnamization;* and *War in Vietnam, Book IV: Fall of Vietnam* (all 1989, available only as a set). (Rev: BL 6/1/89; SLJ 6/89) [959.704]

Geographical Regions

Africa

General

16137 Ayo, Yvonne. *Africa* (4–8). Illus. Series: Eyewitness Books. 1995, Knopf LB $20.99 (0-674-97334-6). 64pp. This introduces the continent of Africa, with its amazing diversity of people, places, wildlife, and cultures. (Rev: BL 12/15/95) [960]

16138 Banting, Erinn. *The Nile River: The Longest River in the World* (3–6). Illus. Series: Natural Wonders. 2004, Weigl LB $18.20 (1-59036-269-1). 32pp. A look at the history of the Nile, the people who live on its banks, the animals and plants it supports, and the environmental threats it faces. (Rev: BL 4/1/04; HBG 3/03; SLJ 4/05)

16139 Barter, James. *The Nile* (5–8). Series: Rivers of the World. 2003, Gale $27.45 (1-56006-935-X). 112pp. An appealing and informative description of the Nile's source, tributaries, and path; history from ancient times; and the long-term environmental problems affecting the river and actions that are being taken to preserve the river. (Rev: SLJ 1/03) [962]

16140 Bingham, Jane. *African Art and Culture* (5–8). Illus. Series: World Art and Culture. 2004, Raintree LB $29.99 (0-7398-6606-0). 56pp. The indigenous art and culture of Africa from prehistoric times to the present are beautifully captured in this handsome and comprehensive overview. (Rev: BL 4/1/04; HBG 4/04; SLJ 2/04) [709]

16141 Bowden, Rob. *The Nile* (5–7). Series: A River Journey. 2003, Raintree LB $28.56 (0-7398-6072-0). 48pp. A trip down the length of East Africa's Nile, from its source to the sea, and a look at its importance to the people who live along it and the challenge of pollution, with photographs, maps, and charts. (Rev: HBG 4/04; SLJ 3/04) [916.2]

16142 Craats, Rennay. *Maasai* (4–6). Illus. Series: Indigenous Peoples. 2005, Weigl $16.95 (1-59036-255-1). 32pp. A fascinating and informative over-view of the Maasai people, covering history, culture, language, and family life.

16143 Cumming, David. *The Nile* (4–7). Series: Great Rivers of the World. 2003, World Almanac LB $26.60 (0-8368-5445-4). 48pp. An exploration of the Nile's flow, history, and animals and plants, with discussion of the settlements along its banks, the industries it supports, recreation on its waters, and environmental threats to the river. (Rev: SLJ 9/03)

16144 Golding, Vivien. *Traditions from Africa* (3–6). Illus. Series: Cultural Journeys. 1999, Raintree $25.69 (0-8172-8382-3). 48pp. This photoessay gives a quick view of some of the cultural characteristics of various African regions. (Rev: BL 5/15/99) [306]

16145 Graf, Mike. *Africa* (K–3). Series: Continents. 2002, Capstone LB $18.60 (0-7368-1414-0). 24pp. With maps and full-color graphics, this is a brief introduction to the geography, history, flora, fauna, and peoples of Africa. (Rev: HBG 3/03; SLJ 4/03)

16146 Halliburton, Warren J. *African Industries* (4–6). Illus. Series: Africa Today. 1993, Macmillan LB $17.95 (0-89686-672-6). 48pp. Since colonialism, Africans have tried to develop such industries as agriculture, fishing, and mining. (Rev: BL 4/15/93) [338]

16147 Halliburton, Warren J. *African Landscapes* (4–6). Illus. Series: Africa Today. 1993, Silver Burdett LB $17.95 (0-89686-673-4). 48pp. From tropical forests to freezing mountain tops and arid deserts, this book describes the African landscape and geography. (Rev: BL 4/15/93) [916]

16148 Halliburton, Warren J. *Africa's Struggle for Independence* (4–6). Illus. Series: Africa Today. 1992, Macmillan LB $13.95 (0-89686-679-3). 48pp. An overview of the people and kingdoms of Africa, slave trade, colonial invasion, and the fight of individual nations for freedom. (Rev: BCCB 2/93; BL 3/1/93; SLJ 2/93) [960]

16149 Halliburton, Warren J. *Africa's Struggle to Survive* (4–6). Illus. 1993, Macmillan LB $17.95 (0-

855

89686-675-0). 48pp. This book describes the natural disasters and forces of nature dictating the lives of the people of Africa. (Rev: BL 4/15/93) [960]

16150 Halliburton, Warren J. *Celebrations of African Heritage* (4–6). Illus. Series: Africa Today. 1992, Macmillan LB $13.95 (0-89686-676-9). 48pp. This book describes African holidays and celebrations and tells how some of these have been brought to America. (Rev: BL 2/15/93; SLJ 2/93) [394.2]

16151 Haskins, Jim, and Kathleen Benson. *African Beginnings* (3–7). Illus. by Floyd Cooper. 1998, Lothrop $18.00 (0-688-10256-5). 48pp. Eleven ancient African cultures, including the Egyptian, are described, beginning with Nubia around 3800 B.C. (Rev: BL 2/15/98; HBG 10/98; SLJ 6/98) [960]

16152 Ibazebo, Isimeme. *Exploration into Africa* (4–6). Illus. Series: Exploration. 1994, New Discovery paper $7.95 (0-382-24732-9). 48pp. An account of the foreign influences in the history of Africa, including the slave trade, and how these have changed its history. (Rev: SLJ 5/95) [960]

16153 Knight, Margy B., and Mark Melnicove. *Africa Is Not a Country* (1–3). Illus. by Anne S. O'Brien. 2000, Millbrook $24.90 (0-7613-1266-8). 40pp. This book celebrates the diversity of the African continent by portraying children from various countries and supplying a vignette about each of them. (Rev: BL 11/15/00; HBG 3/01; SLJ 1/01) [960]

16154 Martell, Hazel M. *Exploring Africa* (4–8). Illus. Series: Voyages of Discovery. 1998, Bedrick $18.95 (0-87226-490-4). Double-page spreads, maps, and illustrations are used in this introduction to the history and geography of Africa, including an overview of early trade, European exploration and colonization, and African independence movements. (Rev: HBG 10/98; SLJ 4/98) [960]

16155 Meister, Cari. *Nile River* (3–4). Series: Rivers and Lakes. 2002, ABDO LB $13.95 (1-57765-098-0). 24pp. A solid introduction to the Nile, its tributaries, flora and fauna, and the ways in which it has influenced human development in the area throughout history. (Rev: HBG 10/02; SLJ 7/02) [960]

16156 Millard, Anne. *Story of the Nile: A Journey Through Time Along the World's Longest River* (3–6). Illus. by Steve Noon. 2003, DK $19.99 (0-7894-9871-5). 31pp. An attractive, richly illustrated expedition down the Nile, visiting notable landmarks and exploring its history. (Rev: HBG 4/04; LMC 3/04; SLJ 12/03) [960]

16157 Pollard, Michael. *The Nile* (4–6). Series: Great Rivers. 1997, Benchmark LB $21.36 (0-7614-0503-8). 45pp. The story of the Nile, the lands through which it flows, its flooding, and its place in history. (Rev: HBG 3/98; SLJ 5/98) [960]

16158 Rich, Susan, et al. *Africa South of the Sahara: Understanding Geography and History Through Art* (5–9). Series: Artisans Around the World. 1999, Raintree LB $27.12 (0-7398-0118-X). 48pp. After a brief overview of the history and geography of southern Africa, this book presents a colorful introduction to such crafts as beadwork from Kenya, a carved wooden mask from Congo, and a wire toy

from South Africa. Most will require adult help or supervision. (Rev: HBG 3/00; SLJ 1/00) [960]

16159 Sheehan, Sean. *Great African Kingdoms* (5–10). Series: Ancient World. 1998, Raintree LB $27.12 (0-8172-5124-3). Coverage of the great African kingdoms includes the spectacular palace of Great Zimbabwe, the majestic sculptures of Benin, and the Zulu empire's struggle for survival. (Rev: BL 1/1–15/99; HBG 3/99) [960]

16160 Weintraub, Aileen. *Discovering Africa's Land, People, and Wildlife* (5–8). Series: Continents of the World. 2004, Enslow/MyReportLinks.com LB $19.95 (0-7660-5204-4). 48pp. An introduction to the geography, history, economy, plants and animals, culture, and peoples of the continent, with discussion of the continuing need for foreign aid in many countries. (Rev: SLJ 11/04) [916]

Central and Eastern Africa

16161 Ayodo, Awuor. *Luo* (4–7). Illus. Series: Heritage Library of African Peoples. 1995, Rosen LB $17.95 (0-8239-1758-4). 64pp. A portrait of the culture, history, and society of the Luo people, who lived on the shores of Lake Victoria in Kenya. (Rev: BL 3/1/96) [967.8]

16162 Bangura, Abdul Karim. *Kipsigis* (5–8). Illus. Series: Heritage Library of African Peoples. 1994, Rosen LB $17.95 (0-8239-1765-7). 64pp. An attractive title that deals with the history and present status of the Kipsigis people of Kenya. (Rev: SLJ 5/95) [967.62]

16163 Baroin, Catherine. *Tubu: The Teda and the Daza* (5–7). Illus. Series: Heritage Library of African Peoples. 1997, Rosen LB $15.95 (0-8239-2000-3). 64pp. The history and contemporary life of these African peoples who now live in Central Africa, including Chad, Libya, Niger, and the Sudan. (Rev: BL 4/15/97) [967.43]

16164 Berg, Elizabeth. *Ethiopia* (2–4). Series: Festivals of the World. 1999, Gareth Stevens LB $15.95 (0-8368-2032-0). 32pp. This account describes Ethiopia's secular and religious holidays and gives instructions for creating the crafts and foods associated with these festivals. (Rev: BL 12/15/99; HBG 10/00) [963]

16165 Bessire, Aimee, and Mark Bessire. *Sukuma* (5–8). Series: Heritage Library of African Peoples. 1997, Rosen LB $17.95 (0-8239-1992-7). Describes the history, culture, leaders, customs, and present situation of the Sukuma people of Tanzania. (Rev: BL 9/15/97) [967.6]

16166 Blauer, Ettagale, and Jason Lauré. *Uganda* (5–8). Illus. Series: Enchantment of the World. 1997, Children's Book Pr. paper $32.00 (0-516-20306-1). 128pp. This introduction to Uganda covers such topics as geography, climate, plants and animals, history, religion, culture, and daily life. (Rev: BL 7/97; HBG 3/98) [967.61]

16167 Broberg, Catherine. *Kenya in Pictures*. Rev. ed. (4–7). Illus. Series: Visual Geography. 2002, Lerner LB $27.93 (0-8225-1957-7). 80pp. Information on all aspects of life in this African country, including extensive coverage of its history, is accompanied by plenty of photographs and a Web site that offers up-to-date links. (Rev: BL 10/15/02; HBG 3/03; SLJ 12/02)

16168 Burnham, Philip. *Gbaya* (5–7). Illus. Series: Heritage Library of African Peoples. 1997, Rosen LB $17.95 (0-8239-1995-1). 64pp. Covers the contemporary culture and the significant history of the Gbaya people, who live in Cameroon, Central African Republic, Congo, and Zaire. (Rev: BL 4/15/97) [967]

16169 Cobb, Vicki. *This Place Is Wild: East Africa* (3–5). Illus. Series: Imagine Living Here. 1998, Walker LB $16.85 (0-8027-8633-2). 32pp. This slim book explores the uniqueness of East Africa, describes its unusual animal and plant life, and introduces the reader to the Masai people. (Rev: BL 4/1/98; HBG 10/98; SLJ 5/98) [599]

16170 Corona, Laurel. *Ethiopia* (5–8). Series: Modern Nations of the World. 2000, Lucent LB $27.45 (1-56006-823-X). 128pp. An attractive, well-organized introduction to Ethiopia that gives its history, geography, and culture plus national statistics, a chronology, and bibliographies. (Rev: BL 3/1/01) [963]

16171 Corona, Laurel. *Kenya* (5–8). Illus. Series: Modern Nations of the World. 1999, Lucent LB $27.45 (1-56006-590-7). 127pp. A profile of this poor African country that is a study in contrasts and cultures, with material on such subjects as geography, economics, people, and current problems. (Rev: BL 2/15/00; HBG 10/00) [967.62]

16172 Deady, Kathleen W. *Rwanda* (2–5). Illus. Series: Questions and Answers: Countries. 2005, Capstone LB $16.95 (0-7368-3759-0). 32pp. Using a question-and-answer format, simple text, large photos, and many factboxes, this is an introduction to Rwanda today, with material on history and traditional culture.

16173 Deer, Victoria. *Kenya* (4–6). Series: Countries of the World. 1999, Gareth Stevens LB $19.95 (0-8368-2311-7). 96pp. An excellent introduction to Kenya with material on history, geography, government, unique customs, language, food, and current conditions. (Rev: BL 12/15/99; HBG 10/00) [967.6]

16174 Delzio, Suzanne. *Ethiopia* (2–3). Illus. Series: Many Cultures, One World. 2004, Capstone LB $17.95 (0-7368-2449-9). 32pp. A brief, accessible introduction to Ethiopia and its people, family life, customs, and legends.

16175 Diouf, Sylviane. *Kings and Queens of Central Africa* (4–7). Series: Watts Library: Africa — Kings and Queens. 2000, Watts LB $24.00 (0-531-20372-7). 64pp. This look at the political and social evolution of central Africa describes some of its important royalty including the 15th-century Afonso and Bolongongo, the legendary Bakuba king, with a final chapter on the region today. (Rev: BL 3/1/01) [960]

16176 Diouf, Sylviane. *Kings and Queens of East Africa* (4–7). Illus. Series: Watts Library: Africa — Kings and Queens. 2000, Watts LB $24.00 (0-531-20373-5). 64pp. This book gives biographical infor-

mation about royalty in East Africa and through these sketches re-creates the history of this part of Africa. (Rev: BL 2/15/01) [967.6]

16177 *Ethiopia in Pictures* (5–8). Illus. Series: Visual Geography. 1994, Lerner LB $21.27 (0-8225-1836-8). 64pp. Land, history and government, culture, education, religion, and health are covered. (Rev: BL 2/1/89) [963]

16178 Fox, Mary V. *Somalia* (5–8). Illus. Series: Enchantment of the World. 1996, Children's Pr. paper $32.00 (0-516-20019-4). An introduction to the land and people of this Muslim republic, which occupies the eastern horn of Africa. (Rev: BL 1/1–15/97) [967.73]

16179 Giles, Bridget. *Kenya* (4–8). Series: Nations of the World. 2001, Raintree LB $34.26 (0-7398-1290-4). 128pp. From snow-capped mountains to scorching deserts, this geographically and culturally diverse African nation is attractively introduced in this volume. (Rev: BL 12/15/01; HBG 3/02; SLJ 12/01) [967.62]

16180 Gish, Steven. *Ethiopia* (4–7). Illus. Series: Cultures of the World. 1996, Marshall Cavendish LB $35.64 (0-7614-0276-4). 128pp. After general background information on Ethiopia, such topics as lifestyles, religion, and language are discussed. (Rev: BL 8/96; SLJ 8/96) [963]

16181 Greenberg, Keith E. *Rwanda: Fierce Clashes in Central Africa* (1–4). Photos by John Isaac. Series: Children in Crisis. 1996, Blackbirch LB $16.95 (1-56711-185-8). 30pp. A harrowing eyewitness account in text and photos of the effects of the war in Rwanda on the lives of children in the refugee camps. (Rev: SLJ 6/97) [967]

16182 Holtzman, Jon. *Samburu* (5–8). Illus. Series: Heritage Library of African Peoples. 1995, Rosen LB $17.95 (0-8239-1759-2). 64pp. A detailed account of the culture, history, and life-styles of these Kenyan people. (Rev: SLJ 5/95) [967.62]

16183 Jones, Schuyler. *Pygmies of Central Africa* (5–8). Illus. 1989, Rourke LB $16.67 (0-86625-268-1). 48pp. A vivid look into the lives of these fascinating people. (Rev: BL 5/15/89) [967.00496]

16184 Kairi, Wambui. *Kenya* (2–4). Series: We Come From. 2000, Raintree LB $22.83 (0-8172-5512-5). 32pp. A young native guide gives basic facts about Kenya, explains how to cook some delicious dishes, and makes simple toys. (Rev: BL 4/15/00; HBG 10/00) [967.62]

16185 *Kenya in Pictures* (5–8). Illus. 1997, Lerner LB $21.27 (0-8225-1830-9). 64pp. Information on all aspects of life in this African country, including extensive coverage of its history. (Rev: BL 4/15/88; SLJ 11/88)

16186 Klyce, Katherine P., and Virginia O. McLean. *Kenya, Jambo!* (2–5). Illus. 1989, Redbird $21.95 (0-9606046-4-2). 36pp. In photos and simple text, a ten-year-old girl tells of her family's vacation in Kenya. (Rev: BL 12/1/89) [916]

16187 Kurtz, Jane. *Ethiopia: The Roof of Africa* (5–8). Illus. Series: Discovering Our Heritage. 1991, Macmillan LB $14.95 (0-87518-483-9). 128pp. Beginning with a map and two pages of basic facts, this is an interesting introduction to the land, people, and modern problems of Ethiopia. (Rev: BL 2/1/92; SLJ 5/92) [963]

16188 Lindblad, Lisa. *The Serengeti Migration: Africa's Animals on the Move* (3–7). Photos by Sven-Olof Lindblad. 1994, Hyperion $15.95 (1-56282-668-9). 40pp. A short text and stunning photos describe the annual migration of zebras and wildebeests through Tanzania and Kenya. (Rev: BCCB 5/94; BL 7/94*; SLJ 5/94) [599.73]

16189 McCollum, Sean. *Kenya* (3–5). Illus. Series: Globe-Trotters Club. 1999, Carolrhoda LB $22.60 (1-57505-105-2). 48pp. This book introduces Kenya, with material on its history, geography, religion, people, culture, and population. (Rev: BL 9/15/99; HBG 10/99) [967.62]

16190 McCollum, Sean. *Kenya* (1–3). Illus. Series: A Ticket To. 1999, Carolrhoda LB $22.60 (1-57505-130-3). 48pp. A basic introduction to this African nation that includes many color photographs. (Rev: BL 9/15/99; HBG 10/99) [967.62]

16191 McNair, Sylvia, and Lynne Mansure. *Kenya* (4–7). Series: Enchantment of the World. 2001, Children's Book Pr. LB $34.50 (0-516-21078-5). A superior introduction to the land and people of Kenya with material on such topics as history, culture, problems, climate, resources, and religion. (Rev: BL 1/1–15/02) [967.62]

16192 McQuail, Lisa. *The Masai of Africa* (4–7). Illus. Series: First Peoples. 2001, Lerner LB $23.93 (0-8225-4855-0). 48pp. McQuail provides information about the Masai people, covering their history, customs, and contemporary daily life, with photographs. (Rev: BL 10/15/01; HBG 3/02; SLJ 3/02) [967.6]

16193 *Malawi in Pictures* (5–8). Illus. Series: Visual Geography. 1989, Lerner LB $25.55 (0-8225-1842-2). 64pp. An overview of climate, history, geography, culture, education, and other aspects of life. (Rev: BL 2/1/89) [968.97]

16194 Ng'weno, Fleur. *Kenya* (4–7). Illus. Series: Focus On. 1992, Trafalgar $22.95 (0-237-60194-X). 32pp. Discusses Kenya's history, peoples, and lifestyles. (Rev: SLJ 8/92) [967.6]

16195 Njoku, Onwuka N. *Mbundu* (5–7). Illus. Series: Heritage Library of African Peoples. 1997, Rosen LB $17.95 (0-8239-2004-6). 64pp. An introduction to the history and contemporary culture of this people of the African republic of Zaire. (Rev: BL 4/15/97) [9678.3]

16196 Nnoromele, Salome. *Somalia* (5–8). Series: Modern Nations of the World. 2000, Lucent LB $27.45 (1-56006-396-3). 112pp. An introduction to this East African country with material on its history and geography and a large section on daily life. (Rev: BL 5/15/00; HBG 10/00) [967.73]

16197 Oghojafor, Kingsley. *Uganda* (5–8). Series: Countries of the World. 2004, Gareth Stevens LB $29.26 (0-8368-3112-8). 96pp. Introduces readers to the African country's geography, history, people, culture, and government and also takes a look at its relations with other countries and contemporary challenges. (Rev: SLJ 8/04) [967.61]

16198 Okeke, Chika. *Kongo* (5–7). Illus. 1997, Rosen LB $15.95 (0-8239-2001-1). 64pp. The Kongo people of Angola, Congo, and Zaire in central Africa are featured, with material on their history and contemporary culture. (Rev: BL 4/15/97) [967]

16199 Parris, Ronald. *Rendille* (5–8). Illus. Series: Heritage Library of African Peoples. 1994, Rosen LB $17.95 (0-8239-1763-0). 64pp. With extensive use of black-and-white and color photographs, introduces the history and customs of the Rendille people of Kenya. (Rev: SLJ 5/95) [967.62]

16200 Pateman, Robert. *Kenya* (4–7). Illus. Series: Cultures of the World. 1993, Marshall Cavendish LB $35.64 (1-85435-572-4). 128pp. The background story of Kenya is revealed through color photographs and a text that also covers present concerns. (Rev: BL 8/93) [967.62]

16201 Schemenauer, Elma. *Ethiopia* (3–5). Series: Countries: Faces and Places. 2000, Child's World LB $25.64 (1-56766-713-9). 32pp. Basic facts and background material about Ethiopia are given in a simple text with color illustrations on each page. (Rev: BL 4/15/01; HBG 3/01) [963]

16202 Schemenauer, Elma. *Somalia* (3–5). Series: Faces and Places. 2001, Child's World LB $25.64 (1-56766-911-5). 32pp. Basic facts about Somalia are given in a simple introduction with large type, many color photographs, and a text that emphasizes the everyday life of the people. (Rev: BL 9/15/01; HBG 3/02; SLJ 12/01) [967.73]

16203 Schemenauer, Elma. *Uganda* (3–5). Series: Countries: Faces and Places. 2003, Child's World LB $25.64 (1-56766-941-X). 32pp. A brief introduction to the geography, history, people, culture, and flora and fauna of this landlocked country. (Rev: SLJ 7/03) [967.61]

16204 Stewart, Judy. *A Family in Sudan* (4–6). Illus. 1988, Lerner LB $18.60 (0-8225-1682-9). 32pp. Customs, work, and play are covered in this look at life in this African land. (Rev: BL 8/88)

16205 *Sudan in Pictures* (5–8). Illus. Series: Visual Geography. 1990, Lerner LB $25.55 (0-8225-1839-2). 64pp. An overview of history, culture, geography, economy, education, and health. (Rev: BL 2/1/89) [962.4]

16206 Swinimer, Ciarunji C. *Pokot* (5–8). Illus. Series: Heritage Library of African Peoples. 1994, Rosen LB $17.95 (0-8239-1756-8). 64pp. Using a good balance of text and visuals, this account describes the history, culture, and present status of the Pokot people of Kenya. (Rev: SLJ 5/95) [967.62]

16207 *Tanzania in Pictures* (5–8). Illus. Series: Visual Geography. 1989, Lerner LB $25.55 (0-8225-1838-4). 64pp. Part of the Visual Geography series, contains information on history, geography, economy, religion, and culture. (Rev: BL 2/1/89) [967.8104]

16208 Twagilimana, Aimable. *Hutu and Tutsi* (5–9). Series: The Heritage Library of African Peoples. 1997, Rosen LB $28.75 (0-8239-1999-4). A large section of this book is devoted to the current struggle between the Hutu and Tutsi people of central

Africa, along with chapters on art and religion. (Rev: BR 9–10/98; SLJ 3/98) [967]

16209 Wangari, Esther. *Ameru* (5–8). Illus. Series: Heritage Library of American Peoples. 1995, Rosen LB $15.95 (0-8239-1766-5). 64pp. A history and description of the culture of the Ameru people of Kenya and the humiliation of being conquered by the British. (Rev: SLJ 11/95) [967.62]

16210 Willis, Terri. *Democratic Republic of the Congo* (4–6). Series: Enchantment of the World. 2004, Scholastic LB $35.00 (0-516-24250-4). 144pp. Contemporary life, history, geography, culture are all covered in this well-illustrated and well-written volume suitable for report writers. (Rev: BL 9/1/04) [967.51]

16211 Zeleza, Tiyambe. *Maasai* (5–8). Illus. Series: Heritage Library of African Peoples. 1994, Rosen LB $17.95 (0-8239-1757-6). 64pp. An introduction to these people of Kenya and Tanzania, their culture, customs, and history. (Rev: SLJ 5/95) [967.62]

16212 Zeleza, Tiyambe. *Mijikenda* (5–8). Illus. Series: Heritage Library of American Peoples. 1995, Rosen LB $15.95 (0-8239-1767-3). 64pp. The history and present-day lifestyle of this group that lives in Kenya and is made up of nine peoples. (Rev: SLJ 11/95) [967.62]

Northern Africa

16213 Blauer, Ettagale, and Jason Lauré. *Morocco* (4–7). Series: Enchantment of the World. 1999, Children's Book Pr. LB $34.50 (0-516-20961-2). 144pp. In this fine introduction to Morocco topics include history, government, economics, people, religion, culture, and the arts. (Rev: BL 9/15/99) [964]

16214 Bowden, Rob. *Settlements of the Nile* (3–5). Illus. Series: Rivers Through Time. 2005, Heinemann LB $20.95 (1-4034-5720-4). 48pp. Traces the history and contemporary life of major settlements along the Nile, discussing environmental and other important issues.

16215 Fox, Mary V. *Tunisia* (5–8). Illus. Series: Enchantment of the World. 1990, Children's Book Pr. paper $32.00 (0-516-02724-7). 128pp. Introduces this North African country. (Rev: BL 1/1/91) [961.1]

16216 Kagda, Falaq. *Algeria* (4–7). Illus. Series: Cultures of the World. 1997, Marshall Cavendish LB $35.64 (0-7614-0680-8). 128pp. This book on Algeria emphasizes the people and how they live. (Rev: BL 8/97) [965]

16217 Malcolm, Peter. *Libya* (4–7). Illus. 1993, Marshall Cavendish LB $35.64 (1-85435-573-2). 128pp. Well-chosen photographs and readable text give good background information as well as material on present problems. (Rev: BL 8/93) [961.2]

16218 Mann, Kenny. *Egypt, Kush, Aksum: Northeast Africa* (4–6). Illus. Series: African Kingdoms of the Past. 1997, Dillon LB $19.95 (0-87518-655-6); paper $7.95 (0-382-39657-X). 105pp. Describes these famous ancient African civilizations as well as

northeast Africa today. Also use *Zenj, Buganda: East Africa.* (Rev: SLJ 9/97) [967]

16219 Merrick, Patrick. *Morocco* (3–5). Series: Countries: Faces and Places. 2000, Child's World LB $25.64 (1-56766-737-6). 32pp. An oversize book filled with color illustrations that describes the history, geography, and people of Morocco. (Rev: BL 4/15/01; HBG 3/01) [964]

16220 Stewart, Judy. *A Family in Morocco* (2–4). Illus. 1986, Lerner LB $18.60 (0-8225-1664-0). 32pp. Basic geography and the facts of daily living, focusing on one child in a family. (Rev: BL 5/15/86; SLJ 10/86)

16221 Weintraub, Aileen. *The Sahara Desert: The Biggest Desert* (3–5). Illus. Series: Great Record Breakers in Nature. 2001, Rosen $18.75 (0-8239-5640-7). 24pp. Informative text and dramatic full-page photographs introduce the world's biggest desert and its composition, extraordinary range of temperatures, residents, and fossil history. (Rev: BL 12/15/01; SLJ 7/01) [966]

Southern Africa

16222 Biesele, Megan, and Kxao Royal. *San* (5–7). Series: Heritage Library of African Peoples. 1997, Rosen LB $15.95 (0-8239-1997-8). 63pp. The San people of Botswana, Namibia, and South Africa are featured in this account that tells of their rich tradition and their struggle for freedom. (Rev: BL 9/15/97) [968.06]

16223 Blauer, Ettagale, and Jason Lauré. *Madagascar* (4–7). Series: Enchantment of the World. 2000, Children's Book Pr. LB $34.50 (0-516-21634-1). 144pp. Madagascar, the island nation off the coast of Africa, is introduced. Topics addressed include its land and people, wildlife, history, traditions, daily life, and economy. (Rev: BL 12/15/00) [969]

16224 Blauer, Ettagale, and Jason Lauré. *Swaziland* (5–8). Illus. Series: Enchantment of the World. 1996, Children's Pr. paper $32.00 (0-516-20020-8). This landlocked kingdom north of South Africa is introduced with material on its physical features, history, and economy. (Rev: BL 1/1–15/97) [968.87]

16225 Bolaane, Maitseo, and Part T. Mgadla. *Batswana* (5–7). Series: Heritage Library of African Peoples. 1997, Rosen LB $15.95 (0-8239-2008-9). 64pp. Discusses the Batswana people, who live in Botswana and South Africa, with material on their history, culture, and present status. (Rev: BL 1/1–15/98) [968]

16226 Brandenburg, Jim. *Sand and Fog: Adventures in Southern Africa* (5–8). Illus. 1994, Walker LB $17.85 (0-8027-8233-7). 44pp. A stunning photoessay about the wildlife found in Namibia. (Rev: BCCB 5/94; BL 3/1/94*; HB 5–6/94; SLJ 5/94) [968.1]

16227 Brownlie, Alison. *South Africa* (2–4). Illus. Series: We Come From. 2000, Raintree $22.83 (0-8172-5221-5). 32pp. Readers are introduced to South Africa, the homeland of this book's 7-year-old narrator, including its geography, food, weather, work, schools, and other topics. (Rev: BL 4/15/00; HBG 10/00; SLJ 10/00) [968]

16228 Dawson, Zoe. *South Africa* (K–3). Illus. Series: Postcards From. 1995, Raintree LB $22.83 (0-8172-4015-2). 32pp. In double-page spreads, points of interest in South Africa are described. (Rev: SLJ 3/96) [968]

16229 Diouf, Sylviane. *Kings and Queens of Southern Africa* (4–7). Illus. Series: Watts Library: Africa — Kings and Queens. 2000, Watts LB $24.00 (0-531-20374-3). 64pp. Through the lives of Shaka the Zulu king, Moshoeshoe of the Sotho kingdom, and others, the reader gets a good history of this region before and during the colonial period. (Rev: BL 2/15/01) [968]

16230 Ellis, Royston, and John R. Jones. *Madagascar* (2–4). Series: Festivals of the World. 1999, Gareth Stevens LB $14.95 (0-8368-2023-1). 32pp. A few craft projects and recipes accompany this description of Madagascar's unique holidays — both religious and secular. (Rev: BL 4/15/98) [969.1]

16231 Flint, David. *South Africa* (5–8). Illus. Series: Modern Industrial World. 1996, Raintree $24.26 (0-8172-4554-5). 48pp. The present economic status of South Africa is studied through personal narratives and case studies. (Rev: BL 2/15/97; SLJ 8/97) [968]

16232 Green, Jen. *South Africa* (4–8). Series: Nations of the World. 2001, Raintree LB $34.26 (0-7398-1282-3). 128pp. A profile of the strongest industrial nation in Africa, with material on its geography, resources, environment, government, economy, and future. (Rev: BL 6/1–15/01; HBG 10/01) [968]

16233 Green, Rebecca L. *Merina* (5–7). Illus. Series: Heritage Library of African Peoples. 1997, Rosen LB $17.95 (0-8239-1991-9). 64pp. This account tells of the life, past and present, of this African tribal group that lives on the island of Madagascar. (Rev: BL 4/15/97) [969.1]

16234 Halvorsen, Lisa. *Letters Home from Zimbabwe* (2–5). Series: Letters Home From. 2000, Blackbirch LB $16.95 (1-56711-412-1). 32pp. Formatted as letters from a child visiting Zimbabwe to a friend back home, this book gives basic information on the country with postcard-like illustrations. (Rev: HBG 3/01; SLJ 11/00) [968.91]

16235 Heale, Jay. *South Africa* (2–3). Illus. Series: Festivals of the World. 1998, Gareth Stevens LB $18.60 (0-8368-2007-X). 32pp. Lists the principal holidays in South Africa, details the main ones, and provides a section on crafts. (Rev: BL 5/15/98; HBG 10/98; SLJ 10/98) [394.2]

16236 Heinrichs, Ann. *South Africa* (2–4). Illus. Series: True Books. 1997, Children's Book Pr. LB $22.00 (0-516-20340-1). 48pp. South Africa is introduced, with material on its history, geography, economy, and peoples. (Rev: BL 9/15/97) [968]

16237 Inserra, Rose, and Susan Powell. *The Kalahari* (5–8). Series: Ends of the Earth. 1997, Heinemann LB $25.45 (0-431-06932-8). An introduction to the history, animal and vegetable life, and future of this desert region of southern Botswana, eastern

Namibia, and western South Africa. (Rev: SLJ 11/97) [968]

16238 Kaschula, Russel. *Xhosa* (5–7). Series: Heritage Library of African Peoples. 1997, Rosen LB $17.95 (0-8239-2013-5). 64pp. The Xhosa people of South Africa are introduced with stunning photos and coverage of their past as well as present culture and lifestyles. (Rev: BL 1/1–15/98) [968]

16239 Langley, Andrew. *Cape Town* (4–7). Illus. Series: Great Cities of the World. 2005, World Almanac LB $22.50 (0-8368-5045-9). 48pp. An informative and appealing overview of this major city, with material on its history, its economy, and what it's like to live there.

16240 Lauré, Jason. *Angola* (5–8). Illus. Series: Enchantment of the World. 1990, Children's Book Pr. paper $32.00 (0-516-02721-2). 128pp. The troubled history of Angola is given, and geography and key people are introduced. (Rev: BL 1/1/91) [967.3]

16241 Lauré, Jason. *Botswana* (5–8). Illus. Series: Enchantment of the World. 1993, Children's Book Pr. paper $32.00 (0-516-02616-X). 128pp. An introduction to this republic that gained independence in 1964 and is famous for its gold and wildlife preserves. (Rev: BL 11/1/93; SLJ 4/94) [968.83]

16242 Lauré, Jason. *Namibia* (5–8). Series: Enchantment of the World. 1993, Children's Pr. paper $32.00 (0-516-02615-1). A description of the land and people of Namibia, which was once administered by South Africa and gained full independence in 1990. (Rev: BL 8/93) [968.81]

16243 Lauré, Jason. *Zambia* (4–6). Illus. Series: Enchantment of the World. 1989, Children's Book Pr. LB $32.00 (0-516-02716-6). 128pp. The land and people of Zambia are covered with special material in a ten-page section of important facts. (Rev: BL 1/1/90) [941.5]

16244 Lauré, Jason. *Zimbabwe* (4–7). Illus. 1989, Children's Book Pr. paper $32.00 (0-516-02704-2). 128pp. The history, culture, people, and customs of this African land. (Rev: BL 8/88) [968.91]

16245 Leigh, Nila K. *Learning to Swim in Swaziland: A Child's-Eye View of a Southern African Country* (2–4). Illus. 1993, Scholastic $15.95 (0-590-45938-4). 48pp. Nila's first-person account of her year in Swaziland. (Rev: BCCB 3/93; BL 1/15/93; SLJ 5/93) [968.8]

16246 *Madagascar in Pictures* (5–8). Illus. Series: Visual Geography. 1988, Lerner LB $25.55 (0-8225-1841-4). 64pp. Covers geography, history, culture, economics, religion, and health. (Rev: BL 2/1/89) [969.1]

16247 Ngwane, Zolani. *Zulu* (5–7). Series: Heritage Library of African Peoples. 1997, Rosen LB $15.95 (0-8239-2014-3). 64pp. Introduces the past history and culture of the Zulus of South Africa. Also use *Sukuma* and *Luba* (both 1997). (Rev: BL 9/15/97) [968.06]

16248 Nwaezeigwe, Nwankwo T. *Ngoni* (5–7). Illus. Series: Heritage Library of African Peoples. 1997, Rosen LB $17.95 (0-8239-2006-2). 64pp. Describes the history, traditions, and struggle for freedom of this African group in Malawi. (Rev: BL 4/15/97) [968.97]

16249 Oluikpe, Benson O. *Swazi* (5–7). Illus. Series: Heritage Library of African Peoples. 1997, Rosen LB $15.95 (0-8239-2012-7). 64pp. The Swazi people live in Swaziland and South Africa, and this book describes their history, traditions, and struggles for freedom. (Rev: BL 4/15/97; SLJ 12/97) [968]

16250 Oluonye, Mary N. *Madagascar* (1–3). Series: Globe-Trotters Club. 2000, Carolrhoda LB $22.60 (1-57505-120-6). 48pp. From the monsoons to the comfortable dry season, this is a simple introduction to the island off the coast of Africa that is known as "a World Apart." (Rev: BL 5/15/00; HBG 10/00) [969]

16251 Oluonye, Mary N. *South Africa* (3–5). Series: Globe-Trotters Club. 1999, Carolrhoda $22.60 (1-57505-116-8). 48pp. Double-page spreads cover standard topics on South Africa and are enhanced with sidebars containing activities and unusual bits of information. (Rev: BL 9/15/99; HBG 3/00; SLJ 3/00) [968]

16252 Oluonye, Mary N. *South Africa* (1–3). Series: A Ticket To. 1999, Carolrhoda LB $22.60 (1-57505-141-9). 48pp. Following a large map of the country, this first look at South Africa introduces the land and its people, using easy-to-understand language and many color pictures. (Rev: BL 9/15/99; HBG 3/00; SLJ 3/00) [968]

16253 Parker, Linda J. *The San of Africa* (4–6). Series: First Peoples. 2002, Lerner LB $23.93 (0-8225-4177-7). This account describes the history and culture of this nomadic people of the Kalahari Desert. (Rev: BL 5/15/02; HBG 10/02) [968]

16254 Rogers, Barbara Radcliffe, and Stillman D. Rogers. *Zimbabwe* (4–7). Series: Enchantment of the World. 2002, Children's Book Pr. LB $34.50 (0-516-21113-7). 144pp. This troubled African land is introduced with material on topics including history, geography, people, government, and resources. (Rev: BL 5/15/02; SLJ 7/02) [968.9]

16255 Rosemarin, Ike. *South Africa* (4–7). Illus. Series: Cultures of the World. 1993, Marshall Cavendish LB $35.64 (1-85435-575-9). 128pp. Historical and modern concerns are covered in this look at South Africa. (Rev: BL 8/93) [968]

16256 Schneider, Elizabeth Ann. *Ndebele* (5–7). Illus. Series: Heritage Library of African Peoples. 1997, Rosen LB $17.95 (0-8239-2009-7). 64pp. Topics covered about the Ndebele people of South Africa include environment, history, religion, social organization, politics, and customs. (Rev: BL 4/15/97) [968]

16257 *South Africa in Pictures* (5–8). Illus. Series: Visual Geography. 1996, Lerner LB $25.55 (0-8225-1835-X). 64pp. Focusing on climate, geography, wildlife, and the history of this troubled country. (Rev: BL 8/88) [968.06]

16258 Stark, Al. *Zimbabwe: A Treasure of Africa* (4–7). Illus. 1986, Macmillan $14.95 (0-87518-308-5). 160pp. The colorful history, culture, wildlife,

geography, and diversity of the people of Zimbabwe are detailed. (Rev: BL 6/15/86; SLJ 5/86) [968]

16259 Stein, R. Conrad. *Cape Town* (5–8). Series: Cities of the World. 1998, Children's Pr. LB $27.00 (0-516-20781-4). A photoessay that shows this modern, multicultural, multiracial South African capital with its rich diversity of people at work, at school, and at play. (Rev: BL 12/15/98; HBG 3/99) [968.7]

16260 Stotko, Mary-Ann. *South Africa* (4–6). Series: Countries of the World. 2002, Gareth Stevens LB $21.95 (0-8368-2347-8). 96pp. This fine, basic introduction to South Africa covers historical subjects as well as contemporary life and problems. (Rev: BL 6/1–15/02; HBG 10/02; SLJ 8/02) [938]

16261 Udechukwu, Ada. *Herero* (5–7). Illus. Series: Heritage Library of African Peoples. 1996, Rosen LB $17.95 (0-8239-2003-8). 64pp. The history, customs, and culture of the Herero people are described. (Rev: BL 3/15/96; SLJ 6/96) [968.8]

16262 Van Wyk, Gary N. *Basotho* (5–7). Illus. Series: Heritage Library of African Peoples. 1996, Rosen LB $17.95 (0-8239-2005-4). 63pp. Describes the Basotho people, who live in Lesotho and South Africa, with simple text on their history, religion, social organization, and customs. (Rev: BL 11/15/96; SLJ 3/97) [968]

16263 Van Wyk, Gary N., and Robert Johnson. *Shona* (5–7). Series: Heritage Library of African Peoples. 1997, Rosen LB $17.95 (0-8239-2011-9). 64pp. The Shona people of Zimbabwe are presented in outstanding photographs, with a text that covers their past, their culture, and their present living conditions and problems. (Rev: BL 1/1–15/98) [968]

16264 Wulfsohn, Gisèle. *A Child's Day in a South African City* (K–3). Illus. Series: A Child's Day. 2003, Marshall Cavendish $15.95 (0-7614-1407-X). 32pp. A black South African child's experiences in his integrated school and blended family, with explanations of his country's customs and culture. (Rev: BL 2/15/03; HBG 3/03; SLJ 2/03) [968]

16265 *Zimbabwe* (5–9). Illus. Series: Major World Nations. 1999, Chelsea LB $19.95 (0-7910-4753-9). A good introduction to Zimbabwe's history, geography, government, people, pastimes, economy, and culture. (Rev: SLJ 8/98) [968]

16266 *Zimbabwe in Pictures* (5–8). Illus. Series: Visual Geography. 1997, Lerner LB $25.55 (0-8225-1825-2). 64pp. Many photographs highlight this overview of Zimbabwe's history, climate, wildlife, and culture. (Rev: BL 4/15/88) [968]

Western Africa

16267 Adeeb, Hassan, and Bonnetta Adeeb. *Nigeria: One Nation, Many Cultures* (4–8). Illus. Series: Exploring Cultures of the World. 1995, Benchmark LB $27.07 (0-7614-0190-3). 64pp. Opening with an account of a legendary figure, this book continues with an introduction to Nigeria that emphasizes its culture and how the people live. (Rev: SLJ 6/96) [966.9]

861

16268 Adeleke, Tunde. *Songhay* (5–7). Illus. Series: Heritage Library of African Peoples. 1996, Rosen LB $28.75 (0-8239-1986-2). 63pp. Both historical information and material on contemporary life are given in this account of the African people who live chiefly in Mali, Niger, and Benin. (Rev: BL 11/15/96) [960]

16269 Ahiagble, Gilbert Bobbo, and Louise Meyer. *Master Weaver from Ghana* (3–5). Photos by Nestor Hernandez. 1998, Open Hand $18.00 (0-940880-61-X). 32pp. Daily life in Ghana is explored in this book about a master weaver, Ahiagble, his techniques, craft, and the culture he represents. (Rev: SLJ 3/99) [966.7]

16270 Anda, Michael O. *Yoruba* (5–7). Illus. Series: Heritage Library of African Peoples. 1996, Rosen LB $15.95 (0-8239-1988-9). 64pp. Looks at the environment, history, religion, social organization, politics, customs, and culture of the Yoruba people. (Rev: BL 3/15/96; SLJ 6/96) [960]

16271 Azuonye, Chukwuma. *Edo: The Bini People of the Benin Kingdom* (5–7). Illus. Series: Heritage Library of African Peoples. 1996, Rosen LB $17.95 (0-8239-1985-4). 64pp. In this discussion of the Edo people of Nigeria, such topics as history, religion, customs, and culture are covered. (Rev: BL 3/15/96) [966.9]

16272 Beaton, Margaret. *Senegal* (5–8). Series: Enchantment of the World. 1997, Children's Pr. paper $32.00 (0-516-20304-5). An introduction to this West African nation, its people, and its cities, including the capital of Dakar. (Rev: BL 7/97; HBG 3/98) [916.63]

16273 Berg, Elizabeth. *Nigeria* (2–4). Series: Festivals of the World. 1998, Gareth Stevens LB $14.95 (0-8368-2017-7). 32pp. A few suitable crafts and recipes accompany this introduction to the land and people of Nigeria, with emphasis on their special holidays and how they are celebrated. (Rev: BL 12/15/98; HBG 10/99) [966.8]

16274 Blauer, Ettagale, and Jason Lauré. *Ghana* (4–7). Series: Enchantment of the World. 1999, Children's Book Pr. LB $34.50 (0-516-20962-0). 144pp. A geographical and cultural exploration of the African nation of Ghana, once a center of the slave trade. (Rev: BL 12/15/99) [966.7]

16275 Blauer, Ettagale, and Jason Lauré. *Nigeria* (4–7). Series: Enchantment of the World. 2001, Children's Book Pr. LB $34.50 (0-516-22281-3). An interesting and well-illustrated introduction to the nation that is dominated by the delta of the Niger River. (Rev: BL 1/1–15/02) [966.9]

16276 Boateng, Faustine Ama. *Asante* (5–7). Illus. Series: Heritage Library of African Peoples. 1996, Rosen LB $17.95 (0-8239-1975-7). 63pp. This African people living in present-day Ghana is described, with information on history, traditions, and lifestyle. (Rev: BL 11/15/96; SLJ 3/97) [966.7]

16277 Bowden, Rob, and Roy Maconachie. *Nigeria* (5–7). Series: The Changing Face Of. 2003, Raintree LB $28.56 (0-7398-6829-2). 48pp. An examination of modern-day Nigeria, with a look at the nation's past difficulties and how it may benefit

from its wealth of natural resources. (Rev: SLJ 4/04) [966.9]

16278 Brace, Steve. *Ghana* (4–8). Illus. Series: Economically Developing Countries. 1995, Thomson Learning LB $24.26 (1-56847-242-0). 48pp. Rich and poor rural and urban families are introduced in this attractive book on Ghana, its past, and its present. (Rev: SLJ 7/95) [966.7]

16279 Brook, Larry. *Daily Life in Ancient and Modern Timbuktu* (5–7). Illus. 1999, Lerner LB $25.26 (0-8225-3215-8). 64pp. A fascinating look at this ancient West African city that was once a center of commerce and learning. (Rev: BL 9/1/99; HBG 10/99; SLJ 7/99) [966.23]

16280 Brownlie, Alison. *Nigeria* (2–4). Series: We Come From. 2000, Raintree LB $22.83 (0-8172-5513-3). 32pp. Using a native child as a guide, this introduction to Nigeria gives basic information on the country plus such specialized coverage as a trip to local markets, making a fish stew, a game of hide and seek, and several recipes. (Rev: BL 4/15/00; HBG 10/00; SLJ 10/00) [966.9]

16281 Brownlie, Alison. *West Africa* (3–5). Series: Foods and Festivals. 1999, Raintree LB $22.83 (0-8172-5552-4). 32pp. Recipes for festival dishes enhance this account of life in West Africa as seen through its various holidays. (Rev: BL 5/15/99; HBG 10/99; SLJ 7/99) [966]

16282 Chambers, Catherine. *West African States: 15th Century to the Colonial Era* (5–8). Series: Looking Back. 1999, Raintree $19.98 (0-8172-5427-7). A brief overview of the history and culture of the great empires of West Africa and how they disappeared with the arrival of the Europeans. (Rev: BL 5/15/99) [966.2]

16283 Chicoine, Stephen D. *A Liberian Family* (3–5). Photos by Stephen Chicoine. Series: Journey Between Two Worlds. 1997, Lerner LB $22.60 (0-8225-3411-8); paper $8.95 (0-8225-0975-6). 64pp. Explains why a family was forced to leave Liberia to escape persecution. Also gives a history of this land and its people. (Rev: HBG 3/98; SLJ 2/98) [966]

16284 Chocolate, Deborah M. *Kente Colors* (PS–3). Illus. by John Ward. 1996, Walker LB $16.85 (0-8027-8389-9). 32pp. The history and traditions of kente cloth of Ghana are told, along with a description of its meaning and colors. (Rev: BL 2/15/96; SLJ 6/96) [391]

16285 *Cote d'Ivoire (Ivory Coast) in Pictures* (5–8). Illus. Series: Visual Geography. 1988, Lerner LB $25.55 (0-8225-1828-7). 64pp. Covering all aspects of life in this overview, with pictorial emphasis and coverage of possible future developments. (Rev: BL 4/15/88; SLJ 11/88) [966.68]

16286 Diouf, Sylviane. *Kings and Queens of West Africa* (4–7). Series: Watts Library: Africa — Kings and Queens. 2000, Watts LB $24.00 (0-531-20375-1). 64pp. Some of the royal figures covered in this historical survey of West Africa are Emperor Mansa Musa of Mali and Nsate Yalla Mbodj, queen of the Walo of Senegal. (Rev: BL 3/1/01) [960]

16287 Dubois, Muriel L. *Liberia* (2–5). Illus. Series: Questions and Answers: Countries. 2005, Capstone LB $16.95 (0-7368-3755-8). 32pp. Using a question-and-answer format, simple text, large photos, and many factboxes, this is an introduction to Liberia today, with material on history and traditional culture.

16288 *Ghana* (5–9). Illus. Series: Major World Nations. 1999, Chelsea LB $21.95 (0-7910-4739-3). Basic facts about Ghana's history, geography, politics, government, economy, natural resources, education, and people. (Rev: HBG 9/98; SLJ 8/98) [966.7]

16289 Hathaway, Jim. *Cameroon in Pictures* (5–8). Illus. Series: Visual Geography. 1992, Lerner LB $25.55 (0-8225-1857-0). 64pp. With numerous charts, maps, and photographs, the country of Cameroon is introduced. (Rev: BL 9/15/89) [967]

16290 Heale, Jay. *Democratic Republic of the Congo* (5–9). Series: Cultures of the World. 1998, Marshall Cavendish LB $35.64 (0-7614-0874-6). A history of this nation that has been stricken with civil wars and political instability, with descriptions of its history, economy, government, people, and culture. (Rev: HBG 9/99; SLJ 6/99) [967]

16291 Heinrichs, Ann. *Niger* (4–7). Series: Enchantment of the World. 2001, Children's Book Pr. LB $34.50 (0-516-21633-3). Niger, a predominately Muslim country that is one of the hottest places in the world, is described in this attractive volume with material on topics such as resources, history, and culture. (Rev: BL 1/1–15/02) [967]

16292 Hetfield, Jamie. *The Yoruba of West Africa* (PS–2). Illus. Series: Celebrating the Peoples and Civilizations of Africa. 1996, Rosen LB $13.95 (0-8239-2332-0). 24pp. A simple introduction to the Yoruba people of West Africa, with material on their culture, food, rituals, and lifestyle. (Rev: SLJ 11/96) [966.9]

16293 Ismail, Yinka. *Nigeria* (4–6). Series: Countries of the World. 2001, Gareth Stevens LB $21.95 (0-8368-2337-0). 96pp. This general introduction to Nigeria is presented in concise, well-organized text and many colorful illustrations and maps. (Rev: BL 12/15/01; HBG 3/02; SLJ 1/02) [966.9]

16294 Koslow, Philip. *Dahomey: The Warrior Kings* (5–8). Illus. Series: The Kingdoms of Africa. 1996, Chelsea LB $20.85 (0-7910-3137-3); paper $8.95 (0-7910-3138-1). 63pp. A history of the West African kingdom that flourished in the 17th and 18th centuries, describing how the slave trade affected it. (Rev: BR 11–12/96; SLJ 12/96) [960]

16295 Kummer, Patricia K. *Cote d'Ivoire* (5–8). Illus. Series: Enchantment of the World. 1996, Children's Book Pr. paper $32.00 (0-516-02641-0). 124pp. An introduction to the small French-speaking African republic of Ivory Coast, which gained its freedom in 1960 and is now known as Cote d'Ivoire. (Rev: BL 7/96) [966.68]

16296 Kushner, Nina. *The Democratic Republic of the Congo* (4–6). Series: Countries of the World. 2000, Gareth Stevens LB $26.60 (0-8368-2330-3). 96pp. Details the history of this African republic

once controlled by the French, along with material on geography, government, lifestyles, food, economy, and current problems. (Rev: BL 3/15/01; HBG 10/01) [967]

16297 Levy, Patricia. *Nigeria* (4–7). Illus. Series: Cultures of the World. 1993, Marshall Cavendish LB $35.64 (1-85435-574-0). 128pp. Information on history, geography, lifestyles, people, and culture. (Rev: BL 8/93) [966.9]

16298 *Liberia in Pictures* (5–8). Illus. Series: Visual Geography. 1996, Lerner LB $25.55 (0-8225-1837-6). 64pp. Covers climate, geography, wildlife, vegetation, and natural resources. (Rev: BL 8/88) [966.62]

16299 MacDonald, Fiona. *Ancient African Town* (4–7). Illus. by Gerald Wood. Series: Metropolis. 1998, Watts LB $25.00 (0-531-14480-1). 45pp. Using a well-written text and colorful drawings, this work describes life in a 17th-century African community based on Benin City of the Edo empire in present-day Nigeria. (Rev: HBG 3/99; SLJ 1/99) [966.9]

16300 Mack-Williams, Kibibi V. *Mossi* (5–7). Illus. Series: Heritage Library of African Peoples. 1996, Rosen LB $17.95 (0-8239-1984-6). 64pp. The history, social organization, and culture of the Mossi people of West Africa are described. (Rev: BL 3/15/96) [966.25]

16301 Mann, Kenny. *Ghana, Mali, Songhay: The Western Sudan* (4–8). Series: African Kingdoms of the Past. 1996, Silver Burdett $15.95 (0-87518-656-4); paper $7.95 (0-382-39176-4). An eloquently written book about the once powerful empires of Ghana, Mali, and Songhay, with information on the beginnings of Islam Africa and how the slave trade gradually took over. (Rev: SLJ 9/96) [960]

16302 Murphy, Patricia J. *Nigeria* (3–5). Illus. Series: Discovering Cultures. 2004, Benchmark LB $17.95 (0-7614-1795-8). 48pp. An attractive introduction to Nigeria, covering land, people, daily life, education, food, and celebrations, with discussion of the relationships among the many tribes. (Rev: SLJ 6/05)

16303 *Nigeria in Pictures* (5–8). Illus. Series: Visual Geography. 1995, Lerner LB $25.55 (0-8225-1826-0). 64pp. A visual focus on this African land. (Rev: BL 8/88) [966.9]

16304 Nnoromele, Salome. *Life Among the Ibo Women of Nigeria* (4–7). Illus. 1998, Lucent LB $27.45 (1-56006-344-0). 96pp. A beautifully written account of women's role in Nigeria's Ibo society, tracing the country's history, social structure, and changes brought about by contacts with Western culture. (Rev: BL 9/1/98) [305.48]

16305 Nwanunobi, C. O. *Malinke* (5–7). Illus. Series: Heritage Library of African Peoples. 1996, Rosen LB $28.75 (0-8239-1979-X). 63pp. Features the culture, history, and contemporary lifeways of the Malinke people, now living along the western coast of Africa. (Rev: BL 11/15/96) [966.23]

16306 Nwanunobi, C. O. *Soninke* (5–7). Illus. Series: Heritage Library of African Peoples. 1996, Rosen LB $28.75 (0-8239-1978-1). 63pp. A discussion of the African people found in such countries as Ghana, Mali, Nigeria, and Senegal, with material on history, customs, and present living conditions. (Rev: BL 11/15/96) [966]

16307 Ogbaa, Kalu. *Igbo* (5–8). Illus. Series: Heritage Library of American Peoples. 1995, Rosen LB $15.95 (0-8239-1977-3). 64pp. An introduction to the Igbo people, who are one of the three most important ethnic groups in Nigeria. (Rev: SLJ 11/95) [966.9]

16308 Onyefulu, Ifeoma. *Here Comes Our Bride! An African Wedding Story* (K–3). Illus. 2004, Lincoln $15.95 (1-84507-047-X). 32pp. A Nigerian wedding comes to life in this attractive photoessay that captures all the local traditions and rituals before, during, and after the marriage ceremony. (Rev: BL 9/1/04) [392.5]

16309 Onyefulu, Ifeoma. *Ogbo: Sharing Life in an African Village* (1–5). Illus. 1996, Harcourt $15.00 (0-15-200498-X). 32pp. In a Nigerian village, people in the same age group, called ogbo, work together for the good of the community. (Rev: BCCB 4/96; BL 4/15/96; HB 9–10/96; SLJ 4/96*) [306]

16310 Onyefulu, Ifeoma. *Saying Good-Bye: A Special Farewell to Mama Nkwelle* (PS–2). Illus. 2001, Millbrook $21.91 (0-7613-1965-4). 32pp. A young boy describes the two weeks of mourning and the traditional Nigerian village funeral that take place on his great-grandmother's death. (Rev: BL 5/1/01; HB 7–8/01; HBG 10/01; SLJ 7/01) [393.9]

16311 Onyefulu, Ifeoma. *Welcome Dede! An African Naming Ceremony* (K–3). Illus. 2005, Frances Lincoln paper $7.95 (1-84507-311-8). 32pp. A dazzling photoessay of a traditional ceremony in a Ghanaian village. (Rev: BL 2/1/05) [392.1]

16312 Parris, Ronald. *Hausa* (5–7). Illus. Series: Heritage Library of African Peoples. 1996, Rosen LB $28.75 (0-8239-1983-8). 63pp. A look at the Hausa people of Niger and Nigeria, with material on history and contemporary life. (Rev: BL 11/15/96) [966]

16313 Peffer-Engels, John. *The Benin Kingdom of West Africa* (K–2). Illus. Series: Celebrating the Peoples and Civilizations of Africa. 1996, Rosen LB $13.95 (0-8239-2334-7). 24pp. This account describes the Benin kingdom, the Edo people, how many were enslaved and taken to the United States, and their present culture and lifestyle. (Rev: SLJ 1/97) [966.9]

16314 Provencal, Francis, and Catherine McNamara. *A Child's Day in a Ghanaian City* (1–3). Series: A Child's Day. 2001, Benchmark LB $15.95 (0-7614-1223-9). 32pp. A 7-year-old escorts readers through a typical day in this book that ends with brief information on history, geography, people, religion, and language. (Rev: BL 11/15/01; SLJ 3/02) [966.7]

16315 Reef, Catherine. *This Our Dark Country: The American Settlers of Liberia* (5–10). 2002, Clarion $17.00 (0-618-14785-3). 136pp. This chronological account of Liberia's history makes good use of excerpts from letters and diaries. (Rev: BL 11/15/02; HBG 3/03; SLJ 12/02)

16316 Sallah, Tijan M. *Wolof* (5–7). Illus. Series: Heritage Library of African Peoples. 1996, Rosen LB $17.95 (0-8239-1987-0). 64pp. Using maps, many color illustrations, and text, the Wolof people of Africa are introduced. (Rev: BL 3/15/96; SLJ 7/96) [966.3]

16317 *Senegal in Pictures* (5–8). Illus. Series: Visual Geography. 1989, Lerner LB $25.55 (0-8225-1827-9). 64pp. A look at the geography, history, culture, and economics of Senegal. (Rev: BL 4/15/89; SLJ 11/88) [966.3]

16318 Sheehan, Patricia. *Côte d'Ivoire* (5–8). 1999, Marshall Cavendish LB $35.64 (0-7614-0980-7). 128pp. The Ivory Coast is presented with coverage of its geography, history, government, economy, and social and cultural life. (Rev: HBG 10/00; SLJ 4/00) [966.68]

16319 Tenquist, Alasdair. *Nigeria* (5–8). Illus. Series: Economically Developing Countries. 1996, Raintree LB $24.26 (0-8172-4527-8). This introduction to Nigeria emphasizes present-day government and economic conditions. (Rev: BL 3/1/97; SLJ 9/97) [330.9669]

16320 Zimmermann, Robert. *The Gambia* (5–8). Illus. Series: Enchantment of the World. 1994, Children's Book Pr. paper $32.00 (0-516-02625-9). 128pp. This tiny West African country is introduced in text and color photographs that cover all major topics related to this nation. (Rev: BL 12/15/94; SLJ 4/95) [966.51]

Asia

General

16321 Barber, Nicola. *Hong Kong* (3–6). Series: Great Cities of the World. 2004, World Almanac LB $30.00 (0-8368-5038-6). 48pp. Hong Kong's history, geography, and economy are described, as are shopping and leisure attractions and the life of the city. (Rev: SLJ 4/05)

16322 Bowden, Rob. *Settlements of the Indus River* (3–5). Illus. Series: Rivers Through Time. 2005, Heinemann LB $20.95 (1-4034-5718-2). 48pp. Traces the history and contemporary life of major settlements along the Indus, discussing environmental and other important issues.

16323 Bramwell, Martyn. *Southern and Eastern Asia* (4–8). Illus. Series: The World in Maps. 2001, Lerner LB $23.93 (0-8225-2916-5). 48pp. For each country in these geographical areas, readers will find a color map, the flag, a box containing important facts, and brief discussions of geography, industry, and economy. Also use *Northern and Western Asia* (2001). (Rev: HBG 10/01; SLJ 7/01) [915]

16324 Dramer, Kim. *The Mekong River* (4–8). Series: Watts Library. 2001, Watts LB $24.00 (0-531-11854-1). 63pp. A fact-filled introduction to the history of the Mekong and to the landscape and industry found along it. (Rev: SLJ 5/01) [959.7]

16325 Greenblatt, Miriam. *Genghis Khan and the Mongol Empire* (5–8). Series: Rulers and Their

Times. 2001, Marshall Cavendish LB $28.50 (0-7614-1027-9). This handsomely illustrated book presents, in three parts, a life of Genghis Khan, a section on conditions in Russia during his reign, and a selection of documents of the time. (Rev: BL 1/1–15/02; HBG 3/02; SLJ 2/02) [947]

16326 Hammond, Paula. *China and Japan* (4–8). Illus. Series: Cultures and Costumes: Symbols of Their Period. 2003, Mason Crest LB $19.95 (1-59084-436-X). 64pp. A detailed survey of the history of garments and accessories worn by people of all classes in these two Asian nations prior to the 20th century. (Rev: HBG 4/04; SLJ 3/04) [391]

16327 Kalz, Jill. *Mount Everest* (4–6). Illus. Series: Natural Wonders of the World. 2004, Creative Education LB $18.95 (1-58341-325-1). 32pp. After establishing this important mountain's location, this oversized picture book full of color photographs looks at geology, climate, wildlife, people, and other pertinent facts. (Rev: SLJ 1/05) [915.496]

16328 Kilgallon, Conor. *India and Sri Lanka* (4–8). Illus. Series: Cultures and Costumes: Symbols of Their Period. 2003, Mason Crest LB $19.95 (1-59084-443-2). 64pp. A look at the history of garments and accessories worn by all classes of people in India and Sri Lanka up to the end of the 19th century. (Rev: HBG 4/04; SLJ 3/04) [391]

16329 Lobaido, Anthony C., and Yumi Ng. *The Kurds of Asia* (4–6). Illus. Series: First Peoples. 2002, Lerner LB $23.93 (0-8225-0664-5). 48pp. Traditional and contemporary lifestyles are both included in this presentation of the Kurd people, the territory in which they live, and their history, culture, and economy. (Rev: HBG 3/03; SLJ 2/03)

16330 Major, John S., and Betty J. Belanus. *Caravan to America: Living Arts of the Silk Road* (5–8). Illus. 2002, Cricket $24.95 (0-8126-2666-4); paper $15.95 (0-8126-2677-X). 144pp. The traditions and skills emanating from the ancient trade routes are shown as surviving today in the work of a rug restorer in New York, an artist-monk in Los Angeles, a cook from Iran, and other examples in this fascinating approach to an interesting subject. (Rev: BL 11/1/02; HB 1–2/03; HBG 3/03; SLJ 2/03) [745]

16331 Sayre, April Pulley. *Asia* (5–8). Illus. Series: Seven Continents. 1999, Twenty-First Century LB $25.90 (0-7613-1368-0). 64pp. Using maps, photographs, and sidebars, this concise work discusses Asia's people, geography and geology, climate and oceans, flora and fauna. (Rev: BL 8/99; HBG 3/00) [915]

16332 Wilkinson, Philip, and Michael Pollard. *The Magical East* (4–7). Illus. by Robert Ingpen. Series: Mysterious Places. 1994, Chelsea LB $21.95 (0-7910-2754-6). 92pp. An oversize volume that highlights several places and cities of importance in the history of the Orient. (Rev: BL 1/15/94; SLJ 4/94) [930.1]

China

16333 Andersen, Dale. *Ancient China* (3–5). Illus. Series: History in Art. 2004, Raintree LB $29.93 (1-

4109-0519-5). 48pp. Examples of the era's art and sculpture accompany brief accounts of successive Chinese dynasties, pointing out what art can reveal about the life of the time. (Rev: BL 2/1/05; SLJ 4/05) [709]

16334 Baldwin, Robert F. *Daily Life in Ancient and Modern Beijing* (4–7). Illus. by Ray Webb. Series: Cities Through Time. 1999, Runestone LB $25.26 (0-8225-3214-X). 64pp. Topics introduced in this contrast between Beijing past and present include the arts, religion, school, history, and daily life. (Rev: HBG 10/99; SLJ 7/99) [951]

16335 Barber, Nicola. *Beijing* (4–7). Illus. Series: Great Cities of the World. 2004, World Almanac LB $29.26 (0-8368-5028-9). 48pp. In addition to the usual information on history and people, this attractive volume describes living conditions and leisure time and provides maps and sidebars about contemporary environmental and political issues. (Rev: BL 4/15/04) [951]

16336 Barter, James. *The Yangtze* (4–7). Series: Rivers of the World. 2003, Gale/Lucent LB $21.96 (1-59018-370-3). 112pp. A look at China's Yangtze river, illustrated with maps and black-and-white photographs, concentrating on its exploitation and development over the past half-century. (Rev: SLJ 3/04) [951]

16337 Behnke, Alison. *China in Pictures*. Rev. ed. (4–8). Illus. Series: Visual Geography. 2002, Lerner LB $27.93 (0-8225-0370-0). 80pp. An excellent introduction to China that includes material on geography, history, people, economy, and culture with maps, photographs, and illustrations. (Rev: BL 10/15/02; HBG 3/03; SLJ 3/03)

16338 Bowden, Rob. *The Yangtze* (5–7). Series: A River Journey. 2003, Raintree LB $28.56 (0-7398-6074-7). 48pp. A well-illustrated trip along China's Yangtze River, concentrating on mankind's influence on the river and vice versa, with photographs, maps, and charts. (Rev: HBG 4/04; SLJ 3/04) [915.1]

16339 Brown, Don. *Far Beyond the Garden Gate: Alexandra David-Neel's Journey to Lhasa* (PS–2). Illus. 2002, Houghton Mifflin $16.00 (0-618-08364-2). 32pp. This is the dramatic story of the long, intrepid travels of the first Western woman to visit the holy city of Lhasa (in 1924) and of her intense interest in Buddhism. (Rev: BL 10/1/02; HB 9–10/02; HBG 3/03; SLJ 10/02) [915.1]

16340 *China in Pictures* (5–8). Illus. 1994, Lerner LB $21.27 (0-8225-1859-7). 64pp. Covers history and government, cities, minerals, vegetation, and wildlife. (Rev: BL 5/1/89)

16341 Cole, Joanna. *Imperial China* (1–3). Illus. by Bruce Degen. Series: Ms. Frizzle's Adventures. 2005, Scholastic $16.95 (0-590-10822-0). 48pp. From Chinatown, Frizzle and friends are transported by dragon to 11th-century China in this information-packed yet appealing volume combining fact and fiction. (Rev: BL 6/1–15/05) [951]

16342 Costain, Meredith, and Paul Collins. *Welcome to China* (3–5). Illus. Series: Countries of the World. 2001, Chelsea LB $16.95 (0-7910-6548-0).

32pp. A very basic overview of the country with information on plants and animals, culture, sports, and schooling. (Rev: HBG 3/02; SLJ 2/02)

16343 Deedrick, Tami. *China* (3–6). Series: Ancient Civilizations. 2001, Raintree LB $15.98 (0-7398-3580-7). 48pp. Deedrick covers the Song, Yuan, and Ming dynasties of the Imperial period, giving good, clear information on history, daily life, culture, and inventions. (Rev: HBG 3/02; SLJ 9/01) [951]

16344 Dramer, Kim. *People's Republic of China* (4–7). Series: Enchantment of the World. 1999, Children's Book Pr. LB $34.50 (0-516-21077-7). 144pp. A revision of a standard source on China, including its history, government, people, languages, culture, and current conditions. (Rev: BL 9/15/99) [951]

16345 DuTemple, Lesley A. *The Great Wall of China* (4–7). Illus. Series: Great Building Feats. 2003, Lerner LB $27.93 (0-8225-0377-8). 80pp. This absorbing account tells the story of the building and importance of the Great Wall of China, with a good selection of illustrations, sidebar features, and maps. (Rev: BL 1/1–15/03; HBG 10/03; SLJ 4/03*) [931]

16346 Ferroa, Peggy. *China* (4–7). Illus. Series: Cultures of the World. 1991, Marshall Cavendish LB $35.64 (1-85435-399-3). 128pp. Unusual facts highlight this look at China, with emphasis on culture. (Rev: BL 2/15/92; SLJ 3/92) [951]

16347 Field, Catherine. *China* (4–8). Illus. Series: Nations of the World. 2000, Raintree LB $34.26 (0-8172-5781-0). 128pp. This is a fine introduction to China's past and present that supplies even more interesting information through the use of sidebars. (Rev: BL 10/15/00; HBG 10/00) [951.21]

16348 Flint, David. *China* (2–4). Series: On the Map. 1994, Raintree LB $22.83 (0-8114-3421-4). 32pp. Alternating a page of color photos with a page of text, such topics as China's geography, education, industry, and family life are covered. (Rev: BL 2/1/94; SLJ 7/94) [951]

16349 Goh, Sui Noi. *China* (4–8). Series: Countries of the World. 1998, Gareth Stevens LB $29.26 (0-8368-2124-6). An overview of the country's history, government, economy, geography, people, and the arts, followed by a "Closer Look" section that examines contemporary issues such as the role of women, secret societies, Tibet, Tiananman Square, and a final section on relations with North America. (Rev: BL 12/15/98; HBG 10/99; SLJ 6/99) [951]

16350 Goh, Sui Noi, and Lim Bee Ling. *Welcome to China* (2–4). Series: Welcome to My Country. 1999, Gareth Stevens LB $16.95 (0-8368-2395-8). 48pp. With an illustration on each page, this introduction to China covers such topics as geography, history, government, everyday life, language, and food. (Rev: SLJ 3/00) [951]

16351 Gresko, Marcia S. *Letters Home from China* (3–5). Illus. Series: Letters Home From. 1999, Blackbirch LB $16.95 (1-56711-400-8). 32pp. Written from the viewpoint of a young tourist, this book of letters introduces China, its land, people, and his-

tory. (Rev: BL 11/15/99; HBG 3/00; SLJ 1/00) [915.104]

16352 Harkonen, Reijo. *The Children of China* (4–6). Illus. by Matti Pitkanen. Series: The World's Children. 1990, Carolrhoda LB $23.93 (0-87614-394-X). 40pp. A travelogue narrative with striking color photos. (Rev: BL 6/15/90; SLJ 9/90) [951]

16353 Haskins, Jim. *Count Your Way Through China* (3–5). Illus. 1987, Carolrhoda LB $19.93 (0-87614-302-8); Lerner paper $5.95 (0-87614-486-5). 24pp. Concepts about China are introduced with the use of numbers 1 through 10. (Rev: BL 10/15/87; SLJ 9/87)

16354 Heinrichs, Ann. *China* (2–4). Illus. Series: True Books. 1997, Children's Book Pr. LB $22.00 (0-516-20329-0). 48pp. This introduction to China includes material on the land, people, history, and culture. (Rev: BL 9/15/97; SLJ 11/97) [951]

16355 Kagda, Falaq. *Hong Kong* (5–8). Series: Cultures of the World. 1998, Marshall Cavendish LB $35.64 (0-7614-0692-1). 128pp. An attractive book that introduces us to Hong Kong's history and geography, its people, and their culture and lifestyles. (Rev: HBG 3/98; SLJ 6/98) [951]

16356 Lazo, Caroline. *The Terra Cotta Army of Emperor Qin* (5–8). Illus. 1993, Macmillan LB $14.95 (0-02-754631-4). 80pp. The story of the 7,500 terracotta figures that guard the tomb of China's first emperor. (Rev: BL 7/93; SLJ 8/93) [931]

16357 McLenighan, Valjean. *China: A History to 1949* (5–8). Illus. 1983, Children's Book Pr. paper $32.00 (0-516-02754-9). 128pp. China from its earliest days to the founding of the People's Republic in 1949. [951]

16358 McMahon, Patricia. *Six Words, Many Turtles, and Three Days in Hong Kong* (4–6). Illus. 1997, Houghton Mifflin $16.00 (0-395-68621-0). 64pp. A photoessay about middle-class life in modern Hong Kong. (Rev: BL 7/97; HBG 3/98; SLJ 12/97) [306.85]

16359 Malaspina, Ann. *The Chinese Revolution and Mao Zedong in World History* (5–8). Series: World History. 2004, Enslow LB $20.95 (0-7660-1935-7). 128pp. After a brief overview of Chinese history, Malaspina provides a well-researched introduction to Chinese communism under Mao Zedong, from the early days of the party in the 1920s to the post-Mao reforms of recent times. (Rev: SLJ 3/04) [951]

16360 Mann, Elizabeth. *The Great Wall: The Story of Thousands of Miles of Earth and Stone* (4–8). Illus. Series: Wonders of the World. 1997, Mikaya $19.95 (0-9650493-2-9). The story behind the building of this massive structure, which began as far back as 200 B.C. and involves historical battles for land and power between the Chinese and the nomadic Mongols. (Rev: BL 1/1–15/98; SLJ 12/97) [951]

16361 March, Michael. *China* (2–5). Series: Country File. 2003, Smart Apple Media LB $16.95 (1-58340-236-5). 32pp. An introductory guide to China and its people, well illustrated with maps, charts, and photographs. (Rev: SLJ 3/04) [951]

16362 Martell, Hazel M. *The Ancient Chinese* (4–6). Illus. Series: World of the Past. 1993, Macmillan LB $14.95 (0-02-730653-4). 64pp. A history of early China with emphasis on culture and accomplishments. (Rev: BL 8/93) [951]

16363 Meister, Cari. *Yangtze River* (3–4). Series: Rivers and Lakes. 2002, ABDO LB $13.95 (1-57765-103-0). 24pp. A solid introduction to the Yangtze, its tributaries, flora and fauna, and the ways in which it has influenced human development in the area throughout history. (Rev: HBG 10/02; SLJ 7/02)

16364 Michels, Dia L. *Visiting China* (PS). Photos by Michael J. N. Bowles. Series: Look What I See! Where Can I Be? 2003, Platypus Media $16.95 (1-930775-15-6). Through the eyes of an infant, readers visit China in this unusual interactive book. (Rev: SLJ 4/04) [915.104]

16365 Minnis, Ivan. *You Are in Ancient China* (3–6). Series: You Are There! 2004, Raintree LB $18.45 (1-4109-0619-1). 32pp. Double-page spreads with plenty of illustrations and a low readling level introduce readers to the culture and lifestyle of the Han Dynasty. (Rev: BL 12/1/04; SLJ 2/05) [931]

16366 O'Connor, Jane. *The Emperor's Silent Army: Terracotta Warriors of Ancient China* (4–6). 2002, Viking $17.99 (0-670-03512-2). 48pp. The beautifully packaged story of the amazing discovery of an army of life-size terracotta soldiers in a field in China in 1974, with information about the emperor who oversaw their construction. (Rev: BL 4/15/02*; HBG 10/02; SLJ 4/02) [931]

16367 Odijk, Pamela. *The Chinese* (4–7). Illus. Series: Ancient World. 1991, Silver Burdett LB $14.95 (0-382-09894-3). 47pp. Brief, informative, and eye-catching treatment of the Chinese, including their influences on medicine and architecture. (Rev: BL 1/15/92) [951]

16368 Olson, Kay Melchisedech. *China* (2–3). Illus. Series: Many Cultures, One World. 2003, Capstone LB $22.60 (0-7368-1531-7). 32pp. A brief, accessible introduction to China and its people, family life, customs, and legends. (Rev: BL 10/15/03; HBG 10/03; SLJ 12/03) [951]

16369 Olson, Nathan. *China* (3–4). Illus. Series: Fact Finders: Questions and Answers. 2004, Capstone LB $22.60 (0-7368-2687-4). 32pp. Using a question-and-answer format, this title introduces China's history, government, economy, education, culture, sports, and lifestyle. (Rev: SLJ 1/05) [951]

16370 Patent, Dorothy Hinshaw. *The Incredible Story of China's Buried Warriors* (4–7). Series: Frozen in Time. 1999, Benchmark LB $27.07 (0-7614-0783-9). 64pp. This book explores the mystery of the creation of China's buried warriors, the thousands of terracotta statues that belonged to the first emperor of China and were uncovered in 1974. (Rev: BL 2/1/00; HBG 10/00; SLJ 3/00) [951]

16371 Pollard, Michael. *The Yangtze* (5–7). Series: Great Rivers. 1997, Benchmark LB $22.79 (0-7614-0505-4). 45pp. Covers historical and geographical aspects of the Yangtze River and discusses current dam-building projects. (Rev: HBG 3/98; SLJ 4/98) [951]

16372 Prior, Katherine. *The History of Emigration from China and Southeast Asia* (4–7). Series: Origins. 1997, Watts LB $21.00 (0-531-14442-9). 32pp. Outlines the political, social, and economic conditions in China that led to people leaving during different periods in its history, as well as material on where they went and their reception. (Rev: BL 12/15/97; HBG 3/98; SLJ 2/98) [951]

16373 Roop, Peter, and Connie Roop. *China* (1–3). Series: A Visit To. 1998, Heinemann LB $19.92 (1-57572-123-6). 32pp. An introduction to China in double-page spreads covering the land, its history and geography, culture, language, and transportation. (Rev: SLJ 7/98) [951]

16374 Schomp, Virginia. *The Ancient Chinese* (4–7). Series: People of the Ancient World. 2004, Watts LB $29.50 (0-531-11817-7). 112pp. Emperors, artisans, inventors, and healers are among the people presented in this overview of life in ancient China. (Rev: SLJ 2/05) [931]

16375 Shemie, Bonnie. *Houses of China* (4–7). Illus. Series: Native Dwellings. 1996, Tundra $13.95 (0-88776-369-3). 24pp. The various cultures of China, past and present, are introduced through an examination of 10 traditional houses. (Rev: SLJ 2/97) [951]

16376 Shui, Amy, and Stuart Thompson. *China* (3–5). Illus. Series: Foods and Festivals. 1999, Raintree $22.83 (0-8172-5757-8). 32pp. A few suitable recipes accompany descriptions of such Chinese festivals as New Year's, the Dragon-Boat festival, and the Moon festival. (Rev: BL 5/15/99; HBG 10/99) [394.1]

16377 So, Sungwan. *In a Chinese City* (2–4). 2001, Benchmark LB $15.95 (0-7614-1224-7). 32pp. A 7-year-old escorts readers through a typical day in this book that ends with brief information on history, geography, people, religion, and language. (Rev: HBG 3/02; SLJ 3/02)

16378 Stepanchuk, Carol. *Red Eggs and Dragon Boats: Celebrating Chinese Festivals* (3–6). Illus. 1994, Pacific View $16.95 (1-881896-08-0). 48pp. Five traditional Chinese festivals, including the Dragon Boat Festival and Moon Festival, are introduced, with details on customs and traditions plus recipes for food. (Rev: BL 3/15/94; SLJ 4/94) [394]

16379 Tao, Wang. *Exploration into China* (4–7). Illus. Series: Exploration. 1996, Dillon LB $15.95 (0-02-718087-5); paper $7.95 (0-382-39185-3). 48pp. The story of Chinese history until the opening up of the country by Europeans is given, with a brief overview of its recent history and contemporary life. (Rev: BL 8/96) [951]

16380 Teague, Ken. *Growing Up in Ancient China* (3–5). Illus. Series: Growing Up In. 1993, Troll paper $4.95 (0-8167-2716-3). 32pp. An introduction to life in ancient China, with information on history, customs, schooling, food, clothing, and daily activities. (Rev: BL 1/15/94) [931]

16381 Walker, Kathryn. *Shanghai* (4–7). Illus. Series: Great Cities of the World. 2005, World

Almanac LB $22.50 (0-8368-5046-7). 48pp. An informative and appealing overview of this important Chinese city, with material on its history, its economy, and what it's like to live there.

16382 Waterlow, Julia. *China* (4–7). Illus. Series: Country Insights. 1997, Raintree LB $27.12 (0-8172-4787-4). 48pp. Compares the social conditions — home life, employment, schooling, and recreation — in a large city and a rural village in China. (Rev: BL 7/97; SLJ 8/97) [951]

16383 Waterlow, Julia. *China* (2–4). Series: We Come From. 1999, Raintree LB $22.83 (0-8172-5219-3). 32pp. As well as a little information on Chinese home life, schools, and daily activities, this short book discusses geography and weather and gives a single recipe. (Rev: HBG 3/00; SLJ 3/00) [951]

16384 Waterlow, Julia. *The Yangtze* (4–7). Series: Great Rivers of the World. 2003, World Almanac LB $26.60 (0-8368-5447-0). 48pp. An exploration of the Yangtze's flow, history, and animals and plants, with discussion of the settlements along its banks, the industries it supports, recreation on its waters, and environmental threats to the river. (Rev: SLJ 9/03) [951]

16385 Williams, Suzanne. *Made in China: Ideas and Inventions from Ancient China* (4–6). Illus. 1997, Pacific View LB $19.95 (1-881896-14-5). 48pp. Covers such topics as papermaking, medicine, and inventions as they were developed in ancient China. (Rev: BL 2/1/97; SLJ 7/97) [931]

16386 Zhang, Song Nan. *The Children of China* (3–6). Illus. 1996, Tundra $17.95 (0-88776-363-4). 32pp. Children of nomadic minorities in China (e.g., Mongolians) are highlighted in this well-illustrated account. (Rev: BL 2/1/96) [759.11]

16387 Zhang, Song Nan. *Cowboy on the Steppes* (4–7). Illus. 1997, Tundra $15.95 (0-88776-410-X). 32pp. The true story of an 18-year-old Chinese boy and the first eight months he spent living in the steppes of Mongolia, where he has been sent during the Cultural Revolution to herd sheep. (Rev: BL 2/15/98; HBG 3/98; SLJ 2/98) [951.7]

India

16388 Arora Lal, Sunandini. *India* (4–5). Series: Countries of the World. 1999, Gareth Stevens LB $18.95 (0-8368-2262-5). 95pp. A colorful introduction to India, covering its geography, history, government, culture, and current problems. (Rev: BL 9/15/99; SLJ 10/99) [954]

16389 Bowden, Rob. *The Ganges* (5–7). Series: A River Journey. 2003, Raintree LB $28.56 (0-7398-6070-4). 48pp. A detailed look at India's most famous river, its importance to the people who live along it, and the challenge of pollution, with photographs, maps, and charts. (Rev: HBG 4/04; SLJ 3/04) [915.4]

16390 Chatterjee, Manini, and Anita Roy. *India* (4–8). Illus. Series: Eyewitness Books. 2002, DK paper $19.99 (0-7894-9029-3). 64pp. An informative and attractive overview of all aspects of India's

history and culture. (Rev: HBG 3/03; SLJ 12/02) [954.002]

16391 Cumming, David. *The Ganges Delta and Its People* (5–8). Illus. Series: People and Places. 1994, Thomson Learning LB $24.26 (1-56847-168-8). 48pp. An introduction to the Ganges delta, the people who live there, the economy it supports, and the tragedy of its frequent flooding. (Rev: BL 10/15/94) [954]

16392 Cumming, David. *India* (2–4). Series: We Come From. 1999, Raintree LB $22.83 (0-8172-5213-4). 32pp. A short book that gives an introduction to daily life in India plus some material on cities, weather, land features, and a recipe. (Rev: HBG 3/00; SLJ 3/00) [954]

16393 Cumming, David. *India* (4–7). Illus. Series: Our Country. 1998, Raintree LB $27.12 (0-8172-4797-1). 48pp. Several young inhabitants introduce India and describe life, customs, food, and their homes. (Rev: BL 12/1/89; HBG 10/98; SLJ 3/92) [954]

16394 Dalal, Anita. *India* (4–8). Series: Nations of the World. 2001, Raintree LB $34.26 (0-7398-1289-0). 128pp. A fine introduction to this vast, populous country with chapters on the land and cities, past and present, the economy, arts and living, and the future. (Rev: BL 12/15/01; HBG 3/02) [954]

16395 Das, Prodeepta. *I Is for India* (2–5). Photos by author. 1996, Silver Pr. LB $14.95 (0-382-39278-7). Using an alphabet book format, this account describes India and its geography, culture, religions, and peoples. (Rev: SLJ 11/96) [954]

16396 Dhanjal, Beryl. *Amritsar* (3–6). Illus. Series: Holy Cities. 1994, Dillon LB $21.00 (0-87518-571-1). 46pp. A colorful introduction to the holy city of Amritsar in northern India and to the religion of Sikhism. (Rev: SLJ 8/94) [915.404]

16397 DuTemple, Lesley A. *The Taj Mahal* (4–7). Series: Great Building Feats. 2003, Lerner LB $27.93 (0-8225-4692-0). 96pp. Using many illustrations, this account traces the building of the magnificent tomb that was inspired by one man's love for his wife. (Rev: BL 11/15/03) [954]

16398 Ganeri, Anita. *Exploration into India* (4–6). Illus. Series: Exploration. 1994, New Discovery $19.95 (0-02-718082-4); paper $7.95 (0-382-24733-7). 48pp. A history of India and its people that focuses on the outside individuals and empires that were influences through exploration and exploitation. (Rev: SLJ 5/95) [954]

16399 Goodwin, William. *India* (5–8). Series: Modern Nations of the World. 2000, Lucent LB $27.45 (1-56006-598-2). 112pp. An admirable introduction to India that gives material on the land and its past but concentrates on today's population, living conditions, and problems. (Rev: BL 3/15/00; HBG 10/00) [954]

16400 Gresko, Marcia S. *India* (3–5). Series: Letters Home From. 1999, Blackbirch LB $16.95 (1-56711-403-2). 32pp. Basic material on India's land, history, people, religion, and cities is given in a series of letters addressed home by a young American traveler. (Rev: BL 2/15/00; HBG 3/00) [954]

16401 Guile, Melanie. *Culture in India* (4–7). Illus. Series: Culture In. 2005, Raintree LB $27.79 (1-4109-1134-9). 32pp. Customs, holidays, clothing, food, and arts and crafts are well covered in this volume that also provides basic information needed for reports and interesting sidebar features on such topics as ancestor worship and celebrities. (Rev: SLJ 5/05) [954]

16402 Haskins, Jim. *Count Your Way Through India* (3–5). Illus. by Liz B. Dodson. Series: Count Your Way. 1990, Carolrhoda LB $19.93 (0-87614-414-8). 24pp. Using a numbers approach, this book introduces the culture, climate, and people of India. (Rev: BL 4/1/91) [954]

16403 Hermes, Jules. *The Children of India* (3–6). Illus. Series: World's Children. 1994, Carolrhoda LB $23.93 (0-87614-759-7). 48pp. A brief look at the diversity of children and their cultures in the vast subcontinent of India. (Rev: BCCB 4/94; BL 2/1/94) [305.23]

16404 Hirst, Mike. *A Flavor of India* (3–5). Series: Foods and Festivals. 1999, Raintree LB $22.83 (0-8172-5551-6). 32pp. Various festivals and holidays observed in India are discussed, with four simple recipes for the dishes associated with them. (Rev: BL 5/15/99; HBG 10/99) [954]

16405 Lewin, Ted. *Sacred River* (2–4). Illus. 1995, Clarion $14.95 (0-395-69846-4). 32pp. In a series of beautiful watercolors and brief text, the holy city of Benares (Varanasi) and its dominating force, the River Ganges, are introduced. (Rev: BL 6/1–15/95; SLJ 8/95) [954.1]

16406 McNair, Sylvia. *India* (5–8). Illus. Series: Enchantment of the World. 1991, Children's Book Pr. paper $32.00 (0-516-02719-0). 128pp. Such topics as civilization, ethnic groups, and history are treated in this lively introduction to India. (Rev: SLJ 5/91) [954]

16407 Nagda, Ann Whitehead. *Snake Charmer* (2–5). Illus. 2002, Holt $16.95 (0-8050-6499-0). 32pp. Readers of this fascinating photoessay about young Vishnu and his snake charmer father will learn much about life in rural India. (Rev: BL 7/02; HBG 10/02; SLJ 7/02) [791.8]

16408 Olson, Nathan. *India: A Question And Answer Book* (2–5). Illus. Series: Questions and Answers: Countries. 2005, Capstone LB $16.95 (0-7368-3751-5). 32pp. Using a question-and-answer format, simple text, large photos, and many factboxes, this is an introduction to India today, with material on history and traditional culture. (Rev: SLJ 6/05)

16409 Pollard, Michael. *The Ganges* (5–7). Series: Great Rivers. 1997, Benchmark LB $22.79 (0-7614-0504-6). 45pp. This work describes the course of the Ganges from the Himalayas to its muddy delta, covers its history, and touches on the poverty and pollution that is found around it today. (Rev: HBG 3/98; SLJ 4/98) [954]

16410 Prior, Katherine. *Indian Subcontinent* (4–7). Illus. Series: Origins. 1997, Watts LB $21.00 (0-531-14418-6). 32pp. Describes the conditions in India, Pakistan, and Bangladesh that led to emigration, where their people went, and their reception in

such countries as the United States and Great Britain. (Rev: BL 4/15/97; SLJ 7/97) [304.8]

16411 Rowe, Percy, and Patience Coster. *Delhi* (4–7). Illus. Series: Great Cities of the World. 2005, World Almanac LB $22.50 (0-8368-5037-8). 48pp. An informative and appealing overview of this major Indian city, with material on its history, its economy, and what it's like to live there.

16412 Spilsbury, Richard. *Settlements of the Ganges River* (3–5). Illus. Series: Rivers Through Time. 2005, Heinemann LB $20.95 (1-4034-6526-6). 48pp. Traces the history and contemporary life of major settlements along the Ganges, discussing environmental and other important issues.

16413 Srinivasan, Radhika, and Leslie Jermyn. *India*. 2nd ed. (4–8). Illus. Series: Cultures of the World. 2001, Benchmark LB $35.64 (0-7614-1354-5). 144pp. An updated edition of the 1990 title, covering the history, geography, politics, people, arts, culture, and environmental concerns of India. (Rev: HBG 3/02; SLJ 3/02) [954]

16414 Swan, Erin Pembrey. *India* (4–7). Series: Enchantment of the World. 2002, Children's Book Pr. LB $34.50 (0-516-21121-8). 144pp. This visually attractive introduction to the past and present of India includes coverage of languages, culture, the people, economy, and government. (Rev: BL 5/15/02) [954]

Japan

16415 Avikian, Monique. *The Mejii Restoration and the Rise of Modern Japan* (5–8). Illus. Series: Turning Points. 1991, Silver Burdett LB $14.95 (0-382-24132-0); paper $7.95 (0-382-24139-8). 64pp. The major factors that led to Japan's economic superiority are discussed. (Rev: BL 3/15/92) [952.03]

16416 Baines, John. *Japan* (3–5). Illus. Series: Country Facts Files. 1994, Raintree LB $27.12 (0-8114-1847-2). 45pp. Contemporary Japan is introduced under such headings as landscape, climate, trade, and daily life. (Rev: SLJ 10/94) [952]

16417 Barber, Nicola. *Tokyo* (4–6). Series: Great Cities of the World. 2004, World Almanac LB $29.26 (0-8368-5033-5). 48pp. Report writers will find useful information on the Japanese capital's history, culture, and lifestyle. (Rev: SLJ 7/04) [952]

16418 Blumberg, Rhoda. *Commodore Perry in the Land of the Shogun* (5–8). Illus. 1985, Lothrop $18.95 (0-688-03723-2). 128pp. Japan was a mysterious country when Perry arrived in 1853 to open its harbors to American ships. (Rev: BL 11/1/85; SLJ 10/85) [952.025]

16419 Boraas, Tracey. *Japan* (3–6). Illus. Series: Countries and Cultures. 2001, Capstone LB $17.95 (0-7368-0770-5). 64pp. An overview of history, geography, government, economy, and culture that will be useful for students preparing reports. (Rev: HBG 3/02; SLJ 4/02)

16420 Bornoff, Nick. *Japan* (4–7). Illus. Series: Country Insights. 1997, Raintree LB $27.12 (0-8172-4786-6). 48pp. This description of modern life in the city of Okazaki and in the village of Narai compares home life, employment, schooling, and recreation. (Rev: BL 7/97; SLJ 8/97) [952]

16421 Burgan, Michael. *Japan* (2–5). Illus. Series: Questions and Answers: Countries. 2004, Capstone LB $16.95 (0-7368-2478-2). 32pp. Using a question-and-answer format, simple text, large photos, and many factboxes, this is an introduction to Japan today, with material on history and traditional culture.

16422 Cobb, Vicki. *This Place Is Crowded: Japan* (3–5). Illus. by Barbara Lavallee. Series: Imagine Living Here. 1992, Walker LB $15.85 (0-8027-8146-2). 32pp. The focus is on the concept of space in this book that provides basic information about living in a highly populated nation of islands. (Rev: BL 9/1/92; SLJ 8/92) [952.04]

16423 Costain, Meredith, and Paul Collins. *Welcome to Japan* (3–5). Illus. Series: Countries of the World. 2001, Chelsea LB $16.95 (0-7910-6541-3). 32pp. A basic overview that covers history, government, culture, transportation, plants and animals, sports, and schooling. (Rev: HBG 3/02; SLJ 2/02) [952]

16424 Green, Jen. *Japan* (4–8). Series: Nations of the World. 2001, Raintree LB $34.26 (0-8172-5783-7). 128pp. An attractive, fact-filled introduction to this island nation, its rich culture, advanced technology, and wealthy economy. (Rev: BL 6/1–15/01; HBG 10/01) [952]

16425 Gresko, Marcia. *Letters Home from Japan* (3–5). Series: Letters Home From. 2000, Blackbirch LB $16.95 (1-56711-409-1). 32pp. Using a chatty, letter-from-a-friend format, this book covers the basic facts about Japan and its people. (Rev: BL 5/15/00; HBG 10/00) [952]

16426 Haskins, Jim. *Count Your Way Through Japan* (3–5). Illus. 1987, Carolrhoda LB $19.93 (0-87614-301-X); paper $5.95 (0-87614-485-7). 24pp. "Two chopsticks" and other numbers help to introduce the culture of Japan. (Rev: BL 10/15/87; SLJ 9/87)

16427 Heinrichs, Ann. *Japan* (4–6). Series: True Books. 1997, Children's Book Pr. LB $22.00 (0-516-20336-3). 48pp. This simple, colorful photoessay includes material on Japanese geography, history, culture, and how the people live. (Rev: BL 9/15/97; SLJ 11/97) [952]

16428 Kent, Deborah. *Tokyo* (3–6). Illus. 1996, Children's Book Pr. LB $26.50 (0-516-00354-2). 64pp. An introduction in text and many pictures to the principal sights of the capital of Japan. (Rev: BL 11/1/96; SLJ 10/96) [952]

16429 Littlefield, Holly. *Colors of Japan* (3–4). Illus. by Helen Byers. 1997, Carolrhoda $19.93 (0-87614-885-2); paper $5.95 (1-57505-215-6). 24pp. A picture book that uses different colors to explore various aspects of Japanese culture. (Rev: HBG 3/98; SLJ 1/98) [952]

16430 MacMillan, Dianne M. *Japanese Children's Day and the Obon Festival* (3–5). Series: Best Holiday. 1997, Enslow LB $18.95 (0-89490-818-9). 48pp. The origins of these closely related Japanese holidays are described, with material on how they are celebrated. (Rev: BL 12/15/97; HBG 3/98; SLJ 8/97) [952]

16431 Metcalf, Florence E. *A Peek at Japan: A Lighthearted Look at Japan's Language and Culture* (3–6). Illus. by Tomoko. 1992, Metco paper $14.95 (0-9631684-3-6). 136pp. After a section on Japanese language and vocabulary, this book deals with Japan's culture, games, origami, and unusual facts. (Rev: SLJ 7/92) [952]

16432 Netzley, Patricia D. *Japan* (5–8). Series: Modern Nations of the World. 1999, Lucent LB $27.45 (1-56006-599-0). 112pp. Background historic and geographic information is given in this introduction to Japan, but the emphasis is on modern history, the people today, and current living conditions and problems. (Rev: BL 2/15/00; HBG 10/00) [952]

16433 Odijk, Pamela. *The Japanese* (4–7). Illus. Series: Ancient World. 1991, Silver Burdett LB $14.95 (0-382-09898-6). 47pp. This brief, informative volume includes sections on famous figures and places. (Rev: BL 1/15/92) [952]

16434 Patchett, Kaye. *The Akashi Kaikyo Bridge* (5–8). Illus. Series: Building World Landmarks. 2004, Gale/Blackbirch LB $18.96 (1-4103-0140-0). 48pp. A concise account of the amazing construction of the bridge that links Shikoku and Honshu islands. (Rev: BL 4/1/04; SLJ 4/05)

16435 Pilbeam, Mavis. *Japan Under the Shoguns, 1185–1868* (5–8). Series: Looking Back. 1999, Raintree $19.98 (0-8172-5431-5). A handsome, detailed overview of the shogun society of Japan from 1185 to 1868, featuring color photographs and reproductions of original art. (Rev: BL 5/15/99) [452]

16436 Poisson, Barbara Aoki. *The Ainu of Japan* (4–6). Series: First Peoples. 2002, Lerner LB $23.93 (0-8225-4176-9). The Ainu of Japan have shared their homeland with the Japanese for centuries and continue to retain their independent culture. (Rev: BL 5/15/02; HBG 10/02; SLJ 8/02) [952]

16437 Say, Allen. *Tea with Milk* (4–8). Illus. 1999, Houghton Mifflin LB $17.00 (0-395-90495-1). 32pp. A picture book about the author's mother, who was forced by her father to leave her California residence and return to the family's original home in Japan. (Rev: BCCB 6/99; BL 3/15/99*; HB 7–8/99; HBG 10/99; SLJ 5/99) [952]

16438 Schemenauer, Elma. *Japan* (2–3). Illus. Series: Faces and Places. 1997, Child's World LB $22.79 (1-56766-371-0). 32pp. A simple introduction to Japan, with many color photos and basic information on geography, history, people, and customs. (Rev: BL 2/1/98) [952]

16439 Schomp, Virginia. *Japan in the Days of the Samurai* (5–8). Illus. Series: Cultures of the Past. 2001, Marshall Cavendish LB $28.50 (0-7614-0304-3). 80pp. A well-illustrated look at the history of Japan, including information on such cultural topics as the tea ceremony and samurai women. (Rev: BL 2/15/02; HBG 3/02; SLJ 3/02) [952]

16440 Shelley, Rex, and Teo Chuu Yong. *Japan*. 2nd ed. (5–8). Illus. Series: Cultures of the World. 2001, Benchmark LB $35.64 (0-7614-1356-1). 144pp. An updated edition of the 1996 title, covering the history, geography, politics, people, arts, culture, and environmental concerns of Japan. (Rev: HBG 3/02; SLJ 3/02) [952]

16441 Takabayashi, Mari. *I Live in Tokyo* (1–3). Illus. 2001, Houghton Mifflin $16.00 (0-618-07702-2). 32pp. Readers learn about the customs, traditions, and everyday activities that are part of a 7-year-old Japanese girl's life. (Rev: BL 9/15/01; HB 11–12/01*; HBG 3/02; SLJ 10/01) [952]

16442 Tames, Richard. *Exploration into Japan* (5–7). Illus. Series: Exploration. 1996, Dillon LB $15.95 (0-02-751390-4); paper $7.95 (0-382-39186-1). 48pp. A brief history of Japan is given, including the effects of early Western influences. (Rev: BL 8/96) [952]

16443 Tyler, Deborah. *Japan* (3–5). Illus. Series: Discovering. 1993, Crestwood LB $17.95 (0-89686-773-0). 32pp. A brief introduction to modern Japan that stresses its distinctive culture and modern accomplishments. (Rev: BL 2/1/94) [952]

16444 Whyte, Harlinah. *Japan* (4–8). Series: Countries of the World. 1998, Gareth Stevens LB $29.26 (0-8368-2126-2). After a section that presents standard introductory information about Japan, this account describes interesting aspects of Japanese culture including sumo wrestling, sushi, and etiquette. (Rev: BL 12/15/98; HBG 9/99; SLJ 6/99) [952]

16445 Zurlo, Tony. *Japan: Superpower of the Pacific* (5–8). Illus. Series: Discovering Our Heritage. 1991, Macmillan LB $14.95 (0-87518-480-4). 128pp. A book that highlights aspects of Japan's history and culture as well as its economic growth and living conditions to 1990. (Rev: BL 2/1/92; SLJ 4/92) [952]

Other Asian Lands

16446 *Afghanistan in Pictures* (5–8). Illus. Series: Visual Geography. 1997, Lerner LB $25.55 (0-8225-1849-X). 64pp. Includes sections on vegetation and wildlife, minerals, cities, history, and government. (Rev: BL 5/1/89) [958.1]

16447 Ali, Sharifah Enayat. *Afghanistan* (4–7). Illus. Series: Cultures of the World. 1995, Marshall Cavendish LB $35.64 (0-7614-0177-6). 128pp. After general background information, this account focuses on the arts, leisure activities, and festivals of the people of Afghanistan. (Rev: BL 1/1–15/96; SLJ 4/96) [958.1]

16448 Ansary, Mir T. *Afghanistan: Fighting for Freedom* (5–8). Illus. Series: Discovering Our Heritage. 1991, Macmillan LB $14.95 (0-87518-482-0). 128pp. In text and pictures, this account gives some background information, but concentrates on modern Afghanistan. (Rev: BL 2/1/92; SLJ 3/92) [958.1]

16449 Baker, James Michael, and Junia Marion Baker. *Singapore* (4–6). Series: Countries of the World. 2002, Gareth Stevens LB $21.95 (0-8368-2346-X). 96pp. An attractive introduction to the

people, land, and culture of this prosperous island nation. (Rev: BL 6/1–15/02; HBG 10/02) [959.57]

16450 Barber, Nicola. *Singapore* (4–7). Illus. Series: Great Cities of the World. 2005, World Almanac LB $22.50 (0-8368-5047-5). 48pp. An informative and appealing overview of one of the world's most famous cities, with material on its history, its economy, and what it's like to live there.

16451 Behnke, Alison. *Afghanistan in Pictures*. Rev. ed. (5–9). Illus. Series: Visual Geography. 2003, Lerner LB $27.93 (0-8225-4683-3). 80pp. This substantially revised profile of Aghanistan covers the history, geography, culture, and lifestyle and also reflects changes since the post-9/11 invasion by U.S. troops. (Rev: HBG 10/03; SLJ 7/03) [958.1]

16452 Bennett, Gay. *A Family in Sri Lanka* (3–6). Illus. 1985, Lerner LB $18.60 (0-8225-1661-6). 32pp. The focus is on one family member in this look at the everyday life of a family in this small nation. (Rev: BL 11/15/85)

16453 Boraas, Tracey. *Thailand* (4–6). Series: Countries and Cultures. 2002, Capstone LB $23.93 (0-7368-0940-6). 64pp. The land and people of Thailand are introduced with material on climate, landforms, history, traditions, people, and even a recipe. (Rev: BL 1/1–15/03; HBG 3/03; SLJ 2/03) [959.3]

16454 Brace, Steve. *Bangladesh* (4–8). Illus. Series: Economically Developing Countries. 1995, Thomson Learning LB $24.26 (1-56847-243-9). 48pp. An overview of life in Bangladesh told in a simple, large-print text and many color photographs. (Rev: SLJ 7/95) [954.9]

16455 Brill, Marlene T. *Mongolia* (5–8). Illus. Series: Enchantment of the World. 1992, Children's Book Pr. LB $32.00 (0-516-02605-4). 128pp. This little-known and isolated Asian country is introduced with material on its history, people, and geography. (Rev: BL 6/1/92) [951.7]

16456 Brown, Marion M. *Singapore* (4–6). Illus. Series: Enchantment of the World. 1989, Children's Book Pr. LB $32.00 (0-516-02715-8). 128pp. In this introduction, topics covered include geography, history, key attractions, and important people. (Rev: BL 1/1/90; SLJ 4/90) [959.57]

16457 Burbank, Jon. *Nepal* (4–7). Illus. Series: Cultures of the World. 1991, Marshall Cavendish LB $35.64 (1-85435-401-9). 128pp. The emphasis is on culture as well as the basics of geography, history, government, and people. (Rev: BL 2/15/92) [954.96]

16458 Cha, Dia. *Dia's Story Cloth* (3–5). Illus. by Chue Cha and Nhia Thao Cha. 1996, Lee & Low $15.95 (1-880000-34-2). 32pp. The story of the author's family, who fled first from Laos and then from Thailand to settle in the United States. (Rev: BCCB 7–8/96; BL 6/1–15/96; SLJ 7/96) [973]

16459 Clifford, Mary Louise. *The Land and People of Afghanistan* (5–7). Illus. 1989, HarperCollins LB $14.89 (0-397-32339-5). 240pp. An introduction to past life in this central Asian country. A reissue. [958.1]

16460 Condra-Peters, Amy. *Vietnam* (4–6). Series: Countries of the World. 2002, Gareth Stevens LB

$21.95 (0-8368-2348-6). 96pp. An introduction to this Asian nation that emphasizes the progress made since the war. (Rev: BL 6/1–15/02; HBG 10/02) [959.7]

16461 Cromie, Alice. *Taiwan* (5–8). Illus. Series: Enchantment of the World. 1994, Children's Pr. paper $32.00 (0-516-02627-5). An attractive introduction, with many color photographs, to Taiwan's history, government, people, and economy. (Rev: BL 12/15/94) [951.24]

16462 De Capua, Sarah. *Korea* (3–5). Illus. Series: Discovering Cultures. 2004, Benchmark LB $17.95 (0-7614-1794-X). 48pp. An attractive introduction to the Korean peninsula, covering land, people, daily life, education, food, and celebrations, with discussion of the differences between North and South. (Rev: SLJ 6/05)

16463 Ericson, Alex. *Thailand* (3–5). Series: Faces and Places. 2001, Child's World LB $25.64 (1-56766-913-1). 32pp. This oversize volume presents basic facts on Thailand with an emphasis on the people and how they live. (Rev: BL 9/15/01; HBG 3/02) [959.3]

16464 Fiscus, James W. *America's War in Afghanistan* (5–9). Illus. Series: War and Conflict in the Middle East. 2004, Rosen LB $19.95 (0-8239-4552-9). 64pp. A well-organized, balanced account of the war between the United States and Afghanistan in the aftermath of the 2001 terrorist attacks on New York and Washington, D.C.

16465 Fisher, Frederick. *Indonesia* (4–6). Series: Countries of the World. 2000, Gareth Stevens LB $19.95 (0-8368-2317-6). 96pp. Colored illustrations and maps, a glossary, and a clear text make this is a fine introduction to Indonesia and its people. (Rev: BL 6/1–15/00; HBG 10/00; SLJ 12/00) [959.8]

16466 Fordyce, Deborah. *Welcome to Afghanistan* (3–5). Series: Welcome to My Country. 2004, Gareth Stevens LB $25.26 (0-8368-2557-8). 48pp. Introduces readers to Afghanistan's geography, history, people, culture, family life, government, religion, and language. (Rev: SLJ 7/04) [958.1]

16467 Foster, Leila M. *Afghanistan* (5–8). Illus. Series: Enchantment of the World. 1996, Children's Book Pr. LB $32.00 (0-516-20017-8). 127pp. This introduction to the troubled land torn by civil war emphasizes its history, geography, and people. (Rev: BL 1/1–15/97) [958.1]

16468 Garland, Sherry. *Vietnam: Rebuilding a Nation* (4–6). Illus. 1990, Macmillan $19.95 (0-87518-422-7). 127pp. This overview of Vietnam describes landscape, people, history, and culture. (Rev: BL 4/1/90*) [959.7]

16469 Gogol, Sara. *A Mien Family* (4–7). Illus. Series: Journey Between Two Worlds. 1996, Lerner LB $22.60 (0-8225-3407-X); paper $8.95 (0-8225-9745-4). 64pp. The story of a refugee family from the mountainous area of Laos and their journey to the United States. (Rev: BL 11/15/96; SLJ 1/97) [306.85]

16470 Goodman, Jim. *Thailand* (5–9). Series: Cultures of the World. 1991, Marshall Cavendish LB $35.64 (1-85435-402-7). Thailand's history, land, and culture. (Rev: BL 3/15/92) [959.3]

16471 Goodman, Susan. *Chopsticks for My Noodle Soup: Eliza's Life in Malaysia* (1–3). Illus. by Michael Doolittle. 2000, Millbrook LB $21.40 (0-7613-1552-7). 32pp. A kindergartner from Connecticut visits a Malaysian village with her parents and comments on its daily life and customs in an account illustrated with her father's photographs. (Rev: BL 3/15/00; HBG 10/00; SLJ 5/00) [959.5]

16472 Goom, Bridget. *A Family in Singapore* (3–4). Illus. 1986, Lerner LB $18.60 (0-8225-1663-2). 32pp. With the focus on one child in one family, readers discover what life is like in Singapore. (Rev: BL 5/15/86; SLJ 10/86)

16473 Green, Robert. *Cambodia* (5–9). Series: Modern Nations of the World. 2003, Gale LB $27.45 (1-59018-109-3). 112pp. As well as general material on Cambodia including geography, history and culture, this account gives a detailed chronology, national statistics, and extensive sidebars. (Rev: BL 11/15/03; SLJ 8/03) [959.5]

16474 Green, Robert. *Taiwan* (5–8). Series: Modern Nations of the World. 2001, Lucent LB $27.45 (1-56006-819-1). 112pp. Once known as Formosa, this island nation is introduced with material on its history, geography, climate, people, and economy. (Rev: BL 6/1–15/01) [951.24]

16475 Greenblatt, Miriam. *Afghanistan* (4–8). Series: Enchantment of the World. 2003, Children's Pr. LB $34.50 (0-516-22696-7). 144pp. A visually attractive book that covers such topics as the geography, history, government, culture, and people, with a timeline, fast facts, and a recipe. (Rev: SLJ 1/04) [958.1]

16476 Guile, Melanie. *Culture in Malaysia* (4–7). Illus. Series: Culture In. 2005, Raintree LB $27.79 (1-4109-1133-0). 32pp. Customs, holidays, clothing, food, and arts and crafts are well covered in this volume that also provides basic information needed for reports and interesting sidebar features. (Rev: SLJ 5/05)

16477 Guile, Melanie. *Culture in Vietnam* (3–5). Illus. Series: Culture In. 2005, Raintree LB $19.45 (1-4109-1135-7). 32pp. Vietnam's people, language, celebrations and customs are covered, with photographs and maps adding to the appeal. (Rev: BL 3/1/05; SLJ 5/05) [306]

16478 Guruswamy, Krishnan. *Sri Lanka* (4–8). Series: Countries of the World. 2002, Gareth Stevens LB $29.27 (0-8368-2354-0). 96pp. History, geography, government, and people are all covered here, with special sections on such topics as the status of women and relations with the United States. Also use *South Korea* (2002). (Rev: HBG 3/03; SLJ 2/03) [954.93]

16479 Haberle, Susan E. *North Korea* (2–5). Illus. Series: Questions and Answers: Countries. 2005, Capstone LB $16.95 (0-7368-3756-6). 32pp. Using a question-and-answer format, simple text, large photos, and many factboxes, this is an introduction to North Korea today, with material on history and traditional culture.

16480 Haberle, Susan E. *South Korea* (2–5). Illus. Series: Questions and Answers: Countries. 2005, Capstone LB $16.95 (0-7368-3761-2). 32pp. Using a question-and-answer format, simple text, large photos, and many factboxes, this is an introduction to South Korea today, with material on history and traditional culture.

16481 Hansen, Ole Steen. *Vietnam* (5–8). Illus. Series: Economically Developing Countries. 1996, Raintree LB $24.26 (0-8172-4526-X). 48pp. This introduction to Vietnam includes background information and material on its emerging economy. (Rev: BL 3/1/97) [959.7]

16482 Haque, Jameel. *Pakistan* (4–8). Series: Countries of the World. 2002, Gareth Stevens LB $29.27 (0-8368-2352-4). 96pp. A useful source of the standard information on Pakistan plus a discussion of relations with the United States and some interesting sidebar features on such topics as pollution and cricket. (Rev: HBG 3/03; SLJ 1/03) [954.91]

16483 Heinrichs, Ann. *Nepal* (5–8). Illus. Series: Enchantment of the World. 1996, Children's Pr. paper $32.00 (0-516-02642-9). Using color photographs on each page, this attractive book introduces the history, geography, and people of Nepal. (Rev: BL 7/96) [954.96]

16484 Heinrichs, Ann. *Pakistan* (2–3). Series: A True Book. 2004, Children's Pr. LB $24.00 (0-516-22813-7). 47pp. Geography, history, and daily life are covered in this attractive introduction to Pakistan. (Rev: SLJ 11/04) [954.9]

16485 Heinrichs, Ann. *Tibet* (5–8). Illus. Series: Enchantment of the World. 1996, Children's Pr. LB $32.00 (0-516-20155-7). An introduction to the history, people, and geography of this country, now occupied by China. (Rev: BL 1/1–15/97) [951]

16486 Hill, Valerie. *Korea* (3–6). Illus. Series: Ask About Asia. 2002, Mason Crest LB $18.95 (1-59084-206-5). 47pp. Geography, history, culture, government, and daily life are presented in double-page spreads with plenty of photographs, reproductions, and maps. (Rev: SLJ 4/03) [951]

16487 Ho, Siow Yen. *South Korea* (2–4). Illus. Series: Festivals of the World. 1998, Gareth Stevens LB $14.95 (0-8368-2019-3). 32pp. Although this book focuses on national holidays, including Buddha's Birthday, Tan-O Day, and Sokchonje Rites, and describes a number of related craft projects, it also provides background information on South Korea. (Rev: BL 12/15/98; HBG 10/99) [394.26]

16488 Holmes, Jim, and Tom Morgan. *A Child's Day in a Vietnamese City* (K–3). Series: A Child's Day. 2002, Marshall Cavendish LB $15.95 (0-7614-1409-6). 32pp. Present-day Vietnam is introduced through the everyday experiences of a Vietnamese child. (Rev: BL 2/15/03; HBG 3/03) [959.7]

16489 Huynh, Quang Nhuong. *Water Buffalo Days* (4–6). Illus. 1997, HarperCollins LB $13.00 (0-06-024958-7). 128pp. This is a story of growing up in rural Vietnam in the late 1940s and of a family's water buffalo, Tank. (Rev: BL 11/15/97; SLJ 2/98*) [636.2]

16490 Jacobs, Judy. *Indonesia: A Nation of Islands* (4–8). Illus. Series: Discovering Our Heritage. 1990, Macmillan LB $14.95 (0-87518-423-5). 127pp. History and geography of the major Indonesian islands. (Rev: SLJ 9/90) [959.8]

16491 Jung, Sung-Hoon. *South Korea* (5–8). Series: Economically Developing Countries. 1997, Raintree LB $24.26 (0-8172-4530-8). This overview of economic conditions in South Korea describes the country's success with electronic exports and provides case studies of family-run companies. (Rev: BL 5/15/97) [951.95]

16492 Karkonen, Reijo. *The Children of Nepal* (4–6). Illus. by Matti Pitkanen. Series: World's Children. 1990, Carolrhoda LB $23.93 (0-87614-395-8). 40pp. Comments on life in Nepal, with striking color photos. (Rev: BL 6/15/90; SLJ 8/90) [954.96]

16493 Kazem, Halima. *Afghanistan* (4–8). Illus. 2003, Gareth Stevens LB $29.26 (0-8368-2357-5). 96pp. Afghanistan's geography, history, government, people, and culture are introduced, with material on women, sports, and clothing, a map, and a glossary. (Rev: HBG 10/03; SLJ 7/03) [58.1]

16494 Kendra, Judith. *Tibetans* (5–8). Series: Threatened Cultures. 1994, Thomson Learning LB $24.25 (1-56847-152-1). Discusses Tibetan culture and religion, with emphasis on the denial by China of Tibetans' rights. Follows the daily lives of two Tibetan children, one living in the country, one in the city. (Rev: BL 7/94) [951]

16495 Khan, Aisha. *A Historical Atlas of Uzbekistan* (5–9). Series: Historical Atlases of South Asia, Central Asia and the Middle East. 2003, Rosen LB $30.60 (0-8239-3868-9). 64pp. This attractive profile that includes many maps and photographs traces the central Asian country's development from prehistoric times to the present, with emphasis on relations with Russia. (Rev: SLJ 8/03)

16496 Khng, Pauline. *Myanmar* (4–6). Series: Countries of the World. 2000, Gareth Stevens LB $19.95 (0-8368-2320-6). 96pp. This introduction to Myanmar (formerly Burma) includes coverage of such topics as history, geography, people, form of government, current concerns, and relations with Canada and the U.S. (Rev: BL 6/1–15/00; HBG 10/00; SLJ 12/00) [954.9]

16497 Knox, Barbara. *Afghanistan* (2–4). Series: Many Cultures, One World. 2004, Capstone LB $23.93 (0-7368-2448-0). 32pp. An interesting introduction to Afghanistan, covering city and country life, family life, laws and customs, seasons, important sights, and even favorite pets. (Rev: SLJ 8/04) [958.1]

16498 Koh, Frances M. *Korean Holidays and Festivals* (2–5). Illus. by Liz B. Dodson. 1990, East-West LB $15.00 (0-9606090-5-9). 32pp. Nine holidays and cultural festivals that are celebrated in South Korea are described. (Rev: BL 3/1/91; SLJ 6/91) [394.25]

16499 Kummer, Patricia. *Tibet* (4–8). Series: Enchantment of the World. 2003, Children's Pr. LB $34.50 (0-516-22693-2). 144pp. A visually attractive book that covers such topics as the geography, history, government, culture, and people, with a timeline, fast facts, and a recipe. (Rev: SLJ 1/04) [951]

16500 Lauré, Jason. *Bangladesh* (5–8). Series: Enchantment of the World. 1992, Children's Pr. paper $32.00 (0-516-02609-7). The history, culture, and economic problems of this crowded Asian land are covered. (Rev: BL 12/15/92; SLJ 1/93) [954.9]

16501 Layton, Lesley. *Singapore* (5–8). Illus. Series: Cultures of the World. 1990, Marshall Cavendish LB $35.64 (1-85435-295-4). 128pp. As well as history and economy, this introduction to Singapore includes coverage of lifestyles and current problems. (Rev: BL 3/1/91; SLJ 6/91) [959.57]

16502 Levy, Patricia. *Tibet* (4–7). Illus. Series: Cultures of the World. 1996, Marshall Cavendish LB $35.64 (0-7614-0277-2). 128pp. Tibet is introduced with general background information, followed by material on its people and their culture, festivals, and food. (Rev: BL 8/96; SLJ 9/96) [951.1]

16503 Liberman, Sherri. *Historical Atlas of Azerbaijan* (4–6). Illus. 2004, Rosen LB $22.95 (0-8239-4497-2). 64pp. Liberman traces the turbulent history of Azerbaijan in this slim volume, concentrating mainly on politics and the ethnic groups that make up the population. (Rev: BL 12/1/04; SLJ 11/04) [911]

16504 Lorbiecki, Marybeth. *Children of Vietnam* (4–7). Photos by Paul P. Rome. Series: The World's Children. 1997, Carolrhoda LB $28.75 (1-57505-034-X). 45pp. Beginning in the north and working south, this photoessay describes the people of Vietnam and the lives of their children. (Rev: HBG 3/98; SLJ 2/98) [959.7]

16505 McNair, Sylvia. *Indonesia* (5–8). Illus. Series: Enchantment of the World. 1993, Children's Book Pr. LB $33.00 (0-516-02618-6). 128pp. Introduces the history, geography, and peoples of this vast country, the world's largest island group. (Rev: BL 11/1/93; SLJ 3/94) [959.8]

16506 McNair, Sylvia. *Korea* (4–6). Illus. 1986, Children's Book Pr. LB $32.00 (0-516-02771-9). 127pp. Geography, culture, economy, and history are featured, as well as tourist sights. (Rev: BL 8/15/86; SLJ 10/86)

16507 McNair, Sylvia. *Malaysia* (4–7). Series: Enchantment of the World. 2002, Children's Book Pr. LB $34.50 (0-516-21009-2). 144pp. This Southeast Asian nation is presented in text and many color photographs that introduce its history, geography, people, culture, and present status. (Rev: BL 9/15/02) [959.505]

16508 *Malaysia in Pictures* (5–8). Illus. Series: Visual Geography. 1997, Lerner LB $25.55 (0-8225-1854-6). 64pp. A basic, visual overview of this nation and its people. (Rev: BL 5/1/89) [959.5]

16509 Merrick, Patrick. *Vietnam* (3–5). Series: Countries: Faces and Places. 2000, Child's World LB $25.64 (1-56766-740-6). 32pp. With color pictures on each page, this basic introduction to Vietnam covers geography, history, culture, and everyday life. (Rev: BL 4/15/01; HBG 3/01) [959.7]

16510 Millett, Sandra. *The Hmong of Southeast Asia* (4–6). Series: First Peoples. 2001, Lerner LB $23.93 (0-8225-4852-6). 48pp. This attractive introduction to the Hmong people and their native region and culture also contrasts traditional and modern lifestyles. (Rev: HBG 3/02; SLJ 3/02) [305.895]

16511 Mirpuri, Gouri, and Robert Cooper. *Indonesia.* 2nd ed. (5–8). Illus. Series: Cultures of the World. 2001, Marshall Cavendish LB $35.64 (0-7614-1355-3). 144pp. An encompassing look at the history, culture, society, and geography of Indonesia. (Rev: BL 3/1/02; HBG 3/02; SLJ 4/02) [959.8]

16512 Moiz, Azra. *Taiwan* (4–7). Illus. Series: Cultures of the World. 1995, Marshall Cavendish LB $35.64 (0-7614-0180-6). 128pp. The accomplishments, lifestyle, and religious festivals of the people of Taiwan are covered, along with its history and geography. (Rev: BL 1/1–15/96; SLJ 9/96) [957.24]

16513 Munan, Heidi. *Malaysia* (5–8). Illus. Series: Cultures of the World. 1990, Marshall Cavendish LB $35.64 (1-85435-296-2). 128pp. Cultural diversity and lifestyles of the people are two topics covered in this introduction to Malaysia. (Rev: BL 3/1/91) [959.5]

16514 O'Connor, Karen. *Vietnam* (3–5). Series: Globe-Trotters Club. 1999, Carolrhoda LB $22.60 (1-57505-117-6). 48pp. Sidebars and stunning color photos bring to life the land and people of Vietnam in an entertaining and instructive manner. (Rev: BL 11/15/99; HBG 3/00; SLJ 2/00) [959.7]

16515 O'Connor, Karen. *Vietnam* (1–3). Series: A Ticket To. 1999, Carolrhoda LB $22.60 (1-57505-142-7). 48pp. This first look at Vietnam introduces the land, people, culture, customs, and famous sights with a simple, large-type text, color photos, and well-organized topics. (Rev: BL 11/15/99; HBG 3/00; SLJ 2/00) [959.7]

16516 Olson, Gillia M. *Afghanistan: A Question and Answer Book* (2–5). Series: Fact Finders. 2004, Capstone LB $16.95 (0-7368-2685-8). 32pp. Double-page spreads use simple text, factboxes, and plenty of color photographs to answer pertinent questions about the country's history, geography, government, and culture. (Rev: BL 11/15/04; SLJ 3/05) [958.1]

16517 *Pakistan in Pictures* (5–8). Illus. Series: Visual Geography. 1996, Lerner LB $25.55 (0-8225-1850-3). 64pp. Photographs, charts, and maps help to introduce the country of Pakistan. (Rev: BL 9/15/89) [954.9]

16518 Pang, Guek-Cheng. *Mongolia* (5–8). Series: Cultures of the World. 1999, Marshall Cavendish LB $35.64 (0-7614-0954-8). 128pp. A clear, well-illustrated introduction to this remote land that includes good background information as well as coverage of modern life. (Rev: HBG 10/99; SLJ 10/99) [957]

16519 Park, Frances, and Ginger Park. *My Freedom Trip* (K–4). Illus. by Debra R. Jenkins. 1998, Boyds Mills $15.95 (1-56397-468-1). 32pp. A true story about the authors' mother, Soo, and her escape with her father from North Korea on the eve of the Korean War, leaving behind a mother she would never see again. (Rev: BL 9/1/98; HBG 3/99; SLJ 1/99) [951.93]

16520 Pascoe, Elaine, ed. *Into Wild Borneo* (3–6). Series: The Jeff Corwin Experience. 2004, Gale/ Blackbirch LB $19.96 (1-56711-859-3). 48pp. Jeff Corwin of the Animal Planet television series interacts with elephants, apes, and much smaller creatures in Borneo. (Rev: SLJ 4/04) [591.9598]

16521 Petersen, David. *Thailand* (3–5). 2001, Children's Book Pr. paper $6.95 (0-516-27361-2). 48pp. A colorful overview of Thailand's geography, government, and customs. (Rev: BL 2/1/02) [959.3]

16522 Ramulshah, Mano. *Pakistan* (3–8). Illus. 1992, Viking $22.95 (0-237-60193-1). 32pp. Famous landmarks, social and political life, and history are discussed. (Rev: SLJ 8/92) [954]

16523 Romano, Amy. *A Historical Atlas of Afghanistan* (4–6). Illus. Series: Historical Atlases of South Asia, Central Asia and the Middle East. 2003, Rosen LB $30.60 (0-8239-3863-8). 64pp. This attractive profile that includes many maps and photographs traces Afghanistan's development from prehistoric times to the present. (Rev: SLJ 8/03)

16524 Roop, Peter, and Connie Roop. *Vietnam* (1–3). Series: A Visit To. 1998, Heinemann LB $19.92 (1-57572-120-1). 32pp. Introduces us to the land and people of Vietnam, showing how they live, work, and celebrate their festivals. (Rev: SLJ 7/98) [959.7]

16525 Rowell, Jonathan. *Malaysia* (5–8). Illus. Series: Economically Developing Countries. 1997, Raintree LB $24.26 (0-8172-4531-6). 48pp. The growth and development of Malaysia are traced, with material on its high-tech sector. (Rev: BL 5/15/97) [959.505]

16526 Schmidt, Jeremy, and Ted Wood. *Two Lands, One Heart: An American Boy's Journey to His Mother's Vietnam* (3–5). Illus. 1995, Walker LB $18.85 (0-8027-8358-9). 48pp. A young boy is introduced to the culture and life of contemporary Vietnam when he visits his mother's homeland. (Rev: BCCB 6/95; BL 5/1/95; SLJ 4/95) [915.97]

16527 Schwabach, Karen. *Thailand: Land of Smiles* (5–8). Illus. Series: Discovering Our Heritage. 1991, Macmillan LB $14.95 (0-87518-454-5). 128pp. Explores the land and people of Thailand, with a chapter on the immigrants who have come to the United States. (Rev: BL 4/1/91; SLJ 7/91) [959.3]

16528 Sheehan, Sean. *Cambodia* (4–7). Illus. Series: Cultures of the World. 1996, Marshall Cavendish LB $35.64 (0-7614-0281-0). 128pp. The troubled land of Cambodia is introduced, with emphasis on its people, their lifestyles, and culture. (Rev: BL 8/96; SLJ 9/96) [959]

16529 Sheehan, Sean, and Shahrezad Samiuddin. *Pakistan* (5–9). Illus. Series: Cultures of the World. 2004, Benchmark LB $25.95 (0-7614-1787-7). 144pp. Pakistan's geography, history, economy, and people are all examined, with discussion of interesting aspects of Pakistani culture. (Rev: SLJ 2/05) [954.9]

16530 Simpson, Judith. *Indonesia* (3–6). Illus. Series: Ask About Asia. 2002, Mason Crest LB

$18.95 (1-59084-208-1). 47pp. Geography, history, culture, government, and daily life are presenetd in double-page spreads with plenty of photographs, reproductions, and maps. (Rev: HBG 10/03; SLJ 4/03) [959.8]

16531 *South Korea in Pictures* (5–7). Series: Visual Geography. 1997, Lerner LB $25.55 (0-8225-1868-6). 64pp. An introduction to South Korea that focuses on its politics and economy. (Rev: SLJ 5/90) [951.9]

16532 Stevens, Kathryn. *Afghanistan* (2–4). Series: Faces and Places. 2003, Child's World LB $25.64 (1-56766-181-5). 32pp. This introduction to Afghanistan covers the central Asian country's geography, history, people, culture, government, and economy. (Rev: SLJ 8/03) [958.1]

16533 Stickler, John, and Soma Han Stickler. *Land of Morning Calm: Korean Culture Then and Now* (3–5). Illus. by authors. 2003, Shen's $16.95 (1-885008-22-8). 32pp. An excellent introduction to Korea for young readers, this attractive book covers the history and geography of the peninsula and also examines various cultural aspects. (Rev: BL 10/15/03; SLJ 12/03)

16534 Taus-Bolstad, Stacy. *Pakistan in Pictures*. Rev. ed. (5–9). Illus. Series: Visual Geography. 2003, Lerner LB $27.93 (0-8225-4682-5). 80pp. This substantially revised volume covers Pakistan's history, geography, culture, and lifestyle. (Rev: HBG 10/03; SLJ 7/03) [954.9]

16535 Thomas, Matt. *Singapore* (3–5). Series: Faces and Places. 2001, Child's World LB $25.64 (1-56766-910-7). 32pp. The prosperous, tiny nation of Singapore is presented in a simple text, oversize format, and many attractive color photographs. (Rev: BL 9/15/01; HBG 3/02; SLJ 1/02) [959.57]

16536 Thomson, Ruth, and Neil Thomson. *A Family in Thailand* (4–6). Illus. 1988, Lerner LB $18.60 (0-8225-1684-5). 32pp. Thai children point out the characteristics of life in their country. (Rev: BL 8/88)

16537 Tull, Mary, et al. *Northern Asia* (4–7). Illus. Series: Artisans Around the World. 1990, Raintree LB $27.12 (0-7398-0119-8). 48pp. This book introduces Mongolia and its neighbors, with descriptions of arts and crafts and many projects. (Rev: BL 10/15/99; HBG 3/00; SLJ 1/00) [745.5]

16538 *Vietnam in Pictures* (5–8). Illus. Series: Visual Geography. 1994, Lerner LB $25.55 (0-8225-1909-7). 64pp. This well-illustrated account of Vietnam covers its history, geography, people, government, and economy. (Rev: BL 11/1/94) [915.97]

16539 Wanasundera, Nanda P. *Sri Lanka* (4–7). Illus. Series: Cultures of the World. 1991, Marshall Cavendish LB $213.86 (1-85435-397-7). 128pp. The history, geography, and culture of Sri Lanka are introduced with an emphasis on contemporary problems. (Rev: BL 2/15/92) [954.93]

16540 Whyte, Harlinah. *Thailand* (2–4). Series: Festivals of the World. 1998, Gareth Stevens LB $18.60 (0-8368-2009-6). 32pp. Discusses the major holidays celebrated in Thailand and provides some related craft projects, recipes, and general informa-

875

tion about the country. (Rev: BL 5/15/98; HBG 10/98) [959.3]

16541 Whyte, Mariam. *Bangladesh* (5–9). Series: Cultures of the World. 1998, Marshall Cavendish LB $35.64 (0-7614-0869-X). A sympathetic look at the history and geography of Bangladesh, with details of the country's rich background and current problems. (Rev: HBG 10/99; SLJ 6/99) [954.9]

16542 Willis, Karen. *Vietnam* (5–8). Illus. Series: Modern Nations of the World. 2000, Lucent LB $27.45 (1-56006-635-0). 126pp. A thorough history of Vietnam, this work also focuses on progress after the war and daily life in modern Vietnam. (Rev: BL 9/15/00; HBG 3/01) [959.7]

16543 Willis, Terri. *Vietnam* (4–7). Series: Enchantment of the World. 2002, Children's Book Pr. LB $34.50 (0-516-22150-7). 144pp. This attractive volume presents basic material on Vietnam's history, geography, and culture, with an emphasis on progress after the war. (Rev: BL 9/15/02; SLJ 12/02) [959.7]

16544 Withington, William A. *Southeast Asia* (5–8). Illus. 1988, Gateway $16.95 (0-934291-32-2). 160pp. Sections on lifestyle, land and climate, history and government, festivals, sports, arts, and crafts. (Rev: BL 12/1/88)

16545 Wright, David K. *Brunei* (5–8). Illus. Series: Enchantment of the World. 1991, Children's Book Pr. LB $32.00 (0-516-02602-X). 128pp. The country of Brunei is introduced with many photographs covering its geography, history, and culture. (Rev: BL 2/1/92) [959.55]

16546 Wright, David K. *Burma* (5–8). Illus. Series: Enchantment of the World. 1991, Children's Book Pr. paper $32.00 (0-516-02725-5). 128pp. The land and people of Myanmar (Burma), together with its culture and history, are covered in this colorful introduction. (Rev: BL 8/91; SLJ 9/91) [788.9]

16547 Wright, David K. *Vietnam* (4–7). Illus. 1989, Children's Book Pr. paper $32.00 (0-516-02712-3). 128pp. Standard information is highlighted by color illustrations and war coverage. (Rev: BL 8/89; SLJ 1/90) [959.7]

16548 Yin, Saw Myat. *Myanmar*. Rev. ed. (4–8). Illus. Series: Cultures of the World. 2001, Benchmark LB $35.64 (0-7614-1353-7). 144pp. An introduction to every aspect of Myanmar with useful information on daily life and phonetic pronunciations of many foreign words. Also use *Indonesia* (2001). (Rev: HBG 3/02; SLJ 4/02) [959.1]

16549 Yu, Ling. *Taiwan in Pictures* (5–8). Illus. Series: Visual Geography. 1997, Lerner LB $25.55 (0-8225-1865-1). 64pp. The history and geography of Taiwan are introduced, with coverage of cities, culture, religion, and economy. (Rev: BL 9/15/89) [915.1]

16550 Yusufali, Jabeen. *Pakistan: An Islamic Treasure* (4–8). Illus. Series: Discovering Our Heritage. 1990, Macmillan LB $14.95 (0-87518-433-2). 128pp. This book covers the country of Pakistan from its foundation in 1947 to the present, with coverage of economy, geography, and more. (Rev: BL 7/90; SLJ 8/90) [954.91]

16551 Zimmermann, Robert. *Sri Lanka* (5–8). Illus. Series: Enchantment of the World. 1992, Children's Book Pr. LB $32.00 (0-516-02606-2). 128pp. In addition to background information on the history and geography of Sri Lanka, this book provides material on its current problems. (Rev: BL 6/1/92) [954.93]

Australia and the Pacific Islands

16552 Alter, Judy. *Discovering Australia's Land, People, and Wildlife* (5–8). Series: Continents of the World. 2004, Enslow/MyReportLinks.com LB $19.95 (0-7660-5207-9). 48pp. An introduction to the geography, history, economy, plants and animals, culture, and people of the continent, showing the contrast between the urban centers on the coasts and the rugged interior. (Rev: SLJ 11/04) [994]

16553 Arnold, Caroline. *Easter Island: Giant Stone Statues Tell of a Rich and Tragic Past* (4–7). Illus. 2000, Clarion LB $15.00 (0-395-87609-5). 48pp. This chronological history of Easter Island tells how the stone statues got there and what they mean. (Rev: BCCB 4/00; BL 3/15/00; HB 5–6/00; HBG 10/00; SLJ 4/00) [996.1]

16554 Arnold, Caroline. *Uluru: Australia's Aboriginal Heart* (4–8). Illus. by Arthur Arnold. 2003, Clarion $16.00 (0-618-18181-4). 64pp. Uluru, formerly known as Ayers Rock, is a giant sandstone monolith that changes color in the setting sun and is a spiritual landmark for the native people of the central Australian desert. (Rev: BCCB 12/03; BL 12/15/03; HB 11–12/03; HBG 11–12/03; SLJ 1/04) [994.01]

16555 Arnold, Caroline. *A Walk on the Great Barrier Reef* (4–7). Illus. 1988, Lerner LB $23.93 (0-87614-285-4). 48pp. Exploring one of the great natural wonders of the world. (Rev: BL 7/88; SLJ 8/88) [574.91943]

16556 Banting, Erinn. *The Great Barrier Reef: The Largest Coral Reef in the World* (3–6). Illus. Series: Natural Wonders. 2004, Weigl LB $18.20 (1-59036-272-1). 32pp. A look at this giant reef, the living creatures found there, and the dangers it faces. (Rev: SLJ 4/05) [919.43]

16557 Bartlett, Anne. *The Aboriginal Peoples of Australia* (4–7). Illus. Series: First Peoples. 2001, Lerner LB $23.93 (0-8225-4854-2). 48pp. An introduction to the indigenous people of Australia, including their history, customs, and daily life, with photographs. (Rev: BL 10/15/01; HBG 3/02; SLJ 3/02) [994]

16558 Browne, Rollo. *An Aboriginal Family* (3–6). Illus. 1985, Lerner LB $18.60 (0-8225-1655-1). 32pp. A taste of aboriginal culture is highlighted with color photos. (Rev: BCCB 6/85; BL 6/15/85; SLJ 10/85)

16559 Coffey, Maria, and Debora Pearson. *Jungle Islands: My South Sea Adventure* (4–6). Illus. 2000, Annick LB $26.95 (1-55037-597-0); paper $14.95 (1-55037-596-2). 88pp. The waters, land, people, and history of the Solomon Islands are presented in vibrant photos and an interesting narrative. (Rev: BL 1/1–15/01; HBG 3/01; SLJ 12/00) [919.59]

16560 Cooper, Rod, and Emilie Cooper. *Journey Through Australia* (3–5). Illus. Series: Journey Around the World. 1994, Troll LB $18.60 (0-8167-2757-0). 32pp. This brief tour of Australia introduces its most important regions and cities. (Rev: SLJ 8/94) [919.4]

16561 Darian-Smith, Kate. *Exploration into Australia* (5–7). Illus. Series: Exploration. 1996, Dillon LB $15.95 (0-02-718088-3); paper $7.95 (0-382-39227-2). 48pp. Descriptions are given of the prehistory of Australia and the changes made after European exploration. (Rev: BL 8/96; SLJ 9/96) [994]

16562 Darian-Smith, Kate, and David Lowe. *The Australian Outback and Its People* (4–7). Illus. Series: People and Places. 1995, Thomson Learning LB $24.26 (1-56847-337-0). 48pp. A well-organized guide to the Australian outback, its exploration and history, flora and fauna, mining, environmental issues, and people. (Rev: SLJ 7/95) [994]

16563 Darlington, Robert. *Australia* (4–8). Series: Nations of the World. 2001, Raintree LB $34.26 (0-7398-1280-7). 128pp. Australia, the world's largest island, is introduced in this attractive volume that gives material on geography, climate, terrain, history, economy, and lifestyles. (Rev: BL 6/1–15/01; HBG 10/01) [994]

16564 Ercelawn, Ayesha. *New Zealand* (4–6). Series: Countries of the World. 2000, Gareth Stevens LB $26.60 (0-8368-2332-X). 96pp. As well as the geography, history, system of government, and lifestyles of New Zealand, this book covers the country's unique customs and its current concerns. (Rev: BL 3/15/01; HBG 10/01) [992]

16565 Fox, Mary V. *New Zealand* (5–8). Illus. Series: Enchantment of the World. 1991, Children's Book Pr. paper $32.00 (0-516-02728-X). 128pp. This island country is introduced in text and pictures that cover geography, history, the people, and key attractions. (Rev: BL 10/1/91) [992]

16566 Franklin, Sharon, et al. *Southwest Pacific* (4–7). Series: Artisans Around the World. 1999, Raintree LB $27.12 (0-7398-0120-1). 48pp. The influence of traditions and geography is shown in this survey of folk art from Australia, New Guinea, New Zealand, and Indonesia, with directions for projects such as a Maori woven band and a batik wall hanging. (Rev: BL 10/15/99; HBG 3/00; SLJ 1/00) [994]

16567 Gonzalez, Joaquin L. *The Philippines* (4–6). Series: Countries of the World. 2000, Gareth Stevens LB $26.60 (0-8368-2334-6). 96pp. The Philippine Islands are introduced with material on the geography, history, government, lifestyle, language, food, unique customs, and current issues. (Rev: BL 3/15/01; HBG 10/01) [959.9]

16568 Grabowski, John F. *Australia* (5–8). Series: Modern Nations of the World. 2002, Gale LB $27.45 (1-56006-566-4). 112pp. The continent Down Under is introduced with coverage of history,

natural resources, landmarks, economy, and people. (Rev: BL 12/15/02) [994]

16569 Griffith, Jonathan. *New Zealand* (2–4). Series: Festivals of the World. 1999, Gareth Stevens LB $15.95 (0-8368-2033-9). 32pp. An introduction to the major festivals celebrated in New Zealand, this account also describes Maori culture and traditions, takes the reader to sheep-shearing competitions, and gives directions for creating one's own celebration. (Rev: BL 12/15/99; HBG 10/00) [993.1]

16570 Griffiths, Diana. *Australia* (2–4). Series: Festivals of the World. 1999, Gareth Stevens LB $14.95 (0-8368-2021-5). 32pp. Introduces the land and people of Australia, describes their main holidays, and offers craft projects and tasty recipes for these celebrations. (Rev: BL 4/15/98; SLJ 8/99) [919.4]

16571 Grupper, Jonathan. *Destination: Australia* (4–6). Illus. 2000, National Geographic $16.95 (0-7922-7165-3). 32pp. This stunningly illustrated introduction to Australia covers many subjects but concentrates on its unusual animals. (Rev: BL 6/1–15/00; HBG 10/00; SLJ 5/00) [591]

16572 Hermes, Jules. *The Children of Micronesia* (4–6). Illus. Series: World's Children. 1994, Carolrhoda LB $23.93 (0-87614-819-4). 48pp. A look at growing up in these South Pacific islands, including the Caroline, Gilbert, and Marshall island groups. (Rev: BCCB 9/94; BL 9/15/94) [996.5]

16573 Keyworth, Valerie. *New Zealand: Land of the Long White Cloud* (4–7). Illus. Series: Discovering Our Heritage. 1990, Macmillan LB $14.95 (0-87518-414-6). 111pp. New Zealand is introduced with information on people, history, culture, and geography. (Rev: SLJ 1/91) [993.1]

16574 Krasno, Rena. *Kneeling Carabao and Dancing Giants: Celebrating Filipino Festivals* (4–6). Illus. by Ileana C. Lee. 1997, Pacific View $19.95 (1-881896-15-3). 48pp. Contains information on Filipino festivals, customs, folktales, games, and activities. (Rev: BL 12/1/97; HBG 3/98) [394]

16575 Lepthien, Emilie U. *The Philippines* (4–7). 1986, Children's Book Pr. paper $32.00 (0-516-02782-4). 128pp. These islands are introduced through a discussion of their history, geography, and culture.

16576 Lester, Alison. *Are We There Yet?* (2–4). Illus. 2005, Kane/Miller $15.95 (1-929132-73-5). 32pp. A family of five has a great time touring Australia, seeing its sights and enjoying its unique experiences over the course of six months. (Rev: BL 3/15/05; SLJ 4/05) [823.3]

16577 Lewin, Ted, and Betsy Lewin. *Top to Bottom Down Under* (2–4). Illus. 2005, HarperCollins LB $16.89 (0-688-14114-5). 40pp. With plenty of Australian-speak, the Lewins offer an eye-catching adventure- and animal-filled tour down under. (Rev: BL 1/1–15/05; SLJ 3/05) [919.4]

16578 Lowe, David, and Andrea Shimmen. *Australia* (4–8). Illus. Series: Modern Industrial World. 1996, Raintree LB $24.26 (0-8172-4553-7). Australia's economic status, living standards, educational system, and industry are covered. (Rev: BL 2/15/97) [919.4]

16579 McCollum, Sean. *Australia* (3–5). Series: Globe-Trotters Club. 1999, Carolrhoda $22.60 (1-57505-104-4). 48pp. Each of the colorful two-page spreads covers a different topic about Australia, including the people, major sights, and unusual animals. (Rev: BL 9/15/99; HBG 10/99; SLJ 11/99) [994]

16580 McCollum, Sean. *Australia* (1–3). Series: A Ticket To. 1999, Carolrhoda LB $22.60 (1-57505-129-X). 48pp. For beginning readers, this is a first look at Australia, its people, chief attractions, and landscape. (Rev: BL 9/15/99; HBG 10/99; SLJ 11/99) [994]

16581 Macdonald, Robert. *Islands of the Pacific Rim and Their People* (5–8). Illus. Series: People and Places. 1994, Thomson Learning LB $24.26 (1-56847-167-X). 48pp. An overview of the islands of the Pacific Ocean and their people, different environments, and economies. (Rev: BL 10/15/94; SLJ 10/94) [990]

16582 Marshall, Diana. *Aboriginal Australians* (3–5). Series: Indigenous Peoples. 2004, Weigl LB $18.20 (1-59036-121-0). 32pp. A fascinating and informative overview of Australia's aboriginals, covering history, culture, language, and family life. (Rev: SLJ 7/04) [305.89]

16583 Meisel, Jacqueline D. *Australia: The Land Down Under* (3–5). Illus. Series: Exploring Cultures of the World. 1997, Marshall Cavendish LB $27.07 (0-7614-0139-3). 64pp. A description of various aspects of life in Australia, with material on the range of races and lifestyles. (Rev: BL 7/97; SLJ 4/98) [994]

16584 Mendoza, Lunita. *Philippines* (2–4). Series: Festivals of the World. 1999, Gareth Stevens LB $14.95 (0-8368-2025-8). 32pp. Contemporary photographs and a simple text introduce the Philippines, the people, and the holidays they celebrate, plus step-by-step craft projects and some tasty recipes. (Rev: BL 4/15/98) [959.9]

16585 NgCheong-Lum, Roseline. *Tahiti* (4–7). Illus. Series: Cultures of the World. 1997, Marshall Cavendish LB $35.64 (0-7614-0682-4). 128pp. Background material on history and geography is given, with information on how Tahitians live today. (Rev: BL 8/97; HBG 3/98) [919.62]

16586 Nile, Richard. *Australian Aborigines* (4–7). Illus. Series: Threatened Cultures. 1993, Raintree LB $24.26 (0-8114-2303-4). 48pp. The aboriginal culture of Australia is presented. (Rev: BL 8/93; SLJ 8/93) [305]

16587 North, Peter. *Australia* (4–6). Series: Countries of the World. 1998, Gareth Stevens LB $25.26 (0-8368-2122-X). 96pp. This broad introduction to Australia covers its history, geography, government, and culture. (Rev: BL 12/15/98; HBG 10/99; SLJ 2/99) [994]

16588 North, Peter, and Susan McKay. *Welcome to Australia* (2–4). Series: Welcome to My Country. 1999, Gareth Stevens LB $16.95 (0-8368-2393-1). 48pp. An attractive introduction to Australia with

material on its geography, history, government, people, recreation, and food. (Rev: HBG 10/00; SLJ 1/00) [994]

16589 Oleksy, Walter. *The Philippines* (4–7). Series: Enchantment of the World. 2000, Children's Book Pr. LB $34.50 (0-516-21010-6). 144pp. These South Pacific islands are presented with coverage of history, geography, economy, the people, current problems, culture, and recreation. (Rev: BL 7/00) [959.9]

16590 Olson, Nathan. *Australia: A Question And Answer Book* (2–5). Illus. Series: Questions and Answers: Countries. 2005, Capstone LB $16.95 (0-7368-3747-7). 32pp. Using a question-and-answer format, simple text, large photos, and many factboxes, this is an introduction to Australia today, with material on history and traditional culture.

16591 Pelta, Kathy. *Rediscovering Easter Island* (5–9). Series: How History Is Invented. 2001, Lerner LB $28.75 (0-8225-4890-9). 112pp. An assortment of illustrations, maps, and inserts add to this exploration of the mysteries of Easter Island. (Rev: BCCB 7–8/01; HBG 10/01; SLJ 2/02) [996.18]

16592 Rajendra, Vijeya, and Sundran Rajendra. *Australia* (4–7). Illus. Series: Cultures of the World. 1991, Marshall Cavendish LB $35.64 (1-85435-400-0). 128pp. Beyond the basics, this volume highlights contemporary problems and concerns in the Land Down Under. (Rev: BL 2/15/92; SLJ 3/92) [994]

16593 Schroeder, Holly. *New Zealand ABCs: A Book About the People and Places of New Zealand* (2–4). Illus. by Claudia Wolf. Series: Country ABCs. 2004, Picture Window LB $23.93 (1-4048-0178-2). 32pp. Young researchers will find useful facts in this alphabetically organized volume. (Rev: SLJ 8/04) [992]

16594 Sharp, Anne Wallace. *Australia* (5–9). Series: Indigenous Peoples of the World. 2003, Gale $27.45 (1-59018-091-7). 112pp. In addition to discussing the customs and traditions of the aboriginal people of Australia, the author looks at their harsh treatment by the European settlers. (Rev: SLJ 1/03) [305.89915]

16595 Shepherd, Donna Walsh. *New Zealand* (4–7). Series: Enchantment of the World. 2002, Children's Book Pr. LB $34.50 (0-516-21099-8). 144pp. Some of the subjects covered in this fine introduction to New Zealand are history, people and languages, economy, government, culture, natural resources, and climate. (Rev: BL 5/15/02; SLJ 10/02) [992]

16596 Steele, Philip. *Sydney* (4–6). Series: Great Cities of the World. 2004, World Almanac LB $29.26 (0-8368-5032-7). 48pp. A profile of Australia's oldest and biggest city, well illustrated with photographs. (Rev: SLJ 6/04) [994]

16597 Sullivan, Margaret. *The Philippines: Pacific Crossroads* (4–8). Illus. Series: Discovering Our Heritage. 1993, Macmillan LB $14.95 (0-87518-548-7). 127pp. A history with a focus on relations with the United States and current developments. (Rev: SLJ 8/93) [959.9]

16598 Theunissen, Steve. *The Maori of New Zealand* (4–6). Illus. Series: First Peoples. 2002, Lerner LB $23.93 (0-8225-0665-3). 48pp. Full of photographs, this is a wide-ranging introduction to the history and culture of the Polynesian people who settled in New Zealand centuries before the Europeans arrived. (Rev: HBG 3/03; SLJ 6/03) [993]

16599 Tope, Lily R. *Philippines* (4–7). Illus. Series: Cultures of the World. 1991, Marshall Cavendish LB $35.64 (1-85435-403-5). 128pp. With emphasis on contemporary problems and concerns, the land and culture of the Philippines are introduced in text and well-chosen color photographs. (Rev: BL 2/15/92) [959.9]

16600 Underwood, Deborah. *The Easter Island Statues* (3–6). Illus. Series: Wonders of the World. 2004, Gale/KidHaven LB $23.70 (0-7377-3065-X). 31pp. Underwood discusses the construction and symbolism of these famous statues, and includes material on the island's geography, history, and people. (Rev: SLJ 6/05) [996.1]

16601 Webster, Christine. *Polynesians* (4–6). Illus. Series: Indigenous Peoples. 2004, Weigl LB $18.20 (1-59036-123-7). 32pp. Historical and contemporary issues are both covered in this detailed portrait of life among the Polynesian people and how they've endured and adapted to dramatic changes in their homelands. (Rev: BL 4/1/04; SLJ 7/04) [996]

16602 Wilson, Barbara K. *Acacia Terrace* (2–4). Illus. by David Fielding. 1990, Scholastic $13.95 (0-590-42885-3). 40pp. This is the story of an Australian family's fortunes and misfortunes through the years. (Rev: BL 2/15/90) [994.4]

Europe

General and Miscellaneous

16603 Allan, Tony. *The Rhine* (4–7). Series: Great Rivers of the World. 2003, World Almanac LB $26.60 (0-8368-5446-2). 48pp. An exploration of the Rhine's flow, history, and animals and plants, with discussion of the settlements along its banks, the industries it supports, recreation on its waters, and environmental threats to the river. (Rev: SLJ 9/03) [943]

16604 Baralt, Luis A. *Turkey* (5–8). Illus. Series: Enchantment of the World. 1997, Children's Book Pr. paper $32.00 (0-516-20305-3). 128pp. A visually attractive book that covers such topics as Turkey's population, natural resources, historic landmarks, and people. (Rev: BL 8/97; HBG 3/98) [915.61]

16605 Bramwell, Martyn. *Europe* (4–6). Illus. Series: World in Maps. 2000, Carolrhoda $23.93 (0-8225-2913-0). 48pp. Portrays the countries of Europe in a series of maps and accompanying text that supply information on such topics as population, government, geography, cities, and notable physical features. (Rev: BL 10/15/00; HBG 10/01; SLJ 1/01) [940]

16606 *Cyprus in Pictures* (5–8). Illus. Series: Visual Geography. 1992, Lerner LB $25.55 (0-8225-1910-

0). 64pp. The divided island of Cyprus is introduced, with good background information and material on the standoff between Greece and Turkey up to 1992. (Rev: BL 2/1/93) [956.45]

16607 Feinstein, Steve. *Turkey in Pictures* (5–8). Illus. 1989, Lerner LB $25.55 (0-8225-1831-7). 64pp. An overview of Turkey and its people that includes lots of images. (Rev: BL 8/88) [956.1]

16608 Fox, Mary V. *Cyprus* (5–8). Illus. Series: Enchantment of the World. 1993, Children's Book Pr. paper $32.00 (0-516-02617-8). 128pp. An introduction to this Mediterranean island, its troubled history, and its present division between Turkey and Greece. (Rev: BL 11/1/93; SLJ 3/94) [956.93]

16609 Kallen, Stuart A. *The Rhine* (5–8). Series: Rivers of the World. 2003, Gale LB $27.45 (1-59018-062-3). 112pp. A comprehensive look at this important river's history, geology, agricultural and industrial significance, environmental problems, and the floods that threaten surrounding communities. (Rev: SLJ 9/03) [943]

16610 Nerman, Kemal, and Selina Kuo. *Turkey* (4–6). Series: Countries of the World. 2001, Gareth Stevens LB $21.95 (0-8368-2341-9). 96pp. A recommended introduction to Turkey that includes material on its people, traditions, geography, history, and current affairs. (Rev: BL 12/15/01; HBG 3/02) [956.1]

16611 Orr, Tamra. *Turkey* (5–8). Illus. Series: Enchantment of the World, Second Series. 2003, Children's Book Pr. LB $34.00 (0-516-22679-7). 144pp. A visually attractive book that covers such topics as the geography, history, government, culture, and people, with a timeline, fast facts, and a recipe. (Rev: SLJ 5/03) [915]

16612 O'Shea, Maria. *Turkey* (2–4). Series: Festivals of the World. 1999, Gareth Stevens LB $15.95 (0-8368-2037-1). 32pp. This book introduces the land and people of Turkey through their national holidays, such as the Festival of Sacrifice and the Kirkpinar wrestling competition. Instructions for crafts and related foods are included. (Rev: BL 12/15/99; HBG 10/00) [956.1]

16613 Pollard, Michael. *The Rhine* (5–8). Series: Great Rivers. 1997, Benchmark LB $22.79 (0-7614-0500-3). After explaining how the Rhine was formed, this attractive book describes its history, importance, tributaries, tourism, and present-day role. (Rev: HBG 3/98; SLJ 3/98) [943]

16614 Sheehan, Sean. *Malta* (5–9). Series: Cultures of the World. 2000, Marshall Cavendish LB $35.64 (0-7614-0993-9). 128pp. This work covers the culture, geography, and history of Malta with material on such subjects as government, economy, people, lifestyles, and leisure. (Rev: HBG 10/00; SLJ 11/00) [945]

16615 Sheehan, Sean. *Turkey* (4–7). Illus. Series: Cultures of the World. 1993, Marshall Cavendish LB $35.64 (1-85435-576-7). 128pp. This introduction to Turkey covers history, culture, economics, and present-day concerns. (Rev: BL 8/93) [956.1]

Central and Eastern Europe

16616 Andryszewski, Tricia. *Kosovo: The Splintering of Yugoslavia* (5–8). Illus. Series: Headliners. 2000, Millbrook LB $25.90 (0-7613-1750-3). 64pp. Introduced by refugees' accounts of the horror in Kosovo, this book traces the origins of ethnic conflicts in Yugoslavia, with a concentration on events of the past 10 years. (Rev: BL 6/1–15/00; HBG 10/00; SLJ 6/00) [949.7]

16617 Burke, Patrick. *Eastern Europe: Bulgaria, Czech Republic, Hungary, Poland, Romania, Slovakia* (5–8). Series: Country Fact Files. 1997, Raintree LB $27.12 (0-8172-4628-2). In chapters two to four pages long, the impact of geography on the landscape, daily life, natural resources, transportation, and other aspects of life is examined for these six countries. (Rev: SLJ 8/97) [947]

16618 Carran, Betty B. *Romania* (4–7). Illus. 1988, Children's Book Pr. paper $32.00 (0-516-02703-4). 124pp. Coverage includes geography, culture, history, and politics. (Rev: BL 8/88) [949.8]

16619 Clemmons, Brad, and Pamela K. Harris. *Switzerland* (3–5). Series: Faces and Places. 2001, Child's World LB $25.64 (1-56766-912-3). 32pp. In a series of short chapters with accompanying large color photographs, basic material on Switzerland is given, including facts on people, their work, the land, food, and everyday life. (Rev: BL 9/15/01; HBG 3/02; SLJ 12/01) [949.4]

16620 Corona, Laurel. *Poland* (5–8). Illus. Series: Modern Nations of the World. 2000, Lucent LB $27.45 (1-56006-600-8). 126pp. A good history of Poland that also covers Polish achievements and daily life. (Rev: BL 9/15/00; HBG 3/01) [943.8]

16621 Denenberg, Barry. *Elisabeth: The Princess Bride* (4–8). Series: Royal Diaries. 2003, Scholastic $10.95 (0-439-26644-0). 160pp. Princess Elisabeth of mid-19th-century Austria describes to her diary how her life changes when Emperor Franz Joseph I chooses her as his bride-to-be. (Rev: HBG 10/03; SLJ 4/03)

16622 Englar, Mary. *Turkey* (2–5). Illus. Series: Questions and Answers: Countries. 2005, Capstone LB $16.95 (0-7368-3762-0). 32pp. Using a question-and-answer format, simple text, large photos, and many factboxes, this is an introduction to Turkey today, with material on history and traditional culture.

16623 Gabrielpillai, Matilda. *Bosnia and Herzegovina* (4–6). Series: Countries of the World. 2000, Gareth Stevens LB $26.60 (0-8368-2329-X). 96pp. Describes the history, government, geography, and current concerns of this troubled area, once part of Yugoslavia. (Rev: BL 3/15/01; HBG 10/01) [949.703]

16624 Ganeri, Anita. *I Remember Bosnia* (3–6). Illus. Series: Why We Left. 1995, Raintree LB $22.83 (0-8114-5607-2). 32pp. An introduction to Bosnia that gives good background material and an explanation of the recent political and military problems. (Rev: BCCB 3/95; SLJ 6/95) [949.702]

16625 Grajnert, Paul. *Poland* (4–6). Series: Countries of the World. 2002, Gareth Stevens LB $21.95 (0-8368-2345-1). 96pp. Along with basic background material, this colorful introduction to Poland covers contemporary life. (Rev: BL 6/1–15/02; HBG 10/02; SLJ 5/02) [943.8]

16626 Hintz, Martin. *Switzerland* (4–6). Illus. 1986, Children's Book Pr. LB $32.00 (0-516-02790-5). 128pp. Standard, useful information highlighted by color photos. (Rev: BL 4/1/87; SLJ 5/87)

16627 *Hungary in Pictures* (5–8). Illus. Series: Visual Geography. 1993, Lerner LB $25.55 (0-8225-1883-X). 64pp. Concise text and extensive photographs introduce the land, history, and people of Hungary. (Rev: BL 12/1/93; SLJ 12/93) [943.9]

16628 Kinkade, Sheila. *Children of Slovakia* (2–5). Photos by Elaine Little. Series: The World's Children. 2001, Carolrhoda LB $23.93 (1-57505-446-9). 48pp. The daily lives of children in Slovakia are used to introduce the history, geography, and culture of the country, with appealing full-color illustrations, a pronunciation guide, and map. (Rev: HBG 10/01; SLJ 6/01) [943.7305]

16629 Levy, Patricia. *Switzerland* (4–6). Illus. Series: Cultures of the World. 1994, Marshall Cavendish LB $35.64 (1-85435-591-0). 128pp. This attractive introduction to Switzerland includes material on lifestyles, economy, geography, arts, and leisure. (Rev: SLJ 7/94) [949.4]

16630 Lundrigan, Nicole. *Hungary* (4–6). Series: Countries of the World. 2002, Gareth Stevens LB $21.95 (0-8368-2344-3). 96pp. A well-illustrated introduction to the past and present of Hungary with an emphasis on how people live. (Rev: BL 6/1–15/02; HBG 10/02; SLJ 5/02) [943.9]

16631 McCollum, Sean. *Poland* (1–3). Series: A Ticket To. 1999, Carolrhoda LB $22.60 (1-57505-131-1). 48pp. Easy-to-understand language and a large map enhance this beginning account of the land, people, and main cultural features of Poland. (Rev: BL 9/15/99; HBG 3/00; SLJ 10/00) [943.8]

16632 McCollum, Sean. *Poland* (3–5). Series: Globe-Trotters Club. 1999, Carolrhoda LB $16.95 (1-57505-106-0). 48pp. After a brief history, this book focuses on modern life covering topics including religion, food, education, and family life. (Rev: BL 9/15/99; HBG 3/00; SLJ 2/00) [943.8]

16633 McKay, Susan. *Switzerland* (2–4). Series: Festivals of the World. 1999, Gareth Stevens LB $14.95 (0-8368-2027-4). 32pp. Switzerland's uniqueness is stressed in this description of its chief holidays, with craft projects and recipes to help readers celebrate. (Rev: BL 4/15/98; SLJ 8/99) [949.4]

16634 Marx, Trish. *One Boy from Kosovo* (3–6). Illus. 2000, HarperCollins LB $15.89 (0-688-17733-6). 32pp. Using a case study of an Albanian family in Kosovo and their son Edi, the author discusses the conflict in Kosovo, its causes, its course, and its consequences. (Rev: BL 6/1–15/00; HB 7–8/00; HBG 10/00; SLJ 6/00) [305.9]

16635 Milivojevic, JoAnn. *Bosnia and Herzegovina* (4–6). Series: Enchantment of the World. 2004,

Scholastic LB $35.00 (0-516-24247-4). 144pp. Contemporary life, history, geography, culture are all covered in this well-illustrated and well-written volume suitable for report writers. (Rev: BL 9/1/04; SLJ 7/04) [949.742]

16636 Netzley, Patricia D. *Switzerland* (5–8). Series: Modern Nations of the World. 2001, Lucent LB $27.45 (1-56006-821-3). 112pp. Interesting sidebars, a chronology, and excellent photographs supplement informative text introducing this small country. (Rev: BL 6/1–15/01) [949.3]

16637 Nollen, Tim. *Czech Republic* (2–4). Series: Festivals of the World. 1999, Gareth Stevens LB $15.95 (0-8368-2031-2). 32pp. This description of Czech festivals such as the *slavnost* and the Burning of the Witches also includes instructions for staging one's own *slavnost*. (Rev: BL 12/15/99; HBG 10/00) [943.7]

16638 Orr, Tamra. *Slovenia* (5–8). Series: Enchantment of the World. 2004, Children's Pr. LB $34.50 (0-516-24249-0). 144pp. Introduces the history, geography, people, and culture of Slovenia, with plenty of clear photographs and an emphasis on contemporary life. (Rev: SLJ 7/04) [949.73]

16639 Pfeiffer, Christine. *Poland: Land of Freedom Fighters* (5–8). Illus. 1991, Macmillan LB $14.95 (0-87518-464-2). 144pp. An introduction to the land and people of Poland and of their migration to the United States. [943.8]

16640 Ricchiardi, Sherry. *Bosnia: The Struggle for Peace* (5–8). Illus. 1996, Millbrook LB $25.90 (0-7613-0031-7). An account that gives background information but concentrates on the recent (through 1995) history of Bosnia. (Rev: BL 7/96; SLJ 7/96) [949.702]

16641 Rogers, Lura. *Switzerland* (4–7). Series: Enchantment of the World. 2001, Children's Book Pr. LB $34.50 (0-516-21080-7). A highly visual introduction to Switzerland that covers such topics as people and languages, history, natural resources, and climate. (Rev: BL 1/1–15/02) [949.4]

16642 *Romania in Pictures* (5–8). Illus. Series: Visual Geography. 1993, Lerner LB $25.55 (0-8225-1894-5). 64pp. In addition to background material on history and geography, this account gives a good picture of contemporary life in Romania. (Rev: BL 9/1/93) [949.8]

16643 Ryan, Patrick. *Poland* (3–5). Illus. Series: Faces and Places. 2000, Child's World LB $25.64 (1-56766-716-3). 32pp. A general introduction to Poland that uses double-page spreads to cover such topics as geography, history, animals, people, food, and holidays. (Rev: BL 3/1/01; HBG 3/01) [943.8]

16644 Schrepfer, Margaret. *Switzerland: The Summit of Europe* (4–7). Illus. Series: Discovering Our Heritage. 1989, Macmillan LB $14.95 (0-87518-405-7). 142pp. Four ethnic groups plus Switzerland's ancient and modern history are covered in this introduction. (Rev: BL 7/89; SLJ 10/89) [949.4]

16645 Sheehan, Sean. *Austria* (4–7). Illus. Series: Cultures of the World. 1992, Marshall Cavendish LB $35.64 (1-85435-454-X). 128pp. This introduction to Austria covers its history, lifestyles of the

people, and contemporary problems. (Rev: BL 10/15/92) [943.6]

16646 Stein, R. Conrad. *Austria* (4–7). Series: Enchantment of the World. 2000, Children's Book Pr. LB $34.50 (0-516-21049-1). 144pp. A thorough introduction to Austria with material on such subjects as history, the land, government, people, culture, cities, and daily life. (Rev: BL 1/1–15/01) [943.6]

16647 Steins, Richard. *Hungary: Crossroads of Europe* (3–5). Illus. Series: Exploring Cultures of the World. 1997, Marshall Cavendish LB $27.07 (0-7614-0141-5). 64pp. Current conditions in Hungary are covered, along with good background information about its people, culture, and history. (Rev: BL 7/97; SLJ 1/98) [943.9]

16648 *Switzerland in Pictures* (5–8). Series: Visual Geography. 1996, Lerner LB $25.55 (0-8225-1895-3). With a generous number of color pictures, this account traces the history and geography of Switzerland, with emphasis on the modern nation and its people. (Rev: BL 9/15/96; SLJ 8/98) [949.4]

16649 Willis, Terri. *Romania* (4–7). Series: Enchantment of the World. 2001, Children's Book Pr. LB $34.50 (0-516-21635-X). Packed with photographs, original maps, and browser-friendly sidebars, this is a fine introduction to Romania that explores a number of aspects of the past and present of this country. (Rev: BL 1/1–15/02) [949.8]

16650 Zwierzynska-Coldicott, Aldona Maria. *Poland* (2–4). Series: Festivals of the World. 1998, Gareth Stevens LB $14.95 (0-8368-2018-5). 32pp. Discusses Poland and its people, with emphasis on its unique holidays, crafts, and food. (Rev: BL 12/15/98; HBG 10/99) [947]

France

16651 Arnold, Helen. *France* (1–3). Illus. Series: Postcards From. 1995, Raintree LB $21.40 (0-8172-4004-7). 32pp. France is introduced through a series of postcards written by fictitious children. (Rev: SLJ 2/96) [944]

16652 Bader, Philip. *France* (3–5). Series: Dropping In On. 2001, Rourke LB $25.27 (1-55916-280-5). 32pp. A brief tour of France in a hot-air balloon — with stops at interesting places — that includes material on landmarks, the people, food, and growing up. (Rev: SLJ 1/01) [944]

16653 Bailey, Linda. *Adventures in the Ice Age* (3–6). Illus. by Bill Slavin. Series: Good Times Travel Agency. 2004, Kids Can paper $8.95 (1-55337-504-1). 48pp. In this sixth installment, the Binkerton children are whisked off to Ice Age France, where they learn facts about life at that time while continuing their fictional adventure. (Rev: BL 11/1/04) [559.9]

16654 Benedict, Kitty C. *The Fall of the Bastille* (5–8). Series: Turning Points in World History. 1991, Silver Burdett LB $14.95 (0-382-24129-0); paper $7.95 (0-382-24135-5). A study of the event that symbolized a tremendous change in French society. (Rev: BL 3/15/92) [944.04]

16655 Boast, Clare. *France* (2–4). Series: Next Stop. 1998, Heinemann LB $19.92 (1-57572-565-7). 32pp. A lively introduction to France that covers its history, geography, and people. (Rev: SLJ 6/98) [944]

16656 Butler, Daphne. *France* (2–4). Illus. Series: On the Map. 1993, Raintree LB $22.83 (0-8114-3675-6). 32pp. An overview of life in France, with coverage of geogrphy, industry, customs, and landmarks. (Rev: BL 9/1/93) [944]

16657 Corona, Laurel. *France* (5–8). Series: Modern Nations of the World. 2002, Gale LB $27.45 (1-56006-760-8). 112pp. A comprehensive introduction to the land and people of France with material on history, geography, culture, and lifestyles. (Rev: BL 12/15/02) [944]

16658 Costain, Meredith, and Paul Collins. *Welcome to France* (3–5). Illus. Series: Countries of the World. 2001, Chelsea LB $16.95 (0-7910-6551-0). 32pp. Young Gregoire introduces daily life, schooling, sports, transport, important places, and so forth, with interesting color photographs. (Rev: HBG 3/02; SLJ 10/01) [944]

16659 Dunford, Mick. *France* (5–8). Illus. Series: Modern Industrial World. 1994, Thomson Learning LB $24.26 (1-56847-263-3). 48pp. An introduction to modern France that gives information about government, people, economic conditions, and recent history. (Rev: BL 1/15/95) [944]

16660 Fisher, Teresa. *France* (3–6). Series: Foods and Festivals. 1999, Raintree LB $22.83 (0-8172-5550-8). 32pp. This book gives an overview of the celebrations and holidays of France, with material on related food crops and special dishes plus many simple recipes. (Rev: HBG 10/99; SLJ 7/99) [944]

16661 Fisher, Teresa. *France* (2–4). Series: We Come From. 1999, Raintree LB $22.83 (0-8172-5212-6). 32pp. This book gives a little information on daily life in France, plus some coverage of its geography, cities, and weather, and a recipe. (Rev: HBG 3/00; SLJ 3/00) [944]

16662 Fisher, Teresa. *France: City and Village Life* (4–7). Illus. Series: Country Insights. 1997, Raintree LB $27.12 (0-8172-4788-2). 48pp. A specific city and village are used to compare and contrast two lifestyles in contemporary France. (Rev: SLJ 8/97) [944]

16663 Gamgee, John. *Journey Through France* (K–3). Illus. Series: Journey Around the World. 1994, Troll LB $18.60 (0-8167-2759-7). 32pp. An introduction to contemporary life in France using color photos and a brief text. (Rev: SLJ 9/94) [914.4]

16664 Gilbert, Adrian. *The French Revolution* (4–6). Series: Revolution! 1995, Thomson Learning LB $24.26 (1-56847-390-7). 48pp. Beginning with the execution of Louis XVI in 1793, this account moves back in time to trace the history of the French Revolution. (Rev: SLJ 2/96) [944]

16665 Gofen, Ethel C. *France* (4–7). Illus. Series: Cultures of the World. 1992, Marshall Cavendish LB $35.64 (1-85435-449-3). 128pp. This account provides information on the history, culture, and

people of France and discusses the current problems and concerns. (Rev: BL 10/15/92) [944]

16666 Haskins, Jim, and Kathleen Benson. *Count Your Way Through France* (2–4). Illus. by Andrea Shine. Series: Count Your Way. 1996, Carolrhoda LB $19.93 (0-87614-874-7); paper $5.95 (0-87614-972-7). 24pp. Using the numbers 1 through 10, each page contains useful information about the history, traditions, and people of France. (Rev: BL 9/15/96; SLJ 8/96) [944]

16667 Hoban, Sarah. *Daily Life in Ancient and Modern Paris* (4–7). Illus. 2000, Runestone LB $25.26 (0-8225-3222-0). 64pp. This well-illustrated history of Paris is divided chronologically into seven sections, beginning with early Paris and working through the Middle Ages to World War II and the Paris of today. (Rev: BL 2/1/01; HBG 3/01; SLJ 2/01) [944]

16668 Ingham, Richard. *France* (4–8). Illus. 2000, Raintree LB $34.26 (0-8172-5782-9). 128pp. A fine introduction to France — its past, its present, and its people — that is particularly noteworthy for its use of graphics. (Rev: BL 10/15/00; HBG 10/00; SLJ 7/00) [944]

16669 McKay, Susan. *France* (2–4). Series: Festivals of the World. 1998, Gareth Stevens LB $18.60 (0-8368-2003-7). 32pp. Bastille Day is only one of several French national holidays discussed in this colorful book containing craft projects and recipes. (Rev: BL 5/15/98; HBG 10/98; SLJ 6/98) [944]

16670 Nardo, Don. *France* (4–7). Series: Enchantment of the World. 2000, Children's Book Pr. LB $34.50 (0-516-21052-1). 144pp. This attractively formatted and illustrated new edition gives solid information about France, its land, and its people. (Rev: BL 7/00) [944]

16671 NgCheong-Lum, Roseline. *France* (5–7). Series: Countries of the World. 1999, Gareth Stevens LB $29.26 (0-8368-2260-9). 96pp. A wide range of topics including history, government, people, customs, and geography are covered in this colorful introduction to France. (Rev: BL 9/15/99; SLJ 8/99) [944]

16672 Plain, Nancy. *Louis XVI, Marie-Antoinette and the French Revolution* (5–8). Series: Rulers and Their Times. 2001, Marshall Cavendish LB $28.50 (0-7614-1029-5). In three well-illustrated parts, this book offers a biography of Marie Antoinette, a history of France and its people during the French Revolution, and a generous selection of original documents of the period. (Rev: BL 1/1–15/02; HBG 3/02; SLJ 3/02) [944]

16673 Powell, Jillian. *A History of France Through Art* (5–8). Illus. Series: History Through Art. 1996, Thomson Learning LB $5.00 (1-56847-441-5). The basic history of France is covered in 21 double-page spreads, each dealing with an important event or subject and each containing works of art and informative background text. (Rev: BL 3/1/96; SLJ 2/96) [944]

16674 Shuter, Jane, ed. *Helen Williams and the French Revolution* (5–8). Illus. Series: History Eyewitness. 1996, Raintree LB $24.26 (0-8114-8287-

1). 48pp. An abridged, well-illustrated firsthand account describes the causes and the course of the French Revolution. (Rev: BL 5/15/96; SLJ 6/96) [944.04]

16675 Spengler, Kremena. *France* (2–5). Illus. Series: Questions and Answers: Countries. 2004, Capstone LB $16.95 (0-7368-2689-0). 32pp. Using a question-and-answer format, simple text, large photos, and many factboxes, this is an introduction to France today, with material on history and traditional culture.

16676 Stacey, Gill. *Paris* (4–7). Illus. 2004, World Almanac LB $29.26 (0-8368-5030-0). 48pp. This attractive introduction to Paris covers the French capital's history and examines some of its modern-day problems. (Rev: BL 4/15/04) [944]

16677 Stevens, Kathryn. *France* (3–5). Series: Countries: Faces and Places. 2000, Child's World LB $25.64 (1-56766-714-7). 32pp. This basic introduction to France, its history, people, and culture uses simple text, color photographs on each page, and an oversize format. (Rev: BL 4/15/01; HBG 3/01) [944]

16678 Sturges, Jo. *France* (3–5). Illus. Series: Discovering. 1993, Crestwood LB $13.95 (0-89686-778-1). 32pp. This brief review of French life covers geography, history, holidays, food, entertainment, and landmarks. (Rev: BL 2/1/94; SLJ 12/93) [944]

16679 Wright, Rachel. *Paris 1789: A Guide to Paris on the Eve of the Revolution* (4–7). Series: Sightseers. 1999, Kingfisher $8.95 (0-7534-5183-2). 31pp. Using the format of a tourist guide, this book tells you what to see, eat, wear, and buy in the Paris of the late 18th century. (Rev: HBG 10/99; SLJ 8/99) [944]

16680 Yuan, Margaret Speaker. *The Arc de Triomphe* (5–8). Series: Building World Landmarks. 2004, Gale/Blackbirch LB $18.96 (1-4103-0138-9). 48pp. A concise account of the design and construction of this arch, which met financial, political, and technical difficulties. (Rev: SLJ 4/05)

Germany

16681 Ayer, Eleanor. *Germany: In the Heartland of Europe* (4–6). Illus. Series: Exploring Cultures of the World. 1996, Benchmark LB $27.07 (0-7614-0189-X). 64pp. Good background material on Germany is presented, with special emphasis on the arts, sports, leisure, holidays, and festivals. (Rev: SLJ 6/96) [943]

16682 Barber, Nicola. *Berlin* (4–7). Illus. Series: Great Cities of the World. 2005, World Almanac LB $22.50 (0-8368-5043-2). 48pp. An informative and appealing overview of one of the world's most famous cities, with material on its history, its economy, and what it's like to live there.

16683 Fuller, Barbara. *Germany* (4–7). Illus. Series: Cultures of the World. 1992, Marshall Cavendish LB $35.64 (1-85435-530-9). 128pp. In addition to the usual information on the history and geography

of Germany, this account stresses how the people live and their traditions. (Rev: BL 1/1/93) [943]

16684 *Germany in Pictures* (5–8). Illus. Series: Visual Geography. 1994, Lerner LB $21.27 (0-8225-1873-2). 64pp. The new united Germany is introduced with a basic text and copious illustrations, including maps, charts, and attractive photographs. (Rev: BL 1/15/95) [943]

16685 Gray, Susan H. *Germany* (1–3). Series: A True Book. 2003, Children's Pr. LB $23.50 (0-516-22673-8); paper $6.95 (0-516-27753-7). 48pp. A blend of easy-to-understand text and colorful illustrations make this overview suitable for beginning readers. (Rev: SLJ 10/03) [943]

16686 Hargrove, Jim. *Germany* (5–8). Illus. Series: Enchantment of the World. 1991, Children's Book Pr. paper $32.00 (0-516-02601-1). 128pp. German geography, people, culture, and history through reunification are covered in text and pictures. (Rev: BL 2/1/92) [943]

16687 Haskins, Jim. *Count Your Way Through Germany* (2–4). Illus. by Helen Byers. Series: Count Your Way. 1990, Carolrhoda LB $19.93 (0-87614-407-5). The reader is introduced to Germany through numbers. (Rev: SLJ 8/90) [943]

16688 Levy, Debbie. *The Berlin Wall* (5–8). Series: Building World Landmarks. 2004, Gale/Blackbirch LB $18.96 (1-4103-0137-0). 48pp. A concise account of the wall's history and its importance in the struggle between East and West; with a timeline. (Rev: SLJ 4/05)

16689 Lord, Richard. *Germany* (3–5). Illus. Series: Festivals of the World. 1997, Gareth Stevens LB $21.27 (0-8368-1682-X). 32pp. Such German festivals as St. Martin's Day, Karneval, St. Nikolaus Day and Christmas, Oktoberfest, and Walpurgis Night are introduced and described. (Rev: SLJ 1/98) [943]

16690 Lord, Richard. *Germany* (4–5). Series: Countries of the World. 1999, Gareth Stevens LB $18.95 (0-8368-2261-7). 95pp. Vivid color photos and an up-to-date text are used in this comprehensive introduction to Germany. (Rev: BL 9/15/99) [943]

16691 Mirable, Lisa. *The Berlin Wall* (5–8). Series: Turning Points. 1991, Silver Burdett LB $14.95 (0-382-24133-9); paper $7.95 (0-382-24140-1). 64pp. How the fall of the Berlin Wall dramatically changed German history. (Rev: BL 3/15/92) [943.1]

16692 Nickles, Greg, and Niki Walker. *Germany* (4–8). Series: Nations of the World. 2001, Raintree LB $34.26 (0-7398-1285-8). 128pp. A profile of this recently united, highly industrialized, and urbanized country, with material on its past, present, and future. (Rev: BL 6/1–15/01; HBG 10/01) [943]

16693 Spengler, Kremena. *Germany* (2–5). Illus. Series: Questions and Answers: Countries. 2004, Capstone LB $16.95 (0-7368-2690-4). 32pp. Using a question-and-answer format, simple text, large photos, and many factboxes, this is an introduction to Germany today, with material on history and traditional culture.

16694 Steele, Philip. *Germany* (3–5). Illus. Series: Discovering. 1993, Crestwood LB $13.95 (0-89686-

777-3). 32pp. A brief introduction to modern Germany, with good background material on its culture and reunification. (Rev: BL 2/1/94; SLJ 2/94) [943]

16695 Stein, R. Conrad. *Berlin* (3–6). Series: Cities of the World. 1997, Children's Book Pr. LB $26.50 (0-516-20582-X). 64pp. Describes present-day Berlin, Germany, its landmarks, people, geography, and history, including the division during the Communist period. (Rev: BL 1/1–15/98; HBG 3/98) [943]

Great Britain and Ireland

16696 Allan, Tony. *The Irish Famine: The Birth of Irish America* (4–9). Illus. by Stefan Chabluk. Series: Point of Impact. 2001, Heinemann LB $24.22 (1-58810-077-4). 32pp. Allan traces the causes of the crisis that started in Ireland in 1845, the subsequent wave of emigration to the United States, and the ill feelings created between Britain and Ireland. (Rev: HBG 10/01; SLJ 7/01) [941.5081]

16697 Almond, David. *Counting Stars* (5–9). 2002, Delacorte LB $18.99 (0-385-90034-1). 205pp. In a series of vignettes based on personal experience, a man recalls growing up in a poor mining town in northern England. (Rev: BCCB 3/02; BL 1/1/02; HB 3–4/02; HBG 10/02; SLJ 3/02)

16698 Ashby, Ruth. *Elizabethan England* (5–9). Series: Cultures of the Past. 1998, Benchmark LB $28.50 (0-7614-0269-1). 80pp. Ashby looks at the cultural aspects of Elizabethan England, providing material on the art and literature of the period plus coverage of daily life, religion, and major personalities. (Rev: BL 12/15/98; BR 5–6/99; HBG 10/99; SLJ 2/99) [942]

16699 Ashby, Ruth. *Victorian England* (5–8). Series: Cultures of the Past. 2002, Marshall Cavendish $19.95 (0-7614-1493-2). 80pp. The political, historical, and cultural aspects of life in England during the reign of Victoria are covered in this handsome volume. (Rev: BL 1/1–15/03; HBG 3/03) [942]

16700 Bell, Rachael. *Ireland* (1–3). Series: A Visit To. 1999, Heinemann LB $13.95 (1-57572-847-8). 32pp. Double-page spreads present information on Ireland's geography, landmarks, homes, work, food, schools, and celebrations. (Rev: HBG 10/99; SLJ 10/99) [941.5]

16701 Blashfield, Jean F. *England* (4–7). Illus. Series: Enchantment of the World. 1997, Children's Book Pr. LB $34.50 (0-516-20471-8). 144pp. This fine introduction to England gives material on its history, politics, the royal family, religion, and daily life. (Rev: BL 2/1/98; HBG 10/98) [942]

16702 Blashfield, Jean F. *Ireland* (4–7). Series: Enchantment of the World. 2002, Children's Book Pr. LB $34.50 (0-516-21127-7). 144pp. Using many visual aids and a lively text, this is an introduction to Ireland — the land, the people, and the culture. (Rev: BL 5/15/02; SLJ 12/02) [941.5]

16703 Boraas, Tracey. *England* (4–6). Series: Countries and Cultures. 2002, Capstone LB $23.93 (0-7368-0937-6). 64pp. Using devices such as timelines, maps, sidebars, and a recipe, English history, geog-

raphy, and culture are introduced. (Rev: BL 1/1–15/03; HBG 3/03; SLJ 7/03) [942]

16704 Brassey, Richard, and Stewart Ross. *The Story of Ireland* (3–5). Illus. 2002, Trafalgar $19.95 (1-85881-848-6); paper $9.95 (1-85881-849-4). 40pp. Fast-paced narrative and brief biographies tell the history of Ireland from prehistoric times. (Rev: BL 3/1/02) [941.5]

16705 Burgan, Michael. *England* (2–4). Series: True Books. 1999, Children's Book Pr. LB $21.00 (0-516-21187-0). 47pp. An attractive introduction to England with a text that covers such topics as history, geography, climate, people, and culture. (Rev: HBG 10/99; SLJ 10/99) [942]

16706 Buscher, Sarah, and Bettina Ling. *Mairead Corrigan and Betty Williams: Making Peace in Northern Ireland* (5–8). Illus. 1999, Feminist Pr. $19.95 (1-55861-200-9); paper $9.95 (1-55861-201-7). 112pp. The story of the two women in Northern Ireland who won the Nobel Peace Prize for their efforts to help end the civil strife in their country. (Rev: BL 3/15/00; SLJ 2/00) [941]

16707 Chrisp, Peter. *Welcome to the Globe! The Story of Shakespeare's Theater* (3–5). Illus. 2000, DK $12.95 (0-7894-6641-4); paper $3.95 (0-7894-6640-6). 48pp. The Globe is presented through the words of a variety of characters, real and fictitious, working there and through detailed illustrations. (Rev: HBG 3/01; SLJ 4/01) [792]

16708 Cole, Joanna. *Ms. Frizzle's Adventures: Medieval Castle* (2–5). Illus. by Bruce Degen. Series: The Magic School Bus. 2003, Scholastic $15.95 (0-590-10820-4). 40pp. Ms. Frizzle is on the move again in this amusing and informative large-format volume, this time traveling back in time to medieval England with her student Arnold. (Rev: BL 7/03; HBG 4/04; SLJ 7/03) [728.8]

16709 Corona, Laurel. *Scotland* (5–8). Series: Modern Nations of the World. 2000, Lucent LB $27.45 (1-56006-703-9). 128pp. The history, geography, and culture of Scotland are discussed along with material on daily life in modern Scotland. (Rev: BL 3/1/01) [941]

16710 Dahl, Michael. *England* (3–4). Illus. Series: Fact Finders: Questions and Answers. 2004, Capstone LB $22.60 (0-7368-2477-4). 32pp. Using a question-and-answer format, this title introduces England's history, government, economy, education, culture, sports, and lifestyle. (Rev: SLJ 1/05) [942]

16711 Davis, Kenneth C. *Don't Know Much About the Kings and Queens of England* (4–7). Illus. by S. D. Schindler. Series: Don't Know Much About. 2002, HarperCollins LB $15.89 (0-06-028612-1). 48pp. Humorous questions and answers supply information that browsers will enjoy. (Rev: HBG 10/02; SLJ 7/02) [941.0099]

16712 Dumas, Philippe. *A Farm* (3–6). Illus. 1999, Creative $29.95 (1-56846-169-0). 42pp. The inner workings of a 19th-century English farm are revealed in this oversize book containing extraordinary illustrations. (Rev: BL 12/1/99) [630.42]

16713 Flint, David. *Great Britain* (5–8). Illus. Series: Modern Industrial World. 1996, Raintree LB $24.26 (0-8172-4555-3). Modern Great Britain is the focus of this volume, which concentrates on the economy and industrial development. (Rev: BL 2/15/96; SLJ 8/97) [330.941]

16714 Flint, David. *The United Kingdom* (3–6). Illus. Series: Country Facts Files. 1994, Raintree LB $27.12 (0-8114-1849-9). 48pp. A fact-filled introduction to the United Kingdom, with coverage of such topics as its economy, daily life, climate, and traditions. (Rev: BL 9/1/94; SLJ 7/94) [941]

16715 Fradin, Dennis B. *The Republic of Ireland* (4–7). Illus. 1984, Children's Book Pr. paper $32.00 (0-516-02767-0). 128pp. An introduction to this country that touches briefly on many subjects. [941]

16716 Fuller, Barbara. *Britain* (4–6). Illus. Series: Cultures of the World. 1994, Marshall Cavendish LB $35.64 (1-85435-587-2). 128pp. This fact-filled, heavily illustrated account gives a good overview of life in Great Britain today. (Rev: SLJ 7/94) [941.06]

16717 Gottfried, Ted. *Northern Ireland: Peace in Our Time?* (5–8). Series: Headliners. 2002, Millbrook LB $25.90 (0-7613-2252-3). This attractive book gives current and background information on the struggles within Northern Ireland and the causes and possible solutions. (Rev: BL 4/15/02; HBG 10/02; SLJ 3/02) [941]

16718 Greenblatt, Miriam. *Elizabeth I and Tudor England* (5–8). Series: Rulers and Their Times. 2001, Marshall Cavendish LB $28.50 (0-7614-1028-7). After a biography of Elizabeth I, this colorful account traces everyday life in Elizabethan times and supplies a selection of primary documents. (Rev: BL 1/1–15/02; HBG 3/02; SLJ 3/02) [942.1]

16719 Gresko, Marcia. *Letters Home from Scotland* (3–5). Series: Letters Home From. 2000, Blackbirch LB $16.95 (1-56711-408-3). 32pp. With postcard-style color illustrations and a chatty text, this first-person account introduces important topics about Scotland, such as the land, people, cities, food, and daily life. (Rev: BL 5/15/00; HBG 10/00) [941.106]

16720 Griffith, Jonathan. *Scotland* (2–4). Series: Festivals of the World. 1999, Gareth Stevens LB $15.95 (0-8368-2034-7). 32pp. A description of Scotland's holidays — both secular and religious — is accompanied by a section on related crafts and recipes. (Rev: BL 12/15/99; HBG 10/00) [941.1]

16721 Haskins, Jim, and Kathleen Benson. *Count Your Way Through Ireland* (2–4). Illus. by Beth Wright. Series: Count Your Way. 1996, Carolrhoda LB $19.93 (0-87614-872-0); paper $5.95 (0-87614-974-3). 24pp. After a brief introduction, each double-page spread, numbered from 1 to 10, gives interesting facts about Ireland. (Rev: BL 9/15/96; SLJ 8/96) [941.5]

16722 Hestler, Anna. *Wales* (5–9). Illus. Series: Cultures of the World. 2001, Marshall Cavendish LB $35.64 (0-7614-1195-X). 128pp. Geography, history, government, arts and culture, and lifestyle are all covered in this interesting and attractive volume. (Rev: HBG 10/01; SLJ 11/01) [942.9]

16723 Hirst, Mike. *The History of Emigration from Scotland* (4–7). Series: Origins. 1997, Watts LB $21.00 (0-531-14441-0). 32pp. Details on the political, social, and economic conditions in Scotland through various periods in its history that led to emigration to the United States and other lands. (Rev: BL 12/15/97; HBG 3/98; SLJ 2/98) [941.106]

16724 Hull, Lisa. *Scotland* (4–6). Series: Countries of the World. 2001, Gareth Stevens LB $21.95 (0-8368-2339-7). 96pp. The history, geography, people, customs, and present status of Scotland are covered in this well-illustrated introduction. (Rev: BL 12/15/01; HBG 3/02) [941.1]

16725 Innes, Brian. *United Kingdom* (4–8). Series: Nations of the World. 2001, Raintree LB $34.26 (0-7398-1288-1). 128pp. An in-depth look at the nation's geography, climate. terrain, history, government, and lifestyles. (Rev: BL 12/15/01) [941]

16726 *Ireland in Pictures* (5–8). Illus. Series: Visual Geography. 1997, Lerner LB $25.55 (0-8225-1878-3). 64pp. Contemporary Ireland is highlighted in this illustrated account. (Rev: BL 12/1/90) [941.5]

16727 January, Brendan. *Ireland* (2–4). Series: True Books. 1999, Children's Book Pr. LB $21.00 (0-516-21186-2). 47pp. A large-print text and many color illustrations introduce the history, geography, people, climate, and culture of Ireland. (Rev: HBG 10/99; SLJ 10/99) [941]

16728 Kent, Deborah. *Dublin* (3–6). Illus. Series: Cities of the World. 1997, Children's Book Pr. LB $26.50 (0-516-20302-9). 64pp. This introduction to the Irish capital introduces its history, people, and famous sights. (Rev: BL 8/97) [941.8]

16729 Killeen, Richard. *The Easter Rising* (4–6). Illus. Series: Revolution! 1995, Thomson Learning LB $24.26 (1-56847-391-5). 48pp. Presents, in a well-paced text, the story of the 1916 Irish Easter Rebellion, during which the Fenians fought for independence from British rule. (Rev: SLJ 2/96) [941.508]

16730 Levy, Patricia. *Ireland* (4–7). Illus. Series: Cultures of the World. 1993, Marshall Cavendish LB $35.64 (1-85435-580-5). 128pp. An account that traces the role of women in Irish history to the present day. (Rev: SLJ 2/94) [941]

16731 Lister, Maree, and Marti Sevier. *England* (5–8). Series: Countries of the World. 1998, Gareth Stevens LB $29.26 (0-8368-2125-4). In addition to basic information on the geography, history, economy, culture, and people of England, this book has a special section that describes characteristics that make this country unique, including particular places, people, and traditions. (Rev: BL 12/15/98; HBG 9/99; SLJ 2/99) [941]

16732 Lister, Maree, and Marti Sevier. *Welcome to England* (2–4). Series: Welcome to My Country. 1999, Gareth Stevens LB $16.95 (0-8368-2396-6). 48pp. England is introduced with separate chapters on land, history, government and economy, people, language, arts, leisure, and food. (Rev: HBG 10/00; SLJ 1/00) [942]

16733 Lyons, Mary E., ed. *Feed the Children First: Irish Memories of the Great Hunger* (4–8). Illus.

2002, Simon & Schuster $17.00 (0-689-84226-0). 48pp. Text, full-color reproductions, and occasional photographs clearly document the suffering of ordinary people during the Irish potato famine. (Rev: BL 12/15/01; HB 3–4/02; HBG 10/02; SLJ 3/02*) [941.5081]

16734 McKay, Patricia. *Ireland* (2–4). Series: Festivals of the World. 1998, Gareth Stevens LB $18.60 (0-8368-2004-5). 32pp. A brief introduction to the land and people of Ireland is followed by a discussion of why and how such holidays as St. Patrick's Day are celebrated. A few background craft projects and recipes are included. (Rev: BL 5/15/98; HBG 10/98; SLJ 8/98) [941.5]

16735 McMahon, Patricia. *One Belfast Boy* (4–6). Illus. 1999, Houghton Mifflin $16.00 (0-395-68620-2). 64pp. This photoessay tells about the daily life of an Irish Catholic boy growing up in violence-torn Northern Ireland. (Rev: BCCB 7–8/99; BL 3/15/99; HBG 10/99; SLJ 5/99) [941]

16736 Mitchell, Graham. *The Napoleonic Wars* (5–9). Illus. 1990, Batsford $19.95 (0-7134-5729-5). This British import tells about the war chiefly from the British point of view and uses many quotations from original sources. (Rev: BR 3–4/90; SLJ 3/90) [944.05]

16737 *Northern Ireland in Pictures* (5–8). Series: Visual Geography. 1991, Lerner LB $25.55 (0-8225-1898-8). This beautiful but troubled land is introduced in text and pictures. (Rev: BL 2/15/92) [941.6]

16738 O'Sullivan, MaryCate. *Scotland* (3–5). Series: Faces and Places. 2001, Child's World LB $25.64 (1-56766-909-3). 32pp. The land and people of Scotland are introduced using a simple text, large type, and color pictures on each page. (Rev: BL 9/15/01; HBG 3/02) [941.1]

16739 Oxlade, Chris, and Anita Ganeri. *England* (1–3). Series: A Visit To. 2003, Heinemann LB $22.79 (1-4034-0965-X). 32pp. Full of photographs, this is a useful and interesting overview of the country's geography, history, and culture, suitable for beginning readers. Also use *Scotland* and *Wales* (both 2003). (Rev: HBG 10/03; SLJ 7/03) [942]

16740 Prior, Katherine. *Ireland* (4–7). Illus. Series: Origins. 1997, Watts LB $21.00 (0-531-14415-1). 32pp. Tells of the conditions in Ireland that led to emigration, where the Irish went, and their reception in Great Britain, the United States, and elsewhere. (Rev: BL 4/15/97) [941.5]

16741 Ross, Michael Elsohn. *Children of Ireland* (4–6). Series: The World's Children. 2001, Carolrhoda LB $23.93 (1-57505-521-X). Outstanding photographs of children are used to introduce this land and the daily lives of its people. (Rev: BL 1/1–15/02; HBG 3/02) [951.5]

16742 Ross, Michael Elsohn. *Children of Northern Ireland* (2–5). Photos by Felix Rigau. Series: The World's Children. 2001, Carolrhoda LB $23.93 (1-57505-433-7). 48pp. This look at the daily lives of children in Northern Ireland introduces the history, geography, and culture of the country, with appeal-

ing full-color illustrations, a pronunciation guide, and map. (Rev: HBG 10/01; SLJ 6/01) [941.6]

16743 Schemenauer, Elma. *England* (3–5). Series: Countries: Faces and Places. 2000, Child's World LB $25.64 (1-56766-735-X). 32pp. Basic information about the past and present of England and its people is given in an attractive volume with large type and many color photographs. (Rev: BL 4/15/01; HBG 3/01) [942]

16744 Shuter, Jane. *Carisbrooke Castle* (4–6). Series: Visiting the Past. 1999, Heinemann LB $16.95 (1-57572-857-5). 32pp. This book covers the history of this stronghold on the Isle of Wight, including the construction of the castle after the Norman conquest, its uses through the centuries, and its restoration in 1896. (Rev: SLJ 3/00) [942]

16745 Spencer, Shannon. *Ireland* (4–6). Series: Countries of the World. 2000, Gareth Stevens LB $19.95 (0-8368-2318-4). 96pp. A fine, colorful introduction that includes the standard coverage plus material on such topics as folklore, food, and unique customs. (Rev: BL 6/1–15/00; HBG 10/00) [941.7]

16746 Sproule, Anna. *Great Britain: The Land and Its People* (4–6). Illus. 1991, Silver Burdett LB $14.95 (0-382-24243-2). 48pp. An overview of history, people, religion, and industry is highlighted by numerous illustrations. (Rev: BL 11/15/87)

16747 Stacey, Gill. *London* (4–8). Series: Great Cities of the World. 2003, World Almanac LB $29.26 (0-8368-5022-X). 48pp. In an appealing blend of text, photographs, quotations, and sidebar features, this volume introduces readers to some of London's history and attractions. (Rev: SLJ 1/04) [942.1]

16748 Stein, R. Conrad. *Scotland* (4–7). Series: Enchantment of the World. 2001, Children's Book Pr. LB $34.50 (0-516-21112-9). Numerous pictures, charts, maps, and drawings contribute to a fascinating portrait of Scotland's past and present. (Rev: BL 1/1–15/02) [931]

16749 Sutherland, Dorothy B. *Wales* (4–6). Illus. 1987, Children's Book Pr. LB $32.00 (0-516-02794-8). 128pp. Color photos help to explain the history, geography, and culture of Wales. (Rev: BL 10/15/87)

16750 Toht, Betony, and David Toht. *Daily Life in Ancient and Modern London* (4–8). Illus. by Ray Webb. Series: Cities Through Time. 2001, Runestone LB $25.26 (0-8225-3223-9). 64pp. London's evolution from earliest times to today is presented in double-page spreads, with information on political, social, and religious life. (Rev: BL 4/15/01; HBG 10/01; SLJ 7/01)

16751 *Wales in Pictures* (5–8). Illus. 1994, Lerner LB $25.55 (0-8225-1877-5). 64pp. Wales is introduced and material is given on history and current conditions. (Rev: BL 12/1/90) [942.9]

Greece and Italy

16752 Allard, Denise. *Greece* (K–2). Illus. Series: Postcards From. 1996, Raintree LB $22.83 (0-8172-

4022-5). 32pp. Using a postcard format, this book supplies a brief overview of the geography, culture, and sights of Greece. (Rev: SLJ 2/97) [938]

16753 Barber, Nicola. *Rome* (4–7). Illus. Series: Great Cities of the World. 2005, World Almanac LB $22.50 (0-8368-5040-8). 48pp. An informative and appealing overview of one of the world's most famous cities, with material on its history, its economy, and what it's like to live there.

16754 Barghusen, Joan. *Daily Life in Ancient and Modern Rome* (3–6). Illus. by Ray Webb. Series: Cities Through Time. 1999, Runestone LB $17.95 (0-8225-3213-1). 64pp. Daily life and the culture of ancient and modern Rome are covered in double-page spreads illustrated with original drawings and photographs. (Rev: HBG 10/99; SLJ 6/99) [945]

16755 Behnke, Alison. *Italy in Pictures*. Rev. ed. (4–8). Illus. Series: Visual Geography. 2002, Lerner LB $27.93 (0-8225-0368-9). 80pp. An excellent introduction to Italy that includes material on geography, history, people, economy, and culture with maps, photographs, and illustrations. (Rev: HBG 3/03; SLJ 3/03) [914.5]

16756 Blashfield, Jean F. *Italy* (4–7). Series: Enchantment of the World. 1999, Children's Book Pr. LB $34.50 (0-516-20960-4). 144pp. The topics covered in this book about Italy range from history, geography, and government to mythology, culture, daily life, and sports. (Rev: BL 1/1–15/00) [945]

16757 Britton, Tamara L. *Greece* (2–4). Series: Countries. 2000, ABDO LB $14.95 (1-57765-385-8). 40pp. A workable introduction to Greece with a focus on modern times. (Rev: HBG 10/01; SLJ 3/01) [949.5]

16758 Butler, Daphne. *Italy* (2–4). Illus. 1992, Raintree LB $22.83 (0-8114-3677-2). 32pp. A broad overview of Italy, described in terms of topography and lifestyle. (Rev: BL 3/15/93) [945]

16759 Cassidy, Picot. *Italy* (4–8). Series: Nations of the World. 2001, Raintree LB $34.26 (0-7398-1287-4). 128pp. A fine overall picture of Italy, its past, its land, its people, its culture, and present-day problems. (Rev: BL 12/15/01; HBG 3/02) [945]

16760 Costain, Meredith, and Paul Collins. *Welcome to Greece* (1–4). Illus. Series: Countries of the World. 2001, Chelsea LB $16.95 (0-7910-6545-6). 32pp. An attractive introduction to the land and people of Greece, with a recipe, a craft, a brief page of facts, and many illustrations. (Rev: HBG 3/02; SLJ 12/01)

16761 De Capua, Sarah E. *Italy* (2–4). Illus. Series: First Reports. 2003, Compass Point LB $21.26 (0-7565-0425-2). 48pp. In this attractive title from the First Reports series, author Sarah E. De Capua introduces readers to the geography, history, people, and culture of Italy. (Rev: SLJ 10/03)

16762 Dubois, Jill. *Greece* (4–7). Illus. Series: Cultures of the World. 1992, Marshall Cavendish LB $35.64 (1-85435-450-7). 128pp. This book supplies an introduction to Greece with emphasis on its culture and lifestyles. (Rev: BL 10/15/92) [949.5]

16763 Dubois, Jill, and Xenia Skoura. *Greece*. 2nd ed. (5–8). Illus. Series: Cultures of the World. 2003,

Benchmark LB $24.95 (0-7614-1499-1). 143pp. In addition to coverage of the geography, history, and economics of Greece, this volume looks at the people and the culture of this Mediterranean nation and provides recipes. (Rev: HBG 10/03; SLJ 8/03) [949.5]

16764 Ferro, Jennifer. *Italian Foods and Culture* (3–5). Series: Festive Foods and Celebrations. 1999, Rourke LB $19.45 (1-57103-302-5). 48pp. Saint Joseph's Day, Christmas, and the Festival of Santa Rosalia are three of the Italian celebrations that are covered in this book that also contains recipes. (Rev: SLJ 2/00) [945]

16765 Foster, Leila M. *Italy* (5–9). Series: Modern Nations of the World. 1998, Lucent LB $27.45 (1-56006-481-1). 112pp. A fine introduction to Italy's past and present with an overview of its amazing history, modern popular culture, achievements, daily life, and geography. (Rev: SLJ 5/99) [945]

16766 Frank, Nicole, and Josephine Sander Hausam. *Welcome to Italy* (2–4). Illus. Series: Welcome to My Country. 2000, Gareth Stevens $22.60 (0-8368-2510-1). Full-page illustrations on every page and a simple text are used to introduce modern Italy and its people to young readers. (Rev: HBG 10/01; SLJ 1/01) [945]

16767 Frank, Nicole, and Yeoh Hong Nam. *Welcome to Greece* (2–4). Series: Welcome to My Country. 2000, Gareth Stevens LB $22.60 (0-8368-2509-8). 48pp. A simple introduction to Greece and its people with many color illustrations. (Rev: HBG 10/01; SLJ 1/01) [949.5]

16768 *Greece in Pictures* (5–8). Illus. Series: Visual Geography. 1996, Lerner LB $25.55 (0-8225-1882-1). 64pp. Photographs, maps, charts, and concise text introduce the land and people of Greece. (Rev: BL 10/1/92) [949.5]

16769 Gresko, Marcia S. *Letters Home from Greece* (3–5). Illus. 1999, Blackbirch LB $16.95 (1-56711-406-7). 32pp. Through a series of letters, the land, people, and history of Greece are seen from the standpoint of a young tourist. (Rev: BL 11/15/99; HBG 3/00; SLJ 1/00) [914.950]

16770 Haskins, Jim. *Count Your Way Through Italy* (2–4). Illus. by Beth Wright. Series: Count Your Way. 1990, Carolrhoda LB $19.93 (0-87614-406-7). Introduces the geography and culture of Italy through numbers. (Rev: SLJ 8/90) [945]

16771 Haskins, Jim, and Kathleen Benson. *Count Your Way Through Greece* (2–4). Illus. by Janice L. Porter. Series: Count Your Way. 1996, Carolrhoda LB $19.93 (0-87614-875-5); paper $5.95 (0-87614-973-5). 24pp. Greece is introduced in a counting book that goes from 1 to 10. (Rev: BL 9/15/96; SLJ 8/96) [949.5]

16772 Hausam, Josephine Sanders. *Italy* (4–6). Series: Countries of the World. 1999, Gareth Stevens LB $19.95 (0-8368-2310-9). 96pp. A broad introduction to Italy — its history and geography, its language and lifestyle, its government and culture. (Rev: BL 12/15/99; HBG 10/00; SLJ 1/00) [945]

16773 Heinrichs, Ann. *Greece* (4–7). Series: Enchantment of the World. 2002, Children's Book Pr. LB $34.50 (0-516-22271-6). 144pp. With many color illustrations, this book gives a fascinating portrait of Greece's past and present with coverage of topics including natural resources, culture, climate, and religion. (Rev: BL 9/15/02; SLJ 12/02) [949.5]

16774 Hinds, Kathryn. *Venice and Its Merchant Empire* (5–8). Illus. Series: Cultures of the Past. 2001, Marshall Cavendish LB $28.50 (0-7614-0305-1). 80pp. A well-illustrated overview of the history of Venice with a focus on the city's glory during the Renaissance. (Rev: BL 2/15/02; HBG 3/02) [945]

16775 Hull, Robert. *Greece* (5–10). Series: Ancient World. 1998, Raintree LB $27.12 (0-8172-5055-7). 64pp. This brief introduction to ancient Greece touches on its religion and mythology, its great philosophers, important historical events, and its contributions to world culture. (Rev: BL 1/1–15/99; HBG 3/99) [938]

16776 Kotapish, Dawn. *Daily Life in Ancient and Modern Athens* (5–8). Illus. by Bob Moulder. Series: Cities Through Time. 2000, Runestone LB $25.26 (0-8225-3216-6). 64pp. Kotapish explores everyday life, government, and culture in Athens through the ages. (Rev: HBG 3/01; SLJ 5/01) [949.5]

16777 Langley, Andrew. *Athens* (4–8). Series: Great Cities of the World. 2003, World Almanac LB $29.26 (0-8368-5021-1). 48pp. An attractive introduction to the Greek capital's history, people, culture, and attractions. (Rev: SLJ 1/04) [938]

16778 Macaulay, David. *Rome Antics* (5–8). Illus. 1997, Houghton Mifflin $18.00 (0-395-82279-3). The reader gets a pigeon-eye view of vistas and buildings as the bird flies over Rome. (Rev: BL 9/15/97; SLJ 11/97*) [945]

16779 Martin, Fred. *Italy* (5–8). Series: Country Studies. 1999, Heinemann LB $27.07 (1-57572-894-X). Using double-page spreads filled with charts, graphs, drawings, maps, and photographs, this book provides basic material about Italy with a focus on contemporary issues. (Rev: BL 8/99; SLJ 8/99) [945]

16780 Nardo, Don. *Greece* (5–8). Series: Modern Nations of the World. 2000, Lucent LB $27.45 (1-56006-587-7). 128pp. Although there is coverage of ancient Greece, this account stresses modern history, the people today, and current living conditions and problems. (Rev: BL 2/15/00; HBG 10/00; SLJ 6/00) [949.5]

16781 Olson, Nathan. *Italy* (2–5). Illus. Series: Questions and Answers: Countries. 2005, Capstone LB $16.95 (0-7368-3754-X). 32pp. Using a question-and-answer format, simple text, large photos, and many factboxes, this is an introduction to Italy today, with material on history and traditional culture.

16782 Pirotta, Saviour. *Rome* (4–6). Illus. Series: Holy Cities. 1993, Dillon LB $17.95 (0-87518-570-3). 46pp. This account focuses on Rome as the center of the pagan religion during the ancient empire

and its evolution into the heart of the largest Christian denomination in the world. (Rev: BL 9/15/93; SLJ 8/93) [263]

16783 Riehecky, Janet. *Greece* (1–3). Series: Countries of the World. 2000, Bridgestone LB $17.26 (0-7368-0628-8). 24pp. Full-page photos and current information are the highlights of this basic introduction to Greece. (Rev: HBG 3/01; SLJ 3/01) [949.5]

16784 Sioras, Efstathia. *Greece* (2–4). Series: Festivals of the World. 1998, Gareth Stevens LB $14.95 (0-8368-2014-2). 32pp. This description of Greek traditions and holidays includes an introduction to the land and people and some related recipes and craft projects. (Rev: BL 12/15/98; HBG 10/99) [949.5]

16785 Stein, R. Conrad. *Athens* (3–6). Illus. Series: Cities of the World. 1997, Children's Book Pr. LB $26.50 (0-516-20300-2). 64pp. A heavily illustrated account that describes Athens, gives a brief history, tells about its famous landmarks, and introduces its people. (Rev: BL 8/97) [949.5]

16786 Stein, R. Conrad. *Greece* (4–7). Illus. 1988, Children's Book Pr. paper $32.00 (0-516-02759-X). 128pp. Photographs and maps highlight this overview of an ancient land. (Rev: BL 5/15/88) [938]

16787 Winter, Jane K. *Italy* (5–8). Illus. Series: Cultures of the World. 1992, Marshall Cavendish LB $35.64 (1-85435-453-1). 128pp. Gives geographic and historical information about Italy and tells about its people and their concerns. (Rev: BL 10/15/92) [945]

16788 Yeoh, Hong Nam. *Greece* (4–6). Series: Countries of the World. 1999, Gareth Stevens LB $19.95 (0-8368-2309-5). 96pp. A look at life in present-day Greece that also examines its past. (Rev: BL 12/15/99; HBG 10/00; SLJ 1/00) [949.5]

16789 Zinovieff, Sofka. *Greece* (4–7). Illus. Series: Origins. 1997, Watts LB $21.00 (0-531-14417-8). 32pp. A look at the conditions in Greece at various times in history that led to emigration to the United States and Canada, and the experiences of these immigrants. (Rev: BL 4/15/97) [949.5]

Low Countries

16790 Burgan, Michael. *Belgium* (4–7). Series: Enchantment of the World. 2000, Children's Book Pr. LB $34.50 (0-516-21006-8). 144pp. This new edition of a standard title contains up-to-date material on such topics as geography and climate, plants and animals, people and culture, the arts, and sports. (Rev: BL 7/00) [949.3]

16791 De Capua, Sarah E. *Netherlands* (2–4). Illus. Series: First Reports. 2003, Compass Point LB $21.26 (0-7565-0426-0). 48pp. Simple text introduces readers to basic information on the Netherlands and its geography, history, people, and culture. (Rev: SLJ 10/03)

16792 Heinrichs, Ann. *The Netherlands* (1–3). Series: A True Book. 2003, Children's Pr. LB $23.50 (0-516-22675-4); paper $6.95 (0-516-27750-2). 48pp. A blend of easy-to-understand text and colorful illustrations make this overview suitable for beginning readers. (Rev: SLJ 10/03) [949.2]

16793 Hintz, Martin. *The Netherlands* (4–7). Series: Enchantment of the World. 1999, Children's Book Pr. LB $34.50 (0-516-21053-X). 144pp. An up-to-date, well-illustrated, and comprehensive introduction to the Netherlands. (Rev: BL 12/15/99) [949.2]

16794 Kent, Deborah. *Amsterdam* (3–6). Illus. Series: Cities of the World. 1997, Children's Book Pr. LB $26.50 (0-516-20299-5). 64pp. In this introduction to Amsterdam, readers are given a tour of the city, told about its history, and given a picture of its people. (Rev: BL 8/97; SLJ 2/98) [949.2]

16795 NgCheong-Lum, Roseline. *The Netherlands* (4–6). Series: Countries of the World. 2001, Gareth Stevens LB $21.95 (0-8368-2336-2). 96pp. As well as the people, traditions, and lifestyles, this well-illustrated account provides general material on history and geography. (Rev: BL 12/15/01; HBG 3/02) [949.2]

16796 Pateman, Robert. *Belgium* (4–7). Illus. Series: Cultures of the World. 1995, Marshall Cavendish LB $35.64 (0-7614-0176-8). 128pp. After a brief introduction to the history and geography of Belgium, this book focuses on the populace, how they live, and their major contributions to the world. (Rev: BL 1/1–15/96; SLJ 9/96) [949.3]

16797 Sheehan, Patricia. *Luxembourg* (4–7). Illus. Series: Cultures of the World. 1997, Marshall Cavendish LB $35.64 (0-7614-0685-9). 128pp. Includes information on this tiny European country's history, culture, and lifestyles. (Rev: BL 8/97) [914.935]

16798 Van Fenema, Joyce. *Netherlands* (2–4). Illus. Series: Festivals of the World. 1998, Gareth Stevens LB $14.95 (0-8368-2016-9). 32pp. Introduces Netherlands festivals such as Sinterklaas, Carnaval, and Queensday, along with basic facts about the country and a few related craft projects. (Rev: BL 12/15/98; HBG 10/99) [394.26]

Russia and the Former Soviet States

16799 *Armenia* (5–8). Series: Then and Now. 1992, Lerner LB $23.93 (0-8225-2806-1). The story up to 1991 of the former Soviet republic that faced many internal problems after it gained independence. (Rev: BL 2/1/93; SLJ 3/93) [956.6]

16800 Arnold, Helen. *Russia* (1–3). Illus. Series: Postcards From. 1995, Raintree LB $22.83 (0-8172-4006-3). 32pp. In this quick overview of Russia, such topics as food, shopping, transportation, money, and language are covered. (Rev: SLJ 2/96) [947]

16801 *Azerbaijan* (5–8). Series: Then and Now. 1993, Lerner LB $23.93 (0-8225-2810-X). This book introduces the small republic of Azerbaijan, once the Soviet Union's most important oil producing area. (Rev: BL 2/15/93) [947]

16802 Bassis, Volodymyr. *Ukraine* (2–4). Series: Festivals of the World. 1998, Gareth Stevens LB $18.60 (0-8368-2010-X). 32pp. A colorful look at the people and customs of the Ukraine as seen

through their holidays, with related crafts and recipes included. (Rev: BL 5/15/98; HBG 10/98; SLJ 6/98) [947]

16803 Bassis, Volodymyr. *Ukraine* (4–7). Illus. Series: Cultures of the World. 1997, Marshall Cavendish LB $35.64 (0-7614-0684-0). 128pp. An introduction to this former Soviet state, with emphasis on current history and culture. (Rev: BL 8/97; SLJ 10/97) [947.7]

16804 *Belarus* (5–8). Series: Then and Now. 1993, Lerner LB $23.93 (0-8225-2811-8). An introduction to the history and status as of 1993 of the former Soviet republic of Belarus, which borders on Ukraine. (Rev: BL 5/15/93) [947]

16805 Boast, Clare. *Russia* (2–4). Series: Next Stop. 1998, Heinemann LB $19.92 (1-57572-569-X). 32pp. A general introduction to Russia, its history, geography, people, and current living standards. (Rev: SLJ 6/98) [947]

16806 Carrion, Esther. *The Empire of the Czars* (4–7). Illus. Series: World Heritage. 1994, Children's Book Pr. LB $15.00 (0-516-08319-0). 34pp. An overview of Russian history from early times to the breakup of the Soviet Union, with special material on Russia's famous sights, such as Red Square, the Kremlin, and St. Petersburg. (Rev: SLJ 5/95) [947.07]

16807 Corona, Laurel. *Ukraine* (5–8). Series: Modern Nations of the World. 2001, Lucent LB $27.45 (1-56006-737-3). 112pp. This well-illustrated introduction to the former Soviet republic presents material on the people, culture, economy, history, and physical features. (Rev: BL 6/1–15/01) [947]

16808 Cumming, David. *Russia* (5–8). Illus. Series: Modern Industrial World. 1994, Thomson Learning LB $24.26 (1-56847-240-4). 48pp. An introduction to Russia that stresses the economic upheaval caused by the breakup of the USSR. (Rev: BL 1/15/95; SLJ 3/95) [947]

16809 Dhilawala, Sakina. *Armenia* (4–7). Illus. Series: Cultures of the World. 1997, Marshall Cavendish LB $35.64 (0-7614-0683-2). 128pp. An introduction to this troubled land that describes how its people live, their lifestyles, and culture. (Rev: BL 8/97; HBG 3/98) [945.56]

16810 *Estonia* (5–8). 1992, Lerner LB $23.93 (0-8225-2803-7). Following an introduction about the fall of communism, the book provides an overview of the land and its peoples. (Rev: BL 2/1/93; SLJ 12/92) [914.7]

16811 Frost, Helen. *A Look at Russia* (K–2). Illus. Series: Our World. 2001, Capstone LB $10.95 (0-7368-0986-4). 24pp. Brief text and full-page color photographs give a basic introduction to Russia's land, people, and animals. (Rev: HBG 3/02; SLJ 12/01)

16812 *Georgia* (5–8). Illus. Series: Then and Now. 1994, Lerner LB $23.93 (0-8225-2807-X). This former Soviet republic is introduced, with information on its geography, ethnic makeup, history, economy, and future challenges. (Rev: BL 2/1/94; SLJ 3/94) [947]

16813 Gresko, Marcia. *Letters Home from Russia* (3–5). Series: Letters Home From. 2000, Blackbirch LB $16.95 (1-56711-411-3). 32pp. A first-person account that introduces Russia and presents such topics as the history, land, and people from a child's point of view. (Rev: BL 5/15/00; HBG 10/00; SLJ 6/00) [947]

16814 Haskins, Jim. *Count Your Way Through Russia* (3–5). Illus. 1987, Carolrhoda LB $19.93 (0-87614-303-6); paper $5.95 (0-87614-488-1). Snowshoes and folk dancers are two of the concepts used with numbers to highlight Russian culture. (Rev: BL 10/15/87; SLJ 9/87)

16815 Ilyin, Andrey. *A Child's Day in a Russian City* (1–3). Illus. Series: A Child's Day. 2001, Marshall Cavendish $15.95 (0-7614-1222-0). 32pp. The events in a typical day for Polina, a 7-year-old Russian girl living in St. Petersburg, with color photographs, sections on history and culture, and other background material. (Rev: BL 11/15/01; HBG 3/02; SLJ 3/02) [947.086]

16816 Kagda, Sakina. *Lithuania* (4–7). Illus. Series: Cultures of the World. 1997, Marshall Cavendish LB $35.64 (0-7614-0681-6). 128pp. An introduction to Lithuania, with material on geography, history, government, culture, daily life, and festivals. (Rev: BL 8/97; SLJ 10/97) [947.93]

16817 *Kazakhstan* (5–8). Series: Then and Now. 1993, Lerner LB $23.93 (0-8225-2815-0). An introduction to the second-largest republic in the former USSR, with information on its status as of 1993. (Rev: BL 9/1/93; SLJ 9/93) [958]

16818 Khan, Aisha. *A Historical Atlas of Kyrgyzstan* (4–6). Illus. Series: Historical Atlases of South Asia, Central Asia and the Middle East. 2004, Rosen LB $22.95 (0-8239-4499-9). 64pp. This attractive profile that includes many maps and photographs traces Kyrgyzstan's development from prehistoric times to the present. (Rev: SLJ 11/04)

16819 Kummer, Patricia. *Ukraine* (4–7). Series: Enchantment of the World. 2001, Children's Book Pr. LB $34.50 (0-516-21101-3). A fine introduction to the past and present of the Ukraine with well-chosen illustrations and material on such topics as resources, daily life, landmarks, languages, and economy. (Rev: BL 1/1–15/02; SLJ 12/01) [947.7]

16820 *Latvia* (5–8). 1992, Lerner LB $23.93 (0-8225-2802-9). Following an introduction about the fall of communism, this book provides an overview of the land and its peoples. (Rev: BL 2/1/93; SLJ 12/92) [947]

16821 *Lithuania* (5–8). Series: Then and Now. 1992, Lerner LB $23.93 (0-8225-2804-5). This Baltic Sea republic is described, including its history, people, and conditions in the period immediately following its independence in 1990. (Rev: BL 2/1/93) [947]

16822 *Moldova* (5–8). Series: Then and Now. 1992, Lerner LB $23.93 (0-8225-2809-6). The history of this small, landlocked republic, parts of which at one time or another have belonged to the Ottoman Turks, Romania, Russia, and the USSR, and which is now independent. (Rev: BL 2/1/93; SLJ 3/93) [947]

16823 Resnick, Abraham. *The Commonwealth of Independent States: Russia and the Other Republics* (5–8). Illus. Series: Enchantment of the World. 1993, Children's Book Pr. paper $32.00 (0-516-02613-5). 144pp. Following a description of the fall of Communism, this title introduces the geography, history, society, and economies of each of the independent republics. (Rev: SLJ 9/93) [947]

16824 Rice, Terence M. G. *Russia* (4–5). Series: Countries of the World. 1999, Gareth Stevens LB $18.95 (0-8368-2263-3). 95pp. Vivid color photos and an up-to-date text introduce the land and people of Russia; special sections on unique customs and current issues are included. (Rev: BL 9/15/99; SLJ 8/99) [947]

16825 Rogers, Stillman D. *Russia* (4–7). Series: Enchantment of the World. 2002, Children's Book Pr. LB $34.50 (0-516-22494-8). 144pp. This portrait of Russia in text and illustrations covers such basic subjects as history, resources, geography, people, problems, economy, and culture. (Rev: BL 9/15/02; SLJ 10/02) [947]

16826 *Russia* (5–8). Series: Then and Now. 1992, Lerner LB $23.93 (0-8225-2805-3). A brief history of Russia with emphasis on its status in the period immediately following the fall of the USSR in 1991. (Rev: BL 2/1/93; SLJ 12/92) [947]

16827 Sallnow, John, and Tatyana Saiko. *Russia* (5–8). Series: Country Fact Files. 1997, Raintree LB $27.12 (0-8172-4625-8). The impact of geography on different aspects of life in Russia, including natural resources, daily life, the landscape, and transportation, is explored. (Rev: SLJ 8/97) [947]

16828 Schomp, Virginia. *Russia: New Freedoms, New Challenges* (4–6). Illus. Series: Exploring Cultures of the World. 1996, Benchmark LB $27.07 (0-7614-0186-5). 64pp. As well as providing background information on Russia, this account stresses current conditions, with an emphasis on culture and the arts. (Rev: SLJ 6/96) [947]

16829 Sheehan, Patricia. *Moldova* (5–9). Series: Cultures of the World. 2000, Marshall Cavendish LB $35.64 (0-7614-0997-1). 128pp. This book on the former Soviet republic that borders on the Ukraine covers such topics as culture, land, people, history, resources, and government. (Rev: HBG 10/00; SLJ 11/00) [947]

16830 Spengler, Kremena. *Russia* (2–5). Illus. Series: Questions and Answers: Countries. 2004, Capstone LB $16.95 (0-7368-2692-0). 32pp. Using a question-and-answer format, simple text, large photos, and many factboxes, this is an introduction to Russia today, with material on history and traditional culture.

16831 Steele, Philip. *Moscow* (3–6). Series: Great Cities of the World. 2003, World Almanac LB $29.26 (0-8368-5024-6). 48pp. A visit to the Russian capital, well illustrated with photographs, covering the city's history, economy, and people. (Rev: SLJ 3/04) [947]

16832 *Tajikistan* (5–8). Illus. Series: Then and Now. 1993, Lerner LB $23.93 (0-8225-2816-9). An introduction to the land and people of this remote former

Soviet republic located north of Afghanistan. (Rev: BL 10/15/93; SLJ 11/93) [958.6]

16833 *Ukraine* (5–8). Series: Then and Now. 1992, Lerner LB $23.93 (0-8225-2808-8). The history of this Black Sea republic and its status in the period immediately following its independence in 1991. (Rev: BCCB 3/93; BL 2/1/93; SLJ 3/93) [947]

16834 *Uzbekistan* (5–8). Series: Then and Now. 1993, Lerner LB $23.93 (0-8225-2812-6). A history of this Muslim republic, its economic situation, and prospects for the future as of 1993. (Rev: BL 5/15/93) [958.7]

16835 Wilson, Neil. *Russia* (4–8). Series: Nations of the World. 2001, Raintree LB $34.26 (0-7398-1281-5). 128pp. Colorful photographs, charts, and maps enrich chapters on Russia's past and present, land and cities, economy, art and culture, and possible future developments. (Rev: BL 6/1–15/01; HBG 10/01) [947]

Scandinavia, Iceland, Greenland, and Finland

16836 Alatalo, Jaakko. *A Child's Day in a Nordic Village* (K–3). Series: A Child's Day. 2002, Marshall Cavendish LB $15.95 (0-7614-1411-8). 32pp. This book takes a Scandinavian child through a typical day, showing the reader about family, friends, culture, and language. (Rev: BL 2/15/03; HBG 3/03) [948]

16837 Berger, Melvin, and Gilda Berger. *The Real Vikings: Craftsmen, Traders, and Fearsome Raiders* (4–8). Illus. 2003, National Geographic $18.95 (0-7922-5132-6). 64pp. A highly illustrated introduction to the Vikings and their world, with information on their political and social ideals — including democracy — as well as their more fearsome and acquisitive traits. (Rev: BL 12/1/03; HBG 4/04; SLJ 1/04) [948]

16838 Blashfield, Jean F. *Norway* (4–7). Series: Enchantment of the World. 2000, Children's Book Pr. LB $34.50 (0-516-20651-6). 144pp. An introduction to Norway that covers such subjects as geography and climate, history and government, mythology and culture, and people and economy. (Rev: BL 7/00) [948.1]

16839 Boraas, Tracey. *Sweden* (4–6). Series: Countries and Cultures. 2002, Capstone LB $23.93 (0-7368-0939-2). 64pp. This introduction to the land and people of Sweden explores topics including history, landforms, government, economics, and traditions. (Rev: BL 1/1–15/03; HBG 3/03) [948.5]

16840 Butler, Robbie. *Sweden* (4–8). Series: Nations of the World. 2001, Raintree LB $34.26 (0-8172-5784-5). 128pp. Colorful maps, charts and graphs, and photographs supplement the text in this fine profile of Sweden. (Rev: BL 6/1–15/01; HBG 10/01) [948.5]

16841 Carlsson, Bo Kage. *Sweden* (5–8). Series: Modern Industrial World. 1995, Thomson Learning LB $24.26 (1-56847-436-9). A survey of modern Sweden and its industries, economy, resources, and people. (Rev: BL 12/15/95) [949.4]

16842 Clare, John D., ed. *The Vikings* (3–6). Illus. 1992, Harcourt $16.95 (0-15-200512-9). 64pp. Period costumes and period settings help to dramatize this historical era. (Rev: BL 12/1/92; SLJ 11/92) [948]

16843 Corona, Laurel. *Norway* (5–8). Series: Modern Nations of the World. 2000, Lucent LB $27.45 (1-56006-647-4). 128pp. Norway is introduced with coverage of history, geography, and culture plus material on everyday modern life. (Rev: BL 3/1/01) [948.1]

16844 *Denmark in Pictures* (5–8). Illus. Series: Visual Geography. 1997, Lerner LB $25.55 (0-8225-1880-5). 64pp. In photographs, maps, charts, and concise text, the land of Denmark and its people are introduced. (Rev: BL 4/1/91; SLJ 7/91) [948]

16845 Dupre, Kelly. *The Raven's Gift: A True Story from Greenland* (K–3). Illus. 2001, Houghton Mifflin $15.00 (0-618-01171-4). 32pp. An encounter with a raven inspires two men to continue their journey around Greenland, in this effectively illustrated story of an expedition taken by the author's husband. (Rev: BL 8/01; HBG 3/02; SLJ 9/01) [919.82]

16846 DuTemple, Lesley A. *Sweden* (5–8). Series: Modern Nations of the World. 2000, Lucent LB $27.45 (1-56006-588-5). 112pp. A general introduction to Sweden that includes its history and geography but stresses today's living conditions and the people's lifestyles. (Rev: BL 3/15/00; HBG 10/00) [948.5]

16847 Franklin, Sharon, et al. *Scandinavia* (4–7). Series: Artisans Around the World. 1999, Raintree LB $27.12 (0-7398-0122-8). 48pp. This book, which contains many hands-on activities, surveys Scandinavian crafts and shows how geography has influenced this area's artisans. (Rev: BL 10/15/99; HBG 3/00; SLJ 1/00) [948]

16848 Gan, Delice. *Sweden* (4–7). Illus. Series: Cultures of the World. 1992, Marshall Cavendish LB $35.64 (1-85435-452-3). 128pp. This introduction to Sweden gives special coverage of the people and their lifestyles. (Rev: BL 10/15/92) [948.5]

16849 Grant, Neil. *The Vikings* (3–6). Illus. Series: Spotlights. 1998, Oxford $10.95 (0-19-521393-9). 46pp. Traces the history of the Vikings and covers their culture, customs, and contributions. (Rev: BL 12/1/98; SLJ 10/98) [948]

16850 Gravett, Christopher. *Going to War in Viking Times* (4–6). Illus. 2001, Watts LB $23.00 (0-531-14592-1). 32pp. Examines war in Viking times from many perspectives, including strategy, weapons, and the impact on society. (Rev: BL 3/1/02; SLJ 10/01) [355]

16851 Hansen, Ole Steen. *Denmark* (4–7). Series: Country Insights. 1998, Raintree LB $27.12 (0-8172-4794-7). 48pp. This book provides a broad description of the country — its lifestyle, culture, and traditions — and contrasts Denmark's rural and urban environments. (Rev: BL 6/1–15/98; HBG 10/98) [948]

16852 Hintz, Martin. *Norway* (4–6). Illus. 1982, Children's Book Pr. LB $32.00 (0-516-02780-8).

128pp. The land and the people of Norway are introduced in text and pictures.

16853 Hopkins, Andrea. *Viking Explorers and Settlers* (3–6). Illus. Series: The Viking Library. 2001, Rosen LB $19.50 (0-8239-5816-7). 24pp. Beginning report writers will find basic historical information with illustrations, maps, and documents in this slim volume. Also use *Viking Gods and Legends* and *Vikings: The Norse Discovery of America* (both 2002). (Rev: SLJ 6/02) [938]

16854 *Iceland in Pictures* (5–8). Illus. Series: Visual Geography. 1996, Lerner LB $25.55 (0-8225-1892-9). 64pp. The history, government, people, and economy of the northern republic of Iceland are covered in words and pictures. (Rev: BL 8/91) [949.12]

16855 James, Louise. *The Vikings* (3–6). Illus. Series: How We Know About. 1997, Bedrick LB $17.95 (0-87226-535-8). 32pp. Using both contemporary photos and many reconstructions, the everyday life of the Vikings is described, with information on how archaeologists determined these facts. (Rev: BL 12/15/97; HBG 3/98; SLJ 10/97) [948.022]

16856 Jovinelly, Joann, and Jason Netelkos. *The Crafts and Culture of the Vikings* (5–8). Series: Crafts of the Ancient World. 2002, Rosen LB $29.25 (0-8239-3514-0). 48pp. In addition to giving a tour of ancient Scandinavia, this book outlines such craft projects as designing a battle shield and helmet, minting coins, and playing an ancient board game. (Rev: BL 5/15/02) [948]

16857 Kagda, Sakina. *Norway* (4–7). Illus. Series: Cultures of the World. 1995, Marshall Cavendish LB $35.64 (0-7614-0181-4). 128pp. After general information on Norway's geography and history, this account concentrates on the Norwegian people, how they live, and their artistic accomplishments. (Rev: BL 1/1–15/96; SLJ 9/96) [948.1]

16858 Kopka, Deborah. *Norway* (1–3). Series: Globe-Trotters Club. 2000, Carolrhoda LB $22.60 (1-57505-123-0). 48pp. Double-page spreads with stunning photographs introduce the land and people of Norway, with material on the Vikings, fjords, and skiing. (Rev: BL 10/15/00; HBG 3/01) [948.1]

16859 Lee, Tan Chung. *Finland* (2–4). Series: Festivals of the World. 1998, Gareth Stevens LB $14.95 (0-8368-2013-4). 32pp. Introduces the festivals and traditions of Finland, with some coverage on the land, people, and related craft projects. (Rev: BL 12/15/98; HBG 10/99) [984.97]

16860 Lee, Tan Chung. *Finland* (4–7). Illus. Series: Cultures of the World. 1996, Marshall Cavendish LB $35.64 (0-7614-0280-2). 128pp. The small country of Finland with its thousands of lakes is introduced, with emphasis on the people and how they live. (Rev: BL 8/96; SLJ 7/96) [984.97]

16861 Lepthien, Emilie U. *Iceland* (4–6). Illus. 1987, Children's Book Pr. LB $32.00 (0-516-02775-1). 128pp. Life in Iceland is portrayed in straight text and color photos and maps. (Rev: BL 10/15/87)

16862 McMillan, Bruce. *Going Fishing* (2–4). Illus. 2005, Houghton Mifflin $16.00 (0-618-47201-0). 32pp. Photographs capture a boy and his grandfa-

thers as they fish for cod and lumpfish in Iceland. (Rev: BL 3/1/05; SLJ 5/05) [799.16]

16863 Martell, Hazel M. *The Vikings and Jorvik* (4–7). Illus. Series: Hidden Worlds. 1993, Dillon LB $13.95 (0-87518-541-X). 32pp. A detailed account of how the Vikings lived, based on sound archaeological research. (Rev: BL 10/15/93; SLJ 8/93) [942.8]

16864 Meichun, Zhong. *Finland* (4–6). Series: Countries of the World. 2000, Gareth Stevens LB $26.60 (0-8368-2331-1). 96pp. The history of this northern nation is given plus material on its land and people, the economy, unique customs, current concerns, and relations with the United States and Canada. (Rev: BL 3/15/01; HBG 10/01) [984.97]

16865 Morley, Jacqueline. *How Would You Survive as a Viking?* (4–7). Illus. Series: How Would You Survive? 1995, Watts LB $25.00 (0-531-14344-9). 48pp. The way Vikings lived in A.D. 1000 is discussed, with information on such topics as their food, forms of worship, and how they settled disputes. (Rev: BL 6/1–15/95; SLJ 8/95) [948]

16866 Odijk, Pamela. *The Vikings* (4–7). Illus. Series: Ancient World. 1990, Silver Burdett LB $14.95 (0-382-09893-5). 48pp. The exploits, explorations, and contributions of the Vikings. (Rev: BL 7/90; SLJ 8/90) [936]

16867 Pitkanen, Matti A. *The Grandchildren of the Vikings* (3–6). Illus. Series: World's Children. 1996, Carolrhoda LB $23.93 (0-87614-889-5). 47pp. A photo-essay that explores family life in five areas settled by the Vikings, including the Faeroe Islands, Iceland, Gotland, Aland, and Lofoten. (Rev: SLJ 2/97) [949]

16868 Rabe, Monica. *Sweden* (2–4). Series: Festivals of the World. 1998, Gareth Stevens LB $18.60 (0-8368-2008-8). 32pp. This work introduces the Swedes, describes their distinctive holidays, and provides some related crafts. (Rev: BL 5/15/98; HBG 10/98; SLJ 8/98) [949.4]

16869 Robinson, Deborah B. *The Sami of Northern Europe* (4–6). Series: First Peoples. 2002, Lerner LB $23.93 (0-8225-4175-0). This book describes the life and culture of the Sami, once known as Lapps, who were once primarily reindeer herders. (Rev: BL 5/15/02; HBG 10/02; SLJ 8/02) [948]

16870 *Sweden in Pictures* (5–8). Illus. Series: Visual Geography. 1993, Lerner LB $21.27 (0-8225-1872-4). 64pp. Gives the background geography and history of Sweden, along with contemporary material. (Rev: BL 12/1/90) [948.5]

16871 Tweddle, Dominic. *Growing Up in Viking Times* (3–5). Illus. by Angus McBride. Series: Growing Up In. 1993, Troll paper $4.95 (0-8167-2726-0). 32pp. The upbringing of Viking children is the focus of this account that also describes everyday life in a Viking community. (Rev: BL 1/15/94) [948]

16872 Wagner, Michele. *Sweden* (4–6). Series: Countries of the World. 2001, Gareth Stevens LB $21.95 (0-8368-2340-0). 96pp. In an attractive format with many illustrations, this basic account covers general topics such as geography, people, lifestyle, economy, history, and traditions. (Rev: BL 12/15/01; HBG 3/02; SLJ 2/02) [948.5]

16873 Wilcox, Jonathan. *Iceland* (4–7). Series: Cultures of the World. 1996, Marshall Cavendish LB $35.64 (0-7614-0279-9). The history, geography, people, and culture of this remote island republic are introduced, with many color photographs. (Rev: SLJ 7/96) [949.12]

16874 Yanuck, Debbie L. *Sweden* (2–3). Illus. Series: Many Cultures, One World. 2004, Capstone LB $17.95 (0-7368-2452-9). 32pp. A brief, accessible introduction to Sweden and its people, family life, customs, and legends. (Rev: SLJ 10/04)

Spain and Portugal

16875 Anderson, Wayne. *The ETA: Spain's Basque Terrorists* (4–8). Series: Inside the World's Most Infamous Terrorist Organizations. 2003, Rosen LB $26.50 (0-8239-3818-2). 64pp. This is the history and present status of the violent organization committed to creating an ethnic homeland separate from Spain. (Rev: BL 10/15/03; SLJ 9/03) [946]

16876 Anno, Mitsumasa. *Anno's Spain* (2–8). Illus. by author. 2004, Philomel $17.99 (0-399-24238-4). Anno's signature pen-and-ink and watercolor drawings illustrate this wordless tour of Spain that includes country scenes, architectural scenes, flamenco dancers, religious processions, and so forth. (Rev: SLJ 11/04) [946]

16877 Blauer, Ettagale, and Jason Lauré. *Portugal* (4–7). Series: Enchantment of the World. 2002, Children's Book Pr. LB $34.50 (0-516-21109-9). 144pp. This highly visual introduction to Portugal includes accessible information on topics including history, people and language, customs, and economy. (Rev: BL 9/15/02) [946.9]

16878 Champion, Neil. *Portugal* (5–8). Illus. Series: Modern Industrial World. 1995, Thomson Learning LB $24.26 (1-56847-435-0). 48pp. Modern Portugal is highlighted in text and pictures, with coverage of its economy, industries, and resources. (Rev: BL 12/15/95) [946.904]

16879 Chicoine, Stephen D. *Spain: Bridge Between Continents* (3–5). Illus. Series: Exploring Cultures of the World. 1997, Marshall Cavendish LB $27.07 (0-7614-0143-1). 64pp. This introduction to Spain covers geography, history, the people, family life, the arts, festivals, and recreation. (Rev: BL 7/97; SLJ 1/98) [946]

16880 Goodman, Joan Elizabeth. *A Long and Uncertain Journey: The 27,000-Mile Voyage of Vasco da Gama* (4–8). Illus. by Tom McNeely. 2001, Mikaya $19.95 (0-9650493-7-X). 48pp. Details of Vasco da Gama's explorations and their historical context are accompanied by biographical information, illustrations, journal entries, a map, and a timeline. (Rev: BL 9/1/01; HBG 10/01; SLJ 6/01*) [910]

16881 Grabowski, John F. *Spain* (5–8). Series: Modern Nations of the World. 1999, Lucent LB $27.45 (1-56006-602-4). 112pp. This fact-filled introduction to Spain emphasizes both history and current life and contains black-and-white photographs and

interesting sidebars. (Rev: BL 2/15/00; HBG 10/00) [946]

16882 Grinsted, Katherine. *Spain* (4–6). Series: Countries of the World. 1999, Gareth Stevens LB $19.95 (0-8368-2312-5). 96pp. A broad introduction to Spain that focuses on both its past and its present. (Rev: BL 12/15/99; HBG 10/00) [946]

16883 Heale, Jay. *Portugal* (5–8). Illus. Series: Cultures of the World. 1995, Marshall Cavendish LB $35.64 (0-7614-0169-5). 128pp. Present-day conditions in Portugal are emphasized in this account, which also covers history, geography, and culture. (Rev: SLJ 11/95) [914.9]

16884 Humble, Richard, and Mark Bergin. *A 16th Century Galleon* (4–6). Illus. Series: Inside Story. 1995, Bedrick LB $18.95 (0-87226-372-X). 48pp. A richly illustrated volume that begins with the construction of the galleon from massive tree trunks and continues through its launching and techniques of ocean navigation. (Rev: BL 8/95) [623.8]

16885 Kohen, Elizabeth. *Spain* (4–7). Illus. Series: Cultures of the World. 1992, Marshall Cavendish LB $35.64 (1-85435-451-5). 128pp. With text, photographs, maps, and fact sheets, the land and people of Spain are introduced. (Rev: BL 10/15/92) [946]

16886 Leahy, Philippa. *Spain* (3–5). Illus. Series: Discovering. 1993, Crestwood LB $17.95 (0-89686-772-2). 32pp. An introduction to Spain that covers geography, history, landmarks, language, customs, food, and entertainment. (Rev: BL 2/1/94; SLJ 11/93) [946]

16887 McKay, Susan. *Spain* (2–4). Series: Festivals of the World. 1999, Gareth Stevens LB $14.95 (0-8368-2035-5). 32pp. A brief introduction to Spain and its people, focusing on the major festivals and holidays celebrated there and accompanied by a few craft projects and recipes. (Rev: BL 4/15/98) [946]

16888 Mann, Kenny. *Isabel, Ferdinand and Fifteenth-Century Spain* (5–8). Series: Rulers and Their Times. 2001, Marshall Cavendish LB $28.50 (0-7614-1030-9). Following biographies of these great Spanish rulers, there is a section on the life and culture of their times plus a generous selection of original documents of the period. (Rev: BL 1/1–15/02; HBG 3/02; SLJ 3/02) [946]

16889 Millar, Heather. *Spain in the Age of Exploration* (5–8). Series: Cultures of the Past. 1998, Benchmark LB $28.50 (0-7614-0303-5). 80pp. This book covers Spanish history from the time of Columbus to about 1700, with an emphasis on art and literature plus material on daily life and major personalities. (Rev: BL 12/15/98; BR 5–6/99; HBG 10/99; SLJ 2/99) [946]

16890 Miller, Arthur. *Spain* (4–6). Illus. 1989, Chelsea LB $16.95 (1-55546-795-4). 112pp. Culture, history, geography, and daily lifestyles are covered in this introduction. (Rev: BL 4/1/89; SLJ 5/89)

16891 *Portugal in Pictures* (5–8). Illus. Series: Visual Geography. 1996, Lerner LB $25.55 (0-8225-1886-4). 64pp. Current conditions and problems in Portugal are introduced along with the standard material on history, geography, and social conditions. (Rev: BL 12/15/91) [946.9]

16892 Rogers, Lura. *Spain* (4–7). Series: Enchantment of the World. 2001, Children's Book Pr. LB $34.50 (0-516-21123-4). A well-designed book that uses clear text, numerous charts, maps, drawings, and photographs to introduce a number of topics related to Spain and its people. (Rev: BL 1/1–15/02) [946]

16893 Selby, Anna. *Spain* (4–7). Illus. Series: Country Fact Files. 1994, Raintree LB $27.12 (0-8114-1848-0). 45pp. A well-illustrated introduction to Spain, with coverage of such subjects as current social conditions, the economy, food and farming, and the environment. (Rev: SLJ 7/94) [946]

16894 *Spain in Pictures* (5–8). Illus. Series: Visual Geography. 1995, Lerner LB $25.55 (0-8225-1887-2). 64pp. Modern Spain is the focus of this introduction, which includes many photographs, charts, and maps. (Rev: BL 11/15/95) [914.6]

16895 Yanuck, Debbie L. *Spain* (2–3). Illus. Series: Many Cultures, One World. 2004, Capstone LB $17.95 (0-7368-2451-0). 32pp. A brief, accessible introduction to Spain and its people, family life, customs, and legends.

The Middle East

General

16896 Broyles, Matthew. *The Six-Day War* (5–9). Illus. Series: War and Conflict in the Middle East. 2004, Rosen LB $19.95 (0-8239-4549-9). 64pp. A well-organized, balanced account of the 1973 war between Israel and its Arab neighbors Egypt, Jordan, and Syria. (Rev: SLJ 1/05)

16897 Due, Andrea. *The Atlas of the Bible Lands: History, Daily Life and Traditions* (4–9). Illus. 1999, Bedrick $19.95 (0-87226-559-5). This atlas presents an encyclopedic amount of information on the history and culture of the Middle East from prehistory to modern times, with maps supplemented by clearly written text and extensive artwork. (Rev: BR 9–10/99; HBG 10/99; SLJ 3/99) [956]

16898 Fiscus, James W. *The Suez Crisis* (5–9). Illus. Series: War and Conflict in the Middle East. 2004, Rosen LB $19.95 (0-8239-4550-2). 64pp. Examines the 1956 conflict over control of the canal, involving Egypt, Israel, Britain, and France.

16899 Ford, Nick. *Jerusalem Under Muslim Rule in the Eleventh Century: Christian Pilgrims Under Islamic Government* (5–9). Series: The Library of the Middle Ages. 2004, Rosen LB $29.25 (0-8239-4216-3). 64pp. Useful for report writers, this volume looks at life in Jerusalem for people of all religions, providing details from primary sources. (Rev: SLJ 8/04) [956.94]

16900 Gay, Kathlyn, and Martin Gay. *Persian Gulf War* (5–8). Illus. Series: Voices from the Past. 1996, Twenty-First Century LB $18.90 (0-8050-4102-8). 63pp. A clearly written, objective overview of the Gulf War that gives material on the recent history of

Iraq and Saddam Hussein's rise to power. (Rev: SLJ 2/97) [956.704]

16901 Hancock, Lee. *Saladin and the Kingdom of Jerusalem: The Muslims Recapture the Holy Land in AD 1187* (5–9). Series: The Library of the Middle Ages. 2004, Rosen LB $29.25 (0-8239-4217-1). 64pp. Useful for report writers, this volume looks at life in Jerusalem under the Crusaders, providing details from primary sources. (Rev: SLJ 8/04) [956]

16902 Hilliam, Paul. *Islamic Weapons, Warfare, and Armies: Muslim Military Operations Against the Crusaders* (5–9). Series: The Library of the Middle Ages. 2004, Rosen LB $29.25 (0-8239-4215-5). 64pp. Useful for report writers, this volume looks at the spread of Islam and the conflicts with the Crusaders. (Rev: SLJ 8/04) [355]

16903 King, John. *Bedouin* (4–6). Illus. Series: Threatened Cultures. 1992, Raintree LB $24.26 (0-8114-2304-2). 48pp. This book presents the life and culture of the nomadic Bedouins. (Rev: BCCB 7–8/93; BL 8/93; SLJ 9/93) [961]

16904 Long, Cathryn J. *The Middle East in Search of Peace*. Rev. ed. (4–7). Illus. Series: Headliners. 1996, Millbrook LB $25.90 (0-7613-0105-4). 64pp. An objective account of the conflict between Arabs and Jews in the Middle East, with good historical information and a description of various peace plans. (Rev: SLJ 1/97) [956]

16905 Losleben, Elizabeth. *The Bedouin of the Middle East* (4–6). Series: First Peoples. 2002, Lerner LB $23.93 (0-8225-0663-7). 48pp. Traditional and contemporary lifestyles are included in this presentation of the Bedouin people, the territory in which they live, and their history, culture, and economy. (Rev: HBG 3/03; SLJ 2/03) [961]

16906 MacDonald, Fiona. *A 16th Century Mosque* (4–6). Illus. Series: Inside Story. 1995, Bedrick $18.95 (0-87226-310-X). 48pp. After a discussion of the fundamentals of the Muslim faith, this account graphically covers the construction of the Sulemaniye mosque in Constantinople in 1557. (Rev: BL 4/15/95) [297]

16907 Murdico, Suzanne J. *The Gulf War* (5–9). Illus. Series: War and Conflict in the Middle East. 2004, Rosen LB $19.95 (0-8239-4551-0). 64pp. Examines the 1991 war between Iraq and a coalition of nations. [956.7]

16908 Nardo, Don. *The War Against Iraq* (5–8). Series: American War. 2000, Lucent LB $19.96 (1-56006-715-2). 112pp. An nonjudgmental account of the Gulf War that includes a good final chapter on the results of the war. (Rev: BL 3/1/01; SLJ 3/01) [956.704]

16909 Rivera, Sheila. *Women of the Middle East* (4–6). Series: World in Conflict. 2004, ABDO LB $17.95 (1-59197-415-1). 48pp. For reluctant readers, this title studies the status of contemporary women in Saudi Arabia, Afghanistan, Iran, Egypt, and Israel, looking at the role of religion, politics, and local custom in their lives. (Rev: SLJ 3/04) [305.42]

16910 Santella, Andrew. *The Persian Gulf War* (3–6). Illus. Series: We the People. 2004, Compass

Point LB $16.95 (0-7565-0612-3). 48pp. Provides a concise description of the fall of Kuwait, the formation of the Desert Storm coalition, and the aftermath. [956.7]

16911 Senker, Cath. *The Arab-Israeli Conflict* (5–8). Series: Questioning History. 2004, Smart Apple Media LB $28.50 (1-58340-441-4). 64pp. A clear and balanced discussion of the history and current status of relations between Arabs and Israelis, with a timeline, glossary, and detailed index. (Rev: SLJ 2/05) [956.04]

16912 Whitcraft, Melissa. *The Tigris and Euphrates Rivers* (4–8). Series: Watts Library. 1999, Watts LB $24.00 (0-531-11741-3). 64pp. Describes the historical importance of these rivers and their ancient civilizations and traces their course today through Turkey, Iraq, and Syria. (Rev: BL 1/1–15/00; SLJ 2/00) [956]

16913 Wingate, Katherine. *The Intifadas* (5–9). Illus. Series: War and Conflict in the Middle East. 2004, Rosen LB $19.95 (0-8239-4546-4). 64pp. An even-handed overview of the events leading up to the Palestinian uprisings, with statistics, maps, photographs, and profiles of leaders. (Rev: BL 11/1/04) [956.95]

Egypt

16914 Barghusen, Joan. *Daily Life in Ancient and Modern Cairo* (4–8). Illus. by Bob Moulder. Series: Cities Through Time. 2001, Runestone LB $25.26 (0-8225-3221-2). 63pp. Cairo's evolution from earliest times to today is presented in double-page spreads with information on political, social, and religious life as well as women's issues, with a timeline and quotations. (Rev: BL 4/15/01; HBG 10/01; SLJ 7/01) [962]

16915 Bennett, Olivia. *A Family in Egypt* (3–6). Illus. 1985, Lerner LB $18.60 (0-8225-1652-7). 32pp. Color photos highlight the life of a family in this Middle East land. (Rev: BL 6/15/85; SLJ 10/85)

16916 Bowden, Rob, and Roy Maconachie. *Cairo* (4–7). Illus. Series: Great Cities of the World. 2005, World Almanac LB $22.50 (0-8368-5035-1). 48pp. An informative and appealing overview of one of the world's most famous cities, with material on its history, its economy, and what it's like to live there.

16917 Deady, Kathleen W. *Egypt* (1–3). Series: Countries of the World. 2000, Bridgestone LB $17.26 (0-7368-0626-1). 24pp. A very basic introduction to Egypt that contains current facts and full-page photos. (Rev: HBG 3/01; SLJ 3/01) [962]

16918 Diamond, Arthur. *Egypt: Gift of the Nile* (5–9). Series: Discovering Our Heritage. 1992, Dillon $14.95 (0-87518-511-8). An introduction to Egypt that includes history, culture, folktales, maps, recipes, and a discussion of Egyptian immigrants in the United States. (Rev: BL 8/92; SLJ 11/92) [962]

16919 Draper, Allison Stark. *Historical Atlas of Egypt* (4–6). Illus. Series: Historical Atlases of South Asia, Central Asia and the Middle East. 2004, Rosen LB $22.95 (0-8239-4498-0). 64pp. This attractive profile that includes many maps and pho-

tographs traces Egypt's development from prehistoric times to the present.

16920 Eldash, Khaled, and Dalia Khattab. *A Child's Day in an Egyptian City* (K–3). Series: A Child's Day. 2002, Marshall Cavendish LB $15.95 (0-7614-1410-X). 32pp. An accessible introduction to present-day Egypt through the daily life of its children. (Rev: BL 2/15/03; HBG 3/03) [962]

16921 Feinstein, Steve. *Egypt in Pictures* (5–8). Illus. 1992, Lerner LB $21.27 (0-8225-1840-6). 64pp. Covers all areas of life in this Middle East land. (Rev: BL 2/1/89)

16922 Flint, David. *Egypt* (2–4). Illus. Series: On the Map. 1993, Raintree LB $22.83 (0-8114-3420-6). 32pp. Using many color photos, this account covers briefly such topics related to Egypt as geography, religion, history, and landmarks. (Rev: BL 2/1/94) [954.9]

16923 Frank, Nicole, and Susan L. Wilson. *Welcome to Egypt* (2–4). Series: Welcome to My Country. 2000, Gareth Stevens LB $22.60 (0-8368-2494-6). 48pp. Brilliantly colored photos on each page are the highlight of this brief introduction to Egypt past and present and the way people live today. (Rev: HBG 10/00; SLJ 3/01) [962]

16924 Gresko, Marcia S. *Letters Home from Egypt* (3–5). Series: Letters Home From. 1999, Blackbirch LB $16.95 (1-56711-401-6). 32pp. A series of letters written home by a young traveler present basic facts about Egypt and its people, land, cities, food, and daily life. (Rev: BL 2/15/00; HBG 3/00; SLJ 2/00) [962]

16925 Harkonen, Reijo. *The Children of Egypt* (4–6). Illus. by Matti Pitkanen. Series: The World's Children. 1991, Carolrhoda LB $23.93 (0-87614-396-6). 40pp. In this profile, two of the children highlighted guide tourists to the pyramids, and another is a brickmaker. (Rev: BL 6/1/91) [962]

16926 Heinrichs, Ann. *Egypt* (4–7). Illus. Series: Enchantment of the World. 1997, Children's Book Pr. LB $34.50 (0-516-20470-X). 144pp. This fine introduction to Egypt gives substantial information on ancient and modern history, with coverage of religion, daily life, politics, and relations with Israel. (Rev: BL 2/1/98; HBG 10/98; SLJ 5/98) [962]

16927 Hooper, Meredith. *Who Built the Pyramid?* (3–5). Illus. by Robin Heighway-Bury. 2001, Candlewick $15.99 (0-7636-0786-X). 40pp. A combination of fact and fiction is used to describe the roles of various participants — from the king of Egypt to the designer to the water carrier — in the construction of a pyramid 4,000 years ago. (Rev: BCCB 1/02; BL 1/1–15/02; HB 1–2/02; HBG 3/02; SLJ 1/02) [932.013]

16928 Kallen, Stuart A. *Egypt* (4–8). Series: Modern Nations of the World. 1999, Lucent LB $27.45 (1-56006-535-4). 111pp. Sidebars are used for specialized topics in this overview that is particularly strong on the history of Egypt. (Rev: HBG 3/00; SLJ 10/99) [962]

16929 King, David C. *Egypt: Ancient Traditions, Modern Hopes* (3–5). Illus. Series: Exploring Cultures of the World. 1997, Marshall Cavendish LB

$27.07 (0-7614-0142-3). 64pp. Describes various aspects of life in modern Egypt, with comparisons and contrasts made to past conditions. (Rev: BL 7/97; SLJ 1/98) [932]

16930 Loveridge, Emma. *Egypt* (5–8). Series: Country Fact Files. 1997, Raintree LB $27.12 (0-8172-4626-6). This book gives standard basic information about Egypt, including its climate, landscape, trade, industry, and daily life. (Rev: SLJ 9/97) [962]

16931 Moscovitch, Arlene. *Egypt, the Land* (4–6). Series: Lands, Peoples, and Cultures. 2000, Crabtree LB $15.45 (0-86505-232-8); paper $7.16 (0-86505-312-X). 32pp. This book concentrates on the use of land and water in modern Egypt and the growth of cities like Cairo and Alexandria. Also use in the same series *Egypt, the People* (2000). (Rev: SLJ 7/00) [962]

16932 Orr, Tamra. *Egyptian Islamic Jihad* (4–8). Series: Inside the World's Most Infamous Terrorist Organizations. 2003, Rosen LB $26.50 (0-8239-3819-0). 64pp. Dedicated to the overthrow of the secular Egyptian government, this terrorist organization has links to the Al Qaeda terrorist network. (Rev: BL 10/15/03) [962]

16933 Parks, Peggy J. *The Aswan High Dam* (5–8). Series: Building World Landmarks. 2004, Gale/Blackbirch LB $18.96 (1-56711-329-X). 48pp. This is the fascinating story of the construction of the huge dam on the Nile and the immense technical and social challenges involved. (Rev: SLJ 6/04) [627]

16934 Pateman, Robert. *Egypt* (4–7). Illus. Series: Cultures of the World. 1992, Marshall Cavendish LB $35.64 (1-85435-535-X). 128pp. Egypt past and present is introduced in this account that stresses how the people live. (Rev: BL 1/1/93) [962]

16935 Roop, Peter, and Connie Roop. *Egypt* (2–4). Series: A Visit To. 1998, Heinemann LB $19.92 (1-57572-122-8). 32pp. An attractive introduction to modern Egypt, covering its geography, history, cities, people, and culture. (Rev: SLJ 9/98) [967]

16936 Streissguth, Thomas. *Egypt* (3–5). Series: Globe-Trotters Club. 1999, Carolrhoda $16.95 (1-57505-110-9). 48pp. Two-page spreads present a variety of topics related to Egypt, including its geography, history, the people, religion, schools, food, and government. (Rev: BL 9/15/99; HBG 3/00; SLJ 12/99) [962]

16937 Streissguth, Thomas. *Egypt* (1–3). Series: A Ticket To. 1999, Carolrhoda LB $22.60 (1-57505-135-4). 48pp. This heavily illustrated first look at Egypt covers the land, its people, and its main ethnic and cultural features. (Rev: BL 9/15/99; HBG 3/00; SLJ 12/99) [962]

16938 Tenquist, Alasdair. *Egypt* (5–7). Illus. Series: Economically Developing Countries. 1995, Thomson Learning LB $24.26 (1-56847-385-0). 48pp. A look at present-day conditions in Egypt and its concerns and problems. (Rev: SLJ 2/96) [962]

16939 Wilson, Neil. *Egypt* (4–8). Series: Nations of the World. 2001, Raintree LB $34.26 (0-7398-1283-1). 128pp. An excellent introduction to the country that housed one of the world's oldest civilizations

and is currently a center of Islamic culture and religion. (Rev: BL 6/1–15/01; HBG 10/01) [962]

16940 Wilson, Susan. *Egypt* (4–5). Series: Countries of the World. 1999, Gareth Stevens LB $18.95 (0-8368-2259-5). 95pp. Geography, history, lifestyle, art, food, and government are some of the topics covered in this introduction to Egypt, which also discusses current problems. (Rev: BL 9/15/99; SLJ 10/99) [962]

16941 Zuehlke, Jeffrey. *Egypt in Pictures*. Rev. ed. (4–8). Illus. Series: Visual Geography. 2002, Lerner LB $27.93 (0-8225-0367-0). 80pp. Covers Egypt's geography, history, people, economy, and culture with maps, photographs, and illustrations. (Rev: SLJ 3/03) [962]

Israel

16942 Bernards, Neal. *The Palestinian Conflict: Identifying Propaganda Techniques* (4–7). Illus. 1990, Greenhaven LB $22.45 (0-89908-602-0). 32pp. Such skills as distinguishing between fact and fiction and detecting bias are stressed in this book. (Rev: BL 6/15/91) [956.04]

16943 Boraas, Tracey. *Israel* (4–6). Series: Countries and Cultures. 2002, Capstone LB $23.93 (0-7368-0938-4). 64pp. This introduction to Israel includes basic material on history, wildlife, government, geography, and economics. (Rev: BL 1/1–15/03; HBG 3/03; SLJ 4/03) [956.54]

16944 Dubois, Jill. *Israel* (4–7). Illus. Series: Cultures of the World. 1992, Marshall Cavendish LB $35.64 (1-85435-531-7). 128pp. This introduction to Israel emphasizes its culture and the lifestyles of the people. (Rev: BL 1/1/93) [956.94]

16945 Feinstein, Steve. *Israel in Pictures* (5–8). Illus. 1992, Lerner LB $25.55 (0-8225-1833-3). 64pp. An overview of geography, climate, wildlife, and vegetation with photographs, maps, and charts. (Rev: BL 8/88) [956.9405]

16946 Fisher, Frederick. *Israel* (4–6). Series: Countries of the World. 2000, Gareth Stevens LB $19.95 (0-8368-2319-2). 96pp. This well-illustrated guide to Israel covers its geography, history, government, current problems, language, food, and relations with Canada and the United States. (Rev: BL 6/1–15/00; HBG 10/00) [956.94]

16947 Green, Jen. *Israel* (4–8). Series: Nations of the World. 2001, Raintree LB $34.26 (0-7398-1286-6). 128pp. A fine, attractive introduction to the land and people of Israel, the nation that was created as a homeland for the Jewish people after World War II. (Rev: BL 6/1–15/01; HBG 10/01) [956.94]

16948 Gresko, Marcia S. *Israel* (1–3). Series: Globe-Trotters Club. 2000, Carolrhoda LB $22.60 (1-57505-118-4). 48pp. From the rocky Negev Desert to the Sea of Galilee, the state of Israel is brought to life in this account that introduces the country through double-page spreads on a variety of subjects. (Rev: BL 5/15/00; HBG 3/01) [956.94]

16949 Gresko, Marcia S. *Letters Home from Israel* (3–5). Series: Letters Home From. 1999, Blackbirch LB $16.95 (1-56711-404-0). 32pp. Basic facts about

Israel — its land, people, daily life, and history — are given in a series of letters written by a young traveler, illustrated with postcard-style photographs. (Rev: BL 2/15/00; HBG 3/00; SLJ 2/00) [956.94]

16950 Grossman, Laurie M. *Children of Israel* (2–5). Photos by author. Series: The World's Children. 2001, Carolrhoda LB $23.93 (1-57505-448-5). 48pp. This look at the daily lives of children in Israel introduces the history, geography, and culture of the country with appealing full-color illustrations, a pronunciation guide, and map. (Rev: HBG 10/01; SLJ 6/01)

16951 Gunderson, Cory. *The Israeli-Palestinian Conflict* (4–6). Series: World in Conflict. 2004, ABDO LB $17.95 (1-59197-416-X). 48pp. A politically balanced introduction to the ongoing conflict between the Israelis and Palestinians, aimed at reluctant readers, with numerous photographs and maps. (Rev: SLJ 3/04) [956.04]

16952 Haskins, Jim. *Count Your Way Through Israel* (2–4). Illus. by Rick Handson. Series: Count Your Way. 1990, Carolrhoda LB $19.93 (0-87614-415-6). Using the format of counting from 1 to 10 in Hebrew, the land and people of Israel are introduced. (Rev: SLJ 2/91) [956.94]

16953 Hayhurst, Chris. *Israel's War of Independence* (5–9). Illus. Series: War and Conflict in the Middle East. 2004, Rosen LB $19.95 (0-8239-4548-0). 64pp. An even-handed overview of Israel's struggle for independence and the ensuing years of violence, with statistics, maps, photographs, and profiles of leaders. (Rev: BL 11/1/04; SLJ 1/05) [956.04]

16954 Kuskin, Karla. *Jerusalem, Shining Still* (3–5). Illus. by David Frampton. 1987, HarperCollins paper $5.50 (0-06-443243-2). 32pp. The history of Jerusalem is briefly told in lyrical prose and touches of verse. (Rev: BL 10/1/87; HB 11–12/87; SLJ 11/87)

16955 Paris, Alan. *Jerusalem 3000: Kids Discover the City of Gold!* (4–6). Illus. by Peter Gandolfi. 1995, Pitspopany $16.95 (0-943706-59-9). 47pp. This fine introduction to Jerusalem includes material on its history as determined by archaeological research. (Rev: SLJ 12/95) [956.94]

16956 Patterson, Jose. *Israel* (3–6). Illus. Series: Country Facts Files. 1997, Raintree LB $27.12 (0-8172-4627-4). 45pp. This account covers modern-day Israel and its political and economic status, resources, and people. (Rev: BL 7/97) [956.94]

16957 Pirotta, Saviour. *Jerusalem* (4–6). Illus. Series: Holy Cities. 1993, Dillon LB $17.95 (0-87518-569-X). 46pp. An oversize volume that introduces Jerusalem, its buildings, holy sites, and the facts and legends surrounding them. (Rev: BL 9/15/93; SLJ 8/93) [956.94]

16958 Scharfstein, Sol. *Understanding Israel* (5–7). Illus. 1994, KTAV paper $14.95 (0-88125-428-2). 144pp. A heavily illustrated introduction to Israel that covers history, religion, government, culture, and current concerns. (Rev: SLJ 10/94) [956.94]

16959 Sherman, Josepha. *Your Travel Guide to Ancient Israel* (4–8). Illus. Series: Passport to History. 2003, Lerner LB $26.60 (0-8225-3072-4). 80pp.

An illustrated visit to Israel in the time of King Solomon, with description of foods, housing, clothing, customs, and notable people of that era. (Rev: HBG 4/04; SLJ 4/04) [933]

16960 Silverman, Maida. *Israel: The Founding of a Modern Nation* (4–7). Illus. 1998, Dial LB $15.00 (0-8034-2136-6). 112pp. This account covers 3,000 years of Jewish history, with emphasis on recent centuries, and includes a timeline showing Israel's history from 1948 to 1998. (Rev: BL 5/1/98) [956.94]

16961 Spengler, Kremena. *Israel* (2–5). Illus. Series: Questions and Answers: Countries. 2005, Capstone LB $16.95 (0-7368-3753-1). 32pp. Using a question-and-answer format, simple text, large photos, and many factboxes, this is an introduction to Israel today, with material on history and traditional culture.

16962 Taitz, Emily, and Sondra Henry. *Israel: A Sacred Land* (5–7). Illus. 1988, Macmillan LB $14.95 (0-87518-364-6). 160pp. The focus is on everyday life in this Middle East land. (Rev: BL 2/15/88) [956.94054]

16963 *Three Wishes: Palestinian and Israeli Children Speak* (5–12). 2004, Groundwood $16.95 (0-88899-554-7). 144pp. In an evenhanded presentation that offers an introductory historical overview, 20 first-person accounts relate the experiences of Christian, Jewish, and Muslim young people during the ongoing conflict between Israelis and Palestinians. (Rev: BL 9/1/04*; SLJ 10/04) [956.04]

16964 Waldman, Neil. *The Golden City: Jerusalem's 3,000 Years* (4–6). Illus. 1995, Simon & Schuster $15.00 (0-689-80080-0). 32pp. Beginning with Moses, this account traces the important events in the history of Jerusalem during its 3,000-year existence. (Rev: BL 9/1/95; SLJ 11/95) [965.94]

Other Middle Eastern Lands

16965 Anderson, Laurie Halse. *Saudi Arabia* (1–3). Series: Globe-Trotters Club. 2000, Lerner LB $22.60 (1-57505-121-4). 48pp. An introduction to this country on the Arabian Peninsula that tells about its landmarks, ethnic groups, oil riches, ancient traditions, and modern conveniences. (Rev: BL 12/15/00; HBG 3/01; SLJ 1/01) [953]

16966 Augustin, Byron. *United Arab Emirates* (4–7). Series: Enchantment of the World. 2002, Children's Book Pr. LB $34.50 (0-516-20473-4). 144pp. This important nation is introduced with material on topics including history, natural resources, climate, and people. (Rev: BL 5/15/02; SLJ 9/02) [953]

16967 Augustin, Byron, and Rebecca A. Augustin. *Qatar* (5–8). Illus. Series: Enchantment of the World. 1997, Children's Book Pr. LB $32.00 (0-516-20303-7). 128pp. An introduction to the small oil-producing country on the Persian Gulf that describes its history under British rule and how the people now live. (Rev: BL 7/97; HBG 3/98) [953.63]

16968 Bader, Philip. *Iran* (3–5). Illus. Series: Dropping In On. 2001, Rourke $25.27 (1-55916-285-6). This brief tour of Iran via hot-air balloon includes material on geography, famous sights, and the people. (Rev: SLJ 1/01) [955]

16969 Balcavage, Dynise. *Iraq* (5–8). Illus. Series: Countries of the World. 2003, Gareth Stevens LB $29.27 (0-8368-2359-1). 96pp. Report writers will find solid information on Iraq's history, geography, government, and society in this volume that includes discussion of Iraq's relations with the United States. (Rev: BL 5/1/03; HBG 10/03) [956.7]

16970 Balcavage, Dynise. *Saudi Arabia* (4–6). Series: Countries of the World. 2001, Gareth Stevens LB $21.95 (0-8368-2338-9). 96pp. A fine introduction to Saudi Arabia told in a simple, well-organized text with many accompanying color photographs. (Rev: BL 12/15/01; HBG 3/02) [953.8]

16971 Bauer, Brandy. *Iran: A Question And Answer Book* (2–5). Illus. Series: Questions and Answers: Countries. 2005, Capstone LB $16.95 (0-7368-3752-3). 32pp. Using a question-and-answer format, simple text, large photos, and many factboxes, this is an introduction to Iran today, with material on history and traditional culture.

16972 Byers, Ann. *Lebanon's Hezbollah* (4–8). Series: Inside the World's Most Infamous Terrorist Organizations. 2003, Rosen LB $26.50 (0-8239-3821-2). 64pp. This is the story of the Lebanese terrorist organization dedicated to installing a conservative Islamic government in Lebanon and to the destruction of Israel. (Rev: BL 10/15/03; SLJ 9/03) [956.92]

16973 Cartlidge, Cherese. *Iran* (5–8). Series: Modern Nations of the World. 2002, Gale LB $27.45 (1-56006-971-6). 112pp. This colorful account gives a comprehensive overview of Iran, including history, geography, and culture. (Rev: BL 12/15/02; SLJ 1/03) [955]

16974 Deady, Kathleen W. *Saudi Arabia* (2–5). Illus. Series: Questions and Answers: Countries. 2005, Capstone LB $16.95 (0-7368-3760-4). 32pp. Using a question-and-answer format, simple text, large photos, and many factboxes, this is an introduction to Saudi Arabia today, with material on history and traditional culture. (Rev: HBG 3/02)

16975 Dutton, Roderic. *An Arab Family* (3–6). Illus. 1985, Lerner LB $18.60 (0-8225-1660-8). 32pp. The author focuses mainly on one family member to give fascinating details of life, noting how the discovery of oil has influenced daily activities. (Rev: BL 11/15/85)

16976 Eboch, Chris. *Turkey* (5–9). Series: Modern Nations of the World. 2003, Gale LB $27.45 (1-59018-122-0). 112pp. This account presents a broad spectrum of material about Turkey including history, geography, and culture. (Rev: BL 11/15/03; SLJ 6/03) [961]

16977 Ferguson, Amanda. *The Attack on U.S. Servicemen in Saudi Arabia on June 25, 1996* (4–7). Series: Terrorist Attacks. 2003, Rosen LB $26.50 (0-8239-3861-1). 64pp. This thoughtful account of the 1996 terrorist bombing of the Khobar Towers discusses the history of U.S.-Saudi relations and the terrorist movement within the desert kingdom. (Rev: SLJ 10/03) [953.8]

16978 Foster, Leila M. *Jordan* (5–8). Illus. Series: Enchantment of the World. 1991, Children's Book Pr. paper $32.00 (0-516-02603-8). 128pp. An introduction in text and pictures to the geography, history, culture, and important people of Jordan. (Rev: BL 2/1/92) [956.95]

16979 Foster, Leila M. *Kuwait* (5–10). Series: Enchantment of the World. 1998, Children's Book Pr. LB $34.50 (0-516-20604-4). 143pp. An introduction to Kuwait for older readers, with extensive coverage of the Gulf War. (Rev: SLJ 11/98) [956]

16980 Foster, Leila M. *Oman* (4–7). Series: Enchantment of the World. 1999, Children's Book Pr. LB $34.50 (0-516-20964-7). 144pp. A fine introduction to this oil-producing country, covering topics such as history, geography, government, religion, and the economy. (Rev: BL 9/15/99) [956]

16981 Foster, Leila M. *Saudi Arabia* (5–8). Series: Enchantment of the World. 1993, Children's Pr. paper $32.00 (0-516-02611-9). The huge, oil-rich Middle Eastern kingdom of Saudi Arabia is presented, with material on its economic conditions, relationship with the West, and social and religious beliefs. (Rev: BL 8/93; SLJ 8/93) [953.8]

16982 Fox, Mary V. *Bahrain* (5–8). Series: Enchantment of the World. 1992, Children's Pr. paper $32.00 (0-516-02608-9). An in-depth introduction to Bahrain, including geological, meteorological, historical, and engineering aspects. (Rev: BL 12/15/92; SLJ 1/93) [953.65]

16983 Fox, Mary V. *Iran* (5–8). Illus. Series: Enchantment of the World. 1991, Children's Book Pr. paper $32.00 (0-516-02727-1). 128pp. The history of the country once known as Persia is presented along with discussion of conditions at the end of the 1980s and brief biographies of famous people. (Rev: BL 10/1/91) [955]

16984 Goodwin, William. *Saudi Arabia* (5–8). Series: Modern Nations of the World. 2001, Lucent LB $27.45 (1-56006-763-2). 112pp. The land ruled by the Saud dynasty is presented with details on history, government, geography, resources, and world importance. (Rev: BL 6/1–15/01) [953.8]

16985 Greenblatt, Miriam. *Iran* (5–9). Illus. 2003, Children's Book Pr. LB $34.00 (0-516-22375-5). 144pp. Iran's geography, history, economy, religion, culture, lifestyle, and people are among the topics covered in this comprehensive volume that will be useful for reports. (Rev: SLJ 11/03) [955]

16986 Haskins, Jim. *Count Your Way Through the Arab World* (3–5). Illus. 1987, Carolrhoda LB $19.93 (0-87614-304-4); Lerner paper $5.95 (0-87614-487-3). 24pp. "Muslims pray to Mecca 5 times a day" and other numbers help to introduce the culture of the Arab world. (Rev: BL 10/15/87; SLJ 9/87)

16987 Hassig, Susan M. *Iraq* (4–7). Illus. Series: Cultures of the World. 1992, Marshall Cavendish LB $35.64 (1-85435-533-3). 128pp. This introduction stresses the lifestyles of the people, their religion, and culture. (Rev: BL 1/1/93) [956.7]

16988 Heinrichs, Ann. *Saudi Arabia* (4–7). Series: Enchantment of the World. 2002, Children's Book

Pr. LB $34.50 (0-516-22287-2). 144pp. Topics covered in the highly visual introduction to Saudi Arabia include history, religion, language, economy, and government. (Rev: BL 9/15/02) [953.8]

16989 Hestler, Anna. *Yemen* (5–8). Series: Cultures of the World. 1999, Marshall Cavendish LB $35.64 (0-7614-0956-4). 128pp. A fine introduction to this country on the Gulf of Aden with good background information and an overview of modern life. (Rev: HBG 10/99; SLJ 10/99) [956]

16990 *Iran in Pictures* (5–8). Illus. Series: Visual Geography. 1992, Lerner LB $21.27 (0-8225-1848-1). 64pp. Basic coverage on this Middle Eastern land and its people. (Rev: BL 5/1/89) [955]

16991 Isaac, Michael. *Historical Atlas of Oman* (4–6). Illus. Series: Historical Atlases of South Asia, Central Asia and the Middle East. 2004, Rosen LB $22.95 (0-8239-4500-6). 64pp. This attractive profile that includes many maps and photographs traces Oman's development from prehistoric times to the present.

16992 Janin, Hunt. *Saudi Arabia* (4–7). Illus. Series: Cultures of the World. 1992, Marshall Cavendish LB $35.64 (1-85435-532-5). 128pp. The history, geography, economy, language, and people are discussed in this book about Saudi Arabia. (Rev: BL 1/1/93) [953.8]

16993 *Jordan in Pictures* (5–8). Illus. 1992, Lerner LB $25.55 (0-8225-1834-1). 64pp. Young readers learn what life is like in this Middle East land. (Rev: BL 2/1/89; SLJ 2/89) [956.9504]

16994 *Lebanon in Pictures* (5–8). Illus. Series: Visual Geography. 1992, Lerner LB $25.55 (0-8225-1832-5). 64pp. A country torn apart by strife is the focus of this edition. (Rev: BL 2/1/89) [956.9204]

16995 Malhotra, Sonali. *Welcome to Iraq* (3–5). Series: Welcome to My Country. 2004, Gareth Stevens LB $25.26 (0-8368-2559-4). 48pp. Introduces readers to Iraq's geography, history, people, culture, family life, government, religion, and language. (Rev: SLJ 7/04) [956.7]

16996 Marcovitz, Hal. *Kuwait* (5–8). Illus. Series: Modern Middle East Nations. 2003, Mason Crest LB $24.95 (1-59084-510-2). 112pp. A thorough introduction to the geography, history, and people of Kuwait, whose wealth makes it an unusual country. (Rev: BL 6/1–15/03; HBG 4/04; SLJ 10/03) [953.67]

16997 Marston, Elsa. *Lebanon: New Light in an Ancient Land* (5–8). Illus. Series: Discovering Our Heritage. 1994, Dillon LB $14.95 (0-87518-584-3). 124pp. A well-organized, readable introduction to the history, geography, and people of Lebanon, together with material on the impact of Lebanese immigration on the United States. (Rev: SLJ 7/94) [956]

16998 Moktefi, Mokhtar. *The Arabs in the Golden Age* (4–6). Illus. by Veronique Ageorges. 1992, Millbrook LB $22.40 (1-56294-201-8). 64pp. This book takes the reader back to the 8th through mid-13th centuries. (Rev: BL 10/15/92) [909]

16999 O'Shea, Maria. *Saudi Arabia* (2–4). Series: Festivals of the World. 1999, Gareth Stevens LB

$15.95 (0-8368-2026-6). 32pp. The major holidays celebrated in Saudi Arabia are highlighted, including *eid,* a hajj pilgrimage to the holy city of Mecca, and the ways Muslims observe the founding of Islam. (Rev: BL 12/15/99; HBG 10/00) [953.8]

17000 Rajendra, Vijeya, and Gisela Kaplan. *Iran* (4–7). Illus. Series: Cultures of the World. 1992, Marshall Cavendish LB $35.64 (1-85435-534-1). 128pp. As well as standard introductory information about Iran, this book tells about how the people live and what the country's present problems are. (Rev: BL 1/1/93) [955]

17001 Reed, Jennifer Bond. *The Saudi Royal Family* (5–8). Illus. Series: Major World Leaders. 2002, Chelsea $23.95 (0-7910-7063-8); paper $9.95 (0-7910-7187-1). 112pp. Saudi Arabia's ruling royal family is profiled, detailing its rise to power, its Islamic policies, and the various individual rulers, with a look at the contrast between the family's extravagant lifestyle and its religious beliefs. (Rev: BL 1/1–15/03; SLJ 4/03) [953.8]

17002 Romano, Amy. *A Historical Atlas of the United Arab Emirates* (4–6). Illus. 2004, Rosen LB $22.95 (0-8239-4501-4). 64pp. A useful supplement to more detailed books on the United Arab Emirates, this title chronicles the country's history from the time of its earliest known settlements to the present. (Rev: BL 12/1/04) [911]

17003 Romano, Amy. *Historical Atlas of Yemen* (4–6). Illus. Series: Historical Atlases of South Asia, Central Asia and the Middle East. 2004, Rosen LB $22.95 (0-8239-4502-2). 64pp. This attractive profile that includes many maps and photographs traces Yemen's development from prehistoric times to the present.

17004 Schemenauer, Elma. *Iran* (3–5). Illus. Series: Faces and Places. 2000, Child's World LB $25.64 (1-56766-738-4). 32pp. An introduction to Iran that covers topics including geography, history, people, customs, pastimes, and religion as well as material on politics past and present. (Rev: BL 3/1/01; HBG 3/01) [955]

17005 Sheehan, Sean. *Lebanon* (5–10). Series: Cultures of the World. 1996, Marshall Cavendish LB $35.64 (0-7614-0283-7). A lively, well-written introduction to this war-ravaged country with details on history, economy, culture, religion and foods, including a recipe for a typical dish. (Rev: SLJ 6/97) [569.2]

17006 South, Coleman. *Jordan* (5–10). Series: Cultures of the World. 1996, Marshall Cavendish LB $35.64 (0-7614-0287-X). Everyday life in Jordan is the focus of this book that also covers history, religion, culture, geography, festivals, and foods; a single recipe is included. (Rev: SLJ 6/97) [569.5]

17007 Spengler, Kremena. *Iraq: A Question and Answer Book* (2–5). Illus. Series: Fact Finders. 2004, Capstone LB $16.95 (0-7368-2691-2). 32pp. Double-page spreads use simple text, factboxes, and plenty of color photographs to answer pertinent questions about the country's history, geography, government, and culture. (Rev: BL 11/15/04; SLJ 3/05) [956.7]

17008 Stein, R. Conrad. *The Iran Hostage Crisis* (3–5). Illus. Series: Cornerstones of Freedom. 1994, Children's Book Pr. LB $18.70 (0-516-06681-1). 32pp. This international incident that brought humiliation to the United States and helped cause the fall of a president are vividly re-created. (Rev: BL 1/15/95; SLJ 4/95) [955.05]

17009 Temple, Bob. *Saudi Arabia* (3–5). Series: Countries: Faces and Places. 2000, Child's World LB $25.64 (1-56766-717-1). 32pp. Using a simple text, short chapters, and plenty of color illustrations, basic facts about Saudi Arabia and its present-day status are given. (Rev: BL 4/15/01; HBG 3/01) [953]

17010 Webster, Christine. *Egypt* (2–5). Illus. Series: Questions and Answers: Countries. 2004, Capstone LB $16.95 (0-7368-2688-2). 32pp. Using a question-and-answer format, simple text, large photos, and many factboxes, this is an introduction to Egypt today, with material on history and traditional culture.

17011 Wills, Karen. *Jordan* (5–8). Series: Modern Nations of the World. 2001, Lucent LB $27.45 (1-56006-822-1). 112pp. A good profile of Jordan is presented, with basic background material and information on present conditions and the people today. (Rev: BL 6/1–15/01) [956.95]

17012 Winter, Jeanette. *The Librarian of Basra: A True Story from Iraq* (3–5). Illus. 2005, Harcourt $16.00 (0-15-205445-6). 32pp. This is the inspiring, true story of an Iraqi librarian's efforts to save the 30,000 books in Basra's library collection from destruction as invading forces neared the city in 2003. (Rev: BL 12/1/04; SLJ *1/05) [020]

17013 *Yemen in Pictures* (5–8). Illus. Series: Visual Geography. 1993, Lerner LB $25.55 (0-8225-1911-9). 64pp. In introduction to this Muslim republic on the Gulf of Aden, with material on its economic and social conditions. (Rev: BL 12/1/93; SLJ 12/93) [953.3]

North and South America (Excluding the United States)

North and South America

17014 Alter, Judy. *Discovering North America's Land, People, and Wildlife* (5–8). Series: Continents of the World. 2004, Enslow/MyReportLinks.com LB $19.95 (0-7660-5206-0). 48pp. An introduction to the geography, history, economy, plants and animals, culture, and people of the continent, with brief coverage of the Caribbean and Central America. (Rev: SLJ 11/04) [917]

17015 Bramwell, Martyn. *North America and the Caribbean* (4–6). Series: World in Maps. 2000, Lerner LB $23.93 (0-8225-2911-4). 48pp. A comprehensive and well-illustrated treatment of all the countries that make up North America, from Canada to Mexico and the Caribbean islands. (Rev: BL 10/15/00; HBG 10/01) [970]

Canada

17016 Barlas, Bob, and Norman Tompsett. *Welcome to Canada* (2–4). Series: Welcome to My Country. 1999, Gareth Stevens LB $16.95 (0-8368-2394-X). 48pp. An overview that contain separate chapters on Canada's history, government and economy, people, language, arts, leisure, and food. (Rev: HBG 10/00; SLJ 1/00) [971.9]

17017 Barlas, Robert, and Norman Tompsett. *Canada* (5–8). Series: Countries of the World. 1998, Gareth Stevens LB $29.26 (0-8368-2123-8). Using maps, illustrations, concise text, and a quick facts section, this book gives basic information about Canada, with particular attention to education and politics. (Rev: BL 12/15/98; HBG 9/99; SLJ 2/99) [971]

17018 Beattie, Owen, and John Geiger. *Buried in Ice: The Mystery of a Lost Arctic Expedition* (4–7). Illus. by Janet Wilson. Series: Time Quest. 1993, Scholastic paper $6.95 (0-590-43849-2). 64pp. The story of Sir John Franklin's unsuccessful 1845 expedition from England to find the Northwest Passage. (Rev: BCCB 3/92; BL 4/1/92; SLJ 4/92*) [919.804]

17019 Bowers, Vivien. *Wow Canada! Exploring This Land from Coast to Coast to Coast* (4–6). Illus. 2000, Firefly $29.95 (1-895688-93-0); paper $19.95 (1-895688-94-9). 160pp. A family travels across Canada visiting important sites and gathering material on the land and its people in this relaxed travelogue. (Rev: BL 2/15/00; HBG 10/00; SLJ 4/00) [917.104]

17020 Braun, Eric. *Canada in Pictures*. Rev. ed. (5–9). Illus. Series: Visual Geography. 2003, Lerner LB $27.93 (0-8225-4679-5). 80pp. An informative and interesting overview of Canada's history, geography, government, economy, and people suitable for both research and browsing. (Rev: HBG 10/03; SLJ 7/03) [971.064]

17021 Butler, Geoff. *Ode to Newfoundland* (1–6). Illus. by author. 2003, Tundra $19.95 (0-88776-631-5). 32pp. A picture-book celebration of Newfoundland, with historical notes, lyrics, and music appended. (Rev: HBG 4/04; SLJ 1/04) [971.8]

17022 Campbell, Kumari. *Prince Edward Island* (3–6). Illus. Series: Hello Canada. 1996, Lerner LB $19.93 (0-8225-2762-6). 72pp. This volume highlights Canada's island province, its inhabitants, history, famous people, and economy. (Rev: BL 4/15/96) [971.7]

17023 *Canada in Pictures* (4–6). Series: Visual Geography. 1993, Lerner LB $21.27 (0-8225-1870-8). 64pp. In four separate sections that explore the land, the history and government, the people, and the economy, the basic facts about Canada and Canadians are presented. (Rev: SLJ 2/90) [971]

17024 *Christmas in Canada: Christmas Around the World from World Book* (4–6). Illus. 1994, World Book $18.50 (0-7166-0894-4). 80pp. An overview of how several ethnic groups in Canada spend their Christmas, with asides about special rituals and traditions. (Rev: BL 12/15/94) [394.26]

17025 Cooper, Michael. *Klondike Fever: The Famous Gold Rush of 1898* (5–8). Illus. 1990, Houghton Mifflin paper $6.95 (0-395-54784-9). 80pp. The events that turned a remote part of the Yukon into a three-ring circus of gold-hungry prospectors. (Rev: BCCB 1/90; BL 11/15/89; HB 1–2/90) [971.9]

17026 Coulter, Tony. *Jacques Cartier, Samuel de Champlain, and the Explorers of Canada* (5–8). Illus. Series: World Explorers. 1993, Chelsea LB $21.95 (0-7910-1298-0). This book about the early exploration of Canada includes material on Cartier, Champlain, Cabot, and Hudson, among others. (Rev: BL 1/1/93) [971]

17027 Daitch, Richard W. *Northwest Territories* (3–6). Illus. Series: Hello Canada. 1996, Lerner $19.93 (0-8225-2761-8). 72pp. A remote northern part of Canada is featured in this book, with material on its people, history, government, and economy. (Rev: BL 4/15/96) [971.9]

17028 Ekoomiak, Normee. *Arctic Memories* (3–5). Illus. 1990, Holt paper $5.95 (0-8050-2347-X). 32pp. Memories of an Inuit artist who was raised in the James Bay area of Arctic Quebec. (Rev: BCCB 3/90; BL 3/1/90; HB 5–6/90; SLJ 4/90) [998]

17029 Grabowski, John. *Canada* (5–8). Illus. Series: Overview: Modern Nations of the World. 1997, Lucent LB $27.45 (1-56006-520-6). A fine introduction to Canada and its people with coverage of major cities, industry, art and culture, government, and the separatist movement in Quebec. (Rev: BL 6/1–15/98; SLJ 8/98) [971]

17030 Greenwood, Barbara. *Gold Rush Fever: A Story of the Klondike, 1898* (4–7). Illus. by Heather Collins. 2001, Kids Can $18.95 (1-55074-852-1); paper $12.95 (1-55074-850-5). 160pp. Thirteen-year-old Tim and his older brother trek to the Yukon to try to win their fortune in this account that interweaves fact and fiction, with many details about the hardships the miners faced. (Rev: BL 12/15/01; HBG 10/02; SLJ 10/01) [971.91]

17031 Gresko, Marcia. *Letters Home from Canada* (3–5). Series: Letters Home From. 2000, Blackbirch LB $16.95 (1-56711-410-5). 32pp. Using full-color photos on every page and a letter format, this book covers basic topics about Canada, including the land, people, cities, wildlife, and history. (Rev: BL 5/15/00; HBG 10/00) [971]

17032 Hamilton, Janice. *Canada* (3–5). Illus. Series: Globe-Trotters Club. 1999, Carolrhoda LB $22.60 (1-57505-108-7). 48pp. A fine introduction to Canada for young readers that includes material on history, geography, culture, religion, and present-day conditions. (Rev: BL 9/15/99; HBG 10/99) [971]

17033 Hamilton, Janice. *Canada* (1–3). Illus. Series: A Ticket To. 1999, Carolrhoda LB $22.60 (1-57505-133-8). 48pp. A basic, well-illustrated introduction to Canada, the land and its people. (Rev: BL 9/15/99; HBG 10/99) [971]

17034 Hamilton, Janice. *Quebec* (3–6). Illus. Series: Hello Canada. 1996, Lerner LB $19.93 (0-8225-2766-9). 72pp. This Canadian province, currently divided about its political future, is featured, with

material on its heritage, geography, and economy. (Rev: BL 4/15/96) [971.4]

17035 Hancock, Lyn. *Nunavut* (3–6). Illus. Series: Hello Canada. 1995, Lerner LB $19.93 (0-8225-2758-8). 76pp. Basic information is given on this Canadian territory founded in 1993 from the eastern part of the Northwest Territories. (Rev: BL 12/15/95) [971.9]

17036 Harrison, Ted. *O Canada* (2–5). Illus. 1993, Ticknor $14.95 (0-395-66075-0). 32pp. A brief province-by-province tour of Canada, with paintings by the author. (Rev: BCCB 9/93; BL 10/15/93; SLJ 8/93) [971]

17037 Haugen, Brenda. *Canada ABCs: A Book About the People and Places of Canada* (2–4). Illus. by David Shaw. Series: Country ABCs. 2004, Picture Window LB $23.93 (1-4048-0285-1). 32pp. Young researchers will find useful facts in this alphabetically organized volume. (Rev: SLJ 8/04) [971]

17038 Hughes, Susan. *Let's Call It Canada: Amazing Stories of Canadian Place Names* (3–6). Illus. by Clive Dobson and Jolie Dobson. 2003, Maple Tree $26.95 (1-894379-49-7); paper $16.95 (1-894379-50-0). 96pp. A topically organized compendium of Canadian place names and the interesting stories behind them. (Rev: SLJ 7/03) [917.1]

17039 Jackson, Lawrence. *Newfoundland and Labrador* (3–6). Illus. Series: Hello Canada. 1995, Lerner LB $19.93 (0-8225-2757-X). 72pp. A slim volume that presents a guided tour of these regions of Canada, with coverage on history, economic development, principal cities, and important residents, past and present. (Rev: BL 12/15/95) [971.8]

17040 Kalman, Bobbie. *Canada: The Culture*. Rev. ed. (4–6). Series: The Lands, Peoples, and Cultures. 2001, Crabtree LB $15.45 (0-7787-9360-5); paper $7.16 (0-7787-9728-7). 32pp. This revised and updated edition includes Native, French, and English perspectives as well as discussion of refugees. Also use *Canada: The Land* and *Canada: The People* (both 2002). (Rev: SLJ 6/02)

17041 Kalman, Bobbie. *Canada Celebrates Multiculturalism* (3–5). Illus. Series: Lands, Peoples, and Cultures. 1993, Crabtree LB $20.60 (0-86505-220-4); paper $7.95 (0-86505-300-6). 32pp. Some topics covered are the beginnings of multiculturalism in Canada, religious and heritage days, cross-cultural festivals, and the traditions of various ethnic groups. (Rev: BL 2/1/94) [971]

17042 Major, Kevin. *Eh? to Zed* (2–4). Illus. 2001, Red Deer $16.95 (0-88995-222-1). 32pp. Canadian history and diverse culture are presented in an alphabet running from "Arctic, apple, aurora, Anik" to "Zamboni, zipper, zinc, zed." (Rev: BL 6/1–15/01; SLJ 7/01) [421.1]

17043 Marx, David F. *Canada* (1–2). Illus. Series: Rookie Readers. 2000, Children's Book Pr. LB $19.00 (0-516-21550-7); paper $6.95 (0-516-27083-4). 32pp. This book for beginning readers gives a quick introduction to Canada, its history, people, and languages. (Rev: BL 12/1/00) [971]

17044 Newhouse, Maxwell. *The RCMP Musical Ride* (4–6). Illus. by author. 2004, Tundra $15.95 (0-88776-683-8). A lively, behind-the-scenes look at the horseback displays performed by the Royal Canadian Mounted Police. (Rev: SLJ 9/04) [363.2]

17045 Olson, Nathan. *Canada* (3–4). Illus. Series: Fact Finders: Questions and Answers. 2004, Capstone LB $22.60 (0-7368-2686-6). 32pp. Using a question-and-answer format, this title introduces Canada's history, government, economy, education, culture, sports, and lifestyle. (Rev: SLJ 1/05) [971]

17046 Pang, Guek-Cheng. *Canada.* 2nd ed. (5–9). Illus. Series: Cultures of the World. 2004, Benchmark LB $25.95 (0-7614-1788-5). 144pp. History, geography, and culture are all covered in this useful volume that attempts to impart a comprehensive understanding of life in all parts of Canada. (Rev: SLJ 2/05) [971]

17047 Quigley, Mary. *Canada* (1–3). Illus. Series: A Visit To. 2003, Heinemann LB $22.79 (1-4034-0964-1). 32pp. Full of photographs, this is a useful and interesting overview of the country's geography, history, and culture, suitable for beginning readers. (Rev: HBG 10/03; SLJ 7/03) [971]

17048 Richardson, Gillian. *Saskatchewan* (3–6). Illus. Series: Hello Canada. 1995, Lerner LB $19.93 (0-8225-2760-X). 72pp. This introduction to Canada's midwestern province and bread basket includes material on history, geography, resources, and famous people. (Rev: BL 12/15/95) [971.24]

17049 Robinson, Deborah B. *The Cree of North America* (4–6). Series: First Peoples. 2002, Lerner LB $23.93 (0-8225-4178-5). This book describes the culture and history of the Cree of North America, who are found primarily in subarctic Canada. (Rev: BL 5/15/02; HBG 10/02) [971]

17050 Rogers, Barbara Radcliffe, and Stillman D. Rogers. *Canada* (4–7). Series: Enchantment of the World. 2000, Children's Book Pr. LB $34.50 (0-516-21076-9). 144pp. This fine introduction to Canada, its land and its people, also contains coverage of its history, economy, plants and animals, languages, sports, and the arts. (Rev: BL 1/1–15/01) [971]

17051 Rowe, Percy. *Toronto* (3–6). Series: Great Cities of the World. 2003, World Almanac LB $29.26 (0-8368-5026-2). 48pp. Color photographs enliven this in-depth look at Canada's most populous city, with detailed information on its history, economy, and the lives of its residents. (Rev: SLJ 3/04) [971.3]

17052 Rowe, Percy, and Patience Coster. *Montreal* (3–6). Series: Great Cities of the World. 2004, World Almanac LB $30.00 (0-8368-5039-4). 48pp. Montreal's history, geography, and economy are described, as are shopping and leisure attractions and the life of the city. (Rev: SLJ 4/05)

17053 Shepherd, Jennifer. *Canada* (4–7). Illus. 1988, Children's Book Pr. paper $32.00 (0-516-02757-3). 128pp. Geography, history, climate, and people are discussed in this look at the northern U.S. neighbor. (Rev: BL 5/15/88; SLJ 8/88) [971]

17054 Siy, Alexandra. *The Eeyou: People of Eastern James Bay* (4–7). Illus. Series: Global Villages. 1993, Macmillan $14.95 (0-87518-549-5). 80pp. Introduces the Indian culture of the Eeyou, a people with their own writing system. (Rev: BCCB 7–8; SLJ 8/93) [970]

17055 Strudwick, Leslie. *Inuit* (4–6). Illus. Series: Indigenous Peoples. 2004, Weigl LB $18.20 (1-59036-149-0). 32pp. Historical and contemporary issues are both covered in this detailed portrait of life among the Inuit. (Rev: BL 4/1/04) [971.9004]

17056 Thompson, Alexa. *Nova Scotia* (4–8). Series: Hello Canada. 1995, Lerner LB $19.93 (0-8225-2759-6). Nova Scotia's history, geography, and the economy are covered, with material on the various peoples and cultures. (Rev: SLJ 3/96) [971.6]

17057 Whitcraft, Melissa. *The Niagara River* (4–8). Series: Watts Library. 2001, Watts LB $24.00 (0-531-11903-3). 63pp. This absorbing and readable account with maps and historical and contemporary photographs looks at the river's history, industry, and impact on the surrounding region. (Rev: SLJ 5/01) [971.3]

17058 Williams, Suzanne M. *The Inuit* (4–6). Series: Watts Library. 2003, Watts LB $24.00 (0-531-12172-0); paper $8.95 (0-531-16235-4). 63pp. The author profiles an Inuit family in Canada's far north, showing how they combine aspects of traditional and modern life. (Rev: SLJ 5/04) [971.9]

17059 Yates, Sarah. *Alberta* (4–8). Series: Hello Canada. 1995, Lerner LB $19.93 (0-8225-2763-4). A colorful, slim volume that crams many facts about this western Canadian province's culture, history, geography, and resources into a few attractive pages. (Rev: BL 12/15/95; SLJ 3/96) [971.23]

Mexico

17060 Ancona, George. *The Fiestas* (3–6). Illus. Series: Viva Mexico! 2001, Marshall Cavendish LB $16.95 (0-7614-1327-8). 48pp. One in a series of visually exciting photoessay books for older readers about Mexican culture and traditions that also includes *The Folk Arts* and *The Foods* (both 2001). (Rev: BL 3/1/02; HBG 3/02; SLJ 2/02) [394.26972]

17061 Ancona, George. *Pablo Remembers: The Fiesta of the Day of the Dead* (3–6). Illus. 1993, Lothrop $16.95 (0-688-11249-8). 48pp. The customs and traditions surrounding the three-day Mexican celebration, the Fiesta of the Day of the Dead, are described in this photoessay. A Spanish-language edition is also available. (Rev: BCCB 12/93; BL 2/1/94; SLJ 12/93) [393.9]

17062 Ancona, George. *The Pinata Maker / El Piñatero* (1–3). Illus. 1994, Harcourt $17.00 (0-15-261875-9); paper $9.00 (0-15-200060-7). 40pp. Many Mexican crafts, like the piñata and puppet making, are highlighted when a group of children visit an aged craftsman in this dual-language book. (Rev: BL 2/15/94; HB 7–8/94; SLJ 4/94) [745]

17063 Arnold, Helen. *Mexico* (1–3). Illus. Series: Postcards From. 1995, Raintree LB $22.83 (0-8172-4012-8). 32pp. A quick overview of Mexico is

given through a series of postcards written by fictitious children. (Rev: SLJ 2/96) [972]

17064 Berendes, Mary. *Mexico* (K–3). Illus. Series:
Faces and Places. 1997, Child's World LB $22.79
(1-56766-372-9). 32pp. Concisely describes the
land, plants, animals, history, and culture of Mexico. (Rev: SLJ 2/98) [972]

17065 Bulmer-Thomas, Barbara. *Journey Through
Mexico* (3–5). Illus. by Martin Camm. Series: Journey Around the World. 1990, Troll paper $4.95 (0-
8167-2117-3). 32pp. Mexico, a mix of Native
American traditions and the culture of the conquis-
tadores, is introduced in colorful photos and text.
(Rev: BL 5/15/91) [972]

17066 Burr, Claudia, et al. *When the Viceroy Came*
(3–5). Illus. 1999, Groundwood $15.95 (0-88899-
354-4). 33pp. Told from a young boy's point of
view, this slice of Mexican history relates how the
new Spanish viceroy came to Mexico in 1702. (Rev:
BL 8/99; SLJ 8/99) [972]

17067 Chapman, Gillian. *The Aztecs* (4–8). Series:
Crafts from the Past. 1997, Heinemann LB $25.64
(1-57572-555-X). A craft book with instructions for
a variety of Aztec ornaments and artifacts, including
textiles and statues. (Rev: SLJ 4/98) [745]

17068 Chrisp, Peter. *The Aztecs* (4–6). Series: History Beneath Your Feet. 1999, Raintree LB $25.69 (0-
8172-5753-5). 48pp. Using authentic drawings and
paintings, this account presents the daily life of the
Aztecs and how archaeologists have gathered this
information. (Rev: HBG 10/00; SLJ 3/00) [972]

17069 Conlon, Laura. *People of Mexico* (2–4). Illus.
Series: South of the Border. 1994, Rourke LB
$15.93 (1-55916-052-7). 24pp. Introduces the vari-
ous peoples of Mexico and where they live in a simple text with many attractive color photos. Also use
in this series *Products of Mexico, Visiting Mexico*,
and *Wonders of Mexico* (all 1994). (Rev: SLJ 2/95)
[972]

17070 Cory, Steve. *Daily Life in Ancient and Modern Mexico City* (3–6). Illus. by Ray Webb. Series:
Cities Through Time. 1999, Runestone LB $17.95
(0-8225-3212-3). 64pp. Daily life in Mexico City
during the time of the Aztecs and the Spanish conquest is presented, followed by information on the
city today. (Rev: HBG 10/99; SLJ 6/99) [972]

17071 Dawson, Imogen. *Clothes and Crafts in
Ancient Aztec Times* (4–6). Series: Clothing and
Crafts in History. 2000, Gareth Stevens LB $21.27
(0-8368-2735-X). 32pp. Covers Aztec crafts such as
stoneworking, pottery, basketmaking, metalwork,
weaving, and textiles, as well as outlining several
projects including face painting and making an
Aztec headband. (Rev: BL 1/1–15/01; HBG 3/02)
[972]

17072 Flint, David. *Mexico* (2–4). Illus. Series: On
the Map. 1993, Raintree LB $22.83 (0-8114-3419-
2). 32pp. Such topics as geography, history, customs, lifestyles, and landmarks are covered in this
well-illustrated introduction to Mexico. (Rev: BL
2/1/94) [972]

17073 Franklin, Sharon, et al. *Mexico and Central
America* (4–7). Illus. Series: Artisans Around the

World. 1999, Raintree LB $27.12 (0-7398-0121-X).
48pp. This craft book, with related projects,
describes the folk art of each of the countries in
Central America and Mexico. (Rev: BL 10/15/99;
HBG 3/00; SLJ 1/00) [745.5]

17074 Furlong, Kate A. *Mexico* (2–4). Series: Countries. 2000, ABDO LB $14.95 (1-57765-390-4).
40pp. An adequate, brief introduction to Mexico
that contains excellent photographs, a timeline, and
a recipe. (Rev: HBG 10/01; SLJ 3/01) [972]

17075 Hamilton, Janice. *Mexico in Pictures*. Rev. ed.
(4–8). Illus. Series: Visual Geography. 2002, Lerner
LB $27.93 (0-8225-1960-7). 80pp. An excellent
introduction to Mexico that includes material on
geography, history, people, economy, and culture
with maps, photographs, and illustrations. (Rev:
HBG 3/03; SLJ 3/03) [972]

17076 Heinrichs, Ann. *Mexico* (4–6). Series: True
Books. 1997, Children's Book Pr. LB $22.00 (0-
516-20337-1). 48pp. Basic materials on Mexico —
history, geography, culture, and the people — is
covered in this attractive title with many bright photos and a map. (Rev: BL 9/15/97; HBG 3/98; SLJ
11/97) [972]

17077 Higginson, Mel. *Wildlife of Mexico* (2–4).
Illus. Series: South of the Border. 1994, Rourke LB
$15.93 (1-55916-055-1). 24pp. The flora and fauna
of Mexico are introduced in a heavily illustrated
volume with an easy-to-read text. (Rev: SLJ 2/95)
[972]

17078 Hodgkins, Fran. *Mexico* (2–5). Illus. Series:
Questions and Answers: Countries. 2004, Capstone
LB $16.95 (0-7368-2479-0). 32pp. Using a ques-
tion-and-answer format, simple text, large photos,
and many factboxes, this is an introduction to Mexico today, with material on history and traditional
culture. (Rev: SLJ 3/05)

17079 Hull, Robert. *The Aztecs* (5–10). Series:
Ancient World. 1998, Raintree LB $27.12 (0-8172-
5056-5). 64pp. This history of the Aztecs and their
culture describes their great pyramids, feathered
headdresses, gods, human sacrifices, and the coming of the Spanish. (Rev: BL 1/1–15/99; HBG 3/99)
[972]

17080 Illsley, Linda. *Mexico* (3–5). Series: Foods
and Festivals. 1999, Raintree LB $22.83 (0-8172-
5553-2). 32pp. An overview of festivals celebrated
in Mexico, the special foods associated with each,
and four simple recipes to prepare authentic Mexican holiday food. (Rev: BL 5/15/99; HBG 10/99;
SLJ 7/99) [972]

17081 Jermyn, Leslie. *Mexico* (5–8). Series: Countries of the World. 1998, Gareth Stevens LB $29.26
(0-8368-2127-0). Good basic information about
Mexico, particularly in the areas of education and
politics, is presented through clear text, full-page
illustrations, maps, and a quick facts section. (Rev:
BL 12/15/98; HBG 9/99; SLJ 2/99) [972]

17082 Jermyn, Leslie, and Fiona Conboy. *Welcome
to Mexico* (2–4). Series: Welcome to My Country.
1999, Gareth Stevens LB $16.95 (0-8368-2398-2).
48pp. A heavily illustrated introduction to Mexico
with coverage of the land and its people, history,

daily life, food, and government. (Rev: HBG 10/00; SLJ 3/00) [972]

17083 Jovinelly, Joann, and Jason Netelkos. *The Crafts and Culture of the Aztecs* (5–8). Illus. Series: Crafts of the Ancient World. 2002, Rosen LB $29.25 (0-8239-3512-4). 48pp. The culture of the Aztecs is covered through a discussion of their crafts and a variety of easily accomplished projects related to them. (Rev: BL 4/1/02) [972]

17084 Kent, Deborah. *Mexico: Rich in Spirit and Tradition* (4–8). Series: Exploring Cultures of the World. 1995, Benchmark LB $27.07 (0-7614-0187-3). This book begins with a Mexican folktale, then gives an overview of the country's people, culture, history, and problems. (Rev: SLJ 6/96) [972]

17085 Lasky, Kathryn. *Days of the Dead* (3–6). Illus. by Christopher G. Knight. 1994, Hyperion LB $16.49 (0-7868-2018-7). 48pp. Through the story of a single Mexican family, the customs and significance of the Days of the Dead are revealed. (Rev: BCCB 10/94; BL 10/15/94; SLJ 10/94) [394.2]

17086 Laufer, Peter. *Made in Mexico* (K–4). Illus. by Susan L. Roth. 2000, National Geographic $16.95 (0-7922-7118-1). A beautifully illustrated book that describes the guitar-making business that flourishes in the remote village of Paracho in Mexico. (Rev: HBG 10/00; SLJ 4/00) [972]

17087 Lewington, Anna. *Mexico* (5–8). Illus. Series: Economically Developing Countries. 1996, Raintree LB $24.26 (0-8172-4528-6). A fine general profile of Mexico that includes jobs, industries, and other economic indicators. (Rev: BL 3/15/97; SLJ 2/97) [330.972]

17088 Lewis, Elizabeth. *Mexican Art and Culture* (5–8). Illus. Series: World Art and Culture. 2004, Raintree LB $29.99 (0-7398-6610-9). 56pp. The indigenous art and culture of Mexico from prehistoric times to the present are beautifully captured in this handsome and comprehensive overview. (Rev: BL 4/1/04; HBG 4/04; SLJ 2/04) [709]

17089 Lewis, Thomas P. *Hill of Fire* (1–3). Illus. by Joan Sandin. 1971, HarperCollins LB $15.89 (0-06-023804-6); paper $3.95 (0-06-444040-0). 64pp. The eruption of the volcano Paricutin and its effect on the lives of the people.

17090 Libura, Krystyna, et al. *What the Aztecs Told Me* (4–8). Illus. 1997, Douglas & McIntyre $15.95 (0-88899-305-6); paper $6.95 (0-88899-306-4). Based on an original 12-volume work written in the 16th century, this book describes the Aztec people from observation and eyewitness accounts. (Rev: BL 12/1/97; HB 11–12/97; HBG 3/98; SLJ 12/97) [972]

17091 MacDonald, Fiona. *You Wouldn't Want to Be an Aztec Sacrifice! Gruesome Things You'd Rather Not Know* (4–6). Illus. by David Antram. Series: You Wouldn't Want To. 2001, Watts LB $25.00 (0-531-14602-2); paper $9.95 (0-531-16209-5). 32pp. The circumstances of human sacrifice — and potential ways of avoiding this fate — are discussed with some black humor. (Rev: SLJ 3/02) [972]

17092 MacMillan, Dianne M. *Mexican Independence Day and Cinco de Mayo* (3–5). Series: Best

Holiday. 1997, Enslow LB $18.95 (0-89490-816-2). 48pp. The history of Mexico is interwoven in the description of these related holidays, with material on how they are celebrated. (Rev: BL 12/15/97; HBG 3/98; SLJ 8/97) [972]

17093 Marquez, Heron. *Destination Veracruz* (5–8). Series: Port Cities of North America. 1998, Lerner LB $23.93 (0-8225-2791-X). A description of this port city on the Gulf of Mexico that reviews its history, everyday life, the effects of development on the environment, and the city's economy, including the impact of NAFTA and a discussion of international trade, economic systems, and free trade. (Rev: HBG 3/99; SLJ 3/99) [972]

17094 *Mexico in Pictures* (4–7). Illus. 1994, Lerner LB $21.27 (0-8225-1801-5). 64pp. An introduction to our south-of-the-border neighbor. (Rev: BL 8/87)

17095 Milord, Susan. *Mexico! 50 Activities to Experience Mexico Past and Present* (3–7). Series: A Kaleidoscope Kids Book. 1999, Williamson paper $10.95 (1-885593-22-8). 96pp. The author presents a survey of Mexican history and culture from ancient history through the Spanish conquest to the present day, followed by craft projects that include a piñata, a skull for Day of the Dead, and recipes for salsa, tortillas, and hot chocolate. (Rev: SLJ 5/99) [972]

17096 Odijk, Pamela. *The Aztecs* (4–7). Illus. Series: Ancient World. 1990, Silver Burdett LB $14.95 (0-382-09887-0). 48pp. A well-illustrated account of the rise and fall of the ancient Mexican civilization. (Rev: BL 7/90; SLJ 8/90) [972]

17097 Olawsky, Lynn A. *Colors of Mexico* (2–5). Illus. by Janice L. Porter. Series: Colors of the World. 1997, Carolrhoda LB $20.76 (0-87614-886-0); paper $5.95 (1-57505-216-4). 24pp. Ten different colors are used to introduce facts about Mexico, its history, geography, traditions, and people. (Rev: HBG 3/98; SLJ 10/97) [972]

17098 Rees, Rosemary. *The Aztecs* (3–6). Illus. Series: Understanding People in the Past. 1999, Heinemann LB $15.95 (1-57572-888-5). 64pp. Topics such as Aztec history, culture, floating gardens, food, feasts, and sports are covered in a series of double-page spreads. (Rev: BL 6/1–15/99) [972]

17099 Reilly, Mary J. *Mexico* (5–8). Illus. Series: Cultures of the World. 1991, Marshall Cavendish LB $35.64 (1-85435-385-3). 128pp. This account emphasizes the geography, history, economy, and lifestyles of the Mexican people. (Rev: BL 4/1/91) [972]

17100 Rosenblum, Morris. *Heroes of Mexico* (5–8). 1972, Fleet $9.50 (0-8303-0082-1). A collected group of profiles of people important in the history of Mexico. (Rev: BL 6/87) [972]

17101 Rummel, Jack. *Mexico*. Rev. ed. (4–7). Series: Major World Nations. 1998, Chelsea LB $19.95 (0-7910-4763-6). 128pp. This guide supplies a fine introduction to Mexico, the land and the people, with good coverage on current problems. (Rev: HBG 3/99; SLJ 12/98) [972]

17102 Sanna, Ellyn. *Mexico: Facts and Figures* (5–8). Series: Mexico: Our Southern Neighbor.

2002, Mason Crest LB $19.95 (1-59084-088-7). 64pp. An introduction to Mexico and its states, with material on history, people and culture today, and issues of importance such as poverty. Also use *The Geography of Mexico, The Economy of Mexico,* and *The Government of Mexico*. (Rev: SLJ 12/02) [972]

17103 Shepherd, Donna Walsh. *The Aztecs* (4–6). Illus. 1992, Watts paper $6.95 (0-531-15634-6). 64pp. Covers the history, culture, and society of the ancient Aztec civilization of Mexico and its fate under the Spanish conquerers. (Rev: BL 6/15/92; SLJ 8/92) [972]

17104 Staub, Frank. *The Children of the Sierra Madre* (3–6). Illus. Series: The World's Children. 1996, Carolrhoda LB $14.96 (0-87614-943-4); paper $7.95 (0-87614-967-0). 48pp. The young people of the Sierra Madre and their social conditions are discussed, with additional historical information. (Rev: BL 10/1/96; SLJ 8/96) [972]

17105 Staub, Frank. *Children of Yucatan* (3–6). Illus. Series: The World's Children. 1996, Carolrhoda LB $23.93 (0-87614-984-0). 48pp. The daily activities and social conditions of children in this remote part of Mexico are featured, along with good background information. (Rev: BCCB 11/96; BL 10/1/96; SLJ 10/96) [972]

17106 Stein, R. Conrad. *The Aztec Empire* (5–8). Series: Cultures of the Past. 1995, Benchmark LB $28.50 (0-7614-0072-9). The Aztecs' history, beliefs, and lifestyles are examined in this book, with quotations from original sources and many color photographs of artifacts, monuments, and historical sites. (Rev: BR 9–10/96; SLJ 6/96) [972]

17107 Wolf, Bernard. *Beneath the Stone: A Mexican Zapotec Tale* (4–6). Illus. 1994, Orchard LB $17.99 (0-531-08685-2). 48pp. In photos and text, several months in the life of a Zapotec Indian family in Mexico are followed, with descriptions of their holidays and family business. (Rev: BL 3/15/94; SLJ 8/94) [972]

17108 Wood, Marion. *Growing Up in Aztec Times* (3–5). Illus. by Richard Hook. Series: Growing Up In. 1993, Troll paper $4.95 (0-8167-2724-4). 32pp. Describes Aztec community life and their beliefs, customs, and rituals, with details on the education of children. (Rev: BL 1/15/94) [972]

17109 Wyborny, Sheila. *The Aztec Empire* (4–6). Illus. Series: Life During the Great Civilizations. 2004, Gale/Blackbirch LB $18.96 (1-56711-736-8). 48pp. Wyborny explores day-to-day life among the Aztecs, looking at everything from clothes and jobs to social structures, medicine, and religion. (Rev: BL 5/15/04; SLJ 8/04) [972]

Other Central American Lands

17110 Adams, Faith. *El Salvador: Beauty Among the Ashes* (4–6). Illus. 1986, Macmillan $14.95 (0-87518-309-3). 136pp. Basic facts on geography, culture, and history are combined with a sensitive look at the lives of Salvadorans today. (Rev: BCCB 2/86; BL 3/1/86; SLJ 3/86)

17111 Adams, Faith. *Nicaragua: Struggling with Change* (5–8). Illus. 1987, Macmillan LB $14.95 (0-87518-340-9). 152pp. A balanced telling of a troubled Central American country's story. (Rev: BL 5/15/87; SLJ 8/87) [972.85]

17112 Brill, Marlene T., and Harry R. Targ. *Guatemala* (5–8). Illus. Series: Enchantment of the World. 1993, Children's Book Pr. paper $32.00 (0-516-02614-3). 128pp. This introduction to Guatemala covers history, geography, people, and culture. (Rev: BL 8/93) [972.8]

17113 Coulter, Laurie. *Secrets in Stone: All About Maya Hieroglyphs* (3–6). Illus. by Sarah Jane English. 2001, Little, Brown $17.95 (0-316-15883-6). 48pp. Coulter describes the process through which Mayan hieroglyphs were finally deciphered and explains the Mayan number system and calendar, as well as providing a chart of common glyphs, crafts and activities, and a timeline, glossary, and list of resources. (Rev: BL 12/15/01; HBG 3/02; SLJ 4/02) [497]

17114 Day, Nancy. *Your Travel Guide to Ancient Mayan Civilization* (4–8). Series: Passport to History. 2000, Lerner LB $26.60 (0-8225-3077-5). 96pp. Using the format of a modern-day travel guide, this book explores the ancient Mayan cities of Uzmal, Tikal, Copan, and others to discover the lifestyles of the Maya, their food, clothes, religion, discoveries, and behavior. (Rev: BL 3/1/01; HBG 10/01; SLJ 4/01) [972]

17115 Deady, Kathleen W. *El Salvador* (2–5). Illus. Series: Questions and Answers: Countries. 2005, Capstone LB $16.95 (0-7368-3750-7). 32pp. Using a question-and-answer format, simple text, large photos, and many factboxes, this is an introduction to El Salvador today, with material on history and traditional culture.

17116 Fisher, Frederick. *Costa Rica* (2–4). Series: Festivals of the World. 1999, Gareth Stevens LB $15.95 (0-8368-2022-3). 32pp. Lists the holidays celebrated in Costa Rica, profiles the main ones, and provides related crafts and recipes. (Rev: BL 12/15/99; HBG 10/00) [972.86]

17117 Franklin, Kristine L., and Nancy McGirr, eds. *Out of the Dump: Writings and Photographs by Children from Guatemala* (4–8). Illus. 1996, Lothrop LB $18.93 (0-688-13924-8). 56pp. A photographic essay that focuses on the poor children who exist by scavenging in the garbage dump of Guatemala City. (Rev: BCCB 3/96; BL 3/15/96*; SLJ 4/96*) [861]

17118 Freedman, Russell. *In the Days of the Vaqueros: America's First True Cowboys* (5–9). Illus. 2001, Clarion $18.00 (0-395-96788-0). 70pp. Vivid artwork complements this history of the earliest cowboys, the Central American vaqueros who first rode the range in the late 15th century. (Rev: BL 11/15/01*; HB 1–2/02; HBG 3/02; SLJ 9/01) [636.2]

17119 Gaines, Ann. *The Panama Canal in American History* (4–8). Series: In American History. 1999, Enslow LB $20.95 (0-7660-1216-6). This is a carefully researched history of the building of the Panama Canal, including a review of events before U.S. involvement, how the United States established the country of Panama and gained control of the Canal Zone, details of the many difficulties encountered, and a description of how the canal locks operate. (Rev: BL 3/1/99; HBG 10/99; SLJ 8/99) [972.87]

17120 Garcia, Guy. *Spirit of the Maya: A Boy Explores His People's Mysterious Past* (4–6). Illus. 1995, Walker LB $17.85 (0-8027-8380-5). 48pp. A young Mayan boy discovers his heritage when he explores the ruins at Palenque and learns of the boy-king Pacal, who is buried there. (Rev: BCCB 12/95; BL 10/1/95; SLJ 1/96) [972]

17121 Grandell, Rachel. *Hands of the Maya: Villagers at Work and Play* (K–3). Illus. 2002, Holt $16.95 (0-8050-6687-X). 32pp. This photoessay takes readers through a day in a Mayan town and shows typical activities and recreations. (Rev: BL 5/1/02; HB 9–10/02; HBG 3/03; SLJ 8/02) [972.83]

17122 Greene, Jacqueline D. *The Maya* (3–5). Illus. Series: First Books. 1992, Watts LB $22.50 (0-531-20067-1). 64pp. This account explores the daily life of the Central American civilization that survived for thousands of years. (Rev: BL 6/15/92; SLJ 8/92) [972.81]

17123 Hassig, Susan M. *Panama* (4–7). Illus. Series: Cultures of the World. 1996, Marshall Cavendish LB $35.64 (0-7614-0278-0). 128pp. The troubled history of Panama is covered, with material on geography and the lifestyle and culture of its people. (Rev: BL 8/96) [972.87]

17124 Haverstock, Nathan A. *Nicaragua in Pictures* (5–8). Illus. 1993, Lerner LB $25.55 (0-8225-1817-1). 64pp. A visit to this controversial country is highlighted by color photographs and clear text. (Rev: BL 10/15/87) [972.85]

17125 *Honduras in Pictures* (4–7). Illus. Series: Visual Geography. 1994, Lerner LB $25.55 (0-8225-1804-X). 64pp. Chapters focus on history, culture, education, people, geography, and lifestyles. (Rev: BL 8/87)

17126 Jermyn, Leslie. *Belize* (5–9). Series: Cultures of the World. 2001, Marshall Cavendish LB $35.64 (0-7614-1190-9). 128pp. Geography, history, government, arts and culture, and lifestyle are all covered in this interesting and attractive volume. (Rev: HBG 10/01; SLJ 11/01) [972.82]

17127 Lindop, Edmund. *Panama and the United States: Divided by the Canal* (5–8). Illus. 1997, Twenty-First Century LB $23.40 (0-8050-4768-9). A history of United States-Panama relations, from the building of the canal to the present. (Rev: BL 8/97; BR 11–12/97; SLJ 7/97) [327.7307287]

17128 McGaffey, Leta. *Honduras* (5–9). Series: Cultures of the World. 1999, Marshall Cavendish LB $35.64 (0-7614-0955-6). 128pp. After background material on the history and geography of Honduras, this book focuses on modern times and such topics as the economy, population, religion, holidays, and recreation. (Rev: HBG 10/99; SLJ 11/99) [972.8]

17129 McNeese, Tim. *The Panama Canal* (5–8). Illus. Series: Building History. 1997, Lucent LB $27.45 (1-56006-425-0). 96pp. A description of the

building of the Panama Canal that also supplies valuable insights into the economic and social conditions of the times. (Rev: BL 8/97; BR 1–2/98; HBG 3/98; SLJ 7/97) [386]

17130 Malone, Michael. *A Guatemalan Family* (4–7). Illus. Series: Journey Between Two Worlds. 1996, Lerner paper $8.95 (0-8225-9742-X). 64pp. The story of a refugee family from Guatemala and of its resettlement in the United States. (Rev: BL 11/15/96; SLJ 1/97) [975.9]

17131 Mann, Elizabeth. *The Panama Canal* (4–6). Illus. Series: Wonders of the World. 1998, Mikaya $19.95 (0-9650493-4-5). 48pp. The story of the construction of the Panama Canal from the failed French attempt by Ferdinand de Lesseps to the American success and opening in 1914. (Rev: BL 2/1/99; SLJ 12/98) [972.87]

17132 Mann, Elizabeth. *Tikal: The Center of the Maya World* (4–8). Illus. by Tom McNeely. Series: Wonders of the World. 2002, Mikaya $19.95 (1-931414-05-X). 48pp. Mann provides an overview for older readers of the Mayan city of Tikal, covering the location, the people, the architecture, the culture, and their sometimes bloodthirsty customs. (Rev: BL 12/15/02; HBG 3/03; SLJ 1/03) [972.81]

17133 Markun, Patricia M. *It's Panama's Canal!* (5–9). Illus. 1999, Linnet LB $22.50 (0-208-02499-9). 103pp. This account gives a good background history of the canal plus current information on Panama's control of the zone and its plans for successful management. (Rev: BL 1/1–15/00; HBG 3/00) [972.87]

17134 Morrison, Marion. *Belize* (5–8). Illus. Series: Enchantment of the World. 1996, Children's Book Pr. paper $32.00 (0-516-02639-9). 124pp. An introduction to the small Central American nation, formerly called British Honduras. (Rev: BL 7/96) [972.82]

17135 Morrison, Marion. *Nicaragua* (4–7). Series: Enchantment of the World. 2002, Children's Book Pr. LB $34.50 (0-516-20963-9). 144pp. Such topics as geography, history, people, language, economy, and government are covered in this introduction to Nicaragua. (Rev: BL 5/15/02) [972.8]

17136 Odijk, Pamela. *The Mayas* (4–7). Illus. Series: Ancient World. 1990, Silver Burdett LB $14.95 (0-382-09890-0). 48pp. The history and accomplishments of the Mayas are covered in this illustrated account. (Rev: BL 11/1/90; SLJ 1/91) [972.81]

17137 *Panama in Pictures* (4–7). Illus. Series: Visual Geography. 1996, Lerner LB $25.55 (0-8225-1818-X). 64pp. The life and culture, history, and geography of the people of Panama. (Rev: BL 8/87) [972.87]

17138 Pascoe, Elaine, ed. *Into Wild Panama* (3–6). Series: The Jeff Corwin Experience. 2004, Gale/Blackbirch LB $19.96 (1-56711-856-9). 48pp. Jeff Corwin of TV's Animal Planet series explores the jungles of Panama, where he encounters such creatures as a frog-eating bat. (Rev: SLJ 4/04) [591.9]

17139 Sherrow, Victoria. *The Maya Indians* (3–5). Illus. Series: Junior Library of American Indians. 1993, Chelsea LB $16.95 (0-7910-1666-8). 80pp.

An account of the Mayan culture, principally of the Yucatan area of Mexico and Guatemala, its destruction by the Spaniards, and the present status of the descendants. (Rev: BL 2/15/94; SLJ 2/94) [973.81]

17140 Shields, Charles J. *Belize* (5–7). Illus. Series: Discovering Central America. 2002, Mason Crest LB $19.95 (1-59084-092-5). 64pp. Students needing facts about Belize will find everything here: geography, history, people, and culture, all backed up by maps, photographs, a timeline, and even recipes. (Rev: BL 1/1–15/03) [972.82]

17141 Shields, Charles J. *Central America: Facts and Figures* (5–7). Illus. Series: Discovering Central America. 2002, Mason Crest LB $19.95 (1-59084-099-2). 64pp. This look at Central America as a whole covers history, geography, inhabitants, and cultures. (Rev: BL 1/1–15/03) [972.8]

17142 Silverstone, Michael. *Rigoberta Menchu: Defending Human Rights in Guatemala* (5–8). Illus. 1999, Feminist Pr. $19.95 (1-55861-198-3); paper $9.95 (1-55861-199-1). 112pp. In addition to a biography of Nobel Peace Prize winner Rigoberta Menchu, this account presents Guatemala, its civil war, and the efforts to end it. (Rev: BL 3/15/00) [972.81]

17143 Staub, Frank. *Children of Belize* (3–6). Series: The World's Children. 1997, Carolrhoda $23.93 (1-57505-039-0). 45pp. The reader meets a variety of children from this small Central American country with a unique history and a population of remarkable diversity. (Rev: BL 3/15/98; SLJ 3/98) [972.82]

17144 Turck, Mary. *Mexico and Central America: A Fiesta of Cultures, Crafts, and Activities for Ages 8–12* (3–6). 2004, Chicago Review paper $14.95 (1-55652-525-7). 160pp. Turck provides wide-ranging information on Mexico and the countries of Central America, including items on history, geography, and culture, plus recipes, crafts, and activities. (Rev: BL 8/04; SLJ 8/04) [972]

17145 Vazquez, Ana Maria B. *Panama* (5–8). Illus. Series: Enchantment of the World. 1991, Children's Book Pr. paper $32.00 (0-516-02604-6). 128pp. In addition to historical and geographic information, this book discusses the importance of the canal. (Rev: BL 2/1/92) [972.87]

17146 West, Tracey. *Costa Rica* (3–5). Series: Globe-Trotters Club. 1999, Carolrhoda $22.60 (1-57505-109-5). 48pp. The land of Costa Rica is given a colorful introduction in this informal treatment, which covers the basic topics, with an emphasis on contemporary life. (Rev: BL 9/15/99; HBG 3/00; SLJ 2/00) [972.8]

17147 West, Tracey. *Costa Rica* (1–3). Series: A Ticket To. 1999, Carolrhoda LB $22.60 (1-57505-134-6). 48pp. This beginning glimpse of Costa Rica introduces the country's landscape and its main ethnic and cultural features, using plenty of pictures and a simple text. (Rev: BL 9/15/99; HBG 3/00; SLJ 1/00) [972]

Puerto Rico and Other Caribbean Islands

17148 Ada, Alma F. *Under the Royal Palms: A Childhood in Cuba* (3–6). Illus. 1998, Simon & Schuster $15.00 (0-689-80631-0). 96pp. The story of a little girl growing up in a small town in Cuba is presented in a series of short vignettes. (Rev: BL 11/15/98; HBG 3/99; SLJ 12/98) [813]

17149 Ancona, George. *Cuban Kids* (3–5). Illus. 2000, Marshall Cavendish $15.95 (0-7614-5077-7). 40pp. This photoessay gives a fine picture of contemporary Cuba as seen through the eyes and actions of the country's children at work and at play. (Rev: BL 12/15/00; HBG 3/01; SLJ 1/01) [972.91]

17150 Barlas, Bob. *Jamaica* (2–4). Series: Festivals of the World. 1998, Gareth Stevens LB $18.60 (0-8368-2005-3). 32pp. Introduces the people and culture of Jamaica, describes their most important holidays, and provides related recipes and craft ideas. (Rev: BL 5/15/98; HBG 10/98; SLJ 9/98) [975.9]

17151 Bernier-Grand, Carmen. *Shake It, Morena?* (3–5). Illus. by Lulu Delacre. 2002, Millbrook LB $24.90 (0-7613-1910-7). 48pp. This is a collection of games, songs, riddles, and counting rhymes from Puerto Rico with explanations of origins and cultural backgrounds. (Rev: BL 4/15/02; HBG 10/02) [972.9]

17152 Capek, Michael. *Jamaica* (3–5). Series: Globe-Trotters Club. 1999, Carolrhoda $16.95 (1-57505-112-5). 48pp. Using two-page spreads, this breezy account provides a broad introduction to Jamaica, with many colorful photos, fact boxes, and sidebars. (Rev: BL 9/15/99; HBG 3/00) [972.92]

17153 Capek, Michael. *Jamaica* (1–3). Series: A Ticket To. 1999, Carolrhoda LB $22.60 (1-57505-137-0). 48pp. Color photos and a simple, concise text enhance this first look at Jamaica, which gives basic information about the people and their land. (Rev: BL 9/15/99; HBG 3/00) [972.92]

17154 Cramer, Mark. *Cuba* (4–6). Series: Countries of the World. 2000, Gareth Stevens LB $19.95 (0-8368-2316-8). 96pp. This colorful introduction to Cuba tells about its history, geography, people, current conditions, and relations with the United States and Canada. (Rev: BL 6/1–15/00; HBG 10/00) [972.9]

17155 Davis, Lucile. *Puerto Rico* (5–8). Series: America the Beautiful. 2000, Children's Book Pr. LB $34.00 (0-516-21042-4). 144pp. This introduction to Puerto Rico contains information on the island's history, geography, economy, people, culture, and current concerns. (Rev: BL 5/15/00) [972.95]

17156 Dubois, Muriel L. *Cuba* (2–5). Illus. Series: Questions and Answers: Countries. 2005, Capstone LB $16.95 (0-7368-3749-3). 32pp. Using a question-and-answer format, simple text, large photos, and many factboxes, this is an introduction to Cuba today, with material on history and traditional culture.

17157 Ellis, Royston. *Trinidad* (2–4). Series: Festivals of the World. 1999, Gareth Stevens LB $15.95 (0-8368-2036-3). 32pp. Color photos and a simple text are used to describe the main holidays in Trinidad, how they are celebrated, plus crafts and cooking associated with each. (Rev: BL 12/15/99; HBG 10/00) [972.98]

17158 Englar, Mary. *Dominican Republic* (2–3). Illus. Series: Many Cultures, One World. 2004, Capstone LB $17.95 (0-7368-2453-7). 32pp. A brief, accessible introduction to the Dominican Republic and its people, family life, customs, and legends.

17159 Feeney, Kathy. *Puerto Rico Facts and Symbols* (1–4). Series: States and Their Symbols. 2000, Capstone LB $15.93 (0-7368-0644-X). 24pp. Double-page spreads present illustrations followed by descriptions of pertinent facts including Puerto Rico's flag, flower, animal, seal, and bird. (Rev: BL 3/1/01; HBG 10/01) [972.9]

17160 Furlong, Kate A. *Haiti* (3–5). Illus. Series: The Countries. 2003, ABDO LB $14.95 (1-57765-841-8). 40pp. Full-color photographs add to this well-written introduction to Haiti. (Rev: HBG 10/03; SLJ 10/03) [972.94]

17161 Graves, Kerry A. *Haiti* (4–6). Illus. Series: Countries and Cultures. 2002, Capstone LB $18.60 (0-7368-1078-1). 64pp. An introduction to Haiti's geography, history, and culture, with maps, timelines, and other aids. (Rev: BL 5/15/02; HBG 3/03) [972.94]

17162 Greenberg, Keith E. *A Haitian Family* (4–7). Illus. Series: Journey Between Two Worlds. 1998, Lerner LB $22.60 (0-8225-3410-X). 56pp. The story of the Beaubrun family, the political oppression they suffered in Haiti, and their eventual journey to freedom in the United States. (Rev: BL 3/1/98; HBG 10/98) [305.9]

17163 Haverstock, Nathan A. *Cuba in Pictures* (5–8). Illus. Series: Visual Geography. 1997, Lerner LB $25.55 (0-8225-1811-2). 64pp. A look at America's island neighbor, with color photographs. Also use *Dominican Republic in Pictures* (1997). (Rev: BL 10/15/87) [972.91064]

17164 Hernandez, Romel. *Trinidad and Tobago* (4–6). Series: Discovering the Caribbean. 2003, Mason Crest LB $19.95 (1-59084-304-5). 63pp. An appealing look at the geography, history, plants and animals, economy, and people of these Caribbean islands, with lots of photographs plus recipes and report ideas. (Rev: SLJ 10/03) [972.983]

17165 Illsley, Linda. *The Caribbean* (3–5). Illus. Series: Foods and Festivals. 1999, Raintree $22.83 (0-8172-5758-6). 32pp. Because the Caribbean Islands contain a diverse population, the festivals vary from Hindu and Christian holidays to the special children's carnival in Trinidad and Tobago. (Rev: BL 5/15/99; HBG 10/99) [394.1]

17166 *Jamaica in Pictures* (5–8). Illus. Series: Visual Geography. 1997, Lerner LB $25.55 (0-8225-1814-7). 64pp. Color photographs highlight this visit to a popular and beautiful island. (Rev: BL 10/15/87) [972.92]

17167 Kent, Deborah. *Puerto Rico* (4–6). Illus. Series: America the Beautiful. 1991, Children's Book Pr. LB $28.00 (0-516-00498-0). 144pp. In a fine combination of text and graphics, the history, geography, and culture of Puerto Rico are introduced. (Rev: BL 1/15/92) [972.95]

17168 McCarthy, Pat. *The Dominican Republic* (5–8). Illus. Series: Top Ten Countries of Recent Immigrants. 2004, Enslow/MyReportLinks.com LB $25.26 (0-7660-5179-X). 48pp. Information on the Dominican Republic — culture, history, climate, and people — accompanies an explanation of the reasons for migration to the United States and discussion of the contributions of this community; supported by Web links. (Rev: SLJ 3/05) [304]

17169 Marquez, Heron. *Destination San Juan* (5–8). Series: Port Cities of North America. 1998, Lerner LB $23.93 (0-8225-2792-8). 80pp. A matter-of-fact introduction to San Juan that describes the city, people, economy, and port activities. (Rev: HBG 3/99; SLJ 3/99) [972.95]

17170 Marx, Trish. *Reaching for the Sun: Kids in Cuba* (3–6). Photos by Cindy Karp. 2003, Millbrook LB $25.90 (0-7613-2261-2). 48pp. This attractive photoessay documents a Los Angeles children's arts group's month-long visit to Cuba and the personal interaction between visitors and hosts. (Rev: BL 4/15/03; HBG 10/03; SLJ 7/03) [972.9106]

17171 Milivojevic, JoAnn. *Puerto Rico* (1–3). Series: Globe-Trotters Club. 2000, Carolrhoda LB $22.60 (1-57505-119-2). 48pp. A simple look at the land and people of Puerto Rico, including natural wonders and such attractions as the Arecibo Observatory, home of the world's largest telescope. (Rev: BL 5/15/00; HBG 10/00; SLJ 9/00) [972.95]

17172 Milivojevic, JoAnn. *Puerto Rico* (2–3). Series: A Ticket To. 2000, Lerner LB $22.60 (1-57505-144-3). 48pp. A simple introduction to Puerto Rico that covers basic history, geography, and society. (Rev: HBG 10/00; SLJ 9/00) [972.9]

17173 Morrison, Marion. *Cuba* (4–7). Illus. Series: Country Insights. 1998, Raintree LB $27.12 (0-8172-4796-3). 48pp. An introduction to contemporary life in Cuba, showing the contrast between life in a big city (Havana) and in a country village. (Rev: BL 5/1/98; HBG 10/98) [972.91]

17174 Morrison, Marion. *Cuba* (5–9). Illus. Series: Enchantment of the World. 1999, Children's Book Pr. LB $34.50 (0-516-21051-3). 144pp. A fine, colorful introduction to Cuba past and present, with material on climate, industry, government, daily life, social customs, and religions. (Rev: BL 12/15/99) [972.91]

17175 NgCheong-Lum, Roseline. *Haiti* (2–4). Series: Festivals of the World. 1999, Gareth Stevens LB $15.95 (0-8368-2015-0). 32pp. The people and land of Haiti are introduced through a description of their main holidays, festivals, and voodoo religion, plus sections on related crafts and food. (Rev: BL 12/15/99; HBG 10/00) [972.94]

17176 Orr, Tamra. *Barbados* (3–5). Series: Discovering the Caribbean. 2003, Mason Crest LB $19.95 (1-59084-306-1). 63pp. Introduces readers to the geography, history, people, culture, and attractions of Barbados, with recipes and projects. (Rev: HBG 4/04; SLJ 1/04) [972.981]

17177 Orr, Tamra. *Windward Islands* (4–6). Illus. Series: Discovering the Caribbean. 2003, Mason Crest LB $19.95 (1-59084-305-3). 63pp. An appealing look at the geography, history, plants and animals, economy, and people of these Caribbean islands, with lots of photographs plus recipes and report ideas. (Rev: HBG 4/04; SLJ 10/03) [972.984]

17178 Petersen, Christine, and David Petersen. *Cuba* (3–5). Illus. Series: True Books — Geography. 2001, Children's Book Pr. paper $6.95 (0-516-27358-2). 48pp. A colorful overview of Cuba's history and geography, with a positive slant on Castro's influence. (Rev: BL 2/1/02) [972.91]

17179 *Puerto Rico in Pictures* (4–7). Illus. Series: Visual Geography. 1995, Lerner LB $25.55 (0-8225-1821-X). 64pp. Everyday life, history, culture, and geography are introduced. (Rev: BL 8/87) [972.95]

17180 Rogers, Barbara Radcliffe, and Lure Rogers. *The Dominican Republic* (4–7). Series: Enchantment of the World. 1999, Children's Book Pr. LB $34.50 (0-516-21125-0). 144pp. An introduction to the Dominican Republic with coverage of such topics as history, climate, geography, people, religion, culture, daily life, and landmarks. (Rev: BL 12/15/99) [972.93]

17181 Ross, Michael Elsohn. *Children of Puerto Rico* (4–6). Series: The World's Children. 2001, Carolrhoda LB $23.93 (1-57505-522-8). This handsome volume filled with color photographs of Puerto Rican children describes the daily life of their island home. (Rev: BL 1/1–15/02; HBG 3/02; SLJ 2/02) [972.95]

17182 Schemenauer, Elma. *Haiti* (3–5). Series: Countries: Faces and Places. 2000, Child's World LB $25.64 (1-56766-715-5). 32pp. Basic material about the troubled island nation of Haiti is given in short chapters, simple text, and outstanding color photographs. (Rev: BL 4/15/01; HBG 3/01) [972.94]

17183 Schreier, Alta. *Cuba* (2–4). Series: A Visit To. 2000, Heinemann LB $21.36 (1-57572-380-8). 32pp. An introductory overview of the island nation today, with information on geography, people and culture, language, schools, and transportation presented in large photographs and simple text. (Rev: HBG 10/01; SLJ 4/01) [972.9]

17184 Sheehan, Sean. *Jamaica* (5–8). Illus. Series: Cultures of the World. 1993, Marshall Cavendish LB $35.64 (1-85435-581-3). 128pp. This informative account describes many facets of Jamaican life, including history, religion, and reggae music. (Rev: SLJ 2/94) [972.92]

17185 Staub, Frank. *Children of Cuba* (3–6). Illus. Series: World's Children. 1996, Carolrhoda LB $23.93 (0-87614-989-1). 48pp. Interesting background information on Cuba is introduced through the experiences of several children. (Rev: BL 12/1/96; SLJ 2/97) [972.91]

17186 Staub, Frank. *Children of Dominica* (4–6). Illus. Series: World's Children. 1998, Lerner $22.60

(1-57505-217-2). 48pp. This book introduces the people of Dominica, part of the Lesser Antilles, and tells how they live, their history, and the role of children in their culture. (Rev: BL 4/1/99; SLJ 3/99) [972.9841]

17187 Stevens, Kathryn. *Cuba* (3–5). Series: Faces and Places. 2001, Child's World LB $25.64 (1-56766-906-9). 32pp. The island of Cuba and its people are introduced in this oversize volume with a simple text, short chapters, and color photographs on each page. (Rev: BL 9/15/01; HBG 3/02) [972.91]

17188 Telemaque, Eleanor Wong. *Haiti Through Its Holidays* (4–5). Illus. by Earl Hill. 1980, Blyden Pr. $8.50 (0-685-00779-0). 64pp. An introduction to Haiti through its holidays and customs surrounding them.

17189 Temple, Bob. *Dominican Republic* (3–5). Series: Discovering the Caribbean. 2003, Mason Crest LB $19.95 (1-59084-301-0). 63pp. Introduces readers to the geography, history, people, culture, and attractions of the Dominican Republic, with a focus on music, plus recipes and projects. (Rev: SLJ 1/04) [972.93]

17190 Tuck, Jay, and Norma C. Vergara. *Heroes of Puerto Rico* (5–8). 1969, Fleet $9.50 (0-8303-0070-8). A series of profiles of famous Puerto Ricans. (Rev: BL 6/87) [972.9]

17191 Wagner, Michele. *Haiti* (4–8). 2002, Gareth Stevens LB $29.27 (0-8368-2351-6). 96pp. History, geography, government, and people are all covered here, with special sections on such topics as the status of women and relations with the United States. (Rev: HBG 3/03; SLJ 2/03) [972.94]

17192 Will, Emily Wade. *Haiti* (5–8). Series: Modern Nations of the World. 2001, Lucent LB $27.45 (1-56006-761-6). 112pp. The history, geography, and culture of this island country are presented with colorful prose and pictures plus unusual facts contained in sidebars. (Rev: BL 6/1–15/01) [972.94]

17193 Williams, Colleen Madonna Flood. *The Bahamas* (4–6). Series: Discovering the Caribbean. 2003, Mason Crest LB $19.95 (1-59084-296-0). 63pp. An appealing look at the geography, history, plants and animals, economy, and people of the Bahamas, with lots of photographs plus recipes and report ideas. (Rev: HBG 4/04; SLJ 10/03) [972.96]

South America

17194 Allen, Nancy Kelly. *On the Banks of the Amazon / En las orillas del Amazonas* (K–2). Trans. by Eida de la Vega. Illus. by Elizabeth Driessen. 2003, Raven Tree LB $16.95 (0-9720192-7-8). 31pp. A lively bilingual introduction to the animals of the Amazon rain forest, featuring two wildlife photographers. (Rev: HBG 4/04; SLJ 12/03) [981]

17195 *Argentina in Pictures* (5–8). Illus. Series: Visual Geography. 1994, Lerner LB $25.55 (0-8225-1807-4). 64pp. An overview of climate, wildlife, cities, vegetation, and mineral resources. (Rev: BL 4/15/88; SLJ 5/88) [982]

17196 Augustin, Byron. *Bolivia* (4–7). Series: Enchantment of the World. 2001, Children's Book Pr. LB $34.50 (0-516-21050-5). With each page containing a color illustration, this attractive book introduces the land and people, economy, culture, and natural resources of Bolivia. (Rev: BL 1/1–15/02) [984]

17197 Barter, James. *The Amazon* (5–9). Illus. 2003, Gale $27.45 (1-56006-934-1). 112pp. In addition to covering the river's location and importance, Barter reviews the history of the peoples living along the Amazon, early exploration by outsiders, and the environmental problems of the area. (Rev: BL 3/15/03; SLJ 1/03) [981]

17198 Bauer, Brandy. *Brazil* (2–5). Illus. Series: Questions and Answers: Countries. 2004, Capstone LB $16.95 (0-7368-2481-2). 32pp. Using a question-and-answer format, simple text, large photos, and many factboxes, this is an introduction to Brazil today, with material on history and traditional culture.

17199 Beirne, Barbara. *Children of the Ecuadorean Highlands* (3–6). Illus. Series: The World's Children. 1996, Carolrhoda LB $23.93 (1-57505-000-5). 48pp. Historical and geographical materials are included in this story about young people in Equador. (Rev: BL 10/1/96; SLJ 11/96) [972]

17200 Boraas, Tracey. *Colombia* (4–6). Illus. Series: Countries and Cultures. 2002, Capstone LB $18.60 (0-7368-1076-5). 64pp. An introduction to Colombia that covers many topics including geography, history, and culture, with maps, timelines, and other aids. (Rev: BL 5/15/02; HBG 3/03) [986.1]

17201 Brill, Marlene T. *Guyana* (5–8). Illus. Series: Enchantment of the World. 1994, Children's Book Pr. LB $32.00 (0-516-02626-7). 127pp. With color photos on each page, this account introduces Guyana and supplies material on its geography, history, peoples, culture, and resources. (Rev: BL 12/15/94) [988.1]

17202 Calvert, Patricia. *The Ancient Inca* (5–8). Series: People of the Ancient World. 2004, Watts LB $29.50 (0-531-12358-8). 128pp. This fascinating volume covers the history and culture of the Inca people, looking at childhood and the daily life of people ranging from farmers to priests, warriors, and emperors. (Rev: SLJ 3/05) [985]

17203 Carpenter, Mark L. *Brazil: An Awakening Giant* (5–7). Illus. 1988, Macmillan LB $14.95 (0-87518-366-2). 128pp. A wide range of information is included, with the focus on everyday life. (Rev: BL 2/15/88) [981]

17204 *Colombia in Pictures* (5–8). Illus. Series: Visual Geography. 1996, Lerner LB $25.55 (0-8225-1810-4). 64pp. Many photographs highlight this visit to a South American nation. (Rev: BL 10/15/87) [986.1]

17205 Corona, Laurel. *Brazil* (5–8). Series: Modern Nations of the World. 1999, Lucent LB $27.45 (1-56006-621-0). 128pp. A lively account of Brazil's history, geography, famous people, and conditions today. (Rev: BL 2/15/00; HBG 10/00) [981]

17206 Corona, Laurel. *Peru* (5–8). Series: Modern Nations of the World. 2001, Lucent LB $27.45 (1-56006-862-0). 112pp. Detailed sidebars, a chronology, and national statistics supplement the general information presented in this colorful introduction to Peru. (Rev: BL 6/1–15/01) [985]

17207 Dalal, Anita. *Argentina* (4–8). Series: Nations of the World. 2001, Raintree LB $34.26 (0-7398-1279-3). 128pp. A colorful, interesting introduction to Argentina that covers its land and cities, history, culture, present economic conditions, and possible future developments. (Rev: BL 6/1–15/01; HBG 10/01) [982]

17208 Dalal, Anita. *Brazil* (4–8). Series: Nations of the World. 2001, Raintree LB $34.26 (0-7398-1284-X). 128pp. A profile of the home of Carnival, the Amazon, and Pele with material attractively presented on its past and present, its people, and its culture. (Rev: BL 6/1–15/01; HBG 10/01) [981]

17209 Daniels, Amy S. *Ecuador* (4–6). Series: Countries of the World. 2002, Gareth Stevens LB $21.95 (0-8368-2343-5). 96pp. Using excellent illustrations and a clear text, this is a fine introduction to the land and people of Ecuador. (Rev: BL 6/1–15/02; HBG 10/02) [986.6]

17210 Dubois, Jill. *Colombia* (5–8). Illus. Series: Cultures of the World. 1991, Marshall Cavendish LB $35.64 (1-85435-384-5). 128pp. Background information on Colombia is given as well as coverage of contemporary concerns. (Rev: BL 4/1/91) [986.1]

17211 Dubois, Muriel L. *Peru* (2–5). Illus. Series: Questions and Answers: Countries. 2005, Capstone LB $16.95 (0-7368-3758-2). 32pp. Using a question-and-answer format, simple text, large photos, and many factboxes, this is an introduction to Peru today, with material on history and traditional culture.

17212 Eagen, James. *The Aymara of South America* (4–6). Series: First Peoples. 2002, Lerner LB $23.93 (0-8225-4174-2). This volume describes the history and present status of the Aymara, who live in the high plains of Peru and Bolivia, where they are known for domesticating the potato. (Rev: BL 5/15/02; HBG 10/02) [985]

17213 Fajardo, Dara Andrea. *A Child's Day in a Peruvian City* (K–3). Series: A Child's Day. 2002, Marshall Cavendish LB $15.95 (0-7614-1408-8). 32pp. The reader meets a Peruvian child and learns about culture, work, and play in modern Peru. (Rev: BL 2/15/03; HBG 3/03; SLJ 12/02) [985]

17214 Falconer, Kieran. *Peru* (4–7). Illus. Series: Cultures of the World. 1995, Marshall Cavendish LB $35.64 (0-7614-0179-2). 128pp. The focus of this book is on the people of Peru, their lifestyles, artistic endeavors, religion, and leisure activities. (Rev: BL 1/1–15/96; SLJ 4/96) [985]

17215 Ferro, Jennifer. *Brazilian Foods and Culture* (3–5). Series: Festive Foods and Celebrations. 1999, Rourke LB $19.45 (1-57103-301-7). 48pp. Information on Brazilian history and culture are featured along with a number of recipes and explanations for such celebrations as Carnival, Iemanj, and Saint John's Day. (Rev: SLJ 2/00) [981]

17216 Fitzpatrick, Anne. *Amazon River* (4–6). Illus. Series: Natural Wonders of the World. 2004, Creative Education LB $18.95 (1-58341-322-7). 32pp. After establishing this important river's location, this oversized picture book full of color photographs looks at geology, climate, wildlife, people, and other pertinent facts. (Rev: SLJ 1/05) [918.1]

17217 Foley, Erin. *Ecuador* (5–8). Illus. Series: Cultures of the World. 1995, Marshall Cavendish LB $35.64 (0-7614-0173-3). 128pp. This book supplies good background material on Ecuador but is strongest in describing contemporary conditions. (Rev: SLJ 11/95) [980]

17218 Frank, Nicole. *Argentina* (4–6). Series: Countries of the World. 2000, Gareth Stevens LB $19.95 (0-8368-2315-X). 96pp. A well-illustrated guide to Argentina that includes coverage of the land, economy, history, government, people, customs, and relations with United States and Canada. (Rev: BL 6/1–15/00; HBG 10/00) [982]

17219 Furlong, Arlene. *Argentina* (2–4). Series: Festivals of the World. 1999, Gareth Stevens LB $15.95 (0-8368-2030-4). 32pp. This account describes the people and the land but emphasizes Argentina's main holidays and provides related craft projects and recipes. (Rev: BL 12/15/99; HBG 10/00) [982]

17220 Gofen, Ethel C. *Cultures of the World: Argentina* (5–8). Illus. Series: Cultures of the World. 1991, Marshall Cavendish LB $213.86 (1-85435-380-2). 128pp. This book provides standard information on history and geography and tells about the contemporary lifestyles of the people. (Rev: BL 4/1/91) [962]

17221 Gresko, Marcia S. *Brazil* (3–5). Series: Letters Home From. 1999, Blackbirch LB $16.95 (1-56711-407-5). 32pp. A series of letters written by a young traveler, illustrated in color, presents basic information about Brazil. (Rev: BL 2/15/00; HBG 3/00; SLJ 2/00) [981]

17222 *Guyana in Pictures* (5–8). Illus. Series: Visual Geography. 1997, Lerner LB $25.55 (0-8225-1815-5). 64pp. History, climate, wildlife, and major cities are covered in this overview. (Rev: BL 4/15/88) [988.1]

17223 Haskins, Jim, and Kathleen Benson. *Count Your Way Through Brazil* (2–4). Illus. by Liz B. Dodson. Series: Count Your Way. 1996, Carolrhoda LB $19.93 (0-87614-873-9); paper $5.95 (0-87614-971-9). 24pp. Facts about Brazil are introduced in a counting book that goes from 1 to 10. (Rev: BL 9/15/96; SLJ 8/96) [981]

17224 Haverstock, Nathan A. *Brazil in Pictures* (4–7). Illus. Series: Visual Geography. 1997, Lerner LB $25.55 (0-8225-1802-3). 64pp. Current data on the political scene, plus chapters on history, people, and culture in this revised text. Also use *Chile in Pictures* (1988). (Rev: BL 8/87)

17225 Haverstock, Nathan A. *Paraguay in Pictures* (5–8). Illus. Series: Visual Geography. 1995, Lerner LB $25.55 (0-8225-1819-8). 64pp. This overview of

Paraguay includes its history to 1987 and possible future developments. (Rev: BL 4/15/88) [989.2]

17226 Heinrichs, Ann. *Brazil* (4–6). Series: True Books. 1997, Children's Book Pr. LB $22.00 (0-516-20328-2). 48pp. Short chapters on Brazil cover such topics as land, people, history, homes, and culture. (Rev: BL 9/15/97; HBG 3/98) [981]

17227 Heinrichs, Ann. *Venezuela* (4–6). Series: True Books. 1997, Children's Book Pr. LB $22.00 (0-516-20344-4). 48pp. Venezuela is introduced with a simple text, many color photos, and a map. (Rev: BL 9/15/97; HBG 3/98) [987]

17228 Heisey, Janet. *Peru* (5–8). Illus. Series: Countries of the World. 2001, Gareth Stevens LB $29.26 (0-8368-2333-8). 96pp. An informative overview of Peru's history, geography, government, culture, and relationship with other countries in the Western Hemisphere. (Rev: HBG 10/01; SLJ 4/01) [985]

17229 Hermes, Jules. *The Children of Bolivia* (3–5). Illus. Series: World's Children. 1996, Carolrhoda LB $23.93 (0-87614-935-2). 47pp. By focusing on children in the country and in cities, the two distinct native cultures of Bolivia are explored. (Rev: SLJ 5/96) [984]

17230 Hintz, Martin. *Chile* (4–6). Illus. 1985, Children's Book Pr. LB $32.00 (0-516-02755-7). 128pp. Covers basic aspects of life in this South American land.

17231 Jermyn, Leslie. *Brazil* (4–5). Series: Countries of the World. 1999, Gareth Stevens LB $18.95 (0-8368-2258-7). 95pp. Basic information on the land and its people is supplemented with special sections on unique customs and current problems. (Rev: BL 9/15/99; SLJ 8/99) [981]

17232 Jermyn, Leslie. *Colombia* (4–6). Series: Countries of the World. 1999, Gareth Stevens LB $19.95 (0-8368-2308-7). 96pp. A basic introduction to Colombia that also delves into current problems, lifestyles, language, and culture. (Rev: BL 12/15/99; HBG 10/00) [986]

17233 Jermyn, Leslie. *Paraguay* (5–8). 1999, Marshall Cavendish LB $35.64 (0-7614-0979-3). 128pp. This book about Paraguay covers history, geography, government, and economy as well as such social and cultural topics as religion, the arts, food, and recreation. (Rev: HBG 10/00; SLJ 4/00) [989]

17234 Jermyn, Leslie. *Peru* (2–3). Illus. Series: Festivals of the World. 1998, Gareth Stevens LB $18.60 (0-8368-2006-1). 32pp. Color photos and a simple text are used to describe Peru's religious holidays and those with Inca origins. (Rev: BL 5/15/98; HBG 10/98; SLJ 9/98) [394.2]

17235 Jones, Helga. *Venezuela* (1–3). Series: Globe-Trotters Club. 2000, Carolrhoda LB $22.60 (1-57505-122-2). 48pp. Some of the topics covered in this simple introduction to Venezuela are the land, people, culture, rain forests, and Angel Falls, the highest waterfall in the world. (Rev: BL 5/15/00; HBG 10/00) [987]

17236 Kendall, Sarita. *The Incas* (5–6). Illus. Series: World of the Past. 1992, Macmillan LB $21.00 (0-02-750160-4). 64pp. A history of the Incas before, during, and after the Spanish conquest. (Rev: SLJ 11/92) [940.54]

17237 Knox, Barbara. *Peru* (2–3). Illus. Series: Many Cultures, One World. 2004, Capstone LB $17.95 (0-7368-2450-2). 32pp. A brief, accessible introduction to Peru and its people, family life, customs, and legends.

17238 Lehtinen, Ritva, and Karl E. Nurmi. *The Grandchildren of the Incas* (4–6). Illus. by Matti Pitkanen. Series: The World's Children. 1991, Carolrhoda LB $23.93 (0-87614-397-4). 40pp. Some children herd sheep while others work in the city in this profile of young Incan descendants. (Rev: BL 6/1/91) [980]

17239 Lepthien, Emilie U. *Peru* (5–8). Series: Enchantment of the World. 1992, Children's Pr. paper $32.00 (0-516-02610-0). An illustrated discussion of Peru's history, economy, and politics through 1990. (Rev: BL 2/1/93; SLJ 2/93) [985]

17240 Lewin, Ted. *Lost City: The Discovery of Machu Picchu* (2–4). 2003, Penguin Putnam $16.99 (0-399-23302-4). 48pp. Striking watercolor spreads grab attention in this picture-book account of the discovery of the lost Inca city. (Rev: BL 7/03; HB 9–10/03; HBG 4/04; SLJ 6/03) [985]

17241 Lewington, Anna. *What Do We Know About the Amazonian Indians?* (4–6). Illus. by Ian Thompson. Series: What Do We Know About. 1993, Bedrick LB $18.95 (0-87226-367-3); paper $8.95 (0-87226-262-6). 43pp. Double-page spreads are used to introduce the history, lives, and cultures of the Indians of the Amazon River. (Rev: SLJ 3/94) [981.1]

17242 Lichtenberg, Andre. *Brazil* (2–4). Illus. 2000, Raintree $22.83 (0-8172-5514-1). 32pp. A young Brazilian boy introduces the reader to his homeland, its geography, food, customs, schools, and everyday life. (Rev: BL 4/15/00; HBG 10/00) [981]

17243 Lourie, Peter. *Lost Treasure of the Inca* (4–7). Illus. 1999, Boyds Mills $18.95 (1-56397-743-5). 48pp. A thrilling narrative of a modern search for the gold supposedly hidden by the Incas in the Ecuadorian mountains. (Rev: BCCB 11/99; BL 10/15/99; HBG 3/00; SLJ 11/99) [986.6]

17244 Lourie, Peter. *Tierra del Fuego: A Journey to the End of the Earth* (2–5). Illus. 2002, Boyds Mills $19.95 (1-56397-973-X). 48pp. A fascinating first-person look at Tierra del Fuego, the southernmost island off the coast of South America, including its discovery and the fate of its native peoples. (Rev: BL 10/15/02; HBG 3/03; SLJ 9/02) [918.276]

17245 MacDonald, Fiona. *Inca Town* (4–7). Illus. by Mark Bergin. Series: Metropolis. 1998, Watts LB $25.00 (0-531-14481-X). 45pp. Double-page spreads, a well-organized text, and colorful drawings present life in an Inca town in the 15th century. (Rev: HBG 3/99; SLJ 1/99) [985]

17246 McNair, Sylvia. *Chile* (4–7). Series: Enchantment of the World. 2000, Children's Book Pr. LB $34.50 (0-516-21007-6). 144pp. This attractive new edition of an old title includes material on Chile's land and people, history and government, econom-

ics and landmarks, daily life, and sports. (Rev: BL 7/00) [983]

17247 Mann, Elizabeth. *Machu Picchu* (3–5). Illus. Series: Wonders of the World. 2000, Mikaya $19.95 (0-9650493-9-6). 48pp. Beginning with the discovery of Machu Picchu in 1911, this book goes back to trace its construction and history. (Rev: BL 7/00*; HBG 10/00; SLJ 6/00) [985]

17248 Martell, Hazel M. *Civilizations of Peru, Before 1535* (5–8). Illus. Series: Looking Back. 1999, Raintree $19.98 (0-8172-5428-5). 63pp. This book covers the history and culture of the Inca empire that stretched far beyond the boundaries of Peru. (Rev: BL 5/15/99; SLJ 7/99) [985]

17249 Morrison, Marion. *Brazil* (4–7). Illus. Series: Country Insights. 1997, Raintree LB $27.12 (0-8172-4785-8). 48pp. Compares the home life, employment, schooling, and recreation in a large city and in a small village in Brazil. (Rev: BL 7/97; SLJ 8/97) [918.1]

17250 Morrison, Marion. *Colombia* (4–7). Series: Enchantment of the World. 1999, Children's Book Pr. LB $34.50 (0-516-21106-4). 144pp. A revision of a standard introduction to this South American country that covers such topics as history, government, people, economy, and current issues. (Rev: BL 9/15/99; HBG 3/00) [986.1]

17251 Morrison, Marion. *Ecuador* (4–7). Series: Enchantment of the World. 2000, Children's Book Pr. LB $34.50 (0-516-21544-2). 144pp. This book examines the geography and climate of Ecuador, its history, government, language, economy, and people. (Rev: BL 1/1–15/01) [986]

17252 Morrison, Marion. *Guyana* (5–8). Illus. Series: Enchantment of the World, Second Series. 2003, Children's Book Pr. LB $34.00 (0-516-22377-1). 144pp. A visually attractive book that covers such topics as the geography, history, government, culture, and people with a timeline, fast facts, and a recipe. (Rev: SLJ 5/03) [966.7]

17253 Morrison, Marion. *Indians of the Andes* (4–6). Illus. 1987, Rourke LB $16.67 (0-86625-260-6). 48pp. With attractive design and numerous color photos, the Indians of the Andes are introduced to young readers. (Rev: BL 1/15/88)

17254 Morrison, Marion. *Paraguay* (5–8). Series: Enchantment of the World. 1993, Children's Pr. paper $32.00 (0-516-02619-4). An introduction to Paraguay's history, geography, economy, and culture. (Rev: BL 11/1/93; SLJ 3/94) [989.2]

17255 Morrison, Marion. *Peru* (4–7). Series: Enchantment of the World. 2000, Children's Book Pr. LB $34.50 (0-516-21545-0). 144pp. History, geography and climate, daily life and ancient civilizations, cities, culture, and traditions are some of the topics covered in this attractive introduction to Peru. (Rev: BL 7/00) [985]

17256 Morrison, Marion. *Rio de Janeiro* (4–6). Series: Great Cities of the World. 2004, World Almanac LB $29.26 (0-8368-5031-9). 48pp. Report writers will find useful information on Rio's history, culture, and lifestyle. Also use *Buenos Aires* (2004). (Rev: SLJ 7/04) [981]

17257 Morrison, Marion. *Uruguay* (5–8). Series: Enchantment of the World. 1992, Children's Pr. paper $36.00 (0-516-02607-0). An introduction to Uruguay's people, history, climate, geography, and government. (Rev: BL 6/1/92) [989.5]

17258 Morrison, Marion. *Venezuela* (5–8). Illus. Series: Enchantment of the World. 1989, Children's Book Pr. paper $32.00 (0-516-02711-5). 128pp. Economy, geography, history, and people are some of the topics covered. (Rev: BL 8/89; SLJ 2/90) [987]

17259 Nesbitt, Kris. *My Amazon River Day* (2–5). Illus. 2000, Shedd Aquarium $23.95 (0-9701035-0-6). 48pp. This book chronicles everyday life on the banks of the Amazon River in Peru for Patricia, her family, and her friends. (Rev: BL 10/15/00) [577.098]

17260 Odijk, Pamela. *The Incas* (4–7). Illus. Series: Ancient World. 1990, Silver Burdett LB $14.95 (0-382-09889-7). 48pp. In addition to a history of the civilization that prospered in Peru, there is a timeline, glossary, and list of famous names. (Rev: BL 7/90; SLJ 8/90) [985]

17261 O'Sullivan, MaryCate. *Peru* (3–5). Series: Countries: Faces and Places. 2000, Child's World LB $25.64 (1-56766-739-2). 32pp. This oversize, picture-filled book supplies basic information about the land and people of Peru. (Rev: BL 4/15/01; HBG 3/01) [985]

17262 Parker, Edward. *The Amazon* (5–9). Illus. Series: Great Rivers of the World. 2003, World Almanac LB $29.26 (0-8368-5442-X). 48pp. A comprehensive look at the river, its flora and fauna, its importance to mankind throughout history, and efforts to control outside factors threatening its survival. (Rev: BL 3/15/03) [981]

17263 Parker, Edward. *Peru* (5–8). Illus. 1996, Raintree LB $24.26 (0-8172-4525-1). After a general introduction to Peru, this account discusses such current economic indicators as the job market, industry, and agriculture. (Rev: BL 3/15/97; SLJ 2/97) [985]

17264 Pateman, Robert. *Bolivia* (4–7). Illus. Series: Cultures of the World. 1995, Marshall Cavendish LB $35.64 (0-7614-0178-4). 128pp. The people of Bolivia, how they live, and their traditions are some of the topics covered in this general introduction. (Rev: BL 1/1–15/96; SLJ 4/96) [984]

17265 *Peru in Pictures* (5–8). Illus. Series: Visual Geography. 1997, Lerner LB $25.55 (0-8225-1820-1). 64pp. An introduction to this South American land, highlighted by color photographs. (Rev: BL 10/15/87) [985]

17266 Petersen, David. *South America* (2–4). Illus. 1998, Children's Book Pr. LB $21.00 (0-516-20769-5). 48pp. Topographical features, climate, animals and plants, and the native peoples are covered in this overview of South America that uses maps, satellite photos, and other illustrations. (Rev: BL 1/1–15/99; HBG 3/99) [968]

17267 Pollard, Michael. *The Amazon* (4–6). Series: Great Rivers. 1997, Benchmark LB $21.36 (0-7614-0501-1). 45pp. The story of the river that rises in the

Andes of Peru and flows for almost 4,000 miles to the Atlantic. (Rev: HBG 3/98; SLJ 5/98) [981]

17268 Rawlins, Carol B. *The Orinoco River* (4–7). Illus. Series: World of Water. 1999, Watts LB $24.00 (0-531-11740-5). 64pp. An introduction to this important Venezuelan river, with material on its history and current status and the areas through which it passes. (Rev: BL 1/1–15/00) [987.06]

17269 Rees, Rosemary. *The Incas* (3–6). Illus. 1999, Heinemann LB $15.95 (1-57572-889-3). 64pp. In addition to giving a general history of the Incas, their culture and contributions, this book describes their calendar, family life, and the Spanish conquest. (Rev: BL 6/1–15/99) [985]

17270 Richard, Christopher. *Brazil* (5–8). Illus. Series: Cultures of the World. 1991, Marshall Cavendish LB $35.64 (1-85435-382-9). 128pp. Brazil is introduced with information on such topics as history, economics, people, and modern problems. (Rev: BL 4/1/91) [981]

17271 Robinson, Roger. *Brazil* (5–8). Series: Country Studies. 1999, Heinemann LB $27.07 (1-57572-892-3). Using colorful charts, graphs, drawings, maps, and photographs in double-page spreads, this book provides basic information about Brazil, with emphasis on regional contrasts and contemporary issues, such as population changes and the growth of agribusiness. (Rev: BL 8/99; SLJ 8/99) [981]

17272 Roraff, Susan. *Chile* (2–4). Series: Festivals of the World. 1998, Gareth Stevens LB $14.95 (0-8368-2012-6). 32pp. An introduction to the land and people of Chile, describing its unique traditions and holidays, and giving step-by-step instructions for some related craft projects and recipes. (Rev: BL 12/15/98; HBG 10/99) [983]

17273 St. John, Jetty. *A Family in Chile* (2–4). Illus. 1986, Lerner LB $18.60 (0-8225-1667-5). 32pp. Focusing on one child in a Chilean family, the reader learns of life in this South American land. (Rev: BL 5/15/86; SLJ 10/86)

17274 Sayer, Chloe. *The Incas* (5–10). Series: Ancient World. 1998, Raintree LB $27.12 (0-8172-5125-1). An in-depth look at Inca life, from their beautiful gold ornaments to their unique form of record keeping and impressive citadels and forts. (Rev: BL 1/1–15/99; HBG 3/99) [985]

17275 Siy, Alexandra. *The Waorani: People of the Ecuadoran Rain Forest* (4–7). Illus. Series: Global Villages. 1993, Macmillan LB $14.95 (0-87518-550-9). 80pp. Presents the history, culture, and prospects for the future of these people. (Rev: SLJ 8/93) [980]

17276 Spengler, Kremena. *Chile* (2–5). Illus. Series: Questions and Answers: Countries. 2005, Capstone LB $16.95 (0-7368-3748-5). 32pp. Using a question-and-answer format, simple text, large photos, and many factboxes, this is an introduction to Chile today, with material on history and traditional culture.

17277 Steele, Philip. *The Incas and Machu Picchu* (4–7). Illus. Series: Hidden Worlds. 1993, Dillon LB $13.95 (0-87518-536-3). 32pp. A history of the Inca people and a tour of their ruined fortress city in

Peru are included in this fascinating account. (Rev: BL 12/1/93) [985.37]

17278 Stevens, Kathryn. *Argentina* (3–5). Series: Countries: Faces and Places. 2000, Child's World LB $25.64 (1-56766-712-0). 32pp. Simple text, many color photographs, and an oversize format are used to supply basic background material on the land and people of Argentina. (Rev: BL 4/15/01; HBG 3/01) [982]

17279 Tagliaferro, Linda. *Galapagos Islands: Nature's Delicate Balance at Risk* (4–8). Illus. 2001, Lerner LB $25.26 (0-8225-0648-3). 88pp. This is a detailed but accessible introduction to the history, geology, wildlife, and ecology of the Galapagos Islands, with maps and photographs. (Rev: BL 9/15/01; HBG 3/02; SLJ 11/01) [561.9866]

17280 Tahan, Raya. *The Yanomami of South America* (4–6). Illus. Series: First Peoples. 2001, Lerner $23.93 (0-8225-4851-8). 48pp. This attractive introduction to the Yanomami people and their native region and culture also contrasts traditional and modern lifestyles. (Rev: BL 2/1/02; HBG 3/02; SLJ 3/02) [981.004]

17281 *Venezuela in Pictures* (4–7). Illus. Series: Visual Geography. 1993, Lerner LB $21.27 (0-8225-1824-4). 64pp. The land, people, and government of this oil-rich country are explored in maps, text, and photographs. (Rev: BL 1/1/88) [987]

17282 Watson, Galadriel. *The Amazon Rain Forest: The Largest Rain Forest in the World* (3–6). Illus. Series: Natural Wonders. 2004, Weigl LB $18.20 (1-59036-270-5). 32pp. A look at the history of the rain forest, the people who live there, the animals and plants it supports, and the environmental threats it faces. (Rev: SLJ 4/05)

17283 Webster, Christine. *Yanomami* (3–5). Series: Indigenous Peoples. 2004, Weigl LB $18.20 (1-59036-124-5). 32pp. A fascinating and informative overview of the Yanomami people of the Amazon River basin, covering history, culture, language, and family life. (Rev: SLJ 7/04) [981.0]

17284 Winter, Jane K. *Chile* (5–8). Illus. Series: Cultures of the World. 1991, Marshall Cavendish LB $35.64 (1-85435-383-7). 128pp. The geography, history, government, and economy of Chile are some of the topics covered in this fine introduction. (Rev: BL 4/1/91) [983]

17285 Winter, Jane K. *Venezuela* (5–8). Illus. Series: Cultures of the World. 1991, Marshall Cavendish LB $35.64 (1-85435-386-1). 128pp. In detailed text and color photographs, the land, people, and contemporary problems and concerns of Venezuela are introduced. (Rev: BL 4/1/91) [987]

17286 Yip, Dora, and Janet Heisey. *Welcome to Peru* (3–4). Illus. Series: Welcome to My Country. 2002, Gareth Stevens LB $23.93 (0-8368-2533-0). 48pp. An introduction to the geography, culture, and daily life of Peru, with a map, quick facts, and pronunciation guide for Spanish and Quechua words. (Rev: HBG 3/03; SLJ 4/02)

Polar Regions

17287 Aldis, Rodney. *Polar Lands* (5–8). Series: Ecology Watch. 1992, Dillon LB $13.95 (0-87518-494-4). The lands around both the North and South Poles are introduced, with discussion of their similarities and differences. (Rev: BL 11/1/92) [574.5]

17288 Alexander, Bryan, and Cherry Alexander. *An Eskimo Family* (3–6). Illus. 1985, Lerner LB $18.60 (0-8225-1656-X). 32pp. Young readers get a taste of life in the far north in this look at an Eskimo family. (Rev: BL 6/15/85; SLJ 10/85)

17289 Alexander, Bryan, and Cherry Alexander. *Journey into the Arctic* (1–5). Photos by authors. 2003, Oxford LB $22.00 (0-19-522004-8). 48pp. A fascinating tour of Arctic regions takes readers from a village in Greenland through Arctic Canada and Siberia to the North Pole. (Rev: HBG 4/04; SLJ 1/04)

17290 Bagley, Katie. *Antarctica* (K–3). Series: Continents. 2002, Capstone LB $18.60 (0-7368-1415-9). 24pp. A brief introduction to the geography, history, flora (mostly lichens and moss), and fauna of Antarctica. (Rev: HBG 3/03; SLJ 4/03)

17291 Bial, Raymond. *The Inuit* (5–8). Series: Lifeways. 2001, Marshall Cavendish LB $32.79 (0-7614-1212-3). Using clear language and many intriguing illustrations, this is a fine introduction to the Inuit that begins with a folk story on the origins of the people and continues with material on a variety of basic topics. (Rev: BL 1/1–15/02; HBG 3/02; SLJ 4/02) [979.8]

17292 Billings, Henry. *Antarctica* (5–8). Illus. Series: Enchantment of the World. 1994, Children's Book Pr. paper $32.00 (0-516-02624-0). 127pp. With color photographs on each page, this book explores the history and geography of the Antarctic region, with material on plant and animal life. (Rev: BL 12/15/94) [998.2]

17293 Bocknek, Jonathan. *Antarctica: The Last Wilderness* (5–8). Series: Understanding Global Issues. 2003, Smart Apple $19.95 (1-58340-356-6). 56pp. This nicely-illustrated book introduces Antarctica with material on climate, animals, exploration, and possible future developments. (Rev: BL 11/15/03; HBG 3/02; SLJ 12/03) [998.9]

17294 Bredeson, Carmen. *After the Last Dog Died: The True-Life, Hair-Raising Adventures of Douglas Mawson and his 1911–1914 Antarctic Expedition* (5–8). Illus. 2003, National Geographic $18.95 (0-7922-6140-2). 64pp. This enthralling story of courage in the face of starvation and harsh conditions draws on primary materials including the writings of expedition leader Mawson himself. (Rev: BL 11/1/03; HBG 4/04; SLJ 1/04*) [919.8]

17295 Byles, Monica. *Life in the Polar Lands* (2–5). Illus. by Francis Mosley. 2000, Two-Can LB $9.95 (1-58728-557-6); paper $4.95 (1-58728-572-X). 31pp. This is a basic introduction to how plants, animals, and humans manage to survive in the Arctic and Antarctic. (Rev: SLJ 4/01) [508.311]

17296 Cerullo, Mary M. *Life Under Ice* (3–5). Illus. by Bill Curtsinger. 2004, Tilbury House $16.95 (0-88448-246-4). 40pp. Plant and animal life above and below the waters of Antarctica are shown in eye-catching color photographs. (Rev: BL 9/15/03; HBG 4/04; SLJ 10/03) [578.777]

17297 Conlan, Kathy. *Under the Ice* (4–6). Illus. 2002, Kids Can $16.95 (1-55337-001-5). 56pp. This photoessay relates the author's exciting experiences doing underwater marine biology research in Antarctica. (Rev: BL 11/1/02; HBG 3/03; SLJ 12/02) [578.77]

17298 Cordoba, Yasmine A. *Igloo* (3–5). Illus. by Kimberly L. Dawson Kurnizki. Series: Native American Homes. 2001, Rourke LB $25.27 (1-55916-277-5). 32pp. Using well-chosen photos and a good text, this book explains the construction of the igloo, its uses, and its place in the culture of the Inuit. (Rev: SLJ 3/01) [979.8]

17299 Corriveau, Danielle. *The Inuit of Canada* (4–6). Illus. Series: First Peoples. 2001, Lerner $23.93 (0-8225-4850-X). 48pp. This attractive introduction to the Inuit people and their native region and culture also contrasts traditional and modern lifestyles. (Rev: BL 2/1/02; HBG 3/02; SLJ 3/02) [979.8]

17300 Curlee, Lynn. *Into the Ice: The Story of Arctic Exploration* (4–6). Illus. by author. 1998, Houghton Mifflin $16.00 (0-395-83013-3). 40pp. Attractive acrylic paintings are used to illustrate this history of Arctic exploration, emphasizing the motivation behind the fearless explorers who venture into this cold, hostile environment. (Rev: BCCB 6/98; BL 4/1/98; HB 5–6/98; HBG 10/98; SLJ 5/98) [998]

17301 Darling, Kathy. *Arctic Babies* (K–3). Illus. by Tara Darling. 1996, Walker LB $16.85 (0-8027-8414-3). 32pp. Using full-color photos of each animal, the author introduces a variety of babies from a lynx kitten to a baby beluga whale. (Rev: BL 4/15/96; SLJ 4/96) [591.9]

17302 Dewey, Jennifer O. *Antarctic Journal: Four Months at the Bottom of the World* (4–6). Illus. 2001, HarperCollins LB $16.89 (0-06-028587-7). 64pp. A travel diary kept by the award-winning author and illustrator when she spent four months at Palmer Station on Anvers Island in Antarctica. (Rev: BCCB 2/01; BL 2/15/01; HB 5–6/01; HBG 10/01; SLJ 3/01) [919.8]

17303 Esbensen, Barbara J. *The Night Rainbow* (1–4). Illus. by Helen K. Davie. 2000, Orchard LB $17.99 (0-531-33244-6). 32pp. A poetic picture book that discusses the Northern Lights and the many images from different folk traditions that are associated with this phenomenon. (Rev: BL 3/1/00; HBG 10/00; SLJ 4/00) [538.768]

17304 Foran, Jill. *Search for the Northwest Passage* (5–8). Series: Great Journeys. 2004, Weigl LB $.00 (1-59036-205-5). Colorful illustrations and an attractive format will appeal to browsers seeking information about the search for a sea route to the West; a useful timeline and links to Web sites are included. (Rev: BL 11/1/04) [910]

17305 Gray, Susan H. *Tundra* (2–5). Series: First Reports. 2000, Compass Point LB $15.95 (0-7565-0024-9). 48pp. An informative introduction to the ecosystem, with material on plants and animals, the conditions there, the importance of the biome to the global environment, and features such as the discovery of a woolly mammoth in the permafrost in Russia. (Rev: SLJ 5/01) [577.5]

17306 Green, Jen. *Exploring the Polar Regions* (4–8). Illus. by David Antram. Series: Voyages of Discovery. 1998, Bedrick $18.95 (0-87226-489-0). 48pp. After an introduction to the polar regions, this book covers the exploration of these areas from the days of Eric the Red in A.D. 998 through 1993. (Rev: HBG 10/98; SLJ 4/98) [998]

17307 Green, Jen. *On the Tundra* (2–5). Illus. Series: Small World. 2002, Crabtree LB $15.96 (0-7787-0139-5); paper $8.06 (0-7787-0153-0). 32pp. This book for younger readers takes a close look at the creatures that are found in the tundra, and how plant and animal life coexist there. (Rev: BL 10/15/02; SLJ 8/02) [577.5]

17308 Hooper, Meredith. *Antarctic Journal: The Hidden Worlds of Antarctica's Animals* (5–7). Illus. by Lucia deLeiris. 2001, National Geographic $16.95 (0-7922-7188-2). An exciting account of a summer the author spent at Palmer Station in the Antarctic and the wildlife there. (Rev: BL 6/1–15/01; HBG 10/01; SLJ 3/01) [988]

17309 Hoyt-Goldsmith, Diane. *Arctic Hunter* (3–6). 1992, Holiday House LB $16.95 (0-8234-0972-4). 32pp. Ten-year-old Reggie and his family travel to their camp north of the Arctic Circle to add to their food supply. (Rev: BL 12/15/92; HB 1–2/93; SLJ 11/92*) [979.8]

17310 Johnson, Rebecca L. *A Walk in the Tundra* (2–4). Illus. Series: Biomes of North America. 2000, Carolrhoda LB $23.93 (1-57505-157-5). 48pp. A lively account that uses maps, pictures, and text to describe the climate, flora and fauna, and the people of the tundra regions of North America. (Rev: BL 10/15/00; HBG 3/01; SLJ 12/00) [577.5]

17311 Kaplan, Elizabeth. *Tundra* (4–6). Illus. Series: Biomes of the World. 1995, Marshall Cavendish LB $25.64 (0-7614-0080-X). 64pp. Material is given on the location of this frigid biome and the life it supports. (Rev: BL 12/15/95; SLJ 3/96) [551.4]

17312 Kendall, Russ. *Eskimo Boy: Life in an Inupiag Eskimo Village* (2–4). Illus. 1992, Scholastic $15.95 (0-590-43695-3). 40pp. An informal photoessay that focuses on seven-year-old Norman Kokeok, who lives on the remote Alaskan island of Shishmaref. (Rev: BCCB 2/92; BL 1/15/92; SLJ 4/92) [979.8]

17313 Kimmel, Elizabeth C. *Ice Story: Shackleton's Lost Expedition* (4–7). Illus. 1999, Clarion $18.00 (0-395-91524-4). 120pp. A fine, accurate, and engrossing description of Shackleton's Imperial Transatlantic Expedition to the Antarctic — one of the great survival stories of all time. (Rev: BL 4/1/99; HBG 10/99; SLJ 4/99) [910.9]

17314 Lambert, David. *Polar Regions* (5–8). Illus. 1988, Silver Burdett LB $12.95 (0-382-09502-2). 48pp. Striking color photographs, maps, and diagrams highlight this description of the world's polar regions. (Rev: BL 4/1/88) [919.8]

17315 Lassieur, Allison. *The Inuit* (2–4). Illus. Series: Native Peoples. 2000, Bridgestone LB $15.93 (0-7368-0498-6). 24pp. Such topics as history, housing, government, culture, and daily life are covered in this simple introduction to the Inuit people. (Rev: BL 10/1/00; HBG 10/00; SLJ 12/00) [971.9]

17316 Levinson, Nancy Smiler. *North Pole South Pole* (1–2). Illus. by Diane D. Hearn. 2002, Holiday House $14.95 (0-8234-1737-9). 40pp. Basic facts about the two poles for beginning readers. (Rev: HB 1–2/03; HBG 3/03; SLJ 12/02) [574]

17317 Love, Ann, and Jane Drake. *The Kids Book of the Far North* (2–4). Illus. 2000, Kids Can $15.95 (1-55074-563-8). 48pp. Topics covered in this introduction to the Arctic include climate and landscape, natural resources, exploration and settlement, and the life, past and present, of the native people. (Rev: BL 9/15/00; SLJ 1/01) [909]

17318 Lynch, Wayne. *Arctic Alphabet: Exploring the North from A to Z* (3–5). Illus. 1999, Firefly $19.95 (1-55209-336-0); paper $6.95 (1-55209-334-4). 32pp. Using an alphabetical arrangement, the author/photographer introduces Arctic wildlife as well as the aurora borealis, glaciers, hibernation, and the Inuit. (Rev: BL 2/1/00; HBG 3/00; SLJ 2/00) [577]

17319 McCurdy, Michael. *Trapped by the Ice: Shackleton's Amazing Antarctic Adventure* (3–5). Illus. 1997, Walker LB $17.85 (0-8027-8439-9). 40pp. The breathtaking account of Shackleton's six-month ordeal living on the ice after his ship sank in the Arctic. (Rev: BL 9/15/97; HBG 3/98; SLJ 10/97) [919.9804]

17320 McMillan, Bruce. *Summer Ice: Life Along the Antarctic Peninsula* (4–6). Illus. 1995, Houghton Mifflin $16.00 (0-395-66561-2). 48pp. A photoessay that describes the geography and the plants and animals that live on the Antarctic Peninsula. (Rev: BL 11/1/95; SLJ 9/95) [508]

17321 Markle, Sandra. *Super Cool Science: South Pole Stations Past, Present, and Future* (3–5). Illus. 1998, Walker LB $17.85 (0-8027-8471-2). 32pp. After describing the first research station at the South Pole built in 1956, the author describes the present facilities and their uses, with coverage on plans for a newer, larger station in the future. (Rev: BL 3/15/98; HBG 10/98; SLJ 4/98) [507]

17322 Martin, Jacqueline B. *The Lamp, the Ice, and the Boat Called Fish* (2–4). Illus. 2000, Houghton Mifflin $15.00 (0-618-00341-X). 48pp. The story of the personnel aboard a research boat named Fish and how they survived with the help of some natives after they were trapped in the ice during an Arctic expedition. (Rev: BCCB 2/01; BL 3/1/01; HB 3–4/01; HBG 10/01) [919.804]

17323 Matsen, Brad. *An Extreme Dive Under the Antarctic Ice* (4–6). Series: Incredible Deep-Sea Adventures. 2003, Enslow LB $18.95 (0-7660-2190-4). 48pp. Readers follow environmental scientists under the cold ice of the Antarctic and discover

pollution and other threats. (Rev: HBG 4/04; SLJ 1/04) [551.46]

17324 Miller, Debbie S. *Arctic Lights, Arctic Nights* (2–4). Illus. by Jon Van Zyle. 2003, Walker $17.85 (0-8027-8857-2). 32pp. Brief text and double-page paintings explore life during the seasons of an Arctic year. (Rev: BL 10/1/03; HBG 10/03; SLJ 8/03)

17325 Newman, Shirlee P. *The Inuits* (4–6). Illus. Series: First Books. 1993, Watts LB $22.00 (0-531-20073-6). 64pp. A vivid account of Inuit, or Eskimo, life that supplies information on their homes, food, clothing, family life, and social structure. (Rev: BL 12/1/93) [973]

17326 Oberman, Sheldon. *The Shaman's Nephew: A Life in the Far North* (4–8). Illus. 2000, Stoddart $18.95 (0-7737-3200-4). 56pp. This first-person narrative explores Inuit art and culture as experienced by Tookoome, an Inuit artist, who reflects on the daily life, beliefs, and myths of his people as presented in his work. (Rev: BL 6/1–15/00; SLJ 7/00) [971.9]

17327 Penner, Lucille Recht. *Ice Wreck* (2–4). Illus. Series: Road to Reading. 2001, Golden Books $11.99 (0-307-46408-3); paper $3.99 (0-307-26408-4). 48pp. An absorbing narrative about Shackleton's disastrous expedition and exciting rescue. (Rev: BL 7/01; HBG 3/02) [919.8]

17328 Penny, Malcolm. *The Polar Seas* (4–6). Illus. Series: Seas and Oceans. 1997, Raintree $27.12 (0-8172-4513-8). 48pp. An overview of the history and importance of the polar seas, as well as the dangers that tourism and the search for natural resources now pose. (Rev: BL 7/97) [551.46]

17329 Pipes, Rose. *Tundra and Cold Deserts* (2–4). Series: World Habitats. 1998, Raintree LB $15.98 (0-8172-5010-7). 32pp. The world's tundra areas are introduced along with their physical characteristics, wildlife, climate, and uses. (Rev: BL 3/15/99; HBG 3/99) [574.5]

17330 Rootes, David. *The Arctic* (3–6). Illus. Series: Endangered People and Places. 1996, Lerner LB $22.60 (0-8225-2776-6). 48pp. A glimpse of the Arctic region and the people who live in this hostile environment. (Rev: BL 11/15/96; SLJ 1/97) [333.73]

17331 Sayre, April P. *Antarctica* (5–8). Series: Seven Continents. 1998, Twenty-First Century LB $25.90 (0-7613-3227-8). A well-written and well-illustrated introduction to the Antarctic environment, including its geology, plants, animals, and research facilities. (Rev: BL 2/1/99; HBG 9/99; SLJ 4/99) [919.89]

17332 Scott, Elaine. *Poles Apart: Why Penguins and Polar Bears Will Never Be Neighbors* (4–8). Illus. 2004, Viking $17.99 (0-670-05925-0). 64pp. This fascinating overview of the two polar regions examines their physical characteristics, seasons, wildlife, magnetism, exploration, and the effects of global warming. (Rev: BL 12/1/04; SLJ 12/04) [909]

17333 Shemie, Bonnie. *Houses of Snow, Skin and Bones* (3–6). Illus. 1989, Tundra $13.95 (0-88776-240-9). 24pp. Covers a variety of dwellings used by people of the extreme north. (Rev: BCCB 12/89; BL 12/15/89; SLJ 4/90) [392.36]

17334 Steele, Philip. *Tundra* (3–5). Illus. Series: Geography Detectives. 1997, Carolrhoda LB $19.93 (1-57505-040-4). 32pp. The treeless plains of the Arctic and parts of Antarctica are introduced, with material on the people who live there and how these areas have changed through the centuries. (Rev: BL 8/97; SLJ 1/98) [574.5]

17335 Steger, Will, and Jon Bowermaster. *Over the Top of the World: Explorer Will Steger's Trek Across the Arctic* (4–7). Illus. 1997, Scholastic paper $17.95 (0-590-84860-7). 64pp. Describes the grueling, dangerous adventures involved in a journey across the Arctic Ocean. (Rev: BCCB 2/97; BL 4/15/97; SLJ 4/97*) [919.804]

17336 Stone, Lynn. *Tundra* (1–3). Illus. Series: Biomes of North America. 2003, Rourke $20.64 (1-58952-687-2). 24pp. For young researchers, this is an excellent introduction to this biome, with clear, simple text, photographs, and maps. (Rev: BL 10/15/03) [577.5]

17337 Theodorou, Rod. *From the Arctic to Antarctica* (2–4). Series: Amazing Journeys. 2000, Heinemann LB $15.95 (1-57572-485-5). 32pp. Both the Arctic and Antarctic regions are described in this brief overview that also introduces plant and animal life. (Rev: HBG 3/01; SLJ 7/00) [998]

17338 Wadsworth, Ginger. *Tundra Discoveries* (PS–3). Illus. by John Carrozza. 1999, Charlesbridge LB $15.95 (0-88106-875-6); paper $6.95 (0-88106-876-4). 32pp. Each double-page spread chronicles a different month in the Arctic tundra and describes the changes in both animals and plants. (Rev: BL 9/1/99; HBG 3/00; SLJ 8/99) [591.75]

17339 Wallace, Mary. *The Inuksuk Book* (4–6). Illus. 1999, Firefly LB $19.95 (1-895688-90-6). 64pp. The daily life of the Inuit are described in this illustrated account that emphasizes *inuksuk,* the stone structures these people build for a variety of reasons. (Rev: BL 9/1/99; HBG 10/99; SLJ 6/99) [306]

17340 Wheeler, Sara. *Greetings from Antarctica* (1–5). Photos by author. 1999, Bedrick $15.95 (0-87226-295-2). 45pp. An attractive, lively introduction to Antarctica with coverage of geography, geology, ecology, history, and climate. (Rev: HBG 3/00; SLJ 8/99) [998.2]

17341 Winckler, Suzanne. *Our Endangered Planet: Antarctica* (4–7). Illus. Series: Our Endangered Planet. 1992, Lerner LB $27.15 (0-8225-2506-2). 72pp. Introduces the continent of Antarctica, including current environmental concerns. (Rev: BL 5/15/92) [918.8]

17342 Winner, Cherie. *Life in the Tundra* (5–8). Series: Ecosystems in Action. 2003, Lerner LB $26.60 (0-8225-4686-8). 72pp. In text and pictures, the Arctic tundra is presented with material on the organisms that live there and how human life has changed this ecosystem. (Rev: BL 9/15/03; HBG 10/03) [551.4]

17343 Yolen, Jane. *Welcome to the Ice House* (PS–3). Illus. by Laura Regan. 1998, Penguin Putnam $15.99 (0-399-23011-4). 32pp. Using illustrations that portray the bleak Arctic landscapes, the poet introduces various animals that live in this inhos-

pitable climate. (Rev: BL 2/15/98; HBG 10/98; SLJ 3/98*) [591.7586]

17344 Yue, Charlotte, and David Yue. *The Igloo* (3–6). Illus. 1988, Houghton Mifflin $16.00 (0-395-44613-9); paper $6.95 (0-395-62986-1). 128pp. Describes the construction and function of igloos. (Rev: BCCB 1/89; BL 9/1/88; SLJ 12/88)

United States

General

17345 Arnosky, Jim. *Under the Wild Western Sky* (2–4). Illus. 2005, HarperCollins LB $16.89 (0-688-17122-2). 32pp. In first-person narrative and eye-catching illustrations, Arnosky introduces readers to the wildlife and grandeur of the West. (Rev: BL 6/1–15/05) [578.74]

17346 Ayer, Eleanor. *Our National Monuments* (4–6). Illus. Series: I Know America. 1992, Millbrook LB $20.90 (1-56294-078-3). 48pp. The most important of our national monuments are highlighted and their history explained in this well-illustrated account. (Rev: BL 9/1/92; SLJ 10/92) [973]

17347 Brent, Lynnette R. *At School: Long Ago and Today* (2–4). Series: Times Change. 2003, Heinemann LB $24.22 (1-4034-4533-8). 32pp. This book, illustrated with period and contemporary photographs, contrasts a day in school today and a century or so ago. (Rev: SLJ 5/04) [372.973]

17348 Brent, Lynnette R. *Going Shopping: Long Ago and Today* (2–4). Series: Times Change. 2003, Heinemann LB $24.22 (1-4034-4535-4). 32pp. A comparison of what it was like to go shopping more than 100 years ago with what it's like today, illustrated with contemporary and period photographs. (Rev: SLJ 5/04) [380.1]

17349 Deangelis, Therese. *Blackout! Cities in Darkness* (4–8). Series: American Disasters. 2003, Enslow LB $18.95 (0-7660-2110-6). 48pp. This book chronicles the events and people involved in some of the important blackouts that have crippled America's cities. (Rev: BL 11/15/03; HBG 4/04) [307.7]

17350 Haskins, Lori. *Spooky America: Four Real Ghost Stories* (2–3). Series: Step into Reading. 2003, Golden Books paper $3.99 (0-375-82500-2). 48pp. Truth and legend are intertwined in these illustrated stories set in Massachusetts, Virginia, Colorado, and California. (Rev: BL 10/1/03; HBG 4/04) [133.1]

17351 Johnson, Linda C. *Our National Symbols* (4–6). Illus. Series: I Know America. 1992, Millbrook LB $20.90 (1-56294-108-9). 48pp. American symbols — historical and current, such as yellow ribbons during the Persian Gulf War — are discussed. (Rev: BL 5/15/92; SLJ 7/93) [929.9]

17352 Keenan, Sheila. *O, Say Can You See? America's Symbols, Landmarks, and Important Words* (2–5). Illus. by Ann Boyajian. 2004, Scholastic $16.95 (0-439-42450-X). 64pp. The bald eagle, the Pledge of Allegiance, and Veteran's Day are among the holidays, landmarks, symbols, and sayings included in this attractive guide. (Rev: BL 10/15/04) [973]

17353 Locker, Thomas. *Home: A Journey Through America* (4–6). Illus. 1998, Harcourt $16.00 (0-15-201473-X). 32pp. Using excerpts from poems, letters, and novels, plus outstanding full-page oil paintings, this book celebrates the beauty of various American landscapes. (Rev: BL 11/1/98; HBG 3/99; SLJ 10/98) [810.8]

17354 Saller, Carol. *Working Children* (3–6). Illus. Series: Picture the American Past. 1998, Carolrhoda LB $22.60 (1-57505-276-8). 48pp. This work supplies a history of child labor, particularly in this country, and efforts to stop it. (Rev: BL 3/1/99; HBG 3/99; SLJ 1/99) [331.3]

17355 Sis, Peter. *The Train of States* (K–3). 2004, Greenwillow LB $18.89 (0-06-057839-4). 64pp. Eye-catching circus wagons representing each of the 50 states (the District of Columbia gets the caboose) are arranged in chronological order and accompanied by pertinent facts. (Rev: BL 10/15/04; SLJ 11/04*) [973]

17356 Stone, Tanya L. *America's Top 10 National Monuments* (3–6). Illus. Series: America's Top 10. 1997, Blackbirch LB $16.95 (1-56711-194-7). 24pp. Presidential memorials in Washington, D.C., and the Mesa Verde National Park are some of the monuments introduced in a series of two-page spreads. (Rev: HBG 3/98; SLJ 1/98) [973]

17357 West, Delno C., and Jean M. West. *Uncle Sam and Old Glory: Symbols of America* (2–5). Illus. 2000, Simon & Schuster $17.00 (0-689-82043-7). 40pp. From the bald eagle and the Liberty Bell to Smokey the Bear, this is a history of 15 symbols, their origins, and meanings. (Rev: BCCB 1/00; BL 12/15/99; HBG 10/00; SLJ 1/00) [929.9]

General History and Geography

17358 Andryszewski, Tricia. *Step by Step Along the Appalachian Trail* (4–8). 1998, Twenty-First Century LB $24.90 (0-7613-0273-5). A state-by-state tour of the Appalachian Trail, with material on the terrain, elevations, landmarks, and sites along the way. (Rev: BL 3/1/99; HBG 9/99; SLJ 4/99) [973]

17359 Baines, John. *The United States* (4–8). Illus. Series: Country Fact Files. 1994, Raintree LB $27.12 (0-8114-1857-X). 45pp. In a series of double-page spreads, basic information about the United States is given, including geography, economy, population, industry, education, government, and environment. (Rev: SLJ 7/94) [973]

17360 Beckett, Harry. *Lake Erie* (3–5). Series: Great Lakes of North America. 1999, Rourke LB $17.45 (0-86593-527-0). 32pp. This book introduces the history of Lake Erie as well as its geography and industries. (Rev: SLJ 2/00) [973]

17361 Beckett, Harry. *Lake Superior* (3–5). Series: Great Lakes of North America. 1999, Rourke LB $17.45 (0-86593-528-9). 32pp. Maps, graphs, and photographs illustrate this introduction to Lake Superior, its history, geography, and commercial value. (Rev: SLJ 2/00) [973]

17362 Beckett, Harry. *Waterways to the Great Lakes* (3–5). Series: Great Lakes of North America. 1999, Rourke LB $17.45 (0-86593-529-7). 32pp. This book discusses how the Great Lakes were formed, the fur trade, the lock system, and current environmental problems. (Rev: SLJ 2/00) [973]

17363 Berg, Elizabeth. *USA* (4–6). Series: Countries of the World. 1999, Gareth Stevens LB $19.95 (0-8368-2313-3). 96pp. This introduction to the geography and history of the U.S. gives additional information on government, lifestyles, art, food, and unique holidays and customs. (Rev: BL 12/15/99; HBG 10/00; SLJ 1/00) [973]

17364 Berg, Elizabeth. *USA* (2–4). Series: Festivals of the World. 1999, Gareth Stevens LB $15.95 (0-8368-2028-2). 32pp. After listing both secular and religious holidays celebrated in the United States, the most important are described and related craft projects and recipes supplied. (Rev: BL 12/15/99; HBG 10/00) [973]

17365 Bial, Raymond. *One-Room School* (3–6). Illus. 1999, Houghton Mifflin $15.00 (0-395-90514-1). 48pp. This photoessay gives a history of the rural one-room schoolhouse in America from the 1700s through the 1950s. (Rev: BCCB 10/99; BL 11/1/99; HBG 3/00; SLJ 10/99) [370]

17366 Bockenhauer, Mark H., and Stephen F. Cunha. *Our Fifty States* (4–10). Illus. 2004, National Geographic LB $45.90 (0-7922-6992-6). 239pp. Maps of the states are accompanied by basic facts, photographs, and archival reproductions of key historical events; also includes the U.S. territories. (Rev: SLJ 1/05) [973]

17367 Bowden, Rob. *Settlements of the Mississippi River* (3–5). Illus. Series: Rivers Through Time. 2005, Heinemann LB $20.95 (1-4034-5719-0). 48pp. Traces the history and contemporary life of major settlements along the Mississippi, discussing the development of industry and the importance of environmental factors.

17368 Brent, Lynnette R. *At Home: Long Ago and Today* (2–4). Series: Times Change. 2003, Heinemann LB $24.22 (1-4034-4531-1). 32pp. A look at how things were "at home" a century or more ago compared with today. (Rev: SLJ 5/04) [690]

17369 Brexel, Bernadette. *The Knights of Labor and the Haymarket Riot: The Fight for an Eight-Hour Workday* (5–8). Illus. Series: America's Industrial Society in the 19th Century. 2004, Rosen LB $21.25 (0-8239-4028-4). 32pp. For reluctant readers, this overview of the struggle to improve working conditions features large print and short chapters. Also use *The Populist Party: A Voice for the Farmers in an Industrial Society* (2004).

17370 Brown, Gene. *Conflict in Europe and the Great Depression: World War I (1914–1940)* (5–8). Series: First Person America. 1994, Twenty-First Century LB $20.90 (0-8050-2585-5). The period from 1914 to 1940 is re-created through excerpts from original source material and texts describing events and social conditions. (Rev: BL 5/15/94; SLJ 11/94) [973.9]

17371 Brownell, Barbara. *Spin's Really Wild U.S.A. Tour* (K–4). Illus. 1996, National Geographic paper $7.95 (0-7922-3422-7). An introduction to the geography of the United States that highlights the flora, fauna, and land formations, conducted by Spin from the National Geographic TV series. (Rev: SLJ 6/96) [910]

17372 Burleigh, Robert. *American Moments: Scenes from American History* (3–6). Trans. and illus. by Bruce Strachan. 2004, Holt $18.95 (0-8050-7082-6). 48pp. Eighteen chapters present scenes from American history that may lack detail but will arouse interest. (Rev: BL 7/04; SLJ 6/04) [973]

17373 Butler, Daphne. *U.S.A.* (2–4). Illus. 1992, Raintree LB $23.83 (0-8114-3676-4). 32pp. Color photos aid in a broad overview of the United States, described in terms of topography and lifestyle. (Rev: BL 3/15/93) [973]

17374 Collier, Christopher, and James Lincoln Collier. *The Rise of the Cities: 1820–1920* (5–8). Illus. Series: The Drama of American History. 2001, Marshall Cavendish LB $29.93 (0-7614-1051-1). 96pp. In this highly illustrated volume, the Colliers paint a broad picture of the process of urbanization in the United States, tracing the problems involved and the growing prominence of cities in American life. (Rev: BL 3/15/01; HBG 10/01; SLJ 7/01) [973]

17375 Collier, Christopher, and James Lincoln Collier. *The United States Enters the World Stage: From the Alaska Purchase Through World War I* (5–8). Series: The Drama of American History. 2001, Marshall Cavendish LB $29.93 (0-7614-1053-8). Covering the years 1867 through 1918, this well-illustrated account traces America's emergence as a world power. (Rev: BL 3/15/01; HBG 10/01) [973.9]

17376 Colman, Penny. *Girls: A History of Growing Up Female in America* (5–8). Illus. 2000, Scholastic paper $18.95 (0-590-37129-0). 192pp. Using diaries, memoirs, letters, magazine articles, and other sources, the author presents a history of girls in America from the first females to cross the Bering Strait to the present day. (Rev: BCCB 2/00; BL 2/1/00; HBG 10/00; SLJ 3/00) [305.23]

17377 Cooper, Jason. *Árboles / Trees* (4–8). Trans. by Blanca Rey. Illus. Series: La Guía de Rourke Para los Símbolos de los Estados/Rourke's Guide to State Symbols. 2002, Rourke LB $29.93 (1-58952-399-7). 63pp. The 50 state trees are introduced in bilingual text and illustrations. Also use *Aves / Birds, Banderas / Flags*, and *Flores / Flowers*. (Rev: SLJ 3/03) [582]

17378 Costain, Meredith, and Paul Collins. *Welcome to the United States of America* (3–5). Illus. Series: Countries of the World. 2001, Chelsea LB $16.95 (0-7910-6542-1). 32pp. This basic introduction to the land, people, and culture of the United States will be useful in work with new immigrants and ESL students. (Rev: HBG 3/02; SLJ 2/02)

17379 Currie, Stephen. *The Mississippi* (5–8). Series: Rivers of the World. 2003, Gale LB $27.45 (1-59018-061-5). 112pp. A comprehensive look at this important river's history, geology, agricultural and industrial significance, environmental problems, and the floods that threaten surrounding communities. (Rev: SLJ 9/03) [977]

17380 Davis, Kenneth C. *Don't Know Much About American History* (4–7). Illus. by Matt Faulkner. Series: Don't Know Much About. 2003, HarperCollins LB $20.89 (0-06-028604-0); paper $6.99 (0-06-440836-1). 224pp. Davis brings wit and reason to this fact-filled, question-and-answer approach to American history, arranged in chronological order. (Rev: HBG 10/03; SLJ 5/03) [973]

17381 Davis, Kenneth C. *Don't Know Much About the 50 States* (3–5). Illus. by Renee W. Andriani. Series: Don't Know Much About. 2001, HarperCollins LB $15.89 (0-06-028608-3). 61pp. Each state gets its own page packed with facts, statistics, stories, and cartoon drawings, in addition to the standard fare of map, nickname, date of statehood, capital, and major state symbols. (Rev: HBG 3/02; SLJ 9/01)

17382 Davis, Todd, and Marc Frey. *The New Big Book of America* (3–5). 2002, Running Press $9.98 (0-7624-1263-1). 56pp. The 50 states are organized in alphabetical order, giving an overview of history, geography, and culture with a map, a list of basic facts, and topics of particular interest. (Rev: HBG 3/03; SLJ 1/03)

17383 Dolan, Edward F. *The American Indian Wars* (5–8). Illus. 2003, Millbrook LB $29.90 (0-7613-1968-9). 112pp. Four hundred years of conflict are covered in this volume that looks at the causes, details the key battles and events, and provides portraits of the key participants. (Rev: BL 12/1/03) [973.04]

17384 English, June A., and Thomas D. Jones. *Scholastic Encyclopedia of the United States at War* (5–8). 1998, Scholastic paper $18.95 (0-590-59959-3). A heavily illustrated volume that traces America's wars from the Revolution to the Gulf War, with each chapter including a timeline, a map, and a discussion of causes, battles, new technologies, and the aftermath. (Rev: BL 10/15/98; SLJ 2/99) [973]

17385 Feinstein, Stephen. *The 1910s: From World War I to Ragtime Music* (5–8). Series: Decades of the 20th Century. 2001, Enslow LB $17.95 (0-7660-1611-0). 64pp. The events of the 1910s are covered in chapters on lifestyle and fashion, arts and entertainment, sports, politics, and science, technology, and medicine. Also use *The 1920s: From Prohibition to Charles Lindbergh* (2001). (Rev: HBG 10/02; SLJ 2/02) [973.9]

17386 Feinstein, Stephen. *The 1940s: From World War II to Jackie Robinson* (5–8). Illus. Series: Decades of the 20th Century. 2000, Enslow LB $17.95 (0-7660-1428-2). 64pp. A lively look at events of the 1940s, covering everything from fashion and fads to politics, science, technology, medicine, and sports. Also use *The 1930s: From the Great Depression to the Wizard of Oz* (2001) and *The 1950s: From the Korean War to Elvis* (2000). (Rev: HBG 3/01; SLJ 5/01) [973.9]

17387 Feinstein, Stephen. *The 1960s: From the Vietnam War to Flower Power* (4–7). Illus. Series:

Decades of the 20th Century. 2000, Enslow LB $17.95 (0-7660-1426-6). 64pp. An account of America's turbulent 1960s that includes lifestyles, politics, fashion, fads, and entertainment. (Rev: BL 10/15/00; HBG 3/01; SLJ 12/00) [973.92]

17388 Feinstein, Stephen. *The 1970s: From Watergate to Disco* (4–7). Series: Decades of the 20th Century. 2000, Enslow LB $17.95 (0-7660-1425-8). 64pp. This book covers the people and events of the 1970s along with developments in such areas as politics, science, and sports. (Rev: BL 10/15/00; HBG 3/01; SLJ 12/00) [973.9]

17389 Feinstein, Stephen. *The 1990s: From the Persian Gulf War to Y2K* (5–8). Series: Decades of the 20th Century. 2001, Enslow LB $17.95 (0-7660-1613-7). 64pp. The events of the 1990s are covered in chapters on lifestyle and fashion; arts and entertainment; sports; politics; and science, technology, and medicine. (Rev: HBG 10/02; SLJ 2/02) [973.9]

17390 Fischer, Maureen M. *Nineteenth Century Lumber Camp Cooking* (4–7). Series: Exploring History Through Simple Recipes. 2000, Capstone LB $22.60 (0-7368-0604-0). 32pp. After describing life in a lumber camp more than a hundred years ago, this book supplies some authentic recipes. (Rev: BL 3/1/01; HBG 10/01; SLJ 4/01) [973.8]

17391 Foster, Genevieve, and Joanna Foster. *George Washington's World*. Rev. ed. (5–8). Illus. 1997, Beautiful Feet paper $15.95 (0-9643803-4-X). 357pp. A new edition of this 50-year-old book that re-creates what was happening in the world during Washington's life, now with expanded coverage on minorities. (Rev: SLJ 3/98) [909]

17392 Frank, Nicole, and Elizabeth Berg. *Welcome to the USA* (2–4). Illus. Series: Welcome to My Country. 2000, Gareth Stevens $22.60 (0-8368-2513-6). With color pictures on each page and a simple text, this is a basic introduction to the United States, its geography, and its people. (Rev: HBG 10/01; SLJ 1/01) [973]

17393 Haban, Rita D. *How Proudly They Wave: Flags of the Fifty States* (4–9). Illus. 1989, Lerner LB $23.93 (0-8225-1799-X). Pictures of the state flags are accompanied by background information. (Rev: BL 12/15/89; SLJ 3/90) [929.9]

17394 Hakim, Joy. *An Age of Extremes*. 2nd ed. (5–8). Series: A History of Us. 1999, Oxford LB $19.95 (0-19-512765-X); paper $13.95 (0-19-512766-8). 205pp. A thorough and accurate history of the United States' coming of age after Reconstruction — from 1870 through World War I. (Rev: BL 12/15/99) [973.8]

17395 Hakim, Joy. *War, Peace, and All That Jazz*. 2nd ed (5–8). Series: A History of Us. 1999, Oxford LB $19.95 (0-19-512767-6). 206pp. Political, social, and cultural events and developments are traced in this fascinating account of life in the United States between the world wars and through World War II, with coverage of the Jazz Age, the Great Depression, and the war itself. (Rev: BL 12/15/99) [973.9]

17396 Hamilton, John. *Everglades National Park* (4–6). Series: National Parks. 2005, ABDO LB $16.94 (1-59197-424-0). 32pp. Full-color photographs illustrate the information on the Everglades's history, ecosystem, geology, and wildlife, plus discussion of development of this area. Also use *Glacier National Park*, *Grand Canyon National Park*, and *Great Smoky Mountains National Park* (2005). (Rev: SLJ 6/05) [975.9]

17397 Holling, Holling C. *Paddle-to-the-Sea* (3–6). Illus. by author. 1980, Houghton Mifflin $20.00 (0-395-15082-5); paper $10.00 (0-395-29203-4). From Ontario to the Atlantic in a toy canoe, in this classic juvenile tale.

17398 Hoobler, Dorothy, and Thomas Hoobler. *Real American Girls Tell Their Own Stories* (4–7). Illus. 1999, Simon & Schuster $12.95 (0-689-82083-6). 112pp. Excerpts from personal diaries and autobiographies are used to introduce a number of young American girls from colonial times to the 1950s. (Rev: BCCB 12/99; BL 10/15/99; HBG 3/00; SLJ 12/99) [305.23]

17399 Hudson, Wade. *Powerful Words* (5–9). Illus. by Sean Qualls. 2004, Scholastic $19.95 (0-439-40969-1). 192pp. Excerpts from the writings and speeches of both well-known and less-familiar African Americans are accompanied by notes on the context and the writer. (Rev: BL 2/15/04; SLJ 2/04) [081]

17400 Isaacs, Sally Senzell. *America in the Time of Franklin Delano Roosevelt: The Story of Our Nation from Coast to Coast, from 1929 to 1948* (4–8). Series: America in the Time Of. 1999, Heinemann LB $30.35 (1-57572-761-7). 48pp. Using the life of Roosevelt as a framework, this account describes life in America during the Great Depression and World War II. (Rev: SLJ 5/00) [973.9]

17401 Isaacs, Sally Senzell. *America in the Time of Susan B. Anthony: The Story of Our Nation from Coast to Coast, from 1845 to 1928* (4–8). 1999, Heinemann LB $30.35 (1-57572-763-3). 48pp. Using the life of Susan B. Anthony as a framework, this work covers topics including woman's suffrage, poverty, and World War I. (Rev: SLJ 5/00) [973.9]

17402 Johnston, Robert D. *The Making of America* (5–8). Illus. 2002, National Geographic $29.95 (0-7922-6944-6). 224pp. An informative and balanced overview of American history, this appealing volume divides American history into eight periods; in addition to the narrative, each period includes profiles of two major figures and examines important issues of the time. (Rev: BL 1/1–15/03; HBG 3/03; SLJ 12/02*) [973]

17403 Kalman, Bobbie, and Greg Nickles. *Spanish Missions* (4–7). Illus. Series: Historic Communities. 1996, Crabtree LB $21.28 (0-86505-436-3); paper $7.95 (0-86505-466-5). 32pp. In double-page spreads, this book covers the building of the mission in the southern United States and of its functions: teaching Christianity, educating children, and supplying housing and food. (Rev: SLJ 4/97) [973]

17404 King, David C. *First Facts About U.S. History* (4–8). Illus. Series: First Facts. 1996, Blackbirch $34.94 (1-56711-168-8). A brief chronological survey of major events in U.S. history. (Rev: BL 7/96; SLJ 7/96) [973]

17405 Kroll, Steven. *Ellis Island: Doorway to Freedom* (3–5). Illus. by Karen Ritz. 1995, Holiday House LB $16.95 (0-8234-1192-3). 32pp. This history, beginning with colonial times, concentrates on the period when Ellis Island's immigration center processed millions of immigrants. (Rev: BL 11/15/95; SLJ 1/96) [325.73]

17406 Leacock, Elspeth, and Susan Buckley. *Journeys in Time: A New Atlas of American History* (4–6). Illus. 2001, Houghton Mifflin $15.00 (0-395-97956-0). 48pp. Twenty dramatic stories of "journeys" drawn from true accounts serve to introduce the history of America in an unusual and effective way. (Rev: BL 6/1–15/01; HB 7–8/01; HBG 10/01; SLJ 6/01) [973]

17407 Leacock, Elspeth, and Susan Buckley. *Places in Time: A New Atlas of American History* (4–6). Illus. 2001, Houghton Mifflin $15.00 (0-395-97958-7). 48pp. In this companion to *Journeys in Time*, 20 significant sites — towns, battlefields, Ellis Island, even a tract house — are used to convey essential elements of American history. (Rev: BL 6/1–15/01; HB 7–8/01; HBG 10/01; SLJ 6/01) [911]

17408 Leedy, Loreen. *Celebrate the 50 States!* (1–3). Illus. 1999, Holiday House $16.95 (0-8234-1431-0). 32pp. Each page in this simple geography book introduces two states and gives basic information such as capitals, state symbols, and bits of state lore. (Rev: BL 9/1/99; HBG 3/00; SLJ 9/99) [973]

17409 Lourie, Peter. *Mississippi River* (3–5). Illus. 2000, Boyds Mills $17.95 (1-56397-756-7). 48pp. While describing his trip on the Mississippi from Minnesota to Louisiana, the author gives facts about the waterway and the life that surrounds it. (Rev: BCCB 10/00; BL 10/1/00; HBG 3/01; SLJ 10/00) [976.81]

17410 Lourie, Peter. *On the Trail of Lewis and Clark: A Journey Up the Missouri River* (3–5). Illus. 2002, Boyds Mills $19.95 (1-56397-936-5). 48pp. Lourie connects his own trip up the Missouri River to the more famous journey that Lewis and Clark took years before. (Rev: BL 4/1/02; HBG 10/02; SLJ 6/02) [917.804]

17411 Lourie, Peter. *Rio Grande: From the Rocky Mountains to the Gulf of Mexico* (4–6). Illus. 1999, Boyds Mills $17.95 (1-56397-706-0). 46pp. In dramatic prose and stunning photos, the course of the Rio Grande and its place in American history are covered. (Rev: BCCB 4/99; BL 2/15/99; HBG 10/99; SLJ 6/99) [917.3]

17412 McCormick, Anita Louise. *The Industrial Revolution in American History* (5–8). Illus. Series: In American History. 1998, Enslow LB $20.95 (0-89490-985-1). A description of the causes of the Industrial Revolution and the changes that it brought to the United States up to 1946. (Rev: BL 9/1/98; BR 11–12/98) [338.0973]

17413 Miller, Marilyn. *Words That Built a Nation: A Young Person's Collection of Historic American Documents* (4–8). Illus. 1999, Scholastic paper $18.95 (0-590-29881-X). 176pp. A collection of 37

documents important in American history — from the Mayflower Compact and the Declaration of Independence to Hillary Rodham Clinton's address to the United Nations Conference on Women and Malcolm X's "The Ballot or the Bullet" speech. (Rev: BL 10/15/99; HBG 3/00; SLJ 2/00) [973]

17414 Miller, Millie, and Cyndi Nelson. *The United States of America: A State-by-State Guide* (3–6). Illus. 1999, Scholastic $14.95 (0-590-04374-9). 64pp. A state-by-state guide to the U.S. and Puerto Rico that supplies basic information, including a map and population figures for each. (Rev: BL 11/15/99; HBG 3/00; SLJ 12/99) [973]

17415 Miller, Page Putnam. *Landmarks of American Women's History* (5–8). 2004, Oxford LB $30.00 (0-19-514501-1). 143pp. Landmarks — all on the National Register of Historic Places — highlighted for their importance in women's history include Taos Pueblo, New Mexico, chosen for the strong Native American women who lived there; the Wesleyan Chapel at Seneca Falls, where the first women's rights conference was held; and the Boardinghouse at Boott Cotton Mill in Lowell, Massachusetts, home to many young women who worked in the textile industry. (Rev: SLJ 9/04) [973]

17416 Nash, Gary B. *Landmarks of the American Revolution* (5–8). Series: American Landmarks. 2003, Oxford LB $30.00 (0-19-512849-4). 158pp. Landmark sites such as Independence Hall, Valley Forge National Historic Park, Faneuil Hall, and Yorktown Battlefield are introduced with excerpts from primary documents such as letters and broadsides. (Rev: SLJ 8/03) [973.3]

17417 Nelson, Robin. *School* (3–6). Series: First Step Nonfiction. 2003, Lerner LB $15.93 (0-8225-4640-X). 24pp. Ideal for new readers, this book looks at how early schools differed from those we know today. Also in this series, use *Toys and Games* (2003). (Rev: BL 11/15/03; HBG 4/04; SLJ 12/03)

17418 Pollard, Michael. *The Mississippi* (5–8). Illus. Series: Great Rivers. 1997, Benchmark LB $22.79 (0-7614-0502-X). 45pp. A history of this great river and its influence on American history, with photographs, maps, and diagrams. (Rev: HBG 3/98; SLJ 3/98) [917.7]

17419 Prevost, John. *Mississippi River* (3–4). Series: Rivers and Lakes. 2002, ABDO LB $13.95 (1-57765-102-2). 24pp. A solid introduction to the Mississippi, its tributaries, flora and fauna, and the ways in which it has influenced human development in the area throughout history. (Rev: HBG 10/02; SLJ 7/02) [976.81]

17420 Rawlins, Carol B. *The Colorado River* (4–8). Series: Watts Library. 1999, Watts LB $24.00 (0-531-11738-3). 64pp. With full-color photographs and maps that complement the text, this book traces the famous Rocky Mountain waterway from north-central Colorado through the Southwest into the Gulf of California and covers its history and uses. (Rev: BL 1/1–15/00; SLJ 2/00) [973]

17421 Roop, Peter, and Connie Roop. *A Farm Album* (2–3). Series: Long Ago and Today. 1998, Heinemann LB $13.95 (1-57572-601-7). 24pp. Pairing old illustrations with modern photographs, this work compares life on a farm today with that of 100 years ago. (Rev: BL 12/15/98) [973]

17422 Roop, Peter, and Connie Roop. *A Home Album* (2–3). Series: Long Ago and Today. 1998, Heinemann LB $13.95 (1-57572-602-5). 24pp. American home life today and 100 years ago are compared through a simple text and contrasting photographs. (Rev: BL 12/15/98) [973]

17423 Rubel, David. *Scholastic Atlas of the United States* (3–5). 2000, Scholastic $19.95 (0-590-72562-9). 144pp. Arranged by region and then by state, this atlas also contains a text that gives good background on each state plus maps that indicate principal towns, highways, natural resources, national parks, etc. (Rev: HBG 3/01; SLJ 2/01) [917.3]

17424 Sabuda, Robert. *America the Beautiful* (2–4). Illus. by author. 2004, Simon & Schuster $26.95 (0-689-84744-0). 16pp. Elaborate pop-up spreads salute natural and man-made landmarks, including Mount Rushmore, New York City, Mesa Verde, and the Golden Gate Bridge, and the verses of the well-known song. (Rev: BL 11/15/04; SLJ 11/04) [811]

17425 Sandak, Cass R. *The United States* (4–8). Illus. Series: Modern Industrial World. 1996, Raintree LB $24.26 (0-8172-4556-1). An examination of the economic and industrial situation in the United States, with additional information on education, living standards, and related subjects. (Rev: BL 2/15/97; SLJ 8/97) [973]

17426 Sanders, Nancy I. *A Kid's Guide to African American History: More Than 70 Activities* (4–6). Illus. 2000, Chicago Review paper $14.95 (1-55652-417-X). 242pp. Along with a history of African Americans from slavery through the civil rights movement and hopes for the future, there are more than 70 activities and crafts including recipes, making a bead necklace, constructing a star-watching chart, and crafts about Kwanzaa. (Rev: BL 2/15/01) [973]

17427 Sandler, Martin W. *America's Great Disasters* (4–6). 2003, HarperCollins LB $18.89 (0-06-029108-7). 96pp. Among the disasters covered here (along with their effects on building codes, safety procedures, and so forth) are the Johnstown (PA) flood, the influenza epidemic of 1918–1919, the San Francisco earthquake of 1906, and the eruption of Mount St. Helens. (Rev: BL 6/1–15/03; HBG 10/03; SLJ 8/03) [973]

17428 Siebert, Diane. *Mississippi* (3–5). Illus. 2001, HarperCollins LB $16.89 (0-688-16446-3). 40pp. This volume uses free-verse to describe the history associated with the Mississippi River as well as its course from its beginnings in the north to its mouth on the Gulf of Mexico. (Rev: BL 3/15/01; HBG 10/01) [976.2]

17429 Sills, Leslie. *From Rags to Riches: A History of Girls' Clothing in America* (4–7). Illus. 2005, Holiday House $16.95 (0-8234-1708-5). 48pp. Changes in clothing over the centuries are linked to the social mores of the time in this appealing volume. (Rev: BL 5/1/05) [391]

17430 Smith-Baranzini, Marlene, and Howard Egger-Bovet. *Brown Paper School USKids History: Book of the New American Nation* (5–7). Illus. 1995, Little, Brown paper $14.95 (0-316-22206-2). 96pp. From George Washington to the building of the Erie Canal, key issues and people in American history are introduced. (Rev: BL 8/95; SLJ 8/95) [973.5]

17431 Sonneborn, Liz. *The Pledge of Allegiance: The Story Behind Our Patriotic Promise* (3–5). Illus. Series: America in Words and Song. 2004, Chelsea House LB $14.95 (0-7910-7336-X). 32pp. This slim volume provides the history of the pledge and the changes it has undergone over the years. (Rev: BL 4/1/04; SLJ 5/04) [323.0]

17432 Stanley, George E. *The New Republic (1763–1815)* (5–8). Illus. Series: A Primary Source History of the United States. 2005, World Almanac LB $22.50 (0-8368-5825-5). 48pp. A simple narrative links well-chosen primary sources documenting the key events of the revolutionary period.

17433 Stevenson, Harvey. *Looking at Liberty* (3–5). Illus. by author. 2003, HarperCollins LB $17.89 (0-06-000101-1). 40pp. This artful blend of poetry, eye-catching artwork, and concise facts recounts the story behind the construction of the Statue of Liberty — a gift from the people of France to the people of the United States. (Rev: BL 10/1/03; HBG 10/03; SLJ 6/03)

17434 Stewart, Gail B. *1900s* (5–8). Illus. Series: Timelines. 1990, Macmillan LB $11.95 (0-89686-471-5). 48pp. Events and trivia of the decade, with many illustrations. Also use *1910s; 1920s; 1930s* (all 1989). (Rev: SLJ 6/90) [973.9]

17435 Stienecker, David L. *First Facts About the States* (4–8). Series: First Facts. 1996, Blackbirch $34.94 (1-56711-166-1). Using a double-page spread for each state, this account gives basic information on such topics as state symbols, mottos, history, geography, and landmarks. (Rev: SLJ 7/96) [973]

17436 Stienecker, David L. *States* (2–5). Illus. Series: Discovering Geography. 1997, Marshall Cavendish LB $22.79 (0-7614-0541-0). 32pp. Using a question-and-answer approach, this book teaches youngsters how to read maps that show topics such as terrain, weather, landmarks, population, capitals and products. (Rev: BL 2/1/98; HBG 3/98) [917.3]

17437 Tackach, James. *The Abolition of American Slavery* (5–9). Series: World History. 2002, Gale LB $27.45 (1-59018-002-X). 112pp. A comprehensive survey of slavery and the abolition movement in the United States, with closing information on segregation and the civil rights movement of the 20th century. (Rev: BL 8/02; SLJ 9/02)

17438 Telford, Carole, and Rod Theodorou. *Down a River* (2–6). Illus. by Stephen Lings and Jane Pickering. Series: Amazing Journeys. 1997, Heinemann LB $13.95 (1-57572-153-8). 32pp. This journey of the entire length of the Mississippi and Missouri rivers supplies maps, illustrations and a description of the plants and animals that live in this ecosystem. (Rev: SLJ 5/98) [917.3]

17439 Thro, Ellen, and Andrew K. Frank. *Growing and Dividing* (5–8). Series: The Making of America. 2001, Raintree LB $28.54 (0-8172-5704-7). 96pp. The story of the development of the eastern United States from the early days of the Republic through the clashes that led to the Civil War. (Rev: BL 4/15/01; HBG 10/01) [973.5]

17440 Travis, George. *State Facts* (3–5). Series: The Rourke Guide to State Symbols. 1999, Rourke LB $19.45 (1-57103-297-5). 48pp. Basic information about each state is given including nicknames, size, number of counties, and bordering states, plus colorful topographical maps. (Rev: SLJ 2/00) [973]

17441 *United States in Pictures* (5–8). Illus. Series: Visual Geography. 1995, Lerner LB $25.55 (0-8225-1896-1). 64pp. An attractive basic introduction to the geography, history, and people of the United States. (Rev: BL 8/95) [973]

17442 Van Zandt, Eleanor. *A History of the United States Through Art* (5–8). Illus. Series: History Through Art. 1996, Thomson Learning LB $5.00 (1-56847-443-1). 48pp. American history is covered in 21 double-page spreads that feature text and famous artworks. (Rev: BL 3/1/96; SLJ 2/96) [973]

17443 Wacker, Grant. *Religion in Nineteenth Century America* (5–8). Series: Religion in American Life. 2000, Oxford $28.00 (0-19-511021-8). 183pp. This is the story of how religion in America affected such 19th-century events as the westward movement, the Civil War, and immigration, with additional coverage of the careers of such people as Sojourner Truth and Mary Baker Eddy. (Rev: BL 6/1–15/00; HBG 10/00; SLJ 8/00) [973]

17444 Walsh, Kieran J. *The Mississippi* (4–7). Series: Great Rivers of the World. 2003, World Almanac LB $26.60 (0-8368-5444-6). 48pp. An exploration of the Mississippi's flow, history, and animals and plants, with discussion of the settlements along its banks, the industries it supports, recreation on its waters, and environmental threats to the river. (Rev: SLJ 9/03) [977]

17445 Webb, Marcus. *The United States* (5–8). Series: Modern Nations of the World. 2000, Lucent LB $27.45 (1-56006-663-6). 112pp. A mature look at the past and present United States with an extended section on modern culture. (Rev: BL 5/15/00; HBG 10/00) [973]

17446 Wilbur, Keith C. *Revolutionary Medicine, 1700–1800* (4–8). Illus. Series: Illustrated Living History. 1996, Chelsea $21.95 (0-7910-4532-3). In a large-book format, this account gives a great deal of information — some gruesome, some funny — about medicine in 18th-century America. (Rev: BL 6/1–15/97; SLJ 7/97) [973.3]

Historical Periods

NATIVE AMERICANS

17447 Abbink, Emily. *Colors of the Navajo* (2–4). Illus. by Janice L. Porter. Series: Colors of the World. 1998, Carolrhoda LB $19.93 (1-57505-207-

5); paper $5.95 (1-57505-269-5). 24pp. Ten different colors are used to tie together this book about Navajo life, culture, arts, and traditions. (Rev: SLJ 12/98) [973]

17448 Adams, McCrea. *Tipi* (3–5). Illus. by Kimberly L. Dawson Kurnizki. Series: Native American Homes. 2001, Rourke LB $25.27 (1-55916-275-9). 32pp. This volume discusses Native American tipis and how, why, where, and by whom they were built. (Rev: SLJ 3/01) [973]

17449 Adare, Sierra. *Mohawk* (4–8). Illus. 2003, Gareth Stevens LB $22.60 (0-8368-3665-0). 32pp. An introduction to the history, culture, and current status of the Mohawk people, with photographs, maps, and interesting sidebar features that will be useful for reports. Also use *Apache* and *Nez Perce* (both 2003). (Rev: HBG 10/03; SLJ 9/03) [974.7004]

17450 Alter, Judy. *Native Americans* (3–5). Series: Spirit of America: Our Cultural Heritage. 2002, Child's World LB $27.07 (1-56766-152-1). 32pp. This account gives an overview of the history of Native Americans, their problems, and the impact of their cultures on present-day American society. (Rev: BL 10/15/02) [973]

17451 Anderson, Dale. *The Anasazi Culture at Mesa Verde* (5–8). Series: Landmark Events in American History. 2003, World Almanac LB $26.60 (0-8368-5371-7). 48pp. The story of the native people from the region around the Four Corners and of their many cultural accomplishment including basketry, pottery, and urban architecture. (Rev: BL 10/15/03) [973]

17452 Andryszewski, Tricia. *The Seminoles: People of the Southeast* (3–6). Illus. Series: Native Americans. 1995, Millbrook LB $21.90 (1-56294-530-0). 64pp. As well as giving a history of the Seminoles, this account tells about their culture and traditions and includes a recipe, a legend, and instructions for the Seminole pole-ball game. (Rev: SLJ 1/96) [973]

17453 Arnold, Caroline. *The Ancient Cliff Dwellers of Mesa Verde* (4–7). Illus. by Richard Hewett. 1992, Houghton Mifflin $16.00 (0-395-56241-4). 64pp. This is the fascinating story of the Anasazi of southwestern Colorado, who made their homes in the cliffs of steep canyons and later abandoned them. (Rev: BL 5/1/92; SLJ 7/92*) [978.8]

17454 Baylor, Byrd. *The Desert Is Theirs* (2–4). Illus. by Peter Parnall. 1987, Macmillan $16.00 (0-684-14266-X); paper $5.95 (0-689-71105-0). 32pp. Through colorful, strong pictures and a lyric text, the life of the Papago Indians and their reverence for the desert are revealed.

17455 Bealer, Alex W. *Only the Names Remain: The Cherokees and the Trail of Tears* (4–6). Illus. by William Sauts Bock. 1996, Little, Brown paper $5.95 (0-316-08519-7). A history of the Cherokees, with emphasis on their tragic exile west of the Mississippi River in 1839.

17456 Beres, Cynthia Breslin. *Longhouse* (3–5). Illus. by Kimberly L. Dawson Kurnizki. 2001, Rourke LB $25.27 (1-55916-247-3). 32pp. This book describes the building and uses of the Native

American longhouses and the part they played in the culture. (Rev: SLJ 3/01) [973]

17457 Bial, Raymond. *The Apache* (5–8). Series: Lifeways. 2000, Benchmark LB $32.79 (0-7614-0939-4). 128pp. Presents the dramatic, often tragic history of the Apache Indians, with biographies of leaders such as Geronimo and a description of the social and cultural life of these nomadic people. (Rev: BL 11/15/00; HBG 3/01; SLJ 3/01) [973]

17458 Bial, Raymond. *The Cheyenne* (5–8). Series: Lifeways. 2000, Benchmark LB $32.79 (0-7614-0938-6). 128pp. Part of the Great Plains Indian group, the Cheyenne's daily life, religious beliefs, social system, and history are introduced in this book. (Rev: BL 11/15/00; HBG 3/01; SLJ 3/01) [973]

17459 Bial, Raymond. *The Comanche* (4–8). Series: Lifeways. 1999, Benchmark LB $32.79 (0-7614-0864-9). 127pp. This impressive volume gives an accurate picture of the social and political life of the Comanche from their early history to the present day. (Rev: BL 3/15/00; HBG 10/00; SLJ 3/00) [973]

17460 Bial, Raymond. *The Haida* (5–8). Series: Lifeways. 2000, Benchmark LB $32.79 (0-7614-0937-8). 128pp. This book describes these Native Americans of the Northwest and introduces their artistic and carving skills, their social system, beliefs, history, and daily life. (Rev: BL 11/15/00; HBG 3/01; SLJ 3/01) [973]

17461 Bial, Raymond. *The Huron* (5–8). Series: Lifeways. 2000, Benchmark LB $32.79 (0-7614-0940-8). 128pp. Color pictures and clear text describe this Indian group's past and present and give details of their daily life, religion, and rituals. (Rev: BL 11/15/00; HBG 3/01; SLJ 3/01) [973]

17462 Bial, Raymond. *Longhouses* (2–5). Series: American Community. 2004, Children's Pr. LB $28.00 (0-516-23707-1). 48pp. A look at life in the longhouses of the Iroquois living in the Great Lakes region. (Rev: SLJ 1/05) [973]

17463 Bial, Raymond. *The Nez Perce* (5–8). Series: Lifeways. 2001, Marshall Cavendish LB $32.79 (0-7614-1210-7). This attractively illustrated account gives basic material on the historical and social aspects of this Native American tribe, including their food, clothing, and culture. (Rev: BL 1/1–15/02; HBG 3/02; SLJ 4/02) [973]

17464 Bial, Raymond. *The Ojibwe* (5–8). Illus. Series: Lifeways. 1999, Marshall Cavendish LB $32.79 (0-7614-0863-0). 127pp. Topics covered in this introduction to the Ojibwe nation include history, traditions, beliefs, and the nation today. (Rev: BL 3/1/00; HBG 10/00; SLJ 3/00) [977]

17465 Bial, Raymond. *The Powhatan* (5–8). Series: Lifeways. 2001, Marshall Cavendish LB $32.79 (0-7614-1209-3). The story of the Powhatan tribe of Virginia, whose members included Pocahontas, with material on their history and various aspects of their culture. (Rev: BL 1/1–15/02; HBG 3/02) [973]

17466 Bial, Raymond. *The Pueblo* (5–8). Illus. Series: Lifeways. 1999, Marshall Cavendish LB $32.79 (0-7614-0861-4). 127pp. Good photographs and a lucid text combine to produce a fine introduc-

tion to the Pueblo Indians, their history, culture, traditions, present status, and notable members of the nation. (Rev: BL 3/1/00; HBG 10/00; SLJ 3/00) [978.9]

17467 Bial, Raymond. *The Seminole* (4–8). Series: Lifeways. 1999, Benchmark LB $32.79 (0-7614-0862-2). 127pp. Topics covered in this account of the Seminole Indians include history, daily life, religious beliefs, sacred rituals, and attitudes toward themselves. (Rev: BL 3/15/00; HBG 10/00; SLJ 3/00) [973]

17468 Bial, Raymond. *The Shoshone* (5–8). Series: Lifeways. 2001, Marshall Cavendish LB $32.79 (0-7614-1211-5). The story of the Native American tribe of buffalo hunters who lived in the Northwest, with material on their history, culture, language, food, and clothing. (Rev: BL 1/1–15/02; HBG 3/02) [973]

17469 Bial, Raymond. *The Tlingit* (5–9). Series: Lifeways. 2002, Benchmark LB $22.95 (0-7614-1414-2). 128pp. A photo-filled overview of the Tlingit people who live along the northern Pacific Coast of North America, with insights into their folklore, cuisine, and language. (Rev: HBG 3/03; SLJ 6/03) [979.8004]

17470 Birchfield, D. L. *The Trail of Tears* (4–7). Series: Landmark Events in American History. 2003, World Almanac LB $29.26 (0-8368-5381-4). 48pp. A brief account of the tragic forced removal of Native American people from their lands by the U.S. government in the mid-19th century. (Rev: SLJ 6/04) [973.04]

17471 Braine, Susan. *Drumbeat . . . Heartbeat: A Celebration of the Powwow* (4–6). Photos by author. Series: We Are Still Here: Native Americans Today. 1995, Lerner LB $21.27 (0-8225-2656-5); paper $6.95 (0-8225-9711-X). 48pp. An introduction to powwows that explains their history, where they are held, and what they mean to Native Americans today. (Rev: SLJ 9/95) [973]

17472 Brody, J. J. *A Day with a Mimbres* (4–6). Illus. by Giorgio Bacchin. Series: A Day With. 1999, Runestone LB $22.60 (0-8225-1917-8). 48pp. This book explores the history and daily life of this ancient Native American group who lived in the Southwest. (Rev: HBG 10/99; SLJ 10/99) [973]

17473 Broida, Marian. *Projects About American Indians of the Southwest* (3–5). Illus. Series: Hands-On History. 2003, Marshall Cavendish LB $18.95 (0-7614-1602-1). 48pp. The 10 simple projects outlined in this book introduce information about the Navajo, Hopi, Zuni, and Pueblo Indians. (Rev: BL 4/1/04; HBG 4/04; SLJ 4/04) [979.004]

17474 Bruchac, Joseph. *Navajo Long Walk: The Tragic Story of a Proud People's Forced March from Their Homeland* (4–8). Illus. by Shonto Begay. 2002, National Geographic $18.95 (0-7922-7058-4). 34pp. Using revealing words and pictures, this large picture book for older readers re-creates the shameful story of the deadly marches of the Navajo in the 1860s. (Rev: BL 5/1/02; HBG 10/02; SLJ 7/02) [979.1]

924

17475 Bruchac, Joseph. *Seasons of the Circle: A Native American Year* (2–4). Illus. by Robert F. Goetzl. 2002, Troll $15.95 (0-8167-7467-6). 32pp. An overview of Native American activities, lore, and traditions associated with the different seasons, with effective illustrations, a helpful map, and a chart of Native American names of the months. (Rev: BL 10/1/02; HBG 3/03) [391]

17476 Bruchac, Joseph. *The Trail of Tears* (2–4). Illus. by Diana Magnuson. Series: Step into Reading. 1999, Random LB $11.99 (0-679-99052-6); paper $3.99 (0-679-89052-1). 48pp. An easy reader that movingly tells the story of the Cherokees and the bitter 1,200-mile forced journey from Georgia to Oklahoma between 1838 and 1839. (Rev: BL 12/1/99) [973]

17477 Burgan, Michael. *The Trail of Tears* (3–5). Series: We the People. 2001, Compass Point LB $21.26 (0-7565-0101-6). 48pp. A well-illustrated, concise introduction to the Cherokee people and the events leading up to their removal from their lands in 1838. (Rev: SLJ 6/01) [975]

17478 Carew-Miller, Anna. *Native American Cooking* (4–7). Illus. Series: Native American Life. 2002, Mason Crest LB $19.95 (1-59084-131-X). 64pp. The role of the environment in Native American food choices is emphasized in this overview that is organized by region. Also use *Native American Tools and Weapons* and *What the Native Americans Wore* (both 2002). (Rev: SLJ 2/03) [641.5979]

17479 Claro, Nicole. *The Cherokee Indians* (3–5). Illus. Series: Indians of North America. 1991, Chelsea LB $16.95 (0-7910-1652-8). 80pp. The concentration is on the history of the Cherokee since their contact with Europeans. (Rev: BL 10/15/91) [973]

17480 Collins, David R., and Kris Bergren. *Ishi: The Last of His People* (5–8). Illus. 2000, Morgan Reynolds LB $21.95 (1-883846-54-4). 96pp. This is the story of Ishi, the ill-clad and half-starved man who emerged from the wilderness in California in 1911 and who was believed to be a survivor of the lost Yahi tribe. (Rev: BL 12/1/00; HBG 10/00) [979.4004]

17481 Cooper, Michael L. *Indian School: Teaching the White Man's Way* (5–10). Illus. 1999, Clarion $16.00 (0-395-92084-1). 103pp. A moving photoessay about Native American children and how they were removed from their homes and uprooted from their culture to attend Indian boarding schools in an effort to "civilize" them. (Rev: BL 12/1/99; HBG 4/00; SLJ 2/00) [370]

17482 Cory, Steven. *Pueblo Indian* (5–8). Illus. Series: American Pastfinder. 1996, Lerner LB $25.55 (0-8225-2976-9). Color illustrations and maps accompany this account of the Pueblo Indians and the incredible cities they built. (Rev: BL 7/96) [973]

17483 Crewe, Sabrina, and Dale Anderson. *The Anasazi Culture at Mesa Verde* (3–5). Series: Events That Shaped America. 2003, Gareth Stevens LB $22.60 (0-8368-3390-2). 32pp. Explores what we know about the ancient Anasazi culture of the American Southwest and why they chose to settle in Mesa Verde. (Rev: HBG 10/03; SLJ 10/03) [978.8]

17484 Deangelis, Therese. *The Cherokee: Native Basket Weavers* (3–5). Illus. Series: America's First Peoples. 2003, Capstone LB $22.60 (0-7368-1535-X). 32pp. This fascinating overview of the Cherokee provides a basic introduction to the history and culture of the Native American tribe with particular focus on basket weaving skills. (Rev: SLJ 10/03)

17485 Deangelis, Therese. *The Ojibwa: Wild Rice Gatherers* (3–5). Illus. Series: America's First Peoples. 2003, Capstone LB $22.60 (0-7368-1537-6). 32pp. This title from America's First Families series introduces readers to the history and culture of the Ojibwa, an Algonquian-speaking tribe that traditionally lived in the north central United States and nearby Canada. (Rev: HBG 10/03; SLJ 10/03)

17486 Delgado, James P. *Native American Shipwrecks* (5–7). Illus. Series: Watts Library: Shipwrecks. 2000, Watts LB $24.00 (0-531-20379-4); paper $8.95 (0-531-16473-X). 64pp. This book covers the boats that Native Americans made, their uses and voyages, the culture of these peoples, and how underwater archaeologists have explored their wrecks. (Rev: BL 10/15/00) [623.8]

17487 Dennis, Yvonne Wakim, and Arlene Hirschfelder. *Children of Native America Today* (3–6). Illus. 2003, Charlesbridge $19.95 (1-57091-499-0). 64pp. Photos show contemporary Native American young people wearing traditional as well as modern clothes, with maps, reservation locations, and a resource list. (Rev: BL 3/1/03; HBG 10/03; SLJ 10/03) [306]

17488 Denny, Sidney G., and Ernest L. Schusky. *The Ancient Splendor of Prehistoric Cahokia* (4–8). 1997, Ozark paper $3.95 (1-56763-272-6). Using the findings at the Cahokia Mounds in southern Illinois as a beginning, the author re-creates the life and culture of these prehistoric American Indians. (Rev: BL 5/1/97) [977.3]

17489 Elish, Dan. *The Trail of Tears: The Story of the Cherokee Removal* (5–9). Series: Great Journeys. 2001, Benchmark LB $21.95 (0-7614-1228-X). 96pp. The economic and social reasons for the Cherokee's forced exile to lands in the west are presented in text, quotations from primary sources, and many illustrations and maps. (Rev: BL 1/1–15/02; HBG 10/02; SLJ 3/02) [973]

17490 *Enduring Wisdom: Sayings from Native Americans* (3–6). Ed. by Virginia Driving Hawk Sneve. Illus. by Synthia Saint James. 2003, Holiday House $16.95 (0-8234-1455-8). 32pp. A picture-book collection of sayings from 1647 to the present day that are backed up by helpful endnotes. (Rev: BL 3/15/03; HBG 10/03; SLJ 5/03) [970]

17491 Englar, Mary. *The Iroquois: The Six Nations Confederacy* (4–7). Illus. Series: American Indian Nations. 2002, Capstone LB $22.60 (0-7368-1353-5). 48pp. Describes the history, traditions, and current status of the Iroquois, with photographs, reproductions, and a map. (Rev: HBG 3/03; SLJ 6/03) [973]

17492 Englar, Mary. *The Pueblo: Southwestern Potters* (3–5). Illus. Series: America's First Peoples. 2003, Capstone LB $22.60 (0-7368-1538-4). 32pp. This appealing introduction to the Pueblo people of America's Southwest focuses on their traditional pottery. (Rev: HBG 10/03; SLJ 10/03)

17493 Feinstein, Stephen. *California Native Peoples* (4–6). Illus. Series: Heinemann State Studies. 2003, Heinemann LB $27.07 (1-4034-0341-4). 48pp. From prehistory to today, this attractively illustrated volume looks at the lives and culture of California's native peoples, with particular focus on "outside influences" that brought upheavals. (Rev: HBG 4/04; SLJ 11/03) [979.4]

17494 Ferrell, Nancy W. *The Battle of the Little Bighorn* (5–9). Series: In American History. 1996, Enslow LB $20.95 (0-89490-768-9). A detailed account of the Battle of Little Bighorn from various points of view on both sides, along with a review of the conflicts between the U.S. government and Native Americans, the different cultures of various tribes, key figures such as Crazy Horse and Sitting Bull, and the aftermath of the battle. (Rev: BR 1–2/97; SLJ 12/96) [973.8]

17495 Fischer, Laura. *Life on the Trail of Tears* (2–4). Illus. Series: Picture the Past. 2003, Heinemann LB $24.22 (1-4034-3800-5). 32pp. The plight of Cherokee children is highlighted in this attractive introduction to the sad story of forced relocation. (Rev: SLJ 6/04) [973.04]

17496 Fowler, Verna. *The Menominee* (4–7). Series: Indian Nations. 2000, Raintree LB $25.69 (0-8172-5458-7). 48pp. Opening with a folk tale, this book describes the Menominee Indians, their life and culture, and how they were overrun in the 19th century and pushed onto a reservation in northern Wisconsin. (Rev: BL 3/15/01; HBG 10/01) [973]

17497 Fradin, Dennis B. *The Cheyenne* (2–4). Illus. 1988, Children's Book Pr. paper $5.50 (0-516-41211-6). 48pp. History of this Native American tribe called "the people." (Rev: BL 8/88; SLJ 11/88)

17498 Freedman, Russell. *Buffalo Hunt* (4–6). Illus. 1988, Holiday House LB $21.95 (0-8234-0702-0). 52pp. How the Plains Indians worshiped and depended on the buffalo. (Rev: BCCB 10/88; BL 10/1/88; SLJ 10/88)

17499 Freedman, Russell. *An Indian Winter* (4–8). Illus. by Karl Bodmer. 1992, Holiday House $21.95 (0-8234-0930-9). 88pp. A fascinating re-creation of the winter of 1833-34 that the German prince Maximilian and a Swiss artist spent with the Indians in North Dakota. (Rev: HB 7–8/92; SLJ 6/92) [970]

17500 Fulkerston, Chuck. *The Shawnee* (4–6). Illus. by Katherine Ace. Series: Native American People. 1992, Rourke LB $21.27 (0-86625-392-0). 32pp. This account emphasizes the history of the Shawnee and presents material on their everyday life and religion. (Rev: BL 12/15/92) [973]

17501 Gallimard Jeunesse, et al. *Native Americans* (PS–2). Series: First Discovery. 1998, Scholastic $11.95 (0-590-38153-9). 24pp. Using sturdy plastic pages, overlays, and colorful illustrations, this introduction to Native Americans emphasizes the part they have played in U.S. history. (Rev: BL 9/15/98; HBG 10/98) [973]

17502 Gibson, Karen Bush. *The Chickasaw Nation* (2–5). Series: Native Peoples. 2002, Capstone LB $18.60 (0-7368-1365-9). 24pp. A clearly written history of this Native American tribe that lived in the northern Mississippi area. (Rev: BL 3/15/03; SLJ 4/03) [973]

17503 Gibson, Karen Bush. *The Potawatomi* (2–5). Series: Native Peoples. 2002, Capstone LB $18.60 (0-7368-1368-3). 24pp. This history of the noted midwestern Native American group includes material on lifestyle, culture, and present status. (Rev: BL 3/15/03; SLJ 4/03) [973]

17504 Gold, Susan D. *Indian Treaties* (5–8). Illus. Series: Pacts and Treaties. 1997, Twenty-First Century LB $24.90 (0-8050-4813-8). A history of the successive treaties under which the Native Americans gradually lost their homes and livelihood. (Rev: BL 5/15/97; BR 9–10/97; SLJ 6/97) [323.1]

17505 Gorsline, Marie, and Douglas Gorsline. *North American Indians* (5–8). Illus. by Douglas Gorsline. 1978, Random paper $3.25 (0-394-83702-9). Major tribes are identified and briefly described. [973]

17506 Gravelle, Karen. *Growing Up Where the Partridge Drums Its Wings: A Mohawk Childhood* (4–6). Illus. 1997, Watts LB $24.00 (0-531-11453-8). 64pp. This account focuses on Chantelle Francis and her cousin David Francis and their youth on a Mohawk reservation that bridges Canada and the United States. (Rev: BL 1/1–15/98; HBG 3/98; SLJ 3/98) [971.4]

17507 Gray-Kanatiiosh, Barbara A. *Hopi* (2–4). Illus. by Charles Chimerica. Series: Native Americans. 2002, ABDO LB $14.95 (1-57765-598-2). 32pp. An attractive and accessible introduction to the Hopi people that covers homeland, culture, family life, mythology, crafts, war, early contact with the Europeans, and contemporary lifestyle. Also use *Inuit* (2002). (Rev: HBG 10/02; SLJ 8/02) [973]

17508 Greene, Jacqueline D. *Powwow: A Good Day to Dance* (4–6). Illus. 1998, Watts LB $22.00 (0-531-20337-9). 64pp. Ten-year-old Little Man and his family participate in the annual Wampanoag powwow in eastern Massachusetts where they celebrate their culture with family and friends. (Rev: BL 1/1–15/99; HBG 3/99; SLJ 2/99) [394]

17509 Griffin, Lana T. *The Navajo* (4–7). Illus. Series: Indian Nations. 1999, Raintree LB $25.69 (0-8172-5463-3). 48pp. This book describes the history of the Navajo, their everyday life, customs, and tribal government, and includes two Navajo creation stories. (Rev: BL 2/15/00; HBG 10/00; SLJ 4/00) [979.1]

17510 Gunderson, Mary. *American Indian Cooking Before 1500* (4–7). Series: Exploring History Through Simple Recipes. 2000, Capstone LB $22.60 (0-7368-0605-9). 32pp. This book describes the everyday life of Native Americans before Europeans arrived and gives a few simple recipes. (Rev: BL 3/1/01; HBG 10/01; SLJ 7/01) [973]

17511 Haderer, Kurt. *Journey to Native Americans* (2–5). Illus. 1999, Prestel $14.95 (3-7913-2083-1).

30pp. This is a report on Native Americans as studied by German prince Maximilian of Wied and Swiss painter Karl Bodmer in the 1830s. (Rev: BL 11/1/99; SLJ 1/00) [978]

17512 Hahn, Elizabeth. *The Creek* (4–6). Illus. by Katherine Ace. Series: Native American People. 1992, Rourke LB $21.27 (0-86625-393-9). 32pp. History is emphasized in this book that features the point of view of the Native Americans. (Rev: BL 12/15/92) [976]

17513 Hahn, Elizabeth. *The Pawnee* (4–6). Illus. by Katherine Ace. Series: Native American People. 1992, Rourke LB $21.27 (0-86625-391-2). 32pp. Everyday life of the Pawnee, their religion, history, and present-day status are covered in this illustrated account. (Rev: BL 12/15/92) [973]

17514 Hakim, Joy. *The First Americans*. 2nd ed. (5–8). Series: A History of Us. 1999, Oxford LB $19.95 (0-19-512751-X). 177pp. The first volume in this outstanding series traces the history of America from prehistory through the coming of the Europeans, with emphasis on the development of Native American culture. (Rev: BL 12/15/99) [973.1]

17515 Haluska, Vicki. *The Arapaho Indians* (3–5). Illus. Series: Junior Library of American Indians. 1993, Chelsea LB $16.95 (0-7910-1657-9). 80pp. Coverage is given on both the past and the present of this Indian group, with special material on their arts and crafts. (Rev: BL 5/15/93) [973]

17516 Hoyt-Goldsmith, Diane. *Apache Rodeo* (3–5). Photos by Lawrence Migdale. 1995, Holiday House LB $15.95 (0-8234-1164-8). 32pp. The current lifestyles and traditions of the Apache people are revealed through the eyes of young Felicita. (Rev: BCCB 2/95; BL 2/1/95; SLJ 6/95) [973]

17517 Hoyt-Goldsmith, Diane. *Buffalo Days* (3–7). Illus. by Lawrence Migdale. 1997, Holiday House LB $16.95 (0-8234-1327-6). 32pp. By focusing on ten-year-old Clarence Three Irons, Jr., the reader is introduced to the Crow Indians of the present and their heritage, which includes celebrating Buffalo Days. (Rev: BL 11/1/97*; HBG 3/98; SLJ 12/97*) [973]

17518 Hoyt-Goldsmith, Diane. *Potlatch: A Tsimshian Celebration* (4–8). 1997, Holiday House $16.95 (0-8234-1290-3). A 13-year-old boy explains the meaning of potlatch for the Tsimshian tribe in Alaska and describes the many rituals and activities it involves. (Rev: BL 5/1/97; SLJ 6/97) [394.2]

17519 Hoyt-Goldsmith, Diane. *Pueblo Storyteller* (3–5). Illus. by Lawrence Migdale. 1991, Holiday House LB $16.95 (0-8234-0864-7). 32pp. A present-day account of how a Pueblo family in New Mexico lives. (Rev: BCCB 4/91; BL 3/5/91; SLJ 5/91) [978.9]

17520 Hunter, Sally M. *Four Seasons of Corn: A Winnebago Tradition* (3–6). Illus. 1997, Lerner LB $21.27 (0-8225-2658-1); paper $6.95 (0-8225-9741-1). 40pp. The daily life of a boy who assimilates his Anglo-American heritage, along with the traditional activities of his Winnebago people. (Rev: BL 2/1/97; SLJ 3/97) [394.1]

17521 Isaacs, Sally Senzell. *Life in a Hopi Village* (1–3). Series: Picture the Past. 2000, Heinemann $21.36 (1-57572-314-X). A well-organized, visually attractive account that describes daily life in a Hopi village and covers such topics as food, clothing, shelter, and care of children. (Rev: HBG 3/01; SLJ 11/00) [973]

17522 Jemison, Mary. *The Diary of Mary Jemison: Captured by the Indians* (3–6). Ed. by Connie Roop and Peter Roop. Illus. Series: My Own Words. 2000, Marshall Cavendish LB $16.95 (0-7614-1010-4). 64pp. Based on the account published in 1824, this short, nicely illustrated book tells, in a first-person narrative, how Mary Jemison was captured by Indians at age 12 and describes her life with these Native Americans. (Rev: BL 2/15/01; HBG 3/01; SLJ 3/01) [974.7]

17523 Kalman, Bobbie. *Celebrating the Powwow* (2–4). Illus. Series: Crabapples. 1997, Crabtree LB $19.96 (0-86505-640-4); paper $5.95 (0-86505-740-0). 32pp. Using a number of quality photos, this account describes powwows and their various components. (Rev: SLJ 1/98) [973]

17524 Kavasch, E. Barrie. *The Seminoles* (4–7). Illus. Series: Indian Nations. 1999, Raintree LB $25.69 (0-8172-5464-1). 48pp. This account gives a history of the Seminole Indians, with material on their society, customs, festivals, government, present-day conditions, and one of their creation myths. (Rev: BL 2/15/00; HBG 10/00; SLJ 4/00) [975.9]

17525 Keegan, Marcia. *Pueblo Girls: Growing Up in Two Worlds* (3–6). Photos by author. 1999, Clear Light $14.95 (1-57416-020-6). A brief look at how two girls of the San Ildefonso Pueblo in New Mexico are growing up and learning about two cultures, religions, and languages, first their Native American one and secondly that of modern America. (Rev: HBG 3/00; SLJ 10/99) [973]

17526 King, Sandra. *Shannon: An Ojibway Dancer* (4–7). Illus. by Catherine Whipple. 1993, Lerner $19.95 (0-8225-2752-2); paper $11.15 (0-8225-9643-1). 48pp. Thirteen-year-old Shannon Anderson, an Ojibway girl, prepares for the summer powwow and her part in the shawl dance. (Rev: BCCB 1/94; BL 1/15/94; SLJ 2/94) [394]

17527 Kirk, Connie Ann. *The Mohawks of North America* (4–7). Series: First Peoples. 2001, Lerner LB $23.93 (0-8225-4853-4). 32pp. This book focuses on the history and cultural practices of the Mohawk people and their present status in America. (Rev: BL 10/15/01; HBG 3/02) [973]

17528 Krehbiel, Randy. *Little Bighorn* (4–8). Series: Battlefields Across America. 1997, Twenty-First Century LB $26.90 (0-8050-5236-4). A review of the historical background and events leading up to the Battle of Little Bighorn, followed by a description of the battle itself and the site as it is today. (Rev: SLJ 1/98) [973.8]

17529 Krull, Kathleen. *One Nation, Many Tribes: How Kids Live in Milwaukee's Indian Community* (3–7). Illus. Series: A World of My Own. 1995, Dutton $15.99 (0-526-67440-3). 48pp. The story of the daily life and activities of Native American children who are growing up in a community in Milwaukee, Wisconsin. (Rev: BCCB 2/95; BL 2/15/95; SLJ 3/95) [977.5]

17530 Landau, Elaine. *The Ottawa* (4–6). Illus. Series: First Books. 1996, Watts LB $22.00 (0-531-20226-7). 64pp. A description of the history, life, and ways of the Great Lakes Ottawa people. (Rev: BL 8/96; SLJ 1/97) [977]

17531 La Pierre, Yvette. *Native American Rock Art: Messages from the Past* (4–8). Illus. 1994, Thomasson-Grant $16.95 (1-56566-064-1). 48pp. Different types and techniques of Native American rock art are discussed, with additional information on the cultures that produced this phenomenon. (Rev: BL 12/1/94; SLJ 11/94) [709]

17532 Larson, Timothy. *Anasazi* (4–6). Series: Ancient Civilizations. 2001, Raintree LB $15.98 (0-7398-3575-0). 48pp. The history, culture, and daily life of the Anasazi Indians are introduced, with maps and photographs and discussion of archaeological studies and the architecture. (Rev: HBG 3/02; SLJ 6/01) [979]

17533 Lassieur, Allison. *The Apsaalooke (Crow) Nation* (2–5). Series: Native Peoples. 2002, Bridgestone LB $18.60 (0-7368-1103-6). 24pp. This account describes the history and lifestyle of this Native American people who lived on the plains around the Yellowstone River. (Rev: BL 6/1–15/02; HBG 3/03) [973]

17534 Lassieur, Allison. *The Arapaho Tribe* (2–5). Series: Native Peoples. 2001, Bridgestone LB $18.60 (0-7368-0945-7). 24pp. Covers the history, culture, and lifestyle of this Native American tribe from the Colorado-Wyoming region. (Rev: BL 3/15/02; HBG 3/02) [973]

17535 Lassieur, Allison. *The Blackfeet Nation* (2–5). Series: Native Peoples. 2001, Bridgestone LB $18.60 (0-7368-0946-5). 24pp. A brief, colorful introduction to the past and the present of this midwestern Native American nation whose members dyed their moccasins black. (Rev: BL 3/15/02; HBG 3/02) [973]

17536 Lassieur, Allison. *The Choctaw Nation* (2–5). Illus. Series: Native Peoples. 2001, Capstone $12.95 (0-7368-0832-9). 24pp. History and contemporary lifestyle are among the topics covered in this introduction to the Choctaw Indians, the first tribe forced to leave its homeland. Also use *The Shoshone People* (2001). (Rev: BL 5/15/01; HBG 10/01; SLJ 8/01) [973]

17537 Lassieur, Allison. *The Creek Nation* (2–5). Series: Native Peoples. 2001, Bridgestone LB $18.60 (0-7368-0947-3). 24pp. This short history of the Creek people covers present status and conditions as well as offering informative text and full-color historical photographs and illustrations. (Rev: BL 3/15/02; HBG 3/02) [973]

17538 Lassieur, Allison. *The Delaware People* (2–5). Series: Native Peoples. 2002, Bridgestone LB $18.60 (0-7368-1104-4). 24pp. A descrioption of the Native American people who first lived around the Delaware River, and made a famous treaty with William Penn in 1682. (Rev: BL 6/1–15/02) [921]

17539 Lassieur, Allison. *The Hopi* (2–5). Series: Native Peoples. 2002, Bridgestone LB $18.60 (0-7368-1102-8). 24pp. A brief account with many photographs that describes the past and present of this tribe of Pueblo Indians and gives details on the richness of the culture they developed. (Rev: BL 6/1–15/02) [973]

17540 Lassieur, Allison. *The Pequot Tribe* (2–5). Series: Native Peoples. 2001, Bridgestone LB $18.60 (0-7368-0948-1). 24pp. The story of this Eastern Woodlands group of Native Americans is covered briefly in a simple text with many color illustrations. (Rev: BL 3/15/02; HBG 3/02) [973]

17541 Lassieur, Allison. *The Utes* (2–5). Series: Native Peoples. 2002, Bridgestone LB $18.60 (0-7368-1105-2). 24pp. The history and cultural development of the Native American people who began as fierce nomadic horsemen in what is now Colorado and Utah. (Rev: BL 6/1–15/02; HBG 3/03) [973]

17542 Lavender, David. *Mother Earth, Father Sky: Pueblo Indians of the American Southwest* (5–8). Illus. 1998, Holiday House $16.95 (0-8234-1365-9). 117pp. After introducing the geographical area of the Southwest known as Four Corners — where Arizona, New Mexico, Colorado, and Utah meet — this book traces the history and culture of the Pueblo Indians who live there. (Rev: BL 9/1/98; BR 5–6/99; HBG 10/99; SLJ 11/98) [978]

17543 Lee, Georgia. *A Day with a Chumash* (4–6). Illus. by Giorgio Bacchin. Series: A Day With. 1999, Runestone LB $22.60 (0-8225-1918-6). 48pp. Based on archaeological and anthropological findings, this account traces the history and lifestyles of this ancient people of California. (Rev: HBG 10/99; SLJ 10/99) [973]

17544 Limberland, Dennis, and Mary Em Parrilli. *The Cheyenne* (4–7). Series: Indian Nations. 2000, Raintree LB $25.69 (0-8172-5469-2). 48pp. This history of the Cheyenne Indians begins with a folk tale and goes on to describe their lifestyles before and after being sent to reservations in Oklahoma and Montana. (Rev: BL 3/15/01; HBG 10/01) [973]

17545 Liptak, Karen. *North American Indian Survival Skills* (4–6). Illus. Series: First Books. 1990, Watts LB $22.00 (0-531-10870-8). 64pp. An intriguing introduction to survival skills used by various North American tribes. (Rev: BCCB 12/90; BL 2/1/91) [613.6]

17546 Littlefield, Holly. *Children of the Indian Boarding Schools* (3–6). Illus. Series: Picture the American Past. 2001, Carolrhoda LB $22.60 (1-57505-467-1). 48pp. A brief, informative text is accompanied by moving photographs that dramatically tell the sad story of Native American children taken from their homes and sent to boarding schools to learn European customs. (Rev: BL 5/15/01; HBG 10/01; SLJ 7/01) [371.829]

17547 McCarthy, Cathy. *The Ojibwa* (4–7). Series: Indian Nations. 2000, Raintree LB $25.69 (0-8172-5460-9). 48pp. A history of the Ojibwa Indians that includes material on the daily life and traditions of this group that now lives in Minnesota, Wisconsin,

928

and central Canada. (Rev: BL 3/15/01; HBG 10/01) [973]

17548 McCurdy, Michael. *An Algonquian Year: The Year According to the Full Moon* (4–6). Illus. 2000, Houghton Mifflin $15.00 (0-618-00705-9). 32pp. Starting with the full moon in January and progressing through a year of full moons, this handsome book traces the daily activities, shelter, and food of the Algonquian Indians of New England as the seasons change. (Rev: BL 11/1/00; HBG 3/01; SLJ 12/00) [973]

17549 McDaniel, Melissa. *The Sac and Fox Indians* (3–5). Illus. Series: Junior Library of American Indians. 1995, Chelsea LB $16.95 (0-7910-1670-6); paper $9.95 (0-7910-2034-7). 80pp. This account tells of these Wisconsin-based Indians, their near annihilation by the French, and their part in the Black Hawk War. (Rev: BL 1/1–15/96) [977]

17550 McLerran, Alice. *The Ghost Dance* (3–6). Illus. by Paul Morin. 1995, Clarion $15.95 (0-395-63168-8). The story of the hardships inflicted on Native Americans by whites and of the Ghost Dance, which was believed would magically rid their land of these intruders. (Rev: BCCB 11/95; SLJ 11/95*) [973]

17551 McLester, L. Gordon, and Elisabeth Towers. *The Oneida* (4–7). Series: Indian Nations. 2000, Raintree LB $25.69 (0-8172-5457-9). 48pp. The Oneida left their New York lands for Wisconsin and Canada. Beginning with a folk tale, this account describes their past and present with some indication of what the future holds. (Rev: BL 3/15/01; HBG 10/01) [973]

17552 Margolin, Malcolm, and Yolanda Montijo, eds. *Native Ways: California Indian Stories and Memories* (5–8). Illus. 1996, Heyday paper $8.95 (0-930588-73-8). Reminiscences and stories reflect California Indian culture, both past and present. (Rev: BL 7/96) [979.4]

17553 Martell, Hazel M. *Native Americans and Mesa Verde* (4–7). Illus. Series: Hidden Worlds. 1993, Dillon LB $13.95 (0-87518-540-1). 32pp. The history of the Pueblo Indians, their amazing cliff dwellings, and the Mesa Verde National Park. (Rev: BL 10/15/93; SLJ 8/93) [948.8]

17554 May, Robin. *Plains Indians of North America* (4–6). Illus. 1987, Rourke LB $16.67 (0-86625-258-4). 48pp. Lifestyle and customs of the Plains Indians are described in this well-illustrated introduction to these indigenous people, part of the Original Peoples series. (Rev: BL 1/15/88)

17555 Mayfield, Thomas Jefferson. *Adopted by Indians: A True Story* (5–8). Ed. by Malcolm Margolin. Illus. 1997, Heyday paper $10.95 (0-930588-93-2). This is an adaption of the memoirs of a white man who lived with the Choinumne Indians in California for 10 years, beginning in 1850 when he was 8 years old. (Rev: BL 3/1/98) [979.4]

17556 Meli, Franco. *A Day with a Cheyenne* (4–6). Illus. by Giorgio Bacchin. Series: A Day With. 1999, Runestone LB $16.95 (0-8225-1920-8). 48pp. An account of the Cheyenne Indians that gives background historical information and then describes

the daily life of a hunter and his son in the late 1800s. (Rev: HBG 3/00; SLJ 6/00) [973]

17557 Mercredi, Morningstar. *Fort Chipewyan Homecoming: A Journey to Native Canada* (3–6). Photos by Darren McNally. 1997, Lerner LB $21.27 (0-8225-2659-X); paper $6.95 (0-8225-9731-4). 48pp. Twelve-year-old Matthew visits relatives at Fort Chipewyan in Alberta, Canada, and learns a great deal about his Native American heritage. (Rev: SLJ 9/97) [973]

17558 Meyers, Madeleine, ed. *Cherokee Nation: Life Before the Tears* (4–8). Series: Perspectives on History. 1994, Discovery paper $6.95 (1-878668-26-9). 60pp. A history of the Cherokees that emphasizes the leadership of Sequoyah and the life of the tribe before their forced displacement. (Rev: BL 8/94) [970.3]

17559 Miller, Jay. *American Indian Families* (3–5). Illus. Series: True Books. 1996, Children's Book Pr. LB $22.00 (0-516-20133-6). 47pp. Discusses family structure and importance in various Native American tribes. (Rev: SLJ 8/97) [973]

17560 Miller, Jay. *American Indian Festivals* (2–3). Illus. Series: True Books. 1996, Children's Book Pr. LB $22.00 (0-516-20134-4). 47pp. Presents various festivals of Native Americans, like rain dances and thanksgiving celebrations. (Rev: BL 3/1/97; SLJ 8/97) [394.2]

17561 Miller, Jay. *American Indian Foods* (2–3). Illus. Series: True Books. 1996, Children's Book Pr. LB $22.00 (0-516-20135-2). 47pp. The foods eaten by different Native American groups are described by region. (Rev: BL 3/1/97; SLJ 8/97) [641.59]

17562 Miller, Jay. *American Indian Games* (2–3). Illus. Series: True Books. 1996, Children's Book Pr. LB $22.00 (0-516-20136-0). 47pp. With a color photograph on each page and brief text, this title presents the games Native Americans played in the past, like canoe racing and lacrosse, and how they compare with today's interests. (Rev: BL 3/15/97) [394]

17563 Mooney, Martin. *The Comanche Indians* (4–7). Illus. Series: Junior Library of American Indians. 1993, Chelsea LB $19.75 (0-7910-1653-6). 71pp. A historical account of the Comanches from about 1700 to the present. (Rev: SLJ 4/93) [970]

17564 Morris, Ann. *Grandma Maxine Remembers: A Native-American Family Story* (1–3). Series: What Was It Like, Grandma? 2002, Millbrook LB $22.90 (0-7613-2317-1). 32pp. Native American culture is explored through the memories of a grandmother who tells about her experiences as young girl. An appropriate activity, recipe, and game are appended. (Rev: BL 9/15/02; HBG 10/02; SLJ 10/02) [973]

17565 Myers, Arthur. *The Cheyenne* (4–6). Illus. Series: First Books. 1992, Watts paper $6.95 (0-531-15636-2). 64pp. In addition to a description of social organization and customs of the Cheyenne, this book tells of their history, including the Battle of Little Bighorn. (Rev: BL 6/15/92) [970.004]

17566 Naranjo, Tito E. *A Day with a Pueblo* (4–6). Illus. by Giorgio Bacchin. Series: A Day With. 1999, Runestone LB $16.95 (0-8225-1919-4). 48pp.

Historical information is given about the Pueblo Indians followed by an account of an elder today and his daily activities at Taos Pueblo. (Rev: HBG 3/00; SLJ 6/00) [973]

17567 Nelson, Sharlene, and Ted Nelson. *The Makah* (4–6). Series: Watts Library. 2003, Watts LB $24.00 (0-531-12168-2); paper $8.95 (0-531-16215-X). 63pp. An accessible introduction to the Makah people of the Northwest Pacific Coast, with material on their history and culture. (Rev: SLJ 5/04) [979.7]

17568 Netzley, Patricia D. *Apache Warriors* (3–5). Illus. 2003, Gale LB $18.96 (0-7377-0989-8). 48pp. An absorbing look at the Apache warriors in the mid-19th century — with details of housing, clothing, hunting practices, and equipment — that draws on Geronimo's autobiography. (Rev: SLJ 1/03) [979.004]

17569 Newman, Shirlee P. *The Creek* (4–6). Illus. Series: Indians of the Americas. 1996, Watts LB $22.50 (0-531-20236-4); paper $6.95 (0-531-15809-8). 62pp. The history of the Creek (Muskogee) people, who were moved from southeastern United States to Oklahoma. (Rev: BL 12/15/96) [975]

17570 Nobleman, Marc Tyler. *The Battle of the Little Bighorn* (4–6). Series: We the People. 2001, Compass Point LB $21.26 (0-7565-0150-4). 48pp. A basic overview of Custer's last stand and the motivations of both sides in the battle. (Rev: SLJ 1/02) [973.8]

17571 Pasqua, Sandra M. *The Navajo Nation* (2–4). Illus. 2000, Bridgestone LB $15.93 (0-7368-0499-4). 24pp. This introduction to the largest group of Native Americans in the U.S. briefly covers their history, culture, government, and daily life. (Rev: BL 10/1/00; HBG 10/00; SLJ 12/00) [979.1]

17572 Pennington, Daniel. *Itse Selu: Cherokee Harvest Festival* (K–3). Illus. by Don Stewart. 1994, Charlesbridge paper $6.95 (0-88106-850-0). 32pp. Little Wolf and his Cherokee family celebrate the Green Corn Festival with rituals and feasting to acknowledge the ripening of the corn. (Rev: BL 5/15/94; SLJ 7/94) [394.2]

17573 Peters, Russell. *Clambake: A Wampanoag Tradition* (3–5). Illus. by John Madama. Series: We Are Still Here: Native Americans Today. 1992, Lerner LB $21.27 (0-8225-2651-4); paper $6.95 (0-8225-9621-0). 48pp. Origins and present-day observations of the traditional ceremony that we know as a clambake. (Rev: BCCB 11/92; SLJ 12/92) [973]

17574 Philip, Neil, ed. *A Braid of Lives: Native American Childhood* (4–8). Illus. 2000, Clarion $20.00 (0-395-64528-X). 80pp. Twenty vignettes of one or two pages in length give a many-faceted picture of growing up Native American in different parts of the county. (Rev: BL 10/1/00; HBG 10/01; SLJ 6/01) [973]

17575 Philip, Neil, ed. *In a Sacred Manner I Live: Native American Wisdom* (4–8). Illus. 1997, Clarion $20.00 (0-395-84981-0). 93pp. More than 30 Native American leaders — including Geronimo and Cochise — are quoted on topics relating to the conduct of life and their beliefs. (Rev: BL 7/97; BR 5–6/98; HBG 3/98; SLJ 12/97) [973]

17576 Powell, Suzanne. *The Pueblos* (4–7). Illus. Series: First Books. 1993, Watts paper $6.95 (0-531-15703-2). 64pp. Covers the history and present status of the Pueblos and their ability to survive the harsh weather and terrain of the American Southwest. (Rev: BL 2/15/94) [978.9]

17577 Press, Petra. *Indians of the Northwest: Traditions, History, Legends, and Life* (4–6). Illus. Series: Native Americans. 2000, Gareth Stevens LB $17.95 (0-8368-2647-7). 64pp. This account describes the land where many Indian peoples lived for thousands of years and their many earthworks, including the Great Serpent Mound in Ohio. (Rev: BL 5/15/00; HBG 10/00) [979]

17578 Press, Petra. *The Pueblo* (3–6). Series: First Reports. 2001, Compass Point LB $21.26 (0-7565-0082-6). 48pp. An absorbing, well-illustrated account of the Pueblo people that covers religion, society, history, culture, and lifestyle today. (Rev: SLJ 7/01) [978.9]

17579 Rasmussen, R. Kent. *Pueblo* (3–5). Illus. by Kimberly L. Dawson Kurnizki. 2001, Rourke LB $25.27 (1-55916-249-X). 32pp. The amazing clay-based homes and villages of the Pueblo Indians are highlighted in this account that explains how they were built, their parts, and their many uses. (Rev: SLJ 3/01) [973]

17580 Ray, Kurt. *Native Americans and the New American Government: Treaties and Promises* (4–6). Illus. Series: Life in the New American Nation. 2004, Rosen LB $21.25 (0-8239-4035-7). 32pp. The often fractious relations between Native Americans and the federal government are explored. (Rev: BL 6/1–15/04) [323.1]

17581 Remington, Gwen. *The Sioux* (5–9). Series: Indigenous Peoples of North America. 1999, Lucent LB $27.45 (1-56006-615-6). 112pp. A thorough discussion of the history of the Sioux tribe, their origins, and their traditions and culture, with good coverage of conflicts such as Wounded Knee, their forced assimilation, and their style of life since 1920. (Rev: SLJ 3/00) [973.1]

17582 Riehecky, Janet. *The Cree Tribe* (2–5). Series: Native Peoples. 2002, Capstone LB $18.60 (0-7368-1366-7). 24pp. A brief introduction to these Plains Indians with details on their past and present and an emphasis on their place in today's world. (Rev: BL 3/15/03; HBG 3/03) [973]

17583 Riehecky, Janet. *The Osage* (2–5). Series: Native Peoples. 2002, Capstone LB $18.60 (0-7368-1367-5). 24pp. This introduction to these Plains Indians tells about their history, culture, and how they live today. (Rev: BL 3/15/03; HBG 3/03) [973]

17584 Roessel, Monty. *Kinaalda: A Navajo Girl Grows Up* (4–7). Illus. 1993, Lerner LB $25.55 (0-8225-2655-7); paper $11.15 (0-8225-9641-5). 48pp. Celinda McKelvey, a Navajo girl, returns to the reservation to participate in her Kinaalda, the coming-of-age ceremony. (Rev: BCCB 1/94; BL 1/15/94; SLJ 2/94) [392.1]

17585 Roessel, Monty. *Songs from the Loom: A Navajo Girl Learns to Weave* (3–6). Illus. 1995, Lerner LB $21.27 (0-8225-2657-3); paper $6.95 (0-

8225-9712-8). 48pp. A photoessay about weaving the Navajo way that reveals information about the culture and way of life of these people. (Rev: BL 9/15/95; SLJ 11/95) [746.1]

17586 Rose, LaVera. *Grandchildren of the Lakota* (4–6). Illus. Series: World's Children. 1998, Carolrhoda $22.60 (1-57505-279-2). 48pp. An introduction to the Lakota Indians, their history, how they live, and their current struggles with the U.S. government. (Rev: BL 4/1/99; HBG 3/99; SLJ 12/98) [305.23]

17587 Rosinsky, Natalie M. *The Wampanoag and Their History* (3–6). Illus. Series: We the People. 2005, Compass Point LB $22.60 (0-7565-0847-9). 48pp. A concise introduction to the Wampanoag people, their way of life, and the impact of the arrival of the colonists. [974]

17588 Ryan, Marla Felkins, and Linda Schmittroth, eds. *Abenaki* (3–6). Series: Tribes of Native America. 2004, Gale/Blackbirch LB $17.96 (1-56711-574-8). 32pp. A richly illustrated look at the Abenaki people of northern New England and southeastern Canada, their history, and their traditional and contemporary customs. Also use *Chickasaw* and *Chinook* (both 2004). (Rev: SLJ 5/04) [974.004]

17589 Salas, Laura Purdie. *The Trail of Tears, 1838* (4–6). Illus. Series: Let Freedom Ring. 2003, Capstone LB $18.60 (0-7368-1559-7). 48pp. Examines the government's removal of the Cherokee from their homelands, their forced march to reservations in Indian Territory, the challenges they faced their, and their status today. (Rev: HBG 10/03; LMC 11/03; SLJ 12/03) [973.04]

17590 Santella, Andrew. *The Cherokee* (2–3). Series: True Books: American Indians. 2001, Children's Book Pr. LB $22.00 (0-516-22216-3); paper $6.95 (0-516-27315-9). 48pp. This simple, colorful introduction to the Cherokee Indians covers topics such as their homelands, traditions and customs, history, and present status. (Rev: BL 8/1/01) [973]

17591 Schonberg, Marcia. *Ohio Native Peoples* (4–6). Illus. Series: Heinemann State Studies. 2003, Heinemann LB $27.07 (1-4034-0667-7). 48pp. This historical survey of the native peoples who have called Ohio home covers roughly 13,000 years of history. (Rev: HBG 4/04; SLJ 10/03) [977.1]

17592 Schwabacher, Martin. *The Huron Indians* (3–5). Illus. Series: The Junior Library of American Indians. 1995, Chelsea $16.95 (0-7910-2489-X); paper $8.95 (0-7910-2033-9). 80pp. An introduction to the history and culture of the Huron peoples, with material on how they preserve their traditions today. (Rev: BL 7/95) [392.2]

17593 Secakuku, Susan. *Meet Mindy: A Native Girl from the Southwest* (5–8). Photos by John Harrington. Series: My World: Young Native Americans Today. 2003, Beyond Words paper $15.95 (1-58270-091-5). 48pp. A Hopi teen named Mindy talks about her life and heritage in this full-color photoessay. (Rev: BL 4/1/03; HBG 10/03; SLJ 3/03) [979.1004]

17594 Shemie, Bonnie. *Houses of Adobe: Native Dwellings: The Southwest* (3–5). Illus. Series:

Native Dwellings. 1995, Tundra $13.95 (0-88776-330-8); paper $6.99 (0-88776-353-7). 24pp. Various dwellings built by Indians of the Southwest — like pit houses and cliff homes — are described in double-page spreads with detailed drawings. (Rev: BL 9/1/95) [392]

17595 Shemie, Bonnie. *Mounds of Earth and Shell* (3–6). Illus. Series: Native Dwellings. 1993, Tundra $13.95 (0-88776-318-9). 24pp. Explores the mound-building Indians of North America, where the mounds are located, and why they were built. (Rev: BL 1/1/94) [393.1]

17596 Sherrow, Victoria. *The Iroquois Indians* (3–5). Series: Junior Library of American Indians. 1993, Chelsea LB $16.95 (0-7910-1655-2). 82pp. History and culture of Iroquis arts and crafts. Includes an eight-page photoessay. (Rev: BL 11/1/92) [973]

17597 Shuter, Jane, ed. *Francis Parkman and the Plains Indians* (5–8). Illus. Series: History Eyewitness. 1995, Raintree LB $24.26 (0-8114-8280-4). 48pp. An edited and abridged version of Parkman's autobiographical writing about the social customs, family life, and hunting practices of the Plains Indians. (Rev: BL 4/15/95) [978]

17598 Shuter, Jane. *Mesa Verde* (4–6). Series: Visiting the Past. 1999, Heinemann LB $16.95 (1-57572-858-3). 32pp. This work introduces the homes and lifestyle of the ancient Pueblo Indians (A.D. 500 to 1292), with coverage of their clothing, beliefs, trade, farming, and tools. (Rev: SLJ 3/00) [973.1]

17599 Siegel, Beatrice. *Indians of the Northeast Woodlands* (4–8). Illus. by William Sauts Bock. 1991, Walker LB $14.85 (0-8027-8157-8). 96pp. In question-and-answer format — following the original 1972 edition — this volume contains much information on Native Americans in New England. (Rev: BL 11/15/92) [973]

17600 Sita, Lisa. *Indians of the Great Plains: Traditions, History, Legends, and Life* (4–6). Series: The Native Americans. 2000, Gareth Stevens LB $17.95 (0-8368-2645-0). 64pp. Topics covered in this introduction to such tribes as the Pawnee, Blackfoot, Cheyenne, Sioux, and Cree include history, society, government, and cultural traditions. (Rev: BL 5/15/00; HBG 10/00) [973]

17601 Sita, Lisa. *Indians of the Southwest: Traditions, History, Legends, and Life* (4–6). Illus. Series: Native Americans. 2000, Gareth Stevens LB $17.95 (0-8368-2648-5). 64pp. This account traces the history of the many Native American nations that still live in the Southwest today. (Rev: BL 5/15/00; HBG 10/00) [970.4]

17602 Smith, Karla. *Virginia Native Peoples* (4–6). 2003, Heinemann LB $27.07 (1-4034-0363-5). 48pp. Introduces readers to the native peoples who resided in the state before and after the arrival of European settlers. (Rev: HBG 4/04; SLJ 12/03) [975.5004]

17603 Sneve, Virginia Driving Hawk. *The Apaches* (3–6). Illus. by Ronald Himler. Series: First Americans. 1997, Holiday House LB $16.95 (0-8234-1287-3). 32pp. An overview of the six tribes that make up the Apache nation, accompanied by handsome illustrations. (Rev: BL 4/1/97; SLJ 7/97) [973]

17604 Sneve, Virginia Driving Hawk. *The Cherokees* (3–6). Illus. by Ronald Himler. Series: First Americans. 1996, Holiday House $16.95 (0-8234-1214-8). 32pp. The story of this large, important Indian group, its culture, and its present status. (Rev: BCCB 5/96; BL 2/15/96; HB 5–6/96; SLJ 4/96) [973]

17605 Sneve, Virginia Driving Hawk. *The Cheyennes* (K–4). Illus. Series: First Americans. 1996, Holiday House LB $16.95 (0-8234-1250-4). 32pp. The story of the Cheyenne, their history, customs, and how the white man affected their lives. (Rev: BL 9/15/96; SLJ 2/97) [970]

17606 Sneve, Virginia Driving Hawk. *The Hopis* (3–5). Illus. by Ronald Himler. Series: First Americans. 1995, Holiday House LB $16.95 (0-8234-1194-X). 32pp. Details are given of the religion, social structure, history, and lifestyle of the Hopi, along with a creation myth. (Rev: SLJ 10/95) [973]

17607 Sneve, Virginia Driving Hawk. *The Iroquois* (K–4). Illus. by Ronald Himler. Series: A First American Book. 1995, Holiday House LB $16.95 (0-8234-1163-X). 32pp. Provides a history of the Iroquois, as well as their beliefs, way of life, religion, and current situation. (Rev: BL 6/1–15/95; SLJ 7/95) [973]

17608 Sneve, Virginia Driving Hawk. *The Navajos* (K–3). Illus. by Ronald Himler. Series: First Americans. 1993, Holiday House LB $16.95 (0-8234-1039-0). 32pp. After a creation story, the Navajos are introduced with details given on their daily life, society, relations with other Indian groups, and their fortune after the white man came. (Rev: BCCB 10/93; BL 12/15/93; SLJ 10/93) [973]

17609 Sneve, Virginia Driving Hawk. *The Nez Perce* (K–3). Illus. by Ronald Himler. Series: First Americans. 1994, Holiday House LB $16.95 (0-8234-1090-0). 32pp. Beginning with a creation myth, this account continues with an exploration of the daily life and history of the Nez Perce. (Rev: BL 10/1/94) [973]

17610 Sneve, Virginia Driving Hawk. *The Seminoles: A First Americans Book* (3–5). Illus. by Ronald Himler. 1994, Holiday House LB $16.95 (0-8234-1112-5). 32pp. Discusses many aspects of the Seminole history and culture, including the career of Osceola, the Seminole Wars, and their living conditions today. (Rev: BCCB 7–8/94; SLJ 4/94) [973]

17611 Sneve, Virginia Driving Hawk. *The Sioux* (K–3). Illus. by Ronald Himler. Series: First Americans. 1993, Holiday House LB $15.95 (0-8234-1017-X). 32pp. The history of the Sioux Indians is given, with information on their social structure, daily life, ceremonies, and contemporary condition. (Rev: BCCB 10/93; BL 12/15/93; SLJ 10/93) [973]

17612 Sonneborn, Liz. *The Cheyenne Indians* (3–5). Illus. Series: Junior Library of American Indians. 1991, Chelsea LB $16.95 (0-7910-1654-4). 80pp. The history and culture of the Cheyenne are covered in simple text, historic photos, maps, and an eight-

page color section on arts and crafts. (Rev: BL 3/1/92) [973.04973]

17613 Sonneborn, Liz. *The New York Public Library Amazing Native American History: A Book of Answers for Kids* (5–8). 1999, Wiley paper $12.95 (0-471-33204-6). 169pp. Organized by regions and using a question-and-answer approach, this is a fine overview of the history of Native Americans, ending with a chapter on contemporary conditions. (Rev: BL 5/1/00; SLJ 7/00) [970.004]

17614 Spradlin, Michael P. *The Legend of Blue Jacket* (3–6). Illus. by Ronald Himler. 2002, HarperCollins LB $17.89 (0-688-15836-6). 32pp. This book looks at theories about the identity of the Shawnee chief known as Blue Jacket, and whether he might in fact have been the kidnapped son of a pioneer family. (Rev: BL 11/1/02; HBG 3/03; SLJ 11/02) [974.004]

17615 Steele, Philip. *Little Bighorn* (5–8). Illus. by Richard Hook. Series: Great Battles and Sieges. 1992, Macmillan $21.00 (0-02-786885-0). 32pp. How General George Custer was defeated by Cheyenne and Sioux Indians in 1876. (Rev: BL 10/1/92; SLJ 2/93) [973.8]

17616 Stone, Amy M. *Creek* (4–8). Series: Native American Peoples. 2004, Gareth Stevens LB $24.67 (0-8368-4217-0). 32pp. History, tradition, and contemporary life are described with photographs, timeline, fact boxes, and activities. (Rev: SLJ 1/05) [973]

17617 Stout, Mary. *Blackfoot* (4–8). Series: Native American Peoples. 2004, Gareth Stevens LB $24.67 (0-8368-4216-2). 32pp. History, tradition, and contemporary life are described with photographs, timeline, fact boxes, and activities. (Rev: SLJ 1/05) [973]

17618 Stout, Mary A. *Nez Perce* (4–8). Illus. Series: Native American Peoples. 2003, Gareth Stevens LB $22.60 (0-8368-3666-9). 32pp. Introduces readers to the history and culture of the Nez Perce tribe, which traditionally made its home in the American Northwest. (Rev: HBG 10/03; SLJ 9/03) [973]

17619 Strudwick, Leslie. *Inuit* (3–5). Series: Indigenous Peoples. 2004, Weigl LB $18.20 (1-59036-122-9). 32pp. A fascinating and informative overview of the Inuit people, covering history, culture, language, and family life. (Rev: SLJ 7/04) [971.9]

17620 Sundling, Charles W. *Native Americans of the Frontier* (4–6). Illus. Series: Frontier Land. 2000, ABDO $15.95 (1-57765-042-5). 32pp. A simple text and many illustrations are used in this accessible account of the daily life of the American Plains Indians during the 19th century. (Rev: BL 10/15/00; HBG 10/00; SLJ 6/00) [978]

17621 Swentzell, Rina. *Children of Clay: A Family of Pueblo Potters* (3–5). Illus. by Bill Steen. 1992, Lerner LB $21.27 (0-8225-2654-9). 40pp. The family of Gia Rose of Santa Clara Pueblo takes the reader through the ancient process of pottery making. (Rev: BCCB 3/93; BL 1/15/93; SLJ 2/92) [978.9]

17622 Tayac, Gabrielle. *Meet Naiche: A Native Boy from the Chesapeake Bay Area* (3–6). Photos by

John Harrington. Series: My World: Young Native Americans Today. 2002, Beyond Words $15.95 (1-58270-072-9). 48pp. Tayac presents the everyday life of a Native American child of mixed heritage living in rural Maryland today, with descriptions of school and a traditional ceremony. (Rev: BL 4/1/03; HBG 10/03; SLJ 3/03)

17623 Terry, Michael Bad Hand. *Daily Life in a Plains Indian Village: 1868* (3–6). Illus. 1999, Clarion $20.00 (0-395-94542-9). 48pp. This book gives a detailed description of the daily life — including housing, food, clothing, government, and games — of the Northern Cheyenne Indians in 1868, before the Europeans forced them onto reservations. (Rev: BL 2/15/00; HBG 3/00; SLJ 9/99) [978]

17624 Thompson, Linda. *The California People* (4–7). Illus. Series: Native People, Native Lands. 2003, Rourke LB $29.93 (1-58952-753-4). 48pp. One of a well-illustrated series on individual groups of native Americans, with attention to the negative impact of the arrival of European settlers. Other titles in the series include *People of the Northwest and Subarctic, People of the Great Basin, People of the Northeast Woodlands*, and *People of the Plains and Prairies* (all 2003). (Rev: SLJ 4/04) [979.4]

17625 Torr, James D., ed. *Primary Sources* (5–9). Series: Indigenous Peoples of North America. 2002, Gale LB $27.45 (1-59018-010-0). 96pp. An anthology of excerpts from primary documents, with a timeline, that covers Native American history and culture since the arrival of Europeans. (Rev: SLJ 8/02) [970.00497]

17626 Uschan, Michael V. *The Battle of Little Bighorn* (5–8). Illus. Series: Landmark Events in American History. 2003, World Almanac LB $29.26 (0-8368-5338-5). 48pp. The significance and key events of the famous battle are described from both white and Indian points of view, with extracts from primary sources, maps, and many illustrations. (Rev: BL 10/15/03; SLJ 2/03) [973.8]

17627 White Deer of Autumn. *The Native American Book of Knowledge* (5–8). Illus. by Shonto Begay. 1992, Beyond Words paper $5.95 (0-941831-42-6). 88pp. A description of Native American hero figures before Columbus is part of the information in this native view of history and life-styles. (Rev: BL 10/15/92) [970]

17628 White Deer of Autumn. *The Native American Book of Life* (5–8). Illus. by Shonto Begay. 1992, Beyond Words paper $5.95 (0-941831-43-4). 88pp. In this look at lifestyles from the Native American point of view, the focus is on child rearing. (Rev: BL 10/15/92) [970]

17629 Williams, Suzanne Morgan. *Tlingit Indians* (2–4). Illus. Series: Native Americans. 2003, Heinemann LB $24.22 (1-4034-0868-8). 32pp. A look at the Tlingit native people of the northwest Pacific coast and their lives before and after the arrival of white settlers. (Rev: SLJ 5/04) [979.8]

17630 Wittstock, Laura W. *Ininatig's Gift of Sugar: Traditional Native Sugarmaking* (3–5). Illus. by Dale Kakkak. Series: We Are Still Here: Native Americans Today. 1993, Lerner LB $21.27 (0-

8225-2653-0); paper $6.95 (0-8225-9642-3). 48pp. Describes the traditional way of making maple sugar and syrup by Minnesota Indians. (Rev: BL 9/1/93; HB 11–12/93) [338.1]

17631 Wolfson, Evelyn. *Growing Up Indian* (5–7). Illus. 1986, Walker LB $11.85 (0-8027-6644-7). 96pp. What it was like to grow up Indian in traditional American culture before the influence of the white race. (Rev: BL 1/15/87; SLJ 3/87) [306.08997073]

17632 Wood, Leigh. *The Crow Indians* (3–5). Illus. Series: Junior Library of American Indians. 1993, Chelsea LB $16.95 (0-7910-1661-7). 80pp. This account tells about the past, present, and culture of the Crow Indians who now live in southeastern Montana. (Rev: BL 5/15/93) [973]

17633 Wood, Marion, and Brian Williams. *Ancient America*. Rev. ed. (5–8). Illus. Series: Cultural Atlas for Young People. 2003, Facts on File $35.00 (0-8160-5145-3). 96pp. Colorful topical spreads introduce readers to Native American history from the end of the Ice Age to the arrival of European explorers and conquerers. (Rev: SLJ 1/04) [970.01]

17634 Wood, Ted, and Wanbli Numpa Afraid of Hawk. *A Boy Becomes a Man at Wounded Knee* (4–6). Illus. 1992, Walker LB $16.85 (0-8027-8175-6). 42pp. An eight-year-old Lakota boy wants to participate in his ancestor's journey to Wounded Knee. (Rev: BCCB 12/92; BL 9/1/92; SLJ 11/92) [973.8]

17635 Woods, Geraldine. *The Navajo* (5–7). Illus. Series: Watts Library: Indians of the Americas. 2002, Watts LB $24.00 (0-531-13950-6); paper $8.95 (0-531-16227-3). 64pp. This account includes information on history and contemporary issues and covers the Navajo code talkers, land disputes, traditions, housing, and clothing. (Rev: BL 7/02) [979.1]

17636 Young, Robert. *A Personal Tour of Mesa Verde* (4–7). Illus. Series: How It Was. 1999, Lerner LB $30.35 (0-8225-3577-7). 64pp. This book gives a special glimpse into the lives of the Native Americans known as the Puebloans, how they lived, and the culture they developed. (Rev: BL 6/1–15/99; HBG 10/99; SLJ 7/99) [978.8]

17637 Yue, Charlotte, and David Yue. *The Wigwam and the Longhouse* (4–9). Illus. by authors. 2000, Houghton Mifflin $15.00 (0-395-84169-0). 118pp. A well-balanced account that describes the life and history of several tribes of Native Americans from the eastern woodlands. (Rev: HB 7–8/00; HBG 10/00; SLJ 10/00) [973]

DISCOVERY AND EXPLORATION

17638 Arenstam, Peter, et al. *Mayflower 1620: A New Look at a Pilgrim Voyage* (5–9). 2003, National Geographic $17.95 (0-7922-6142-9). 48pp. A large-format photoessay of a voyage of the *Mayflower II* — re-creating the original journey — is the backdrop for detail about the 1620 passengers, supplies, navigation techniques, and the new country they arrived in. (Rev: BL 11/1/03; HBG 4/04; SLJ 11/03) [974.4]

17639 Armentrout, David, and Patricia Armentrout. *The Mayflower Compact* (4–7). 2004, Rourke $.00

(1-59515-229-6). 48pp. The reasons for the creation of this document — a political statement signed by a group of *Mayflower* passengers — are thoroughly explored in concise text, accompanied by an array of maps and illustrations. (Rev: BL 10/15/04) [974.4]

17640 Asikinack, Bill, and Kate Scarborough. *Exploration into North America* (5–7). Illus. Series: Exploration. 1996, Dillon LB $15.95 (0-02-718086-7); paper $7.95 (0-382-39228-0). 48pp. This account tells the history of North America from pre-history to European exploration and settlement. (Rev: BL 8/96; SLJ 9/96) [970]

17641 Aykroyd, Clarissa. *Exploration of the California Coast* (4–7). Series: Exploration and Discovery. 2002, Mason Crest LB $19.95 (1-59084-043-7). 64pp. Explorers such as Cortes and Drake are covered in this look at 16th-century California. (Rev: SLJ 12/02) [917.94041]

17642 Blumberg, Rhoda. *York's Adventures with Lewis and Clark: An African-American's Part in the Great Expedition* (4–8). Illus. 2003, HarperCollins LB $18.89 (0-06-009112-6). 96pp. York, a slave, was the only African American included on Lewis and Clark's trip but is credited with great strength and agility, attributes that impressed the Native Americans. (Rev: BL 12/1/03; SLJ 2/04) [971.804]

17643 Bowen, Andy Russell. *The Back of Beyond: A Story About Lewis and Clark* (3–5). Illus. 1997, Carolrhoda LB $21.27 (1-57505-010-2). 64pp. A gripping account of the journey that took Lewis and Clark to the mouth of the Columbia River in 1805. (Rev: BL 9/1/97; HB 11–12/97; SLJ 3/98) [917.804]

17644 Dell, Pamela. *The Plymouth Colony* (4–6). Series: Let Freedom Ring. 2004, Capstone LB $23.93 (0-7368-2463-4). 48pp. With large type and bright design, this volume explores the hardships and triumphs of the Pilgrims. (Rev: SLJ 8/04) [974.4]

17645 Dyson, John. *Westward with Columbus* (4–6). Illus. by Peter Christopher. 1991, Scholastic paper $6.95 (0-590-43847-6). 64pp. A fictionalized account of the 1492 voyage, theorizing that Columbus used a secret map. (Rev: BL 11/15/91; SLJ 11/91) [910.4]

17646 Faber, Harold. *Lewis and Clark: From Ocean to Ocean* (5–8). Illus. Series: Great Explorations. 2001, Benchmark LB $28.50 (0-7614-1241-7). 80pp. This concise, artfully illustrated volume about the journey of Lewis and Clark includes journal entries, a timeline, and Web site information. (Rev: BL 1/1–15/02; HBG 3/02; SLJ 3/02) [917.804]

17647 Fritz, Jean. *The Lost Colony of Roanoke* (3–5). Illus. by Hudson Talbott. 2004, Penguin Putnam $16.99 (0-399-24027-6). 64pp. Fritz interweaves facts and speculation in this captivating and well-illustrated account of the lost colony. (Rev: BL 4/1/04; HB 5–6/04; SLJ 5/04) [975.6]

17648 Gunderson, Mary. *Cooking on the Lewis and Clark Expedition* (3–6). 2000, Capstone LB $22.60 (0-7368-0354-8). 32pp. As well as historical material on the Lewis and Clark expedition, this book contains a number of modern recipes for food that might have been eaten on this memorable journey. (Rev: HBG 10/00; SLJ 12/00) [978]

17649 Hirschfelder, Arlene B. *Photo Odyssey: Solomon Carvalho's Remarkable Western Adventure, 1853–54* (5–9). 2000, Clarion $18.00 (0-395-89123-X). 118pp. The story of the last westward journey of John C. Fremont as seen through the eyes of a painter/photographer who was a member of this 1853 expedition. (Rev: BCCB 9/00; BL 7/00; HBG 10/00; SLJ 8/00*) [978]

17650 Johmann, Carol A. *The Lewis and Clark Expedition: Join the Corps of Discovery to Explore Uncharted Territory* (4–6). Illus. by Michael Kline. Series: Kaleidoscope Kids. 2002, Williamson paper $12.95 (1-885593-73-2). 112pp. This is a wide-ranging and lively history of the expedition, providing profiles of the explorers, excerpts from journals, lists of resources, and activities. (Rev: BL 1/1–15/03; SLJ 3/03) [917.804]

17651 Kimmel, Elizabeth Cody. *As Far as the Eye Can Reach: Lewis and Clark's Westward Quest* (3–6). Illus. 2003, Random $14.95 (0-375-81348-9). 112pp. The expedition is brought to life in this well-written account that covers the planning stages, meetings with Native Americans, and the skills of the explorers, with journal excerpts, and a lengthy list of resources. (Rev: BL 1/1–15/03; HBG 10/03; SLJ 3/03) [917.804]

17652 Krensky, Stephen. *Christopher Columbus* (1–2). Illus. by Norman Green. 1991, Random paper $3.99 (0-679-80369-6). 32pp. This is an easy-reading book that tells about Columbus's first voyage to America. (Rev: BL 12/1/91; SLJ 12/91) [970.01]

17653 Krensky, Stephen. *Who Really Discovered America?* (4–6). Illus. 1991, Scholastic paper $2.50 (0-590-40854-2). 64pp. A parade of discoverers who came to North or South America are uncovered in the attempt to answer this intriguing question. (Rev: BL 1/15/88; SLJ 4/88) [970.01]

17654 Lasky, Kathryn. *The Journal of Augustus Pelletier: The Lewis and Clark Expedition* (4–6). Series: My Name Is America. 2000, Scholastic $10.95 (0-590-68489-2). 172pp. Fourteen-year-old Augustus Pelletier, half French and half Omaha Indian, relates his adventures into unknown territory. (Rev: HBG 10/01) [978.02]

17655 Lourie, Peter. *On the Trail of Sacagawea* (4–6). Illus. 2001, Boyds Mills $18.95 (1-56397-840-7). 48pp. In this handsome pictorial account of a family trip retracing the steps of Lewis and Clark, the author interweaves their contemporary experiences and historical notes. (Rev: BL 5/1/01; HBG 3/02; SLJ 4/01) [978.004]

17656 McGrath, Patrick. *The Lewis and Clark Expedition* (5–8). Illus. 1986, Silver Burdett LB $14.95 (0-382-06828-9); paper $7.95 (0-382-09899-4). 64pp. A straightforward account illustrated with maps, photographs, paintings, and diary entries. (Rev: BCCB 6/86) [921]

17657 Parker, Nancy Winslow. *Land Ho! Fifty Glorious Years in the Age of Exploration* (3–5). Illus. 2001, HarperCollins LB $15.89 (0-06-027760-2). 40pp. Brief overviews of 12 European explorers and their travels to the New World are accompanied by drawings and maps. (Rev: BL 11/1/01; HBG 3/02; SLJ 8/01) [910.92]

17658 Patent, Dorothy Hinshaw. *Animals on the Trail with Lewis and Clark* (4–8). Illus. by William Muñoz. 2002, Clarion $18.00 (0-395-91415-9). 118pp. A handsome account of the Lewis and Clark expedition with emphasis on the animals that were discovered during the journey. (Rev: BCCB 5/02; BL 4/15/02*; HB 5–6/02; HBG 10/02; SLJ 4/02) [917.804]

17659 Patent, Dorothy Hinshaw. *The Lewis and Clark Trail: Then and Now* (4–8). Illus. by William Muñoz. 2002, Dutton $19.99 (0-525-46912-5). 64pp. The hardships faced by the members of the famous expedition are given a new focus, comparing the conditions and landscapes of today to those Lewis and Clark discovered. (Rev: BL 1/1–15/03; HB 1–2/03; HBG 3/03; SLJ 1/03) [917.804]

17660 Quiri, Patricia R. *The Lewis and Clark Expedition* (3–6). Series: We the People. 2000, Compass Point LB $15.95 (0-7565-0044-3). 48pp. A profusely illustrated, readable account of the Lewis and Clark expedition that makes for a good introductory overview. (Rev: SLJ 2/01) [917.8]

17661 Roberts, Russell. *Pedro Menendez de Aviles* (5–7). Illus. Series: Latinos in American History. 2002, Mitchell Lane LB $19.95 (1-58415-150-1). 48pp. This account of explorer Pedro Menendez de Aviles's efforts to procure Florida for Spain uses some fictionalized narrative to illustrate the times. (Rev: BL 10/15/02; HBG 3/03; SLJ 10/02) [975.9]

17662 Roop, Peter, and Connie Roop, eds. *Off the Map: The Journals of Lewis and Clark* (4–6). Illus. by Tim Tanner. 1993, Walker LB $15.85 (0-8027-8208-6). 40pp. Excerpts from the journals and diaries of Lewis and Clark are used to present a vivid picture of their amazing explorations. (Rev: BL 9/1/93; SLJ 6/93) [917.8]

17663 Schanzer, Rosalyn. *How We Crossed the West: The Adventures of Lewis and Clark* (3–5). Illus. 1997, National Geographic $18.00 (0-7922-3738-2). 48pp. A richly illustrated volume that deals with the expedition of Lewis and Clark as taken from their journals. (Rev: BL 9/15/97; HBG 3/98; SLJ 10/97*) [917.8]

17664 Stefoff, Rebecca. *Exploring the New World* (4–7). Illus. Series: North American Historical Atlases. 2000, Benchmark LB $24.21 (0-7614-1056-2). Using historical maps and reproductions, the important explorers and their accomplishments are covered in this slim, attractive volume. (Rev: HBG 3/01; SLJ 1/01) [970.01]

17665 Stefoff, Rebecca. *Lewis and Clark* (4–7). Illus. 1992, Chelsea LB $18.65 (0-7910-1750-8). 80pp. A simple text and pictures of the Lewis and Clark expedition, which helped open up the West. (Rev: BL 7/92) [978.02]

17666 Steins, Richard. *Exploration and Settlement* (5–8). Illus. Series: Making of America. 2000, Raintree LB $28.54 (0-8172-5700-4). 96pp. This account begins with prehistoric migrations to North America and continues with European explorers, including

the Spanish, English, French, and Dutch. (Rev: BL 5/1/00; HBG 10/00; SLJ 9/00) [970.01]

17667 Whiting, Jim. *Francisco Vasquez de Coronado* (5–7). Illus. Series: Latinos in American History. 2002, Mitchell Lane LB $19.95 (1-58415-146-3). 56pp. This account of Francisco Vasquez de Coronado's search for the lost cities of gold, and his subsequent trial for cruelty to Native Americans, uses some fictionalized narrative. (Rev: BL 10/15/02; HBG 3/03; SLJ 10/02) [979]

17668 Wittmann, Kelly. *The European Rediscovery of America* (4–7). Series: Exploration and Discovery. 2002, Mason Crest LB $19.95 (1-59084-052-6). 64pp. Wittmann looks at the explorers of the 15th and 16th centuries, including Columbus and Cabot. (Rev: SLJ 12/02) [970]

COLONIAL PERIOD

17669 ADC, the Map People Staff. *Virginia* (4–7). Series: Life in the Thirteen Colonies. 2004, Children's Pr. LB $24.95 (0-516-24580-5). This look at colonial Virginia, including the turbulent social and political climate of the period, presents an even-handed portrait of life for both the Indians and the settlers. (Rev: BL 12/15/04)

17670 Allman, Melinda, ed. *Primary Sources* (5–8). Series: Thirteen Colonies. 2002, Gale LB $27.45 (1-59018-011-9). 112pp. A fascinating collection of primary source material for the young researcher. (Rev: BL 9/15/02; SLJ 10/02) [873.2]

17671 Appelbaum, Diana. *Giants in the Land* (2–4). Illus. by Michael McCurdy. 1993, Houghton Mifflin $17.00 (0-395-64720-7). 32pp. An ecological story concerning the forests of giant white pines in New England that were destroyed to build ships for the British in the 18th century. (Rev: BCCB 9/93; BL 10/1/93*; SLJ 11/93*) [634.9]

17672 Barrett, Tracy. *Growing Up in Colonial America* (4–6). Illus. 1995, Millbrook LB $23.40 (1-56294-578-5). 96pp. Colonial settlements in the North and South are contrasted in their theories and practices of child rearing. (Rev: BL 12/15/95; SLJ 12/95) [973]

17673 Bjornlund, Lydia J. *Massachusetts* (5–8). Series: The Thirteen Colonies. 2001, Lucent LB $27.45 (1-56006-879-5). 96pp. The story of the colony of Massachusetts with particular emphasis on its role in the Revolution and creation of a new nation. (Rev: BL 3/15/02) [973.2]

17674 Blohm, Craig E. *New Hampshire* (5–8). Series: Thirteen Colonies. 2002, Gale LB $27.45 (1-56006-991-0). 96pp. Clear writing and reproductions of period illustrations are the highlights of this history of the New Hampshire colony. (Rev: BL 9/15/02; SLJ 4/02) [973.2]

17675 Boraas, Tracey. *The Salem Witch Trials* (4–6). Series: Let Freedom Ring. 2004, Capstone LB $23.93 (0-7368-2464-2). 48pp. A clear explanation of the trials, with background information that aids understanding plus lots of illustrations and a large-size text that will appeal to reluctant readers. (Rev: SLJ 8/04) [974.4]

17676 Britton, Tamara. *The Georgia Colony* (3–4). Series: The Colonies. 2001, ABDO LB $14.95 (1-57765-583-4). 32pp. The history of the colony is presented here, with information on both the settlers and the Native Americans of the area and on housing, clothing, and the economy. Also use *Roanoke: The Lost Colony* (2001). (Rev: HBG 3/02; SLJ 4/02) [975]

17677 Broida, Marian. *Projects About Colonial Life* (3–5). Illus. Series: Hands-On History. 2003, Marshall Cavendish LB $18.95 (0-7614-1603-X). 48pp. The easy-to-follow projects in this slim volume offer students new insights into life in colonial America. (Rev: BL 4/1/04; HBG 4/04; SLJ 3/04) [973.2]

17678 Brown, Gene. *Discovery and Settlement: Europe Meets the New World (1490–1700)* (5–7). Series: First Person America. 1993, Twenty-First Century LB $20.90 (0-8050-2574-X). 64pp. Using excerpts from original documents, this book covers the exploration of the United States, the Puritans, and the role of Native Americans, African Americans, and women in early colonial days. (Rev: SLJ 3/94) [973.2]

17679 Burgan, Michael. *The Boston Massacre* (3–6). Illus. Series: We the People. 2005, Compass Point LB $22.60 (0-7565-0832-0). 48pp. Describes the 1770 protest against the British that ended in violence. [973]

17680 Burgan, Michael. *Maryland* (3–6). Series: Life in the Thirteen Colonies. 2004, Children's Pr. LB $35.00 (0-516-24571-6). 124pp. From the first settlers to the end of the Revolutionary War, this interesting volume covers important events and daily life of the settlers plus information on the Native Amerian tribes. (Rev: SLJ 2/05) [975.2]

17681 Burgan, Michael. *The Salem Witch Trials* (4–6). Series: We the People. 2005, Compass Point LB $22.60 (0-7565-0845-2). 48pp. Details the 1692 trials and places them in historical context. (Rev: SLJ 6/05) [973.2]

17682 Burgan, Michael. *The Stamp Act of 1765* (3–6). Illus. Series: We the People. 2005, Compass Point LB $22.60 (0-7565-0846-0). 48pp. A concise account of the American colonists' rebellion against a new British tax. [973]

17683 Butler, Jon. *Religion in Colonial America* (5–8). Series: Religion in American Life. 2000, Oxford $28.00 (0-19-511998-3). 154pp. This book describes the mix of Catholics, Jews, Africans, Native Americans, Puritans, and various Protestant faiths that coexisted during colonial times. (Rev: BL 6/1–15/00; HBG 10/00) [973.2]

17684 Carlson, Laurie. *Colonial Kids: An Activity Guide to Life in the New World* (4–6). Illus. 1997, Chicago Review paper $12.95 (1-55652-322-X). 160pp. Along with facts about colonial America, this book gives directions for many related projects and activities, like tying sailors' knots, steaming clams, dyeing a shirt, and stitching a sampler. (Rev: BL 2/15/98; SLJ 3/98) [973.2]

17685 Carter, E. J. *The Mayflower Compact* (4–6). Series: Historical Documents. 2003, Heinemann LB $27.07 (1-4034-0803-3). 48pp. A study of the Mayflower Compact, the agreement signed by Pilgrims aboard the *Mayflower* that would effectively form their government in the New World, with suitable illustrations and maps. (Rev: SLJ 5/04) [974.4]

17686 Cobb, Mary. *A Sampler View of Colonial Life: With Projects Kids Can Make* (3–5). Illus. 1999, Millbrook LB $23.90 (0-7613-0372-3). 64pp. This book discusses many of the home crafts of colonial times, with an emphasis on samplers and crafts projects that the reader can make. (Rev: BL 10/15/99; HBG 3/00; SLJ 1/00) [746.44]

17687 Collier, Christopher, and James Lincoln Collier. *Clash of Cultures: Prehistory–1638* (5–8). Illus. Series: Drama of American History. 1998, Marshall Cavendish LB $29.93 (0-7614-0436-8). This well-illustrated examination of the cultures on both sides of the Atlantic — Native American and European — in the years before and during the formation of the colonies. (Rev: BL 4/15/98*; BR 11–12/98; HBG 10/98) [970.00497]

17688 Collier, Christopher, and James Lincoln Collier. *The French and Indian War* (5–8). Illus. Series: Drama of American History. 1998, Marshall Cavendish LB $28.50 (0-7614-0439-2). 96pp. A nicely illustrated book providing a broad perspective on the French and Indian War, and noting the conflict's importance on both sides of the Atlantic. (Rev: BL 4/15/98*; BR 11–12/98; HBG 10/98) [973.2]

17689 Collier, Christopher, and James Lincoln Collier. *The Paradox of Jamestown: 1585–1700* (5–8). Illus. Series: Drama of American History. 1998, Marshall Cavendish LB $29.93 (0-7614-0437-6). The paradox of Jamestown's history is that it gave democratic freedom through its elected legislature while introducing the first African slaves into the colonies. (Rev: BL 4/15/98*; BR 11–12/98; HBG 10/98) [975.5]

17690 Collier, Christopher, and James Lincoln Collier. *Pilgrims and Puritans: 1620–1676* (5–8). Illus. Series: Drama of American History. 1997, Marshall Cavendish LB $29.93 (0-7614-0438-4). 96pp. This volume describes the routes the Pilgrims and Puritans took to America, their beliefs and practices, and how present-day American life continues to be influenced by them. (Rev: BL 4/15/98*; BR 11–12/98; HBG 10/98) [974.4]

17691 Currie, Stephen. *The Salem Witch Trials* (4–6). 2002, Gale LB $23.70 (0-7377-1038-1). 48pp. A brief introduction to the trials that includes color photographs from the 1996 movie *The Crucible*. (Rev: SLJ 11/02)

17692 Daugherty, James. *The Landing of the Pilgrims* (5–7). Illus. by author. 1981, Random paper $5.99 (0-394-84697-4). 160pp. Based on his own writings, this is the story of the Pilgrims from the standpoint of William Bradford. [974.4]

17693 Davis, Kenneth C. *Don't Know Much About the Pilgrims* (3–5). Illus. by S. D. Schindler. Series: Don't Know Much About. 2002, HarperCollins LB $17.89 (0-06-028610-5). 48pp. A lively and informative look at the lives of the pilgrims. (Rev: BL 8/02; HBG 3/03; SLJ 10/02) [974.48]

17694 Day, Nancy. *Your Travel Guide to Colonial America* (4–8). Series: Passport to History. 2000, Lerner LB $26.60 (0-8225-3079-1). 96pp. Using a modern-day guidebook format, this account takes the reader back to colonial times with glimpses of the *Mayflower* and visits to such colonies as Jamestown, Virginia, and Plymouth, Massachusetts. (Rev: BL 3/1/01; HBG 10/01; SLJ 4/01) [973.2]

17695 Dean, Ruth, and Melissa Thomson. *Life in the American Colonies* (4–8). Illus. Series: The Way People Live. 1999, Lucent LB $27.45 (1-56006-376-9). 96pp. A description of life in the American colonies that covers immigrants, slaves, cities, farms, the frontier, home, crafts, professions, science, technology, and encounters with Native Americans. (Rev: BL 5/1/99; SLJ 7/99) [973.2]

17696 De Capua, Sarah E. *The Virginia Colony* (3–6). Series: Our Thirteen Colonies. 2003, Child's World LB $28.50 (1-56766-711-2). 40pp. A profile of colonial-era Virginia, with a concentration on its role in early steps toward U.S. nationhood. (Rev: SLJ 6/04) [975.5]

17697 DeFord, Deborah H. *Massachusetts* (4–7). Illus. Series: Life in the Thirteen Colonies. 2004, Children's Pr. LB $35.00 (0-516-24572-4). 128pp. From the first settlers to the end of the Revolutionary War, this interesting volume covers important events and daily life of the settlers plus information on the Native Amerian tribes.

17698 DeFord, Deborah H. *Pennsylvania* (4–7). Illus. Series: Life in the Thirteen Colonies. 2004, Children's Pr. LB $35.00 (0-516-24577-5). 128pp. From the first settlers to the end of the Revolutionary War, this interesting volume covers important events and daily life of the settlers plus information on the Native Amerian tribes.

17699 Doak, Robin S. *Georgia* (3–6). Series: Life in the Thirteen Colonies. 2004, Children's Pr. LB $35.00 (0-516-24570-8). 124pp. From the first settlers to the end of the Revolutionary War, this interesting volume covers important events and daily life of the settlers plus information on the Native Amerian tribes. (Rev: SLJ 2/05) [975.8]

17700 Doak, Robin S. *Rhode Island* (4–7). Illus. Series: Life in the Thirteen Colonies. 2004, Children's Pr. LB $35.00 (0-516-24578-3). 128pp. From the first settlers to the end of the Revolutionary War, this interesting volume covers important events and daily life of the settlers plus information on the Native Amerian tribes.

17701 Doeden, Matt. *The Boston Tea Party* (4–6). Illus. Series: Graphic History. 2005, Capstone LB $16.95 (0-7368-3846-5). 32pp. An eye-catching and dramatically worded graphic presentation of the tax revolt.

17702 Doherty, Kieran. *Puritans, Pilgrims, and Merchants: Founders of the Northeastern Colonies* (4–8). Illus. 1999, Oliver LB $22.95 (1-881508-50-1). 176pp. A history of each of the northeastern colonies is supplemented with brief biographies of such people as William Bradford, John Winthrop, Peter Stuyvesant, Anne Hutchinson, and William Penn. (Rev: BL 8/99; HBG 3/00; SLJ 1/00) [974]

17703 Doherty, Kieran. *Soldiers, Cavaliers, and Planters: Settlers of the Southeastern Colonies* (4–8). 1999, Oliver LB $22.95 (1-881508-51-X). This book focuses on the early southern colonies and their founders and leaders, among them Captain John Smith, Sir Walter Raleigh, and Pedro Menendez de Aviles. (Rev: BL 8/99; HBG 3/00; SLJ 10/99) [975]

17704 Dosier, Susan. *Colonial Cooking* (4–7). Illus. Series: Exploring History Through Simple Recipes. 2000, Capstone LB $22.60 (0-7368-0352-1). 32pp. This work covers the home life of the colonialists in the North, with material on kitchens, celebrations, food, and some recipes. (Rev: BL 8/00; HBG 10/00) [394.1]

17705 Dunnahoo, Terry. *Boston's Freedom Trail* (4–7). Illus. Series: Places in American History. 1994, Dillon LB $22.00 (0-87518-623-8); paper $7.95 (0-382-24762-0). 72pp. An explanation of the historical events of the colonial period that are commemorated in the famous Boston walking tour. (Rev: BL 1/1/95; SLJ 3/95) [917.4]

17706 Egger-Bovet, Howard, and Marlene Smith-Baranzini. *US Kids History: Book of the American Colonies* (5–7). Illus. Series: Brown Paper School. 1996, Little, Brown paper $14.99 (0-316-22201-1). 96pp. In an informal writing style with plenty of drawings and activities, the American colonial period is introduced. (Rev: BL 8/96; SLJ 8/96) [973.2]

17707 Erickson, Paul. *Daily Life in the Pilgrim Colony 1636* (3–5). Illus. Series: Daily Life. 2001, Clarion $20.00 (0-618-05846-X); paper $9.95 (0-395-98841-1). 48pp. Text, drawings, photographs, and maps describe how the Pilgrims lived at the Plymouth colony in 1636. (Rev: BL 10/1/01; HBG 3/02; SLJ 10/01) [974.4]

17708 Fischer, Laura. *Life in New Amsterdam* (2–4). Illus. Series: Picture the Past. 2003, Heinemann LB $24.22 (1-4034-3798-X). 32pp. A simple, illustrated account of what daily life was like in what is now New York City. (Rev: SLJ 4/04) [974.7]

17709 Fisher, Leonard Everett. *The Hatters* (4–6). Illus. Series: Colonial Craftsmen. 2000, Marshall Cavendish LB $14.95 (0-7614-1146-1). 48pp. This book supplies a glimpse into the hat trade of the 17th and 18th centuries with material on how different hats were made, worn, and marketed. Also use *The Potters* (2000). (Rev: BL 3/15/01; HBG 10/01) [646.5]

17710 Fisher, Leonard Everett. *The Papermakers* (4–6). Series: Colonial Craftsmen. 2000, Marshall Cavendish LB $14.95 (0-7614-1147-X). 48pp. A reissue of this beautifully illustrated work that describes the process of manufacturing, selling, and using paper during colonial times. Also use from the same series *The Tanners* (2000). (Rev: BL 3/15/01; HBG 10/01) [973.2]

17711 Fradin, Dennis Brindell. *The Signers: The 56 Stories Behind the Declaration of Independence* (4–6). Illus. by Michael McCurdy. 2002, Walker $22.95 (0-8027-8849-1). 160pp. Report writers will find plenty of information on the 13 colonies and the important individuals of the time in this lively presentation. (Rev: HB 1–2/03; HBG 3/03; SLJ 11/02)

17712 Gillis, Jennifer Blizin. *Life in Colonial Boston* (2–4). Illus. Series: Picture the Past. 2003, Heinemann LB $24.22 (1-4034-3795-5). 32pp. An introductory look at Boston in the late pre-Revolutionary War era (1760–1773), with information on what life was like for its residents at home, at school, and at work. (Rev: SLJ 4/04) [973]

17713 Gillis, Jennifer Blizin. *Life in New France* (2–4). Illus. Series: Picture the Past. 2003, Heinemann LB $24.22 (1-4034-3799-8). 32pp. A sampling of everyday colonial life in "New France" — the French colonies in eastern Canada and Louisiana — with illustrations, timelines, and maps. (Rev: SLJ 4/04) [971.01]

17714 Girod, Christina M. *Connecticut* (5–8). Illus. Series: Thirteen Colonies. 2001, Lucent LB $27.45 (1-56006-892-2). 96pp. This frank history of the Connecticut area covers the period from 1613 to statehood in 1788, with period illustrations, photographs, a map, source notes, and recommended resources. (Rev: BL 12/1/01) [974.6]

17715 Girod, Christina M. *Georgia* (5–8). Series: The Thirteen Colonies. 2001, Lucent LB $27.45 (1-56006-990-2). 96pp. The story of the last of the 13 colonies to be founded is told in a clear, forthright text with many black-and-white period illustrations. (Rev: BL 3/15/02; SLJ 8/02) [973.2]

17716 Girod, Christina M. *South Carolina* (5–8). Series: Thirteen Colonies. 2002, Gale LB $27.45 (1-56006-994-5). 96pp. A history of the colony of South Carolina and its people from the early settlements to admission into the United States, told in concise prose with numerous black-and-white illustrations. (Rev: BL 9/15/02) [973.2]

17717 Gourley, Catherine. *Welcome to Felicity's World, 1774* (3–6). Illus. 1999, Pleasant Co. $14.95 (1-56247-768-4). 58pp. Using double-page spreads, this book covers everyday life in Colonial Williamsburg in the 1770s, with material on such topics as the plantation village, slave laws, women, and epidemics. (Rev: BCCB 9/99; BL 9/1/99; HBG 3/00; SLJ 10/99) [973.2]

17718 Green, Carl R. *The French and Indian War* (4–6). Illus. Series: U.S. Wars. 2002, Enslow LB $19.95 (0-7660-5090-4). 48pp. Supported by verified and updated Web links, this is a useful overview of the French and Indian Wars. (Rev: BL 10/15/02; HBG 3/03) [973.2]

17719 Hakim, Joy. *From Colonies to Country*. 2nd ed. (5–8). Series: A History of Us. 1999, Oxford LB $19.95 (0-19-512755-2). 208pp. The colonial period and Revolutionary War are covered in this outstanding account that uses many quotations, profiles of personalities, and vivid details. (Rev: BL 12/15/99) [973.2]

17720 Hakim, Joy. *Making Thirteen Colonies*. 2nd ed. (5–8). Illus. Series: A History of Us. 1999, Oxford $19.95 (0-19-512753-6). 160pp. This excellent history of the colonial period is a reissue of the 1993 volume with some revisions and new illustrations. (Rev: BL 12/15/99) [973.2]

17721 Hale, Anna W. *The Mayflower People: Triumphs and Tragedies* (5–8). Illus. 1995, Harbinger $15.95 (1-57140-002-8); paper $9.95 (1-57140-003-6). A human account of the Pilgrims that begins with their departure from Southampton, England, in 1620 and ends two years later in the New World with the death of Squanto. (Rev: BL 1/1–15/96) [974.4]

17722 Hossell, Karen Price. *Virginia* (5–8). Series: Thirteen Colonies. 2002, Gale LB $27.45 (1-56006-995-3). 96pp. A cogently written history of the early years of Virginia, its people, and their lifestyle, plus sketches of their most famous colonial personalities. (Rev: BL 9/15/02) [973.2]

17723 Howarth, Sarah. *Colonial Places* (4–8). Illus. Series: People and Places. 1994, Millbrook LB $22.90 (1-56294-513-0). 48pp. Highlights various places of importance in everyday colonial life, such as the meetinghouse and the church. (Rev: BL 5/15/95; SLJ 3/95) [973]

17724 Hubbard-Brown, Janet. *The Secret of Roanoke Island* (4–7). Illus. 1991, Avon paper $3.50 (0-380-76223-4). 96pp. An intriguing look at this bit of history in colonial times. (Rev: BL 12/15/91) [975.63]

17725 Ichord, Loretta Frances. *Hasty Pudding, Johnnycakes, and Other Good Stuff: Cooking in Colonial America* (3–6). Illus. 1998, Millbrook LB $22.40 (0-7613-0369-3). 64pp. Topics related to colonial life and early Thanksgivings are covered, with background information on colonial cooking and step-by-step recipes (the original and updated versions). (Rev: BL 1/1–15/99; HBG 3/99; SLJ 2/99) [641.5973]

17726 Isaacs, Sally Senzell. *Life in a Colonial Town* (1–3). Series: Picture the Past. 2000, Heinemann LB $21.36 (1-57572-312-3). This well-organized account covers such topics as communication, houses, occupations, education, clothing, and food. Similar coverage for colonial cities is given in *Life in America's First Cities* (2000). (Rev: HBG 3/01; SLJ 11/00) [973.2]

17727 Italia, Bob. *The New York Colony* (3–5). Illus. Series: The Colonies. 2001, ABDO $14.95 (1-57765-589-3). 32pp. An overview for younger readers of the New York colony, including information on early history, settlements, everyday life, and other topics. Also use *Roanoke* (2001). (Rev: BL 1/1–15/02; HBG 3/02; SLJ 2/02) [974.7]

17728 Jackson, Shirley. *The Witchcraft of Salem Village* (4–7). Illus. 1963, Random paper $5.99 (0-394-89176-7). An account of the witch-hunting hysteria that hit Salem Village. [133.43097445]

17729 January, Brendan. *The Jamestown Colony* (3–6). Series: We the People. 2000, Compass Point LB $15.95 (0-7565-0043-5). 48pp. A heavily illustrated account of the Jamestown colony that is simple in appearance and format. (Rev: SLJ 2/01) [973.2]

17730 Kallen, Stuart A. *Delaware* (5–8). Series: Thirteen Colonies. 2002, Gale LB $27.45 (1-56006-989-9). 96pp. This history of colonial Delaware offers a clearly written account plus black-and-white portraits, engravings, paintings, some photographs, and a map of the colonies. (Rev: BL 9/15/02; SLJ 4/02) [973.2]

17731 Kallen, Stuart A. *The Salem Witch Trials* (5–8). Series: World History. 1999, Lucent LB $27.45 (1-56006-544-3). 96pp. After a general history of witch-hunting, this book describes the Salem trials and quotes extensively from firsthand accounts and trial notes. (Rev: BL 9/15/99; SLJ 9/99) [973.2]

17732 Kalman, Bobbie. *The Blacksmith* (3–5). Illus. by Barbara Bedell. Series: Colonial People. 2002, Crabtree LB $15.96 (0-7787-0747-4); paper $7.16 (0-7787-0793-8). 32pp. Photographs of reenactments at Williamsburg and Old Salem, North Carolina, add appeal to this description of the work of a colonial blacksmith and the equipment he used. Also use *The Milliner* and *The Woodworker* (2002). (Rev: SLJ 10/02)

17733 Kalman, Bobbie. *Colonial Crafts* (3–6). Illus. by Antoinette DeBiasi. Series: Historic Communities. 1992, Crabtree LB $20.60 (0-86505-490-8); paper $7.95 (0-86505-510-6). 32pp. This book introduces crafts from colonial America through those found in the many reconstructed craft shops in Williamsburg, Virginia. Two others in this series dealing with colonial life are: *A Colonial Town: Williamsburg* and *Tools and Gadgets* (both 1992). (Rev: SLJ 7/92) [973.2]

17734 Kalman, Bobbie. *Colonial Life* (3–6). Illus. Series: Historic Communities. 1992, Crabtree LB $20.60 (0-86505-491-6); paper $7.95 (0-86505-511-4). 32pp. Using many illustrations and simple text, this book describes how people lived during the colonial period in U.S. history. (Rev: BL 11/1/92) [973.2]

17735 Kalman, Bobbie, and Amanda Bishop. *A Slave Family* (3–5). Illus. Series: Colonial People. 2003, Crabtree LB $15.96 (0-7787-0746-6); paper $8.06 (0-7787-0792-X). 32pp. Describes the lives of slave families during America's colonial period from the early 17th century until the Revolutionary War. (Rev: SLJ 1/04)

17736 Kent, Deborah. *In Colonial New England* (4–8). Series: How We Lived. 1999, Benchmark LB $27.07 (0-7614-0905-X). 72pp. Topics such as home life, childhood, religion, problems, and amusements are covered for the colonial period in New England. Companion volumes are *In the Middle Colonies* and *In the Southern Colonies* (1999). (Rev: HBG 10/00; SLJ 2/00) [973.2]

17737 Kent, Deborah. *Salem, Massachusetts* (4–6). Illus. Series: Places in American History. 1995, Silver Burdett LB $14.95 (0-87518-648-3). 72pp. The place of Salem in the country's history, with special emphasis on the witch trials during the colonial period. (Rev: BL 2/15/96; SLJ 1/96) [133.4]

17738 King, David C. *Colonial Days: Discover the Past with Fun Projects, Games, Activities, and Recipes* (3–6). Illus. 1998, Wiley paper $12.95 (0-471-16168-3). 128pp. Focusing on a year in the lives of a fictional colonial family, this book outlines 40 projects, including making a sundial, dyeing yarn, and dipping candles. (Rev: BL 2/1/98; SLJ 6/98) [973]

17739 Kling, Andrew A. *Rhode Island* (5–8). Series: The Thirteen Colonies. 2001, Lucent LB $27.45 (1-56006-873-6). 112pp. In text and period prints, the story of colonial Rhode Island is told from its beginning to its stormy path to Constitution ratification. (Rev: BL 3/15/02; SLJ 8/02) [973.2]

17740 Knight, James E. *Blue Feather's Vision: The Dawn of Colonial America* (4–6). Illus. by George Guzzi. 1982, Troll paper $3.50 (0-89375-723-3). 32pp. The first volume of a ten-volume set on colonial America. Followed by: *Boston Tea Party: Rebellion in the Colonies; The Farm: Life in Colonial Pennsylvania; Jamestown: New World Adventure; Journey to Monticello: Traveling in Colonial Times; Sailing to America: Colonists at Sea* (all 1982); and four other titles.

17741 Lauren, Emily. *Connecticut* (3–6). Series: Life in the Thirteen Colonies. 2004, Children's Pr. LB $35.00 (0-516-24568-6). 124pp. From the first settlers to the end of the Revolutionary War, this interesting volume covers important events and daily life of the settlers plus information on the Native American tribes. (Rev: SLJ 2/05) [974.6]

17742 McDonald, Megan. *Shadows in the Glasshouse* (4–6). Illus. by Paul Bachem and Laszlo Kubinyi. Series: History Mysteries. 2000, Pleasant Co. $9.95 (1-58485-093-0); paper $5.95 (1-58485-092-2). 163pp. Set in Jamestown in 1621, this is the story of an indentured servant named Mary and her involvement in a mystery concerning someone who is sabotaging the glassblowing shop where she works. (Rev: HBG 10/01; SLJ 2/01)

17743 McGovern, Ann. *If You Lived in Colonial Times* (2–4). Illus. 1992, Scholastic paper $5.99 (0-590-45160-X). A re-creation of incidents and situations that could have occurred in the colonial period.

17744 McGovern, Ann. *If You Sailed on the Mayflower* (3–4). Illus. by Anna Devito. 1991, Scholastic paper $5.99 (0-590-45161-8). 80pp. In a question-and-answer format, information is given on the historic voyage and the settlement in New England.

17745 McKissack, Patricia, and Frederick L. McKissack. *Hard Labor: The First African Americans, 1619* (5–8). Illus. by Joseph Fiedler. Series: Milestone Books. 2004, Simon & Schuster paper $3.99 (0-689-86149-4). 64pp. Drawing on the meager evidence available, the authors reconstruct the story of the first Africans brought to America. (Rev: BL 2/15/04; SLJ 3/04) [306.3]

17746 Maestro, Betsy. *The New Americans: Colonial Times, 1620–1689* (2–5). Illus. by Giulio Maestro. Series: American Story. 1998, Lothrop LB $15.93 (0-688-13449-1). 48pp. Describes the various European immigrants to the United States during the colonial period and tells why they came and where they settled. (Rev: BCCB 5/98; BL 4/1/98; SLJ 3/98) [973.2]

17747 Maestro, Betsy. *Struggle for a Continent: The French and Indian Wars, 1689–1763* (3–6). Illus. Series: American Story. 2000, HarperCollins LB $15.89 (0-688-13451-3). 48pp. This picture book tells of the series of wars that pitted the French and

Algonquins against the English and the Iroquois. (Rev: BL 1/1–15/01; HBG 3/01; SLJ 9/00) [973.2]

17748 Marrin, Albert. *Struggle for a Continent: The French and Indian Wars, 1690–1760* (5–8). Illus. 1987, Macmillan LB $15.95 (0-689-31313-6). 232pp. History comes to life in this story of the events leading to the French and Indian wars and their contribution to independence for the colonists. (Rev: BL 1/15/88)

17749 Masoff, Joy. *Colonial Times, 1600–1700* (4–7). Series: Chronicle of America. 2000, Scholastic paper $16.95 (0-439-05107-X). 48pp. As well as describing why the colonists came to America, this work covers life aboard ships crossing the Atlantic and the challenges these people faced on arrival in the New World. (Rev: BCCB 9/00; HBG 3/01; SLJ 10/00) [973.2]

17750 Miller, Brandon Marie. *Good Women of a Well-Blessed Land: Women's Lives in Colonial America* (5–8). Series: People's History. 2003, Lerner LB $25.26 (0-8225-0032-9). 96pp. The lives and roles of women from all layers of early American society are presented in this well-written account that includes many quotations, maps, and period reproductions. (Rev: BL 5/15/03; HBG 10/03; SLJ 7/03) [305.4]

17751 Miller, Brandon Marie. *Growing Up in a New World* (5–8). Series: Our America. 2002, Lerner LB $31.95 (0-8225-0658-0). 64pp. The thrill of landing in the New World for the first time is re-created through true-life adventures of young people. (Rev: BL 2/15/03; HBG 3/03; SLJ 7/03) [973.2]

17752 Ochoa, George. *The Fall of Quebec and the French and Indian War* (5–7). Illus. Series: Turning Points. 1990, Silver Burdett LB $14.95 (0-382-09954-0); paper $7.95 (0-382-09950-8). 64pp. Illustrated account of the French and Indian Wars and the importance of the defeat of Montcalm and the taking of Quebec under Wolfe. (Rev: BL 3/1/91) [973.2]

17753 Paulson, Timothy J. *New York* (4–7). Illus. Series: Life in the Thirteen Colonies. 2004, Children's Pr. LB $35.00 (0-516-24575-9). 128pp. From the first settlers to the end of the Revolutionary War, this interesting volume covers important events and daily life of the settlers plus information on the Native Amerian tribes.

17754 Riehecky, Janet. *The Settling of Jamestown* (5–8). Series: Landmark Events in American History. 2003, World Almanac LB $26.60 (0-8368-5341-5). 48pp. The story of the first permanent English settlement in North America and how its was established near the mouth of Chesapeake Bay. (Rev: BL 10/15/03) [975.5]

17755 Roop, Connie, and Peter Roop, eds. *Pilgrim Voices: Our First Year in the New World* (4–7). Illus. 1995, Walker LB $17.85 (0-8027-8315-5). 48pp. Using first-person sources, the experiences of the Pilgrims from their sea journey to the first Thanksgiving are re-created. (Rev: BL 2/1/96; SLJ 1/96) [974.4]

17756 St. George, Judith. *The One and Only Declaration of Independence* (1–3). Illus. by Will Hillen-

brand. 2005, Penguin Putnam $16.99 (0-399-23738-0). 48pp. The story of the document's search for a permanent home, presented using questions and answers with cartoon-style illustrations. (Rev: BL 3/1/05; SLJ 6/05) [973.3]

17757 Sateren, Shelley Swanson. *Going to School in Colonial America* (4–6). Series: Going to School in History. 2001, Capstone LB $16.95 (0-7368-0803-5). 32pp. As well as material on schooling in the colonies, this book describes everyday life and the games, crafts, and activities popular at the time. (Rev: BL 10/15/01; HBG 3/02; SLJ 1/02) [973.2]

17758 Sewall, Marcia. *James Towne: Struggle for Survival* (3–5). Illus. 2001, Simon & Schuster $16.00 (0-689-81814-9). 40pp. An 18-year-old carpenter relates his experiences in the colony of Jamestown, sparing little detail of the hardships the settlers faced. (Rev: BL 6/1–15/01; HB 7–8/01; HBG 10/01; SLJ 6/01) [975.5]

17759 Sherrow, Victoria. *Huskings, Quiltings, and Barn Raisings: Work-Play Parties in Early America* (4–7). Illus. by Laura LoTurco. 1992, Walker LB $14.85 (0-8027-8188-8). 78pp. How people in early America helped each other with difficult tasks, such as clearing land and raising barns. (Rev: BL 1/15/93) [973.2]

17760 Sherrow, Victoria. *Pennsylvania* (5–8). Series: Thirteen Colonies. 2002, Gale LB $27.45 (1-56006-993-7). 96pp. The history of the colony of Pennsylvania from early settlements to achieving statehood. (Rev: BL 9/15/02) [973.2]

17761 Slavicek, Louise Chipley. *Life Among the Puritans* (4–8). Series: The Way People Live. 2001, Lucent LB $27.45 (1-56006-869-8). 108pp. Slavicek discusses the religious beliefs of the Puritans and how these affected the everyday life and policies of the Plymouth Colony and Massachusetts Bay Colony. (Rev: SLJ 9/01) [974.02]

17762 Smith, Carter, ed. *The Arts and Sciences: A Sourcebook on Colonial America* (5–8). Illus. Series: American Albums. 1991, Millbrook $25.90 (1-56294-037-6). 96pp. Through many well-captioned illustrations and brief text, this sourcebook traces cultural and scientific life during the U.S. colonial period. (Rev: BL 1/1/92) [973.2]

17763 Smith, Carter. *The Jamestown Colony* (5–7). Illus. Series: Turning Points. 1991, Silver Burdett LB $14.95 (0-382-24121-5); paper $7.95 (0-382-24116-9). 64pp. An introduction in text and excellent illustrations to the ill-fated early colony in Virginia. (Rev: BL 1/15/92) [975.5]

17764 Smolinski, Diane. *Battles of the French and Indian War* (4–7). Illus. Series: Americans at War: The French and Indian War. 2002, Heinemann LB $24.22 (1-4034-0169-1). 32pp. A slim volume with many illustrations, plus timelines of battles and boxed features on casualties and key figures. (Rev: HBG 10/03; SLJ 5/03) [973.2]

17765 Smolinski, Diane. *Soldiers of the French and Indian War* (4–7). Illus. Series: Americans at War: The French and Indian War. 2002, Heinemann LB $24.22 (1-4034-0172-1). 32pp. A slim volume with many illustrations, plus details of equipment and key figures. (Rev: HBG 10/03; SLJ 5/03) [973.2]

17766 Steen, Sandra, and Susan Steen. *Colonial Williamsburg* (4–7). Illus. 1993, Macmillan LB $14.95 (0-87518-546-0). 72pp. The historic town of Williamsburg, the birthplace of the Bill of Rights, has been restored to its colonial state through John D. Rockefeller's generosity. (Rev: BL 5/15/93; SLJ 6/93) [975.5]

17767 Stefoff, Rebecca. *The Colonies* (4–7). Series: North American Historical Atlases. 2000, Benchmark LB $24.21 (0-7614-1057-0). 48pp. A slim, clearly written account that gives a history of the American colonies, important places, and outstanding people. (Rev: HBG 3/01; SLJ 1/01) [973.2]

17768 Stein, R. Conrad. *Spanish Missionaries: Bringing Spanish Culture to the Americas* (3–6). Series: A Proud Heritage. 2005, Child's World LB $28.50 (1-59296-387-0). 40pp. A look at the missions found in various parts of the country and at key missionary leaders. (Rev: SLJ 6/05)

17769 Steins, Richard. *Colonial America* (5–8). Series: Making of America. 2000, Raintree LB $28.54 (0-8172-5701-2). 96pp. A brief history of the colonies from 1607 to 1763 with details of their founding, composition, and history. (Rev: HBG 10/00; SLJ 8/00) [973.2]

17770 Sterngass, Jon, and Matthew Kachur. *New Jersey* (4–7). Illus. Series: Life in the Thirteen Colonies. 2004, Children's Pr. LB $35.00 (0-516-24574-0). 128pp. From the first settlers to the end of the Revolutionary War, this interesting volume covers important events and daily life of the settlers plus information on the Native Amerian tribes.

17771 Stevens, Bernardine S. *Colonial American Craftspeople* (5–8). Series: Colonial America. 1993, Watts LB $24.00 (0-531-12536-X). A description of colonial trades and the apprenticeship system, illustrated with period engravings and paintings. (Rev: BL 1/1/94; SLJ 2/94) [680]

17772 Streissguth, Thomas. *New Jersey* (5–8). Series: Thirteen Colonies. 2002, Gale LB $27.45 (1-56006-872-8). 96pp. Using many well-chosen quotations and interesting black-and-white illustrations, this is a solid account of colonial New Jersey and its people. (Rev: BL 9/15/02) [973.2]

17773 Teitelbaum, Michael. *New Hampshire* (4–7). Illus. Series: Life in the Thirteen Colonies. 2004, Children's Pr. LB $35.00 (0-516-24573-2). 128pp. From the first settlers to the end of the Revolutionary War, this interesting volume covers important events and daily life of the settlers plus information on the Native Amerian tribes.

17774 Terkel, Susan N. *Colonial American Medicine* (5–8). Illus. Series: Colonial America. 1993, Watts LB $24.00 (0-531-12539-4). 112pp. An exploration of the practice of medicine in colonial America, with material on physicians, barbers, midwives, and astrologers. (Rev: BL 1/1/94; SLJ 11/93) [362.1]

17775 Uschan, Michael V. *North Carolina* (5–8). Series: The Thirteen Colonies. 2001, Lucent LB $27.45 (1-56006-885-X). 112pp. A straightforward text is combined with many period illustrations and

lists of related media to tell North Carolina's early history. (Rev: BL 3/15/02) [973.2]

17776 Walker, Niki. *Colonial Women* (3–5). Illus. by Barbara Bedell. Series: Colonial People. 2003, Crabtree LB $15.96 (0-7787-0749-0); paper $8.06 (0-7787-0795-4). 32pp. Examines what life was like for women during America's colonial era. (Rev: SLJ 1/04)

17777 Warner, John F. *Colonial American Home Life* (5–8). Illus. Series: Colonial America. 1993, Watts LB $24.00 (0-531-12541-6). 112pp. Topics covered in this book about colonial life include housing, clothing, food, work, and schools. (Rev: BL 1/1/94; SLJ 2/94) [973.2]

17778 Waters, Kate. *On the Mayflower: Voyage of the Ship's Apprentice and a Passenger Girl* (3–5). Illus. 1996, Scholastic $16.95 (0-590-67308-4). 40pp. A young ship's apprentice on the *Mayflower* tells the story of the historic crossing, with photographs taken during the voyage of *Mayflower II.* (Rev: BL 10/1/96; SLJ 10/96) [973.2]

17779 Waters, Kate. *Sara Morton's Day: A Day in the Life of a Pilgrim Girl* (4–6). Illus. by Russ Kendall. 1989, Scholastic paper $16.95 (0-590-42634-6). 32pp. A typical day in the life of a girl in the Plymouth plantation of 1627. (Rev: BCCB 1/90; BL 10/1/89; SLJ 11/89) [974.4]

17780 Waters, Kate. *Tapenum's Day: A Wampanoag Indian Boy in Pilgrim Times* (3–5). Illus. by Russ Kendall. 1996, Scholastic $16.95 (0-590-20237-5). 40pp. Re-enactment photos of the Plimoth Plantation site in Massachusetts enhance this account of a Wampanoag Indian boy in the 1620s. (Rev: BCCB 3/96; BL 5/1/96; HB 5–6/96; SLJ 5/96) [974.4]

17781 Whitehurst, Susan. *Plymouth: Surviving the First Winter* (2–4). Series: The Library of the Pilgrims. 2001, Rosen LB $19.50 (0-8239-5809-4). 24pp. An accessible account of the pilgrims' hard first winter, with details of housing, food, and illness. Also use *William Bradford and Plymouth: A Colony Grows* (2001). (Rev: SLJ 3/02) [974.4]

17782 Wiener, Roberta, and James R. Arnold. *Connecticut: The History of Connecticut Colony, 1633–1776* (5–8). Series: 13 Colonies. 2004, Raintree LB $31.36 (0-7398-6877-2). 64pp. A fact-filled and balanced discussion of the settlement of this area and the problems — political, social, and religious — that confronted the early European inhabitants. Also use *Delaware* and *Maryland* (both 2004). (Rev: SLJ 4/05) [974.6]

17783 Williams, Jean Kinney. *The Maryland Colony* (3–6). Series: Our Thirteen Colonies. 2003, Child's World LB $28.50 (1-56766-615-9). 40pp. Maps, prints, and other illustrations add to this presentation of Maryland's early history — from its founding in 1634 to early statehood, with coverage of colonial life, relations with Native Americans, and the roles of women and slaves. (Rev: SLJ 6/04) [975.2]

17784 Wilmore, Kathy. *A Day in the Life of a Colonial Innkeeper* (3–5). Illus. Series: Library of Living and Working in Colonial Times. 2000, Rosen $18.60 (0-8239-5430-7). 24pp. In this picture of life at an inn in colonial times, innkeepers Mr. and Mrs.

Watkins go about their daily chores — cooking, minding the horses in the stable, cleaning the rooms, and so forth. (Rev: BL 10/15/00) [973.3]

17785 Wilmore, Kathy. *A Day in the Life of a Colonial Wigmaker* (3–5). Illus. Series: Library of Living and Working in Colonial Times. 2000, Rosen $18.60 (0-8239-5426-9). 24pp. Set in a colonial American wig shop, this account shows how Mr. Hawkins and his staff of wig makers accomplish such tasks as making scull caps, sewing hair onto them, and powdering the finished wigs. (Rev: BL 10/15/00) [973.3]

17786 Woog, Adam. *New York* (5–8). Series: The Thirteen Colonies. 2001, Lucent LB $27.45 (1-56006-992-9). 80pp. Well-chosen quotations as well as black-and-white illustrations and maps help bring to life the story of colonial New York State. (Rev: BL 3/15/02) [973.2]

17787 Worth, Richard. *Delaware* (4–7). Illus. Series: Life in the Thirteen Colonies. 2004, Children's Pr. LB $35.00 (0-516-24569-4). 128pp. From the first settlers to the end of the Revolutionary War, this interesting volume covers important events and daily life of the settlers plus information on the Native Amerian tribes.

17788 Worth, Richard. *North Carolina* (4–7). Illus. Series: Life in the Thirteen Colonies. 2004, Children's Pr. LB $35.00 (0-516-24576-7). 128pp. From the first settlers to the end of the Revolutionary War, this interesting volume covers important events and daily life of the settlers plus information on the Native Amerian tribes.

17789 Wroble, Lisa A. *Kids in Colonial Times* (1–3). Series: Kids Throughout History. 1997, Rosen LB $13.95 (0-8239-5118-9). 24pp. An introduction to daily life and customs in the New England colonies. (Rev: SLJ 4/98) [973.2]

17790 Yolen, Jane, and Heidi Elizabet Yolen-Stemple. *Roanoke the Lost Colony: An Unsolved Mystery from History* (2–5). Illus. by Roger Roth. Series: Unsolved Mystery from History. 2003, Simon & Schuster $16.95 (0-689-82321-5). 32pp. Fact and fiction are cleverly woven together in this picture book for older children about the disappearance of the colonists of Roanoke, narrated by a young girl who aspires to be a detective. (Rev: BL 7/03; HBG 4/04; SLJ 10/03) [975]

REVOLUTIONARY PERIOD

17791 Ammon, Richard. *Valley Forge* (3–6). Illus. by Bill Farnsworth. 2004, Holiday House $16.95 (0-8234-1746-8). 32pp. Details of the hardships suffered by American forces during the winter of 1777–1778 are placed in historical context in this large-format book. (Rev: BL 9/15/04; SLJ 10/04) [973.3]

17792 Amstel, Marsha. *Sybil Ludington's Midnight Ride* (2–4). Illus. by Ellen Beier. 2000, Carolrhoda LB $21.27 (1-57505-211-3); paper $5.95 (1-57505-456-6). 48pp. A readable account of 16-year-old Sybil Ludington's exciting midnight ride to spread the word that the British were attacking Danbury, Connecticut. (Rev: HBG 10/00; SLJ 6/00) [973.3]

17793 Anderson, Dale. *Lexington and Concord, April 19, 1775* (5–7). Series: American Battlefields. 2004, Enchanted Lion $14.95 (1-59270-027-6). 32pp. This volume looks at the April 1775 skirmishes between American patriots and British soldiers at Lexington and Concord that marked the opening of the Revolutionary War; sidebars, illustrations, a timeline, and other features add to the narrative. (Rev: BL 11/1/04) [973]

17794 Beller, Susan Provost. *The Revolutionary War* (5–8). Series: Letters from the Homefront. 2001, Benchmark LB $28.50 (0-7614-1094-5). 96pp. An attractive volume that brings events and living conditions during the Revolution alive through a collection of letters and other personal documents. (Rev: BL 10/15/01; HBG 3/02) [973.3]

17795 Beller, Susan Provost. *Yankee Doodle and the Redcoats: Soldiering in the Revolutionary War* (5–8). Illus. by Larry Day. 2003, Millbrook LB $26.90 (0-7613-2612-X). 96pp. This attractive book covers the plight of the Revolutionary War soldier, with artwork as well as soldiers' letters and other documents adding to the presentation. (Rev: BL 5/15/03; HBG 10/03; SLJ 9/01) [973.3]

17796 Bobrick, Benson. *Fight for Freedom: The American Revolutionary War* (5–8). 2004, Simon & Schuster $22.95 (0-689-86422-1). 96pp. Full-page illustrations face text and "Quick Facts" about topics ranging from the origins and progress of the war to the Continental Congresses, with profiles of key figures and maps. (Rev: BL 11/15/04; SLJ 11/04) [973.3]

17797 Bohannon, Lisa Frederiksen. *The American Revolution* (5–8). Series: Chronicle of America's Wars. 2003, Lerner LB $27.93 (0-8225-4717-1). 88pp. Illustrations and maps enliven this overview of the American colonies' struggle for independence, covering the two decades from the French and Indian War to the Treaty of Paris. (Rev: HBG 4/04; SLJ 3/04) [973.3]

17798 Brennan, Linda Crotta. *The Black Regiment of the American Revolution* (4–6). Illus. by Cheryl Kirk Noll. 2004, Moon Mountain $16.95 (1-931659-06-0). 32pp. This picture book for older readers tells the story of Rhode Island's Black Regiment, composed largely of slaves who were fighting for their own freedom as well as America's independence. (Rev: BL 10/15/04; SLJ 1/05) [973.3]

17799 Brenner, Barbara. *If You Were There in 1776* (4–8). Illus. 1994, Bradbury $17.95 (0-02-712322-7). 112pp. The year 1776 is explored, with particular emphasis on the everyday life of young people in the colonies. (Rev: BCCB 6/94; BL 5/15/94; SLJ 6/94) [973.3]

17800 Cheney, Lynne V. *When Washington Crossed the Delaware: A Wintertime Story for Young Patriots* (2–4). Illus. by Peter M. Fiore. 2004, Simon & Schuster $16.95 (0-689-87043-4). 40pp. The battles of Trenton and Princeton are described in vivid prose with brief eyewitness quotations. (Rev: BL 10/1/04; SLJ 11/04) [973]

17801 Collier, Christopher, and James Lincoln Collier. *The American Revolution: 1763–1783* (5–8).

Series: Drama of American History. 1998, Marshall Cavendish LB $29.93 (0-7614-0440-6). Using period illustrations, this is a basic history of the Revolution, with material on how the colonialists felt, major battles, and major figures. (Rev: BL 4/15/98*; BR 11–12/98; HBG 10/98) [973.3]

17802 Collier, Christopher, and James Lincoln Collier. *Building a New Nation, 1789–1801* (5–8). Illus. Series: Drama of American History. 1998, Marshall Cavendish LB $29.93 (0-7614-0777-4). 89pp. An account of how the Federalists began to use the Constitution as a blueprint for guiding the young nation. (Rev: BL 2/15/99) [973.4]

17803 Collier, Christopher, and James Lincoln Collier. *Creating the Constitution, 1787* (5–8). Illus. Series: Drama of American History. 1998, Marshall Cavendish LB $19.95 (0-7914-0776-6). 89pp. This history of the U.S. Constitution describes the background and importance of the document and the compromises made to ensure ratification. (Rev: BL 2/15/99) [970.00497]

17804 Corey, Shana. *Paul Revere's Ride* (1–3). Illus. by Chris O'Leary. Series: Step into Reading. 2004, Random LB $11.99 (0-375-92836-7); paper $3.99 (0-375-82836-2). 48pp. The story of Revere's historic ride is placed in historical context in this very accessible account. (Rev: BL 2/1/05; SLJ 5/05) [973.3]

17805 Cox, Clinton. *Come All You Brave Soldiers: Blacks in the Revolutionary War* (5–7). Illus. 1999, Scholastic paper $15.95 (0-590-47576-2). 208pp. Beginning with the Boston Massacre and ending with the Battle of Yorktown, this is an exciting account of the participation and contributions of more than 5,000 blacks in the American Revolution. (Rev: BL 2/15/99; HBG 10/99; SLJ 2/99) [973.3]

17806 Crewe, Sabrina, and Dale Anderson. *Lexington and Concord* (4–6). Series: Events That Shaped America. 2004, Gareth Stevens LB $23.93 (0-8368-3398-8). 32pp. The story of the 1775 battle serves as the opening for a well-illustrated and well-organized discussion of the Revolutionary War. (Rev: SLJ 8/04) [973.3]

17807 Dolan, Edward F. *The American Revolution: How We Fought the War of Independence* (5–8). Illus. 1995, Millbrook LB $27.40 (1-56294-521-1). 112pp. An outline of the American Revolution that covers key events and profiles all the familiar historical figures. (Rev: BL 12/15/95; SLJ 1/96) [973.3]

17808 Draper, Allison Stark. *George Washington Elected: How America's First President Was Chosen* (2–4). Illus. Series: Headlines from History. 2001, Rosen LB $19.50 (0-8239-5675-X). 24pp. Newspaper headlines and large type make for easy-reading accounts of significant events leading up to and during Washington's tenure. Also use *The Boston Tea Party: Angry Colonists Dump British Tea* (2001). (Rev: SLJ 8/01) [973.4]

17809 Edwards, Pamela Duncan. *Boston Tea Party* (1–3). Illus. by Henry Cole. 2001, Penguin Putnam $15.99 (0-399-23357-1). 32pp. Rhythmic text presents the key events in the lead-up to the Tea Party,

enlivened by additional commentary from a crew of mice. (Rev: BCCB 6/01; BL 6/1–15/01; HBG 3/02; SLJ 7/01) [973.3]

17810 Erickson, Paul. *Daily Life on a Southern Plantation 1853* (4–7). 1998, Bt. Bound $16.45 (0-613-28459-3). 48pp. Gives an hour-by-hour tour of a Southern plantation in Louisiana in 1853, revealing how both the landowners and the slaves lived. (Rev: HBG 10/98; SLJ 12/98) [973.5]

17811 Ferrie, Richard. *The World Turned Upside Down: George Washington and the Battle of Yorktown* (5–9). Illus. 1999, Holiday House $18.95 (0-8234-1402-7). A lavishly illustrated account of the battle that was the turning point in the Revolution, with details on strategies, personalities, and period warfare. (Rev: BL 9/1/99; HBG 3/00; SLJ 10/99) [973.3]

17812 Fradin, Dennis Brindell. *Let It Begin Here! Lexington and Concord: First Battles of the American Revolution* (2–4). Illus. by Larry Day. 2005, Walker LB $17.85 (0-8027-8946-3). 32pp. The story of the battles that began it all, told in an engaging style to appeal to students; with illustrations and information on key figures of the war. (Rev: BL 4/15/05) [973.3]

17813 Freedman, Russell. *Give Me Liberty! The Story of the Declaration of Independence* (4–7). Illus. 2000, Holiday House $24.95 (0-8234-1448-5). 90pp. Beginning with the Boston Tea Party, this stirring account introduces characters including Patrick Henry and Paul Revere, events such as the battles at Lexington and Concord, and ends with the Continental Congress and the drawing up of the Declaration of Independence. (Rev: BCCB 10/00; BL 10/1/00*; HB 1–2/01; HBG 3/01; SLJ 10/00) [973.3]

17814 Furgang, Kathy. *The Declaration of Independence and John Adams of Massachusetts* (3–4). Illus. Series: Framers of the Declaration of Independence. 2001, Rosen LB $17.25 (0-8239-5590-7). 24pp. Large print and visual interest make this introductory account suitable for reluctant readers. Also use *The Declaration of Independence and Richard Henry Lee of Virginia* and *The Declaration of Independence and Roger Sherman of Connecticut* (both 2002). (Rev: SLJ 5/02)

17815 Furstinger, Nancy. *The Boston Tea Party* (4–6). Illus. Series: Let Freedom Ring. 2002, Capstone LB $22.60 (0-7368-1093-5). 48pp. Furstinger gives a concise account of the event and places it in a simple historical context that will be useful for report writers. Also use *The Boston Massacre* (2002). (Rev: HBG 3/03; SLJ 6/02)

17816 Graves, Kerry A. *The Declaration of Independence: The Story Behind America's Founding Document* (3–5). Series: America in Words and Song. 2003, Chelsea Clubhouse LB $14.95 (0-7910-7334-3). 32pp. Details events leading up to America's political break from Britain and the difficulties in framing the document declaring that independence. (Rev: SLJ 5/04) [973.3]

17817 Green, Carl R. *The Revolutionary War* (4–6). Illus. Series: U.S. Wars. 2002, Enslow LB $19.95

(0-7660-5089-0). 48pp. Supported by verified and updated Web links, this is a useful account of the Revolutionary War. (Rev: BL 10/15/02; HBG 3/03) [973.3]

17818 Harper, Judith E. *African Americans and the Revolutionary War* (4–6). Series: Journey to Freedom. 2000, Child's World LB $25.64 (1-56766-745-7). 40pp. This account traces the contributions of African Americans in the struggle for freedom against the English. (Rev: BL 11/15/00; HBG 3/01; SLJ 3/01) [973.3]

17819 Herbert, Janis. *The American Revolution for Kids* (5–8). Illus. 2002, Chicago Review paper $14.95 (1-55652-456-0). 160pp. A comprehensive look at the American Revolution from its causes through the early 18th century, with biographical information and interesting features. (Rev: BL 10/1/02; SLJ 11/02) [973.3]

17820 Hess, Debra. *The American Flag* (3–5). Series: Symbols of America. 2003, Benchmark LB $17.95 (0-7614-1709-5). 39pp. A look back at the many variations of the Stars and Stripes before and since the first one was made (according to legend) by Betsy Ross during the Revolutionary War. (Rev: HBG 4/04; SLJ 3/04)

17821 Hess, Debra. *The Liberty Bell* (3–5). Series: Symbols of America. 2003, Benchmark LB $17.95 (0-7614-1713-3). 40pp. A look at the Liberty Bell, its role in the Revolution, and why it is cracked. Also use *Statue of Liberty* (2003). (Rev: HBG 4/04; SLJ 3/04)

17822 Hossell, Karen Price. *The Articles of Confederation* (4–6). Series: Historical Documents. 2003, Heinemann LB $27.07 (1-4034-0800-9). 48pp. The story of the Articles of Confederation, which served as the first Constitution of the newly independent United States, with a look at what a primary document is and how original documents are preserved. (Rev: SLJ 5/04) [342.73]

17823 Hughes, Libby. *Valley Forge* (4–6). Illus. Series: Places in American History. 1993, Macmillan LB $18.95 (0-87518-547-9). 72pp. The story of Valley Forge, Pennsylvania, and the terrible winter during the American Revolutionary War when more than 3,000 of General Washington's troops died. (Rev: BL 4/15/93; SLJ 7/93) [973]

17824 Hull, Mary E. *Shays' Rebellion and the Constitution in American History* (5–10). Series: In American History. 2000, Enslow LB $19.95 (0-7660-1418-5). 112pp. Photos and reproductions of documents are used to bring to life this rebellion against the Massachusetts government in 1787. (Rev: BL 2/15/00; HBG 10/00; SLJ 6/00) [973.4]

17825 Ingram, Scott. *The Battle of Long Island* (4–6). Series: Triangle Histories of the American Revolution. 2003, Gale/Blackbirch LB $22.45 (1-56711-776-7). 32pp. A finely detailed, lively account of an early battle of the Revolutionary War, fought in what is now the borough of Brooklyn. (Rev: SLJ 3/04) [973.3]

17826 Ingram, Scott. *The Battle of Valcour Bay* (4–6). Series: Triangle Histories of the American Revolution. 2003, Gale/Blackbirch LB $22.45 (1-56711-778-3). 32pp. A detailed and well-illustrated account of the Revolutionary War battle of Valcour Bay on Lake Champlain. (Rev: SLJ 3/04)

17827 Kent, Deborah. *The American Revolution: "Give Me Liberty, or Give Me Death!"* (5–7). Illus. Series: American War. 1994, Enslow LB $20.95 (0-89490-521-X). 128pp. A succinct history of the Revolution that uses many firsthand quotations and period illustrations and maps. (Rev: BL 7/94; SLJ 7/94) [973.3]

17828 King, David C. *Saratoga* (5–8). Illus. Series: Battlefields Across America. 1998, Twenty-First Century LB $26.90 (0-7613-3011-9). The significance of the battle at Saratoga in 1777, in which General Burgoyne's British army was defeated, and where and how the history of this battle is preserved today. (Rev: HBG 9/98; SLJ 8/98) [973.3]

17829 Kirby, Philippa. *Glorious Days, Dreadful Days: The Battle of Bunker Hill* (4–6). Illus. by John Edens. Series: Stories of America. 1993, Raintree LB $28.55 (0-8114-7226-4). 88pp. Describes the Battle of Bunker Hill and its significance to the Revolution. (Rev: HB 11–12/97; SLJ 9/93) [973.3]

17830 Krensky, Stephen. *Paul Revere's Midnight Ride* (3–5). Illus. by Greg Harlin. 2002, Harper-Collins LB $17.89 (0-688-16410-2). 32pp. This beautifully illustrated picture book places Revere's ride in historical context, helped by a clear and attractive map of his route. (Rev: BL 10/1/02; HBG 3/03; SLJ 9/02) [973.3]

17831 Kroll, Steven. *The Boston Tea Party* (3–6). Illus. by Peter M. Fiore. 1998, Holiday House $16.95 (0-8234-1316-0). 32pp. A mature picture book in which the events leading up to and during the Boston Tea Party are described, with an afterword on its consequences. (Rev: BL 9/15/98; HBG 10/98; SLJ 12/98) [973.3]

17832 Leebrick, Kristal. *The United States Constitution* (3–8). Series: Let Freedom Ring. 2002, Capstone LB $16.95 (0-7368-1094-3). 48pp. James Madison's role in creating the constitution, the Constitutional Convention, and the ratification process are all covered here. Also use *The Declaration of Independence* (2002). (Rev: HBG 3/03; SLJ 7/02) [973.3]

17833 Lilly, Melinda. *The Boston Tea Party* (K–2). Illus. by Patrick O'Brien. Series: Reading American History. 2002, Rourke LB $19.47 (1-58952-357-1). 24pp. A simple account for beginning readers that introduces the key characters behind the rebellion. (Rev: SLJ 3/03) [973.3]

17834 Lunn, Janet. *Charlotte* (4–6). Illus. by Brian Deines. 1998, Tundra $15.95 (0-88776-383-9). 32pp. Based on fact, this picture book for older readers tells the story of Charlotte who, as a child living in New York City during Revolutionary times, is forced to accompany her Loyalist aunt and uncle to Nova Scotia as punishment for disobeying her father. (Rev: BCCB 9/98; BL 8/98; HBG 10/98; SLJ 9/98) [974.7]

17835 Marquette, Scott. *Revolutionary War* (4–7). Illus. Series: America at War. 2002, Rourke LB $27.93 (1-58952-387-3). 48pp. This book for middle graders studies the war itself and the events that led up to it. [973.3]

17836 Martin, Joseph Plumb. *A Revolutionary War Soldier* (3–6). Series: In My Own Words. 2000, Marshall Cavendish LB $16.95 (0-7614-1014-7). 64pp. Sly humor is present in diary excerpts that bring to life stirring moments in America's war for independence. (Rev: BL 3/1/01; HBG 3/01; SLJ 3/01) [973.3]

17837 Miller, Brandon Marie. *Growing Up in the Revolution and the New Nation* (4–7). Illus. Series: Our America. 2002, Lerner LB $31.95 (0-8225-0078-7). 64pp. An in-depth examination of the lives of children during and immediately after the American Revolution, including biographical information about real youngsters. (Rev: BL 10/15/02; HBG 3/03; SLJ 12/02) [973.3]

17838 Murphy, Jim. *A Young Patriot: The American Revolution as Experienced by One Boy* (5–8). Illus. 1996, Clarion $16.00 (0-395-60523-7). The American Revolution as seen through the eyes of a 15-year-old volunteer. (Rev: BCCB 6/96; BL 6/1–15/96*; HB 9–10/96; SLJ 6/96*) [973.3]

17839 Nordstrom, Judy. *Concord and Lexington* (4–6). Illus. Series: Places in American History. 1993, Macmillan LB $14.95 (0-87518-567-3). 72pp. The history and monuments of these two historic towns are covered, plus their place in the history of the Revolution. (Rev: BL 4/15/93; SLJ 7/93) [973.3]

17840 O'Neill, Laurie A. *The Boston Tea Party* (4–8). Series: Spotlight on American History. 1996, Millbrook LB $24.90 (0-7613-0006-6). The causes and effects of the Boston Tea Party are discussed, along with material on the Battles of Lexington and Concord. (Rev: BL 1/1–15/97; SLJ 3/97) [973.3]

17841 Quiri, Patricia R. *The Declaration of Independence* (3–4). Illus. Series: True Books. 1998, Children's Book Pr. LB $21.00 (0-516-20664-8). 48pp. After outlining the colonists' grievances, this account discusses the drafting of the Declaration of Independence and its final congressional approval. (Rev: BL 2/1/99; HBG 3/99) [973.3]

17842 Raatma, Lucia. *The Minutemen* (4–6). Series: We the People. 2005, Compass Point LB $22.60 (0-7565-0842-8). 48pp. Describes the role of the Minutemen and their bravery at the battles of Lexington and Concord. (Rev: SLJ 6/05)

17843 Rappaport, Doreen. *The Boston Coffee Party* (1–3). Illus. by Emily Arnold McCully. 1988, HarperCollins paper $3.95 (0-06-444141-5). 64pp. Angry women force a greedy merchant to turn over coffee in this true Revolutionary War incident. (Rev: BL 4/1/88; HB 9–10/88; SLJ 5/88)

17844 Rappaport, Doreen, and Joan Verniero. *Victory or Death! Stories of the American Revolution* (4–6). Illus. by Greg Call. 2003, HarperCollins LB $17.89 (0-06-029516-3). 128pp. Eight brief chapters tell inspiring stories of heroic acts — some familiar, others less well known — of the American Revolution. (Rev: BL 6/1–15/03; HBG 10/03; SLJ 6/03) [973.3]

17845 Scarbrough, Mary Hertz. *The Battle of Harlem Heights* (4–6). Series: Triangle Histories of the American Revolution. 2003, Gale/Blackbirch LB $22.45 (1-56711-777-5). 32pp. A finely detailed, lively account of an early battle of the Revolutionary War, fought in what is now upper Manhattan. (Rev: SLJ 3/04) [973.3]

17846 Schanzer, Rosalyn. *George vs. George: The Revolutionary War as Seen by Both Sides* (5–7). Illus. 2004, National Geographic $16.95 (0-7922-7349-4). 64pp. The two sides' differences — and commonalities — are portrayed in an appealing combination of well-written text, colorful art, and speech balloons; sensationalist aspects detract from the overall value. (Rev: BL 11/15/04; SLJ 10/04*) [973.3]

17847 Schleifer, Jay. *Our Declaration of Independence* (4–6). Illus. Series: I Know America. 1992, Millbrook LB $20.90 (1-56294-205-0). 48pp. A well-illustrated history of the writing of the Declaration of Independence and its significance. (Rev: BL 9/1/92; SLJ 10/92) [973.3]

17848 Silox-Jarrett, Diane. *Heroines of the American Revolution: America's Founding Mothers* (4–6). Illus. 1998, Green Angel $19.95 (0-9658065-2-0). 94pp. Profiles of 25 important women who championed the colonists' cause during the American Revolution. (Rev: BL 2/15/98) [973.3]

17849 Smith, Carter, ed. *The Revolutionary War: A Sourcebook on Colonial America* (5–8). Series: American Albums. 1991, Millbrook $25.90 (1-56294-039-2). This volume illustrates the major events leading up to the Revolution and the battles and personalities involved. (Rev: BL 1/1/92) [973.38]

17850 Stefoff, Rebecca. *Revolutionary War* (4–7). Illus. Series: North American Historical Atlases. 2000, Benchmark LB $24.21 (0-7614-1058-9). Using historical maps and reproductions plus a clear text, this is a basic account of the American Revolution. (Rev: HBG 3/01; SLJ 1/01) [973.3]

17851 Weber, Michael. *The American Revolution* (5–8). Series: Making of America. 2000, Raintree LB $28.54 (0-8172-5702-0). 96pp. A fine overview of the American Revolution from the French and Indian War to the creation of the United States. (Rev: BL 7/00; HBG 10/00; SLJ 8/00) [973.3]

17852 Weber, Michael. *Yorktown* (4–7). Illus. Series: Battlefields Across America. 1997, Twenty-First Century LB $26.90 (0-8050-5226-7). 63pp. Background material on the Revolutionary War is given, along with details of the battle and the present-day condition of its site. (Rev: SLJ 1/98) [973.3]

17853 Weber, Michael. *The Young Republic* (5–8). Illus. Series: Making of America. 2000, Raintree LB $28.54 (0-8172-5703-9). 94pp. This well-illustrated account begins in the 1780s with the creation of the federal system, the ratification of the Constitution, and the inauguration of Washington as president in 1789. (Rev: BL 5/1/00; HBG 10/00; SLJ 9/00) [973]

17854 Whitelaw, Nancy. *The Shot Heard Round the World: The Battles of Lexington and Concord* (5–8).

Illus. 2001, Morgan Reynolds LB $21.95 (1-883846-75-7). 112pp. Whitelaw details events from the Boston Massacre in 1770 to the first battles of the Revolution in 1775, with profiles of some of the key players. (Rev: BL 5/15/01; HBG 10/01; SLJ 7/01) [973.3]

17855 Wilbur, Keith C. *The Revolutionary Soldier, 1775–1783* (4–8). Series: Illustrated Living History. 1996, Chelsea LB $21.95 (0-7910-4533-1). Topics covered in this book about the Continental Army include clothing, weapons, camp life, food, hospitals, and leisure activities. (Rev: BL 6/1–15/97; SLJ 7/97) [973.3]

17856 Wister, Sally. *A Colonial Quaker Girl: The Diary of Sally Wister, 1777–1778* (4–6). Series: Diaries, Letters, and Memoirs. 2000, Capstone LB $22.60 (0-7368-0349-1). 32pp. This diary of a young girl, kept during the Revolution, reflects everyday family life during this period. (Rev: BL 10/15/00; SLJ 9/00) [973.3]

17857 Young, Robert. *The Real Patriots of the American Revolution* (4–6). Illus. Series: Both Sides. 1997, Dillon LB $18.95 (0-87518-612-2). 72pp. The points of view of Revolutionists, Loyalists, and the British are represented in this account of the causes and important events of the American Revolution. (Rev: BL 9/15/97) [973.3]

17858 Zeinert, Karen. *Those Remarkable Women of the American Revolution* (5–8). Illus. 1996, Millbrook LB $29.90 (1-56294-657-9). A fascinating account of the conditions and status of women in colonial America and their important contributions to the Revolution, from fighting and spying to fund raising. (Rev: BL 12/1/96; SLJ 3/97) [973.3]

THE YOUNG NATION, 1789–1861

17859 Baldwin, Robert F. *New England Whaler* (5–8). Illus. Series: American Pastfinder. 1996, Lerner LB $25.55 (0-8225-2978-5). Life on a 19th-century whaling ship is detailed, with many maps and color photographs. (Rev: BL 7/96; SLJ 6/96) [638.2]

17860 Bial, Raymond. *The Strength of These Arms: Life in the Slave Quarters* (5–8). 1997, Houghton Mifflin $16.00 (0-395-77394-6). This photoessay re-creates daily life in the slave quarters on large plantations, contrasts it with the luxurious lifestyles of the slave holders, and documents how slaves tried to preserve their heritage, dignity, and hope. (Rev: BL 9/15/97; HBG 3/98; SLJ 11/97) [975]

17861 Bial, Raymond. *The Underground Railroad* (4–7). Illus. 1995, Houghton Mifflin $17.00 (0-395-69937-1). 48pp. This photoessay re-creates the places involved in the Underground Railroad and the heroism of the people involved. (Rev: BCCB 3/95; BL 4/1/95; HB 7–8/95; SLJ 4/95) [973.7]

17862 Blumberg, Rhoda. *What's the Deal? Jefferson, Napoleon, and the Louisiana Purchase* (5–9). Illus. 1998, National Geographic $18.95 (0-7922-7013-4). 144pp. A dramatic retelling of the events surrounding the Louisiana Purchase, the people involved, the greed and double-dealing it induced, and what might have happened had Napoleon

refused to sell it. (Rev: BL 11/1/98*; HB 11–12/98; HBG 3/99; SLJ 10/98) [973.4]

17863 Bredeson, Carmen. *The Battle of the Alamo: The Fight for Texas Territory* (5–8). Series: Spotlight on American History. 1996, Millbrook LB $24.90 (0-7613-0019-8). A well-organized account of the causes, events, and campaigns of the war in which much of California, Texas, and the Southwest became part of the United States. (Rev: SLJ 4/97) [973.6]

17864 Britton, Tamara L. *The Alamo* (3–5). Series: Symbols, Landmarks, and Monuments. 2004, ABDO LB $15.95 (1-59197-518-2). 32pp. Historical and contemporary photographs add interest to this presentation of the Alamo's history and significance. (Rev: SLJ 11/04) [976.4]

17865 Burgan, Michael. *The Alamo* (3–6). Series: We the People. 2001, Compass Point LB $21.26 (0-7565-0097-4). 48pp. The major figures are profiled in this overview of the battle, along with maps, photographs, and paintings that bring the story to life. (Rev: SLJ 8/01) [976.4]

17866 Burgan, Michael. *The Louisiana Purchase* (5–8). Series: We the People. 2002, Compass Point LB $27.15 (0-7565-0210-1). 48pp. An accessible, well-illustrated account of the purchase that doubled the size of the United States. (Rev: SLJ 7/02) [973.46]

17867 Cantor, Carrie Nicholas. *The Mexican War: How the United States Gained Its Western Lands* (4–6). Illus. Series: A Proud Heritage: The Hispanic Library. 2003, Child's World LB $28.50 (1-56766-176-9). 40pp. A balanced account of the reasons why the United States went to war and of the progress of the war itself, with material on the prominent individuals, a timeline, and a glossary. (Rev: BL 10/15/03) [973.6]

17868 Chase, John Churchill. *Louisiana Purchase: An American Story.* Rev. ed. (5–8). Illus. 2002, Pelican paper $12.95 (1-58980-084-2). 96pp. The story of the Louisiana Purchase, engagingly told in comic-strip format. (Rev: BL 2/1/03) [973.4]

17869 Collier, Christopher, and James Lincoln Collier. *Andrew Jackson's America, 1824–1850* (5–8). Illus. Series: Drama of American History. 1998, Marshall Cavendish LB $29.93 (0-7614-0779-0). The Colliers trace American history over an eventful 26 years that encompass great change, from the Industrial Revolution to the Trail of Tears. (Rev: BL 2/15/99; HBG 10/99) [973.56]

17870 Collier, Christopher, and James Lincoln Collier. *Hispanic America, Texas and the Mexican War, 1835–1850* (5–8). Illus. Series: Drama of American History. 1998, Marshall Cavendish LB $29.93 (0-7614-0780-4). 89pp. This account covers the history of Europeans in the Southwest, the Hispanic culture in the region, the doctrine of Manifest Destiny, the Mexican War, and the settling of California. (Rev: BL 2/15/99; HBG 10/99; SLJ 4/99) [979]

17871 Collier, Christopher, and James Lincoln Collier. *The Jeffersonian Republicans, 1800–1823* (5–8). Illus. Series: Drama of American History. 1998, Marshall Cavendish LB $29.93 (0-7614-

0778-2). This lively account describes 23 eventful years in our history that include the Louisiana Purchase, the Lewis and Clark Expedition, and the War of 1812. (Rev: BL 2/15/99; HBG 10/99; SLJ 4/99) [973.46]

17872 Collier, Christopher, and James Lincoln Collier. *Slavery and the Coming of the Civil War, 1831–1861* (5–8). Illus. 1999, Marshall Cavendish LB $29.93 (0-7614-0817-7). 87pp. A reliable, interesting account the traces the history of slavery in the United States, with an emphasis on the events leading up to the Civil War. (Rev: BL 2/15/00; HBG 10/00; SLJ 3/00) [973.7]

17873 Currie, Stephen. *Escapes from Slavery* (5–9). Series: Great Escapes. 2003, Gale/Lucent LB $27.45 (1-59018-276-6). 112pp. The stories of six of the approximately 60,000 slaves who escaped from captivity in pre-Civil War America. (Rev: SLJ 4/04) [973.7]

17874 Diouf, Sylviane A. *Growing Up in Slavery* (5–7). 2001, Millbrook LB $24.90 (0-7613-1763-5). 96pp. A compelling account that dispels any myths about happy slave children and describes the hard life and work of life on the plantation as well as the atrocious conditions on slave ships. (Rev: BL 3/1/01; HBG 10/01; SLJ 6/01) [380.1]

17875 Doeden, Matt. *The Battle of the Alamo* (4–6). Illus. Series: Graphic History. 2005, Capstone LB $16.95 (0-7368-3832-5). 32pp. An eye-catching and dramatically worded graphic presentation of the battle. [976]

17876 Doherty, Craig A., and Katherine M. Doherty. *The Erie Canal* (4–7). Illus. Series: Building America. 1996, Blackbirch LB $26.19 (1-56711-112-2). 48pp. Photographs and maps are used effectively in this introduction to the Erie Canal, an engineering marvel. (Rev: BL 2/15/97; SLJ 2/97) [386]

17877 Draper, Charla L. *Cooking on Nineteenth Century Whaling Ships* (4–7). Series: Exploring History Through Simple Recipes. 2000, Capstone LB $22.60 (0-7368-0602-4). 32pp. As well as learning about life on a whaling ship, this book provides a series of simple recipes. (Rev: BL 3/1/01; HBG 10/01; SLJ 4/01) [974.8]

17878 Fischer, Laura. *Life in a Mississippi River Town* (2–4). Illus. Series: Picture the Past. 2003, Heinemann LB $24.22 (1-4034-3797-1). 32pp. A well-illustrated look at life along the Mississippi in the mid-19th century and the busy river's impact on society. (Rev: SLJ 6/04) [977]

17879 Fleischner, Jennifer. *The Dred Scott Case: Testing the Right to Live Free* (5–8). Series: Spotlight on American History. 1997, Millbrook $24.90 (0-7613-0005-8). An account of the life of the slave Dred Scott and the historic court case of 1857 against his owner, John Sanford. (Rev: BL 5/1/97; SLJ 4/97) [342.73]

17880 Forten, Charlotte. *A Free Black Girl Before the Civil War: The Diary of Charlotte Forten, 1854* (4–8). Ed. by Kerry Graves. Illus. Series: Diaries, Letters, and Memoirs. 2000, Capstone LB $22.60 (0-7368-0345-9). 32pp. This first-person account based on actual sources describes, in diary format, the life of a 16-year-old African American girl living in Massachusetts before the Civil War and her participation in the antislavery movement. (Rev: BL 10/15/00; HBG 10/00; SLJ 9/00) [974.4]

17881 Fradin, Dennis B. *Bound for the North Star: True Stories of Fugitive Slaves* (5–9). 2000, Clarion $20.00 (0-395-97017-2). 206pp. This is a gripping narrative that tells the true stories of 12 runaway slaves, including Harriet Tubman, who successfully escaped to the North and freedom. (Rev: BL 1/1–15/01; HB 1–2/01; HBG 3/01; SLJ 11/00) [973.6]

17882 Freedman, Florence B. *Two Tickets to Freedom: The True Story of Ellen and William Craft, Fugitive Slaves* (4–8). Illus. by Ezra Jack Keats. 1971, Bedrick $12.95 (0-87226-330-4); paper $5.95 (0-87226-221-9). 96pp. An exciting story of slavery, escape, and pursuit that is based on fact. A reissue. (Rev: BR 3–4/90) [973.5]

17883 Gaines, Ann. *The Alamo: The Fight Over Texas* (4–6). Illus. Series: A Proud Heritage: The Hispanic Library. 2003, Child's World LB $28.50 (1-56766-173-4). 40pp. An even-handed description of the history of the mission, its use as a fort, and the famous battle fought there. [976.4]

17884 Garland, Sherry. *Voices of the Alamo* (3–6). 2000, Scholastic $16.95 (0-590-98833-6). 40pp. Using a series of first-person narratives, this picture book describes the siege of the Alamo as well as covering the origins of the conflict and its aftermath. (Rev: BL 2/15/00; HBG 10/00; SLJ 6/00) [976.4]

17885 Gay, Kathlyn, and Martin Gay. *War of 1812* (5–8). Series: Voices of the Past. 1995, Twenty-First Century LB $25.90 (0-8050-2846-3). Excerpts from letters, memoirs, and official reports highlight this well-illustrated history of the War of 1812 and its consequences. (Rev: BL 12/15/95; SLJ 3/96) [973.5]

17886 Green, Carl R. *The War of 1812* (4–6). Series: U.S. Wars. 2002, Enslow/MyReportLinks.com LB $19.95 (0-7660-5092-0). 48pp. In addition to a concise discussion of the causes, progress, and resolution of the War of 1812, this book contains a lengthy listing of Web sites where students can find additional material on the subject. (Rev: BL 10/15/02; HBG 3/03) [973.5]

17887 Gunderson, Mary. *Southern Plantation Cooking* (4–7). Illus. 2000, Capstone LB $22.60 (0-7368-0357-2). 32pp. This book explores life on Southern plantations during the days of slavery with emphasis on the importance of food and food preparation. A few representative recipes are provided. (Rev: BL 8/00; HBG 10/00) [394.1]

17888 Hakim, Joy. *Liberty for All?* 2nd ed. (5–8). Series: A History of Us. 1999, Oxford LB $19.95 (0-19-512759-5); paper $13.95 (0-19-512760-9). 204pp. An excellent account of American history from 1800 to the outbreak of the Civil War, with emphasis on the slave economy and events leading up to the war. (Rev: BL 12/15/99) [973.5]

17889 Hakim, Joy. *The New Nation.* 2nd ed. (5–8). Series: A History of Us. 1999, Oxford LB $19.95

(0-19-512757-9). 192pp. Political and social developments, including territorial expansion and pioneer life, are covered in this excellent history of America from 1789 through 1850. (Rev: BL 12/15/99) [973.5]

17890 Hamilton, John. *The Corps of Discovery* (4–7). Series: Lewis and Clark. 2003, ABDO LB $16.95 (1-57765-761-6). 32pp. An interesting overview of the expedition, looking at Jefferson's goals for the mission and at the equipment available at the time. Also in this series about the expedition are *The Missouri River* and *The Mountains* (both 2003). (Rev: HBG 10/03; SLJ 5/03) [917.804]

17891 Hansen, Joyce, and Gary McGowan. *Freedom Roads: Searching for the Underground Railroad* (5–8). Illus. by James Ransome. 2003, Cricket $18.95 (0-8126-2673-7). 176pp. This look at the history of the Underground Railroad emphasizes how much of our knowledge consists of speculation and anecdotal material rather than hard evidence. (Rev: BL 5/1/03; HB 7–8/03; HBG 10/03; SLJ 9/03*) [973.7]

17892 Heinrichs, Ann. *The Underground Railroad* (3–5). Series: We the People. 2001, Compass Point LB $21.26 (0-7565-0102-4). 48pp. Heinrichs gives a clear explanation of the causes for the development of this route to freedom, details how it worked, and profiles key figures. (Rev: SLJ 7/01) [973.7]

17893 Hess, Debra. *The White House* (3–5). Series: Symbols of America. 2003, Benchmark LB $17.95 (0-7614-1712-5). 40pp. The history of the White House, residence of every U.S. president since 1792, and how it has changed over the years. (Rev: HBG 4/04; SLJ 3/04)

17894 Isaacs, Sally Senzell. *The Gold Rush* (4–6). Illus. Series: The American Adventure. 2003, Heinemann LB $25.64 (1-4034-2501-9). 32pp. An accessible account of the "Fortyniners" who thronged to California in the mid-18th century. (Rev: HBG 4/04; SLJ 6/04) [979.4]

17895 Isaacs, Sally Senzell. *Life on a Southern Plantation* (1–3). Series: Picture the Past. 2000, Heinemann $21.36 (1-57572-316-6). A well-organized account that uses double-page spreads to describe life on a southern plantation before the Civil War with coverage of the lives of both the planters and the slaves. (Rev: HBG 3/01; SLJ 11/00) [973.6]

17896 Jacobs, William J. *War with Mexico* (4–6). Illus. Series: Spotlight on American History. 1993, Millbrook LB $21.90 (1-56294-366-9). 64pp. The events of the 1846–1848 war with Mexico are reported, with an objective account of its causes and results. (Rev: BL 12/15/93; SLJ 1/94) [973.6]

17897 Kallen, Stuart A. *Life on the Underground Railroad* (5–8). Series: The Way People Live. 2000, Lucent LB $18.96 (1-56006-667-9). 96pp. After a brief history of slavery in America, this account covers the organization of and people involved in the Underground Railroad, the journeys made on it, and its impact on future history. (Rev: HBG 10/00; SLJ 5/00) [973.6]

17898 Kalman, Bobbie. *The General Store* (3–5). Illus. Series: Historic Communities. 1997, Crabtree LB $20.60 (0-86505-432-0); paper $7.95 (0-86505-462-2). 32pp. Using photos of reconstructions in such places as Old Sturbridge Village, this account describes the importance, contents, and workings of the general store in 18th- and 19th-century America. (Rev: SLJ 7/97) [381]

17899 Kalman, Bobbie. *Life on a Plantation* (3–6). Illus. Series: Historic Communities. 1997, Crabtree LB $20.60 (0-86505-435-5); paper $7.95 (0-86505-465-7). 32pp. Daily life on the plantation for both the owners and their slaves is covered, with details about working in the fields and the roles and duties of various workers. (Rev: BL 7/97) [975]

17900 King, David C. *New Orleans* (5–8). Illus. Series: Battlefields Across America. 1998, Twenty-First Century LB $26.90 (0-7613-3010-0). The story of the famous 1815 battle in New Orleans in which the British were decisively defeated, including the background of the War of 1812, the role of Andrew Jackson, and the significance of this defeat to the British. (Rev: HBG 9/98; SLJ 8/98) [973.6]

17901 Levy, Janey. *The Alamo: A Primary Source History of the Legendary Texas Mission* (5–8). Illus. Series: Primary Sources in American History. 2003, Rosen LB $29.25 (0-8239-3681-3). 64pp. Primary sources — including maps and paintings — tell the story of the Battle of the Alamo. (Rev: BL 5/15/03; SLJ 5/03) [976.4]

17902 Levy, Janey. *The Erie Canal: A Primary Source History of the Canal That Changed America* (5–8). 2003, Rosen LB $29.25 (0-8239-3680-5). 64pp. The story of the construction of the Erie Canal and its impact on commerce is revealed through primary documents and many period illustrations. (Rev: SLJ 5/03) [974.7]

17903 Lourie, Peter. *Erie Canal: Canoeing America's Great Waterway* (5–8). Illus. 1997, Boyds Mills $17.95 (1-56397-669-2). This colorful book about a journey along the Erie Canal also supplies historical facts about its construction and uses. (Rev: BL 7/97; HBG 3/98; SLJ 9/97) [974.7]

17904 McGowen, Tom. *The Alamo* (3–6). Series: Cornerstones of Freedom, Second Series. 2003, Children's Pr. LB $24.00 (0-516-24208-3). 48pp. Background information provides context for the famous events at the Alamo; details of uniforms and weapons add to the picture. (Rev: SLJ 6/03) [976.4]

17905 McKissack, Patricia, and Fredrick McKissack. *Christmas in the Big House, Christmas in the Quarters* (4–6). Illus. by John Thompson. 1994, Scholastic $17.95 (0-590-43027-0). 80pp. This book describes life on a Virginia plantation in 1859 and includes social life and master-slave relations plus material on how Christmas was celebrated. (Rev: BCCB 10/94; BL 8/94; SLJ 10/94*) [975]

17906 McKissack, Patricia, and Fredrick McKissack. *Rebels Against Slavery: American Slave Revolts* (5–8). Illus. 1996, Scholastic paper $15.95 (0-590-45735-7). A fascinating account of the men and women who led revolts against slavery, including Toussaint L'Ouverture, Cinque, Harriet Tubman, and Nat Turner. (Rev: BCCB 6/96; BL 2/15/96; BR 3–4/96; SLJ 3/96) [970]

17907 McNeese, Tim. *America's Early Canals* (4–6). Illus. Series: America on the Move. 1993, Macmillan LB $11.95 (0-89686-730-7). 48pp. An introduction to canals famous in American history, such as the Potomac Canal and the Erie Canal, with discussion of the builders and how the canals were built. (Rev: BL 11/15/93) [386]

17908 Marquette, Scott. *War of 1812* (4–7). Illus. Series: America at War. 2002, Rourke LB $27.93 (1-58952-389-X). 48pp. This book for middle-graders studies the war itself and the events that led up to it. (Rev: BL 10/15/02) [973.5]

17909 Moore, Cathy. *The Daring Escape of Ellen Craft* (1–3). Illus. by Mary O. Young. Series: On My Own History. 2002, Carolrhoda LB $21.27 (0-87614-462-8); paper $6.95 (0-87614-787-2). 48pp. This is the story, based on truth, of two slaves' 1848 journey from Georgia to safety in Philadelphia, the woman disguised as a white slave master. (Rev: HBG 10/02; SLJ 4/02)

17910 Morrison, Taylor. *Coast Mappers* (4–8). Illus. 2004, Houghton Mifflin $16.00 (0-618-25408-0). 48pp. Science and biography are interwoven in this examination of the mid-19th-century mapping of the U.S. Pacific coastline. (Rev: BL 3/15/04; SLJ 5/04) [623.89]

17911 Myers, Walter Dean. *Amistad: A Long Road to Freedom* (5–9). Illus. 1998, Dutton $16.99 (0-525-45970-7). The fascinating story of the 1839 mutiny and its consequences, told in a skillful narrative that emphasizes the courage, strength, and dignity of the mutineers. (Rev: BCCB 5/98; BL 2/15/98; HBG 10/98; SLJ 5/98) [326]

17912 Nofi, Albert A. *The Underground Railroad and the Civil War* (4–8). Series: Untold History of the Civil War. 2000, Chelsea $19.75 (0-7910-5434-9). 64pp. A history of the dangers, devotion, excitement, and daring involved in this collaborative system that was developed to help fugitive Southern slaves reach freedom in the North or in Canada. (Rev: BL 5/15/00; HBG 10/00; SLJ 6/00) [973.7]

17913 Olson, Kay Melchisedech. *Africans in America: 1619–1865* (4–6). Series: Coming to America. 2002, Capstone LB $22.60 (0-7368-1204-0). 32pp. The story of the forced migrations of Africans to America, their life of slavery, their culture and contributions, and information on famous African Americans. (Rev: BL 1/1–15/03; HBG 3/03) [973]

17914 Paulson, Timothy J. *Days of Sorrow, Years of Glory, 1831–1850: From the Nat Turner Revolt to the Fugitive Slave Law* (5–9). Series: Milestones in Black American History. 1994, Chelsea paper $14.93 (0-7910-2552-7). An examination of the Underground Railroad, slave resistance, the Seminole Wars, and the abolition movement. (Rev: BL 11/1/94; SLJ 4/95) [973]

17915 Pelta, Kathy. *Eastern Trails: From Footpaths to Turnpikes* (4–6). Series: American Trails. 1997, Raintree LB $39.75 (0-8172-4071-3). 96pp. Focusing on trails, footpaths, and emerging roads, this account traces the opening up of the American East

to settlers and explorers. Also use *Trails to the West: Beyond the Mississippi* (1997). (Rev: BL 10/15/97; HBG 3/98) [973.6]

17916 Ray, Kurt. *New Roads, Canals, and Railroads in Early-19th-Century America: The Transportation Revolution* (3–5). Illus. Series: Life in the New American Nation. 2004, Rosen LB $15.95 (0-8239-4036-5). 32pp. A look at the growth in transport-related construction in the early 19th century.

17917 Richards, Caroline Cowles. *A 19th Century Schoolgirl: The Diary of Caroline Cowles Richards, 1852–1855* (4–8). Ed. by Kerry Graves. Illus. Series: Diaries, Letters, and Memoirs. 2000, Capstone LB $22.60 (0-7368-0342-4). 32pp. This diary of a young girl living in western New York State in the early 1850s describes her daily life, schooling, and her reaction to the women's rights movement. (Rev: BL 10/15/00; HBG 10/00; SLJ 9/00) [974.7]

17918 Riehecky, Janet. *The Siege of the Alamo* (3–6). Illus. Series: Landmark Events in American History. 2002, World Almanac LB $26.60 (0-8368-5342-3). 48pp. The factors leading up to the siege are detailed in this account that distinguishes legend from reality and explains the historical significance. (Rev: SLJ 2/03) [976.4]

17919 Santella, Andrew. *The Erie Canal* (4–6). Series: We the People. 2004, Compass Point LB $22.60 (0-7565-0679-4). 48pp. Discusses the construction of this canal in the 19th century and its importance in transporting goods. (Rev: SLJ 2/05) [386]

17920 Silverstein, Herma. *The Alamo* (4–6). Illus. Series: Places in American History. 1992, Macmillan LB $14.95 (0-87518-502-9). 72pp. A visual and narrative introduction to the historical site in San Antonio that was besieged by Mexican forces. (Rev: BL 9/1/92; SLJ 8/92) [976]

17921 Simonds, Christopher. *Samuel Slater's Mill and the Industrial Revolution* (5–7). Illus. Series: Turning Points. 1990, Silver Burdett LB $14.95 (0-382-09951-6); paper $7.95 (0-382-09947-8). 64pp. Describes how the pioneer in the cotton textile industry reproduced English machinery and how the Industrial Revolution began in this country. (Rev: BL 3/1/91) [338]

17922 Stefoff, Rebecca. *The War of 1812* (4–7). Illus. Series: North American Historical Atlases. 2000, Benchmark LB $24.21 (0-7614-1060-0). A clearly written text plus historical maps and reproductions are used to give an easy-to-read account of the War of 1812. (Rev: HBG 3/01; SLJ 1/01) [973.8]

17923 Stewart, Mark. *The Alamo, February 23–March 6, 1836* (5–7). Illus. Series: American Battlefields. 2004, Enchanted Lion $14.95 (1-59270-026-8). 32pp. This overview of the Battle of the Alamo offers a clear account of the conflict and an examination of the developments leading up to it; sidebars, illustrations, a timeline, and other features add to the narrative. [976.4]

17924 Toynton, Evelyn. *Growing Up in America: 1830 to 1860* (4–6). Illus. 1995, Millbrook LB $24.90 (1-56294-453-3). 96pp. Describes the life of pre-Civil War children from five social groups, including Native Americans, slaves, and farmers. (Rev: BL 4/15/95; SLJ 4/95) [973.5]

17925 Turner, Glennette Tilley. *The Underground Railroad in Illinois* (5–8). Illus. 2001, Newman Educational paper $16.95 (0-938990-05-5). 320pp. Using a question-and-answer format, this book focuses on the Underground Railroad in Illinois, the historical period, the problems, people who worked on the effort, and the many heroic deeds. (Rev: BL 2/15/01) [973.7]

17926 Wells, Rosemary. *Streets of Gold* (2–5). Illus. by Dan Andreasen. 1999, Dial $16.99 (0-8037-2149-8). 40pp. This picture book for older readers is the biography of a Russian Jewish girl who leaves the old country for a new life in America. (Rev: BCCB 7–8/99; BL 5/1/99; HBG 3/00; SLJ 6/99) [973]

PIONEER LIFE AND WESTWARD EXPANSION

17927 Altman, Linda Jacobs. *The California Gold Rush in American History* (4–8). Illus. Series: In American History. 1997, Enslow LB $20.95 (0-89490-878-2). 128pp. After a brief history of the California Gold Rush, this book covers topics including frontier injustice, racial discrimination, and the place of women. (Rev: BR 1–2/98; HBG 3/98; SLJ 3/98) [979.4]

17928 Ammon, Richard. *Conestoga Wagons* (2–5). Illus. 2000, Holiday House $16.95 (0-8234-1475-2). 32pp. This illustrated account gives the history of the vehicles used for long-distance hauling between 1750 and 1850 and discusses their construction, parts, uses, and the people who drove them. (Rev: BCCB 9/00; BL 10/1/00; HBG 3/01; SLJ 9/00) [388.3]

17929 Anderson, Dale. *Westward Expansion* (5–8). Series: The Making of America. 2001, Raintree LB $28.54 (0-8172-5705-5). 96pp. An attractive, balanced history of the expansion of the United States to the Pacific with many biographies of pioneers given in sidebars. (Rev: BL 4/15/01; HBG 10/01) [978]

17930 Anderson, Joan. *Spanish Pioneers of the Southwest* (3–6). Illus. 1989, Dutton paper $16.00 (0-525-67546-9). 64pp. A photoessay of life in mid-18th-century New Mexico. (Rev: BCCB 4/89; BL 4/15/89; SLJ 5/89)

17931 Bial, Raymond. *Cow Towns* (2–5). Series: American Community. 2004, Children's Pr. LB $28.00 (0-516-23706-3). 48pp. The daily lives of the people — cattlemen and prospectors, for example — who populated the towns of the early West are described plus detailed back matter and many illustrations. Also use *Frontier Settlements* and *Missions and Presidios* (both 2004). (Rev: SLJ 1/05) [978]

17932 Bial, Raymond. *Frontier Home* (3–6). Illus. 1993, Houghton Mifflin $17.00 (0-395-64046-6). 40pp. A description of the exteriors and contents of frontier homes, with many quotes from original sources. (Rev: BCCB 10/93; BL 11/1/93; SLJ 9/93) [978]

17933 Bial, Raymond. *Ghost Towns of the American West* (3–5). Illus. 2001, Houghton Mifflin $16.00 (0-618-06557-1). Several western ghost towns are presented, with pictures of how they looked then and look today and details of why they were abandoned. (Rev: BCCB 2/01; BL 1/1–15/01; HB 3–4/01; HBG 10/01; SLJ 2/01) [978]

17934 Blackwood, Gary L. *Life on the Oregon Trail* (5–8). Series: The Way People Live. 1999, Lucent LB $27.45 (1-56006-540-0). 111pp. Using many excerpts from diaries, this is a thorough, appealing account of life on the Oregon Trail, which took pioneers from Missouri to the Pacific Ocean. (Rev: HBG 3/00; SLJ 8/99) [978]

17935 Blashfield, Jean F. *The California Gold Rush* (3–6). Series: We the People. 2000, Compass Point LB $15.95 (0-7565-0041-9). 48pp. A straightforward account of why and how people traveled to California during the Gold Rush and of the lasting effects this migration had on western history. (Rev: SLJ 3/01) [979.4]

17936 Blashfield, Jean F. *The Oregon Trail* (3–6). 2000, Compass Point LB $15.95 (0-7565-0045-1). 48pp. This book explains the building of the Oregon Trail, its uses, and travel conditions along it. Also use: *The Santa Fe Trail* (2000). (Rev: SLJ 3/01) [978]

17937 Brill, Marlene Targ. *Bronco Charlie and the Pony Express* (2–4). Illus. by Craig Orback. Series: On My Own History. 2004, Carolrhoda LB $27.93 (1-57505-587-2); paper $5.95 (1-57505-618-6). 46pp. Bronco Charlie, 11, became the youngest rider for the Pony Express in 1861 and rode bravely through various dangers. (Rev: SLJ 8/04) [383]

17938 Calabro, Marian. *The Perilous Journey of the Donner Party* (5–8). Illus. 1999, Houghton Mifflin $20.00 (0-395-86610-3). The story of the ill-fated Donner Party, as seen through the eyes of 12-year-old Virginia Reed. (Rev: BL 4/1/99*; HB 5–6/99; SLJ 5/99) [979.4]

17939 Carlson, Laurie. *Westward Ho! An Activity Guide to the Wild West* (4–6). 1996, Chicago Review paper $12.95 (1-55652-271-1). 160pp. Clear directions accompany this introduction to 50 activities — like hooking rugs or keeping a trapper's journal — associated with the westward movement. (Rev: BL 10/1/96; SLJ 12/96) [978]

17940 Cobb, Mary. *The Quilt-Block History of Pioneer Days: With Projects Kids Can Make* (3–6). Illus. 1995, Millbrook LB $23.90 (1-56294-485-1). 64pp. A history of America's Western pioneers as seen through the patterns in their quilts plus a number of related craft projects, such as making bookmarks. (Rev: BL 4/15/95; SLJ 6/95) [746.9]

17941 Collier, Christopher, and James Lincoln Collier. *Indians, Cowboys, and Farmers: And the Battle for the Great Plains* (5–8). Series: The Drama of American History. 2001, Marshall Cavendish LB $29.93 (0-7614-1052-X). This excellently written and illustrated account covers the history of the Great Plains from the end of the Civil War to 1910, by which time the Native Americans had been scattered and the ranchers and farmers had reached a truce. (Rev: BL 3/15/01; HBG 10/01; SLJ 7/01) [973.8]

17942 Comport, Sally Wern. *The Great Expedition of Lewis and Clark: By Private Reubin Field, Member of the Corps of Discovery* (3–4). Illus. by author. 2003, Farrar $17.00 (0-374-38039-2). 40pp. Writing from the point of view of Reubin Field, Edwards gives a lively account of the famous expedition, its principal characters, and its dangers and delights. (Rev: BL 8/03; HBG 4/04; SLJ 11/03) [917.8]

17943 Crewe, Sabrina, and Dale Anderson. *The California Gold Rush* (3–5). Series: Events That Shaped America. 2003, Gareth Stevens LB $22.60 (0-8368-3393-7). 32pp. This brief history of the mid-19th-century California Gold Rush covers the discovery of gold at Sutter's Mill and that event's impact on the state and the nation as a whole. (Rev: HBG 10/03; SLJ 10/03) [979.4]

17944 Davis, Kenneth C. *Don't Know Much About the Pioneers* (3–5). Illus. by Ren e Andriani. Series: Don't Know Much About. 2003, HarperCollins LB $16.89 (0-06-028618-0). 48pp. Quizzes, quotations, feature sidebars, and bright illustrations make this a volume for browsing. (Rev: HBG 10/03; SLJ 6/03) [978]

17945 Dean, Arlan. *The Mormon Pioneer Trail: From Nauvoo, Illinois, to the Great Salt Lake, Utah* (2–4). Illus. Series: Famous American Trails. 2003, Rosen LB $17.25 (0-8239-6476-0). 24pp. For early readers and researchers, this title explores the 1,200-mile trail, providing lots of illustrations and maps. (Rev: SLJ 6/03) [978]

17946 Dean, Arlan. *The Old Spanish Trail: From Santa Fe, New Mexico, to Los Angeles, California* (2–4). Series: Famous American Trails. 2003, Rosen LB $17.25 (0-8239-6480-9). 24pp. This attractive and informative survey for young readers includes maps, photographs, and illustrations. (Rev: SLJ 12/03) [979]

17947 Dean, Arlan. *The Santa Fe Trail: From Independence, Missouri, to Santa Fe, New Mexico* (2–4). Illus. Series: Famous American Trails. 2003, Rosen LB $17.25 (0-8239-6481-7). 24pp. For early readers and researchers, this title explores the historic wagon trail, providing lots of illustrations and maps. (Rev: SLJ 6/03) [978]

17948 DeAngelis, Gina. *The Black Cowboys* (4–8). Illus. Series: Legends of the West. 1997, Chelsea LB $21.95 (0-7910-2589-6); paper $9.95 (0-7910-2590-X). A look at the contributions of African Americans such as Jim Beckwourth and Edward Rose to the exploration and settlement of the American West. (Rev: BL 2/15/98; HBG 3/98) [978]

17949 DeAngelis, Gina. *The Wild West* (5–8). Series: Costume, Tradition, and Culture: Reflecting on the Past. 1998, Chelsea $19.75 (0-7910-5169-2). 64pp. Illustrated with historical collectors' cards, this account relates the legends and stories of the Wild West — its explorers, lawmen, outlaws, and Native Americans. (Rev: BL 3/15/99; HBG 10/99) [978]

17950 Delgado, James P. *Shipwrecks from the Westward Movement* (5–7). Series: Shipwrecks. 2000, Watts LB $24.00 (0-531-20380-8). 64pp. A discussion and exploration of the shipwrecks — from small canoes to steam-powered riverboats — that occurred as European settlers moved across America. (Rev: BL 10/15/00) [978]

17951 Dolan, Edward F. *Beyond the Frontier: The Story of the Trails West* (4–8). Series: Great Journeys. 1999, Benchmark LB $21.95 (0-7614-0969-6). 112pp. As well as describing life on the Santa Fe, Oregon, and California trails, and the sea routes taken west, this account covers such specific topics as the Donner party and life in western settlements. (Rev: BL 1/1–15/00; HBG 3/00; SLJ 2/00) [978]

17952 Duncan, Dayton. *People of the West* (5–10). Illus. 1996, Little, Brown $19.95 (0-316-19627-4). Individual people — both famous and less well known — describe in their own words the opening up of the West. Based on the PBS series. (Rev: BL 8/96; SLJ 10/96) [978]

17953 Fisher, Leonard Everett. *The Oregon Trail* (4–6). Illus. 1990, Holiday House LB $18.95 (0-8234-0833-7). 64pp. A clear, readable account of the westward expansion in the 1800s. (Rev: BCCB 1/91; BL 12/15/90; HB 3–4/91; SLJ 1/91) [979.5]

17954 Freedman, Russell. *Children of the Wild West* (5–9). Illus. 1983, Clarion $18.00 (0-89919-143-6). A look at the life of the children of pioneers. (Rev: BL 1/1/90) [978]

17955 Freedman, Russell. *Cowboys of the Wild West* (5–8). Illus. 1990, Houghton Mifflin paper $9.95 (0-395-54800-4). 128pp. Text and excellent historical photographs describe these romantic figures. (Rev: BCCB 12/85; HB 3–4/86) [978.02]

17956 Galford, Ellen. *The Trail West: Exploring History Through Art* (5–8). Illus. Series: Picture That! 2004, Two-Can $19.95 (1-58728-442-1). 64pp. Paintings serve as the vehicle to draw students into the story of westward expansion. (Rev: BL 11/1/04; SLJ 2/05) [978]

17957 Goldsmith, Connie. *Lost in Death Valley: The True Story of Four Families in California's Gold Rush* (5–8). Illus. 2001, Twenty-First Century LB $24.90 (0-7613-1915-8). 144pp. Using original sources, the author has re-created the story of an ill-fated pioneer trek and the shortcut that led them into Death Valley. (Rev: BL 4/1/01; HBG 10/01; SLJ 4/01) [979.4]

17958 Graves, Kerry A. *Going to School in Pioneer Times* (4–6). Illus. Series: Going to School in History. 2001, Capstone LB $16.95 (0-7368-0804-3). 32pp. Today's students will enjoy this look at the one-room schoolhouse of pioneer days, introduced by historical context and illustrated with period photographs. (Rev: BL 10/15/01; HBG 3/02; SLJ 1/02) [370.977]

17959 Green, Carl R., and William R. Sanford. *The Dalton Gang* (4–8). Illus. Series: Outlaws and Lawmen of the Wild West. 1995, Enslow LB $16.95 (0-89490-588-0). 48pp. The story of the gang of outlaws who roamed the West during pioneer days. (Rev: BL 11/15/95) [978]

951

17960 Gunderson, Mary. *Oregon Trail Cooking* (4–7). Series: Exploring History Through Simple Recipes. 2000, Capstone LB $22.60 (0-7368-0355-6). 32pp. This book tells about journeys on the Oregon Trail, the lifestyles of the pioneers, the foods they ate, and some of the recipes that they used. Also use *Cowboy Cooking* (2000). (Rev: BL 8/00; HBG 10/00; SLJ 12/00) [973.5]

17961 Hatt, Christine. *The American West: Native Americans, Pioneers and Settlers* (4–7). Series: History in Writing. 1999, Bedrick $19.95 (0-87226-290-1). 62pp. A broad overview of frontier life in America with material on such topics as the Louisiana Purchase, Indian relocations, the Gold Rush, and a settler's daily life. (Rev: HBG 3/00; SLJ 5/99) [978]

17962 Hester, Sallie. *A Covered Wagon Girl: The Diary of Sallie Hester, 1849–1850* (4–6). Series: Diaries, Letters, and Memoirs. 2000, Capstone LB $22.60 (0-7368-0344-0). 32pp. Diary entries by a young pioneer girl reveal everyday life on the American frontier. (Rev: BL 10/15/00; HBG 10/00; SLJ 9/00) [978]

17963 Isaacs, Sally Senzell. *The Great Land Rush* (4–6). Illus. Series: The American Adventure. 2003, Heinemann LB $25.64 (1-4034-2505-1). 32pp. The story of the rush to settle land on the American frontier in the late 19th century, including its impact on the native people who already lived there. (Rev: HBG 4/04; SLJ 6/04) [976.6]

17964 Isaacs, Sally Senzell. *The Lewis and Clark Expedition* (4–6). Illus. Series: The American Adventure. 2003, Heinemann LB $25.64 (1-4034-2503-5). 32pp. The impact on the native peoples of the West and Pacific Northwest is one focus of this well-illustrated account. (Rev: HBG 4/04; SLJ 6/04) [917.8]

17965 Isaacs, Sally Senzell. *Life on a Pioneer Homestead* (1–3). Series: Picture the Past. 2000, Heinemann LB $21.36 (1-57572-313-1). Using double-page spreads, this well-organized account covers such basic topics as pioneer food, clothing, and rearing of children. Also use from this series *Life on the Oregon Trail* (2000). (Rev: HBG 3/01; SLJ 11/00) [978]

17966 January, Brendan. *Little Bighorn: June 25, 1876* (5–7). Series: American Battlefields. 2004, Enchanted Lion $14.95 (1-59270-028-4). 32pp. This overview of the Battle of Little Bighorn offers a clear-cut account of the bloody conflict and an examination of the developments leading up to it; sidebars, illustrations, a timeline, and other features add to the narrative. (Rev: BL 11/1/04) [973]

17967 Johmann, Carol A., and Elizabeth J. Rieth. *Going West! Journey on a Wagon Train to Settle a Frontier Town* (3–6). Illus. by Michael Kline. Series: Kaleidoscope Kids. 2000, Williamson paper $10.95 (1-885593-38-4). 96pp. As well as information on wagon trains, this book gives good background history involving the opening up of the West and outlines projects that use the crafts and skills of the pioneers. (Rev: SLJ 1/01) [978]

17968 Josephson, Judith Pinkerton. *Growing up in Pioneer America: 1800 to 1890* (4–6). Series: Our America. 2002, Lerner LB $26.60 (0-8225-0659-9). 64pp. The lives of children in this period are described with many quotations and excerpts from diaries, letter, and memoirs. (Rev: HBG 3/03; SLJ 2/03)

17969 Kallen, Stuart A. *Life on the American Frontier* (5–8). Series: The Way People Live. 1998, Lucent LB $17.96 (1-56006-366-1). 108pp. Thematically arranged chapters offer material on everyday life on the American frontier and on such groups as the trailblazers, the mountain men, the miners, the railroad men, the sodbusters, and the cattlemen. (Rev: SLJ 1/99) [973.5]

17970 Kalman, Bobbie. *Bandannas, Chaps, and Ten-Gallon Hats* (3–6). Series: Life in the Old West. 1999, Crabtree LB $14.37 (0-7787-0073-9); paper $7.16 (0-7787-0105-0). 32pp. An interesting but somewhat disorganized account on the part played by cowboys in the opening up of the West. (Rev: SLJ 9/99) [978]

17971 Kalman, Bobbie. *The Gristmill* (3–6). Illus. Series: Historic Communities. 1991, Crabtree LB $20.60 (0-86505-486-X); paper $7.95 (0-86505-506-8). 32pp. Text and pictures show the construction and operation of the mill as well as the skills of the millers. (Rev: BL 7/91) [664]

17972 Kalman, Bobbie. *Home Crafts* (3–6). Illus. Series: Historic Communities. 1991, Crabtree LB $20.60 (0-86505-485-1); paper $7.95 (0-86505-505-X). 32pp. How early settlers produced wool and other cloth and made quilts, soap, leather goods, and other necessities. (Rev: BL 7/91) [745.5]

17973 Kalman, Bobbie. *In the Barn* (3–6). Illus. Series: Historic Communities. 1997, Crabtree LB $20.60 (0-86505-433-9); paper $7.95 (0-86505-463-0). 32pp. Shows how the barn was the center of activity on a settler's farm and supplies details on its design, barn raising, and all the seasonal activities it housed. (Rev: BL 7/97) [631.2]

17974 Kalman, Bobbie. *The Kitchen* (3–6). Illus. Series: Historic Communities. 1991, Crabtree LB $20.60 (0-86505-484-3); paper $7.95 (0-86505-504-1). 32pp. The kitchen and its utensils as they existed in pioneer times are pictured and described. (Rev: BL 7/91) [643.3]

17975 Kalman, Bobbie. *A One-Room School* (3–5). Illus. Series: Historic Communities. 1994, Crabtree LB $20.60 (0-86505-497-5); paper $7.95 (0-86505-517-3). 32pp. Through pictures and text, the physical plan of a one-room school is presented, with material on supplies, routines, expected conduct, and school rules. (Rev: SLJ 9/94) [371.7]

17976 Kalman, Bobbie. *Settler Sayings* (3–5). Illus. Series: Historic Communities. 1994, Crabtree LB $20.60 (0-86505-498-3); paper $7.95 (0-86505-518-1). 32pp. In a conversational text, sayings popular with settlers are described under such headings as the kitchen and the farm. (Rev: SLJ 7/94) [973.8]

17977 Kalman, Bobbie. *Visiting a Village* (3–6). Illus. Series: Historic Communities. 1991, Crabtree $20.60 (0-86505-487-8); paper $7.95 (0-86505-507-

6). 32pp. Life in a frontier village is described in this well-illustrated account. (Rev: BL 7/91) [971]

17978 Kalman, Bobbie. *Who Settled the West?* (3–6). Series: Life in the Old West. 1999, Crabtree LB $14.37 (0-7787-0075-5); paper $7.16 (0-7787-0107-7). 32pp. An eclectic collection of material about the various groups of pioneers who settled in the West. Also use *Boomtowns of the West*. (Rev: SLJ 9/99) [978]

17979 Kalman, Bobbie, and Kate Calder. *The Life of a Miner* (3–6). Series: Life in the Old West. 1999, Crabtree LB $14.97 (0-7787-0077-1); paper $7.16 (0-7787-0109-3). 32pp. This well-researched title traces the development of the mining industry in the mid-1800s and takes the reader underground to show how miners worked. (Rev: SLJ 5/00) [973.6]

17980 Kalman, Bobbie, and Kate Calder. *Women of the West* (3–6). 1999, Crabtree LB $14.97 (0-7787-0080-1); paper $7.16 (0-7787-0112-3). 32pp. Traces the roles of both white and Native American women in the history of the old West with material on daily life and hardships. (Rev: SLJ 5/00) [973.6]

17981 Kalman, Bobbie, and Tammy Everts. *A Child's Day* (3–5). Illus. by Antoinette DeBiasi. Series: Historic Communities. 1994, Crabtree LB $20.60 (0-86505-494-0); paper $7.95 (0-86505-514-9). 32pp. A day in the life of settlers' children is shown through such activities as doing chores, playing games, going to school, and visiting a fair. (Rev: SLJ 9/94) [978]

17982 Kalman, Bobbie, and Tammy Everts. *Customs and Traditions* (3–5). Illus. Series: Historic Communities. 1994, Crabtree LB $20.60 (0-86505-495-9); paper $7.95 (0-86505-515-7). 32pp. Various customs and traditions from the days of the settlers are described and their origins traced in this heavily illustrated volume. (Rev: SLJ 7/94) [973.8]

17983 Kalman, Bobbie, and David Schimpky. *Fort Life* (3–5). Illus. Series: Historic Communities. 1994, Crabtree LB $20.60 (0-86505-496-7); paper $7.95 (0-86505-516-5). 32pp. This book describes life in a fort, with details on early American defenses and the daily life of soldiers. (Rev: SLJ 9/94) [978]

17984 King, David C. *Pioneer Days: Discover the Past with Fun Projects, Games, Activities, and Recipes* (3–6). Illus. by Bobbie Moore. Series: American Kids in History. 1997, Wiley paper $12.95 (0-471-16169-1). 118pp. In chapters arranged by season, the daily life of pioneers is re-created through an assortment of history, culture, crafts, and stories. (Rev: SLJ 2/98) [973.5]

17985 Klausmeier, Robert. *Cowboy* (4–7). Illus. Series: American Pastfinder. 1996, Lerner LB $25.55 (0-8225-2975-0). 48pp. This account focuses on the huge cattle drives and the men who led them in the years following the Civil War. (Rev: BL 3/1/96; SLJ 3/96) [636.2]

17986 La Pierre, Yvette. *Welcome to Josefina's World, 1824* (3–6). Series: American Girl. 1999, Pleasant Co. $14.95 (1-56247-769-2). 58pp. With excellent illustrations and good historical information, this book uses a series of double-page spreads

to introduce life on the American Southwest frontier in 1824 as experienced by a young girl. (Rev: BL 1/1–15/00; HBG 3/00) [973.4]

17987 Leeper, David R. *The Diary of David R. Leeper: Rush for Gold* (3–6). Ed. by Connie Roop and Peter Roop. Illus. Series: My Own Words. 2000, Marshall Cavendish LB $16.95 (0-7614-1011-2). 64pp. This book, taken from Leeper's memoirs published in 1894, tells how he crossed the country by wagon train and his life as a prospector for gold in California. (Rev: BL 2/15/01; HBG 3/01; SLJ 3/01) [979.4]

17988 Loeper, John J. *Meet the Drakes on the Kentucky Frontier* (3–5). Series: Early American Family. 1998, Marshall Cavendish LB $25.64 (0-7614-0845-2). 64pp. Based on fact, this account depicts the life of the Drake family, who moved to the unsettled Kentucky frontier in 1781. (Rev: HBG 10/99; SLJ 4/99) [973.3]

17989 Loeper, John J. *Meet the Wards on the Oregon Trail* (3–5). Series: Early American Family. 1998, Marshall Cavendish LB $25.64 (0-7614-0844-4). 64pp. Using many authentic details, this is an exciting re-creation of a family's everyday experiences as they travel on the Oregon Trail in the 1850s. (Rev: HBG 10/99; SLJ 4/99) [973.6]

17990 Markel, Rita J. *Your Travel Guide to America's Old West* (4–6). Illus. Series: Passport to History. 2003, Lerner LB $26.60 (0-8225-3074-0). 96pp. Information about the Old West — everything from historical anecdotes to profiles of key individuals to details of dress and behavior — is conveyed in the style of a travel guide complete with photographs and prints. (Rev: BL 2/15/04; HBG 4/04; SLJ 4/04) [917.604]

17991 Miller, Brandon M. *Buffalo Gals: Women of the Old West* (4–7). Illus. 1995, Lerner LB $30.35 (0-8225-1730-2). 88pp. A realistic portrait of the hardships faced by women pioneers during the 19th century on the western frontier. (Rev: BCCB 7–8/95; BL 5/1/95; SLJ 6/95*) [978]

17992 Nelson, Sharlene, and Ted Nelson. *Bull Whackers to Whistle Punks: Logging in the Old West* (4–6). Illus. 1996, Watts LB $22.50 (0-531-20228-3). 63pp. The early days of logging in the West, with descriptions of each of the jobs and the tools used. (Rev: BL 8/96; SLJ 7/96) [634.6]

17993 O'Donnell, Kerri. *The Gold Rush: A Primary Source History of the Search for Gold in California* (4–8). Series: Primary Sources in American History. 2003, Rosen LB $29.25 (0-8239-3682-1). 64pp. Timelines and reproductions of period photographs and relevant items add to the narrative in this introduction to the Gold Rush, the life of the miners, and the lawless character of the West. (Rev: SLJ 5/03) [979.4]

17994 Patent, Dorothy Hinshaw. *Homesteading: Settling America's Heartland* (2–5). Photos by William Munoz. 1998, Walker $16.95 (0-8027-8664-2). 32pp. Building a sod house, farming, housekeeping, schooling, and amusements are some of the subjects in this account of homesteading on the American frontier. (Rev: BL 11/1/98; HBG 10/99; SLJ 10/98) [978]

17995 Patent, Dorothy Hinshaw. *West by Covered Wagon: Retracing the Pioneer Trails* (3–6). Illus. by William Muñoz. 1995, Walker LB $16.85 (0-8027-8378-3). 32pp. A modern covered-wagon trip is compared to the original journeys accomplished by pioneers as they opened up the West. (Rev: BCCB 11/95; BL 11/1/95; SLJ 10/95*) [978]

17996 Paul, Ann W. *The Seasons Sewn: A Year in Patchwork* (4–6). Illus. by Michael McCurdy. 1996, Harcourt $16.00 (0-15-276918-8). 40pp. Various squares on historical patchwork quilts reflect life on the American frontier in the late 19th century. (Rev: BCCB 5/96; BL 4/1/96; SLJ 5/96) [746.46]

17997 Pelta, Kathy. *Cattle Trails: "Get Along Little Dogies"* (5–8). Series: American Trails. 1997, Raintree LB $19.98 (0-8172-4073-X). A discussion of the cattle drives that were part of the history of the American West from 1850 to 1890. (Rev: SLJ 12/97) [978]

17998 Pelta, Kathy. *The Royal Roads: Spanish Trails in North America* (5–8). Series: American Trails. 1997, Raintree LB $19.98 (0-8172-4074-8). The story of the Spanish trails in Florida, California, New Mexico, and Texas, and the people who traveled them looking for spiritual or material gain. (Rev: SLJ 12/97) [970.01]

17999 Raabe, Emily. *Pioneers: Life as a Homesteader* (2–4). Series: Westward Ho! 2003, Rosen LB $17.25 (0-8239-6498-1). 24pp. An overview of what life was like for the men and women who opened up the American West. (Rev: SLJ 12/03) [978]

18000 Randolph, Ryan P. *Frontier Schools and Schoolteachers* (3–5). Illus. Series: The Library of the Westward Expansion. 2003, Rosen LB $19.50 (0-8239-6295-4). 24pp. Historical artwork and "Did You Know" boxes enliven this overview of schools on the American frontier. (Rev: SLJ 10/03) [371.009]

18001 Randolph, Ryan P. *Wild West Lawmen and Outlaws* (3–5). Illus. Series: The Library of the Westward Expansion. 2003, Rosen LB $19.50 (0-8239-6293-8). 24pp. Profiles the men who helped to put the "wild" in Wild West and the law enforcement officers who did their best to keep the peace. (Rev: SLJ 10/03) [978]

18002 Redmond, Shirley Raye. *Lewis and Clark: A Prairie Dog for the President* (1–3). Illus. by John Manders. Series: Step into Reading. 2003, Random LB $11.99 (0-375-81120-6); paper $3.99 (0-375-91120-0). 48pp. This entertaining history for beginning readers uses cartoon-style art to portray Lewis and Clark's efforts to find suitable presents to send back to President Jefferson. (Rev: BL 8/03; HBG 4/04) [917.804]

18003 Ritchie, David. *Frontier Life* (5–7). Illus. Series: Life in America 100 Years Ago. 1995, Chelsea $21.95 (0-7910-2842-9). 104pp. A concise overview of life on the American frontier that does not gloss over the harsh and often violent aspects. (Rev: SLJ 1/96) [973.5]

18004 Ross, Stewart. *Cowboys* (5–7). Illus. Series: Fact or Fiction? 1995, Millbrook LB $26.90 (1-56294-618-8). 48pp. The life of cowboys during the late 1800s is covered, with information that tries to separate fact from fable. (Rev: BL 7/95; SLJ 5/95) [978.02]

18005 Rounds, Glen. *Sod Houses on the Great Plains* (K–3). Illus. 1995, Holiday House LB $16.95 (0-8234-1162-1). 32pp. An illustrated account of the construction and utilization of a sod house, home of many prairie pioneers. (Rev: BCCB 3/95; BL 3/1/95*; HB 5–6/95; SLJ 3/95*) [693]

18006 Russell, Marion. *Along the Santa Fe Trail: Marion Russell's Own Story* (3–5). Adapted by Ginger Wadsworth. Illus. by James Watling. 1993, Whitman LB $16.95 (0-8075-0295-2). 32pp. In a reworking of a memoir of pioneer life, the experiences of a seven-year-old traveling in a wagon train on the Santa Fe Trail are recalled. (Rev: BL 1/15/94; SLJ 12/93) [917.8]

18007 Saffer, Barbara. *The California Gold Rush* (5–7). Series: The American West. 2002, Mason Crest LB $19.95 (1-59084-060-7). 64pp. Reluctant readers will be drawn to this attractive account of the hardships of traveling to California and the life in the mining camps. (Rev: SLJ 4/02) [979.4]

18008 Salas, Laura Purdie. *The Wilderness Road, 1775* (4–6). Illus. Series: Let Freedom Ring. 2003, Capstone LB $18.60 (0-7368-1561-9). 48pp. Tells the story of the building of the Wilderness Road, which opened the way into Kentucky for early American settlers; includes a chapter on Daniel Boone. (Rev: HBG 10/03; SLJ 12/03) [973.2]

18009 Sandler, Martin W. *Vaqueros: America's First Cowboys* (3–8). 2001, Holt $18.00 (0-8050-6019-7). 117pp. A interesting account that traces the role of the *vaquero* — the Hispanic cowboy — in the opening up of the West and in the history of ranch development in the U.S. (Rev: BL 1/1–15/01; HB 1–2/01; HBG 10/01; SLJ 1/01) [978]

18010 Sanford, William R. *The Chisholm Trail in American History* (4–6). Series: In American History. 2000, Enslow LB $19.95 (0-7660-1345-6). 112pp. This book traces the history of the Chisholm Trail, the daily life of the cowboys who used it, and its eventual demise. (Rev: BL 7/00; HBG 3/01; SLJ 12/00) [978]

18011 Savage, Candace. *Born to Be a Cowgirl: A Spirited Ride Through the Old West* (4–8). 2001, Tricycle $15.95 (1-58246-019-1); paper $9.95 (1-58246-020-5). 64pp. An appealing package of fascinating text, excerpts from letters and journals, and period illustrations that introduces female cowhands and their lifestyle. (Rev: BL 5/15/01; HB 7–8/01; HBG 10/01; SLJ 6/01) [978]

18012 Savage, Jeff. *Cowboys and Cow Towns of the Wild West* (4–7). Illus. Series: Trailblazers of the Wild West. 1995, Enslow LB $16.95 (0-89490-603-8). 48pp. Through the experiences of a single cowboy, the reader learns about his equipment, dangers, leisure time, cattle drives, and roundups. (Rev: SLJ 2/96) [978]

18013 Savage, Jeff. *Gunfighters of the Wild West* (3–5). Illus. Series: Trailblazers of the Wild West. 1995, Enslow LB $16.95 (0-89490-600-3). 48pp. This book briefly covers the lives and exploits of such gunslingers as Doc Holliday, the Earps, John Fisher King, Billy the Kid, the Jameses, the Daltons, and the Wild Bunch. (Rev: SLJ 1/96) [973.5]

18014 Savage, Jeff. *Pioneering Women of the Wild West* (3–5). Illus. Series: Trailblazers of the Wild West. 1995, Enslow LB $16.95 (0-89490-604-6). 48pp. The struggles and hardships of women in the Wild West are covered, with particular mention of such famous characters as Calamity Jane and Carrie Nation. (Rev: SLJ 1/96) [973.5]

18015 Schanzer, Rosalyn. *Gold Fever! Tales from the California Gold Rush* (3–5). Illus. 1999, National Geographic $17.95 (0-7922-7303-6). 48pp. Beginning with the discovery of gold nuggets at Sutter's Mill in 1847, this story of the California Gold Rush is told through diaries and original writings. (Rev: BCCB 6/99; BL 4/15/99; HBG 10/99; SLJ 4/99) [979.4]

18016 Schroeder, Lisa Golden. *California Gold Rush Cooking* (4–7). Series: Exploring History Through Simple Recipes. 2000, Capstone LB $22.60 (0-7368-0603-2). 32pp. This book discusses the California Gold Rush and everyday life of the period with details of the kinds of food eaten and some simple recipes. (Rev: BL 3/1/01; HBG 10/01; SLJ 4/01) [979.4]

18017 Sherrow, Victoria. *Life During the Gold Rush* (5–9). Series: The Way People Live. 1998, Lucent LB $27.45 (1-56006-382-3). 96pp. This story of the California Gold Rush, from Sutter's Mill to the advent of huge companies, gives good information on the daily life of the forty-niners. (Rev: BL 8/98; SLJ 12/98) [979.5]

18018 Shuter, Jane, ed. *Sarah Royce and the American West* (5–8). Illus. Series: History Eyewitness. 1996, Raintree LB $24.26 (0-8114-8286-3). The ordeals and achievements of American pioneers are chronicled in this first-person account, accompanied by many splendid illustrations. (Rev: BL 5/15/96; SLJ 6/96) [978]

18019 Sinnott, Susan. *Welcome to Kirsten's World, 1854: Growing Up in Pioneer America* (3–6). Illus. Series: American Girls Collection. 1999, Pleasant Co. $14.95 (1-56247-770-6). 58pp. As seen through the eyes of a family of Swedish immigrants, this account describes frontier life in the Minnesota Territory in the 1840s. (Rev: BL 1/1–15/00; HBG 3/00) [978]

18020 Stanley, Jerry. *Cowboys and Longhorns: A Portrait of the Long Drive* (5–12). Illus. 2003, Crown $18.95 (0-375-81565-1). 128pp. Stanley debunks the popular view of cowboys, using the long cattle drives from Texas to Kansas to illustrate the dangers and discomforts of an unglamorous life on horseback. (Rev: BL 7/03*; HBG 4/04; SLJ 8/03) [636.2]

18021 Steedman, Scott. *A Frontier Fort on the Oregon Trail* (4–6). Illus. Series: Inside Story. 1994, Bedrick $18.95 (0-87226-371-1); paper $10.95 (0-

87226-264-2). 48pp. An examination of both the exterior and interior of a frontier fort, with details on its construction and everyday life in it. (Rev: BL 10/15/94; SLJ 9/94) [978]

18022 Stefoff, Rebecca. *First Frontier* (4–7). Series: North American Historical Atlases. 2000, Benchmark LB $24.21 (0-7614-1059-7). 48pp. This book presents an illustrated view of the western expansion and its effects on Native Americans, frontiersmen, speculators, and soldiers. (Rev: HBG 3/01; SLJ 1/01) [978]

18023 Stefoff, Rebecca. *The Opening of the West* (5–8). 2002, Benchmark LB $22.95 (0-7614-1201-8). 105pp. A collection of primary sources that includes excerpts from letters, newspaper articles, and journal entries commenting on different aspects of frontier life, exploration, and the plight of Native Americans. (Rev: HBG 10/03; SLJ 4/03) [978]

18024 Stein, R. Conrad. *In the Spanish West* (4–8). Series: How We Lived. 1999, Benchmark LB $27.07 (0-7614-0906-8). 72pp. This well-balanced account describes the American West under Spanish control and influence with material on history, social life, agriculture, and home life. (Rev: HBG 10/00; SLJ 3/00) [978]

18025 Stein, R. Conrad. *On the Old Western Frontier* (4–8). Series: How We Lived. 1999, Benchmark LB $27.07 (0-7614-0909-2). 72pp. An interesting book that gives an overview of the history and living conditions on the American frontier with material on everyday life, farming and ranching, social life, religion, Native Americans, and slaves. (Rev: HBG 10/00; SLJ 3/00) [978]

18026 Sundling, Charles W. *Cowboys of the Frontier* (4–6). Illus. Series: Frontier Land. 2000, ABDO $15.95 (1-57765-045-X). 32pp. An accessible text that describes the daily life of hardworking cattle drivers, with emphasis on the second half of the 19th century. (Rev: BL 10/15/00; HBG 10/00; SLJ 7/00) [978]

18027 Sundling, Charles W. *Explorers of the Frontier* (4–6). Series: Frontier Land. 2000, ABDO LB $15.95 (1-57765-044-1). 32pp. Using many easy-to-read maps and a fact-filled text, this book traces the exploits of the explorers who opened up the West. A companion volume is *Mountain Men of the Frontier* (2000). (Rev: BL 10/15/00; HBG 10/00) [978]

18028 Sundling, Charles W. *Pioneers of the Frontier* (4–6). Series: Frontier Land. 2000, ABDO LB $15.95 (1-57765-047-6). 32pp. The day-to-day struggles of the early pioneers of the West are recreated in text and pictures. Also use *Women of the Frontier* (2000). (Rev: BL 10/15/00; HBG 10/00) [978]

18029 Swanson, Wayne. *Why the West Was Wild* (5–8). 2004, Annick $12.95 (1-55037-837-6); paper $12.95 (1-55037-836-8). 48pp. The excitement of the Old West is captured in this lavishly illustrated survey of the region's history during the second half of the 19th century. (Rev: BL 8/04; SLJ 6/04) [978]

18030 Thompson, Linda. *The Transcontinental Railroad* (4–6). Illus. Series: Expansion of America. 2005, Rourke LB $29.93 (1-59515-227-X). 48pp.

The who, what, where, when, and how of the railroad, with background information linking the project to America's expansion. Among the other titles in this series by this author are *The Erie Canal*, *The Mississippi and West*, and *The Oregon Trail* (all 2005). (Rev: BL 4/1/05) [385]

18031 Toht, David W. *Sodbuster* (3–6). Illus. by Richard Erickson. Series: American Pastfinder. 1996, Lerner LB $21.50 (0-8225-2977-7). 48pp. In double-page chapters, the life of early pioneers is described, with many quotes from original sources. (Rev: SLJ 3/96) [973.6]

18032 Wadsworth, Ginger. *Words West: Voices of Young Pioneers* (5–8). 2003, Clarion $18.00 (0-618-23475-6). 208pp. Excerpts from journals and other documents give a clear picture of the experiences of young people traveling west between 1840 and 1870. (Rev: HBG 4/04; SLJ 12/03) [917.804]

18033 Warren, Andrea. *Pioneer Girl: Growing Up on the Prairie* (3–6). 1998, Morrow $15.00 (0-688-15438-7). 96pp. Based on the memoirs of Grace McCance Snyder, this is the true story of a homesteading family in Nebraska during the late 1800s. (Rev: BCCB 12/98; BL 10/1/98; HB 11–12/98; HBG 3/99; SLJ 11/98) [978.2]

18034 Werther, Scott P. *The Donner Party* (5–7). Illus. 2002, Children's Book Pr. LB $20.00 (0-516-23901-5). 48pp. The fate of the Donner Party is described against the backdrop of life in America in the 1840s and the dangers of travel to the West and the Pacific. (Rev: SLJ 10/02) [979.4]

18035 Winslow, Mimi. *Loggers and Railroad Workers* (5–8). Illus. Series: Settling the West. 1995, Twenty-First Century LB $20.40 (0-8050-2997-4). 96pp. The story of the men and machines who settled in the West, cleared the wilderness, and built the railroads that opened the way for agriculture and industry. (Rev: SLJ 9/95) [973.8]

18036 Woog, Adam. *A Cowboy in the Wild West* (3–5). Illus. Series: Daily Life. 2002, Gale LB $21.54 (0-7377-0990-1). 48pp. An information-packed review of a cowboy's daily routine, including material on clothing, trail drives and roundups, and the overall history of cowboys. (Rev: BL 12/1/02; SLJ 8/02) [978]

18037 Worcester, Don. *Cowboy with a Camera, Erwin E. Smith: Cowboy Photographer* (3–5). 1999, Amon Carter Museum $18.95 (0-88360-091-9). 48pp. With photos from the turn of the last century, this book chronicles the life and work of cowboys, including roping, wrangling, and bronco busting. (Rev: BCCB 2/99; BL 1/1–15/99; HBG 10/99) [636.2]

THE CIVIL WAR

18038 Anderson, Dale. *The Causes of the Civil War* (4–6). 2004, World Almanac LB $29.26 (0-8368-5581-7); paper $11.95 (0-8368-5590-6). 48pp. A concise and readable overview of the underlying causes of the Civil War, with material on key individuals, interesting sidebar features, maps, and many appropriate illustrations. Also use *A Soldier's Life in the Civil War*, *The Aftermath of the Civil War*, and *The Union Victory: (July 1863[EN[1865).* (Rev: SLJ 3/05) [973.7]

18039 Anderson, Dale. *The Civil War at Sea* (4–6). Series: World Almanac Library of the Civil War. 2004, World Almanac LB $29.26 (0-8368-5585-X). 48pp. A look at major battles at sea, with period photographs, maps, and sidebars about individuals. Also use in this series: *The Civil War in the East (1861–July 1863)*, *The Civil War in the West (1861–July 1863)*, and *The Home Fronts in the Civil War* (all 2004). (Rev: SLJ 7/04) [973.7]

18040 Armentrout, David, and Patricia Armentrout. *The Emancipation Proclamation* (4–7). Series: Documents That Shaped the Nation. 2004, Rourke $.00 (1-59515-233-4). 48pp. The reasons for the creation of this document and the results of its proclamation are thoroughly explored in concise text, accompanied by an array of maps and illustrations. (Rev: BL 10/15/04) [973.7]

18041 Armstrong, Jennifer. *A Three-Minute Speech: Lincoln's Remarks at Gettysburg* (2–5). Series: Milestone Books. 2003, Aladdin LB $11.89 (0-689-85623-7); paper $3.99 (0-689-85622-9). 96pp. This appealing introduction to the Gettysburg Address provides extensive background information. (Rev: BL 9/1/03; HBG 4/04; SLJ 9/03) [973]

18042 Arnold, James R., and Roberta Wiener. *Divided in Two: The Road to Civil War* (4–7). Series: The Civil War. 2002, Lerner LB $25.26 (0-8225-2312-4). 72pp. A well-designed oversize book that describes the events of 1861 that led to the outbreak of the Civil War. (Rev: BL 10/15/02; HBG 10/02; SLJ 7/02) [973.7]

18043 Arnold, James R., and Roberta Wiener. *Life Goes On: The Civil War at Home* (4–7). Series: The Civil War. 2002, Lerner LB $25.26 (0-8225-2315-9). 72pp. Many easy-to-follow maps and illustrations are used with a simple text to describe life on the home front in both South and North during the Civil War. (Rev: BL 10/15/02; HBG 10/02; SLJ 7/02) [973.7]

18044 Arnold, James R., and Roberta Wiener. *Lost Cause: The End of the Civil War* (4–7). Series: The Civil War. 2002, Lerner LB $25.26 (0-8225-2317-5). 72pp. Beginning with the campaign of 1864, this well-illustrated account traces the Civil War to Appomattox and beyond. (Rev: BL 10/15/02; HBG 10/02; SLJ 6/02) [973.7]

18045 Arnold, James R., and Roberta Wiener. *On to Richmond: The Civil War in the East, 1861–1862* (4–7). Illus. Series: Civil War. 2002, Lerner LB $25.26 (0-8225-2313-2). 72pp. Early battles in the Civil War are the subject of this volume for older readers that includes timelines, notes, and lists of Web sites and battlefields to visit. (Rev: BL 10/15/02; HBG 10/02; SLJ 6/02) [973.7]

18046 Arnold, James R., and Roberta Wiener. *River to Victory: The Civil War in the West* (4–7). Series: The Civil War. 2002, Lerner LB $25.26 (0-8225-2314-0). 72pp. The Civil War in the West from 1861 through 1863 is re-created in text and illustrations with many maps and sidebars on personalities and events. (Rev: BL 10/15/02; HBG 10/02; SLJ 6/02) [973.7]

18047 Arnold, James R., and Roberta Wiener. *This Unhappy Country: The Turn of the Civil War* (4–7). Illus. Series: Civil War. 2002, Lerner LB $25.26 (0-8225-2316-7). 72pp. Maps and other period illustrations flesh out the events of 1863, a pivotal year in the Civil War, in this volume for older readers. (Rev: BL 10/15/02; HBG 10/02; SLJ 7/02) [973.7]

18048 Ashby, Ruth. *Gettysburg* (5–8). Series: Civil War Chronicles. 2002, Smart Apple LB $28.50 (1-58340-186-5). 48pp. The three days of battle are covered in some detail, and the text and photographs convey the horrible conditions. (Rev: HBG 3/03; SLJ 2/03) [973]

18049 Beller, Susan P. *Billy Yank and Johnny Reb: Soldiering in the Civil War* (5–8). Illus. 2000, Twenty-First Century LB $26.90 (0-7613-1869-0). 96pp. Solid, interesting information is provided in this illustrated account that describes the everyday life of soldiers on both sides of the Civil War. (Rev: BL 10/15/00; HBG 3/01; SLJ 12/00) [973.7]

18050 Beller, Susan P. *The Confederate Ladies of Richmond* (5–8). Illus. 1999, Twenty-First Century LB $26.90 (0-7613-1470-9). 96pp. The Civil War seen through the eyes and activities of the upper-class women of Richmond, the capital of the Confederacy. (Rev: BCCB 1/00; BL 12/15/99; HBG 3/00; SLJ 1/00) [973.7]

18051 Beller, Susan Provost. *The Civil War* (5–8). Series: American Voices From. 2002, Benchmark LB $22.95 (0-7614-1204-2). 103pp. A collection of primary sources that includes speeches by Lincoln and Lee and represents people from all walks of life commenting on different aspects of the Civil War. (Rev: HBG 10/03; SLJ 4/03) [973.7]

18052 Berry, Carrie. *A Confederate Girl: The Diary of Carrie Berry, 1864* (4–6). Ed. by Christy Steel and Anne Todd. Series: Diaries, Letters, and Memoirs. 2000, Capstone LB $22.60 (0-7368-0343-2). 32pp. These excerpts from the diary of a 10-year-old Confederate girl describe everyday life and problems behind the front lines and are supplemented by informative sidebars that give good background information. (Rev: BL 10/15/00; HBG 10/00; SLJ 9/00) [973.7]

18053 Bircher, William. *A Civil War Drummer Boy: The Diary of William Bircher, 1861–1865* (4–6). Ed. by Shelley Swanson Sateren. Illus. Series: Diaries, Letters, and Memoirs. 2000, Capstone $22.60 (0-7368-0348-3). Excerpts from a 15-year-old's diary tell what it was like for a young man to face death in the Civil War; this account also contains period photographs, a timeline, maps, and sidebars. (Rev: BL 10/15/00; HBG 10/00; SLJ 9/00) [973.7]

18054 Black, Wallace B. *Blockade Runners and Ironclads: Naval Action in the Civil War* (3–5). Illus. Series: First Books. 1997, Watts $22.50 (0-531-20272-0). 64pp. Introduces naval operations during the Civil War, with material on battles, strategies, shipbuilding, and prominent military personnel. (Rev: BL 2/1/98; HBG 3/98) [973.7]

18055 Black, Wallace B. *Slaves to Soldiers: African-American Fighting Men in the Civil War* (4–6). Series: First Books. 1998, Watts LB $21.00 (0-531-20252-6). 63pp. This story of the African Americans who served during the Civil War discusses the campaigns in which they participated. (Rev: HBG 10/98; SLJ 10/98) [973.7]

18056 Blashfield, Jean F. *Horse Soldiers: Cavalry in the Civil War* (4–6). 1998, Watts LB $22.00 (0-531-20300-X). A history of the the Union and Confederate cavalries, their officers, and their roles in the Civil War. (Rev: BL 8/98; HBG 10/98; SLJ 8/98) [973.7]

18057 Blashfield, Jean F. *Mines and Minie Balls* (4–6). Illus. Series: First Books. 1997, Watts LB $22.50 (0-531-20273-9). 64pp. Discusses Union and Confederate weapons at the beginning of the Civil War and shows how they became more deadly and sophisticated as the war went on. (Rev: BL 1/1–15/98; HBG 3/98) [973.7]

18058 Blashfield, Jean F. *Women at the Front: Their Changing Roles in the Civil War* (4–6). Illus. Series: First Books. 1997, Watts LB $22.50 (0-531-20275-5). 64pp. An introduction to the roles of female nurses, spies, soldiers, and camp followers during the Civil War, with material on women on the home front. (Rev: BL 1/1–15/98; HBG 3/98) [973.7]

18059 Bolotin, Norman. *Civil War A to Z: A Young Reader's Guide to Over 100 People, Places, and Points of Importance* (4–8). Illus. 2002, Dutton $19.99 (0-525-46268-6). 160pp. An encyclopedia-style text on the Civil War, with brief entries on important battles; politicians, generals, and other key figures; and crucial issues of the time, with photographs, a glossary, a timeline, and information on further resources. (Rev: BL 7/02; SLJ 7/02) [973.7]

18060 Brooks, Victor. *African Americans in the Civil War* (4–8). Illus. Series: Untold History of the Civil War. 2000, Chelsea $19.75 (0-7910-5435-7). 64pp. This book describes African American soldiers' roles in the Civil War, on both the Confederate and Union sides. (Rev: BL 5/15/00; HBG 10/00; SLJ 6/00) [355.7]

18061 Brooks, Victor. *Civil War Forts* (4–8). Illus. Series: Untold History of the Civil War. 2000, Chelsea $19.75 (0-7910-5438-1). 64pp. Describes the important roles played by such forts as Fort Sumter and Fort Wagner in South Carolina, Fort Fischer in North Carolina, Fort Henry and Fort Donelson in Tennessee, and the city of Vicksburg, Mississippi. (Rev: BL 5/15/00; HBG 10/00; SLJ 7/00) [973.7]

18062 Brooks, Victor. *Secret Weapons in the Civil War* (4–8). Series: Untold History of the Civil War. 2000, Chelsea $19.75 (0-7910-5433-0). 64pp. Covers such secret weapons and maneuvers as underwater transportation, advanced artillery, communications devices, and explosive materials. (Rev: BL 5/15/00; HBG 10/00; SLJ 7/00) [973.7]

18063 Carey, Charles W. *The Emancipation Proclamation* (4–6). Series: Journey to Freedom. 1999, Child's World LB $16.95 (1-56766-620-5). 32pp. Sepia-toned illustrations enhance this account of the end of slavery, the document's importance in African American history, and the civil war that resulted. (Rev: BL 10/15/99; HBG 3/00) [973.7]

18064 Clinton, Catherine. *Scholastic Encyclopedia of the Civil War* (4–7). Illus. 1999, Scholastic paper $18.95 (0-590-37227-0). 112pp. Using many black-and-white illustrations, this narrative gives a good chronological introduction to the Civil War, with interesting supplementary information. (Rev: BL 1/1–15/00; HBG 3/00; SLJ 5/00) [973.7]

18065 Collier, Christopher, and James Lincoln Collier. *The Civil War, 1860–1865* (5–8). Series: Drama of American History. 1999, Marshall Cavendish LB $29.93 (0-7614-0818-5). 95pp. A dramatic, accurate account that covers causes, leaders, battles, effects, and the immediate aftermath of the Civil War. (Rev: BL 2/15/00; HBG 10/00; SLJ 3/00) [973.7]

18066 Damon, Duane. *Growing Up In the Civil War: 1861 to 1865* (5–8). Series: Our America. 2002, Lerner LB $31.95 (0-8225-0656-4). 64pp. The lives of children in this period are described with many quotations and excerpts from diaries, letters, and memoirs. (Rev: BL 2/15/03; HBG 3/03; SLJ 2/03) [973.7]

18067 Damon, Duane. *When This Cruel War Is Over* (5–8). Illus. 1996, Lerner LB $30.35 (0-8225-1731-0). The human side of the Civil War is stressed as the reader goes behind the scenes at the battlefields and learns about conditions on the home front. (Rev: BL 8/96; SLJ 8/96*) [973.7]

18068 Day, Nancy. *Your Travel Guide to Civil War America* (4–8). Series: Passport to History. 2000, Lerner LB $26.60 (0-8225-3078-3). 96pp. Using the format of a guide book, this account takes the reader back to the Civil War with coverage of topics including food, civil and military clothing, Lincoln's office, Gettysburg, and various battlefields. (Rev: BL 3/1/01; HBG 10/01; SLJ 4/01) [073.7]

18069 Dolan, Edward F. *The American Civil War: A House Divided* (5–8). Illus. 1997, Millbrook LB $29.90 (0-7613-0255-7). A chronologically arranged, well-organized account of the Civil War, beginning with the shots fired at Fort Sumter. (Rev: BL 3/1/98; HBG 3/98; SLJ 3/98) [973.7]

18070 Dosier, Susan. *Civil War Cooking: The Confederacy* (4–7). Series: Exploring History Through Simple Recipes. 2000, Capstone LB $22.60 (0-7368-0350-5). 32pp. As well as simple, authentic recipes of Civil War times, this book tells of customs, family roles, and everyday life during this period. Also use *Civil War Cooking: The Union* (2000). (Rev: BL 8/00; HBG 10/00; SLJ 9/00) [973.7]

18071 Egger-Bovet, Howard, and Marlene Smith-Baranzini. *Book of the American Civil War* (5–7). Illus. by D. J. Simison. Series: Brown Paper School. 1998, Little, Brown paper $12.95 (0-316-22243-7). 95pp. Facts, photographs, illustrations, stories and appealing activities are combined in this overview of the Civil War. (Rev: SLJ 12/98) [973.7]

18072 Feinberg, Barbara S. *Abraham Lincoln's Gettysburg Address: Four Score and More . . .* (4–8).

Illus. 2000, Twenty-First Century LB $24.40 (0-7613-1410-8). 80pp. Illustrated with period photographs, this well-researched volume reveals surprising facts about the Gettysburg Address and its delivery. (Rev: BL 11/15/00) [973.7]

18073 Fleischman, Paul. *Bull Run* (5–8). 1993, HarperCollins LB $14.89 (0-06-021447-3). 102pp. An innovative account of the first great battle of the Civil War. (Rev: BCCB 3/93; BL 5-6/93) [973.7]

18074 Ford, Carin T. *The American Civil War: An Overview* (5–8). Series: The Civil War Library. 2004, Enslow LB $23.93 (0-7660-2255-2). 48pp. This informative general overview of the war features maps, illustrations, and interesting sidebar features. Also use *Lincoln, Slavery, and the Emancipation Proclamation* (2004). (Rev: SLJ 3/05) [973.7]

18075 Ford, Carin T. *The Battle of Gettysburg and Lincoln's Gettysburg Address* (4–6). Series: The Civil War Library. 2004, Enslow LB $23.93 (0-7660-2253-6). 48pp. Background information adds to the coverage of the battle itself and to an understanding of the importance of Lincoln's speech. (Rev: SLJ 1/05) [973]

18076 Ford, Carin T. *Daring Women of the Civil War* (3–5). Series: The Civil War Library. 2004, Enslow LB $23.93 (0-7660-2250-1). 48pp. Primary-source quotations and reproductions add to the discussion of the role of women — from both the Union and the Confederacy — in America's Civil War. (Rev: BL 7/04; SLJ 8/04) [973.7]

18077 Ford, Carin T. *Slavery and the Underground Railroad: Bound for Freedom* (3–5). Series: The Civil War Library. 2004, Enslow LB $23.93 (0-7660-2251-X). 48pp. Primary-source quotations and reproductions add to the discussion of the role of the Underground Railroad and the people involved in its success. (Rev: BL 7/04; SLJ 8/04) [973]

18078 Fraser, Mary Ann. *Vicksburg: The Battle That Won the Civil War* (4–8). Illus. 1999, Holt $17.95 (0-8050-6106-1). 100pp. The focus of this book is the Battle of Vicksburg, the events surrounding it, the participants, and its importance. (Rev: BCCB 1/00; BL 3/1/00; HBG 3/00; SLJ 3/00) [973.7]

18079 Friend, Sandra. *Florida in the Civil War: A State in Turmoil* (5–8). Illus. 2001, Millbrook LB $25.90 (0-7613-1973-5). 80pp. An account of Florida's involvement in the Civil War, with maps and photographs. (Rev: BL 10/15/01; HBG 3/02; SLJ 2/02) [973.7]

18080 Fritz, Jean. *Just a Few Words, Mr. Lincoln: The Story of the Gettysburg Address* (1–3). Illus. by Charles Robinson. 1993, Penguin Putnam paper $3.99 (0-448-40170-3). 48pp. An easy-to-read book that tells the background of the Gettysburg Address and explains its importance. (Rev: BL 10/1/93; SLJ 10/93) [973.7]

18081 Graves, Kerry A. *Going to School During the Civil War: The Confederacy* (4–6). Series: Going to School in History. 2001, Capstone LB $16.95 (0-7368-0802-7). 32pp. A look at schools in the South during the Civil War with information on subjects studied, the length of the school year, classroom materials, and typical activities and games. (Rev: BL 10/15/01; HBG 3/02) [973.7]

18082 Graves, Kerry A. *Going to School During the Civil War: The Union* (4–6). Series: Going to School in History. 2001, Capstone LB $16.95 (0-7368-0801-9). 32pp. Details of school life in the northern states include curriculum, teaching methods, and subjects taught plus sidebars on crafts and games. (Rev: BL 10/15/01; HBG 3/03) [973.7]

18083 Hakim, Joy. *War, Terrible War.* 2nd ed. (5–8). Illus. Series: A History of Us. 1999, Oxford $19.95 (0-19-512761-7). 160pp. This excellent history of the Civil War is basically a reissue of the 1994 edition with a few minor revisions and changes in illustrations. (Rev: BL 12/15/99) [973.7]

18084 Haskins, Jim. *The Day Fort Sumter Was Fired On: A Photo History of the Civil War* (5–8). Illus. 1995, Scholastic paper $6.95 (0-590-46397-7). 96pp. A short, well-illustrated history of the Civil War, with coverage of the roles of women and African Americans. (Rev: BL 7/95) [973.7]

18085 Heinrichs, Ann. *The Emancipation Proclamation* (5–8). Series: We the People. 2002, Compass Point LB $27.15 (0-7565-0209-8). 48pp. An accessible examination of the proclamation's creation that reveals Lincoln's careful attention to detail. (Rev: SLJ 7/02) [973.7]

18086 Herbert, Janis. *The Civil War for Kids: A History with 21 Activities* (4–8). Illus. 1999, Chicago Review paper $14.95 (1-55652-355-6). 166pp. As well as supplying information about leaders, battles, daily life, and the contributions of women and African Americans, this book on the Civil War includes activities such as reenactments of battles, most of which are geared toward groups. (Rev: SLJ 12/99) [973.7]

18087 Holford, David M. *Lincoln and the Emancipation Proclamation in American History* (5–8). Series: In American History. 2002, Enslow LB $20.95 (0-7660-1456-8). 128pp. A well-researched account that gives background material and traces the significance of this document. (Rev: BL 1/1–15/03; HBG 3/03) [973.7]

18088 Hughes, Christopher. *Antietam* (5–8). Series: Battlefields Across America. 1998, Millbrook LB $26.90 (0-7613-3009-7). This book describes the battle at Antietam in detail, discusses its impact on the outcome of the war and on the future of the United States, profiles the major people involved, and provides information on where the history of this battle is preserved. (Rev: HBG 9/98; SLJ 8/98) [973.7]

18089 January, Brendan. *Gettysburg, July 1–3, 1863* (5–7). Illus. Series: American Battlefields. 2004, Enchanted Lion $14.95 (1-59270-025-X). 32pp. This overview of the Battle of Gettysburg offers a clear account of the bloody conflict and an examination of the developments leading up to it; sidebars, illustrations, a timeline, and other features add to the narrative. [973]

18090 Kantor, MacKinlay. *Gettysburg* (5–8). Illus. 1963, Random paper $5.99 (0-394-89181-3). This explains how Gettysburg became the site of the bloodiest Civil War battle; a vivid re-creation of the struggle.

18091 Kent, Zachary. *The Civil War: "A House Divided"* (5–7). Illus. Series: American War. 1994, Enslow LB $20.95 (0-89490-522-8). 128pp. Using many original quotations, period illustrations, and maps, this account gives a concise history of the Civil War. (Rev: BL 7/94; SLJ 9/94) [973.7]

18092 King, Wilma. *Children of the Emancipation* (2–5). Illus. Series: Picture the American Past. 2000, Carolrhoda $22.60 (1-57505-396-9). 48pp. This book covers the years 1860 through 1890 and examines the lives of children born as slaves, and how they fared before the Emancipation Proclamation, during the Civil War, and also during Reconstruction. (Rev: BL 6/1–15/00; HBG 10/00; SLJ 7/00) [973.7]

18093 Lincoln, Abraham. *The Gettysburg Address* (4–6). Illus. by Michael McCurdy. 1995, Houghton Mifflin $14.95 (0-395-69824-3). 32pp. An illustrated edition of the address, with pictures that show the audience and the thoughts they might have had. (Rev: BL 10/15/95; HB 11–12/95; SLJ 9/95*) [973.7]

18094 McKissack, Patricia, and Fredrick McKissack. *Days of Jubilee: The End of Slavery in the United States* (5–8). Illus. 2003, Scholastic $18.95 (0-439-10764-X). 144pp. A moving book on the Civil War and its effect on slaves, based on first-person accounts. With photographs, artwork and other graphic elements. (Rev: BL 2/15/03) [973.7]

18095 Marquette, Scott. *The Civil War* (4–7). Illus. Series: America at War. 2002, Rourke LB $27.93 (1-58952-388-1). 48pp. This book for middle graders introduces in simple terms the causes and events of the Civil War. [973.7]

18096 Morrison, Taylor. *Civil War Artist* (5–7). Illus. 1999, Houghton Mifflin $16.00 (0-395-91426-4). 32pp. Explains the long and complex process involved in transmitting drawings of Civil War scenes from the field to the public via a newspaper. (Rev: BL 4/15/99; HBG 3/00; SLJ 5/99) [070.4]

18097 Nofi, Albert A. *Spies in the Civil War* (5–8). Series: Untold History of the Civil War. 2000, Chelsea $19.75 (0-7910-5427-6). 64pp. In this account readers meet famous spies (including Allan Pinkerton and Belle Boyd) and lesser-known spies of the Civil War. (Rev: HBG 10/00; SLJ 7/00) [973.7]

18098 O'Brien, Patrick. *Duel of the Ironclads: The Monitor vs. the Virginia* (2–6). Illus. 2003, Walker LB $18.85 (0-8027-8843-2). 40pp. A beautifully illustrated account of the battle between two state-of-the-art Civil War ships. (Rev: BL 3/15/03*; HBG 10/03; SLJ 5/03) [973.7]

18099 Ransom, Candice. *Children of the Civil War* (3–6). Series: Picture the American Past. 1998, Carolrhoda LB $19.93 (0-57505-241-5). 48pp. This book, divided into three parts — before, during, and after the Civil War — uses photos to show children in such roles as soldiers, slaves, servants, prisoners, and orphans. (Rev: SLJ 1/99) [973.7]

18100 Reef, Catherine. *Gettysburg* (4–6). Illus. Series: Places in American History. 1992, Macmillan LB $18.95 (0-87518-503-7). 72pp. After background material on the Battle of Gettysburg, this account introduces the national military park of today. (Rev: BL 9/1/92; SLJ 8/92) [973]

18101 Roberts, Russell. *Lincoln and the Abolition of Slavery* (5–12). Series: American War. 1999, Lucent LB $27.45 (1-56006-580-X). 112pp. This gripping, fully documented account describes the events leading to the Civil War and Lincoln's role in these events. (Rev: BL 1/1–15/00; HBG 9/00) [973.7]

18102 Savage, Douglas J. *Ironclads and Blockades in the Civil War* (4–8). Series: Untold History of the Civil War. 2000, Chelsea $19.95 (0-7910-5429-2). 64pp. A clear text and period illustrations introduce the huge ships used in the Union and Confederate navies and their efforts to block different ports during the Civil War. (Rev: BL 7/00; HBG 10/00; SLJ 9/00) [973.7]

18103 Savage, Douglas J. *Prison Camps in the Civil War* (4–8). Series: Untold History of the Civil War. 2000, Chelsea $19.75 (0-7910-5428-4). 64pp. This account describes the prisoner-of-war camps on both sides during the Civil War, the appalling conditions in them, and the acts of heroism that sometimes occurred. (Rev: BL 7/00; HBG 10/00; SLJ 9/00) [973.7]

18104 Savage, Douglas J. *Women in the Civil War* (4–8). Series: Untold History of the Civil War. 2000, Chelsea $19.75 (0-7910-5436-5). 64pp. This book describes the roles played by women in the Civil War as nurses, suppliers of support services, and crusaders for issues including suffrage and abolition. (Rev: BL 7/00; HBG 10/00; SLJ 9/00) [973.7]

18105 Schomp, Virginia. *The Civil War* (5–8). Illus. Series: Letters from the Homefront. 2001, Marshall Cavendish LB $28.50 (0-7614-1095-3). 95pp. After placing the conflict in historical context, Schomp uses excerpts from letters and other accounts that bring the period to life. (Rev: BL 10/15/01; HBG 3/02; SLJ 3/02) [973.7]

18106 Silber, Nina. *Landmarks of the Civil War* (5–8). Series: American Landmarks. 2003, Oxford LB $30.00 (0-19-512920-2). 143pp. The 12 landmarks that played a key role in the Civil War; included are the Gettysburg battlefield, the White House of the Confederacy, the home of Robert E. Lee, and New York City's Cooper Union Building. (Rev: SLJ 11/03) [973.7]

18107 Sinnott, Susan. *Charley Waters Goes to Gettysburg* (3–5). Illus. 2000, Millbrook LB $22.90 (0-7613-1567-5). 48pp. Told from the point of view of an 8-year-old boy who is visiting the Gettysburg battlefield with his parents, this book gives information on the battle and its reenactments. (Rev: BL 3/15/00; HBG 10/00; SLJ 6/00) [973.7]

18108 Sinnott, Susan. *Welcome to Addy's World, 1864* (3–6). Series: American Girl. 1999, Pleasant Co. $14.95 (1-56237-771-4). 58pp. Addy was born a slave and lived on a Southern plantation until age

nine. Through her eyes, life during the last year of the Civil War is re-created in a series of double-page spreads that explore slavery and other social and political topics of the time. (Rev: BL 1/1–15/00) [973.7]

18109 Smith, Carter, ed. *One Nation Again: A Sourcebook on the Civil War* (5–8). Series: American Albums. 1993, Millbrook LB $25.90 (1-56294-266-2). This heavily illustrated sourcebook chronicles the peace at Appomattox and the period immediately following. (Rev: BL 3/1/93) [973.8]

18110 Smith, Carter, ed. *The Road to Appomattox: A Sourcebook on the Civil War* (5–8). Series: American Albums. 1993, Millbrook $25.90 (1-56294-264-6). The last battles of the Civil War are covered in this album that uses period illustrations and excerpts from first-person accounts. (Rev: BL 3/1/93) [973.7]

18111 Somerlott, Robert. *The Lincoln Assassination* (5–8). Series: In American History. 1998, Enslow LB $20.95 (0-89490-886-3). 128pp. Using primary sources, the author has created a gripping story of the causes of the assassination, the shooting itself, and its aftermath. (Rev: BL 7/98; BR 9–10/98; SLJ 6/98) [973.7]

18112 Stanchak, John. *Civil War* (5–8). Illus. Series: Eyewitness Books. 2000, DK paper $15.99 (0-7894-6302-4). 64pp. This highly visual treatment presents topics related to the Civil War such as causes, battles, slavery, states' rights, weapons, and uniforms in a series of double-page spreads. (Rev: BL 1/1–15/01; HBG 3/01; SLJ 12/00) [973.7]

18113 Stanley, George E. *The Crisis of the Union (1815–1865)* (5–8). Illus. Series: A Primary Source History of the United States. 2005, World Almanac LB $22.50 (0-8368-5826-3). 48pp. A simple narrative links well-chosen primary sources documenting the key events of the Civil War.

18114 Sullivan, George. *The Civil War at Sea* (5–8). Illus. 2001, Twenty-First Century LB $27.90 (0-7613-1553-5). 64pp. This book tells of the struggle between the Union and Confederate forces in American bays, harbors, and rivers with material on famous ships and their commanders, important battles, and the daily life of the sailors. (Rev: BL 2/1/01; HBG 10/01; SLJ 3/01) [973.7]

18115 Tanaka, Shelley. *A Day That Changed America: Gettysburg* (4–8). Illus. by David Craig. Series: A Day That Changed America. 2003, Hyperion $16.99 (0-7868-1922-7). 48pp. A brief account of the key battle, with illustrations and diagrams as well as information on Lincoln's famous speech. (Rev: HBG 4/04; SLJ 2/04) [973.7]

18116 Weber, Michael. *Civil War and Reconstruction* (5–8). Series: The Making of America. 2001, Raintree LB $19.98 (0-8172-5707-2). 96pp. Using many illustrations, interesting sidebars, and an accessible text, this is a concise history of the Civil War and its immediate aftermath. (Rev: BL 4/15/01) [973.7]

18117 Yancey, Diane. *Strategic Battles* (5–12). Series: American War. 1999, Lucent LB $27.45 (1-56006-496-X). 128pp. The key battles of the Civil

War are covered in chronological order with maps and other illustrations. (Rev: BL 1/1–15/00; HBG 9/00) [973.7]

18118 Zeinert, Karen. *Those Courageous Women of the Civil War* (5–8). Illus. 1998, Millbrook LB $29.90 (0-7613-0212-3). 96pp. This account relates the contributions of women during the Civil War, with details on how they served as nurses, spies, writers, and workers on the home front. (Rev: BL 6/1–15/98; HBG 3/99) [973.7]

RECONSTRUCTION TO THE KOREAN WAR, 1865–1950

18119 Andrews, Jan. *Pa's Harvest* (3–7). Illus. 2000, Douglas & McIntyre $12.95 (0-88899-405-2). 40pp. Small, framed pictures in sepia tones illustrate this remembrance of the Great Depression and the hardship it brought to one family. (Rev: BL 12/15/00; HBG 10/01; SLJ 2/01) [813]

18120 Arnold, Caroline. *Children of the Settlement Houses* (4–7). Illus. Series: Picture the American Past. 1998, Carolrhoda LB $27.15 (1-57505-242-3). 48pp. Using historical photographs and a simple text, this book introduces the turn-of-the-20th-century settlement house, where the poor and new immigrants found shelter and a place to learn, explore the arts, and develop a sense of belonging. (Rev: BL 9/15/98; HBG 3/99; SLJ 1/99) [362.5]

18121 Axelrod-Contrada, Joan. *The Lizzie Borden "Axe Murder" Trial: A Headline Court Case* (5–9). Series: Headline Court Cases. 2000, Enslow LB $20.95 (0-7660-1422-3). 128pp. A well-documented account of the famous 1892 trial, the events that led up to it, and its aftermath. (Rev: HBG 3/01; SLJ 1/01) [973.8]

18122 Bartoletti, Susan C. *Growing Up in Coal Country* (5–8). Illus. 1996, Houghton Mifflin $17.00 (0-395-77847-6). The life of child laborers in the coal mines of Pennsylvania 100 years ago is covered in this brilliant photoessay. (Rev: BCCB 2/97; BL 12/1/96*; BR 11–12/97; SLJ 2/97*) [331.3]

18123 Bartoletti, Susan C. *Kids on Strike!* (5–8). Illus. 1999, Houghton Mifflin $20.00 (0-395-88892-1). 208pp. This book chronicles the history of child labor in America during the 19th and early 20th centuries and features such personalities as William Randolph Hearst, Pauline Newman, and Mother Jones. (Rev: BCCB 12/99; BL 12/1/99; HBG 3/00; SLJ 12/99*) [973.8]

18124 Black, Wallace B., and Jean F. Blashfield. *America Prepares for War* (5–7). Illus. Series: World War II 50th Anniversary. 1991, Macmillan LB $12.95 (0-89686-554-1). 48pp. The U.S. entry into World War II, with numerous photographs. (Rev: BL 6/15/91; SLJ 9/91) [940.53]

18125 Blackman, Cally. *The 20s and 30s: Flappers and Vamps* (5–10). Series: 20th Century Fashion. 2000, Gareth Stevens LB $25.26 (0-8368-2599-3). 32pp. Social history is combined with fashion and design in this account of the 1920s and 1930s that is illustrated with period photographs and magazine covers. (Rev: HBG 10/00; SLJ 6/00) [973.9]

18126 Brezina, Corona. *America's Political Scandals in the late 1800s: Boss Tweed and Tammany Hall* (5–8). Illus. Series: America's Industrial Society in the 19th Century. 2004, Rosen LB $21.25 (0-8239-4021-7). 32pp. For reluctant readers, this overview of the political scandals of the late 19th century features large print and short chapters.

18127 Brown, Harriet. *Welcome to Kit's World — 1934: Growing Up During America's Great Depression* (3–6). Illus. Series: American Girl. 2002, Pleasant Co. $16.95 (1-58485-359-X). 60pp. Double-page spreads are used in this heavily illustrated volume to describe growing up in 1934 during the Great Depression. (Rev: BL 4/15/02; HBG 10/02; SLJ 7/02) [973.9]

18128 Burgan, Michael. *The Great Depression* (4–6). Series: We the People. 2001, Compass Point LB $21.26 (0-7565-0152-0). 48pp. A basic overview of the causes of the Depression and the programs that were intended to alleviate its impact. (Rev: SLJ 1/02)

18129 Carter, Ron. *The Youngest Drover* (5–9). 1995, Harbour $19.95 (0-9643672-1-1); paper $14.95 (0-9643672-0-3). In 1923, when he was 15, the author's father participated in an exciting cattle drive from Alberta to Montana. (Rev: BL 1/1–15/96) [978]

18130 Cohen, Daniel. *The Alaska Purchase* (4–8). Series: Spotlight on American History. 1996, Millbrook $24.90 (1-56294-528-9). The story of the purchase of Alaska from Russia in 1867 and how it changed the course of American history. (Rev: BL 3/15/96; SLJ 5/96) [979.8]

18131 Collier, Christopher, and James Lincoln Collier. *Progressivism, the Great Depression, and the New Deal* (5–8). Illus. Series: The Drama of American History. 2001, Marshall Cavendish LB $29.93 (0-7614-1054-6). 96pp. A highly readable account that covers such topics as the stock market crash, the reformation of business practices, the Great Depression, and the social policies of the New Deal. (Rev: BL 3/15/01; HBG 10/01) [973.91]

18132 Collier, Christopher, and James Lincoln Collier. *Reconstruction and the Rise of Jim Crow, 1864–1896* (5–8). Series: Drama of American History. 1999, Marshall Cavendish LB $29.93 (0-7614-0819-3). 89pp. A clear, objective account of the problems facing the country after the Civil War and how they were resolved. (Rev: BL 2/15/00; HBG 10/00; SLJ 3/00) [973.8]

18133 Collier, Christopher, and James Lincoln Collier. *The Rise of Industry, 1860–1900* (5–8). Illus. Series: Drama of American History. 1999, Marshall Cavendish LB $29.93 (0-7614-0820-7). 89pp. A readable account of 40 years of industrialism and its effect on the United States. (Rev: BL 2/15/00; HBG 10/00; SLJ 3/00) [338.0973]

18134 Coombs, Karen Mueller. *Children of the Dust Days* (3–6). Illus. Series: Picture the American Past. 2000, Carolrhoda LB $22.60 (1-57505-360-8). 48pp. A mainly illustrated account of the hardships associated with the Dust Bowl and the journeys of many displaced farmers to California. (Rev: BL 4/1/00; HBG 10/00; SLJ 6/00) [978]

18135 Cooper, Michael L. *Dust to Eat: Drought and Depression in the 1930s* (5–8). Illus. 2004, Clarion $15.00 (0-618-15449-3). 96pp. First-person accounts and period photographs convey the hopelessness of those who were caught in the grip of the Depression and the drought in the Midwest. (Rev: BL 7/04; SLJ 9/04) [973.917]

18136 Cooper, Michael L. *Remembering Manzanar: Life in a Japanese Relocation Camp* (4–8). Illus. 2002, Clarion $15.00 (0-618-06778-7). 68pp. This evocative account of life in a Japanese American World War II internment center tells its tale through personal accounts of survivors, quotations from the camp newspaper, and revealing photographs. (Rev: BL 1/1–15/03; HBG 10/03; SLJ 2/03) [940.54]

18137 Cryan-Hicks, Kathryn, ed. *Pride and Promise: The Harlem Renaisssance* (4–8). Illus. Series: Perspectives on History. 1994, Discovery Enterprises paper $6.95 (1-878668-30-7). The story of the great artistic awakening in New York's Harlem and of its many leaders, including Langston Hughes. (Rev: BL 8/94) [305.896]

18138 Dolan, Edward F. *The Spanish-American War* (5–8). Illus. 2001, Millbrook LB $28.90 (0-7613-1453-9). 112pp. This chronological account of the Spanish-American War includes profiles of military personnel, maps, and historical photographs. (Rev: BL 11/1/01; HBG 3/02; SLJ 11/01) [973.8]

18139 Duden, Jane. *1940s* (3–7). Illus. 1989, Macmillan LB $16.95 (0-89686-475-8). 48pp. The eventful decade of the 1940s, which included World War II and adjustments to a peacetime economy, is covered in this well-illustrated book. (Rev: SLJ 4/90) [973.9]

18140 Feinberg, Barbara S. *Black Tuesday: The Stock Market Crash of 1929* (4–7). Illus. Series: Spotlight on American History. 1995, Millbrook LB $24.90 (1-56294-574-2). 64pp. The causes and consequences of the great stock market crash of 1929 are interestingly retold with many photographs and illustrations. (Rev: BL 10/15/95) [338.5]

18141 Ferrell, Claudine L. *Reconstruction* (5–10). Series: Greenwood Guides to Historic Events, 1500–1900. 2003, Greenwood $45.00 (0-313-32062-4). 220pp. Covers key individuals involved in Reconstruction and the speeches, proclamations, and other primary documents that cast light on the events of the time. (Rev: SLJ 6/04) [973.8]

18142 Flanagan, Alice K. *The Buffalo Soldiers* (3–6). Illus. Series: We the People. 2005, Compass Point LB $22.60 (0-7565-0833-9). 48pp. An introduction to the first all-black regiments formed after the Civil War and nicknamed "Buffalo soldiers" by the Kiowa Indians. [973.7]

18143 Freedman, Russell. *Immigrant Kids* (3–7). Illus. 1995, Puffin paper $5.99 (0-140-37594-5). 64pp. An account of the immigration to the United States from 1880 to 1920.

18144 Fremon, David K. *The Jim Crow Laws and Racism in American History* (5–9). 2000, Enslow LB $20.95 (0-7660-1297-2). 128pp. This is a histo-

ry of racism in America from the end of the Civil War to the death of Martin Luther King, Jr., in 1968. (Rev: BL 10/15/00; HBG 3/01; SLJ 12/00) [973]

18145 Gillespie, Sarah. *A Pioneer Farm Girl: The Diary of Sarah Gillespie, 1877–1878* (4–6). Series: Diaries, Letters, and Memoirs. 2000, Capstone LB $22.60 (0-7368-0347-5). 32pp. Told in diary entries, this is the true story of everyday life on a pioneer farm after the Civil War as experienced by a young girl. (Rev: BL 10/15/00; HBG 10/00; SLJ 9/00) [978]

18146 Gourley, Catherine. *Good Girl Work: Factories, Sweatshops, and How Women Changed Their Role in the American Workforce* (4–8). 1999, Millbrook LB $23.40 (0-7613-0951-9). 96pp. A history of female labor in U.S. factories during the late 19th and early 20th centuries with material on the terrible working conditions and the gradual changes that took place. (Rev: SLJ 8/99) [973.8]

18147 Gourley, Catherine. *Welcome to Samantha's World, 1904* (3–6). Series: American Girl. 1999, Pleasant Co. $14.95 (1-56247-772-2). 58pp. Using double-page spreads, this book introduces social and cultural life in America at the beginning of the 20th century. (Rev: BL 1/1–15/00; HBG 3/00) [973.9]

18148 Graves, Kerry A. *Going to School During the Great Depression* (4–6). Series: Going to School in History. 2001, Capstone LB $16.95 (0-7368-0800-7). 32pp. School life during the 1930s and early '40s is covered with material on subjects studied, school supplies, and typical activities and games of the time. (Rev: BL 10/15/01) [973.9]

18149 Green, Carl R. *The Spanish-American War* (4–6). Series: U.S. Wars. 2002, Enslow/MyReportLinks.com LB $19.95 (0-7660-5091-2). 48pp. Preceding a brief history of the Spanish-American War, there is a lengthy section listing Internet sites that offer students additional material on the subject. (Rev: BL 10/15/02; HBG 3/03) [973.8]

18150 Greene, Meg. *Into the Land of Freedom: African Americans in Reconstruction* (5–8). Illus. Series: People's History. 2004, Lerner LB $25.26 (0-8225-4690-6). 112pp. Sepia-toned photographs and historical documents and interviews add to this portrait of the situation of African Americans during Reconstruction. (Rev: BL 2/15/04*; SLJ 5/04) [973]

18151 Hakim, Joy. *Reconstruction and Reform*. 2nd ed. (5–8). Series: A History of Us. 1999, Oxford LB $19.95 (0-19-512763-3); paper $13.95 (0-19-512764-1). 192pp. The years immediately following the Civil War (1865–1896) are covered in this outstanding history that uses many quotes, anecdotes, and excellent illustrations. (Rev: BL 12/15/99) [973.8]

18152 Heinrichs, Ann. *The Dust Bowl* (3–6). Illus. Series: We the People. 2005, Compass Point LB $22.60 (0-7565-0837-1). 48pp. Describes the plight of people living in the Midwest during the long drought of the 1930s. [978]

18153 Hoffman, Nancy. *Eleanor Roosevelt and the Arthurdale Experiment* (5–8). Illus. 2001, Linnet

LB $22.50 (0-208-02504-9). 108pp. Hoffman includes quotations and black-and-white photographs in her account of the story of Arthurdale, a government-planned community of the 1930s. (Rev: BL 10/15/01; HBG 3/02; SLJ 12/01) [975.4]

18154 Holiday, Billie, and Arthur Herzog. *God Bless the Child* (2–5). Illus. by Ierry Pinkney. 2004, HarperCollins $16.99 (0-06-028797-7). 32pp. The lyrics of Billie Holiday's signature song provide the framework for this moving portrait of a black family joining the great migration from the cotton fields of the Deep South to the streets of Chicago; a CD is included. (Rev: BL 2/15/04*; SLJ 2/04) [782.42164]

18155 Houle, Michelle M. *Triangle Shirtwaist Factory Fire: Flames of Labor Reform* (4–6). Illus. Series: American Disasters. 2002, Enslow LB $18.95 (0-7660-1785-0). 48pp. A frank portrayal of the tragic 1911 fire and the impact it had on the labor movement. (Rev: HBG 3/03; SLJ 12/02)

18156 Isaacs, Sally Senzell. *Life in the Dust Bowl* (2–4). Illus. Series: Picture the Past. 2001, Heinemann LB $21.36 (1-58810-248-3). 32pp. A gripping introduction to the hardships of life on the plains in the 1930s, with information on society at the time. (Rev: SLJ 3/02)

18157 Jackson, Robert. *Meet Me in St. Louis: A Trip to the 1904 World's Fair* (4–7). Illus. 2004, HarperCollins $17.99 (0-06-009267-X). 144pp. Jackson beautifully evokes the excitement surrounding the 1904 St. Louis World's Fair, which attracted nearly 20 million people, many of them key figures of the day. (Rev: BL 2/15/04; SLJ 4/04) [907]

18158 Jernegan, Laura. *A Whaling Captain's Daughter: The Diary of Laura Jernegan, 1868–1871* (4–6). Series: Diaries, Letters, and Memoirs. 2000, Capstone LB $22.60 (0-7368-0319-1). Excerpts from a young girl's diary introduce the reader to life ashore and aboard a whaling ship immediately after the Civil War. (Rev: BL 10/15/00; SLJ 9/00) [973.8]

18159 Josephson, Judith Pinkerton. *Growing Up in a New Century* (5–8). Illus. Series: Our America. 2002, Lerner LB $31.95 (0-8225-0657-2). 64pp. A look at the lives of American children of different backgrounds and situations at the dawn of the 20th century. (Rev: BL 2/1/03; HBG 3/03; SLJ 7/03) [973.91]

18160 Josephson, Judith Pinkerton. *Growing Up in World War II* (5–8). Illus. Series: Our America. 2002, Lerner LB $26.60 (0-8225-0660-2). 64pp. A look at the lives of American children of different backgrounds and situations during World War II. (Rev: BL 2/1/03; HBG 3/03) [940.533]

18161 Kalman, Bobbie. *19th Century Girls and Women* (3–5). Illus. 1997, Crabtree LB $20.60 (0-86505-434-7); paper $7.95 (0-86505-464-9). 32pp. A realistic portrait of the life women led in both the working and wealthy classes, with details on home life, chores, health hazards, and stifling clothing. (Rev: BL 7/97; SLJ 8/97) [305.4]

18162 King, David C. *Victorian Days: Discover the Past with Fun Projects, Games, Activities, and Recipes* (4–6). Illus. by Cheryl K. Noll. Series:

American Kids in History. 2000, Wiley paper $12.95 (0-471-33122-8). 96pp. Through an interesting text and more than 30 activities like making paper flowers and shadow puppets and following some delicious recipes, young readers can re-create life in New York in the year 1893. (Rev: SLJ 4/00) [973.8]

18163 King, David C. *World Wars and the Modern Age* (5–8). Illus. Series: American Heritage, American Voices. 2004, Wiley paper $18.99 (0-471-44392-1). 144pp. A concise overview of the profound changes seen in the United States during the decades from 1870 to 1950, with excerpts from primary sources. (Rev: BL 2/1/05; SLJ 5/05) [973]

18164 Komatsu, Kimberly, and Kaleigh Komatsu. *In America's Shadow* (5–8). Illus. 2003, Thomas George $35.00 (0-9709829-0-9). 96pp. This account of the internment of Japanese Americans during World War II draws on the memories and archives of the authors' family. (Rev: BL 4/1/03) [940.531]

18165 Littlefield, Holly. *Children of the Orphan Trains* (3–6). Illus. Series: Picture the American Past. 2001, Carolrhoda LB $22.60 (1-57505-466-3). 48pp. A brief, informative text is accompanied by moving photographs that dramatically tell the sad story of orphan children transported West to find work and homes. (Rev: BL 5/15/01; HBG 10/01) [362.73]

18166 Martin, Bill, Jr., and Michael Sampson. *I Pledge Allegiance* (K–4). Illus. by Chris Raschka. 2002, Candlewick $15.99 (0-7636-1648-6). 40pp. The Pledge of Allegiance, which was adopted in 1892, is explained to young readers in simple language. (Rev: BCCB 10/02; BL 9/1/02; HBG 3/03; SLJ 12/02) [323.6]

18167 Meltzer, Milton. *Driven from the Land: The Story of the Dust Bowl* (4–8). Series: Great Journeys. 1999, Benchmark LB $31.36 (0-7614-0968-8). 111pp. Traces the development of the Dust Bowl, its effects on the land and the people, and how many were forced to leave their farms and seek a new life elsewhere. (Rev: BL 1/1–15/00; HBG 3/00; SLJ 2/00) [973.9]

18168 Miller, Marilyn. *The Transcontinental Railroad* (5–8). Illus. 1987, Silver Burdett paper $12.36 (0-382-09912-5). 64pp. The great event that linked East and West by rail is portrayed with numerous illustrations. (Rev: BL 7/87; SLJ 9/87) [385.0979]

18169 Murphy, Jim. *Blizzard! The Storm that Changed America* (5–9). Illus. 2000, Scholastic paper $18.95 (0-590-67309-2). 136pp. A brilliant narrative about the great storm that hit the Northeast on March 10, 1888, and brought 31 inches of snow and 800 deaths in New York City alone. (Rev: BL 2/15/01*; HB 1–2/01; HBG 3/01; SLJ 12/00) [974.7]

18170 Nardo, Don. *The 1930s* (4–6). Illus. 2003, Gale/KidHaven LB $23.70 (0-7377-1515-4). 48pp. This concise and well-written overview of the 1930s includes discussion of the causes of the Great Depression and the chain of events that led to World War II. (Rev: BL 2/15/04) [973.917]

18171 Nicholson, Dorinda M. *Pearl Harbor Child: A Child's View of Pearl Harbor — from Attack to Peace* (5–8). 1998, Woodson House paper $9.95 (1-892858-00-2). This photoessay describes a child's experience during the bombing of Pearl Harbor, the temporary evacuation, and everyday life growing up in Hawaii during World War II. (Rev: BL 1/1–15/99) [996.9]

18172 Nobisso, Josephine. *John Blair and the Great Hinckley Fire* (1–4). Illus. by Ted Rose. 2000, Houghton Mifflin $15.00 (0-618-01560-4). This is the story of the African American railway porter who was the hero of the forest fire that killed more than 400 people in Minnesota in 1894. (Rev: BCCB 10/00; HBG 3/01; SLJ 12/00) [973.9]

18173 Porterfield, Jason. *Problems and Progress in American Politics: The Growth of the Democratic Party in the Late 1800s* (5–8). Illus. Series: America's Industrial Society in the 19th Century. 2004, Rosen LB $21.25 (0-8239-4026-8). 32pp. For reluctant readers, this overview of the growth of the Democratic Party features large print and short chapters.

18174 Ruth, Amy. *Growing Up in the Great Depression* (5–8). Series: Our America. 2002, Lerner LB $31.95 (0-8225-0655-6). 64pp. With many sidebars and quotations from original sources, this narrative re-creates the despair and courage of children growing up during the Great Depression. (Rev: BL 2/15/03; HBG 3/03) [973.9]

18175 Sandler, Martin A. *Island of Hope: The Story of Ellis Island and the Journey to America* (5–7). Illus. 2004, Scholastic $18.95 (0-439-53082-2). 144pp. Drawing heavily on first-hand accounts, Sandler traces immigrants' progress through the processing at Ellis Island and on into the cities and farms of their new country. (Rev: BL 4/15/04; SLJ 6/04) [304.8]

18176 Schaefer, Adam R. *The Triangle Shirtwaist Factory Fire* (4–7). Series: Landmark Events in American History. 2003, World Almanac LB $29.26 (0-8368-5383-0). 48pp. An accessible account of the tragic 1911 fire in New York City, with material on the horrible working conditions and the resulting reforms in labor law. (Rev: SLJ 6/04) [974.7]

18177 Schomp, Virginia. *World War II* (5–8). Illus. Series: Letters from the Homefront. 2001, Marshall Cavendish LB $28.50 (0-7614-1098-8). 96pp. Schomp uses letters written during World War II, accompanied by relevant illustrations, to give readers a real understanding of the difficulties of life on the homefront. (Rev: BL 10/15/01; HBG 3/02) [940.54]

18178 Sherrow, Victoria. *The Triangle Factory Fire* (5–8). Series: Spotlight on American History. 1995, Millbrook LB $24.90 (1-56294-572-6). The story of the deadly factory fire that exposed the shameful labor exploitation in this country and led to needed reforms. (Rev: BR 1–2/96; SLJ 3/96) [363.37]

18179 Smolinski, Diane. *Battles of the Spanish-American War* (4–7). Series: Americans at War: The Spanish-American War. 2002, Heinemann LB $24.22 (1-4034-0170-5). 32pp. A slim volume with many illustrations, plus timelines of battles and boxed features on casualties and key figures. (Rev: HBG 10/03; SLJ 5/03) [973.8]

18180 Smolinski, Diane. *Soldiers of the Spanish-American War* (4–7). Illus. Series: Americans at War: The Spanish-American War. 2002, Heinemann LB $24.22 (1-4034-0173-X). 32pp. A slim volume with many illustrations, plus details of equipment and key figures. (Rev: HBG 10/03; SLJ 5/03) [973.8]

18181 Spedden, Daisy C. S. *Polar the Titanic Bear* (3–5). Illus. by Laurie McGaw. 1994, Little, Brown $17.95 (0-316-80625-0). 64pp. The true story of a toy bear, his many owners, and his rescue from the Titanic. (Rev: BCCB 12/94; BL 12/1/94*; SLJ 1/95) [910.91]

18182 Splear, Elise Lee. *Growing Seasons* (3–5). Illus. 2000, Penguin Putnam $16.99 (0-399-23460-8). 40pp. This nonfiction book of remembrances paints a vivid picture of growing up in America about 100 years ago. (Rev: BCCB 7–8/00; BL 5/15/00; HBG 10/00; SLJ 7/00) [973.8]

18183 Stanley, George E. *An Emerging World Power (1900–1929)* (5–8). Illus. Series: A Primary Source History of the United States. 2005, World Almanac LB $22.50 (0-8368-5828-X). 48pp. A simple narrative links well-chosen primary sources documenting the key events of the early 20th century. Also use *The Era of Reconstruction and Expansion (1865–1900)* and *The Great Depression and World War II (1929–1949)* (both 2005).

18184 Stewart, Dave. *You Wouldn't Want to Sail on the Titanic! One Voyage You'd Rather Not Make* (4–6). Illus. by David Antram. Series: You Wouldn't Want To. 2001, Watts LB $25.00 (0-531-14604-9); paper $9.95 (0-531-16210-9). 32pp. The uncomfortable opportunity to imagine yourself aboard the *Titanic*. (Rev: SLJ 3/02) [910.91]

18185 Stewart, Gail B. *1920s* (5–9). Illus. 1990, Crestwood LB $11.95 (0-89686-473-1). A chronological description of the Great War and its aftermath plus material on the trivia associated with this period. Also use *1930s* (1990). (Rev: SLJ 6/90) [973.9]

18186 Stites, Bill. *The Republican Party in the Late 1800s: A Changing Role for American Government* (5–8). Illus. Series: America's Industrial Society in the 19th Century. 2004, Rosen LB $21.25 (0-8239-4030-6). 32pp. For reluctant readers, this overview of the growth of the Republican Party features large print and short chapters.

18187 Stone, Tanya Lee. *The Great Depression and World War II* (5–8). Series: Making of America. 2001, Raintree LB $28.54 (0-8172-5710-1). 96pp. Concise text and attractive illustrations re-create the history of America from 1929 through World War II. (Rev: BL 9/15/01; HBG 10/01) [973.9]

18188 Stone, Tanya Lee. *The Progressive Era and World War I* (5–8). Series: Making of America. 2001, Raintree LB $28.54 (0-8172-5709-8). 96pp. Roughly the first 20 years of the 20th century in American history are retold in this history that also looks at home life, culture, and entertainment. (Rev: BL 9/15/01; HBG 10/01; SLJ 6/01) [973.9]

18189 Tanaka, Shelley. *A Day That Changed America: Earthquake!* (3–5). Illus. by David Craig. Series: A Day That Changed America. 2004, Hyperion $16.99 (0-7868-1882-4). 48pp. Four survivors recall the day of the massive earthquake in 1906; sidebars offer information on earthquakes, the Richter scale, and so forth. (Rev: BL 10/15/04; SLJ 10/04) [979.4]

18190 Uschan, Michael V. *The 1940s* (5–10). Series: Cultural History of the United States. 1998, Lucent LB $18.96 (1-56510-554-0). Life at home and abroad during World War II dominate this book, which also discusses the Great Depression, the New Deal, events leading up to U.S. participation in the war, the beginnings of the Cold War, the growth of suburban living, and the rise of television, with sidebars on such topics as the Holocaust, the influences of radio, movies, and comics, 1940s slang, and the first computers. (Rev: SLJ 1/99) [973.9]

18191 Warren, Andrea. *Orphan Train Rider: One Boy's True Story* (4–8). 1996, Houghton Mifflin $17.00 (0-395-69822-7). Between 1854 and 1930, more than 200,000 orphaned and abandoned children from cities on the East Coast were "placed out" to new homes and families in midwestern and western states. This is an account of one of them. (Rev: BL 7/96; SLJ 8/96*) [362.7]

18192 Warren, Andrea. *We Rode the Orphan Trains* (4–8). Illus. 2001, Houghton Mifflin $18.00 (0-618-11712-1). 144pp. Eight moving biographical accounts of men and women, now in their 80s and 90s, who traveled to the Midwest to find new homes and families. (Rev: BCCB 11/01; BL 11/1/01; HBG 3/02; SLJ 11/01) [362.73]

18193 Weber, Valerie, and Valerie Baker. *Traveling in Grandma's Day* (3–4). 2000, Carolrhoda LB $21.27 (1-57505-326-8). 32pp. A nostalgic look at traveling in the 1930s and 1940s told through first-person narratives and plenty of photographs. Also use *School in Grandma's Day*, *Shopping in Grandma's Day*, and *Food in Grandma's Day* (all 2000). (Rev: HBG 10/00; SLJ 6/00) [973.9]

18194 Wells, Donna. *America Comes of Age* (5–8). Series: The Making of America. 2001, Raintree LB $28.54 (0-8172-5708-X). 96pp. A handsomely illustrated account that traces U.S. history from Reconstruction to the beginning of the 20th century. (Rev: BL 4/15/01; HBG 10/01) [973.8]

18195 Wetterer, Margaret K., and Charles M. Wetterer. *The Snow Walker* (2–4). Illus. 1996, Carolrhoda LB $18.60 (0-87614-891-7); paper $5.95 (0-87614-959-X). 48pp. During the terrible blizzard of 1888, Milton Daub unselfishly helped his neighbors in the Bronx by delivering needed supplies. (Rev: BCCB 12/96; BL 2/15/96; SLJ 3/96) [973.9]

18196 Whitman, Sylvia. *Immigrant Children: Late 1800s to Early 1900s* (3–5). Series: Picture the American Past. 2000, Carolrhoda LB $22.60 (1-57505-395-0). 48pp. This book describes the lives of immigrant children who arrived in this country, many to work in mines, factories, or farms but all

trying to get ahead. (Rev: HBG 10/00; SLJ 7/00) [973.9]

18197 Whitman, Sylvia. *V Is for Victory: The American Home Front During World War II* (4–7). Illus. 1993, Lerner LB $30.35 (0-8225-1727-2). 80pp. Rosie the Riveter, ration stamps, and the relocation of Japanese Americans are among the topics covered in this look at the United States in another time. (Rev: BL 2/15/93) [973.9]

18198 Woog, Adam. *A Sweatshop During the Industrial Revolution* (5–9). Series: The Working Life. 2003, Gale LB $21.96 (1-59018-179-4). 112pp. An exploration of daily life for a sweatshop worker during a time of social change, with material on the roles of women, minorities, and organized labor. (Rev: SLJ 5/03) [331.25]

18199 Wroble, Lisa A. *Kids During the Great Depression* (3–5). Series: Kids Throughout History. 1999, Rosen LB $11.95 (0-8239-5255-X). 24pp. This book tells of the events preceding the Depression, its effects on people and particularly children, and the gradual recovery before World War II. (Rev: SLJ 11/99) [973.9]

18200 Wroble, Lisa A. *The New Deal and the Great Depression in American History* (5–8). Series: In American History. 2002, Enslow LB $20.95 (0-7660-1421-5). 128pp. A timeline, maps, chapter notes, and research topics are found in this well-researched account that concentrates on Roosevelt's economic policies during the 1930s. (Rev: BL 1/1–15/03; HBG 3/03) [973.9]

THE 1950S TO THE PRESENT

18201 Anderson, Dale. *America into a New Millennium* (5–8). Series: Making of America. 2001, Raintree LB $28.54 (0-8172-5712-8). 96pp. This last part of a 12-volume series presents American history from the end of the Cold War to the beginning of the 21st century. (Rev: BL 9/15/01; HBG 10/01; SLJ 6/01) [973.9]

18202 Anderson, Dale. *The Cold War Years* (5–8). Series: Making of America. 2001, Raintree LB $28.54 (0-8172-5711-X). 96pp. A concise, easy-to-understand text tells America's story from the end of World War II to the 1990s. (Rev: BL 9/15/01; HBG 10/01; SLJ 6/01) [973.9]

18203 Britton, Tamara L. *The World Trade Center* (3–5). Series: Symbols, Landmarks, and Monuments. 2003, ABDO LB $14.95 (1-57765-850-7). 40pp. The design and construction of New York City's World Trade Center are described along with its destruction on September 11, 2001. (Rev: HBG 10/03; SLJ 10/03) [720]

18204 Brown, Gene. *The Nation in Turmoil: Civil Rights and the Vietnam War (1960–1973)* (5–8). Series: First Person America. 1994, Twenty-First Century LB $20.90 (0-8050-2588-X). An overview of the civil rights movement and the Vietnam War, highlighting excerpts from letters, diaries, and speeches. (Rev: BL 5/15/94) [973.92]

18205 Brown, Gene. *The 1992 Election* (5–8). Illus. Series: Headliners. 1993, Millbrook LB $25.90 (1-56294-080-5). This book presents the issues and highlights of the campaigns and presidential election. (Rev: BL 4/1/93; SLJ 7/93) [973.9]

18206 Campbell, Geoffrey A. *Life of an American Soldier* (5–9). Series: American War Library: The Persian Gulf War. 2001, Lucent LB $27.45 (1-56006-713-6). 128pp. Interviews with Gulf War veterans bring a personal touch to this volume, which includes many photographs of soldiers and equipment along with a history of the war and discussion of the reasons for the conflict. (Rev: SLJ 8/01) [956.7044]

18207 Canwell, Diane, and Jon Sutherland. *African Americans in the Vietnam War* (5–8). Illus. Series: American Experience in Vietnam. 2005, World Almanac LB $30.00 (0-8368-5772-0). 48pp. Personal stories and full-color photographs add to the information on black Americans' contributions to the conflict and the military's efforts toward integration. Also use *American Women in the Vietnam War* (2005). (Rev: BL 2/1/05) [959.705]

18208 Carter, E. J. *The Cuban Missile Crisis* (4–8). Series: 20th Century Perspectives. 2003, Heinemann LB $27.07 (1-4034-3806-4). 48pp. A review of the 1962 crisis in which Cuba secretly installed missiles capable of carrying nuclear warheads. (Rev: SLJ 5/04) [972.9]

18209 Coles, Robert. *The Story of Ruby Bridges* (K–4). Illus. by George Ford. 1995, Scholastic $13.95 (0-590-43967-7). 32pp. A re-creation of the trauma faced by a young African American girl who is the first to integrate an all-white school in New Orleans in 1960. (Rev: BCCB 3/95; BL 1/15/95; SLJ 3/95)

18210 Duden, Jane. *1950s* (3–7). 1989, Macmillan LB $20.00 (0-89686-476-6). 48pp. Events and people associated with this eventful decade come to life in this book that is divided by years. It is continued in *1960s* and *1970s* (both 1989). (Rev: SLJ 4/90) [973.9]

18211 Feinstein, Stephen. *The 1980s: From Ronald Reagan to MTV* (4–7). Series: Decades of the 20th Century. 2000, Enslow LB $17.95 (0-7660-1424-X). 64pp. Presents the decade's major events, important people, and developments in such areas as politics, science, the arts, and sports. (Rev: BL 10/15/00; HBG 10/00; SLJ 12/00) [973.9]

18212 Gard, Carolyn. *The Attack on the Pentagon on September 11, 2001* (4–8). Series: Terrorist Attacks. 2003, Rosen LB $26.50 (0-8239-3858-1). 64pp. In addition to describing the attack itself, Gard looks at the organization of Al-Qaeda. (Rev: SLJ 2/04) [975.5]

18213 Green, Carl R. *The Vietnam War* (4–6). Illus. Series: U.S. Wars. 2003, Enslow LB $19.95 (0-7660-5147-1). 48pp. Supported by verified and updated Web links, this is a useful introduction to the Vietnam War. (Rev: HBG 4/04)

18214 Gresko, Jessica A. *The 1960s* (4–6). Illus. Series: American History by the Decade. 2003, Gale/KidHaven LB $23.70 (0-7377-1748-3). 48pp. This otherwise well-written retrospective on the turbulent 1960s is marred by its limited coverage of

Kennedy's presidency and assassination. (Rev: BL 2/15/04) [973.923]

18215 Hakim, Joy. *All the People*. 2nd ed. (5–8). Series: A History of Us. 1999, Oxford LB $19.95 (0-19-512769-2); paper $13.95 (0-19-512770-6). 235pp. An outstanding history of the political and social events, trends, and developments in the United States from the end of World War II through 1998. (Rev: BL 12/15/99) [973.9]

18216 Hampton, Wilborn. *Kennedy Assassinated! The World Mourns* (5–8). Illus. 1997, Candlewick $17.99 (1-56402-811-9). A gripping first-person account of John Kennedy's assassination by a veteran newspaper reporter who was in Dallas that day. (Rev: BL 9/15/97; BR 3–4/98; HBG 3/98; SLJ 10/97) [364.1]

18217 Isaacs, Sally Senzell. *America in the Time of Martin Luther King Jr.: The Story of Our Nation from Coast to Coast, from 1948 to 1976* (4–8). Series: America in the Time Of. 1999, Heinemann LB $30.35 (1-57572-780-3). 48pp. As well as describing the accomplishment of Martin Luther King, Jr., this account traces important developments during his time including the 1960s peace movement, the Vietnam War, space travel, and the Watergate scandal. (Rev: SLJ 5/00) [973.9]

18218 Kallen, Stuart A. *The 1950s* (5–8). Series: Cultural History of the United States. 1998, Lucent LB $27.45 (1-56006-555-9). Readable text and many photographs are used to survey the contrasting political and cultural trends, events, and movements of the 1950s in the United States and examine what life was like for teenagers at that time. (Rev: BL 1/1–15/99; SLJ 3/99) [973.921]

18219 Kent, Deborah. *The Vietnam War: "What Are We Fighting For?"* (5–7). Illus. Series: American War. 1994, Enslow LB $20.95 (0-89490-527-9). 128pp. An objective overview of this war, its causes, progression, and results. (Rev: BL 10/15/94; SLJ 11/94) [959.704]

18220 Koestler, Rachel. *Going to School During the Civil Rights Movement* (4–6). Illus. Series: Going to School in History. 2001, Capstone LB $16.95 (0-7368-0799-3). 32pp. Koestler explores the difficulties of attending school during segregation. (Rev: BL 10/15/01; HBG 3/02) [379.2]

18221 Levitas, Mitchel, ed. *A Nation Challenged: A Visual History of 9/11 and Its Aftermath: Young Reader's Edition* (4–9). 2002, Scholastic $18.95 (0-439-48803-6). 96pp. This is a selection of material first published in the *New York Times* that has been chosen as suitable for young readers. (Rev: BL 9/1/02; HBG 10/03; SLJ 9/02)

18222 Marquette, Scott. *Korean Conflict* (4–7). Illus. Series: America at War. 2002, Rourke LB $27.93 (1-58952-390-3). 48pp. This book for middle graders explains in simple terms the causes and events of the Korean conflict. [951]

18223 Marquette, Scott. *Vietnam War* (4–7). Illus. Series: America at War. 2002, Rourke LB $27.93 (1-58952-391-1). 48pp. This book for middle graders studies the war itself and the events that led up to it. [959]

18224 *The Montgomery Bus Boycott* (5–8). Series: Landmark Events in American History. 2003, World Almanac LB $26.60 (0-8368-5375-X). 48pp. The story of what happened when Rosa Parks refused to give up her seat on a Montgomery, Alabama, bus in 1955. (Rev: BL 10/15/03; SLJ 9/03) [305.8]

18225 Petersen, Christine. *The Iran-Contra Scandal* (4–6). Series: Cornerstones of Freedom. 2004, Children's Pr. LB $24.00 (0-516-24228-8). 48pp. Petersen offers a fascinating overview of the investigations into Reagan administration activities involving illegal arms sales to Iran. (Rev: SLJ 7/04) [973.927]

18226 Poffenberger, Nancy. *September 11th, 2001: A Simple Account for Children* (PS–2). Illus. 2002, Fun paper $8.95 (0-938293-12-5). 16pp. Drawings by schoolchildren illustrate a straightforward presentation of the events of September 11. (Rev: BL 7/02) [973.931]

18227 Santella, Andrew. *September 11, 2001* (4–6). Series: Cornerstones of Freedom, Second Series. 2002, Children's Book Pr. LB $24.00 (0-516-22692-4). 48pp. This presentation gives the basic facts on the attacks and the U.S. response. (Rev: SLJ 11/02)

18228 Schomp, Virginia. *The Vietnam War* (5–8). Series: Letters from the Homefront. 2001, Benchmark LB $28.50 (0-7614-1099-6). 96pp. Conditions on the home front during the Vietnam War are recreated through primary documents such as letters and period photographs. (Rev: BL 10/15/01; HBG 3/02; SLJ 3/02) [973.9]

18229 Stein, R. Conrad. *The Cold War* (4–6). Series: U.S. Wars. 2002, Enslow/MyReportLinks.com LB $19.95 (0-7660-5095-5). 48pp. In addition to a concise history of the causes and progress of the Cold War, this volume includes a listing of pertinent Web sites where additional material such as maps, documents, and biographies can be found. (Rev: BL 10/15/02; HBG 3/03) [973.9]

18230 Steins, Richard. *The Postwar Years: The Cold War and the Atomic Age (1950–1959)* (5–8). Series: First Person America. 1994, Twenty-First Century LB $20.90 (0-8050-2587-1). Coverage of the 1950s includes first-person material on the Cold War and the Korean conflict. (Rev: BL 5/15/94; SLJ 12/94) [973.92]

18231 Stewart, Gail B. *Terrorism* (4–6). Illus. Series: Understanding Issues. 2002, Gale LB $23.70 (0-7377-1287-2). 48pp. Taking September 11, 2001, as a starting point, this account explores the causes and effects of terrorism and the measures taken to combat it. (Rev: BL 6/1–15/02; SLJ 9/02) [303.6]

18232 Summer, L. S. *The March on Washington* (4–6). Series: Journey to Freedom. 2000, Child's World LB $25.64 (1-56766-718-X). 40pp. The story of the August 28, 1963, march on Washington to support President Kennedy's civil rights legislation, during which Martin Luther King Jr. gave his "I Have a Dream" speech. (Rev: BL 11/15/00; HBG 3/01; SLJ 1/01) [973.9]

18233 Westerfeld, Scott. *Watergate* (5–7). Illus. Series: Turning Points. 1991, Silver Burdett paper $7.95 (0-382-24120-7). 64pp. An objective account in text and pictures of the Watergate break-in during Nixon's presidency and its consequences. (Rev: BL 1/15/92) [364.1]

18234 Wheeler, Jill C. *September 11, 2001: The Day That Changed America* (3–5). Illus. Series: War on Terrorism. 2002, ABDO $16.95 (1-57765-656-3). 64pp. This introductory volume covers the attacks, the rescue efforts, and the initial American response, with lots of photographs. Also use *Ground Zero* and *Heroes of the Day*. (Rev: BL 5/1/02; HBG 10/02; SLJ 6/02) [973.931]

18235 Young, Jeff C. *The Korean War* (4–6). Illus. Series: U.S. Wars. 2003, Enslow LB $19.95 (0-7660-5148-X). 48pp. Supported by verified and updated Web links, this is a useful account of the Korean War. (Rev: HBG 4/04)

18236 Young, Jeff C. *Operation Iraqi Freedom* (4–6). Illus. Series: U.S. Wars. 2003, Enslow LB $19.95 (0-7660-5088-2). 48pp. Supported by verified and updated Web links, this is a useful introduction to Operation Iraqi Freedom. (Rev: HBG 4/04)

18237 Zeinert, Karen. *The Valiant Women of the Vietnam War* (5–8). Illus. 2000, Millbrook LB $29.90 (0-7613-1268-4). 96pp. Provides a good overview of the Vietnam War and highlights the contributions of women at home and abroad during this conflict. (Rev: BL 4/1/00; HBG 10/00; SLJ 5/00) [959.704]

Regions

MIDWEST

18238 Anderson, Kathy P. *Illinois* (3–6). Illus. Series: Hello USA. 1993, Lerner LB $19.93 (0-8225-2723-5). 72pp. Presents the history and geography of this state, and includes biographies of famous native sons and daughters. (Rev: BL 1/15/93) [977.3]

18239 Anderson, Reuben. *Uniquely Oklahoma* (4–7). Illus. Series: Heinemann State Studies. 2004, Heinemann LB $21.95 (1-4034-4658-X). 48pp. In addition to providing the facts necessary for report writers, this volume emphasizes the features that distinguish Oklahoma from its neighbors.

18240 Anderson, Reuben. *Uniquely South Dakota* (4–7). Illus. Series: Heinemann State Studies. 2004, Heinemann LB $21.95 (1-4034-4662-8). 48pp. In addition to providing the facts necessary for report writers, this volume emphasizes the features that distinguish South Dakota from its neighbors.

18241 Armbruster, Ann. *Lake Huron* (2–4). Illus. Series: A True Book. 1996, Children's Book Pr. LB $22.00 (0-516-20012-7). 48pp. An overview of the formation of this lake and the early Indians who lived around it plus additional history and its current importance. Also use *Lake Michigan* and *Lake Superior* (both 1996). (Rev: SLJ 3/97) [917.709]

18242 Armbruster, Ann. *Lake Ontario* (2–4). Illus. Series: A True Book. 1996, Children's Book Pr. LB

$22.00 (0-516-20014-3). 48pp. A history of Lake Ontario, the role it has played in Canadian-American history, and its importance today. Also use *St. Lawrence Seaway* (1996). (Rev: SLJ 4/97) [917.704]

18243 Ash, Stephanie. *Uniquely Minnesota* (4–7). Series: Heinemann State Studies: Uniquely. 2004, Heinemann LB $27.07 (1-4034-4494-3). 48pp. In addition to providing the facts necessary for report writers, this volume emphasizes the features that distinguish Minnesota from its neighbors.

18244 Aylesworth, Thomas G., and Virginia L. Aylesworth. *Eastern Great Lakes: Indiana, Michigan, Ohio* (4–7). Illus. Series: State Reports. 1995, Chelsea $19.95 (0-7910-3409-7). 64pp. Information is given for each of the three states covered, including major cities, history, geography, and climate. (Rev: BL 3/15/92) [977]

18245 Badt, Karin Luisa. *The Mississippi Flood of 1993* (3–5). Illus. Series: Cornerstones of Freedom. 1994, Children's Book Pr. LB $20.50 (0-516-06680-3). 32pp. The causes and effects of this major modern disaster are traced with eyewitness reports. (Rev: BL 1/15/95) [977.033]

18246 Balcavage, Dynise. *Iowa* (5–8). Illus. Series: From Sea to Shining Sea, Second Series. 2002, Children's Book Pr. LB $29.50 (0-516-22481-6). 80pp. An attractive overview of Iowa's land, history, culture, economy, and people. (Rev: SLJ 3/03) [977.7]

18247 Baldwin, Guy. *Oklahoma* (4–8). Series: Celebrate the States. 2000, Marshall Cavendish LB $142.57 (0-7614-1061-9). 144pp. The beauties and hidden treasures of Oklahoma are covered in this colorful introduction to the state, its past, its present, and its people. (Rev: BL 12/15/00) [976.6]

18248 Bennett, Michelle. *Missouri* (4–8). Series: Celebrate the States. 2001, Benchmark LB $35.64 (0-7614-1063-5). 144pp. A logically organized, thorough introduction to Missouri with material on such topics as history, people, landmarks, and famous natives. (Rev: BL 9/15/01; HBG 10/01) [977.8]

18249 Bjorkland, Ruth. *Kansas* (4–8). Series: Celebrate the States. 2000, Marshall Cavendish LB $35.64 (0-7614-0646-8). 143pp. A broad introduction to Kansas — its geography and history, its government and people, its songs and folktales, and a few of its recipes. (Rev: BL 6/1–15/00; HBG 10/00) [978.1]

18250 Blashfield, Jean F. *Wisconsin* (5–8). Series: America the Beautiful. 1998, Children's Book Pr. LB $34.00 (0-516-20640-0). 144pp. Important facts about Wisconsin include its history, famous people, dates, places, and economy. (Rev: BL 1/1–15/99; SLJ 4/99) [977.5]

18251 Boekhoff, P. M., and Stuart A. Kallen. *Illinois* (4–7). Illus. Series: Seeds of a Nation. 2002, Gale LB $30.35 (0-7377-0279-6). 48pp. This is a compact history of the territory that would become Illinois, with fine coverage of Native American culture and history. (Rev: BL 4/1/02; SLJ 3/02) [977.3]

18252 Brandenburg, Jim. *An American Safari: Adventures on the North American Prairie* (4–6).

Illus. 1995, Walker LB $17.85 (0-8027-8320-1). 48pp. This American photographer describes in words and pictures the western prairies and the animals that live there. (Rev: BCCB 6/95; BL 4/15/95; SLJ 8/95) [508.73]

18253 Bratvold, Gretchen. *Wisconsin* (3–6). Illus. Series: Hello USA. 1991, Lerner LB $19.93 (0-8225-2700-6). 72pp. An introduction to the dairy state, with full-color photos. (Rev: BL 4/15/91; SLJ 7/91) [977.5]

18254 Brill, Marlene T. *Illinois* (4–8). Illus. Series: Celebrate the States. 1996, Marshall Cavendish LB $35.64 (0-7614-0113-X). 144pp. Maps, diagrams, and photographs enliven this introduction to Illinois that gives good coverage of history, geography, and social conditions. (Rev: BL 2/1/97; SLJ 2/97) [913.73]

18255 Brill, Marlene T. *Indiana* (4–8). Illus. Series: Celebrate the States. 1997, Marshall Cavendish LB $35.64 (0-7614-0147-4). An introduction to this Midwest state's agriculture, industries, famous natives, history, and geography. (Rev: BL 7/97; SLJ 8/97) [977.2]

18256 Brown, Dottie. *Ohio* (3–6). Illus. Series: Hello USA. 1992, Lerner LB $19.93 (0-8225-2725-1). 72pp. Ohio, the nation's seventh-largest state, is described from the days of the Indians and settlers until today. (Rev: BL 11/15/92) [977.1]

18257 Butler, Dori Hillestad. *M Is for Minnesota* (3–5). Illus. by Janice L. Porter. 1998, Univ. of Minnesota $16.95 (0-8166-3041-0). 32pp. Using an A through Z approach, this picture book covers basic facts about Minnesota. (Rev: BL 1/1–15/99; HBG 3/99; SLJ 3/99) [977.6]

18258 Carlson, Jeffrey D. *A Historical Album of Minnesota* (5–8). Illus. Series: Historical Albums. 1993, Millbrook LB $24.40 (1-56294-006-6). 64pp. A heavily illustrated volume that traces the history of Minnesota from Native American communities through exploration and settlement to present-day concerns. (Rev: SLJ 10/93) [977.6]

18259 Curlee, Lynn. *Rushmore* (4–6). Illus. 1999, Scholastic $17.95 (0-590-22573-1). 49pp. A thorough examination of the creation of this monument in South Dakota, designed by Gutzon Borglum and completed by his son in 1941. (Rev: BCCB 3/99; BL 3/1/99; HB 3–4/99; HBG 10/99; SLJ 3/99) [730]

18260 Deady, Kathleen W. *Kansas Facts and Symbols* (1–4). Series: States and Their Symbols. 2000, Capstone LB $15.93 (0-7368-0638-5). 24pp. As well as state symbols, this book gives a map, a page of fast facts, and a list of places to visit. (Rev: BL 3/1/01) [978.1]

18261 Deinard, Jenny. *How to Draw Illinois' Sights and Symbols* (3–6). Illus. Series: Kid's Guide to Drawing America. 2002, Rosen LB $25.25 (0-8239-6069-2). 32pp. An eclectic mix of drawing exercises and basic facts about Illinois history, geography, demographics, and important features. Also use *How to Draw Missouri's Sights and Symbols* (2001). (Rev: BL 2/15/02; SLJ 7/02) [743]

18262 Doherty, Craig A., and Katherine M. Doherty. *The Gateway Arch* (3–6). Illus. Series: Building

America. 1995, Blackbirch LB $17.95 (1-56711-105-X). 48pp. A description of the construction and parts of this St. Louis landmark. (Rev: BL 9/15/95; SLJ 7/95) [725]

18263 Doherty, Craig A., and Katherine M. Doherty. *Mount Rushmore* (3–6). Illus. Series: Build America. 1995, Blackbirch LB $17.95 (1-56711-108-4). 48pp. The story of the planning through the execution of the four gigantic heads on Mount Rushmore and the controversy concerning taking the land from the Sioux. (Rev: BL 9/15/95; SLJ 7/95) [730]

18264 Doherty, Craig A., and Katherine M. Doherty. *The Sears Tower* (3–6). Illus. Series: Building America. 1995, Blackbirch LB $17.95 (1-56711-109-2). 48pp. The story of the design and construction of the world's tallest building and of some of the wonders found inside. (Rev: BL 9/15/95; SLJ 7/95) [725]

18265 Dornfeld, Margaret. *Wisconsin* (4–7). Series: It's My State! 2003, Marshall Cavendish LB $18.95 (0-7614-1524-6). 80pp. Using many quotations from various sources, this account supplies a basic introduction to Wisconsin, its people, and its past and present. (Rev: BL 9/15/03; HBG 4/04; SLJ 11/03) [977.5]

18266 Edge, Laura B. *A Personal Tour of Hull-House* (4–7). Series: How It Was. 2001, Lerner LB $25.26 (0-8225-3583-3). 64pp. A firsthand account of the settlement house founded in Chicago by Jane Addams. (Rev: BL 8/1/01) [977.3]

18267 Feeney, Kathy. *South Dakota Facts and Symbols* (1–4). Series: States and Their Symbols. 2000, Capstone LB $15.93 (0-7368-0646-6). 24pp. This short book uses double-page spreads to introduce South Dakota's major symbols including the state flower, flag, animal, tree, and seal. (Rev: BL 3/1/01) [978.3]

18268 Ford, Barbara. *Saint Louis* (3–5). Illus. Series: Downtown America. 1989, Macmillan LB $13.95 (0-87518-402-2). 64pp. This introduction includes history, geography, and places to visit. (Rev: BL 8/89; SLJ 11/89) [977.8]

18269 Fradin, Dennis B. *Illinois* (2–5). Illus. Series: From Sea to Shining Sea. 1991, Children's Book Pr. LB $27.00 (0-516-03813-3). 64pp. Many full-color photos add to the attractive coverage of this midwestern state. (Rev: BL 2/1/92) [977.3]

18270 Fradin, Dennis B. *Iowa* (3–5). Illus. Series: From Sea to Shining Sea. 1993, Children's Book Pr. LB $27.00 (0-516-03815-X). 64pp. This midwestern state is examined, with material on its history, geography, people, industries, and famous residents. (Rev: BL 11/1/93) [922.7]

18271 Fradin, Dennis B. *Michigan* (3–5). Illus. Series: From Sea to Shining Sea. 1992, Children's Book Pr. LB $27.00 (0-516-03822-2). 64pp. In addition to material on history and geography, this simple introduction includes a two-page Fact Sheet summary. (Rev: BL 5/1/92) [977.4]

18272 Fradin, Dennis B. *Missouri* (3–5). Illus. Series: From Sea to Shining Sea. 1994, Children's Book Pr. LB $27.00 (0-516-03825-7). 64pp. Some of the topics covered are Missouri's geography, his-

tory, and industries, plus a gallery of famous residents. (Rev: BL 8/94) [977.8]

18273 Fradin, Dennis B. *Ohio* (3–5). Illus. Series: From Sea to Shining Sea. 1993, Children's Book Pr. LB $27.00 (0-516-03835-4). 64pp. Ohio is covered through such topics as geography, history, industries, and cities. (Rev: BL 7/93) [977.1]

18274 Fredeen, Charles. *Kansas* (3–6). Illus. Series: Hello USA. 1992, Lerner LB $19.93 (0-8225-2716-2). 72pp. With excellent color illustrations, this account covers the state of Kansas and includes information on history, geography, and social and economic conditions. (Rev: BL 6/1/92) [978.1]

18275 Gibson, Karen Bush. *North Dakota Facts and Symbols* (1–4). Series: States and Their Symbols. 2000, Capstone LB $15.93 (0-7368-0642-3). 24pp. The flag, flower, seal, tree, bird, and animal that are the state symbols of North Dakota are presented in photographs and text. (Rev: BL 3/1/01) [978.4]

18276 Gibson, Karen Bush. *Oklahoma Facts and Symbols* (1–4). Series: States and Their Symbols. 2000, Capstone LB $15.93 (0-7368-0643-1). 24pp. A page of state facts and another of places to visit are included in this book that focuses on Oklahoma's state symbols, such as its flag, flower, seal, tree, and animal. (Rev: BL 3/1/01) [976.6]

18277 Hahn, Laura. *Mount Rushmore* (4–8). Illus. Series: American Symbols and Their Meanings. 2002, Mason Crest LB $18.95 (1-59084-027-5). 48pp. Hahn describes Gutzon Borglum's struggle to build his monument, with a helpful timeline and many illustrations. (Rev: SLJ 9/02) [730]

18278 Heinrichs, Ann. *Illinois* (3–6). Series: This Land Is Your Land. 2002, Compass Point LB $22.60 (0-7565-0313-2). 48pp. An overview of the geography, history, government, economy, people, and attractions of Illinois. (Rev: SLJ 2/03)

18279 Heinrichs, Ann. *Indiana* (5–8). Series: America the Beautiful. 2000, Children's Book Pr. LB $34.00 (0-516-21038-6). 144pp. Topics covered in this excellent introduction to Indiana include geography, history, government, economy, people, and places. (Rev: BL 5/15/00) [977]

18280 Heinrichs, Ann. *Michigan* (2–5). Illus. Series: This Land Is Your Land. 2003, Compass Point LB $22.60 (0-7565-0323-X). 48pp. For early researchers, this introduction to basic facts about the state and its history, geography, people, government, economy, and attractions includes plenty of photographs and maps. Also use *Ohio* (2003). (Rev: SLJ 7/03) [977.4]

18281 Heinrichs, Ann. *Minnesota* (2–5). Illus. Series: This Land Is Your Land. 2003, Compass Point LB $22.60 (0-7565-0315-9). 48pp. This brightly illustrated profile explores Minnesota's history, people, geography, government, economy, and attractions. Also use *Ohio* and *Wisconsin* (both 2003). (Rev: SLJ 7/03) [977.6]

18282 Heinrichs, Ann. *Ohio* (5–8). Series: America the Beautiful. 1999, Children's Book Pr. LB $34.00 (0-516-20995-7). 144pp. Clear writing plus many color illustrations and maps are used to cover a wide range of topics about Ohio, including history, geography, famous residents, cities, economy, and government. (Rev: BL 11/15/99) [977.1]

18283 Hintz, Martin. *Iowa* (5–8). Series: America the Beautiful. 2000, Children's Book Pr. LB $34.00 (0-516-21070-X). 144pp. This introduction to Iowa includes such topics as its history, government, celebrities, and sports teams. (Rev: BL 5/15/00) [977.8]

18284 Hintz, Martin. *Michigan* (4–6). Series: America the Beautiful. 1998, Children's Book Pr. LB $32.00 (0-516-20636-2). 144pp. A colorful introduction to Michigan, using many maps, photos, and sidebars. (Rev: BL 10/15/98; HBG 3/99) [977.4]

18285 Hintz, Martin. *Minnesota* (5–8). Series: America the Beautiful. 2000, Children's Book Pr. LB $34.00 (0-516-21040-8). 144pp. This revision of the standard work on Minnesota gives expanded coverage and includes a timeline, fact sheets, and extensive lists of outside resources. (Rev: BL 5/15/00) [977.6]

18286 Hintz, Martin. *Missouri* (5–8). Series: America the Beautiful. 1999, Children's Book Pr. LB $34.00 (0-516-20836-5). 144pp. This colorful introduction to Missouri covers such topics as geography, history, government, economy, famous personalities, people, and culture. (Rev: BL 11/15/99) [977.8]

18287 Hintz, Martin. *North Dakota* (5–8). Series: America the Beautiful. 2000, Children's Book Pr. LB $34.00 (0-516-21072-6). 144pp. An introduction to North Dakota that includes the economy, land, people, history, state symbols, and sports teams. (Rev: BL 11/15/00) [978.4]

18288 Jameson, W. C. *Buried Treasures of the Great Plains* (5–8). Series: Buried Treasure. 1997, August House $11.95 (0-87483-486-4). Stories of buried treasure are organized by the individual states of the Great Plains region. (Rev: BR 5–6/99; SLJ 7/97) [977]

18289 Kent, Deborah. *Iowa* (4–6). Illus. Series: America the Beautiful. 1991, Children's Book Pr. LB $29.40 (0-516-00461-1). 144pp. In addition to geography, history, and economics, this state profile includes special fact sections and a list of important people. (Rev: BL 7/91; SLJ 9/91) [977.8]

18290 Knapp, Ron. *North Dakota* (4–8). Series: MyReportLinks: States. 2003, Enslow/MyReportLinks.com LB $19.95 (0-7660-5119-6). 48pp. Covers the state's geography, history, people, and attractions and includes a number of links to related online resources. (Rev: HBG 4/04; SLJ 10/03) [978.4]

18291 Kule, Elaine. *Iowa Facts and Symbols* (1–4). Series: States and Their Symbols. 2000, Capstone LB $15.93 (0-7368-0637-7). 24pp. The state symbols of Iowa including its flower, flag, tree, bird, seal, and animal are presented in double-page spreads with a photo opposite a few lines of explanatory text. (Rev: BL 3/1/01) [977.7]

18292 LaDoux, Rita C. *Iowa* (3–6). Illus. Series: Hello USA. 1992, Lerner LB $19.93 (0-8225-2724-3). 72pp. This introduction to Iowa gives capsule biographies, a timeline, fact sheets, and chapters on

topics like history and geography. (Rev: BL 9/1/92) [977.7]

18293 LaDoux, Rita C. *Missouri* (3–6). Illus. Series: Hello USA. 1991, Lerner LB $19.93 (0-8225-2710-3). 72pp. With timelines, capsule biographies, many fact sheets, and the usual information, the state of Missouri is introduced. (Rev: BL 12/1/91) [977.8]

18294 LaDoux, Rita C. *Oklahoma* (3–6). Illus. Series: Hello USA. 1992, Lerner LB $19.93 (0-8225-2717-0). 72pp. Oklahoma is introduced with topics that include famous inhabitants, timelines, and fact sheets. (Rev: BL 6/1/92) [976.6]

18295 Ling, Bettina. *Wisconsin* (4–6). Series: From Sea to Shining Sea. 2002, Children's Book Pr. LB $29.50 (0-516-22380-1). The state of Wisconsin is introduced through a lively text, many color photographs, maps, a glossary, a timeline, and other attractive features. (Rev: BL 4/15/02) [977.5]

18296 Mader, Jan. *Michigan* (K–2). Series: Rookie Read-about Geography. 2003, Children's Pr. LB $19.00 (0-516-22736-X); paper $5.95 (0-516-27781-2). 31pp. A small-format, basic introduction to the state of Michigan suitable for beginning readers. (Rev: SLJ 10/03) [917.74]

18297 Martin, Michael A. *Ohio: The Buckeye State* (4–7). Series: World Almanac Library of the States. 2002, World Almanac LB $29.26 (0-8368-5124-2). 48pp. Facts, statistics, a pleasing layout, and color photographs make this a useful choice for report writers. Also use *Iowa: The Hawkeye State* (2002). (Rev: SLJ 9/02) [977.1]

18298 Masters, Nancy Robinson. *Kansas* (5–8). Series: America the Beautiful. 1999, Children's Book Pr. LB $34.00 (0-516-20993-0). 144pp. An introduction to Kansas that covers its history and government, geography and people, tourism and state symbols, culture, and celebrities. (Rev: BL 12/15/9) [978.1]

18299 Murphy, Jim. *The Great Fire* (5–9). 1995, Scholastic paper $17.95 (0-590-47267-4). A dramatic re-creation of the great Chicago fire that combines documents, personal accounts, illustrations, photographs, and street maps to give an in-depth view of the disaster. (Rev: BCCB 5/95; BL 6/1–15/95; HB 5–6/95, 9–10/95; SLJ 7/95) [977.3]

18300 Nobleman, Marc Tyler. *Chicago* (3–6). Series: Great Cities of the World. 2004, World Almanac LB $30.00 (0-8368-5036-X). 48pp. Chicago's history, geography, and economy are described, as are shopping and leisure attractions and the life of the city. (Rev: SLJ 4/05)

18301 Olien, Rebecca. *Kansas* (3–5). Illus. Series: Land of Liberty. 2003, Capstone LB $23.93 (0-7368-1584-8). 64pp. Bright illustrations — photographs, reproductions, charts, and maps — add to this overview of the state's geography, climate, history, people, lifestyle, economy, government, and flora and fauna. (Rev: SLJ 10/03) [978.1]

18302 Opat, Jamie Stockman. *Uniquely Nebraska* (4–7). Illus. Series: Heinemann State Studies. 2004, Heinemann LB $21.95 (1-4034-4649-0). 48pp. In addition to providing the facts necessary for report writers, this volume emphasizes the features that distinguish Nebraska from its neighbors.

18303 Pfeffer, Wendy. *The Big Flood* (K–3). Illus. by Vanessa Lubach. 2001, Millbrook LB $23.90 (0-7613-1653-1). 32pp. Young Patti describes the Mississippi flood of 1993 and the way the neighbors worked together to try to avert disaster. (Rev: BL 6/1–15/01; HBG 10/01; SLJ 10/01) [363.34]

18304 Pfeiffer, Christine. *Chicago* (3–6). Illus. 1989, Macmillan LB $17.95 (0-87518-385-9). 60pp. History and modern life in the great midwestern metropolis. (Rev: BL 3/15/89; SLJ 3/89)

18305 Porter, A. P. *Minnesota* (3–6). Illus. Series: Hello USA. 1992, Lerner LB $19.93 (0-8225-2718-9). 72pp. Fact sheets, timelines, and biographies of famous native sons and daughters are included in this introduction to Minnesota. (Rev: BL 6/1/92) [977.6]

18306 Porter, A. P. *Nebraska* (3–6). Illus. Series: Hello USA. 1991, Lerner LB $19.93 (0-8225-2708-1). 72pp. With information on the environment as well as on topics like population, industries, symbols, history, and geography, Nebraska is given good coverage. (Rev: BL 12/1/91) [978.2]

18307 Price-Groff, Claire. *Illinois* (3–6). Illus. Series: It's My State! 2002, Benchmark LB $18.95 (0-7614-1422-3). 80pp. The usual state information — geography, history, government, people, and economy — is presented in an appealing layout and with an activity. (Rev: BL 3/1/03; HBG 10/03; SLJ 2/03)

18308 Redmond, Jim, and D. J. Ross. *Uniquely North Dakota* (4–7). Series: Heinemann State Studies: Uniquely. 2004, Heinemann LB $18.95 (1-4034-4657-1). 48pp. In addition to providing the facts necessary for report writers, this volume emphasizes the features that distinguish North Dakota from its neighbors.

18309 Reedy, Jerry. *Oklahoma* (5–8). Series: America the Beautiful. 1998, Children's Pr. LB $34.00 (0-516-20639-7). Basic material on Oklahoma, plus a special reference section that includes key statistics, important dates, famous people, and maps. (Rev: BL 1/1–15/99; SLJ 2/99) [976.6]

18310 Ross, Jim, and Paul Myers, eds. *Dear Oklahoma City, Get Well Soon* (3–6). Illus. 1996, Walker LB $17.85 (0-8027-8437-2). 48pp. A sampling of the letters and drawings sent by children to victims of the 1995 bombing of the Oklahoma City Federal Building. (Rev: BCCB 6/96; BL 5/15/96; SLJ 5/96) [976.6]

18311 St. Antoine, Sara, ed. *Stories from Where We Live: The Great Lakes* (4–8). Illus. by Trudy Nicholson. 2003, Milkweed $19.95 (1-57131-639-6). 280pp. Fiction, poetry, journal entries, and essays celebrate the flora, fauna, topology, and traditions of the Great Lakes region. (Rev: BL 12/1/03; HBG 4/04) [810.8]

18312 St. Antoine, Sara, ed. *Stories from Where We Live: The Great North American Prairie* (4–8). 2001, Milkweed $19.95 (1-57131-630-2). 264pp. A collection of historical and contemporary stories, poems, essays, and journal entries about life on the prairie, with informative appendixes. (Rev: BL 5/15/01) [978]

18313 Santella, Andrew. *Illinois* (5–8). Illus. Series: America the Beautiful. 1998, Children's Book Pr. LB $34.00 (0-516-20633-8). 144pp. This comprehensive account of Illinois includes its history and geography, principal cities and important landmarks, and culture and people. (Rev: BL 1/1–15/99) [977.3]

18314 Schonberg, Lisa. *People of Ohio* (4–7). Illus. Series: Heinemann State Studies. 2003, Heinemann LB $27.07 (1-4034-0668-5). 48pp. Schonberg looks at groups of Ohioans from the original native peoples to later arrivals and at individuals who have contributed to all fields of endeavor, with many color photographs. (Rev: BL 10/15/03; HBG 4/04; SLJ 10/03) [305.8]

18315 Schonberg, Marcia. *Uniquely Ohio* (4–6). Illus. Series: Heinemann State Studies. 2003, Heinemann LB $27.07 (1-4034-0670-7). 48pp. Full of facts and figures about the people, places, and things that make Ohio "a one-of-a-kind place." (Rev: HBG 4/04; SLJ 10/03) [977.1]

18316 Schwabacher, Martin. *Minnesota* (4–7). Series: Celebrate the States. 1999, Benchmark LB $35.64 (0-7614-0658-1). 144pp. Minnesota is introduced in six chapters that cover history, geography, government and economy, people, achievements, and landmarks. (Rev: HBG 10/99; SLJ 10/99) [977.6]

18317 Sirvaitis, Karen. *Michigan* (3–5). Illus. Series: Hello USA. 1994, Lerner LB $19.93 (0-8225-2722-7). 72pp. With photos on every page, this account supplies a brief trip around Michigan plus historical information and material on resources, cities, and people. (Rev: BL 4/15/94) [977.4]

18318 Somervill, Barbara A. *Illinois* (4–6). Illus. Series: From Sea to Shining Sea. 2001, Children's Book Pr. LB $29.50 (0-516-22320-8). 80pp. A good resource for report writing, this book features historical facts, maps, and information about the governmental structure and the people of Illinois. (Rev: BL 3/15/02) [977.3]

18319 Steele, Christy Lee. *Uniquely Wisconsin* (4–7). Series: Heinemann State Studies: Uniquely. 2004, Heinemann LB $27.07 (1-4034-4499-4). 48pp. In addition to providing the facts necessary for report writers, this volume emphasizes the features that distinguish Wisconsin from its neighbors.

18320 Stein, R. Conrad. *Minnesota* (4–6). Illus. Series: America the Beautiful. 1990, Children's Book Pr. LB $28.00 (0-516-00469-7). 144pp. Historical and geographical coverage, plus a tour of important sites. (Rev: BL 1/1/91) [977.6]

18321 Sturm, Ellen. *Ohio* (3–5). Illus. Series: Land of Liberty. 2003, Capstone LB $23.93 (0-7368-1593-7). 64pp. Bright illustrations — photographs, reproductions, charts, and maps — add to this overview of the state's geography, climate, history, people, lifestyle, economy, government, and flora and fauna. (Rev: SLJ 10/03) [977.1]

18322 Sturman, Susan. *Kansas City* (3–5). Illus. Series: Downtown America. 1990, Macmillan LB

$13.95 (0-87518-432-4). 60pp. The history of Kansas City, Missouri, is covered, with data on sights and cultural life. (Rev: BL 6/1/90) [977.8]

18323 Verba, Joan M. *North Dakota* (2–6). Illus. Series: Hello USA. 1992, Lerner LB $19.93 (0-8225-2746-4). 72pp. This guide to the Flickertail State includes coverage of history, geography, and famous North Dakotans. (Rev: BL 12/15/92) [978.4]

18324 Wills, Charles A. *A Historical Album of Illinois* (4–8). Illus. Series: Historical Albums. 1994, Millbrook LB $24.40 (1-56294-482-7). 64pp. A brief history of Illinois that touches on the most important events from before the white man to the 1990s. (Rev: SLJ 3/95) [977.3]

18325 Wills, Charles A. *A Historical Album of Michigan* (4–7). Illus. Series: Historical Albums. 1996, Millbrook LB $24.40 (0-7613-0036-8). 64pp. Using many archival prints, drawings, photographs, and ample text, the history of Michigan is told. (Rev: BL 10/15/96) [977]

18326 Zimmerman, Chanda K. *Detroit* (3–5). Illus. Series: Downtown America. 1989, Macmillan LB $13.95 (0-87518-409-X). 64pp. Physical features and the history of Detroit are covered. (Rev: BL 8/89; SLJ 11/89) [977.4]

MOUNTAIN STATES

18327 Anderson, Bob. *Nevada* (3–6). Illus. Series: Seeds of a Nation. 2003, Gale/KidHaven LB $23.70 (0-7377-1564-2). 48pp. The history of Nevada is the focus of this brief overview that contains photographs, maps, and an appendix of facts about the modern state. (Rev: SLJ 10/03) [979.3]

18328 Ayer, Eleanor. *Colorado* (4–8). Illus. Series: Celebrate the States. 1997, Marshall Cavendish LB $35.64 (0-7614-0148-2). An introduction to the Centennial State, with information on its history, geography, and people. (Rev: BL 7/97; SLJ 8/97) [978.8]

18329 Ayres, Becky. *Salt Lake City* (3–5). Illus. Series: Downtown America. 1990, Macmillan LB $17.95 (0-87518-436-7). 60pp. Introduces Salt Lake City, its sights, sounds, and history. (Rev: BL 2/1/91) [979.2]

18330 Blashfield, Jean F. *Colorado* (5–8). Series: America the Beautiful. 1999, Children's Book Pr. LB $34.00 (0-516-20684-2). 144pp. A solid introduction to Colorado that contains the standard historical and geographical information plus state symbols, a government chart, about a dozen maps, and a historical timeline. (Rev: BL 11/15/99; HBG 10/99; SLJ 10/99) [978.8]

18331 Bledsoe, Sara. *Colorado* (3–6). Illus. Series: Hello USA. 1993, Lerner LB $19.93 (0-8225-2750-2). 72pp. A small volume that covers Colorado's history, geography, people, industries, and landmarks. (Rev: BL 12/1/93) [978.8]

18332 Bograd, Larry. *Uniquely Wyoming* (4–7). Illus. Series: Heinemann State Studies. 2004, Heinemann LB $21.95 (1-4034-4666-0). 48pp. In addition to providing the facts necessary for report writers,

this volume emphasizes the features that distinguish Wyoming from its neighbors.

18333 Doherty, Craig A., and Katherine M. Doherty. *Hoover Dam* (3–6). Illus. Series: Building America. 1995, Blackbirch LB $17.95 (1-56711-107-6). 48pp. Traces the construction of the Hoover Dam on the Colorado River, from its conception through its completion in 1936 to its present importance. (Rev: BL 9/15/95; SLJ 7/95) [627]

18334 Dubois, Muriel. *Wyoming: Facts and Symbols* (1–4). Series: The States and Their Symbols. 2000, Capstone LB $15.93 (0-7368-0529-X). 24pp. After a few easily read pages of basic facts about Wyoming, this account covers in double-page spreads such topics as the state seal, flag, flower, bird, and animal. (Rev: BL 6/1–15/00; HBG 10/00) [972.95]

18335 Dumas, Bianca, and D. J. Ross. *Uniquely Utah* (4–7). Series: Heinemann State Studies: Uniquely. 2004, Heinemann LB $18.95 (1-4034-4663-6). 48pp. In addition to providing the facts necessary for report writers, this volume emphasizes the features that distinguish Utah from its neighbors.

18336 Feeney, Kathy. *Utah: Facts and Symbols* (1–4). Illus. Series: States and Their Symbols. 2000, Capstone LB $15.93 (0-7368-0526-5). 24pp. This introduction to Utah uses a basic fact sheet followed by information on its state symbols. (Rev: BL 6/1–15/00; HBG 10/00; SLJ 10/00) [979.2]

18337 Feinstein, Stephen. *Utah* (4–8). Series: States. 2003, Enslow/MyReportLinks.com LB $19.95 (0-7660-5097-1). 48pp. A solid introduction to the information report writers need about Utah, with links to online resources. (Rev: HBG 4/04; SLJ 10/03) [979.2]

18338 Foster, Lynne. *Exploring the Grand Canyon: Adventures of Yesterday and Today* (3–6). Illus. by Margaret Sanfilippo. 1990, Grand Canyon Natural History Assn. paper $15.95 (0-938216-33-3). 150pp. This work gives a history of the Grand Canyon, the kinds of people who have been involved with it, and tips for the first-time visitor. (Rev: BL 9/1/90) [917]

18339 Fradin, Dennis B. *Colorado* (3–5). Illus. Series: From Sea to Shining Sea. 1993, Children's Book Pr. LB $27.00 (0-516-03806-0). 64pp. Maps, diagrams, and color photos on each page enliven this introduction to Colorado, its history, geography, landmarks, and people. (Rev: BL 11/1/93; SLJ 1/94) [978.8]

18340 Fradin, Dennis B. *Montana* (3–5). Illus. Series: From Sea to Shining Sea. 1992, Children's Book Pr. LB $27.00 (0-516-03826-5). 64pp. With many color photos, this introduction to Montana includes material on people, industries, and principal cities. (Rev: BL 5/1/92) [978.6]

18341 Fradin, Dennis B. *Utah* (3–5). Illus. Series: From Sea to Shining Sea. 1993, Children's Book Pr. LB $27.00 (0-516-03844-3). 64pp. Coverage includes history, geography, people, and famous places. (Rev: BL 7/93) [979.2]

18342 Fradin, Dennis B., and Judith B. Fradin. *Wyoming* (3–5). Illus. Series: From Sea to Shining Sea. 1994, Children's Book Pr. LB $27.00 (0-516-

03850-8). 64pp. An attractive presentation of the geography, history, and people of Wyoming, with maps, glossary, reference section, and thorough index. (Rev: BL 8/94) [978.7]

18343 Frisch, Carlienne. *Wyoming* (3–6). Illus. Series: Hello USA. 1994, Lerner LB $19.93 (0-8225-2736-7). 72pp. The famous sights and attractions of Wyoming are covered, along with its history, development, and people. (Rev: BL 4/15/94; SLJ 7/94) [978.7]

18344 George, Charles, and Linda George. *Idaho* (5–8). Series: America the Beautiful. 2000, Children's Book Pr. LB $34.00 (0-516-21037-8). 144pp. A fine introduction to Idaho that includes such topics as geography, history, government, landmarks, people, recreation, and culture. (Rev: BL 9/15/00) [978]

18345 George, Charles, and Linda George. *Montana* (5–8). Series: America the Beautiful. 2000, Children's Book Pr. LB $34.00 (0-516-21092-0). 144pp. A broad introduction to the state of Montana, including its history and geography, cities and landmarks, people, and economy. (Rev: BL 11/15/00) [978.6]

18346 Gibson, Karen Bush. *Nevada Facts and Symbols* (1–4). Series: States and Their Symbols. 2000, Capstone LB $15.93 (0-7368-0641-5). 24pp. Following a page of important state facts, this book uses color photos and a brief text to present Nevada's official symbols. (Rev: BL 3/1/01) [979.3]

18347 Graf, Mike. *Montana* (3–5). Illus. Series: Land of Liberty. 2003, Capstone LB $25.26 (0-7368-2184-8). 64pp. An accessible profile of Montana, covering its people, history, topography, climate, economy, and more, together with suggestions for further reading. (Rev: SLJ 3/04) [978.6]

18348 Halvorsen, Lisa. *Letters Home from Grand Canyon* (3–6). Series: Letters Home from Our National Parks. 2000, Blackbirch LB $16.95 (1-56711-463-6). 32pp. An interesting, first-person account of a visit to the Grand Canyon with material on land formations, animals, plants, and sights. Also use *Letters Home from Yosemite* (2000). (Rev: BL 5/15/00; HBG 10/00; SLJ 8/00) [979.1]

18349 Halvorsen, Lisa. *Letters Home from Zion* (2–5). Series: Letters Home From. 2000, Blackbirch LB $16.95 (1-56711-464-4). 32pp. Taking the format of letters to a friend back home, this book describes Zion National Park in Utah with its red cliffs and deep canyons. (Rev: HBG 3/01; SLJ 11/00) [979.2]

18350 Heinrichs, Ann. *Montana* (4–6). Illus. Series: America the Beautiful. 1991, Children's Book Pr. LB $28.00 (0-516-00472-7). 144pp. After an introduction to Montana, there is a special reference section that contains key facts. (Rev: BL 7/91) [978.8]

18351 Herda, D. J. *Environmental America: The Northwestern States* (4–7). Illus. Series: American Scene. 1991, Millbrook LB $22.40 (1-878841-10-6). 64pp. This account presents information on such topics as pollution, waste, logging, and the general condition of the environment in Idaho, Montana,

Oregon, Washington, and Wyoming. (Rev: BL 8/91; SLJ 7/91) [639.9]

18352 Kent, Deborah. *Utah* (5–8). Series: America the Beautiful. 2000, Children's Book Pr. LB $34.00 (0-516-21045-9). 144pp. A guide to this mountain state, covering all the basics plus information on sports, religion, celebrities, and the Indian tribes that lived there. (Rev: BL 5/15/00) [979.2]

18353 Kent, Deborah. *Wyoming* (5–8). Series: America the Beautiful. 2000, Children's Book Pr. LB $34.00 (0-516-21075-0). 144pp. An introduction to Wyoming, including its geography, history, government, economy, people, sports, and celebrities. (Rev: BL 9/15/00) [978.7]

18354 Kule, Elaine. *Idaho Facts and Symbols* (1–4). Series: States and Their Symbols. 2000, Capstone LB $15.93 (0-7368-0636-9). 24pp. This book presents a few basic facts about Idaho followed by double-page spreads that illustrate and describe this state's flag, bird, flower, seal, animal, and tree. (Rev: BL 3/1/01; HBG 10/01) [979.6]

18355 LaDoux, Rita C. *Montana* (3–6). Illus. Series: Hello USA. 1992, Lerner LB $19.93 (0-8225-2714-6). 72pp. In addition to standard introductory material, coverage includes timelines about Montana and biographies of famous residents. (Rev: BL 5/15/92; SLJ 7/92) [978.6]

18356 Lauber, Patricia. *Summer of Fire: Yellowstone 1988* (3–5). Illus. 1991, Orchard $19.95 (0-531-05943-X). 64pp. Striking photos dramatize the fires of 1988 and their aftermath in Yellowstone National Park. (Rev: BCCB 10/91; BL 9/1/91; HB 9–10/91*; SLJ 9/91) [581.5]

18357 Lillegard, Dee, and Wayne Stoker. *Nevada* (4–6). Illus. Series: America the Beautiful. 1990, Children's Book Pr. LB $28.00 (0-516-00474-3). 144pp. This introduction includes history, geography, life today, and statistics. (Rev: BL 1/1/91) [979.3]

18358 McCarthy, Betty. *Utah* (5–7). Illus. Series: America the Beautiful. 1989, Children's Book Pr. LB $28.00 (0-516-00490-5). 144pp. The story of Utah is told in pictures and text covering such topics as economy, history, geography, and recreation. (Rev: BL 1/1/90) [979.2]

18359 Mann, Elizabeth. *Hoover Dam* (3–6). Illus. by Alan Witschonke. Series: Wonders of the World. 2001, Mikaya $19.95 (1-931414-02-5). 48pp. The exciting story of Hoover Dam is presented in a well-designed package with personal anecdotes and an emphasis on the loss of life. (Rev: BL 12/1/01; HB 3–4/02; HBG 10/02; SLJ 12/01) [627]

18360 Maynard, Charles W. *The Rocky Mountains* (2–5). Series: Great Mountain Ranges of the World. 2004, Rosen LB $21.25 (0-8239-6926-6). 24pp. Full-page, full-color photographs grace each spread of this slim volume that introduces the geology, climate, plants, animals, economy, peoples, and exploration of the Rockies, with discussion of environmental issues. (Rev: SLJ 8/04) [917.8]

18361 Meister, Cari. *Grand Canyon* (2–4). Series: Going Places. 2000, ABDO LB $13.95 (1-57765-024-7). 24pp. This well-organized introduction to the Grand Canyon describes the geological formations and supplies material on the plants, animals, and interesting sights in the area. (Rev: HBG 10/00; SLJ 1/01) [917.91]

18362 Meister, Cari. *Yellowstone National Park* (2–4). Illus. Series: Going Places. 2000, ABDO $13.95 (1-57765-026-3). This tour of Yellowstone National Park includes material on history, its things to see and do, and the plants and animals. (Rev: HBG 10/00; SLJ 1/01) [917.8]

18363 Minor, Wendell. *Grand Canyon: Exploring a Natural Wonder* (4–8). Illus. 1998, Scholastic paper $16.95 (0-590-47968-7). In watercolors and lyrical text, the author presents a grand portrait of the Grand Canyon. (Rev: BL 9/15/98; BR 1–2/99; HBG 3/99; SLJ 8/98) [978.8]

18364 O'Connor, Rebecca K., and Dennis Myers. *Uniquely Nevada* (4–7). Illus. Series: Heinemann State Studies. 2004, Heinemann LB $21.95 (1-4034-4650-4). 48pp. In addition to providing the facts necessary for report writers, this volume emphasizes the features that distinguish Nevada from its neighbors.

18365 Petersen, David. *Bryce Canyon National Park* (2–3). Illus. Series: True Books. 1996, Children's Book Pr. LB $22.00 (0-516-20048-8). 48pp. A well-illustrated introduction to this national park and its amazing rock formations. Also use *Death Valley National Park* (1996). (Rev: SLJ 5/97) [917.91]

18366 Powell, John Wesley. *Conquering the Grand Canyon* (3–6). Series: In My Own Words. 2000, Marshall Cavendish LB $16.95 (0-7614-1013-9). 64pp. These excerpts from the writings of John Wesley Powell describe how he felt as the first white man to view the natural wonders of the Grand Canyon. (Rev: BL 3/1/01; HBG 3/01) [978]

18367 Sanders, Doug. *Idaho* (4–6). Illus. Series: It's My State! 2004, Benchmark LB $18.95 (0-7614-1824-5). 80pp. Idaho's geography, wildlife, history, people, government, and natural resources are all covered here, with material on key individuals and famous events. (Rev: SLJ 5/05)

18368 Sirvaitis, Karen. *Utah* (3–6). Illus. Series: Hello USA. 1991, Lerner LB $19.93 (0-8225-2707-3). 72pp. This introduction to Utah features color illustrations on each page, facts-at-a-glance sections, and a historical timeline. (Rev: BL 8/91; SLJ 2/92) [979.2]

18369 Spies, Karen B. *Denver* (3–5). Illus. 1988, Macmillan LB $17.95 (0-87518-386-7). 60pp. Living in Denver as described by a resident. (Rev: BL 1/15/89; SLJ 3/89)

18370 Staub, Frank. *Yellowstone's Cycle of Fire* (3–6). Illus. Series: Earth Watch. 1994, Carolrhoda LB $19.95 (0-87614-778-3). 48pp. The cycle of forest fires and later renewal in Yellowstone Park is described, with major coverage of the huge fire of 1988. (Rev: BL 2/1/94; SLJ 6/94) [574.5]

18371 Stefoff, Rebecca. *Idaho* (4–8). Series: Celebrate the States. 2000, Benchmark LB $35.64 (0-7614-0663-8). Interesting charts, graphs, and maps are used to illustrate such topics as the people, land,

history, and culture of Idaho. (Rev: BL 1/1–15/00; HBG 10/00) [978.8]

18372 Stefoff, Rebecca. *Nevada* (4–8). Series: Celebrate the States. 2001, Benchmark LB $35.64 (0-7614-1073-2). 144pp. This well-organized introduction to Nevada gives general information followed by a timeline and special material on tourist attractions, famous natives of Nevada, and local festivals. (Rev: BL 9/15/01; HBG 10/01) [979.3]

18373 Stefoff, Rebecca. *Utah* (4–8). Series: Celebrate the States. 2000, Marshall Cavendish LB $35.64 (0-7614-1064-3). 144pp. Utah's unique characteristics and places are highlighted in this account that also covers the state's history, geography, and government. (Rev: BL 12/15/00; HBG 3/01; SLJ 2/01) [979.2]

18374 Stein, R. Conrad. *Nevada* (5–8). Series: America the Beautiful. 2000, Children's Book Pr. LB $34.00 (0-516-21041-6). 144pp. A good introduction to Nevada's history and geography, economy, culture, people, sights, and entertainment. (Rev: BL 5/15/00) [979.3]

18375 Wills, Charles A. *A Historical Album of Colorado* (4–7). Illus. Series: Historical Albums. 1996, Millbrook $24.40 (1-56294-592-0); paper $6.95 (1-56294-858-X). 64pp. Using many old engravings and photographs, the history of Colorado is traced, beginning with its Native American population. (Rev: BL 7/96; SLJ 7/96) [978.8]

NORTHEAST

18376 Adams, Barbara J. *New York City* (3–5). Illus. 1988, Macmillan LB $13.95 (0-87518-384-0). 60pp. Explaining the unique character of this city in words and pictures. (Rev: BL 1/15/89; SLJ 5/89)

18377 Ashabranner, Brent. *Badge of Valor: The National Law Enforcement Officers Memorial* (5–8). Illus. 2000, Twenty-First Century LB $25.90 (0-7613-1522-5). 64pp. This history of the memorial, from the original proposal in the 1970s to its opening in 1991, also discusses what it stands for and reveals the heroic deeds of some important law enforcement officers. (Rev: BL 10/1/00; HBG 3/01; SLJ 1/01) [363.2]

18378 Ashabranner, Brent. *A Date with Destiny: The Women in Military Service for America Memorial* (5–8). Illus. 2000, Twenty-First Century LB $25.90 (0-7613-1472-5). 64pp. This book tells the story of the memorial outside Arlington National Cemetery that honors American women in the military and retells some of the stories of these servicewomen. (Rev: BL 2/1/00; HBG 10/00; SLJ 4/00) [355.1]

18379 Ashabranner, Brent. *No Better Hope: What the Lincoln Memorial Means to America* (4–8). Illus. Series: Great American Memorials. 2001, Twenty-First Century LB $25.90 (0-7613-1523-3). 64pp. As well as telling about Lincoln and his importance to the country, this volume describes the building of the memorial and the important events that have occurred on the site. (Rev: BL 3/1/01; HBG 10/01; SLJ 7/01) [975.3]

18380 Ashabranner, Brent. *On the Mall in Washington, D.C.: A Visit to America's Front Yard* (5–7).

Illus. by Jennifer Ashabranner. 2002, Twenty-First Century LB $23.90 (0-7613-2351-1). 64pp. An entertaining and informative tour of the National Mall in Washington, D.C. (Rev: BL 3/15/02; HBG 10/02; SLJ 4/02) [917.5304]

18381 Ashabranner, Brent. *Remembering Korea: The Korean War Veterans Memorial* (4–8). Illus. by Jennifer Ashabranner. Series: Great American Memorials. 2001, Twenty-First Century LB $25.90 (0-7613-2156-X). 64pp. Ashabranner explains who the memorial honors, how much it cost, and what it represents. (Rev: BL 9/15/01; HBG 3/02; SLJ 12/01) [951.904]

18382 Ashabranner, Brent. *The Washington Monument: A Beacon for America* (4–8). Illus. by Jennifer Ashabranner. Series: Great American Memorials. 2002, Millbrook LB $25.90 (0-7613-1524-1). 64pp. Ashabranner presents the story behind the monument, including its planning, design, and construction, with full-color photographs and black-and-white period reproductions. (Rev: BL 9/1/02; HBG 3/03; SLJ 11/02) [975.3]

18383 Avakian, Monique. *A Historical Album of Massachusetts* (4–8). Illus. Series: Historical Albums. 1994, Millbrook LB $24.40 (1-56294-481-9). 64pp. A history of Massachusetts that begins with the Native American culture and ends with the 1900s, including basic material on major events and personalities. (Rev: SLJ 2/95) [974.4]

18384 Avakian, Monique, and Carter Smith, III. *A Historical Album of New York* (5–8). Illus. Series: Historical Albums. 1993, Millbrook $24.40 (1-56294-005-8). 64pp. An overview of New York State history from Native American settlements to the present day, using extensive archival illustrations. (Rev: SLJ 10/93) [974.7]

18385 Aylesworth, Thomas G., and Virginia L. Aylesworth. *Upper Atlantic: New Jersey, New York* (3–8). Illus. 1995, Chelsea LB $19.95 (0-7910-3399-6); paper $9.95 (0-7910-3417-8). 64pp. Encyclopedia-like coverage of New York and New Jersey. (Rev: BL 9/1/87; SLJ 11/87)

18386 Balcer, Bernadette, and Fran O'Byrne-Pelham. *Philadelphia* (3–6). Illus. 1989, Macmillan LB $17.95 (0-87518-388-3). 60pp. All aspects of the old city's history, as well as modern living, are discussed. (Rev: BL 3/15/89; SLJ 3/89)

18387 Barenblat, Rachel. *Massachusetts: The Bay State* (4–7). Series: World Almanac Library of the States. 2002, World Almanac LB $29.26 (0-8368-5123-4). 48pp. History, politics, government, culture, and state symbols are all covered, with charts, maps, photographs, biographical sketches, and a list of important events and attractions. (Rev: SLJ 6/02) [974.4]

18388 Benson, Laura Lee. *Washington, D.C.: A Scrapbook* (2–6). Illus. by Iris Van Rynbach. 1999, Charlesbridge LB $15.95 (0-88106-064-X); paper $6.95 (0-88106-063-1). A young African American student records a class trip to Washington, D.C., where he uses the subway line and visits such landmarks as the White House and the National Zoo. (Rev: HBG 3/00; SLJ 11/99) [975.3]

18389 Bial, Raymond. *Tenement: Immigrant Life on the Lower East Side* (5–8). Illus. 2002, Houghton Mifflin $16.00 (0-618-13849-8). 48pp. Historic photographs complement the simple, descriptive text about life in New York City tenement housing in the late 1800s and early 1900s. (Rev: BL 10/15/02; HB 11–12/02; HBG 3/03; SLJ 9/02) [307.76]

18390 Blashfield, Jean F. *Delaware* (5–8). Series: America the Beautiful. 2000, Children's Book Pr. LB $34.00 (0-516-21090-4). 144pp. Delaware's geography and history are explored in this attractive volume, which also discusses its culture, people, and lifestyle. (Rev: BL 11/15/00) [975.1]

18391 Braithwaite, Jill. *The Statue of Liberty* (K–2). Series: Pull Ahead Books. 2003, Lerner LB $22.60 (0-8225-3802-4); paper $5.95 (0-8225-3756-7). 32pp. For beginning report writers, this is a simple, well-illustrated look at the statue and its symbolism. (Rev: SLJ 1/04) [974.7]

18392 Britton, Tamara L. *The Pentagon* (3–5). Series: Symbols, Landmarks, and Monuments. 2003, ABDO LB $14.95 (1-57765-849-3). 32pp. A brief history of the vast headquarters of the U.S. Department of Defense, covering the terrorist attack of September 11, 2001. (Rev: HBG 10/03; SLJ 10/03) [355.6]

18393 Britton, Tamara L. *The Smithsonian Institution* (3–5). Series: Symbols, Landmarks, and Monuments. 2004, ABDO LB $15.95 (1-59197-521-2). 32pp. An introduction to the history and contemporary importance of the museums that make up this venerable establishment. (Rev: SLJ 11/04) [069]

18394 Britton, Tamara L. *The Vietnam Veterans Memorial* (3–5). Series: Symbols, Landmarks, and Monuments. 2004, ABDO LB $15.95 (1-59197-523-9). 32pp. Explains the importance of this memorial and the story of its design. (Rev: SLJ 11/04) [975.3]

18395 Brown, Dottie. *Delaware* (3–6). Illus. Series: Hello USA. 1994, Lerner LB $19.93 (0-8225-2733-2). 72pp. A compact book that introduces Delaware's history, geography, resources, and famous people. (Rev: BL 4/15/94) [975.1]

18396 Brown, Dottie. *New Hampshire* (3–6). Illus. Series: Hello USA. 1993, Lerner LB $19.93 (0-8225-2730-8). 72pp. A brief, colorful introduction to New Hampshire that takes the reader on a tour of the state, covers its history, tells how the people live, and gives biographies of famous residents. (Rev: BL 12/1/93) [974.2]

18397 Burgan, Michael. *Connecticut* (4–7). Series: It's My State! 2003, Marshall Cavendish LB $18.95 (0-7614-1523-8). 80pp. This New England state is introduced with material on its people, geography, history, cities, products, and resources. (Rev: BL 9/15/03; HBG 4/04) [974.6]

18398 Climo, Shirley. *City! Washington, D.C.* (4–6). 1991, Macmillan LB $16.95 (0-02-719036-6). 64pp. An upbeat look at the nation's capital. (Rev: BL 8/91; SLJ 9/91) [917.5304]

18399 Cotter, Kristin. *New York* (3–5). Illus. Series: From Sea to Shining Sea, Second Series. 2002, Children's Book Pr. LB $29.50 (0-516-22485-9).

80pp. This revision of an earlier title adds information and features that will enhance its appeal to report writers. Also use *Connecticut* and *Delaware* (both 2002). (Rev: SLJ 1/03)

18400 Cowan, Mary Morton. *Timberrr: A History of Logging in New England* (5–8). Illus. 2003, Millbrook LB $25.90 (0-7613-1866-6). 96pp. Cowan highlights timber's historical importance in many walks of life — trade, politics, and construction, for example — and looks at changes brought by new technologies and the impact on ecology and the environment. (Rev: BL 11/15/03; HBG 4/04) [634.9]

18401 Curlee, Lynn. *Brooklyn Bridge* (3–6). Illus. 2001, Simon & Schuster $18.00 (0-689-83183-8). 40pp. The story of the construction of the Brooklyn Bridge with particular emphasis on the role played by the Roebling family. (Rev: BCCB 6/01; BL 4/15/01; HB 7–8/01; HBG 10/01; SLJ 5/01) [624]

18402 Curlee, Lynn. *Capital* (2–5). Illus. 2003, Simon & Schuster $17.95 (0-689-84947-8). 48pp. Stories of five important Washington, D.C., buildings portray much of American history. (Rev: BCCB 2/03; BL 1/1–15/03; HBG 10/03; SLJ 1/03) [975.3]

18403 Curlee, Lynn. *Liberty* (3–8). Illus. by author. 2000, Simon & Schuster $18.00 (0-689-82823-3). 41pp. This slim volume presents, in picture-book format, a history of the Statue of Liberty with material on its construction, its recent restoration, and what it symbolizes. (Rev: BCCB 5/00; HB 5–6/00; HBG 10/00; SLJ 5/00) [974.7]

18404 Cytron, Barry. *Fire! The Library Is Burning* (4–7). Illus. 1988, Lerner LB $15.93 (0-8225-0525-8). 56pp. How workers and volunteers helped to restore the Jewish Theological Seminary in New York City when it was nearly destroyed by fire. (Rev: BL 7/88; SLJ 9/88) [027.63]

18405 Degezelle, Terri. *Ellis Island* (K–2). Series: American Symbols. 2003, Capstone LB $19.93 (0-7368-2292-5). 24pp. A visit to Ellis Island in New York Harbor, the place of entry to the United States for millions of immigrants, with modern and archival photos. (Rev: SLJ 4/04) [304.8]

18406 Deinard, Jenny. *How to Draw Massachusetts's Sights and Symbols* (3–6). Series: Kid's Guide to Drawing America. 2001, Rosen LB $25.25 (0-8239-6077-3). As well as basic facts on key sights and symbols of Massachusetts, clear instructions are given on how to draw the state seal, flag, bird, and so forth. (Rev: BL 4/15/02; SLJ 7/02) [974.4]

18407 Doak, Robin. *New Jersey* (5–8). Illus. Series: Voices from Colonial America. 2005, National Geographic LB $32.90 (0-7922-6680-3). 112pp. A compelling account of life in early New Jersey, from its initial settlement by the Dutch through the adoption of the Constitution. (Rev: BL 6/1–15/05) [974.9]

18408 Doherty, Craig A., and Katherine M. Doherty. *The Statue of Liberty* (3–6). Illus. Series: Building America. 1996, Blackbirch LB $17.95 (1-56711-111-4). 48pp. The Statue of Liberty, from the origi-

nal idea to the finished sculpture. (Rev: BL 11/15/96; SLJ 1/97) [974.7]

18409 Dornfeld, Margaret. *Maine* (4–8). Series: Celebrate the States. 2001, Benchmark LB $35.64 (0-7614-1071-6). 144pp. An attractive, fact-filled introduction to the state of Maine with material on history, famous places and people, and current concerns. (Rev: BL 9/15/01; HBG 10/01) [974.1]

18410 Dubois, Muriel L. *New Hampshire: Facts and Symbols* (1–4). Illus. Series: States and Their Symbols. 2000, Capstone LB $15.93 (0-7368-0524-9). 24pp. A colorfully illustrated guide to New Hampshire that supplements basic facts with information on the state seal, motto, flag, bird, tree, flower, and animal. (Rev: BL 6/1–15/00; HBG 10/00) [974.2]

18411 Elish, Dan. *New York* (4–7). Illus. Series: My State. 2003, Marshall Cavendish $18.95 (0-7614-1419-3). 80pp. Color photographs accompany information on the state's topography, wildlife, climate, population, government, industries, and resources. (Rev: BL 3/1/03; HBG 10/03) [974.7]

18412 Elish, Dan. *Vermont* (4–8). Illus. Series: Celebrate the States. 1997, Marshall Cavendish LB $35.64 (0-7614-0146-6). An introduction to this New England state, including famous sights, history, and how the people live. (Rev: BL 7/97; SLJ 8/97) [974.3]

18413 Elish, Dan. *Washington, D.C.* (5–8). Series: Celebrate the States. 1998, Benchmark LB $35.64 (0-7614-0423-6). 144pp. An attractive introduction to the people and government of the U.S. capital with material on parks, landmarks, history, economics, and racial problems. (Rev: HBG 10/98; SLJ 1/99) [975.3]

18414 Engfer, LeeAnne. *Maine* (3–6). Illus. Series: Hello USA. 1991, Lerner LB $19.93 (0-8225-2701-4). 72pp. With many illustrations, this is a solid introduction to the New England state Maine. (Rev: BL 4/15/91; SLJ 6/91) [974.1]

18415 Feeney, Kathy. *Rhode Island Facts and Symbols* (1–4). Series: States and Their Symbols. 2000, Capstone LB $15.93 (0-7368-0645-8). 24pp. After a few basic facts about Rhode Island, most of this book's contents are devoted to photos and brief explanations of the state's flag, flower, seal, animal, and other symbols. (Rev: BL 3/1/01; HBG 10/01) [974.5]

18416 Feeney, Kathy. *Vermont Facts and Symbols* (1–4). Series: States and Their Symbols. 2000, Capstone LB $15.93 (0-7368-0647-4). 24pp. After a page of basic facts about Vermont, this book introduces, through photos and text, such state symbols as its flag, seal, flower, animal, tree, and bird. (Rev: BL 3/1/01) [974.3]

18417 Feeney, Kathy. *Washington, D.C. Facts and Symbols* (3–4). Series: States and Their Symbols. 2000, Capstone LB $15.93 (0-7368-0527-3). 24pp. A brief account of Washington, D.C., that includes material on the District's symbols including its seal and motto, bird, tree, flower, the national mall, and places to visit. (Rev: HBG 10/00; SLJ 10/00) [975.3]

18418 Fradin, Dennis B. *Maine* (3–5). Illus. Series: From Sea to Shining Sea. 1994, Children's Book Pr. LB $27.00 (0-516-03819-2). 64pp. In addition to providing standard geographical and historical information, this well-illustrated book contains a checklist of important information about Maine, a timeline, maps, and a glossary. (Rev: BL 8/94) [974.1]

18419 Fradin, Dennis B. *Massachusetts* (2–5). Illus. Series: From Sea to Shining Sea. 1991, Children's Book Pr. LB $27.00 (0-516-03821-4). 64pp. An attractive, informative package covering this New England state. (Rev: BL 2/1/92; SLJ 3/92) [974.4]

18420 Fradin, Dennis B. *New Hampshire* (3–5). Illus. Series: From Sea to Shining Sea. 1992, Children's Book Pr. LB $27.00 (0-516-03829-X). 64pp. This introduction to New Hampshire tells about its geography, early history, present status, and state symbols. (Rev: BL 1/15/93) [974.2]

18421 Fradin, Dennis B. *New Jersey* (3–5). Illus. Series: From Sea to Shining Sea. 1993, Children's Book Pr. LB $27.00 (0-516-03830-3). 64pp. A tour of the Garden State is included in this good introduction. (Rev: BL 7/93) [974.9]

18422 Fradin, Dennis B. *New York* (3–5). Illus. Series: From Sea to Shining Sea. 1993, Children's Book Pr. LB $27.00 (0-516-03832-X). 64pp. This account takes one on a tour of the state, highlighting landmarks and geography, with material on history, industries, and famous New Yorkers. (Rev: BL 11/1/93; SLJ 2/94) [974.7]

18423 Fradin, Dennis B. *Pennsylvania* (3–5). Illus. Series: From Sea to Shining Sea. 1994, Children's Book Pr. LB $27.00 (0-516-03838-9). 64pp. An attractive portrait of the past and present of Pennsylvania, with coverage of the people and how they work and play. (Rev: BL 8/94) [974.8]

18424 Fradin, Dennis B. *Vermont* (3–5). Illus. Series: From Sea to Shining Sea. 1993, Children's Book Pr. LB $27.00 (0-516-03845-1). 64pp. Many photographs and simple text introduce the New England state of Vermont. (Rev: BL 7/93) [974.3]

18425 Fradin, Dennis B. *Washington, D.C.* (3–5). Illus. Series: From Sea to Shining Sea. 1992, Children's Book Pr. LB $27.00 (0-516-03851-6). 64pp. This introduction to the nation's capital includes a fact summary and a guide to major monuments. (Rev: BL 5/1/92; SLJ 8/92) [975.3]

18426 Fredeen, Charles. *New Jersey* (3–6). Illus. Series: Hello USA. 1993, Lerner LB $19.93 (0-8225-2732-4). 72pp. The Garden State is introduced with color illustrations and informative text. (Rev: BL 7/93; SLJ 8/93) [974.9]

18427 Gibbons, Gail. *From Path to Highway: The Story of the Boston Post Road* (2–4). Illus. 1986, HarperCollins LB $14.89 (0-690-04514-X). 32pp. A picture-book history of the road used by early travelers and today's citizens when traveling between Boston and New York. (Rev: BCCB 6/86; BL 6/15/86; SLJ 9/86)

18428 Gleman, Amy. *Connecticut* (3–6). Illus. 1991, Lerner LB $19.93 (0-8225-2709-X). 72pp. In text and pictures, this book covers history, economics,

and interesting features and includes a timeline, maps, and charts. (Rev: BL 10/15/91) [974.6]

18429 Goldstein, Ernest. *The Statue of Abraham Lincoln: A Masterpiece by Daniel Chester French* (5–8). Series: Art Beyond Borders. 1998, Lerner LB $28.80 (0-8225-2067-2). 64pp. This book provides a detailed description of the Lincoln Memorial and an introduction to the life and accomplishments of its sculptor, Daniel Chester French. (Rev: SLJ 5/98) [975.3]

18430 Grace, Catherine O'Neill. *The White House: An Illustrated History* (4–8). Illus. 2003, Scholastic $19.95 (0-439-42971-4). 144pp. Plenty of photographs are featured in this attractive and detailed volume devoted to the building's history and its residents over the years, with profiles of the people who work there. (Rev: BL 12/1/03; HBG 4/04; SLJ 12/03) [975.3]

18431 Graham, Amy. *Maine* (4–7). Illus. Series: States. 2002, Enslow/MyReportLinks.com LB $19.95 (0-7660-5017-3). 48pp. This well-illustrated volume offers report writers basic information on the state's land, climate, economy, government, and history, plus recommendations of Web sites that will extend their knowledge. Also use *New York* (2002). (Rev: SLJ 9/02) [974.1]

18432 Gray, Susan H. *The White House* (2–4). Series: Our Nation. 2001, Compass Point LB $18.60 (0-7565-0145-8). 24pp. An introduction to the interior of the executive mansion. (Rev: SLJ 1/02) [975.3]

18433 Guzzetti, Paula. *The White House* (4–6). Illus. Series: Places in American History. 1995, Silver Burdett LB $14.95 (0-87518-650-5). 72pp. A tour of the White House and its history, with brief asides on some of its inhabitants and their effects on the building. (Rev: BL 2/15/96; SLJ 1/96) [975.3]

18434 Haas, Jessie. *Fire! My Parents' Story* (4–6). Illus. 1998, Greenwillow $15.00 (0-688-15203-1). 72pp. Told from the standpoint of an eight-year-old girl, this is the true story of how a fire destroyed a Vermont farm and how the family eventually rebuilt and returned to their property. (Rev: BCCB 3/98; BL 5/1/98; HBG 10/98; SLJ 5/98) [974.3]

18435 Hansen, Joyce, and Gary McGowan. *Breaking Ground, Breaking Silence: The Story of New York's African Burial Ground* (5–9). 1998, Holt $16.95 (0-8050-5012-4). 118pp. The story of the archaeologists' find in New York City — the African Burial Ground — that reveals the part that African Americans have played in the history of New York City, dating back to the Dutch settlers. (Rev: HBG 10/98; SLJ 5/98) [974.7]

18436 Heinrichs, Ann. *Pennsylvania* (2–5). Illus. Series: This Land Is Your Land. 2003, Compass Point LB $22.60 (0-7565-0320-5). 48pp. A brightly illustrated introduction to Pennsylvania's history, people, geography, government, economy, and attractions. (Rev: SLJ 8/03) [974.8]

18437 Heinrichs, Ann. *Pennsylvania* (5–8). Series: America the Beautiful. 2000, Children's Book Pr. LB $34.00 (0-516-20692-3). 144pp. A basic introduction to Pennsylvania that also covers such topics as state symbols, sports teams, and regional food. (Rev: BL 5/15/00) [975]

18438 Heinrichs, Ann. *Rhode Island* (4–6). Illus. Series: America the Beautiful. 1990, Children's Book Pr. LB $28.00 (0-516-00485-9). 144pp. This profile of tiny Rhode Island includes a chronology and map section. (Rev: BL 7/90) [974]

18439 Herda, D. J. *Environmental America: The Northeastern States* (4–7). Illus. Series: American Scene. 1991, Millbrook LB $22.40 (1-878841-06-8). 64pp. This volume discusses the condition of the environment and presents information on such topics as water and land pollution in the northeastern states. (Rev: BL 8/91; SLJ 7/91) [639.9]

18440 Herda, D. J. *Ethnic America: The Northeastern States* (5–7). Illus. Series: American Scene. 1991, Millbrook LB $22.40 (1-56294-014-7). 64pp. In this heavily illustrated account, the ethnic groups of the area, including Native Americans, are described and their accomplishments detailed. (Rev: BL 2/1/92; SLJ 2/92) [572.973]

18441 High, Linda O. *Under New York* (PS–3). Illus. by Robert Rayevsky. 2001, Holiday House $16.95 (0-8234-1551-1). 32pp. A richly illustrated picture book that takes the reader underground in New York City to a world of pipes, power lines, trains, and tunnels. (Rev: BL 3/1/01; HB 7–8/01; HBG 10/01) [974.7]

18442 Hochain, Serge. *Building Liberty: A Statue Is Born* (3–6). Trans. from French by Camilla Bozzoli. Illus. by author. 2004, National Geographic LB $25.90 (0-7922-6969-1). 46pp. The Statue of Liberty's story is told in four parts — design and construction, transportation across the Atlantic, fund-raising for the pedestal, and eventual erection — each involving a boy who plays a role. (Rev: SLJ 8/04) [974.7]

18443 Ingram, Scott. *Pennsylvania: The Keystone State* (4–7). Series: World Almanac Library of the States. 2002, World Almanac LB $29.26 (0-8368-5120-X). 48pp. Facts, statistics, a pleasing layout, and color photographs make this a useful choice for report writers. (Rev: SLJ 9/02) [974.8]

18444 Jacobs, William J. *Ellis Island* (4–6). Illus. 1990, Macmillan $17.00 (0-684-19171-7). 40pp. A well-written introduction to Ellis Island in the you-are-there style. (Rev: BCCB 5/90; BL 4/15/90; SLJ 6/90) [304.8]

18445 Jameson, W. C. *Buried Treasures of New England: Legends of Hidden Riches, Forgotten War Loots, and Lost Ship Treasures* (4–8). Series: Buried Treasure. 1997, August House $11.95 (0-87483-485-6). This account describes how these treasures were amassed and lost, and furnishes maps to indicate their general location. (Rev: BR 5–6/99; SLJ 10/97) [910.4]

18446 Johnston, Joyce. *Washington, D.C.* (3–6). Illus. Series: Hello USA. 1994, Lerner LB $19.93 (0-8225-2751-0). 72pp. This brief introduction to Washington, D.C., tells about its history, local government, landmarks, and daily life. (Rev: BL 2/1/94) [975.3]

18447 Kent, Deborah. *Delaware* (4–6). Illus. Series: America the Beautiful. 1991, Children's Book Pr. LB $28.00 (0-516-00454-9). 144pp. Material on history, geography, and economy, plus a tour of the state. (Rev: BL 6/1/91) [975.1]

18448 Kent, Deborah. *Maine* (5–8). Series: America the Beautiful. 1999, Children's Book Pr. LB $34.00 (0-516-20994-9). 144pp. A standard account of the history, geography, and people of Maine, with additional information on state symbols, famous personalities, annual events, and weather. (Rev: BL 11/15/99) [974.1]

18449 Knox, Barbara. *New Hampshire* (3–5). Illus. Series: Land of Liberty. 2003, Capstone LB $25.26 (0-7368-2187-2). 64pp. A trip to Mount Monadnock opens this survey of New Hampshire, which provides all the material needed for a state report. (Rev: SLJ 2/04) [974.2]

18450 Krementz, Jill. *A Visit to Washington, D.C.* (K–3). Illus. by author. 1987, Scholastic paper $5.95 (0-590-40583-7). 48pp. A six-year-old tells of his home town, the nation's capital city. (Rev: BL 5/15/87; HB 7–8/87; SLJ 5/87)

18451 Kule, Elaine. *Delaware Facts and Symbols* (1–4). Series: States and Their Symbols. 2000, Capstone LB $15.93 (0-7368-0635-0). 24pp. The flag, seal, bird, tree, flower, and animal that are the symbols of Delaware are presented in double-page spreads that consist of a full-page photograph opposite a few lines of simple text. (Rev: BL 3/1/01) [975.1]

18452 Leotta, Joan. *Massachusetts* (4–6). Series: From Sea to Shining Sea. 2001, Children's Book Pr. LB $29.50 (0-516-22486-7). As well as basic coverage on Massachusetts, this book includes interesting sidebars. (Rev: BL 4/15/02) [974.4]

18453 Levert, Suzanne. *Massachusetts* (4–8). Series: Celebrate the States. 2000, Benchmark LB $35.64 (0-7614-0666-2). A fine introduction to the people and places of the Bay State that also includes recipes, folktales, and songs. (Rev: BL 1/1–15/00; HBG 10/00; SLJ 5/00) [974.4]

18454 Locker, Thomas. *In Blue Mountains: An Artist's Return to America's First Wilderness* (4–8). Illus. by author. 2000, Bell Pond $18.00 (0-88010-471-6). This is a personal tour of New York's Hudson Valley with lyrical paintings and prose by the author-artist. (Rev: BL 7/00; SLJ 11/00) [974.7]

18455 Louis, Nancy. *Ground Zero* (4–7). Series: War on Terrorism. 2002, ABDO LB $16.95 (1-57765-675-1). 48pp. This heavily illustrated, factually accurate account describes the search, recovery, and cleanup that took place after September 11, 2001, in New York City. (Rev: BL 5/15/02) [974.7]

18456 McAuliffe, Emily. *Connecticut Facts and Symbols*. Rev. ed. (3–5). Illus. Series: The States and Their Symbols. 2003, Capstone LB $19.93 (0-7368-2237-2). 24pp. A brief, illustrated overview of facts about Connecticut such as the state's nickname, motto, flag, and other symbols. (Rev: SLJ 1/04) [974.6]

18457 McNair, Sylvia. *Connecticut* (5–8). Series: America the Beautiful. 1999, Children's Book Pr.

LB $34.00 (0-516-20832-2). 144pp. Color photographs and about a dozen maps are included in this survey of Connecticut that covers history, geography, economy, famous sights, recreation, and state symbols. (Rev: BL 11/15/99) [974.6]

18458 McNair, Sylvia. *Massachusetts* (5–8). Series: America the Beautiful. 1998, Children's Pr. LB $34.00 (0-516-20635-4). With a special reference section and a fine use of graphics, this book introduces the Bay State's history, geography, and important people. (Rev: BL 1/1–15/99; HBG 3/99) [974.4]

18459 McNair, Sylvia. *New Hampshire* (4–6). Illus. Series: America the Beautiful. 1991, Children's Book Pr. LB $28.00 (0-516-00475-1). 144pp. Topics such as history, geography, industry, and famous residents are covered. (Rev: BL 1/15/92) [972.95]

18460 McNair, Sylvia. *Rhode Island* (5–8). Series: America the Beautiful. 2000, Children's Book Pr. LB $34.00 (0-516-21043-2). 144pp. An accessible fund of knowledge is contained in this book on Rhode Island that gives well-organized, basic information on this tiny state, its past, its present, and its people. (Rev: BL 5/15/00) [974.5]

18461 Marcovitz, Hal. *The Liberty Bell* (4–8). Illus. Series: American Symbols and Their Meanings. 2002, Mason Crest LB $18.95 (1-59084-025-9). 48pp. The history and condition of the bell are presented through text, illustrations, and a useful timeline. Also use *The White House* (2002). (Rev: SLJ 9/02) [974.8]

18462 Marcus, Leonard S. *Storied City: A Children's Book Walking-Tour Guide to New York City* (4–9). 2003, Dutton paper $12.99 (0-525-46924-9). 154pp. This historical and geographic guide to tours of New York City that are based on children's literature features an eclectic mix of fiction, nonfiction, maps, illustrations, and trivia that will enhance the enjoyment of any visit. (Rev: BCCB 6/03; LMC 11–12/03; SLJ 7/03) [016.9747]

18463 Melman, Peter. *Uniquely New Hampshire* (4–7). Series: Heinemann State Studies: Uniquely. 2004, Heinemann LB $18.95 (1-4034-4651-2). 48pp. In addition to providing the facts necessary for report writers, this volume emphasizes the features that distinguish New Hampshire from its neighbors.

18464 Miller, Natalie. *The Statue of Liberty* (3–5). Illus. Series: Cornerstones of Freedom. 1992, Children's Book Pr. LB $20.50 (0-516-06655-2). 32pp. The story of the building of the Statue of Liberty and the place it has taken in American history. (Rev: BL 1/1/93; SLJ 1/93) [974.7]

18465 Monke, Ingrid. *Boston* (3–6). Illus. 1989, Macmillan LB $13.95 (0-87518-382-4). 60pp. History and modern living in the famous old city. (Rev: BL 3/15/89; SLJ 3/89)

18466 Moose, Katherine. *Uniquely Rhode Island* (4–7). Illus. Series: Heinemann State Studies. 2004, Heinemann LB $21.95 (1-4034-4660-1). 48pp. In addition to providing the facts necessary for report writers, this volume emphasizes the features that distinguish Rhode Island from its neighbors.

18467 Moose, Katherine B. *Uniquely Delaware* (4–7). Series: Heinemann State Studies: Uniquely. 2004, Heinemann LB $18.95 (1-4034-4644-X). 48pp. In addition to providing the facts necessary for report writers, this volume emphasizes the features that distinguish Delaware from its neighbors.

18468 Morgane, Wendy. *New Jersey* (4–8). Series: Celebrate the States. 2000, Benchmark LB $35.64 (0-7614-0673-5). This excellent introduction to New Jersey covers its history, land, government, economy, unique characteristics, and famous residents. (Rev: BL 1/1–15/00; HBG 10/00) [974.9]

18469 Nelson, Kristin L. *The Washington Monument* (K–2). Series: Pull Ahead Books. 2003, Lerner LB $22.60 (0-8225-0250-X); paper $5.95 (0-8225-3759-1). 32pp. For beginning report writers, this is a simple, well-illustrated look at the monument and its symbolism. (Rev: SLJ 1/04) [975.3]

18470 *New York*. Rev. ed. (3–5). Series: One Nation. 2002, Capstone LB $22.60 (0-7368-1256-3). 48pp. A chapter on New York City's subways introduces an overview of the state's geography, history, people, lifestyle, economy, and tourist attractions. (Rev: HBG 3/03; SLJ 4/03) [974.7]

18471 Pascoe, Elaine. *The Brooklyn Bridge* (4–6). Illus. Series: Building America. 1999, Blackbirch LB $17.95 (1-56711-173-4). 48pp. The story of the Brooklyn Bridge from the first proposals in 1811 to 1983 when it celebrated its 100th birthday. (Rev: BL 12/1/99; HBG 3/00; SLJ 2/00) [624]

18472 Pascoe, Elaine. *History Around You: A Unique Look at the Past, People, and Places of New York* (4–7). Illus. 2004, Gale/Blackbirch LB $26.20 (1-4103-0490-6). 80pp. Using a news-style format with maps, charts, and illustrations, Pascoe details the history of New York State and profiles famous individuals. (Rev: SLJ 3/05) [974.7]

18473 Peduzzi, Kelli. *Shaping a President: Sculpting for the Roosevelt Memorial* (3–6). Illus. 1997, Millbrook LB $22.40 (0-7613-0207-7); paper $9.95 (0-7613-0325-1). 48pp. This photoessay tells of the work of the sculptor Neil Estrin, who sculpted figures of Franklin, Eleanor, and their dog Fala, for the Roosevelt Memorial in Washington, D.C. (Rev: BL 12/1/97; HBG 3/98; SLJ 3/98) [730]

18474 Peters, Stephen. *Pennsylvania* (4–7). Series: Celebrate the States. 2000, Marshall Cavendish LB $35.64 (0-7614-0644-1). 144pp. An overview of the history, geography, and culture of Pennsylvania with additional material on state symbols, industry, the people, and the economy. (Rev: BL 6/1–15/00; SLJ 9/00) [974.8]

18475 Phillips, Margaret Coull. *Pennsylvania* (3–6). Illus. Series: Seeds of a Nation. 2003, Gale/KidHaven LB $23.70 (0-7377-1023-3). 48pp. The history of Pennsylvania is the focus of this brief overview that contains photographs, maps, and an appendix of facts about the modern state. (Rev: SLJ 10/03) [974.8]

18476 Quiri, Patricia R. *Ellis Island* (2–4). Series: True Books. 1998, Children's Book Pr. LB $21.00 (0-516-20622-2). 47pp. This account covers the history and purposes of Ellis Island and is enhanced by many archival and contemporary photographs. (Rev: HBG 10/98; SLJ 9/98) [974.7]

18477 Quiri, Patricia R. *The White House* (4–8). Series: First Books. 1996, Watts LB $22.00 (0-531-20221-6). A well-illustrated history of the White House, with a description of the exterior design and the rooms inside, interesting items such as the introduction of running water, and information about the families that have lived there. (Rev: BL 6/1–15/96; SLJ 8/96) [975.3]

18478 Raabe, Emily. *Uniquely Vermont* (4–7). Illus. Series: Heinemann State Studies. 2005, Heinemann LB $21.95 (1-4034-4664-4). 48pp. In addition to providing the facts necessary for report writers, this volume emphasizes the features that distinguish Vermont from its neighbors.

18479 Rau, Dana Meachen. *The Statue of Liberty* (2–4). Series: Our Nation. 2001, Compass Point LB $18.60 (0-7565-0143-1). 24pp. An introduction to the statue with information on its history, symbolism, and location. (Rev: SLJ 1/02) [974.7]

18480 Rebman, Renee C. *Life on Ellis Island* (5–8). Series: The Way People Live. 1999, Lucent LB $27.45 (1-56006-533-8). 95pp. With extensive use of firsthand accounts, this book relates the purpose of Ellis Island, the processing of immigrants, and the joys and hardships involved. (Rev: BL 10/15/99; HBG 10/00; SLJ 1/00) [325.1]

18481 Reef, Catherine. *The Lincoln Memorial* (3–6). Illus. Series: Places in American History. 1994, Dillon $14.95 (0-87518-624-6). 71pp. This guide to one of Washington's landmark buildings also touches on the importance of Lincoln, as well as supplying details on the planning and construction of the monument. (Rev: SLJ 8/94) [975.3]

18482 Reef, Catherine. *Washington, D.C.* (3–6). Illus. Series: Downtown America. 1989, Macmillan LB $13.95 (0-87518-411-1). 72pp. This introduction includes a "Fast Facts" section, maps, and a timeline. (Rev: BL 1/1/90; SLJ 4/90) [975.3]

18483 Ross, D. J. *Uniquely Maine* (4–7). Series: Heinemann State Studies: Uniquely. 2004, Heinemann LB $18.95 (1-4034-4655-5). 48pp. In addition to providing the facts necessary for report writers, this volume emphasizes the features that distinguish Maine from its neighbors.

18484 St. Antoine, Sara, ed. *The North Atlantic Coast* (5–8). Illus. Series: Stories from Where We Live. 2000, Milkweed $19.95 (1-57131-627-2). 280pp. This anthology presents stories, essays, folktales, journal entries, songs, and poems related to the north coast of the Atlantic Ocean from Newfoundland to Delaware. (Rev: BL 1/1–15/01) [974]

18485 Sanders, Mark. *The White House* (3–6). Series: American Government Today. 2000, Raintree LB $22.83 (0-7398-1791-4). 48pp. An account that gives a history of the White House, its construction and renovations, plus details on its rooms and offices. (Rev: HBG 10/00; SLJ 8/00) [975]

18486 Schnurnberger, Lynn. *Kids Love New York! The A-to-Z Resource Book* (4–8). Illus. 1990, Congdon & Weed paper $133.65 (0-312-92415-1).

224pp. A group of suggestions for various activities in New York City.

18487 Schomp, Virginia. *New York* (4–8). Illus. Series: Celebrate the States. 1996, Marshall Cavendish LB $37.07 (0-7614-0108-3). 144pp. The Empire State is introduced, with information on history, geography, people, landmarks, and distinguished New Yorkers. (Rev: BL 2/15/97; SLJ 2/97) [917.47]

18488 Schuman, Michael. *Delaware* (4–8). Series: Celebrate the States. 2000, Marshall Cavendish LB $35.64 (0-7614-0645-X). 139pp. Beginning with quotations about Delaware and its people, this account covers the basic topics plus information on folklore, food, and festivals. (Rev: BL 6/1–15/00; HBG 10/00) [975.1]

18489 Somervill, Barbara A. *Pennsylvania* (3–6). Illus. Series: From Sea to Shining Sea. 2003, Children's Pr. LB $29.50 (0-516-22388-7). 80pp. A photo-filled profile covering the state's geography, people, government, lifestyle, and attractions. (Rev: SLJ 8/03) [974.8]

18490 Steen, Sandra, and Susan Steen. *Independence Hall* (3–6). Illus. Series: Places in American History. 1994, Dillon LB $14.95 (0-87518-603-3). 71pp. This introduction to Philadelphia's famous landmark tells about its construction, historical importance, and present status, with material on the State House and the Liberty Bell. (Rev: SLJ 8/94) [974.8]

18491 Stein, R. Conrad. *New Hampshire* (5–8). Series: America the Beautiful. 2000, Children's Book Pr. LB $34.00 (0-516-21071-8). 144pp. A basic introduction to New Hampshire, including its people, history, geography, economy, government, and state symbols. (Rev: BL 11/15/00) [974.2]

18492 Stein, R. Conrad. *New Jersey* (5–8). Series: America the Beautiful. 1998, Children's Book Pr. LB $34.00 (0-516-20637-0). 144pp. Full-color graphics and a clear text highlight this introduction to New Jersey's history, geography, economy, people, and culture. (Rev: BL 1/1–15/99) [974.9]

18493 Stein, R. Conrad. *Washington, D.C.* (5–8). Series: America the Beautiful. 1999, Children's Book Pr. LB $34.00 (0-516-21046-7). 144pp. The District of Columbia is covered in text, color photographs, sidebars, maps, and a timeline, with material on its history, government, people, economy, sights, and related subjects. (Rev: BL 12/15/99) [975.3]

18494 Stewart, Mark. *All Around New Jersey: Regions and Resources* (4–7). Illus. Series: Heinemann State Studies. 2003, Heinemann LB $18.95 (1-4034-0672-3). 48pp. An introduction to New Jersey and its regions and resources, with colorful maps. Also in this series are *New Jersey: History*, *New Jersey: Native Peoples*, *New Jersey: Plants and Animals*, and *People of New Jersey* (all 2004).

18495 Sullivan, George. *How the White House Really Works* (5–8). Illus. 1990, Scholastic paper $3.95 (0-590-43403-9). Home, office, museum, and tourist attraction — how the White House operates. (Rev: BCCB 5/89; BL 5/15/89; HB 7–8/89) [975.3]

18496 Swain, Gwenyth. *Pennsylvania* (3–5). Illus. Series: Hello USA. 1994, Lerner LB $19.93 (0-

8225-2727-8). 72pp. After an introductory trip around Pennsylvania, this concise book covers its history, attractions, environment, and famous people. (Rev: BL 4/15/94; SLJ 8/94) [974.8]

18497 Tagliaferro, Linda. *Destination New York* (4–8). Series: Port Cities of North America. 1998, Lerner LB $23.93 (0-8225-2793-6). Written with a focus on New York's economic life and its handling of goods moving in and out of the port, this book also gives information on the city's history, geography, and daily life. (Rev: HBG 3/99; SLJ 1/99) [974.7]

18498 Thomas, Pamela. *Brooklyn Pops Up* (3–10). Illus. 2000, Simon & Schuster $19.95 (0-689-84019-5). This pop-up book takes you on a tour of this borough of New York City, including visits to Coney Island and the Brooklyn Museum. (Rev: BL 12/1/00; HBG 3/01) [917.47]

18499 Topper, Frank, and Charles A. Wills. *A Historical Album of New Jersey* (3–5). Illus. Series: Historical Album. 1995, Millbrook LB $23.40 (1-56294-505-X). 64pp. Beginning with the Native American culture and ending with the present day, the most important events and people in New Jersey history are touched on in a rapid overview. (Rev: SLJ 7/95) [974.9]

18500 Walsh, Frank. *New York City* (3–6). Series: Great Cities of the World. 2003, World Almanac LB $29.26 (0-8368-5025-4). 48pp. An overview of one of the world's most famous cities, with detail on its history, its economy, and what it's like to live there. (Rev: SLJ 3/04) [974.7]

18501 Warner, J. F. *Rhode Island* (3–6). Illus. Series: Hello USA. 1993, Lerner LB $19.93 (0-8225-2731-6). 72pp. In excellent color illustrations and informative text, Rhode Island and its history, geography, cities, and social and economic life are covered. (Rev: BL 1/15/93) [974]

18502 Warrick, Karen Clemens. *Independence National Historical Park* (5–8). Illus. Series: Virtual Field Trips. 2005, Enslow/MyReportLinks.com LB $25.26 (0-7660-5224-9). 48pp. A visit to Independence Park, using both print and related Web sites, that covers its historical importance, including Independence Hall and the Liberty Bell. (Rev: SLJ 5/05)

18503 Welsbacher, Anne. *New York* (3–4). Series: Checkerboard Geography. 1999, ABDO LB $14.95 (1-56239-891-1). 32pp. By focusing on the people, history, and geography of New York State, this simple book introduces the different regions and supplies such unusual facts as how Uncle Sam originated. (Rev: HBG 10/99; SLJ 8/99) [974.7]

18504 Whitcraft, Melissa. *The Hudson River* (4–7). Illus. Series: World of Water. 1999, Watts LB $24.00 (0-531-11739-1). 64pp. A handsome volume that traces the history of New York State's most important river and how it currently affects people's lives. (Rev: BL 1/1–15/00) [974.7]

18505 Wills, Charles A. *A Historical Album of Pennsylvania* (4–8). Series: Historical Albums. 1996, Millbrook LB $24.40 (1-56294-595-5). Beginning with its Native American origins and settlement by Europeans and the Quakers, this book traces the his-

tory of Pennsylvania from the First Continental Congress and the ratification of the United States Constitution, through the Battle of Gettysburg and President Lincoln's famous Gettysburg Address, and up to today. (Rev: BL 7/96; SLJ 7/96) [974.8]

18506 Yolen, Jane. *House, House* (3–6). Illus. 1998, Marshall Cavendish $15.95 (0-7614-5013-0). 32pp. Life in Hatfield, Massachusetts, in 1900 and 2000 is contrasted in a series of then-and-now photographs and explanatory text. (Rev: BL 5/15/98; HBG 10/98; SLJ 6/98) [974.4]

18507 Zschock, Martha, and Heather Zschock. *Journey Around New York from A to Z* (1–3). Illus. 2002, Commonwealth $17.95 (1-889833-32-0). 32pp. An alphabetical journey around New York that combines information on tourist attractions, history, neighborhoods, and public celebrations. (Rev: BL 6/1–15/02; SLJ 7/02) [917.47]

PACIFIC STATES

18508 Abbink, Emily. *Missions of the Monterey Bay Area* (4–7). Series: California Missions. 1996, Lerner LB $28.75 (0-8225-1928-3). 80pp. Covers the history of the missions at San Carlos Borromeo de Carmelo, San Juan Bautista, and Santa Cruz. (Rev: BL 2/15/97) [979.4]

18509 Altman, Linda J. *California* (4–8). Illus. Series: Celebrate the States. 1996, Marshall Cavendish LB $35.64 (0-7614-0111-3). A richly illustrated book that contains material on California's geography, history, economic life, contemporary challenges, society, contributions, and landmarks. (Rev: BL 2/1/97; SLJ 2/97) [979.4]

18510 Ancona, George. *Barrio: Jose's Neighborhood* (3–6). Illus. 1998, Harcourt $18.00 (0-15-201049-1). 48pp. A year in the life of San Francisco's Mission District as experienced by a Mexican American boy who loves to participate in all the festivities and activities of the community. (Rev: BL 12/1/98; HBG 3/99; SLJ 12/98) [979.4]

18511 Anderson, Dale. *The California Missions* (5–8). Series: Landmark Events in American History. 2003, World Almanac LB $26.60 (0-8368-5339-3). 48pp. The story of the California missions, how they were founded, their purposes, and their contributions to opening up this state. (Rev: BL 10/15/03; SLJ 1/03) [979.4]

18512 Ansary, Mir Tamim. *People of California* (4–7). Illus. Series: Heinemann State Studies. 2003, Heinemann LB $27.07 (1-4034-0342-2). 48pp. Ansary looks at groups of people who have settled in California and offers brief biographies of individuals who have contributed to all fields of endeavor, with many color photographs. (Rev: BL 10/15/03; HBG 4/04; SLJ 11/03) [305.8]

18513 Aylesworth, Thomas G., and Virginia L. Aylesworth. *The Pacific: California, Hawaii* (3–8). Illus. 1995, Chelsea LB $19.95 (0-7910-3407-0); paper $9.95 (0-7910-3425-9). 64pp. People and places are included in this study of the West. (Rev: BL 11/1/87; SLJ 11/95)

18514 Behrens, June. *Missions of the Central Coast* (4–7). Series: California Missions. 1996, Lerner LB

$28.75 (0-8225-1930-5). 80pp. The missions at Santa Barbara, Santa Ines, and La Purisima Concepción are discussed, with material on their history and importance. (Rev: BL 2/15/97) [979.4]

18515 Bjorklund, Ruth. *Alaska* (4–6). Illus. Series: It's My State! 2004, Benchmark LB $18.95 (0-7614-1823-7). 80pp. Alaska's geography, wildlife, history, people, government, and natural resources are all covered here, with material on key individuals and famous events. (Rev: SLJ 5/05) [979.8]

18516 Boekhoff, P. M., and Stuart A. Kallen. *California* (4–7). Illus. Series: Seeds of a Nation. 2002, Gale LB $30.35 (0-7377-0946-4). 48pp. The history of California before statehood is presented with material on Native Americans, missionaries, settlers, and prospectors. (Rev: BL 4/1/02) [979.4]

18517 Bowler, Sarah. *Father Junipero Serra and the California Missions* (4–6). Illus. Series: A Proud Heritage: The Hispanic Library. 2003, Child's World LB $28.50 (1-56766-175-0). 40pp. A balanced account of the building of the missions in California, with discussion of the impact on the Native Americans. (Rev: BL 10/15/03) [979.4]

18518 Bratvold, Gretchen. *Oregon* (3–6). Illus. Series: Hello USA. 1991, Lerner LB $19.93 (0-8225-2704-9). 72pp. Topics include geography; history; and social, economic, and environmental concerns, with full-color photos. (Rev: BL 4/15/91; SLJ 6/91) [979.5]

18519 Bredeson, Carmen. *Fire in Oakland, California: Billion-Dollar Blaze* (4–8). Series: American Disasters. 1999, Enslow LB $18.95 (0-7660-1220-4). 48pp. A high-interest book that tells of the terrible fire in Oakland and the massive destruction it caused. (Rev: BL 10/15/99; HBG 3/00) [976.8]

18520 Britton, Tamara L. *Pearl Harbor* (3–5). Series: Symbols, Landmarks, and Monuments. 2003, ABDO LB $14.95 (1-57765-851-5). 40pp. From the attack in 1941 to the USS Arizona Memorial, this volume provides information that will be useful to report writers. (Rev: HBG 10/03; SLJ 10/03) [940.54]

18521 Brower, Pauline. *Missions of the Inland Valleys* (4–7). Series: California Missions. 1996, Lerner LB $28.75 (0-8225-1929-1). 80pp. Examines four missions, including San Luis Obispo and San Miguel Arcangel, with material on their early history and their impact on the existing cultures. (Rev: BL 2/15/97) [979.4]

18522 Brown, Tricia. *Children of the Midnight Sun: Young Native Voices of Alaska* (4–7). Illus. 1998, Graphic Arts Center $16.95 (0-88240-500-4). 48pp. This illustrated book gives a fine introduction to various aspects of the Alaskan environment, describing the lives of eight preteens from different regions and ethnic backgrounds. (Rev: BL 7/98; HBG 10/98; SLJ 9/98) [979.8]

18523 Chippendale, Lisa A. *The San Francisco Earthquake of 1906* (5–9). Series: Great Disasters: Reforms and Ramifications. 2000, Chelsea LB $19.95 (0-7910-5270-2). 120pp. An interesting account that focuses on the appropriateness of the responses to the disaster by the various authorities

and the lessons learned. (Rev: BL 4/15/01; HBG 10/01; SLJ 6/01)

18524 Corral, Kimberly. *A Child's Glacier Bay* (4–8). Illus. 1998, Graphic Arts Center $15.95 (0-88240-503-9). A photoessay chronicling a three-week kayak trip in Alaska's Glacier Bay, told from the perspective of a 13-year-old girl. (Rev: BL 7/98; HBG 10/98; SLJ 8/98) [978.652]

18525 Covert, Kim. *Washington* (3–5). Illus. Series: Land of Liberty. 2003, Capstone LB $25.26 (0-7368-2203-8). 64pp. A profile of the state of Washington, covering everything from climate and topography to people and economy, with fast facts, a recipe, and other useful material at the end. (Rev: SLJ 3/04) [979.7]

18526 Crewe, Sabrina. *Los Angeles* (4–6). Series: Great Cities of the World. 2004, World Almanac LB $29.26 (0-8368-5029-7). 48pp. Report writers will find useful information on Los Angeles's history, culture, lifestyle, and current problems such as traffic congestion, smog, and water shortages. (Rev: SLJ 7/04) [979.4]

18527 Doherty, Craig A., and Katherine M. Doherty. *The Golden Gate Bridge* (3–6). Illus. Series: Building America. 1995, Blackbirch LB $17.95 (1-56711-106-8). 48pp. From concept to completion, this is a thorough, engrossing description of the Golden Gate Bridge in San Francisco. (Rev: BL 9/15/95; SLJ 7/95) [624]

18528 Dubois, Muriel. *Alaska: Facts and Symbols* (1–4). Series: The States and Their Symbols. 2000, Capstone LB $15.93 (0-7368-0522-2). 24pp. An easily read introduction to Alaska that covers its history, geography, and major state symbols. (Rev: BL 6/1–15/00; HBG 10/00; SLJ 10/00) [979.8]

18529 Feeney, Stephanie. *Hawaii Is a Rainbow* (2–6). Illus. 1985, Univ. of Hawaii Pr. $12.95 (0-8248-1007-4). 64pp. Color photos present the people and land of Hawaii as they present the colors of the rainbow. (Rev: BL 2/1/85; SLJ 1/86)

18530 Fradin, Dennis B. *Alaska* (3–5). Illus. Series: From Sea to Shining Sea. 1993, Children's Book Pr. LB $27.00 (0-516-03802-8). 64pp. With color photos on each page, this attractive account supplies basic information about Alaska, its past and present, and unusual facts that make it unique. (Rev: BL 3/1/94) [979.8]

18531 Fradin, Dennis B. *California* (3–5). Illus. Series: From Sea to Shining Sea. 1992, Children's Book Pr. LB $27.00 (0-516-03805-2). 64pp. History, geography, famous names, and a chronology are presented in this introduction to California. (Rev: BL 2/1/93; SLJ 4/93) [976.8]

18532 Fradin, Dennis B. *Hawaii* (3–5). Illus. Series: From Sea to Shining Sea. 1994, Children's Book Pr. LB $27.00 (0-516-03811-7). 64pp. Among the topics covered in this introduction to Hawaii are its natural wonders, economy, history, and people. (Rev: BL 8/94; SLJ 11/94) [996.9]

18533 Fradin, Dennis B., and Judith B. Fradin. *Oregon* (3–5). Illus. Series: From Sea to Shining Sea. 1995, Children's Book Pr. LB $27.00 (0-516-03837-0). 64pp. This guide to the Beaver State presents Oregon's geography, history, climate, wildlife, history, and people. (Rev: SLJ 8/95) [917.95]

18534 Fremon, David K. *The Alaska Purchase in American History* (5–8). Series: In American History. 1999, Enslow LB $19.95 (0-7660-1138-0). 128pp. This account covers both the purchase of Alaska in 1867 and an early history of the Native Americans who lived there. (Rev: BL 11/15/99; HBG 3/00; SLJ 3/00) [979.8]

18535 Goh, Geok Yian. *Uniquely Hawaii* (4–7). Illus. Series: Heinemann State Studies. 2004, Heinemann LB $21.95 (1-4034-4645-8). 48pp. In addition to providing the facts necessary for report writers, this volume emphasizes the features that make Hawaii unique.

18536 Goldberg, Jake. *Hawaii* (5–8). Series: Celebrate the States. 1998, Benchmark LB $35.64 (0-7614-0203-9). 144pp. Using fine illustrations, fact boxes, graphs, and maps, this attractive book gives an excellent introduction to Hawaii, with the added bonus of a recipe and two songs. (Rev: HBG 10/98; SLJ 1/99) [996.9]

18537 Grabowski, John, and Patricia Grabowski. *The Northwest: Alaska, Idaho, Oregon, Washington* (3–6). Series: State Reports. 1995, Chelsea LB $19.95 (0-7910-3406-2); paper $9.95 (0-7910-3424-0). 64pp. History, geography, state symbols, capitals, principal cities, and places to visit are some of the topics covered in this introduction to these four states. (Rev: SLJ 9/92) [978]

18538 Green, Carl R. *The Mission Trails in American History* (5–8). Series: In American History. 2001, Enslow LB $20.95 (0-7660-1349-9). 128pp. Green traces the creation of these routes, the reasons for building the missions, and the confrontations between newcomers and the Native Americans. (Rev: BL 12/15/01; HBG 3/02; SLJ 3/02)

18539 Haddock, Patricia. *San Francisco* (3–6). Illus. 1989, Macmillan LB $17.95 (0-87518-383-2). 60pp. A close-up look at life in one of America's favorite cities. (Rev: BL 3/15/89)

18540 Halvorsen, Lisa. *Letters Home from Yosemite* (3–5). Series: Letters Home From. 2000, Blackbirch LB $16.95 (1-56711-462-8). 32pp. Using a letter format and captioned snapshots, this first-person account describes Yosemite National Park's attractions, history, wildlife, and conservation efforts. (Rev: BL 5/15/00; HBG 10/00; SLJ 8/00) [979.4]

18541 Harder, Dan, and Lawrence Migdale. *A Child's California* (2–4). Illus. 2000, Graphic Arts $15.95 (1-55868-520-0). 48pp. This introduction to California covers topics of particular interest to children and emphasizes the state's diversity and contrasts. (Rev: BL 2/1/01; SLJ 1/01) [917.94]

18542 Heinrichs, Ann. *California* (2–4). Illus. Series: This Land Is Your Land. 2002, Compass Point LB $22.60 (0-7565-0308-6). 48pp. Simple text with age-appropriate language and good illustrations introduce the history, geography, culture, famous people, and attractions of California. (Rev: SLJ 1/03)

18543 Heinrichs, Ann. *California* (5–8). Series: America the Beautiful. 1998, Children's Book Pr.

LB $34.00 (0-516-20631-1). 144pp. A fine introduction to California's history, geography, economy, arts, and recreation. (Rev: BL 1/1–15/99; HBG 3/99; SLJ 2/99) [979.4]

18544 Heinrichs, Ann. *The California Missions* (5–8). Series: We the People. 2002, Compass Point LB $27.15 (0-7565-0208-X). 48pp. An accessible, well-illustrated account of the creation of Spanish missions in California and the impact on the native peoples of the region. (Rev: SLJ 7/02) [979.402]

18545 Henry, Judy. *Uniquely Alaska* (4–7). Illus. Series: Heinemann State Studies. 2005, Heinemann LB $21.95 (1-4034-4642-3). 48pp. In addition to providing the facts necessary for report writers, this volume emphasizes the features that make Alaska unique.

18546 Hintz, Martin. *Hawaii* (5–8). Series: America the Beautiful. 1999, Children's Book Pr. LB $34.00 (0-516-20686-9). 144pp. An introduction to Hawaii — its land and people, its government and economy, its state symbols and famous sights. (Rev: BL 11/15/99; HBG 10/99) [996.9]

18547 Ingram, W. Scott. *Oregon* (5–8). Series: America the Beautiful. 2000, Children's Book Pr. LB $34.00 (0-516-20996-5). 144pp. An attractive guide to Oregon that is packed with facts about its history, geography, population, economy, culture, cities, and recreation. (Rev: BL 5/15/00) [979.5]

18548 Isaacs, Sally Senzell. *Life in San Francisco's Chinatown* (2–4). Illus. Series: Picture the Past. 2002, Heinemann LB $22.79 (1-58810-692-6). 32pp. A look at life in San Francisco for Chinese immigrants in the years from the Gold Rush through the early 20th century. (Rev: HBG 3/03; SLJ 3/03) [979.4]

18549 Jaskol, Julie, and Brian Lewis. *City of Angels* (3–6). Illus. 1999, Dutton $16.99 (0-525-46214-7). 48pp. A delightful introduction to 20 Los Angeles neighborhoods and their interesting sights. (Rev: BL 12/1/99; HBG 3/00; SLJ 12/99) [979.4]

18550 Johnston, Joyce. *Alaska* (3–6). Illus. Series: Hello USA. 1994, Lerner LB $19.93 (0-8225-2735-9). 72pp. This introduction to Alaska features a trip around the state, historical information, and material on the life-styles of its people. (Rev: BL 4/15/94; SLJ 8/94) [979.8]

18551 Kennedy, Teresa. *California* (4–6). Series: From Sea to Shining Sea. 2001, Children's Book Pr. LB $29.50 (0-516-22309-7). This attractive, oversize volume includes material on the land, history, people, and lifestyle of California. (Rev: BL 4/15/02) [979.4]

18552 Kimmel, Elizabeth C. *Balto and the Great Race* (3–5). Illus. 1999, Random LB $11.99 (0-679-99198-0); paper $3.99 (0-679-89198-6). 112pp. The true story set of a dog team, led by a Siberian husky, that delivered medicine to sick children in Alaska in 1925. (Rev: BL 10/15/99; HBG 10/00; SLJ 3/00) [636.73]

18553 Lemke, Nancy. *Missions of the Southern Coast* (4–7). Illus. Series: California Missions. 1996, Lerner LB $28.75 (0-8225-1925-9). 80pp. The three missions described here are San Diego de

Alcala, San Luis Rey de Francia, and San Juan Capistrano. (Rev: BL 9/15/96; SLJ 8/96) [979.4]

18554 Levi, Steven C. *Cowboys of the Sky: The Story of Alaska's Bush Pilots* (5–9). Illus. 1996, Walker LB $18.85 (0-8027-8332-5). The exciting life of the people who deliver medical supplies, mail, and passengers to remote areas in Alaska is vividly re-created. (Rev: BL 6/1–15/96; BR 9–10/96; SLJ 7/96) [629.13]

18555 Levinson, Nancy Smiler. *Death Valley: A Day in the Desert* (2–3). Illus. by Diane D. Hearn. 2001, Holiday House $14.95 (0-8234-1566-X). 32pp. In this easily read book, Death Valley and its plants and animals are introduced with excellent drawings. (Rev: BL 4/15/01; HBG 10/01; SLJ 4/01) [508.794]

18556 McMillan, Bruce. *Salmon Summer* (K–3). Illus. 1998, Houghton Mifflin $16.00 (0-395-84544-0). 32pp. An outstanding photoessay about 9-year-old Alex, an Aleut boy, and his summer at his family's salmon fishing camp. (Rev: BCCB 5/98; BL 4/1/98; HB 5–6/98; HBG 10/98; SLJ 5/98) [639.2]

18557 MacMillan, Dianne. *Destination Los Angeles* (4–6). Illus. Series: Port Cities of North America. 1998, Lerner LB $23.93 (0-8225-2786-3). 80pp. Describes Los Angeles and its history but concentrates on the harbor, trade, and the cargo shipped in and out. (Rev: HBG 10/98; SLJ 3/98) [917.94]

18558 MacMillan, Dianne. *Missions of the Los Angeles Area* (4–7). Illus. Series: California Missions. 1996, Lerner LB $28.75 (0-8225-1927-5). 80pp. This volume gives a description and history of three missions: San Gabriel Arcangel, San Fernando Rey de España, and San Buenaventura. (Rev: BL 9/15/96; SLJ 8/96) [979.4]

18559 Markle, Sandra. *After the Spill: The Exxon Valdez Disaster Then and Now* (3–5). Illus. 1999, Walker $15.95 (0-8027-8610-3). 32pp. A photoessay that describes the oil spill and events through mid-1999 involving the cleanup. (Rev: BL 8/99; HBG 10/99; SLJ 9/99) [363.738]

18560 Miller, Debbie S. *Disappearing Lake: Nature's Magic in Denali National Park* (K–3). Illus. by Jon Van Zyle. 1997, Walker $15.95 (0-8027-8474-7). 32pp. The story of an area in Alaska's Denali National Park, which is transformed annually into a lake and then, as the waters recede, into a flowering meadow. (Rev: BCCB 2/97; BL 3/15/97; SLJ 4/97*) [508.798]

18561 Miller, Debbie S. *River of Life* (K–3). Illus. by Jon Van Zyle. 2000, Clarion $15.00 (0-395-96790-2). 32pp. Realistic oil paintings are used to illustrate this book that describes a year in the life of an Alaskan river and the wildlife surrounding it. (Rev: BL 3/15/00; HBG 10/00; SLJ 7/00) [577.6]

18562 Neri, P. J. *Hawaii* (3–6). Illus. Series: From Sea to Shining Sea, Second Series. 2003, Children's Pr. LB $29.50 (0-516-22383-6). 80pp. A revised, photo-filled introduction to the Aloha State's geography, history, people, culture, and economy. (Rev: SLJ 12/03) [919.6]

18563 Oberle, Joseph. *Anchorage* (3–5). Illus. Series: Downtown America. 1990, Macmillan LB $17.95 (0-87518-420-0). 60pp. The sights and sounds of Anchorage are captured, along with the city's colorful history and people. (Rev: BL 6/1/90; SLJ 11/90) [979]

18564 O'Connor, Karen. *San Diego* (3–5). Illus. Series: Downtown America. 1990, Macmillan LB $17.95 (0-87518-439-1). 60pp. In color photos and brief text, the city of San Diego, California, is introduced. (Rev: BL 2/1/91) [974.94]

18565 Oliver, Marilyn Tower. *Alcatraz Prison* (4–8). Series: In American History. 1998, Enslow LB $20.95 (0-89490-990-8). After years as first a settlement and then a fort and a lighthouse, the "Rock" became a military and federal prison. This is its history, including famous prisoners, escape attempts, and its evolution into a top tourist attraction. (Rev: HBG 3/99; SLJ 1/99) [979.4]

18566 Otfinoski, Steve. *Washington* (4–7). Series: It's My State! 2003, Marshall Cavendish LB $18.95 (0-7614-1522-X). 80pp. The state of Washington, its geography, history, people, and economic development are some of the topics covered in this introduction to this Pacific state. (Rev: BL 9/15/03; HBG 4/04) [979.9]

18567 Pelta, Kathy. *California* (3–5). Illus. Series: Hello USA. 1994, Lerner LB $19.93 (0-8225-2738-3). 72pp. This small book is crammed with basic information about California, including its history, famous attractions, and important residents. (Rev: BL 4/15/94) [979.4]

18568 Penisten, John. *Honolulu* (3–6). Illus. Series: Downtown America. 1989, Macmillan LB $12.95 (0-87518-416-2). 72pp. Included in this introduction are maps, a timeline, and lists of places to visit. (Rev: BL 1/1/90; SLJ 5/90) [996.9]

18569 Quasha, Jennifer. *How to Draw California's Sights and Symbols* (3–6). Illus. Series: Kid's Guide to Drawing America. 2002, Rosen LB $25.25 (0-8239-6059-5). 32pp. An eclectic mix of California history, geography, demographics, and state sights and symbols. (Rev: BL 2/15/02; SLJ 7/02) [743]

18570 Rice, Oliver D. *Lone Woman of Ghalas-Hat* (5–7). Illus. by Charles Zafuto. 1993, California Weekly LB $13.00 (0-936778-52-0); paper $6.00 (0-936778-51-2). 32pp. The true story of the Indian woman who lived alone on a California island for 18 years. This was the basis of *Island of the Blue Dolphins*. A reissue. [979.7]

18571 St. Antoine, Sara, ed. *Stories from Where We Live: The California Coast* (4–7). Illus. by Trudy Nicholson. 2001, Milkweed $19.95 (1-57131-631-0). 288pp. A compilation of poetry and prose focusing on the California coastal region and its plant and animal life. (Rev: BL 1/1–15/02; HBG 10/02) [979.4]

18572 Seibold, J. Otto, and Vivian Walsh. *Going to the Getty: A Book About the Getty Center in Los Angeles* (4–7). Illus. 1997, Getty Museum $16.95 (0-89236-493-9). 32pp. This introduction to the Getty Museum in Los Angeles is a patchwork of impressions, photographs, drawings, and reproductions of artworks. (Rev: BL 2/15/98; HBG 10/98) [708]

18573 Sherrow, Victoria. *The Exxon Valdez: Tragic Oil Spill* (4–8). Series: American Disasters. 1998, Enslow LB $18.95 (0-7660-1058-9). 48pp. The dramatic story of the *Exxon Valdez* oil spill and the damage it caused to the Alaskan coast and its wildlife. (Rev: BL 1/1–15/99; BR 5–6/99; HBG 3/99; SLJ 3/99) [979.8]

18574 Sherrow, Victoria. *San Francisco Earthquake, 1989: Death and Destruction* (4–8). Illus. Series: American Disasters. 1998, Enslow LB $18.95 (0-7660-1060-0). 48pp. This account of the San Francisco earthquake incorporates many eyewitness reports. (Rev: BL 1/1–15/99; HBG 3/99; SLJ 6/99) [363.34]

18575 Snelson, Karin. *Seattle* (3–5). Illus. Series: Downtown America. 1992, Macmillan LB $13.95 (0-87518-509-6). 64pp. This introduction to Seattle includes its history, ethnic life, and places to visit. (Rev: BL 6/1/92) [979.7]

18576 Staub, Frank. *Children of Hawaii* (4–6). Series: The World's Children. 1999, Carolrhoda $16.95 (1-57505-253-9). 48pp. Through enticing photographs of Hawaiian children, the reader learns about the history, geography, and culture of the 50th U.S. state. (Rev: BL 7/99; HBG 10/99) [996.9]

18577 Staub, Frank. *Children of the Tlingit* (3–6). Illus. Series: The World's Children. 1999, Carolrhoda LB $21.27 (1-57505-333-0). 48pp. A look at the daily life of several children who belong to the Tlingit people of southeastern Alaska. (Rev: BL 6/1–15/99; HBG 10/99; SLJ 10/99) [979.8]

18578 Stefoff, Rebecca. *Oregon* (4–8). Illus. Series: Celebrate the States. 1997, Marshall Cavendish LB $35.64 (0-7614-0145-8). 140pp. A look at life in this Pacific state, along with its history, famous sights, cities, and industries. (Rev: BL 7/97; SLJ 7/97) [917.95]

18579 Stein, R. Conrad. *Oregon* (4–6). Illus. Series: America the Beautiful. 1989, Children's Book Pr. LB $28.00 (0-516-00483-2). 144pp. The Pacific state of Oregon is highlighted, covering history, geography, famous people, and important sites. (Rev: BL 7/89) [979.5]

18580 Stepanchuk, Carol. *Exploring Chinatown* (4–8). Illus. by Leland Wong. 2002, Pacific View LB $22.95 (1-881896-25-0). 64pp. This "walk" through San Francisco's Chinatown explores the Chinese culture and customs, and offers historical facts as well as a few hands-on projects. (Rev: BL 8/02; SLJ 9/02) [305.8951073]

18581 Uschan, Michael V. *The California Gold Rush* (5–8). Series: Landmark Events in American History. 2003, World Almanac LB $26.60 (0-8368-5374-1). 48pp. An attractive account of the California gold rush, famous people involved, and its consequences. (Rev: BL 10/15/03) [979.4]

18582 Webster, Christine. *Washington* (3–6). Illus. Series: From Sea to Shining Sea. 2003, Children's Pr. LB $29.50 (0-516-22386-0). 80pp. This photo-filled overview provides all the information on the Pacific Northwest state that report writers need. (Rev: SLJ 9/03) [979.7]

18583 Whitcraft, Melissa. *Seward's Folly* (3–6). Series: Cornerstones of Freedom, Second Series. 2002, Children's Book Pr. LB $24.00 (0-516-22525-1). 48pp. An attractive account of the purchase of the Alaskan territory. (Rev: SLJ 12/02)

18584 White, Tekla N. *Missions of the San Francisco Bay Area* (4–7). Illus. Series: California Missions. 1996, Lerner LB $28.75 (0-8225-1926-7). 80pp. The history of five Spanish missions in the San Francisco Bay Area, including Santa Clara de Asis and San Rafael Arcangel. (Rev: BL 9/15/96; SLJ 8/96) [979.4]

18585 Wills, Charles A. *A Historical Album of California* (4–8). Illus. Series: Historical Albums. 1994, Millbrook LB $24.40 (1-56294-479-7). 64pp. A slim volume that covers the basic history of California, with material on major events and important personalities. (Rev: SLJ 3/95) [979.4]

18586 Wills, Charles A. *A Historical Album of Oregon* (4–8). Series: Historical Albums. 1995, Millbrook $24.40 (1-56294-594-7). A good, broad overview of Oregon's history and current political and economic situation, places to see, and other information, with many illustrations. (Rev: BL 12/15/95; SLJ 1/96) [979.5]

18587 Young, Robert. *A Personal Tour of La Purisima* (4–7). Series: How It Was. 1999, Lerner LB $30.35 (0-8225-3576-9). 64pp. A you-are-there visit to La Purisima — one of the 21 missions built by the Spanish in California — in which the reader experiences life in the mission as it was in 1820. (Rev: BL 6/1–15/99; HBG 10/99) [979.4]

SOUTH

18588 Alex, Nan. *North Carolina* (4–6). Series: From Sea to Shining Sea. 2001, Children's Book Pr. LB $29.50 (0-516-22487-5). An attractive, well-organized volume that introduces the land and people of North Carolina. Also use *Florida, Georgia, Kentucky,* and *Tennessee* (all 2001). (Rev: BL 4/15/02) [975.6]

18589 Altman, Linda Jacobs. *Arkansas* (4–8). Series: Celebrate the States. 2000, Benchmark LB $35.64 (0-7614-0672-7). An broad introduction to the culture, land, government, history, and unique characteristics of Arkansas, with emphasis on its inhabitants. (Rev: BL 1/1–15/00; HBG 10/00) [976.7]

18590 Aylesworth, Thomas G., and Virginia L. Aylesworth. *The Southeast: Georgia, Kentucky, Tennessee* (3–8). Illus. 1995, Chelsea LB $19.95 (0-7910-3411-9); paper $8.95 (0-7910-3429-1). 64pp. An inviting look at this region, with color photos and map. (Rev: BL 11/1/87; SLJ 11/87)

18591 Barrett, Tracy. *Kentucky* (4–7). Series: Celebrate the States. 1999, Benchmark LB $35.64 (0-7614-0657-3). 144pp. An attractive, concise introduction to Kentucky that covers geography, history, government and economy, people, achievements, and landmarks. (Rev: HBG 10/99; SLJ 10/99) [976.9]

18592 Barrett, Tracy. *Virginia* (4–8). Illus. Series: Celebrate the States. 1996, Marshall Cavendish LB $35.64 (0-7614-0110-5). An introduction to Virginia, including its history, culture, famous sites, and important Virginians. (Rev: BL 2/15/97; SLJ 6/97) [975.5]

18593 Bial, Raymond. *Cajun Home* (4–7). Illus. 1998, Houghton Mifflin $16.00 (0-395-86095-4). 48pp. This is the story of the people who left France to find freedom in Canada, only to be transported to Louisiana where they settled in the backwood swamp areas. (Rev: BL 3/15/98; HB 5–6/98; HBG 10/98; SLJ 5/98) [976.3]

18594 Blashfield, Jean F. *Virginia* (5–8). Series: America the Beautiful. 1999, Children's Book Pr. LB $34.00 (0-516-20831-4). 144pp. A solid account of the land and people of Virginia, with full-color maps, sidebars, a timeline, and a discussion of its state symbols. (Rev: BL 11/15/99) [975.5]

18595 Brown, Dottie. *Kentucky* (3–6). Illus. Series: Hello USA. 1992, Lerner LB $19.93 (0-8225-2715-4). 72pp. The visual beauty of the Bluegrass State is captured in text and pictures in this introductory volume. (Rev: BL 5/15/92; SLJ 7/92) [976.9]

18596 Burgan, Michael. *Maryland* (5–8). Series: America the Beautiful. 1999, Children's Book Pr. LB $34.00 (0-516-21039-4). 144pp. History and government, economy and population, famous sights, and annual events are only a few of the topics covered in this fine introduction to Maryland. (Rev: BL 11/15/99) [975]

18597 Chang, Perry. *Florida* (5–8). Series: Celebrate the States. 1998, Benchmark LB $35.64 (0-7614-0420-1). A fine introduction to the history, geography, people, landmarks, and government of Florida, with material on the cultural diversity of its people. (Rev: HBG 9/98; SLJ 1/99) [975.9]

18598 Cocke, William. *A Historical Album of Virginia* (4–8). Series: Historical Albums. 1995, Millbrook paper $6.95 (1-56294-856-3). A broad overview of Virginia's history, using many period prints and paintings, with equal space given to past and current events, and including general information on the state. (Rev: SLJ 1/96) [975.5]

18599 Coleman, Wim, and Pat Perrin. *Colonial Williamsburg* (5–8). Illus. Series: Virtual Field Trips. 2005, Enslow/MyReportLinks.com LB $25.26 (0-7660-5220-6). 48pp. A visit to Williamsburg, using both print and related Web sites, that covers its historical importance and its portrayal of colonial life. (Rev: SLJ 5/05)

18600 Cribben, Patrick. *Uniquely West Virginia* (4–7). Illus. Series: Heinemann State Studies. 2005, Heinemann LB $21.95 (1-4034-4665-2). 48pp. In addition to providing the facts necessary for report writers, this volume emphasizes the features that distinguish West Virginia from its neighbors.

18601 Davis, Lucile. *Alabama* (4–10). Series: America the Beautiful. 1999, Children's Book Pr. LB $32.00 (0-516-20683-4). 144pp. A well-organized, appealing introduction to Alabama, the land, its history, the people, and contemporary life. (Rev: HBG 3/00; SLJ 1/00) [976.1]

18602 Deady, Kathleen W. *Kentucky Facts and Symbols* (1–4). Series: States and Their Symbols. 2000, Capstone LB $15.93 (0-7368-0639-3). 24pp. A beginner's book that displays and describes Ken-

tucky's state flag, seal, bird, tree, flower, and animal. (Rev: BL 3/1/01; HBG 10/01) [976.9]

18603 Dubois, Muriel. *Maryland: Facts and Symbols* (1–4). Series: The States and Their Symbols. 2000, Capstone LB $15.93 (0-7368-0523-0). 24pp. An attractive and useful book that presents important social studies material on geography and history in addition to coverage of Maryland's state symbols. (Rev: BL 6/1–15/00; HBG 10/00) [975]

18604 Fazio, Wende. *West Virginia* (5–8). Series: America the Beautiful. 2000, Children's Book Pr. LB $34.00 (0-516-21074-2). 144pp. As well as the standard information on history, geography, and the people, this colorful introduction covers topics such as state symbols and famous West Virginians. (Rev: BL 5/15/00) [975.5]

18605 Feeney, Kathy. *Tennessee: Facts and Symbols* (1–4). Illus. Series: States and Their Symbols. 2000, Capstone LB $15.93 (0-7368-0525-7). 24pp. This basic account of Tennessee also includes a map and its state symbols. (Rev: BL 6/1–15/00; HBG 10/00) [976]

18606 Feeney, Kathy. *West Virginia: Facts and Symbols* (1–4). Series: The States and Their Symbols. 2000, Capstone LB $15.93 (0-7368-0528-1). 24pp. An easily read, basic introduction to West Virginia that also includes its state symbols. (Rev: BL 6/1–15/00; HBG 10/00) [975.4]

18607 Fischer, Marsha. *Miami* (3–5). Illus. Series: Downtown America. 1990, Macmillan LB $13.95 (0-87518-428-6). 60pp. This introduction to Miami includes a map, a historical timeline, and places to visit. (Rev: BL 6/1/90) [975.9]

18608 Fisher, Leonard Everett. *Monticello* (4–7). Illus. by author. 1988, Holiday House $18.95 (0-8234-0688-1). 64pp. Touring the famous home of the third president. (Rev: BCCB 6/88; BL 6/1/88; SLJ 6–7/88) [973.46]

18609 Fradin, Dennis B. *Alabama* (3–5). Illus. Series: From Sea to Shining Sea. 1993, Children's Book Pr. LB $27.00 (0-516-03801-X). 64pp. A good introduction to this southern state. (Rev: BL 7/93) [976.1]

18610 Fradin, Dennis B. *Georgia* (3–5). Illus. Series: From Sea to Shining Sea. 1991, Children's Book Pr. LB $27.00 (0-516-03810-9). 64pp. A simple, attractive look at geography, early history, and current status of this southern state. (Rev: BL 2/1/92) [975.8]

18611 Fradin, Dennis B. *Kentucky* (3–5). Illus. Series: From Sea to Shining Sea. 1993, Children's Book Pr. LB $27.00 (0-516-03817-6). 64pp. A fine introduction to the Bluegrass State. (Rev: BL 7/93) [976.9]

18612 Fradin, Dennis B. *North Carolina* (3–5). Illus. Series: From Sea to Shining Sea. 1992, Children's Book Pr. LB $27.00 (0-516-03833-8). 64pp. This introduction to North Carolina includes history, geography, and a trip through the state. (Rev: BL 5/1/92) [917.5]

18613 Fradin, Dennis B. *Tennessee* (3–5). Illus. Series: From Sea to Shining Sea. 1992, Children's Book Pr. LB $27.00 (0-516-03842-7). 64pp. Tennessee is introduced with coverage of geography, history, people, and their work. (Rev: BL 2/1/93; SLJ 4/93) [976.8]

18614 Fradin, Dennis B. *Virginia* (3–5). Illus. Series: From Sea to Shining Sea. 1992, Children's Book Pr. LB $27.00 (0-516-03846-X). 64pp. This introduction to Virginia includes standard information on history and geography and an imaginary trip through the state. (Rev: BL 2/1/93) [975.5]

18615 Fradin, Dennis B., and Judith B. Fradin. *Arkansas* (3–5). Illus. Series: From Sea to Shining Sea. 1994, Children's Book Pr. LB $27.00 (0-516-03804-4). 64pp. A nicely illustrated introduction to Arkansas past and present, with information on natural resources, its cities, and its people. (Rev: BL 8/94) [976.7]

18616 Gaines, Ann Graham. *Kentucky* (4–7). Series: It's My State! 2003, Marshall Cavendish LB $18.95 (0-7614-1525-4). 80pp. Full-color photographs, trivia, and recipes and crafts are included along with the standard information required for reports. (Rev: BL 9/15/03; HBG 4/04; SLJ 9/03) [976.9]

18617 George, Jean Craighead. *Everglades* (2–4). Illus. by Wendell Minor. 1995, HarperCollins LB $15.89 (0-06-021229-2). 32pp. A storyteller explains to five children the origins and characteristics of the Everglades and the destruction that humans have caused to this ecosystem. (Rev: BCCB 7–8/95; BL 6/1–15/95; SLJ 6/95*) [975.9]

18618 Gibson, Karen Bush. *Mississippi Facts and Symbols* (1–4). Series: States and Their Symbols. 2000, Capstone LB $15.93 (0-7368-0640-7). 24pp. Color photos and brief text introduce Mississippi's state flower, flag, seal, animal, tree, and other symbols. (Rev: BL 3/1/01) [976.2]

18619 Gravelle, Karen. *Growing Up in a Holler in the Mountains: An Appalachian Childhood* (4–6). Illus. Series: Growing Up in America. 1997, Watts LB $24.00 (0-531-11452-X). 64pp. This account focuses on the unique aspects of growing up in the Appalachian mountains by focusing on the childhood of Joseph Ratliff in Kentucky. (Rev: BL 1/1–15/98; HBG 3/98; SLJ 3/98) [974]

18620 Gravelle, Karen, and Sylviane Diouf. *Growing Up in Crawfish Country: A Cajun Childhood* (3–6). Illus. Series: Growing Up in America. 1998, Watts LB $24.00 (0-531-11535-6). 64pp. Cajun culture, including food, music, and architecture, is described through the eyes of children in the Bayou country. (Rev: BL 12/1/98; HBG 3/99; SLJ 1/99) [976.3]

18621 Heinrichs, Ann. *Florida* (4–8). Series: America the Beautiful. 1998, Children's Pr. LB $34.00 (0-516-20632-X). This book provides background on the history, geography, and economy of Florida and describes the recent influx of people there, its major cities, and endangered wildlife. (Rev: BL 10/15/98; SLJ 1/99) [975.9]

18622 Heinrichs, Ann. *Kentucky* (2–5). Illus. Series: This Land Is Your Land. 2003, Compass Point LB $22.60 (0-7565-0322-1). 48pp. Introduces readers to the geography, history, government, economy, and famous citizens of the Bluegrass State. (Rev: SLJ 8/03)

18623 Heinrichs, Ann. *Maryland* (2–5). Illus. Series: This Land Is Your Land. 2003, Compass Point LB $22.60 (0-7565-0348-5). 48pp. An attractive introduction to Maryland with plenty of photographs and accessible information for report writers. (Rev: SLJ 8/03) [975]

18624 Heinrichs, Ann. *Tennessee* (2–5). Illus. Series: This Land Is Your Land. 2003, Compass Point LB $22.60 (0-7565-0319-1). 48pp. This brightly illustrated profile explores Tennessee's history, people, geography, government, economy, and attractions. (Rev: SLJ 7/03) [976.8]

18625 Heinrichs, Ann. *Virginia* (2–4). Illus. Series: This Land Is Your Land. 2002, Compass Point LB $22.60 (0-7565-0310-8). 48pp. Simple text and good illustrations introduce the history, geography, culture, famous people, and attractions of Virginia. (Rev: SLJ 1/03)

18626 Herda, D. J. *Environmental America: The South Central States* (4–7). Illus. Series: American Scene. 1991, Millbrook LB $22.40 (1-878841-09-2). 64pp. This account discusses the general state of the environment and presents information on animal species, pollution, waste, and urban sprawl for 10 states, including Georgia, Kansas, Missouri, and Texas. (Rev: BL 8/91; SLJ 7/91) [639.9]

18627 Hess, Debra. *Florida* (4–7). Series: It's My State! 2003, Marshall Cavendish LB $18.95 (0-7614-1527-0). 80pp. Products, resources, plants and animals, and important background material are some of the topics covered in this general introduction to Florida. (Rev: BL 9/15/03; HBG 4/04; SLJ 9/03) [975.9]

18628 Hintz, Martin. *Louisiana* (5–8). Series: America the Beautiful. 1998, Children's Book Pr. LB $34.00 (0-516-20634-6). 144pp. With a good use of graphics and clear writing, this book provides a wealth of information about Louisiana, past and present. (Rev: BL 1/1–15/99; SLJ 2/99) [975.6]

18629 Hintz, Martin, and Stephen Hintz. *North Carolina* (5–8). Illus. Series: America the Beautiful. 1998, Children's Book Pr. LB $34.00 (0-516-20638-9). 144pp. A revised edition of a comprehensive introduction to North Carolina's history and geography, natural resources and industry, people and landmarks. (Rev: BL 1/1–15/99; SLJ 4/99) [975.6]

18630 Hoffman, Nancy. *South Carolina* (4–8). Series: Celebrate the States. 2000, Marshall Cavendish LB $35.64 (0-7614-1065-1). 144pp. An interesting introduction to South Carolina, with material on its land and waterways, history, government, economy, landmarks, and success stories. (Rev: BL 12/15/00; HBG 3/01) [975.7]

18631 Johnston, Joyce. *Maryland* (3–6). Illus. Series: Hello USA. 1992, Lerner LB $19.93 (0-8225-2713-8). 72pp. In this overview on Maryland, there are chapters on history and geography, as well as social and economic conditions. (Rev: BL 5/15/92; SLJ 10/92) [975]

18632 Kule, Elaine. *Arkansas Facts and Symbols* (1–4). Series: States and Their Symbols. 2000, Capstone LB $15.93 (0-7368-0634-2). 24pp. A page of basic facts about Arkansas and another page of places to visit are included in this book whose main body consists of pictures and text describing such state symbols as the flag, seal, tree, flower, and bird. (Rev: BL 3/1/01) [976.7]

18633 LaDoux, Rita C. *Georgia* (3–6). Illus. Series: Hello USA. 1991, Lerner LB $19.93 (0-8225-2703-0). 72pp. Geography, economics, history, and the environment are some of the topics covered in this look at a southern state. (Rev: BL 4/15/91; SLJ 6/91) [975.8]

18634 La Doux, Rita C. *Louisiana*. Rev. ed. (3–5). Illus. Series: Hello U.S.A. 2001, Lerner LB $25.26 (0-8225-4065-7); paper $6.95 (0-8225-4145-9). 84pp. This revision of the 1993 edition features a more spacious layout and some expanded content. (Rev: SLJ 2/02) [976]

18635 Leese, Jennifer. *Uniquely Maryland* (4–7). Series: State Studies. 2004, Heinemann LB $27.07 (1-4034-4493-5). 48pp. History, industry, tourism, and culture are among the highlights of this survey of Maryland and its characteristics. (Rev: BL 4/1/04) [975.2]

18636 Levert, Suzanne. *Louisiana* (4–8). Illus. Series: Celebrate the States. 1997, Marshall Cavendish LB $35.64 (0-7614-0112-1). An interesting introduction that covers the standard material needed for reports. (Rev: BL 7/97; SLJ 7/97) [976.3]

18637 Lynch, Amy. *Nashville* (3–5). Illus. Series: Downtown America. 1990, Macmillan LB $17.95 (0-87518-453-7). 60pp. The sights and people of the nation's country music capital are introduced. (Rev: BL 2/1/91) [976.8]

18638 Lynn, Vyvyan. *Georgia* (3–5). Series: Seeds of a Nation. 2003, Gale/KidHaven LB $18.96 (0-7377-1018-7). 48pp. An attractive profile of early Georgia, from the colonial era through statehood and the Civil War. (Rev: SLJ 4/04) [975.8]

18639 MacAulay, Ellen. *Arkansas* (3–5). Illus. 2002, Children's Book Pr. LB $29.50 (0-516-22296-1). 80pp. This revision of an earlier title adds information and features that will enhance its appeal to report writers. (Rev: SLJ 1/03)

18640 McAuliffe, Emily. *Florida Facts and Symbols*. Rev. ed. (3–5). Illus. Series: The States and Their Symbols. 2003, Capstone LB $19.93 (0-7368-2239-9). 24pp. A brief, illustrated overview of facts about Florida such as the state's nickname, motto, flag, and other symbols. (Rev: SLJ 1/04) [975.9]

18641 McAuliffe, Emily. *Georgia Facts and Symbols*. Rev. ed. (3–5). Illus. Series: The States and Their Symbols. 2003, Capstone LB $19.93 (0-7368-2240-2). 24pp. A brief overview that will serve as a source of limited facts about the state. (Rev: SLJ 1/04) [975.8]

18642 McClellan, Adam, and Martin Wilson. *Uniquely North Carolina* (4–7). Series: Heinemann State Studies: Uniquely. 2004, Heinemann LB $18.95 (1-4034-4653-9). 48pp. In addition to providing the facts necessary for report writers, this volume emphasizes the features that distinguish North Carolina from its neighbors.

18643 Martin, Michael A. *Alabama: The Heart of Dixie* (4–7). Series: World Almanac Library of the States. 2002, World Almanac LB $29.26 (0-8368-

5127-7). 48pp. Full-color photographs and graphic elements this informative introduction to the state. Also use *Virginia* (2002). (Rev: SLJ 2/03) [976.1]

18644 Morgan, Cheryl Koenig. *The Everglades* (3–5). Illus. 1990, Troll paper $3.95 (0-8167-1734-6). 32pp. A description of the Everglades with emphasis on ecology. (Rev: SLJ 8/90) [975.9]

18645 Nichols, Joan Kane. *New Orleans* (3–5). Illus. Series: Downtown America. 1989, Macmillan LB $13.95 (0-87518-403-0). 64pp. History, neighborhoods, and unique features of New Orleans are covered. (Rev: BL 8/89; SLJ 1/90) [976.3]

18646 Odinoski, Steve. *Georgia* (4–8). Series: Celebrate the States. 2000, Marshall Cavendish LB $35.64 (0-7614-1062-7). 144pp. An informative, attractive introduction to Georgia with material on its land, history, people, social issues, and hidden treasures. (Rev: BL 12/15/00; HBG 3/01; SLJ 2/01) [975.8]

18647 Otfinoski, Steve. *Maryland* (3–6). Illus. Series: It's My State! 2002, Benchmark LB $18.95 (0-7614-1421-5). 80pp. The usual state information — geography, history, government, people, and economy — is presented in an appealing layout. (Rev: HBG 10/03; SLJ 2/03)

18648 Owens, Lisa. *Uniquely Missouri* (4–7). Series: Heinemann State Studies: Uniquely. 2004, Heinemann LB $27.07 (1-4034-4495-1). 48pp. In addition to providing the facts necessary for report writers, this volume emphasizes the features that distinguish Missouri from its neighbors.

18649 Rauth, Leslie. *Maryland* (5–9). Series: Celebrate the States. 1999, Benchmark LB $35.64 (0-7614-0671-9). 144pp. This book explores Maryland with material on topics including land and waterways, government, economy, festivals, and people. (Rev: BL 1/1–15/00; HBG 10/00; SLJ 5/00) [975.2]

18650 Ready, Anna. *Mississippi* (3–6). Illus. Series: Hello USA. 1993, Lerner LB $19.93 (0-8225-2743-X). 72pp. Such topics as geography, culture, history, and economics are covered in this introduction. (Rev: BL 7/93) [976.2]

18651 Reef, Catherine. *Arlington National Cemetery* (4–6). Illus. Series: Places in American History. 1991, Macmillan $18.95 (0-87518-471-5). 72pp. The history and development of this cemetery known as "America's greatest national shrine." (Rev: BL 2/15/92; SLJ 3/92) [975.5]

18652 Reef, Catherine. *Monticello* (4–6). Illus. Series: Places in American History. 1991, Macmillan LB $14.95 (0-87518-472-3). 72pp. Through pictures and text, the fascinating home of President Thomas Jefferson is introduced. (Rev: BL 2/15/92) [973.4]

18653 Reef, Catherine. *Mount Vernon* (4–6). Illus. Series: Places in American History. 1992, Macmillan LB $18.95 (0-87518-474-X). 72pp. This account not only introduces the home of this first president, but also tells about the life of George Washington. (Rev: BL 9/1/92) [973]

18654 Sanford, William R. *The Natchez Trace Historic Trail in American History* (5–8). Series: In American History. 2001, Enslow LB $20.95 (0-7660-1344-8). 112pp. Sanford looks at the history of this ancient Native American trail, the people who used it, and confrontations between newcomers and the indigenous people. (Rev: BL 12/15/01; HBG 3/02; SLJ 3/02) [976]

18655 Santella, Andrew. *Mount Vernon* (4–6). Series: We the People. 2004, Compass Point LB $22.60 (0-7565-0682-4). 48pp. A look at George Washington's home, with discussion of its role as a plantation and of the slaves who worked there. (Rev: SLJ 2/05) [973]

18656 Schulz, Andrea. *North Carolina* (3–6). Illus. Series: Hello USA. 1994, Lerner LB $19.93 (0-8225-2744-8). 72pp. A colorful introduction to North Carolina's history, geography, landmarks, and life-styles. (Rev: BL 2/1/94) [975.6]

18657 Sherrow, Victoria. *Uniquely South Carolina* (4–7). Illus. Series: Heinemann State Studies. 2005, Heinemann LB $21.95 (1-4034-4661-X). 48pp. In addition to providing the facts necessary for report writers, this volume emphasizes the features that distinguish South Carolina from its neighbors.

18658 Shirley, David. *Alabama* (4–8). Series: Celebrate the States. 2000, Marshall Cavendish LB $35.64 (0-7614-0648-4). 141pp. An introduction to Alabama that covers its land and waterways; its history, government, and economy; and its culture and success stories. (Rev: BL 6/1–15/00; HBG 10/00) [976.1]

18659 Shirley, David. *North Carolina* (4–8). Series: Celebrate the States. 2001, Benchmark LB $35.64 (0-7614-1072-4). 144pp. A fine introduction to the land, history, economy, and people of North Carolina. (Rev: BL 9/15/01; HBG 10/01) [975.6]

18660 Sirvaitis, Karen. *Florida* (3–5). Illus. Series: Hello USA. 1994, Lerner LB $19.93 (0-8225-2728-6). 72pp. With photos on every page, this compact book contains basic background information about Florida, including its history, famous sights, and important residents. (Rev: BL 4/15/94) [973]

18661 Sirvaitis, Karen. *Tennessee* (3–6). Illus. Series: Hello USA. 1991, Lerner LB $19.93 (0-8225-2711-1). 72pp. This book covers the geography, history, and socioeconomic conditions, along with timelines and biographies of famous residents. (Rev: BL 12/1/91) [976.8]

18662 Sirvaitis, Karen. *Virginia* (3–6). Illus. Series: Hello USA. 1991, Lerner LB $19.93 (0-8225-2702-2). 72pp. With full-color photos, this is a good, fact-filled introduction to Virginia. (Rev: BL 4/15/91; SLJ 6/91) [975.5]

18663 Smith, Karla. *Virginia* (4–6). Series: Heinemann State Studies. 2003, Heinemann LB $27.07 (1-4034-0361-9). 48pp. A useful overview of Virginia's geography, history, people, culture, and attractions. (Rev: HBG 4/04; SLJ 12/03) [975.5]

18664 Smith, Karla. *Virginia History* (4–6). 2003, Heinemann LB $27.07 (1-4034-0362-7). 48pp. A useful overview of the history of Virginia. (Rev: HBG 4/04; SLJ 12/03) [975.5]

18665 Snow, Pegeen. *Atlanta* (3–6). Illus. 1989, Macmillan LB $13.95 (0-87518-389-1). 60pp. History and modern life in this growing southern city. (Rev: BL 3/15/89; SLJ 5/89)

18666 Stein, R. Conrad. *South Carolina* (5–8). Series: America the Beautiful. 1999, Children's Book Pr. LB $34.00 (0-516-20997-3). 144pp. A comprehensive and well-illustrated introduction to South Carolina — its history and geography, its government and economy, its people and important places. (Rev: BL 11/15/99) [975.2]

18667 Stein, R. Conrad. *West Virginia* (4–6). Illus. Series: America the Beautiful. 1990, Children's Book Pr. LB $28.00 (0-516-00494-8). 144pp. The small state of West Virginia is introduced with coverage on government, history, economy, and geography. (Rev: BL 1/1/91) [975.4]

18668 Stout, Mary. *Atlanta* (4–7). Illus. Series: Great Cities of the World. 2005, World Almanac LB $22.50 (0-8368-5042-4). 48pp. Report writers will find useful information on Atlanta's history, culture, lifestyle, and current problems.

18669 Streissguth, Thomas. *Maryland* (5–8). Series: The Thirteen Colonies. 2001, Lucent LB $27.45 (1-56006-871-X). 96pp. Source notes, annotated bibliographies, and lists of Internet resources complement this history of Maryland from its beginnings to statehood. (Rev: BL 3/15/02) [973.2]

18670 Valzania, Kimberly. *Tennessee* (K–2). Series: Rookie Read-about Geography. 2003, Children's Pr. LB $19.00 (0-516-22699-1); paper $5.95 (0-516-27843-6). 31pp. For beginning readers, this is a useful introduction to Tennessee, covering the Volunteer State's geography, people, industry, agriculture, and recreation. (Rev: SLJ 10/03) [917.68]

18671 Weatherford, Carole Boston. *Sink or Swim: African-American Lifesavers of the Outer Banks* (4–8). Illus. 1999, Coastal Carolina $15.95 (1-928556-01-9); paper $12.95 (1-928556-03-5). 80pp. A history of the African Americans who participated in lifesaving efforts on the Outer Banks of North Carolina, known as "the graveyard of the Atlantic." (Rev: BL 12/15/99) [363.28]

18672 Wills, Charles A. *A Historical Album of Alabama* (4–8). Series: Historical Albums. 1995, Millbrook LB $23.40 (1-56294-591-2); paper $6.95 (1-56294-854-7). Using many period prints and engravings, the author traces the history of Alabama from prehistoric days to today, including the impact of the shift away from cotton as a main crop, the civil rights movement, and the importance of football in the state. (Rev: BL 12/15/95; SLJ 1/96) [976.1]

18673 Wills, Charles A. *A Historical Album of Florida* (4–8). Illus. Series: Historical Albums. 1994, Millbrook LB $24.40 (1-56294-480-0). 64pp. This compressed history of Florida deals with major events from prehistory through the 1990s. (Rev: SLJ 2/95) [975.9]

18674 Wills, Charles A. *A Historical Album of Georgia* (4–7). Illus. Series: Historical Albums. 1996, Millbrook LB $24.40 (0-7613-0035-X). 64pp. With many period illustrations, some in color, and a simple text, the history and geography of Georgia are presented. (Rev: BL 12/15/96) [975.8]

18675 Wilson, Martin. *Uniquely Alabama* (4–7). Series: Heinemann State Studies: Uniquely. 2004, Heinemann LB $27.07 (1-4034-4485-4). 48pp. In addition to providing the facts necessary for report writers, this volume emphasizes the features that distinguish Alabama from its neighbors.

18676 Wilson, Martin. *Uniquely Mississippi* (4–7). Illus. Series: Heinemann State Studies. 2004, Heinemann LB $21.95 (1-4034-4656-3). 48pp. In addition to providing the facts necessary for report writers, this volume emphasizes the features that distinguish Mississippi from its neighbors.

18677 Wyborny, Sheila. *Kentucky* (3–5). Series: Seeds of a Nation. 2003, Gale/KidHaven LB $18.96 (0-7377-1446-8). 48pp. Kentucky's early days and its quest for statehood are detailed in this well-illustrated volume. (Rev: SLJ 4/04) [976.9]

18678 Yolen, Jane. *Welcome to the River of Grass* (PS–3). Illus. by Laura Regan. 2001, Penguin Putnam $15.99 (0-399-23221-4). 32pp. Yolen examines the animal and plant life of the Everglades — and the perils the area faces — in rhythmic text accompanied by excellent illustrations. (Rev: BCCB 2/02; BL 10/1/01; HBG 3/02; SLJ 11/01) [577.68]

18679 Young, Robert. *A Personal Tour of Monticello* (4–7). Illus. Series: How It Was. 1999, Lerner LB $30.35 (0-8225-3575-0). 64pp. Through the eyes of Jefferson, his daughter, and one of his slaves, the reader is introduced to the home of the third president of the United States. (Rev: BL 6/1–15/99; HBG 10/99; SLJ 7/99) [975.5]

SOUTHWEST

18680 Alter, Judy. *New Mexico* (4–7). Illus. Series: MyReportLinks.com. 2002, Enslow LB $19.95 (0-7660-5098-X). 48pp. An introduction to the government, geography, and history of the state, with helpful Web sites. (Rev: BL 2/1/03; SLJ 4/03) [978.9]

18681 Alter, Judy. *Texas* (5–8). Series: States. 2002, Enslow/MyReportLinks.com LB $19.95 (0-7660-5018-1). 48pp. This photo-filled guide to the state of Texas offers links to online resources for students who would like to learn more. (Rev: HBG 3/03; SLJ 4/03) [976.4]

18682 Anderson, Joan. *Cowboys* (4–6). Illus. by George Ancona. 1996, Scholastic $16.95 (0-590-48424-9). 48pp. All of the Eby family, including their young sons and hired cowboys, work during the spring roundup. (Rev: BL 3/15/96*; HB 5–6/96; SLJ 3/96*) [978]

18683 Aylesworth, Thomas G., and Virginia L. Aylesworth. *The Southwest: Colorado, New Mexico, Texas* (3–6). Illus. 1995, Chelsea LB $19.95 (0-7910-3412-7); paper $9.95 (0-7910-3430-5). 64pp. An easy-to-use study of three southwestern states. (Rev: BL 8/88; SLJ 11/88)

18684 Bjorklund, Ruth. *New Mexico* (4–7). Series: It's My State! 2003, Marshall Cavendish LB $18.95 (0-7614-1526-2). 80pp. Actual quotations from both famous and unknown residents of New Mexico are used to introduce this state, its people, history, wildlife, and resources. (Rev: BL 9/15/03; HBG 4/04) [978.9]

18685 Blashfield, Jean F. *Arizona* (5–8). Series: America the Beautiful. 2000, Children's Book Pr.

LB $34.00 (0-516-21068-8). 144pp. This excellent guide to Arizona covers all the basic topics about the southwestern state. (Rev: BL 9/15/00) [979.1]

18686 Bredeson, Carmen. *The Spindletop Gusher: The Story of the Texas Oil Boom* (4–7). Illus. Series: Spotlight on American History. 1996, Millbrook LB $24.90 (1-56294-916-0). 64pp. A discussion of the Texas oil boom, its effects on the state and its economy, and the present status of the oil industry. (Rev: BL 3/15/96) [338.4]

18687 Bredeson, Carmen. *Texas* (4–8). Illus. Series: Celebrate the States. 1996, Marshall Cavendish LB $35.64 (0-7614-0109-1). Basic information about Texas is presented in an attractive format with many color photographs, maps, and diagrams. (Rev: BL 2/15/97; SLJ 6/97) [976.4]

18688 Coleman, Wim, and Pat Perrin. *The Alamo* (5–8). Illus. Series: Virtual Field Trips. 2005, Enslow/MyReportLinks.com LB $25.26 (0-7660-5221-4). 48pp. A visit to the Alamo, using both print and related Web sites, that covers its historical importance and introduces key figures. (Rev: SLJ 5/05)

18689 Corrick, James. *Uniquely Arizona* (4–7). Series: Heinemann State Studies: Uniquely. 2004, Heinemann LB $27.07 (1-4034-4486-2); paper $8.50 (104304-4501-X). 48pp. In addition to providing the facts necessary for report writers, this volume emphasizes the features that distinguish Arizona from its neighbors.

18690 Early, Theresa S. *New Mexico* (3–6). Illus. Series: Hello USA. 1993, Lerner LB $19.93 (0-8225-2748-0). 72pp. An introduction to New Mexico that includes geography, history, and social and economic conditions. (Rev: BL 7/93; SLJ 8/93) [978.9]

18691 Fradin, Dennis B. *Arizona* (3–5). Illus. Series: From Sea to Shining Sea. 1993, Children's Book Pr. LB $27.00 (0-516-03803-6). 64pp. This account takes the reader on a trip around Arizona, as well as covering its basic history and geography. (Rev: BL 11/1/93; SLJ 1/94) [979.1]

18692 Fradin, Dennis B. *Texas* (3–5). Illus. Series: From Sea to Shining Sea. 1992, Children's Book Pr. LB $27.00 (0-516-03843-5). 64pp. A chronology of Texas history and a state map are included in this account. (Rev: BL 2/1/93; SLJ 4/93) [976.4]

18693 Fradin, Judith B., and Dennis B. Fradin. *New Mexico* (3–5). Illus. Series: From Sea to Shining Sea. 1993, Children's Book Pr. LB $27.00 (0-516-03831-1). 64pp. Includes material on such topics as the land, people, history, important sights, and economy. (Rev: BL 11/1/93) [978.9]

18694 Garza, Carmen Lomas, and Harriet Rohmer. *Magic Windows: Ventanas Magicas* (3–7). Illus. 1999, Children's Book Pr. $15.95 (0-89239-157-X). 32pp. This bilingual book introduces Mexican American culture and lifestyle through an examination of *papel picado* (cut-paper art). Also see *Making Magic Windows*. (Rev: BL 5/1/99; HBG 10/99; SLJ 7/99) [745.54]

18695 Gibson, Karen Bush. *Oklahoma Facts and Symbols*. Rev. ed. (3–5). Illus. Series: The States and Their Symbols. 2003, Capstone LB $19.93 (0-

7368-2266-6). 24pp. A brief overview that will serve as a source of limited facts about the state. (Rev: SLJ 1/04) [976.6]

18696 Hanson-Harding, Alexandra. *Texas* (4–6). Illus. Series: From Sea to Shining Sea. 2001, Children's Book Pr. LB $29.50 (0-516-22322-4). 80pp. A good resource for report writing, this book features historical facts, maps, and information about the governmental structure and the people of Texas. (Rev: BL 3/15/02) [976.4]

18697 Heinrichs, Ann. *Arizona* (4–6). Illus. Series: America the Beautiful. 1991, Children's Book Pr. LB $28.00 (0-516-00449-2). 144pp. This introduction to Arizona includes a chronology, maps, and biographies of important people. (Rev: BL 7/91) [979.1]

18698 Heinrichs, Ann. *Oklahoma* (2–5). Illus. Series: This Land Is Your Land. 2003, Compass Point LB $22.60 (0-7565-0330-2). 48pp. This brightly illustrated profile explores Oklahoma's history, people, geography, government, economy, and attractions. (Rev: SLJ 7/03) [976.6]

18699 Heinrichs, Ann. *Texas* (2–4). Illus. Series: This Land Is Your Land. 2002, Compass Point LB $22.60 (0-7565-0312-4). 48pp. Simple text with age-appropriate language and good illustrations introduce the history, geography, culture, famous people, and attractions of Texas. (Rev: SLJ 1/03)

18700 Heinrichs, Ann. *Texas* (5–8). Series: America the Beautiful. 1999, Children's Book Pr. LB $34.00 (0-516-20998-1). 144pp. Photographs and maps illustrate this account of Texas — its history and geography, economy and government, people and resources. (Rev: BL 11/15/99) [976.4]

18701 Herda, D. J. *Environmental America: The Southwestern States* (4–7). Illus. Series: American Scene. 1991, Millbrook LB $22.40 (1-878841-11-4). 64pp. This account, which discusses the state of the environment and how it can be changed for the better, covers Arizona, California, Colorado, Nevada, New Mexico, and Utah. (Rev: BL 8/91; SLJ 7/91) [639.9]

18702 Kent, Deborah. *New Mexico* (4–10). Series: America the Beautiful. 1999, Children's Book Pr. LB $32.00 (0-516-20690-7). 144pp. New Mexico is introduced with material on the land, its people, history, and current conditions in this fine revision of an earlier edition. (Rev: HBG 3/00; SLJ 1/00) [978.9]

18703 Lee, Sally. *San Antonio* (4–7). Illus. Series: Downtown America. 1992, Macmillan LB $13.95 (0-87518-510-X). 63pp. This introduction to San Antonio covers history, people, festivals, and interesting landmarks such as the Alamo, the river walk, and Spanish missions. (Rev: BL 4/15/92; SLJ 5/92) [976]

18704 Lourie, Peter. *The Lost World of the Anasazi: Exploring the Mysteries of Chaco Canyon* (5–8). Illus. 2003, Boyds Mills $19.95 (1-56397-972-1). 48pp. With many full-color photographs, the author describes his trip to the ruins of Chaco Canyon and discusses the mysterious disappearance of its

Anasazi residents. (Rev: BL 9/1/03; HBG 4/04; SLJ 1/04) [978.9]

18705 McDaniel, Melissa. *Arizona* (4–8). Series: Celebrate the States. 2000, Marshall Cavendish LB $35.64 (0-7614-0647-6). 139pp. This introduction to Arizona discusses its land, history, economy, festivals, cultural diversity, and landmarks. (Rev: BL 6/1–15/00; HBG 10/00; SLJ 9/00) [979.1]

18706 Marcovitz, Hal. *The Alamo* (4–8). Illus. Series: American Symbols and Their Meanings. 2002, Mason Crest LB $18.95 (1-59084-037-2). 48pp. A basic and readable introduction to the history of the Alamo and its importance to Americans, with illuminating illustrations and inset features. (Rev: SLJ 9/02) [976]

18707 Munro, Roxie. *The Inside-Outside Book of Texas* (K–3). Illus. Series: Inside-Outside. 2001, North-South LB $16.88 (1-58717-051-5). 48pp. Some of the most famous places and landmarks in Texas are pictured in this attractive book with a minimum of text. (Rev: BL 4/1/01; HB 5–6/01; HBG 10/01; SLJ 6/01) [976.4]

18708 Peifer, Charles. *Houston* (3–5). Illus. 1988, Macmillan $17.95 (0-87518-387-5). 60pp. A look at life in this big Texas city. (Rev: BL 1/15/89; SLJ 5/89)

18709 Pelta, Kathy. *Texas*. Rev. ed. (3–5). Illus. Series: Hello U.S.A. 2001, Lerner LB $25.26 (0-8225-4064-9); paper $6.95 (0-8225-4142-4). 84pp. This revision of a 1993 edition features a more spacious layout and some expanded content. (Rev: HBG 3/02; SLJ 2/02) [976.4]

18710 Tweit, Susan J. *Meet the Wild Southwest: Land of Hoodoos and Gila Monsters* (4–8). Illus. 1996, Alaska Northwest paper $14.95 (0-88240-468-7). 124pp. An impressive collection of facts and curiosities about the natural history of the Southwest, with many appendixes that supply more-traditional information. (Rev: BL 3/1/96) [508.79]

18711 Wade, Mary Dodson. *All Around Texas: Regions and Sources* (4–7). Illus. Series: Heinemann State Studies. 2003, Heinemann LB $18.95 (1-4034-0686-3). 48pp. A general introduction to the regions of Texas and their valuable resources, with colorful maps. Also in this series are *Texas: Plants and Animals*, *Texas: History*, *Texas: Native Peoples*, and *People of Texas* (all 2003). (Rev: HBG 4/04)

18712 Weintraub, Aileen. *The Grand Canyon: The Widest Canyon* (3–5). Illus. Series: Great Record Breakers in Nature. 2001, Rosen $18.75 (0-8239-5641-5). 24pp. Jam-packed with facts, this book takes readers on a word and photo tour of the formation, history, and appeal of one of the world's natural wonders. (Rev: BL 12/15/01; SLJ 7/01) [979.1]

18713 Wills, Charles A. *A Historical Album of Texas* (4–7). Illus. Series: Historical Albums. 1995, Millbrook LB $24.40 (1-56294-504-1). 64pp. This account of the history of Texas from earliest times to today is also particularly noteworthy for its many illustrations. (Rev: SLJ 6/95) [976.4]

Social Institutions and Issues

Business and Economics

General

18714 Adams, Barbara J. *The Go-Around Dollar* (2–4). Illus. by Joyce A. Zarins. 1992, Macmillan LB $16.00 (0-02-700031-1). 32pp. The dollar is introduced within the framework of a story and the look of a picture book. (Rev: BCCB 2/92; BL 2/15/92; SLJ 5/92) [332.4]

18715 Berger, Melvin, and Gilda Berger. *Round and Round the Money Goes: What Money Is and How We Use It* (1–3). Illus. by Jane McCreary. Series: Discovery Readers. 1993, Ideals paper $4.50 (0-8249-8598-2). 48pp. Many topics about money are briefly introduced in this beginner's account, including the forms money takes, why it is necessary, world monetary units, and how banks work. (Rev: SLJ 12/93) [332]

18716 Burns, Peggy. *Money* (3–5). Illus. Series: Stepping Through History. 1995, Thomson Learning LB $5.00 (1-56847-248-X). 32pp. As well as a history of coins and paper money, this account tells of the development of banks, credit cards, and foreign exchange. (Rev: BL 4/15/95; SLJ 6/95) [332.4]

18717 Caes, Charles J. *The Young Zillionaire's Guide to the Stock Market* (5–8). Series: Be a Zillionaire. 2000, Rosen LB $23.95 (0-8239-3265-6). 48pp. Basic information on the inner workings of the stock market is presented with many examples from the corporate world. (Rev: HBG 10/01; SLJ 3/01) [332.6]

18718 Condon, Daniel. *Playing the Market: Stocks and Bonds* (3–5). Series: Everyday Economics. 2004, Heinemann LB $27.07 (1-5881-0495-8). 48pp. Condon discusses savings and investment, stocks and bonds, interest rates, and the role of the government and the Federal Reserve. (Rev: SLJ 6/04) [332.63]

18719 Cooper, Jason. *Around the World with Money* (2–4). Series: Money Power. 2002, Rourke LB $19.27 (1-58952-212-5). 24pp. This brief, small-format overview introduces the currencies of Cana-

da, Mexico, the United States, and Europe. Also use *Money Through the Ages* (2002), which looks at the history of money. (Rev: SLJ 4/03) [332.4]

18720 de Ruiz, Dana C., and Richard Larios. *La Causa: The Migrant Farmworkers' Story* (4–7). Illus. by Rudy Gutierrez. 1992, Raintree LB $30.40 (0-8114-7231-0). 92pp. The story of the founding of the United Farm Workers highlights the work of Cesar Chavez and Dolores Huerta. (Rev: BL 6/1–15/93) [331]

18721 Downing, David. *Capitalism* (5–8). Series: Political and Economic Systems. 2002, Heinemann LB $28.50 (1-40340-315-5). 64pp. In an attractive format, this book explains the capitalistic economic system, its history, key thinkers, and present status. (Rev: BL 1/1–15/03; HBG 3/03; SLJ 2/03) [330.12]

18722 Downing, David. *Communism* (5–8). Series: Political and Economic Systems. 2002, Heinemann LB $28.50 (1-40340-316-3). 64pp. The theoretical basis of communism is explained with material on its application, history, important thinkers and leaders, and different movements. (Rev: BL 1/1–15/03; HBG 3/03; SLJ 2/03) [335.43]

18723 Drobot, Eve. *Money, Money, Money: Where It Comes From, How to Save It, Spend It, and Make It* (4–6). Illus. by Claudia Davila. 2004, Maple Tree $19.95 (1-897066-10-4); paper $12.95 (1-897066-11-2). 96pp. Useful both for browsing and research, this accessible volume covers such fundamentals as the history of currency, banks and savings, credit cards, the stock market, and identity theft. (Rev: BL 1/1–15/05; SLJ 1/05) [332.4]

18724 Firestone, Mary. *Earning Money* (K–3). Illus. Series: Learning About Money. 2004, Capstone LB $15.95 (0-7368-2639-4). 24pp. A simple introduction to the reasons why people want to earn money and how prices of goods are established. Also use *Saving Money* and *Spending Money* (both 2004). (Rev: BL 10/15/04) [650.1]

18725 Firestone, Mary. *What Is Money?* (K–3). Series: Learning About Money. 2004, Capstone LB $15.95 (0-7368-2642-4). 24pp. Informative and attractive, this volume explains the basics of currency in clear text and covers such topics as bartering and the minting of new money. Also use *Earning Money* (2004), which explores ways of acquiring money and its relative worth. (Rev: BL 10/15/04) [332.4]

18726 Giesecke, Ernestine. *Your Money at Work: Taxes* (3–5). Series: Everyday Economics. 2004, Heinemann LB $27.07 (1-5881-0494-X). 48pp. Introduces the principle of taxation, why it's necessary, different forms of taxation, and how the money collected is spent. (Rev: SLJ 6/04) [336.73]

18727 Graydon, Shari. *Made You Look: How Advertising Works and Why You Should Know* (5–9). Illus. by Warren Clark. 2003, Annick $24.95 (1-55037-815-5); paper $14.95 (1-55037-814-7). 120pp. The 8- to 14-year-old age group is an advertising target, and this title teaches readers to recognize the various techniques used and to assess products' value. (Rev: BL 12/1/03*; SLJ 12/03) [659.1]

18728 Green, Meg. *The Young Zillionaire's Guide to Investments and Savings* (5–8). Series: Be a Zillionaire. 2000, Rosen LB $23.95 (0-8239-3261-3). 48pp. A guide to the investment markets and methods of saving with good use of examples and case studies. (Rev: HBG 10/01; SLJ 3/01) [338.5]

18729 Hall, Margaret. *Credit Cards and Checks* (3–5). Illus. Series: Earning, Saving, Spending. 2000, Heinemann $14.95 (1-57572-232-1). 32pp. Using double-page spreads, this colorful book describes what checks and credit cards are, how they are used, and how they can become a substitute for money. (Rev: BL 10/15/00) [332.76]

18730 Hall, Margaret. *Money* (3–5). Illus. Series: Earning, Saving, Spending. 2000, Heinemann $14.95 (1-57572-233-X). 32pp. This history of coins and paper money also discusses their value and uses and how people earn and spend money. (Rev: BL 10/15/00) [332.4]

18731 Harman, Hollis Page. *Money $ense for Kids!* 2nd ed. (4–7). Illus. 2004, Barron's paper $10.95 (0-7641-2894-9). 180pp. Explains the basics of money and currency and of earning, saving, and investing, with exercises at the end of each chapter and a "Money Games" section. (Rev: SLJ 11/04) [332.024]

18732 Kummer, Patricia K. *Currency* (4–8). Series: Inventions That Shaped the World. 2004, Watts LB $29.50 (0-531-12341-3). 80pp. After looking at the nature of currency, this title discusses modern forms and the role of currency in our lives. (Rev: SLJ 2/05) [332.4]

18733 McGillian, Jamie Kyle. *The Kids' Money Book: Earning, Saving, Spending, Investing, Donating* (5–8). Illus. by Ian Phillips. 2003, Sterling $17.95 (0-8069-8223-3). 96pp. After a brief history of money, this volume covers topics including earning, budgeting, saving, and spending money. (Rev: HBG 4/04; SLJ 10/03) [332.024]

18734 McGowan, Eileen Nixon, and Nancy Lagow Dumas. *Stock Market Smart* (5–8). Illus. 2002, Millbrook LB $23.90 (0-7613-2113-6). 64pp. An accessible question-and-answer presentation on the stock

market and different types of investors, with illustrations, tips on saving, activities, a glossary, and list of resources. (Rev: BL 9/1/02; HBG 3/03; SLJ 10/02) [332.63]

18735 McKissack, Patricia, and Fredrick McKissack. *A Long Hard Journey* (5–9). Illus. 1989, Walker LB $18.85 (0-8027-6885-7). A 150-year saga of the organization of porters into the first black American union, the Brotherhood of Sleeping Car Porters. (Rev: BL 9/15/89; SLJ 1/90) [331]

18736 Maestro, Betsy. *The Story of Money* (2–4). Illus. by Giulio Maestro. 1993, Houghton Mifflin $17.00 (0-395-56242-2). 48pp. The story of the ancient Sumerians who invented the idea of making money. (Rev: BCCB 3/93; BL 3/1/93; SLJ 4/93) [332.4]

18737 Seidman, David. *The Young Zillionaire's Guide to Supply and Demand* (5–7). Series: Be a Zillionaire. 2000, Rosen LB $23.95 (0-8239-3264-8). 48pp. The basic principles of supply and demand are explained, with information on how they are influenced by producers and consumers and how they help create economic conditions. (Rev: SLJ 2/01) [330]

18738 Simonds, Patricia. *The Founding of the AFL and the Rise of Organized Labor* (5–7). Illus. Series: Turning Points. 1991, Silver Burdett LB $14.95 (0-382-24123-1); paper $7.95 (0-382-24118-5). 64pp. The inspiring story of the beginning of the labor movement in the United States and its impact on American history and society. (Rev: BL 1/15/92) [331.88]

18739 *Sold! The Origins of Money and Trade* (5–8). Series: Buried Worlds. 1994, Runestone LB $28.75 (0-8225-3206-9). Explains the world origins of commerce and money, with coverage of how the earliest coins were made in the West and how other cultures developed unique forms of currency. (Rev: BL 9/15/94; SLJ 9/94) [737.4]

18740 Thomas, Keltie. *The Kids Guide to Money Cent$* (4–7). Illus. by Stephen MacEachern. 2004, Kids Can $14.95 (1-55337-389-8); paper $7.95 (1-55337-390-1). 56pp. Readers follow three children — the Money Cent$ Gang — who join together to investigate the ins and outs of banking, credit, investment, and money making; quizzes and examples make the content clear and comic-strip scenes add appeal. (Rev: SLJ 7/04) [332.02]

18741 Wilson, Antoine. *The Young Zillionaire's Guide to Distributing Goods and Services* (5–7). Series: Be a Zillionaire. 2000, Rosen LB $23.95 (0-8239-3259-1). 48pp. This book explains how goods and services are distributed, the importance of retailing and wholesaling, how transportation affects prices and availability, and how the Internet might change these conditions. (Rev: SLJ 2/01) [330]

18742 Young, Robert. *Money* (3–6). Illus. Series: Household History. 1998, Carolrhoda LB $16.95 (1-57505-070-6). 48pp. A breezy account of the history of money in its various forms, including counterfeiting, credit, and even some magic tricks with coins and bills. (Rev: BL 9/1/98; HBG 9/98; SLJ 7/98) [332.4]

Consumerism

18743 Bendick, Jeanne, and Robert Bendick. *Markets: From Barter to Bar Codes* (3–5). Illus. 1997, Watts LB $22.00 (0-531-20263-1). 64pp. Illustrates the history of trade in the Western world by viewing a number of different markets. (Rev: BL 9/1/97; SLJ 1/98) [380.1]

18744 Burns, Peggy. *Stores and Markets* (3–5). Illus. Series: Stepping Through History. 1995, Thomson Learning LB $5.00 (1-56847-344-3). 32pp. A history of the distribution of goods from ancient markets and bazaars to today's shopping malls. (Rev: BL 7/95) [381]

18745 Miller, Marilyn. *Behind the Scenes at the Shopping Mall* (PS–3). Illus. Series: Behind the Scenes. 1996, Raintree LB $21.40 (0-8172-4088-8). 32pp. Using many leading questions and cartoon-style illustrations, this book provides an inside look at the activities that make a shopping mall work. (Rev: BL 4/15/96; SLJ 12/96) [381]

18746 Yardley, Thompson. *Buy Now, Pay Later: Smart Shopping Counts* (2–3). Illus. by author. Series: Lighter Look. 1992, Millbrook LB $20.90 (1-56294-149-6). 39pp. In an entertaining format, facts about smart shopping and recycling are given. (Rev: SLJ 6/92) [640.73]

Money-Making Ideas and Budgeting

18747 Barkin, Carol, and Elizabeth James. *The New Complete Babysitter's Handbook* (5–7). Illus. 1995, Clarion paper $7.95 (0-395-66558-2). 164pp. A fine manual that covers such topics as first aid, ways to amuse children, and how to get jobs baby sitting. (Rev: BL 5/1/95; SLJ 6/95) [649.1]

18748 Byers, Patricia, and Julia Preston. *The Kids' Money Book* (2–6). Illus. 1983, Liberty paper $4.95 (0-89709-041-1). A number of ways kids can make money.

18749 Drew, Bonnie, and Noel Drew. *Fast Cash for Kids* (4–7). Illus. 1995, Career Pr. paper $13.99 (1-564-14154-3). 168pp. The authors present a variety of possible ways to make money. (Rev: BL 6/15/87) [658.041]

18750 Hall, Margaret. *Your Allowance* (3–5). Illus. Series: Earning, Saving, Spending. 2000, Heinemann $14.95 (1-57572-234-8). 32pp. This book looks seriously at budgeting one's allowance, at good consumer practices, savings accounts, and gifts to charity. (Rev: BL 10/15/00) [332.024]

18751 Halperin, Wendy A. *Once upon a Company: A True Story* (1–5). Illus. 1998, Orchard LB $17.99 (0-531-33089-3). 40pp. A winningly illustrated picture book about the three Halperin children who raised money for their college fund by creating and selling Christmas wreaths and, in the summer, opening a food stand. (Rev: BCCB 9/98; BL 9/1/98*; HBG 3/99; SLJ 9/98) [658]

18752 Kiefer, Jeanne. *Jobs for Kids: A Smart Kid's Q & A Guide* (4–8). Illus. by Carol Nicklaus. 2003, Millbrook LB $25.90 (0-7613-2611-1). 112pp. A detailed and brightly illustrated guide to five popular ways to make money — baby sitting, pet care, and so forth — using a question-and-answer format and including useful forms and tips. (Rev: SLJ 7/03)

18753 Nathan, Amy. *The Kids' Allowance Book* (4–7). Illus. 1998, Walker $15.95 (0-8027-8651-0). 96pp. Children ages 9 to 14 present the pros and cons of allowances and money management. (Rev: BCCB 6/98; BL 7/98; HBG 9/98; SLJ 10/98) [332.02]

18754 Otfinoski, Steven. *The Kid's Guide to Money: Earning It, Saving It, Spending It, Growing It, Sharing It* (4–8). Illus. 1996, Scholastic paper $4.95 (0-590-53853-5). This practical guide for kids on how to earn money and manage it responsibly includes budgeting, standard consumer advice, basic information about the stock market, credit cards, and sharing. (Rev: BL 4/1/96; SLJ 6/96) [332.4]

18755 Weintraub, Aileen. *Everything You Need to Know About Being a Baby-Sitter: A Teen's Guide to Responsible Child Care* (5–8). 2000, Rosen LB $25.25 (0-8239-3085-8). 64pp. This book covers all facets of baby-sitting from preparation, responsibilities, and safety precautions to employment opportunities. (Rev: SLJ 7/00) [649]

18756 Zakarin, Debra M. *The Ultimate Baby-Sitter's Handbook: So You Wanna Make Tons of Money?* (4–8). Illus. 1997, Price Stern Sloan paper $4.99 (0-8431-7936-8). A practical, easily read guide to baby-sitting and setting up a business. (Rev: BL 9/15/97; SLJ 12/97) [649]

Retail Stores and Other Workplaces

18757 Krull, Kathleen. *Supermarket* (K–3). Illus. by Melanie Hope Greenberg. 2001, Holiday House $16.95 (0-8234-1546-5). 32pp. This is a fascinating and stimulating overview of what you'll find in the supermarket and how it gets there, including material on the history of shopping from barter onward and lots of interesting tidbits. (Rev: BL 9/15/01; HBG 3/02; SLJ 10/01) [381]

Ecology and Environment

General

18758 Ansary, Mir Tamim. *Earth Day* (2–3). Illus. Series: Holiday Histories. 2002, Heinemann LB $14.95 (1-58810-220-3). 32pp. The author traces the history of the Earth and its natural resources, man's misappropriation of them, and the founding of Earth Day. (Rev: BL 2/1/02) [333.7]

18759 Ballard, Carol. *The Search for Better Conservation* (4–7). Illus. Series: Science Quest. 2005, Gareth Stevens LB $18.50 (0-8368-4553-6). 32pp. A look at how lack of conservation affects us, and what scientists are doing to tackle this problem.

18760 Bowden, Rob. *Water Supply: Our Impact on the Planet* (5–8). Illus. Series: 21st Century Debates. 2003, Raintree LB $28.56 (0-7398-5506-9). 64pp. A thought-provoking examination of the status of the world's water supply, predictions of a looming water crisis, and measures that could be taken to avert this. (Rev: BL 8/03; HBG 10/03) [363.6]

18761 Burnie, David. *Endangered Planet* (4–8). Illus. Series: Kingfisher Knowledge. 2004, Kingfisher $11.95 (0-7534-5776-8). 63pp. This volume looks at how human requirements threaten the flora, fauna, and resources of our planet. (Rev: SLJ 1/05) [333.95]

18762 Dalgleish, Sharon. *Protecting Wildlife* (4–6). Illus. Series: Our World: Our Future. 2002, Chelsea LB $18.95 (0-7910-7021-2). 32pp. The role of humans is emphasized in this look at the impact on wildlife of vanishing habitats and changes in the weather, and simple actions that children can take are suggested. Also use *Saving Our Water* (2002). (Rev: HBG 3/03; SLJ 1/03)

18763 Ditchfield, Christin. *Oil* (2–5). Illus. Series: True Books — Natural Resources. 2002, Children's Book Pr. LB $23.50 (0-516-22343-7); paper $6.95 (0-516-29367-2). 48pp. This book discusses oil, its procurement and processing, and the environmental impact of using oil as fuel, with simple text and excellent photographs. (Rev: BL 10/15/02) [553.2]

18764 Ditchfield, Christin. *Water* (2–5). Illus. Series: True Books — Natural Resources. 2002, Children's Book Pr. LB $23.50 (0-516-22345-3); paper $6.95 (0-516-29369-9). 48pp. Ditchfield discusses water as a natural resource, covering in simple text and excellent photographs the forms of water, the water cycle, and the ways in which we use water. (Rev: BL 10/15/02) [553.7]

18765 Domeniconi, David. *M Is for Majestic: A National Parks Alphabet* (1–5). Illus. by Pam Carroll. 2003, Sleeping Bear $17.95 (1-58536-138-0). In a blend of rhyming verse and stunning artwork, young readers are introduced to America's national parks from Acadia to Zion. (Rev: HBG 4/04; SLJ 12/03) [333.78]

18766 Hill, Lee S. *Parks Are to Share* (1–3). Series: Building Blocks Books. 1997, Carolrhoda $21.27 (1-57505-068-4). 32pp. This book explores all kinds of parks and their care and uses, from Yosemite National Park to Central Park in New York City. (Rev: BL 3/15/98; HBG 3/98) [363.6]

18767 Holmes, Anita. *I Can Save the Earth: A Kid's Handbook for Keeping Earth Healthy and Green* (4–6). Illus. by David Neuhaus. 1993, Simon & Schuster LB $13.98 (0-671-74544-1); paper $7.95 (0-671-74545-X). 96pp. A practical guide that offers many suggestions on ways for young people to actively help in conservation. (Rev: SLJ 7/93) [320.5]

18768 Javna, John. *50 Simple Things Kids Can Do to Save the Earth* (3–6). Illus. by Michele Montez. 1990, Andrews & McMeel paper $6.95 (0-8362-2301-2). 156pp. This book shows how small changes can help to save the environment. (Rev: BL 6/15/90; SLJ 9/90) [333.7]

18769 Johnson, Rebecca L. *Investigating the Ozone Hole* (5–8). 1994, Lerner LB $28.75 (0-8225-1574-1). Using interviews, documents, and firsthand research, the author charts the development and possible consequences of an ozone hole above the Antarctic. (Rev: BL 3/1/94) [551.5]

18770 Juettner, Bonnie. *Energy* (5–8). Illus. Series: Our Environment. 2004, Gale/KidHaven LB $23.70 (0-7377-1821-8). 48pp. Answers such questions as "How is energy managed?" and "Are we running out of energy?" in four chapters that feature many illustrations and large type. (Rev: SLJ 4/05) [333.79]

18771 Kerley, Barbara. *A Cool Drink of Water* (PS–3). Illus. 2002, National Geographic $16.95 (0-7922-6723-0). 32pp. A series of beautiful photographs with minimal text show how water is collected and carried by people throughout the world. (Rev: BL 3/15/02; HBG 10/02; SLJ 4/02*) [363.6]

18772 Krensky, Stephen. *Four Against the Odds: The Struggle to Save Our Environment* (5–8). 1992, Scholastic paper $2.99 (0-590-44743-2). Introduces the work of four individuals who fought to raise public awareness about important environmental issues: John Muir, Chico Mendes, Rachel Carson, and Lois Gibb. (Rev: BL 6/1/92; SLJ 10/92) [363.7]

18773 Lester, Julius. *From Slave Ship to Freedom Road* (5–10). Illus. 1998, Dial $17.99 (0-8037-1893-4). This book combines art, history, and commentary to produce a graphically gripping history of slavery. (Rev: BL 2/15/98; HBG 9/98; SLJ 2/98*) [759.13]

18774 Levine, Shar, and Allison Grafton. *Projects for a Healthy Planet: Simple Environmental Experiments for Kids* (3–7). Illus. by Terry Chui. 1992, Wiley paper $10.95 (0-471-55484-7). 64pp. A worthy addition to the many ecology books on the market. (Rev: BL 8/92; SLJ 8/92) [628]

18775 Lowery, Linda, and Marybeth Lorbiecki. *Earthwise at Home* (3–5). Illus. by David Mataya. 1993, Carolrhoda LB $19.95 (0-87614-730-9). 48pp. This book gives tips on how to recycle, reuse, and preserve materials at home. Others in this series are *Earthwise at Play* and *Earthwise at School* (both 1993). (Rev: SLJ 5/93) [320]

18776 Mattson, Mark. *Scholastic Environmental Atlas of the United States* (3–6). Illus. 1993, Scholastic $14.95 (0-590-49354-X). 80pp. In this atlas, natural resources and ecological threats like water pollution and toxic dumps are pictured globally. (Rev: BL 10/15/93; SLJ 4/94) [333.7]

18777 Oxlade, Chris. *Global Warming* (5–7). Illus. Series: Our Planet in Peril. 2002, Capstone LB $22.60 (0-7368-1361-6). 32pp. Attractive double-page spreads explore the concern about global warning, its causes, and options for the future. Also use *Nuclear Waste* (2003). (Rev: HBG 3/03; SLJ 4/03) [363.738]

18778 Parker, Janice, ed. *The Disappearing Forests* (5–8). Illus. Series: Understanding Global Issues. 2002, Smart Apple LB $19.95 (1-58340-168-7). 56pp. A great deal of information about forest use, abuse, and conservation is packed into double-paged spreads with color illustrations. (Rev: BL 10/15/02; HBG 3/03; SLJ 12/02) [634.9]

18779 Parks, Peggy J. *Global Warming* (5–8). Illus. Series: Our Environment. 2004, Gale/KidHaven LB $23.70 (0-7377-1822-6). 48pp. Answers such ques-tions as "Caused by humans or caused by nature?" and "What can be done?" in four chapters that feature many illustrations and large type. (Rev: SLJ 4/05) [363.738]

18780 Penny, Malcolm. *Our Environment* (2–3). Series: Talking About. 1999, Raintree LB $15.98 (0-8172-5889-2). 32pp. A simple format and many illustrations enhance this beginner's book on conservation and environmental protection, using such everyday examples as littering. (Rev: BL 2/15/00; HBG 9/00) [333.75]

18781 Peters, Celeste, ed. *The Energy Dilemma* (5–8). Illus. Series: Understanding Global Issues. 2002, Smart Apple LB $19.95 (1-58340-169-5). 56pp. The information about energy sources, use, and conservation packed into these double-paged spreads with color illustrations will spark debate. (Rev: BL 10/15/02) [333.79]

18782 Pringle, Laurence. *Global Warming: The Threat of Earth's Changing Climate* (4–8). Illus. 2001, North-South $16.95 (1-58717-009-4). 48pp. A straightforward account that covers topics including the causes of global warming, the signs that it is occurring, and possible solutions. (Rev: BL 4/1/01; HBG 10/01; SLJ 6/01) [363.738]

18783 Pringle, Laurence. *Vanishing Ozone: Protecting Earth from Ultraviolet Radiation* (4–8). Illus. Series: Save-the-Earth Books. 1995, Morrow LB $15.89 (0-688-04158-2). 64pp. The exciting but disturbing story of the thinning ozone layer and the conflicts it is producing among governments, environmentalists, and industry. (Rev: SLJ 9/95*) [363.73]

18784 Seibert, Patricia. *Toad Overload: A True Tale of Nature Knocked Off Balance in Australia* (K–3). Illus. by Jan Davey Ellis. 1996, Millbrook LB $21.90 (1-56294-613-7). 32pp. The balance of nature in Australia is upset when large toads are imported to eat marauding beetles. (Rev: BCCB 2/96; BL 2/15/96; SLJ 4/96) [597.8]

18785 Sheehan, Sean. *Greenpeace* (5–8). Series: World Watch. 2004, Raintree LB $27.14 (0-7398-6612-5). 47pp. A thorough review of the sometimes controversial conservationist organization since its founding in 1970, with some graphic photographs. (Rev: BL 4/1/04; SLJ 3/04) [333.7]

18786 Suzuki, David, and Kathy Vanderlinden. *Eco-Fun* (5–8). Illus. 2001, Douglas & McIntyre paper $10.95 (1-55054-823-9). 128pp. The activities in this collection reinforce some basic scientific concepts about air, water, earth, and fire, and encourage young readers to think about environmental issues and avoid pollution. (Rev: BL 6/1–15/01; SLJ 8/01) [577]

18787 Taylor, Barbara. *How to Save the Planet* (3–6). Illus. by Scoular Anderson. Series: How To. 2001, Watts LB $14.00 (0-531-14640-5); paper $4.95 (0-531-14821-1). 96pp. Experiments back up the concepts introduced in this discussion of global warming, pollution, future energy needs, and other important topics. (Rev: SLJ 4/02) [363.7]

18788 VanCleave, Janice. *Janice VanCleave's Ecology for Every Kid* (4–7). Illus. 1996, Wiley paper

$10.95 (0-471-10086-2). 240pp. Clear instructions and many diagrams introduce a series of experiments that highlight environmental issues. (Rev: BL 3/1/96; SLJ 4/96) [574.5]

18789 Whitman, Sylvia. *This Land Is Your Land: The American Conservation Movement* (5–7). Illus. 1994, Lerner LB $30.35 (0-8225-1729-9). 88pp. A history of the conservation movement from its beginnings in 1870 when there were efforts to save Yellowstone and ending with today's major problems such as oil spills and trash disposal. (Rev: BL 12/15/94; HB 3–4/94; SLJ 12/94) [363.7]

Cities

18790 Aldis, Rodney. *Towns and Cities* (5–8). Series: Ecology Watch. 1992, Dillon LB $13.95 (0-87518-496-0). A discussion of urban life and environmental problems that it creates. (Rev: BL 12/15/92) [574.5]

18791 Matsen, Bradford. *Go Wild in New York City* (4–6). Illus. 2005, National Geographic $16.95 (0-7922-7982-4). 80pp. Skippy the squirrel guides readers through the nature to be found in the urban landscape of New York City, with chapters on its flora and fauna, water, rocks, and air. (Rev: BL 3/15/05; SLJ 5/05) [508.747]

18792 Parker, Philip. *Global Cities* (4–6). Illus. Series: Project Eco-City. 1995, Thomson Learning LB $7.95 (1-56847-286-2). 48pp. This account concentrates on the ecology and balance of nature found in large cities. (Rev: BL 6/1–15/95) [307.76]

18793 Sammis, Fran. *Cities and Towns* (2–5). Illus. Series: Discovering Geography. 1997, Marshall Cavendish LB $22.79 (0-7614-0540-2). 32pp. Using a question-and-answer approach, this account introduces cities and towns and outlines projects in map making, including finding houses along a newspaper route or stores in a mall. (Rev: BL 2/1/98; HBG 3/98; SLJ 4/98) [307.76]

Garbage and Waste Recycling

18794 Burton, Jane, and Kim Taylor. *The Nature and Science of Waste* (3–6). Series: Exploring the Science of Nature. 1999, Gareth Stevens LB $14.95 (0-8368-2186-6). 32pp. Different kinds of waste and their disposal techniques and problems are discussed in this well-illustrated account that includes a special activities section. (Rev: BL 7/99; SLJ 1/00) [363.7]

18795 Coombs, Karen Mueller. *Flush! Treating Wastewater* (3–6). Illus. 1995, Carolrhoda LB $22.60 (0-87614-879-8). 56pp. A history of sanitation through the centuries is given, plus a description of present-day water purification systems. (Rev: BCCB 1/96; BL 12/1/95; SLJ 12/95) [628.3]

18796 Hall, Eleanor J. *Garbage* (5–8). Illus. Series: Overview. 1997, Lucent LB $27.45 (1-56006-188-X). A history of how waste disposal has been han-

dled, and current ecological and environmental approaches, including recycling. (Rev: BL 8/97; HBG 3/98) [363.72]

18797 Hall, Eleanor J. *Recycling* (5–8). Illus. Series: Our Environment. 2004, Gale/KidHaven LB $23.70 (0-7377-1517-0). 48pp. Answers such questions as "What is recycling?" and "What does the future hold?" in four chapters that feature many illustrations and large type. (Rev: SLJ 4/05) [363.72]

18798 Heilman, Joan R. *Tons of Trash: Why You Should Recycle and What Happens When You Do* (3–5). 1992, Avon paper $3.50 (0-380-76379-6). 80pp. This lively tour of processing plants shows how garbage is recycled. (Rev: BL 4/15/92) [363.72]

18799 Ring, Elizabeth. *What Rot! Nature's Mighty Recycler* (3–5). Illus. 1996, Millbrook LB $23.40 (1-56294-671-4). 32pp. Numerous photos and a lively text describe how nature provides organisms and processes to decompose materials naturally. (Rev: BL 2/15/96; SLJ 4/96) [574.2]

18800 Snodgrass, Mary Ellen. *Solid Waste* (4–6). Illus. Series: Environmental Awareness. 1991, Bancroft-Sage LB $14.95 (0-944280-28-5). 48pp. The techniques and problems of waste removal and recycling, with many color illustrations. Also use: *Water Pollution* (1991). (Rev: BL 2/15/92) [363.73]

18801 Wilcox, Charlotte. *Trash!* (3–5). Illus. 1988, Carolrhoda LB $16.95 (0-87614-311-7); Lerner paper $5.95 (0-87614-511-X). 40pp. What happens to garbage after it's collected. (Rev: BL 12/1/88; HB 1–2/89; SLJ 1/89)

Pollution

18802 Berger, Melvin. *Oil Spill!* (K–3). Illus. by Paul Mirocha. 1994, HarperCollins paper $4.95 (0-06-445121-6). 32pp. After a description of the *Exxon Valdez* catastrophe, general material on oil spills is presented, including their causes, effects, and how they can be prevented. (Rev: BL 6/1–15/94) [363.73]

18803 Brown, Paul. *Global Pollution* (5–8). Illus. Series: Face the Facts. 2003, Raintree LB $28.56 (0-7398-6433-5). 56pp. The effects of pollution on the environment are described in understandable terms, and practical responses from young people are suggested. (Rev: BL 11/15/03; HBG 10/03; SLJ 9/03) [303.73]

18804 Bryan, Nichol. *Danube: Cyanide Spill* (4–6). Series: Environmental Disasters. 2003, World Almanac LB $29.26 (0-8368-5505-1). 48pp. This entry in a series on environmental disasters chronicles a cyanide spill in the Danube in 2000 that affected wildlife and people in four countries. (Rev: SLJ 3/04)

18805 Bryan, Nichol. *Exxon Valdez: Oil Spill* (4–8). Illus. Series: Environmental Disasters. 2003, World Almanac LB $29.26 (0-8368-5506-X). 48pp. The environmental impact of the 1989 Exxon Valdez oil spill in Alaska's Prince William Sound is thoughtfully explored in this slim volume about the disaster. (Rev: BL 2/1/04; SLJ 3/04) [363.738]

18806 Bryan, Nichol. *Love Canal: Pollution Crisis* (4–8). Illus. Series: Environmental Disasters. 2003, World Almanac LB $29.26 (0-8368-5508-6). 48pp. A look at the dumping of hazardous industrial wastes in upstate New York and the devastating effects on the area's environment. (Rev: BL 2/1/04; SLJ 3/04) [303.738]

18807 Chapman, Matthew, and Rob Bowden. *Air Pollution* (5–8). Series: 21st Century Debates. 2002, Raintree LB $27.12 (0-7398-4874-7). 64pp. The causes of air pollution, the present situation, and possible future solutions are presented in this well-illustrated book that presents various points of view and offers topics for debate. (Rev: BL 6/1–15/02) [363.73]

18808 Cherry, Lynne. *A River Ran Wild* (1–3). Illus. 1992, Harcourt $16.00 (0-15-200542-0). 40pp. Tracing the environmental history and present status of the Nashua River, which runs through New Hampshire and Massachusetts. (Rev: BL 3/15/92; HB 5–6/92; SLJ 5/92) [974.4]

18809 Cole, Joanna. *The Magic School Bus: At the Water Works* (2–5). Illus. by Bruce Degen. 1995, Scholastic $14.95 (0-614-03341-1); paper $4.99 (0-590-40360-5). 40pp. Scientific fun with Ms. Frizzle, the world's strangest teacher and an unflappable naturalist. (Rev: BL 11/15/86; SLJ 1/87)

18810 Collinson, Alan. *Pollution* (5–8). Series: Repairing the Damage. 1992, Macmillan LB $21.00 (0-02-722995-5). A historical overview of nuclear waste, river pollution, overpopulation, and other aspects of pollution. (Rev: BL 9/15/92) [363.73]

18811 Hoff, Mary, and Mary M. Rodgers. *Our Endangered Planet: Groundwater* (4–7). Illus. Series: Our Endangered Planet. 1991, Lerner LB $22.60 (0-8225-2500-3). 64pp. A discussion of the supply, access, uses, and pollution of groundwater around the world. (Rev: BL 6/15/91; SLJ 5/91) [333.91]

18812 O'Neill, Mary. *Air Scare* (4–7). Illus. by John Bindon. Series: SOS Planet Earth. 1991, Troll paper $5.95 (0-8167-2083-5). 32pp. An oversize book that deals with the important environmental issue of air pollution. (Rev: BL 6/15/91) [363]

18813 Parks, Peggy. *Global Warming* (5–8). Illus. Series: Lucent Library of Science and Technology. 2004, Gale/Lucent LB $27.45 (1-59018-319-3). 112pp. Explores the controversies surrounding the theory of global warming and the potential consequences of the Earth's rising temperature.

18814 Pringle, Laurence. *Oil Spills: Damage, Recovery, and Prevention* (5–8). 1993, Morrow LB $14.89 (0-688-09861-4). A discussion of damage caused by oil spills, cleanup, and prevention efforts, with a description of how petroleum forms, how it is removed from the ground, and its uses as background. (Rev: BL 9/15/93) [363.73]

18815 Snodgrass, Mary Ellen. *Acid Rain* (4–6). Illus. Series: Environmental Awareness. 1991, Bancroft-Sage LB $14.95 (0-944280-30-7). 48pp. Basic, up-to-date information on acid rain. Also use: *Toxic Waste* (1991). (Rev: BL 2/15/92) [363.73]

18816 Snodgrass, Mary Ellen. *Air Pollution* (4–6). Illus. Series: Environmental Awareness. 1991, Bancroft-Sage LB $14.95 (0-944280-31-5). 48pp. Using color photos, diagrams, and straightforward information, the problems of air pollution are introduced, along with possible solutions. Also use: *Land Pollution* (1991). (Rev: BL 2/15/92) [363.73]

18817 Zipko, Stephen J. *Toxic Threat: How Hazardous Substances Poison Our Lives* (5–7). Illus. by Malle N. Whitaker. 1990, Simon & Schuster paper $5.95 (0-671-69331-X). 249pp. Many environmental pollutants, including radon and PCBs, are introduced. (Rev: SLJ 8/90) [363.7]

Population

18818 Bowden, Rob. *An Overcrowded World?* (5–8). Series: 21st Century Debates. 2002, Raintree LB $27.12 (0-7398-4872-0). 64pp. Using a well-organized text, plus sidebars for additional facts and statements of opinion, this colorfully illustrated volume explores the current problems of overpopulation and the dire strain it causes on the earth's supplies. (Rev: BL 6/1–15/02) [304.6]

18819 Gedatus, Gus. *Violence in Public Places* (5–8). Series: Perspectives on Violence. 2000, Capstone LB $23.93 (0-7368-0428-5). 64pp. This examines violence in public places from hate crimes to road rage. Also use in the same series *Violence in the Media* (2000). (Rev: HBG 9/00; SLJ 8/00) [362]

18820 Gellman, Marc, and Thomas Hartman. *Bad Stuff in the News: A Family Guide to Handling the Headlines* (4–7). 2002, North-South $14.95 (1-58717-132-5). 120pp. A reassuring book about difficult current issues, including terrorism, accidents, school violence, and more. (Rev: BL 5/15/02; HBG 10/02; SLJ 3/02) [302.23]

18821 Smith, David J. *If the World Were a Village* (3–5). Illus. by Shelagh Armstrong. 2002, Kids Can $15.95 (1-55074-779-7). 32pp. By condensing the world's population to a "village" of 100 people, this book makes data and statistics more comprehensible — and more fascinating — for younger readers. (Rev: BL 3/1/02; HB 5–6/02; HBG 10/02; SLJ 5/02) [304.6]

18822 Winckler, Suzanne, and Mary M. Rodgers. *Our Endangered Planet: Population Growth* (4–7). Illus. Series: Our Endangered Planet. 1991, Lerner LB $27.15 (0-8225-2502-X). 64pp. A discussion of the effects that rapid population growth has had on the environment. (Rev: BL 6/15/91; SLJ 5/91) [304.6]

Government and Politics

Courts and the Law

18823 Anderson, Wayne. *Brown v. Board of Education: The Case Against School Segregation* (5–8). Series: Supreme Court Cases Through Primary Sources. 2004, Rosen LB $29.25 (0-8239-4009-8). 64pp. Primary sources — photographs, police records, newspaper clippings, and court documents — provide details of the case and the narrative discusses the historical and social context. Also use *Plessy v. Ferguson: Legalizing Segregation* (2004). (Rev: SLJ 6/04) [345.73]

18824 Beaudry, Jo, and Lynne Ketchum. *Carla Goes to Court* (3–6). Illus. 1983, Human Sciences $16.95 (0-89885-088-6); paper $10.95 (0-89885-354-0). 32pp. The court process is explored through Carla's experience after she witnesses a burglary.

18825 Burnett, Betty. *The Trial of Julius and Ethel Rosenberg: A Primary Source Account* (5–8). Illus. Series: Great Trials of the Twentieth Century. 2004, Rosen LB $21.95 (0-8239-3976-6). 64pp. Primary sources — photographs, original transcripts, quotations, and so forth — give depth to this compelling account of the complex trial. (Rev: SLJ 10/04)

18826 Crewe, Sabrina, and Michael V. Uschan. *The Scottsboro Case* (4–7). Illus. Series: Events That Shaped America. 2005, Gareth Stevens LB $18.50 (0-8368-3407-0). 32pp. A thorough and thought-provoking look at the infamous Scottsboro case in which nine young African Americans were accused of raping two white women. (Rev: BL 1/1–15/05; SLJ 3/05) [345.73]

18827 De Capua, Sarah E. *Serving on a Jury* (2–5). Series: True Books — Civics. 2002, Children's Book Pr. LB $23.00 (0-516-22329-1); paper $6.95 (0-516-27364-7). 48pp. Chapters in this simple book on the jury system include material on what is a jury, who can serve, how members are selected, and what they do. (Rev: BL 6/1–15/02; SLJ 10/02) [347.73]

18828 Deegan, Paul J. *Supreme Court Book* (4–6). Illus. Series: Supreme Court Justices. 1992, ABDO LB $19.99 (1-56239-097-X). 50pp. This account explains the various functions of the court and how they have changed from George Washington's time to the present. (Rev: BL 6/1–15/93) [347]

18829 Donnelly, Karen. *Cruzan v. Missouri: The Right to Die* (5–7). Illus. Series: Supreme Court Cases through Primary Sources. 2004, Rosen LB $31.95 (0-8239-4014-4). 64pp. The lengthy legal battle for a patient's right to die is chronicled in this account of the Supreme Court's decision in Cruzan v. Missouri. (Rev: BL 6/1–15/04; SLJ 6/04) [344.73]

18830 Donovan, Sandy. *Making Laws: A Look at How a Bill Becomes a Law* (4–6). Illus. Series: How Government Works. 2003, Lerner LB $25.26 (0-8225-1346-3). 56pp. An easily understood explanation of how an idea (the example is banning school on Fridays) can become a bill and then a law. (Rev: SLJ 3/04) [328.7]

18831 Dudley, Mark E. *Engel v. Vitale (1962): Religion and the Schools* (5–9). Series: Supreme Court Decisions. 1995, Twenty-First Century LB $25.90 (0-8050-3916-3). The story of the Supreme Court case on school prayer that originated with two Jewish youngsters who objected to being forced to pray every morning in a New York City school. (Rev: BL 11/15/95; SLJ 1/96) [347]

18832 Goldish, Meish. *Our Supreme Court* (4–6). Illus. Series: I Know America. 1994, Millbrook LB $21.90 (1-56294-445-2). 48pp. An introduction to the Supreme Court that gives its history, composition, and a few historic decisions. (Rev: BL 11/15/94; SLJ 1/95) [347.73]

18833 Grabowski, John F. *The Death Penalty* (5–8). Series: Overview. 1999, Lucent LB $27.45 (1-56006-371-8). 96pp. A fair, unbiased review of the history, pro and con arguments, and present status of the death penalty in America. (Rev: BL 8/99) [364.6]

18834 Himton, Kerry. *The Trial of Sacco and Vanzetti: A Primary Source Account* (5–8). Illus. Series:

Great Trials of the Twentieth Century. 2004, Rosen LB $21.95 (0-8239-3973-1). 64pp. Primary sources — photographs, original transcripts, quotations, and so forth — give depth to this compelling account of the complex trial. (Rev: SLJ 6/04)

18835 Horn, Geoffrey M. *The Supreme Court* (5–8). Series: World Almanac Library of American Government. 2003, World Almanac LB $26.60 (0-8368-5459-4). 48pp. An excellent introduction to the U.S. Supreme Court and the important role it plays in interpreting the laws of the land. (Rev: SLJ 1/04)

18836 Linz, Kathi. *Chickens May Not Cross the Road and Other Crazy (But True) Laws* (2–4). Illus. by Tony Griego. 2002, Houghton Mifflin $16.00 (0-618-11257-X). 32pp. A compilation of silly laws ("no tying crocodiles to fire hydrants," "no donkeys in bathtubs") from cities across the United States, each with a cartoon illustration. (Rev: BL 9/1/02; HBG 3/03; SLJ 11/02) [348.73]

18837 Naden, Corinne J., and Rose Blue. *Dred Scott: Person or Property?* (5–8). Illus. Series: Supreme Court Milestones. 2005, Benchmark LB $25.95 (0-7614-1841-5). 144pp. The Supreme Court's 1857 Dred Scott decision, arguably the high court's most misguided ruling ever, is examined in detail. (Rev: BL 2/1/05) [342.7]

18838 Olson, Steven P. *The Trial of John T. Scopes: A Primary Source Account* (5–8). Series: Great Trials of the Twentieth Century. 2004, Rosen LB $29.25 (0-8239-3974-X). 64pp. Primary sources — photographs, original transcripts, quotations, and so forth — give depth to this compelling account of the complex trial. (Rev: SLJ 8/04) [344.73]

18839 Payment, Simone. *Roe v. Wade: The Right to Choose* (5–7). Illus. Series: Supreme Court Cases Through Primary Sources. 2004, Rosen LB $31.95 (0-8239-4012-8). 64pp. Illustrations are used to good effect in this overview of the issues raised in the Supreme Court's landmark decision. (Rev: BL 6/1–15/04; SLJ 6/04) [342.73]

18840 Payment, Simone. *The Trial of Leopold and Loeb: A Primary Source Account* (5–8). Illus. Series: Great Trials of the Twentieth Century. 2004, Rosen LB $21.95 (0-8239-3970-7). 64pp. Primary sources — photographs, original transcripts, quotations, and so forth — give depth to this compelling account of the complex trial. (Rev: SLJ 6/04)

18841 Reef, Catherine. *The Supreme Court* (4–7). Illus. Series: Places in American History. 1994, Dillon paper $7.95 (0-382-24722-1). 72pp. An introduction to the Supreme Court, its powers, composition, and landmark decisions. (Rev: BL 1/1/95) [347.73]

18842 Roensch, Greg. *The Lindbergh Baby Kidnapping Trial: A Primary Source Account* (5–8). Series: Great Trials of the Twentieth Century. 2004, Rosen LB $29.25 (0-8239-3971-5). 64pp. Primary sources — photographs, original transcripts, handwriting samples, and so forth — give depth to this account of this controversial trial. (Rev: SLJ 8/04) [345.73]

18843 Scheppler, Bill. *The Mississippi Burning Trial: A Primary Source Account* (5–8). Illus. Series: Great Trials of the Twentieth Century. 2004,

Rosen LB $21.95 (0-8239-3972-3). 64pp. Primary sources — photographs, original transcripts, quotations, and so forth — give depth to this compelling account of the complex trial. (Rev: SLJ 10/04)

18844 Sonneborn, Liz. *Miranda v. Arizona: The Rights of the Accused* (5–8). Series: Supreme Court Cases Through Primary Sources. 2004, Rosen LB $29.25 (0-8239-4010-1). 64pp. Primary sources — photographs, police records, newspaper clippings, and court documents — provide details of the case and the narrative discusses the historical and social context. (Rev: SLJ 6/04) [345.73]

United Nations and International Affairs

18845 Burger, Leslie, and Debra L. Rahm. *Red Cross / Red Crescent: When Help Can't Wait* (5–7). Illus. 1996, Lerner $22.60 (0-8225-2698-0). 80pp. The story of the Red Cross and the role it plays in helping people today. (Rev: BL 1/1–15/97; SLJ 1/97) [361.7]

18846 Castle, Caroline. *For Every Child: The UN Convention on the Rights of the Child in Words and Pictures* (1–4). Illus. 2001, Penguin Putnam $16.99 (0-8037-2650-3). 40pp. Based on the principles adopted by the United Nations, this book presents 14 rights of children each with a painting by a distinguished artist. (Rev: BL 2/1/01; HBG 10/01; SLJ 3/01) [346.01]

18847 Giesecke, Ernestine. *Governments Around the World* (3–5). Series: Kids' Guide. 2000, Heinemann $21.36 (1-57572-511-8). 32pp. This book explains different kinds of governments — democracies, communist and socialist states, monarchies, and other systems. (Rev: HBG 3/01; SLJ 10/00) [320]

18848 Grant, R. G. *Genocide* (5–10). Illus. Series: Talking Points. 1999, Raintree LB $27.12 (0-8172-5314-9). This book covers the Holocaust in World War II as well as more recent massacres in Cambodia, Rwanda, and Bosnia, and probes such controversies as who is guilty of genocide — the person who pulls the trigger or those who plan and organize it, and what about the bystander? (Rev: BL 9/1/99) [304.6]

18849 Maddocks, Steven. *UNICEF* (5–8). Series: World Watch. 2004, Raintree LB $27.14 (0-7398-6617-6). 48pp. Introduces UNICEF's history, organization, and work on behalf of the world's children; sidebars provide key facts and relevant quotations. (Rev: SLJ 6/04) [362.7]

18850 Melvern, Linda. *United Nations* (3–5). Illus. Series: World Organizations. 2001, Watts LB $23.00 (0-531-14624-3); paper $6.95 (0-531-14814-9). 32pp. An overview of the United Nations, for younger readers, that outlines the organization's history and goals as well as the problems it faces. (Rev: BL 1/1–15/02) [341.23]

18851 Ostopowich, Melanie. *Greenpeace* (4–8). Series: International Organizations. 2002, Weigl LB $24.25 (1-59036-020-6). 32pp. An introduction to the goals, structure, members, and volunteers who work with this international organization. Also use *Peace Corps* (2003). (Rev: HBG 3/03; SLJ 4/03) [333.72]

18852 Powell, Jillian. *World Wildlife Fund* (3–5). Illus. Series: World Organizations. 2001, Watts LB $23.00 (0-531-14626-X); paper $6.95 (0-531-14816-5). 32pp. This volume for younger readers describes the mission, projects, and problems of the World Wildlife Fund. (Rev: BL 1/1–15/02) [639.9]

18853 Radunsky, Vladimir. *What Does Peace Feel Like?* (PS–3). Illus. by author. 2004, Simon & Schuster $14.95 (0-689-86676-3). 24pp. Students at an international school in Rome imagine what peace looks, sounds, tastes, feels, and smells like. (Rev: BL 11/1/04; SLJ 1/05) [303.6]

18854 Ross, Stewart. *United Nations* (5–8). Illus. Series: World Watch. 2004, Raintree LB $18.99 (0-7398-6616-8). 48pp. Ross explains the role of the United Nations as an international watchdog and provides a brief review of its history and organization. (Rev: BL 4/1/04) [341.23]

18855 Spies, Karen B. *Isolation vs. Intervention: Is America the World's Police Force?* (4–6). Illus. Series: Issues of Our Time. 1995, Twenty-First Century LB $18.90 (0-8050-3880-9). 64pp. Objectively presents arguments, pro and con, concerning involvement in the political and economic problems of other countries. (Rev: SLJ 2/96) [327.73]

18856 Stearman, Kaye. *Homelessness* (5–10). Illus. Series: Talking Points. 1999, Raintree LB $27.12 (0-8172-5312-2). 64pp. A worldwide view of homelessness, its causes — including eviction, natural disasters, and war — and international efforts to combat it. (Rev: BL 9/1/99; SLJ 8/99) [363.5]

18857 Suen, Anastasia. *Doctors Without Borders* (1–2). Series: Helping Organizations. 2002, Rosen LB $16.00 (0-8239-6002-1). 24pp. As well as giving a history of this humanitarian organization, this simple account describes how it works and the good work it accomplishes. (Rev: BL 6/1–15/02; SLJ 4/02) [361.7]

18858 Suen, Anastasia. *The Red Cross* (1–2). Illus. Series: Helping Organizations. 2002, Rosen LB $16.00 (0-8239-6003-X). 24pp. This basic introduction to the Red Cross explains how it was formed and the work it does around the world. (Rev: BL 6/1–15/02) [361.7]

18859 Suen, Anastasia. *UNICEF* (1–2). Illus. 2002, Rosen LB $16.00 (0-8239-6005-6). 24pp. This introduction to UNICEF and its mission also tells how volunteers can help and how youngsters can raise money to aid its programs. (Rev: BL 6/1–15/02; SLJ 3/02) [362.7]

United States

Civil Rights

18860 Adams, Colleen. *Women's Suffrage: A Primary Source History of the Women's Rights Movement in America* (5–8). Illus. Series: Primary Sources in American History. 2003, Rosen LB $29.25 (0-8239-

3685-6). 64pp. Primary sources — including pamphlets and newspaper articles — tell the story of the women's rights movement in America. (Rev: BL 5/15/03) [305.42]

18861 Bradley, Catherine. *Freedom of Movement* (5–8). Illus. Series: What Do We Mean by Human Rights? 1998, Watts LB $23.00 (0-531-14447-X). This lavishly illustrated book uses double-page spreads to explore immigration, nationalism, and refugees. (Rev: BL 4/1/98; HBG 9/98) [323]

18862 Bradley, David, and Shelley Fisher Fishkin, eds. *The Encyclopedia of Civil Rights in America* (5–10). 1997, Sharpe Reference $299.00 (0-7656-8000-9). This three-volume set contains 683 alphabetically arranged articles that explore the history, meaning, and application of civil rights issues in the United States. (Rev: BL 2/15/98; SLJ 5/98) [323]

18863 Bridges, Ruby. *Through My Eyes* (3–9). Illus. 1999, Scholastic $16.95 (0-590-18923-9). 64pp. Ruby Bridges tells what it was like to be the first African American child at an integrated school in 1960; photographs add to the attractive presentation. (Rev: BCCB 1/00*; BL 11/15/99*; HBG 4/00; SLJ 12/99*) [379.2]

18864 Brill, Marlene T. *Let Women Vote!* (4–6). Illus. Series: Spotlight on American History. 1995, Millbrook LB $15.90 (0-56294-589-0). 64pp. The history of the struggle to gain the vote for U.S. women and of the key personalities involved. (Rev: BL 12/15/95; SLJ 1/96) [324.6]

18865 Crewe, Sabrina, and Dale Anderson. *The Seneca Falls Women's Rights Convention* (3–5). Series: Events that Shaped America. 2005, Gareth Stevens LB $24.67 (0-8368-3408-9). 32pp. A simple, straightforward account of the 1848 convention featuring direct quotations, editorial cartoons, photographs, reproductions, and newspaper clippings. (Rev: SLJ 3/05) [305.42]

18866 Davidson, Tish. *Prejudice* (4–8). Series: Life Balance. 2003, Watts LB $19.50 (0-531-12252-2); paper $6.95 (0-531-15572-2). 80pp. This book explore the causes, types, and effects of prejudice, how it can change a person's mental health, and how it has influenced human history. (Rev: BL 10/15/03) [305.8]

18867 De Capua, Sarah E. *Abolitionists: A Force for Change* (4–7). Series: Journey to Freedom. 2002, Child's World LB $28.50 (1-56766-644-2). 40pp. An overview of the efforts of abolitionists in America from the 17th through 19th centuries. (Rev: SLJ 12/02) [326.80973]

18868 Ditchfield, Christin. *Knowing Your Civil Rights* (3–5). Series: A True Book. 2004, Children's Pr. LB $23.50 (0-516-22800-5). 47pp. A straightforward introduction to the concept of civil rights, this title looks at the freedoms guaranteed to all Americans under the Bill of Rights and provides a brief overview of the struggles of women and African Americans for equal rights. (Rev: SLJ 8/04) [342.7]

18869 Gold, Susan D. *In Re Gault (1967): Juvenile Justice* (5–9). Series: Supreme Court Decisions. 1995, Twenty-First Century LB $25.90 (0-8050-3917-1). Inequalities in juvenile sentencing were the

1004

subject of this Supreme Court case, an appeal of a six-year reform school sentence given to a juvenile for making an obscene phone call. (Rev: BL 11/15/95; SLJ 1/96) [347]

18870 Good, Diane L. *Brown v. Board of Education* (4–6). Series: Cornerstones of Freedom. 2004, Children's Pr. LB $24.00 (0-516-24225-3). 48pp. A nicely presented examination of the Supreme Court's 1954 ruling against school segregation. (Rev: SLJ 7/04) [344.73]

18871 Greenberg, Keith E. *Adolescent Rights: Are Young People Equal Under the Law?* (5–8). Illus. Series: Issues of Our Time. 1995, Twenty-First Century LB $22.90 (0-8050-3877-9). 64pp. This unbiased account of the controversial subject encourages readers to form their own conclusions. (Rev: SLJ 9/95) [323]

18872 Harvey, Miles. *Women's Voting Rights* (3–5). Illus. Series: Cornerstones of Freedom. 1996, Children's Book Pr. LB $20.50 (0-516-20003-8). 32pp. With illustrations on each page (many in color), this account traces the history of women's suffrage and the important people who were active in the movement. (Rev: BL 12/15/96; SLJ 2/97) [324.6]

18873 Haskins, Jim. *The Day Martin Luther King, Jr., Was Shot: A Photo History of the Civil Rights Movement* (4–9). 1992, Scholastic paper $5.99 (0-590-43661-9). A photographic history of the African American struggle from the time of slavery to the early 1990s. (Rev: BL 2/1/92; SLJ 5/92) [323.4]

18874 Haskins, Jim. *Freedom Rides: Journey for Justice* (5–7). Illus. 1995, Hyperion LB $15.49 (0-7868-2037-3). 128pp. This account focuses on a single dramatic aspect of the civil rights movement: the integration of buses and trains. (Rev: BL 1/1/95; SLJ 4/95) [323.1]

18875 Heinrichs, Ann. *The Ku Klux Klan: A Hooded Brotherhood* (4–7). Series: Journey to Freedom. 2002, Child's World LB $28.50 (1-56766-646-9). 40pp. This brief introduction to the Klan covers the group's origins and history, and touches on the Internet's role in spreading hate messages. (Rev: SLJ 12/02) [322.4]

18876 Hirst, Mike. *Freedom of Belief* (4–8). Illus. Series: What Do We Mean by Human Rights? 1997, Watts LB $23.00 (0-531-14435-6). An information-packed overview of religious and political freedom and the people who fought and sometimes died for it. (Rev: BL 1/1–15/98; HBG 3/98) [323.44]

18877 Hu, Evaleen. *A Level Playing Field: Sports and Race* (5–8). Illus. Series: Sports Issues. 1995, Lerner LB $28.75 (0-8225-3302-2). A frank, thorough examination of the problems involving race in sports and how different athletes have dealt with them. (Rev: BL 1/1–15/96; SLJ 9/95) [796]

18878 Isler, Claudia. *The Right to Free Speech* (4–6). Series: Individual Rights and Civic Responsibility. 2001, Rosen LB $19.95 (0-8239-3234-6). 128pp. The history of the first amendment is followed by information on sedition, protest, obscenity, symbolic speech, and hate speech. (Rev: SLJ 2/02) [342.0853]

18879 Johnston, Norma. *Remember the Ladies: The First Women's Rights Convention* (4–6). Illus. 1995, Scholastic paper $3.50 (0-590-47086-8). 169pp. The story of the 1848 Women's Rights Convention in Seneca Falls, New York, includes biographies of its leaders, like Elizabeth Cady Stanton and Lucretia Mott. (Rev: BL 5/1/95) [323.34]

18880 Kelso, Richard. *Walking for Freedom: The Montgomery Bus Boycott* (3–5). Illus. by Michael Newton. 1993, Raintree LB $27.12 (0-8114-7218-3). 52pp. The events and personalities associated with the Montgomery bus boycott are noted. (Rev: SLJ 8/93) [323.4]

18881 Kendall, Martha E. *Failure Is Impossible: The History of American Women's Rights* (5–8). Illus. Series: People's History. 2001, Lerner LB $30.35 (0-8225-1744-2). 96pp. The status of women in the United States is discussed from the time of the Puritans to the present, including information on life for slaves, Native American women, and mill girls, and on equal pay and equal opportunity. (Rev: BL 5/1/01; HBG 10/01; SLJ 6/01) [305.42]

18882 King, David C. *Freedom of Assembly* (4–8). Series: Land of the Free. 1997, Millbrook LB $22.90 (0-7613-0064-3). This book covers this basic civil right with examples throughout U.S. history and landmark court cases that helped define its limits. (Rev: BL 5/15/97; SLJ 10/97) [342.73]

18883 King, David C. *The Right to Speak Out* (4–8). Series: Land of the Free. 1997, Millbrook LB $22.90 (0-7613-0063-5). Background material on the freedom of speech is given, its use and abuse, and landmark courts cases that have defined it. (Rev: BL 5/15/97; SLJ 10/97) [351.81]

18884 King, Martin Luther, Jr. *I Have a Dream* (4–8). Illus. 1997, Scholastic paper $16.95 (0-590-20516-1). The full text of Dr. King's speech is reprinted, with illustrations by 15 award-winning African American artists. (Rev: BL 2/15/98; HBG 3/98; SLJ 11/97) [305.896]

18885 Kops, Deborah. *Women's Suffrage* (5–8). Illus. Series: People at the Center. 2004, Gale/Blackbirch LB $18.96 (1-56711-772-4). 48pp. This brief but fact-filled volume introduces key leaders in the women's suffrage movement in America. (Rev: BL 5/15/04; SLJ 9/04) [324.6]

18886 Landau, Elaine. *The Civil Rights Movement in America* (3–5). Series: Cornerstones of Freedom. 2003, Children's Pr. LB $24.00 (0-516-24219-9). 48pp. A brief, well-illustrated history of the troubled race relations in the United States and the concerted drive for equality beginning with the U.S. Supreme Court finding that school segregation was unconstitutional. (Rev: SLJ 2/04) [323]

18887 Lucas, Eileen. *Civil Rights: The Long Struggle* (5–8). Illus. Series: Issues in Focus. 1996, Enslow LB $19.95 (0-89490-729-8). 112pp. After a discussion of the first ten amendments to the U.S. Constitution, this account focuses on the civil rights struggles of African Americans. (Rev: SLJ 12/96) [323]

18888 Lucas, Eileen. *Cracking the Wall: The Struggles of the Little Rock Nine* (3–5). Illus. 1998, Carolrhoda $21.27 (0-87614-990-5). 48pp. A simple narrative that tells of the desegregation of Central High School in Little Rock, Arkansas, and gives background information on the 1953 Supreme Court decision. (Rev: BCCB 3/98; BL 2/15/98; HBG 9/98; SLJ 6/98) [379.2]

18889 McKissack, Patricia C., and Frederick L. McKissack. *Days of Jubilee: The End of Slavery in the United States* (5–8). 2003, Scholastic $18.95 (0-590-10764-X). 134pp. A combination of clear, interesting narrative, relevant quotations from primary sources, thorough historical approach, and well-chosen illustrations make this a worthwhile volume on the gradual end of slavery. (Rev: BCCB 4/03; BL 5/15/03; HBG 10/03; SLJ 5/03) [973.7]

18890 Meyers, Madeleine, ed. *Forward into Light: The Struggle for Woman's Suffrage* (4–8). Illus. Series: Perspectives on History. 1994, Discovery paper $6.95 (1-878668-25-0). 64pp. The story of the long struggle for women's right to vote, including the contributions of Elizabeth Cady Stanton, Susan B. Anthony, Sojourner Truth, and other leaders. (Rev: BL 8/94) [324.6]

18891 Miller, Jake. *The Montgomery Bus Boycott: Integrating Public Buses* (2–4). Series: The Library of the Civil Rights Movement. 2004, Rosen LB $19.95 (0-8239-6251-2). 24pp. Full of photographs, this is an accessible account of the major events of the bus boycott. Also use *Sit-Ins and Freedom Rides: The Power of Nonviolent Resistance* and *The March from Selma to Montgomery: African Americans Demand the Vote* (both 2004). (Rev: SLJ 6/04) [323.1]

18892 Morrison, Toni. *Remember: The Journey to School Integration* (5–12). Illus. 2004, Houghton Mifflin $18.00 (0-618-39740-X). 80pp. With striking archival photographs and a fictionalized narrative based on historical fact, this fascinating book explores the impact of the American struggle for civil rights on the children who were often at its center. (Rev: BL 4/15/04; SLJ 6/04) [379.2]

18893 O'Connor, Maureen. *Equal Rights* (5–8). Illus. Series: What Do We Mean by Human Rights? 1998, Watts LB $23.00 (0-531-14448-8). Uses an illustrated, double-page format to explore subjects including racism, freedom, and various types of prejudice. (Rev: BL 4/1/98) [323]

18894 Pacoe, Elaine. *The Right to Vote* (4–6). Illus. Series: Land of the Free. 1997, Millbrook LB $19.90 (0-7613-0066-X). 48pp. Explores the principles behind the right to vote and how it was gradually awarded to all citizens. (Rev: BL 5/15/97; SLJ 5/97) [324.6]

18895 Parks, Rosa, and Gregory J. Reed. *Dear Mrs. Parks: A Dialogue with Today's Youth* (5–8). 1996, Lee & Low $16.95 (1-880000-45-8). This book contains a sampling of the thousands of letters sent to civil rights leader Rosa Parks and her replies. (Rev: BL 12/1/96; SLJ 12/96) [323]

18896 Quiri, Patricia R. *The Bill of Rights* (3–4). Illus. Series: True Books. 1998, Children's Book Pr. LB $21.00 (0-516-20661-3). 48pp. An examination of the Bill of Rights, a discussion of the difficulties

encountered in writing the document, and paraphrases of each of its ten amendments. (Rev: BL 2/1/99; HBG 3/99) [323]

18897 Rappaport, Doreen. *The School Is Not White!* (2–4). Illus. by Curtis James. 2005, Hyperion $16.99 (0-7868-1838-7). 32pp. This inspiring true story chronicles the courageous 1960s campaign by Mae Bertha and Matthew Carter, African American sharecroppers, to ensure that their children receive a quality education. (Rev: BL 2/1/05) [323.1]

18898 Rossi, Ann. *Created Equal: Women Campaign for the Right to Vote, 1* (4–6). Series: Crossroads America. 2005, National Geographic LB $21.90 (0-7922-8285-X). 40pp. The campaign for women's right to vote is placed in historical context through period photographs, cartoons, and primary source material; biographical information is provided for key individuals. (Rev: SLJ 4/05) [324.6]

18899 Rossi, Ann. *Freedom Struggle: The Anti-Slavery Movement in America, 1830–1865* (4–6). Series: Crossroads America. 2005, National Geographic LB $21.90 (0-7922-8061-X). 40pp. Efforts to abolish slavery in the mid-19th century are placed in historical context through period photographs, cartoons, and primary source material; biographical information is provided for key individuals. (Rev: SLJ 4/05) [323]

18900 Seidman, David. *Civil Rights* (4–6). Series: Individual Rights and Civic Responsibility. 2001, Rosen LB $19.95 (0-8239-3231-1). 128pp. Covers civil rights issues involving African Americans, women, Native Americans, immigrants, prisoners, and gays and lesbians. (Rev: BL 3/15/02; SLJ 2/02) [323]

18901 Sherrow, Victoria. *Freedom of Worship* (4–6). Illus. Series: Land of the Free. 1997, Millbrook LB $19.90 (0-7613-0065-1). 48pp. As well as discussing the right to worship as one pleases, this account covers the religious right, religious intolerance, school prayer, and cults. (Rev: BL 5/15/97; SLJ 5/97) [323.44]

18902 Sullivan, George. *The Day the Women Got the Vote: A Photo History of the Women's Rights Movement* (5–8). Illus. 1994, Scholastic paper $6.95 (0-590-47560-6). 96pp. The history of the struggle for women's rights is covered in a series of 24 short photoessays. (Rev: BL 6/1–15/94; SLJ 7/94) [323.34]

18903 Turck, Mary C. *The Civil Rights Movement for Kids: A History with 21 Activities* (4–8). 2000, Chicago Review paper $14.95 (1-55652-370-X). 189pp. The story of the civil rights movement with coverage of key events and personalities plus a number of related activities. (Rev: SLJ 10/00) [973.9]

18904 Venable, Rose. *The Civil Rights Movement* (4–6). Series: Journey to Freedom: The African American Library. 2001, Child's World LB $17.95 (1-56766-917-4). 40pp. An oversize, attractive volume that supplies details on the 20th-century civil rights movement in the United States, its leaders, and their accomplishments. (Rev: BL 12/15/01; HBG 3/02; SLJ 1/02) [323]

18905 Welch, Catherine A. *Children of the Civil Rights Era* (3–6). Series: Picture the American Past. 2001, Carolrhoda LB $22.60 (1-57505-481-7). 48pp. Large historical photographs and a simple text are used to describe how young people participated in America's civil rights movement. (Rev: BL 6/1–15/01; HBG 10/01) [323]

18906 Wilson, Reginald. *Think About Our Rights: Civil Liberties and the United States* (5–8). Illus. 1991, Walker LB $15.85 (0-8027-8127-6); paper $9.95 (0-8027-7371-0). 128pp. The focus is on such civil rights questions as integration, affirmative action, and women's rights. (Rev: SLJ 1/92) [323.4]

Constitution

18907 Burgan, Michael. *The Bill of Rights* (4–6). Series: We the People. 2001, Compass Point LB $21.26 (0-7565-0151-2). 48pp. Burgan discusses the reasons behind the creation of the Bill of Rights, with paintings, maps, and documents. (Rev: SLJ 1/02) [342.73]

18908 Catrow, David. *We the Kids* (PS–3). Illus. 2002, Dial $16.99 (0-8037-2553-1). 32pp. A visually engaging, straightforward interpretation of the constitution for young readers. (Rev: BL 3/15/02; HBG 10/02; SLJ 5/02) [342.73]

18909 Collier, Christopher, and James L. Collier. *Creating the Constitution, 1787* (5–8). Illus. Series: Drama of American History. 1998, Marshall Cavendish LB $29.93 (0-7614-0776-6). 89pp. This history of the U.S. Constitution describes the background and importance of the document and the compromises made to win ratification. (Rev: BL 2/15/99; HBG 9/99) [342.73029]

18910 Feinberg, Barbara S. *Constitutional Amendments* (5–8). Series: Inside Government. 1996, Twenty-First Century LB $22.40 (0-8050-4619-4). After presenting a brief history of the Constitution, this work examines the Bill of Rights and then covers the remaining amendments in chapters arranged by topic. (Rev: SLJ 12/96) [342.73]

18911 Freedman, Russell. *In Defense of Liberty: The Story of America's Bill of Rights* (5–10). 2003, Holiday House $24.95 (0-8234-1585-6). 196pp. A succinct explanation of the history of the Bill of Rights, discussing each amendment in turn and its particular relevance to today's controversies, with many references to cases involving young people. (Rev: BCCB 10/03*; BL 10/1/03*; HB 9–10/03*; HBG 4/04; SLJ 10/03*) [342.73]

18912 Grodin, Elissa. *D is for Democracy: A Citizen's Alphabet* (5–8). Illus. by Victor Juhasz. 2004, Sleeping Bear $16.95 (1-58536-234-4). 40pp. From "Amendment" to "Zeitgeist," this is an exploration of key concepts, people, places, and things, with the emphasis on the United States. (Rev: BL 1/1–15/05; SLJ 10/04) [320.973]

18913 Horn, Geoffrey M. *The Bill of Rights and Other Amendments* (5–8). Series: World Almanac Library of American Government. 2004, World Almanac LB $29.26 (0-8368-5475-6). 48pp. A thorough and detailed examination of the process of changing the Constitution and the issues underlying the various amendments. (Rev: SLJ 9/04) [342.73]

18914 Hudson, David L. *The Bill of Rights* (5–8). Illus. Series: The Constitution. 2002, Enslow LB $20.95 (0-7660-1903-9). 128pp. A look at the first ten amendments to the Constitution and how they have affected the citizens of the United States. (Rev: BL 2/15/03; HBG 3/03) [342.73]

18915 Hudson, David L. *The Fourteenth Amendment: Equal Protection Under the Law* (5–8). Illus. Series: The Constitution. 2002, Enslow LB $20.95 (0-7660-1904-7). 128pp. What the 14th amendment to the Constitution entails and how it has affected the citizens of the United States. (Rev: BL 2/15/03; HBG 10/03) [342.73]

18916 Johnson, Linda C. *Our Constitution* (4–6). Illus. Series: I Know America. 1992, Millbrook LB $20.90 (1-56294-090-2). 48pp. This history of our Constitution includes an explanation of its important parts. (Rev: BL 9/1/92; SLJ 10/92) [342.73]

18917 Krull, Kathleen. *A Kids' Guide to America's Bill of Rights: Curfews, Censorship, and the 100-Pound Giant* (5–8). Illus. 1999, Avon $15.99 (0-380-97497-5). 224pp. After a description of the first 10 amendments, this book details famous court cases and what each amendment means to young people. (Rev: BL 12/1/99; HBG 4/00) [342.73]

18918 Levert, Suzanne. *The Constitution* (2–5). Series: Kaleidoscope. 2002, Benchmark LB $15.95 (0-7614-1452-5). 48pp. An accessible overview of the Constitution, its history, and its impact on the government of the United States. (Rev: HBG 3/03; SLJ 4/03) [342.73]

18919 Levy, Elizabeth. *If You Were There When They Signed the Constitution* (2–4). Illus. 1992, Scholastic paper $5.99 (0-590-45159-6). 80pp. All about the delegates and the U.S. Constitution. (Rev: BL 9/15/87; SLJ 11/87)

18920 Maestro, Betsy, and Giulio Maestro. *A More Perfect Union: The Story of Our Constitution* (2–4). Illus. 1987, Lothrop LB $15.93 (0-688-06840-5); Morrow paper $7.95 (0-688-10192-5). 48pp. The U.S. Constitution is explained for young readers. (Rev: BCCB 10/87; BL 9/1/87; SLJ 9/87)

18921 Nardo, Don. *The U.S. Constitution* (5–8). Illus. Series: History of the World. 2001, Gale LB $23.70 (0-7377-0776-3). 48pp. A history of the Constitution and the Bill of Rights is given plus a discussion of their importance today. (Rev: BL 4/1/02) [342.73]

18922 Sobel, Syl. *The U.S. Constitution and You* (3–5). Illus. by Denise Gilgannon. 2001, Barron's paper $6.95 (0-7641-1707-6). 48pp. Clear text and pen-and-ink sketches provide a concise look at the importance of the Constitution, with chapters on checks and balances and the rights of the people and of the states. (Rev: SLJ 8/01) [342.73]

18923 Weidner, Daniel. *The Constitution: The Preamble and the Articles* (5–8). Series: The Constitution. 2002, Enslow LB $20.95 (0-7660-1906-3). 112pp. The history of the U.S. Constitution and its meanings are explored through personal stories and examples. (Rev: BL 2/15/03; HBG 3/03; SLJ 1/03) [342.73]

18924 Weidner, Daniel. *Creating the Constitution: The People and Events That Formed the Nation* (5–8). Series: The Constitution. 2002, Enslow LB $20.95 (0-7660-1905-5). 112pp. This informative volume describes how the U.S. Constitution was written and the debates that preceded its adoption. (Rev: BL 2/15/03; HBG 3/03; SLJ 1/03) [342.73]

Crime and Criminals

18925 Aaseng, Nathan. *Treacherous Traitors* (5–9). Series: Profiles. 1997, Oliver LB $19.95 (1-881508-38-2). This book profiles 12 Americans who were tried for treason, including Benedict Arnold, John Brown, Alger Hiss, Julius and Ethel Rosenberg, and Aldrich Ames. (Rev: SLJ 2/98) [355.3]

18926 Anderson, Wayne. *The Chicago Black Sox Trial: A Primary Source Account* (5–8). Illus. Series: Great Trials of the Twentieth Century. 2003, Rosen LB $31.95 (0-8239-3969-3). 64pp. This is a detailed, readable account of the 1919 Chicago Black Sox scandal and the plot to fix the World Series. (Rev: BL 4/1/04; SLJ 6/04) [796.357]

18927 Blackwood, Gary L. *Gangsters* (4–7). Series: Bad Guys. 2001, Benchmark LB $28.50 (0-7614-1016-3). 72pp. Al Capone is just one of the evildoers profiled in this volume that gives historical context for each "bad guy." Also use *Outlaws* and *Highwaymen* (both 2001). (Rev: HBG 3/02; SLJ 1/02) [364.106]

18928 Bourgeois, Paulette. *Police Officers* (1–3). Series: Kids Can Read. 2004, Kids Can $5.95 (1-55337-742-7); paper $3.95 (1-55337-743-5). 32pp. After describing a fictional police investigation, Bourgeois moves on to discuss police duties and children's safety. (Rev: BL 11/15/04) [363.2]

18929 Dahl, Michael. *Computer Evidence* (4–8). Illus. Series: Forensic Crime Solvers. 2004, Capstone LB $16.95 (0-7368-2698-X). 32pp. After a story that draws the readers in, Dahl looks at the use of computer evidence in tracking down and convicting criminals. Also use *Poison Evidence* (2004).

18930 Dickson, Louise. *Lu and Clancy's Crime Science* (2–4). Illus. by Pat Cupples. Series: Lu and Clancy. 1999, Kids Can paper $5.95 (1-55074-552-2). 40pp. While solving a mystery about missing pups, a Scotch terrier and a basset hound teach readers about observational skills, how to take finger and lip prints, how to analyze footprints and teeth prints, and how to perform other procedures in criminal science. (Rev: SLJ 11/99) [364]

18931 Draper, Allison Stark. *The Assassination of Malcolm X* (5–8). Series: The Library of Political Assassinations. 2002, Rosen LB $26.50 (0-8239-3542-6). 64pp. A description of the assassination and its aftermath is followed by information on Malcolm X's life and beliefs. Also use *The Assassination of Medgar Evers, The Assassination of Abraham Lincoln, The Assassination of Martin Luther King Jr.,* and *The Assassination of Robert F. Kennedy* (all 2002). (Rev: BL 2/15/02; SLJ 7/02)

18932 Farman, John. *The Short and Bloody History of Spies* (5–8). Illus. 2002, Lerner LB $23.95 (0-8225-0845-1); paper $9.55 (0-8225-0846-X). 96pp. A witty and fascinating account of the intriguing lives of spies, with descriptions of spying techniques and gadgets. (Rev: BL 1/1–15/03; HBG 3/03) [327.12]

18933 Friedlander, Mark P., Jr., and Terry M. Phillips. *When Objects Talk: Solving a Crime with Science* (5–8). Illus. Series: Discovery! 2001, Lerner LB $26.60 (0-8225-0649-1). 120pp. A fictional mystery serves to introduce criminal investigation techniques such as fingerprints and DNA. (Rev: HBG 3/02; SLJ 2/02) [363.25]

18934 Gifford, Clive. *Spies* (5–9). Illus. Series: Kingfisher Knowledge. 2004, Kingfisher LB $11.95 (0-7534-5777-6). 64pp. Stories of notable espionage achievements are included along with brisk facts, plenty of high-interest illustrations, a history of spying, and discussion of the future of this field. (Rev: SLJ 5/05)

18935 Goldentyer, Debra. *Street Violence* (4–8). Series: Preteen Pressures. 1998, Raintree LB $25.69 (0-8172-5028-X). This book discusses types of street violence and how young people can protect themselves, as well as gang issues and alternatives to participation. (Rev: BL 5/15/98; HBG 9/98; SLJ 6/98) [364]

18936 Graham, Ian. *Crime-Fighting* (5–8). Illus. Series: Science Spotlight. 1995, Raintree LB $24.26 (0-8114-3840-6). 46pp. A discussion of scientific methods used in analyzing evidence at crime scenes, such as DNA testing. (Rev: SLJ 7/95) [364]

18937 Graham, Ian. *Fakes and Forgeries* (5–8). Illus. Series: Science Spotlight. 1995, Raintree LB $24.26 (0-8114-3843-0). 46pp. Examines famous scandals in history involving such fakes as the Loch Ness monster, counterfeit money, and the forged Hitler diaries. (Rev: SLJ 7/95) [364]

18938 Greenberg, Keith E. *Out of the Gang* (5–8). Illus. 1992, Lerner LB $19.93 (0-8225-2553-4). 40pp. A realistic portrait of gang life, revealed by a man who escaped it and a boy who managed to stay out of it. (Rev: BCCB 6/92; BL 6/15/92; SLJ 9/92) [364.1]

18939 Hjelmeland, Andy. *Prisons: Inside the Big House* (4–8). Illus. Series: Pro/Con Issues. 1996, Lerner LB $30.35 (0-8225-2607-7). Opposing viewpoints are presented on the purposes of prisons, prison conditions, and alternate forms of rehabilitation. (Rev: BL 8/96; SLJ 9/96) [365]

18940 Jackson, Donna M. *The Bone Detectives: How Forensic Anthropologists Solve Crimes and Uncover Mysteries of the Dead* (5–9). 1996, Little, Brown $17.95 (0-316-82935-8). A look at the role of forensic anthropologists in solving crimes including murder. (Rev: BCCB 4/96; BL 4/1/96; HB 5–6/96; SLJ 5/96*) [363.2]

18941 Johnson, Julie. *Why Do People Join Gangs?* (5–8). Series: Exploring Tough Issues. 2001, Raintree LB $25.69 (0-7398-3236-0). 48pp. Johnson looks at gangs — who joins them and why, and how to get out of one — in the United States and abroad, and includes a chapter on dealing with bullies. Also use *Why Do People Fight Wars?* and *Why Are People Prejudiced?* (both 2002). (Rev: SLJ 11/01) [364.1]

18942 Lane, Brian. *Investigation of Murder* (4–6). Illus. Series: Crimebusters. 1996, Millbrook LB $20.90 (0-7613-0527-0). 32pp. A fictitious murder is used as the framework for this discussion of the work of police and forensic experts. (Rev: BL 1/1–15/97; SLJ 1/97) [363.2]

18943 Larsen, Anita. *Psychic Sleuths* (5–7). 1994, Macmillan LB $14.95 (0-02-751645-8). 112pp. Pros and cons concerning the use of psychics in solving crimes are discussed, with many case studies. (Rev: BL 10/1/94; SLJ 11/94) [363.2]

18944 Monroe, Judy. *The Susan B. Anthony Women's Voting Rights Trial: A Headline Court Case* (5–9). Series: Headline Court Cases. 2002, Enslow LB $20.95 (0-7660-1759-1). 112pp. Monroe explores the fight for women's suffrage and the trial of Susan B. Anthony for voting illegally in the 1872 election. (Rev: BL 3/15/03; HBG 3/03; SLJ 12/02)

18945 Oliver, Marilyn Tower. *Gangs: Trouble in the Streets* (5–8). 1995, Enslow LB $20.95 (0-89490-492-2). Discusses the roots of gangs in the 19th century, aspects of modern gang life, and how members manage to quit gangs. (Rev: BL 8/95) [364.1]

18946 Oxlade, Chris. *Crime Detection* (3–5). Illus. Series: Science Encounters. 1997, Rigby $22.79 (1-57572-090-6). 32pp. An introduction to detective work that covers forensic science, security, fingerprints, and how evidence is chemically treated. (Rev: SLJ 11/97) [364]

18947 Pentland, Peter, and Pennie Stoyles. *Forensic Science* (4–6). Illus. Series: Science and Scientists. 2002, Chelsea House LB $18.95 (0-7910-7010-7). 32pp. An overview of how blood types, fingerprints, and DNA profiling figure in forensic science, and of the career itself, with illustrations and interesting sidebars. (Rev: HBG 3/03; SLJ 4/03) [363.25]

18948 Platt, Richard. *Spy* (4–7). Illus. 1996, Knopf LB $20.99 (0-679-98123-7). 64pp. All aspects of spying, including equipment and techniques, are described, along with profiles of famous spies. (Rev: BL 12/1/96; SLJ 6/97) [327.12]

18949 Powell, Jillian. *Drug Trafficking* (4–6). Illus. Series: Crimebusters. 1997, Millbrook LB $20.90 (0-7613-0555-6). 32pp. Using a fabricated crime as a focus, this book describes the many avenues of drug trafficking in the United States and how various agencies are combating it. (Rev: BL 6/1–15/97) [364.1]

18950 Rainis, Kenneth G. *Crime-Solving Science Projects: Forensic Science Experiments* (5–9). 2000, Enslow LB $20.95 (0-7660-1289-1). 128pp. After defining forensic science, this book contains experiments and projects involving such areas as fingerprints, inks, writing samples, fibers, forgeries, and blood evidence. (Rev: HBG 10/01; SLJ 2/01) [363.2]

18951 Rollins, Barbara B., and Michael Dahl. *Ballistics* (4–7). Series: Edge Books, Forensic Crime Solvers. 2004, Capstone LB $22.60 (0-7368-2421-

9). 32pp. Report writers and reluctant readers will be attracted to this brief, concise discussion of the science of ballistics. (Rev: SLJ 8/04) [363.25]

18952 Rollins, Barbara B., and Michael Dahl. *Blood Evidence* (4–8). Illus. Series: Forensic Crime Solvers. 2004, Capstone LB $22.60 (0-7368-2418-9). 32pp. Reluctant readers will be attracted to the gruesome nature of the subject matter and the often lurid presentation of facts. (Rev: BL 5/1/04; SLJ 8/04) [363.25]

18953 Rollins, Barbara B., and Michael Dahl. *Cause of Death* (4–8). Illus. Series: Forensic Crime Solvers. 2004, Capstone LB $22.60 (0-7368-2420-0). 32pp. This look at how crime scene technicians and medical examiners determine cause of death will draw in reluctant readers. (Rev: BL 5/1/04; SLJ 8/04) [614]

18954 Rollins, Barbara B., and Michael Dahl. *Fingerprint Evidence* (4–7). Series: Edge Books, Forensic Crime Solvers. 2004, Capstone LB $22.60 (0-7368-2419-7). 32pp. After a story that draws the readers in, the authors describe the features of fingerprints and discusses their use in solving crimes. (Rev: SLJ 8/04) [363.25]

18955 Ross, Stewart. *Spies and Traitors* (5–8). Series: Fact or Fiction? 1995, Millbrook LB $26.90 (1-56294-648-X). A history of the people who have placed themselves above their country in the dangerous game of espionage and betrayal. (Rev: BL 11/15/95; SLJ 3/96) [355.3]

18956 Salak, John. *Violent Crime: Is It Out of Control?* (6–8). Illus. Series: Issues of Our Time. 1995, Twenty-First Century LB $18.90 (0-8050-4239-3). 64pp. An honest presentation of why violent crimes are committed more frequently and how young people are becoming increasingly involved in them. (Rev: BL 2/1/96; SLJ 2/96) [364.1]

18957 Schroeder, Andreas. *Scams!* (5–8). Series: True Stories from the Edge. 2004, Annick $18.95 (1-55037-853-8); paper $7.95 (1-55037-852-X). 154pp. Ten stories reveal daring trickery, con jobs, and scams, including the 1938 radio broadcast of *War of the Worlds* that terrified millions of Americans and the baseless claim that a tribe of cavemen had been found living in a remote corner of the Philippines. (Rev: SLJ 8/04) [364.16]

18958 Sorensen, Lita. *The Scottsboro Boys Trial: A Primary Source Account* (5–8). Illus. 2003, Rosen LB $31.95 (0-8239-3975-8). 64pp. Sorensen dissects the sensational Scottsboro Boys rape case in Alabama that attracted media attention from around the globe. (Rev: BL 4/1/04) [345.761]

18959 Steele, Philip. *Smuggling* (5–9). Series: Past and Present. 1993, Macmillan LB $20.00 (0-02-786884-2). A colorful history of smuggling through the ages. (Rev: BL 8/93) [364.1]

18960 Stewart, Gail B. *Gangs* (5–8). Illus. Series: The Other America. 1996, Lucent LB $17.96 (1-56006-340-8). 96pp. This account describes past and present gangs, discusses causes for their formation, tells about their characteristics, and profiles several members. (Rev: SLJ 3/97) [394.3]

18961 Trapani, Margi. *Working Together Against Gang Violence* (4–8). Series: The Library of Social Activism. 1996, Rosen LB $16.95 (0-8239-2260-X). After a general discussion on gang behavior, the author gives pointers to help young people cope with the threat of gangs and suggestions for working with others against gang violence. (Rev: SLJ 2/97) [302.3]

18962 Wiese, Jim. *Detective Science: 40 Crime-Solving, Case-Breaking, Crook-Catching Activities for Kids* (4–7). 1996, Wiley paper $12.95 (0-471-11980-6). 128pp. Presents 40 experiments and activities that illustrate techniques in forensic science related to observing, collecting, and analyzing evidence. (Rev: BL 4/15/96; SLJ 6/96) [363.2]

18963 Williams, Stanley, and Barbara C. Becnel. *Gangs and Drugs* (3–5). Illus. Series: Tookie Speaks Out. 1996, Rosen LB $13.95 (0-8239-2348-7). 24pp. A former gang leader and current prison inmate, Tookie Williams tells about the part drugs play in the gang scene. (Rev: BL 2/15/97) [364.1]

18964 Williams, Stanley, and Barbara C. Becnel. *Gangs and the Abuse of Power* (4–8). Series: Tookie Speaks Out. 1996, Rosen LB $17.25 (0-8239-2346-0). A former active gang member in Los Angeles tells what his life was like as a member and how to avoid his mistakes. Also use in this series *Gangs and Wanting to Belong* (1996). (Rev: SLJ 1/97) [302.3]

18965 Williams, Stanley, and Barbara C. Becnel. *Gangs and Weapons* (4–8). Series: Tookie Speaks Out. 1996, Rosen LB $17.25 (0-8239-2342-8). The use of weapons in gangs to gain and maintain power and how they are obtained are two of the topics covered in this cautionary account written by a former gang member who was seriously wounded in a shootout. Also use *Gangs and Your Friends* (1996). (Rev: SLJ 1/97) [302.3]

18966 Williams, Stanley, and Barbara C. Becnel. *Gangs and Your Neighborhood* (4–8). Series: Tookie Speaks Out. 1996, Rosen LB $17.25 (0-8239-2347-9). How gangs grow in neighborhoods and how they change them are two of the topics covered in this book about the dangers of gangs and how to avoid joining one. (Rev: SLJ 1/97) [302.3]

18967 Winkleman, Katherine K. *Police Patrol* (PS–3). Illus. by John S. Winkleman. 1996, Walker LB $16.85 (0-8027-8454-2). 32pp. Activities in a police station and the duties of police are described in words and photos. (Rev: BCCB 1/97; BL 1/1–15/97; SLJ 12/96) [363.2]

18968 Woodford, Chris. *Criminal Investigation* (4–8). Illus. Series: Science Fact Files. 2001, Raintree LB $27.12 (0-7398-1016-2). 45pp. A concise introduction to the forensic science with information on the newest equipment and techniques. (Rev: HBG 10/01; SLJ 1/02) [363.2]

18969 Yaffe, Rebecca M., and Lonnie F. Hoade. *When a Parent Goes to Jail: A Comprehensive Guide for Counseling Children of Incarcerated Parents* (3–5). Illus. by Barbara S. Moody. 2000, Rayve $49.95 (1-877810-08-8). 45pp. This book about adults in trouble with the law goes through the incarceration process from arrest to sentencing. (Rev: SLJ 12/00) [363.2]

Elections and Political Parties

18970 Ansary, Mir Tamim. *Election Day* (2–3). Illus. Series: Holiday Histories. 2002, Heinemann LB $14.95 (1-58810-221-1). 32pp. A brief history and overview of the U.S. presidential election system. (Rev: BL 2/1/02) [324.973]

18971 Audryszewski, Tricia. *The Reform Party* (5–8). Series: Headliners. 2000, Millbrook LB $25.90 (0-7613-1906-9). 64pp. This book describes the formation of the Reform Party and highlights the work of Ross Perot, Pat Buchanan, and Jesse Ventura. (Rev: BL 8/00; HBG 10/01; SLJ 1/01) [324.273]

18972 Christelow, Eileen. *Vote!* (2–5). 2003, Houghton Mifflin LB $16.00 (0-618-24754-8). 48pp. A mayoral campaign — with comic-book style art and commentary by politically minded dogs — serves to illustrate the voting process and teach helpful lessons about such related issues as voting rights, registration, fund raising, and ballot recounts. (Rev: BL 11/1/03; HBG 4/04; SLJ 12/03)

18973 Cunningham, Kevin. *Power to the People: How We Elect the President and Other Officials* (3–6). Illus. Series: Our Government and Citizenship. 2004, Child's World LB $27.07 (1-59296-322-6). 32pp. An excellent step-by-step introduction to the American election process and the importance of casting a vote. (Rev: BL 10/15/04; SLJ 1/05) [324.6]

18974 De Capua, Sarah E. *Running for Public Office* (2–5). Series: True Books — Civics. 2002, Children's Book Pr. LB $23.00 (0-516-22333-X); paper $6.95 (0-516-27368-X). 48pp. A simple, large-type text and many photographs are used to introduce the positions open in public office and the steps in running for these positions, including campaigning and elections. (Rev: BL 6/1–15/02; SLJ 10/02) [324.7]

18975 De Capua, Sarah E. *Voting* (2–5). Series: True Books — Civics. 2002, Children's Book Pr. LB $23.00 (0-516-22330-5); paper $6.95 (0-516-27365-5). 48pp. The election system is introduced in simple, large-type text with plenty of attractive color photographs. (Rev: BL 6/1–15/02) [324]

18976 Donovan, Sandy. *Running for Office: A Look at Political Campaigns* (4–6). Illus. Series: How Government Works. 2004, Lerner LB $25.26 (0-8225-4700-7). 56pp. The fictional tale of Samantha Brown's campaign for election as a state senator serves as a framework for details about all aspects of electioneering. (Rev: BL 5/1/04; HBG 4/04) [324.7]

18977 Gottfried, Ted. *The 2000 Election* (5–8). Illus. 2002, Millbrook LB $25.90 (0-7613-2406-2). 64pp. A well-designed and detailed look at the controversial presidential election of 2000, with background information, sidebars on important people, and an electoral map and other graphics. (Rev: BL 7/02; HBG 10/02; SLJ 4/02) [324.973]

18978 Granfield, Linda. *America Votes: How Our President Is Elected* (4–6). 2003, Kids Can $16.95

(1-55337-086-4); paper $9.95 (1-55337-087-2). 64pp. This is an appealing and clear explanation of the American presidential election process, from qualifications for voting through such issues as election fraud and the role of television. (Rev: BL 9/15/03; HBG 4/04; SLJ 12/03) [324.6]

18979 Henry, Christopher. *The Electoral College* (4–6). Illus. Series: First Books. 1996, Watts LB $22.00 (0-531-20218-6). 63pp. Introduces the electoral college, its origins, composition, and functions. (Rev: BL 9/1/96; SLJ 10/96) [324.6]

18980 Henry, Christopher. *Presidential Conventions* (4–6). Illus. Series: First Books. 1996, Watts LB $22.00 (0-531-20219-4). 62pp. Discusses the purpose of political party conventions and their place in the election process. (Rev: BL 9/1/96; SLJ 10/96) [324.6]

18981 Hewson, Martha S. *The Electoral College* (5–9). 2002, Chelsea $19.75 (0-7910-6790-4). 64pp. Covers the history of the electoral college and details of elections of particular interest, including the 2000 Bush–Gore decision. (Rev: HBG 3/03; SLJ 2/03) [324.6]

18982 Horn, Geoffrey M. *Political Parties, Interest Groups, and the Media* (5–8). Series: World Almanac Library of American Government. 2004, World Almanac LB $29.26 (0-8368-5478-0). 48pp. An engaging introduction to the world of politics, the importance of money and lobbying, and the role of the press. (Rev: SLJ 9/04) [324]

18983 Landau, Elaine. *Friendly Foes: A Look at Political Parties* (4–6). Illus. Series: How Government Works. 2003, Lerner LB $25.26 (0-8225-1349-8). 56pp. Discusses the two major political parties in the United States, with an eye to their differences in such areas as the role of government in society; minority parties are mentioned in a final chapter. (Rev: HBG 4/04; SLJ 3/04) [324.273]

18984 Landau, Elaine. *The 2000 Presidential Election* (2–5). Series: Cornerstones of Freedom, Second Series. 2002, Children's Book Pr. LB $24.00 (0-516-22527-8). 48pp. A timeline and informative text help to unravel the events between the 2000 election and Gore's concession speech. (Rev: SLJ 3/03)

18985 Levert, Suzanne. *The Electoral College* (3–6). Series: Watts Library. 2004, Watts LB $24.50 (0-531-12292-1). 63pp. Describes the role of the Electoral College and the confusion surrounding the 2000 presidential election. (Rev: SLJ 3/05) [324.6]

18986 Lindop, Edmund. *Political Parties* (5–8). Series: Inside Government. 1996, Twenty-First Century LB $24.90 (0-8050-4618-6). This work traces the origins of political parties and the role they play in presidential elections. (Rev: BL 9/15/96; SLJ 12/96) [324.273]

18987 Lutz, Norma Jean. *The History of Third Parties* (4–6). Series: Your Government: How It Works. 2000, Chelsea LB $17.95 (0-7910-5541-8). 64pp. The Abolitionists, Liberty Party, Southern Democrats, Nativists, Prohibitionists, Socialists, and Reform Party are a few of the American third parties discussed here. (Rev: HBG 9/00; SLJ 8/00) [324.273]

18988 Murphy, Patricia. *Election Day* (PS–2). Series: Rookie Read-About Holidays. 2003, Children's Book Pr. LB $19.00 (0-516-22663-0); paper $5.95 (0-516-27488-0). 32pp. In very simple words and pictures, this book describes the activities that occur on the first Tuesday after the first Monday in November. (Rev: BL 3/15/03) [324]

18989 Murphy, Patricia J. *Voting and Elections* (K–2). Series: Let's See. 2001, Compass Point LB $18.60 (0-7565-0144-X). 24pp. A simple introduction to the voting process and how you register to vote. (Rev: SLJ 1/02) [324.7]

18990 Payan, Gregory. *The Federalists and Anti-Federalists: How and Why Political Parties Were Formed in Young America* (4–6). Illus. Series: Life in the New American Nation. 2004, Rosen LB $21.25 (0-8239-4038-1). 32pp. The evolution of political parties in America is chronicled from the close of the Constitutional Convention to the present. (Rev: BL 6/1–15/04) [324.2732]

18991 Santella, Andrew. *U.S. Presidential Inaugurations* (3–6). Series: Cornerstones of Freedom, Second Series. 2002, Children's Book Pr. LB $24.00 (0-516-22533-2). 48pp. Inaugural addresses, inaugural balls, and inaugural weather are the focus of this narrative, which also explains the role of the Electoral College and its part in the Gore-Bush presidential election. (Rev: SLJ 12/02)

18992 Steins, Richard. *Our Elections* (4–6). Illus. 1994, Millbrook LB $20.90 (1-56294-446-0). 48pp. The process of being elected to office (primarily at the national level) is outlined in text, pictures, and diagrams. (Rev: BL 11/15/94; SLJ 12/94) [324.6]

18993 Zeinert, Karen. *Women in Politics: In the Running* (5–9). 2002, Twenty-First Century LB $29.90 (0-7613-2253-1). 112pp. From 1774 to the present, the author looks at women who have been elected to office or who have been influential in the political field, and discusses the possibility of a woman president. (Rev: BL 12/1/02; HBG 3/03; SLJ 11/02) [320]

Federal Government and Agencies

18994 Bausum, Ann. *Our Country's Presidents* (5–8). Illus. 2005, National Geographic LB $45.90 (0-7922-9330-4). 208pp. Full of interesting facts, quotations, and illustrations, this new edition has been extended with information on vice presidents, the Electoral College, and presidential security. (Rev: BL 5/15/05; SLJ 4/05) [973]

18995 Bay, Ann Phillips. *The Kid's Guide to the Smithsonian* (4–6). Illus. by Steven Rotblatt. 1996, Smithsonian Institution $26.95 (1-56098-734-0); paper $15.95 (1-56098-693-X). 160pp. A handy guide to historical information on many of the treasures of the Smithsonian. (Rev: BL 9/1/96) [069]

18996 Berger, Melvin, and Gilda Berger. *Where Does the Mail Go? A Book About the Postal System* (K–3). Illus. by Geoffrey Brittingham. Series: Discovery Readers. 1994, Ideals paper $4.50 (1-57102-

006-3). 48pp. Explores the U.S. Postal Service by tracing a letter from posting to delivery. (Rev: SLJ 9/94) [353]

18997 Bolick, Nancy O. *Mail Call! The History of the U.S. Postal Service* (4–6). Illus. Series: First Books. 1995, Watts LB $22.50 (0-531-20170-8). 64pp. From colonial days to the present, this is a chronological survey of the history of the U.S. Postal Service. (Rev: BL 2/15/95; SLJ 6/95) [383]

18998 Burns, Peggy. *The Mail* (3–5). Illus. Series: Stepping Through History. 1995, Thomson Learning LB $19.92 (1-56847-249-8). 32pp. A broad history of mail service, beginning with the ancient Persians and including material on today's computerized mail sorting and the hobby of stamp collecting. (Rev: BL 4/15/95; SLJ 6/95) [383]

18999 Cunningham, Kevin. *The U. S. Congress: Who Represents You* (3–6). Illus. Series: Our Government and Citizenship. 2004, Child's World LB $18.95 (1-59296-327-7). 32pp. A concise explanation of the makeup of the U.S. Congress and its role in government.

19000 De Capua, Sarah. *How People Immigrate* (3–5). Series: A True Book. 2004, Children's Pr. LB $23.50 (0-516-22799-8). 47pp. The process of immigration into the United States is examined in simple, large text, with clear explanations of the differences between non-immigrants and permanent residents. (Rev: SLJ 8/04) [325.73]

19001 De Capua, Sarah E. *Becoming a Citizen* (2–5). Illus. Series: True Books — Civics. 2002, Children's Book Pr. LB $23.00 (0-516-22331-3); paper $6.95 (0-516-27366-3). 48pp. This work describes the requirements for becoming a U.S. citizen and the steps one must take to become naturalized. (Rev: BL 6/1–15/02; SLJ check) [342.73]

19002 De Capua, Sarah E. *Paying Taxes* (2–5). Illus. Series: True Books — Civics. 2002, Children's Book Pr. LB $23.00 (0-516-22332-1); paper $6.95 (0-516-27367-1). 48pp. This account explains the taxes people pay, their history, and what the money is used for. (Rev: BL 6/1–15/02; SLJ check) [336.2]

19003 Donovan, Sandy. *Protecting America: A Look at the People Who Keep Our Country Safe* (4–6). Illus. Series: How Government Works. 2003, Lerner LB $25.26 (0-8225-1345-5). 56pp. A look at the U.S. armed forces and at security agencies including the FBI and CIA, all from a post-September 11 vantage point. (Rev: HBG 4/04; SLJ 3/04)

19004 Feinberg, Barbara S. *The Cabinet* (4–6). Illus. Series: Inside Government. 1995, Twenty-First Century LB $18.90 (0-8050-3421-8). 64pp. The history and changing composition of the cabinet are traced, with an explanation of each member's duties. (Rev: BL 9/1/95; SLJ 10/95) [353.04]

19005 Feinberg, Barbara S. *The National Government* (4–8). Illus. Series: First Books. 1993, Watts LB $22.00 (0-531-20155-4). 64pp. After an introduction to the federal government, this book explains the functions of each department and how they work together. (Rev: SLJ 1/94) [336.73]

19006 Feinberg, Barbara S. *Term Limits for Congress?* (4–6). Illus. Series: Inside Government.

1996, Twenty-First Century LB $18.90 (0-8050-4099-4). 64pp. A clear and concise overview of the arguments for and against congressional term limits. (Rev: BL 5/15/96; SLJ 8/96) [328.73]

19007 Feldman, Ruth Tenzer. *How Congress Works: A Look at the Legislative Branch* (4–6). Illus. Series: How Government Works. 2004, Lerner LB $25.26 (0-8225-1347-1). 56pp. An easily understood explanation of the roles of the two houses of the legislative branch.

19008 Friedman, Mark. *Government: How Local, State, and Federal Government Works* (3–6). Illus. Series: Our Government and Citizenship. 2004, Child's World LB $18.95 (1-59296-323-4). 32pp. An excellent step-by-step introduction to the concept of democracy and the various levels of government that coexist in the United States. (Rev: BL 10/15/04) [320.473]

19009 Gibbons, Gail. *The Post Office Book: Mail and How It Moves* (K–3). Illus. by author. 1982, HarperCollins LB $14.89 (0-690-04199-3); paper $5.95 (0-06-446029-0). 32pp. A simple description of how the post office works.

19010 Giesecke, Ernestine. *National Government* (3–5). Series: Kids' Guide. 2000, Heinemann $21.36 (1-57572-510-X). 32pp. A simple explanation of the three branches of government in the U.S. and the duties and responsibilities of each. (Rev: HBG 3/01; SLJ 10/00) [320]

19011 Greenberg, Judith E. *Young People's Letters to the President* (4–6). Series: In Their Own Voices. 1998, Watts LB $22.00 (0-531-11435-X). An anthology of 23 letters sent to presidents from Lincoln to Clinton that also includes six replies. (Rev: HBG 3/99; SLJ 4/99) [973]

19012 Horn, Geoffrey M. *The Presidency* (5–8). Series: World Almanac Library of American Government. 2003, World Almanac LB $26.60 (0-8368-5458-6). 48pp. Information on the first lady, the White House, and key presidents add to the coverage here, which includes primary sources as well as many photographs and statistics. (Rev: SLJ 1/04) [973]

19013 January, Brendan. *The CIA* (4–6). Illus. Series: Watts Library: U.S. Government and Military. 2002, Watts LB $24.00 (0-531-12034-1); paper $8.95 (0-531-16600-7). 64pp. A brief history and overview of the CIA from its conception to September 11, 2001, including photographs and a timeline. (Rev: BL 10/15/02; SLJ 1/03) [327.1273]

19014 January, Brendan. *The FBI* (4–6). Illus. Series: Watts Library: U.S. Government and Military. 2002, Watts LB $24.00 (0-531-12033-3); paper $8.95 (0-531-16601-5). 64pp. An overview of the FBI and its activities from the agency's conception up to September 11, 2001, including photographs and a timeline. (Rev: BL 10/15/02; SLJ 1/03) [363.25]

19015 January, Brendan. *The Presidency* (3–6). Series: Watts Library. 2004, Watts LB $24.50 (0-531-12293-X). 63pp. Presents the history of the office, its constitutional role, and key events and office holders. (Rev: SLJ 3/05) [973]

19016 Kassinger, Ruth. *U.S. Census: A Mirror of America* (5–8). Illus. 1999, Raintree $28.54 (0-7398-1217-3). 80pp. Written before the 2000 census began, this book describes the history of the census and the methods used to count Americans. (Rev: BL 12/15/99; HBG 4/00) [304]

19017 Kowalski, Kathiann M. *A Balancing Act: A Look at Checks and Balances* (4–6). Illus. Series: How Government Works. 2004, Lerner LB $25.26 (0-8225-1350-1). 56pp. An easily understood explanation of the principle intended to ensure that the three branches of government share power. (Rev: HBG 4/04)

19018 Kule, Elaine A. *The U.S. Mail* (2–4). Series: Transportation and Communication. 2002, Enslow LB $18.95 (0-7660-1892-X). 48pp. A history of the U.S. Postal Service from colonial days to the present, with material on how it works, its possible future uses, and people important in its development. (Rev: BL 9/15/02; HBG 3/03) [353]

19019 Landau, Elaine. *The President's Work: A Look at the Executive Branch* (4–6). Illus. Series: How Government Works. 2004, Lerner LB $25.26 (0-8225-0811-7). 56pp. A look at the president's responsibilities, enhanced by interesting sidebars and photographs. (Rev: BL 5/1/04; HBG 4/04; SLJ 3/04) [352.23]

19020 Levert, Suzanne. *The Congress* (2–5). Series: Kaleidoscope. 2002, Benchmark LB $15.95 (0-7614-1451-7). 48pp. An inside look at the inner workings of the House and Senate, with a description of the life of a piece of legislation, from introduction to passage. (Rev: HBG 3/03; SLJ 4/03) [328.73]

19021 Levert, Suzanne. *Congress* (3–6). Series: Watts Library. 2004, Watts LB $24.50 (0-531-12291-3). 63pp. Describes the activities of the two houses of Congress, how a bill becomes a law, and how citizens become involved. (Rev: SLJ 3/05) [328.73]

19022 McCave, Marta E. *Counting Heads, and More: The Work of the U.S. Census Bureau* (3–5). Illus. 1998, Twenty-First Century LB $22.40 (0-7613-3017-8). 64pp. An introduction to the U.S. Census Bureau, with information on its history, organization, functions, and the day-to-day work of its employees. (Rev: BL 12/15/98) [352.7]

19023 Maestro, Betsy. *The Voice of the People: American Democracy in Action* (3–5). Illus. by Giulio Maestro. 1996, Lothrop LB $15.93 (0-688-10679-X). 48pp. The election process and the three branches of government are two of the topics covered in this overview of our government. (Rev: BCCB 5/96; BL 4/1/96; SLJ 6/96) [324.973]

19024 Murphy, Patricia J. *The Presidency* (K–2). Series: Let's See. 2001, Compass Point LB $18.60 (0-7565-0142-3). 24pp. A simple introduction in double-page spreads to the office of the president that includes material on the vice president and first lady. (Rev: SLJ 1/02) [353.03]

19025 Patrick, Diane. *The Executive Branch* (4–6). Illus. Series: First Books. 1995, Watts LB $22.00 (0-531-20179-1). 64pp. An introduction to the exec-utive wing, the cabinet, and the duties of the U.S. president. (Rev: BL 3/1/95) [353]

19026 Peters, Celeste. *Peace Corps* (4–8). Series: International Organizations. 2002, Weigl LB $24.25 (1-59036-023-0). 32pp. The history, mission, key issues, and current initiatives of the Corps are covered in a volume that includes photographs, maps, and case sturies. (Rev: HBG 3/03; SLJ 4/03) [361.6]

19027 Phillips, Louis. *Ask Me Anything About the Presidents* (5–8). Illus. by Valeria Costantino. 1992, Avon paper $5.99 (0-380-76426-1). 130pp. A collection of unusual facts about various aspects of the U.S. presidency, presented in a question-and-answer format. (Rev: BL 4/15/92) [920]

19028 Ricciuti, Edward R. *Wildlife Special Agent: Protecting Endangered Species* (3–5). Illus. Series: Risky Business. 1996, Blackbirch LB $16.95 (1-56711-160-2). 32pp. A look at the exciting work of the people involved in the Law Enforcement Division of the U.S. Fish and Wildlife Service and how it helps protect endangered species. (Rev: SLJ 2/97) [363.11]

19029 Robb, Don. *Hail to the Chief: The American Presidency* (3–5). Illus. by Alan Witschonke. 2000, Charlesbridge LB $16.95 (0-88106-392-4); paper $7.95 (0-88106-939-2). 31pp. In 14 double-page spreads, the office of the presidency is introduced with material on duties, responsibilities and powers plus coverage of some men who have held the office and changed its character. (Rev: HBG 3/01; SLJ 3/01) [353.03]

19030 Rubel, David. *Scholastic Encyclopedia of the Presidents and Their Times*. Rev. ed. (4–8). Illus. 1997, Scholastic paper $18.95 (0-590-49366-3). 232pp. This fine reference book introduces each of the presidents and his administration and supplies material on related historical events, movements, and personalities. (Rev: SLJ 5/97) [920]

19031 St. George, Judith. *So You Want to Be President?* (3–5). Illus. by David Small. 2000, Penguin Putnam $17.99 (0-399-23407-1). 56pp. A delightful, lively compendium of facts about the presidency and the presidents covering such topics as favorite sports, appearance, pets, musical abilities, ages, and personalities. (Rev: BCCB 7–8/00; BL 7/00*; HB 7–8/00; HBG 3/01; SLJ 8/00) [324.6]

19032 Sandak, Cass R. *Congressional Committees* (4–6). Illus. Series: Inside Government. 1995, Twenty-First Century LB $18.90 (0-8050-3425-0). 64pp. The purposes, structure, and functions of congressional committees are covered in this illustrated account. (Rev: BL 12/15/95) [328.73]

19033 Sandak, Cass R. *Lobbying* (4–6). Illus. Series: Inside Government. 1995, Twenty-First Century LB $18.90 (0-8050-3424-2). 64pp. An objective account that discusses the history, purposes, and results of lobbying in the U.S. Congress. (Rev: BL 12/15/95; SLJ 1/96) [324]

19034 Sandak, Cass R. *The National Debt* (5–8). Series: Inside Government. 1996, Twenty-First Century LB $22.40 (0-8050-3423-4). The origins and causes of the national debt are covered, with options for the future. (Rev: BL 5/15/96; SLJ 8/96) [336.3]

19035 Shea, Pegi Deitz. *The Impeachment Process* (4–6). Series: Your Government: How It Works. 2000, Chelsea LB $17.95 (0-7910-5538-8). 64pp. Beginning with the Watergate and Clinton scandals, this account traces the impeachment process and why the Constitution was written as it was. (Rev: HBG 9/00; SLJ 8/00) [320]

19036 Smith, Carter, ed. *Presidents in a Time of Change: A Sourcebook on the U.S. Presidency* (5–8). Illus. Series: American Albums. 1993, Millbrook $25.90 (1-56294-362-6). 96pp. A heavily illustrated, attractive review of the presidency from Truman to Clinton. (Rev: BL 12/1/93; SLJ 4/94) [973.92]

19037 Smith, Carter, ed. *Presidents of a Divided Nation: A Sourcebook on the U.S. Presidency* (5–8). Series: American Albums. 1993, Millbrook $25.90 (1-56294-360-X). A visual sourcebook about the presidents during the Civil War and immediately after, from the Library of Congress collection on U.S. presidents. Also use *Presidents of a Growing Country*. (Rev: BL 12/1/93) [973.8]

19038 Smith, Carter, ed. *Presidents of a Growing Country: A Sourcebook on the U.S. Presidency* (5–8). Illus. Series: American Albums. 1993, Millbrook $25.90 (1-56294-358-8). 96pp. Through extensive use of pictorials, a thorough timeline, and concise text, this attractive book traces the presidency from Hayes through McKinley. (Rev: BL 12/1/93; SLJ 4/94) [973.8]

19039 Smith, Carter, ed. *Presidents of a Young Republic: A Sourcebook on the U.S. Presidency* (5–8). Illus. Series: American Albums. 1993, Millbrook $25.90 (1-56294-359-6). 96pp. A well-illustrated account that traces U.S. history from the presidency of John Quincy Adams through James Buchanan. (Rev: BL 12/1/93; SLJ 4/94) [973.5]

19040 Stein, R. Conrad. *The National Archives* (4–6). Series: Watts Library: U.S. Government and Military. 2002, Watts LB $24.00 (0-531-13032-5); paper $8.95 (0-531-16602-3). 64pp. This account presents in text and pictures a visit to the National Archives, a treasure trove that holds millions of American documents including the original Declaration of Independence. (Rev: BL 10/15/02) [069]

19041 Stier, Catherine. *If I Were President* (1–3). Illus. by DyAnne DiSalvo-Ryan. 1999, Whitman $14.95 (0-8075-3541-9). An easy picture book that explains in simple terms what the duties of the president are — including tossing the first pitch of the baseball season. (Rev: BL 10/1/99; HBG 4/00; SLJ 10/99) [352.23]

19042 Suen, Anastasia. *The Peace Corps* (1–2). Series: Helping Organizations. 2002, Rosen LB $16.00 (0-8239-6001-3). 24pp. As well as a brief description of the history and activities of the Peace Corps, this beginning reader tells how youngsters can become involved. (Rev: BL 6/1–15/02) [361.6]

19043 Sullivan, George. *Presidents at Play* (4–6). Illus. 1995, Walker LB $16.85 (0-8027-8334-1). 176pp. An unusual side of U.S. presidents is explored: the sports and other recreational activities they engaged in. (Rev: BL 1/1/95; SLJ 2/95) [973]

State Government and Agencies

19044 Armentrout, David, and Patricia Armentrout. *State Seals* (3–5). Illus. Series: The Rourke Guide to State Symbols. 2001, Rourke LB $27.93 (1-58952-087-4). 48pp. Brief, large-print text explains the history and design of each state's seal. (Rev: SLJ 5/02) [973]

19045 Feinberg, Barbara S. *State Governments* (4–8). Illus. Series: First Books. 1993, Watts LB $22.00 (0-531-20154-6). 64pp. Introduces the various parts of a state government, explains how each works, and stresses the need for cooperation among the components. (Rev: SLJ 1/94) [320]

19046 Giesecke, Ernestine. *State Government* (3–5). Series: Kids' Guide. 2000, Heinemann $21.36 (1-57572-513-4). 32pp. An appealing, simple account that discusses the structure of state governments in the U.S. and the responsibilities involved. (Rev: HBG 3/01; SLJ 10/00) [320]

19047 Ventura, Jesse, and Heron Marquez. *Jesse Ventura Tells It Like It Is: America's Most Outspoken Governor Speaks Out About Government* (5–8). Illus. 2002, Lerner LB $19.15 (0-8225-0385-9). 64pp. A look at the U.S. government and politicians from the viewpoint of wrestler-turned-Minnesota-governor Jesse Ventura. (Rev: BL 8/02; HBG 3/03; SLJ 9/02) [977.6]

Municipal Government and Agencies

19048 Giesecke, Ernestine. *Local Government* (3–5). Series: Kids' Guide. 2000, Heinemann $21.36 (1-57572-512-6). 32pp. The functions of city, country, and school district governments are explained with material on duties and responsibilities. (Rev: HBG 3/01; SLJ 10/00) [320.8]

Social Problems and Solutions

19049 Ajmera, Maya, and John D. Ivanko. *Be My Neighbor* (PS–2). Illus. 2004, Charlesbridge $15.95 (1-57091-504-0). 32pp. Observations from the late Fred Rogers open this appealing introduction to the concepts of community and neighborhood, presented on horizontal spreads with photographs depicting many environments. (Rev: BL 1/1–15/05; SLJ 1/05) [307.3]

19050 Ditchfield, Christin. *Serving Your Community* (3–5). Series: True Book. 2004, Children's Pr. LB $23.50 (0-516-22802-1). 47pp. The concept of volunteerism is introduced, with discussion of what young people can do to improve the quality of life in their communities. (Rev: SLJ 8/04) [361.3]

19051 Green, Jen. *Dealing with Racism* (2–4). Photos by Roger Vlitos. Illus. by Chris O'Neill. Series: How Do I Feel About. 1998, Millbrook LB $19.90 (0-7613-0810-5). 24pp. Using the words of children, this book defines racism, gives examples of, and makes suggestions on how to stop it. (Rev: HBG 9/98; SLJ 7/98) [305.8]

19052 Green, Jen. *Racism* (2–3). Series: Talking About. 1999, Raintree LB $15.98 (0-7398-1375-7). 32pp. In this simple, attractive book, several examples of racism are given, with ways of dealing with them and tips on how to get along in a multicultural society. (Rev: BL 2/15/00; HBG 9/00; SLJ 7/00) [305.42]

19053 Hurwitz, Eugene, and Sue Hurwitz. *Working Together Against Homelessness* (4–6). Illus. Series: Library of Social Activism. 1995, Rosen LB $16.95 (0-8239-1772-X). 64pp. A history of homelessness both nationally and globally, its present frequency, and possible solutions. (Rev: BL 2/15/95; SLJ 12/94) [362.5]

19054 Katella-Cofrancesco, Kathy. *Children's Causes* (4–6). Illus. Series: Celebrity Activist. 1998, Twenty-First Century LB $23.40 (0-7613-3013-5). 64pp. Each chapter in this book examines the contributions made by a celebrity to a cause involving children. (Rev: BL 8/98; HBG 9/98) [361.7]

19055 Katella-Cofrancesco, Kathy. *Economic Causes* (4–6). Illus. Series: Celebrity Activist. 1998, Twenty-First Century LB $23.40 (0-7613-3014-3). 64pp. Focuses on how celebrities, including Sharon Stone (Planet Hope) and former President Carter (Habitat for Humanity), support causes involving poverty and related problems. (Rev: BL 8/98; HBG 9/98) [361.7]

19056 Rondeau, Amanda. *Do Something in Your Community* (K–2). Illus. Series: Do Something About It! 2004, ABDO LB $19.93 (1-59197-572-7). 24pp. Photographs of people who contribute to the community — doctors and firefighters, for example — are accompanied by short descriptions of their roles. Also use *Do Something in Your Family* (2004). (Rev: BL 11/1/04) [361]

19057 Rondeau, Amanda. *Volunteering* (1–3). 2003, ABDO LB $12.95 (1-57765-882-5). 24pp. Numer-

ous examples of volunteer activities are shown in full-color photographs and simple text. (Rev: HBG 10/03; SLJ 6/03) [361.3]

19058 Rozakis, Laurie. *Homelessness: Can We Solve the Problem?* (5–8). Illus. Series: Issues of Our Time. 1995, Twenty-First Century LB $18.90 (0-8050-3878-7). 64pp. A history of homelessness is given, with various opinions and possible solutions. (Rev: SLJ 9/95) [362.5]

19059 Siegel, Danny. *Mitzvah Magic: What Kids Can Do to Change the World* (3–8). Illus. by Naomi Eisenberger. 2002, Kar-Ben paper $8.95 (1-58013-034-8). 64pp. Siegel has amassed a large number of suggestions for children who want to help others. (Rev: BL 10/1/02) [302]

19060 Siegel, Danny. *Tell Me a Mitzvah: Little and Big Ways to Repair the World* (3–6). Illus. by Judith Friedman. 1993, Kar-Ben paper $7.95 (0-929371-78-X). 64pp. Profiles of 12 people who have made the world a better place by performing mitzvahs, or good deeds. (Rev: SLJ 3/94) [307.1]

19061 Steins, Richard. *Censorship: How Does It Conflict with Freedom?* (5–9). Series: Issues of Our Time. 1995, Twenty-First Century LB $22.90 (0-8050-3879-5). A clearly written introduction to censorship, its history, and the various positions possible toward it. (Rev: BL 7/95; SLJ 9/95) [363.3]

19062 Suen, Anastasia. *Habitat for Humanity* (1–2). Series: Helping Organizations. 2002, Rosen LB $16.00 (0-8239-6006-4). 24pp. A beginning reader that describes how this organization provides housing for the poor and tells how such people as President Carter participate in its work. (Rev: BL 6/1–15/02; SLJ 3/02) [361.7]

19063 Wolf, Bernard. *Homeless* (2–4). Illus. 1995, Orchard LB $17.99 (0-531-08736-0). 46pp. The plight of a homeless family caught up in the New York City welfare system is the subject of this affecting picture book. (Rev: BCCB 3/95; BL 2/15/95; HB 5–6/95; SLJ 4/95) [362.5]

Religion and Holidays

General and Miscellaneous

19064 Aaseng, Rolfe E. *Augsburg Story Bible* (4–8). Illus. by Annegert Fuchshuber. 1992, Augsburg LB $19.99 (0-8066-2607-0). 270pp. This copiously illustrated version of the Bible is only slightly abridged. (Rev: SLJ 7/92) [222]

19065 Alexander, Cecil Frances. *All Things Bright and Beautiful* (PS–3). Illus. by Anna Vojtech. 2004, North-South LB $16.50 (0-7358-1893-2). A beautifully — and inventively — illustrated version of this 19th-century song. (Rev: SLJ 11/04) [264]

19066 Banks, William H., Jr. *The Black Muslims* (5–10). Series: African-American Achievers. 1996, Chelsea LB $21.95 (0-7910-2593-4); paper $9.95 (0-7910-2594-2). The story of the founding of the Nation of Islam, its leaders, the Million Man March, and the reign of Louis Farrakhan. (Rev: SLJ 5/97) [323]

19067 Baring-Gould, Sabine. *Now the Day Is Over* (PS–2). Illus. by Preston McDaniels. 2001, Morehouse $17.95 (0-8192-1868-5). 32pp. Graceful illustrations of a little boy, animals, and angels accompany the four verses of the song. (Rev: BL 6/1–15/01) [242]

19068 Batchelor, Mary, ed. *Children's Prayers: From Around the World* (4–7). Illus. 1995, Augsburg $13.99 (0-8066-2830-8). 93pp. Two hundred prayers for children from many sources worldwide, with some for special holidays and holy days. (Rev: BL 9/1/95) [242]

19069 Bedard, Michael. *The Wolf of Gubbio* (2–4). Illus. 2001, Stoddart $15.95 (0-7737-3250-0). 24pp. The story of Saint Francis of Assisi and how his ability to talk to animals saved the city of Gubbio from a hungry wolf is retold through the voice of a young child. (Rev: BCCB 6/01; BL 4/15/01) [398.22]

19070 Bennett, Helen. *Humanism, What's That? A Book for Curious Kids* (3–5). Illus. 2005, Prometheus $18.00 (1-59102-229-0). 69pp. This introduction to secular humanism is presented in the form of a lively classroom discussion between Mrs. Green, a humanist science teacher, and her students. (Rev: BL 2/15/05) [211]

19071 Bial, Raymond. *Amish Home* (3–6). Illus. by author. 1993, Houghton Mifflin $17.00 (0-395-59504-5). 40pp. A haunting photoessay of Amish life without the Amish themselves because their religious doctrine forbids portraiture. (Rev: BCCB 5/93; BL 2/15/93; SLJ 5/93) [973.08]

19072 Birdseye, Debbie H., and Tom Birdseye. *What I Believe: Kids Talk About Faith* (4–7). 1996, Holiday House $15.95 (0-8234-1268-7). 32pp. Children from six faiths explain what their religion means to them. (Rev: BL 12/15/96; SLJ 2/97) [200]

19073 Bolden, Tonya. *Rock of Ages* (K–4). Illus. by R. Gregory Christie. 2001, Knopf LB $18.99 (0-679-99485-8). 32pp. Rhythmic text and striking art present the importance of religion in African American life, from slavery through the civil rights movement to the present. (Rev: BL 10/1/01; HB 1–2/02; HBG 3/02; SLJ 1/02*) [811.5]

19074 Bolick, Nancy O., and Sallie G. Randolph. *Shaker Inventions* (4–6). Illus. by Melissa Francisco. 1990, Walker LB $14.85 (0-8027-6934-9). 96pp. A rundown on many inventions by the Shakers, and a general introduction to their way of life. (Rev: SLJ 9/90) [289]

19075 Bolick, Nancy O., and Sallie G. Randolph. *Shaker Villages* (4–8). Illus. by Laura LoTurco. 1993, Walker LB $13.85 (0-8027-8210-8). 79pp. A history of the Shaker movement. (Rev: SLJ 6/93) [289]

19076 Borchard, Therese. *Taste and See: The Goodness of the Lord* (PS–K). Illus. by Phyllis V. Saroff. 2000, Paulist Press $9.95 (0-8091-6665-8). 32pp. With images that use the five senses, children are made to feel that God is everywhere and in all living things. (Rev: BL 10/1/00; HBG 3/01) [231]

19077 Brown, Alan, and Andrew Langley. *What I Believe: A Young Person's Guide to the Religions of the World* (4–7). Illus. 1999, Millbrook LB $24.90

(0-7613-1501-2). 64pp. Young people of eight major faiths explain their religion's principal tenets, rituals, holy days, and celebrations. (Rev: BL 10/1/99; HBG 4/00; SLJ 2/00) [291]

19078 Brunelli, Roberto. *A Family Treasury of Bible Stories: One for Each Week of the Year* (4–8). Illus. 1997, Abrams $24.95 (0-8109-1248-7). A collection of 52 short stories from the Old and New Testaments. (Rev: BL 10/1/97; SLJ 2/98) [220.9]

19079 Capek, Michael. *A Personal Tour of a Shaker Village* (4–7). Series: How It Was. 2001, Lerner LB $30.35 (0-8225-3584-X). 64pp. An account of life in a Shaker village, seen through the eyes of people who lived there. (Rev: BL 8/1/01; SLJ 8/01) [289.8]

19080 Carew-Miller, Anna. *Buddha: Father of Buddhism* (2–5). Illus. by Paolo d'Altan. Series: Great Names. 2002, Mason Crest LB $19.95 (1-59084-137-9). This account of Buddha's life blends fact and fiction and conveys information on the religion as well as the man. (Rev: SLJ 8/03) [294.3]

19081 Carlstrom, Nancy White. *Does God Know How to Tie Shoes?* (PS–K). Illus. by Lori McElrath-Eslick. 1993, Eerdmans $15.00 (0-8028-5074-X). 32pp. A child questions her parents about the nature of God, and the answers are correlated with passages from the Bible. (Rev: BL 12/1/93; SLJ 3/94)

19082 Chaikin, Miriam. *Angels Sweep the Desert Floor: Bible Legends About Moses in the Wilderness* (4–7). Illus. by Alexander Koshkin. 2002, Clarion $19.00 (0-395-97825-4). 102pp. This collection of stories mixes religious history and rabbinic literature to tell the story of the Israelites' 40 years in the wilderness. (Rev: BL 10/1/02; HB 11–12/02; HBG 3/03; SLJ 9/02) [296.1]

19083 Chaikin, Miriam. *Menorahs, Mezuzas, and Other Jewish Symbols* (5–9). 1990, Clarion $17.00 (0-89919-856-2). A Jewish historian explains some of the symbols of the faith. (Rev: BL 1/15/91; HB 5–6/91; SLJ 1/91) [296.4]

19084 Chalfonte, Jessica. *I Am Muslim* (1–4). Illus. Series: Religions of the World. 1996, Rosen LB $15.93 (0-8239-2375-4). 24pp. An introduction to the Muslim religion and the world of Islam as seen through the eyes of Ahmet, a boy living in Detroit. (Rev: SLJ 2/97) [297]

19085 *The Children's Book of Faith* (4–6). Ed. by William J. Bennett. Illus. by Michael Hague. 2000, Doubleday $24.95 (0-385-32771-4). 112pp. A collection of poems, Bible stories, proverbs, short stories, and pieces of nonfiction that have a moral purpose chiefly from a Christian point of view. (Rev: BL 10/1/00; HBG 3/01; SLJ 12/00) [248]

19086 Cole, Michael D. *The Siege at Waco: Deadly Inferno* (5–9). Series: American Disasters. 1999, Enslow LB $18.95 (0-7660-1218-2). The story of the disaster that ended the 51-day siege at Waco and resulted in the deaths of cult leader David Koresh and 73 of his followers. (Rev: BL 2/15/99; HBG 9/99) [976.4]

19087 Conover, Sarah, and Freda Crane. *Beautiful Signs / Ayat Jamilah: A Treasury of Islamic Wisdom for Children and Parents* (5–7). Illus. by Valerie Wahl. Series: Little Light of Mine. 2004, Eastern

Washington Univ. paper $19.95 (0-910055-94-7). 200pp. Muslim folktales, fables, stories from the Koran, and historic tales originate from countries around the world. (Rev: BL 10/15/04; SLJ 8/04) [297.1]

19088 Cooper, Ilene. *The Dead Sea Scrolls* (5–8). Illus. 1997, Morrow $15.00 (0-688-14300-8). An account of the discovery of the Dead Sea Scrolls, their contents, and their archaeological importance. (Rev: BCCB 5/97; BL 3/1/97; HB 9–10/97; SLJ 6/97) [296.1]

19089 David, Jo, and Daniel B. Syme. *The Book of the Jewish Life* (5–8). Illus. 1997, UAHC paper $12.95 (0-8074-0628-7). This book explores common Jewish traditions in such areas as birth and naming, religious schools, bar/bat mitzvahs, confirmation, marriage, and mourning. (Rev: SLJ 9/98) [296]

19090 Demi. *Buddha* (4–6). Illus. 1996, Holt $18.95 (0-8050-4203-2). 32pp. In this picture book for older children, the story of Buddha's life and teachings is effectively retold. (Rev: BCCB 6/96; BL 4/1/96; HB 9–10/96; SLJ 6/96) [294.3]

19091 Demi. *Buddha Stories* (3–6). Illus. 1997, Holt $16.95 (0-8050-4886-3). 32pp. Ten of the author's favorite Buddha stories, or jakatas, are elegantly retold with excellent illustrations. (Rev: BCCB 4/97; BL 2/15/97; SLJ 6/97) [294.3]

19092 Demi. *The Legend of St. Nicholas* (2–5). Illus. by author. 2003, Simon & Schuster $19.95 (0-689-84681-9). 40pp. Young readers will be fascinated by this beautifully illustrated biography of the real St. Nicholas, who devoted his life to relieving the suffering of others. (Rev: BL 10/1/03; HBG 4/04; SLJ 10/03)

19093 Dhanjal, Beryl. *What Do We Know About Sikhism?* (3–6). Illus. Series: What Do We Know About. 1997, Bedrick LB $18.95 (0-87226-387-8). 45pp. The history of Sikhism is covered, along with material on its founder, Guru Nanak; the ten succeeding Gurus; the Sikh Holy Book; and the Golden Temple at Amritsar. (Rev: SLJ 3/97) [294.6]

19094 Dillon, Leo, and Diane Dillon. *To Every Thing There Is a Season: Verses from Ecclesiastes* (4–7). Illus. 1998, Scholastic paper $16.95 (0-590-47887-7). 40pp. Using verses from Ecclesiastes such as "A time to be born and a time to die," the artists have created a stunning picture book on the cycle of life. (Rev: BCCB 11/98; BL 10/1/98*; HB 9–10/98; HBG 3/99; SLJ 9/98) [223]

19095 Dineen, Jacqueline. *Births* (3–6). Series: Ceremonies and Celebrations. 2001, Raintree LB $17.98 (0-7398-3267-0). 32pp. Traditions surrounding births are explored in six major religions, covering topics from circumcision, baptism, and naming ceremonies to gifts, clothing, food, and horoscopes. Also use *Weddings* (2001). (Rev: SLJ 9/01) [392.12]

19096 Douglass, Susan L. *Ramadan* (1–3). Series: On My Own Holidays. 2003, Carolrhoda LB $22.60 (0-87614-932-8); paper $5.95 (1-57505-584-8). 48pp. An excellent introduction to the holy month of fasting observed by Muslims each year, with helpful information about the basic beliefs and practices of Islam. (Rev: BL 10/15/03; HBG 4/04; SLJ 8/03)

19097 Egan, Andrew. *Islam* (5–8). Illus. Series: Living Religions. 2003, Raintree LB $28.56 (0-7398-6385-1). 62pp. This overview of Islam provides valuable insights into the core beliefs and rituals of the religion as well as its adherents' views on such contemporary issues as women's rights. (Rev: HBG 10/03; SLJ 10/03) [297]

19098 Faber, Doris. *The Amish* (3–5). Illus. by Michael Erkel. 1990, Doubleday $17.95 (0-385-44518-0). An enlightening look at the people, who live plainly, in harmony with nature. (Rev: BL 1/15/91) [973.08]

19099 Feinstein, Edward. *Tough Questions Jews Ask: A Young Adult's Guide to Building a Jewish Life* (5–7). 2003, Jewish Lights $14.95 (1-58023-139-X). 128pp. Rabbi Feinstein effectively answers hypothetical questions posed by an imagined class of thoughtful young students. (Rev: BL 4/1/03) [296.7]

19100 Fisher, James T. *Catholics in America* (5–9). Illus. Series: Religion in American Life. 2000, Oxford $28.00 (0-19-511179-6). 176pp. This account traces the history of Roman Catholicism in America, its adherents, their role in public affairs, and debates over topics such as abortion. (Rev: BL 6/1–15/00; SLJ 12/00) [282]

19101 Fisher, Leonard E. *To Bigotry No Sanction: The Story of the Oldest Synagogue in America* (5–8). Illus. 1998, Holiday House $16.95 (0-8234-1401-9). Beginning with the expulsion of the Jews from Spain in 1492, the author traces the history of Jews in America, including the 1763 building — with George Washington's blessing — of the Touro Synagogue. (Rev: BCCB 4/99; BL 2/1/99; SLJ 3/99) [296.097457]

19102 Fitch, Florence Mary. *A Book About God* (PS–3). Illus. by Henri Sorensen. 1999, Lothrop LB $15.93 (0-688-16129-4). 24pp. A new edition of a book originally published in 1953 that tries to explain the nature of God and how this spirit is found everywhere. (Rev: BL 4/1/99; HBG 9/99; SLJ 5/99) [231]

19103 Ganeri, Anita. *Buddhism* (3–6). Series: World of Beliefs. 2001, McGraw-Hill $16.95 (0-87226-685-0). 46pp. With a large-format, short paragraphs, and a copious assortment of illustrations, this book gives a brief introduction to Buddhism and its beliefs. (Rev: BL 12/15/01; HBG 3/02; SLJ 11/01) [294]

19104 Ganeri, Anita. *Growing Up: From Child to Adult* (4–6). Series: Life Times. 1999, Bedrick LB $15.95 (0-87226-287-1). 32pp. This book describes rites of passage from child to adult as practiced in six major religions, including Buddhism, Christianity, Judaism, and Hinduism. (Rev: BL 5/15/99; HBG 9/99; SLJ 3/99) [291]

19105 Ganeri, Anita. *What Do We Know About Buddhism?* (4–7). Illus. Series: What Do We Know About. 1997, Bedrick $18.95 (0-87226-389-4). 45pp. Using double-page spreads, basic facts about Buddha's life and teachings are covered, with infor-

mation on Buddhist beliefs, sacred texts, festivals, and the art and folk literature connected with this religion. (Rev: HBG 3/98; SLJ 10/97) [294]

19106 Gellman, Marc. *And God Cried, Too: A Kid's Book of Healing and Hope* (2–5). Illus. by Harry Bliss. 2002, HarperCollins LB $17.89 (0-06-009887-2); paper $5.99 (0-06-009886-4). 128pp. A fictional story about a young angel-in-training opens this thought-provoking book that deals with questions that challenge faith. (Rev: BL 10/1/02; SLJ 12/02) [291.2]

19107 Gellman, Marc. *God's Mailbox: More Stories About Stories in the Bible* (4–7). Illus. by Debbie Tilley. 1996, Morrow $15.00 (0-688-13169-7). 92pp. Some stories retold from the Bible, including the Creation, Garden of Eden, Jacob's ladder, the Exodus, and Moses receiving the Ten Commandments. (Rev: BCCB 5/96; SLJ 3/96) [222]

19108 Gellman, Marc, and Thomas Hartman. *How Do You Spell God? Answers to the Big Questions from Around the World* (5–8). Illus. by Joseph A. Smith. 1995, Morrow $17.99 (0-688-13041-0). 224pp. A priest and a rabbi have written this introduction to the world's most important religions: Judaism, Christianity, Islam, Buddhism, and Hinduism. (Rev: BCCB 7–8/95; BL 6/1–15/95; SLJ 5/95) [200]

19109 George, Charles. *Buddhist* (3–5). Series: What Makes Me A? 2004, Gale $23.70 (0-7377-2269-X). 48pp. This is a straightforward and attractively designed introduction to the beliefs and practice of Buddhism, with a listing of print and online resources for further research. Also use *What Makes Me a Hindu?* (2004). (Rev: BL 10/15/04*; SLJ 11/04) [294.3]

19110 Gershator, Phillis, and Alexa Ginsburg. *Wise . . . and Not So Wise: Ten Tales from the Rabbis* (3–6). Series: New Children's Titles. 2004, Jewish Publication Soc. $15.95 (0-8276-0755-5). 120pp. Ten stories drawn from traditional Jewish sources present interesting situations and are followed by questions that will provoke thoughtful analysis of their meaning and relevance today. (Rev: BL 10/1/04; SLJ 1/05) [296.1]

19111 Gibson, Lynne. *Hinduism* (5–8). Illus. Series: Living Religions. 2003, Raintree LB $28.56 (0-7398-6384-3). 62pp. Gibson describes Hinduism's core beliefs and rituals and examines some contemporary controversies. (Rev: HBG 10/03; SLJ 10/03) [294.5]

19112 Glossop, Jennifer. *The Kids Book of World Religions* (3–6). Illus. by John Mantha. 2003, Kids Can $15.95 (1-55074-959-5). 64pp. Students writing reports will find this a useful source of information on the basic tenets of the world's major religions. (Rev: BL 4/15/03; HBG 10/03; SLJ 4/03) [291]

19113 Gold, Susan D. *Religions of the Western Hemisphere* (5–8). Illus. Series: Comparing Continents. 1997, Twenty-First Century $23.40 (0-8050-5603-3). This work explores the history and influence of religions, beliefs, and customs on life in the United States, Canada, and Latin America, with discussion of the roles of religious leaders in government, economy, and everyday life. (Rev: BL 2/1/98; SLJ 3/98) [200]

19114 Goldin, Barbara D. *Journeys with Elijah: Eight Tales of the Prophet* (4–7). Illus. by Jerry Pinkney. 1999, Harcourt $20.00 (0-15-200445-9). 96pp. Eight tales depict the prophet Elijah in his many roles as teacher, miracle worker, and mysterious stranger. (Rev: BCCB 4/99; BL 4/15/99; HB 3–4/99; HBG 9/99; SLJ 6/99) [222]

19115 Goodnough, David. *Cult Awareness: A Hot Issue* (5–8). Series: Hot Issues. 2000, Enslow LB $21.95 (0-7660-1196-8). 64pp. This book explains the nature of cults and how they differ as well as giving information on many groups including Jehovah's Witnesses, Unification Church, Hare Krishna, Shakers, Mormons, and Church of Scientology. (Rev: BL 6/1–15/00; HBG 9/00; SLJ 6/00) [291.9]

19116 Griffith, Linda Hill. *Blessings and Prayers for Little Bears* (PS–K). Illus. 2002, HarperCollins $15.95 (0-06-623689-4). 32pp. Traditional children's prayers are illustrated with full-page paintings of teddy bears involved in everyday activities. (Rev: BL 1/1–15/02; HBG 10/02; SLJ 7/02) [242]

19117 Grimes, Nikki. *At Break of Day* (PS–3). Illus. by Paul Morin. 1999, Eerdmans $17.00 (0-8028-5104-5). 32pp. In this version of the creation story, God and his Son work together to produce the universe and its wonders. (Rev: BL 10/1/99; HBG 4/00; SLJ 1/00)

19118 Gunderson, Cory. *Religions of the Middle East* (3–5). Series: World in Conflict: The Middle East. 2004, ABDO LB $17.95 (1-59197-412-7). 48pp. A comparative description of the major religions of the Middle East — Islam, Judaism, Christianity, Druze, and Hinduism. (Rev: SLJ 5/04) [200]

19119 Hodges, Margaret. *The Legend of Saint Christopher* (3–6). Illus. by Richard J. Watson. 2002, Eerdmans $18.00 (0-8028-5077-4). 32pp. Hodges retells the story of how Saint Christopher got the name that means "Christ bearer." (Rev: BCCB 12/02; BL 10/1/02; HBG 3/03; SLJ 11/02) [242]

19120 Hoffman, Lawrence A., and Wolfson Ron. *What You Will See Inside a Synagogue* (3–5). Illus. 2004, Skylight Paths $17.99 (1-59473-012-1). 32pp. Introduces readers to the rituals and places of worship of three branches of American Judaism — Conservative, Reconstruction, and Reform. (Rev: BL 1/1–15/05; SLJ 2/05) [296.4]

19121 *I Believe: The Nicene Creed* (1–3). Illus. by Pauline Baynes. 2004, Eerdmans $16.00 (0-8028-5258-0). 32pp. The Nicene Creed, a basic outline of Christian doctrine used by Eastern Orthodox, Roman Catholic, and most Protestant denominations, is examined line by line in this beautifully illustrated book. (Rev: BL 7/03; HBG 4/04; SLJ 11/03) [238]

19122 Israel, Fred L. *The Amish* (5–8). Illus. Series: Immigrant Experience. 1996, Chelsea LB $21.95 (0-7910-3368-6). The story of this conservative division of the Mennonites, why they settled in the United States, and their contributions to the nation. (Rev: BL 7/96; SLJ 10/96) [305.6]

19123 Jaffe, Nina. *The Mysterious Visitor: Stories of the Prophet Elijah* (4–6). Illus. 1997, Scholastic $19.95 (0-590-48422-2). 112pp. Eight Jewish stories that involve the prophet Elijah are retold. (Rev: BCCB 6/97; BL 5/1/97; HBG 3/98; SLJ 6/97*) [222]

19124 Johari, Harish, and Vatsala Sperling. *How Ganesh Got His Elephant Head* (1–4). Illus. by Pieter Weltevrede. 2003, Bear & Company $15.95 (1-59143-021-6). 32pp. Traditional illustrations highlight the Hindu story of how Ganesh got his elephant head, which is amplified with a tale of Ganesh's rivalry with his brother. (Rev: BL 12/1/03; SLJ 1/04)

19125 John Paul II. *Every Child a Light: The Pope's Message to Young People* (4–7). Ed. by Jerome M. Vereb. Illus. 2002, Boyds Mills $16.95 (1-56397-090-2). 48pp. Using photographs and snippets from Pope John Paul II's writings for children and teens, this is an inspirational book of comments and advice for youngsters. (Rev: BL 6/1–15/02; SLJ 5/02) [248.8]

19126 Kanitkar, V. P. *Hinduism* (4–6). Illus. 1986, Dufour paper $21.00 (1-871402-09-3). History, major tenets, and an explanation of holidays and festivals. (Rev: BL 12/15/86)

19127 Kaur-Singh, Kanwaljit. *Sikh Gurdwara* (1–3). Series: Places of Worship. 2000, Gareth Stevens LB $15.95 (0-8368-2610-8). 32pp. This book explores the gurdwara, where Sikhs worship God and show respect for the Guru Granth Sahib, and also tells about the the basic beliefs and practices of the Sikh faith. (Rev: BL 6/1–15/00; HBG 9/00) [294.6]

19128 Keane, Michael. *What You Will See Inside a Catholic Church* (3–6). Illus. 2002, Skylight Paths $17.95 (1-893361-54-3). 32pp. Readers are introduced to the layout, ceremonies, and rituals of a Roman Catholic church. (Rev: BL 3/15/03; SLJ 9/03) [264]

19129 Kenna, Kathleen. *A People Apart* (5–8). Illus. 1995, Houghton Mifflin $18.00 (0-395-67344-5). A thoughtful photoessay on the lives of the Mennonites by a woman who attended the church as a child. Interviews and the history of the group flesh out the text. (Rev: BL 11/1/95*; SLJ 12/95*) [289.7]

19130 Khan, Rukhsana. *Muslim Child: Understanding Islam Through Stories and Poems* (4–6). Illus. by Patty Gallinger. 2002, Whitman $14.95 (0-8075-5307-7). 104pp. A series of vignettes told by children about living as a Muslim in various countries around the world. (Rev: BL 2/15/02; HBG 10/02; SLJ 2/02) [297]

19131 Kimmel, Eric A. *Brother Wolf, Sister Sparrow: Stories About Saints and Animals* (3–6). Illus. by John Winch. 2003, Holiday House $18.95 (0-8234-1724-7). 64pp. This collection of well-illustrated stories explores several saints' relationships with animals and includes the tale of a bargain Francis of Assisi struck with a wolf and an account of how angels helped Saint Brigid to replace the butter and milk she'd given to the needy. (Rev: BL 4/1/03; HBG 10/03; SLJ 5/03) [398.22]

19132 Krishnaswami, Uma. *The Broken Tusk: Stories of the Hindu God Ganesha* (4–6). Illus. 1996, Linnet LB $21.50 (0-208-02442-5). 98pp. A collection of folktales about the elephant-headed Hindu god Ganesha, the god of good beginnings. (Rev: BCCB 10/96; BL 10/1/96; SLJ 7/97) [294.5]

19133 Kroll, Virginia. *I Wanted to Know All About God* (PS–1). Illus. by Debra R. Jenkins. 1994, Eerdmans $15.00 (0-8028-5078-2). 32pp. A book about the nature of God that emphasizes human relationships and the wonders of nature. (Rev: BL 2/15/94; SLJ 8/94) [231.2]

19134 Krull, Kathleen, ed. *Songs of Praise* (PS–1). Illus. by Kathryn Hewitt. 1989, Harcourt paper $5.95 (0-15-277109-3). 32pp. A collection of 15 hymns. (Rev: BCCB 9/88; BL 11/15/88)

19135 Kushner, Lawrence, and Karen Kushner. *Because Nothing Looks Like God* (PS–2). Illus. by Dawn Majewski. 2001, Jewish Lights $16.95 (1-58023-092-X). 32pp. The concept of God is explored in this picture book filled with paintings of nature scenes. (Rev: BL 1/1–15/01; SLJ 2/01) [291.2]

19136 Lehman-Wilzig, Tami. *Keeping the Promise: A Torah's Journey* (1–5). Illus. by Craig Orback. 2004, Lerner LB $16.95 (1-58013-117-4); paper $6.95 (1-58013-118-2). The story of a tiny Torah scroll that is passed from a Dutch rabbi to a young boy in Bergen-Belsen who years later gives it to Ilan Ramon, the Israeli astronaut, who took it with him on the tragic *Columbia* mission. (Rev: BCCB 4/04; SLJ 8/04) [296.4]

19137 Lester, Julius. *When the Beginning Began: Stories About God, the Creatures, and Us* (4–8). Illus. 1999, Harcourt $17.00 (0-15-201138-9). Using parts of Genesis and creation stories from Jewish legends, this wondrous retelling adds thought-provoking human interest to the stories that end with Adam and Eve. (Rev: BL 4/15/99*; SLJ 5/99) [296.1]

19138 *Let There Be Light: Poems and Prayers for Repairing the World* (2–6). Ed. by Jane Breskin Zalben. Illus. 2002, Dutton $16.99 (0-525-46995-8). 32pp. Zalben has chosen a selection of spiritual passages from sources ranging from the Bible and Koran to Native American peoples and Mahatma Gandhi. (Rev: BL 10/1/02*; HBG 3/03; SLJ 11/02) [242.8]

19139 Lincoln, Frances. *A Family Treasury of Prayers* (4–8). 1996, Simon & Schuster $16.00 (0-689-80956-5). Classic art works illustrate this lovely collection of prayers from famous sources. (Rev: BL 10/1/96; SLJ 10/96) [242]

19140 Lindbergh, Reeve. *The Circle of Days* (PS–3). Illus. by Cathie Felstead. 1998, Candlewick $15.99 (0-7637-0357-0). 32pp. This adaptation of the writings of St. Francis of Assisi translates the cycle of creation, life, and death in nature into simple, flowing prose and detailed illustrations. (Rev: BL 4/1/98*) [242]

19141 Llewellyn, Claire. *Saints and Angels* (3–6). 2003, Houghton Mifflin $14.95 (0-7534-5588-9). 64pp. This lushly illustrated book focuses primarily on the Christian saints — organized into such logical groups as martyrs, thinkers, and disciples — but also devotes a section to angels. (Rev: BL 10/1/03; HBG 4/04)

19142 Lutz, Norma Jean. *The History of the Black Church* (5–8). Illus. Series: African American Achievers. 2001, Chelsea $21.95 (0-7910-5822-0); paper $9.95 (0-7910-5823-9). 112pp. Historical and contemporary photographs illustrate this history of African American religious life and institutions. (Rev: BL 10/1/01; SLJ 12/01) [277.3]

19143 McFarlane, Marilyn. *Sacred Myths: Stories of World Religions* (4–7). 1996, Sibyl $26.95 (0-9638327-7-8). 110pp. A collection of myths from a number of religions, including Judaism, Christianity, Islam, and Hinduism. (Rev: BL 10/1/96; SLJ 1/97) [291.1]

19144 MacMillan, Dianne M. *Diwali: Hindu Festival of Lights* (4–8). Series: Best Holiday Books. 1997, Enslow LB $18.95 (0-89490-817-0). This book on the Hindu Diwali festival discusses its significance and relationship to the history, culture, and people of India, and includes material on the food, crafts, instruments, and costumes of the festival. (Rev: SLJ 8/97) [294.5]

19145 Maestro, Betsy. *The Story of Religion* (4–7). Illus. by Giulio Maestro. 1996, Clarion LB $16.00 (0-395-62364-2). 46pp. Traces the history of religion from the beliefs of primitive peoples to the development of such modern religions as Islam and Christianity. (Rev: BL 10/1/96; SLJ 9/96*) [291]

19146 Manushkin, Fran. *Daughters of Fire* (4–7). Illus. by Uri Shulevitz. 2001, Harcourt $20.00 (0-15-201869-7). 88pp. Rich, striking illustrations accompany a selection of stories about biblical women. (Rev: BL 12/15/01; HBG 3/02; SLJ 10/01) [221.9]

19147 Mayled, Jon. *Sikhism* (5–8). Illus. Series: Living Religions. 2003, Raintree LB $28.56 (0-7398-6387-8). 62pp. Examines Sikhism's core beliefs and rituals and looks at its views on contemporary issues. (Rev: HBG 10/03; SLJ 10/03) [294.6]

19148 Moehn, Heather. *World Holidays: A Watts Guide for Children* (3–6). Illus. 2000, Watts LB $32.00 (0-531-11714-6); paper $19.95 (0-531-16490-X). 128pp. The origins and methods of celebrating more than 100 world holidays, both religious and secular, are included in this illustrated book. (Rev: BL 9/1/00; SLJ 7/00) [394.26]

19149 Morris, Neil. *Islam* (3–6). Illus. Series: World of Beliefs. 2001, McGraw-Hill $16.95 (0-87226-693-1). 46pp. A large-format introduction to the religion of Islam both in history and today that touches on the role of women, with concise text and lots of photographs and illustrations. (Rev: BL 10/1/01; HBG 3/02; SLJ 11/01) [297]

19150 Mulvihill, Margaret. *The Treasury of Saints and Martyrs* (5–7). Illus. 1999, Viking $19.99 (0-670-88789-7). 80pp. A handsome, oversize book about the lives of 40 saints from the beginning of Christianity to the present day. (Rev: BL 10/1/99; SLJ 3/00) [270.029]

19151 Nomura, Noriko S. *I Am Shinto* (K–3). Illus. Series: Religions of the World. 1996, Rosen LB $15.93 (0-8239-2380-0). 24pp. In double-page spreads, various aspects of the Shinto religion are introduced, including Dami spirits, shrines, and purification rituals. (Rev: SLJ 11/96) [299]

19152 Novesky, Amy. *Elephant Prince: The Story of Ganesh* (PS–2). Illus. by Belgin K. Wedman. 2004, Mandala $16.95 (1-886069-16-6). 32pp. A beautifully illustrated story of how the Hindu god Ganesh acquired his elephant head. (Rev: BL 1/1–15/05; SLJ 2/05) [294.5]

19153 Paterson, John, and Katherine Paterson. *Images of God: Views of the Invisible* (5–8). Illus. 1998, Houghton Mifflin $20.00 (0-395-70734-X). After explaining the differences between the Hebrew and the Christian Bibles, the authors describe the images of God in these texts, as well as the portrayal of such elements as light, water, wind, fire, rocks, and clouds. (Rev: BL 5/1/98; HBG 9/98; SLJ 4/98) [231]

19154 Paul, John. *For the Children: Words of Love and Inspiration from His Holiness John Paul II* (4–7). Illus. 2000, Scholastic paper $16.95 (0-439-14902-9). 32pp. Letters and speeches by Pope John Paul II and photographs of children from around the world are used to illustrate inspirational messages about such subjects as hope, faith, and school. (Rev: BL 3/1/00; SLJ 3/00) [248.8]

19155 Pilling, Ann. *A Kingfisher Treasury of Bible Stories, Poems, and Prayers for Bedtime* (3–6). Illus. 2000, Kingfisher $18.95 (0-7534-5329-0). 96pp. Poetry, songs, and Bible stories from the Old and New Testaments are included in this anthology aimed at Christian children. (Rev: BL 10/1/00; HBG 10/01) [242]

19156 Raimondo, Lois. *The Little Lama of Tibet* (K–4). Illus. 1994, Scholastic $15.95 (0-590-46167-2). 40pp. This photoessay deals with the everyday life of Ling Rinpoche, a six-year-old high lama in the Tibetan Buddhist religion. (Rev: BCCB 1/94; BL 1/1/94; HB 9–10/94; SLJ 3/94) [294.3]

19157 Ross, Lillian H. *Daughters of Eve: Strong Women of the Bible* (5–7). Illus. 2000, Barefoot $19.99 (1-902283-82-1). 96pp. Fictionalized accounts that expand on the material given in the Bible and Apocrypha about 12 strong women and their deeds. (Rev: BL 10/1/00; SLJ 11/00) [220.9]

19158 Rushton, Lucy. *Birth Customs* (4–6). Illus. Series: Religions. 1993, Thomson Learning LB $19.92 (1-56847-030-4). 32pp. This book examines the rituals and customs associated with birth as found in many of the world's religions. A companion volume is: *Death Customs* (1993). (Rev: BL 6/1–15/93; SLJ 7/93) [291.2]

19159 Sasso, Sandy Eisenberg. *God in Between* (PS–3). Illus. by Sally Sweetland. 1998, Jewish Lights $16.95 (1-879045-86-9). 32pp. Two townspeople are disappointed when their journey to find God ends unsuccessfully — until they realize that God is found while reaching out to others in need. (Rev: BL 10/15/98; HBG 9/98; SLJ 9/98) [211]

19160 Schwartz, Howard. *Invisible Kingdoms: Jewish Tales of Angels, Spirits, and Demons* (3–5). Illus. by Stephen Fieser. 2002, HarperCollins LB $18.89 (0-06-027856-0). 80pp. Schwartz retells nine varied tales peopled with angels, ghosts, and demons. (Rev: BL 10/1/02; HB 11–12/02; HBG 3/03; SLJ 10/02) [398.2]

19161 Senker, Cath. *Judaism* (3–6). Illus. Series: World of Beliefs. 2001, McGraw-Hill $16.95 (0-87226-684-2). 46pp. Concise text and plentiful photographs and illustrations are used in this introduction to the history and current practice of Judaism that covers the creation of the state of Israel. (Rev: BL 10/1/01; HBG 3/02; SLJ 12/01) [296]

19162 Sevastiades, Philemon D. *I Am Eastern Orthodox* (1–4). Illus. Series: Religions of the World. 1996, Rosen LB $16.95 (0-8239-2377-0). 24pp. The unique qualities of this church are covered through the story of Anastasia and her brother, who is the priest of her church in Chicago. (Rev: SLJ 2/97) [291]

19163 Sevastiades, Philemon D. *I Am Protestant* (1–4). Illus. Series: Religions of the World. 1996, Rosen LB $15.93 (0-8239-2378-9). 24pp. Focusing on Yvonne, a Southern African American girl who is an Evangelical Protestant, this and other branches of Protestantism and their beliefs are covered. (Rev: SLJ 2/97) [280]

19164 Sevastiades, Philemon D. *I Am Roman Catholic* (K–3). Illus. Series: Religions of the World. 1996, Rosen LB $17.26 (0-8239-2376-2). 24pp. Such Roman Catholic institutions, beliefs, and rituals as the Trinity, the Pope, baptism, Mass, confession, communion, and confirmation are discussed. (Rev: SLJ 11/96) [282]

19165 Sita, Lisa. *Worlds of Belief: Religion and Spirituality* (5–8). Series: Our Human Family. 1995, Blackbirch LB $31.19 (1-56711-125-4). Using many illustrations, this book gives a tour of the world's religions, with an emphasis on the similarities rather than the differences. (Rev: SLJ 1/96) [200]

19166 Stanton, Sue. *Child's Guide to the Mass* (PS–3). Illus. by H. M. Alan. 2001, Paulist Press $9.95 (0-8091-6682-8). 32pp. Using a lighthearted approach, this book explains the parts of the Roman Catholic Mass and what each means. (Rev: BL 3/15/01; HBG 10/01) [264]

19167 Stauffacher, Sue. *The Angel and Other Stories* (2–6). Illus. by Leonid Gore. 2002, Eerdmans $20.00 (0-8028-5203-3). 80pp. Stauffacher retells 10 stories that reflect on faith and prayer written by authors including Hans Christian Andersen, Fyodor Dostoyevsky, and Oscar Wilde. (Rev: BCCB 11/02; BL 10/1/02; HBG 3/03; SLJ 1/03) [242]

19168 *Stories Told by Mother Teresa* (2–4). Ed. by Edward Le Joly and Jaya Chaliha. Illus. by Allan Drummond. 2000, Element Books $15.95 (1-90261-865-3). 32pp. These 11 moving stories derived from the personal experiences of Mother Teresa describe acts of sacrifice, faith, and devotion by ordinary people. (Rev: BL 3/15/00; HBG 9/00) [271.97]

1021

19169 Sturges, Philemon. *Sacred Places* (4–6). Illus. 2000, Penguin Putnam $16.99 (0-399-23317-2). 40pp. This general introduction to religion describes different places of worship including a pagoda, mosque, synagogue, church, and Hindu temple. (Rev: BCCB 12/00; BL 10/1/00; HBG 3/01; SLJ 12/00) [291.3]

19170 Sugarman, Joan G., and Grace R. Freeman. *Inside the Synagogue* (K–3). Illus. 1984, UAHC paper $7.00 (0-8074-0268-0). In text and photos, the Jewish house of worship is introduced. (Rev: SLJ 3/85)

19171 Teece, Geoff. *Christianity* (3–7). Illus. Series: Religion in Focus. 2004, Smart Apple Media LB $18.95 (1-58340-465-1). This slim, photo-filled volume introduces the history, beliefs, and practices of Christianity, covering festivals, sacred places, and a list of denominations. Also use *Buddhism* (2004). (Rev: BL 10/1/04) [202]

19172 Tompert, Ann. *Saint Nicholas* (2–4). Illus. 2000, Boyds Mills $15.95 (1-56397-844-X). 32pp. A retelling of the legends surrounding St. Nicholas and the attributes that made him one of the most beloved of all saints. (Rev: BCCB 10/00; BL 10/1/00; HBG 3/01) [398.2]

19173 Visconte, Guido. *Clare and Francis* (4–7). Illus. by Bimba Landmann. 2004, Eerdmans $20.00 (0-8028-5269-6). 40pp. Eye-catching artwork highlights the inspiring stories of saints Clare and Francis in this picture book for older readers. (Rev: BL 2/1/04*; SLJ 6/04) [270]

19174 Waldman, Neil. *The Promised Land: The Birth of the Jewish People* (4–7). Illus. 2002, Boyds Mills $21.95 (1-56397-332-4). 40pp. Waldman interweaves information on religious tradition and the experiences of the Jewish people over time in this handsome volume. (Rev: BL 10/1/02; HBG 3/03; SLJ 9/02) [909]

19175 Weiss, Bernard P. *I Am Jewish* (1–4). Illus. Series: Religions of the World. 1996, Rosen LB $13.95 (0-8239-2349-5). 24pp. This explanation of Judaism shows the links between the religion, Jewish history, and the country of Israel. (Rev: SLJ 2/97) [296]

19176 *What You Will See Inside a Mosque* (3–6). Series: What You Will See Inside. 2003, Skylight Paths $16.95 (1-893361-60-8). 32pp. Two small New York mosques are featured in this introduction to the fundamentals of Islam and how and where Muslims worship. (Rev: BL 10/1/03; SLJ 2/04) [297.3]

19177 Wilkinson, Philip. *Buddhism* (5–8). Illus. 2003, DK $15.99 (0-7894-9833-2). 64pp. An attractive, well-illustrated overview of the teachings and symbols of Buddhism, with information on history, different forms, important sites, and art and artifacts. (Rev: BL 1/1–15/04; HBG 4/04) [294.3]

19178 Wood, Angela. *Buddhist Temple* (1–3). Series: Places of Worship. 2000, Gareth Stevens LB $15.95 (0-8368-2605-1). 32pp. A description of a Buddhist temple and an explanation of the basic beliefs and practices of this Eastern religion. (Rev: BL 6/1–15/00; HBG 9/00) [294.3]

19179 Wood, Angela. *Christian Church* (1–3). Illus. Series: Places of Worship. 2000, Gareth Stevens LB $15.95 (0-8368-2606-X). 32pp. This book introduces Christian churches and describes the structure and contents of many. (Rev: BL 6/1–15/00; HBG 9/00) [262]

19180 Wood, Angela. *Hindu Mandir* (1–3). Series: Places of Worship. 2000, Gareth Stevens LB $15.95 (0-8368-2607-8). 32pp. This book introduces the reader to the beliefs and practices of Hinduism and describes home shrines and the parts of a Hindu mandir. (Rev: BL 6/1–15/00; HBG 9/00) [294.5]

19181 Wood, Angela. *Jewish Synagogue* (1–3). Illus. 2000, Gareth Stevens LB $15.95 (0-8368-2608-6). 32pp. An introduction to a synagogue, with information about rabbis, the Torah scrolls, and other important aspects. (Rev: BL 6/1–15/00; HBG 9/00; SLJ 8/00) [296.6]

19182 Wood, Angela. *Judaism* (5–8). Illus. Series: World Religions. 1995, Thomson Learning LB $24.26 (1-56847-376-1). 48pp. An informative, clearly written text on Judaism, with a glossary, bibliography, and map of regions in which the religion flourishes. (Rev: BL 9/1/95; SLJ 11/95) [296]

19183 Wood, Angela. *Muslim Mosque* (1–3). Illus. 2000, Gareth Stevens LB $15.95 (0-8368-2609-4). 32pp. A typical mosque is presented, with material on its functions and on the Koran. (Rev: BL 6/1–15/00; HBG 9/00; SLJ 8/00) [297.3]

Bible Stories

19184 Alexander, Pat. *My First Bible* (PS–1). Illus. by Leon Baxter. 2002, Good Books $17.99 (1-56148-360-5). 480pp. A collection of more than 60 stories from the Old and New Testaments, with amusing, cartoon-style illustrations. (Rev: SLJ 12/02)

19185 Barner, Bob. *To Everything* (K–2). Illus. by author. 1998, Chronicle $14.95 (0-8118-2086-6). Stylized illustrations are used to present ten familiar verses from Ecclesiastes about time's cycle. (Rev: HBG 3/99; SLJ 11/98) [222]

19186 Beneduce, Ann Keay. *Moses: The Long Road to Freedom* (2–4). Illus. by Gennady Spirin. 2004, Scholastic $16.95 (0-439-35225-8). 32pp. The striking artwork of Gennady Spirin enhances this retelling of the story of Moses and how he led his people out of Egypt to freedom. (Rev: BL 4/1/04; SLJ 3/04) [222]

19187 Bible. *And It Was Good* (PS–2). Illus. by Harold H. Nofziger. 1993, Herald Pr. $12.99 (0-8361-3634-9). The Creation story is reproduced with brightly colored collages and a text from the New Revised Standard Version of the Bible. (Rev: SLJ 12/93) [222]

19188 Bible. *The Ark* (PS–2). Illus. by Arthur Geisert. 1988, Houghton Mifflin $18.00 (0-395-43078-X). 48pp. A richly detailed account that includes both well-known and unusual animals. (Rev: HB 11–12/89)

19189 Bogot, Howard I., and Mary K. Bogot, retellers. *Seven Animal Stories for Children* (K–3). Illus. by Harry Araten. 1997, Pitspopany $16.95 (0-943706-40-8); paper $9.95 (0-943706-41-6). 45pp. A collection of Bible stories and Jewish folktales that tell about such people as Noah, Solomon, David, and Jonah. (Rev: HBG 3/98; SLJ 12/97) [226]

19190 Boroson, Martin. *Becoming Me* (K–3). Illus. by Christopher Gilvan-Cartwright. 2000, Skylight Paths $16.95 (1-893361-11-X). 32pp. The Bible creation story as told from the standpoint of God. (Rev: BL 7/00; SLJ 10/00) [291.2]

19191 Boss, Sarah Jane. *Mary's Story* (3–5). Illus. by Helen Cann. 1999, Barefoot $16.95 (1-901223-44-2). 48pp. Using biblical sources as well as folk traditions, this book re-creates the life of Mary, the mother of Jesus. (Rev: BL 10/1/99; SLJ 10/99) [224]

19192 Brett, Jan. *On Noah's Ark* (PS–1). Illus. by author. 2003, Penguin Putnam $16.99 (0-399-24028-4). Noah's granddaughter is the focus of this beautifully illustrated retelling with detailed watercolors of the ark's occupants. (Rev: HBG 4/04; SLJ 9/03)

19193 Chaikin, Miriam, adapt. *Exodus* (3–5). Illus. by Charles Mikolaycak. 1987, Holiday House LB $14.95 (0-8234-0607-5). 32pp. The story of the Israelites' flight out of Egypt. (Rev: BCCB 5/87; BL 5/15/87; HB 5–6/87)

19194 Chancellor, Deborah, retel. *DK Children's Everyday Bible: A Bible Story for Every Day of the Year* (K–4). Illus. by Anna C. Leplar. 2002, DK $19.99 (0-7894-8858-2). 383pp. Retellings of Old and New Testament stories for each day of the year. (Rev: HBG 10/03; SLJ 12/02)

19195 Clements, Andrew. *Noah and the Ark and the Animals* (PS–2). Illus. 1992, Scholastic paper $4.95 (0-590-44457-3). 28pp. Subdued watercolors enhance this retelling.

19196 Connolly, Sean. *New Testament Miracles* (5–10). Series: Art Revelations. 2004, Enchanted Lion $18.95 (1-59270-012-8). 32pp. Presents brief retellings of 12 miracles performed by Jesus Christ, each illustrated by a well-known painting by an eminent artist, such as Rembrandt, El Greco, and Tintoretto. (Rev: SLJ 8/04) [226.7]

19197 Crossley-Holland, Kevin. *How Many Miles to Bethlehem?* (1–3). Illus. by Peter Malone. 2004, Scholastic LB $16.95 (0-439-67642-8). 32pp. Illustrations with a Renaissance flavor form a backdrop for the characters who introduce themselves and their role in the story of the Nativity. (Rev: BL 10/1/04; SLJ 10/04) [232.92]

19198 dePaola, Tomie. *Mary: The Mother of Jesus* (K–3). Illus. 1995, Holiday House LB $16.95 (0-8234-1018-8). 32pp. This account combines stories from the Bible with popular legends to create a life of Mary. (Rev: BCCB 11/95; BL 9/1/95; SLJ 12/95) [232.91]

19199 dePaola, Tomie. *The Miracles of Jesus* (3–6). Illus. by author. 1987, Holiday House LB $16.95 (0-8234-0635-0). 32pp. These one-page adaptations from the New Testament include the 12 miracles of Jesus. (Rev: BL 11/1/87; SLJ 10/87)

19200 dePaola, Tomie. *The Parables of Jesus* (3–6). Illus. by author. 1987, Holiday House LB $16.95 (0-8234-0636-9). 32pp. Seven retellings of the parables of Jesus, such as "The Good Samaritan" and "The Mustard Seed." (Rev: BL 11/1/87; SLJ 10/87)

19201 dePaola, Tomie. *Tomie dePaola's Book of Bible Stories* (K–3). Illus. 1990, Penguin Putnam $24.99 (0-399-21690-1). 128pp. A collection of stories from the Old and New Testaments. (Rev: BCCB 11/90; BL 10/15/90; SLJ 12/90*) [220]

19202 De Regniers, Beatrice S. *David and Goliath* (1–3). Illus. by Scott Cameron. 1996, Orchard LB $16.99 (0-531-08796-4). 32pp. The story of the shepherd boy David and his deadly confrontation with Goliath. (Rev: BL 3/15/96; SLJ 3/96) [222]

19203 Devon, Paddie. *The Grumpy Shepherd* (PS–2). Illus. 1995, Abingdon paper $7.00 (0-687-00129-3). 32pp. A grumpy shepherd named Joram changes his attitude when he meets Jesus. (Rev: BL 12/1/95)

19204 Downey, Lynn. *This Is the Earth That God Made* (PS–1). Illus. by Benrei Huang. 2000, Augsburg $8.99 (0-8066-3960-1). In this good-natured look at the Creation, images such as mountains, fountains, seas, winds, animals, and bees gradually appear, ending with a human family giving thanks. (Rev: SLJ 9/00) [224]

19205 Feiler, Bruce S. *Walking the Bible: An Illustrated Journey for Kids Through the Greatest Stories Ever Told* (5–8). Illus. by Sasha Meret. 2004, HarperCollins LB $17.89 (0-06-051118-4). 112pp. Feiler's interesting descriptions of his travels to biblical sites throughout the Middle East are accompanied by photographs and maps. (Rev: BL 10/1/04; SLJ 11/04) [222]

19206 Fisher, Leonard Everett. *David and Goliath* (K–3). Illus. 1993, Holiday House LB $15.95 (0-8234-0997-X). 32pp. An expertly illustrated retelling of the Bible story of the brave lad who saved the land of the Israelites. (Rev: BL 5/1/93*; SLJ 6/93) [222]

19207 Fisher, Leonard Everett. *Moses* (PS–4). Illus. 1995, Holiday House LB $15.95 (0-8234-1149-4). 32pp. The life of Moses and the salvation of the Jewish people are portrayed in double-page spreads. (Rev: BCCB 5/95; BL 5/15/95; SLJ 5/95) [222]

19208 Gellman, Marc. *Does God Have a Big Toe? Stories About Stories in the Bible* (4–6). Illus. by Oscar de Mejo. 1989, HarperCollins $16.00 (0-060-22432-0); paper $7.95 (0-064-40453-6). 96pp. A look at familiar tales in the Bible through new eyes. (Rev: BL 10/15/89; HB 3–4/90; SLJ 12/89) [221]

19209 Gilles-Sebaoun, Elisabeth, retel. *A Young Child's Bible* (PS–3). Trans. from French by Joan Robins. Illus. by Charlotte Roederer. 2001, HarperCollins $12.95 (0-06-029464-7). 87pp. This is a lively, conversational retelling of 30 of the most important stories of both Testaments with rich full-color illustrations. (Rev: HBG 10/01; SLJ 8/01) [224]

19210 Goble, Paul. *Song of Creation* (K–3). Illus. by author. 2004, Eerdmans $16.00 (0-8028-5271-8).

32pp. This richly illustrated celebration of God and the wonders of nature draws on *The Book of Common Prayer*. (Rev: BL 10/1/04; SLJ 10/04) [242]

19211 Goodhart, Pippa. *Noah Makes a Boat* (PS–2). Illus. by Bernard Lodge. 1997, Houghton Mifflin $15.00 (0-395-86957-9). 32pp. A picture book that humanizes the story of Noah building the ark and of the flood that covered the earth. (Rev: BL 10/1/97; HB 9–10/97; HBG 3/98; SLJ 9/97) [222]

19212 Graham, Lorenz. *How God Fix Jonah* (3–5). Illus. 2000, Boyds Mills $17.95 (1-56397-698-6). 156pp. This collection of biblical-story poems contains tales from both the Testaments told from a West African native's viewpoint. (Rev: BL 10/1/00; HBG 10/01; SLJ 12/00) [220.9]

19213 Greenberg, Blu, and Linda Tarry. *King Solomon and the Queen of Sheba* (2–5). Illus. by Avi Katz. 1997, Pitspopany $16.95 (0-943706-90-4). 48pp. The biblically based story of the Ethiopian queen, her love for the wise, Jewish king, Solomon, and their child. (Rev: SLJ 5/98)

19214 Greene, Rhonda Gowler. *The Beautiful World That God Made* (PS–1). Illus. by Anne Wilson. 2002, Eerdmans $16.00 (0-8028-5213-0). 32pp. A creation story in cumulative verse illustrated with colorful collages. (Rev: BL 2/1/02; HBG 10/02; SLJ 9/02) [231.7]

19215 Greenfield, Karen R. *Sister Yessa's Story* (2–5). Illus. by Claire Ewart. 1992, HarperCollins $15.00 (0-06-020278-5). As she walks through the woods, Yessa gathers animals for her brother's ark. (Rev: SLJ 8/92)

19216 Grindley, Sally. *The Life of Jesus* (3–6). Illus. by Chris Molan. 2003, DK $17.99 (0-7894-8884-1). 32pp. New Testament stories are illustrated with dramatic watercolors in an oversize, horizontal format. (Rev: BL 5/1/03; HBG 10/03) [232.9]

19217 Grindley, Sally, and Jan Barger. *Bible Stories for the Young* (PS–2). Illus. 1998, Little Tiger $16.95 (1-888444-42-8). 96pp. Twenty well-known stories from the Old and New Testaments are presented in language and pictures suitable for a young audience. (Rev: BCCB 2/99; BL 10/1/98; HBG 9/99; SLJ 10/98) [220.9]

19218 Harik, Ramsay M. *Jesus of Nazareth: Teacher and Prophet* (5–8). Illus. Series: Book Report Biographies. 2001, Watts paper $6.95 (0-531-15552-8). 128pp. Harik presents the life and ministry of Jesus. (Rev: BL 8/01) [232.9]

19219 Harrison, James. *My Very First Bible* (PS–2). Illus. by Diana Mayo. 2005, DK $12.99 (0-7566-0983-6). 80pp. Twenty-five key stories from both Testaments are told in clear prose and appealing illustrations. (Rev: BL 3/1/04; SLJ 5/05) [220.9]

19220 Hoffman, Mary, reteller. *A First Bible Story Book* (K–2). Illus. by Julie Downing. 1998, DK $12.95 (0-7894-1555-0). 80pp. A basic Bible storybook that contains easy-to-read narratives from both the Old and New Testaments. (Rev: HBG 9/99; SLJ 2/99) [221.9]

19221 Johnson, James W. *The Creation* (K–4). Illus. by James E. Ransome. 1994, Holiday House LB $16.95 (0-8234-1069-2). 32pp. The story of the first

seven days of the world is told in the paintings and a poem by a famous African American writer. (Rev: BL 4/15/94; HB 9–10/94; SLJ 5/94*) [811]

19222 Jonas, Ann. *Aardvarks, Disembark!* (PS). Illus. 1990, Greenwillow $15.93 (0-688-07207-0). 40pp. Happy rhymes and songs with appealing design. (Rev: BCCB 11/90; BL 11/15/90; HB 11–12/90*; SLJ 10/90*) [222]

19223 Kimmel, Eric. *Why the Snake Crawls on Its Belly* (K–3). Illus. by Allen Davis. 2001, Pitspopany $14.95 (1-930143-20-6). 32pp. This very readable pourquoi story relates how God punishes the snake for tempting Adam and Eve in the garden of Eden. (Rev: BL 10/1/01; HBG 3/02; SLJ 12/01)

19224 Koralek, Jenny. *The Coat of Many Colors* (PS–2). Illus. by Pauline Baynes. 2004, Eerdmans $16.00 (0-8028-5277-7). 32pp. The Old Testament story of Joseph is retold in a lively way and enhanced with art that evokes the time and the setting. (Rev: BL 10/15/04; SLJ 11/04) [224]

19225 Koralek, Jenny. *The Moses Basket* (3–5). Illus. by Pauline Baynes. 2003, Eerdmans $16.00 (0-8028-5251-3). This beautifully realized retelling relates how Moses's mother gave up her infant son rather than see him killed. (Rev: HBG 4/04; SLJ 10/03) [221.9]

19226 Kuskin, Karla. *The Animals and the Ark* (PS–3). Illus. by Michael Grejniec. 2002, Simon & Schuster $16.95 (0-689-83095-5). 40pp. A secular version of the story of Noah and the ark. (Rev: BCCB 3/02; BL 1/1–15/02; HB 3–4/02; HBG 10/02; SLJ 4/02) [222]

19227 Le Tord, Bijou. *Noah's Tree* (PS–2). Illus. 1999, HarperCollins LB $15.89 (0-06-028527-3). 40pp. Noah is hoping to pass on his lovely forest to his sons but God instructs him to cut down the trees and make an ark. (Rev: BL 10/15/99; HBG 4/00; SLJ 12/99)

19228 *The Lord Is My Shepherd* (PS–2). Illus. by Anne Wilson. 2003, Eerdmans $16.00 (0-8028-5250-5). 32pp. The 23rd psalm is accompanied by expressive art. (Rev: BL 2/1/03; HBG 10/03; SLJ 7/03) [223]

19229 Lottridge, Celia B. *Stories from Adam and Eve to Ezekiel: Retold from the Bible* (4–7). Illus. by Gary Clement. 2004, Groundwood $24.95 (0-88899-490-7). 192pp. Some of the best-loved stories from the Hebrew Bible are engagingly adapted in this attractively illustrated volume. (Rev: BL 10/1/04; SLJ 4/05) [220]

19230 Lottridge, Celia Baker. *Stories from the Life of Jesus* (5–7). Illus. by Linda Wolfsgruber. 2004, Douglas & McIntyre $24.95 (0-88899-497-4). 128pp. Lottridge draws on the first four books of the New Testament for this illustrated collection of stories. (Rev: BL 5/1/04; HB 7–8/04; SLJ 11/04) [232.9]

19231 Lucado, Max. *Small Gifts in God's Hands* (K–3). Illus. by Cheri Bladholm. 2000, Nelson/Tommy Nelson $14.99 (0-8499-5842-3). 32pp. A poor boy offers Jesus his humble bread and fishes, and from these He feeds the multitude. (Rev: BL 2/1/01) [224]

19232 McCarthy, Michael, retel. *The Story of Daniel in the Lions' Den* (PS–3). Illus. by Giuliano Ferri. 2003, Barefoot $16.99 (1-84148-209-9). The Old Testament story is retold in rhyme in this beautifully illustrated picture book. (Rev: BL 6/1–15/03; HBG 10/03; SLJ 5/03) [224.5]

19233 McCarthy, Michael. *The Story of Noah and the Ark* (PS–K). Illus. by Giuliano Ferri. 2001, Barefoot $16.99 (1-84148-361-3). 32pp. Wonderful illustrations show the animals arrayed around the decks, the roiling seas, and the arrival of the dove. (Rev: BL 10/1/01; HBG 3/02; SLJ 11/01) [222]

19234 McGee, Marni. *The Colt and the King* (PS–3). Illus. by John Winch. 2002, Holiday House $16.95 (0-8234-1695-X). 32pp. Told from the standpoint of the donkey that carried Jesus into Jerusalem on Palm Sunday, this is a beautifully illustrated retelling of a Bible story. (Rev: BCCB 4/02; BL 4/1/02; HB 3–4/02; HBG 10/02; SLJ 4/02)

19235 Marzollo, Jean, retel. *Daniel in the Lion's Den* (PS–4). Illus. by Jean Marzollo. 2004, Little, Brown $14.95 (0-316-74132-9). The story of Daniel is retold in a lively manner, with childlike illustrations and commentary from little ants at the bottom of the pages. Also use *Miriam and Her Brother Moses* and *Jonah and the Whale (and the Worm): A Bible Story* (both 2004). (Rev: SLJ 8/04)

19236 Marzollo, Jean, retel. *David and Goliath* (PS–3). Illus. by Jean Marzollo. Series: Bible Story. 2004, Little, Brown $15.95 (0-316-74138-8). One of a series of author-illustrated stories intended to introduce beginning readers to characters from the Old Testament. Also use *Ruth and Naomi* (2005). (Rev: SLJ 6/04) [222.430]

19237 Matthews, Caitlin. *The Blessing Seed: A Creation Myth for the New Millennium* (1–5). Illus. by Alison Dexter. 1998, Barefoot $14.95 (1-901223-28-0). 32pp. An enthralling new version of the world's beginnings, using the Judeo-Christian creation story as a basis, supplemented with mystical interpretations. (Rev: BL 10/15/98; SLJ 9/98) [291.2]

19238 Mayer, Marianna. *Young Jesus of Nazareth* (2–4). Illus. 1999, Morrow LB $15.93 (0-688-16728-4). 32pp. From the Nativity to the Sermon on the Mount, this is a retelling of stories about the youthful Jesus. (Rev: BCCB 11/99; BL 10/1/99; HBG 4/00; SLJ 12/99) [232.92]

19239 Oberman, Sheldon. *The Wisdom Bird: A Tale of Solomon and Sheba* (K–4). Illus. by Neil Waldman. 2000, Boyds Mills $15.95 (1-56397-816-4). 32pp. Drawing on many sources, including the Bible, African folklore, and Jewish tales, this is the story of Sheba's request that Solomon build her a palace out of bird's beaks. (Rev: BCCB 10/00; BL 10/1/00; HBG 3/01; SLJ 10/00)

19240 *Paradise* (2–5). Illus. by Fiona French. 2004, Frances Lincoln $15.95 (1-84507-007-0). An eye-catching version of the Creation story, based on the King James translation of the Bible. (Rev: SLJ 6/04) [222.1]

19241 Paterson, Katherine. *The Angel and the Donkey* (1–4). Illus. by Alexander Koshkin. 1996, Clari-on $15.95 (0-395-68969-4). 34pp. Based on passages in the Hebrew Bible, this is the story of Pethor, a soothsayer, and his encounter with Moses. (Rev: BCCB 4/96; BL 3/1/96; SLJ 3/96) [222]

19242 Pinkney, Jerry. *Noah's Ark* (2–5). Illus. 2002, North-South LB $16.50 (1-58717-202-X). 40pp. Pinkney offers a fresh take on the popular story while keeping his narrative fairly close to the standard version. (Rev: BCCB 1/03; BL 10/1/02; HB 1–2/03; HBG 3/03; SLJ 11/02*) [222]

19243 *Psalm Twenty-Three* (PS–3). Illus. by Tim Ladwig. 1997, Eerdmans $16.00 (0-8028-5160-6); paper $8.00 (0-8028-5163-0). 32pp. This version of the famous psalm pictures two African American children growing up in a bleak, urban neighborhood. (Rev: BL 10/1/97; HBG 3/98) [123.2]

19244 Ray, Jane. *Adam and Eve and the Garden of Eden* (K–3). Illus. 2005, Eerdmans $17.00 (0-8028-5278-5). 32pp. A beautiful picture-book presentation of the story of the creation and fall of the first humans. (Rev: BL 4/1/05; SLJ 5/05) [222]

19245 Rock, Lois. *Everlasting Stories: A Family Bible Treasury* (3–5). Illus. by Christina Balit. 2001, Chronicle $24.95 (0-8118-3258-9). 224pp. One hundred biblical stories told in simple narrative surrounded by vibrant illustrations. (Rev: BL 1/1–15/02; HBG 3/02; SLJ 4/02) [220.9]

19246 Sasso, Sandy Eisenberg. *Adam and Eve's First Sunset: God's New Day* (K–4). Illus. by Joani Keller Rothenberg. 2003, Jewish Lights $17.95 (1-58023-177-2). 32pp. Based on a Talmudic lesson, this is the story of how God helped Adam and Eve build a fire on their first night in the Garden of Eden. (Rev: BL 1/1–15/04; SLJ 3/04) [222]

19247 Sasso, Sandy Eisenberg. *But God Remembered: Stories of Women from Creation to the Promised Land* (3–6). Illus. by Bethanne Andersen. 1995, Jewish Lights $16.95 (1-879045-43-5). 32pp. In this picture book, the stories of several almost-forgotten women in the Old Testament are retold. (Rev: BL 9/1/95*; SLJ 12/95) [221.9]

19248 Sasso, Sandy Eisenberg. *Cain and Abel: Finding the Fruits of Peace* (K–3). Illus. by Joani Keller Rothenberg. 2001, Jewish Lights $16.95 (1-58023-123-3). 32pp. This retelling of a biblical parable encourages children to think about the harmful consequences of jealousy and anger. (Rev: BL 11/15/01; HBG 10/02; SLJ 2/02) [222.1]

19249 Sasso, Sandy Eisenberg. *Naamah, Noah's Wife* (PS–K). Illus. by Bethanne Andersen. 2002, Jewish Lights $7.95 (1-893361-56-X). 24pp. This board-book version of *Noah's Wife: The Story of Naamah* (2002) shows Naamah gathering seeds and planting them aboard the ark, and then restocking the earth's plant life after the flood. (Rev: BL 1/1–15/03) [222]

19250 Schmidt, Gary D., retel. *The Blessing of the Lord: Stories from the Old and New Testaments* (5–8). Illus. 1997, Eerdmans $20.00 (0-8028-3789-1). Using 25 Old and New Testament stories as a focus, these insightful accounts describe how biblical personalities react to such events as Daniel's struggle with the lions and Jesus causing nets to be filled with fish. (Rev: BL 11/1/97; SLJ 10/97) [222]

19251 Spier, Peter, reteller. *Noah's Ark* (PS–K). Illus. by Peter Spier. 1977, Dell paper $7.99 (0-440-40693-5). 44pp. Vital, humorous, detailed pictures present a panorama of the animals and their voyage in the ark. Caldecott Medal winner, 1978.

19252 Stickney, Anne Elizabeth. *The Loving Arms of God* (3–6). Illus. 2001, Eerdmans $22.00 (0-8028-5171-1). 164pp. An appealing collection of Bible stories that progresses from the Old to the New Testament. (Rev: BL 6/1–15/01; HBG 3/02; SLJ 8/01) [220.9]

19253 *Stories from the Bible* (5–7). Illus. by Lisbeth Zwerger. 2002, North-South $19.95 (0-7358-1413-9). 160pp. Sophisticated paintings illustrate verbatim excerpts from the King James version of both the Old and New Testaments. (Rev: BCCB 9/02; BL 4/1/02; HB 7–8/02; SLJ 5/02) [220.5]

19254 *The Story of Noah and the Ark: According to the Book of Genesis: From the King James Bible* (3–5). Illus. by Gennady Spirin. 2004, Holt $18.95 (0-8050-6181-9). 32pp. This retelling of the bible story of Noah's Ark is set apart by Spirin's strikingly beautiful oil illustrations. (Rev: BL 4/15/04; HB 7–8/04; SLJ 4/04) [222]

19255 Topek, Susan Remick. *Ten Good Rules* (PS–K). Illus. by Rosalyn Schanzer. 1992, Kar-Ben paper $5.95 (0-929371-28-3). In modern language, the Ten Commandments and their meanings are presented in an attractive concept book. (Rev: SLJ 7/92) [222]

19256 Wallis, Diz. *One More River: Noah's Ark in Song* (PS–2). Illus. by author. 2003, Ragged Bear $16.95 (1-929927-45-2). With rich and entertaining illustrations, this retelling is based on the African American spiritual. (Rev: HBG 10/03; SLJ 10/03) [782.42]

19257 Ward, Elaine. *Old Testament Women* (5–10). Series: Art Revelations. 2004, Enchanted Lion $18.95 (1-59270-011-X). 32pp. Large paintings by masters accompany stories about 18 women including Rachel, Ruth, and Bathsheba. (Rev: SLJ 8/04) [224]

19258 Watts, Murray. *The Bible for Children* (K–4). Illus. by Helen Cann. 2002, Good Books $23.99 (1-56148-362-1). 352pp. Watts vividly retells more than 200 stories from both Old and New Testaments in this handsome volume that includes a map, a glossary, and indexes of people and places. (Rev: BL 10/1/02; HBG 3/03; SLJ 1/03) [220.9]

19259 Wildsmith, Brian. *Exodus* (3–5). Illus. 1999, Eerdmans $20.00 (0-8028-5175-4). 36pp. A lushly illustrated and detailed life of Moses, from his beginnings in Egypt to his arrival in the promised land. (Rev: BL 2/15/99; HBG 9/99; SLJ 1/99) [222]

19260 Wildsmith, Brian. *Jesus* (PS–3). Illus. 2000, Eerdmans $20.00 (0-8028-5212-2). 32pp. Using quotes from the four gospels, the illustrator covers the important incidents in the life of Jesus beginning with the Nativity story and ending with Jesus' death and resurrection. (Rev: BCCB 1/01; BL 2/1/01; HBG 10/01) [224]

19261 Wildsmith, Brian. *Joseph* (K–4). Illus. 1997, Eerdmans $20.00 (0-8028-5161-4). 40pp. A handsome, well-told version of the biblical story of Joseph. (Rev: BL 2/1/98; HBG 3/98) [222]

19262 Wildsmith, Brian. *Mary* (PS–3). Illus. 2002, Eerdmans $20.00 (0-8028-5231-9). 30pp. Using legends and excerpts from the Bible, the noted illustrator re-creates the life of Mary and the role she played in the life of Jesus. (Rev: BL 4/1/02; SLJ 6/02) [232.91]

19263 Williams, Marcia. *God and His Creations: Tales from the Old Testament* (K–2). Illus. 2004, Candlewick $15.99 (0-7636-2211-7). 40pp. Comic-strip interpretations make accessible several well-known Old Testament stories. (Rev: BL 3/15/04; SLJ 5/04) [221.9]

19264 Winch, John. *Two by Two* (PS). 2004, Holiday House $16.95 (0-8234-1840-5). 32pp. This retelling of the story of Noah's Ark, recounted in a lush blend of poetic narrative and detailed artwork, focuses on the flood itself and not the spiritual aspects of the Bible story. (Rev: BL 10/1/04; SLJ 10/04)

19265 Winthrop, Elizabeth, adapt. *He Is Risen: The Easter Story* (4–7). Illus. by Charles Mikolaycak. 1985, Holiday House $16.95 (0-8234-0547-8). 32pp. The Easter story taken from parts of the King James version of the Bible and dramatically illustrated. (Rev: BCCB 4/85; HB 7–8/85; SLJ 4/85)

19266 *Words of Gold: A Treasury of Bible Poetry and Wisdom* (4–6). Ed. by Lois Rock. Illus. 2000, Eerdmans $18.00 (0-8028-5199-1). 48pp. Using 22 double-page spreads, this book contains passages from the Old and New Testaments covering the story of the Jewish people from Abraham to Revelations. (Rev: BL 4/1/00; HBG 9/00; SLJ 9/00) [220.9]

Holidays and Holy Days

General and Miscellaneous

19267 Ancona, George. *Fiesta U.S.A.* (3–6). Illus. 1995, Dutton $16.99 (0-525-67498-5). 48pp. Various Latin American festivals — like Three Kings' Day and the Day of the Dead — are pictured as they are celebrated in various parts of the United States. (Rev: BL 10/1/95; HB 11–12/95; SLJ 9/95) [394.2]

19268 Ansary, Mir T. *Columbus Day* (K–2). Series: Holiday Histories. 1998, Heinemann LB $13.95 (1-57572-702-1). 32pp. Though somewhat oversimplified, this is a history of Columbus Day and the celebration of the discovery of America. (Rev: SLJ 2/99) [394]

19269 Ansary, Mir T. *Labor Day* (2–3). Illus. Series: Holiday Histories. 1998, Heinemann LB $13.95 (1-57572-703-X). 32pp. This holiday book explains how workers banded together to fight poor working conditions and how, in time, this national holiday was born. (Rev: BL 1/1–15/99; SLJ 2/99) [394.264]

19270 Ansary, Mir T. *Martin Luther King Jr. Day* (2–3). Series: Holiday Histories. 1998, Heinemann LB $13.95 (1-57572-873-7). 32pp. This easy reader examines the history of Martin Luther King Day, tells how it is celebrated, and why it is important. (Rev: BL 12/15/98) [394.2]

19271 Ansary, Mir T. *Memorial Day* (2–3). Series: Holiday Histories. 1998, Heinemann LB $13.95 (1-57572-874-5). 32pp. Gives the history of Memorial Day, explaining how and why we celebrate it. (Rev: BL 12/15/98) [394.2]

19272 Ansary, Mir T. *Veterans Day* (2–3). Illus. Series: Holiday Histories. 1998, Heinemann LB $13.95 (1-57572-876-1). 32pp. A discussion of Veterans Day — its origins, history, and its growing importance after World Wars I and II. (Rev: BL 1/1–15/99) [394.264]

19273 Barner, Bob. *Parade Day: Marching Through the Calendar Year* (PS–1). Illus. 2003, Holiday House $16.95 (0-8234-1690-9). 32pp. A parade for each month — some for holidays, others (such as a pet parade) just for fun. (Rev: BL 2/15/03; HBG 10/03; SLJ 4/03)

19274 Barrett, Anna Pearl. *Juneteenth: Celebrating Freedom in Texas* (3–6). Illus. by Gary Laronde. 1999, Eakin $12.95 (1-57168-180-9). 80pp. This book tells how the author and her family celebrated in 1945 the 80th Juneteenth, the holiday that celebrates the emancipation of African Americans from slavery. (Rev: SLJ 8/99)

19275 Behrens, June. *Gung Hay Fat Choy: Happy New Year* (2–4). Illus. 1982, Children's Book Pr. paper $4.95 (0-516-48842-2). A description of the Chinese New Year and how it is celebrated.

19276 Bennett, Kelly. *Flag Day* (PS–2). Series: Rookie Read-About Holidays. 2003, Children's Book Pr. LB $19.00 (0-516-22862-5); paper $5.95 (0-516-27755-3). 32pp. An easy-to-read book that introduces the holiday celebrated on June 14, with details on its origin and observances. (Rev: BL 3/15/03) [394]

19277 Brady, April A. *Kwanzaa Karamu: Cooking and Crafts for a Kwanzaa Feast* (4–6). Illus. 1995, Carolrhoda LB $21.27 (0-87614-842-9); paper $6.95 (0-87614-633-7). 64pp. Following a general introduction to Kwanzaa, this book introduces crafts and gives 18 recipes for appropriate food. (Rev: BL 4/15/95) [641.59]

19278 Brill, Marlene Targ. *Veterans Day* (1–3). Illus. Series: On My Own Holidays. 2005, Carolrhoda LB $23.93 (1-57505-699-2); paper $5.95 (1-57505-766-2). 48pp. The origins and traditions of Veterans Day are introduced with many illustrations and a short glossary.

19279 Brown, Tricia. *Chinese New Year* (3–5). Illus. 1997, Holt paper $6.95 (0-8050-5544-4). 48pp. A description of this centuries-old spring holiday that families celebrate in different ways. (Rev: BL 12/1/87; SLJ 12/87)

19280 Campbell, Louisa. *A World of Holidays! Family Festivities All Over the World!* (3–5). Illus. by Michael Bryant. Series: Family Ties. 1993, Silver Moon LB $14.95 (1-881889-08-4). 60pp. Using a ficticious framework, five holidays from such places as Pakistan, Japan, and Namibia are introduced. (Rev: SLJ 2/94) [394.2]

19281 Chambers, Catherine. *Carnival* (4–6). Illus. Series: World of Holidays. 1998, Raintree LB $22.11 (0-8172-4613-4). 32pp. Reveals the African influences that have shaped the pre-Lenten celebration of Carnival and provides suitable activities such as recipes and mask-making. (Rev: BL 5/1/98; HBG 9/98) [394.25]

19282 Chambers, Catherine. *Chinese New Year* (3–5). Illus. Series: World of Holidays. 1997, Raintree LB $25.69 (0-8172-4605-3). 31pp. With many color photos and several craft ideas, this book supplies background information on this spring celebration of good fortune and success and the rituals that surround it. (Rev: BL 6/1–15/97) [394.261]

19283 Chandler, Clare. *Harvest Celebrations* (2–4). Illus. Series: Festivals. 1998, Millbrook LB $20.90 (0-7613-0964-0). 32pp. This book outlines the best-known and most popular harvest celebrations around the world. (Rev: BL 3/1/99; HBG 3/99; SLJ 4/99) [394.264]

19284 Chocolate, Deborah M. *My First Kwanzaa Book* (PS–2). Illus. by Cal Massey. 1992, Scholastic $10.95 (0-590-45762-4). 32pp. A celebration of African American cultural heritage for the very young. (Rev: BCCB 2/93; BL 9/1/92) [394.2]

19285 Cooper, Jason. *Arbor Day* (1–3). Illus. Series: Holiday Celebrations. 2003, Rourke LB $19.27 (1-58952-217-6). 24pp. An attractive and informative overview of Arbor Day, the holiday's origins, and the contributions trees make to a healthy environment. (Rev: BL 4/1/03) [394.26]

19286 Ditchfield, Christin. *Memorial Day* (2–4). Series: A True Book. 2003, Children's Pr. LB $23.50 (0-516-22783-1); paper $6.95 (0-516-27821-5). 48pp. A concise look at Memorial Day (formerly known as Decoration Day) and the various ways in which it is observed. (Rev: SLJ 1/04) [394.262]

19287 Ditchfield, Christin. *Presidents' Day* (2–4). Series: A True Book. 2003, Children's Pr. LB $23.50 (0-516-22784-X); paper $6.95 (0-516-27817-7). 48pp. A history of the holiday created to celebrate the birthdays of Washington and Lincoln, with information on how we recognize this day today. (Rev: SLJ 1/04) [394.261]

19288 Erlbach, Arlene. *Happy Birthday, Everywhere!* (3–5). Illus. 1997, Millbrook LB $23.90 (0-7613-0007-4). 48pp. With accompanying food and craft projects, this book describes birthday celebrations around the world. (Rev: BL 12/1/97; HBG 3/98; SLJ 2/98) [394.2]

19289 Erlbach, Arlene. *Happy New Year, Everywhere!* (K–3). Illus. by Sharon L. Holm. 2000, Millbrook LB $23.90 (0-7613-1707-4). 48pp. Lavish double-page spreads introduce New Year celebrations in 20 countries, including Belgium, Haiti, Iran, and Israel. (Rev: BL 11/1/00; HBG 3/01; SLJ 12/00) [394.261]

19290 Fradin, Dennis B. *Columbus Day* (2–4). Illus. Series: Best Holiday Books. 1990, Enslow LB $18.95 (0-89490-233-4). 48pp. Highlights of the explorer's life and his four voyages. (Rev: BL 5/1/90) [970.01]

1027

19291 Freeman, Dorothy R. *St. Patrick's Day* (3–5). Illus. Series: Best Holiday Books. 1992, Enslow LB $18.95 (0-89490-383-7). 48pp. This easily read account describes the origins of St. Patrick's Day and how it is celebrated. (Rev: BL 10/1/92) [394.2]

19292 Freeman, Dorothy R., and Dianne M. MacMillan. *Kwanzaa* (3–5). Illus. Series: Best Holiday Books. 1992, Enslow LB $18.95 (0-89490-381-0). 48pp. A full treatment of this African American holiday. (Rev: BL 10/1/92) [394.2]

19293 Ganeri, Anita. *Hindu Festivals Throughout the Year* (3–6). Illus. Series: A Year of Festivals. 2003, Smart Apple Media LB $16.95 (1-58340-372-8). 30pp. After a short introduction to the religion, chronological chapters explain the origins and customs of the major festivals of Hinduism. Also use *Muslim Festivals Throughout the Year* (2003). (Rev: SLJ 12/03) [294.5]

19294 Ganeri, Anita. *Journey's End: Death and Mourning* (4–6). Illus. 1999, Bedrick LB $15.95 (0-87226-289-8). 32pp. This book looks at death rituals in six major religions: Hinduism, Buddhism, Sikhism, Islam, Judaism, and Christianity. (Rev: BL 5/15/99; HBG 9/99; SLJ 3/99) [291.3]

19295 Ganeri, Anita. *New Beginnings: Celebrating Birth* (4–6). Series: Life Times. 1999, Bedrick LB $15.95 (0-87226-286-3). 32pp. Rites and rituals associated with birth and early childhood are outlined in six religions: Buddhism, Christianity, Hinduism, Judaism, Islam, and Sikhism. (Rev: BL 5/15/99; HBG 9/99; SLJ 3/99) [291]

19296 Ganeri, Anita. *Wedding Days: Celebrations of Marriage* (4–6). Illus. 1999, Bedrick LB $15.95 (0-87226-288-X). 32pp. Covers marriage and marriage customs in six religions: Hinduism, Buddhism, Sikhism, Islam, Judaism, and Christianity. (Rev: BL 5/15/99; SLJ 3/99) [291.3]

19297 Gardeski, Christina Mia. *Diwali* (PS–2). Illus. Series: Rookie Read-About Holidays. 2001, Children's Book Pr. LB $19.00 (0-516-22372-0); paper $5.95 (0-516-26311-0). 32pp. A basic introduction to the Hindu festival of Diwali and the way it is celebrated. (Rev: BL 12/1/01) [294.5]

19298 Gelber, Carol. *Love and Marriage Around the World* (5–7). 1998, Millbrook LB $23.90 (0-7613-0102-X). 72pp. From courtship to the wedding, this book introduces marriage customs from around the world and among different ethnic groups. (Rev: BCCB 7–8/98; HBG 9/98; SLJ 6/98) [392]

19299 Gibbons, Gail. *St. Patrick's Day* (2–4). Illus. 1994, Holiday House LB $16.95 (0-8234-1119-2). 32pp. As well as telling the story of St. Patrick's life, this simple account describes how we celebrate his day and the symbols connected with it. (Rev: BCCB 2/94; BL 2/1/94; SLJ 4/94) [394.2]

19300 Gnojewski, Carol. *Cinco de Mayo: Celebrating Hispanic Pride* (3–5). Illus. Series: Finding Out About Holidays. 2002, Enslow LB $18.95 (0-7660-1575-0). 48pp. Simple text and colorful photographs cover many aspects of Cinco de Mayo, from its history to the way it is celebrated today. (Rev: BL 12/15/02; HBG 3/03; SLJ 11/02) [394.26972]

19301 Gnojewski, Carol. *Day of the Dead: A Latino Celebration of Family and Life* (3–5). Illus. Series: Finding Out About Holidays. 2005, Enslow LB $17.95 (0-7660-1780-X). 48pp. A history of this Mexican holiday, with discussion of how it is celebrated today and its emphasis on family. (Rev: BL 6/1–15/05) [394.264]

19302 Gnojewski, Carol. *Martin Luther King, Jr., Day: Honoring a Man of Peace* (2–4). Series: Finding Out About Holidays. 2002, Enslow LB $18.95 (0-7660-1574-2). 48pp. Information on the holiday and how it is celebrated follows a brief introduction to King's life. (Rev: HBG 3/03; SLJ 12/02)

19303 Gogerly, Liz. *Autumn* (2–4). Series: Holidays Around the World. 2004, Rourke $.00 (1-59515-198-2). The holidays of September to November — and how they're celebrated in different parts of the globe — are profiled with many photographs. Also use *Spring* (2004). (Rev: BL 11/15/04) [394.264]

19304 Graham-Barber, Lynda. *Mushy! The Complete Book of Valentine Words* (4–8). Illus. by Betsy Lewin. 1993, Avon paper $3.50 (0-380-71650-X). 122pp. An explanation of the words, symbols, and customs concerning Valentine's Day. (Rev: BCCB 3/91; BL 2/15/91; SLJ 5/91) [394.2]

19305 Harris, Zoe, and Suzanne Williams. *Pinatas and Smiling Skeletons* (4–8). Illus. 1998, Pacific View LB $19.95 (1-881896-19-6). This book introduces six festivals celebrated in Mexico: the Feast of the Virgin of Guadalupe, Christmas, Carnaval, Corpus Christi, Independence Day, and the Day of the Dead. (Rev: BL 3/15/99; HBG 3/99; SLJ 3/99) [394.2]

19306 Hoyt-Goldsmith, Diane. *Celebrating a Quinceañera: A Latina's 15th Birthday Celebration* (3–6). Photos by Lawrence Migdale. 2002, Holiday House $16.95 (0-8234-1693-3). 30pp. A detailed description of a young woman's preparations for and celebration of her quinceanera, the ritual coming of age at 15. (Rev: HBG 3/03; SLJ 9/02) [395.24]

19307 Hoyt-Goldsmith, Diane. *Celebrating Chinese New Year* (3–5). Illus. 1998, Holiday House $16.95 (0-8234-1393-4). 32pp. A richly illustrated book that traces the activities of a Chinese American family in San Francisco as they prepare for and participate in Chinese New Year. (Rev: BL 12/1/98; HBG 3/99; SLJ 2/99) [394.261]

19308 Hoyt-Goldsmith, Diane. *Celebrating Kwanzaa* (4–6). Illus. by Lawrence Migdale. 1993, Holiday House LB $16.95 (0-8234-1048-X). 32pp. A photoessay about a Chicago family's celebration of Kwanzaa that explains the origins and meanings of the Seven Principles. (Rev: BCCB 11/93; BL 10/1/93*) [394.2]

19309 Hoyt-Goldsmith, Diane. *Celebrating Ramadan* (2–5). Illus. by Lawrence Migdale. 2001, Holiday House $16.95 (0-8234-1581-3). 32pp. This informative picture-book introduction to Islam and the month of Ramadan features a fourth-grade New Jersey boy named Ibraheem. (Rev: BCCB 12/01; BL 10/1/01; HB 1–2/02; HBG 3/02; SLJ 8/01) [297]

19310 Hoyt-Goldsmith, Diane. *Mardi Gras: A Cajun Country Celebration* (4–6). Illus. 1995, Holiday House LB $15.95 (0-8234-1184-2). 32pp. A story of the rituals of Mardi Gras plus a history of the Cajun people and even a recipe for gumbo. (Rev: BL 10/1/95; SLJ 11/95) [394.2]

19311 Hoyt-Goldsmith, Diane. *Three Kings Day: A Celebration at Christmastime* (2–5). Illus. by Lawrence Migdale. 2004, Holiday House $16.95 (0-8234-1839-1). 32pp. Dia de los Tres Reyes is seen from the point of view of a 10-year-old girl living in New York's Puerto Rican community. (Rev: BL 9/15/04; SLJ 10/04) [263]

19312 Jackson, Ellen. *The Autumn Equinox: Celebrating the Harvest* (2–5). Illus. by Jan Davey Ellis. 2000, Millbrook LB $22.90 (0-7613-1354-0). Harvest festivals, past and present, from around the world are described with attractive craft projects, games, and recipes. (Rev: HBG 3/01; SLJ 11/00) [394.3]

19313 Jackson, Ellen. *Here Come the Brides* (3–5). Illus. by Carol Heyer. 1998, Walker LB $16.85 (0-8027-8469-0). 32pp. Brides, wedding customs, symbols, and attire are a few of the topics covered in this overview of wedding practices in different cultures. (Rev: BL 5/1/98; HBG 9/98; SLJ 4/98) [392.5]

19314 Jackson, Ellen. *The Spring Equinox: Celebrating the Greening of the Earth* (3–5). Illus. by Jan Davey Ellis. 2002, Millbrook LB $22.90 (0-7613-1955-7). 32pp. Many of the holidays associated with spring — including Passover, Easter, Earth Day, and Holi — are highlighted in a series of illustrated double-page spreads. (Rev: BL 4/15/02; HBG 10/02; SLJ 6/02) [394.262]

19315 Jango-Cohen, Judith. *Chinese New Year* (1–3). Illus. by Jason Chin. Series: On My Own Holidays. 2005, Carolrhoda LB $22.60 (1-57505-653-4); paper $5.95 (1-57505-763-8). 48pp. The origins and traditions of the Chinese New Year are introduced with many illustrations and a short glossary. (Rev: BL 1/1–15/05) [394.261]

19316 Johnson, Dolores. *The Children's Book of Kwanzaa: A Guide to Celebrating the Holiday* (4–7). Illus. 1996, Simon & Schuster $16.00 (0-689-80864-X). 159pp. This account discusses African American history and the origins of Kwanzaa, its meaning, and its rituals. (Rev: BCCB 11/96; BL 9/1/96) [394.2]

19317 Jones, Amy Robin. *Kwanzaa* (4–6). Series: Journey to Freedom. 2000, Child's World LB $25.64 (1-56766-719-8). 40pp. Sepia-toned pictures and a lively text present the origins, festivities, and customs of Kwanzaa. (Rev: BL 11/15/00; HBG 10/01) [394.2]

19318 Jones, Lynda. *Kids Around the World Celebrate! The Best Feasts and Festivals from Many Lands* (3–6). Illus. by Michelle Nidenoff. Series: Kids Around the World. 1999, Wiley paper $12.95 (0-471-34527-X). 124pp. Each chapter covers the customs of different cultures organized by themes, like giving thanks and celebrating New Year; for

each there are a number of hands-on activities. (Rev: SLJ 2/00) [394.3]

19319 Jordan, Denise M. *Juneteenth* (1–3). Series: Holiday Histories. 2003, Heinemann LB $22.79 (1-4034-3505-7). 32pp. The story of the unofficial holiday (June 19th) that celebrates the end of slavery. (Rev: SLJ 5/04) [394.263]

19320 Kadodwala, Dilip. *Divali* (4–6). Illus. Series: World of Holidays. 1998, Raintree LB $22.11 (0-8172-4616-9). 32pp. Discusses the origins, methods of celebrating, and the many gods and goddesses involved in the Hindu holiday of Diwali. (Rev: BL 5/1/98; HBG 9/98) [294.5]

19321 Kadodwala, Dilip. *Holi* (3–5). Illus. Series: World of Holidays. 1997, Raintree LB $25.69 (0-8172-4610-X). 31pp. A description of this joyous Hindu spring festival and how it is observed. (Rev: BL 6/1–15/97) [294.5]

19322 Kaplan, Leslie C. *Chinese New Year* (2–4). Series: Library of Holidays. 2004, Rosen LB $18.75 (0-8239-6658-5). 24pp. Brief, illustrated chapters introduce the history and traditions of this month-long holiday. (Rev: SLJ 8/04) [394.261]

19323 Kaplan, Leslie C. *Cinco de Mayo* (2–4). Series: Library of Holidays. 2004, Rosen LB $18.75 (0-8239-6662-3). 24pp. A brief introduction to Cinco de Mayo, with information on history and tradition paired with full-page photographs. (Rev: SLJ 8/04) [394.26972]

19324 Kaplan, Leslie C. *Flag Day* (2–4). Series: Library of Holidays. 2004, Rosen LB $18.75 (0-8239-6659-3). 24pp. A brief introduction to the patriotic holiday, with information on history and tradition paired with full-page photographs. (Rev: SLJ 8/04) [394.263]

19325 Katz, Karen. *My First Chinese New Year* (PS–K). Illus. 2004, Holt $14.95 (0-8050-7076-1). 32pp. A young girl and her family prepare for the annual celebration in this simple introduction. (Rev: BL 2/1/05) [394.2]

19326 Kerven, Rosalind. *Id-ul-Fitr* (3–5). Illus. Series: World of Holidays. 1997, Raintree LB $25.69 (0-8172-4609-6). 31pp. After giving a brief introduction to Islam, describes the celebration that marks the end of the sacred month of Ramadan. (Rev: BL 6/1–15/97) [297]

19327 Kindersley, Barnabas, and Anabel Kindersley. *Celebrations!* (2–6). Illus. Series: Children Just Like Me. 1997, DK $17.95 (0-7894-2027-9). 63pp. Using double-page spreads, a number of holidays from around the world are featured, such as Christmas in Germany and Diwali in India. (Rev: HBG 3/98; SLJ 1/98) [394.2]

19328 Krasno, Rena. *Floating Lanterns and Golden Shrines: Celebrating Japanese Festivals* (3–5). Illus. by Toru Sugita. 2000, Pacific View $19.95 (1-881896-21-8). 49pp. Important celebrations for both Japanese and Japanese Americans are covered in this attractive book. (Rev: HBG 9/00; SLJ 6/00) [394.2]

19329 Krishnaswami, Uma. *Holi* (K–2). Illus. Series: Rookie Read-About Holidays. 2003, Children's Pr. LB $19.00 (0-516-22863-3). 32pp. For beginning readers, this is a well-illustrated basic description of the Hindu festival of Holi. (Rev: BL 5/1/03; SLJ 6/03) [294.5]

19330 Landau, Elaine. *Columbus Day — Celebrating a Famous Explorer* (3–6). Series: Finding Out About Holidays. 2001, Enslow LB $18.95 (0-7660-1573-4). 48pp. After introducing Christopher Columbus, this account describes the history of the holiday that honors him and tells how it is celebrated. (Rev: BL 9/15/01; HBG 3/02; SLJ 9/01) [394.2]

19331 Landau, Elaine. *Earth Day: Keeping Our Planet Clean* (3–6). Series: Finding Out About Holidays. 2002, Enslow LB $18.95 (0-7660-1778-8). 48pp. A look at the founding of Earth Day in 1970 by Senator Gaylord Nelson and how Earth Day is observed today. (Rev: BL 7/02; HBG 10/02; SLJ 7/02) [333.7]

19332 Landau, Elaine. *Independence Day: Birthday of the United States* (3–6). Series: Finding Out About Holidays. 2001, Enslow LB $18.95 (0-7660-1571-8). 48pp. Short chapters and plenty of color photographs introduce the history of the July 4th holiday and how it is celebrated today. (Rev: BL 9/15/01; HBG 3/02; SLJ 9/01) [394]

19333 Landau, Elaine. *Mardi Gras: Parades, Costumes, and Parties* (3–6). Series: Finding Out About Holidays. 2002, Enslow LB $18.95 (0-7660-1776-1). 48pp. The origins of Mardi Gras are explained, with material on how the holiday is observed in locations including New Orleans. (Rev: BL 7/02; HBG 10/02; SLJ 8/02) [394.2]

19334 Landau, Elaine. *St. Patrick's Day: Parades, Shamrocks, and Leprechauns* (3–6). Series: Finding Out About Holidays. 2002, Enslow LB $18.95 (0-7660-1777-X). 48pp. SaintPatrick is introduced along with material on the symbols connected with this holiday and ways it is observed. (Rev: BL 7/02; HBG 3/03; SLJ 10/02) [394.2]

19335 Landau, Elaine. *Veteran's Day: Remembering Our War Heroes* (3–6). Series: Finding Out About Holidays. 2002, Enslow LB $18.95 (0-7660-1775-3). 48pp. Landau traces the origins of this holiday and details how it is observed across the United States. (Rev: BL 7/02; HBG 10/02) [394.264]

19336 Lankford, Mary D. *Birthdays Around the World* (2–4). Illus. by Karen M. Dugan. 2002, HarperCollins LB $17.89 (0-688-15432-8). 32pp. Presents the customs surrounding birthday celebrations in seven countries, with ideas for an around-the-world birthday party. (Rev: BL 2/1/03; HBG 3/03; SLJ 1/03) [394.2]

19337 Liestman, Vicki. *Columbus Day* (2–3). Illus. by Rick Hanson. Series: On My Own. 1991, Carolrhoda LB $21.27 (0-87614-444-X). 56pp. The history of this holiday, plus the life of the explorer, illustrated with colorful paintings. (Rev: BCCB 10/91; BL 9/1/91; SLJ 9/91) [970.01]

19338 Livingston, Myra Cohn. *Festivals* (K–3). Illus. by Leonard Everett Fisher. 1996, Holiday House $16.95 (0-8234-1217-2). 32pp. Fourteen of the world's festivals, both common and obscure, are introduced in poetry and paintings. (Rev: BCCB 5/96; BL 5/1/96; SLJ 7/96) [811]

19339 Lowery, Linda. *Day of the Dead* (K–3). Illus. by Barbara Knutson. Series: On My Own Holidays. 2003, Carolrhoda LB $22.60 (0-87614-914-X); paper $5.95 (1-57505-581-3). 48pp. A lively, easy-reader introduction to the Mexican holiday. (Rev: HBG 4/04; SLJ 11/03) [394.266]

19340 Luenn, Nancy. *Celebrations of Light: A Year of Holidays Around the World* (3–5). Illus. 1998, Simon & Schuster $16.00 (0-689-31986-X). 32pp. Describes 12 festivals of light, including Christmas, Hanukkah, Buddha's Birthday, and the Swedish Luciadagen. (Rev: BL 9/15/98; HBG 3/99; SLJ 12/98) [394.2]

19341 MacMillan, Dianne M. *Mardi Gras* (3–5). Series: Best Holiday. 1997, Enslow LB $18.95 (0-89490-819-7). 48pp. Gives a description and history of this holiday with religious roots, with details on how it is celebrated around the world, particularly in New Orleans. (Rev: BL 12/15/97; HBG 3/98; SLJ 8/97) [394.2]

19342 MacMillan, Dianne M. *Martin Luther King, Jr. Day* (3–5). Illus. Series: Best Holiday Books. 1992, Enslow LB $18.95 (0-89490-382-9). 48pp. This easy-to-read book describes how Martin Luther King, Jr. Day originated and how it is celebrated in schools and towns. (Rev: BL 10/1/92; SLJ 1/93) [323]

19343 MacMillan, Dianne M. *Presidents Day* (3–5). Illus. Series: Best Holiday. 1997, Enslow LB $18.95 (0-89490-820-0). 48pp. An introduction to the day on which Americans pay tribute to their presidents and a discussion of the ways in which it is celebrated. (Rev: BL 7/97) [973.4]

19344 Marchant, Kerena. *Id-Ul-Fitr* (3–5). Series: Festivals. 1998, Millbrook LB $20.90 (0-7613-0963-2). 32pp. An explanation of this Muslim festival is followed by colorful descriptions of how it is celebrated around the world. (Rev: HBG 3/99; SLJ 4/99) [297]

19345 Martinet, Jeanne, comp. *The Year You Were Born, 1986* (2–6). Illus. by Judy Lanfredi. Series: Day-By-Day Record Of. 1993, Tambourine paper $7.95 (0-688-11968-9). This book, like the others in the series, gives facts and assorted trivia for each day of the featured year. (Rev: SLJ 2/94) [793.21]

19346 Marx, David F. *Chinese New Year* (PS–1). Series: Rookie Read-about Holidays. 2002, Children's Book Pr. LB $19.00 (0-516-22267-8); paper $5.95 (0-516-27375-2). 32pp. An introduction for very young readers to the rituals of the Chinese New Year. Also use *Ramadan*. (Rev: SLJ 9/02) [394.2]

19347 Murray, Julie. *Kwanzaa* (1–3). Illus. Series: Holidays. 2003, ABDO LB $14.95 (1-57765-955-4). 24pp. Examines Kwanzaa's adaptation from an African harvest festival and looks at some of the activities associated with the holiday. (Rev: HBG 10/03; SLJ 10/03) [394.261]

19348 Nobleman, Marc Tyler. *Election Day* (1–3). Series: Let's See. 2004, Compass Point LB $19.93 (0-7565-0644-1). 24pp. Using a question-and-answer format, large print, and many illustrations, this small book introduces the American election process. (Rev: BL 10/15/04) [324.6]

19349 Nobleman, Marc Tyler. *Martin Luther King Jr. Day* (1–3). Series: Let's See. 2004, Compass Point LB $19.93 (0-7565-0646-8). 24pp. For young researchers, this is an introduction to this holiday, using questions as chapter headings. (Rev: SLJ 1/05) [394.261]

19350 Penner, Lucille R. *Celebration: The Story of American Holidays* (3–5). Illus. by Ib Ohlsson. 1993, Macmillan LB $15.95 (0-02-770903-5). 79pp. A discussion of the origins of and celebrations associated with 13 important American holidays, e.g., Columbus Day, Veterans Day, Martin Luther King Day, Halloween, and New Year's Day. (Rev: SLJ 11/93) [394.2]

19351 Perl, Lila. *Pinatas and Paper Flowers: Holidays of the Americas in English and Spanish* (4–8). Illus. by Victoria de Larrea. 1985, Houghton Mifflin paper $7.95 (0-89919-155-X). 91pp. Eight Hispanic holidays are highlighted in this bilingual volume.

19352 Porter, A. P. *Kwanzaa* (2–4). Illus. by Janice L. Porter. 1991, Carolrhoda LB $21.27 (0-87614-668-X). 56pp. African Americans celebrate their rich history and culture by observing Kwanzaa. (Rev: BCCB 12/91; BL 12/1/91) [394.2]

19353 Robinson, Fay. *Chinese New Year: A Time for Parades, Family, and Friends* (3–6). Illus. Series: Finding Out About Holidays. 2001, Enslow LB $18.95 (0-7660-1631-5). 48pp. This detailed account gives the history behind this traditional holiday and explains how Chinese Americans celebrate it. (Rev: BL 9/15/01; HBG 3/02; SLJ 1/02) [394.261]

19354 Roop, Connie, and Peter Roop. *Let's Celebrate Earth Day* (1–3). Illus. by Gwen Connelly. 2001, Millbrook LB $21.90 (0-7613-1812-7). 32pp. Information on the history and purpose of Earth Day is presented in a question-and-answer format. (Rev: BL 5/1/01; HBG 10/01) [363.7]

19355 Rosinsky, Natalie M. *Juneteenth* (1–3). Series: Let's See. 2004, Compass Point LB $19.93 (0-7565-0770-7). 24pp. For young researchers, this is an introduction to this holiday, using questions as chapter headings. (Rev: SLJ 1/05) [394.2]

19356 Rosinsky, Natalie M. *Presidents' Day* (1–3). Illus. Series: Let's See. 2004, Compass Point LB $19.93 (0-7565-0773-1). 24pp. Using a question-and-answer format, large print, and many illustrations, this small book discusses the history of Presidents' Day and how it honors Washington and Lincoln. (Rev: BL 10/15/04) [394.201]

19357 Ross, Kathy. *The Best Birthday Parties Ever! A Kid's Do-It-Yourself Guide* (2–5). Illus. by Sharon L. Holm. 1999, Millbrook LB $23.90 (0-7613-1410-5). 78pp. This do-it-yourself guide to great birthday parties includes instructions on invitations, hats, decorations, cakes, favors, and games. (Rev: HBG 4/00; SLJ 11/99) [394.2]

19358 Saint James, Synthia. *It's Kwanzaa Time! A Lift-the-Flap Story* (PS–2). Illus. by author. 2001, Simon & Schuster paper $5.99 (0-689-84163-9). A simple introduction to the traditions of Kwanzaa

that uses flaps to reveal the important principles. (Rev: SLJ 10/01)

19359 San Vicente, Luis. *The Festival of Bones / El Festival de las Calaveras: The Little-Bitty Book for the Day of the Dead* (PS–3). Illus. by author. 2002, Cinco Puntos $14.95 (0-938317-67-9). Dancing skeletons accompany the text describing the Mexican festival known as the Day of the Dead, or el Día de los Muertos. (Rev: HBG 3/03; SLJ 3/03) [394.266]

19360 Schaefer, Lola M. *Chinese New Year* (PS–2). Series: Holidays and Celebrations. 2000, Capstone LB $13.25 (0-7368-0660-1). 24pp. A simple beginning reader that introduces the traditions and meaning behind the Chinese New Year. (Rev: HBG 3/01; SLJ 12/00) [394.2]

19361 Schaefer, Lola M. *Cinco de Mayo* (PS–2). Series: Holidays and Celebrations. 2000, Capstone LB $13.25 (0-7368-0661-X). 24pp. The traditions and customs surrounding the Mexican Independence Day are outlined in this simple book for beginning readers. (Rev: HBG 3/01; SLJ 12/00) [394.2]

19362 Schuh, Mari C. *Flag Day* (PS–2). Series: National Holidays. 2003, Capstone LB $14.60 (0-7368-1652-6). 24pp. For beginning readers, this is an introduction to Flag Day and its history. (Rev: HBG 10/03; SLJ 9/03) [394.203]

19363 Schuh, Mari C. *Labor Day* (PS–2). Series: National Holidays. 2003, Capstone LB $14.60 (0-7368-1653-4). 24pp. For beginning readers, this is an introduction to Labor Day and its history. (Rev: HBG 10/03) [394.204]

19364 Schuh, Mari C. *New Year's Day* (K–2). Series: Holidays and Celebrations. 2002, Capstone LB $14.60 (0-7368-1446-9). 24pp. Double-page spreads with bright full-page photographs on the left and a brief text on the right introduce the history, traditions, and celebrations that surround New Year's Day. (Rev: BL 1/1–15/03; HBG 3/03) [394.2]

19365 Schuh, Mari C. *St. Patrick's Day* (K–2). Illus. Series: Holidays and Celebrations. 2002, Capstone $14.60 (0-7368-1447-7). 24pp. This small, square book about Saint Patrick's Day includes discussion of the holiday's symbols and traditions and includes reference sources and a glossary. (Rev: BL 1/1–15/03; HBG 3/03) [296.4]

19366 Scott, Geoffrey. *Labor Day* (1–4). Illus. by Cherie R. Wyman. 1982, Carolrhoda LB $17.50 (0-87614-178-5). 48pp. A simple book about the first Labor Day.

19367 Senker, Cath. *Winter* (2–4). Illus. Series: Holidays Around the World. 2004, Rourke $19.95 (1-59515-199-0). Holidays that take place from December to February are included here, with Christmas in Zimbabwe and Id ul-Fitr in Canada among those featured; a chart lists dates through 2006. Also use *Summer* (2004). (Rev: BL 11/15/04) [394.261]

19368 Simonds, Nina, et al. *Moonbeams, Dumplings and Dragon Boats: A Treasury of Chinese Holiday Tales, Activities and Recipes* (4–6). Illus. by Meilo So. 2002, Harcourt $20.00 (0-15-201983-9). 80pp.

This vibrantly illustrated book for older readers examines five Chinese holidays and includes stories, recipes, and crafts related to each. (Rev: BL 10/15/02; HBG 3/03; SLJ 11/02*) [394.26]

19369 Sita, Lisa. *Coming of Age* (2–5). Series: World Celebrations and Ceremonies. 1998, Blackbirch LB $15.95 (1-56711-276-5). 24pp. Presenting facts and maps about each country highlighted, this account describes the ceremonies associated with the rites of passage that lead to adulthood in ten countries on six continents. (Rev: HBG 3/99; SLJ 4/99) [612]

19370 Spirn, Michele. *Birth* (2–5). Series: World Celebrations and Ceremonies. 1998, Blackbirch LB $15.95 (1-56711-277-3). 24pp. Outlines the rituals and traditions surrounding the birth of a child in 15 countries in six continents. (Rev: HBG 3/99; SLJ 4/99) [392]

19371 Spirn, Michele. *New Year* (3–5). Series: World Celebrations and Ceremonies. 1998, Blackbirch LB $14.95 (1-56711-249-8). 24pp. Introduces New Year's celebrations in Brazil, China, England, India, Israel, Mexico, Nigeria, Puerto Rico, Russia, and the United States. (Rev: HBG 3/99; SLJ 1/99) [394]

19372 Tabor, Nancy María Grande. *Celebrations / Celebraciones* (PS–3). Illus. 2004, Charlesbridge $16.95 (1-57091-575-X). 32pp. Shared holidays and individual Mexican and U.S. holidays are introduced in both Spanish and English. (Rev: BL 3/1/04; SLJ 4/04) [394.26972]

19373 Taylor, Charles A. *Juneteenth: A Celebration of Freedom* (5–8). Illus. by author. 2002, Open Hand $19.95 (0-940880-68-7). 32pp. A well-organized account of this holiday, which celebrates emancipation, with a discussion of the history of slavery. (Rev: SLJ 11/02) [394.2]

19374 Thompson, Jan. *Christian Festivals* (3–6). Illus. Series: Celebrate! 1997, Heinemann $19.92 (0-431-06961-1). 48pp. Familiar Christian holidays such as Christmas, Lent, Ascension Day, and Easter are explained through the experiences of three children. (Rev: BL 8/97; SLJ 12/97) [263]

19375 Verma, Jatinder. *The Story of Divaali* (1–3). Illus. by Nilesh Mistry. 2002, Barefoot $16.99 (1-84148-936-0). 40pp. Verma effectively retells the complex story, based on the Sanskrit *Ramayana*, of the lighting of lamps that started the celebration of the Hindu festival of Diwali. (Rev: BL 1/1–15/03; HBG 3/03; SLJ 11/02) [294.5]

19376 Viesti, Joe, and Diane Hall. *Celebrate! In South Asia* (2–5). Illus. 1996, Lothrop LB $15.93 (0-688-13775-X). 32pp. Nine holidays as celebrated on the Indian subcontinent are introduced. (Rev: BCCB 10/96; BL 9/1/96; SLJ 9/96) [394.2]

19377 Viesti, Joe, and Diane Hall. *Celebrate! In Southeast Asia* (2–5). Illus. 1996, Lothrop LB $15.93 (0-688-13489-0). 32pp. Such countries as Vietnam, Thailand, Malaysia, and the Philippines are represented in this explanation of nine celebrations. (Rev: BCCB 10/96; BL 9/1/96; SLJ 9/96) [394.2]

19378 Wade, Mary Dodson. *Cinco de Mayo* (K–2). Illus. Series: Rookie Read-About Holidays. 2003, Children's Pr. LB $19.00 (0-516-22664-9). 32pp. For beginning readers, this slim volume tells the story behind the Mexican holiday and describes the contemporary celebrations. (Rev: BL 5/1/03) [394.26972]

19379 Wallace, Paula S. *The World of Birthdays* (2–4). Illus. Series: Life Around the World. 2003, Gareth Stevens LB $21.26 (0-8368-3659-6). 48pp. Describes birthday traditions in 10 countries, including Australia, Brazil, Egypt, Japan, and South Africa. (Rev: HBG 10/03; SLJ 10/03)

19380 Walsh, Kieran. *Chinese New Year* (2–3). Series: Holiday Celebrations. 2003, Rourke LB $19.27 (1-58952-215-X). 24pp. Provides basic information about how the holiday began and how it is celebrated. Also use *Cinco de Mayo* (2003). (Rev: BL 9/15/03; SLJ 1/03) [394.261]

19381 Walsh, Kieran. *Cinco de Mayo* (1–3). Illus. Series: Holiday Celebrations. 2003, Rourke LB $19.27 (1-58952-221-4). 24pp. The Mexican holiday comes to life with discussions of the festivities that take place as well as the origin of the celebration. (Rev: BL 4/1/03) [394.26972]

19382 Walter, Mildred P. *Kwanzaa: A Family Affair* (PS–2). Illus. by Cheryl Carrington. 1995, Lothrop $15.00 (0-688-11553-5). 80pp. Background material, ways of celebrating the holiday, and crafts and gifts are all covered in this introduction to Kwanzaa. (Rev: BL 9/15/95) [394.2]

19383 Waters, Kate, and Madeline Slovenz-Low. *Lion Dancer: Ernie Wan's Chinese New Year* (PS–3). 1990, Scholastic paper $4.99 (0-590-43047-5). 32pp. This account describes how a Chinese-American family celebrates the lunar New Year. (Rev: HB 7–8/90; SLJ 2/90) [391.2]

19384 Wilcox, Jane. *Why Do We Celebrate That?* (4–6). Illus. Series: Why Do We? 1996, Watts LB $20.00 (0-531-14393-7). 31pp. This book looks at various cultures, their holidays and festivals, and how they observe birthdays, weddings, and funeral rites. (Rev: SLJ 8/97) [394.2]

19385 Wilkinson, Philip. *A Celebration of Customs and Rituals of the World* (5–8). Illus. 1996, Facts on File $44.00 (0-8160-3479-6). A discussion of customs and rituals connected with birth, death, marriage, and coming-of-age. (Rev: BL 4/1/96) [394.2]

19386 Wilson, Sule Greg C. *Kwanzaa! Africa Lives in a New World Festival* (4–7). Series: The Library of African American Arts and Culture. 1999, Rosen LB $31.95 (0-8239-1857-2). 64pp. This book begins with a history of slavery and the civil rights movement, then explains the origins and meaning of Kwanzaa. (Rev: SLJ 10/99) [641.59]

Christmas

19387 Bible. *The Nativity* (PS–3). Illus. by Julie Vivas. 1988, Harcourt $13.95 (0-15-200535-8). 34pp. A retelling using Bible verses and earthy, sometimes humorous illustrations. A reissue. (Rev: HB 11–12/88)

19388 Chambers, Catherine. *Christmas* (3–5). Illus. Series: World of Holidays. 1997, Raintree LB $25.69 (0-8172-4608-8). 31pp. This book explains the origins of Christmas and how it is observed around the world, along with decorating ideas and some craft projects. (Rev: BL 6/1–15/97) [394.2]

19389 *Christmas in Colonial and Early America* (4–7). Illus. 1996, World Book $19.00 (0-7166-0875-8). 80pp. The evolution of Christmas celebrations is traced through more than 100 years of American history to the end of the 19th century. (Rev: BL 11/1/96) [394.26]

19390 *Christmas in Greece* (5–10). Illus. Series: Christmas Around the World. 2000, World Book $19.00 (0-7166-0859-6). 80pp. This account focuses on the religious practices of the Greek Orthodox Church at Christmastime, which begins with a long fasting period. (Rev: BL 9/1/00) [398.2]

19391 *Christmas in Switzerland* (4–6). Illus. 1995, World Book $18.50 (0-7166-0895-2). 80pp. This book introduces Swiss customs and traditional activities surrounding Christmas. (Rev: BL 9/15/95) [394.26]

19392 *Christmas Soul: African American Holiday Memories* (PS–4). Ed. by Allison Samuels. Illus. by Michele Wood. 2000, Hyperion $17.99 (0-7868-0521-8). 48pp. A number of African American celebrities, including Debbie Allen, Whitney Houston, and Aretha Franklin, recall family gatherings and gift exchanges. (Rev: BL 9/15/00) [394.2]

19393 Davis, Katherine, et al. *The Little Drummer Boy* (K–3). Illus. by Kristina Rodanas. 2001, Clarion $15.00 (0-395-97015-6). 32pp. An attractive rendering of the traditional Christmas song about the little boy and the value of gifts. (Rev: BL 9/1/01; HBG 3/02; SLJ 10/01) [782.42]

19394 Erlbach, Arlene. *Christmas — Celebrating Life, Giving, and Kindness* (3–6). Series: Finding Out About Holidays. 2001, Enslow LB $18.95 (0-7660-1576-9). 48pp. In a series of short chapters that include many attractive color photographs, this book explores the history of Christmas and tells how it is observed in the United States. (Rev: BL 9/15/01; HBG 3/02; SLJ 10/01) [394.2]

19395 Erlbach, Arlene, and Herb Erlbach. *Merry Christmas, Everywhere!* (K–2). Illus. by Sharon L. Holm. 2002, Millbrook $23.90 (0-7613-1956-5); paper $8.95 (0-7613-1699-X). 48pp. Fine illustrations and maps introduce Christmas traditions in countries around the world, accompanied by illustrations, recipes, and crafts. (Rev: BL 9/15/02; HBG 3/03; SLJ 10/02) [394.2663]

19396 *The First Christmas* (3–7). Illus. 1992, Simon & Schuster paper $17.00 (0-671-79364-0). 30pp. This Christmas story, in the words of Isaiah, St. Matthew, and St. Luke, is illustrated with the work of such artists as Botticelli and Fra Filippo Lippi. (Rev: BL 11/1/92) [226]

19397 Flanagan, Alice K. *Christmas* (2–3). Series: Holidays and Festivals. 2001, Compass Point LB $22.60 (0-7565-0085-0). 32pp. An easy-to-read picture book that describes the origins of Christmas

and the many ways in which it is celebrated. (Rev: BL 10/15/01; SLJ 10/01) [394]

19398 Foreman, Michael. *Michael Foreman's Christmas Treasury* (3–6). 2000, Pavilion $22.95 (1-86205-197-6). 124pp. A delightful collection of songs, stories, poems, and carols. (Rev: BL 12/1/00) [394.26]

19399 French, Fiona. *Bethlehem* (PS–3). Illus. 2001, HarperCollins $15.95 (0-06-029623-2). 32pp. Stained-glass style illustrations illuminate the story of the first Christmas as told in the King James version of the gospels of St. Luke and St. Matthew. (Rev: BL 10/15/01; HBG 3/02; SLJ 10/01) [226]

19400 Graham, Ruth B. *One Wintry Night* (4–6). Illus. by Richard J. Watson. 1995, Baker $12.97 (0-8010-3848-0). 72pp. A woman tells an injured mountain boy the story of the importance of Christmas after she rescues him from a snowstorm. (Rev: BL 9/1/95)

19401 Graham-Barber, Lynda. *Ho Ho Ho! The Complete Book of Christmas Words* (4–6). Illus. by Betsy Lewin. 1993, Bradbury $16.00 (0-02-736933-1). 128pp. A collection of words associated with Christmas, with their definitions and derivations. (Rev: BL 10/1/93) [394.2]

19402 Hickman, Martha W. *A Baby Born in Bethlehem* (K–5). Illus. by Giuliano Ferri. 1999, Whitman $15.95 (0-8075-5522-3). 32pp. Simplified biblical verses tell the story of Jesus' birth and the visits by the shepherds and the magi. (Rev: BCCB 11/99; BL 9/1/99; HBG 4/00; SLJ 10/99) [232]

19403 Hoyt-Goldsmith, Diane. *Las Posadas: An Hispanic Christmas Celebration* (3–6). Illus. 1999, Holiday House $16.95 (0-8234-1449-3). 32pp. Using a Hispanic American family as a focus, this book explains the nine-night celebration known as Las Posadas, which tells the story of Mary and Joseph's journey to Bethlehem and the birth of Jesus. (Rev: BL 10/1/99; HBG 4/00; SLJ 10/99) [394.266]

19404 Jeffers, H. Paul. *Legends of Santa Claus* (4–7). Series: A&E Biography. 2000, Lucent LB $25.26 (0-8225-4983-2). 112pp. This book recounts the tales, legends, and myths about Santa Claus and sorts the truth from the fiction. (Rev: BL 12/15/00) [394.2]

19405 Kelley, Emily. *Christmas Around the World.* Rev. ed. (2–3). Illus. by Joni Oeltjenbruns. Series: On My Own Holidays. 2003, Carolrhoda LB $22.60 (0-87614-915-8); paper $5.95 (1-57505-580-5). 48pp. This revised edition introduces young readers to Christmas traditions in Australia, China, Ethiopia, Germany, Lebanon, Mexico, Russia, and Sweden. (Rev: HBG 4/04; SLJ 10/03)

19406 Kurelek, William. *A Northern Nativity: Christmas Dreams of a Prairie Boy* (1–3). Illus. by author. 1976, Tundra paper $9.95 (0-88776-099-6). Twenty paintings of the Holy Family transferred to various locales, accompanied by a lyrical text.

19407 Lankford, Mary D. *Christmas Around the World* (2–5). Illus. 1995, Morrow $15.93 (0-688-12167-5). 48pp. An examination of Christmas traditions in 12 countries. (Rev: BL 9/15/95) [394.2]

19408 Mayer, Marianna. *The Real Santa Claus* (3–6). Illus. 2001, Penguin Putnam $17.99 (0-8037-2624-4). 32pp. The poem "A Visit from Saint Nicholas" is followed by the story of the real Saint Nicholas, illustrated with reproductions of Renaissance art. (Rev: BCCB 11/01; BL 10/1/01; HBG 3/02; SLJ 10/01) [394.26]

19409 Murray, Julie. *Christmas* (1–3). Series: Holidays. 2003, ABDO LB $14.95 (1-57765-951-1). 24pp. Explores the origins of the holiday, as well as many of the activities, foods, and customs associated with it. (Rev: HBG 10/03; SLJ 10/03) [394.2663]

19410 Ouwendijk, George. *Santas of the World* (3–6). Series: Looking Into the Past: People, Places, and Customs. 1998, Chelsea LB $16.95 (0-7910-4678-8). 64pp. A overview of the Santa Claus legend is followed by an examination of Christmas gift-giving customs in 24 countries and regions. (Rev: HBG 9/98; SLJ 10/98) [394.26]

19411 Pingry, Patricia A. *Joseph's Story* (1–3). Illus. by George Hinke. 1998, Ideals $16.95 (0-8249-4092-X). The traditional stories surrounding the birth of Jesus are retold from the standpoint of Joseph, Mary's husband. (Rev: SLJ 10/98) [394.2]

19412 Rollins, Charlemae Hill, ed. *Christmas Gif': An Anthology of Christmas Poems, Songs, and Stories* (5–10). Illus. 1993, Morrow $14.00 (0-688-11667-1). A reissue of this Christmas anthology of African American songs, stories, poems, spirituals, and recipes, newly illustrated by Ashley Bryan. (Rev: BL 7/93) [810.8]

19413 Roop, Peter, and Connie Roop. *Let's Celebrate Christmas* (3–5). Illus. 1997, Millbrook LB $19.90 (0-7613-0115-1). 32pp. As well as a history of the customs surrounding Christmas, this book contains crafts, puzzles, and riddles. (Rev: BL 9/1/97; HBG 3/98; SLJ 10/97) [394]

19414 Ross, Michael Elsohn. *A Mexican Christmas* (K–3). Photos by Felix Rigau. 2002, Carolrhoda LB $23.93 (0-87614-601-9). 40pp. Christmas customs in Oaxaca are described in text and photographs. (Rev: HBG 3/03; SLJ 10/02) [394.2663]

19415 Schuh, Mari C. *Christmas* (PS–2). Series: Holidays and Celebrations. 2002, Capstone LB $14.60 (0-7368-0979-1). 24pp. An overview of holiday traditions in the United States for beginning readers. (Rev: HBG 3/02; SLJ 10/02)

19416 Steiner, Joan. *Look-Alikes Christmas* (K–4). Photos by Ogden Gigli. 2003, Little, Brown $14.95 (0-316-81187-4). Challenges young readers to name the everyday objects that have been used to construct nine three-dimensional holiday scenes, including Santa's workshop, a cathedral, and a scene from the *Nutcracker* ballet. (Rev: HB 11–12/03; HBG 4/04; SLJ 10/03) [793.73]

19417 *'Tis the Season: A Classic Illustrated Christmas Treasury* (3–7). 2003, Chronicle $19.95 (0-8118-3768-8). 80pp. Vintage illustrations add to the appeal of this collection of Christmas songs, poems, and stories, including the perennial favorite, "A Visit from St. Nicholas." (Rev: BL 11/15/03; HBG 4/04; SLJ 10/03)

Easter

19418 Chambers, Catherine. *Easter* (4–6). Series: A World of Holidays. 1998, Raintree LB $22.11 (0-8172-4615-0). 32pp. Tells the story of Easter and Christ's resurrection, and covers the secular aspects of this spring celebration, such as Easter eggs, bunnies, and baskets. (Rev: BL 6/1–15/98; HBG 9/98) [394.2]

19419 Kennedy, Pamela. *An Easter Celebration: Traditions and Customs from Around the World* (4–6). Illus. 1991, Ideals $10.95 (0-8249-8506-0). 32pp. Color photos and historical drawings add to this handy volume on Easter celebrations. (Rev: BL 3/15/91) [394.2]

19420 Knudsen, Shannon. *Easter Around the World* (1–3). Illus. Series: On My Own Holidays. 2005, Carolrhoda LB $22.60 (1-57505-655-0). 48pp. The origins and traditions of Easter are introduced with many illustrations and a short glossary.

19421 Landau, Elaine. *Easter: Parades, Chocolates, and Celebration* (2–5). Illus. Series: Finding Out About Holidays. 2004, Enslow LB $23.93 (0-7660-2172-6). 48pp. Informative text and colorful photographs present the history and religious significance of Easter, plus traditional symbols and contemporary ways of celebrating this holiday. (Rev: SLJ 4/05)

19422 Merrick, Patrick. *Easter Bunnies* (2–3). Series: Holiday Symbols. 1999, Child's World LB $15.95 (1-56766-639-6). 32pp. This account tells how rabbits became associated with Easter and also discusses several traditions connected to the holiday. (Rev: HBG 4/00; SLJ 1/00) [394.2]

19423 Schuh, Mari C. *Easter* (K–2). Series: Holidays and Celebrations. 2002, Capstone LB $14.60 (0-7368-1445-0). 24pp. This small, square book uses full-page photographs and a brief text to present the meaning of Easter, its symbols, celebrations, and importance. (Rev: BCCB 2/02; BL 1/1–15/03; HBG 3/03) [394.2]

19424 Stalcup, Ann. *Ukrainian Egg Decoration: A Holiday Tradition* (3–5). Series: Crafts of the World. 1999, Rosen $19.33 (0-8239-5335-1). 24pp. This photoessay covers the history and lore of the Ukrainian tradition of creating beautifully patterned eggs at Easter. Also features one craft project. (Rev: SLJ 4/99) [394.2]

Halloween

19425 Bull, Jane. *The Halloween Book: 50 Creepy Crafts for a Hair-Raising Halloween* (2–5). Photos by Andy Crawford. 2000, DK $12.95 (0-7894-6655-4). 48pp. This book includes crafts, costumes, food, and party ideas for Halloween in an attractive, well-illustrated format. (Rev: HBG 3/01; SLJ 9/00) [745.5]

19426 Chambers, Catherine. *All Saints, All Souls, and Halloween* (3–5). Illus. Series: World of Holidays. 1997, Raintree LB $25.69 (0-8172-4606-1). 31pp. An explanation of the origins of this holiday as an observance for the spirits of the dead, customs associated with it, and a number of craft activities. (Rev: BL 6/1–15/97) [394.2]

19427 Flanagan, Alice K. *Halloween* (2–3). Series: Holidays and Festivals. 2001, Compass Point LB $22.60 (0-7565-0086-9). 32pp. An attractive picture book that describes the origins of Halloween and how it is celebrated by youngsters today. (Rev: BCCB 10/02; BL 10/15/01; SLJ 1/02) [745.5]

19428 Gibbons, Gail. *Halloween* (PS–1). Illus. by author. 1984, Holiday House LB $16.95 (0-8234-0524-9); paper $6.95 (0-8234-0577-X). 32pp. Halloween history and traditions are explained in this simple picture book.

19429 Gibbons, Gail. *Halloween Is . . .* (PS–2). Illus. 2002, Holiday House $16.95 (0-8234-1758-1). 32pp. A larger, revised version with new, enhanced illustrations of the 1984 *Halloween*, describing the holiday's history and traditions. (Rev: BL 9/15/02; HBG 3/03) [394.2646]

19430 Greene, Carol. *The Story of Halloween* (3–5). Illus. by Linda Bronson. 2004, HarperCollins LB $16.89 (0-06-029560-0). 40pp. The history of Halloween is covered from its origins in the Celtic festival of Samhain to present-day problems with trick-or-treating. (Rev: BL 9/1/04; SLJ 8/04) [394]

19431 Limburg, Peter R. *Weird! The Complete Book of Halloween Words* (4–7). Illus. by Betsy Lewin. 1989, Macmillan LB $13.95 (0-02-759050-X). 128pp. This book defines 41 words and expressions, such as trick or treat, associated with Halloween. (Rev: BL 9/1/89; SLJ 9/89) [394]

19432 Parker, Toni Trent. *Sweets and Treats* (PS). Photos by Earl Anderson. 2002, Scholastic $6.95 (0-439-33871-9). Babies, toddlers, and preschoolers are portrayed in full costume, ready to hit Halloween streets. (Rev: HBG 3/03; SLJ 9/02)

19433 Robinson, Fay. *Halloween — Costumes and Treats on All Hallows' Eve* (3–6). Series: Finding Out About Holidays. 2001, Enslow LB $18.95 (0-7660-1632-3). 48pp. The origins of Halloween are described, with material on how this holiday has evolved and how it is currently celebrated in the United States. (Rev: BL 9/15/01; HBG 3/02; SLJ 9/01) [745.5]

19434 Roop, Peter, and Connie Roop. *Let's Celebrate Halloween* (3–5). Illus. 1997, Millbrook LB $19.90 (0-7613-0113-5); paper $5.95 (0-7613-0284-0). 32pp. Includes a number of crafts, like making a haunted house and different masks, as well as a history of Halloween and its significance. (Rev: BL 9/1/97; HBG 3/98; SLJ 8/97) [745.5]

19435 Stevens, Kathryn. *Halloween Jack-o'-Lanterns* (2–3). Series: Holiday Symbols. 1999, Child's World LB $15.95 (1-56766-641-8). 32pp. This book gives a history of Halloween and jack-o'-lanterns in a clear, well-organized text. (Rev: HBG 4/00; SLJ 1/00) [394.2]

19436 Trumbauer, Lisa. *Computer Fun Halloween* (2–5). Illus. by Sydney Wright. Series: Click It! 1999, Millbrook LB $21.90 (0-7613-1560-8). 32pp. These projects involving a computer and a paint program give directions on how to make decorations, masks and costumes, party invitations, place

cards, and more. (Rev: HBG 4/00; SLJ 2/00) [745.5]

19437 Wolff, Ferida, and Dolores Kozielski. *Halloween Fun for Everyone* (1–6). Illus. by Judy Lanfredi. 1997, Morrow paper $7.95 (0-688-15257-0). 79pp. After a history of Halloween, this book gives directions on how to make costumes, games, decorations, and holiday food. (Rev: SLJ 1/98) [745.5]

Jewish Holy Days and Celebrations

19438 Adler, David A. *The Kids' Catalog of Jewish Holidays* (4–7). Illus. 1996, Jewish Publication Soc. paper $15.95 (0-8276-0581-1). 244pp. Thirteen major and several minor Jewish holidays are introduced, along with activities, songs, and recipes. (Rev: BL 12/15/96; SLJ 3/97) [296.4]

19439 Berger, Gilda. *Celebrate! Stories of the Jewish Holidays* (3–5). Illus. 1998, Scholastic $17.95 (0-590-93503-8). 128pp. Eight different Jewish holidays, including Shabbat, Rosh Hashanah, Yom Kippur, and Hanukkah are introduced and explained, with suggested activities and crafts for each. (Rev: BL 10/1/98; HBG 3/99; SLJ 2/99) [296.4]

19440 Brinn, Ruth Esrig. *Jewish Holiday Crafts for Little Hands* (PS–4). Illus. by Katherine J. Kahn. 1993, Kar-Ben paper $10.95 (9-929371-47-X). 127pp. Using 11 different Jewish holidays as a focus, this unique craft book gives an average of a dozen simple projects for each. (Rev: SLJ 10/93) [296.4]

19441 Burstein, Chaya M. *The Jewish Kids Catalog* (3–7). Illus. by author. 1983, Jewish Publication Soc. paper $14.95 (0-8276-0215-4). 224pp. An introduction to Jewish holidays, traditions, and crafts.

19442 Clark, Anne, et al. *Hanukkah* (4–6). Series: A World of Holidays. 1998, Raintree LB $22.11 (0-8172-4614-2). 32pp. Tells the story of Hanukkah, its traditions, symbols, and heroes, such as Judah Maccabee and others who faced incredible odds. (Rev: BL 6/1–15/98; HBG 9/98) [296.4]

19443 Cohn, Janice. *The Christmas Menorahs: How a Town Fought Hate* (3–5). Illus. 1995, Whitman LB $16.95 (0-8075-1152-8). 40pp. The true story about the people of Billings, Montana, who put menorahs in their windows to fight bigotry. (Rev: BL 9/15/95) [305]

19444 Cone, Molly. *The Story of Shabbat* (2–5). Illus. 2000, HarperCollins LB $15.89 (0-06-027945-1). 40pp. A discussion of the weekly Jewish holiday — its history, customs, and such practices as abstaining from work and studying the Torah. (Rev: BL 4/1/00; HBG 9/00; SLJ 8/00) [296.4]

19445 Cooper, Ilene. *Jewish Holidays All Year Round: A Family Treasury* (3–5). Illus. by Elivia Savadier. 2002, Abrams $18.95 (0-8109-0550-7). 80pp. Details of the rituals that take place at home and in the synagogue are given in this overview of the holidays of the Jewish year, with an activity and recipe for each celebration. (Rev: HBG 3/03; SLJ 3/03) [296.4]

19446 Corwin, Judith Hoffman. *Jewish Holiday Fun* (4–6). Illus. by author. 1987, Silver Burdett paper $5.95 (0-671-60127-X). 64pp. All sorts of ways to celebrate plus an explanation of the meaning of each holiday in this reissued book.

19447 Ferro, Jennifer. *Jewish Foods and Culture* (3–5). Series: Festive Foods and Celebrations. 1999, Rourke LB $19.45 (1-57103-303-3). 48pp. Bar and bat mitzvahs, Passover, and Purim are three facets of Jewish life that are featured, along with recipes, in this book that also discusses Jewish history and culture. (Rev: SLJ 2/00) [296.4]

19448 Fishman, Cathy Goldberg. *Hanukkah* (2–3). Illus. by Mary O'Keefe Young. Series: On My Own Holidays. 2003, Carolrhoda LB $22.60 (1-57505-195-8); paper $5.95 (1-57505-583-X). 48pp. A simple history of the Jewish holiday, with a look at how it is celebrated today and instructions on how to play dreidel. (Rev: HBG 4/04; SLJ 10/03) [296.4]

19449 Freedland, Sara. *Hanukkah! A Three-Dimensional Celebration* (3–5). Illus. by Sue Clark. 1999, Candlewick $18.99 (0-7636-0890-4). Using three-dimensional illustrations, this book covers the history of Hanukkah and provides recipes and games. (Rev: BL 12/15/99; HBG 4/00) [296.4]

19450 Goldin, Barbara, D. *Ten Holiday Jewish Children's Stories* (K–3). Illus. by Jeffrey Allon. 2000, Pitspopany $16.95 (0-943706-47-5); paper $9.95 (0-943706-48-3). 48pp. A lively collection of ten stories, each of which stems from a tradition or practice associated with a Jewish holiday. (Rev: BL 10/1/00)

19451 Groner, Judye, and Madeline Wikler. *All About Passover* (2–4). Illus. by Kinny Kreiswirth. 2000, Kar-Ben paper $5.95 (1-58013-060-7). 32pp. A concise guide to this holiday, with a summary of the Passover story, details on suitable preparations, including cooking the seder meal, and a description of the seder itself. (Rev: BL 10/1/00) [296.4]

19452 Groner, Judye, and Madeline Wikler. *All About Sukkot* (1–5). Illus. by Kinny Kreiswirth. 1998, Kar-Ben paper $4.95 (1-58013-018-6). 32pp. This book gives information on the origins and history of this Jewish festival, on how it is celebrated and the connection between Sukkot and Thanksgiving, and provides suitable prayers, a story, and some poems. (Rev: SLJ 3/99) [296.4]

19453 Hesse, Karen. *The Stone Lamp: Eight Stories of Hanukkah Through History* (4–6). Illus. by Brian Pinkney. 2003, Hyperion $18.99 (0-7868-0619-2). 40pp. In free verse, Hesse highlights eight painful episodes in the history of the Jews, presenting them through the eyes of a child at Hanukkah. (Rev: BL 10/1/03; HB 11–12/03; HBG 4/04; SLJ 10/03) [811]

19454 Hildebrandt, Ziporah. *This Is Our Seder* (PS–2). Illus. by Robin Roraback. 1999, Holiday House $15.95 (0-8234-1436-1). 32pp. Wonderful illustrations and a simple text introduce each of the items associated with a Passover seder. (Rev: BL 3/1/99; HBG 9/99; SLJ 4/99) [296.4]

19455 Hoyt-Goldsmith, Diane. *Celebrating Hanukkah* (3–6). Illus. by Lawrence Migdale. 1996, Holiday House $16.95 (0-8234-1252-0). 32pp. A photoessay

about Hanukkah and how it is celebrated in the United States. (Rev: BCCB 11/96; BL 9/1/96) [296.4]

19456 Hoyt-Goldsmith, Diane. *Celebrating Passover* (2–5). Illus. 2000, Holiday House $16.95 (0-8234-1420-5). 32pp. A 9-year-old boy explains the origins of Passover and how he and his extended family celebrate it. (Rev: BL 5/1/00; HBG 9/00; SLJ 6/00) [296.4]

19457 Jaffe, Nina. *The Uninvited Guest and Other Jewish Holiday Tales* (4–6). Illus. by Elivia. 1993, Scholastic $16.95 (0-590-44653-3). 80pp. Seven Jewish holidays, including Rosh Hashanah, Yom Kippur, and Passover, are highlighted in these delightful folktales. (Rev: BL 11/15/93; SLJ 2/94) [296.4]

19458 Kimmel, Eric A., ed. *A Hanukkah Treasury* (5–8). 1998, Holt $19.95 (0-8050-5293-3). A diverse collection of Hanukkah stories, songs, poems, and activities, such as making a menorah, playing dreidel games, and cooking special foods associated with the holiday. (Rev: BL 12/1/98; SLJ 10/98) [296.4]

19459 Kimmel, Eric A. *Wonders and Miracles: A Passover Companion* (4–8). Illus. 2004, Scholastic $18.95 (0-439-07175-5). 144pp. In addition to a description of the holiday and its rituals, Kimmel provides stories, songs, prayers, poems, and recipes. (Rev: BL 2/15/04*; SLJ 2/04) [296.4]

19460 Kolatch, Alfred J. *The Jewish Child's First Book of Why* (PS–4). Illus. by Harry Araten. 1992, Jonathan David $14.95 (0-8246-0354-0). 32pp. Fifteen questions and answers dealing mainly with Jewish holidays. (Rev: BL 4/15/92) [296.4]

19461 Kropf, Latifa Berry. *It's Challah Time!* (PS–1). Illus. by Tod Cohen. 2002, Kar-Ben LB $10.95 (1-58013-036-4). 24pp. Color photographs show happy young children making challah for the Sabbath, singing blessings, and tasting the final product. (Rev: BL 10/1/02; HBG 3/03; SLJ 12/02) [641.5]

19462 Manushkin, Fran. *Miriam's Cup: A Passover Story* (2–4). Illus. by Bob Dacey. 1998, Scholastic $15.95 (0-590-67720-9). 32pp. An account of the origins of Passover in ancient Egypt and of the role played by Miriam, Moses' sister. (Rev: BL 2/1/98; HBG 9/98; SLJ 2/98) [222]

19463 Murray, Julie. *Hanukkah* (1–3). Series: Holidays. 2003, ABDO LB $14.95 (1-57765-953-8). 24pp. Provides a brief history of the holiday as well as a look at some of the associated traditions. (Rev: HBG 10/03; SLJ 10/03) [296.4]

19464 Musleah, Rahel. *Why on This Night? A Passover Haggadah for Family Celebration* (3–6). Illus. by Louise August. 2000, Simon & Schuster $24.95 (0-689-81356-2). 112pp. Using linocuts and poetic explanations, the author and illustrator introduce the seder, home service, and festive meal that begin Passover, with additional folk stories and a brief play. (Rev: BL 1/1–15/00*; HB 3–4/00; HBG 9/00; SLJ 2/00) [296.4]

19465 Musleah, Rahel, and Michael Klayman. *Sharing Blessings: Children's Stories for Exploring the*

Spirit of the Jewish Holidays (3–5). Illus. 1997, Jewish Lights $18.95 (1-879045-71-0). 64pp. Through the observances of a single family, all the major Jewish holidays are introduced and explained. (Rev: BL 10/1/97; HBG 3/98; SLJ 9/97) [296.4]

19466 Podwal, Mark. *A Sweet Year: A Taste of the Jewish Holidays* (K–6). Illus. by author. 2003, Doubleday LB $14.99 (0-385-90869-5). Lyrical prose and striking artwork offer an excellent introduction to the traditions and foods of the Jewish holidays. (Rev: HBG 4/04; SLJ 8/03) [296.4]

19467 Rose, David, and Gill Rose. *Passover* (3–5). Illus. Series: World of Holidays. 1997, Raintree LB $25.69 (0-8172-4607-X). 31pp. This book explains the origins of Passover and the Seder that accompanies it, along with many activities and craft projects. (Rev: BL 6/1–15/97) [296.4]

19468 Ross, Kathy. *Crafts for Hanukkah* (2–4). Illus. 1996, Millbrook LB $21.90 (1-56294-919-5); paper $6.95 (0-7613-0078-3). 48pp. Outlines crafts associated with Hanukkah, like making dreidels and menorahs. (Rev: BL 9/1/96) [745.594]

19469 Roth, Susan L. *Hanukkah, Oh Hanukkah* (PS–3). 2004, Penguin Putnam $10.99 (0-8037-2843-3). 24pp. This guide to the songs, games, and traditions of Hanukkah features mice as the main characters. (Rev: BL 9/1/04; SLJ 10/04)

19470 Rush, Barbara, and Cherie Karo Schwartz. *The Kids' Catalog of Passover: A Worldwide Celebration of Stories, Songs, Customs, Crafts, Food, and Fun* (K–5). 2000, Jewish Publication Soc. paper $15.95 (0-8276-0687-7). 223pp. A mixed bag of songs, stories, riddles, recipes, crafts, and other activities related to Passover plus background information on the holiday and how it is observed around the world. (Rev: SLJ 7/00) [296.4]

19471 Scharfstein, Sol. *Understanding Jewish Holidays and Customs: Historical and Contemporary* (4–7). Illus. 1999, KTAV $27.50 (0-88125-634-X); paper $18.95 (0-88125-626-9). 186pp. From ancient Jewish traditions to the present day, this highly visual volume describes the history, customs, and teaching of Judaism. (Rev: BL 10/1/99; SLJ 2/00) [296.4]

19472 Schecter, Ellen. *The Family Haggadah* (3–6). Illus. 1999, Viking $13.99 (0-670-88341-7). 80pp. For use by both parents and children, this guide to a Passover seder has instructions for table settings, a version of the service, and some traditional prayers and music. (Rev: BCCB 3/99; BL 5/15/99; SLJ 6/99) [296.4]

19473 Schuh, Mari C. *Passover* (K–2). Illus. Series: Holidays and Celebrations. 2002, Capstone $14.60 (0-7368-1448-5). 24pp. Colorful photographs and simple text explain the meaning, history, and traditions of the Passover celebration in this small, square book. (Rev: BL 1/1–15/03; HBG 3/03) [394.262]

19474 Siegel, Bruce H. *The Magic of Kol Nidre: A Yom Kippur Story* (1–4). Illus. by Shelly O. Haas. 1998, Kar-Ben $16.95 (1-58013-003-8); paper $6.95 (1-58013-002-X). The meanings behind Kol Nidre, the opening prayer of the Yom Kippur eve

service, are explored in this book illustrated with realistic watercolors. (Rev: HBG 3/99; SLJ 3/99) [296.4]

19475 Techner, David, and Judith Hirt-Manheimer. *A Candle for Grandpa* (K–3). Illus. by Joel Iskowitz. 1993, UAHC $11.95 (0-8074-0507-8). Using the first anniversary of the death of a boy's grandfather as a focus, this book presents Jewish funeral practices. (Rev: SLJ 10/93) [296.4]

19476 Wood, Angela. *Jewish Festivals* (4–6). Illus. Series: Celebrate! 1997, Heinemann $22.79 (0-431-06962-X). 48pp. A boy in Jerusalem and a girl in Chicago explain how their families celebrate a number of Jewish holidays and holy days. (Rev: SLJ 12/97) [221.6]

Thanksgiving

19477 Anderson, Laurie Halse. *Thank You, Sarah: The Woman Who Saved Thanksgiving* (K–3). Illus. by Matt Faulkner. 2002, Simon & Schuster $16.95 (0-689-84787-4). 40pp. Humorous illustrations accompany this true tale of a woman who campaigned for almost four decades to make Thanksgiving a national holiday. (Rev: BL 12/15/02; HBG 3/03; SLJ 12/02) [394.2649]

19478 Bruchac, Joseph. *Squanto's Journey: The Story of the First Thanksgiving* (4–8). Illus. by Greg Shed. 2000, Harcourt $16.00 (0-15-201817-4). 32pp. A picture book for older readers about the Pilgrims, the first Thanksgiving, and the important role played by the Paluxet Indian Squanto in helping the colony survive. (Rev: BL 9/1/00; HBG 3/01; SLJ 11/00) [394.2]

19479 Corwin, Judith Hoffman. *Harvest Festivals Around the World* (4–6). Illus. 1995, Messner LB $6.95 (0-671-87240-0). 48pp. Fifteen projects, like mask and doll making, that celebrate harvests and thanksgiving globally. (Rev: BL 2/1/96; SLJ 5/96) [394.2]

19480 Corwin, Judith Hoffman. *Thanksgiving Fun* (2–4). Illus. 1984, Silver Burdett paper $5.95 (0-671-50849-0). 64pp. A number of Thanksgiving projects are outlined, including a big dinner.

19481 Fink, Deborah F. *It's a Family Thanksgiving! A Celebration of an American Tradition for Children and Their Families* (K–4). Illus. by Kinny Kreiswirth. 2000, Harmony Hearth paper $9.95 (0-9678871-0-0). 32pp. History, foods, and traditions are covered in this book about Thanksgiving that also contains recipes and craft projects. (Rev: BL 9/15/00) [394.2]

19482 Flanagan, Alice K. *Thanksgiving* (2–4). Illus. by Kathi Kelleher. Series: Holidays and Festivals. 2001, Compass Point LB $22.60 (0-7565-0087-7). 32pp. The history behind Thanksgiving, with information about how we celebrate the holiday today. (Rev: BL 10/15/01; SLJ 1/02) [394.2]

19483 Gibbons, Gail. *Thanksgiving Day* (PS–2). Illus. by author. 1983, Holiday House LB $16.95 (0-8234-0489-7); paper $6.95 (0-8234-0576-1). 32pp. A very simple introduction to Thanksgiving Day.

19484 Grace, Catherine O'Neill, and Margaret M. Bruchac. *1621: A New Look at Thanksgiving* (K–4). Illus. by Sisse Brimberg and Cotton Coulson. 2001, National Geographic $17.95 (0-7922-7027-4). 48pp. This appealing and informative photoessay presents the historically correct story of the first Thanksgiving, as reenacted at the Plimoth Plantation. (Rev: BL 9/1/01; HBG 10/02; SLJ 9/01*) [394.2649]

19485 Graham-Barber, Lynda. *Gobble! The Complete Book of Thanksgiving Words* (4–6). Illus. by Betsy Lewin. 1993, Avon paper $3.99 (0-380-71963-0). 128pp. In readable fashion, all the words associated with this holiday are featured. (Rev: BL 1/1/91; SLJ 11/91) [394.2]

19486 Greenwood, Barbara. *A Pioneer Thanksgiving: A Story of Harvest Celebrations in 1841* (3–6). Illus. by Heather Collins. 1999, Kids Can $12.95 (1-55074-744-4); paper $5.95 (1-55074-574-3). 48pp. This book about a family's Thanksgiving celebration in 1841 includes recipes, craft projects, and games. (Rev: BCCB 11/99; BL 9/1/99; HBG 4/00; SLJ 9/99) [394]

19487 Hayward, Linda. *The First Thanksgiving* (1–3). Illus. by James Watling. Series: Step into Reading. 1990, Random LB $11.99 (0-679-90218-X); paper $3.99 (0-679-80218-5). 48pp. This easy-to-read book tells about the journey of the Pilgrims and of their first colony. (Rev: BCCB 11/90; BL 12/1/90) [394.2]

19488 Landau, Elaine. *Thanksgiving Day: A Time to Be Thankful* (3–6). Illus. Series: Finding Out About Holidays. 2001, Enslow LB $18.95 (0-7660-1572-6). 48pp. A general introduction to this traditional American holiday, its history, and how it is celebrated. (Rev: BL 9/15/01; HBG 3/02; SLJ 1/02) [394.2649]

19489 MacMillan, Dianne M. *Thanksgiving Day* (4–8). Series: Best Holiday Books. 1997, Enslow LB $18.95 (0-89490-822-7). In spite of a dull format, this book gives solid information about Thanksgiving, its history, common traditions, and modern observances. (Rev: SLJ 8/97) [394.2]

19490 Markham, Lois. *Harvest* (3–5). Series: World Celebrations and Ceremonies. 1998, Blackbirch LB $14.95 (1-56711-275-7). 23pp. Harvest festivals are described in such countries as Brazil, China, England, India, Israel, Mexico, and the United States. (Rev: HBG 3/99; SLJ 1/99) [394.2]

19491 Miller, Marilyn. *Thanksgiving* (4–6). Series: A World of Holidays. 1998, Raintree LB $22.11 (0-8172-4612-6). 32pp. This book discusses America's Thanksgiving Day and compares it with similar harvest festivals in such countries as the Czech Republic and Sierra Leone. (Rev: BL 6/1–15/98; HBG 9/98) [394.2]

19492 Schuh, Mari C. *Thanksgiving Day* (PS–1). Series: National Holidays. 2003, Capstone LB $14.60 (0-7368-1654-2). 24pp. This slim title examines the history of Thanksgiving Day, which was declared a national holiday in the 1860s. (Rev: HBG 10/03; SLJ 9/03) [394.2]

Valentine's Day

19493 Bulla, Clyde Robert. *The Story of Valentine's Day* (3–5). Illus. by Susan Estelle Kwas. 1999, HarperCollins LB $14.89 (0-06-027884-6). 40pp. This well-illustrated volume discusses the origins of Valentine's Day, shows how it is celebrated, and presents a few related projects. (Rev: BL 2/1/99; HBG 9/99; SLJ 6/99) [394.2618]

19494 Flanagan, Alice K. *Valentine's Day* (2–4). Illus. by Shelley Dieterichs. Series: Holidays and Festivals. 2001, Compass Point LB $22.60 (0-7565-0088-5). 32pp. Flanagan tells readers about the origins of Valentine's Day (as a Roman festival) and details how we celebrate the holiday today. (Rev: BL 10/15/01; SLJ 1/02) [394.2618]

19495 Fradin, Dennis B. *Valentine's Day* (3–5). Illus. 1990, Enslow LB $18.95 (0-89490-237-7). 48pp. A look at how this holiday has been celebrated over the years. (Rev: BL 8/90; SLJ 2/91) [394.2]

19496 Gibbons, Gail. *Valentine's Day* (PS–1). Illus. by author. 1986, Holiday House LB $16.95 (0-8234-0572-9); paper $6.95 (0-8234-0764-0). 32pp. History, meaning, and customs of Valentine's Day with simple drawings in bright colors. (Rev: BCCB 2/86; BL 12/15/85)

19497 Kessel, Joyce K. *Valentine's Day* (2–4). Illus. by Karen Ritz. 1981, Carolrhoda LB $21.27 (0-87614-166-1); Lerner paper $5.95 (0-87614-502-0). 48pp. An easily read account of the origins of this holiday and the traditions surrounding it.

19498 Landau, Elaine. *Valentine's Day: Candy, Love, and Hearts* (3–6). Series: Finding Out About Holidays. 2002, Enslow LB $18.95 (0-7660-1779-6). 48pp. Material on Saint Valentine is included with information on the symbols connected with the holiday and the ways in which it is celebrated. (Rev: BL 7/02; HBG 10/02; SLJ 10/02) [394.2]

19499 Sabuda, Robert. *Saint Valentine* (K–4). Illus. 1992, Macmillan $16.95 (0-689-31762-X). 32pp. Mosaiclike illustrations accompany the story of the gentle Christian physician and priest who lived in Rome during the Christian persecutions. (Rev: BL 11/15/92; SLJ 11/92) [270.1]

Prayers

19500 Beckett, Wendy. *A Child's Book of Prayer in Art* (3–6). Illus. 1995, DK $14.95 (1-56458-875-0). 32pp. Using the work of 15 artists, from Michelangelo to Millet, the editor shows how the act of praying has been represented in art. (Rev: BL 9/1/95*; SLJ 8/95) [242]

19501 Bible. *Give Us This Day: The Lord's Prayer* (PS–4). Illus. by Tasha Tudor. 1989, Penguin Putnam $12.95 (0-399-21442-9). Children in New England a century ago highlight the lovely paintings that illustrate the words of this Christian prayer. (Rev: BL 2/1/88)

19502 Carlstrom, Nancy White. *Glory* (PS–2). Illus. by Debra R. Jenkins. 2001, Eerdmans $17.00 (0-8028-5143-6). 32pp. Animals — and one little girl

— joyfully reflect the glory of God in this prayer with bright, bold illustrations. (Rev: BL 10/1/01; HBG 3/02; SLJ 12/01) [811]

19503 *The Children's Book of Poems, Prayers and Meditations* (4–6). Ed. by Liz Attenborough. Illus. 1998, Element Books $19.95 (1-90188-185-7). 128pp. From St. Francis of Assisi to Bob Dylan and Maya Angelou, this is a fine collection of meditative poems dealing with such topics as the nature of time and brotherly love. (Rev: BL 12/15/98; HBG 3/99; SLJ 1/99) [808.81]

19504 Cuthbert, Susan, comp. *The Classic Treasury of Children's Prayers* (K–5). Illus. by Alison Jay. 2000, Augsburg $19.99 (0-8066-4070-7). 223pp. A well-chosen collection of prayers with an emphasis on Christian ones that deal with such subjects as animals, seasons, festivals, forgiveness, virtues, and blessings. (Rev: SLJ 3/01) [242]

19505 Dearborn, Sabrina, ed. *A Child's Book of Blessings* (3–6). Illus. 1999, Barefoot $16.95 (1-84148-010-X). 40pp. A collection of simple blessings from various world cultures and religions. (Rev: BL 10/1/99; SLJ 2/00) [291.43]

19506 Emerson, Ralph Waldo. *Father, We Thank You* (PS–3). Illus. by Mark Graham. 2001, North-South LB $15.88 (1-58717-073-6). 32pp. Based on Emerson's classic poem, this beautiful book is a paean to God for flowers, grass, birds' songs, and other phenomena found in nature. (Rev: BL 4/1/01; HBG 10/01; SLJ 6/01) [811]

19507 Field, Rachel. *Prayer for a Child* (1–3). Illus. by Elizabeth Orton Jones. 1968, Macmillan LB $14.00 (0-02-735190-4); paper $5.99 (0-02-043070-1). 32pp. A prayer bespeaking the faith, hope, and love of little children. Caldecott Medal winner, 1945.

19508 Groner, Judye, and Madeline Wikler. *Thank You, God! A Jewish Child's Book of Prayers* (PS–2). Illus. by Shelly O. Haas. 1994, Kar-Ben $16.95 (0-929371-65-8). 32pp. A series of blessings and prayers involving Jewish traditions, written in Hebrew letters with an English translation. (Rev: BL 3/15/94; SLJ 4/94) [296.7]

19509 Hennessy, B. G. *My Book of Thanks* (PS). Illus. 2002, Candlewick $12.00 (0-7636-1523-4). 32pp. Vivid watercolor illustrations accompany these short, sweet prayers for very young children. (Rev: BL 12/15/02; HBG 3/03; SLJ 4/03) [242]

19510 *In Every Tiny Grain of Sand: A Child's Book of Prayers and Praise* (3–6). Ed. by Reeve Lindbergh. Illus. 2000, Candlewick $21.99 (0-7636-0176-4). 80pp. A marvelous collection of 77 poems and prayers drawn from many cultures, including Native American, Jewish, Muslim, Buddhist, African, and Celtic sources. (Rev: BCCB 12/00; BL 11/1/00*; HBG 3/01; SLJ 12/00) [291.4]

19511 Knowlton, Laurie L. *God Be in My Heart: Poems and Prayers for Children* (K–3). Illus. 1999, Boyds Mills $9.95 (1-56397-646-3). 32pp. A charming collection of 11 Christian prayers — some from history and others written by the author. (Rev: BL 4/1/99; HBG 9/99; SLJ 4/99) [291.4]

19512 Ladwig, Tim. *The Lord's Prayer* (PS–4). 2000, Eerdmans $17.00 (0-8028-5180-0). 32pp.

Full-page paintings are used with the text of the Lord's Prayer to tell the story of an African American father and daughter who help an elderly neighbor. (Rev: BCCB 12/00; BL 10/1/00; SLJ 1/01) [226.9]

19513 Maccarone, Grace. *A Child's Good Night Prayer* (PS). Illus. by Sam Williams. 2001, Scholastic $10.95 (0-439-23505-7). 32pp. Children of different ethnic backgrounds ask for nighttime blessings for their favorite things in this appealing picture book with rhyming text. (Rev: BL 10/1/01; HBG 10/02; SLJ 10/01) [291.4]

19514 O'Keefe, Susan Heyboer. *Angel Prayers: Prayers for All Children* (PS–1). Illus. by Sophia Suzan. 1999, Boyds Mills $15.95 (1-56397-683-8). A warm, gentle collection of prayers addressed to God and angels, plus several blessings. (Rev: HBG 4/00; SLJ 12/99) [242]

19515 Rock, Lois, comp. *My Very First Prayers* (PS–2). Illus. by Alex Ayliffe. 2003, Good Books $14.99 (1-56148-371-0). 159pp. This collection of prayers covers family, friends, pets, holidays, love, nature, and the seasons. (Rev: SLJ 1/04) [242]

19516 Rylant, Cynthia. *Bless Us All: A Child's Yearbook of Blessings* (PS–K). Illus. 1998, Simon & Schuster $14.00 (0-689-82370-3). 32pp. This book features 12 rhymed blessings — one for each month — each illustrated with childlike paintings. (Rev: BCCB 2/99; BL 11/1/98; HBG 3/99; SLJ 12/98) [291.4]

19517 Rylant, Cynthia. *Give Me Grace: A Child's Daybook of Prayers* (PS–K). Illus. 1999, Simon & Schuster $12.00 (0-689-82293-6). 32pp. A simple book of seven prayers, one for each day of the week. (Rev: BL 10/1/99; HBG 4/00; SLJ 12/99) [291.4]

19518 *A Small Child's Book of Prayers* (PS–1). Ed. by Cyndy Szekeres. Illus. 1999, Scholastic $6.95 (0-590-38363-9). 32pp. A fine collection of prayers that also includes poems about God and nature. (Rev: BL 2/1/99; HBG 9/99; SLJ 4/99) [242]

19519 Staub, Leslie. *Bless This House: A Bedtime Prayer for the Whole World* (PS). Illus. 2000, Harcourt $16.00 (0-15-201984-7). 32pp. A bedtime prayer that asks for blessings on all living creatures. (Rev: BL 10/1/00; HBG 3/01; SLJ 1/01) [242]

19520 Wheeler, Susan. *Holly Pond Hill: A Child's Book of Prayers* (PS–K). Illus. 2000, Dutton $9.99 (0-525-46187-6). 22pp. This charming board book includes six famous prayers and two selections from the Bible. (Rev: BL 3/15/00) [242]

19521 Willard, Nancy. *The Good-Night Blessing Book* (K–3). Illus. 1996, Scholastic $15.95 (0-590-62393-1). 32pp. This is a good-night prayer illustrated with the author's photographs. (Rev: BL 10/1/96; SLJ 10/96) [811]

19522 Winter, Rebecca. *Prayers for Children* (2–4). Illus. by Helen Cann. 2005, Good Books $14.99 (1-56148-470-9). 160pp. More than 200 prayers, traditional and new, come from different countries and cover a wide variety of subjects. (Rev: BL 6/1–15/05) [242]

Social Groups

Ethnic Groups

19523 Aliotta, Jerome J. *The Puerto Ricans* (5–8). Series: Land of Immigrants. 1995, Chelsea LB $21.95 (0-7910-3360-0). This account provides an extensive history of Puerto Ricans living in the United States, their struggles, traditions, and way of life. (Rev: BL 10/15/95) [305.868]

19524 Alter, Judy. *Mexican Americans* (3–5). Series: Spirit of America: Our Cultural Heritage. 2002, Child's World LB $27.07 (1-56766-156-4). 32pp. A useful overview of the history of Mexican Americans, their immigration to the United States, and their contributions to the nation's culture. (Rev: BL 10/15/02; SLJ 12/02) [973]

19525 Ashabranner, Brent. *The New African Americans* (5–9). Illus. 1999, Linnet LB $22.50 (0-208-02420-4). 105pp. After a brief history of early African immigration and slavery, this account focuses on present-day immigrants — where they come from and their reception in the United States. (Rev: BCCB 12/99; BL 10/15/99; HB 11–12/99; HBG 4/00) [304.87]

19526 Bandon, Alexandra. *Asian Indian Americans* (5–8). Illus. Series: Footsteps to America. 1995, New Discovery LB $13.95 (0-02-768144-0). 111pp. An account of the conditions that have caused emigration from India and a description of life in the United States for the immigrants. (Rev: SLJ 8/95) [973]

19527 Bandon, Alexandra. *Dominican Americans* (5–8). Illus. Series: Footsteps to America. 1995, New Discovery $22.00 (0-02-768152-1). 111pp. A readable account of why many residents of the Dominican Republic left their country to come to the United States and the conditions they found. (Rev: SLJ 8/95) [973]

19528 Bandon, Alexandra. *West Indian Americans* (5–10). Series: Footsteps to America. 1994, Silver Burdett LB $13.95 (0-02-768148-3). Describes why some West Indians left their islands to come to the United States, their reception, and their present lifestyles and contributions to their new nation. (Rev: BL 10/15/94; SLJ 12/94) [973]

19529 Behnke, Alison. *Mexicans in America* (4–8). Series: In America. 2004, Lerner LB $27.93 (0-8225-3955-1). 80pp. The reasons for Mexican migration to the United States and the life the newcomers find when they arrive are discussed in engaging narrative, with personal stories, notes on key figures, illustrations, and a timeline. (Rev: SLJ 3/05) [304.8]

19530 Berger, Melvin, and Gilda Berger. *Where Did Your Family Come From? A Book About Immigrants* (2–3). Illus. by Robert Quackenbush. Series: Discovery Readers. 1993, Ideals paper $4.50 (0-8249-8610-5). 48pp. A simple text about the waves of immigration to the United States. (Rev: BCCB 4/93; BL 7/93; SLJ 6/93) [325.73]

19531 Bial, Raymond. *The Mandan* (5–9). Series: Lifeways. 2002, Benchmark LB $22.95 (0-7614-1415-0). 126pp. Two traditional stories, a recipe, and a language guide accompany information on the history, culture, beliefs, and key figures of the Mandan people. (Rev: HBG 3/03; SLJ 6/03) [978.004]

19532 Bierman, Carol, and Barbara Hehner. *Journey to Ellis Island: How My Father Came to America* (2–5). Illus. by Laurie McGaw. 1998, Hyperion $17.95 (0-7868-0377-0). 48pp. Based on real-life experiences, this is the story of 11-year-old Yehuda Weinstein and his detention on Ellis Island because of an injured arm. (Rev: SLJ 5/99) [304.8]

19533 Binns, Tristan Boyer. *Chinese Americans* (3–5). Series: We Are America. 2003, Heinemann LB $24.22 (1-4034-0162-4). 32pp. Binns explores the challenges and hardships faced by Chinese immigrants to America and the many contributions they have made to society as a whole. Also use *Mexican Americans* (2003). (Rev: HBG 10/03; SLJ 8/03) [973]

19534 Birdseye, Debbie H., and Tom Birdseye. *Under Our Skin: Kids Talk About Race* (4–8). 1997, Holiday House $15.95 (0-8234-1325-X). In separate chapters, six eighth-grade students in Oregon from different racial and ethnic backgrounds talk about race and what racism means to them. (Rev: HBG 3/98; SLJ 4/98) [572.973]

19535 Bolden, Tonya. *Tell All the Children Our Story: Memories and Mementos of Being Young and Black in America* (4–8). Illus. 2002, Abrams $24.95 (0-8109-4496-0). 128pp. From the first recorded birth of a black child in the United States to the Million Man March, this book describes the African American experience through both personal and historical accounts, using a scrapbook format. (Rev: BL 2/15/02; HB 3–4/02; HBG 10/02; SLJ 3/02*) [973]

19536 Bryan, Nichol. *Haitian Americans* (3–5). Series: One Nation. 2004, ABDO LB $15.95 (1-57765-982-1). 32pp. A look at immigration from Haiti (both legal and illegal), the reasons behind it, what happens to the immigrants once they are in the United States, and the contributions they make to the culture in their new country. Also use *Mexican Americans* (2004). (Rev: HBG 4/04; SLJ 3/04) [973]

19537 Burgan, Michael. *African Americans* (3–5). Illus. Series: Our Cultural Heritage. 2004, Child's World LB $18.95 (1-59296-012-X). 32pp. Covers migration from America to the United States, emphasizing that in the early years few came by choice, with material on native culture, ethnic background, and contributions to present-day American society. [973]

19538 Burgan, Michael. *Italian Immigrants* (5–8). Series: Immigration to the United States. 2004, Facts on File $35.00 (0-8160-5681-1). 96pp. After an overview of the reasons underlying immigration in general, this illustrated volume looks at the circumstances of migrants from Italy, the group's history in the United States, and the contemporary situation, with sidebar features, a timeline, and a glossary. (Rev: SLJ 4/05)

19539 Cannarella, Deborah. *Cuban Americans* (3–5). Illus. Series: Our Cultural Heritage. 2004, Child's World LB $18.95 (1-59296-013-8). 32pp. Covers Cuban migration to the United States, with material on native culture, ethnic background, and the impact on present-day American society.

19540 Catalano, Julie. *The Mexican Americans* (5–8). Illus. Series: Immigrant Experience. 1995, Chelsea LB $21.95 (0-7910-3359-7); paper $9.95 (0-7910-3381-3). 100pp. This book traces the reasons for leaving Mexico, the immigrants' reception in the United States, and their contributions and achievements. (Rev: BL 11/15/95; SLJ 1/96) [973]

19541 Cavan, Seamus. *The Irish-American Experience* (5–7). Illus. Series: Coming to America. 1993, Millbrook LB $23.40 (1-56294-218-2). 64pp. Beginning with the potato famine that forced millions of Irish to come to America, this is the story of the rise of Irish Americans to positions of prominence. (Rev: BCCB 4/93; BL 6/1–15/93) [973]

19542 Clinton, Catherine. *The Black Soldier: 1492 to the Present* (5–8). Illus. 2000, Houghton Mifflin $17.00 (0-395-67722-X). 128pp. This history of

African Americans in the army begins with colonial slaves who were given muskets to fight the Indians and continues through each of America's wars to the present with emphasis on the slow progress toward equality in the ranks. (Rev: BCCB 10/00; BL 9/15/00; HBG 3/01; SLJ 10/00) [355]

19543 Cole, Harriette, and John Pinderhuges. *Coming Together: Celebrations for African American Families* (4–12). Illus. 2003, Hyperion $22.99 (0-7868-0753-9). 128pp. Traditions surrounding celebrations including Christmas, Kwanzaa, and naming ceremonies are covered here, with accompanying crafts, menu suggestions, and activities. (Rev: BL 12/15/03; HBG 4/04) [306.8]

19544 Cole, Melanie, et al. *Famous People of Hispanic Heritage* (4–7). Series: Contemporary American Success Stories. 1997, Mitchell Lane LB $21.95 (1-883845-44-0); paper $12.95 (1-883845-43-2). 96pp. This useful series, now in nine volumes, profiles famous Hispanics, past and present, from around the world. (Rev: BL 3/15/98; HBG 3/98) [920]

19545 Cole, Michael D. *The Los Angeles Riots: Rage in the City of Angels* (5–9). Series: American Disasters. 1999, Enslow LB $18.95 (0-7660-1219-0). An account of the police beating of Rodney King in Los Angeles and the subsequent riots, the worst in U.S. history. (Rev: BL 2/1/99; HBG 9/99; SLJ 6/99) [979.494053]

19546 Coleman, Lori. *Vietnamese in America* (4–8). Series: In America. 2004, Lerner LB $27.93 (0-8225-3951-9). 72pp. The reasons for Vietnamese migration to the United States and the life the newcomers find when they arrive are discussed in engaging narrative, with personal stories, notes on key figures, illustrations, and a timeline. Also use *Koreans in America* (2004). (Rev: SLJ 3/05) [973]

19547 Cunningham, Kevin. *Canadian Americans* (3–5). Illus. Series: Our Cultural Heritage. 2004, Child's World LB $18.95 (1-59296-178-9). 32pp. Covers Canadian migration to the United States, with material on native culture, ethnic background, and contributions to present-day American society.

19548 Daley, William. *The Chinese Americans* (5–8). Illus. 1995, Chelsea LB $21.95 (0-7910-3357-0); paper $9.95 (0-7910-3379-1). 112pp. The background and culture of this group are explained, as well as its adjustment to life in America. (Rev: BL 1/1/88) [973.04951]

19549 De Capua, Sarah E. *Irish Americans* (3–5). Series: Spirit of America: Our Cultural Heritage. 2002, Child's World LB $27.07 (1-56766-155-6). 32pp. De Capua discusses the reasons for Irish migration to the United States and the lasting contributions this group has made. (Rev: BL 10/15/02) [973]

19550 Di Franco, J. Philip. *The Italian Americans* (5–8). Illus. 1995, Chelsea LB $21.95 (0-791-03353-8); paper $9.95 (0-7910-3375-9). 112pp. A heavily illustrated discussion of the culture that Italian immigrants left behind and their contributions to American life. (Rev: BL 1/1/88) [973.0451]

19551 Feelings, Tom. *Tommy Traveler in the World of Black History* (5–8). 1991, Black Butterfly $13.95 (0-86316-202-9). A history of African Americans seen through the eyes of a boy who imagines himself participating in the important events. (Rev: BL 9/15/91; SLJ 2/92) [973]

19552 Fitterer, C. Ann. *Arab Americans* (3–5). Illus. Series: Spirit of America: Our Cultural Heritage. 2002, Child's World LB $27.07 (1-56766-150-5). 32pp. An overview of the Arab American experience, including the history of Arab immigration, post 9/11 discrimination, and the contributions of Arab Americans to society as a whole. (Rev: BL 10/15/02; SLJ 2/03) [973]

19553 Fitterer, C. Ann. *German Americans* (3–5). Series: Spirit of America: Our Cultural Heritage. 2002, Child's World LB $27.07 (1-56766-151-3). 32pp. Fitterer discusses German migration to the United States and the contributions of this community. (Rev: BL 10/15/02; SLJ 2/03) [973]

19554 Fitterer, C. Ann. *Russian Americans* (3–5). Series: Spirit of America: Our Cultural Heritage. 2002, Child's World LB $27.07 (1-56766-158-0). 32pp. Russian migration to the United States is discussed in this richly illustrated account that includes material on famous immigrants. (Rev: BL 10/15/02; SLJ 12/02) [973]

19555 Fitterer, C. Ann. *Vietnamese Americans* (3–5). Series: Spirit of America: Our Cultural Heritage. 2002, Child's World LB $27.07 (1-56766-160-2). 32pp. A history of recent migration to the United States by the Vietnamese is accompanied by material on this group's reception, contributions, and assimilation. (Rev: BL 10/15/02; SLJ 12/02) [973]

19556 Franchino, Vicky. *Italian Americans* (3–5). Series: Spirit of America: Our Cultural Heritage. 2002, Child's World LB $27.07 (1-56766-153-X). 32pp. How Italian immigrants changed American life is one of the topics discussed in this simple account of why and how they came to this country, their reception, and a rundown of famous Italian Americans. Also use *British Americans* and *Spanish Americans* (both 2002). (Rev: BL 10/15/02) [973]

19557 Freeman, Dena. *How People Live* (3–6). 2003, DK $29.99 (0-7894-9867-7). 304pp. Organized by continent, this ambitious volume full of photographs explores many different cultures and is suitable for browsing. (Rev: HBG 4/04; SLJ 2/04) [306]

19558 Frost, Helen. *German Immigrants, 1820–1920* (4–6). Illus. Series: Coming to America. 2001, Capstone LB $16.95 (0-7368-0794-2). 32pp. A look at German immigrants to the United States, including why they migrated, where they settled, and their customs, with historical photographs and features such as maps, crafts, and recipes. Also use *Norwegian, Swedish, and Danish Immigrants, 1820–1920* (2001). (Rev: BL 10/15/01; HBG 3/02) [973.04]

19559 Frost, Helen. *Russian Immigrants: 1860–1915* (4–6). Series: Coming to America. 2002, Capstone LB $22.60 (0-7368-1209-1). 32pp. After a look at why Russians left their country to migrate to the United States, this account covers their destinations,

culture, and contributions. (Rev: BL 1/1–15/03; HBG 3/03; SLJ 3/03) [973]

19560 Gabor, A. *Polish Americans* (4–6). Illus. Series: Cultures of America. 1995, Marshall Cavendish $19.95 (1-7614-0154-7). 80pp. After a description of life in Poland, this account describes the history of Polish Americans and various aspects of their culture. (Rev: BL 7/95) [305.89]

19561 Galicich, Anne. *The German Americans* (5–8). Illus. Series: Immigrant Experience. 1995, Chelsea LB $19.95 (0-7910-3362-7); paper $9.95 (0-7910-3384-8). 120pp. This account traces the history of German Americans, from their reasons for leaving Germany and their initial reception in the United States to their present status. (Rev: BL 4/1/89) [973]

19562 Gernand, Renee. *The Cuban Americans* (5–8). Illus. 1995, Chelsea LB $21.95 (0-791-03354-6); paper $9.95 (0-791-03376-7). 112pp. The contributions of Cuban Americans and reasons why they came to America. (Rev: BL 2/1/89) [973.0468729]

19563 Giff, Patricia Reilly. *Don't Tell the Girls: A Family Memoir* (4–7). Illus. 2005, Holiday House $16.95 (0-8234-1813-8). 144pp. The author tells of the search for her family's roots that led her to Ireland. (Rev: BL 3/1/05) [813]

19564 Goldish, Meish. *Immigration: How Should It Be Controlled?* (4–6). Illus. Series: Issues of Our Time. 1994, Twenty-First Century LB $18.90 (0-8050-3182-0). 64pp. Contains historical information about immigration plus material on citizenship laws, illegal aliens, and the pros and cons of allowing more immigrants into the United States. (Rev: SLJ 7/94) [304.8]

19565 Goldstein, Margaret J. *Irish in America* (5–8). Series: In America. 2004, Lerner LB $27.93 (0-8225-3950-0). 80pp. This overview of Irish migration to the United States looks at the underlying reasons for the exodus and explores the lives of the new arrivals and the traditions they maintained. (Rev: BL 11/15/04) [973]

19566 Greene, Meg. *Slave Young, Slave Long: The American Slave Experience* (5–8). Illus. Series: People's History. 1999, Lerner LB $30.35 (0-8225-1739-6). Using quotations from both victims and perpetrators, and illustrated by historical prints and photographs, this book presents the story of slavery in the United States. (Rev: BL 4/1/99; HBG 9/99; SLJ 10/99) [973.0496]

19567 Greenfield, Eloise, and Lessie Jones Little. *Childtimes: A Three-Generation Memoir* (5–8). Illus. by Jerry Pinkney. 1979, HarperCollins LB $16.89 (0-690-03875-5); paper $9.99 (0-06-446134-3). 160pp. The childhoods of three generations of African American women.

19568 Haberle, Susan E. *Jewish Immigrants: 1880–1924* (4–6). Series: Coming to America. 2002, Capstone LB $22.60 (0-7368-1207-5). 32pp. A brief overview of why Jews left Europe, plus an account of where they settled in America, their cultural contributions, and a list of famous Jewish Americans. (Rev: BL 1/1–15/03; HBG 3/03) [973]

19569 Hamanaka, Sheila. *The Journey: Japanese Americans, Racism and Renewal* (5–9). Illus. by author. 1990, Orchard LB $20.99 (0-531-08449-3). 39pp. With brief text, this book is a series of paintings from a large mural that describes the injustices suffered by Japanese Americans at the beginning of World War II. (Rev: BL 3/15/90; HB 5–6/90; SLJ 5/90) [940.54]

19570 Hamilton, Virginia. *Many Thousand Gone: African Americans from Slavery to Freedom* (5–9). Illus. 1993, Random LB $18.99 (0-394-92873-3). Combining history with personal slave narratives and biography, Hamilton tells of the famous — Douglass, Truth, Tubman — and the unknown — slaves, rebels, and conductors. (Rev: BL 12/1/92*; SLJ 5/93*) [973.7]

19571 Harkrader, Lisa. *South Korea* (5–8). Illus. Series: Top Ten Countries of Recent Immigrants. 2004, Enslow/MyReportLinks.com LB $25.26 (0-7660-5181-1). 48pp. Information on South Korea — culture, history, climate, and people — accompanies an explanation of the reasons for migration to the United States and discussion of the contributions of this community; supported by Web links. (Rev: SLJ 3/05) [304]

19572 Hatt, Christine. *Slavery: From Africa to the Americas* (5–8). 1998, Bedrick $19.95 (0-87226-552-8). 63pp. A broad overview of slavery in America that covers slave ships, plantation life, abolitionism, the Civil War, and Reconstruction, with maps, illustrations, and reproductions of documents. (Rev: HBG 9/98; SLJ 5/98) [973]

19573 Heinrichs, Ann. *French Americans* (3–5). Illus. Series: Our Cultural Heritage. 2004, Child's World LB $18.95 (1-59296-180-0). 32pp. Covers French migration to the United States, with material on the group's native culture, ethnic background, and the impact they have had on present-day American society.

19574 Heinrichs, Ann. *Norwegian Americans* (3–5). Illus. Series: Our Cultural Heritage. 2004, Child's World LB $18.95 (1-59296-182-7). 32pp. Covers Norwegian migration to the United States, with material on the group's native culture, ethnic background, and the impact they have had on present-day American society.

19575 *Honoring Our Ancestors: Stories and Pictures by Fourteen Artists* (3–6). Ed. by Harriet Rohmer. Illus. 1999, Children's Book Pr. $15.95 (0-89239-158-8). 32pp. A diverse group of artists from various ethnic groups honor family members and describe how they succeeded in America. (Rev: BCCB 3/99; BL 2/1/99; HBG 9/99; SLJ 6/99) [759.13]

19576 Hopkinson, Deborah. *Shutting Out the Sky* (5–12). Illus. 2003, Scholastic $17.95 (0-439-37590-8). 144pp. Five personal stories of young immigrants, striking photographs, and excerpts from primary documents form the backbone of this history of immigration to New York City in the late 19th century. (Rev: BL 11/1/03*; HBG 4/04; SLJ 12/03*) [307.76]

19577 Horton, Casey. *The Jews* (4–8). Series: We Came to North America. 2000, Crabtree LB $21.28 (0-7787-0187-5); paper $8.95 (0-7787-0201-4). 32pp. As well as discussing the reasons why Jews left Europe, this account describes the trip across the Atlantic, reception in America, and the many contributions to the United States. (Rev: SLJ 10/00) [973]

19578 Hossell, Karen Price. *Pakistani Americans* (3–5). Series: We Are America. 2004, Heinemann LB $24.22 (1-4034-5023-4). 32pp. A story about a young Pakistani's arrival in America introduces this overview of immigration from Pakistan that looks at history, cultural life, and contributions to the United States, with a map, a chart, and a timeline. (Rev: SLJ 11/04) [973]

19579 Hoyt-Goldsmith, Diane. *Hoang Anh: A Vietnamese-American Boy* (3–5). Illus. by Lawrence Migdale. Series: Cornerstones of Freedom. 1992, Holiday House LB $16.95 (0-8234-0948-1). 32pp. Color photos and a first-person narrative describe the life of a Vietnamese boy living in California. (Rev: BCCB 4/92; BL 4/15/92; HB 5–6/92; SLJ 4/92) [378.1]

19580 Hull, Mary. *Ethnic Violence* (5–8). Illus. Series: Overview. 1997, Lucent LB $27.45 (1-56006-184-7). 112pp. Gives a history of racial prejudice that has led to violence and discusses decisions and policies that currently guide our behavior and attitudes toward this problem. (Rev: BL 8/97; SLJ 9/97) [305.8]

19581 Ingram, W. Scott. *Greek Immigrants* (5–8). Series: Immigration to the United States. 2004, Facts on File $35.00 (0-8160-5689-7). 96pp. After an overview of the reasons underlying immigration in general, this illustrated volume looks at the circumstances of migrants from Greece, the group's history in the United States, and the contemporary situation, with sidebar features, a timeline, and a glossary. Also use *Japanese Immigrants* and *Polish Immigrants* (both 2004). (Rev: BL 4/1/04; HB 3–4/04; SLJ 4/05)

19582 James, Barbara. *Animal Rights* (5–10). Series: Talking Points. 1999, Raintree LB $27.12 (0-8172-5317-3). 64pp. Various aspects of the animal rights controversy are explored in an objective, straightforward manner. (Rev: BL 8/99) [179.3]

19583 Kitano, Harry. *The Japanese Americans*. 2nd ed. (5–8). Photos by Richard Hewett. Series: Land of Immigrants. 1995, Chelsea LB $19.95 (0-7910-3358-9); paper $9.95 (0-7910-3380-5). 92pp. The story of Japanese Americans and their traditions and contributions to American life and culture. (Rev: BL 10/15/95) [305]

19584 Koenig, Angela T. *Pakistani Americans* (3–5). Series: Spirit of America: Our Cultural Heritage. 2003, Child's World LB $27.07 (1-59296-017-0). 32pp. Explores the history behind immigration to the United States from Pakistan, the influences this ethnic group has had on American culture, and life today. (Rev: SLJ 2/04) [973]

19585 Kroll, Virginia. *With Love, to Earth's Endangered Peoples* (3–6). Illus. by Roberta Collier-

Morales. 1998, Dawn $17.95 (1-883220-83-1); paper $8.95 (1-883220-82-3). This book deals with such endangered peoples as the Australian aborigine, the Inuit, the Toda of India, and the Ainu of Japan. (Rev: HBG 3/99; SLJ 12/98) [910]

19586 Kuropas, Myron B. *Ukrainians in America* (5–7). Illus. Series: In America. 1996, Lerner LB $19.93 (0-8225-1043-X). 80pp. The story of Ukrainian immigrants to the United States, their cultural traditions, and their contributions to American life. (Rev: BL 3/15/96; SLJ 3/96) [973]

19587 Leder, Jane. *A Russian Jewish Family* (5–8). Series: Journey Between Two Worlds. 1996, Lerner LB $22.60 (0-8225-3401-0); paper $8.95 (0-8225-9744-6). This account compares the living conditions of a Jewish family in Russia and in their new American home. (Rev: BL 11/1/96; SLJ 11/96) [977.3]

19588 Levine, Ellen. *If Your Name Was Changed at Ellis Island* (3–5). Illus. by Wayne Parmenter. 1993, Scholastic $15.95 (0-590-46134-6). 80pp. Informative and lively case histories highlight the stories of the millions who passed through Ellis Island for a new life in America. (Rev: BCCB 4/93; BL 3/1/93; SLJ 3/93) [325.1]

19589 Lingen, Marissa. *The Jewish Americans* (4–7). Illus. Series: We Came to America. 2002, Mason Crest LB $19.95 (1-59084-109-3). 64pp. Lingen traces the history of Jewish migration to the United States and provides a list of Jewish Americans of note. (Rev: SLJ 9/02) [973.049]

19590 Lock, Donna. *The Polish Americans* (5–8). Illus. Series: We Came to America. 2002, Mason Crest LB $19.95 (1-59084-112-3). 64pp. A look at the customs and contributions of this ethnic group, including information on famous Polish Americans, with a bibliography, glossary, timeline, and resources for tracing ancestors. (Rev: BL 7/02) [305.891]

19591 Lomas Garza, Carmen. *Family Pictures / Cuadros de Familia* (3–7). Illus. 1990, Children's Book Pr. $15.95 (0-89239-050-6); paper $7.95 (0-89239-108-1). 32pp. A Mexican American artist shares memories of her childhood in Texas. (Rev: BCCB 10/90; BL 6/1/90; SLJ 11/90*) [306]

19592 McDaniel, Melissa. *Japanese Americans* (3–5). Series: Spirit of America: Our Cultural Heritage. 2002, Child's World LB $27.07 (1-56766-154-8). 32pp. The history of Japanese migration to the United States is discussed, with material on the the discrimination the new citizens faced and the many ways in which they have changed American culture. (Rev: BL 10/15/02; SLJ 12/02) [973]

19593 McGill, Allyson. *The Swedish Americans* (5–8). Series: Immigrant Experience. 1997, Chelsea $19.95 (0-7910-4551-X); paper $9.95 (0-7910-4552-8). 107pp. Explains why Swedes have emigrated from their homeland, their reception in the United States, and their contributions to the nation. (Rev: BL 10/15/97) [322.4]

19594 Maestro, Betsy. *Coming to America: The Story of Immigration* (K–3). Illus. by Susannah Ryan. 1996, Scholastic $15.95 (0-590-44151-5). 40pp. A picture-book introduction to what the many waves of immigrants have meant to the United States. (Rev: BCCB 2/96; BL 2/1/96; SLJ 5/96) [304]

19595 Magocsi, Paul R. *The Russian Americans* (5–8). Illus. Series: Immigrant Experience. 1995, Chelsea LB $21.95 (0-7910-3367-8). 110pp. Coverage includes reasons for leaving Russia, customs and traditions, contributions to their new nation, and famous Russian Americans. (Rev: BL 11/15/95; SLJ 1/96) [973]

19596 Mendez, Adriana. *Cubans in America* (5–7). Illus. Series: In America. 1994, Lerner LB $19.93 (0-8225-1953-4). 80pp. An account that describes why Cubans left their homeland, where they live in the United States, their lifestyles, and their contributions to society. (Rev: BL 8/94; SLJ 8/94) [973]

19597 Morris, Ann. *Grandma Esther Remembers: A Jewish-American Family Story* (1–3). Series: What Was It Like, Grandma? 2002, Millbrook LB $22.90 (0-7613-2318-X). 32pp. In double-page spreads (with a picture opposite a page of simple text), a Jewish American grandmother describes her life in the old country and her early experiences in the United States. (Rev: BL 9/15/02; HBG 10/02; SLJ 6/02) [973]

19598 Morris, Ann. *Grandma Francisca Remembers: A Mexican-American Family Story* (1–3). Illus. by Peter Linenthal. Series: What Was It Like, Grandma? 2002, Millbrook LB $22.90 (0-7613-2315-5). 32pp. Some Spanish vocabulary, a recipe for stew, and instructions for making a sock doll accompany this account of the activities of a young Mexican American girl and her grandmother. (Rev: BL 2/15/02; HBG 10/02; SLJ 4/02) [973]

19599 Morris, Ann. *Grandma Lai Goon Remembers: A Chinese-American Family Story* (1–3). Series: What Was It Like, Grandma? 2002, Millbrook LB $22.90 (0-7613-2314-7). 32pp. Activities such as making a Chinese doll, making Chinese buns, and playing a Chinese game complement the story of a Chinese American grandmother's life. (Rev: BL 9/15/02; HBG 10/02; SLJ 6/02) [973]

19600 Morris, Ann. *Grandma Lois Remembers: An African-American Family Story* (1–3). Series: What Was It Like, Grandma? 2002, Millbrook LB $22.90 (0-7613-2316-3). 32pp. An African American grandmother tells the family history to her grandson, with appended activities and games. (Rev: BL 9/15/02; HBG 10/02; SLJ 3/02) [976.1]

19601 Morris, Ann. *Grandma Susan Remembers: A British-American Family Story* (1–3). Series: What Was It Like, Grandma? 2002, Millbrook LB $22.90 (0-7613-2319-8). 32pp. A grandmother who was born in Britain recalls her childhood and the culture of the land she left. Activities are appended. (Rev: BL 9/15/02; HBG 10/02; SLJ 6/02) [973]

19602 Muggamin, Howard. *The Jewish Americans* (5–8). Series: Immigrant Experience. 1995, Chelsea LB $19.95 (0-7910-3365-1); paper $9.95 (0-7910-3387-2). An examination of Jewish Americans, their history of immigration and their reception in this country, and their achievements and contributions. (Rev: BL 11/15/95) [973]

19603 Newman, Shirlee P. *Slavery in the United States* (4–7). Series: Watts Library: History of Slavery. 2000, Watts LB $24.00 (0-531-11695-6). 64pp. This account covers the shameful American record concerning slavery with coverage from the African slave trade through plantation life, the Underground Railroad, and abolitionists to the Civil War and emancipation. (Rev: BL 3/1/01) [973]

19604 Ochoa, George. *The New York Public Library Amazing Hispanic American History: A Book of Answers for Kids* (4–9). 1998, Wiley paper $12.95 (0-471-19204-X). Using a question-and-answer format, this work explores such topics as Hispanic American identity and history, cultural groups, accomplishments, and immigrant experiences. (Rev: BL 12/1/98; SLJ 11/98) [973]

19605 O'Hara, Megan. *Irish Immigrants: 1840–1920* (4–6). Series: Coming to America. 2001, Capstone LB $16.95 (0-7368-0795-0). 32pp. This account, complete with many reader activities, takes a quick look at Irish history, explains why the migrants left their country, and describes their reception in the United States and their contributions to American life. (Rev: BL 10/15/01; HBG 3/02; SLJ 1/02) [973]

19606 Olson, Kay Melchisedech. *Chinese Immigrants: 1850–1900* (4–6). Series: Coming to America. 2001, Capstone LB $16.95 (0-7368-0793-4). 32pp. Using many sidebars, recipes, and suggested activities, this book tells how and why the Chinese originally came to the United States and the contributions they have made to American culture. (Rev: BL 10/15/01; HBG 3/02) [973]

19607 Olson, Kay Melchisedech. *French Immigrants: 1840–1940* (4–6). Series: Coming to America. 2002, Capstone LB $22.60 (0-7368-1205-9). 32pp. Covers the reasons why French citizens left their country for America and gives details of their struggle to retain their traditions, of their contributions, and the lives of famous immigrants and their descendants. (Rev: BL 1/1–15/03; HBG 3/03) [973]

19608 Omoto, Susan. *Hmong Milestones in America: Citizens in a New World* (5–8). Illus. 2003, John Gordon Burke $27.00 (0-934272-57-3); paper $15.00 (0-934272-56-5). 64pp. The author introduces the Hmong people's history and traditions and traces the steps of Hmong refugees who migrated to the United States, profiling five individuals who have found success in their new country. (Rev: BL 4/15/03) [973]

19609 Parker, Lewis K. *Why Japanese Immigrants Came to America* (2–5). Series: Coming to America. 2003, Rosen LB $17.25 (0-8239-6463-9). 24pp. A brief overview of the experience of Japanese immigrants to America, the first major wave of whom arrived in Hawaii in 1885. (Rev: SLJ 10/03) [973]

19610 Parker, Lewis K. *Why Mexican Immigrants Came to America* (2–5). Series: Coming to America. 2003, Rosen LB $17.25 (0-8239-6459-0). 24pp. Examines the reasons underlying Mexican immigration to the United States and the contributions this group has made to American society. (Rev: SLJ 10/03) [304.8]

19611 Parker, Lewis K. *Why Vietnamese Immigrants Came to America* (2–5). Series: Coming to America. 2003, Rosen LB $17.25 (0-8239-6461-2). 24pp. Focuses on the influx of Vietnamese immigrants that began in the 1960s, emphasizing the contributions this group has made to American society. (Rev: SLJ 10/03) [304.8]

19612 Patrick, Diane. *The New York Public Library Amazing African American History: A Book of Answers for Kids* (5–9). Illus. 1998, Wiley paper $12.95 (0-471-19217-1). Using a question-and-answer format, this book traces the history of African Americans from slavery to the present day. (Rev: BL 2/15/98; SLJ 4/98) [973]

19613 Paulson, Timothy J. *Irish Immigrants* (5–8). Series: Immigration to the United States. 2004, Facts on File $35.00 (0-8160-5682-X). 96pp. After an overview of the reasons underlying immigration in general, this illustrated volume looks at the circumstances of migrants from Ireland, the group's history in the United States, and the contemporary situation, with sidebar features, a timeline, and a glossary. (Rev: SLJ 4/05)

19614 Perl, Lila. *North Across the Border: The Story of the Mexican Americans* (5–9). Series: Great Journeys. 2001, Benchmark LB $31.36 (0-7614-1226-3). 112pp. The economic and social reasons for Mexican migration to the north through history are presented in text, quotations from primary sources, and many illustrations and maps. (Rev: BL 1/1–15/02; HBG 10/02; SLJ 3/02) [973.0468]

19615 Peterson, Tiffany. *Greek Americans* (3–5). Series: We Are America. 2004, Heinemann LB $24.22 (1-4034-5021-8). 32pp. A personal story introduces this overview of immigration from Greece that looks at history, cultural life, and contributions to the United States, with a map, a chart, and a timeline. Also use *Japanese Americans* (2004), which includes material on internment. (Rev: SLJ 11/04) [973]

19616 Press, Petra. *Puerto Ricans* (4–6). Illus. Series: Cultures of America. 1996, Marshall Cavendish LB $19.95 (0-7614-0160-0). 80pp. A nicely illustrated description of the island of Puerto Rico details the customs, traditions, and contributions of its people. (Rev: BL 5/15/96) [973]

19617 Raatma, Lucia. *Chinese Americans* (3–5). Illus. Series: Spirit of America: Our Cultural Heritage. 2002, Child's World LB $27.07 (1-56766-149-1). 32pp. An overview of the Chinese American experience that includes maps, timelines, and other visuals. (Rev: BL 10/15/02) [973]

19618 Raatma, Lucia. *Polish Americans* (3–5). Series: Spirit of America: Our Cultural Heritage. 2002, Child's World LB $27.07 (1-56766-157-2). 32pp. Provides a history of Polish migration to this country, with emphasis on the many contributions this group has made to American life and culture. (Rev: BL 10/15/02) [973]

19619 Raatma, Lucia. *Swedish Americans* (3–5). Series: Spirit of America: Our Cultural Heritage. 2002, Child's World LB $27.07 (1-56766-159-9). 32pp. Swedish migration to the United States is the topic of this work, with material on the group's native culture, ethnic background, and the impact they have had on present-day American society. (Rev: BL 10/15/02) [973]

19620 Rappaport, Doreen. *Free at Last! Stories and Songs of Emancipation* (4–8). Illus. by Shane W. Evans. 2004, Candlewick $19.99 (0-7636-1440-8). 64pp. First-hand accounts form the basis of this portrait of the black experience from emancipation to the 1954 Supreme Court decision declaring school segregation illegal. (Rev: BL 2/15/04*; HB 5–6/04; SLJ 2/04) [973]

19621 Rappaport, Doreen. *No More! Stories and Songs of Slave Resistance* (4–7). Illus. by Shane W. Evans. 2002, Candlewick $17.99 (0-7636-0984-6). 64pp. A collection of narratives, prose, poetry, and songs that describe the African slave experience and the various forms of rebellion that took place. (Rev: BCCB 4/02; BL 2/15/02; HB 3–4/02; HBG 10/02; SLJ 2/02*) [306.3]

19622 Rosenberg, Pam. *Jewish Americans* (3–5). Illus. Series: Our Cultural Heritage. 2004, Child's World LB $18.95 (1-59296-181-9). 32pp. Covers Jewish migration to the United States, with material on the group's native culture, ethnic background, and the impact they have had on present-day American society.

19623 Sawyers, June S. *Famous Firsts of Scottish-Americans* (4–8). Illus. 1996, Pelican $13.95 (1-56554-122-7). Brief biographies of 30 Americans of Scottish descent, including Neil Armstrong, Alexander Calder, Herman Melville, and Patrick Henry. (Rev: BL 6/1–15/97) [920]

19624 Schanzer, Rosalyn. *Escaping to America: A True Story* (K–4). Illus. by author. 2000, Harper-Collins LB $15.89 (0-688-16990-2). This book tells how and why the author's Jewish grandparents left Poland in 1921 and describes their journey and arrival in America. (Rev: BL 8/00; HBG 3/01; SLJ 9/00) [973]

19625 Schouweiler, Thomas. *Germans in America* (5–7). Illus. Series: In America. 1994, Lerner LB $19.93 (0-8225-0245-3). 72pp. The causes and results of German immigration to the United States are outlined, with good coverage of their contributions and important figures. (Rev: BL 1/15/95; SLJ 12/94) [973]

19626 Shalant, Phyllis. *Look What We've Brought You from Vietnam: Crafts, Games, Recipes, Stories, and Other Cultural Activities from New Americans* (3–6). Illus. 1988, Simon & Schuster paper $6.95 (0-671-65978-2). 48pp. Activities to foster an appreciation of Vietnamese culture. (Rev: BL 9/1/88)

19627 Silverman, Robin L. *A Bosnian Family* (4–7). Illus. Series: Journey Between Two Worlds. 1997, Lerner LB $27.15 (0-8225-3404-5); paper $8.95 (0-8225-9754-3). 64pp. The story of Velma Dusper, her homeland of Bosnia, and her journey with her family to freedom and a new home in North Dakota. (Rev: BL 6/1–15/97; SLJ 7/97) [304.8]

19628 Smith, Charles R., Jr. *I Am America* (1–3). Photos by author. 2003, Scholastic $14.95 (0-439-

43179-4). Striking color photographs and simple text show children of multiple races and ethnicities. (Rev: HBG 4/04; SLJ 11/03) [305.23]

19629 Stanek, Muriel. *We Came from Vietnam* (4–6). Illus. 1985, Whitman LB $11.95 (0-8075-8699-4). 48pp. Photos and text focus on the Nguyen family from Vietnam, now settled in Chicago. (Rev: BCCB 11/85; BL 11/1/85)

19630 Straub, Deborah G., ed. *African American Voices* (5–8). Illus. 1996, Gale $105.00 (0-8103-9497-9). 320pp. This is a collection of excerpts from important speeches delivered by a vast array of African Americans, past and present. (Rev: SLJ 2/97) [973]

19631 Sullivan, Charles, ed. *Children of Promise: African-American Literature and Art for Young People* (4–8). Illus. 1991, Abrams $24.95 (0-8109-3170-2). 126pp. Through poems, songs, literary excerpts, and illustrations, the history of African Americans is traced. (Rev: BL 11/16/91; SLJ 1/92) [973]

19632 Taus-Bolstad, Stacy. *Puerto Ricans in America* (5–8). Series: In America. 2004, Lerner LB $27.93 (0-8225-3953-5). 80pp. This overview of Puerto Rican migration to the United States looks at the motivations for moving and explores the lives of the new arrivals and the traditions they maintained. (Rev: BL 11/15/04) [304.8]

19633 Teitelbaum, Michael. *Chinese Immigrants* (5–8). Series: Immigration to the United States. 2004, Facts on File $35.00 (0-8160-5687-0). 96pp. After an overview of the reasons underlying immigration in general, this illustrated volume looks at the circumstances of migrants from China, the group's history in the United States, and the contemporary situation, with sidebar features, a timeline, and a glossary. (Rev: SLJ 4/05)

19634 Temple, Bob. *The Arab Americans* (5–8). Illus. Series: We Came to America. 2002, Mason Crest LB $19.95 (1-59084-102-6). 64pp. Temple reviews the history of Arab immigration to North America, the group's customs and contributions, and famous Arab Americans, with the aid of photographs, a timeline, and glossary. (Rev: BL 7/02; SLJ 9/02) [305.892]

19635 Todd, Anne M. *Italian Immigrants: 1880–1920* (4–6). Series: Coming to America. 2001, Capstone LB $16.95 (0-7368-0796-9). 32pp. The rich heritage and cultural contributions of Italian Americans are covered in this book that also explores why and how they came to the United States. (Rev: BL 10/15/01; HBG 3/02) [973]

19636 Trumbauer, Lisa. *German Immigrants* (5–8). Series: Immigration to the United States. 2004, Facts on File $35.00 (0-8160-5683-8). 96pp. After an overview of the reasons underlying immigration in general, this illustrated volume looks at the circumstances of migrants from Germany, the group's history in the United States, and the contemporary situation, with sidebar features, a timeline, and a glossary. Also use *Russian Immigrants* (2004). (Rev: SLJ 4/05)

19637 Wallner, Rosemary. *Greek Immigrants: 1890–1920* (4–6). Series: Coming to America. 2002, Capstone LB $22.60 (0-7368-1206-7). 32pp. Using many primary sources, this book traces the causes of Greek immigration and provides information on the Greek immigrants' journeys, culture, integration, and contributions. (Rev: BL 1/1–15/03; HBG 3/03; SLJ 3/03) [973]

19638 Wallner, Rosemary. *Japanese Immigrants: 1850–1950* (4–6). Series: Coming to America. 2001, Capstone LB $16.95 (0-7368-0797-9). 32pp. A century of Japanese migration to the United States is detailed with material on their contributions, cultural heritage, and treatment on arrival. (Rev: BL 10/15/01) [973]

19639 Wallner, Rosemary. *Polish Immigrants: 1890–1920* (4–6). Series: Coming to America. 2002, Capstone LB $22.60 (0-7368-1208-3). 32pp. The exodus from Poland to America is traced through text, timelines, maps, and personal memoirs, with material on such topics as Polish culture, contributions to American life, and famous Polish Americans. (Rev: BL 1/1–15/03; HBG 3/03) [973]

19640 Watts, J. F. *The Irish Americans* (5–8). Series: Immigrant Experience. 1995, Chelsea paper $9.95 (0-7910-3388-0). A lively, informative account of why the Irish came to America, the conditions they found here, and how they have fared. (Rev: BL 10/15/95) [973]

19641 *We Are All Related: A Celebration of Our Cultural Heritage* (3–6). Illus. 1997, Orca paper $15.95 (0-9680479-0-4). 64pp. Reproduces the collages created by students at a Vancouver, B.C., elementary school during a yearlong arts program that focused on intercultural and intergenerational studies. (Rev: BL 8/97) [704]

19642 Weitzman, Elizabeth. *I Am Jewish American* (K–3). Series: Our American Family. 1998, Rosen LB $13.95 (0-8239-5006-9). 24pp. A young girl living in Chicago describes her feelings about her family and the Jewish American community of which she is a part. (Rev: SLJ 9/98) [973]

19643 Williams, Jean Kinney. *Asian Indian Americans* (3–5). Series: Spirit of America: Our Cultural Heritage. 2003, Child's World LB $27.07 (1-59296-015-4). 32pp. A brief look at the history of Indian immigration to the United States and an assessment of the community's contributions to American culture and society. (Rev: SLJ 2/04) [973]

19644 Wolf, Bernard. *Coming to America: A Muslim Family's Story* (3–5). Illus. 2003, Lee & Low $17.95 (1-58430-086-8); paper $7.95 (1-58430-177-5). 48pp. This bright photoessay offers useful insights into Islam and its adherents as it tells the story of a Muslim family's migration from Egypt to the United States. (Rev: BL 4/1/03; HB 5–6/03; HBG 10/03; SLJ 5/03) [305.892]

19645 Worth, Richard. *Mexican Immigrants* (5–8). Series: Immigration to the United States. 2004, Facts on File $35.00 (0-8160-5690-0). 96pp. After an overview of the reasons underlying immigration in general, this illustrated volume looks at the circumstances of migrants from Mexico, the group's

history in the United States, and the contemporary situation, with sidebar features, a timeline, and a glossary. Also use *Jewish Immigrants* and *Africans in America* (both 2004). (Rev: SLJ 4/05) [304.8]

19646 Wu, Dana Ying-Hul, and Jeffrey Dao-Sheng Tung. *The Chinese-American Experience* (5–7). Illus. Series: Coming to America. 1993, Millbrook LB $22.40 (1-56294-271-9). 64pp. The story of Chinese immigration to the United States, from exploitation, prejudice, and discrimination to gradual acceptance. (Rev: BL 6/1–15/93) [973]

19647 Yoder, Carolyn P. *Asian Indian Americans* (3–5). Series: We Are America. 2003, Heinemann LB $24.22 (1-4034-0167-5). 32pp. Yoder explores the challenges and hardships faced by Indian immigrants to America and the many contributions they have made to society as a whole. Also use *Italian Americans* (2003). (Rev: HBG 10/03; SLJ 8/03) [973]

Terrorism

19648 Bingley, Richard. *Terrorism* (5–9). Series: Face the Facts. 2003, Raintree LB $28.56 (0-7398-6852-7). 56pp. An examination of terrorism, its causes, and the efforts being made to combat it. (Rev: SLJ 4/04) [303.6]

19649 Buell, Tonya. *The Crash of United Flight 93 on September 11, 2001* (4–7). Series: Terrorist Attacks. 2003, Rosen LB $26.50 (0-8239-3857-3). 64pp. Buell focuses on the courage of the passengers and crew members who foiled the terrorist hijackers' plan to crash Flight 93 into a landmark in the nation's capital. (Rev: SLJ 10/03) [974.8]

19650 Hamilton, John. *Behind the Terror* (4–7). Series: War on Terrorism. 2002, ABDO LB $16.95 (1-57765-679-8). 48pp. Using an accessible text and color photographs, this book reports on various international terrorist organizations, their leaders, and their tactics. (Rev: BL 5/15/02) [909.9]

19651 Hamilton, John. *Operation Enduring Freedom* (4–7). Series: War on Terrorism. 2002, ABDO LB $25.65 (1-57765-665-2). 48pp. Using many color photographs and a matter-of-fact text, this book covers various aspects of the U.S. war against terrorism. (Rev: BL 5/15/02; HBG 10/02) [973.9]

19652 Hamilton, John. *Operation Noble Eagle* (4–7). Series: War on Terrorism. 2002, ABDO LB $25.65 (1-57765-664-4). 48pp. A look at U.S. efforts to police and defend its borders as part of the war on terroism. (Rev: BL 5/15/02; HBG 10/02) [973.9]

19653 Lalley, Patrick. *9.11.01: Terrorists Attack the U.S* (4–7). Illus. 2002, Raintree LB $31.40 (0-7398-6021-6). 48pp. A compact look at the terrorist attacks of September 11, 2001, their causes, the world of Islam, the history of the World Trade Center, and personal stories related to the attacks. (Rev: BL 4/1/02; HBG 10/02; SLJ 5/02) [303.6250]

19654 Louis, Nancy. *Heroes of the Day* (4–7). Series: War on Terrorism. 2002, ABDO LB $25.65 (1-57765-658-X). 48pp. This account of September 11, 2001, describes through pictures and case studies the gallant feats of firefighters, police, and those who fought back on Flight 93. (Rev: BL 5/15/02; HBG 10/02; SLJ 6/02) [973.9]

19655 Louis, Nancy. *United We Stand* (4–7). Series: War on Terrorism. 2002, ABDO LB $25.65 (1-57765-660-1). 48pp. In text and pictures, this account describes the support offered to the victims of the terrorist attacks of September 11, 2001, and their families. (Rev: BL 5/15/02; HBG 10/02) [909.9]

19656 Margulies, Phillip. *Al-Qaeda: Osama Bin Laden's Army of Terrorists* (5–7). Illus. Series: Inside the World's Most Infamous Terrorist Organizations. 2003, Rosen LB $26.50 (0-8239-3817-4). 64pp. Al-Qaeda's history, missions, methods, and structure are described, with a detailed profile of Osama Bin Laden. (Rev: BL 10/15/03) [973.93]

19657 Marquette, Scott. *America Under Attack* (4–7). Illus. Series: America at War. 2002, Rourke LB $27.93 (1-58952-386-5). 48pp. This book for middle graders explains in simple terms the September 11, 2001 attacks and other acts of terrorism against the United States, as well as discussing resulting legislation and changing opinions in America. (Rev: BL 10/15/02) [973.931]

19658 Roden, Katie. *Terrorism* (4–6). Illus. Series: Crimebusters. 1997, Millbrook LB $20.90 (0-7613-

0556-4). 32pp. Using many text boxes, photos, diagrams, file folder formats, and a fabricated crime to set the stage, this book studies the causes and effects of terrorism. (Rev: BL 6/1–15/97; SLJ 9/97) [363.2]

19659 Rosaler, Maxine. *Hamas: Palestinian Terrorists* (5–7). Illus. Series: Inside the World's Most Infamous Terrorist Organizations. 2003, Rosen LB $26.50 (0-8239-3820-4). 64pp. Hamas's history, missions, methods, and structure are described, with profiles of key figures. (Rev: BL 10/15/03) [950.940]

19660 Sherrow, Victoria. *The Oklahoma City Bombing: Terror in the Heartland* (4–8). Illus. Series: American Disasters. 1998, Enslow LB $18.95 (0-7660-1061-9). 48pp. Using many first-person descriptions, this account of the Oklahoma City bombing ends with the sentencing of Timothy McVeigh and Terry Nichols. (Rev: BL 1/1–15/99; BR 5–6/99; HBG 3/99; SLJ 3/99) [364.16]

19661 Sherrow, Victoria. *The World Trade Center Bombing: Terror in the Towers* (4–8). Illus. Series: American Disasters. 1998, Enslow LB $18.95 (0-7660-1056-2). An illustrated discussion of the events and individuals leading up to the 1993 World Trade Center bombing. (Rev: BL 1/1–15/99; BR 5–6/99; HBG 3/99; SLJ 3/99) [363.2]

Personal Development

Behavior

1051

General

19662 Andrews, Linda Wasmer. *Meditation* (3–6). Illus. Series: Life Balance. 2004, Watts LB $19.50 (0-531-12219-0). 79pp. Explores different forms of meditation, including yoga, zen, and transcendental meditation, and discusses how they can be used to reduce stress and improve mental well-being. (Rev: SLJ 7/04) [158.1]

19663 Barron, T. A. *The Hero's Trail: A Guide for Heroic Life* (4–7). Illus. 2002, Penguin Putnam $14.99 (0-399-23860-3). 160pp. This collection of anecdotes about both real and fictional characters aims to define heroism, and explores how one can lead a heroic life. (Rev: BL 10/15/02; HBG 3/03; SLJ 12/02) [170]

19664 Berger, Terry. *I Have Feelings* (1–5). Illus. 1971, Human Sciences $18.95 (0-87705-021-X); paper $10.95 (0-89885-342-7). 32pp. Text and photos show children that their feelings and emotions — good and bad — are natural.

19665 Borden, Sara, et al. *Middle School: How to Deal* (4–6). Illus. by Yuki Hatori. 2005, Chronicle LB $15.50 (0-8118-4845-0); paper $9.95 (0-8118-4497-8). 96pp. Advice from five 7th-grade girls on everything academic and social, with a dictionary of online chat conventions. (Rev: BL 6/1–15/05) [373.236]

19666 Damm, Antje. *Ask Me* (PS–3). Trans. from German by Doris Orgel. Illus. by author. 2003, Millbrook $14.95 (0-7613-1845-3). 220pp. This is a compilation of questions, ranging from the fairly basic to the thought-provoking and accompanied by imaginative illustrations, that can be used to prompt discussion. (Rev: BCCB 3/03; BL 4/1/03; HBG 10/03; SLJ 3/03) [306.874]

19667 Dee, Catherine, ed. *The Girls' Book of Friendship: Cool Quotes, True Stories, Secrets and More* (5–9). Illus. by Ali Douglass. 2001, Little, Brown paper $8.95 (0-316-16818-1). 194pp. A well-organized collection of humorous and affecting entries encompassing material from celebrities and everyday teens. (Rev: SLJ 11/01) [177]

19668 Doak, Robin. *Caring* (3–6). Series: Character Education. 2003, Raintree LB $24.26 (0-7398-5778-9). 32pp. Photographs and text illustrate the importance of compassion and caring. (Rev: HBG 3/03; SLJ 4/03)

19669 Dylan, Matthew. *Respect* (3–6). Series: Character Education. 2003, Raintree LB $24.26 (0-7398-5780-0). 32pp. This slim book examines respect from a number of points of view, including respect for authority, self, others, women, property rights, and the environment. (Rev: HBG 3/03; SLJ 4/03) [179]

19670 Erlbach, Arlene. *Worth the Risk: True Stories About Risk Takers, Plus How You Can Be One, Too* (5–9). Illus. 1999, Free Spirit paper $12.95 (1-57542-051-1). 127pp. These are 20 case studies of teenagers who took risks, from defying the dominant cliques in school to entering a burning house to save siblings. (Rev: BL 5/1/99; SLJ 8/99) [158]

19671 Fleming, Robert. *Rescuing a Neighborhood: The Bedford-Stuyvesant Volunteer Ambulance Corps* (4–8). Illus. 1995, Walker LB $16.85 (0-8027-8330-9). 48pp. The story of how two determined, dedicated men organized emergency response services in their inner-city neighborhood. (Rev: BL 5/1/95; SLJ 9/95) [362]

19672 Frost, Helen. *Feeling Angry* (PS–1). Series: Emotions. 2000, Capstone LB $13.25 (0-7368-0668-7). 24pp. Nine full-color photos and nine short sentences are used to illustrate anger. Others in the series are *Feeling Happy* and *Feeling Scared* (both 2000). (Rev: HBG 3/01; SLJ 1/01) [152.4]

19673 Gardner, Richard A. *The Girls and Boys Book About Good and Bad Behavior* (3–6). Illus. by Al Lowenheim. 1990, Creative Therapeutics paper $17.00 (0-933812-21-3). 221pp. This book talks about ethics and values. (Rev: SLJ 12/90) [155.5]

19674 Holyoke, Nancy. *A Smart Girl's Guide to Boys: Surviving Crushes, Staying True to Yourself, and Other Love Stuff* (4–6). Illus. 2001, Pleasant Co.

$9.95 (1-58485-368-9). 112pp. Age-appropriate advice on dealing with boys, first kisses, and balancing friends and boyfriends is interwoven with magazine-style quizzes and letters from girls. (Rev: BL 8/01; SLJ 9/01) [305.23]

19675 Hovanec, Erin M. *Get Involved! A Girl's Guide to Volunteering* (5–8). Series: Girls' Guides. 1999, Rosen LB $23.95 (0-8239-2985-X). 48pp. Two case studies of successful volunteers are given in this account that explains where to volunteer, how to approach organizations, and how to determine one's interests. (Rev: HBG 9/00; SLJ 1/00) [361]

19676 Hubbard, Woodleigh Marx. *All That You Are* (K–3). Illus. 2000, Penguin Putnam $12.99 (0-399-23364-4). 32pp. Various qualities that make a child special, such as loyalty and confidence, are pictured in this book about admirable human characteristics. (Rev: BL 3/1/00; HBG 3/01; SLJ 4/00) [158]

19677 Hughes, Monica. *First Day at School* (PS–2). Series: My First. 2004, Raintree LB $18.56 (1-4109-0643-4); paper $5.50 (1-4109-0669-8). 24pp. Simple language introduces young readers to what happens on the first day of school — coatrooms, classrooms, playtime, and so forth. Also use *First Vacation* (2004). [371]

19678 Inwald, Robin. *Cap It Off with a Smile: A Guide for Making Friends* (K–3). Illus. by author. 1994, Hilson Pr. $16.95 (1-885738-00-5). This book offers practical tips to young people on how they can make friends. (Rev: SLJ 12/94) [158]

19679 Jackson, Ellen. *Sometimes Bad Things Happen* (PS–2). Photos by Shelley Rotner. 2002, Millbrook LB $22.90 (0-7613-2810-6); paper $7.95 (0-7613-1734-1). Children are reassured that while bad things do happen, there are ways to cope and people who will want to help. (Rev: BL 11/15/02; HBG 3/03; SLJ 2/03)

19680 James, Elizabeth, and Carol Barkin. *How to Be School Smart: Secrets of Successful Schoolwork* (4–6). Illus. 1988, Morrow $15.00 (0-688-16130-8); Lothrop paper $4.95 (0-688-16139-1). Getting better grades is made easier in this easily read practical guide. (Rev: BL 3/15/88; SLJ 5/88)

19681 Johnston, Marianne. *Dealing with Anger* (2–4). Illus. Series: Conflict Resolution Library. 1996, Rosen LB $13.95 (0-8239-2325-8). 24pp. This simple introduction to anger defines it, explains its different forms, and tells how to handle it. (Rev: SLJ 9/96) [152.4]

19682 Karnes, Frances A., and Suzanne M. Bean. *Girls and Young Women Leading the Way: 20 True Stories About Leadership* (5–8). Illus. 1993, Free Spirit paper $12.95 (0-915793-52-0). 160pp. Contains case histories of 20 girls who changed their communities by starting projects such as collecting food for the homeless or starting a recycling program. (Rev: SLJ 12/93) [307.1]

19683 Kevi. *Don't Talk to Strangers* (K–3). Illus. Series: Hip Kid Hop. 2003, Scholastic $13.95 (0-439-31385-6). This attractive title, packaged with an audio CD, uses a rap rhyme to teach young readers

how to recognize and behave around strangers. (Rev: HBG 10/03; SLJ 9/03)

19684 Kincher, Jonni. *Psychology for Kids II: 40 Fun Experiments That Help You Learn About Others* (4–6). Illus. 1995, Free Spirit paper $17.95 (0-915793-83-0). 157pp. This second volume supplies more activities and projects to help explore the world of human behavior. (Rev: BL 7/95) [155.2]

19685 Klingel, Cynthia, and Robert B. Noyed. *Friendship* (K–3). Series: Wonder Books. 2002, Child's World LB $21.36 (1-56766-088-6). 32pp. A series of vignettes give everyday examples of how to make friends and how to be a friend. Also use *Honesty* and *Respect* (both 2002). (Rev: SLJ 12/02) [177]

19686 Lester, Julius. *Let's Talk About Race* (K–3). Illus. by Karen Barbour. 2005, HarperCollins LB $16.89 (0-06-028598-2). 32pp. Lester emphasizes that racial identity is only one of the many elements in an individual's makeup. (Rev: BL 2/1/05; SLJ 1/05) [305.8]

19687 Lewis, Barbara A. *The Kid's Guide to Service Projects: Over 500 Service Ideas for Young People Who Want to Make a Difference* (4–7). 1995, Free Spirit paper $12.95 (0-915793-82-2). 175pp. After an introduction on how to organize and conduct service projects, this book gives details on 500 ideas from running errands for seniors to working for voter registration. (Rev: SLJ 7/95) [307]

19688 Lewis, Barbara A. *The Kid's Guide to Social Action: How to Solve the Social Problems You Choose — and Turn Creative Thinking into Positive Action.* Rev. ed. (4–8). 1998, Free Spirit paper $18.95 (1-57542-038-4). An inspirational guide that shows how young people can make a difference by becoming involved in social action, such as instigating a cleanup of toxic waste, lobbying, or youth rights campaigns. (Rev: SLJ 1/99) [361.6]

19689 Lewis, Barbara S. *Being Your Best: Character Building for Kids 7–10* (4–6). Illus. 1999, Free Spirit paper $14.95 (1-57542-063-5). 148pp. A child-centered book that presents ten positive character traits and suggests practical ways and activities to develop and strengthen them. (Rev: BL 5/15/00) [155.2]

19690 Lound, Karen. *Girl Power in the Family: A Book About Girls, Their Rights, and Their Voice* (5–10). Series: Girl Power. 2000, Lerner LB $30.35 (0-8225-2692-1). 80pp. A book that explores the problems of growing up female today with material on gender roles, biases, and relationships. (Rev: HBG 10/00; SLJ 6/00) [303.6]

19691 MacGregor, Cynthia. *Think for Yourself: A Kid's Guide to Solving Life's Dilemmas and Other Sticky Problems* (3–6). Illus. by Susan Norberg Farias. 2003, Lobster paper $7.95 (1-894222-73-3). 96pp. Readers learn to identify problems and to work out solutions for themselves. (Rev: SLJ 2/04) [170]

19692 Madison, Lynda. *The Feelings Book: The Care and Keeping of Your Emotions* (4–6). Illus. by Norm Bendell. 2002, Pleasant Co. paper $8.95 (1-58485-528-2). 104pp. Madison tackles the topic of the emotional upheavals that many youngsters experience as they near their teens and offers tips on identifying and coping with strong feelings. (Rev: BL 12/1/02; SLJ 10/02) [155.43]

19693 Meiners, Cheri J. *Be Polite and Kind* (PS–1). Illus. by Meredith Johnson. 2004, Free Spirit paper $10.95 (1-57542-151-8). 40pp. This attractive picture book is designed to teach the simple virtues of courtesy and kindness. (Rev: BL 5/1/04; SLJ 8/04) [177]

19694 Meiners, Cheri J. *Join In and Play* (PS–1). Illus. by Meredith Johnson. 2004, Free Spirit paper $10.95 (1-57542-152-6). 40pp. The basic skills children need to interact happily with others are clearly communicated in this attractive picture book. (Rev: BL 5/1/04; SLJ 8/04) [790]

19695 *The Milestones Project: Celebrating Childhood Around the World* (PS–2). Photos by Richard Steckel and Michele Steckel. Illus. 2004, Tricycle $17.95 (1-58246-132-5). 64pp. Children around the world are shown in "milestone moments" — birthdays, losing a tooth, haircuts, playing with toys, and so forth. (Rev: BL 1/1–15/05; SLJ 11/04) [305.23]

19696 Montanari, Donata. *Children Around the World* (PS–K). Illus. by author. 2001, Kids Can $14.95 (1-55337-064-3). Readers are introduced to children in countries around the world who describe their lives in simple sentences that highlight their similarities and differences. (Rev: HBG 3/02; SLJ 12/01) [390.083]

19697 Murkoff, Heidi. *What to Expect at Preschool* (PS–K). Illus. by Laura Rader. Series: What to Expect. 2001, HarperCollins $7.99 (0-694-01326-9). 32pp. A dog named Angus addresses the concerns of anxious preschoolers in the question-and-answer format of the What to Expect series. (Rev: BL 11/15/01; HBG 3/02; SLJ 12/01) [372.21]

19698 Navarra, Tova. *The Kids' Guidebook: Great Advice to Help Kids Cope.* Rev. ed. (4–6). Illus. by Tom Kerr. 2002, Barron's paper $10.95 (0-7641-2066-2). 128pp. Advice on coping with difficult situations, from power outages and dealing with strangers to the death of a loved one. (Rev: SLJ 3/03)

19699 Nelson, Robin. *Being a Leader* (K–1). Illus. Series: First Step Nonfiction: Citizenship. 2003, Lerner LB $15.93 (0-8225-1287-4). 23pp. A basic look at what it takes to be a leader and how to become a good leader at home, school, and in the community. (Rev: HBG 4/04; SLJ 11/03) [303.3]

19700 Payne, Lauren M. *We Can Get Along: A Child's Book of Choices* (PS–2). Illus. by Claudia Rohling. 1997, Free Spirit paper $9.95 (1-57542-013-9). 36pp. A simple guide on getting along with others and how to be aware of other people's feelings. (Rev: BL 8/97; SLJ 4/97) [302]

19701 Peacock, Judith. *Anger Management* (5–8). Illus. Series: Perspectives on Mental Health. 2000, Capstone LB $23.93 (0-7368-0433-1). 64pp. A discussion of anger, its various types, its causes, its effects on the body and on others, and how and when to control it. (Rev: BL 8/00; HBG 9/00; SLJ 8/00) [152.4]

19702 Pendleton, Scott. *The Ultimate Guide to Student Contests, Grades K–6* (4–6). 1998, Walker paper $14.95 (0-8027-7513-6). 208pp. A directory of organizations that sponsor student competitions or reward outstanding student work, arranged by subject. (Rev: BL 3/15/98; SLJ 9/98) [370]

19703 Raatma, Lucia. *Determination* (2–4). Series: Character Education. 2002, Capstone LB $18.60 (0-7368-1387-X). 24pp. The characteristic is described, with examples of how to show determination and a famous person who exhibits it. Also use *Loyalty* and *Leadership* (both 2002). (Rev: HBG 3/03; SLJ 2/03)

19704 Robson, Pam. *Body Language* (2–5). Illus. Series: Hello Out There. 1997, Watts LB $20.00 (0-531-14468-2). 32pp. As well as giving good advice on reading the body signals of others, this book includes examples from the animal kingdom and a number of suggested activities. (Rev: BL 1/1–15/98; HBG 3/98; SLJ 3/98) [153.6]

19705 Romain, Trevor. *How to Do Homework Without Throwing Up* (3–6). Illus. by author. 1997, Free Spirit paper $8.95 (1-57542-011-2). 67pp. Using humorous text and drawings, this work supplies a positive approach to homework with many tips on how to do it efficiently. (Rev: SLJ 5/97) [371.3]

19706 Rotner, Shelley, and Sheila Kelly. *What Can You Do? A Book About Discovering What You Do Well* (PS–1). Photos by Shelley Rotner. Illus. 2001, Millbrook LB $21.90 (0-7613-2119-5). 24pp. With illustrations and text that show a variety of activities and talents, the authors ask readers to determine what they can do best. (Rev: BL 4/15/01; HBG 10/01; SLJ 9/01) [153.9]

19707 Salzmann, Mary Elizabeth. *I Am a Good Citizen* (K–2). Series: Building Character. 2003, ABDO LB $12.95 (1-57765-825-6). 23pp. A simple explanation of the character traits and behavior that make a good citizen. Also use *I Am Fair* (2003). (Rev: HBG 10/03; SLJ 9/03) [323.6]

19708 Sanders, Pete, and Steve Myers. *Feeling Violent* (3–6). Illus. by Mike Lacey. Series: What Do You Know About. 1997, Millbrook LB $20.90 (0-7613-0700-1). 32pp. This book explores violence, its different forms, its causes, and how to handle it. (Rev: HBG 9/98; SLJ 4/98) [616.8]

19709 Scheunemann, Pam. *Patriotism* (1–3). Series: United We Stand. 2003, ABDO LB $12.95 (1-57765-880-9). 24pp. A look at pride in one's country, with simple text and relevant, multicultural photographs. (Rev: HBG 10/03; SLJ 6/03) [323.6]

19710 Schuette, Sarah L. *I Am Cooperative* (PS–2). Series: Character Values. 2002, Capstone LB $14.60 (0-7368-1439-6). 24pp. Photographs and simple text are used to explain how to be cooperative. Also use *I Am Honest, I Am Respectful*, and *I Am Responsible*. (Rev: HBG 3/03; SLJ 3/03)

19711 Schuette, Sarah L. *Soy bondadosa / I Am Caring* (PS–2). Trans. by Martin Luis Guzman Ferrer. Series: Pebble Bilingual Books. 2003, Capstone LB $15.93 (0-7368-2301-8). 24pp. Good, caring behavior is illustrated and described in English and Spanish. Also use *Soy respetuoso/I Am Respectful, Soy cooperativa/I Am Cooperative*, and *Soy respons-*

able/I Am Responsible (all 2003). (Rev: SLJ 4/04) [395]

19712 Sheindlin, Judy. *Judge Judy Sheindlin's You Can't Judge a Book by Its Cover: Cool Rules for School* (2–5). Illus. by Bob Tore. 2001, Harper-Collins LB $14.89 (0-06-029484-1). Judge Judy looks at common choices young students have to make, presenting a range of possible decisions, some sensible and some clearly not. (Rev: HBG 10/01; SLJ 7/01) [170]

19713 Sheindlin, Judy. *Win or Lose by How You Choose!* (2–6). Illus. by Bob Tore. 2000, Harper-Collins LB $14.89 (0-06-028474-9). Television's Judge Judy offers questions and answers on issues involving character and value judgments. (Rev: HBG 9/00; SLJ 6/00) [305.2]

19714 Sherman, Joanne. *Because It's My Body!* (PS–2). Illus. by John S. Gurney. Series: Keep `em Safe. 2002, S.A.F.E. for Children paper $14.95 (0-9711735-0-8). 30pp. This text presents clear strategies for dealing with unwelcome attention, even from friends and family. (Rev: SLJ 12/02)

19715 Silverman, Robin L. *Reaching Your Goals* (4–8). Illus. Series: Life Balance. 2004, Watts LB $19.50 (0-531-12342-1); paper $6.95 (0-531-16691-0). 80pp. Practical advice on building self-confidence, making smart decisions, and focusing on achievable goals.

19716 Swain, Gwenyth. *Smiling* (PS–1). Illus. Series: Small Worlds. 1999, Carolrhoda $14.95 (1-57505-256-3). 24pp. Children from around the world, including China, Australia, Sudan, and Mexico, display a variety of smiles in this happy book about childhood. (Rev: BL 6/1–15/99; HBG 9/99; SLJ 6/99) [153.6]

19717 Waber, Bernard. *Courage* (K–3). Illus. 2002, Houghton Mifflin $12.00 (0-618-23855-7). 40pp. Waber introduces the concept of courage with amusing illustrations and examples that younger readers can understand. (Rev: BCCB 2/03; BL 12/15/02; HBG 3/03; SLJ 12/02) [179]

19718 Waters, Jennifer. *Be a Good Friend!* (K–1). Series: Spyglass Books. 2002, Compass Point LB $18.60 (0-7565-0376-0). 24pp. For beginning readers, this book lists the qualities that make a good friend. Also use *Be a Good Sport!* (2002). (Rev: SLJ 1/03)

19719 Williams, Venus, and Serena Williams. *Venus and Serena: Serving from the Hip* (5–8). Illus. 2005, Houghton Mifflin paper $14.00 (0-618-57653-3). 144pp. The successful Williams sisters offer practical advice on self-respect, friendship, financial security, and other pertinent topics. (Rev: BL 5/15/05; SLJ 4/05) [796.342]

Etiquette

19720 Aliki. *Manners* (K–3). Illus. 1990, Greenwillow $15.89 (0-688-09199-7). 32pp. Cartoon-style characters help make manners accessible to young readers. (Rev: BL 10/1/90; SLJ 11/90*) [395]

19721 Best, Alyse. *Miss Best's Etiquette for Young People: Manners for Real People in Today's World* (3–7). Illus. 1991, PEP paper $9.95 (0-945033-02-8). 137pp. Advice is given to young people on proper behavior for both formal and informal social events. (Rev: BL 9/15/91) [395]

19722 Cabot, Meg. *Princess Lessons* (5–7). Illus. by Chesley McLaren. Series: Princess Diaries. 2003, HarperCollins LB $14.89 (0-06-052678-5). 144pp. Princess Mia gives lighthearted tips and often quite practical tips on behaving like a real princess. (Rev: BL 5/15/03; HBG 10/03) [646.7]

19723 Doudna, Kelly. *Excuse Me* (PS–1). Series: Good Manners. 2001, ABDO LB $12.95 (1-57765-574-5). 24pp. Simple text suitable for beginning readers introduces the basic concept, accompanied by illustrations of children in appropriate situations. Also in this series are *Please* and *Thank You.* (Rev: HBG 3/02; SLJ 4/02) [395.1]

19724 Dougherty, Karla. *The Rules to Be Cool: Etiquette and Netiquette* (5–9). Series: Teen Issues. 2001, Enslow LB $17.95 (0-7660-1607-2). 64pp. Respect and consideration for others are the key elements of Dougherty's rules of behavior, with an emphasis on politeness, kindness, and courtesy, on the Internet as well as at home and at school. (Rev: HBG 3/02; SLJ 10/01) [395]

19725 Gibbs, Lynne. *Don't Slurp Your Soup! A First Guide to Letter Writing, E-Mail Etiquette, and Other Everyday Manners* (K–2). Illus. by John Eastwood. 2003, McGraw-Hill $14.95 (1-57768-556-3). 32pp. A lighthearted introduction to the basic rules of behavior, this guide covers table manners, party invitations, and phone etiquette. (Rev: BL 4/1/03; HBG 4/04; SLJ 8/03) [390]

19726 Holyoke, Nancy. *Oops! The Manners Guide for Girls* (3–7). Illus. by Debbie Tilley. Series: American Girl. 1997, Pleasant Co. paper $7.95 (1-56247-530-4). 116pp. An amusing book of manners aimed at girls that covers almost any situation. (Rev: SLJ 3/98) [393]

19727 James, Elizabeth, and Carol Barkin. *Social Smarts: Manners for Today's Kids* (4–7). Illus. 1996, Clarion paper $6.95 (0-395-81312-3). 103pp. Table manners and responsible, appropriate public behavior are two topics covered. (Rev: BL 9/1/96; SLJ 9/96) [395]

19728 Kirtland, Mark. *Why Do We Do That?* (4–6). Illus. Series: Why Do We? 1996, Watts LB $20.00 (0-531-14394-5). 31pp. Using cross-cultural and historical approaches, this book explores etiquette and protocol around the world. (Rev: SLJ 8/97) [395]

19729 Lauber, Patricia. *What You Never Knew About Fingers, Forks, and Chopsticks* (2–5). Illus. by John Manders. 1999, Simon & Schuster $16.00 (0-689-80479-2). 40pp. An amusing, fascinating look at manners and eating utensils, from the Stone Age to the present. (Rev: BCCB 12/99; BL 9/1/99*; HBG 4/00; SLJ 9/99) [394.1]

19730 Levitin, Sonia. *When Kangaroo Goes to School* (PS–1). Illus. by Jeff Seaver. 2001, Rising Moon $15.95 (0-87358-791-X). A guide to correct behavior at school designed to ease the fears of first-time students. (Rev: HBG 3/02; SLJ 12/01)

19731 Post, Peggy, and Cindy Post Senning. *Emily Post's The Guide to Good Manners for Kids* (4–7). Illus. by Steve Bjorkman. 2004, HarperCollins LB $16.89 (0-06-057197-7). 144pp. A useful guide to good manners, covering such fundamentals as thank-you notes, Internet safety, cell phone etiquette, and table manners. (Rev: BL 1/1–15/05; SLJ 12/04) [395.1]

19732 Raatma, Lucia. *Politeness* (K–2). Series: Character Education. 2002, Capstone LB $18.60 (0-7368-1134-6). 24pp. A how-to guide for the very young that provides a definition of politeness, shows how to display it, and offers some practice ideas. Also use *Self-Respect* and *Sportsmanship* (2002). (Rev: SLJ 6/02) [395.1]

19733 Smith, Mavis. *Mind Your Manners, Ben Bunny: A Lift-the-Flap Book About Table Manners* (PS–K). Illus. by author. 1998, Scholastic $8.95 (0-590-06844-X). This book uses flaps and advice from a crow to teach Ben Bunny and two friends proper table manners. (Rev: HBG 3/99; SLJ 7/98) [395]

19734 Stewart, Marjabelle Young, and Ann Buchwald. *What to Do When and Why* (4–7). 1988, Luce $14.95 (0-88331-105-4). An easily read introduction to the basics of good manners and behavior.

Family Relationships

19735 Aldape, Virginia Totorica. *David, Donny, and Darren: A Book About Identical Triplets* (2–4). Illus. Series: Meeting the Challenge. 1997, Lerner LB $21.27 (0-8225-2584-4). 40pp. Using a first-person narrative, this is the story of an identical triplet and how his life is different from those of average kids. (Rev: BL 3/15/98; HBG 3/98) [306.875]

19736 Bingham, Jane. *Why Do Families Break Up?* (4–8). Series: Exploring Tough Issues. 2004, Raintree LB $29.93 (0-7398-6683-4). 48pp. Every member of the family is considered in this comprehensive examination of divorce and how individuals of different ages cope. (Rev: SLJ 2/05) [306.8]

19737 Bode, Janet. *For Better, For Worse: A Guide to Surviving Divorce for Preteens and Their Families* (5–8). Illus. 2001, Simon & Schuster $16.00 (0-689-81945-5). 162pp. Using extensive interviews with preteens, this is a practical guide to handling divorce. Half of the book is for preteens, the other half for parents. (Rev: BCCB 2/01; BL 1/1–15/01; HBG 10/01; SLJ 2/01) [306.89]

19738 Brown, Laurie Krasny, and Marc Brown. *Dinosaurs Divorce: A Guide for Changing Families* (PS–3). Illus. by Marc Brown. 1988, Little, Brown $15.95 (0-316-11248-8); paper $7.95 (0-316-10996-7). 32pp. These green, somewhat crocodilian dinosaurs demonstrate all the feelings and problems children encounter with divorce in the family. (Rev: SLJ 10/86)

19739 Charlish, Anne. *Divorce* (5–10). Series: Talking Points. 1999, Raintree LB $27.12 (0-8172-5310-6). 64pp. An overview of the causes of divorce, the legal aspects, and the difficult adjustments that must be made. (Rev: BL 8/99; BR 9–10/99) [306.89]

19740 Cole, Joanna. *The New Baby at Your House.* Rev. ed. (PS–1). Illus. by Margaret Miller. 1998, Morrow $15.93 (0-688-13898-5). 48pp. A revision of the standard account on adjustments that are made in a family when a new baby arrives. (Rev: BL 3/1/98; HBG 9/98; SLJ 4/98) [306.875]

19741 Cooper, Kay. *Where Did You Get Those Eyes? A Guide to Discovering Your Family History* (5–7). Illus. by Anthony Accardo. 1988, Walker LB $14.85 (0-8027-6803-2). A helpful guide for researching the family tree. (Rev: BCCB 11/88; BL 1/15/89; SLJ 2/89)

19742 Currie, Stephen. *Adoption* (5–8). Illus. Series: Overview. 1997, Lucent LB $27.45 (1-56006-183-9). 96pp. A well-illustrated account of the history of adoption and present-day practices, procedures, and problems. (Rev: BL 5/15/97; SLJ 4/97) [362.7]

19743 Douglas, Ann. *The Family Tree Detective: Cracking the Case of Your Family's Story* (4–8). Illus. 1999, Owl paper $9.95 (1-895688-89-2). In 16 compact chapters, this book covers the basics of genealogical research — gathering information, using appropriate organizations, forms for making a family tree, and recording family facts. (Rev: SLJ 6/99) [929]

19744 Drescher, Joan. *Your Family, My Family* (K–3). Illus. by author. 1980, Walker LB $13.85 (0-8027-6383-9). 32pp. All kinds of family arrangements, such as single parents and working mothers, are described.

19745 Gardner, Richard A. *Boys and Girls Book About Divorce* (5–8). Illus. 1992, Bantam paper $6.99 (0-553-27619-0). 160pp. A self-help book written for adolescents trying to cope with parental marriage problems. [306.8]

19746 Gellman, Marc. *"Always Wear Clean Underwear!" and Other Ways Parents Say "I Love You"* (4–7). 1997, Morrow $14.95 (0-688-14492-6). 128pp. Some kids think that the expressions featured in this book are parental nagging, but the message really is that parents care. (Rev: BL 10/1/97; HBG 3/98; SLJ 11/97) [306.874]

19747 Goldentyer, Debra. *Divorce* (4–8). Series: Preteen Pressures. 1998, Raintree LB $25.69 (0-8172-5030-1). 48pp. This work discusses the reasons for divorce, the legal aspects, the effect on children, remarriage, and relationships with new family members. (Rev: BL 5/15/98; HBG 9/98; SLJ 6/98) [306.8]

19748 Greenberg, Keith E. *Family Abuse: Why Do People Hurt Each Other?* (3–6). Illus. 1994, Twenty-First Century LB $18.90 (0-8050-3183-9). 64pp. An easily read book that explores physical, emotional, and sexual abuse of children as well as neglect and abuse of spouses, the elderly, and the disabled. (Rev: SLJ 9/94) [362.7]

19749 Greenberg, Keith E. *Zack's Story: Growing Up with Same-Sex Parents* (5–7). Illus. Series: Meeting the Challenge. 1996, Lerner LB $25.55 (0-8225-2581-X). 32pp. A true account of 11-year-old

Zack, who is growing up with his lesbian mother and her lover, whom he has grown to regard as a second mother. (Rev: BL 10/15/96; SLJ 3/97) [306]

19750 Havelin, Kate. *Child Abuse: Why Do My Parents Hit Me?* (4–10). Series: Perspectives on Relationships. 1999, Capstone LB $16.95 (0-7368-0287-8). 64pp. This book defines the forms of child abuse, explains its causes and characteristics, and offers advice on handling it. (Rev: SLJ 5/00) [362.7]

19751 Havelin, Kate. *Family Violence: My Parents Hurt Each Other!* (4–10). 1999, Capstone LB $16.95 (0-7368-0286-X). 64pp. Examines causes and forms of domestic violence and offers coping strategies. (Rev: SLJ 5/00) [364.3]

19752 Holyoke, Nancy. *Help! A Girl's Guide to Divorce and Stepfamilies* (3–6). Illus. 1999, Pleasant Co. paper $8.95 (1-56247-749-8). 128pp. An upbeat account about divorce and stepfamilies, including topics such as fear, guilt, anger, money, violence, and parents' dating. (Rev: BL 2/1/00; SLJ 11/99) [306.89]

19753 Hughes, Monica. *First Brother or Sister* (PS–2). Series: My First. 2004, Raintree LB $18.56 (1-4109-0644-2). 24pp. Color photographs and simple narrative are tailor-made for only children whose families are awaiting the arrival of a new baby. (Rev: BL 4/1/04) [306.875]

19754 Isler, Claudia. *Caught in the Middle: A Teen Guide to Custody* (5–8). Series: The Divorce Resource. 2000, Rosen LB $26.50 (0-8239-3109-9). 64pp. This book about divorce uses many actual case histories to explore such questions as what happens to the children when parents divorce and whether grandparents get visitation rights. (Rev: SLJ 6/00) [306.8]

19755 Johnson, Julie. *My Stepfamily* (2–4). Series: How Do I Feel About. 1998, Millbrook LB $19.90 (0-7613-0868-7). 24pp. Four children explain their feelings about being part of a stepfamily and how they have dealt with various situations. (Rev: HBG 9/99; SLJ 4/99) [646.7]

19756 Kandel, Bethany. *Trevor's Story: Growing Up Biracial* (2–4). Illus. Series: Meeting the Challenge. 1997, Lerner LB $21.27 (0-8225-2583-6). 40pp. A first-person narrative in which a boy talks about the racism he has had to face growing up with a white mother and an African American father. (Rev: BL 3/15/98; HBG 3/98) [362.1]

19757 Koh, Frances M. *Adopted from Asia: How It Feels to Grow Up in America* (5–8). 1993, East-West $16.95 (0-9606090-6-7). 95pp. The author has gathered stories, impressions, and opinions from 11 young people who were born in Korea and adopted by Caucasian Americans. (Rev: BL 2/15/94) [306.874]

19758 Krementz, Jill. *How It Feels to Be Adopted* (5–8). Illus. 1988, Knopf paper $15.00 (0-394-75853-6). Interviews with 19 young people, ages 8 to 16, on how it feels to be adopted. [362.7]

19759 Krementz, Jill. *How It Feels When Parents Divorce* (4–8). Illus. 1988, Knopf paper $15.00 (0-394-75855-2). Boys and girls, ages 8 to 16, share their experiences with divorced parents. [306.8]

19760 Krohn, Katherine. *Everything You Need to Know About Birth Order* (5–9). Series: Need to Know Library. 2000, Rosen LB $18.95 (0-8239-3228-1). 64pp. An interesting book that looks at a number of theories about how birth order affects people. (Rev: SLJ 12/00) [306.85]

19761 Krohn, Katherine. *You and Your Parents' Divorce* (5–8). Series: Family Matters. 2001, Rosen LB $23.95 (0-8239-3354-7). 48pp. Krohn writes about the practicalities and emotional problems of divorce in a style suitable for reluctant readers. (Rev: SLJ 8/01) [155.44]

19762 Landau, Elaine. *Sibling Rivalry: Brothers and Sisters at Odds* (3–6). Illus. 1994, Millbrook LB $19.90 (1-56294-328-6). 64pp. Factors that influence sibling rivalry, such as family size, gender, and divorce, are discussed, with tips on how to understand and lessen the problem. (Rev: BL 5/1/94; SLJ 4/94) [306]

19763 Leibowitz, Julie. *Finding Your Place: A Teen Guide to Life in a Blended Family* (5–8). 2000, Rosen LB $26.50 (0-8239-3114-5). 64pp. This book explores possible problems and solutions for members of blended families. (Rev: SLJ 6/00) [645.7]

19764 Lindsay, Jeanne W. *Do I Have a Daddy? A Story About a Single-Parent Child* (PS–2). Illus. by Jami Moffett. 2000, Morning Glory $14.95 (1-885356-62-5); paper $7.95 (1-885356-63-3). 48pp. A single mother reassures her son that, although he does not have a father, his uncle and grandfather will be there to help him. (Rev: BL 5/15/00; HBG 9/00; SLJ 7/00) [306.85]

19765 MacGregor, Cynthia. *The Divorce Helpbook for Kids* (4–7). 2001, Impact paper $12.95 (1-886230-39-0). 112pp. In this candid, honest book, a divorced mother gives advice to children about how to survive their parent's divorce. (Rev: BL 2/1/02; SLJ 3/02) [306.89]

19766 Morris, Ann. *The Daddy Book* (PS). Illus. Series: The World's Family. 1995, Silver Burdett $13.95 (0-382-24695-0); paper $5.95 (0-382-24697-7). 32pp. In this photograph album, all kinds of daddies engage in everyday activities, like going fishing and telling stories. (Rev: BL 2/15/96; SLJ 5/96) [306]

19767 Morris, Ann. *Families* (PS–1). Illus. 2000, HarperCollins LB $15.89 (0-688-17199-0). 32pp. Different kinds of families around the world are introduced in this photo-essay that uses very little text. (Rev: BL 5/15/00; HBG 9/00; SLJ 5/00) [306.85]

19768 Morris, Ann. *Loving* (PS–2). Illus. by Ken Heyman. 1990, Lothrop LB $15.93 (0-688-06341-1). 32pp. Clear photos focus on children, their families, and their pets. Also use *On the Go* (1990). (Rev: BL 1/1/91; SLJ 1/91) [306.7]

19769 Morris, Ann. *The Mommy Book* (PS). Illus. Series: The World's Family. 1995, Silver Burdett LB $22.00 (0-382-24693-4); paper $5.95 (0-382-24694-2). 32pp. Photographs from around the world depict mothers and children in a variety of shared experiences. (Rev: BL 2/15/96; SLJ 5/96) [306]

19770 Powell, Jillian. *Adoption* (2–3). Series: Talking About. 1999, Raintree LB $15.98 (0-8172-5890-6). 32pp. Stories with happy endings enhance this simple account of adoptions — their meaning, reasons, and effects on children's feelings. (Rev: BL 2/15/00; HBG 9/00) [362.7]

19771 Powell, Jillian. *Family Breakup* (1–3). Photos by Martyn F. Chillmaid. Series: Talking About. 1999, Raintree LB $22.83 (0-8172-5542-7). 32pp. Covers children's concerns when a family is breaking up — why this happens, what becomes of the children, who one can talk to, and what a stepfamily is. (Rev: HBG 9/99; SLJ 7/99) [306.8]

19772 Roca, Nuria. *La Familia: Del Pequeño al Mayor / Family: From the Youngest to the Oldest* (K–3). Illus. by Rosa Maria Curto. 2000, Barron's paper $6.95 (0-7641-1688-6). 36pp. The message of this book, originally published in Spain, is that families come in many different forms. (Rev: BL 10/1/01)

19773 Rosenberg, Maxine B. *Living with a Single Parent* (4–7). 1992, Macmillan $14.95 (0-02-777915-7). 160pp. In interview format, this topic is presented through the opinions of youngsters from eight to 13. (Rev: BCCB 2/93; BL 11/15/92; SLJ 12/92) [306.85]

19774 Rotner, Shelley, and Sheila Kelly. *Lots of Grandparents* (PS–1). Illus. 2001, Millbrook $23.90 (0-7613-2313-9). 24pp. A collection of color photographs showing grandparents of various ethnicities engaged in many activities. (Rev: BL 9/1/01; HBG 3/02; SLJ 9/01) [306.874]

19775 Rubel, Nicole. *Twice As Nice: What It's Like to Be a Twin* (3–5). 2004, Farrar $16.50 (0-374-31836-0). 32pp. An entertaining exploration of the biology, psychology, and advantages and disadvantages of being — and parenting — a twin. (Rev: BL 11/15/04; SLJ 11/04) [306.875]

19776 Sanders, Pete, and Steve Myers. *Divorce and Separation* (4–8). Illus. Series: What Do You Know About. 1997, Millbrook LB $23.90 (0-7613-0574-2). An introduction to separation and divorce, with an emphasis on tips to help youngsters adjust and cope. (Rev: SLJ 10/97) [306.8]

19777 Schwartz, Perry. *Carolyn's Story: A Book About an Adopted Girl* (5–7). Illus. Series: Meeting the Challenge. 1996, Lerner LB $25.55 (0-8225-2580-1). 40pp. Using fictional case histories, various aspects of adoption are explored. (Rev: BL 10/15/96; SLJ 4/97) [362.7]

19778 Shaggy. *Hope* (K–3). Illus. by Jr Buckingham, Joseph. Series: Hip Kid Hop. 2003, Scholastic $13.95 (0-439-38048-0). In this inspiring story, packaged with an audio CD, popular reggae singer Shaggy tells how his mother's love guided him through childhood hardships and put him on the road to a successful life. (Rev: HBG 10/03; SLJ 9/03)

19779 Simon, Norma. *All Kinds of Families* (4–6). Illus. by Joe Lasker. 1976, Whitman LB $14.95 (0-8075-0282-0). 40pp. Explores various kinds of families and their problems.

19780 Snow, Judith E. *How It Feels to Have a Gay or Lesbian Parent: A Book by Kids for Kids of All Ages* (5–8). 2004, Haworth $19.95 (1-56023-419-9); paper $12.95 (1-56023-420-2). 110pp. Diverse reflections on what it means to have a gay or lesbian parent come from children, young adults, and adults (up to age 31). (Rev: BL 1/1–15/05; SLJ 10/04) [306.874]

19781 Stein, Sara Bonnett. *On Divorce* (2–4). Illus. 1979, Walker $10.95 (0-8027-6344-8); paper $4.95 (0-8027-7226-9). Photographs and text cover this subject in an elementary fashion.

19782 Thomas, Pat. *My Family's Changing* (PS–2). Illus. by Lesley Harker. 1999, Barron's paper $5.95 (0-7641-0995-2). 32pp. A beginning book about divorce and how it affects different members of the family. (Rev: BL 5/15/99; SLJ 6/99) [306.89]

19783 Tym, Kate, and Penny Worms. *Coping with Families: A Guide to Taking Control of Your Life* (5–8). Series: Get Real. 2004, Raintree LB $29.93 (1-4109-0574-8). 48pp. Expert advice and case studies are presented in an appealing format, plus a list of hotline numbers. Also use *Coping with Friends* (2004). (Rev: SLJ 5/05)

19784 Weitzman, Elizabeth. *Let's Talk About Foster Homes* (K–2). Illus. Series: Let's Talk. 1996, Rosen LB $15.93 (0-8239-2310-X). 24pp. After defining what a foster home is, this title explains why some children are placed in one and the adjustments that they must make. Other family problems are explored in *Let's Talk About Staying in a Shelter, Let's Talk About When a Parent Dies,* and *Let's Talk About Your Parents' Divorce* (all 1996). (Rev: SLJ 12/96) [362.7]

19785 Wolfman, Ira. *Climbing Your Family Tree: Online and Off-Line Genealogy for Kids.* Rev. ed. (5–9). Illus. by Tim Robinson. 2002, Workman paper $13.95 (0-7611-2539-6). 228pp. A wide-ranging look at genealogy and the ways of tracing family names through document research, interviews, and the World Wide Web. (Rev: SLJ 2/03) [929]

Personal Problems and Relationships

19786 Adams, Lisa K. *Dealing with Teasing* (K–4). Series: Conflict Resolution Library. 1997, Rosen LB $13.95 (0-8239-5070-0). 24pp. This book explains the different kinds of teasing — from the innocent to the harmful — and how to cope when teasing gets out of hand. (Rev: SLJ 4/98) [152.4]

19787 Arredia, Joni. *Sex, Boys, and You: Be Your Own Best Girlfriend* (5–9). Illus. 1998, Perc Publg. paper $15.95 (0-9653203-2-4). A self-help book for younger teen girls with advice on how to accept oneself, when to say "no" to sex, how to assess one's strengths and weaknesses, and how to develop healthy relationships with boys. (Rev: SLJ 10/98) [305.23]

19788 Ayer, Eleanor. *Homeless Children* (5–8). Illus. Series: Overview. 1997, Lucent LB $27.45 (1-56006-177-4). The causes and consequences of homelessness are explored, with a focus on children and the ways the problem is being handled. (Rev: BL 3/15/97) [362.7]

19789 Brown, Laurie Krasny. *When Dinosaurs Die: A Guide to Understanding Death* (K–3). Illus. by Marc Brown. 1996, Little, Brown $14.95 (0-316-10917-7). 32pp. A beginner's book about death and its meaning. (Rev: BCCB 3/96; BL 4/1/96; HB 9–10/96; SLJ 4/96) [155.9]

19790 Cohen-Posey, Kate. *How to Handle Bullies, Teasers and Other Meanies: A Book That Takes the Nuisance out of Name Calling and Other Nonsense* (4–7). 1995, Rainbow paper $8.95 (1-56825-029-0). 91pp. A practical book that offers useful suggestions on how to handle bullies. (Rev: BCCB 12/95; BL 11/15/95) [646.7]

19791 Cordes, Helen. *Girl Power in the Classroom: A Book About Girls, Their Fears, and Their Future* (5–8). Illus. 2000, Lerner LB $30.35 (0-8225-2693-X). 112pp. This book of personal guidance for girls describes how to conquer fears and cope with difficult situations at school. (Rev: BL 5/15/00; HBG 9/00; SLJ 5/00) [373.1822]

19792 Cordes, Helen. *Girl Power in the Mirror: A Book About Girls, Their Bodies, and Themselves* (5–8). Illus. 2000, Lerner LB $30.35 (0-8225-2691-3). 112pp. This book for girls explains proper attitudes about appearance and gives coping strategies concerning pressures about one's looks. (Rev: BL 5/15/00; HBG 9/00; SLJ 5/00) [306.4]

19793 Crist, James J. *What to Do When You're Scared and Worried: A Guide for Kids* (5–8). Illus. by Michael Chesworth. 2004, Free Spirit paper $9.95 (1-57542-153-4). 123pp. Reassuring words and sound advice for young people troubled by such diverse issues as school exams, bullies, terrorism, nightmares, monsters, and the dark. (Rev: SLJ 7/04) [152.4]

19794 Dee, Catherine, ed. *The Girls' Book of Wisdom: Empowering, Inspirational Quotes from Over 400 Fabulous Females* (5–8). Illus. by Lou M. Pollack. 1999, Little, Brown paper $8.95 (0-316-17956-6). 192pp. A collection of quotations from more than 400 famous women grouped by such subjects as "Friends," "Happiness," and "Leadership." (Rev: SLJ 12/99) [305.23]

19795 Erlbach, Arlene. *The Middle School Survival Guide* (5–7). Illus. by Helen Flook. 2003, Walker $16.95 (0-8027-8852-1); paper $8.95 (0-8027-7657-4). 160pp. The author offers tips on a wide variety of topics of interest to this age group (homework, drugs, sex, and so forth), interspersed with advice from students themselves. (Rev: BL 9/15/03; HBG 4/04; SLJ 9/03) [373.18]

19796 Fisher, Enid. *Emotional Ups and Downs* (4–6). Series: Good Health Guides. 1998, Gareth Stevens LB $14.95 (0-8368-2179-3). 32pp. A heavily illustrated account that covers such topics as handling emotions such as shyness and anger; dealing with bullies, death of a loved one, and divorce; and coping with difficult family situations and with problems involving personal relationships. (Rev: HBG 9/99; SLJ 6/99) [362]

19797 Foltz, Linda Lee. *Kids Helping Kids: Break the Silence of Sexual Abuse* (4–9). 2003, Lighthouse Point $21.95 (0-9637966-8-2); paper $14.95 (0-9637966-9-0). 141pp. Personal stories from young people and adults who suffered abuse as children illustrate the guilt and shame typically experienced and show how to get help. (Rev: SLJ 9/03) [362.7]

19798 Goldentyer, Debra. *Child Abuse* (4–8). Series: Preteen Pressures. 1998, Raintree LB $25.69 (0-8172-5032-8). 48pp. This work describes the types, causes, and effects of child abuse and supplies material on how to change an abusive situation. (Rev: BL 5/15/98; HBG 9/98) [362.7]

19799 Greenberg, Judith E. *A Girl's Guide to Growing Up: Making the Right Choices* (5–8). Illus. 2000, Watts LB $23.00 (0-531-11592-5). 144pp. Lots of personal stories are quoted in this guidance book for preteen and teenage girls dealing with such subjects as school, risky behaviors, dating, sex, self-esteem, eating disorders, and cliques. (Rev: BL 2/15/01; SLJ 4/01) [305.23]

19800 Gurian, Michael. *From Boys to Men: All About Adolescence and You* (5–7). Illus. by Brian Floca. Series: Plugged In. 1999, Price Stern Sloan paper $4.99 (0-8431-7483-8). 86pp. Using a conversational tone, the author covers preteen emotional and physical changes and discusses topics including friendship, social and sexual relationships, peer pressure, and keeping healthy as they relate to boys. (Rev: SLJ 7/99) [605.23]

19801 Halperin, Wendy A. *Love Is . . .* (PS–3). Illus. 2001, Simon & Schuster $16.00 (0-689-82980-9). 32pp. Different kinds of love are explored in this unusually beautiful picture book. (Rev: BL 1/1–15/01*; HBG 10/01; SLJ 2/01) [242]

19802 Hartman, Holly, ed. *Girlwonder: Every Girl's Guide to the Fantastic Feats, Cool Qualities, and Remarkable Abilities of Women and Girls* (4–8). Illus. 2003, Houghton Mifflin paper $9.95 (0-618-31939-5). 234pp. A browsable look at famous women and their accomplishments, interspersed with information and advice on topics ranging from romance to fashion. (Rev: SLJ 5/04) [305.235]

19803 Heegaard, Mary E. *Coping with Death and Grief* (4–6). 1990, Lerner LB $19.93 (0-8225-0043-4). 64pp. This account helps children understand how the grieving process promotes emotional growth. (Rev: BL 11/1/90; SLJ 11/90) [155.6]

19804 Hyde, Margaret O. *Know About Abuse* (5–7). Illus. 1992, Walker LB $14.85 (0-8027-8177-2). 93pp. Various kinds of abuse in the home are described and information on how to get help is given. (Rev: SLJ 9/92) [362.7]

19805 Johnson, Julie. *Bullies and Gangs* (2–4). Photos by Roger Vlitos. Illus. by Chris O'Neill. Series: How Do I Feel About. 1998, Millbrook LB $19.90 (0-7613-0807-5). 24pp. This work describes how and why bullies behave the way they do and how to cope with them. (Rev: HBG 9/98; SLJ 7/98) [646.7]

19806 Johnston, Marianne. *Dealing with Bullying* (K–3). Illus. Series: Conflict Resolution Library. 1996, Rosen LB $15.93 (0-8239-2374-6). 24pp. A helpful book that helps young people understand bullies and offers techniques for self-protection. (Rev: SLJ 1/97) [155.5]

19807 Johnston, Marianne. *Let's Talk About Being Shy* (4–8). Illus. Series: Let's Talk. 1996, Rosen LB $17.25 (0-8239-2304-5). 24pp. The causes and possible cures of shyness are covered in this straightforward discussion. Also use *Let's Talk About Being Afraid* (1996). (Rev: BL 3/15/97) [155.4]

19808 Kent, Susan. *Let's Talk About Needing Extra Help at School* (3–5). Series: Let's Talk. 2000, Rosen LB $17.26 (0-8239-5422-6). 24pp. Using actual cases and realistic photos, this book explores the many reasons why kids might need extra help at school and what they can do about it. (Rev: SLJ 2/01) [371.2]

19809 Levete, Sarah. *Being Jealous* (1–3). Illus. by Chris O'Neill. Series: How Do I Feel About. 1999, Millbrook LB $19.90 (0-7613-0911-X). 24pp. The experiences of five youngsters in the same class are used to explore the concept of jealousy. (Rev: BL 9/15/99; HBG 9/99; SLJ 12/99) [152.4]

19810 McIntyre, Tom. *The Behavior Survival Guide for Kids: How to Make Good Choices and Stay out of Trouble* (4–7). Illus. by Chris Sharp. 2003, Free Spirit paper $12.95 (1-57542-132-1). 167pp. This accessible guide offers concrete suggestions for dealing with behavior disorders and improving relations with teachers, family members, and friends. (Rev: SLJ 1/04) [649]

19811 Middleton, Don. *Dealing with Competitiveness* (2–4). Series: Conflict Resolution Library. 1999, Rosen $17.26 (0-8239-5267-3). 24pp. An attractive introduction to this difficult subject that uses fictional anecdotes to explain the nature of competitiveness and its problems and solutions. Also use (from the same series and author) *Dealing with Secrets* (1998). (Rev: SLJ 4/99) [155]

19812 Moehn, Heather. *Everything You Need to Know About Cliques* (5–8). Series: Need to Know Library. 2001, Rosen LB $25.25 (0-8239-3326-1). 64pp. Moehn uses first-person narratives to introduce such topics as making friends, peer pressure, bullies, insecurity, and popularity, with a look at how cliques continue after high school. (Rev: SLJ 12/01) [158.25]

19813 Monson-Burton, Marianne, comp. *Girls Know Best 2: Tips On Life and Fun Stuff to Do!* (5–8). Series: Girl Power. 1998, Beyond Words paper $8.95 (1-885223-84-6). 152pp. Girls ages 10 to 16 give hundreds of tips, bits of advice, and projects concerning adolescent problems both serious and trivial. (Rev: SLJ 1/99) [155]

19814 Nichelason, Margery G. *Homeless or Hopeless?* (5–8). Illus. Series: Pro/Con Issues. 1994, Lerner LB $30.35 (0-8225-2606-9). 112pp. After an explanation of the roots and causes of homelessness, clearly written statements debate who is responsible for homelessness and how it should be handled. (Rev: BL 6/1–15/94; SLJ 7/94) [362.5]

19815 O'Neill, Terry. *The Homeless: Distinguishing Between Fact and Opinion* (4–7). Illus. Series: Opposing Viewpoints Juniors. 1991, Greenwillow LB $16.20 (0-89908-605-5). 32pp. Homelessness is

explored, with different points of view on how serious the problem is and who is to blame. (Rev: BL 6/15/91) [362.5]

19816 Peacock, Carol Antoinette. *Death and Dying* (4–8). Illus. Series: Life Balance. 2004, Watts LB $19.50 (0-531-12370-7); paper $6.95 (0-531-16728-3). 80pp. A practical guide to dealing with death and dying, with advice on seeking help when necessary.

19817 Polland, Barbara K. *We Can Work it Out: Conflict Resolution for Children* (K–3). Illus. by Craig DeRoy. 2000, Tricycle $13.95 (1-58246-031-0). 64pp. This book poses questions about various kinds of behavioral problems (e.g., teasing, poor sportsmanship) and enables children to solve these problems through self-direction. (Rev: BL 1/1–15/01; HBG 10/01) [303.6]

19818 Powell, Jillian. *Talking About Bullying* (2–3). Illus. Series: Talking About. 1999, Raintree LB $22.83 (0-8172-5535-4). 32pp. This book explains to young children why kids become bullies and how to cope with them. (Rev: BL 7/99; HBG 9/99; SLJ 7/99) [371.58]

19819 Radabaugh, Melinda. *Sleeping Over* (PS–1). Series: First Time. 2003, Heinemann LB $18.50 (1-4034-0231-0). 24pp. Reassuring text and photographs introduce various kinds of sleepovers. (Rev: HBG 10/03; SLJ 9/03) [793.2]

19820 Rimm, Sylvia. *See Jane Win for Girls: A Smart Girl's Guide to Success* (5–9). Illus. 2003, Free Spirit paper $13.95 (1-57542-122-4). 131pp. Rimm offers practical advice on social and academic achievement and general life skills, with quizzes, activities, and success stories. (Rev: SLJ 6/03) [305.235]

19821 Roehm, Michelle, comp. *Girls Know Best: Advice for Girls from Girls on Just About Everything!* (5–9). 1997, Beyond Words paper $8.95 (1-885223-63-3). In 26 topically arranged chapters, girls ranging in age from 7 to 16 give advice on such matters as life's embarrassments, difficult parents, volunteerism, boys, depression, divorce, backyard camping, and saving the environment. (Rev: SLJ 12/97) [305.23]

19822 Romain, Trevor. *Bullies Are a Pain in the Brain* (3–7). Illus. by author. 1997, Free Spirit paper $9.95 (1-57542-023-6). 105pp. Explains why bullies act the way they do, types of bullying, and ways to cope with it. (Rev: SLJ 2/98) [371.5]

19823 Romain, Trevor. *Cliques, Phonies, and Other Baloney* (3–8). Illus. by author. 1998, Free Spirit paper $9.95 (1-57542-045-7). 136pp. This book deals with social groups centered around friendships (many false and destructive) and suggests ways to form and hold solid friendships. (Rev: SLJ 4/99) [177]

19824 Ross, Dave. *A Book of Friends* (PS–3). Illus. by Laura Rader. 1999, HarperCollins LB $12.89 (0-06-028362-9). This simple picture book shows in words and pictures how to be a good friend. (Rev: HBG 9/99; SLJ 7/99) [177]

19825 Sanders, Pete, and Steve Myers. *It's My Life* (5–9). Illus. Series: Life Education. 1997, Watts paper $19.00 (0-531-14429-1). This book of practical advice focuses on the emotional changes that accompany the onset of puberty and adolescence, including relationships with families and friends, lifestyle choices, peer pressure, drugs, and making decisions. (Rev: BCCB 3/98; HBG 3/98; SLJ 1/98) [305.23]

19826 Seymour-Jones, Carole. *Homelessness* (5–9). Series: Past and Present. 1993, Macmillan $20.00 (0-02-786882-6). A discussion of the causes of homelessness, the extent of the problem and who is affected, and ways to end it. (Rev: BL 8/93) [362.5]

19827 Spelman, Cornelia Maude. *Your Body Belongs to You* (K–3). Illus. by Teri Weidner. 1997, Whitman LB $13.95 (0-8075-9474-1). 24pp. An introduction to child sexual abuse, with a special section of advice for parents. (Rev: BL 9/1/97; HBG 3/98; SLJ 9/97) [613.6]

19828 Stearman, Kaye. *Why Do People Live on the Streets?* (5–7). Series: Exploring Tough Issues. 2001, Raintree LB $25.69 (0-7398-3232-8). 48pp. Among reasons given for homelessness are poverty and discrimination. (Rev: HBG 10/01; SLJ 7/01) [305.569]

19829 Waldman, Jackie. *Teens with the Courage to Give: Young People Who Triumphed Over Tragedy and Volunteered to Make a Difference* (4–10). 2000, Conari paper $15.95 (1-57324-504-6). 240pp. A compelling set of narratives in which 30 teens describe how they conquered various personal problems, such as loss of a limb or drug addiction, and went on to help others solve their problems. (Rev: BL 4/1/00) [179]

19830 Weston, Carol. *For Girls Only: Wise Words, Good Advice* (4–8). 1998, Avon paper $5.99 (0-380-79538-8). Arranged by broad topics — friendship, love, and family, for example — this is a collection of quotations from people ranging from Aesop and Socrates to Oprah Winfrey and Madonna. (Rev: SLJ 7/98) [305.23]

19831 Weston, Carol. *Private and Personal: Questions and Answers for Girls Only* (5–7). 2000, HarperCollins paper $10.99 (0-380-81025-5). 272pp. Using categories such as family, friendship, boyfriends, and growing up, this book consists of letters requesting advice and the author's responses to these letters. (Rev: BL 5/1/00; SLJ 7/00) [158]

19832 Worth, Richard. *Poverty* (5–8). Illus. Series: Overview. 1997, Lucent LB $27.45 (1-56006-192-8). A carefully researched title that gives a history of poverty in America, changing attitudes toward it, and current policies and practices. (Rev: BL 8/97; SLJ 9/97) [362.5]

Careers

General and Miscellaneous

19833 Bauld, Jane Scoggins. *We Need Librarians* (PS–1). Series: Helpers in Our Schools. 2000, Capstone LB $13.25 (0-7368-0531-1). 24pp. The many roles of school librarians are discussed in this beginning reader. (Rev: HBG 9/00; SLJ 10/00) [027]

19834 Bauld, Jane Scoggins. *We Need Principals* (PS–1). Series: Helpers in Our Schools. 2000, Capstone LB $13.25 (0-7368-0532-X). 24pp. For beginning readers, this is a book about school principals and what they do. (Rev: HBG 9/00; SLJ 10/00) [371]

19835 Bourgeois, Paulette. *Garbage Collectors* (PS–2). Illus. by Kim LaFave. Series: In My Neighborhood. 1998, Kids Can $12.95 (1-55074-440-2). 32pp. Using realistic paintings as illustrations, this book describes the duties of garbage collectors and how waste is recycled. (Rev: BL 4/15/98; HBG 10/98; SLJ 6/98) [363.72]

19836 Bourgeois, Paulette. *Postal Workers* (PS–2). Illus. by Kim LaFave. 1999, Kids Can $12.95 (1-55074-504-2). 32pp. This work introduces the many types of postal workers — from those who work in the post office to mail carriers. (Rev: BL 7/99; HBG 9/99; SLJ 7/99) [383.4973]

19837 Cefrey, Holly. *Archaeologists: Life Digging Up Artifacts* (5–10). Series: Extreme Careers. 2004, Rosen LB $19.95 (0-8239-3963-4). 64pp. This is an introduction to the field of archeology, its problems, its opportunities, and its rewards. (Rev: BL 5/15/04) [930]

19838 Croce, Nicholas. *Detectives: Life Investigating Crimes* (5–10). Series: Extreme Careers. 2003, Rosen LB $26.50 (0-8239-3796-8). 64pp. As well as exploring the exciting side of detective work, this account explains the qualifications and training needed and the techniques that help do this job well. (Rev: BL 9/15/03) [340]

19839 Duvall, Jill D. *Chef Ki Is Serving Dinner!* (1–2). Illus. Series: Our Neighborhood. 1997, Children's Book Pr. LB $19.50 (0-516-20313-4). 32pp. In a photojournalistic style, readers are introduced to a chef who cooks Oriental food. Also use *Mr. Duvall Reports the News* and *Ms. Moja Makes Beautiful Clothes* (both 1997). (Rev: BL 8/97) [641.59519]

19840 Flanagan, Alice K. *A Day in Court with Mrs. Trinh* (1–2). Series: Our Neighborhood. 1997, Children's Book Pr. LB $19.50 (0-516-20008-9). 32pp. This career book describes the legal profession through the day-to-day activities of a real-life lawyer. (Rev: BL 12/15/97; SLJ 1/98) [340]

19841 Flanagan, Alice K. *Exploring Parks with Ranger Dockett* (1–2). Series: Our Neighborhood. 1997, Children's Book Pr. LB $19.50 (0-516-20496-3). 32pp. The work of National Park Service personnel is highlighted in this account that features a real member of the force, Ranger Dockett. (Rev: BL 12/15/97) [363.6]

19842 Flanagan, Alice K. *Mayors* (1–3). Series: Community Workers. 2001, Compass Point LB $19.93 (0-7565-0064-8). 32pp. This is an easily read introduction to the work of mayors, the skills and training required, and their contributions to the community. Also use *Teachers* (2001). (Rev: SLJ 5/01) [352.23]

19843 Flanagan, Alice K. *Raising Cows on the Koebel's Farm* (PS–1). Series: Our Neighborhood. 1999, Children's Book Pr. LB $19.50 (0-516-21133-1). 32pp. A simple, direct text and many illustrations tell this story of life on a cattle farm. (Rev: BL 7/99; HBG 9/99; SLJ 9/99) [631.2]

19844 Flanagan, Alice K. *The Zieglers and Their Apple Orchard* (PS–1). Series: Our Neighborhood. 1999, Children's Book Pr. LB $19.50 (0-516-21134-X). 32pp. A simple text and pictures introduce the work, duties, and lifestyle of a couple who operate an apple orchard. (Rev: BL 7/99; HBG 9/99) [631.2]

19845 Giacobello, John. *Bodyguards: Life Protecting Others* (5–10). Series: Extreme Careers. 2003, Rosen LB $26.50 (0-8239-3795-X). 64pp. This book explores the duties and responsibilities of a bodyguard and includes information how to stay safe on the job and get ahead in this profession. (Rev: BL 9/15/03; SLJ 11/03) [340]

19846 Gibson, Karen Bush. *Child Care Workers* (K–3). Series: Community Helpers. 2000, Bridgestone LB $17.26 (0-7368-0622-9). 24pp. A solid introduction to various people who are involved in child care. (Rev: HBG 3/01; SLJ 2/01) [649]

19847 Gorman, Jacqueline Laks. *Librarian / El Bibliotecario* (PS–2). Photos by Gregg Andersen. Series: People in My Community/La Gente de Mi Comunidad. 2002, Gareth Stevens LB $18.60 (0-8368-3310-4). 24pp. Full-color photographs and single-sentence descriptions, in English and in Spanish, introduce various aspects of a librarian's job. (Rev: SLJ 3/03)

19848 Greenberg, Keith E. *Window Washer: At Work Above the Clouds* (2–5). Illus. Series: Risky Business. 1995, Blackbirch LB $16.95 (1-56711-154-8). 32pp. The dangers involved and the safety measures required are stressed in this career book about two men who wash windows at the World Trade Center in New York City. (Rev: SLJ 8/95) [646.2]

19849 Greene, Meg. *Careers in the National Guard's Search and Rescue Unit* (5–9). Series: Careers in Search and Rescue Operations. 2003, Rosen LB $26.50 (0-8239-3836-0). 64pp. This account describes the vital role that citizen-soldiers play in the line of defense and tells of the their search and rescue activities during the terrorist attacks of September 11, 2001. (Rev: BL 10/15/03; SLJ 4/04) [335]

19850 Hayhurst, Chris. *Astronauts: Life Exploring Outer Space* (4–7). Series: Extreme Careers. 2001, Rosen LB $26.50 (0-8239-3364-4). 64pp. A high-interest look at the extensive skills required to become an astronaut, with brief coverage of space exploration and profiles of astronauts. (Rev: SLJ 1/02) [629]

19851 Hurwitz, Jane. *Choosing a Career in Animal Care* (4–8). Illus. Series: World of Work. 1996, Rosen LB $17.95 (0-8239-2268-5). 64pp. Various careers in working with animals are described, along with the education required, desirable character traits, and ways to break into the field. (Rev: SLJ 8/97) [371.7]

19852 Jacobs, Shannon K. *Healers of the Wild: People Who Care for Injured and Orphaned Wildlife* (4–7). Illus. 1998, Coyote Moon paper $19.95 (0-9661070-0-4). 212pp. The process of helping orphaned, injured, or displaced wildlife is covered thoroughly under three operational headings: rescue, rehabilitation, and release. (Rev: BL 10/1/98) [339.946]

19853 Jaspersohn, William. *A Week in the Life of an Airline Pilot* (4–8). Illus. 1991, Little, Brown $14.95 (0-316-45822-8). 96pp. A close-up look at the duties and lives of members of an airline crew. (Rev: BL 3/15/91; HB 5–6/91; SLJ 5/91) [629.132]

19854 Johnson, Neil. *All in a Day's Work: Twelve Americans Talk About Their Jobs* (5–7). Illus. 1989, Little, Brown $14.95 (0-316-46957-2). 89pp. People in various occupations — such as farmer, musician, and judge — show that work can be fun. (Rev: BCCB 2/90; BL 1/15/90; HB 3–4/90) [331.7]

19855 Lee, Barbara. *Working with Animals* (4–8). Illus. Series: Exploring Careers. 1996, Lerner LB $28.75 (0-8225-1759-0). 112pp. Profiles of 12 careers involving animals, such as veterinarian, animal shelter worker, or pet sitter. (Rev: BL 2/15/97) [591]

19856 L'Hommedieu, Arthur J. *Working at a Museum* (1–3). Photos by Judith Angel. Series: Working Here. 1998, Children's Book Pr. LB $23.00 (0-516-20748-2). 32pp. Brief text and pictures show various workers at the Brooklyn Children's Museum and what they do. (Rev: HBG 3/99; SLJ 3/99) [562]

19857 Liebman, Dan. *I Want to Be a Teacher* (K–2). Series: I Want to Be. 2001, Firefly LB $14.95 (1-55209-572-X). 24pp. A teacher's typical working day is described with a color photograph and two or three lines of text on each page in this easily read book. (Rev: BL 12/15/01; HBG 10/01) [371.1]

19858 Manley, Claudia B. *Secret Agents: Life as a Professional Spy* (4–7). Series: Extreme Careers. 2001, Rosen LB $26.50 (0-8239-3369-5). 64pp. A high-interest look at the extensive skills required to become an intelligence agent and the kinds of intelligence that are gathered (strategic, tactical, counterintelligence), with material on the history of espionage and on real-life and fictional spies. (Rev: SLJ 1/02) [327.12]

19859 Monroe, Judy. *A Day in the Life of a Librarian* (K–3). Series: First Facts: Community Helpers at Work. 2004, Capstone LB $21.26 (0-7368-2630-0). 24pp. Using a question-and-answer format and full-color photos, this volume looks at the tasks a librarian performs. (Rev: SLJ 1/05)

19860 Morris, Ann. *That's Our Librarian!* (K–3). Photos and illus. by Peter Linenthal. Series: That's Our School. 2003, Millbrook LB $22.90 (0-7613-2400-3). Readers are introduced to elementary school librarian Maria Rodriguez and all the responsibilities of her job. Also use *That's Our Teacher!* (2003). (Rev: HBG 4/04; SLJ 11/03) [027.8]

19861 Murdico, Suzanne J. *Bomb Squad Experts: Life Defusing Explosive Devices* (5–10). Series: Extreme Careers. 2004, Rosen LB $19.95 (0-8239-3968-5). 64pp. A look at the career opportunities in bomb squads, with material on training, salaries, and working conditions. (Rev: BL 5/15/04) [363]

19862 O'Brien, John, and Maxi Bilkins. *The Beach Patrol* (PS–2). Trans. and illus. by John O'Brien. 2004, Holt $15.95 (0-8050-6911-9). 32pp. The day-to-day life and responsibilities of beach lifeguards are outlined by two real-life practitioners. (Rev: BL 7/04; HB 5–6/04; SLJ 7/04)

19863 Pasternak, Ceel. *Cool Careers for Girls with Animals* (5–8). Series: Cool Careers for Girls. 1998, Impact $19.95 (1-57023-108-7); paper $12.95 (1-57023-105-2). Veterinarian, pet sitter, bird handler, animal trainer, and horse-farm owner are among the careers covered, supplemented by interviews with women who work in each field. (Rev: SLJ 4/99) [371.7]

19864 Pasternak, Ceel, and Linda Thornburg. *Cool Careers for Girls in Food* (5–10). Series: Cool Careers for Girls. 2000, Impact $19.95 (1-57023-127-3); paper $12.95 (1-57023-120-6). 128pp. The 11 women featured in this book are involved in various aspects of the food industry such as cheese making, baking, wine making, selling health food, and cooking for the military. (Rev: SLJ 2/00) [641]

19865 Pasternak, Ceel, and Linda Thornburg. *Cool Careers for Girls in Sports* (5–10). Series: Cool Careers for Girls. 1999, Impact $19.95 (1-57023-107-9); paper $12.95 (1-57023-104-4). 120pp. A golf pro, basketball player, ski instructor, sports broadcaster, trainer, sports psychologist, and athletic director are among the 10 women profiled in this overview of careers for women in sports. (Rev: SLJ 7/99) [796]

19866 Reeves, Diane Lindsey. *Career Ideas for Kids Who Like Math* (4–8). Illus. by Nancy Bond. 2000, Facts on File $23.00 (0-8160-4095-8). 186pp. Presents an amazing array of careers available for the mathematically inclined, arranged alphabetically with good solid information on each. (Rev: HBG 9/00; SLJ 9/00) [510]

19867 Reeves, Diane Lindsey. *Career Ideas for Kids Who Like Talking* (5–9). Illus. by Nancy Bond. Series: Career Ideas for Kids. 1998, Facts on File $23.00 (0-8160-3683-7); paper $12.95 (0-8160-3689-6). 154pp. This is a guide to careers in communications, from hotel manager to publicist to broadcaster, with reports from people in the field, tests to check one's aptitude, and lists of resources. (Rev: SLJ 10/98) [331.7]

19868 Reeves, Diane Lindsey, and Nancy Heubeck. *Career Ideas for Kids Who Like Adventure* (5–8). Illus. by Nancy Bond. Series: Career Ideas for Kids. 2001, Facts on File $23.00 (0-8160-4321-3). 170pp. An attractive introduction to careers such as fire fighting, scuba diving, oil rig work, and piloting, with personal profiles of individuals in the various fields and attractive cartoons. Also use *Career Ideas for Kids Who Like Money* (2001). (Rev: BL 7/01; HBG 3/02; SLJ 8/01) [331.7]

19869 Ring, Susan. *Animal Watch* (2–4). Series: On the Job. 2003, Chelsea Clubhouse LB $13.95 (0-7910-7409-9). 24pp. Explores three jobs that involve the study of animals: zoologist, entomologist, and ornithologist. (Rev: HBG 10/03; SLJ 10/03) [590]

19870 Rosenberg, Aaron. *Cryptologists: Life Making and Breaking Codes* (5–10). Series: Extreme Careers. 2004, Rosen LB $19.95 (0-8239-3965-0). 64pp. After some background material on the history of codes, this volume discusses career opportunities as a cryptologist. (Rev: BL 5/15/04; SLJ 5/90) [410]

19871 Rotner, Shelley, and Ken Kreisler. *Everybody Works* (PS–1). Photos by Shelley Rotner. 2003, Millbrook LB $23.90 (0-7613-1751-1). In addition to jobs that interest youngsters — police, firefighters, and so forth — this book looks at lower-profile

occupations and at volunteerism, hobbies, and even working animals. (Rev: HBG 10/03; SLJ 7/03) [331.7]

19872 Roza, Greg. *Careers in the Coast Guard's Search and Rescue Unit* (5–9). Series: Careers in Search and Rescue Operations. 2003, Rosen LB $26.50 (0-8239-3835-2). 64pp. This book covers the search and rescue operations involving the Coast Guard with particular emphasis on their vital role during the September 11, 2001 attacks. (Rev: BL 10/15/03; SLJ 4/04) [355]

19873 Schomp, Virginia. *If You Were a Farmer* (3–4). Series: If You Were A. 2000, Benchmark LB $15.95 (0-7614-1001-5). 32pp. The daily routines of a farmer and the equipment used are included in this simple career book. (Rev: BL 11/15/00; HBG 3/01; SLJ 3/01) [631]

19874 Schomp, Virginia. *If You Were a Teacher* (1–3). Series: If You Were A. 1999, Benchmark LB $15.95 (0-7614-0916-5). 32pp. After a brief history of teaching, there is coverage of various kinds of teachers in this attractive book. (Rev: HBG 9/00; SLJ 3/00) [371.7]

19875 Schomp, Virginia. *If You Were an Astronaut* (3–4). Series: If You Were A. 1997, Marshall Cavendish LB $22.79 (0-7614-0618-2). 32pp. Covers the education, training, and duties of astronauts. (Rev: BL 2/15/98; HBG 3/98; SLJ 2/98) [629]

19876 Seidman, David. *Secret Service Agents* (5–10). Illus. Series: Extreme Careers. 2003, Rosen LB $26.50 (0-8239-3636-8). 64pp. A look at the professional life of a Secret Service agent and the training and education required for the job. (Rev: BL 5/15/03) [363.28]

19877 Sommers, Michael A. *Wildlife Photographers: Life Through a Lens* (5–10). Series: Extreme Careers. 2003, Rosen LB $26.50 (0-8239-3638-4). 64pp. A concise explanation of the work of wildlife photographers, the attributes needed, and the training and tenacity required to enter this field. (Rev: BL 9/15/03; SLJ 5/03) [771]

19878 Stockdale, Linda. *ABC Career Book for Girls / El Libro de Carreras para Niñas* (K–3). Illus. by John Schafer. 1996, Columbia Univ. Pr. paper $9.95 (1-884830-00-5). 31pp. Using the letters of the alphabet, this book describes a wide range of occupations in English and Spanish. (Rev: SLJ 2/97) [331.7]

19879 Talbert, Marc. *Holding the Reins: A Ride Through Cowgirl Life* (5–7). Photos by Barbara Van Cleve. 2003, HarperCollins LB $17.89 (0-06-029256-3). 105pp. The demanding but exhilarating lives of modern-day cowgirls are shown here as the author follows four teens through the seasons. (Rev: BCCB 4/03; BL 1/1–15/03; HBG 10/03; SLJ 4/03) [978]

19880 Turner, Chérie. *Adventure Tour Guides: Life on Extreme Outdoor Adventures* (5–10). Series: Extreme Careers. 2003, Rosen LB $26.50 (0-8239-3793-3). 64pp. A look at the profession of tour guiding on excursions such as white-water rafting and mountain climbing, with material on qualifications and future possibilities. (Rev: BL 9/15/03) [908]

19881 White, Katherine. *Oil Rig Workers: Life Drilling for Oil* (5–10). Series: Extreme Careers. 2003, Rosen LB $26.50 (0-8239-3797-6). 64pp. A look at the lives of oil rig workers and day-to-day activities on a rig. (Rev: BL 9/15/03) [665.5]

19882 Willett, Edward. *Careers in Outer Space: New Business Opportunities* (4–9). Series: The Career Resource Library. 2002, Rosen LB $25.25 (0-8239-3358-X). 92pp. An interesting look at opportunities in the fields of science, math, engineering, technology, communication, and, of course, aeronautics, with information on required skills and training and on the pros and cons of working in the public and private sectors. (Rev: SLJ 6/02) [629.4]

19883 *Yikes! A Smart Girl's Guide to Surviving Tricky, Sticky, Icky Situations* (4–8). Illus. by Bonnie Timmons. Series: American Girl Library. 2002, Pleasant Co. paper $8.95 (1-58485-530-4). 87pp. Advice on everything from dealing with teachers and friends to coping with embarrassing situations and dangerous incidents. (Rev: SLJ 12/02) [305.23]

Arts and Entertainment

19884 Aaseng, Nathan. *Wildshots: The World of the Wildlife Photographer* (5–8). Illus. 2001, Millbrook LB $29.90 (0-7613-1551-9). 80pp. This account describes the work of a wildlife photographer and tells exciting stories about unusual encounters. (Rev: BL 3/1/01*; HBG 10/01; SLJ 3/01) [778.9]

19885 *Art* (4–8). Illus. Series: Discovering Careers for Your Future. 2001, Ferguson LB $15.95 (0-89434-388-2). 92pp. A useful introduction to career opportunities in art, with information on the skills required, potential earnings, and job outlook. (Rev: SLJ 11/01) [702.373]

19886 Burton, Marilee. *Artists at Work* (2–4). Series: On the Job. 2003, Chelsea Clubhouse LB $13.95 (0-7910-7410-2). 24pp. Introduces young readers to theatrical producer/costume designer Julie Taymor, architect/sculptor Maya Lin, and jazz trumpeter Wynton Marsalis. (Rev: HBG 10/03; SLJ 10/03) [700]

19887 Christelow, Eileen. *What Do Illustrators Do?* (2–4). Illus. 1999, Clarion $15.00 (0-395-90230-4). 40pp. Showing two illustrators — both working on a version of *Jack and the Beanstalk* — this book explores the illustration process and its finished product. (Rev: BCCB 5/99; BL 3/1/99; HB 5–6/99; HBG 9/99; SLJ 11/99) [741.6]

19888 Dubois, Muriel L. *I Like Music* (1–3). 2000, Bridgestone LB $17.26 (0-7368-0632-6). 24pp. Opposite each full-page photo, there is a description of a music-related occupation such as composer, conductor, sound engineer, or disc jockey. (Rev: HBG 3/01; SLJ 2/01) [780]

19889 Dubois, Muriel L. *I Like Sports* (1–3). Series: What Can I Be? 2000, Bridgestone LB $17.26 (0-7368-0633-4). 24pp. A beginning career book that talks about sports broadcasters, referees, coaches,

and players and gives instructions on how to make a racket-and-ball game. (Rev: HBG 3/01; SLJ 2/01) [796]

19890 Flanagan, Alice K. *Mrs. Scott's Beautiful Art* (PS–1). Series: Our Neighborhood. 1999, Children's Book Pr. LB $19.50 (0-516-21135-8). 32pp. A photo-filled account and a simple text introduce a woman who works with fabrics and weaving. (Rev: BL 7/99; HBG 9/99) [746.1]

19891 Johnson, Marlys H. *Careers in the Movies* (5–9). Series: Career Resource Library. 2001, Rosen LB $18.95 (0-8239-3186-2). 122pp. Job descriptions and qualifications are clearly laid out in this guide for aspiring filmmakers that also discusses the history of the industry and the basic steps in film production. (Rev: SLJ 8/01) [791.43]

19892 Lee, Barbara. *Working in Sports and Recreation* (5–9). Illus. Series: Exploring Careers. 1996, Lerner LB $28.75 (0-8225-1762-0). Twelve people involved in careers related to sports and recreation talk candidly about their professions. (Rev: BL 2/15/97) [796]

19893 Lehn, Barbara. *What Is an Artist?* (PS–2). Illus. by Carol Krauss. 2002, Millbrook LB $21.90 (0-7613-2259-0). 32pp. An introduction of the concept of "artist," presented in a friendly format for younger readers. (Rev: BL 12/15/02; HBG 3/03) [709]

19894 Libal, Joyce, and Rae Simons. *Professional Athlete and Sports Official* (5–9). Series: Careers with Character. 2003, Mason Crest LB $22.95 (1-59084-321-5). 90pp. The importance of character traits such as integrity, respect, fairness, and self-discipline when seeking careers in sports is emphasized here. (Rev: HBG 10/03; SLJ 4/03) [796]

19895 Lyon, George E. *A Sign* (K–4). Illus. by Chris K. Soentpiet. 1998, Orchard $15.95 (0-531-30073-0). 32pp. As a child, the author wanted to pursue many different careers, but finally she decided that the best one would be writing. (Rev: BL 2/15/98; HBG 9/98; SLJ 3/98) [813]

19896 McLaglen, Mary, et al. *You Can Be a Woman Movie Maker* (4–8). Series: You Can Be a Woman. 2003, Cascade Pass $19.95 (1-880599-64-3); paper $14.95 (1-880599-63-5). 71pp. Three women — a producer, an independent filmmaker, and an executive producer — talk about their jobs, how they got into the movie industry, and what a day on the job is like. Interviews and film clips are on an accompanying DVD. (Rev: SLJ 4/04) [791.43]

19897 Maze, Stephanie. *I Want to Be a Dancer* (4–6). Illus. Series: I Want to Be. 1997, Harcourt $16.00 (0-15-201299-0). 48pp. Careers in dance are examined, with information on education, training, the history of dance, famous people, and special terms. (Rev: BL 2/1/98; HBG 3/98; SLJ 12/97) [792.8]

19898 Nathan, Amy. *The Young Musician's Survival Guide: Tips from Teens and Pros* (5–8). 2000, Oxford $18.95 (0-19-512611-4); paper $9.95 (0-19-512612-2). 126pp. A thorough study of how to break into the music world, with information on working with music teachers, conductors, and peers, and tips on practicing, choosing an instrument, and handling fears and frustrations. (Rev: BL 4/1/00; HBG 9/00; SLJ 6/00) [780]

19899 Parks, Peggy J. *Musician* (4–7). Illus. Series: Exploring Careers. 2004, Gale/KidHaven LB $18.96 (0-7377-2067-0). 48pp. In addition to a description of the work that musicians (including DJs) do, there is a frank assessment of the opportunities available. (Rev: BL 3/15/04) [780]

19900 Parks, Peggy J. *Writer* (4–7). Illus. Series: Exploring Careers. 2004, Gale/KidHaven LB $18.96 (0-7377-2069-7). 48pp. The ups and downs of a career in writing are frankly discussed in this slim guide. (Rev: BL 3/15/04) [808]

19901 Reeves, Diane L. *Career Ideas for Kids Who Like Writing* (5–9). Illus. Series: Career Ideas for Kids Who Like. 1998, Facts on File $23.00 (0-8160-3685-3); paper $12.95 (0-8160-3691-8). A look at 15 careers related to writing, among them advertising copywriter, author, bookseller, editor, grant writer, journalist, librarian, literary agent, and publicist, with a self-test for each one and a profile of a person working in the field. (Rev: SLJ 3/99) [808]

19902 Reeves, Diane L., and Peter Kent. *Career Ideas for Kids Who Like Sports* (5–9). Illus. Series: Career Ideas for Kids Who Like. 1998, Facts on File $23.00 (0-8160-3684-5); paper $12.95 (0-8160-3690-X). The 15 sports-related careers highlighted in this volume include coach, athlete, agent, sportscaster, and sports equipment manufacturer, with accompanying material on necessary skills, opportunities, duties, and a report from someone in the field. (Rev: SLJ 6/99) [796]

19903 Schomp, Virginia. *If You Were a Ballet Dancer* (3–4). Illus. Series: If You Were A. 1997, Marshall Cavendish LB $22.79 (0-7614-0616-6). 32pp. This introduction to a career in ballet tells about practicing, performing, styles of dance, costumes, and terminology. (Rev: BL 2/15/98; HBG 3/98; SLJ 2/98) [792.8]

19904 Schomp, Virginia. *If You Were a Musician* (3–4). Series: If You Were A. 2000, Benchmark LB $15.95 (0-7614-1002-3). 32pp. Using color photos and a simple text, this career book covers a typical day in the life of a musician. (Rev: BL 11/15/00; HBG 3/01; SLJ 3/01) [780]

19905 Vitkus-Weeks, Jessica. *Television* (4–8). Illus. Series: Now Hiring. 1994, Crestwood LB $14.95 (0-89686-783-8). 48pp. Using real people as case histories, this book describes such TV careers as grip, camera operator, production assistant, costume designer, and actor. (Rev: SLJ 8/94) [621.388]

19906 Wessling, Katherine. *Backstage at a Movie Set* (4–8). Series: Backstage Pass. 2003, Children's Pr. LB $20.00 (0-516-24325-X); paper $6.95 (0-516-24387-X). 48pp. A photo-filled glimpse behind the scenes of a movie in production, with advice on how to become involved. (Rev: SLJ 10/03) [791.43]

Engineering, Technology, and Trades

19907 Brown, Marty. *Webmaster* (4–8). Series: Coolcareers.com. 2000, Rosen LB $23.95 (0-8239-3111-0). 44pp. This volume describes a Web page, types of networks, servers, browsers, and protocols and introduces some careers in Web-related areas. (Rev: SLJ 6/00) [004]

19908 *Computers* (4–8). Illus. Series: Discovering Careers for Your Future. 2001, Ferguson LB $15.95 (0-89434-389-0). 92pp. A useful introduction to the career opportunities in this field, with information on the skills required, potential earnings, and job outlook. (Rev: SLJ 11/01) [004.02373]

19909 Frew, Katherine. *Plumber* (5–8). Series: Great Jobs. 2004, Children's Pr. LB $20.00 (0-516-24088-9); paper $6.95 (0-516-25935-0). 48pp. This appealing, photo-filled title focuses on the plumbing trade, looking at job requirements, training, and tools, as well as providing a history of the plumbing business and a look at a typical day at work. (Rev: SLJ 7/04) [696]

19910 Hovanec, Erin M. *Careers as a Content Provider for the Web* (5–8). Series: The Library of E-Commerce and Internet Careers. 2001, Rosen LB $19.95 (0-8239-3418-7). 64pp. A basic guide to career opportunities in the high-tech sector, with personal stories, information on skills needed and how to get started, and lists of recommended resources, many of which are on the Web. Also use *E-Tailing: Careers Selling Over the Web* (2001). (Rev: SLJ 4/02) [004]

19911 McGinty, Alice B. *Software Designer* (4–8). Series: Coolcareers.com. 2000, Rosen LB $23.95 (0-8239-3149-8). 48pp. This book explains what a software engineer does, the skills required, education needed, and future prospects. (Rev: SLJ 6/00) [004]

19912 Maupin, Melissa. *Computer Engineer* (4–6). Series: Career Exploration. 2000, Capstone LB $21.26 (0-7368-0591-5). 48pp. Readers follow the events of a typical day for a computer engineer and learn the skills and temperament required for such a job, with full-color photographs, charts, and fast facts that include salary ranges and job outlook. Also use *Police Detective* and *Human Services Worker* (both 2000). (Rev: SLJ 5/01) [004]

19913 Maze, Stephanie. *I Want to Be an Engineer* (4–6). Illus. Series: I Want to Be. 1997, Harcourt $16.00 (0-15-201298-2). 48pp. Engineering and its various branches are introduced, along with the education and training necessary, terms used, and famous engineers. (Rev: BL 2/1/98; HBG 3/98; SLJ 12/97) [620]

19914 Mazor, Barry. *Multimedia and New Media Developer* (4–8). Series: Coolcareers.com. 2000, Rosen LB $23.95 (0-8239-3102-1). 45pp. This work explains the nature of multimedia careers, the training and skills necessary, and the job opportunities. (Rev: SLJ 6/00) [004]

19915 O'Donnell, Annie. *Computer Animator* (4–8). Series: Coolcareers.com. 2000, Rosen LB $23.95

(0-8239-3101-3). 44pp. This book gives a brief history of animation and explains how it is used today, the specialized roles of animators, educational requirements, and the future of the industry. (Rev: SLJ 6/00) [004]

19916 Oleksy, Walter. *Video Game Designer* (4–8). Series: Coolcareers.com. 2000, Rosen LB $23.95 (0-8239-3117-X). 47pp. This account explains how video games work and how they are designed, with material on the careers involved and the qualifications necessary. (Rev: SLJ 6/00) [794.8]

19917 Oleksy, Walter. *Web Page Designer* (4–8). Series: Coolcareers.com. 2000, Rosen LB $23.95 (0-8239-3112-9). 47pp. This well-illustrated account, which features case studies of several teenagers, gives information on Web page construction, what a designer does, the training required, and the job outlook. (Rev: SLJ 6/00) [004]

19918 Overcamp, David. *Electrician* (5–8). Series: Great Jobs. 2004, Children's Pr. LB $20.00 (0-516-24086-2); paper $6.95 (0-516-25924-5). 48pp. This appealing, photo-filled title focuses on the work of an electrician, looking at job requirements, training, and tools, as well as providing a history of the field and a look at a typical day at work. (Rev: SLJ 7/04) [621.3]

19919 Pasternak, Ceel, and Linda Thornburg. *Cool Careers for Girls in Computers* (5–8). 1999, Impact $19.95 (1-57023-106-0); paper $12.95 (1-57023-103-6). 121pp. This book introduces ten women of various ages and ethnic backgrounds who have been successful in different aspects of the computer industry. (Rev: SLJ 4/00) [004]

19920 Reeves, Diane Lindsey, and Peter Kent. *Career Ideas for Kids Who Like Computers* (5–9). Illus. by Nancy Bond. Series: Career Ideas for Kids. 1998, Facts on File $23.00 (0-8160-3682-9); paper $12.95 (0-8160-3688-8). 167pp. An upbeat, breezy introduction to careers related to computers, providing aptitude tests and information on educational requirements, working conditions, activities, etc. (Rev: SLJ 6/99) [004]

19921 Schomp, Virginia. *If You Were a Construction Worker* (3–4). Illus. Series: If You Were A. 1997, Marshall Cavendish LB $22.79 (0-7614-0617-4). 32pp. This title describes the different jobs involved in a construction project, the various kinds of buildings these people work on, and some of the world's great structures, such as the Empire State Building and the pyramids. (Rev: BL 2/15/98; HBG 3/98) [624]

19922 Weintraub, Aileen. *Auto Mechanic* (5–8). Series: Great Jobs. 2004, Children's Pr. LB $20.00 (0-516-24090-0); paper $6.95 (0-516-25922-9). 48pp. This appealing, photo-filled title focuses on the work of an auto mechanic, looking at job requirements, training, and tools, as well as providing a history of the trade and a look at a typical day at work. (Rev: SLJ 7/04) [629.28]

Health and Medicine

19923 Asher, Dana. *Epidemiologists: Life Tracking Deadly Diseases* (5–10). Series: Extreme Careers. 2003, Rosen LB $26.50 (0-8239-3633-3). 64pp. A concise explanation of the work of epidemiologists, the history of this discipline, and the training required to enter this field, with a case study. (Rev: BL 5/15/03; SLJ 5/03) [614.4]

19924 Brill, Marlene Targ. *Doctors* (K–2). Series: Pull Ahead Books. 2004, Lerner LB $22.60 (0-8225-1689-6). The important role that doctors play in maintaining a healthy community is shown in brief text and and full-color photographs in this small-format book. (Rev: BL 10/15/04) [610]

19925 Flanagan, Alice K. *Ask Nurse Pfaff, She'll Help You!* (1–2). Series: Our Neighborhood. 1997, Children's Book Pr. LB $19.50 (0-516-20495-5). 32pp. The life story of a nurse is given in this simple book that tells about nurses and their contributions to a community. (Rev: BL 12/15/97) [610]

19926 Flanagan, Alice K. *Dr. Kanner, Dentist with a Smile* (1–2). Series: Our Neighborhood. 1997, Children's Book Pr. LB $20.00 (0-516-20493-9). 32pp. What dentists do and their contributions to a community are covered in this book highlighting the work of an actual dentist, Dr. Kanner. (Rev: BL 12/15/97; SLJ 1/98) [617]

19927 Fluet, Connie. *A Day in the Life of a Nurse* (K–3). Series: First Facts: Community Helpers at Work. 2004, Capstone LB $21.26 (0-7368-2631-9). 24pp. Using a question-and-answer format and full-color photos, Fluet looks at the tasks a nurse performs. (Rev: SLJ 1/05) [610]

19928 Gibson, Karen Bush. *Emergency Medical Technicians* (K–3). Series: Community Helpers. 2000, Bridgestone LB $17.26 (0-7368-0623-7). 24pp. A solid introduction to emergency medical technicians, their work, training, and rewards. (Rev: HBG 3/01; SLJ 2/01) [610]

19929 Gorman, Jacqueline Laks. *Dentist / El Dentista* (PS–2). Photos by Gregg Andersen. Series: People in My Community/La Gente de Mi Comunidad. 2002, Gareth Stevens LB $18.60 (0-8368-3307-4). 24pp. Full-color photographs and single-sentence descriptions, in English and in Spanish, introduce various aspects of a dentist's work. Also use *Doctor / El Medico* (2002). (Rev: HBG 3/03; SLJ 3/03)

19930 Kalman, Bobbie. *Hospital Workers in the Emergency Room* (1–4). Illus. Series: My Community and Its Helpers. 2004, Crabtree LB $16.95 (0-7787-2095-0); paper $8.06 (0-7787-2123-X). 32pp. A simple review of the tasks assigned to emergency room workers and the education necessary for a career in this field. (Rev: BL 5/1/04; SLJ 6/05)

19931 Lee, Barbara. *Working in Health Care and Wellness* (4–8). Illus. Series: Exploring Careers. 1996, Lerner LB $28.75 (0-8225-1760-4). This book profiles 12 people who are in health care professions, and includes the pros and cons of each career. (Rev: BL 2/15/97) [610.69]

19932 Liebman, Dan. *I Want to Be a Doctor* (PS–1). Illus. Series: I Want to Be. 2000, Firefly LB $14.95 (1-55209-463-4); paper $3.99 (1-55209-461-8). 24pp. Using a simple text and many full-color photos, this book introduces the medical profession. (Rev: BL 9/15/00; HBG 9/00; SLJ 9/00) [610]

19933 Liebman, Dan. *I Want to Be a Nurse* (K–2). Series: I Want to Be. 2001, Firefly LB $14.95 (1-55209-568-1). 24pp. With color photographs and two or three lines of simple text on each page, the working day of a nurse is described. (Rev: BL 12/15/01; HBG 10/01) [610]

19934 Pasternak, Ceel, and Linda Thornburg. *Cool Careers for Girls in Health* (5–9). Series: Cool Careers for Girls. 1999, Impact $19.95 (1-57023-125-7); paper $12.95 (1-57023-118-4). 160pp. This book describes health-related careers for girls — as doctors, nurses, dentists, personal trainers, medical technologists, physical therapists, and dietitians. (Rev: SLJ 10/99) [610]

19935 Schomp, Virginia. *If You Were a Doctor* (3–4). Series: If You Were A. 2000, Benchmark LB $15.95 (0-7614-1000-7). 32pp. Full-color photographs and an easy text are used to describe the daily routines of a doctor. (Rev: BL 11/15/00; HBG 3/01) [610]

Police and Fire Fighters

19936 Binney, Greg A. *Careers in the Federal Emergency Management Agency's Search and Rescue Unit* (5–9). Illus. Series: Careers in Search and Rescue Operations. 2003, Rosen LB $26.50 (0-8239-3832-8). 64pp. Starting with September 11, 2001, this volume explores the work of the teams that specialize in search and rescue after disasters such as tornadoes, hazardous materials spills, and building collapses, with material on the training required. (Rev: BL 10/15/03) [363.3]

19937 Bourgeois, Paulette. *Fire Fighters* (PS–2). Illus. by Kim LaFave. Series: In My Neighborhood. 1998, Kids Can $12.95 (1-55074-438-0). 32pp. This book about fire fighters and their duties highlights fires in various settings and the ways fire fighters approach them. (Rev: BL 4/15/98; HBG 10/98; SLJ 6/98) [363.37]

19938 Bourgeois, Paulette. *Police Officers* (PS–2). Illus. by Kim LaFave. Series: My Neighborhood. 1999, Kids Can $12.95 (1-55074-502-6). 32pp. This picture book explains the basic duties of neighborhood police officers. (Rev: BL 7/99; HBG 9/99; SLJ 7/99) [363.2]

19939 Demarest, Chris L. *Hotshots!* (K–2). Illus. 2003, Simon & Schuster $17.95 (0-689-84816-1). 48pp. Dramatic text and vivid illustrations deliver a compelling profile of "hotshots," the brave men and women who each year battle western wildfires. (Rev: BL 4/15/03; HBG 10/03; SLJ 8/03) [634.9]

19940 Fall, Mitchell. *Careers in Fire Departments' Search and Rescue Unit* (5–9). Series: Careers in Search and Rescue Operations. 2003, Rosen LB $26.50 (0-8239-3833-6). 64pp. This account pays tribute to the heroism of fire departments' search and rescue operations particularly during the September 11, 2001 attacks and also gives a career guide to this occupation. (Rev: BL 10/15/03) [363]

19941 Fine, Jil. *Bomb Squad Specialist* (4–8). Series: Danger Is My Business. 2003, Children's Pr. LB $20.00 (0-516-24340-3); paper $6.95 (0-516-27864-9). 48pp. An illustrated glimpse of the perilous life of a bomb squad member in an age of terrorism, including information on how bombs work and how they are detected and disarmed. (Rev: SLJ 3/04) [363.2]

19942 Flanagan, Alice K. *Ms. Murphy Fights Fires* (1–2). Series: Our Neighborhood. 1997, Children's Book Pr. LB $20.00 (0-516-20494-7). 32pp. A modern fire fighter is the focus of this book, which describes what these people do and their contributions to a neighborhood. (Rev: BL 12/15/97; SLJ 1/98) [363.77]

19943 Fortney, Mary T. *Fire Station Number 4: The Daily Life of Firefighters* (2–4). Illus. 1998, Carolrhoda LB $22.60 (1-57505-089-7). 48pp. Using the fire station at Livermore, a suburb of San Francisco, as home base, this photo-essay clearly details the day-to-day activities in a fire station and the duties and responsibilities of typical fire fighters. (Rev: BL 10/1/98; HBG 3/99; SLJ 1/99) [363.37]

19944 Freedman, Jeri. *Careers in Emergency Medical Response Team's Search and Rescue Unit* (5–9). Illus. Series: Careers in Search and Rescue Operations. 2003, Rosen LB $26.50 (0-8239-3831-X). 64pp. Starting with September 11, 2001, this volume explores the various roles played by emergency response teams, the use of equipment including helicopters and ambulances, and the training required. (Rev: BL 10/15/03) [616.0]

19945 Gorman, Jacqueline Laks. *Firefighter / El Bombero* (PS–2). Photos by Gregg Andersen. Series: People in My Community/La Gente de Mi Comunidad. 2002, Gareth Stevens LB $18.60 (0-8368-3309-0). 24pp. Full-color photographs and single-sentence descriptions, in English and in Spanish, introduce various aspects of a fire fighter's job. Also use *Police Officer / El Policía* (2002). (Rev: SLJ 3/03)

19946 Gorrell, Gena K. *Catching Fire: The Story of Firefighting* (4–6). Illus. 1999, Tundra $16.95 (0-88776-430-4). 144pp. After giving a history of fire fighting, this account describes different kinds of fires and the methods used to combat them. (Rev: BCCB 5/99; BL 6/1–15/99) [363.37]

19947 Greenberg, Keith E. *Bomb Squad Officer: Expert with Explosives* (2–4). Illus. Series: Risky Business. 1995, Blackbirch LB $16.95 (1-56711-155-6). 32pp. A career book, set in New Jersey, that explains the work of the men who remove and dismantle or detonate suspicious objects. (Rev: SLJ 2/96) [363]

19948 Greenberg, Keith E. *Smokejumper: Firefighter from the Sky* (2–5). Illus. Series: Risky Business. 1995, Blackbirch LB $16.95 (1-56711-153-X). 32pp. This career book gives details on the training and skills needed to become a smoke jumper — a person who parachutes into wildfires. (Rev: SLJ 8/95) [634.9]

19949 Hayward, Linda. *A Day in the Life of a Fire-fighter* (PS–K). Series: Dorling Kindersley Readers: Jobs People Do. 2001, DK $12.95 (0-7894-7366-6); paper $3.95 (0-7894-7365-8). 32pp. In this beginning reader that uses a limited vocabulary and simple sentences, the daily life of a fire fighter is portrayed. (Rev: BL 8/1/01; HBG 10/01) [363]

19950 Kalman, Bobbie. *Firefighters to the Rescue!* (1–4). Illus. Series: My Community and Its Helpers. 2004, Crabtree LB $16.95 (0-7787-2096-9); paper $8.06 (0-7787-2124-8). 32pp. A simple review of the work of fire fighters and the education necessary for a career in this field. (Rev: BL 5/1/04; SLJ 6/05) [363.37]

19951 Knudsen, Shannon. *Police Officers* (K–2). 2004, Lerner LB $16.95 (0-8225-1693-4). 32pp. The important role that police officers play in the community is shown in brief text and and full-color photographs in this small-format book. (Rev: BL 10/15/04) [363.2]

19952 Landau, Elaine. *Smokejumpers* (3–6). Illus. 2002, Millbrook LB $23.90 (0-7613-2324-4). 48pp. An excellent tribute to the life and work of the gallant men and women who jump from planes to fight forest fires. (Rev: BCCB 3/02; BL 6/1–15/02; HBG 10/02; SLJ 7/02) [634.9]

19953 Liebman, Dan. *I Want to Be a Police Officer* (PS–1). Illus. Series: I Want to Be. 2000, Firefly LB $14.95 (1-55209-467-7); paper $3.99 (1-55209-465-0). 24pp. Full-color photographs and a brief text introduce police officers and what they do. (Rev: BL 6/1–15/00; SLJ 9/00) [363.2]

19954 Maass, Robert. *Fire Fighters* (2–3). Illus. 1989, Scholastic paper $4.99 (0-590-41460-7). 32pp. Photos of fire fighters in training, relaxing, and working a fire. (Rev: BCCB 2/89; BL 4/1/89)

19955 Masoff, Joy. *Fire!* (3–7). Illus. 1998, Scholastic $16.95 (0-590-97872-1). 48pp. The facts about and excitement of fire fighting are covered in this fast-paced book filled with pictures, sidebars, and extensive captions. (Rev: BCCB 4/98; BL 2/1/98; HB 3–4/98; HBG 9/98; SLJ 3/98) [363.37]

19956 Meltzer, Milton. *Case Closed: The Real Scoop on Detective Work* (5–9). Illus. 2001, Scholastic paper $18.95 (0-439-29315-4). 96pp. Meltzer introduces the methods that detectives (both police and private) use to investigate crimes and provides case studies and a look at the history of detective agencies. (Rev: BL 9/15/01; HBG 10/02; SLJ 9/01) [363.25]

19957 Plum, Jennifer. *Careers in Police Departments' Search and Rescue Unit* (5–9). Series: Careers in Search and Rescue Operations. 2003, Rosen LB $26.50 (0-8239-3834-4). 64pp. This account highlights the role of police officers in search and rescue operations particularly their acts of heroism during the attacks of September 11, 2001. (Rev: BL 10/15/03) [363]

19958 Royston, Angela. *Fire Fighters* (1–3). Illus. Series: Eyewitness Reader. 1998, DK paper $3.95 (0-7894-2960-8). 32pp. Using photographs and a

simple text, this easy reader describes a house fire and the role of fire fighters in controlling it. (Rev: BL 7/98) [628.9]

19959 Ruth, Maria Mudd. *Firefighting: Behind the Scenes* (3–5). Illus. 1998, Houghton Mifflin $17.00 (0-395-70129-5). 64pp. This book discusses the tools, training, and procedures of today's fire fighters and various specializations such as dispatcher and pump operator. (Rev: BL 10/15/98; HB 9–10/98; HBG 3/99; SLJ 9/98) [628.9]

19960 Schomp, Virginia. *If You Were a Firefighter* (3–4). Series: If You Were A. 1997, Marshall Cavendish LB $22.79 (0-7614-0615-8). 32pp. In this simple career book, the training and responsibilities of fire fighters are introduced. (Rev: BL 2/15/98; HBG 3/98) [363]

19961 Schomp, Virginia. *If You Were a Police Officer* (3–4). Series: If You Were A. 1997, Marshall Cavendish LB $22.79 (0-7614-0614-X). 32pp. The everyday activities of a police officer are described in this simple career book. (Rev: BL 2/15/98; HBG 3/98) [363]

19962 Winkleman, Katherine K. *Firehouse* (2–4). Illus. by John S. Winkleman. 1994, Walker $15.85 (0-8027-8317-1). 32pp. Facts about firehouses, past and present, and how they operate are presented in this fascinating behind-the-scenes look. (Rev: BCCB 10/94; BL 10/1/94; SLJ 1/95) [363.37]

Science

19963 Collard, Sneed B., III. *A Firefly Biologist at Work* (4–6). Illus. Series: Wildlife Conservation Society. 2001, Watts LB $22.50 (0-531-11798-7); paper $6.95 (0-531-16568-X). 48pp. Readers learn about the career of a firefly researcher, with information both about fireflies themselves and about the life and interests of a biologist. (Rev: BL 12/1/01; SLJ check) [595.7]

19964 Duvall, Jill D. *Who Keeps the Water Clean? Ms. Schindler!* (1–2). Illus. Series: Our Neighborhood. 1997, Children's Book Pr. LB $20.00 (0-516-20315-0). 32pp. This unusual book looks at the life and career of a worker in a water treatment plant. (Rev: BL 5/15/97; SLJ 7/97) [628.1]

19965 Ghez, Andrea Mia, and Judith Cohen. *You Can Be a Woman Astronomer* (3–5). Illus. by David Katz. 1995, Cascade Pass paper $6.00 (1-880599-17-1). 38pp. A career book in which the author tells how she became a scientist and of the excitement and wonder of using telescopes and other tools of the astronomer. (Rev: SLJ 1/96) [520]

19966 Greenberg, Keith E. *Marine Biologist: Swimming with the Sharks* (2–4). Illus. Series: Risky Business. 1995, Blackbirch LB $16.95 (1-56711-156-4). 32pp. A career book that focuses on the work of marine biologist Sonny Gruber, who has studied sharks for the past 30 years. (Rev: SLJ 2/96) [574.92]

19967 Hammonds, Heather. *Geologists* (4–6). 2004, Smart Apple Media LB $18.95 (1-58340-543-7). 32pp. Following an overview of the science and its history, this volume discusses geology today, the duties of geologists and equipment used, the future of the profession, and how to become a geologist. (Rev: BL 10/15/04; SLJ 2/05) [551]

19968 Haydon, Julie. *Astronomers* (4–6). Illus. Series: Scientists at Work. 2004, Smart Apple Media LB $18.95 (1-58340-541-0). 32pp. Following an overview of the science and its history, this volume discusses astronomy today, the duties of astronomers and equipment used, the future of the profession, and how to become an astronomer. (Rev: BL 10/15/04; SLJ 2/05) [520]

19969 Hayhurst, Chris. *Arctic Scientists: Life Studying the Arctic* (5–10). Series: Extreme Careers. 2003, Rosen LB $26.50 (0-8239-3794-1). 64pp. This guide to the life and work of Arctic scientists indicates exciting areas of research such as the plant and animal life and the effects of global warming. (Rev: BL 9/15/03; SLJ 11/03) [500]

19970 Hayhurst, Chris. *Volcanologists: Life Exploring Volcanoes* (5–10). Series: Extreme Careers. 2003, Rosen LB $26.50 (0-8239-3637-6). 64pp. This career guide explains what is necessary to become a serious student of volcanoes and what to expect when one becomes a volcanologist. (Rev: BL 9/15/03) [551.2]

19971 Higginson, Mel. *Scientists Who Study Ancient Temples and Tombs* (1–2). Illus. Series: Scientists. 1994, Rourke LB $10.95 (0-86593-376-6). 24pp. A simple introduction to archaeologists, what they do, the education necessary, and some of their important discoveries. (Rev: SLJ 2/95) [930]

19972 Higginson, Mel. *Scientists Who Study Fossils* (1–2). Illus. Series: Scientists. 1994, Rourke LB $10.95 (0-86593-375-8). 24pp. This basic book describes what paleontologists do, what sort of education and training they require, and some of their important accomplishments. (Rev: SLJ 2/95) [560]

19973 Higginson, Mel. *Scientists Who Study Ocean Life* (1–2). Illus. Series: Scientists. 1994, Rourke LB $10.95 (0-86593-371-5). 24pp. Describes the science of oceanography, as well as the training required and discoveries of these scientists who study the oceans. (Rev: SLJ 2/95) [551.46]

19974 Higginson, Mel. *Scientists Who Study the Earth* (1–2). Illus. Series: Scientists. 1994, Rourke LB $10.95 (0-86593-372-3). 24pp. A basic introduction to the work that geologists do and how they prepare for it. (Rev: SLJ 2/95) [557]

19975 Higginson, Mel. *Scientists Who Study Wild Animals* (1–2). Illus. Series: Scientists. 1994, Rourke LB $10.95 (0-86593-374-X). 24pp. Careers in animal biology are introduced briefly, with a description of the education and training necessary. (Rev: SLJ 2/95) [591]

19976 Lehn, Barbara. *What Is a Scientist?* (K–2). 1998, Millbrook $19.90 (0-7613-1272-2). 32pp. Outlines the various steps in the scientific method — designing experiments, making observations, and so forth — and introduces the work of different kinds of scientists. (Rev: HBG 3/99; SLJ 4/99) [500]

19977 McElroy, Lisa Tucker. *Meet My Grandmother: She's a Deep Sea Explorer* (2–4). Series: Grandmothers at Work. 2000, Millbrook LB $22.90 (0-7613-1720-1). 32pp. A young boy introduces his grandmother, Sylvia Earle, who regularly swims with sharks as she explores the ocean's depths. (Rev: BL 9/15/00; HBG 3/01; SLJ 1/01) [551.46]

19978 McGlone, Catherine. *Visiting Volcanoes with a Scientist* (1–3). Illus. Series: I Like Science! 2004, Enslow LB $16.95 (0-7660-2269-2). 24pp. Readers follow a volcanologist through work in the field and learn how to make a model volcano using everyday materials. (Rev: BL 4/1/04; SLJ 2/05) [551.21]

19979 Murdico, Suzanne J. *Forensic Scientists: Life Investigating Sudden Death* (5–12). Series: Extreme Careers. 2004, Rosen LB $19.95 (0-8239-3966-9). 64pp. A look at this rapidly growing science and the career opportunities offered. (Rev: BL 5/15/04) [363.2]

19980 Paige, David. *A Day in the Life of a Marine Biologist* (4–6). Illus. 1981, Troll paper $3.95 (0-89375-447-1). 32pp. Colorful pictures and brief text are used to describe the daily tasks of a marine biologist.

19981 Pasternak, Ceel, and Linda Thornburg. *Cool Careers for Girls in Engineering* (5–8). Series: Cool Careers for Girls. 1999, Impact $19.95 (1-57023-126-5); paper $12.95 (1-57023-119-2). 132pp. Examines engineering specializations — such as computer, biomedical, civil, and agricultural — and the opportunities for women in these fields. (Rev: SLJ 1/00) [620]

19982 Reeves, Diane Lindsey. *Career Ideas for Kids Who Like Science* (5–9). Illus. by Nancy Bond. Series: Career Ideas for Kids. 1998, Facts on File $23.00 (0-8160-3680-2); paper $12.95 (0-8060-3686-1). 165pp. An upbeat, breezy introduction to 15 careers, providing aptitude tests and information on educational requirements, working conditions, activities, etc. (Rev: SLJ 9/98) [500]

19983 Swinburne, Stephen R. *The Woods Scientist* (4–8). Photos by Susan C. Morse. Illus. Series: Scientists in the Field. 2003, Houghton Mifflin $16.00 (0-618-04602-X). 48pp. Swinburne describes his fascinating expeditions in the company of a conservationist and ecologist in the woods of Vermont, and provides lots of information on risks to wildlife. (Rev: BCCB 3/03; BL 3/15/03; HBG 10/03; SLJ 4/03) [591.73]

19984 Williams, Judith. *Discovering Dinosaurs with a Fossil Hunter* (1–3). Illus. by Michael W. Skrepnick. Series: I Like Science! 2004, Enslow LB $16.95 (0-7660-2267-6). 24pp. Readers follow a paleontologist through work in the field and learn how to re-create a plant fossil. (Rev: BL 4/1/04; SLJ 2/05) [567.9]

Transportation

19985 Flanagan, Alice K. *Flying an Agricultural Plane with Mr. Miller* (PS–1). Series: Our Neighborhood. 1999, Children's Book Pr. LB $19.50 (0-

516-21132-3). 32pp. The various duties of an agricultural airplane pilot, such as crop spraying, are covered in this photo-filled book with a simple text. (Rev: BL 7/99; HBG 9/99) [629.13]

19986 Gorman, Jacqueline Laks. *Bus Driver / El Conductor del Autobús* (PS–2). Photos by Gregg Andersen. Series: People in My Community/La Gente de Mi Comunidad. 2002, Gareth Stevens LB $18.60 (0-8368-3306-6). 24pp. Full-color photographs and single-sentence descriptions, in English and in Spanish, introduce various aspects of a bus driver's job. (Rev: HBG 3/03; SLJ 3/03)

19987 Liebman, Dan. *I Want to Be a Truck Driver* (K–2). Series: I Want to Be. 2001, Firefly LB $14.95 (1-55209-576-2). 24pp. The daily life of a truck driver is described using a brief text and color photographs on each page. (Rev: BL 12/15/01; HBG 10/01) [629.24]

19988 Royston, Angela. *Truck Trouble* (1–3). Illus. Series: Eyewitness Reader. 1998, DK paper $3.95 (0-7894-2958-6). 32pp. This easy reader describes the problems — a flat tire and a rainstorm — encountered by a truck driver who is making a special delivery to a children's hospital. (Rev: BL 7/98) [629.2]

19989 Schomp, Virginia. *If You Were a Pilot* (1–3). Series: If You Were A. 1999, Benchmark LB $15.95 (0-7614-0919-X). 32pp. A brief, attractive introduction to what a pilot does, plus a discussion of different kinds of planes. (Rev: HBG 9/00; SLJ 3/00) [629.132]

19990 Schomp, Virginia. *If You Were a Truck Driver* (3–4). Series: If You Were A. 2000, Benchmark LB $15.95 (0-7614-1003-1). 32pp. Covers the daily life of a truck driver, with information on the care and handling of trucks. (Rev: BL 11/15/00; HBG 3/01) [629.24]

Veterinarians

19991 Bryant, Jennifer. *Jane Sayler: Veterinarian* (3–5). Illus. Series: Working Moms. 1991, Children's Book Pr. LB $21.27 (0-516-07378-8). 40pp. Combining the jobs of mother and animal doctor is the focus of this career book. (Rev: BL 6/15/91; SLJ 6/91) [636]

19992 Davis, Wendy. *Working at a Marine Institute* (1–3). Series: Working Here. 1998, Children's Book Pr. LB $23.00 (0-516-21223-0). 32pp. Different workers at the Marine Resources Development Foundation in Key Largo, Florida, are introduced with a description of their jobs and a picture of each. (Rev: HBG 3/99; SLJ 3/99) [636]

19993 Ermitage, Kathleen. *Veterinarian* (2–4). Series: Workers You Know. 2000, Raintree LB $25.59 (0-8172-5592-3). 32pp. Describes a day in the life of a vet, including routine diagnoses, emergency procedures, and follow-up activities. (Rev: HBG 9/00; SLJ 11/00) [636.089]

19994 Flanagan, Alice K. *Dr. Friedman Helps Animals* (1–2). Series: Our Neighborhood. 1999, Children's Book Pr. LB $19.50 (0-516-21138-2). 32pp. Colorful illustrations and large-type text introduce the reader to veterinary medicine, through the daily experiences of a female vet. (Rev: BL 10/15/99) [636]

19995 Kalman, Bobbie. *Veterinarians Help Keep Animals Healthy* (1–4). Illus. Series: My Community and Its Helpers. 2004, Crabtree LB $16.95 (0-7787-2097-7); paper $8.06 (0-7787-2125-6). 32pp. A simple review of the work of veterinarians and the education necessary for a career in this field. (Rev: SLJ 6/05) [636]

19996 Knight, Bertram T. *Working at a Zoo* (1–3). Photos by Tom Stack and Therisa Stack. Series: Working Here. 1998, Children's Book Pr. LB $23.00 (0-516-20751-2). 32pp. Various workers at the zoo in Miami are introduced with descriptions of their jobs and how they keep the animals healthy and happy. (Rev: HBG 3/99; SLJ 3/99) [590]

19997 Leboutillier, Nate. *A Day in the Life of a Zookeeper* (K–3). Series: First Facts: Community Helpers at Work. 2004, Capstone LB $21.26 (0-7368-2632-7). 24pp. Using a question-and-answer format and full-color photos, this volume looks at the tasks a zookeeper performs. (Rev: SLJ 1/05) [636]

19998 Liebman, Dan. *I Want to Be a Vet* (PS–1). Illus. Series: I Want to Be. 2000, Firefly LB $14.95 (1-55209-471-5); paper $3.99 (1-55209-469-3). 24pp. A very simple introduction to what veterinarians do and how they are prepared for their jobs. (Rev: BL 9/15/00; HBG 9/00; SLJ 2/01) [636]

19999 Maze, Stephanie, and Catherine O. Grace. *I Want to Be a Veterinarian* (3–5). Illus. Series: I Want to Be. 1997, Harcourt $16.00 (0-15-201296-6). 48pp. Describes the responsibilities of a veterinarian, educational requirements for the profession, and how to make a start toward getting into the field. (Rev: BCCB 5/97; BL 4/15/97; HB 5–6/97; SLJ 4/97) [636]

20000 Owen, Ann. *Caring for Your Pets: A Book About Veterinarians* (PS–3). Illus. by Eric Thomas. Series: Community Workers. 2004, Picture Window LB $21.26 (1-4048-0087-5). 24pp. A simple, first look at the many tasks of veterinarians as they work with pets, livestock, and wild animals. (Rev: SLJ 4/04) [636]

20001 Patrick, Jean L. S. *Cows, Cats, and Kids: A Veterinarian's Family at Work* (3–6). Illus. by Alvis Upitis. 2003, Boyds Mills $17.95 (1-56397-111-9). 48pp. A rural vet's wife describes the family's love of animals and the ways in which her children are able to help their father. (Rev: BL 3/1/03; HBG 10/03; SLJ 4/03) [636.089]

20002 Schomp, Virginia. *If You Were a Veterinarian* (3–4). Series: If You Were A. 1997, Marshall Cavendish LB $22.79 (0-7614-0613-1). 32pp. In this simple career book, the everyday activities of a veterinarian are described, with some information on the educational background necessary. (Rev: BL 2/15/98; HBG 3/98; SLJ 2/98) [636]

Health and the Human Body

Aging and Death

20003 Dennison, Amy, and Allie Dennison. *Our Dad Died: The True Story of Three Kids Whose Lives Changed* (3–7). Illus. by authors. 2003, Free Spirit paper $9.95 (1-57542-135-6). 107pp. Three young siblings recount their initial reaction to the sudden and unexpected death of their father and how, with support from their mother, they learned to live with this loss. (Rev: SLJ 1/04) [155.9]

20004 Helmer, Diana Star. *Let's Talk About When Someone You Know Is in a Nursing Home* (PS–2). Photos by Seth Dinnerman. Series: Let's Talk. 1999, Rosen LB $11.95 (0-8239-5190-1). 24pp. A simply written account that answers questions that children might have about nursing homes, including how to be comfortable when visiting. (Rev: SLJ 12/99) [362]

20005 Hyde, Margaret O., and Lawrence E. Hyde. *Meeting Death* (5–8). 1989, Walker LB $15.85 (0-8027-6874-1). After a history of how various cultures regard death, the authors discuss this phenomenon, the concept of grieving, and how to face death. (Rev: BL 1/1/90; SLJ 11/89) [306.9]

20006 Jackson, Aariane R. *Can You Hear Me Smiling? A Child Grieves a Sister* (2–4). Series: New Child and Family Press Titles 2004, Child Welfare League of America $9.95 (0-87868-835-8). 40pp. Nine-year-old Aariane discusses the conflicting emotions she experienced after the sudden death of her older sister in this story that will be helpful for counselors. (Rev: BL 7/04) [155.9]

20007 Johnston, Marianne. *Let's Talk About Going to a Funeral* (1–4). Series: Let's Talk. 1998, Rosen LB $13.95 (0-8239-5038-7). 24pp. This book describes what happens before, during, and after a funeral and discusses grieving, the cemetery, the grave, and cremation. (Rev: SLJ 7/98) [393]

20008 Krementz, Jill. *How It Feels When a Parent Dies* (4–7). Illus. 1988, Knopf paper $15.00 (0-394-

75854-4). 128pp. Eighteen experiences of parental death are recounted.

20009 LeShan, Eda. *Learning to Say Good-bye: When a Parent Dies* (5–7). Illus. by Paul Giovanopoulos. 1976, Avon paper $8.00 (0-380-40105-3). 96pp. A sympathetic explanation of the many reactions children have to death.

20010 Perl, Lila. *Dying to Know . . .: About Death, Funeral Customs, and Final Resting Places* (5–7). Illus. 2001, Twenty-First Century LB $25.90 (0-7613-1564-0). 95pp. Ancient and contemporary funeral and burial practices are covered in this book that ends with a selection of humorous epitaphs. (Rev: BL 12/1/01; HBG 10/02; SLJ 12/01) [393]

20011 Rebman, Renee C. *Euthanasia and the "Right to Die": A Pro/Con Issue* (5–8). Illus. Series: Pro/Con Issues. 2002, Enslow LB $21.95 (0-7660-1816-4). 64pp. An objective examination of both sides of the issue of euthanasia. (Rev: BL 9/1/02; HBG 3/03) [179.7]

20012 Stalfelt, Pernilla. *The Death Book* (2–4). Illus. 2002, Groundwood $15.95 (0-88899-482-6). 32pp. A straightforward yet lighthearted look at death, including the customs surrounding it, what might happen when we die, and an "interview" with a ghost. (Rev: BL 2/1/03; HBG 3/03; SLJ 8/03) [306.9]

20013 Walker, Richard. *A Right to Die?* (4–8). Series: Viewpoints. 1997, Watts LB $23.00 (0-531-14413-5). This objective book discusses traditional views of death, describes the impact of modern medicine on life spans, and presents different points of view on suicide, euthanasia, life-support systems, doctors' duties and responsibilities in terminal situations, hospice programs, living wills, and funeral choices. (Rev: SLJ 5/97) [306.88]

20014 Wilson, Antoine. *You and a Death in Your Family* (5–8). Series: Family Matters. 2001, Rosen LB $23.95 (0-8239-3355-5). 48pp. Wilson provides concise, readable advice on coping with the death of a relative or pet and stresses that youngsters should seek help when necessary. (Rev: SLJ 8/01) [155.9]

Alcohol, Drugs, and Smoking

20015 Algeo, Philippa. *Acid and Hallucinogens* (5–8). Illus. 1990, Watts paper $20.80 (0-531-10932-1). This book discusses the composition and effects of such drugs as LSD, mescaline, marijuana, and angel dust. (Rev: BL 8/90; SLJ 10/90) [615]

20016 Boyd, George A. *Drugs and Sex* (5–10). Illus. Series: Drug Abuse Prevention Library. 1994, Rosen LB $17.95 (0-8239-1538-7). A careful examination of the hazards of combining drugs and sex, including unsafe sex, pregnancy, AIDS, and other sexually transmitted diseases. (Rev: BL 6/1–15/94; SLJ 5/94) [613.9]

20017 Bryant-Mole, Karen. *Drugs* (2–3). Series: Talking About. 1999, Raintree LB $15.98 (0-8172-5887-6). 32pp. Large pages, large type, big color photos, and short sentences introduce, from a child's point of view, drugs and their use and misuse. (Rev: BL 2/15/00; HBG 9/00; SLJ 5/00) [362.29]

20018 Clayton, Lawrence. *Alcohol Drug Dangers* (4–7). Illus. Series: Drug Dangers. 1999, Enslow LB $21.95 (0-7660-1159-3). 64pp. Using real-life case histories, this book describes the effects of alcohol on the body and mind. (Rev: BL 8/99; HBG 9/99) [362.292]

20019 Clayton, Lawrence. *Diet Pill Drug Dangers* (5–9). Series: Drug Dangers. 1999, Enslow LB $19.95 (0-7660-1158-5). With liberal use of case histories, this book explores the dangers of diet pill use, their effects on the human body, and prevention techniques. (Rev: HBG 9/99; SLJ 9/99) [362.29]

20020 Galas, Judith C. *Drugs and Sports* (5–8). Illus. Series: Overview. 1997, Lucent LB $27.45 (1-56006-185-5). A look at the kinds of illegal drugs taken by athletes, the reasons for their use, and the ways in which their use can be detected. (Rev: BL 3/15/97) [362.29]

20021 Green, Jen. *Alcohol* (2–3). Series: Talking About. 1999, Raintree LB $15.98 (0-8172-5888-4). 32pp. A simple but colorfully illustrated introduction to alcohol — what it is and how it affects the human body. (Rev: BL 2/15/00; HBG 9/00) [613.8]

20022 Grosshandler-Smith, Janet. *Working Together Against Drinking and Driving* (4–8). Series: The Library of Social Activism. 1996, Rosen LB $16.95 (0-8239-2259-6). With an emphasis on prevention, the author presents a general discussion on drinking and driving and its consequences, followed by pointers on how to avoid embarrassing situations, how to handle peer pressure about drinking. (Rev: SLJ 2/97) [613.8]

20023 Hanan, Jessica. *When Someone You Love Is Addicted* (5–9). Series: Drug Abuse Prevention Library. 1999, Rosen LB $17.95 (0-8239-2831-4). A short book that begins with teenage case histories and then discusses treatments and resources for young people with drug problems. (Rev: SLJ 7/99) [362.29]

20024 Haughton, Emma. *Alcohol* (5–10). Series: Talking Points. 1999, Raintree $27.11 (0-8172-

5317-1). 64pp. A candid look at the use and abuse of alcohol and its physical and emotional effects. (Rev: BL 8/99) [613.8]

20025 Haughton, Emma. *A Right to Smoke?* (4–8). Series: Viewpoints. 1997, Watts LB $23.00 (0-531-14412-7). Using double-page spreads, this book offers different viewpoints on who smokes, why they start, the physical dangers, second-hand smoke, the tobacco industry giants, taxes on cigarettes, advertising, and programs to discourage people from smoking. (Rev: BL 6/1–15/97; SLJ 5/97) [362.2]

20026 Hirschfelder, Arlene. *Kick Butts! A Kid's Action Guide to a Tobacco-Free America* (5–8). Illus. 1998, Silver Burdett $19.95 (0-382-39632-4); paper $9.95 (0-382-39633-2). 160pp. A look at the history of smoking in the United States and its connection with various diseases, followed by examples of steps taken by young activists to create a smoke-free environment. (Rev: BL 6/1–15/98; HBG 9/98; SLJ 7/98) [613.8]

20027 Hyde, Margaret O. *Know About Drugs*. 4th ed. (5–8). 1995, Walker LB $15.85 (0-8027-8395-3). 93pp. An introduction to drugs including marijuana, alcohol, PCP, inhalants, crack/cocaine, heroin, and nicotine. (Rev: BL 7/90; SLJ 3/96) [362.2]

20028 Hyde, Margaret O. *Know About Smoking*. Rev. ed. (5–8). Illus. 1995, Walker LB $14.85 (0-8027-8400-3). 100pp. After a history of tobacco and nicotine, this book describes their effects on the body, addiction prevention, and the role of advertising in smoking. (Rev: BL 7/90; SLJ 9/95) [362.2]

20029 Hyde, Margaret O., and John F. Setaro. *Alcohol 101: An Overview for Teens* (5–10). 1999, Twenty-First Century LB $24.90 (0-7613-1274-9). 128pp. Kinds of alcohol and their effects are described, with material on alcoholism and binge drinking. (Rev: HBG 3/00; SLJ 3/00) [613.8]

20030 Kreiner, Anna. *Let's Talk About Drug Abuse* (1–4). Illus. Series: Let's Talk. 1996, Rosen LB $13.95 (0-8239-2302-9). 24pp. Various kinds of drugs and their effects on the human body are introduced. (Rev: BL 3/1/97; SLJ 12/96) [362.29]

20031 Landau, Elaine. *Hooked: Talking About Addiction* (5–10). Illus. 1995, Millbrook LB $22.90 (1-56294-469-X). 64pp. This account defines addiction broadly — from use of alcohol and drugs to various forms of compulsive behavior — and gives suggestions for recovery. (Rev: BL 1/1–15/96; SLJ 1/96) [362.29]

20032 Lawler, Jennifer. *Drug Testing in Schools: A Pro/Con Issue* (5–8). Series: Hot Issues. 2000, Enslow LB $21.95 (0-7660-1367-7). 64pp. The pros and cons of drug testing in schools are presented in an unbiased manner with sections on methods of drug testing, policies of various organizations, and the opinions of students, teachers, and parents. (Rev: HBG 3/01; SLJ 12/00) [362.29]

20033 Lee, Mary Price, and Richard S. Lee. *Drugs and the Media* (5–10). Illus. Series: Drug Abuse Prevention Library. 1994, Rosen LB $17.95 (0-8239-1537-9). This book shows that the media often unintentionally glamorize drug use and describes how teens can evaluate the media's mixed messages. (Rev: BL 6/1–15/94; SLJ 5/94) [070.4]

20034 Littell, Mary Ann. *Heroin Drug Dangers* (5–8). Series: Drug Dangers. 1999, Enslow LB $21.95 (0-7660-1156-9). A short, well-illustrated book that describes the physiological effects of heroin, the dangers of its use, and how to resist its temptations. (Rev: BL 9/15/99; HBG 4/00) [362.29]

20035 McGuire, Paula. *Alcohol* (4–8). Illus. Series: Preteen Pressures. 1998, Raintree LB $25.69 (0-8172-5026-3). 48pp. Topics discussed in this practical account include peer pressure to drink, the physical effects of alcohol, underage drinking, alcoholic parents, and ways to seek help. (Rev: BL 4/15/98; HBG 9/98) [362.29]

20036 Monroe, Judy. *Inhalant Drug Dangers* (5–9). 1999, Enslow LB $21.95 (0-7660-1153-4). Using case histories — such as the story of Ian, who is addicted to inhaling fabric protector — this slim volume tells of the effects and dangers of inhalants. (Rev: BL 8/99; HBG 9/99; SLJ 9/99) [362.29]

20037 Monroe, Judy. *Steroid Drug Dangers* (5–8). Illus. Series: Drug Dangers. 1999, Enslow LB $21.95 (0-7660-1154-2). Case histories, facts, and statistics introduce the reader to steroid drugs and their legal and illegal uses, their effects and dangers, and the organizations that promote safe usage. (Rev: BL 9/15/99; HBG 4/00) [362.29]

20038 Murdico, Suzanne J. *Drug Abuse* (4–8). Series: Preteen Pressures. 1998, Raintree LB $25.69 (0-8172-5027-1). 48pp. This work discusses drug abuse, with emphasis on healthy alternatives and solutions to typical drug-related problems faced by many young people. (Rev: BL 5/15/98; HBG 9/98) [362.2]

20039 Pringle, Laurence. *Smoking: A Risky Business* (5–10). 1996, Morrow $16.00 (0-688-13039-9). After a history of tobacco, this book describes the dangers of smoking and the advertising strategies used to get people to smoke. (Rev: BL 12/1/96; SLJ 1/97) [362.2]

20040 Robbins, Paul R. *Crack and Cocaine Drug Dangers* (5–9). Series: Drug Dangers. 1999, Enslow LB $21.95 (0-7660-1155-0). Charts, photographs, fact boxes, and a succinct text are used to discuss crack cocaine, its effects, and how to avoid its use. (Rev: BL 9/15/99; HBG 4/00) [362.29]

20041 Salak, John. *Drugs in Society: Are They Our Suicide Pill?* (5–8). Illus. Series: Issues of Our Time. 1993, Twenty-First Century LB $18.90 (0-8050-2572-3). 64pp. A slim, easily read account that describes the history of drug abuse, its unfortunate byproducts, and important cases involving such people as Manuel Noriega. (Rev: SLJ 2/94) [616]

20042 Sanders, Pete. *Smoking* (4–7). Illus. Series: What Do You Know About. 1996, Millbrook LB $23.90 (0-7613-0536-X). 32pp. Covers the effects of smoking and ways in which youngsters can avoid getting hooked. (Rev: SLJ 3/97) [362.2]

20043 Sanders, Pete, and Steve Myers. *Drinking Alcohol* (4–8). Illus. Series: What Do You Know About. 1997, Millbrook LB $23.90 (0-7613-0573-

4). An introduction to alcohol use and abuse, with material on how alcohol affects the body and behavior. (Rev: SLJ 10/97) [613.8]

20044 Schleifer, Jay. *Methamphetamine: Speed Kills* (5–9). Series: Drug Abuse Prevention Library. 1999, Rosen LB $17.95 (0-8239-2512-9). An introduction to this drug, its effects, the crime and violence associated with it, and agencies and organizations where help is available. (Rev: SLJ 7/99) [362.29]

20045 Sherry, Clifford J. *Drugs and Eating Disorders* (5–10). Illus. Series: Drug Abuse Prevention Library. 1994, Rosen LB $17.95 (0-8239-1540-9). Shows how diet pills and other weight-loss products can lead to drug abuse and, in some cases, addiction. (Rev: BL 6/1–15/94; SLJ 6/94) [616.85]

20046 Sherry, Clifford J. *Inhalants* (5–10). 1994, Rosen LB $17.95 (0-8239-1704-5). A look at inhalants, where they are found, and how they affect the body. (Rev: BL 2/15/95; SLJ 3/95) [362.29]

20047 Simpson, Carolyn. *Methadone* (5–9). Series: Drug Abuse Prevention Library. 1997, Rosen LB $17.95 (0-8239-2286-3). The dangers of heroin are discussed, followed by an objective discussion of the pros and cons of methadone, the legal drug used to combat heroin addiction. (Rev: SLJ 11/97) [362.29]

20048 Somdahl, Gary L. *Marijuana Drug Dangers* (5–8). Series: Drug Dangers. 1999, Enslow LB $21.95 (0-7660-1214-X). 64pp. After introducing marijuana and its effects, this account covers its misuse and abuse and ways to resist it. (Rev: BL 11/15/99; HBG 4/00) [362.29]

20049 Taylor, Clark. *The House That Crack Built* (3–8). Illus. by Jan T. Dicks. 1992, Chronicle paper $6.95 (0-8118-0123-3). 36pp. An old children's rhyme is turned into a dark verse, with a relentless rap beat, about drugs. (Rev: BL 4/15/92; SLJ 6/92) [362.29]

20050 Washburne, Carolyn K. *Drug Abuse* (5–8). Illus. Series: Overview. 1996, Lucent LB $27.45 (1-56006-169-3). 112pp. A carefully researched account that gives important background information on drug abuse and present-day practices and problems. (Rev: BL 1/1–15/96) [362.29]

20051 Wax, Wendy. *Say No and Know Why: Kids Learn About Drugs* (4–7). Illus. by Toby McAfee. 1992, Walker LB $13.85 (0-8027-8141-1). 80pp. A serious look at drug problems as a 6th-grade class in the Bronx, New York, gets a visit from a local nurse and an assistant district attorney. (Rev: BL 1/15/93; SLJ 10/92) [362.29]

20052 Weitzman, Elizabeth. *Let's Talk About Smoking* (4–8). Illus. Series: Let's Talk. 1996, Rosen LB $17.25 (0-8239-2307-X). 24pp. This book explains why people smoke, its effects, and ways to avoid starting, with tips on how to give up. (Rev: BL 3/15/97; SLJ 1/97) [362.29]

20053 Westcott, Patsy. *Why Do People Take Drugs?* (5–7). Series: Exploring Tough Issues. 2001, Raintree LB $25.69 (0-7398-3231-X). 48pp. Drugs from caffeine to cocaine are explored, with discussion of society's attitudes toward drugs, legal issues, and the reasons some people are more tempted to abuse substances. (Rev: HBG 10/01; SLJ 7/01) [362.29]

Bionics and Transplants

20054 Beecroft, Simon. *Super Humans: A Beginner's Guide to Bionics* (5–7). Illus. by Ian Thompson and Stephen Sweet. Series: Future Files. 1998, Millbrook LB $23.40 (0-7613-0621-8). 32pp. This work explores such futuristic topics as cloning humans, gene manipulation, electronic body parts, and life extension. (Rev: HBG 9/98; SLJ 10/98) [617.9]

20055 Fullick, Ann. *Rebuilding the Body* (5–8). Illus. Series: Science at the Edge. 2002, Heinemann LB $27.86 (1-58810-700-0). 64pp. An insightful volume about transplant procedures, including a section on how the organs of the body function and a discussion about ethics. (Rev: BL 10/15/02; HBG 3/03; SLJ 4/03) [617.9]

20056 Rosaler, Maxine. *Bionics* (5–9). Series: Science on the Edge. 2003, Gale LB $20.95 (1-56711-784-8). 48pp. This account explores the science of fusing artificial parts with human parts to aid body functions and comments on the controversy surround this new science. (Rev: BL 10/15/03; SLJ 3/04) [174]

Disabilities, Physical and Mental

20057 Abeel, Samantha. *What Once Was White* (5–8). Illus. by Charles R. Murphy. 1993, Village Pr. $19.95 (0-941653-13-7). The author is a 13-year-old learning-disabled student who can't tell time but writes sensitive interpretations of a group of watercolor paintings. (Rev: SLJ 9/93*) [618.62]

20058 Alexander, Sally H. *Do You Remember the Color Blue? And Other Questions Kids Ask About Blindness* (5–8). Illus. 2000, Viking $16.99 (0-670-88043-4). 80pp. The writer, a blind person, tells about her daily life — how she tells time and works with her guide dog and how she and others have reacted to her disability. (Rev: BCCB 3/00; BL 3/15/00; HBG 9/00; SLJ 4/00) [305.9]

20059 Aseltine, Lorraine, et al. *I'm Deaf and It's Okay* (3–5). Illus. by Helen Cogancherry. 1986, Whitman LB $13.95 (0-8075-3472-2). 40pp. A boy copes with the frustrations of deafness. (Rev: BL 5/15/86; SLJ 8/86)

20060 Baldwin, Carol. *Autism* (4–6). Illus. Series: Health Matters. 2002, Heinemann LB $22.79 (1-4034-0250-7). 32pp. Examines the causes and symptoms of autism and offers an inspiring profile of Scottish artist Richard Wawro, who has become world-famous despite his autism. (Rev: HBG 10/03; SLJ 5/03) [616.8]

20061 Brown, Fern G. *Special Olympics* (4–7). Illus. 1992, Watts paper $22.00 (0-531-20062-0). 64pp. The history of the Special Olympics, which began

in 1963. (Rev: BCCB 5/92; BL 6/1/92; SLJ 7/92) [796]

20062 Dendy, Chris A. Zeigler, and Alex Zeigler. *A Bird's-Eye View of Life with ADD and ADHD: Advice from Young Survivors* (5–9). 2003, Cherish the Children paper $19.95 (0-9679911-3-7). 180pp. A guide to ADD and ADHD, written by a dozen teenagers with these disorders with the aim of helping others cope, with advice on succeeding in school, medication, driving, and so forth. (Rev: SLJ 4/04) [618.9]

20063 Dinner, Sherry H. *Nothing to Be Ashamed Of: Growing Up with Mental Illness in Your Family* (5–10). 1989, Lothrop LB $12.93 (0-688-08482-6). A psychologist gives good advice to those who live with a mentally ill person. (Rev: BL 6/1/89; BR 11–12/89; SLJ 4/89) [616.89]

20064 Dwight, Laura. *We Can Do It!* (PS–3). Illus. 1992, Checkerboard $7.95 (1-56288-301-1). 36pp. Children with various disabilities are shown at home, at play, at school. (Rev: BL 1/15/93) [305]

20065 Dwyer, Kathleen M. *What Do You Mean I Have a Learning Disability?* (3–6). 1991, Walker LB $15.85 (0-8027-8103-9). 48pp. Feelings of inferiority are related in this story of a ten-year-old boy who fails in school. (Rev: BCCB 9/91; BL 9/1/91; SLJ 11/91) [371.9]

20066 Dwyer, Kathleen M. *What Do You Mean I Have Attention Deficit Disorder?* (4–6). Illus. 1996, Walker LB $15.85 (0-8027-8393-7). 128pp. Patrick doesn't know why he can't pay attention in school until he is diagnosed as having ADD. (Rev: BCCB 9/96; BL 8/96; SLJ 8/96) [618.92]

20067 Gordon, Melanie Apel. *Let's Talk About Dyslexia* (2–4). Series: Let's Talk. 1999, Rosen LB $13.95 (0-8239-5199-5). 24pp. This book describes problems with reading and gives several examples of reading difficulties. (Rev: SLJ 3/99) [371.92]

20068 Gray, Shirley W. *Good Mental Health* (2–4). Illus. Series: Living Well. 2003, Child's World LB $25.64 (1-59296-082-0). 32pp. Worry, stress, depression, and other mental problems are discussed. (Rev: SLJ 2/04) [616.89]

20069 Heelan, Jamee Riggio. *Can You Hear a Rainbow? The Story of a Deaf Boy Named Chris* (K–3). Illus. by Nicola Simmonds. 2002, Peachtree $14.95 (1-56145-268-8). Chris tells the reader how sign language and other aids help him to cope with his deafness. (Rev: HBG 10/02; SLJ 9/02) [362.42]

20070 Heelan, Jamee Riggio. *The Making of My Special Hand: Madison's Story* (PS–3). Photos by author. Illus. by Nicola Simmonds. 2000, Peachtree $14.95 (1-56145-186-X). Described the process of making a prosthesis for a girl who was born with one hand, from taking a plaster cast to connecting the electrode and battery and giving occupational therapy. (Rev: BL 4/1/00; HBG 3/01; SLJ 9/00) [617.5]

20071 Heelan, Jamee Riggio. *Rolling Along: The Story of Taylor and His Wheelchair* (PS–4). Illus. by Nicola Simmonds. 2000, Peachtree $14.95 (1-56145-219-X). 32pp. The true story of Taylor, who was born with cerebral palsy and uses a wheelchair. (Rev: BL 9/1/00; HBG 3/01; SLJ 12/00) [616.6]

20072 Kent, Deborah. *American Sign Language* (5–7). Series: Watts Library: Disabilities. 2003, Watts LB $24.00 (0-531-12018-X); paper $8.95 (0-531-16662-7). 64pp. This work covers the history of sign language, explains how it works, and tells how it has help countless deaf people. (Rev: BL 10/15/03; SLJ 6/03) [001.56]

20073 Kent, Susan. *Let's Talk About Stuttering* (3–5). Series: Let's Talk. 2000, Rosen LB $17.26 (0-8239-5423-4). 24pp. As well as explaining what causes stuttering and who is most likely to stutter, this book tells how to deal with teasing and how to get help. (Rev: SLJ 2/01) [616.85]

20074 Landau, Elaine. *Blindness* (4–7). Illus. Series: Understanding Illness. 1994, Twenty-First Century LB $24.90 (0-8050-2992-3). 64pp. Both the emotional and scientific aspects of blindness are covered, with an excellent chapter on prevention. (Rev: BL 12/15/94; SLJ 2/95) [617.7]

20075 Landau, Elaine. *Deafness* (4–7). Illus. Series: Understanding Illness. 1994, Twenty-First Century LB $24.90 (0-8050-2993-1). 64pp. Beginning with the story of a deaf child, this book explores the causes of deafness, the scientific and emotional factors involved, treatments, and problems in adjusting. (Rev: BL 12/15/94; SLJ 2/95) [617.8]

20076 Landau, Elaine. *Dyslexia* (3–6). Series: Life Balanc. 2004, Watts LB $19.50 (0-531-12217-4). 79pp. An informative and practical guide that describes dyslexia and talks about ways to cope with the problem, mentioning famous people who have dealt with this "learning difference." (Rev: SLJ 7/04) [616.85]

20077 Landau, Elaine. *Schizophrenia* (4–8). Illus. Series: Life Balance. 2004, Watts LB $19.50 (0-531-12215-8); paper $6.95 (0-531-16614-7). 80pp. An overview of the causes, symptoms, and treatment of this mental condition, with true stories of sufferers.

20078 Leigh, Vanora. *Mental Illness* (5–10). Series: Talking Points. 1999, Raintree LB $27.12 (0-8172-5311-4). 64pp. This book defines mental illness, gives examples, and discusses causes, treatments, and how to stay mentally healthy. (Rev: BL 8/99; BR 9–10/99; SLJ 8/99) [362.2]

20079 MacKinnon, Christy. *Silent Observer* (K–4). Illus. 1993, Gallaudet Univ. $15.95 (1-56368-022-X). 48pp. The journal of a young deaf girl growing up in Nova Scotia at the end of the 19th century and her experiences at a boarding school. (Rev: BL 1/15/94; SLJ 3/94) [362.4]

20080 McMahon, Patricia. *Dancing Wheels* (3–7). Illus. 2000, Houghton Mifflin $16.00 (0-395-88889-1). 48pp. Founded by a woman born with spina bifida, the Dancing Wheels project teaches people to "dance" from their wheelchairs. (Rev: BL 10/1/00; HBG 3/01; SLJ 11/00) [792.8]

20081 McNey, Martha. *Leslie's Story: A Book About a Girl with Mental Retardation* (3–5). Illus. 1996, Lerner LB $21.27 (0-8225-2576-3). 32pp. The

lifestyle and limitations of a mentally retarded girl are explained. (Rev: BL 7/96; SLJ 9/96) [362.3]

20082 McCarthy-Tucker, Sherri. *Coping with Special-Needs Classmates* (5–8). 1993, Rosen LB $25.25 (0-8239-1598-0). 115pp. First-person accounts describe physical, mental, and emotional problems faced by some young people. (Rev: SLJ 8/93) [616]

20083 Meyer, Donald, ed. *Views from Our Shoes: Growing Up with a Brother or Sister with Special Needs* (4–6). Illus. 1997, Woodbine paper $14.95 (0-933149-98-0). 106pp. Using the words of 45 youngsters ages four to 18 as a focus, this book tells what it is like living with a sibling who has a physical or mental disability. (Rev: BL 1/1–15/98; SLJ 4/98) [362.1]

20084 Nemiroff, Marc A., and Jane Annunziata. *Help Is on the Way: A Child's Book About ADD* (K–3). Illus. by Margaret Scott. 1998, Magination $19.95 (1-55798-505-7). 60pp. A picture book for children who suffer from attention deficit disorder, with material on its symptoms, the emotions it causes, and treatments that are available. (Rev: SLJ 9/98) [371.9]

20085 Pigache, Philippa. *ADHD* (4–8). Series: Just the Facts. 2004, Heinemann LB $27.07 (1-4034-5142-7). 56pp. The symptoms, causes, and treatment of attention deficit hyperactivity disorder are described, with discussion of continuing research. (Rev: SLJ 5/05)

20086 Powell, Jillian. *Talking About Disability* (2–3). Illus. Series: Talking About. 1999, Raintree LB $22.83 (0-8172-5537-0). 32pp. Large pages, big type, and color photographs introduce children to physical and mental disabilities. (Rev: BL 7/99; HBG 9/99) [362.4]

20087 Riggs, Stephanie. *Never Sell Yourself Short* (3–6). Illus. 2001, Whitman $15.95 (0-8075-5563-0). 32pp. Through text and photographs, readers learn how Josh, a 14-year-old dwarf, enjoys his life despite obstacles. (Rev: BCCB 1/02; BL 9/1/01; HBG 3/02; SLJ 11/01) [618.92]

20088 Rotner, Shelley, and Sheila Kelly. *The A.D.D. Book for Kids* (K–3). Illus. 2000, Millbrook LB $22.90 (0-7613-1722-8). 32pp. This photo-essay describes attention deficit disorder and its various symptoms and coping mechanisms. (Rev: BL 4/15/00; HBG 9/00; SLJ 7/00) [618.9]

20089 Silverstein, Alvin, et al. *Dyslexia* (3–5). Series: My Health. 2001, Watts LB $23.00 (0-531-11862-2). This account describes dyslexia, its symptoms, its diagnosis, and how to get help, and provides material on brain structure and famous dyslexics. (Rev: BL 1/1–15/02; SLJ 10/01) [371.92]

20090 Silverstein, Alvin, et al. *Scoliosis* (3–5). Series: My Health. 2002, Watts LB $24.00 (0-531-12046-5); paper $6.95 (0-531-16639-2). 48pp. The causes of this abnormal curvature of the spine are covered with material on how it affects young people and how it can be treated. (Rev: BL 12/15/02) [616]

20091 Silverstein, Alvin, and Virginia Silverstein. *Attention Deficit Disorder* (3–5). Series: My Health.

2001, Watts LB $23.00 (0-531-11778-2). With many color photographs, this account discusses ADD, its causes, symptoms, and treatment. (Rev: BL 1/1–15/02; SLJ 5/01) [618.92]

20092 Stein, Sara Bonnett. *About Handicaps* (2–3). Illus. 1974, Walker $14.95 (0-8027-6174-7); paper $8.95 (0-8027-7225-0). 48pp. A book about learning to accept people who have physical handicaps.

20093 Trueit, Trudi Strain. *ADHD* (3–6). Illus. Series: Life Balance. 2004, Watts LB $19.50 (0-531-12261-1). 79pp. Trueit looks at the learning and behavioral problems faced by children — and adults — who suffer from the disorder and discusses some of the more popular methods of treatment. (Rev: SLJ 7/04) [618.92]

20094 Westcott, Patsy. *Living with Blindness* (3–5). 1999, Raintree LB $22.83 (0-8172-5741-1). 32pp. This book shows how blind people go about their daily lives and informs the reader about how the eye functions, kinds of visual impairment, and the causes of cataracts, glaucoma, and other conditions. (Rev: HBG 9/00; SLJ 4/00) [617.7]

Disease and Illness

20095 Abramovitz, Melissa. *Leukemia* (5–8). Illus. Series: Diseases and Disorders. 2002, Gale LB $27.45 (1-56006-863-9). 112pp. A look at the different types of leukemia, the possible causes, diagnosis, treatment, and the serious nature of the disease. (Rev: SLJ 3/03) [616.99419]

20096 Abrams, Liesa. *Chronic Fatigue Syndrome* (5–7). Illus. Series: Diseases and Disorders. 2003, Gale LB $27.45 (1-59018-039-9). 96pp. The symptoms of and treatments for this mysterious condition and related medical problems are covered here, along with the research being undertaken. (Rev: SLJ 7/03) [616]

20097 Aldape, Virginia Totorica. *Nicole's Story: A Book About a Girl with Juvenile Rheumatoid Arthritis* (3–5). Illus. 1996, Lerner LB $21.27 (0-8225-2578-X). 40pp. The case history of a young girl who has rheumatoid arthritis. (Rev: BL 7/96; SLJ 9/96) [362.1]

20098 Arnold, Lynda. *My Mommy Has AIDS* (PS–3). Illus. by Rosemont School of the Holy Child Students. 1998, Dream $18.95 (1-892073-01-3). 32pp. This story about a boy and his sick mother is a first-person narrative describing AIDS, how to avoid infection, and current treatments. (Rev: SLJ 5/99) [616.97]

20099 Baldwin, Carol. *Asthma* (4–6). Illus. Series: Health Matters. 2002, Heinemann LB $22.79 (1-4034-0248-5). 32pp. Examines the causes and symptoms of asthma and offers an inspiring profile of Olympic gold medalist Jackie Joyner-Kersee. (Rev: HBG 10/03; SLJ 5/03) [616.2]

20100 Baldwin, Carol. *Sickle Cell Disease* (4–6). Illus. Series: Health Matters. 2002, Heinemann LB $22.79 (1-4034-0252-3). 32pp. Examines the causes and symptoms of this disease and describes the condition of Rev. Jesse Jackson, who carries the genetic

trait for this disease. (Rev: HBG 10/03; SLJ 5/03) [616.1]

20101 Bee, Peta. *Living with Asthma* (3–5). Illus. Series: Living With. 1999, Raintree $22.83 (0-8172-5568-0). 32pp. This work discusses the causes and nature of asthma, various medications and treatments, and gives advice on how friends and family can help. (Rev: BL 8/99; HBG 9/99) [618.92]

20102 Berger, Melvin. *Germs Make Me Sick!* Rev. ed. (K–3). Illus. by Marylin Hafner. Series: Let's-Read-and-Find-Out. 1995, HarperCollins LB $15.89 (0-06-024250-7); paper $4.95 (0-06445-154-2). 32pp. In this easily read book, germs and viruses and their effects on the human body are introduced. (Rev: BL 10/1/95; SLJ 3/96) [616.9]

20103 Bjorklund, Ruth. *Asthma* (4–7). Illus. Series: Health Alert. 2004, Benchmark LB $19.95 (0-7614-1803-2). 64pp. In addition to describing the causes and treatment of asthma, this attractive title opens with a case history and also includes lists of famous people who suffer from the condition. (Rev: SLJ 5/05)

20104 Blake, Claire, et al. *The Paper Chain* (PS–2). Illus. by Kathy Parkinson. 1998, Health paper $8.95 (0-929173-28-7). 30pp. As seen through the eyes of Marcus and Ben, this book deals with breast cancer and what happens when their mother undergoes surgery, chemotherapy, and radiation. (Rev: SLJ 6/98) [616.99]

20105 Bowman-Kruhm, Mary. *Everything You Need to Know About Down Syndrome* (4–7). Series: Need to Know Library. 2000, Rosen LB $25.25 (0-8239-2949-3). 63pp. Describes the causes, symptoms, and treatment of Down syndrome, and looks at the education and family life of individuals with this condition. (Rev: HBG 9/00; SLJ 3/00) [362.1]

20106 Bridge, Chris. *Andrew's Story: A Book About a Boy Who Beat Cancer* (2–4). Illus. 2001, Lerner LB $21.27 (0-8225-2587-9). 32pp. A straightforward account of a boy's battle with cancer written in a 9-year-old's voice. (Rev: BL 1/1–15/02; HBG 3/02; SLJ 12/01) [362.1]

20107 Brill, Marlene Targ. *Alzheimer's Disease* (4–7). Illus. Series: Health Alert. 2004, Benchmark LB $19.95 (0-7614-1799-0). 64pp. In addition to describing the diagnosis and treatment of Alzheimer's disease, this attractive title opens with a case history and also includes lists of famous people who suffer from the condition. (Rev: SLJ 5/05) [362.19]

20108 Bryan, Jenny. *Asthma* (5–10). Illus. Series: Just the Facts. 2004, Heinemann LB $27.07 (1-4034-4599-0). 56pp. A well-organized explanation of asthma, illustrated with numerous color photographs and providing material on how air pollution and smoking are factors in causing or aggravating the disease. (Rev: SLJ 6/04) [616.2]

20109 Bryan, Jenny. *Diabetes* (5–10). Illus. Series: Just the Facts. 2004, Heinemann LB $27.07 (1-4034-4600-8). 56pp. An illustrated overview of the disease, including causes and treatments and the effects of diet and cultural factors. (Rev: SLJ 6/04) [616.4]

20110 Bryan, Jenny. *What's Wrong with Me? What Happens When You're Sick, and Ways to Stay Healthy* (2–4). Illus. 1995, Thomson Learning LB $5.00 (1-56847-199-8). 32pp. In this book about illnesses, double-page spreads reveal possible causes and treatments for various symptoms. (Rev: BL 3/15/95) [616]

20111 Bueche, Shelley. *The Ebola Virus* (4–7). Illus. Series: Parasites. 2003, Gale/KidHaven LB $22.45 (0-7377-1780-7). 32pp. Although it's part of the Parasites series, this book focuses on the Ebola virus, which causes an infectious illness and is found widely in Central Africa. (Rev: BL 3/1/04; SLJ 6/04) [616.9]

20112 Burnfield, Alexander. *Multiple Sclerosis* (5–8). Series: Just the Facts. 2004, Heinemann LB $27.07 (1-4034-4602-4). 56pp. An accessible explanation of multiple sclerosis, its symptoms, treatment, and the efforts being made to find new treatments and a cure. (Rev: SLJ 6/04) [616.8]

20113 Caffey, Donna. *Yikes — Lice!* (PS–4). Illus. by Patrick Girouard. 1998, Whitman $13.95 (0-8075-9374-5). 32pp. Uses rhymed couplets and cartoon illustrations to introduce head lice and their control. (Rev: BCCB 6/98; BL 4/15/98; HBG 9/98; SLJ 5/98) [616.5]

20114 Carson, Mary Kay. *Epilepsy* (4–8). Series: Diseases and People. 1998, Enslow LB $18.95 (0-7660-1049-X). 112pp. Traces the history of epilepsy and gives details on symptoms, diagnosis, and current treatments. (Rev: SLJ 9/98) [616.8]

20115 Carter, Alden R. *I'm Tougher than Diabetes!* (2–4). Illus. 2001, Whitman $14.95 (0-8075-1572-8). 32pp. A first-person account from the perspective of a pre-teen girl about the management of Type 1 diabetes, with color photographs and frequently asked questions. (Rev: BL 1/1–15/02; HBG 3/02; SLJ 5/02) [616.4]

20116 Cefrey, Holly. *Coping with Cancer* (5–10). Series: Coping. 2000, Rosen LB $18.95 (0-8239-2849-7). 138pp. As well as discussing how cancer develops in various parts of the body, this book gives self-help advice for anyone who is diagnosed with the disease. (Rev: BL 1/1–15/01; SLJ 12/00) [616.99]

20117 Cefrey, Holly. *Syphilis and Other Sexually Transmitted Diseases* (5–8). Illus. Series: Epidemics. 2001, Rosen LB $19.95 (0-8239-3488-8). 64pp. Cefrey describes historic outbreaks and treatments, as well as the symptoms and cure, of syphilis and other sexually transmitted diseases. (Rev: BL 3/15/02) [616.95]

20118 Cefrey, Holly. *Yellow Fever* (5–8). Series: Epidemics. 2002, Rosen LB $19.95 (0-8239-3489-6). 64pp. Yellow fever, spread by mosquitoes, was the cause of several epidemics in American cities during the 19th century before a cure was found by dedicated doctors who risked their lives. (Rev: BL 8/02) [616]

20119 Connelly, John P., and Leonard Berlow. *You're Too Sweet: A Guide for the Young Diabetic* (4–6). Illus. 1968, Astor-Honor $14.95 (0-8392-

1173-2). The cause and treatment of diabetes from the standpoint of a 9-year-old boy.

20120 DerKazarian, Susan. *You Have Head Lice!* (PS–2). Illus. Series: Rookie Read-About Health. 2005, Children's Pr. LB $19.50 (0-516-25879-6); paper $5.95 (0-516-27920-3). 32pp. A small-format, matter-of-fact look at head lice and their transmission and treatment. (Rev: BL 6/1–15/05) [616.5]

20121 Donnellan, William L. *The Miracle of Immunity* (5–8). Illus. Series: The Story of Science. 2002, Benchmark LB $19.95 (0-7614-1425-8). 79pp. A history of mankind's discoveries about diseases and about the body's vulnerabilities and abilities to fend off infections, from the earliest times through AIDS. (Rev: HBG 3/03; SLJ 5/03) [616.07]

20122 Donnelly, Karen. *Everything You Need to Know About Lyme Disease* (5–8). Illus. Series: Need to Know Library. 2000, Rosen LB $25.25 (0-8239-3216-8). 64pp. This book explains how Lyme disease was discovered, how it is transmitted, its symptoms, and its treatments. (Rev: BL 12/1/00) [616.9]

20123 Donnelly, Karen. *Leprosy (Hansen's Disease)* (5–8). Series: Epidemics. 2002, Rosen LB $19.95 (0-8239-3498-5). 64pp. This is the story of leprosy, the disease that created social outcasts of its victims, and of a man named Hansen who discovered an effective treatment. (Rev: BL 8/02) [616.9]

20124 Draper, Allison Stark. *Ebola* (5–8). Illus. Series: Epidemics. 2002, Rosen LB $19.95 (0-8239-3496-9). 64pp. Discusses the Ebola virus in both scientific and human terms. Also use *Mad Cow Disease* (2002). (Rev: BL 8/02; SLJ 6/02) [616.9]

20125 Fassler, David, and Kelly McQueen. *What's a Virus, Anyway? The Kids' Book About AIDS* (K–4). 1993, Waterfront $10.95 (0-914525-14-X). 67pp. This book describes what AIDS is through an explanation of what a virus is and how some viruses attack our immune system. A reissue. (Rev: BL 6/1/90) [616]

20126 Favor, Lesli J. *Bacteria* (5–8). Illus. Series: Germs: The Library of Disease-Causing Organisms. 2004, Rosen LB $25.25 (0-8239-4491-3). 48pp. An informative, illustrated discussion of bacteria, covering their discovery, how they survive, and the dangers they pose to humans. (Rev: SLJ 1/05) [616]

20127 Fleischman, John. *Phineas Gage: A Gruesome but True Story About Brain Science* (5–10). Illus. 2002, Houghton Mifflin $16.00 (0-618-05252-6). 86pp. This riveting story of the amiable man whose personality changed when an iron rod shot through his brain presents lots of information on brain science and medical knowledge in the 19th century. (Rev: BL 3/1/02; HB 5–6/02; HBG 10/02; SLJ 3/02) [362.1]

20128 Foley, Ronan. *World Health: The Impact on Our Lives* (5–8). Illus. Series: 21st Century Debates. 2003, Raintree LB $28.56 (0-7398-5507-7). 64pp. A thorough and thought-provoking exploration of the health status of countries around the world and the reasons for the wide disparity between wealthy and poor nations. (Rev: BL 8/03; HBG 10/03; SLJ 7/03) [362.1]

20129 Forbes, Anna. *Kids with AIDS* (2–5). Illus. Series: AIDS Awareness Library. 1996, Rosen LB $13.95 (0-8239-2372-X). 24pp. Essential facts about AIDS are presented simply, with a focus on living with the disease and that being with AIDS- or HIV-infected individuals need not involve a health risk. (Rev: SLJ 1/97) [616.97]

20130 Forbes, Anna. *When Someone You Know Has AIDS* (3–5). Illus. Series: The AIDS Awareness Library. 1996, Rosen LB $13.95 (0-8239-2369-X). 24pp. A simple introduction to AIDS that covers its causes, effects, and treatments. Also use *Where Did AIDS Come From?* (1996). (Rev: SLJ 12/96) [616.97]

20131 Getz, David. *Purple Death: The Mysterious Flu of 1918* (3–5). Illus. 2000, Holt $16.00 (0-8050-5751-X). 86pp. This account describes the deadliest six months in human history — the 1918 flu epidemic that infected 2 billion people. (Rev: BCCB 12/00; BL 12/1/00; HBG 3/01; SLJ 2/01) [614.5]

20132 Gillie, Oliver. *Cancer* (5–8). Series: Just the Facts. 2004, Heinemann LB $27.07 (1-4034-5144-3). 56pp. Provides accessible explanations of cancer itself, plus the symptoms, diagnosis, and surgery, chemotherapy, and ratiation involved in its treatment. (Rev: SLJ 2/05) [616.99]

20133 Gillie, Oliver. *Sickle Cell Disease* (5–8). Series: Just the Facts. 2004, Heinemann LB $27.07 (1-4034-4603-2). 56pp. An examination of sickle cell anemia presented in an accessible style, with coverage of symptoms, treatment, and research. (Rev: SLJ 6/04) [616.1]

20134 Gilman, Laura Anne. *Coping with Cerebral Palsy* (5–9). Series: Coping. 2001, Rosen LB $25.25 (0-8239-3150-1). 92pp. This is a self-help book that looks at ways to deal with school, work, and travel as well as coping with other people and their attitudes. (Rev: SLJ 2/02) [616.836]

20135 Gold, Susan D. *Alzheimer's Disease* (4–7). Illus. Series: Health Watch. 1995, Silver Burdett LB $15.95 (0-89686-857-5). 48pp. Using a case study as the focus, this account introduces Alzheimer's disease, its treatment, and current research. (Rev: BL 5/15/96; SLJ 1/96) [362.19]

20136 Gold, Susan Dudley. *Sickle Cell Disease* (4–7). Illus. Series: Health Watch. 2001, Enslow LB $18.95 (0-7660-1662-5). 48pp. Readers are introduced to the symptoms and treatment of this disease through the true story of a young African American boy called Keone who received a successful stem-cell transplant. (Rev: HBG 3/02; SLJ 12/01) [616.1]

20137 Goldstein, Margaret J. *Everything You Need to Know About Multiple Sclerosis* (5–8). Series: Need to Know Library. 2001, Rosen LB $25.25 (0-8239-3292-3). 64pp. An introduction to multiple sclerosis, its symptoms and treatment, and how it affects the nervous system, along with information on the importance of treating the emotional impact of this disease. (Rev: SLJ 5/01) [616]

20138 Goodnough, David. *Eating Disorders: A Hot Issue* (5–8). Series: Hot Issues. 1999, Enslow LB $21.95 (0-7660-1336-7). 64pp. This is a clear introduction to anorexia nervosa, bulimia, and binge eating with material and case studies on symptoms, causes, and consequences but little coverage of prevention and treatment. (Rev: HBG 4/00; SLJ 1/00) [618.92]

20139 Gordon, Melanie Apel. *Let's Talk About Head Lice* (2–4). Series: Let's Talk. 1999, Rosen LB $13.95 (1-56838-276-6). 24pp. The habits of head lice are covered plus material on how they are transmitted and how to get rid of them. (Rev: SLJ 3/99) [595.7]

20140 Gray, Shirley Wimbish. *Living with Asthma* (3–5). Illus. Series: Living Well. 2002, Child's World LB $25.64 (1-56766-100-9). 32pp. Explains various aspects of asthma, from why attacks occur to treatment of this chronic illness. Other titles in this series include *Living with Diabetes*, *Living with Epilepsy*, and *Living with Cerebral Palsy* (all 2002). (Rev: BL 10/15/02; SLJ 1/03) [618.92]

20141 Gray, Susan H. *Living with Cystic Fibrosis* (3–5). Series: Living Well. 2002, Child's World LB $25.64 (1-56766-105-X). 32pp. The nature of cystic fibrosis is discussed with details on how it affects the body, its causes, and how to live with it, plus anecdotes from people who suffer from the illness. Also use *Living with Cerebral Palsy* (2002). (Rev: BL 10/15/02) [616]

20142 Gray, Susan H. *Living with Juvenile Rheumatoid Arthritis* (3–5). Illus. Series: Living Well. 2002, Child's World LB $25.64 (1-56766-104-1). 32pp. First-hand accounts from children with juvenile rheumatoid arthritis enhance the information on the disease, from diagnosis to treatment. (Rev: BL 10/15/02; SLJ 3/03) [618.92]

20143 Gutman, Bill. *Harmful to Your Health* (5–8). Illus. Series: Focus on Safety. 1996, Twenty-First Century LB $24.90 (0-8050-4144-3). This volume outlines the problems inherent in drugs, alcohol, AIDS, steroids, and sexual abuse, with material on how to be alert to their dangers. (Rev: BL 2/1/97; SLJ 2/97) [616.86]

20144 Haney, Johannah. *Juvenile Diabetes* (4–7). Illus. Series: Health Alert. 2004, Benchmark LB $19.95 (0-7614-1798-2). 63pp. In addition to describing the treatment and possible complications of juvenile diabetes, this attractive title opens with a case history and also includes lists of famous people who suffer from the condition. (Rev: SLJ 5/05)

20145 Hawkins, Trisha. *Everything You Need to Know About Measles and Rubella* (4–8). Series: Need to Know Library. 2001, Rosen LB $25.25 (0-8239-3322-9). 64pp. Simple text and photographs describe the diseases and methods of prevention and treatment, and discuss public-health issues. Also use *Everything You Need to Know About Chicken Pox and Shingles* (2001). (Rev: SLJ 8/01) [616.9]

20146 Hayhurst, Chris. *Cholera* (5–9). Series: Epidemics. 2001, Rosen LB $26.50 (0-8239-3345-8). 64pp. In a readable style, Hayhurst discusses the history of cholera, formerly a deadly disease, and explains how its treatment was developed. Also use *Polio* and *Smallpox* (both 2001). (Rev: SLJ 7/01) [616.9]

20147 Hayhurst, Chris. *E. Coli* (4–7). Series: Epidemics. 2004, Rosen LB $26.50 (0-8239-4201-5). 64pp. A look at the transmission, treatment, and prevention of this bacterium, with an emphasis on the importance of washing hands and food before eating. (Rev: SLJ 8/04) [616.9]

20148 Hirschmann, Kris. *Salmonella* (4–7). Illus. Series: Parasites. 2003, Gale/KidHaven LB $22.45 (0-7377-1785-8). 32pp. This fascinating examination of Salmonella bacteria, responsible for a wide variety of illnesses in the United States and elsewhere, is supplemented with numerous photos and microscopic views of the title bacteria. (Rev: BL 3/1/04) [615.4]

20149 Huegel, Kelly. *Young People and Chronic Illness: True Stories, Help, and Hope* (5–9). 1998, Free Spirit paper $14.95 (1-57542-041-4). 199pp. This book highlights ten case histories of young people with such medical problems as hemophilia, diabetes, epilepsy, asthma, cancer, heart problems, and lupus. (Rev: SLJ 10/98) [362.1]

20150 Hyde, Margaret O., and Elizabeth Forsyth. *Diabetes* (4–7). Illus. 2003, Watts LB $25.00 (0-531-12209-3). 96pp. Case studies of young people add to the easy-to-understand coverage of the disease, its different types, causes, symptoms, and popular methods of treatment. (Rev: SLJ 2/04) [616.4]

20151 Hyde, Margaret O., and Elizabeth Forsyth. *The Disease Book: A Kid's Guide* (5–8). Illus. 1997, Walker LB $17.85 (0-8027-8498-4). A simple, straightforward overview of the causes, symptoms, and treatments of more than 100 physical and mental diseases. (Rev: BL 9/15/97; HBG 3/98; SLJ 11/97) [616]

20152 Hyde, Margaret O., and Elizabeth Forsyth. *Living with Asthma* (4–6). Illus. 1995, Walker LB $15.85 (0-8027-8287-6). 96pp. The physical and emotional aspects of asthma are introduced, with several case histories of people who cope with this condition. (Rev: BL 6/1–15/95; SLJ 7/95) [362]

20153 Isle, Mick. *Everything You Need to Know About Food Poisoning* (4–8). Illus. Series: Need to Know Library. 2001, Rosen LB $25.25 (0-8239-3396-2). 64pp. Safe ways to prepare food are the main focus of this book, which also describes the symptoms and treatment of food poisoning. (Rev: SLJ 10/01) [615.954]

20154 Jukes, Mavis, and Lilian Cheung. *Be Healthy! It's a Girl Thing: Food, Fitness, and Feeling Great* (5–8). Illus. by Debra Ziss. 2003, Crown LB $18.99 (0-679-99029-1); paper $12.95 (0-679-89029-7). 160pp. The authors take a matter-of-fact, motivational approach to changes that arrive with puberty and the steps girls can take to be healthy and avoid weight gain and eating disorders. (Rev: BL 1/1–15/04; SLJ 12/03) [613]

20155 Katz, Bobbi. *Germs! Germs! Germs!* (1–2). Illus. by Steve Bjorkman. Series: Beginning Reader: Science. 1996, Scholastic $3.99 (0-590-67295-9). 40pp. The contributions and havoc caused by germs are revealed from their point of view. (Rev: BL 2/1/97) [616]

20156 Katz, Bobbi. *Lots of Lice* (1–3). Illus. by Steve Bjorkman. Series: Hello Reader! 1998, Scholastic paper $3.99 (0-590-10834-4). 40pp. A funny and informative book for beginning readers that tells about lice, how one gets them, and what to do about them — as told from the standpoint of one of the lice. (Rev: BL 11/1/98; SLJ 2/99) [613]

20157 Kehret, Peg. *Small Steps: The Year I Got Polio* (3–5). 1996, Whitman LB $14.95 (0-8075-7457-0). 179pp. The author describes seven months in her life when, at age 12, she was stricken with polio. (Rev: BCCB 11/96; BL 11/1/96; SLJ 11/96*) [362.1]

20158 Lamb, Kirsten. *Cancer* (5–8). Series: Health Issues. 2002, Raintree LB $28.54 (0-7398-5219-1). 64pp. An informative account that covers various kinds of cancer, giving real-life stories, and also deals with issues and choices facing teens today. (Rev: BL 12/15/02; HBG 3/03; SLJ 3/03) [616.99]

20159 Landau, Elaine. *Allergies* (4–7). Illus. Series: Understanding Illness. 1994, Twenty-First Century LB $24.90 (0-8050-2989-3). 64pp. After a case history that explores allergies in personal terms, an objective presentation is given of their causes, effects, and treatment. (Rev: BL 12/15/94; SLJ 2/95) [616.97]

20160 Landau, Elaine. *Cancer* (4–7). Illus. Series: Understanding Illness. 1994, Twenty-First Century LB $24.90 (0-8050-2990-7). 64pp. This book explains the many types of cancer, their causes, present-day treatments, and possible developments in the future. (Rev: BL 12/15/95; SLJ 2/95) [616.99]

20161 Landau, Elaine. *Epilepsy* (4–7). Illus. Series: Understanding Illness. 1994, Twenty-First Century LB $24.90 (0-8050-2991-5). 64pp. Following the story of a youngster who has epilepsy, this account describes the disorder, its emotional and medical aspects, and treatments. (Rev: BL 12/15/94; SLJ 2/95) [616.8]

20162 Lassieur, Allison. *Head Lice* (3–5). Illus. Series: My Health. 2000, Watts LB $22.50 (0-531-11624-7); paper $6.95 (0-531-16450-0). 48pp. Using amazing photos taken with microscopes, this account introduces head lice, their physical characteristics, how they are transmitted, and how to get rid of them. (Rev: BL 6/1–15/00) [616.5]

20163 Lennard-Brown, Sarah. *Asthma* (5–8). Illus. Series: Health Issues. 2002, Raintree LB $28.54 (0-7398-5218-3). 64pp. Color photographs and straightforward text explain the symptoms, diagnosis, and treatment of asthma. (Rev: BL 12/15/02; HBG 3/03) [616.2]

20164 Lennard-Brown, Sarah. *Autism* (5–8). Illus. Series: Health Issues. 2003, Raintree LB $28.56 (0-7398-6422-X). 64pp. An in-depth introduction to autism, with attention to the difficulties people with autism face and what is being done to help them. (Rev: HBG 4/04; SLJ 5/04) [616.89]

20165 McGuire, Paula. *AIDS* (4–8). Series: Preteen Pressures. 1998, Raintree LB $25.69 (0-8172-5025-5). 48pp. Straight facts and statistics are given on AIDS, including methods of prevention and stories of people with HIV/AIDS, such as Magic Johnson and the late Ryan White. (Rev: BL 5/15/98; HBG 9/98) [616,97]

20166 Manning, Karen. *AIDS: Can This Epidemic Be Stopped?* (6–8). Illus. Series: Issues of Our Time. 1995, Twenty-First Century LB $18.90 (0-8050-4240-7). 64pp. A frank, objective account of how AIDS is transmitted and present treatment strategies. (Rev: BL 2/1/96; SLJ 2/96) [616.97]

20167 Margulies, Phillip. *Creutzfeldt-Jakob Disease* (4–7). Series: Epidemics. 2004, Rosen LB $26.50 (0-8239-4199-X). 64pp. Examines the history and current state of knowledge about this rare disorder that affects the brain and is related to Mad Cow Disease. Also use *West Nile Virus* (2004). (Rev: SLJ 8/04) [616.8]

20168 Margulies, Phillip. *Everything You Need to Know About Rheumatic Fever* (5–8). Series: The Need to Know Library. 2004, Rosen LB $25.25 (0-8239-4509-X). 64pp. After a brief history of the disease and the discovery of its cause, this volume discusses symptoms, treatment, and the concern that the disease may become more prevalent as bacteria develop resistance to antibiotics. (Rev: SLJ 4/05)

20169 Marrin, Albert. *Dr. Jenner and the Speckled Monster: The Search for the Smallpox Vaccine* (4–8). Illus. 2002, Dutton $17.99 (0-525-46922-2). 96pp. This highly readable and detailed account describes the impact of smallpox from the time of the Aztecs, major outbreaks over the years, the way the virus works, the work of Jenner in developing a vaccine, and the virus's potential as a weapon of mass destruction. (Rev: BL 11/15/02; HB 11–12/02; HBG 3/03; SLJ 1/03) [614.5]

20170 Marx, Trish, and Dorita Beh-Eger. *I Heal: The Children of Chernobyl in Cuba* (3–6). Illus. 1996, Lerner LB $21.27 (0-8225-4897-6). 48pp. This book contains the story of two young victims of the Chernobyl nuclear disaster and of their medical treatment in Cuba. (Rev: BCCB 12/96; BL 12/1/96; SLJ 10/96) [618.92]

20171 Massari, Francesca. *Everything You Need to Know About Cancer* (5–9). Series: Need to Know Library. 2000, Rosen LB $25.25 (0-8239-3164-1). 64pp. This book defines what cancer is and looks at its causes, prevention, symptoms, diagnosis, and treatment. (Rev: HBG 9/00; SLJ 8/00) [616.99]

20172 Moehn, Heather. *Everything You Need to Know When Someone You Know Has Leukemia* (5–10). Series: Need to Know Library. 2000, Rosen LB $25.25 (0-8239-3121-8). 64pp. The basic facts about leukemia are covered with material on its various types and treatments, possible causes, and the emotional aspects of the illness. (Rev: SLJ 9/00) [616.99]

20173 Monroe, Judy. *Cystic Fibrosis* (5–9). Illus. Series: Perspectives on Disease and Illness. 2001, Capstone LB $23.93 (0-7368-1026-9). 64pp. A straightforward account of the symptoms, diagnosis, and treatment of this disease, with discussion of the impact on the life of the patient and other family members. Also use *Breast Cancer* (2001). (Rev: HBG 3/02; SLJ 3/02) [616.3]

20174 Moragne, Wendy. *Allergies* (5–8). Series: Twenty-First Century Medical Library. 1999, Twenty-First Century LB $26.90 (0-7613-1359-1). 128pp. After general material on allergies, their causes and treatment, this account describes specific allergies involving food, skin, rhinitis, drugs, and insects. (Rev: HBG 4/00; SLJ 3/00) [616.97]

20175 Morgan, Sally. *Germ Killers: Fighting Disease* (5–8). Series: Science at the Edge. 2002, Heinemann LB $27.86 (1-58810-699-3). 64pp. Current advances in fighting disease are outlined with their current applications and future possibilities. (Rev: BL 10/15/02; HBG 3/03) [616]

20176 Nardo, Don. *Germs* (4–5). Illus. Series: Kidhaven Science Library. 2002, Gale LB $23.70 (0-7377-0943-X). 48pp. This volume covers a broad spectrum of germs including viruses, bacteria, microscopic fungi, and some algae, with information on their structure and functions. (Rev: BL 5/1/02) [579]

20177 Nye, Bill, and Kathleen W. Zoehfeld. *Bill Nye the Science Guy's Great Big Book of Tiny Germs* (4–7). Illus. by Bryn Barnard. 2005, Hyperion $16.99 (0-7868-0543-9). 48pp. Solid information on bacteria and viruses is presented in an appealing and lively format. (Rev: BL 6/1–15/05) [579]

20178 Peacock, Carol Antoinette. *Sugar Was My Best Food: Diabetes and Me* (3–6). Illus. 1998, Whitman $12.95 (0-8075-7646-8). 55pp. An 11-year-old boy describes his daily experiences in coping with diabetes, which he has had since age nine. (Rev: BL 8/98; HBG 9/98; SLJ 6/98) [362.1]

20179 Pincus, Dion. *Everything You Need to Know About Cerebral Palsy* (4–7). Series: Need to Know Library. 2000, Rosen LB $25.25 (0-8239-2960-4). 64pp. The causes and characteristics of cerebral palsy are discussed with material on the treatments and the daily life of those affected. (Rev: HBG 9/00; SLJ 3/00) [618.92]

20180 Pirner, Connie W. *Even Little Kids Get Diabetes* (PS–2). Illus. by Nadine Bernard Westcott. 1991, Whitman LB $13.95 (0-8075-2158-2). 24pp. A young girl tells of her life with diabetes. (Rev: BL 3/1/91; SLJ 4/91) [616.4]

20181 Ramen, Fred. *Sleeping Sickness and Other Parasitic Tropical Diseases* (5–8). Series: Epidemics. 2002, Rosen LB $26.50 (0-8239-3499-3). 64pp. After a history of parasitic diseases around the globe and the role played by bloodsucking killers like the tsetse fly, this account describes the treatments now available. (Rev: BL 8/02; SLJ 7/02) [616]

20182 Ray, Kurt. *Typhoid Fever* (5–8). Illus. Series: Epidemics. 2002, Rosen LB $19.95 (0-8239-3572-8). 64pp. An introduction to the history and treatment of typhoid fever, including coverage of Typhoid Mary. (Rev: BL 3/15/02) [614.5]

20183 Romano, Amy. *Germ Warfare* (5–8). Illus. Series: Germs: The Library of Disease-Causing Organisms. 2004, Rosen LB $25.25 (0-8239-4493-X). 48pp. An informative, illustrated overview of the history and current status of germ warfare, with discussion of what we can do to protect ourselves. (Rev: SLJ 1/05) [358]

20184 Rosaler, Maxine. *Botulism* (4–7). Series: Epidemics. 2004, Rosen LB $26.50 (0-8239-4197-3). 64pp. A look at outbreaks of botulism and their causes and prevention. (Rev: SLJ 8/04) [614.5]

20185 Routh, Kristina. *Down Syndrome* (5–8). Series: Just the Facts. 2004, Heinemann LB $27.07 (1-4034-5145-1). 56pp. An informative overview of this disease and its diagnosis and treatment, stressing the individuality of children with the syndrome. (Rev: SLJ 2/05) [362.1]

20186 Routh, Kristina. *Meningitis* (5–8). Illus. Series: Just the Facts. 2004, Heinemann LB $27.07 (1-4034-5146-X). 56pp. The symptoms of meningitis are provided along with a thorough explanation of the disease and its diagnosis and treatment. (Rev: SLJ 2/05)

20187 Roy, Jennifer Rozines. *Depression* (4–7). Illus. Series: Health Alert. 2004, Benchmark LB $19.95 (0-7614-1800-8). 64pp. In addition to describing the causes and treatment of depression, this attractive title opens with a case history and also includes lists of famous people who suffer from the condition. (Rev: SLJ 5/05)

20188 Royston, Angela. *Why Do My Eyes Itch? And Other Questions About Allergies* (3–5). Illus. Series: Body Matters. 2002, Heinemann LB $22.79 (1-4034-0207-8). 32pp. All kinds of allergies are introduced in concise, simple text with many illustrations. (Rev: SLJ 4/03) [616.97]

20189 Sanders, Pete, and Steve Myers. *Anorexia and Bulimia* (4–8). Illus. by Mike Lacy and Liz Sawyer. Series: What Do You Know About. 1999, Millbrook LB $23.90 (0-7613-0914-4). 32pp. Using an actual case study as a beginning, this book explores the causes, effects, and treatment of these eating disorders and covers the behavioral patterns of those afflicted. (Rev: HBG 9/99; SLJ 10/99) [618.92]

20190 Schwartz, Robert H., and Peter M. G. Deane. *Coping with Allergies* (4–7). Series: Coping. 1999, Rosen LB $25.25 (0-8239-2511-0). 160pp. After a rundown of the types and causes of allergies, this account describes their physical and emotional impact and current treatments. (Rev: BL 2/15/00) [616.97]

20191 Senker, Cath. *World Health Organization* (5–8). Series: World Watch. 2004, Raintree LB $27.14 (0-7398-6614-1). 48pp. The world's health problems and what is being done to combat them are the focus of this somber title, which looks at both the developing world and the wealthiest of nations. (Rev: SLJ 3/04) [362.1]

20192 Sheen, Barbara. *Diabetes* (5–7). Illus. Series: Diseases and Disorders. 2003, Gale LB $27.45 (1-59018-244-8). 112pp. The symptoms of and treatments for diabetes are covered here, with discussion of alternative treatments, how diabetics manage their disease, and the research being undertaken. (Rev: SLJ 7/03) [616.4]

20193 Shein, Lori. *AIDS* (5–8). Series: Overview. 1998, Lucent LB $27.45 (1-56006-193-6). A concise overview of the AIDS epidemic in the late 20th

century, the attempts to treat and restrict the spread of the disease, and the controversies surrounding it. (Rev: BL 8/98) [616.99]

20194 Sherrow, Victoria. *Polio Epidemic: Crippling Virus Outbreak* (4–7). Series: American Disasters. 2001, Enslow LB $18.95 (0-7660-1555-6). 48pp. In this readable account, Sherrow looks at the history of polio, its treatment, the epidemic in the United States that started in 1952, and the creation of the polio vaccine. (Rev: HBG 3/02; SLJ 3/02) [362.1]

20195 Silverstein, Alvin, et al. *Allergies* (3–5). Series: My Health. 1999, Watts LB $22.50 (0-531-11581-X). 48pp. This simple work with entertaining drawings and photos explains, from a child's point of view, what allergies are, the different kinds, and how they can be treated. (Rev: BL 10/15/99; HBG 4/00; SLJ 12/99) [616]

20196 Silverstein, Alvin, et al. *Asthma* (3–5). Series: My Health. 2002, Watts LB $24.00 (0-531-12048-1); paper $6.95 (0-531-16637-6). 48pp. Using many color photographs and cartoons, this brief account explains asthma's causes, symptoms, effects, and the methods of treatment. Also use *Diabetes* and *What Are Germs?* (Rev: BL 12/15/02; SLJ 4/03) [616.2]

20197 Silverstein, Alvin, et al. *Chickenpox* (3–5). Series: My Health. 2001, Watts LB $23.00 (0-531-11782-0). The disease chickenpox is introduced with discussion of its causes, symptoms, dangers, treatment, and immunization. (Rev: BL 1/1–15/02; SLJ 8/01) [616.9]

20198 Silverstein, Alvin, et al. *Common Colds* (3–5). Illus. Series: My Health. 1999, Watts LB $22.50 (0-531-11579-8). 48pp. This book explains the symptoms of the common cold, how people catch and pass colds along, and how they are treated. (Rev: BL 10/15/99; HBG 4/00) [616.2]

20199 Silverstein, Alvin, et al. *Headaches* (3–5). Series: My Health. 2001, Watts LB $23.00 (0-531-11872-X). Different types of headaches are introduced, with their causes, treatment, and prevention. (Rev: BL 1/1–15/02; SLJ 12/01) [616.8]

20200 Silverstein, Alvin, et al. *Lyme Disease* (3–5). Series: My Health. 2001, Watts LB $23.00 (0-531-11638-7). Covers the symptoms, causes, prevention, and treatment of this disease named after Lyme, Connecticut, where it was first identified. (Rev: BL 1/1–15/02; SLJ 12/01) [616]

20201 Silverstein, Alvin, et al. *Lyme Disease* (4–7). Illus. 2000, Watts LB $24.00 (0-531-11751-0); paper $8.95 (0-531-16531-0). 64pp. This book introduces Lyme disease, its symptoms, history, the tick that carries it, prevention, and treatments. (Rev: BL 10/15/00) [616.9]

20202 Silverstein, Alvin, et al. *Sickle Cell Anemia* (4–8). Illus. Series: Diseases and People. 1997, Enslow LB $20.95 (0-89490-711-5). 112pp. The symptoms, treatment, and screening of this hereditary disorder are explained in a clear, well-organized text. (Rev: SLJ 2/97) [616]

20203 Silverstein, Alvin, et al. *Sore Throats and Tonsillitis* (3–5). Series: My Health. 2000, Watts LB $22.50 (0-531-11640-9). 48pp. Photos, medical information, and amusing cartoons are used to describe throat problems — their causes and cures. (Rev: BL 11/15/00) [616.3]

20204 Silverstein, Alvin, and Virginia Silverstein. *Diabetes* (3–5). Illus. Series: My Health. 2002, Watts LB $24.00 (0-531-12049-X); paper $6.95 (0-531-16638-4). 48pp. The symptoms and causes of the disease, the differences between type 1 and type 2 diabetes, and common forms of treatment are all described in this succinct text with helpful illustrations. (Rev: SLJ 4/03) [616.4]

20205 Silverstein, Alvin, and Virginia Silverstein. *Parkinson's Disease* (4–6). Illus. Series: Diseases and People. 2002, Enslow LB $20.95 (0-7660-1593-9). 128pp. Actor Michael J. Fox's diagnosis of Parkinson's serves as an introduction to the history, causes, symptoms, and treatment of this disease. (Rev: HBG 3/03; SLJ 12/02)

20206 Silverstein, Alvin, and Virginia Silverstein. *Vaccinations* (3–5). Series: My Health. 2002, Watts LB $23.00 (0-531-11874-6); paper $6.95 (0-531-15564-1). 48pp. Using many visuals and a clear, simple text, this book describes how vaccinations were developed, how they work, and the various types. (Rev: BL 6/1–15/02; SLJ 8/02) [614.4]

20207 Simpson, Carolyn. *Everything You Need to Know About Asthma* (5–10). Illus. Series: Need to Know Library. 1998, Rosen LB $25.25 (0-8239-2567-6). Vital background information is given about the causes and effects, symptoms, and treatments of asthma. (Rev: SLJ 10/98) [616.2]

20208 Smart, Paul. *Everything You Need to Know About Mononucleosis* (5–9). Series: Need to Know Library. 1998, Rosen LB $25.25 (0-8239-2550-1). 64pp. A straightforward presentation about the "kissing disease," which is often undiagnosed or mistaken for the flu and which requires long periods of rest for recovery. (Rev: SLJ 10/98) [616]

20209 Spray, Michelle. *Growing Up with Scoliosis: A Young Girl's Story* (5–9). Illus. by author. 2002, Book Shelf paper $12.95 (0-9714160-3-6). 119pp. An autobiographical account of the treatment of scoliosis and the emotional impact on the patient, with clear illustrations. (Rev: SLJ 12/02) [362.19673]

20210 Stewart, Gail B. *Sleep Disorders* (5–8). Illus. Series: Diseases and Disorders. 2002, Gale LB $27.45 (1-56006-909-0). 112pp. Insomnia, narcolepsy, apnea, and night terrors are among the problems discussed here, with material on treatments, new research, and attitudes toward people who are always tired. (Rev: SLJ 3/03) [616.8498]

20211 Susman, Edward. *Multiple Sclerosis* (4–7). Series: Diseases and People. 1999, Enslow LB $20.95 (0-7660-1185-2). 128pp. A description of this debilitating disease that attacks the nervous system. (Rev: HBG 4/00; SLJ 2/00) [616]

20212 Tsubakiyama, Margaret. *Lice Are Lousy! All About Headlice* (3–5). Illus. 1999, Millbrook $19.90 (0-7613-1316-8). 32pp. A breezy but fact-filled introduction to head lice, their habits, how you get them, and how to get rid of them. (Rev: BL 8/99; HBG 9/99; SLJ 9/99) [616.5]

20213 Veggeberg, Scott. *Lyme Disease* (4–8). Series: Diseases and People. 1998, Enslow LB $18.95 (0-7660-1052-X). 104pp. Describes the symptoms of Lyme disease, discusses how it is diagnosed and treated, and emphasizes the importance of prevention. (Rev: HBG 9/98; SLJ 9/98) [616]

20214 Viegas, Jennifer. *Parasites* (5–8). Illus. Series: Germs: The Library of Disease-Causing Organisms. 2004, Rosen LB $25.25 (0-8239-4494-8). 48pp. An informative, illustrated discussion of parasites, covering how they survive and the dangers they pose to humans. (Rev: SLJ 1/05) [574.5]

20215 Wainwright, Tabitha. *You and an Illness in Your Family* (5–8). Series: Family Matters. 2001, Rosen LB $23.95 (0-8239-3352-0). 48pp. Concise, readable advice is accompanied by full-page photographs of young teens and the recommendation to seek help when necessary. (Rev: SLJ 8/01) [610]

20216 Ward, Brian. *Epidemic* (4–7). Illus. Series: Eyewitness Books. 2000, DK $15.95 (0-7894-6296-6). 64pp. This book covers the nature of epidemics, their causes, how they are spread and contained, and gives examples from history. (Rev: BL 12/1/00; HBG 10/01) [614.4]

20217 Weiss, Jonathan H. *Breathe Easy: Young People's Guide to Asthma* (4–7). Illus. 1994, Magination paper $9.95 (0-945354-62-2). 64pp. Describes the causes of asthma, what happens during an attack, and how to manage this condition. (Rev: BL 2/15/95) [618.92]

20218 Weitzman, Elizabeth. *Let's Talk About When Someone You Love Has Alzheimer's Disease* (1–4). Illus. Series: Let's Talk. 1996, Rosen LB $15.93 (0-8239-2306-1). 24pp. A discussion of the nature of Alzheimer's disease, the changes it causes, and how to adjust to it. (Rev: BL 3/1/97; SLJ 8/96) [618.97]

20219 Westcott, Patsy. *Living with Epilepsy* (3–5). Series: Living With. 1999, Raintree LB $22.83 (0-8172-5570-2). 32pp. This book introduces epilepsy and explains the causes, different kinds of seizures, and treatment options. (Rev: BL 8/99; HBG 9/99) [616.8]

20220 Whelan, Jo. *Diabetes* (5–8). Series: Health Issues. 2002, Raintree LB $28.54 (0-7398-5220-5). 64pp. Case histories of youngsters with diabetes are used to explain the nature of this disease, the problems it produces, and the treatments available. (Rev: BL 12/15/02; HBG 3/03) [616.4]

20221 Wiener, Lori S., et al. *Be a Friend: Children Who Live with HIV Speak* (1–4). Illus. 1994, Whitman LB $14.95 (0-8075-0590-0). 40pp. The nature of AIDS is made dramatically clear through the voices of several youthful sufferers and their families. (Rev: BCCB 4/94; BL 3/15/94; SLJ 4/94) [362.1]

20222 Woolf, Alex. *Death and Disease* (5–8). Series: Medieval Realms. 2004, Gale/Lucent LB $27.45 (1-59018-533-1). 48pp. Black Death, leprosy, and other diseases are discussed, with their impact on society, and the practice of medicine in general is described. (Rev: BL 4/1/04; SLJ 3/05) [610]

20223 Yount, Lisa. *Cancer* (5–8). Series: Overview. 1999, Lucent LB $27.45 (1-56006-363-7). 111pp. This objective overview explains how cancer cells develop, types of cancer, causes, and past and present treatments, both traditional and alternative. (Rev: BL 9/15/99; HBG 4/00; SLJ 7/99) [616.994]

20224 Zonta, Pat. *Jessica's X-Ray* (2–5). Illus. by Clive Dobson. 2002, Firefly $19.95 (1-52297-578-9); paper $8.95 (1-55297-577-0). 28pp. When Jessica breaks her arm, the doctor orders X-rays and the reader is introduced to the whys and hows of this diagnostic tool. (Rev: BL 5/1/02; HBG 10/02; SLJ check) [616.0750]

Doctors and Medicine

20225 Casanellas, Antonio. *Great Discoveries and Inventions That Improved Human Health* (3–5). Illus. 2000, Gareth Stevens $21.27 (0-8368-2585-3). Using double-page spreads this book discusses such inventions as radioisotopes, DNA, and genetic engineering. (Rev: HBG 10/01; SLJ 1/01) [610]

20226 Casterline, Linda. *Natural-born Killers: A Chapter Book* (3–7). Series: True Tales. 2004, Children's Pr. LB $21.50 (0-516-23725-X). 48pp. Discusses various poisonous plants and animals that have been used in modern medicine to save lives. (Rev: SLJ 2/05) [578.6]

20227 Dowswell, Paul. *Medicine* (5–8). Illus. Series: Great Inventions. 2001, Heinemann LB $25.64 (1-58810-213-0). 48pp. A chronological look at new medical instruments and procedures over the ages, with diagrams and information on the inventors. (Rev: HBG 3/02; SLJ 2/02) [610]

20228 Green, Jen. *Medicine* (4–7). Illus. Series: Routes of Science. 2004, Gale/Blackbirch LB $23.70 (1-4103-0168-0). 40pp. A look at the history of medicine and the scientific process, with profiles of key individuals and their discoveries, a chronology, and discussion of future advances. (Rev: SLJ 5/05)

20229 Hughes, Monica. *First Visit to the Dentist* (PS–2). Series: My First. 2004, Raintree LB $18.56 (1-4109-0645-0); paper $5.50 (1-4109-0671-X). 24pp. Simple language introduces young readers to what happens at the dentist — waiting rooms, examination, cleaning and polishing, and so forth.

20230 Ichord, Loretta Frances. *Toothworms and Spider Juice: An Illustrated History of Dentistry* (5–8). Illus. 2000, Millbrook LB $24.90 (0-7613-1465-2). 96pp. A history of dentistry that reveals many of the barbaric treatments of the past and how superstition and ignorance gradually gave way to modern practices. (Rev: BCCB 2/00; BL 2/15/00; HBG 9/00; SLJ 2/00) [617.6]

20231 Jacobs, Lee. *The Orthopedist* (3–5). Illus. Series: Doctors in Action. 1998, Blackbirch LB $14.95 (1-56711-236-6). 24pp. Using many color photos and a reassuring text, this book gives a candid look at what specialists in muscle and bone deformities do — especially when they work with children. (Rev: BL 12/15/98; HBG 3/99) [616.7]

20232 Jefferis, David. *Bio Tech: Frontiers of Medicine* (4–8). Illus. Series: Megatech. 2001, Crabtree LB $22.60 (0-7787-0051-8); paper $8.95 (0-7787-0061-5). 32pp. An eye-catching look at future medical possibilities such as artificial body parts, enhanced use of robots, special foods, and so forth. (Rev: SLJ 6/02) [660.6]

20233 Lindsay, Judy. *The Story of Medicine: From Acupuncture to X Rays* (4–6). Illus. 2003, Oxford LB $21.95 (0-19-521984-8). 40pp. The history of medicine, from ancient times to the modern day, is presented in this lively and accessible book full of reproductions. (Rev: HBG 4/04; SLJ 4/04) [610]

20234 Manson, Ainslie. *House Calls: The True Story of a Pioneer Doctor* (3–6). Illus. by Mary Jane Gerber. 2001, Groundwood $15.95 (0-88899-446-X). 56pp. Though the narrator of this book is a fictional girl, the story details the real life of an early 19th-century rural Canadian doctor with information on tools and treatment. (Rev: BL 2/1/02; HBG 3/02; SLJ 12/01) [610.92]

20235 Masoff, Joy. *Emergency!* (4–8). 1999, Scholastic paper $16.95 (0-590-97898-5). In a series of double-page spreads, this book explores various aspects of a medical emergency, from getting help to victims with an explanation of what goes on in an emergency room to giving advice on precautions youngsters can take to be prepared for an emergency. (Rev: BCCB 2/99; BL 1/1–15/99; HB 3–4/99; HBG 9/99; SLJ 8/99) [362.1]

20236 Miller, Brandon M. *Just What the Doctor Ordered: The History of American Medicine* (5–8). Series: People's History. 1997, Lerner LB $30.35 (0-8225-1737-X). A history of American medicine from early Indian ceremonies and remedies to today's use of laser surgery, placing medical developments in a historical context, such as the role disease played in the Revolutionary and Civil Wars. (Rev: SLJ 5/97*) [610.9]

20237 Murphy, Patricia J. *Everything You Need to Know About Staying in the Hospital* (5–8). Series: Need to Know Library. 2001, Rosen LB $25.25 (0-8239-3325-3). 64pp. This volume explains the basic hospital process from admission to discharge and follows a patient through a typical day. (Rev: HBG 10/03; SLJ 5/01) [362.1]

20238 Nichols, Catherine. *Medical Marvels: A Chapter Book* (2–4). Series: True Tales — Science. 2004, Scholastic LB $21.50 (0-516-24686-0). 48pp. Nichols uses stories about a handful of humans who have survived catastrophic medical challenges to document progress made by the medical profession. (Rev: BL 12/1/04) [610.28]

20239 Snedden, Robert. *Medical Ethics: Changing Attitudes 1900–2000* (4–7). 1999, Raintree LB $28.54 (0-8172-5893-0). 64pp. Beginning with Hippocrates, this book gives a history of bioethics and follows with coverage of topics including reproductive rights, euthanasia, organ donation, psychiatry, eugenics, and cloning. (Rev: HBG 9/00; SLJ 5/00) [616]

20240 Stone, Tanya L. *Medical Causes* (5–10). Series: Celebrity Activists. 1997, Twenty-First Century LB $25.90 (0-8050-5233-X). The contributions of such celebrity activists as Elizabeth Taylor, Elton John, Paul Newman, Jerry Lewis, and Linda Eller-bee to various medical causes are highlighted, with material on each of their causes. (Rev: BR 3–4/98; SLJ 1/98) [616]

20241 Tesar, Jeremy. *Stem Cells* (5–9). Illus. Series: Science on the Edge. 2003, Gale $20.95 (1-56711-787-2). 48pp. Clear, accessible text and photographs describe stems cells and present the pros and cons of their use. (Rev: BL 10/15/03; SLJ 2/04) [616]

20242 Townsend, John. *Scalpels, Stitches and Scars: A History of Surgery* (4–7). Illus. Series: A Painful History of Medicine. 2005, Raintree LB $21.95 (1-4109-1332-5). 56pp. Gory it may be but this title conveys accurate facts and the eye-catching illustrations will entice browsers. (Rev: BL 5/15/05) [617]

20243 Van Steenwyk, Elizabeth. *Frontier Fever: The Silly, Superstitious — and Sometimes Sensible — Medicine of the Pioneers* (5–8). Illus. 1995, Walker LB $16.85 (0-8027-8403-8). 160pp. A history of medicine in the United States from colonial times through the 19th century, including information on the training of caregivers. (Rev: BL 7/95; SLJ 12/95) [610]

20244 Ward, Sally G. *The Anesthesiologist* (3–5). Series: Doctors in Action. 1998, Blackbirch LB $14.95 (1-56711-233-1). 24pp. A behind-the-scenes look at these medical specialists, with coverage on the problems and procedures they face each day. (Rev: BL 12/15/98; HBG 3/99) [610]

20245 Winkler, Kathy. *Radiology* (4–8). Series: Inventors and Inventions. 1996, Benchmark LB $25.64 (0-7614-0075-3). This work outlines the history of radiology, provides short profiles of leaders in the field, and describes the effects of too many x-rays on tissue, how x-rays are made, their use in diagnosis and treatment, and other medical imaging such as ultrasound and MRIs. (Rev: BL 7/96; SLJ 9/96) [616.07]

20246 Woods, Samuel. *The Pediatrician* (3–5). Illus. Series: Doctors in Action. 1998, Blackbirch LB $14.95 (1-56711-237-4). 24pp. Introduces the branch of medicine that deals with children and their health problems, and provides many examples of good patient-doctor relationships. (Rev: BL 12/15/98; HBG 3/99) [618.92]

Genetics

20247 Allan, Tony. *Understanding DNA: A Breakthrough in Medicine* (5–8). Illus. Series: Point of Impact. 2002, Heinemann LB $25.64 (1-58810-557-1). 32pp. A history of genetics with profiles of the important scientists and discussion of future uses of this knowledge in cloning, medicine, and production of food. (Rev: SLJ 9/02) [572.8609]

20248 Beatty, Richard. *Genetics* (4–8). Illus. Series: Science Fact Files. 2001, Raintree LB $27.12 (0-7398-1015-4). 42pp. Cells, chromosomes, genes, and genetic engineering are covered here, with pro-

files of key scientists. (Rev: HBG 10/01; SLJ 1/02) [660]

20249 Bornstein, Sandy. *What Makes You What You Are: A First Look at Genetics* (5–8). Illus. by Frank Cecala. 1989, Silver Burdett paper $6.95 (0-671-68650-X). 115pp. This book affords a fine introduction to cell structure, dominant and recessive traits, and heredity. (Rev: SLJ 1/90) [573.2]

20250 Butterfield, Moira. *Genetics* (5–8). Illus. Series: 21st Century Science. 2003, Smart Apple LB $18.95 (1-58340-350-7). 44pp. An accessible, large-format volume on genetics, cloning, and the use of genes in medicine and food engineering, with attractive full-color photographs. (Rev: BL 12/1/03; HBG 4/04) [576.5]

20251 Gallant, Roy A. *The Treasure of Inheritance* (5–8). Illus. Series: The Story of Science. 2002, Benchmark LB $19.95 (0-7614-1426-6). 78pp. A history of mankind's discoveries about genetics and heredity, starting with the earliest efforts to improve crops and animals, with material on today's and future genetic engineering and the mapping of the human genome. (Rev: HBG 3/03; SLJ 5/03) [576.5]

20252 George, Linda. *Gene Therapy* (5–9). Series: Science on the Edge. 2003, Gale LB $20.95 (1-56711-786-4). 48pp. This book explain how genetic engineering can not only have applications in health and industry but also can arouse a great deal of controversy. (Rev: BL 10/15/03) [660]

20253 Jefferis, David. *Cloning: Frontiers of Genetic Engineering* (5–7). Series: Megatech. 1999, Crabtree LB $22.60 (0-7787-0048-8); paper $8.95 (0-7787-0058-5). 32pp. This account discusses the history of genetic discoveries and theories, cell reproduction, and the present and possible future of genetic engineering with plants, animals, and humans. (Rev: SLJ 9/99) [174.957]

20254 Morgan, Sally. *Body Doubles: Cloning Plants and Animals* (5–8). Illus. Series: Science at the Edge. 2002, Heinemann LB $27.86 (1-58810-698-5). 64pp. A discussion of the scientific and ethical issues of cloning, with excellent diagrams. (Rev: BL 10/15/02; HBG 3/03) [660.6]

20255 Nardo, Don. *Cloning* (5–9). Illus. Series: Science on the Edge. 2003, Gale $20.95 (1-56711-782-1). 48pp. A concise overview of the techniques involved in cloning and the ways this science can be applied, with a balanced presentation of the pro and con arguments. (Rev: BL 10/15/03; SLJ 2/04) [660.6]

20256 Nicolson, Cynthia Pratt. *Baa! The Most Interesting Book You'll Ever Read About Genes and Cloning* (4–6). Illus. by Rose Cowles. Series: Mysterious You. 2001, Kids Can $14.95 (1-55074-856-4); paper $6.95 (1-55074-886-6). 40pp. Nicolson provides succinct definitions and descriptions of genetics and cloning-related issues in an easy-to-read volume. (Rev: BL 1/1–15/02; HBG 3/02) [572.8]

20257 Silverstein, Alvin, et al. *DNA* (4–8). Series: Science Concepts. 2002, Millbrook LB $26.90 (0-7613-2257-4). 64pp. This book examines the structure of DNA and clearly explains its components and functions and includes current topics such as the genome project, genetic engineering, gene therapy, and cloning. (Rev: BL 9/15/02; HBG 3/03; SLJ 11/02) [574.87]

20258 Taylor, Robert. *Genetics* (5–8). Illus. Series: Lucent Library of Science and Technology. 2004, Gale/Lucent LB $27.45 (1-59018-103-4). 112pp. Describes the basic scientific principles involved in genetics and discusses practical applications. (Rev: SLJ 3/04)

20259 Wells, Donna. *Biotechnology* (3–6). Illus. Series: Inventors and Inventions. 1996, Marshall Cavendish LB $25.64 (0-7614-0046-X). 63pp. Cell structure, DNA, and ways of altering genetic make-up are discussed, with short profiles of past and current leaders in the field. (Rev: BL 7/96; SLJ 9/96) [660]

Hospitals

20260 Amos, Janine. *The Hospital* (1–4). Photos by Angela Hampton. Illus. by Gwen Green. Series: Separations. 2002, Gareth Stevens LB $21.26 (0-8368-3091-1). 31pp. Letters, stories, and informational text will help a child to prepare for a visit to a hospital. The same format is used in *Death* and *Divorce* (both 2002). (Rev: HBG 10/02; SLJ 6/02) [362.1]

20261 Brink, Benjamin. *David's Story: A Book About Surgery* (3–5). Illus. 1996, Lerner LB $21.27 (0-8225-2577-1). 32pp. A step-by-step account of a boy undergoing surgery. (Rev: BL 12/1/96; SLJ 10/96) [617.5]

20262 Dooley, Virginia. *Tubes in My Ears: My Trip to the Hospital* (PS–1). Illus. by Miriam Katin. 1996, Mondo paper $4.95 (1-57255-118-6). 32pp. The experiences of a young boy when he goes to a hospital for the first time to treat an ear infection. (Rev: BL 5/1/96; SLJ 6/96) [362.1]

20263 Howe, James. *The Hospital Book*. Rev. ed. (2–6). Illus. by Mal Warshaw. 1994, Morrow $16.00 (0-688-12731-2). 96pp. This book filled with photos explains hospital procedures to young patients and tries to lessen any fears they might have about hospitals. (Rev: BL 4/1/94; HB 7–8/94) [362.1]

20264 Johnston, Marianne. *Let's Talk About Going to the Hospital* (1–4). Series: Let's Talk. 1998, Rosen LB $13.95 (0-8239-5036-0). 24pp. Two-page sections cover such hospital-related topics as admission, meals, IV tubes, blood tests, anesthesia, and surgery. (Rev: SLJ 4/98) [362.1]

20265 Miller, Marilyn. *Behind the Scenes at the Hospital* (PS–3). Illus. 1996, Raintree LB $21.40 (0-8172-4087-X). 32pp. The workers and activities that make hospitals function are introduced in a simple question-and-answer format. (Rev: BL 4/15/96; SLJ 12/96) [362.1]

20266 Pascoe, Elaine, ed. *Crash: The Body in Crisis* (5–8). Illus. Series: Body Story. 2003, Gale/Blackbirch LB $23.70 (1-4103-0062-5). 48pp. Two people are badly hurt in a car crash — he is uncon-

scious, she has a ruptured spleen — and readers accompany them to the emergency room and the operating room as they fight for their lives. (Rev: SLJ 4/04) [617.1]

20267 Rosenberg, Maxine B. *Mommy's in the Hospital Having a Baby* (PS–1). Illus. by Robert Maass. 1997, Clarion $15.00 (0-395-71813-9). 29pp. Questions are answered about what happens in a hospital when mommy is having a baby, including "How do I behave on visits?" (Rev: BL 4/1/97; SLJ 5/97) [618.4]

20268 Stein, Sara Bonnett. *A Hospital Story* (1–3). Illus. 1984, Walker paper $8.95 (0-8027-7222-6). A fine introduction to hospitals and what a hospital stay involves.

The Human Body

General

20269 Aliki. *My Feet* (PS–1). Illus. Series: Let's-Read-and-Find-Out. 1990, HarperCollins LB $16.89 (0-690-04815-7). 32pp. Children are asked to consider the uniqueness of their feet. (Rev: BL 10/1/90; HB 11–12/90; SLJ 11/90) [612]

20270 Aliki. *My Hands* (1–3). Illus. by author. 1990, HarperCollins LB $15.89 (0-690-04880-7); paper $4.95 (0-06-445096-1). 32pp. The structure and uses of our hands are presented.

20271 Allison, Linda. *Blood and Guts: A Working Guide to Your Own Little Insides* (5–8). 1976, Little, Brown paper $14.99 (0-316-03443-6). An off-putting title but a fine explanation of the functions of the human body.

20272 Balkwill, Fran. *Cells Are Us* (4–5). Illus. by Mic Rolph. 1993, Carolrhoda LB $19.93 (0-87614-762-7). 32pp. This book introduces the many types of cells found in the human body. Other related books by the same author are: *Cell Wars* and *DNA Is Here to Stay* (both 1993). (Rev: SLJ 4/93) [611]

20273 Batten, Mary. *Who Has a Belly Button?* (K–4). Illus. by Higgins Bond. 2004, Peachtree $15.95 (1-56145-235-1). All about belly buttons — what they are, where they come from, what animals' belly buttons are like, and so forth. (Rev: SLJ 5/04) [612.6]

20274 Berger, Melvin, and Gilda Berger. *Why Don't Haircuts Hurt? Questions and Answers About the Human Body* (3–5). Series: Question and Answer. 1999, Scholastic $12.95 (0-590-13079-X); paper $5.95 (0-590-08569-1). 48pp. Using questions that children might ask about the human body, this account supplies concise, well-organized answers, which are illustrated with many original paintings. (Rev: BL 11/15/99; SLJ 12/99) [612]

20275 Berger, Melvin, and Gilda Berger. *You're Tall in the Morning but Shorter at Night and Other Amazing Facts About the Human Body* (2–5). Illus. Series: Speedy Facts. 2004, Scholastic paper $7.99 (0-439-62536-X). 48pp. An entertaining and lively presentation of amazing and informative facts about the human body. [611]

20276 Borenstein, Gerri. *Therapy* (4–8). Illus. Series: Life Balance. 2003, Watts LB $19.50 (0-531-12269-7); paper $6.95 (0-531-15585-4). 80pp. This friendly, reassuring introduction explains what therapy consists of, the different kinds of professionals involved, and the ways in which privacy is maintained. (Rev: BL 10/15/03; SLJ 12/03) [616.89]

20277 Cole, Joanna. *The Magic School Bus: Inside the Human Body* (2–5). Illus. by Bruce Degen. 1989, Scholastic $15.95 (0-590-41426-7); paper $4.99 (0-590-41427-5). Ms. Frizzle's class goes on a guided tour of the human body. (Rev: BCCB 4/89; BL 4/15/89; HB 5–6/89)

20278 Cole, Joanna. *Your Insides* (PS–1). Illus. by Paul Meisel. 1998, Penguin Putnam paper $9.99 (0-698-11675-5). Clear overlays help to explain the workings of the human body for the young reader. (Rev: BL 12/1/92) [612]

20279 Darling, Kathy. *There's a Zoo on You!* (3–5). Illus. 2000, Millbrook LB $24.90 (0-7613-1357-5). 48pp. The supermagnified photographs in this book are of the bacteria, fungi, and other organisms that live in or on the human body. (Rev: BL 11/1/00; HBG 9/00; SLJ 7/00) [579]

20280 Davidson, Sue, and Ben Morgan. *Human Body Revealed* (5–8). Illus. 2002, DK paper $12.99 (0-7894-8882-5). 38pp. Overlays, cutaway photographs, diagrams, and captions are all used effectively to give a picture of what's contained in various parts of the body. (Rev: BL 12/1/02; HBG 3/03) [611]

20281 Ewald, Wendy. *The Best Part of Me: Children Talk About Their Bodies in Pictures and Words* (1–3). Illus. 2001, Little, Brown $16.95 (0-316-70306-0). 32pp. In their own words, youngsters describe what they like best about their bodies. (Rev: BL 9/1/01; HBG 3/02; SLJ 10/01) [810.8]

20282 Fisher, Gary L., and Rhoda Woods Cummings. *The Survival Guide for Kids with LD (Learning Differences)* (5–8). Illus. 1990, Free Spirit paper $9.95 (0-915793-18-0). A book that explains various kinds of learning disabilities and how to cope with them. (Rev: BL 7/90; SLJ 6/90) [371.9]

20283 Fowler, Allan. *Arms and Legs and Other Limbs* (1–2). Series: Rookie Readers. 1999, Children's Book Pr. LB $18.50 (0-516-20809-8). 32pp. This small book, with many pictures and large print, introduces arms and legs as found in various animals, including humans. (Rev: BL 7/99; HBG 9/99) [612]

20284 Gardner, Robert. *Science Projects About the Human Body* (5–7). 1992, Enslow LB $20.95 (0-89490-443-4). 104pp. Simple experiments and activities are used to illustrate various areas of the human body, such as the senses, bones, teeth, and hair. (Rev: SLJ 11/93) [612]

20285 Giacobello, John. *Everything You Need to Know About Anxiety and Panic Attacks* (5–9). Series: Need to Know Library. 2000, Rosen LB $25.25 (0-8239-3219-2). 64pp. This book explains anxiety attacks' causes, symptoms, and treatments in a reassuring tone. (Rev: SLJ 1/01) [616]

20286 Gold, Susan D. *Attention Deficit Disorder* (4–8). Series: Health Watch. 2000, Enslow LB $18.95 (0-7660-1657-9). 48pp. This account focuses on one boy from childhood to college and how he coped with attention deficit disorder. Several young people are profiled in the companion volume *Bipolar Disorder and Depression* (2000). (Rev: HBG 10/01; SLJ 2/01) [618.92]

20287 Gold, Susan Dudley. *The Musculoskeletal System and the Skin* (5–10). Illus. Series: Human Body Library. 2003, Enslow LB $18.95 (0-7660-2023-1). 48pp. Gold uses a conversational style to introduce detailed facts about the skeletal system, with useful graphics and some practical advice. (Rev: BL 4/15/03; HBG 10/03; SLJ 10/03) [612.7]

20288 Gregson, Susan R. *Stress Management: Managing and Reducing Stress* (5–8). Series: Perspectives on Mental Health. 2000, Capstone LB $23.93 (0-7368-0432-3). 64pp. This book discusses the causes of stress, explains its positive and negative effects on the body and mind, and outlines strategies for reducing and managing it. (Rev: HBG 9/00; SLJ 8/00) [152.4]

20289 Hall, David E. *Living with Learning Disabilities: A Guide for Students* (5–8). 1993, Lerner LB $19.93 (0-8225-0036-1). This book explains what learning disabilities are, what causes them, how they can be detected, and today's techniques for treatment. (Rev: BL 1/1/94; SLJ 4/94) [371.9]

20290 Hawcock, David. *The Amazing Pop-Up Pull-Out Body in a Book* (2–4). Illus. 1997, DK $19.95 (0-7894-2052-X). 9pp. Unfolding pages in this book brings out a full-length 3-D skeleton, accompanied by facts about the human body. (Rev: BL 12/15/97) [612]

20291 Hindley, Judy. *Eyes, Nose, Fingers, and Toes: A First Book All About You* (PS). Illus. by Brita Granström. 1999, Candlewick $15.99 (0-7636-0440-2). 32pp. A delightful activity book for toddlers that points out parts of the body. (Rev: BL 6/1–15/99*; HBG 9/99; SLJ 7/99) [612]

20292 Jackson, Donna. *In Your Face: The Facts About Your Features* (5–8). 2004, Viking $17.99 (0-670-03657-9). 48pp. Just about everything one might want to know about faces can be found in this fascinating volume, from study of individual features to ornamentation to face recognition by computer. (Rev: BL 10/15/04; SLJ 11/04) [611]

20293 Jefferis, David. *Human Body* (3–6). Illus. Series: Record Breakers. 2003, Raintree LB $25.69 (0-7398-6322-3). 32pp. An attractively illustrated collection of fascinating trivia about the human body. (Rev: HBG 10/03; SLJ 7/03)

20294 Kahn, Ada P., and Ronald M. Doctor. *Phobias* (4–8). Series: Life Balance. 2003, Watts LB $19.50 (0-531-12256-5); paper $6.95 (0-531-15575-7). 80pp. This book discusses the causes of phobias, the different types, how they affect people, and their treatment. (Rev: BL 10/15/03) [616.85]

20295 Kim, Melissa L. *The Endocrine and Reproductive Systems* (5–10). Illus. Series: Human Body Library. 2003, Enslow LB $18.95 (0-7660-2020-7). 48pp. Kim uses a conversational style to introduce detailed facts about these two body systems, with useful graphics and some practical advice. (Rev: BL 4/15/03; HBG 10/03) [612.4]

20296 Klingel, Cynthia, and Robert B. Noyed. *Feet* (PS–1). Photos by Gregg Andersen. Series: Let's Read About Our Bodies. 2002, Gareth Stevens LB $18.60 (0-8368-3064-4). 24pp. Full-page, full-color close-ups and minimal text present toes, feet, and shoes. Also use *Nose* and *Skin* (2002). (Rev: HBG 10/02; SLJ 5/02) [612.98]

20297 Kroll, Virginia. *Hands!* (PS–1). Illus. by Cathryn Falwell. 1997, Boyds Mills $7.95 (1-56397-051-1). 32pp. In this unusual picture book, hands are seen fulfilling a variety of tasks. (Rev: BL 9/15/97; HBG 3/98; SLJ 12/97) [612]

20298 Lauren, Jill. *Succeeding with LD: 20 True Stories About Real People with LD* (5–8). Illus. 1997, Free Spirit paper $14.95 (1-57542-012-0). 160pp. Case studies of 20 people ages 10 to 61 who have overcome various learning difficulties. (Rev: BL 6/1–15/97; SLJ 7/97) [371.92]

20299 Lee, Mary Price, and Richard S. Lee. *Everything You Need to Know About Natural Disasters and Post-Traumatic Stress Disorder* (5–9). Series: Need to Know Library. 1996, Rosen LB $17.95 (0-8239-2053-4). This book explains how such disasters as hurricanes, floods, and earthquakes can cause post-traumatic stress disorder and how to get help and counseling. (Rev: SLJ 6/96) [155.5]

20300 Macnair, Patricia Ann. *Life Cycle* (3–5). Series: Bodyscope. 2004, Houghton Mifflin $9.95 (0-7534-5780-6). 40pp. From egg to child to aging adult, the human life cycle is described in straightforward and clear terms, plus many illustrations. (Rev: BL 10/15/04) [612.6]

20301 Parker, Steve. *Allergies* (5–8). Series: Just the Facts. 2004, Heinemann LB $27.07 (1-4034-4598-2). 56pp. A comprehensive and accessible overview of allergies, their causes, symptoms, and treatment. (Rev: SLJ 6/04) [616.97]

20302 Pascoe, Elaine, ed. *Out of Control: Brain Function and Immune Reactions* (5–8). Illus. Series: Body Story. 2003, Gale/Blackbirch LB $23.70 (1-4103-0063-3). 48pp. This fact-packed book looks first at a baby's brain function, before and after birth, and how its capabilities grow as he learns, then traces the reaction of a young woman's immune system as it copes with a severe allergic reaction to a wasp sting. (Rev: SLJ 4/04) [612.8]

20303 Peacock, Judith. *Bipolar Disorder: A Roller Coaster of Emotions* (5–8). Series: Perspectives on Mental Health. 2000, Capstone LB $23.93 (0-7368-0434-X). 64pp. Manic depression is defined with material on its various types and how it is diagnosed and treated in both youngsters and adults. (Rev: HBG 9/00; SLJ 8/00) [616.85]

20304 Peacock, Judith. *Depression* (5–8). Illus. Series: Perspectives on Mental Health. 2000, Capstone LB $23.93 (0-7368-0435-8). 64pp. The causes and effects of mental depression are introduced, with material on how to handle it and its effects on the human body. (Rev: BL 8/00; HBG 9/00; SLJ 8/00) [616.85]

20305 Perols, Sylvaine. *The Human Body* (PS–1). Trans. from French by Jennifer Riggs. Illus. by author. Series: First Discovery. 1996, Scholastic $12.95 (0-590-73876-3). With the uses of transparencies, the skeleton and different systems and organs of the human body are introduced. (Rev: BL 10/15/96; SLJ 2/97) [612]

20306 Powell, Jillian. *Moving* (1–3). Series: The Body in Action 2004, Smart Apple Media LB $18.95 (1-58340-437-6). 32pp. Powell explores human movement and explains the parts of the body involved in various activities and how injuries can occur. (Rev: BL 11/1/04) [612.7]

20307 Pringle, Laurence. *Everybody Has a Bellybutton* (PS–3). Illus. by Clare Wood. 1997, Boyds Mills $14.95 (1-56397-009-0). 32pp. A simple account of the growth of a fetus from a single cell to the birth of a baby. (Rev: BL 9/15/97; HBG 3/98; SLJ 10/97) [612]

20308 Rosenberg, Marsha Sarah. *Everything You Need to Know When a Brother or Sister Is Autistic* (5–9). Series: Need to Know Library. 2000, Rosen LB $25.25 (0-8239-3123-4). 64pp. Autism is defined and described, with material on its diagnosis and treatment plus coverage of how this condition can affect other members of the family. (Rev: SLJ 8/00) [616.8]

20309 Ross, Michael Elsohn. *Body Cycles* (PS–1). Illus. by Gustav Moore. Series: Cycles. 2002, Millbrook LB $22.40 (0-7613-1816-X). Young readers are introduced to the ways in which the body uses oxygen, blood, and nutrients. (Rev: HBG 10/02; SLJ 8/02) [612]

20310 Saltz, Gail. *Amazing You! Getting Smart About Your Private Parts* (PS–2). Illus. by Lynne Cravath. 2005, Button $15.99 (0-525-47389-0). 32pp. Cheerful cartoons and straightforward text offer age-appropriate information about reproduction, birth, development, and the difference between boys' and girls' bodies. (Rev: BL 6/1–15/05; SLJ 5/05) [612.6]

20311 Sanders, Pete, and Steve Myers. *Dyslexia* (4–8). Illus. by Mike Lacy and Liz Sawyer. Series: What Do You Know About. 1999, Millbrook LB $23.90 (0-7613-0915-2). 32pp. Using a case study, this book explores one boy's problems with dyslexia, its causes, symptoms, and treatment. (Rev: HBG 9/99; SLJ 10/99) [617.7]

20312 Seuling, Barbara. *From Head to Toe: The Amazing Human Body and How It Works* (3–4). Illus. by Edward Miller. 2002, Holiday House $16.95 (0-8234-1699-2). 32pp. An accessible overview of the various body systems, omitting reproduction, with clear illustrations and several experiments. (Rev: SLJ 11/02) [612]

20313 Sprung, Barbara. *Stress* (4–8). Illus. Series: Preteen Pressures. 1998, Raintree LB $25.69 (0-8172-5033-6). 48pp. A concise, practical account of the types and causes of stress in young people and how to manage it. (Rev: BL 4/15/98; HBG 9/98; SLJ 6/98) [155.4]

20314 Stangl, Jean. *What Makes You Cough* (3–5). Series: My Health. 2000, Watts LB $22.50 (0-531-

20382-4). 48pp. The full title of this book is *What Makes You Cough, Sneeze, Burp, Hiccup, Yawn, Blink, Sweat, and Shiver?* (Rev: BL 11/15/00) [612]

20315 Szpirglas, Jeff. *Gross Universe: Your Guide to All Disgusting Things Under the Sun* (3–6). Illus. by Michael Cho. 2004, Maple Tree $21.95 (1-894379-64-0); paper $12.95 (1-894379-65-9). 64pp. Cartoon characters add details to the entertaining narrative about various bodily unpleasantnesses. (Rev: BCCB 5/04; SLJ 11/04) [612]

20316 VanCleave, Janice. *The Human Body for Every Kid: Easy Activities That Make Learning Science Fun* (5–7). Illus. Series: Science for Every Kid. 1995, Wiley $32.50 (0-471-02413-9); paper $12.95 (0-471-02408-2). 240pp. The various systems in the human body are introduced and decribed, with many projects and experiments. (Rev: BL 4/15/95; SLJ 5/95) [612]

20317 Walker, Richard. *Body: Bones, Muscle, Blood and Other Body Bits* (4–8). Series: Secret Worlds. 2001, DK $14.99 (0-7894-7967-2); paper $5.95 (0-7894-7968-0). 96pp. A lively, unusual introduction to human anatomy that uses attractive layouts and lively text as well as providing a listing of tested Web sites and a special reference section. (Rev: BL 10/15/01; HBG 3/02) [612]

20318 Walker, Richard. *The Kingfisher First Human Body Encyclopedia* (3–5). 1999, Kingfisher $16.95 (0-7534-5177-8). 112pp. Using a topical arrangement, this book offers an outstanding look at the inside and outside of the human body. (Rev: HBG 4/00; SLJ 11/99) [612]

20319 Waters, Jennifer. *All Kinds of People: What Makes Us Different* (K–2). Illus. Series: Spyglass Books. 2002, Compass Point LB $18.60 (0-7565-0377-9). 24pp. Eight spreads look at how people differ in physical appearance, personality, and ways of moving and communicating. (Rev: SLJ 4/03)

20320 Wiese, Jim. *Head to Toe Science: Over 40 Eye-Popping, Spine-Tingling, Heart-Pounding Activities That Teach Kids* (4–8). Illus. 2000, Wiley paper $12.95 (0-471-33203-8). 120pp. A collection of experiments and projects that is arranged by body systems (e.g., nervous, digestive), accompanied by good instructions and scientific explanations. (Rev: BL 7/00; SLJ 7/00) [612]

20321 Wiltshire, Paula. *Dyslexia* (5–8). Illus. Series: Health Issues. 2002, Raintree $28.54 (0-7398-5221-3). 64pp. Color photographs and straightforward text introduce dyslexia's symptoms and treatment and explain how it affects learning, with tips on how to cope with the disability. (Rev: BL 12/15/02; HBG 3/03; SLJ 3/03) [616.85]

20322 Winston, Robert M. L. *What Makes Me Me?* (4–6). 2004, DK $15.99 (0-7566-0325-0). 96pp. In this creative approach to human biology, full of questions and activities, Winston takes readers on a fascinating journey through the body and then concentrates on the mind. (Rev: BL 12/1/04) [612]

20323 Wolf, Allan. *The Blood-Hungry Spleen: And Other Poems About Our Parts* (3–5). Illus. by Greg Clarke. 2003, Candlewick $17.99 (0-7636-1565-X). 56pp. This poetic look at human anatomy, written by a former life science teacher, will both entertain and educate young readers. (Rev: BL 10/15/03; HBG 4/04)

20324 Woog, Adam. *Suicide* (5–8). Illus. Series: Overview. 1997, Lucent LB $27.45 (1-56006-187-1). An in-depth view of suicide, including causes, frequency, consequences, and detectable warning signs. (Rev: BL 3/15/97; SLJ 4/97) [362.2]

20325 Zucker, Faye. *Depression* (4–8). Series: Life Balance. 2003, Watts LB $19.50 (0-531-12259-X); paper $6.95 (0-531-15578-1). 80pp. This friendly, reassuring introduction explains the causes, diagnosis, and treatment of depression. (Rev: BL 10/15/03; SLJ 12/03) [616.85]

Circulatory System

20326 Ballard, Carol. *The Heart and Circulatory System* (5–8). Illus. Series: The Human Body. 1997, Raintree LB $18.98 (0-8172-4800-5). Topics discussed in this nicely illustrated volume include how blood is made, how it is pumped through the body, and how the heart and circulation system work together. (Rev: BL 6/1–15/97; SLJ 8/97) [612.1]

20327 Bryan, Jenny. *The Pulse of Life: The Circulatory System* (4–6). Illus. Series: Body Talk. 1993, Dillon LB $18.95 (0-87518-566-5). 48pp. A clear, concise introduction to the circulatory system and an explanation of current concerns and research. (Rev: SLJ 10/93) [612]

20328 Frost, Helen. *The Circulatory System* (K–2). Illus. Series: Human Body Systems. 2000, Capstone LB $13.25 (0-7368-0648-2). 24pp. A small-format, basic introduction for beginning readers. (Rev: HBG 10/01; SLJ 4/01) [612.1]

20329 Gray, Susan H. *The Circulatory System* (3–6). Illus. Series: The Human Body. 2003, Child's World LB $27.07 (1-59296-036-7). 32pp. A clear and detailed description of the functions of the circulatory system, using a child-friendly approach. (Rev: BL 2/1/04) [612.1]

20330 Parker, Steve. *Heart, Lungs, and Blood* (5–9). Illus. Series: Our Bodies. 2004, Raintree LB $19.99 (0-7398-6621-4). 48pp. Details of the human body's circulatory system are accompanied by information on keeping them healthy. [612.1]

20331 Parramon, Merce. *How Our Blood Circulates* (5–7). Illus. by Marcel Socias. Series: Invisible World. 1994, Chelsea LB $17.55 (0-7910-2127-0). 31pp. Double-page spreads introduce the circulatory system and discuss such topics as blood cells, clotting, the heart and its functions, and the lymphatic system. (Rev: SLJ 8/94) [612]

20332 Rau, Dana Meachen. *My Heart and Blood* (PS–3). Illus. Series: Bookworms: What's Inside Me? 2004, Benchmark LB $14.95 (0-7614-1779-6). 31pp. A simple overview of the circulatory system, with photographs, diagrams, and X-rays. (Rev: SLJ 2/05) [612]

20333 Sandeman, Anna. *Blood* (1–3). Illus. Series: Body Books. 1996, Millbrook LB $18.90 (0-7613-0477-0). 32pp. An introduction to the composition and function of blood and the circulatory system, with clearly labeled artwork. (Rev: BL 4/15/96; SLJ 4/96) [612.1]

20334 Showers, Paul. *A Drop of Blood* (K–2). Illus. by Edward Miller. Series: Let's Read-and-Find-Out. 2004, HarperCollins LB $16.89 (0-06-009110-X); paper $4.99 (0-06-009109-6). 128pp. This updated edition features a new, vampire slant and retains the earlier clear overview of blood and the human circulatory system. (Rev: BL 8/04; SLJ 7/04) [612]

20335 Showers, Paul. *Hear Your Heart* (2–5). Illus. by Holly Keller. Series: Let's-Read-and-Find-Out. 2001, HarperCollins LB $15.89 (0-06-025411-4); paper $4.95 (0-06-445139-9). 32pp. An amusing introduction to the human heart accompanied by activities such as making a stethoscope, taking a pulse, and listening to heartbeats. (Rev: BL 1/1–15/01; HBG 10/01) [612.1]

20336 Simon, Seymour. *The Heart: Our Circulatory System* (3–6). Illus. 1996, Morrow $15.93 (0-688-11408-3). 32pp. An excellent introduction to the circulatory system, with illustrations on each page. (Rev: BCCB 10/96; BL 7/96*; HB 9–10/96; SLJ 8/96) [612.1]

20337 Stille, Darlene R. *The Circulatory System* (2–4). Illus. Series: True Books. 1997, Children's Book Pr. LB $22.00 (0-516-20438-6). 48pp. This account tells how the heart works, what blood does, the flow of blood through the body, and how to keep the heart healthy. (Rev: BL 12/1/97; HBG 3/98; SLJ 2/98) [612.1]

20338 Viegas, Jennifer. *The Heart: Learning How Our Blood Circulates* (5–9). Illus. Series: 3-D Library of the Human Body. 2002, Rosen LB $26.50 (0-8239-3532-9). 48pp. An introduction to the anatomy and function of the human heart and the circulatory system that includes illustrations, diagrams, a glossary, and other aids. (Rev: BL 7/02) [612.1]

Digestive and Excretory Systems

20339 Ballard, Carol. *The Stomach and Digestive System* (5–8). Illus. Series: The Human Body. 1997, Raintree LB $25.68 (0-8172-4801-3). Topics discussed in this nicely illustrated volume include the digestive organs, how they work together, how food is tasted, and where nutrients are stored. (Rev: BL 6/1–15/97; SLJ 8/97) [612.3]

20340 Bryan, Jenny. *Digestion: The Digestive System* (4–6). Illus. Series: Body Talk. 1993, Dillon LB $13.95 (0-87518-564-0). 48pp. A clear, informative text and large captioned illustrations tell about the digestive system and related topics. (Rev: SLJ 10/93) [612]

20341 Brynie, Faith Hickman. *101 Questions About Food and Digestion That Have Been Eating at You . . . Until Now* (5–8). Illus. 2002, Millbrook LB $27.90 (0-7613-2309-0). 176pp. A question-and-answer format succeeds in conveying lots of food for thought, with details on digestive functions, digestive disorders, food safety, fat cells, Mad Cow disease, vitamins, and so forth. (Rev: BL 1/1–15/03; HBG 3/03; SLJ 3/03) [612.3]

20342 Burgess, Jan. *Food and Digestion* (5–8). Illus. Series: How Our Bodies Work. 1988, Silver Burdett LB $12.95 (0-382-09704-1). 48pp. Advice for staying healthy is provided in this addition to the How Our Bodies Work series. (Rev: BL 4/15/89) [612.3]

20343 Cho, Shinta. *The Gas We Pass: The Story of Farts* (PS–2). Trans. by Amanda Mayer Stinchecum. Illus. 1994, Kane/Miller $11.95 (0-916291-52-9). 28pp. This book tells about the causes, production, and effects of farts in a variety of animals, mainly humans. (Rev: BL 10/1/94; SLJ 11/94) [612.3]

20344 Davies, Nicola. *Poop: A Natural History of the Unmentionable* (2–5). Illus. by Neal Layton. 2005, Candlewick $12.99 (0-7636-2437-3). 64pp. Animal droppings are the main focus of this frank discussion with light-hearted cartoon illustrations. (Rev: BL 10/15/04) [573.4]

20345 Frost, Helen. *The Digestive System* (K–2). Illus. Series: Human Body Systems. 2000, Capstone LB $13.25 (0-7368-0649-0). 24pp. This is a simple introduction to the digestive system that includes clearly labeled diagrams and full-color photographs. (Rev: HBG 10/01; SLJ 4/01) [612.3]

20346 Goodman, Susan E. *The Truth About Poop* (4–6). Illus. by Elwood H. Smith. 2004, Viking $15.99 (0-670-03674-9). 40pp. Cartoon artwork accompanies matter-of-fact information about human and animal waste and the history of toilets and sewage. (Rev: BL 5/15/04; SLJ 7/04) [612.3]

20347 Holub, Joan. *I Have a Weird Brother Who Digested a Fly* (K–3). Illus. by Patrick Girouard. 1999, Whitman LB $13.95 (0-8075-3506-0). A whimsical tour of the digestive system that follows a fly from ingestion to elimination. (Rev: HBG 4/00; SLJ 12/99) [612.3]

20348 Lambourne, Mike. *Down the Hatch: Find Out About Your Food* (2–3). Illus. by Thompson Yardley. Series: Lighter Look. 1992, Millbrook LB $20.90 (1-56294-150-X). 39pp. In simple text and cartoonlike illustrations, the story of food and nutrition is presented. (Rev: SLJ 6/92) [641]

20349 Llewellyn, Claire. *Eating* (1–3). Series: Body in Action. 2004, Smart Apple Media LB $.00 (1-58340-436-8). The digestive system, senses of smell and taste, the body's use of nutrients, and various types of food are all covered here, along with information on healthy eating and food allergies. (Rev: BL 11/1/04) [612.3]

20350 Parker, Steve. *Digestion* (5–9). Illus. Series: Our Bodies. 2004, Raintree LB $19.99 (0-7398-6620-6). 48pp. Details of the human body's digestive system are accompanied by information on keeping them healthy. [612]

20351 Rau, Dana Meachen. *My Stomach* (PS–3). Illus. Series: Bookworms: What's Inside Me? 2004, Benchmark LB $14.95 (0-7614-1782-6). 31pp. A simple overview of the stomach's role in digestion, with photographs, diagrams, and X-rays. (Rev: SLJ 2/05) [612.3]

20352 Royston, Angela. *Why Do I Vomit? And Other Questions About Digestion* (3–5). Illus. Series: Body Matters. 2002, Heinemann LB $22.79 (1-

4034-0206-X). 32pp. In easy-to-understand language and many illustrations, Royston gives an inside look at the gastrointestinal system and some of its most obvious manifestations. (Rev: HBG 10/03; SLJ 4/03) [612.3]

20353 Showers, Paul. *What Happens to a Hamburger?* (K–3). Illus. by Edward Miller. Series: Let's-Read-and-Find-Out Science. 2001, HarperCollins LB $15.89 (0-06-027948-6); paper $4.95 (0-06-445183-6). 32pp. A new edition of this interesting easy reader that explains the mysteries of digestion. (Rev: BL 4/15/01; HBG 10/01) [612.3]

20354 Silverstein, Alvin, et al. *The Excretory System* (5–8). Illus. Series: Human Body Systems. 1994, Twenty-First Century LB $29.90 (0-8050-2834-X). A discussion on the human system of waste elimination. (Rev: BL 3/15/95; SLJ 3/95) [612.4]

20355 Simon, Seymour. *Guts: Our Digestive System* (5–8). Illus. 2005, HarperCollins LB $16.89 (0-06-054652-2). 32pp. Photographs and straightforward yet fascinating text present the digestive system. (Rev: BL 3/1/05; SLJ 4/05) [612.3]

20356 Stille, Darlene R. *The Digestive System* (2–4). Illus. Series: True Books. 1997, Children's Book Pr. LB $22.00 (0-516-20439-4). 47pp. Explains the process of digestion and the organs involved, with special coverage on topics like ulcers, diet, and the importance of cleanliness. (Rev: HBG 3/98; SLJ 2/98) [612]

20357 Toriello, James. *The Stomach: Learning How We Digest* (5–9). Series: 3-D Library of the Human Body. 2002, Rosen LB $26.50 (0-8239-3536-1). 48pp. Using outstanding diagrams and clear explanations, the digestive system is highlighted with material on each of its parts and their functions. (Rev: BL 7/02; SLJ 7/02) [612.3]

Nervous System

20358 Andrews, Linda Wasmer. *Intelligence* (4–8). Series: Life Balance. 2003, Watts LB $19.50 (0-531-12220-4); paper $6.95 (0-531-16608-2). 80pp. This book explores the concept of intelligence, how it is measured, and how it affects daily life. (Rev: BL 10/15/03) [612]

20359 Ballard, Carol. *How Do We Think?* (3–5). Series: How Your Body Works. 1998, Raintree LB $22.11 (0-8172-4740-8). 32pp. This book includes material on learning, memory, information processing, and message transmittal and provides activities on mental reactions and memory testing. (Rev: BL 5/15/98; HBG 9/98; SLJ 7/98) [612.8]

20360 Brynie, Faith Hickman. *The Physical Brain* (5–9). Illus. Series: The Amazing Brain. 2001, Blackbirch LB $21.95 (1-56711-424-5). 64pp. Photographs and absorbing text introduce the physical characteristics of the brain. Also use *Neurological Disorders* (2001). (Rev: BL 10/15/01; HBG 3/02; SLJ 9/01) [612.8]

20361 Degezelle, Terri. *Your Brain* (K–2). Illus. Series: The Bridgestone Science Library. 2002, Capstone LB $13.95 (0-7368-1147-8). 24pp. An attractive, basic overview of the brain with "Fun Facts" and an easy activity. (Rev: SLJ 7/02) [612.8]

20362 Garfield, Patricia. *The Dream Book: A Young Person's Guide to Understanding Dreams* (5–8). 2002, Tundra paper $9.95 (0-88776-594-7). 124pp. The author, a psychologist, explains the meanings of common (and uncommon) dreams and suggests how to use dreams to good effect. (Rev: BL 9/15/02; SLJ 9/02) [154.6]

20363 Gray, Susan H. *The Nervous System* (3–6). Illus. Series: The Human Body. 2003, Child's World LB $27.07 (1-59296-039-1). 32pp. A clear and detailed description of the human nervous system, using a child-friendly approach. (Rev: BL 2/1/04) [612.8]

20364 Hayhurst, Chris. *The Brain and Spinal Cord: Learning How We Think, Feel, and Move* (5–9). Series: 3-D Library of the Human Body. 2002, Rosen LB $26.50 (0-8239-3528-0). 48pp. Exceptional illustrations and a clear text are used to explain the composition of the brain with explanations of how it works and how emotions influence our thoughts. (Rev: BL 7/02; SLJ 7/02) [612.8]

20365 Innes, Brian. *Powers of the Mind* (4–7). Series: Unsolved Mysteries. 1999, Raintree LB $25.69 (0-8172-5488-9). 48pp. A balanced account that explores the powers of the brain in such controversial areas as moving objects, planting thoughts, and predicting events. (Rev: BL 5/15/99; HBG 9/99) [612.8]

20366 Lambert, Mark. *The Brain and Nervous System* (5–7). Illus. 1988, Silver Burdett LB $12.95 (0-382-09703-3). 48pp. Diagrams and photographs highlight this description. (Rev: BL 4/1/89) [612.8]

20367 Nettleton, Pamela Hill. *Think, Think, Think: Learning About Your Brain* (K–3). Illus. by Becky Shipe. Series: The Amazing Body. 2004, Picture Window LB $21.26 (1-4048-0252-5). 24pp. A simple explanation of how the brain works, with an activity and discussion of protective gear and brain scans. (Rev: SLJ 11/04) [612.8]

20368 Newquist, H. P. *The Great Brain Book: An Inside Look at the Inside of Your Head* (5–8). Illus. by Keith Kasnot. 2005, Scholastic $18.95 (0-439-45895-1). 160pp. The structure of the brain, its inner workings, and the history of our knowledge of this organ are all discussed in detail; interesting anecdotes add to the presentation. (Rev: BL 6/1–15/05) [612.8]

20369 Parker, Steve. *Brain and Nerves* (4–6). Illus. by Ian Thompson. Series: Look at Your Body. 1998, Millbrook LB $20.90 (0-7613-0812-1). 31pp. This explanation of the nervous system covers the brain, spinal cord, and nerves, with additional material on such topics as memory, headaches, and meningitis. (Rev: HBG 9/98; SLJ 10/98) [612]

20370 Parker, Steve. *The Brain and Nervous System* (5–9). Illus. Series: Our Bodies. 2004, Raintree LB $19.99 (0-7398-6619-2). 48pp. Details of the human body's brain and nervous system are accompanied by information on keeping them healthy.

20371 Parker, Steve. *The Brain and the Nervous System* (5–8). Series: The Human Body. 1997, Raintree

LB $18.98 (0-8172-4802-1). Double-page spreads introduce parts of the brain and their functions, brain waves, the nature of sleep and dreams, and other aspects of the brain and the nervous system. (Rev: BL 6/1–15/97; SLJ 8/97) [612.8]

20372 Routh, Kristina. *Epilepsy* (5–10). Illus. Series: Just the Facts. 2004, Heinemann LB $27.07 (1-4034-4601-6). 56pp. An overview of epilepsy, with attention to its effect on individuals when it comes to driving, sports, education, and employment. (Rev: SLJ 6/04) [616.8]

20373 Sandeman, Anna. *Brain* (1–2). Illus. Series: Body Books. 1996, Millbrook LB $18.90 (0-7613-0490-8). 32pp. With a simple text and full-color photos and diagrams, the brain is explored and explanations are given on how it works. (Rev: BL 10/15/96; SLJ 1/97) [612]

20374 Showers, Paul. *Sleep Is for Everyone* (PS–1). Illus. by Wendy Watson. Series: Let's-Read-and-Find-Out. 1997, HarperCollins LB $14.89 (0-06-025393-2). 32pp. This simple science book explains what sleep is, why it is necessary, and what happens if we do without it. (Rev: BL 8/97; SLJ 8/97) [612.8]

20375 Silverstein, Alvin, et al. *The Nervous System* (5–8). Illus. Series: Human Body Systems. 1994, Twenty-First Century LB $28.90 (0-8050-2835-8). 96pp. The human nervous system and how it functions and can malfunction are described, with information on the systems of other animals. (Rev: BL 3/15/95; SLJ 5/95) [612.8]

20376 Simon, Seymour. *The Brain: Our Nervous System* (3–6). Illus. 1997, Morrow $15.89 (0-688-14641-4). 32pp. The anatomy and functions of the nervous system and brain are carefully explained and illustrated with photos and diagrams. (Rev: BL 8/97; HB 9–10/97; HBG 3/98; SLJ 8/97) [612.8]

20377 Smith, Kathie Billingslea, and Victoria Crenson. *Thinking* (1–3). Illus. 1988, Troll LB $15.85 (0-8167-1016-3). 24pp. How the brain works is the focus of this simple introduction. (Rev: BL 3/15/88)

20378 Stille, Darlene R. *The Nervous System* (3–5). Illus. 1997, Children's Book Pr. LB $22.00 (0-516-20445-9). 48pp. In this introduction to the nervous system, the brain, nerve cells, and muscles are featured, with information on how they interact. (Rev: BL 2/15/98; HBG 3/98) [612.8]

Respiratory System

20379 Bryan, Jenny. *Breathing: The Respiratory System* (4–6). Illus. Series: Body Talk. 1993, Dillon LB $18.95 (0-87518-563-0). 48pp. Large captioned photos are used to explain what happens when we breathe plus giving information on health problems associated with the respiratory system. (Rev: SLJ 10/93) [612]

20380 Frost, Helen. *The Respiratory System* (K–2). Illus. Series: Human Body Systems. 2000, Capstone LB $13.25 (0-7368-0652-0). 24pp. Simple, brief text introduces the respiratory system, with clearly labeled diagrams and full-color photographs. (Rev: HBG 10/01; SLJ 4/01) [612]

20381 Furgang, Kathy. *My Lungs* (K–3). Illus. Series: My Body. 2001, Rosen LB $19.50 (0-8239-5575-3). 24pp. A basic overview of the lungs, their anatomy, how they function, and diseases of the lung, with helpful illustrations. (Rev: SLJ 9/01) [612.2]

20382 Hayhurst, Chris. *The Lungs: Learning How We Breathe* (5–9). Series: 3-D Library of the Human Body. 2002, Rosen LB $26.50 (0-8239-3534-5). 48pp. Amazing computer graphics are used to explain the composition of the lungs, how they work, and what keeps them healthy. (Rev: BL 7/02) [612.6]

20383 Lambert, Mark. *The Lungs and Breathing* (5–7). Illus. 1988, Silver Burdett LB $12.95 (0-382-09701-7). Profusely illustrated addition to the How Our Bodies Work series. (Rev: BL 4/15/89)

20384 Nettleton, Pamela Hill. *Breathe in, Breathe Out: Learning About Your Lungs* (K–3). Illus. by Becky Shipe. Series: The Amazing Body. 2004, Picture Window LB $21.26 (1-4048-0254-1). 24pp. A simple explanation of how the lungs work, with breathing activities and discussion of asthma and inhalers. (Rev: SLJ 11/04) [612.2]

20385 Parker, Steve. *Lungs* (4–6). Illus. Series: Look at Your Body. 1996, Millbrook LB $20.90 (0-7613-0530-0). 32pp. A well-organized, clearly illustrated description of lungs and their functions. (Rev: BL 11/1/96) [612.2]

20386 Parker, Steve. *The Lungs and Respiratory System* (5–8). Illus. Series: The Human Body. 1997, Raintree LB $18.98 (0-8172-4803-X). This nicely illustrated volume examines the organs used in breathing, tells how the respiratory system works, and explains what happens when it fails. (Rev: BL 6/1–15/97; SLJ 8/97) [612.2]

20387 Silverstein, Alvin, et al. *The Respiratory System* (5–8). Illus. Series: Human Body Systems. 1994, Twenty-First Century LB $29.90 (0-8050-2831-5). The purpose and process of breathing are discussed, with the text and illustrations focusing on the human respiratory system. (Rev: BL 3/15/95; SLJ 4/95) [612.2]

20388 Stille, Darlene R. *The Respiratory System* (2–4). Illus. Series: True Books. 1997, Children's Book Pr. LB $22.00 (0-516-20448-3). 47pp. Explains the process of respiration and the role of the lungs, with additional material on topics like asthma, tuberculosis, lung cancer, and emphysema. (Rev: HBG 3/98; SLJ 2/98) [612]

Senses

20389 Aliki. *My Five Senses* (PS–1). Illus. by author. 1989, HarperCollins paper $4.95 (0-06-445083-X). 32pp. A young boy finds that he is learning about the world through the marvels of his five senses. (Rev: SLJ 1/90) [152.1]

20390 Ballard, Carol. *How Do Our Ears Hear?* (3–5). Illus. Series: How Your Body Works. 1998, Raintree LB $22.11 (0-8172-4737-8). 32pp. Using attractive double-page spreads, this book explains the anatomy of the ear, its role in hearing and balance, and methods for coping with a hearing loss. (Rev: BL 4/15/98; HBG 9/98) [612.8]

20391 Ballard, Carol. *How Do Our Eyes See?* (3–5). Illus. Series: How Your Body Works. 1998, Raintree LB $22.11 (0-8172-4736-X). 32pp. Double-page spreads and clearly labeled diagrams introduce the structure and functions of the eyes along with material on optical illusions, optometry, and vision problems. (Rev: BL 4/15/98; HBG 9/98) [612.8]

20392 Ballard, Carol. *How Do We Feel and Touch?* (3–5). Series: How Your Body Works. 1998, Raintree LB $22.11 (0-8172-4739-4). 32pp. Informative photos and drawings help explain the sense of touch, with added activities such as creating a "feely" box and using a test to determine different degrees of sensitivity. (Rev: BL 5/15/98; HBG 9/98) [612.8]

20393 Ballard, Carol. *How Do We Taste and Smell?* (3–5). Series: How Your Body Works. 1998, Raintree LB $22.11 (0-8172-4738-6). 32pp. Good explanations, fine diagrams and photos, and a few related activities are used to explain how we are able to smell and taste. (Rev: BL 5/15/98; HBG 9/98; SLJ 7/98) [612.8]

20394 Bryan, Jenny. *Smell, Taste and Touch: The Sensory Systems* (4–6). Illus. Series: Body Talk. 1994, Dillon LB $13.95 (0-87518-590-8). 48pp. An illustrated introduction to three of the senses and how they function. Also use *Sound and Vision* (1994). (Rev: SLJ 8/94) [612.8]

20395 Byles, Monica. *Experiment with Senses* (2–5). Illus. Series: Science Experiments. 1994, Lerner LB $19.93 (0-8225-2455-4). 32pp. Fifteen experiments explain the senses, how they operate, and how they send messages to the brain. (Rev: BL 3/1/94; SLJ 4/94) [612.8]

20396 Cobb, Vicki. *Follow Your Nose: Discover Your Sense of Smell* (3–5). Illus. Series: Five Senses. 2000, Millbrook LB $21.90 (0-7613-1521-7). 32pp. This book blends facts and humor in an exploration of the sense of smell and also offers suggestions for easy experiments. (Rev: BL 11/15/00; HBG 3/01) [612.8]

20397 Cobb, Vicki. *Open Your Eyes: Discover Your Sense of Sight* (2–5). Illus. by Cynthia C. Lewis. Series: The Five Senses. 2002, Millbrook LB $22.90 (0-7613-1705-8). An appealing look at the eye, the parts of the eye, and how the eye works, with easy experiments and optical illusions. (Rev: HBG 10/02; SLJ 5/02) [612.84]

20398 Cobb, Vicki. *Perk up Your Ears: Discover Your Sense of Hearing* (3–6). Illus. by Cynthia C. Lewis. Series: The Five Senses. 2001, Millbrook LB $22.90 (0-7613-1704-X). An entertaining overview of hearing that encourages children to do lots of experimenting. (Rev: HBG 3/02; SLJ 4/02) [612.8]

20399 Cobb, Vicki. *Your Tongue Can Tell: Discover Your Sense of Taste* (3–5). Illus. Series: Five Senses. 2000, Millbrook LB $21.90 (0-7613-1473-3). 32pp. As well as giving an entertaining introduction to the sense of taste, this book supplies many ideas for activities and simple projects. (Rev: BL 11/15/00; HBG 3/01) [612.8]

20400 Cole, Joanna. *The Magic School Bus Explores the Senses* (2–4). Illus. by Bruce Degen. 1999, Scholastic $15.95 (0-590-44697-5). 48pp. The Magic School Bus travels with its passengers through an eye, an ear, a nose, and a mouth as it explores the human senses. (Rev: BL 2/15/99; HB 7–8/99; HBG 9/99; SLJ 2/99) [612.8]

20401 Cole, Joanna. *You Can't Smell a Flower with Your Ear! All About Your Five Senses* (1–3). Illus. by Mavis Smith. 1994, Penguin Putnam paper $3.99 (0-448-40469-9). 48pp. Using everyday experiences as examples, the five senses are introduced in this easy-to-read book. (Rev: BL 1/1/95) [612.8]

20402 Fowler, Allan. *Knowing About Noses* (1–2). Series: Rookie Readers. 1999, Children's Book Pr. LB $18.50 (0-516-20810-1). 32pp. This attractive beginning science book explains the functions of noses and explores the sense of smell. (Rev: BL 7/99; HBG 9/99) [612.8]

20403 Furgang, Kathy. *My Ears* (K–3). Illus. Series: My Body. 2001, Rosen LB $19.50 (0-8239-5572-9). 24pp. A basic overview of the ears, their anatomy, how they function, and diseases of the ear, with helpful illustrations. (Rev: SLJ 9/01) [612.8]

20404 Gordon, Sharon. *Seeing* (1–2). Illus. Series: Rookie Read-About Health. 2001, Children's Book Pr. $19.00 (0-516-22291-0); paper $5.95 (0-516-25990-3). 32pp. Very young readers are encouraged to think about their eyes and their ability to see. Also use *Smelling* (2001). (Rev: BL 12/1/01) [612.8]

20405 Hewitt, Sally. *The Five Senses* (K–3). Series: It's Science! 1999, Children's Book Pr. LB $20.00 (0-516-21179-X). 30pp. A very basic introduction to the senses with a few simple activities included. (Rev: SLJ 5/99) [612]

20406 Isadora, Rachael. *I See* (PS). Illus. by Rachel Isadora. 1985, Greenwillow $14.89 (0-688-04060-8). 32pp. A little girl sees objects — her ball, her teddy bear. (Rev: BCCB 6/85; BL 3/15/85; SLJ 4/85)

20407 Isadora, Rachael. *I Touch* (PS). Illus. by Rachel Isadora. 1991, Greenwillow paper $6.95 (0-688-10524-6). 32pp. "I touch my bear, he's soft" says this book that calls attention to tactile sensations. (Rev: BL 11/15/85; SLJ 2/86)

20408 Johnson, Jinny. *Senses* (K–3). Illus. Series: Kingfisher Young Knowledge. 2004, Kingfisher $8.95 (0-7534-5771-7). 47pp. Using two-page chapters with large text and eye-catching photographs, Johnson introduces the five senses. (Rev: SLJ 4/05) [612]

20409 Levine, Shar, and Leslie Johnstone. *Super Senses* (K–3). Illus. by Steve Harpster. Series: First Science Experiments. 2003, Sterling LB $12.95 (0-8069-7247-5). 48pp. This cartoon-illustrated exploration of the five senses includes experiments that provide insight. (Rev: HBG 10/03; SLJ 10/03) [612.8]

20410 Litchfield, Ada B. *A Button in Her Ear* (1–3). Illus. by Eleanor Mill. 1976, Whitman LB $14.95 (0-8075-0987-6). 32pp. A simple introduction to hearing problems and correctional devices such as the hearing aid.

20411 Martin, Paul D. *Messengers to the Brain: Our Fantastic Five Senses* (4–6). Illus. 1984, National Geographic LB $12.50 (0-87044-504-9). 104pp. A well-illustrated explanation of how the organs of the human body send messages to the brain, which acts as a message center.

20412 Murphy, Patricia J. *Hearing* (2–4). Illus. Series: A True Book. 2003, Children's Pr. LB $23.50 (0-516-22599-5); paper $6.95 (0-516-26970-4). 47pp. A simple, large-print look at the ear and our sense of hearing. Also use *Taste* and *Touch* (both 2003). (Rev: SLJ 7/03) [612.8]

20413 O'Brien-Palmer, Michelle. *Sense-Abilities: Fun Ways to Explore the Senses: Activities for Children 4 to 8* (PS–2). Illus. by Fran Lee. 1998, Chicago Review paper $12.95 (1-55652-327-1). 166pp. With a single chapter devoted to each of the senses, this activity book contains facts and experiments that explore various sensory experiences. (Rev: SLJ 1/99) [612.8]

20414 Parker, Steve. *The Senses* (5–9). Illus. Series: Our Bodies. 2004, Raintree LB $19.99 (0-7398-6624-9). 48pp. Details of the human senses are accompanied by information on keeping them healthy. [612]

20415 Parker, Steve. *Senses* (4–6). Series: Look at Your Body. 1997, Millbrook LB $20.90 (0-7613-0602-1). 32pp. In this visually appealing, clearly written book, the five senses are introduced and explored, with interesting accompanying activities. (Rev: BL 1/1–15/98; HBG 3/98) [612]

20416 Parramon, J. M., and J. J. Puig. *Hearing* (PS–1). Illus. by Maria Rius. 1985, Barron's paper $6.95 (0-8120-3563-1). 32pp. An easy introduction to the sense of hearing. (Rev: BL 9/1/85)

20417 Parramon, J. M., and J. J. Puig. *Sight* (PS–1). Illus. by Maria Rius. 1985, Barron's paper $6.95 (0-8120-3564-X). 32pp. The sense of sight is explained to young readers. (Rev: BL 9/1/85; SLJ 11/85)

20418 Parramon, J. M., and J. J. Puig. *Smell* (PS–1). Illus. by Maria Rius. 1985, Barron's paper $6.95 (0-8120-3565-8). 32pp. An easy explanation of the sense of smell. (Rev: BL 9/1/85)

20419 Parramon, J. M., and J. J. Puig. *Taste* (PS–1). Illus. by Maria Rius. 1985, Barron's paper $6.95 (0-8120-3566-6). 32pp. Easy reading about the sense of taste. (Rev: BL 9/1/85)

20420 Parramon, J. M., and J. J. Puig. *Touch* (PS–1). Illus. by Maria Rius. 1985, Barron's paper $6.95 (0-8120-3567-4). 32pp. An easy-to-read explanation of the sense of touch. (Rev: BL 9/1/85)

20421 Pringle, Laurence. *Hearing* (3–6). Illus. Series: Explore Your Senses. 1999, Marshall Cavendish LB $15.95 (0-7614-0735-9). 32pp. Using a large format and clear diagrams, this book discusses the structure of the ear, how it operates, possible malfunctions, and how to preserve hearing. (Rev: BL 2/1/00; HBG 9/00; SLJ 3/00) [612.8]

20422 Pringle, Laurence. *Smell* (3–6). Series: Explore Your Senses. 1999, Marshall Cavendish LB $15.95 (0-7614-0737-5). 32pp. A clear text, diagrams, and

photographs are used to explain how the sense of smell works, problems that can occur, and the differences between animals and humans. (Rev: BL 2/15/00; HBG 9/00; SLJ 3/00) [612]

20423 Pringle, Laurence. *Taste* (3–6). Illus. Series: Explore Your Senses. 1999, Marshall Cavendish LB $15.95 (0-7614-0736-7). 32pp. The structure of the tongue, taste buds, taste cells, and the relationship between smell and taste are some of the subjects covered in this large-format book. (Rev: BL 2/1/00; HBG 9/00; SLJ 3/00) [612.8]

20424 Pringle, Laurence. *Touch* (3–6). Series: Explore Your Senses. 1999, Marshall Cavendish LB $15.95 (0-7614-0738-3). 32pp. A fresh look at the sense of touch that uses many color diagrams, photos, and an accessible text. (Rev: BL 2/15/00; HBG 9/00) [612]

20425 Sandeman, Anna. *Senses* (1–2). Illus. Series: Body Books. 1995, Millbrook LB $18.90 (1-56294-944-6). 32pp. Body organs that are involved with the senses, like eyes, are discussed in this simple introduction that also mentions such topics as color blindness and the ears' role in balance. (Rev: BL 12/15/95; SLJ 2/96) [612.8]

20426 Sherman, Josepha. *The Ear: Learning How We Hear* (5–9). Series: 3-D Library of the Human Body. 2002, Rosen LB $26.50 (0-8239-3529-9). 48pp. Using amazing illustrations and clear explanations, Sherman introduces the ear, its anatomy, uses, operation, and problems that can develop. (Rev: BL 7/02) [612.8]

20427 Showers, Paul. *Look at Your Eyes* (PS–2). Illus. by True Kelley. Series: Let's-Read-and-Find-Out. 1992, HarperCollins LB $15.89 (0-06-020189-4). 32pp. A little boy looks in the bathroom mirror and begins to think about his eyes. (Rev: BL 1/1/93) [612.8]

20428 Sideri, Simona. *Let's Look at Eyes* (PS–K). Illus. by Sheilagh Noble. Series: Let's Look At. 2004, Smart Apple Media LB $22.80 (1-58340-495-3). 30pp. Young children compare their eyes and sight with those of animals, including owls, eagles, camels, lobsters, and wasps. Also use *Let's Look at Feet* (2004). (Rev: BL 1/1–15/05) [573.8]

20429 Silverstein, Alvin, et al. *Can You See the Chalkboard?* (3–5). Series: My Health. 2001, Watts LB $23.00 (0-531-11783-9). Problems with vision are discussed with material on the structure of the eye, diagnosis of these problems, and treatments available. (Rev: BL 1/1–15/02; SLJ 8/01) [612.8]

20430 Silverstein, Alvin, and Virginia Silverstein. *Earaches* (3–5). Series: My Health. 2002, Watts LB $23.00 (0-531-11873-8); paper $6.95 (0-531-15562-5). 48pp. This book describes, in a simple text and many pictures, how the ear functions, what can cause earaches, and how to treat them. (Rev: BL 6/1–15/02) [612.8]

20431 Silverstein, Alvin, and Virginia Silverstein. *Smelling and Tasting* (4–6). Illus. by Anne Canevari Green. Series: Senses and Sensors. 2002, Twenty-First Century LB $25.90 (0-7613-1667-1). 64pp. Human and animal senses of smell and taste are covered in this well-organized and readable volume.

Also use *Touching and Feeling* (2002). (Rev: BL 3/15/02; HBG 10/02; SLJ 8/02)

20432 Simon, Seymour. *Eyes and Ears* (5–8). Illus. 2003, HarperCollins LB $16.89 (0-688-15304-6). 32pp. Simon explains in clear, straightforward terms our ability to see and hear. (Rev: BL 3/15/03*; HBG 10/03; SLJ 6/03) [612.8]

20433 Suhr, Mandy. *Taste* (PS–1). Illus. by Mike Gordon. Series: I'm Alive. 1994, Carolrhoda LB $19.93 (0-87614-836-4). 32pp. Why and how we taste is covered in a nontechnical way, with simple activities and projects to amplify the text. From the same series, also use *Touch* (1994). (Rev: SLJ 12/94) [152.1]

20434 Viegas, Jennifer. *The Eye: Learning How We See* (5–9). Illus. Series: 3-D Library of the Human Body. 2002, Rosen LB $26.50 (0-8239-3530-2). 48pp. This volume on the anatomy and function of the human eye includes illustrations, diagrams, a glossary, and other aids. (Rev: BL 7/02) [612.8]

20435 Viegas, Jennifer. *The Mouth and Nose: Learning How We Taste and Smell* (5–9). Series: 3-D Library of the Human Body. 2002, Rosen LB $26.50 (0-8239-3535-3). 48pp. The mouth and nose are featured in this heavily illustrated account that covers their composition, functions, and how they work together. (Rev: BL 7/02) [612]

20436 Ziefert, Harriet. *You Can't Taste a Pickle with Your Ear* (K–2). Illus. by Amanda Haley. 2002, Blue Apple $15.95 (1-929766-68-8). 40pp. The five senses are explored in humorous style as Ziefert blends facts, goofy rhymes, cartoons, and questions that will spur further investigation. (Rev: BL 1/1–15/03; SLJ 1/03) [612.8]

Skeletal-Muscular System

20437 Arnold, Caroline. *The Skeletal System* (3–4). Illus. 2004, Lerner LB $25.26 (0-8225-5140-3). 48pp. The skeleton and bones are introduced in simple, concise text. (Rev: SLJ 2/05) [612.7]

20438 Balestrino, Philip. *The Skeleton Inside You* (2–4). Illus. by True Kelley. 1989, HarperCollins paper $4.95 (0-06-445087-2). 32pp. Color illustrations help to explain the body's structure. (Rev: BL 6/15/89)

20439 Ballard, Carol. *How Do We Move?* (3–5). Series: How Your Body Works. 1998, Raintree LB $22.11 (0-8172-4741-6). 32pp. This book explains how the skeletal and muscular systems work and includes activities such as creating a model of a muscle. (Rev: BL 5/15/98; HBG 9/98) [612]

20440 Ballard, Carol. *The Skeleton and Muscular System* (5–8). Illus. Series: Human Body. 1997, Raintree $18.98 (0-8172-4805-6). 48pp. This well-organized book introduces in text and pictures such topics as muscles and how they work, joint diseases, bones, and skeletal diseases. (Rev: SLJ 2/98) [612]

20441 Barner, Bob. *Dem Bones* (K–3). Illus. 1996, Chronicle $14.95 (0-8118-0827-0). 32pp. The human skeleton is introduced by using the words of the old song "Dem Dry Bones." (Rev: BL 12/1/96; SLJ 11/96) [611]

20442 Bryan, Jenny. *Movement: The Muscular and Skeletal System* (4–6). Illus. Series: Body Talk. 1993, Dillon LB $18.95 (0-87518-565-7). 48pp. This clear introduction to muscles and bones also discusses such topics as running, weightlessness, joint replacement, genetic engineering, and artificial limbs. (Rev: SLJ 10/93) [612]

20443 Degezelle, Terri. *Your Bones* (K–2). Illus. Series: The Bridgestone Science Library. 2002, Capstone LB $13.95 (0-7368-1146-X). 24pp. An attractive, basic overview of bones with "Fun Facts" and an easy activity. (Rev: SLJ 7/02) [612.7]

20444 Dineen, Jacqueline. *The Skeleton and Movement* (5–7). Illus. 1988, Silver Burdett $12.95 (0-382-09702-5). An explanation of human body movement. (Rev: BL 4/15/89) [612.75]

20445 Frost, Helen. *The Muscular System* (K–2). Illus. Series: Human Body Systems. 2000, Capstone LB $13.25 (0-7368-0650-4). 24pp. Short, simple text introduces the muscular system, accompanied by full-color illustrations. (Rev: HBG 10/01; SLJ 4/01) [612]

20446 Johnson, Rebecca L. *The Muscular System* (2–4). Series: Early Bird Body Systems. 2004, Lerner LB $25.26 (0-8225-1248-3). Photographs and diagrams add to the easy-to-understand text; a word list starts the book and print and Web resources are appended. (Rev: BL 10/15/04; SLJ 2/05) [612.7]

20447 Macnair, Patricia Ann. *Movers and Shapers* (3–5). Series: Bodyscope. 2004, Houghton Mifflin $9.95 (0-7534-5791-1). 40pp. The importance of physical fitness is emphasized in this attractive overview of the musculoskeletal system. (Rev: BL 10/15/04) [612.7]

20448 Oleksy, Walter. *The Head and Neck: Learning How We Use Our Muscles* (5–9). Series: 3-D Library of the Human Body. 2002, Rosen LB $26.50 (0-8239-3531-0). 48pp. The muscles of the head and neck and their roles in controlling the sense organs, chewing and swallowing, facial expressions, and conveying emotions are explained in this well-illustrated account. (Rev: BL 7/02) [612.7]

20449 Parker, Steve. *Skeleton* (4–6). Illus. Series: Look at Your Body. 1996, Millbrook LB $20.90 (0-7613-0529-7). 32pp. The human skeleton, its composition, and its uses are covered, with extensive, unusual illustrations like X-rays and CAT scans. (Rev: BL 11/1/96) [611]

20450 Parker, Steve. *The Skeleton and Muscles* (5–9). Illus. Series: Our Bodies. 2004, Raintree LB $28.56 (0-7398-6622-2). 48pp. Details of the human body's skeletal and muscular systems are accompanied by information on keeping them healthy. (Rev: BL 8/04) [612.7]

20451 Rau, Dana Meachen. *My Bones and Muscles* (PS–3). Illus. Series: Bookworms: What's Inside Me? 2004, Benchmark LB $14.95 (0-7614-1777-X). 31pp. A simple overview of bones, skeleton, and muscles, with photographs, diagrams, and X-rays. (Rev: SLJ 2/05) [612.7]

20452 Saunderson, Jane. *Muscles and Bones* (3–6). Illus. by Robina Green. Series: You and Your Body.

1992, Troll LB $18.60 (0-8167-2088-6); paper $3.95 (0-8167-2089-4). 32pp. The structure and function of human muscles in a well-designed book. (Rev: BL 5/15/92) [612.7]

20453 Sherman, Josepha. *The Upper Limbs: Learning How We Use Our Arms, Elbows, Forearms, and Hands* (5–9). Series: 3-D Library of the Human Body. 2002, Rosen LB $26.50 (0-8239-3537-X). 48pp. The parts of the arm and hand are examined with illustrated material on how the muscles in these areas function and receive support from the skeletal structure. (Rev: BL 7/02) [612.7]

20454 Silverstein, Alvin, et al. *Broken Bones* (3–5). Series: My Health. 2001, Watts LB $23.00 (0-531-11781-2). This book describes what happens when bones get broken, the causes, treatments available, and how mending takes place. (Rev: BL 1/1–15/02; SLJ 8/01) [612.7]

20455 Silverstein, Alvin, et al. *The Muscular System* (5–8). Illus. Series: Human Body Systems. 1994, Twenty-First Century $29.90 (0-8050-2836-6). Full-color diagrams, drawings, and photographs highlight this survey of the human muscular system. (Rev: BL 3/15/95; SLJ 5/95) [612.7]

20456 Simon, Seymour. *Bones: Our Skeletal System* (3–6). Illus. 1998, Morrow LB $15.93 (0-688-14645-7). 32pp. This book describes the human skeleton and explains the structure of bones, their important groups, how they connect, and how they move. (Rev: BCCB 9/98; BL 9/1/98; HBG 3/99; SLJ 12/98) [612.7]

20457 Viegas, Jennifer. *The Lower Limbs: Learning How We Use Our Thighs, Knees, Legs, and Feet* (5–9). Series: 3-D Library of the Human Body. 2002, Rosen LB $26.50 (0-8239-3533-7). 48pp. The bones and muscles of the legs and feet and their functions are described in a clear text and exceptional illustrations. (Rev: BL 7/02; SLJ 7/02) [612.7]

Skin and Hair

20458 Dawson, Mildred L. *Beauty Lab: How Science Is Changing the Way We Look* (5–10). 1997, Silver Moon $14.95 (1-881889-84-X). This work on health and hygiene contains chapters on skin, eyes, teeth, fitness, and hair. (Rev: BR 5–6/97; SLJ 3/97) [613.7]

20459 Kinch, Michael P. *Warts* (3–5). Illus. Series: My Health. 2000, Watts LB $22.50 (0-531-11625-5); paper $6.95 (0-531-16453-5). 48pp. Different kinds of warts are discussed, with material and activities related to how they are transmitted, how they grow, and how they can be eliminated. (Rev: BL 6/1–15/00) [616.5]

20460 Tyler, Michael. *The Skin You Live In* (PS–2). Illus. by David Lee Csicsko. 2005, Chicago Children's Museum $14.95 (0-9759580-0-3). Skin's physical properties and different shades are among the features explored in rhyming verse. (Rev: SLJ 5/05)

20461 Radabaugh, Melinda. *Getting a Haircut* (PS–1). Series: First Time. 2003, Heinemann LB

$18.50 (1-4034-0225-6). 24pp. Reasons for getting a haircut and the experiences involved are emploerd in simple, reassuring text plus pictures and a quiz. (Rev: HBG 10/03; SLJ 9/03) [646.7]

20462 Sandeman, Anna. *Skin, Teeth, and Hair* (1–2). Illus. Series: Body Books. 1996, Millbrook LB $18.90 (0-7613-0489-4). 32pp. For beginning readers, this colorful account explains the composition and use in the human body of skin, teeth, and hair. (Rev: BL 10/15/96; SLJ 1/97) [612]

20463 Showers, Paul. *Your Skin and Mine* (PS–3). Illus. by Kathleen Kuchera. Series: Let's-Read-and-Find-Out. 1991, HarperCollins paper $5.95 (0-06-445102-X). 32pp. A look at skin, with simple experiments to show skin reactions. (Rev: BL 10/15/91; SLJ 8/91) [612.7]

20464 Silverstein, Alvin, et al. *Cuts, Scrapes, Scabs, Scars* (3–5). Series: My Health. 1999, Watts LB $22.50 (0-531-11582-8). 48pp. Using colored medical illustrations, photos, and amusing cartoons, this book describes various skin injuries and how the body heals itself and produces new skin. (Rev: BL 10/15/99; HBG 4/00) [612.7]

20465 Silverstein, Alvin, et al. *Is That a Rash?* (3–5). Illus. Series: My Health. 2000, Watts LB $22.50 (0-531-11637-9); paper $6.95 (0-531-16451-9). 48pp. With many suggested activities and excellent color photos, this account introduces skin problems — their causes and treatments. (Rev: BL 6/1–15/00) [616.5]

20466 Silverstein, Alvin, and Virginia Silverstein. *Burns and Blisters* (3–5). Series: My Health. 2002, Watts LB $23.00 (0-531-11871-1); paper $6.95 (0-531-15561-7). 48pp. Using photographs, cartoons, and other visuals as well as a lively text, this book explains what happens when the skin becomes burned and blistered. (Rev: BL 6/1–15/02; SLJ 8/02) [612.7]

20467 Yagyu, Genichiro. *All About Scabs* (K–3). Trans. by Amanda Mayer Stinchecum. Illus. 1998, Kane/Miller $11.95 (0-916291-82-0). 28pp. This attention-getting book tells what a scab is, how it is formed, its uses, and what eventually happens to it. (Rev: BL 1/1–15/99; HBG 3/99; SLJ 2/99) [617.1]

Teeth

20468 Copeland, Cynthia L. *The Tooth Fairy Tells All* (K–3). Illus. by author. Series: Silly Millies. 2002, Millbrook LB $17.90 (0-7613-2805-X); paper $4.99 (0-7613-1785-6). 31pp. This gentle exchange between the Tooth Fairy and the Wisdom Tooth, provides useful information about teeth — including the different types — and how best to care for them. (Rev: HBG 3/03; SLJ 8/03)

20469 Keller, Laurie. *Open Wide: Tooth School Inside* (2–4). Illus. 2000, Holt $16.95 (0-8050-6192-4). 32pp. A fun book that explores the different kinds of teeth, dental care, and the causes of tooth decay. (Rev: BCCB 9/00; BL 5/1/00; HB 5–6/00; HBG 9/00; SLJ 5/00) [617.6]

20470 Lee, Jordan. *Coping with Braces and Other Orthodontic Work* (4–9). Series: Coping. 1998,

Rosen LB $25.25 (0-8239-2721-0). 95pp. A book about braces, their purposes, and the problems they can cause. (Rev: SLJ 11/98) [612.3]

20471 McGinty, Alice B. *Staying Healthy: Dental Care* (K–3). Series: The Library of Healthy Living. 1998, Rosen LB $15.95 (0-8239-5139-1). 24pp. A fine introduction to teeth that covers such topics as different types of teeth, parts of a tooth, dental hygiene, and problems such as decay and cavities. (Rev: SLJ 9/98) [612.3]

20472 Murkoff, Heidi. *What to Expect When You Go to the Dentist* (1–3). Illus. by Laura Rader. Series: What To Expect Kids. 2002, HarperCollins $7.99 (0-694-01328-5). 32pp. Angus the dog gives good advice and some projects to prepare youngsters for their first visit to a dentist. (Rev: BL 6/1–15/02; HBG 10/02) [617.601]

20473 Rockwell, Harlow. *My Dentist* (1–2). Illus. 1975, Morrow paper $4.95 (0-688-07040-X). 32pp. A matter-of-fact, informative book about dentists and the instruments they use.

20474 Showers, Paul. *How Many Teeth?* (PS–2). Illus. by True Kelley. Series: Let's-Read-and-Find-Out. 1991, HarperCollins paper $4.95 (0-06-445098-8). 32pp. A full-color, funny, informative book showing a multiracial classroom. (Rev: BL 6/15/91; SLJ 10/91) [612.3]

20475 Silverstein, Alvin, et al. *Tooth Decay and Cavities* (3–5). Illus. Series: My Health. 1999, Watts LB $22.50 (0-531-11580-1). 48pp. Discusses the structure and functions of teeth, how decay occurs, and how it can be prevented. (Rev: BL 10/15/99; HBG 4/00; SLJ 12/99) [617.6]

Hygiene, Physical Fitness, and Nutrition

20476 Baptiste, Baron. *My Daddy Is a Pretzel* (PS–3). Illus. by Sophie Fatus. 2004, Barefoot $16.99 (1-84148-151-3). 48pp. An attractive introduction to basic yoga poses. (Rev: BL 10/15/04; SLJ 1/05) [613]

20477 Brown, Laurie Krasny, and Marc Brown. *Dinosaurs Alive and Well! A Guide to Good Health* (PS–3). Illus. 1990, Little, Brown paper $6.95 (0-316-11009-4). 32pp. Using dinosaurs, the basic principles of nutrition and hygiene are covered. Also use *Dinosaurs Travel* (1990). (Rev: BCCB 5/90; BL 5/15/90; HB 5–6/90; SLJ 4/90*) [613]

20478 Crump, Marguerite. *Don't Sweat It! Every Body's Answers to Questions You Don't Want to Ask: A Guide for Young People* (5–9). Illus. by Chris Sharp. 2002, Free Spirit paper $13.95 (1-57542-114-3). 118pp. Crump tackles potentially embarrassing questions about personal hygiene. (Rev: SLJ 1/03) [613.0433]

20479 De Brunhoff, Laurent. *Babar's Yoga for Elephants* (2–4). Illus. 2002, Abrams $16.95 (0-8109-1021-7). 48pp. The sage elephant Babar re-creates yoga poses, which kids may be tempted to do as well, in this nonfiction book best read with an adult

nearby. (Rev: BL 10/15/02; HBG 3/03; SLJ 4/03) [613.7]

20480 Ehrlich, Fred. *Does a Lion Brush?* (PS). Illus. by Emily Bolam. Series: Early Experiences. 2002, Handprint $10.95 (1-929766-64-5). This small-format picture book gives a humorous introduction to tooth brushing. Also use *Does a Pig Flush?* (2002). (Rev: SLJ 3/03)

20481 Feeney, Kathy. *Get Moving: Tips on Exercise* (K–3). Series: Your Health. 2001, Capstone LB $13.95 (0-7368-0973-2). 24pp. The importance of exercise is stressed through simple text and an activity pyramid. (Rev: HBG 3/02; SLJ 4/02) [613.7]

20482 Frost, Helen. *Drinking Water* (K–2). 2000, Capstone LB $13.25 (0-7368-0534-6). 24pp. This book explains simply why drinking water is a necessary part of one's diet. (Rev: HBG 9/00; SLJ 10/00) [613.2]

20483 Frost, Helen. *Eating Right* (K–2). Series: Food Guide Pyramid. 2000, Capstone LB $13.25 (0-7368-0535-4). 24pp. A very simple introduction to nutrition and the food pyramid. (Rev: HBG 9/00; SLJ 10/00) [613.2]

20484 Frost, Simon. *Fitness for Young People* (4–8). Series: Flowmotion. 2003, Sterling paper $9.95 (0-8069-9373-1). 96pp. Using a number of excellent stop-action photographs, the routines, techniques, and exercises involved with young people keeping fit are presented. (Rev: BL 10/15/03) [613]

20485 Gedatus, Gus. *Exercise for Weight Management* (4–7). Series: Nutrition and Fitness. 2001, Capstone LB $23.93 (0-7368-0706-3). 64pp. As well as outlining a simple, practical exercise program, this volume stresses good nutrition and contains some healthy recipes. (Rev: BL 9/15/01; HBG 10/01) [613.7]

20486 Glibbery, Caroline. *Join the Total Fitness Gang* (4–6). Series: Good Health Guides. 1998, Gareth Stevens LB $14.95 (0-8368-2181-5). 32pp. In this guide to good health, topics covered include personal hygiene, weight control, sleep habits, dental and eye care, first aid, and drugs and smoking. (Rev: HBG 9/99; SLJ 6/99) [613]

20487 Gordon, Sharon. *Exercise* (3–5). Series: Rookie Read-About Health. 2002, Children's Book Pr. LB $19.00 (0-516-22571-5); paper $5.95 (0-516-26950-X). 32pp. This easy-reader explains how exercise builds strong muscles and shows how children can have fun while doing favorite activities. (Rev: BL 12/15/02) [613.7]

20488 Gordon, Sharon. *Keeping Clean* (3–5). Series: Rookie Read-About Health. 2002, Children's Book Pr. LB $19.00 (0-516-22572-3); paper $5.95 (0-516-26951-8). 32pp. From bathing after exercise to washing one's hand before eating, this is a simple guide to personal hygiene and on how to keep germs from spreading. (Rev: BL 12/15/02) [613]

20489 Gordon, Sharon. *You Are What You Eat* (3–5). Series: Rookie Read-About Health. 2002, Children's Book Pr. LB $19.00 (0-516-22573-1); paper $5.95 (0-516-26952-6). 32pp. This book uses simple language to explain such nutritional facts as why breakfast is the most important meal of the day and why an apple is a better snack than potato chips. (Rev: BL 12/15/02) [613]

20490 Gray, Shirley W. *Exercising for Good Health* (2–4). Illus. Series: Living Well. 2003, Child's World LB $25.64 (1-59296-081-2). 32pp. Outlines the many benefits of regular exercise and describes the effects of specific activities on overall health. (Rev: SLJ 2/04) [613.7]

20491 Green, Tamara. *Exercise Is Fun!* (4–6). Series: Good Health Guides. 1998, Gareth Stevens LB $14.95 (0-8368-2180-7). 32pp. Many illustrations are included in this beginner's guide to exercise that includes material on yoga, breathing and posture exercises, dancing, jumping rope, and jogging. (Rev: HBG 9/99; SLJ 6/99) [613.7]

20492 King, Hazel. *Carbohydrates for a Healthy Body* (4–6). Illus. Series: Body Needs. 2003, Heinemann LB $27.07 (1-4034-0756-8). 48pp. A clearly written and well illustrated introduction to the role and value of carbohydrates in nutrition. (Rev: HBG 10/03; SLJ 4/04) [612.3]

20493 Landau, Elaine. *A Healthy Diet* (4–7). Series: Watts Library. 2003, Watts LB $24.00 (0-531-12027-9); paper $8.95 (0-531-16668-6). 63pp. Landau explains the basics of good nutrition; the benefits of vitamins, minerals, and exercise; and the dangers of fad diets. (Rev: SLJ 9/03) [613.2]

20494 Luby, Thia. *Children's Book of Yoga: Games and Exercises Mimic Plants and Animals and Objects* (PS–7). 1998, Clear Light $14.95 (1-57416-003-6). 112pp. Brief, clear instructions are used to introduce yoga exercises — from the very easy to the more complex. (Rev: SLJ 10/98) [181.45]

20495 Lukes, Bonnie L. *How to Be a Reasonably Thin Teenage Girl: Without Starving, Losing Your Friends or Running Away from Home* (5–8). Illus. 1986, Macmillan $15.00 (0-689-31269-5). 96pp. A commonsense guide that addresses the particular weight problems of young teenagers. (Rev: BCCB 10/86; BL 1/1/87; SLJ 11/86) [613.2]

20496 Mainland, Pauline. *A Yoga Parade of Animals: A First Fun Picture Book of Yoga* (2–6). Photos by Katie Vandyck. Illus. by Chris Perry. 1998, Element Books $15.95 (1-90188-165-2). This book shows children how they can assume the shapes and positions of various animals and supplies information about yoga and its history. (Rev: HBG 3/99; SLJ 11/98) [613.7]

20497 Parker, Steve. *Professor Protein's Fitness, Health, Hygiene and Relaxation Tonic* (4–6). Illus. by Rob Shone. 1996, Millbrook LB $23.90 (0-7613-0494-0). 48pp. A witty presentation of material about fitness, health, and hygiene, with accompanying humorous cartoons. (Rev: SLJ 1/97) [613]

20498 Parsons, Alexandra. *Fit for Life* (3–6). Illus. by John Shackell and Stuart Harrison. Series: Life Education. 1996, Watts LB $19.00 (0-531-14372-4). 32pp. A beginner's guide to nutrition, hygiene, and exercise, with coverage of the effects of drugs, smoking, and alcohol. (Rev: SLJ 10/96) [613.2]

20499 Pascoe, Elaine, ed. *Spreading Menace: Salmonella Attack and the Hunger Craving* (5–8). Illus. Series: Body Story. 2003, Gale/Blackbirch LB

$23.70 (1-4103-0064-1). 48pp. Two stories show how the body can react to food — Mike is infected with salmonella, and George's hunger is giving him a weight problem. (Rev: SLJ 4/04) [615.9]

20500 Petrie, Kristin. *The Food Pyramid* (2–4). Illus. Series: Nutrition. 2004, ABDO LB $15.95 (1-59197-403-8). 32pp. A look at food groups, nutrition, serving sizes, and healthy eating in general, illustrated with photographs and other graphics. (Rev: HBG 4/04; SLJ 4/04) [613.2]

20501 Petrie, Kristin. *Nutrition Anyone?* (2–4). Illus. Series: Nutrition. 2004, ABDO LB $15.95 (1-59197-404-6). 32pp. Clear text and graphics introduce good nutrition and why it is necessary. (Rev: HBG 4/04; SLJ 4/04) [613.2]

20502 Petrie, Kristin. *Vitamins Are Vital* (2–4). Illus. Series: Nutrition. 2004, ABDO LB $15.95 (1-59197-406-2). 32pp. An exploration of the role of vitamins and minerals in nutrition, aimed at helping children have a healthful and balanced diet. (Rev: HBG 4/04; SLJ 4/04) [613.2]

20503 Powell, Jillian. *Exercise and Your Health* (2–5). Illus. Series: Health Matters. 1997, Raintree LB $25.69 (0-8172-4927-3). 32pp. Explains how exercise affects good health and gives tips on types of exercises, warming-up and cooling activities, proper dress, and ways to design a personalized program. (Rev: HBG 3/98; SLJ 2/98) [613.7]

20504 Powell, Jillian. *Food and Your Health* (2–5). Illus. Series: Health Matters. 1997, Raintree LB $25.69 (0-8172-4925-7). 32pp. Explains how food is digested, what constitutes good nutrition, problem foods, and data on proper body weight. (Rev: HBG 3/98; SLJ 2/98) [613.2]

20505 Rockwell, Lizzy. *The Busy Body Book: A Kid's Guide to Fitness* (PS–1). Illus. by author. 2004, Crown LB $17.99 (0-375-92203-2). Children of diverse backgrounds are shown in activities from yoga to rollerblading, and there is information on how the body works and the important role of exercise. (Rev: SLJ 1/04) [612]

20506 Rockwell, Lizzy. *Good Enough to Eat: A Kid's Guide to Food and Nutrition* (K–4). Illus. 1999, HarperCollins $14.95 (0-06-027434-4). 40pp. A nutritional guide for preschoolers that tells them about food groups, good eating habits, and how proper nutrition can keep them healthy and growing. (Rev: BL 1/1–15/99; HBG 9/99; SLJ 1/99) [613.2]

20507 Royston, Angela. *Eat Well* (K–2). Series: Safe and Sound. 1999, Heinemann LB $13.95 (1-57572-982-2). 32pp. This basic book on nutrition explains the food pyramid and the nutrients that are essential for good health. Exercise is given a similar treatment in the author's *A Healthy Body* (1999). (Rev: SLJ 1/00) [613]

20508 Royston, Angela. *Get Some Exercise!* (1–3). Series: Look After Yourself. 2003, Heinemann LB $22.79 (1-4034-4440-4). 32pp. The mechanics and benefits of exercise are clearly explained in easy-to-understand text. Also use *Get Some Rest!* (2003). (Rev: SLJ 2/04) [613.7]

20509 Royston, Angela. *Proteins for a Healthy Body* (4–6). Illus. Series: Body Needs. 2003, Heinemann

LB $27.07 (1-4034-0759-2). 48pp. A description of the various types of proteins — hormones, antibodies, and enzymes — and how they are important in nutrition, with a look at how vegetarians can get enough of them on a restricted diet. (Rev: HBG 10/03; SLJ 4/04) [612.3]

20510 Royston, Angela. *Vitamins and Minerals for a Healthy Body* (4–6). Illus. Series: Body Needs. 2003, Heinemann LB $27.07 (1-4034-0758-4). 48pp. A look at the importance of vitamins and minerals in maintaining a healthy body, and at their role in preventing disease. (Rev: HBG 10/03; SLJ 4/04) [612.3]

20511 Savage, Jeff. *Aerobics* (4–6). Illus. Series: Working Out. 1995, Silver Burdett LB $17.95 (0-89686-853-2); paper $7.95 (0-382-24945-3). 48pp. This book describes the nature and benefits of aerobic exercise, how to get started, and how to develop a routine. (Rev: SLJ 10/95) [613.7]

20512 Savage, Jeff. *Fundamental Strength Training* (5–9). Photos by Jimmy Clarke. Series: Fundamental Sports. 1998, Lerner LB $26.40 (0-8225-3461-4). 64pp. This beginner's manual discusses weight machines, training without weights, and various exercises for developing specific parts of the body. (Rev: HBG 9/99; SLJ 2/99) [613.7]

20513 Schwartz, Ellen. *I'm a Vegetarian: Amazing Facts and Ideas for Healthy Vegetarians* (5–8). Illus. by Farida Zaman. 2002, Tundra paper $9.95 (0-88776-588-2). 112pp. The social aspects of being a vegetarian are handled here with humor and sensitivity. (Rev: BL 7/02; SLJ 9/02) [613.2]

20514 Serafin, Kim. *Everything You Need to Know About Being a Vegetarian* (5–8). Series: Need to Know Library. 1999, Rosen LB $25.25 (0-8239-2951-5). 64pp. This book explains vegetarianism and its various varieties, the reasons why people become vegetarians, the nature of their diets, social problems involved, and names celebrities who are vegetarians. (Rev: SLJ 1/00) [613.2]

20515 Silverstein, Alvin, et al. *Eat Your Vegetables! Drink Your Milk!* (3–5). Series: My Health. 2000, Watts LB $22.50 (0-531-11635-2); paper $6.95 (0-531-16507-8). 48pp. This is a beginner's guide to nutrition and the part played by foods in maintaining a healthy body. (Rev: BL 9/15/00) [613]

20516 Silverstein, Alvin, and Virginia Silverstein. *Physical Fitness* (3–5). Series: My Health. 2002, Watts LB $23.00 (0-531-11860-6); paper $6.95 (0-531-15563-3). 48pp. Using photographs, cartoons, and other visuals plus a simple text, this book describes the importance of physical fitness and how to maintain it. (Rev: BL 6/1–15/02) [613.7]

20517 Turck, Mary. *Food and Emotions* (4–7). Series: Nutrition and Fitness. 2001, Capstone LB $23.93 (0-7368-0711-X). 64pp. This book explains the relationship between nutrition and a healthy emotional life and gives many tips and recipes for healthy living. (Rev: BL 9/15/01; HBG 10/01; SLJ 7/01) [613.2]

20518 Turck, Mary. *Healthy Eating for Weight Management* (4–7). Series: Nutrition and Fitness. 2001, Capstone LB $23.95 (0-7368-0709-8). 64pp. Good

nutrition is emphasized as an effective method of controlling one's weight, and readers will find a fitness plan and several tempting recipes. (Rev: BL 9/15/01; HBG 10/01; SLJ 7/01) [613.2]

20519 Turck, Mary. *Healthy Snack and Fast-Food Choices* (4–7). Series: Nutrition and Fitness. 2001, Capstone LB $23.93 (0-7368-0710-1). 64pp. Making healthy eating decisions is the focus of this guide to good nutrition that contains some delicious recipes. (Rev: BL 9/15/01; HBG 10/01) [613.2]

20520 VanCleave, Janice. *Janice VanCleave's Food and Nutrition for Every Kid: Easy Activities That Make Learning Science Fun* (4–8). Illus. Series: Science for Every Kid. 1999, Wiley $32.50 (0-471-17666-4); paper $12.95 (0-471-17665-6). Each of the 25 chapters in this book contains information about food, including food groups, the relationship between energy and food, how to read nutrition labels, and vitamins and minerals, plus dozens of easily performed projects that demonstrate these facts and concepts. (Rev: SLJ 8/99) [641.3]

20521 Weiss, Stefanie Iris. *Everything You Need to Know About Being a Vegan* (5–8). Series: Need to Know Library. 1999, Rosen LB $25.25 (0-8239-2958-2). 64pp. This book discusses vegans, people who do not eat or use animal products (usually for religious reasons), their lifestyles, diets, and possible social problems. (Rev: SLJ 1/00) [613.2]

Safety and Accidents

20522 Boelts, Maribeth. *A Kid's Guide to Staying Safe Around Water* (K–3). Series: The Kids' Library of Personal Safety. 1997, Rosen LB $13.95 (0-8239-5078-6). 24pp. This simple book on water safety presents basic rules for situations in a pool, lake, or ocean, plus coverage on swimming lessons, sunscreen, and what to do if someone is in trouble. (Rev: SLJ 4/98) [613.7]

20523 Boelts, Maribeth, and Darwin Boelts. *Kids to the Rescue! First Aid Techniques for Kids* (3–6). Illus. by Marina Megale. 1992, Parenting LB $20.00 (0-943990-83-1). 72pp. This book helps children react properly to 14 different medical emergencies and includes directions for appropriate actions in each case. (Rev: SLJ 9/92) [616.04]

20524 Chaiet, Donna, and Francine Russell. *The Safe Zone: A Kid's Guide to Personal Safety* (4–7). Illus. 1998, Morrow paper $6.95 (0-688-16091-3). 160pp. This book alerts youngsters to danger signs, gives advice on body language and self-esteem, and offers tips on how to avoid threatening situations. (Rev: BL 4/1/98; HBG 10/98) [613.6]

20525 Gale, Karen Buhler. *The Kids' Guide to First Aid: All About Bruises, Burns, Stings, Sprains and Other Ouches* (4–6). Illus. by Michael Kline. 2002, Williamson paper $12.95 (1-885593-58-9). 128pp. Readers learn to distinguish between situations they can handle and when they need to call for help, and gain useful information on stopping bleeding, applying bandages, and dealing with choking. (Rev: SLJ 4/02) [616.04]

20526 Gordon, Sharon. *Bruises* (1–2). Series: Rookie Read-About Health. 2002, Children's Book Pr. LB $19.00 (0-516-22568-5); paper $5.95 (0-516-26872-4). 31pp. Readers learn why bruises change color and how to treat them, with reminders of the protection that proper clothing can offer. Also use *Cuts and Scrapes* (2001). (Rev: SLJ 8/02) [616.04]

20527 Gutman, Bill. *Be Aware of Danger* (5–8). Illus. Series: Focus on Safety. 1996, Twenty-First Century LB $24.90 (0-8050-4142-7). Situations that could be dangerous to young people are highlighted and preventive measures outlined. (Rev: BL 2/1/97; SLJ 2/97) [613.6]

20528 Gutman, Bill. *Hazards at Home* (4–8). Series: Focus on Safety. 1996, Twenty-First Century LB $24.90 (0-8050-4141-9). A look at sources of potential accidents in the home with information on prevention and first-aid procedures. (Rev: SLJ 9/96) [363.1]

20529 Gutman, Bill. *Recreation Can Be Risky* (4–8). Series: Focus on Safety. 1996, Holt LB $24.90 (0-8050-4143-5). The author gives practical suggestions for enjoying such activities as baseball, biking, or hiking while also keeping safe through warm-up exercises, proper equipment, correct clothing, etc. (Rev: BL 7/96; SLJ 9/96) [790]

20530 MacGregor, Cynthia. *Ten Steps to Staying Safe* (2–4). Illus. Series: Abduction Prevention Library. 1998, Rosen LB $11.95 (0-8239-5248-7). 24pp. This book focuses on the inherent dangers of being with strangers and how to protect oneself in these situations. (Rev: BL 2/1/99) [613.6]

20531 MacGregor, Cynthia. *What to Do If You Get Lost* (2–4). Illus. Series: Abduction Prevention Library. 1998, Rosen LB $11.95 (0-8239-5250-9). 24pp. This is a practical guide for children who get separated from familiar places and people, telling how they can get help. (Rev: BL 2/1/99) [613.6]

20532 Mattern, Joanne. *Safety at School* (K–3). Series: Safety First. 1999, ABDO LB $13.95 (1-57765-070-0). 24pp. This book tells youngsters how to stay safe at school. Also use *Safety in Public Places* (1999). (Rev: HBG 4/00; SLJ 1/00) [613.6]

20533 Mattern, Joanne. *Safety on the Go* (K–3). Series: Safety First. 1999, ABDO LB $13.95 (1-57765-075-1). 24pp. This account tells children how to remain safe while using public transportation. Also use *Safety in the Water* and *Safety on Your Bicycle* (both 1999). (Rev: HBG 4/00; SLJ 1/00) [613.6]

20534 Raatma, Lucia. *Bicycle Safety* (2–4). Illus. Series: Living Well. 2003, Child's World LB $25.64 (1-59296-085-5). 32pp. A simple story about a child riding a bicycle is followed by easy-to-understand safety rules. Also use *School Safety* and *Internet Safety* (both 2003). (Rev: SLJ 3/04) [796.6]

20535 Raatma, Lucia. *Fire Safety* (2–4). Series: Living Well. 2003, Child's World LB $25.64 (1-59296-086-3). 32pp. Illustrated with photographs, this book on fire safety includes information about how fires start, how to guard against them, and how to escape if caught in one. (Rev: SLJ 3/04)

20536 Roberts, Robin. *Sports Injuries: How to Stay Safe and Keep on Playing* (5–8). Series: Get in the Game! With Robin Roberts. 2001, Millbrook LB $23.90 (0-7613-2116-0). 48pp. This general sports book that targets girls as a primary audience discusses safety in a variety of sports and how to cope with injuries. (Rev: BL 9/15/01; HBG 3/02; SLJ 1/02) [790]

20537 Silverstein, Alvin, et al. *Bites and Stings* (3–5). Series: My Health. 2001, Watts LB $23.00 (0-531-11861-4). Insect and animal bites and stings are discussed with material on why they occur and on their prevention and treatment. (Rev: BL 1/1–15/02; SLJ 10/01) [617.1]

20538 Silverstein, Alvin, et al. *Staying Safe* (3–5). Series: My Health. 2000, Watts LB $22.50 (0-531-11639-5). 48pp. This is an amusing, accurate look at accidents and their prevention, along with tips on safety. (Rev: BL 11/15/00) [613.6]

Sleep and Dreams

20539 Feeney, Kathy. *Sleep Well: Why You Need to Rest* (K–3). Series: Your Health. 2001, Capstone LB $13.95 (0-7368-0970-8). 24pp. Simple text and illustrations stress the importance of sleep and discuss sleepwalking and nightmares. (Rev: HBG 3/02; SLJ 4/02) [612.82]

20540 Gordon, Sharon. *A Good Night's Sleep* (3–5). Series: Rookie Read-About Health. 2002, Children's Book Pr. LB $19.00 (0-516-22570-7); paper $5.95 (0-516-26874-0). 32pp. After explaining the reasons why sleep is important, this easy-reader gives a few hints on how to fall asleep fast. (Rev: BL 12/15/02) [616.5]

20541 Mcphee, Andrew T. *Sleep and Dreams* (5–8). Illus. 2001, Watts LB $24.00 (0-531-11735-9). 111pp. Normal sleep patterns, sleep deprivation, and sleep disorders (sleep walking and sleep apnea) are discussed along with the nature and symbolism of dreams. (Rev: BL 6/1–15/01; SLJ 8/01) [616.8]

20542 Romanek, Trudee. *Zzz . . .: The Most Interesting Book You'll Ever Read About Sleep* (3–6). Illus. by Rose Cowles. 2002, Kids Can $14.95 (1-55074-944-7); paper $6.95 (1-55074-946-3). 40pp. With lively, amusing illustrations and an interesting text, this book covers such topics related to sleep as REM sleep, dreams, sleep cycles, snoring, and yawning. (Rev: BL 6/1–15/02; HBG 10/02; SLJ 6/02) [612.8]

20543 Swain, Ruth Freeman. *Bedtime!* (PS–3). Illus. by Cat B. Smith. 1999, Holiday House $15.95 (0-8234-1444-2). This history of beds highlights simple mats, dorm bunks, hammocks, Pullman sleepers, Murphy beds, and so on. (Rev: BL 9/15/99; HBG 3/00; SLJ 11/99) [392.3]

20544 Trueit, Trudi Strain. *Dreams and Sleep* (4–8). Illus. Series: Life Balance. 2004, Watts LB $19.50 (0-531-12260-3); paper $6.95 (0-531-15579-X). 80pp. Discusses why we dream and what dreams mean and gives advice on getting a good night's sleep. [616.5]

Sex Education and Reproduction

Babies

20545 Anderson, Rachel. *Hello Peanut* (PS). Illus. by Debbie Harter. Series: Hodder Toddler. 2004, Hodder paper $8.95 (0-340-85248-8). A toddler follows the progress of her mother's pregnancy with great interest. (Rev: SLJ 2/04)

20546 Bernhard, Emery. *A Ride on Mother's Back: A Day of Baby Carrying Around the World* (K–2). Illus. by Durga Bernhard. 1996, Harcourt $16.00 (0-15-200870-5). 40pp. Various ways of carrying babies reflect cultural differences around the world. (Rev: BL 10/15/96; SLJ 10/96) [392]

20547 Cole, Joanna. *When You Were Inside Mommy* (PS). Illus. by Maxie Chambliss. 2001, Harper-Collins $5.95 (0-688-17043-9). 32pp. Basic facts about a child's development are presented in this small-format picture book. (Rev: BL 8/01; HBG 3/02; SLJ 12/01) [612.6]

20548 Davis, Jennifer. *Before You Were Born* (PS–2). Illus. by Laura Cornell. 1998, Workman $10.95 (0-7611-1200-6). 24pp. The nine months of prenatal development are chronicled in a simple text with thumbnail drawings and told from a pregnant woman's point of view. (Rev: HBG 3/99; SLJ 9/98) [612]

20549 Dilley, Becki, and Keith Dilley. *Sixty Fingers, Sixty Toes: See How the Dilley Sextuplets Grow* (PS). Photos by E. Anthony Valainis. 1998, Walker $15.95 (0-8027-8613-8). 32pp. In a series of photographs, the life and activities of the Dilley sextuplets are covered from infancy through age four. (Rev: HBG 9/98; SLJ 7/98) [305]

20550 Douglas, Ann. *Baby Science: How Babies Really Work!* (PS–2). Illus. by Helene Desputeaux. 1998, Firefly $17.95 (1-895688-83-3). 32pp. The behavioral habits of babies during the first year of life are explored in this colorful picture book. (Rev: BL 1/1–15/99; SLJ 12/98) [305.232]

20551 Heiligman, Deborah. *Babies: All You Need to Know* (K–2). Illus. by Laura Freeman. Series: Jump into Science. 2002, National Geographic $16.95 (0-7922-8205-1). 32pp. Young readers learn how babies grow, what they eat, how they learn, and so forth. (Rev: BCCB 10/02; BL 10/1/02; HBG 3/03; SLJ 10/02) [612.6]

20552 Johnson, Kelly. *Look at the Baby* (PS). Photos by author. 2002, Holt $14.95 (0-8050-6522-9). Photographs of multicultural babies look at noses, fingers, toes, and so forth. (Rev: BCCB 1/03; HBG 3/03; SLJ 12/02)

20553 Lasky, Kathryn. *Love That Baby! A Book About Babies for New Brothers, Sisters, Cousins, and Friends* (PS–1). Illus. by Jennifer Plecas. 2004, Candlewick $14.99 (1-56402-679-5). Useful for children expecting a new sibling, this guide describes important aspects of infant care and behavior, including how babies look, play, eat, and sleep. (Rev: SLJ 1/04) [305.232]

20554 Morris, Ann. *The Baby Book* (PS). Illus. Series: World's Family. 1995, Silver Burdett $13.95 (0-382-24698-5); paper $5.95 (0-382-24700-0). 32pp. Full-color photographs show infants from around the world, with ethnic backgrounds explained at the back of the book. (Rev: BL 2/15/96) [305.23]

20555 Murkoff, Heidi. *What to Expect When the New Baby Comes Home* (PS–K). Illus. by Laura Rader. 2001, HarperCollins $7.99 (0-694-01327-7). 32pp. Angus the Answer Dog guides readers through answers to such questions as "What do new babies eat?" and "Can I play with the new baby?" (Rev: BL 7/01; HBG 10/01; SLJ 6/01) [305.232]

20556 Nanao, Jun. *Contemplating Your Bellybutton* (PS–K). Trans. by Amanda Mayer Stinchecum. Illus. by Tomoko Hasegawa. 1995, Kane/Miller $11.95 (0-916291-60-X). 32pp. Young Tettchan is told how he got his belly button and the purpose it serves. (Rev: BL 1/1–15/96; SLJ 12/95) [611.95]

20557 Sears, William, et al. *Baby on the Way* (K–3). Illus. by Renee W. Andriani. 2001, Little, Brown $12.95 (0-316-78767-1). 32pp. A reassuring, colorfully illustrated book that tells young children about the effects of pregnancy on the mother. (Rev: BL 9/15/01; HBG 3/02; SLJ 10/01) [618.2]

20558 Sears, William, et al. *What Baby Needs* (K–3). Illus. by Renee W. Andriani. 2001, Little, Brown $12.95 (0-316-78828-7). 32pp. A readable look at the changes boys and girls can expect when they become big brothers or sisters. (Rev: BL 9/15/01; HBG 3/02; SLJ 10/01) [649]

20559 Stein, Sara Bonnett. *Oh, Baby!* (PS–1). Illus. by Holly Anne Shelowitz. 1993, Walker LB $15.85 (0-8027-8262-0). 32pp. Using a series of baby pictures, physical and mental developments during the first year of a child's life are outlined. (Rev: BL 3/1/94*; SLJ 12/93*) [305]

20560 Thomas, Shelley M. *A Baby's Coming to Your House!* (PS–1). Illus. by Eric Futran. 2001, Whitman $15.95 (0-8075-0502-1). 32pp. Using funny family pictures as illustrations, this book explains to youngsters the changes that take place when a new baby enters the house — like the appearance of high chairs and messy diapers. (Rev: BL 3/15/01; HBG 10/01) [305.2]

Reproduction

20561 Audry, Andrew C., and Steven Schepp. *How Babies Are Made* (K–3). Illus. 1984, Little, Brown paper $12.95 (0-316-04227-7). 80pp. Explaining intercourse, pregnancy, and birth — using flowers, animals, and humans.

20562 Butler, Dori Hillestad. *My Mom's Having a Baby!* (2–4). Illus. by Carol Thompson. 2005, Whitman $15.95 (0-8075-5344-1). 32pp. For children who are ready for a detailed treatment of intercourse, conception, gestation, and birth, this book discusses it all and is enhanced with cartoon-style illustrations. (Rev: BL 4/1/05; SLJ 5/05) [618.2]

20563 Cole, Babette. *Mommy Laid an Egg!* (K–3). Illus. 1993, Chronicle $13.95 (0-8118-0350-3). 30pp. After parents try to explain where babies come from, the children tell them the truth. (Rev: BL 7/93) [649]

20564 Cole, Joanna. *How You Were Born* (PS–3). Illus. by Margaret Miller. 1993, Morrow paper $5.95 (0-688-12061-X). 48pp. Fetal development is tracked in text and color pictures, plus tips are given on how to use this book with children. (Rev: BL 6/1–15/93; SLJ 4/93*) [612]

20565 Fullick, Ann. *Test Tube Babies: In Vitro Fertilization* (5–8). Series: Science at the Edge. 2002, Heinemann LB $27.86 (1-58810-703-5). 64pp. This attractive book balances hard science with thought-provoking discussion on this controversial topic. (Rev: BL 10/15/02; HBG 3/03; SLJ 4/03) [613.9]

20566 Girard, Linda Walvoord. *You Were Born on Your Very First Birthday* (PS). Illus. by Christa Kieffer. 1983, Whitman paper $5.95 (0-8075-9456-3). 32pp. A simple introduction to pregnancy and birth.

20567 Jackson, Donna M. *Twin Tales: The Magic and Mystery of Multiple Birth* (5–8). Illus. 2001, Little, Brown $16.95 (0-316-45431-1). 48pp. A

clear account of current scientific knowledge about multiple births, with anecdotes from children of multiple births and their families. (Rev: BCCB 2/01; BL 5/15/01; HB 3–4/01; HBG 10/01; SLJ 5/01*) [618.2]

20568 Orr, Tamra B. *Test Tube Babies* (5–9). Series: Science on the Edge. 2003, Gale LB $20.95 (1-56711-788-0). 48pp. This book discusses in vitro fertilization, and how it has helped many but also caused a great deal of controversy. (Rev: BL 10/15/03; SLJ 3/04) [612]

20569 Overend, Jenni. *Welcome with Love* (1–3). Illus. by Julie Vivas. 2000, Kane/Miller $15.95 (0-916291-96-0). 32pp. A direct, graphic treatment of childbirth showing the members of a close family participating in a home delivery. (Rev: BCCB 6/00; BL 3/15/00; HBG 9/00; SLJ 4/00) [618.4]

20570 Parker, Steve. *Reproduction* (5–9). Illus. Series: Our Bodies. 2004, Raintree LB $28.56 (0-7398-6623-0). 48pp. Details of the human body's reproductive organs and how they function are accompanied by information on keeping them healthy. (Rev: BL 8/04) [612.6]

20571 Parker, Steve. *The Reproductive System* (5–8). Illus. Series: Human Body. 1997, Raintree LB $18.98 (0-8172-4806-4). 48pp. A well-organized, straightforward account that covers male and female anatomy, genes, fertility problems, contraception, STDs, and human development from conception to adolescence. (Rev: SLJ 2/98) [613.9]

20572 Sandeman, Anna. *Babies* (2–4). Illus. Series: Body Books. 1996, Millbrook LB $18.90 (0-7613-0478-9). 31pp. Clear information is given on conception, pregnancy, childbirth, and the growth of babies. (Rev: SLJ 6/96) [613.9]

20573 Schnitter, Jane T. *Let Me Explain: A Story About Donor Insemination* (2–4). Illus. by Joanne Bowring. 1995, Perspectives $14.00 (0-944934-12-9). 32pp. A young girl tells how much she adores her father and also explains that she was the product of artificial insemination. (Rev: SLJ 7/95) [618]

20574 Silverstein, Alvin, et al. *The Reproductive System* (5–8). Illus. Series: Human Body Systems. 1994, Twenty-First Century LB $16.95 (0-8050-2838-2). Reproduction in the plant and animal worlds is introduced, focusing on the human system and body parts. (Rev: BL 3/15/95) [612.6]

20575 Taylor, Nicole. *Baby* (3–5). Illus. Series: Images. 1994, Creative Ed. LB $25.30 (0-88682-595-4). The process of conception is described in text and photos, along with a month-by-month depiction of fetal development and pictures of a birth. (Rev: SLJ 12/94) [306]

Sex Education and Puberty

20576 Bailey, Jacqui. *Sex, Puberty and All That Stuff: A Guide to Growing Up* (5–10). Illus. by Jan McCafferty. 2004, Barron's paper $12.95 (0-7641-2992-9). 112pp. In this comprehensive volume full of lighthearted illustrations, Bailey covers the wide range of changes that affect young people, emphasizing the individual's right to choose and the need to resist peer pressure. (Rev: SLJ 1/05) [613.9]

20577 Blackstone, Margaret, and Elissa Haden Guest. *Girl Stuff: A Survival Guide to Growing Up* (5–7). Illus. 2000, Harcourt $14.95 (0-15-201830-1); paper $8.95 (0-15-202644-4). 144pp. Coverage of such topics as puberty, physical changes, sex, birth control, and sexually transmitted diseases helps girls learn about becoming young women. (Rev: BL 5/15/00; HBG 9/00; SLJ 6/00) [613]

20578 Brewer, Janet Neff. *In God's Image* (PS–K). Illus. 1998, Bridge Resources $14.95 (1-57895-055-4). 32pp. Using a Christian framework that stresses God's love, this book on sex education explains to the very young how babies grow inside mothers, the differences between a boy's and a girl's body, what "bad" touching is about, and how to cope with various emotions. (Rev: BL 10/1/98) [241]

20579 Brody, Janis. *Your Body: The Girls' Guide* (5–10). 2000, St. Martin's paper $4.99 (0-312-97563-5). 256pp. This book on puberty and body changes covers such subjects as self-image, menstruation, sexuality, sports participation, nutrition, eating disorders, substance abuse, and counseling. (Rev: SLJ 10/00) [612]

20580 Brown, Laurie Krasny. *What's the Big Secret? Talking About Sex with Girls and Boys* (2–4). Illus. by Marc Brown. 1997, Little, Brown $15.95 (0-316-10915-0). 32pp. This picture book on sex education discusses sexuality, gender roles, reproduction, and the issue of privacy. (Rev: BL 10/1/97; HBG 3/98; SLJ 3/98) [613]

20581 Cole, Babette. *Hair in Funny Places* (3–5). Illus. 2000, Hyperion $15.99 (0-7868-0590-0). 32pp. A simple introduction to puberty and the changes Mr. and Mrs. Hormone produce in the body, with coverage of menstruation and ejaculation. (Rev: BL 7/00; HBG 9/00; SLJ 7/00) [612]

20582 Dickerson, Karle. *On the Spot: Real Girls on Periods, Growing Up, and Finding Your Groove* (4–7). 2005, Adams paper $8.95 (1-59337-215-9). 192pp. The former managing editor of *Teen Magazine* offers upbeat advice on the important physical and emotional changes that pre-adolescent girls can expect. (Rev: BL 2/15/05; SLJ 5/05) [612.6]

20583 Feinmann, Jane. *Everything a Girl Needs to Know About Her Periods* (5–9). Illus. 2003, Ronnie Sellers paper $14.95 (1-56906-555-1). 144pp. This useful and reassuring guide to the female body changes of puberty focuses largely on the menstrual cycle. (Rev: BL 2/1/04) [618.083]

20584 Girard, Linda Walvoord. *My Body Is Private* (PS–3). Illus. by Rodney Pate. 1984, Whitman LB $13.95 (0-8075-5320-4); paper $5.95 (0-8075-5319-0). 32pp. A girl of seven or eight talks about unwarranted touching of one's body by another in this lesson on prevention of sexual abuse.

20585 Gordon, Sol, and Judith Gordon. *A Better Safe Than Sorry Book: A Family Guide for Sexual Assault Prevention* (PS–1). Illus. 1992, Prometheus paper $10.00 (0-87975-768-X). A book that approaches the subjects of sexual abuse and threats from strangers in a nonscary manner. (Rev: BL 11/15/85)

20586 Gordon, Sol, and Judith Gordon. *Did the Sun Shine Before You Were Born? A Sex Education Primer* (PS–3). Illus. 1974, Okpaku $12.00 (0-89388-179-1); Prometheus paper $9.95 (0-879-75723-X). A self-styled sex education manual for the very young.

20587 Gravelle, Karen, and Nick Castro. *What's Going on Down There? Answers to Questions Boys Find Hard to Ask* (5–10). Illus. by Robert Leighton. 1998, Walker paper $8.95 (0-8027-7540-3). 128pp. Straightforward information for boys covers such topics as physical changes, sexual intercourse, peer pressure, and pregnancy and birth. (Rev: BL 11/1/98; BR 5–6/99; HB 1–2/99; HBG 3/99; SLJ 12/98) [613]

20588 Harris, Robie H. *It's So Amazing: A Book About Eggs, Sperm, Birth, Babies, and Families* (2–5). Illus. by Michael Emberley. 1999, Candlewick $21.99 (0-7636-0051-2). 80pp. An outstanding book that explains human reproduction and birth in straightforward prose and bold, colorful illustrations. (Rev: BCCB 2/00; BL 1/1–15/00*; HBG 4/00; SLJ 2/00) [612.6]

20589 Johnson, Eric W. *People, Love, Sex, and Families: Answers to Questions That Preteens Ask* (5–8). Illus. 1985, Walker LB $14.85 (0-8027-6605-6). 144pp. Based on the results of a survey of 1,000 preteens, this book covers a broad range of topics, from sexual abuse to venereal disease to divorce and incest. (Rev: BL 3/15/86) [306.707]

20590 Kemp, Kristen. *Healthy Sexuality* (5–10). Illus. Series: Life Balance. 2004, Watts LB $19.50 (0-531-12336-7); paper $6.95 (0-531-16689-9). 80pp. Covering both boys and girls, this easy-to-understand volume looks at physical and emotional changes and provides practical tips on handling difficult decisions and confusing feelings. (Rev: SLJ 4/05)

20591 Kleven, Sandy. *The Right Touch: A Read-Aloud Story to Help Prevent Child Sexual Abuse* (PS–3). Illus. by Jody Bergsma. 1998, Illumination Arts $15.95 (0-935699-10-4). 32pp. This book instructs children on how to deal with unwanted and inappropriate touching. (Rev: SLJ 7/98) [306]

20592 Loulan, JoAnn, and Bonnie Worthen. *Period: A Girl's Guide to Menstruation with a Parent's Guide*. Rev. ed. (5–7). Illus. 2001, Book Peddlers $15.95 (0-916773-97-3); paper $9.99 (0-916773-96-5). 96pp. This practical guide to menstruation is arranged by such questions as "What do I do when I get my first period?" and "What kind of exercise can I do?" (Rev: BL 2/1/01; HBG 10/01) [612.6]

20593 Madaras, Lynda. *Ready, Set, Grow! A "What's Happening to My Body?" Book for Younger Girls* (2–5). Illus. by Linda Davick. 2003, Newmarket $22.00 (1-55704-587-9); paper $12.00 (1-55704-565-8). 125pp. This spin-off guide to puberty is aimed at the girls who are now going through this experience at a younger age and includes medical tips and upbeat discussion. (Rev: HBG 4/04; SLJ 11/03) [612.6]

20594 Madaras, Lynda, and Area Madaras. *The What's Happening to My Body? Book for Boys: A Growing Up Guide for Parents and Sons.* 3rd ed. (4–8). Illus. 2001, Newmarket $22.95 (1-55704-447-3); paper $12.95 (1-55704-443-0). 238pp. This new edition of the classic guide has been recast to suit today's children and their earlier puberty. (Rev: BL 9/1/01) [613.9]

20595 Marsh, Carole. *AIDS to Zits: A "Sextionary" for Kids* (3–7). 1987, Gallopade $29.95 (1-55609-263-6); paper $19.95 (1-55609-210-5). 28pp. This dictionary contains definitions of about 100 words related to sexuality. (Rev: BL 12/1/89) [613.951]

20596 Mosatche, Harriet S., and Karen Unger. *Too Old for This, Too Young for That! Your Survival Guide for the Middle-School Years* (5–8). Illus. 2000, Free Spirit paper $14.95 (1-57542-067-8). 200pp. This guide to the early years of puberty contains material on self-esteem, family relationships, friendships, and activities; also included is a lengthy section on bodily changes and such events as the onset of menstruation, erections, and ejaculation. (Rev: BL 7/00; SLJ 9/00) [646.7]

20597 Nardo, Don. *Teen Sexuality* (5–8). Illus. Series: Overview. 1997, Lucent LB $27.45 (1-56006-189-8). This book traces changing attitudes toward sex and looks at what's considered acceptable today. (Rev: BL 3/15/97; SLJ 2/97) [362.29]

20598 Pascoe, Elaine, ed. *Teen Dreams: The Journey Through Puberty* (5–8). Illus. Series: Body Story. 2003, Gale/Blackbirch LB $23.70 (1-4103-0061-7). 48pp. Puberty and the many changes it brings are the topic of this arresting and informative book, seen from the points of view of a teenage boy and girl. (Rev: SLJ 4/04) [612.6]

20599 Rozakis, Laurie. *Teen Pregnancy: Why Are Kids Having Babies?* (5–8). Illus. Series: Issues of Our Time. 1993, Twenty-First Century LB $22.90 (0-8050-2569-3). 64pp. A slim, easily read account that explains birth control and deplores the fact that teens do not have access to information about it. (Rev: SLJ 2/94) [612.6]

Physical and Applied Sciences

General Science

Miscellaneous

20600 Aaseng, Nathan. *Yearbooks in Science: 1930–1939* (5–8). Illus. Series: Yearbooks in Science. 1995, Twenty-First Century LB $22.90 (0-8050-3433-1). 80pp. An overview of the accomplishments in science in the 1930s arranged by such divisions as physics and chemistry. (Rev: BL 12/1/95; SLJ 1/96) [609]

20601 Aaseng, Nathan. *Yearbooks in Science: 1940–1949* (5–8). Illus. Series: Yearbooks in Science. 1995, Twenty-First Century LB $22.90 (0-8050-3434-X). An important decade in scientific discovery is chronicled, with emphasis on the impact of these advances on society. (Rev: BL 1/1–15/96; SLJ 5/96) [609]

20602 Bridgman, Roger. *1000 Inventions and Discoveries* (5–9). Illus. 2002, DK paper $24.99 (0-7894-8826-4). 256pp. A heavily illustrated overview of scientific discoveries, arranged chronologically with a timeline of concurrent historical and cultural events. (Rev: SLJ 3/03) [609]

20603 Bruno, Leonard C. *Science and Technology Breakthroughs: From the Wheel to the World Wide Web* (5–8). 1997, Gale LB $158.40 (0-7876-1927-2). This expanded version contains more than 1,200 paragraph-long entries in 12 chronologically arranged chapters: agriculture and everyday life; astronomy; biology; chemistry; communications; computers; earth sciences; energy, power systems, and weaponry; mathematics; medicine; physics; and transportation. (Rev: BL 3/1/98; BR 5–6/98; SLJ 5/98) [509]

20604 Day, Trevor. *Genetics* (4–7). Illus. Series: Routes of Science. 2004, Gale/Blackbirch LB $23.70 (1-4103-0301-2). 40pp. A detailed examination of the development of genetics as a science, with profiles of key individuals and their discoveries, a chronology, and discussion of future advances. (Rev: SLJ 5/05)

20605 *The DK Science Encyclopedia*. Rev. ed. (4–8). 1998, DK paper $39.99 (0-7894-2190-9). Using one- or two-page articles and a profusion of illustrations, this topically arranged encyclopedia gives an overview of the field of science, emphasizing its interconnectedness with technology, under such headings as weather, ecology, and reactions. (Rev: BL 12/1/98; SLJ 2/99) [500]

20606 Dolan, Graham. *The Greenwich Guide to Time and the Millennium* (4–7). Illus. by Jeff Edwards. 1999, Heinemann $16.95 (1-57572-802-8). 48pp. Covers such subjects as time zones, calendars, centuries, and longitude. (Rev: SLJ 9/99) [529]

20607 Duffy, Trent. *The Clock* (5–9). Illus. by Toby Welles. Series: Turning Points. 2000, Simon & Schuster $17.95 (0-689-82814-4). 80pp. After a general introduction to the concept of time, this visually interesting volume tells how time has been measured with a special focus on clocks and watches and a foldout on how a clock works. (Rev: BCCB 5/00; HBG 9/00; SLJ 5/00) [529]

20608 Ehrlich, Robert. *What If? Mind-Boggling Science Questions for Kids* (4–6). Illus. 1998, Wiley paper $12.95 (0-471-17608-7). 192pp. Chapters on such subjects as time, the earth, and the planets provide explanations for intriguing science puzzlers. (Rev: BL 6/1–15/98; SLJ 10/98) [500]

20609 Ganeri, Anita, and Chris Oxlade. *The Kingfisher First Science Encyclopedia* (2–4). Illus. 1997, Kingfisher $16.95 (0-7534-5089-5). 112pp. This alphabetically arranged book covers about 75 topics in science, such as color, calculators, television, and physics. (Rev: SLJ 11/97) [500]

20610 Gutfreund, Geraldine M. *Yearbooks in Science: 1970–1979* (5–8). Illus. Series: Yearbooks in Science. 1995, Twenty-First Century LB $22.90 (0-8050-3437-4). A decade of new scientific concepts and inventions is discussed, with profiles of the scientists behind them. (Rev: BL 1/1–15/96; SLJ 5/96) [609]

20611 Hickman, Pamela. *The Night Book: Exploring Nature After Dark with Activities, Experiments and*

Information (3–6). Illus. 1999, Kids Can $12.95 (1-55074-318-X); paper $6.95 (1-55074-306-6). 48pp. This is a collection of activities exploring the night world, including starlight, stargazing, night vision, and such nocturnal creatures as owls and fireflies. (Rev: BL 2/15/99; SLJ 8/99) [591.5]

20612 Hoyt, Beth Caldwell, and Erica Ritter. *The Ultimate Girls' Guide to Science: From Backyard Experiments to Winning the Nobel Prize!* (4–8). Illus. 2004, Beyond Words paper $9.95 (1-58270-092-3). 128pp. Designed to pique girls' interest in the study of science, this attractive title offers brief profiles of famous female scientists as well as the major branches of science and also provides instructions for a number of scientific experiments. (Rev: SLJ 8/04) [500]

20613 Koss, Amy Goldman. *Where Fish Go in Winter and Other Great Mysteries* (PS–2). Illus. by Laura J. Bryant. Series: Dial Easy-to-Read. 2002, Dial $13.99 (0-8037-2704-6). 32pp. Beginning readers will enjoy these poetic answers to such questions as why onions make people cry and how cats purr. (Rev: BL 1/1–15/03; HBG 3/03; SLJ 1/03) [500]

20614 Kramer, Stephen. *Hidden Worlds: Looking Through a Scientist's Microscope* (4–7). Illus. Series: Scientists in the Field. 2001, Houghton Mifflin $16.00 (0-618-05546-0). 61pp. Striking photographs, mostly taken with electron microscopes by scientist Dennis Kunkel, serve to illustrate this explanation of how scientists use microscopes in their work. (Rev: BL 8/01; HB 1–2/02; HBG 3/02; SLJ 9/01*) [570]

20615 Kramer, Stephen. *How to Think Like a Scientist: Answering Questions by the Scientific Method* (3–5). Illus. 1987, HarperCollins LB $15.89 (0-690-04565-4). 48pp. An intriguing account of the ways in which questions are asked, and how scientists try to make sure they are answered correctly. (Rev: BCCB 1/87; BL 5/15/87; SLJ 5/87)

20616 Krautwurst, Terry. *Night Science for Kids: Exploring the World After Dark* (3–7). 2003, Lark Books $19.95 (1-57990-411-4). 144pp. This beautifully illustrated, large-format guide takes readers out into the night and explores everything from owls' eyes to individual stars. (Rev: BL 12/1/03; SLJ 3/04)

20617 McGowen, Tom. *The Beginnings of Science* (5–8). Illus. 1998, Twenty-First Century LB $26.90 (0-7613-3016-X). 80pp. Beginning with primitive people and their use of magic, fire, counting, writing, and astronomy, this book traces the history of science up to the 16th century. (Rev: BL 12/1/98; HBG 3/99) [509]

20618 McGowen, Tom. *Yearbooks in Science: 1900–1919* (5–8). Illus. Series: Yearbooks in Science. 1995, Twenty-First Century LB $22.90 (0-8050-3431-5). 80pp. An overview of human achievements in science and technology during the first 20 years of the 20th century, how they helped humanity, and the men and women involved. (Rev: BL 12/1/95; SLJ 1/96) [609]

20619 McGowen, Tom. *Yearbooks in Science: 1960–1969* (5–8). Illus. Series: Yearbooks in Science. 1996, Twenty-First Century LB $22.90 (0-8050-3436-6). Developments in the history of science and technology during the 1960s are covered in an exciting step-by-step approach. (Rev: BL 1/1–15/96; SLJ 5/96) [609]

20620 Martin, Paul D. *Science: It's Changing Your World* (5–8). Illus. 1985, National Geographic LB $12.50 (0-87044-521-9). 104pp. An overview of the science field today, crediting computers and lasers with the vast growth of scientific information. (Rev: BL 9/15/85; SLJ 10/85) [500]

20621 Masoff, Joy. *Oh, Yuck! The Encyclopedia of Everything Nasty* (4–8). Illus. by Terry Sirrell. 2001, Workman paper $14.95 (0-7611-0771-1). 212pp. This unsavory, fact-filled look at smells, noises, creepy-crawlies, toilets, and other fascinating topics even includes some suitably gross experiments. (Rev: SLJ 5/01) [031.02]

20622 Myers, Jack. *On the Trail of the Komodo Dragon: And Other Explorations of Science in Action* (3–6). Illus. 1999, Boyds Mills $17.95 (1-56397-761-3). 63pp. A collection of 11 "Science Reporting" columns from *Highlights for Children* that explore unusual topics, such as how horses sleep and why cats can often fall safely. (Rev: BL 2/15/99; HBG 9/99; SLJ 4/99) [591]

20623 Newton, David E. *Yearbooks in Science: 1920–1929* (5–8). Illus. Series: Yearbooks in Science. 1995, Twenty-First Century LB $22.90 (0-8050-3432-3). 80pp. The history of scientific advances in the 1920s, with chapters on various fields that explain the breakthroughs, how they helped humanity, and the scientists involved. (Rev: BL 12/1/95; SLJ 1/96) [609]

20624 Pentland, Peter, and Pennie Stoyles. *Kitchen Science* (4–6). Illus. Series: Science and Scientists. 2002, Chelsea House LB $18.95 (0-7910-7014-X). 32pp. A clear overview of the scientific phenomena involved in basic foodstuffs as well as the various ways in which they are prepared and preserved, with illustrations, interesting sidebars, and information on careers in kitchen science. Also use *Party Science* and *Toy and Game Science* (both 2002). (Rev: HBG 3/03; SLJ 4/03) [641.5]

20625 Rice, David L. *Lifetimes* (3–6). Illus. 1997, Dawn $16.95 (1-883220-58-0); paper $7.95 (1-883220-59-9). 32pp. Various activities are interspersed with facts about a number of animals, plants, and astronomical bodies. (Rev: BL 6/1–15/97; SLJ 2/98) [574.3]

20626 Robinson, Richard. *Science Magic in the Bedroom: Amazing Tricks with Ordinary Stuff* (4–7). Illus. by Alan Rowe. Series: Science Magic. 2002, Simon & Schuster paper $4.99 (0-689-84335-6). 95pp. Robinson presents tricks that fool the sight, hearing, and touch and explains the underlying science and physiology. (Rev: SLJ 7/02) [507.8]

20627 Rosinsky, Natalie M. *How Scientists Work* (3–5). Series: Simply Science. 2004, Compass Point LB $21.26 (0-7565-0596-8). 32pp. Introduces readers to the scientific method of research. (Rev: SLJ 8/04) [507]

20628 Ross, Michael Elsohn. *Re-Cycles* (K–2). Illus. by Gustav Moore. 2002, Millbrook LB $22.90 (0-7613-1818-6). 32pp. Readers learn how water and soil are constantly being recycled for reuse, and how humans can contribute to nature's efforts. (Rev: BL 11/1/02; HBG 3/03; SLJ 1/03) [551.3]

20629 Schwartz, David M. *Q Is for Quark: A Science Alphabet Book* (4–9). Illus. by Kim Doner. 2001, Tricycle $15.95 (1-58246-021-3). 64pp. An entertaining and informative alphabet book from atom to Zzzzzzzz that doesn't hesitate to tackle difficult topics. (Rev: HBG 3/02; SLJ 11/01) [500]

20630 Shields, Carol Diggory. *Brain Juice: Science, Fresh Squeezed!* (4–7). Illus. by Richard Thompson. 2003, Handprint $14.95 (1-59354-005-1). 64pp. A humorous, rhyming look at grade-school science with appealing illustrations and useful mnemonic devices. (Rev: HBG 4/04; SLJ 3/04) [500]

20631 Silverstein, Herma. *Yearbooks in Science: 1990 and Beyond* (5–8). Illus. Series: Yearbooks in Science. 1995, Twenty-First Century LB $22.90 (0-8050-3439-0). The final volume in this series not only traces recent developments in science and technology but also presents the challenges of the future. (Rev: BL 1/1–15/96) [609]

20632 Simon, Seymour. *Out of Sight: Pictures of Hidden Worlds* (3–6). Illus. 2000, North-South $15.88 (1-58717-012-4). 48pp. A book of unusual pictures of phenomena — such as the operation of the human heart, Jupiter's red spot, and a racing bullet — that can only be seen using scientific instruments. (Rev: BL 10/1/00; HBG 3/01; SLJ 11/00) [612.8]

20633 Simon, Seymour, and Nicole Fauteux. *Let's Try It Out with Towers and Bridges* (PS–2). Illus. by Doug Cushman. 2003, Simon & Schuster $14.95 (0-689-82923-X). 32pp. Basic principles of engineering and construction are laid out in this colorful picture book that suggests various activities using readily available materials — corrugated cardboard, building blocks, and modeling clay, for instance. (Rev: BL 4/1/03; HBG 10/03) [624.1]

20634 Stein, Sara Bonnett. *The Science Book* (4–8). Illus. by author. 1980, Workman paper $9.95 (0-89480-120-1). 288pp. A whole-earth approach to strange and fascinating science facts.

20635 Swanson, Diane. *Nibbling on Einstein's Brain* (5–8). Illus. by Warren Clark. 2001, Firefly $24.95 (1-55037-687-X); paper $14.95 (1-55037-686-1). 112pp. Swanson looks at "bad" science and examines the difference between sound scientific theory and hype, teaching kids how to ask the right questions when analyzing advertisers' claims. (Rev: BL 2/15/02; HBG 3/02; SLJ 11/01) [507.2]

20636 Swanson, Diane. *Turn It Loose: The Scientist in Absolutely Everybody* (4–6). Illus. by Warren Clark. 2004, Annick $29.95 (1-55037-851-1); paper $14.95 (1-55037-850-3). 120pp. Swanson offers activities to help young people polish their scientific skills and profiles a number of scientists and others who have demonstrated scientific thinking. (Rev: BL 6/1–15/04; SLJ 6/04) [500]

20637 Tocci, Salvatore. *Experiments with Magic* (2–4). Illus. Series: A True Book. 2003, Children's Pr. LB $23.50 (0-516-22788-2); paper $6.95 (0-516-27808-8). 48pp. Basic scientific principles are demonstrated through "magic" tricks in this attractive book that is suitable for beginning readers. (Rev: SLJ 4/04) [507.8]

20638 Wilkes, Angela. *Your World: A First Encyclopedia* (K–2). 1999, Kingfisher $24.95 (0-7534-5217-0). 320pp. Questions and answers are given on such topics as the universe, the environment, prehistoric life, plants, animals, the human body, people, and places. (Rev: BL 12/1/99; HBG 4/00; SLJ 2/00) [030]

20639 Wollard, Kathy. *How Come?* (5–9). 1993, Workman paper $12.95 (1-56305-324-1). Provides answers to some common and not-so-common questions about ordinary things. (Rev: BL 5/1/94) [500]

20640 Wollard, Kathy. *How Come Planet Earth?* (4–7). Illus. by Debra Solomon. 1999, Workman paper $12.95 (0-7611-1239-1). 332pp. This book contains 125 science questions asked by children involving subjects such as warts, dust, cholesterol, and volcanoes. (Rev: SLJ 5/00) [500]

Experiments and Projects

20641 *The Big Book of Nature Projects* (4–6). Illus. 1997, Thames & Hudson paper $16.95 (0-500-01773-5). 128pp. An attractive large-format paperback that introduces a wide variety of nature projects for both indoors and outdoors with easy instructions. (Rev: BL 7/97; SLJ 1/98) [507.8]

20642 Bonnet, Bob, and Dan Keen. *Science Fair Projects: Chemistry* (4–6). Illus. by Frances Zweifel. 2000, Sterling $17.95 (0-8069-7771-X). 95pp. A book of 47 experiments and projects including growing crystals, testing acids and bases, and separating liquids by density. (Rev: SLJ 1/01) [509]

20643 Carrow, Robert. *Put a Fan in Your Hat! Inventions, Contraptions, and Gadgets Kids Can Build* (5–8). Illus. by Rick Brown. 1997, McGraw-Hill paper $14.95 (0-07-011658-X). 139pp. Interesting projects include making a natural battery, building a motor, and creating a hat with a cooling fan. (Rev: BL 4/15/97; SLJ 5/97) [507]

20644 Chapman, Gillian, and Pam Robson. *Exploring Time* (3–5). Illus. 1995, Millbrook LB $19.90 (1-56294-559-9). 32pp. Fourteen projects of varying difficulty related to time, such as creating a timeline and a sundial. (Rev: BL 11/1/95; SLJ 3/96) [529]

20645 Cobb, Vicki. *I Get Wet* (PS–2). Illus. by Julia Gorton. Series: Science Play. 2002, HarperCollins LB $17.89 (0-688-17839-1). 40pp. An introduction to the properties of water that includes bright illustrations and simple experiments sure to stimulate the curiosity of younger readers. Also use *I See Myself* (2002), an introduction to the properties of light. (Rev: BL 8/02; HB 11–12/02; HBG 3/03; SLJ 10/02) [546]

20646 Cobb, Vicki. *See for Yourself: More Than 100 Experiments for Science Fairs and Projects* (3–8). Illus. by Dave Klug. 2001, Scholastic $16.95 (0-439-09010-5); paper $7.95 (0-439-09011-3). 192pp. A collection of experiments and activities arranged by topic, with a notation of the level of difficulty. (Rev: HBG 10/02; SLJ 3/02) [507.8]

20647 Cobb, Vicki, and Kathy Darling. *Wanna Bet? Science Challenges to Fool You* (3–6). Illus. by Meredith Johnson. 1993, Lothrop $15.00 (0-688-11213-7). 128pp. This book of experiments and projects for young people covers such areas as physics, chemistry, mathematics, physiology, and electricity. (Rev: BL 5/1/93; SLJ 8/93) [793]

20648 Cobb, Vicki, and Kathy Darling. *You Gotta Try This! Absolutely Irresistible Science* (4–8). Illus. 1999, Morrow $15.99 (0-688-15740-8). An easy, enjoyable book of 50 experiments, that gives clear directions, lists of materials, and an explanation of the concepts involved. Some require adult assistance. (Rev: BCCB 5/99; BL 8/99; HBG 4/00; SLJ 8/99) [507]

20649 Coulter, George, and Shirley Coulter. *Science in Art* (3–4). Illus. Series: Science Projects. 1995, Rourke LB $23.93 (0-86625-519-2). 32pp. Six science activities are included in this volume, each of which explores some aspect of art, color, or artists' materials. Companion volumes are *Science in Food* and *Science in History* (both 1995). (Rev: SLJ 1/96) [507]

20650 Diehn, Gwen, et al. *Nature Smart: Awesome Projects to Make with Mother Nature's Help* (3–6). Illus. 2003, Main Street paper $19.95 (1-4027-0515-8). 398pp. More than 150 projects that offer insight into the natural world are accompanied by relevant facts and easy instructions. (Rev: SLJ 10/03) [745.5]

20651 Diehn, Gwen, et al. *Science Smart: Cool Projects for Exploring the Marvels of the Planet Earth* (4–7). Illus. 2003, Sterling paper $19.95 (1-4027-0514-X). 400pp. This richly illustrated collection of 150 crafts and experiments will provide readers with hours of science fun, including such diverse projects as building a station for observing wildlife and creating a fossil that looks like the real thing. (Rev: SLJ 12/03) [550]

20652 Duensing, Edward. *Talking to Fireflies, Shrinking the Moon: Nature Activities for All Ages* (5–9). Illus. 1997, Fulcrum paper $15.95 (1-55591-310-5). More than 40 nature activities are included in this volume, including how to hypnotize a frog, weave a daisy chain, and whistle for woodchucks. [507]

20653 *Experiments You Can Do in Your Backyard* (5–8). Illus. Series: Science Experiments. 2003, McGraw-Hill $16.95 (1-57768-624-1). 96pp. The 50-plus backyard experiments and activities outlined in this book come with straightforward instructions and clear explanations of nature and scientific principles. (Rev: HBG 4/04; SLJ 2/04) [507]

20654 Falk, John H., et al. *Bubble Monster: And Other Science Fun* (PS–3). Illus. by Charles C. Somerville. 1996, Chicago Review paper $17.95 (1-55652-301-7). 168pp. Five scientific areas — patterns, matter, communication, the human body, and technology — are covered in a series of activities that require some adult help. (Rev: SLJ 4/97) [507]

20655 Gardner, Robert. *Kitchen Chemistry: Science Experiments to Do at Home* (4–8). Illus. 1989, Silver Burdett paper $4.95 (0-671-67576-1). 136pp. These entertaining and instructive experiments can be performed in the kitchen with everyday equipment and supplies. [542]

20656 Gardner, Robert. *Projects in Space Science* (4–8). Illus. 1988, Silver Burdett paper $5.95 (0-671-65993-6). 136pp. Science projects involving space travel and astronomy. (Rev: BL 1/15/89; SLJ 2/89) [500.2]

20657 Gardner, Robert. *Science Around the House* (4–6). Illus. 1989, Silver Burdett paper $4.95 (0-671-68139-7). 136pp. Simple experiments using everyday objects are detailed in this reissued project book.

20658 Gibson, Gary. *Making Shapes* (3–5). Photos by Roger Vlitos. Illus. by Tony Kenyon. Series: Science for Fun. 1995, Millbrook LB $20.90 (1-56294-631-5). 32pp. In double-page spreads, experiments in shape making and shifting are described, as well as how they illustrate various principles of science. (Rev: SLJ 3/96) [507]

20659 Gibson, Gary. *Making Things Change* (3–5). Illus. Series: Science for Fun. 1995, Millbrook LB $20.90 (1-56294-645-5). 32pp. Double-page spreads are used to introduce a series of experiments and projects that illustrate how objects and materials can change their forms and structures. (Rev: BL 12/15/95) [507.8]

20660 Graham, John, et al. *Hands-On Science* (4–6). Illus. by David Le Jars. Series: Hands-On. 2002, Kingfisher paper $10.95 (0-7534-5440-8). 160pp. More than 100 easy-to-follow, nicely presented experiments teach students about basic science concepts. (Rev: SLJ 8/02)

20661 Haduch, Bill. *Science Fair Success Secrets: How to Win Prizes, Have Fun, and Think Like a Scientist* (5–8). Illus. by Philip Scheuer. 2002, Dutton paper $10.99 (0-525-46534-0). 128pp. A handy and appealing introduction to how to conduct a science experiment, with examples of award-winning projects, a list of ideas, and metric conversion tables. (Rev: BL 12/1/02; SLJ 3/03) [507]

20662 Hartzog, John Daniel. *Everyday Science Experiments in the Kitchen* (PS–3). Series: Science Suprises. 2000, Rosen $19.33 (0-8239-5456-0). 24pp. Eight simple experiments are outlined from using lemon juice to shine a penny to creating a celery straw. (Rev: SLJ 9/00) [509]

20663 Hauser, Jill F. *Gizmos and Gadgets: Creating Science Contraptions That Work (and Knowing Why)* (4–7). Illus. by Michael Kline. Series: Kids Can! 1999, Williamson paper $12.95 (1-885593-26-0). 144pp. Outlines the construction of all sorts of gadgets from objects found in kitchen and garage closets and relates each to such scientific topics as motion, energy, balancing, and gravity. (Rev: SLJ 1/00) [745]

20664 Hauser, Jill F. *Science Play! Beginning Discoveries for 2- to 6-Year-Olds* (PS–K). Illus. by Michael Kline. Series: Little Hands. 1998, Williamson paper $12.95 (1-885593-20-1). 135pp. Basic science concepts are taught in this book for preschoolers that contains 65 simple activities. (Rev: SLJ 1/99) [507.8]

20665 Hirschfeld, Robert, and Nancy White. *The Kids' Science Book: Creative Experiences for Hands-on Fun* (2–5). Illus. by Loretta Braren. Series: Kids Can! 1995, Williamson paper $12.95 (0-913589-88-8). 157pp. An interesting collection of games, experiments, and activities that illustrate various principles of science and are fun to perform. (Rev: SLJ 12/95) [507]

20666 Kramer, Alan. *How to Make a Chemical Volcano and Other Mysterious Experiments* (4–7). Illus. by Paul Harvey. 1991, Watts paper $6.95 (0-531-15610-9). 111pp. Thirty experiments for "detectives of chemistry" by a 13-year-old student. (Rev: BCCB 2/90; BL 12/15/89; SLJ 3/90) [532]

20667 Levine, Shar, and Leslie Johnstone. *Bathtub Science* (2–6). Photos by Jeff Connery. Illus. by Dave Garbot. 2001, Sterling $19.95 (0-8069-7185-1). 80pp. Thirty-five experiments and activities that involve water — such as learning how a submarine works and making paper flowers that absorb moisture — are accompanied by colorful photographs, cartoons, and advice on safety. (Rev: HBG 10/01; SLJ 8/01) [532]

20668 Levine, Shar, and Leslie Johnstone. *Everyday Science: Fun and Easy Projects for Making Practical Things* (4–6). Illus. by Ed Shems. 1995, Wiley paper $9.95 (0-471-11014-0). 97pp. The science behind everyday objects is explored in this book of 25 simple projects under such headings as Light and Optics, Heat, Earth Science, Electricity, and Chemistry. (Rev: SLJ 8/95) [507]

20669 Levine, Shar, and Leslie Johnstone. *Kitchen Science* (3–5). Illus. 2004, Sterling $19.95 (1-4027-0332-5). 64pp. More than 30 science experiments are described and illustrated, all of them involving materials (from chocolate to cabbage) found in most home kitchens. (Rev: SLJ 4/04) [507]

20670 Levine, Shar, and Leslie Johnstone. *Science Around the World: Travel Through Time and Space with Fun Experiments and Projects* (3–6). Illus. by Laurel Aiello. 1996, Wiley paper $10.95 (0-471-11916-4). 84pp. This project book presents activities from ten countries around the world, including making paper and creating a sand timer. (Rev: SLJ 7/96) [507]

20671 Markle, Sandra. *Exploring Autumn: A Season of Science Activities, Puzzlers, and Games* (4–7). Illus. Series: Exploring Seasons. 1991, Avon paper $3.50 (0-380-71910-X). 160pp. Science, history, myth, quizzes, and more combined in this book on seasonal activities in the classroom and home. (Rev: BL 1/1/91; SLJ 1/92) [574.5]

20672 Markle, Sandra. *Super Science Secrets: Exploring Nature Through Games, Puzzles and*

Activities (1–3). Illus. 1997, Longstreet $14.95 (1-56352-396-5). 36pp. Scientific topics like evaporation, static electricity, and animal defenses are examined, with follow-up questions and simple experiments. (Rev: SLJ 9/97) [507]

20673 Mason, Adrienne. *Living Things* (K–4). Series: Starting with Science. 1998, Kids Can LB $10.95 (1-55074-343-0). 32pp. Basic science concepts about life are examined, using 13 simple experiments such as "worm farming," "hairy egg heads," and "baking beasts." (Rev: BL 5/15/98; HBG 9/98; SLJ 5/98) [507.8]

20674 Maynard, Chris. *Kitchen Science* (3–5). Illus. 2001, DK $12.95 (0-7894-6972-3). 48pp. A humorous and attractive collection of projects that include creating emulsions, observing mold, and making fizzy and bubbly concoctions. Also use *Backyard Science* (2001). (Rev: HBG 10/03; SLJ 12/01) [507.8]

20675 Muller, Eric. *While You're Waiting for the Food to Come* (4–6). Illus. 1999, Orchard $15.95 (0-531-30199-0); paper $8.95 (0-531-07144-8). 96pp. An appealing experiment book that contains simple projects, arranged like a menu, designed to be performed where food is served. (Rev: BCCB 9/99; BL 1/1–15/00; HBG 4/00; SLJ 10/99) [507]

20676 Murphy, Pat, et al. *The Science Explorer Out and About: Fantastic Science Experiments Your Family Can Do Anywhere!* (3–8). Illus. by Jason Gorski. Series: Exploratorium Science-at-Home Book. 1997, Holt paper $12.95 (0-8050-4537-6). 127pp. A wide variety of science experiments are outlined, many that can be performed alone and others that require adult help. (Rev: SLJ 2/98) [507]

20677 Nye, Bill. *Bill Nye the Science Guy's Big Blast of Science* (5–8). Illus. 1993, Addison-Wesley paper $16.00 (0-201-60864-2). 172pp. Matter, heat, light, electricity, magnetism, weather, and space are among the topics introduced in this quick and entertaining tour of the world of science. (Rev: BL 2/15/94) [507.8]

20678 Parker, Steve. *Shocking, Slimy, Stinky, Shiny Science Experiments* (3–5). Illus. 1999, Sterling $19.95 (0-8069-6295-X). 96pp. Using carefully laid-out steps and sharp photographs, this book provides 73 simple experiments covering basic concepts in light, electricity, and the properties of common household objects. (Rev: BL 5/15/99; HBG 9/99; SLJ 4/99) [507.8]

20679 Potter, Jean. *Science in Seconds with Toys: Over 100 Experiments You Can Do in Ten Minutes or Less* (2–5). 1998, Wiley paper $12.95 (0-471-17900-0). 131pp. Each page contains a separate easy-to-perform activity that answers a question involving a simple scientific principle. (Rev: SLJ 4/98) [507.8]

20680 Press, H. J. *Giant Book of Science Experiments* (3–6). 1998, Sterling paper $14.95 (0-8069-8139-3). 352pp. This collection of experiments contains 325 simple activities, each outlined on a single page and most using easy-to-find materials. (Rev: SLJ 7/98) [507]

20681 Rhatigan, Joe, and Rain Newcomb. *Prize-Winning Science Fair Projects for Curious Kids* (5–8). Illus. 2004, Lark Books $19.95 (1-57990-478-5). 112pp. Clear graphics and practical tips add to the stimulating text in this guide to science fair projects. (Rev: BL 12/1/04; SLJ 1/05) [507]

20682 Richards, Roy. *101 Science Surprises: Exciting Experiments with Everyday Materials* (3–5). Illus. 1993, Sterling $17.95 (0-8069-8822-3). 104pp. The activities and experiments presented in this book represent various branches of science and vary in difficulty. (Rev: BL 9/1/93; SLJ 6/93) [507.8]

20683 Richards, Roy. *101 Science Tricks: Fun Experiments with Everyday Materials* (4–8). Illus. by Alex Pang. 1992, Sterling $16.95 (0-8069-8388-4). 104pp. Interesting, easy-to-do science and math activities emphasize the underlying principles. (Rev: BL 2/1/92; SLJ 1/92) [507.8]

20684 Ross, Michael E. *Sandbox Scientist: Real Science Activities for Little Kids* (PS–2). Illus. by Mary Anne Lloyd. 1995, Chicago Review paper $12.95 (1-55652-248-7). 206pp. Simple experiments and activities introduce young children to the principles involving such components as light and water. (Rev: BL 2/1/96) [372.3]

20685 Ross, Michael Elsohn. *Toy Lab* (4–6). Illus. by Tim Seeley. Series: You Are the Scientist. 2002, Carolrhoda LB $23.93 (0-87614-456-3). 48pp. Toys such as slinkies, silly putty, frisbees, and blocks are all put to good use as readers learn about gravity, flight, motion, and other basic concepts. (Rev: HBG 3/03; SLJ 2/03)

20686 Rybolt, Thomas R., and Leah M. Rybolt. *Science Fair Success with Scents, Aromas, and Smells* (5–8). Series: Science Fair Success. 2002, Enslow LB $20.95 (0-7660-1625-0). 112pp. Several science fair projects using the sense of smell are presented with clear instructions and easy-to-find materials. (Rev: BL 5/15/02; HBG 10/02; SLJ 11/02) [507]

20687 *Science Fairs: Ideas and Activities* (4–8). 1998, World Book $15.00 (0-7166-4498-3). Using many diagrams and logical step-by-step explanations, this work offers science projects in such areas as space, earth science, geology, botany, and machines. (Rev: SLJ 1/99) [507]

20688 Smith, Norman F. *How to Do Successful Science Projects.* Rev. ed. (5–8). Illus. 1990, Messner paper $5.95 (0-671-70686-1). This guide gives many fine tips and concentrates on the applications of the scientific method. (Rev: BL 7/90) [507.8]

20689 Sobey, Ed. *Wrapper Rockets and Trombone Straws: Science at Every Meal* (4–7). Illus. 1996, McGraw-Hill paper $14.95 (0-07-021745-9). 137pp. Using simple items found in restaurants such as glasses, straws, and napkins, a number of simple tricks and experiments are introduced. (Rev: BL 3/1/97; SLJ 6/97) [500]

20690 Tocci, Salvatore. *Experiments with Sports* (2–4). Illus. Series: True Books. 2003, Children's Pr. LB $23.50 (0-516-22789-0); paper $6.95 (0-516-27807-X). 48pp. A book of experiments that

demonstrate how basic scientific principles apply to sports. (Rev: SLJ 4/04) [507.8]

20691 Tocci, Salvatore. *Science Fair Success in the Hardware Store* (5–8). Series: Science Fair Success. 2000, Enslow LB $20.95 (0-7660-1287-5). 128pp. A group of science fair projects that use materials and objects found in a hardware store, with clear explanations of the scientific principles behind each project. (Rev: BL 4/15/00; HBG 9/00) [507]

20692 Tocci, Salvatore. *Science Fair Success Using Supermarket Products* (5–8). Series: Science Fair Success. 2000, Enslow LB $20.95 (0-7660-1288-3). 128pp. Using common items found in a supermarket, this work outlines a number of excellent science projects that demonstrate important scientific principles. (Rev: BL 4/15/00; HBG 9/00; SLJ 4/00) [507]

20693 Tocci, Salvatore. *Using Household Products* (5–8). Series: Science Fair Success. 2002, Enslow LB $20.95 (0-7660-1626-9). This useful volume outlines a number of science fair projects that can be done using materials found around the house. (Rev: BL 4/15/02; HBG 10/02) [509]

20694 UNESCO. *700 Science Experiments for Everyone* (5–8). Illus. 1964, Doubleday $19.95 (0-385-05275-8). 252pp. An excellent collection of experiments, noted for its number of entries and breadth of coverage.

20695 VanCleave, Janice. *Janice VanCleave's Animals* (4–6). Illus. Series: Spectacular Science Projects. 1992, Wiley paper $10.95 (0-471-55052-3). 84pp. This book contains many easy-to-follow projects involving animals. (Rev: BL 1/1/93; SLJ 2/93) [591]

20696 VanCleave, Janice. *Janice VanCleave's Biology for Every Kid: 101 Easy Experiments That Really Work* (4–7). Illus. 1989, Wiley paper $12.95 (0-471-50381-9). 224pp. This book outlines simple experiments that use readily available equipment and supplies. (Rev: BL 2/15/90) [574]

20697 VanCleave, Janice. *Janice VanCleave's Guide to More of the Best Science Fair Projects* (4–8). 2000, Wiley paper $14.95 (0-471-32627-5). 156pp. After general information about the scientific method, research, and presentation, this book outlines about 50 projects in the areas of astronomy, biology, earth science, engineering, physical science, and mathematics. (Rev: SLJ 5/00) [509]

20698 VanCleave, Janice. *Janice VanCleave's Guide to the Best Science Fair Projects* (3–6). Illus. 1997, Wiley paper $14.95 (0-471-14802-4). 144pp. An excellent experiment book that covers 50 science projects in the life and physical sciences, astronomy, mathematics, and engineering. (Rev: BL 3/15/97; SLJ 4/97) [507.8]

20699 VanCleave, Janice. *Janice VanCleave's 203 Icy, Freezing, Frosty, Cool and Wild Experiments* (4–7). 1999, Wiley paper $12.95 (0-471-25223-9). 122pp. An excellent book filled with easily performed experiments in such areas as biology, chemistry, earth science, and physics. (Rev: SLJ 4/00) [507.8]

20700 VanCleave, Janice. *Janice VanCleave's 202 Oozing, Bubbling, Dripping and Bouncing Experi-*

ments (4–6). Illus. 1996, Wiley paper $12.95 (0-471-14025-2). 120pp. Fun and learning are combined in these experiments that investigate astronomy, biology, chemistry, earth science, and physics. (Rev: SLJ 2/97) [507]

20701 Vecchione, Glen. *100 First Prize Make It Yourself Science Fair Projects* (4–8). Illus. 1998, Sterling $19.95 (0-8069-0703-7). The projects outlined in this good resource for project ideas range from the simple to complex and cover a wide range of branches of science. (Rev: SLJ 4/99) [507]

20702 Voth, Danna. *Kidsource: Science Fair Handbook* (5–8). Illus. 1998, Lowell House paper $9.95 (1-56565-514-1). This source provides excellent advice on selecting, preparing, and presenting science projects, with material on choosing workable topics, equipment needed, safety, measuring devices, and record keeping. (Rev: BL 2/15/99; SLJ 5/99) [507]

20703 Wiese, Jim. *Magic Science: 50 Jaw-Dropping, Mind-Boggling, Head-Scratching Activities for Kids* (4–6). Illus. 1998, Wiley paper $12.95 (0-471-18239-7). 128pp. The author explains the science behind 50 magic tricks, which are divided into six categories: matter, reactions, water, air, force and energy, and electricity and magnetism. (Rev: BL 5/15/98) [507.8]

20704 Wiese, Jim. *Rocket Science: 50 Flying, Floating, Flipping, Spinning Gadgets Kids Create Themselves* (3–6). Illus. 1995, Wiley paper $12.95 (0-471-11357-3). 128pp. Principles related to physics, electricity, optics, acoustics, and other branches of science are explored in a number of interesting projects and experiments. (Rev: BL 12/1/95; SLJ 3/96) [507.8]

20705 Willow, Diane, and Emily Curran. *Science Sensations* (3–5). Illus. by Lady McCrady. Series: Boston Children's Museum Activity Books. 1990, Addison-Wesley paper $11.00 (0-201-07189-4). 95pp. A simple child-tested experiment book using everyday objects. (Rev: SLJ 6/90) [507]

20706 Wyatt, Valerie. *The Science Book for Girls and Other Intelligent Beings* (3–5). Illus. by Pat Cupples. 1997, Kids Can paper $8.95 (1-55074-113-6). 80pp. Introduces various science experiments from different branches of science, as well as several female scientists, like Mary Leakey and Sally Ride. (Rev: SLJ 10/97) [509]

20707 Wyler, Rose. *Science Fun with Peanuts and Popcorn* (2–4). Illus. 1986, Simon & Schuster paper $4.95 (0-671-62452-0). 48pp. Simple experiments that explain scientific principles. Also use: *Science Fun with Mud and Dirt* (1986). (Rev: BL 7/86; SLJ 11/86)

20708 Wyler, Rose. *Science Fun with Toy Boats and Planes* (2–4). Illus. 1986, Simon & Schuster paper $4.95 (0-671-62453-9). 48pp. Experiments that explain the forces that move these vehicles. Also use: *Science Fun with Toy Cars and Trucks* (1988). (Rev: BL 7/86; SLJ 10/86)

Astronomy

General

20709 Asimov, Isaac. *The Birth of Our Universe* (5–8). Illus. Series: Isaac Asimov's 21st Century Library of the Universe. 2005, Gareth Stevens LB $18.50 (0-8368-3964-1). 32pp. This is an update of a 1995 edition on the origins of the universe, with illustrations and photographs. (Rev: BL 3/1/05) [523.1]

20710 Becklake, Sue. *All About Space* (2–5). Series: Scholastic First Encyclopedia. 1999, Scholastic $14.95 (0-590-10471-3). 77pp. This book crams an amazing amount of important information about space into a few pages with coverage of such topics as the solar system, telescopes, stars, space travel, space exploration, and space programs. (Rev: SLJ 6/99) [528]

20711 Berger, Melvin, and Gilda Berger. *Do Stars Have Points? Questions and Answers About Stars and Planets* (3–5). Illus. Series: Question and Answer. 1999, Scholastic $12.95 (0-590-13080-3); paper $5.95 (0-590-08570-5). 48pp. Using a question-and-answer format, this book covers important facts in astronomy involving the solar system and the universe. (Rev: BL 11/1/99; SLJ 2/00) [523]

20712 Bonnet, Bob, and Dan Keen. *Science Fair Projects: Flight, Space and Astronomy* (4–6). Illus. by Frances Zweifel. 1997, Sterling $17.95 (0-8069-9450-9). 95pp. A collection of 53 clever astronomy-related experiments that vary considerably in difficulty and in the nature of the equipment involved. (Rev: SLJ 2/98) [520]

20713 Bortz, Fred. *Collision Course! Cosmic Impacts and Life on Earth* (4–7). Illus. 2001, Millbrook LB $25.90 (0-7613-1403-2). 72pp. A straightforward discussion of an intriguing subject that includes material on past collisions and on detecting and perhaps deflecting future "near Earth objects." (Rev: BL 5/1/01; HBG 10/01; SLJ 5/01) [523.44]

20714 Campbell, Ann-Jeanette. *The New York Public Library: Amazing Space: A Book of Answers for Kids* (5–8). Illus. 1997, Wiley paper $12.95 (0-471-14498-3). This question-and-answer book introduces space exploration, the solar system, individual planets, galaxies, and related phenomena. (Rev: SLJ 7/97) [523]

20715 Carruthers, Margaret W. *The Hubble Space Telescope* (5–7). Series: Watts Library. 2003, Watts LB $24.00 (0-531-12279-4). 64pp. Excellent photographs enhance this history of the telescope and explanation of how it works and its importance to our knowledge of space. (Rev: SLJ 2/04) [522]

20716 Cole, Michael D. *Hubble Space Telescope: Exploring the Universe* (4–7). Illus. Series: Countdown to Space. 1999, Enslow LB $18.95 (0-7660-1120-8). 48pp. This close-up look at the Hubble space telescope covers its parts, uses, problems, and photographs that the telescope has sent back to earth. (Rev: BL 2/1/99; HBG 9/99) [522]

20717 Davis, Kenneth C. *Don't Know Much About Space* (3–7). Illus. by Sergio Ruzzier. Series: Don't Know Much About. 2001, HarperCollins LB $19.89 (0-06-028602-4); paper $6.95 (0-06-440835-3). 144pp. An entertaining, informal, question-and-answer introduction to astronomy. (Rev: BL 9/15/01; HBG 3/02; SLJ 8/01) [520]

20718 Delafosse, Claude, et al. *Hidden World: Space* (PS–2). Series: First Discovery. 2000, Scholastic $12.95 (0-439-14826-X). 24pp. For the very young, this is a colorful, well-illustrated introduction to space and what it means. (Rev: BL 8/00) [523]

20719 Gallant, Roy A. *The Life Stories of Stars* (5–7). Series: Story of Science. 2000, Benchmark LB $19.95 (0-7614-1152-6). 80pp. This is a history of astronomy with coverage of how our attitudes about the heavens have changed over the years as well as our methods of studying the sky. (Rev: BL 12/15/00; HBG 10/01; SLJ 2/01) [523]

20720 Gifford, Clive. *The Kingfisher Facts and Records Book of Space: The Ultimate Information Database* (4–6). Illus. 2001, Kingfisher $14.95 (0-7534-5363-0). 64pp. Among the topics covered in this fact-packed volume are the solar system, the

Milky Way and other galaxies, astronomical equipment, and man's journeys into space. (Rev: HBG 10/02; SLJ 12/01) [520]

20721 Graun, Ken, and Suzanne Maly. *Our Galaxy and the Universe* (4–6). Illus. Series: 21st Century Astronomy. 2002, Ken Pr. $15.95 (1-928771-08-4). 36pp. Excellent illustrations add to the appeal of this look at the stars. (Rev: SLJ 12/02)

20722 Gustafson, John. *Planets, Moons and Meteors: The Young Stargazer's Guide to the Galaxy* (4–8). Illus. 1992, Simon & Schuster LB $12.95 (0-671-72534-3); paper $6.95 (0-671-72535-1). 64pp. This guidebook tells how and when to observe the solar system and provides basic information about the planets. (Rev: BL 11/1/92) [523]

20723 Halpern, Paul. *Faraway Worlds: Planets Beyond Our Solar System* (3–6). Illus. by Lynette R. Cook. 2004, Charlesbridge $16.95 (1-57091-616-0); paper $6.95 (1-57091-617-9). 32pp. This strikingly illustrated slim volume looks at planets exising beyond our solar system and discusses how they are studied by scientists. (Rev: BL 8/04; SLJ 3/05) [523.2]

20724 Hirst, Robin, and Sally Hirst. *My Place in Space* (3–4). Illus. by Roland Harvey. 1992, Orchard paper $6.95 (0-531-07030-1). 40pp. A sky show from earth to solar system to the outer reaches of the universe. (Rev: BCCB 3/90; BL 4/1/90; HB 5–6/91; SLJ 4/90) [520]

20725 Jackson, Ellen. *Looking for Life in the Universe: The Search for Extraterrestrial Intelligence* (4–7). Illus. by Nic Bishop. 2002, Houghton Mifflin $16.00 (0-618-12894-8). 64pp. Jackson examines the possibility of life elsewhere and profiles Dr. Jill Tarter, a research astrophysicist, as she searches for traces of an extraterrestrial signal. (Rev: BL 12/1/02; HB 1–2/03; HBG 3/03; SLJ 12/02*) [576.8]

20726 Kerrod, Robin. *Starwatch: A Month-by-Month Guide to the Night Sky* (5–8). Illus. 2003, Barron's $18.95 (0-7641-5666-7). 96pp. An appealing introduction to astronomy with illustrations that make it easy to identify stellar objects from both northern and southern hemispheres. (Rev: BL 12/1/03; HBG 4/04) [523]

20727 Love, Ann, and Jane Drake. *The Kids' Book of the Night Sky* (4–6). Illus. by Heather Collins. 2004, Kids Can $19.95 (1-55337-357-X). 144pp. The authors offer a potpourri of basic astronomy facts, sky folklore, charts, and suggestions for art and science projects, leavened with light humor and helpful illustrations. (Rev: BL 4/15/04; SLJ 7/04) [520]

20728 Macy, Sue. *Are We Alone? Scientists Search for Life in Space* (4–8). Illus. 2004, National Geographic $18.95 (0-7922-6567-X). 96pp. Modern scientific efforts to find extraterrestrial life are discussed along with the popularity of flying saucer, crop circle, and other theories. (Rev: BL 10/1/04; SLJ 12/04*) [001.9]

20729 Maynard, Christopher. *The Young Scientist Book of Stars and Planets* (4–7). Illus. 1978, EDC LB $14.95 (0-88110-313-6); paper $6.95 (0-86020-

094-9). 32pp. Attractive illustrations and plentiful experiments and projects add to this book's appeal.

20730 Mechler, Gary. *National Audubon Society First Field Guide: Night Sky* (4–6). Series: First Field Guide. 1999, Scholastic $17.95 (0-590-64085-2); paper $11.95 (0-590-64086-0). 160pp. This atlas to the night sky identifies and gives information on the most common stars and constellations. (Rev: BL 10/15/99) [523]

20731 Miles, Lisa, and Alastair Smith. *The Usborne Complete Book of Astronomy and Space* (3–4). Illus. by Gary Bines and Peter Bull. 1998, EDC paper $14.95 (0-7460-3104-1). 96pp. A clear introduction to astronomy and famous astronomers, plus tips for stargazers and sky photographers. (Rev: SLJ 1/99) [523]

20732 Miotto, Enrico. *The Universe: Origins and Evolution* (5–8). Series: Beginnings. 1995, Raintree LB $24.26 (0-8114-3334-X). This basic outline of the history of the universe begins with the Big Bang theory and finishes with the "Big Crunch" that may end time. (Rev: BL 4/15/95) [523.1]

20733 Moeschl, Richard. *Exploring the Sky: 100 Projects for Beginning Astronomers* (5–8). Illus. 1992, Chicago Review paper $16.95 (1-55652-160-X). 320pp. Many ideas for experiments and observations in an information-packed book. (Rev: BL 5/1/89)

20734 Oleksy, Walter. *Mapping the Skies* (5–7). Series: Watts Library: Geography. 2002, Watts LB $24.00 (0-531-12031-7); paper $8.95 (0-531-16635-X). 64pp. From the ancient Greeks and Romans through Galileo to astronomers today, this is a history of how the stars, planets, and space have been mapped. (Rev: BL 10/15/02) [520]

20735 Orr, Tamra. *The Telescope* (4–8). Series: Inventions That Shaped the World. 2004, Watts LB $29.50 (0-531-12344-8). 80pp. Describes the invention of the telescope, the impact of the knowledge imparted, and future possibilities. (Rev: BL 4/1/04; SLJ 2/05) [522]

20736 Oxlade, Chris. *The Mystery of Black Holes* (4–6). Series: Can Science Solve? 1999, Heinemann LB $15.95 (1-57572-808-7). 32pp. Using a dynamic format, this book supplies a brief overview of theories concerning the existence of black holes. (Rev: SLJ 1/00) [523]

20737 Petty, Kate. *The Sun Is a Star: And Other Amazing Facts About the Universe* (1–3). Illus. by Francis Phillips and Ian Thompson. Series: I Didn't Know That. 1997, Millbrook LB $19.90 (0-7613-0567-X). 32pp. As well as introducing the sun, this book describes other parts of the solar system, black holes, the Milky Way, and other parts of the universe. (Rev: SLJ 9/97) [523]

20738 Rabe, Tish. *There's No Place Like Space: All About Our Solar System* (K–3). Illus. by Aristides Ruiz. Series: The Cat in the Hat's Learning Library. 1999, Random LB $11.99 (0-679-99115-8). 44pp. Using rhyming couplets and cartoon-like illustrations, this is a basic introduction to space and the solar system. (Rev: HBG 9/00; SLJ 3/00) [523]

1115

20739 Redfern, Martin. *The Kingfisher Young People's Book of Space* (4–6). 1998, Kingfisher $19.95 (0-7534-5136-0). 95pp. This work contains a short history of astronomy, a tour of the universe with material on galaxies and the solar system, a rundown on space exploration, and a list of questions about space still to be answered. (Rev: HBG 3/99; SLJ 2/99) [523]

20740 Rhatigan, Joe, and Rain Newcomb. *Out-of-This-World Astronomy: 50 Amazing Activities and Projects* (5–8). Illus. 2003, Sterling $19.95 (1-57990-410-6). 128pp. Strong background information adds to the value of this collection of interesting, well-presented activities. (Rev: SLJ 4/04) [520]

20741 Rockwell, Anne. *Our Stars* (PS–4). Illus. 1999, Harcourt $13.00 (0-15-201868-9). 24pp. A stylish picture book that introduces a young audience to the stars, planets, comets, and meteors. (Rev: BL 3/1/99; HBG 9/99; SLJ 5/99) [523.8]

20742 Roza, Greg. *The Incredible Story of Telescopes* (3–6). Illus. Series: A Kid's Guide to Incredible Technology. 2004, Rosen LB $19.95 (0-8239-6715-8). 24pp. The history and technology of telescopes are discussed in concise terms, with material on Hubble and on future developments. (Rev: SLJ 2/05) [681]

20743 Ruiz, Andres L. *The Origin of the Universe* (4–9). Series: Sequences of Earth and Space. 1997, Sterling $12.95 (0-8069-9744-3). In simple, concise language, this work discusses various theories concerning the origin of the universe, including the Big Bang theory. (Rev: BL 12/15/97; HBG 3/98) [523]

20744 Simon, Seymour. *Destination: Space* (3–5). Illus. Series: Destination. 2002, HarperCollins LB $15.89 (0-688-16290-8). 32pp. An attractive collection of pictures from the Hubble Space Telescope with explanations of what these images from space mean. (Rev: BL 6/1–15/02; HB 9–10/02; HBG 3/03; SLJ 5/02) [520]

20745 Simon, Seymour. *The Universe* (3–6). 1998, Morrow LB $15.93 (0-688-15302-X). In a series of double-page spreads, this book introduces topics related to the universe, including nebulas, galaxies, the Big Bang, quasars, stars, and planets. (Rev: HBG 3/99; SLJ 5/98) [523]

20746 Sipiera, Diane M., and Paul P. Sipiera. *The Hubble Space Telescope* (2–4). Illus. Series: True Books. 1997, Children's Book Pr. LB $22.00 (0-516-20442-4). 48pp. As well as describing the Hubble Space Telescope and its uses, this account tells about space explorations that are unsafe for both humans and telescopes. (Rev: BL 12/1/97; HBG 3/98) [522]

20747 Spangenburg, Ray, and Kit Moser. *The Hubble Space Telescope* (5–9). Illus. Series: Out of This World. 2002, Watts LB $33.50 (0-531-11894-0); paper $14.95 (0-531-15565-X). 128pp. A look at the telescope itself, its development and launch, the subsequent problems, and the information it has provided to scientists. (Rev: SLJ 12/02) [522]

20748 Steele, Philip. *Astronomy* (4–8). Illus. Series: Pocket Facts. 1991, Macmillan LB $11.95 (0-89686-586-X). 32pp. A concise introduction to

astronomy, complemented by color photographs and drawings. (Rev: BL 3/15/92) [520]

20749 Stott, Carole. *Astronomy* (4–6). Illus. 2003, Kingfisher $16.95 (0-7534-5582-X). 64pp. This engaging introduction to astronomy explores the history of the science, how the universe was viewed by earlier civilizations, and the tools of the astronomer. (Rev: HBG 4/04; SLJ 11/03) [520]

20750 Verdet, Jean-Pierre. *The Universe* (PS–2). Illus. Series: First Discovery. 1997, Scholastic $11.95 (0-590-96212-4). 24pp. From the endless cosmos to exploding stars and a view of our blazing sun, this brilliantly illustrated book introduces the universe. (Rev: BL 2/1/98) [520]

20751 Vogt, Gregory L. *Deep Space Astronomy* (5–8). Illus. 1999, Twenty-First Century LB $25.90 (0-7613-1369-9). 80pp. This look beyond our own star system covers such topics as the development of space-based detectors, information-gathering techniques, and recent discoveries. (Rev: BL 1/1–15/00; HBG 4/00; SLJ 2/00) [520]

20752 Wiese, Jim. *Cosmic Science: Over 40 Gravity-Defying, Earth-Orbiting, Space-Cruising Activities for Kids* (4–6). Illus. 1997, Wiley paper $12.95 (0-471-15852-6). 128pp. Principles of astronomy and space technology are explored through a series of engaging projects with common materials that involve topics like gravity, orbits, planets, and space travel. (Rev: BL 7/97; SLJ 7/97) [929.4]

20753 Wills, Susan, and Steven Wills. *Astronomy: Looking at the Stars* (5–8). Illus. Series: Innovators. 2001, Oliver $21.95 (1-881508-76-5). 144pp. A good starting point for research into astronomy, with profiles of individuals including Ptolemy, Copernicus, Galileo, and Newton. (Rev: HBG 10/02; SLJ 2/02) [520.922]

20754 Wyler, Rose. *The Starry Sky* (K–4). Illus. by Steven J. Petruccio. Series: Outdoor Science. 1989, Simon & Schuster paper $4.95 (0-671-66349-6). 48pp. This book introduces such topics as the earth's rotation, planets, stars, and the phases of the moon. (Rev: SLJ 9/89) [523]

Earth

20755 Adamson, Thomas K. *Earth* (1–2). Illus. Series: Pebble Plus: Exploring the Galaxy. 2003, Capstone LB $17.26 (0-7368-2111-2). 24pp. A very basic introduction to Earth and its place in the solar system. Also use *Jupiter* and *Mars* (both 2003). (Rev: SLJ 4/04) [525]

20756 Alessandrello, Anna. *The Earth: Origins and Evolution* (4–8). Illus. Series: Beginnings — Origins and Evolution. 1995, Raintree LB $24.26 (0-8114-3331-5). 48pp. An oversize book with lavish illustrations that discusses the theories concerning the formation of the earth, its structure and composition, and ways in which it is changing. (Rev: BL 4/15/95; SLJ 6/95) [550]

20757 Bailey, Jacqui. *Sun Up, Sun Down: The Story of Day and Night* (2–4). Illus. by Matthew Lilly. Series: Science Works. 2004, Picture Window LB

$22.60 (1-4048-0567-2). 31pp. A clear and attractive look at the Earth's rotation and the changes in light, explaining how light rays travel, how shadows are formed, and so forth. (Rev: SLJ 8/04) [525.35]

20758 Branley, Franklyn M. *What Makes Day and Night?* (1–3). Illus. by Arthur Dorros. 1986, HarperCollins paper $4.95 (0-06-445050-3). 32pp. A clear, simple explanation of the rotation of the earth. (Rev: BL 3/15/86; SLJ 9/86)

20759 Brimner, Larry. *Earth* (2–5). Illus. Series: True Books. 1998, Children's Book Pr. LB $21.00 (0-516-20620-6). 48pp. Using a chronological approach, this book describes what we have found out about our planet, its composition, layers, and its rotational calendar. (Rev: BL 12/1/98; HBG 3/99) [550]

20760 Davis, Kenneth C. *Don't Know Much About Planet Earth* (3–6). Illus. by Tom Bloom. Series: Don't Know Much About. 2001, HarperCollins LB $19.89 (0-06-028600-8); paper $6.95 (0-06-440834-5). 144pp. A question-and-answer format with cartoonlike drawings makes an attractive backdrop for this overview of the earth's physical and environmental features, as well as today's political divisions and a timeline of historical highlights. (Rev: BL 12/15/01; HBG 3/02; SLJ 8/01) [910]

20761 Gallant, Roy A. *Earth's Place in Space* (5–8). Series: The Story of Science. 1999, Benchmark LB $28.50 (0-7614-0963-7). 80pp. Using a chronological approach, this account traces our knowledge of the earth and its place in the solar system and space. (Rev: BL 2/15/00; HBG 4/00; SLJ 2/00) [525]

20762 Karas, G. Brian. *On Earth* (K–3). Illus. 2005, Penguin Putnam $16.99 (0-399-24025-X). 32pp. Large double-page spreads featuring attractive illustrations discuss the passage of time, the seasons, and the Earth's obit, rotation, and tilt. (Rev: BL 5/1/05; SLJ 5/05) [525]

20763 Kerrod, Robin. *Planet Earth* (4–6). Series: Planet Library. 2000, Lerner LB $21.27 (0-8225-3902-0). 32pp. This book discusses the earth's formation, its journey through space, its drifting continents, its waters and weather, and its many forms of life. (Rev: BL 10/15/00; HBG 3/01) [525]

20764 Miller, Ron. *Earth and the Moon* (5–7). Illus. Series: Worlds Beyond. 2003, Twenty-First Century LB $25.90 (0-7613-2358-9). 96pp. NASA photographs and computer-generated images are used throughout this account of the origin, composition, and evolution the Earth and its moon. (Rev: HBG 10/03; SLJ 8/03) [525]

20765 Nicolson, Cynthia P. *The Earth* (2–5). Illus. Series: Starting with Space. 1997, Kids Can $14.95 (1-55074-314-7). 40pp. Appropriate folktales and projects are included, along with information about the earth and night and day. (Rev: BL 9/1/97; SLJ 9/97) [525]

20766 Patent, Dorothy Hinshaw. *Shaping the Earth* (4–7). Illus. 2000, Clarion $18.00 (0-395-85691-4). 88pp. The evolution of the earth is traced in this compelling book that describes how the surface has changed and continues to change, with coverage of plate tectonics, ice ages, natural disasters, and

descriptions of its natural wonders. (Rev: BL 3/15/00; HBG 9/00; SLJ 4/00) [550]

20767 Pettigrew, Mark. *Planet Earth* (3–6). Series: Science World. 2004, Stargazer Books LB $18.95 (1-932799-28-1). 32pp. Basic facts about the Earth — its structure, movement, atmosphere, and so forth — are introduced in concise text with good diagrams, photographs, and a project, all presented in picture-book format. (Rev: BL 12/1/04) [551]

20768 Riley, Peter D. *Earth* (4–5). Series: Cycles in Science. 1998, Heinemann LB $21.36 (1-57572-620-3). 32pp. This colorfully illustrated book looks at the earth's major cycles, including orbits, rotations, seasons, time zones, and the sun's life. (Rev: SLJ 7/98) [525]

20769 Ross, Michael E. *Earth Cycles* (1–3). Illus. by Gustav Moore. 2001, Millbrook $22.40 (0-7613-1815-1). 32pp. The earth's rotation pattern is described with material on the reasons for night and day and the causes of seasons, plus why the moon appears to change shape during a lunar month. (Rev: BL 1/1–15/01; HBG 10/01) [525]

20770 Vogt, Gregory L. *Earth* (2–4). Illus. Series: Gateway Solar System. 1996, Millbrook LB $19.90 (1-56294-602-1). 32pp. A beginning introduction to the planet, its composition, and its place in the solar system. (Rev: BL 4/15/96; SLJ 5/96) [550]

20771 Whitehouse, Patricia. *The Earth* (2–4). Illus. Series: Space Explorer. 2004, Heinemann LB $16.95 (1-4034-5150-8). 32pp. A slim overview of the Earth, discussing its composition, axis, and rotation, with fascinating photographs from space and final Earth facts. [550]

Moon

20772 Bourgeois, Paulette. *The Moon* (3–4). Illus. by Bill Slavin. Series: Starting with Space. 1997, Kids Can $12.95 (1-55074-157-8). 40pp. This introduction to the moon includes material on its features, phases, and tides, important lunar landings, and legends about the moon from around the world. (Rev: SLJ 9/97) [523.3]

20773 Branley, Franklyn M. *What the Moon Is Like* (1–3). Illus. by True Kelley. Series: Let's-Read-and-Find-Out. 2000, HarperCollins LB $15.89 (0-06-027993-1). 40pp. An updated version of this standard title that includes important new material about the moon and its composition. (Rev: BL 6/1–15/00; HBG 9/00; SLJ 7/00) [559.9]

20774 Bredeson, Carmen. *The Moon* (3–5). Illus. Series: First Books. 1998, Watts LB $21.00 (0-531-20308-5). 64pp. In this fine introduction to the moon, topics covered include its composition, lunar exploration, moon rocks, superstitions and legends concerning the moon, and the effect of the moon on the earth. (Rev: BL 5/1/98; HBG 9/98) [523.3]

20775 Cole, Michael D. *The Moon: Earth's Companion in Space* (3–7). Series: Countdown to Space. 2001, Enslow LB $18.95 (0-7660-1510-6). 48pp. Handsomely illustrated with color and black-and-white photographs, this is a good introduction to the moon, its evolution, composition, and exploration. (Rev: BL 6/1–15/01; HBG 10/01) [523.3]

20776 Fowler, Allan. *So That's How the Moon Changes Shape!* (1–2). Illus. Series: Rookie Readers. 1991, Children's Book Pr. LB $19.00 (0-516-04917-8). 32pp. The phases of the moon are introduced in minimal text and many color photographs. (Rev: BL 4/1/92) [523.3]

20777 Gardner, Robert. *Science Project Ideas About the Moon* (4–7). Illus. Series: Science Project Ideas. 1997, Enslow LB $19.95 (0-89490-844-8). 96pp. After giving basic information about the moon, this book outlines projects involving ways of observing the moon and how to make models to show its movements. (Rev: BL 12/1/97; HBG 3/98) [523.3]

20778 Gibbons, Gail. *The Moon Book* (2–4). Illus. 1997, Holiday House LB $16.95 (0-8234-1297-0). 32pp. An introductory description of the moon, its orbit and phases, its place in eclipses, and its effects of the earth's oceans. (Rev: BCCB 7–8/97; BL 5/1/97; SLJ 4/97) [523.3]

20779 Graham, Ian. *The Best Book of the Moon* (2–5). Series: The Best Book Of. 1999, Kingfisher $10.95 (0-7534-5174-3). 31pp. A fine introduction to the moon with material on its composition, exploration including the *Apollo* and recent *Prospector* missions, and lunar and solar eclipses. (Rev: HBG 9/99; SLJ 5/99) [523.3]

20780 Kerrod, Robin. *The Moon* (4–6). Series: Planet Library. 2000, Lerner LB $21.27 (0-8225-3900-4). 32pp. The moon's formation, history, orbit, and makeup are covered, plus material on the moon landing. (Rev: BL 10/15/00; HBG 3/01; SLJ 11/00) [523.3]

20781 Krupp, E. C. *The Moon and You* (3–6). Illus. by Robin R. Krupp. 1993, Macmillan LB $15.00 (0-02-751142-1). 48pp. In picture-book format, this account covers all the basic facts about the moon, including its formation, phases, and exploration. (Rev: BL 11/1/93; SLJ 2/94) [523.3]

20782 Lassieur, Allison. *The Moon* (2–4). Series: True Books. 2000, Children's Book Pr. LB $22.00 (0-516-22001-2). 48pp. A well-illustrated introduction to our moon, the myths that surround it, its composition and exploration, and the effect it has on life on earth. (Rev: BL 3/1/01) [523.3]

20783 *Our Satellite: The Moon* (3–6). Illus. Series: Window on the Universe. 1994, Barron's $12.95 (0-8120-6369-4). 32pp. In double-page spreads, features of the moon are explained, such as lunar eclipses and the appearance of the moon's far side. (Rev: BL 4/15/94; SLJ 5/94) [523.3]

20784 Rosen, Sidney. *Where Does the Moon Go?* (2–4). Illus. 1992, Carolrhoda LB $19.95 (0-87614-685-X). 40pp. In excellent photos, clever illustrations, and simple text, the moon and its phases are introduced. (Rev: SLJ 11/92) [523.3]

20785 Simon, Seymour. *The Moon* (2–4). 2003, Simon & Schuster $17.95 (0-689-83563-9). 32pp. This revised edition adds new photographs and color reproductions. (Rev: BL 10/15/03; SLJ 1/04) [559.9]

20786 Siy, Alexandra. *Footprints on the Moon* (3–5). Illus. 2001, Charlesbridge $16.95 (1-57091-408-7). 32pp. This heavily illustrated book covers human fascination with the moon throughout history and then focuses on Project Apollo and the moon landings. (Rev: BL 2/1/01; HBG 10/01; SLJ 2/01) [629.45]

20787 Tomecek, Steve. *Moon* (K–3). Illus. by Lisa Chauncy Guida. Series: Jump into Science. 2005, National Geographic LB $25.90 (0-7922-8304-X). 32pp. An entertaining introduction to the moon for young children. (Rev: BL 3/1/05) [523.3]

20788 Whitehouse, Patricia. *The Moon* (2–4). Illus. Series: Space Explorer. 2004, Heinemann LB $16.95 (1-4034-5152-4). 32pp. A slim overview of the moon, covering topics including its size, composition, climate, and different phases. (Rev: BL 7/02; HBG 10/02) [523.3]

Planets

20789 Berger, Melvin. *Discovering Jupiter: The Amazing Collision in Space* (3–6). Illus. by Tom Leonard. 1995, Scholastic paper $4.95 (0-590-48824-4). 55pp. After covering the general facts we know about Jupiter, this account tells of the Comet Shoemaker-Levy 9 and its crash into the planet. (Rev: SLJ 3/96) [523.4]

20790 Bortolotti, Dan. *Exploring Saturn* (4–8). Illus. 2003, Firefly $19.95 (1-55297-766-8); paper $9.95 (1-55297-765-X). 64pp. This highly visual volume with readable text presents facts about Saturn, explains how and when we acquired this knowledge, and looks at the Cassini-Huygens mission, scheduled to reach the planet in 2004. (Rev: BL 12/1/03; SLJ 5/04) [523.46]

20791 Branley, Franklyn M. *The Planets in Our Solar System* (K–2). Illus. by Kevin O'Malley. Series: Let's-Read-and-Find-Out. 1998, HarperCollins LB $15.89 (0-06-027770-X); paper $4.95 (0-06-445178-X). 31pp. The planets of our solar system are described — their similarities, differences, and distinctive characteristics. (Rev: SLJ 6/98) [523.4]

20792 Brimner, Larry. *Jupiter* (2–5). Series: True Books. 1999, Children's Book Pr. LB $21.00 (0-516-21153-6). 48pp. An attractive introduction to the largest planet of the solar system, what we know about it, and the space probes that have added to our knowledge. (Rev: BL 7/99; HBG 9/99; SLJ 9/99) [523.4]

20793 Brimner, Larry. *Mars* (2–4). Series: True Books. 1998, Children's Book Pr. LB $21.00 (0-516-20618-4). 48pp. This richly illustrated account reports on recent findings about the Red Planet. (Rev: BL 9/15/98; HBG 3/99) [523.4]

20794 Brimner, Larry. *Mercury* (2–4). Series: True Books. 1998, Children's Book Pr. LB $21.00 (0-516-20619-2). 48pp. A colorful introduction to Mercury, the planet closest to the sun. (Rev: BL 9/15/98; HBG 3/99) [523.4]

20795 Brimner, Larry. *Neptune* (2–5). Series: True Books. 1999, Children's Book Pr. LB $21.00 (0-516-21157-9). 48pp. An interesting overview of the distant planet Neptune, from its discovery in 1846 to the present day. (Rev: BL 7/99; HBG 9/99) [523.4]

20796 Brimner, Larry. *Pluto* (2–5). Series: True Books. 1999, Children's Book Pr. LB $21.00 (0-516-21155-2). 48pp. This attractive, well-illustrated book takes the reader on a tour of Pluto, the outermost known planet of our solar system. (Rev: BL 7/99; HBG 9/99) [523.4]

20797 Brimner, Larry. *Saturn* (2–5). Series: True Books. 1999, Children's Book Pr. LB $21.00 (0-516-21154-4). 48pp. Using recently discovered data and pictures, this is a solid introduction to Saturn, the sixth planet from the sun, which is noted for the broad flat rings circling it. (Rev: BL 7/99; HBG 9/99; SLJ 9/99) [523.4]

20798 Brimner, Larry. *Uranus* (2–5). Series: True Books. 1999, Children's Book Pr. LB $21.00 (0-516-21156-0). 48pp. An interesting, heavily illustrated account that introduces Uranus and describes recent findings about this planet, discovered in 1781, which is one of the most distant in the solar system. (Rev: BL 7/99; HBG 9/99) [523.4]

20799 Brimner, Larry. *Venus* (2–5). Illus. Series: True Books. 1998, Children's Book Pr. LB $21.00 (0-516-21158-7). 48pp. This book summarizes what we know about the planet Venus, its composition, structure, rotation patterns, and distance from the sun. (Rev: BL 12/1/98) [523.42]

20800 Cole, Michael D. *Living on Mars: Mission to the Red Planet* (4–6). Illus. Series: Countdown to Space. 1999, Enslow LB $18.95 (0-7660-1121-6). 48pp. This book covers our findings through the late 1990s from the exploration of Mars and discusses the possibility of visiting and colonizing this planet in the future. (Rev: BL 12/1/98; HBG 9/99; SLJ 4/99) [919.9]

20801 Dickinson, Terence. *Other Worlds: A Beginner's Guide to Planets and Moons* (4–8). Illus. 1995, Firefly paper $9.95 (1-895565-70-7). 64pp. An entertaining, well-illustrated introduction to the solar system, the planets, important moons, comets, brown dwarfs, and the search for evidence of other planetary systems. (Rev: BL 11/15/95; SLJ 1/96) [523.4]

20802 Fowler, Allan. *The Sun's Family of Planets* (1–2). Illus. Series: Rookie Readers. 1992, Children's Book Pr. LB $19.00 (0-516-06004-X); paper $4.95 (0-516-46004-8). 32pp. The planets are introduced in full-color photos and minimal text. This simple book is also available in an oversized "Big Book" edition. (Rev: BL 12/15/92) [523.4]

20803 Fradin, Dennis B. *The Planet Hunters: The Search for Other Worlds* (5–8). Illus. 1997, Simon & Schuster $19.95 (0-689-81323-6). This well-researched book traces the search for other worlds from the time of early civilization and the discovery of each of the planets, including the difficulty scientists had convincing the world that the Earth is also

a planet. (Rev: BL 12/1/97*; BR 3–4/98; HBG 3/98; SLJ 1/98) [523.4]

20804 Gallant, Roy A. *Planets* (2–4). Illus. Series: Kaleidoscope. 2000, Marshall Cavendish LB $15.95 (0-7614-1033-3). 48pp. With colorful illustrations, each of the planets of our solar system is introduced with a brief descriptive text. (Rev: BL 1/1–15/01; HBG 10/01) [523.4]

20805 Getz, David. *Life on Mars* (3–5). Illus. Series: Redfeather. 1997, Holt $14.95 (0-8050-3708-X). 70pp. A simple description of a trip to Mars and what the reader would find there. (Rev: BL 5/15/97; SLJ 6/97) [574]

20806 Gibbons, Gail. *The Planets* (K–3). Illus. 1993, Holiday House LB $16.95 (0-8234-1040-4). 32pp. In a well-illustrated format, this is a good introduction to the planets of our solar system. (Rev: BL 12/15/93; SLJ 10/93) [523.4]

20807 Gifford, Clive. *How to Live on Mars* (3–6). Illus. by Scoular Anderson. Series: How To. 2001, Watts LB $14.00 (0-531-14647-2); paper $4.95 (0-531-16201-X). 96pp. Experiments back up the concepts introduced in this discussion of the possibilities of traveling to and living on Mars. (Rev: SLJ 4/02) [523.4]

20808 Goldstein, Margaret J. *Uranus* (2–3). Illus. Series: Our Universe. 2003, Lerner LB $22.60 (0-8225-4654-X). 32pp. This solid introduction to Uranus examines the huge planet's physical characteristics, distance from the sun, rotation axis, and 15 moons. Also use *Saturn* and *Venus* (both 2003). (Rev: SLJ 1/04) [523.47]

20809 Harris, Nicholas. *The Incredible Journey to the Planets: Close Encounters with Our Neighbors in Space* (4–6). Illus. by Sebastian Quigley and Gary Hincks. 1999, Bedrick $18.95 (0-87226-600-1). 32pp. A tour of the planets that allows readers to see planets from different directions by using die-cut holes in the pages. (Rev: HBG 4/00; SLJ 10/99) [523]

20810 Kelch, Joseph W. *Millions of Miles to Mars: A Journey to the Red Planet* (4–6). Illus. by Connell P. Byrne. 1995, Messner $18.95 (0-671-88249-X); paper $9.95 (0-671-88250-3). 121pp. A make-believe journey to the Red Planet reveals what we know and do not know about Mars. (Rev: SLJ 9/95) [523.4]

20811 Kerrod, Robin. *Jupiter* (4–6). Illus. Series: Planet Library. 2000, Lerner $21.27 (0-8225-3907-1). 32pp. Jupiter, the largest of the planets, is presented in text and pictures with material on its formation, makeup, atmosphere, and the space probes that have gathered information about it. Two others in this series are *Mars* and *Mercury and Venus*. (Rev: BL 10/15/00; HBG 3/01) [523.45]

20812 Kerrod, Robin. *Saturn* (4–6). Series: Planet Library. 2000, Lerner LB $21.27 (0-8225-3909-8). 32pp. Breathtaking photographs and a clear text introduce Saturn, the planet of swirling clouds, bright rings, and 18 moons. (Rev: BL 10/15/00; HBG 3/01; SLJ 1/01) [523.4]

20813 Kerrod, Robin. *Uranus, Neptune, and Pluto* (4–6). Series: Planet Library. 2000, Lerner LB

$21.27 (0-8225-3908-X). 32pp. An exploration of the planets on the edge of our solar system, beginning with the ringed gas giants, Uranus and Neptune, and ending with mysterious Pluto. (Rev: BL 10/15/00; HBG 3/01; SLJ 1/01) [513.4]

20814 Landau, Elaine. *Jupiter* (5–7). Series: Watts Library. 1999, Watts LB $24.00 (0-531-20387-5). 63pp. This is an update of the fine earlier book, with material on the Ulysses and Galileo probes. (Rev: SLJ 2/00) [523.4]

20815 Landau, Elaine. *Mars* (5–7). Series: Watts Library. 1999, Watts LB $24.00 (0-531-20388-3). 63pp. This updated version of an earlier title is a fine introduction to the planet Mars with new material on the *Pathfinder* landing that launched little *Sojourner* in 1993. (Rev: SLJ 2/00) [523.4]

20816 Landau, Elaine. *Neptune* (4–6). Illus. Series: First Books. 1991, Watts LB $22.00 (0-531-20014-0). 64pp. Using information from the 1989 *Voyager II* mission, this account introduces this distant planet and its surrounding moons. (Rev: BL 6/15/91; SLJ 8/91) [523.4]

20817 Landau, Elaine. *Saturn* (4–6). Series: Watts Library. 1999, Watts LB $24.00 (0-531-20389-1). 63pp. This revision of the 1991 volume includes recent material gathered by the Hubble Space Telescope and a report on the current Cassini/Huygens probe. (Rev: SLJ 11/99) [523.4]

20818 Miller, Ron. *Jupiter* (5–8). Series: Worlds Beyond. 2002, Millbrook LB $25.90 (0-7613-2356-2). 64pp. An excellent oversize volume that explores the largest of the planets with amazing full-page color illustrations and a detailed text. Also use *Venus* (2002). (Rev: BL 8/02; HBG 3/03; SLJ 8/02) [523.4]

20819 Miller, Ron. *Mercury and Pluto* (5–8). Series: Worlds Beyond. 2003, Millbrook LB $25.90 (0-7613-2361-9). 80pp. Information on these planets and their discoveries is presented clearly, with helpful illustrations. Also use *Saturn* (2003). (Rev: BL 11/15/03; HBG 4/04; SLJ 12/03) [523.4]

20820 Miller, Ron. *Saturn* (5–8). Series: Worlds Beyond. 2003, Millbrook LB $25.90 (0-7613-2360-0). 80pp. A colorful volume that describes the discovery of the solar system and supplies details about the planet Saturn and its many rings. (Rev: BL 11/15/03; HBG 4/04; SLJ 12/03) [523.4]

20821 Miller, Ron. *The Sun* (5–8). Illus. Series: Worlds Beyond. 2002, Millbrook LB $25.90 (0-7613-2355-4). 64pp. Miller explores the nature and structure of the sun and the importance of solar energy. (Rev: BL 4/1/02; HBG 10/02; SLJ 5/02) [523.7]

20822 Miller, Ron. *Uranus and Neptune* (5–7). Illus. Series: Worlds Beyond. 2003, Twenty-First Century LB $25.90 (0-7613-2357-0). 80pp. NASA photographs and computer-generated images are used throughout this account of the discovery and exploration of these two planets and what we know about their origin, composition, and evolution. (Rev: HBG 10/03; SLJ 8/03) [523.47]

20823 Moore, Patrick. *The Planets* (K–3). Illus. Series: Starry Sky. 1995, Millbrook LB $18.90 (1-56294-624-2). 24pp. The size and makeup of the planets are discussed in this beginning astronomy book that also looks at the possibility of interplanetary travel. (Rev: SLJ 7/95) [523.4]

20824 Nicolson, Cynthia P. *The Planets* (2–5). Series: Starting with Space. 1998, Kids Can $12.95 (1-55074-512-3). Using a question-and-answer format and NASA mission photos, this concise book introduces the planets to a young audience. (Rev: BL 8/98; HBG 3/99; SLJ 10/98) [523.4]

20825 Rau, Dana Meachen. *Jupiter* (3–5). Illus. Series: Our Solar System. 2002, Compass Point LB $15.95 (0-7565-0198-9). 32pp. An appealing introduction to the planet, with large photographs. Also use *Mars, Mercury,* and *Venus* (all 2002). (Rev: BL 5/15/02; SLJ 7/02) [523.45]

20826 Ride, Sally, and Tam O'Shaughnessy. *Exploring Our Solar System* (4–8). Illus. 2003, Crown LB $21.99 (0-375-91568-0). 112pp. This enthralling look at each of the planets includes excellent images and charts. (Rev: BL 12/1/03; HB 1–2/04; HBG 4/04; SLJ 10/03) [523.2]

20827 Shepherd, Donna Walsh. *Uranus* (4–6). Illus. Series: First Books. 1994, Watts LB $22.00 (0-531-20167-8). 64pp. From its discovery in 1787 to present-day findings, this book looks at the seventh planet in our solar system. (Rev: BL 10/15/94) [523.4]

20828 Simon, Charnan. *Jupiter* (3–4). Illus. Series: Our Galaxy and Beyond. 2003, Child's World LB $27.07 (1-59296-049-9). 32pp. A quick overview of Jupiter and its many moons, with plenty of color photographs and simple, direct text. Also use *Saturn* (2003). (Rev: SLJ 1/04) [523.45]

20829 Simon, Seymour. *Destination: Jupiter.* Rev. ed. (3–5). Illus. 1998, Morrow $16.00 (0-688-15620-7). 32pp. This update of the 1985 edition includes information on the findings of the Hubble space telescope, material on the *Galileo* space probe, and basic information about the planet. (Rev: BL 4/15/98; HBG 9/98; SLJ 5/98) [523.45]

20830 Simon, Seymour. *Destination: Mars* (3–5). Illus. 2000, HarperCollins LB $15.89 (0-688-15771-8). 32pp. This new edition of the well-received 1987 book now contains pictures from the Orbiter camera, the Hubble space telescope, and the *Pathfinder* lander. (Rev: BL 5/1/00; HB 7–8/00; HBG 9/00) [523.43]

20831 Simon, Seymour. *Jupiter* (2–4). Illus. 1988, Morrow paper $5.95 (0-688-08403-6). 32pp. A detailed look at Jupiter, enhanced by photographs taken mostly from unmanned spacecraft. (Rev: BCCB 12/85; BL 9/15/85; SLJ 10/85)

20832 Simon, Seymour. *Mars* (2–5). Illus. 1987, Morrow paper $6.95 (0-688-09928-9). 32pp. Lucid text and spectacular photos highlight this detailed study of the Red Planet. (Rev: BL 10/15/87; HB 11–12/87; SLJ 12/87)

20833 Simon, Seymour. *Neptune* (4–8). Illus. 1991, Morrow $17.89 (0-688-09632-8). 32pp. The voyage of *Voyager II* as it swept past Neptune provided scientists with more information on this planet than they had ever had. (Rev: BCCB 4/91; BL 2/15/91; HB 5–6/91; SLJ 4/91) [523.4]

20834 Simon, Seymour. *Planets Around the Sun* (1–3). Series: See More Readers. 2002, North-South $13.95 (1-58717-145-7); paper $3.95 (1-58717-146-5). 32pp. The plants and the solar system are introduced in this beginning reader. (Rev: BL 7/02; HBG 10/02; SLJ 6/02) [523.2]

20835 Simon, Seymour. *Saturn* (2–4). Illus. 1985, Morrow $15.93 (0-688-05799-3); paper $6.95 (0-688-08404-4). 32pp. Lots of information about Saturn and its rings, enhanced with color photographs. (Rev: BL 9/15/85; HB 1–2/86; SLJ 10/85)

20836 Simon, Seymour. *Uranus* (2–5). Illus. 1987, Morrow paper $6.95 (0-688-09929-7). 32pp. Descriptions and photos of its five moons highlight this look at Uranus, which was not recognized as a planet until 1781. (Rev: BL 10/15/87; HB 11–12/87; SLJ 12/87)

20837 Skurzynski, Gloria. *Discover Mars* (4–6). 1998, National Geographic $17.95 (0-7922-7099-1). 44pp. An overview of what we know about Mars, a rundown on space probes in the area, and plenty of illustrations — some in 3–D that require special glasses, which are provided. (Rev: SLJ 11/98) [523.4]

20838 Stefoff, Rebecca. *Pluto* (3–5). Illus. Series: Blastoff. 2003, Marshall Cavendish LB $18.95 (0-7614-1404-5). 64pp. A fascinating, well-illustrated account of the discovery of the planet Pluto and the continuing scientific debate about whether it is a true planet or not. (Rev: BL 4/1/03; HBG 3/03) [523.48]

20839 Stille, Darlene R. *Mars* (3–4). Illus. Series: Our Galaxy and Beyond. 2003, Child's World LB $27.07 (1-59296-050-2). 32pp. A quick overview of Mars, with plenty of color photographs and simple, direct text. (Rev: SLJ 1/04) [523.43]

20840 Stone, Tanya Lee. *Mercury* (3–5). Illus. Series: Blastoff. 2003, Marshall Cavendish LB $18.95 (0-7614-1403-7). 64pp. Stone explains the history of our knowledge of Mercury and what we may learn from new expeditions to the planet; a glossary, bibliography, and list of Web sites follow the text. (Rev: BL 4/1/03; HBG 3/03) [523.41]

20841 Vogt, Gregory L. *Jupiter* (3–4). Series: Galaxy. 2000, Capstone LB $15.93 (0-7368-0512-5). 24pp. This book and the others listed cover basic facts and material on atmospheres, rings, physical features, and moons. Others are *Neptune*, *Pluto*, and *Uranus* (all 2000). (Rev: HBG 9/00; SLJ 9/00) [523.4]

20842 Vogt, Gregory L. *Mars* (3–6). Illus. Series: Gateway Solar System. 1994, Millbrook LB $19.90 (1-56294-392-8). 31pp. Color and black-and-white photos and drawings highlight this introduction to Mars and its geography. Also use *Pluto* (1994). (Rev: BL 7/94; SLJ 5/94) [523.4]

20843 Vogt, Gregory L. *Mercury* (3–6). Illus. Series: Gateway Solar System. 1994, Millbrook LB $19.90 (1-56294-390-1). 32pp. A useful introduction to the planet Mercury that includes material on Project

Mariner and its findings. (Rev: BL 7/94; SLJ 5/94) [523.4]

20844 Vogt, Gregory L. *Pluto* (2–4). Illus. Series: Gateway Solar System. 1994, Millbrook LB $19.90 (1-56294-393-6). 32pp. This introduction to Pluto describes its origins plus a history of what we know about it and things we should find out in the future. Also use *Venus* (1994). (Rev: BL 7/94; SLJ 5/94) [523.1]

20845 Vogt, Gregory L. *Saturn* (3–5). Illus. Series: Gateway Solar System. 1993, Millbrook LB $19.90 (1-56294-332-4). 32pp. This introduction to Saturn includes material on its cloud layers, magnetic field, and thousands of rings. (Rev: SLJ 11/93) [523.2]

20846 Vogt, Gregory L. *Uranus* (3–5). Illus. Series: Gateway Solar System. 1993, Millbrook LB $19.90 (1-56294-330-8). 32pp. Sharp, full-color illustrations and a brief text introduce the salient features of Uranus, including its moons, rings, and atmosphere. (Rev: SLJ 11/93) [523.2]

Solar System

20847 Aronson, Billy. *Meteors: The Truth Behind Shooting Stars* (4–6). Illus. 1996, Watts LB $22.50 (0-531-20242-9). 63pp. A useful manual that explains the differences between meteors, meteorites, and meteoroids, with general information on their composition and when they can be seen. (Rev: BL 2/15/97; SLJ 3/97) [523.5]

20848 Asimov, Isaac. *How Did We Find Out About Comets?* (5–7). Illus. 1975, Walker LB $10.85 (0-8027-6204-2). 64pp. An introduction to comets and our knowledge and attitudes about them since ancient times. [523.6]

20849 Bonar, Samantha. *Asteroids* (4–6). Series: Watts Library. 1999, Watts LB $24.00 (0-531-20367-0). 63pp. This book describes the various kinds of rocky debris that are found in the solar system and the possible problems they can cause. (Rev: SLJ 11/99) [523]

20850 Bonar, Samantha. *Comets* (3–5). Series: First Books. 1998, Watts LB $22.00 (0-531-20301-8). 63pp. A history of what we know about comets from the ancient Greeks to Halley, with material on their composition, frequency, and where and how they can be seen. (Rev: HBG 9/98; SLJ 6/98) [523.5]

20851 Branley, Franklyn M. *The Sun and the Solar System* (4–6). Illus. Series: Secrets of Space. 1996, Twenty-First Century LB $20.40 (0-8050-4475-2). 80pp. Traces the origin of the solar system and the place of the earth and its moon within it. (Rev: BL 12/15/96; SLJ 1/97) [523.2]

20852 Cole, Joanna. *The Magic School Bus Lost in the Solar System* (3–5). Illus. by Bruce Degen. 1990, Scholastic $15.95 (0-590-41428-3). 40pp. Basic facts about the cosmos are revealed in this fantasy. (Rev: BCCB 10/90; BL 11/15/90; HB 1–2/91; SLJ 8/90*) [523.4]

20853 Gallan, Roy. *Comets, Asteroids, and Meteorites* (2–4). Series: Kaleidoscope. 2000, Marshall

Cavendish LB $15.95 (0-7614-1034-1). 48pp. An up-to-date account that combines good visuals with an exciting text in this examination of these visitors from space. (Rev: BL 1/1–15/01; HBG 10/01) [523]

20854 Goldsmith, Mike. *Solar System* (K–3). Series: Kingfisher Young Knowledge. 2004, Kingfisher $8.95 (0-7534-5773-3). 47pp. Using two-page chapters with large text and eye-catching photographs, planets, asteroids, comets, and meteoroids are introduced. (Rev: SLJ 4/05) [523.4]

20855 Graun, Ken. *Our Earth and the Solar System* (4–6). Illus. 2001, Ken Pr. $15.95 (1-928771-02-5). 36pp. A large-format, interesting guide to the solar system that also looks at the equipment we use to look at these bodies. (Rev: BL 5/1/01; SLJ 6/01) [523.2]

20856 Hansen, Rosanna, and Robert A. Bell. *My First Book About Space* (3–6). Illus. 1985, Simon & Schuster $13.00 (0-671-60262-4). The solar system is explained, including each planet, discussed in terms of appearance, atmosphere, orbit, and revolutions. (Rev: BCCB 7–8/86; BL 12/1/85; SLJ 2/86)

20857 Jenkins, Alvin. *Next Stop Neptune: Experiencing the Solar System* (2–5). Illus. by Steve Jenkins. 2004, Houghton Mifflin $16.00 (0-618-41603-X). 40pp. Colorful collage illustrations subsitute for photographs in this well-written introduction to the solar system. (Rev: BL 10/15/04; SLJ 10/04) [523.2]

20858 Kerrod, Robin. *Asteroids, Comets, and Meteors* (4–6). Series: Planet Library. 2000, Lerner LB $21.27 (0-8225-3905-5). 32pp. This book explores the smallest members of the solar system and tells how they were formed, how they shaped the surface of the planets and moons, and how they sometimes light up our sky. (Rev: BL 10/15/00; HBG 3/01) [523.4]

20859 Kerrod, Robin. *The Solar System* (4–6). Illus. Series: Planet Library. 2000, Lerner $21.27 (0-8225-3903-9). 32pp. A discussion on the formation of the sun, the planets, their moons, and the asteroid belt is followed by additional coverage of topics such as orbiting stars, space exploration, and the search for extraterrestrial life. (Rev: BL 10/15/00; HBG 3/01; SLJ 11/00) [523.3]

20860 Koppes, Steven N. *Killer Rocks from Outer Space: Asteroids, Comets, and Meteorites* (5–8). Series: Discovery! 2003, Lerner LB $26.60 (0-8225-2861-4). 112pp. An examination of what might happen if a large asteroid, meteorite, or comet collided with Earth, based in part on evidence of past collisions. (Rev: BL 1/1–15/04; HBG 4/04; SLJ 3/04) [523.5]

20861 Leedy, Loreen. *Postcards from Pluto: A Tour of the Solar System* (1–3). Illus. 1993, Holiday House LB $16.95 (0-8234-1000-5). 32pp. A group of children are introduced to the solar system via a spaceship tour conducted by a robot, Dr. Quasar. (Rev: BL 10/15/93; SLJ 10/93) [523.2]

20862 Marsh, Carole. *Asteroids, Comets, and Meteors* (4–6). Illus. Series: Secrets of Space. 1996, Twenty-First Century LB $20.40 (0-8050-4473-6). 64pp. The history of our knowledge of these bodies

from outer space is traced, with descriptions of the nature of each. (Rev: BL 12/15/96; SLJ 1/97) [523.4]

20863 Moore, Patrick. *The Sun and Moon* (K–3). Illus. Series: Starry Sky. 1995, Millbrook LB $18.90 (1-56294-622-6). 24pp. A description of the sun and moon is given, with an explanation of their movements and eclipses. (Rev: SLJ 7/95) [523]

20864 Peddicord, Jane Ann. *Night Wonders* (2–4). Illus. 2005, Charlesbridge paper $6.95 (1-57091-878-3). 32pp. Eye-catching full-color images of the moon, sun, stars, and planets are paired with appealing verse and brief descriptive narrative. (Rev: SLJ 4/05) [523]

20865 Poynter, Margaret. *Killer Asteroids* (3–6). Illus. Series: Weird and Wacky Science. 1996, Enslow LB $18.95 (0-89490-616-X). 48pp. Violent clashes involving asteroids and the earth are described, along with coverage of the recent encounter of a comet with Jupiter. (Rev: SLJ 5/96) [551.3]

20866 Rau, Dana Meachen. *The Solar System* (2–3). 2000, Compass Point LB $14.95 (0-7565-0036-2). 32pp. After discussing the sun, the author conducts a quick tour of the solar system including meteors, comets, and moons. (Rev: SLJ 2/01) [523.4]

20867 Rosen, Sidney. *Can You Hitch a Ride on a Comet?* (1–3). Illus. by Dean Lindberg. Series: A Question of Science. 1993, Carolrhoda LB $19.95 (0-87614-773-2). 40pp. Using a question-and-answer format, all sorts of information is given about comets, including their formation, discovery, and tracking. (Rev: BL 10/15/93) [525.6]

20868 Simon, Seymour. *Comets, Meteors, and Asteroids* (3–5). Illus. 1994, Morrow LB $14.93 (0-688-12710-X). 32pp. These three space bodies are described, with material on their composition and differences. (Rev: BL 9/15/94; SLJ 8/94) [523.6]

20869 Simon, Seymour. *Our Solar System* (2–6). Illus. 1992, Morrow $19.93 (0-688-09993-9). 72pp. A quick tour of the solar system, with many of NASA's striking photos. (Rev: BL 10/15/92; HB 11–12/92; SLJ 10/92) [523.2]

20870 Sipiera, Paul P. *Comets and Meteor Showers* (2–4). Illus. Series: True Books. 1997, Children's Book Pr. LB $22.00 (0-516-20330-4). 48pp. Large print and clear diagrams highlight this description of comets and the way they have been regarded through history. (Rev: BL 9/15/97) [523.6]

20871 Sipiera, Paul P. *The Solar System* (2–4). Illus. Series: True Books. 1997, Children's Book Pr. $22.00 (0-516-20339-8). 48pp. A brief informative introduction to the solar system, with excellent graphics and a large-print text. (Rev: BL 9/15/97) [523.2]

20872 Theodorou, Rod. *Across the Solar System* (2–4). Series: Amazing Journeys. 2000, Heinemann LB $15.95 (1-57572-486-3). 32pp. In this journey into outer space there are double-page spreads with information on each planet including distance from the sun, size, and length of a day and year. (Rev: HBG 3/01; SLJ 7/00) [523.4]

20873 VanCleave, Janice. *Janice VanCleave's Solar System: Mind-Boggling Experiments You Can Turn into Science Fair Projects* (4–6). Illus. by Laurel Aiello. Series: Spectacular Science Projects. 2000, Wiley paper $10.95 (0-471-32204-0). 90pp. Twenty interesting experiments involving the solar system are outlined with material on how to turn them into science projects. (Rev: SLJ 6/00) [523.4]

20874 Vogt, Gregory L. *Asteroids, Comets, and Meteors* (2–4). Illus. Series: Gateway Solar System. 1996, Millbrook LB $19.90 (1-56294-601-3). 32pp. A beginning introduction to these celestial bodies and their characteristics. (Rev: BL 4/15/96; SLJ 5/96) [523.6]

20875 Whitehouse, Patricia. *The Planets* (2–4). Illus. Series: Space Explorer. 2004, Heinemann LB $16.95 (1-4034-5153-2). 32pp. A slim survey of the solar system and the individual planets, defining what makes a planet and ending with a listing of quick facts.

20876 Wilsdon, Christina. *The Solar System: An A–Z Guide* (4–7). 2000, Watts LB $32.00 (0-531-11710-3). 96pp. An alphabetically arranged book that covers many aspect of the solar system including planets, space probes and missions, famous personalities, and such phenomena as greenhouse effect and solar wind. (Rev: SLJ 7/00) [523.4]

Stars

20877 Asimov, Issac. *The Life and Death of Stars* (5–8). Illus. Series: Isaac Asimov's 21st Century Library of the Universe. 2005, Gareth Stevens LB $18.50 (0-8368-3967-6). 32pp. A revised, well-illustrated edition of a previously published book, this discusses the birth of stars, profiles different types of stars, and looks at the future of our Sun. Also in this series: *Black Holes, Pulsars, and Quasars*, *The Milky Way and Other Galaxies*, *Our Planetary System*, and *Comets and Meteors* (all 2005).

20878 Bendick, Jeanne. *The Stars: Lights in the Night Sky* (2–4). Illus. by Chris Forsey. Series: Early Bird Astronomy. 1991, Millbrook LB $19.90 (1-878841-00-9). 32pp. Ideas and theories about stars and their formation are presented in a clear and simple text and with many diagrams. (Rev: BL 9/1/91; SLJ 8/91) [523.8]

20879 Berger, Melvin, and Gilda Berger. *Where Are the Stars During the Day? A Book About Stars* (3–5). Illus. by Blanche Sims. Series: Discovery Readers. 1993, Ideals paper $4.50 (0-8249-8607-5). 48pp. An easy-to-read book that introduces the stars, sun, and constellations. (Rev: BCCB 4/93; SLJ 5/93) [523]

20880 Branley, Franklyn M. *The Big Dipper* (K–2). Illus. by Ed Emberley. 1991, HarperCollins paper $4.95 (0-06-445100-3). 32pp. An introduction to the composition, mythology, and location of the Big and Little Dippers.

20881 Branley, Franklyn M. *The Sky Is Full of Stars* (2–4). Illus. by Felicia Bond. 1981, HarperCollins paper $4.95 (0-06-445002-3). 40pp. A simple introduction to constellations and star watching.

20882 Branley, Franklyn M. *Star Guide* (4–6). Illus. by Ellen Eagle. 1997, Macmillan paper $9.10 (0-028-62019-4). 64pp. An exploration of what stars are made of, how they change, and how they are formed. (Rev: BL 8/87; SLJ 9/87)

20883 Croswell, Ken. *See the Stars* (4–8). Illus. 2000, Boyds Mills $16.95 (1-56397-757-5). 32pp. Twelve constellations are introduced in double-page spreads, with material on where and when to look for them. (Rev: BL 11/1/00; HBG 3/01; SLJ 10/00) [523]

20884 Gallan, Roy. *Stars* (2–4). Series: Kaleidoscope. 2000, Marshall Cavendish LB $15.95 (0-7614-1036-8). 48pp. This book introduces stars, how they are born and die, and their constellations. (Rev: BL 1/1–15/01; HBG 10/01) [523]

20885 Gibbons, Gail. *Stargazers* (1–3). Illus. 1992, Holiday House LB $16.95 (0-8234-0983-X). 32pp. With full-color artwork, the author explains what stars are and how we look at them. (Rev: BCCB 1/93; BL 10/15/92; SLJ 10/92) [520]

20886 Gustafson, John. *Stars, Clusters and Galaxies* (5–8). Illus. Series: Young Stargazer's Guide to the Galaxy. 1993, Simon & Schuster LB $18.95 (0-671-72536-X); paper $6.95 (0-671-72537-8). 64pp. Introduces stars, binary stars, star clusters, nebulae, and galaxies, and provides tips for viewing the night sky through binoculars and telescopes. (Rev: BL 7/93; SLJ 6/93) [523.8]

20887 Mitton, Jacqueline. *Once upon a Starry Night: A Book of Constellations* (K–4). Illus. by Christina Balit. 2004, National Geographic $16.95 (0-7922-6332-4). 26pp. Ten brief, richly illustrated tales about the constellations are drawn from the mythology of ancient Greece and Rome. (Rev: BL 1/1–15/04; SLJ 1/04) [523.8]

20888 Mitton, Jacqueline. *Zoo in the Sky: A Book of Animal Constellations* (K–3). Illus. by Christina Balit. 1998, National Geographic $17.95 (0-7922-7069-X). 32pp. This attractive introduction to the animal constellations uses sparkling silver stars to outline each of them in the night sky. (Rev: BL 11/1/98; HBG 3/99; SLJ 12/98) [523.8]

20889 Moore, Patrick. *The Stars* (K–3). Illus. Series: Starry Sky. 1995, Millbrook LB $18.90 (1-56294-623-4). 24pp. A beginning astronomy book that describes the birth and death of stars and the composition of the Milky Way and other galaxies. (Rev: SLJ 7/95) [523.8]

20890 Nicolson, Cynthia P. *The Stars* (4–6). 1998, Kids Can $12.95 (1-55074-524-7). The stars are introduced in a question-and-answer format with good photographs and a glossary of terms. (Rev: BL 8/98; HBG 3/99; SLJ 10/98) [523.8]

20891 Pearce, Q. L. *The Stargazer's Guide to the Galaxy* (4–8). Illus. by Mary Ann Fraser. 1991, Tor paper $6.99 (0-812-59423-1). 60pp. In this introduction to star gazing in the Northern Hemisphere, material covered includes a look at the night sky in each of the four seasons. (Rev: SLJ 12/91) [523]

20892 Rey, H. A. *Find the Constellations* (5–7). Illus. 1976, Houghton Mifflin LB $20.00 (0-395-24509-5); paper $9.95 (0-395-24418-8). 80pp. Through clear text and illustrations, the reader is helped to recognize stars and constellations in the northern United States. Also use *The Stars: A New Way to See Them* (1973).

20893 Rosen, Sidney. *Where's the Big Dipper?* (2–4). Illus. by Dean Lindberg. Series: A Question of Science. 1996, Carolrhoda $14.95 (0-87614-883-6). 40pp. In a question-and-answer format, this book supplies a simple introduction to deep space, with a focus on the Big Dipper. (Rev: SLJ 4/96) [523]

20894 Simon, Seymour. *Galaxies* (2–5). Illus. 1988, Morrow paper $6.95 (0-688-10992-6). 32pp. Engrossing photographs highlight this look at galaxies. (Rev: BCCB 4/88; BL 3/1/88; SLJ 5/88)

20895 Simon, Seymour. *The Stars* (3–5). Illus. 1986, Morrow $16.93 (0-688-05856-6); paper $6.95 (0-688-09237-3). 32pp. Large photos and diagrams highlight the story of the life cycles of stars, giving a sense of their great numbers and relationship to earth. (Rev: BCCB 10/86; BL 9/1/86; SLJ 12/86)

20896 Sipiera, Diane M., and Paul P. Sipiera. *Constellations* (2–4). Series: True Books. 1997, Children's Book Pr. LB $22.00 (0-516-20331-2). 48pp. A simple, basic introduction to constellations in a highly accessible format. Also use *Black Holes, Galaxies,* and *Stars* (all 1997). (Rev: BL 9/15/97) [523]

20897 Tomecek, Steve. *Stars* (K–3). Illus. by Sachiko Yoshikawa. 2003, National Geographic $16.95 (0-7922-6955-1). 32pp. A boy introduces young readers to the stars in this book that includes a star activity. (Rev: BL 2/1/03; HBG 10/03; SLJ 5/03) [523.8]

20898 Whitehouse, Patricia. *The Stars* (2–4). Illus. Series: Space Explorer. 2004, Heinemann LB $16.95 (1-4034-5156-7). 32pp. A slim overview of stars, looking at the Milky Way and other galaxies, the ways in which stars are born and grow, and the changing night sky. [523.8]

Sun and the Seasons

20899 Bourgeois, Paulette. *The Sun* (2–5). Illus. Series: Starting with Space. 1997, Kids Can $12.95 (1-55074-158-6). 40pp. As well as providing information about the sun, stars, and the seasons, this work contains folktales and projects. (Rev: BL 9/1/97; SLJ 9/97) [523.7]

20900 Branley, Franklyn M. *The Sun: Our Nearest Star* (1–3). Illus. by Don Madden. 1988, HarperCollins LB $14.89 (0-690-04678-2). 32pp. An easily read book about the sun and its importance in our lives. Update of 1962 edition.

20901 Branley, Franklyn M. *Sunshine Makes the Seasons* (3–4). Illus. by Giulio Maestro. 1988, HarperCollins paper $4.95 (0-06-445019-8). 32pp. A very simple account that explains the seasons by exploring the relationship of the sun to the earth and its orbit. Update of 1974 edition.

20902 Burton, Jane, and Kim Taylor. *The Nature and Science of Autumn* (3–6). Series: Exploring the Science of Nature. 1999, Gareth Stevens LB $15.95 (0-8368-2190-4). 32pp. This book explains the causes of autumn, its weather, and the animal and plant changes that occur during this season. A special activities section is included. Also use *The Nature and Science of Spring, The Nature and Science of Summer,* and *The Nature and Science of Winter* (all 1999). (Rev: BL 12/15/99; HBG 9/00) [525]

20903 Dolan, Graham. *The Greenwich Guide to the Seasons* (3–6). Illus. Series: Greenwich Guide To. 2001, Heinemann LB $22.79 (1-58810-044-8). 32pp. Color photographs and clear text introduce the seasons, with a glossary and other aids. (Rev: BL 10/15/01) [525]

20904 Fowler, Allan. *How Do You Know It's Fall?* (1–2). Illus. Series: Rookie Readers. 1992, Children's Book Pr. LB $19.00 (0-516-04922-4). 32pp. For beginning readers, the season of autumn is introduced in many color photos and brief text. (Rev: BL 6/15/92) [508]

20905 Fowler, Allan. *How Do You Know It's Summer?* (1–2). Illus. Series: Rookie Readers. 1992, Children's Book Pr. LB $19.00 (0-516-04923-2). 32pp. Summer and its characteristics are introduced in many color illustrations and minimal text. (Rev: BL 6/15/92) [508]

20906 Fowler, Allan. *The Sun Is Always Shining Somewhere* (1–2). Illus. Series: Rookie Readers. 1991, Children's Book Pr. LB $19.00 (0-516-04906-2). 32pp. This simple introduction to astronomy tells about the sun and the earth's rotation around it. (Rev: BL 8/91) [523.7]

20907 Glaser, Linda. *It's Fall!* (2–4). Illus. by Susan Swan. 2001, Millbrook $21.90 (0-7613-1758-9). 32pp. A young boy observes the changes that occur in nature in the fall, with suggested nature activities for the season. (Rev: BL 9/15/01; HBG 3/02; SLJ 10/01)

20908 Jackson, Ellen. *The Summer Solstice* (2–4). Illus. 2001, Millbrook LB $21.90 (0-7613-1623-X). 32pp. An attractive resource that explains the summer solstice, why it is the longest day of the year, and its cultural significance. (Rev: BL 4/1/01; HBG 10/01; SLJ 5/01) [394.263]

20909 Jackson, Ellen. *The Winter Solstice* (2–4). Illus. 1994, Millbrook LB $23.40 (1-56294-400-2). 32pp. The customs and beliefs surrounding the winter solstice are explored in many cultures, e.g., the ancient Britons, Romans, and Peruvians. (Rev: BL 2/15/94; SLJ 4/94) [394.2]

20910 Kerrod, Robin. *The Sun* (4–6). Series: Planet Library. 2000, Lerner LB $21.27 (0-8225-3901-2). 32pp. This work explains how the sun was formed, its role in the solar system, in the galaxy, and beyond, and what the future holds. (Rev: BL 10/15/00; HBG 3/01; SLJ 1/01) [523.7]

20911 Lassieur, Allison. *The Sun* (2–4). Series: True Books. 2000, Children's Book Pr. LB $22.00 (0-516-22002-0). 48pp. This book explains the functions of the sun, its composition, and its importance in our lives. (Rev: BL 10/15/00) [523.7]

20912 Markle, Sandra. *Exploring Winter* (3–6). Illus. by author. 1984, Avon paper $2.99 (0-380-71321-7). 160pp. Science and recreation are mixed in this book about winter and activities that are associated with it.

20913 Meyer, Mary L. *Spring* (2–3). Series: Seasons. 2002, Smart Apple LB $21.35 (1-58340-143-1). 24pp. The weather, animals, plants, and activities of spring are presented in concise text with attractive full-color photographs. Also use *Fall* (2002). (Rev: HBG 10/03; SLJ 2/03)

20914 Pfeffer, Wendy. *The Shortest Day: Celebrating the Winter Solstice* (K–4). Illus. by Jesse Reisch. 2003, Dutton $17.99 (0-525-46968-0). History and astronomy are combined in this easy-to-understand overview of the winter landmark. (Rev: HBG 4/04; SLJ 9/03) [394.261]

20915 Pipe, Jim. *The Sun* (3–5). Illus. Series: Earthwise. 2004, Stargazer Books LB $18.95 (1-932799-46-X). 32pp. An excellent introduction to the sun and its energy, this attractively illustrated volume supplements its facts and figures with suggested activities. (Rev: BL 10/15/04) [523.7]

20916 Rockwell, Anne. *Four Seasons Make a Year* (K–2). Illus. by Megan Halsey. 2004, Walker $15.95 (0-8027-8883-1). 32pp. A young girl on a farm guides readers through the seasons, following the progress of a sunflower she planted in spring. (Rev: BL 2/15/04; SLJ 4/04) [508]

20917 Simon, Seymour. *Spring Across America* (3–5). Illus. 1996, Hyperion LB $16.49 (0-7868-2056-X). 32pp. A book about spring as it develops in various sections of our country. A sequel to *Autumn Across America* (1993) and *Winter Across America* (1994). (Rev: BL 3/1/96; SLJ 4/96) [508.73]

20918 Simon, Seymour. *The Sun* (3–5). Illus. 1986, Morrow paper $5.95 (0-688-09236-5). 32pp. A look at the structure and atmosphere of this "middle-size" star. (Rev: BCCB 10/86; BL 9/1/86; SLJ 12/86)

20919 Vogt, Gregory L. *The Sun* (2–4). Illus. Series: Gateway Solar System. 1996, Millbrook LB $19.90 (1-56294-600-5). 32pp. An introduction to the star of our solar system and its life-sustaining force. (Rev: BL 4/15/96; SLJ 7/96) [523.7]

20920 Whitehouse, Patricia. *The Sun* (2–4). Illus. Series: Space Explorer. 2004, Heinemann LB $16.95 (1-4034-5157-5). 32pp. A slim overview of the sun and its composition, size, and temperature, with material on solar flares, eclipses, and solar wind. [523.7]

Biological Sciences

General

20921 Arnold, Katya. *Let's Find It! My First Nature Guide* (PS–1). Illus. 2002, Holiday House $16.95 (0-8234-1539-2). 32pp. Young readers search for plants and animals in painted scenes of habitats in this colorful introduction to nature. (Rev: BL 8/02; HBG 3/03; SLJ 10/02) [570]

20922 Batten, Mary. *Aliens from Earth: When Animals and Plants Invade Other Ecosystems* (3–5). Illus. by Beverly J. Doyle. 2003, Peachtree $15.95 (1-56145-236-X). 32pp. A narrative overview of the results of animal and plant migrations to new home ecosystems, with full-page illustrations. (Rev: BL 3/1/03; HBG 10/03; SLJ 5/03) [577]

20923 Biesiot, Elizabeth. *Natural Treasures Field Guide for Kids* (3–6). Illus. 1996, Roberts Rinehart paper $12.95 (1-57098-082-9). 64pp. A paperback that explains the lives of wild animals by examining such evidence as paw prints, nests, and night sounds. (Rev: BL 9/1/96; SLJ 7/96) [591]

20924 Bottone, Frank G., Jr. *The Science of Life: Projects and Principles for Beginning Biologists* (5–8). Illus. 2001, Chicago Review paper $14.95 (1-55652-382-3). 126pp. Twenty-five projects introduce readers to the basics of biology and the rigors of scientific research. (Rev: SLJ 11/01) [570.78]

20925 Brimner, Larry. *Unusual Friendships: Symbiosis in the Animal World* (4–6). Illus. 1993, Watts LB $22.50 (0-531-20106-6). 64pp. This book presents the various plant and animal relationships in nature in which the host, the guest, or both benefit. (Rev: BL 8/93) [591]

20926 Burnie, David. *How Nature Works* (3–8). Illus. 1991, Reader's Digest $24.00 (0-89577-391-0). 190pp. Well-organized science topics give young readers solid explanations at their fingertips. (Rev: BL 11/15/91*; SLJ 12/91*) [508]

20927 Burton, Jane, and Kim Taylor. *The Nature and Science of Survival* (3–6). Series: Exploring the Science of Nature. 2001, Gareth Stevens LB $21.27

(0-8368-2211-0). 32pp. This book, which contains a projects and activities section, shows how various animals and plants adapt and survive. (Rev: BL 3/15/01; HBG 10/01) [574]

20928 *DK Nature Encyclopedia* (5–8). 1998, DK paper $29.99 (0-7894-3411-3). A browsable reference book that covers topics including classification of living things, ecology, the origins and evolution of life, specific animal and plant groups, and the inner workings of plants and animals, all in a series of beautifully illustrated double-page spreads. (Rev: BL 12/1/98; SLJ 2/99) [574]

20929 Doris, Ellen. *Woods, Ponds, and Fields* (4–7). Illus. Series: Real Kids Real Science. 1994, Thames & Hudson $16.95 (0-500-19006-2). 64pp. A book that gives background essays as well as step-by-step directions for nature study projects in all seasons. (Rev: BL 9/1/94) [508]

20930 Emory, Jerry. *Dirty, Rotten, Dead? A Worm's-eye View of Death, Decomposition . . . and Life* (5–8). Illus. 1996, Harcourt paper $15.00 (0-15-200695-8). Along with a number of experiments and ecological projects, this book discusses death and recycling in nature, including such topics as the parts of the human body that become waste (e.g. hair, nails, skin), digestion and human excretion, processing of sewage, water pollution, diseases of the immune system, and contemporary mortician practices. (Rev: SLJ 8/96) [628.4]

20931 Gallant, Roy A. *The Wonders of Biodiversity* (5–8). Illus. Series: The Story of Science. 2002, Benchmark $19.95 (0-7614-1427-4). 80pp. Gallant discusses the importance of biodiversity, the plight of species that are affected by loss of habitat and other environmental factors, and species interdependence. (Rev: HBG 3/03; SLJ 2/03) [578]

20932 Gifford, Clive, and Jerry Cadle. *The Kingfisher Young People's Book of Living Worlds* (5–7). Illus. Series: Kingfisher Young People's Book Of. 2002, Kingfisher $21.95 (0-7534-5390-8). 80pp. Habitats and ecosystems are covered in an attractive, fact-filled format that looks at man's impact on nature. (Rev: HBG 3/03; SLJ 12/02) [577]

20933 Goodman, Susan E. *Nature Did It First!* (PS–2). Illus. 2003, Millbrook LB $21.90 (0-7613-2413-5). 24pp. This attractive picture book teaches younger children about everyday products and processes that have their roots in nature. (Rev: BL 5/1/03; HBG 10/03) [508]

20934 Green, Jen. *In a Backyard* (2–5). Illus. Series: Small World. 2002, Crabtree LB $15.96 (0-7787-0141-7); paper $8.06 (0-7787-0155-7). 32pp. This book for younger readers takes a close look at the creatures that might be found in a backyard, and how plant and animal life coexist there. (Rev: BL 10/15/02) [591.75]

20935 Hoff, Mary, and Mary M. Rodgers. *Life on Land* (4–7). Illus. Series: Our Endangered Planet. 1992, Lerner LB $27.15 (0-8225-2507-0). 72pp. This account covers such topics as the interdependence of all living things, pollution, and necessary food sources. (Rev: BL 1/15/93; SLJ 2/93) [333]

20936 Jones, Jennifer Berry. *Who Lives in the Snow?* (PS–3). Illus. by Consie Powell. 2001, Court Wayne $15.95 (1-57098-287-2). 32pp. Cutaway illustrations give young readers a glimpse below the surface of a snowy meadow to see what happens to plants, insects, and animals during winter. (Rev: BL 11/15/01) [591.4]

20937 Kalman, Bobbie. *Forest Food Chains* (2–4). Illus. Series: Food Chains. 2004, Crabtree LB $16.95 (0-7787-1943-X); paper $6.26 (0-7787-1989-8). 32pp. All about the dynamics of food chains and food webs in the forest. (Rev: BL 3/15/05) [577.3]

20938 Kalman, Bobbie, and Jacqueline Langille. *What Are Food Chains and Webs?* (3–5). Series: Science of Living Things. 1998, Crabtree LB $14.37 (0-86505-876-8); paper $5.36 (0-86505-888-1). 32pp. This book uses clear photographs, illustrations, charts, and short chapters to describe food chains and explain their various levels and types. A game is included to enhance the learning process. (Rev: SLJ 11/98) [574.5]

20939 Kalman, Bobbie, and Jacqueline Langille. *What Is a Life Cycle?* (3–5). Series: Science of Living Things. 1998, Crabtree LB $14.37 (0-86505-874-1); paper $5.36 (0-86505-886-5). 32pp. Using many visuals and a concise text, this book traces life cycles from birth to adulthood of a number of plants and animals, including humans. (Rev: SLJ 11/98) [508]

20940 Knight, Tim. *Dramatic Displays* (3–5). Series: Amazing Nature. 2003, Heinemann LB $24.22 (1-4034-0721-5). 32pp. An attractive look at nature's use of camouflage, mimicry, and brilliant color displays, more suitable for browsers than for report writers. Also use *Ferocious Fighters* and *Fantastic Feeders*(2003). (Rev: HBG 10/03; SLJ 7/03) [591.4]

20941 Knight, Tim. *Super Survivors* (3–5). Series: Amazing Nature. 2003, Heinemann LB $24.22 (1-4034-0723-1). 32pp. How plants and animals adapt to their surroundings in order to survive and thrive

is the subject of this photo-illustrated volume. Also in this series is *Incredible Life Cycles* (2003), which looks at the more unusual features of the life cycles of plants and animals. (Rev: HBG 4/04; SLJ 3/04) [578.4]

20942 Maynard, Caitlin, and Thane Maynard. *Rain Forests and Reefs: A Kid's-Eye View of the Tropics* (4–8). Illus. 1996, Watts LB $24.00 (0-531-11281-0). The flora and fauna of rain forests and coral reefs in Belize are described in text and stunning photographs. (Rev: BL 2/15/97; SLJ 3/97*) [574.5]

20943 Morrison, Gordon. *Nature in the Neighborhood* (2–5). Illus. 2004, Houghton Mifflin $16.00 (0-618-35215-5). 32pp. This attractively illustrated title introduces readers to the abundance of plant and animal life that can be found in areas ranging from their own backyards to train tracks and vacant lots. (Rev: BL 12/1/04; SLJ 10/04) [508]

20944 Parker, Steve. *Survival and Change* (4–7). Series: Life Processes. 2001, Heinemann LB $21.36 (1-57572-340-9). 32pp. Parker considers how organisms evolve and looks at how species behave under threat and the origin of new species in this concise book with diagrams, charts, and color photographs. (Rev: HBG 10/01; SLJ 7/01) [578.4]

20945 Peters, Lisa Westberg. *Our Family Tree: An Evolution Story* (K–3). Illus. by Lauren Stringer. 2003, Harcourt $17.00 (0-15-201772-0). This oversize picture book, with conversational text and many bright illustrations, is fairly successful in its ambitious mission; adults may want to explain the timeline and final notes. (Rev: BL 3/15/03; HBG 10/03; SLJ 5/03) [576.8]

20946 Quinlan, Susan E. *The Case of the Monkeys That Fell from the Trees: And Other Mysteries in Tropical Nature* (5–8). Illus. 2003, Boyds Mills $15.95 (1-56397-902-0). 171pp. Quinlan introduces plant and animal mysteries in South and Central American tropical forests and shows how scientists approached solving them. (Rev: BL 3/1/03; HBG 10/03; SLJ 3/03) [508.313]

20947 Rockwell, Anne. *Growing Like Me* (PS–K). Illus. by Holly Keller. 2001, Harcourt $14.00 (0-15-202202-3). 24pp. This simple book about change and development in the plant and animal world shows an organism on one page and what it becomes on the next (e.g., a caterpillar and then a butterfly). (Rev: BL 3/1/01; HB 9–10/01; HBG 3/02) [571.8]

20948 Ross, Michael Elsohn. *Life Cycles* (2–4). Illus. by Gustav Moore. 2001, Millbrook LB $22.40 (0-7613-1817-8). 32pp. Young readers are introduced to the concept of life cycles through the stories a sunflower, a mushroom, and a grasshopper. (Rev: BL 8/01; HBG 3/02; SLJ 1/02) [571.8]

20949 Silverstein, Alvin, et al. *Symbiosis* (5–9). Series: Science Concepts. 1998, Twenty-First Century LB $26.90 (0-7613-3001-1). 64pp. The concept of cooperation in nature for mutual benefit is explored, with explanations of various forms of symbiotic partnerships including the relationships humans have with animals, plants, fungi, and microorganisms. (Rev: HBG 3/99; SLJ 2/99) [574.5]

20950 Smith, Karla. *Virginia: Plants and Animals* (4–6). 2003, Heinemann LB $27.07 (1-4034-0360-0). 48pp. Part of the Heinemann State Studies series, this overview of Virginia's natural life offers an excellent introduction to the flora and fauna native to the Old Dominion State. (Rev: HBG 4/04; SLJ 12/03) [578]

20951 Squire, Ann. *101 Questions and Answers About Backyard Wildlife* (5–8). Illus. 1996, Walker LB $16.85 (0-8027-8458-5). Using a question-and-answer format, this work provides fascinating information about common insects, birds, mammals, and reptiles. (Rev: SLJ 1/97) [574]

20952 Strauss, Rochelle. *Tree of Life: The Incredible Biodiversity of Life on Earth* (3–6). Illus. by Margot Thompson. 2004, Kids Can $16.95 (1-55337-669-2). 40pp. This large-format book presents a visual representation — using the branches of a tree — of the diversity of species, from bacteria on up. (Rev: BL 12/1/04; SLJ 10/04) [578]

20953 Thornhill, Jan. *Before and After: A Book of Nature Timescapes* (PS–3). Illus. 1997, National Geographic $16.00 (0-7922-7093-2). 32pp. Using different habitats, this book pictures a variety of animals and plants using a single dramatic incident, like the charge of a lioness, to show before-and-after situations. (Rev: BL 10/1/97; HBG 3/98; SLJ 9/97) [577]

20954 Wallace, Holly. *Classification* (4–7). Series: Life Processes. 2001, Heinemann LB $21.36 (1-57572-337-9). 32pp. A concise look at the system that we use for classifying plants and animals, with diagrams, charts, and color photographs. Also use *Adaptation* and *Cells and Systems* (both 2001). (Rev: HBG 10/01; SLJ 7/01) [570]

Animal Life

General

20955 Aaseng, Nathan. *Invertebrates* (5–8). Illus. 1993, Watts LB $22.00 (0-531-12550-5). 112pp. Describes the varieties of life forms without backbones, including insects, and how they have diversified through the ages. (Rev: BL 3/15/94; SLJ 3/94) [592]

20956 Aaseng, Nathan. *Nature's Poisonous Creatures* (5–9). Series: Scientific American Sourcebooks. 1997, Twenty-First Century LB $28.90 (0-8050-4690-9). After a general introduction to animal poisons, why they are produced, and their composition, this book devotes separate chapters to such venom-bearing vertebrates and invertebrates as sea wasps, blue-ringed octopi, African killer bees, and marine toads. (Rev: BL 2/1/98; SLJ 8/98) [591.6]

20957 Armentrout, David, and Patricia Armentrout. *Animals* (PS–2). Series: 50 Words About. 2002, Rourke LB $26.60 (1-58952-341-5). 32pp. Simple definitions are given for 50 words about animals (camouflage, extinct, and so forth), along with a sentence that includes the word. (Rev: SLJ 3/03) [590]

20958 Arnold, Caroline. *Australian Animals* (1–3). 2000, HarperCollins LB $15.89 (0-688-16767-5). 48pp. Seventeen Australian animals are introduced in four sections that represent individual biomes. (Rev: HBG 3/01; SLJ 10/00) [591]

20959 Arnosky, Jim. *Field Trips: Bug Hunting, Animal Tracking, Bird-Watching, Shore Walking* (3–5). Illus. by author. 2002, HarperCollins LB $15.89 (0-688-15173-6). 96pp. Young people heading on an expedition will find safety measures, guidance on observing and identifying animals, and advice on leaving nature unaltered, all in an appealing format with useful charts and notes. (Rev: HB 7–8/02; HBG 10/02; SLJ 6/02) [508]

20960 *Atlas of Animals* (PS–2). Illus. Series: First Discovery. 1996, Scholastic $12.95 (0-590-58280-1). 24pp. Using a highly visual approach, this short book discusses the animals found in the basic regions of the world. (Rev: BL 10/15/96) [591]

20961 Barrow, Lloyd H. *Science Fair Projects Investigating Earthworms* (5–8). Series: Science Fair Success. 2000, Enslow LB $20.95 (0-7660-1291-3). 104pp. This book contains a fascinating number of experiments involving earthworms, with very explicit directions and explanations of the scientific principles behind each project. (Rev: BL 4/15/00; HBG 9/00) [595.1]

20962 Berger, Melvin, and Gilda Berger. *Do Tarantulas Have Teeth? Questions and Answers About Poisonous Creatures* (3–5). Illus. by Jim Effler. Series: Scholastic Question and Answer. 2000, Scholastic $14.95 (0-439-09578-6); paper $5.95 (0-439-14877-4). 48pp. Using a question-and-answer format and bright, realistic illustrations, this title presents information on the methods poisonous animals use to inject their venom, how they hunt and feed, and their physical characteristics. (Rev: HBG 3/01; SLJ 5/01) [591]

20963 Bial, Raymond. *A Handful of Dirt* (3–5). Photos by author. 2000, Walker $16.95 (0-8027-8698-7). 32pp. This set of photographs with accompanying text examines life found underground from invertebrates to the mammals and reptiles that burrow into the earth. (Rev: BCCB 5/00; HBG 9/00; SLJ 4/00) [591]

20964 Bishop, Nic. *Backyard Detective: Critters Up Close* (1–3). Illus. 2002, Scholastic $16.95 (0-439-17478-3). 48pp. Photographic collages show "life-sized" animals and insects found in backyards across the United States, along with two pages of informational text about each and a section of nature projects. (Rev: BL 10/15/02; HBG 3/03; SLJ 10/02) [591.75]

20965 Browning, Bel. *Animal Welfare* (5–8). Illus. Series: Face the Facts. 2003, Raintree LB $28.56 (0-7398-6430-0). 56pp. Hot issues in animal protection such as whaling, intensive farming, and zoos are discussed, and practical responses from young people are suggested. (Rev: BL 11/15/03; HBG 10/03) [364.1]

20966 Cassie, Brian. *Say It Again* (1–3). Illus. by David Mooney. 2000, Charlesbridge LB $16.95 (0-88106-341-X); paper $6.95 (0-88106-342-8). This unusual animal book features, in picture and text, 12 creatures whose names involve a repetitive sound, such as a killy-killy and a caracara. (Rev: HBG 9/00; SLJ 3/00) [591]

20967 Cobb, Allan B. *Super Science Projects About Animals and Their Habitats* (4–8). Series: Psyched for Science. 2000, Rosen LB $23.95 (0-8239-3175-7). 48pp. Six hand-on activities are introduced to help children observe animals and to study their adjustments to climate, habitat, and food. (Rev: SLJ 9/00) [591]

20968 Crenson, Victoria. *Horseshoe Crabs and Shorebirds: The Story of a Food Web* (2–4). Illus. by Annie Cannon. 2003, Marshall Cavendish $16.95 (0-7614-5115-3). 32pp. Wildlife on the Delaware Bay is the focus of this informative picture-book exploration full of attractive and atmospheric paintings. (Rev: BL 11/1/03; HBG 4/04; SLJ 12/03)

20969 *Do Bears Give Bear Hugs? First Questions and Answers About Animals* (PS–1). Series: Library of First Questions and Answers. 1994, Time-Life $14.95 (0-7835-0870-0). 47pp. A fun book that explores some common questions about animals. (Rev: SLJ 8/94) [591]

20970 Donovan, Sandra. *Animals of Rivers, Lakes, and Ponds* (2–4). Series: Animals of the Biomes. 2003, Raintree LB $24.26 (0-7398-5690-1). 48pp. The great blue heron, giant water bugs, raccoons, and snapping turtles are featured in this introduction. Also use *Desert Animals*, which looks at roadrunners, scorpions, camels, and Gila monsters. (Rev: HBG 3/03; SLJ 2/03)

20971 Doris, Ellen. *Meet the Arthropods* (4–7). 1996, Thames & Hudson $16.95 (0-500-19010-0). 64pp. Such arthropods as the horseshoe crab, potato beetle, and praying mantis are introduced with photographs and activities. (Rev: BL 10/15/96) [595.2]

20972 DuQuette, Keith. *They Call Me Woolly: What Animal Names Can Tell You* (K–4). Illus. 2002, Penguin Putnam $15.99 (0-399-23445-4). 32pp. Younger readers will discover how animal names — polar bear, zebra butterfly — reflect their traits in this informative and well-illustrated book. (Rev: BL 1/1–15/02; HBG 10/02; SLJ 2/02) [590]

20973 Elliott, Leslee. *Mind-Blowing Mammals* (3–6). Illus. Series: Amazing Animals. 1995, Sterling $12.95 (0-8069-1270-7); paper $9.95 (0-8069-1271-5). 64pp. Introduces some amazing mammals with full-color photos on each page. (Rev: SLJ 4/95) [591]

20974 Fowler, Allan. *Animals Under the Ground* (1–3). Series: Rookie Readers. 1997, Children's Book Pr. $19.00 (0-516-20427-0). 32pp. An easy-to-read science book that introduces basic material about such animals as moles. (Rev: BL 12/15/97; HBG 3/98) [591]

20975 Fredericks, Anthony D. *Fearsome Fangs* (4–6). Illus. Series: Watts Library. 2002, Watts LB $24.00 (0-531-11966-1); paper $8.95 (0-531-16597-3). 63pp. Animals with alarming teeth — including some prehistoric beasts — are profiled here, with information on physical features, behavior, distribu-tion, habitat, prey, and relationship with humans. (Rev: SLJ 1/03) [591.47]

20976 Ganeri, Anita. *Animal Life Cycles* (K–3). Illus. Series: Nature's Patterns. 2005, Heinemann LB $24.21 (1-4034-5894-4). 32pp. In simple language, this volume introduces the life cycles of reptiles, insects, mammals, and amphibians. (Rev: SLJ 6/05)

20977 Ganeri, Anita. *The Hunt for Food* (1–5). Illus. Series: Life Cycle. 1997, Millbrook LB $21.40 (0-7613-0304-9). 32pp. This book deals with animals in a meadow and their feeding habits throughout the four seasons. (Rev: BL 12/1/97; HBG 3/98; SLJ 1/98) [577.4]

20978 George, Jean Craighead. *Morning, Noon, and Night* (PS–3). Illus. by Wendell Minor. 1999, HarperCollins LB $15.89 (0-06-023629-9). 32pp. An easy-reader about a full day from Maine to California and the activities of such animals as antelopes, lizards, and cardinals. (Rev: HBG 9/99; SLJ 4/99) [591]

20979 Glassman, Jackie. *Amazing Arctic Animals* (K–3). Illus. by Lisa Bonforte. Series: All Aboard Science Reader. 2002, Grosset LB $13.89 (0-448-42876-8); paper $3.99 (0-448-42844-X). 48pp. Animals including the polar bear, arctic tern, caribou, snowy owl, and arctic fox are introduced with colored illustrations. (Rev: SLJ 6/03) [591.7]

20980 Gordon, Sharon. *Guess Who Grabs* (K–2). Series: Bookworms: Guess Who. 2003, Benchmark LB $14.95 (0-7614-1557-2). 31pp. Young readers are challenged to identify an animal that "grabs" (an octopus), with clues about characteristics, habitat, and so forth. Also use *Guess Who Changes* and *Guess Who Hides* (both 2003). (Rev: HBG 4/04; SLJ 4/04)

20981 Guiberson, Brenda Z. *Exotic Species: Invaders in Paradise* (4–6). Illus. 1999, Twenty-First Century LB $23.90 (0-7613-1319-2). 80pp. Using examples including starlings, kudzu, and zebra mussels, this account reveals the disastrous results that occur when a foreign species is introduced into a different ecosystem. (Rev: BL 7/99; HBG 4/00; SLJ 9/99) [577]

20982 Halfmann, Janet. *Life in a Garden* (5–7). Photos by David Liebman. 2000, Creative LB $22.60 (1-58341-072-4). This book explores such life forms found in a garden as fungi, beetles, slugs, snails, and aphids. (Rev: SLJ 8/00) [635]

20983 Halliburton, Warren J. *African Wildlife* (4–6). Illus. Series: Africa Today. 1992, Macmillan LB $13.95 (0-89686-674-2). 48pp. Color photos complement this look at four areas — savanna, forest, wetlands, and desert — of wildlife habitat in Africa. (Rev: BL 3/1/93) [591]

20984 Hanly, Sheila. *The Big Book of Animals* (PS–2). Illus. 1997, DK $14.95 (0-7894-1485-6). 48pp. In a book arranged by habitat, more than 300 familiar or little-known animals are introduced and pictured. (Rev: BL 7/97; HBG 3/98) [590]

20985 Hanna, Jack, and Rick A. Prebeg. *Jungle Jack Hanna's Safari Adventure* (3–5). Illus. 1996, Scholastic $12.95 (0-590-67322-X). 44pp. The animals of Kenya and Uganda are introduced in this handsomely illustrated account. (Rev: BL 10/15/96; SLJ 11/96) [591.96]

20986 Hansen, Rosanna. *Caring Animals* (2–4). Illus. Series: True Tales. 2003, Children's Pr. LB $21.50 (0-516-22912-5); paper $5.95 (0-516-24603-8). 48pp. Introduces animals that help people, from dolphins to a seeing-eye horse. (Rev: BL 1/1–15/04) [362.404]

20987 Heller, Ruth. *"Galápagos" Means "Tortoises"* (3–5). Illus. by author. 2000, Sierra Club $14.95 (0-87156-917-5). 41pp. The animals and birds of the Galapagos Islands are described in this book of rhymes and accompanying realistic paintings. (Rev: SLJ 3/01) [985]

20988 Hiller, Ilo. *Introducing Mammals to Young Naturalists* (5–9). Illus. 1990, Texas A & M Univ. Pr. $9.00 (0-89096-427-0). An introduction to a number of mammals, from the common squirrel to the exotic armadillo. (Rev: BL 7/90) [599]

20989 Hodgkins, Fran. *Animals Among Us: Living with Suburban Wildlife* (5–8). Illus. 2000, Linnet LB $19.50 (0-208-02478-6). 116pp. This book discusses the behavior and lifestyles of animals such as deer, coyotes, bears, skunks, and bats that live in suburbs, close to their original haunts. (Rev: BL 6/1–15/00; HB 7–8/00; HBG 9/00; SLJ 9/00) [591.7]

20990 Jackson, Donna M. *The Wildlife Detectives: How Forensic Scientists Fight Crimes Against Nature* (3–7). Illus. 2000, Houghton Mifflin $16.00 (0-395-86976-5). 48pp. This book introduces the forensic scientists who track down criminals who harm wild animals. (Rev: BL 4/1/00; HBG 9/00; SLJ 7/00) [363.28]

20991 Jefferis, David. *Animal Kingdom* (3–6). Illus. Series: Record Breakers. 2003, Raintree LB $25.69 (0-7398-6321-5). 32pp. Good for browsing, this attractive volume identifies such animal record-holders as the smallest bird, largest sea creature, longest migrator, best camouflage, and so forth. (Rev: HBG 10/03; SLJ 7/03) [591]

20992 Jenkins, Steve. *Actual Size* (1–3). Illus. 2004, Houghton Mifflin $16.00 (0-618-37594-5). 32pp. Striking cut-paper collages portray animals — and parts of animals — in real size, so that an earthworm appears in full size while only the eyes of a giant squid can be accommodated. (Rev: BL 5/15/04; HB 5–6/04; SLJ 6/04) [591.4]

20993 Jenkins, Steve. *Biggest, Strongest, Fastest* (PS–3). Illus. 1995, Ticknor $14.95 (0-395-69701-8). 32pp. Double-page collages illustrate some of the animal kingdom's record holders. (Rev: BCCB 6/95; BL 2/1/95*; HB 7–8/95; SLJ 5/95*) [591]

20994 Jenkins, Steve, and Robin Page. *What Do You Do with a Tail Like This?* (PS–2). Illus. 2003, Houghton Mifflin $15.00 (0-618-25628-8). 32pp. The tails, mouths, and other parts of different animals are rendered in cut paper, illustrating interesting animal facts. (Rev: BCCB 3/03; BL 2/15/03*; HBG 10/03; SLJ 3/03) [573.8]

20995 Johnson, Sylvia A. *Silkworms* (4–7). Illus. 1982, Lerner paper $9.55 (0-8225-9557-5). 48pp.

The life cycle of the silkworm, told in text and striking color pictures. [595.78]

20996 Jolivet, Jo'lle. *Zoo-ology* (PS–3). Illus. by author. 2003, Millbrook LB $24.90 (0-7613-2780-0). 33pp. This beautifully illustrated, large-format book introduces young readers to more than 300 different animals, which are cleverly grouped by such characteristics as appearance, habitat, and size. (Rev: HBG 4/04; SLJ 11/03) [590]

20997 Kalman, Bobbie. *Food Chains and You* (2–4). Illus. Series: Food Chains. 2004, Crabtree LB $16.95 (0-7787-1942-1); paper $6.26 (0-7787-1988-X). 32pp. A simple look at the relationship between producers and consumers of energy (both herbivores and carnivores), with discussion of humans' food choices.

20998 Kaner, Etta. *Animals at Work: How Animals Build, Dig, Fish and Trap* (2–4). Illus. by Pat Stephens. 2001, Kids Can $10.95 (1-55074-673-1); paper $5.95 (1-55074-675-8). 40pp. Activities, a game, and a quiz are provided in this basic look at the work various animals have to do to find food, shelter, and mates. (Rev: HBG 3/02; SLJ 10/01) [591.5]

20999 Knapp, Ron. *Bloodsuckers* (3–6). Illus. Series: Weird and Wacky Science. 1996, Enslow LB $18.95 (0-89490-614-3). 48pp. An interesting look at such creatures as vampire bats, leeches, fleas, lice, mosquitoes, and lampreys. (Rev: SLJ 6/96) [591]

21000 Kneidel, Sally. *Slugs, Bugs, and Salamanders: Discovering Animals in Your Garden* (5–7). Illus. by Anna-Maria L. Crum. 1997, Fulcrum paper $16.95 (1-55591-313-X). 120pp. As well as introducing backyard insects and other small creatures, this account gives a number of tips on growing healthy flowers and vegetables. (Rev: SLJ 10/97) [595.7]

21001 Kratter, Paul. *The Living Rain Forest: An Animal Alphabet* (PS–2). Illus. 2004, Charlesbridge $17.95 (1-57091-603-9). 64pp. Striking acrylic-and-watercolor illustrations introduces 26 animals of the rain forest. (Rev: BL 2/1/04; SLJ 4/04) [591.734]

21002 Landstrom, Lee Ann, and Karen I. Shragg. *Nature's Yucky! Gross Stuff That Helps Nature Work* (3–4). Illus. by Constance R. Bergum. 2003, Mountain paper $10.00 (0-87842-474-1). For browsers, this is a compendium of examples — many of them scatalogical — of animal behaviors. (Rev: SLJ 11/03) [591.5]

21003 Lauber, Patricia. *Fur, Feathers, and Flippers: How Animals Live Where They Do* (4–8). Illus. 1994, Scholastic paper $4.95 (0-590-45072-7). 48pp. Using various habitats such as the grasslands of East Africa as examples, this photoessay describes how animals have adapted to their different environments. (Rev: BL 12/1/94*; SLJ 12/94) [591.5]

21004 Lesinski, Jeanne M. *Exotic Invaders: Killer Bees, Fire Ants, and Other Alien Species Are Infesting America!* (4–6). Illus. 1996, Walker LB $17.85 (0-8027-8391-0). 49pp. In separate chapters, five pests — sea lampreys, fire ants, zebra mussels, starlings, and African honeybees — are featured, with a description of the harm they do. (Rev: SLJ 5/96) [591]

21005 Martin, James W. R. *In a House* (2–5). Series: Small World. 2002, Crabtree LB $15.96 (0-7787-0140-9); paper $8.06 (0-7787-0154-9). 32pp. From bugs and rodents to insects and worms, this is a run-down of the animal life that can be found inside a house. (Rev: BL 10/15/02) [591]

21006 Maynard, Christopher. *Micromonsters: Life Under the Microscope* (3–5). Illus. Series: Eyewitness Reader. 1999, DK LB $12.95 (0-7894-4757-6); paper $3.95 (0-7894-4756-8). 48pp. Tapeworms, fleas, and lice are among the monsters introduced in this book illustrated with magnifications of microscope photographs. (Rev: BL 12/15/99; HBG 4/00) [595]

21007 Maze, Stephanie, ed. *Beautiful Moments in the Wild: Animals and Their Colors* (PS–K). Series: Moments in the Wild. 2002, Moonstone $15.00 (0-9707768-7-X). An attractive picture book showing the diversity of animal colors in full-color shots. (Rev: SLJ 3/03)

21008 Miles, Victoria. *Wild Science: Amazing Encounters Between Animals and the People Who Study Them* (5–8). Series: Scientists in the Field. 2004, Raincoast paper $18.95 (1-55192-618-0). 168pp. This photo-filled volume introduces readers to scientists who study animals and describes memorable moments with animals in the wilderness. (Rev: BL 12/1/04; SLJ 12/04) [591.68]

21009 Palazzo, Tony. *The Biggest and the Littlest Animals* (4–7). Illus. by author. 1973, Lion LB $13.95 (0-87460-225-4). 40pp. Many ways of comparing animals, including size and mobility, are explored.

21010 Pascoe, Elaine. *Earthworms* (4–7). Illus. Series: Nature Close-Up. 1996, Blackbirch LB $27.44 (1-56711-177-7). 48pp. An account of the anatomy of earthworms and how they live, as well as how to collect and care for them. (Rev: BL 12/1/96) [595.1]

21011 Pascoe, Elaine, ed. *Into Wild California* (3–6). Series: The Jeff Corwin Experience. 2004, Gale/Blackbirch LB $19.96 (1-56711-858-5). 48pp. In a spin-off of his Animal Planet TV series, Corwin introduces such creatures as bears, snakes, sea otters, and bobcats that make California their home. (Rev: SLJ 4/04) [591.9]

21012 Pascoe, Elaine, ed. *Into Wild Madagascar* (3–6). Series: The Jeff Corwin Experience. 2004, Gale/Blackbirch LB $19.96 (1-56711-855-0). 48pp. Jeff Corwin of television's Animal Planet is the "host" for this survey of the threatened wildlife of Madagascar, from chameleons to lemurs. (Rev: SLJ 4/04) [591.9]

21013 Pascoe, Elaine. *Snails and Slugs* (4–7). Series: Nature Close-Up. 1998, Blackbirch LB $27.44 (1-56711-181-5). 48pp. Outstanding photographs, an interesting text, and several easy-to-do projects highlight this introduction to snails and slugs. (Rev: BL 9/15/98; HBG 3/99) [594.3]

21014 Paul, Tessa. *In Fields and Meadows* (2–5). Illus. Series: Animal Trackers. 1997, Crabtree LB

$20.60 (0-86505-585-8); paper $7.95 (0-86505-593-9). 32pp. Using evidence like footprints, teeth marks, holes, nests, and hair or fur, about a dozen creatures that live in fields and meadows are described. (Rev: HBG 3/98; SLJ 10/97) [591]

21015 Pearce, Q. L. *Piranhas and Other Wonders of the Jungle* (3–6). Illus. by Mary Ann Fraser. Series: Amazing Science. 1990, Simon & Schuster paper $5.95 (0-671-70690-X). 64pp. Sketches of animals found in the jungle, such as driver ants and vampire bats. (Rev: SLJ 2/91) [591]

21016 Perham, Molly, and Julian Rowe. *Wildlife* (4–6). Illus. Series: Mapworlds. 1997, Watts LB $20.00 (0-531-14388-0). 32pp. Using an atlaslike format, this work shows where a variety of animals, birds, and insects are found in the world, with details on their habits and habitats. (Rev: BL 4/15/97) [591.9]

21017 Pfeffer, Wendy. *Icy Antarctic Waters* (3–5). Series: Living on the Edge. 2002, Benchmark LB $16.95 (0-7614-1438-X). 40pp. The Weddell seal, emperor penguin, and minke whale are highlighted in this colorful, easy-to-read overview of Antarctic animals. (Rev: HBG 10/03; SLJ 6/03) [591.77]

21018 Pope, Joyce. *Living Fossils: Animals Unchanged by Time* (3–6). Illus. by Stella Stilwell and Helen Ward. Series: Curious Creatures. 1992, Raintree LB $5.00 (0-8114-3151-7). 46pp. Many examples of animals that exist in prehistoric form, from dragonflies to horseshoe crabs, are explored in this volume. A companion volume is *Two Lives: Metamorphosis in the Natural World* (1992). (Rev: SLJ 5/92) [591]

21019 Powell, Jillian. *Animal Rights* (2–3). Series: Talking About. 1999, Raintree LB $15.98 (0-7398-1374-9). 32pp. This simple account shows how society's use of animals can conflict with the animals' needs and how this dilemma can be tackled. (Rev: BL 2/15/00; HBG 9/00) [346]

21020 Presnall, Judith J. *Animals That Glow* (5–7). Illus. Series: First Books. 1993, Watts LB $23.00 (0-531-20071-X). 64pp. From fireflies to tiny sea creatures, this book covers the amazing phenomenon of bioluminescence. (Rev: BL 5/15/93; SLJ 6/93) [591]

21021 Presnall, Judith Janda. *Animal Actors* (4–6). Series: Animals with Jobs. 2002, Gale LB $23.70 (0-7377-0934-0). 48pp. Animals that work in television and movies are profiled here with information on their training and care. Also use *Navy Dolphins* (2002). (Rev: SLJ 3/02) [791.43]

21022 Presnall, Judith Janda. *Circus Animals* (4–7). Series: Animals with Jobs. 2002, Gale LB $23.70 (0-7377-1360-7). 48pp. This colorful book describes the training and performance of such circus animals as elephants, lions, tigers, and horses. (Rev: BL 2/15/03) [791.3]

21023 Pringle, Laurence. *Animal Monsters: The Truth About Scary Creatures* (4–6). Illus. 1997, Marshall Cavendish $15.95 (0-7614-5003-3). 64pp. The truth about such feared animals as alligators, killer bees, and tarantulas — and why they are not as dangerous as many believe. (Rev: BL 9/1/97; HBG 3/98; SLJ 10/97) [591]

21024 Renne. *Animal Males and Females* (1–3). Trans. by Alison Taurel. Illus. by author. 2000, Gareth Stevens LB $21.27 (0-8368-2712-0). 38pp. Using stunning photographs, the differences between the males and females of a species are vividly presented. (Rev: HBG 10/01; SLJ 2/01) [591]

21025 Ross, Michael E. *Rolypolyology* (4–6). Illus. Series: Backyard Creatures. 1996, Carolrhoda LB $19.95 (0-87614-862-3). 48pp. Several common backyard creatures and their habits are described with interesting accompanying activities. (Rev: BL 3/15/96; SLJ 7/96) [595.3]

21026 Ruiz, Andres L. *Metamorphosis* (3–5). Illus. by Francisco Arredondo. Series: Cycles of Life. 1997, Sterling $12.95 (0-8069-9325-1). 32pp. In double-page spreads, explains how some creatures transform themselves into another life form, such as tadpoles becoming frogs. (Rev: SLJ 6/97) [591]

21027 Ruurs, Margriet. *Wild Babies* (PS–2). Illus. by Andrew Kiss. 2003, Tundra $14.95 (0-88776-627-7). 32pp. Young animals and birds found in a North American forest are shown in lush, detailed paintings that provide intriguing hints of the next animal. (Rev: HBG 10/03; SLJ 2/03)

21028 Sateren, Shelley Swanson. *The Humane Societies: A Voice for the Animals* (4–6). Illus. 1996, Silver Burdett LB $14.95 (0-87518-622-X); paper $7.95 (0-382-39309-0). 80pp. Introduces animal rights groups and humane societies and the work they do, including prevention of cruelty to animals and ways of controlling pet populations. (Rev: SLJ 11/96) [179.3]

21029 Schubert, Ingrid, and Dieter Schubert. *Amazing Animals* (1–3). Trans. from Dutch by Leigh Sauerwein. 1995, Front Street $15.95 (1-886910-05-7). Using catchy rhymes and pleasant illustrations, this book shows how common animals live, reproduce, and deal with danger. (Rev: SLJ 1/96) [591]

21030 Setford, Steve. *Predator: Animals with the Skill to Kill* (4–8). Series: Secret Worlds. 2003, DK LB $14.99 (0-7894-9705-0); paper $5.99 (0-7894-9224-5). 96pp. A lively, unusual introduction to animal predators with attractive layouts and a listing of tested Web sites. (Rev: HBG 10/03)

21031 Shedd, Warner. *The Kids' Wildlife Book: Exploring Animal Worlds Through Indoor/Outdoor Experiences* (2–6). Illus. by Loretta Braren. Series: Kids Can! 1994, Williamson paper $12.95 (0-913589-77-2). 156pp. This book of projects and experiments features common mammals, amphibians, and birds of Canada and the United States. (Rev: SLJ 8/94) [591]

21032 Silver, Donald M. *Extinction Is Forever* (2–3). Illus. by Patricia J. Wynne. 1995, Simon & Schuster $19.95 (0-671-86769-5); paper $7.95 (0-671-86770-9). 48pp. Beginning with the end of dinosaurs during the Ice Ages and ending with the present, this account traces the reasons why various species have become extinct. (Rev: SLJ 2/96) [575.7]

21033 Silverstein, Alvin, et al. *Vertebrates* (3–6). Illus. Series: Kingdoms of Life. 1996, Twenty-First

Century LB $21.40 (0-8050-3517-6). 64pp. Vertebrates — animals with enclosed spinal cords — are introduced, with many color photos. (Rev: BL 6/1–15/96) [596]

21034 Squire, Ann O. *African Animals* (2–3). Series: True Books — Animals. 2001, Children's Book Pr. LB $23.00 (0-516-22186-6). 48pp. A compact guide to the most common animals of Africa is presented in a simple text with color photographs on each page. (Rev: BL 12/15/01) [599]

21035 Stetson, Emily. *Kids' Easy-to-Create Wildlife Habitats* (2–5). Illus. by J. Susan Stone. Series: Quick Starts for Kids! 2004, Williamson/Kids Can paper $12.95 (0-8249-8665-2). 128pp. Offering solid information, illustrations, and activities, this wide-format book introduces the wildlife found in many communities and the foods that may bring them into the open. (Rev: BL 12/1/04; SLJ 3/05) [639.9]

21036 Stewart, Melissa. *Life Without Light* (5–8). Illus. 1999, Watts LB $23.00 (0-531-11529-1). 128pp. This book explores the world of nature that exists without sun, including creatures discovered during research on hydrothermal vents, caves, aquifers, and rocks. (Rev: BL 7/99; SLJ 8/99) [577]

21037 Suen, Anastasia. *ASPCA* (1–2). Series: Helping Organizations. 2002, Rosen LB $16.00 (0-8239-6004-8). 24pp. As well as a history of this organization, this easily read account describes how it works and how young people can get involved. (Rev: BL 6/1–15/02; SLJ 4/02) [179.3]

21038 Wadsworth, Ginger. *River Discoveries* (2–4). Illus. by Paul Kratter. 2002, Charlesbridge $16.95 (1-57091-418-4); paper $6.95 (1-57091-419-2). 32pp. An introduction to the varied wildlife that surrounds and depends on a river, describing the activities of 13 types of animals over a 24-hour period. (Rev: BL 9/15/02; HBG 3/03; SLJ 8/02) [591.76]

21039 Whyman, Kate. *The Animal Kingdom* (5–8). Illus. 1999, Raintree LB $27.12 (0-8172-5885-X). 48pp. A valuable account that introduces animal classification basics through text, sidebars, diagrams, and many eye-catching color photographs. (Rev: BL 2/1/00) [596]

21040 Woods, Geraldine. *Animal Experimentation and Testing: A Pro/Con Issue* (5–8). Series: Hot Issues. 1999, Enslow LB $21.95 (0-7660-1191-7). 64pp. The controversial subject of using animals in experiments is discussed with a history of the problem, arguments for and against, and a summary of important actions taken by government and individual groups. (Rev: HBG 4/00; SLJ 3/00) [179.3]

21041 Wu, Norbert, and Jim Mastro. *Antarctic Ice* (2–4). 2003, Holt $16.95 (0-8050-6517-2). 32pp. This attractive, well-illustrated guide to Antarctic wildlife focuses on four animal species — the orca, Weddell seal, and Adelie and emperor penguins. (Rev: BL 12/1/03; HBG 4/04; SLJ 11/03)

Amphibians and Reptiles

GENERAL AND MISCELLANEOUS

21042 Allen, Nancy Kelly. *Whose Food Is This: A Look at What Animals Eat — Seeds, Bugs, and Nuts* (PS–2). Illus. by Derrick Alderman and Denise Shea. Series: Whose Is It? 2004, Picture Window LB $22.60 (1-4048-0607-5). 24pp. Rhythmic question-and-answer format and colorful collages introduce the wide variety of foods that animals eat. Also use *Whose Sound Is This? A Look at Animal Noises — Chirps, Clicks, and Hoots* (2004). (Rev: BL 11/1/04) [591.5]

21043 Behler, John L. *National Audubon Society First Field Guide: Reptiles* (4–8). 1999, Scholastic $17.95 (0-590-05467-8); paper $11.95 (0-590-05487-2). This richly illustrated manual discusses common characteristics of North American reptiles, then presents individual species under four groups: crocodiles, turtles, lizards, and snakes. (Rev: BL 3/15/99; SLJ 7/99) [597.9]

21044 Brenner, Barbara, and Bernice Chardiet. *Where's That Reptile?* (2–4). Illus. Series: Hide and Seek. 1993, Scholastic $10.95 (0-590-45212-6). 32pp. An interactive book that introduces a variety of reptiles to primary-age children. (Rev: BL 10/15/93; SLJ 1/94) [597.9]

21045 Burns, Diane L. *Frogs, Toads and Turtles* (3–6). Illus. 1997, NorthWord paper $6.95 (1-55971-593-6). 48pp. A paperback field guide that introduces the world of 30 amphibians, with coverage of their habitats, food, and appearance. (Rev: BL 8/97) [597.8]

21046 Cassie, Brian. *National Audubon Society First Field Guide: Amphibians* (4–6). Series: First Field Guide. 1999, Scholastic $17.95 (0-590-63982-X); paper $11.95 (0-590-64008-9). 160pp. This field guide, with more than 450 full-color illustrations, introduces 50 easily found amphibians, with material on their characteristics and habitats. (Rev: BL 10/15/99) [597.5]

21047 Chermayeff, Ivan. *Scaly Facts* (PS–1). Illus. 1995, Harcourt $11.00 (0-15-200109-3). 32pp. Reptiles are introduced through brief, simple text and dynamic illustrations. (Rev: BL 4/1/95; SLJ 7/95) [597.9]

21048 Dennard, Deborah. *Reptiles* (5–7). Illus. by Jennifer Owings Dewey. Series: Our Wild World. 2004, NorthWord $16.95 (1-55971-880-3). 191pp. A compilation of four shorter books published by NorthWord in 2003, this volume examines the physical characteristics, natural habitat, diet, and behavior of alligators, crocodiles, lizards, snakes, and turtles. (Rev: SLJ 8/04) [597.9]

21049 Fridell, Ron. *Amphibians in Danger: A Worldwide Warning* (5–9). 1999, Watts LB $22.50 (0-531-11373-5). 96pp. This book identifies the amphibians that are in danger, explains the reasons why, and outlines various efforts to save them. (Rev: SLJ 8/99) [597.9]

21050 Holub, Joan. *Why Do Snakes Hiss? And Other Questions About Snakes, Lizards, and Turtles* (1–2). Illus. by Anna DiVito. Series: Easy-to-Read. 2004, Penguin Putnam $14.99 (0-8037-3000-4). 48pp. Using an attractive question-and-answer format, this volume explores the characteristics and behavior of the reptile family. (Rev: BL 11/1/04; SLJ 11/04) [597.9]

21051 Jango-Cohen, Judith. *Desert Iguanas* (PS–2). Series: Pull Ahead Books. 2001, Lerner LB $22.95 (0-8225-3635-8). 32pp. A color photograph and two lines of simple text are found on each page of this attractive basic introduction to these desert reptiles. (Rev: BL 6/1–15/01; HBG 10/01) [597.9]

21052 Kalman, Bobbie, and Jacqueline Langille. *What Is an Amphibian?* (2–5). Series: Science of Living Things. 1999, Crabtree LB $14.97 (0-86505-934-9); paper $5.36 (0-86505-952-7). 32pp. Amphibians and their general characteristics, habits, and habitats are covered plus material on some specific members of the group in this lavishly illustrated book. (Rev: SLJ 3/00) [597.8]

21053 Llewellyn, Claire. *Question Time: Reptiles* (3–5). Illus. Series: Question Time. 2002, Kingfisher $11.95 (0-7534-5451-3); paper $6.95 (0-7534-5463-7). 32pp. Topics covered in a question-and-answer format include the different types of reptiles, and their characteristics, habitat, and defense mechanisms. (Rev: HBG 3/03; SLJ 2/03)

21054 Miller, Ruth. *Reptiles* (4–6). Series: Animal Kingdom. 2004, Raintree LB $32.79 (1-4109-1052-0). 64pp. The common characteristics of reptiles are explained, followed by descriptions of various orders of reptiles and selected specific species plus discussion of endangered status and evolution. Also use *Amphibians* (2004). (Rev: BL 5/1/04; SLJ 6/05)

21055 Miller, Sara S. *Salamanders: Secret Silent Lives* (3–5). Series: Animals in Order. 1999, Watts LB $23.00 (0-531-11568-2). 48pp. This book discusses the amphibian class known as salamanders and gives a pictorial glimpse into their types, lives, structure, habits, and homes. (Rev: BL 12/15/99; HBG 4/00) [597.6]

21056 Miller, Sara S. *Snakes and Lizards: What They Have in Common* (3–5). Series: Animals in Order. 2000, Watts LB $23.00 (0-531-16448-9). 48pp. A brief introduction to animal classification is followed by a description of reptiles, with many examples in text and pictures. (Rev: BL 4/15/00) [597.9]

21057 Murray, Peter. *Amphibians* (3–6). Series: Science Around Us. 2004, Child's World LB $27.07 (1-59296-271-8). 32pp. Eye-catching photographs and interesting "Did You Know?" features draw the reader into this overview of amphibians. (Rev: SLJ 3/05) [597.8]

21058 Murray, Peter. *Reptiles* (3–6). Series: Science Around Us. 2004, Child's World LB $27.07 (1-59296-218-1). 32pp. Eye-catching photographs and interesting "Did You Know?" features draw the reader into this overview of reptiles. (Rev: SLJ 3/05) [597.9]

21059 Pascoe, Elaine, ed. *Into Wild Louisiana* (3–6). Series: The Jeff Corwin Experience. 2004, Gale/Blackbirch LB $19.96 (1-41030-060-9). 48pp. Readers visit the swamp creatures of backwoods

Louisiana, from alligators to frogs, guided by Jeff Corwin of TV's *Animal Planet*. (Rev: SLJ 4/04)

21060 *Reptiles* (3–5). Ed. by Simon Holland. 2002, DK LB $17.95 (0-7894-8555-9). 48pp. This is a visually stunning introduction to all kinds of reptiles with details on their characteristics, habits, and habitats. (Rev: BL 6/1–15/02; HBG 10/02) [597.96]

21061 Savage, Stephen. *Amphibians* (2–4). Series: What's the Difference? 2000, Raintree LB $25.69 (0-7398-1359-5). 32pp. This book introduces a number of amphibians that live on water, land, or both. (Rev: BL 10/15/00; HBG 3/01) [597.6]

21062 Savage, Stephen. *Reptiles* (2–4). Series: What's the Difference? 2000, Raintree LB $25.69 (0-7398-1358-7). 32pp. This book explores the similarities and differences in the class known as reptiles and introduces such creatures as crocodiles, rattlesnakes, and tortoises. (Rev: BL 10/15/00; HBG 3/01; SLJ 1/01) [597.96]

21063 Sill, Cathryn. *About Amphibians: A Guide for Children* (PS–2). Illus. by John Sill. 2001, Peachtree $14.95 (1-56145-234-3). 40pp. An introduction for young children that has colorful, realistic paintings facing brief text. (Rev: BL 5/15/01; HBG 10/01; SLJ 6/01) [597.8]

21064 Sill, Cathryn. *About Reptiles: A Guide for Children* (PS–2). Illus. by John Sill. 1999, Peachtree $14.95 (1-56145-183-5). 40pp. This introduction to reptiles in general and snakes in particular is aimed at young children and has a colorful, realistic painting on one page followed by brief text on the facing page. (Rev: BL 6/1–15/99; HBG 9/99; SLJ 7/99) [597.9]

21065 Spilsbury, Richard, and Louise Spilsbury. *Classifying Reptiles* (4–6). Series: Classifying Living Things. 2003, Heinemann LB $24.22 (1-4034-0848-3). 32pp. This title in the Classifying Living Things series examines the scientific classification of reptiles, including identification of the phyllum, class, and order of different types of reptiles. (Rev: HBG 10/03; SLJ 11/03) [597.9]

21066 Spilsbury, Richard, and Louise Spilsbury. *The Life Cycle of Amphibians* (3–5). Illus. Series: From Egg to Adult. 2003, Heinemann LB $24.22 (1-4034-0785-1). 32pp. A brief overview of amphibians, examining the creatures' physical characteristics, habitat, diet, and life cycle. (Rev: HBG 4/04; SLJ 10/03) [597.8]

21067 Stewart, Melissa. *Amphibians* (2–3). Series: True Books — Animals. 2001, Children's Book Pr. LB $23.00 (0-516-22037-3). 48pp. In this colorful, simple volume, a variety of amphibians are introduced with material on their appearance, habits, and distinctive characteristics. (Rev: BL 12/15/01) [597.6]

21068 Theodorou, Rod. *Amphibians* (2–4). Series: Animal Babies. 1999, Heinemann LB $14.95 (1-57572-950-4). 32pp. The babies of about half a dozen species of amphibians are presented, with material on their anatomy, life cycles, and habits. (Rev: SLJ 4/00) [597.6]

21069 Winner, Cherie. *Everything Reptile: What Kids Really Want to Know About Reptiles* (3–5).

2004, NorthWord $10.95 (1-55971-146-9); paper $7.95 (1-55971-164-7). 63pp. A basic introduction, using a question-and-answer format with plenty of photographs. (Rev: SLJ 11/04) [597.9]

21070 Winner, Cherie. *Salamanders* (3–6). Illus. Series: Nature Watch. 1993, Carolrhoda LB $23.93 (0-87614-757-0). 48pp. Various kinds of salamanders are introduced, with material given on life cycle, habits, and endangered status. (Rev: BL 8/93) [597.6]

ALLIGATORS AND CROCODILES

21071 Bare, Colleen S. *Never Kiss an Alligator!* (2–4). Illus. 1994, Puffin paper $4.99 (0-140-55257-X). 32pp. Sharp color photos highlight this close-up look at the alligator. (Rev: BCCB 9/89; BL 9/1/89; SLJ 8/89) [597.98]

21072 Clarke, Ginjer L. *Baby Alligator* (1–3). Illus. by Neecy Twinem. 2000, Penguin Putnam $13.89 (0-448-41851-7); paper $3.99 (0-448-42095-3). 48pp. For beginning readers, this is a simple introduction to alligators that traces the life cycle from hatching from an egg in the spring to waiting out the winter in a dark tunnel. (Rev: BL 7/00; HBG 9/00) [597.98]

21073 Fitzgerald, Patrick J. *Croc and Gator Attacks* (4–7). Series: Animal Attack! 2000, Children's Book Pr. LB $20.00 (0-516-23314-9); paper $6.95 (0-516-23514-1). 48pp. Aimed at the reluctant reader, this book tells true stories of attacks by crocodiles and alligators and gives information about these species and their differences. (Rev: SLJ 2/01) [597.98]

21074 Jango-Cohen, Judith. *Crocodiles* (4–6). Series: Animals Animals. 2002, Benchmark LB $15.95 (0-7614-1446-0). 48pp. This is an oversize book filled with excellent photographs and text covering the anatomy, habits, food, and habitats of crocodiles. (Rev: BL 12/15/02; HBG 3/03; SLJ 2/03) [597.98]

21075 Jango-Cohen, Judith. *Crocodiles* (5–8). Series: AnimalWays. 2000, Marshall Cavendish LB $28.50 (0-7614-1136-4). 112pp. This book examines the habitat, range, classification, evolution, anatomy, behavior, and endangered status of the crocodile. (Rev: BL 1/1–15/01; HBG 3/01) [597.98]

21076 Kallen, Stuart A., and P. M. Boekhoff. *Alligators* (4–6). Series: Nature's Predators. 2002, Gale LB $23.70 (0-7377-0642-2). Color photographs are used with a simple text to describe characteristics of alligators and their habitats, with coverage on how they kill their prey and how they also are hunted. (Rev: BL 1/1–15/02; SLJ 6/02) [597.98]

21077 Llewellyn, Claire. *Crocodile* (PS–3). Illus. by Simon Mendez. Series: Starting Life. 2004, NorthWord $16.95 (1-55971-900-1). 23pp. On pages that grow progressively wider, the stages of a crocodile's development are traced, with information on such topics as habitat, diet, and predatory behavior plus realistic illustrations. (Rev: SLJ 11/04) [597.98]

21078 London, Jonathan. *Crocodile: Disappearing Dragon* (1–3). Illus. by Paul Morin. 2001, Candlewick $15.99 (1-56402-634-5). 32pp. The tale of a mother alligator's encounter with a hunter lays the scene for a thoughtful account of the plight of the nearly extinct species, including facts about its life cycle and habitat. (Rev: BL 12/1/01; HBG 3/02; SLJ 11/01) [596.698]

21079 Markle, Sandra. *Crocodiles* (2–5). Illus. Series: Animal Predators. 2004, Carolrhoda LB $25.26 (1-57505-726-3). 40pp. Concise text and clear, full-page photographs introduce the life cycle of the crocodile and its physical characteristics, habitat, diet, and predatory behavior. (Rev: BL 9/15/04; SLJ 10/04) [597.98]

21080 Muñoz, William. *Waiting Alligators* (PS–2). Series: Pull Ahead Books. 1999, Lerner LB $15.95 (0-8225-3615-3). 32pp. Using interactive material, this simple science book introduces alligators and includes many photos, a map, a body diagram, glossary, and index. (Rev: BL 8/99; HBG 9/99) [597.98]

21081 Noonan, Diana. *The Crocodile* (2–4). Illus. Series: Life Cycles. 2002, Chelsea LB $14.95 (0-7910-6964-8). 32pp. Handsome photographs and simple text describe the life cycle, habitat, appearance, and predators of the crocodile, in a small, square, photo-essay format. (Rev: BL 1/1–15/03; HBG 3/03) [597.98]

21082 Perry, Phyllis J. *The Crocodilians: Reminders of the Age of Dinosaurs* (4–6). Illus. Series: First Books. 1997, Watts LB $22.50 (0-531-20254-2). 64pp. Although the dinosaurs are gone, their descendants — the alligator, gavial, caiman, and crocodile — are still here, and this book describes them and how they live. (Rev: BL 8/97; SLJ 8/97) [597.98]

21083 Robinson, Claire. *Crocodiles* (2–3). Illus. Series: In the Wild. 1997, Heinemann $19.92 (1-57572-133-3). 24pp. A simple introduction to crocodiles that tells how they live, communicate, find food, and raise their young. (Rev: BL 2/1/98; SLJ 4/98) [597.98]

21084 Simon, Seymour. *Crocodiles and Alligators* (3–6). Illus. 1999, HarperCollins LB $15.89 (0-06-027474-3). 32pp. Basic information about alligators and crocodiles is given, including their history, differences, habitats, food, reproduction, and endangered status. (Rev: BL 4/1/99; HBG 9/99; SLJ 6/99) [597.98]

21085 Souza, D. M. *Roaring Reptiles: A Book About Crocodilians* (3–5). Illus. Series: Creatures All Around Us. 1992, Carolrhoda LB $19.95 (0-87614-710-4). 40pp. Close-up photographs and lively text introduce the types of crocodilians found in North America. (Rev: BL 10/1/92; SLJ 12/92) [597.98]

21086 Spilsbury, Richard. *Alligator* (4–6). Illus. Series: Animals Under Threat. 2004, Heinemann LB $18.95 (1-4034-4857-4). 48pp. The life cycle of the alligator and threats to its survival are explored in this blend of narrative and eye-catching color photography.

21087 Staub, Frank. *Alligators* (2–4). Photos by author. Illus. Series: Early Bird Nature Books. 1995, Lerner LB $22.60 (0-8225-3007-4). 48pp. Discusses the appearance and habits of alligators, as well as

the role they play in their environment. (Rev: SLJ 8/95) [597.6]

21088 Walker, Sally M. *Crocodiles* (4–6). Illus. Series: Nature Watch. 2003, Lerner LB $23.93 (1-57505-345-4). 48pp. An attractive introduction to crocodiles, how and where they live, and their life cycle. (Rev: HBG 4/04)

FROGS AND TOADS

21089 Arnosky, Jim. *All About Frogs* (2–4). Illus. Series: All About. 2002, Scholastic $15.95 (0-590-48164-9). 32pp. Excellent illustrations accompany the in-depth information about the anatomy and habitats of various species of frogs in this book for younger readers. (Rev: BL 2/1/02; HB 3–4/02; HBG 10/02; SLJ 3/02) [597.8]

21090 Back, Christine. *Tadpole and Frog* (1–3). Illus. 1986, Silver Burdett LB $15.95 (0-382-09285-6); paper $3.95 (0-382-24021-9). 24pp. A basic science book in full color explaining the reproductive cycle of the frog. (Rev: BL 1/1/87)

21091 Berman, Ruth. *Climbing Tree Frogs* (PS–2). Series: Pull Ahead Books. 1998, Lerner LB $21.27 (0-8225-3605-6). 32pp. This unusual branch of the frog family is introduced with a series of thoughtful questions, color photos, maps, and simple text. (Rev: BL 2/15/99; HBG 3/99; SLJ 6/99) [597.8]

21092 Chinery, Michael. *Frog* (3–5). Illus. by Martin Camm. Series: Life Story. 1990, Troll LB $17.25 (0-8167-2102-5); paper $4.95 (0-8167-2103-3). 32pp. The life cycle of the frog is revealed through detailed text, color photographs, and other illustrations. (Rev: BL 4/1/91) [597.8]

21093 Chrustowski, Rick. *Hop Frog* (PS–3). Illus. by author. 2003, Holt $15.95 (0-8050-6688-8). The life cycle of a leopard frog is told in an entertaining narrative. (Rev: HBG 10/03; SLJ 5/03) [597.8]

21094 Cowley, Joy. *Red-Eyed Tree Frog* (PS–K). Illus. by Nic Bishop. 1999, Scholastic $16.95 (0-590-87175-7). 32pp. In this stunning work, the feeding habits of several animals in a rain forest in Central America are described from a tree frog's point of view. (Rev: BCCB 3/99; BL 5/15/99*; HB 3–4/99; HBG 9/99; SLJ 3/99) [597.8]

21095 Delafosse, Claude. *Frogs* (PS–2). Illus. Series: First Discovery. 1997, Scholastic $12.95 (0-590-93782-0). 24pp. With a highly visual approach, this book introduces frogs using excellent drawings and a brief text. (Rev: BL 2/15/97) [597.8]

21096 Dell'Oro, Suzanne Paul. *Hiding Toads* (PS–2). Series: Pull Ahead Books. 1999, Lerner $21.27 (0-8225-3626-9); paper $6.95 (0-8225-3630-7). 32pp. Using questions and plenty of close-up photos to produce interest, this simple science book introduces the behavior and physical characteristics of toads and provides a map that shows where they live. (Rev: BL 12/15/99; HBG 4/00) [597.8]

21097 Dewey, Jennifer O. *Poison Dart Frogs* (K–3). Illus. 1998, Boyds Mills $15.95 (1-56397-655-2). This introduction to the many kinds of poison dart frogs of Latin American rain forests explains how they release a poison through their skin that is used by hunters on blowpipe darts. (Rev: BCCB 4/98;

BL 3/1/98; HB 3–4/98; HBG 9/98; SLJ 4/98) [597.8]

21098 Fowler, Allan. *Frogs and Toads and Tadpoles Too!* (1–2). Illus. Series: Rookie Readers. 1992, Children's Book Pr. LB $19.00 (0-516-04925-9). 32pp. In minimal text and many color photos, the life cycle of frogs and toads is introduced. (Rev: BL 6/15/92) [597.8]

21099 Gibbons, Gail. *Frogs* (K–3). Illus. 1993, Holiday House LB $16.95 (0-8234-1052-8). 32pp. Colorful water scenes and a simple text depict frogs in all stages of development from spawn to maturity. (Rev: BL 10/15/93; SLJ 12/93) [597.8]

21100 Glaser, Linda. *Fabulous Frogs* (PS–1). Illus. by Loretta Krupinski. 1999, Millbrook LB $21.90 (0-7613-0424-X). An enjoyable picture book that presents the life of a frog from mating to birth and growth, plus material on such varieties as the leopard frog, spring peeper, and bullfrog. (Rev: HBG 9/99; SLJ 5/99) [597.8]

21101 Godwin, Sam. *The Trouble with Tadpoles: A First Look at the Life Cycle of a Frog* (K–1). Illus. Series: First Look: Science. 2004, Picture Window LB $16.95 (1-4048-0654-7). 32pp. In simple language with cartoon-style illustrations, this volume describes the life cycle of frogs.

21102 Greenberg, Dan. *Frogs* (5–8). Series: AnimalWays. 2000, Marshall Cavendish LB $28.50 (0-7614-1138-0). 112pp. As well as chapters devoted to the amazing variety of frogs, this book discusses their anatomy, habits, and survival skills. (Rev: BL 1/1–15/01; HBG 3/01) [597.8]

21103 Hawes, Judy. *Why Frogs Are Wet* (K–3). Illus. by Mary Ann Fraser. Series: Let's-Read-and-Find-Out. 2000, HarperCollins LB $15.89 (0-06-028162-6); paper $4.95 (0-06-445195-X). 40pp. The physical characteristics, life cycle, evolution, and behavior of frogs are introduced in this revision of the 1968 title. (Rev: BL 9/15/00; HBG 3/01) [597.8]

21104 Hickman, Pamela. *A New Frog: My First Look at the Life Cycle of an Amphibian* (PS–2). Illus. by Heather Collins. Series: My First Look At. 1999, Kids Can $6.95 (1-55074-615-4). 20pp. A beginning science book that explains the life cycle of a frog, using rhymes, factual text, and watercolor paintings. (Rev: BL 6/1–15/99; HBG 9/99; SLJ 8/99) [571.8]

21105 Johnson, Sylvia A. *Tree Frogs* (4–6). Illus. 1986, Lerner LB $22.60 (0-8225-1467-2). 48pp. A look at the characteristics, environment, breeding, and life cycles of the tree frog. (Rev: BL 10/1/86; SLJ 11/86)

21106 Magloff, Lisa. *Watch Me Grow: Frog* (PS–2). Series: Watch Me Grow. 2003, DK $7.99 (0-7894-9629-1). 24pp. This attractive title provides a close-up look — from the perspective of the animal — at the early life cycle of a frog from the tadpole stage. (Rev: BL 10/15/03) [597.8]

21107 Mara, William P. *The Fragile Frog* (3–6). Illus. 1996, Whitman LB $16.95 (0-8075-2580-4). 48pp. A description is given of the life cycle of this tiny frog, whose existence is now threatened. (Rev: BL 11/1/96; SLJ 11/96) [597.8]

21108 Miller, Sara S. *Frogs and Toads: The Leggy Leapers* (3–5). Series: Animals in Order. 2000, Watts LB $23.00 (0-531-11632-8). 48pp. A brief introduction to animal classification is followed by a description of frogs and toads, their similarities, differences, and life cycles. (Rev: BL 10/15/00) [597.8]

21109 Netherton, John. *Red-Eyed Tree Frogs* (2–3). Series: Early Bird Nature Books. 2000, Lerner LB $22.60 (0-8225-3037-6). 48pp. An introduction to these colorful rain forest amphibians — with their orange feet, lime green skin, blue stripes, and big red eyes. (Rev: BL 7/00; HBG 3/01) [597.8]

21110 Noonan, Diana. *The Frog* (2–4). Series: Life Cycles. 2002, Chelsea LB $14.95 (0-7910-6966-4). 32pp. This account follows the life cycle of this amphibian from egg to tadpole and finally the growth of lungs and legs needed to live on land. (Rev: BL 12/15/02; HBG 3/03) [597.8]

21111 O'Hare, Jeffrey. *Frogs and Toads* (4–6). Series: Nature's Predators. 2003, Gale/KidHaven LB $23.70 (0-7377-1388-7). 48pp. This short book, suitable for new readers, packs in a good deal of information about frogs and toads, including their physical characteristics, where they live, what they eat, and how they hunt their prey. (Rev: BL 11/15/03)

21112 Pascoe, Elaine. *Tadpoles* (3–6). Photos by Dwight Kuhn. Series: Nature Close-up. 1996, Blackbirch LB $18.95 (1-56711-179-3). 48pp. A frog book that concentrates on the growth and development of tadpoles, using excellent color photos. (Rev: SLJ 10/96) [597.8]

21113 Pfeffer, Wendy. *From Tadpole to Frog* (PS–1). Illus. by Holly Keller. Series: Let's-Read-and-Find-Out. 1994, HarperCollins paper $4.95 (0-06-445123-2). 32pp. This simple science book shows one year in the life cycle of a frog, beginning with the end of its hibernation in the spring. (Rev: BL 8/94; HB 7–8/94; SLJ 11/94) [597.8]

21114 Robinson, Fay. *Fantastic Frogs* (1–2). Illus. by Jean Cassels. Series: Hello Reader! 2000, Scholastic paper $3.99 (0-590-52269-8). 32pp. Different varieties of frogs like brown, green, and jungle frogs are introduced in this beginning reader with material on their looks and behavior. (Rev: BL 2/15/01) [597.8]

21115 Royston, Angela. *Life Cycle of a Frog* (2–3). Illus. Series: Life Cycle. 1998, Heinemann $13.95 (1-57572-613-0). 32pp. Using a color photograph and a continuing timeline on each page, the development of a frog is traced from egg to full-grown adult, who, in turn, produces eggs. (Rev: BL 4/15/98; SLJ 7/98) [597.8]

21116 Souza, D. M. *Frogs, Frogs Everywhere* (3–5). Illus. Series: Creatures All Around Us. 1995, Carolrhoda LB $22.60 (0-87614-825-9). 40pp. Physical and behavioral characteristics of frogs are attractively presented, along with various species and habitats. (Rev: BL 4/15/95; SLJ 9/95) [597.8]

21117 Starosta, Paul. *The Frog: Natural Acrobat* (3–6). Photos by author. Series: Animal Close-Ups. 1996, Charlesbridge paper $6.95 (0-88106-437-8). 27pp. A simple account with plenty of photos that tells about the various species, habitats, life cycles, and behavior of frogs. (Rev: SLJ 1/97) [597.8]

21118 Stone, Tanya. *Toads* (3–5). Series: Wild America. 2002, Gale LB $24.94 (1-56711-646-9). 24pp. A close-up look at these amphibians that gives material on where they live and their physical features, life cycle, and habits. (Rev: BL 10/15/02) [597.8]

21119 Tagholm, Sally. *The Frog* (2–3). Illus. by Bert Kitchen. Series: Animal Lives. 2000, Kingfisher $9.95 (0-7534-5215-4). 32pp. After a series of pictures depicting the daily activities of a frog and its mating procedures, this account focuses on the development of an egg to adulthood. (Rev: BL 5/15/00; HBG 3/01; SLJ 8/00) [597.8]

21120 Wallace, Karen. *Tale of a Tadpole* (PS–2). Series: Eyewitness Reader. 1998, DK $3.95 (0-7894-3437-7); paper $12.95 (0-7894-3761-9). 32pp. The growth cycle of a frog from egg to mature adult is traced in a spare text with well-chosen photographs. (Rev: HBG 3/99; SLJ 4/99) [597.8]

21121 Wechsler, Doug. *Bullfrogs* (3–6). Series: The Really Wild Life of Frogs. 2002, Rosen LB $18.75 (0-8239-5855-8). 24pp. The bullfrog's physical characteristics, habitat, diet, predators, and so forth are presented with close-up photographs and boxed features. Also use *Leopard Frogs*, *Treefrogs*, and *Wood Frogs* (all 2002). (Rev: SLJ 5/02) [597.89]

21122 White, William. *All About the Frog* (4–8). Illus. Series: Sterling Color Nature. 1992, Sterling $14.95 (0-8069-8274-8). 72pp. A brief history of the frog and a discussion of its anatomy, reproduction, food, adaptations, and likely future. (Rev: BL 7/92; SLJ 9/92) [597.8]

21123 Winer, Yvonne. *Frogs Sing Songs* (PS–3). Illus. by Tony Oliver. 2003, Charlesbridge $16.95 (1-57091-548-2); paper $6.95 (1-57091-549-0). 32pp. Frogs and their sounds are presented in a lyrical text combined with realistic watercolor illustrations and a strong environmental message. (Rev: BL 4/1/03; HBG 10/03; SLJ 7/03) [597.8]

LIZARDS

21124 Cowley, Joy. *Chameleon, Chameleon* (K–2). Illus. 2005, Scholastic $16.95 (0-439-66653-8). 32pp. The panther chameleon of Madagascar is the focus of this compelling photoessay. (Rev: BL 2/15/05; SLJ 4/05) [597.95]

21125 Darling, Kathy. *Chameleons: On Location* (3–6). Illus. by Tara Darling. 1997, Lothrop LB $15.93 (0-688-12538-7). 40pp. An introduction to chameleons in their natural habitat in Madagascar that tells about their lives, habits, diets, and mating. (Rev: BCCB 5/97; BL 4/1/97; SLJ 4/97) [597.95]

21126 Darling, Kathy. *Komodo Dragon: On Location* (4–6). Illus. by Tara Darling. Series: On Location. 1997, Lothrop LB $16.89 (0-688-13777-6). 40pp. Color photographs enliven the description of this reptile, its habits, and its habitat on Komodo Island. (Rev: BCCB 5/97; BL 2/15/97; SLJ 4/97) [597.95]

21127 Facklam, Margery. *Lizards: Weird and Wonderful* (5–8). Illus. by Alan Male. Series: Around

the World. 2003, Little, Brown $15.95 (0-316-17346-0). 32pp. Colorful illustrations and anecdotes add to the factual information about 13 types of lizards, including the Komodo dragon, horned lizard, and basilisk. (Rev: BL 6/1–15/03; HBG 10/03; SLJ 6/03) [597.9]

21128 Kalman, Bobbie. *Endangered Komodo Dragons* (3–5). Illus. Series: Earth's Endangered Animals. 2004, Crabtree $16.95 (0-7787-1857-3); paper $6.26 (0-7787-1903-0). 32pp. In addition to discussion of their endangered status, this volume covers these animals' habitat, behavior, life cycle, and so forth. (Rev: SLJ 6/05)

21129 Mattern, Joanne. *Lizards* (3–6). Series: Animals, Animals. 2001, Benchmark LB $15.95 (0-7614-1259-X). 48pp. In addition to describing physical characteristics, behavior, habitat, and so forth of more than two dozen species, Mattern looks at related folklore and at the animals' relationship with humans. (Rev: HBG 10/02; SLJ 6/02) [597.95]

21130 Pipe, Jim. *The Giant Book of Snakes and Slithery Creatures* (4–8). Illus. 1998, Millbrook LB $27.90 (0-7613-0804-0). This richly illustrated, oversize volume contains details about snakes, lizards, and amphibians. (Rev: BL 8/98; HBG 9/98; SLJ 12/98) [597.9]

21131 Schafer, Susan. *The Komodo Dragon* (3–5). Illus. Series: Remarkable Animals. 1992, Macmillan LB $13.95 (0-87518-504-5). 60pp. Evolution, adaptation, habitat and behavior are covered, as well as why this animal is in danger of extinction. (Rev: BL 11/1/92; SLJ 10/92) [597.95]

21132 Schnieper, Claudia. *Chameleons* (3–6). Illus. by Max Meier. Series: Nature Watch. 1989, Carolrhoda LB $19.95 (0-87614-341-9). 48pp. Introduces the life cycle, physical characteristics, and habits of chameleons. (Rev: BL 9/15/89; HB 11–12/89; SLJ 10/89) [597.95]

21133 Schnieper, Claudia. *Lizards* (3–6). Illus. by Max Meier. Series: Nature Watch. 1990, Carolrhoda LB $19.95 (0-87614-405-9). 48pp. Characteristics and reproductive patterns are covered, with color photos. (Rev: BCCB 10/90; BL 6/15/90; SLJ 9/90) [597.95]

21134 Sherrow, Victoria. *The Gecko* (4–6). Illus. 1990, Macmillan LB $13.95 (0-87518-441-3). 60pp. Color photos highlight this introduction to the gecko. (Rev: BL 1/1/90; SLJ 2/91) [597.95]

21135 Stefoff, Rebecca. *Chameleon* (2–4). Illus. Series: From the Living Things. 1996, Marshall Cavendish LB $22.79 (0-7614-0118-0). 32pp. The African chameleon, its life history, and its habits are presented in brief text and colorful photos. (Rev: BL 2/1/97; SLJ 3/97) [597.95]

21136 Welsbacher, Anne. *Komodo Dragons* (3–5). Series: Predators in the Wild. 2002, Capstone LB $21.26 (0-7368-1066-8). 32pp. Basic information about the komodo dragon's life, habitat, diet, and endangered status is presented in a format that will suit both browsers and report writers. (Rev: SLJ 8/02) [597.95]

SNAKES

21137 Arnosky, Jim. *All About Rattlesnakes* (3–5). Illus. 1997, Scholastic $15.95 (0-590-46794-8). 32pp. This account is filled with information about snakes, from their physical structure to how they behave, with special material on rattlesnakes. (Rev: BL 12/1/97; HB 9–10/97; HBG 3/98; SLJ 10/97) [597.96]

21138 Behler, Deborah, and John Behler. *Snakes* (5–8). Series: AnimalWays. 2001, Marshall Cavendish LB $28.50 (0-7614-1265-4). 112pp. Brilliant photographs highlight this fine introduction to snakes, their habitats, behavior, species, evolution, and anatomy. (Rev: BL 3/15/02; HBG 10/02) [597.96]

21139 Berman, Ruth. *Buzzing Rattlesnakes* (PS–2). Series: Pull Ahead Books. 1998, Lerner LB $21.27 (0-8225-3603-X). 32pp. An innovative book that uses questions to introduce the topic of rattlesnakes, their homes, food, and habits. (Rev: BL 2/15/99; HBG 3/99; SLJ 1/99) [597.96]

21140 Demuth, Patricia. *Snakes* (1–3). Illus. by Judith Moffatt. 1993, Penguin Putnam paper $3.99 (0-448-40513-X). 48pp. An introduction to snakes, their habits, size, and food. (Rev: BL 7/93; SLJ 7/93) [597.66]

21141 Editors of Time for Kids. *Snakes!* (1–3). Illus. Series: Time For Kids Science Scoops. 2005, HarperCollins $14.99 (0-06-057637-5); paper $3.99 (0-06-057636-7). 32pp. Simple text suitable for beginning readers and bright illustrations present basic information on snakes, plus a profile of a scientist who works with them.

21142 Feldman, Heather. *Cottonmouths* (3–5). Series: The Really Wild Life of Snakes. 2004, Rosen LB $18.75 (0-8239-6722-0). 24pp. The behavior, physical characteristics, and habitat of the cottonmouth are featured in this colorfully illustrated account. Also use *Diamondbacks* and *Milk Snakes* (both 2004). (Rev: SLJ 2/05) [597.96]

21143 Greenaway, Theresa. *Snakes* (4–7). Series: The Secret World Of. 2001, Raintree LB $18.98 (0-7398-3510-6). 48pp. An accessible, attractive volume about ants and their physical characteristics, behavior, food, and habitats. (Rev: HBG 3/02)

21144 Greenaway, Theresa. *Snakes* (4–7). Series: The Secret World Of. 2001, Raintree LB $18.98 (0-7368-3510-6). 48pp. A look at the world of snakes with material on their structure, habitats, behavior, food, mating habits, and enemies. (Rev: BL 10/15/01) [597.96]

21145 Ling, Mary, and Mary Atkinson. *The Snake Book* (4–6). Illus. 1997, DK $12.95 (0-7894-1526-7). 32pp. A fascinating book that introduces 12 varieties of snakes, with a four-panel foldout of a python. (Rev: BCCB 5/97; BL 7/97; SLJ 9/97) [597.96]

21146 Llewellyn, Claire. *Some Snakes Spit Poison and Other Amazing Facts About Snakes* (2–4). Illus. Series: I Didn't Know That. 1997, Millbrook LB $19.90 (0-7613-0561-0). 32pp. Strange facts about unusual snakes and their behavior are given along with basic facts about the life span, food, and repro-

duction of snakes. (Rev: HBG 3/98; SLJ 10/97) [597.96]

21147 McDonald, Mary Ann. *Boas* (3–5). Illus. Series: Naturebooks. 1996, Child's World LB $22.79 (1-56766-212-9). 32pp. This account features in text and photos the large snake that crushes its prey. (Rev: BL 12/15/96) [597.96]

21148 Mason, Adrienne. *Snakes* (2–4). Illus. by Nancy Gray Ogle. Series: Wildlife. 2005, Kids Can $10.95 (1-55337-627-7); paper $6.95 (1-55337-628-5). 32pp. In addition to introducing the physical characteristics and behavior of snakes, this overview discusses their usefulness to humans and the reasons why people are afraid of snakes. (Rev: BL 5/1/05; SLJ 6/05) [597.96]

21149 Montgomery, Sy. *The Snake Scientist* (5–8). Series: Scientists in the Field. 1999, Houghton Mifflin $16.00 (0-395-87169-7). This account captures the excitement of scientific discovery by focusing on a zoologist and young students who are studying the red-sided garter snake in Canada. (Rev: BCCB 4/99; BL 2/15/99; HB 7–8/99; HBG 9/99; SLJ 5/99) [597.96]

21150 Pascoe, Elaine, ed. *Into Wild Arizona* (3–6). Series: The Jeff Corwin Experience. 2004, Gale/Blackbirch LB $19.96 (1-41030-058-7). 48pp. Jeff Corwin of TV's *Animal Planet* guides a tour of the wildlife of Arizona, concentrating on its snakes. (Rev: SLJ 4/04)

21151 Patent, Dorothy Hinshaw. *Slinky Scaly Slithery Snakes* (K–3). Illus. by Kendahl J. Jubb. 2000, Walker LB $17.85 (0-8027-8744-4). 32pp. This colorful introduction to snakes explains how they move, their body parts, where they live, and how they can eat animals larger than themselves. (Rev: BL 12/1/00; HBG 3/01; SLJ 3/01) [597.96]

21152 Penner, Lucille R. *S-S-Snakes!* (1–2). Illus. by Peter Barrett. Series: Step into Reading. 1994, Random LB $9.99 (0-679-94777-9); paper $3.99 (0-679-84777-4). 32pp. An easy-to-read book about snakes, their structure, and their habits. (Rev: BL 1/1/95; SLJ 2/95) [597.96]

21153 Pringle, Laurence P. *Snakes! Strange and Wonderful* (2–5). Illus. by Meryl Henderson. Series: Strange and Wonderful. 2004, Boyds Mills $15.95 (1-59078-003-5). 32pp. Realistic illustrations and lively, concise text present an interesting and fact-filled introduction to snakes and their diverse behaviors. (Rev: BL 12/1/04*; SLJ 9/04) [597.96]

21154 Robinson, Fay. *Great Snakes!* (2–3). Illus. by Jean Day Zallinger. 1996, Scholastic paper $3.99 (0-590-26243-2). 32pp. In an easily read format, this counting book introduces various snakes. (Rev: BL 11/15/96) [597.96]

21155 Ruth, Maria Mudd. *Snakes* (3–6). Series: Animals, Animals. 2001, Benchmark LB $15.95 (0-7614-1262-X). 48pp. In addition to describing physical characteristics, behavior, habitat, locomotion, and so forth of more than a dozen species, Mattern looks at related folklore and at the animals' relationship with humans. (Rev: HBG 10/02; SLJ 6/02) [597.96]

21156 Schnieper, Claudia. *Snakes: Silent Hunters* (3–5). Illus. Series: Nature Watch. 1995, Carolrhoda LB $23.93 (0-87614-881-X); paper $7.95 (0-87614-952-2). 48pp. An introduction to snakes organized under such headings as physical characteristics, reproduction, hunting, and self-defense. (Rev: BL 10/1/95; SLJ 12/95) [597.96]

21157 Welsbacher, Anne. *Anacondas* (3–6). Series: Predators in the Wild. 2001, Capstone LB $15.95 (0-7368-0785-3). 32pp. Myths about the anaconda are presented along with facts in this general introduction to the snake's characteristics and habitat. (Rev: HBG 10/01; SLJ 1/02) [597.96]

TURTLES AND TORTOISES

21158 Arnosky, Jim. *All About Turtles* (1–3). Illus. Series: All About. 2000, Scholastic $15.95 (0-590-48149-5). 32pp. This brief, well-illustrated account introduces turtles and touches on such topics as how and where they live, their shells, feeding habits, and reproductive cycle. (Rev: BL 2/1/00; HBG 9/00; SLJ 4/00) [597.92]

21159 Bair, Diane, and Pamela Wright. *Sea Turtle Watching* (2–5). Series: Wildlife Watching. 1999, Capstone $19.93 (0-7368-0323-8). 48pp. A description of sea turtles, their habits, and habitats that also provides special tips for successful turtle watching. (Rev: BL 2/15/00) [597.92]

21160 Baskin-Salzberg, Anita, and Allen Salzberg. *Turtles* (3–7). Illus. 1996, Watts LB $22.50 (0-531-20220-8). 64pp. From tiny bog turtles to giant sea turtles, many species are presented, along with their habitats and life-styles. (Rev: BL 9/1/96) [597.92]

21161 Cerullo, Mary M. *Sea Turtles: Ocean Nomads* (3–6). Photos by Jeffrey L. Rotman. Illus. 2003, Dutton $17.99 (0-525-46649-5). 32pp. A handsome photoessay on these endangered animals and their fascinating lives. (Rev: BL 5/15/03; HBG 10/03; SLJ 7/03) [597.92]

21162 Cooper, Jason. *Loggerhead Turtle* (1–3). Series: Life Cycles. 2002, Rourke LB $23.93 (1-58952-354-7). 24pp. Handsome photographs and simple text describe the life cycle, habitat, appearance, and behavior of these animals. (Rev: SLJ 12/02) [597.92]

21163 Davies, Nicola. *One Tiny Turtle* (PS–4). Illus. by Janet Chapman. 2001, Candlewick $15.99 (0-7636-1549-8). 32pp. An appealing overview of the loggerhead sea turtle, introduced by the story of one turtle's life from hatching to laying her own eggs on the beach of her birth. (Rev: BCCB 11/01; BL 12/1/01; HBG 3/02; SLJ 12/01) [597.92]

21164 Fowler, Allan. *Turtles Take Their Time* (1–2). Illus. Series: Rookie Readers. 1992, Children's Book Pr. LB $19.00 (0-516-06005-8). 32pp. For young children, turtles are introduced with a large color photo on each page and very brief text. (Rev: BL 12/15/92) [597.92]

21165 Gibbons, Gail. *Sea Turtles* (2–4). Illus. 1995, Holiday House LB $16.95 (0-8234-1191-5). 32pp. This account covers the anatomy, life cycle, diet, and habitat of the sea turtle and how it differs from other members of its reptile family. (Rev: BL 10/1/95; SLJ 10/95) [597.92]

21166 Guiberson, Brenda Z. *Into the Sea* (2–4). Illus. by Alix Berenzy. 1996, Holt $16.95 (0-8050-2263-5). 28pp. The life of a sea turtle from being hatched to becoming an egg-laying adult. (Rev: BCCB 9/96; BL 9/15/96; HB 11–12/96; SLJ 9/96*) [597.92]

21167 Holling, Holling C. *Minn of the Mississippi* (4–6). Illus. by author. 1951, Houghton Mifflin $20.00 (0-395-17578-X); paper $11.95 (0-395-27399-4). A snapping turtle's trip down the Mississippi.

21168 Jacobs, Francine. *Lonesome George, the Giant Tortoise* (2–3). Illus. by Jean Cassels. 2003, Walker LB $17.85 (0-8027-8865-3). This is the moving and true story of a giant saddleback tortoise, George, believed to be the last of his kind and apparently choosy about a suitable mate. (Rev: BL 1/1–15/04; HBG 4/04; SLJ 12/03) [597]

21169 Jacobs, Lee. *Turtles* (3–5). Series: Wild America. 2003, Gale/Blackbirch LB $23.70 (1-56711-571-3). 24pp. A brief and basic introduction to turtles and their habitat, diet, physical appearance, and behavior. (Rev: SLJ 11/03) [597.92]

21170 Kalman, Bobbie. *The Life Cycle of a Sea Turtle* (2–4). Illus. Series: The Life Cycle. 2001, Crabtree LB $15.45 (0-7787-0652-4); paper $5.36 (0-7787-0682-6). 32pp. After a general description of the sea turtle, the author clearly explains its life cycle and discusses what can be done to curb human encroachment. (Rev: SLJ 6/02) [597.92]

21171 Korman, Susan. *Box Turtle at Silver Pond Lake* (K–3). Illus. by Stephen Marchesi. Series: Smithsonian Backyard. 2001, Smithsonian Institution $15.95 (1-56899-860-0). 32pp. A female box turtle's daily life is presented in simple text with realistic illustrations. (Rev: BL 9/15/01; HBG 10/01; SLJ 8/01)

21172 Laskey, Elizabeth. *Sea Turtles* (4–6). Illus. Series: Sea Creatures. 2003, Heinemann LB $24.22 (1-4034-0962-5). 32pp. A clear overview of sea turtles and their lives, using a question-and-answer format. (Rev: HBG 10/03; SLJ 11/03) [597.9]

21173 Lasky, Kathryn. *Interrupted Journey* (3–6). Illus. 2001, Candlewick $16.99 (0-7636-0635-9). 32pp. Beginning with a boy and his mother finding an injured Kemp's ridley turtle, this outstanding photo-essay explores the endangered animal — its life cycle, hazards it faces, and the miracle of its survival. (Rev: BL 12/1/00*; HB 7–8/01; HBG 10/01) [639.9]

21174 Lepthien, Emilie U. *Sea Turtles* (3–4). Illus. Series: True Books. 1996, Children's Book Pr. LB $22.00 (0-516-20161-1). 48pp. An introduction to sea turtles that covers their environment, physiology, feeding, mating, nesting, and current endangered status. (Rev: SLJ 6/97) [597.92]

21175 Martin-James, Kathleen. *Sturdy Turtles* (PS–2). Series: Pull Ahead Books. 1999, Lerner $21.27 (0-8225-3627-7); paper $6.95 (0-8225-3631-5). 32pp. This book uses provocative questions, outstanding photos, and simple text to describe turtles, their habits, and habitats. (Rev: BL 12/15/99; HBG 4/00) [597.92]

21176 Noonan, Diana. *The Green Turtle* (2–4). Series: Life Cycles. 2002, Chelsea LB $14.95 (0-7910-6967-2). 32pp. The story of this endangered reptile that lives and mates in the sea is told with material on how the female goes ashore to lay her eggs and what happens when the young hatch. (Rev: BL 12/15/02; HBG 3/03) [597.92]

21177 Sayre, April Pulley. *Turtle, Turtle, Watch Out!* (PS–2). Illus. by Lee Christiansen. 2000, Orchard LB $17.99 (0-531-33285-3). 32pp. A lovely nature book with some fictional touches that covers the life cycle of a sea turtle and how a boy protected one turtle's eggs so they could hatch. (Rev: BL 8/00; HBG 3/01; SLJ 10/00) [597.92]

21178 Schafer, Susan. *The Galapagos Tortoise* (3–5). Illus. Series: Remarkable Animals. 1992, Macmillan LB $18.95 (0-87518-544-4). 64pp. With text, pictures, and maps, the story of the endangered Galapagos tortoise is told with information on habitat and behavior. (Rev: BL 12/1/92; SLJ 3/93) [597.92]

21179 Schafer, Susan. *Turtles* (2–5). Series: Perfect Pets. 1998, Benchmark LB $15.95 (0-7614-0796-0). 31pp. This book deals with turtles as pets and gives material on physical characteristics, behavior patterns, and tips on caring and raising them. (Rev: HBG 9/99; SLJ 5/99) [597.92]

21180 Souza, D. M. *What's Under That Shell? A Book About Turtles* (3–5). Illus. Series: Creatures All Around Us. 1992, Carolrhoda LB $19.95 (0-87614-712-0). 40pp. Various varieties of turtles and tortoises are introduced in color photographs and a lively text. (Rev: BL 10/1/92; SLJ 12/92) [597.92]

21181 Theodorou, Rod. *Leatherback Sea Turtle* (2–4). Illus. Series: Animals in Danger. 2001, Heinemann LB $21.36 (1-57572-272-0). 32pp. Basic information about the sea turtle and its endangered status. (Rev: BL 7/01; HBG 10/01) [597.2]

Animal Behavior and Anatomy

GENERAL

21182 Arnold, Caroline. *Did You Hear That? Animals with Super Hearing* (3–5). Illus. by Cathy Trachok. 2001, Charlesbridge $16.95 (1-57091-404-4). 32pp. This book full of color pictures introduces bats' and dolphins' echolocation skills, rhinos' ability to communicate over long distances, and other facts to do with animal hearing. (Rev: BL 12/1/01; HBG 3/02; SLJ 8/01) [591.59]

21183 Arnold, Caroline. *Mealtime for Zoo Animals* (PS–3). Illus. by Richard Hewett. Series: Zoo Animals. 1999, Carolrhoda LB $15.95 (1-57505-286-5). 32pp. Unusual color photographs and a simple text show a variety of zoo animals and how and what they eat. (Rev: BL 6/1–15/99; HBG 9/99) [636.088]

21184 Arnold, Caroline. *Noisytime for Zoo Animals* (PS–3). Illus. by Richard Hewett. Series: Zoo Animals. 1999, Carolrhoda LB $15.95 (1-57505-289-X). 32pp. All sorts of noises made by zoo animals

are portrayed in lively photographs and a simple text. (Rev: BL 6/1–15/99; HBG 9/99) [636.088]

21185 Arnold, Caroline. *Playtime for Zoo Animals* (PS–3). Series: Zoo Animals. 1999, Carolrhoda LB $15.95 (1-57505-287-3); paper $9.95 (1-57505-391-8). 32pp. A very simple text identifies 15 zoo animals shown at play in full-page illustrations, and stresses similarities between human and animal behavior. (Rev: BL 6/1–15/99; HBG 9/99) [591.51]

21186 Arnold, Caroline. *Sleepytime for Zoo Animals* (PS–3). Series: Zoo Animals. 1999, Carolrhoda LB $15.95 (1-57505-290-3); paper $9.95 (1-57505-393-4). 32pp. The sleeping habits of zoo animals are shown in full-page color photos and a brief text. (Rev: BL 6/1–15/99; HBG 9/99; SLJ 8/99) [591]

21187 Arnold, Caroline. *Splashtime for Zoo Animals* (PS–3). Series: Zoo Animals. 1999, Carolrhoda LB $15.95 (1-57505-288-1); paper $9.95 (1-57505-394-2). 32pp. A simple, engaging text and full-page color photos of zoo animals show that animals bathe in ways often similar to their human counterparts. (Rev: BL 6/1–15/99; HBG 9/99; SLJ 8/99) [591]

21188 Aruego, Jose, and Ariane Dewey. *Weird Friends: Unlikely Allies in the Animal Kingdom* (1–3). Illus. 2002, Harcourt $16.00 (0-15-202128-0). 40pp. Fourteen symbiotic relationships among animals are explained and brightly illustrated. (Rev: BL 5/15/02; HBG 10/02; SLJ 4/02) [577.8]

21189 Bancroft, Henrietta, and Richard G. Van Gelder. *Animals in Winter* (PS–1). Illus. by Helen K. Davie. Series: Let's-Read-and-Find-Out. 1997, HarperCollins LB $15.89 (0-06-027158-2). 32pp. An easily read title that describes how some animals prepare for winter and how others don't. (Rev: BL 12/1/96; SLJ 3/97) [591.54]

21190 Barre, Michel. *Animal Senses* (3–6). Series: Animal Survival. 1998, Gareth Stevens LB $19.93 (0-8368-2078-9). 48pp. This well-organized account explains how animals use their senses on land, in the sea, and in the air. (Rev: HBG 9/98; SLJ 7/98) [591]

21191 Bonsignore, Joan. *Stick Out Your Tongue! Fantastic Facts, Features, and Functions of Animal and Human Tongues* (2–3). Illus. by John T. Ward. 2001, Peachtree $15.95 (1-56145-230-0). 32pp. A look at how animals of all kinds use their tongues with comparisons to similar human behavior. (Rev: BL 8/01; HBG 3/02; SLJ 11/01) [612.8]

21192 Butler, John. *Can You Cuddle Like a Koala?* (PS). Illus. by author. 2003, Peachtree $15.95 (1-56145-298-X). In this enchanting blend of rhyming text and colorful artwork, young readers will learn how various animals move. (Rev: HBG 4/04; SLJ 1/04)

21193 Challoner, Jack. *Wet and Dry* (K–4). Illus. Series: Start-Up Science. 1996, Raintree LB $24.26 (0-8172-4322-4). 32pp. Using both text and experiments, discusses the different habitats of water and land and the creatures that exist in/on them. (Rev: SLJ 2/97) [530]

21194 Collard, Sneed B. *Animals Asleep* (PS–3). Illus. by Anik McGrory. 2004, Houghton Mifflin $15.00 (0-618-27697-1). 32pp. Readers can choose between brief, large-print information and more detailed smaller text in this chatty overview of animals' sleeping habits. (Rev: BL 3/1/04; SLJ 5/04) [591.56]

21195 Collard, Sneed B., III. *Leaving Home* (PS–3). Illus. by Joan Dunning. 2002, Houghton Mifflin $15.00 (0-618-11454-8). 32pp. This unique book for younger readers explores the various ways in which animals leave their homes upon maturation. (Rev: BL 3/1/02; HBG 10/02; SLJ 4/02) [591.5]

21196 Crump, Donald J., ed. *How Animals Behave: A New Look at Wildlife* (5–8). Illus. 1984, National Geographic LB $12.50 (0-87044-505-7). 104pp. A general, colorful introduction to why and how animals perform such functions as courting, living together, and caring for their young. [591.5]

21197 Crump, Donald J., ed. *Secrets of Animal Survival* (4–8). Illus. 1983, National Geographic LB $12.50 (0-87044-431-X). 104pp. The survival tactics of animals in five geographical environments are discussed.

21198 Dossenbach, Monika, and Hans D. Dossenbach. *EyeOpeners! All About Animal Vision* (3–5). Illus. 1998, Blackbirch LB $16.95 (1-56711-216-1). 32pp. Describes the characteristics and functions of vision in various animals. (Rev: BL 12/1/98; HBG 3/99; SLJ 3/99) [573.8]

21199 Facklam, Margery. *Bugs for Lunch* (PS–3). Illus. by Sylvia Long. 1999, Charlesbridge LB $15.95 (0-88106-271-5); paper $6.95 (0-88106-272-3). 32pp. This work highlights the creatures that eat insects, including bats, bears, aardvarks, rainbow trout, praying mantises, and Venus's-flytraps. (Rev: BL 2/1/99; HBG 9/99; SLJ 3/99) [591.5]

21200 Flegg, Jim. *Animal Movement* (4–7). Illus. by David Hosking. Series: Wild World. 1991, Millbrook LB $17.90 (1-878137-21-2). 32pp. Various ways animals move and at what speeds are discussed in this well-illustrated book. (Rev: BL 1/1/91; SLJ 2/92) [591.18]

21201 Fowler, Allan. *Animals on the Move* (1–2). Series: Rookie Readers. 2000, Children's Book Pr. LB $19.00 (0-516-21589-2). 32pp. This is a simple introduction to animal and bird migration that explains why and where they go. (Rev: BL 4/15/00) [591]

21202 Fowler, Allan. *How Animals See Things* (1–2). Series: Rookie Readers. 1998, Children's Book Pr. LB $18.50 (0-516-20797-0). 32pp. Minimal text and full-page color photographs are used to explain sight in animals. (Rev: BL 9/15/98; HBG 9/99) [591]

21203 Fraser, Mary Ann. *Where Are the Night Animals?* (PS–1). Illus. Series: Let's-Read-and-Find-Out. 1999, HarperCollins LB $15.89 (0-06-027718-1). 32pp. Several nocturnal animals are introduced, including the coyote, skunk, harvest mouse, barn owl, opossum, raccoon, bat, and tree frog. (Rev: BL 2/15/99; HBG 9/99; SLJ 1/99) [591.5]

21204 Fredericks, Anthony D. *Animal Sharpshooters* (5–7). Illus. Series: Watts Library: Animals. 1999, Watts LB $24.00 (0-531-11700-6). 64pp. This book focuses on the strange adaptations some animals

have made to protect themselves and to find food. (Rev: BL 12/1/99; SLJ 12/99) [591.47]

21205 Fredericks, Anthony D. *Cannibal Animals: Animals That Eat Their Own Kind* (5–7). Illus. Series: Watts Library: Animals. 1999, Watts LB $24.00 (0-531-11701-4). 64pp. A book that focuses on such animals as the female praying mantis, sharks, gerbils, and Tyrannosaurus rex, and how they have been accused of cannibalism. (Rev: BL 12/1/99; SLJ 12/99) [591.5]

21206 Funston, Sylvia. *Animal Feelings* (3–5). Illus. by Pat Stephens. Series: The Secret Life of Animals. 1998, Owl $19.95 (1-895688-82-5); paper $9.95 (1-895688-81-7). 48pp. An investigation of emotions in both wild and domestic animals is included in this book that also emphasizes that animals should be treated with compassion and respect. (Rev: SLJ 3/99) [591]

21207 Funston, Sylvia. *Animal Smarts* (4–6). Illus. 1997, Firefly $19.95 (1-895688-66-3); paper $9.95 (1-895688-67-1). 48pp. Explores the levels of intelligence in various mammals, birds, and insects, with material on how they think, solve problems, and understand human language. (Rev: BL 2/1/98; SLJ 4/98) [591.5]

21208 Gardner, Robert, and David Webster. *Science Project Ideas About Animal Behavior* (4–8). Illus. Series: Science Project Ideas. 1997, Enslow LB $19.95 (0-89490-842-1). A workmanlike compilation of projects involving animal behavior, such as the language of honeybees, with full background information and clear instructions. (Rev: BL 12/15/97; BR 5–6/98; HBG 3/98; SLJ 2/98) [591]

21209 Goodman, Susan E. *Claws, Coats, and Camouflage: The Ways Animals Fit into Their World* (2–5). Illus. by Michael Doolittle. 2001, Millbrook $22.90 (0-7613-1865-8). 48pp. The ways in which animals (and finally, humans) adapt to their worlds are presented in broad categories with brief text and photographs. (Rev: BL 12/1/01; HBG 3/02; SLJ 1/02) [591.4]

21210 Greenaway, Theresa. *Paws and Claws* (3–5). Illus. by Ann Savage, et al. Series: Head to Tail. 1995, Raintree LB $5.00 (0-8114-8266-9). 39pp. An appealing introduction to various kinds of animal feet and their uses for movement, digging, climbing, etc. (Rev: SLJ 5/95) [591]

21211 Hartley, Karen, and Chris Macro. *Hearing in Living Things* (K–2). Series: Sense. 2000, Heinemann LB $13.95 (1-57572-246-1). 32pp. An overview that explains hearing in animals and uses as examples such animals as bats, frogs, insects, owls, elephants, and humans. Also use *Tasting in Living Things* (2000). (Rev: HBG 3/01; SLJ 8/00) [591]

21212 Hickman, Pamela. *Animal Senses: How Animals See, Hear, Taste, Smell and Feel* (3–5). Illus. 1998, Kids Can $10.95 (1-55074-423-2). 40pp. In double-page spreads with text and accompanying activities, this book explores the senses of such animals as frogs, bats, butterflies, and deer. (Rev: BL 5/15/98; HBG 9/98; SLJ 5/98) [573.8]

21213 Hickman, Pamela. *Animals Eating* (3–5). Illus. 2001, Kids Can $10.95 (1-55074-577-8); paper $5.95 (1-55074-579-4). 40pp. After a general discussion of animal mouths, tongues, and teeth, this book explains how various animals eat and drink. It also gives a number of interesting simple activities. (Rev: BL 3/15/01; HBG 10/01) [591.5]

21214 Hickman, Pamela. *Animals in Motion: How Animals Swim, Jump, Slither and Glide* (3–5). Illus. 2000, Kids Can $10.95 (1-55074-573-5); paper $5.95 (1-55074-575-1). 40pp. This book on animal locomotion classifies animals by how they move — running, hopping, slipping, swimming, and climbing, for example. (Rev: BL 5/1/00; HBG 9/00; SLJ 9/00) [573.7]

21215 Hirschi, Ron. *When Morning Comes* (1–4). Photos by Thomas D. Mangelsen. 2000, Boyds Mills $15.95 (1-56397-767-2). Using striking photographs, this book on nature study shows various forms of wildlife in the morning. A companion volume is *When Night Comes* (2000). (Rev: BL 10/15/00; HBG 3/01; SLJ 12/00) [508]

21216 Hirschi, Ron. *When Night Comes* (1–3). Illus. by Thomas D. Mangelsen. 2000, Boyds Mills $15.95 (1-56397-766-4). 32pp. The activities of such animals as otters, raccoons, and coyotes at night are described in excellent photos and a simple text. (Rev: BL 10/15/00; HBG 3/01; SLJ 12/00) [591.5]

21217 Jenkins, Steve, and Robin Page. *Animals in Flight* (PS–3). Illus. by Steve Jenkins. 2001, Houghton Mifflin $16.00 (0-618-12351-2). 32pp. The wonder of flight is explained in simple prose and sensational cut-paper collages. (Rev: BCCB 12/01; BL 12/15/01; HBG 3/02; SLJ 11/01) [573.7]

21218 Kajikawa, Kimiko. *Sweet Dreams: How Animals Sleep* (PS–1). Illus. 1999, Holt $15.95 (0-8050-5890-7). Animals including a chipmunk, flamingo, bear, and bat are pictured and described while asleep. (Rev: BL 4/1/99; HBG 9/99; SLJ 4/99) [591.5]

21219 Kalman, Bobbie. *How Do Animals Adapt?* (1–3). Series: Science of Living Things. 2000, Crabtree LB $14.97 (0-86505-980-2); paper $5.36 (0-86505-957-8). 32pp. This beginning science book on animal adaptations includes camouflage, hibernation, and migration. (Rev: SLJ 11/00) [591]

21220 Kalman, Bobbie. *How Do Animals Find Food?* (2–4). Illus. Series: The Science of Living Things. 2001, Crabtree LB $14.97 (0-86505-986-1); paper $5.36 (0-86505-963-2). 32pp. Colorful illustrations present details of animals of various kinds and their ways of killing and devouring their prey. (Rev: SLJ 12/01) [591.5]

21221 Kaner, Etta. *Animal Groups: How Animals Live Together* (K–3). Illus. by Pat Stephens. 2004, Kids Can $10.95 (1-55337-337-5); paper $5.95 (1-55337-338-3). 40pp. For browsers, this is an interesting introduction to how animals behave, from hunting to grooming to raising young. (Rev: SLJ 5/04) [591.56]

21222 Kenah, Katherine. *Predator Attack!* (K–2). Illus. Series: Extreme Readers. 2004, McGraw-Hill

paper $4.99 (0-7696-3176-2). 32pp. This photo-filled book introduces, with drama, such predators as the shark, tiger, alligator, cheetah, and polar bear. (Rev: BL 4/15/04) [591.5]

21223 MacDonald, Suse. *Peck Slither and Slide* (PS–1). Illus. 1997, Harcourt $15.00 (0-15-200079-8). 48pp. The ways that animals move and travel are illustrated, and the words that describe their motions — for example, *wade* and *slither* — are explained. (Rev: BL 4/1/97; SLJ 4/97) [591]

21224 McGrath, Susan. *The Amazing Things Animals Do* (4–7). Illus. 1989, National Geographic $8.95 (0-87044-709-2). 96pp. Unusual animal behavior is shown in such areas as communication, motion, raising young, and survival. (Rev: SLJ 2/90) [591.5]

21225 Manning, Mick, and Brita Granström. *My Body, Your Body* (PS–2). Illus. by authors. Series: Wonderwise. 1997, Watts LB $21.00 (0-531-14486-0). 31pp. An easy science book that explains various parts of human anatomy and compares each with similar parts of animals' bodies. (Rev: HBG 3/98; SLJ 6/98) [591]

21226 Matero, Robert. *Animals Asleep* (3–6). Illus. 2000, Millbrook LB $25.90 (0-7613-1652-3). 80pp. Covers the sleep and rest habits of humans and animals, including bears, woodchucks, bats, hummingbirds, lobsters, and frogs. (Rev: BL 11/1/00; HBG 3/01; SLJ 2/01) [579.5]

21227 Moses, Brian. *Winking, Blinking, Wiggling, and Waggling* (2–3). Illus. Series: Eyewitness Reader. 2000, DK $12.95 (0-7894-5414-9); paper $3.95 (0-7894-5413-0). 32pp. This book for beginning readers describes fascinating facts about animals that have unusual eyes and ears. (Rev: BL 4/15/00; HBG 9/00; SLJ 8/00) [573.8]

21228 Mostue, Trude. *Wild About Animals: A Book of Beastly Behaviour* (4–6). 2000, Madcap $24.95 (0-233-99684-2). 112pp. A total of 26 mammals — some familiar, like the elephant, and others not so, like the hyrax — are introduced with four-page descriptions of each animal, its habits, and habitats. (Rev: SLJ 1/01) [591]

21229 Myers, Jack. *How Dogs Came from Wolves: And Other Explorations of Science in Action* (3–6). Illus. by John Rice. 2001, Boyds Mills $17.95 (1-56397-411-8). 64pp. A professor of zoology presents 12 fascinating animal abilities and adaptations, such as elephant "speech" and dog domestication. (Rev: BL 9/15/01; HBG 3/02; SLJ 10/01) [590]

21230 Myers, Jack. *What Happened to the Mammoths? And Other Explorations of Science in Action* (4–6). Illus. 2000, Boyds Mills $17.95 (1-56397-801-6). 64pp. A collection of articles from *Highlights for Children* magazine that explores such aspects of animal behavior as the seal's ability to dive and the cat's purr. (Rev: BL 3/1/00; HBG 9/00; SLJ 6/00) [591]

21231 Nail, Jim. *Whose Tracks Are These? A Clue Book of Familiar Forest Animals* (PS–3). Illus. by Hyla Skudder. 1994, Roberts Rinehart $13.95 (1-879373-89-0). Presents six guessing games in which readers are challenged to identify various common forest creatures through their tracks and a description of their habits. (Rev: SLJ 9/94) [591]

21232 Nichols, Catherine. *Animal Masterminds: A Chapter Book* (2–5). Series: True Tales. 2003, Children's Pr. LB $21.50 (0-516-22913-3). 48pp. Four animals with amazing abilities are the focus of this appealing volume that introduces new terms with care. (Rev: SLJ 1/04) [591.5]

21233 Pearce, Q. L. *Great Predators of the Land* (3–5). Illus. by Ed Yakovetic. 1999, Tor paper $12.95 (0-312-85981-3). 57pp. A mostly pictorial presentation that deals with various methods used to capture prey and highlights animals including tigers and eagles. Also use *Great Predators of the Sea* (1999). (Rev: SLJ 3/00) [591]

21234 Pipe, Jim. *The Giant Book of Creatures of the Night* (3–5). Illus. 1998, Millbrook LB $25.90 (0-7613-0858-X). 32pp. An entertaining, oversize book with copious illustrations and lots of information about night creatures, including various insects as well as birds and animals. (Rev: BL 12/15/98; HBG 3/99) [591.5]

21235 Renne. *Animals Trails and Tracks* (1–3). Trans. by Alison Taurel. Illus. by author. Series: Animals Up Close. 2000, Gareth Stevens LB $21.27 (0-8368-2713-9). 38pp. A brief text and many full-color pictures are used to introduce different animals and their tracks. (Rev: HBG 10/01; SLJ 2/01) [591]

21236 Riha, Susanne. *Animal Journeys: Life Cycles and Migrations* (4–6). Illus. by author. Series: Animals in the Wild. 1999, Blackbirch LB $16.95 (1-56711-426-1). 30pp. This colorful book describes the life cycle and migration patterns of both land and water animals. (Rev: HBG 4/00; SLJ 4/00) [591.52]

21237 Riha, Susanne. *Animals at Rest: Sleeping Patterns and Habitats* (4–6). Illus. by author. Series: Animals in the Wild. 1999, Blackbirch LB $16.95 (1-56711-425-3). 30pp. This book covers sleeping and resting patterns in a number of birds, fish, and mammals. (Rev: HBG 4/00; SLJ 4/00) [154.6]

21238 Savage, Stephen. *Skin* (2–4). Illus. Series: Adaptation for Survival. 1995, Thomson Learning LB $5.00 (1-56847-353-2). 32pp. Describes the skin covering on a variety of animals, including humans and other mammals, reptiles, birds, fish, and shellfish. (Rev: SLJ 3/96) [591]

21239 Sayre, April Pulley. *Home at Last: A Song of Migration* (PS–4). Illus. by Alix Berenzy. 1998, Holt $15.95 (0-8050-5154-6). Fish, birds, butterflies, whales, lobsters, and other animals are used to explain and explore the mystery of animal migration. (Rev: BL 12/1/98; HBG 3/99; SLJ 12/98) [591.56]

21240 Sayre, April Pulley. *Splish! Splash! Animal Baths* (PS–1). Illus. 2000, Millbrook LB $21.90 (0-7613-1821-6). 32pp. Lots of photos and a spare text are used to introduce unusual grooming techniques in the animal kingdom, such as chimpanzees picking fleas off each other. (Rev: BL 4/1/00; HBG 9/00; SLJ 5/00) [591.56]

21241 Settel, Joanne. *Exploding Ants: Amazing Facts About How Animals Adapt* (4–8). Illus. 1999, Simon & Schuster $16.00 (0-689-81739-8). 40pp. Lurid details of animal life, such as predatory fireflies, regurgitating birds, and bloodsuckers, are presented in this attention-getting collection of biological facts. (Rev: BCCB 3/99; BL 4/15/99; HBG 9/99; SLJ 4/99) [591.5]

21242 Shalev, Zahavit. *Water Hole* (3–5). Illus. Series: 24 Hours. 2005, DK $12.99 (0-7566-1126-1). 48pp. A colorful and information-packed look at the animals — elephants, giraffes, wildebeest, hawks, and so forth — that use a water hole over a 24-hour period. (Rev: BL 5/15/05) [591.74]

21243 Singer, Marilyn. *Bottoms Up!* (3–6). Illus. by Patrick O'Brien. 1998, Holt $14.95 (0-8050-4246-6). 32pp. A book about the behinds of animals and humans, their various uses, and variations in color, size and structure. (Rev: BL 3/15/98; HBG 9/98; SLJ 7/98) [591.5]

21244 Singer, Marilyn. *A Pair of Wings* (2–3). Illus. by Anne Wertheim. 2001, Holiday House $16.95 (0-8234-1547-3). 32pp. A fascinating introduction to all the ways in which animals' wings are used in addition to simple flying. (Rev: BL 5/15/01; HBG 10/01; SLJ 6/01) [591.47]

21245 Singer, Marilyn. *Prairie Dogs Kiss and Lobsters Wave: How Animals Say Hello* (2–4). Illus. 1998, Holt $15.95 (0-8050-3703-9). An informal look at how animals greet each other, including bears circling, zebras chewing, and elephants touching. (Rev: BL 12/1/98; HBG 3/99; SLJ 12/98) [591.59]

21246 Smith, Katherine. *Why Don't Elephants Live in the City?* (K–3). Series: Animal Puzzlers. 2004, McGraw-Hill $12.95 (1-57768-948-8). 32pp. Effective illustrations accompany questions such as "why don't tigers have spots?"; the text supplies information on concepts including camouflage. Also use *Why Don't Gorillas Lay Eggs?*, *Why Don't Polar Bears Have Stripes?*, and *Why Don't Tigers Eat Bananas?* (all 2004). (Rev: SLJ 8/04) [599.67]

21247 Stockdale, Susan. *Nature's Paintbrush: The Patterns and Colors Around You* (K–2). Illus. 1999, Simon & Schuster $15.00 (0-689-81081-4). 32pp. With a series of clear color drawings, the author shows how animals use their coloration for a variety of purposes — hiding, escaping, reproducing, and repelling enemies. (Rev: BL 7/99; HBG 9/99; SLJ 6/99) [578.4]

21248 Stockland, Patricia M. *Red Eyes or Blue Feathers: A Book About Animal Colors* (K–2). Illus. Series: Animal Wise. 2005, Picture Window LB $22.60 (1-4048-0931-7). 24pp. With color photographs, this volume introduces the varied colors found in animals and the ways in which they enable survival. Also use *Pointy, Long or Round: A Book About Animal Shapes*, *Strange Dances and Long Flights: A Book About Animal Behaviors*, and *Stripes, Spots, or Diamonds: A Book About Animal Patterns* (all 2005).

21249 Sussman, Susan, and Robert James. *Lies (People Believe) About Animals* (3–6). Illus. 1987, Whitman LB $13.95 (0-8075-4530-9). 48pp. A snake's skin is not wet and slimy; this is typical of the fascinating science facts included here. (Rev: BCCB 7–8/87; BL 8/87; SLJ 11/87)

21250 Swanson, Diane. *Animals Can Be So Playful* (K–1). Illus. by Rose Cowles. Series: Animals Can Be So. 2002, Douglas & McIntyre $10.95 (1-55054-900-6). 24pp. Various animals are seen at play in a series of excellent color photographs and an accompanying simple text. (Rev: BL 4/1/02) [591.5]

21251 Swanson, Diane. *Animals Eat the Weirdest Things* (3–6). Illus. 1998, Holt $16.95 (0-8050-5846-X). 64pp. The eating habits of animals, from carrion scavenging and cannibalism to sucking blood and chewing wood, are covered in this fascinating book on animal behavior. (Rev: BL 1/1–15/99; HBG 3/99; SLJ 1/99) [591.5]

21252 Swanson, Diane. *Feet That Suck and Feed* (2–4). Illus. Series: Up Close. 2000, Greystone $9.95 (1-55054-767-4); paper $5.95 (1-55054-769-0). 32pp. Excellent close-up photos are used to show a number of animal feet that are used to absorb food. (Rev: BL 10/15/00) [573.9]

21253 Swanson, Diane. *Headgear That Hides and Plays* (2–4). Series: Up Close. 2001, Greystone $9.95 (1-55054-819-0). 32pp. This interesting science book starts with the human skin and then describes the outer coverings of different animals, from the armored skin of an African rhino to the poison-packed needles on the back of a red lionfish. (Rev: BL 8/1/01; SLJ 1/02) [591]

21254 Swanson, Diane. *Noses That Plow and Poke* (2–4). Series: Up Close. 2000, Greystone $9.95 (1-55054-715-1). 30pp. A colorful, well-organized book that examines noses on a number of animals and their uses beyond breathing. (Rev: HB 7–8/03; HBG 10/03; SLJ 4/00) [591]

21255 Swanson, Diane. *Skin That Slimes and Scares* (2–4). Series: Up Close. 2001, Greystone $9.95 (1-55054-817-4). 32pp. Beginning with the human skull, this book describe the head structure of a number of animals from birds to the musk ox and tells how their heads help them to compete, court, and defend themselves. (Rev: BL 8/1/01; SLJ 1/02) [591]

21256 Swanson, Diane. *Tails That Talk and Fly* (2–4). Series: Up Close. 2000, Greystone $9.95 (1-55054-717-8). 30pp. This book presents a variety of animal tails and explains their many uses in a well-organized book with good photos and captions. (Rev: SLJ 4/00) [591]

21257 Swanson, Diane. *Teeth That Stab and Grind* (2–4). Illus. Series: Up Close. 2000, Greystone $9.95 (1-55054-768-2); paper $5.95 (1-55054-770-4). 32pp. Teeth that are used for protection and processing food are shown in a series of close-up photographs that picture. (Rev: BL 10/15/00; SLJ 11/00) [573.3]

21258 Swinburne, Stephen R. *Safe, Warm, and Snug* (PS–2). Illus. by Jose Aruego and Ariane Dewey. 1999, Harcourt $16.00 (0-15-201734-8). 40pp. A book that highlights in illustrations and rhyming couplets how a number of animals protect and nur-

ture their young. (Rev: BL 6/1–15/99; HBG 9/99; SLJ 6/99) [591.56]

21259 Walker, Niki, and Bobbie Kalman. *How Do Animals Move?* (1–3). Series: Science of Living Things. 2000, Crabtree LB $14.97 (0-86505-981-0); paper $5.36 (0-86505-958-6). 32pp. Using pictures and a very simple text, this book introduces such forms of animal locomotion as swimming, running, flying, and jumping. (Rev: SLJ 11/00) [591]

21260 Wells, Robert E. *What's Faster Than a Speeding Cheetah?* (K–4). Illus. 1997, Whitman LB $14.95 (0-8075-2280-5); paper $6.95 (0-8075-2281-3). 32pp. The author explores the concept of speed in the animal kingdom by focusing on the cheetah, the fastest animal. (Rev: BL 10/1/97; HBG 3/98; SLJ 1/98) [531]

21261 Woelfle, Gretchen. *Animal Families, Animal Friends* (1–3). Illus. by Robert Hynes. 2005, North-Word $15.95 (1-55971-901-X). Animal relationships are explored in three areas: parent-child, family group or pack, and larger communities. (Rev: LMC 10/05; SLJ 5/05)

BABIES

21262 Arnold, Caroline. *Mother and Baby Zoo Animals* (PS–3). Series: Zoo Animals. 1999, Carolrhoda LB $15.95 (1-57505-285-7); paper $9.95 (1-57505-390-X). 32pp. Similarities between human and animal behavior are stressed in this delightful book that introduces several zoo animals and how they care for their young. (Rev: BL 6/1–15/99; HBG 9/99) [591.3]

21263 Ashman, Linda. *Babies on the Go* (PS–2). Illus. by Jane Dyer. 2003, Harcourt $16.00 (0-15-201894-8). 32pp. This beautiful picture book looks at the diverse ways in which animal mothers — including humans — transport their young from one place to another. (Rev: BL 5/1/03; HBG 10/03; SLJ 5/03) [591.56]

21264 Batten, Mary. *Hey, Daddy! Animal Fathers and Their Babies* (K–3). Illus. by Higgins Bond. 2002, Peachtree $15.95 (1-56145-272-6). 32pp. Detailed illustrations are paired with descriptive text to introduce animal fathers that share in parenting. (Rev: BL 10/1/02; HBG 3/03; SLJ 12/02) [591.56]

21265 Bentley, Dawn. *Busy Little Beaver* (PS–2). Illus. by Beth Stover. Series: Read-and-Discover Atlantic Wilderness Adventures. 2003, Soundprints paper $3.95 (1-59249-011-5). 48pp. This appealing book follows a male beaver as he prepares a suitable home for his mate and the new babies that are soon to arrive. (Rev: SLJ 1/04)

21266 Bull, Schuyler. *Crocodile Crossing* (K–4). Illus. by Alan Male. Series: Amazing Animal Adventures. 2003, Soundprints $15.95 (1-59249-051-4); paper $6.95 (1-59249-052-2). 27pp. A Nile crocodile waits for her hatchlings to emerge from the egg and then tries to protect them from the multiple threats around the waterhole. (Rev: HBG 4/04; SLJ 2/04) [597.98]

21267 Collard, Sneed B. *Animal Dads* (PS–2). Illus. by Steve Jenkins. 1997, Houghton Mifflin $15.95 (0-395-83621-2). 32pp. The role of fathers in the animal kingdom is presented in large type and beautiful collages. (Rev: BCCB 5/97; BL 5/15/97; SLJ 6/97*) [591.56]

21268 Darling, Kathy. *Desert Babies* (3–5). Illus. by Tara Darling. 1997, Walker LB $16.85 (0-8027-8480-1). 32pp. An introduction to deserts, with a focus on the young animals found there, their size, food, enemies, and world location. (Rev: BCCB 3/97; BL 4/1/97; SLJ 3/97) [591.909]

21269 Dewey, Jennifer O. *Family Ties: Raising Wild Babies* (4–6). Illus. 1998, Marshall Cavendish $15.95 (0-7614-5037-8). 80pp. Using case histories involving five different animals, these accounts demonstrate the strong — often fierce — drive to protect the family. (Rev: BL 10/1/98; HBG 3/99; SLJ 10/98) [591.5]

21270 Fraser, Mary Ann. *How Animal Babies Stay Safe* (PS–1). Illus. Series: Let's-Read-and-Find-Out Science. 2002, HarperCollins $15.95 (0-06-028803-5). 40pp. An introduction to the many ways in which nature protects baby animals, from camouflage to parental supervision. (Rev: BL 2/1/02; HBG 10/02; SLJ 2/02) [591.56]

21271 Hickman, Pamela. *Animals and Their Young: How Animals Produce and Care for Their Babies* (3–5). Illus. by Pat Stephens. 2003, Kids Can $10.95 (1-55337-061-9); paper $5.95 (1-55337-062-7). 40pp. This picture-book-format account shows animals' reproductive habits and care of the young. (Rev: BL 3/1/03; HBG 10/03; SLJ 6/03) [591.56]

21272 Maze, Stephanie, ed. *Tender Moments in the Wild: Animals and Their Babies* (PS–2). 2001, Moonstone $15.00 (0-9707768-0-2). Adult animals caring for their young are shown in attractive spreads with minimal text. (Rev: SLJ 12/01)

21273 Priddy, Roger. *Baby's Book of Animals* (PS). 1993, DK $9.95 (1-56458-278-7). 21pp. An album of photos that contains pictures of 70 animals and their babies. (Rev: SLJ 4/94) [591]

21274 Schofield, Jennifer. *Animal Babies in Ponds and Rivers* (PS–K). Illus. Series: Animal Babies. 2004, Kingfisher $7.95 (0-7534-5790-3). 32pp. Using a simple question-and-answer format that involves young readers, this volume introduces seven baby animals found in ponds and rivers. Also use *Animal Babies in Grasslands*. (Rev: BL 4/1/04; SLJ 10/04) [591.76]

21275 Simon, Seymour. *Baby Animals* (1–3). Series: See More Readers. 2002, North-South $13.95 (1-58717-170-8); paper $3.95 (1-58717-171-6). 32pp. Double-page spreads containing a brief text opposite a color photograph introduce a number of different baby animals with material on how they are raised. (Rev: BL 7/02; HBG 3/03; SLJ 10/02) [591.3]

21276 Singer, Marilyn. *Tough Beginnings: How Baby Animals Survive* (2–4). Illus. by Anna Vojtech. 2001, Holt $16.95 (0-8050-6164-9). 32pp. The chances of survival for some animal babies — and the very varied threats — are the subject of this interesting book that combines straightforward text and appealing illustrations. (Rev: BL 8/01; HB 9–10/01; HBG 3/02; SLJ 8/01) [591.3]

21277 Squire, Ann O. *Animal Babies* (2–3). Series: True Books — Animals. 2001, Children's Book Pr. LB $23.00 (0-516-22188-4). 48pp. The young of many species are presented in colorful pictures and simple text. (Rev: BL 12/15/01) [591.3]

21278 Stockdale, Susan. *Carry Me! Animal Babies on the Move* (PS–2). Illus. 2005, Peachtree $15.95 (1-56145-328-5). 32pp. Bright illustrations show how 14 varied animals — including a baboon and an alligator — carry their young. (Rev: BL 5/1/05; SLJ 4/05) [591.56]

21279 Wallace, Karen. *Wild Baby Animals* (K–3). Illus. Series: Eyewitness Reader. 2000, DK $12.95 (0-7894-5420-3); paper $3.95 (0-7894-5419-X). 32pp. Beginning readers will enjoy this book on various animal babies, their body parts, behavior, protection, and diet. (Rev: BL 7/00; HBG 9/00) [591.3]

CAMOUFLAGE

21280 Fowler, Allan. *Hard-to-See Animals* (1–2). Series: Rookie Readers. 1997, Children's Book Pr. LB $19.00 (0-516-20548-X). 32pp. This book introduces animal camouflage, with striking photos and minimal text, suitable for beginning readers. (Rev: BL 11/15/97; HBG 3/98; SLJ 10/97) [591]

21281 Holmes, Anita. *Can You Find Us?* (1–2). Illus. 2000, Benchmark $14.95 (0-7614-1108-9). 32pp. A beginner reader that explores animal camouflage and challenges children to find small animals hidden in their surroundings. (Rev: BL 12/1/00; HBG 3/01; SLJ 2/01) [591.47]

21282 Kalman, Bobbie. *What Are Camouflage and Mimicry?* (2–4). Illus. Series: The Science of Living Things. 2001, Crabtree LB $14.97 (0-86505-985-3); paper $5.36 (0-86505-962-4). 32pp. Dramatic close-up photographs with informative captions accompany details of animals' efforts to become invisible. (Rev: SLJ 12/01) [591]

21283 Patent, Dorothy Hinshaw. *Bold and Bright: Black-and-White Animals* (K–3). Illus. by Kendahl J. Jubb. 1998, Walker LB $16.85 (0-8027-8673-1). 32pp. This work presents a number of black-and-white animals, such as the skunk and the penguin, and shows how this coloration has helped them survive. (Rev: BL 9/1/98; HBG 3/99; SLJ 10/98) [591.42]

21284 Perry, Phyllis J. *Hide and Seek: Creatures in Camouflage* (3–5). Illus. Series: First Books. 1997, Watts $22.50 (0-531-20306-9). 63pp. Describes animal camouflage in various groups of animals, including mammals, birds, insects, reptiles, and ocean life. (Rev: HBG 3/98; SLJ 2/98) [591]

21285 Stone, Tanya Lee. *Living in a World of Green: Where Survival Means Blending In* (2–4). Series: Living in a World Of. 2001, Gale LB $17.95 (1-56711-583-7). 24pp. A look at animal camouflage in temperate and tropical areas, with photographs, facts, and clear, spare text. Also use *Living in a World of White: Where Survival Means Blending In* (2001). (Rev: HBG 3/02; SLJ 1/02) [591]

21286 Swanson, Diane. *Animals Can Be So Hard to See* (K–1). Illus. by Rose Cowles. Series: Animals

Can Be So. 2002, Douglas & McIntyre $10.95 (1-55054-901-4). 24pp. Using double-page spreads with a color photograph on one side and simple text on the other, the camouflaging abilities of a variety of animals are explored. (Rev: BL 4/1/02; SLJ 8/02) [591.47]

21287 Weber, Belinda. *Animal Disguises* (K–3). Illus. Series: Kingfisher Young Knowledge. 2004, Kingfisher $8.95 (0-7534-5772-5). 47pp. Using two-page chapters with large text and eye-catching photographs, Weber introduces camouflage and the various animals that use this disguise. (Rev: BL 4/15/04*; SLJ 4/05) [591]

COMMUNICATION

21288 Jenkins, Steve. *Slap, Squeak, and Scatter: How Animals Communicate* (K–3). Illus. 2001, Houghton Mifflin $16.00 (0-618-03376-9). 48pp. An introduction to the many wonderful ways in which animals communicate with each other. (Rev: BL 5/15/01; HBG 10/01; SLJ 5/01) [591.59]

21289 Kalman, Bobbie. *How Animals Communicate* (2–4). Illus. Series: Crabapples. 1996, Crabtree LB $19.96 (0-86505-635-8); paper $5.95 (0-86505-735-4). 32pp. Discusses sound, scent, touch, color, and movement in such animals as elephants, giraffes, and honeybees. (Rev: SLJ 6/97) [591]

21290 Kaner, Etta. *Animal Talk: How Animals Communicate Through Sight, Sound and Smell* (2–4). Illus. by Greg Douglas. 2002, Kids Can $10.95 (1-55074-982-X); paper $5.95 (1-55074-984-6). 40pp. Double-page spreads with photographs and original artwork explain how a variety of animals communicate through smell, sound, and body language. (Rev: BL 4/15/02; HBG 10/02; SLJ 7/02) [581.59]

21291 McDonnell, Janet. *Animal Communication* (K–2). Illus. Series: Animal Behavior. 1997, Child's World LB $22.79 (1-56766-401-6). 32pp. The ways that animals communicate through sounds and movements are explored in this simple science book. (Rev: SLJ 2/98) [591.59]

21292 Sayre, April Pulley. *Secrets of Sound: Studying the Calls and Songs of Whales, Elephants, and Birds* (4–7). Illus. 2002, Houghton Mifflin $16.00 (0-618-01514-0). 64pp. Fascinating profiles of scientists who study animal sounds serve to introduce readers to a number of scientific concepts. (Rev: BL 12/1/02; HB 9–10/02; HBG 3/03; SLJ 10/02) [559.159]

21293 Schlein, Miriam. *Hello, Hello!* (K–2). Illus. by Daniel Kirk. 2002, Simon & Schuster $16.95 (0-689-83435-7). 32pp. This simple picture book shows how different animals greet each other. (Rev: BL 6/1–15/02; HB 7–8/02; HBG 10/02; SLJ 7/02) [591.59]

DEFENSES

21294 Barre, Michel. *How Animals Protect Themselves* (3–6). Series: Animal Survival. 1998, Gareth Stevens LB $19.93 (0-8368-2080-0). 48pp. Animal protection is discussed in this well-organized book that explains defenses, camouflage, and how homes

are used for safety. (Rev: HBG 9/98; SLJ 7/98) [591.47]

21295 Bennett, Paul. *Escaping from Enemies* (1–4). Illus. Series: Nature's Secrets. 1995, Thomson Learning LB $21.40 (1-56847-358-3). 32pp. Describes how animals defend themselves by fighting, running, or resorting to trickery. (Rev: SLJ 8/95) [591]

21296 Jenkins, Steve. *What Do You Do When Something Wants to Eat You?* (PS–3). Illus. 1997, Houghton Mifflin $16.00 (0-395-82514-8). 32pp. In this thrilling science book illustrated with paper collages, 14 different animals employ unusual tricks of nature to escape their predators. (Rev: BL 12/1/97; HBG 3/98; SLJ 11/97) [591.47]

21297 Kaner, Etta. *Animal Defenses: How Animals Protect Themselves* (2–5). Illus. by Pat Stephens. 1999, Kids Can $10.95 (1-55074-419-4). 40pp. Each section of this book is devoted to a particular type of defense, with several animals used as examples. (Rev: BL 4/15/99; HBG 9/99; SLJ 6/99) [591.47]

21298 Perry, Phyllis J. *Armor to Venom: Animal Defenses* (3–5). Illus. Series: First Books. 1997, Watts $22.50 (0-531-20299-2). 63pp. This book explores animal defenses and survival mechanisms, from camouflage to venom production. (Rev: HBG 3/98; SLJ 12/97) [591]

HIBERNATION

21299 Berger, Melvin, and Gilda Berger. *What Do Animals Do in Winter? How Animals Survive the Cold* (2–4). Illus. Series: Discovery Readers. 1995, Ideals paper $4.50 (1-57102-041-1). 48pp. Such winter survival tactics as hibernation and migration are presented with many examples. (Rev: BL 12/1/95; SLJ 2/96) [591.54]

21300 Ganeri, Anita. *Hibernation* (K–3). Series: Nature's Patterns. 2005, Heinemann LB $24.21 (1-4034-5895-2). 32pp. In simple langue, this volume introduces the stages of animal hibernation. (Rev: SLJ 6/05)

21301 Seuling, Barbara. *Winter Lullaby* (PS–1). Illus. by Greg Newbold. 1998, Harcourt $16.00 (0-15-201403-9). 32pp. Poetic language and colorful acrylic paintings are used to tell where such animals as bees, ducks, and mice spend the winter. (Rev: BL 9/1/98; HBG 3/99; SLJ 9/98) [591.54]

HOMES

21302 Crump, Donald J., ed. *Animal Architects* (3–8). Illus. 1987, National Geographic LB $12.50 (0-87044-617-7). 104pp. Chapters on animal builders are divided according to techniques — mound builders, weavers, excavators, and so on. (Rev: BL 12/15/87)

21303 Gregoire, Elizabeth. *Whose House Is This? A Look at Animal Homes — Webs, Nests, and Shells* (PS–2). Illus. by Derrick Alderman and Denise Shea. Series: Whose Is It? 2004, Picture Window LB $22.60 (1-4048-0608-3). 24pp. Rhythmic question-and-answer format and colorful collages introduce a wide variety of animal habitats. (Rev: BL 11/1/04) [591.56]

21304 Jenkins, Steve, and Robin Page. *I See a Kookaburra! Discovering Animal Habitats Around the World* (K–3). Illus. by Steve Jenkins. 2005, Houghton Mifflin $16.00 (0-618-50764-7). A bright I Spy game that introduces six habitats — the American Southwest, an English coastal tide pool, the Amazon rain forest, African grasslands, an Australian forest, and a Midwest pond — and the wildlife found there. (Rev: BCCB 5/05; BL 8/05; HB 5-6/05; SLJ 5/05) [591]

21305 Nicholson, John. *Animal Architects* (3–5). Illus. 2005, Allen & Unwin $15.95 (1-86508-955-9). 32pp. Animal burrowers, weavers, carpenters, and bricklayers are shown, with illustrations of their constructions. (Rev: BL 3/15/05) [591.564]

21306 Robinson, W. Wright. *How Mammals Build Their Amazing Homes* (5–8). Illus. by Carlyn Iverson. Series: Animal Architects. 1999, Blackbirch LB $27.44 (1-56711-381-8). 64pp. After defining what a mammal is, this account shows the homes of animals including beavers, chimpanzees, squirrels, prairie dogs, and moles, and describes how they are constructed. (Rev: HBG 4/00; SLJ 5/00) [591.56]

21307 Ryan, Pam M. *Armadillos Sleep in Dugouts: And Other Places Animals Live* (K–2). Illus. by Diane De Groat. 1997, Hyperion LB $14.89 (0-7868-2222-8). About 30 animal homes, from a beaver lodge to a woody thicket for deer, are described in text and pictures in this simple science book. (Rev: HBG 3/98; SLJ 12/97) [591]

21308 Shields, Carol Diggory. *Homes* (PS–3). Illus. by Svjetlan Junakovic. Series: Animagicals. 2001, Handprint $9.95 (1-929766-27-0). 32pp. Rhyming riddles give clues about animal homes hidden under the flaps in this tall-format picture book. (Rev: BL 2/1/02; HBG 3/02; SLJ 2/02) [811]

21309 Squire, Ann O. *Animal Homes* (2–3). Series: True Books — Animals. 2001, Children's Book Pr. LB $23.00 (0-516-22189-2). 48pp. Various kinds of animal homes are presented with well-captioned color pictures on each page plus a few lines of accompanying text. (Rev: BL 12/15/01) [591.56]

21310 Stockland, Patricia M. *Sand, Leaf, or Coral Reef: A Book About Animal Habitats* (K–2). Illus. Series: Animal Wise. 2005, Picture Window LB $16.95 (1-4048-0932-5). 24pp. With color photographs, this volume introduces the varied places where animals make their homes.

21311 Zoehfeld, Kathleen W. *What Lives in a Shell?* (PS–1). Illus. by Helen K. Davie. Series: Let's-Read-and-Find-Out. 1994, HarperCollins paper $4.95 (0-06-445124-0). 32pp. A simple science book that introduces such creatures as snails, turtles, crabs, and oysters, that use their shells as homes. (Rev: BL 8/94; HB 11–12/94; SLJ 9/94) [591.4]

REPRODUCTION

21312 Collard, Sneed B. *Making Animal Babies* (1–4). Illus. by Steve Jenkins. 2000, Houghton Mifflin $16.00 (0-395-95317-0). 32pp. This beginning science book explains how animals reproduce —

from budding and splitting to sexual reproduction — and provides material on the strategies used to mate. (Rev: BCCB 9/00; BL 5/1/00; HBG 9/00; SLJ 7/00) [571.8]

21313 Gill, Shelley. *The Egg* (K–3). Illus. by Jo-Ellen Bosson. 2001, Charlesbridge $16.95 (1-57091-377-3). 32pp. A fact-filled book about eggs and egg-bearers with attractive illustrations and humorous text. (Rev: BCCB 2/01; BL 11/1/01; HBG 3/02; SLJ 7/01) [591.4]

21314 Hickman, Pamela. *Animals and Their Mates: How Animals Attract, Fight for and Protect Each Other* (2–5). Illus. by Pat Stephens. 2004, Kids Can $10.95 (1-55337-546-7). 40pp. A broad range of mating rituals — many involving unexpected behaviors — are presented. (Rev: BL 10/15/04) [591.56]

Animal Species
GENERAL AND MISCELLANEOUS

21315 Arnold, Caroline. *Zebra* (3–7). Illus. 1993, Morrow paper $5.95 (0-688-12273-6). 48pp. Characteristics and behavior of zebras just like Punda, who lives in an animal park in New Jersey. (Rev: BL 9/1/87; SLJ 9/87)

21316 Arnosky, Jim. *Raccoons and Ripe Corn* (PS–1). Illus. by author. 1991, Morrow paper $4.95 (0-688-10489-4). 32pp. An autumn night with mother and baby raccoon eating corn in the field. (Rev: BL 9/1/87; SLJ 9/87)

21317 Berman, Ruth. *American Bison* (3–6). Illus. by Cheryl Walsh Bellville. Series: Nature Watch. 1992, Carolrhoda LB $23.93 (0-87614-697-3). 48pp. The lifestyle, habitat, and current status of the American buffalo is covered in text and pictures. (Rev: BL 8/92; SLJ 10/82) [599.73]

21318 Brimner, Larry. *Polar Mammals* (3–4). Illus. Series: A True Book. 1996, Children's Book Pr. LB $22.00 (0-516-20042-9). 48pp. An introduction to the Arctic biome, followed by general information on the many different mammals that live there. (Rev: SLJ 4/97) [590]

21319 Butler, John. *Whose Baby Am I?* (PS). Illus. 2001, Viking $10.99 (0-670-89683-7). 24pp. Nine animal babies ask "Whose baby am I?" and the answer is found by turning the page. (Rev: BL 6/1–15/01; HBG 10/01; SLJ 7/01) [591.39]

21320 Butterfield, Moira. *Fast, Strong, and Striped: What Am I?* (PS–3). Illus. by Wayne Ford. Series: What Am I? 1997, Raintree LB $22.83 (0-8172-4583-9); paper $5.95 (0-8172-7229-1). 32pp. Using double-page spreads, clues are given about an animal by introducing its physical characteristics, habitat, and diet and then identifying it. Also use *Brown, Fierce, and Furry: What Am I?* (1997). (Rev: SLJ 7/97) [591]

21321 Clarke, Ginjer L. *Platypus!* (PS–1). Illus. by Paul Mirocha. Series: Step into Reading. 2004, Random LB $11.99 (0-375-92417-5); Random paper $3.99 (0-375-82417-0). 32pp. This friendly introduction to the platypus provides simple, engaging text and close-up illustrations. (Rev: BL 7/04) [599.2]

21322 Cole, Melissa. *Rhinos* (3–5). Series: Wild Africa. 2002, Gale LB $19.95 (1-56711-633-7). 24pp. An introduction to the life and habits of this heavy pachyderm that, in spite of its reputation, is a peaceful herbivore now facing extinction in many parts of Asia and Africa. Also use *Hippos, Wildebeest,* and *Zebras* (all 2002). (Rev: BL 10/15/02) [599.72]

21323 Crump, Donald J., ed. *Amazing Animals of Australia* (5–8). Illus. 1985, National Geographic LB $12.50 (0-87044-520-0). 104pp. Creatures of the rain forest, ocean, outback, and Tasmania are highlighted with color photos. (Rev: BL 6/1/85)

21324 Delafosse, Claude. *Under the Ground: Hidden World* (PS–2). Series: First Discovery. 1999, Scholastic $12.95 (0-590-43813-1). 24pp. For young children, this colorful, well-illustrated account introduces underground animals such as moles and worms. (Rev: BL 6/1–15/99; SLJ 7/99) [591]

21325 Dossenbach, Hans D. *Beware! We Are Poisonous: How Animals Defend Themselves* (4–6). Illus. 1998, Blackbirch LB $16.95 (1-56711-215-3). 40pp. Many poisonous animals are discussed including some that are relatively harmless, such as the tarantula, and others that mimic poisonous ones to avoid predators. (Rev: BL 12/1/98; HBG 3/99) [591.6]

21326 Everts, Tammy, and Bobbie Kalman. *Really Weird Animals* (2–5). Illus. Series: Crabapples. 1995, Crabtree LB $19.96 (0-86505-627-7); paper $5.95 (0-86505-727-3). 32pp. A brief introduction to 13 strange animals, including the armadillo, tarsier, hagfish, and the smelliest animal in the world, the zorilla. (Rev: SLJ 6/96) [591]

21327 Fontanel, Beatrice. *Monsters: The World's Most Incredible Animals* (3–6). Illus. 2000, Bedrick $19.95 (0-87226-605-2). 94pp. Strange animals such as a transparent frog and a mole with a tentacled snout are highlighted in this beautifully illustrated volume that includes descriptions of their appearance, movement, and reproduction. (Rev: BL 12/1/00; HBG 3/01) [596]

21328 Fowler, Allan. *The Biggest Animal on Land* (PS–3). Illus. Series: Rookie Readers. 1996, Children's Book Pr. LB $19.00 (0-516-06050-3). 31pp. This easy-to-read science book describes some of the world's largest animals, like the elephant, and includes full-color pictures of each. (Rev: SLJ 8/96) [591]

21329 Fowler, Allan. *It Could Still Be a Mammal* (1–2). Illus. Series: Rookie Readers. 1990, Children's Book Pr. LB $19.00 (0-516-04903-8). 32pp. The nature of mammals and some examples are covered in this easily read science book. (Rev: BL 2/1/91) [599]

21330 Fowler, Allan. *Raccoons* (1–2). Series: Rookie Readers. 2000, Children's Book Pr. LB $19.00 (0-516-21590-6). 32pp. A basic introduction to raccoons, their behavior, and appearance, with full-color photos on one page and six or seven lines of

simple text on the facing page. (Rev: BL 4/15/00) [599.74]

21331 Fredericks, Anthony D. *Zebras* (2–3). Series: Early Bird Nature Books. 2000, Lerner LB $22.60 (0-8225-3043-0). 48pp. A fact-filled text and amazing color photos explore how zebras live and grow in their native Africa or in zoos around the world. (Rev: BL 7/00; HBG 3/01) [599.72]

21332 Gibbons, Gail. *Pigs* (PS–2). Illus. 1999, Holiday House $16.95 (0-8234-1441-8). This book introduces various breeds of pigs, their physical characteristics, their history and habits, and common myths about them. (Rev: BL 3/15/99; HBG 9/99; SLJ 5/99) [636.4]

21333 Grassy, John, and Chuck Keene. *National Audubon Society First Field Guide: Mammals* (4–8). Series: Audubon Society First Field Guide. 1998, Scholastic paper $17.95 (0-590-05471-6). 160pp. An attractive guide to mammals, with maps showing habitats, a picture of each animal, and basic descriptive text. (Rev: SLJ 4/99) [599]

21334 Harman, Amanda. *Rhinoceroses* (3–5). Illus. Series: Endangered! 1996, Benchmark LB $22.79 (0-7614-0290-X). 32pp. The ferocious rhinoceros is described, with material on its habits, habitats, and why it is on the endangered list. (Rev: SLJ 2/97) [599.72]

21335 Hoban, Tana. *A Children's Zoo* (PS). Illus. 1985, Greenwillow $16.89 (0-688-05204-5). 24pp. Appealing portraits of 11 common zoo animals. (Rev: BCCB 10/85; BL 9/1/85; SLJ 10/85)

21336 Jacobs, Lee. *Raccoon* (3–5). Illus. Series: Wild America. 2002, Gale LB $19.95 (1-56711-644-2). 24pp. Packed with colorful photographs, this volume is filled with information about the life of the raccoon. (Rev: BL 10/15/02; SLJ 2/03) [599.76]

21337 Jango-Cohen, Judith. *Camels* (3–6). Illus. Series: Animals, Animals. 2004, Benchmark $17.95 (0-7614-1750-8). 47pp. A well-written overview of these animals, providing all the information needed for report writing plus additional material of interest. (Rev: BL 3/15/04; SLJ 2/05) [599.63]

21338 Jango-Cohen, Judith. *Rhinoceroses* (3–6). Illus. Series: Animals, Animals. 2004, Benchmark $17.95 (0-7614-1753-2). 47pp. A well-written overview of these animals, providing all the information needed for report writing plus additional material of interest. (Rev: BL 4/15/04; HB 3–4/04; SLJ 2/05) [599.72]

21339 Jarrow, Gail. *Rhinos* (3–6). Series: Animals Attack. 2003, Gale/KidHaven LB $23.70 (0-7377-1543-X). 48pp. Accounts — some of them firsthand — of attacks on people by enraged rhinos, carefully documented and illustrated and accompanied by maps and charts. (Rev: SLJ 4/04) [599.66]

21340 Jarrow, Gail, and Paul Sherman. *Naked Mole-Rats* (4–7). Illus. Series: Nature Watch. 1996, Carolrhoda LB $28.75 (0-87614-995-6). 48pp. An informative introduction to the naked mole-rat, a most unusual animal that seems to copy habits from a variety of other species. (Rev: SLJ 10/96) [599.32]

21341 Johnson, Sylvia A. *Ferrets* (3–6). Illus. 1997, Carolrhoda LB $23.93 (1-57505-014-5). 48pp. Several types of wild and domestic ferrets and their cousins, including otters and skunks, are introduced, with a concentration on efforts to save the black-footed ferret. (Rev: BL 7/97; HBG 3/98; SLJ 8/97) [636]

21342 Kalbacken, Joan. *Badgers* (3–4). Illus. Series: A True Book. 1996, Children's Book Pr. LB $22.00 (0-516-20157-3). 48pp. In text and photos, the badger is introduced, with material on its physical characteristics, life-style, breeding, and survival. (Rev: SLJ 4/97) [599.74]

21343 LaBonte, Gail. *The Llama* (4–6). Illus. 1989, Macmillan $13.95 (0-87518-393-X). 60pp. Introducing this gentle-natured member of the camel family. (Rev: BL 3/1/89)

21344 Lang, Aubrey. *Baby Ground Squirrel* (2–4). Photos by Wayne Lynch. Series: Nature Babies. 2004, Fitzhenry & Whiteside $11.95 (1-55041-797-5); paper $5.95 (1-55041-799-1). 36pp. Full-color photographs follow the development of a litter of baby ground squirrels on the Western Canadian prairie. (Rev: BCCB 7-8/04; SLJ 2/05)

21345 Lang, Aubrey. *Baby Sloth* (1–4). Photos by Wayne Lynch. Series: Nature Babies. 2005, Fitzhenry & Whiteside $11.95 (1-55041-825-4); paper $5.95 (1-55041-827-0). 36pp. After a fascinating account of their trip to Panama's rain forests, the authors supply basic information on baby sloths — habitat, diet, relationship with their mothers, and so forth. (Rev: SLJ 4/05)

21346 Lepthien, Emilie U. *Llamas* (3–4). Illus. Series: True Books. 1996, Children's Book Pr. LB $22.00 (0-516-20160-3). 48pp. An introduction to llamas and their relatives that tells about body structure, wool, and habits. (Rev: SLJ 6/97) [599.7]

21347 MacKen, JoAnn Early. *Zebras* (K–2). Series: Animals I See at the Zoo. 2002, Gareth Stevens LB $18.60 (0-8368-3277-9). 24pp. Large type and clear pictures make this introduction appealing to beginning readers. (Rev: SLJ 2/03) [599.72]

21348 Markert, Jenny. *Zebras* (2–4). Series: Naturebooks. 2001, Child's World LB $24.21 (1-56766-883-6). 32pp. Double-page spreads (color photograph on one page, simple text on the other) are used to introduce this animal and its habitats. Also use *Rhinos* (2001). (Rev: BL 9/15/01; HBG 10/01) [599.72]

21349 Midge, Tiffany. *Buffalo* (PS–3). Illus. by Diana Magnuson. Series: Animal Lore and Legend. 1995, Scholastic $4.95 (0-590-22489-1). 32pp. The food, habitats, and behavior of buffalo are described, along with three Indian folktales about them. (Rev: SLJ 3/96) [591.52]

21350 Miller, Sara S. *Horses and Rhinos: What They Have in Common* (3–5). Series: Animals in Order. 1999, Watts LB $23.00 (0-531-11586-0). 48pp. After a general introduction to animal classification, this beautifully illustrated book discusses horses and rhinos — how they are considered alike and how they differ. (Rev: BL 12/15/99; HBG 4/00) [591]

21351 Miller, Sara Swan. *Moles and Hedgehogs: What They Have in Common* (3–5). Series: Animals in Order. 2001, Watts LB $23.00 (0-531-11633-6). 32pp. Using two-page spreads (a color photograph on one side and text on the other), the world of these related mammals is explored. (Rev: BL 6/1–15/01) [599.3]

21352 Moore, Heidi. *A Mob of Meerkats* (3–5). Series: Animal Groups. 2004, Heinemann LB $24.22 (1-4034-4694-6). 32pp. A basic introduction to the animal and its characteristics, using a question-and-answer format and including color close-ups. (Rev: SLJ 9/04)

21353 Morgan, Ben. *DK Guide to Mammals: A Wild Journey with These Extraordinary Beasts* (4–6). Illus. 2003, DK $15.99 (0-7894-9581-3). 64pp. For browsers, an excellent overview of mammals, covering topics from the purely physical to the social — "Urban Living," for example. (Rev: HBG 4/04; SLJ 1/04) [599]

21354 Nelson, Kristin L. *Clever Raccoons* (PS–2). Series: Pull Ahead Books. 2000, Lerner LB $21.27 (0-8225-3763-X); paper $6.95 (0-8225-3644-7). 32pp. This simple science book covers raccoons — their homes, when they are active, and how they use their paws. (Rev: BL 9/15/00; HBG 3/01) [599.32]

21355 Nelson, Kristin L. *Spraying Skunks* (2–3). Series: Pull Ahead Books. 2003, Lerner LB $22.60 (0-8225-4670-1); paper $5.95 (0-8225-3598-X). 32pp. An introduction to skunks and their habits that contains many color photographs and a map activity. (Rev: BL 3/15/03; HBG 10/03) [599.74]

21356 Nicholson, Darrel. *Wild Boars* (2–4). Illus. 1987, Carolrhoda LB $23.93 (0-87614-308-7). 48pp. Full-color photos highlight the habits and characteristics of the boar, introduced in the United States 100 years ago. (Rev: BCCB 9/87; BL 7/87; SLJ 9/87)

21357 Older, Jules. *Pig* (K–3). Illus. by Lyn Severance. 2004, Charlesbridge paper $6.95 (0-88106-110-7). 32pp. Children will enjoy browsing through the pages of this colorfully illustrated introduction to pigs and their place in the world. (Rev: BL 8/04; SLJ 9/04) [636.4]

21358 Pearce, Q. L. *Armadillos and Other Unusual Animals* (4–6). Illus. by Mary Ann Fraser. Series: Amazing Science. 1989, Simon & Schuster paper $5.95 (0-671-68645-3). 64pp. Unusual animals and their habits are introduced in this well-organized volume. (Rev: SLJ 4/90) [599]

21359 Pembleton, Seliesa. *The Armadillo* (2–5). Illus. Series: Amazing Animals. 1992, Macmillan LB $13.95 (0-87518-507-X). 60pp. The story of the armed mammal, the armadillo, telling where and how it lives and why it is presently endangered. (Rev: BL 11/1/92; SLJ 10/92) [599.3]

21360 Penny, Malcolm. *Black Rhino* (3–6). Illus. Series: Natural World. 2001, Raintree LB $18.98 (0-7398-4438-5). 48pp. A fine guide to the black rhinoceros with accessible text, memorable photographs, a glossary, and list of Web sites. (Rev: BL 12/15/01; HBG 10/02) [599.66]

21361 *Polar Animals* (PS–2). Illus. by Paul Hess. 1996, De Agostini $6.95 (1-899883-36-3). Humorous rhymes accompany paintings that describe eight animals from the polar regions. (Rev: SLJ 12/96) [591]

21362 Pringle, Laurence. *Strange Animals, New to Science* (4–7). Illus. 2002, Marshall Cavendish $16.95 (0-7614-5083-1). 112pp. The results of scientists' efforts to discover new animal species are presented here, with color photographs and coverage of the reasons behind disappearing habitats. (Rev: BCCB 9/02; BL 7/02; HBG 10/02; SLJ 8/02) [591.68]

21363 Ransford, Sandy. *The Otter* (K–3). Illus. by Bert Kitchen. Series: Animal Lives. 1999, Kingfisher $9.95 (0-7534-5176-X). 32pp. Using a story format, this charming book traces the life of a female otter as she hunts, mates, and raises her young. (Rev: HBG 9/99; SLJ 8/99) [599]

21364 Ring, Susan. *Project Hippopotamus* (3–6). Illus. Series: Zoo Life. 2002, Weigl LB $15.95 (1-59036-013-3). 32pp. This volume looks at both the good and bad aspects of raising hippopotamuses in zoos, and discusses their natural habitat, physiology, and so forth, using color photographs and featured sidebars. (Rev: BL 12/15/02; HBG 3/03) [599.63]

21365 Robbins, Ken. *Thunder on the Plains: The Story of the American Buffalo* (3–5). Illus. 2001, Simon & Schuster $16.00 (0-689-83025-4). 32pp. An introduction to the American buffalo, its place in American history, and why its population went from 50 million to near extinction. (Rev: BL 12/1/00; HBG 10/01; SLJ 3/01) [599.64]

21366 Royer, Anne. *Little Marmots* (3–5). Illus. Series: Born to Be Wild. 2005, Gareth Stevens LB $16.50 (0-8368-4439-4). 24pp. A simply worded look at young marmots and their lives, with large photographs.

21367 Savage, Stephen. *Mammals* (2–4). Illus. Series: What's the Difference? 2000, Raintree $25.69 (0-7398-1354-4). 32pp. This book reveals common characteristics and differences among mammals and discusses habitats, babies, food, and locomotion. (Rev: BL 10/15/00; HBG 3/01) [599]

21368 Schlaepfer, Gloria G., and Mary Lou Samuelson. *The African Rhinos* (3–5). Illus. Series: Remarkable Animals. 1992, Macmillan LB $18.95 (0-87518-505-3). 60pp. Full-color photos help tell the story of this great animal and why it is in danger of extinction. (Rev: BL 11/1/92; SLJ 10/92) [599]

21369 Sherrow, Victoria. *The Porcupine* (4–6). Illus. Series: Remarkable Animals. 1991, Macmillan LB $18.95 (0-87518-442-1). 60pp. The life cycle and habits of the porcupine are explored in colorful photographs and informative text. (Rev: BL 8/91; SLJ 1/92) [599.32]

21370 Short, Joan, et al. *Platypus* (3–4). Illus. by Andrew Wichlinski. 1997, Mondo paper $4.95 (1-57255-195-X). 22pp. There is coverage on the anatomy, habits, and habitat of this unusual animal, with a cross-section drawing of its underground burrow. (Rev: SLJ 8/97) [599]

21371 Sill, Cathryn. *About Mammals: A Guide for Children* (1–2). Illus. by John Sill. 1997, Peachtree $14.95 (1-56145-141-X). 32pp. In this very simple volume with full-color paintings, several mammals and their habits are introduced to young children. (Rev: BL 6/1–15/97; SLJ 6/97) [500]

21372 Souza, D. M. *Skunks Do More Than Stink!* (3–5). Illus. 2002, Millbrook LB $21.90 (0-7613-2503-4). 32pp. This volume is filled with photographs and easily understandable text about the lives of skunks. (Rev: BL 3/1/02; HBG 10/02; SLJ 3/02) [599.76]

21373 Spilsbury, Richard. *Black Rhino* (4–6). Illus. Series: Animals Under Threat. 2004, Heinemann LB $27.07 (1-4034-4859-0); paper $8.50 (1-4034-5433-7). 48pp. The rhinoceros and its characteristics are described before discussion of poaching, relocation, tourism, and other environmental concerns. (Rev: SLJ 1/05) [599.66]

21374 Spilsbury, Richard, and Louise Spilsbury. *A Mob of Kangaroos* (3–5). Series: Animal Groups. 2004, Heinemann LB $24.22 (1-4034-4690-3). 32pp. A basic introduction to the animal and its characteristics, using a question-and-answer format and including color close-ups. (Rev: SLJ 9/04)

21375 Squire, Ann O. *Anteaters, Sloths, and Armadillos* (3–5). Series: Animals in Order. 1999, Watts LB $22.00 (0-531-11515-1). 48pp. After a general introduction to animal classification, this book discusses three oddities of the animal world. (Rev: BL 8/99; HBG 9/99) [591]

21376 Staub, Frank. *Mountain Goats* (2–5). Photos by author. Series: Early Bird Nature Books. 1994, Lerner LB $22.60 (0-8225-3000-7). 48pp. A simple text and excellent photos are used to introduce mountain goats of the American Northwest. (Rev: SLJ 8/94) [599]

21377 Stewart, Melissa. *Hippopotamuses* (2–3). Series: Animals. 2002, Children's Book Pr. LB $23.00 (0-516-22200-7); paper $6.95 (0-516-26991-7). 48pp. The anatomy, life cycle, and habits of the hippopotamus are covered in a simple, large-type text and many color photographs. Also use *Rhinoceroses* and *Zebras* (both 2002). (Rev: BL 8/02) [599.63]

21378 Stewart, Melissa. *Mammals* (2–3). Series: True Books. 2001, Children's Book Pr. LB $22.00 (0-516-22035-7). 48pp. Common characteristics of mammals are pointed out in this simple book that shows many different mammals and covers similarities as well as differences. (Rev: BL 3/15/01) [599]

21379 Stone, Tanya. *Skunk* (3–5). Series: Wild America. 2002, Gale LB $24.94 (1-56711-641-8). 24pp. A photo-essay on this much-shunned animal with material on its appearance, unusual abilities, food, and life cycle. (Rev: BL 10/15/02; SLJ 2/03) [599.74]

21380 Stuart, Dee. *The Astonishing Armadillo* (3–6). Illus. Series: Nature Watch. 1993, Carolrhoda LB $23.93 (0-87614-769-4). 48pp. The amazing armadillo is featured in text and sharp color photos. (Rev: BL 8/93) [599.3]

21381 Swan, Erin Pembrey. *Camels and Pigs: What They Have in Common* (3–5). Series: Animals in Order. 1999, Watts LB $23.00 (0-531-11585-2). 47pp. This title deals with 14 specific animals from the Artiodactyla, or "even-toed," order, which includes camels, llamas, deer, and pigs. (Rev: SLJ 11/99) [599]

21382 Swan, Erin Pembrey. *Land Predators of North America* (2–4). Series: Animals in Order. 1999, Watts LB $22.00 (0-531-11451-1). 47pp. After an examination of animal classification, a number of land predators are introduced with material on lifestyles, appearance, homes, and food. (Rev: HBG 9/99; SLJ 5/99) [599]

21383 Swanson, Diane. *Skunks* (2–4). Series: Welcome to the World of Animals. 2002, Gareth Stevens LB $22.60 (0-8368-3317-1). 32pp. A slim volume that provides information on the animal's home, diet, communication, and lifestyle. (Rev: HBG 3/03; SLJ 3/03) [599.74]

21384 Theodorou, Rod. *Black Rhino* (K–2). Illus. Series: Animals in Danger. 2000, Heinemann LB $21.36 (1-57572-262-3). 32pp. The endangered black rhino is introduced, with information on diet, habitat, life cycle, and so on, as well as the reasons why the animal is imperiled. (Rev: HBG 10/03; SLJ 4/01) [599]

21385 Toda, Kyoko. *Animal Faces* (PS). Trans. from Japanese by Amanda Mayer Stinchecum. Photos by Akira Satoh. 1996, Kane/Miller $16.95 (0-916291-62-6). 53pp. This book shows how animal faces differ, even within a particular species. (Rev: SLJ 11/96) [591]

21386 Walker, Sally M. *Hippos* (4–6). Illus. Series: Nature Watch. 1998, Carolrhoda LB $14.95 (1-57505-078-1). 48pp. Two types of hippos are introduced, with material on physical characteristics, life cycles, habits, communication, and habitats. (Rev: BL 5/1/98; HBG 9/98; SLJ 4/98) [599.63]

21387 Walker, Sally M. *Rhinos* (4–6). Illus. 1996, Carolrhoda LB $23.93 (1-57505-008-0). 48pp. An introduction to rhinos that stresses their present near extinction and conservation efforts. (Rev: BL 12/1/96; SLJ 12/96*) [599.72]

21388 Webber, Desiree Morrison. *The Buffalo Train Ride* (4–7). Illus. by Sandy Shropshire. 1999, Eakin $14.95 (1-57168-275-9). 91pp. This is a history of the American buffalo, how it was hunted to near extinction, and the modern efforts to make sure it survives, with special attention to the work of William Hornaday. (Rev: HBG 4/00; SLJ 3/00) [591.52]

APE FAMILY

21389 Ashby, Ruth. *The Orangutan* (4–6). Illus. Series: Remarkable Animals. 1994, Dillon LB $18.95 (0-87518-600-9). 60pp. As well as a description of the orangutan and its environment, this account discusses conservation efforts being undertaken to save this endangered species. (Rev: SLJ 8/94) [599.88]

21390 Climo, Shirley. *Monkey Business: Stories from Around the World* (3–5). Illus. by Erik Brooks.

2005, Holt $18.95 (0-8050-6392-7). 128pp. Climo has gathered monkey-related folktales, proverbs, historical facts, and scientific information in one entertaining volume. (Rev: BL 5/15/05; SLJ 6/05) [599.8]

21391 Darling, Kathy. *Lemurs on Location* (3–5). Illus. Series: On Location. 1998, Lothrop $16.00 (0-688-12539-5). 32pp. Three species of Madagascar lemurs are introduced in text and color illustrations, with material on their physical characteristics, habits, diet, and social organization. (Rev: BL 4/15/98; HBG 3/99; SLJ 5/98) [599.8]

21392 Darling, Tara, and Kathy Darling. *How to Babysit an Orangutan* (2–4). Illus. 1996, Walker LB $16.85 (0-8027-8467-4). 32pp. The description of the activities and functions of Camp Leakey on Borneo, where orphaned orangutans are cared for. (Rev: BL 12/15/96; HB 11–12/96; SLJ 10/96) [599.88]

21393 Fleisher, Paul. *Gorillas* (5–8). Illus. Series: AnimalWays. 2000, Marshall Cavendish LB $28.50 (0-7614-1140-2). 104pp. Color photographs and clear text introduce gorillas, their scientific classification, physical and behavioral characteristics, and relationship to humans. (Rev: BL 1/1–15/01; HBG 3/01) [599.884]

21394 Gallimard Jeunesse. *Monkeys and Apes* (PS–2). Series: First Discovery. 1999, Scholastic $12.95 (0-590-87610-4). 24pp. Using many color photos and a brief text, this colorful book introduces different members of the ape family and explains their differences. (Rev: BL 6/1–15/99; HBG 9/99; SLJ 8/99) [599.88]

21395 Gelman, Rita G. *Monkeys and Apes of the World* (2–5). Illus. 1990, Watts LB $24.00 (0-531-10749-3). 64pp. Apes and monkeys are compared and contrasted in this well-illustrated study. (Rev: BL 7/90; SLJ 8/90) [599.8]

21396 Goodall, Jane. *The Chimpanzee Family Book* (4–6). Illus. 1997, North-South paper $8.95 (1-558-58803-5). 72pp. Illustrated with photographs, this is an affectionate portrayal of a family of chimps. (Rev: BL 7/89; HB 7–8/89; SLJ 6/89) [599.88]

21397 Goodall, Jane. *The Chimpanzees I Love: Saving Their World and Ours* (5–8). Illus. 2001, Scholastic paper $17.95 (0-439-21310-X). 80pp. Jane Goodall combines details of her own life researching chimpanzees with fact-filled descriptions of the animals' behavior and a cry for chimpanzee protection. (Rev: BL 12/1/01; HB 1–2/02; HBG 3/02; SLJ 9/01*) [599]

21398 Green, Carl R. *The Gorilla: A MyReportLinks.com Book* (3–7). Series: Endangered and Threatened Animals. 2004, Enslow LB $25.26 (0-7660-5060-2). 48pp. Supplemented by a lengthy list of links to online resources, this overview of the gorilla explores its behavior and physical characteristics, as well as the threats it faces. (Rev: BL 6/1–15/04)

21399 Harman, Amanda. *South American Monkeys* (4–6). Illus. Series: Endangered! 1996, Benchmark LB $22.79 (0-7614-0218-7). 32pp. The monkeys of South America are introduced, with material on how they differ from their African counterparts and why they are endangered. (Rev: SLJ 8/96) [599.88]

21400 Horton, Casey. *Apes* (3–6). Illus. Series: Endangered! 1996, Benchmark LB $22.79 (0-7614-0212-8). 32pp. Several species of great and lesser apes are introduced, with material on habitats, physical traits, behavior, and endangered status. (Rev: SLJ 3/96) [599.88]

21401 Jango-Cohen, Judith. *Gorillas* (4–6). Series: Animals Animals. 2002, Benchmark LB $15.95 (0-7614-1444-4). 48pp. The world of the giant gorilla is explored in this volume that covers topics including physical characteristics, habitat, care of the young, food, and social life. (Rev: BL 12/15/02; HBG 3/03) [599.884]

21402 Kalman, Bobbie. *Endangered Mountain Gorillas* (3–5). Illus. Series: Earth's Endangered Animals. 2004, Crabtree LB $16.95 (0-7787-1855-7); paper $6.26 (0-7787-1901-4). 32pp. In addition to discussion of their endangered status, this volume covers these animals' habitat, behavior, life cycle, and so forth. (Rev: SLJ 6/05) [599.884]

21403 Kalman, Bobbie, and Heather Levigne. *What Is a Primate?* (3–5). Illus. by Barbara Bedell. Series: Science of Living Things. 1999, Crabtree LB $14.37 (0-86505-922-5); paper $5.36 (0-86505-950-0). 32pp. Double-page spreads are used to introduce primates of different species like gorillas, gibbons, orangutans, chimpanzees, and bonobos. (Rev: SLJ 12/99) [599.8]

21404 Kane, Karen. *Mountain Gorillas* (2–3). Series: Early Bird Nature Books. 2001, Lerner LB $22.60 (0-8225-3040-6). 48pp. An easy-to-read text and numerous color photographs highlight this introduction to mountain gorillas that covers their life cycle, habits, anatomy, and habitats. (Rev: BL 8/1/01) [599.884]

21405 Kendell, Patricia. *Gorillas* (K–2). Series: In the Wild. 2003, Raintree LB $25.70 (0-7398-5497-6). 32pp. Designed for beginning readers, this colorfully illustrated book provides a basic overview of gorillas, including their habitat, diet, behavior, and the reasons the species is endangered. (Rev: HBG 10/03; SLJ 10/03) [599.8]

21406 Lewin, Ted, and Betsy Lewin. *Gorilla Walk* (4–8). 1999, Lothrop LB $16.89 (0-688-16510-9). A beautifully illustrated book about the Lewins' trip to Uganda to study mountain gorillas. (Rev: BL 8/99; HBG 4/00; SLJ 9/99) [599.8]

21407 Martin, Patricia A. *Chimpanzees* (3–5). Series: True Books. 2000, Children's Book Pr. LB $21.50 (0-516-24013-3). 48pp. Large text and color photos introduce chimpanzees, their habits, food, and homes. (Rev: BL 5/15/00) [599.88]

21408 Martin, Patricia A. *Gorillas* (3–5). Series: True Books. 2000, Children's Book Pr. LB $21.50 (0-516-21570-1). 48pp. Colorful photographs illustrate this book on gorillas, their physical characteristics, habitats, and endangered status. (Rev: BL 5/15/00) [599.8]

21409 Martin, Patricia A. *Lemurs, Lorises, and Other Lower Primates* (3–5). Series: True Books. 2000, Children's Book Pr. LB $21.50 (0-516-21575-2). 48pp. The lemur of Madagascar and the

tailless loris are two of the lower primates presented in this colorful account. (Rev: BL 5/15/00) [599.8]

21410 Martin, Patricia A. *Monkeys of Asia and Africa* (3–5). Series: True Books. 2000, Children's Book Pr. LB $21.50 (0-516-21573-6). 48pp. Large type, simple text, and full-color photos are used to introduce these monkeys from Asia and Africa. Also use *Monkeys of Central and South America* (2000). (Rev: BL 5/15/00) [599.88]

21411 Martin, Patricia A. *Orangutans* (3–5). Series: True Books. 2000, Children's Book Pr. LB $21.50 (0-516-21571-X). 48pp. This is a simple introduction to these tree-living primates native to Borneo and Sumatra. (Rev: BL 5/15/00) [599.8]

21412 Milton, Joyce. *Gorillas: Gentle Giants of the Forest* (1–3). Illus. by Bryn Barnard. Series: Step into Reading. 1997, Random paper $3.99 (0-679-87284-1). 48pp. This easy-to-read account introduces gorillas, where they live, what they eat, and how they move. (Rev: BL 5/1/97; SLJ 8/97) [598.98]

21413 Orme, David. *Orangutan* (4–6). Illus. Series: Animals Under Threat. 2005, Heinemann LB $20.95 (1-4034-5586-4). 48pp. The life cycle of the orangutan and threats to its survival are explored in this blend of narrative and eye-catching color photography.

21414 Powzyk, Joyce. *In Search of Lemurs: My Days and Nights in a Madagascar Rain Forest* (4–7). Illus. 1998, National Geographic $17.95 (0-7922-7072-X). 48pp. The author describes and illustrates her journey into the wilds of Madagascar and the many animals, plants, and birds she encountered, culminating in the elusive lemur. (Rev: BL 9/15/98; HBG 3/99; SLJ 10/98) [599.8]

21415 Robinson, Claire. *Chimpanzees* (2–3). Illus. Series: In the Wild. 1997, Heinemann $21.36 (1-57572-136-8). 24pp. A simple introduction to chimpanzees with close-up views of family life, information on how apes use tools, and material about their endangered status. (Rev: BL 2/1/98) [599.885]

21416 Saign, Geoffrey. *The Great Apes* (3–5). Illus. Series: First Books. 1998, Watts LB $21.00 (0-531-20361-1). 64pp. Introduces gorillas, chimpanzees, bonobos, and orangutans, noting their similarities to humans and describing the status of conservation efforts. (Rev: BL 5/15/98; HBG 9/98) [599.8]

21417 Spilsbury, Richard, and Louise Spilsbury. *A Troop of Chimpanzees* (3–5). Series: Animal Groups. 2003, Heinemann LB $24.22 (1-4034-0746-0). 32pp. This photo-filled overview of chimpanzees looks at behavior, diet, habitat, physical appearance, and social structure. (Rev: HBG 10/03; SLJ 9/03) [599.885]

21418 Stefoff, Rebecca. *Chimpanzees* (4–7). Illus. Series: AnimalWays. 2003, Benchmark LB $21.95 (0-7614-1579-3). 112pp. A richly illustrated look at chimpanzees, from their physiology to their interaction with humans. (Rev: HBG 4/04; SLJ 3/04)

21419 Stone, Lynn M. *Baboons* (1–3). Illus. Series: Monkey Discovery Library. 1991, Rourke LB $10.95 (0-86593-067-8). 24pp. A brief introduction to baboons: physical traits, behavior, and habitats.

1152

Also use: *Chimpanzees; Gorillas;* and *Snow Monkeys* (all 1990). (Rev: SLJ 6/91) [599.8]

21420 Taylor, Marianne. *Mountain Gorilla* (4–6). Illus. Series: Animals Under Threat. 2004, Heinemann LB $27.07 (1-4034-4861-2); paper $8.50 (1-4034-5435-3). 48pp. The mountain gorilla and its characteristics are described before discussion of problems with habitat, tourism, and conservation. (Rev: SLJ 1/05) [599.884]

21421 Thomson, Sarah L. *Amazing Gorillas!* (K–2). Illus. Series: I Can Read. 2005, HarperCollins LB $16.89 (0-06-054460-0). 32pp. Close-up color photographs add to the simple text in this informative introduction that looks at gorillas and their diet, habitat, physical characteristics, and endangered status. (Rev: BL 5/1/05) [599.884]

21422 Turner, Pamela S. *Gorilla Doctors: Saving Endangered Great Apes* (3–5). Illus. Series: Scientists in the Field. 2005, Houghton Mifflin $17.00 (0-618-44555-2). 48pp. Exciting accounts of real events add drama to this exploration of the work of veterinarians in east central Africa. (Rev: BL 6/1–15/05) [333.95]

BATS

21423 Bair, Diane, and Pamela Wright. *Bat Watching* (2–5). Series: Wildlife Watching. 1999, Capstone $19.93 (0-7638-0318-1). 48pp. An introduction to bats, their habits, habitats, and practical advice on how, when, and where to observe them. (Rev: BL 2/15/00) [599.4]

21424 Berman, Ruth. *Squeaking Bats* (PS–2). Series: Pull Ahead Books. 1998, Lerner LB $21.27 (0-8225-3602-1). 32pp. An interactive text, color photos, and a body diagram are used to explore the fascinating world of bats. (Rev: BL 2/15/99; HBG 3/99; SLJ 1/99) [599.4]

21425 Earle, Ann. *Zipping, Zapping, Zooming Bats* (2–3). Illus. by Henry Cole. 1995, HarperCollins LB $15.89 (0-06-023480-6). 32pp. Coverage is given on various types of bats and their body structure, senses, eating habits, and homes. (Rev: BCCB 2/96; BL 8/95; SLJ 8/95) [599.4]

21426 Gibbons, Gail. *Bats* (K–3). Illus. 1999, Holiday House $16.95 (0-8234-1457-4). 32pp. An introduction to bats that discusses their physical characteristics, habits, food, and lifestyle. (Rev: BL 9/1/99; HBG 4/00; SLJ 1/00) [599.4]

21427 Glaser, Linda. *Beautiful Bats* (PS–K). Illus. by Sharon L. Holm. 1997, Millbrook LB $21.40 (0-7613-0254-9). Basic information about bats is given in the body of this simple science book, with six pages of additional details at the back of the book. (Rev: HBG 3/98; SLJ 12/97) [599.4]

21428 Greenaway, Theresa. *The Secret Life of Bats* (4–7). Series: The Secret World Of. 2002, Raintree LB $27.12 (0-7398-4982-4). 48pp. An accessible, attractive volume that begins with little-known facts about bats and continues with information on their structure, habits, food, and habitats. (Rev: BL 8/02) [599.4]

21429 Haffner, Marianne, and Hans-Peter B. Stutz. *Bats! Amazing and Mysterious Creatures of the*

Night (3–4). Illus. 1998, Blackbirch LB $16.95 (1-56711-214-5). 40pp. Using text and well-captioned photos, this account describes the anatomy, habits, and habitats of several species of bats, with emphasis on the mouse-eared variety. (Rev: BL 12/1/98; HBG 3/99) [599.4]

21430 Heinrichs, Ann. *Bats* (1–3). Illus. Series: Nature's Friends. 2004, Compass Point LB $15.95 (0-7565-0591-7). 32pp. Basic facts about bats — and myths about their abilities — are presented in an appealing design. (Rev: BL 5/15/04) [599.4]

21431 Johnson, Sylvia A. *Bats* (4–7). Illus. 1985, Lerner paper $9.55 (0-8225-9500-1). 48pp. Characteristics and behavior patterns of this flying mammal. (Rev: BCCB 3/86; BL 4/15/86; SLJ 2/86) [599.4]

21432 McNulty, Faith. *When I Lived with Bats* (1–4). Illus. by Lena Shiffman. Series: Hello Reader! 1999, Scholastic paper $3.99 (0-590-04980-1). Basic information about bats is given by an author who studied them while living one summer in a house filled with them. (Rev: HB 7–8/99; HBG 9/99; SLJ 8/99) [599.4]

21433 Maestro, Betsy. *Bats: Night Fliers* (K–3). Illus. by Giulio Maestro. 1994, Scholastic $15.95 (0-590-46150-8). 32pp. An attractive picture book that exposes the myths concerning this night flier and replaces them with the truth. (Rev: SLJ 12/94) [599.4]

21434 Milton, Joyce. *Bats: Creatures of the Night* (1–3). Illus. by Judith Moffatt. 1993, Penguin Putnam paper $3.95 (0-448-40193-2). 48pp. Simple vocabulary and short sentences are used to convey basic information about bats and their habits. (Rev: BL 12/1/93; SLJ 2/94) [599.4]

21435 Penny, Malcolm. *How Bats "See" in the Dark* (3–5). Illus. Series: Nature's Mysteries. 1996, Benchmark LB $22.79 (0-7614-0455-4). 32pp. The facts about bats are interestingly presented with details on how we uncovered their secrets and what questions remain unanswered. (Rev: SLJ 2/97) [599.4]

21436 Perry, Phyllis J. *Bats: The Amazing Upside-Downers* (3–6). Illus. Series: First Books. 1998, Watts LB $21.00 (0-531-20342-5). 64pp. This introduction to the world of bats describes varieties, how they live, feed, raise their young, and contribute to the world's ecology. (Rev: BL 5/1/98; HBG 3/98) [599.4]

21437 Pringle, Laurence. *Bats! Strange and Wonderful* (3–5). 2000, Boyds Mills $15.95 (1-56397-327-8). 32pp. This book gives basic information about various types of bats and their habitats and lifestyles, and exposes popular myths about these misunderstood mammals. (Rev: BCCB 4/00; BL 3/15/00; HBG 9/00; SLJ 6/00) [599.4]

21438 Ruff, Sue, and Don E. Wilson. *Bats* (5–8). Series: AnimalWays. 2000, Marshall Cavendish LB $28.50 (0-7614-1137-2). 112pp. Some of the topics that are covered include anatomy, habits, range, classification, habitats, evolution, and survival skills. (Rev: BL 1/1–15/01; HBG 3/01) [599.4]

21439 Stuart, Dee. *Bats: Mysterious Flyers of the Night* (3–6). Illus. Series: Nature Watch. 1994, Carolrhoda LB $27.75 (0-87614-814-3). 48pp. With outstanding photographs, this is a fine introduction to bats and their habits, food, and habitats. (Rev: BL 9/15/94; SLJ 10/94) [599.4]

21440 Welsbacher, Anne. *Vampire Bats* (3–6). Series: Predators in the Wild. 2001, Capstone LB $15.95 (0-7368-0787-X). 32pp. Myths about the vampire bat are presented along with facts in this general introduction to the animal's characteristics and habitat. (Rev: HBG 10/01; SLJ 1/02) [599.4]

BEARS

21441 Berman, Ruth. *Fishing Bears* (PS–2). Series: Pull Ahead Books. 1998, Lerner LB $21.27 (0-8225-3601-3). 32pp. For beginning readers, this introduction to bears, their habits, and habitats uses color photographs, questions and answers, and an easy-to-read text. (Rev: BL 2/15/99; HBG 3/99; SLJ 1/99) [599.74]

21442 Calabro, Marian. *Operation Grizzly Bear* (5–8). Illus. 1989, Macmillan $13.95 (0-02-716241-9). An account by two naturalists on a 12-year study of silvertip bears in Yellowstone Park. (Rev: BL 3/15/90) [599.74]

21443 Deady, Kathleen W. *Grizzly Bears* (3–5). Series: Predators in the Wild. 2002, Capstone LB $21.26 (0-7368-1063-3). 32pp. Basic information about grizzly bears' lives, habitat, diet, and endangered status is presented in a format that will suit both browsers and report writers. (Rev: SLJ 8/02) [599.74]

21444 DuTemple, Lesley A. *Polar Bears* (2–3). Series: Early Bird Nature Books. 1998, Lerner LB $22.60 (0-8225-3025-2). 48pp. An easily read, extremely attractive introduction to polar bears that covers their life cycle and habitats. (Rev: BL 3/15/98; HBG 9/98; SLJ 7/98) [599.74]

21445 Fertl, Dagmar, et al. *Bears* (4–6). Illus. 2001, Sterling $17.95 (0-8069-6541-X). 80pp. This overview of bears presents a wealth of information on such topics as habitat, physical characteristics, eating, mating, defenses, and sleeping behavior. (Rev: BL 2/1/01; HBG 10/01) [599.78]

21446 Fitzgerald, Patrick J. *Bear Attacks* (4–7). Series: Animal Attack! 2000, Children's Book Pr. LB $20.00 (0-516-23312-2); paper $6.95 (0-516-23512-5). 48pp. Along with reasons why bears attack people and animals, this account describes their habitats, preferred food, and survival techniques. (Rev: SLJ 3/01) [599.7]

21447 Fraggalosch, Audrey. *Great Grizzly Wilderness: A Story of the Pacific Rain Forest* (K–3). Illus. by Donald G. Eberhart. Series: Habitats. 2000, Soundprints $15.95 (1-56899-838-4). This highly pictorial account traces one year in the lives of a British Columbia grizzly bear and her cubs. (Rev: HBG 3/01; SLJ 1/01) [599.7]

21448 Gibbons, Gail. *Grizzly Bears* (K–4). Illus. by author. 2003, Holiday House $16.95 (0-8234-1793-X). All about grizzly bears — where they live, what they eat, and what's being done to protect them. (Rev: HBG 4/04; SLJ 3/04) [599.7]

21449 Gibbons, Gail. *Polar Bears* (2–4). Illus. 2001, Holiday House $16.95 (0-8234-1593-7). 32pp. An accessible, nicely illustrated introduction to the habitat, behavior, diet, and anatomy of the polar bear. (Rev: BL 9/15/01; HBG 3/02; SLJ 9/01) [599.786]

21450 Gilks, Helen. *Bears* (2–5). Illus. by Andrew Bale. 1993, Ticknor $15.95 (0-395-66899-9). 32pp. Besides giving basic information about bears and where they live, this account introduces eight different types. (Rev: BL 7/93; SLJ 8/93) [599.72]

21451 Hall, Eleanor J. *Grizzly Bears* (4–6). Series: Nature's Predators. 2002, Gale LB $23.70 (0-7377-0941-3). As well as introducing grizzly bears and their anatomy, habits, and habitats, this account explains how they hunt and kill their prey. Also use *Polar Bears* (2001). (Rev: BL 1/1–15/02; SLJ 6/02) [599.74]

21452 Hodge, Deborah. *Bears: Polar Bears, Black Bears and Grizzly Bears* (K–3). Illus. by Pat Stephens. Series: Wildlife. 1997, Kids Can $10.95 (1-55074-269-8). 32pp. Discusses bears' food, habitats, hibernation, and life cycle. (Rev: BL 9/15/97; SLJ 9/97) [599.78]

21453 Horton, Casey. *Bears* (3–5). Illus. Series: Endangered! 1996, Benchmark LB $22.79 (0-7614-0211-X). 32pp. Different species of bears are introduced, with their habitats, physical traits, behavior, and endangered status. (Rev: SLJ 3/96) [599.74]

21454 Jarrow, Gail. *Bears* (3–6). Series: Animals Attack. 2003, Gale/KidHaven LB $23.70 (0-7377-1525-1). 48pp. True stories about attacks by bears on humans, including firsthand accounts, illustrated with photographs, charts, and maps. (Rev: SLJ 4/04) [599.7]

21455 Kulling, Monica. *Bears: Life in the Wild* (2–3). Illus. Series: Road to Reading. 1998, Golden Books paper $3.99 (0-307-26303-7). 32pp. In a book for beginning readers, several different species of bears are introduced with material on what they eat and how they hibernate and behave. (Rev: BL 3/15/99) [599.78]

21456 Lang, Aubrey. *The Adventures of Baby Bear* (K–2). Illus. by Wayne Lynch. Series: Nature Babies. 2001, Fitzhenry & Whiteside $11.95 (1-55041-670-7). 28pp. Readers accompany two young bear cubs from birth to adolescence, in a photographic presentation with simple text and a page of facts. (Rev: BL 12/15/01; SLJ 2/02) [599.78]

21457 Leeson, Tom, and Pat Leeson. *Black Bear* (2–4). Series: Wild Bears! 2000, Blackbirch LB $16.95 (1-56711-343-5). 24pp. This book describes the black bear — its habitat, survival techniques, reproduction, and interaction with humans. (Rev: BL 12/15/00; HBG 3/01) [599.7]

21458 Lepthien, Emilie U. *Grizzlies* (3–4). Illus. Series: A True Book. 1996, Children's Book Pr. LB $22.00 (0-516-20159-X). 48pp. Many photos and a large typeface are used in this book introducing grizzly bears, their characteristics and habitats. (Rev: SLJ 4/97) [599.74]

21459 McDonald, Mary Ann. *Grizzlies* (3–5). Illus. Series: Naturebooks. 1996, Child's World LB $22.79 (1-56766-213-7). 32pp. This fierce North American bear is highlighted in full-page pictures and large-print text. (Rev: BL 12/15/96) [599.74]

21460 Magloff, Lisa. *Bear* (1–2). Illus. Series: Watch Me Grow. 2004, DK $7.99 (0-7566-0194-0). 24pp. An appealing look at how bears develop, with eye-catching illustrations.

21461 Markle, Sandra. *Polar Bears* (3–7). Series: Animal Predators. 2004, Carolrhoda LB $25.26 (1-57505-730-1). 40pp. Describes the life of a female polar bear in the Arctic — behavior, diet, communication, life cycle, and so forth. (Rev: SLJ 1/05) [599.786]

21462 Montgomery, Sy. *Search for the Golden Moon Bear: Science and Adventure in the Asian Tropics* (5–9). 2004, Houghton Mifflin $17.00 (0-618-35650-9). 80pp. Nature writer Montgomery describes her search across war-torn Southeast Asia for the elusive golden moon bear. (Rev: BL 12/1/04; SLJ 12/04) [599.78]

21463 Murray, Julie. *Black Bears* (2–3). Illus. Series: Animal Kingdom. 2005, ABDO LB $14.95 (1-59197-302-3). 24pp. For beginning readers, this is an introduction to the black bear and its physical characteristics, habitat, and diet. (Rev: SLJ 5/05) [599]

21464 Murray, Julie. *Grizzly Bears* (1–3). Illus. Series: Animal Kingdom. 2002, ABDO LB $14.95 (1-57765-715-2). 24pp. For beginning readers, this photo-filled book offers a basic introduction to the life of the grizzly bear. (Rev: SLJ 4/03) [599.784]

21465 Patent, Dorothy Hinshaw. *Great Ice Bear: The Polar Bear and the Eskimo* (3–5). Illus. 1999, Morrow LB $15.93 (0-688-13768-7). 48pp. An appealing account of the characteristics, habits, and habitats of the polar bear. (Rev: BL 12/1/99; HBG 4/00; SLJ 10/99) [599.786]

21466 Patent, Dorothy Hinshaw. *Looking at Bears* (2–5). Photos by William Munoz. 1994, Holiday House LB $15.95 (0-8234-1139-7). 40pp. An attractive book on bears that covers such subjects as classification, behavior, food, reproduction, hibernation, and evolution. (Rev: BL 12/1/94; SLJ 1/95) [599.74]

21467 Patent, Dorothy Hinshaw. *A Polar Bear Biologist at Work* (4–6). Series: Wildlife Conservation Society. 2001, Watts LB $22.50 (0-531-11850-9). 48pp. Basic information on polar bears is enlivened by the portrayal of biologist Chuck Jonkel at work and by his comments on bears and the environment. (Rev: SLJ 11/01) [599.786]

21468 Patent, Dorothy Hinshaw. *Polar Bears* (3–6). Series: Nature Watch. 2000, Carolrhoda $22.60 (1-57505-020-X). 48pp. The biggest and strongest animal of the arctic, the polar bear is the subject of this simple science book that contains outstanding color photographs. (Rev: BL 3/15/00; HBG 9/00; SLJ 7/00) [599.78]

21469 Penny, Malcolm. *Polar Bear* (2–4). Series: Natural World. 2000, Raintree LB $25.69 (0-7398-1060-X). 48pp. This fine introduction to the polar bear, with clear photos and a good layout, covers

topics including appearance, life cycle, mating, food, and habits. (Rev: HBG 9/00; SLJ 7/00) [599.7]

21470 Pfeffer, Wendy. *Polar Bears* (K–3). Illus. 1996, Dillon LB $14.95 (0-382-39327-9); paper $5.95 (0-382-39326-0). 32pp. An account of the first two years of a polar bear's life, with material on its habitat. (Rev: BCCB 10/96; BL 8/96; SLJ 9/96) [599]

21471 Preston-Mafham, Rod. *The Secret Life of Bears* (4–7). Series: The Secret World Of. 2002, Raintree LB $27.12 (0-7398-4983-2). 48pp. In this attractive volume readers learn why bears behave as they do, how they feed, communicate, and reproduce, and what dangers face their future. (Rev: BL 8/02) [599.74]

21472 Robinson, Claire. *Bears* (2–3). Series: In the Wild. 1997, Heinemann $21.36 (1-57572-134-1). 24pp. In this simple introduction to bears, such topics as food, care of cubs, and communication are covered. (Rev: BL 2/15/98) [599.74]

21473 Silverstein, Alvin, et al. *The Grizzly Bear* (3–6). Illus. Series: Endangered in America. 1998, Millbrook LB $22.40 (0-7613-0265-4). 64pp. This book describes the life cycle, physical characteristics, and habits of the grizzly and why it is now considered an endangered animal. (Rev: BL 9/1/98; HBG 9/98) [639.97]

21474 Stefoff, Rebecca. *Bears* (5–8). Series: AnimalWays. 2001, Marshall Cavendish LB $28.50 (0-7614-1268-9). 112pp. Various species of bears are introduced in text and color photographs with additional material on their location, anatomy, habits, and behavior. (Rev: BL 3/15/02; HBG 10/02) [599.74]

21475 Stone, Jason, and Jody Stone. *Grizzly Bear* (2–4). Illus. 2000, Blackbirch $16.95 (1-56711-342-7). 24pp. Striking photos and a straightforward text are used to introduce grizzly bears, their physical characteristics, habits, hibernation, food, and habitats. (Rev: BL 12/15/00; HBG 3/01) [599.784]

21476 Stone, Jason, and Jody Stone. *Polar Bear* (2–4). Series: Wild Bears! 2000, Blackbirch LB $16.95 (1-56711-344-3). 24pp. This stunningly illustrated book describes the physical characteristics and homes of the polar bear, its food, mating, care of young, and interaction with humans. (Rev: BL 12/15/00; HBG 3/01) [599.7]

21477 Stone, Lynn M. *Grizzlies* (3–6). Illus. Series: Nature Watch. 1993, Carolrhoda LB $23.93 (0-87614-800-3). 48pp. Outstanding color photos and clear text are used to introduce grizzlies, their habitats, food, and family life. (Rev: BL 1/15/94; SLJ 2/94) [599.74]

21478 Swinburne, Stephen R. *Black Bear: North America's Bear* (3–4). 2003, Boyds Mills $15.95 (1-59078-023-X). 32pp. This comprehensive, photo-filled overview covers the black bear's habitat, diet, and behavior, looks at the bear's history in Yellowstone, and clears up some common misconceptions. (Rev: BL 1/1–15/04; HBG 4/04; SLJ 11/03) [599.78]

21479 Tracqui, Valerie. *The Brown Bear: Giant of the Mountains* (3–5). Illus. Series: Animal Close-

Ups. 1998, Charlesbridge paper $6.95 (0-88106-439-4). 32pp. Introduces brown bears and discusses their habitats, characteristics, habits, and life cycles. (Rev: BL 5/15/98) [599.74]

BIG CATS

21480 Aaseng, Nathan. *Cheetahs* (4–6). Series: Nature's Predators. 2002, Gale LB $23.70 (0-7377-0700-3). An attractive introduction to cheetahs, how they hunt and kill prey, and how they, in turn, are hunted. (Rev: BL 1/1–15/02) [599.74]

21481 Arnold, Caroline. *Bobcats* (2–3). Series: Early Bird Nature Books. 1998, Lerner LB $22.60 (0-8225-3021-X). 48pp. A very attractive introduction to the world of the bobcat and its life cycle. (Rev: BL 3/15/98; HBG 9/98; SLJ 3/98) [599.74]

21482 Arnold, Caroline. *Lion* (3–6). Photos by Richard Hewett. 1995, Morrow LB $15.93 (0-688-12693-6). 48pp. The physical features of lions are discussed, with material on their habitats, behavior, and family life. (Rev: BL 9/15/95; SLJ 12/95) [599.74]

21483 Ball, Jacqueline A., and Kit Carlson. *The Leopard Son: A True Story* (3–5). Illus. 1996, McGraw-Hill $14.95 (0-07-016061-9). 32pp. The animals and vegetation of the Serengeti are seen through the eyes of a young leopard. (Rev: BL 11/1/96; SLJ 1/97) [599.74]

21484 Barfuss, Matto H. *My Cheetah Family* (4–6). Trans. by Amy Gelman. Illus. by author. 1999, Carolrhoda LB $17.95 (1-57505-377-2). 48pp. This photo-essay chronicles the life of a female cheetah and her cubs on the Serengeti Plain. (Rev: HBG 4/00; SLJ 12/99) [599.74]

21485 Barrett, Jalma. *Bobcat* (3–5). Series: Wildcats of North America. 1998, Blackbirch LB $14.95 (1-56711-257-9). 24pp. Excellent photographs and an appealing, simple text are used to introduce the North American bobcat, its habits, and habitats. (Rev: BL 12/15/98; HBG 3/99; SLJ 11/98) [599.74]

21486 Barrett, Jalma. *Cougar* (3–5). Illus. Series: Wildcats of North America. 1998, Blackbirch LB $14.95 (1-56711-258-7). 24pp. A discussion of the cougar — also known as the panther, puma, or mountain lion — that includes material on its life cycle and physical features. (Rev: BL 12/1/98; HBG 3/99) [599.73]

21487 Barrett, Jalma. *Feral Cat* (3–5). Series: Wildcats of North America. 1998, Blackbirch LB $14.95 (1-56711-260-9). 24pp. The world of the feral cat is explored in photographs and an appealing text. (Rev: BL 12/15/98; HBG 3/99; SLJ 11/98) [599.74]

21488 Barrett, Jalma. *Lynx* (3–5). Illus. Series: Wildcats of North America. 1998, Blackbirch LB $14.95 (1-56711-259-5). 24pp. Introduces the lynx, with material on its habits, habitats, and physical features. (Rev: BL 12/1/98; HBG 3/99; SLJ 11/98) [599.75]

21489 *Big Cats* (3–5). Ed. by Sarah Walker. Series: Eye Wonder. 2002, DK LB $17.95 (0-7894-8549-4); paper $9.95 (0-7894-8548-6). 48pp. A brilliantly illustrated look at tigers, lions, and other big cats

and how and where they live. (Rev: BL 6/1–15/02; HBG 10/02) [599.74]

21490 Bortolotti, Dan. *Tiger Rescue: Changing the Future for Endangered Wildlife* (3–8). Series: Firefly Animal Rescue. 2003, Firefly LB $19.95 (1-55297-599-1); paper $9.95 (1-55297-558-4). 64pp. A look at how and why tigers are an endangered species and what can be done to help them, with profiles of some of the people involved in the effort. (Rev: BL 1/1–15/04; SLJ 4/04) [333.9]

21491 Chancellor, Deborah. *Tiger Tales: And Big Cat Stories* (2–4). Illus. by Peter Dennis. Series: Eyewitness Reader. 2000, DK $12.95 (0-7894-5424-6); paper $3.95 (0-7894-5423-8). 48pp. A beginning reader that features lions, tigers, and other big cats and incidents in which they clash with humans. (Rev: HBG 9/00; SLJ 7/00) [599.74]

21492 Chottin, Ariane. *Little Leopards* (3–5). Illus. Series: Born to Be Wild. 2005, Gareth Stevens LB $16.50 (0-8368-4438-6). 24pp. A simply worded look at young leopards and their lives, with large photographs.

21493 Costello, Emily. *Realm of the Panther: A Story of South Florida's Forests* (K–3). Illus. by Wes Siegrist. Series: Habitats. 2000, Soundprints $15.95 (1-56899-847-3). A richly illustrated account that focuses on a pair of yearling panthers in the Big Cypress National Preserve in Florida. (Rev: HBG 3/01; SLJ 1/01) [599.74]

21494 Darling, Kathy. *Lions* (3–6). Series: Nature Watch. 2000, Carolrhoda $22.60 (1-57505-404-3). 48pp. The unique life of the lion is described in this simple book that contains a wealth of attention-getting color photographs. (Rev: BL 3/15/00; HBG 9/00) [599.74]

21495 DuTemple, Lesley A. *Tigers* (2–4). Photos by Lynn M. Stone. Series: Early Bird Nature Books. 1996, Lerner LB $22.60 (0-8225-3010-4). 48pp. Beginning readers will find this an interesting introduction to tigers, their characteristics, and their endangered status. (Rev: SLJ 9/96) [599.74]

21496 Estigarribia, Diana. *Cheetahs* (3–6). Illus. Series: Animals, Animals. 2004, Benchmark $17.95 (0-7614-1749-4). 46pp. A well-written overview of these animals, providing all the information needed for report writing plus additional material of interest. (Rev: SLJ 2/05) [599.74]

21497 Gallimard Jeunesse, et al. *Lions* (PS–2). Series: First Discovery. 2000, Scholastic $12.95 (0-439-14824-3). 24pp. A beginner's look at lions in a heavily illustrated book that presents their physical characteristics, homes, and family life. (Rev: BL 8/00; HBG 3/01) [599.74]

21498 Greenberg, Dan. *Leopards* (4–6). Series: Animals Animals. 2002, Benchmark LB $15.95 (0-7614-1448-7). 48pp. This simple introduction to leopards examines, in text and photographs, their anatomy, habitats, behavior, and eating habits. (Rev: BL 12/15/02; HBG 3/03) [599.6]

21499 Harman, Amanda. *Leopards* (3–5). Illus. Series: Endangered! 1996, Benchmark LB $22.79 (0-7614-0223-3). 32pp. Introduces the three species of leopards and their characteristics and describes the circumstances that have caused them to be placed on the endangered list. (Rev: SLJ 8/96) [599.74]

21500 Harman, Amanda. *Tigers* (4–6). Illus. Series: Endangered! 1996, Benchmark LB $22.79 (0-7614-0215-2). 32pp. The world of the tiger is introduced, with material on its hunting skills, habitats, parenting habits, and endangered status. (Rev: SLJ 4/96) [599.74]

21501 Hewitt, Joan. *A Tiger Cub Grows Up* (1–3). Series: Baby Animals. 2001, Carolrhoda LB $21.27 (1-57505-163-X); paper $6.95 (0-8225-0089-2). 32pp. For beginning readers, this colorful account describes the youth of a tiger cub in a brief, simple text. (Rev: BL 10/15/01; HBG 3/02; SLJ 10/01) [599.74]

21502 Hirschman, Kris. *Lions* (4–6). Series: Nature's Predators. 2002, Gale LB $23.70 (0-7377-0540-X). Members of the lion family are described, with material on how and where they live and how they hunt their prey. Also use *Tigers* (2002). (Rev: BL 1/1–15/02) [599.757]

21503 Hodge, Deborah. *Wild Cats: Cougars, Bobcats and Lynx* (K–3). Illus. by Nancy Gray Ogle. Series: Wildlife. 1997, Kids Can $10.95 (1-55074-267-1). 32pp. Double-page spreads cover such topics about these big cats as their homes, food, habits, and relations with humans. (Rev: BL 9/15/97; SLJ 9/97) [599.75]

21504 Jordan, Billy. *Lion* (3–5). Illus. Series: Natural World. 1999, Raintree $25.69 (0-7398-1057-X). 48pp. This book, illustrated with many stunning photographs, introduces the lion and how it lives. (Rev: BL 10/15/99; HBG 4/00) [599.757]

21505 Kendell, Patricia. *Leopards* (K–2). Series: In the Wild. 2003, Raintree LB $25.70 (0-7398-5496-8). 32pp. Designed for beginning readers, this photo-filled overview of leopards provides basic information about the big cat's habitat, diet, behavior, and how it raises its young. (Rev: HBG 10/03; SLJ 10/03) [599.7]

21506 Landau, Elaine. *Fierce Cats* (3–5). Illus. Series: Fearsome, Scary, and Creepy Animals. 2003, Enslow LB $18.95 (0-7660-2062-2). 48pp. Landau offers a dramatic overview of the fierce behavior of leopards, cheetahs, and other big cats and documents some real-life attacks on humans. (Rev: BL 10/15/03; HBG 4/04) [599.7]

21507 Levine, Stuart P. *Tigers* (4–6). Illus. Series: Nature's Predators. 2002, Gale LB $23.70 (0-7377-1007-1). 48pp. Members of the tiger family are described, with material on how and where they live and how they hunt their prey.

21508 London, Jonathan. *Panther: Shadow of the Swamp* (1–3). Illus. by Paul Morin. 2000, Candlewick $15.99 (1-56402-623-X). Oil paintings and free verse illustrate a panther's daily activities, looking for food for her cubs. (Rev: BL 1/1–15/01; HBG 3/01; SLJ 1/01) [599.74]

21509 Lumpkin, Susan. *Small Cats* (5–8). Series: Great Creatures of the World. 1993, Facts on File $17.95 (0-8160-2848-6). A handsome oversized

volume about the smaller wild cats, with many photographs and charts. (Rev: BL 2/15/93) [599.74]

21510 McDonald, Mary Ann. *Leopards* (2–4). Series: Naturebooks. 2001, Child's World LB $24.21 (1-56766-886-0). 32pp. An attractive introduction to leopards and their lives, which consists of full-page color photographs facing a few lines of text. Also use *Cheetahs* and *Jaguars* (both 2001). (Rev: BL 9/15/01) [599.74]

21511 MacKen, JoAnn Early. *Tigers* (K–2). Series: Animals I See at the Zoo. 2002, Gareth Stevens LB $18.60 (0-8368-3276-0). 24pp. Large type and clear pictures make this introduction appealing to beginning readers. (Rev: HBG 3/03; SLJ 2/03)

21512 MacMillan, Dianne M. *Cheetahs* (3–5). Illus. Series: Nature Watch. 1998, Carolrhoda $23.93 (1-57505-044-7). 48pp. An attractive title that introduces the cheetah and tells about its anatomy, habitats, behavior, and its endangered status. (Rev: BL 2/15/98; HBG 9/98) [599.74]

21513 Markle, Sandra. *Lions* (2–5). Illus. Series: Animal Predators. 2004, Carolrhoda LB $25.26 (1-57505-727-1). Concise text and clear, full-page photographs introduce the life cycle of the lion and its physical characteristics, habitat, diet, and predatory behavior. (Rev: BL 9/15/04; SLJ 10/04) [599.757]

21514 Markle, Sandra. *Outside and Inside Big Cats* (2–4). Series: Outside Inside. 2003, Simon & Schuster $16.95 (0-689-82299-5). 40pp. This overview of the big cats, including cougars, leopards, lions, and tigers, looks in particular at their predatory characteristics. (Rev: BL 10/1/03; HB 7–8/03; HBG 4/04; SLJ 8/03) [599.75]

21515 Middleton, Don. *Jaguars* (2–4). Illus. Series: Big Cats. 1998, Rosen $17.27 (0-8239-5210-X). 24pp. A simple, easy-to-read introduction to jaguars that describes their characteristics, habits, and danger of extinction. (Rev: BL 2/1/99) [599.75]

21516 Middleton, Don. *Tigers* (2–4). Illus. Series: Big Cats. 1998, Rosen $17.27 (0-8239-5213-4). 24pp. The appearance, behavior, and mating habits of tigers are introduced along with a discussion of their endangered status. (Rev: BL 2/1/99) [599.756]

21517 Milton, Joyce. *Big Cats* (1–3). Illus. by Silvia Duran. Series: All Aboard Reading. 1994, Penguin Putnam paper $3.95 (0-448-40564-4). 48pp. An easy-to-read book that introduces such big cats as leopards, tigers, lions, jaguars, cougars, and cheetahs. (Rev: BCCB 4/95; BL 1/1/95; HB 3–4/94; SLJ 2/95) [599.74]

21518 Montgomery, Sy. *The Man-Eating Tigers of Sundarbans* (4–7). Illus. 2001, Houghton Mifflin $16.00 (0-618-07704-9). 64pp. This oversize volume introduces the savage tigers found in the Sundarbans Tiger Reserve on the border between India and Bangladesh and gives details on their behavior, food, and physical characteristics. (Rev: BCCB 2/01; BL 3/1/01*; HB 3–4/01; HBG 10/01; SLJ 3/01) [599.756]

21519 Robinson, Claire. *Lions* (2–3). Series: In the Wild. 1997, Heinemann $18.50 (1-57572-132-5). 24pp. A heavily illustrated introduction to lions that uses double-page spreads to cover such topics as behavior, food, habitats, and care of young. (Rev: BL 2/15/98) [599.74]

21520 Schafer, Susan. *Tigers* (3–5). Illus. Series: Animals, Animals. 2000, Benchmark LB $15.95 (0-7614-1170-4). 48pp. Color photographs and brief, readable text introduce these big cats and their anatomy, behavior, diet, reproduction, and so on. Also use *Lions* (2000). (Rev: HBG 3/01; SLJ 7/01) [599.756]

21521 Schlaepfer, Gloria G. *Cheetahs* (5–8). Series: AnimalWays. 2001, Marshall Cavendish LB $28.50 (0-7614-1266-2). 112pp. Cheetahs are introduced with material on anatomy, species identification, habitats, behavior, and endangered status. (Rev: BL 3/15/02; HBG 10/02) [599.7]

21522 Schneider, Jost. *Lynx* (4–7). Illus. 1994, Carolrhoda LB $28.75 (0-87614-844-5). 48pp. The life cycle, habits, and behavior of the lynx are described. (Rev: BL 1/15/95; SLJ 3/95) [599.74]

21523 Silverstein, Alvin, et al. *The Florida Panther* (4–7). Illus. Series: Endangered in America. 1997, Millbrook $24.90 (0-7613-0049-X). 64pp. Explains why the Florida panther has become endangered, with material on its life cycle and behavior and the efforts being made to save it. (Rev: BL 3/15/97; SLJ 6/97) [599.74]

21524 Simon, Seymour. *Big Cats* (K–3). 1991, HarperCollins LB $16.89 (0-06-021647-6). 40pp. The life and characteristics of big cats all over the world, with large color photos. (Rev: BCCB 6/91; BL 5/1/91; SLJ 5/91) [599.74]

21525 Spilsbury, Richard. *Bengal Tiger* (4–6). Illus. Series: Animals Under Threat. 2004, Heinemann LB $31.43 (1-4034-4858-2). 48pp. The life cycle of the threatened Bengal tiger is explored in this blend of narrative and eye-catching color photography. (Rev: BL 8/04; SLJ 1/05) [599.756]

21526 Squire, Ann O. *Cheetahs* (2–4). Illus. Series: True Book. 2005, Children's Pr. LB $24.00 (0-516-22792-0); paper $6.95 (0-516-27932-7). 48pp. An appealing look at the cheetah and its characteristics, with discussion of its endangered status and plenty of arresting color photographs. (Rev: BL 6/1–15/05) [599.759]

21527 Stone, Lynn M. *Cougars* (2–3). Series: Early Bird Nature Books. 1997, Lerner LB $22.60 (0-8225-3013-9). 48pp. These large cats, noted for their speed and ferocity, are introduced with stunning photos and a simple text. (Rev: BL 9/15/97; SLJ 10/97) [599.74]

21528 Stone, Lynn M. *Cougars* (3–6). Illus. Series: Nature Watch. 1999, Carolrhoda LB $22.60 (1-57505-050-1). 48pp. Topics discussed in this colorful volume include the cougar's structure, habitats, reproduction, hunting, and relations with humans. (Rev: BL 9/1/99; HBG 9/99) [599.75]

21529 Sullivan, Jody. *Cheetahs: Spotted Speedsters* (1–3). Illus. Series: Wild World of Animals. 2002, Capstone LB $18.60 (0-7368-1393-4). 24pp. Facts about the fleet-footed cheetah include habitat, reproduction, behavior, and physical characteristics. (Rev: BL 1/1–15/03; HBG 3/03) [599]

21530 Swinburne, Stephen R. *Bobcat: North America's Cat* (3–6). Illus. 2001, Boyds Mills $15.95 (1-56397-843-1). 32pp. Using a first-person narrative, the author describes his encounters with the bobcat and gives many background facts about this animal. (Rev: BL 4/1/01; HBG 10/01; SLJ 8/01) [599.75]

21531 Taylor, Bonnie Highsmith. *Ezra: A Mountain Lion* (3–5). Illus. Series: Cover-to-Cover Books. 2000, Perfection Learning $14.95 (0-7807-9313-7); paper $8.95 (0-7891-5166-9). 56pp. The reader learns through text and color photos about the life cycle of a mountain lion named Ezra. (Rev: BL 2/1/01) [599.75]

21532 Thapar, Valmik. *Tiger* (3–5). Illus. Series: Natural World. 1999, Raintree $25.69 (0-7398-1055-3). 48pp. This book introduces the tiger, labels the parts of its body, and explains how it lives. (Rev: BL 10/15/99; HBG 4/00) [599.766]

21533 Theodorou, Rod. *Bengal Tiger* (K–2). Illus. Series: Animals in Danger. 2000, Heinemann LB $21.36 (1-57572-267-4). 32pp. A look at the Bengal tiger and its life cycle, habitat, habits, and diet, with a section on its endangered status and efforts to save the species. (Rev: HBG 3/01; SLJ 4/01) [599.756]

21534 Thompson, Sharon E. *Built for Speed: The Extraordinary, Enigmatic Cheetah* (5–8). Illus. 1998, Lerner LB $23.93 (0-8225-2854-1). 88pp. The habits and lifestyle of this endangered animal are introduced with full-color illustrations. (Rev: BL 6/1–15/98; HBG 9/98) [599.75]

21535 Thomson, Sarah L. *Tigers* (1–2). Series: An I Can Read Book. 2004, HarperCollins $16.89 (0-06-054451-1). 32pp. In easy-to-understand, concise language, the author provides an overview of tigers and their habitat, characteristics, and endangered status. (Rev: BL 7/04; SLJ 9/04) [599.756]

COYOTES, FOXES, AND WOLVES

21536 Bailey, Jill. *Gray Wolf* (4–6). Illus. Series: Animals Under Threat. 2005, Heinemann LB $20.95 (1-4034-5583-X). 48pp. The life cycle of the gray wolf and threats to its survival are explored in this blend of narrative and eye-catching color photography.

21537 Berman, Ruth. *Watchful Wolves* (PS–2). Illus. by William Muñoz. Series: Pull Again Books. 1998, Lerner LB $21.27 (0-8225-3600-5). 32pp. Questions with answers and colorful photos are used to explore the world of wolves with material on their habits, habitats, and social behavior. (Rev: BL 2/1/99; HBG 3/99; SLJ 1/99) [599.773]

21538 Brandenburg, Jim. *To the Top of the World: Adventures with Arctic Wolves* (5–7). Illus. 1993, Walker LB $17.85 (0-8027-8220-5). 44pp. Amazing color photographs highlight this account of a photographer's experiences living near a pack of Arctic wolves. (Rev: BCCB 11/93; BL 1/1/94*; SLJ 12/93*) [599.74]

21539 Chottin, Ariane. *Little Foxes* (3–5). Illus. Series: Born to Be Wild. 2005, Gareth Stevens LB $16.50 (0-8368-4435-1). 24pp. A simply worded look at young foxes and their lives, with large photographs.

1158

21540 Gentle, Victor, and Janet Perry. *Wolves* (2–4). Series: Wild Dogs. 2002, Gareth Stevens LB $19.93 (0-8368-3099-7). 24pp. A brief introduction to the life of the wolf, with appealing illustrations and plenty of photographs. Also use *Jackals* and *Dingoes* (both 2002). (Rev: HBG 10/02; SLJ 6/02) [599.773]

21541 George, Michael. *Wolves* (3–5). Series: Naturebooks: Animals. 1999, Child's World LB $15.95 (1-56766-584-5). 32pp. The world of the wolf is introduced in 15 full-page, full-color illustrations and a concise, simple text. (Rev: BL 10/15/99; HBG 4/00; SLJ 2/00) [599.74]

21542 Gibbons, Gail. *Wolves* (2–4). Illus. 1994, Holiday House LB $16.95 (0-8234-1127-3). 32pp. The habitat, life cycle, and habits of the gray (timber) wolf are explored in large color drawings and a detailed text. (Rev: BL 9/15/94; SLJ 9/94) [599.74]

21543 Greenaway, Theresa. *Wolves, Wild Dogs, and Foxes* (4–7). Illus. Series: Secret World Of. 2001, Raintree LB $27.12 (0-7398-3507-6). 48pp. Report writers will find information here about wolves, wild dogs, and foxes, including their diet, habitat, and behavior, with photographs and interesting facts. (Rev: BL 10/15/01; HBG 3/02; SLJ 1/02) [599.77]

21544 Greenberg, Dan. *Wolves* (4–6). Series: Animals Animals. 2002, Benchmark LB $15.95 (0-7614-1447-9). 48pp. A colorful introduction to wolves, their physical characteristics, social behavior, and hunting strategies. (Rev: BL 12/15/02; HBG 3/03) [599.773]

21545 Gunzi, Christiane. *The Best Book of Wolves and Wild Dogs* (3–5). Illus. by Mike Rowe. 2003, Kingfisher $12.95 (0-7534-5574-9). 31pp. Young dog lovers will delight in this richly illustrated overview of wild canines, including African wild dogs, gray wolves of North America, Australian dingoes, and the jackals of southern Europe. (Rev: HBG 10/03; SLJ 11/03) [599.773]

21546 Harrington, Fred H. *The Ethiopian Wolf* (2–4). Series: The Library of Wolves and Wild Dogs. 2002, Rosen LB $18.75 (0-8239-5767-5). 24pp. Basic information about this wolf is accompanied by full-page photographs. Also use *The Dingo* and *The African Wild Dog* (2002). (Rev: SLJ 6/02)

21547 Havard, Christian. *The Fox: Playful Prowler* (PS–3). Illus. Series: Animal Close-Ups. 1995, Charlesbridge paper $6.95 (0-88106-434-3). 28pp. Using clear, colorful photos and a simple text, this is an attractive introduction to foxes and their lifestyle. (Rev: BL 4/15/95) [599.74]

21548 Heinz, Brian J. *The Wolves* (K–3). Illus. by Bernie Fuchs. 1996, Dial LB $15.89 (0-8037-1636-9). 32pp. The life of wolves and the activities of the pack are chronicled in this entertaining picture book. (Rev: BL 9/15/96*; SLJ 10/96) [599.74]

21549 Hodge, Deborah. *Wild Dogs: Wolves, Coyotes and Foxes* (K–3). Series: Wildlife. 1997, Kids Can $10.95 (1-55074-360-0). 32pp. Effective illustrations highlight these double-page spreads introducing these "wild dogs" and their lives, food, habits, and sleep. (Rev: BL 9/15/97; SLJ 11/97) [599.74]

21550 Horton, Casey. *Wolves* (3–5). Illus. Series: Endangered! 1996, Benchmark LB $22.79 (0-7614-0213-6). 32pp. Different species of wolves are discussed, with material on habitats, physical traits, behavior, and endangered status. (Rev: SLJ 3/96) [599.74]

21551 Johnson, Sylvia A., and Alice Aamodt. *Wolf Pack: Tracking Wolves in the Wild* (5–8). Illus. 1985, Lerner paper $11.15 (0-8225-9526-5). 96pp. Fascinating details of the lives of these animals that travel in packs and share hunting, raising the young, and protection. (Rev: BCCB 12/85; BL 2/1/86; SLJ 1/86) [599.74442]

21552 Kalman, Bobbie. *Endangered Wolves* (3–5). Illus. Series: Earth's Endangered Animals. 2004, Crabtree LB $16.95 (0-7787-1854-9); paper $6.26 (0-7787-1900-6). 32pp. In addition to discussion of their endangered status, this volume covers these animals' habitat, behavior, life cycle, and so forth. (Rev: SLJ 6/05) [599.74]

21553 Kalman, Bobbie, and Amanda Bishop. *The Life Cycle of a Wolf* (2–5). Illus. by Margaret Amy Reiach. Series: The Life Cycle. 2002, Crabtree LB $15.45 (0-7787-0657-5); paper $5.36 (0-7787-0687-7). 32pp. Report writers and browsers will find value in this easily read account of the life and habits of wolves that includes plenty of illustrations. (Rev: SLJ 10/02)

21554 Lang, Aubrey. *Baby Fox* (1–3). Photos by Wayne Lynch. Series: Nature Babies. 2002, Fitzhenry & Whiteside $11.95 (1-55041-688-X). 36pp. Browsers will enjoy following the story of a female fox finding a mate, giving birth to pups, and rearing them. (Rev: SLJ 12/02)

21555 Markle, Sandra. *Growing Up Wild: Wolves* (2–4). Illus. Series: Growing Up Wild. 2001, Simon & Schuster $16.00 (0-689-81886-6). 32pp. Beginning with a wolf's birth, this account describes the physical features, habits, and food of wolf pups. (Rev: BL 4/1/01; HB 3–4/01; HBG 10/01; SLJ 9/01) [599.773]

21556 Markle, Sandra. *Wolves* (3–6). Illus. Series: Animal Predators. 2004, Carolrhoda LB $21.96 (1-57505-732-8). 40pp. Concise text and clear, full-page photographs introduce the life cycle of the wolf and its physical characteristics, habitat, diet, and predatory behavior. (Rev: SLJ 10/04) [599.74]

21557 Martin, Patricia A. Fink. *Gray Wolves* (2–3). Series: Animals. 2002, Children's Book Pr. LB $23.50 (0-516-22162-0); paper $6.95 (0-516-27472-4). 48pp. An attractive, well-designed beginning chapter book that introduces gray wolves, their social life, habits, homes, and food. (Rev: BL 8/02) [599.773]

21558 Mason, Cherie. *Wild Fox* (3–5). Illus. by JoEllen M. Stammen. 1993, Down East $15.95 (0-89272-319-X). 32pp. This picture book tells about the author's encounter with a lame red fox. (Rev: BL 6/1–15/93; SLJ 8/93*) [599.7]

21559 Montardre, Helene. *Little Wolves* (3–5). Illus. Series: Born to Be Wild. 2005, Gareth Stevens LB $16.50 (0-8368-4440-8). 24pp. A simply worded look at young wolves and their lives, with large photographs.

21560 Murdico, Suzanne J. *Coyote Attacks* (4–7). 2000, Children's Book Pr. LB $20.00 (0-516-23313-0); paper $6.95 (0-516-23513-3). 48pp. As well as covering the causes of coyote attacks on animals and humans, this account gives basic information on coyotes, their habitat, survival techniques, behavior, and preferred food. (Rev: SLJ 3/01) [599.74]

21561 Parker, Barbara Keevil. *North American Wolves* (4–6). Illus. Series: Nature Watch. 1998, Carolrhoda LB $21.27 (1-57505-095-1). 48pp. A superior account that describes the North American wolf's physical characteristics, habitat, social behavior, hunting habits, family care, and means of communication. (Rev: BL 12/1/98; HBG 3/99; SLJ 11/98) [599.773]

21562 Patent, Dorothy Hinshaw. *Gray Wolf, Red Wolf* (4–7). Illus. by William Muñoz. 1990, Houghton Mifflin $16.00 (0-89919-863-5). 64pp. Two native species of North American wolf are covered. (Rev: BL 12/1/90; HB 1–2/91) [777.74]

21563 Perry, Phyllis J. *Crafty Canines* (3–5). Illus. 1999, Watts LB $24.00 (0-531-11680-8). 64pp. An introduction to the physical characteristics, behavior, and habitats of North American coyotes, foxes, and wolves. (Rev: BL 11/1/99; HBG 4/00) [599.77]

21564 Samuelson, Mary Lou, and Gloria G. Schlaepfer. *The Coyote* (3–5). Illus. Series: Remarkable Animals. 1993, Dillon LB $13.95 (0-87518-560-6). 60pp. An introduction to this renegade of the dog family, its habits, anatomy, and family life. (Rev: BL 11/1/93) [599.74]

21565 Silverstein, Alvin, et al. *The Red Wolf* (4–8). Illus. Series: Endangered Species. 1994, Millbrook LB $24.90 (1-56294-416-9). 48pp. The story of the red wolf, once thought to have become extinct in the United States, and the recent efforts to reintroduce it in North Carolina. (Rev: BL 4/15/95) [333.95]

21566 Swanson, Diane. *Coyotes* (2–4). Series: Welcome to the World of Animals. 2002, Gareth Stevens LB $22.60 (0-8368-3313-9). 32pp. A slim volume that provides information on the animal's home, diet, communication, and lifestyle. (Rev: SLJ 3/03)

21567 Swinburne, Stephen R. *Coyote: North America's Dog* (4–6). Illus. 1999, Boyds Mills $15.95 (1-56397-765-6). 32pp. The author, a veteran park ranger who knows these animals well, describes the coyote and supplies details on the animals' life and habits. (Rev: BL 10/15/99; HBG 4/00; SLJ 11/99) [599.77]

21568 Swinburne, Stephen R. *Once a Wolf: How Wildlife Biologists Fought to Bring Back the Gray Wolf* (5–8). Illus. 1999, Houghton Mifflin $16.00 (0-395-89827-7). 48pp. This work chronicles the 25-year struggle to reintroduce the gray wolf to Yellowstone Park. (Rev: BCCB 7–8/99; BL 3/1/99; HB 7–8/99; HBG 9/99; SLJ 5/99) [333.95]

21569 van Frankenhuyzen, Robbyn Smith. *Saving Samantha: A True Story* (K–2). Illus. by Gijsbert van Frankenhuyzen. 2004, Sleeping Bear $17.95 (1-

58536-220-4). 48pp. A fox pup named Samantha is the focus of this frank story about rehabilitating animals and returning them to the wild. (Rev: BL 7/04; SLJ 9/04) [599.775]

21570 Weide, Bruce, and Patricia Tucker. *There's a Wolf in the Classroom!* (3–5). Illus. 1995, Carolrhoda LB $22.60 (0-87614-939-5). 56pp. After a general introduction to gray wolves, this book gives details on raising Koani, from cub to an adult wolf that can be taken into classrooms. (Rev: BCCB 12/95; BL 9/1/95; SLJ 10/95) [599.74]

21571 Winner, Cherie. *Coyotes* (3–6). Illus. Series: Nature Watch. 1995, Carolrhoda LB $23.93 (0-87614-938-7). 48pp. With color photos on each page and an interesting text, the world of the coyote is introduced, with material on its habitats, family life, and place in America's folklore. (Rev: BL 10/15/95) [599.74]

DEER FAMILY

21572 Arnold, Caroline. *Tule Elk* (3–6). Illus. by Richard Hewett. Series: Nature Watch. 1989, Carolrhoda LB $19.95 (0-87614-343-5). 48pp. This account is highlighted with data on structure, habits, and preservation techniques on this nearly extinct species of elk. (Rev: BL 9/15/89; HB 11–12/89; SLJ 9/89) [599.73]

21573 Bair, Diane, and Pamela Wright. *Deer Watching* (2–5). Illus. Series: Wildlife Watching. 1999, Capstone $19.93 (0-7368-0321-1). 48pp. As well as material on how, when, and where to observe deer, this book explains some of the behavioral characteristics of this animal. (Rev: BL 2/15/00) [599.65]

21574 Berendes, Mary. *Deer* (3–5). Series: Naturebooks: Animals. 1999, Child's World LB $15.95 (1-56766-586-1). 32pp. Using a question-and-answer approach and large color photographs, deer are introduced with material on such topics as food, habitat, and breeding. (Rev: BL 10/15/99; HBG 4/00; SLJ 2/00) [599.73]

21575 DuTemple, Lesley A. *North American Moose* (3–6). Series: Nature Watch. 2000, Carolrhoda LB $22.60 (1-57505-426-4). 48pp. An introduction to these gentle giants of the north, how and where they live, and their life cycle. (Rev: BL 5/15/00; HBG 10/01) [599.73]

21576 Guiberson, Brenda Z. *Teddy Roosevelt's Elk* (2–4). Illus. by Patrick O'Brien. 1997, Holt paper $15.95 (0-8050-4296-2). 32pp. A book that combines information about Teddy Roosevelt, the elk named after him, and national parks. (Rev: BL 9/15/97; HBG 3/98; SLJ 10/97) [599.65]

21577 Hinshaw Patent, Dorothy. *White-Tailed Deer* (2–4). Series: Early Bird Nature Books. 2004, Lerner LB $25.26 (0-8225-3052-X). This engaging overview ntroduces early readers to the white-tailed deer's physical characteristics, habitat, diet, behavior, and life cycle. (Rev: BL 12/15/04)

21578 Hiscock, Bruce. *The Big Caribou Herd: Life in the Arctic National Wildlife Refuge* (2–5). Illus. 2003, Boyds Mills $16.95 (1-59078-010-8). 32pp. Beautiful watercolor paintings illustrate this account of a caribou herd's migration through Alaska's Arctic National Wildlife Refuge. (Rev: BL 2/1/03; HBG 10/03; SLJ 3/03) [599.73]

21579 Hodge, Deborah. *Deer, Moose, Elk and Caribou* (3–5). Illus. Series: Wildlife. 1998, Kids Can $10.95 (1-55074-435-6). 32pp. Using colorful pictures, diagrams, and sidebars, this work introduces the moose, its habitats, life cycle, survival techniques, and reproductive process. (Rev: BL 1/1–15/99; HBG 3/99; SLJ 2/99) [599.65]

21580 Patent, Dorothy Hinshaw. *Deer and Elk* (4–6). Photos by William Munoz. 1994, Clarion $15.95 (0-395-52003-7). 78pp. The deer family and its branches are described, with coverage of mating, caring for young, overpopulation, hunting, and harvesting. (Rev: BL 5/1/94; HB 7–8/94; SLJ 6/94) [599.73]

21581 Stewart, Melissa. *Antelope* (2–3). Series: Animals. 2002, Children's Book Pr. LB $23.00 (0-516-22198-1); paper $6.95 (0-516-26989-5). 48pp. An attractively designed beginning chapter book that introduces the antelope, its life cycle, and how and where it lives. (Rev: BL 8/02) [599.73]

21582 Stone, Tanya. *Deer* (3–5). Series: Wild America. 2002, Gale LB $24.94 (1-56711-643-4). 24pp. A photo-essay showing the life cycle and habits of the deer using short chapters and many color photographs. (Rev: BL 10/15/02) [599.65]

21583 Sullivan, Jody. *Deer: Graceful Grazers* (1–3). Series: Wild World of Animals. 2002, Capstone LB $18.60 (0-7368-1394-2). 24pp. Using a simple text, colorful images, and large type, this is a beginner's introduction to the world of the deer. (Rev: BL 1/1–15/03; HBG 3/03) [599.73]

ELEPHANTS

21584 Buckley, Carol. *Travels with Tarra* (3–5). Illus. 2002, Tilbury House $16.95 (0-88448-241-3). 40pp. Buckley tells the story of Tarra, the elephant she trained to do circus acts before creating an elephant sanctuary for Tarra's retirement. (Rev: BL 10/1/02; HBG 3/03) [599.67]

21585 Cole, Melissa. *Elephants* (3–5). Series: Wild Africa. 2002, Gale LB $19.95 (1-56711-638-8). 24pp. Lavish color photographs and a brief text introduce the world's largest and heaviest land mammal, with material on its habits and habitats. (Rev: BL 10/15/02) [599.6]

21586 Darling, Kathy. *The Elephant Hospital* (3–5). Illus. by Tara Darling. 2002, Millbrook LB $23.90 (0-7613-1723-6). 40pp. This is the story of a hospital for sick elephants that was founded in Thailand in 1994. (Rev: BCCB 7–8/02; BL 4/15/02; HBG 10/02; SLJ 4/02) [636.9]

21587 Douglas-Hamilton, Oria. *The Elephant Family Book* (3–5). Illus. 1996, North-South paper $8.95 (1-558-58549-4). 60pp. A beautifully illustrated book about this endangered species. (Rev: BL 1/1/91; HB 9–10/90; SLJ 4/91) [599.6]

21588 Harman, Amanda. *Elephants* (3–5). Illus. Series: Endangered! 1996, Benchmark LB $22.79 (0-7614-0221-7). 32pp. After an introduction to the two species of elephants and their characteristics,

this book describes why they are considered endangered. (Rev: SLJ 8/96) [599.6]

21589 Jenkins, Martin. *Grandma Elephant's in Charge* (K–2). Illus. by Ivan Bates. 2003, Candlewick $15.99 (0-7636-2074-2). 29pp. An appealing picture-book introduction to the African elephant and its large size and large family. (Rev: HB 9–10/03; HBG 4/04; SLJ 12/03) [599.67]

21590 Jonas, Anne. *Little Elephants* (3–5). Illus. Series: Born to Be Wild. 2005, Gareth Stevens LB $16.50 (0-8368-4434-3). 24pp. A simply worded look at young elephants and their lives, with large color photographs.

21591 MacMillan, Dianne M. *Elephants: Our Last Land Giants* (3–6). Illus. Series: Nature Watch. 1993, Lerner LB $19.95 (0-87614-770-8). 48pp. A well-organized look at the animal's physical, social, and behavioral characteristics, with excellent full-color photos. (Rev: BL 1/15/94; SLJ 2/94) [599.6]

21592 Magloff, Lisa. *Elephant* (1–2). Illus. Series: Watch Me Grow. 2005, DK $7.99 (0-7566-1155-5). 24pp. An appealing look at how elephants develop, with eye-catching illustrations.

21593 Morgan, Jody. *Elephant Rescue: Changing the Future for Endangered Wildlife* (4–7). Illus. Series: Firefly Animal Rescue. 2005, Firefly $19.95 (1-55297-595-9); paper $9.95 (1-55297-594-0). 64pp. This photo-filled book documents the many threats facing the world's remaining herds of African and Asian elephants, and discusses elephant physiology, behavior, and habitat. (Rev: BL 2/15/05; SLJ 5/05) [599.67]

21594 Murray, Julie. *Elephants* (2–3). Illus. Series: Animal Kingdom. 2005, ABDO LB $14.95 (1-59197-314-7). 24pp. For beginning readers, this is an introduction to the elephant and its physical characteristics, habitat, and diet. (Rev: SLJ 5/05) [599.6]

21595 Overbeck, Cynthia. *Elephants* (4–7). Illus. 1981, Lerner LB $22.60 (0-8225-1452-4). 48pp. Elephants and their life cycle and habitats are discussed in this well-illustrated volume. [599]

21596 Ring, Susan. *Project Elephant* (3–6). Illus. Series: Zoo Life. 2002, Weigl LB $15.95 (1-59036-016-8). 32pp. Ring looks at elephants born in captivity and at the good and bad aspects of being raised in a zoo, with information on the animals' natural habitat and physiology. (Rev: BL 12/15/02; HBG 3/03) [599.67]

21597 Robinson, Claire. *Elephants* (2–3). Series: In the Wild. 1997, Heinemann $21.36 (1-57572-135-X). 24pp. A heavily illustrated introduction to elephants that covers topics like how they move, find food, and raise their young. (Rev: BL 2/15/98) [599.6]

21598 Schlaepfer, Gloria G. *Elephants* (5–9). Illus. Series: AnimalWays. 2003, Marshall Cavendish $20.95 (0-7614-1390-1). 112pp. In addition to material on physical characteristics, behavior, habitats, and threats, Schlaepfer touches on the animal's roles in history, mythology, religion, and literature. (Rev: BL 3/15/03; HBG 3/03) [599.67]

21599 Schmidt, Jeremy. *In the Village of the Elephants* (3–6). Illus. by Ted Wood. 1994, Walker LB

$16.85 (0-8027-8227-2). 32pp. This book focuses on an elephant keeper who works with other mahouts and their elephants in a wildlife sanctuary in India. (Rev: BCCB 3/94; BL 4/15/94; SLJ 5/94) [636]

21600 Schwabacher, Martin. *Elephants* (4–6). Illus. 2000, Marshall Cavendish LB $15.95 (0-7614-1168-2). 32pp. A useful volume that describes the physical structure of the elephant and gives coverage on its habitats, behavior, mating habits, life cycle, and food. (Rev: BL 3/15/01; HBG 3/01) [599.67]

21601 Smith, Roland. *African Elephants* (2–4). Photos by Gerry Ellis. Illus. Series: Early Bird Nature Books. 1995, Lerner LB $22.60 (0-8225-3006-6). 48pp. Beginning with a map of Africa, this account describes the African elephant, its habits and habitats, and why it is scarce and valuable. (Rev: SLJ 8/95) [599.6]

21602 Sobol, Richard. *An Elephant in the Backyard* (PS–2). Illus. 2004, Penguin Putnam $17.99 (0-525-47288-6). 32pp. A 4-year-old elephant is the focus of this photoessay about elephants' roles in the everyday life of a Thai village. (Rev: BL 6/1–15/04; SLJ 7/04) [636.9]

21603 Stewart, Melissa. *Elephants* (2–3). Series: Animals. 2002, Children's Book Pr. LB $23.00 (0-516-22199-X); paper $6.95 (0-516-26990-9). 48pp. This beginning chapter book uses attractive color photographs and a simple text to introduce the elephant and explain where and how it lives and raises its family. (Rev: BL 8/02) [599.6]

21604 Travers, Will. *Elephant* (3–5). Series: Natural World. 1999, Raintree $25.69 (0-7398-1056-1). 48pp. Through amazing photos and brief text, this book traces the life cycle of the elephant from its first steps in the African savanna through learning essential skills to finally taking its place as an adult in the herd. (Rev: BL 10/15/99; HBG 4/00) [599.6]

21605 Turner, Matt. *Asian Elephant* (4–6). Illus. Series: Animals Under Threat. 2005, Heinemann LB $20.95 (1-4034-5581-3). 48pp. The life cycle of the Asian elephant and threats to its survival are explored in this blend of narrative and eye-catching color photography.

GIRAFFES

21606 Cole, Melissa. *Giraffes* (3–5). Illus. by Tom Leeson and Pat Leeson. Series: Wild Africa. 2002, Gale LB $19.95 (1-56711-634-5). 24pp. Packed with colorful photographs, this book is filled with information about the life of a giraffe. (Rev: BL 10/15/02) [599.638]

21607 Jango-Cohen, Judith. *Giraffes* (3–5). Illus. Series: Animals, Animals. 2001, Benchmark LB $15.95 (0-7614-1258-1). 48pp. In addition to the usual information on the species, this book discusses the giraffe's discovery and naming, and its relationship with humans. (Rev: HBG 10/02; SLJ 2/02) [599.638]

21608 Leach, Michael. *Giraffe* (3–6). Illus. Series: Natural World. 2001, Raintree LB $18.98 (0-7398-4435-0). 48pp. Fascinating facts about giraffes are expressed in breezy, clear terms, with memorable close-up photographs, a glossary, and a list of Web sites. (Rev: BL 12/15/01; HBG 10/02) [599.638]

21609 Lepthien, Emilie U. *Giraffes* (3–4). Illus. Series: True Books. 1996, Children's Book Pr. LB $22.00 (0-516-20158-1). 48pp. This introduction to giraffes includes coverage on its physiology, habitat, food, and lifestyle. (Rev: SLJ 6/97) [599.7]

21610 Marie, Christian. *Little Giraffes* (3–5). Illus. Series: Born to Be Wild. 2005, Gareth Stevens LB $16.50 (0-8368-4436-X). 24pp. A simply worded look at young giraffes and their lives, with large color photographs.

21611 Markert, Jenny. *Giraffes* (K–4). Series: Naturebooks. 2001, Child's World LB $24.21 (1-56766-879-8). 32pp. Concise text and full-page photographs present basic information on the giraffe in a friendly, question-and-answer format. (Rev: HBG 10/01; SLJ 8/01) [599.7]

21612 Parker, Barbara Keevil. *Giraffes* (4–6). Illus. Series: Nature Watch. 2003, Lerner LB $23.93 (1-57505-346-2). 48pp. An attractive introduction to these long-necked animals, how and where they live, and their life cycle. (Rev: HBG 4/04)

INVERTEBRATES

21613 Blaxland, Beth. *Annelids: Earthworms, Leeches, and Sea Worms* (3–5). Illus. Series: Invertebrates. 2002, Chelsea LB $17.95 (0-7910-6993-1). 32pp. Close-up photographs, straightforward text, and an enticing layout introduce the annelid invertebrates. Also use *Cephalopods: Octopuses, Squids, and Their Relatives* and *Myriapods: Centipedes, Millipedes, and Their Relatives* (2002). (Rev: BL 12/1/02; HBG 3/03) [592]

21614 *Invertebrates* (4–6). Illus. Series: Discovery Channel School Science: The Plant and Animal Kingdoms. 2002, Gareth Stevens LB $22.60 (0-8368-3216-7). 32pp. An attractive, fact-filled yet accessible introduction with many full-color photographs and charts. (Rev: HBG 3/03; SLJ 2/03)

MARSUPIALS

21615 Burt, Denise. *Kangaroos* (3–6). Series: Nature Watch. 2000, Carolrhoda $22.60 (1-57505-388-8). 48pp. This attractive volume uses a number of color photos to introduce the kangaroo, its physical characteristics, habits, and homes. (Rev: BL 3/15/00; HBG 9/00) [599.2]

21616 Burt, Denise. *Koalas* (3–6). Illus. Series: Nature Watch. 1999, Carolrhoda $22.60 (1-57505-380-2). 48pp. Colorful photographs and clear text introduce koalas, their food, physical characteristics, lifestyles, habitats, and mating habits. (Rev: BL 12/15/99; HBG 4/00) [599.2]

21617 Dennard, Deborah. *Koala Country: The Story of an Australian Eucalyptus Forest* (2–4). Illus. Series: Wild Habitat. 2001, Soundprints $15.95 (1-56899-887-2). 32pp. An appealing look at a day in the life of a koala, covering the animal's diet, habitat, and nocturnal and reproductive activities. (Rev: BL 6/1–15/01; HBG 10/01; SLJ 11/01) [599.1]

21618 Dolbear, Emily J., and E. Russell Primm. *Kangaroos Have Joeys* (K–2). Series: Animals and Their Young. 2001, Compass Point LB $18.60 (0-7565-0061-3). 24pp. Close-up color photographs accompany information on gestation, birth, and growth, along with a lighthearted "Did You Know?" facts section. Also use *Pandas Have Cubs* (2001). (Rev: SLJ 11/01) [599.2]

21619 Hewett, Joan. *A Kangaroo Joey Grows Up* (1–3). Illus. by Richard Hewett. Series: Baby Animals. 2001, Lerner LB $21.27 (1-57505-165-6); paper $6.95 (0-8225-0091-4). 32pp. Beginning readers will enjoy this basic book about a young kangaroo joey. (Rev: BL 10/15/01; HBG 3/02; SLJ 10/01) [599.2]

21620 Inskipp, Carol. *Koala* (4–6). Illus. Series: Animals Under Threat. 2005, Heinemann LB $20.95 (1-4034-5585-6). 48pp. The life cycle of the koala and threats to its survival are explored in this blend of narrative and eye-catching color photography. [599.1]

21621 Jacobs, Lee. *Opossum* (3–5). Series: Wild America. 2003, Gale/Blackbirch LB $23.70 (1-56711-570-5). 24pp. A colorful, basic introduction to the opossum and its physical appearance, diet, habitat, and behavior. (Rev: SLJ 11/03) [599.2]

21622 Kalman, Bobbie. *The Life Cycle of a Koala* (2–4). Illus. Series: The Life Cycle. 2001, Crabtree LB $15.45 (0-7787-0655-9); paper $5.36 (0-7787-0685-0). 32pp. After a general description of the koala bear, the author clearly explains its life cycle and discusses what can be done to curb human encroachment. (Rev: SLJ 6/02) [599.1]

21623 Kalman, Bobbie, and Heather Levigne. *What Is a Marsupial?* (1–3). Series: Science of Living Things. 2000, Crabtree LB $14.97 (0-86505-978-0); paper $5.36 (0-86505-955-1). 32pp. This beginning science book introduces in text and pictures such marsupials as the kangaroo, koala, and opossum. (Rev: SLJ 11/00) [599.1]

21624 Lang, Aubrey. *Baby Koala* (K–3). Illus. Series: Nature Babies. 2005, Fitzhenry & Whiteside $11.95 (1-55041-874-2); paper $5.95 (1-55041-876-9). 36pp. This appealing photo-essay follows a koala mother and baby as they browse on eucalyptus in an Australian forest. (Rev: BL 2/1/05; SLJ 4/05) [599.25]

21625 Levine, Michelle. *Jumping Kangaroos* (K–2). Illus. Series: Pull Ahead Books. 2005, Lerner LB $22.60 (0-8225-2421-X); paper $5.95 (0-8225-2440-6). 32pp. All about kangaroos, their behavior and habitat, designed for the beginning reader. (Rev: BL 3/15/05) [599.2]

21626 Noonan, Diana. *The Kangaroo* (2–4). Illus. Series: Life Cycles. 2002, Chelsea LB $14.95 (0-7910-6968-0). 32pp. Handsome images and simple text describe the life cycle, habitat, appearance, and predators of the kangaroo, in a small, square, photo-essay format. (Rev: BL 1/1–15/03; HBG 3/03) [599.2]

21627 Penny, Malcolm. *The Secret Life of Kangaroos* (4–7). Series: The Secret World Of. 2002, Raintree LB $27.12 (0-7398-4986-7). 48pp. A visu-

ally interesting look at the world of the kangaroo with material on behavior, anatomy, reproduction, and how pollution and habitat destruction have affected these animals. (Rev: BL 8/02) [599.2]

21628 Royston, Angela. *Life Cycle of a Kangaroo* (PS–3). Series: Life Cycle. 1998, Heinemann LB $13.95 (1-57572-615-7). 32pp. Using a color photo and four lines of text per page, this book introduces the kangaroo and its life cycle. (Rev: BL 5/15/98; SLJ 6/98) [599]

21629 Sotzek, Hannelore, and Bobbie Kalman. *A Koala Is Not a Bear!* (1–3). Illus. by Barbara Bedell. Series: Crabapples. 1997, Crabtree LB $19.96 (0-86505-639-0); paper $5.95 (0-86505-739-7). 32pp. After distinguishing between this marsupial and bears, this book introduces their subspecies and traits and habits. (Rev: SLJ 9/97) [599.1]

21630 Swan, Erin Pembrey. *Kangaroos and Koalas: What They Have in Common* (3–5). Series: Animals in Order. 2000, Watts LB $23.00 (0-531-11593-3). 48pp. After describing how animals are classified, this book concentrates on marsupials and features the two most famous members of this group — the kangaroo and the koala. (Rev: BL 4/15/00) [599.1]

21631 Swan, Erin Pembrey. *Meat-Eating Marsupials* (3–5). Series: Animals in Order. 2002, Watts LB $24.00 (0-531-11628-X). 48pp. After a general introduction to these pouched animals, individual species are featured in descriptive text and striking color photographs. (Rev: BL 3/15/02) [599.1]

21632 Tesar, Jenny. *What on Earth Is a Quokka?* (3–4). Illus. Series: What on Earth? 1996, Blackbirch LB $17.95 (1-56711-104-1). 32pp. Describes the characteristics and habitat of this cat-sized marsupial that lives in Australia. (Rev: SLJ 3/97) [599.1]

21633 Theodorou, Rod. *Koala* (2–4). Illus. Series: Animals in Danger. 2001, Heinemann LB $21.36 (1-57572-271-2). 32pp. Basic information about the koala and its endangered status. (Rev: BL 7/01; HBG 10/01) [599.2]

21634 Twinem, Neecy. *High in the Trees* (PS–3). Illus. by author. Series: Animal Clues Board Books. 1996, Charlesbridge $4.95 (0-88106-940-X). Close-up pictures of parts of an animal are revealed to be those of a koala in this picture puzzle book. (Rev: SLJ 12/96) [599.74]

PANDAS

21635 Bortolotti, Dan. *Panda Rescue: Changing the Future for Endangered Wildlife* (3–8). Series: Firefly Animal Rescue. 2003, Firefly LB $19.95 (1-55297-598-3); paper $9.95 (1-55297-557-6). 64pp. Threats to the panda's survivial and efforts to protect them from extinction are examined in detail, with profiles of some of the key individuals involved. (Rev: BL 1/1–15/04; SLJ 4/04) [599.789]

21636 Claybourne, Anna. *Giant Panda* (4–6). Illus. Series: Animals Under Threat. 2005, Heinemann LB $20.95 (1-4034-5582-1). 48pp. The life cycle of the giant panda and threats to its survival are explored in this blend of narrative and eye-catching color photography. [599.74]

1163

21637 Dudley, Karen. *Giant Pandas* (3–6). Illus. Series: Untamed World. 1997, Raintree LB $28.95 (0-8172-4566-9). 64pp. This presentation includes material on the panda's classification, life span, behavior, and endangered status, plus the myths and legends that surround this animal. (Rev: SLJ 8/97) [599.74]

21638 Fowler, Allan. *Giant Pandas: Gifts from China* (1–2). Illus. Series: Rookie Readers. 1995, Children's Book Pr. LB $19.00 (0-516-06031-7). 32pp. The life of the giant panda is explored, with information about its habitats, food, and endangered-species status. (Rev: BL 7/95) [599.74]

21639 Gibbons, Gail. *Giant Pandas* (K–3). Illus. 2002, Holiday House $16.95 (0-8234-1761-1). 32pp. Simple text and watercolors introduce facts about pandas in the wild and in zoos. (Rev: BL 1/1–15/03; HBG 10/03; SLJ 12/02) [599.789]

21640 Green, Carl R. *The Giant Panda: A MyReportLinks. com Book* (3–7). Series: Endangered and Threatened Animals. 2004, Enslow LB $25.26 (0-7660-5061-0). 48pp. Supplemented by a lengthy list of links to online resources, this overview of the giant panda explores its behavior and physical characteristics, as well as the threats it faces. (Rev: BL 6/1–15/04) [599.789]

21641 Jiguang, Xin, and Markus Kappeler. *The Giant Panda* (5–7). Trans. by Noel Simon. Illus. 1984, China Books paper $9.95 (0-8351-1388-4). 118pp. China's giant panda is introduced in its natural habitat. (Rev: BL 12/15/86; HB 1–2/87; SLJ 12/86) [599]

21642 Leeson, Tom, and Pat Leeson. *Panda* (2–4). Illus. Series: Wild Bears! 2000, Blackbirch $16.95 (1-56711-341-9). 24pp. Using a direct text and quality photos, this book covers topics related to pandas, such as the world population, physical characteristics, behavior, diet, and endangered status. (Rev: BL 12/15/00; HBG 3/01) [599.789]

21643 Martin, Patricia A. Fink. *Giant Pandas* (2–3). Series: Animals. 2002, Children's Book Pr. LB $23.50 (0-516-22165-5); paper $6.95 (0-516-27471-6). 48pp. The giant panda, its anatomy, habits, food, and habitats are introduced in a simple text with many color illustrations. (Rev: BL 8/02) [599.74]

21644 Penny, Malcolm. *Giant Panda* (2–4). Series: Natural World. 2000, Raintree LB $25.69 (0-7398-1063-4). 48pp. Clear photos and a good layout distinguish this book about the giant panda, its habitat, mating, diet, and endangered status. (Rev: HBG 9/00; SLJ 7/00) [599.74]

21645 Ryder, Joanne. *Little Panda* (K–3). Illus. 2001, Simon & Schuster $16.95 (0-689-84310-0). 32pp. This photo-essay chronicles the birth and early life of Hua Mei, a panda born at the San Diego Zoo. (Rev: BL 4/15/01; HB 5–6/01; HBG 10/01; SLJ 7/01*) [599.789]

RODENTS

21646 Bastian, Lois Brunner. *Chipmunk Family* (3–5). Illus. Series: Wildlife Conservation Society Books. 2000, Watts LB $22.50 (0-531-11683-2). 48pp. Photographed in the author's backyard in New Jersey, this is a stunning book that focuses on a mother chipmunk and how she raises her brood. (Rev: BL 2/15/01) [599.36]

21647 Becker, John E. *The North American Beaver* (3–6). Illus. Series: Returning Wildlife. 2002, Gale LB $23.70 (0-7377-1011-X). 48pp. Becker covers historic and contemporary threats to the beaver's survival, with full-color photographs and a glossary and bibliography. (Rev: BL 12/1/02; SLJ 1/03) [599.37]

21648 Conniff, Richard. *Rats! The Good, the Bad, and the Ugly* (3–5). Illus. 2002, Crown $15.95 (0-375-81207-5). 37pp. A volume packed with information, anecdotes, and color photographs covering the biology, mythology, and history of rats. (Rev: BCCB 12/02; BL 12/15/02; HBG 3/03; SLJ 1/03) [599.35]

21649 Fowler, Allan. *Of Mice and Rats* (1–2). Series: Rookie Readers. 1998, Children's Book Pr. LB $18.50 (0-516-20800-4). 32pp. These rodents are introduced through full-page illustrations and minimal text. (Rev: BL 9/15/98; HBG 9/99) [599.32]

21650 Gallagher, Kristin Ellersbusch. *Cottontail Rabbits* (PS–2). Series: Pull Ahead Books. 2000, Lerner LB $21.27 (0-8225-3617-X); paper $6.95 (0-8225-3623-4). 32pp. Using many questions built into the text, this attractive easy reader introduces the cottontail rabbit, its physical characteristics, habits, food, and habitats. (Rev: BL 8/00; HBG 3/01) [599.32]

21651 Hipp, Andrew. *The Life Cycle of a Mouse* (PS–2). Illus. by Dwight Kuhn. Series: Life Cycle Of. 2002, Rosen LB $18.76 (0-8239-5866-3). 24pp. This book for beginning readers follows the life of a mouse from conception to adulthood. (Rev: BL 12/15/02) [599.35]

21652 Hodge, Deborah. *Beavers* (3–5). Illus. Series: Wildlife. 1998, Kids Can $10.95 (1-55074-429-1). 32pp. As well as the habitats, appearance, survival techniques, and life cycle of the beaver, this work discusses the animal's incredible building skills. (Rev: BL 1/1–15/99; HBG 3/99; SLJ 2/99) [599.37]

21653 Holub, Joan. *Why Do Rabbits Hop?* (K–2). Illus. 2003, Dial $13.99 (0-8037-2771-2); paper $6.99 (0-14-230120-5). 48pp. An interesting introduction to rabbits in a question-and-answer format for beginning readers. (Rev: BL 11/15/02; HBG 10/03; SLJ 2/03) [636.9]

21654 Jacobs, Lee. *Beaver* (3–5). Series: Wild America. 2003, Gale/Blackbirch LB $23.70 (1-56711-566-7). 24pp. This photo-filled volume in the Wild America series introduces young readers to the beaver, examining the toothful creature's physical characteristics, habitat, and behavior. (Rev: SLJ 11/03) [599.37]

21655 Kalman, Bobbie, and Jacqueline Langille. *What Is a Rodent?* (2–5). Series: Science of Living Things. 1999, Crabtree LB $14.97 (0-86505-923-3); paper $5.36 (0-86505-951-9). 32pp. Excellent photos and an informative text introduce rodents, their characteristics, and habitat, as well as giving information on specific members of the group. (Rev: SLJ 3/00) [599.32]

21656 Lorbiecki, Marybeth. *Prairie Dogs* (2–4). Illus. Series: Our Wild World. 2004, NorthWord $10.95 (1-55971-883-8). 48pp. This photo-filled book dramatizes the plight of prairie dogs, facing increasing pressure from the rapid spread of human development into their habitat. (Rev: BL 3/15/04; SLJ 10/04) [599.36]

21657 Markle, Sandra. *Outside and Inside Rats and Mice* (2–4). Illus. Series: Outside and Inside. 2001, Simon & Schuster $16.00 (0-689-82301-0). 40pp. Facts about rats and mice and their "outsides" (diet, habitat, behavior, etc.) and "insides" (anatomy and physiology) are paired with excellent color photographs and questions and answers. (Rev: BL 9/15/01; HB 9–10/01; HBG 3/02; SLJ 11/01) [599.35]

21658 Martin-James, Kathleen. *Building Beavers* (PS–2). Series: Pull Ahead Books. 1999, Lerner $21.27 (0-8225-3628-5); paper $6.95 (0-8225-3632-3). 32pp. This introduction to the physical characteristics and habits of the beaver includes a map activity, a body diagram, and many close-up color photos. (Rev: BL 12/15/99; HBG 4/00; SLJ 3/00) [599.32]

21659 Miller, Sara S. *Rodents: From Mice to Muskrats* (3–5). Illus. Series: Animals in Order. 1998, Watts LB $22.00 (0-531-11488-0). 48pp. Using a scientific classification, this book describes, in photos and text, 14 species of rodents, their various habitats, and ways to observe these creatures. (Rev: BL 9/15/98; HBG 3/99) [599.35]

21660 Miller, Sara Swan. *Rabbits, Pikas, and Hares* (3–5). Series: Animals in Order. 2002, Watts LB $24.00 (0-531-11634-4). 48pp. Following a general explanation of animal classification, this attractive volume describes in text and color photographs several species of rabbits and related animals. (Rev: BL 3/15/02) [599.32]

21661 Old, Wendie. *The Groundhog Day Book of Facts and Fun* (K–3). Illus. by Paige Billin-Frye. 2004, Whitman LB $15.95 (0-8075-3066-2). 40pp. Punxsutawney Phil, groundhogs in general, and information on other animal forecasters around the world are all included in this volume. (Rev: BL 12/15/04; SLJ 1/05)

21662 Powell, Sandy. *Rats* (2–4). Illus. 1994, Lerner LB $22.60 (0-8225-3003-1). 48pp. The characteristics, habits, and life cycle of various species of rats are described. (Rev: BL 1/1/95) [599.32]

21663 Ricciuti, Edward R. *What on Earth Is a Capybara?* (3–5). Illus. Series: What on Earth? 1995, Blackbirch LB $17.95 (1-56711-097-5). 32pp. The habitat, characteristics, and behavior of this unusual rodent are described in pictures and text. (Rev: SLJ 11/95) [636.3]

21664 Richardson, Adele D. *Groundhogs: Woodchuck, Marmots, and Whistle Pigs* (1–3). Illus. Series: Wild World of Animals. 2002, Capstone LB $18.60 (0-7368-1397-7). 24pp. A simple introduction to the groundhog's appearance, behavior, and other basic facts, is followed by a glossary and list of resources. Also use *Beavers* (2002). (Rev: BL 1/1–15/03; HBG 3/03; SLJ 4/03) [599]

21665 Rounds, Glen. *Beaver* (PS–2). Illus. by author. 1999, Holiday House $15.95 (0-8234-1440-X). With text and drawings, this book shows many beaver activities including tree cutting, bark eating, and dam building. (Rev: BCCB 6/99; HB 5–6/99; HBG 9/99; SLJ 7/99*) [599.32]

21666 Souza, D. M. *What's a Lemming?* (4–5). Series: Creatures All Around Us. 1998, Carolrhoda $22.60 (1-57505-088-9). 40pp. This book on the tiny rodents found in subarctic regions tells of their appearance, mating, life cycle, habits, and food. (Rev: HBG 3/99; SLJ 1/99) [599.32]

21667 Staub, Frank. *Prairie Dogs* (2–3). Series: Early Bird Nature Books. 1998, Lerner $22.60 (0-8225-3038-4). 48pp. This work introduces the prairie dog, its habitat, and its unique burrows. (Rev: BL 10/15/98; HBG 3/99; SLJ 1/99) [599.32]

21668 Stone, Tanya. *Rabbits* (3–5). Series: Wild America. 2002, Gale LB $24.94 (1-56711-645-0). 24pp. Rabbits in the wild are featured in this picture-filled account that describes appearance, life cycle, food, and survival skills. Also use *Squirrels* (2002). (Rev: BL 10/15/02) [599.32]

21669 Tagholm, Sally. *The Rabbit* (2–3). Illus. by Bert Kitchen. Series: Animal Lives. 2000, Kingfisher $9.95 (0-7534-5214-6). 32pp. After a description of the daily routines of a rabbit and its mating habits, this account details the building of a nest by the female, the birth of little rabbits, and their care until adulthood. (Rev: BL 5/15/00; HBG 3/01; SLJ 8/00) [599.32]

21670 Zuchora-Walske, Christine. *Peeking Prairie Dogs* (PS–2). Series: Pull Ahead Books. 1999, Lerner $21.27 (0-8225-3616-1); paper $6.95 (0-8225-3622-6). 32pp. The prairie dog's physical characteristics, habitats, and habits are introduced in a simple text with a color picture on each page. (Rev: BL 12/15/99; HBG 4/00; SLJ 3/00) [599.32]

Birds

GENERAL AND MISCELLANEOUS

21671 Arnold, Caroline. *Birds: Nature's Magnificent Flying Machines* (3–4). Illus. by Patricia J. Wynne. 2003, Charlesbridge $16.95 (1-57091-516-4); paper $6.95 (1-57091-572-5). 32pp. Arnold take a close look at the physical mechanics behind birds' flight, examining such topics as taking off, hovering, gliding, altering direction, soaring, and landing. (Rev: BL 6/1–15/03; HBG 4/04; SLJ 12/03) [598]

21672 Arnold, Caroline. *House Sparrows Everywhere* (3–6). Illus. Series: Nature Watch. 1992, Carolrhoda LB $23.93 (0-87614-696-5). 48pp. Gives details on the house sparrow's life cycle, how it was introduced into the United States, and how its population has grown. (Rev: BL 7/92) [598.8]

21673 Arnold, Caroline. *Ostriches and Other Flightless Birds* (3–6). Illus. by Richard Hewett. Series: Nature Watch. 1990, Carolrhoda LB $23.93 (0-87614-377-X). 48pp. Smooth text and sharp photos tell of the amazing ostrich and other flightless birds. (Rev: BL 3/1/90; SLJ 7/90) [598.5]

21674 Arnosky, Jim. *All About Turkeys* (1–4). Illus. Series: All About. 1998, Scholastic $15.95 (0-590-48147-9). 32pp. Using double-page spreads, this book introduces wild turkeys, their bodies, habitats, behavior, and food. (Rev: BL 10/15/98; HBG 3/99; SLJ 11/98) [598.6]

21675 Arnosky, Jim. *Watching Water Birds* (1–4). Illus. 1997, National Geographic $16.00 (0-7922-7073-8). 32pp. An informal introduction to such diving birds as loons, grebes, mallards, wood ducks, Canada geese, gulls, and herons. (Rev: BL 10/1/97; SLJ 10/97*) [598.179]

21676 Aziz, Laurel. *Hummingbirds: A Beginner's Guide* (5–8). Illus. 2002, Firefly LB $19.95 (1-55209-487-1); paper $9.95 (1-55209-374-7). 64pp. This heavily illustrated book offers a great deal of information about hummingbirds, including their bills, metabolism, flight, nesting, and migration. (Rev: BL 6/1–15/02; HBG 10/02) [598.7]

21677 Bailey, Jill, and David Burnie. *Birds* (4–6). Illus. Series: Eyewitness Explorers. 1997, DK paper $5.95 (0-7894-2212-3). 64pp. This book includes general information on avian biology and behavior. (Rev: BL 2/1/93; SLJ 8/92) [598]

21678 Berman, Ruth. *Peacocks* (2–5). Photos by Richard Hewett. Series: Early Bird Nature Books. 1996, Lerner LB $22.60 (0-8225-3009-0). 47pp. A clear, succinct text and full-color photographs are used to introduce the members of the peafowl family. (Rev: SLJ 5/96) [598]

21679 *Birds* (PS–3). Illus. by Rene Mettler. Series: First Discovery. 1993, Scholastic $12.95 (0-590-46367-5). 29pp. Includes basic information about birds — including their beaks, claws, nests, feathers, and food — in a series of transparencies in a spiral-bound book. (Rev: BL 10/1/93; SLJ 8/93) [598.2]

21680 *Birds* (3–5). Ed. by Samantha Gray and Sarah Walker. 2002, DK LB $17.95 (0-7894-8551-6). 48pp. A visually striking introduction to a variety of birds and their anatomies, habitats, and habits. (Rev: BL 6/1–15/02; HBG 10/02) [598]

21681 Bishop, Nic. *The Secrets of Animal Flight* (3–6). Illus. 1997, Houghton Mifflin $16.00 (0-395-77848-4). 32pp. An explanation of why birds fly is followed by a discussion of how they do it, different types of wings, and various modes of flight. (Rev: BCCB 6/97; BL 3/15/97; HB 5–6/97; SLJ 4/97*) [591.9]

21682 Carney, Margaret. *Where Does a Tiger-Heron Spend the Night?* (PS–1). Illus. by Melanie Watt. 2002, Kids Can $15.95 (1-55337-022-8). 32pp. Rhyming text, rich acrylic artwork, and a lift-the-flap format combine to present facts about birds for younger readers. (Rev: BCCB 9/02; BL 3/15/02; HBG 10/02; SLJ 5/02) [598]

21683 Chermayeff, Ivan. *Feathery Facts* (PS–1). Illus. 1995, Harcourt $11.00 (0-15-200110-7). 32pp. Short, simple text and attractive illustrations are used to introduce the world of birds. (Rev: BL 4/1/95; SLJ 7/95) [598]

21684 Chrustowski, Rick. *Blue Sky Bluebird* (1–3). 2004, Holt $16.95 (0-8050-7104-0). 32pp. This overview of the bluebird's physical characteristics, diet, mating habits, and migratory patterns includes vivid and detailed illustrations. (Rev: BL 8/04; SLJ 4/04) [598.8]

21685 Collard, Sneed B., III. *Beaks!* (K–3). Illus. by Robin Brickman. 2002, Charlesbridge $16.95 (1-57091-387-0); paper $6.95 (1-57091-388-9). 32pp. Striking artwork and engrossing text about birds and their beaks will fascinate younger readers. (Rev: BL 8/02; HBG 3/03; SLJ 8/02) [573.3]

21686 Copeland, Cynthia L., and Alexandra P. Lewis. *Funny Faces, Wacky Wings, and Other Silly Big Bird Things* (K–3). Series: Silly Millies. 2002, Millbrook LB $17.90 (0-7613-2863-7); paper $4.99 (0-7613-1788-0). 28pp. This overview of the world of big birds looks at the physical characteristics and behavior of such creatures as the ostrich, penguin, and bustard in an appealing blend of colorful illustrations and easy-to-read narrative. (Rev: HBG 3/03; SLJ 8/03)

21687 Demuth, Patricia. *Cradles in the Trees: The Story of Bird Nests* (1–3). Illus. by Suzanne Barnes. 1994, Macmillan LB $14.95 (0-02-728466-2). 32pp. Describes and pictures a number of different bird nests and the way in which each meets the special needs of a species. (Rev: BL 9/15/94; SLJ 11/94) [598.2]

21688 Dewey, Jennifer Owings. *Paisano, the Road-runner* (4–6). Illus. by Wyman Meinzer. 2002, Millbrook LB $23.90 (0-7613-1250-1). 48pp. The author relates — in photographs, diary entries, and narrative — her experiences with a roadrunner she named "Paisano." (Rev: BCCB 9/02; BL 5/15/02; HB 7–8/02; HBG 10/02; SLJ 8/02) [598.7]

21689 Doris, Ellen. *Ornithology* (4–7). Illus. Series: Real Kids Real Science. 1994, Thames & Hudson $16.95 (0-500-19008-9). 64pp. An excellent manual on how to study birds in their natural habitats, with accompanying activities for all seasons. (Rev: BL 9/1/94) [598]

21690 DuTemple, Lesley A. *North American Cranes* (3–6). Illus. Series: Nature Watch. 1999, Carolrhoda $15.95 (1-57505-302-0). 48pp. Includes material on the physical characteristics and life cycles of the sandhill crane and the whooping crane. (Rev: BL 5/1/99; HBG 9/99; SLJ 4/99) [598.3]

21691 Fowler, Allan. *The Chicken or the Egg?* (1–2). Illus. Series: Rookie Readers. 1993, Children's Book Pr. LB $19.00 (0-516-06008-2). 31pp. This small-format book with large print and color photos on each page traces the development of an egg and the hatching of a chick. (Rev: BL 9/1/93; SLJ 9/93) [636.5]

21692 Fowler, Allan. *These Birds Can't Fly* (1–2). Series: Rookie Readers. 1998, Children's Book Pr. LB $18.50 (0-516-20798-9). 32pp. Color photographs and a few lines of text introduce penguins and other flightless birds. (Rev: BL 9/15/98; HBG 9/99) [598.2]

21693 Friedman, Judi. *Operation Siberian Crane: The Story Behind the International Effort to Save an Amazing Bird* (4–7). 1992, Macmillan LB $13.95 (0-87518-515-0). 96pp. Ron Sauey and George

Archibald founded the International Crane Foundation and concentrated on the most endangered species. (Rev: BL 1/15/93; SLJ 1/93*) [639.9]

21694 Gans, Roma. *How Do Birds Find Their Way?* (PS–3). Illus. by Paul Mirocha. Series: Let's-Read-and-Find-Out. 1996, HarperCollins LB $15.89 (0-06-020225-4); paper $4.95 (0-06-445150-X). 32pp. Various kinds of birds that migrate are introduced and the mysteries connected with their semiannual flights are explored. (Rev: BL 2/1/96; SLJ 4/96) [598.2]

21695 Garelick, May. *What Makes a Bird a Bird?* (K–3). Illus. 1995, Mondo paper $4.95 (1-57255-008-2). 32pp. In a series of questions and answers, the distinctive characteristics of birds are enumerated. (Rev: BL 8/95) [598.2]

21696 Guiberson, Brenda Z. *Mud City: A Flamingo Story* (K–3). Illus. 2005, Holt $16.95 (0-8050-7177-6). 32pp. From egg through mating and having a chick, this volume follows the life cycle of a flamingo. (Rev: BL 5/15/05; SLJ 5/05) [598.3]

21697 Harrison, George H. *Backyard Bird Watching for Kids* (2–5). Illus. 1997, Willow Creek $14.95 (1-57223-089-4). 64pp. Describes the joys of bird watching and introduces 20 popular backyard birds, with material on their calls, food, and habitats. (Rev: BL 12/1/97) [598]

21698 Haus, Robyn. *Make Your Own Birdhouses and Feeders* (3–6). Illus. Series: Quick Starts for Kids! 2001, Williamson paper $7.95 (1-885593-55-4). 64pp. A detailed guide for younger readers to feeding and providing shelter for wild birds. (Rev: BL 2/15/02; SLJ 12/01) [690]

21699 Herkert, Barbara. *Birds in Your Backyard* (K–3). Illus. by author. Series: A Sharing Nature with Children Book. 2001, Dawn $17.95 (1-58469-026-7); paper $8.95 (1-58469-025-9). 35pp. Tips on attracting birds to your backyard, instructions for building a birdhouse, and advice on binoculars accompany descriptions of a variety of birds and maps showing birds commonly found in North America. (Rev: HBG 3/02; SLJ 5/02) [598]

21700 Hewitt, Joan. *A Flamingo Chick Grows Up* (1–3). Series: Baby Animals. 2001, Carolrhoda LB $21.27 (1-57505-164-8); paper $6.95 (0-8225-0090-6). 32pp. Using excellent photographs, short sentences, large print, and simple vocabulary, this attractive book describes a flamingo chick's growth to adulthood. (Rev: BL 10/15/01; HBG 3/02; SLJ 10/01) [598]

21701 Hickman, Pamela. *Starting with Nature Bird Book* (2–4). Illus. by Heather Collins. Series: Starting with Nature. 2000, Kids Can $12.95 (1-55074-471-2); paper $5.95 (1-55074-810-6). 32pp. An introduction to birds that gives basic material on species, homes, migration, songs, and banding as well as advice to bird watchers and a series of activities including making a birdhouse. (Rev: HBG 9/00; SLJ 7/00) [598]

21702 Holub, Joan. *Why Do Birds Sing?* (1–2). Illus. by Anna DiVito. Series: Dial Easy-to-Read. 2004, Penguin Putnam paper $3.99 (0-8037-2999-5). 48pp. Using an attractive question-and-answer for-

mat, this volume explores the characteristics and behavior of birds. (Rev: BL 11/1/04; SLJ 11/04) [598]

21703 Hoose, Phillip M. *The Race to Save the Lord God Bird* (5–8). 2004, Farrar $20.00 (0-374-36173-8). 208pp. The sad tale of the ivory-billed woodpecker's decline is interwoven with discussion of the scientific and sociological implications. (Rev: BL 6/1–15/04; SLJ 9/04) [598.7]

21704 Horton, Casey. *Parrots* (3–6). Illus. Series: Endangered! 1996, Benchmark LB $22.79 (0-7614-0222-5). 32pp. This account focuses on eight species of parrots from around the world and why they are endangered. (Rev: SLJ 9/96) [598.71]

21705 Jango-Cohen, Judith. *Hovering Hummingbirds* (2–3). Series: Pull Ahead Books. 2003, Lerner LB $22.60 (0-8225-4666-3). 32pp. In this book, ideal for beginning readers, author Judith Jango-Cohen examines the life cycle, physical characteristics, behavior, and habitat of hummingbirds. (Rev: BL 11/15/03; HBG 10/03)

21706 Jenkins, Priscilla B. *A Nest Full of Eggs* (1–3). Illus. by Lizzy Rockwell. 1995, HarperCollins LB $15.89 (0-06-023442-3). 32pp. By observing a pair of robins build a nest and raise a family, two youngsters learn about birds and their habits. (Rev: BCCB 7–8/95; BL 6/1–15/95; SLJ 8/95) [598.8]

21707 Johnson, Sylvia A. *Albatrosses of Midway Island* (3–6). Illus. by Frans Lanting. 1990, Carolrhoda LB $22.60 (0-87614-391-5). 48pp. Amazing facts and statistics about the wondrous albatross. (Rev: BL 3/1/90; SLJ 7/90) [598.4]

21708 Johnson, Sylvia A. *Crows* (4–6). Illus. Series: Nature Watch. 2004, Carolrhoda LB $25.26 (1-57505-628-3). Along with information on the crow's habitat, diet, behavior, migratory patterns, and life cycle, this photo-filled overview discusses West Nile virus and crows' increasing taste for city dwelling. (Rev: BL 12/1/04; SLJ 4/05) [598.8]

21709 Kelly, Irene. *It's a Hummingbird's Life* (1–3). Illus. 2003, Holiday House $16.95 (0-8234-1658-5). 32pp. An appealing look at a year in the life of the ruby-throated hummingbird, including its annual migration south in search of warmer weather. (Rev: BL 4/1/03; HBG 10/03; SLJ 6/03) [598.7]

21710 Kittinger, Jo S. *Birds of North America: East* (5–8). Series: Smithsonian Kids' Field Guides. 2001, DK paper $9.95 (0-7894-7899-4). 160pp. An introduction to the birds found in the eastern United States, with clear photographs of the male and female, information on size and habitat, and a description of special features. Also use *Birds of North America: West* (2001). (Rev: BL 10/15/01) [598]

21711 Klein, Tom. *Loon Magic for Kids* (2–4). Illus. 1990, NorthWord paper $6.95 (1-55971-121-3). 48pp. This colorful account includes information on the behavior and life cycle of the loon. (Rev: BL 6/1/90; SLJ 3/91) [598.4]

21712 Kuchalla, Susan. *Birds* (K–3). Illus. by Gary Britt. 1982, Troll paper $3.50 (0-89375-657-1). 32pp. A simple introduction with a few short sentences and many illustrations.

21713 Latimer, Jonathan P., and Karen Stray Nolting. *Bizarre Birds* (3–6). Series: Peterson Field Guides for Young Naturalists. 1999, Houghton Mifflin $15.00 (0-395-95213-1); paper $5.95 (0-395-92279-8). 48pp. Using double-page spreads, this field guide describes and pictures a number of birds that are unusual for their appearance, habits, mating rituals, habitats, or other considerations. (Rev: BL 6/1–15/99; SLJ 8/99) [598]

21714 Latimer, Jonathan P., and Karen Stray Nolting. *Shorebirds* (3–6). Illus. Series: Peterson Field Guides for Young Naturalists. 1999, Houghton Mifflin $15.00 (0-395-95212-3); paper $5.95 (0-395-92278-X). 48pp. A wide variety of shore birds that live near fresh water as well as oceans and the Gulf of Mexico are described in a series of colorful double-page spreads. (Rev: BL 6/1–15/99; SLJ 8/99) [598.3]

21715 Llamas, Andreu. *Birds Conquer the Sky* (4–8). Illus. by Miriam Ferrón and Miguel Ferrón. Series: Development of the Earth. 1996, Chelsea LB $17.55 (0-7910-3455-0). 32pp. A science book that explains the evolution of birds from prehistoric land birds onward and defines their characteristics. (Rev: SLJ 7/96) [598]

21716 London, Jonathan. *Gone Again Ptarmigan* (K–3). Illus. by Jon Van Zyle. 2001, National Geographic $16.95 (0-7922-7561-6). 32pp. The life cycle of the Arctic ptarmigan is covered in this picture book that shows how its feathers change color to offer camouflage in both winter and summer. (Rev: BL 1/1–15/01; HBG 10/01) [598.6]

21717 Lynne, Cherry. *Flute's Journey: The Life of a Wood Thrush* (K–3). Illus. 1997, Harcourt $15.00 (0-15-292853-7). 40pp. The story of a single wood thrush's journey from Maryland to a Central American rain forest and back. (Rev: BCCB 5/97; BL 4/1/97; SLJ 7/97) [599.8]

21718 McMillan, Bruce. *A Beach for the Birds* (4–6). Illus. 1993, Houghton Mifflin $16.00 (0-395-64050-4). 32pp. This book introduces the sea swallow and discusses its life cycle, behavior, and habitats. Information is also given on its endangered status. (Rev: BCCB 6/93; BL 4/1/93; SLJ 4/93) [598.3]

21719 McMillan, Bruce. *Puffins Climb, Penguins Rhyme* (PS–1). Illus. 1995, Harcourt $16.00 (0-15-200362-2). 32pp. A rhyming text is used to describe various activities of penguins and puffins. (Rev: BL 4/1/95; SLJ 5/95) [598.3]

21720 McMillan, Bruce. *Wild Flamingos* (3–5). Illus. 1997, Houghton Mifflin $15.00 (0-395-84545-9). 32pp. Introduces the flamingos of Bonaire in the Caribbean using clear text and spectacular photos. (Rev: BL 7/97; HB 9–10/97; SLJ 8/97*) [598.3]

21721 McNulty, Faith. *Peeping in the Shell: A Whooping Crane Is Hatched* (2–4). Illus. by Irene Brady. 1986, HarperCollins $11.95 (0-06-024134-9). 64pp. The process of hatching a whooping crane egg, with a personal narrative. (Rev: BCCB 10/86; BL 1/1/87; SLJ 12/86)

21722 Mania, Cathy, and Robert Mania. *Woodpecker in the Backyard* (3–5). Series: Wildlife Conserva-tion Society Books. 2000, Watts LB $22.50 (0-531-11799-5). 48pp. A heavily illustrated book that describes the physical characteristics of the woodpecker and gives material on its habits, lifestyle, food, and homes. (Rev: BL 3/15/01) [598]

21723 Martin, Gilles. *Birds* (5–8). Illus. 2005, Abrams $18.95 (0-8109-5878-3). 80pp. An oversize book full of color photographs of birds, plus watercolor sketches and brief, quite advanced text that comments on various aspects of the birds. (Rev: BL 5/1/05; SLJ 5/05) [598.22]

21724 Martin, Patricia A. Fink. *California Condors* (2–3). Series: Animals. 2002, Children's Book Pr. LB $23.50 (0-516-22161-2); paper $6.95 (0-516-27470-8). 48pp. With a color photograph on almost every page and large type throughout, this is a simple but informative introduction to the California condor. (Rev: BL 8/02) [598.9]

21725 Miller, Sara S. *Perching Birds of North America* (2–4). Series: Animals in Order. 1999, Watts LB $22.00 (0-531-11520-8). 47pp. This book explains animal classification and then introduces a group of perching birds, their characteristics, appearance, habits, and habitats. (Rev: HBG 9/99; SLJ 5/99) [598]

21726 Miller, Sara S. *Shorebirds: From Stilts to Sanderlings* (3–5). Illus. Series: Animals in Order. 2000, Watts LB $23.00 (0-531-11596-8); paper $6.95 (0-531-16498-5). 48pp. Introductory material on animal classification is followed by an overview of shorebirds, their varieties, habits, structure, and care of young. (Rev: BL 9/15/00) [598.29]

21727 Miller, Sara Swan. *Wading Birds: From Herons to Hammerheads* (3–5). Series: Animals in Order. 2001, Watts LB $23.00 (0-531-11630-1). 32pp. The traits and behavior of wading birds are discussed with full color photographs of various species and a simple text. (Rev: BL 6/1–15/01) [598.3]

21728 Miller, Sara Swan. *Woodpeckers, Toucans, and Their Kin* (4–6). Series: Animals in Order. 2003, Watts LB $25.00 (0-531-12243-3); paper $6.95 (0-531-16661-9). 47pp. Introduces readers to birds that are members of the piciforme order, with information on representative species and their habitats. (Rev: SLJ 7/03) [598]

21729 Parker, Edward. *Birds* (5–8). Photos by author. Series: Rain Forest. 2003, Raintree LB $27.12 (0-7398-5239-6). 48pp. Birds that are found in rain forests are the topic of this overview that describes the dangers posed by humans through hunting, pollution, and agriculture. (Rev: HBG 3/03; SLJ 1/03) [598]

21730 Patent, Dorothy Hinshaw. *Pigeons* (3–6). Illus. 1997, Clarion $16.00 (0-395-69848-0). 78pp. An introduction to pigeons that covers their history, homes, uses, and intelligence. (Rev: BL 9/1/97; SLJ 10/97) [598.6]

21731 Patent, Dorothy Hinshaw. *Wild Turkeys* (2–3). Series: Early Bird Nature Books. 1999, Lerner LB $16.95 (0-8225-3026-0). 48pp. A well-written, handsomely illustrated guide to the life cycle, habits, and physical characteristics of wild turkeys. (Rev: BL 8/99; HBG 9/99; SLJ 5/99) [598]

21732 Pembleton, Seliesa. *The Pileated Woodpecker* (3–5). Illus. 1989, Macmillan LB $13.95 (0-87518-392-1). 60pp. A report on the physical characteristics and life cyle of this large woodpecker. (Rev: BL 2/1/89; SLJ 4/89)

21733 Posada, Mia. *Robins: Songbirds of Spring* (K–3). Illus. by author. 2004, Carolrhoda LB $16.95 (1-57505-615-1). After a description in rhyming text of the life cycle of the American robin and its migratory and other behaviors, a detailed section gives additional facts and tips. (Rev: SLJ 5/04) [598.8]

21734 Powell, Jillian. *Eggs* (3–5). Illus. Series: Everyone Eats. 1997, Raintree LB $25.69 (0-8172-4759-9). 32pp. This book introduces eggs — their sizes, from caviar to ostrich; the construction, production, and nutritional value of chickens' eggs; rituals connected with eggs; and two recipes. (Rev: SLJ 8/97) [598.6]

21735 Pringle, Laurence. *Crows! Strange and Wonderful* (2–4). Illus. by Bob Marstall. 2002, Boyds Mills $15.95 (1-56397-899-7). 32pp. This is an absorbing, well-illustrated account of the life and behavior of the crow, showing the bird's intelligence, adaptability, and amazing ability to communicate. (Rev: BCCB 12/02; BL 11/1/02; HBG 3/03; SLJ 9/02) [598.964]

21736 Rauzon, Mark. *Hummingbirds* (4–6). Illus. Series: First Books. 1997, Watts LB $22.50 (0-531-20260-7). 63pp. Describes the anatomy and characteristics of the smallest and most active bird and introduces various species, such as the rufous, sword-billed, and ruby-throated hummingbird. (Rev: BL 8/97; SLJ 8/97) [598.8]

21737 Rauzon, Mark. *Parrots* (4–6). Illus. 1996, Watts LB $22.50 (0-531-20244-5). 62pp. Types of parrots, their mating and nesting habits, and their life cycles are discussed. (Rev: BL 1/1–15/97; SLJ 4/97) [598.7]

21738 Rauzon, Mark. *Vultures* (4–6). Illus. Series: First Books. 1997, Watts LB $22.50 (0-531-20271-2). 63pp. Discusses the important role these scavengers play and describes various species, such as the condor, lammergeier, and Egyptian vulture. (Rev: BL 8/97) [598.9]

21739 Rauzon, Mark J. *Parrots Around the World* (3–5). Series: Animals in Order. 2001, Watts LB $23.00 (0-531-11688-3). 32pp. Following a discussion of the parrot family, various species are introduced through color photographs and a brief text that describes anatomy, habits, and habitats. Also use *Pelicans, Cormorants, and Their Kin* (2002). (Rev: BL 6/1–15/01) [598.71]

21740 Ricciuti, Edward R. *Birds* (4–6). Illus. Series: Our Living World. 1993, Blackbirch LB $19.95 (1-56711-038-X). 64pp. This introduction covers general topics related to birds. (Rev: SLJ 8/93) [598]

21741 Robinson, Fay. *Singing Robins* (PS–2). Series: Pull Ahead Books. 2000, Lerner $21.27 (0-8225-3641-2). 32pp. With four lines of simple text and a color photo on each page, this book tells of the bird

with the beautiful orange breast feathers and the pretty blue eggs. (Rev: BL 5/15/00; HBG 9/00) [598.8]

21742 Roop, Peter, and Connie Roop. *Seasons of the Crane* (2–6). Illus. 1989, Walker LB $15.85 (0-8027-6860-1). 48pp. With outstanding photos and lucid text, the migratory habits of this endangered bird are described. (Rev: BL 8/89; SLJ 9/89) [598.31]

21743 Savage, Stephen. *Birds* (2–4). Illus. Series: What's the Difference? 2000, Raintree $25.69 (0-7398-1356-0). 32pp. A most attractive volume that presents a number of different birds and explains their common characteristics, along with material on their nests, food, and how they care for their young. (Rev: BL 10/15/00; HBG 3/01) [598]

21744 Sayre, April Pulley. *The Hungry Hummingbird* (K–3). Illus. by Gay W. Holland. 2001, Millbrook LB $22.90 (0-7613-1951-4). 32pp. A hungry little hummingbird searches for food in this beautifully illustrated book. (Rev: BL 11/15/01; HBG 3/02; SLJ 11/01) [598.7]

21745 Sill, Cathryn. *About Birds: A Guide for Children* (3–6). Illus. by John Sill. 1991, Peachtree $14.95 (1-56145-028-6). 40pp. This very simple introduction to birds describes common species and their characteristics. (Rev: BL 12/15/91; SLJ 2/92*) [598]

21746 Smith, Roland. *Vultures* (2–3). Series: Early Bird Nature Books. 1998, Lerner LB $22.60 (0-8225-3011-2). 48pp. A sympathetic, easily read introduction to the world of the vulture, including the ways they find and eat their food, their life cycle, and habitats. (Rev: BL 3/15/98; HBG 9/98; SLJ 3/98) [598]

21747 Spaulding, Dean T. *Feeding Our Feathered Friends* (4–6). Series: Birder's Bookshelf. 1997, Lerner LB $19.93 (0-8225-3175-5). 56pp. This book covers many aspects of backyard bird feeding, like how to build bird feeders, where and when to hang them, their contents, and how to keep squirrels away. (Rev: BL 3/15/98; HBG 3/98; SLJ 4/98) [598]

21748 Spaulding, Dean T. *Housing Our Feathered Friends* (4–6). Illus. Series: Birder's Bookshelf. 1997, Lerner LB $19.93 (0-8225-3176-3). 56pp. As well as supplying information on nests and other conveniences birds use as homes, this book gives directions on how to make a number of birdhouses. Also use: *Protecting Our Feathered Friends* (1997). (Rev: BL 10/15/97; HBG 3/98; SLJ 9/97) [690]

21749 Spaulding, Dean T. *Watching Our Feathered Friends* (4–6). Series: Birder's Bookshelf. 1997, Lerner LB $19.93 (0-8225-3177-1). 56pp. This book introduces the hobby of bird watching, with material on its history, how to use a field guide, the best times and places for birding, and the necessary equipment. (Rev: BL 3/15/98; HBG 3/98) [598]

21750 Spilsbury, Richard, and Louise Spilsbury. *A Murder of Crows* (3–5). Series: Animal Groups. 2003, Heinemann LB $24.22 (1-4034-0742-8). 32pp. In this attractively illustrated book readers learn about the crow's habitat, diet, hierarchical social structure, and behavior in groups. (Rev: HBG 10/03; SLJ 9/03) [598.8]

21751 Staub, Frank. *Herons* (2–5). Illus. Series: Early Bird. 1997, Lerner LB $22.60 (0-8225-3017-1). 48pp. Text and wonderful photos introduce a variety of heron species and their behavior and habitats. (Rev: BL 7/97; SLJ 8/97) [598.3]

21752 Stewart, Melissa. *Birds* (2–3). Series: True Books. 2001, Children's Book Pr. LB $22.00 (0-516-22039-X). 48pp. This beginning look at birds includes basic material on their structure, how they fly, their homes, and how they care for their young. (Rev: BL 3/15/01) [598]

21753 Stone, Lynn M. *Sandhill Cranes* (2–3). Series: Early Bird Nature Books. 1998, Lerner LB $22.60 (0-8225-3027-9). 48pp. This easily read, beautifully illustrated account introduces the sand hill crane and its life cycle, with material on its habitat, food, and enemies. (Rev: BL 3/15/98; HBG 9/98; SLJ 7/98) [597]

21754 Swinburne, Stephen R. *Unbeatable Beaks* (PS–3). Illus. by Joan Paley. 1999, Holt $15.95 (0-8050-4802-2). Using colorful collages and a singsong verse, this book introduces 39 birds each with a distinctive beak and also includes a quiz to match the birds with their beaks. (Rev: BCCB 11/99; HBG 4/00; SLJ 11/99) [598]

21755 Tesar, Jenny. *What on Earth Is a Bustard?* (3–5). Illus. Series: What on Earth? 1996, Blackbirch LB $17.95 (1-56711-102-5). 32pp. Examines the world of the bustard, a ground-dwelling bird found in grasslands on several continents. (Rev: SLJ 2/97) [598]

21756 Townsend, Emily Rose. *Woodpeckers* (PS–2). 2004, Capstone LB $15.93 (0-7368-2070-1). 24pp. Presents basic information on woodpeckers in a small format with brief text facing full-color close-up photographs. (Rev: SLJ 8/04) [598]

21757 Voeller, Edward. *The Red-Crowned Crane* (3–6). Illus. 1989, Macmillan LB $13.95 (0-87518-417-0). 60pp. A book about the amazing Japanese red-crowned crane and a retelling of the folktale it inspired, The Grateful Crane. (Rev: BL 12/15/89; SLJ 3/90) [598.31]

21758 Wechsler, Doug. *Bizarre Birds* (3–5). Illus. 1999, Boyds Mills $17.95 (1-56397-760-5). 48pp. This description of birds with unique habits — such as strange food preferences — offers scientific explanations for their behavior. (Rev: BL 1/1–15/00; HBG 4/00; SLJ 11/99) [598]

21759 Weidensaul, Scott, ed. *National Audubon Society First Field Guide: Birds* (4–8). Illus. 1998, Scholastic paper $17.95 (0-590-05446-5). After a general introduction to ornithology, this guide describes and pictures several species of birds, including markings, eating, mating and nesting habits, migration, and endangered status. (Rev: BL 8/98; SLJ 10/98) [598]

21760 Welsbacher, Anne. *Wading Birds* (K–2). Photos by John Netherton. Series: Pull Ahead Books. 1999, Lerner LB $15.95 (0-8225-3614-5). 32pp. This book focuses on herons as wading birds and describes their physical characteristics, food, where they live, and how they bring up their young. (Rev: HBG 9/99; SLJ 5/99) [598]

21761 Wilkes, Angela. *Question Time: Birds* (3–5). Illus. Series: Question Time. 2002, Kingfisher $11.95 (0-7534-5450-5); paper $6.95 (0-7534-5462-9). 32pp. Topics covered in a question-and-answer format include the different types of birds, and their characteristics, habitat, and defense mechanisms. (Rev: HBG 3/03; SLJ 2/03)

21762 Williams, Nick. *How Birds Fly* (3–5). Illus. Series: Nature's Mysteries. 1996, Benchmark LB $22.79 (0-7614-0454-6). 32pp. The flight of birds is explained through an investigation of the internal and external design of their bodies in this book that gives many different examples and descriptions to amplify the text. (Rev: SLJ 2/97) [598]

21763 Willis, Nancy C. *The Robins in Your Backyard* (K–3). Illus. 1996, Cucumber Island Storytellers $15.95 (1-887813-21-7). 32pp. The life of robins is covered, with material on mating habits and nest building. (Rev: BCCB 6/97; BL 1/1–15/97; SLJ 7/97) [598.8]

21764 Winner, Cherie. *Woodpeckers* (3–6). Series: Nature Watch. 2000, Carolrhoda LB $23.93 (1-57505-445-0). 48pp. This colorful introduction to the varieties of woodpeckers explains why they tap holes in wood. (Rev: BL 7/00; HBG 10/01) [598]

21765 Zim, Herbert S., and Ira N. Gabrielson. *Birds* (5–8). Illus. 1991, Western paper $21.27 (0-307-64053-1). A guide to the most commonly seen birds, with accompanying illustrations and basic materials. [598]

BEHAVIOR

21766 Back, Christine, and Jens Olesen. *Chicken and Egg* (1–3). Illus. 1986, Silver Burdett LB $15.95 (0-382-09284-8); paper $3.95 (0-382-09959-1). Basic science explaining how the reproductive cycle operates. (Rev: BL 1/1/87)

21767 Bash, Barbara. *Urban Roosts: Where Birds Nest in the City* (3–5). Illus. 1992, Little, Brown paper $6.95 (0-316-08312-7). 32pp. This unusual nature study shows that wildlife can thrive in an urban setting. (Rev: BCCB 3/91; BL 1/1/91*; HB 1–2/91; SLJ 11/90*) [598]

21768 Johnson, Sylvia A. *Inside an Egg* (5–8). Illus. 1982, Lerner LB $31.95 (0-8225-1472-9); paper $9.55 (0-8225-9522-2). 48pp. An excellently illustrated account tracing the growth of a chicken in an egg until it is hatched. [598]

21769 Johnson, Sylvia A. *Songbirds: The Language of Song* (3–6). Series: Nature Watch. 2000, Carolrhoda LB $23.70 (1-57505-483-3). 48pp. This book introduces a number of songbirds and describes their songs. (Rev: BL 3/1/01; HBG 10/01) [598]

21770 Lerner, Carol. *On the Wing: American Birds in Migration* (3–6). Illus. 2001, HarperCollins $16.95 (0-688-16649-0). 48pp. Lerner looks at all aspects of bird migration — the reasons why, how they navigate, and the impact of environmental change — in clear text, attractive paintings, and useful maps. (Rev: BL 6/1–15/01; HB 9–10/01; HBG 3/02; SLJ 9/01*) [598.156]

21771 Selsam, Millicent E. *Egg to Chick* (K–3). Illus. by Barbara Wolff. 1970, HarperCollins paper $3.95 (0-06-444113-X). 64pp. A concise guide to how an egg develops.

21772 Stevens, Ann Shepard. *Strange Nests* (2–5). Illus. by Jennifer Owings Dewey. 1998, Millbrook LB $20.40 (0-7613-0413-4). 31pp. Covers the nests and building habits of 11 common North American birds, including robins, swallows, eagles, wrens, house sparrows, Baltimore orioles, and crows. (Rev: HBG 9/99; SLJ 7/99) [598]

21773 Winer, Yvonne. *Birds Build Nests* (PS–3). Illus. by Tony Oliver. 2002, Charlesbridge $16.95 (1-57091-500-8); paper $6.95 (1-57091-501-6). 32pp. A lovely book of poetic text and beautiful, realistic illustrations that introduces the nesting habits of various species of birds to younger readers. (Rev: BL 3/1/02; HBG 10/02; SLJ 3/02) [598.156]

DUCKS, GEESE, AND SWANS

21774 Cooper, Jason. *Canada Goose* (1–3). Series: Life Cycles. 2002, Rourke LB $23.93 (1-58952-351-2). 24pp. Handsome photographs and simple text describe the life cycle, habitat, appearance, and behavior of these animals. (Rev: SLJ 12/02)

21775 Goldin, Augusta. *Ducks Don't Get Wet* (PS–2). Illus. Series: Let's-Read-and-Find-Out. 1999, HarperCollins LB $15.89 (0-06-027882-X); paper $4.95 (0-06-445187-9). 32pp. Explains why ducks don't get wet in water and introduces several types of wild ducks, their habits, diet, migration, and habitats. (Rev: BL 8/99*; HBG 9/99; SLJ 6/99) [598.4]

21776 Hickman, Pamela. *A New Duck: My First Look at the Life Cycle of a Bird* (PS–K). Illus. by Heather Collins. Series: My First Look At. 1999, Kids Can $6.95 (1-55074-613-8). The nesting habits of a pair of mallards and the hatching and growth of their ducklings are covered in attractive pictures and simple text. (Rev: HBG 9/99; SLJ 8/99) [598.4]

21777 Hipp, Andrew. *The Life Cycle of a Duck* (PS–2). Illus. by Dwight Kuhn. Series: Life Cycle Of. 2002, Rosen LB $18.76 (0-8239-5868-X). 24pp. This book for beginning readers follows the life of a duck from conception to adulthood. (Rev: BL 12/15/02) [598.4]

21778 Horton, Tom. *Swanfall: Journey of the Tundra Swans* (4–6). Illus. by David Harp. 1991, Walker LB $16.85 (0-8027-8107-1). 48pp. All about migration and the life of a swan family for one year. (Rev: BCCB 2/92; BL 12/15/91) [598.4]

21779 Llewellyn, Claire. *Duck* (K–3). Illus. by Simon Mendez. Series: Starting Life. 2004, North-Word $16.95 (1-55971-878-1). 32pp. An innovative picture-book layout enhances the journey of the mallard duck from egg to adult. (Rev: BL 4/15/04; SLJ 11/04) [598.4]

21780 Loomis, Jennifer A. *A Duck in a Tree* (K–3). Illus. 1996, Stemmer $18.95 (0-88045-136-X). 40pp. A year in the lives of two wood ducks includes raising a family and migrating to Florida. (Rev: BL 2/1/97) [598.4]

21781 McMillan, Bruce. *Days of the Ducklings* (K–3). Illus. 2001, Houghton Mifflin $16.00 (0-618-04878-2). 32pp. This eye-catching book of photography and spare text records a young Icelandic girl's efforts to reintroduce wild eider ducklings to her island. (Rev: BCCB 12/01; BL 9/15/01; HB 1–2/02; HBG 3/02; SLJ 9/01) [598.4]

21782 Magloff, Lisa. *Watch Me Grow: Duckling* (1–2). Series: Watch Me Grow. 2003, DK $7.99 (0-7894-9628-3). 24pp. This attractive title provides a close-up look — from the perspective of the animal — at the development of a duckling from the time it hatches until it becomes self-sufficient. (Rev: BL 10/15/03) [598.4]

21783 Miller, Sara S. *Waterfowl: From Swans to Screamers* (3–5). Series: Animals in Order. 1999, Watts LB $23.00 (0-531-11584-4). 48pp. After a discussion of animal classification, water birds are introduced and several are pictured and described. (Rev: BL 12/15/99; HBG 4/00) [598.4]

21784 Osborn, Elinor. *Project UltraSwan* (3–6). Illus. 2002, Houghton Mifflin $16.00 (0-618-14528-1). 64pp. This is a fascinating and readable account of how scientists using ultralight aircraft are working to help trumpeter swans to rediscover their migratory routes. (Rev: BCCB 12/02; BL 12/15/02; HB 1–2/03; HBG 3/03; SLJ 6/03) [598.4]

21785 Pfeffer, Wendy. *Mute Swans* (PS–3). Illus. Series: Creatures in White. 1996, Silver Pr. LB $14.95 (0-382-39325-2). Using two-page spreads, the reader follows two swans through nest building, protecting the eggs, raising their young, and migrating. (Rev: SLJ 2/97) [598.4]

21786 Savage, Stephen. *Duck* (K–2). Illus. by Stephen Lings. Series: Observing Nature. 1995, Thomson Learning LB $21.20 (1-56847-328-1). 32pp. Using double-page spreads, very basic information is given on the life cycle of the mallard duck. (Rev: SLJ 10/95) [598.4]

21787 Stone, Lynn M. *Swans* (2–3). Series: Early Bird Nature Books. 1997, Lerner LB $22.60 (0-8225-3019-8). 48pp. A well-written introduction for beginners to these handsome birds, with a simple text and many color photos. (Rev: BL 9/15/97; SLJ 10/97) [598.4]

21788 Wallace, Karen. *Duckling Days* (1). Illus. Series: Eyewitness Reader. 1999, DK $12.95 (0-7894-3995-6); paper $3.95 (0-7894-3994-8). 32pp. Six ducks hatch from mother duck's eggs, one of them a loner in this easily read book. (Rev: BL 5/15/99; HBG 9/99) [598.4]

21789 Watts, Barrie. *Duck* (K–3). Illus. 2002, Smart Apple LB $16.95 (1-58340-197-0). 32pp. This easy-to-read book about ducks includes loads of facts and excellent photography. (Rev: BL 10/15/02; HBG 3/03) [598.4]

EAGLES, HAWKS, AND OTHER BIRDS OF PREY

21790 Arnold, Caroline. *Saving the Peregrine Falcon* (4–6). Illus. 1985, Lerner paper $7.95 (0-87614-523-3). 48pp. Once threatened because its eggs were weakened by the pesticide DDT, the peregrine falcon can now be seen in American cities. The story of their comeback. (Rev: BCCB 3/85; BL 4/1/85; SLJ 3/85)

21791 Bailey, Jill. *Birds of Prey* (5–8). Illus. 1988, Facts on File $17.55 (0-8160-1655-0). In brief, lavishly illustrated chapters, various characteristics of birds of prey are explored and the most important types are described. (Rev: SLJ 1/89) [598]

21792 Bailey, Jill. *The Secret Life of Falcons* (4–7). Series: The Secret World Of. 2002, Raintree LB $27.12 (0-7398-4985-9). 48pp. This book describes the anatomy and habits of the falcon with material on how they feed, communicate, and reproduce. (Rev: BL 8/02) [598.9]

21793 Bair, Diane, and Pamela Wright. *Eagle Watching* (2–5). Series: Wildlife Watching. 1999, Capstone $19.93 (0-7368-0322-X). 48pp. An introduction to the world of the eagle, with special information on how to observe these birds. (Rev: BL 2/15/00) [598.9]

21794 Becker, John E. *The Bald Eagle* (3–6). Illus. Series: Returning Wildlife. 2002, Gale LB $23.70 (0-7377-1279-1). 32pp. Covers the bald eagle's place in American history and new threats to its livelihood, with lots of photographs, a useful bibliography, and a glossary. (Rev: BL 12/1/02) [598.9]

21795 Bernhard, Emery. *Eagles: Lions of the Sky* (PS–3). Illus. by Durga Bernhard. 1994, Holiday House LB $15.95 (0-8234-1105-2). 32pp. Many aspects of the life of eagles, including mating, eating, flying, hunting, and parenting, are discussed in this richly illustrated book. (Rev: BL 2/1/94; HB 5–6/94; SLJ 5/94) [598.9]

21796 Collard, Sneed B. *Birds of Prey: A Look at Daytime Raptors* (4–7). Illus. 1999, Watts LB $24.00 (0-531-20363-8). 64pp. Eagles, hawks, ospreys, falcons, and vultures of North America are introduced with material on the appearance and habits of each. (Rev: BL 10/15/99; HBG 4/00) [598.9]

21797 Gibbons, Gail. *Soaring with the Wind: The Bald Eagle* (3–5). Illus. 1998, Morrow $16.00 (0-688-13730-X). 32pp. Excellent full-color illustrations dominate this account of the bald eagle, its characteristics, behavior, life cycle, struggle for survival, and its emergence as a national symbol. (Rev: BL 4/15/98; HBG 3/99; SLJ 4/98) [598.9]

21798 Grambo, Rebecca L. *Eagles* (5–8). Series: World Life Library. 1999, Voyageur paper $16.95 (0-89658-363-5). This beautifully illustrated book describes the legends and lore surrounding eagles, their physical characteristics, behavior, habitats, and different species. (Rev: BL 8/99) [598.9]

21799 Haugen, Hayley Mitchell. *Eagles* (4–6). Series: Nature's Predators. 2002, Gale LB $23.70 (0-7377-1004-7). 48pp. In four brief chapters, the lives of eagles are explored with material on the food they eat and how they catch it. (Rev: BL 8/02) [598.8]

21800 Hodge, Deborah. *Eagles* (2–5). Illus. Series: Kids Can! 2000, Kids Can $10.95 (1-55074-715-0); paper $5.95 (1-55074-717-7). 32pp. After a general look at eagles around the world, this account focus-

es on two American breeds and gives information on their habitats, food, physical characteristics, flight, behavior, and young. (Rev: BL 11/1/00; HBG 3/01) [598.9]

21801 Horton, Casey. *Eagles* (4–6). Illus. Series: Endangered! 1996, Benchmark LB $22.79 (0-7614-0214-4). 32pp. The endangered eagle is presented, with individual chapters on eight species. (Rev: SLJ 4/96) [598.9]

21802 Latimer, Jonathan P., and Karen Stray Nolting. *Birds of Prey* (3–6). Illus. Series: Peterson Field Guides for Young Naturalists. 1999, Houghton Mifflin $15.00 (0-395-95211-5); paper $5.95 (0-395-92277-1). 48pp. A general introduction to birds of prey is followed by 20 double-page spreads that introduce the appearance and habits of such birds as eagles, hawks, falcons, and owls. (Rev: BL 6/1–15/99; SLJ 8/99) [598.9]

21803 Laubach, Christyna, et al. *Raptor! A Kid's Guide to Birds of Prey* (4–7). Illus. 2002, Storey $21.95 (1-58017-475-2); paper $14.95 (1-58017-445-0). 128pp. A large-format treasure trove of facts about raptors, with information on individual species, identification, habits, habitat, range maps, and so forth. (Rev: BL 12/1/02; HBG 3/03; SLJ 10/02) [598.9]

21804 Martin-James, Kathleen. *Soaring Bald Eagles* (PS–2). Series: Pull Ahead Books. 2001, Lerner LB $22.95 (0-8225-3636-6). 32pp. A few lines of simple text plus a color photograph on each page present the world of bald eagles to beginning readers. (Rev: BL 6/1–15/01; HBG 10/01) [598.9]

21805 Morrison, Gordon. *Bald Eagle* (PS–4). Illus. 1998, Houghton Mifflin $16.00 (0-395-87328-2). 32pp. Using watercolor paintings that trace the life cycle of two bald eagles, from hatching to producing an egg of their own, this is a fine introduction to these majestic birds of prey. (Rev: BL 6/1–15/98; HBG 3/99; SLJ 5/98) [598.9]

21806 Patent, Dorothy Hinshaw. *The Bald Eagle Returns* (4–8). Illus. 2000, Clarion $15.00 (0-395-91416-7). 68pp. This book not only discusses the successful efforts to save the bald eagle but also gives material on its anatomy, habitats, mating, and behavior. (Rev: BCCB 1/01; BL 10/15/00; HBG 10/01; SLJ 11/00) [598.9]

21807 Patent, Dorothy Hinshaw. *Eagles of America* (4–6). Photos by William Munoz. 1995, Holiday House $15.95 (0-8234-1198-2). 40pp. Bald and golden eagles are described, with information on their habits and endangered status. (Rev: BL 3/1/96; SLJ 2/96) [598.9]

21808 Povey, Karen D. *Falcons* (4–6). Illus. Series: Nature's Predators. 2005, Gale LB $18.96 (0-7377-2347-5). 48pp. In four brief chapters, the lives of falcons are explored with material on the food they eat and how they catch it.

21809 Priebe, Mac. *The Peregrine Falcon* (2–5). Illus. by Jennifer Priebe. 1999, Mindfull $15.95 (0-9669551-9-6). 32pp. This environmental success story tells how the peregrine falcon was saved from extinction by the banning of the pesticide DDT. (Rev: SLJ 4/00) [598.9]

1172

21810 Rauzon, Mark. *Golden Eagles of Devil Mountain* (3–5). Series: Wildlife Conservation Society Books. 2000, Watts LB $22.50 (0-531-11787-1). 48pp. The golden eagle is introduced, with material on its anatomy, behavioral patterns, life cycle, and habitat. (Rev: BL 3/15/01) [598.9]

21811 Silverstein, Alvin, et al. *The California Condor* (3–6). Illus. Series: Endangered in America. 1998, Millbrook LB $22.40 (0-7613-0264-6). 64pp. In addition to a description of the characteristics and habits of the California condor, this book explains why the species has declined in number and outlines efforts to save it. (Rev: BL 9/1/98; HBG 9/98) [639.97]

21812 Stone, Lynn M. *Vultures* (3–6). Illus. Series: Nature Watch. 1993, Carolrhoda LB $19.95 (0-87614-768-6). 48pp. The life cycle of the vulture is covered, and material is given on its habitat and food. (Rev: BL 8/93; SLJ 8/93*) [598.9]

21813 Swinburne, Stephen R. *In Good Hands: Behind the Scenes at a Center for Orphaned and Injured Birds* (3–6). Illus. 1998, Sierra Club $16.95 (0-87156-397-5). 32pp. A behind-the-scenes visit to the Vermont Raptor Center where orphaned or injured birds of prey, such as owls and eagles, are cared for. (Rev: BL 7/98; HBG 3/99; SLJ 8/98) [639.9]

21814 Unwin, Mike. *Peregrine Falcon* (4–6). Illus. Series: Animals Under Threat. 2004, Heinemann LB $18.95 (1-4034-4862-0). 48pp. The life cycle of the peregrine falcon and threats to its survival are explored in this blend of narrative and eye-catching color photography.

GULLS AND OTHER SEA BIRDS

21815 Bentley, Dawn. *Welcome Back, Puffin!* (PS–2). Illus. by Beth Stover. Series: Read-and-Discover Atlantic Wilderness Adventures. 2003, Soundprints paper $3.95 (1-59249-009-3). 48pp. This appealing title follows a female puffin and her mate as they make their annual visit to an island; soon after they arrive, the female lays a single egg, and she and her mate keep it warm until it hatches, after which they're kept busy gathering food for the hatchling that eats ten times a day. (Rev: SLJ 1/04)

21816 Gibbons, Gail. *Gulls . . . Gulls . . . Gulls* (3–5). Illus. 1997, Holiday House LB $15.95 (0-8234-1323-3). 32pp. Brief text and watercolor pictures are used to explore the world of the gull, its structure, diet, habits, mating behavior, and migration. (Rev: BL 9/1/97; HBG 3/98; SLJ 9/97) [598.3]

21817 Holling, Holling C. *Seabird* (4–6). 1978, Houghton Mifflin $20.00 (0-395-18230-1); paper $10.00 (0-395-26681-5). A gull accompanies a whaling expedition.

21818 Kress, Stephen W., and Pete Salmansohn. *Project Puffin: How We Brought Puffins Back to Egg Rock* (3–6). Illus. 1997, Tilbury House $16.95 (0-88448-170-0). 40pp. A first-person narrative about the project starting in 1973 that had as a goal bringing puffins back to Eastern Egg Rock off the Maine coast. (Rev: BCCB 7–8/97; BL 8/97) [636.9]

21819 McMillan, Bruce. *Nights of the Pufflings* (2–4). Illus. 1995, Houghton Mifflin $15.00 (0-395-70810-9). 32pp. On an island off the coast of Iceland, children help young puffins succeed in their first flight. (Rev: BCCB 3/95; BL 3/15/95; SLJ 3/95*) [598.3]

21820 O'Connor, Karen. *The Herring Gull* (3–5). Illus. Series: Amazing Animals. 1992, Macmillan $18.95 (0-87518-506-1). 60pp. This introduction to the herring gull discusses its evolution, habitat, behavior, and the reasons why it is endangered. (Rev: BL 11/1/92) [598]

21821 Quinlan, Susan E. *Puffins* (3–5). Illus. 1999, Lerner LB $22.60 (1-57505-090-0). 48pp. Three species of puffins are introduced, with material on their life cycles, habits, and habitats. (Rev: BL 1/1–15/99; HBG 9/99; SLJ 2/99) [598.3]

21822 Taylor, Kenny. *Puffins* (5–9). Series: World-Life Library. 1999, Voyageur paper $16.95 (0-89658-419-4). 72pp. Outstanding photographs and conservation awareness are highlights of this introduction to puffins, their characteristics, habitats, and habits. (Rev: BL 8/99) [598.3]

21823 Webb, Sophie. *Looking for Seabirds: Journal from an Alaskan Voyage* (4–6). Illus. 2004, Houghton Mifflin $16.00 (0-618-21235-3). 48pp. The author conveys the excitement of research in this fact-filled account of a shipboard bird-counting expedition. (Rev: BL 4/15/04; HB 5–6/04; SLJ 5/04) [598.177]

21824 Welsbacher, Anne. *Flying Brown Pelicans* (K–2). Photos by John Netherton. Series: Pull Ahead Books. 1999, Lerner LB $15.95 (0-8225-3613-7). 32pp. A colorful introduction to pelicans that includes material on appearance, habits, habitats, a map, and a physiological diagram. (Rev: HBG 9/99; SLJ 5/99) [598]

OWLS

21825 Arnosky, Jim. *All About Owls* (K–3). Illus. Series: All About. 1995, Scholastic $15.95 (0-590-46790-5). 32pp. The physical features of owls and their habits are discussed, with an introduction to some common species. (Rev: BL 9/1/95; SLJ 10/95*) [598.9]

21826 Browne, Vee. *Owl* (PS–3). Illus. by Diana Magnuson. Series: Animal Lore and Legend. 1995, Scholastic paper $4.95 (0-590-22488-3). 32pp. Factual information is given about owls on their characteristics, habitats, species, and food, as well as three folktales. (Rev: SLJ 3/96) [598.9]

21827 Epple, Wolfgang. *Barn Owls* (3–6). Illus. by Manfred Rogl. Series: Nature Watch. 1992, Carolrhoda LB $23.93 (0-87614-742-2). 48pp. This informative book looks at the life cycle, habitat, and feeding habits of the barn owl. (Rev: BCCB 1/93*; BL 10/1/92; SLJ 1/93) [598.97]

21828 Esbensen, Barbara J. *Tiger with Wings: The Great Horned Owl* (3–5). Illus. by Mary B. Brown. 1991, Orchard $16.95 (0-531-05940-5); paper $5.95 (0-531-07071-9). 32pp. This deadly hunter, with stripes and a catlike face, is known as a tiger with wings. (Rev: BL 9/1/91; HB 9–10/91; SLJ 8/91*) [598.97]

21829 Gibbons, Gail. *Owls* (K–3). Illus. 2005, Holiday House $16.95 (0-8234-1880-4). 32pp. All about the owls that are native to North America, with watercolor illustrations and a section about an owl family. (Rev: BL 3/15/05; SLJ 4/05) [598.9]

21830 Jarvis, Kila, and Denver W. Holt. *Owls: Whoo Are They?* (3–5). Illus. 1996, Mountain paper $12.00 (0-87842-336-2). 64pp. This introduction to owls includes descriptions of the 19 species found in North America. (Rev: BL 8/96; SLJ 12/96) [598.9]

21831 Lang, Aubrey. *Baby Owl* (1–3). Photos by Wayne Lynch. Series: Nature Babies. 2004, Fitzhenry & Whiteside $11.95 (1-55041-796-5); paper $5.95 (1-55041-798-3). 36pp. Full-color photographs follow the development of three baby great horned owls from hatching to independence. (Rev: SLJ 2/05) [598.9]

21832 Markle, Sandra. *Owls* (3–6). Illus. Series: Animal Predators. 2004, Carolrhoda LB $21.96 (1-57505-729-8). 40pp. Concise text and clear, full-page photographs introduce the life cycle of the owl and its physical characteristics, habitat, diet, and predatory behavior. (Rev: SLJ 12/04)

21833 Miller, Sara S. *Owls: The Silent Hunters* (3–5). Series: Animals in Order. 2000, Watts LB $23.00 (0-531-11595-X). 48pp. This book describes how animals are classified and then tells about different kinds of owls, their physical characteristics, food, habits, and habitats. (Rev: BL 10/15/00) [598.9]

21834 Richardson, Adele D. *Owls: Flat-Faced Flyers* (1–3). Series: Wild World of Animals. 2002, Capstone LB $18.60 (0-7368-1396-9). 24pp. For beginning readers, this is an attractive introduction to owls, their appearance, habits, care of young, and habitats. (Rev: BL 1/1–15/03; HBG 3/03) [598.9]

21835 Sattler, Helen R. *The Book of North American Owls* (3–6). Illus. 1995, Clarion $17.00 (0-395-60524-5). 64pp. After a general introduction to owls, their habits, and habitats, there is a rundown on 21 species. (Rev: BCCB 5/95; BL 4/15/95; HB 5–6/95; SLJ 5/95) [598]

21836 Silverstein, Alvin, et al. *The Spotted Owl* (4–8). Illus. Series: Endangered Species. 1994, Millbrook LB $24.90 (1-56294-415-0). 48pp. The story of the spotted owl, its endangered status, efforts to protect it, and the conflicts with the timber industry. (Rev: BL 4/15/95) [333.95]

21837 Stefoff, Rebecca. *Owl* (K–3). Series: Living Things. 1997, Marshall Cavendish LB $22.79 (0-7614-0443-0). 32pp. This simple introduction to the owl contains short bits of basic information and many colorful photos. (Rev: BL 2/15/98; HBG 3/98) [598.9]

21838 Townsend, Emily Rose. *Owls* (PS–2). Series: Woodland Animals. 2004, Capstone LB $15.93 (0-7368-2068-X). 24pp. Presents basic information on owls in a small format with brief text facing full-color close-up photographs. (Rev: SLJ 8/04) [598]

PENGUINS

21839 Bonners, Susan. *A Penguin Year* (K–4). Illus. by author. 1981, Delacorte $9.43 (0-440-00170-6). 48pp. An introduction to the lifestyle of penguins of the South Pole.

21840 Fontanel, Beatrice. *The Penguin: A Funny Bird* (2–4). Illus. by Andre Fatras. 1992, Charlesbridge paper $6.95 (0-88106-426-2). 28pp. The growth, development, and behavior of this "funny bird" are presented in color photos and large format. (Rev: BL 2/1/93) [598]

21841 Gibbons, Gail. *Penguins!* (2–4). Illus. 1998, Holiday House $16.95 (0-8234-1388-8). With pen-and-ink and watercolor paintings, the author introduces different species of penguins and describes their characteristics, food, habits, and enemies. (Rev: BL 11/1/98; HBG 3/99; SLJ 11/98) [598.47]

21842 Guiberson, Brenda Z. *The Emperor Lays an Egg* (K–3). Illus. by Joan Paley. 2001, Holt $16.95 (0-8050-6204-1). 32pp. Colorful text and lovely collages depict a year in the life of a family of emperor penguins, showing the father's incredible care for the egg, the necessary swimming skills, and the struggle to stay warm in the frigid air. (Rev: BL 12/1/01; HB 1–2/02; HBG 3/02; SLJ 12/01*) [598.47]

21843 Jango-Cohen, Judith. *Penguins* (3–5). Illus. Series: Animals, Animals. 2001, Benchmark LB $15.95 (0-7614-1260-3). 48pp. In addition to the usual information on the species, this book discusses the penguin's discovery and naming, and its relationship with humans. (Rev: HBG 10/02; SLJ 2/02) [598.47]

21844 Jenkins, Martin. *The Emperor's Egg* (PS–1). Illus. by Jane Chapman. 1999, Candlewick $16.99 (0-7636-0557-3). 32pp. A simple introduction to the emperor penguin that stresses the role played by the father in hatching the egg. (Rev: BCCB 1/00; BL 1/1–15/00; HBG 4/00; SLJ 12/99) [598.42]

21845 Johnson, Sylvia A. *Penguins* (4–7). Illus. 1981, Lerner LB $22.60 (0-8225-1453-2). 48pp. Handsome photographs enliven the text of this introduction to penguins and their habitats. [598]

21846 Kalman, Bobbie. *Penguins* (2–4). Illus. Series: Crabapples. 1995, Crabtree LB $19.96 (0-86505-624-2); paper $5.95 (0-86505-724-9). 32pp. Color photos and text are used to give basic facts about the habits, anatomy, food, and enemies of penguins. (Rev: SLJ 5/96) [598.4]

21847 Lang, Aubrey. *Baby Penguin* (K–2). Illus. by Wayne Lynch. Series: Nature Babies. 2001, Fitzhenry & Whiteside $11.95 (1-55041-675-8). 28pp. Excellent photographs and a brief text present young penguins from birth to adolescence. (Rev: BL 12/15/01; SLJ 2/02) [598.47]

21848 Lepthien, Emilie U. *Penguins* (1–4). Illus. 1983, Children's Book Pr. paper $5.50 (0-516-41683-9). 48pp. This account is distinguished by a simple text and fine color photographs.

21849 Lynch, Wayne. *Penguins!* (4–7). Illus. 1999, Firefly LB $19.95 (1-55209-421-9); paper $9.95 (1-55209-424-3). 64pp. An appealing book that introduces penguins and their various species with coverage of their evolution, food, life cycle, habits, and habitats. (Rev: BCCB 12/99; BL 9/15/99; HBG 4/00) [598.47]

21850 McMillan, Bruce. *Penguins at Home: Gentoos of Antarctica* (3–6). Illus. 1993, Houghton Mifflin $17.00 (0-395-66560-4). 32pp. A photo-essay on the Gentoo penguins of Antarctica that describes their anatomy, behavior, and mating cycle. (Rev: BCCB 9/93; BL 11/15/93; SLJ 12/93) [598]

21851 Noonan, Diana. *The Emperor Penguin* (2–4). Series: Life Cycles. 2002, Chelsea LB $14.95 (0-7910-6965-6). 32pp. This account covers the life cycle of the Antarctic emperor penguin and how these animals grow, mate, incubate their eggs, and feed their chicks. (Rev: BL 12/15/02; HBG 3/03) [598.42]

21852 Patent, Dorothy Hinshaw. *Looking at Penguins* (3–5). Illus. by Graham Robertson. 1993, Holiday House LB $16.95 (0-8234-1037-4). 40pp. Various kinds of penguins are introduced, with material on their world habitats and on the endangered emperor penguin. (Rev: BL 1/1/94; SLJ 1/94*) [598]

21853 *Penguins* (PS–2). Illus. Series: First Discovery. 1996, Scholastic $12.95 (0-590-73877-1). 24pp. Using interactive techniques and interesting visuals, answers basic questions about penguins, such as where they live. (Rev: BL 10/15/96) [598.441]

21854 Raatma, Lucia. *Penguins* (2–4). Series: First Reports. 2001, Compass Point LB $21.26 (0-7565-0058-3). 48pp. Young report writers will quickly find basic information on penguins here. (Rev: HBG 4/04; SLJ 7/01) [598]

21855 Robinson, Claire. *Penguin* (3–5). Illus. Series: Life Story. 1993, Troll paper $4.95 (0-8167-2772-4). 32pp. The habits and habitats of penguins are covered in this brief, illustrated volume. (Rev: BL 2/1/94) [594.4]

21856 Robinson, Claire. *Penguins* (2–3). Series: In the Wild. 1997, Heinemann $18.50 (1-57572-137-6). 24pp. A heavily illustrated introduction to penguins that uses double-page spreads to cover such topics as behavior, food, habitats, and care of young. (Rev: BL 2/15/98; SLJ 4/98) [598.4]

21857 Schlein, Miriam. *What's a Penguin Doing in a Place Like This?* (3–5). Illus. 1997, Millbrook LB $23.90 (0-7613-0003-1). 48pp. A guide to 17 species of penguins, arranged by habitat. (Rev: BL 6/1–15/97; SLJ 7/97) [598.4]

21858 Spilsbury, Richard, and Louise Spilsbury. *A Rookery of Penguins* (3–5). Illus. Series: Animal Groups. 2004, Heinemann LB $24.22 (1-4034-4691-1). 32pp. Easy-to-understand narrative and plenty of color photographs provide a good overview of penguins and their behaviors and habitats. (Rev: BL 4/15/04; SLJ 9/04) [598.47]

21859 Stefoff, Rebecca. *Penguin* (K–3). Series: Living Things. 1997, Marshall Cavendish LB $22.79 (0-7614-0446-5). 32pp. Using double-page spreads and many color photos, the habits, homes, and behavior of penguins are introduced very simply. (Rev: BL 2/15/98; HBG 3/98) [598.4]

21860 Stone, Lynn M. *Penguins* (2–4). Series: Bird Discovery Library. 1989, Rourke LB $14.60 (0-86592-325-6). 24pp. Introduces penguins, with brief text, color photos, and a glossary on the effects of pollution on penguins. Also use: *Vultures* (1989). (Rev: SLJ 11/89) [598.4]

21861 Stone, Lynn M. *Penguins* (2–4). Illus. Series: Early Bird Nature Books. 1998, Lerner LB $22.60 (0-8225-3022-8). 48pp. Questions are used throughout this book to explain important facts about penguins, their habits, family life, and homes. (Rev: BL 12/1/98; HBG 3/99) [598.47]

21862 Tatham, Betty. *Penguin Chick* (2–3). Illus. by Helen K. Davie. Series: Let's-Read-and-Find-Out Science. 2002, HarperCollins $15.95 (0-06-028594-X); paper $4.95 (0-06-445206-9). 40pp. An account for younger readers of an emperor penguin chick's survival in an often ruthless habitat. (Rev: BL 3/1/02; HB 5–6/02; HBG 10/02; SLJ 3/02) [598.47]

21863 Webb, Sophie. *My Season with Penguins: An Antarctic Journal* (4–8). Illus. by author. 2000, Houghton Mifflin $15.00 (0-395-92291-7). 48pp. Journal entries plus effective drawings show the joys and tribulations of a two-month stay in the Antarctic studying penguins and their behavior. (Rev: HB 11–12/00; HBG 3/01; SLJ 12/00) [598]

Conservation of Endangered Species

21864 Astorga, Amalia, and Gary Paul Nabhan. *Efrain of the Sonoran Desert: A Lizard's Life Among the Seri People* (2–6). Illus. by Janet K. Miller. 2001, Cinco Puntos $15.95 (0-938317-55-5). 32pp. The fascinating story of how an endangered lizard can flourish within a special community. (Rev: BL 12/15/01; HBG 3/02; SLJ 12/01) [305.8975]

21865 Barnes, Simon. *Planet Zoo* (4–7). Illus. 2001, Orion $29.95 (1-85881-488-X). 264pp. An overview of 100 endangered species that conveys information in a conversational manner. (Rev: BL 8/01; SLJ 8/01) [578.68]

21866 Becker, John E. *The North American Bison* (4–6). Illus. Series: Returning Wildlife. 2003, Gale LB $18.96 (0-7377-1380-1). 48pp. The bison's recovery from near-extinction and its importance to Native Americans are detailed here. (Rev: BL 1/1–15/03) [599.64]

21867 Casterline, Linda. *Rare Animals: A Chapter Book* (2–5). Series: True Tales. 2003, Children's Pr. LB $21.50 (0-516-22914-1). 48pp. Written in simple language, this volume introduces four endangered animals — the whooping crane, elephant, monk seal, and polar bear — and discusses what is being done to protect them. (Rev: SLJ 2/04) [591.68]

21868 Chandler, Gary, and Kevin Graham. *Guardians of Wildlife* (4–8). Illus. Series: Making a Better World. 1996, Twenty-First Century LB $25.90 (0-8050-4626-7). 64pp. Solutions to overhunting, poaching, and overfishing are explored, as well as new wildlife management techniques. (Rev: BL 12/15/96; SLJ 4/97) [639.9]

21869 Dobson, David. *Can We Save Them? Endangered Species of North America* (4–5). Illus. by James M. Needham. 1997, Charlesbridge $16.95 (0-88106-823-3); paper $6.95 (0-88106-822-5). 32pp. Features 12 North American species of endangered wildlife, including Florida panthers, tree snails, gray bats, peregrine falcons, and wildflowers. (Rev: BL 4/1/97; SLJ 7/97) [591.52]

21870 Fowler, Allan. *It Could Still Be Endangered* (K–2). Illus. Series: Rookie Readers. 2000, Children's Book Pr. $19.00 (0-516-21208-7). 32pp. Full-page colors photos introduce the concept of endangerment and introduce several animals large and small that are on the endangered list. (Rev: BL 1/1–15/01) [333.95]

21871 Gutfreund, Geraldine M. *Vanishing Animal Neighbors* (4–6). Illus. 1993, Watts LB $22.00 (0-531-20060-4). 64pp. Five different endangered species are introduced, with a discussion of why they are decreasing and what their loss can mean. (Rev: BL 7/93; SLJ 6/93) [591]

21872 Kendell, Patricia. *WWF* (5–8). Series: World Watch. 2004, Raintree LB $27.14 (0-7398-6615-X). 48pp. Introduces the World Wildlife Fund's history, organization, and work on behalf of the endangered animals; sidebars provide key facts and relevant quotations. (Rev: SLJ 6/04) [333.95]

21873 Lessem, Don. *Dinosaurs to Dodos: An Encyclopedia of Extinct Animals* (4–7). Illus. 1999, Scholastic paper $16.95 (0-590-31684-2). 112pp. Moving through 12 time periods, this book describes each period and how geological changes caused the extinction of certain species and the creation of new ones. (Rev: BL 11/1/99; HBG 4/00; SLJ 11/99) [560]

21874 Lovett, Sarah. *Extremely Weird Endangered Species* (3–6). Illus. by Mary Sundstrom and Sally Blakemore. Series: Extremely Weird. 1997, Davidson LB $21.27 (1-884756-26-3); John Muir paper $5.95 (0-56261-280-8). 48pp. This colorful book introduces such unusual endangered species as manatees, bats, guans, rhinos, and condors. (Rev: SLJ 7/92) [574]

21875 McClung, Robert M. *Lost Wild America: The Story of Our Extinct and Vanishing Wildlife*. Rev. ed. (5–8). Illus. 1993, Shoe String LB $30.00 (0-208-02359-3). A history of American wildlife management from pioneer days to the present, with information on extinct and endangered species. (Rev: BL 1/1/94; SLJ 2/94*) [591.5]

21876 Nirgiotis, Nicholas, and Theodore Nigiortis. *No More Dodos: How Zoos Help Endangered Wildlife* (5–8). Illus. 1996, Lerner LB $23.93 (0-8225-2856-8). An introduction to the many organizations that are trying to protect and preserve endangered wildlife worldwide. (Rev: BCCB 2/97; BL 2/15/97; SLJ 2/97) [639.9]

21877 O'Neill, Mary. *Nature in Danger* (4–7). Illus. by John Bindon. Series: SOS Planet Earth. 1991, Troll paper $5.95 (0-8167-2286-2). 32pp. Background information and history lead into the problem of animals in danger. (Rev: BL 6/15/91) [333.7]

21878 Penny, Malcolm. *Endangered Species* (5–8). Series: 21st Century Debates. 2002, Raintree LB $27.12 (0-7398-4873-9). 64pp. Topics covered in this well-illustrated book include a history of conservation, how species become endangered, methods for protection such as captive breeding, and saving habitats. (Rev: BL 6/1–15/02) [591]

21879 Radley, Gail. *Forests and Jungles* (2–5). Illus. by Jean Sherlock. Series: Vanishing From. 2001, Carolrhoda LB $22.60 (1-57505-405-1); paper $6.95 (1-57505-567-8). 32pp. The plight of endangered species as humans threaten their habitats serves as an introduction to double-page spreads about specific animals. Also use *Grasslands and Deserts* and *The Skies* (both 2001). (Rev: HBG 3/02; SLJ 10/01) [591]

21880 Salmansohn, Pete, and Stephen W. Kress. *Saving Birds: Heroes Around the World* (4–7). Illus. 2003, Tilbury House $16.95 (0-88448-237-5). 40pp. Efforts to save endangered bird species are detailed in informative text and arresting, full-color photographs. (Rev: BL 3/15/03; HBG 10/03; SLJ 5/03) [333.95]

21881 Stuart, Gene S. *Wildlife Alert: The Struggle to Survive* (3–6). Illus. 1980, National Geographic LB $12.00 (0-87044-323-2). 104pp. This book outlines the steps being taken to help endangered animals around the world.

21882 Taylor, Dave. *Endangered Forest Animals* (3–5). Illus. Series: Endangered Animals. 1992, Crabtree LB $19.96 (0-86505-529-7); paper $7.95 (0-86505-539-4). 32pp. In this heavily illustrated book, several endangered animals and forest ecology are highlighted. (Rev: BL 11/15/92) [591]

21883 Taylor, Dave. *Endangered Grassland Animals* (3–5). Series: Endangered Animals. 1992, Crabtree LB $19.96 (0-86505-528-9); paper $7.95 (0-86505-538-6). 32pp. Animals of the African, Australian, and North American grasslands are introduced, with many full-color photos. (Rev: BL 12/15/92) [591]

21884 Taylor, Dave. *Endangered Wetland Animals* (3–5). Illus. Series: Endangered Animals. 1992, Crabtree LB $19.96 (0-86505-530-0); paper $7.95 (0-86505-540-8). 32pp. Wetlands are described, and several wetlands animals currently considered endangered are pictured. Also use *Endangered Mountain Animals* (1992). (Rev: BL 11/15/92; SLJ 11/92) [591]

21885 Thomas, Peggy. *Big Cat Conservation* (5–8). Illus. Series: Science of Saving Animals. 2000, Twenty-First Century LB $25.90 (0-7613-3231-6). 64pp. This book focuses on seven species, including panthers, cheetahs, and tigers, and discusses wildlife conservation programs, challenges, and successes. (Rev: BL 6/1–15/00; HBG 9/00; SLJ 7/00) [333.95]

21886 Thomas, Peggy. *Bird Alert* (5–8). Series: The Science of Saving Animals. 2000, Twenty-First Century LB $25.90 (0-7613-1457-1). 64pp. This book discusses conservation programs designed to save endangered bird species and tells how youngsters can get involved in saving birds. (Rev: BL 10/15/00; HBG 10/01; SLJ 12/00) [591.52]

21887 Thomas, Peggy. *Marine Mammal Preservation* (5–8). Series: The Science of Saving Animals. 2000, Twenty-First Century LB $25.90 (0-7613-1458-X). 64pp. Focuses on endangered marine mammals and describes a wide range of conservation programs. (Rev: BL 10/15/00; HBG 10/01; SLJ 1/01) [574.92]

21888 Thomas, Peggy. *Reptile Rescue* (5–8). Illus. Series: Science of Saving Animals. 2000, Twenty-First Century LB $25.90 (0-7613-3232-4). 64pp. A description of various conservation programs and how they operate in relation to several reptile species, including tortoises, crocodiles, and snakes. (Rev: BL 6/1–15/00; HBG 9/00; SLJ 7/00) [333.95]

21889 Turbak, Gary. *Mountain Animals in Danger* (1–4). Illus. by Lawrence Ormsby. 1994, Northland LB $14.95 (0-87358-573-9). 32pp. Introduces ten endangered species, like the gray wolf, bald eagle, and spotted owl. (Rev: BL 2/1/95; SLJ 2/95) [599]

21890 Vergoth, Karin, and Christopher Lampton. *Endangered Species*. Rev. ed. (5–7). Illus. 1999, Watts LB $25.00 (0-531-11480-5). 112pp. A valuable overview of the subject that updates the 1988 edition with good, comprehensive lists of endangered species. (Rev: BL 2/1/00) [578.68]

Insects and Arachnids

GENERAL AND MISCELLANEOUS

21891 Allen, Judy. *Are You a Dragonfly?* (PS–1). Series: Backyard Books. 2002, Kingfisher $9.95 (0-7534-5346-0). 32pp. This book describes life from a dragonfly's point-of-view with information on its life cycle and behavior. Also use *Are You a Grasshopper?* (2002). (Rev: BL 2/15/03) [595.7]

21892 Anderson, Margaret J. *Bizarre Insects* (3–6). Illus. Series: Weird and Wacky Science. 1996, Enslow LB $19.95 (0-89490-613-5). 48pp. Fascinating facts and lots of pictures highlight this account of unusual insects and their habits. (Rev: SLJ 6/96) [595.7]

21893 Ashley, Susan. *Fireflies* (1–4). Series: Let's Read About Insects. 2004, Weekly Reader LB $18.60 (0-8368-4053-4); paper $5.95 (0-8368-4060-7). 24pp. The life cycle of fireflies is described in small-format, easy-to-read text with close-up photographs. (Rev: SLJ 2/05)

21894 Bailey, Jill. *Mosquito* (1–3). Illus. by Alan Male. Series: Bug Books. 1998, Heinemann LB $19.92 (1-57572-663-7). 32pp. Large photos of mosquitoes accompanied by short paragraphs of text introduce such subjects as mating, physical structure, life cycle, and diet. (Rev: HBG 9/99; SLJ 1/99) [595.77]

21895 Barner, Bob. *Bug Safari* (1–3). Illus. 2004, Holiday House $16.95 (0-8234-1707-7). 32pp. In this colorful journey into the world of insects, a young boy follows a trail of ants and discovers an alternative perspective on a picnic lunch. (Rev: BL 4/15/04; SLJ 3/04) [595.7]

21896 Barner, Bob. *Bugs! Bugs! Bugs!* (PS–1). Illus. 1999, Chronicle $12.95 (0-8118-2238-9). 32pp. A rhyming text and bold color illustrations effectively introduce the world of bugs. (Rev: BL 7/99; SLJ 8/99) [595.7]

21897 Berger, Melvin. *Buzz! A Book About Insects* (1–2). Illus. 2000, Scholastic $3.99 (0-439-08748-1). 40pp. This easy-to-read science book uses color photographs to introduce various insects, explain their physical characteristics, and show the changes from caterpillar to butterfly. (Rev: BL 10/1/00) [595.7]

21898 Berger, Melvin. *Killer Bugs* (4–8). Illus. 1990, Avon paper $3.50 (0-380-76036-3). 88pp. This account explores the world of killer bees, fire ants, and other such bugs. (Rev: BL 12/15/90) [595.7]

21899 Berger, Melvin, and Gilda Berger. *How Do Flies Walk Upside Down? Questions and Answers About Insects* (3–5). Illus. Series: Question and Answer. 1999, Scholastic $12.95 (0-590-13082-X); paper $5.95 (0-590-08572-1). 48pp. An attractive book that describes the characteristics of insects in a question-and-answer format. (Rev: BL 11/1/99; SLJ 12/99) [595.7]

21900 Brenner, Barbara, and Bernice Chardiet. *Where's That Insect?* (2–4). Illus. by Carol Schwartz. 1995, Scholastic paper $4.99 (0-590-45211-8). 32pp. Simple facts are presented about 14 kinds of insects. (Rev: BL 8/93; SLJ 3/93) [595.7]

21901 Brimner, Larry. *Cockroaches* (3–5). Series: True Books. 1999, Children's Book Pr. LB $21.50 (0-516-21159-5). 48pp. This squarish book with large print and many captioned photographs gives basic information about the cockroach, its structure, habits, life cycle, and habitats. (Rev: BL 11/15/99) [595.7]

21902 Brimner, Larry. *Flies* (3–5). Series: True Books. 1999, Children's Book Pr. LB $21.50 (0-516-21161-7). 48pp. Different kinds of flies are introduced with material on their structure, life cycles, habits, food, and habitats. (Rev: BL 11/15/99) [595.7]

21903 Brimner, Larry. *Praying Mantises* (3–5). Series: True Books. 1999, Children's Book Pr. LB $21.50 (0-516-21163-3). 48pp. This carnivorous insect — named because the position of its forelegs suggests hands in prayer — is introduced in a large-type text and numerous captioned photos. (Rev: BL 11/15/99) [959.7]

21904 *Bugs* (3–5). Ed. by Penelope York. 2002, DK LB $17.95 (0-7894-8553-2). 48pp. A colorful introduction to insects, their characteristics, life cycles, habitats, and varieties. (Rev: BL 6/1–15/02; HBG 10/02) [595.7]

21905 Dewey, Jennifer O. *Bedbugs in Our House: True Tales of Insect, Bug, and Spider Discovery* (4–6). Illus. 1997, Marshall Cavendish $14.95 (0-7614-5006-8). 64pp. Using personal encounters with insects as a focus, the author presents details about all sorts of creatures, including fireflies, locusts, and spiders. (Rev: BL 1/1–15/98; HBG 9/98) [595.7]

21906 Doris, Ellen. *Entomology* (4–6). Illus. by Len Rubenstein. 1993, Thames & Hudson $16.95 (0-500-19004-6). 64pp. In this project book, the classification of insects is covered, along with their habitats and metamorphosis and ideas for field trips and collecting specimens. (Rev: BL 10/1/93; SLJ 9/93) [595.7]

21907 Dussling, Jennifer. *Bugs! Bugs! Bugs!* (2–4). Series: Eyewitness Reader. 1998, DK $12.95 (0-7894-3762-7); paper $3.95 (0-7894-3438-5). 32pp. Using lavish illustrations, a chatty text, information boxes, and fact pages, this book introduces a variety of insects, their physical characteristics, habits, food, and life cycles. (Rev: HBG 3/99; SLJ 1/99) [595.7]

21908 Fischer-Nagel, Heiderose, and Andreas Fischer-Nagel. *The Housefly* (3–6). Illus. Series: Nature Watch. 1990, Carolrhoda LB $19.95 (0-87614-374-5). 48pp. A well-organized text with many details about the housefly. (Rev: BL 6/15/90; SLJ 9/90) [595.7]

21909 Fleisher, Paul. *Ants* (5–8). Series: Animal-Ways. 2001, Marshall Cavendish LB $28.50 (0-7614-1269-7). 112pp. This introduction to ants and their habits and habitats also includes fine color images and material on species identification, anatomy, and classification. (Rev: BL 3/15/02; HBG 10/02) [595.79]

21910 Fowler, Allan. *It's a Good Thing There Are Insects* (1–2). Illus. Series: Rookie Readers. 1990, Children's Book Pr. LB $19.00 (0-516-04905-4). 32pp. Insects and their characteristics are introduced in this beginner's science book. (Rev: BL 2/1/91) [595.7]

21911 Frost, Helen. *Praying Mantises* (PS–3). Series: Insects. 2001, Capstone LB $9.95 (0-7368-0853-1). 24pp. Spare text and full-page color photographs — often close-up shots — offer basic information on praying mantises. Also use *Walking-sticks* (2001). (Rev: HBG 3/02; SLJ 9/01) [959.7]

21912 Goldsen, Louise. *The Ladybug and Other Insects* (PS–2). Illus. by Sylvaine Perols. Series: First Discovery. 1991, Scholastic $12.95 (0-590-45235-5). Through painted overlays, the transformation of a larva to a ladybug is depicted, and information is given on the habits and habitats of this and other insects. (Rev: SLJ 6/92) [595.7]

21913 Green, Jen. *Insects* (3–6). Series: Young Scientist Concepts and Projects. 1999, Gareth Stevens LB $16.95 (0-8368-2266-8). 64pp. This illustrated book of easy-to-do projects — including how to make an ant colony — introduces children to the secret world of insects. (Rev: BL 4/15/98) [595.7]

21914 Greenaway, Theresa. *Ants* (4–7). Series: The Secret World Of. 2001, Raintree LB $18.98 (0-7368-3511-4). 48pp. After presenting interesting and unusual facts about ants, this book examines their structure, homes, behavior, and enemies. (Rev: BL 10/15/01) [595.79]

21915 Hartley, Karen, et al. *Centipede* (K–3). Series: Heinemann First Library. 1999, Heinemann LB $13.95 (1-57572-796-X). 32pp. Using color photos and a brief text, this book introduces a variety of centipedes and explains locomotion and how and where they live. (Rev: BL 6/1–15/99; HBG 9/99) [595.7]

21916 Hartley, Karen, et al. *Cockroach* (K–3). Series: Heinemann First Library. 1999, Heinemann LB $13.95 (1-57572-797-8). 32pp. Through amazing color photos and a simple text, the cockroach is introduced, with material on types, food, habitats, and life cycle. (Rev: BL 6/1–15/99; HBG 9/99) [595.7]

21917 Hartley, Karen, et al. *Fly* (1–4). Illus. Series: Bug Books. 2000, Heinemann LB $19.92 (1-57572-548-7). 32pp. Traces the life cycle of the fly, with illustrations and text that also cover its habitats and food. (Rev: BL 7/00) [595.77]

21918 Hartley, Karen, et al. *Grasshopper* (K–3). Illus. Series: Heinemann First Library. 1999, Heinemann LB $13.95 (1-57572-798-6). 32pp. A large labeled drawing of a grasshopper's body is accompanied by descriptions in pictures and text of its life cycle, habits, habitats, and unique characteristics. (Rev: BL 6/1–15/99; HBG 9/99) [595]

21919 Hartley, Karen, et al. *Head Louse* (1–4). Illus. Series: Bug Books. 2000, Heinemann LB $19.92 (1-57572-549-5). 32pp. Close-up photos are used to introduce the life cycle of the head louse, its food, and habits. (Rev: BL 7/00) [616.5]

21920 Hartley, Karen, et al. *Termite* (K–3). Series: Heinemann First Library. 1999, Heinemann LB $13.95 (1-57572-800-1). 32pp. The termite is introduced in stunning photographs and a simple text that gives basic information about varieties, habits, habitats, and their destructive behavior. (Rev: BL 6/1–15/99; HBG 9/99) [595.7]

21921 Hawes, Judy. *Fireflies in the Night* (PS–3). Illus. by Ellen Alexander. Series: Let's-Read-and-Find-Out. 1991, HarperCollins $13.95 (0-06-022484-3); paper $4.95 (0-06-445101-1). 32pp. Full-color illustrations help to explain the world of fireflies. A remake of the original 1963 edition. (Rev: BL 11/15/91; SLJ 3/92) [595.76]

21922 Heinrichs, Ann. *Fireflies* (1–3). Illus. Series: Nature's Friends. 2004, Compass Point LB $15.95 (0-7565-0588-7). 32pp. Fireflies' anatomy and life cycle are covered in simple text and clear close-up photographs.

21923 Heinrichs, Ann. *Grasshoppers* (2–4). Series: Nature's Friends. 2002, Compass Point LB $21.26 (0-7565-0166-0). 32pp. Grasshoppers, their anatomy and life cycle, and their relationship to humans are covered in simple text and clear close-up photographs. (Rev: SLJ 7/02) [595.7]

21924 Hickman, Pamela. *Bug Book* (3–5). Illus. Series: Starting with Nature. 1999, Kids Can $12.95 (1-55074-475-5). 32pp. Using double-page spreads and fact boxes, this is an attractive introduction to insects including beetles, moths, termites, and butterflies. (Rev: BL 2/1/99; HBG 9/99) [595.7]

21925 Hipp, Andrew. *Orchid Mantises* (3–5). Series: The Really Wild Life of Insects. 2003, Rosen LB $18.75 (0-8239-6239-3). 24pp. Mantises that can mimic the flower of an orchid are the focus of this interesting, well-illustrated volume. (Rev: SLJ 1/04) [595.7]

21926 Hipp, Andrew. *Peanut-Head Bugs* (3–5). Series: The Really Wild Life of Insects. 2003,

Rosen LB $18.75 (0-8239-6242-3). 24pp. An excellent overview of members of the Fulgoridae family, found throughout much of Latin America and commonly called peanut-head bugs. (Rev: SLJ 1/04) [595.7]

21927 Hirschmann, Kris. *Lice* (4–6). Illus. Series: Parasites. 2003, Gale/KidHaven LB $22.45 (0-7377-1784-X). 32pp. The physical and behavioral characteristics of lice are introduced, with information on how they spread disease to humans. (Rev: SLJ 6/04) [614.4]

21928 Holland, Gay W. *Look Closer: An Introduction to Bug-Watching* (1–4). Illus. 2003, Millbrook LB $22.90 (0-7613-2664-2). 32pp. Aphids, spittlebugs, and dragonflies are among the bugs introduced in this guide that combines realistic illustrations with easy-to-read text. (Rev: BL 6/1–15/03; HBG 10/03; SLJ 9/03) [595.7]

21929 Holmes, Anita. *Insect Detector* (1–2). Illus. Series: We Can Read About — Nature! 2000, Benchmark $14.95 (0-7614-1110-0). 32pp. A beginning reader that defines the characteristics of an insect and asks if particular creatures such as a scorpion or a spider would meet these criteria. (Rev: BL 12/1/00; HBG 3/01; SLJ 2/01) [595.7]

21930 Hughes, Monica. *Pill Bugs* (PS–2). Illus. Series: Creepy Creatures. 2003, Raintree LB $18.56 (1-4109-0624-8). 24pp. A close-up look at the diet, anatomy, habitat, and life cycle of pill bugs, for beginning readers. (Rev: BL 2/15/04) [595.3]

21931 *Insects* (4–6). Illus. Series: Discovery Channel School Science: The Plant and Animal Kingdoms. 2002, Gareth Stevens LB $22.60 (0-8368-3215-9). 32pp. An attractive, fact-filled yet accessible introduction with many full-color photographs and charts. (Rev: HBG 3/03; SLJ 2/03)

21932 Jackson, Donna. *The Bug Scientists* (4–7). Illus. Series: Scientists in the Field. 2002, Houghton Mifflin $16.00 (0-618-10868-8). 48pp. In addition to describing a variety of professional jobs related to insects, this colorful volume presents excellent information about insects and how they live. (Rev: BCCB 6/02; BL 4/1/02; HB 5–6/02; HBG 10/02; SLJ 4/02) [595.7]

21933 Jarrow, Gail. *Chiggers* (4–6). Series: Parasites. 2003, Gale/KidHaven LB $22.45 (0-7377-1778-5). 32pp. A close-up look at these tiny bloodsucking mites, with color photographs and first-person accounts of chigger encounters. (Rev: SLJ 6/04) [616.9]

21934 Johnson, Jinny. *Children's Guide to Insects and Spiders* (3–5). Illus. 1997, Simon & Schuster $19.95 (0-689-81163-2). 64pp. Using a large format, the author identifies and describes families of insects and spiders and furnishes drawings and photos of body parts and stages of life cycles. (Rev: BL 5/1/97; SLJ 11/97) [595.7]

21935 Johnson, Sylvia A. *Beetles* (4–7). Illus. 1982, Lerner LB $22.60 (0-8225-1476-1). 48pp. Color photography highlights this account that concentrates on the scarab beetle.

21936 Johnson, Sylvia A. *Fireflies* (4–6). 1986, Lerner LB $22.60 (0-8225-1485-0). 48pp. Life cycle, breeding, environment, and characteristics of the firefly. (Rev: BL 10/1/86; SLJ 11/86)

21937 Johnson, Sylvia A. *Water Insects* (3–6). Illus. by Modoki Masuda. 1989, Lerner LB $22.60 (0-8225-1489-3). 48pp. Various kinds of aquatic insects are pictured and described. (Rev: BL 2/15/90; SLJ 4/90) [595]

21938 Kite, L. Patricia. *Cockroaches* (2–3). Series: Early Bird Nature Books. 2001, Lerner LB $22.60 (0-8225-3046-5). 48pp. Using a simple text and color photographs on each page, this book effectively introduces the life cycle of the cockroach with material on its habits, anatomy, and homes. Also use *Fireflies* (2001). (Rev: BL 8/1/01; HBG 10/01) [595.7]

21939 Kite, L. Patricia. *Insect: Facts and Folklore* (3–6). Illus. 2001, Millbrook LB $27.90 (0-7613-1822-4). 80pp. Fascinating information (mixing facts, folklore, and interesting anecdotes) about insects, all colorfully presented. (Rev: BL 9/1/01; HBG 3/02; SLJ 10/01) [595.7]

21940 Kneidel, Sally. *Pet Bugs: A Kid's Guide to Catching and Keeping Touchable Insects* (4–6). Illus. 1994, Wiley paper $12.95 (0-471-31188-X). 117pp. Describes 25 insects; how they live, eat, and reproduce; and how they can be kept as specimens. (Rev: BL 7/94; SLJ 9/94) [638]

21941 Lavies, Bianca. *Compost Critters* (3–5). Illus. 1993, Dutton $15.99 (0-525-44763-6). 32pp. Amazing photos and simple text introduce such organisms as mites, various bugs, and snails in compost piles. (Rev: BCCB 6/93; BL 7/93*; SLJ 7/93*) [591]

21942 Llewellyn, Claire. *The Best Book of Bugs* (3–5). 1998, Kingfisher $10.95 (0-7534-5118-2). 33pp. A lavishly illustrated book that introduces insects and spiders and describes more than 20 different species, including information on the life cycles of honeybees, dragonflies, and butterflies. (Rev: HBG 9/98; SLJ 7/98) [595.7]

21943 Llewellyn, Claire. *Some Bugs Glow in the Dark: And Other Amazing Facts About Insects* (1–3). Illus. by Mike Taylor, et al. Series: I Didn't Know That. 1997, Millbrook LB $19.90 (0-7613-0562-9). 32pp. As well as explaining what insects are, this book covers amazing facts about their speed, size, weight, metamorphosis, and unusual behavior. (Rev: SLJ 9/97) [595.7]

21944 McEvey, Shane F. *Beetles* (3–5). Series: Insects and Spiders. 2001, Chelsea LB $16.95 (0-7910-6600-2). 32pp. Beetle facts of all kinds are amplified by information on how scientists collect and study them and by tips on keeping beetles as pets. Also use *Bugs* (2001). (Rev: HBG 3/02; SLJ 2/02) [595.76]

21945 McLaughlin, Molly. *Dragonflies* (2–6). Illus. 1988, Walker LB $15.85 (0-8027-6847-4). 48pp. The life cycle of dragonflies plus information on different varieties are provided with outstanding photographs. (Rev: BCCB 10/89; BL 8/89*; SLJ 9/89) [595.7]

21946 Markle, Sandra. *Creepy, Crawly Baby Bugs* (3–5). Illus. 1996, Walker LB $16.85 (0-8027-8444-5). 32pp. The growth cycle of insects is explored, with emphasis on each infant stage. (Rev: BL 11/15/96; SLJ 4/97*) [595.7]

21947 Meister, Cari. *Mosquitoes* (2–4). Illus. Series: Checkerboard Science and Nature Library: Insects. 2001, ABDO LB $13.95 (1-57765-464-1). 24pp. An introduction to mosquitoes and their structure, diet, habitat, and habits. (Rev: BL 10/15/01; HBG 10/01) [595.77]

21948 Merrick, Patrick. *Centipedes* (1–4). Series: Naturebooks. 2003, Child's World LB $25.64 (1-56766-978-6). 32pp. This photo-filled overview of centipedes examines the insect's physical appearance, habitat, diet, behavior, and defense mechanisms. (Rev: SLJ 12/03) [595.6]

21949 Merrick, Patrick. *Cockroaches* (1–4). Series: Naturebooks. 2003, Child's World LB $25.64 (1-56766-206-4). 32pp. Large-print text and close-up photographs explore the cockroach's physical characteristics, habitat, diet, and behavior. (Rev: SLJ 12/03) [595.7]

21950 Miller, Sara S. *Flies: From Flower Flies to Mosquitoes* (3–5). Illus. Series: Animals in Order. 1998, Watts LB $22.00 (0-531-11486-4). 48pp. After an explanation of the classification of living things, this book profiles 14 different flies commonly found in America and gives details on the life cycle, habits, physical characteristics, and behavior of each. (Rev: BL 1/1–15/99; HBG 3/99; SLJ 12/98) [595.77]

21951 Miller, Sara S. *True Bugs: When Is a Bug Really a Bug?* (3–5). Illus. Series: Animals in Order. 1998, Watts LB $22.00 (0-531-11479-1). 48pp. The classification of animals is explained, followed by a profile of 14 common insects with material on their physical characteristics, behavior, and life cycles. (Rev: BL 1/1–15/99; HBG 3/99) [595.7]

21952 Miller, Sara Swan. *Ants, Bees, and Wasps of North America* (4–6). Series: Animals in Order. 2003, Watts LB $25.00 (0-531-12244-1); paper $6.95 (0-531-16658-9). 47pp. This overview of the hymenoptera order gives a close-up look at the lives of ants, bees, and wasps and gives tips on their habitat and observation. (Rev: SLJ 7/03) [595.79]

21953 Miller, Sara Swan. *Grasshoppers and Crickets of North America* (3–5). Series: Animals in Order. 2002, Watts $25.00 (0-531-12170-4). 48pp. This colorful volume explores insect jumpers of the orthopteran order, which includes grasshoppers, crickets, and katydids. (Rev: BL 9/15/02) [595]

21954 Murawski, Darlyne A. *Bug Faces* (K–4). Illus. 2000, National Geographic $16.95 (0-7922-7557-8). 32pp. Huge, sometimes scary photographs in gorgeous color show close-up views of such creatures as a spider, cockroach, bumblebee, deer fly, and weevil. (Rev: BL 11/15/00; HBG 3/01; SLJ 11/00) [595.7]

21955 Nathan, Emma. *What Do You Call a Group of Butterflies? And Other Insect Groups* (3–5). Illus. 2000, Blackbirch LB $15.95 (1-56711-359-1). 24pp. This simple science book uses questions and answers to give basic facts about insects and to reveal each one's group name, such as a colony of ants. (Rev: BL 12/1/00; HBG 3/01) [595.7]

21956 Needham, Karen, and Launi Lucas. *Strange Beginnings* (K–2). Illus. by Launi Lucas. 2002, Tradewind paper $6.95 (1-896580-11-4). An attractive introduction to the various insects that emerge from water to spend their often brief adult lives in the air. (Rev: SLJ 9/02) [595.7176]

21957 Oppenheim, Joanne. *Have You Seen Bugs?* (K–3). Illus. by Ron Broda. 1998, Scholastic $15.95 (0-590-05963-7). 32pp. A series of charming verses and paper sculptures introduce moths, bees, spiders, and several insects, and describe their life cycles and characteristics. (Rev: BL 4/1/98; HBG 9/98; SLJ 9/98) [595.7]

21958 Parker, Janice. *Cockroaches, Cocoons, and Honeycombs: The Science of Insects* (3–5). Series: Science@Work. 1999, Raintree LB $25.69 (0-7398-0135-X). 48pp. This book about insects presents interesting facts, diagrams, and lots of appended information, along with material on careers related to the study of insects. (Rev: SLJ 3/00) [595.7]

21959 Parker, Janice. *The Science of Insects* (2–5). Series: Living Science. 1999, Gareth Stevens LB $14.95 (0-8368-2466-0). 32pp. In double-page spreads, different types of insects are introduced, with material on their life cycles and habitats. (Rev: HBG 9/00; SLJ 1/00) [595.7]

21960 Parker, Nancy W., and Joan Richards Wright. *Bugs* (K–3). Illus. by Nancy Winslow Parker. 1987, Morrow paper $4.95 (0-688-08296-3). A picture-book format provides solid facts on bugs — including 16 common insects. (Rev: BL 11/1/87; SLJ 10/87)

21961 Pascoe, Elaine. *Ant Lions and Lacewings* (4–8). Photos by Dwight Kuhn. Series: Nature Close-Up. 2005, Gale/Blackbirch LB $18.96 (1-4103-0310-1). 48pp. Eye-catching close-ups illustrate information on these insects' life cycles and eating habits. Also use *Mantids and Their Relatives* (2005). (Rev: SLJ 6/05)

21962 Pascoe, Elaine. *Ants* (4–7). Series: Nature Close-Up. 1998, Blackbirch LB $27.44 (1-56711-183-1). 48pp. Using outstanding photographs, this book introduces ants and a series of projects designed to teach more about these creatures. (Rev: BL 9/15/98; HBG 3/99; SLJ 3/99) [595.78]

21963 Pascoe, Elaine. *Beetle* (4–7). Series: Nature Close-Up. 2000, Blackbirch LB $27.44 (1-56711-175-0). 48pp. Outstanding photographs grace this simple introduction to beetles that discusses their anatomy, habits, and food. (Rev: BL 4/15/00; HBG 3/01; SLJ 9/00) [595.76]

21964 Pascoe, Elaine. *Crickets and Grasshoppers* (4–7). Series: Nature Close-Up. 1998, Blackbirch LB $27.44 (1-56711-176-9). 48pp. Easy projects introduce youngsters to these insects in this book illustrated with color photographs. (Rev: BL 9/15/98; HBG 3/99) [595.7]

21965 Pascoe, Elaine. *Flies* (4–7). Series: Nature Close-Up. 2000, Blackbirch LB $27.44 (1-56711-149-1). 48pp. This introduction to flies uses stunning photographs and text to describe their body parts, life cycle, and how to observe them; a few focused experiments are also included. (Rev: BL 4/15/00; HBG 3/01; SLJ 9/00) [595.7]

21966 Pascoe, Elaine. *Spittlebugs: And Other Sap Tappers* (3–5). Photos by Dwight Kuhn. Series: Nature Close-up. 2003, Gale/Blackbirch LB $27.45 (1-56711-430-X). 48pp. A close-up study, with eye-catching photographs, of the insect order Homoptera, covering life cycle, behavior, characteristics, and how they may be harmful or beneficial. (Rev: SLJ 3/04) [595.7]

21967 Pipe, Jim. *The Giant Book of Bugs and Creepy Crawlies* (4–8). Illus. 1998, Millbrook LB $27.90 (0-7613-0716-8). Exotic and common insects and spiders are presented in this oversize book with eye-catching pictures and fascinating text. (Rev: BL 8/98) [595.7]

21968 Pringle, Laurence. *A Dragon in the Sky: The Story of a Green Darner Dragonfly* (3–5). Illus. 2001, Scholastic $18.95 (0-531-30315-2). 64pp. The reader follows a green darner from egg to mating in this attractive, large-format book. (Rev: BL 6/1–15/01; HB 7–8/01; HBG 10/01; SLJ 8/01) [595.7]

21969 Pyers, Greg. *Grasshoppers up Close* (2–4). Illus. Series: Minibeasts Up Close. 2005, Raintree LB $18.45 (1-4109-1529-8). 32pp. A simple introduction to grasshoppers and their physical characteristics, habitat, senses, locomotion, and reproduction, with large-scale color photographs.

21970 Rabe, Tish. *On Beyond Bugs! All About Insects* (K–3). Series: The Cat in the Hat's Learning Library. 1999, Random LB $11.99 (0-679-97303-6). 45pp. A beginning reader that contains basic facts about insects in rhyming couplets. (Rev: HBG 9/00; SLJ 3/00) [595.7]

21971 Reinhart, Matthew. *Insect-lo-pedia: Young Naturalist's Handbook* (2–6). Illus. by author. 2003, Hyperion $15.99 (0-7868-0559-5). 47pp. This accessible guide includes lots of facts about insect life and is suitable for browsers. (Rev: HBG 4/04; SLJ 12/03) [595.7]

21972 Riley, Joelle. *Buzzing Bumblebees* (2–3). Series: Pull Ahead Books. 2003, Lerner LB $22.60 (0-8225-4668-X). 32pp. An excellent introduction to the physical characteristics, behavior, and life cycle of the bumblebee, this book is suitable for beginning readers. (Rev: BL 11/15/03; HBG 10/03)

21973 Robertson, Matthew. *Insects and Spiders* (4–8). Illus. Series: Pathfinders. 2000, Reader's Digest $16.99 (1-57584-375-7). 64pp. This oversize, attractive volume uses double-page spreads to introduce various insects and spiders, their physical characteristics, habits, and habitats. (Rev: BL 9/15/00; HBG 3/01; SLJ 2/01) [595.7]

21974 Robinson, W. Wright. *How Insects Build Their Amazing Homes* (5–8). Illus. by Carlyn Iverson. Series: Animal Architects. 1999, Blackbirch LB $27.44 (1-56711-375-3). 64pp. After defining what an insect is, this book shows how termites, wasps, ants, and bees construct their houses and nests. (Rev: HBG 4/00; SLJ 5/00) [595.7]

21975 Rockwell, Anne. *Bugs Are Insects* (K–3). Illus. by Steve Jenkins. Series: Let's-Read-and-Find-Out Science. 2001, HarperCollins $15.95 (0-06-028568-0); paper $15.89 (0-06-028569-9). 32pp. Rockwell makes clear the distinctions between insects and spiders and the characteristics of bugs and beetles. (Rev: BCCB 7–8/01; BL 5/1/01; HB 9–10/01; HBG 3/02; SLJ 10/01) [595.7]

21976 Ross, Michael E. *Cricketology* (4–6). Illus. Series: Backyard Buddies. 1996, Carolrhoda LB $19.95 (0-87614-985-9). 48pp. The classification, life cycle, and habits of crickets are discussed in this science activity book. (Rev: BL 7/96; SLJ 8/96) [595.7]

21977 Savage, Stephen. *Insects* (2–4). Series: What's the Difference? 2000, Raintree LB $25.69 (0-7398-1355-2). 32pp. This book points out similar characteristics among insects — such as the three parts of their bodies — but also shows how they can differ in size, color, and shape. (Rev: BL 10/15/00; HBG 3/01; SLJ 1/01) [595.7]

21978 Schaffer, Donna. *Pillbugs* (2–4). Illus. Series: Life Cycle. 1999, Capstone LB $14.00 (0-7368-0212-6). 24pp. This book introduces pillbugs (also known as rolypolies or wood lice) and explains their structure, habits, habitats, and reproductive cycle. (Rev: BL 7/99) [595.3]

21979 Schaffer, Donna. *Silkworms* (2–4). Illus. Series: Life Cycle. 1999, Capstone LB $14.00 (0-7368-0213-4). 24pp. Covers the life story of the silkworm, with material on how the cocoons are used to produce silk thread. (Rev: BL 7/99) [595.78]

21980 Selsam, Millicent E., and Ron Goor. *Backyard Insects* (K–3). Illus. 1988, Scholastic paper $4.99 (0-590-42256-1). 40pp. How backyard insects camouflage themselves for protection.

21981 Sill, Cathryn. *About Arachnids: A Guide for Children* (PS–2). Illus. by John Sill. 2003, Peachtree $15.95 (1-56145-038-8). 40pp. Clear simple sentences and naturalistic paintings present basic information about arachnids. (Rev: BL 3/1/03) [595.4]

21982 Sill, Cathryn. *About Insects: A Guide for Children* (PS–2). Illus. by John Sill. Series: About Books. 2000, Peachtree $14.95 (1-56145-207-6). 48pp. Naturalistic paintings present several insects and their characteristics. (Rev: BL 2/1/00; HBG 9/00; SLJ 7/00) [595.7]

21983 Siy, Alexandra. *Mosquito Bite* (2–4). Illus. by Dennis Kunkel. 2005, Charlesbridge $15.95 (1-57091-591-1). 32pp. Information on the mosquito is presented within the framework of a story about children playing outside on a summer night; arresting magnified photographs show the insect and its parts. (Rev: BL 6/1–15/05) [595.77]

21984 Solway, Andrew. *Classifying Insects* (4–6). Series: Classifying Living Things. 2003, Heinemann LB $24.22. (1-4034-0849-1). 32pp. This introduction to the scientific classification of animals provides an overview of the ways in which insects differ from other animals and also how different insect species differ from each other; among the insects examined are ants, butterflies, bees, dragonflies, cockroaches, and grasshoppers. (Rev: HBG 10/03; SLJ 11/03) [595.7]

21985 Souza, D. M. *Insects Around the House* (3–5). Illus. Series: Creatures All Around Us. 1991, Carolrhoda LB $22.60 (0-87614-438-5). 40pp. Describes household insects, from termites under the front steps to caterpillars in the carpet. Also use: *Insects in the Garden* (1991). (Rev: BL 4/15/91; SLJ 7/91) [595.7]

21986 Souza, D. M. *What Bit Me?* (3–5). Illus. Series: Creatures All Around Us. 1991, Carolrhoda LB $22.60 (0-87614-440-7). 40pp. In pictures and text, this book introduces creatures that can bite and sting, such as water bugs, ticks, and mosquitoes. (Rev: BL 4/15/91; SLJ 7/91) [595.7]

21987 Spilsbury, Richard, and Louise Spilsbury. *The Life Cycle of Insects* (3–5). Illus. Series: From Egg to Adult. 2003, Heinemann LB $24.22 (1-4034-0786-X). 32pp. This overview of insect life looks at where they live, what they eat, and how they differ from other types of animals. (Rev: HBG 4/04; SLJ 10/03) [595.7]

21988 Stewart, Melissa. *Insects* (2–3). Series: True Books. 2001, Children's Book Pr. LB $22.00 (0-516-22040-3). 48pp. Introduces the basic characteristics of all insects and then introduces specific insects and explains how they live. (Rev: BL 3/15/01) [595.7]

21989 Stewart, Melissa. *Maggots, Grubs, and More: The Secret Lives of Young Insects* (4–6). 2003, Millbrook LB $24.90 (0-7613-2658-8). 63pp. This photo-filled look at the world of insects details the life cycles of more than 20 insect species, including ants, mosquitoes, and yellow jackets. (Rev: HBG 4/04; SLJ 1/04) [595.7]

21990 Telford, Carole, and Rod Theodorou. *Through a Termite City* (3–5). Series: Amazing Journeys. 1997, Heinemann LB $13.95 (1-57572-155-4). 32pp. Organized like a journey, this trek through a termite mound in Africa reveals details on termite life, food, and society. (Rev: SLJ 4/98) [595.7]

21991 Theodorou, Rod. *Insects* (2–4). Series: Animal Babies. 1999, Heinemann LB $14.95 (1-57572-880-X). 32pp. Several insect species are introduced with material on their characteristics, habits, habitats, and life cycles. (Rev: SLJ 4/00) [595.7]

21992 VanCleave, Janice. *Bugs C* (PS–2). Series: Play and Find Out. 1999, Wiley $29.95 (0-471-17664-8). 121pp. A series of entertaining experiments and projects that explores such topics as life cycles, movement, communication, feeding, and camouflage. (Rev: HBG 9/99; SLJ 4/99) [595.7]

21993 VanCleave, Janice. *Janice VanCleave's Insects and Spiders: Mind-Boggling Experiments You Can Turn into Science Fair Projects* (3–5). Illus. by Doris Ettlinger. Series: Spectacular Science Projects. 1998, Wiley paper $10.95 (0-471-16396-1). 92pp. Divided into 20 chapters arranged by specific questions about insects and spiders, each supplying a step-by-step activity to answer the question, with variations on that project and ways of turning it into a science fair entry. (Rev: SLJ 6/98) [595]

21994 Wangberg, James K. *Do Bees Sneeze? And Other Questions Kids Ask About Insects* (4–6). Illus.

1997, Fulcrum paper $17.95 (1-55591-963-4). 194pp. A noted entomologist answers 200 questions about insects that were actually asked him by children, like "Do bugs have emotions?" (Rev: BL 1/1–15/98; SLJ 4/98) [595.7]

21995 Wilsdon, Christina, ed. *National Audubon Society First Field Guide: Insects* (4–8). Illus. 1998, Scholastic paper $17.95 (0-590-05447-3). Following a general introduction to entomology, specific insects are pictured and information is given on such topics as their eating, mating and social habits, physical structure, habitats, and identification markings. (Rev: BL 8/98; SLJ 10/98) [595]

21996 Winner, Cherie. *Everything Bug: What Kids Really Want to Know About Insects and Spiders* (3–6). Series: Kids' FAQs. 2004, North Word $10.95 (1-55971-890-0). 64pp. In a question-and-answer format, this compendium of facts is suitable for browsing. (Rev: BL 2/15/04; SLJ 7/04) [595]

21997 Woodward, John. *What Lives in the Garden?* (3–6). Illus. 2002, Barron's paper $7.95 (0-7641-2108-1). 48pp. The many small creatures that are found in gardens — grasshoppers, earwigs, and termites, to name just a few — are profiled in text and interesting sidebars and shown in dramatic close-up photographs. Also use *What Lives Under the Carpet?* (2002). (Rev: SLJ 10/02)

21998 *The World in Your Backyard: And Other Stories of Insects and Spiders* (3–5). Illus. 1990, Zaner-Bloser $10.95 (0-88309-132-1). 63pp. Eighteen articles and stories from *Highlights for Children* magazine. (Rev: SLJ 6/90) [595.7]

21999 Zakowski, Connie. *The Insect Book: A Basic Guide to the Collection and Care of Common Insects for Young Children* (3–5). Illus. 1996, Rainbow paper $8.95 (1-56825-037-1). 64pp. A practical beginner's guide to collecting, caring for, and studying insects. (Rev: BL 12/1/96; SLJ 5/97) [595.7]

22000 Zuchora-Walske, Christine. *Leaping Grasshoppers* (PS–2). Series: Pull Ahead Books. 2000, Lerner $21.27 (0-8225-3634-X). 32pp. This simple, colorful introduction to grasshoppers explains the reasons why they hop: to find food, to avoid predators, and to find mates. (Rev: BL 5/15/00; HBG 9/00) [595.7]

ANTS

22001 Allen, Judy. *Are You an Ant?* (PS–1). Series: Backyard Books. 2002, Kingfisher $9.95 (0-7534-5365-7). 32pp. A young ant faces many challenges on the road to adulthood in this beginning science book. (Rev: BL 6/1–15/02; SLJ 7/02) [595.79]

22002 Berman, Ruth. *Ants* (2–3). Illus. Series: Early Bird Nature Books. 1996, Lerner LB $22.60 (0-8225-3012-0). 48pp. The formica ant and its community are described in this introduction to the ant world. (Rev: BL 8/96; SLJ 7/96) [595.78]

22003 Brenner, Barbara. *Thinking About Ants* (2–3). Illus. by Carol Schwartz. 1997, Mondo $15.95 (1-57255-210-7). 32pp. In a readable style, 11 types of ants are introduced, with material on their bodies, colors, diet, colonies, and enemies. (Rev: BL 6/1–15/97; SLJ 10/97) [595.79]

22004 Chinery, Michael. *Ant* (3–5). Illus. by Nichola Armstrong. Series: Life Story. 1997, Troll paper $4.95 (0-8167-2099-1). 32pp. Life in an anthill is introduced in this informative text with color photographs. (Rev: BL 4/1/91) [595.79]

22005 Dorros, Arthur. *Ant Cities* (K–2). Illus. by author. 1987, HarperCollins LB $15.89 (0-690-04570-0); paper $4.95 (0-06-445079-1). 32pp. A simplified explanation of the ant world: jobs of worker ants, operation of the ant hill, social divisions of the ant colony. (Rev: BCCB 3/87; BL 2/15/87; SLJ 8/87)

22006 Gomel, Luc. *The Ant: Energetic Worker* (3–6). Illus. by Remy Amann and Dominique Stoffell. Series: Face-to-Face. 2001, Charlesbridge $9.95 (1-57091-451-6). 32pp. This is a detailed look at ants and the ant world, with arresting photographs. (Rev: BL 10/15/01; HBG 3/02) [595.79]

22007 Greenaway, Theresa. *Ants* (4–7). Series: The Secret World Of. 2001, Raintree LB $18.98 (0-7398-3511-4). 48pp. An accessible, attractive volume about ants and their structure, habits, food, and habitats. (Rev: HBG 3/02)

22008 Heinrichs, Ann. *Ants* (1–3). Illus. Series: Nature's Friends. 2002, Compass Point LB $15.95 (0-7565-0164-4). 32pp. Ants' anatomy and life cycle are covered in simple text and clear close-up photographs.

22009 Hodge, Deborah. *Ants* (1–3). Illus. Series: Denver Museum of Nature and Science. 2004, Kids Can $14.95 (1-55337-066-X). 32pp. Simple narrative and detailed photographs combine to offer young readers an introduction to the world of ants; instructions for three related projects are included. (Rev: BL 4/1/04; SLJ 6/04) [595.79]

22010 Micucci, Charles. *The Life and Times of the Ant* (1–4). Illus. 2003, Houghton Mifflin $16.00 (0-618-00559-5). 32pp. Micucci provides an impressive amount of information about the life and physique of the ant in a brightly illustrated picture-book format. (Rev: BL 4/15/03; HB 5–6/03; HBG 10/03; SLJ 5/03) [595.79]

22011 Morris, Ting. *Ant* (2–4). Illus. by Desiderio Sanzi. Series: Creepy Crawly World. 2004, Smart Apple Media LB $27.10 (1-58340-376-0). 32pp. Introduces ants' characteristics, habitat, diet, defense mechanisms, and life cycle, using realistic paintings and diagrams. (Rev: HB 11–12/96; SLJ 6/05)

22012 Orr, Tamra B. *Fire Ants* (3–6). Series: Animals Attack. 2003, Gale/KidHaven LB $23.70 (0-7377-1526-X). 48pp. True stories of attacks on humans by fire ants, some of them firsthand, add to the appeal of this entry in a series on conflict between man and animal. (Rev: SLJ 4/04) [595.78]

22013 Orr, Tamra B. *Fire Ants* (4–6). Series: Nature's Predators. 2002, Gale LB $18.96 (0-7377-1389-5). 48pp. In four fascinating chapters with numerous illustrations, the life and habits of these insects are introduced. (Rev: BL 2/15/03; SLJ 10/03) [595.78]

22014 Sabin, Francene. *Amazing World of Ants* (1–3). Illus. by Eulala Conner. 1982, Troll paper

$3.50 (0-89375-559-1). 32pp. An examination of an ant colony, its inhabitants, and construction.

22015 Sayre, April Pulley. *Army Ant Parade* (PS–2). Illus. by Rick Chrustowski. 2002, Holt $16.95 (0-8050-6353-6). 32pp. This beautifully illustrated book for younger readers gives a detailed description of an army ant swarm in a Central American jungle. (Rev: BCCB 3/02; BL 3/1/02; HB 9–10/02; HBG 3/03; SLJ 5/02) [595.79]

22016 Stefoff, Rebecca. *Ant* (K–3). Series: Living Things. 1997, Marshall Cavendish LB $22.79 (0-7614-0447-3). 32pp. A colorful introduction to the world of ants that describes colonies, homes and food. (Rev: BL 2/15/98; HBG 3/98; SLJ 3/98) [595.79]

BEES AND WASPS

22017 Allen, Judy. *Are You a Bee?* (PS–1). Series: Backyard Books. 2002, Kingfisher $9.95 (0-7534-5345-2). 32pp. This simple science book describes life as experienced by a bee and, with interesting color drawings, portrays the bee's life cycle and social life. (Rev: BL 2/15/03) [595.79]

22018 Ashley, Susan. *Bees* (1–3). Series: Let's Read About Insects. 2004, Weekly Reader LB $18.60 (0-8368-4051-8); paper $5.95 (0-8368-4058-5). 24pp. The life cycle of bees is described in small-format, easy-to-read text with close-up photographs. (Rev: SLJ 2/05) [595.79]

22019 Brimner, Larry. *Bees* (3–5). Series: True Books. 1999, Children's Book Pr. LB $21.50 (0-516-21160-9). 48pp. The structure, varieties, behavior, social nature, and uses of bees are presented in a book with large print and plenty of captioned photographs. (Rev: BL 11/15/99) [595.79]

22020 Chinery, Michael. *How Bees Make Honey* (3–5). Illus. Series: Nature's Mysteries. 1996, Benchmark LB $22.79 (0-7614-0453-8). 32pp. In this introduction to bees, such topics as a bee's anatomy, life cycle, enemies, nectar gathering, and honey production are covered. (Rev: SLJ 2/97) [595.79]

22021 Cole, Joanna. *The Magic School Bus Inside a Beehive* (3–5). Illus. by Bruce Degen. 1996, Scholastic $15.95 (0-590-44684-3). 48pp. Mrs. Frizzle's school bus becomes a beehive in this exploration of the anatomy, activities, and social structure of bees. (Rev: BCCB 10/96; BL 9/1/96; HB 11–12/96; SLJ 10/96) [585.79]

22022 Davis, Kathleen, and Dave Mayes. *Killer Bees* (3–5). Illus. Series: Remarkable Animals. 1993, Dillon LB $18.95 (0-87518-582-7). 60pp. This well-illustrated account explains where these Africanized honeybees come from, their habits, and the damage they can cause. (Rev: BL 11/1/93) [599.79]

22023 Delafosse, Claude. *Bees* (PS–2). Illus. Series: First Discovery. 1997, Scholastic $12.95 (0-590-93780-4). 24pp. Basic information about bees and their colonies is given concisely in this interactive book with overlays. (Rev: BL 2/15/97) [595.79]

22024 Fischer-Nagel, Heiderose, and Andreas Fischer-Nagel. *Life of the Honeybee* (2–5). Illus. 1986, Carolrhoda paper $7.95 (0-87614-470-9). 48pp. A simply written science book showing the work of three kinds of bees. (Rev: BCCB 4/86; BL 4/15/86; SLJ 2/86)

22025 Gibbons, Gail. *The Honey Makers* (1–4). Illus. 1997, Morrow $15.93 (0-688-11387-7). 32pp. An informative picture book that introduces honeybees and their society. (Rev: BCCB 4/97; BL 3/15/97; SLJ 5/97) [595.79]

22026 Glaser, Linda. *Brilliant Bees* (K–3). Illus. by Gay W. Holland. 2003, Millbrook LB $22.90 (0-7613-2670-7); paper $8.95 (0-7613-1943-3). A young girl looks at bees' behavior and habits in simple text and large colored pictures; four pages at the back of the book add factual information. (Rev: HBG 4/04; SLJ 1/04) [595.79]

22027 Guidoux, Valerie. *Little Bees* (3–5). Illus. Series: Born to Be Wild. 2005, Gareth Stevens LB $16.50 (0-7368-4433-5). 32pp. A simply worded look at young bees and their lives, with large color photographs.

22028 Heinrichs, Ann. *Bees* (1–3). Illus. Series: Nature's Friends. 2002, Compass Point LB $15.95 (0-7565-0165-2). 32pp. Bees' anatomy and life cycle are covered in simple text and clear close-up photographs.

22029 Helligman, Deborah. *Honeybees* (K–3). Illus. by Carla Golembe. Series: Jump into Science. 2002, National Geographic $16.95 (0-7922-6678-1). 32pp. Paintings and lucid text introduce honeybees and their hives, division of labor, life cycle, and behavior. (Rev: BCCB 9/02; BL 5/1/02; HBG 10/02; SLJ 5/02) [595.79]

22030 Hodge, Deborah. *Bees* (1–3). Illus. Series: Denver Museum of Nature and Science. 2004, Kids Can $14.95 (1-55337-065-1). 32pp. Suggestions for simple projects supplement this attractive examination of the life cycle of bees. (Rev: BL 4/1/04; SLJ 6/04) [595.79]

22031 Johnson, Sylvia A. *Wasps* (4–6). Illus. 1984, Lerner LB $22.60 (0-8225-1460-5). 48pp. A year in the life of a wasp is presented in a clear text and fascinating illustrations.

22032 Landau, Elaine. *Killer Bees* (4–6). Series: Fearsome, Scary, and Creepy Animals. 2003, Enslow LB $18.95 (0-7660-2061-4). 48pp. Landau offers a dramatic overview of killer bees and documents some real-life attacks on humans. (Rev: BL 10/15/03; HBG 10/03; SLJ 2/04) [595.79]

22033 Markle, Sandra. *Outside and Inside Killer Bees* (3–6). Illus. 2004, Walker LB $18.85 (0-8027-8907-2). 40pp. In this compelling photoessay, Markle traces the northward progress of the so-called killer bees that escaped from a Brazilian research project nearly half a century ago. (Rev: BL 12/1/04*; SLJ 1/05) [595.79]

22034 Sayre, April Pulley. *The Bumblebee Queen* (1–3). Illus. by Patricia J. Wynne. 2005, Charlesbridge $14.95 (1-57091-362-5). 32pp. The life of a bumblebee queen, accompanied by additional bee information and detailed watercolor illustrations. (Rev: BL 3/1/05; SLJ 4/05) [595.79]

22035 Watts, Barrie. *Honeybee* (PS–3). Illus. Series: Stopwatch. 1990, Silver Burdett LB $15.95 (0-382-

24011-1). 25pp. The life of the honeybee, beginning with newly laid eggs, is revealed in clear photos and text. (Rev: BL 6/15/90) [595]

BEETLES

22036 Allen, Judy. *Are You a Ladybug?* (PS–1). Illus. by Tudor Humphries. Series: Backyard Books. 2000, Kingfisher $9.95 (0-7534-5241-3). 32pp. A beginner's book that explains in text and pictures what a ladybug is, what it eats, and how it grows from egg to first flight. (Rev: BL 5/15/00; HBG 3/01; SLJ 9/00) [595.76]

22037 Ashley, Susan. *Ladybugs* (1–4). Series: Let's Read About Insects. 2004, Weekly Reader LB $18.60 (0-8368-4055-0); paper $5.95 (0-8368-4062-3). 24pp. The life cycle of ladybugs is described in small-format, easy-to-read text with close-up photographs. (Rev: SLJ 2/05) [595.76]

22038 Chrustowski, Rick. *Bright Beetle* (PS–2). Illus. 2000, Holt $15.95 (0-8050-6058-8). 32pp. The life cycle of the ladybug, its habits, and physical characteristics are covered in this good introduction for beginning scientists. (Rev: BL 6/1–15/00; HBG 9/00; SLJ 5/00) [595.76]

22039 Fischer-Nagel, Heiderose, and Andreas Fischer-Nagel. *Life of the Ladybug* (2–5). Illus. 1986, Carolrhoda LB $22.60 (0-87614-240-4). 48pp. The life cycle of the ladybug with full-color, informative photographs. (Rev: BCCB 3/86; BL 5/15/86; SLJ 4/86)

22040 Hartley, Karen, and Chris Macro. *Ladybug* (1–3). Illus. by Alan Male. Series: Bug Books. 1998, Heinemann LB $19.92 (1-57572-662-9). 32pp. Double-page spreads, each with a large photo of a ladybug, introduce such topics as structure, behavior, enemies, food, and life cycle. (Rev: HBG 9/99; SLJ 1/99) [595.7]

22041 Heinrichs, Ann. *Ladybugs* (1–3). Illus. Series: Nature's Friends. 2002, Compass Point LB $15.95 (0-7565-0167-9). 32pp. Ladybugs' anatomy and life cycle are covered in simple text and clear close-up photographs.

22042 Jango-Cohen, Judith. *Hungry Ladybugs* (2–3). Series: Pull Ahead Books. 2003, Lerner LB $22.60 (0-8225-4667-1). 32pp. The life cycle and physical characteristics of the ladybird beetle, one of nature's most efficient pest-killers and commonly known as the ladybug, is explored in this short book suitable for beginning readers. (Rev: BL 11/15/03; HBG 10/03)

22043 Johnson, Sylvia A. *Ladybugs* (5–8). Illus. by Yuko Sato. 1983, Lerner LB $22.60 (0-8225-1481-8). 48pp. A description of the ladybug, its habits, behavior, and uses. [595.7]

22044 Llewellyn, Claire. *Ladybug* (PS–3). Illus. by Simon Mendez. Series: Starting Life. 2004, NorthWord $16.95 (1-55971-892-7). 23pp. On pages that grow progressively wider, the stages of a ladybug's development are traced, with information on such topics as habitat and diet plus realistic illustrations. (Rev: SLJ 11/04) [595.76]

22045 Mason, Adrienne. *Mealworms: Raise Them, Watch Them, See Them Change* (3–5). Illus. 1998,

Kids Can $10.95 (1-55074-448-8). 24pp. Gives the life story of mealworms (the larval stage of the darkling beetle) and tips on how to raise and observe them. (Rev: BL 6/1–15/98; HBG 9/98; SLJ 9/98) [638.5]

22046 Miller, Sara Swan. *Beetles: The Most Common Insects* (3–5). Series: Animals in Order. 2001, Watts LB $23.00 (0-531-11629-8). 32pp. After an overview of animal classification, this book describes in text and color photographs a variety of beetles and their anatomy, traits, and behavior. (Rev: BL 6/1–15/01) [595.76]

22047 Murray, Peter. *Beetles* (1–4). Series: Naturebooks. 2003, Child's World LB $25.64 (1-56766-976-X). 32pp. Large-print text and close-up photographs explore beetles' many varieties, physical characteristics, habitat, diet, and behavior. (Rev: SLJ 12/03) [595.76]

22048 Pallotta, Jerry. *The Beetle Alphabet Book* (PS–2). Illus. by David Biedrzycki. 2004, Charlesbridge $16.95 (1-57091-551-2). 32pp. An arresting alphabet of bugs, providing brightly illustrated information with a dollop of humor. (Rev: BL 2/1/04; SLJ 5/04) [595.76]

22049 Posada, Mia. *Ladybugs: Red, Fiery, and Bright* (PS–2). Illus. by author. 2002, Carolrhoda LB $15.95 (0-87614-334-6). A rhythmic look at ladybugs and their life cycle and behavior. (Rev: HBG 10/02; SLJ 5/02) [595.7]

22050 Pyers, Greg. *Ladybugs up Close* (2–4). Illus. Series: Minibeasts Up Close. 2005, Raintree LB $18.45 (1-4109-1530-1). 32pp. A simple introduction to ladybugs and their physical characteristics, habitat, senses, and reproduction, with large-scale color photographs.

22051 Ross, Michael E. *Ladybugology* (3–5). Photos by Brian Grogan. Illus. by Darren Erickson. Series: Backyard Buddies. 1998, Carolrhoda $19.93 (1-57505-051-X). 48pp. This introduction to ladybugs describes their structure and habits and outlines a number of activities that involve capturing and observing them. (Rev: BL 7/98; SLJ 3/98) [595.7]

22052 Tracqui, Valerie. *Face-to-Face with the Ladybug* (3–6). Series: Face-to-Face. 2002, Charlesbridge $9.95 (1-57091-453-2). 32pp. The physical characteristics, habits, life cycle, and habitats of the industrious, colorful ladybug are featured in this attractive volume. (Rev: BCCB 10/02; BL 9/15/02; HBG 3/03) [595.76]

CATERPILLARS, BUTTERFLIES, AND MOTHS

22053 Allen, Judy. *Are You a Butterfly?* (PS–1). Illus. by Tudor Humphries. Series: Backyard Books. 2000, Kingfisher $9.95 (0-7534-5240-5). 32pp. By allowing the child to imagine that he or she is the insect discussed, this simple book goes through the stages of growth from egg and caterpillar to chrysalis and butterfly. (Rev: BL 10/15/00; HBG 10/01) [544.2]

22054 Bair, Diane, and Pamela Wright. *Butterfly Watching* (2–5). Series: Wildlife Watching. 1999, Capstone $19.93 (0-7368-0320-3). 48pp. As well as

giving good basic information about butterflies, this book is a practical guide to butterfly watching with plenty of tips for the amateur naturalist. (Rev: BL 2/15/00) [595.78]

22055 Brimner, Larry. *Butterflies and Moths* (3–5). Series: True Books. 1999, Children's Book Pr. LB $21.50 (0-516-21162-5). 48pp. Butterflies and moths are introduced in this book that discusses life cycles, varieties, structure, habitats, and behavior in a simple text with splendid photos. (Rev: BL 11/15/99) [595.78]

22056 Cassie, Brian, and Jerry Pallotta. *The Butterfly Alphabet Book* (PS–2). Illus. by Mark Astrella. 1995, Charlesbridge paper $6.95 (0-88106-894-2). From an Apollo butterfly to a Zephyr Metalmark, this alphabet book features amazing butterflies with descriptions of their characteristics. (Rev: SLJ 12/95) [595.78]

22057 Delafosse, Claude. *Butterflies* (PS–2). Illus. Series: First Discovery. 1997, Scholastic $12.95 (0-590-93781-2). 24pp. The life cycle of butterflies and their movements are pictured in this beginning book with impressive pictures. (Rev: BL 2/15/97) [595.78]

22058 Ehlert, Lois. *Waiting for Wings* (PS–1). Illus. 2001, Harcourt $17.00 (0-15-202608-8). 38pp. Using a short rhyming text and glowing illustrations, this book covers the life cycle of the butterfly, with information on physical characteristics, diet, and behavior. (Rev: BL 3/1/01*; HB 5–6/01; HBG 10/01) [595.78]

22059 Fischer-Nagel, Heiderose, and Andreas Fischer-Nagel. *Life of the Butterfly* (4–6). Illus. 1987, Lerner paper $7.95 (0-87614-484-9). 48pp. Clear, readable text and color photos detail the life of a peacock butterfly. (Rev: BL 4/1/87; SLJ 5/87)

22060 Frost, Helen. *Moths* (PS–3). Series: Insects. 2001, Capstone LB $9.95 (0-7368-0852-3). 24pp. Spare text and full-page color photographs — often close-up shots — offer basic information on moths. (Rev: HBG 3/02; SLJ 9/01) [595.78]

22061 Gibbons, Gail. *Monarch Butterfly* (1–3). Illus. 1989, Holiday House LB $16.95 (0-8234-0773-X). 32pp. The basic life cycle of the monarch butterfly from egg to adult. (Rev: BCCB 12/89; BL 11/1/89; HB 11–12/89; SLJ 12/89) [595.78]

22062 Glaser, Linda. *Magnificent Monarchs* (K–3). Illus. by Gay Holland. 2000, Millbrook LB $21.40 (0-7613-1700-7). This is a very attractive work on monarch butterflies and their amazing lives and migrations. (Rev: HBG 10/01; SLJ 1/01) [595.78]

22063 Hamilton, Kersten. *The Butterfly Book: A Kid's Guide to Attracting, Raising, and Keeping Butterflies* (3–6). Illus. 1997, John Muir paper $8.95 (1-56261-309-X). 40pp. Introduces 20 species of butterflies and how to attract and keep them, as well as describing their life cycle, anatomy, and habits. (Rev: BL 7/97) [595.78]

22064 Hariton, Anca. *Butterfly Story* (2–4). Illus. 1995, Dutton $15.99 (0-525-45212-5). 32pp. The five-week process of turning a caterpillar into a butterfly is described in words and pictures. (Rev: BL 1/15/95; SLJ 4/95) [595.78]

22065 Hartley, Karen, et al. *Caterpillar* (K–3). Series: Heinemann First Library. 1999, Heinemann LB $13.95 (1-57572-795-1). 32pp. Different kinds of caterpillars are introduced, with material on lifestyles and habitats, richly illustrated with full-page color photographs that accompany a simple text. (Rev: BL 6/1–15/99; HBG 9/99) [595.78]

22066 Heiligman, Deborah. *From Caterpillar to Butterfly* (PS–1). Illus. by Bari Weissman. Series: Let's-Read-and-Find-Out. 1996, HarperCollins LB $15.89 (0-06-024268-X); paper $4.95 (0-06-445129-1). 31pp. Using a classroom setting, this book shows children watching the miracle of the metamorphosis from caterpillar to butterfly. (Rev: SLJ 8/96) [595.78]

22067 Kalman, Bobbie. *The Life Cycle of a Butterfly* (2–4). Illus. Series: The Life Cycle. 2001, Crabtree LB $15.45 (0-7787-0650-8); paper $5.36 (0-7787-0680-X). 32pp. After a general description of the butterfly, the author clearly explains the stages of its life cycle and discusses what can be done to curb human encroachment. (Rev: SLJ 6/02) [595.789]

22068 Lasky, Kathryn. *Monarchs* (4–6). Illus. by Christopher G. Knight. 1993, Harcourt paper $11.00 (0-15-255297-9). 64pp. The life cycle of the monarch butterfly is presented with details of its mammoth migration. Also tells how communities have helped preserve this species. (Rev: BCCB 11/93; BL 11/15/93; HB 11–12/93; SLJ 9/93*) [595.78]

22069 Lerner, Carol. *Butterflies in the Garden* (2–4). Illus. 2002, HarperCollins LB $16.89 (0-688-17479-5). 32pp. Using beautiful watercolors and simple explanations, the author describes the characteristics of butterflies and their life cycle. (Rev: BL 6/1–15/02; HB 7–8/02; HBG 10/02; SLJ 5/02) [595.78]

22070 List, Ilka Katherine. *Moths and Butterflies of North America* (3–5). Series: Animals in Order. 2002, Watts LB $24.00 (0-531-11597-6). 48pp. After a general discussion of animal classification, this book describes in words and pictures 15 species of moths and butterflies that live in North America. (Rev: BL 3/15/02) [595.78]

22071 Llewellyn, Claire. *Butterfly* (K–4). Illus. by Simon Mendez. Series: Starting Life. 2003, North-Word $16.95 (1-55971-868-4). 23pp. The life cycle of a butterfly is detailed in words and paintings, together with a combined glossary and index; the unusual graduated page sizes add appeal. (Rev: SLJ 4/04) [595.78]

22072 Meister, Cari. *Butterflies* (2–4). Illus. Series: Checkerboard Science and Nature Library: Insects. 2001, ABDO LB $13.95 (1-57765-459-5). 24pp. This is an attractive, basic introduction to butterflies. (Rev: BL 10/15/01; HBG 10/01) [595.78]

22073 Morris, Ting. *Butterfly* (2–4). Illus. by Desiderio Sanzi. Series: Creepy Crawly World. 2004, Smart Apple Media LB $27.10 (1-58340-379-5). 32pp. Introduces butterflies' characteristics, habitat, diet, defense mechanisms, and life cycle, using realistic paintings and diagrams. (Rev: SLJ 6/05)

22074 Noonan, Diana. *The Butterfly* (2–4). Series: Life Cycles. 2002, Chelsea LB $14.95 (0-7910-6963-X). 32pp. Full-color illustrations show the various stages in the life cycle of the butterfly from egg to caterpillar and pupa to the mature butterfly. (Rev: BL 12/15/02; HBG 3/03) [595.78]

22075 Pascoe, Elaine. *Butterflies and Moths* (3–6). Photos by Dwight Kuhn. Illus. Series: Nature Close-up. 1996, Blackbirch LB $18.95 (1-56711-180-7). 48pp. After a general introduction to butterflies and moths, this book shows how they can be caught, housed, fed, and observed. (Rev: SLJ 4/97) [595.78]

22076 Patent, Dorothy Hinshaw. *Fabulous Fluttering Tropical Butterflies* (1–3). Illus. by Kendal Jan Jubb. 2003, Walker LB $17.85 (0-8027-8839-4). 32pp. With bright illustrations, this book describes tropical butterflies' life cycles and looks at individual species and at butterflies' lives in the rainforest and in zoos. (Rev: BL 5/1/03; HBG 10/03; SLJ 5/03) [595.78]

22077 Preston-Mafham, Rod. *The Secret Life of Butterflies and Moths* (4–7). Series: The Secret World Of. 2002, Raintree LB $27.12 (0-7398-4984-0). 48pp. Beginning with little-known facts about butterflies and moths, this book explores their life cycles, behavior, mating habits, enemies, food, and habitats. (Rev: BL 8/02) [595.78]

22078 Pringle, Laurence. *An Extraordinary Life: The Story of a Monarch Butterfly* (3–6). Illus. by Bob Marstall. 1997, Orchard LB $19.99 (0-531-33002-8). 32pp. The life cycle of a single monarch butterfly and its migration from Massachusetts to Mexico. (Rev: BCCB 5/97; BL 3/15/97*; HB 5–6/97; SLJ 5/97) [595.78]

22079 Pyers, Greg. *Butterflies up Close* (2–4). Illus. Series: Minibeasts Up Close. 2005, Raintree LB $18.45 (1-4109-1528-X). 32pp. A simple introduction to butterflies and their physical characteristics, habitat, senses, and reproduction, with large-scale color photographs.

22080 Ring, Elizabeth. *Night Flier* (1–3). Photos by Dwight Kuhn. 1994, Millbrook LB $21.90 (1-56294-467-3). 32pp. The life cycle of the cecropia moth is chronicled from its hatching. (Rev: BL 10/1/94; SLJ 12/94) [595.78]

22081 Rockwell, Anne. *Becoming Butterflies* (PS–2). Illus. by Megan Halsey. 2002, Walker LB $16.85 (0-8027-8798-3). 32pp. The story of the metamorphosis of monarch butterflies is told in a clear, concise manner for young readers. (Rev: BCCB 5/02; BL 3/15/02; HBG 10/02; SLJ 3/02) [595.78]

22082 Rosenblatt, Lynn. *Monarch Magic! Butterfly Activities and Nature Discoveries* (3–6). Illus. Series: Good Times! 1998, Williamson paper $12.95 (1-885593-23-6). 96pp. This work covers many topics involving the monarch butterfly, including physical characteristics, feeding habits, habitats, and migratory patterns plus material on how to raise them and protect them from extinction. (Rev: BL 12/1/98; SLJ 4/99) [595.78]

22083 Ross, Michael E. *Caterpillarology* (3–5). Photos by Brian Grogan. Illus. by Darren Erickson. Series: Backyard Buddies. 1998, Carolrhoda LB

$19.93 (1-57505-055-2). 48pp. A great deal of scientific information is presented about caterpillars in an entertaining way, with experiments and instructions on how to capture and release them. (Rev: BL 7/98; SLJ 3/98) [595.78]

22084 Sabin, Louis. *Amazing World of Butterflies and Moths* (1–3). Illus. by Jean Helmer. 1982, Troll paper $3.50 (0-89375-561-3). 32pp. A simple account for young readers with brief text and many illustrations.

22085 Waxman, Laura Hamilton. *Monarch Butterflies* (2–3). Series: Pull Ahead Books. 2003, Lerner LB $22.60 (0-8225-4669-8). 32pp. Suitable for beginning readers, this book follows the beautiful monarch butterfly through each stage of its life cycle. (Rev: BL 11/15/03; HBG 10/03)

22086 Wilner, Yvonne. *Butterflies Fly* (2–5). Illus. by Karen Lloyd-Jones. 2001, Charlesbridge LB $16.95 (1-57091-446-X). 32pp. A poetic text with large illustrations shows butterflies of the world in their natural habitats. (Rev: BL 2/15/01; HBG 10/01; SLJ 2/01) [595.78]

22087 Zemlicka, Shannon. *From Egg to Butterfly* (K–2). Series: Start to Finish. 2003, Lerner LB $18.60 (0-8225-0713-7). 24pp. Full of photographs, this basic introduction suitable for beginning readers follows the life cycle of a butterfly. (Rev: SLJ 9/03) [595.78]

SPIDERS AND SCORPIONS

22088 Allen, Judy. *Are You a Spider?* (PS–1). Illus. by Tudor Humphries. Series: Backyard Books. 2000, Kingfisher $9.95 (0-7534-5243-X). 32pp. The reader becomes a newly hatched spider and learns how to spin threads, make webs, and watch out for dangers such as birds. (Rev: BL 10/15/00; HBG 10/01) [595.4]

22089 Back, Christine. *Spider's Web* (1–3). Illus. 1986, Silver Burdett paper $3.95 (0-382-24020-0). 25pp. How the garden spider spins its web and uses it as a food trap. (Rev: BL 1/1/87)

22090 Bailey, Jill. *How Spiders Make Their Webs* (3–5). Illus. Series: Nature's Mysteries. 1996, Benchmark LB $22.79 (0-7614-0456-2). 32pp. Using a large number of illustrations, this account describes a variety of spider constructions and how they are made. (Rev: SLJ 2/97) [595.4]

22091 Berger, Melvin. *Spinning Spiders* (K–4). Illus. by S. D. Schindler. Series: Let's-Read-and-Find-Out Science. 2003, HarperCollins LB $16.89 (0-06-028697-0); paper $4.99 (0-06-445207-7). 33pp. The differences between arachnids and insects are clearly explained, and five types of spiders are profiled with full-color illustrations. (Rev: HBG 10/03; SLJ 9/03) [595.4]

22092 Berger, Melvin, and Gilda Berger. *Do All Spiders Spin Webs? Questions and Answers About Spiders* (3–5). Illus. by Roberto Osti. Series: Scholastic Question and Answer. 2000, Scholastic $14.95 (0-439-09586-7); paper $5.95 (0-439-14881-2). 48pp. The authors give informative answers to such questions as "What happens when an enemy bites off a

spider's leg?" Also use *Tarantulas* (2001). (Rev: HBG 3/01; SLJ 5/01) [595.4]

22093 Berman, Ruth. *Spinning Spiders* (PS–2). Illus. by David T. Roberts. Series: Pull Ahead Books. 1998, Lerner LB $21.27 (0-8225-3604-8). 32pp. Using questions within the text, this book introduces spiders and their habits along with information on the differences between spiders and insects, spider webs, egg sacs, and spiderlings. (Rev: BL 2/1/99; HBG 3/99; SLJ 6/99) [595.4]

22094 Chinery, Michael. *Spider* (3–5). Illus. by Alan Male. Series: Life Story. 1990, Troll paper $4.95 (0-8167-2109-2). 32pp. The life of the common spider is introduced in detailed text and unusual photos. (Rev: BL 4/1/91) [595.4]

22095 Facklam, Margery. *Spiders and Their Web Sites* (5–8). Illus. by Alan Male. 2001, Little, Brown $15.95 (0-316-27329-5). 32pp. This book takes a look at 12 kinds of spiders, with material on webs, lifestyles, and reproduction. (Rev: BL 3/15/01; HB 5–6/01; HBG 10/01; SLJ 8/01) [595.4]

22096 Fowler, Allan. *Spiders Are Not Insects* (PS–3). Illus. Series: Rookie Readers. 1996, Children's Book Pr. LB $19.00 (0-516-06054-6). 31pp. A beginning reader that introduces spiders and features such species as the tarantula, bird spider, and the black widow. (Rev: SLJ 8/96) [595.4]

22097 Gibbons, Gail. *Spiders* (1–2). Illus. 1993, Holiday House LB $16.95 (0-8234-1006-4). 32pp. An introductory account with stunning drawings of spiders, plus their structure, behavior, and important species. (Rev: BL 4/15/93; SLJ 7/93) [595.4]

22098 Glaser, Linda. *Spectacular Spiders* (K–2). Illus. by Gay Holland. 1998, Millbrook LB $21.40 (0-7613-0353-7). 32pp. A young girl explains the habits and behavior of garden spiders, including their diet and how they spin webs. (Rev: BL 1/1–15/99; HBG 3/99; SLJ 3/99) [595.4]

22099 Greenaway, Theresa. *Spiders* (4–7). Series: The Secret World Of. 2001, Raintree LB $18.98 (0-7398-3509-2). 48pp. An accessible, attractive volume about spiders and their physical characteristics, behavior, food, and habitats. (Rev: HBG 3/02)

22100 Greenaway, Theresa. *Spiders* (4–7). Series: The Secret World Of. 2001, Raintree LB $18.98 (0-7368-3509-2). 48pp. An information-crammed text and attractive illustrations introduce spiders, how and where they live, and their behavior. (Rev: BL 10/15/01) [595.4]

22101 Hartley, Karen, et al. *Spider* (K–3). Series: Heinemann First Library. 1999, Heinemann LB $13.95 (1-57572-799-4). 32pp. Different kinds of spiders are pictured in full-color photos with textual material on habits, physical characteristics, and life cycles. (Rev: BL 6/1–15/99; HBG 9/99) [595.4]

22102 Heinrichs, Ann. *Spiders* (1–3). Illus. Series: Nature's Friends. 2004, Compass Point LB $15.95 (0-7565-0590-9). 32pp. Basic facts about spiders are presented in an appealing design. (Rev: BL 5/15/04) [595.4]

22103 Himmelman, John. *A House Spider's Life* (K–2). Illus. by author. Series: Nature Upclose. 1999, Children's Book Pr. LB $24.00 (0-516-

21185-4). Using realistic paintings (one per page), this simple account traces the life cycle of the common spider. (Rev: SLJ 3/00) [595.4]

22104 Hughes, Monica. *Spiders* (PS–2). Illus. 2003, Raintree LB $18.56 (1-4109-0622-1). 24pp. A close-up look at the diet, anatomy, habitat, and life cycle of spiders, for beginning readers. (Rev: BL 2/15/04) [595.4]

22105 Kallen, Stuart A. *Spiders* (4–6). Illus. Series: Nature's Predators. 2001, Gale LB $23.70 (0-7377-0630-9). 48pp. Spiders' methods of hunting, catching, and eating their prey are presented, with illustrations. (Rev: BL 10/15/01) [595.4]

22106 Kalman, Bobbie. *Web Weavers and Other Spiders* (2–5). Illus. Series: Crabapples. 1997, Crabtree LB $19.96 (0-86505-632-3); paper $5.95 (0-86505-732-X). 32pp. A description of how spiders live is given, with material on physical characteristics, web building, defenses, and mating behavior. (Rev: BL 7/97; SLJ 7/97) [595.4]

22107 Lassieur, Allison. *Scorpions: The Sneaky Stingers* (3–5). Illus. Series: Animals in Order. 2000, Watts LB $23.00 (0-531-11651-4); paper $6.95 (0-531-16497-7). 48pp. After a general introduction to animal classification, this book describes scorpions, their structure, where they live, and their habits. (Rev: BL 9/15/00) [595.7]

22108 McGinty, Alice B. *The Jumping Spider* (3–6). 2001, Rosen LB $18.75 (0-8239-5568-0). 24pp. Two-page chapters with arresting photographs discuss topics such as the spider's anatomy, behavior, habitat, and relationship to humans. Other titles in this series include *The Black Widow* and *The Tarantula* (both 2001). (Rev: SLJ 3/02) [595.4]

22109 Montgomery, Sy. *The Tarantula Scientist* (4–7). Photos by Nic Bishop. Series: Scientists in the Field. 2004, Houghton Mifflin $18.00 (0-618-14799-3). 80pp. This informative, photo-filled book chronicles the day-to-day field work of arachnologist Sam Marshall as he searches for tarantulas in the French Guianan rain forest. (Rev: BL 3/15/04; HB 7–8/04; SLJ 5/04) [595.4]

22110 Murawski, Darlyne. *Spiders and Their Webs* (2–5). 2004, National Geographic $16.95 (0-7922-6979-9). 32pp. Dramatic telephoto shots of spiders are paired with basic facts and information on unusual behaviors. (Rev: BL 12/1/04; SLJ 3/05) [595.4]

22111 Murray, Peter. *Scorpions* (3–5). Illus. Series: Naturebooks. 1996, Child's World LB $22.79 (1-56766-217-X). 32pp. This book features in color photos and simple text this spiderlike creature with a sting in its tail. (Rev: BL 12/15/96) [595.4]

22112 Murray, Peter. *Spiders and Scorpions* (3–6). Series: Science Around Us. 2004, Child's World LB $27.07 (1-59296-273-4). 32pp. Eye-catching photographs and interesting "Did You Know?" features draw the reader into this overview of spiders and scorpions. (Rev: SLJ 3/05) [595.4]

22113 Ross, Michael E. *Spiderology* (3–6). Illus. 2000, Carolrhoda LB $19.93 (1-57505-387-X); paper $6.95 (1-57505-438-8). 48pp. After describing how to collect and observe spiders humanely,

this book suggests a number of activities to learn more about them. (Rev: BL 5/15/00; HBG 9/00; SLJ 7/00) [595.4]

22114 Schnieper, Claudia. *Amazing Spiders* (3–6). Illus. by Max Meier. 1989, Carolrhoda LB $23.93 (0-87614-342-7). 48pp. In often startling photos and a clear text, spiders are introduced. (Rev: BL 9/15/89; HB 11–12/89; SLJ 8/89) [595.4]

22115 Simon, Seymour. *Spiders* (2–5). 2003, HarperCollins LB $16.89 (0-06-028392-0). 32pp. Stunning photographs and smooth, informative text make this guide to spiders a browsing pleasure as well as a resource for reports. (Rev: BL 12/1/03; HB 11–12/03; HBG 4/04; SLJ 1/04)

22116 Souza, D. M. *Eight Legs* (3–5). Illus. Series: Creatures All Around Us. 1991, Carolrhoda LB $22.60 (0-87614-441-5). 40pp. Close-up photographs and clear explanations introduce spiders, scorpions, and other crawling creatures with eight legs. (Rev: BL 4/15/91; SLJ 7/91) [595.4]

22117 Squire, Ann O. *Spiders of North America* (3–5). Series: Animals in Order. 2000, Watts LB $23.00 (0-531-11516-X). 48pp. This book explains the animal classification system and then goes on to describe arachnids and introduce different varieties of spiders and their behavior. (Rev: BL 4/15/00) [595.4]

22118 Storad, Conrad J. *Tarantulas* (2–3). Series: Early Bird Nature Books. 1998, Lerner LB $22.60 (0-8225-3024-4). 48pp. This easily read, beautifully illustrated account introduces the tarantula, its life cycle, and its feeding habits. (Rev: BL 3/15/98; HBG 9/98; SLJ 7/98) [595.4]

22119 Time for kids eds., and Nicole Iorio. *Spiders!* (2–3). Illus. Series: Time for Kids Science Scoops. 2005, HarperCollins $14.99 (0-06-057635-9); paper $3.99 (0-06-057634-0). 48pp. Simple text suitable for beginning readers and bright illustrations present basic information on spiders, plus a profile of a scientist who works with them. (Rev: SLJ 3/05) [595.4]

22120 Winer, Yvonne. *Spiders Spin Webs* (PS–3). Illus. by Karen Lloyd-Jones. 1998, Charlesbridge $15.95 (0-88106-983-3); paper $6.95 (0-88106-984-1). 32pp. This visually exciting field guide introduces 15 types of spiders and their characteristics. (Rev: BL 7/98; HBG 3/99; SLJ 11/98) [595.4]

Land Invertebrates

22121 Allen, Judy. *Are You a Snail?* (PS–1). Illus. by Tudor Humphries. Series: Backyard Books. 2000, Kingfisher $9.95 (0-7534-5242-1). 32pp. An introduction to snails that discusses their appearance, food, and how they grow from egg to adult. (Rev: BL 5/15/00; HBG 3/01; SLJ 9/00) [594]

22122 Buholzer, Theres. *Life of the Snail* (2–5). Illus. 1987, Carolrhoda LB $22.60 (0-87614-246-3). 48pp. Close-up photos highlight the story of this small, fascinating animal. (Rev: BL 3/15/87; SLJ 6–7/87)

22123 Dell'Oro, Suzanne Paul. *Tunneling Earthworms* (PS–2). Series: Pull Ahead Books. 2000,

Lerner LB $21.27 (0-8225-3762-1). 32pp. A lavishly illustrated book that introduces the earthworm, its anatomy, food, and how it is able to move through earth. (Rev: BL 3/1/01; HBG 10/01) [595]

22124 Fowler, Allan. *A Snail's Pace* (1–2). Illus. Series: Rookie Readers. 1999, Children's Book Pr. LB $18.50 (0-516-20812-8). 32pp. This introduction to snails and slugs features large type, many color pictures, and a small format. (Rev: BL 7/99; HBG 9/99) [594]

22125 Fredericks, Anthony D. *Slugs* (2–3). Series: Early Bird Nature Books. 2000, Lerner LB $22.60 (0-8225-3041-4). 48pp. A beginning science book that describes, in pictures and text, what a slug looks like, where it lives, how it reproduces, and how it survives in spite of predators. (Rev: BL 5/15/00; HBG 9/00) [595]

22126 Glaser, Linda. *Wonderful Worms* (PS–2). Illus. by Loretta Krupinski. 1992, Millbrook LB $21.90 (1-56294-062-7). 32pp. A close peek at the wriggly world of earthworms. (Rev: BL 1/15/93; SLJ 3/93) [595]

22127 Hartley, Karen, and Chris Macro. *Snail* (1–3). Illus. by Alan Male. Series: Bug Books. 1998, Heinemann LB $19.92 (1-57572-664-5). 32pp. Large color photos of snails and short paragraphs of text are used to explain the physical structure, behavior, food, and life cycle of the snail. (Rev: HBG 9/99; SLJ 1/99) [594.3]

22128 Heinrichs, Ann. *Worms* (1–3). Illus. Series: Nature's Friends. 2004, Compass Point LB $15.95 (0-7565-0589-5). 32pp. Worms' anatomy and life cycle are covered in simple text and clear close-up photographs.

22129 Himmelman, John. *An Earthworm's Life* (K–2). Series: Nature Upclose. 2000, Children's Book Pr. LB $24.00 (0-516-21164-1). 32pp. Original watercolor paintings are used to illustrate this simple introduction to earthworms, their habits, where they live, and their life cycle. (Rev: BL 10/15/00) [595]

22130 Johnson, Sylvia A. *Snails* (4–6). Illus. 1982, Lerner LB $22.60 (0-8225-1475-3). 48pp. The structure, habits, and life cycle of a snail.

22131 Knudsen, Michelle. *A Slimy Story* (K–2). Illus. by Paige Billin-Frye. Series: Science Solves It! 2004, Kane paper $4.99 (1-57565-144-0). 32pp. Dan can't think what he can give his mother for her birthday until he realizes that earthworms are the perfect present for a gardener; scientific facts are interwoven into the text. (Rev: SLJ 1/05) [595]

22132 McLaughlin, Molly. *Earthworms, Dirt, and Rotten Leaves: An Exploration in Ecology* (4–6). Illus. 1986, Avon paper $3.50 (0-380-71074-9). 96pp. Activities that lead to an understanding of the behavior and appearance of earthworms. (Rev: BCCB 2/87; BL 2/1/87; SLJ 3/87)

22133 Miller, Ruth. *Arthropods* (4–6). Series: Animal Kingdom. 2004, Raintree LB $32.79 (1-4109-1049-0). 64pp. The common characteristics of arthropods are explained, followed by descriptions of various orders of arthropods and selected specific

species plus discussion of endangered status and evolution. (Rev: SLJ 6/05)

22134 Pfeffer, Wendy. *Wiggling Worms at Work* (K–3). Illus. by Steve Jenkins. Series: Let's-Read-and-Find-Out Science. 2004, HarperCollins $15.99 (0-06-028448-X). 40pp. Solid information on the earthworm and its characteristics are followed by advice on observing worms in their native habitat. (Rev: BL 2/15/04; SLJ 3/04) [592]

22135 Ross, Michael E. *Millipedeology* (3–6). Illus. Series: Backyard Buddies. 2000, Carolrhoda LB $19.93 (1-57505-398-5); paper $6.95 (1-57505-436-1). 48pp. This book shows how to collect and humanely study millipedes, with experiments that can be performed to learn more about them. (Rev: BL 5/15/00; HBG 9/00; SLJ 7/00) [595.6]

22136 Ross, Michael E. *Snailology* (4–6). Illus. Series: Backyard Buddies. 1996, Carolrhoda LB $19.95 (0-87614-894-1). 48pp. Various types of snails are introduced, with material on their classification, physical structure, and habits. (Rev: BL 7/96; SLJ 8/96) [594]

22137 Ross, Michael E. *Wormology* (4–6). Illus. 1996, Carolrhoda LB $14.95 (0-87614-937-9). 48pp. Worms and their classification, structure, and habits are introduced, with several activities and experiments. (Rev: BL 3/15/96; SLJ 7/96) [595.1]

Marine and Freshwater Life

GENERAL AND MISCELLANEOUS

22138 Armstrong, Pam. *Young Explorer's Guide to Undersea Life* (3–5). Illus. 1996, Monterey Bay $16.95 (1-878244-10-8). 64pp. Some plants and about 20 animals that live in or around the sea are described. (Rev: BL 9/15/96; SLJ 9/96) [574.92]

22139 Batten, Mary. *The Winking, Blinking Sea: All About Bioluminescence* (3–5). 2000, Millbrook LB $20.90 (0-7613-1550-0). Large photos of 11 bioluminescent sea creatures are presented opposite a paragraph or two of descriptive text. (Rev: BCCB 6/00; HBG 9/00; SLJ 7/00) [591.92]

22140 Berger, Melvin. *Dive! A Book of Deep-Sea Creatures* (1–2). Illus. Series: Hello Reader! 2000, Scholastic $3.99 (0-439-08747-3). 40pp. This easy reader introduces the marine life found on the ocean floor, with color photographs mostly at a close range. (Rev: BL 10/1/00) [591.77]

22141 Berger, Melvin, and Gilda Berger. *Do Whales Have Belly Buttons? Questions and Answers About Whales and Dolphins* (3–5). Series: Question and Answer. 1999, Scholastic $12.95 (0-590-13081-1); paper $5.95 (0-590-08571-3). 48pp. Simple questions related to whales and dolphins are asked and answered in a clear and precise way in this book illustrated with dramatic, often beautiful, paintings. (Rev: BL 11/15/99; SLJ 12/99) [599.5]

22142 Berger, Melvin, and Gilda Berger. *Fish Sleep but Don't Shut Their Eyes And Other Amazing Facts About Ocean Creatures* (2–5). Illus. Series: Speedy Facts. 2004, Scholastic paper $7.99 (0-439-62533-5). 48pp. An entertaining and lively presentation of amazing and informative facts about fish and marine creatures.

22143 Cerullo, Mary. *The Octopus: Phantom of the Sea* (4–8). Illus. 1997, Dutton $18.99 (0-525-65199-3). 64pp. The life cycle of this mysterious sea creature is described, with illustrations of its anatomy and of its relatives, such as the squid. (Rev: BCCB 2/97; BL 2/1/97; SLJ 12/97*) [594]

22144 Cerullo, Mary. *Sea Soup: Phytoplankton* (4–7). Illus. 1999, Tilbury House $16.95 (0-88448-208-1). 40pp. An introduction to the microscopic world of tiny plants known as phytoplankton and their contributions to life on this planet. (Rev: BL 3/15/00; SLJ 5/00) [578.77]

22145 Cerullo, Mary M. *Sea Soup: Zooplankton* (4–7). Illus. by Bill Curtsinger. 2001, Tilbury House $16.95 (0-88448-219-7). 48pp. An inviting introduction to the world of tiny drifting animals known as zooplankton, with intriguing photographs. (Rev: BL 7/01; HBG 10/01; SLJ 8/01) [592.1776]

22146 Cerullo, Mary M. *The Truth About Dangerous Sea Creatures* (3–5). Photos by Jeffrey L. Rotman. Illus. by Michael Wertz. 2003, Chronicle $15.95 (0-8118-4050-6). 46pp. The dangers posed by jellyfish, giant squid, sharks, octopi, and other marine animals are examined in text and illustrations. (Rev: SLJ 12/03) [591.77]

22147 Darling, Kathy. *Seashore Babies* (3–5). Illus. by Tara Darling. 1997, Walker LB $16.85 (0-8027-8477-1). 32pp. Seashores are introduced, with details of the young of the creatures found there and their lives and enemies. (Rev: BL 4/1/97; SLJ 3/97) [591.3]

22148 Delafosse, Claude. *Under the Sea: Hidden World* (PS–2). Series: First Discovery. 1999, Scholastic $12.95 (0-590-10992-8). 24pp. This beginning science book explores life in the ocean depths through many color pictures and a simple text. (Rev: BL 6/1–15/99; SLJ 7/99) [591]

22149 Demuth, Patricia. *Way Down Deep: Strange Ocean Creatures* (1–3). Illus. by Jim Deal. Series: All Aboard Reading. 1995, Penguin Putnam paper $3.99 (0-448-40851-1). 48pp. This easy-to-read science book introduces youngsters to the amazing creatures found at the bottom of the ocean. (Rev: BL 1/1–15/96; SLJ 6/96) [551.46]

22150 Earle, Sylvia A. *Dive! My Adventures in the Deep Frontier* (3–7). Illus. 1999, National Geographic $18.95 (0-7922-7144-0). 64pp. This photoessay contains a spectacular view of underwater life as experienced by the author, an eminent marine biologist. (Rev: BCCB 6/99; BL 2/15/99*; HBG 9/99; SLJ 3/99) [627]

22151 Earle, Sylvia A. *Sea Critters* (1–4). Illus. by Wolcott Henry. 2000, National Geographic $16.95 (0-7922-7181-5). 32pp. Color photos and a lyrical text are used to introduce such unusual sea creatures as Christmas-tree worms, sea squirts, sponges, and moray eels. (Rev: BL 11/1/00; HBG 3/01; SLJ 9/00) [591.7]

22152 Feeney, Stephanie, and Ann Fielding. *Sand to Sea: Marine Life of Hawaii* (2–4). Illus. by Ed Robinson. 1989, Univ. of Hawaii Pr. $13.95 (0-8248-1180-1). 64pp. A look at the fascinating sea life in Hawaii. (Rev: BL 11/1/89) [574]

22153 Gowell, Elizabeth T. *Whales and Dolphins: What They Have in Common* (3–5). Series: Animals in Order. 2000, Watts LB $23.00 (0-531-20396-4). 48pp. After material on animal classification, this book explains how dolphins and whales are related and goes on to present their individual characteristics. (Rev: BL 4/15/00; SLJ 7/00) [591.9]

22154 Grupper, Jonathan. *Destination: Deep Sea* (1–4). 2000, National Geographic $16.95 (0-7922-7693-0). 31pp. A beautiful collection of photographs and informative text present many sea creatures, from the inhabitants of coral reefs to dolphins, whales, and sea otters. (Rev: BL 10/15/00; HBG 3/01; SLJ 9/00) [591.92]

22155 Halfmann, Janet. *Life in the Sea* (5–7). Series: LifeViews. 2000, Creative LB $22.60 (1-58341-074-0). 25pp. All life in the sea is discussed with a focus on the tiniest — plankton, algae, sea spiders, coral, and worms. (Rev: SLJ 8/00) [591.92]

22156 Hirschmann, Kris. *Moray Eels* (4–6). Illus. Series: Creatures of the Sea. 2003, Gale LB $18.96 (0-7377-0985-5). 48pp. Introduces the moray eel, with color photographs and readable text. (Rev: SLJ 3/03) [597]

22157 Johnson, Jinny. *Simon and Schuster Children's Guide to Sea Creatures* (4–7). 1998, Simon & Schuster $19.95 (0-689-81534-4). 80pp. This book contains broad coverage of the invertebrates, birds, mammals, and fish found in various parts of the oceans and their shores. (Rev: HBG 9/98; SLJ 5/98) [591]

22158 Kalman, Bobbie. *AB Sea* (K–3). Illus. Series: Crabapples. 1995, Crabtree LB $19.96 (0-86505-625-0); paper $5.95 (0-86505-725-7). 32pp. An alphabet book that uses full-color pictures of marine life to illustrate the ABCs. (Rev: SLJ 4/96) [574.92]

22159 Kalman, Bobbie, and Heather Levigne. *What Is a Whale?* (2–4). Series: Science of Living Things. 1999, Crabtree LB $14.97 (0-86505-935-7); paper $5.36 (0-86505-953-5). 32pp. This introduction to whales, dolphins, and other cetaceans is well illustrated and informative. (Rev: SLJ 4/00) [599]

22160 Llewellyn, Claire. *Frog* (K–4). Illus. by Simon Mendez. Series: Starting Life. 2003, North-Word $16.95 (1-55971-869-2). 23pp. A look at the life cycle of a frog, from egg to tadpole to adult, and the environment in which frogs live. (Rev: SLJ 4/04) [597.8]

22161 Markle, Sandra. *Outside and Inside Giant Squid* (3–5). 2003, Walker LB $17.85 (0-8027-8873-4). 40pp. Markle is careful to convey how much of the available information about the giant squid has been determined by scientific methods rather than through study of a live animal. (Rev: BL 9/15/03; HBG 4/04; SLJ 12/03) [594]

22162 Pallotta, Jerry. *The Freshwater Alphabet Book* (1–4). Illus. by David Biedrzycki. 1996, Charlesbridge $15.95 (0-88106-901-9). Freshwater fish and crustaceans are used, along with a mythical monster or two, in this nicely illustrated alphabet book. (Rev: SLJ 4/96) [597]

22163 Pascoe, Elaine. *Pill Bugs and Sow Bugs* (4–7). Series: Nature Close-Up. 2001, Blackbirch LB $27.44 (1-56711-473-3). 32pp. This informative book of facts and easy-to-do projects introduces some small land crustacea found under stones and in other damp places. (Rev: BL 9/15/01; HBG 3/02) [595.3]

22164 Perry, Phyllis J. *Freshwater Giants* (3–5). Illus. 1999, Watts LB $24.00 (0-531-11681-6). 64pp. For each "giant," such as the hippopotamus, dolphin, and manatee, details are given on its characteristics, behavior, and habitat. (Rev: BL 11/1/99; HBG 4/00) [599.176]

22165 Redmond, Shirley Raye. *Tentacles! Tales of the Giant Squid* (1–3). Illus. by Bryn Barnard. Series: Step into Reading. 2003, Random LB $11.99 (0-375-91307-6); paper $3.99 (0-375-81307-1). 48pp. For beginning readers, facts and myths about the giant squid are presented with photographs and paintings. (Rev: BL 7/03; HBG 4/04) [594]

22166 Savage, Stephen. *Animals of the Oceans* (2–6). Illus. Series: Animals by Habitat. 1997, Raintree LB $22.83 (0-8172-4753-X). 32pp. Readers are taken on a tour of vast underwater habitats and encounter such animals as the moray eel, green turtle, and sea anemone. (Rev: BL 5/15/97; SLJ 8/97) [591.9]

22167 Sheather, Allan. *Neptune's Nursery* (2–3). Illus. by Kim Michelle Toft. 2000, Charlesbridge LB $16.95 (1-57091-391-9); paper $6.95 (1-57091-392-7). 32pp. A rhyming text and stunning paintings introduce a number of marine animals and their young. (Rev: BL 12/15/00; HBG 3/01; SLJ 10/00) [591.77]

22168 Sibbald, Jean H. *Strange Eating Habits of Sea Creatures* (4–8). Illus. 1987, Macmillan LB $13.95 (0-87518-349-2). 112pp. Eating habits of numerous creatures of the sea are divided into techniques — grazers, gulpers, poisoners, and so on. (Rev: BL 12/1/86; SLJ 2/87)

22169 Souza, D. M. *Sea Snakes* (2–3). Illus. Series: Creatures All Around Us. 1998, Carolrhoda LB $19.93 (1-57505-263-6). 40pp. An illustrated study of the habits, life cycles, and reproductive behavior of sea snakes and sea kraits, including a fact summary and glossary. (Rev: BL 12/1/98; HBG 3/99; SLJ 3/99) [597.96]

22170 Squire, Ann O. *Animals of the Sea and Shore* (2–3). Series: True Books — Animals. 2001, Children's Book Pr. LB $23.00 (0-516-22190-6). 48pp. A variety of common marine animals are introduced with well-captioned color pictures on each page and a concise text. (Rev: BL 12/15/01) [591.32]

22171 Stone, Lynn M. *The Food Chain* (2–4). Illus. Series: Under the Sea Discovery Library. 2001, Rourke LB $18.60 (1-58952-113-7). 24pp. A look at how food is used to provide energy and at the structure of the food chain found in the underwater world. (Rev: BL 12/15/01; SLJ 3/02) [577.7]

22172 Stone, Lynn M. *Getting Around* (2–3). Series: Under the Sea. 2001, Rourke LB $18.60 (1-58952-110-2). 24pp. Text and full-page color photographs provide a simple introduction to the locomotion of various sea animals. (Rev: BL 3/15/02; SLJ 3/02) [591.7]

22173 Stone, Lynn M. *Life of the Kelp Forest* (2–3). Series: Under the Sea. 2001, Rourke LB $18.60 (1-58952-112-9). 24pp. The vegetation and marine life found in an ocean kelp forest are introduced with simple text and full-page photographs. (Rev: BL 3/15/02; SLJ 2/02) [589.4]

22174 Stone, Lynn M. *Partners* (2–4). Illus. Series: Under the Sea Discovery Library. 2001, Rourke LB $18.60 (1-58952-114-5). 24pp. Underwater partnerships such as parasites and symbiotic relationships are the focus of this slim volume with full-color double-page spreads. (Rev: BL 12/15/01; SLJ 2/02) [591.77]

22175 Treat, Rose. *The Seaweed Book: How to Find and Have Fun with Seaweed* (4–7). Illus. 1995, Star Bright paper $5.95 (1-887724-00-7). 32pp. The identification, collection, and preservation of various kinds of seaweed. (Rev: BL 2/1/96) [589.45]

22176 Vogel, Carole G. *Ocean Wildlife* (5–9). Series: The Restless Sea. 2003, Watts LB $29.50 (0-531-12324-3); paper $12.95 (0-531-16681-3). 95pp. A thorough examination of marine life, from algae to whales, with an emphasis on those species facing extinction through pollution, overfishing, and other manmade threats. (Rev: SLJ 3/04) [591.77]

CORALS AND JELLYFISH

22177 Buttfield, Helen. *The Secret Life of Fishes: From Angels to Zebras on the Coral Reef* (5–8). Illus. by author. 2000, Abrams $19.95 (0-8109-3933-9). 72pp. As well as introducing the fish found on coral reefs, this handsome book talks about the reef itself and other creatures found there such as the octopus and sea star. (Rev: SLJ 7/00) [574.97]

22178 Cerullo, Mary. *Coral Reef: A City That Never Sleeps* (5–8). Illus. 1996, Dutton $18.99 (0-525-65193-4). Exceptional photographs highlight this account of coral reefs and the life they support. (Rev: BL 3/1/96; SLJ 1/96*) [574.9]

22179 Collard, Sneed B. *Lizard Island: Science and Scientists on Australia's Great Barrier Reef* (5–7). Illus. 2000, Watts LB $25.00 (0-531-11719-7); paper $12.95 (0-531-16519-1). 144pp. A lively and absorbing description of the work of scientists studying the forms of life on the Great Barrier Reef. (Rev: BL 2/1/01; SLJ 5/01) [577.7]

22180 Collard, Sneed B. *One Night in the Coral Sea* (3–5). Illus. by Robin Brickman. 2005, Charlesbridge $15.95 (1-57091-389-7). 32pp. Collard describes a unique spawning of millions of eggs by the coral of the Great Barrier Reef. (Rev: BL 5/15/05) [593.6]

22181 Earle, Sylvia A. *Coral Reefs* (K–2). Illus. by Bonnie Matthews. Series: Jump into Science. 2003, National Geographic $16.95 (0-7922-6953-5). 32pp. A young swimmer describes the passing world of a coral reef, explaining its ecology, plants, and sea life, illustrated by vivid paintings and accompanied by a map and an activity. (Rev: BL 1/1–15/03; HBG 10/03; SLJ 5/03) [577.7]

22182 Earle, Sylvia A. *Hello, Fish! Visiting the Coral Reef* (PS–4). Photos by Wolcott Henry. 1999, National Geographic $15.95 (0-7922-7103-3). Stunning photography is featured in a series of double-page spreads that introduce 12 fish that live in the waters around coral reefs. (Rev: BCCB 6/99; HBG 9/99; SLJ 3/99) [574]

22183 Fleisher, Paul. *Coral Reef* (3–5). Series: Webs of Life. 1997, Marshall Cavendish LB $22.79 (0-7614-0432-5). 40pp. This look at life in a coral reef explains how they are formed and the kinds of life found within them. (Rev: BL 2/15/98; HBG 3/98; SLJ 4/98) [574.9]

22184 Furgang, Kathy. *Let's Take a Field Trip to a Coral Reef* (3–5). Illus. Series: Neighborhoods in Nature. 2000, Rosen LB $18.60 (0-8239-5445-5). 24pp. This book looks at the formation of coral reefs, the types of plants and animals found there, and the impact of human activities. (Rev: SLJ 4/01) [574.9]

22185 George, Twig C. *Jellies: The Life of Jellyfish* (K–3). Illus. 2000, Millbrook LB $21.90 (0-7613-1659-0). 32pp. Handsome photographs introduce jellyfish, their many varieties, special features, and beauty. (Rev: BL 5/1/00; HBG 9/00; SLJ 8/00) [593.5]

22186 Green, Jen. *A Coral Reef* (2–5). Series: Small World. 2002, Crabtree LB $15.96 (0-7787-0138-7); paper $8.06 (0-7787-0152-2). 32pp. The variety of life found in a coral reef is described in a simple text with stunning pictures. (Rev: BL 10/15/02; SLJ 8/02) [574.5]

22187 Johnson, Rebecca L. *The Great Barrier Reef: A Living Laboratory* (5–8). 1992, Lerner LB $28.75 (0-8225-1596-2). A look at the world's largest coral reef, off the coast of Australia. (Rev: BL 5/15/92; SLJ 7/92) [574.9943]

22188 Kalman, Bobbie. *Life in the Coral Reef* (2–5). Illus. Series: Crabapples. 1997, Crabtree LB $19.96 (0-86505-629-3); paper $5.95 (0-86505-729-X). 32pp. A description of how coral reefs are formed, their interdependence with other animals and plants, and methods used to save them. (Rev: BL 7/97) [574.5]

22189 Landau, Elaine. *Jellyfish* (3–5). Illus. Series: True Books. 1999, Children's Book Pr. LB $21.00 (0-516-20676-1). 48pp. With plenty of captioned photographs, this work describes the structure, variety, and unique features of jellyfish. (Rev: BL 6/1–15/99; HBG 9/99) [593.5]

22190 Martin-James, Kathleen. *Floating Jellyfish* (PS–2). Series: Pull Ahead Books. 2001, Lerner LB $22.95 (0-8225-3766-4). 32pp. Each page contains two lines of simple text and a color photograph in this introduction to jellyfish for beginning readers. (Rev: BL 6/1–15/01; HBG 10/01) [593.5]

22191 Patent, Dorothy Hinshaw. *Colorful Captivating Coral Reefs* (1–3). Illus. by Kendahl Jan Jubb. 2003, Walker LB $18.85 (0-8027-8863-7). The life cycle of corals and the ways in which humans benefit from and cause damage to reefs are covered in interesting text and attractive illustrations. (Rev: BL 1/1–15/04; HBG 4/04; SLJ 11/03) [577.7]

22192 Pyers, Greg. *Coral Reef Explorer* (2–4). Illus. Series: Perspectives: Habitat Explorer. 2004, Raintree LB $25.70 (1-4109-0515-2). 32pp. This photo-filled exploration of Australia's Great Barrier Reef and other reefs offers readers important information about coral reefs, the abundant life found there, and their fragility. (Rev: BL 4/1/04) [577.7]

22193 Sharth, Sharon. *Sea Jellies: From Corals to Jellyfish* (3–5). Series: Animals in Order. 2002, Watts LB $24.00 (0-531-11867-3). 48pp. An amazing diversity of sea jellies and their individual characteristics and habitats are described in text with color photographs. (Rev: BL 3/15/02; SLJ 7/02) [593.5]

22194 Siy, Alexandra. *The Great Astrolabe Reef* (5–8). Illus. Series: Circle of Life. 1992, Macmillan $14.95 (0-87518-499-5). 80pp. Color photographs help to tell the story of this delicate coral ecosystem. (Rev: BL 9/1/92; SLJ 11/92) [574.5]

22195 Telford, Carole, and Rod Theodorou. *Inside a Coral Reef* (2–6). Illus. by Stephen Lings and Jane Pickering. Series: Amazing Journeys. 1997, Heinemann LB $13.95 (1-57572-154-6). 32pp. Using a journey format with maps and other illustrations, this account introduces readers to the Great Barrier Reef and its flora and fauna. (Rev: SLJ 5/98) [574.9]

CRUSTACEANS

22196 Blaxland, Beth. *Crustaceans: Crabs, Crayfishes, and Their Relatives* (4–6). Series: Invertebrates. 2002, Chelsea LB $18.95 (0-7910-6994-X). 32pp. Blaxland defines crustaceans and describes their physical characteristics, life cycles, habitats, senses, food, and means of self-defense. (Rev: HBG 3/03; SLJ 1/03)

22197 Day, Nancy. *The Horseshoe Crab* (3–5). Illus. Series: Remarkable Animals. 1992, Macmillan $13.95 (0-87518-545-2). 60pp. The evolution of the horseshoe crab is given, plus material on its structure, habitats, and behavior. (Rev: BL 12/1/92; SLJ 3/93) [595.3]

22198 Fowler, Allan. *Shellfish Aren't Fish* (1–2). Series: Rookie Readers. 1998, Children's Book Pr. LB $18.50 (0-516-20802-0). 32pp. An interesting introduction to shrimps, crabs, and other crustaceans. (Rev: BL 9/15/98; HBG 9/99) [595.3]

22199 Greenaway, Theresa. *Crabs* (4–6). Illus. Series: The Secret World Of. 2001, Raintree LB $18.98 (0-7398-3506-8). 48pp. An attractive, well-organized account of the life cycle, anatomy, and habits of the crab, with information on the animal's place in the ecosystem and interesting material on peculiar features or unusual subspecies. (Rev: BL 10/15/01; HBG 3/02; SLJ 1/02) [595.3]

22200 Grimm, Phyllis W. *Crayfish* (2–3). Series: Early Bird Nature Books. 2000, Lerner LB $22.60 (0-8225-3030-9). 48pp. A look at this unusual sea creature that has eight legs, two large claws, four antennae, and many mouth parts. (Rev: BL 10/15/00; HBG 3/01; SLJ 2/01) [595.3]

22201 Holling, Holling C. *Pagoo* (4–6). Illus. 1957, Houghton Mifflin $20.00 (0-395-06826-6); paper

$10.00 (0-395-53964-1). 96pp. Life cycle of the hermit crab.

22202 Johnson, Sylvia A. *Crabs* (4–6). Illus. 1982, Lerner LB $22.60 (0-8225-1471-0). 48pp. A look at the structure and life cycle of various crabs.

22203 Kite, Patricia. *Down in the Sea: The Crab* (2–4). Illus. 1994, Whitman LB $14.95 (0-8075-1709-7). 32pp. Photographs and simple text introduce the crab, with interesting material on how they communicate. (Rev: BL 6/1–15/94; SLJ 5/94) [595.3]

22204 Sill, Cathryn. *About Crustaceans: A Guide for Children* (PS–2). Illus. by John Sill. Series: About . . . 2004, Peachtree $15.95 (1-56145-301-3). 40pp. Brief, large-print text and precise watercolor paintings introduce the world of crustaceans, including barnacles, crabs, and lobsters. (Rev: BL 5/1/04; SLJ 6/04) [595.3]

DOLPHINS AND PORPOISES

22205 Cerullo, Mary. *Dolphins: What They Can Teach Us* (4–6). Photos by Jeffrey L. Rotman. 1999, Dutton $16.99 (0-525-65263-9). 42pp. This account concentrates on the behavior of dolphins and the research centers where these popular animals are studied. (Rev: BCCB 2/99; HBG 9/99; SLJ 3/99) [599.5]

22206 Cole, Melissa. *Dolphins* (4–6). Photos by Brandon Cole. Series: Wild Marine Animals! 2001, Gale LB $17.95 (1-56711-443-1). 24pp. Basic information on dolphins and their distribution in the world's waters is enhanced by many large color photographs. (Rev: HBG 3/02; SLJ 3/02) [599.53]

22207 Crisp, Marty. *Everything Dolphin: What Kids Really Want to Know About Dolphins* (3–5). 2004, NorthWord $10.95 (1-55971-042-X); paper $7.95 (1-55971-049-7). 63pp. A basic introduction, using a question-and-answer format with plenty of photographs. (Rev: SLJ 11/04) [599.5]

22208 Dudzinski, Kathleen. *Meeting Dolphins: My Adventures in the Sea* (3–6). Illus. 2000, National Geographic $17.95 (0-7922-7129-7). 64pp. Using her own experiences and scientific research, the author introduces the reader to dolphins, their appearance, behavior, and life cycle. (Rev: BL 5/15/00; HBG 9/00; SLJ 7/00) [599.53]

22209 Fowler, Allan. *Friendly Dolphins* (1–2). Series: Rookie Readers. 1997, Children's Book Pr. LB $19.00 (0-516-20428-9). 32pp. Introduces dolphins with striking photos and minimal text suitable for beginning readers. (Rev: BL 11/15/97; HBG 3/98; SLJ 10/97) [599.5]

22210 Hirschi, Ron. *Dolphins* (4–6). Series: Animals Animals. 2002, Benchmark LB $15.95 (0-7614-1443-6). 48pp. An oversize book filled with excellent photographs and a simple text that introduces dolphins and their structure, habits, and homes. (Rev: BL 12/15/02; HBG 3/03) [599.5]

22211 Horton, Casey. *Dolphins* (3–5). Illus. Series: Endangered! 1996, Benchmark LB $22.79 (0-7614-0216-0). 32pp. A basic introduction to dolphins, their characteristics, habitats, and structure is given

through text and full-color photos. (Rev: SLJ 3/96) [599.5]

22212 Morris, Robert A. *Dolphin* (K–3). Illus. by Mamoru Funai. 1975, HarperCollins $6.93 (0-06-024337-6). 64pp. A simple account of the first five months of this lovable sea mammal.

22213 Pascoe, Elaine, adapt. *Animal Intelligence: Why Is This Dolphin Smiling?* (5–8). 1997, Blackbirch $17.95 (1-56711-226-9). This book reports on the scientific research on communication between dolphins and humans, with reports on such projects as one by John Lilly to create, via computer, dolphin equivalents of human words. (Rev: HBG 3/98; SLJ 12/97) [599.5]

22214 Pfeffer, Wendy. *Dolphin Talk: Whistles, Clicks, and Clapping Jaws* (1–2). Illus. by Helen K. Davie. Series: Let's-Read-and-Find-Out Science. 2003, HarperCollins LB $16.89 (0-06-028802-7); paper $4.99 (0-06-445210-7). 33pp. Dolphins' many ways of communicating are conveyed in understandable text. (Rev: HBG 4/04; SLJ 1/04) [599.53]

22215 Read, Andrew. *Porpoises* (5–8). Illus. Series: WorldLife Library. 1999, Voyageur paper $16.95 (0-89658-420-8). 72pp. With many color illustrations and large print, this book introduces porpoises, their characteristics, behavior, habitats, and how humans study them. (Rev: BL 8/99) [599.53]

22216 Rinard, Judith E. *Amazing Animals of the Sea* (5–8). Illus. 1981, National Geographic LB $12.50 (0-87044-387-9). 104pp. Whales, dolphins, sea otters, sea lions, seals, manatees, and other marine mammals are described.

22217 Schomp, Virginia. *The Bottlenose Dolphin* (3–5). Illus. 1994, Silver Burdett LB $13.95 (0-87518-605-X). 60pp. Fact and mythology mingle in this account of the dolphin, its life cycle, and its habitats. (Rev: BL 3/1/95) [599.5]

22218 Spilsbury, Richard, and Louise Spilsbury. *A School of Dolphins* (3–5). Illus. Series: Animal Groups. 2004, Heinemann LB $24.22 (1-4034-4692-X). 32pp. Easy-to-understand narrative and plenty of color photographs provide a good overview of dolphins and their behaviors and habitats. (Rev: BL 4/15/04) [599.53]

22219 Stahl, Dean. *Dolphins* (2–4). Illus. 2001, Child's World LB $24.21 (1-56766-889-5). 32pp. Concise text and full-page photographs present basic information on the dolphin in a friendly, question-and-answer format. (Rev: BL 7/01; HBG 10/01) [599.53]

22220 Sweeney, Diane, and Michelle Reddy. *Dolphin Babies: Making a Splash* (4–6). Photos by Jeff Smith. Illus. by Jim Corey. 1998, Roberts Rinehart paper $14.95 (1-57098-194-9). 64pp. Using remarkable photos and a brief text, this book chronicles the pregnancy of four dolphins and the subsequent births at the Dolphin Learning Center in Hawaii. (Rev: SLJ 9/98) [599.5]

22221 Walker, Sally M. *Dolphins* (3–6). Illus. Series: Nature Watch. 1999, Carolrhoda LB $22.60 (1-57505-221-0). 48pp. This attractive introduction to dolphins includes material on their physical characteristics, communication, behavior, life cycle, and relations with people. (Rev: BL 9/1/99; HBG 9/99) [599.53]

FISH

22222 Arnold, Caroline. *Shockers of the Sea and Other Electrical Animals* (1–3). Illus. by Crista Forest. 1999, Charlesbridge $15.95 (0-88106-873-X); paper $6.95 (0-88106-874-8). 32pp. Covers electric fish and how they use this attribute for purposes such as getting food, defense, and communication. (Rev: BL 10/15/99; HBG 4/00; SLJ 1/00) [597]

22223 Arnosky, Jim. *Crinkleroot's 25 Fish Every Child Should Know* (PS–3). Illus. 1993, Bradbury LB $12.95 (0-02-705844-1). 32pp. A picture-book field guide that introduces with paintings and brief text 25 common species of fish. (Rev: BL 9/1/93; SLJ 9/93) [597]

22224 Bailey, Jill. *How Fish Swim* (3–5). Illus. by Colin Newman. Series: Nature's Mysteries. 1996, Benchmark LB $22.79 (0-7614-0451-1). 32pp. This work covers how fish and other aquatic animals move and the different anatomical specializations that make locomotion possible. (Rev: SLJ 2/97) [597]

22225 Berendes, Mary. *Piranhas* (PS–3). Series: Naturebooks. 1999, Child's World LB $15.95 (1-56766-493-8). 32pp. Amazing full-page photographs opposite one or two short paragraphs of text are used to introduce these savage marine creatures. (Rev: BL 6/1–15/99; HBG 9/99; SLJ 9/99) [597]

22226 Cole, Joanna. *A Fish Hatches* (3–5). Illus. 1978, Morrow $14.89 (0-688-32153-4). 40pp. The story of a trout, from egg to fully grown fish, in text and photographs.

22227 Eastman, David. *What Is a Fish?* (K–3). Illus. by Lynn Sweat. 1982, Troll LB $17.25 (0-89375-660-1); paper $3.50 (0-89375-661-X). 32pp. A simple account that shows various kinds of fish.

22228 Gallimard Jeunesse. *Fish* (PS–2). Illus. Series: First Discovery. 1998, Scholastic $11.95 (0-590-38155-5). 24pp. Using overlays and colorful illustrations, this book introduces several types of fish and describes how fish breathe, reproduce, eat, and protect themselves. (Rev: BL 9/15/98; HBG 9/98) [579]

22229 Grossman, Susan. *Piranhas* (4–6). Illus. Series: Remarkable Animals. 1994, Dillon LB $13.95 (0-87518-593-2). 60pp. An introduction to piranhas that points out their value to fisherman and that the harm they do to humans is exaggerated. (Rev: SLJ 8/94) [597]

22230 Hirschi, Ron. *Salmon* (3–6). Series: Nature Watch. 2000, Carolrhoda LB $23.93 (1-57505-482-5). 48pp. Amazing photos and a clear text describe how salmon change from egg to fry to grown fish that then complete the cycle by making a journey upstream to reproduce. (Rev: BL 10/15/00; HBG 10/01) [597.55]

22231 Hirschmann, Kris. *Rays* (4–7). Illus. 2003, Gale LB $23.70 (0-7377-0988-X). 48pp. Hirschmann presents basic information about the ray's anatomy, movement, feeding, defense, reproduc-

tion, and man's fascination with this fish. (Rev: BL 3/1/03) [597.3]

22232 Hodge, Deborah. *Salmon* (3–5). Illus. by Nancy Gray Ogle. Series: Wildlife. 2002, Kids Can $10.95 (1-55074-961-7); paper $5.95 (1-55074-963-3). 32pp. Atlantic and Pacific salmon are covered along with subspecies in a flowing text and detailed paintings. (Rev: HBG 10/02; SLJ 7/02) [597.56]

22233 Jango-Cohen, Judith. *Clinging Sea Horses* (PS–2). Series: Pull Ahead Books. 2000, Lerner LB $21.27 (0-8225-3764-8); paper $6.95 (0-8225-3767-2). 32pp. Stunning underwater photos bring to life this unique fish whose young grow in a pouch on the father's body. (Rev: BL 8/00; HBG 3/01; SLJ 1/01) [597]

22234 Kurlansky, Mark. *The Cod's Tale* (3–5). Illus. by S. D. Schindler. 2001, Penguin Putnam $16.99 (0-399-23476-4). 48pp. Kurlansky looks at the surprisingly fascinating relationship between cod and humans, presenting basic facts about the fish itself (including how to cook it) and exploring its importance throughout history. (Rev: BCCB 10/01; BL 12/1/01; HB 11–12/01; HBG 3/02; SLJ 10/01) [639.2]

22235 Landau, Elaine. *Angelfish* (3–5). Series: A True Book. 1999, Children's Book Pr. LB $21.00 (0-516-20660-5). 48pp. A brief introduction to angelfish and their appearance and life cycle, along with instructions for caring for them in an aquarium. (Rev: BL 8/99; HBG 9/99) [597]

22236 Landau, Elaine. *Electric Fish* (3–5). Series: A True Book. 1999, Children's Book Pr. LB $21.00 (0-513-20660-4). 48pp. With stunning photos and a simple text, this account introduces fish that produce electricity and explains the causes and effects of this phenomenon. (Rev: BL 8/99) [597]

22237 Landau, Elaine. *Piranhas* (3–5). Series: True Books. 1999, Children's Book Pr. LB $21.00 (0-516-20673-7). 48pp. Using a square format, large type, and plenty of captioned photographs, this account introduces the piranha, its physical characteristics, habits, and why it is dreaded. (Rev: BL 6/1–15/99; HBG 9/99; SLJ 8/99) [597]

22238 Landau, Elaine. *Sea Horses* (3–5). Series: True Books. 1999, Children's Book Pr. LB $21.00 (0-516-20675-3). 48pp. The fascinating sea horse and its habits, habitats, and life cycle are introduced in this square-shaped book that contains many excellent color illustrations. (Rev: BL 6/1–15/99; HBG 9/99; SLJ 8/99) [597]

22239 Landau, Elaine. *Siamese Fighting Fish* (3–5). Illus. Series: True Books. 1999, Children's Book Pr. LB $21.00 (0-516-20678-8). 48pp. Describes the varieties of Siamese fighting fish with a number of color photographs and a brief text. (Rev: BL 6/1–15/99; HBG 9/99; SLJ 8/99) [639.3]

22240 Laskey, Elizabeth. *Seahorses* (4–6). Series: Sea Creatures. 2003, Heinemann LB $24.22 (1-40340-963-3). 32pp. Examines the tiny marine animal's physical characteristics, habitat, diet, and behavior. (Rev: HBG 10/03; SLJ 11/03) [597]

22241 Miller, Sara Swan. *Seahorses, Pipefishes, and Their Kin* (3–5). Series: Animals in Order. 2002,

Watts $25.00 (0-531-12171-2). 48pp. The sea horse, banded pipefish, cornetfish, and brook stickleback, all members of the gasterosteiforme order, are described in a simple text and excellent photographs. (Rev: BL 9/15/02; SLJ 10/02) [597]

22242 Pascoe, Elaine. *Freshwater Fish* (4–8). Photos by Dwight Kuhn. Series: Nature Close-Up. 2005, Gale/Blackbirch LB $18.96 (1-4103-0308-X). 48pp. Eye-catching close-ups illustrate information on the life cycles and eating habits of freshwater fish. (Rev: SLJ 6/05)

22243 Ricciuti, Edward R. *What on Earth Is a Pout?* (3–5). Illus. Series: What on Earth? 1996, Blackbirch LB $17.95 (1-56711-103-3). 32pp. An introduction to the pout, a bottom-dwelling fish of the Atlantic, covering its appearance, lifestyle, and habits. (Rev: SLJ 2/97) [597]

22244 Royston, Angela. *Life Cycle of a Salmon* (PS–3). Series: Life Cycle. 2000, Heinemann LB $19.92 (1-57572-212-7). 32pp. From egg to adult, this book explains the life cycle of a salmon, using a simple text and full-color photos on each page. (Rev: BL 5/15/00; HBG 3/01) [597.55]

22245 Savage, Stephen. *Fish* (2–4). Series: What's the Difference? 2000, Raintree LB $25.69 (0-7398-1357-9). 32pp. Fish can be as different as a goldfish and a shark, but this book points out their common features (e.g., gills) as well as salient differences. (Rev: BL 10/15/00; HBG 3/01) [597]

22246 Sill, Cathryn. *About Fish: A Guide for Children* (PS–1). Illus. by John Sill. 2002, Peachtree $14.95 (1-56145-256-4). 40pp. Watercolor illustrations and simple text describe for preschoolers how fish live and move. Also use *About Amphibians* (2001). (Rev: BL 3/1/02; HBG 10/02; SLJ 6/02) [597]

22247 Spilsbury, Richard, and Louise Spilsbury. *Classifying Fish* (4–6). Series: Classifying Living Things. 2003, Heinemann LB $24.22 (1-4034-0846-7). 32pp. The principles of scientific classification are covered along with an introduction to some of the many groupings of fish. (Rev: HBG 10/03; SLJ 11/03) [597]

22248 Spilsbury, Richard, and Louise Spilsbury. *The Life Cycle of Fish* (3–5). Illus. Series: From Egg to Adult. 2003, Heinemann LB $24.22 (1-4034-0783-5). 32pp. A photo-filled overview of the life cycle of fish, with material on habitat, diet, and life expectancy. (Rev: HBG 4/04; SLJ 10/03) [597]

22249 Stefoff, Rebecca. *Sea Horse* (2–4). Illus. Series: From the Living Things. 1996, Marshall Cavendish LB $22.79 (0-7614-0116-4). 32pp. Various kinds of sea horses are described, along with their habits and life cycles. (Rev: BL 2/1/97; SLJ 3/97) [597]

22250 Stewart, Melissa. *Fishes* (2–3). Series: True Books. 2001, Children's Book Pr. LB $22.00 (0-516-22038-1). 48pp. This book looks at a number of kinds of fish and points out similarities as well as differences. (Rev: BL 3/15/01) [597]

22251 Stone, Lynn M. *Ocean Hunters* (2–3). Series: Under the Sea. 2001, Rourke LB $18.60 (1-58952-111-0). 24pp. A basic introduction to various sea animals and how they find, kill, and eat their food. (Rev: BL 3/15/02) [597]

22252 Walker, Sally M. *Fossil Fish Found Alive: Discovering the Coelacanth* (5–8). Illus. 2002, Carolrhoda LB $21.55 (1-57505-536-8). 64pp. An engaging look at the search for and study of coelacanths, a fish believed to be extinct until 1938. (Rev: BL 3/15/02; HB 1–2/03; HBG 3/03; SLJ 5/02*) [597.3]

22253 Walker, Sally M. *Sea Horses* (2–4). Series: Early Bird Nature Books. 2003, Lerner LB $23.93 (0-8225-3051-1). 48pp. Newly independent readers will enjoy this basic introduction to the life cycle of the sea horse, covering habitat, diet, and reproduction. (Rev: HBG 4/04; SLJ 11/03) [597]

22254 Walker, Sally M. *Sea Horses* (3–6). Illus. Series: Nature Watch. 1999, Lerner $16.95 (1-57505-317-9). 48pp. The sea horse is introduced with many color photographs and material on its physical characteristics, bonding rituals, classification, and the mythology surrounding these small animals. (Rev: BL 5/1/99; HBG 9/99; SLJ 11/99) [597]

22255 Walker, Sally M. *Seahorse Reef: A Story of the South Pacific* (1–3). Illus. by Steven J. Petruccio. Series: Smithsonian Oceanic. 2001, Smithsonian Institution $15.95 (1-56899-869-4). 32pp. Information about the sea horse — behavior, habitat, and reproduction — is presented through the story of one sea horse and his mate. (Rev: BL 9/15/01; HBG 10/01; SLJ 8/01) [597]

22256 Winkelman, Barbara Gaines. *Puffer's Surprise* (2–3). 2005, Soundprints $15.95 (1-59249-032-8); paper $8.95 (1-59249-034-4). 32pp. A fascinating day in the life of a tiny puffer fish is chronicled in beautiful illustratations and simple but detailed text. (Rev: BL 12/1/03; HBG 4/04)

22257 Zim, Herbert S., and Hurst H. Shoemaker. *Fishes* (5–8). Illus. by James G. Irving. 1991, Western paper $21.27 (0-307-64059-0). 160pp. This is a basic guide to both fresh and saltwater species.

MOLLUSKS, SPONGES, AND STARFISH

22258 Blaxland, Beth. *Echinoderms: Sea Stars, Sea Urchins, and Their Relatives* (4–6). Series: Invertebrates. 2002, Chelsea LB $18.95 (0-7910-6996-6). 32pp. Blaxland defines echinoderms and describes their physical characteristics, life cycles, habitats, senses, food, and means of self-defense. (Rev: HBG 3/03; SLJ 1/03)

22259 Esbensen, Barbara J. *Sponges Are Skeletons* (1–4). Illus. by Holly Keller. Series: Let's-Read-and-Find-Out. 1993, HarperCollins LB $15.89 (0-06-021037-0). 32pp. This account tells about the original bath sponges and how they originated on the ocean floor. (Rev: BL 12/1/93; SLJ 2/94) [593.4]

22260 Fowler, Allan. *Star of the Sea* (1–2). Series: Rookie Readers. 2000, Children's Book Pr. LB $19.00 (0-516-21214-1). 32pp. Using a full-page picture opposite six or seven lines of simple text, this beginning science book introduces starfish, explains their physical characteristics, and describes their food and habitats. (Rev: BL 4/15/00) [593.9]

22261 Hirschmann, Kris. *Sea Stars* (4–6). Illus. Series: Creatures of the Sea. 2003, Gale LB $18.96 (0-7377-1362-3). 48pp. Introduces the marine invertebrate also known as the starfish. (Rev: SLJ 3/03)

22262 Morgan, Sally. *Sponges and Other Minor Phyla* (4–6). Series: Animal Kingdom. 2004, Raintree LB $32.79 (1-4109-1053-9). 64pp. The common characteristics of sponges and other minor phyla are explained, followed by descriptions of various orders within this classification and selected specific species, plus discussion of endangered status and evolution. (Rev: SLJ 6/05)

22263 Sill, Cathryn. *About Mollusks: A Guide for Children* (K–2). Illus. by John Sill. 2005, Peachtree $15.95 (1-56145-331-5). A simple introduction to mollusks, with large, realistic watercolors. (Rev: BL 2/1/04; HB 5–6/04; SLJ 4/05)

22264 Zuchora-Walske, Christine. *Spiny Sea Stars* (PS–2). Series: Pull Ahead Books. 2001, Lerner LB $22.95 (0-8225-3765-6). 32pp. A variety of starfish and their habits and habitats are presented with a simple, basic text and attractive color photographs. (Rev: BL 6/1–15/01; HBG 10/01) [593.9]

OCTOPUS

22265 Hirschi, Ron. *Octopuses* (3–6). Series: Nature Watch. 2000, Carolrhoda $22.60 (1-57505-386-1). 48pp. An informative text about the octopus, its daily life, and how it uses its eight arms for swimming, eating, catching prey, and even tasting food. (Rev: BL 3/15/00; HBG 9/00; SLJ 7/00) [594]

22266 Matsen, Brad. *The Incredible Hunt for the Giant Squid* (4–6). Illus. Series: Incredible Deep-Sea Adventures. 2003, Enslow LB $18.95 (0-7660-2192-0). 48pp. An engaging overview of what is known about the mysterious creature, focusing primarily on efforts to track down the elusive squid in its deep habitat. (Rev: HBG 4/04; SLJ 1/04) [594]

22267 Souza, D. M. *Sea Creatures with Many Arms* (2–3). Illus. Series: Creatures All Around Us. 1998, Carolrhoda LB $19.93 (1-57505-262-8). 40pp. The life cycle, habits, and reproduction of squid, octopuses, cuttlefish, and chambered nautiluses are introduced through color photos and clear captions. (Rev: BL 12/1/98; HBG 3/99; SLJ 3/99) [594]

22268 Stefoff, Rebecca. *Octopus* (K–3). Illus. Series: Living Things. 1996, Marshall Cavendish LB $22.79 (0-7614-0119-9). 32pp. This colorful introduction to the octopus uses short bits of information and many illustrations on double-page spreads. Also use in this series *Starfish, Giant Turtle,* and *Praying Mantis.* (Rev: BL 3/15/97; SLJ 3/97) [597.92]

22269 Trueit, Trudi Strain. *Octopuses, Squids, and Cuttlefish* (3–5). Series: Animals in Order. 2002, Watts $25.00 (0-531-11930-0). 48pp. A look at how these animals change color, camouflage themselves, and display a remarkable intelligence. (Rev: BL 9/15/02; SLJ 10/02) [594]

22270 Zuchora-Walske, Christine. *Giant Octopuses* (PS–2). Series: Pull Ahead Books. 1999, Lerner $21.27 (0-8225-3633-1); paper $6.95 (0-8225-3637-

4). 32pp. The physical characteristics and habits of the octopus are covered with a brief text and a color photo on each page plus a body diagram, map, glossary, and simple index. (Rev: BL 12/15/99; HBG 4/00) [594.56]

SEA MAMMALS

22271 Becker, John E. *North American River Otters* (4–6). Illus. Series: Returning Wildlife. 2002, Gale LB $23.70 (0-7377-0755-0). 48pp. The reasons why the otter became endangered are described, followed by a discussion of the animal's habitat and habits, and descriptions of efforts to reintroduce otters to their native environment. (Rev: SLJ 1/03)

22272 Boyle, Doe. *Otter on His Own: The Story of a Sea Otter.* 2nd ed. (K–2). Illus. by Robert Lawson. 2002, Soundprints $15.95 (1-56899-129-0); paper $5.95 (1-931465-53-3). 31pp. A revision of the exciting story of an otter pup's childhood, with plenty of facts about sea otters. (Rev: HBG 3/03; SLJ 11/02) [599.74]

22273 Cossi, Olga. *Harp Seals* (3–6). Illus. 1991, Carolrhoda LB $23.93 (0-87614-437-7). 48pp. The life cycle, migratory patterns, and behavior of the Arctic harp seal are described. (Rev: BCCB 4/91; BL 5/5/91; SLJ 6/91) [599.74]

22274 Darling, Kathy. *Walrus: On Location* (1–4). Illus. by Tara Darling. Series: On Location. 1991, Lothrop $14.95 (0-688-09032-Y). 40pp. Watching the walrus who come to shore every year on Round Island off the coast of Alaska. (Rev: BL 8/91; SLJ 12/91) [599.74]

22275 Grace, Eric S. *Seals* (4–6). Illus. by Fred Bruemmer. Series: Sierra Club Wildlife Library. 1994, Little, Brown paper $7.95 (0-316-32291-1). 62pp. This slim, oversized volume supplies an attractive, well-organized introduction to seals and their cousins, sea lions and walruses. (Rev: BL 1/15/92; SLJ 2/92*) [599.74]

22276 Harman, Amanda. *Manatees and Dugongs* (3–5). Illus. Series: Endangered! 1996, Benchmark LB $22.79 (0-7614-0294-2). 32pp. These endangered sea creatures are described in text and pictures, with material on their habitats, lifestyles, and how they can be helped. (Rev: SLJ 2/97) [599.5]

22277 Hewett, Joan. *A Harbor Seal Grows Up* (1–3). Illus. by Richard Hewett. Series: Baby Animals. 2001, Lerner LB $21.27 (1-57505-166-4); paper $6.95 (0-8225-0092-2). 32pp. A book for beginning readers about a baby harbor seal being raised in captivity. (Rev: BL 10/15/01; HBG 3/02; SLJ 10/01) [599.79]

22278 Hirschi, Ron. *Seals* (4–6). Series: Animals Animals. 2002, Benchmark LB $15.95 (0-7614-1445-2). 48pp. Pictures and text present these animals' anatomy, diet, habits, and social interactions. (Rev: BL 12/15/02; HBG 3/03; SLJ 2/03) [599.74]

22279 Hodgkins, Fran. *Andre: The Famous Harbor Seal* (K–3). Illus. by Yetti Frenkel. 2003, Down East $16.95 (0-89272-594-X). 32pp. The real-life story of Andre the harbor seal traces the animal's life from its 1961 adoption as a pup by a Maine harbormaster to its death in 1986. (Rev: SLJ 1/04) [599.79]

22280 Hurd, Edith Thacher. *The Song of the Sea Otter* (4–6). Illus. by Jennifer Dewey. 1989, Sierra Club paper $5.95 (0-316-38323-6). 40pp. In a harbor on the Pacific coast, a baby sea otter explores his world. A reissue.

22281 Jenkins, Priscilla B. *A Safe Home for Manatees* (PS–3). Illus. by Martin Classen. Series: Let's-Read-and-Find-Out. 1997, HarperCollins LB $14.89 (0-06-027150-7); paper $4.95 (0-06-445164-X). 32pp. An introduction to Florida's sea cows, or manatees, their habits, why they are facing extinction, and the efforts being made to save them. (Rev: BL 12/1/97; HBG 3/98; SLJ 10/97) [599.5]

22282 Johnson, Sylvia A. *Elephant Seals* (3–6). Illus. 1989, Lerner LB $22.60 (0-8225-1487-7). 48pp. The story of these animals, hunted almost to extinction, along the California and Mexico coasts. (Rev: BL 3/1/89)

22283 Lepthien, Emilie U. *Walruses* (3–4). Illus. Series: True Books. 1996, Children's Book Pr. LB $22.00 (0-516-20162-X). 48pp. Introduces the walrus and its life at sea, anatomy, food, child rearing, and habits. (Rev: SLJ 6/97) [599.7]

22284 Martin, Patricia A. Fink. *Manatees* (2–3). Series: Animals. 2002, Children's Book Pr. LB $23.50 (0-516-22163-9); paper $6.95 (0-516-27473-2). 48pp. Color photographs on almost every page and large-type text are used to introduce these endangered sea mammals and explain their life cycle, habits, and habitats. (Rev: BL 8/02) [599.5]

22285 Meeker, Clare Hodgson. *Lootas, Little Wave Eater: An Orphaned Sea Otter's Story* (3–5). Photos by C. J. Casson. 1999, Sasquatch paper $12.95 (1-57061-164-5). 43pp. Describes the early life of a young sea otter and how she was rescued after a boating accident and raised in the Seattle Aquarium. (Rev: SLJ 1/00) [599.74]

22286 Richardson, Adele D. *Manatees: Peaceful Plant-Eaters* (1–3). Series: Wild World of Animals. 2002, Capstone LB $18.60 (0-7368-1395-0). 24pp. This endangered aquatic mammal is introduced with many color photographs, large type, and simple language. (Rev: BL 1/1–15/03; HBG 3/03) [599.55]

22287 Rotter, Charles. *Seals* (K–3). Series: Naturebooks. 2001, Child's World LB $24.21 (1-56766-891-7). 32pp. Concise text and full-page photographs present basic information on seals in a friendly, question-and-answer format. Also use *Walruses* (2001). (Rev: HBG 10/01; SLJ 7/01) [599.79]

22288 Sibbald, Jean H. *The Manatee* (4–7). Illus. 1990, Macmillan LB $13.95 (0-87518-429-4). 60pp. The life of this gentle sea mammal is examined, along with material on how its survival is threatened by humans. (Rev: BL 6/15/90; SLJ 8/90) [599.5]

22289 Silverstein, Alvin, et al. *The Manatee* (4–7). Illus. Series: Endangered in America. 1995, Millbrook LB $24.90 (1-56294-551-3). 64pp. A profile of this sea creature, its lifestyle and habits, and how it became an endangered species. (Rev: BL 10/15/95; SLJ 1/96) [599.5]

22290 Staub, Frank. *Manatees* (2–3). Series: Early Bird Nature Books. 1998, Lerner $22.60 (0-8225-3023-6). 48pp. Good illustrations and simple text are used to introduce this endangered sea mammal. (Rev: BL 10/15/98; HBG 3/99; SLJ 1/99) [599.5]

22291 Staub, Frank. *Sea Lions* (2–3). Series: Early Bird Nature Books. 2000, Lerner LB $22.60 (0-8225-3018-X). 48pp. This simple introduction to the California sea lion covers its habitat, appearance, behavior, and the dangers it faces. (Rev: BL 5/15/00; HBG 9/00) [599]

22292 Stille, Darlene R. *I Am a Seal: The Life of an Elephant Seal* (K–3). Illus. by Todd Ouren. Series: I Live in the Ocean. 2004, Picture Window LB $22.60 (1-4048-0598-2). 24pp. An elephant seal describes its life — diet, activities, and so forth. (Rev: SLJ 1/05) [599.74]

22293 Swanson, Diane. *Otters* (2–4). Series: Welcome to the World of Animals. 1998, Gareth Stevens LB $14.95 (0-8368-2214-5). 32pp. A slim volume that offers information on the homes, diet, communication, and lifestyles of both sea and river otters. (Rev: HBG 9/99; SLJ 5/99) [599.74]

22294 Theodorou, Rod. *Florida Manatee* (K–2). Illus. Series: Animals in Danger. 2000, Heinemann LB $21.36 (1-57572-265-8). 32pp. This is an introductory overview of the manatee, with basic information on the animal, its diet and habitat, and the reasons it is endangered. (Rev: HBG 3/01; SLJ 4/01) [599.5]

22295 Walker, Sally M. *Manatees* (3–6). Illus. Series: Nature Watch. 1999, Carolrhoda $22.60 (1-57505-299-7). 48pp. Amazing photographs are used to illustrate this introduction to the manatee, its physical characteristics, lifestyle, habits, and habitats. (Rev: BL 12/15/99; HBG 4/00) [599.55]

22296 Weber, Valerie. *Squids* (2–4). Illus. Series: Weird Wonders of the Deep. 2005, Gareth Stevens LB $16.50 (0-8368-4564-1). 24pp. A small-format but informative introduction to the many types of squid and their characteristics. (Rev: BL 5/1/05) [594]

SHARKS

22297 Arnosky, Jim. *All About Sharks* (1–4). Illus. by author. Series: All About. 2003, Scholastic $15.95 (0-590-48166-5). Easy-to-understand text and attractive illustrations present facts about sharks in an accessible manner. (Rev: BL 7/03; HBG 4/04; SLJ 6/03) [597.3]

22298 Berger, Melvin. *Chomp! A Book About Sharks* (1–3). Series: Hello Reader! 1999, Scholastic paper $3.99 (0-590-52298-1). Lots of introductory information about sharks is given in this book for beginning readers. (Rev: SLJ 7/99) [597.31]

22299 Burnham, Brad. *The Hammerhead Shark* (1–4). Illus. Series: Underwater World of Sharks. 2001, Rosen LB $18.75 (0-8239-5584-2). 24pp. A fact-filled, easy-to-read book about the odd-looking hammerhead shark, with full-color photographs and a list of Web sites. (Rev: BL 12/15/01) [597.3]

22300 Cerullo, Mary. *The Truth About Great White Sharks* (4–7). Illus. 2000, Chronicle $14.95 (0-

8118-2467-5). 48pp. A fascinating account with excellent underwater photographs that explores such topics about sharks as physical characteristics, behavior, feeding habits, and the difficulty of studying them. (Rev: BL 4/1/00; SLJ 7/00) [597.3]

22301 Cole, Joanna. *Hungry, Hungry Sharks* (1–3). Illus. by Patricia J. Wynne. 1986, Random paper $3.99 (0-394-87471-4). 48pp. Different kinds of sharks are explained in simple terms. (Rev: BL 8/86)

22302 Cole, Melissa. *Sharks* (4–6). Photos by Brandon Cole. Series: Wild Marine Animals! 2001, Gale LB $17.95 (1-56711-442-3). 24pp. Basic information on sharks and their distribution in the world's waters is enhanced by many large color photographs. (Rev: HBG 3/02; SLJ 3/02) [597]

22303 Davies, Nicola. *Surprising Sharks* (1–3). Illus. by James Croft. 2003, Candlewick $15.99 (0-7636-2185-4). 29pp. Shows sharks' wide diversity of size and shape and emphasizes that they have more to fear from humans than vice versa. (Rev: HBG 4/04; SLJ 10/03) [597.3]

22304 Del Prado, Dana. *Terror Below! True Shark Stories* (2–3). Illus. by Stephen Marchesi. Series: All Aboard Reading. 1997, Grosset paper $3.99 (0-448-41124-5). 47pp. Three true stories about encounters with sharks in which the victims lived to tell their stories. (Rev: SLJ 10/97) [597.31]

22305 Fowler, Allan. *The Best Way to See a Shark* (1–2). Illus. Series: Rookie Readers. 1995, Children's Book Pr. LB $19.00 (0-516-06032-5). 32pp. In a small format, this colorful book introduces sharks and their bodies, types, and habits. (Rev: BL 7/95) [596.31]

22306 Gentle, Victor, and Janet Perry. *Killer Sharks, Killer People* (2–4). Series: Sharks: An Imagination Library. 2001, Gareth Stevens LB $19.93 (0-8368-2826-7). 24pp. This slim volume presents the many ways in which sharks are useful to people, providing materials that can be used as food, medicine, tools, clothing, even weapons. Other titles in the series include *Baby Sharks*, *Chasing Sharks*, and *Shark Camouflage and Armour* (all 2001). (Rev: HBG 10/01; SLJ 6/01) [597.3]

22307 Gibbons, Gail. *Sharks* (2–4). Illus. 1992, Holiday House LB $16.95 (0-8234-0960-0). For the primary level, this account presents basic general facts as well as specific data on 12 common sharks. (Rev: BL 5/1/92; SLJ 7/92) [597.31]

22308 Harman, Amanda. *Sharks* (4–6). Illus. Series: Endangered! 1996, Benchmark LB $15.95 (0-7614-0220-9). 32pp. This account concentrates on three kinds of sharks — the great white, the whale, and the basking — and tells about the differences in their anatomies and why they are endangered. (Rev: SLJ 8/96) [597]

22309 Hirschmann, Kris. *Sharks* (4–6). Series: Nature's Predators. 2002, Gale LB $23.70 (0-7377-1005-5). 48pp. The shark is introduced in four brief chapters, with information on how they hunt and kill their prey and on how they, in turn, become prey. (Rev: BL 8/02) [597.31]

22310 Johnston, Marianne. *Sharks Past and Present* (3–5). Illus. 2000, Rosen LB $18.60 (0-8239-5206-1). 24pp. The shark's anatomy is discussed, as well as its 400-million-year history and why it has changed so little during that time. (Rev: BL 12/1/00) [567.3]

22311 Llewellyn, Claire. *The Best Book of Sharks* (3–5). Illus. by Ray Grinaway and Roger Stewart. Series: The Best Book Of. 1999, Kingfisher $12.95 (0-7534-5173-5). 31pp. A book about sharks that contains information on body structure, teeth, species, life cycle, and shark attacks. (Rev: HBG 4/00; SLJ 2/00) [597]

22312 Maestro, Betsy. *A Sea Full of Sharks* (3–6). Illus. by Giulio Maestro. 1997, Scholastic paper $5.99 (0-590-43101-3). 32pp. An informative look at this feared but fascinating creature. (Rev: BL 1/1/91; SLJ 10/90) [597.31]

22313 Mallory, Kenneth. *Swimming with Hammerhead Sharks* (3–7). Illus. Series: Scientists in the Field. 2001, Houghton Mifflin $16.00 (0-618-05543-6). 48pp. Vivid photographs and first-person narrative depict the excitement of swimming with sharks and describe this creature of the deep. (Rev: BL 4/1/01; HB 7–8/01; HBG 10/01; SLJ 7/01*) [597.3]

22314 Markle, Sandra. *Great White Sharks* (3–6). Illus. Series: Animal Predators. 2004, Carolrhoda LB $21.96 (1-57505-731-X). 40pp. Concise text and clear, full-page photographs introduce the life cycle of the great white shark and its physical characteristics, habitat, diet, and predatory behavior. (Rev: SLJ 12/04) [597]

22315 Nelson, Kristin L. *Hunting Sharks* (2–3). Series: Pull Ahead Books. 2003, Lerner LB $22.60 (0-8225-4671-X). 32pp. This fascinating book explores the physical characteristics, behavior, and life cycle of the shark and is suitable for beginning readers. (Rev: BL 11/15/03; HBG 10/03)

22316 Parker, Steve. *Sharks* (3–5). Illus. Series: What If. 1996, Millbrook LB $19.90 (0-7613-0456-8); paper $6.95 (0-7613-0471-1). 32pp. Using questions and answers, various characteristics of sharks are highlighted. (Rev: SLJ 6/96) [597.13]

22317 Pringle, Laurence. *Sharks! Strange and Wonderful* (3–5). Illus. 2001, Boyds Mills $15.95 (1-56397-863-6). 32pp. A picture book for older children that explains the shark's anatomy and habits, and introduces several different species. (Rev: BL 4/15/01; HBG 10/01; SLJ 8/01) [597.3]

22318 Raatma, Lucia. *Sharks* (2–4). Series: First Reports. 2001, Compass Point LB $21.26 (0-7565-0056-7). 48pp. Young report writers will quickly find basic information on sharks here. (Rev: SLJ 7/01) [597.3]

22319 Rockwell, Anne. *Little Shark* (K–2). Illus. by Megan Halsey. 2005, Walker $15.95 (0-8027-8955-2). Readers follow the growth and maturing of a baby blue shark in this simple text with pertinent facts presented in bubbles. (Rev: BL 2/1/04*; SLJ 4/05) [597]

22320 Sharth, Sharon. *Sharks and Rays: Underwater Predators* (3–5). Series: Animals in Order. 2002,

Watts LB $24.00 (0-531-11868-1). 48pp. After an introduction to animal classification, a variety of sharks and rays are featured, each with a color photograph and descriptive materials on appearance, habits, and habitats. (Rev: BL 3/15/02) [597]

22321 Sieswerda, Paul L. *Sharks* (5–8). Series: AnimalWays. 2001, Marshall Cavendish LB $28.50 (0-7614-1267-0). 112pp. Photographs, maps, and text introduce many species of sharks, their behavior, anatomy, and habitats. (Rev: BL 3/15/02; HBG 10/02) [597.31]

22322 Simon, Seymour. *Sharks* (2–4). Illus. 1995, HarperCollins LB $15.89 (0-06-023032-0). 32pp. Basic information about sharks, including life cycles, anatomy, and habits, is given with full-color illustrations. (Rev: BL 10/15/95; HB 11–12/95; SLJ 9/95) [597]

22323 Spilsbury, Richard. *Great White Shark* (4–6). Illus. Series: Animals Under Threat. 2004, Heinemann LB $31.43 (1-4034-4860-4). 48pp. Striking color photographs enhance this overview of the great white shark and the environmental threats it faces. (Rev: BL 8/04) [597.3]

22324 Stille, Darlene R. *I Am a Shark: The Life of a Hammerhead Shark* (K–3). Illus. by Todd Ouren. Series: I Live in the Ocean. 2004, Picture Window LB $22.60 (1-4048-0599-0). 24pp. A hammerhead shark describes its life — diet, activities, and so forth. (Rev: SLJ 1/05) [597]

22325 Strong, Mike. *Shark! The Truth Behind the Terror* (4–6). Series: High Five Reading. 2002, Capstone LB $22.60 (0-7368-9547-7). 48pp. The combination of simple text describing sharks and shark attacks plus eye-catching photographs will attract reluctant readers. (Rev: HBG 10/03; SLJ 5/03) [597.3]

22326 Troll, Ray. *Sharkabet: A Sea of Sharks from A to Z* (2–4). Illus. 2002, Graphic Arts paper $8.95 (1-55868-519-7). 40pp. From angel sharks to zebra sharks (and including some non-shark species), Troll includes many interesting shark facts in this unusual and beautifully illustrated alphabet book. (Rev: BL 9/1/02; HBG 10/02; SLJ 5/02) [597.3]

22327 Ward, Nathalie. *Do Sharks Ever . . .?* (3–4). Illus. by Tessa Morgan. 1999, Down East paper $9.95 (0-89272-438-2). Using a question-and-answer format, this book covers topics related to sharks including physical characteristics, species, life cycle, food, and mating. (Rev: SLJ 2/00) [597.31]

22328 Zoehfeld, Kathleen W. *Great White Shark: Ruler of the Sea* (PS–3). Illus. by Steven J. Petruccio. Series: Smithsonian Oceanic. 1995, Soundprints $15.95 (1-56899-122-3). 31pp. The life cycle of a great white shark, the Ruler of the Sea, which grows to 20 feet in length in adulthood. (Rev: SLJ 6/95) [597]

SHELLS

22329 Berkes, Marianne. *Seashells by the Seashore* (PS–2). Illus. by Robert Noreika. 2002, Dawn $16.95 (1-58469-035-6); paper $8.95 (1-58469-034-8). 32pp. Using rhyme and lovely illustrations, this picture book combines a lesson in counting with a lesson in seashell identification. (Rev: BL 3/1/02; HBG 10/02; SLJ check) [594.147]

22330 Burton, Jane, and Kim Taylor. *The Nature and Science of Shells* (3–6). Series: Exploring the Science of Nature. 1999, Gareth Stevens LB $14.95 (0-8368-2185-8). 32pp. The composition of shells, different varieties, their uses, and location are some of the topics discussed in this volume that contains a special activity and project section. (Rev: BL 7/99; SLJ 1/00) [594]

22331 Cassie, Brian. *Shells* (4–6). Series: National Audubon Society First Field Guides. 2000, Scholastic $17.95 (0-590-64233-2); paper $8.95 (0-590-64258-8). 160pp. With more than 450 color photographs, this attractive volume focuses on about 50 of the most easily found shells and their characteristics. (Rev: BL 8/00; SLJ 1/01) [591]

22332 Lember, Barbara Hirsch. *The Shell Book* (K–3). Photos by author. 1997, Houghton Mifflin $17.00 (0-395-72030-3). 32pp. Two-page layouts are used to introduce and describe several seashells that are found along the North American coastline. (Rev: SLJ 4/97) [594]

WHALES

22333 Arnold, Caroline. *Killer Whale* (3–5). Illus. by Richard Hewett. 1994, Morrow $14.93 (0-688-12030-X). 48pp. Using the facilities of Sea World in California, the anatomy and behavior of killer whales are examined in the wild and in captivity. (Rev: BL 9/15/94; HB 11–12/94; SLJ 10/94) [599.5]

22334 Arnold, Caroline, and Richard Hewett. *Baby Whale Rescue: The True Story of J. J.* (2–4). Illus. 1999, Troll $15.95 (0-8167-4961-2). 32pp. This real-life adventure tells how J. J., a baby gray whale, was rescued and brought back to health at Sea World in California. (Rev: BL 3/1/99; SLJ 3/99) [599.5]

22335 Bair, Diane, and Pamela Wright. *Whale Watching* (2–5). Series: Wildlife Watching. 1999, Capstone $19.93 (0-7368-0325-4). 48pp. After a general introduction to whales, the different types, and their habits, this book explains how and where whales can be seen in their natural habitats. (Rev: BL 2/15/00) [599.5]

22336 Carrick, Carol. *Whaling Days* (3–6). Illus. by David Frampton. 1993, Houghton Mifflin $15.95 (0-395-50948-3). 40pp. With an emphasis on conservation, this is a history of whaling, from ancient times to the present. (Rev: BCCB 7–8/93; BL 5/1/93*; HB 5–6/93; SLJ 5/93*) [639.2]

22337 Carwardine, Mark. *Killer Whale* (3–5). Series: Natural World. 1999, Raintree $25.69 (0-7398-1058-8). 48pp. Illustrated with brilliant color photos, this book describes the life cycle of the killer whale from being a 400-pound baby, to learning to hunt with other members of the pod, and finally reaching maturity. (Rev: BL 10/15/99; HBG 4/00) [599.5]

22338 Chrisp, Peter. *The Whalers* (4–6). Illus. 1995, Thomson Learning LB $24.26 (1-56847-421-0).

48pp. A history of whaling from ancient to modern times, with information on present-day efforts to protect whales. (Rev: BL 2/15/96; SLJ 3/96) [639.2]

22339 Collard, Sneed B. *A Whale Biologist at Work* (3–5). Illus. Series: Wildlife Conservation Society Books. 2000, Watts LB $22.50 (0-531-11786-3). 48pp. This book focuses on a marine biologist's observations of humpback and blue whales off the Pacific coast of North America. (Rev: BL 2/15/01; SLJ 3/01) [578.77]

22340 Delafosse, Claude, and Ute Fuhr. *Whales* (PS–3). Illus. Series: First Discovery. 1993, Scholastic $12.95 (0-590-47130-9). 24pp. This interactive, highly visual beginner's book introduces whales, how and where they live, and what they eat. (Rev: BL 11/15/93; HB 3–4/93; SLJ 4/94) [599.5]

22341 DuTemple, Lesley A. *Whales* (2–3). Illus. Series: Early Bird Nature Books. 1996, Lerner LB $22.60 (0-8225-3008-2). 48pp. Several kinds of whales are introduced, with descriptions of their appearance and behavior. (Rev: BL 8/96; SLJ 7/96) [599.5]

22342 Esbensen, Barbara J. *Baby Whales Drink Milk* (PS–1). Illus. by Lambert Davis. Series: Let's-Read-and-Find-Out. 1994, HarperCollins paper $4.95 (0-06-445119-4). 32pp. This book explains why whales are not fish and in so doing covers the characteristics of mammals. (Rev: BL 2/15/94; SLJ 3/94) [599.5]

22343 Fowler, Allan. *The Biggest Animal Ever* (1–2). Illus. Series: Rookie Readers. 1992, Children's Book Pr. paper $4.95 (0-516-46001-3). 32pp. With many color photos and sparse text, whales are introduced to very young readers. (Rev: BL 12/15/92; SLJ 2/93) [599.5]

22344 Gibbons, Gail. *Whales* (PS–1). Illus. 1991, Holiday House LB $16.95 (0-8234-0900-7). 32pp. The world of the fascinating whale, with good photos. (Rev: BL 10/15/91; HB 11–12/91; SLJ 12/91) [599.5]

22345 Greenaway, Theresa. *Whales* (4–7). Illus. Series: Secret World Of. 2001, Raintree LB $27.12 (0-7398-3508-4). 48pp. A look at whales' diet, habitat, and behavior, with photographs and interesting facts. (Rev: BL 10/15/01; HBG 3/02) [599.5]

22346 Greenberg, Dan. *Whales* (5–9). Illus. Series: AnimalWays. 2003, Marshall Cavendish $20.95 (0-7614-1389-8). 110pp. In addition to material on physical characteristics, behavior, habitats, and threats, Greenberg touches on the animal's roles in history, mythology, religion, and literature. (Rev: BL 3/15/03; HBG 3/03) [599.5]

22347 Greenberg, Dan. *Whales* (4–6). Illus. Series: Animals Animals. 2000, Marshall Cavendish LB $15.95 (0-7614-1167-4). 32pp. A useful book that introduces several types of whales and supplies information on their habitats, mating habits, structure, and behavior. (Rev: BL 3/15/01; HBG 3/01) [599.5]

22348 Harman, Amanda. *Whales* (4–6). Illus. Series: Endangered! 1996, Benchmark LB $22.79 (0-7614-0219-5). 32pp. Different species of whales are introduced, with coverage on why they have been hunted

to near extinction and the efforts being made to save them. (Rev: SLJ 8/96) [599.5]

22349 Hirschmann, Kris. *Humpback Whales* (4–7). Illus. Series: Creatures of the Sea. 2003, Gale LB $23.70 (0-7377-0984-7). 48pp. Hirschmann presents basic information about the humpback whale's anatomy, movement, feeding, defense, reproduction, endangered status, and means of communication, with lots of clear photographs. (Rev: BL 3/1/03) [599.5]

22350 Hodge, Deborah. *Whales: Killer Whales, Blue Whales and More* (K–3). Series: Wildlife. 1997, Kids Can $14.95 (1-55074-356-2). 32pp. In a series of double-page spreads, various whales are introduced, with material on food, habitats, and mobility. (Rev: BL 9/15/97; SLJ 11/97) [599.5]

22351 Hopkins, Ellen. *Orcas: High Seas Supermen* (3–7). Illus. 2000, Perfection Learning $13.95 (0-7807-9670-5); paper $8.95 (0-7891-5258-4). 56pp. For reluctant readers, this attractive book introduces different species of whales, their habitats, food, and methods of communication. (Rev: BL 11/1/00) [599.5]

22352 Hoyt, Erich. *Meeting the Whales: The Equinox Guide to Giants of the Deep* (5–10). Illus. 1991, Camden House paper $9.95 (0-921820-23-2). This guide to 19 whale species describes their origins and habits. Includes a discussion on whale watching and photography. (Rev: BL 8/91) [599.5]

22353 Hoyt, Erich. *Whale Rescue: Changing the Future for Endangered Wildlife* (4–6). Illus. Series: Animal Rescue. 2005, Firefly $19.95 (1-55297-601-7); paper $9.95 (1-55297-600-9). 64pp. This photo-filled book documents the threats facing the world's remaining whales, discusses whale behavior and relationship with humans, and profiles whale researchers. (Rev: BCCB 9/05; BL 8/05) [599.5]

22354 Inskipp, Carol. *Killer Whale* (4–6). Illus. Series: Animals Under Threat. 2005, Heinemann LB $20.95 (1-4034-5584-8). 48pp. The life cycle of the killer whale and threats to its survival are explored in this blend of narrative and eye-catching color photography.

22355 Kelsey, Elin. *Finding Out About Whales* (4–8). Illus. Series: Science Explorers. 1998, Owl $19.95 (1-895688-79-5); paper $9.95 (1-895688-80-9). This book discusses how information is gathered about whales and introduces five different species: blue, humpback, beluga, gray, and killer. (Rev: BL 3/1/99; SLJ 3/99) [595.5]

22356 Kurth, Linda Moore. *Keiko's Story: A Killer Whale Goes Home* (4–6). 2000, Millbrook $23.90 (0-7613-1500-4). 72pp. An informative, enjoyable read about Keiko, the killer whale who played in the movie *Free Willy* and the efforts to return him to the wild. (Rev: HBG 4/04; SLJ 9/00) [595.5]

22357 McMillan, Bruce. *Going on a Whale Watch* (PS–3). Illus. 1993, Scholastic $19.95 (0-590-72826-1). 40pp. Readers go on a whale watch and watch two children watching the whales. (Rev: BL 10/15/92; SLJ 4/93) [599.5]

22358 McNulty, Faith. *How Whales Walked into the Sea* (2–4). Illus. by Ted Rand. 1999, Scholastic

$16.95 (0-590-89830-2). 32pp. The evolution of whales from land to sea mammals is traced, with a survey of several kinds of modern whales. (Rev: BL 1/1–15/99; HB 3–4/99; HBG 9/99; SLJ 2/99) [599.5]

22359 Markle, Sandra. *Killer Whales* (3–6). Series: Animal Predators. 2004, Carolrhoda LB $25.26 (1-57505-728-X). The killer whale's skill as a hunter is emphasized in this attractive overview. (Rev: BL 12/1/04; SLJ 1/05) [599.53]

22360 Posell, Elsa. *Whales and Other Sea Mammals* (1–4). Illus. 1982, Children's Book Pr. paper $5.50 (0-516-41663-4). A description of these sea animals in large type and many color illustrations.

22361 Pringle, Laurence. *Whales! Strange and Wonderful* (3–5). Illus. by Meryl Henderson. 2003, Boyds Mills $15.95 (1-56397-439-8). 32pp. Whales and their physical and behavioral characteristics are introduced, with brief information on whaling history and current conservation efforts. (Rev: BL 3/15/03; HBG 10/03; SLJ 4/03) [599.53]

22362 Reiter, Chris. *The Blue Whale* (4–7). Series: Endangered and Threatened Animals. 2003, Enslow/MyReportLinks.com LB $19.95 (0-7660-5055-6). 48pp. Standard information on the blue whale and its endangered status is accompanied by links to Web sites for further research. (Rev: HBG 10/03; SLJ 6/03) [599.5]

22363 Short, Joan, and Bettina Bird. *Whales* (3–5). Illus. by Deborah Savin. 1997, Mondo paper $4.95 (1-57255-190-9). 31pp. Colorful illustrations are used to cover such particulars about whales as anatomy, swimming, breathing, feeding, and communication. (Rev: SLJ 9/97) [599.5]

22364 Simon, Seymour. *Killer Whales* (1–3). Series: See More Readers. 2002, North-South $13.95 (1-58717-141-4); paper $3.95 (1-58717-142-2). 32pp. Stunning photographs placed opposite a few lines of text give basic information about killer whales in this beginning reader. (Rev: BL 7/02; HBG 10/02; SLJ 4/02) [599.5]

22365 Skerry, Brian. *A Whale on Her Own: The True Story of Wilma the Beluga Whale* (3–4). Photos by author. 2000, Blackbirch LB $18.95 (1-56711-431-8). 32pp. This true story tells of the friendly relationship that developed between a diver and a beluga whale in Chedabucto Bay, Nova Scotia. (Rev: HBG 9/00; SLJ 10/00) [595.5]

22366 Smyth, Karen C. *Crystal: The Story of a Real Baby Whale* (3–6). Illus. 1986, Down East paper $10.95 (0-89272-327-0). 96pp. The first year in the life of a humpback whale. (Rev: BL 8/86; SLJ 4/87)

22367 Sobol, Richard. *Adelina's Whales* (2–5). Illus. 2003, Penguin Putnam $17.99 (0-525-47110-3). 32pp. Readers meet 10-year-old Adelina, who lives in a simple home in Baja California and each winter awaits the arrival of gray whales in the lagoon — and of the tourists who watch them; facts about the gray whale and a foreword about protectionist efforts accompany this photoessay. (Rev: BL 7/03; HBG 10/03; SLJ 9/03) [639]

22368 Stille, Darlene R. *I Am a Whale: The Life of a Humpback Whale* (K–3). Illus. by Todd Ouren.

Series: I Live in the Ocean. 2004, Picture Window LB $22.60 (1-4048-0600-8). 24pp. A humpback whale describes its life — diet, activities, and so forth. (Rev: SLJ 1/05) [599.5]

22369 Stonehouse, Bernard. *Whales: A Visual Introduction to Whales, Dolphins, and Porpoises* (4–6). Illus. Series: Animal Watch. 1998, Facts on File LB $16.95 (0-8160-3922-4). 48pp. Maps, photos, paintings, and double-page spreads are used to introduce readers to the world of cetaceans. (Rev: BL 12/1/98) [599.5]

22370 Stoops, Erik D., et al. *Whales* (3–6). Illus. 1995, Sterling $17.95 (0-8069-0566-2). 80pp. Using a question-and-answer format, this book provides basic facts about whales, including why they don't drown. (Rev: BL 12/1/95; SLJ 1/96) [599.5]

22371 Thomson, Sarah L. *Amazing Whales!* (1–3). Illus. Series: I Can Read! 2005, HarperCollins LB $16.89 (0-06-054466-X). 32pp. Simple, easy-reader text introduces blue whales, killer whales, sperm whales, dolphins, and porpoises and their characteristics, communication, and endangered status. (Rev: BL 5/15/05; SLJ 1/05) [599.5]

22372 Woog, Adam. *Killer Whales* (4–6). Series: Nature's Predators. 2002, Gale LB $23.70 (0-7377-0702-X). Woog presents the life cycle of the killer whale and describes how they hunt and kill their prey, and how, they in turn, become prey. (Rev: BL 1/1–15/02) [599.5]

Microscopes and Microbiology

22373 Bleifeld, Maurice. *Experimenting with a Microscope* (5–9). Illus. 1988, Watts paper $22.50 (0-531-10580-6). The story of the microscope plus many experiments and projects involving its use. (Rev: BL 1/15/89; BR 3–4/89; SLJ 2/89) [578]

22374 Levine, Shar, and Leslie Johnstone. *The Microscope Book* (5–8). Illus. 1997, Sterling $19.95 (0-8069-4898-1); paper $10.95 (0-8069-4899-X). An excellent introduction to microscopes, with material on parts of the microscope, lenses, how to focus and produce slides, and tips on keeping a journal. (Rev: SLJ 7/97) [502]

22375 Rogers, Kirsteen. *The Usborne Complete Book of the Microscope* (4–8). Illus. 1999, EDC paper $14.95 (0-7460-3106-8). Objects and organisms that can be viewed with a microscope are pictured and described in a series of double-page spreads, along with material on the parts and uses of different kinds of microscopes. (Rev: SLJ 7/99) [535]

22376 Selsam, Millicent E. *Greg's Microscope* (K–3). Illus. by Arnold Lobel. 1963, HarperCollins paper $3.95 (0-06-444144-X). 64pp. Greg and his parents observe small household items through a microscope.

22377 Silverstein, Alvin, et al. *Cells* (4–8). Series: Science Concepts. 2002, Millbrook LB $26.90 (0-7613-2254-X). 64pp. The functions and components of plant and animal cells are discussed along with such topics as cloning, cell fusion, and stem cell research. (Rev: BL 9/15/02; HBG 3/03) [574.87]

22378 Stewart, Gail B. *Microscopes* (4–6). Illus. Series: Kidhaven Science Library. 2003, Gale/Kidhaven LB $23.70 (0-7377-0945-6). 48pp. This brief overview chronicles the evolution of microscopes and their refinement from the primitive devices of the 16th and 17th centuries to the sophisticated electronic instruments in use today. (Rev: SLJ 1/04) [502.8]

22379 Stwertka, Eve, and Albert Stwertka. *Microscope: How to Use It and Enjoy It* (5–9). Illus. 1989, Silver Burdett LB $9.95 (0-671-63705-3); paper $4.95 (0-671-67060-3). A fine introduction that covers such topics as the parts of the microscope, techniques for use, and how to prepare slides. (Rev: BL 3/1/89; BR 9–10/89; SLJ 4/89) [502.8]

22380 Thomas, Peggy. *Bacteria and Viruses* (5–8). Illus. Series: Lucent Library of Science and Technology. 2005, Gale/Lucent LB $26.96 (1-59018-438-6). 112pp. Introduces the scientists who discovered bacteria and viruses and how we fight ones that harm us and attempt to use others to our benefit.

22381 Walker, Richard. *Microscopic Life* (4–8). Illus. Series: Kingfisher Knowledge. 2004, Kingfisher $11.95 (0-7534-5778-4). 63pp. A well-illustrated look at the tiniest living things — bacteria, viruses, mites, fungi, and molds, for example — and how we study them and attempt to use them to our benefit. (Rev: SLJ 1/05) [579]

Oceanography

GENERAL

22382 Berger, Melvin, and Gilda Berger. *What Makes an Ocean Wave? Questions and Answers About Oceans and Ocean Life* (3–6). Illus. 2001, Scholastic $14.95 (0-439-09588-3). 48pp. In question-and-answer format, this title tackles topics of interest both to browsers and report writers. (Rev: BL 7/01; HBG 10/01) [551.46]

22383 Burleigh, Robert, adapt. *The Sea: Exploring Life on an Ocean Planet* (5–12). Photos by Philip Plisson. Illus. by Emmanuel Cerisier. 2003, Abrams $14.95 (0-8109-4591-6). 79pp. The power, economic importance, and fragility of the sea are shown in this oversized photoessay with an ecological emphasis. (Rev: HBG 4/04; SLJ 12/03) [551]

22384 Castaldo, Nancy F. *Oceans: An Activity Guide for Ages 6–9* (3–5). Illus. 2002, Chicago Review paper $14.95 (1-55652-443-9). 134pp. All about the world's oceans, including their plant and animal life, folklore, and currents and tides, with related crafts and experiments. (Rev: BL 5/15/02; SLJ 3/02) [372.3]

22385 Chambers, Catherine. *Oceans and Seas* (3–5). Series: Mapping Earthforms. 2000, Heinemann LB $14.95 (1-57572-526-6). 32pp. A basic overview that describes the characteristics of oceans and seas, life within them, and how environmental factors like global warming affect them. (Rev: HBG 3/01; SLJ 8/00) [551.46]

22386 Cobb, Allan B. *Super Science Projects About Oceans* (4–7). Series: Psyched for Science. 2000, Rosen LB $23.95 (0-8239-3174-9). 48pp. Although the format is unattractive, this book contains six fine experiments that explore concepts involving the ocean. (Rev: SLJ 7/00) [551.46]

22387 Cole, Joanna. *The Magic School Bus on the Ocean Floor* (3–5). Illus. by Bruce Degen. 1992, Scholastic $15.95 (0-590-41430-5). 48pp. Miss Frizzle's class takes a class trip down to the ocean floor to study the animals and plants that live there. (Rev: BCCB 12/92; BL 6/15/92; SLJ 8/92*) [591.92]

22388 Davies, Nicola. *Oceans and Seas* (K–3). Series: Kingfisher Young Knowledge. 2004, Houghton Mifflin $8.95 (0-7534-5758-X). 48pp. Attractive double-page spreads with many illustrations and diagrams present basic information on salt water, tides, and marine plants and animals and the dangers they face. (Rev: BL 9/1/04) [551.46]

22389 Ganeri, Anita. *I Wonder Why the Sea Is Salty: And Other Questions About the Oceans* (PS–2). Illus. by Tony Kenyon, et al. Series: I Wonder Why. 1995, Kingfisher $11.95 (1-85697-549-5); paper $6.95 (0-85697-664-5). 32pp. Amazing and commonplace facts about marine life are presented in a question-and-answer format with entertaining drawings. (Rev: SLJ 7/95) [551.46]

22390 Gibbons, Gail. *Exploring the Deep, Dark Sea* (3–5). Illus. 1999, Little, Brown $14.95 (0-316-30945-1). 32pp. This book describes in pictures and text each level or zone on the way to the ocean's bottom, with additional material on the history of deep sea diving. (Rev: BCCB 4/99; BL 4/1/99; HB 3–4/99; HBG 9/99; SLJ 6/99) [551.46]

22391 Gray, Samantha. *Ocean* (3–5). Illus. Series: Eye Wonder. 2001, DK LB $17.95 (0-7894-8180-4); paper $9.95 (0-7894-7852-8). 48pp. The ocean, marine animals, and marine research are among the topics tackled in this fact-filled book. (Rev: BL 12/1/01; HBG 3/02) [591.77]

22392 Harrison, David L. *Oceans: The Vast, Mysterious Deep* (2–3). Illus. by Cheryl Nathan. Series: Earthworks. 2003, Boyds Mills $15.95 (1-59078-018-3). 32pp. The oceans, their movement, and the life they support are shown in bright illustrations and brief, informative text. (Rev: BL 1/1–15/04; HBG 4/04; SLJ 1/04) [577.7]

22393 Hoff, Mary, and Mary M. Rodgers. *Our Endangered Planet: Oceans* (4–6). Illus. Series: Our Endangered Planet. 1992, Lerner LB $22.60 (0-8225-2505-4); paper $8.95 (0-8225-9628-8). 72pp. This volume gives a good overview of oceans and the major environmental concerns they present. (Rev: BL 5/15/92; SLJ 7/92) [551.46]

22394 Kraske, Robert. *The Voyager's Stone* (4–6). Illus. 1995, Orchard LB $16.99 (0-531-08740-9). 96pp. The framework of a message in a bottle cast into the sea is used to introduce oceanography, currents, and sea life. (Rev: BCCB 3/95; BL 3/1/95; SLJ 3/95) [551.46]

22395 Lambert, David. *The Kingfisher Young People's Book of Oceans* (4–6). Illus. 1997, Kingfisher $21.95 (0-7534-5098-4). 95pp. A colorful look at oceans and marine biology is given in a series of double-page spreads. (Rev: HBG 3/98; SLJ 3/98) [551.46]

22396 Lambert, David. *The Mediterranean Sea* (4–6). Illus. Series: Seas and Oceans. 1997, Raintree LB $24.26 (0-8172-4512-X). 48pp. Describes the role of the Mediterranean throughout history, its features and formations, and the plant and animal life it supports. (Rev: BL 7/97) [551.46]

22397 Lambert, David. *The Pacific Ocean* (4–6). Illus. Series: Seas and Oceans. 1996, Raintree LB $27.12 (0-8172-4507-3). 48pp. Ocean life, currents, the formation of islands, and pollution are a few of the topics discussed in this introduction to the Pacific Ocean. (Rev: BL 1/1–15/97) [551.46]

22398 Lambert, David. *Seas and Oceans* (5–8). Illus. 1988, Silver Burdett LB $12.95 (0-382-09503-0). 48pp. Covers waves, tides, currents, underwater exploration, and ocean life. (Rev: BL 4/1/88) [551.46]

22399 Littlefield, Cindy A. *Awesome Ocean Science!* (3–5). Illus. by Sarah Rakitin. Series: Kids Can. 2003, Williamson paper $12.95 (1-885593-71-6). 120pp. This informative book looks at the water cycle, the oceans and their animal life, and at conservation, and provides simple projects that illustrate or reinforce some of the basic concepts. (Rev: BL 1/1–15/03; SLJ 5/03) [551.46]

22400 Markle, Sandra. *Down, Down, Down in the Ocean* (3–5). Illus. by Bob Marstall. 1999, Walker LB $17.85 (0-8027-8655-3). 32pp. This is a dramatic journey through the different levels of life in the ocean told in double-page spreads. (Rev: HBG 4/00; SLJ 11/99) [551.46]

22401 Morgan, Nina. *The Caribbean and the Gulf of Mexico* (4–6). Illus. Series: Seas and Oceans. 1996, Raintree LB $27.12 (0-8172-4508-1). 48pp. For these two bodies of water, material is presented on such topics as ocean life, shipping, tourism, currents, and people. (Rev: BL 1/1–15/97) [917.29]

22402 Morgan, Nina. *The North Sea and the Baltic Sea* (4–6). Illus. Series: Seas and Oceans. 1996, Raintree LB $27.12 (0-8172-4510-3). 48pp. These two European bodies of water are introduced, with coverage on their importance, history, shipping routes, and plant and animal life. (Rev: BL 1/1–15/97) [551.46]

22403 Penny, Malcolm. *The Indian Ocean* (4–6). Illus. Series: Seas and Oceans. 1997, Raintree LB $24.26 (0-8172-4514-6). 48pp. The history of the world's third-largest ocean, the migration and exploration paths that people took from Europe to Asia, and the marine life it supports. (Rev: BL 7/97) [551.46]

22404 Pyers, Greg. *Ocean Explorer* (2–4). Illus. Series: Habitat Explorer. 2004, Raintree LB $18.45 (1-4109-0510-1). 32pp. This photo-filled exploration of oceans looks at the plants and animals found there, plus environmental threats posed by pollution and development.

22405 Ricciuti, Edward R. *Ocean* (4–6). Illus. Series: Biomes of the World. 1995, Marshall Cavendish LB $25.64 (0-7614-0079-6). 64pp. With clear explanations and full-color photos, the world's

ocean environment and its animal and plant life are introduced. (Rev: BL 12/15/95) [551.46]

22406 Robinson, W. Wright. *Incredible Facts About the Ocean: The Land Below, the Life Within*, Vol. 2 (4–8). Illus. 1987, Macmillan LB $13.95 (0-87518-358-1). 120pp. Maps, diagrams, color photographs, and a glossary add to this detailed explanation. (Rev: BL 11/1/87; SLJ 10/87)

22407 Sabin, Louis. *Wonders of the Sea* (1–3). Illus. by Bert Dodson. 1982, Troll paper $3.50 (0-89375-579-6). 32pp. An easy-to-read account for primary grades that covers basic topics.

22408 Sauvain, Philip. *Oceans* (3–5). Illus. Series: Geography Detectives. 1997, Carolrhoda LB $19.93 (1-57505-043-9). 32pp. This account identifies and describes the world's oceans, explains the saltwater ecosystem, and explores coastlines, the ocean floor, tides, and marine plant and animal life. (Rev: BL 8/97; SLJ 1/98) [551.46]

22409 Sayre, April Pulley. *Ocean* (4–7). Illus. Series: Exploring Earth's Biomes. 1996, Twenty-First Century LB $25.90 (0-8050-4084-6). 80pp. An introduction to the nature and composition of oceans and the animal and plant life that they support. (Rev: BL 10/15/96; SLJ 1/97) [551.46]

22410 *Scholastic Atlas of Oceans* (4–7). Illus. 2004, Scholastic $18.95 (0-439-56128-0). 96pp. Full of illustrations, diagrams, and feature sidebars, this attractive, information-packed volume looks at the five oceans and five major seas and their marine life and vulnerability to human activities. (Rev: SLJ 4/05) [551.46]

22411 Simon, Seymour. *How to Be an Ocean Scientist in Your Own Home* (5–8). Illus. 1988, HarperCollins $15.89 (0-397-32292-5). A great deal of information about oceans and life in them is imparted through a series of simple experiments and activities. (Rev: BCCB 11/88; BL 10/1/88) [551.46]

22412 Stille, Darlene R. *Oceans* (2–4). Series: True Books. 1999, Children's Book Pr. LB $21.50 (0-516-21510-8). 48pp. Oceans and the life found in them are introduced briefly in this book that is heavily illustrated with color photos. (Rev: BL 10/15/99) [591.92]

22413 Stone, Lynn. *Oceans* (1–3). Illus. Series: Biomes of North America. 2003, Rourke $20.64 (1-58952-686-4). 24pp. For young researchers, this is an excellent introduction to this biome, with clear, simple text, photographs, and maps. (Rev: BL 10/15/03) [577.7]

22414 Taylor, Leighton. *The Atlantic Ocean* (4–7). Series: Life in the Sea. 1999, Blackbirch LB $26.19 (1-56711-246-3). 48pp. In 20 short chapters, this book introduces the Atlantic Ocean and life forms found in it at various levels. (Rev: HBG 4/00; SLJ 2/00) [551.46]

22415 Taylor, Leighton. *The Mediterranean Sea* (4–7). Series: Life in the Sea. 1999, Blackbirch LB $26.19 (1-56711-247-1). 48pp. This account introduces the Mediterranean Sea, its geography, life forms, uses, and pollution. (Rev: HBG 4/00; SLJ 2/00) [551.46]

1203

22416 Twist, Clint. *Seas and Oceans* (5–8). Illus. Series: Ecology Watch. 1991, Macmillan LB $13.95 (0-87518-491-X). 45pp. Ethical issues are discussed in this attractive, oversize volume dealing with problems of the earth's seas and oceans. (Rev: BL 3/1/92) [333.95]

22417 VanCleave, Janice. *Janice VanCleave's Oceans for Every Kid: Easy Activities That Make Learning Science Fun* (5–7). Illus. Series: Science for Every Kid. 1996, Wiley paper $12.95 (0-471-12453-2). 256pp. This book gives good background information about oceans plus a number of entertaining and instructive projects and activities. (Rev: BL 4/15/96; SLJ 5/96) [551.46]

22418 Vieira, Linda. *The Seven Seas: Exploring the World Ocean* (2–5). Illus. by Higgins Bond. 2003, Walker LB $17.85 (0-8027-8834-3). Double-page chapters present information on the history of the oceans, their importance in our life, and the environmental threats they face. (Rev: HBG 10/03; SLJ 7/03) [910]

22419 Vogel, Carole G. *Dangerous Crossings* (5–8). Illus. Series: The Restless Sea. 2003, Watts LB $29.50 (0-531-12325-1); paper $12.95 (0-531-16679-1). 79pp. Ranging widely from tales of endurance at sea to pirates and problems created by global warming, this is an arresting account. (Rev: BL 1/1/04; SLJ 1/04) [910.4]

22420 Vogel, Carole G. *Human Impact* (5–9). Series: The Restless Sea. 2003, Watts LB $29.50 (0-531-12323-5); paper $12.95 (0-531-16680-5). 95pp. An examination of how mankind is endangering the sea and its creatures through activities including coastal development, global warming, and oil spills. (Rev: SLJ 3/04) [333.91]

22421 Waterlow, Julia. *The Atlantic Ocean* (4–6). Illus. Series: Seas and Oceans. 1996, Raintree LB $27.12 (0-8172-4509-X). 48pp. Such topics as geography, currents, history, and economic and recreational importance are covered in relation to the Atlantic Ocean. (Rev: BL 1/1–15/97) [551.46]

22422 Waterlow, Julia. *The Red Sea and the Arabian Gulf* (4–6). Illus. Series: Seas and Oceans. 1997, Raintree LB $27.12 (0-8172-4515-4). 48pp. An overview of the history and importance of these bodies of water, with information on the coral reefs and animals of the Red Sea and oil reserves of the Arabian Gulf. (Rev: BL 7/97) [551.46]

22423 Zubrowski, Bernie. *Making Waves: Finding Out About Rhythmic Motion* (4–8). Illus. Series: Boston Children's Museum Activity Books. 1994, Morrow LB $14.89 (0-688-11787-2). 96pp. Step-by-step instructions are given for creating a wave machine, plus activities that show waves in various media. (Rev: BL 7/94; SLJ 8/94) [532]

COMMERCIAL FISHING

22424 Love, Ann, and Jane Drake. *Fishing* (2–4). Illus. by Pat Cupples. Series: America at Work. 1999, Kids Can $12.95 (1-55074-457-7). 31pp. This book introduces the fishing industry on both coasts by visiting a fish farm, taking a voyage on a trawler,

and studying the life cycles and habitats of various fish. (Rev: HBG 4/00; SLJ 11/99) [639]

CURRENTS, TIDES, AND WAVES

22425 Lampton, Christopher. *Tidal Wave* (4–6). Illus. Series: Disaster! 1992, Houghton Mifflin paper $5.70 (0-395-62464-9). 40pp. This explanation of the causes and effects of tidal waves includes many color photos and detailed descriptions of important tidal-wave disasters of the past. (Rev: BL 3/15/92) [363.3]

22426 Vogel, Carole G. *Savage Waters* (5–8). Illus. Series: The Restless Sea. 2003, Watts LB $29.50 (0-531-12321-9); paper $12.95 (0-531-16682-1). 79pp. An entertaining and attractive discussion of the origins of the world's oceans and seas and the forces that influence waves, tides, and tsunamis. Also use *Shifting Shores* (2003). (Rev: BL 1/1/04; SLJ 1/04) [551.46]

SEASHORES AND TIDAL POOLS

22427 Arnosky, Jim. *Beach Combing: Exploring the Seashore* (PS–2). 2004, Penguin Putnam $15.99 (0-525-47104-9). 32pp. Arnosky explores the wonders of a tropical beach and its wildlife. (Rev: BL 7/04; SLJ 7/04) [578.769]

22428 Arnosky, Jim. *Following the Coast* (3–5). Illus. 2004, HarperCollins $15.99 (0-688-17117-6). 32pp. The life and landmarks of the salt marshes of the Atlantic Coast, from Florida northward to Delaware, are the focus of this attractive blend of narrative and artwork. (Rev: BL 2/15/04; SLJ 5/04) [591.769]

22429 Bair, Diane, and Pamela Wright. *Tide Pool Life Watching* (2–5). Illus. Series: Wildlife Watching. 1999, Capstone $19.93 (0-7368-0324-6). 48pp. As well as introducing the flora and fauna in tidal pools, this book explains how and when to observe these life forms in their natural habitat. (Rev: BL 2/15/00) [591.769]

22430 Bredeson, Carmen. *Tide Pools* (3–6). Illus. Series: First Books. 1999, Watts LB $22.00 (0-531-20368-9). 64pp. A discussion of tide pools, how they are formed, and the plant and animal life found there. (Rev: BL 5/1/99; HBG 9/99) [577.69]

22431 Brenner, Barbara. *One Small Place by the Sea* (2–4). Illus. by Tom Leonard. 2004, HarperCollins $15.99 (0-688-17182-6). 32pp. The abundant life in a tidal pool is explored in accessible text and realistic illustrations. (Rev: BL 3/1/04; SLJ 4/04) [577.69]

22432 Cohat, Elisabeth. *The Seashore* (PS–2). Illus. by Pierre de Hugo. Series: First Discovery. 1995, Scholastic $12.95 (0-590-20303-7). A spiral-bound book with transparencies that show the many organisms found in tidal pools. (Rev: SLJ 9/95) [591]

22433 Cooper, Ann. *Along the Seashore* (3–5). Illus. Series: Wild Wonders. 1997, Roberts Rinehart paper $9.95 (1-57098-121-2). 46pp. A little book that introduces animals associated with seas and seashores: the seal, cormorant, hermit crab, raccoon, osprey, sea star, dolphin, gull, and sea trout. (Rev: BL 7/97; SLJ 8/97) [577.7]

22434 Fleisher, Paul. *Tide Pool* (3–5). Illus. Series: Webs of Life. 1997, Marshall Cavendish LB $22.79 (0-7614-0431-7). 40pp. This wet-and-dry environment is introduced, along with the animals and plants that thrive under conditions where flooding occurs twice a day. (Rev: BL 2/15/98; HBG 3/98; SLJ 4/98) [574.5]

22435 Giesecke, Ernestine. *Seashore Plants* (K–3). Illus. Series: Heinemann First Library. 1999, Heinemann $13.95 (1-57572-828-1). 32pp. Ten plants, six from sandy shores such as sea oats and eelgrass and four from rocky shores including kelp and rock weed, are introduced in full-page photos and a brief text. (Rev: BL 6/1–15/99; SLJ 8/99) [581.769]

22436 Hunter, Anne. *What's in the Tide Pool?* (K–2). Illus. 2000, Houghton Mifflin $4.95 (0-618-01510-8). 32pp. Ten animals that live in tidal pools, such as the sea anemone, herring gull, hermit crab, and barnacle, are introduced in this little book. (Rev: BL 9/15/00; HBG 3/01) [578.769]

22437 Malnig, Anita. *Where the Waves Break: Life at the Edge of the Sea* (3–5). Illus. 1985, Carolrhoda LB $19.93 (0-87614-226-9); Lerner paper $7.95 (0-87614-477-6). 48pp. An introduction to life at the sea's edge, including descriptions of starfish, brittle stars, snails, and seaweed. (Rev: BL 6/1/85; HB 9–10/85; SLJ 5/85)

22438 Paul, Tessa. *By the Seashore* (2–5). Illus. Series: Animal Trackers. 1997, Crabtree LB $20.60 (0-86505-587-4); paper $7.95 (0-86505-595-5). 32pp. Ten creatures found at the seashore are introduced and identified by the evidence they leave behind, like prints, holes, nests, and hair or fur. (Rev: HBG 3/98; SLJ 10/97) [591]

22439 Pipes, Rose. *Coasts and Shores* (2–4). Series: World Habitats. 1998, Raintree LB $15.98 (0-8172-5008-5). 32pp. This book describes the physical features of coastal regions with material on climates, wildlife, human interaction, and the need for protection. (Rev: BL 3/15/99; HBG 3/99) [591]

22440 Pringle, Laurence. *Come to the Ocean's Edge* (K–3). Illus. by Michael Chesworth. 2003, Boyds Mills $15.95 (1-56397-779-6). 32pp. Watercolor paintings depict the shoreline and the wildlife found there in daytime and at night. (Rev: BL 2/1/04; HBG 4/04; SLJ 10/03) [577.7]

22441 Sayre, April Pulley. *Seashore* (4–7). Illus. Series: Exploring Earth's Biomes. 1996, Twenty-First Century LB $25.90 (0-8050-4085-4). 80pp. The composition of seashores and the life that they support are covered in this nicely illustrated account. (Rev: BL 10/15/96; SLJ 1/97) [574.5]

22442 Silverstein, Alvin, and Virginia Silverstein. *Life in a Tidal Pool* (4–6). Illus. by Pamela Carroll and Walter Carroll. 1990, Little, Brown $14.95 (0-316-79120-2). 60pp. The tidal pool habitat is explored. (Rev: SLJ 10/90) [574]

22443 Theodorou, Rod. *Along the Seashore* (2–4). Series: Amazing Journeys. 2000, Heinemann LB $15.95 (1-57572-483-9). 32pp. This brief overview of seashores focuses on several specific plants and

animals found there. (Rev: HBG 3/01; SLJ 7/00) [591]

22444 Wright-Frierson, Virginia. *An Island Scrapbook: Dawn to Dusk on a Barrier Island* (2–5). Illus. 1998, Simon & Schuster $16.00 (0-689-81563-8). 40pp. The author and her young daughter have recorded in text and drawings the flora and fauna of a barrier island off the coast of Virginia. (Rev: BL 8/98; HBG 3/99; SLJ 8/98) [508.75]

22445 Zim, Herbert S., and Lester Ingle. *Seashores* (5–8). Illus. 1991, Western $21.27 (0-307-64496-0). 160pp. This is a guide to animals and plants found along the beaches.

UNDERWATER EXPLORATION

22446 Ballard, Robert D. *Exploring the Titanic* (4–8). Illus. by Ken Marschall. 1988, Scholastic $15.95 (0-590-41953-6). A compelling description of the undersea search for the ocean liner. (Rev: BCCB 10/88; BL 1/15/89; HB 5–6/89; SLJ 11/88) [363.1]

22447 Collard, Sneed B., III. *The Deep-Sea Floor* (2–4). Illus. by Gregory Wenzel. 2003, Charlesbridge $16.95 (1-57091-402-8); paper $6.95 (1-57091-403-6). 32pp. A look at the amazing discoveries gleaned from the exploration of the deep-sea floor, including plant and animal life and geologic finds, with watercolor illustrations. (Rev: BL 2/1/03; HBG 10/03; SLJ 7/03) [591.779]

22448 Gibbons, Gail. *Sunken Treasure* (2–5). Illus. 1988, HarperCollins LB $15.89 (0-690-04736-3); paper $6.95 (0-06-446097-5). 32pp. Searching for the cargo of the Atocha, a Spanish galleon sunk off Florida in 1622. (Rev: BCCB 10/88; BL 10/15/88; HB 9–10/88)

22449 Harris, Nicholas. *The Incredible Journey to the Depths of the Ocean: An Epic Voyage from the Seashore to the Bottom of the Deepest Trench* (4–6). Illus. 2000, Bedrick $18.95 (0-87226-601-X). 32pp. Using double-page spreads, this book starts with a seashore and coral reef and moves down through six depths to the deepest ocean floor. (Rev: BL 3/15/01; HBG 3/01) [551.46]

22450 Malam, John. *Titanic: Shipwrecks and Sunken Treasure* (5–9). Illus. 2003, DK $14.99 (0-7894-9704-2); paper $5.99 (0-7894-9225-3). 96pp. Disasters that befell all types of seagoing vessels, tales of pirates and treasures, survivor stories, and details of salvaging techniques are all covered in this colorful and dramatic volume. (Rev: HBG 10/03; SLJ 9/03) [904]

22451 Matsen, Brad. *The Incredible Record-Setting Deep-Sea Dive of the Bathysphere* (4–6). Series: Incredible Deep-Sea Adventures. 2003, Enslow LB $18.95 (0-7660-2188-2). 48pp. An attractive look at early bathyspheres and undersea discoveries. Also use *The Incredible Submersible Alvin Discovers a Strange Deep-Sea World* (2003), about more recent explorations. (Rev: HBG 4/04; SLJ 1/04) [551.46]

22452 Pitkin, Linda. *Journey Under the Sea* (3–6). Illus. 2003, Oxford $18.95 (0-19-521972-4). 48pp. In words and pictures, marine photographer Pitkin paints a vivid portrait of her visit to coral reefs off the coast of Indonesia. (Rev: BL 2/15/04; HBG 4/04) [578]

22453 Platt, Richard. *Shipwreck* (4–9). Series: Eyewitness Books. 1997, Knopf LB $20.99 (0-679-98569-X). An overview of the causes and consequences of the world's most famous maritime disasters. (Rev: BL 12/15/97; BR 1–2/98) [387.2]

22454 Sloan, Frank. *Titanic*. Rev. ed. (5–8). 1998, Raintree $19.98 (0-8172-4091-8). This thorough account of the *Titanic* and its sinking covers the structure of the ship, why it sank, the inquiries that followed, the many attempts to find and explore the wreckage, and movies and plays inspired by it. (Rev: BL 9/1/98; HBG 9/99; SLJ 2/99) [910]

22455 Sullivan, George. *To the Bottom of the Sea: The Exploration of Exotic Life, the Titanic, and Other Secrets of the Oceans* (4–6). Illus. 1999, Twenty-First Century LB $24.90 (0-7613-0352-9). 80pp. A history of underwater exploration with fascinating information on contemporary accomplishments and discoveries such as locating the *Titanic*. (Rev: BL 10/1/99; HBG 4/00; SLJ 10/99) [551.46]

22456 *Sunk! Exploring Underwater Archaeology* (5–8). Series: Buried Worlds. 1994, Lerner LB $28.75 (0-8225-3205-0). Provides a general overview of how archaeologists interpret underwater discoveries to learn about aspects of ancient trade, commerce, and history. (Rev: BL 10/15/94; SLJ 9/94) [930.1]

Pets

GENERAL AND MISCELLANEOUS

22457 Altman, Linda Jacobs. *Parrots* (4–6). Illus. Series: Perfect Pets. 2000, Marshall Cavendish LB $15.95 (0-7614-1102-X). 32pp. Full-color photographs and accessible text introduce parrots, their physical characteristics, and how to care for them. (Rev: BL 3/15/01; HBG 3/01) [636.6]

22458 Barnes, Julia. *101 Facts About Terrarium Pets* (2–4). Series: 101 Facts About Pets. 2002, Gareth Stevens LB $21.26 (0-8368-3021-0). 32pp. Facts about snakes, lizards, salamanders, and other animals will help readers decide if they will make a suitable pet. (Rev: HBG 10/02; SLJ 8/02)

22459 Curran, Wanda L. *Your Guinea Pig: A Kid's Guide to Raising and Showing* (4–6). Illus. 1995, Storey paper $14.95 (0-88266-889-7). 160pp. Topics in this book on how to keep guinea pigs as pets include selecting, feeding, mating, and showing. (Rev: BL 9/1/95) [636]

22460 Davis, Kathryn Gibbs. *Wacky White House Pets* (2–4). Illus. by David Johnson. 2004, Scholastic LB $16.95 (0-439-44373-3). 48pp. Presidential pets have included John Quincy Adam's alligator, Reagan's First Fish, and Coolidge's raccoon; all White House occupants are mentioned in the appendix to this entertaining book. (Rev: BL 10/1/04; SLJ 11/04) [636.088]

22461 Engfer, LeeAnne. *My Pet Lizards* (3–6). Photos by Andy King. Series: All About Pets. 1999, Lerner LB $16.95 (0-8225-2263-2). 64pp. An unusual book that deals with lizards as pets with material on how to acquire them, care for them, feed them, handle them, and detect health problems. (Rev: HBG 9/99; SLJ 8/99) [597.95]

22462 Ganeri, Anita. *Guinea Pigs* (1–3). Series: A Pet's Life. 2003, Heinemann LB $22.79 (1-4034-3996-6). 32pp. All about pet guinea pigs and how to care for them, with detailed information on their physiology and life cycle. (Rev: SLJ 6/04) [636.9]

22463 Ganeri, Anita. *Hamsters* (1–3). Series: A Pet's Life. 2003, Heinemann LB $22.79 (1-4034-3997-4). 32pp. Presents clear information on hamsters and their physiology, habits, and care and feeding; suitable for beginning readers. (Rev: SLJ 6/04) [636.9]

22464 Ganeri, Anita. *Rabbits* (1–3). Series: A Pet's Life. 2003, Heinemann LB $22.79 (1-4034-3995-8). 32pp. A book on keeping rabbits as pets, with help on their care and feeding, habits, and physiology. (Rev: SLJ 6/04) [636.9]

22465 Gelman, Amy. *My Pet Ferrets* (2–5). Photos by Andy King. Series: All About Pets. 2000, Lerner LB $22.60 (0-8225-2264-0). 64pp. The care and feeding of ferrets are covered in this book that also gives details on grooming, bathing, and even litter-box training. (Rev: BL 1/1–15/01; HBG 3/01; SLJ 11/00) [636]

22466 Gibbons, Gail. *Rabbits, Rabbits and More Rabbits!* (K–3). Illus. 2000, Holiday House $16.95 (0-8234-1486-8). 32pp. Simple text and colored drawings introduce different types of rabbits, their physical characteristics, habits, behavior, and how to care for them. (Rev: BCCB 3/00; BL 1/1–15/00; HBG 9/00; SLJ 3/00) [636.9]

22467 Gutman, Bill. *Adopting Pets: How to Choose Your New Best Friend* (3–6). Illus. by Anne Canevari Green. Series: Pet Friends. 2001, Millbrook LB $22.90 (0-7613-1863-1). 64pp. This book gives special tips on choosing a pet with attention to topics such as the kind of home and food it will need and the attention required. (Rev: BCCB 3/01; BL 3/1/01; HBG 10/01) [636]

22468 Gutman, Bill. *Becoming Best Friends with Your Hamster, Guinea Pig, or Rabbit* (3–6). Illus. 1997, Millbrook LB $21.90 (0-7613-0201-8). 64pp. Practical advice on the care of these pets, with tips on how to make their lives comfortable. (Rev: BCCB 6/97; BL 8/97; SLJ 7/97) [636]

22469 Gutman, Bill. *Becoming Best Friends with Your Iguana, Snake, or Turtle* (3–6). Illus. by Anne Canevari Green. Series: Pet Friends. 2001, Millbrook LB $22.90 (0-7613-1862-3). 64pp. Explains the special needs of reptiles that are kept as pets. (Rev: BL 3/1/01; HBG 10/01) [636]

22470 Hamilton, Lynn. *Caring for Your Bird* (3–5). Illus. 2002, Weigl LB $24.95 (1-59036-037-0). 32pp. A guide to choosing and looking after a feathered pet with information on different avian breeds. (Rev: BL 12/1/02; HBG 3/03) [636.6]

22471 Hansen, Elvig. *Guinea Pig* (3–6). Illus. 1992, Carolrhoda LB $23.93 (0-87614-681-7). 48pp. Charming, informative photos explore the life and care of guinea pigs. (Rev: BL 6/15/92; SLJ 8/92) [636]

22472 Hansen, Rosanna. *Animal Rescuers: A Chapter Book* (2–5). Series: True Tales. 2003, Children's Pr. LB $21.50 (0-516-22915-X). 48pp. Heroic animals featured in these four tales include the guide dog named Salty that led his owner from the World Trade Center on 9/11. (Rev: SLJ 1/04) [636.088]

22473 Hernandez-Divers, Sonia. *Geckos* (4–8). Illus. Series: Keeping Unusual Pets. 2003, Heinemann LB $25.64 (1-40340-282-5). 48pp. An appealing and informative introduction to geckos that provides much practical guidance on actually keeping one as a pet. Also use *Chinchillas, Ferrets, Snakes* (all 2002), and *Rats* (2003). (Rev: BL 3/15/03; HBG 10/03; SLJ 4/03) [639.3]

22474 Hinds, Kathryn. *Hamsters and Gerbils* (4–6). Illus. Series: Perfect Pets. 2000, Marshall Cavendish LB $15.95 (0-7614-1104-6). 32pp. Gives tips on housing, feeding, training, and keeping these pets safe. (Rev: BL 3/15/01; HBG 3/01) [636]

22475 Hinds, Kathryn. *Rabbits* (2–5). Series: Perfect Pets. 1998, Benchmark LB $15.95 (0-7614-0793-6). 32pp. The physical characteristics of rabbits, how they live, and tips on caring for them are given in this simple book with color photos. (Rev: HBG 9/99; SLJ 5/99) [636.932]

22476 Horton-Bussey, Claire. *101 Facts About Ferrets* (2–4). Series: 101 Facts About Pets. 2002, Gareth Stevens LB $21.26 (0-8368-3016-4). 32pp. Readers learn about the history of ferrets and how to care for them and train them. (Rev: HBG 10/02; SLJ 8/02) [636]

22477 Kent, Deborah. *Animal Helpers for the Disabled* (5–7). Illus. Series: Watts Library: Disabilities. 2003, Watts LB $24.00 (0-531-12017-1); paper $8.95 (0-531-16663-5). 64pp. Stories of animal accomplishments draw readers into this account, which covers the history of service animals, the kinds of animals used, and the training they undergo. (Rev: BL 10/15/03; LMC 11–12/03; SLJ 9/03) [636.08]

22478 McKay, Sindy. *About Pets* (K–2). Series: We Both Read. 2003, Treasure Bay $7.99 (1-891327-41-0). 40pp. Designed to be read together by a child and an adult, this book looks at what's involved in caring for a pet. (Rev: HBG 10/03; SLJ 7/03) [636.088]

22479 McNicholas, June. *Ferrets* (3–6). Series: Keeping Unusual Pets. 2002, Heinemann LB $24.22 (1-4034-0281-7). 48pp. A pratical, no-nonsense guide to the choice of and responsibilities of caring for such a pet. (Rev: HBG 10/03; SLJ 4/03) [636.9]

22480 Miller, Michaela. *Guinea Pigs* (K–2). Series: Pets. 1997, Heinemann LB $18.50 (1-57572-575-4). 24pp. A simple introduction to guinea pigs, their care and feeding, and how to treat them as pets. (Rev: SLJ 4/98) [636]

22481 Nelson, Robin. *Pet Frog* (PS). Series: Classroom Pets. 2002, Lerner LB $15.93 (0-8225-1271-8). 24pp. With only a few sentences of text and full-page color illustrations, this book introduces the frog as a pet and describes its care and feeding. Also use *Pet Guinea Pig, Pet Hamster,* and *Pet Hermit*

Crab (all 2002). (Rev: BL 10/15/02; HBG 3/03; SLJ 10/02) [597.8]

22482 Nelson, Robin. *Pet Hamster* (PS–K). Illus. Series: Classroom Pets. 2002, Lerner LB $15.93 (0-8225-1269-6). 24pp. A preschooler's introduction to the care and feeding of classroom hamsters, with relevant facts, a glossary, and an index. Also use *Pet Guinea Pig* (2002). (Rev: BL 10/15/02; HBG 3/03) [636.9]

22483 Nelson, Robin. *Pet Hermit Crab* (PS–K). Illus. Series: Classroom Pets. 2002, Lerner LB $15.93 (0-8225-1270-X). 24pp. A preschooler's introduction to the care and feeding of classroom hermit crabs, with relevant facts, a glossary, and an index. (Rev: HBG 3/03)

22484 Rayner, Matthew. *Hamster* (2–4). Photos by Frank Greenaway. Series: I Am Your Pet. 2004, Gareth Stevens LB $22.60 (0-8368-4104-2). 32pp. Practical information on selecting and caring for a hamster is presented in clear text with dialogue bubbles giving the hamster's point of view plus colorful fact boxes. (Rev: SLJ 8/04) [636]

22485 Rockwell, Anne. *My Pet Hamster* (K–2). Illus. by Bernice Lum. Series: Let's-Read-and-Find-Out Science. 2002, HarperCollins LB $17.89 (0-06-028565-6); paper $4.99 (0-06-445205-0). 33pp. Facts about hamsters blend easily with the text about a young girl selecting, looking after, and playing with her pet. (Rev: HBG 3/03; SLJ 12/02) [636]

22486 Ross, Veronica. *My First Hamster* (K–2). Illus. Series: My First Pet. 2002, Thameside LB $16.95 (1-930643-75-6). 32pp. A basic guide to caring for a hamster, with information on diet and hygiene. (Rev: BL 3/1/03) [636.935]

22487 Royston, Angela. *Life Cycle of a Guinea Pig* (PS–3). Series: Life Cycle. 1998, Heinemann LB $13.95 (1-57572-614-9). 32pp. With a color photo and four or five lines of text per page, this book explains the life cycle of the guinea pig and gives a timeline to help identify stages of development. (Rev: BL 5/15/98; SLJ 6/98) [636]

22488 Schafer, Susan. *Lizards* (4–6). Series: Perfect Pets. 2000, Marshall Cavendish LB $15.95 (0-7614-1103-8). 32pp. History, folklore, and practical tips are included in this introduction to the care, feeding, and raising of pet lizards. (Rev: BL 3/15/01; HBG 3/01) [595.95]

22489 Silverstein, Alvin, et al. *Snakes and Such* (3–6). Illus. Series: What a Pet! 1999, Twenty-First Century LB $21.40 (0-7613-3229-4). 48pp. In pictures and text, this book explores the idea that such reptiles and amphibians as chameleons, geckos, iguanas, as well as frogs and toads, can be kept as pets. (Rev: BL 8/99; HBG 4/00; SLJ 10/99) [639.3]

22490 Simon, Seymour. *Pets in a Jar: Collecting and Caring for Small Wild Animals* (4–6). Illus. by Betty Fraser. 1979, Puffin paper $6.99 (0-14-049186-4). How to catch and care for such small wild creatures as snails, toads, and ants.

22491 Starosta, Paul. *Face-to-Face with the Hamster* (3–4). Photos by author. Series: Face-to-Face. 2004, Charlesbridge $9.95 (1-57091-456-7). 25pp. Colorful photographs accompany bright text on the characteristics and care of hamsters. (Rev: SLJ 2/05) [636]

22492 Watts, Barrie. *Hamster* (1–3). Illus. 1986, Silver Burdett LB $15.95 (0-382-09281-3); paper $3.95 (0-382-09957-5). 28pp. Well-organized, basic scientific information, with full-color photos. (Rev: BL 1/1/87)

22493 Wexler, Jerome. *Pet Hamsters* (3–6). Illus. 1992, Whitman LB $15.95 (0-8075-6525-3). 48pp. Personal advice from a hamster raiser on the care and handling of these pets. (Rev: BCCB 2/93; BL 2/15/93; SLJ 2/93) [636]

CATS

22494 Arnold, Caroline. *Cats: In from the Wild* (4–7). Photos by Richard Hewett. 1993, Carolrhoda LB $19.93 (0-87614-692-2). 48pp. Domestic and wild cats are highlighted with comparisons and contrasts. (Rev: BL 8/93) [636.8]

22495 Cole, Joanna. *My New Kitten* (PS–1). Illus. by Margaret Miller. 1995, Morrow $14.93 (0-688-12902-1). 40pp. A photoessay about a young girl getting to know and love her new kitten. (Rev: BCCB 6/95; BL 3/1/95; HB 5–6/95; SLJ 4/95) [636.8]

22496 Fowler, Allan. *It Could Still Be a Cat* (1–2). Illus. Series: Rookie Readers. 1993, Children's Book Pr. LB $19.00 (0-516-06015-5). 32pp. The cat family is introduced in this easy-to-read book for beginners. (Rev: BL 3/1/94) [636.8]

22497 George, Jean Craighead. *How to Talk to Your Cat* (2–4). Illus. by Paul Meisel. 2000, HarperCollins LB $9.89 (0-06-027969-9). 40pp. After a history of the domestication of cats, this account tells how and what they communicate with humans. (Rev: BCCB 4/00; BL 12/15/99; HB 3–4/00; HBG 9/00; SLJ 2/00) [636.8]

22498 Gibbons, Gail. *Cats* (PS–2). Illus. by author. 1996, Holiday House LB $16.95 (0-8234-1253-9). Watercolor illustrations are used to introduce a number of breeds of cats, their characteristics, and behavior. (Rev: SLJ 12/96) [636.8]

22499 Gutman, Bill. *Becoming Your Cat's Best Friend* (3–6). Illus. Series: Pet Friends. 1997, Millbrook LB $21.90 (0-7613-0200-X). 64pp. This book expresses the cat's point of view and gives advice on how to make the pet and its owner happy with the relationship. (Rev: BCCB 6/97; BL 8/97; SLJ 7/97) [636.8]

22500 Hinds, Kathryn. *Cats* (2–5). Series: Perfect Pets. 1998, Benchmark LB $15.95 (0-7614-0794-4). 31pp. As well as a history of cats and their role in mythology, this simple book describes their physical characteristics and how to take care of them. (Rev: HBG 9/99; SLJ 5/99) [636.8]

22501 Holub, Joan. *Why Do Cats Meow?* (1–2). Illus. Series: Easy-to-Read. 2001, Dial $13.99 (0-8037-2503-5); paper $3.99 (0-14-056788-7). 48pp. This informative, easy-to-read book, with many photos and cartoons, discusses behavioral traits of cats and provides material on breeds and their characteristics. (Rev: BCCB 2/01; BL 2/15/01) [636.8]

22502 Hubbell, Patricia. *I Like Cats* (PS). Illus. by Pamela Paparone. 2003, North-South LB $16.50 (0-7358-1775-8). 32pp. Vivid illustrations of all kinds of domestic cats are accompanied by simple, rhyming descriptions of their varied activities. (Rev: HBG 4/04; SLJ 1/04)

22503 Jeffrey, Laura S. *Cats: How to Choose and Care for a Cat* (3–5). Illus. Series: American Humane Pet Care Library. 2004, Enslow LB $23.93 (0-7660-2516-0). 48pp. Offers a wide array of information on cats and their care, including tips on selecting the right cat, steps to prevent the loss of a pet, cat allergies, and how to cope with feline misbehavior. (Rev: BL 10/15/04; SLJ 2/05) [636.8]

22504 Mattern, Joanne. *The American Shorthair Cat* (4–7). Illus. Series: Learning About Cats. 2002, Capstone LB $21.26 (0-7368-1300-4). 48pp. Beautiful photographs of frisky felines are accompanied by data about the physical characteristics and personality, with a glossary, bibliography, and lists of addresses and Web sites. Also use *The Manx Cat* (2002). (Rev: BL 12/1/02; HBG 3/03) [636.8]

22505 Meadows, Graham. *Cats* (PS–2). Photos by author. Series: Animals Are Not Like Us. 1999, Gareth Stevens LB $13.95 (0-8368-2251-X). 24pp. Very basic information about cats — material on their senses, communication, and appearance, for example — is given with comparisons to humans. (Rev: HBG 9/99; SLJ 7/99) [636.8]

22506 Overbeck, Cynthia. *Cats* (4–6). Illus. by Shin Yoshino. 1983, Lerner LB $22.60 (0-8225-1480-X). 48pp. This work concentrates on domestic cats and their habits and appearance.

22507 Quasha, Jennifer. *The Manx: The Cat with No Tail* (2–4). Illus. Series: Kids Can! 2000, Rosen LB $18.60 (0-8239-5512-5). 24pp. Many color close-ups are used to present the Manx cat, its characteristics, habits, and the myth about how it lost its tail. (Rev: BL 10/15/00) [636.8]

22508 Quasha, Jennifer. *Shorthaired Cats in America* (2–4). Illus. 2000, Rosen LB $18.60 (0-8239-5513-3). 24pp. This is a general book about cats that covers American attitudes toward them, their history from the Mayflower to today, their part in the Salem witch trials, and similar material. (Rev: BL 10/15/00) [636.8]

22509 Rayner, Matthew. *Cat* (2–4). Photos by Jane Burton. Series: I Am Your Pet. 2004, Gareth Stevens LB $22.60 (0-8368-4102-6). 32pp. Practical information on selecting and caring for a cat is presented in clear text with dialogue bubbles giving the cat's point of view plus colorful fact boxes. (Rev: SLJ 8/04) [636.8]

22510 Ring, Susan. *Caring for Your Cat* (3–5). Illus. 2002, Weigl LB $24.95 (1-59036-032-X). 32pp. A detailed introduction to the various breeds of cat and how to care for one — in more than the strict physical sense — with photographs and a list of relevant Web sites. (Rev: BL 12/1/02; HBG 3/03) [636.8]

22511 Rosen, Michael J., ed. *Purr . . . Children's Book Illustrators Brag About Their Cats* (2–5). Illus. 1996, Harcourt $18.00 (0-15-200837-3). 48pp. Paintings and text illustrate the moods and activities of a variety of cats. (Rev: BL 4/1/96; SLJ 5/96) [636.8]

22512 Ross, Veronica. *My First Cat* (K–2). Illus. Series: My First Pet. 2002, Thameside LB $16.95 (1-930643-72-1). 32pp. A basic guide to choosing and caring for a cat. (Rev: BL 3/1/03; HBG 3/03) [636.8]

22513 Selsam, Millicent E. *How Kittens Grow* (1–2). Illus. by Esther Bubley. 1992, Scholastic paper $3.25 (0-590-44784-X). Photographs and simply written text describe the stages in a kitten's growth.

22514 Simon, Seymour. *Cats* (2–3). Illus. 2004, HarperCollins $15.99 (0-06-028940-6). 40pp. Full-color photographs and clear text explore basic facts about cats — breeds, intelligence, diet, and so forth. (Rev: BL 3/15/04; SLJ 6/04) [599.75]

22515 Stefoff, Rebecca. *Cats* (4–7). Series: Animal-Ways. 2003, Benchmark LB $21.95 (0-7614-1577-7). 112pp. A well-illustrated study of cats, their evolution, behavior, and human attitudes toward them. (Rev: HBG 4/04; SLJ 3/04) [636.8]

22516 Tildes, Phyllis L. *Calico's Cousins: Cats from Around the World* (K–3). Illus. 1999, Charlesbridge LB $15.95 (0-88106-648-6); paper $6.95 (0-88106-649-4). 32pp. General information about different breeds of cats is given in this book that features beautiful watercolor art. (Rev: BL 2/1/99; HBG 9/99; SLJ 3/99) [636.8]

DOGS

22517 Ajmera, Maya, and Alex Fisher. *A Kid's Best Friend* (1–3). Illus. 2002, Charlesbridge $15.95 (1-57091-513-X); paper $6.95 (1-57091-514-8). 32pp. Photographs of children and their dogs show that dogs are friends and helpers everywhere in the world. (Rev: BL 9/1/02; HBG 3/03; SLJ 8/02) [636.7]

22518 Altman, Linda Jacobs. *Big Dogs* (4–6). Series: Perfect Pets. 2000, Marshall Cavendish LB $15.95 (0-7614-1101-1). 32pp. Filled with historical and factual material, this book introduces several breeds of large dogs and gives tips for raising and caring for them. (Rev: BL 3/15/01; HBG 3/01) [636.7]

22519 Altman, Linda Jacobs. *Small Dogs* (2–5). Series: Perfect Pets. 1998, Benchmark LB $15.95 (0-7614-0795-2). 32pp. Young dog lovers will enjoy this simple introduction to dogs that gives some history plus behavioral traits and tips on caring for them. (Rev: HBG 9/99; SLJ 5/99) [636.7]

22520 Arnold, Caroline. *A Guide Dog Puppy Grows Up* (3–5). Photos by Richard Hewett. 1991, Harcourt $16.95 (0-15-232657-X); paper $7.00 (0-15-201557-4). 48pp. The life and training of a golden retriever named Honey. (Rev: BCCB 3/91; BL 4/15/91; HB 5–6/91; SLJ 5/91) [362.4]

22521 Benjamin, Carol Lea. *Dog Training for Kids*. Rev. ed. (5–8). Illus. 1988, Howell Book House $17.95 (0-87605-541-2). A simple guide to dog training that emphasizes the goal of having fun with a dog you are proud of. (Rev: SLJ 4/89) [636.7]

22522 Calmenson, Stephanie. *Rosie: A Visiting Dog's Story* (PS–3). Illus. by Justin Sutcliffe. 1994, Houghton Mifflin $16.00 (0-395-65477-7). 48pp. The true story of the dog Rosie, who is being trained to be a visiting dog to help those who are sad or lonely. (Rev: BL 4/15/94; HB 7–8/94; SLJ 4/94) [636.7]

22523 Calmenson, Stephanie. *Shaggy, Waggy Dogs (and Others)* (K–3). Illus. by Justin Sutcliffe. 1998, Clarion $15.00 (0-395-77605-8). 48pp. Twenty canine breeds are introduced in a series of four-line poems and clear color photographs. (Rev: BL 5/1/98; HBG 9/98; SLJ 7/98) [636.7]

22524 Crisp, Marty. *Everything Dog: What Kids Really Want to Know About Dogs* (2–5). 2003, NorthWord $9.95 (1-55971-839-0); paper $6.95 (1-55971-854-4). 64pp. Friendly and attractive, this is nonetheless a fact-filled volume suitable for browsing. (Rev: BL 5/15/03; SLJ 6/03) [636.7]

22525 Darling, Kathy. *ABC Dogs* (PS–3). Illus. by Tara Darling. 1997, Walker LB $16.85 (0-8027-8635-9). 32pp. This ABC book introduces various breeds of dogs and shows them in photographs, both as puppies and as adults. (Rev: BL 10/15/97; HBG 3/98; SLJ 10/97) [636.7]

22526 Feldman, Heather. *The Story of the Golden Retriever* (2–4). Illus. Series: Dogs Throughout History. 2000, Rosen $18.60 (0-8239-5514-1). 24pp. This history of the golden retriever also describes its physical characteristics and its roles in rescue missions and as a guide dog. (Rev: BL 10/15/00) [636.752]

22527 Flowers, Pam, and Ann Dixon. *Big-Enough Anna: The Little Sled Dog Who Braved the Arctic* (PS–3). Illus. by Bill Farnsworth. 2003, Alaska Northwest $15.95 (0-88240-577-2); paper $8.95 (0-88240-580-2). In this inspiring real-life story, Anna, a sled dog that was the runt of her litter, takes over as lead dog on an arduous journey across the North American Arctic. (Rev: HBG 4/04; SLJ 1/04) [636.73]

22528 Gallimard Jeunesse. *Dogs* (PS–2). Series: First Discovery. 1999, Scholastic $12.95 (0-590-87608-2). 24pp. A heavily illustrated, simple introduction to dogs, their characteristics, and some of the important breeds. (Rev: BL 6/1–15/99; HBG 9/99) [636.7]

22529 George, Jean Craighead. *How to Talk to Your Dog* (2–4). Illus. by Sue Truesdell. 2000, HarperCollins LB $9.89 (0-06-027093-4). 40pp. Jean Craighead George teaches us what dogs are trying to tell us — and how to communicate back — as well as giving a history of how dogs were domesticated. (Rev: BCCB 4/00; BL 12/15/99; HBG 9/00; SLJ 2/00) [636.7]

22530 Gibbons, Gail. *Dogs* (K–2). Illus. by author. 1996, Holiday House LB $16.95 (0-8234-1226-1). An easy-to-read overview of dogs and their history, breeds, and anatomy. (Rev: BCCB 5/96; HB 5–6/96; SLJ 9/96) [636.7]

22531 Gorrell, Gena K. *Working Like a Dog: The Story of Working Dogs Through History* (4–8). Illus. 2003, Tundra $16.95 (0-88776-589-0). 160pp. A comprehensive and very appealing look at dogs' services to man throughout history — as hunters and trackers, bomb sniffers, guide dogs, and companions, to name but a few. (Rev: BL 11/1/03; SLJ 12/03) [636.73]

22532 Jackson, Donna M. *Hero Dogs: Courageous Canines in Action* (2–5). Illus. by author. 2003, Little, Brown $16.95 (0-316-82681-2). 48pp. The dogs celebrated in this photoessay range from 9/11 search-and-rescue and bomb-sniffing dogs to companion animals and other working dogs. (Rev: BL 7/03; HBG 4/04; SLJ 9/03) [636.7]

22533 Jeffrey, Laura S. *Dogs: How to Choose and Care for a Dog* (2–5). Illus. Series: American Humane Pet Care Library. 2004, Enslow LB $23.93 (0-7660-2520-9). 48pp. Appealing full-color photographs accompany advice on choosing and caring for a dog. (Rev: SLJ 2/05) [636.7]

22534 Kehret, Peg. *Shelter Dogs: Amazing Stories of Adopted Strays* (3–5). Illus. 1999, Whitman $14.95 (0-8075-7334-5). 134pp. A collection of eight true stories about shelter dogs that went on to great things — starring on TV, for example. (Rev: BCCB 4/99; BL 5/1/99; HBG 9/99; SLJ 10/99) [636.7]

22535 Kirk, Daniel F. *Dogs Rule!* (3–5). Illus. by author. 2003, Disney $18.99 (0-7868-1949-9). 48pp. In this large-format collection of dog-related poetry and accompanying CD, Kirk manages to celebrate just about every aspect of canine behavior. (Rev: BL 10/15/03; HBG 4/04; SLJ 12/03)

22536 Lauber, Patricia. *The True-or-False Book of Dogs* (1–3). Illus. by Rosalyn Schanzer. 2003, HarperCollins $15.99 (0-06-029767-0). 32pp. This brightly illustrated book uses a true-or-false format to convey a wide range of facts and figures about dogs and their history. (Rev: BL 11/1/03; HBG 4/04; SLJ 12/03)

22537 Lawrenson, Diana. *Guide Dogs: From Puppies to Partners* (4–6). 2002, Allen & Unwin paper $7.95 (1-86508-246-5). 32pp. The breeding, care, and training of guide dogs are covered in this title from Australia, with profiles of several dogs and their partners and an interesting chart of commands. (Rev: SLJ 10/02)

22538 Meadows, Graham. *Dogs* (PS–2). Photos by author. Series: Animals Are Not Like Us. 1999, Gareth Stevens LB $13.95 (0-8368-2252-8). 24pp. Very basic information about dogs — material on their senses, communication, and appearance, for example — is given with comparisons with humans. (Rev: HBG 9/99; SLJ 7/99) [636.7]

22539 Meister, Cari. *Basset Hounds* (3–5). Series: Dogs. 2001, ABDO $13.95 (1-57765-478-1). 24pp. A simple colorful introduction to this breed of dog that describes its physical and behavioral characteristics and gives tips on proper care. Other titles in this series include *Boxers*, *Greyhounds*, and *Saint Bernards* (all 2001). (Rev: BL 12/15/01; HBG 3/02) [636.7]

22540 Meister, Cari. *Bulldogs* (3–5). Series: Dogs. 2001, ABDO $13.95 (1-57765-476-5). 24pp. Attractive color photographs show bulldogs playing, eating, and sleeping, and a simple text describes the breed, its many varieties, and its characteristics. (Rev: BL 12/15/01; HBG 3/02) [636.7]

22541 Moore, Eva. *Buddy: The First Seeing Eye Dog* (2–3). Illus. by Don Bolognese. 1996, Scholastic paper $3.99 (0-590-26585-7). 48pp. In simple prose, this book traces the beginning of the Seeing Eye movement in the 1930s. (Rev: BL 11/15/96) [392.4]

22542 Mulvany, Martha. *The Story of the Boxer* (2–4). Illus. Series: Dogs Throughout History. 2000, Rosen $18.60 (0-8239-5519-2). 24pp. This history of the boxer also describes its physical characteristics and its reputation for loyalty and courage. (Rev: BL 10/15/00) [636.73]

22543 O'Neill, Amanda. *Dogs* (3–5). 1999, Kingfisher $15.95 (0-7534-5175-1). 63pp. This oversize introduction to dogs covers such topics as physical features, evolution, history, breeds, behavior, and care. (Rev: HBG 9/99; SLJ 7/99) [636.7]

22544 Otto, Carolyn. *Our Puppies Are Growing* (1). Illus. by Mary Morgan. Series: Let's-Read-and-Find-Out. 1998, HarperCollins LB $15.89 (0-06-027272-4); paper $4.95 (0-06-445169-0). 32pp. In this book for beginning readers, the experiences of a preschooler whose dog has five puppies help readers learn about the dog's pregnancy, the birth process, and the care of the newborn puppies. (Rev: BL 11/1/98; HBG 3/99; SLJ 7/99) [636.7]

22545 Patent, Dorothy Hinshaw. *Dogs: The Wolf Within* (3–6). Illus. by William Muñoz. 1993, Carolrhoda LB $19.95 (0-87614-691-4); paper $7.95 (0-87614-604-3). 48pp. This book describes the relationship between the habits of the domesticated dog and its distant ancestor, the wolf. (Rev: BCCB 7–8/93; BL 6/1–15/93) [599]

22546 Patent, Dorothy Hinshaw. *Right Dog for the Job: Ira's Path from Service Dog to Guide Dog* (3–5). 2004, Walker $16.95 (0-8027-8915-3). 32pp. A puppy's training to be a guide dog is followed in loving detail in this appealing and informative photoessay. (Rev: BL 6/1–15/04; SLJ 6/04)

22547 Paulsen, Gary. *My Life in Dog Years* (5–10). Illus. 1998, Delacorte $15.95 (0-385-32570-3). The famous novelist tells about eight wonderful dogs that he has known and loved over the years. (Rev: BCCB 3/98; BL 1/1–15/98; SLJ 3/98) [636.7]

22548 Petersen-Fleming, Judy, and Bill Fleming. *Puppy Care and Critters, Too!* (1–3). Illus. by Debra Reingold-Reiss. 1994, Morrow $15.00 (0-688-12563-8). 40pp. This manual focuses on raising, feeding, and caring for a puppy, with material on other kinds of pets. (Rev: BL 4/1/94; SLJ 6/94) [636.7]

22549 Presnall, Judith Janda. *Police Dogs* (4–7). Illus. Series: Animals with Jobs. 2002, Gale LB $23.70 (0-7377-0631-7). 48pp. This well-illustrated account describes the various ways in which dogs are used to fight crime. (Rev: BL 4/1/02) [363.2]

22550 Presnall, Judith Janda. *Rescue Dogs* (4–6). Series: Animals with Jobs. 2002, Gale/KidHaven LB $23.70 (0-7377-1361-5). 48pp. Individual rescue dogs are profiled in this well-written overview of these animals and their training. (Rev: SLJ 9/03) [636.7]

22551 Rayner, Matthew. *Dog* (2–4). Photos by Jane Burton. Series: I Am Your Pet. 2004, Gareth

Stevens LB $22.60 (0-8368-4103-4). 32pp. Practical information on selecting and caring for a dog is presented in clear text with dialogue bubbles giving the dog's point of view plus colorful fact boxes. (Rev: SLJ 8/04) [636.7]

22552 Rock, Maxine. *Totally Fun Things to Do with Your Dog* (3–6). Illus. 1998, Wiley paper $12.95 (0-471-19754-X). 128pp. An informative manual for young dog owners on training, suitable activities, and building bonds of trust and friendship between owner and dog. (Rev: BL 6/1–15/98) [636]

22553 Rosenthal, Lisa. *A Dog's Best Friend: An Activity Book for Kids and Their Dogs* (4–7). Illus. by Bonnie Matthews. 1999, Chicago Review paper $12.95 (1-55652-362-9). 181pp. This book that gives hints on how to choose a dog and care for a puppy offers 60 projects related to these subjects including crafts, recipes, and games. (Rev: SLJ 1/00) [636.7]

22554 Ross, Veronica. *My First Dog* (PS–2). Series: My First. 2002, Raintree LB $16.95 (1-930643-71-3). 32pp. Simple language introduces young readers to dogs and their care. (Rev: HBG 3/03)

22555 Rossiter, Nan P. *Rugby and Rosie* (1–3). Illus. by author. 1997, Dutton $14.99 (0-525-45484-5). Background information about guide dogs is given in this story about a young boy who keeps a puppy for a year before it leaves to be trained as a guide dog. (Rev: BCCB 3/97; SLJ 2/97) [636.7]

22556 Royston, Angela. *Life Cycle of a Dog* (PS–3). Series: Life Cycle. 2000, Heinemann LB $19.92 (1-57572-209-7). 32pp. This book describes a dog's life cycle with a simple text and color photos on each page. (Rev: BL 5/15/00; HBG 3/01) [636.7]

22557 Seibert, Patricia. *Mush! Across Alaska in the World's Longest Sled-Dog Race* (2–4). Illus. 1992, Houghton Mifflin paper $5.70 (0-395-64537-9). 32pp. Focusing on the work dogs of the 1,000-plus-mile Iditarod race from Anchorage to Nome. (Rev: BL 9/15/92; SLJ 11/92) [798.8]

22558 Selsam, Millicent E. *How Puppies Grow* (1–2). Illus. 1990, Scholastic paper $2.99 (0-590-42736-9). 32pp. The stages in a puppy's life — from birth through walking, seeing, eating, and playing — described in excellent photographs and simple text.

22559 Selsam, Millicent E., and Joyce Hunt. *A First Look at Dogs* (1–3). Illus. by Harriett Springer. 1981, Walker LB $9.85 (0-8027-6421-5). 32pp. A history of dogs and an introduction to present breeds.

22560 Silverstein, Alvin, et al. *Different Dogs* (4–7). Series: What a Pet! 2000, Twenty-First Century LB $23.90 (0-7613-1371-0). 48pp. Several different breeds of dogs are introduced in pictures and text plus information on cost, food, housing, and training. (Rev: HBG 9/00; SLJ 5/00) [636.7]

22561 Silverstein, Alvin, and Virginia Silverstein. *Dogs: All About Them* (5–8). Illus. 1986, Lothrop $16.00 (0-688-04805-6). 256pp. After a history of dogs from the Stone Age on, the authors cover such topics as breeds, uses, and care of dogs. (Rev: BCCB 11/86; BL 3/1/86; SLJ 9/86) [599.74]

22562 Simon, Seymour. *Dogs* (2–3). Illus. 2004, HarperCollins $15.99 (0-06-028942-2). 40pp. Full-color photographs and clear text explore basic facts about dogs — breeds, intelligence, diet, and so forth. (Rev: BL 3/15/04; SLJ 6/04) [636.7]

22563 Singer, Marilyn. *A Dog's Gotta Do What a Dog's Gotta Do* (3–6). Illus. 2000, Holt $16.00 (0-8050-6074-X). 86pp. This book on working dogs includes material on their roles as defenders, herders, detectives, rescuers, and entertainers. (Rev: BCCB 11/00; BL 11/15/00; HBG 3/01; SLJ 2/01) [636.7]

22564 Stone, Lynn M. *Beagles* (K–2). Series: Eye to Eye with Dogs. 2002, Rourke LB $23.93 (1-58952-325-3). 24pp. From puppyhood to adult status, this is an introduction to beagles and their behavior, characteristics, and care. Other titles in this series include *German Shepherds*, *Golden Retrievers*, *Labrador Retrievers*, and *Poodles* (all 2002). (Rev: BL 10/15/02) [636.7]

22565 Stone, Lynn M. *Dachshunds* (K–2). Series: Eye to Eye with Dogs. 2002, Rourke LB $23.93 (1-58952-326-1). 24pp. The five short sections in this simple book give information on dachshunds' characteristics, history, appearance, and care, and discuss how dachshunds help people. (Rev: BL 10/15/02) [636.7]

22566 Storer, Pat. *Your Puppy, Your Dog: A Kid's Guide to Raising a Happy, Healthy Dog* (4–6). Illus. 1997, Storey paper $14.95 (0-88266-959-1). 172pp. Chapters in this complete dog care manual cover such subjects as feeding, walking, playing, grooming, and toilet needs. (Rev: BL 12/15/97) [636.7]

22567 Temple, Bob. *Chihuahuas* (3–5). Series: Dogs. 2000, ABDO LB $13.95 (1-57765-419-6). 24pp. This heavily illustrated book covers the history of this breed, its structure, habits, and required care and feeding. Also use from the same series: *Pugs*, *Scottish Terriers*, and *Shih Tzus* (all 2000). (Rev: BL 3/15/01; HBG 3/01) [636.7]

22568 Temple, Bob. *Jack Russell Terriers* (3–5). Illus. Series: Dogs. 2000, ABDO $13.95 (1-57765-424-2). 24pp. This book introduces terriers, their physical characteristics, habits, how to care for them, and their special needs. Similar material is found in *Siberian Huskies* (2000). (Rev: BL 3/15/01; HBG 3/01) [636.755]

22569 Tracqui, Valerie. *The Dog: Loyal Companion* (2–4). Trans. from French by Lisa Laird. Photos by Marie-Luce Hubert and Jean-Louis Klein. Series: Face-to-Face. 2002, Charlesbridge $9.95 (1-57091-452-4). 32pp. A celebration of dogs' relationship with humans, their ability to follow commands, and their contributions to the lost and handicapped. (Rev: SLJ 8/02) [636.7]

22570 Turner, Pamelas. *Hachiko: The True Story of a Loyal Dog* (1–3). Illus. by Yan Nascimbene. 2004, Houghton Mifflin $15.00 (0-618-14094-8). 32pp. This small-format picture book tells the moving story of Hachiko, the devoted dog who spent nearly 10 years at a Tokyo train station, waiting in vain for the return of his dead master. (Rev: BL 4/15/04*; HB 7–8/04; SLJ 5/04) [636.7]

22571 Urbigkit, Cat. *Brave Dogs, Gentle Dogs: How They Guard Sheep* (K–2). Illus. 2005, Boyds Mills $15.95 (1-59078-317-4). 32pp. Photographs of Wyoming ranch dogs accompany the text on guardian dogs, trained to tend and protect flocks of sheep. (Rev: BL 3/1/05; SLJ 3/05) [636.737]

22572 White, Nancy. *Why Do Dogs Do That?* (2–4). Illus. by Gioia Fiammenghi. 1995, Scholastic paper $4.99 (0-590-26597-0). 32pp. Through answers to 24 simple questions, such common canine behavior as tail wagging is explained. (Rev: BL 2/15/96) [599]

22573 Wood, Ted. *Bear Dogs: Canines with a Mission* (4–6). Illus. Series: Canines with a Mission. 2001, Walker LB $17.85 (0-8027-8759-2). 32pp. These dogs are trained to bark and chase bears, frightening them back to their natural habitats and saving their lives. (Rev: BL 4/1/01; HBG 10/01; SLJ 7/01) [636.7]

FISH

22574 Coleman, Lori. *My Pet Fish* (3–6). Illus. Series: All About Pets. 1998, Lerner LB $16.95 (0-8225-2262-4). 64pp. This book supplies basic information on aquariums, the equipment involved, and the problems of maintenance. (Rev: BL 9/1/98; HBG 9/98) [639.34]

22575 Nelson, Robin. *Pet Fish* (PS–K). Illus. Series: Classroom Pets. 2002, Lerner LB $15.93 (0-8225-1267-X). 24pp. A preschooler's introduction to the care and feeding of classroom fish, with fish facts, a glossary, and an index. (Rev: BL 10/15/02; HBG 3/03) [639.34]

HORSES AND PONIES

22576 Ancona, George. *Man and Mustang* (3–6). Illus. 1992, Macmillan LB $15.95 (0-02-700802-9). 48pp. Black-and-white photos help to tell the story of how the Bureau of Land Management manages the growing population of wild mustangs. (Rev: BCCB 4/92; BL 3/15/92; HB 7–8/92; SLJ 4/92) [636.1]

22577 Arnosky, Jim. *Wild Ponies* (PS–3). Illus. by author. Series: One Whole Day. 2002, National Geographic $16.95 (0-7922-7121-1). Bright illustrations and simple rhyming text introduce the small ponies of Assateague Island and the other animals that live there. (Rev: HBG 3/03; SLJ 10/02)

22578 Budd, Jackie. *The Best Book of Ponies* (2–3). Series: The Best Book Of. 1999, Kingfisher $10.95 (0-7534-5172-7). 32pp. A beginning chapter book with attractive double-page spreads on such topics as horses and ponies of the world, bridles and bits, learning to ride, and going to a show. (Rev: HBG 9/99; SLJ 7/99) [636.1]

22579 Budd, Jackie. *Horse and Pony Breeds* (4–8). Series: The Complete Guides to Horses and Ponies. 1998, Gareth Stevens LB $25.26 (0-8368-2046-0). 64pp. Each type of horse is profiled with action photographs, fact boxes, checklists, and a clear text. (Rev: HBG 9/98; SLJ 7/98) [636.1]

22580 Budd, Jackie. *Horse and Pony Care* (4–8). Series: The Complete Guides to Horses and Ponies. 1998, Gareth Stevens LB $26.60 (0-8368-2047-9). 64pp. This book discusses such topics related to horse and pony care as feeding, stables, grooming, shoeing, and common ailments. (Rev: HBG 9/98; SLJ 7/98) [636.1]

22581 Budd, Jackie. *Horses* (3–8). Illus. 1995, Kingfisher $15.95 (1-85697-566-5). 64pp. Drawings and text cover such subjects related to horses as anatomy, breeds, care, and grooming. (Rev: BL 10/1/95; SLJ 12/95) [636.1]

22582 Budd, Jackie. *Learning to Ride Horses and Ponies* (4–8). Series: The Complete Guides to Horses and Ponies. 1998, Gareth Stevens LB $25.26 (0-8368-2045-2). 64pp. This book supplies basic information that prospective young riders need to know including gear, types of lessons, and attitudes. (Rev: HBG 9/98; SLJ 7/98) [636.1]

22583 Budiansky, Stephen. *The World According to Horses: How They Run, See, and Think* (4–8). Illus. 2000, Holt $17.95 (0-8050-6054-5). 101pp. This book explores horses' behavior — such as their sight and thinking powers — and goes on to explain how this knowledge was gained through observation and experiments. (Rev: BCCB 5/00; BL 3/1/00; HB 5–6/00; HBG 9/00; SLJ 7/00) [636.1]

22584 Dubowski, Kathy East, and Mark Dubowski. *A Horse Named Seabiscuit* (2–4). Illus. by Mark Rowe. Series: All Aboard Reading. 2003, Grosset LB $13.89 (0-448-43343-5); paper $3.99 (0-448-43342-7). 47pp. The story of the famous Depression-era race horse is told in lively, well-illustrated narrative. (Rev: BL 1/1–15/04; HBG 4/04; SLJ 4/04) [636.1]

22585 Farley, Walter. *Man O' War* (4–6). Illus. 1983, Random paper $4.99 (0-394-86015-2). 352pp. The story of the famous racehorse.

22586 Fowler, Allan. *Horses, Horses, Horses* (1–2). Illus. Series: Rookie Readers. 1992, Children's Book Pr. LB $19.00 (0-516-04921-6). 32pp. With a minimum of text and lots of pictures, this account introduces various kinds of horses and tells how they help people. (Rev: BL 7/92) [636.1]

22587 Gentle, Victor, and Janet Perry. *Florida Cracker Horses* (3–5). Series: Great American Horses. 2001, Gareth Stevens LB $19.93 (0-8368-2936-0). 24pp. The physical features, history, and primary use of these horses are presented along with illustrations of famous horses of the breed. Also see *Chincoteague Ponies, Miniature Horses, Saddlebreds, Standardbreds,* and *Tennessee Walking Horses.* (Rev: HBG 3/02; SLJ 3/02) [636.1]

22588 Gibbons, Gail. *Horses!* (K–3). Illus. by author. 2003, Holiday House $16.95 (0-8234-1703-4). Browsers and report writers will enjoy Gibbons's exploration of horses' history, physical characteristics and breeds, life cycle, and care and grooming. (Rev: HBG 4/04; SLJ 12/03) [636.1]

22589 Hayden, Kate. *Horse Show* (1–3). Series: Dorling Kindersley Readers. 2001, DK $12.95 (0-7894-7372-0); paper $3.95 (0-7894-7371-2). 32pp. An introduction to gymkhanas and the preparations that horses and riders undergo, for beginning readers. (Rev: HBG 10/01; SLJ 6/01) [798.24]

22590 Henry, Marguerite. *Album of Horses* (5–8). Illus. by Wesley Dennis. 1951, Macmillan paper $11.99 (0-689-71709-1). 112pp. A beautifully illustrated guide to 20 breeds of horses.

22591 Hill, Cherry. *Horse Care for Kids* (4–8). Illus. 2002, Storey $23.95 (1-58017-476-0); paper $16.95 (1-58017-407-8). 128pp. A very practical guide for young horse lovers and their parents using clear prose and topnotch illustrations to cover everything from selecting a horse and instructor to proper care and equine psychology. (Rev: BL 12/1/02; HBG 3/03; SLJ 1/03) [636.1]

22592 Holub, Joan. *Why Do Horses Neigh?* (K–2). Illus. Series: Dial Easy-to-Read. 2003, Dial $13.99 (0-8037-2770-4); paper $6.99 (0-14-230119-1). 48pp. Beginning readers will enjoy this introduction to horses that presents interesting material in a question-and-answer format. (Rev: BL 11/15/02; HBG 10/03; SLJ 2/03) [636.1]

22593 Isenbart, Hans-Heinrich. *Birth of a Foal* (2–5). Illus. 1986, Carolrhoda LB $22.60 (0-87614-239-0). 48pp. Complemented by color photos, the phases of fetal development and the birth process are detailed. (Rev: BL 4/1/86; HB 5–6/86; SLJ 3/86)

22594 Jauck, Andrea. *Assateague: Island of the Wild Ponies* (2–4). Illus. 1997, Sierra Club paper $7.95 (0-939365-59-6). 32pp. A color photo-essay to interest horse fans. (Rev: BCCB 5/93; BL 3/15/93; SLJ 6/93) [599.72]

22595 Jeffrey, Laura S. *Horses: How to Choose and Care for a Horse* (3–5). Illus. Series: American Humane Pet Care Library. 2004, Enslow LB $23.93 (0-7660-2519-5). 48pp. This helpful guide to horses and their care offers tips on selecting the right breed for your needs and on grooming, housing, and diet. (Rev: BL 10/15/04; SLJ 2/05) [636.1]

22596 Jurmain, Suzanne. *Once upon a Horse: A History of Horses and How They Shaped Our History* (5–9). Illus. 1989, Lothrop $15.95 (0-688-05550-8). A history of the horse and how it has been domesticated and used by humans. (Rev: BL 12/15/89; BR 3–4/90; SLJ 1/90) [636.1]

22597 Kelley, Brent. *Horse Breeds of the World* (4–8). Series: Horse Library. 2001, Chelsea $19.75 (0-7910-6652-5). 64pp. In addition to basic facts about nearly 40 types of horses around the world, this account looks briefly at the horse's evolutionary history and related species. (Rev: HBG 3/02; SLJ 3/02) [636.1]

22598 LaBonte, Gail. *The Miniature Horse* (3–5). Illus. 1990, Macmillan LB $13.95 (0-87518-424-3). 60pp. The origin of these tiny horses, some no more than 25 inches tall. (Rev: BCCB 4/90; BL 4/1/90; SLJ 7/90) [636.1]

22599 Lauber, Patricia. *The True-or-False Book of Horses* (2–3). Illus. by Rosalyn Schanzer. 2000, HarperCollins LB $16.99 (0-688-16920-1). 32pp. Using a question-and-answer format, this book covers topics about horses including their physical

characteristics, behavior, and history. (Rev: BL 4/15/00; HBG 9/00; SLJ 6/00) [636.1]

22600 Libby, Barbara M. *I Rode the Red Horse: Secretariat's Belmont Race* (1–3). Illus. by author. 2003, Blood-Horse $16.95 (1-58150-096-3). 32pp. Triple Crown-winner Secretariat's victory at the Belmont Stakes in 1973 is told in the words of jockey Ron Turcotte. (Rev: BL 7/03; HBG 10/03) [798.4]

22601 McMillan, Bruce. *My Horse of the North* (K–3). Illus. 1997, Scholastic $15.95 (0-590-97205-7). 32pp. Three Icelandic youngsters tell about the horses that were originally brought there by the Vikings. (Rev: BL 9/1/97; HB 9–10/97; HBG 3/98; SLJ 9/97) [636.3]

22602 Meadows, Graham. *Horses* (PS–2). Photos by author. Series: Animals Are Not Like Us. 1999, Gareth Stevens LB $13.95 (0-8368-2253-6). 24pp. This is a very simple introduction to horses, their appearance, senses, and behavior, with some comparisons with humans. (Rev: HBG 9/99; SLJ 7/99) [636.1]

22603 Parker, Jane. *The Fantastic Book of Horses* (4–6). Illus. Series: Fantastic Book Of. 1997, Millbrook LB $22.40 (0-7613-0566-1). 40pp. The care, uses, and breeds of horses are introduced in this copiously illustrated book with foldout sections. (Rev: SLJ 8/97) [636.1]

22604 Patent, Dorothy Hinshaw. *Horses* (3–5). Illus. by William Muñoz. 1994, Carolrhoda LB $19.93 (0-87614-766-X). 48pp. This excellent introduction to the world of horses includes material on their history, types, behavior, and current uses. (Rev: BCCB 3/94; BL 4/1/94; SLJ 3/94) [636.1]

22605 Patent, Dorothy Hinshaw. *Horses* (2–3). Series: Early Bird Nature Books. 2001, Lerner LB $22.60 (0-8225-3045-7). 48pp. With color photographs on each page and a simple text, this book introduces the life cycle of the horse with material on its anatomy, habits, and relationship to humans. (Rev: BL 8/1/01; HBG 10/01) [636.1]

22606 Penny, Malcolm. *The Secret Life of Wild Horses* (4–7). Series: The Secret World Of. 2002, Raintree LB $27.12 (0-7398-4987-5). 48pp. A page of little-known facts about wild horses introduces this book that explores the horse's life, habits, mating, behavior, and threats to its future. (Rev: BL 8/02) [636.1]

22607 Peterson, Chris. *Wild Horses* (3–8). Illus. 2003, Boyds Mills $16.95 (1-56397-745-1). 32pp. Peterson presents photographs of and information about the horses living in the Wild Horse Sanctuary in the Black Hills of South Dakota. (Rev: BL 2/15/03; HBG 10/03; SLJ 3/03) [599.665]

22608 Peterson, Cris. *Horsepower: The Wonder of Draft Horses* (K–4). Photos by Alvis Upitis. 1997, Boyds Mills $16.95 (1-56397-626-9). A photoessay that introduces the history, physical characteristics, and functions of the draft horse, with special coverage on Belgians, Percherons, and Clydesdales. (Rev: BCCB 4/97; SLJ 4/97) [636.1]

22609 Presnall, Judith Janda. *Horse Therapists* (4–7). Illus. Series: Animals with Jobs. 2002, Gale

LB $23.70 (0-7377-0615-5). 48pp. Numerous photographs show how horses are used in various therapeutic situations including exercise for people with physical and mental disabilities. (Rev: BL 4/1/02; SLJ 3/02) [636.1]

22610 Price, Steven D. *The Kids' Book of the American Quarter Horse* (3–5). Illus. 2000, Lyons Pr. paper $19.95 (1-55821-975-7). 159pp. As well as telling how to choose, care for, and ride quarter horses, this account tells their history and explains the functions of the American Quarter Horse Association. (Rev: BL 2/1/00) [636.1]

22611 Ransford, Sandy. *Horse and Pony Breeds* (3–5). Photos by Bob Langrish. Series: Kingfisher Riding Club. 2003, Kingfisher $14.95 (0-7534-5575-7). 64pp. An attractive guide to horse and pony breeds from around the world. (Rev: HBG 10/03; SLJ 7/03) [636.1]

22612 Ransford, Sandy. *Horse and Pony Care* (4–7). Illus. by Bob Langrish. 2002, Kingfisher $14.95 (0-7534-5439-4). 64pp. A well-illustrated account that gives clear instructions on such topics as washing and clipping a pony, exercise routines, and caring for pastureland. (Rev: BL 5/1/02; SLJ 7/02) [636.1]

22613 Ransford, Sandy. *The Kingfisher Illustrated Horse and Pony Encyclopedia* (4–8). Photos by Bob Langrish. Illus. 2004, Kingfisher $24.95 (0-7534-5781-4). 224pp. After describing the history and various breeds of horses, this comprehensive and highly illustrated volume explains how to care for horses and how to ride them well and safely. (Rev: BL 3/1/05; SLJ 1/05) [636.1]

22614 Richter, Judy. *Riding for Kids* (4–8). 2003, Storey Kids $23.95 (1-58017-511-2); paper $16.95 (1-58017-510-4). 128pp. An introduction to horsemanship, from caring for horses and riding equipment to advice on safety, showing, and jumping. (Rev: SLJ 3/04) [798.2]

22615 Ryden, Hope. *Wild Horses I Have Known* (4–8). 1999, Clarion $18.00 (0-395-77520-5). This photoessay about the wild mustangs that live around the Wyoming-Montana border details their behavior, social structure, and survival methods. (Rev: BCCB 4/99; BL 4/15/99; HB 3–4/99; HBG 9/99; SLJ 4/99) [636.1]

22616 Silverstein, Alvin, et al. *The Mustang* (4–8). Series: Endangered in America. 1997, Millbrook $24.90 (0-7613-0048-1). Examines the life cycle and behavior of the mustang, the reasons it has become endangered, and the measures being taken to ensure its survival. (Rev: BL 3/15/97; SLJ 6/97) [636.1]

22617 Stefoff, Rebecca. *Horses* (5–8). Illus. Series: AnimalWays. 2000, Marshall Cavendish LB $28.50 (0-7614-1139-9). 112pp. A well-illustrated account that describes the physical and behavioral characteristics of horses, their place in the classification system, and their relationships with humans. (Rev: BL 1/1–15/01) [599.884]

22618 Tracqui, Valerie. *The Horse: Faster Than the Wind* (3–6). Illus. by Gilles Delaborde. Series: Face-to-Face. 2001, Charlesbridge $9.95 (1-57091-450-8). 32pp. Clear text and photographs introduce the

horse, with information on habitat, behavior, and reproduction. (Rev: BL 10/15/01; HBG 3/02) [599.665]

22619 van der Linde, Laurel. *From Mustangs to Movie Stars: Five True Horse Legends of Our Time* (4–7). Illus. 1995, Millbrook LB $24.40 (1-56294-456-8). 71pp. Biographies of five famous horses are recounted, from the racer Native Dancer to Cass Olé, who was the star of the film *The Black Stallion*. (Rev: BCCB 12/95; SLJ 12/95) [636.1]

22620 *The Visual Dictionary of the Horse* (5–8). Illus. Series: Eyewitness Visual Dictionaries. 1994, DK paper $18.99 (1-56458-504-2). 64pp. This pictorial study includes information on anatomy, breeds, grooming, racing, jumping, and equipment. (Rev: BCCB 7–8/94; SLJ 7/94) [636]

22621 Vogel, Julia. *Wild Horses* (2–4). Illus. 2004, NorthWord $10.95 (1-55971-881-1). 48pp. Vogel examines the threats facing the last remaining herds of wild mustangs roaming the western United States. (Rev: BL 3/15/04; SLJ 10/04) [599.665]

Zoos and Marine Aquariums

22622 Aliki. *My Visit to the Zoo* (PS–2). Illus. 1997, HarperCollins LB $15.89 (0-06-024943-9). 40pp. A young girl acts as guide in a zoo and introduces the purposes of zoos as well as many of the animals that are kept there. (Rev: BL 7/97; HB 9–10/97; HBG 3/98; SLJ 10/97) [590]

22623 Altman, Joyce. *Dear Bronx Zoo* (3–6). Illus. by Sue Goldberg. 1992, Avon paper $3.50 (0-380-71649-6). 102pp. The answers to questions most frequently asked by Bronx Zoo visitors. (Rev: BL 1/1/91; SLJ 3/91) [590.74]

22624 Altman, Joyce. *Lunch at the Zoo: What Zoo Animals Eat and Why* (3–6). Illus. 2001, Holt $16.00 (0-8050-6070-7). 88pp. This outstanding science book goes behind the scenes at a zoo to show the care and medical expertise that goes into preparing and feeding the different animals. (Rev: BCCB 2/01; BL 12/1/00*; HBG 10/01; SLJ 2/01) [636]

22625 Hanna, Jack. *Jungle Jack Hanna's What Zookeepers Do* (2–3). Illus. by Rick A. Prebeg. Series: Hello Reader! 1998, Scholastic paper $3.99 (0-590-67324-6). 48pp. A fascinating subject and dramatic photos make this easy-to-read book a popular one on zookeepers and their duties, such as feeding the tigers and caring for newly hatched eagle chicks. (Rev: BL 11/1/98) [636.088]

22626 McMillan, Bruce. *The Baby Zoo* (1–6). 1995, Scholastic paper $3.95 (0-590-44635-5). 40pp. A survey of 16 baby animals in two American zoos. (Rev: HB 3–4/92; SLJ 5/92) [599]

22627 Morecroft, Richard, and Alison Mackay. *Zoo Album* (3–5). Illus. by Karen Lloyd-Diviny. 2004, Enchanted Lion $17.95 (1-59270-032-2). 48pp. Vivid artwork and an easy-to-follow narrative introduce animals in Australian zoos, with interesting anecdotes by caretakers. (Rev: BL 12/1/04; SLJ 2/05) [590.73]

22628 Nagda, Ann Whitehead, and Cindy Bickel. *Tiger Math* (3–6). Illus. 2000, Holt $16.00 (0-8050-

6248-3). 30pp. This account traces the growth and maturation of a Siberian tiger cub who was cared for at the Denver Zoo after his mother died when he was only ten weeks old. (Rev: BCCB 9/00; BL 10/1/00; HBG 3/01; SLJ 10/00) [511]

22629 Patent, Dorothy Hinshaw. *Back to the Wild* (4–6). Photos by William Munoz. 1997, Harcourt $18.00 (0-15-200280-4). 69pp. This account shows how present-day zoos are helping save endangered animals and gives four case studies where tamarins, red wolves, lemurs, and the black-footed ferret have been rescued. (Rev: SLJ 4/97) [590]

22630 Pfeffer, Wendy. *Popcorn Park Zoo: A Haven with a Heart* (3–6). Illus. by J. Gerard Smith. 1992, Simon & Schuster paper $16.95 (0-671-74589-1). 64pp. A unique zoo in New Jersey that cares for animals that are sick, old, hurt, abused, or unwanted. (Rev: BL 6/1/92; SLJ 7/92) [590]

22631 Ricciuti, Edward R. *A Pelican Swallowed My Head and Other Zoo Stories* (4–8). 2002, Simon & Schuster $17.00 (0-689-82532-3). 222pp. Anecdotes about a variety of animals and their keepers serve as a framework for information on the Bronx Zoo's innovative approach to designing animal-friendly, environmentally appropriate habitats. (Rev: HBG 3/03; SLJ 10/02) [590.74]

22632 Rinard, Judith E. *Zoos Without Cages* (5–8). Illus. 1981, National Geographic LB $12.50 (0-87044-340-2). 104pp. A description of the new zoos that strive to reproduce the natural habitat of the enclosed animals. [590.74]

22633 Yancey, Diane. *Zoos* (5–8). Series: Overview. 1995, Lucent LB $27.45 (1-56006-163-4). Discusses the history of zoos, the controversy surrounding them, and species survival plans. (Rev: BL 6/1–15/95; SLJ 3/95) [590]

Botany

General and Miscellaneous

22634 Ganeri, Anita. *Plant Life Cycles* (K–3). Series: Nature's Patterns. 2005, Heinemann LB $24.21 (1-4034-5896-0). 32pp. In simple langue, this volume introduces the life cycles of plants. (Rev: SLJ 6/05)

22635 Greenaway, Theresa. *The Plant Kingdom* (5–8). Illus. 1999, Raintree LB $27.12 (0-8172-5886-8). 48pp. Using diagrams, sidebars, and color photographs, this account introduces the basics of plant classification while also covering such topics as photosynthesis and plant reproduction. (Rev: BL 2/1/00) [580]

22636 Murphy, Patricia J. *Peeking at Plants with a Scientist* (1–3). Series: I Like Science! 2004, Enslow LB $16.95 (0-7660-2266-8). 24pp. The work of a botanist is portrayed in question-and-answer format and many photographs. (Rev: SLJ 8/04) [580]

22637 Patent, Dorothy Hinshaw. *Plants on the Trail with Lewis and Clark.* (5–8). Photos by William Muñoz. 2003, Clarion $18.00 (0-618-06776-0). 102pp. This introduction to the trees and plants seen by Lewis and Clark also discusses Lewis's training

as a botanist and his contributions to the field. (Rev: BL 3/1/03; HBG 10/03; SLJ 5/03) [581.978]

22638 Schaeffer, Lola M. *Pick, Pull, Snap! Where Once a Flower Bloomed* (PS–1). Illus. by Lindsay Barrett George. 2003, Greenwillow $15.99 (0-688-17834-0). 32pp. Attractively illustrated flaps and fold-outs add to the appeal of this introduction to the basics of plant growth. (Rev: BL 5/1/03; HBG 10/03; SLJ 7/03) [571.8]

22639 Silverstein, Alvin, et al. *Photosynthesis* (5–9). Series: Science Concepts. 1998, Twenty-First Century LB $26.90 (0-7613-3000-3). 63pp. Photosynthesis is explained, with a history of the discoveries about the process and material on related issues including acid rain and the greenhouse effect. (Rev: HBG 3/99; SLJ 2/99) [581.1]

Flowers

22640 *Flowers* (PS–3). Illus. Series: First Discovery. 1993, Scholastic $11.95 (0-590-46383-7). 30pp. In this interactive book, various kinds of flowers and their parts are introduced. (Rev: BL 10/1/93; SLJ 8/93) [582.13]

22641 Holmes, Anita. *Flowers and Friends* (K–2). Series: We Can Read About — Science! 2000, Benchmark LB $14.95 (0-7614-1113-5). 32pp. An easy-to-read book that describes the process of pollination through the perception of various creatures. (Rev: HBG 3/01; SLJ 2/01) [582]

22642 Hood, Susan, ed. *Wildflowers* (5–8). Illus. 1998, Scholastic paper $17.95 (0-590-05464-3). Fifty common wildflowers are pictured and described, along with information on what equipment to use and what to look for to observe and study wildflowers (leaves, blooms, habitat, height, range). (Rev: BL 8/98; SLJ 8/98) [583]

22643 Johnson, Sylvia A. *Morning Glories* (4–7). Illus. 1985, Lerner LB $22.60 (0-8225-1462-1). 48pp. Color photographs display the stages of this plant's development. (Rev: BCCB 3/86; BL 4/15/86; SLJ 4/86)

22644 Lerner, Carol. *Cactus* (4–7). Illus. 1992, Morrow LB $14.89 (0-688-09637-9). 32pp. After explaining the parts of the cactus and how it can exist in near-waterless environments, this account describes different species. (Rev: BCCB 10/92; HB 1–2/93; SLJ 12/92) [635.7]

22645 Nielsen, Nancy J. *Carnivorous Plants* (4–8). Illus. 1992, Watts paper $6.95 (0-531-15644-3). 64pp. A look, with the help of color photographs, at flesh-eating plants, such as the Venus's-flytrap. (Rev: BL 6/1/92; SLJ 7/92) [581.5]

22646 Overbeck, Cynthia. *Carnivorous Plants* (4–8). Illus. by Kiyashi Shimizu. 1982, Lerner LB $31.95 (0-8225-1470-2). 48pp. A survey of these plants and how they evolved. [581.5]

22647 Pascoe, Elaine. *Flowers* (3–5). Photos by Dwight Kuhn. Series: Nature Close-Up. 2003, Gale/Blackbirch LB $27.45 (1-56711-432-6). 48pp. Beautiful photographs of flowering plants are accompanied by introductory information on their importance to ecology and their usefulness to mankind. (Rev: SLJ 3/04) [575.6]

22648 Ryden, Hope. *Wildflowers Around the Year* (4–6). Illus. 2001, Clarion $17.00 (0-395-85814-3). 48pp. A handsome book on wildflowers that gives details on characteristics, uses in food or medicine, and fertilization. (Rev: BL 3/1/01; HB 3–4/01; HBG 10/01) [582.13]

22649 Souza, D. M. *Freaky Flowers* (4–7). Series: Watts Library. 2002, Watts LB $24.00 (0-531-11981-5). 64pp. Flowering plants are the main focus in this discussion of basic botany, the ways in which flowers attract pollinators, and the environmental dangers plants are facing. (Rev: SLJ 7/02) [582]

22650 Winner, Cherie. *The Sunflower Family* (4–7). Illus. 1996, Carolrhoda LB $23.93 (1-57505-007-2); paper $7.95 (1-57505-029-3). 48pp. Growth patterns, structures, and reproduction are topics covered in this account of the sunflower family, including thistles, daisies, and asters. (Rev: BL 10/1/96; SLJ 10/96) [583]

Foods and Farming

GENERAL

22651 Bial, Raymond. *Portrait of a Farm Family* (4–7). Illus. 1995, Houghton Mifflin $17.00 (0-395-69936-3). 48pp. A behind-the-scenes look at a dairy farm in Illinois that gives details on day-to-day operations and problems. (Rev: BCCB 10/95; BL 9/1/95*; HB 11–12/95; SLJ 12/95) [338.1]

22652 Bowden, Rob. *Food and Farming* (5–8). Illus. Series: Sustainable World. 2004, Gale/KidHaven LB $23.70 (0-7377-1899-4). 48pp. Bowden looks at conventional methods of farming and at the new focus on sustainable agriculture, providing lots of facts and statistics and highlighting choices we all can make that may improve the future. (Rev: BL 4/15/04; SLJ 10/04) [338]

22653 Hughes, Meredith S. *Glorious Grasses: The Grains* (5–8). Series: Plants We Eat. 1999, Lerner LB $26.60 (0-8225-2831-2). A description of the history, cultivation, processing, and dietary importance of wheat, rice, corn, millet, barley, oats, and rye, plus recipes and activities. (Rev: BL 7/99; HBG 9/99; SLJ 8/99) [633.1]

22654 Lampton, Christopher. *Famine* (4–6). Illus. Series: Disaster Book. 1994, Millbrook LB $19.90 (1-56294-317-0). 48pp. The causes and effects of famines are covered, with information on some historic disasters. (Rev: BL 6/1–15/94; SLJ 4/94) [363.8]

22655 Olney, Ross R. *The Farm Combine* (4–8). Illus. 1984, Walker LB $10.85 (0-8027-6568-8). 64pp. The development of the reaper and thrasher is discussed, with information on today's combine harvester.

22656 Tesar, Jenny. *Food and Water: Threats, Shortages and Solutions* (5–9). Series: Our Fragile Planet. 1992, Facts on File LB $21.95 (0-8160-2495-2). A discussion of the world's water and food supplies, threats to them, and possible solutions. (Rev: BL 6/1/92) [333.91]

FARMS, RANCHES, AND FARM ANIMALS

22657 Artley, Bob. *Once Upon a Farm* (4–9). Illus. by author. 2000, Pelican $21.95 (1-56554-753-5). 127pp. Fine watercolors accompany a readable look at the seasons as experienced by the author while growing up on a farm in Iowa. (Rev: SLJ 12/00) [630]

22658 Bell, Rachael. *Cows* (K–3). Series: Farm Animals. 2000, Heinemann LB $13.95 (1-57572-529-0). 32pp. Using double-page spreads, this book introduces cows and their uses as a source of meat and milk. Also use *Pigs* (2000). (Rev: HBG 3/01; SLJ 7/00) [630]

22659 Bial, Raymond. *The Farms* (4–7). Photos by author. Illus. Series: Building America. 2001, Benchmark LB $25.64 (0-7614-1332-4). 56pp. An interesting, beautifully illustrated look at the ways in which farms developed in America, with information on their structure and significance to the country as a whole. Also use *The Mills* (2001). (Rev: HBG 3/02; SLJ 2/02*) [630]

22660 Damerow, Gail. *Your Chickens: A Kid's Guide to Raising and Showing* (4–7). Illus. 1993, Storey paper $14.95 (0-88266-823-4). 160pp. A straightforward, practical guide on raising prize-winning chickens that is both thorough and filled with information. (Rev: BL 5/15/94; SLJ 1/94) [636.5]

22661 Damerow, Gail. *Your Goats: A Kid's Guide to Raising and Showing* (4–7). Illus. 1993, Storey paper $14.95 (0-88266-825-0). 176pp. This is a complete guide to raising, breeding, and showing goats, with many useful tips and helpful illustrations. (Rev: BL 5/15/94; SLJ 1/94) [636.3]

22662 Drake, Jane, and Ann Love. *Farming* (3–4). Illus. by Pat Cupples. Series: America at Work. 1998, Kids Can $12.95 (1-55074-451-8). 31pp. Factual information about a vegetable farm and a cattle ranch, including chores, processes, and equipment, is introduced by fictional children who live on these farms and ranches. (Rev: HBG 3/99; SLJ 12/98) [630]

22663 Feldman, Thea. *Who You Callin' Chicken?* (3–5). Photos by Stephen Green-Armytage. 2003, Abrams $14.95 (0-8109-4593-2). Chickens of all kinds feature in this lively photographic survey. (Rev: HBG 4/04; SLJ 12/03) [636.5]

22664 Fowler, Allan. *If It Weren't for Farmers* (1–2). Illus. Series: Rookie Readers. 1993, Children's Book Pr. LB $19.00 (0-516-06009-0). 32pp. For beginning readers, this is an introduction to what farmers do and how various foods are grown. (Rev: BL 3/1/94) [630]

22665 Fowler, Allan. *Thanks to Cows* (1–2). Illus. Series: Rookie Readers. 1992, Children's Book Pr. LB $19.00 (0-516-04924-0). 32pp. With large color photos and simple text, this book introduces cattle and their importance. (Rev: BL 6/15/92) [636.2]

22666 Fowler, Allan. *Woolly Sheep and Hungry Goats* (1–2). Illus. Series: Rookie Readers. 1993, Children's Book Pr. LB $19.00 (0-516-06014-7). 32pp. Sheep and goats and their habits are introduced with a simple text, color pictures on each page, and a small format. (Rev: BL 9/1/93; SLJ 9/93) [636.3]

22667 Geisert, Bonnie, and Arthur Geisert. *Haystack* (K–3). Illus. 1995, Houghton Mifflin $15.95 (0-395-69722-0). 32pp. The story of how haystacks are made and of their uses on farms. (Rev: BCCB 10/95; BL 9/15/95; HB 11–12/95; SLJ 9/95) [633.2]

22668 Gibbons, Gail. *Chicks and Chickens* (1–3). Illus. by author. 2003, Holiday House $16.95 (0-8234-1700-X). Using cartoon illustrations and simple narrative, Gibbons examines the life cycle of chickens. (Rev: HBG 10/03; SLJ 7/03) [636.5]

22669 Gibbons, Gail. *Farming* (PS–2). Illus. by author. 1988, Holiday House LB $16.95 (0-8234-0682-2); paper $6.95 (0-8234-0797-7). 32pp. Farm landscapes through the seasons. (Rev: BL 6/1/88; SLJ 8/88)

22670 Graff, Nancy P. *The Strength of the Hills: A Portrait of a Family Farm* (4–6). Illus. by Richard Howard. 1989, Little, Brown $14.95 (0-316-32277-6). 80pp. This account highlights life on a family dairy farm in Vermont. (Rev: BL 11/15/89; SLJ 4/90*) [338.1]

22671 Hill, Lee S. *Farms Feed the World* (1–3). Series: Building Blocks Books. 1997, Carolrhoda LB $21.27 (1-57505-075-7). 32pp. This book takes the reader on a visit to many kinds of farms around the world, from a wheat field in Montana to a rice paddy in Indonesia. (Rev: BL 3/15/98; HBG 3/98) [630]

22672 Kalman, Bobbie. *Hooray for Sheep Farming!* (K–3). Series: Hooray for Farming! 1997, Crabtree LB $19.96 (0-86505-655-2); paper $7.95 (0-86505-669-2). 32pp. This book describes the habits and physical structure of sheep, different kinds of wool, and the everyday routines on a sheep farm. (Rev: HBG 3/98; SLJ 4/98) [630]

22673 Klingel, Cynthia, and Robert B. Noyed. *Farmers* (K–1). Series: Wonder Books. 2001, Child's World LB $21.36 (1-56766-940-9). 24pp. This book for beginning readers gives basic information about farms and farmers. (Rev: HBG 3/02; SLJ 2/02) [630]

22674 Miller, Sara S. *Chickens* (2–3). Series: True Books. 2000, Children's Book Pr. LB $22.00 (0-516-21576-0). 32pp. A simple introduction to chickens that describes their anatomy, uses, homes, and habits. (Rev: BL 1/1–15/01) [636.5]

22675 Miller, Sara S. *Cows* (2–3). Illus. Series: True Books. 2000, Children's Book Pr. LB $22.00 (0-516-21577-9). 48pp. Covers dairy cows and their domestication as well as giving information on dairy products and life on a dairy farm. (Rev: BL 1/1–15/01) [636.3]

22676 Miller, Sara S. *Goats* (2–3). Series: True Books. 2000, Children's Book Pr. LB $22.00 (0-516-21578-7). 32pp. A look at the life cycle of the goat, its habits, and its uses. (Rev: BL 1/1–15/01) [636.3]

22677 Miller, Sara S. *Pigs* (2–3). Series: True Books. 2000, Children's Book Pr. LB $22.00 (0-516-21579-5). 32pp. Using colorful pictures and a minimum of text, this farm animal is introduced with

material on its anatomy, habits, and uses. (Rev: BL 1/1–15/01) [636.3]

22678 Miller, Sara S. *Sheep* (2–3). Illus. Series: True Books. 2000, Children's Book Pr. LB $22.00 (0-516-21580-9). 48pp. This book introduces sheep and sheep farming with material on the animal's use both for food and wool. (Rev: BL 1/1–15/01) [636.3]

22679 Morck, Irene. *Old Bird* (2–4). Illus. by Muriel Wood. 2003, Fitzhenry & Whiteside $15.95 (1-55041-695-2). 32pp. An aging horse named Bird is determined to prove she can pull her weight around the farm in this novel based on a true story. (Rev: SLJ 10/03) [813]

22680 Munro, Roxie. *Ranch* (2–4). 2004, Bright Sky $16.95 (1-931721-37-8). 36pp. Readers are introduced to all aspects of a cattle ranch and the people who work there. (Rev: BL 7/04; SLJ 9/04) [636.2]

22681 Peterson, Chris. *Amazing Grazing* (3–5). Illus. by Alvis Upitis. 2002, Boyds Mills $16.95 (1-56397-942-X). 32pp. Color photographs and a lucid text show how three Montana cattle ranchers are using environment-friendly practices. (Rev: BL 4/1/02; HBG 10/02; SLJ 4/02) [636.0845]

22682 Peterson, Cris. *Century Farm: One Hundred Years on a Family Farm* (2–4). Illus. 1999, Boyds Mills $16.95 (1-56397-710-9). 32pp. Traces the changes in farm life over a century and includes material on the machinery used, the tasks performed, and the different farm animals. (Rev: BCCB 3/99; BL 3/1/99; HBG 9/99; SLJ 4/99) [636.2]

22683 Powell, Jillian. *From Calf to Cow* (PS–3). Series: How Do They Grow? 2001, Raintree LB $17.98 (0-7398-4426-1). 32pp. Brief text and large, full-color photographs follow calves through birth and growth. Also use *From Chick to Chicken* and from *From Piglet to Pig* (both 2001). (Rev: HBG 3/02; SLJ 1/02) [636.2]

22684 Rendon, Marcie, and Cheryl Walsh Bellville. *Farmer's Market: Families Working Together* (4–6). Illus. 2001, Carolrhoda $23.93 (1-57505-462-0). 48pp. A look at truck farming and the sale of the produce at farmers' markets, with profiles of two Midwest families. (Rev: BL 5/1/01; HBG 10/01) [635]

22685 Rogers, Hal. *Milking Machines* (PS–K). Series: Farm Machines at Work. 2000, Child's World LB $21.36 (1-56766-753-8). 24pp. Color pictures and a brief text introduce milking machines, their parts, and their uses. Also use from the same series: *Combines*, *Plows*, and *Tractors* (all 2000). (Rev: BL 1/1–15/01; HBG 10/01; SLJ 1/01) [621]

22686 Schuh, Mari C. *Chickens on the Farm* (PS–2). Series: On the Farm. 2001, Capstone LB $10.95 (0-7368-0991-0). 24pp. Spare text and full-color photographs convey simple facts about chickens. Also use *Pigs on the Farm* and *Sheep on the Farm* (both 2001). (Rev: HBG 3/02; SLJ 1/02) [636.5]

22687 Sklansky, Amy E. *Where Do Chicks Come From?* (K–2). Illus. by Pam Paparone. Series: Let's-Read-and-Find-Out. 2005, HarperCollins LB $16.89 (0-06-028893-0); paper $4.99 (0-06-445212-3).

40pp. Follows the development of a chick from the moment of fertilization until it hatches from the egg roughly three weeks later. (Rev: BL 2/1/05; SLJ 2/05) [636.5]

22688 Webber, Desiree Morrison. *Bone Head: Story of the Longhorn* (4–7). Illus. by Sandy Shropshire. 2003, Eakin $16.95 (1-57168-763-7). 74pp. The longhorn's characteristics and the reasons for its early success but decline with the arrival of the railroad are explored in appealing text and archival photographs. (Rev: HBG 4/04; SLJ 2/04) [636.2]

22689 Wolfman, Judy. *Life on a Cattle Farm* (4–6). Illus. by David Lorenz Winston. Series: Life on a Farm. 2001, Carolrhoda LB $23.93 (1-57505-516-3). 48pp. A photo-illustrated look at activities on a Pennsylvania cattle farm, told from a teenager's point of view. Also use *Life on a Crop Farm, Life on a Goat Farm*, and *Life on a Horse Farm* (all 2001). (Rev: BL 11/15/01; HBG 3/02; SLJ 11/01) [636.2]

22690 Wolfman, Judy. *Life on a Pig Farm* (3–5). Illus. 1998, Carolrhoda $22.60 (1-57505-237-7). 48pp. This photoessay describes life on a pig farm, as experienced by three sisters. (Rev: BL 10/15/98; HBG 3/99; SLJ 3/99) [636.4]

FOODS

22691 Allen, Nancy Kelly. *Whose Work Is This? A Look at Things Animals Make-Pearls, Milk, and Honey* (PS–2). Illus. Series: Whose Is It? Science. 2004, Picture Window LB $16.95 (1-4048-0612-1). 24pp. A rhythmic question-and-answer format and colorful collages introduce the wide variety of foods that animals produce.

22692 Back, Christine. *Bean and Plant* (1–3). Illus. 1986, Silver Burdett LB $15.95 (0-382-09286-4); paper $3.95 (0-382-24014-6). 25pp. A basic science book in full color telling how beans grow. (Rev: BL 1/1/87)

22693 Bryant-Mole, Karen. *Food* (PS–3). Illus. Series: Picture This! 1997, Rigby $18.50 (1-57572-150-3). 24pp. Various kinds of food are introduced, cooking methods are discussed, and the principles of good nutrition are mentioned. (Rev: BL 10/15/97; SLJ 12/97) [641.3]

22694 Burleigh, Robert. *Chocolate: Riches from the Rainforest* (3–6). Illus. 2002, Abrams $16.95 (0-8109-5734-5). 40pp. Traces the rich history of chocolate, from the Aztecs to Hershey's. (Rev: BL 3/1/02; HBG 10/02; SLJ 4/02) [641.3]

22695 Burns, Diane L. *Cranberries: Fruit of the Bogs* (3–5). Illus. by Cheryl Walsh Bellville. 1994, Carolrhoda LB $22.60 (0-87614-822-4). 48pp. A book about cranberry growing and activities during and after harvesting. (Rev: BL 12/1/94; SLJ 3/95) [633.76]

22696 Burns, Diane L. *Sugaring Season: Making Maple Syrup* (1–5). Illus. 1990, Carolrhoda $22.60 (0-87614-420-2); paper $5.95 (0-87614-554-3). 32pp. Crisp photos and good diagrams help to explain the maple syrup process. (Rev: BL 11/1/90; SLJ 12/90) [664]

22697 Chandler, Gary, and Kevin Graham. *Natural Foods and Products* (4–8). Illus. Series: Making a Better World. 1996, Twenty-First Century LB $25.90 (0-8050-4623-2). This work discusses genetically engineered foods, safe eco-friendly methods of growing crops, and companies that engage in safe practices. (Rev: BL 12/15/96; SLJ 1/97) [333.76]

22698 Charles, Oz. *How Does Soda Get into the Bottle?* (2–4). Illus. 1996, Silver Burdett paper $4.95 (0-382-24375-7). 32pp. A brief photo-essay on this manufacturing process that takes the reader into a bottling plant. (Rev: BL 4/15/88)

22699 Charlip, Remy. *Peanut Butter Party: Including the History, Uses, and Future of Peanut Butter* (K–4). Illus. by author. 1999, Tricycle $14.95 (1-883672-69-4). Peanut butter is celebrated in a book that covers its history and outlines such activities as recipes for foods with peanut butter, edible arts and crafts, riddles, games, a one-act play on the subject, and a series of clever illustrations. (Rev: BCCB 7–8/99; HBG 9/99; SLJ 6/99) [641.3]

22700 Cooper, Jason. *Beef* (1–3). Series: Farm to Market. 1997, Rourke LB $14.60 (0-86625-617-2). 24pp. This book describes how North American beef cattle are raised, slaughtered, processed, and marketed. (Rev: SLJ 6/98) [641]

22701 Cooper, Jason. *Dairy Products* (1–3). Series: Farm to Market. 1997, Rourke LB $14.60 (0-86625-619-9). 24pp. After a description of how dairy cattle are raised, this book covers their products, how they are processed, and how they are marketed. (Rev: SLJ 6/98) [637]

22702 Cooper, Jason. *Poultry* (1–3). Series: Farm to Market. 1997, Rourke LB $14.60 (0-86625-618-0). 24pp. This book shows how different types of poultry are raised, processed, and marketed. (Rev: SLJ 6/98) [598]

22703 D'Amico, Joan, and Karen Eich Drummond. *The Science Chef: 100 Fun Food Experiments and Recipes for Kids* (4–6). Illus. 1994, Wiley paper $12.95 (0-471-31045-X). 192pp. Simple experiments introduce various properties of foods and give youngsters a chance to be cooks. (Rev: BL 11/1/94; SLJ 12/94) [641.3]

22704 dePaola, Tomie. *The Popcorn Book* (1–3). Illus. 1978, Holiday House LB $15.95 (0-8234-0314-9); paper $6.95 (0-8234-0533-8). 32pp. While Tony makes a plate of popcorn, Tiny relates interesting facts about this delicious food.

22705 Erdosh, George. *The African American Kitchen: Food for Body and Soul* (4–7). Series: The Library of African American Arts and Culture. 1999, Rosen LB $17.95 (0-8239-1850-5). 64pp. Traces the origins and evolution of "soul food" in American culture and includes a number of recipes. (Rev: SLJ 8/99) [394.1]

22706 Erlbach, Arlene. *Soda Pop* (3–6). Illus. 1994, Lerner LB $19.93 (0-8225-2386-8). 48pp. Tells about the origins, history, and manufacture of soda pop, with recipes for making various kinds at home. Also use *Peanut Butter* (1994). (Rev: BL 5/1/94) [663]

22707 Fleisher, Paul. *Ice Cream Treats: The Inside Scoop* (4–6). Photos by David O. Saunders. 2001, Carolrhoda LB $23.93 (1-57505-268-7). 48pp. This is an appealing overview of the history of ice cream, with a tour of a factory and a few simple recipes. (Rev: HBG 10/01; SLJ 7/01) [641.8]

22708 Frost, Helen. *The Grain Group* (K–2). Series: Food Guide Pyramid. 2000, Capstone LB $13.25 (0-7368-0538-9). 24pp. This text for beginning readers introduces different grains and explains their importance in the food pyramid. (Rev: HBG 9/00; SLJ 10/00) [633.1]

22709 Gelman, Rita G. *Rice Is Life* (1–4). Illus. by Yangsook Choi. 2000, Holt $15.95 (0-8050-5719-6). 32pp. In original poems and nonfiction vignettes, the author tells of the importance of rice in the life and culture of the Balinese. (Rev: BL 5/15/00; HBG 9/00; SLJ 6/00) [633.1]

22710 Greenstein, Elaine. *Ice-Cream Cones for Sale!* (K–2). Illus. 2003, Scholastic $15.95 (0-439-32728-8). 32pp. Greenstein tells the "real" story behind the ice-cream cone, taking care to delineate the boundaries between known fact and speculative fiction. (Rev: BL 5/1/03; HB 9–10/03; HBG 4/04; SLJ 9/03) [637.4]

22711 Harbison, Elizabeth M. *Loaves of Fun: A History of Bread with Activities and Recipes from Around the World* (3–6). Illus. 1997, Chicago Review paper $12.95 (1-55652-311-4). 91pp. A history of bread from ancient times to the present day, with several activities and 24 recipes. (Rev: BL 5/1/97; SLJ 9/97) [641.8]

22712 Hartzog, John Daniel. *Everyday Science Experiments with Food* (PS–3). 2000, Rosen $19.33 (0-8239-5460-9). 24pp. The eight projects outlined in this simple science book include recipes for making butter and homemade soda. (Rev: SLJ 9/00) [641.3]

22713 Hausherr, Rosmarie. *What Food Is This?* (1–3). Illus. 1994, Scholastic $14.95 (0-590-46583-X). 40pp. Questions about common foods we eat are answered in simple text and luscious photos. (Rev: BCCB 5/94; BL 4/15/94; SLJ 5/94) [641.3]

22714 Hughes, Meredith S. *Flavor Foods: Spices and Herbs* (5–8). Series: Plants We Eat. 2000, Lerner LB $26.60 (0-8225-2835-5). 88pp. This book explains how roots, leaves, flowers, seeds, fruit, and bark of some plants are transformed in the seasonings that flavor so many dishes. (Rev: BL 7/00; HBG 9/00) [633.8]

22715 Johnson, Sylvia A. *Wheat* (4–6). Illus. by Masaharu Susuki. 1990, Lerner LB $21.50 (0-8225-1490-7). 48pp. The life cycle of the wheat plant is described, with material on harvesting and processing. (Rev: BL 4/15/90; SLJ 8/90) [633.1]

22716 Jones, Carol. *Cheese* (4–7). Illus. Series: From Farm to You. 2002, Chelsea $17.95 (0-7910-7005-0). 32pp. This is an absorbing account of the techniques used in manufacturing cheese and the history of cheese, with an overview of the many varieties and a map of cheese eating around the world. Also use *Pasta and Noodles* (2002). (Rev: BL 11/1/02; HBG 3/03) [641.3]

22717 Keller, Kristin Thoennes. *From Maple Trees to Maple Syrup* (1–3). Series: First Facts: From Farm to Table. 2004, Capstone LB $21.26 (0-7368-2634-3). 24pp. This easy-reader traces the various steps involved in the production of maple syrup and includes a simple recipe. Also use *From Oranges to Orange Juice* and *From Peanuts to Peanut Butter* (both 2004). (Rev: SLJ 2/05) [641.3]

22718 Keller, Stella. *Ice Cream* (PS). Illus. by John Holm. Series: Real Readers. 1989, Raintree LB $21.40 (0-8172-3523-X). 32pp. This easily read account describes the history of ice cream. (Rev: BL 2/1/90) [637.4]

22719 King, Hazel. *Milk and Yogurt* (3–5). Series: Food in Focus. 1998, Heinemann LB $15.95 (1-57572-657-2). 32pp. This work gives a history of milk and yogurt, plus material on their processing, nutritional value, nutrients, and related experiments and recipes. (Rev: SLJ 2/99) [636.2]

22720 Landau, Elaine. *Popcorn!* (2–4). Illus. by Brian Lies. 2003, Charlesbridge $16.95 (1-57091-442-7); paper $6.95 (1-57091-443-5). 32pp. An entertaining look at the history of the popular snack, with humorous illustrations. (Rev: BL 2/1/03; HBG 10/03; SLJ 4/03) [646.6]

22721 Landau, Elaine. *Wheat* (2–4). Series: True Books. 1999, Children's Book Pr. LB $21.50 (0-516-21029-7). 48pp. Where wheat is grown, its appearance, uses, and nutritional value are topics covered in this colorful introduction. (Rev: BL 10/15/99) [633.1]

22722 Lasky, Kathryn. *Sugaring Time* (4–7). Illus. 1998, Center for Applied Research paper $4.95 (0-87628-350-4). 64pp. Through photographs and text, the process of maple sugar production in New England is described.

22723 Levenson, George. *Bread Comes to Life: A Garden of Wheat and a Loaf to Eat* (PS–1). 2004, Tricycle $15.95 (1-58246-114-7). 32pp. All kinds of bread feature in this rhythmic and appetizing volume. (Rev: BL 10/1/04) [641.8]

22724 Mandell, Muriel. *Simple Kitchen Experiments: Learning Science with Everyday Foods* (4–6). Illus. 1994, Sterling paper $4.95 (0-8069-8415-5). 128pp. The kitchen becomes a chemistry lab in this book of simple experiments and projects, such as degassing beans. (Rev: BL 5/1/94; SLJ 8/93) [641.3]

22725 Martino, Teresa. *Pizza!* (PS). Illus. by Brigid Faranda. Series: Real Readers. 1989, Raintree LB $21.40 (0-8172-3533-7). 32pp. This easy-to-read account describes the development of pizza from its beginnings 1,000 years ago. (Rev: BL 2/1/90) [641.8]

22726 Mayo, Gretchen Will. *Milk* (1–3). Illus. Series: Where Does Our Food Come From? 2004, Weekly Reader LB $18.60 (0-8368-4067-4). 24pp. This small-format volume shows how milk from dairy cows makes its way to the family dinner table in a variety of processed forms. Also use *Orange Juice* and *Apple Sauce* (2004). (Rev: BL 4/1/04) [637]

22727 Mayo, Gretchen Will. *Pasta* (1–3). Illus. Series: Where Does Our Food Come From? 2004, Weekly Reader LB $18.60 (0-8368-4069-0). 24pp. From fields of wheat to the dinner table, this small-format volume looks at the making of pasta and its many forms. (Rev: BL 4/1/04) [664]

22728 Meltzer, Milton. *Food* (4–8). Illus. 1998, Millbrook LB $24.90 (0-7613-0354-5). 96pp. A fascinating history of food and how it affects our lives. (Rev: BL 1/1–15/99; HBG 3/99; SLJ 1/99) [641.3]

22729 Morgan, Sally. *Superfoods: Genetic Modification of Foods* (5–8). Series: Science at the Edge. 2002, Heinemann LB $27.86 (1-58810-702-7). 64pp. A look at the history and genetic alteration of foods, with discussion of the controversy this has created. (Rev: BL 10/15/02; HBG 3/03; SLJ 4/03) [174.957]

22730 Nelson, Robin. *From Flower to Honey* (K–2). Series: Start to Finish. 2003, Lerner LB $18.60 (0-8225-0717-X). 24pp. Full of photographs, this basic introduction suitable for beginning readers follows the cycle of honey creation. (Rev: HBG 3/03; SLJ 9/03) [638]

22731 Nottridge, Rhoda. *Sugars* (3–6). Illus. Series: Food Facts. 1993, Carolrhoda LB $19.93 (0-87614-796-1). 32pp. Covers such topics as the various forms of sugars, the ways they are made, and their uses, with some simple recipes and activities. (Rev: SLJ 10/93) [613.2]

22732 Older, Jules. *Ice Cream* (3–6). Illus. by Lyn Severance. 2002, Charlesbridge $16.95 (0-88106-111-5); paper $6.95 (0-88106-112-3). 32pp. A fact-packed, colorful, and lighthearted book about the history of ice cream and important ice cream inventions, such as the cone and the banana split. (Rev: BL 2/15/02; HBG 10/02; SLJ 5/02) [641.8]

22733 Paulsen, Gary. *The Tortilla Factory* (1–4). Illus. by Ruth W. Paulsen. 1995, Harcourt $16.00 (0-15-292876-6). 32pp. Simple text and paintings show how kernels of corn become flour and eventually tortillas. (Rev: BL 6/1–15/95; HB 7–8/95; SLJ 7/95) [641.8]

22734 Peters, Celeste A. *Peppers, Popcorn, and Pizza: The Science of Food* (3–5). Series: Science@Work. 1999, Raintree LB $25.69 (0-7398-0136-8). 48pp. This account illustrates how food is related to everyday life through technology, careers, society, and the environment. (Rev: SLJ 3/00) [641]

22735 Peterson, Cris. *Harvest Year* (1–3). Illus. by Alvis Upitis. 1996, Boyds Mills $15.95 (1-56397-571-8). 28pp. Using a month-by-month arrangement, various crops grown in the United States are highlighted. (Rev: BL 9/15/96; SLJ 11/96) [641]

22736 Polin, C. J. *The Story of Chocolate* (2–4). Illus. Series: DK Readers. 2004, DK $12.99 (0-7566-0991-7); paper $3.99 (0-7566-0992-5). 48pp. From harvesting of beans to production of candy bars, this is a simple introduction to chocolate and its history. (Rev: BL 2/1/05) [641.3]

22737 Powell, Jillian. *Milk* (3–5). Illus. Series: Everyone Eats. 1997, Raintree LB $25.69 (0-8172-4766-1). 32pp. This book introduces milk from different animals, but it focuses on the production, uses, and nutritional value of cow's milk. (Rev: SLJ 8/97) [636.2]

22738 Powell, Jillian. *Pasta* (1–4). Illus. Series: Everyone Eats. 1997, Raintree LB $25.69 (0-8172-4760-2). 32pp. A tour of a pasta-producing facility and a guide to the various shapes of pasta highlight this account, which includes a few tasty recipes. (Rev: SLJ 7/97) [664]

22739 Ridgewell, Jenny. *Fruit and Vegetables* (3–5). Series: Food in Focus. 1998, Heinemann LB $15.95 (1-57572-656-4). 32pp. A history of fruits and vegetables is given with material on their cultivation, food value, and processing as well as recipes and a few experiments. (Rev: SLJ 2/99) [634]

22740 Scott, Janine. *Let's Eat: Foods of Our World* (K–2). Series: Spyglass Books. 2002, Compass Point LB $18.60 (0-7565-0365-5). 24pp. A basic look, for beginning readers, at the kinds of foods people eat around the world. (Rev: SLJ 3/03)

22741 Solheim, James. *It's Disgusting — and We Ate It! True Food Facts from Around the World — and Throughout History!* (4–6). Illus. by Eric Brace. 1998, Simon & Schuster $16.00 (0-689-80675-2). 48pp. With zany illustrations and some poems and recipes, this book explores food trivia and uncovers little-known facts such as the use of seaweed in ice cream. (Rev: BCCB 4/98; BL 4/1/98; HBG 9/98; SLJ 6/98) [641.3]

22742 Swain, Ruth Freeman. *How Sweet It Is (and Was): The History of Candy* (1–3). Illus. by John O'Brien. 2003, Holiday House $16.95 (0-8234-1712-3). 32pp. This entertaining, illustrated history of sugary delights includes anecdoes, facts, a timeline, recipes, and a bibliography. (Rev: BL 10/15/03; HBG 4/04; SLJ 11/03)

22743 Thomas, Ann. *Dairy Products* (K–4). Series: Food. 2002, Chelsea Clubhouse LB $14.95 (0-7910-6980-X). 32pp. A simple introduction to milk (including goat and soy milks), cheese, yogurt, and other dairy products. Also use *Meat and Protein* and *Vegetables* (both 2002). (Rev: HBG 3/03; SLJ 2/03)

22744 Thomson, Peggy. *Siggy's Spaghetti Works* (1–3). Illus. by Gloria Kamen. 1993, Morrow $13.93 (0-688-11374-5). 32pp. During a tour of a spaghetti factory, seven kids learn how pasta is made. (Rev: BL 10/1/93; SLJ 1/94) [664]

22745 Thomson, Ruth. *Rice* (3–5). Illus. by Prodeepta Das. Series: Threads. 1990, Garrett LB $15.93 (0-944483-71-2). 26pp. The story of rice, from its growth in paddies to its uses in many cultures. (Rev: BL 2/1/91; SLJ 5/91) [633.1]

22746 Wardlaw, Lee. *Bubblemania* (4–8). 1997, Simon & Schuster paper $4.99 (0-689-81719-3). A thorough history of chewing gum, including descriptions of how gum is made, marketed, and distributed. (Rev: BL 10/1/97; SLJ 1/98) [641.3]

22747 Wardlaw, Lee. *We All Scream for Ice Cream: The Scoop on America's Favorite Dessert* (4–7). Illus. by Sandra Forrest. 2000, HarperCollins paper $4.95 (0-380-80250-3). 216pp. A history of this frozen dessert from ancient times to the present with a concentration on modern times and such variations as Eskimo pies and the Good Humor business. (Rev: SLJ 11/00) [637]

22748 Watts, Barrie. *Tomato* (PS–3). Illus. 1990, Silver Burdett LB $15.95 (0-382-24008-1). 25pp. The growth of a tomato plant is shown above and below ground. (Rev: BL 6/15/90; SLJ 9/90) [635]

22749 *What Makes Popcorn Pop? First Questions and Answers About Food* (K–2). Series: Library of First Questions and Answers. 1994, Time-Life $14.95 (0-7835-0862-X). 47pp. Cartoonlike illustrations help answer such questions about food as how potato chips are made and why Swiss cheese has holes. (Rev: SLJ 8/94) [641]

22750 Woods, Samuel G. *Chocolate: From Start to Finish* (3–5). Photos by Gale Zucker. Series: Made in the USA. 1999, Blackbirch LB $16.95 (1-56711-391-5). 32pp. An attractive book that takes the reader to a chocolate factory in Pennsylvania where they see the manufacturing process from raw material to finished product. (Rev: HBG 4/00; SLJ 2/00) [633.7]

22751 Young, Robert. *The Chewing Gum Book* (3–5). Illus. 1989, Macmillan LB $12.95 (0-87518-401-4). 72pp. Some related topics include history, production, ingredients, and effects on health. (Rev: BL 9/1/89; SLJ 11/89) [664]

22752 Zubrowski, Bernie. *Soda Science: Designing and Testing Soft Drinks* (5–8). Illus. 1997, Morrow LB $14.89 (0-688-13917-5). More than 50 experiments explore the properties of soft drinks and give directions for producing and bottling one's own product. (Rev: BL 8/97; SLJ 10/97) [641.8]

FRUITS

22753 Coldrey, Jennifer. *Strawberry* (K–3). Illus. 1989, Silver Burdett LB $15.95 (0-382-09801-3). 25pp. This simple account traces the development of the strawberry and describes how the use of runners creates new plants. (Rev: SLJ 1/90) [582]

22754 Frost, Helen. *The Fruit Group* (K–2). Series: Food Guide Pyramid. 2000, Capstone LB $13.25 (0-7368-0537-0). 24pp. This easy-to-read guide to good health through eating properly introduces the fruit group and gives examples. (Rev: HBG 9/00; SLJ 10/00) [634]

22755 Gibbons, Gail. *Apples* (2–3). Illus. 2000, Holiday House $16.95 (0-8234-1497-3). 32pp. This introduction to apples includes information on their history, varieties, parts, and development from blossom to fruit. (Rev: BL 8/00; HBG 3/01; SLJ 9/00) [634]

22756 Gibbons, Gail. *The Berry Book* (PS–2). Illus. 2002, Holiday House $16.95 (0-8234-1697-6). 32pp. A well-illustrated introduction to North American berries, including a few simple recipes. (Rev: BL 3/1/02; HBG 10/02; SLJ 3/02) [634]

22757 Goldsen, Louise. *Fruit* (PS–2). Illus. by P. M. Valet. Series: First Discovery. 1991, Scholastic paper $12.95 (0-590-45233-9). Through the use of overlays, several kinds of fruit are depicted in various stages, such as the ripening of an apple. (Rev: SLJ 6/92) [641]

22758 Hubbell, Will. *Apples Here!* (PS–1). Illus. 2002, Whitman $15.95 (0-8075-0397-5). 32pp. The life of apples, from buds to blossoms to fruit, is the subject of this informative book. (Rev: BL 10/15/02; HBG 3/03; SLJ 9/02) [634.11]

22759 Hughes, Meredith S. *Yes, We Have Bananas: Fruits from Shrubs and Vines* (5–8). Series: Plants We Eat. 1999, Lerner LB $26.60 (0-8225-2836-3). 80pp. A fascinating introduction to bananas, pineapples, grapes, berries, and melons with material on how and where they grow, their cultivation and marketing, plus fun recipes and activities. (Rev: BL 11/15/99; HBG 4/00; SLJ 3/00) [641]

22760 Klingel, Cynthia, and Robert B. Noyed. *Fruit* (PS–1). Photos by Gregg Andersen. Series: Let's Read About Food. 2002, Gareth Stevens LB $18.60 (0-8368-3057-1). 24pp. The importance of fruit as part of a healthy diet is emphasized in this attractive volume. (Rev: HBG 10/02; SLJ 7/02) [641.34]

22761 Landau, Elaine. *Apples* (2–4). Illus. Series: True Books. 1999, Children's Book Pr. LB $21.50 (0-516-21024-6). 48pp. This book gives a history of apples, shows how they grow, introduces different species, and supplies a few simple recipes. (Rev: BL 10/15/99) [634]

22762 Landau, Elaine. *Bananas* (2–4). Series: True Books. 2000, Children's Book Pr. paper $6.95 (0-516-26574-1). 48pp. Color photos and a simple text are used to introduce bananas, where they are grown, and their nutritional value. (Rev: BL 10/15/99) [641]

22763 Lember, Barbara Hirsch. *A Book of Fruit* (PS–K). Illus. 1994, Ticknor $14.95 (0-395-66989-8). 32pp. Expressive photographs are used to introduce 14 fruits and where they grow. (Rev: BCCB 2/95; BL 7/94; SLJ 9/94) [634]

22764 Pfeffer, Wendy. *From Seed to Pumpkin* (PS–2). Illus. by James Graham Hale. Series: Let's-Read-and-Find-Out Science. 2004, HarperCollins LB $16.89 (0-06-445190-9); paper $4.99 (0-06-028039-5). 40pp. Children watch a pumpkin grow from seed to maturity; two activities round out this volume for beginning readers. (Rev: BL 10/1/04; SLJ 10/04) [583]

22765 Powell, Jillian. *Fruit* (1–4). Illus. Series: Everyone Eats. 1997, Raintree LB $25.69 (0-8172-4765-3). 32pp. Describes how fruit are grown, and some of the varieties, legends, and traditional customs surrounding them, with a few tasty recipes. (Rev: SLJ 7/97) [634]

22766 Robbins, Ken. *Apples* (2–4). Photos by author. 2002, Simon & Schuster $15.95 (0-689-83024-6). 32pp. An appealing account of apples — how they are grown, harvested, and consumed — with information on apples in history, in literature, and in language. (Rev: BCCB 12/02; HBG 3/03; SLJ 9/02) [634.11]

22767 Robinson, Fay. *We Love Fruit!* (1–2). Illus. Series: Rookie Readers. 1992, Children's Book Pr. LB $19.00 (0-516-06006-6). 32pp. Various kinds of fruit are pictured in color photos and identified in a simple text. An oversized edition of this title is available. (Rev: BL 12/15/92; SLJ 2/93) [641.3]

22768 Watts, Barrie. *Apple Tree* (PS–2). Illus. 1987, Silver Burdett LB $15.95 (0-382-09436-0). 24pp. Photos help to show the annual cycle of an apple tree. (Rev: BL 11/15/87)

22769 Weninger, Brigitte. *Little Apple: A Book of Thanks* (PS–1). Illus. by Anne Moller. 2001, North-South LB $13.88 (0-7358-1427-9). 32pp. The life cycle of an apple is told in bold, clear illustrations and a simple text. (Rev: BL 4/1/01; HBG 10/01; SLJ 6/01) [634]

NUTRITION

22770 Inglis, Jane. *Fiber* (4–6). Illus. Series: Food Facts. 1993, Carolrhoda LB $19.93 (0-87614-793-7). 32pp. This nutrition book focuses on the natural fiber the body needs and how to obtain it. (Rev: BL 11/15/93; SLJ 10/93) [613.2]

22771 Kalbacken, Joan. *The Food Pyramid* (2–4). Illus. Series: True Books. 1998, Children's Book Pr. LB $21.00 (0-516-20756-3). 48pp. This book explains the various levels of the food pyramid and its use in meal planning. (Rev: BL 7/98; HBG 9/98; SLJ 8/98) [613.2]

22772 Kalbacken, Joan. *Food Safety* (2–4). Illus. Series: True Books. 1998, Children's Book Pr. LB $21.00 (0-516-20757-1). 48pp. This book describes various food-borne illnesses, such as salmonella and trichinosis, and shows how proper food preparation can prevent these illnesses. (Rev: BL 7/98; HBG 9/98) [615.9]

22773 Kalbacken, Joan. *Vitamins and Minerals* (2–4). Illus. Series: True Books. 1998, Children's Book Pr. LB $21.00 (0-516-20758-X). 48pp. This book describes vitamins and minerals, their nutritional importance, and the various foods in which they are found. (Rev: BL 7/98; HBG 9/98; SLJ 8/98) [613.2]

22774 Leedy, Loreen. *The Edible Pyramid: Good Eating Every Day* (K–2). Illus. 1994, Holiday House LB $16.95 (0-8234-1126-5). 30pp. A waiter in a restaurant introduces the nutritional pyramid that the U.S. Department of Agriculture has developed. (Rev: BCCB 2/95; BL 11/15/94; SLJ 4/95) [613.2]

22775 Nottridge, Rhoda. *Additives* (4–6). Illus. Series: Food Facts. 1993, Carolrhoda LB $19.93 (0-87614-794-5). 32pp. The value of such food additives as preservatives and flavorings is discussed, with an analysis of their possible harmful effects. (Rev: BL 11/15/93; SLJ 10/93) [664]

22776 Nottridge, Rhoda. *Fats* (4–6). Illus. Series: Food Facts. 1993, Lerner LB $19.93 (0-87614-779-1). 32pp. Introduces saturated and unsaturated fats and tells how much should be consumed in the daily diet. (Rev: BL 11/15/93; SLJ 10/93) [613.2]

22777 Nottridge, Rhoda. *Vitamins* (3–6). Illus. Series: Food Facts. 1993, Carolrhoda LB $19.93 (0-87614-795-3). 32pp. This book introduces the classification of vitamins, where they are found, their properties and uses, and some experiments and recipes connected with vitamins. (Rev: SLJ 10/93) [613.2]

VEGETABLES

22778 Aliki. *Corn Is Maize: The Gift of the Indians* (2–4). Illus. by author. 1976, HarperCollins LB $15.89 (0-690-00975-5); paper $4.95 (0-06-445026-0). 40pp. A simply written, comprehensive treatment of corn, its origins, how it is husbanded and harvested, and its many uses.

22779 Bial, Raymond. *Corn Belt Harvest* (4–6). Illus. 1991, Houghton Mifflin $17.00 (0-395-56234-1). 48pp. A photo-essay about how corn is grown and harvested. (Rev: BCCB 1/92; BL 12/15/91; SLJ 2/92) [633.1]

22780 Cook, Deanna F. *Kids' Pumpkin Projects* (3–6). Illus. 1998, Williamson paper $9.95 (1-885593-21-X). 104pp. Discusses the planting and cultivating of pumpkins and contains craft and cooking ideas arranged by the seasons. (Rev: BL 10/15/98; SLJ 9/98) [745.5]

22781 De Bourgoing, Pascale, and Gallimard Jeunesse. *Vegetables in the Garden* (PS–3). Illus. by Gilbert Houbre. Series: First Discovery. 1994, Scholastic $11.95 (0-590-48326-7). 24pp. In this well-illustrated interactive book, small children learn about gardens and different kinds of vegetables and how they grow. (Rev: BL 11/15/94) [635]

22782 Farmer, Jacqueline. *Pumpkins!* (1–3). Illus. by Phyllis L. Tildes. 2004, Charlesbridge paper $6.95 (1-57091-558-X). 32pp. Facts about pumpkins are followed by instructions for cooking and carving them and interesting tidbits such as world pumpkin records. (Rev: BL 8/04; SLJ 7/04) [635]

22783 Fowler, Allan. *Corn — On and Off the Cob* (1–2). Illus. Series: Rookie Readers. 1994, Children's Book Pr. LB $19.00 (0-516-06027-9). 32pp. An easily read science book about different kinds of corn and their uses. (Rev: BL 4/15/95) [633.1]

22784 Fowler, Allan. *Taking Root* (1–2). Series: Rookie Readers. 2000, Children's Book Pr. LB $19.00 (0-516-21591-4). 32pp. This simple science book introduces taproots that we eat including carrots, beets, and radishes. (Rev: BL 4/15/00) [641.6]

22785 Gibbons, Gail. *The Pumpkin Book* (K–3). Illus. 1999, Holiday House $16.95 (0-8234-1465-5). 32pp. After a discussion of how pumpkins grow and reproduce, the author explains their roles in Halloween and Thanksgiving celebrations and gives some craft projects. (Rev: BL 9/1/99; HBG 4/00; SLJ 9/99) [635]

22786 Hughes, Meredith S. *Cool as a Cucumber, Hot as a Pepper* (5–8). Series: Foods We Eat. 1999, Lerner LB $26.60 (0-8225-2832-0). This lively book on vegetables gives botanical information, details on growing and harvesting, the history of many of these plants, and a number of mouth-watering recipes. (Rev: BL 7/99; HBG 9/99; SLJ 8/99) [635]

22787 Hughes, Meredith S. *Spill the Beans and Pass the Peanuts: Legumes* (5–8). Series: Plants We Eat. 1999, Lerner LB $31.95 (0-8225-2834-7). 80pp. Peas and beans are two of the legumes introduced in this book that explains, in an entertaining way, their origins, how they grow, their appearance, and nutritional value, plus giving the occasional recipe or activity. (Rev: BL 10/15/99; HBG 4/00; SLJ 12/99) [641.6]

22788 Hughes, Meredith S. *Stinky and Stringy* (5–8). Series: Plants We Eat. 1999, Lerner LB $31.95 (0-8225-2833-9). 88pp. Stem and bulb vegetables onions and garlic are introduced with interesting historical information, details about their cultivation, harvesting and marketing, and a few tempting recipes. (Rev: BL 7/99; HBG 9/99; SLJ 8/99) [635]

22789 Hughes, Meredith S., and E. Thomas Hughes. *Buried Treasure: Roots and Tubers* (4–7). Series: Plants We Eat. 1998, Lerner LB $26.60 (0-8225-2830-4). 96pp. Covering such vegetables as potatoes, sweet potatoes, carrots, turnips, beets, and radishes, this account describes the origin, history, cultivation, and importance of each. (Rev: HBG 3/99; SLJ 4/99) [635]

22790 Klingel, Cynthia, and Robert B. Noyed. *Vegetables* (PS–1). Photos by Gregg Andersen. Series: Let's Read About Food. 2002, Gareth Stevens LB $18.60 (0-8368-3060-1). 24pp. The importance of vegetables as part of a healthy diet is emphasized in this attractive volume. (Rev: HBG 10/02; SLJ 7/02) [613.262]

22791 Kudlinski, Kathleen V. *Popcorn Plants* (2–3). Series: Early Bird Nature Books. 1998, Lerner $22.60 (0-8225-3014-7). 48pp. The life cycle of the popcorn plant is traced in excellent photos and simple text. (Rev: BL 10/15/98; HBG 3/99; SLJ 1/99) [633.1]

22792 Landau, Elaine. *Corn* (2–4). Illus. 1999, Children's Book Pr. LB $21.50 (0-516-21026-2). 48pp. A history of corn is accompanied by descriptions of different species and how they grow plus a few simple tasty recipes. (Rev: BL 10/15/99) [633.1]

22793 Levenson, George. *Pumpkin Circle: The Story of a Garden* (PS–3). Illus. 1999, Tricycle $14.95 (1-58246-004-3). 40pp. This book, illustrated with excellent photographs, traces the life cycle of a pumpkin from seed to a mature plant that produces more seeds. (Rev: BL 10/15/99; HB 11–12/99; HBG 4/00; SLJ 10/99) [635]

22794 Nelson, Robin. *From Kernel to Corn* (PS–2). Illus. Series: Start to Finish. 2003, Lerner $18.60 (0-8225-4659-0). 24pp. This small, colorful picture book uses simple language to describe corn's progress from initial planting to delivery to market. (Rev: BL 4/15/03; HBG 10/03; SLJ 7/03) [633.1]

22795 Robinson, Fay. *Vegetables, Vegetables!* (1–2). Illus. Series: Rookie Readers. 1994, Children's Book Pr. LB $19.00 (0-516-06030-9). 32pp. An easily read book that introduces various vegetables and shows ways in which they are prepared as food. (Rev: BL 4/15/95) [635]

22796 Watts, Barrie. *Potato* (1–3). Illus. 1988, Silver Burdett LB $15.95 (0-382-09527-8); paper $3.95 (0-382-24018-9). How a potato grows and is harvested. (Rev: BL 10/1/88; SLJ 10/88)

22797 Watts, Barrie. *Pumpkin* (K–3). Illus. 2002, Smart Apple LB $16.95 (1-58340-199-7). 32pp. This easy-to-read book about pumpkins includes lots of facts and excellent photography. Also use

Bean (2002). (Rev: BL 10/15/02; HBG 3/03; SLJ 2/03) [635]

Fungi

22798 Royston, Angela. *Life Cycle of a Mushroom* (PS–3). Series: Life Cycle. 2000, Heinemann LB $19.92 (1-57572-210-0). 32pp. Using a color photo and four or five lines of text on each page, this book describes different mushrooms and gives their basic life cycle. (Rev: BL 5/15/00; HBG 3/01) [589.2]

22799 Souza, D. M. *What Is a Fungus?* (4–7). Series: Watts Library. 2002, Watts LB $24.00 (0-531-11979-3); paper $8.95 (0-531-16223-0). 63pp. In readable and appealing text, Souza explains what a fungus is and how it lives, eats, and reproduces. (Rev: SLJ 8/02) [579.5]

22800 Tesar, Jenny. *Fungi* (5–7). Illus. Series: Our Living World. 1994, Blackbirch LB $27.44 (1-56711-044-4). 64pp. A volume that explains what a fungus is, how the various types reproduce and grow, their unique characteristics, and how they fit into food webs and chains. (Rev: BL 12/1/94) [589.2]

Leaves and Trees

22801 Brenner, Barbara. *One Small Place in a Tree* (2–4). Illus. by Tom Leonard. 2004, HarperCollins $15.99 (0-688-17180-X). 32pp. The abundant life found in a single tree is captured in easy-to-understand narrative and realistic artwork. (Rev: BL 3/1/04; SLJ 4/04) [577.3]

22802 Bulla, Clyde Robert. *A Tree Is a Plant* (PS–1). Illus. by Stacey Schuett. Series: Let's-Read-and-Find-Out Science. 2001, HarperCollins LB $4.95 (0-06-445196-8); paper $15.89 (0-06-028172-3). 34pp. Vivid paintings grace this new version of the book first published in 1960 that portrays the life cycle of an apple tree and discusses how the different parts of a tree work. (Rev: BL 12/15/01; HBG 10/02; SLJ 11/01) [583]

22803 Cassie, Brian. *National Audubon Society First Field Guide: Trees* (4–8). 1999, Scholastic $17.95 (0-590-05472-4); paper $8.95 (0-590-05490-2). After a general, illustrated introduction to the characteristics and types of North American trees, this field guide then categorizes the trees according to the shape of their leaves. (Rev: BL 3/15/99; SLJ 7/99) [582.16]

22804 Dorros, Arthur. *A Tree Is Growing* (2–4). Illus. by S. D. Schindler. 1997, Scholastic $15.95 (0-590-45300-9). 32pp. In double-page spreads, various types of trees and leaves are introduced, with material on how trees grow. (Rev: BCCB 6/97; BL 2/1/97; SLJ 3/97) [582.16]

22805 Fischer-Nagel, Heiderose, and Andreas Fischer-Nagel. *Fir Trees* (3–6). Illus. Series: Nature Watch. 1989, Carolrhoda LB $19.93 (0-87614-340-0). 48pp. The development and growth of the conifers. (Rev: BL 10/15/89; SLJ 1/90) [585.2]

22806 Fleisher, Paul. *Oak Tree* (3–5). Illus. Series: Webs of Life. 1997, Marshall Cavendish LB $22.79

(0-7614-0434-1). 40pp. Describes an Eastern decid-uous forest and the plant and animal life that sur-rounds an oak tree. (Rev: BL 2/15/98; HBG 3/98) [583]

22807 Fowler, Allan. *It Could Still Be a Tree* (1–2). Illus. Series: Rookie Readers. 1990, Children's Book Pr. LB $19.00 (0-516-04904-6). 32pp. With simple text and many photos, the characteristics of trees are introduced. (Rev: BL 2/1/91) [582.12]

22808 Fowler, Allan. *Maple Trees* (1–2). Series: Rookie Read-About Science. 2001, Children's Book Pr. LB $19.00 (0-516-21684-8). 32pp. For begin-ning readers, a simple text with color illustrations introduces trees, their varieties, parts, and growth cycles. (Rev: BL 1/1–15/02) [582.16]

22809 Gardner, Robert, and David Webster. *Science Project Ideas About Trees* (5–8). Illus. Series: Sci-ence Project Ideas. 1997, Enslow LB $19.95 (0-89490-846-4). The parts of trees and their functions are described, with activities involving leaves, seeds, flowers, roots, and twigs. (Rev: BL 12/1/97; BR 5–6/98; HBG 3/98; SLJ 2/98) [582.16]

22810 Gerber, Carole. *Leaf Jumpers* (PS–1). Illus. by Leslie Evans. 2004, Charlesbridge $15.95 (1-57091-497-4). 32pp. The leaves of eight common trees — including the red maple, birch, and ginkgo — are introduced in simple, lyrical text and striking autumnal colors. (Rev: BL 9/1/04; SLJ 8/04) [575.5]

22811 Gibbons, Gail. *Tell Me, Tree: All About Trees for Kids* (PS–3). Illus. 2002, Little, Brown $15.95 (0-316-30903-6). 32pp. An oversize basic guide that introduces different kinds of trees, and explains their parts and how each operates. (Rev: BL 4/1/02; HB 7–8/02; HBG 10/02; SLJ 3/02) [582.16]

22812 Godwin, Sam. *From Little Acorns: A First Look at the Life Cycle of a Tree* (K–1). Illus. by Simone Abel. Series: First Look : Science. 2004, Picture Window LB $22.60 (1-4048-0658-X). 32pp. In simple language with cartoon-style illustrations, a mother squirrel and her babies discuss how an oak tree grows. (Rev: BL 10/15/04; SLJ 3/05) [571.8]

22813 Hickman, Pamela. *Tree Book* (3–5). Illus. 1999, Kids Can $12.95 (1-55074-485-2). 32pp. An introduction to trees, how they grow and reproduce, and their parts, plus a few related activities and proj-ects. (Rev: BL 2/1/99; HBG 9/99) [582.16]

22814 Holmes, Bonnie. *Quaking Aspen* (2–4). Series: Nature Watch. 1999, Carolrhoda $16.95 (1-57505-351-9). 48pp. This illustrated book about the aspen tree includes material on its location, characteristics, ecology, and possible future endangerments. (Rev: BL 10/1/99; HBG 4/00) [583]

22815 Hughes, Meredith S. *Tall and Tasty: Fruit Trees* (5–8). Series: Plants We Eat. 2000, Lerner LB $31.95 (0-8225-2837-1). 80pp. This book explores the world of apples, peaches, mangoes, and other fruits that grow on trees and explains each one's life cycle, and how the fruit has migrated during its his-tory. (Rev: BL 4/15/00; HBG 9/00) [641.3]

22816 Johnson, Sylvia A. *Apple Trees* (5–8). Illus. by Hiro Koike. 1983, Lerner LB $31.95 (0-8225-

1479-6). 48pp. The story of the apple tree and seed and fruit formation.

22817 Johnson, Sylvia A. *How Leaves Change* (3–5). Illus. 1986, Lerner LB $22.60 (0-8225-1483-4); paper $5.95 (0-8225-9513-3). 48pp. Explains how and why leaves change color in the fall. (Rev: BCCB 4/87; BL 1/15/87; SLJ 3/87)

22818 Jorgensen, Lisa. *Grand Trees of America: Our State and Champion Trees* (4–7). Illus. 1992, Roberts Rinehart paper $8.95 (1-879373-15-7). 120pp. This book describes the official tree of each state and introduces the National Register of Big Trees. (Rev: BL 2/15/93) [582.16]

22819 Lauber, Patricia. *Be a Friend to Trees* (2–4). Illus. by Holly Keller. Series: Let's-Read-and-Find-Out. 1994, HarperCollins LB $15.89 (0-06-021529-1). 32pp. The many uses of trees — such as provid-ing homes for birds and supplying wood for construction — are outlined, with material on trees' structure, parts, and how their leaves make food. (Rev: BCCB 1/94; BL 6/1–15/94; SLJ 3/94) [582.16]

22820 Llewellyn, Claire. *Tree* (K–3). Illus. by Simon Mendez. 2004, NorthWord $16.95 (1-55971-879-X). 32pp. An innovative picture-book layout chroni-cles the life cycle of an apple tree, tracing its progress from seedling to a mature, fruit-bearing adult. (Rev: BL 4/15/04; SLJ 11/04) [634]

22821 Maestro, Betsy. *Why Do Leaves Change Color?* (K–4). Illus. by Loretta Krupinski. Series: Let's-Read-and-Find-Out. 1994, HarperCollins LB $15.89 (0-06-022874-1). 32pp. This book explains the process that causes leaf color change in the autumn and why leaves fall from the trees. (Rev: BCCB 11/94; BL 11/15/94; SLJ 7/95) [582.16]

22822 Miller, Cameron, and Dominique Falla. *Woodlore* (3–5). Illus. 1995, Ticknor $14.95 (0-395-72034-6). 32pp. Various kinds of wood and their uses are explored in text and full-color illustrations. (Rev: BCCB 3/95; BL 3/1/95; SLJ 3/95) [674.8]

22823 Miller, Debbie S. *Are Trees Alive?* (K–3). Illus. by Stacey Schuett. 2002, Walker LB $17.85 (0-8027-8802-5). 32pp. This colorful picture book explains how trees live and survive in different environments. (Rev: BL 6/1–15/02; HBG 10/02; SLJ 5/02) [582.16]

22824 Morrison, Gordon. *Oak Tree* (4–6). Illus. 2000, Houghton Mifflin $16.00 (0-395-95644-7). 32pp. A year in the life of an oak tree is described in this appealing account that uses a picture-book for-mat. (Rev: BL 3/1/00; HBG 9/00; SLJ 6/00) [583]

22825 Pascoe, Elaine. *The Ecosystem of a Fallen Tree* (3–5). Photos by Dwight Kuhn. Series: The Library of Small Ecosystems. 2003, Rosen LB $20.65 (0-8239-6308-X). 32pp. In this photo-filled overview of the plant and animal life that can be sustained in the remains of a downed tree, students will learn that ecosystems come in all sizes. (Rev: SLJ 11/03) [577]

22826 Pascoe, Elaine. *The Ecosystem of an Apple Tree* (3–5). Photos by Dwight Kuhn. Series: The Library of Small Ecosystems. 2003, Rosen LB $20.65 (0-8239-6304-7). 32pp. An overview of the animal and plant life associated with the apple tree. (Rev: SLJ 11/03) [577]

22827 Pascoe, Elaine. *Leaves and Trees* (4–7). Series: Nature Close-Up. 2001, Blackbirch LB $27.44 (1-56711-474-1). 32pp. Easy projects and a simple text are used to introduce the nature of trees and leaves and the living processes involved. (Rev: BL 9/15/01; HBG 3/02) [582.16]

22828 Patent, Dorothy Hinshaw. *Apple Trees* (2–3). Series: Early Bird Nature Books. 1998, Lerner LB $22.60 (0-8225-3020-1). 48pp. An easily read introduction to the apple tree and its life cycle, told in a simple text with attractive color photographs. (Rev: BL 3/15/98; HBG 9/98; SLJ 4/98) [582.16]

22829 Patent, Dorothy Hinshaw. *Fire: Friend or Foe* (4–8). 1998, Clarion $16.00 (0-395-73081-3). Using a concise text and excellent photographs, the author describes the causes of forest fires, their effect on the land, and the equipment and practices used by firefighters, and discusses the growing belief that fire is part of the natural cycle of renewal and scientific evidence refuting the concept that fire is deadly to all wildlife. (Rev: BL 11/15/98; HB 1–2/99; HBG 3/99; SLJ 12/98) [577.2]

22830 Pfeffer, Wendy. *A Log's Life* (K–3). Illus. by Robin Brickman. 1997, Simon & Schuster paper $16.00 (0-689-80636-1). 32pp. The life cycle of an oak tree and its many roles in the forest ecology. (Rev: BL 9/15/97; HBG 3/98; SLJ 9/97) [574.5]

22831 Reed-Jones, Carol. *The Tree in the Ancient Forest* (K–3). Illus. by Christopher Canyon. 1995, Dawn $16.95 (1-883220-32-7); paper $7.95 (1-883220-31-9). 32pp. The food cycle of interdependence that involves both plants and animals and a 300-year-old fir tree is the subject of this stunning picture book. (Rev: BL 7/95; SLJ 9/95) [574]

22832 Royston, Angela. *Life Cycle of an Oak Tree* (PS–3). Series: Life Cycle. 2000, Heinemann LB $19.92 (1-57572-211-9). 32pp. From acorn to giant oak, this book describes the life cycle of an oak tree using a few lines of text and a color photo on each page. (Rev: BL 5/15/00; HBG 3/01) [583]

22833 Souza, D. M. *Wacky Trees* (3–6). Series: Watts Library. 2003, Watts LB $24.00 (0-531-12210-7); paper $8.95 (0-531-16246-X). 63pp. The oddities of the tree world, including such giants as the sequoia and the baobab, are examined in this illustrated work. (Rev: SLJ 4/04) [582.16]

22834 Spicer, Maggee, and Richard Thompson. *We'll All Go Exploring* (PS–1). Illus. by Kim LaFave. 2003, Fitzhenry & Whiteside $16.95 (1-55041-732-0). 36pp. Three young explorers find out about different kinds of trees and the wildlife found near them in this lively rhyming-text picture book. (Rev: BL 5/1/03; SLJ 5/03) [811]

22835 Vieira, Linda. *The Ever-Living Tree: The Life and Times of a Coast Redwood* (2–5). Illus. by Christopher Canyon. 1994, Walker LB $15.85 (0-8027-8278-7). 32pp. The life of a 2,000-year-old redwood, with details of some important events that occurred during its life. (Rev: BL 3/1/94; SLJ 5/94) [584]

22836 Wadsworth, Ginger. *Giant Sequoia Trees* (2–4). Photos by Frank Staub. Series: Early Bird Nature Books. 1995, Lerner LB $22.60 (0-8225-3001-5). 48pp. A photo-essay about the world's largest tree, the sequoia, with details on its parts, environment, and life cycle. (Rev: SLJ 10/95) [582]

22837 Zim, Herbert S., and Alexander C. Martin. *Trees* (5–8). Illus. 1991, Western paper $21.27 (0-307-64056-6). 160pp. A small, handy volume packed with information and color illustrations that help identify our most important trees. [582.16]

Plants

22838 Aaseng, Nathan. *Meat-Eating Plants* (3–6). Illus. Series: Weird and Wacky Science. 1996, Enslow LB $18.95 (0-89490-617-8). 48pp. Such plants as bladderworts, sundews, pitcher plants, and Venus's-flytraps are described, along with their methods of obtaining food. (Rev: SLJ 5/96) [581.5]

22839 Ardley, Neil. *The Science Book of Things That Grow* (3–6). Illus. Series: Science Books. 1991, Harcourt $9.95 (0-15-200586-2). 29pp. With everyday equipment and step-by-step procedures, the process of plant growth is explained. (Rev: BL 10/15/91) [581]

22840 *Atlas of Plants* (1–3). Illus. by Sylvaine Perols. Series: First Discovery Atlases. 1996, Scholastic $11.95 (0-590-58113-9). Using extensive captions and maps, this atlas tells where plants come from. (Rev: SLJ 9/96) [581.5]

22841 Bash, Barbara. *Desert Giant: The World of the Saguaro Cactus* (3–6). Illus. 1989, Little, Brown paper $5.95 (0-685-33583-6). 32pp. The Tohono O'odham Indians — the Desert People — gather the fruit of the saguaro in a centuries-old harvest ritual. (Rev: BL 3/15/89; HB 3–4/89)

22842 Bocknek, Jonathan. *The Science of Plants* (2–5). Series: Living Science. 1999, Gareth Stevens LB $14.95 (0-8368-2467-9). 32pp. Different kinds of plants are presented in double-page spreads with activities and coverage on their life cycles, habitats, and products. (Rev: HBG 9/00; SLJ 1/00) [581]

22843 Coil, Suzanne M. *Poisonous Plants* (3–6). Illus. Series: First Books. 1992, Watts paper $6.95 (0-531-15647-8). 64pp. An attractive format with lots of information about these plants and with many illustrations. (Rev: BL 5/15/91; SLJ 7/91) [582]

22844 Fowler, Allan. *Ferns* (1–2). Series: Rookie Read-About Science. 2001, Children's Book Pr. LB $19.00 (0-516-25984-9). 32pp. In this beginning science reader, different ferns are introduced in color photographs and a simple text. (Rev: BL 1/1–15/02) [587]

22845 Garassino, Alessandro. *Plants: Origins and Evolution* (4–8). Illus. Series: Beginnings — Origins and Evolution. 1995, Raintree LB $24.26 (0-8114-3332-3). 48pp. This treatment of plant evolution includes good factual data and discussion of several important concepts. (Rev: BL 4/15/95) [581.3]

22846 Gardner, Robert. *Science Projects About Plants* (5–8). Illus. Series: Science Projects. 1999, Enslow LB $20.95 (0-89490-952-5). 112pp. This book contains a series of fascinating experiments and projects involving seeds, leaves, roots, stems, flowers, and whole plants. (Rev: BL 2/15/99; BR 5–6/99; SLJ 5/99) [580]

22847 Godwin, Sam. *A Seed in Need: A First Look at the Plant Cycle* (K–1). Illus. Series: First Look: Science. 2004, Picture Window LB $16.95 (1-4048-0920-1). 32pp. In simple language with cartoon-style illustrations, this volume describes the life cycle of plants.

22848 Goodman, Susan E. *Seeds, Stems, and Stamens: The Ways Plants Fit into Their World* (2–4). Illus. by Michael Doolittle. 2001, Millbrook LB $22.90 (0-7613-1874-7). 48pp. A clear look at how plants adapt to their environments, with stunning photographs and questions to stimulate investigation. (Rev: BL 9/15/01; HBG 3/02; SLJ 11/01) [581.4]

22849 Griswell, Kim T. *Carnivorous Plants* (4–6). Series: Nature's Predators. 2002, Gale LB $18.96 (0-7377-1387-9). 48pp. An introduction to many kinds of carnivorous plants with material on how they trap, kill, and eat their prey. (Rev: BL 2/15/03; SLJ 10/03) [581.5]

22850 Guiberson, Brenda Z. *Cactus Hotel* (PS–3). Illus. by Megan Lloyd. 1991, Holt $16.95 (0-8050-1333-4). 32pp. The life cycle of the giant saguaro cactus. (Rev: BL 6/15/91; SLJ 7/91) [574.5]

22851 Halfmann, Janet. *Plant Tricksters* (3–6). Series: Watts Library. 2003, Watts LB $24.00 (0-531-12278-6); paper $8.95 (0-531-16371-7). 63pp. With plenty of close-up photographs, this is a study of the unusual mechanisms by which some plants survive — from being unusually smelly to trying to fool the eye. (Rev: SLJ 4/04) [581.4]

22852 Hickman, Pamela. *Starting with Nature Plant Book* (2–4). Illus. by Heather Collins. Series: Starting with Nature. 2000, Kids Can $12.95 (1-55074-483-6); paper $5.95 (1-55074-812-2). 32pp. This introductory account describes groups of plants and plant parts and gives material on state flowers, endangered plants, and outlines of several related activities. (Rev: HBG 9/00; SLJ 7/00) [581]

22853 Himmelman, John. *A Dandelion's Life* (K–2). Illus. Series: Nature Upclose. 1998, Children's Book Pr. LB $24.00 (0-516-21177-3). 32pp. Beginning with a seed floating in the air, this illustrated book traces the life of a dandelion plant. (Rev: BL 12/1/98; HBG 3/99) [583]

22854 Kalman, Bobbie. *How a Plant Grows* (3–5). Illus. by Barbara Bedell. Series: Crabapples. 1996, Crabtree LB $19.96 (0-86505-628-5); paper $5.95 (0-86505-728-1). 32pp. An introduction to plants that covers topics like structure, photosynthesis, pollination, carnivorous plants, and the importance of plants in the food chain. (Rev: SLJ 7/97) [581.5]

22855 Kite, L. Patricia. *Dandelion Adventures* (PS–2). Illus. by Anca Hariton. 1998, Millbrook $20.90 (0-7613-0037-6); paper $6.95 (0-7613-0377-4). 32pp. This appealing picture book describing the life cycle of a dandelion begins with the landing of seed parachutes and ending with new plants producing their own flowers and seeds. (Rev: BL 3/15/98; HBG 3/99; SLJ 7/98) [583]

22856 Kudlinski, Kathleen V. *Dandelions* (2–3). Series: Early Bird Nature Books. 1999, Lerner LB $22.60 (0-8225-3016-3). 48pp. This attractive account, suitable for beginning readers, describes the characteristics of a dandelion and outlines its life cycle. (Rev: BL 10/15/99; HBG 4/00; SLJ 1/00) [583]

22857 Kudlinski, Kathleen V. *Venus Flytraps* (2–5). Illus. Series: Early Bird Nature Books. 1998, Lerner LB $22.60 (0-8225-3015-5). 48pp. This photo-essay uses amazing color photos and a simple text to describe the habitats of the Venus's-flytrap and how and why it kills insects. (Rev: BL 12/1/98; HBG 3/99; SLJ 3/99) [583]

22858 Landau, Elaine. *Endangered Plants* (4–6). Illus. Series: First Books. 1992, Watts paper $6.95 (0-531-15645-1). 64pp. Color photos enhance this look at plants in danger of extinction. (Rev: BL 6/1/92; SLJ 7/92) [581.5]

22859 Llamas, Andreu. *Plants Under the Sea* (4–6). Illus. by Luis Rizo. Series: Incredible World of Plants. 1996, Chelsea LB $15.95 (0-7910-3468-2). 32pp. Familiar and less common ocean plants are described and pictured, along with their relation to aquatic animal life. Also use *The Vegetation of Rivers, Lakes, and Swamps* (1996). (Rev: SLJ 7/96) [581]

22860 Lucht, Irmgard. *The Red Poppy* (K–3). Trans. by Frank Jacoby-Nelson. Illus. 1995, Hyperion LB $14.49 (0-7868-2043-8). 32pp. A year in the life of a poppy plant is explored in this large-format picture book. (Rev: BCCB 6/95; BL 4/1/95; SLJ 6/95*) [583]

22861 Overbeck, Cynthia. *Cactus* (3–6). Illus. by Shabo Hans. 1982, Lerner paper $5.95 (0-8225-9556-7). 48pp. A description of the cactus and how it lives.

22862 Pascoe, Elaine. *The Ecosystem of a Milkweed Patch* (3–5). Photos by Dwight Kuhn. Series: The Library of Small Ecosystems. 2003, Rosen LB $20.65 (0-8239-6309-8). 32pp. Introduces the animals and plants that live within a milkweed patch and also to the ways in which they interact. (Rev: SLJ 11/03) [577.4]

22863 Penny, Malcolm. *How Plants Grow* (3–5). Illus. by Stuart Lafford. Series: Nature's Mysteries. 1996, Benchmark LB $22.79 (0-7614-0452-X). 32pp. Topics like flowering, pollination, seed production, and growth are covered in this elementary book about plants. (Rev: SLJ 2/97) [581.5]

22864 *Plants* (K–4). Series: Starting with Science. 1998, Kids Can LB $10.95 (1-55074-193-4). 32pp. Thirteen safe and simple experiments with plants, such as creating "super soil," are presented in this beginning science activity book. (Rev: BL 5/15/98; HBG 9/98; SLJ 5/98) [581]

22865 Posada, Mia. *Dandelions: Stars in the Grass* (PS–2). Illus. by author. 2000, Carolrhoda LB $15.95 (1-57505-383-7). The life cycle of a dandelion is covered in bright acrylic illustrations and a text that includes unusual facts and a recipe for dandelion salad. (Rev: HBG 9/00; SLJ 5/00) [581]

22866 Rockwell, Anne. *One Bean* (PS–2). Illus. by Megan Halsey. 1998, Walker LB $15.85 (0-8027-8649-9). 32pp. This book shows, with step-by-step instructions, how to grow a bean plant and gives details on other bean activities. (Rev: BL 4/15/98; HBG 9/98; SLJ 5/98) [635]

22867 Royston, Angela. *Flowers, Fruits, and Seeds* (K–3). Series: Heinemann First Library. 1999, Heinemann LB $13.95 (1-57572-822-2). 32pp. Through color photos and a brief text, this book introduces the life cycle of various fruits from pollination of flowers through development of the fruit and production of seeds. Also use the companion book by the same author, *How Plants Grow.* (Rev: BL 6/1–15/99; SLJ 1/00) [634]

22868 Royston, Angela. *Life Cycle of a Bean* (2–3). Illus. Series: Life Cycle. 1998, Heinemann $13.95 (1-57572-612-2). 32pp. Using a colorful photograph and a timeline on each page, this book describes the stages in the maturation of a bean plant and its eventual production of a new seed. (Rev: BL 4/15/98; SLJ 7/98) [583]

22869 Royston, Angela. *Plants and Us* (K–3). Series: Heinemann First Library. 1999, Heinemann LB $13.95 (1-57572-825-7). 32pp. Attractive illustrations and a short text are used to explain the relationship between plants and humankind, with material on plants' various uses in everyday life. Also use *Strange Plants* by the same author. (Rev: BL 6/1–15/99) [581]

22870 Silverstein, Alvin, et al. *Plants* (3–6). Illus. Series: Kingdoms of Life. 1996, Twenty-First Century LB $21.40 (0-8050-3519-2). 64pp. Scientific classification of life on earth is explained, focusing on the world of plants and its diversity. (Rev: BL 6/1–15/96; SLJ 7/96) [581]

22871 Souza, D. M. *Plant Invaders* (3–6). Series: Watts Library. 2003, Watts LB $24.00 (0-531-12211-5); paper $8.95 (0-531-16247-8). 63pp. An illustrated look at invasive plants, such as kudzu, that spread widely and pose a significant threat to the ecosystem. (Rev: SLJ 4/04) [581.6]

22872 VanCleave, Janice. *Janice VanCleave's Plants: Mind-Boggling Experiments You Can Turn into Science Fair Projects* (3–7). Illus. 1997, Wiley paper $10.95 (0-471-14687-0). 96pp. Twenty projects and experiments involving plants, their parts, and their growth cycles are presented with clear, easy-to-follow instructions. (Rev: BL 2/15/97; SLJ 3/97) [581]

22873 Watts, Barrie. *Dandelion* (PS–3). Illus. 1987, Silver Burdett LB $9.95 (0-382-09438-7); paper $3.95 (0-382-24016-2). 24pp. The simple dandelion in close-up photography. (Rev: BL 12/1/87)

22874 Wexler, Jerome. *Queen Anne's Lace* (3–6). Illus. 1994, Whitman LB $14.95 (0-8075-6710-8). 32pp. An examination of this common weed, exploring its structure, roots, seeds, and flowers. (Rev: BCCB 6/94; BL 4/15/94; SLJ 6/94) [583]

Seeds

22875 Burns, Diane L. *Berries, Nuts and Seeds* (4–7). Illus. by John F. McGee. 1996, NorthWord paper $7.95 (1-55971-573-1). 42pp. Each page in this guide is devoted to a description of a single berry, nut, or seed. (Rev: BL 2/15/97) [582.13]

22876 Burton, Jane, and Kim Taylor. *The Nature and Science of Seeds* (3–6). Series: Exploring the Science of Nature. 1999, Gareth Stevens LB $14.95 (0-8368-2184-X). 32pp. The composition and functions of seeds are explored in this well-illustrated book that contains a special section of projects and activities involving seeds and plant growth. (Rev: BL 7/99) [582]

22877 Gibbons, Gail. *From Seed to Plant* (PS–3). Illus. 1991, Holiday House LB $16.95 (0-8234-0872-8). 32pp. How seeds grow into plants and how flowering plants produce seeds. (Rev: BL 3/1/91; HB 7–8/91; SLJ 7/91) [581.3]

22878 Jordan, Helene J. *How a Seed Grows* (3–6). Illus. by Loretta Krupinski. Series: Let's-Read-and-Find-Out. 1992, HarperCollins LB $15.89 (0-06-020185-1); paper $4.95 (0-06-445107-0). 32pp. A boy and a girl plant seeds and watch them grow. (Rev: BL 8/92; SLJ 7/92) [582]

22879 Kuchalla, Susan. *All About Seeds* (K–3). Illus. by Jane McBee. 1982, Troll paper $3.50 (0-89375-659-8). 32pp. A simple account that explains how and where seeds grow.

22880 Pascoe, Elaine. *Plants with Seeds* (2–5). Photos by Dwight Kuhn. Series: A Kid's Guide to the Classification of Living Things. 2003, Rosen LB $20.65 (0-8239-6314-4). 32pp. A richly illustrated, slim guide to plants that use seeds to reproduce, with color photographs and a useful glossary. Also use *Plants Without Seeds* (2003). (Rev: SLJ 7/03) [580]

22881 Pascoe, Elaine. *Seeds and Seedlings* (4–7). Illus. Series: Nature Close-Up. 1996, Blackbirch LB $27.44 (1-56711-178-5). 48pp. The growth cycle of seeds is explained, with many projects on how to plant and raise seedlings. (Rev: BL 12/1/96; SLJ 3/97) [582]

22882 Richards, Jean. *A Fruit Is a Suitcase for Seeds* (PS–2). Illus. by Anca Hariton. 2002, Millbrook LB $21.90 (0-7613-1622-1). An accessible and very visual introduction to seeds and how they are dispersed. (Rev: HBG 10/02; SLJ 5/02) [581.467]

Chemistry

22883 Angliss, Sarah. *Gold* (4–8). Series: The Elements. 1999, Marshall Cavendish LB $22.79 (0-7614-0887-8). 32pp. Easy-to-follow diagrams, fact boxes, and color illustrations accompany an informative text that introduces gold, where it is mined and processed, its properties, value, and uses. (Rev: BL 2/15/00; HBG 9/00) [546]

22884 Baxter, Roberta. *Chemical Reaction* (4–8). Illus. Series: The Kidhaven Science Library. 2004, Gale/KidHaven LB $23.70 (0-7377-2072-7). 48pp. Clear, concise text, supported by full-color photographs and diagrams, describes many types of reactions — oxidation and photosynthesis, for example — and discusses their uses. (Rev: SLJ 6/05)

22885 Beatty, Richard. *Copper* (4–8). Series: The Elements. 2000, Marshall Cavendish LB $22.79 (0-7614-0945-9). 32pp. This book identifies the element copper, defines its properties and describes its uses in everyday life, especially in electrical cables. (Rev: BL 1/1–15/01; HBG 10/01; SLJ 2/01) [546]

22886 Beatty, Richard. *Maganese* (5–8). Illus. Series: The Elements. 2004, Marshall Cavendish LB $17.95 (0-7614-1813-X). 32pp. Easy-to-follow diagrams, fact boxes, and color illustrations accompany an informative text that introduces manganese and its properties, value, and uses.

22887 Beatty, Richard. *Phosphorous* (4–8). Series: The Elements. 2000, Marshall Cavendish LB $22.79 (0-7614-0946-7). 32pp. This book describes this nonmetallic element, lists its properties, tells how it behaves, and discusses such uses as matches and fertilizers. (Rev: BL 1/1–15/01; HBG 10/01; SLJ 2/01) [546]

22888 Beatty, Richard. *Sulfur* (4–8). Series: The Elements. 2000, Marshall Cavendish LB $22.79 (0-7614-0948-3). 32pp. Introduces this nonmetallic element, its characteristics, various compounds, and uses in everyday life, with color photographs, easy-to-follow diagrams, fact boxes, and a clear text. (Rev: BL 1/1–15/01; HBG 10/01; SLJ 2/01) [546]

22889 Brandolini, Anita. *Fizz, Bubble and Flash! Element Explorations and Atom Adventures for Hands-On Science Fun!* (4–7). Illus. by Michael Kline. Series: Kids Can! 2003, Williamson paper $12.95 (1-885593-83-X). 127pp. A friendly narrative and cartoon-style drawing present activities that illustrate basic scientific concepts. (Rev: BL 1/1–15/04; SLJ 11/03) [546]

22890 Burton, Jane, and Kim Taylor. *The Nature and Science of Fire* (3–6). Series: Exploring the Science of Nature. 2001, Gareth Stevens LB $21.27 (0-8368-2198-X). 32pp. An introduction to fire and the chemical processes involved with some safe activities appended. (Rev: BL 3/15/01; HBG 10/01) [530]

22891 Farndon, John. *Aluminum* (4–8). Series: The Elements. 2000, Marshall Cavendish LB $22.79 (0-7614-0947-5). 32pp. This silvery, metallic element is introduced, with material on its individual characteristics, how it behaves, and its many uses in everyday life. (Rev: BL 1/1–15/01; HBG 10/01) [546]

22892 Farndon, John. *Calcium* (5–8). 1999, Benchmark LB $22.79 (0-7614-0888-6). 32pp. An attractive, readable book that explains calcium's atomic structure, where and how it occurs in nature, its reactions, compounds, and uses. (Rev: BL 2/15/00; HBG 9/00; SLJ 6/00) [540]

22893 Farndon, John. *Chemicals* (3–6). Series: Science Experiments. 2002, Marshall Cavendish LB $16.95 (0-7614-1466-5). 32pp. Simple experiments with easy-to-follow instructions explore the nature and properties of chemicals. (Rev: BL 12/15/02; HBG 3/03; SLJ 4/03) [540]

22894 Farndon, John. *Hydrogen* (5–8). Illus. Series: Elements. 1999, Marshall Cavendish LB $22.79 (0-7614-0886-X). 32pp. As well as explaining hydrogen's place on the periodic table, this account traces the history of its discovery, its properties, reactive combinations, and uses. (Rev: BL 2/15/00; HBG 9/00; SLJ 6/00) [546]

22895 Farndon, John. *Nitrogen* (5–8). Series: The Elements. 1998, Benchmark LB $22.79 (0-7614-0877-0). An informative science book that introduces nitrogen's properties, reactions, place in the periodic table, and importance in the human body and the environment, and environmental issues relating to nitrogen such as pollution from noxious gases and acid rain. (Rev: HBG 9/99; SLJ 2/99) [540]

22896 Farndon, John. *Oxygen* (5–8). Series: The Elements. 1998, Benchmark LB $22.79 (0-7614-0879-7). 32pp. Oxygen, its properties, uses, and various chemical combinations are covered in this informative text that also discusses the ozone layer. (Rev: HBG 9/99; SLJ 2/99) [540]

22897 Fitzgerald, Karen. *The Story of Iron* (5–8). Series: First Books: Chemical Elements. 1997, Watts LB $23.00 (0-531-20270-4). This volume outlines the discovery, uses, and chemistry of iron, with explanations of its importance throughout history and the role it plays in our lives today. (Rev: BL 9/1/97; SLJ 10/97) [669]

22898 Fitzgerald, Karen. *The Story of Nitrogen* (5–8). Series: First Books: Chemical Elements. 1997, Watts LB $23.00 (0-531-20248-8). Nitrogen is introduced, with information on its atomic structure, properties, uses, and production. (Rev: BL 9/1/97; SLJ 10/97) [546]

22899 Fitzgerald, Karen. *The Story of Oxygen* (5–8). 1996, Watts LB $22.50 (0-531-20225-9). A discussion of the discovery of oxygen, its role in nature, and its chemistry. (Rev: BL 10/15/96; SLJ 9/96) [546]

22900 Gray, Leon. *Iodine* (5–8). Series: Elements (Group 7). 2004, Marshall Cavendish $17.95 (0-7614-1812-1). This introduction to iodine examines the importance of this substance to body chemistry, as well as how it was discovered, where it is found, and its physical characteristics. (Rev: BL 12/1/04) [546]

22901 Madgwick, Wendy. *Super Materials* (K–3). Series: Science Starters. 1999, Raintree LB $15.98 (0-8172-5555-9). 32pp. The properties of various materials are explored in a dozen simple projects using everyday materials: for example, how crystals are formed, why sugar disappears in water, and where metals come from. (Rev: BL 6/1–15/99; HBG 9/99) [540]

22902 Mebane, Robert C., and Thomas R. Rybolt. *Salts and Solids* (4–6). Illus. Series: Everyday Material Science Experiments. 1995, Twenty-First Century LB $18.90 (0-8050-2841-2). 64pp. Each of the experiments that explore the properties of salts and solids is accompanied by an explanation of what should happen and why. (Rev: BL 9/15/95; SLJ 8/95) [530]

22903 O'Daly, Anne. *Sodium* (4–8). Series: The Elements. 2001, Marshall Cavendish LB $22.79 (0-7614-1271-9). 32pp. Diagrams and full-color illustrations are used to introduce sodium and its characteristics and importance in everyday life. (Rev: BL 3/15/02; HBG 3/02) [546]

22904 Richards, Jon. *Chemicals and Reactions* (3–6). Illus. 2000, Millbrook LB $21.90 (0-7613-1160-2). 32pp. Using common household items, experiments involving chemical reactions are accompanied with sidebars that explain how each works. (Rev: BL 8/00; HBG 3/01) [540]

22905 Sparrow, Giles. *Nickel* (5–8). Illus. Series: The Elements. 2004, Marshall Cavendish LB $17.95 (0-7614-1811-3). 32pp. Easy-to-follow diagrams, fact boxes, and color illustrations accompany an informative text that introduces nickel and its properties, value, and uses.

22906 Thomas, Jens. *Silicon* (4–8). Series: The Elements. 2001, Marshall Cavendish LB $22.79 (0-7614-1274-3). 32pp. Thomas introduces this important element and its origins, discovery, and many uses. (Rev: BL 3/15/02; HBG 3/02) [546]

22907 Tocci, Salvatore. *Carbon* (2–3). Illus. Series: True Book - Elements. 2004, Children's Pr. LB $24.00 (0-516-22828-5); paper $6.95 (0-516-27848-7). 48pp. An exploration of the characteristics of carbon and what makes it special. Also use *Calcium* and *Nitrogen* (both 2004).

22908 Tocci, Salvatore. *The Periodic Table* (2–3). Illus. Series: True Book - Elements. 2004, Children's Pr. LB $24.00 (0-516-22833-1); paper $6.95 (0-516-27852-5). 48pp. Introduces the periodic table, how it was developed, and how it is organized, with some fun facts at the end. [546.8]

22909 Uttley, Colin. *Magnesium* (4–8). Series: The Elements. 1999, Marshall Cavendish LB $22.79 (0-7614-0889-4). 32pp. This book explores magnesium, a silvery metallic element important in living organisms, and explains its place in the periodic table, as well as its forms, uses, and properties. (Rev: BL 2/15/00; HBG 9/00) [546]

22910 VanCleave, Janice. *Janice VanCleave's Molecules* (4–6). Illus. 1992, Wiley paper $10.95 (0-471-55054-X). 86pp. The principles of cohesion, adhesion, density, diffusion, and emulsion are explored, with clear line drawings. (Rev: BL 1/15/93; SLJ 2/93) [540]

22911 Watt, Susan. *Chlorine* (4–8). Series: The Elements. 2001, Marshall Cavendish LB $22.79 (0-7614-1272-7). 32pp. Using diagrams, photographs, and a concise text, this book introduces this active, nonmetallic element with material on its composition, characteristics, and many uses — including as a disinfectant and in water purification. (Rev: BL 3/15/02; HBG 3/02) [546]

22912 Watt, Susan. *Lead* (4–8). Series: The Elements. 2001, Marshall Cavendish LB $22.79 (0-7614-1273-5). 32pp. Explores the history, origins, discovery, characteristics, and uses of this heavy metallic element in everyday life. (Rev: BL 3/15/02; HBG 3/02) [546]

22913 Watt, Susan. *Mercury* (5–8). Illus. Series: The Elements. 2004, Marshall Cavendish LB $17.95 (0-7614-1814-8). 32pp. Easy-to-follow diagrams, fact boxes, and color illustrations accompany an informative text that introduces mercury and its properties, value, and uses.

22914 Watt, Susan. *Silver* (4–8). Illus. Series: The Elements. 2002, Benchmark LB $15.95 (0-7614-1464-9). 32pp. A concise introduction to this element, its history, where it is found and how it is mined, and its many uses. (Rev: HBG 3/03; LMC 4–5/03; SLJ 4/03) [546]

22915 Woodford, Chris. *Potassium* (4–8). Illus. Series: The Elements. 2002, Benchmark LB $15.95 (0-7614-1463-0). 32pp. A concise introduction to this element, its history, where it is found and how it is mined, and its many uses. (Rev: HBG 3/03; SLJ 4/03) [546]

Geology and Geography

22916 Allaby, Michael. *The Environment* (4–7). Series: Inside Look. 2000, Gareth Stevens LB $25.26 (0-8368-2725-2). 48pp. Topics covered in this brief overview of the natural systems of our planet include the ozone layer, greenhouse effect, plant life and food webs, ecosystems and biomes, the water cycle, soil life, and rivers. (Rev: HBG 10/01; SLJ 3/01) [550]

22917 Arnold, Caroline. *Coping with Natural Disasters* (5–7). Illus. 1988, Walker LB $14.85 (0-8027-6717-6). 128pp. How a community returns to life after a natural disaster. (Rev: BCCB 6/88; BL 6/15/88)

22918 Bailey, Jacqui. *The Birth of the Earth* (3–5). Illus. by Matthew Lilly. Series: Cartoon History of the Earth. 2001, Kids Can $16.95 (1-55337-071-6); paper $7.95 (1-55337-080-5). 32pp. A comic-book-style presentation of the origin of the planet. (Rev: BL 10/15/01; HBG 3/02; SLJ 1/02) [523.1]

22919 Bannan, Jan G. *Letting Off Steam* (3–7). Illus. 1989, Carolrhoda LB $21.27 (0-87614-300-1). 48pp. This book explains and illustrates how underground heat can cause hot springs, geysers, and other phenomena. (Rev: BCCB 12/89; BL 9/15/89; HB 9–10/89; SLJ 9/89) [551.3]

22920 Blobaum, Cindy. *Geology Rocks! 50 Hands-On Activities to Explore the Earth* (4–6). Illus. by Michael Kline. Series: A Kaleidoscope Kids Book. 2000, Williamson paper $10.95 (1-885593-29-5). 96pp. Each chapter introduces a different concept in geology with accompanying projects and plenty of sidebars to furnish interesting information on geologists, land formations, the scientific method, etc. (Rev: SLJ 3/00) [551]

22921 Burton, Virginia Lee. *Life Story* (3–5). Illus. by author. 1989, Houghton Mifflin $20.00 (0-395-16030-8); paper $9.95 (0-395-52017-7). A work about the changes that have taken place on the earth and in its flora and fauna, from the beginning of time until the present.

22922 Campbell, Ann-Jeanette, and Ronald Rood. *The New York Public Library Incredible Earth: A Book of Answers for Kids* (4–7). Illus. 1996, Wiley paper $12.95 (0-471-14497-5). 192pp. Questions and answers involving science, collected from the reference department of the New York Public Library. (Rev: BL 9/15/96; SLJ 1/97) [550]

22923 Christian, Spencer, and Antonia Felix. *What Makes the Grand Canyon Grand? The World's Most Awe-Inspiring Natural Wonders* (4–6). Series: Spencer Christian's World of Wonders. 1998, Wiley paper $12.95 (0-471-19617-7). 116pp. Chapters on canyons, wild waters, caves, mountains, forests, glaciers, and icebergs are accompanied by many experiments and projects in this book on the world's geographical wonders. (Rev: SLJ 4/98) [550]

22924 Coady, Christopher, and Meredith Hooper. *The Island That Moved* (3–5). 2004, Penguin Putnam $16.99 (0-670-05882-3). An imaginary island off the coast of Antarctica serves as the focus for an exploration of geologic and climate change, continental drift, and plate tectonics. (Rev: BL 8/04; SLJ 12/04) [551.1]

22925 Cole, Joanna. *The Magic School Bus: Inside the Earth* (2–5). Illus. by Bruce Degen. 1987, Scholastic $15.95 (0-590-40759-7); paper $4.99 (0-590-40760-0). 48pp. In picture-book format, geology is introduced as a school bus journeys to the center of the earth. (Rev: BL 1/1/88)

22926 Dewey, Jennifer O. *Mud Matters* (4–6). 1998, Marshall Cavendish $14.95 (0-7416-5014-9). 65pp. The author, a native of the Southwest, describes all kinds of mud, its characteristics, uses, and the part it played in her childhood, when she became acquainted with flash floods, sinkholes, and other manifestations of mud. (Rev: BL 8/98*) [553.6]

22927 Downs, Sandra. *Shaping the Earth: Erosion* (5–8). Series: Exploring Planet Earth. 2000, Twenty-First Century LB $24.90 (0-7613-1414-8). 64pp. This book explores the force of erosion and how such phenomena as wind, waves, floods, rain, acid rain, freezing, and thawing can change the face of the land. (Rev: HBG 9/00; SLJ 7/00) [551]

22928 Gallant, Roy A. *Dance of the Continents* (5–8). Series: The Story of Science. 1999, Benchmark LB $28.50 (0-7614-0962-9). 80pp. This book covers geological theory from the ancient Greeks to modern plate tectonics with material on earthquakes, volcanoes, geysers, and other phenomena. (Rev: BL 2/15/00; HBG 4/00; SLJ 3/00) [551]

22929 George, Linda. *Plate Tectonics* (4–9). Illus. 2003, Gale LB $23.70 (0-7377-1405-0). 48pp. Concise information on the movement of continents, the formation of mountains, and volcanic and earthquake activity is presented with full-color photographs and diagrams. (Rev: SLJ 10/03) [551.1]

22930 Gibbons, Gail. *Planet Earth/Inside Out* (2–4). Illus. 1995, Morrow $15.93 (0-688-09681-6). 32pp. Theories about the earth's formation are discussed and information about the earth's interior is given. (Rev: BCCB 9/95; BL 8/95; SLJ 10/95) [550]

22931 Goodman, Billy. *Natural Wonders and Disasters* (4–7). Illus. Series: Planet Earth. 1991, Little, Brown $17.95 (0-316-32016-1). 96pp. Full-color photographs help to explain the earth's natural wonders as well as such disasters as floods and typhoons. (Rev: BL 12/1/91; SLJ 1/92) [550]

22932 Goodwin, Peter. *Landslides, Slumps, and Creep* (4–6). Illus. Series: First Books. 1997, Watts LB $22.50 (0-531-20332-8). 64pp. Different types of landslides and avalanches are introduced, with material on their causes and effects and an account of some of the major ones. (Rev: BL 11/1/97; HBG 3/98; SLJ 1/98) [551.3]

22933 Henderson, Doug. *Asteroid Impact* (3–5). Illus. 2000, Dial $16.99 (0-8037-2500-0). 40pp. A fascinating account that traces the history of the world before, during, and after a trillion-ton asteroid struck about 65 million years ago causing the death of many plants and animals including the dinosaurs. (Rev: BL 11/1/00*; HB 11–12/00; HBG 3/01; SLJ 11/00) [567.9]

22934 Hooper, Meredith. *The Pebble in My Pocket: A History of Our Earth* (3–5). Illus. by Chris Coady. 1996, Viking $14.99 (0-670-86259-2). 40pp. From molten rock to the formation of mountains, this is a concise history of the earth. (Rev: BL 7/96; SLJ 4/96) [552]

22935 McNulty, Faith. *How to Dig a Hole to the Other Side of the World* (2–4). Illus. by Marc Simont. 1979, HarperCollins paper $5.95 (0-06-443218-1). 32pp. A journey to the center of the earth.

22936 O'Neill, Catherine. *Natural Wonders of North America* (4–6). Illus. 1984, National Geographic LB $12.50 (0-87044-519-7). 104pp. Many of the wonders of North America, such as a Mexican volcano and life far north in Alaska, are shown in color photographs.

22937 Pellant, Chris. *Rocks and Fossils* (K–3). Series: Kingfisher Young Knowledge. 2003, Kingfisher $8.95 (0-7534-5619-2). 47pp. Bright, clear photographs and easy-to-read text convey informa-

tion on rocks and fossils, crystals, and erosion, plus suggested activities. (Rev: HBG 4/04; SLJ 4/04) [552]

22938 Perham, Molly, and Julian Rowe. *Resources* (4–6). Illus. Series: Mapworlds. 1997, Watts LB $20.00 (0-531-14387-2). 32pp. Using an atlaslike format, this work shows where such natural resources as minerals, oil, and coal are found in the world. (Rev: BL 4/15/97) [333.7]

22939 Redfern, Martin. *The Kingfisher Young People's Book of Planet Earth* (4–8). 1999, Kingfisher $21.95 (0-7534-5180-8). 96pp. A useful, enjoyable look at the earth's geology, atmosphere, and weather. (Rev: HBG 9/00; SLJ 2/00) [525]

22940 Redmond, Jim, and Ronda Redmond. *Landslides and Avalanches* (3–5). Illus. Series: Nature on the Rampage. 2001, Raintree LB $15.98 (0-7398-4704-X). 32pp. The authors look at our knowledge of landslides and avalanches and their causes, and discuss the ways in which we can protect ourselves from danger. (Rev: HBG 3/02; SLJ 2/02) [551.3]

22941 Robson, Pam. *Mountains and Our Moving Earth* (2–4). Illus. by Tony Kenyon. Series: Geography for Fun. 2001, Millbrook LB $22.90 (0-7613-2166-7). 32pp. Step-by-step instructions for projects that reinforce the information given here on geology, weather and erosion, and earthquakes and volcanoes. (Rev: HBG 10/01; SLJ 9/01) [551.43]

22942 Rockwell, Anne. *Our Earth* (PS–1). Illus. 1998, Harcourt $13.00 (0-15-201679-1). 24pp. This book introduces very young children to the physical features of the earth, as well as different land formations and landscapes. (Rev: BL 11/1/98; HBG 3/99; SLJ 4/99) [910]

22943 Savan, Beth. *Earthwatch: Earthcycles and Ecosystems* (3–7). Illus. by Pat Cupples. 1992, Addison-Wesley paper $9.95 (0-201-58148-5). 96pp. Earth cycles — such as those of water, earth, and air — are explained; contemporary ecology problems are introduced; and simple activities are outlined. (Rev: SLJ 7/92) [550]

22944 Silverstein, Alvin, et al. *Plate Tectonics* (5–8). Illus. Series: Science Concepts. 1998, Twenty-First Century LB $26.90 (0-7613-3225-1). 64pp. An account that includes an introduction to the earth's crust and mantle, an explanation of plate tectonics theory, and information on the prediction of volcanic eruptions and earthquakes. (Rev: BL 2/1/99; HBG 9/99; SLJ 5/99) [555.1]

22945 VanCleave, Janice. *Janice VanCleave's A+ Projects in Earth Science: Winning Experiments for Science Fairs and Extra Credit* (5–10). Illus. 1999, Wiley $32.50 (0-471-17769-5); paper $12.95 (0-471-17770-9). 240pp. Thirty projects varying in complexity are included in this exploration of topography, minerals, atmospheric composition, the ocean floor, and erosion. (Rev: BL 12/1/98; SLJ 6/99) [550]

22946 VanCleave, Janice. *Janice VanCleave's Gravity* (4–6). Illus. 1992, Wiley paper $10.95 (0-471-55050-7). 86pp. Problems that explain how gravity affects the environment, with clear line drawings. (Rev: BL 1/15/93; SLJ 2/93) [531]

22947 Verdet, Jean-Pierre. *Atlas of the Earth* (PS–2). Illus. Series: First Discovery. 1997, Scholastic $12.95 (0-590-96211-6). 24pp. This atlas introduces the different surfaces and regions of the earth, from the ocean floor to the dry stretches of the Sahara desert. (Rev: BL 2/1/98; HBG 3/98) [550]

22948 Williams, Brian. *Earth Time* (4–6). Series: About Time. 2002, Smart Apple LB $24.25 (1-58340-210-1). 32pp. An exploration of geologic and evolutionary time that looks at the forms of life appearing in each era. (Rev: HBG 3/03; SLJ 12/02)

22949 Zike, Dinah. *The Earth Science Book: Activities for Kids* (3–6). Illus. by Jessie J. Flores. 1993, Wiley paper $12.95 (0-471-57166-0). 119pp. Earth science concepts and environmental issues are presented. (Rev: SLJ 7/93) [551]

Earthquakes and Volcanoes

22950 Archer, Jules. *Earthquake!* (5–7). Illus. Series: Nature's Disasters. 1991, Macmillan LB $16.95 (0-89686-593-2). 48pp. This colorful account discusses the causes and effects of earthquakes and includes a list of famous quakes of the past. (Rev: BCCB 7–8/91; BL 8/91) [551.2]

22951 Asimov, Isaac. *How Did We Find Out About Volcanoes?* (5–7). Illus. by David Wool. 1981, Avon paper $1.95 (0-380-59626-1). 64pp. An overview of volcanoes, from Pompeii to Mount St. Helens. [550]

22952 Berger, Melvin, and Gilda Berger. *Why Do Volcanoes Blow Their Tops?* (3–5). Series: Scholastic Question and Answer. 2000, Scholastic LB $14.95 (0-439-09580-8). 48pp. Answers basic questions about volcanoes and earthquakes with plenty of eye-catching illustrations. (Rev: BL 12/15/00; HBG 3/01; SLJ 2/01) [551.2]

22953 Booth, Basil. *Earthquakes and Volcanoes* (5–8). Illus. Series: Repairing the Damage. 1992, Macmillan LB $13.95 (0-02-711735-9). 46pp. A well-organized photoessay that explains the interrelationship between earthquakes and volcanoes. (Rev: BL 9/15/92; SLJ 10/92) [551.2]

22954 Branley, Franklyn M. *Earthquakes* (K–3). Illus. by Megan Lloyd. Series: Let's-Read-and-Find-Out Science. 2005, HarperCollins LB $16.89 (0-06-028009-3); paper $4.99 (0-06-445188-7). 40pp. An update of the 1990 edition, with photographs and diagrams of what happens when earthquakes strike. (Rev: BL 3/1/05; SLJ 4/05) [551.22]

22955 Branley, Franklyn M. *Volcanoes* (1–3). Illus. by Marc Simont. 1986, HarperCollins paper $4.95 (0-06-445059-7). 32pp. A simple look at the whys and hows of volcanoes. (Rev: BL 6/15/89; HB 5–6/85; SLJ 9/85)

22956 Bunce, Vincent. *Volcanoes* (4–6). Series: Restless Planet. 2000, Raintree LB $25.69 (0-7398-1327-7). 48pp. Different volcanic landforms are illustrated and explained, along with various kinds of eruptions, their effects, and disaster relief efforts. (Rev: HBG 9/00; SLJ 12/00) [551.2]

22957 Burleigh, Robert, adapt. *Volcanoes: Journey to the Crater's Edge* (5–9). Photos by Philippe Bourseiller. Illus. by David Giraudon. 2003, Abrams $14.95 (0-8109-4590-8). 75pp. Volcanoes, lava lakes, ash plumes, and other related phenomena are beautifully illustrated in this oversized photoessay. (Rev: BL 1/1–15/04; HBG 4/04; SLJ 12/03) [550]

22958 Challen, Paul. *Volcano Alert!* (4–6). Illus. Series: Disaster Alert! 2004, Crabtree LB $16.95 (0-7787-1570-1); paper $8.06 (0-7787-1602-3). 32pp. In addition to describing volcanoes, there is colorfully presented material on early beliefs and myths associated with them, discussion of advances in predicting eruptions, tips on staying safe, and an experiment. (Rev: SLJ 3/05) [551.2]

22959 Drohan, Michele Ingber. *Earthquakes* (2–4). Illus. Series: Natural Disasters. 1999, Rosen $13.50 (0-8239-5285-1). 24pp. Full-page photographs and large type are used in this book that explains the causes and effects of earthquakes. (Rev: BL 9/15/99) [551.22]

22960 Elting, Mary, et al. *Volcanoes and Earthquakes* (4–7). Illus. by Courtney. 1990, Simon & Schuster $9.95 (0-671-67217-7). 40pp. Disasters are covered with a you-are-there approach. (Rev: BL 2/1/91) [551.2]

22961 Harrison, David L. *Earthquakes: Earth's Mightiest Moments* (K–3). Illus. by Cheryl Nathan. Series: Earthworks. 2004, Boyds Mills $15.95 (1-59078-243-7). After a dramatic account of an 1811 earthquake in Missouri, Harrison presents clear, reader-friendly explanations of plate tectonics and the study of earthquakes. (Rev: SLJ 11/04) [551.2]

22962 Harrison, David L. *Volcanoes: Nature's Incredible Fireworks* (1–3). Illus. by Cheryl Nathan. Series: Earthworks. 2002, Boyds Mills $15.95 (1-56397-996-9). 32pp. The forces underlying volcanic eruptions are discussed here, with rich and informative illustrations. (Rev: BL 7/02; HBG 3/03; SLJ 9/02) [551.21]

22963 Lindop, Laurie. *Probing Volcanoes* (5–8). Illus. Series: Science on the Edge. 2003, Millbrook LB $26.90 (0-7613-2700-2). 80pp. A lively introduction to the history of volcanoes and eruptions, the scientists who dare to study volcanoes, and techniques for collecting data and forecasting volcanic activity. (Rev: BL 12/1/03; HBG 4/04; SLJ 1/04) [551.21]

22964 Maslin, Mark. *Earthquakes* (4–6). Series: Restless Planet. 2000, Raintree LB $25.69 (0-7398-1328-5). 48pp. This book explains the causes, measurement, hazards, and effects of both earthquakes and tsunamis. (Rev: HBG 9/00; SLJ 12/00) [551.2]

22965 Mehta-Jones, Shilpa. *Earthquake Alert!* (4–6). Illus. Series: Disaster Alert! 2004, Crabtree LB $16.95 (0-7787-1572-8); paper $8.06 (0-7787-1604-X). 32pp. In addition to describing earthquakes, there is colorfully presented material on early beliefs and myths associated with them, discussion of advances in predicting events, tips on staying safe, and an experiment. (Rev: SLJ 3/05) [551.2]

22966 Meister, Cari. *Earthquakes* (4–6). Illus. Series: Nature's Fury. 1999, ABDO LB $14.95 (1-57765-083-2). 32pp. This account presents a history of earthquakes, how they are predicted, and how to stay safe. Also use *Volcanoes* (1999). (Rev: HBG 4/00; SLJ 12/99) [551.2]

22967 Nicholson, Cynthia Pratt. *Volcano!* (2–5). Illus. Series: Disaster. 2001, Kids Can $14.95 (1-55074-908-0); paper $6.95 (1-55074-966-8). 32pp. A tabloid-style format with sensational headlines draws attention to this survey of volcanoes, famous volcanic eruptions, and the work of volcanologists. (Rev: BL 12/1/01; HBG 3/02) [551.21]

22968 Nicolson, Cynthia Pratt. *Earthquake!* (3–6). Illus. 2002, Kids Can $14.95 (1-55074-949-8); paper $6.95 (1-55074-968-4). 32pp. Using double-page spreads that contain concise text and dramatic photographs, various aspects of earthquakes and their causes and effects are covered. (Rev: BL 5/1/02; HBG 10/02; SLJ 5/02) [551.22]

22969 Prager, Ellen. *Earthquakes* (K–3). Illus. by Susan Greenstein. Series: Jump into Science. 2002, National Geographic $16.95 (0-7922-8202-7). 32pp. This is a colorful book that explains simply what earthquakes are, where and why they occur, and their effects. (Rev: BL 6/1–15/02; HBG 10/02) [551.22]

22970 Reed, Jennifer. *Earthquakes: Disaster and Survival, 2005* (4–7). Illus. Series: Disaster and Survival. 2005, Enslow LB $17.95 (0-7660-2381-8). 48pp. Major earthquakes and their effects are detailed in text and personal accounts, with a chapter devoted to the December 2004 Asian tsunami. (Rev: BL 5/1/05) [363.34]

22971 Rogers, Daniel. *Earthquakes* (3–4). Series: Geography Starts Here. 1999, Raintree LB $22.83 (0-8172-5546-X). 32pp. Covers many topics including faults, plate movement, shock waves, methods of measurement, and kinds of destruction. (Rev: HBG 9/99; SLJ 7/99) [551.2]

22972 Rogers, Daniel. *Volcanoes* (3–4). Series: Geography Starts Here. 1999, Raintree LB $22.83 (0-8172-5547-8). 32pp. The causes of volcanic eruptions are covered along with how they occur, their effects, and the ecological consequences. (Rev: HBG 9/99; SLJ 7/99) [551.2]

22973 Ruiz, Andres L. *Volcanoes and Earthquakes* (4–7). Series: Sequences of Earth and Space. 1997, Sterling $13.95 (0-8069-9745-1). 32pp. This book covers such topics as tectonic plates, quakes, and tsunamis plus the formation, structure, and eruption of volcanoes. (Rev: BL 12/1/97; HBG 3/98) [551.21]

22974 Simon, Seymour. *Danger! Earthquakes* (1–3). Illus. Series: SeeMore Readers. 2002, North-South LB $13.95 (1-58717-139-2); paper $3.95 (1-58717-140-6). 32pp. Double-page spreads that use color photographs and diagrams explain the causes and impact of earthquakes. (Rev: BL 4/15/02; HBG 10/02; SLJ 3/02) [551.22]

22975 Simon, Seymour. *Danger! Volcanoes* (1–3). Series: See More Readers. 2002, North-South $13.95 (1-58717-181-3); paper $3.95 (1-58717-182-1). 32pp. Outstanding pictures and a brief, simple text are the highlights in this first reader that explores the world of volcanoes. (Rev: BL 7/02; HBG 3/03; SLJ 8/02) [551.2]

22976 Simon, Seymour. *Volcanoes* (1–3). Illus. 1988, Morrow LB $15.88 (0-688-07412-X). 32pp. How volcanoes are formed and erupt, with well-known examples. (Rev: BCCB 10/88; HB 9–10/88; SLJ 12/88)

22977 Sutherland, Lin. *Earthquakes and Volcanoes* (4–8). Illus. Series: Pathfinders. 2000, Reader's Digest $16.99 (1-57584-374-9). 64pp. An oversize volume that uses double-page spreads to introduce earthquakes and volcanoes along with material on major disasters, their causes, and their effects. (Rev: BL 9/15/00; HBG 3/01) [551.2]

22978 Thomas, Margaret. *Volcano!* (5–7). Illus. Series: Nature's Disasters. 1991, Macmillan LB $12.95 (0-89686-595-9). 48pp. This book gives solid information about the causes of volcanic eruptions and their effects and includes famous volcanic disasters of the past. (Rev: BL 8/91) [551.2]

22979 VanCleave, Janice. *Earthquakes: Mind-Boggling Experiments You Can Turn into Science Fair Projects* (4–6). Illus. Series: Spectacular Science Projects. 1993, Wiley paper $10.95 (0-471-57107-5). 88pp. This is a collection of projects involving the movements of the earth, along with good scientific explanations and simple directions. (Rev: BL 5/1/93; SLJ 7/93) [551.2]

22980 VanCleave, Janice. *Janice VanCleave's Volcanoes: Mind-Boggling Experiments You Can Turn into Science Fair Projects* (4–7). Illus. 1994, Wiley paper $10.95 (0-471-30811-0). 89pp. Twenty experiments that explore the properties of erupting volcanoes using simple materials that can often be found around the house. (Rev: BL 7/94; SLJ 8/94) [551.2]

22981 Walker, Sally M. *Earthquakes* (3–6). Illus. Series: Earth Watch. 1996, Carolrhoda LB $21.27 (0-87614-888-7). 48pp. A clearly written text and powerful color photos highlight this award-winning book. (Rev: BL 4/15/96; SLJ 6/96) [551.2]

22982 Walker, Sally M. *Volcanoes: Earth's Inner Fire* (3–6). Illus. Series: Earth Watch. 1994, Carolrhoda LB $21.27 (0-87614-812-7). 56pp. Many color photographs and clear text are used to explain the causes, locations, and effects of volcanoes. (Rev: BL 1/15/95) [551.2]

22983 Watson, Nancy. *Our Violent Earth* (4–8). Illus. 1982, National Geographic LB $12.50 (0-87044-388-7). 104pp. A discussion of such phenomena as earthquakes, volcanoes, and floods. [363.3]

Icebergs and Glaciers

22984 Bundey, Nikki. *Ice and the Earth* (3–5). Series: The Science of Weather. 2000, Carolrhoda LB $21.27 (1-57505-472-8). 32pp. Along with some interesting experiments, this book describes how ice affects the earth, how it is created, and what would happen if there was no ice on the earth. Also use a companion work *Ice and People* (2000). (Rev: BL 12/15/00; HBG 3/01) [551.3]

22985 Fowler, Allan. *Icebergs, Ice Caps, and Glaciers* (1–3). Series: Rookie Readers. 1997, Children's Book Pr. LB $19.00 (0-516-20429-7). 32pp. Large type and color illustrations are used to introduce these ice formations, with material on how glaciers move and how pieces of ice caps become icebergs. (Rev: BL 11/15/97; HBG 3/98) [551.31]

22986 Gallant, Roy A. *Glaciers* (3–5). Illus. Series: First Books. 1999, Watts LB $22.00 (0-531-20390-5). 64pp. This book explains the nature of glaciers, how they are formed and move, and how they have changed the face of the earth. (Rev: BL 4/15/99; HBG 9/99) [551.31]

22987 George, Michael. *Glaciers* (3–8). Illus. 1991, Creative Ed. LB $25.30 (0-88682-401-X). 40pp. Formations and types of glaciers, as well as their future effects, are explained. (Rev: BL 12/15/91; SLJ 3/92) [551.3]

22988 Walker, Sally M. *Glaciers: Ice on the Move* (4–7). Illus. 1990, Carolrhoda LB $19.93 (0-87614-373-7). 48pp. This book explains how glaciers are formed, where they are found, and how they move. (Rev: BCCB 9/90; BL 6/15/90; SLJ 8/90) [551.3]

Physical Geography

General and Miscellaneous

22989 Armbruster, Ann. *Wildfires* (4–6). Illus. Series: First Books. 1996, Watts LB $22.50 (0-531-20250-X). 63pp. Introduces types of wildfires, their causes, effects, and possible prevention. (Rev: BL 1/1–15/97) [363.37]

22990 Arnosky, Jim. *Wild and Swampy* (3–5). Illus. 2000, HarperCollins LB $15.89 (0-688-17120-6). 32pp. Paintings and drawings are used effectively to introduce the flora and fauna of a swamp. (Rev: BL 11/1/00; HBG 3/01; SLJ 10/00) [591.768]

22991 Baldwin, Carol. *Living in the Tundra* (3–6). Series: Living Habitats. 2003, Heinemann LB $24.22 (1-4034-2991-X). 32pp. The plants and animals of the tundra are presented in question-and-answer format, with brief discussion of human interference. (Rev: HBG 4/04; SLJ 2/04) [577.5]

22992 Blaustein, Daniel. *The Everglades and the Gulf Coast* (4–7). 1999, Benchmark LB $27.07 (0-7614-0896-7). 64pp. In addition to a tour of the wetlands of the southeastern United States, this book describes how the plants and animals there interact and how this changes human life. (Rev: HBG 9/00; SLJ 4/00) [574.5]

22993 Burnie, David. *Shrublands* (5–8). Series: Biomes Atlases. 2003, Raintree LB $31.42 (0-7398-5514-X). 64pp. This comprehensive overview of shrublands describes the climate, flora and fauna, people, and future of these areas, and includes good maps. (Rev: SLJ 9/03) [577.3]

22994 Collard, Sneed B. *Our Natural Homes* (3–6). Illus. by James M. Needham. Series: Our Perfect Planet. 1996, Charlesbridge paper $6.95 (0-88106-928-0). An introduction to the plant and animal life found in such North and South American biomes as tundra, boreal forest, mountains, grasslands, deserts, rain forests, and chaparral. (Rev: SLJ 10/96) [910]

22995 Cone, Patrick. *Wildfire* (3–7). Illus. 1996, Carolrhoda $19.95 (0-87614-936-0); paper $7.95 (1-57505-027-7). 48pp. After a general description of wildfires, discusses their causes, effects, and possible preventive measures that can be taken. (Rev: BL 2/15/97; SLJ 1/97) [574.5]

22996 Fowler, Allan. *Life in a Wetland* (1–2). Series: Rookie Readers. 1998, Children's Book Pr. LB $18.50 (0-516-20799-7). 32pp. Three or four lines of text facing a full-page photo form the basis of this book that explains what a wetland is and the life found in it. (Rev: BL 9/15/98; HBG 9/99) [574.5]

22997 Fowler, Allan. *The Wonder of a Waterfall* (1–2). Series: Rookie Readers. 1999, Children's Book Pr. LB $18.50 (0-516-20813-6). 32pp. In stunning photographs and large-type text, this book introduces waterfalls, their nature, uses, and beauty. (Rev: BL 7/99; HBG 9/99; SLJ 6/99) [551.48]

22998 Gallant, Roy A. *Limestone Caves* (4–7). Series: First Books. 1998, Watts LB $23.00 (0-531-20293-3). 63pp. Following a general history of caves and their different types, this account focuses on the limestone variety, how they are formed, where they are found, and the creatures that live within them. (Rev: HBG 9/98; SLJ 9/98) [551.4]

22999 Gibbons, Gail. *Marshes and Swamps* (2–3). Illus. 1998, Holiday House LB $16.95 (0-8234-1347-0). 32pp. Fresh and saltwater wetlands are introduced, as well as the amazing variety of animals and plants that are found in them. (Rev: BCCB 4/98; BL 3/15/98; HBG 9/98; SLJ 5/98) [551.41]

23000 Godkin, Celia. *Sea Otter Inlet* (1–3). Illus. by author. 1998, Fitzhenry & Whiteside $15.95 (1-55041-080-6). Ecosystems and the balance of nature are explored in this account of what happens to a kelp bed when the otters are killed or driven off by hunters. (Rev: SLJ 1/99) [574]

23001 Guiberson, Brenda Z. *Spoonbill Swamp* (1–3). Illus. by Megan Lloyd. 1995, Holt paper $6.95 (0-8050-3385-8). 32pp. This story depicts a day in the lives of a mother spoonbill and a mother alligator in a southern swamp. (Rev: BL 3/15/92; SLJ 3/92) [591.5]

23002 Harrison, David L. *Caves: Mysteries Beneath Our Feet* (1–3). Illus. by Cheryl Nathan. 2001, Boyds Mills $15.95 (1-56397-915-2). 32pp. A general discussion of caves follows the story of the discovery of New York's Howe Caverns in 1842. (Rev: BL 9/15/01; HBG 3/02; SLJ 10/01) [551.447]

23003 Hewitt, Sally. *All Kinds of Habitats* (K–3). Series: It's Science! 1999, Children's Book Pr. LB $20.00 (0-516-21181-1). 30pp. Basic information is given in double-page spreads on a variety of habitats including rain forests and grasslands, with material on the plants and animals found in them. (Rev: SLJ 5/99) [574]

23004 Jenkins, Steve. *Hottest, Coldest, Highest, Deepest* (PS–3). Illus. 1998, Houghton Mifflin $16.00 (0-395-89999-0). 32pp. A geographical picture book describing superlative locations — the deepest lake, highest mountain, and places that are the hottest, coldest, windiest, etc. (Rev: BCCB 1/99; BL 8/98; HBG 3/99; SLJ 8/98) [910]

23005 Jennings, Terry. *Coasts and Islands* (3–6). Illus. Series: Restless Earth. 2003, Thameside LB $24.25 (1-931983-18-6). 32pp. Diagrams, photographs, and paintings combine with the text to illustrate how islands, coral reefs, and atolls are created and how water and earth interact. (Rev: BL 12/1/02; HBG 3/03) [551.457]

23006 Johansson, Philip. *The Frozen Tundra: A Web of Life* (3–5). Illus. Series: World of Biomes. 2004, Enslow LB $18.95 (0-7660-2176-9). 48pp. Plants and animals of the tundra are introduced here, along with information on the climate and seasons and the cycle of life. (Rev: BL 4/1/04) [577.5]

23007 Johnson, Rebecca L. *A Journey into a Wetland* (3–6). Illus. by Phyllis V. Saroff. Series: Biomes of North America. 2004, Lerner LB $23.93 (1-57505-593-7). 48pp. This appealing blend of easy-to-understand narrative and colorful illustrations explores the plants and animals found in and around a wetlands habitat. (Rev: BL 5/1/04) [577.68]

23008 Kalman, Bobbie, and Jacqueline Langille. *What Is a Biome?* (3–5). Series: Science of Living Things. 1998, Crabtree LB $14.37 (0-86505-875-X); paper $5.36 (0-86505-887-3). 32pp. Different types of ecological communities such as grasslands and deserts are described, with maps, photographs, charts, and short, interesting chapters. (Rev: SLJ 11/98) [591]

23009 Kramer, Stephen. *Caves* (3–6). Photos by Kenrick L. Day. Series: Caves. 1995, Carolrhoda LB $19.95 (0-87614-447-4); paper $7.95 (0-87614-896-8). 48pp. Using color photos, diagrams, and maps plus an interesting text, this book supplies a fascinating introduction to caves and their exploration. (Rev: BCCB 7–8/95; BL 4/15/95; SLJ 7/95) [557.4]

23010 Lye, Keith. *Coasts* (4–7). Illus. 1989, Silver Burdett LB $12.95 (0-382-09790-4). 48pp. An explanation of the effects of receding and advancing coastlines. (Rev: BL 5/1/89)

23011 Marx, Irish. *Everglades Forever: Restoring America's Great Wetland* (3–5). Illus. 2004, Lee & Low $17.95 (1-58430-164-3). 40pp. A Florida fifth-grade class's exploration of the Everglades serves as an appealing framework for information on this ecosystem and the perils it faces. (Rev: BL 2/1/05; SLJ 1/05) [508.759]

23012 Perenyi, Constance. *Wild Wild West: Wildlife Habitats of Western North America* (K–3). Illus. 1993, Sasquatch paper $8.95 (0-912365-90-0). 32pp. Ten geographical areas, including the Arctic tundra, Rocky Mountains, Sonoran Desert, and a coral reef, are described and pictured in colorful collages. (Rev: BL 12/15/93; SLJ 12/93) [508.78]

23013 Pipes, Rose. *Islands* (2–4). Series: World Habitats. 1998, Raintree LB $15.98 (0-8172-5009-3). 32pp. The physical characteristics of islands are presented with material on shore life, general geog-

raphy, and various kinds of wildlife. (Rev: BL 3/15/99; HBG 3/99) [551.4]

23014 Pipes, Rose. *Wetlands* (2–4). Series: World Habitats. 1998, Raintree LB $22.11 (0-8172-5001-8). 32pp. A nicely illustrated and well-laid out book on the ecology of wetlands, their climate, physical features, and plant and animal life. (Rev: BL 5/15/98; HBG 9/98) [574.5]

23015 Quigley, Mary. *Wetlands Explorer* (2–4). Illus. Series: Habitat Explorer. 2004, Raintree LB $18.45 (1-4109-0514-4). 32pp. This photo-filled exploration of wetlands looks at the plants and animals found there, plus environmental threats posed by pollution and development.

23016 Regan, Colm. *People of the Islands* (4–6). Series: Wide World. 1998, Raintree LB $25.69 (0-8172-5064-6). 48pp. Island environments are introduced with material on their geography and ecology and how humans live in these environments. (Rev: HBG 3/99; SLJ 2/99) [551.4]

23017 Ricciuti, Edward R. *Chaparral* (5–7). Illus. Series: Biomes of the World. 1996, Benchmark LB $25.64 (0-7614-0137-7). 64pp. An examination of the climate, vegetation, and life cycles of the chaparral, the biome situated between desert and grassland or forest and grassland, as in western North America from Oregon to Baja California. (Rev: SLJ 7/96) [574.5]

23018 Sauvain, Philip. *Rivers and Valleys* (4–7). Illus. Series: Geography Detectives. 1996, Carolrhoda LB $23.95 (0-87614-996-4). 32pp. In two-page spreads, rivers and valleys are introduced, with material on geology, flood control, wildlife, and tourism. (Rev: SLJ 3/97) [551.48]

23019 Sayres, Meghan Nuttall. *The Shape of Betts Meadow: A Wetlands Story* (K–3). Illus. by Joanne Friar. 2002, Millbrook LB $22.90 (0-7613-2115-3). 32pp. A stunning picture book set in Washington State that shows how a local doctor purchased a dry meadow and restored it to its original condition as a wetland. (Rev: BL 6/1–15/02; HBG 10/02; SLJ 4/02) [333.91]

23020 Siebert, Diane. *Cave* (2–4). Illus. 2000, HarperCollins LB $16.89 (0-688-16448-X). 32pp. In the form of a poem, this account describes caves, their formation, animal life, and such phenomena as stalactites and stalagmites. (Rev: BL 10/1/00; HBG 3/01; SLJ 10/00) [551.44]

23021 Staub, Frank. *America's Wetlands* (4–6). Illus. 1995, Carolrhoda LB $21.27 (0-87614-827-5). 48pp. The ecology of wetlands is described, with emphasis on their importance for the survival of wildlife. (Rev: BL 4/1/95; SLJ 5/95) [574.5]

23022 Steele, Philip. *Islands* (3–5). Illus. Series: Geography Detectives. 1996, Carolrhoda LB $19.95 (0-87614-997-2). 32pp. Double-page spreads introduce islands, their composition, and how they have been changed by humankind. (Rev: BL 9/1/96; SLJ 9/96) [551.4]

23023 Stille, Darlene R. *Wetlands* (2–4). Illus. Series: True Books. 1999, Children's Book Pr. LB $21.50 (0-516-21512-4). 48pp. A simple text and many photographs are used to introduce wetlands, their climate and geography, and the plants and animals that exist there. (Rev: BL 10/15/99) [578.768]

23024 Stone, Lynn M. *Wetlands* (1–3). Illus. Series: Biomes of North America. 2003, Rourke LB $20.64 (1-58952-688-0). 24pp. For young researchers, this is an excellent introduction to this biome, with clear, simple text, photographs, and maps. [574.5]

23025 Young, Allen M. *Lives Intertwined: Relationships Between Plants and Animals* (4–6). Illus. Series: A First Book. 1996, Watts LB $22.50 (0-531-20251-8). 63pp. Using the Central American rain forest as a lab, this account explores the complex relationships and interdependence of its plant and animal life. (Rev: SLJ 4/97) [574.5]

Deserts

23026 Arnold, Caroline. *Watching Desert Wildlife* (3–6). Photos by Arthur Arnold. 1994, Carolrhoda LB $23.93 (0-87614-841-0). 48pp. The desert environment is first explained, and then its wildlife is introduced in text and excellent photographs. (Rev: BL 12/1/94; SLJ 1/95) [574.5]

23027 Brown, John. *Journey into the Desert* (3–6). 2003, Oxford LB $18.95 (0-19-515777-X). 48pp. A camping trip forms the backdrop for a photo-filled introduction to the landscape, plants, and wildlife of the Sonoran Desert. (Rev: HBG 10/03; SLJ 8/03) [508.3154]

23028 Chambers, Catherine. *Deserts* (3–5). Series: Mapping Earthforms. 2000, Heinemann LB $14.95 (1-57572-522-3). 32pp. Deserts and desert life plus environmental factors that affect deserts are introduced in a large, bold text and numerous illustrations. (Rev: HBG 3/01; SLJ 8/00) [574.5]

23029 Fleisher, Paul. *Saguaro Cactus* (3–5). Series: Webs of Life. 1997, Marshall Cavendish LB $15.95 (0-7614-0433-3). 40pp. An introduction to this gigantic cactus found in the Southwest, with material on how it survives in a hostile environment. (Rev: BL 2/15/98; HBG 3/98) [635.9]

23030 Fredericks, Anthony D. *Around One Cactus: Owls, Bats and Leaping Rats* (K–4). Illus. by Jennifer DiRubbio. Series: Sharing Nature with Children. 2003, Dawn $16.95 (1-58469-051-8); paper $7.95 (1-58469-052-6). A cumulative tale, told in verse, about the natural life surrounding a Saguaro cactus, colorfully illustrated with detailed drawings. (Rev: HBG 4/04; SLJ 4/04) [591.754]

23031 Giesecke, Ernestine. *Desert Plants* (K–3). Series: Heinemann First Library. 1999, Heinemann LB $13.95 (1-57572-821-4). 32pp. A colorful beginning book that introduces desert plants and explains a little about their ecosystem and how they have adapted. (Rev: BL 6/1–15/99; SLJ 8/99) [574.4]

23032 Green, Jen. *A Saguaro Cactus* (2–4). Series: Small Worlds. 1999, Crabtree LB $15.96 (0-7787-0134-4); paper $8.06 (0-7787-0148-4). 32pp. The desert ecosystem of the Sonoran Desert is introduced with material on the plants and animals found there. (Rev: SLJ 2/00) [574.5]

23033 Jenkins, Martin. *Deserts* (3–6). Illus. Series: Endangered People and Places. 1996, Lerner LB $22.60 (0-8225-2775-8). 48pp. In this account that combines geography and sociology, deserts and the survival of their inhabitants are described. (Rev: BL 11/15/96; SLJ 11/96) [333.73]

23034 Jernigan, Gisela. *Sonoran Seasons: A Year in the Desert* (3–6). Illus. by E. Wesley Jernigan. 1994, Harbinger paper $10.95 (0-943173-91-4). For every month of the year, a different plant from the Sonoran Desert is introduced, most of them edible. (Rev: SLJ 6/94) [581.5]

23035 Johnson, Rebecca L. *A Walk in the Desert* (2–5). Illus. by Phyllis V. Saroff. Series: Biomes of North America. 2001, Carolrhoda LB $23.93 (1-57505-152-4). 48pp. As well as the climate of the desert, this account covers its flora and fauna and their interactions. (Rev: HBG 10/01; SLJ 3/01) [574.5]

23036 Lambert, David. *People of the Deserts* (4–6). Series: Wide World. 1998, Raintree LB $25.69 (0-8172-5063-8). 48pp. The physical geography and ecology of desert regions are discussed with material on the human cultures in these areas. (Rev: HBG 3/99; SLJ 2/99) [551.4]

23037 Landau, Elaine. *Desert Mammals* (1–3). Illus. Series: A True Book. 1996, Children's Book Pr. LB $22.00 (0-516-20038-0). 48pp. After brief coverage on what and where deserts are, this account describes some indigenous mammals, like camels, kangaroo rats, antelope jack rabbits, and addaxes. (Rev: SLJ 3/97) [591]

23038 Lazaroff, David. *Correctamundo! Prickly Pete's Guide to Desert Facts and Cactifracts* (K–3). Illus. by Preston Neel. 2001, Arizona-Sonora Desert Museum paper $9.95 (1-886679-17-7). A bright, lively question-and-answer introduction to desert plants and animals, conducted by a packrat named Prickly Pete. (Rev: SLJ 8/01) [574.5]

23039 Le Rochais, Marie-Ange. *Desert Trek: An Eye-Opening Journey Through the World's Driest Places* (3–5). Trans. by George L. Newman. Illus. 2001, Walker LB $18.85 (0-8027-8766-5). 40pp. Dramatic spreads and brief text show the diversity of desert landscapes around the world, with features ranging from plants, animals, and oases to people hunting and working. (Rev: BL 6/1–15/01; HBG 10/01; SLJ 9/01) [577.54]

23040 Lesser, Carolyn. *Storm on the Desert* (K–3). Illus. by Ted Rand. 1997, Harcourt $16.00 (0-15-272198-3). 40pp. Pictures and text depict what happens in a desert before, during, and after a violent storm. (Rev: BL 5/1/97; SLJ 5/97) [574.5]

23041 Low, Robert. *Peoples of the Desert* (2–5). Illus. Series: People and Their Environments. 1996, Rosen LB $10.46 (0-8239-2296-0). 24pp. Two nomadic tribes, one from the Sahara and the other from the Kalahari, are featured in this discussion of human life in a desert environment. (Rev: BL 10/15/96; SLJ 1/97) [966]

23042 Lye, Keith. *Deserts* (4–6). Illus. 1987, Silver Burdett LB $12.95 (0-382-09501-4). 48pp. A well-illustrated survey that describes the locations, climate, evolution of, and plant and animal life in the world's deserts. (Rev: BL 2/1/88)

23043 Patent, Dorothy Hinshaw. *Life in a Desert* (5–8). Series: Ecosystems in Action. 2003, Lerner LB $26.60 (0-8225-2140-7). 72pp. This account explores the plant and animal life in deserts and how human intervention has changed this ecosystem. (Rev: BL 9/15/03; HBG 10/03) [574.5]

23044 Pfeffer, Wendy. *Hot Deserts* (3–5). Series: Living on the Edge. 2002, Benchmark LB $16.95 (0-7614-1440-1). 40pp. This easy-to-read overview of the animals and plants that flourish in desert climates opens with a map. (Rev: HBG 10/03; SLJ 6/03) [577.54]

23045 Pipes, Rose. *Hot Deserts* (2–4). Illus. Series: World Habitats. 1998, Raintree LB $22.11 (0-8172-5004-2). 32pp. Color photos and a large, clear text introduce deserts, their climate, vegetation, and the people and animals populating them. (Rev: BL 4/15/98; HBG 9/98) [577.54]

23046 Pratt-Serafini, Kristin Joy. *Saguaro Moon: A Desert Journal* (3–6). Illus. 2002, Dawn $16.95 (1-58469-037-2); paper $7.95 (1-58469-036-4). 32pp. In this hybrid, factual information about desert plant and animal life is presented in the form of a nature journal written by a girl named Megan, who has recently moved to Arizona. (Rev: BL 10/15/02; HBG 3/03; SLJ 9/02) [508.3154]

23047 Pyers, Greg. *Desert Explorer* (2–4). Illus. Series: Habitat Explorer. 2004, Raintree LB $25.70 (1-4109-0507-1). 32pp. This photo-filled exploration of deserts looks at the plants and animals found there, plus environmental threats to this habitat.

23048 Ricciuti, Edward R. *Desert* (4–6). Illus. Series: Biomes of the World. 1996, Benchmark LB $25.64 (0-7614-0134-2). 64pp. Deserts of the world are identified and described, with coverage on their plant and animal life. (Rev: SLJ 7/96) [574.9]

23049 Ruth, Maria Mudd. *The Deserts of the Southwest* (5–8). Series: Ecosystems of North America. 1998, Benchmark LB $27.07 (0-7614-0899-1). After an overview of the deserts of the Southwest and how they were formed, this book introduces desert plants and wildlife, how they interact, adaptations they have made to the desert environment, and the impact of human development. (Rev: BR 5–6/99; HBG 9/99; SLJ 2/99) [591]

23050 Sabin, Louis. *Wonders of the Desert* (1–3). Illus. by Pamela Baldwin Ford. 1982, Troll LB $17.25 (0-89375-574-5); paper $2.50 (0-89375-575-3). 32pp. A fine array of desert flora and fauna is simply introduced.

23051 Salzmann, Mary Elizabeth. *In the Desert* (K–1). Illus. Series: What Do You See? 2001, ABDO LB $12.95 (1-57765-564-8). 24pp. Colorful double-page spreads introduce the desert in simple language for beginning readers. (Rev: HBG 3/02; SLJ 3/02) [577.54]

23052 Savage, Stephen. *Animals of the Desert* (3–6). Illus. Series: Animals by Habitat. 1997, Raintree LB $22.83 (0-8172-4750-5). 32pp. After a discussion of the world's deserts and how they differ, this book

introduces five basic animals groups found in deserts, like mammals, birds, and reptiles. (Rev: BL 5/15/97; SLJ 8/97) [591.5]

23053 Sayre, April Pulley. *Desert* (4–7). Illus. Series: Exploring Earth's Biomes. 1994, Twenty-First Century LB $25.90 (0-8050-2825-0). 64pp. After a general introduction to deserts, a specific one is explored in brief chapters with excellent illustrations. (Rev: BL 1/1/95*; SLJ 1/95) [574.5]

23054 Steele, Philip. *Deserts* (4–6). Illus. Series: Geography Detectives. 1996, Carolrhoda LB $19.95 (0-87614-998-0). 32pp. This introduction to deserts and the life found in them discusses such topics as the differences between hot and cold deserts, their landscape features, and how they are still being created. (Rev: SLJ 9/96) [574.5]

23055 Steele, Philip. *Deserts* (5–8). Series: Pocket Facts. 1991, Macmillan LB $11.95 (0-89686-588-6). A concise introduction to deserts, featuring easily understand facts and photographs. (Rev: BL 3/15/92) [508.315]

23056 Stille, Darlene R. *Deserts* (2–4). Series: True Books. 1999, Children's Book Pr. LB $21.50 (0-516-21508-6). 48pp. A color photo with six lines of simple text on each page is used to introduced deserts and their characteristics, location, and flora and fauna. (Rev: BL 10/15/99) [574.5]

23057 Stone, Lynn M. *Deserts* (1–3). Illus. Series: Biomes of North America. 2003, Rourke LB $20.64 (1-58952-683-X). 24pp. For young researchers, this is an excellent introduction to this biome, with clear, simple text, photographs, and maps. [574.5]

23058 Storad, Conrad J. *Saguaro Cactus* (3–5). Photos by Paula Jansen. Series: Early Bird Nature Books. 1994, Lerner LB $22.60 (0-8225-3002-3). 48pp. After a general introduction to cacti, this account focuses on the physical appearance and life cycle of the saguaro. (Rev: SLJ 8/94) [583]

23059 Twist, Clint. *Deserts* (5–8). Series: Ecology Watch. 1991, Dillon LB $13.95 (0-87518-490-1). Traces the evolution of deserts, explains why they are threatened, and offers possible solutions to specific problems. (Rev: BL 3/1/92; SLJ 4/92) [574.5]

23060 Wallace, Marianne D. *America's Deserts: Guide to Plants and Animals* (3–5). Illus. 1996, Fulcrum paper $15.95 (1-55591-268-0). 48pp. After a general discussion of the flora and fauna of deserts, this account focuses on specific deserts, like Mojave and Death Valley. (Rev: BL 4/1/96; SLJ 7/96) [574.973]

Forests and Rain Forests

23061 Aldis, Rodney. *Rainforests* (5–8). Illus. Series: Ecology Watch. 1991, Macmillan LB $13.95 (0-87518-495-2). 45pp. In an attractive, oversized format, this book discusses how rain forests evolved, why they are threatened, and the plants and animals found in them. (Rev: BL 3/1/92; SLJ 4/92) [574.5]

23062 Art, Henry W., and Michael W. Robbins. *Woods Walk* (4–6). Illus. 2003, Storey $21.95 (1-58017-477-9); paper $14.95 (1-58017-452-3). 128pp. A broad overview of the plants and animals found in the woodlands of the eastern and western United States. (Rev: HBG 4/04; SLJ 6/03) [508.352]

23063 Baldwin, Carol. *Living in a Rain Forest* (3–6). Series: Living Habitats. 2003, Heinemann LB $24.22 (1-4034-2992-8). 32pp. The plants and animals of the rain forest are presented in question-and-answer format, with brief discussion of human interference. (Rev: HBG 4/04; SLJ 2/04) [577.34]

23064 Baldwin, Carol. *Living in the Taiga* (3–6). Series: Living Habitats. 2003, Heinemann LB $24.22 (1-4034-2994-4). 32pp. The plants and animals of the taiga are presented in question-and-answer format, with brief discussion of human interference. (Rev: HBG 4/04; SLJ 2/04) [577.3]

23065 Bishop, Nic. *Forest Explorer: A Life-Size Field Guide* (K–4). Photos by author. 2004, Scholastic $17.95 (0-439-17480-5). 48pp. An attractive introductory guide to the trees and animal life found in deciduous forests. (Rev: BL 1/1–15/04; SLJ 3/04) [591.734]

23066 Butterfield, Moira. *Animals in Trees* (K–3). Series: Looking At. 1999, Raintree LB $22.83 (0-7398-0110-4). 32pp. For beginning readers, this book introduces in a simple text and pictures such animals as the squirrel, marmoset, macaw, and ocelot. (Rev: HBG 9/00; SLJ 3/00) [591]

23067 Castaldo, Nancy F. *Rainforests: An Activity Guide for Ages 6–9* (2–6). Illus. 2003, Chicago Review paper $14.95 (1-55652-476-5). 133pp. This engaging collection of resources and activities is designed to help young readers gain a better understanding of the different types of rainforests and the animals and plants that are common to each. (Rev: SLJ 11/03) [577.34]

23068 Chinery, Michael. *Poisoners and Pretenders* (5–8). Series: Secrets of the Rainforests. 2000, Crabtree LB $21.28 (0-7787-0219-7); paper $7.95 (0-7787-0229-4). 32pp. After a brief description of a rain forest, this book looks at animals found there and their mimicry, camouflage, venom, natural selection, and adaptation to the environment. Also use *Predators and Prey* (2000). (Rev: SLJ 2/01) [574.5]

23069 Cole, Melissa. *Forests* (3–6). Photos by Tom Leeson and Pat Leeson. Series: Wild America Habitats. 2003, Gale/Blackbirch LB $19.95 (1-56711-802-X). 24pp. Describes the unique characteristics of the forest habitat and the plants and animals that thrive within it. Also use *Rain Forests* (2003). (Rev: SLJ 2/04) [577.3]

23070 Collard, Sneed B. *The Forest in the Clouds* (2–4). Illus. by Michael Rothman. 2000, Charlesbridge $16.95 (0-88106-985-X); paper $6.95 (0-88106-986-8). 32pp. In double-page spreads, the Monteverde Cloud Forest in Costa Rica is introduced with material on its climate, animals, and plants. (Rev: BL 6/1–15/00; HBG 3/01; SLJ 8/00) [577.34]

23071 Crump, Donald J., ed. *Explore a Tropical Forest* (K–3). Illus. by Barbara Gibson. Series: National Geographic Action Books. 1989, National Geographic $16.00 (0-87044-757-2). Pop-ups and flaps are used to give a three-dimensional look at a

tropical rain forest and its flora and fauna. (Rev: SLJ 3/90) [574.5]

23072 Darling, Kathy. *Rain Forest Babies* (K–3). Illus. by Tara Darling. 1996, Walker LB $16.85 (0-8027-8412-7). 32pp. All kinds of baby animals found in the rain forest are introduced in text and full-page color photographs. (Rev: BL 4/15/96; SLJ 4/96) [591]

23073 Dorros, Arthur. *Rain Forest Secrets* (3–5). Illus. 1990, Scholastic $15.95 (0-590-43369-5). 32pp. A picture-book introduction to rain forests. (Rev: BCCB 9/90; BL 9/1/90; SLJ 2/91) [574.5]

23074 Drake, Jane, and Ann Love. *Forestry* (3–4). Illus. by Pat Cupples. Series: America at Work. 1998, Kids Can $12.95 (1-55074-462-3). 31pp. A young boy is taken into a forest where he learns about forestry, the lumbering industry, and associated environmental concerns. (Rev: HBG 3/99; SLJ 12/98) [574.5]

23075 Fowler, Allan. *Our Living Forests* (1–2). Illus. Series: Rookie Readers. 1999, Children's Book Pr. LB $18.50 (0-516-20811-X). 32pp. With a small format, large type, and color pictures, this book introduces different kinds of forests, and tells how climate affects the kinds of trees and other plant life that grow in them. (Rev: BL 7/99; HBG 9/99) [578.73]

23076 George, Jean Craighead. *One Day in the Tropical Rain Forest* (3–6). Illus. by Gary Allen. 1990, HarperCollins $15.95 (0-690-04767-3). 64pp. The tropical rain forest is introduced in a narrative that proceeds through the course of a day. (Rev: BCCB 3/90; BL 4/15/90; HB 5–6/90; SLJ 8/90) [508]

23077 Gibbons, Gail. *Nature's Green Umbrella: Tropical Rain Forests* (3–5). Illus. 1994, Morrow $15.93 (0-688-12354-6). 32pp. The ecosystem of the rain forest is explained, with material on how these resources should be protected and preserved. (Rev: BL 6/1–15/94; SLJ 7/94) [574.5]

23078 Giesecke, Ernestine. *Forest Plants* (K–3). Series: Heinemann First Library. 1999, Heinemann LB $13.95 (1-57572-823-0). 32pp. Different plants that grow in forests are presented with a full-color photo followed by a few lines of explanatory text. (Rev: BL 6/1–15/99) [574]

23079 Goodman, Susan E. *Bats, Bugs, and Biodiversity: Adventures in the Amazonian Rain Forest* (4–8). Illus. 1995, Simon & Schuster $16.00 (0-689-31942-6). Some junior high students learn firsthand about the Amazon rain forest and its endangered ecology. (Rev: BL 12/1/97) [508]

23080 Green, Jen. *A Dead Log* (2–4). Series: Small Worlds. 1999, Crabtree LB $15.96 (0-7787-0136-0); paper $8.06 (0-7787-0150-6). 32pp. This book presents the animals and plants that might be associated with a fallen log in a North American deciduous forest. (Rev: SLJ 2/00) [574.5]

23081 Green, Jen. *Rain Forests* (3–6). Illus. Series: Young Scientist Concepts and Projects. 1999, Gareth Stevens LB $16.95 (0-8368-2268-4). 64pp. This work discusses rain forests, where they are found, and the life on a rain forest floor, and outlines several related projects. (Rev: BL 4/15/99) [577.34]

23082 Grupper, Jonathan. *Destination: Rain Forest* (4–6). Illus. 1997, National Geographic $16.00 (0-7922-7018-5). 32pp. Using brilliant photos, this book introduces the rain forest as a habitat, as well as the animals found there. (Rev: BL 11/1/97; HBG 3/98; SLJ 10/97) [578.734]

23083 Guiberson, Brenda Z. *Rain, Rain, Rainforest* (K–3). Illus. by Steve Jenkins. 2004, Holt $16.95 (0-8050-6582-2). 32pp. Basic information on day-to-day life and survival in the rain forest is conveyed in an attractive blend of picturesque narrative and colorful paper-cut collages. (Rev: BL 5/1/04; HB 7–8/04; SLJ 6/04) [577.34]

23084 Haugen, Hayley Mitchell. *Life in a Forest* (4–6). Illus. Series: Ecosystems. 2005, Gale/KidHaven LB $18.96 (0-7377-3080-3). 48pp. An excellent overview of the six kinds of forests found around the world, their composition, the animals that live in them, and the dangers posed by environmental changes. (Rev: BL 6/1–15/05) [577.3]

23085 Hickman, Pamela. *In the Woods* (3–5). Series: See, Make and Do. 1998, Formac paper $9.95 (0-88780-412-8). 64pp. A book about woodland exploration and the animals and plants one might encounter, with several suggestions for craft projects. (Rev: BL 12/1/98) [557.3]

23086 Jackson, Tom. *Tropical Forests* (5–8). Series: Biomes Atlases. 2003, Raintree LB $31.42 (0-7398-5250-7). 64pp. This comprehensive overview of tropical forests describes the climate, flora and fauna, people, and future of these areas, and includes good maps. (Rev: SLJ 9/03) [577.34]

23087 Johanasen, Heather, and Sindy McKay. *About the Rain Forest* (1–2). Illus. Series: We Both Read. 2000, Treasure Bay $7.99 (1-891327-23-2); paper $3.99 (1-891327-24-0). 44pp. Using side-by-side texts, one for adults and the other for children, this book introduces the rain forest, its climate, ecosystem, and animals. (Rev: BL 7/00) [574.5]

23088 Johansson, Philip. *The Dry Desert: A Web of Life* (3–5). Illus. Series: A World of Biomes. 2004, Enslow LB $17.95 (0-7660-2200-5). 48pp. An engaging introduction to the flora and fauna of the desert and to the work of the scientists who study the biome.

23089 Johansson, Philip. *The Forested Taiga: A Web of Life* (3–6). Illus. Series: A World of Biomes. 2004, Enslow LB $18.95 (0-7660-2197-1). 48pp. Introduces readers to the physical characteristics, climate, flora, and fauna of the forested taiga, a vast subpolar region dominated by conifers. (Rev: SLJ 8/04) [577.3]

23090 Johansson, Philip. *The Temperate Forest: A Web of Life* (3–5). Illus. Series: World of Biomes. 2004, Enslow LB $18.95 (0-7660-2198-X). 48pp. A biologist's interest in a black bear in North Carolina serves as an introduction to this study of plant and animal interaction in temperate forests. (Rev: BL 4/1/04; SLJ 8/04) [577.3]

23091 Johansson, Philip. *The Tropical Rain Forest: A Web of Life* (3–6). Illus. Series: World of Biomes.

2004, Enslow LB $18.95 (0-7660-2199-8). 48pp. An engaging introduction to the flora and fauna of the rain forest and to the work of the scientists who study the biome. (Rev: SLJ 8/04) [577.34]

23092 Johnson, Linda Carlson. *Rain Forests: A Pro/Con Issue* (4–8). Series: Hot Issues. 1999, Enslow LB $21.95 (0-7660-1202-6). 64pp. This book describes the rain forests of the world, how political and economic interests are destroying them, efforts to save them, and the pros and cons of conserving them. (Rev: HBG 9/00; SLJ 4/00) [574.5]

23093 Johnson, Rebecca L. *A Walk in the Boreal Forest* (2–4). Illus. by Phyllis V. Saroff. Series: Biomes of North America. 2000, Carolrhoda LB $23.95 (1-57505-156-7). 48pp. This book takes the reader to a forest of tall conifers and tells about its plants and animals and their interdependence. (Rev: BL 10/15/00; HBG 3/01; SLJ 3/01) [574.5]

23094 Johnson, Rebecca L. *A Walk in the Rain Forest* (2–5). Illus. by Phyllis V. Saroff. Series: Biomes of North America. 2001, Carolrhoda LB $23.93 (1-57505-154-0). 48pp. Examines the climate of the rain forest and its flora and fauna. (Rev: HBG 10/01; SLJ 3/01) [574.5]

23095 Kaplan, Elizabeth. *Taiga* (5–7). Illus. Series: Biomes of the World. 1996, Benchmark LB $25.64 (0-7614-0135-0). 64pp. This account discusses the climate, animal and plant life, soil, and seasonal changes in the taiga, the extensive forest in the Northern Hemisphere. (Rev: SLJ 7/96) [574.5]

23096 Kaplan, Elizabeth. *Temperate Forest* (4–6). Illus. Series: Biomes of the World. 1995, Marshall Cavendish LB $25.64 (0-7614-0082-6). 64pp. Four types of temperate forests are introduced, with material on locations, animals, plants, and possible future problems. (Rev: BL 12/15/95; SLJ 3/96) [574.5]

23097 Knapp, Brian. *What Do We Know About Rainforests?* (4–6). Illus. Series: Caring for Environments. 1992, Bedrick LB $15.95 (0-87226-358-4). 40pp. A colorful book that surveys the location, terrain, ecology, and importance of rain forests. (Rev: BL 2/15/93; SLJ 1/93) [574]

23098 Knight, Tim. *Journey into the Rainforest* (3–5). Illus. by Juan Pablo Moreiras and Tim Knight. 2001, Oxford $18.95 (0-19-521751-9). 48pp. Readers take a colorful tour through a rain forest, observing the vegetation and wildlife as they go and learning about the ecosystem's intricacies and endangered status. (Rev: BL 9/15/01; HBG 3/02; SLJ 10/01) [577.34]

23099 Landau, Elaine. *Temperate Forest Mammals* (3–4). Illus. Series: A True Book. 1996, Children's Book Pr. LB $22.00 (0-516-20043-7). 48pp. General information on forests found in temperate climates is followed by material of specific mammals. (Rev: SLJ 4/97) [591]

23100 Lasky, Kathryn. *The Most Beautiful Roof in the World: Exploring the Rainforest Canopy* (3–5). Illus. 1997, Harcourt $18.00 (0-15-100893-4). The canopy of plants and animals found in the rain forest of Belize is explored by the author, a biologist, and her assistant. (Rev: BL 4/1/97*; HB 5–6/97) [574.5]

23101 Lasky, Kathryn. *The Most Beautiful Roof in the World: Exploring the Rainforest Canopy* (5–8). 1997, Harcourt $18.00 (0-15-200893-4); paper $9.00 (0-15-200897-7). The canopy of plants and animals found in the rain forest of Belize is explored by the author, a biologist, who also explains the methods scientists use to conduct research in this environment, sometimes under extremely difficult conditions. (Rev: BL 4/1/97; SLJ 4/97) [574.5]

23102 Lewington, Anna. *Antonio's Rain Forest* (3–5). Illus. by Edward Parker. 1993, Carolrhoda LB $22.60 (0-87614-749-X). 48pp. A first-person narrative by an 8-year-old boy of the rain forest. (Rev: BL 3/1/93; SLJ 3/93) [338]

23103 Lewington, Anna, and Edward Parker. *People of the Rain Forests* (4–7). Series: Wide World. 1998, Raintree $18.98 (0-8172-5061-1). 48pp. As well as introducing rain forests, this book describes the people who live there, their tribal customs, their homes — including cities — and their everyday lives. (Rev: HBG 3/99; SLJ 1/99) [574.5]

23104 Low, Robert. *Peoples of the Rain Forest* (2–5). Illus. Series: People and Their Environments. 1996, Rosen LB $15.93 (0-8239-2297-9). 24pp. Human lifestyles in a rain forest environment are introduced, with examples from peoples in Africa, South America, and Borneo. (Rev: BL 10/15/96; SLJ 11/96) [304.2]

23105 MacMillan, Dianne M. *Life in a Deciduous Forest* (5–8). Series: Ecosystems in Action. 2003, Lerner LB $26.60 (0-8225-4684-1). 72pp. This book explores the ecosystem, its flora and fauna, where trees shed their leaves in autumn. (Rev: BL 9/15/03; HBG 10/03) [574.5]

23106 Mania, Robert, and Cathy Mania. *A Forest's Life: From Meadow to Mature Woodland* (4–6). Illus. Series: First Books. 1997, Watts LB $22.50 (0-531-20319-0). 64pp. Traces the gradual transformation of a meadow into a forest and of the plants and animals involved. (Rev: BL 12/15/97; SLJ 10/97) [577.3]

23107 Montgomery, Sy. *Encantado: Pink Dolphin of the Amazon* (5–8). Illus. by Diane Taylor-Snow. 2002, Houghton Mifflin $18.00 (0-618-13103-5). 80pp. The author describes the flora and fauna of the South American rain forest seen in her unsuccessful journey to locate the encantado, the elusive pink dolphin. (Rev: BL 4/1/02; HB 7–8/02; HBG 10/02; SLJ 5/02*) [599.53]

23108 Morrison, Marion. *The Amazon Rain Forest and Its People* (5–8). Series: People and Places. 1993, Thomson Learning LB $24.26 (1-56847-087-8). After a general history and a description of the region's plants, animals, and people, the author discusses the dangers developers pose to this rain forest. (Rev: BL 11/1/93) [333.75]

23109 Moss, Miriam. *Jungle Song* (PS–2). Illus. by Adrienne Kennaway. 2004, Lincoln $15.95 (1-84507-039-9). 32pp. A young tapir is lured away from his mother by a spider and explores the lush

and busy South American rain forest. (Rev: BL 10/1/04; SLJ 10/04)

23110 Mutel, Cornelia F., and Mary M. Rodgers. *Our Endangered Planet: Tropical Rain Forests* (4–7). Illus. Series: Our Endangered Planet. 1991, Lerner LB $27.15 (0-8225-2503-8); paper $8.95 (0-8225-9629-6). 64pp. Describes tropical rain forests and the environmental threats they face. (Rev: BL 6/15/91; SLJ 5/91) [333]

23111 O'Hare, Ted. *Vanishing Rain Forest* (1–3). Photos by Lynn M. Stone. Series: Rain Forests Today. 2005, Rourke LB $20.64 (1-59515-156-7). 24pp. An attractive introduction to the threats to world's rain forests from pollution and wholesale deforestation. Other titles in this series include *Animals of the Rain Forest*, *Plants of the Rain Forest*, and *People of the Rain Forest* (all 2005). (Rev: BL 1/1–15/05) [333.75]

23112 Oldfield, Sara. *Rain Forests* (3–6). Illus. Series: Endangered People and Places. 1996, Lerner LB $22.60 (0-8225-2778-2). 48pp. The location, geography, and natural life of rain forests are described, plus material on the threats to these regions and how conservation efforts are proceeding. (Rev: BL 11/15/96; SLJ 1/97) [333.75]

23113 Parker, Edward. *People* (5–8). Photos by author. Series: Rain Forest. 2003, Raintree LB $27.12 (0-7398-5242-6). 48pp. An introduction to the various peoples of the rain forest. (Rev: HBG 3/03; SLJ 1/03) [304.2]

23114 Parker, Edward. *Rain Forest Mammals* (5–9). Illus. Series: Rain Forest. 2002, Raintree LB $27.12 (0-7398-5241-8). 48pp. Mammals of the rain forest and the importance of preserving their habitat are introduced in close-up color photographs and a catchy layout, with a glossary, bibliography, and list of related organizations. Also use *Rain Forest Reptiles and Amphibians* (2002). (Rev: BL 12/1/02; HBG 3/03) [599]

23115 Pascoe, Gwen. *Deep in a Rainforest* (PS–1). Illus. by Veronica Jefferis. 1999, Gareth Stevens LB $14.95 (0-8368-2149-1). 32pp. Picture puzzles and double-page spreads introduce the plants and animals of the rain forest to a young audience. (Rev: BL 5/1/99) [578.734]

23116 Pipes, Rose. *Forests and Woodlands* (2–4). Series: World Habitats. 1998, Raintree LB $15.98 (0-8172-5007-7). 32pp. A general description of the physical features of forests is followed by material on climate, wildlife, uses, and protection efforts. (Rev: BL 3/15/99; HBG 3/99) [574.5]

23117 Pipes, Rose. *Rain Forests* (2–4). Illus. Series: World Habitats. 1998, Raintree LB $22.11 (0-8172-5003-4). 32pp. Rain forests are introduced in color photographs and clear text, with material on animal and plant life, climate, and conservation. (Rev: BL 4/15/98; HBG 9/98) [577.4]

23118 Pirotta, Saviour. *People in the Rain Forest* (2–4). Illus. Series: Deep in the Rain Forest. 1998, Raintree LB $15.98 (0-8172-5137-5). 32pp. Rain forests in Peru, Indonesia, and New Guinea are highlighted in this account of the various peoples of the rain forest, their different habitats, how they live, and how their environments are being threatened. (Rev: BL 1/1–15/99; HBG 3/99) [304.2]

23119 Pyers, Greg. *Forest Explorer* (2–4). Illus. Series: Habitat Explorer. 2004, Raintree LB $25.70 (1-4109-0508-X). 32pp. This photo-filled exploration of forests looks at the plants and animals found there, plus environmental threats posed by pollution and development. Also use *Rain Forest Explorer* (2004).

23120 Rapp, Valerie. *Life in an Old Growth Forest* (5–8). Series: Ecosystems in Action. 2002, Lerner LB $26.60 (0-8225-2135-0). 72pp. In pictures and text, this book introduces life in an established forest with material on the interdependence of organisms there, and how human intervention has changed this ecosystem. (Rev: BL 12/15/02; HBG 3/03; SLJ 2/03) [574.5]

23121 Ricciuti, Edward R. *Rainforest* (4–6). Illus. Series: Biomes of the World. 1995, Marshall Cavendish LB $25.64 (0-7614-0081-8). 64pp. The world's rain forest biome is described, with material on this ecological system, its animals, plants, and current threats of destruction. (Rev: BL 12/15/95) [574.5]

23122 Ross, Suzanne. *What's in the Rainforest?* (3–5). Illus. by author. 1991, Enchanted Rainforest paper $5.95 (0-9629895-0-9). 48pp. Using an alphabetical approach, this is a well-organized introduction to the plants and animals found in a rain forest. (Rev: SLJ 3/92) [574.5]

23123 Sabin, Francene. *Wonders of the Forest* (1–3). Illus. by Michael Willard. 1982, Troll paper $3.50 (0-89375-573-7). 32pp. An introduction to the trees of the forest in text and pictures. Also use: *Wonders of the Pond* (1982).

23124 Sauvain, Philip. *Rain Forests* (3–5). Illus. Series: Geography Detectives. 1997, Carolrhoda LB $19.93 (1-57505-041-2). 32pp. Identifies and describes the world's rain forests and the lush plants and diverse peoples and animals that live in them, with information on the many industrial threats to rain forests' survival. (Rev: BL 8/97) [574.5]

23125 Savage, Stephen. *Animals of the Rain Forest* (3–6). Illus. Series: Animals by Habitat. 1997, Raintree LB $22.83 (0-8172-4751-3). 32pp. The rain forest habitat is introduced, with focus on the five categories of animal life found there, such as mammals, birds, and amphibians. (Rev: BL 5/15/97) [591.9]

23126 Sayre, April Pulley. *Taiga* (4–7). Illus. Series: Exploring Earth's Biomes. 1994, Twenty-First Century LB $25.90 (0-8050-2830-7). 64pp. This book clearly describes the swampy, carnivorous forest and the wildlife found, for example, in northern Canada, where the tundra ends. (Rev: BL 1/15/95; SLJ 2/95) [574.5]

23127 Sayre, April Pulley. *Temperate Deciduous Forest* (4–7). Illus. Series: Exploring Earth's Biomes. 1994, Twenty-First Century LB $25.90 (0-8050-2828-5). 64pp. Deciduous forests are introduced with material on their composition, uses, and the animal and other plant life found within their community. (Rev: BL 1/1/95*; SLJ 1/95) [574.5]

23128 Sayre, April Pulley. *Tropical Rain Forest* (4–7). Illus. Series: Exploring Earth's Biomes. 1994, Twenty-First Century LB $25.90 (0-8050-2826-9). 64pp. The structure and contents of rain forests are explored with information on the plants, animals, and people that exist in this habitat. (Rev: BL 1/1/95; SLJ 1/95) [574.5]

23129 Silver, Donald M. *Why Save the Rain Forest?* (3–5). Illus. by Patricia J. Wynne. 1993, Messner LB $23.00 (0-671-86609-5); paper $6.95 (0-671-86610-9). 48pp. A handsome volume that shows the amazing diversity of life in a rain forest and the consequences of destroying this environment. (Rev: SLJ 3/94) [574.5]

23130 Staub, Frank. *America's Forests* (3–6). Illus. 1999, Carolrhoda $15.95 (1-57505-265-2). 48pp. Different types of forests that exist in North America are introduced with material on kinds of trees and a basic woodland ecosystem. (Rev: BL 5/1/99; HBG 9/99; SLJ 7/99) [577.3]

23131 Stille, Darlene R. *Tropical Rain Forests* (2–4). Illus. 1999, Children's Book Pr. LB $21.50 (0-516-21511-6). 48pp. The climate and geography of tropical rain forests are discussed with coverage on their plants and animals. (Rev: BL 10/15/99) [578.734]

23132 Stone, Lynn M. *Forests* (1–3). Illus. Series: Biomes of North America. 2003, Rourke LB $20.64 (1-58952-684-8). 24pp. For young researchers, this is an excellent introduction to this biome, with clear, simple text, photographs, and maps. [574.5]

23133 Telford, Carole, and Rod Theodorou. *Up a Rainforest Tree* (3–5). Series: Amazing Journeys. 1997, Heinemann LB $13.95 (1-57572-156-2). 32pp. This trek through the layers of the Amazon rain forest is well organized, but the illustrations are often too small for clarity. (Rev: SLJ 4/98) [574.5]

23134 Welsbacher, Anne. *Life in a Rainforest* (5–8). Series: Ecosystems in Action. 2003, Lerner LB $26.60 (0-8225-4685-X). 72pp. This illustrated account covers the plant and animal life in rain forests and explains how human intervention has changed, and often endangered, this ecosystem. (Rev: BL 9/15/03; HBG 10/03) [574.5]

23135 Woods, Mae. *Insects of the Rain Forest* (2–4). Series: Rain Forest. 1999, ABDO LB $13.95 (1-57765-023-9). 24pp. This book presents the insects found in the rain forest with outstanding photos and an interesting text. Also use *People of the Rain Forest* and *Protecting the Rain Forest* (both 1999). (Rev: HBG 4/00; SLJ 1/00) [574.5]

23136 Wright-Frierson, Virginia. *A North American Rain Forest Scrapbook* (3–5). Illus. 1999, Walker LB $16.89 (0-8027-8680-4). 40pp. Double-page spreads introduce the rain forest on Washington's Olympic Peninsula and discuss its flora and fauna. (Rev: BCCB 6/99; BL 11/1/99; HBG 9/99; SLJ 6/99) [577.34]

Mountains

23137 Chambers, Catherine. *Mountains* (3–5). Series: Mapping Earthforms. 2000, Heinemann LB $14.95 (1-57572-525-8). 32pp. A basic overview of mountains presented in double-page spreads illustrated with photographs, maps, and charts. (Rev: HBG 3/01; SLJ 8/00) [551.4]

23138 Cobb, Vicki. *This Place Is High* (3–5). Illus. by Barbara Lavallee. Series: Imagine Living Here. 1989, Walker LB $13.85 (0-8027-6883-0). Set in the high Andes, this is a book on an unusual climate zone in South America. A companion volume is *This Place Is Wet* (1989), about the rain forest of the Amazon River. (Rev: SLJ 10/89) [551.4]

23139 Collinson, Alan. *Mountains* (5–8). Series: Ecology Watch. 1992, Dillon LB $13.95 (0-87518-493-6). A discussion of the formation of mountains, how they are gradually being eroded, the flora and fauna of these regions, and the need for preservation. (Rev: BL 11/1/92) [574.5]

23140 Cumming, David. *Mountains* (5–8). Illus. Series: Habitats. 1995, Thomson Learning LB $24.26 (1-56847-388-5). 48pp. Material covered includes the geology of mountains, their formation, and the life they support, and the effects of industry, tourism, and transportation. (Rev: BL 2/1/96) [551.4]

23141 Green, Jen. *People of the Mountains* (4–6). Series: Wide World. 1998, Raintree LB $25.69 (0-8172-5062-X). 48pp. The geography and ecology of mountain environments are discussed plus material on the human cultures in these areas. (Rev: HBG 3/99; SLJ 2/99) [551.4]

23142 Grupper, Jonathan. *Rocky Mountains* (4–6). Series: Destination. 2001, National Geographic LB $16.95 (0-7922-7722-8). 32pp. This book introduces the Rockies, how they were formed, their composition, and their animals and plants. (Rev: BL 3/1/01; HBG 10/01) [978]

23143 Jennings, Terry. *Mountains* (3–6). Illus. 2003, Thameside LB $24.25 (1-931983-19-4). 32pp. Vivid photographs help to explain how mountains are formed and eroded, their importance in our climate, and the kind of life there. (Rev: BL 12/1/02; HBG 3/03) [551.432]

23144 Landau, Elaine. *Mountain Mammals* (3–4). Illus. Series: A True Book. 1996, Children's Book Pr. LB $22.00 (0-516-20040-2). 48pp. General information on mountain environments is presented, and several typical mammals found in this biome are introduced. (Rev: SLJ 4/97) [591]

23145 Locker, Thomas. *Mountain Dance* (K–4). Illus. by author. 2001, Harcourt $16.00 (0-15-202622-3). Verse and oil paintings describe various kinds of mountains and how they were formed, in an informative combination that appends additional details. (Rev: BCCB 2/02; HBG 3/02; SLJ 10/01) [551.4]

23146 Low, Robert. *Peoples of the Mountains* (2–4). Illus. Series: Peoples and Their Environments. 1996, Rosen LB $15.93 (0-8239-2298-7). 24pp. After a definition of a mountain environment, this book tells about people who live in the Himalayas, Andes, and the mountains of China. (Rev: SLJ 1/97) [551.4]

23147 Lye, Keith. *Mountains* (4–6). Illus. 1987, Silver Burdett LB $12.95 (0-382-09498-0). 48pp. Full-

color photos, maps, and diagrams highlight this survey of the world's mountains. (Rev: BL 2/1/88)

23148 Maynard, Charles W. *The Appalachians* (2–5). Series: Great Mountain Ranges of the World. 2004, Rosen LB $21.25 (0-8239-6695-X). 24pp. Geology, history, climate, flora and fauna, and economy are all discussed in this easy-to-read, large-format volume. (Rev: SLJ 8/04) [917.4]

23149 Maynard, Charles W. *The Himalayas* (2–5). Series: Great Mountain Ranges of the World. 2004, Rosen LB $21.25 (0-8239-6694-1). 24pp. Geology, history, climate, flora and fauna, and economy are all discussed in this easy-to-read, large-format volume. (Rev: SLJ 8/04) [915.496]

23150 Pipes, Rose. *Mountains and Volcanoes* (2–4). Series: World Habitats. 1998, Raintree LB $22.11 (0-8172-5006-9). 32pp. This work discusses mountains — their geographic features, evolution, weather, wildlife, and human life — and volcanoes. (Rev: BL 5/15/98; HBG 9/98) [551.4]

23151 Pyers, Greg. *Mountain Explorer* (2–4). Illus. Series: Habitat Explorer. 2004, Raintree LB $18.45 (1-4109-0509-8). 32pp. This photo-filled exploration of mountains looks at the plants and animals found there, plus environmental threats posed by pollution and development.

23152 Rotter, Charles. *Mountains* (5–8). Illus. Series: Images. 1994, Creative Editions LB $23.95 (0-88682-596-2). 40pp. How mountains are formed is discussed, with material on how they change and the life they support. (Rev: SLJ 12/94) [551.4]

23153 Rotter, Charles. *Mountains: The Towering Sentinels* (4–6). Series: Lifeviews. 2002, Creative Editions LB $24.25 (1-58341-123-2). 32pp. The various types of mountains are detailed, with information on climate, ecosystems, and environmental concerns. (Rev: HBG 3/03; SLJ 1/03)

23154 Steele, Philip. *Mountains* (5–8). Series: Pocket Facts. 1991, Macmillan LB $11.95 (0-89686-587-8). Easy-to-understand facts about mountains, with many photographs. (Rev: BL 3/15/92) [910]

23155 Stronach, Neil. *Mountains* (4–8). Series: Endangered People and Places. 1996, Lerner LB $27.15 (0-8225-2777-4). Geological aspects of mountains are covered, as well as the adjustments people make to live in mountainous regions. (Rev: SLJ 11/96) [333.73]

Ponds, Rivers, and Lakes

23156 Amos, William Hopkins. *Life in Ponds and Streams* (PS–3). Illus. 1981, National Geographic LB $16.95 (0-87044-404-2). 32pp. Simple descriptions of pond life, plus outstanding photographs.

23157 Bains, Rae. *Wonders of Rivers* (1–3). Illus. by Yoshi Miyake. 1982, Troll paper $3.50 (0-89375-571-0). 32pp. An explanation of what rivers are and their role in our world.

23158 Baron, Robert. *Hudson: The Story of a River* (2–5). Illus. by Thomas Locker. 2004, Fulcrum $17.95 (1-55591-512-4). 32pp. Breathtaking landscape paintings bring this natural history of the

Hudson River Valley to life. (Rev: BL 5/15/04; SLJ 6/04) [974.7]

23159 Cooper, Ann. *Around the Pond* (3–5). Illus. Series: Wild Wonders. 1998, Roberts Rinehart paper $9.95 (1-57098-223-6). 48pp. Using a series of four-page sections, this book describes such pond life as the bullfrog, blackbird, skunk, heron, dragonfly, grebe, turtle, diving beetle, and muskrat. (Rev: BL 12/1/98; SLJ 6/99) [591.763]

23160 Cumming, David. *Rivers and Lakes* (5–8). Series: Habitats. 1995, Thomson Learning LB $24.26 (1-56847-389-3). The plant and animal life that is supported by lakes and rivers is introduced, with accompanying information on geology and pollution. (Rev: BL 2/1/96) [551.48]

23161 Ganeri, Anita. *Rivers, Ponds and Lakes* (5–8). Series: Ecology Watch. 1992, Dillon LB $13.95 (0-87518-497-9). A discussion of these water environments and how they are threatened by various forms of pollution. (Rev: BL 11/1/92) [574.5]

23162 Giesecke, Ernestine. *Pond Plants* (K–3). Series: Heinemann First Library. 1999, Heinemann LB $13.95 (1-57572-826-5). 32pp. Each of the ten pond plants that are introduced are illustrated with a full-color photo plus a few lines of large-print text. (Rev: BL 6/1–15/99) [574]

23163 Giesecke, Ernestine. *River Plants* (K–3). Series: Heinemann First Library. 1999, Heinemann LB $13.95 (1-57572-827-3). 32pp. Color photos and a few lines of simple text are used to introduce about ten plants that are found in rivers. (Rev: BL 6/1–15/99) [574]

23164 Giesecke, Ernestine. *Wetland Plants* (K–3). Series: Heinemann First Library. 1999, Heinemann LB $13.95 (1-57572-830-3). 32pp. About ten common plants found in wetlands are identified and, for each, there is a color photograph and a few lines of explanatory text. (Rev: BL 6/1–15/99; SLJ 8/99) [574]

23165 Gilpin, Daniel. *The Snake River* (4–8). Illus. Series: Rivers of North America. 2003, Gareth Stevens LB $23.93 (0-8368-3761-4). 32pp. Following the course of the Snake RIver in the Northwestern United States, with attention to the plant and animal life along it and its role in history. (Rev: SLJ 3/04)

23166 Gray, Leon. *The Missouri River* (4–8). Illus. Series: Rivers of North America. 2003, Gareth Stevens LB $23.93 (0-8368-3758-4). 32pp. A trip along the Missouri, the longest river in the United States, from its source to its confluence with the Mississippi, with a look at the history that has been made on its banks. (Rev: SLJ 3/04)

23167 Harris, Tim. *The Mackenzie River* (4–8). Illus. Series: Rivers of North America. 2003, Gareth Stevens LB $23.93 (0-8368-3756-8). 32pp. A vist to the Mackenzie River in Canada's Northwest Territories and the people, plants, and animals who have lived along it. (Rev: SLJ 3/04)

23168 Harrison, David L. *Rivers: Nature's Wondrous Waterways* (K–3). Illus. by Cheryl Nathan. 2002, Boyds Mills $15.95 (1-56397-968-3). 32pp. Using verse and color illustrations, this basic sci-

ence book explains how rivers are formed, how they support life, and their importance in conservation and pollution. (Rev: BL 4/1/02; HBG 10/02; SLJ 5/02) [551.48]

23169 Hawkes, Steve. *The Tennessee River* (4–8). Illus. Series: Rivers of North America. 2003, Gareth Stevens LB $23.93 (0-8368-3763-0). 32pp. A trip along the length of the Tennessee River, with information on its history, natural attributes, and its effect on the people who live along its path. (Rev: SLJ 3/04)

23170 Heinz, Brian J. *Butternut Hollow Pond* (2–4). Illus. by Bob Marstall. 2000, Millbrook LB $22.90 (0-7613-0268-9). 32pp. This beautiful study of a day and night on a pond introduces many forms of animal life and demonstrates the food chain and the interdependence of creatures. (Rev: BL 1/1–15/01*; HBG 3/01; SLJ 3/01) [591.763]

23171 Himmelman, John. *Frog in a Bog* (PS–2). Illus. 2004, Charlesbridge $15.95 (1-57091-517-2). 32pp. A detailed and colorful look at life in a bog, for frogs and for all the other plants and animals found there. (Rev: BL 2/15/04; SLJ 3/04) [591.76]

23172 Hiscock, Bruce. *The Big Rivers: The Missouri, the Mississippi, and the Ohio* (3–5). Illus. 1997, Simon & Schuster $16.00 (0-689-80871-2). 32pp. As well as examining these three rivers, this book gives details on the causes and effects of flooding, with special material on the 1993 floods. (Rev: BL 6/1–15/97; SLJ 7/97) [551.48]

23173 Hoff, Mary, and Mary M. Rodgers. *Our Endangered Planet: Rivers and Lakes* (4–7). Illus. Series: Our Endangered Planet. 1991, Lerner LB $22.60 (0-8225-2501-1). 64pp. The causes and possible cures of water pollution are examined. (Rev: BL 6/15/91; SLJ 5/91) [363.73]

23174 Hunter, Anne. *What's in the Pond?* (PS–2). Illus. by author. 1999, Houghton Mifflin $4.95 (0-395-91224-5). Attractive color drawings are used to introduce pond life including several insects, a bluegill, a red-winged blackbird, a painted turtle, a frog, a tadpole, and a muskrat. Also use *What's Under the Log?* (1999). (Rev: HBG 4/00; SLJ 11/99) [574]

23175 Jackson, Tom. *The Arkansas River* (4–8). Illus. Series: Rivers of North America. 2003, Gareth Stevens LB $23.93 (0-8368-3752-5). 32pp. Tracing the Arkansas River its entire length of nearly 1,500 miles, with coverage of the people who have lived along it over the centuries and its importance to them. (Rev: SLJ 3/04)

23176 Jackson, Tom. *The Ohio River* (4–8). Illus. Series: Rivers of North America. 2003, Gareth Stevens LB $23.93 (0-8368-3759-2). 32pp. Following the Ohio River from Pittsburgh to its confluence with the Mississippi at Cairo, Illinois, with material on the people and places found along its banks. (Rev: SLJ 3/04)

23177 Johnson, Rebecca L. *A Journey into a Lake* (3–6). Illus. by Phyllis V. Saroff. Series: Biomes of North America. 2004, Lerner LB $23.93 (1-57505-594-5). 48pp. The flora and fauna found in and around lakes are clearly described in striking text and illustrations that will please report writers and browsers. (Rev: BL 5/1/04) [577.63]

23178 Kirkpatrick, Rena K. *Look at Pond Life* (K–2). Illus. 1978, Raintree paper $7.00 (0-8114-6901-8). 32pp. An introduction to the subject through brief text and many illustrations.

23179 Morrison, Gordon. *Pond* (3–6). Illus. 2002, Houghton Mifflin $16.00 (0-618-10271-X). 32pp. Wonderful watercolors, descriptive text, and detailed insets show life in and around a pond through the seasons of the year. (Rev: BL 1/1–15/03; HBG 3/03; SLJ 10/02) [577.63]

23180 Pipes, Rose. *Rivers and Lakes* (2–4). Series: World Habitats. 1998, Raintree LB $22.11 (0-8172-5002-6). 32pp. The geographical features of rivers and lakes are introduced with material on plant and animal life found in and around them, and how to protect them in the future. (Rev: BL 5/15/98; HBG 9/98) [574.5]

23181 Pollard, Nik. *The River* (K–2). Illus. by author. 2003, Millbrook LB $22.90 (0-7613-2858-0). This charming picture book traces the journey of a river from its beginnings in the mountains to where it empties into the sea, documenting how it is used by humans and wildlife. (Rev: HBG 10/03; SLJ 8/03)

23182 Pyers, Greg. *River Explorer* (2–4). Illus. Series: Habitat Explorer. 2004, Raintree LB $25.70 (1-4109-0512-8). 32pp. This photo-filled exploration of rivers looks at the plants and animals found in and around them, plus environmental threats posed by pollution and development.

23183 Rapp, Valerie. *Life in a River* (5–8). Illus. Series: Ecosystems in Action. 2002, Lerner LB $26.60 (0-8225-2136-9). 72pp. The first title in a new series about ecosystems, this volume uses the example of the Columbia River to explain the concept and the interrelationship of rivers, animals, and humans. (Rev: BL 10/15/02; HBG 3/03; SLJ 1/03) [577.6]

23184 *The River* (PS–3). Illus. Series: First Discovery. 1993, Scholastic $12.95 (0-590-47128-7). 24pp. Using drawings, overlays, and a concise text, this book for small children describes a river and the life it supports. (Rev: BL 1/1/94) [574.5]

23185 Rowland-Entwistle, Theodore. *Rivers and Lakes* (4–6). Illus. 1987, Silver Burdett LB $20.00 (0-382-09499-9). 48pp. A fact-filled book that emphasizes the need for conservation and care of these important physical features. (Rev: BL 2/1/88)

23186 Sayre, April Pulley. *Lake and Pond* (4–7). Illus. Series: Exploring Earth's Biomes. 1996, Twenty-First Century LB $25.90 (0-8050-4089-7). 80pp. A colorful introduction to lake and pond habitats and the life forms found within them. (Rev: BL 6/1–15/96; SLJ 6/96) [574.05]

23187 Sayre, April Pulley. *River and Stream* (4–7). Illus. Series: Exploring Earth's Biomes. 1996, Twenty-First Century LB $25.90 (0-8050-4088-9). 80pp. In a clearly written, informative style, this book presents material on rivers and streams, their ecology, and the various creatures and plants living

in and around them. (Rev: BL 6/1–15/96; SLJ 6/96) [574.5]

23188 Stewart, Melissa. *Life in a Lake* (5–8). Series: Ecosystems in Action. 2002, Lerner LB $26.60 (0-8225-2138-5). 72pp. The diversity and interdependence of life in a typical lake are introduced with material on how this ecosystem works and how man's interference has changed the balance of nature. (Rev: BL 12/15/02; HBG 3/03) [551.48]

23189 Walker, Sally M. *Life in an Estuary* (5–8). Series: Ecosystems in Action. 2002, Lerner LB $26.60 (0-8225-2137-7). 72pp. A look at life at the tidal mouths of rivers and the diversity of life in these areas, its interdependence, the balance of nature, and how human interaction has changed this ecosystem. (Rev: BL 12/15/02; HBG 3/03; SLJ 2/03) [574]

Prairies and Grasslands

23190 Bannatyne-Cugnet, Jo. *Heartland: A Prairie Sampler* (3–5). Illus. by Yvette Moore. 2002, Tundra $18.95 (0-88776-567-X). 40pp. Life on the prairie — weather, geography, nature, people, economy, and even cuisine — is detailed in bright, realistic paintings and informative text. (Rev: BL 1/1–15/03; HBG 10/03; SLJ 4/03) [971.2]

23191 Bannatyne-Cugnet, Jo. *A Prairie Year* (3–5). Illus. by Yvette Moore. 1994, Tundra $16.95 (0-88776-334-0). 32pp. A month-by-month account of the experiences and activities involved in prairie life. (Rev: BL 1/15/95; SLJ 2/95) [630]

23192 Butterfield, Moira. *Animals on Plains and Prairies* (K–3). Series: Looking At. 1999, Raintree LB $22.83 (0-7398-0109-0). 32pp. Such grassland animals as the giraffe, termite, vulture, and agama lizard are introduced in this beginning reader. (Rev: HBG 9/00; SLJ 3/00) [574.5]

23193 Cole, Melissa. *Prairies* (3–6). Photos by Tom Leeson and Pat Leeson. Series: Wild America Habitats. 2003, Gale/Blackbirch LB $19.95 (1-56711-807-0). 24pp. Examines the overall ecology and climate of the prairie, as well as the specific plant and animal species that flourish there. (Rev: SLJ 2/04) [577.4]

23194 Collard, Sneed B. *The Prairie Builders: Reconstructing America's Lost Grasslands* (5–8). Illus. 2005, Houghton Mifflin $17.00 (0-618-39687-X). 72pp. This wide-format look at a project to regenerate tallgrass prairie and populate it with native plants and animals includes excellent photographs. (Rev: BL 6/1–15/05) [635.9]

23195 Collinson, Alan. *Grasslands* (5–8). Illus. Series: Ecology Watch. 1992, Macmillan $13.95 (0-87518-492-8). 46pp. The flora and fauna and ecological balance of a grassland environment are introduced. (Rev: BL 11/15/92) [574.5]

23196 Fowler, Allan. *Lands of Grass* (K–2). Illus. Series: Rookie Readers. 2000, Children's Book Pr. LB $19.00 (0-516-21213-3). 32pp. This heavily illustrated, simple book introduces different kinds of grasslands, shows animals found there, and makes a plea for conservation. (Rev: BL 1/1–15/01) [577.4]

23197 Green, Jen. *Under a Stone* (2–4). Series: Small Worlds. 1999, Crabtree LB $15.96 (0-7787-0137-9); paper $8.06 (0-7787-0151-4). 32pp. Highlights the animals and plants found on a North American prairie. (Rev: SLJ 2/00) [574.5]

23198 Himmelman, John. *Mouse in a Meadow* (PS–2). Illus. 2005, Charlesbridge $15.95 (1-57091-250-2); paper $6.95 (1-57091-521-0). 32pp. A close-up view of wildlife in a typical North American meadow. (Rev: BL 3/1/05; SLJ 5/05) [578.74]

23199 Hoare, Ben. *Temperate Grasslands* (5–8). Series: Biomes Atlases. 2003, Raintree LB $31.42 (0-7398-5249-3). 64pp. This comprehensive overview of grasslands describes the climate, flora and fauna, people, and future of these areas, and includes good maps. (Rev: SLJ 9/03) [577.4]

23200 Hunter, Anne. *What's in the Meadow?* (K–2). Illus. 2000, Houghton Mifflin $4.95 (0-618-01512-4). 32pp. Ten animals that live in meadows — including the woolly bear caterpillar, spittlebug, firefly, and meadowlark — are introduced with material on this habitat. (Rev: BL 9/15/00; HBG 3/01) [591.74]

23201 Johansson, Philip. *The Wide Open Grasslands: A Web of Life* (3–5). Illus. Series: A World of Biomes. 2004, Enslow LB $17.95 (0-7660-2201-3). 48pp. An engaging introduction to the flora and fauna of the grasslands and to the work of the scientists who study the biome. [577.4]

23202 Knapp, Brian. *What Do We Know About Grasslands?* (4–6). Illus. 1992, Bedrick LB $15.95 (0-87226-359-2). 40pp. Among the topics covered are the importance of grasslands and their locations, ecology, and outlook. (Rev: BL 2/15/93; SLJ 1/93) [574]

23203 Landau, Elaine. *Grassland Mammals* (1–3). Illus. Series: A True Book. 1996, Children's Book Pr. LB $22.00 (0-516-20039-9). 48pp. After grasslands are defined and located in the world, this book introduces such indigenous mammals as African elephants, prairie dogs, giraffes, and kangaroos. (Rev: SLJ 3/97) [591]

23204 Low, Robert. *Peoples of the Savanna* (2–5). Illus. Series: People and Their Environments. 1996, Rosen LB $15.93 (0-8239-2299-5). 24pp. Describes life in a grassland habitat and how this environment has shaped the lifestyles of the people who live there. (Rev: BL 11/15/96; SLJ 1/97) [304.2]

23205 Ormsby, Alison. *The Prairie* (5–8). Series: Ecosystems of North America. 1998, Benchmark LB $27.07 (0-7614-0897-5). A description of the prairie ecosystem and an examination of how the plants and animals in prairies affect one another and their environments. (Rev: BR 5–6/99; HBG 9/99; SLJ 2/99) [551.4]

23206 Patent, Dorothy Hinshaw. *Life in a Grassland* (5–8). Series: Ecosystems in Action. 2002, Lerner LB $26.60 (0-8225-2139-3). 72pp. Using excellent pictures and a clear text, this volume explores the flora and fauna of different kinds of grasslands, with material on conservation. (Rev: BL 12/15/02; HBG 3/03) [574.5]

23207 Patent, Dorothy Hinshaw. *Prairies* (3–6). Illus. by William Muñoz. 1996, Holiday House LB $15.95 (0-8234-1277-6). 40pp. The ecology of prairie environments is covered, with striking photos and clear text. (Rev: BCCB 2/97; BL 11/1/96; SLJ 2/97) [574.5]

23208 Pipes, Rose. *Grasslands* (2–4). Series: World Habitats. 1998, Raintree LB $22.11 (0-8172-5005-0). 32pp. A well-organized account that explains the grassland ecology and gives examples of it around the world using text and pictures. (Rev: BL 5/15/98; HBG 9/98) [574.5]

23209 Quigley, Mary. *Prairie Explorer* (2–4). Illus. Series: Habitat Explorer. 2004, Raintree LB $18.45 (1-4109-0513-6). 32pp. This photo-filled exploration of prairies looks at the plants and animals found there, plus environmental threats posed by pollution and development.

23210 Ricciuti, Edward R. *Grassland* (4–6). Illus. Series: Biomes of the World. 1996, Benchmark LB $25.64 (0-7614-0136-9). 64pp. The world's grasslands are identified and described, with material on their vegetation and animal life and the environmental threats they face. (Rev: SLJ 7/96) [574.5]

23211 Rotter, Charles. *The Prairie* (5–8). Illus. Series: Images. 1994, Creative Editions LB $17.95 (0-88682-598-9). 40pp. The nature of prairie grasslands is introduced, with material on the animals and plants found there. (Rev: SLJ 12/94) [574.5]

23212 Savage, Stephen. *Animals of the Grasslands* (2–6). Illus. Series: Animals by Habitat. 1997, Raintree LB $22.83 (0-8172-4752-1). 32pp. Worldwide locations and characteristics of grasslands are highlighted, with material on such animals as coyotes, zebras, prairie dogs, emus, and termites. (Rev: BL 5/15/97) [591.9]

23213 Sayre, April Pulley. *Grassland* (4–7). Illus. Series: Exploring Earth's Biomes. 1994, Twenty-First Century LB $25.90 (0-8050-2827-7). 64pp. A well-organized, clearly written account that explains what grasslands are and where they exist and the interaction of the creatures who live in this biome. (Rev: BL 1/15/95; SLJ 2/95) [574.5]

23214 Staub, Frank. *America's Prairies* (3–6). Illus. Series: Earth Watch. 1994, Carolrhoda LB $21.27 (0-87614-781-3). 48pp. The three kinds of prairies found in the United States are introduced, with coverage of the animals and plants found in each and the environmental hazards. (Rev: BL 2/1/94) [574.5]

23215 Steele, Philip. *Grasslands* (3–5). Illus. Series: Geography Detectives. 1997, Carolrhoda LB $19.93 (1-57505-042-0). 32pp. Discusses the grassland ecosystem in both temperate and tropical areas, with coverage on how they have been changed by agriculture and urbanization. (Rev: BL 8/97) [574.5]

23216 Stille, Darlene R. *Grasslands* (2–4). Series: True Books. 1999, Children's Book Pr. LB $21.50 (0-516-21509-4). 48pp. Grasslands and prairies are introduced in a book that contains a color picture and six lines of text on each page. (Rev: BL 10/15/99) [574.5]

23217 Stone, Lynn M. *Grasslands* (1–3). Illus. Series: Biomes of North America. 2003, Rourke LB $20.64 (1-58952-685-6). 24pp. For young researchers, this is an excellent introduction to this biome, with clear, simple text, photographs, and maps. [574.5]

Rocks, Minerals, and Soil

23218 Bocknek, Jonathan. *The Science of Soil* (2–5). Series: Living Science. 1999, Gareth Stevens LB $14.95 (0-8368-2468-7). 32pp. Various types of soil are introduced with materials on the animals that live in them and the nutrients they contain. (Rev: HBG 9/00; SLJ 1/00) [631.5]

23219 Bourgeois, Paulette. *The Amazing Dirt Book* (3–5). Illus. by Craig Terlson. Series: Children's Activities. 1990, Addison-Wesley paper $8.95 (0-201-55096-2). 80pp. Facts on such appealing matters as dust mites and worms. (Rev: BL 12/1/90; SLJ 3/91) [631.4]

23220 Burton, Jane. *The Nature and Science of Rocks* (3–6). Series: Exploring the Science of Nature. 1998, Gareth Stevens LB $18.60 (0-8368-1945-4). 32pp. An imaginatively illustrated book on how rocks are formed, their different types, their uses, and how they become soil. (Rev: BL 6/1–15/98; HBG 9/98) [552]

23221 Ditchfield, Christin. *Soil* (2–5). Series: True Books — Natural Resources. 2002, Children's Book Pr. LB $23.50 (0-516-22344-5); paper $6.95 (0-516-29368-0). 48pp. This book covers such topics as how soil is formed, what it is made of, what it's used for, and how we can protect this important resource. (Rev: BL 10/15/02) [631.5]

23222 Eid, Alain. *1000 Photos of Minerals and Fossils* (5–9). Photos by Michel Viard. 2000, Barron's paper $24.95 (0-7641-5218-1). 127pp. An oversized, nicely illustrated volume that introduces minerals in their natural and refined states with material on sites, fossils, and jewelry. (Rev: SLJ 10/00) [548]

23223 Farndon, John. *Rocks and Minerals* (3–6). Series: Science Experiments. 2002, Marshall Cavendish LB $16.95 (0-7614-1468-1). 32pp. Clear illustrations and good step-by-step instructions are used to present a series of experiments that reveal the nature and properties of rocks and minerals. (Rev: BL 12/15/02; HBG 3/03; SLJ 4/03) [552]

23224 Flanagan, Alice K. *Rocks* (2–3). Series: Simply Science. 2000, Compass Point LB $14.95 (0-7565-0033-8). 32pp. This book explains how the three types of rocks are formed with examples of each as well as information on erosion and how to be a rock hound. (Rev: SLJ 2/01) [552]

23225 Friend, Sandra. *Sinkholes* (4–7). Illus. 2002, Pineapple $18.95 (1-56164-258-4). 96pp. This volume uncovers the geological and ecological causes of sinkholes, holes in the earth's surface that occur naturally, sometimes with devastating consequences. (Rev: BL 8/02; HBG 10/02) [551.44]

23226 Gallant, Roy A. *Minerals* (3–5). Illus. Series: Kaleidoscope. 2000, Marshall Cavendish $15.95 (0-7614-1039-2). 48pp. An interesting look at minerals and rocks that begins with simple material and moves on to more complex topics such as mineral replacement. (Rev: BL 2/1/01; HBG 3/01) [549]

23227 Gallant, Roy A. *Rocks* (5–8). Series: Earth Sciences. 2000, Marshall Cavendish LB $22.79 (0-7614-1042-2). 48pp. Illustrations and full-spread diagrams introduce rocks and minerals and their properties, forms, and uses. (Rev: BL 3/1/01; HBG 3/01; SLJ 3/01) [552.2]

23228 Gallant, Roy A. *Sand on the Move: The Story of Dunes* (4–6). Illus. Series: First Books. 1997, Watts LB $22.50 (0-531-20334-4). 64pp. Explains where sand comes from, how and why dunes are formed, and what animals and plants live on them. (Rev: BL 12/1/97; HBG 3/98; SLJ 1/98) [551.3]

23229 Gans, Roma. *Let's Go Rock Collecting* (2–4). Illus. by Holly Keller. 1997, HarperCollins LB $15.89 (0-06-027283-X); paper $4.95 (0-06-445170-4). 32pp. An introduction to rocks, how they were formed, their composition, their uses, and how to collect them. (Rev: BL 5/15/97; SLJ 8/97) [552]

23230 Kallen, Stuart A. *Gems* (4–7). Illus. Series: Wonders of the World. 2003, Gale LB $18.96 (0-7377-1028-4). 48pp. The formation of precious stones, their mining, and individual stones of note are all covered here. (Rev: BL 5/1/03) [553.8]

23231 Klein, James. *Gold Rush! The Young Prospector's Guide to Striking It Rich* (3–6). Illus. 1998, Tricycle paper $8.95 (1-883672-64-3). 96pp. This book provides a history of gold and gold prospecting and gives tips on good prospecting locations, tools, and what to do if you hit pay dirt. (Rev: BL 4/15/98) [622]

23232 Marzollo, Jean. *I Am a Rock* (1). Illus. by Judith Moffatt. Series: Hello Reader! 1998, Scholastic paper $3.50 (0-590-37222-X). 32pp. In this easy reader, a child named Marble visits the Rock Hall of Fame where one can identify 12 different rocks. (Rev: BL 7/98) [552]

23233 Milne, Jean. *The Story of Diamonds* (5–8). 2000, Linnet LB $21.50 (0-208-02476-X). 113pp. A book that explains where diamonds are found and how they are mined, evaluated, cut, polished, and used as jewels or in industry. (Rev: BL 2/1/00; HBG 9/00; SLJ 6/00) [553.8]

23234 Oxlade, Chris. *Rock* (2–3). Series: Materials, Materials, Materials. 2002, Heinemann LB $21.36 (1-58810-585-7). 32pp. Using a few lines of text and a color picture on each page, this is a simple introduction to rocks, their composition, structure, and uses. (Rev: BL 6/1–15/02) [552]

23235 Oxlade, Chris. *Soil* (2–3). Series: Materials, Materials, Materials. 2002, Heinemann LB $21.36 (1-58810-587-3). 32pp. The composition of soil and its properties, uses, and formation are topics covered in this easily-read beginning science book. (Rev: BL 6/1–15/02) [631.5]

23236 Ricciuti, Edward R., ed. *National Audubon Society First Field Guide: Rocks and Minerals*

(5–8). Illus. 1998, Scholastic paper $17.95 (0-590-05463-5). A guide to equipment and techniques for observation and general information on geology, followed by an examination of 50 common rocks, their composition, texture, color, and environment. (Rev: BL 8/98; SLJ 8/98) [552]

23237 Richardson, Adele D. *Rocks* (2–4). Illus. Series: The Bridgestone Science Library. 2001, Capstone LB $13.95 (0-7368-0953-8). 24pp. Rock types, rock formation, and the Mohs scale of hardness are covered in this slim volume. (Rev: HBG 3/02; SLJ 2/02) [552]

23238 Spickert, Diane Nelson. *Earthsteps: A Rock's Journey Through Time* (3–6). Illus. 2000, Fulcrum $17.95 (1-55591-986-3). 32pp. The story of a rock and its transformation over 250 million years to a grain of sand. (Rev: BL 1/1–15/01; SLJ 1/01) [551.3]

23239 Staedter, Tracy. *Rocks and Minerals* (4–8). Series: Reader's Digest Pathfinders. 1999, Reader's Digest $16.99 (1-57584-290-4). 64pp. An outstanding introduction to geology is organized in three sections — "Rocks," "Minerals," and "Collecting Rocks and Minerals" — with "discovery paths" featuring personal accounts, hands-on activities, vocabulary, and facts. (Rev: SLJ 11/99) [552]

23240 Thorson, Kristine, and Robert Thorson. *Stone Wall Secrets* (3–5). Illus. by Gustav Moore. 1998, Tilbury House $16.95 (0-88448-195-6). A history

and geology lesson on rocks and their uses, from the shale formed eons ago in prehistoric seas to the construction of a stone fence surrounding a New England farm. (Rev: SLJ 11/98) [552]

23241 Tomecek, Steve. *Dirt* (1–3). Illus. by Nancy Woodman. Series: Jump into Science. 2002, National Geographic $16.95 (0-7922-8204-3). 31pp. This discussion of soil's composition, inhabitants, and uses combines scientific fact with appealing humor. (Rev: BCCB 11/02; HBG 3/03; SLJ 10/02) [631.5]

23242 Trueit, Trudi Strain. *Rocks, Gems, and Minerals* (4–7). Series: Watts Library. 2003, Watts LB $24.00 (0-531-12195-X); paper $8.95 (0-531-16241-9). 63pp. This attractive volume introduces readers to rocks, gems, and minerals and examines the natural forces that created them. (Rev: SLJ 1/04) [552]

23243 VanCleave, Janice. *Rocks and Minerals* (4–6). Illus. Series: Spectacular Science Projects. 1996, Wiley paper $10.95 (0-471-10269-5). 96pp. In easy-to-follow steps, a series of experiments and other activities illustrate the properties and uses of rocks and minerals. (Rev: BL 3/15/96; SLJ 3/96) [552]

23244 Winckler, Suzanne, and Mary M. Rodgers. *Soil* (4–7). Illus. Series: Our Endangered Planet. 1994, Lerner LB $27.15 (0-8225-2508-9). 72pp. The depletion of our soil resources is the focus of this book, with emphasis on causes and possible solutions. (Rev: BL 5/15/94) [631.4]

Mathematics

General

23245 Aber, Linda Williams. *Who's Got Spots?* (2–3). Illus. by Gioia Fiammenghi. Series: Math Matters. 2000, Kane paper $4.95 (1-57565-099-1). 32pp. In this early math book, there is an outbreak of chicken pox and kids use this opportunity to create charts and graphs to record who has been sick and predict who will stay well. (Rev: SLJ 2/01) [001.4]

23246 Adler, David A. *Fraction Fun* (2–4). Illus. by Nancy Tobin. 1996, Holiday House LB $16.95 (0-8234-1259-8). A clear, concise introduction to fractions using plenty of real-life situations as examples and for fun. (Rev: BCCB 12/96; SLJ 11/96) [513.2]

23247 Axelrod, Amy. *Pigs at Odds: Fun with Math and Games* (2–4). Illus. by Sharon McGinley-Nally. 2000, Simon & Schuster $14.00 (0-689-81566-2). In this entertaining concept book starring the Pig family at a carnival, the concept of probability is explored. (Rev: HBG 3/01; SLJ 1/01)

23248 Bruce, Sheila. *Everybody Wins!* (2–3). Illus. by Paige Billin-Frye. Series: Math Matters. 2001, Kane paper $4.95 (1-57565-101-7). 32pp. Readers learn the usefulness of math skills as they see friends agreeing to share. Also use *Keep Your Distance*. (Rev: SLJ 12/01) [513]

23249 Caron, Lucille, and Philip M. St. Jacques. *Fractions and Decimals* (4–8). Illus. Series: Math Success. 2000, Enslow LB $17.95 (0-7660-1430-4). 64pp. Many examples accompany explanations of how to add, subtract, multiply, and divide fractions and decimals. Also use *Addition and Subtraction* (2001). (Rev: HBG 3/01; SLJ 7/01) [513.2]

23250 Daniels, Teri. *Math Man* (1–3). Illus. by Timothy Bush. 2001, Scholastic $16.95 (0-439-29308-1). 32pp. Marnie's class takes a trip to the supermarket where they meet a math whiz stock boy, who takes them on a "math-in-action" tour. (Rev: BL 11/1/01; HBG 3/02; SLJ 1/02)

23251 Day, Eileen M. *I'm Good at Math* (PS–1). Series: I'm Good At. 2003, Heinemann LB $18.50 (1-4034-0901-3). 24pp. Basic mathematical skills, from counting to measuring, are introduced with large photographs. (Rev: HBG 4/04; SLJ 4/04) [510]

23252 Dobson, Christina. *The Pizza Counting Book* (1–3). Illus. by Matthew Holmes. 2004, Charlesbridge $16.95 (0-88106-338-X); paper (0-88106-339-8). 32pp. Pizzas and their toppings are used to teach young readers such basic mathematical concepts as fractions, large numbers, addition, and subtraction. (Rev: BL 8/03; HBG 4/04; SLJ 11/03) [513.2]

23253 Gifford, Scott. *Piece = Part = Portion: Fractions = Decimals = Percents* (3–5). 2004, Tricycle $14.95 (1-58246-102-3). 32pp. A strong visual approach enhances clear explanations of the relationships between various mathematical concepts. (Rev: BL 12/15/03; HBG 4/04; SLJ 11/03)

23254 Haven, Kendall. *Marvels of Math: Fascinating Reads and Awesome Activities* (5–8). Illus. 1998, Teacher Ideas paper $23.50 (1-56308-585-2). This book chronicles 16 turning points in the history of mathematics, including the discovery of zero and the story of the first female to become a professor of mathematics. (Rev: BR 5–6/99) [510]

23255 Ho, Oliver. *Amazing Math Magic* (3–6). Illus. 2001, Sterling $14.95 (0-8069-6017-5). 96pp. Card, coin, and number tricks abound in this guide for mathematically inclined young magicians. (Rev: BL 7/01; HBG 3/02) [793.8]

23256 Holub, Joan. *Riddle-Iculous Math* (2–5). Illus. by Regan Dunnick. 2003, Whitman $15.95 (0-8075-4996-7). 32pp. Puns, rhymes, jokes, and cartoons add appeal to learning basic mathematical tasks. (Rev: BL 10/15/03; HBG 4/04; SLJ 3/04)

23257 King, Andrew. *Exploring Shapes* (2–5). Illus. Series: Math for Fun. 1998, Millbrook LB $20.90 (0-7613-0851-2). 32pp. Various shapes are introduced in this mathematics book with projects for each shape. (Rev: BL 1/1–15/99; HBG 3/99; SLJ 2/99) [516]

23258 Leedy, Loreen. *Measuring Penny* (2–4). Illus. 1998, Holt $16.95 (0-8050-5360-3). 32pp. An attractively illustrated introduction to the world of measurement. (Rev: BL 4/1/98*; HB 7–8/98; HBG 9/98; SLJ 4/98) [530.8]

23259 Leedy, Loreen. *Mission Addition* (PS–3). Illus. 1997, Holiday House LB $16.95 (0-8234-1307-1). 32pp. Through many practical applications, the animal creatures of Miss Prime's class explore the mysteries of addition. (Rev: BL 10/15/97; HBG 3/98; SLJ 8/97) [513.2]

23260 Littlefield, Cindy A. *Real-World Math for Hands-On Fun!* (3–5). Illus. by Michael Kline. Series: A Williamson Kids Can! Book. 2001, Williamson paper $12.95 (1-885593-51-1). 128pp. Numbers, shapes, measurements, time, probability, and money are all discussed here, with puzzles, activities, and experiments that include a water clock, a pyramid of clay, and a pendulum made from a plastic bottle. (Rev: SLJ 3/02) [510]

23261 Lobosco, Michael L. *Mental Math Challenges* (5–10). 1999, Sterling $17.95 (1-895569-50-8). 80pp. The 37 projects in this fascinating collection involve construction of different mathematical applications, models, games, and drawings and are grouped under such headings as "Solitaire Games," "Math in Everyday Life Situations," and "Instant Calculations and Mind Reading." (Rev: SLJ 8/99) [510]

23262 Lobosco, Michael L. *Mental Math Workout* (3–7). 1998, Sterling $16.95 (1-895569-27-3). 80pp. There are 34 projects in this book, each of which interestingly explores a different idea or concept in mathematics. (Rev: SLJ 10/98) [510]

23263 Long, Lynette. *Dazzling Division: Games and Activities That Make Math Easy and Fun* (2–5). Illus. 2000, Wiley $12.95 (0-471-36983-7). 122pp. A large-format book that explains division and outlines many activities that explore this concept. (Rev: BL 12/15/00; SLJ 1/01) [513]

23264 Long, Lynette. *Fabulous Fractions: Games and Activities that Make Math Easy and Fun* (2–6). Illus. 2001, Wiley $12.95 (0-471-36981-0). 128pp. Games and projects are used to teach youngsters the nature of fractions and how they can be manipulated. (Rev: BL 4/1/01; SLJ 7/01) [513.2]

23265 Long, Lynette. *Marvelous Multiplication: Games and Activities That Make Math Easy and Fun* (2–5). Illus. 2000, Wiley $12.95 (0-471-36982-9). 122pp. Multiplication is explained in this large-format paperback with cheerful drawings and a number of related activities. (Rev: BL 12/15/00) [513.2]

23266 Losi, Carol A. *The 512 Ants on Sullivan Street* (1–2). Illus. by Patrick Merrell. Series: Hello Math Reader. 1997, Scholastic $1.50 (0-590-30876-9). 32pp. A girl watches ants in a mathematical doubling series (e.g., 1, 2, 4, 8, etc.) as they walk off with picnic food in this easily read math book. (Rev: BL 2/1/98; SLJ 1/98)

23267 Murphy, Stuart J. *Betcha!* (1–3). Illus. by S. D. Schindler. Series: MathStart. 1997, Harper-Collins LB $15.89 (0-06-026769-0). 40pp. The mathematical skill of estimating is introduced in this concept book about guessing the number of jelly beans in a jar. Other skills are explored in *Elevator Magic* and *Just Enough Carrots* (both 1997). (Rev: BL 10/1/97; HBG 3/98; SLJ 1/98) [519.5]

23268 Murphy, Stuart J. *Bigger, Better, Best!* (K–3). Illus. by Marsha Winborn. Series: MathStart. 2002, HarperCollins LB $17.89 (0-06-028919-8); paper $4.99 (0-06-446247-1). 33pp. A story of siblings choosing rooms in a new house is a backdrop for math instruction. (Rev: HBG 3/03; SLJ 1/03)

23269 Murphy, Stuart J. *Captain Invincible and the Space Shapes* (1–4). Illus. by Remy Simard. Series: MathStart. 2001, HarperCollins LB $15.89 (0-06-028023-9); paper $4.95 (0-06-446731-7). 40pp. Astronaut Captain Invincible and his dog Comet introduce three-dimensional shapes as they travel through space in this Mathstart series book featuring bright, attractive cartoons. (Rev: BL 11/15/01; HBG 3/02; SLJ 10/01) [516]

23270 Murphy, Stuart J. *Lemonade for Sale* (1–3). Illus. by Tricia Tusa. Series: MathStart. 1998, HarperCollins LB $14.89 (0-06-027441-7); paper $4.95 (0-06-446715-5). 31pp. Four children operate a lemonade stand and use a bar graph to chart their progress in this simple introduction to graphs. (Rev: SLJ 5/98)

23271 Murphy, Stuart J. *Safari Park* (1–4). Illus. by Steve Bjorkman. Series: MathStart. 2002, Harper-Collins LB $4.95 (0-06-446245-5); paper $15.89 (0-06-028915-5). 40pp. On a visit to an amusement park, children must figure out how many tickets they need for each activity. (Rev: BL 2/1/02; HBG 10/02; SLJ 8/02) [512.9]

23272 Murphy, Stuart J. *The Sundae Scoop* (1–3). Illus. by Cynthia Jabar. 2003, HarperCollins LB $16.89 (0-06-028925-2); paper $4.99 (0-06-446250-1). 40pp. A story of the various flavor combinations available at an ice-cream booth illustrates a basic math concept in a way sure to appeal. (Rev: BL 1/1–15/03; HBG 10/03) [511]

23273 Murphy, Stuart J. *Too Many Kangaroo Things to Do!* (1–3). Illus. by Kevin O'Malley. Series: MathStart. 1996, HarperCollins LB $14.89 (0-06-025884-5). 40pp. Addition and multiplication are introduced through the antics of several animals. (Rev: BL 10/15/96; SLJ 12/96) [513.2]

23274 Nagda, Ann Whitehead, and Cindy Bickel. *Polar Bear Math: Learning About Fractions from Klondike and Snow* (3–5). Illus. 2004, Holt $16.95 (0-8050-7301-9). 29pp. The care of two polar bears cubs, Klondike and Snow, is used as a way to introduce fractions — looking at such topics as milk consumption, polar bear weight, and so forth. (Rev: SLJ 9/04) [513.2]

23275 Neuschwander, Cindy. *Sir Cumference and the Great Knight of Angleland: A Math Adventure* (1–4). Illus. by Wayne Geehan. 2001, Charlesbridge LB $16.95 (1-57091-170-3); paper $7.95 (1-57091-169-X). 32pp. The pun-full exploits of Radius, son of Sir Cumference and Lady Di of Ameter, involve the mastery of angles, squares, circles, and so forth, in this story that can be read on several levels. (Rev: HBG 3/02; SLJ 2/02) [516]

23276 Penner, Lucille R. *Clean-Sweep Campers* (2–3). Illus. by Paige Billin-Frye. Series: Math Matters. 2000, Kane paper $4.95 (1-57565-096-7). 32pp. Using a story about a messy cabin at summer camp, this book effectively introduces fractions. (Rev: SLJ 2/01) [513.2]

23277 Pistoia, Sara. *Counting* (1–3). Illus. Series: Mighty Math. 2002, Child's World LB $24.21 (1-56766-114-9). 24pp. Counting by fives and tens is shown with clear examples and advice from cartoon character Math Mutt. Also use *Money*, which discusses counting change. (Rev: SLJ 3/03)

23278 Schwartz, David M. *G Is For Googol: A Math Alphabet Book* (3–5). Illus. 1998, Tricycle $15.95 (1-883672-58-9). 56pp. An alphabet book that uses terms in mathematics, from abacus to zillion, for each letter. (Rev: BL 10/15/98; HBG 3/99) [510]

23279 Skinner, Daphne. *Tightwad Tod* (1–3). Illus. by John Nez. Series: Math Matters. 2001, Kane paper $4.95 (1-57565-109-2). 32pp. Tod has $20 to spend, and the story follows his purchases and deducts the amounts spent, in this book that includes three math problems. (Rev: SLJ 1/02) [512.9]

23280 Stienecker, David L. *Addition* (3–5). Illus. by Richard Maccabe. Series: Discovering Math. 1995, Benchmark LB $22.79 (0-7614-0593-3). 32pp. An introductory math book that explains the principles of addition and gives puzzles and exercises on applying these concepts. Also use *Division, Fractions*, and *Multiplication* (all 1995). (Rev: SLJ 4/96) [510]

23281 Tang, Greg. *The Best of Times: Math Strategies That Multiply* (2–3). Illus. by Harry Briggs. 2002, Scholastic $16.95 (0-439-21044-5). 32pp. A rhyming approach to remembering the multiplication tables from one to ten. (Rev: BL 11/1/02; HBG 3/03; SLJ 9/02) [513.2]

23282 Tang, Greg. *Math-Terpieces* (2–4). 2003, Scholastic $16.95 (0-439-44388-1). 32pp. The paintings of 12 great artists are used in exercises that develop mathematics problem-solving skills. (Rev: BL 7/03; HBG 4/04; SLJ 8/03) [510]

23283 Townsend, Donna. *Apple Fractions* (1–2). Series: Rookie Read-About Math. 2004, Scholastic LB $19.50 (0-516-24670-4). 32pp. Using apples and apple muffins as examples, author Donna Townsend introduces beginning readers to the concept of fractions. (Rev: BL 10/15/04)

23284 Vorderman, Carol. *How Math Works* (5–8). Illus. 1996, Reader's Digest $24.00 (0-89577-850-5). A survey of the history of mathematics and the major concepts involved, with a variety of interesting activities. (Rev: BL 11/1/96) [510]

23285 Wells, Rosemary. *Adding It Up* (PS–K). Illus. by Michael Koelsch. Series: Get Set for Kindergarten! 2001, Viking paper $5.99 (0-14-230040-3). 24pp. Familiar characters tackle basic math skills —

adding, subtracting, counting, sorting, and graphs. (Rev: HBG 3/02; SLJ 3/02) [513.211]

23286 Woods, Mary B., and Michael Woods. *Ancient Computing: From Counting to Calendars* (5–8). Series: Ancient Technologies. 2000, Runestone LB $25.26 (0-8225-2997-1). 88pp. From the invention of the abacus and sundials to the creation of calculators and computers, this is a history of counting with material on the development of the calendar. (Rev: BL 9/15/00; HBG 3/01; SLJ 1/01) [510]

23287 Wyatt, Valerie. *The Math Book for Girls and Other Beings Who Count* (3–6). Illus. 2000, Kids Can $14.95 (1-55074-830-0); paper $9.95 (1-55074-584-0). 64pp. A well-organized, cheerful book that introduces such math concepts as proportion in an entertaining way. (Rev: BCCB 11/00; BL 2/15/01; HBG 10/01; SLJ 11/00) [510.8]

23288 Zaslavsky, Claudia. *Number Sense and Nonsense: Building Math Creativity and Confidence Through Number Play* (3–6). Illus. 2001, Chicago Review paper $14.95 (1-55652-378-5). 120pp. Readers are encouraged to develop "number sense" rather than learning by rote, in chapters that introduce mathematical concepts, look at money and measurement, and provide puzzles, games, and some history. (Rev: SLJ 7/01) [510]

23289 Ziefert, Harriet. *Rabbit and Hare Divide an Apple* (1–2). Illus. by Emily Bolam. Series: Viking Math Easy-to-Read. 1998, Viking paper $3.99 (0-14-038820-6). 32pp. In this easy reader, the math concept of fractions is taught through a story about Rabbit, Hare, and wily Mr. Raccoon. (Rev: BL 2/1/98; HBG 9/98; SLJ 2/98)

Geometry

23290 King, Andrew. *Plotting Points and Position* (2–5). Illus. Series: Math for Fun. 1998, Millbrook LB $20.90 (0-7613-0852-0). 32pp. An activity book that explores plotting coordinates, measuring angles, and different kinds of symmetry. (Rev: BL 1/1–15/99; HBG 3/99; SLJ 2/99) [516.16]

23291 Riggs, Sandy. *Circles* (2–4). Illus. by Richard Maccabe. Series: Discovering Shapes. 1996, Benchmark LB $22.79 (0-7614-0458-9). 32pp. Circles are introduced through a series of games, puzzles, and crafts. Also use *Triangles* (1996). (Rev: SLJ 2/97) [516]

23292 Stienecker, David L. *Rectangles* (2–4). Series: Discovering Shapes. 1996, Benchmark LB $22.79 (0-7614-0460-0). 32pp. A slim volume in which rectangles are explored through games, art ideas, and problems to solve. Also use *Patterns, Polygons*, and *Three-Dimensional Shapes* (all 1996). (Rev: SLJ 2/97) [516]

23293 VanCleave, Janice. *Geometry for Every Kid: Easy Activities That Make Learning Geometry Fun* (4–6). Illus. Series: Science for Every Kid. 1994, Wiley $29.95 (0-471-31142-1); paper $12.95 (0-471-31141-3). 221pp. Through interesting activities, this book explains geometry from simple shapes and angles to coordinate graphing. (Rev: BL 10/15/94; SLJ 12/94) [516]

Mathematical Puzzles

23294 Adler, David A. *Calculator Riddles* (3–5). Illus. by Cynthia Fisher. 1995, Holiday House $14.95 (0-8234-1186-9). 42pp. A series of clever riddles and problems in arithmetic that can be answered using a calculator. (Rev: BL 11/1/95; SLJ 11/95) [513.2]

23295 Adler, David A. *Easy Math Puzzles* (2–5). Illus. by Cynthia Fisher. 1997, Holiday House LB $15.95 (0-8234-1283-0). 32pp. A book of challenging, often very tricky math puzzles that sometimes involve the quirks of language and logic. (Rev: BCCB 5/97; BL 3/1/97; SLJ 6/97) [818]

23296 Barber, Patti. *First Number Book* (PS–1). Illus. by Mandy Stanley. 2001, Kingfisher $12.95 (0-7534-5338-X). 48pp. More than a counting book, this brightly illustrated guide also looks at shapes and sizes and addition and subtraction and includes beginning mathematical puzzles and exercises. (Rev: BL 10/1/01; SLJ 7/01) [513.2]

23297 Blum, Raymond. *Math Tricks, Puzzles and Games* (4–7). Illus. 1994, Sterling $14.95 (0-8069-0582-4). 96pp. Kids who like math will particularly enjoy these tricks, mathematical games and puzzles, and calculator riddles. (Rev: BL 11/1/94) [793.7]

23298 Blum, Raymond. *Mathemania* (3–6). Illus. by Jeff Sinclair. 2001, Sterling $14.95 (0-8069-2399-7). 96pp. Thirty-four math-based tricks are shown with clear directions and explanations of why the trick works. (Rev: HBG 3/02; SLJ 3/02) [793.74]

23299 Burns, Marilyn. *The I Hate Mathematics! Book* (5–8). Illus. by Martha Hairston. 1975, Little, Brown paper $14.99 (0-316-11741-2). 128pp. A lively collection of puzzles and other mind stretchers that illustrate mathematical concepts.

23300 Cushman, Jean. *Do You Wanna Bet? Your Chance to Find Out About Probability* (3–6). Illus. by Martha Weston. 1991, Houghton Mifflin $16.00 (0-395-56516-2). 102pp. A slight plot line aids in the explanation of probability and moves on to guessing games, coin tossing, and breaking codes. (Rev: BCCB 2/92; BL 1/1/92; SLJ 12/91) [519.2]

23301 Ferris, Julie. *Galaxy Getaway: A Math Puzzle Adventure* (2–4). Series: Math for Martians. 2000, Larousse paper $5.95 (0-7534-5276-6). 32pp. Zeno, a young Martian, must solve a number of math problems and decipher codes in order to rescue a pet. Also use: *Planet Omicron: A Math Puzzle Adventure* (2000). (Rev: SLJ 9/00) [793.7]

23302 Gardner, Martin. *Perplexing Puzzles and Tantalizing Teasers* (4–7). Illus. by Laszlo Kubinyi. 1988, Dover paper $6.95 (0-486-25637-5). 256pp. An assortment of math problems, visual teasers, and tricky questions to challenge young, alert minds; perky drawings. [793.73]

23303 Lewis, J. Patrick. *Arithme-Tickle: An Even Number of Odd Riddle-Rhymes* (2–4). Illus. by Frank Remkiewicz. 2002, Harcourt $16.00 (0-15-

216418-9). 32pp. A book of puzzles and problems that entertain while testing elementary mathematics skills, with illustrations. (Rev: BL 5/15/02; HBG 10/02; SLJ 4/02) [513]

23304 Phillips, Louis. *263 Brain Busters: Just How Smart Are You, Anyway?* (4–6). Illus. by James Stevenson. 1985, Puffin paper $4.99 (0-14-031875-5). 87pp. A knowledge of elementary algebra will be helpful in solving some of these brain busters, not all of which are brain twisters. (Rev: BL 2/15/86; SLJ 2/86)

23305 Salvadori, Mario, and Joseph P. Wright. *Math Games for Middle School: Challenges and Skill-Builders for Students at Every Level* (5–8). Illus. 1998, Chicago Review paper $14.95 (1-55652-288-6). 176pp. After explaining the concepts involved in such mathematical areas as geometry, arithmetic, graphing, and linear equations, this work presents a series of puzzles for readers to solve. (Rev: BL 11/1/98) [510]

23306 Sharp, Richard M., and Seymour Metzner. *The Sneaky Square and 113 Other Math Activities for Kids* (4–8). Illus. 1990, TAB $15.95 (0-8306-8474-3); paper $8.95 (0-8306-3474-6). 134pp. Readers are challenged to solve classic as well as new math and logic problems. (Rev: BL 1/1/91) [793.7]

23307 Tang, Greg. *The Grapes of Math: Mind-Stretching Math Riddles* (3–5). Illus. by Harry Briggs. 2001, Scholastic $16.95 (0-439-21033-X). Each riddle and the rhyming clues that accompany it, can be answer by applying simple math skills like adding, subtracting, and multiplying. (Rev: BCCB 3/01; HBG 10/01; SLJ 3/01) [793.7]

23308 Tang, Greg. *Math Appeal: Mind-Stretching Math Riddles* (2–4). Illus. by Harry Briggs. 2003, Scholastic $16.95 (0-439-21046-1). 40pp. Counting and adding puzzles encourage children to find answers in creative ways. (Rev: BL 2/15/03; HBG 10/03; SLJ 2/03) [510]

23309 Tang, Greg. *Math for All Seasons: Mind-Stretching Math Riddles* (1–3). Illus. by Harry Briggs. 2002, Scholastic $16.95 (0-439-21042-9). 40pp. Each spread of this book for younger readers features a different math riddle, as well as clues to counting in different ways. (Rev: BL 2/1/02; HBG 10/02; SLJ 3/02) [513]

23310 Wells, Alison. *Subtraction* (3–5). Illus. by Richard Maccabe. Series: Discovering Math. 1995, Benchmark LB $22.79 (0-7614-0594-1). 32pp. Principles of subtraction are introduced, with many puzzles and games that apply these concepts in problem-solving situations. (Rev: SLJ 4/96) [510]

23311 Wise, Bill. *Whodunit Math Puzzles* (5–8). Illus. 2001, Sterling $14.95 (0-8069-5896-0). 96pp. Cal Q. Leiter tests his wit in a number of pesky puzzles. (Rev: BL 6/1–15/01; HBG 10/01) [793.7]

23312 Wyler, Rose, and Mary Elting. *Math Fun: Test Your Luck* (4–6). Illus. by Patrick Girouard. Series: Math Fun. 1992, Simon & Schuster LB $10.95 (0-671-74311-2). This book of tricks covers number theory, magic squares, and probabilities. A companion book is: *Math Fun with a Pocket Calculator* (1992). (Rev: SLJ 12/92) [513]

23313 Wyler, Rose, and Mary Elting. *Math Fun with Money Puzzlers* (3–6). Illus. by Patrick Girouard. Series: Math Fun. 1992, Simon & Schuster paper $5.95 (0-671-74314-7). 64pp. Math activities and concepts are presented in a playful way, with cartoonlike artwork. Also use: *Math Fun with Tricky Lines and Shapes* (1992). (Rev: BL 1/15/93) [513]

23314 Zaslavsky, Claudia. *More Math Games and Activities from Around the World* (3–7). Illus. 2003, Chicago Review paper $14.95 (1-55652-501-X). 160pp. More than 70 inventive math games and activities are accompanied by historical background. (Rev: SLJ 1/04) [793.7]

Numbers and Number Systems

23315 Adler, David A. *Roman Numerals* (2–4). Illus. by Byron Barton. 1977, HarperCollins LB $15.89 (0-690-01302-7). 40pp. The principles involved in Roman numerals and how to write them are detailed.

23316 Anno, Mitsumasa. *Anno's Mysterious Multiplying Jar* (4–6). Illus. by author. 1983, Penguin Putnam $19.99 (0-399-20951-4). 48pp. Everyday objects are used to explain factorials.

23317 Burton, Jane, and Kim Taylor. *The Nature and Science of Numbers* (3–6). Series: Exploring the Science of Nature. 2001, Gareth Stevens LB $21.27 (0-8368-2193-9). 32pp. Explores the history of numbers and numbering and counting systems, with well thought-out activities and projects. (Rev: BL 3/15/01; HBG 10/01) [512]

23318 Geisert, Arthur. *Roman Numerals I to MM: Numberabillia Romana Uno ad Duo Mila* (2–4). Illus. 1996, Houghton Mifflin $16.00 (0-395-74519-5). 32pp. Using groups of pigs as examples, Roman numerals are introduced, and later other objects test the reader's knowledge. (Rev: BCCB 3/96; BL 5/1/96; HB 9–10/96; SLJ 9/96) [513.5]

23319 Massin. *Fun with Numbers* (2–4). Illus. by Les Chats Pelés. 1995, Harcourt $22.65 (0-15-200962-0). A boy and his dog travel through time from ancient Egypt, Mesopotamia, and Rome, to India and Europe to trace the origins and development of numbers and our counting system. (Rev: SLJ 2/96) [512]

23320 Murphy, Stuart J. *Coyotes All Around* (1–3). Illus. by Steve Bjorkman. Series: MathStart. 2003, HarperCollins $15.99 (0-06-051529-5); paper $4.99 (0-06-051531-7). 31pp. The concept of rounding is introduced through a western setting. (Rev: HBG 4/04; SLJ 2/04) [519.5]

23321 Murphy, Stuart J. *100 Days of Cool* (K–3). Illus. by John Bendall-Brunello. Series: MathStart. 2004, HarperCollins $15.99 (0-06-000121-6). 40pp. When students come to school in their hippest gear for "the first day of cool," they are challenged to extend their "coolness" for a full 100 days in this enticing approach to basic math concepts. (Rev: BL 4/1/04; SLJ 3/04) [513.2]

23322 Murphy, Stuart J. *Shark Swimathon* (2–4). Illus. by Lynne W. Cravath. Series: MathStart. 2001, HarperCollins LB $15.89 (0-06-028031-X); paper $4.95 (0-06-446735-X). 40pp. In this number book, a shark swim team practices subtraction of two-digit numbers while trying to reach a goal of 75 laps. (Rev: BL 2/1/01; HBG 10/01; SLJ 3/01) [513.2]

23323 Schmandt-Besserat, Denise. *The History of Counting* (3–5). Illus. by Michael Hays. 1999, Morrow $17.00 (0-688-14118-8). 48pp. This oversize book traces the history of numbers and counting from primitive people through the Sumerians, Greeks, and Romans to the Arabs who brought Hindu numbers to Europe where this Arabic system was adopted. (Rev: BCCB 11/99; BL 8/99*; HBG 4/00; SLJ 8/99) [513.5]

23324 Schwartz, David M. *How Much Is a Million?* (K–3). Illus. by Steven Kellogg. 1985, Lothrop LB $16.89 (0-688-04050-0); Morrow paper $5.95 (0-688-09933-5). 40pp. Using images that children can enjoy — such as "one million kids standing on each other's shoulders would be taller than . . ." — the concepts of million, billion, and trillion are explained. (Rev: BCCB 7/85; BL 6/15/85; HB 7–8/85)

23325 Schwartz, David M. *If You Made a Million* (2–5). Illus. by Steven Kellogg. 1989, Lothrop LB $16.93 (0-688-07018-3). 40pp. Exploring mathematical concepts in a delightful way. (Rev: BL 6/15/89)

23326 Schwartz, David M. *On Beyond a Million: An Amazing Math Journey* (2–5). Illus. 1999, Doubleday $15.95 (0-385-32217-8). 32pp. Double-page spreads are used to introduce counting by 10s and give facts about such large numbers as millions, trillions, and ever larger numbers. (Rev: BL 11/1/99; HBG 4/00; SLJ 10/99) [513.5]

23327 Stienecker, David L. *Numbers* (3–5). Illus. by Richard Maccabe. Series: Discovering Math. 1995, Benchmark LB $22.79 (0-7614-0597-6). 32pp. This introductory math book introduces the world of numbers and supplies many problems, with answers at the back of the book. (Rev: SLJ 4/96) [512]

Statistics

23328 Long, Lynette. *Great Graphs and Sensational Statistics: Games and Activities That Make Math Easy and Fun* (4–7). Illus. 2004, Wiley paper $12.95 (0-471-21060-9). 118pp. The games and activities in this large-format paperback will give new insights into the value of statistics and graphs and how the latter can be used to visually represent the former. (Rev: BL 5/1/04; SLJ 11/04) [372.7]

23329 Nechaev, Michelle Wagner. *Making Graphs* (PS–1). Illus. Series: I Can Do Math. 2004, Gareth Stevens LB $19.93 (0-8368-4111-5). 24pp. A question-and-answer format and abundant photographs introduce the use of graphs to visually represent different characteristics. (Rev: BL 4/1/04) [001.4]

Time, Clocks, and Calendars

23330 Cobb, Annie. *The Long Wait* (1–3). Illus. by Liza Woodruff. Series: Math Matters. 2000, Kane paper $4.95 (1-57565-094-0). 32pp. Introduces the concept of estimating time, using a simple easy-to-read story about two boys waiting in line for a thrill ride. (Rev: SLJ 6/00)

23331 Dolan, Graham. *The Greenwich Guide to Day and Night* (3–6). Illus. Series: Greenwich Guide To. 2001, Heinemann LB $22.79 (1-58810-042-1). 32pp. Dolan explains how day becomes night, with photographs, a glossary, and other aids. Also use *The Greenwich Guide to Measuring Time* (2001). (Rev: BL 10/15/01) [525]

23332 Farndon, John. *Time* (3–6). Series: Science Experiments. 2002, Marshall Cavendish LB $16.95 (0-7614-1470-3). 32pp. Through simple experiments using common household objects, the nature and properties of time are explored. (Rev: BL 12/15/02; HBG 3/03) [529]

23333 Koscielniak, Bruce. *About Time: A First Look at Time and Clocks* (2–5). Illus. 2004, Houghton Mifflin $16.00 (0-618-39668-3). 32pp. After a general discussion of the basic concepts of time, Koscielniak traces the development of clocks from sundials onward. (Rev: BL 12/1/04; SLJ 11/04) [529.7]

23334 Kummer, Patricia K. *The Calendar* (5–8). Illus. Series: Inventions That Shaped the World. 2005, Watts LB $29.50 (0-531-12340-5). 80pp. Traces the development of calendars from prehistoric times, with period and contemporary illustrations, lists of recommended resources, and a calendar. (Rev: BL 5/15/05) [529]

23335 Maestro, Betsy. *The Story of Clocks and Calendars: Marking a Millennium* (3–5). Illus. by Giulio Maestro. 1999, Lothrop LB $15.93 (0-688-14549-3). 48pp. This book about time explains the various world calendars, past and present, tells how the day got their names, and gives a history of clocks. (Rev: BCCB 5/99; BL 6/1–15/99; HBG 9/99; SLJ 4/99) [909.83]

23336 Murphy, Stuart J. *Get Up and Go!* (1–3). Illus. by Diane Greenseid. Series: MathStart. 1996, HarperCollins LB $15.89 (0-06-025882-9). 40pp. The concept of time as measured by minutes is explored in this imaginative picture book. (Rev: BL 10/15/96; SLJ 12/96) [513.2]

23337 Nagda, Ann Whitehead, and Cindy Bickel. *Chimp Math: Learning About Time from a Baby Chimpanzee* (2–5). Illus. 2002, Holt $16.95 (0-8050-6674-8). 32pp. This is a delightful and effective combination, presenting both the story of young chimp Jiggs being raised by humans and the various methods of timekeeping — clocks, calendars, timelines, charts — that recorded his growth and development. (Rev: BL 11/1/02; HB 9–10/02; HBG 3/03; SLJ 9/02) [529]

23338 Older, Jules. *Telling Time* (PS–2). Illus. by Megan Halsey. 2000, Charlesbridge $16.95 (0-88106-396-7); paper $6.95 (0-88106-397-5). 32pp.

As well as exploring the concept of time, this picture book explains ways in which it is measured and covers topics including how to tell time, calendars, and different kinds of numbers. (Rev: BL 3/1/00; HBG 9/00; SLJ 3/00) [529]

23339 Richards, Kitty. *It's About Time, Max!* (1–3). Illus. by Gioia Fiammenghi. Series: Math Matters. 2000, Kane paper $4.95 (1-57565-088-6). 32pp. After losing his digital watch, a young boy must learn how to tell time using analog timepieces in this easy-to-read concept book. (Rev: SLJ 6/00)

23340 Skurzynski, Gloria. *On Time: From Seasons to Split Seconds* (2–5). Illus. 2000, National Geographic $17.95 (0-7922-7503-9). 48pp. This heavily illustrated book discusses time and seasons, years, months, and days, with additional coverage on the development of clocks and calendars. (Rev: BL 3/1/00; HBG 9/00; SLJ 7/00) [529]

23341 Verdet, Andre. *All About Time* (PS–2). Illus. by Celine Bour-Chollet, et al. Series: First Discovery. 1995, Scholastic $12.95 (0-590-42795-4). This book about time includes material on clocks and watches, time zones, seasons, phases of the moon, months of the year, and how a person can budget time. (Rev: SLJ 3/96) [529]

23342 Wells, Robert E. *How Do You Know What Time It Is?* (2–5). Illus. 2002, Whitman $14.95 (0-8075-7939-4); paper $6.95 (0-8075-7940-8). 32pp. In picture-book format, the author traces the history of timekeeping — from sundials to quartz crystals, from lunar and solar calendars to the one we know today. (Rev: BL 12/1/02; HBG 3/03; SLJ 1/03) [529]

23343 Williams, Brian. *Calendars* (4–6). Series: About Time. 2002, Smart Apple LB $24.25 (1-58340-207-1). 32pp. The need for keeping time and the various methods used over the centuries are explained in text and illustrations. (Rev: HBG 3/03; SLJ 12/02) [909.83]

Weights and Measures

23344 Cato, Sheila. *Measuring* (1–4). Illus. by Sami Sweeten. Series: A Question of Math Book. 1999, Carolrhoda LB $18.95 (1-57505-323-3). 32pp. The concept of measurement, what it involves, and several types are covered briefly in a series of double-page spreads each containing a problem. (Rev: HBG 4/00; SLJ 11/99) [530.8]

23345 Gresko, Marcia S. *Measuring* (PS–1). Illus. Series: I Can Do Math. 2004, Gareth Stevens LB $19.93 (0-8368-4112-3). 24pp. A question-and-answer format and abundant photographs introduce the concept of measurement and the various standards that are used to measure height, weight, length, temperature, and time. (Rev: BL 4/1/04) [530.8]

23346 King, Andrew. *Measuring Weight and Time* (2–5). Series: Math for Fun. 1998, Millbrook LB $20.90 (0-7613-0854-7); paper $5.95 (0-7613-0748-6). 32pp. Using interactive games, projects, and colorful artwork, this book explains how we measure weight and time. (Rev: BL 2/15/99; HBG 9/99) [530.8]

23347 Long, Lynette. *Measurement Mania: Games and Activities that Make Math Easy and Fun* (2–6). Illus. 2001, Wiley $12.95 (0-471-36980-2). 128pp. Forty activities are outlined, such as measuring the length of a smile, in this entertaining book that teaches the rudiments of measurement. (Rev: BL 4/1/01; SLJ 7/01) [513.2]

23348 Loughran, Donna. *How Long Is It?* (1–2). Series: Rookie Read-About Math. 2004, Scholastic LB $19.50 (0-516-24671-2). 32pp. Photographs and brief text introduce linear measures and the use of rulers. (Rev: BL 10/15/04)

23349 Murphy, Stuart J. *Room for Ripley* (2–4). Illus. by Sylvie Wickstrom. Series: MathStart. 1999, HarperCollins LB $15.89 (0-06-446724-4). 33pp. This simple story about a boy filling a fish tank introduces such liquid measurements as a pint and a quart. (Rev: HBG 4/00; SLJ 12/99) [530.8]

23350 Schwartz, David M. *Millions to Measure* (1–4). Illus. by Steven Kellogg. 2003, HarperCollins LB $17.89 (0-06-623784-X). 40pp. Marvelosissimo the Mathematical Magician explains the history of measures and measurement (with an appendix on the metric system) in this informative and entertaining book. (Rev: BL 2/1/03*; HB 3–4/03; HBG 10/03; SLJ 3/03) [530.8]

23351 Scott, Janine. *Why We Measure* (K–2). Illus. 2003, Compass Point LB $18.60 (0-7565-0449-X). 24pp. Introduces the concept of measurement and the various tools that can be used to gauge length, weight, speed, and quantity. (Rev: SLJ 12/03) [530.8]

Meteorology

General

23352 Locker, Thomas. *Cloud Dance* (3–5). Illus. 2000, Harcourt $16.00 (0-15-202231-7). 32pp. This picture book for older readers is a mixture of fiction, science, and art as it describes the beauty of the sky during the different seasons. (Rev: BL 10/1/00; HBG 3/01; SLJ 11/00) [551.5]

23353 Smith, Trevor. *Earth's Changing Climate* (5–8). Series: Understanding Global Issues. 2003, Smart Apple $19.95 (1-58340-358-2). 56pp. Topics including global warming are discussed in this well-organized look at the world's climate, how it is gradually changing, and what can be done about it. (Rev: BL 11/15/03; SLJ 12/03) [551.6]

23354 Staub, Frank. *The Kids' Book of Clouds and Sky* (5–7). Photos by author. Illus. 2004, Sterling $14.95 (0-8069-7879-1). 79pp. Organized in question-and-answer format, this attractively illustrated book provides an overview of clouds and such subjects as lightning and thunder, fog, storms, the atmosphere, and air pollution. (Rev: SLJ 7/04) [551.57]

23355 Vogel, Carole G. *Nature's Fury: Eyewitness Reports of Natural Disasters* (3–6). Illus. 2000, Scholastic $16.95 (0-590-11502-2). 128pp. Taken from historical archives and newspapers, this book features 13 eyewitness accounts of 13 disasters including flash floods, earthquakes, blizzards, and tornadoes. (Rev: BL 12/15/00; HBG 3/01) [551]

Air

23356 Bauer, Marion Dane. *Wind* (K–2). Illus. by John Wallace. Series: Ready-to-Read. 2003, Simon & Schuster LB $11.89 (0-689-85442-0); paper $3.99 (0-689-85443-9). 32pp. For beginning readers, this is an attractively illustrated simple introduc-tion to wind and its properties. (Rev: HBG 4/04; SLJ 1/04) [551.51]

23357 Branley, Franklyn M. *Air Is All Around You* (PS–2). Illus. by Holly Keller. 1986, HarperCollins paper $4.95 (0-06-445048-1). 32pp. Cheery children and an orange cat demonstrate the properties of air. (Rev: BL 4/15/86; SLJ 12/86)

23358 Bundey, Nikki. *Wind and People* (3–5). Series: The Science of Weather. 2000, Carolrhoda LB $21.27 (1-57505-495-7). 32pp. This book, which contains some simple experiments, shows how wind affects our lives — from causing snow-drifts and sandstorms to powering sailboats and cre-ating energy. (Rev: BL 12/15/00; HBG 3/01) [551.5]

23359 Cobb, Vicki. *I Face the Wind* (PS–2). Illus. by Julia Gorton. Series: Vicki Cobb Science Play. 2003, HarperCollins LB $16.89 (0-688-17841-3). For beginning readers, Cobb explains the properties of wind and suggests appropriate demonstrations. (Rev: HB 7–8/03; HBG 10/03; SLJ 8/03) [551.51]

23360 Fowler, Allan. *Can You See the Wind?* (1–2). Series: Rookie Readers. 1999, Children's Book Pr. LB $18.50 (0-516-20814-4). 32pp. With many color pictures and large type, this book explains what the wind is and how it changes life on earth. (Rev: BL 7/99; HBG 9/99) [551.5]

23361 Friend, Sandra. *Earth's Wild Winds* (5–8). Illus. Series: Exploring Planet Earth. 2002, Twenty-First Century LB $24.90 (0-7613-2673-1). 63pp. Report writers will find good material in this attrac-tively presented coverage of all kinds of winds that also looks at the ways in which humans have attempted to harness wind power. (Rev: HBG 3/03; SLJ 10/02) [551.518]

23362 Gallant, Roy A. *Atmosphere: Sea of Air* (4–8). Illus. Series: Earthworks. 2003, Marshall Cavendish $19.95 (0-7614-1366-9). 80pp. An intriguing and well-presented look at how changes in the atmos-phere affect us — from storms to beautiful rainbows and sunsets — and how we affect the atmosphere. (Rev: BL 3/15/03; HBG 3/03) [551.51]

23363 Gardner, Robert. *Science Project Ideas About Air* (4–7). Series: Science Project Ideas. 1997, Enslow LB $19.95 (0-89490-838-3). 96pp. The properties of air are explored in a series of experiments and projects with easy-to-follow directions. (Rev: BL 12/15/97; BR 5–6/98; HBG 3/98; SLJ 4/98) [678.5]

23364 Gardner, Robert, and David Webster. *Experiments with Balloons* (4–7). Illus. Series: Getting Started in Science. 1995, Enslow LB $20.95 (0-89490-669-0). 104pp. More than a dozen experiments explore balloons and the properties of air. (Rev: BL 12/1/95; SLJ 3/96) [507.8]

23365 Hoff, Mary, and Mary M. Rodgers. *Atmosphere* (4–7). Illus. Series: Our Endangered Planet. 1995, Lerner LB $27.15 (0-8225-2509-7). 72pp. This account describes the atmosphere and current threats including the ozone layer problem. (Rev: BL 8/95; SLJ 12/95) [363.73]

23366 Madgwick, Wendy. *Up in the Air* (K–3). Illus. Series: Science Starters. 1999, Raintree $15.98 (0-8172-5325-4). 32pp. Concepts and activities related to air are presented in large double-page spreads that deal with topics including air pressure, wind, and how to make a paper airplane. (Rev: BL 6/1–15/99; HBG 9/99) [553]

23367 Murphy, Bryan. *Experiment with Air* (2–4). Illus. Series: Science Experiments. 1992, Lerner LB $19.93 (0-8225-2452-X). 32pp. Introduces, in simple terms, concepts involving air pressure, how things fly, and how sound waves travel. (Rev: BL 6/15/92; SLJ 10/92) [533.6]

23368 Murray, Peter. *Professor Solomon Snickerdoodle's Air Science Tricks* (1–3). Illus. by Penny Dann. 1998, Child's World LB $21.36 (1-56766-082-7). 29pp. Professor Snickerdoodle helps a young friend perform several science tricks involving air and follows each with an explanation that shows the property of air. (Rev: SLJ 5/98) [553.6]

23369 Stewart, Melissa. *Air Is Everywhere* (2–4). Illus. Series: Investigate Science. 2004, Compass Point LB $21.26 (0-7565-0638-7). 32pp. The characteristics of air are introduced through text, illustrations, and activities. (Rev: SLJ 3/05) [533]

23370 Yount, Lisa, and Mary M. Rodgers. *Our Endangered Planet: Air* (4–7). Illus. Series: Our Endangered Planet. 1995, Lerner LB $27.15 (0-8225-2510-0). 72pp. The emphasis in this book is on how air pollution has become a major environmental issue and how everyone can take action to improve air quality. (Rev: BL 10/15/95) [363.73]

Storms

23371 Adamson, Thomas K. *Tsunamis* (2–4). Illus. 2005, Capstone LB $15.95 (0-7368-5248-4). 24pp. This volume, which explores the causes and destructive capacities of tsunamis, includes information on the December 26, 2004, tragedy. (Rev: BL 6/1–15/05) [551.40]

23372 Allaby, Michael. *Tornadoes and Other Dramatic Weather Systems* (4–8). Series: Secret Worlds.

2001, DK paper $5.95 (0-7894-7980-X). 96pp. Unusual page design and attractive illustrations are found in this book on violent weather systems with an emphasis on tornadoes, how they are formed and tracked, and their effects when they strike. (Rev: BL 10/15/01; HBG 3/02) [551.5]

23373 Archer, Jules. *Hurricane!* (5–7). Illus. Series: Nature's Disasters. 1991, Macmillan LB $12.95 (0-89686-597-5). 48pp. In addition to many real-life examples, this book covers the causes of hurricanes and how we can protect ourselves against them. (Rev: BL 8/91) [551.51]

23374 Archer, Jules. *Tornado!* (5–7). Illus. Series: Nature's Disasters. 1991, Macmillan LB $12.95 (0-89686-594-0). 48pp. Full-color photographs add to the drama of this weather phenomenon. (Rev: BL 8/91) [551.55]

23375 Armbruster, Ann. *Floods* (4–6). Illus. Series: First Books. 1996, Watts LB $22.50 (0-531-20239-9). 63pp. Describes various kinds of floods and preventive measures against them. (Rev: BL 1/1–15/97) [551.48]

23376 Armbruster, Ann, and Elizabeth Taylor. *Tornadoes* (3–5). Illus. Series: First Books. 1993, Watts paper $6.95 (0-531-15666-4). 64pp. A solid introduction to these fearsome storms, including tracking and safety measures. (Rev: BL 12/1/89; SLJ 12/89) [551.55]

23377 Berger, Melvin, and Gilda Berger. *Do Tornadoes Really Twist?* (3–5). Series: Scholastic Question and Answer. 2000, Scholastic LB $14.95 (0-439-09584-0). 48pp. Using a question-and-answer format and lots of excellent illustrations, this book covers children's basic concerns about tornadoes and hurricanes. (Rev: BL 12/15/00; HBG 3/01; SLJ 2/01) [551.5]

23378 Berger, Melvin, and Gilda Berger. *Hurricanes Have Eyes but Can't See and Other Amazing Facts About Wild Weather* (2–5). Illus. Series: Speedy Facts. 2004, Scholastic paper $7.99 (0-439-62534-3). 48pp. An entertaining and lively presentation of amazing and informative facts about storms.

23379 Boskey, Madeline. *Natural Disasters: A Chapter Book* (2–5). Series: True Tales. 2003, Children's Pr. LB $21.50 (0-516-22918-4). 48pp. This imaginative overview of natural disasters transports reluctant readers into the eye of the storm on a hurricane hunter plane, to the edge of a volcano that may erupt at any moment, and into a truck chasing tornadoes. (Rev: SLJ 2/04) [904]

23380 Branley, Franklyn M. *Flash, Crash, Rumble, and Roll* (K–3). Illus. by True Kelley. Series: Let's-Read-and-Find-Out. 1999, HarperCollins LB $15.89 (0-06-027859-5); paper $4.95 (0-06-445179-8). 32pp. A new edition of the classic science book that explains the causes and effects of storms to youngsters and contains accompanying activities. Also use: *Rain and Hail* (1983). (Rev: BL 7/99; HBG 9/99; SLJ 6/99) [551.55]

23381 Branley, Franklyn M. *Tornado Alert* (K–4). Illus. by Giulio Maestro. 1988, HarperCollins LB $15.89 (0-690-04688-X); paper $4.95 (0-06-445094-5). 32pp. An explanation of these powerful storms that hold great fear and fascination for children. (Rev: BCCB 9/88; BL 9/1/88; SLJ 11/88)

23382 Bredeson, Carmen. *The Mighty Midwest Flood: Raging Rivers* (4–8). Series: American Disasters. 1999, Enslow LB $18.95 (0-7660-1221-2). 48pp. This account describes the terrible midwestern flood of 1993 and gives background information on the Mississippi River complex and on the causes of floods. (Rev: BL 10/15/99; HBG 4/00) [363.4]

23383 Burby, Liza N. *Tornadoes* (2–3). Illus. Series: Extreme Weather. 1999, Rosen $12.95 (0-8239-5289-4). 24pp. Using amazing photographs, this book introduces tornadoes with material on their causes, their impact, the possibility of prediction, and where they are commonly found. (Rev: BL 9/15/99) [551.55]

23384 Challen, Paul. *Hurricane and Typhoon Alert!* (4–6). Illus. Series: Disaster Alert! 2004, Crabtree LB $16.95 (0-7787-1575-2); paper $8.06 (0-7787-1607-4). 32pp. In addition to describing hurricanes and typhoons, there is colorfully presented material on early beliefs and myths associated with them, discussion of advances in predicting storms, tips on staying safe, and an experiment. (Rev: SLJ 3/05) [551.5]

23385 Cole, Joanna. *The Magic School Bus Inside a Hurricane* (2–4). Illus. by Bruce Degen. 1995, Scholastic $15.95 (0-590-44686-X). 48pp. Ms. Frizzle takes her busload of youngsters into the clouds to show where hurricanes come from. (Rev: BCCB 10/95; BL 6/1–15/95; HB 11–12/95; SLJ 9/95) [551.55]

23386 De Hahn, Tracee. *The Blizzard of 1888* (5–9). Series: Great Disasters: Reforms and Ramifications. 2000, Chelsea LB $19.95 (0-7910-5787-9). 104pp. De Hahn looks at the impact of this famous blizzard and at the changes in infrastructure and services that resulted from it. (Rev: BL 4/15/01; HBG 10/01; SLJ 6/01) [974.7]

23387 Drohan, Michele Ingber. *Floods* (2–4). Illus. Series: Natural Disasters. 1999, Rosen $13.50 (0-8239-5288-6). 24pp. The causes of floods are explained and their effect on people and places covered in this simple introduction that uses many color photographs. (Rev: BL 9/15/99) [551.48]

23388 Fowler, Allan. *When a Storm Comes Up* (1–2). Illus. Series: Rookie Readers. 1995, Children's Book Pr. LB $19.00 (0-516-06035-X). 32pp. With large type, color photos, and a small format, this effectively introduces storms to young people. (Rev: BL 7/95) [551.55]

23389 Gow, Mary. *Johnstown Flood: The Day the Dam Burst* (4–8). Series: American Disasters. 2003, Enslow LB $18.95 (0-7660-2109-2). 48pp. The story of the terrible Pennsylvania flood of 1889 that resulted in more than 2,000 deaths. (Rev: BL 11/15/03; HBG 10/03) [973.8]

23390 Greenberg, Keith E. *Storm Chaser: Into the Eye of a Hurricane* (4–7). Series: Risky Business. 1997, Blackbirch LB $24.94 (1-56711-161-0). 48pp. Tells about the people who track the paths of hurricanes and the dangers they often face. (Rev: BL 10/15/97; HBG 3/98; SLJ 12/97) [551.55]

23391 Hayden, Kate. *Twisters!* (2–3). Illus. Series: DK Readers. 2000, DK $12.95 (0-7894-5708-3); paper $3.95 (0-7894-5709-1). 32pp. An easy reader that uses a story about Rob, a farmer in Texas, to explain the causes, characteristics, and effects of tornadoes. (Rev: BL 10/1/00; HBG 3/01; SLJ 1/01) [551.55]

23392 Hopping, Lorraine Jean. *Wild Weather: Blizzards!* (2–3). Illus. by Jody Wheeler. Series: Hello Reader! 1999, Scholastic paper $3.99 (0-590-39730-3). 48pp. After describing several terrible blizzards, there is a discussion of what causes blizzards in this easy reader. (Rev: BCCB 1/99; BL 5/15/99; SLJ 5/99) [551.55]

23393 Hopping, Lorraine Jean. *Wild Weather: Lightning!* (1–4). Illus. by Jody Wheeler. Series: Hello Reader! 1999, Scholastic paper $3.99 (0-590-52285-X). 47pp. The story of lightning from classical mythology to its study using modern computer technology, with tales from survivors of lightning strikes. (Rev: SLJ 8/99) [551.5]

23394 Kahl, Jonathan D. *Storm Warning: Tornadoes and Hurricanes* (3–6). Illus. Series: How's the Weather? 1993, Lerner LB $21.27 (0-8225-2527-5). 64pp. An introduction to tornadoes and hurricanes with information on their causes, characteristics, and effects. (Rev: BL 5/15/93) [551]

23395 Kramer, Stephen. *Lightning* (3–6). Illus. by Warren Faidley. Series: Nature in Action. 1992, Carolrhoda LB $19.95 (0-87614-659-0). 48pp. A clear text and many full-color photos explain the hows and whys of lightning. (Rev: BCCB 9/92; BL 6/15/92; SLJ 7/92*) [551.5]

23396 Kramer, Stephen. *Tornado* (3–6). Illus. Series: Nature in Action. 1992, Carolrhoda LB $19.95 (0-87614-660-4). 48pp. This book shows how and where tornadoes usually form and the damage they can cause. (Rev: BL 11/1/92; SLJ 11/92) [551.53]

23397 Lauber, Patricia. *Hurricanes: Earth's Mightiest Storms* (4–8). Illus. 1996, Scholastic paper $17.95 (0-590-47406-5). 64pp. Beginning with an actual hurricane that ravaged Long Island in 1938, this account discusses the causes and effects of these mighty storms and how they are tracked. (Rev: BCCB 10/96; BL 10/1/96; HB 9–10/96; SLJ 9/96*) [363.3]

23398 Lindop, Laurie. *Chasing Tornadoes* (5–8). Illus. Series: Science on the Edge. 2003, Millbrook LB $26.90 (0-7613-2703-7). 80pp. A lively introduction to tornadoes, the scientists who dare to study them, and techniques for collecting data and forecasting tornado activity. (Rev: BL 12/1/03; HBG 4/04; SLJ 1/04) [551.55]

23399 Meister, Cari. *Hurricanes* (4–6). Illus. Series: Nature's Fury. 1999, ABDO LB $14.95 (1-57765-080-8). 32pp. A history of hurricanes is included along with material on their causes, effects, and how to stay safe during one. (Rev: HBG 4/00; SLJ 12/99) [551.5]

23400 Murray, Peter. *Floods* (3–5). Illus. Series: Naturebooks: Natural Disasters. 1996, Child's World LB $22.79 (1-56766-214-5). 32pp. Basic information about floods is given, with full-page color photographs facing each page of text. (Rev: BL 1/1–15/97) [363.3]

23401 Murray, Peter. *Lightning* (3–5). Illus. Series: Naturebooks: Natural Disasters. 1996, Child's World LB $22.79 (1-56766-215-3). 32pp. The causes and effects of lightning are covered, with many full-page illustrations. (Rev: BL 1/1–15/97) [551.5]

23402 Nicolson, Cynthia Pratt. *Hurricane!* (4–8). Illus. Series: Disaster. 2002, Kids Can $14.95 (1-55074-906-4); paper $6.95 (1-55074-970-6). 32pp. An accessible text and many photographs provide information on hurricane formation and intensity, on the preparations for major hurricanes, and on famous storms of the past. (Rev: HBG 3/03; SLJ 12/02) [551.552]

23403 Nicolson, Cynthia Pratt. *Tornado!* (3–6). Illus. 2003, Kids Can $14.95 (1-55337-951-X); paper $6.95 (1-55337-972-2). 32pp. The nature and power of tornadoes are described in this oversize volume that includes easy experiments and accounts of notable tornadoes. (Rev: BL 4/1/03) [551.55]

23404 Nicolson, Cynthia Pratt. *Tornado!* (4–8). Illus. Series: Disaster. 2003, Kids Can $14.95 (1-55074-951-X); paper $6.95 (1-55074-972-2). 32pp. Full of illustrations and with concise text, this oversize volume covers the basics of tornadoes and includes experiments. (Rev: HBG 10/03; SLJ 5/03) [551.55]

23405 Otfinoski, Steven. *Blizzards* (4–6). Illus. Series: When Disaster Strikes! 1994, Twenty-First Century LB $18.90 (0-8050-3093-X). 64pp. This book explains why blizzards occur, provides safety tips, and tells about famous storms of the past. (Rev: BL 10/15/94; SLJ 9/94) [363.3]

23406 Penner, Lucille R. *Twisters!* (2–3). Illus. by Kazushige Nitta. 1996, Random LB $11.99 (0-679-98271-X); paper $3.99 (0-679-88271-5). An easy-to-read introduction to the causes and effects of tornadoes and hurricanes. (Rev: BL 11/15/96) [551.5]

23407 Rotter, Charles. *Hurricanes: Storms of the Sea* (4–6). Series: Lifeviews. 2002, Creative Editions LB $24.25 (1-58341-020-1). 32pp. A revised edition with updated text and new photographs that describes hurricanes and their causes and includes two projects. (Rev: HBG 3/03; SLJ 1/03) [551.5]

23408 Rozens, Aleksandrs. *Floods* (4–6). Illus. Series: When Disaster Strikes! 1994, Twenty-First Century LB $22.90 (0-8050-3097-2). 64pp. A history of famous floods is given, plus an account of their causes and effects and survival tips. (Rev: BL 10/15/94; SLJ 9/94) [363.3]

23409 Scavuzzo, Wendy. *Tornado Alert!* (4–6). Illus. Series: Disaster Alert! 2004, Crabtree LB $16.95 (0-7787-1571-X); paper $8.06 (0-7787-1603-1). 32pp. In addition to describing tornadoes, there is colorfully presented material on early beliefs and myths associated with them, discussion of advances in predicting storms, tips on staying safe, and an experiment. (Rev: SLJ 3/05) [551.55]

23410 Sherrow, Victoria. *Hurricane Andrew: Nature's Rage* (4–8). Series: American Disasters. 1998, Enslow LB $18.95 (0-7660-1057-0). The story of the storm that caused millions of dollars of damage on the Atlantic Coast, told in dramatic text and pictures. (Rev: BL 1/1–15/99; BR 5–6/99; HBG 3/99) [551.5]

23411 Sherrow, Victoria. *Plains Outbreak Tornadoes: Killer Twisters* (4–8). Series: American Disasters. 1998, Enslow LB $18.95 (0-7660-1059-7). The causes and effects of the giant tornadoes that occur in the Midwest, with details of some of the most horrendous. (Rev: BL 1/1–15/99; BR 5–6/99; HBG 3/99) [551.55]

23412 Simon, Seymour. *Hurricanes* (3–4). Illus. 2003, HarperCollins LB $16.89 (0-688-16292-4). 32pp. This blend of easy-to-understand text and colorful illustrations provides an excellent introduction to hurricanes and similar storms. (Rev: BL 8/03; HBG 4/04; SLJ 1/04) [551.55]

23413 Simon, Seymour. *Lightning* (3–6). Illus. 1997, Morrow $15.93 (0-688-14639-2). 32pp. A dramatic, fact-packed description of the causes of lightning, different types, and its effects. (Rev: BL 3/15/97*; SLJ 5/97) [551.319]

23414 Simon, Seymour. *Storms* (3–5). Illus. 1989, Morrow LB $15.93 (0-688-07414-6); paper $5.95 (0-688-11708-2). 32pp. Explaining how storms occur. (Rev: BCCB 3/89; BL 3/1/89; SLJ 4/89)

23415 Simon, Seymour. *Super Storms* (1–3). Series: See More Readers. 2002, North-South $13.95 (1-58717-137-6); paper $3.95 (1-58717-138-4). 32pp. Violent storms and their causes are covered in this beginning reader that uses double-page spreads consisting each of a large color picture opposite a few lines of text. (Rev: BL 7/02; HBG 10/02) [551.5]

23416 Simon, Seymour. *Tornadoes* (4–8). 1999, Morrow LB $16.89 (0-688-14647-3). Well-organized text discusses the weather conditions that give rise to tornadoes, how they form, where they are most likely to occur, and how scientists predict and track them, supplemented by large, riveting photographs showing meteorologists at work, a variety of tornadoes, and the devastation caused by major tornadoes. (Rev: BCCB 4/99; BL 5/99; HBG 9/99; SLJ 6/99) [551.55]

23417 Souza, D. M. *Hurricanes* (3–6). Illus. Series: Nature in Action. 1996, Carolrhoda LB $19.95 (0-87614-861-5); paper $7.95 (0-87614-955-7). 48pp. The causes and effects of hurricanes are covered, as well as forecasting devices. (Rev: BL 8/96; SLJ 11/96) [551.55]

23418 Souza, D. M. *Powerful Waves* (3–6). Illus. 1992, Carolrhoda LB $19.95 (0-87614-661-2). 48pp. Deals with tsunamis — misnamed tidal waves — how they develop, and the disasters they cause. (Rev: BL 11/1/92; SLJ 11/92) [551]

23419 Steele, Christy. *Tsunamis* (3–5). Illus. 2001, Raintree LB $15.98 (0-7398-4706-6). 32pp. The authors look at our knowledge of tidal waves and their causes, and discuss the ways in which we can protect ourselves from danger. (Rev: HBG 3/02; SLJ 2/02) [551.55]

23420 Thompson, Luke. *Tsunamis* (4–10). Series: Natural Disasters. 2000, Children's Book Pr. LB $19.00 (0-516-23368-8); paper $6.95 (0-516-23568-0). 48pp. Using a number of eyewitness accounts, this book tells how tsunamis are created, their movements, and the damage they cause. (Rev: SLJ 3/01) [551.55]

23421 Wade, Mary Dodson. *Tsunami: Monster Waves* (4–8). Series: American Disasters. 2002, Enslow LB $18.95 (0-7660-1786-9). 48pp. This book explains in photographs and text how these giant sea swells are created, how they are tracked, and their effects. (Rev: BL 6/1–15/02; HBG 10/02; SLJ 10/02) [551.55]

23422 Walters, John. *Flood!* (5–7). Illus. Series: Nature's Disasters. 1991, Macmillan LB $12.95 (0-89686-596-7). 48pp. A dramatic account of floods is enhanced by full-color photographs. (Rev: BL 8/91) [551.48]

Water

23423 Ardley, Neil. *The Science Book of Water* (3–6). Illus. Series: Science Books. 1991, Harcourt $9.95 (0-15-200575-7). 28pp. Sinking, floating, and displacement are some of the science projects presented in this full-color book. (Rev: BL 3/1/91; SLJ 5/90) [532]

23424 Asch, Frank. *Water* (PS–1). Illus. 1995, Harcourt $15.00 (0-15-200189-1). 32pp. A simple explanation of the nature of water and its uses, from tears to floodwaters. (Rev: BCCB 4/95; BL 4/15/95; HB 3–4/95; SLJ 5/95) [553.7]

23425 Bauer, Marion Dane. *Snow* (K–2). Illus. by John Wallace. Series: Ready to Read. 2003, Simon & Schuster LB $11.89 (0-689-85436-6); paper $3.99 (0-689-85437-4). 31pp. Facts about snow become part of this gentle story about a child and dog enjoying a wintry day. (Rev: HBG 4/04; SLJ 1/04) [551.57]

23426 Berger, Melvin, and Gilda Berger. *Water, Water Everywhere: A Book About the Water Cycle* (2–4). Illus. Series: Discovery Readers. 1995, Ideals paper $4.50 (1-57102-042-X). 48pp. In addition to the water cycle, this book discusses a city's water system, sewage, and how to conserve water. (Rev: BL 12/1/95; SLJ 2/96) [551.48]

23427 Bundey, Nikki. *Rain and People* (3–5). Illus. Series: Science of Weather. 2000, Carolrhoda $21.27 (1-57505-494-9). 32pp. This volume describes how fresh water and rain are involved in health, agriculture, construction, and power. A companion volume *Rain and the Earth* (2000), discusses the water cycle, clouds, water pollution, and ecosystems. (Rev: BL 10/15/00; HBG 3/01) [551.57]

23428 Bundey, Nikki. *Snow and the Earth* (3–5). Series: The Science of Weather. 2000, Carolrhoda LB $21.27 (1-57505-471-X). 32pp. This account, with a few experiments, shows how important snow is to the well-being of the earth and its people, animals, and plants. (Rev: BL 12/15/00; HBG 3/01) [551.57]

23429 Cobb, Vicki. *Squirts and Spurts: Science Fun with Water* (3–6). Illus. 2000, Millbrook LB $23.40 (0-7613-1572-1). 48pp. The mechanics behind hydraulics, vacuum pressure, and other forms of

moving water are explored in this entertaining activity book that uses a cartoon format. (Rev: BCCB 11/00; BL 10/15/00; HBG 3/01; SLJ 3/01) [507.8]

23430 Farndon, John. *Water* (3–6). Series: Science Experiments. 2000, Marshall Cavendish LB $16.95 (0-7614-1087-2). 32pp. Covers the properties of water, its three states, and the ways it can be manipulated, along with related experiments and projects. (Rev: BL 3/15/01; HBG 3/01) [553.7]

23431 Fiarotta, Noel, and Phyllis Fiarotta. *Great Experiments with H²O* (4–6). Illus. 1997, Sterling paper $9.95 (0-8069-4259-5). 80pp. These simple hands-on experiments demonstrate why water freezes, rises as steam, condenses, and evaporates. (Rev: BL 12/1/97) [553.7]

23432 Fowler, Allan. *It Could Still Be Water* (1–2). Illus. Series: Rookie Readers. 1992, Children's Book Pr. LB $19.00 (0-516-06003-1). 32pp. This is a simple introduction to water and its many uses. It is also available in an oversized "Big Book" edition. (Rev: BL 12/15/92) [553.7]

23433 Gallant, Roy A. *Water* (5–8). Series: Earth Sciences. 2000, Marshall Cavendish LB $22.79 (0-7614-1040-6). 48pp. This work introduces the importance of water on the earth, its three states, and the water cycle. (Rev: BL 3/1/01; HBG 3/01; SLJ 5/01) [551.57]

23434 Gallant, Roy A. *Water: Our Precious Resource* (4–8). Illus. Series: Earthworks. 2003, Marshall Cavendish $19.95 (0-7614-1365-0). 80pp. A thought-provoking and well-presented overview of the sources of water; the ways in which we use, misuse, and recycle water; and efforts to preserve this vital natural resource. (Rev: BL 3/15/03; HBG 3/03; SLJ 2/03) [553.7]

23435 Godwin, Sam. *The Drop Goes Plop: A First Look at the Water Cycle* (K–1). Illus. by Simone Abel. Series: First Look : Science. 2004, Picture Window LB $22.60 (1-4048-0657-1). 32pp. In simple language with cartoon-style illustrations, a mother bird explains to her baby how a single drop of water fits into the water cycle. (Rev: BL 10/15/04) [551.48]

23436 Hamilton, Kersten. *This Is the Ocean* (PS–2). Illus. by Lorianne Siomades. 2001, Boyds Mills $15.95 (1-56397-890-3). 32pp. Using rhyming couplets and lovely three-dimensional collages, this book presents the water cycle to a young audience. (Rev: BL 4/15/01; HBG 10/01; SLJ 6/01) [551.46]

23437 Locker, Thomas. *Water Dance* (3–5). Illus. 1997, Harcourt $16.00 (0-15-201284-2). 32pp. Using a fictionalized format, this account poetically traces the phases of the water cycle. (Rev: BCCB 5/97; BL 3/1/97; SLJ 4/97) [551]

23438 Madgwick, Wendy. *Water Play* (K–3). Illus. Series: Science Starters. 1999, Raintree $15.98 (0-8172-5326-2). 32pp. The composition, states, and uses of water are explored in large double-page spreads with activities such as constructing a rain measure, observing surface tension, and making a bubble wand. (Rev: BL 6/1–15/99; HBG 9/99) [532]

23439 Marzollo, Jean. *I Am Water* (1–2). Illus. by Judith Moffatt. 1996, Scholastic paper $3.99 (0-590-26587-3). 32pp. In a beginning reader, the various forms of water are introduced. (Rev: BL 9/15/96*) [553.7]

23440 Morgan, Sally, and Adrian Morgan. *Water* (4–7). Illus. Series: Designs in Science. 1994, Facts on File $23.00 (0-8160-2982-2). 48pp. The importance and uses of water are described, with information on water storage, filtering, and conservation, plus activities and experiments. (Rev: BL 7/94) [533.7]

23441 Nelson, Robin. *We Use Water* (PS–K). Illus. Series: First Step Nonfiction: Water. 2003, Lerner LB $15.93 (0-8225-4594-2). 24pp. This introduction for beginning readers to the properties and uses of water looks at familiar scenarios such as hand washing, fire fighting, and ice cubes. Also use *Where Is Water?* (2003). (Rev: BL 10/15/03; HBG 4/04) [553.7]

23442 O'Neill, Mary. *Water Squeeze* (4–7). Illus. by John Bindon. Series: SOS Planet Earth. 1991, Troll paper $5.95 (0-8167-2081-9). 32pp. Recent problems, such as a massive die-off of seals, are discussed in this look at the threats to our water supply. (Rev: BL 6/15/91) [363.73]

23443 Oxlade, Chris. *Water* (2–3). Series: Materials, Materials, Materials. 2002, Heinemann LB $21.36 (1-58810-588-1). 32pp. Color photographs and an easy text are used to introduce water, its properties, and its uses. (Rev: BL 6/1–15/02) [533.7]

23444 Robinson, Fay. *Where Do Puddles Go?* (1–2). Illus. Series: Rookie Readers. 1995, Children's Book Pr. LB $19.00 (0-516-06036-8). 32pp. In very simple language and many color photographs, the water cycle is introduced to young children. (Rev: BL 7/95) [551.57]

23445 Schaefer, Lola M. *This Is the Rain* (PS–1). Illus. by Jane Wattenberg. 2001, Greenwillow LB $15.89 (0-688-17040-4). 32pp. Simple, rhythmic text echoes the movement of water through its cycle from sea to sky to streams in this book with inventive illustrations. (Rev: BCCB 10/01; BL 12/15/01; HBG 3/02; SLJ 9/01) [551]

23446 Seuling, Barbara. *Drip! Drop! How Water Gets to Your Tap* (K–2). Illus. by Nancy Tobin. 2000, Holiday House $15.95 (0-8234-1459-0). After describing the water cycle, this concise account tells how reservoir water is collected, filtered, and sent through a water-treatment plant before reaching houses and apartments. (Rev: BCCB 1/01; HBG 10/01; SLJ 2/01) [546]

23447 Stewart, Melissa. *The Wonders of Water* (2–4). Illus. Series: Investigate Science. 2004, Compass Point LB $21.26 (0-7565-0637-9). 32pp. Text, illustrations, and activities introduce the characteristics and importance of water. (Rev: SLJ 3/05) [553.7]

23448 Waldman, Neil. *The Snowflake: A Water Cycle Story* (1–5). Illus. by author. 2003, Millbrook LB $23.90 (0-7613-1762-7). This beautiful overview follows a single drop of water from snowflake

through the entire water cycle and back to snowflake. (Rev: BL 11/1/03; HBG 4/04; SLJ 12/03) [551.48]

23449 Walker, Sally M. *Water Up, Water Down: The Hydrologic Cycle* (3–6). Illus. Series: Earth Watch. 1992, Carolrhoda LB $21.27 (0-87614-695-7). 48pp. This includes a description of the water cycle and material on erosion, flooding, caves, and other interesting aspects. (Rev: BL 1/15/93; SLJ 12/92) [551]

23450 Wick, Walter. *A Drop of Water* (3–6). Illus. 1997, Scholastic $16.95 (0-590-22197-3). 40pp. The properties of water are explored in amazing photographs and activities. (Rev: BCCB 2/97; BL 2/1/97*; HB 3–4/97; SLJ 3/97) [546]

23451 Wyler, Rose. *Raindrops and Rainbows* (K–4). Illus. by Steven J. Petruccio. Series: Outdoor Science. 1989, Simon & Schuster paper $4.95 (0-671-66350-X). 48pp. Many aspects of water and refraction are covered in this simple science book. (Rev: SLJ 9/89) [551.4]

Weather

23452 Allaby, Michael. *Guide to Weather* (3–6). Illus. 2000, DK $19.95 (0-7894-6500-0). 64pp. An oversize book with large illustrations that explores various facets of weather including lightning, tornadoes, and wildfires in a series of attractive double-page spreads. (Rev: BL 12/1/00; HBG 3/01) [551.6]

23453 Armentrout, David, and Patricia Armentrout. *Weather* (PS–2). Illus. 2002, Rourke LB $26.60 (1-58952-346-6). 32pp. Simple definitions are given for 50 words about weather (arid, breeze, and so forth), along with a sentence that includes the word. (Rev: HBG 3/03; SLJ 3/03)

23454 Arnold, Caroline. *El Niño: Stormy Weather for People and Wildlife* (4–8). Illus. 1998, Clarion $16.00 (0-395-77602-3). A brief overview of El Niño, its causes and history, and how tracking and forecasting are used to make predictions. (Rev: BL 10/1/98; BR 5–6/99; HBG 9/99; SLJ 12/98) [551.6]

23455 Berger, Melvin, and Gilda Berger. *Can It Rain Cats and Dogs? Questions and Answers About Weather* (3–5). Series: Question and Answer. 1999, Scholastic $12.95 (0-590-13083-8); paper $5.95 (0-590-08573-X). 148pp. Basic facts about weather are introduced using a question-and-answer format and entertaining illustrations. (Rev: BL 11/15/99; SLJ 2/00) [551.5]

23456 Berger, Melvin, and Gilda Berger. *How's the Weather? A Look at Weather and How It Changes* (K–2). Illus. by John E. Cymerman. Series: Discovery Readers. 1993, Ideals paper $4.50 (0-8249-8599-0). 48pp. A basic introduction to weather that touches on such topics as air pressure, water vapor, weather maps, lightning, hurricanes, and tornadoes. (Rev: SLJ 3/94) [551.5]

23457 Branley, Franklyn M. *It's Raining Cats and Dogs: All Kinds of Weather and Why We Have It* (3–6). Illus. 1987, Houghton Mifflin $16.00 (0-395-33070-X). 128pp. Strange happenings, such as pink and green snowstorms, are mixed in with scientific accounts of the weather. (Rev: BL 7/87; HB 9–10/87)

23458 Bredeson, Carmen. *El Nino and La Nina: Deadly Weather* (4–8). Series: American Disasters. 2002, Enslow LB $18.95 (0-7660-1551-3). 48pp. A well-researched account of these two weather phenomena, their effects, and how they can be traced. (Rev: BL 6/1–15/02; HBG 10/02; SLJ 6/02) [551.6]

23459 Breen, Mark, and Kathleen Friestad. *The Kids' Book of Weather Forecasting* (3–5). Illus. Series: Kids Can! 2000, Williamson paper $12.95 (1-885593-39-2). 140pp. This book explains the complex subject of weather forecasting and includes such activities as making a barometer, a rain gauge, and a tornado. (Rev: BL 2/1/01; SLJ 1/01) [551.63]

23460 Brotak, Edward. *Wild About Weather: 50 Wet, Windy and Wonderful Activities* (3–6). 2004, Lark Books $19.95 (1-57990-468-8). 128pp. In addition to 50 activities with clear instructions, Brotak provides lots of entertainingly presented facts, diagrams, and photographs. (Rev: BL 12/1/04) [551.6]

23461 Burby, Liza N. *Heat Waves and Droughts* (2–3). Illus. Series: Extreme Weather. 1999, Rosen $12.95 (0-8239-5292-4). 24pp. Dramatic photographs illustrate this beginning book on heat waves and droughts and their causes and effects. (Rev: BL 9/15/99) [551.5]

23462 Christian, Spencer, and Antonia Felix. *Can It Really Rain Frogs? The World's Strangest Weather Events* (3–7). Series: Spencer Christian's World of Wonders. 1997, Wiley paper $12.95 (0-471-15290-0). 115pp. Strange facts about the weather are combined with many related activities, experiments, and projects. (Rev: SLJ 4/98) [551.5]

23463 Cobb, Allan B. *Weather Observation Satellites* (5–9). Series: The Library of Satellites. 2003, Rosen LB $26.50 (0-8239-3856-5). 64pp. This book shows how the development of satellites from the 1960s on has provided us with clear weather observations and accurate forecasts. (Rev: BL 11/15/03) [551.6]

23464 DeWitt, Lynda. *What Will the Weather Be?* (K–3). Illus. by Carolyn Croll. Series: Let's-Read-and-Find-Out. 1993, HarperCollins paper $4.95 (0-06-445113-5). 32pp. An illustrated introduction to weather forecasting. (Rev: BCCB 6/91; BL 5/1/91; SLJ 7/91) [551.6]

23465 DiSpezio, Michael A. *Weather Mania: Discovering What's Up and What's Coming Down* (3–5). Illus. by Dave Garbot. 2003, Sterling $19.95 (0-8069-7745-0). 80pp. An introduction to basic weather facts and concepts that includes activities using everyday materials. (Rev: BL 3/15/03; HBG 10/03; SLJ 7/03) [551.5]

23466 Drake, Jane, and Ann Love. *Snow Amazing: Cool Facts and Warm Tales* (3–5). Illus. by Mark Thurman. 2004, Tundra $19.95 (0-88776-670-6). 80pp. Snow lore and facts are at the center of this compendium of diverse facts, figures, and folktales, including details of the animals that inhabit arctic regions. (Rev: BL 2/1/05; SLJ 12/04) [551.57]

23467 Facklam, Howard, and Margery Facklam. *Avalanche!* (5–7). Illus. Series: Nature's Disasters.

1991, Macmillan LB $12.95 (0-89686-598-3). 48pp. Real-life examples and full-color photographs add to the drama of this weather phenomenon. (Rev: BL 8/91) [551.3]

23468 Farndon, John. *Weather* (3–6). Illus. Series: Science Experiments. 2000, Marshall Cavendish LB $16.95 (0-7614-1089-9). 32pp. In addition to material on topics including sunlight, winds, clouds, and storms, this book outlines such projects as making a rain gauge and a weather vane. (Rev: BL 3/15/01; HBG 3/01) [551.6]

23469 Fowler, Allan. *What Do You See in a Cloud?* (PS–3). Illus. Series: Rookie Readers. 1996, Children's Book Pr. LB $19.00 (0-516-06056-2). 31pp. Various kinds of clouds and what each signifies are covered in this easy-to-read science book. (Rev: SLJ 8/96) [551.6]

23470 Fowler, Allan. *What's the Weather Today?* (1–3). Illus. Series: Rookie Readers. 1991, Children's Book Pr. LB $18.50 (0-516-04918-6). 32pp. Various kinds of weather are identified in a series of color photographs. (Rev: SLJ 2/92) [551.6]

23471 Gardner, Robert. *Science Project Ideas About Rain* (4–7). Series: Science Project Ideas. 1997, Enslow LB $19.95 (0-89490-843-X). 96pp. Clear explanations and functional drawings and diagrams for a number of activities that study rain, its causes, and its effects. (Rev: BL 12/15/97; HBG 3/98; SLJ 1/98) [551.55]

23472 Gibbons, Gail. *Weather Words and What They Mean* (1–3). Illus. by author. 1990, Holiday House LB $16.95 (0-8234-0805-1). Various broad terms — such as temperature, air pressure, moisture, and wind — are defined, with breakdowns into more-specific terms. (Rev: BCCB 4/90; SLJ 5/90) [551.6]

23473 Gold, Susan D. *Blame It on El Niño* (5–9). 1999, Raintree LB $28.54 (0-7398-1376-5). 96pp. Covers El Niño, La Niña, how scientists predict and track them, and the effects of each globally. (Rev: HBG 4/00; SLJ 4/00) [551.6]

23474 Goldsen, Louise. *Weather* (K–2). Illus. by Sophie Kniffke. 1991, Scholastic $12.95 (0-590-45234-7). Various changes in the weather are illustrated through the use of overlays. (Rev: SLJ 5/92) [551.6]

23475 Harper, Suzanne. *Clouds: From Mare's Tails to Thunderheads* (4–6). Illus. Series: First Books. 1997, Watts LB $22.00 (0-531-20291-7). 64pp. As well as discussing the types of clouds and how they affect climate, this book tells how to predict weather by studying cloud patterns. (Rev: BL 5/15/97) [551.57]

23476 Kahl, Jonathan D. *Hazy Skies: Weather and the Environment* (4–6). Illus. 1998, Lerner LB $21.27 (0-8225-2530-5). 64pp. After providing a history of air pollution, this book links it to such weather-related topics as the ozone layer and global warming. (Rev: BL 3/15/98; HBG 9/98) [363.73]

23477 Kahl, Jonathan D. *Weather Watch: Forecasting the Weather* (5–8). Series: How's the Weather? 1996, Lerner LB $21.27 (0-8225-2529-1). This work provides basic information on weather systems, maps, and forecasting tools, the history of weather forecasting and keeping weather records, and directions for making a weather station. (Rev: BL 6/1–15/96; SLJ 6/96) [551.6]

23478 Kahl, Jonathan D. *Weatherwise: Learning About the Weather* (4–6). Illus. 1992, Lerner LB $21.27 (0-8225-2525-9). 64pp. Topics covered include atmosphere, winds, storms, and forecasting. (Rev: SLJ 8/92) [551.6]

23479 Kramer, Stephen. *Avalanche* (3–6). Illus. by Patrick Cone. Series: Nature in Action. 1992, Carolrhoda LB $19.95 (0-87614-422-9). 48pp. Examining different types of snowslides, and how and when they occur. (Rev: BCCB 9/92; BL 6/15/92; SLJ 9/92) [551.57]

23480 Levine, Shar, and Leslie Johnstone. *Wonderful Weather* (2–4). Illus. by Steve Harpster. 2003, Sterling $12.95 (0-8069-7249-1). 48pp. Simple experiments are provided in answer to such questions as "Why is the sky blue?" (Rev: HBG 10/03; SLJ 2/04) [551.5]

23481 Markle, Sandra. *A Rainy Day* (K–3). Illus. by Cathy Johnson. 1993, Orchard LB $16.99 (0-531-08576-7). 32pp. A simple explanation of how clouds form and why rain falls. (Rev: BCCB 3/93; BL 3/1/93; SLJ 7/93) [551]

23482 Nelson, Robin. *A Rainy Day* (PS–1). Illus. Series: Weather. 2001, Lerner LB $15.93 (0-8225-0173-2); paper $3.95 (0-8225-1962-3). 23pp. In a small format for beginning readers, some simple facts about rainy days are accompanied by bold illustrations. Also use *A Snowy Day* and *A Sunny Day* (both 2001). (Rev: HBG 3/02; SLJ 4/02) [551.57]

23483 Pipe, Jim. *Weather* (3–5). Illus. Series: Earthwise. 2004, Stargazer Books LB $18.95 (1-932799-47-8). 32pp. An excellent introduction to the forces that create our weather, this attractively illustrated volume supplements its facts and figures with suggested activities. (Rev: BL 10/15/04) [551.5]

23484 Rodgers, Alan, and Angella Streluk. *Cloud Cover* (3–6). Illus. Series: Measuring the Weather. 2002, Heinemann LB $22.79 (1-58810-686-1). 32pp. Fog, ultraviolet radiation, types of cloud, and cloud cover in itself are all discussed — with their benefits and potential dangers — in this attractive titles. (Rev: HBG 3/03; SLJ 4/03) [551.5]

23485 Rodgers, Alan, and Angella Streluk. *Forecasting the Weather* (3–6). Illus. Series: Measuring the Weather. 2002, Heinemann LB $22.79 (1-58810-687-X). 32pp. Many of the tools used by meteorologists are examined here. Also use *Wind and Air Pressure* (2002). (Rev: HBG 3/03; SLJ 4/03) [551.6]

23486 Rupp, Rebecca. *Weather! Watch How Weather Works* (4–8). Illus. 2003, Storey Kids $21.95 (1-58017-469-8); paper $14.95 (1-58017-420-5). 136pp. A well-illustrated and appealing introduction to the science of weather, with numerous experiments and projects. (Rev: SLJ 5/04) [551.6]

23487 Saunders-Smith, Gail. *La lluvia / Rain* (K–2). Trans. by Mart'n Luis Guzm n Ferrer. Series: Pebble Bilingual Books. 2003, Capstone LB $15.93 (0-7368-2309-3). 24pp. An introduction to rain and

rainstorms in English and Spanish, illustrated with photographs. (Rev: SLJ 4/04) [551.5]

23488 Sayre, April Pulley. *El Nino and La Nina: Weather in the Headlines* (4–8). Illus. 2000, Twenty-First Century LB $25.90 (0-7613-1405-9). 80pp. An exploration of this complex Pacific Ocean phenomenon that produces unusual weather conditions that affect the entire world. (Rev: BL 9/15/00; HBG 3/01) [551.6]

23489 *Scholastic Atlas of Weather* (4–7). Illus. 2004, Scholastic $17.95 (0-439-41902-6). 80pp. Full of illustrations, diagrams, and feature sidebars, this volume covers a variety of weather phenomena in attractive, information-packed spreads. (Rev: SLJ 4/05) [551.5]

23490 Silverstein, Alvin, et al. *Weather and Climate* (4–7). Illus. Series: Science Concepts. 1998, Twenty-First Century LB $26.90 (0-7613-3223-5). 64pp. This book introduces weather by explaining earth's atmosphere, rotation, and different climates with material on air and water movements, cloud formation, and recent climate changes. (Rev: BL 5/1/99; HBG 9/99) [551.5]

23491 Singer, Marilyn. *On the Same Day in March: A Tour of the World's Weather* (1–3). Illus. by Frane Lessac. 2000, HarperCollins LB $15.89 (0-06-028188-X). 40pp. The weather in 17 different places around the world on the same day in March is described in this introduction to climate and seasonal differences. (Rev: BCCB 3/00; BL 2/15/00; HBG 9/00; SLJ 4/00) [551.6]

23492 Souza, D. M. *Northern Lights* (5–7). Illus. 1994, Carolrhoda LB $23.95 (0-87614-799-6); paper $12.75 (0-87614-629-9). 48pp. A description of the northern lights and an explanation of what causes them. (Rev: BL 1/15/94) [538]

23493 Stein, Paul. *Forecasting the Climate of the Future* (5–7). Series: The Library of Future Weather and Climate. 2001, Rosen LB $26.50 (0-8239-3413-6). 64pp. A fascinating, well-organized account that looks at long-range weather predictions and at the use and accuracy of computer models in forecasting future weather patterns, especially with regard to global warming. Also use *Storms of the Future* (2001), which looks at whether global warming might cause stronger storms. (Rev: SLJ 4/02) [551.5]

23494 Stein, Paul. *Ice Ages of the Future* (5–7). Series: The Library of Future Weather and Climate. 2001, Rosen LB $26.50 (0-8239-3415-2). 64pp. A look at the possibility that the greenhouse effect and other factors could in fact cause a wave of colder rather than warmer air. (Rev: SLJ 11/01) [551.6]

23495 Stewart, Melissa. *What's the Weather?* (2–4). Illus. Series: Investigate Science. 2004, Compass Point LB $21.26 (0-7565-0639-5). 32pp. The various kinds of weather are introduced through text, illustrations, and activities. (Rev: SLJ 3/05) [551.6]

23496 Stonehouse, Bernard. *Snow, Ice and Cold* (5–7). 1993, Macmillan LB $21.00 (0-02-788530-5). 45pp. This work tells about how cultures and individuals have adjusted to severe cold climates. (Rev: SLJ 7/93) [551.6]

23497 VanCleave, Janice. *Janice VanCleave's Weather: Mind-Boggling Experiments You Can Turn into Science Fair Projects* (3–6). Illus. Series: Janice VanCleave's Spectacular Science Projects. 1995, Wiley paper $10.95 (0-471-03231-X). 89pp. Intriguing questions about the weather are answered in 20 easily performed experiments and projects. (Rev: SLJ 8/95) [551.6]

23498 Vogel, Carole Garbuny. *Weather Legends: Native American Lore and the Science of Weather* (4–8). Illus. 2001, Millbrook LB $29.90 (0-7613-1900-X). 80pp. Native American weather myths are paired with scientific information about actual weather phenomena. (Rev: BL 9/1/01; HBG 3/02; SLJ 10/01) [398.2]

23499 Williams, Judith. *How Does the Sun Make Weather?* (1–3). Illus. Series: I Like Weather! 2005, Enslow LB $15.95 (0-7660-2317-6). 24pp. Preceded by a glossary and using questions as most chapter headers, this volume introduces the sun's influence on our weather. Also use: *Why Is It Raining?* and *Why Is It Windy?* (2005). (Rev: BL 4/1/05) [551.6]

23500 Williams, Terry Tempest, and Ted Major. *The Secret Language of Snow* (4–8). Illus. by Jennifer Dewey. 1984, Pantheon $10.95 (0-394-96574-X). 144pp. Different words for snow in the Eskimo language are used to explore this phenomenon.

23501 Wills, Susan, and Steven Wills. *Meteorology: Predicting the Weather* (5–7). Series: Innovators. 2004, Oliver LB $21.95 (1-881508-61-7). 144pp. Introduces seven scientists who have made substantial contributions to the science of meteorology. (Rev: SLJ 7/04) [920]

23502 *Wind and Weather* (4–6). Illus. Series: Voyages of Discovery. 1995, Scholastic $19.95 (0-590-47646-7). 45pp. Using die-cut pages, transparencies, foldouts, and stickers, this attractively illustrated book explains the atmosphere, weather, storms, climates, and precipitation. (Rev: SLJ 5/96) [551.5]

23503 Wyatt, Valerie. *FAQ Weather* (4–6). Illus. by Brian Share. 2000, Kids Can $12.95 (1-55074-582-4); paper $6.95 (1-55074-815-1). 40pp. Using a question-and-answer format, this book covers many aspects of weather including winds, clouds, precipitation, and global warming. (Rev: SLJ 8/00) [551.6]

Physics

General

23504 Bonnet, Bob, and Dan Keen. *Science Fair Projects: Physics* (4–7). Illus. 2000, Sterling $17.95 (0-8069-0707-X). 96pp. This large-format book presents 47 projects demonstrating concepts in physics and using common materials as equipment. (Rev: BL 2/1/00; SLJ 4/00) [530]

23505 Burton, Jane, and Kim Taylor. *The Nature and Science of Bubbles* (3–6). Illus. Series: Exploring the Science of Nature. 1998, Gareth Stevens LB $18.60 (0-8368-1939-X). 32pp. Large type, color photographs, and a lively text are used to explain the nature and composition of various kinds of bubbles. (Rev: BL 6/1–15/98; HBG 9/98) [530.4]

23506 Challoner, Jack. *Big and Small* (K–4). Illus. Series: Start-Up Science. 1996, Raintree LB $24.26 (0-8172-4319-4). 32pp. Information and experiments are combined in this attractive beginner's science book about size. (Rev: SLJ 2/97) [153.7]

23507 Challoner, Jack. *Floating and Sinking* (K–4). Illus. Series: Start-Up Science. 1996, Raintree LB $24.26 (0-8172-4317-8). 32pp. The concepts of floating and sinking are explored in a simple, conversational text with many attractive pictures. (Rev: SLJ 2/97) [530]

23508 Durant, Penny R. *Bubblemania! Learn the Secrets to Creating Millions of Spectacular Bubbles!* (4–8). 1994, Avon paper $3.99 (0-380-77373-2). 86pp. Through a series of easy experiments, surface tension, bubble formation, and the uses of bubbles are explained. (Rev: SLJ 7/94) [530]

23509 Evans, Neville. *The Science of Gravity* (5–8). Illus. Series: Science World. 2000, Raintree LB $25.69 (0-7398-1323-4). 32pp. Explores the force of gravity and how it affects our lives, with additional material on air resistance, mass, and invisible forces. (Rev: BL 9/15/00; HBG 9/00) [531]

23510 Farndon, John. *Buoyancy* (3–6). Series: Science Experiments. 2002, Marshall Cavendish LB $16.95 (0-7614-1467-3). 32pp. The nature of buoyancy is explained through a simple text, color photographs, and an explanatory experiment in each chapter. (Rev: BL 12/15/02; HBG 3/03) [530]

23511 Gallant, Roy A. *The Ever-Changing Atom* (5–8). Series: The Story of Science. 1999, Benchmark LB $28.50 (0-7614-0961-0). 80pp. Using a chronological approach, this book traces how and what we have found out about the atom and its structure. (Rev: BL 2/15/00; HBG 4/00; SLJ 2/00) [539]

23512 Gardner, Robert. *Experiments with Bubbles* (4–7). Illus. Series: Getting Started in Science. 1995, Enslow LB $20.95 (0-89490-666-6). 104pp. The properties of bubbles are explored in a series of experiments, each a little more complex than the last. (Rev: BL 12/1/95; SLJ 3/96) [530.4]

23513 Goodstein, Madeline. *Fish Tank Physics Projects* (5–8). Series: Science Fair Success. 2002, Enslow LB $20.95 (0-7660-1624-2). 112pp. Using a common fish tank and its contents, various aspects of laws of physics are presented in the form of science fair projects. (Rev: BL 5/15/02; HBG 10/02; SLJ 11/02) [621.9]

23514 Goodstein, Madeline. *Sports Science Projects: The Physics of Balls in Motion* (5–8). Illus. Series: Science Fair Success. 1999, Enslow LB $20.95 (0-7660-1174-7). 128pp. This book contains 40 projects that use the properties of different sports balls to demonstrate principles of physics. (Rev: BL 2/15/00; HBG 9/00; SLJ 3/00) [530]

23515 Hodge, Deborah, and Adrienne Mason. *Solids, Liquids, and Gases* (K–4). Illus. Series: Starting with Science. 1998, Kids Can $10.95 (1-55074-195-0). 32pp. Uses simple science activities to demonstrate the three states of matter and such phenomena as air pressure and condensation. (Rev: BL 4/15/98; HBG 9/98; SLJ 6/98) [530.4]

23516 Juettner, Bonnie. *Molecules* (4–8). Illus. 2004, Gale/KidHaven LB $23.70 (0-7377-2076-X). 48pp. Clear, concise text, supported by full-color photographs and diagrams, describes the characteristics of atoms and molecules. (Rev: SLJ 6/05)

23517 McGrath, Susan. *Fun with Physics* (5–9). Illus. 1986, National Geographic LB $12.50 (0-87044-581-2). An introduction to physics that uses everyday situations as examples and supplies a smattering of experiments. (Rev: SLJ 6/87) [530]

23518 Morgan, Sally, and Adrian Morgan. *Materials* (4–7). Illus. Series: Designs in Science. 1994, Facts on File $23.00 (0-8160-2985-7). 48pp. Basic properties of matter and materials are explored in a series of experiments using everyday materials. (Rev: BL 7/94) [620.1]

23519 Parker, Barry. *The Mystery of Gravity* (5–8). Illus. Series: The Story of Science. 2002, Benchmark $19.95 (0-7614-1428-2). 78pp. Parker traces our understanding of gravity from the early Greek philosophers through Einstein and Hubble, with discussion of the Big Bang theory and black holes. (Rev: HBG 3/03; SLJ 2/03) [531]

23520 Rosinsky, Natalie M. *Sinking and Floating* (3–5). Series: Simply Science. 2004, Compass Point LB $21.26 (0-7565-0598-4). 32pp. Rosinsky examines why some objects float while others sink, looking in detail at such scientific principles as water displacement and density. (Rev: SLJ 8/04) [532]

23521 Stille, Darlene R. *Solids, Liquids, and Gas* (2–4). Illus. Series: Science Around Us. 2004, Child's World LB $27.07 (1-59296-225-4). 32pp. In simple, easy-to-understand language supplemented by bright photographs, Stille introduces readers to the differences between the three basic states of matter. (Rev: BL 11/1/04) [530.4]

23522 Stringer, John. *The Science of a Spring* (5–8). Illus. Series: Science World. 2000, Raintree LB $25.69 (0-7398-1322-6). 32pp. Leaf and coil springs are introduced as well as the balance of forces in physics, the limits of springs, and their uses in such common objects as staplers. (Rev: BL 9/1/00; HBG 9/00; SLJ 8/00) [531]

23523 Tiner, John Hudson. *Gravity* (4–7). Series: Understanding Science. 2002, Smart Apple $24.25 (1-58340-157-1). 32pp. Through a number of simple projects, colorful illustrations, and a clear text, the fundamentals of gravity are explored. (Rev: BL 3/15/03; HBG 3/03) [531]

23524 Woodford, Chris, and Martin Clowes. *Atoms and Molecules* (4–7). Illus. Series: Routes of Science. 2004, Gale/Blackbirch LB $23.70 (1-4103-0295-4). 40pp. A detailed examination of the scientific study of atoms and molecules, with profiles of key individuals and their discoveries, a chronology, and discussion of future advances. (Rev: SLJ 5/05)

Energy and Motion

General

23525 Ardley, Neil. *The Science Book of Motion* (3–6). Illus. Series: Science Books. 1992, Harcourt $9.95 (0-15-200622-2). 28pp. This attractive book of experiments discusses the types and characteristics of motion and includes 12 projects to illustrate each. (Rev: BL 10/15/92; SLJ 1/93) [531]

23526 Asimov, Isaac. *How Did We Find Out About Solar Power?* (5–8). Illus. by David Wool. 1981, Walker LB $12.85 (0-8027-6423-1). 64pp. An explanation of how man has benefited from solar power from the earliest time until today. [621.47]

23527 Bonnet, Bob, and Dan Keen. *Science Fair Projects: Energy* (4–6). Illus. 1998, Sterling $16.95 (0-8069-9793-1). 96pp. Such sources of energy as sunlight, batteries, microwave ovens, and lightbulbs are used in this collection of 55 simple activities about energy and the various forms it takes. (Rev: BL 3/1/98; SLJ 6/98) [531]

23528 Bowden, Rob. *Energy* (5–8). Illus. Series: Sustainable World. 2004, Gale/KidHaven LB $23.70 (0-7377-1897-8). 48pp. The present status and possible future uses of sustainable energy sources (such as wind, water, and sun) are covered in succinct and interesting fashion, and energy choices we all can make are introduced. Also use *Cities, Environments, Transportation,* and *Waste* (all 2004). (Rev: BL 4/15/04) [333.79]

23529 Bradley, Kimberly Brubaker. *Energy Makes Things Happen* (1–3). Illus. by Paul Meisel. Series: Let's-Read-and-Find-Out Science. 2003, HarperCollins LB $16.89 (0-06-028909-0); paper $4.99 (0-06-445213-1). 40pp. An entertaining introduction to energy and its sources and uses, for young readers. (Rev: BL 2/1/03; HBG 10/03; SLJ 1/03) [531]

23530 Burton, Jane. *The Nature and Science of Energy* (3–6). Series: Exploring the Science of Nature. 1998, Gareth Stevens LB $18.60 (0-8368-1941-1). 32pp. Using large type, color photographs, and clear captioning, this work explores the meaning of energy, its various forms, and its uses. (Rev: BL 6/1–15/98; HBG 9/98) [531]

23531 Cobb, Vicki. *I Fall Down* (PS–1). Illus. by Julia Gorton. Series: Science Play. 2004, HarperCollins LB $16.89 (0-688-17843-X). 40pp. Exercises introduce the concept of gravity. (Rev: BL 2/1/05) [531]

23532 Cobb, Vicki. *Whirlers and Twirlers: Science Fun with Spinning* (3–5). Illus. by Steve Haefele. 2001, Millbrook LB $23.40 (0-7613-1573-X). 64pp. A lighthearted introduction to the physics involved in the motion of spinning, with experiments with tops, pinwheels, and other objects. (Rev: BL 10/15/01; HBG 3/02; SLJ 1/02) [531]

23533 Cruden, Gabriel. *Energy Alternatives* (5–8). Illus. Series: Lucent Library of Science and Technology. 2005, Gale/Lucent LB $26.96 (1-59018-530-7). 112pp. A look at the importance of finding alternatives to existing energy sources, covering such technologies as solar, wind, and geothermal power.

23534 Dann, Sarah. *The Science of Energy* (2–4). 2000, Gareth Stevens LB $19.93 (0-8368-2571-3). 32pp. This book defines energy and describes the energy chain and how energy is transformed into electricity, wind, water, and solar power as well as giving some simple activities. (Rev: HBG 9/00; SLJ 9/00) [531.6]

23535 Darling, David J. *Between Fire and Ice: The Science of Heat* (4–8). Illus. Series: Experiment!

1992, Macmillan LB $13.95 (0-87518-501-0). 60pp. After a discussion of the scientific method, characteristics of heat are described and simple experiments are given to demonstrate these properties. (Rev: BL 10/1/92; SLJ 11/92) [536]

23536 de Pinna, Simon. *Forces and Motion* (3–5). Series: Science Projects. 1998, Raintree $25.69 (0-8172-4962-1). 48pp. A brief explanation of force and motion is followed by a series of activities, with each double-page spread dealing with a different aspect of the subject. (Rev: BL 3/15/98; HBG 9/98) [531.6]

23537 DiSpezio, Michael. *Awesome Experiments in Force and Motion* (5–8). Illus. Series: Awesome Experiments. 1999, Sterling $17.95 (0-8069-9821-0). Inertia, buoyancy, surface tension, air pressure, and propulsion are covered in more than 70 well-presented experiments using available materials and supplemented with background material on the concepts involved. (Rev: HBG 9/99; SLJ 7/99) [531]

23538 Doherty, Paul, and Don Rathjen. *The Spinning Blackboard and Other Dynamic Experiments on Force and Motion* (4–8). Illus. Series: Exploratorium Science Snackbook. 1996, Wiley paper $11.95 (0-471-11514-2). The many activities in this well-organized, attractive book reveal important characteristics of force and motion. (Rev: BL 4/15/96; SLJ 6/96) [531]

23539 Driscoll, Laura. *Slow Down, Sara!* (1–3). Illus. by Page Eastburn O'Rourke. Series: Science Solves It! 2003, Kane paper $4.99 (1-57565-125-4). 32pp. This appealing title from the Science Solves It! series focuses on the principle of friction and its impact on speed; young Sara has a need for speed, but she discovers that sometimes it makes sense to slow down. (Rev: SLJ 10/03)

23540 Farndon, John. *Energy* (3–6). Series: Science Experiments. 2002, Marshall Cavendish LB $16.95 (0-7614-1469-X). 32pp. The nature and forms of energy are introduced through a series of easy-to-follow experiments and a simple explanatory text with many color photographs and diagrams. (Rev: BL 12/15/02; HBG 3/03) [531.6]

23541 Farndon, John. *Motion* (3–6). Series: Science Experiments. 2002, Marshall Cavendish LB $16.95 (0-7614-1471-1). 32pp. The properties of motion are revealed to the young scientist through several easy-to-follow activities using common household materials. (Rev: BL 12/15/02; HBG 3/03) [531]

23542 Gardner, Robert. *Experiments with Motion* (5–8). Series: Getting Started in Science. 1995, Enslow LB $20.95 (0-89490-667-4). Projects using simple equipment illustrate the laws of motion and the ways in which motion differs in various situations. (Rev: BL 2/1/96; SLJ 2/96) [531]

23543 Gardner, Robert. *Science Project Ideas About the Sun* (4–7). Series: Science Project Ideas. 1997, Enslow LB $19.95 (0-89490-845-6). 96pp. The sun and solar energy are the subjects of this book that illustrates important concepts through a number of interesting projects and experiments. (Rev: BL 12/15/97; HBG 3/98; SLJ 1/98) [697.78]

23544 Gutnik, Martin J., and Natalie B. Gutnik. *Projects That Explore Energy* (5–8). Illus. Series: Investigate! 1994, Millbrook LB $21.40 (1-56294-334-0). 72pp. A lucid, well-organized series of projects and experiments that explore power, force, and energy sources and resources. (Rev: BL 8/94; SLJ 6/94) [333.79]

23545 Madgwick, Wendy. *On the Move* (K–3). Series: Science Starters. 1999, Raintree LB $15.98 (0-8172-5333-5). 32pp. Energy and motion are explored in this book through a dozen simple activities that use items found in the home to answer questions like why running shoes increase speed, how you keep your balance, and why ice is slippery. (Rev: BL 6/1–15/99; HBG 9/99) [531]

23546 Petersen, Christine. *Wind Power* (3–5). Illus. Series: True Book (Environment and Conservation). 2004, Children's Pr. LB $24.00 (0-516-22809-9); paper $6.95 (0-516-21943-X). 48pp. This thought-provoking look at at the potential of wind power discusses current and future uses of the technology. (Rev: BL 6/1–15/04) [621.31]

23547 Riley, Peter D. *Energy* (4–5). Series: Cycles in Science. 1998, Heinemann LB $21.36 (1-57572-617-3). 32pp. An overview of the world of energy that touches on topics such as kinds of energy, how potential energy becomes kinetic, nuclear energy, electricity, magnetism, and ecological issues. (Rev: SLJ 7/98) [531.6]

23548 Rybolt, Thomas R., and Robert C. Mebane. *Environmental Experiments About Renewable Energy* (3–5). Illus. Series: Science Experiments for Young People. 1994, Enslow LB $19.95 (0-89490-579-1). 96pp. This book contains 16 easy experiments to answer questions about renewable energy. (Rev: SLJ 2/95) [531]

23549 Silverstein, Alvin, et al. *Energy* (4–7). Illus. Series: Science Concepts. 1998, Twenty-First Century LB $26.90 (0-7613-3222-7). 64pp. Photographs, diagrams, and illustrations help to introduce six types of energy: electrical, magnetic, light, heat, sound, and nuclear. (Rev: BL 5/1/99; HBG 9/99) [621.042]

23550 Stille, Darlene R. *Energy* (2–4). Series: Science Around Us. 2004, Child's World LB $27.07 (1-59296-220-3). 32pp. Information on the generation, storage, and distribution of energy is followed by discussion of air pollution and energy conservation. Also use *Motion* (2004). (Rev: BL 11/1/04) [621.042]

23551 Woelfle, Gretchen. *The Wind at Work: An Activity Guide to Windmills* (4–8). 1997, Chicago Review paper $14.95 (1-55652-308-4). The history, types, and uses of windmills are covered, with many activities and a discussion of the future of wind power. (Rev: BL 9/1/97; SLJ 10/97*) [621.4]

23552 Woodruff, John. *Energy* (3–5). Series: Science Projects. 1998, Raintree $25.69 (0-8172-4961-3). 48pp. The properties, uses, and kinds of energy are covered in a series of double-page spreads that give brief explanations followed by simple activities. (Rev: BL 3/15/98; HBG 9/98) [333]

1266

Coal, Gas, and Oil

23553 Ditchfield, Christin. *Coal* (2–5). Series: True Books — Natural Resources. 2002, Children's Book Pr. LB $23.50 (0-516-22342-9); paper $6.95 (0-516-29366-4). 48pp. This simple introduction to coal explains how it is formed, where it is found, how it is used, and how it affects our environment. (Rev: BL 10/15/02) [622]

Nuclear Energy

23554 Cole, Michael D. *Three Mile Island: Nuclear Disaster* (4–8). Series: American Disasters. 2002, Enslow LB $18.95 (0-7660-1556-4). 48pp. An informative, well-researched account of the disaster that affected the development of nuclear power plants in this country. (Rev: BL 6/1–15/02; HBG 10/02; SLJ 6/02) [621.48]

23555 Holland, Gini. *Nuclear Energy* (3–6). Illus. Series: Inventors and Inventions. 1996, Marshall Cavendish LB $25.64 (0-7614-0047-8). 63pp. The story of the discoverers of nuclear energy, its uses, and current problems and possibilities are covered, with many color photos. (Rev: BL 7/96; SLJ 9/96) [333.692]

23556 O'Neill, Mary. *Power Failure* (4–7). Illus. by John Bindon. Series: SOS Planet Earth. 1991, Troll paper $4.95 (0-8167-2289-7). 32pp. The Chernobyl nuclear disaster is just one of the problems discussed in this look at an environmental danger. (Rev: BL 6/15/91) [333.79]

23557 Scarborough, Kate. *Nuclear Waste* (5–7). Illus. Series: Our Planet in Peril. 2002, Capstone LB $22.60 (0-7368-1362-4). 32pp. Report writers will appreciate this well-organized introduction to nuclear waste and its implications for the environment. (Rev: HBG 3/03; SLJ 4/03)

23558 Wilcox, Charlotte. *Powerhouse: Inside a Nuclear Power Plant* (4–8). Illus. 1996, Carolrhoda LB $27.15 (0-87614-945-X); paper $7.95 (0-87614-979-4). 48pp. A history of nuclear energy is followed by a description of how a power plant operates and the dangers that are present. (Rev: BL 10/1/96; SLJ 9/96) [621.48]

Solar Energy

23559 Fowler, Allan. *Energy from the Sun* (1–3). Series: Rookie Readers. 1997, Children's Book Pr. LB $19.00 (0-516-20432-7). 32pp. An easy-to-read science book that introduces solar energy and how it is captured and used. (Rev: BL 12/15/97; HBG 3/98) [697.78]

23560 Petersen, Christine. *Solar Power* (3–5). Illus. Series: True Book (Environment and Conservation). 2004, Children's Pr. LB $24.00 (0-516-22807-2); paper $6.95 (0-516-21941-3). 48pp. The energy of the sun and its potential as a source of power are eplored in this photo-filled, small-format book. (Rev: BL 6/1–15/04) [612.47]

Heat and Fire

23561 Craats, Rennay. *The Science of Fire* (3–5). Series: Living Science. 2000, Gareth Stevens LB $19.93 (0-8368-2680-9). 32pp. This basic book on fire covers chemical basics, fire fighting, conservation issues, and uses of fire in a series of two-page spreads. (Rev: HBG 10/01; SLJ 3/01) [536]

23562 Gardner, Robert, and Eric Kemer. *Science Projects About Temperature and Heat* (4–8). Series: Science Projects. 1994, Enslow LB $20.95 (0-89490-534-1). 128pp. Using household materials, this book clearly outlines procedures and results involving projects that explore heat and temperature. (Rev: SLJ 1/95) [536]

Light and Color

23563 Ardley, Neil. *The Science Book of Color* (3–6). Illus. Series: Science Books. 1991, Harcourt $9.95 (0-15-200576-5). 28pp. Clear color photos enhance the step-by-step directions for science experiments involving color. (Rev: BL 3/1/91; SLJ 5/91) [535.6]

23564 Asimov, Isaac. *How Did We Find Out About Lasers?* (5–7). Illus. by Erika Kors. 1990, Walker LB $13.85 (0-8027-6936-5). 64pp. A readable introduction to laser science by the veteran writer. (Rev: BL 8/90; SLJ 11/90) [621.36]

23565 Bang, Molly. *My Light* (1–3). Illus. 2004, Scholastic $16.95 (0-439-48961-X). 48pp. Highly visual and accessible, this picture book introduces four ways of making electricity and explores the energy provided by the sun. (Rev: BL 2/1/04*; HB 5–6/04; SLJ 4/04) [621]

23566 Boekhoff, P. M., and Stuart A. Kallen. *Lasers* (4–5). Illus. Series: Kidhaven Science Library. 2002, Gale LB $23.70 (0-7377-0944-8). 48pp. A discussion of the discovery of lasers and of their uses today in such fields as industry, medicine, recreation, and the armed forces. (Rev: BL 5/1/02; SLJ 9/02) [621.36]

23567 Branley, Franklyn M. *Day Light, Night Light: Where Light Comes From* (K–3). Illus. by Stacey Schuett. Series: Let's-Read-and-Find-Out. 1998, HarperCollins LB $15.89 (0-06-027295-3). 32pp. In this book about light, topics like darkness, heat, light sources, reflection, vision, and the speed of light are discussed. (Rev: BL 12/1/97; HBG 9/98; SLJ 2/98) [535]

23568 Burton, Jane, and Kim Taylor. *The Nature and Science of Color* (3–6). Illus. Series: Exploring the Science of Nature. 1998, Gareth Stevens LB $18.60 (0-8368-1940-3). 32pp. The nature and composition of color and colors are explained in a lively, large-type text and color photographs. (Rev: BL 6/1–15/98; HBG 9/98) [535]

23569 Burton, Jane, and Kim Taylor. *The Nature and Science of Reflections* (3–6). Series: Exploring the Science of Nature. 2001, Gareth Stevens LB

$21.27 (0-8368-2194-7). 32pp. Light, mirrors, and reflection are topics explored in this basic physics book that also contains activities and projects to demonstrate various principles. (Rev: BL 3/15/01; HBG 10/01) [535]

23570 Darling, David J. *Making Light Work: The Science of Optics* (3–6). Illus. Series: Experiment! 1991, Macmillan LB $17.95 (0-87518-476-6). 64pp. An introduction, with experiments, to the principles of light. (Rev: BL 6/1/92) [535]

23571 Day, Trevor. *Light* (3–5). Illus. Series: Science Projects. 1998, Raintree $25.69 (0-8172-4943-5). 48pp. With explanatory text and simple activities, this account covers such topics as the nature of light, vision, shadows, photography, reflections, refraction, and color. (Rev: BL 3/15/98; HBG 9/98) [538]

23572 Farndon, John. *Color* (3–6). Illus. Series: Science Experiments. 2000, Marshall Cavendish LB $16.95 (0-7614-1092-9). 32pp. Topics covered include the spectrum, primary colors, pigment, mixing colors, and color blindness, with many interesting activities such as making a color wheel and creating a spectrum. (Rev: BL 3/15/01; HBG 3/01) [535.6]

23573 Farndon, John. *Lights and Optics* (3–6). Series: Science Experiments. 2000, Marshall Cavendish LB $16.95 (0-7614-1090-2). 32pp. Explores properties of light and optics and outlines projects that apply the principles established. (Rev: BL 3/15/01; HBG 3/01) [535]

23574 Fowler, Allan. *All the Colors of the Rainbow* (1–2). Series: Rookie Readers. 1998, Children's Book Pr. LB $18.50 (0-516-20801-2). 32pp. Using color photographs and three lines of text per page, this book introduces the concept of color to very young readers. (Rev: BL 9/15/98; HBG 9/99) [535]

23575 Fox, Mary V. *Lasers* (3–6). Illus. Series: Inventors and Inventions. 1996, Benchmark LB $25.64 (0-7614-0067-2). 63pp. The history of laser technology, with profiles of several scientists involved in this branch of science and its effects in such areas as medicine. (Rev: BL 3/15/96; SLJ 6/96) [621.36]

23576 Gardner, Robert. *Experiments with Light and Mirrors* (4–7). Illus. 1995, Enslow LB $20.95 (0-89490-668-2). 112pp. Properties of light are explained and demonstrated using equipment such as mirrors and cardboard. (Rev: BL 2/1/96; SLJ 3/96) [535.2]

23577 Gardner, Robert. *Science Projects About Light* (4–8). Series: Science Projects. 1994, Enslow LB $20.95 (0-89490-529-5). 128pp. This project book contains a wealth of demonstrations that explain the basic principles of light. (Rev: SLJ 1/95) [535]

23578 Krupp, E. C. *The Rainbow and You* (2–3). Illus. by Robin R. Krupp. 2000, HarperCollins LB $15.89 (0-688-15602-9). 32pp. The causes of rainbows are discussed (with directions on how to make your own) plus material on double rainbows, folklore surrounding rainbows, and Isaac Newton's work with them. (Rev: BL 8/00; HBG 9/00; SLJ 5/00) [551.56]

23579 Levine, Shar, and Leslie Johnstone. *The Optics Book: Fun Experiments with Light, Vision and Color* (5–8). Illus. 1999, Sterling $21.95 (0-8069-9947-0). This book contains experiments and projects using easily obtained materials demonstrate reflection, refraction, color, polarization, vision, and light rays. (Rev: BL 3/1/99; SLJ 7/99) [535]

23580 Madgwick, Wendy. *Light and Dark* (K–3). Series: Science Starters. 1999, Raintree LB $15.98 (0-8172-5556-7). 32pp. Double-page spreads introduce about a dozen projects that explore the topic of light including demonstrations on how rainbows are formed, why shadows change, and how lenses work. (Rev: BL 6/1–15/99; HBG 9/99) [535.2]

23581 Murray, Peter. *Professor Solomon Snickerdoodle's Light Science Tricks* (1–3). Illus. by Penny Dann. 1998, Child's World LB $21.36 (1-56766-148-3). 29pp. This book presents amazing science tricks involving light and explanations that demonstrate its properties. (Rev: SLJ 5/98) [535]

23582 Stille, Darlene R. *Light* (2–4). Illus. Series: Science Around Us: Physics. 2004, Child's World LB $18.95 (1-59296-221-1). 32pp. Eye-catching photographs and interesting "Did You Know?" features draw the reader into this overview of light.

23583 Tocci, Salvatore. *Experiments with Colors* (2–4). Illus. Series: A True Book. 2003, Children's Pr. LB $23.50 (0-516-22785-8); paper $6.95 (0-516-27804-5). 48pp. A simple and attractive explanation of what creates color, how we perceive it, and how optical illusions work. (Rev: SLJ 4/04) [535.6]

23584 Trumbauer, Lisa. *All About Light* (PS–1). Series: Rookie Read-About Science. 2004, Scholastic LB $19.50 (0-516-25842-7). 31pp. Simple text and color photographs introduce beginning readers to the concept of light, including its sources and basic characteristics. (Rev: BL 9/1/04) [535]

23585 Wick, Walter. *Walter Wick's Optical Tricks* (4–8). 1998, Scholastic paper $13.95 (0-590-22227-9). A stimulating collection of photographs that present unusual optical illusions, with their secrets revealed in subsequent pages. (Rev: BCCB 10/98; BL 8/98; HB 9–10/98*; HBG 3/99; SLJ 9/98) [152]

23586 Zubrowski, Bernie. *Mirrors: Finding Out About the Properties of Light* (4–7). Illus. by Roy Doty. 1992, Morrow LB $13.89 (0-688-10592-0). 112pp. In this hands-on approach, games and activities entice the reader to learn more. (Rev: BL 7/92; SLJ 8/92) [535]

Magnetism and Electricity

23587 Ardley, Neil. *Electricity* (4–6). Illus. 1992, Macmillan $22.00 (0-02-705665-1). 48pp. This book tells about the types of electricity and how they are produced. (Rev: SLJ 8/92) [537]

23588 Ardley, Neil. *The Science Book of Electricity* (3–6). Illus. Series: Science Books. 1991, Harcourt $9.95 (0-15-200583-8). 29pp. Full-page spreads show step-by-step procedures for projects involving electricity. (Rev: BL 10/15/91) [535]

23589 Ardley, Neil. *The Science Book of Magnets* (3–6). Illus. Series: Science Books. 1991, Harcourt $9.95 (0-15-200581-1). 29pp. Basic properties of magnets and magnetism are explored through a series of projects with clear directions and attractive illustrations. (Rev: BL 10/15/91) [528.4]

23590 Bartholomew, Alan. *Electric Mischief* (4–7). Series: Kids Can Do It! 2002, Kids Can $12.95 (1-55074-923-4); paper $5.95 (1-55074-925-0). 48pp. An activity book that outlines simple, safe experiments with electricity. (Rev: BL 3/15/03; HBG 3/03; SLJ 12/02) [537]

23591 Berger, Melvin. *Switch On, Switch Off* (K–3). Illus. by Carolyn Croll. 1989, HarperCollins LB $15.89 (0-690-04786-X); paper $4.95 (0-06-445097-X). 32pp. Explaining the mysteries of electricity. (Rev: BL 4/15/89; HB 5–6/89)

23592 Bocknek, Jonathan. *The Science of Magnets* (2–4). Series: Living Science. 1999, Gareth Stevens LB $19.93 (0-8368-2572-1). 32pp. Different kinds of magnets, magnetic poles and properties, electromagnets, and magnetic animals and medicine are introduced in a series of double-page spreads with some appended activities. (Rev: HBG 9/00; SLJ 9/00) [538.4]

23593 Cole, Joanna. *The Magic School Bus and the Electric Field Trip* (2–4). Illus. by Bruce Degen. Series: Magic School Bus. 1997, Scholastic $15.95 (0-590-44682-7). 56pp. Mrs. Frizzle's class visits a power plant to find out how electricity is made in this entertaining science book filled with facts, jokes, and puns. (Rev: BL 10/15/97; HBG 3/98; SLJ 11/97) [621.3]

23594 Cosner, Sharon. *The Light Bulb* (4–6). Illus. 1984, Walker LB $10.85 (0-8027-6527-0). 64pp. A history of various forms of lighting, the light bulb, and the electrical industry.

23595 de Pinna, Simon. *Electricity* (3–5). Series: Science Projects. 1998, Raintree $24.26 (0-8172-4945-1). 48pp. The properties of electricity are covered in a series of double-page spreads, each of which covers a different aspect of the subject and outlines three or four simple acitivities. (Rev: BL 3/15/98; HBG 9/98) [621.3]

23596 Evans, Neville. *The Science of a Light Bulb* (5–8). Illus. Series: Science World. 2000, Raintree LB $25.69 (0-7398-1325-0). 32pp. This work explains how Edison invented the light bulb, describes its parts, and tells how light is produced and how we see it. (Rev: BL 9/15/00; HBG 9/00) [535]

23597 Farndon, John. *Electricity* (3–6). Series: Science Experiments. 2000, Marshall Cavendish LB $16.95 (0-7614-1086-4). 32pp. Each chapter contains information on different aspects and applications of electricity plus experiments that illustrate key principles. (Rev: BL 3/15/01; HBG 3/01) [537]

23598 Fowler, Allan. *What Magnets Can Do* (1–2). Illus. Series: Rookie Readers. 1995, Children's Book Pr. LB $19.00 (0-516-06034-1). 32pp. A basic introduction to magnets and magnetism, with photos, large type, and coverage of interesting topics. (Rev: BL 7/95) [538]

23599 Gardner, Robert. *Science Projects About Electricity and Magnets* (4–8). Series: Science Projects. 1994, Enslow LB $20.95 (0-89490-530-9). 128pp. A wealth of projects that cover the basic principles of electricity and magnetism. (Rev: SLJ 1/95) [537]

23600 Good, Keith. *Zap It! Exciting Electricity Activities* (3–7). Series: Design It! 2000, Lerner LB $21.27 (0-8225-3565-3). 30pp. An activity book that explores concepts in electricity and contains projects involving electric circuits, pressure pads, and different kinds of switches. (Rev: HBG 9/00; SLJ 6/00) [537]

23601 Madgwick, Wendy. *Magnets and Sparks* (K–3). Series: Science Starters. 1999, Raintree LB $15.98 (0-8172-5328-9). 32pp. A basic introduction to electricity and magnetism that includes more than a dozen activities using items found in the home to explore topics such as how electricity travels, what magnets attract, and how flashlights work. (Rev: BL 6/1–15/99; HBG 9/99) [537]

23602 Nankivell-Aston, Sally, and Dorothy Jackson. *Science Experiments with Electricity* (3–6). Series: Science Experiments. 2000, Watts LB $20.00 (0-531-14580-8); paper $6.95 (0-531-15443-2). 32pp. This book of simple electricity projects includes building simple switches and circuits with additional material on scientific method and safety. (Rev: SLJ 3/01) [537]

23603 Seuling, Barbara. *Flick a Switch: How Electricity Gets to Your Home* (1–3). Illus. by Nancy Tobin. 2003, Holiday House $16.95 (0-8234-1729-8). 32pp. An easy-to-understand narrative is combined with bright cartoon illustrations to help young readers learn some basics about electricity — where it comes from and how it gets to where it's needed. (Rev: BL 9/1/03; HBG 4/04; SLJ 11/03)

23604 Stille, Darlene R. *Magnetism* (2–4). Illus. Series: Science Around Us: Physics. 2004, Child's World LB $18.95 (1-59296-222-X). 32pp. Eye-catching photographs and interesting "Did You Know?" features draw the reader into this overview of magnetism. [538]

23605 Tiner, John Hudson. *Magnetism* (4–7). Series: Understanding Science. 2002, Smart Apple LB $24.25 (1-58340-158-X). 32pp. Using clear explanations, simple projects, and good illustrations, the concept of magnetism is introduced. (Rev: BL 3/15/03; HBG 3/03) [538.4]

23606 VanCleave, Janice. *Janice VanCleave's Electricity: Mind-Boggling Experiments You Can Turn into Science Fair Projects* (5–7). Illus. 1994, Wiley paper $10.95 (0-471-31010-7). 96pp. As well as providing a discussion on the nature of electricity, this book offers 20 informative experiments that move from the very simple to the more complex. (Rev: BL 12/1/94; SLJ 11/94) [537]

23607 VanCleave, Janice. *Magnets: Mind-Boggling Experiments You Can Turn into Science Fair Projects* (4–6). Illus. Series: Spectacular Science Projects. 1993, Wiley paper $10.95 (0-471-57106-7). 88pp. Using magnets and the principles of magnetism, this book offers clear directions in developing many interesting science projects. Also use: *Ani-*

mals; Gravity; and *Molecules* (all 1993). (Rev: BL 5/1/93; SLJ 7/93) [538]

23608 Whalley, Margaret. *Experiment with Magnets and Electricity* (2–5). Illus. Series: Experiment With. 1994, Lerner LB $19.93 (0-8225-2457-0). 32pp. Principles of magnetism and electricity are covered through a series of simple, fun-to-do experiments using everyday materials. (Rev: BL 3/1/94; SLJ 5/94) [537]

23609 Woodford, Chris, and Martin Clowes. *Electricity* (4–7). Illus. 2004, Gale/Blackbirch LB $23.70 (1-4103-0165-6). 40pp. A detailed examination of the development of electricity, with profiles of key individuals and their discoveries, a chronology, and discussion of future advances. (Rev: SLJ 5/05)

Optical Illusions

23610 Churchill, E. Richard. *Optical Illusion Tricks and Toys* (4–7). Illus. by James Michaels. 1989, Sterling $12.95 (0-8069-6868-0). 128pp. Sixty-plus opportunities to demonstrate that things look different from what they really are. (Rev: BL 7/89) [152.1]

23611 DiSpezio, Michael A. *Eye-Popping Optical Illusions* (3–6). Illus. 2001, Sterling $17.95 (0-8069-6641-6). 80pp. A bright and absorbing look at illusions found in geometric patterns, 3-D photography, shading and light, and other tricks that fool the eye, with scientific explanations and a few projects. (Rev: BL 8/01; HBG 10/01; SLJ 7/01) [152.14]

23612 DiSpezio, Michael A. *Simple Optical Illusion Experiments with Everyday Materials* (3–6). Illus. 2001, Sterling $14.95 (0-8069-6635-1). 128pp. A collection of optical tricks that range from the simple to the complex, with full explanations of the underlying science. (Rev: BL 7/01; HBG 10/01; SLJ 8/01) [152.14]

23613 Simon, Seymour. *Now You See It, Now You Don't: The Amazing World of Optical Illusions.* Rev. ed. (3–6). Illus. 1998, Morrow $15.00 (0-688-16152-9). 96pp. This interesting discussion of optical illusions uses good illustrations and clear explanations. (Rev: BL 10/15/98; HBG 3/99) [152.14]

23614 Simon, Seymour. *The Optical Illusion Book* (4–6). Illus. by Constance Flera. 1976, Morrow paper $6.95 (0-688-03254-0). 80pp. In addition to illustrations that show several optical illusions, there are explanations for each illusion and a chapter on illusion in art.

23615 Westray, Kathleen. *Picture Puzzler* (3–7). Illus. 1994, Ticknor $13.95 (0-395-70130-9). 32pp. An oversize book that depicts a number of optical illusions and shows how proper focusing can produce different visual patterns. (Rev: BCCB 10/94; BL 7/94; HB 11–12/94; SLJ 8/94*) [152.14]

Simple Machines

23616 Armentrout, David, and Patricia Armentrout. *An Inclined Plane* (1–3). Illus. Series: How Can I Experiment With . . . ? 2002, Rourke LB $26.60 (1-58952-333-4). 32pp. This volume teaches younger readers, through illustration, narrative, and experimentation, about inclined planes. Other titles in this series include *A Lever, A Screw, A Wedge,* and *A Wheel* (all 2002). (Rev: BL 10/15/02; SLJ 3/03) [621.8]

23617 Fowler, Allan. *Simple Machines* (1–2). Illus. Series: Rookie Read-About Science. 2001, Children's Book Pr. $19.00 (0-516-21680-5). 32pp. A basic introduction to the lever, inclined plane, pulley, and wheel and axle. (Rev: BL 7/01) [621.8]

23618 Good, Keith. *Gear Up! Marvelous Machine Projects* (3–7). Series: Design It! 2000, Lerner LB $21.27 (0-8225-3566-1). 30pp. Simple machines like pulleys, levers, crankshafts, gear wheels, and conveyor belts are explored in this book of projects that apply the principles behind these machines. (Rev: HBG 9/00; SLJ 6/00) [621.8]

23619 Hodge, Deborah, and Adrienne Mason. *Simple Machines* (K–4). Illus. Series: Starting with Science. 1998, Kids Can $10.95 (1-55074-311-2). 32pp. This activity book uses double-page spreads to present science activities involving pulleys, levers, and other simple machines. (Rev: BL 4/15/98; HBG 9/98; SLJ 6/98) [621.8]

23620 Oxlade, Chris. *Levers* (K–2). Illus. Series: Useful Machines. 2003, Heinemann LB $22.79 (1-4034-3662-2). 32pp. Information on how these simple machines work are followed by illustrations of levers in action in everyday situations. Also use *Pulleys* (2003). (Rev: BL 2/15/04) [021.8]

23621 Royston, Angela. *Screws* (2–4). Illus. Series: Machines in Action. 2000, Heinemann LB $21.36 (1-57572-322-0). 32pp. An easy-to-read introduction to how screws work and the different kinds of screws we find in objects all around us. Also use *Springs* (2000). (Rev: HBG 3/01; SLJ 4/01) [621.8]

23622 Walker, Sally M., and Roseann Feldmann. *Inclined Planes and Wedges* (2–4). Photos by Andy King. 2001, Lerner LB $23.93 (0-8225-2221-7). 47pp. A concise explanation of these simple machines, that increases in complexity as the reader progresses through the book, with simple experiments and clear illustrations. Also use *Pulleys* and *Wheels and Axles* (both 2001). (Rev: HBG 3/02; SLJ 2/02) [621.8]

23623 Welsbacher, Anne. *Inclined Planes* (K–3). Series: Understanding Simple Machines. 2000, Capstone LB $17.26 (0-7368-0610-5). 24pp. As well as showing many examples of inclined planes, this simple physics book outlines activities that apply this knowledge. (Rev: BL 10/15/00; HBG 3/01; SLJ 12/00) [621.8]

23624 Welsbacher, Anne. *Levers* (2–3). Illus. Series: Understanding Simple Machines. 2000, Capstone $17.26 (0-7368-0611-3). 24pp. This work discusses the parts of a lever, the classes of levers, and how these simple machines are used. (Rev: BL 12/1/00; HBG 3/01) [621.8]

23625 Welsbacher, Anne. *Pulleys* (K–3). Series: Understanding Simple Machines. 2000, Capstone LB $17.26 (0-7368-0612-1). 24pp. Gives many examples of pulleys, such as on a flagpole, along with an explanation of their uses and some simple activities. (Rev: BL 10/15/00; HBG 3/01) [621.8]

23626 Welsbacher, Anne. *Screws* (K–3). Series: Understanding Simple Machines. 2000, Capstone LB $17.26 (0-7368-0613-X). 24pp. This simple book on physics explains, with many examples, how screws work and outlines a few hands-on activities. (Rev: BL 10/15/00; HBG 3/01) [621.8]

23627 Welsbacher, Anne. *Wedges* (2–3). Illus. Series: Understanding Simple Machines. 2000, Capstone $17.26 (0-7368-0614-8). 24pp. This book introduces wedges, their parts, and how they are used in axes, knives, scissors, doorstops, and zippers. (Rev: BL 12/1/00; HBG 3/01; SLJ 12/00) [621.8]

23628 Welsbacher, Anne. *Wheels and Axles* (K–3). Series: Understanding Simple Machines. 2000, Capstone LB $17.26 (0-7368-0615-6). 24pp. After showing many examples of wheels (e.g., a steering wheel on a car) and axles (e.g., those found on a wagon), this book explains how they work and their many applications. (Rev: BL 10/15/00; HBG 3/01) [6621.8]

23629 Whittle, Fran, and Sarah Lawrence. *Simple Machines* (3–5). Illus. Series: Design and Create. 1997, Raintree $25.69 (0-8172-4889-7). 32pp. How to make a cookie crusher and a bubble machine are among the 12 projects nicely presented in double-page spreads to outline each activity and give background information. (Rev: BL 2/1/98; HBG 3/98) [621.8]

Sound

23630 Cobb, Vicki. *Bangs and Twangs: Science Fun with Sound* (3–6). Illus. 2000, Millbrook LB $23.40 (0-7613-1571-3). 48pp. Using a cartoon format, this lively activity book explores different aspects of sound including pitch and the physiology of hearing. (Rev: BCCB 11/00; BL 10/15/00; HBG 3/01; SLJ 3/01) [534.078]

23631 Craats, Rennay. *The Science of Sound* (3–5). Series: Living Science. 2000, Gareth Stevens LB $14.95 (0-8368-2682-5). 32pp. Basic information is given on such sound-related topics as musical instruments, nature's sounds, sounds that people can't hear, echoes, sonar, and sound careers. (Rev: HBG 10/01; SLJ 3/01) [534]

23632 Darling, David J. *Sounds Interesting: The Science of Acoustics* (3–6). Illus. 1992, Macmillan LB $17.95 (0-87518-477-4). 64pp. A straightforward text provides an in-depth exploration of the science of sound. (Rev: BL 5/1/92) [523]

23633 de Pinna, Simon. *Sound* (3–5). Series: Science Projects. 1998, Raintree $25.69 (0-8172-4944-3). 48pp. The properties of sound are explored in a

series of double-page spreads that give simple explanations followed by three or four simple activities. (Rev: BL 3/15/98; HBG 9/98) [534]

23634 Dreier, David Louis. *Sound* (2–4). Illus. Series: Science Around Us: Physics. 2004, Child's World LB $18.95 (1-59296-226-2). 32pp. Eye-catching photographs and interesting "Did You Know?" features draw the reader into this overview of sound. [534]

23635 Farndon, John. *Sound and Hearing* (3–6). Series: Science Experiments. 2000, Marshall Cavendish LB $16.95 (0-7614-1091-0). 32pp. The properties of sound and the process of hearing are explored with a series of experiments to illustrate different concepts and applications. (Rev: BL 3/15/01; HBG 3/01) [534]

23636 Gibson, Gary. *Hearing Sounds* (3–5). Illus. Series: Science for Fun. 1995, Millbrook LB $20.90 (1-56294-614-5). 32pp. Basic concepts involving sound are introduced through a series of simple activities and projects, with simple instructions and clear, often amusing illustrations. (Rev: BL 7/95) [534]

23637 Kaner, Etta. *Sound Science* (3–5). Illus. by Louise Phillips. 1992, Addison-Wesley paper $11.00 (0-201-56758-X). 96pp. The 40-plus experiments and projects in this book, which can be done with easily obtained materials, explore various aspects of sound. (Rev: SLJ 6/92) [530]

23638 Madgwick, Wendy. *Super Sound* (K–3). Series: Science Starters. 1999, Raintree LB $15.98 (0-8172-5327-0). 32pp. The properties of sound are explored in this book of simple projects that include topics such as how sound travels, whether two ears are better than one, and the possibility of trapping sound. (Rev: BL 6/1–15/99; HBG 9/99) [534]

23639 Morgan, Sally, and Adrian Morgan. *Using Sound* (4–7). Illus. Series: Designs in Science. 1994, Facts on File $23.00 (0-8160-2981-4). 48pp. The properties of sound and their relation to everyday life are covered in the text and a number of experiments using readily available materials. (Rev: BL 7/94) [534]

23640 Pfeffer, Wendy. *Sounds All Around* (PS–2). Illus. by Holly Keller. Series: Let's-Read-and-Find-Out. 1999, HarperCollins LB $15.89 (0-06-027712-2). 32pp. This book about sound covers such topics as decibels, vibration, communication, and radar with examples for the animal kingdom and suggested activities. (Rev: BL 3/1/99; HBG 9/99; SLJ 1/99) [534]

23641 Trumbauer, Lisa. *All About Sound* (PS–1). Series: Rookie Read-About Science. 2004, Scholastic LB $19.50 (0-516-25847-8). 31pp. Simple text and color photographs introduce beginning readers to the basic characteristics of sound. (Rev: BL 9/1/04) [534]

23642 Wright, Lynne. *The Science of Noise* (5–8). Illus. Series: Science World. 2000, Raintree LB $25.69 (0-7398-1324-2). 32pp. This account describes how sound is produced, how it travels, how we hear it, and how it can be changed. (Rev: BL 9/1/00; HBG 9/00; SLJ 8/00) [534]

Space Exploration

23643 *The Amazing International Space Station* (4–6). Illus. by Rose Cowles. 2003, Kids Can $15.95 (1-55337-380-4); paper $8.95 (1-55337-523-8). 48pp. An appealing, highly visual and information-packed look at life aboard the International Space Station. (Rev: HBG 4/04; SLJ 4/04) [629.44]

23644 Angliss, Sarah. *Cosmic Journeys: A Beginner's Guide to Space and Time Travel* (5–7). Illus. by Alex Pang, et al. Series: Future Files. 1998, Millbrook LB $23.90 (0-7613-0620-X). 32pp. This book explores such topics as traveling to other solar systems, time travel, black holes, and parallel universes. (Rev: HBG 9/98; SLJ 10/98) [629.4]

23645 Barter, James. *Space Stations* (5–8). Illus. Series: Lucent Library of Science and Technology. 2005, Gale/Lucent LB $26.96 (1-59018-106-9). 112pp. Explores the space stations that have been used for many years as medical laboratories and platforms for space study.

23646 Berger, Melvin, and Gilda Berger. *Can You Hear a Shout in Space? Questions and Answers About Space Exploration* (3–6). Illus. 2001, Scholastic $14.95 (0-439-09582-4); paper $5.95 (0-439-14879-0). 48pp. In question-and-answer format, this title tackles topics of interest both to browsers and report writers. (Rev: BL 7/01; HBG 10/01) [629.4]

23647 Berliner, Don. *Living in Space* (4–6). Illus. 1993, Lerner LB $22.60 (0-8225-1599-7). 72pp. The living conditions of travelers in space are covered. (Rev: BL 7/93) [629.47]

23648 Beyer, Mark. *Crisis in Space: Apollo 13* (3–4). Illus. Series: Survivor. 2002, Children's Book Pr. LB $19.00 (0-516-23903-1); paper $6.95 (0-516-23485-4). 48pp. A suspenseful account of the problems encountered on the *Apollo 13* mission and the dangers the astronauts faced. (Rev: SLJ 6/02) [629.45]

23649 Blackwood, Gary L. *Alien Astronauts* (4–6). Series: Secrets of the Unexplained. 1998, Benchmark LB $19.95 (0-7614-0469-4). 80pp. As well as a historical look at UFO sightings, this book covers

the types of sightings and the most common varieties. (Rev: HBG 9/99; SLJ 3/99) [001.9]

23650 Bond, Peter. *DK Guide to Space: A Photographic Journey Through the Universe* (4–6). Illus. 1999, DK $19.95 (0-7894-3946-8). 64pp. In double-page spreads this visually exciting work takes the readers on a trip through the solar system and beyond, covering such topics as the Milky Way, space stations, and extraterrestrial life. (Rev: BL 7/99; HBG 4/00; SLJ 9/99) [520]

23651 Branley, Franklyn M. *Floating in Space* (K–3). Illus. by True Kelley. Series: Let's-Read-and-Find-Out. 1998, HarperCollins LB $15.89 (0-06-025433-5). 32pp. Life in space is covered in this book describing weightlessness, space suits, the food astronauts eat, and the activities aboard a space shuttle. (Rev: BCCB 4/98; BL 12/1/97; HBG 9/98; SLJ 2/98) [629.47]

23652 Branley, Franklyn M. *Is There Life in Outer Space?* (PS–3). Illus. by Edward Miller. Series: Let's-Read-and-Find-Out. 1999, HarperCollins LB $15.89 (0-06-028145-6); paper $4.95 (0-06-445192-5). 31pp. A beginning science book that explores what we know about life on the planets and in outer space. (Rev: HBG 4/00; SLJ 10/99) [523]

23653 Bredeson, Carmen. *The Challenger Disaster: Tragic Space Flight* (4–8). Series: American Disasters. 1999, Enslow LB $18.95 (0-7660-1222-0). 48pp. An account of the 1986 tragedy. (Rev: BL 10/15/99; HBG 4/00) [629.5]

23654 Bredeson, Carmen. *John Glenn Returns to Orbit: Life on the Space Shuttle* (4–7). Series: Countdown to Space. 2000, Enslow LB $18.95 (0-7660-1304-9). 48pp. This is the story of John Glenn, now a famous politician, his return to space, and the different conditions he encountered. (Rev: BL 8/00; HBG 9/00) [629.4]

23655 Bredeson, Carmen. *NASA Planetary Spacecraft: Galileo, Magellan, Pathfinder, and Voyager* (4–7). Series: Countdown to Space. 2000, Enslow LB $18.95 (0-7660-1303-0). 48pp. This gives a good rundown on the NASA spacecraft used to explore planets, their individual missions, and their findings. (Rev: BL 9/15/00; HBG 10/01) [629.4]

23656 Bredeson, Carmen. *Our Space Program* (3–5). Series: I Know America. 1999, Millbrook LB $20.90 (0-7613-0952-7). 48pp. This history of the first 50 years of the space program contains material on the space race with the Soviet Union, prominent astronauts, and major successes, failures, and disasters. (Rev: HBG 9/99; SLJ 5/99) [629.45]

23657 Brenner, Barbara. *Planetarium: The Museum That Explores the Many Wonders of Our Solar System* (1–4). Illus. by Ron Miller. Series: Bank Street Museum Book. 1993, Bantam LB $9.50 (0-533-35428-0). 48pp. On a trip to a planetarium, the reader visits outer space and learns about the solar system. (Rev: BL 9/1/93; SLJ 8/93) [520]

23658 Briggs, Carole S. *Women in Space* (4–7). Series: A&E Biography. 1999, Lerner LB $25.26 (0-8225-4937-9). 112pp. Includes profiles of astronauts including Sally Ride, Mae Jemison, Shannon Lucid, Eileen Collins, and two of their Russian counterparts. (Rev: SLJ 5/99) [629.45]

23659 Casanellas, Antonio. *Great Discoveries and Inventions That Helped Explore Earth and Space* (3–5). Illus. Series: Great Discoveries and Inventions. 2000, Gareth Stevens $21.27 (0-8368-2584-5). In two-page spreads, great inventions such as the Saturn 5 rocket and the seismograph are introduced along with four projects for the young space explorer. (Rev: HBG 10/01; SLJ 1/01) [629.4]

23660 Charleston, Gordon. *Armstrong Lands on the Moon* (3–6). Illus. Series: Great 20th Century Expeditions. 1994, Dillon LB $20.00 (0-87518-530-4). 32pp. This handy account covers a history of space exploration from the first rockets to the moon landing. (Rev: SLJ 11/94) [523]

23661 Clay, Rebecca. *Space Travel and Exploration* (4–8). Illus. Series: Secrets of Space. 1995, Twenty-First Century LB $23.90 (0-8050-4474-4). A history of modern space exploration, covering manned flights, space stations, space probes, and telescopes. (Rev: BL 7/97; SLJ 1/98) [629.5]

23662 Cole, Michael D. *Astronauts: Training for Space* (4–7). Illus. Series: Countdown to Space. 1999, Enslow LB $18.95 (0-7660-1116-X). 48pp. Focusing mainly on Sally Ride, this account describes the rigorous training of NASA astronauts. (Rev: BL 2/1/99; HBG 9/99) [629.45]

23663 Cole, Michael D. *Challenger: America's Space Tragedy* (4–6). Illus. Series: Countdown to Space. 1995, Enslow LB $18.95 (0-89490-544-9). 48pp. This tragic event is movingly described. Two other titles in this series are *Friendship 7: First American in Orbit* and *Vostok 1: First Human in Space* (both 1995). (Rev: SLJ 2/96) [523]

23664 Cole, Michael D. *Galileo Spacecraft: Mission to Jupiter* (4–7). Series: Countdown to Space. 1999, Enslow LB $18.95 (0-7660-1119-4). 48pp. *Galileo's* journey to Jupiter is described with details of the preparations for the flight and its findings. Photographs, a glossary, and Web sites round out the coverage. (Rev: BL 2/15/99; HBG 9/99; SLJ 5/99) [629.45]

23665 Cole, Michael D. *Moon Base: First Colony on Space* (4–7). Series: Countdown to Space. 1999, Enslow LB $18.95 (0-7660-1118-6). 48pp. A futuristic look at what a space colony on the moon might look like and the problems involved in creating it. (Rev: BL 2/15/99; HBG 9/99; SLJ 5/99) [629.45]

23666 Cole, Michael D. *NASA Space Vehicles: Capsules, Shuttles, and Space Stations* (4–7). Series: Countdown to Space. 2000, Enslow LB $18.95 (0-7660-1308-1). 48pp. Gives a rundown on these specialized vehicles plus a description of space stations and how they operate, with full-color photographs and clear, readable text. (Rev: BL 5/15/00; HBG 9/00; SLJ 12/00) [629.4]

23667 Cole, Michael D. *Space Emergency: Astronauts in Danger* (4–8). Illus. Series: Countdown to Space. 2000, Enslow LB $18.95 (0-7660-1307-3). 48pp. An explosion on the command module of *Apollo 13* and a faulty landing bag on *Friendship 7* are two of the emergencies described in this book on crises in space exploration. (Rev: BL 2/1/00; HBG 9/00; SLJ 12/00) [629.45]

23668 Cole, Michael D. *Space Launch Disaster: When Liftoff Goes Wrong* (4–7). Series: Countdown to Space. 2000, Enslow LB $18.95 (0-7660-1309-X). 48pp. This is a rundown of problems that can occur during the liftoff of space vehicles, with examples of actual disasters, many caught on camera. (Rev: BL 3/15/00; HBG 9/00; SLJ 8/00) [629]

23669 Davis, Amanda. *Extraterrestrials: Is There Life in Outer Space?* (2–4). Series: Exploring Space. 1997, Rosen LB $15.95 (0-8239-5058-1). 24pp. Colorful illustrations enliven this explanation of the conditions that led to life on earth and to our current quest for proof of life on other planets. (Rev: SLJ 4/98) [001.9]

23670 Dyson, Marianne J. *Home on the Moon: Living on a Space Frontier* (5–8). Illus. 2003, National Geographic $18.95 (0-7922-7193-9). 64pp. Dyson, a former NASA mission controller, discusses the resources available on the moon, explores the possibilities of building facilities there, and suggests activities. (Rev: BL 7/03; HBG 10/03; SLJ 9/03) [919.91]

23671 Dyson, Marianne J. *Space Station Science: Life in Free Fall* (4–7). Illus. 1999, Scholastic paper $16.95 (0-590-05889-4). 128pp. Written by a former member of a NASA control team, this work explores living and working in space including details on a space station bathroom. (Rev: BL 11/15/99; HBG 9/00; SLJ 12/99) [629.45]

23672 Engelbert, Phillis. *Astronomy and Space: From the Big Bang to the Big Crunch* (4–8). Illus. 1997, Gale LB $232.00 (0-7876-0942-0). 600pp. Some 300 alphabetically arranged entries consider space exploration, the laws and features of the universe, the history of astronomy, important astronauts, famous observatories, and the greenhouse effect. (Rev: BL 5/1/97; BR 5–6/97; SLJ 5/97) [523]

23673 English, June A., and Thomas D. Jones. *Mission: Earth: Voyage to the Home Planet* (4–7). Illus. 1996, Scholastic paper $16.95 (0-590-48571-7).

48pp. The space program is introduced, with special coverage of the flights of the shuttle *Endeavor* in 1994 and its environmental studies. (Rev: BL 10/15/96; SLJ 10/96) [550]

23674 Fallen, Anne-Catherine. *USA from Space* (4–7). Illus. 1997, Firefly LB $19.95 (1-55209-159-7); paper $7.95 (1-55209-157-0). 48pp. Excellent satellite pictures of parts of the earth are contained in this book, which also explains the value of satellite imagery in tracking pollution, population, and natural disasters. (Rev: BL 3/1/98; SLJ 12/97) [917.3]

23675 Farbman, Melinda, and Frye Gaillard. *Space-chimp: NASA's Ape in Space* (4–7). Series: Countdown to Space. 2000, Enslow LB $18.95 (0-7660-1478-9). 48pp. The story of how animals in general have helped the space program and how one chimp's voyage into space contributed to progress. (Rev: BL 8/00; HBG 9/00) [629.4]

23676 Feldman, Heather. *Dennis Tito: The First Space Tourist* (2–3). Series: Space Firsts. 2003, Rosen LB $19.50 (0-8239-6249-0). 24pp. The true story of a 60-year-old man who paid a reported $20 million to spend a week aboard the International Space Station. (Rev: SLJ 3/04) [910]

23677 Feldman, Heather. *Skylab: The First American Space Station* (2–3). Series: Space Firsts. 2003, Rosen LB $19.50 (0-8239-6248-2). 24pp. An interesting look at Skylab and its significance in space exploration. (Rev: SLJ 3/04) [629.44]

23678 Fox, Mary V. *Rockets* (3–6). Illus. Series: Inventors and Inventions. 1996, Benchmark LB $25.64 (0-7614-0063-X). 63pp. Rocket pioneers are profiled, along with their discoveries and the changes these have caused in the modern world. (Rev: BL 3/15/96; SLJ 3/96) [621.43]

23679 Fox, Mary V. *Satellites* (3–6). Illus. Series: Inventors and Inventions. 1996, Marshall Cavendish LB $25.64 (0-7614-0049-4). 63pp. Details in an informal text and many interesting photos the story of satellites, their uses, and their creators. (Rev: BL 7/96; SLJ 8/96) [629.43]

23680 Gaffney, Timothy R. *Secret Spy Satellites: America's Eyes in Space* (4–7). Series: Countdown to Space. 2000, Enslow LB $18.95 (0-7660-1402-9). 48pp. With sharp illustrations and a strong narrative, this book describes U.S. spy satellites, their purposes, and findings. (Rev: BL 9/15/00; HBG 10/01) [629.4]

23681 Gallant, Roy A. *Space Stations* (2–4). Illus. Series: Kaleidoscope. 2000, Marshall Cavendish LB $15.95 (0-7614-1035-X). 48pp. This account briefly covers, in text and color pictures, space stations *Salyut, Skylab,* and *Mir* with a little information on the International Space Station. (Rev: BL 1/1–15/01; HBG 10/01) [629.44]

23682 Goodman, Susan E. *Ultimate Field Trip 5: Blasting Off to Space Academy* (3–5). Illus. Series: Ultimate Field Trip. 2001, Simon & Schuster $17.00 (0-689-83044-0). 48pp. This book follows 16 young people through a week-long training session at the U.S. Space Academy and includes the

children's own comments and some space facts. (Rev: BL 5/1/01; HBG 10/01; SLJ 6/01) [629.45]

23683 Graham, Ian. *The Best Book of Spaceships* (1–4). Illus. 1998, Kingfisher $10.95 (0-7534-5133-6). 33pp. This introduction to space exploration pictures various space vehicles, the Hubble telescope, parts of a space suit, and everyday life in space, while also giving simple explanations of gravity and the solar system. (Rev: BL 12/15/98; HBG 3/99; SLJ 3/99) [629.47]

23684 Hansen, Ole Steen. *Space Flight* (4–7). Illus. Series: The Story of Flight. 2003, Crabtree $17.94 (0-7787-1207-9). 32pp. Double-page spreads present text, feature sidebars, and color photographs covering the people and key events of space flight.

23685 Harris, Alan, and Paul Weissman. *The Great Voyager Adventure: A Guided Tour Through the Solar System* (4–8). Illus. 1990, Simon & Schuster paper $16.95 (0-671-72538-6). 80pp. Two scientists introduce the missions, paths, and discoveries of the Voyager spacecraft. (Rev: BL 2/1/91; SLJ 2/91) [523.4]

23686 Hawcock, David. *The Amazing Pop-Up, Pull-Out Space Shuttle* (3–5). Illus. 1998, DK $19.95 (0-789-43457-1). More for display than circulation, this interactive book about space shuttles contains a four-foot, fold-out model. (Rev: BL 1/1–15/99) [629.5]

23687 Holden, Henry M. *The Tragedy of the Space Shuttle Challenger* (4–8). Illus. Series: Space Flight Adventures and Disasters. 2004, Enslow/MyReportLinks.com LB $25.26 (0-7660-5165-X). 48pp. An account of the ill-fated *Challenger* mission, backed up by a list of Web sites that provide additional information. (Rev: SLJ 2/05) [629.5]

23688 Jefferis, David. *Alien Lifesearch: Quest for Extraterrestrial Organisms* (4–6). Illus. Series: Megatech. 1999, Crabtree LB $14.37 (0-7787-0049-6). 32pp. This work explores the possibility of planets supporting life, alien searches, and UFO mysteries. (Rev: BL 8/99) [516.8]

23689 Johnstone, Michael. *The History News in Space* (3–6). Illus. Series: History News. 1999, Candlewick $16.99 (0-7636-0490-9). 32pp. In a newspaper format, this oversize work covers important news about space and space exploration starting with the ancient Greeks and ending with contemporary achievements. (Rev: BL 10/1/99; HBG 9/99; SLJ 6/99) [629.4]

23690 Kennedy, Gregory. *The First Men in Space* (5–7). Illus. Series: World Explorers. 1991, Chelsea LB $21.95 (0-7910-1324-3). 111pp. This book covers the early years and accomplishments of both Soviet and American space programs. (Rev: SLJ 8/91) [629.44]

23691 Kerrod, Robin. *Dawn of the Space Age* (5–7). Illus. Series: The History of Space Exploration. 2005, World Almanac LB $30.00 (0-8368-5705-4). 48pp. A well-illustrated history of space exploration, from the ideas of Cyrano de Bergerac to the modern Mars probes. Also recommended in this series are *Space Probes, Space Shuttles,* and *Space Stations* (all 2004). (Rev: SLJ 3/05) [629.4]

23692 Kettelkamp, Larry. *ETs and UFOs: Are They Real?* (5–8). Illus. 1996, Morrow $16.00 (0-688-12868-8). Kettelkamp explores the evidence supporting extraterrestrial beings and unidentified flying objects. (Rev: BL 12/15/96; SLJ 1/97) [001.9]

23693 Kettelkamp, Larry. *Living in Space* (5–7). Illus. 1993, Morrow $14.00 (0-688-10018-X). 128pp. Tells how astronauts live in space and discusses plans for space exploration in the future. (Rev: BL 10/1/93; SLJ 9/93) [629.4]

23694 Kupperberg, Paul. *Spy Satellites* (4–8). Illus. Series: Library of Satellites. 2003, Rosen LB $26.50 (0-8239-3854-9). 64pp. The author discusses the history of U.S. spy satellites and how the country has used the information they have gleaned. (Rev: BL 5/15/03; SLJ 1/04) [327.1273]

23695 Landau, Elaine. *Space Disasters* (5–7). Illus. Series: Watts Library. 1999, Watts LB $24.00 (0-531-20345-X); paper $8.95 (0-531-16431-4). 64pp. This work covers four space disasters *Apollo 1, Soyuz 1, Apollo 13,* and the *Challenger.* (Rev: BL 2/1/00; SLJ 2/00) [363.12]

23696 Lassieur, Allison. *Astronauts* (2–4). Series: True Books. 2000, Children's Book Pr. LB $22.00 (0-516-22000-4). 48pp. Explains how astronauts are chosen and what training they receive, provides material on their duties, and profiles some famous astronauts. (Rev: BL 10/15/00) [629.4]

23697 Lassieur, Allison. *The Space Shuttle* (2–4). Series: True Books. 2000, Children's Book Pr. LB $22.00 (0-516-22003-9). 48pp. This book explains what a space shuttle is, its functions, and how it is operated. (Rev: BL 10/15/00) [629.4]

23698 Markle, Sandra. *Pioneering Space* (5–8). 1992, Atheneum LB $14.95 (0-689-31748-4). A look at space travel and how people may succeed in living in space. (Rev: BL 9/1/92; SLJ 2/93) [629.4]

23699 Marsh, Carole. *Unidentified Flying Objects and Extraterrestrial Life* (5–8). Series: Secrets of Space. 1996, Twenty-First Century LB $25.90 (0-8050-4472-8). This book touches on a wide range of topics associated with UFOs, including a history of famous sightings, but the emphasis is on major SETI (Search for Extra Terrestrial Intelligence) projects undertaken to detect alien radio signals. The author concludes that there is no definitive proof of the existence of intelligent life outside Earth. (Rev: BL 12/1/96; SLJ 12/96) [001.9]

23700 Mason, Paul. *Space Race* (3–5). Series: Space Busters. 2002, Raintree LB $17.98 (0-7398-4851-8). 32pp. The Apollo Program is the major focus of this look at efforts to win the space competition. (Rev: HBG 10/02; SLJ 4/02) [629.45]

23701 Murphy, Patricia J. *Exploring Space with an Astronaut* (1–3). Series: I Like Science! 2004, Enslow LB $21.26 (0-7660-2268-4). 24pp. In addition to a discussion of life in space, this title introduces readers to an astronaut and offers a night sky activity. (Rev: SLJ 2/05) [629.5]

23702 Nicolson, Cynthia P. *Exploring Space* (3–5). Illus. Series: Starting with Space. 2000, Kids Can $12.95 (1-55074-711-8). 40pp. A basic book that covers the huge topic of space exploration in a clear, well-organized way. (Rev: BL 12/1/00; HBG 10/01) [629.4]

23703 Ride, Sally, and Susan Okie. *To Space and Back* (3–7). Illus. 1986, Lothrop $19.00 (0-688-06159-1); Morrow paper $12.95 (0-688-09112-1). 96pp. The first American woman in space describes her experiences aboard the shuttle. (Rev: BCCB 10/86; BL 11/1/86; SLJ 11/86)

23704 Schyffert, Bea Uusma. *Man Who Went to the Far Side of the Moon* (3–6). 2003, Chronicle $14.95 (0-8118-4007-7). 80pp. With scrapbook-style illustrations and fascinating details, this story of astronaut Michael Collins, who circled the moon while fellow astronauts Neil Armstrong and Buzz Aldrin walked on its surface, is full of tension and suspense. (Rev: BL 11/1/03; HBG 4/04; SLJ 10/03)

23705 Sherman, Josepha. *Deep Space Observation Satellites* (4–8). Illus. Series: Library of Satellites. 2003, Rosen LB $26.50 (0-8239-3852-2). 64pp. The author discusses the history of U.S. observation satellites and how the country has benefited from their discoveries. (Rev: BL 5/15/03; SLJ 9/01) [522]

23706 Sipiera, Diane M., and Paul P. Sipiera. *Project Apollo* (2–4). Illus. Series: True Books. 1997, Children's Book Pr. LB $22.00 (0-516-20435-1). 48pp. Using large type and many photos, this book chronicles one of the landmark space projects. (Rev: BL 12/1/97; HBG 3/98) [629.45]

23707 Sipiera, Diane M., and Paul P. Sipiera. *Project Mercury* (2–4). Illus. Series: True Books. 1997, Children's Book Pr. $22.00 (0-516-20443-2). 48pp. An account of this space venture told in large type with many clear photos. (Rev: BL 12/1/97; HBG 3/98; SLJ 1/98) [629.45]

23708 Sipiera, Diane M., and Paul P. Sipiera. *Space Stations* (2–4). Illus. 1997, Children's Book Pr. $22.00 (0-516-20450-5). 48pp. This simple account explains what space stations are, their history, the *Mir* station, and plans for the future. (Rev: BL 2/1/98; HBG 3/98) [629.44]

23709 Spangenburg, Ray, and Kit Moser. *Life on Other Worlds* (5–9). Illus. Series: Out of This World. 2002, Watts LB $33.50 (0-531-11895-9); paper $14.95 (0-531-15566-8). 112pp. The possibilities of extraterrestrial life and the efforts to intercept any communications are discussed in this narrative, along with the origins of the solar system and the composition of the planet Mars. (Rev: SLJ 12/02) [001.9]

23710 Steele, Philip. *Space Travel* (4–8). Illus. Series: Pocket Facts. 1991, Macmillan LB $11.95 (0-89686-585-1). 32pp. An introduction to space exploration, packed with basic facts and color illustrations. (Rev: BL 3/15/92) [629.4]

23711 Sullivan, George. *The Day We Walked on the Moon: A Photo History of Space Exploration* (5–8). Illus. 1990, Scholastic paper $4.95 (0-685-58532-8). 80pp. The history of U.S. space exploration, showing the accomplishments of both the United States and the Soviet Union. (Rev: BL 9/1/90; SLJ 2/91) [629.4]

23712 Vogt, Gregory L. *Apollo Moonwalks: The Amazing Lunar Missions* (4–7). Series: Countdown to Space. 2000, Enslow LB $18.95 (0-7660-1306-5). 48pp. This account focuses on the moonwalks during the *Apollo 11* expedition and details what was found. (Rev: BL 8/00; HBG 9/00) [629.4]

23713 Vogt, Gregory L. *Disasters in Space Exploration*. rev. ed. (5–8). 2003, Millbrook LB $25.90 (0-7613-2895-5). 79pp. An illustrated survey of serious accidents that have befallen the U.S. and Soviet space programs, what caused them, and what was learned from them. This revised edition includes the *Columbia* space shuttle disaster of February 2003. (Rev: HBG 4/04; SLJ 3/04) [363.12]

23714 Vogt, Gregory L. *Disasters in Space Exploration* (5–8). Illus. 2001, Millbrook LB $25.90 (0-7613-1920-4). 72pp. Accidents and failures that have marred the success rates of the American and Soviet space programs are covered in interesting detail with many photographs. (Rev: BL 10/1/01; HBG 3/02; SLJ 8/01*) [363.12]

23715 Vogt, Gregory L. *Spacewalks: The Ultimate Adventures in Orbit* (4–7). Series: Countdown to Space. 2000, Enslow LB $18.95 (0-7660-1305-7). 48pp. This gives a history of spacewalks, tells who were the pioneers, and explains their purpose. (Rev: BL 8/00; HBG 9/00) [629.4]

23716 Whitehouse, Patricia. *Working in Space* (1–3). Illus. Series: Space Explorer. 2004, Heinemann LB $24.21 (1-4034-5158-3); paper $6.95 (1-4034-5662-3). 32pp. For young readers, this is a colorful introduction to the kind of work carried out in space. Companion books are *Space Equipment* and *Living in Space* (both 2004). (Rev: SLJ 2/05) [629]

23717 Woodford, Chris. *Space Dramas* (3–5). Illus. Series: Space Busters. 2002, Raintree LB $17.98 (0-7398-4850-X). 32pp. Natural space events such as comet collisions are described along with disasters that have hit manned and unmanned missions outside our atmosphere. (Rev: HBG 10/02; SLJ 4/02) [629.45]

23718 Wunsch, Susi Trautmann. *The Adventures of Sojourner: The Mission to Mars that Thrilled the World* (5–9). 1998, Mikaya LB $22.95 (0-9650493-5-3); paper $9.95 (0-9650493-6-1). 60pp. This book describes the construction of the *Sojourner* rover and its performance on Mars after landing on July 4, 1997. (Rev: SLJ 2/99*) [629.5]

Technology, Engineering, and Industry

General and Miscellaneous Industries and Inventions

23719 Alphin, Elaine M. *Irons* (3–6). Series: Household History. 1998, Carolrhoda LB $16.95 (1-57505-238-5). 48pp. This book traces the history of this important household appliance and its many uses. (Rev: HBG 9/98; SLJ 7/98) [643]

23720 Alphin, Elaine M. *Toasters* (3–6). Series: Household History. 1998, Carolrhoda LB $16.95 (1-57505-243-1). 48pp. A history of toasters, how they operate, and how they are used. (Rev: HBG 9/98; SLJ 7/98) [643]

23721 Alphin, Elaine M. *Vacuum Cleaners* (3–5). Illus. Series: Household History. 1997, Carolrhoda $22.60 (1-57505-018-8). 48pp. A fascinating history of the vacuum cleaner with an explanation of how it works. (Rev: BL 1/1–15/98; HBG 3/98) [683]

23722 Baker, Christopher W. *A New World of Simulators: Training with Technology* (5–8). Illus. 2001, Millbrook LB $23.90 (0-7613-1352-4). 48pp. An introduction to the uses of simulators and their importance in training workers who operate complex technologies such as those found in airplanes, ships, and nuclear power plants. (Rev: BL 8/01; HBG 3/02; SLJ 8/01) [003]

23723 Bredeson, Carmen. *Liftoff!* (K–2). Series: Rookie Read-about Science. 2003, Children's Pr. LB $19.00 (0-516-22499-9); paper $4.95 (0-516-26954-2). 31pp. Conveys all the excitement of the final preparations for the launch of a space shuttle flight. (Rev: SLJ 10/03) [629.4]

23724 Bryant-Mole, Karen. *Toys* (PS–3). Series: Picture This! 1997, Rigby $18.50 (1-57572-057-4). 24pp. Many toys are shown in this heavily illustrated, interactive book. Also use *Games* (1997). (Rev: BL 10/15/97; SLJ 12/97) [745.592]

23725 Casanellas, Antonio. *Great Discoveries and Inventions That Advanced Industry and Technology* (3–5). Illus. by Ali Garousi. Series: Great Discoveries and Inventions. 2000, Gareth Stevens LB $21.27 (0-8368-2583-7). 32pp. A simple overview of inventions that have changed industrial life plus five backup activities. (Rev: HBG 10/01; SLJ 1/01) [608]

23726 *CDs, Super Glue, and Salsa Series 2: How Everyday Products Are Made* (5–10). 1996, Gale LB $158.40 (0-7876-0870-X). This two-volume set tells how 30 everyday products are made, including air bags, bungee cords, contact lenses, ketchup, pencils, soda bottles, and umbrellas. (Rev: BR 1–2/97; SLJ 8/97) [658.5]

23727 Colman, Penny. *Toilets, Bathtubs, Sinks, and Sewers: A History of the Bathroom* (5–8). 1994, Atheneum $16.00 (0-689-31894-4). A fascinating look at sanitation systems and inventions related to personal hygiene from ancient times to the present. (Rev: BCCB 2/95; BL 1/1/95; SLJ 3/95) [643]

23728 Cooper, Elisha. *Ice Cream* (1–3). Illus. 2002, HarperCollins LB $15.89 (0-06-001424-5). 40pp. An entertaining look at the production of ice cream, tracing its way from cow to consumer. (Rev: BL 5/15/02; HB 5–6/02; HBG 10/02; SLJ 5/02) [637.4]

23729 Crump, Donald J., ed. *How Things Work* (5–7). Illus. 1984, National Geographic LB $12.50 (0-87044-430-1). 104pp. A handsome volume that explains the mechanics of a variety of objects from toasters to space shuttles. [600]

23730 Ditchfield, Christin. *Wood* (2–5). Series: True Books — Natural Resources. 2002, Children's Book Pr. LB $23.50 (0-516-22346-1); paper $6.95 (0-516-29370-2). 48pp. This simple account shows the importance of wood in such industries as building and paper-making, and tells how we can protect this resouce from forest fires and pollution. (Rev: BL 10/15/02) [674]

23731 Drake, Jane, and Ann Love. *Mining* (2–4). Illus. by Pat Cupples. Series: America at Work. 1999, Kids Can $12.95 (1-55074-508-5). 31pp. Trish and Jamie learn how the steel blades on their ice skates were made by visiting a mine and then a steel mill and observing the processes in each. (Rev: HBG 4/00; SLJ 11/99) [672]

23732 Englart, Mindi Rose. *Pens* (3–5). Series: Made in the USA. 2002, Gale LB $21.54 (1-56711-487-3). 32pp. The evolution of writing pens is described along with a detailed view of how they are made today. (Rev: BL 9/15/02) [681]

23733 Erlbach, Arlene. *The Kids' Invention Book* (4–6). Illus. 1997, Lerner LB $22.60 (0-8225-2414-7). 64pp. Beginning with 15-year-old Chester Greenwood, who invented earmuffs in 1873, this book introduces over a dozen young people and their inventions. (Rev: BL 2/1/98; HBG 3/98) [608]

23734 Erlbach, Arlene. *Teddy Bears* (3–5). Illus. 1997, Carolrhoda $22.60 (1-57505-019-6); paper $7.95 (1-57505-222-9). 48pp. Provides the history of the teddy bear, discusses the problem of identifying the first maker, and describes the industry today. (Rev: BL 1/1–15/98; HBG 3/98) [745.594]

23735 *Fantastic Feats and Failures* (4–8). Illus. by Jane Kurisu. 2004, Kids Can paper $7.95 (1-55337-634-X). 52pp. Highs and lows of engineering (the Brooklyn Bridge in the first category, for example, and the Tacoma Narrows in the latter) are reviewed in this fascinating large-format book. (Rev: BL 9/15/04) [624.1]

23736 Goldberg, Jan. *Earth Imaging Satellites* (5–9). Series: The Library of Satellites. 2003, Rosen LB $26.50 (0-8239-3853-0). 64pp. A survey of the various satellites and how their images of the earth's surface measure pollution, locate forest fires, find earthquake faults, and measure the size of polar caps. (Rev: BL 11/15/03) [629.46]

23737 Harper, Charise Mericle. *Imaginative Inventions* (2–4). Illus. 2001, Little, Brown $14.95 (0-316-34725-6). 32pp. An imaginative look at the origins of products ranging from chewing gum and doughnuts to roller skates and high-heeled shoes. (Rev: BL 12/15/01; HBG 3/02; SLJ 10/01) [609]

23738 Jones, Charlotte F. *Mistakes That Worked* (4–6). Illus. by John O'Brien. 1994, Doubleday paper $11.95 (0-385-32043-4). 82pp. An entertaining look at successful mistakes, such as the ice cream vendor who ran out of dishes and invented the cone. (Rev: BCCB 10/91; BL 10/15/91*; SLJ 10/91) [609]

23739 Jones, George. *My First Book of How Things Are Made: Crayons, Jeans, Peanut Butter, Guitars and More* (3–5). Illus. 1995, Scholastic $12.95 (0-590-48004-9). 64pp. The manufacturing process of eight objects common in children's lives — including grape jelly, footballs, orange juice, blue jeans, and books — are enumerated. (Rev: SLJ 2/96) [658.5]

23740 Karnes, Frances A., and Suzanne M. Bean. *Girls and Young Women Inventing: Twenty True Stories About Inventors Plus How You Can Be One Yourself* (4–8). Illus. 1995, Free Spirit paper $12.95 (0-915793-89-X). 168pp. The story of Jennifer Donabar and her electric clock invention plus material on other inventions by young women. (Rev: SLJ 12/95) [658.5]

23741 Kassinger, Ruth G. *Iron and Steel: From Thor's Hammer to the Space Shuttle* (5–7). Illus. Series: Material World. 2003, Millbrook LB $25.90 (0-7613-2111-X). 80pp. The different ways in which humans have used and processed iron and steel through the ages is the focus of this book. (Rev: BL 5/15/03; HBG 10/03; SLJ 1/04) [669]

23742 Kerrod, Robin. *New Materials: Present Knowledge, Future Trends* (5–9). Illus. Series: 21st Century Science. 2003, Smart Apple Media LB $18.95 (1-58340-353-1). 44pp. Numerous diagrams, photographs, and drawings help to explain the processing of raw materials and the need to conserve our limited resources. (Rev: SLJ 1/04) [620.11]

23743 Kuklin, Susan. *From Head to Toe: How a Doll Is Made* (1–3). Illus. 1994, Hyperion $15.95 (1-56282-666-2). 32pp. The step-by-step creation of a doll is shown using imaginative photos and a text that introduces each worker. (Rev: BCCB 5/94; BL 5/1/94*; HB 5–6/94; SLJ 5/94) [688.7]

23744 Lampton, Christopher. *Chemical Accident* (4–6). Illus. Series: Disaster Book. 1994, Millbrook LB $19.90 (1-56294-316-2). 48pp. Introduces the chemical industry and explains what happens when chemical accidents occur, their effects, and how to prevent them. (Rev: BL 6/1–15/94; SLJ 4/94) [363.17]

23745 Llewellyn, Claire. *Paper* (2–4). Series: Material World. 2002, Watts LB $23.00 (0-531-14629-4); paper $6.95 (0-531-14831-9). 30pp. A well-illustrated look at paper and the ways it is used; with "Fast Facts," related activities, and a glossary. (Rev: SLJ 5/03) [620.1]

23746 Lockie, Mark. *Biometric Technology* (5–8). Series: Science at the Edge. 2002, Heinemann LB $27.86 (1-58810-701-9). 64pp. Lockie explores the study of biometry and its applications in such areas as voice-speaker identification and facial recognition. (Rev: BL 10/15/02; HBG 3/03) [609]

23747 Macaulay, David. *The New Way Things Work* (4–10). Illus. by author. 1998, Houghton Mifflin $35.00 (0-395-93847-3). 400pp. A popular guide that explains the workings of such machines as telephones, parking meters, bicycles, brakes, automobiles, and all the components used in a computer setup. (Rev: HBG 9/99; SLJ 12/98) [621]

23748 *Machines and Inventions* (5–9). Series: Understanding Science and Nature. 1993, Time-Life $17.95 (0-8094-9704-2). Using a question-and-answer format, double-page spreads look at a variety of inventions including the box camera, printing press, and dynamite. (Rev: BL 1/15/94; SLJ 6/94) [621.8]

23749 Markle, Sandra. *Science Surprises* (4–5). Illus. by June Otani. 1996, Scholastic paper $2.99 (0-590-48401-X). 63pp. Six science surprises — like the invention of photography and the discoveries of penicillin and Velcro/TM — are described, along with 11 fascinating experiments to expand on scientific principles. (Rev: SLJ 7/97) [507]

23750 Mitgutsch, Ali. *From Rubber Tree to Tire* (K–2). Illus. by author. 1986, Carolrhoda LB $18.60

(0-87614-297-8). 24pp. The production of rubber explained in easy text. (Rev: BL 12/15/86)

23751 Mitgutsch, Ali. *From Wood to Paper* (K–2). Illus. by author. 1986, Carolrhoda LB $18.60 (0-87614-296-X). 24pp. Full-color illustrations and easy text explain how paper is made. (Rev: BL 12/15/86)

23752 Nelson, Robin. *From Wax to Crayon* (1–3). Series: Start to Finish. 2003, Lerner LB $18.60 (0-8225-4660-4). 24pp. Traces the creation of a crayon, full-page color photographs. (Rev: HBG 10/03; SLJ 8/03) [741.2]

23753 Nobleman, Marc Tyler. *The Telephone* (2–4). Series: Fact Finders: Great Inventions. 2003, Capstone LB $22.60 (0-7368-2218-6). 32pp. A simple and attractive introduction to the invention of the telephone, how it works, and the effect it has had on society, ending with instructions for making a phone with cups and string. (Rev: SLJ 6/04) [621.385]

23754 Oxlade, Chris. *Glass* (2–3). Series: Materials, Materials, Materials. 2001, Heinemann LB $21.36 (1-58810-154-1). 32pp. Though in a compact format, this book contains lots of information about how glass is manufactured, its history, forms, and uses. (Rev: BL 10/15/01) [666]

23755 Oxlade, Chris. *Paper* (2–3). Series: Materials, Materials, Materials. 2001, Heinemann LB $21.36 (1-58810-156-8). 32pp. An attractive, introductory look at paper, how it is produced, its uses, and its recycling and conservation. (Rev: BL 10/15/01) [676]

23756 Oxlade, Chris. *Plastic* (2–3). Series: Materials, Materials, Materials. 2001, Heinemann LB $21.36 (1-58810-157-6). 32pp. Using a compact format with a color illustration and text on each page, this introductory work explains what plastics are, how they are made, their uses, and their role in conservation. (Rev: BL 10/15/01) [547.7]

23757 Oxlade, Chris. *Rubber* (2–3). Series: Materials, Materials, Materials. 2002, Heinemann LB $21.36 (1-58810-586-5). 32pp. This book provides a simple, clear introduction to rubber, its properties, where it comes from, and its uses in everyday life. (Rev: BL 6/1–15/02) [633.8]

23758 Oxlade, Chris. *Wood* (2–3). Illus. Series: Materials, Materials, Materials. 2001, Heinemann LB $21.36 (1-58810-158-4). 32pp. A discussion of where wood comes from and how it is made into products we use, with photographs. (Rev: BL 10/15/01) [674]

23759 Packard, Mary. *High-tech Inventions: A Chapter Book* (3–7). Series: True Tales. 2004, Children's Pr. LB $21.50 (0-516-23728-4). 48pp. A clear and attractive look at the history of computers and at new and future developments, such as a cockroach that might be used for search-and-rescue operations. (Rev: SLJ 2/05) [004]

23760 Rocker, Megan. *How It Happens at the Fireworks Factory* (K–3). Illus. Series: How It Happens. 2005, Oliver/Clara House $19.95 (1-881508-97-8). 32pp. An inside look at the operation of a factory. Also use *How It Happens at the Cereal Company* (2005).

23761 Romanek, Trudee, and Pat Cupples. *The Technology Book for Girls: And Other Advanced Beings* (3–6). 2001, Kids Can $14.95 (1-55074-936-6); paper $8.95 (1-55074-619-7). 56pp. The workings of a variety of everyday items — remote controls, smoke detectors, lasers, and so forth — are detailed in this lighthearted book that also profiles women with science-based careers. (Rev: HBG 10/01; SLJ 6/01) [604.83]

23762 St. George, Judith. *So You Want to Be an Inventor?* (3–5). Illus. by David Small. 2002, Penguin Putnam $16.99 (0-399-23593-0). 56pp. A spirited and informative look at inventors and their inventions with eye-catching and amusing illustrations. (Rev: BCCB 10/02; BL 8/02; HB 9–10/02; HBG 3/03; SLJ 9/02) [608]

23763 Sandler, Martin W. *Inventors* (5–8). Series: Library of Congress Books. 1996, HarperCollins $24.95 (0-06-024923-4). Concentrating on the late 19th and 20th centuries, the book is divided into sections on inventors, transportation, communication, and entertainment. (Rev: SLJ 2/96) [608]

23764 Skurzynski, Gloria. *Almost the Real Things: Simulation in Your High Tech World* (5–8). 1991, Macmillan LB $16.95 (0-02-778072-4). 64pp. Skurzynski explains how engineers and scientists simulate events from weightlessness to complex animation. (Rev: BCCB 10/91; BL 10/15/91; HB 11–12/91; SLJ 10/91) [620]

23765 Smith, Elizabeth Simpson. *Paper* (4–8). Illus. 1984, Walker LB $10.85 (0-8027-6569-6). 64pp. An exploration of the manufacture and use of paper.

23766 Soucie, Gary. *What's the Difference Between . . . Lenses and Prisms and Other Scientific Things?* (3–6). Illus. by Jeff Domm. 1995, Wiley paper $9.95 (0-471-08626-6). 85pp. This book describes the differences in technology between two similar commodities, e.g., soap and detergent; iron and steel. (Rev: SLJ 2/96) [609]

23767 Stone, Tanya. *Snowboards: From Start to Finish* (3–5). Series: Made in the USA. 2000, Blackbirch LB $16.95 (1-56711-480-6). 32pp. A behind-the-scenes look at how snowboards are made and how special problems with their manufacture were solved. (Rev: BL 9/15/00; HBG 3/01; SLJ 12/00) [796.9]

23768 Stone, Tanya. *Teddy Bears: From Start to Finish* (3–5). Series: Made in the USA. 2000, Blackbirch LB $16.95 (1-56711-479-2). 32pp. This book shows how teddy bears are manufactured and how the finished product is put together and marketed. (Rev: BL 9/15/00; HBG 3/01) [688.7]

23769 Stone, Tanya Lee. *Toothpaste: From Start to Finish* (3–5). Series: Made in the USA. 2001, Blackbirch $16.95 (1-56711-481-4). 32pp. A behind-the-scenes look at a factory where toothpaste is made, with information on the entire manufacturing process from raw materials to finished product. (Rev: BL 8/1/01; HBG 3/02) [668]

23770 Taylor, Barbara. *Be an Inventor* (5–9). Illus. 1987, Harcourt $11.95 (0-15-205950-4); paper $7.95 (0-15-205951-2). A discussion of the process of invention and some examples plus coverage of entries in a *Weekly Reader* invention contest. (Rev: BL 12/15/87; SLJ 3/88) [608]

23771 Thimmesh, Catherine. *Girls Think of Everything* (4–7). Illus. 2000, Houghton Mifflin $16.00 (0-395-93744-2). 64pp. A fresh, breezy account about women whose inventions include the windshield wiper, chocolate chip cookies, and Glo-paper. (Rev: BCCB 5/00; BL 3/15/00; HB 5–6/00; HBG 9/00; SLJ 4/00) [609.2]

23772 Tomecek, Stephen M. *What a Great Idea! Inventions That Changed the World* (3–6). Illus. by Dan Stuckenschneider. 2003, Scholastic $18.95 (0-590-68144-3). 128pp. This attractively illustrated chronology — divided into five time periods — identifies the major inventions of human civilization from the hand axe and wheel to the airplane and computer. (Rev: BL 4/1/03; HBG 10/03; SLJ 4/03) [609]

23773 Wilcox, Jane. *Why Do We Use That?* (4–6). Illus. Series: Why Do We? 1996, Watts LB $20.00 (0-531-14395-3). 31pp. Explains the origin of such common household items as toothbrushes, pencils, garden tools, games, and toys. (Rev: SLJ 3/97) [608]

23774 Wilkinson, Philip, and Jacqueline Dineen. *Art and Technology Through the Ages* (5–8). Illus. Series: Ideas That Changed the World. 1995, Chelsea LB $21.95 (0-7910-2769-4). A survey of the evolution of art and communications, from cave paintings through advanced digital recording and computer graphics. (Rev: BR 5–6/96; SLJ 11/95) [501.4]

23775 Woods, Samuel. *Recycled Paper* (3–5). Series: Made in the USA. 2000, Blackbirch LB $16.95 (1-56711-395-8). 32pp. The process of recycling paper is covered from the collection of old paper to the production of new paper. (Rev: BL 12/15/00; HBG 3/01; SLJ 12/00) [686.2]

23776 Woods, Samuel G. *Crayons: From Start to Finish* (3–5). Photos by Gale Zucker. Series: Made in the USA. 1999, Blackbirch LB $16.95 (1-56711-390-7). 32pp. A visit to the Crayola crayon factory in Pennsylvania where the reader learns about the production of crayons from basic raw material to the finished boxed product. (Rev: HBG 4/00; SLJ 2/00) [681]

23777 Wulffson, Don L. *The Kid Who Invented the Trampoline* (3–6). Illus. 2001, Dutton $15.99 (0-525-46654-1). 128pp. Fifty inventions, arranged alphabetically, range from disposable diapers and Post-It Notes to parking meters and trampolines. (Rev: BL 7/01; HBG 3/02; SLJ 10/01) [609]

23778 Wyatt, Valerie. *Inventions* (3–5). Illus. by Matthew Fernandes. Series: Frequently Asked Questions. 2003, Kids Can $12.95 (1-55337-403-7); paper $6.95 (1-55337-404-5). 40pp. A bright question-and-answer format is used to present information about a variety of inventions. (Rev: HBG 10/03; SLJ 7/03) [608]

Aeronautics and Airplanes

23779 Barton, Byron. *Airplanes* (PS). Illus. by author. 1986, HarperCollins LB $15.89 (0-690-04532-8). 32pp. Simple words and brightly colored artwork portray the roles of airplanes. (Rev: BL 8/86; SLJ 9/86)

23780 Berliner, Don. *Aviation: Reaching for the Sky* (5–8). Illus. Series: Innovators. 1997, Oliver LB $21.95 (1-881508-33-1). 144pp. A thorough history of aviation, beginning with early hot-air balloons and dirigibles and continuing through the Wright Brothers and Sikorsky's helicopter to supersonic jets. (Rev: BL 5/1/97; BR 9–10/97; SLJ 7/97) [629.133]

23781 Bingham, Caroline. *Big Book of Airplanes* (2–5). Illus. 2001, DK $14.95 (0-7894-6521-3). 32pp. A stunning fact-filled picture book about all kinds of planes, from jumbo jets to the tiny "Gee Bee" and the space plane X-33. (Rev: BL 3/1/01; HBG 10/01) [629.133]

23782 Bredeson, Carmen. *Getting Ready for Space* (K–2). Series: Rookie Read-About Science. 2003, Children's Pr. LB $19.00 (0-516-22498-0); paper $4.95 (0-516-26953-4). 31pp. A fascinating look, for beginning readers, at the training involved in preparing astronauts for flights into space. (Rev: SLJ 10/03) [629.45]

23783 Bredeson, Carmen. *Living on a Space Shuttle* (K–2). Series: Rookie Read-about Science. 2003, Children's Pr. LB $19.00 (0-516-22528-6); paper $4.95 (0-516-26955-0). 31pp. Beginning readers will enjoy this overview of what life's like aboard the space shuttle. (Rev: SLJ 10/03) [629.45]

23784 Britton, Tamara L. *Air Force One* (3–5). Series: Symbols, Landmarks, and Monuments. 2004, ABDO LB $15.95 (1-59197-520-4). 32pp. A look at the aircraft that have been used to transport the president, especially Air Force One, which has become a symbol of the office itself. (Rev: SLJ 11/04) [387.7]

23785 Carson, Mary Kay. *The Wright Brothers for Kids: How They Invented the Airplane: 21 Activities Exploring the Science and History of Flight* (4–8). Illus. by Laura D'Argo. 2003, Chicago Review paper $14.95 (1-55652-477-3). 146pp. After an account of the achievements of the Wrights and other early airplane enthusiasts, 21 activities allow readers to investigate some of the basic principles and to learn about equipment and means of communication. (Rev: SLJ 6/03) [629.13]

23786 Cole, Michael D. *TWA Flight 800: Explosion in Midair* (4–8). Series: American Disasters. 1999, Enslow LB $18.95 (0-7660-1217-4). A dramatic account of the air tragedy. (Rev: BL 1/1–15/99; HBG 9/99) [629.136]

23787 Crewe, Sabrina, and Dale Anderson. *The First Moon Landing* (4–6). Series: Events That Shaped America. 2004, Gareth Stevens LB $23.93 (0-8368-3397-X). 32pp. The story of the first moon landing serves as the opening for a well-illustrated and well-organized discussion of America's space program and space exploration in general. (Rev: SLJ 8/04) [629.45]

23788 Darling, David J. *Up and Away: The Science of Flight* (3–6). Illus. 1992, Macmillan LB $17.95 (0-87518-479-0). 64pp. Color photos, clear text, and in-depth experiments explain the science of flight. (Rev: BL 5/1/92; SLJ 3/92) [629.19]

23789 Davis, Meredith. *Up and Away! Taking a Flight* (2–4). Illus. by Ken Dubrowski. 1997, Mondo paper $4.95 (1-57255-214-X). 23pp. An international flight is covered from entering the airport to reaching the final destination. (Rev: SLJ 1/98) [629.133]

23790 Feldman, Heather. *Sputnik: The First Satellite* (2–3). Series: Space Firsts. 2003, Rosen LB $19.50 (0-8239-6244-X). 24pp. An ideal choice for young readers with no memory of the race for space between the Soviet Union and the United States, this book profiles the Soviets' Sputnik 1, the first satellite to be launched into space by humans. (Rev: SLJ 11/03) [629.46]

23791 Feldman, Heather. *Yuri Gagarin: The First Man in Space* (2–3). Series: Space Firsts. 2003, Rosen LB $19.50 (0-8239-6245-8). 24pp. This brief biography includes information (Rev: SLJ 11/03) [629.45]

23792 Gaffney, Timothy R. *Hurricane Hunters* (4–7). Series: Aircraft. 2001, Enslow LB $18.95 (0-7660-1569-6). 48pp. Information on the planes that investigate hurricanes is accompanied by quotations from the pilots and scientists who fly in them. (Rev: HBG 3/02; SLJ 2/02) [551.55]

23793 Green, Carl R. *Apollo 11 Rockets to First Moon Landing: A MyReportLinks. com Book* (4–6). Illus. Series: Space Flight Adventures and Disasters. 2004, Enslow LB $25.26 (0-7660-5164-1). 48pp. Thorough chapter notes support this well-researched account of the dramatic story; Web links extend the book. Also use *The Gemini 4 Spacewalk Mission* (2004). (Rev: BL 10/1/04; SLJ 1/05) [029.45]

23794 Hansen, Ole Steen. *Amazing Flights: The Golden Age* (4–7). Illus. Series: The Story of Flight. 2003, Crabtree LB $23.92 (0-7787-1202-8); paper $8.95 (0-7787-1218-4). 32pp. Double-page spreads present text, feature sidebars, color photographs, and paintings on the people and events of flying after World War I — air races, barnstormers, Lindbergh, and more. (Rev: BL 10/15/03) [629.13]

23795 Hansen, Ole Steen. *Commercial Aviation* (4–7). Series: The Story of Flight. 2003, Crabtree $23.93 (0-7787-1205-2). 32pp. The history and development of airlines and other forms of commercial aviation are discussed with coverage of present-day problems. (Rev: BL 10/15/03) [629.13]

23796 Hansen, Ole Steen. *Flying for Fun* (4–7). Illus. Series: The Story of Flight. 2003, Crabtree $17.94 (0-7787-1211-7). 32pp. Double-page spreads present text, feature sidebars, and color photographs covering recreational flying.

23797 Hansen, Ole Steen. *Helicopters* (4–7). Illus. Series: The Story of Flight. 2003, Crabtree $17.94 (0-7787-1208-7). 32pp. Double-page spreads present helicoptes in text, feature sidebars, and color

photographs. Also use *Weird and Wonderful Aircraft* (2003).

23798 Hansen, Ole Steen. *Modern Military Aircraft* (4–7). Illus. Series: The Story of Flight. 2003, Crabtree LB $23.92 (0-7787-1204-4); paper $8.95 (0-7787-1220-6). 32pp. A highly visual overview of military aircraft since World War II, with a spotter's guide. Also use *Air Combat* and *Seaplanes and Naval Aviation* (both 2003). (Rev: BL 10/15/03) [623.7]

23799 Hart, Philip S. *Flying Free: America's First Black Aviators* (5–9). 1992, Lerner LB $22.60 (0-8225-1598-9). The contributions of African Americans who succeeded against great odds to become aerial performers, combat pilots, and aviation instructors. (Rev: BL 10/15/92; SLJ 1/93) [629.13]

23800 Haskins, Jim. *Black Eagles: African Americans in Aviation* (5–8). Illus. 1995, Scholastic paper $14.95 (0-590-45912-0). 176pp. This account traces the contributions made to aviation history by African Americans from before World War I to the astronaut Mae Jemison. (Rev: BL 2/15/95; SLJ 4/95) [629]

23801 Holden, Henry M. *Living and Working Aboard the International Space Station: A MyReportLinks. com Book* (4–6). Series: Space Flight Adventures and Disasters. 2004, Enslow LB $25.26 (0-7660-5168-4). 48pp. This inside look at space station is supported by thorough chapter notes and extended by Web links. (Rev: BL 10/1/04; SLJ 2/05) [029.44]

23802 Homan, Lynn M., and Thomas Reilly. *Women Who Fly* (5–8). Illus. by Rosalie M. Shepherd. 2004, Pelican $14.95 (1-58980-160-1). 104pp. Women's efforts to establish a foothold in the male-dominated field of aviation are recounted in this book that is suitable for browsers. (Rev: BL 7/04; SLJ 9/04) [629.13]

23803 Hunter, Ryan Ann. *Into the Air: A Timeline of Flight* (2–4). 2003, National Geographic $16.95 (0-7922-5120-2). 48pp. Hunter reaches way back in history to begin her beautifully illustrated history of flight, starting with prehistory's flying reptiles and continuing through the ages to the developments of human flight. (Rev: BL 12/15/03; HBG 4/04)

23804 Hunter, Ryan Ann. *Take Off!* (PS–1). Illus. by Edward Miller. 2000, Holiday House $15.95 (0-8234-1466-3). 32pp. All kinds of airplanes — from the Wright brothers' craft to the 1,000-seat plane of the future — are introduced in this brightly illustrated volume that ends with directions on making a paper airplane. (Rev: BCCB 7–8/00; BL 2/15/00; HBG 9/00; SLJ 9/00) [629.13]

23805 Jefferis, David. *Flight: Fliers and Flying Machines* (3–6). Illus. 1991, Watts $13.95 (0-531-15233-2). 48pp. Beginning with the legend of Icarus, this book chronicles flight to modern times. (Rev: BL 12/15/91; SLJ 3/92) [629.13]

23806 Landau, Elaine. *Air Crashes* (4–7). Series: Watts Library. 1999, Watts LB $24.00 (0-531-20346-8). 63pp. With photographs on almost every page, this book re-creates such air disasters as the Hindenburg, the 1960 Christmas crash, United Airlines Flight 232, and TWA Flight 800. (Rev: SLJ 2/00) [629.136]

23807 Malam, John. *Airport: Behind the Scenes, Check-in to Take-off* (3–5). Illus. Series: Building Works. 2000, Bedrick $16.95 (0-87226-586-2). 32pp. This book supplies an illustrated guided tour of an airport and its facilities plus a history of airports and a glossary of terms. (Rev: BL 7/00; HBG 9/00) [387.7]

23808 Masters, Nancy Robinson. *The Airplane* (4–8). Series: Inventions That Shaped the World. 2004, Watts LB $29.50 (0-531-12360-X). 80pp. An interesting overview of the discovery and development of flight, with discussion of its impact on our lives today and in the future. (Rev: SLJ 2/05) [629.13]

23809 Mayell, Mark. *Tragedies of Space Exploration* (5–8). Illus. Series: Man-Made Disasters. 2004, Gale/Lucent LB $21.96 (1-59018-508-0). 112pp. Interesting details add depth to this account that covers not only the *Challenger* and *Columbia* disasters but also several Russian tragedies. (Rev: SLJ 7/04) [363.12]

23810 Maynard, Chris. *Aircraft* (5–8). Illus. Series: Need for Speed. 1999, Lerner LB $23.93 (0-8225-2485-6); paper $12.75 (0-8225-9855-8). 32pp. Using double-page spreads, this work introduces high-speed aircraft. (Rev: BL 1/1–15/00; HBG 4/00; SLJ 2/00) [629.133]

23811 Miller, Marilyn. *Behind the Scenes at the Airport* (PS–3). Illus. 1996, Raintree LB $21.40 (0-8172-4086-1). 32pp. Using a question-and-answer approach, the activities that make an airport work are pictured. (Rev: BL 4/15/96; SLJ 12/96) [387.7]

23812 Millspaugh, Ben. *Aviation and Space Science Projects* (5–8). Illus. 1992, TAB paper $9.95 (0-8306-2156-3). 133pp. The principles of flight are explored in 19 projects that vary in difficulty and complexity. (Rev: BL 1/15/92; SLJ 6/92) [629.1]

23813 Molzahn, Arlene Bourgeois. *Airplanes* (2–4). Illus. Series: Transportation and Communication. 2003, Enslow LB $18.95 (0-7660-2026-6). 48pp. An easy-to-read history of airplanes and their use in enabling various forms of communication. Also use Ships and Boats (2003). (Rev: HBG 10/03)

23814 O'Brien, Patrick. *Fantastic Flights: One Hundred Years of Flying on the Edge* (3–6). 2003, Walker $17.95 (0-8027-8880-7); paper (0-8027-8881-5). 40pp. Seventeen significant flights — from Otto Lilienthal's glider experiments to the landing of the spacecraft Pathfinder on Mars — are introduced in colorful spreads. (Rev: BL 9/1/03; HBG 4/04; SLJ 11/03) [629.13]

23815 O'Brien, Patrick. *The Hindenburg* (3–6). Illus. 2000, Holt $17.00 (0-8050-6415-X). 32pp. In this picture book for older readers, the story of the Hindenburg dirigible, its designer, Hugo Eckener, and its ultimate destruction are covered effectively. (Rev: BCCB 9/00; BL 9/1/00; HB 9–10/00; HBG 3/01; SLJ 10/00) [629.133]

23816 Old, Wendie. *To Fly: The Story of the Wright Brothers* (3–5). Illus. by Robert Andrew Parker. 2002, Clarion $16.00 (0-618-13347-X). 48pp. An

attractive, large-format introduction to the brothers and their accomplishments with good coverage of the basic principles of flight. (Rev: BL 10/1/02; HB 11–12/02; HBG 3/03; SLJ 10/02) [629.13]

23817 Otfinoski, Steven. *Taking Off: Planes Then and Now* (2–4). Illus. Series: Here We Go! 1996, Benchmark LB $22.79 (0-7614-0407-4). 32pp. A history of airplanes that is notable for its informative large-print text and spectacular photos. (Rev: SLJ 2/97) [629.133]

23818 Oxlade, Chris. *Plane* (4–6). Series: Take It Apart. 2002, Thameside $16.95 (1-930643-95-0). 32pp. Readers get an inside look at the various parts of a plane with cutaway illustrations, in-depth diagrams, and fact boxes. (Rev: BL 1/1–15/03; HBG 3/03) [629.133]

23819 Pallotta, Jerry, and Fred Pallotta. *The Airplane Alphabet Book* (2–4). Illus. by Rob Bolster. 1997, Charlesbridge $16.95 (0-88106-907-8). 32pp. Presents 26 airplanes plus information about the history of flight. (Rev: BL 2/1/97; SLJ 7/97) [629]

23820 Parker, Steve. *What's Inside Airplanes?* (4–8). Illus. Series: What's Inside? 1995, Bedrick LB $17.95 (0-87226-394-0). 45pp. Elaborate illustrations show various types of airplanes and describe their parts, including pistons, propellers, fuel tanks, and landing gear. (Rev: SLJ 12/95) [629.133]

23821 Provensen, Alice, and Martin Provensen. *The Glorious Flight Across the Channel with Louis Bleriot* (1–5). Illus. by authors. 1983, Puffin paper $4.95 (0-317-63651-0). 40pp. The story of a historic flight by a French aviation pioneer. Caldecott Medal winner, 1984.

23822 Rinard, Judith E. *Book of Flight* (4–8). Illus. 2001, Firefly $24.95 (1-55209-619-X); paper $14.95 (1-55209-599-1). 128pp. Significant moments in man's quest for flight each cover a two-page spread in this book based on the Smithsonian's Air and Space Museum collection. (Rev: BL 11/1/01; HBG 3/02; SLJ 12/01) [629.1309]

23823 Rinard, Judith E. *The Story of Flight* (3–6). Illus. 2002, Firefly $16.95 (1-55297-642-4); paper $8.95 (1-55297-694-7). 64pp. From balloon travel to possible manned space flights to Mars, this well-illustrated overview of the history of flight was published in cooperation with the National Air and Space Museum. (Rev: BL 12/15/02; HBG 3/03; SLJ 12/02) [629.1]

23824 Rogers, Hal. *Airplanes* (PS–1). Series: Machines at Work. 2001, Child's World LB $21.36 (1-56766-962-X). 32pp. A beginning reader that uses a simple text and many color photographs to introduce the world of airplanes. (Rev: BL 6/1–15/01; HBG 10/01) [629.133]

23825 Ross, Wilma S. *X-15 Rocket Plane* (3–5). Illus. Series: Those Daring Machines. 1995, Macmillan LB $17.95 (0-89686-831-1). 48pp. A brief history of rocket aircraft is given, with details on the *X-15* and its career. (Rev: BL 2/15/95) [629.133]

23826 Santella, Andrew. *Air Force One* (4–7). Illus. 2003, Millbrook LB $24.90 (0-7613-2617-0). 48pp. An overview of the aircraft that have transported United States presidents, with an inside look at today's Air Force One. (Rev: BL 2/15/03; HBG 10/03; SLJ 8/03) [387.7]

23827 Sherrow, Victoria. *The Hindenburg Disaster: Doomed Airship* (4–8). Series: American Disasters. 2002, Enslow LB $18.95 (0-7660-1554-8). 48pp. Excellent illustrations and a clear text are used to tell the story of the destruction of the mighty German dirigible. (Rev: BL 6/1–15/02; HBG 10/02; SLJ 6/02) [629.133]

23828 Simon, Seymour. *Amazing Aircraft* (1–3). Illus. Series: See More Readers. 2002, North-South $13.95 (1-58717-179-1); paper $3.95 (1-58717-180-5). 32pp. Simon uses concise text and colorful photographs to present information about different types of aircraft from the earliest to Concorde and the Stealth fighter. (Rev: BL 7/02; HBG 3/03; SLJ 8/02) [629.133]

23829 Stein, R. Conrad. *The Spirit of St. Louis* (3–5). Illus. Series: Cornerstones of Freedom. 1994, Children's Book Pr. LB $20.50 (0-516-06682-X). 32pp. The record-breaking, trans-Atlantic flight of Lindbergh is re-created with details on the airplane that he flew. (Rev: BL 1/15/95) [629.13]

23830 Stille, Darlene R. *Airplanes* (2–4). Illus. Series: True Books. 1997, Children's Book Pr. LB $22.00 (0-516-20325-8). 48pp. After a short history of flight, this book describes many airplanes and explains how they work. (Rev: BL 9/15/97) [629.133]

23831 Stille, Darlene R. *Blimps* (2–4). Series: True Books. 1997, Children's Book Pr. LB $22.00 (0-516-20327-4). 48pp. A simple introduction to dirigibles and how they work. (Rev: BL 9/15/97) [629]

23832 Stille, Darlene R. *Helicopters* (2–4). Series: True Books. 1997, Children's Book Pr. LB $22.00 (0-516-20335-5). 48pp. A number of types of helicopters are introduced in a simple format with an explanation of how they work. (Rev: BL 9/15/97) [629]

23833 *The Story of Flight* (4–6). Illus. Series: Voyages of Discovery. 1995, Scholastic $19.95 (0-590-47643-2). 45pp. Using die-cut pages, transparencies, foldouts, and stickers, this attractive book traces the history of flight and airplanes from ancient times to the present. (Rev: SLJ 5/96) [629]

23834 Taylor, Richard L. *The First Unrefueled Flight Around the World: The Story of Dick Rutan and Jeana Yeager* (4–6). Illus. 1994, Watts LB $22.00 (0-531-20176-7). 64pp. The story of this remarkable flight around the world during 1986 in a specially designed plane. (Rev: BL 3/15/95; SLJ 3/95) [629.13]

23835 Tocci, Salvatore. *NASA* (5–7). Illus. Series: Watts Library. 2003, Watts LB $24.00 (0-531-12282-4). 64pp. An accessible introduction to the space agency and its work. (Rev: SLJ 2/04) [629.4]

23836 Weitzman, David. *Jenny: The Airplane That Taught America to Fly* (2–4). Illus. 2002, Millbrook LB $22.90 (0-7613-2565-4). 40pp. Weitzman uses the story of a former pilot telling her grandchildren about their great-grandmother's adventures as a flyer to introduce detailed information about her

early plane and how it was constructed. (Rev: BL 12/1/02; HBG 3/03; SLJ 2/03) [629.133]

23837 Whitehouse, Patricia. *Space Travel* (2–4). Illus. Series: Space Explorer. 2004, Heinemann LB $16.95 (1-4034-5155-9). 32pp. A brief introduction to space travel, with lots of photographs, short paragraphs, and large type. (Rev: BL 1/1–15/05; SLJ 2/05) [910]

23838 Wilkey, Michael. *They Never Gave Up: Adventures in Early Airation* (5–8). Illus. 1998, Orca paper $9.95 (1-55143-077-0). This history of early aviation in North America emphasizes Canadian pioneers, their fortitude, setbacks, and lasting contributions. (Rev: SLJ 9/98) [629.133]

23839 Younkin, Paula. *Spirit of St. Louis* (3–5). Illus. Series: Those Daring Machines. 1995, Macmillan LB $17.95 (0-89686-832-X). 48pp. A description of Lindbergh's airplane and the trans-Atlantic flight that made history. (Rev: BL 2/15/95) [629.13]

23840 Zaunders, Bo. *Feathers, Flaps, and Flops: Fabulous Early Fliers* (3–5). Illus. by Roxie Munro. 2001, Dutton $17.99 (0-525-46466-2). 48pp. After a fascinating introductory chapter that starts with very early and fanciful attempts at flight and ends with the lunar landing, the author profiles lesser-known pioneers including the Montgolfier brothers, Alberto Santos-Dumont, and Jimmy Doolittle. (Rev: BL 8/01; HB 7–8/01; HBG 10/01; SLJ 7/01*) [629.13]

Building and Construction

General

23841 Adam, Robert. *Buildings: How They Work* (4–6). Illus. 1996, Sterling $14.95 (0-8069-0958-7). 48pp. This well-illustrated volume discusses dwellings, from primitive caves to skyscrapers, and their design, materials, and uses. (Rev: BL 2/15/96) [721]

23842 Adkins, Jan. *Bridges: From My Side to Yours* (4–8). Illus. 2002, Millbrook LB $25.90 (0-7613-2510-7). 96pp. An illustrated and very readable history of bridge building — from the Stone Age to the modern age — with information on materials and techniques used and with detailed sketches. (Rev: BL 7/02; HB 7–8/02; HBG 10/02; SLJ 7/02) [624]

23843 *Architecture and Construction* (4–6). Illus. Series: Voyages of Discovery. 1995, Scholastic $19.95 (0-590-47644-0). 45pp. An introduction to architecture that spans the subject from simple shelters to such constructions as a Japanese paper house, skyscrapers, castles, and Frank Lloyd Wright's Fallingwater, with brief text and many illustrations, transparencies, foldouts, stickers, and a spiral binding. (Rev: SLJ 5/96) [720]

23844 Ardagh, Philip. *A Hole in the Road* (PS–K). Illus. by Tig Sutton. Series: British Mighty Machines. 2003, Thameside LB $24.25 (1-931983-02-X). 32pp. A burst water pipe causes a hole in the road and a great deal of digging, earth moving, and paving involving a variety of large machines. (Rev: BL 12/1/02; HBG 3/03) [621.8]

23845 Bial, Raymond. *The Houses* (4–8). Illus. Series: Building America. 2001, Marshall Cavendish LB $25.64 (0-7614-1335-9). 56pp. A history of different types of housing in the United States that includes excellent photographs and drawings. (Rev: BL 3/1/02; HBG 3/02) [392.3]

23846 Boring, Mel. *Incredible Constructions: And the People Who Built Them* (4–7). Illus. 1985, Walker LB $13.85 (0-8027-6560-2). Hoover Dam, the Statue of Liberty, and other structures are featured in this history of engineering marvels. (Rev: BL 6/1/85; SLJ 8/86) [620]

23847 Cash, Terry. *Bricks* (3–5). Illus. by Ed Barber. Series: Threads. 1990, Garrett LB $15.93 (0-944483-68-2). 26pp. The history of bricks, how they are made, and their many uses are explored. (Rev: BL 2/1/91; SLJ 5/91) [666]

23848 Cooper, Elisha. *Building* (K–2). Illus. 1999, Greenwillow $16.00 (0-688-16494-3). 40pp. A small picture book that portrays the process of changing a vacant city lot into an attractive building. (Rev: BCCB 4/99; BL 6/1–15/99; HB 5–6/99; HBG 9/99; SLJ 5/99) [690]

23849 Darling, David. *Spiderwebs to Skyscrapers: The Science of Structures* (5–8). 1991, Dillon LB $13.95 (0-87518-478-2). Discusses foundations, building materials, and styles of construction, in nature and technology, with experiments and color illustrations. (Rev: BL 6/1/92; SLJ 3/92) [624.1]

23850 Delafosse, Claude. *Construction* (PS–2). Illus. Series: First Discovery. 1997, Scholastic paper $12.95 (0-590-93783-9). 24pp. Various forms of building and their processes are introduced simply with interesting visuals that encourage interaction. (Rev: BL 2/15/97) [338.476]

23851 *Do Buildings Have Bones? First Questions and Answers About Buildings* (PS–3). Illus. Series: Time-Life Library of First Questions and Answers. 1995, Time-Life $14.95 (0-7835-0900-6). 48pp. A series of questions and answers supplies basic information about buildings and construction. (Rev: BL 8/95) [720]

23852 Donovan, Sandy. *The Channel Tunnel* (4–7). Series: Great Building Feats. 2003, Lerner LB $27.93 (0-8225-4692-2). 96pp. Using many black-and-white illustrations, diagrams, and maps, this is the exciting story of the underwater engineering marvel that links England and France. (Rev: BL 11/15/03; HBG 10/03; SLJ 11/03) [624.1]

23853 DuTemple, Lesley A. *The Hoover Dam* (4–7). Series: Great Building Feats. 2003, Lerner LB $27.93 (0-8225-4691-4). 96pp. This story traces the dam's construction from the planning stages through its technically difficult and dangerous construction and places this impressive structure in historical context. (Rev: BL 11/15/03; HBG 10/03; SLJ 11/03) [627]

23854 Farbman, Melinda. *Bridges* (2–4). Series: Transportation and Communication. 2001, Enslow LB $18.95 (0-7660-1647-1). 48pp. Basic facts are given on the history of bridges and their present-day construction in this heavily illustrated volume. (Rev: BL 3/15/02; HBG 3/02) [624]

23855 Good, Keith. *Build It! Activities for Setting Up Super Structures* (3–7). Series: Design It! 2000, Lerner LB $21.27 (0-8225-3567-X). 30pp. This book of projects explores ideas for bridges, domes, structures that collapse, and pop-ups in a clear format with good directions. (Rev: HBG 9/00; SLJ 6/00) [624]

23856 Goodman, Susan E. *Skyscraper* (2–5). 2004, Knopf $18.99 (0-375-91309-2). 40pp. The myriad details involved in designing and building a skyscraper are accompanied by personal stories that draw the reader into the process. (Rev: BL 12/1/04*; SLJ 2/05) [720]

23857 Greene, Meg. *The Eiffel Tower* (5–8). Series: Building World Landmarks. 2004, Gale/Blackbirch LB $18.96 (1-56711-315-X). 48pp. The story of the construction of the Eiffel Tower, which when completed in 1899 was the tallest human-made structure in the world. (Rev: SLJ 7/04) [725]

23858 Gresko, Marcia S. *The Grand Coulee Dam* (4–6). Illus. Series: Building America. 1999, Blackbirch LB $17.95 (1-56711-174-2). 48pp. The story of the construction of the Grand Coulee Dam, the largest single producer of hydroelectric power in the U.S. since World War II. (Rev: BL 12/1/99; HBG 4/00; SLJ 2/00) [627]

23859 Hill, Lee S. *Bridges Connect* (1–3). Illus. Series: Building Blocks Books. 1997, Carolrhoda $21.27 (1-57505-021-8). 32pp. Using color photos and a simple text, the structure of bridges is introduced. Also use *Canals Are Water Roads* and *Dams Give Us Power* (both 1997). (Rev: BL 9/15/97; SLJ 7/97) [624]

23860 Hill, Lee S. *Monuments Help Us Remember* (1–3). Illus. Series: Building Blocks Books. 2000, Carolrhoda $21.27 (1-57505-475-2). 32pp. This simple book takes the reader on a tour of the world's most famous monuments, including the Statue of Liberty. (Rev: BL 9/15/00; HBG 3/01) [720]

23861 Hill, Lee S. *Roads Take Us Home* (1–3). Illus. Series: Building Blocks Books. 1997, Carolrhoda LB $21.27 (1-57505-022-6). 32pp. Types of roads and their construction are introduced in color photos and a simple text. Also use *Towers Reach High* (1997). (Rev: BL 9/15/97; SLJ 7/97) [388.1]

23862 Hill, Lee S. *Tunnels Go Underground* (1–3). Illus. Series: Building Blocks Books. 2000, Carolrhoda $21.27 (1-57505-429-9). 32pp. Many different kinds of tunnels are covered, from mining tunnels in Pennsylvania to the tunnel that runs under the English Channel. (Rev: BL 9/15/00; HBG 3/01) [725]

23863 Hunter, Ryan Ann. *Cross a Bridge* (PS–2). Illus. by Edward Miller. 1998, Holiday House LB $15.95 (0-8234-1340-3). A simple picture book that describes various kinds of bridges. (Rev: BL 4/1/98; HBG 9/98; SLJ 3/98) [625]

23864 Hunter, Ryan Ann. *Dig a Tunnel* (PS–2). Illus. by Edward Miller. 1999, Holiday House $15.95 (0-8234-1391-8). 24pp. Beginning with the tunnels dug by animals like moles, this book continues with explanations of how humans have dug tunnels throughout history and the tools they used. (Rev: BCCB 5/99; BL 3/15/99; HBG 9/99; SLJ 4/99) [624.1]

23865 Hunter, Ryan Ann. *Into the Sky* (PS–2). Illus. by Edward Miller. 1998, Holiday House $15.95 (0-8234-1372-1). 32pp. This is a heavily illustrated history of the skyscraper (ending with Japan's planned 196-floor Sky City 1000), with details on how they are built and problems encountered during construction. (Rev: BL 9/15/98; HBG 3/99; SLJ 9/98) [720]

23866 Jefferis, David. *Megastructures* (3–6). Series: Record Breakers. 2003, Raintree LB $25.69 (0-7398-6324-X). 32pp. In this overview of large-scale structures, part of the Record Breakers series, author David Jefferis looks at massive tunnels, bridges, castles, and domes. (Rev: HBG 10/03; SLJ 7/03)

23867 Johmann, Carol A., and Elizabeth J. Rieth. *Bridges! Amazing Structures to Design, Build and Test* (4–6). Illus. Series: Kaleidoscope Kids. 1999, Williamson paper $10.95 (1-885593-30-9). 96pp. Bridge construction, design, mechanics, and maintenance are covered in this paperback that also contains several interesting projects. (Rev: BL 1/1–15/00; SLJ 3/00) [624]

23868 Kent, Peter. *Great Building Stories of the Past* (4–7). Illus. 2002, Oxford $18.95 (0-19-521846-9). 48pp. Provides information on famous architectural marvels (the Great Pyramid, the Great Wall of China, Beauvais Cathedral, the Panama Canal, and others) and how they were built. (Rev: BL 5/15/02; HBG 10/02; SLJ 10/02) [720]

23869 Kirkwood, Jon. *The Fantastic Cutaway Book of Giant Buildings* (4–7). Illus. 1997, Millbrook paper $9.95 (0-7613-0629-3). 40pp. Using double-page spreads, outstanding graphics, and many fact boxes, this book features a wide variety of structures including the Statue of Liberty, the pyramids, the Colosseum, churches, operas houses, Grand Central Station, Munich's Olympic stadium, and skyscrapers. (Rev: BL 4/1/98; HBG 9/98) [720]

23870 Macaulay, David. *Building Big* (5–10). Illus. by author. 2000, Houghton Mifflin $30.00 (0-395-96331-1). 192pp. This book explains the problems posed by ambitious construction projects such as tunnels, bridges, dams, domes, and skyscrapers. (Rev: BL 12/15/00; HB 1–2/01; HBG 3/01; SLJ 11/00) [720]

23871 Macaulay, David. *Unbuilding* (5–8). Illus. by author. 1980, Houghton Mifflin $18.00 (0-395-29457-6); paper $6.95 (0-395-45360-7). 128pp. A book that explores the concept of tearing down the Empire State Building.

23872 Malam, John. *Hospital: From Accident and Emergency to X-ray* (3–5). Series: Building Works. 2000, Bedrick $16.95 (0-87226-585-4). 32pp. Beginning with a large double gatefold that shows a detailed cutaway illustration of a hospital, this heavily illustrated book proceeds to show every part of the hospital in a series of double-page spreads. (Rev: BL 7/00; HBG 9/00; SLJ 9/00) [725]

23873 Malam, John. *Library: From Ancient Scrolls to the World Wide Web* (3–5). Series: Building

Works. 2000, Bedrick $16.95 (0-87226-587-0). 32pp. An outstanding book that first shows the inner workings of a library in a huge double foldout and then proceeds in double-page spreads to describe in detail each part of a library and give a guided tour behind the scenes. (Rev: BL 7/00; HBG 3/01; SLJ 11/00) [027]

23874 Mann, Elizabeth. *The Brooklyn Bridge* (4–7). Illus. Series: Wonders of the World. 1996, Mikaya $19.95 (0-9650493-0-2). 48pp. The story of the building of the Brooklyn Bridge is told through the eyes of a family. (Rev: BL 2/1/97; SLJ 6/97*) [624]

23875 Mann, Elizabeth. *Empire State Building* (3–8). Illus. by Alan Witschonke. Series: Wonders of the World Books. 2003, Mikaya $19.95 (1-931414-06-8). 48pp. With a four-page foldout, period photographs, and full-color illustrations, this story of the skyscraper's construction will please both browsers and report writers. (Rev: BL 2/1/04; SLJ 4/04) [974.7]

23876 Mattern, Joanne. *The Chunnel* (5–8). Series: Building World Landmarks. 2004, Gale/Blackbirch LB $18.96 (1-56711-301-X). 48pp. The story of the long delays and eventual construction of the tunnel under the English Channel, linking England and France, with a focus on the new technology involved. (Rev: SLJ 7/04) [624.1]

23877 Mellentin, Kath. *Let's Build an Airport* (K–3). Illus. 1998, Zero to Ten LB $14.95 (1-84089-026-6). 32pp. From the decision to build an airport to the opening day celebrations this is a step-by-step account of how an airport is built. (Rev: BL 3/1/99; HBG 3/99) [629.136]

23878 Millard, Anne. *Pyramids* (4–6). Illus. 1996, Kingfisher $16.95 (1-85697-674-2). 64pp. The design, construction, and use of pyramids are explained, primarily those found in Egypt. (Rev: BL 5/1/96; SLJ 6/96) [932]

23879 Murray, Julie. *Golden Gate Bridge* (2–3). Illus. Series: All Aboard America. 2003, ABDO LB $14.95 (1-57765-672-5). 24pp. A brief history of the huge San Francisco suspension bridge. (Rev: HBG 10/03; SLJ 11/03) [624]

23880 Neumann, Dietrich. *Joe and the Skyscraper: The Empire State Building in New York City* (2–4). Illus. Series: Where We Live. 2000, Prestel $14.95 (3-7913-2103-X). 32pp. Seen through the eyes of a 16-year-old waterboy, this is the story of the construction of the Empire State Building. (Rev: BL 4/15/00*; SLJ 4/00) [720.483]

23881 Owens, Thomas S. *Football Stadiums* (5–8). Illus. Series: Sports Palaces. 2001, Millbrook LB $25.90 (0-7613-1764-3). 64pp. Rather than highlighting individual stadiums, this book covers general topics such as their design, replacement, funding, amenities, and history. (Rev: BL 4/1/01; HBG 10/01; SLJ 4/01) [796.332]

23882 Oxlade, Chris. *Skyscrapers* (3–5). Series: Building Amazing Structures. 2000, Heinemann LB $14.95 (1-57572-278-X). 32pp. This colorful book introduces skyscrapers and describes their construction, materials, and functions with many examples of historical and contemporary buildings. Also use

Stadiums and *Tunnels* (both 2000). (Rev: HBG 10/01; SLJ 3/01) [720.4]

23883 Ricciuti, Edward R. *America's Top 10 Bridges* (3–7). Illus. Series: America's Top 10. 1997, Blackbirch LB $16.95 (1-56711-197-1). 24pp. Using double-page spreads, this book describes such famous American bridges as the Golden Gate. (Rev: BL 1/1–15/98; HBG 3/98; SLJ 2/98) [388]

23884 Richards, Jon. *Diggers and Other Construction Machines* (1–3). Illus. 1999, Millbrook LB $23.90 (0-7613-0905-5). 40pp. An informative book that highlights all kinds of diggers and allied machinery, along with details of tunnel construction. (Rev: BL 8/99; HBG 9/99) [624.1]

23885 Roza, Greg. *The Incredible Story of Skyscrapers* (3–6). Illus. Series: A Kid's Guide to Incredible Technology. 2004, Rosen LB $19.95 (0-8239-6716-6). 24pp. Discusses the challenges and techniques of building skyscrapers, with a look at some famous buildings and at the potential size of future ones. (Rev: SLJ 2/05) [720]

23886 Severance, John B. *Skyscrapers: How America Grew Up* (5–9). Illus. 2000, Holiday House $18.95 (0-8234-1492-2). 96pp. Beginning with an explanation of the architectural breakthroughs that made the building of skyscrapers possible, this account traces the construction of these buildings from 1851 to the end of the 20th century. (Rev: BL 6/1–15/00; HB 9–10/00; HBG 9/00; SLJ 7/00) [720]

23887 Stone, Lynn M. *Bridges* (3–5). Illus. Series: How Are They Built? 2001, Rourke LB $26.60 (1-58952-135-8). 48pp. How, why, and where bridges are built, with photographs, a glossary, and other features. Also use *Dams* (2001). (Rev: BL 10/15/01) [624]

23888 Stone, Lynn M. *Roads and Highways* (3–5). Series: How Are They Built? 2001, Rourke LB $19.95 (1-58952-138-2). 48pp. Following information on the history of roads, this book gives details on highway construction today, the materials used, and the techniques employed. (Rev: BL 10/15/01) [625.7]

23889 Stone, Lynn M. *Skyscrapers* (3–5). Series: How Are They Built? 2001, Rourke LB $19.95 (1-58952-139-0). 48pp. Background material on skyscrapers is followed by coverage of how they are built, their design, materials used, and present-day practices and concerns. (Rev: BL 10/15/01) [720]

23890 Sturges, Philemon. *Bridges Are to Cross* (3–6). Illus. by Giles Laroche. 1998, Penguin Putnam $15.99 (0-399-23174-4). 32pp. A series of double-page spreads show the beauty and usefulness of bridges — from the Brooklyn Bridge to Chenonceau, where a bridge is part of the castle. (Rev: BL 12/15/98) [624.2]

23891 Woods, Mary B., and Michael Woods. *Ancient Construction: From Tents to Towers* (5–8). Illus. Series: Ancient Technologies. 2000, Runestone LB $25.26 (0-8225-2998-X). 88pp. From Stonehenge and the Colosseum to the Eiffel Tower and the Golden Gate Bridge, this is a history of building and construction. (Rev: BL 9/15/00; HBG 3/01; SLJ 1/01) [720]

23892 Yuan, Margaret Speaker. *The Royal Gorge Bridge* (5–8). Series: Building World Landmarks. 2004, Gale/Blackbirch LB $18.96 (1-56711-352-4). 48pp. Examines the engineering and construction challenges involved in the 1929 construction of Colorado's Royal Gorge Bridge. (Rev: SLJ 7/04) [624.2]

23893 Zaunders, Bo. *The Great Bridge-Building Contest* (3–5). Illus. by Roxie Munro. 2004, Abrams $16.95 (0-8109-4929-6). 32pp. With fine illustrations, this is the story of 19th-century cabinetmaker Lemuel Chenoweth's successful bid to design a bridge. (Rev: BL 12/1/04; SLJ 3/05) [624.2]

Houses

23894 Andersen, Jenna. *How It Happens at the Building Site* (K–3). Illus. Series: How It Happens. 2004, Oliver/Clara House $19.95 (1-881508-95-1). 32pp. An inside look at the work that goes into the construction of a home. (Rev: BL 1/1–15/05) [690]

23895 Gallimard Jeunesse, and Claude Delafosse. *Houses* (PS–2). Series: First Discovery. 1998, Scholastic $11.95 (0-590-38152-0). 24pp. Sturdy plastic pages and overlays are used to describe the construction of a house and its parts. (Rev: BL 9/15/98; HBG 9/98) [690]

23896 Gustafson, Angela. *Imagine a House: A Journey to Fascinating Houses Around the World* (2–5). Illus. 2003, Out of the Box $16.95 (0-9726849-0-5). 32pp. A dozen houses around the world serve as examples of the diversity of architecture and creativity. (Rev: SLJ 2/04) [392.3]

23897 Hill, Lee S. *Homes Keep Us Warm* (1–3). Illus. Series: Building Blocks Books. 2000, Carolrhoda $21.27 (1-57505-430-2). 32pp. This book explores all kinds of homes, from huts made with animal skins to city apartments, farmhouses, and bungalows. (Rev: BL 9/15/00; HBG 3/01) [690]

23898 Komatsu, Yoshio. *Wonderful Houses Around the World* (3–5). Trans. from Japanese by Katy Bridges and Naoko Amemiya. Photos by author. Illus. by Akira Nishiyama. 2004, Shelter $14.95 (0-936070-35-8); paper $8.95 (0-936070-34-X). 43pp. A Mongolian yurt, a Chinese circular tulou, and a Tunisian underground home are among the 10 houses included, with cutaway diagrams and information on decor and inhabitants. (Rev: SLJ 4/05)

23899 Stone, Lynn M. *Houses* (3–5). Series: How Are They Built? 2001, Rourke LB $19.95 (1-58952-137-5). 48pp. After some historical material, this book describes how houses are built today and the materials used. (Rev: BL 10/15/01) [690]

23900 Waters, Jennifer. *Right at Home* (K–2). Illus. Series: Spyglass Books. 2002, Compass Point LB $18.60 (0-7565-0380-9). 24pp. From apartments to grass houses, this is a simple survey of the wide variety in types of housing. (Rev: SLJ 4/03) [690]

1286

Clothing, Textiles, and Jewelry

23901 Bryant-Mole, Karen. *Clothes* (K–3). Illus. Series: Picture This! 1997, Rigby $18.50 (1-57572-149-X). 24pp. This book shows what clothes are made of and which should be worn on different occassions. (Rev: BL 10/15/97) [646]

23902 Carlson, Laurie. *Boss of the Plains: The Hat That Won the West* (K–4). Illus. by Holly Meade. 1998, DK $16.95 (0-7894-2479-7). 32pp. The story of John Batterson Stetson and the broad-brimmed hat he produced to protect himself from the sun and the rain in California. (Rev: BCCB 7–8/98; BL 3/1/98; HB 5–6/98*; HBG 9/98; SLJ 4/98) [338.7]

23903 Carlson, Laurie. *Queen of Inventions: How the Sewing Machine Changed the World* (3–5). Illus. 2003, Millbrook LB $22.90 (0-7613-2706-1). 32pp. The history of the sewing machine and its impact on home and commercial garment-making, with illustrations and photographs. (Rev: BL 2/15/03; HBG 10/03; SLJ 4/03) [681]

23904 Cole, Trish. *Why Do We Wear That?* (4–6). Illus. Series: Why Do We? 1996, Watts LB $19.00 (0-531-14396-1). 31pp. An overview of fashion in clothes from World War II to the present. (Rev: SLJ 3/97) [646]

23905 Dixon, Annabelle. *Wool* (3–5). Illus. by Ed Barber. Series: Threads. 1990, Garrett LB $15.93 (0-944483-73-9). 26pp. The nature of wool, its origins, and its uses are explored in text and pictures. (Rev: BL 2/1/91) [677.31]

23906 Greenberg, Keith E. *Bill Bowerman and Phil Knight: Building the Nike Empire* (3–4). Illus. by Dick Smolinski. Series: Partners. 1994, Blackbirch LB $9.95 (1-56711-085-1). 47pp. The story of the pair who created the Nike empire and the production of the first "waffle sole" using a waffle iron. (Rev: SLJ 1/95) [391]

23907 Hoobler, Dorothy, and Tom Hoobler. *Vanity Rules: A History of American Fashion and Beauty* (5–8). Illus. 2000, Twenty-First Century LB $28.90 (0-7613-1258-7). 160pp. From the painted bodies of early Native Americans to today's body piercing, this is a history of the quest for personal beauty in America. (Rev: BL 4/1/00; HBG 9/00; SLJ 5/00) [391]

23908 Kalman, Bobbie. *18th Century Clothing* (3–6). Illus. Series: Historic Communities. 1993, Crabtree LB $20.60 (0-86505-492-4); paper $7.95 (0-86505-512-2). 32pp. Many illustrations and simple text show how people of all levels of society dressed in the 18th century. A companion volume is: *19th Century Clothing* (1993). (Rev: BL 8/93; SLJ 9/93) [391]

23909 Lattimore, Deborah N. *I Wonder What's Under There? A Brief History of Underwear* (2–4). Illus. by David A. Carter. 1998, Harcourt $15.95 (0-15-276652-9). Using a number of lift-the-flaps, this work gives a history of Western underwear with a few samples from other cultures. (Rev: BL 1/1–15/99; HBG 3/99) [646]

23910 Lawlor, Laurie. *Where Will This Shoe Take You? A Walk Through the History of Footwear* (5–8). Illus. 1996, Walker LB $18.85 (0-8027-8435-6). 144pp. This is a history of footwear, from sandals worn by the ancients to the sneakers popular today. (Rev: BCCB 1/97; BL 11/15/96; SLJ 5/97) [391]

23911 Llewellyn, Claire. *Silk* (2–4). Illus. Series: Material World. 2002, Watts LB $23.00 (0-531-14630-8); paper $6.95 (0-531-14836-X). 30pp. A well-illustrated look at silk, how it is manufactured, and the various types; with "Fast Facts," related activities, and a glossary. (Rev: SLJ 5/03) [677]

23912 MacDonald, Fiona. *Clothing and Jewelry* (5–8). Illus. Series: Discovering World Cultures. 2001, Crabtree paper $8.95 (0-7787-0246-4). 38pp. Readers will enjoy browsing through this heavily illustrated guide that includes fashion, religious garb, and jewelry from around the world. (Rev: SLJ 5/02) [391]

23913 Maze, Stephanie. *I Want to Be a Fashion Designer* (3–6). Illus. Series: I Want to Be. 2000, Harcourt $18.00 (0-15-201862-8); paper $9.00 (0-15-201938-3). 48pp. This large-format book uses double-page spreads to explore the world of fashion design and covers such topics as trade shows, education, and how a designer works. (Rev: BL 3/1/00; SLJ 4/00) [746.9]

23914 Miller, Brandon M. *Dressed for the Occasion: What Americans Wore, 1620–1970* (5–8). 1999, Lerner LB $30.35 (0-8225-1738-8). A fascinating look at men's and women's fashions throughout history and how they reflect society's culture and values. (Rev: BCCB 5/99; BL 4/1/99; SLJ 9/99) [391]

23915 Morris, Ann. *Shoes, Shoes, Shoes* (PS–2). Illus. 1995, Lothrop LB $15.00 (0-688-13667-2). 32pp. Thirty-one shoes from a variety of cultures are identified and pictured. (Rev: BCCB 10/95; BL 10/1/95; SLJ 1/96) [391]

23916 Nelson, Robin. *From Cotton to T-Shirt* (PS–2). Illus. Series: Start to Finish. 2003, Lerner $18.60 (0-8225-4661-2). 24pp. This colorful picture book traces the production of a T-shirt from the picking of the cotton that will be its main ingredient through each step of the manufacturing process. (Rev: BL 4/15/03; HBG 10/03; SLJ 7/03) [633.5]

23917 Nelson, Robin. *From Sheep to Sweater* (1–3). Series: Start to Finish. 2003, Lerner LB $18.60 (0-8225-0716-1). 24pp. This accessible overview follows the process of a wool sweater's creation from shearing of the sheep to finished product. (Rev: HBG 10/03; SLJ 8/03) [746.43]

23918 Nichelason, Margery G. *Shoes* (3–5). Illus. 1997, Carolrhoda $22.60 (1-57505-047-1). 48pp. From the first shoes worn by the Egyptians to today's latest trends, this is the surprising history of footwear through the years. (Rev: BL 1/1–15/98; HB 5–6/97; HBG 3/98) [391.4]

23919 Oxlade, Chris. *Cotton* (2–3). Series: Materials, Materials, Materials. 2002, Heinemann LB $21.36 (1-58810-584-9). 32pp. With a color picture and brief text on each page, this is a basic introduction to cotton and how it is grown, processed, and made into other things. (Rev: BL 6/1–15/02) [633.5]

23920 Oxlade, Chris. *Wool* (2–3). Illus. Series: Materials, Materials, Materials. 2001, Heinemann LB $21.36 (1-58810-159-2). 32pp. Photographs accompany detailed information about where wool comes from and how it is made into products we use. (Rev: BL 10/15/01) [677]

23921 Reynolds, Helen. *Jewelry and Accessories* (3–8). Illus. Series: A Fashionable History of Costume. 2003, Raintree LB $25.70 (1-4109-0029-0). 32pp. Traces the evolution of accessories and jewelry from the beginning of recorded history to the present. (Rev: HBG 10/03; SLJ 9/03) [391.4]

23922 Reynolds, Helen. *The Shoe* (3–8). Illus. Series: A Fashionable History of Costume. 2003, Raintree LB $25.70 (1-4109-0027-4). 32pp. Traces the evolution of footwear from the beginning of recorded history to the present. (Rev: HBG 10/03; SLJ 9/03) [391.4]

23923 Scott, Janine. *Let's Get Dressed: What People Wear* (K–2). Series: Spyglass Books. 2002, Compass Point LB $18.60 (0-7565-0366-3). 24pp. A basic look, for beginning readers, at clothing around the world with information on customs such as wearing black at funerals. (Rev: SLJ 3/03)

23924 Smith, Elizabeth Simpson. *Cloth* (5–8). Illus. 1985, Walker LB $10.85 (0-8027-6577-7). 60pp. The discovery of fiber and how cloth is made. (Rev: BL 8/85; SLJ 11/85) [677.02864]

23925 Straus, Lucy. *The Story of Shoes* (PS). Illus. by Mas Miyamoto. Series: Real Readers. 1989, Raintree LB $19.97 (0-8172-3534-5). 32pp. This easily read account describes how shoes evolved from ancient times. (Rev: BL 2/1/90) [391]

23926 Tythacott, Louise. *Jewelry* (4–8). Illus. Series: Traditions Around the World. 1995, Thomson Learning LB $24.26 (1-56847-229-3). 48pp. A history of jewelry, why it is worn, and the variety of materials and designs used. (Rev: SLJ 7/95) [739.27]

23927 Weaver, Janice. *From Head to Toe: Bound Feet, Bathing Suits, and Other Bizarre and Beautiful Things* (5–8). Illus. by Francis Blake. 2003, Tundra paper $16.95 (0-88776-654-4). 80pp. History and culture are interwoven in this account of fashion fads over the years, mostly in the West. (Rev: SLJ 2/04) [391]

23928 Whitty, Helen. *Protective Clothing* (3–8). Illus. Series: Clothing. 2001, Chelsea LB $17.95 (0-7910-6574-X). 32pp. An interesting look at apparel that includes aprons, armor, firefighting suits, and space suits. Also use *You Are What You Wear* and *Underwear* (both 2001). (Rev: HBG 3/02; SLJ 12/01) [745]

23929 Woods, Samuel G. *Kids' Clothes from Start to Finish* (3–5). Series: Made in the USA. 2001, Blackbirch LB $17.95 (1-56711-483-0). 32pp. The steps in the manufacture of children's clothing from design to finished product are discussed in this colorful, easily read account. (Rev: BL 3/15/02; HBG 3/02) [687]

23930 Woods, Samuel G. *Sneakers: From Start to Finish* (3–5). Illus. Series: Made in the USA. 1999, Blackbirch LB $16.95 (1-56711-393-1). 32pp. The manufacture of sneakers is covered in this book that gives a tour of the New Balance Athletic Shoe factory in Lawrence, Massachusetts. (Rev: BL 12/1/99; HBG 4/00; SLJ 3/00) [685]

23931 Young, Robert. *Sneakers: The Shoes We Choose* (3–5). Illus. 1991, Macmillan LB $14.95 (0-87518-460-X). 64pp. A discussion of the history, development, manufacture, and promotion of the shoes that everybody wears. (Rev: BL 6/1/91; SLJ 7/91) [685.31]

23932 Yue, Charlotte, and David Yue. *Shoes: Their History in Words and Pictures* (5–8). Illus. 1997, Houghton Mifflin $16.00 (0-395-72667-0). 96pp. An in-depth survey of footwear through the ages with emphasis on Western cultures. (Rev: BL 4/1/97; HB 5–6/97; SLJ 4/97) [391]

Computers and Automation

23933 Ahmad, Nyla. *CyberSurfer: The OWL Internet Guide for Kids* (4–7). Illus. 1996, Firefly $19.95 (1-895688-50-7). 72pp. Using cartoons, a fast-paced text, and a demonstration disc, the author introduces the Internet, its functions, and important addresses. (Rev: BL 4/1/96; SLJ 9/96) [004.6]

23934 Baker, Christopher W. *Let There Be Life! Animating with the Computer* (4–6). Illus. 1997, Walker LB $17.85 (0-8027-8473-9). 48pp. An overview of the basics of computer animation, illustrated with stills from feature films, shorts, and commercials. (Rev: BL 1/1–15/98; HBG 3/98) [778.2]

23935 Baker, Christopher W. *Robots Among Us: The Challenges and Promises of Robotics* (5–8). Illus. Series: New Century Technology. 2002, Millbrook LB $23.90 (0-7613-1969-7). 48pp. A lavishly illustrated account that describes the science of robotics, current developments, and what might be expected in the future. (Rev: BL 6/1–15/02; HBG 10/02; SLJ 9/02) [629.8]

23936 Baker, Christopher W. *Scientific Visualization: The New Eyes of Science* (5–8). Illus. Series: New Century Technology. 2000, Millbrook LB $23.90 (0-7613-1351-6). 48pp. This book explores the ways in which computers enable scientists to study the universe and simulate events such as the creation of a black hole. (Rev: BL 4/1/00; HBG 3/01; SLJ 6/00) [507.2]

23937 Brimner, Larry. *E-Mail* (2–5). Illus. Series: True Books. 1997, Children's Book Pr. LB $22.00 (0-516-20332-0). 47pp. A basic introduction to electronic mail that covers topics like what it is, how it works, advantages and disadvantages, symbols, and acronyms. (Rev: SLJ 11/97) [004]

23938 Chorlton, Windsor. *The Invention of the Silicon Chip: A Revolution in Daily Life* (5–8). Series: Point of Impact. 2002, Heinemann LB $25.64 (1-58810-554-7). 32pp. Chorlton explores computers before and after the invention of the chip, introduces key players in the field, and discusses the impact of this new technology on society. (Rev: SLJ 9/02) [621.3815]

23939 Cook, Peter, and Scott Manning. *Why Doesn't My Floppy Disk Flop? And Other Kids' Computer Questions Answered by the CompuDudes* (3–5). Illus. 1999, Wiley paper $12.95 (0-471-18429-2). 90pp. Using a question-and-answer approach, this book covers hardware, software, the Internet, good computer practices, and the future of computers. (Rev: BL 9/1/99) [004]

23940 Douglas, Julie. *The Internet* (2–4). Series: Transportation and Communication. 2002, Enslow LB $18.95 (0-7660-1889-X). 48pp. A basic introduction to the Internet that supplies material on what it is, its history, people behind it, safety while online, and possible future developments. (Rev: BL 9/15/02; HBG 3/03) [004]

23941 Drake, Jim. *Computers All Around Us* (2–4). Illus. Series: Log On to Computers. 1999, Heinemann LB $14.95 (1-57572-784-6). 32pp. An easily read oversize book that explains the many uses of computers in such places as grocery stores, factories, and offices. (Rev: BL 7/99; SLJ 11/99) [004]

23942 Drake, Jim. *Computers and School* (2–4). Series: Log on to Computers. 1999, Heinemann LB $14.95 (1-57572-785-4). 32pp. Large color photographs and a concise text are used to explore the ways computers can be used to gather information to help in school assignments and other related activities. (Rev: BL 7/99; SLJ 12/99) [004]

23943 Drake, Jim. *Play with Computers* (2–4). Series: Log on to Computers. 1999, Heinemann LB $14.95 (1-57572-786-2). 32pp. Double-page spreads featuring large print and bright photographs explore various ways children can use the computer for recreation. (Rev: BL 7/99; SLJ 11/99) [004]

23944 Drake, Jim. *What Is a Computer?* (2–4). Illus. Series: Log on to Computers. 1999, Heinemann LB $14.95 (1-57572-787-0). 32pp. A large-size book that gives a history of computers, explains software and hardware, and relates computers to the everyday life of youngsters. (Rev: BL 7/99; SLJ 12/99) [004]

23945 Fowler, Allan. *It Could Still Be a Robot* (1–3). Illus. Series: Rookie Readers. 1997, Children's Book Pr. LB $19.00 (0-516-20431-9). 32pp. In this easy-to-read book, robots are introduced, along with the tasks they can and cannot do. (Rev: BL 12/1/97; HBG 3/98) [629.8]

23946 Fritz, Sandy. *Robotics and Artificial Intelligence* (5–10). Illus. Series: Hot Science. 2003, Smart Apple LB $19.95 (1-58340-364-7). 48pp. After describing robots' contributions in space, in the workplace, in danger spots, and in medicine, Fritz speculates on the future possibilities. (Rev: BL 12/1/03; HBG 4/04; SLJ 4/04) [629.8]

23947 Gallimard Jeunesse, et al. *Internet* (PS–2). Series: First Discovery. 2000, Scholastic $12.95 (0-439-14825-1). 24pp. A beginning look at computers and the Internet with large illustrations and clear, simple explanations. (Rev: BL 8/00; HBG 3/01; SLJ 11/00) [004]

23948 Gascoigne, Marc. *You Can Surf the Net!* (4–7). Illus. 1996, Penguin Putnam paper $3.99 (0-14-038265-9). 153pp. After introductory material on how to connect into the Internet, there is an annotated directory of Web sites. (Rev: BL 12/15/96) [004.6]

23949 Graham, Ian. *The World of Computers and Communications* (4–7). Series: Inside Look. 2000, Gareth Stevens LB $25.26 (0-8368-2727-9). 48pp. As well as computers, computer peripherals, and networking, this overview of electronic communications touches on recordings, radar, and calculators. (Rev: HBG 10/01; SLJ 3/01) [004]

23950 Herumin, Wendy. *Censorship on the Internet: From Filters to Freedom of Speech* (5 Up). Series: Issues in Focus. 2004, Enslow LB $20.95 (0-7660-1946-2). 128pp. A look at the various ways we restrict the free exchange of information over the Internet and the pros and cons of doing so. (Rev: SLJ 4/04) [303.48]

23951 Hunter, Ryan Ann. *Robots Slither* (K–2). Illus. by Julia Gorton. 2004, Penguin Putnam $14.99 (0-399-23774-7). Introduces in rhyming text and more detailed sidebars various types of robots and the work they can perform today and potentially in the future. (Rev: SLJ 11/04) [629.8]

23952 Jefferis, David. *Artificial Intelligence: Robotics and Machine Evolution* (5–7). Series: Megatech. 1999, Crabtree LB $22.60 (0-7787-0046-1); paper $8.95 (0-7787-0056-9). 32pp. This is a survey of the variety of robotic devices in use at the end of the 20th century, some of the advances that are being made, and a glimpse into the future. (Rev: SLJ 9/99) [004]

23953 Jefferis, David. *Cyber Space: Virtual Reality and the World Wide Web* (4–6). Illus. 1999, Crabtree LB $14.37 (0-7787-0057-7). 32pp. Discusses the world of virtual reality, its uses, applications, and the World Wide Web. (Rev: BL 8/99; SLJ 9/99) [004]

23954 Jefferis, David. *Internet: Electronic Global Village* (4–8). Illus. Series: Megatech. 2001, Crabtree LB $22.60 (0-7787-0052-6); paper $8.95 (0-7787-0062-3). 32pp. An eye-catching look at the development of the Internet and the World Wide Web and their uses in communication and commerce. (Rev: SLJ 6/02)

23955 Jortberg, Charles A. *The Internet* (4–6). Illus. Series: Kids and Computers. 1997, ABDO LB $15.95 (1-56239-727-3). 38pp. A history of the Internet, how to use it, and a listing of important sites for kids. (Rev: BL 6/1–15/97; HBG 3/98) [004.6]

23956 Jortberg, Charles A. *Virtual Reality and Beyond* (4–6). Illus. Series: Kids and Computers. 1997, ABDO LB $22.83 (1-56239-728-1). 38pp. An explanation of virtual reality, its uses at present and in the future, and career possibilities. (Rev: BL 6/1–15/97) [006]

23957 Kazunas, Charnan, and Tom Kazunas. *The Internet for Kids* (2–5). Illus. Series: True Books. 1997, Children's Book Pr. LB $22.00 (0-516-20334-7). 47pp. An easy and attractive introduction that covers such topics as search-and-retrieval tools, networks, addresses, and parts of the Internet, like e-mail and newsgroups. (Rev: SLJ 10/97) [004]

23958 Kazunas, Charnan, and Tom Kazunas. *Personal Computers* (2–4). Illus. Series: True Books. 1997, Children's Book Pr. LB $22.00 (0-516-20338-X). 47pp. Such computer topics as hardware, software, and peripherals are covered, as well as a history of computers from the room-sized ENIAC to modern laptops. (Rev: SLJ 1/98) [004]

23959 Kazunas, Charnan, and Tom Kazunas. *The World Wide Web* (2–4). Illus. Series: True Books. 1997, Children's Book Pr. LB $22.00 (0-516-20345-2). 47pp. Terms like *bookmarks, search engines, hyperlinks,* and *Internet service providers* are explained in this excellent introduction to the World Wide Web. (Rev: SLJ 1/98) [004]

23960 Knittel, John, and Michael Soto. *Everything You Need to Know About the Dangers of Computer Hacking* (5–8). Illus. 2000, Rosen LB $25.25 (0-8239-3034-3). 64pp. This book points out the differences between a hacker and a cracker and, through this, discusses beneficial and harmful computer actions and how to avoid the latter. (Rev: BL 4/1/00; SLJ 5/00) [364.16]

23961 Lampton, Christopher. *Home Page: An Introduction to Web Page Design* (4–8). 1997, Watts LB $23.00 (0-531-20255-0). The author explains to youngsters clearly and simply how they can design their own Web pages using offline time. (Rev: BL 7/97; SLJ 2/98) [005.7]

23962 Lampton, Christopher. *The World Wide Web* (4–8). 1997, Watts LB $23.00 (0-531-20262-3). Aspects of the World Wide Web that would be of value and interest to children are covered, with practical suggestions for effective searching. (Rev: BL 7/97; SLJ 2/98) [025.04]

23963 Lauber, Patricia. *Get Ready for Robots!* (K–3). Illus. by True Kelley. 1987, HarperCollins $12.95 (0-690-04576-X). 32pp. An introduction to robots that work in space, under water, and in factories. (Rev: BCCB 3/87; BL 2/15/87; SLJ 6–7/87)

23964 Lawler, Jennifer. *Cyberdanger and Internet Safety: A Hot Issue* (5–10). Series: Hot Issues. 2000, Enslow LB $21.95 (0-7660-1368-5). 64pp. As well as introducing the Internet, this account explains how people abuse it with hidden identities, threatening or obscene material, loss of privacy, hacking, con tricks, pranks, and hoaxes. (Rev: HBG 3/01; SLJ 1/01) [004.6]

23965 Lindsay, Dave. *Dave's Quick 'n' Easy Web Pages: An Introductory Guide to Creating Web Sites.* 2nd ed. (5–9). Illus. by Sean Lindsay. 2001, Erin $11.95 (0-9690609-8-X). 116pp. Young Dave, Webmaster of the popular Redwall site, gives good, basic information on HTML coding and Web page design. (Rev: SLJ 8/01) [005.7]

23966 Lindsay, Dave, and Bruce Lindsay. *Dave's Quick 'n' Easy Web Pages* (5–9). Illus. 1999, Erin paper $14.95 (0-9690609-7-1). 128pp. Dave, the 14-year-old webmaster of the popular Redwall Abbey Homepage, gives simple, practical, easy-to-follow directions for creating a personal Web page using hypertext markup language (HTML). (Rev: BL 8/99) [005.7]

23967 Loughran, Donna. *Using the Internet Safely* (3–5). Series: Technology and You. 2003, Raintree LB $27.12 (0-7398-4697-3). 48pp. A guide to avioding the pitfalls of the Web, with diagrams and "Techno Tips." (Rev: HBG 10/03; SLJ 4/03) [004.67]

23968 McCormick, Anita Louise. *The Internet: Surfing the Issues* (5–10). Series: Issues in Focus. 1998, Enslow LB $20.95 (0-89490-956-8). 128pp. A guide to the history, mechanics, and use of the Internet that also covers such topics as surfing, child pornography, hate groups, and censorship. (Rev: BL 10/1/98; SLJ 12/98) [004]

23969 Macdonald, Joan Vos. *Cybersafety: Surfing Safely Online* (5–7). Illus. Series: Teen Issues. 2001, Enslow LB $17.95 (0-7660-1580-7). 64pp. Various dangers of venturing online are covered, from viruses and other problems that can infect your computer to activities such as hacking, cyberstalking, and copying software illegally. (Rev: HBG 3/02; SLJ 12/01) [004.6]

23970 Menhard, Francha Roff. *Internet Issues: Pirates, Censors, and Cybersquatters* (5–8). Series: Issues in Focus. 2001, Enslow LB $20.95 (0-7660-1687-0). 128pp. Menhard's overview of problems with filtering, copyright, privacy, and piracy will serve as a good starting point for students, who may need to turn to the Web for the most recent information. (Rev: BL 2/1/02; HBG 10/02; SLJ 2/02) [384.33]

23971 Pascoe, Elaine, adapt. *Virtual Reality: Beyond the Looking Glass* (4–6). Series: New Explorers. 1997, Blackbirch LB $16.95 (1-56711-228-5). 48pp. An interesting look at virtual reality, its nature, history, uses, and future. (Rev: HBG 3/98; SLJ 6/98) [006]

23972 Perry, Robert L. *Build Your Own Website* (4–7). Illus. Series: Watts Library: Computer Science. 2000, Watts LB $24.00 (0-531-11756-1); paper $8.95 (0-531-16469-1). 64pp. Clear, jargon-free language is used to explain the basics of Web site construction under various conditions and for various purposes. (Rev: BL 10/15/00) [005.7]

23973 Perry, Robert L. *Personal Computer Communications* (4–7). Illus. Series: Watts Library: Computer Science. 2000, Watts LB $24.00 (0-531-11758-8); paper $8.95 (0-531-16483-7). 64pp. This work covers such topics as modems, networks, satellite and wireless technology, and the future of communications. (Rev: BL 10/15/00) [004.16]

23974 Roza, Greg. *The Incredible Story of Computers and the Internet* (3–6). Illus. Series: A Kid's Guide to Incredible Technology. 2004, Rosen LB $19.95 (0-8239-6717-4). 24pp. The structure of the Internet and the technology of accessing it are explained in concise terms, with discussion of safe behavior and future developments. (Rev: SLJ 2/05) [004.67]

23975 Sabbeth, Carol. *Kids' Computer Creations: Using Your Computer for Art and Craft Fun* (3–6). Illus. by Loretta Braren. Series: Kids Can! 1995, Williamson paper $12.95 (0-913589-92-6). 158pp. An interesting collection of computer activities grouped by subjects like "Around the House," "Fun and Games," and "Wearable Art." (Rev: SLJ 6/96) [005.1]

23976 Salzman, Marian, and Robert Pondiscio. *Kids On-Line: 150 Ways for Kids to Surf the Net for Fun and Information* (5–9). 1995, Avon paper $5.99 (0-380-78231-6). A leap into cyberspace for both adults and youth, with valuable information plus etiquette for Internet users. (Rev: BL 10/15/95) [004.69]

23977 Selfridge, Benjamin, and Peter Selfridge. *A Kid's Guide to Creating Web Pages for Home and School* (5–10). Illus. 2004, Chicago Review paper $19.95 (1-56976-180-9). 110pp. Simple instructions on creating Web pages using HTML are accompanied by helpful illustrations and sample finished pages. (Rev: SLJ 2/05) [005.7]

23978 Sherman, Josepha. *The History of the Internet* (3–5). Series: Watts Library. 2003, Watts LB $24.00 (0-531-12164-X); paper $8.95 (0-531-16211-7). 63pp. A balanced and attractively illustrated history of the Internet plus discussion of possible future developments. Also use *Internet Safety* (2003). (Rev: SLJ 7/03) [004.67]

23979 Skurzynski, Gloria. *Robots: Your High-Tech World* (4–7). Illus. 1990, Macmillan LB $16.95 (0-02-782917-0). 64pp. An overview of robotics and history and an explanation of how robots work. (Rev: BL 11/15/90; HB 1–2/91; SLJ 9/90) [629.8]

23980 Sonenklar, Carol. *Robots Rising* (3–5). Illus. 1999, Holt $15.95 (0-8050-6096-0). 99pp. A fascinating survey of robotics that includes material on current types of robots and their uses. (Rev: BL 1/1–15/00; HB 3–4/00; HBG 4/00; SLJ 1/00) [629.8]

23981 Spangenburg, Ray, and Kit Moser. *Savvy Surfing on the Internet: Searching and Evaluating Web Sites* (5–8). Illus. Series: Issues in Focus. 2001, Enslow LB $20.95 (0-7660-1590-4). 112pp. Readers are encouraged to view much of the information on the Internet with healthy suspicion and are given advice on efficient searching for and assessment of Web sites. (Rev: HBG 3/02; SLJ 12/01) [004.6]

23982 Steinhauser, Peggy L. *Mousetracks: A Kid's Computer Idea Book* (K–5). Illus. 1997, Tricycle paper $12.95 (1-883672-48-1). 94pp. The 70 projects in this book are designed to help youngsters develop their computer skills. (Rev: SLJ 8/97) [004]

23983 Thomas, Peggy. *Artificial Intelligence* (5–8). Illus. Series: Lucent Library of Science and Technology. 2005, Gale/Lucent LB $22.96 (1-59018-437-8). 112pp. An interesting overview of progress in efforts to create machines that can think like humans. [004]

23984 Trumbauer, Lisa. *Computer Fun Math* (3–5). Illus. by Sydney Wright. Series: Click It! 1999, Millbrook LB $20.90 (0-7613-1504-7); paper $5.95 (0-7613-0996-9). 32pp. This book explains how to create simple graphs, charts, and measuring tools, and how to understand math concepts using the computer. Adult help may be required to understand the directions. Also use *Computer Fun Science.* (Rev: HBG 4/00; SLJ 12/99) [004]

23985 Trumbauer, Lisa. *Free Stuff for Kids on the Net* (3–8). Series: Cool Sites. 1999, Millbrook LB $15.90 (0-7613-1508-X); paper $4.95 (0-7613-1025-8). 74pp. A directory of sites that offer free stuff. Also use *Super Sports for Kids on the Net* (1999). (Rev: HBG 4/00; SLJ 11/99) [004]

23986 Trumbauer, Lisa. *Homework Help for Kids on the Net* (4–8). Series: Cool Sites. 2000, Millbrook LB $17.90 (0-7613-1655-8). 75pp. This useful book lists and describes key sites covering general reference, math, language arts, history, geography, and science. (Rev: HBG 9/00; SLJ 7/00) [004]

23987 Wallace, Mark. *101 Things to Do on the Internet* (4–8). Illus. by Isaac Quaye and Ze Wray. Series: Usborne Computer Guides. 1999, EDC paper $10.95 (0-7460-3294-3). 64pp. Each of the double-page spreads in this book focuses on a single subject or theme to be explored on the Internet such as space, music, games, movies, or weather. (Rev: HBG 9/99; SLJ 6/99) [004]

23988 Ward-Johnson, Chris. *Computers: A Magic Mouse Guide* (1–4). Illus. Series: Magic Mouse Guides. 2003, Enslow LB $17.95 (0-7660-2263-3). 32pp. Suitable for beginners, this basic guide is presented in the form of a story about Ben, Liza, and Hari, who are learning to use a computer. (Rev: HBG 4/04; SLJ 8/03) [004]

23989 Ward-Johnson, Chris. *E-mail: A Magic Mouse Guide* (1–4). Illus. Series: Magic Mouse Guides. 2003, Enslow LB $17.95 (0-7660-2261-7). 32pp. Ben and Hari learn to communicate electronically in this attractive and informative volume for beginners. Also use *Internet* (2003). (Rev: HBG 4/04; SLJ 8/03) [004.692]

23990 Whyborny, Sheila. *Virtual Reality* (5–9). Series: Science on the Edge. 2003, Gale LB $20.95 (1-56711-789-9). 48pp. This book examines the use of sophisticated computer technology to create virtual reality and discusses applications in education, engineering, law, medicine, and entertainment. (Rev: BL 10/15/03; SLJ 2/04) [004]

23991 Williams, Brian. *Computers* (5–8). Illus. Series: Great Inventions. 2001, Heinemann LB $25.64 (1-58810-210-6). 48pp. A chronological look at computers and their predecessors, from the abacus onward, with diagrams and information on the inventors. (Rev: HBG 3/02; SLJ 2/02) [004]

23992 Wolinsky, Art. *Communicating on the Internet* (4–8). Series: The Internet Library. 1999, Enslow LB $17.95 (0-7660-1260-3). 64pp. This book on how to communicate safely and effectively on the Internet includes material on e-mail problems, computer etiquette, chat rooms, and newsgroups. (Rev: HBG 4/00; SLJ 3/00) [004]

23993 Wolinsky, Art. *Creating and Publishing Web Pages on the Internet* (4–8). Series: The Internet Library. 1999, Enslow LB $17.95 (0-7660-1262-X). 64pp. Using many example Web pages, this book gives practical advice on how to create an interesting, well-organized, safe Web page with links to sites for further information. (Rev: HBG 9/00; SLJ 3/00) [004]

23994 Wolinsky, Art. *The History of the Internet and the World Wide Web* (5–9). Illus. Series: Internet Library. 1999, Enslow LB $17.95 (0-7660-1261-1). 64pp. This volume explains how the Internet evolved during the Cold War and how it transfers and distributes information. (Rev: BL 12/15/99; HBG 4/00; SLJ 1/00) [004.67]

23995 Wolinsky, Art. *Internet Power Research Using the Big6 Approach* (4–8). Illus. Series: The Internet Library. 2002, Enslow LB $17.95 (0-7660-2094-0). 64pp. Readers accompany young researchers as they conduct searches using the Big6 method. (Rev: HBG 3/03; SLJ 12/02) [025.04]

23996 Wolinsky, Art. *Locating and Evaluating Information on the Internet* (5–9). Illus. 1999, Enslow LB $17.95 (0-7660-1259-X). 64pp. As well as directions on how to complete successful searches on the Internet, this work tells how to determine the usefulness and credibility of Web pages. (Rev: BL 12/15/99; HBG 4/00; SLJ 1/00) [025.04]

23997 Wolinsky, Art. *Safe Surfing on the Internet* (4–8). Illus. 2003, Enslow LB $17.95 (0-7660-2030-4). 64pp. Wolinksy presents information on safe use of the Internet and topics including proper use of language, copyright, privacy, and plagiarism. (Rev: HBG 10/03; LMC 8–9/03; SLJ 7/03) [004.67]

23998 Woods, Samuel. *Computer Animation* (3–5). Series: Made in the USA. 2000, Blackbirch LB $16.95 (1-56711-396-6). 32pp. This book explains how computers are used to create animation while tracing the production of a computer-animated commercial from start to completion. (Rev: BL 12/15/00; HBG 3/01; SLJ 12/00) [004]

23999 Worland, Gayle. *The Computer* (2–4). Series: Fact Finders: Great Inventions. 2003, Capstone LB $22.60 (0-7368-2215-1). 32pp. An introduction to computers — how they came to be, how they work, and how they have changed daily life — with a final page of facts and an activity (writing a message in binary code). (Rev: SLJ 6/04) [004]

24000 Wright, David. *Computers* (5–8). Series: Inventors and Inventions. 1995, Benchmark LB $25.64 (0-7614-0064-8). A look at the development of the computer, with brief profiles of important people in its history and an examination of the uses of computers in the world today. (Rev: SLJ 6/96) [004]

24001 Yount, Lisa. *Virtual Reality* (5–8). Illus. Series: Lucent Library of Science and Technology. 2004, Gale/Lucent LB $21.96 (1-59018-107-7). 112pp. An interesting exploration of the evolution and potential of virtual reality technology. (Rev: BL 1/1–15/05) [006.8]

Electronics

24002 Bridgman, Roger. *Electronics* (4–8). Illus. Series: Eyewitness Science. 1993, DK LB $15.95 (1-56458-325-4). 64pp. The field of electronics is introduced through full-color graphics, 3-D models, and detailed captions that explain important experi-

ments, equipment, and concepts. (Rev: BL 11/15/93; SLJ 12/93) [621.38]

24003 Hoare, Stephen. *Digital Revolution* (3–6). Series: 20th Century Inventions. 1998, Raintree LB $24.26 (0-8172-4897-8). 48pp. This work introduces digital technology and such applications as compact discs, television, telephones, DVDs, watches, and cameras. (Rev: HBG 3/99; SLJ 2/99) [621.38]

Machinery

24004 Barton, Byron. *Machines at Work* (PS). Illus. 1987, HarperCollins LB $15.89 (0-690-04573-5). 32pp. All sorts of workers — men and women — with picks and drills and cranes and steamrollers parade across the pages. (Rev: BL 10/1/87)

24005 Berger, Melvin, and Gilda Berger. *Telephones, Televisions and Toilets: How They Work and What Can Go Wrong* (2–3). Illus. by Don Madden. Series: Discovery Readers. 1993, Ideals paper $4.50 (0-8249-8608-3). 48pp. Cartoons and simple text explain the inner workings of these three machines. (Rev: BL 7/93) [632.6]

24006 Budd, E. S. *Street Cleaners* (PS–K). Illus. Series: Machines at Work. 2000, Child's World LB $21.36 (1-56766-757-0). 24pp. This simple, informative book pictures street cleaning machinery, shows the inside and outside of this equipment, explains how they keep the streets clean, and tells what happens with the dirt they pick up. (Rev: BL 1/1–15/01; HBG 10/01) [628.4]

24007 Eick, Jean. *Diggers* (PS). Series: Big Machines at Work. 1999, Child's World LB $13.95 (1-56766-529-2). 32pp. Large, clear pictures and a short, simple text explain the parts and uses of diggers. (Rev: BL 4/15/98; HBG 9/99) [629]

24008 Kassinger, Ruth G. *Iron and Steel: From Thor's Hammer to the Space Shuttle* (5–7). Illus. Series: Material World. 2003, Millbrook LB $25.90 (0-7613-21 U-X). 80pp. This interesting title traces the important contributions these metals have made to our civilization and discusses how they are refined and used. (Rev: BL 5/15/03) [669]

24009 Mitchell, Joyce Slayton. *Knuckleboom Loaders Load Logs: A Trip to the Sawmill* (K–3). Illus. 2003, Overlook $14.95 (1-58567-368-4). 40pp. This feast of powerful machines used in the harvesting, hauling, and processing of forest products will appeal to the big-truck crowd. (Rev: BL 2/1/04; HBG 4/04; SLJ 3/04) [634]

24010 Rogers, Hal. *Snowplows* (PS–K). Series: Machines at Work. 2000, Child's World LB $21.36 (1-56766-756-2). 24pp. This book introduces snowplows, their uses, and parts, in a series of clear pictures and a short, simple text. (Rev: BL 1/1–15/01; HBG 10/01) [621]

24011 VanCleave, Janice. *Machines: Mind-Boggling Experiments You Can Turn into Science Fair Projects* (4–6). Illus. Series: Spectacular Science Projects. 1993, Wiley paper $10.95 (0-471-57108-3). 88pp. Simple machines that can be made and operated are featured in this collection of fascinating science projects. (Rev: BL 5/1/93; SLJ 7/93) [521.8]

24012 Wallace, Karen. *Big Machines* (K–2). Series: Eyewitness Reader. 2000, DK LB $12.95 (0-7894-5412-2); paper $3.95 (0-7894-5411-4). 32pp. This book presents pictures and text on such big machines as a crane, a bulldozer, a front loader, a dump truck, and an excavator. (Rev: HBG 9/00; SLJ 7/00) [621.8]

Metals

24013 Oxlade, Chris. *Metal* (2–3). Series: Materials, Materials, Materials. 2001, Heinemann LB $21.36 (1-58810-155-X). 32pp. With color photographs and brief text on each page, the story of what metals are is covered plus where they are found and extracted, and their uses in everyday life. (Rev: BL 10/15/01) [669]

Telegraph, Telephone, and Telecommunications

24014 Byers, Ann. *Communications Satellites* (5–9). Series: The Library of Satellites. 2003, Rosen LB $26.50 (0-8239-3851-4). 64pp. From the first important communications satellites launched in 1962, this account traces the growth of this technology and its possible future developments. (Rev: BL 11/15/03; SLJ 1/04) [001.51]

24015 Hegedus, Alannah, and Kaitlin Rainey. *Bleeps and Blips to Rocket Ships: Great Inventions in Communications* (5–9). Illus. by Bill Slavin. 2001, Tundra paper $17.95 (0-88776-452-5). 88pp. This is a fact-packed and appealing look at the field of communications, with information on history and inventors and inventions as well as suggested activities. (Rev: SLJ 8/01) [609.71]

24016 Maddison, Simon. *Telecoms: Present Knowledge, Future Trends* (5–9). Illus. Series: 21st Century Science. 2003, Smart Apple Media LB $18.95 (1-58340-352-3). 44pp. Numerous diagrams, photographs, and drawings add to this overview of the history of telecommunications and the status of current technology. (Rev: SLJ 1/04) [384]

24017 Mattern, Joanne. *From Radio to the Wireless Web* (2–4). Series: Transportation and Communication. 2002, Enslow LB $18.95 (0-7660-1893-8). 48pp. This book explains the development of telecommunications, present uses, possible future developments, and people involved in its history. (Rev: BL 9/15/02; HBG 10/02) [384]

24018 Mattern, Joanne. *Telephones* (2–4). Series: Transportation and Communication. 2002, Enslow LB $18.95 (0-7660-1888-1). 48pp. From Alexander Graham Bell to the cell phones of today, this is the history of the telephone with material on how it works and possible future developments. (Rev: BL 9/15/02; HBG 10/02) [384.6]

24019 Nelson, Robin. *Communication* (3–6). Series: First Step Nonfiction. 2003, Lerner LB $15.93 (0-8225-4638-8). 24pp. For beginning readers, old and new in the field of communication are paired to good effect on double-page spreads. (Rev: BL 11/15/03; HBG 4/04; SLJ 12/03)

24020 Oxlade, Chris. *Telecommunications* (3–6). Illus. Series: 20th Century Inventions. 1997, Raintree LB $27.12 (0-8172-4813-7). 48pp. After a brief introduction to telecommunications, this account focuses on such topics as the telephone, telegraph, radio, television, and computers. (Rev: BL 6/1–15/97) [384]

24021 Streissguth, Thomas. *Communications: Sending the Message* (5–8). Series: Innovators. 1997, Oliver LB $21.95 (1-881508-41-2). A compact, easy-to-understand history of communication from earliest times, through Gutenberg, Edison, and Marconi, to the present "information highway." (Rev: BR 3–4/98; SLJ 2/98) [001.51]

24022 Wilson, Anthony. *Communications* (4–7). Illus. Series: How the Future Began. 1999, Kingfisher $15.95 (0-7534-5179-4). 64pp. An engaging look at the past, present, and future of communications technologies. (Rev: BL 11/15/99; HBG 4/00) [621.382]

Television, Motion Pictures, Radio, and Recording

24023 Abraham, Philip. *Television and Movies* (4–7). Illus. Series: American Pop Culture. 2004, Children's Pr. LB $22.00 (0-516-24074-9); paper $6.95 (0-516-25946-6). 48pp. Traces the technological and cultural development of TV and movies in the United States. (Rev: SLJ 1/05)

24024 Anderson, Carol D., and Robert Sheely. *Techno Lab: How Science Is Changing Entertainment* (4–6). Illus. 1995, Silver Moon $14.95 (1-881889-63-7). 64pp. This fascinating book traces the influence of science and technology on movies, recorded music, television, video games, and virtual reality. (Rev: BL 1/1–15/96; SLJ 12/95) [791.4]

24025 Biel, Jackie. *Video* (3–6). Illus. Series: Inventors and Inventions. 1996, Marshall Cavendish LB $25.64 (0-7614-0048-6). 63pp. The story of this important modern invention and the people who brought it into being. (Rev: BL 7/96; SLJ 8/96) [621.388]

24026 Dowd, Ned. *That's a Wrap: How Movies Are Made* (5–7). Illus. 1991, Silver Burdett paper $4.95 (0-382-24376-5). 62pp. A behind-the-scenes look at the process of making a movie. (Rev: BCCB 1/92; BL 1/1/92) [791.43]

24027 Englart, Mindi Rose. *Music CDs from Start to Finish* (3–5). Series: Made in the USA. 2001, Blackbirch LB $17.95 (1-56711-485-7). 32pp. From raw material to finished product, this is a behind-the-scenes look at how music compact discs are made. (Rev: BL 3/15/02; HBG 3/02; SLJ 3/02) [321.389]

24028 Feeney, Kathy. *Television* (2–4). Series: Transportation and Communication. 2001, Enslow LB $18.95 (0-7660-1644-7). 48pp. A simple, well-illustrated volume on the history of television, its development, and its many uses. (Rev: BL 3/15/02; HBG 3/02) [384.55]

24029 Hahn, Don. *Disney's Animation Magic: A Behind-the-Scenes Look at How an Animated Film Is Made* (4–6). Illus. 1996, Disney $16.89 (0-7868-5041-8). 96pp. Using a team from the Disney studio as case studies, this book traces the various steps and processes involved in creating an animated film. (Rev: BL 9/1/96; SLJ 10/96) [791.43]

24030 Hamilton, Jake. *Special Effects: In Film and Television* (4–8). Illus. 1998, DK $17.95 (0-7849-2813-X). This is an intriguing glimpse at special effects in film and television, using double-page spreads that each focus on a different aspect of production, such as storyboards, makeup, and stunts. (Rev: BCCB 9/98; BL 8/98) [791.43]

24031 Mattern, Joanne. *The History of Radio* (2–4). Illus. Series: Transportation and Communication. 2002, Enslow LB $18.95 (0-7660-2027-4). 48pp. An easy-to-read account of the invention and long popularity of radio. (Rev: HBG 10/03) [621]

24032 Oxlade, Chris. *Movies* (3–5). Illus. Series: Science Encounters. 1997, Rigby $22.79 (1-57572-088-4). 32pp. An introduction to movie making that gives a basic history of motion pictures, tells how the film camera works, and covers stunts, different types of film, animation, and computer enhancement. (Rev: SLJ 11/97) [791]

24033 Riehecky, Janet. *Television* (3–6). Illus. Series: Inventors and Inventions. 1996, Marshall Cavendish LB $25.64 (0-7614-0045-1). 63pp. The history of television and the people behind its development are chronicled, with many photographs and an informal text. (Rev: BL 7/96; SLJ 8/96) [384.55]

24034 Scott, Elaine. *Movie Magic: Behind the Scenes with Special Effects* (4–7). Illus. 1995, Morrow $16.00 (0-688-12477-1). 96pp. The techniques used to produce special effects in movies are explained, with special material on the use of computers. (Rev: BL 2/15/96) [791.43]

24035 Stwertka, Eve, and Albert Stwertka. *Tuning In: The Sounds of the Radio* (3–5). Illus. by Mena Dolobowsky. Series: At Home with Science. 1993, Simon & Schuster paper $5.95 (0-671-69466-9). 40pp. A history of radio technology. (Rev: SLJ 8/93) [621]

24036 Worland, Gayle. *The Radio* (2–4). Series: Fact Finders: Great Inventions. 2003, Capstone LB $22.60 (0-7368-2217-8). 32pp. A basic history of radio — how it works, who its pioneers were, and the impact it has had on civilization. (Rev: SLJ 6/04) [621.384]

Transportation

General

24037 Bial, Raymond. *The Canals* (4–8). Illus. Series: Building America. 2001, Marshall Caven-

dish LB $25.64 (0-7614-1336-7). 56pp. This history of the U.S. canal system and how it works includes excellent photographs and illustrations that help to explain the technical aspects of canals. (Rev: BL 3/1/02; HBG 3/02; SLJ 2/02*) [386]

24038 Bridges, Sarah. *I Drive a Bulldozer* (PS–2). Illus. by Derrick Alderman and Denise Shea. Series: Working Wheels. 2004, Picture Window $22.60 (1-4048-0613-X). 24pp. A large-format volume that shows a bulldozer driver day at work. Also use *I Drive a Dump Truck* and *I Drive a Snowplow* (2004). (Rev: SLJ 3/05) [621.8]

24039 Brimner, Larry Dane. *Subway: A Brief History of Underground Mass Transit* (3–6). Illus. by Neil Waldman. 2004, Boyds Mills $15.95 (1-59078-176-7). 32pp. This attractively illustrated overview explores the history of New York City's century-old subway, the forces behind its development, and the impact it had on the city. (Rev: BL 10/15/04; SLJ 3/05) [388.4]

24040 Burns, Peggy, and Peter Chrisp. *Travel* (3–5). Illus. Series: Stepping Through History. 1995, Thomson Learning LB $5.00 (1-56847-343-5). 32pp. A history of travel and transportation from ancient days to the superjets of today. (Rev: BL 7/95) [629]

24041 DuTemple, Lesley A. *New York Subways* (4–7). Illus. Series: Great Building Feats. 2003, Lerner LB $27.93 (0-8225-0378-6). 80pp. DuTemple presents the history of the subway system with details of its difficult construction, continuing financial problems, and the damage caused in the destruction of the World Trade Center. (Rev: BL 1/1–15/03; HBG 10/03) [388.4]

24042 Francis, Dorothy. *Our Transportation System* (3–4). Illus. Series: I Know America. 2002, Millbrook LB $23.90 (0-7613-2366-X). 48pp. A historical look at transportation in the United States, from roads to rail, water, and air. (Rev: BL 2/1/02; HBG 10/02) [388]

24043 Goodman, Susan. *Choppers!* (K–2). Photos by Michael J. Doolittle. Series: Step into Reading. 2004, Random LB $11.99 (0-375-92517-1); paper $3.99 (0-375-82517-7). 48pp. For beginning readers, a look at the history and uses of helicopters. (Rev: SLJ 5/05)

24044 Hamilton, John. *Transportation: A Pictorial History of the Past One Thousand Years* (4–7). Illus. Series: The Millennium. 2000, ABDO LB $25.65 (1-57765-361-0). 48pp. A history of 1,000 years of transportation that includes animals, ships, trains, bicycles, motorcycles, cars, airplanes, and spacecraft. (Rev: BL 7/00; HBG 9/00; SLJ 10/00) [388.21]

24045 Macaulay, David. *Underground* (5–10). Illus. by author. 1983, Houghton Mifflin $18.00 (0-395-24739-X); paper $9.95 (0-395-34065-9). An exploration in text and detailed drawings of the intricate network of systems under city streets. [624]

24046 McKendry, Joe. *Beneath the Streets of Boston: Building America's First Subway* (3–5). Illus. 2005, Godine $19.95 (1-56792-284-8). 48pp. A fascinating and detailed look at America's first subway and the social and technical issues surrounding it. (Rev: BL 6/1–15/05) [625.4]

24047 Maynard, Christopher. *Extreme Machines* (3–6). Series: Eyewitness Reader. 2000, DK $12.95 (0-7894-5418-1); paper $3.95 (0-7894-5417-3). 48pp. A visually appealing book that looks at machines from drag cars to helicopters. (Rev: HBG 9/00; SLJ 8/00) [629.04]

24048 Mayo, Margaret. *Choo Choo Clickety-Clack!* (PS–K). Illus. by Alex Ayliffe. 2005, Carolrhoda $14.95 (1-57505-819-7). 32pp. Brightly colored pages with eye-catching graphics and lively words introduce various modes of transportation. (Rev: BL 2/15/05; SLJ 5/05) [629]

24049 Mayo, Margaret. *Dig Dig Digging* (PS). Illus. by Alex Ayliffe. 2002, Holt $14.95 (0-8050-6840-6). 32pp. A rhyming book, with illustrations, about tractors, fire engines, helicopters, and other favorite vehicles. (Rev: BL 5/15/02; HBG 10/02; SLJ 5/02) [629.225]

24050 Nelson, Robin. *Transportation* (3–6). Series: First Step Nonfiction. 2003, Lerner LB $15.93 (0-8225-4636-1). 24pp. Suitable for beginning readers, this book uses double-page spreads to show how transportation has changed over the years. (Rev: BL 11/15/03; HBG 4/04; SLJ 12/03)

24051 Oxlade, Chris. *Fantastic Transport Machines* (3–8). Illus. by David Salariya. Series: X-Ray Picture Books. 1995, Watts LB $25.00 (0-531-14351-1). 48pp. Introduces in double-page spreads such transport machines as motorcycles, cars, trains, ships, submarines, airplanes, and space vehicles. (Rev: SLJ 12/95) [629]

24052 Richards, Julie. *Canals and Aqueducts* (4–6). Illus. Series: Smart Structures. 2003, Smart Apple Media LB $16.95 (1-58340-347-7). 32pp. The science and history of canals, from Venice to Panama, is explored in this well-illustrated book. (Rev: SLJ 3/04) [627]

24053 Sandler, Martin W. *Straphanging in the USA: Trolleys and Subways in American Life* (5–8). Illus. Series: Transportation in America. 2003, Oxford LB $19.95 (0-19-513229-7). 61pp. An interesting, well-illustrated look at urban transportation since the early 19th century. (Rev: HBG 4/04; SLJ 1/04) [388.4]

24054 Tong, Willabel L. *Cars, Boats, Trains, and Planes* (PS). Illus. by Jeff Cummins. 1998, Orchard $12.95 (0-531-30058-7). In this interactive book, all kinds of transportation vehicles pop-out at the reader. (Rev: BL 1/1–15/99) [629.04]

24055 Vandewarker, Paul. *The Big Dig: Reshaping an American City* (5–8). Illus. 2001, Little, Brown $17.95 (0-316-60598-0). 56pp. This is a fascinating and informative account of Boston's massive effort to overhaul its transportation infrastructure. (Rev: BL 10/1/01; HB 1–2/02; HBG 3/02; SLJ 12/01) [624]

24056 Wilkinson, Philip, and Jacqueline Dineen. *Transportation* (5–8). Illus. 1995, Chelsea LB $21.95 (0-7910-2768-6). An informative, simple overview of inventions and changes that created the modern transportation systems of today. (Rev: BR 5–6/96) [629]

Automobiles and Trucks

24057 Anderson, Jenna. *How It Happens at the Truck Plant* (1–3). Photos by Bob Wolfe and Diane Wolfe. Series: How It Happens. 2002, Oliver LB $19.95 (1-881508-93-5). 32pp. How trucks are manufactured is described in text and photographs. (Rev: HBG 10/02; SLJ 12/02) [629]

24058 Barton, Byron. *Trucks* (PS). Illus. by author. 1986, HarperCollins LB $15.89 (0-690-04530-1). 32pp. Bright colors and simple text describe the role of trucks. (Rev: BL 8/86; SLJ 9/86)

24059 Bingham, Caroline. *Big Book of Rescue Vehicles* (PS–3). Illus. 2000, DK $14.95 (0-7894-5454-8). 32pp. An oversize picture book that features such vehicles as fire engines, ambulances, rescue helicopters, lifeboats, and airport fire trucks. (Rev: BL 4/15/00; HBG 9/00) [629.04]

24060 Bingham, Caroline. *Monster Machines* (PS–1). Illus. 1998, DK $14.95 (0-7894-2796-6). 32pp. Double-page spreads feature such monster machines as tow trucks, tractors, jumbo jets, fire engines, and tractor trailers. (Rev: BL 4/1/98; HBG 9/98) [621.8]

24061 Boucher, Jerry. *Fire Truck Nuts and Bolts* (K–3). Illus. 1993, Carolrhoda LB $22.60 (0-87614-783-X); paper $5.95 (0-87614-619-1). 40pp. An examination of the construction of a fire truck and its many parts. (Rev: BL 11/1/93; SLJ 12/93) [629.255]

24062 Burgan, Michael. *The World's Fastest Cars* (3–8). Illus. Series: Built for Speed. 2000, Capstone LB $21.26 (0-7368-0570-2). 48pp. Dragsters, Indie 500 race cars, and other fast automobiles are covered in this visually appealing account that will be attractive to reluctant readers. (Rev: HBG 10/01; SLJ 6/01) [629.228]

24063 Collicutt, Paul. *This Truck* (PS–1). Illus. by author. 2004, Farrar $15.00 (0-374-37496-1). From the front endpapers showing vintage models to the back endpapers' contemporary examples, this is an appealing and colorful look at big rigs. (Rev: SLJ 7/04) [629.224]

24064 Eick, Jean. *Dump Trucks* (PS). Illus. Series: Big Machines at Work. 1999, Child's World LB $13.95 (1-56766-526-8). 32pp. Using many double-page spreads, this work explains the main parts of a dump truck and its functions, particularly in construction. (Rev: BL 4/15/99; HBG 9/99; SLJ 6/99) [732.1]

24065 Eick, Jean. *Forklifts* (PS). Illus. Series: Big Machines at Work. 1999, Child's World LB $13.95 (1-56766-530-6). 32pp. Color photographs and double-page spreads introduce forklifts and the jobs they do. (Rev: BL 4/15/99; HBG 9/99; SLJ 6/99) [621.8]

24066 Eick, Jean. *Garbage Trucks* (PS). Series: Big Machines at Work. 1999, Child's World LB $13.95 (1-56766-528-4). 32pp. This well-illustrated book explores the world of garbage trucks — how they are constructed and how they work. (Rev: BL 4/15/98; HBG 9/99) [629]

24067 Flammang, James M. *Cars* (2–4). Illus. Series: Transportation and Communication. 2001, Enslow LB $18.95 (0-7660-1646-3). 48pp. Car lovers will enjoy this easy-reading look at automobiles past and present with black-and-white and color photographs, a timeline, a glossary, and lists of further resources. (Rev: BL 10/15/01; HBG 3/02) [629.222]

24068 Guttmacher, Peter. *Jeep* (4–6). Illus. Series: Those Daring Machines. 1995, Macmillan LB $17.95 (0-89686-830-3). 48pp. A history of this vehicle and its evolution into today's popular sports automobile. (Rev: BL 2/15/95) [629]

24069 Italia, Bob. *Great Auto Makers and Their Cars* (4–6). Illus. 1993, Oliver LB $18.95 (1-881508-08-0). 160pp. The founders of ten automobile companies — like Henry Ford, Horace Dodge, Karl Benz, Soichiro Honda, and Ferruccio Lamborghini — are profiled with details on the obstacles they overcame. (Rev: SLJ 11/93) [629.2]

24070 Jango-Cohen, Judith. *Dump Trucks* (2–3). Series: Pull Ahead Books. 2002, Lerner LB $22.60 (0-8225-0688-2); paper $5.95 (0-8225-0602-5). 32pp. This colorful account introduces dump trucks, explains their parts, tells how they work, and describes their functions. (Rev: BL 8/02; HBG 3/03) [629.224]

24071 Jango-Cohen, Judith. *Fire Trucks* (2–3). Series: Pull Ahead Books. 2002, Lerner LB $22.60 (0-8225-0077-9); paper $5.95 (0-8225-0604-1). 32pp. After describing the parts of a fire truck in text and pictures, this book explains how they work and the jobs they do. (Rev: BL 8/02; HBG 3/03) [629.255]

24072 Johnstone, Mike. *Monster Trucks* (5–8). Series: Need for Speed. 2002, Lerner LB $28.75 (0-8225-0388-3). 32pp. In stunning action-filled text and pictures, this book highlights huge trucks that weigh thousands of pounds and stand more than 10 feet high. (Rev: BL 8/02; HBG 10/02; SLJ 7/02) [629.225]

24073 Kilby, Don. *On the Road* (PS–K). Illus. 2003, Kids Can $14.95 (1-55337-379-0). 24pp. Double-page spreads show bright illustrations of a variety of trucks and tractors at work. (Rev: BL 5/1/03; HBG 10/03; SLJ 5/03) [629.224]

24074 Levinson, Nancy Smiler. *Cars: A Holiday House Reader, Level 2* (1–3). Trans. and illus. by Jacqueline Rogers. Series: Holiday House Reader. 2004, Holiday House $14.95 (0-8234-1614-3). 32pp. Benz, Daimler, and Ford are among the prominent names in this overview for beginning readers of the early days of the automobile. (Rev: BL 11/15/04) [629.2]

24075 Lichtenheld, Tom. *Everything I Know About Cars: A Collection of Made-up Facts, Educated Guesses, and Silly Pictures About Cars, Trucks, and Other Zoomy Things* (2–4). Illus. 2005, Simon & Schuster $16.95 (0-689-74382-8). 40pp. In this humorous blend of fact and fiction, author-illustrator Tom Lichtenheld offers a compendium of trivia

about real and imaginary cars. (Rev: BL 1/1–15/05) [388.3]

24076 Lichtenheld, Tom. *Everything I Know About Cars: A Collection of Made-Up Facts, Educated Guesses, and Silly Pictures About Cars, Trucks, and Other Zoomy Things* (2–4). Illus. by author. 2005, Simon & Schuster $16.95 (0-689-84382-8). A zany, large-format introduction to cars and car parts, with some facts and some fake facts plus lots of cartoons and good advice on drawing cars. (Rev: BCCB 4/05; BL 1/1–15/05; SLJ 5/05) [388.3]

24077 McKenna, A. T. *Corvette* (5–7). Series: Ultimate Car. 2000, ABDO LB $24.21 (1-57765-127-8). 32pp. This introduction to this famous sports car includes material on its design, construction, and records it has broken. Similar material appears in companion books *Ferrari, Jaguar, Lamborghini, Mustang,* and *Porsche* (all 2000). (Rev: BL 3/1/01; HBG 10/01) [629]

24078 McKenna, A. T. *Jaguar* (5–7). Illus. Series: Ultimate Car. 2000, ABDO LB $15.95 (1-57765-122-7). 32pp. This book traces the history of the Jaguar from 1921 to 2000 with emphasis on current models and how they are made. Also use *Lamborghini* (2000). (Rev: BL 1/1–15/01; HBG 10/01) [629.222]

24079 McKenna, A. T. *Lamborghini* (4–7). Series: Ultimate Car. 2000, ABDO LB $15.95 (1-57765-125-1). 32pp. Car lovers and reluctant readers will enjoy the gleaming photographs of vintage and contemporary Lamborghini and the information on the car's design, engine, and performance. Also use *Porsche* (2000). (Rev: BL 1/01; HBG 10/01; SLJ 5/01) [629.222]

24080 Maurer, Tracy. *License Plates* (3–5). Series: The Rourke Guide to State Symbols. 1999, Rourke LB $19.45 (1-57103-298-3). 48pp. In addition to showing three or four historic and modern license plates for each state, this book includes a few interesting facts and the state motto. (Rev: SLJ 2/00) [629.2]

24081 Mitchell, Joyce Slayton. *Crashed, Smashed, and Mashed* (1–3). Illus. by Steven Borns. 2001, Tricycle $14.95 (1-58246-034-5). 32pp. Photos and text show an automobile junkyard and describe what happens to old cars when they are recycled. (Rev: BL 3/15/01; HBG 10/01) [629.2]

24082 Mitchell, Joyce Slayton. *Tractor-Trailer Trucker: A Powerful Truck Book* (2–5). Illus. 2000, Tricycle $14.95 (1-58246-010-8). 40pp. Written like a manual, this book gives detailed instructions on how to drive and care for a big rig. (Rev: BL 4/1/00; HBG 9/00; SLJ 8/00) [629.2844]

24083 Mitton, Tony. *Cool Cars* (PS–3). Illus. by Ant Parker. 2005, Kingfisher $9.95 (0-7534-5802-0). Rhyming text and cartoon animal drivers add to the appeal of this text about cars of all kinds — race cars, family cars, convertibles, taxis. (Rev: SLJ 6/05)

24084 Molzahn, Arlene Bourgeois. *Fire Engines* (2–4). Illus. Series: Transportation and Communication. 2001, Enslow LB $18.95 (0-7660-1643-9). 48pp. The ever-popular fire engine is featured here, with photographs of vehicles past and present, a timeline, a glossary, and lists of further resources. (Rev: BL 10/15/01; HBG 3/02) [628.9]

24085 Molzahn, Arlene Bourgeois. *Highways and Freeways* (2–4). Series: Transportation and Communication. 2002, Enslow LB $18.95 (0-7660-1891-1). 48pp. This book traces the development of road transportation, how networks developed, their importance, and possible future developments. (Rev: BL 9/15/02; HBG 3/03) [388.11]

24086 Molzahn, Arlene Bourgeois. *Police and Emergency Vehicles* (2–4). Series: Transportation and Communication. 2002, Enslow LB $18.95 (0-7660-1890-3). 48pp. Various kinds of emergency vehicles are presented with background history, details of people who were important in their development, and potential future improvements. (Rev: BL 9/15/02; HBG 3/03) [629.04]

24087 Nelson, Kristin L. *Farm Tractors* (2–3). Series: Pull Ahead Books. 2002, Lerner LB $22.60 (0-8225-0690-4); paper $5.95 (0-8225-0607-6). 32pp. Farm tractors are introduced with many photographs and large-type text and coverage is given on the jobs they do like towing a plow, seed drill, or a mower. (Rev: BL 8/02; HBG 3/03; SLJ 10/02) [621.8]

24088 Nelson, Kristin L. *Monster Trucks* (2–3). Series: Pull Ahead Books. 2002, Lerner LB $22.60 (0-8225-0691-2); paper $5.95 (0-8225-0605-X). 32pp. The world of monster trucks is introduced in color photographs and a simple text with material on their structure and functions such as heavy towing. (Rev: BL 8/02; HBG 3/03) [629.225]

24089 Otfinoski, Steven. *Around the Track: Race Cars Then and Now* (2–4). Series: Here We Go! 1997, Benchmark LB $21.36 (0-7614-0608-5). 32pp. A colorful introduction to race cars, including Grand Prix cars, dragsters, carts, and a few of historical importance. (Rev: HBG 3/98; SLJ 4/98) [629.2]

24090 Otfinoski, Steven. *Behind the Wheel: Cars Then and Now* (2–4). Illus. Series: Here We Go! 1996, Benchmark LB $22.79 (0-7614-0403-1). 32pp. A simple text and spectacular photos are used to give a brief history of cars — past, present, and future. (Rev: SLJ 2/97) [629.27]

24091 Oxlade, Chris. *Car* (4–6). Illus. Series: Take It Apart. 2002, Thameside $16.95 (1-930643-94-2). 32pp. The mechanically minded will particularly enjoy this look at cars that uses cutaways and detailed diagrams to show its major parts. (Rev: BL 1/1–15/03; HBG 3/03) [629.222]

24092 Raby, Philip. *Racing Cars* (5–8). Series: Need for Speed. 1999, Lerner LB $23.93 (0-8225-2487-2). 32pp. Using an attention-getting format with plenty of color, action photographs, and sidebars, this book covers such topics as Le Mans, dragsters, the Camel T, dune buggies, and carting. (Rev: BL 1/1–15/00; HBG 4/00; SLJ 2/00) [623.8]

24093 Relf, Patricia. *Tonka Trucks Night and Day* (PS–2). Illus. by Thomas La Padula. 2000, Scholastic $12.95 (0-439-12196-5). 35pp. This book of trucks covers vehicles that are found on a farm, ones

that are used for moving, and those that are found at an airport. (Rev: HBG 9/00; SLJ 9/00) [629.24]

24094 Robbins, Ken. *Trucks* (PS–2). Illus. 1999, Simon & Schuster $16.00 (0-689-82664-8). 32pp. This book highlights the massive 18-wheelers known as "big rigs" and describes the work of their drivers. (Rev: BCCB 12/99; BL 9/15/99; HB 9–10/99; HBG 4/00) [629.224]

24095 Rogers, Hal. *Buses* (PS–1). Series: Machines at Work. 2001, Child's World LB $21.36 (1-56766-963-8). 32pp. Large type and many full-color illustrations are used in this beginning reader to present different kinds of buses, their structures, and their uses. (Rev: BL 6/1–15/01; HBG 10/01) [629]

24096 Rogers, Hal. *Cars* (PS–1). Series: Machines at Work. 2001, Child's World LB $21.36 (1-56766-964-6). 32pp. An oversize volume that presents different cars and their parts through a simple text, large type, and many attractive photographs. (Rev: BL 6/1–15/01; HBG 10/01) [629]

24097 Sandler, Martin W. *Driving Around the USA: Automobiles in American Life* (4–6). Series: Transportation in America. 2003, Oxford LB $21.95 (0-19-513230-0). 63pp. An examination of the evolution and influence of the automobile through the century that it has been a main feature of American life. (Rev: HBG 4/04; SLJ 4/04) [388.3]

24098 Savage, Jeff. *Demolition Derby* (3–6). Illus. Series: Action Events. 1996, Crestwood LB $14.95 (0-89686-891-5); paper $4.95 (0-382-39294-9). 48pp. Large action photos are used to convey the thrills of this event, which also highlights car designs and builders and members of the driver's team. Also use *Monster Trucks* and *Trucks and Tractor Pullers* (both 1996). (Rev: SLJ 2/97) [629.23]

24099 Schaefer, Margaret A. *Let's Build a Car* (3–5). Illus. by Patrick T. McRae. 1992, Ideals paper $4.95 (0-8249-8536-2). 32pp. Every page shows a step in car production. (Rev: BL 12/1/90) [629.23]

24100 Simon, Seymour. *Seymour Simon's Book of Trucks* (K–4). 2000, HarperCollins LB $15.89 (0-06-028481-1). A highly appealing book that contains pictures and information on a large number of trucks and the various jobs they do. (Rev: HBG 9/00; SLJ 7/00) [629.28]

24101 Simonds, Christopher. *The Model T Ford* (5–7). Illus. Series: Turning Points. 1991, Silver Burdett LB $17.95 (0-382-24122-3); paper $11.00 (0-382-24117-7). 64pp. The invention and development of the Model T and its impact on America. (Rev: BL 1/15/92) [629.222]

24102 Steele, Philip. *Cars and Trucks* (3–4). Illus. Series: Pocket Facts. 1991, Macmillan $15.95 (0-89686-521-5). 32pp. An illustrated compendium of basic facts about cars and trucks. (Rev: SLJ 9/91) [629.28]

24103 Stickland, Paul. *Big Dig: A Pop-Up Construction!* (PS–K). Illus. 2002, Ragged Bear $17.95 (1-929927-41-X). 16pp. This pop-up picture book presents construction trucks readying a site for a new building. (Rev: BL 8/02)

24104 Stille, Darlene R. *Race Cars* (K–2). Illus. Series: Transportation. 2001, Compass Point LB $19.93 (0-7565-0149-0). 32pp. Children's go-karts and adult racing cars zoom past in this overview that includes vivid photographs, basic information, and a glossary. (Rev: BL 12/15/01) [629.228]

24105 Stille, Darlene R. *Trucks* (2–4). Series: True Books. 1997, Children's Book Pr. LB $22.00 (0-516-20343-6). 48pp. A simple but informative guide to various kinds of trucks and their uses with a list of places, including Web sites, to get further information. (Rev: BL 9/15/97) [629.24]

24106 Sturges, Philemon. *I Love Trucks!* (PS). Illus. by Shari Halpern. 1999, HarperCollins $12.95 (0-06-027819-6). 32pp. A number of trucks in action are pictured in this simple introduction. (Rev: BCCB 3/99; BL 2/1/99; HBG 9/99; SLJ 3/99) [629.224]

24107 Walker, Sloan, and Andrew Vasey. *The Only Other Crazy Car Book* (3–6). Illus. 1984, Walker LB $11.85 (0-8027-6517-3). 48pp. There is usually one "oddball" auto to a page, including origins and special features, such as the "Roach Coach," which looks like a giant insect.

24108 Whitman, Sylvia. *Get Up and Go! The History of American Road Travel* (5–8). Illus. 1996, Lerner LB $30.35 (0-8225-1735-3). 88pp. From primitive pathways to modern superhighways, this is a history of American roads and the vehicles that traveled them. (Rev: BL 10/15/96; SLJ 10/96) [388.1]

24109 Wright, David K. *The Story of Chevy Corvettes* (1–3). Series: Classic Cars. 2002, Gareth Stevens LB $19.93 (0-8368-3189-6). 24pp. The Chevrolet Corvette is introduced in color photographs and a simple text that describes its history and design. (Rev: BL 10/15/02; HBG 3/03) [629]

24110 Wright, David K. *The Story of Chevy Impalas* (1–3). Illus. Series: Classic Cars. 2002, Gareth Stevens LB $19.93 (0-8368-3190-X). 24pp. Young automobile enthusiasts will enjoy seeing how the Impala has changed over the years. (Rev: BL 10/15/02; HBG 3/03) [629.222]

24111 Wright, David K. *The Story of Ford Thunderbirds* (1–3). Series: Classic Cars. 2002, Gareth Stevens LB $19.93 (0-8368-3191-8). 24pp. The history of the legendary Ford Thunderbird is told with bright full-page photographs and a simple text. (Rev: BL 10/15/02; HBG 3/03) [629]

24112 Wright, David K. *The Story of Model T Fords* (1–3). Series: Classic Cars. 2002, Gareth Stevens LB $19.93 (0-8368-3192-6). 24pp. The Model T Ford holds a unique position in the history of the automobile. Its story is told here in beginning text and many pictures. (Rev: BL 10/15/02; HBG 3/03) [639]

24113 Wright, David K. *The Story of Porsches* (1–3). Series: Classic Cars. 2002, Gareth Stevens LB $19.93 (0-8368-3193-4). 24pp. The story of this pioneering European automobile is told in full-page color pictures and a beginning-reader text. (Rev: BL 10/15/02; HBG 3/03) [629]

24114 Wright, David K. *The Story of Volkswagen Beetles* (1–3). Illus. Series: Classic Cars. 2002, Gareth Stevens LB $19.93 (0-8368-3194-2). 24pp. Traces the history of the Volkswagen Beetle, from its inception in the 1930s to its revival in the 1990s. (Rev: BL 10/15/02; HBG 3/03) [629.222]

Railroads

24115 Anderson, Peter. *The Transcontinental Railroad* (3–5). Illus. Series: Cornerstones of Freedom. 1996, Children's Book Pr. LB $20.50 (0-516-06635-8). 30pp. The story of building the transcontinental railroad, its many tragedies, and final triumph, with numerous illustrations. (Rev: BL 8/96) [385]

24116 Barton, Byron. *Trains* (PS). Illus. by author. 1986, HarperCollins LB $14.89 (0-690-04534-4). 32pp. Explaining the role of trains for the youngest readers. (Rev: BL 8/86; SLJ 9/86)

24117 *Big Book of Trains: National Railway Museum, York, England* (3–5). Illus. 1998, DK $14.95 (0-7894-3436-9). 32pp. This book begins with the early steam locomotives in England and America and ends with today's bullet trains and monorails. In addition to highlighting in pictures 50 different trains, there is a pullout section on the Channel Tunnel. (Rev: BL 1/1–15/99; HBG 3/99) [625.1]

24118 Cefrey, Holly. *High Speed Trains* (4–7). Illus. Series: Built for Speed. 2001, Children's Book Pr. LB $20.00 (0-516-23157-X); paper $6.95 (0-516-23260-6). 48pp. Train fans will enjoy this attractive overview of high-speed rail in various countries, with information on history, design, and future trends. (Rev: BL 12/1/01) [385]

24119 Crews, Donald. *Freight Train* (PS–K). Illus. by author. 1978, Greenwillow $15.93 (0-688-84165-1); Morrow paper $5.95 (0-688-11701-5). 32pp. A description in text and pictures of the various cars included in a freight train, from engine to caboose.

24120 Gallimard Jeunesse. *Trains* (PS–2). Illus. Series: First Discovery. 1998, Scholastic $11.95 (0-590-38156-3). 24pp. This colorful book uses a number of overlays to answer basic questions about a variety of trains. (Rev: BL 9/15/98; HBG 9/98) [625.1]

24121 Gibbons, Gail. *Trains* (PS–1). Illus. by author. 1987, Holiday House LB $16.95 (0-8234-0640-7); paper $6.95 (0-8234-0699-7). 32pp. Describing the essentials of train transportation. (Rev: BL 5/1/87; SLJ 5/87)

24122 Houghton, Gillian. *The Transcontinental Railroad: A Primary Source History of America's First Coast-to-Coast Railroad* (4–8). Series: Primary Sources in American History. 2003, Rosen LB $29.25 (0-8239-3684-8). 64pp. Timelines and reproductions of period photographs and relevant items add to the narrative in this introduction to the planning and construction of the railroad in the mid-19th century. (Rev: SLJ 5/03) [385]

24123 Kay, Verla. *Iron Horses* (K–4). Illus. by Michael McCurdy. 1999, Penguin Putnam $15.99

(0-399-23119-6). 32pp. In double-page spreads, illustrated with scratchboard drawings, this picture book portrays the labor, hardships, and excitement of constructing the transcontinental railroad. (Rev: BCCB 7–8/99; BL 6/1–15/99; HB 7–8/99; HBG 9/99; SLJ 7/99) [625.4]

24124 McNeese, Tim. *America's First Railroads* (4–8). Illus. by Chris Duke. Series: Americans on the Move. 1993, Macmillan LB $11.95 (0-89686-729-3). 48pp. A history of early railroads and their impact on U.S. history. (Rev: SLJ 8/93) [385]

24125 Maynard, Chris. *High-Speed Trains* (5–8). Series: Need for Speed. 2002, Lerner LB $28.75 (0-8225-0387-5). 32pp. This action-packed book looks at fast trains from around the world, propelled by steam, oil, magnets, and electricity. (Rev: BL 8/02; HBG 10/02) [625.1]

24126 Meltzer, Milton. *Hear That Train Whistle Blow! How the Railroad Changed the World* (5–9). Series: Landmark Books. 2004, Random LB $20.95 (0-375-91563-X). 176pp. In this fascinating historical survey full of period drawings and photographs, Meltzer examines the dramatic ways in which the railroad affected our lives and questions whether the progress achieved was worth the suffering caused. (Rev: BL 9/15/04; SLJ 10/04) [385]

24127 Murphy, Jim. *Across America on an Emigrant Train* (5–8). Illus. 1993, Clarion $17.00 (0-395-63390-7). 150pp. The cross-country train trip by Robert Louis Stevenson in 1879 is used to present material about the history of railroads. (Rev: BCCB 1/94; BL 12/1/93; SLJ 12/93*) [828]

24128 O'Brien, Patrick. *Steam, Smoke, and Steel: Back in Time with Trains* (K–2). Illus. 2000, Charlesbridge $16.95 (0-88106-969-8); paper $6.95 (0-88106-972-8). 32pp. A boy describes the different trains driven by six generations of his family in this history of railroads and trains. (Rev: BL 7/00; HBG 3/01; SLJ 8/00) [385]

24129 Perry, Phyllis. *Trains* (2–4). Series: Transportation and Communication. 2001, Enslow LB $18.95 (0-7660-1645-5). 32pp. In an attractive format, this book supplies information on the history, development, and use of trains in North America. (Rev: BL 10/15/01; HBG 3/02) [625.1]

24130 Petty, Kate. *Some Trains Run on Water: And Other Amazing Facts About Rail Transportation* (1–3). Illus. by Ross Walton and Jo Moore. Series: I Didn't Know That. 1997, Millbrook LB $19.90 (0-7613-0609-9). 32pp. Strange-but-true facts involving trains, past and present, presented with several projects that don't require adult supervision. (Rev: HBG 9/98; SLJ 3/98) [625.2]

24131 Rogers, Hal. *Trains* (PS–1). Series: Machines at Work. 2001, Child's World LB $21.36 (1-56766-965-4). 32pp. Trains, their types, parts and uses, are concisely presented in a beginning-reader text and many color photographs. (Rev: BL 6/1–15/01; HBG 10/01) [625.1]

24132 Sandler, Martin W. *Riding the Rails in the USA: Trains in American Life* (5–8). Series: Transportation in America. 2003, Oxford LB $21.95 (0-19-513228-9). 63pp. This well-researched overview looks at the history of rail transportation and the economic impact of this method of moving both goods and people. (Rev: SLJ 11/03) [385]

24133 Simon, Seymour. *Seymour Simon's Book of Trains* (PS–3). Illus. 2002, HarperCollins LB $16.89 (0-06-028476-5). 40pp. An oversized volume with striking photographs of trains coupled with simple but fascinating information ranging from early steam locomotives to today's high-speed trains. (Rev: BCCB 3/02; BL 2/15/02; HB 5–6/02; HBG 10/02; SLJ 5/02) [385]

24134 Steele, Philip. *Trains* (3–4). Illus. Series: Pocket Facts. 1991, Macmillan LB $15.95 (0-89686-523-1). 32pp. The history of trains plus material on parts, bridges, subways, and the English Channel tunnel. (Rev: SLJ 9/91) [625.2]

24135 Stille, Darlene R. *Freight Trains* (K–2). Illus. Series: Transportation. 2001, Compass Point LB $19.93 (0-7565-0148-2). 32pp. Simple descriptions and an attractive layout will appeal to young train fans. (Rev: BL 12/15/01) [625.1]

24136 Stille, Darlene R. *Trains* (2–4). Illus. Series: True Books. 1997, Children's Book Pr. LB $22.00 (0-516-20342-8). 48pp. A history of railroading is followed by a description of various trains, how they operate, and the men who work on them. (Rev: BL 9/15/97) [625.1]

24137 Uschan, Michael V. *The Transcontinental Railroad* (4–7). Series: Landmark Events in American History. 2003, World Almanac LB $29.26 (0-8368-5382-2). 48pp. In accessible language and with plenty of illustrations, this is the story of the railroad that spanned the nation. (Rev: SLJ 6/04) [385]

24138 Weitzman, David. *The John Bull* (4–7). Illus. 2004, Farrar $16.00 (0-374-38037-6). 40pp. The John Bull, one of the first steam locomotives to travel America's rails, was built in England and shipped across the Atlantic in pieces. (Rev: BL 2/15/04; SLJ 3/04) [625.26]

24139 Yancey, Diane. *Camels for Uncle Sam* (4–7). Illus. 1995, Hendrick-Long $16.95 (0-937460-91-5). 92pp. The story of the experiment that involved importing camels to the Southwest in the 1850s to help in railroad construction. (Rev: BL 9/15/95) [357]

24140 Young, Robert. *The Transcontinental Railroad: America at Its Best?* (4–6). Illus. Series: Both Sides. 1997, Dillon LB $18.95 (0-87518-611-4). 72pp. Various point of view — including those of the workers, business people, and American Indians — are included in this history of the transcontinental railroad. (Rev: BL 9/15/97) [385]

24141 Zimmermann, Karl. *Steam Locomotives: Whistling, Chugging, Smoking Iron Horses of the Past* (4–8). Illus. 2004, Boyds Mills $19.95 (1-59078-165-1). 48pp. Informative and photo-filled, this is an appealing history of steam engines. (Rev: BL 2/1/04; SLJ 7/04) [625.26]

Ships, Boats, and Lighthouses

24142 Ardagh, Philip. *All at Sea* (PS–K). Illus. by Tig Sutton. Series: British Mighty Machines. 2003, Thameside LB $24.25 (1-931983-04-6). 32pp. Young boat lovers will enjoy the parade of yachts, submarines, aircraft carrier, hovercraft, ferry, and other vessels portrayed here in bright illustrations and simple words. (Rev: BL 12/1/02; HBG 3/03) [387.2]

24143 Asimov, Isaac, and Elizabeth Kaplan. *How Do Big Ships Float?* (K–3). Illus. Series: Ask Isaac Asimov. 1992, Gareth Stevens LB $21.27 (0-8368-0802-9). 24pp. This book explains simply how gravity and buoyancy keep ships afloat. (Rev: BL 6/1–15/93) [623.4]

24144 Ballard, Robert D., and Rick Archbold. *Ghost Liners* (5–9). Illus. 1998, Little, Brown $19.95 (0-316-08020-9). The discoverer of the *Titanic* describes this adventure and discusses other ship disasters including the *Lusitania* and the *Andrea Doria.* (Rev: BL 8/98; HBG 3/99; SLJ 9/98) [363]

24145 Barton, Byron. *Boats* (PS). Illus. by author. 1986, HarperCollins LB $14.89 (0-690-04536-0). 32pp. Recreational and functional roles of boats are explained in simple text and bright colors. (Rev: BL 8/86; SLJ 9/86)

24146 *Boats* (PS–3). Illus. Series: First Discovery. 1993, Scholastic $12.95 (0-590-47131-7). 24pp. A book for small children that introduces boats from around the world and explains their differences. (Rev: BL 1/1/94) [623.8]

24147 *Boats and Ships* (4–6). Illus. 1996, Scholastic $19.95 (0-590-47647-5). 48pp. Transparencies, flaps, and windows are used to introduce various ships and boats. (Rev: BL 12/15/96) [623]

24148 Bornhoft, Simon. *High Speed Boats* (5–8). Series: Need for Speed. 1999, Lerner LB $23.93 (0-8225-2488-0). 32pp. Using a jazzy, attention-getting format with action photographs, sidebars with statistics and interesting facts, and different type sizes, this book covers present and future speedboats. (Rev: BL 1/1–15/00; HBG 4/00) [629.222]

24149 Burgan, Michael. *The Titanic* (3–6). Illus. Series: We the People. 2004, Compass Point LB $22.60 (0-7565-0614-X). 48pp. This entry in the We the People series chronicles the tragic history of the *Titanic* from the construction of the mammoth ocean liner through its ill-fated encounter with a North Atlantic iceberg to the discovery of its remains on the ocean floor in the mid-1980s. (Rev: BL 5/1/04) [910]

24150 Collicutt, Paul. *This Boat* (PS–3). Illus. 2001, Farrar $15.00 (0-374-37495-3). 32pp. A number of different boats are presented in this picture book, including sailboats, paddle-powered riverboats, a submarine, and an aircraft carrier. (Rev: BL 3/15/01; HBG 10/01) [623.8]

24151 Cook, Nick. *The World's Fastest Boats* (3–8). Illus. Series: Built for Speed. 2000, Capstone LB $21.26 (0-7368-0569-9). 48pp. Catamarans, hydrofoils, and jetboats are all included in this visually appealing account that will be attractive to reluctant readers. (Rev: HBG 10/01; SLJ 6/01) [623.8]

24152 Delgado, James P. *Wrecks of American Warships* (5–7). Series: Shipwrecks. 2000, Watts LB $24.00 (0-531-20376-X). 64pp. This book describes how underwater archaeologists have discovered and explored such warships as the *Constitution, Philadelphia, Alabama,* and *Arizona.* (Rev: BL 10/15/00) [623.8]

24153 Doeden, Matt. *The Sinking of the Titanic* (3–5). Illus. Series: Graphic History. 2005, Capstone LB $22.60 (0-7368-3834-1). 32pp. An eye-catching and dramatically worded presentation of the sinking. (Rev: BL 2/1/05) [910]

24154 Fine, Jil. *The Whaleship Essex: The True Story of Moby Dick* (5–8). 2003, Children's Pr. LB $20.00 (0-516-24328-4); paper $6.95 (1-516-27872-X). 48pp. In 1820 the whaleship *Essex* sank after being rammed by an enraged sperm whale in the South Pacific, sending its crew of 20 on a nightmare voyage in small boats; this accessible account includes numerous photographs, maps, and other illustrations. (Rev: SLJ 3/04) [910]

24155 Frederick, Dawn. *How It Happens at the Boat Factory* (1–3). Photos by Bob Wolfe and Diane Wolfe. Series: How It Happens. 2002, Oliver LB $19.95 (1-881508-90-0). 32pp. How boats are manufactured is described in text and photographs. (Rev: HBG 10/02; SLJ 12/02)

24156 Gibbons, Gail. *Beacons of Light: Lighthouses* (1–3). Illus. 1990, Morrow $15.95 (0-688-07379-4). 32pp. The development of the lighthouse from a hilltop bonfire to the electronic wonders of today. (Rev: BCCB 3/90; BL 2/15/90; HB 3–4/90; SLJ 4/90) [387.1]

24157 Houghton, Gillian. *The Wreck of the Andrea Gail: Three Days of a Perfect Storm* (4–6). 2003, Rosen LB $23.95 (0-8239-3677-5). 48pp. This account of the 1991 loss of the fishing boat *Andrea Gail,* featured in the film *Perfect Storm,* examines possible causes. (Rev: SLJ 9/03) [910]

24158 Hubble, Richard. *Ships: Sailors and the Sea* (3–6). Illus. Series: Timelines. 1991, Watts $13.95 (0-531-15234-0). 48pp. Includes cutaway views of such ships as the *Titanic* and a modern destroyer. (Rev: BL 12/15/91; SLJ 3/92) [387.2]

24159 Kalman, Maira. *Fireboat: The Heroic Adventures of the John J. Harvey* (2–6). Illus. 2002, Penguin Putnam $16.99 (0-399-23953-7). 48pp. A beautifully and sensitively presented account of the work of the *John J. Harvey* fireboat, from its launch in 1931 through its restoration in the 1990s and its role in fighting fires in New York City on September 11, 2001. (Rev: BL 9/1/02; HB 9–10/02*; HBG 3/03; SLJ 9/02*) [974.71044]

24160 Kently, Eric. *The Story of the Titanic* (4–8). Illus. by Steve Noon. 2001, DK paper $17.99 (0-7894-7943-5). 32pp. Details of life aboard ship, double-page spreads, cutaways and cross-sections, facts and trivia, and a well-designed layout are just a few of the features of this beautifully designed large-format book. (Rev: BL 12/15/01; HBG 3/02; SLJ 12/01) [363.1]

24161 Lewis, Thomas P. *Clipper Ship* (1–3). Illus. by Joan Sandin. 1992, HarperCollins paper $3.95 (0-06-444160-1). 64pp. An easily read account of our sailing ships.

24162 Macaulay, David. *Ship* (5–8). 1993, Houghton Mifflin $19.95 (0-395-52439-3). A fictional caravel is featured in this exploration of historical seagoing vessels and the work of underwater archaeologists. (Rev: BCCB 11/93; BL 10/15/93*; SLJ 11/93) [387.2]

24163 McNeese, Tim. *Clippers and Whaling Ships* (4–8). Illus. by Chris Duke. Series: Americans on the Move. 1993, Macmillan LB $11.95 (0-89686-735-8). 48pp. Early American shipping and commerce are discussed. Also use *West by Steamboat* (1993). (Rev: SLJ 8/93) [623.8]

24164 Maestro, Betsy, and Giulio Maestro. *Ferryboat* (PS–1). Illus. by Giulio Maestro. 1986, HarperCollins LB $15.89 (0-690-04520-4). 32pp. The story of ferryboats, centered around one river crossing. (Rev: BCCB 7–8/86; BL 6/15/86; HB 5–6/86)

24165 Matsen, Brad. *The Incredible Search for the Treasure Ship Atocha* (4–6). Series: Incredible Deep-Sea Adventures. 2003, Enslow LB $18.95 (0-7660-2193-9). 48pp. This is the detailed story of the discovery of the wreck of the Spanish treasure ship *Nuestra Señora de Atocha* that sank in a hurricane in 1622. (Rev: HBG 4/04; SLJ 3/04) [909]

24166 Mayell, Hillary. *Shipwrecks* (5–8). Illus. Series: Man-Made Disasters. 2004, Gale/Lucent LB $21.96 (1-59018-058-5). 112pp. Period photographs enhance the impact of stories of shipwrecks of all kinds — from fishing boats to luxury liners — during the 19th and 20th centuries. (Rev: SLJ 7/04) [910.4]

24167 O'Brien, Patrick. *The Great Ships* (3–6). Illus. 2001, Walker LB $17.85 (0-8027-8775-4). 40pp. From an ancient Viking ship to the doomed *Titanic* and beyond, this volume introduces 17 historically significant vessels in gorgeous double-page spreads. (Rev: BCCB 2/02; BL 1/1–15/02; HBG 3/02; SLJ 9/01) [387.2]

24168 Otfinoski, Steven. *Into the Wind: Sailboats Then and Now* (2–4). Illus. Series: Here We Go! 1996, Benchmark LB $22.79 (0-7614-0405-8). 32pp. This simple, well-illustrated account gives a history of sailboats and shows many types and sizes from all over the world, with details on their important features. (Rev: HB 9–10/96; SLJ 2/97) [623.8]

24169 Rotner, Shelley. *Boats Afloat* (PS–K). Illus. 1998, Orchard $15.95 (0-531-30112-5). 32pp. Colorful photographs introduce various types of boats to very young children. (Rev: BL 11/1/98; HBG 3/99; SLJ 11/98) [623.8]

24170 *Sailing Ships: A Lift-the-Flap Discovery* (3–6). Illus. by Thomas Bayley. 1998, Orchard $16.95 (0-531-30065-X). This interactive book contains fold-outs of many sailing ships including the *Mayflower* and the *Santa Maria*. (Rev: BL 1/1–15/99; HBG 9/98) [623.8]

24171 Schaefer, Lola M. *Tugboats* (1–3). Series: Transportation Library. 2000, Bridgestone LB $15.93 (0-7368-0505-2). 24pp. A simple description

of tugboats, what they do, their parts, and how they operate. (Rev: HBG 9/00; SLJ 8/00) [387.2]

24172 Sherrow, Victoria. *Titanic* (2–4). Series: Scholastic History Readers. 2002, Scholastic paper $3.99 (0-439-26706-4). 48pp. First-person accounts enliven this illustrated account for beginning readers. (Rev: SLJ 4/03) [910]

24173 Van Rynbach, Iris. *Safely to Shore: America's Lighthouses* (3–5). Illus. by author. 2003, Charlesbridge $16.95 (1-57091-434-6); paper $6.95 (1-57091-435-4). 32pp. Twenty-two of the most famous American lighthouses are profiled, with information on equipment, history, and keepers. (Rev: HBG 4/04; SLJ 1/04) [387.1]

24174 Wargin, Kathy-Jo. *The Edmund Fitzgerald: The Song of the Bell* (K–3). Illus. by Gisjbert van Frankenhuyzen. 2003, Sleeping Bear $17.95 (1-58536-126-7). The bell that was retrieved from the *Edmund Fitzgerald* after it sank in Lake Superior in 1975 brings immediacy to this narrative and poem about the storm that took the sailors' lives. (Rev: BL 1/1/04; HBG 4/04; SLJ 2/04) [917.74]

24175 Wilkinson, Phillip. *Ships* (4–7). Illus. 2000, Kingfisher $16.95 (0-7534-5280-4). 64pp. Straightforward text and handsome illustrations cover maritime history from the earliest sailing ships and discuss piracy, the slave trade, and superstitions about the sea. (Rev: BL 2/1/01; HBG 10/01; SLJ 1/01) [623.8]

Weapons, Submarines, and the Armed Forces

24176 Aaseng, Nathan. *The Marine Corps in Action* (4–8). Series: U.S. Military Branches and Careers. 2001, Enslow LB $20.95 (0-7660-1637-4). 128pp. An attractive introduction to all aspects of the Marine Corps that looks at the future of this military branch and the number of women and minorities included. (Rev: HBG 3/02; SLJ 4/02) [359.9]

24177 Adams, Simon. *Castles and Forts* (5–8). Illus. Series: Kingfisher Knowledge. 2003, Kingfisher $11.95 (0-7534-5620-6). 63pp. From Norman mottes to Masada to the Great Wall of China, this is an illustrated exploration of castles, forts, and fortifications, their construction, and their purpose. (Rev: HBG 4/04; SLJ 12/03) [355.7]

24178 Benson, Michael. *The U.S. Army* (4–6). Illus. Series: U.S. Armed Forces. 2004, Lerner LB $25.26 (0-8225-1645-4). 64pp. An introductory overview of the Army and its history, recruitment and training, equipment, and day-to-day routines. (Rev: BL 1/1–15/05; SLJ 3/05) [355]

24179 Benson, Michael. *The U.S. Marine Corps* (4–7). Illus. Series: U.S. Armed Forces. 2004, Lerner LB $25.26 (0-8225-1648-9). 64pp. Introduces the history of the Marine Corps, followed by information on recruitment, training, and daily life. (Rev: SLJ 3/05) [359.6]

24180 Demarest, Chris L. *Mayday! Mayday! A Coast Guard Rescue* (K–2). Illus. by author. 2004, Simon

& Schuster $16.95 (0-689-85161-8). 40pp. Rhyming text and eye-catching illustrations follow a Coast Guard helicopter team as it locates a yacht in trouble and rescues everybody aboard. (Rev: BL 9/1/04; SLJ 7/04) [303.12]

24181 Donovan, Sandy. *The U.S. Air Force* (4–7). Illus. Series: U.S. Armed Forces. 2004, Lerner LB $25.26 (0-8225-1436-2). 64pp. Introduces the history of the Air Force, followed by information on recruitment, training, and daily life. Also use *U.S. Air Force Special Operations* (2004). (Rev: SLJ 3/05) [358.4]

24182 Fein, Eric. *The USS Greeneville Submarine Disaster* (4–6). Series: When Disaster Strikes! 2003, Rosen LB $23.95 (0-8239-3676-7). 48pp. This description of the 2001 collision off Hawaii between a U.S. Navy submarine and a Japanese fishing boat includes a brief history of submarines. (Rev: SLJ 9/03) [363.1]

24183 Gartman, Gene. *Life in Army Basic Training* (4–6). Illus. Series: On Duty. 2000, Children's Book Pr. LB $19.00 (0-516-23347-5); paper $6.95 (0-516-23547-8). 48pp. Written by a man who served in the military, this book goes through the routines and demands of basic training with information on weapons and various fitness programs. (Rev: BL 2/1/01) [355.5]

24184 Goldberg, Jan. *Green Berets: The U.S. Army Special Forces* (5–7). Series: Inside Special Operations. 2003, Rosen LB $19.95 (0-8239-3808-5). 64pp. An overview of the history, mission, training, and equipment of the Special Forces. (Rev: BL 7/03) [356]

24185 Gonen, Rivka. *Charge! Weapons and Warfare in Ancient Times* (5–8). Illus. 1993, Lerner LB $23.93 (0-8225-3201-8). 72pp. A look at the development of weapons from sticks and stones to battering rams. (Rev: BCCB 12/93; BL 2/1/94; SLJ 2/94) [355.8]

24186 Gurstelle, William. *The Art of the Catapult: Build Greek Ballistae, Roman Onagers, English Trebuchets, and More Ancient Artillery* (5 Up). Illus. 2004, Chicago Review paper $14.95 (1-55652-526-5). 172pp. Information on history, physics, and military tactics, plus step-by-step instructions for the construction of 10 working catapults. (Rev: SLJ 11/04) [623.4]

24187 Hamilton, John. *Armed Forces* (4–7). Illus. Series: War on Terrorism. 2002, ABDO LB $25.65 (1-57765-674-1). 48pp. An introduction to the U.S. military and the roles these services play in protecting the country, with color photographs, a glossary, and list of Web sites. (Rev: BL 8/02; HBG 10/02) [355]

24188 Hamilton, John. *Weapons of War* (4–7). Illus. Series: War on Terrorism. 2002, ABDO LB $25.65 (1-57765-673-3). 48pp. This account describes the weapons currently available to U.S. military personnel, including fighter planes, bombers, helicopters, bombs, missiles, and ships. (Rev: BL 5/1/02; HBG 10/02) [623.4]

24189 Hamilton, John. *Weapons of War: A Pictorial History of the Past One Thousand Years* (4–7).

Illus. Series: The Millennium. 2000, ABDO LB $25.65 (1-57765-362-9). 48pp. In a short space, this book traces 1,000 years of weapons including small weaponry, ships, firearms, military airplanes, tanks, missiles, and bombs. (Rev: BL 7/00; HBG 9/00; SLJ 10/00) [623.4]

24190 Hasan, Tahara. *Anthrax Attacks Around the World* (4–8). Series: Terrorist Attacks. 2003, Rosen LB $26.50 (0-8239-3859-X). 64pp. Examines the use of anthrax as a terrorist weapon and includes accounts of its use in Japan, the Soviet Union, and the United States. (Rev: SLJ 2/04) [303.6]

24191 Hibbert, Adam. *Chemical and Biological Warfare* (5–9). Series: Face the Facts. 2003, Raintree LB $28.56 (0-7398-6847-0). 56pp. Part of a series on international issues, this volume examines the powers and dangers of chemical and biological weapons. (Rev: SLJ 4/04) [358]

24192 Hughes, Libby. *West Point* (4–6). Illus. Series: Places in American History. 1993, Macmillan LB $18.95 (0-87518-529-0). 72pp. The story of the military academy founded in 1802 and of the life of cadets trained there. (Rev: BL 4/15/93; SLJ 7/93) [355]

24193 Humble, Richard. *A World War Two Submarine* (3–6). Illus. by Mark Bergin. Series: Inside Story. 1991, Bedrick LB $26.50 (0-87226-351-7). 48pp. This account explores the design, construction, and parts of a World War II submarine. (Rev: BL 12/1/91; SLJ 1/92) [359.9]

24194 Keeler, Barbara, and Don Keeler. *Sailing Ship Eagle* (3–5). Illus. Series: Those Daring Machines. 1995, Macmillan paper $5.95 (0-382-24751-5). 48pp. A brief look at the construction and exploits of the U.S. Coast Guard ship. (Rev: BL 2/15/95) [359.9]

24195 Kennedy, Robert C. *Life as a Paratrooper* (4–7). Series: On Duty. 2000, Children's Book Pr. LB $20.00 (0-516-23344-0). 48pp. An easily read account that describes the work, responsibilities, and opportunities of a paratrooper. Also use *Life as an Air Force Fighter Pilot* (2000). (Rev: BL 3/1/01) [358.4]

24196 Kennedy, Robert C. *Life as an Army Demolition Expert* (4–6). Illus. Series: On Duty. 2000, Children's Book Pr. LB $19.00 (0-516-23346-7); paper $6.95 (0-516-23546-7). 48pp. This work gives historical background plus an explanation of work today in this specialized area of the U.S. Army. (Rev: BL 2/1/01) [358]

24197 Kennedy, Robert C. *Life in the Army Special Forces* (4–7). Series: On Duty. 2000, Children's Book Pr. LB $20.00 (0-516-23350-5). 48pp. The work, responsibilities, and career possibilities of members of this special army unit are described in this well-illustrated book. (Rev: BL 3/1/01; SLJ 3/01) [335]

24198 Kennedy, Robert C. *Life in the Marines* (4–7). Series: On Duty. 2000, Children's Book Pr. LB $20.00 (0-516-23348-3). 48pp. This branch of the military is examined with material on the special training and responsibilities involved. (Rev: BL 3/1/01) [359.6]

24199 Kennedy, Robert C. *Life with the Navy Seals* (4–7). Series: On Duty. 2000, Children's Book Pr. LB $20.00 (0-516-23351-3). 48pp. A look at this special branch of the U.S. Navy with material on its responsibilities, training, and career opportunities. (Rev: BL 3/1/01) [359]

24200 Moran, Tom. *The U.S. Army* (4–8). Illus. 1990, Lerner LB $23.93 (0-8225-1434-6). 88pp. A solid overview of the development of the U.S. Army. (Rev: BL 1/1/91) [335]

24201 Myers, Walter Dean. *USS Constellation: Pride of the American Navy* (4–8). 2004, Holiday House $16.95 (0-8234-1816-2). 86pp. Myers presents the colorful history of the *USS Constellation,* the last of America's all-sail fighting ships, in this volume with extensive illustrations and other materials. (Rev: BL 7/04; HB 7–8/04; SLJ 8/04) [359.8]

24202 Payan, Gregory, and Alexander Guelke. *Life on a Submarine* (4–6). Illus. Series: On Duty. 2000, Children's Book Pr. LB $19.00 (0-516-23349-1); paper $6.95 (0-516-23549-4). 48pp. The glamorous and arduous aspects of life aboard a navy submarine are covered, including exercise and sleeping arrangements. (Rev: BL 2/1/01) [359.9]

24203 Pelta, Kathy. *The U.S. Navy* (5–7). Illus. 1990, Lerner LB $23.93 (0-8225-1435-4). 88pp. A look at the history and present status and activities of the U.S. Navy. (Rev: BL 12/1/90) [359]

24204 Richie, Jason. *Weapons: Designing the Tools of War* (5–10). Illus. 2000, Oliver LB $21.95 (1-881508-60-9). 144pp. Using separate chapters for different categories of weapons — for example, submarines, battleships, and tanks — this is a history of the development of weaponry from 300 B.C. to today. (Rev: BL 5/1/00; HBG 10/00; SLJ 8/00) [623]

24205 Roza, Greg. *The Incredible Story of Aircraft Carriers* (3–6). Illus. Series: A Kid's Guide to Incredible Technology. 2004, Rosen LB $19.95 (0-8239-6714-X). 24pp. A concise look at how and why aircraft carriers are built and at the role they play and the planes they carry, with a layout dia-

gram and discussion of the future for these huge ships. (Rev: SLJ 2/05) [359.9]

24206 Stein, R. Conrad. *The Manhattan Project* (3–5). Illus. Series: Cornerstones of Freedom. 1993, Children's Book Pr. LB $20.50 (0-516-06670-6). 32pp. The history of the development of the atomic bomb in this country, culminating in its use in World War II. (Rev: BL 11/1/93) [355.8]

24207 Thompson, Gare. *The Monitor: The Iron Warship that Changed the World* (2–4). Series: All Aboard Reading. 2003, Penguin Putnam LB $13.89 (0-448-43283-8); paper $3.99 (0-448-43245-5). 48pp. This fascinating book recounts not only the Civil War history of the ironclad *Monitor* but also the successful 20th-century search for its underwater wreck site. (Rev: BL 12/15/03; HBG 4/04)

24208 Warner, J. F. *The U.S. Marine Corps* (4–8). Illus. Series: Armed Services. 1991, Lerner LB $22.95 (0-8225-1432-X). 88pp. From how to enlist to a discussion of the new technology, this is a well-organized introduction to the U.S. Marine Corps. (Rev: BL 2/1/92; SLJ 2/92) [359.6]

24209 Weiss, Harvey. *Submarines and Other Underwater Craft* (3–7). Illus. 1990, HarperCollins LB $13.89 (0-690-04761-4). 64pp. A good history of submarines that explains many peacetime uses. (Rev: BCCB 6/90; BL 7/90; HB 7–8/90; SLJ 5/90) [359.3]

24210 Wolny, Philip. *Weapons Satellites* (5–9). Series: The Library of Satellites. 2003, Rosen LB $26.50 (0-8239-3855-7). 64pp. This account explores the growing technology of weapon satellites that are capable of knocking out enemies' satellites, and launching attacks from outer space. (Rev: BL 11/15/03; SLJ 1/04) [629.46]

24211 Woods, Mary B., and Michael Woods. *Ancient Warfare: From Clubs to Catapults* (5–8). Series: Ancient Technologies. 2000, Runestone LB $25.26 (0-8225-2999-8). 96pp. The weaponry of ancient civilizations including Greece and China. (Rev: BCCB 12/00; BL 9/15/00; HBG 3/01; SLJ 1/01) [623]

Recreation

Crifts

Crafts

General and Miscellaneous

24212 Albregts, Lisa, and Elizabeth Cape. *Best Friends: Tons of Crazy, Cool Things to Do with Your Girlfriends* (4–8). Illus. 1998, Chicago Review paper $12.95 (1-55652-326-2). Arranged by seasons, this activity book contains crafts, games, dances, snacks, and skits to amuse girls when they get together. (Rev: BL 3/1/99; SLJ 1/99) [796.083]

24213 Birdseye, Tom. *A Kids' Guide to Building Forts* (5–8). Illus. by Bill Klein. 1993, Harbinger paper $11.95 (0-943173-69-8). 62pp. A guide to the building of 19 kinds of forts, from the very simple to the more complex, some of which can be turned into clubhouses. (Rev: SLJ 9/93) [745.5]

24214 Blanchette, Peg, and Terri Thibault. *Really Cool Felt Crafts* (3–5). Illus. Series: Quick Starts for Kids! 2002, Williamson paper $7.95 (1-885593-80-5). 64pp. This book of easy-to-make felt projects includes instructions accompanied by drawings, and a section of full-sized templates. (Rev: BL 12/15/02; SLJ 1/03) [746]

24215 Bledsoe, Karen E. *Chinese New Year Crafts* (K–5). Illus. Series: Fun Holiday Crafts Kids Can Do! 2005, Enslow LB $22.60 (0-7660-2347-8). 32pp. The ten crafts presented use everyday materials and include a dragon-streamer puppet, a ribbon lantern, and Chinese zodiac pictures. (Rev: SLJ 6/05) [394.261]

24216 Bose, Terri. *Craft Adventures* (4–6). Illus. Series: Creative Kids. 2003, North Light paper $12.99 (1-58180-374-5). 64pp. Fourteen craft projects that can be made with readily available materials are laid out with clear instructions. (Rev: SLJ 6/03) [745]

24217 Braman, Arlette N. *Create! The Best Crafts and Activities from Many Lands* (3–6). Illus. by Jo-Ellen Bosson. Series: Kids Around the World. 1999, Wiley paper $12.95 (0-471-29005-X). 116pp. From Amish quilts to Zulu woven baskets this craft book includes both ancient and modern crafts from a vari-

ety of cultures, all introduced with clear directions. (Rev: SLJ 12/99) [745]

24218 Browning, Marie. *Totally Cool Soapmaking for Kids* (4–7). 2004, Sterling $19.95 (1-4027-0641-3). 96pp. Many of the soapmaking projects in this photo-filled guide require adult supervision for at least part, if not all, of the activity. (Rev: BL 8/04) [668]

24219 Brownrigg, Sheri. *Hearts and Crafts* (4–8). Illus. 1995, Tricycle paper $9.95 (1-883672-28-7). Clear instructions show how to complete a variety of Valentine's Day projects, including making necklaces and candles. (Rev: BL 3/1/96; SLJ 3/96) [745.5]

24220 Bruder, Mikyla. *Button Girl: More than 20 Cute-as-a-Button Projects* (4–7). Photos by Scott M. Nobles. 2005, Chronicle $12.95 (0-8118-4553-2). 64pp. A spiral-bound guide providing 23 ideas for pretty projects — jewelry, belts, and so forth. (Rev: BL 5/1/05) [745.5]

24221 Caney, Steven. *Steven Caney's Playbook* (3–5). Illus. 1975, Workman paper $9.95 (0-911104-38-0). 240pp. All sorts of activities involving discarded or inexpensive materials, thoroughly and clearly presented.

24222 Carlson, Laurie. *EcoArt! Earth-Friendly Art and Craft Experiences for 3- to 9-Year-Olds* (K–4). Illus. by Loretta Braren. 1993, Williamson paper $12.95 (0-913589-68-3). 160pp. Over 100 arts and crafts activities using natural, recyclable, or reusable materials. (Rev: BL 2/15/93; SLJ 4/93) [745.5]

24223 Castaldo, Nancy F. *Winter Day Play! Activities, Crafts, and Games for Indoors and Out* (PS–3). Illus. 2001, Chicago Review paper $13.95 (1-55652-381-5). 161pp. The more than 70 suggested activities range from scientific projects and artistic endeavors to parties and cooking. (Rev: SLJ 12/01) [790]

24224 Castaldo, Nancy Fusco. *Rainy Day Play! Explore, Create, Discover, Pretend* (PS–1). Illus. by Loretta Braren. Series: A Little Hands Book. 1996, Williamson paper $12.95 (1-885593-00-7). 142pp.

A collection of 64 ideas for activities, crafts, and games that are attractively presented and will afford hours of enjoyment. (Rev: SLJ 2/97) [745.5]

24225 Chapman, Gillian, and Pam Robson. *Art from Fabric: With Projects Using Rags, Old Clothing and Remnants* (3–5). Illus. Series: Salvaged! 1995, Thomson Learning LB $21.40 (1-56847-381-8). 32pp. This book contains several creative projects and crafts using old fabrics or fibers, on double-page spreads. (Rev: SLJ 1/96) [745.5]

24226 Check, Laura. *Create Your Own Candles: 30 Easy-to-Make Designs* (5–8). Illus. by Norma Jean Martin-Jourdenais. 2004, Williamson paper $8.95 (0-8249-8663-6). 61pp. Safety is stressed in this guide to exciting (and complex) candle creations. (Rev: SLJ 11/04) [745.593]

24227 Cherkerzian, Diane, and Colleen Van Blaricom. *Merry Things to Make* (3–5). Illus. 1999, Boyds Mills paper $7.95 (1-56397-838-5). 64pp. A wide range of craft ideas using simple materials are presented with good step-by-step instructions. (Rev: BL 9/1/99; SLJ 10/99) [745.59]

24228 Civardi, Anne, and Penny King. *Festival Decorations* (2–6). Series: Craft Workshop. 1998, Crabtree LB $22.95 (0-86505-780-X); paper $10.95 (0-86505-790-7). 32pp. These well-organized craft projects include decorations and other items used in a variety of celebrations and ceremonies around the world. (Rev: SLJ 10/98) [745]

24229 Corwin, Judith Hoffman. *Christmas Fun* (3–6). Illus. by author. 1982, Silver Burdett paper $5.95 (0-671-49583-6). 64pp. A collection of simple projects that are useful for this holiday, including designs for gifts and decorations.

24230 Corwin, Judith Hoffman. *Easter Crafts* (K–3). Illus. by author. Series: Holiday Crafts. 1994, Watts LB $21.00 (0-531-11145-8). 48pp. A collection of Easter crafts in which bunnies star. (Rev: SLJ 8/94) [745]

24231 Corwin, Judith Hoffman. *Easter Fun* (2–4). Illus. by author. 1984, Silver Burdett paper $5.95 (0-671-53108-5). 64pp. Foods and crafts associated with this holiday are highlighted.

24232 Corwin, Judith Hoffman. *Halloween Crafts: A Holiday Craft Book* (3–5). Illus. Series: Holiday Crafts. 1995, Watts LB $21.00 (0-531-11148-2). 48pp. Following a brief history of Halloween, the author outlines related crafts, including decorations, foods, and costumes. (Rev: BL 9/15/95) [745.594]

24233 Corwin, Judith Hoffman. *Halloween Fun* (3–6). Illus. 1983, Silver Burdett paper $5.95 (0-671-49756-1). 64pp. A wide variety of holiday activities, including party hints and projects.

24234 Corwin, Judith Hoffman. *Valentine Fun* (3–6). Illus. by author. 1983, Silver Burdett paper $5.95 (0-671-49755-3). 64pp. Recipes and craft projects highlight this book of activities.

24235 Dall, Mary Doerfler. *Little Hands Create! Art and Activities for Kids Ages 3 to 6* (PS–2). Illus. by Sarah Rakitin. 2004, Williamson paper $12.95 (0-8249-8664-4). 120pp. Children will need help with these activities, most of which — egg-carton boats

and twisted-paper jewelry, for example, use everyday materials. (Rev: BL 1/1–15/05) [745.5]

24236 Darsie, Richard. *String Games* (3–6). 2003, Sterling $14.95 (0-8069-7735-3). 96pp. This photo-filled introduction to string art provides step-by-step instructions for making string figures and also offers a brief history of this craft. (Rev: HBG 10/03; SLJ 11/03) [793.9]

24237 Deshpande, Chris. *Festival Crafts* (4–7). Illus. Series: World Wide Crafts. 1994, Gareth Stevens LB $23.93 (0-8368-1153-4). 32pp. Thirteen craft projects that relate to such multicultural festivals as Mardi Gras and Mexico's All Souls Day. (Rev: BL 3/1/95; SLJ 1/95) [745.5]

24238 Dorling Kindersley Publishing Staff. *The Crafty Art Book* (3–6). Series: DK Eyewitness Books. 2004, DK $12.99 (0-7566-0550-4). 48pp. Fifty designs for "perfect presents" involve needlework, knitting, printing, paper folding, and so forth. (Rev: BL 12/15/04)

24239 Drake, Jane, and Ann Love. *The Kids Summer Handbook* (4–7). Illus. by Heather Collins. 1994, Ticknor $15.95 (0-395-68711-X). 208pp. A guide to all sorts of outdoor crafts and activities, with several involving whittling, weaving, and knotting. (Rev: BL 4/1/94; SLJ 6/94) [790.1]

24240 Drake, Jane, and Ann Love. *The Kids Winter Handbook* (3–5). Illus. by Heather Collins. 2001, Kids Can $18.95 (1-55337-033-3); paper $12.95 (1-55074-969-2). 127pp. Crafts, recipes, games, and other activities are geared to indoor and outdoor winter entertainment. (Rev: HBG 3/02; SLJ 11/01) [790.1]

24241 Ehlert, Lois. *Snowballs* (PS–3). Illus. 1995, Harcourt $16.00 (0-15-200074-7). 32pp. All kinds of materials are used to create and decorate a snow family in this book of craft ideas. (Rev: BCCB 11/95; BL 12/1/95; SLJ 11/95)

24242 Freixenet, Anna. *Creating with Mosaics* (3–6). Series: Crafts for All Seasons. 2000, Blackbirch LB $18.95 (1-56711-440-7). 32pp. This appealing craft book shows how to create attractive mosaics using items like beads, balls of aluminum foil, beans, seeds, and buttons. (Rev: SLJ 2/01) [745]

24243 *Fun-to-make Crafts for Easter* (3–6). 2005, Boyds Mills $15.95 (1-59078-340-9); paper $7.95 (1-59078-365-4). 64pp. Greeting cards, holiday decorations, and clothing are among the 150 crafts suggested. Also use *Fun-to-Make Crafts for Every Day* (2005). (Rev: SLJ 6/05)

24244 Furstinger, Nancy. *Creative Crafts for Critters* (2–4). Illus. by Philippe Beha. 2001, Stoddart paper $8.95 (0-7737-6135-7). 48pp. Pet lovers will find lots of craft ideas for animal toys, clothing, and nutrition. (Rev: SLJ 1/02) [745.5]

24245 Gessat, Audrey. *Crafts from Salt Dough* (2–4). Trans. from French by Cheryl L. Smith. Series: Step by Step. 2002, Capstone LB $22.60 (0-7368-1475-2). 32pp. Tips on working with dough accompany instructions for making items including a candleholder and a clown pencil. Also use *Crafts* *from Felt* and *Crafts from Modeling Clay* (both 2002). (Rev: HBG 3/03; SLJ 2/03)

24246 Gnojewski, Carol. *Cinco de Mayo Crafts* (K–5). Illus. Series: Fun Holiday Crafts Kids Can Do! 2005, Enslow LB $22.60 (0-7660-2344-3). 32pp. The ten crafts presented use everyday materials and include a sombrero and a paper poncho. (Rev: SLJ 6/05)

24247 Goodman, Polly. *Space and Art Activities* (2–4). Illus. Series: Arty Facts. 2002, Crabtree LB $17.95 (0-7787-1112-9); paper $8.06 (0-7787-1140-4). 48pp. Double-page spreads give factual information on the left and creative ideas on the right. Also use *Structures, Materials and Art Activities* (2002). (Rev: SLJ 9/02) [745.5]

24248 Gould, Roberta. *Kidtopia: 'Round the Country and Back Through Time in 60 Projects* (2–7). 2000, Tricycle paper $13.95 (1-58246-026-4). 152pp. Divided into sections that cover American history and geography, this book contains many related projects, crafts, party ideas, and games. (Rev: SLJ 12/00) [745]

24249 Gould, Roberta. *Making Cool Crafts and Awesome Art: A Kids' Treasure Trove of Fabulous Fun* (2–5). Photos by author. 1998, Williamson paper $12.95 (1-885593-11-2). 160pp. This welcome addition to craft collections includes simple instructions to make a variety of objects from easy-to-find materials. Many of the projects represent foreign cultures and, in these cases, background material is given. (Rev: SLJ 4/98) [745.5]

24250 Halls, Kelly Milner, ed. *Look What You Can Make with Craft Sticks: Over 80 Pictured Crafts and Dozens of Other Ideas* (2–4). Photos by Hank Schneider. 2002, Boyds Mills paper $5.95 (1-56397-997-7). 48pp. Younger children may need help with some of the projects here, which use everyday materials to make a wide variety of items. Also use *Look What You Can Make with Plastic Bottles and Tubs: Over 80 Pictured Crafts and Dozens of Other Ideas* (2002). (Rev: SLJ 4/02) [745.5]

24251 Halls, Kelly Milner, ed. *Look What You Can Make with Plastic-Foam Trays: Over 90 Pictured Crafts and Dozens of Other Ideas* (K–3). Illus. 2003, Boyds Mills paper $5.95 (1-59078-078-7). 48pp. Child-friendly ideas for using plastic-foam trays in a variety of inventive ways. (Rev: SLJ 2/03)

24252 Hauser, Elizabeth Ingrid. *Princess Crafts* (2–5). Illus. by Lisa Parett. 2004, Sterling $14.95 (0-8069-7116-9). 96pp. For aspiring princesses, designs for clothes, jewelry, hair accessories, and wings are organized under such headings as "Classic Princess," "Snow White," and "Hawaiian Princess." (Rev: SLJ 11/04)

24253 Hauser, Jill Frankel. *Little Hands Celebrate America! Learning About the U.S.A. Through Crafts and Activities* (K–5). Illus. by Michael Kline. Series: A Williamson Little Hands Book. 2004, Williamson paper $12.95 (1-885593-93-7). 128pp. Easy projects and activities introduce American symbols, sights, traditions, and holidays. (Rev: SLJ 11/04) [973]

24254 Hebert, Holly. *60 Super Simple Crafts* (3–6). Illus. by Leo Abbett. 1996, Lowell House paper $6.95 (1-56565-385-8). 80pp. Simple instructions are given for 60 crafts projects, most of which involve material found in the home or at local craft shops. (Rev: SLJ 2/97) [745.5]

24255 Hendry, Linda. *Cat Crafts* (4–6). Illus. Series: Kids Can Do It! 2002, Kids Can $12.95 (1-55074-964-1); paper $5.95 (1-55074-921-8). 40pp. Using double-page spreads, this book outlines 17 cat-related projects. (Rev: BL 4/1/02; HBG 10/02; SLJ 6/02) [745.5]

24256 Hendry, Linda. *Dog Crafts* (4–6). Illus. Series: Kids Can Do It! 2002, Kids Can $12.95 (1-55074-960-9); paper $5.95 (1-55074-962-5). 40pp. Seventeen projects, such as making jewelry and toys, and all related to dogs, are presented in double-page spreads with easy-to-follow instructions. (Rev: BL 4/1/02; HBG 10/02; SLJ 6/02) [745.5]

24257 Hendry, Linda. *Making Gift Boxes* (4–8). Illus. by author. Series: Kids Can! 1999, Kids Can paper $5.95 (1-55074-503-4). 40pp. The 14 boxes included in this fine craft book with clear instructions include a photo box, a garden box to grow seeds, a box for storing CDs, and a treasure box with false compartments. (Rev: SLJ 12/99) [745]

24258 Henry, Sandi. *Kids' Art Works! Creating with Color, Design, Texture and More* (K–5). Illus. by Norma Jean Martin-Jourdenais. Series: A Williamson Kids Can! Book. 2000, Williamson paper $12.95 (1-885593-35-X). 138pp. Sixty artistic creations using household materials; for example, a pasta fish, a Swiss cheese candle, and a sandpaper relief print. (Rev: SLJ 3/00) [745]

24259 *Holiday and Everyday Projects: Festive and Fun Creations* (2–5). Illus. Series: Crafty Kids. 2003, McGraw-Hill $12.95 (1-57768-528-8). 48pp. Projects for Easter, Halloween, and Mother's Day are among those included in this volume with easy-to-follow instructions and illustrations. (Rev: HBG 4/04; SLJ 12/03) [745.5]

24260 Hunter, Dette. *38 Ways to Entertain Your Grandparents* (K–2). Illus. by Deirdre Betteridge. 2002, Annick LB $19.95 (1-55037-749-3); paper $9.95 (1-55037-748-5). 48pp. Hunter deftly interweaves Sarah's story of all the entertaining things she does with her grandparents with instructions for young readers to do likewise, including rules for games, recipes, and craft projects. (Rev: BL 12/1/02; HBG 3/03; SLJ 4/03) [793]

24261 Irvin, Christine M. *Egg Carton Mania* (2–4). Illus. Series: Craft Mania. 2002, Children's Book Pr. LB $22.00 (0-516-22277-5); paper $6.95 (0-516-27758-8). 32pp. Projects using egg cartons range from finger puppets to a double-decker bus. (Rev: BL 1/1–15/03; SLJ check) [745.5]

24262 Johnson, Ginger. *Make Your Own Christmas Ornaments* (3–5). Illus. by Norma Jean Martin-Jordenais. Series: Quick Starts for Kids! 2002, Williamson paper $7.95 (1-885593-79-1). 64pp. A collection of 25 ornaments with clear instructions and photographs of finished products. (Rev: BL 12/15/02; SLJ 10/02)

24263 Kerina, Jane. *African Crafts* (5–8). Illus. by Tom Feelings and Marylyn Katzman. 1970, Lion LB $13.95 (0-87460-084-7). Many projects arranged geographically by the region in Africa where they originated.

24264 Kilby, Janice Eaton, and Deborah Morgenthal. *The Book of Wizard Craft: In Which the Apprentice Finds Spells, Potions, Fantastic Tales and 50 Enchanting Things to Make* (4–6). Illus. by Lindy Burnett. 2001, Sterling $19.95 (1-57990-206-5). 144pp. An ancient wizard reveals the recipes for potions and instructions for crafts and skills (making a wizard's robe, reading tea leaves), some of which will require help from an adult. (Rev: HBG 10/01; SLJ 6/01) [745.5]

24265 Kimble-Ellis, Sonya. *Traditional African American Arts and Activities* (3–7). Illus. Series: Celebrating Our Heritage. 2002, Wiley paper $12.95 (0-471-41046-2). 120pp. The projects featured in this title will teach students something about traditional culture, foods, holidays, crafts, and games. (Rev: SLJ 8/02)

24266 King, Penny, and Clare Roundhill. *Out of This World: Lots of Space Pictures to Make* (2–6). Illus. Series: Making Pictures. 1997, Rigby $14.95 (1-57572-193-7). 29pp. This craft book introduces 12 space-related activities, like making a rocket from a cardboard tube. Others in the series are *Secrets of the Sea: Lots of Underwater Pictures to Make* and *Spooky Things: Lots of Spooky Pictures to Make* (both 1997). (Rev: SLJ 12/97) [745.5]

24267 *Kit's Friendship Fun* (3–5). Illus. 2002, Pleasant Co. paper $12.95 (1-58485-415-4). 96pp. After a discussion of family life during the Depression, recipes, crafts, and games typical of the era are introduced. (Rev: SLJ 2/03)

24268 Kohl, MaryAnn F., and Jean Potter. *Global Art: Activities, Projects, and Inventions from Around the World* (3–6). Illus. by Rebecca Van Slyke. 1998, Gryphon paper $14.95 (0-87659-190-X). 189pp. A series of crafts that vary in difficulty, are arranged by continent, and explore the world's different cultures and habitats. (Rev: SLJ 10/98) [745]

24269 Kranz, Linda. *Let's Rock! Rock Painting for Kids* (1–6). Illus. 2003, NorthWord paper $11.95 (1-55971-870-6). 48pp. A comprehensive introduction to rock painting, including recommendations for the best kinds of rocks and paint to use, painting techniques, and special designs. (Rev: SLJ 10/03) [751.4]

24270 Lehne, Judith Logan. *The Never-Be-Bored Book: Quick Things to Make When There's Nothing to Do* (4–6). Illus. by Morissa Lipstein. 1993, Sterling $17.95 (0-8069-1254-5). 128pp. Over 40 projects are included in this useful craft book, plus recipes for many ingredients including clay, dough, and natural dyes. (Rev: BL 5/15/93) [745.5]

24271 Levine, Shar, and Michael Ouchi. *The Ultimate Balloon Book* (5–8). Illus. 2001, Sterling paper $9.95 (0-8069-2959-6). 96pp. A guide to balloon creations that progresses from the simple (dachs-

hunds) to the advanced. (Rev: BL 8/01; SLJ 10/01) [745.594]

24272 Lewis, Amanda. *Making Memory Books* (3–6). Illus. by Esperanca Melo. Series: Kids Can! 1999, Kids Can paper $5.95 (1-55074-567-0). 40pp. This craft book shows how to create a book for memorabilia with instructions on creating stencils, decorations, different types of lettering, templates, stamps, etc. (Rev: SLJ 2/00) [745]

24273 *Look What You Can Make with Dozens of Household Items!* (4–6). Ed. by Kathy Ross. Photos by Hank Schneider. Series: Look What You Can Make With. 2003, Boyds Mills $24.99 (1-59078-058-2). 384pp. Common household items are used to create a wide range of crafts. (Rev: BL 12/15/02) [745]

24274 Love, Ann, and Jane Drake. *Kids and Grandparents: An Activity Book* (3–6). Illus. by Heather Collins. 2000, Kids Can $17.95 (1-55074-784-3); paper $10.95 (1-55074-492-5). 160pp. A collection of over 90 games, crafts, recipes, and activities for children and their grandparents together with a "Making Memories" section on creating a memory book, a relative map, and a family tree. (Rev: HBG 10/00; SLJ 5/00) [745]

24275 McGraw, Sheila. *Gifts Kids Can Make* (4–8). Photos by Sheila McGraw and Joy von Tiedemann. 1994, Firefly paper $9.95 (1-895565-35-9). 96pp. A craft book that gives directions for making 14 simple gifts, such as a cotton sock doll and a hobby horse, using easily obtainable materials. (Rev: SLJ 12/94) [745]

24276 MacLeod, Elizabeth. *Gifts to Make and Eat* (4–7). Illus. by June Bradford. Series: Kids Can Do It! 2001, Kids Can $12.95 (1-55074-956-0); paper $5.95 (1-55074-958-7). 40pp. Kids learn through step-by-step instructions how to make an array of edible and craft gifts. (Rev: BL 11/1/01; HBG 3/02; SLJ 2/02) [641.5]

24277 Martin, Laura C. *Nature's Art Box: From T-Shirts to Twig Baskets, 65 Cool Projects for Crafty Kids to Make with Natural Materials You Can Find Anywhere* (4–8). Illus. by David Cain. 2003, Storey $23.95 (1-58017-503-1); paper $16.95 (1-58017-490-6). 215pp. These projects use natural materials such as twigs, moss, gourds, stones, shells, flowers, and leaves to make articles including wreaths, necklaces, and a chess set. (Rev: HBG 10/03; SLJ 8/03*) [745.5]

24278 Martin, Laura C. *Recycled Crafts Box* (3–7). Illus. 2004, Storey Kids $19.95 (1-58017-523-6). 96pp. A craft book with an environmental twist, this volume offers great project ideas plus information on recycling and the history of trash. (Rev: BL 3/15/04; SLJ 7/04) [363.72]

24279 Merrill, Yvonne Y. *Hands-On America: Art Activities About Vikings, Woodland Indians and Early Colonists*, Vol. 1 (4–7). Illus. Series: Hands-On America. 2001, Kits paper $20.00 (0-9643177-6-1). 92pp. Varied and relatively easy activities focusing on early America will entertain at the same time as enhancing students' knowledge of historical events and concepts. (Rev: SLJ 3/02) [745.5]

24280 Merrill, Yvonne Y. *Hands-On Latin America: Art Activities for All Ages* (4–8). Illus. Series: Hands-On. 1998, Kits paper $20.00 (0-9643177-1-0). 84pp. A collection of 30 interesting, affordable arts and crafts projects inspired by the ancient cultures of Latin America. (Rev: BL 9/1/98; SLJ 8/98) [980.07]

24281 Milord, Susan. *Hands Around the World: 365 Creative Ways to Build Cultural Awareness and Global Respect* (3–6). Illus. 1992, Williamson paper $12.95 (0-913589-65-9). 160pp. One craft, recipe, or project is offered for each day of the year. (Rev: BL 1/1/93; SLJ 1/93) [306]

24282 Moffatt, Judith. *Snow Shapes: A Read-and-Do Book* (1–2). Illus. Series: Hello Reader! 2000, Scholastic $3.99 (0-439-09858-0). 32pp. This beginning reader is also a craft book filled with simple winter projects like making paper snowflakes, snowman ornaments, and a paper chain of squirrels. (Rev: BL 12/1/00) [745.594]

24283 Monaghan, Kathleen, and Hermon Joyner. *You Can Weave! Projects for Young Weavers* (4–7). Illus. 2001, Sterling $19.95 (0-87192-493-5). 104pp. Step-by-step instructions and photographs guide young crafters through weaving projects of varying complexity. (Rev: BL 11/1/01) [746.41]

24284 Mueller, Stephanie R., and Ann E. Wheeler. *101 Great Gifts from Kids: Fabulous Gifts Every Child Can Make* (PS–3). Illus. 2002, Gryphon House paper $14.95 (0-87659-279-5). 174pp. Gift ideas that vary in difficulty and may require some adult help are accompanied by line drawings of the process involved and the end product. (Rev: SLJ 9/02) [745.5]

24285 The Muppet Workshop, and Stephanie St. Pierre. *The Muppets Big Book of Crafts: 100 Great Projects to Snip, Sculpt, Stitch, and Stuff* (2–6). Photos by John E. Barrett. Illus. by Stephanie Osser and Matthew Fox. 2000, Workman paper $18.95 (0-7611-0526-3). 322pp. With projects that progress from the easy to the difficult, this amazing book outlines 100 great craft projects arranged by a particular medium (e.g. paper) or technique. (Rev: SLJ 3/00) [745]

24286 National Wildlife Federation. *Wild and Crafty* (1–7). Series: Ranger Rick's NatureScope. 1999, Chelsea LB $19.95 (0-7910-4884-5). 94pp. Step-by-step directions are given for 31 nature crafts (mostly model or puppet making) each with an assigned grade level. (Rev: SLJ 5/99) [745.5]

24287 O'Sullivan, Joanne. *Girls' World: Making Cool Stuff for Your Room, Your Friends and You* (3–6). Illus. 2002, Sterling paper $12.95 (1-57990-291-X). 112pp. Items to make range from gifts for friends and animals to room decorations and school supplies, all with clear instructions and lists of materials that are available in craft and fabric stores. (Rev: SLJ 7/02) [745.5]

24288 Otten, Jack. *Watch Me Make a Bird Feeder* (PS–2). Series: Making Things. 2002, Children's Book Pr. LB $13.50 (0-516-23943-0); paper $4.95 (0-516-23497-8). 24pp. The process of making a bird feeder is simply explained in language that will

suit challenged early readers. Also use *Watch Me Plant a Garden* (2002). (Rev: SLJ 6/02) [690.89]

24289 Pensiero, Janet. *Totally Cool Journals, Notebooks and Diaries* (4–8). Illus. 2004, Sterling $19.95 (1-4027-0341-4). 96pp. A well-illustrated primer on designing and creating an artistic personal journal. (Rev: SLJ 6/04) [686]

24290 Phillips, Matt. *Make Your Own Fun Frames!* (3–6). Illus. by Stan Jaskiel. 2001, Williamson paper $7.95 (1-885593-64-3). 63pp. Basic instructions for making frames and matting, cropping photographs, and hanging frames are accompanied by design suggestions using a variety of everyday materials. (Rev: SLJ 6/02) [749.7]

24291 Powell, Michelle. *Beadwork* (3–5). Illus. Series: Step-by-Step. 2002, Heinemann LB $24.22 (1-4034-0696-0). 32pp. Color photographs show each step in creating beadwork projects. (Rev: BL 12/15/02; HBG 3/03) [745.58]

24292 Powell, Michelle. *Mosaics* (4–7). Series: Step-by-Step. 2001, Heinemann LB $24.22 (1-57572-332-8). 32pp. A number of fascinating projects creating mosaics are described with step-by-step instructions and many colorful illustrations. (Rev: BL 8/1/01; HBG 10/01; SLJ 10/01) [745]

24293 Press, Judy. *All Around Town: Exploring Your Community Through Craft Fun* (PS–3). Illus. Series: Little Hands. 2002, Williamson paper $12.95 (1-885593-68-6). 128pp. Projects using everyday materials that will introduce youngsters to community institutions such as schools, libraries, and gas stations are shown with instructions and illustrations. (Rev: BL 1/1–15/03; SLJ 4/03) [307]

24294 Press, Judy. *Around-the-World Art and Activities: Visiting the 7 Continents Through Craft Fun* (PS–2). Illus. by Betsy Day. Series: Little Hands. 2001, Williamson paper $12.95 (1-885593-45-7). 128pp. Activities, which are coded by level of difficulty, include making travel-related items such as a passport and suitcase, and cultural items such as totem poles, leis, nesting Russian dolls, gaucho belts, and Korean drums. (Rev: SLJ 5/01) [745]

24295 Press, Judy. *ArtStarts for Little Hands! Fun and Discoveries for 3- to 7-Year-Olds* (PS–2). Illus. by Karol Kaminski. 2000, Williamson paper $12.95 (1-885593-37-6). 118pp. A fresh and amusing book that presents simple activities using everyday materials under such themes as animals, seasons, transportation, colors, and gardens. (Rev: SLJ 10/00) [745]

24296 Press, Judy. *At the Zoo: Explore the Animal World with Craft Fun* (PS–3). Illus. by Jenny Campbell. Series: A Little Hands Book. 2002, Williamson paper $12.95 (1-885593-61-9). 126pp. Crafts using widely available materials are grouped in broad categories such as "African Safari" and "Tropical Forest" that are introduced by a map and brief general information, followed by individual animal projects. (Rev: SLJ 8/02)

24297 Press, Judy. *Vroom! Vroom! Making 'Dozers, 'Copters, Trucks, and More* (2–6). Illus. by Michael Kline. Series: Little Hands. 1997, Williamson paper $12.95 (1-885593-04-X). 160pp. Both craft and transportation enthusiasts can use this simple guide to making several vehicles with ordinary materials and good step-by-step directions. (Rev: SLJ 8/97) [745.5]

24298 Price, Pam. *Cool Rubber Stamp Art* (4–6). Illus. Series: Cool Crafts. 2005, ABDO LB $15.95 (1-59197-743-6). 32pp. A terra-cotta flowerpot, wrapping paper, and a canvas beach bag are among the projects shown, with advice on safety, creativity, and seeking help from adults. Also use *Cool Scrapbooks* (2005). (Rev: SLJ 6/05)

24299 *Recyclables* (4–6). Trans. from Spanish by Colleen Coffey. Series: Let's Create! 2004, Gareth Stevens LB $22.60 (0-8368-4018-6). 32pp. Projects using recyclables — cardboard, paper, and plastic, in particular — include a milk-carton cow and an egg-carton tree. (Rev: SLJ 11/04) [745.5]

24300 Rhatigan, Joe. *Soapmaking: 50 Fun and Fabulous Soaps to Melt and Pour* (4–6). Series: Kids' Crafts. 2003, Lark Books $19.95 (1-57990-416-5). 112pp. More than 50 diverse soap projects follow basic information and are accompanied by tips for budding entrepreneurs. (Rev: BL 12/15/03; SLJ 6/04)

24301 Rhatigan, Joe, and Rain Newcomb. *Paper Fantastic: 50 Creative Projects to Fold, Cut, Glue, Paint and Weave* (3–7). Illus. Series: Lark Kids' Crafts. 2004, Sterling $19.95 (1-57990-476-9). 111pp. Interesting, practical projects feature papier mâché, origami, mosaics, and stamp-making. (Rev: SLJ 6/04) [745]

24302 Rhatigan, Joe, and Rain Newcomb. *Stamp It! 50 Amazing Projects to Make* (3–7). Illus. Series: Lark Kids' Crafts. 2004, Sterling $19.95 (1-57990-504-8). 112pp. Lots of ideas for making stamps out of all sorts of things, from potatoes to cardboard, in a format designed to foster creativity and imagination. (Rev: SLJ 6/04) [761]

24303 Rhodes, Vicki. *Pumpkin Decorating* (4–8). 1997, Sterling $10.95 (0-8069-9574-2). Clear directions and full-color photographs demonstrate more than 80 designs for pumpkins. (Rev: SLJ 12/97) [745.5]

24304 Rice, Melanie. *The Complete Book of Children's Activities* (PS–K). Illus. by Chris Barker. 1993, Kingfisher paper $9.95 (1-85697-907-5). 120pp. For the very young, this is a collection of learning activities, games, and construction projects. (Rev: BL 5/1/93) [372]

24305 Robinson, Fay. *Halloween Crafts* (3–5). Illus. Series: Fun Holiday Crafts Kids Can Do! 2004, Enslow LB $17.95 (0-7660-2236-6). 32pp. Ten craft ideas that involve easily found, inexpensive materials are shown with simple instructions. (Rev: SLJ 7/04) [745.594]

24306 Roche, Denis. *Art Around the World: Loo-Loo, Boo, and More Art You Can Do* (2–4). Illus. 1998, Houghton Mifflin $15.00 (0-395-85597-7). 32pp. Eleven art projects, using simple materials (many somewhat difficult for young children to execute), explore the history and geography of areas such as Peru, Java, Bali, and Togo. (Rev: BL 4/1/98; HBG 10/98; SLJ 8/98) [745.5]

24307 Roche, Denis. *Loo-Loo, Boo, and Art You Can Do* (1–4). Illus. 1996, Houghton Mifflin $14.95 (0-395-75921-8). 32pp. Eleven art projects are introduced by Loo-Loo and her dog, Boo. (Rev: BCCB 9/96; BL 9/15/96; SLJ 8/96) [704]

24308 Ross, Kathy. *All New Crafts for Valentine's Day* (1–3). Illus. by Barbara Leonard. 2002, Millbrook LB $23.90 (0-7613-2553-0); paper $7.95 (0-7613-1576-4). 48pp. Easy crafts are accompanied by step-by-step instructions and bright watercolor paintings. (Rev: HBG 3/03; SLJ 11/02) [745.594]

24309 Ross, Kathy. *Christmas Decorations Kids Can Make* (3–5). Illus. 1999, Millbrook $23.40 (0-7613-1565-9). 64pp. An old-fashioned craft book that uses ordinary materials to create such seasonal gifts and ornaments as figures of the three kings. (Rev: BL 12/15/99; HBG 3/00) [594]

24310 Ross, Kathy. *Christmas Ornaments Kids Can Make* (2–5). Illus. 1998, Millbrook LB $23.40 (0-7613-0366-9). 64pp. Thirty projects for making Christmas ornaments are well-presented in this easy-to-follow craft book. (Rev: BL 10/15/98; HBG 3/99; SLJ 10/98) [745.594]

24311 Ross, Kathy. *Christmas Presents Kids Can Make* (4–6). Illus. by Sharon L. Holm. 2001, Millbrook LB $24.40 (0-7613-1754-6). 64pp. The author provides new ideas for 29 creative Christmas gifts using everyday items. (Rev: BL 9/15/01; HBG 3/02; SLJ 10/01) [745.5]

24312 Ross, Kathy. *Crafts for All Seasons* (3–5). Illus. 2000, Millbrook $19.95 (0-7613-1346-X). 176pp. Drawing widely on the material in the author's four seasonal craft books, this spiral-bound volume contains 80 projects with clear instructions. (Rev: BL 10/15/00; HBG 10/01) [745.5]

24313 Ross, Kathy. *Crafts for Christian Values* (K–4). Illus. by Sharon L. Holm. 2000, Millbrook LB $24.90 (0-7613-1618-3). 63pp. A book of 28 craft projects, each related to a particular Christian value — such as a bookmark that honors one's parents. (Rev: HBG 10/01; SLJ 2/01) [745]

24314 Ross, Kathy. *Crafts for Kids Who Are Wild About Deserts* (3–5). Illus. Series: Kids Who Are Wild About. 1998, Millbrook LB $22.40 (0-7613-0954-3). 48pp. A book of ingenious craft projects related to deserts, such as an egg-carton rattlesnake and a sand art necklace. (Rev: BL 3/15/99; HBG 10/99; SLJ 4/99) [745.5]

24315 Ross, Kathy. *Crafts for Kids Who Are Wild About Dinosaurs* (3–5). Illus. Series: Crafts for Kids Who Are Wild About. 1997, Millbrook LB $22.40 (0-7613-0053-8); paper $8.95 (0-7613-0177-1). 48pp. Twenty projects involving dinosaurs and using everyday objects are described. (Rev: BL 2/1/97; SLJ 6/97) [745.5]

24316 Ross, Kathy. *Crafts for Kids Who Are Wild About Oceans* (3–5). Illus. Series: Crafts for Kids Who Are Wild About. 1998, Millbrook LB $22.40 (0-7613-0262-X); paper $7.95 (0-7613-0331-6). 48pp. Using excellent illustrations and clear instructions, this book describes a series of ocean-related craft projects such as making a clam puppet and a water-spouting whale. (Rev: BL 4/15/98; HBG 10/98; SLJ 5/98) [745.5]

24317 Ross, Kathy. *Crafts for Kids Who Are Wild About Outer Space* (3–5). Illus. Series: Crafts for Kids Who Are Wild About. 1997, Millbrook LB $22.40 (0-7613-0054-6); paper $7.95 (0-7613-0176-3). 48pp. Various aspects of outer space are presented in 20 craft projects that use commonplace items. (Rev: BL 2/1/97; SLJ 6/97) [745.5]

24318 Ross, Kathy. *Crafts for Kids Who Are Wild About Polar Life* (3–5). Illus. Series: Kids Who Are Wild About. 1998, Millbrook LB $22.40 (0-7613-0955-1). 48pp. A penguin pin, a walrus mask, and an arctic fox cup puppet are three of the clever craft projects related to the Arctic that are found in this volume. (Rev: BL 3/15/99; HBG 10/99; SLJ 4/99) [745.5]

24319 Ross, Kathy. *Crafts for Kids Who Are Wild About Reptiles* (3–5). Illus. Series: Crafts for Kids Who Are Wild About. 1998, Millbrook LB $22.40 (0-7613-0263-8); paper $7.95 (0-7613-0332-4). 48pp. Twenty reptile-related projects such as making a shedding snake and constructing a tiny turtle are included in this clearly written and well-illustrated craft book. (Rev: BL 4/15/98; HBG 10/98; SLJ 5/98) [745.59]

24320 Ross, Kathy. *Crafts for Valentine's Day* (2–5). Illus. by Sharon L. Holm. Series: Holiday Crafts. 1995, Millbrook LB $21.90 (1-56294-489-4). 47pp. Twenty simple holiday projects using readily available materials are described on double-page spreads, with color illustrations and step-by-step instructions. (Rev: SLJ 4/95) [745.5]

24321 Ross, Kathy. *Crafts from Your Favorite Bible Stories* (3–5). Illus. 2000, Millbrook LB $24.90 (0-7613-1619-1). 64pp. Using simple materials such as lunch bags and pipe cleaners, this book offers 27 craft projects from both the Old and New Testaments such as making Noah's ark or Joseph's coat of many colors. (Rev: BL 6/1–15/00; HBG 10/00; SLJ 8/00) [268]

24322 Ross, Kathy. *Crafts from Your Favorite Children's Songs* (PS–2). Illus. by Vicky Enright. 2001, Millbrook LB $24.40 (0-7613-1912-3). 47pp. Crafts designed to accompany familiar songs are presented with simple instructions. (Rev: HBG 10/01; SLJ 5/01) [745.5]

24323 Ross, Kathy. *Crafts from Your Favorite Children's Stories* (1–4). Illus. by Elaine Garvin. 2001, Millbrook LB $24.40 (0-7613-1772-4). 47pp. Young children may need help with some of these projects, which include a "Bear Hug Puppet," a spinning Dorothy house on its way to Oz, and a Sourdough Sam. (Rev: HBG 3/02; SLJ 9/01) [745.5]

24324 Ross, Kathy. *Crafts from Your Favorite Nursery Rhymes* (3–5). Illus. by Elaine Garvin. 2002, Millbrook LB $24.90 (0-7613-2523-9); paper $8.95 (0-7613-1589-6). 48pp. Simple directions and clear illustrations accompany projects of varying difficulty; young children will need some help with these activities related to popular rhymes. (Rev: BL 1/1–15/03; HBG 3/03; SLJ 12/02) [745.5]

24325 Ross, Kathy. *Crafts to Celebrate God's Creation* (3–5). Illus. 2001, Millbrook LB $24.90 (0-7613-1621-3). 64pp. Using the creation story in Genesis as a focus, this craft book gives directions for making such items as a "sunrise puppet," flying birds, and a beaded pin in the shape of a cross. (Rev: BL 1/1–15/01; HBG 10/01) [268.432]

24326 Ross, Kathy. *Crafts to Make in the Fall* (3–5). Illus. by Vicky Enright. Series: Crafts for All Seasons. 1998, Millbrook LB $23.40 (0-7613-0318-9); paper $8.95 (0-7613-0335-9). 63pp. Twenty-nine craft projects, with a wide range of difficulty, are included in this book that involves autumn themes and holidays like Columbus Day and Thanksgiving. (Rev: HBG 3/99; SLJ 2/99) [745]

24327 Ross, Kathy. *Crafts to Make in the Spring* (K–4). Illus. by Vicky Enright. 1998, Millbrook LB $23.40 (0-7613-0316-2); paper $8.95 (0-7613-0333-2). 63pp. This book contains 29 simple crafts described in double-page spreads and inspired by spring and such holidays as Passover and Easter. (Rev: HBG 10/98; SLJ 6/98) [745]

24328 Ross, Kathy. *Crafts to Make in the Winter* (K–3). Illus. by Vicky Enright. Series: Crafts for All Seasons. 1999, Millbrook LB $23.40 (0-7613-0319-7). 64pp. The use of accessible materials and good step-by-step instructions make this a fine craft book about making things that are winter-related. (Rev: BL 12/15/99; HBG 3/00; SLJ 1/00) [745.5]

24329 Ross, Kathy. *Every Day Is Earth Day* (2–4). Illus. by Sharon L. Holm. Series: Holiday Crafts. 1995, Millbrook LB $21.90 (1-56294-490-8). 47pp. After a general discussion of Earth Day, presents 20 crafts that reflect an interest in conserving natural resources and recycling materials. (Rev: SLJ 5/95) [745.5]

24330 Ross, Kathy. *Kathy Ross Crafts Numbers* (PS–1). Illus. by Jan Barger. Series: Learning Is Fun! 2003, Millbrook LB $23.90 (0-7613-2105-5); paper $7.95 (0-7613-1697-3). 48pp. Numbers and the ways they are used in everyday life form the central theme of this large-format collection of crafts; included among the simple projects are a birthday cake pin, a toy alarm clock, and playing-card counters. (Rev: BL 4/15/03; HBG 10/03) [745.5]

24331 Ross, Kathy. *Kathy Ross Crafts Triangles, Rectangles, Circles, and Squares* (PS–1). Illus. by Jan Barger. Series: Learning Is Fun! 2002, Millbrook LB $23.90 (0-7613-2104-7); paper $7.95 (0-7613-1696-5). 48pp. Projects that introduce basic geometric shapes include puppets, jewelry, games, and hanging objects. (Rev: HBG 3/03; SLJ 1/03)

24332 Ross, Kathy. *Make Yourself a Monster! A Book of Creepy Crafts* (2–5). Illus. by Sharon Hawkins Vargo. 1999, Millbrook LB $22.90 (0-7613-1556-X). 45pp. Twenty 20 monster-themed crafts include making a slimy monster mitt puppet and a Dracula soap dispenser. (Rev: HBG 3/00; SLJ 4/00) [745]

24333 Ross, Kathy. *Play-Doh Animal Fun* (K–4). Illus. by Sharon Hawkins Vargo. 2002, Millbrook LB $24.40 (0-7613-2506-9). 48pp. Twenty animals to make with play-doh range from simple clams to a rattlesnake with a rattle. Also use *Play-Doh Art Projects* (2002). (Rev: HBG 10/02; SLJ 5/02) [745.5]

24334 Ross, Kathy. *Star-Spangled Crafts* (4–6). Illus. by Sharon Lane Holm. 2003, Millbrook LB $23.90 (0-7613-2853-X). 48pp. Twenty-two crafts with patriotic themes include an American eagle magnet and an Uncle Sam tissue box. (Rev: HBG 10/03; SLJ 7/03)

24335 Sadler, Judy Ann. *Christmas Crafts from Around the World* (4–6). 2003, Kids Can $12.95 (1-55337-427-4); paper $6.95 (1-55337-428-2). 40pp. This guide offers step-by-step instructions for making 17 Christmas crafts with origins in countries around the world. (Rev: BL 12/15/03; HBG 4/04; SLJ 10/03)

24336 Sadler, Judy Ann. *Jumbo Book of Easy Crafts* (3–5). Illus. 2001, Kids Can $14.95 (1-55074-811-4). 208pp. Crafts using everyday items — paper plates, popsicle sticks, aluminum foil, beans, beads, and so forth — are arranged by type of material. (Rev: BL 6/1–15/01; SLJ 7/01) [745.5]

24337 Sadler, Judy Ann. *The Kids Can Press Jumbo Book of Crafts* (2–6). Illus. by Caroline Price. 1998, Kids Can paper $12.00 (1-55074-375-9). 208pp. This book contains an array of easy and inexpensive craft projects, including making papier-mâché bowls, cord-covered bottles, and collage frames. (Rev: SLJ 12/98) [745]

24338 Sanders, Nancy I. *Old Testament Days: An Activity Guide* (4–6). Illus. 1999, Chicago Review paper $14.95 (1-55652-354-8). 144pp. This craft book contains 80 projects related to incidents in the Old Testament, such as making a sleeping mat similar to that used by Abraham. (Rev: BL 10/15/99; SLJ 12/99) [372.89]

24339 Schwarz, Renée. *Birdhouses* (4–7). Illus. Series: Kids Can Do It! 2005, Kids Can $12.95 (1-55337-549-1); paper $6.95 (1-55337-550-5). 40pp. Nine different birdhouse projects for children to tackle, with illustrated instructions and photographs of the finished products. (Rev: BL 4/1/05; SLJ 5/05) [690]

24340 Schwarz, Renée. *Funky Junk* (4–7). Series: Kids Can Do It! 2002, Kids Can $12.95 (1-55337-387-1); paper $5.95 (1-55337-388-X). 48pp. Using easily found materials, this craft book supplies details on how to make unusual conversation pieces. (Rev: BL 3/15/03; HBG 10/03; SLJ 4/03) [745.5]

24341 Simons, Robin. *Recyclopedia: Games, Science Equipment and Crafts from Recycled Materials* (5–8). Illus. by author. 1976, Houghton Mifflin paper $13.95 (0-395-59641-6). Clear directions complemented by good illustrations characterize this book of interesting projects using waste materials.

24342 Smith, Heather, and Joe Rhatigan. *Earth-Friendly Crafts for Kids* (3–6). Illus. 2002, Sterling $24.95 (1-57990-340-1). 144pp. Instructions for crafts made from recyclable materials, with further "Earth-friendly" ideas. (Rev: BL 2/15/03; HBG 3/03; SLJ 1/03) [745.5]

24343 Sohi, Morteza E. *Look What I Did with a Leaf!* (3–6). Illus. Series: Nature Craft. 1993, Walker LB $15.85 (0-8027-8216-7). Combines nature crafts with field guide material and explains how to make collage animals out of leaves. (Rev: SLJ 12/93) [745]

24344 Sohi, Morteza E. *Look What I Did with a Shell!* (3–6). Illus. 2000, Walker LB $16.85 (0-8027-8723-1). 32pp. Shells are introduced with information on sizes, shapes, color, and contrasts, followed by a series of interesting projects and tips on working with shells. (Rev: BL 7/00; HBG 10/00; SLJ 7/00) [745.55]

24345 Solga, Kim, and Priscilla Hershberger. *Craft Fun!* (2–6). Photos by Pamela Monfort. Series: Art and Activities for Kids. 1997, North Light paper $19.99 (0-89134-834-4). 216pp. This activity book introduces crafts projects on a variety of topics, including card making, costumes, and clothes. (Rev: SLJ 1/98) [745.5]

24346 Souter, Gillian. *Holiday Handiworks* (3–6). Illus. Series: Handy Crafts. 2002, Gareth Stevens LB $23.93 (0-8368-3050-4). 48pp. A well-organized collection of crafts with clear instructions, aimed at holidays including Easter, Passover, Kwanzaa, and Chinese New Year. Also use *Rainy Day Fun* and *Terrific Toys* (both 2002). (Rev: HBG 10/02; SLJ 6/02) [745.5]

24347 Souter, Gillian. *Perfect Parties* (2–5). Photos by Andre Martin. Illus. by Clare Watson. Series: Handy Crafts. 2001, Gareth Stevens LB $22.60 (0-8368-2822-4). 48pp. A useful party checklist precedes discussion of each important consideration and step-by-step instructions for creating a wide selection of decorations and games and some foods. Also use *Great Gifts* and *Beads 'n' Bangles* (both 2001). (Rev: HBG 10/01; SLJ 7/01) [793.2]

24348 Steele, Philip. *Clothes and Crafts in Victorian Times* (4–6). Series: Clothing and Crafts in History. 2000, Gareth Stevens LB $21.27 (0-8368-2738-4). 32pp. Nineteenth-century crafts including handmade woolens, lace embroidery, wood carvings, and pottery are described; projects include making a Victorian valentine and a Punch and Judy puppet. (Rev: BL 1/1–15/01; HBG 3/02) [940]

24349 Stetson, Emily, and Vicky Congdon. *Little Hands Fingerplays and Action Songs: Seasonal Rhymes and Creative Play for 2- to 6-Year-Olds* (PS–1). Illus. by Betsy Day. Series: Little Hands. 2001, Williamson paper $12.95 (1-885593-53-8). 128pp. Suggestions for songs, games, and crafts are organized by season and accompanied by brief facts and short reading lists. (Rev: SLJ 11/01) [793.4]

24350 Taylor, Maureen. *Through the Eyes of Your Ancestors: A Step-by-Step Guide to Uncovering Your Family's History* (5–9). Illus. 1999, Houghton Mifflin $17.00 (0-395-86980-3); paper $8.95 (0-395-86982-X). Budding researchers learn how to investigate family history, from conducting interviews to visiting genealogical libraries. (Rev: BCCB 5/99; BL 3/1/99; HB 5–6/99; HBG 10/99; SLJ 5/99) [929.1]

24351 Temko, Florence. *Traditional Crafts from Africa* (2–5). Illus. 1996, Lerner LB $23.93 (0-8225-2936-X). 64pp. Clear instructions and excellent illustrations are used in the presentation of several African craft projects. (Rev: BL 9/1/96; SLJ 10/96) [745]

24352 Temko, Florence. *Traditional Crafts from China* (5–7). Illus. Series: Culture Crafts. 2001, Lerner LB $23.93 (0-8225-2939-4). 64pp. After a few words about crafts in general, this volume carefully outlines a number of projects relating to Chinese culture, including instructions for picture scrolls and tanagrams. (Rev: BL 2/15/01; HBG 10/01; SLJ 4/01) [745]

24353 Temko, Florence. *Traditional Crafts from Japan* (3–5). Illus. by Randall Gooch. Series: Culture Crafts. 2001, Lerner LB $23.93 (0-8225-2938-6). 64pp. Eight traditional Japanese handicrafts are presented with instructions for making them and explanations of their significance in Japanese culture. (Rev: HBG 10/01; SLJ 4/01) [745]

24354 Temko, Florence. *Traditional Crafts from Mexico and Central America* (3–6). Photos by Robert L. Wolfe and Diane Wolfe. Illus. by Randall Gooch. Series: Culture Crafts. 1996, Lerner LB $23.93 (0-8225-2935-1). 64pp. After a brief introduction to the area, this book describes eight traditional crafts with clear instructions and a number of helpful illustrations. (Rev: BCCB 2/97; SLJ 12/96) [745.5]

24355 Temko, Florence. *Traditional Crafts from the Caribbean* (5–7). Illus. Series: Culture Crafts. 2001, Lerner LB $23.93 (0-8225-2937-8). 64pp. Step-by-step instructions with clear diagrams are given for a number of craft projects relating to Caribbean culture including yarn dolls, Puerto Rican masks, and metal cutouts. (Rev: BL 2/15/01; HBG 10/01; SLJ 4/01) [745]

24356 Thomas, John E., and Danita Pagel. *The Ultimate Book of Kid Concoctions* (PS–4). Illus. by Robb Durr and Zachariah Durr. 1998, Kid Concoctions paper $14.95 (0-9661088-0-9). 80pp. Features about 65 recipes and activities using common kitchen supplies to make items like sidewalk chalk, finger paints, and scratch-and-sniff stickers. (Rev: SLJ 3/98) [745.5]

24357 Torres, Laura. *Best Friends Forever! 199 Projects to Make and Share* (5–8). Illus. 2004, Workman paper $13.95 (0-7611-3274-0). 148pp. Craft ideas that will appeal to young teens — bracelets, key chains, picture frames, and so forth — are clearly explained and organized into chapters such as "Cool Notes" and "Home and School." (Rev: SLJ 2/05) [745.5]

24358 Trottier, Maxine. *Native Crafts: Inspired by North America's First Peoples* (3–6). Illus. 2000, Kids Can $12.95 (1-55074-854-8); paper $5.95 (1-55074-549-2). 40pp. Sixteen projects (all requiring adult help) from the traditional arts and crafts of Native Americans are presented with step-by-step instructions and pictures of the finished products. (Rev: BL 7/00; HBG 10/00; SLJ 6/00) [745.5]

24359 Wagner, Lisa. *Cool Painted Stuff* (4–6). Illus. Series: Cool Crafts. 2005, ABDO LB $15.95 (1-59197-742-8). 32pp. A fancy flowerpot and a mini-tote are among the projects shown, with advice on safety, creativity, and seeking help from adults. (Rev: SLJ 6/05)

24360 Wallace, Mary. *I Can Make That! Fantastic Crafts for Kids* (K–5). Illus. Series: I Can Make That. 2002, Maple Tree $19.95 (1-894379-41-1). 160pp. This compilation of five earlier I Can Make That! books contains step-by-step instructions and photographs to help children create their own toys, games, and other crafts. (Rev: BL 10/15/02; SLJ 11/02) [745.5]

24361 Warwick, Ellen. *Stuff for Your Space* (4–6). Series: Kids Can Do It! 2004, Kids Can $12.95 (1-55337-398-7). 40pp. Well-illustrated advice and instructions for boys and girls on decorating their individual living spaces. (Rev: BL 2/15/04; SLJ 4/04) [745]

24362 West, Robin. *My Very Own Birthday: A Book of Cooking and Crafts* (2–4). Photos by Robert L. Wolfe and Diane Wolfe. Illus. by Jackie Urbanovic. Series: My Very Own Holiday. 1996, Carolrhoda LB $21.27 (0-87614-980-8). 64pp. Five birthday parties using different themes are described, along with recipes and craft projects. (Rev: SLJ 5/96) [745.5]

24363 West, Robin. *My Very Own Christmas: A Book of Cooking and Crafts* (PS–1). Illus. by Susan S. Burke. 1993, Carolrhoda LB $21.27 (0-87614-722-8). 64pp. This book contains a variety of Christmas crafts and a number of recipes. (Rev: BL 8/93) [394.2]

24364 White, Linda. *Haunting on a Halloween* (5–7). Illus. by Fran Lee. 2002, Gibbs Smith paper $9.95 (1-58685-112-8). 64pp. Everything young party planners need to host a Halloween get-together, with instructions for crafts, food, decorations, and costumes. (Rev: BL 9/15/02) [745.594]

24365 Williams, Joy. *Nature Crafts* (4–6). Photos by Christine Polomsky. Series: Creative Kids. 2002, North Light paper $12.99 (1-58180-292-7). 64pp. A guide to making a variety of crafts using natural materials whenever possible. (Rev: SLJ 9/02) [745.5]

24366 *A World of Things to Do* (2–5). Illus. 1987, National Geographic LB $12.50 (0-87044-615-0). 104pp. All sorts of activities for even the most hard to please, from kitchen science experiments to holiday ideas. (Rev: BL 5/15/87)

24367 Zakarin, Debra Mostow. *Happening Hanukkah: Creative Ways to Celebrate* (4–6). Illus. by Amanda Haley. 2002, Grosset paper $5.99 (0-448-42869-5). 64pp. A treasure trove of Hanukkah gift ideas plus suggestions for parties, food, and games. (Rev: SLJ 10/02)

American Historical Crafts

24368 *Addy's Craft Book: A Look at Crafts from the Past with Projects You Can Make Today* (3–5).

Illus. Series: American Girls Pastimes. 1994, Pleasant Co. paper $5.95 (1-56247-124-4). 44pp. A book of handicrafts that re-creates projects popular in 19th-century America during the days of slavery. (Rev: BL 12/15/94) [745.5]

24369 Beard, D. C. *The American Boys' Handy Book: What to Do and How to Do It* (5–7). Illus. 1983, Godine paper $12.95 (0-87923-449-0). 392pp. A facsimile edition of a manual first published in 1882. [790.194]

24370 Broida, Marian. *Projects About Plantation Life* (3–5). Series: Hands-On History. 2003, Benchmark LB $18.95 (0-7614-1605-6). 48pp. Introduced by appropriate background, illustrations, and maps, this book offers detailed instructions on re-creating things from the period — from crafts to recipes. Also use *Projects About Westward Expansion* (2003). (Rev: BL 2/15/04; HBG 4/04; SLJ 3/04)

24371 Caney, Steven. *Steven Caney's Kids' America* (4–7). Illus. 1978, Workman paper $14.95 (0-911104-80-1). 416pp. Activities that focus on getting children to rediscover parts of America's past.

24372 D'Amato, Janet, and Alex D'Amato. *Indian Crafts* (1–4). Illus. by authors. 1968, Lion LB $16.50 (0-87460-088-X). An excellent introduction to Indian crafts through projects and activities.

24373 *Felicity's Craft Book: A Look at Crafts from the Past with Projects You Can Make Today* (3–5). Illus. Series: American Girls Pastimes. 1994, Pleasant Co. paper $5.95 (1-56247-121-X). 44pp. This craft book outlines projects that were current during the American colonial period. (Rev: BL 12/15/94) [745.5]

24374 Greenwood, Barbara. *Pioneer Crafts* (4–8). Illus. 1997, Kids Can paper $4.95 (1-55074-359-7). This guide gives directions for 17 projects such as candle making, soap carving, and basket weaving. (Rev: BL 9/15/97; SLJ 9/97) [745.5]

24375 Kalman, Bobbie. *Pioneer Projects* (3–6). Illus. by Marc Crabtree. Series: Historic Communities. 1997, Crabtree LB $20.60 (0-86505-437-1); paper $7.95 (0-86505-467-3). 32pp. Authentic crafts and activities engaged in by early American settlers are outlined, including step-by-step directions for building a model of a pioneer town. (Rev: BL 7/97; SLJ 8/97) [745.5]

24376 *Kirsten's Craft Book: A Look at Crafts from the Past with Projects You Can Make Today* (3–5). Illus. Series: American Girls Pastimes. 1994, Pleasant Co. paper $5.95 (1-56247-112-0). 45pp. Outlines a number of craft projects that pioneer children enjoyed, like making a calendar stick and a yarn doll. (Rev: BL 12/15/94; SLJ 12/94) [680]

24377 Merrill, Yvonne Y. *Hands-On Rocky Mountains: Art Activities About Anasazi, American Indians, Settlers, Trappers, and Cowboys* (4–8). Illus. 1996, Kits paper $16.95 (0-9643177-2-9). Historical groups from the Rocky Mountain region — early people, American Indians, trappers, settlers, and cowboys — are introduced and, for each, a series of craft projects is outlined. (Rev: BL 1/1–15/97; SLJ 4/97) [745.5]

24378 *Molly's Craft Book: A Look at Crafts from the Past with Projects You Can Make Today* (3–5). Illus. Series: American Girls Pastimes. 1994, Pleasant Co. paper $5.95 (1-56247-118-X). 44pp. Through a series of craft projects, life between the world wars is re-created. (Rev: BL 12/15/94) [745.5]

24379 *Samantha's Craft Book: A Look at Crafts from the Past with Projects You Can Make Today* (3–5). Illus. Series: American Girls Pastimes. 1994, Pleasant Co. paper $5.95 (1-56247-115-5). 44pp. Twentieth-century American history is reflected in a series of interesting craft projects. (Rev: BL 12/15/94) [745.5]

24380 Temko, Florence. *Traditional Crafts from Native North America* (2–4). Illus. Series: Culture Crafts. 1997, Lerner LB $23.93 (0-8225-2934-3). 64pp. Introduces the major cultural areas of North American Indians and gives directions for making such objects as baskets, cornhusk dolls, and dream catchers. (Rev: BL 10/1/97; SLJ 7/97) [745.5]

24381 Tull, Mary, et al. *North America* (4–7). Series: Artisans Around the World. 1999, Raintree LB $27.12 (0-7398-0117-1). 48pp. North American folk art is surveyed, from peoples including the Haida of western Canada, New Mexico's Pueblos, the Pennsylvanian German Americans, and African Americans. (Rev: BL 10/15/99; HBG 3/00) [970]

24382 Yamane, Linda. *Weaving a California Tradition: A Native American Basketmaker* (3–6). Illus. Series: We Are Still Here: Native Americans Today. 1996, Lerner $21.27 (0-8225-2660-3); paper $6.95 (0-8225-9730-6). 48pp. The story of California basket weaving, its present status, and the people who engage in it. (Rev: BL 1/1–15/97; SLJ 2/97) [746.41]

Clay and Other Modeling Crafts

24383 Arima, Elaine. *The Kids 'n' Clay Ceramics Book: HandBuilding and Wheel-Throwing Projects from the Kids 'N' Clay Pottery Studio* (3–8). Illus. 2000, Tricycle paper $16.95 (1-883672-89-9). 128pp. A ceramic project book for middle and junior high grades that involves creating both handmade and wheel-thrown objects including a breakfast bowl, bookends, and a porcupine. (Rev: BL 3/1/00; SLJ 8/00) [738]

24384 Carlson, Maureen. *Clay Characters for Kids* (3–8). Photos by author. 2003, North Light paper $12.99 (1-58180-286-2). 79pp. This photo-filled guide to modeling figures out of polymer clay outlines 30 projects that will require a degree of adult supervision. (Rev: SLJ 12/03) [731.4]

24385 *Clay* (3–6). Series: Let's Create! 2003, Gareth Stevens LB $22.60 (0-8368-3746-0). 32pp. This plentifully illustrated primer on working creatively with clay details a dozen projects, with suggestions for further reading and a list of Web resources. (Rev: SLJ 4/04) [738]

24386 Dean, Irene Semanchuk. *Polymer Clay: 30 Terrific Projects to Roll, Mold and Squish* (5–8).

Illus. Series: Kids' Crafts. 2003, Sterling $19.95 (1-57990-350-9). 112pp. Step-by-step instructions are provided for a variety of decorative objects to make from polymer clay. (Rev: HBG 4/04; SLJ 9/03) [731.4]

24387 Dixon, Annabelle. *Clay* (3–5). Illus. by Ed Barber. Series: Threads. 1990, Garrett LB $15.93 (0-944483-69-0). 26pp. The nature of clay, where it is found, and its uses in pottery and model crafts are discussed. (Rev: BL 2/1/91; SLJ 4/91) [553.6]

24388 Ellis, Mary. *Ceramics for Kids: Creative Clay Projects to Pinch, Roll, Coil, Slam and Twist* (3–6). Illus. 2002, Sterling $24.95 (1-57990-198-0). 144pp. Ceramics projects for older readers, organized by the skill required and growing in complexity as readers progress through the book, are outlined step-by-step. (Rev: BL 12/15/02; HBG 3/03; SLJ 1/03) [738.1]

24389 Good, Keith. *Shape It! Magnificent Projects for Molding Materials* (3–7). Series: Design It! 2000, Lerner LB $21.27 (0-8225-3568-8). 30pp. This is a book of craft projects that involve molding materials such as salt dough, plaster, air-drying clay, and edible materials like cookie dough. (Rev: HBG 10/00; SLJ 6/00) [745.5]

24390 Reid, Barbara. *Fun with Modeling Clay* (1–4). Illus. 1998, Kids Can paper $5.95 (1-55074-510-7). 40pp. After such basics as modeling balls, pancakes, and snakes from clay, this craft book goes on to such projects as fruit baskets, cars and trains, and underwater scenes. (Rev: BL 9/1/98) [731.4]

24391 Ross, Kathy. *Play-Doh Fun and Games* (K–4). Illus. by Sharon Vargo. Series: Play-Doh Fun. 2003, Millbrook LB $24.90 (0-7613-2507-7). 48pp. Detailed instructions for 20 game and toy projects that can be made using Play-Doh and/or other readily available materials. (Rev: HBG 10/03; SLJ 6/03)

24392 Rowe, Christine. *The Children's Book of Pottery* (4–7). Illus. 1989, Trafalgar $24.95 (0-7134-5995-6). 64pp. A good British import about pottery making. (Rev: BL 12/1/89) [738.1]

24393 Speechley, Greta. *Clay Modeling* (3–6). Series: Step-by-Step. 2000, Heinemann LB $22.75 (1-57572-326-3). 32pp. This book shows how to create figures including a cat, a tiger, a flowerpot, and a bowl using air-drying clay. (Rev: BL 10/15/00; HBG 10/01; SLJ 12/00) [745.5]

Costume and Jewelry Making

24394 Baker, Diane. *Jazzy Jewelry: Power Beads, Crystals, Chokers, and Illusion and Tattoo Styles* (5–9). Illus. by Alexandra Michaels. 2001, Williamson paper $12.95 (1-885593-47-3). 144pp. Jewelry projects for bead lovers include chokers, headbands, and bobby pins, all presented with black-and-white line drawings and guidance on color choice, clasps and knots, and proper storage. (Rev: SLJ 7/01) [745.594]

24395 Baker, Diane. *Make Your Own Hairwear: Beaded Barrettes, Clips, Dangles and Headbands*

(4–8). Illus. by Alexandra Michaels. 2001, Williamson paper $8.95 (1-885593-63-5). 63pp. Easy instructions guide readers through the steps of making hair accessories using beads, shells, rhinestones, and other materials. (Rev: SLJ 4/02) [745.58]

24396 Casey, Moe. *The Most Excellent Book of Dress Up* (3–5). Illus. Series: Most Excellent Book Of. 1997, Millbrook LB $19.90 (0-7613-0550-5); paper $6.95 (0-7613-0575-0). 32pp. Using many photos and drawings, this colorful book gives easy, step-by-step instructions for making various costumes. (Rev: BL 6/1–15/97; SLJ 8/97) [646.4]

24397 Cummings, Richard. *101 Costumes for All Ages, All Occasions* (5–9). Illus. 1987, Plays paper $12.95 (0-8238-0286-8). A variety of easily made costumes are described from Frankenstein and Captain Hook to Cleopatra and even a tube of toothpaste. (Rev: BL 1/1/88; BR 3–4/88) [792.026]

24398 Gayle, Katie. *Snappy Jazzy Jewelry* (4–7). Illus. 1996, Sterling $14.95 (0-8069-3854-4). 48pp. Making necklaces and earrings are two of the craft projects described, with many helpful photographs. (Rev: BL 5/15/96; SLJ 6/96) [745.594]

24399 Gryski, Camilla. *Friendship Bracelets* (3–6). Illus. 1993, Morrow paper $6.95 (0-688-12437-2). 48pp. Instructions are given on how to make friendship bracelets from different materials, plus material on creating other forms of jewelry. (Rev: BL 10/1/93; SLJ 9/93) [746]

24400 MacLeod-Brudenell, Iain. *Costume Crafts* (4–7). Illus. Series: World Wide Crafts. 1994, Gareth Stevens LB $22.60 (0-8368-1152-6). 32pp. Multicultural projects involving dress and body decoration are featured in this easily followed craft book. (Rev: BL 3/1/95; SLJ 1/95) [745.5]

24401 Newcomb, Rain. *Girls' World Book of Jewelry: 50 Cool Designs to Make* (5–8). Series: Kids Crafts. 2004, Lark Books paper $14.95 (1-57990-473-4). 128pp. Up-to-date designs are accompanied by well-thought-out instructions and advice in this large-format volume. (Rev: BL 12/15/04; SLJ 4/05)

24402 Sadler, Judy Ann. *Beading: Bracelets, Earrings, Necklaces and More* (4–8). Illus. Series: Kids Can! 1998, Kids Can paper $5.95 (1-55074-338-4). 40pp. Using photographs and simple instructions, directions are given for making a simple beading loom and creating necklaces and bracelets. (Rev: BL 5/15/98) [745.594]

24403 Sadler, Judy Ann. *Easy Braids, Barrettes and Bows* (3–7). Illus. 1997, Kids Can paper $5.95 (1-55074-325-2). 40pp. Discusses various hairstyles, like cornrows and ponytails, and gives instructions on making pieces of hair jewelry. (Rev: BL 10/15/97; SLJ 11/97) [646.7]

24404 Sadler, Judy Ann. *Hemp Jewelry* (4–7). Illus. Series: Kids Can Do It! 2005, Kids Can $12.95 (1-55337-774-5); paper $6.95 (1-55337-775-3). 40pp. Sixteen projects for boys and girls using hemp, with drawings and photographs to illustrate the steps and the results. (Rev: BL 3/15/05; SLJ 5/05) [746.4]

24405 Sensier, Danielle. *Costumes* (5–7). Illus. Series: Traditions Around the World. 1994, Thomson Learning LB $24.26 (1-56847-227-7). 48pp.

The rituals and uses involved in costumes are introduced, as well as a general discussion of clothing in various regions and cultures. (Rev: BL 2/1/95; SLJ 3/95) [391]

24406 Wallace, Mary. *I Can Make Jewelry* (2–4). Illus. 1997, Firefly $17.95 (1-895688-62-0); paper $6.95 (1-895688-63-9). 32pp. Rings, beads, hair decorations, and necklaces are some of the jewelry for which there are directions to make and wear. (Rev: BL 8/97) [745.5]

24407 Wilkes, Angela. *Dazzling Disguises and Clever Costumes* (4–6). Illus. 1996, DK $14.95 (0-7894-1001-X). 48pp. Step-by-step instructions on how to make a variety of costumes, the materials needed, and information on clever disguises. (Rev: BCCB 11/96; BL 10/1/96; SLJ 12/96) [646.8]

Drawing and Painting

24408 Ames, Lee J. *Draw Fifty Airplanes, Aircraft and Spacecraft* (3–7). Illus. by author. 1987, Doubleday paper $8.95 (0-385-23629-8). 64pp. Simple directions for drawing various airborne articles, from the Wright brothers' plane to the Saturn V rocket. Also use: *Draw Fifty Boats, Ships, Trucks and Trains* (1976); *Draw Fifty Vehicles* (1997); *Draw Fifty Buildings and Other Structures* (1980).

24409 Ames, Lee J. *Draw Fifty Baby Animals: The Step-by-Step Way to Draw Kittens, Lambs, Chicks, and Other Adorable Offspring* (3–5). Illus. by author. 2003, Broadway $13.95 (0-7679-1283-7); paper $8.95 (0-7679-1284-5). In this step-by-step guide, author Lee J. Ames shows young readers how to draw pictures of baby animals — both wild and domesticated. (Rev: SLJ 11/03) [743.6]

24410 Ames, Lee J. *Draw Fifty Cats* (4–7). Illus. 1986, Doubleday paper $8.95 (0-385-24640-4). 64pp. Step-by-step ways of drawing different breeds and poses of cats. Also use *Draw Fifty Holiday Decorations* (1987). (Rev: BL 11/15/86) [743.69752]

24411 Ames, Lee J. *Draw Fifty Dogs* (4–6). Illus. by author. 1981, Doubleday paper $8.95 (0-385-23431-7). 64pp. Six steps are used to draw several species. Also use: *Draw Fifty Animals* (1985); *Draw Fifty Dinosaurs and Other Prehistoric Animals* (1977); *Draw Fifty Horses* (1984).

24412 Ames, Lee J. *Draw Fifty Famous Cartoons* (4–6). Illus. by author. 1985, Doubleday paper $8.95 (0-385-19521-4). 64pp. How to draw such characters as Dick Tracy and the Flintstones.

24413 Ames, Lee J. *Draw Fifty Monsters, Creeps, Superheroes, Demons, Dragons, Nerds, Dirts, Ghouls, Giants, Vampires, Zombies and Other Curiosa* (4–6). Illus. by author. 1986, Doubleday paper $8.95 (0-385-17639-2). 64pp. How to draw a variety of curiosities.

24414 Ames, Lee J., and Ric Estrada. *Draw Fifty Aliens, UFOs, Galaxy Ghouls, Milky Way Marauders, and Other Extraterrestrial Creatures* (3–5). Illus. Series: Draw 50. 1998, Doubleday paper $8.95 (0-385-49145-X). A step-by-step guide to drawing 50 creatures and objects from outer space. (Rev: BL 1/1–15/99; SLJ 6/99) [743]

24415 Arnosky, Jim. *Sketching Outdoors in Summer* (4–7). Illus. 1988, Lothrop $12.95 (0-688-06286-5). 48pp. The artist's appreciation of nature can inspire young enthusiasts. Also use: *Sketching Outdoors in Spring* (1987). (Rev: BL 6/15/88; HB 7–8/88; SLJ 6–7/88)

24416 Balchin, Judy. *Creative Lettering* (4–7). Series: Step-by-Step. 2001, Heinemann LB $24.22 (1-57572-331-X). 32pp. Using easy-to-find materials, this craft book gives clear directions for several fascinating lettering projects. (Rev: BL 8/1/01; HBG 10/01) [745.6]

24417 Balchin, Judy. *Decorative Painting* (4–7). Series: Step-by-Step. 2001, Heinemann LB $24.22 (1-57572-330-1). 32pp. With easy-to-follow directions and illustrations that describe each step, this colorful book contains a number of simple projects that decorate with paints. (Rev: BL 8/1/01; HBG 10/01; SLJ 10/01) [745]

24418 Baron, Nancy. *Getting Started in Calligraphy* (5–8). 1979, Sterling paper $13.95 (0-8069-8840-1). This well-organized text shows how to draw letters with beauty and grace. [745.6]

24419 Barr, Steve. *1-2-3 Draw Cartoon Aliens and Space Stuff: A Step-by-Step Guide* (3–6). Illus. by author. 2003, Peel paper $8.99 (0-939217-71-6). 62pp. Easy-to-follow instructions show progressively difficult drawings first in black-and-white and finally in color. Also use *1-2-3 Draw Cartoon Wildlife* (2003). (Rev: SLJ 5/03) [741.5]

24420 Barr, Steve. *1-2-3 Draw Cartoon Animals* (2–5). Illus. 2002, Peel paper $8.99 (0-939217-48-1). 64pp. Easy, step-by-step directions guide budding young artists to draw a variety of animals using a cartoon style. Also use *1-2-3 Draw Cartoon Faces* and *1-2-3 Draw Cartoon People* (both 2002). (Rev: BL 1/1–15/03) [741.5]

24421 Butterfield, Moira. *Fun with Paint* (4–8). Illus. Series: Creative Crafts. 1994, Random paper $6.99 (0-679-83942-3). 47pp. This simple introduction to painting covers various media and a number of creative projects, including making your own paints. (Rev: SLJ 3/94) [745]

24422 Carreiro, Carolyn. *Hand-Print Animal Art* (3–5). Illus. by Carolyn Carreiro and A. J. Greenwood. Series: Kids Can! 1997, Williamson paper $14.95 (1-885593-09-0). 144pp. Instructions are given for creating 63 animal shapes by placing paint on one's hands and fingers and stamping them on paper. (Rev: BCCB 3/98; SLJ 4/98) [745.5]

24423 *Cartoon Magic* (2–6). Illus. 2001, North Light paper $12.99 (1-58180-229-3). 64pp. Readers will learn to draw people and animals, to show movement and use perspective, and to use color and word balloons to best effect. Also use *Drawing Magic* (2001). (Rev: SLJ 11/01) [741.2]

24424 ComicsKey Staff. *How to Draw Kung Fu Comics* (4–8). 2004, ComicsOne Corporation paper $19.95 (1-58899-394-9). 160pp. Cheung's instructions on creating architecture and perspective are particularly valuable. (Rev: BL 8/04) [741.5]

24425 Court, Rob. *How to Draw Cars and Trucks* (4–6). Illus. Series: The Scribbles Institute. 2005, Child's World LB $14.95 (1-59296-148-7). 32pp. In addition to introducing the basics, Court focuses readers on the composition and purpose of the objects they are drawing. Also use *How to Draw Dinosaurs* (2005). (Rev: BL 4/1/05) [743]

24426 DuBosque, Doug. *Draw Desert Animals* (3–6). Illus. 1996, Peel paper $8.95 (0-939217-26-0). 64pp. Beginning with simple shapes like circles and squares, teaches the reader to draw a variety of desert animals. (Rev: BL 12/15/96; SLJ 3/97) [743]

24427 DuBosque, Doug. *Draw Dinosaurs*. Rev. ed. (3–6). Illus. 1997, Peel paper $8.95 (0-939217-22-8). 64pp. A fine art book that presents easily followed directions for drawing a wide variety of dinosaurs, with interesting facts about each. (Rev: BL 12/15/97) [743.6]

24428 DuBosque, Doug. *Draw! Grassland Animals: A Step-by-Step Guide* (4–7). Illus. by author. 1996, Peel paper $8.99 (0-939217-25-2). 63pp. A step-by-step description of how to draw 31 animals from grasslands around the world. (Rev: SLJ 9/96) [741]

24429 DuBosque, Doug. *Draw Insects* (4–8). 1997, Peel paper $8.99 (0-939217-28-7). A carefully constructed drawing book that gives simple directions for drawing more than 80 insects, including millipedes, ticks, and spiders. (Rev: SLJ 6/98) [741.2]

24430 DuBosque, Doug. *Draw 3-D: A Step-by-Step Guide to Perspective Drawing* (4–9). Illus. by author. 1999, Peel paper $8.99 (0-939217-14-7). 63pp. Using easy-to-follow sketches, the author introduces the techniques of 3-D drawing, beginning with basic concepts involving depth and progressing to more difficult areas such as multiple vanishing points. (Rev: SLJ 5/99) [741.2]

24431 DuBosque, Doug. *Learn to Draw Now!* (5–8). Illus. by author. Series: Learn to Draw. 1991, Peel paper $8.99 (0-939217-16-3). 64pp. A simple, easily followed manual on how to draw that contains many interesting practice exercises. (Rev: SLJ 8/91) [743]

24432 Emberley, Ed. *Ed Emberley's Drawing Book: Make a World* (2–4). Illus. by author. 1972, Little, Brown paper $6.95 (0-316-23644-6). Illustrations and examples on how to draw objects from flags to faces.

24433 Emberley, Ed. *Ed Emberley's Drawing Book of Faces* (2–5). Illus. 1992, Little, Brown paper $6.95 (0-316-23655-1). 32pp. Step-by-step instructions on how to produce an amusing character from a simple shape.

24434 Emberley, Ed. *Ed Emberley's Drawing Book of Weirdos* (1–4). Illus. by author. 2002, Little, Brown paper $7.95 (0-316-23314-5). Werewolves, skeletons, ghosts, vampires, goblins, and witches are all here with step-by-step instructions. (Rev: HBG 3/03; SLJ 1/03) [741.2]

24435 Emberley, Ed. *Ed Emberley's Fingerprint Drawing Book* (1–3). Illus. 2001, Little, Brown $15.95 (0-316-23638-1); paper $6.95 (0-316-23319-6). 48pp. Emberley gives step-by-step instructions for making fingerprint images, progressing from the

most basic to advanced complete pictures. (Rev: BL 6/1–15/01; HBG 3/02; SLJ 7/01) [741.2]

24436 Ewing, Patrick Aloysius, and Linda L. Louis. *In the Paint* (2–5). Illus. 1999, Abbeville $15.95 (0-7892-0542-4). 64pp. Patrick Ewing talks about his favorite pastime — painting — and how young people can use color, shapes, and texture to create their own works. (Rev: BL 7/99; HBG 10/99; SLJ 11/99) [751]

24437 Foster, Patience. *Guide to Drawing* (5–8). Illus. 1981, Usborne LB $14.95 (0-88110-025-0); paper $6.95 (0-86020-540-1). This book covers such topics as color, media, and perspective while dealing with a large number of subjects. Also use *Guide to Painting* (1981). [741]

24438 Hart, Christopher. *Kids Draw Anime* (4–8). Illus. 2002, Watson-Guptill paper $10.95 (0-8230-2690-6). 128pp. Instructions on how to draw anime (Japanese cartoons) characters, with many colorful examples. (Rev: BL 2/1/03; SLJ 11/02) [741.5]

24439 Hart, Christopher. *Kids Draw Funny and Spooky Holiday Characters* (3–6). Illus. by author. 2001, Watson-Guptill paper $10.95 (0-8230-2626-4). 64pp. Cartoon drawing for Halloween and Christmas are the focus of this guide that covers the basic principles of showing movement and good positioning of characters. (Rev: SLJ 9/01) [741.5]

24440 Hart, Christopher. *Kids Draw Manga* (3–8). Illus. by author. Series: Kids Draw. 2004, Watson-Guptill paper $10.95 (0-8230-2623-X). 64pp. For beginners, this is a guide to the basics of manga, showing how to draw a number of characters, poses, and action moves. (Rev: SLJ 9/04) [741.5]

24441 Hart, Christopher. *Manga Mania: How to Draw Japanese Comics* (5–9). Illus. 2001, Watson-Guptill paper $19.95 (0-8230-3035-0). 144pp. Hart looks at the techniques for drawing typical Japanese comic characters and animals, providing examples of published manga along with an introduction to the various genres of manga and an interview with a manga publisher. (Rev: BL 7/01; SLJ 7/01) [741.5]

24442 Hart, Christopher. *Mecha Mania: How to Draw the Battling Robots, Cool Spaceships, and Military Vehicles of Japanese Comics* (4–8). Illus. 2002, Watson-Guptill paper $19.95 (0-8230-3056-3). 128pp. Instructions on how to draw the high-tech, scary, fanciful machines and weapons that fill the pages of Japanese comic books. (Rev: BL 2/1/03; SLJ 4/03) [741.5]

24443 Hart, Christopher. *Kids Draw Animals* (3–6). Illus. by author. Series: Kids Draw. 2003, Watson-Guptill paper $10.95 (0-8230-2631-0). 64pp. Organized by topics, this is an easy-to-understand, step-by-step guide to drawing cartoons of animals. (Rev: SLJ 11/03) [743.6]

24444 Henson, Paige. *Drawing with Charcoal and Pastels* (3–5). Series: How to Paint and Draw. 1999, Rourke LB $18.45 (1-57103-313-0). 32pp. This book gives background information on charcoal and pastels, shows techniques for using them, suggests ideas and projects, and explains how to clean up when you're finished. Also use *Drawing with Mark-*

ers and *Painting with Face Paints* (both 1999). (Rev: SLJ 1/00) [741.2]

24445 Henson, Paige. *Drawing with Pencils* (1–3). Series: How to Paint and Draw. 1999, Rourke LB $18.45 (1-57103-310-6). 32pp. This book contains a little history, information about supplies, and plenty of easy art projects for budding artists. Also use *Painting with Tempera* and *Painting with Watercolors* (both 1999). (Rev: SLJ 2/00) [742]

24446 Hodge, Anthony. *Drawing* (4–8). Series: Mastering Art. 2004, Stargazer Books LB $.00 (1-932799-01-X). 32pp. Along with basic information on materials, colors, and techniques, this slim volume looks at drawing the human body. Also use *Painting* (2004). (Rev: BL 11/1/04) [741.2]

24447 Kallen, Stuart A. *Eco-Arts and Crafts* (3–4). Illus. Series: Target Earth. 1993, ABDO LB $15.98 (1-56239-208-5). 46pp. In these recycling projects, youngsters are taught how to create their own art supplies, including paper. (Rev: SLJ 3/94) [745]

24448 Lacey, Sue. *Animals* (2–5). Series: Start with Art. 1999, Millbrook LB $21.90 (0-7613-3263-4). 32pp. Various step-by-step projects are introduced using actual artworks to inspire creativity, such as Picasso's model of a goat or a Stubbs painting of a horse. Also use in the same series: *People* (1999). (Rev: HBG 3/00; SLJ 1/00) [741.2]

24449 Leroux-Hugon, Helene. *I Can Draw Polar Animals* (3–5). Trans. from French by Valerie J. Weber. Illus. by author. Series: I Can Draw Animals! 2001, Gareth Stevens LB $21.27 (0-8368-2840-2). 40pp. Three-step instructions for a line drawing of an animal are paired with a completed, color illustration of the animal and simple facts about it, all preceded by encouragement to be observant and to practice drawing. Also use *I Can Draw Wild Animals* (2001). (Rev: HBG 10/01; SLJ 9/01) [743.6]

24450 Levin, Freddie. *1-2-3 Draw: Cars, Trucks, and Other Vehicles* (3–5). Illus. 2002, Peel paper $8.99 (0-939217-43-0). 64pp. A large-format paperback that shows how to draw 24 vehicles including a race car, cement truck, and a school bus. (Rev: BL 4/15/02; SLJ 7/02) [743]

24451 Levin, Freddie. *1-2-3 Draw: Dinosaurs and Other Prehistoric Animals: A Step by Step Guide* (1–5). Illus. by author. 2000, Peel paper $8.95 (0-939217-41-4). 64pp. Using three basic shapes — circles, ovals, and eggs — the author shows how to draw 24 different prehistoric animals. The same techniques are applied in *1-2-3-Draw: Pets and Farm Animals* (2000). (Rev: SLJ 3/01) [742]

24452 Lewis, Amanda. *Lettering: Make Your Own Cards, Signs, Gifts and More* (4–8). Illus. 1997, Kids Can paper $5.95 (1-55074-232-9). This book describes calligraphy and gothic lettering techniques, covering such topics as typefaces, displays, types of pens to purchase, how to determine pen size, and how to use pens, as well as explaining how to make letterhead stationery and newsletters on the computer. (Rev: BL 10/15/97; SLJ 1/98) [745.6]

24453 Luxbacher, Irene. *The Jumbo Book of Art* (3–8). Illus. by author. 2003, Kids Can paper $14.95 (1-55074-762-2). 208pp. Drawing, use of color, sculpting, and mixed media are the focus of this book full of interesting art projects. (Rev: SLJ 11/03) [701]

24454 Lynn, Sara, and Diane James. *Play with Paint* (PS–3). Illus. 1993, Carolrhoda LB $19.93 (0-87614-755-4). 24pp. This beginning craft book contains simple projects with brief explanations using everyday materials. A companion volume is: *Play with Paper* (1993). (Rev: BL 5/1/93) [750]

24455 McGillian, Jamie Kyle. *Sidewalk Chalk: Outdoor Fun and Games* (1–6). Illus. by Blanche Sims. 2002, Sterling $17.95 (0-8069-7905-4). 80pp. Plenty of inventive ideas for the sidewalk set, including making your own chalk. (Rev: HBG 10/02; SLJ 12/02)

24456 Mayne, Don. *Draw Your Own Cartoons* (3–8). Illus. by author. 2001, Williamson paper $7.95 (1-885593-76-7). 64pp. A cartoon-like atmosphere prevails in this guide that teaches readers to draw characters. (Rev: SLJ 6/01) [741.5]

24457 Mayne, Don. *Drawing Horses (That Look Real)* (4–8). Illus. by author. Series: Quick Starts for Kids! 2002, Williamson paper $7.95 (1-885593-74-0). 64pp. Cartoonlike instructions take young artists step by step through using basic shapes to draw horses and to show movement and character. (Rev: SLJ 4/03) [743.6]

24458 Murawski, Laura. *How to Draw Cats* (2–5). Illus. by author. Series: A Kid's Guide to Drawing. 2001, Rosen LB $21.25 (0-8239-5549-4). 24pp. Information about each breed precedes instructions on how to draw it in stages that begin with basic shapes and proceed to add details. Also use *How to Draw Dogs* (2001). (Rev: SLJ 8/01) [741]

24459 *Paper and Paint: Hands-on Crafts for Everyday Fun* (2–5). Illus. Series: Crafty Kids. 2003, McGraw-Hill $12.95 (1-57768-527-X). 48pp. Paper and paint projects that may need adult help are included in this volume with easy-to-follow instructions and illustrations. (Rev: HBG 4/04; SLJ 12/03) [745.54]

24460 Pellowski, Michael M. *The Art of Making Comic Books* (4–8). Illus. 1995, Lerner LB $25.55 (0-8225-2304-3). A history of comic books, plus drawing techniques and advice on how to become a comic book artist. (Rev: BCCB 2/96; BL 1/1–15/96; SLJ 1/96) [741.5]

24461 Peterson, Tiffany. *Watercraft* (3–6). Series: Draw It! 2003, Heinemann LB $24.22 (1-40340-214-0). 32pp. Author Tiffany Peterson offers guidance for drawing and painting pictures of various watercraft, including jet skis, river boats, and sailing ships. Also in this series are *Sports Stars*, *Fashion Design*, and *Sea Creatures* (both 2003). (Rev: BL 11/15/03; HBG 10/03; SLJ 10/03)

24462 Reinagle, Damon J. *Draw! Medieval Fantasies* (4–8). Illus. 1995, Peel paper $8.99 (0-939217-30-9). 64pp. A how-to drawing book that gives simple instructions on creating such medieval subjects as dragons and castles. (Rev: BL 1/1–15/96; SLJ 3/96) [743]

1320

24463 Reinagle, Damon J. *Draw Alien Fantasies* (3–6). Illus. 1996, Peel paper $8.99 (0-939217-31-7). 64pp. Easy-to-follow directions are given for drawing a number of creatures from outer space. (Rev: BL 12/15/96; SLJ 3/97) [741.2]

24464 Reinagle, Damon J. *Draw Sports Figures* (4–8). Illus. 1997, Peel paper $8.99 (0-939217-32-5). In six chapters arranged by sport or sports category, the author gives easy-to-follow instructions on how to draw action figures. (Rev: SLJ 6/98) [742]

24465 Robins, Deri. *Painting* (2–5). Illus. Series: Learn Art. 2004, QEB LB $27.10 (1-59566-046-1). 32pp. Creativity is emphasized in this look at how colors interact and the various techniques for applying them. (Rev: SLJ 4/05) [750]

24466 Robins, Deri. *Special Effects* (3–5). Series: QEB Learn Art. 2004, QEB LB $18.95 (1-59566-047-X). 32pp. Using glitter paint and making mosaics and collages are among the projects presented here with clear step-by-step directions. (Rev: BL 11/1/04; SLJ 4/05) [741.2]

24467 Russon, Jacqueline. *Face Painting* (1–4). Photos by Steve Shott. Illus. by Mei Lim. Series: First Craft Books. 1998, Carolrhoda LB $12.95 (1-57505-099-4). 22pp. There are ten simple craft projects in this book that give directions for painting faces to resemble a cat, mermaid, teddy bear, bunny, etc. (Rev: HBG 10/98; SLJ 4/98) [741.2]

24468 Russon, Jacqueline. *Face Painting* (3–7). Illus. Series: First Arts and Crafts. 1994, Thomson Learning LB $21.40 (1-56847-197-1). 32pp. An amazing number of ideas for creative face painting, with clear instructions and many illustrations. (Rev: BL 1/1/95; SLJ 12/94) [745.5]

24469 Sabbeth, Carol. *Crayons and Computers: Computer Art Activities for Kids Ages 4 to 8* (PS–4). 1998, Chicago Review paper $16.95 (1-55652-289-4). 159pp. Using a PC or Mac, any type of printer, and software such as Windows Paintbrush, ClarisWorks, or Kid Pix, this book gives instructions on over 50 craft and project ideas, including using the computer to draw a picture and, after printing it, coloring it. (Rev: SLJ 7/98) [741]

24470 Silver, Patricia. *Face Painting* (1–4). Illus. by Louise Phillips. 2000, Kids Can $12.95 (1-55074-845-9); paper $5.95 (1-55074-689-8). 40pp. A fine introduction to face painting that includes 16 of the most commonly requested faces with rules for safety and cleanup tips. (Rev: BL 9/15/00; SLJ 10/00) [745.5]

24471 Solga, Kim, et al. *Art Fun!* (1–6). Photos by Pamela Monfort. Illus. Series: Art and Activities for Kids. 1997, North Light paper $19.99 (0-89134-833-6). 216pp. This activity book introduces projects involving painting, drawing, printmaking, and sculpting. (Rev: SLJ 1/98) [741.2]

24472 Souter, Gillian. *Paints Plus* (2–5). Photos by Andre Martin. Illus. by Clare Watson. Series: Handy Crafts. 2001, Gareth Stevens LB $22.60 (0-8368-2821-6). 48pp. Lively spreads full of color and practical directions introduce painting equipment and ways to decorate a variety of everyday materials. (Rev: HBG 10/01; SLJ 7/01) [745.7]

24473 Tecco, Betsy Dru. *How to Draw Egypt's Sights and Symbols* (3–6). Illus. Series: A Kid's Guide to Drawing the Countries of the World. 2004, Rosen LB $26.50 (0-8239-6682-8). 48pp. After background information on Egypt, step-by-step instructions guide readers through sketching scenes including a camel, a date palm, a pyramid, and the mask of King Tut. Also use *How to Draw France's Sights and Symbols* and *How to Draw Japan's Sights and Symbols* (both 2004). (Rev: SLJ 3/05) [743]

24474 Temple, Kathryn. *Drawing* (5–8). Illus. Series: Art for Kids. 2005, Sterling $17.95 (1-57990-587-0). 112pp. A comprehensive and clearly written guide to equipment and techniques, with useful illustrations and practical exercises at the end of each section. (Rev: BL 5/1/05) [741.2]

24475 Wallace, Mary. *I Can Make Art* (4–8). Series: I Can Make. 1997, Firefly $17.95 (1-895688-64-7); paper $6.95 (1-895688-65-5). Art and crafts are combined in these 12 projects involving such techniques as watercolor, still life, chalk drawing, print making, and collage. (Rev: SLJ 12/97) [741.2]

24476 Walsh, Patricia. *Aircraft* (3–6). Illus. Series: Draw It! 2000, Heinemann LB $21.36 (1-57572-347-6). 32pp. From the Wright brothers' flying machine to a modern Bell JetRanger helicopter, this chronologically arranged book describes aircraft and gives directions for sketching them. (Rev: BL 2/1/01; HBG 10/01) [743]

24477 Walsh, Patricia. *Cars* (3–6). Series: Draw It! 2000, Heinemann LB $21.36 (1-57572-348-4). 32pp. Using colored lines to show each step, this book shows how to draw cars in six easy steps. Also use from the same art series: *Dinosaurs, Space Vehicles,* and *Wild Animals* (all 2000). (Rev: BL 3/1/01; HBG 10/01) [741.2]

24478 Walsh, Patricia. *Woodland Animals* (3–6). Illus. 2000, Heinemann LB $21.36 (1-57572-352-2). 32pp. Introducing a single animal per double-page spread, this book describes such animals as the skunk, woodpecker, and porcupine with clear instructions on how to draw each. (Rev: BL 2/1/01; HBG 10/01; SLJ 2/01) [743]

24479 Wellford, Lin. *Painting on Rocks for Kids* (K–3). Illus. 2002, North Light paper $12.99 (1-58180-255-2). 64pp. Step-by-step instructions and tips on technique accompany ideas for making cars, flowers, dinosaurs, fish, food, and other items from painted stones and rocks. (Rev: SLJ 1/03) [745.7]

Masks and Mask Making

24480 Beaton, Clare. *Masks* (2–4). Illus. Series: Make and Play. 1995, Fitzgerald LB $15.95 (1-887238-02-6). 24pp. Step-by-step directions for making seven different masks. (Rev: BL 1/1/91; SLJ 2/91) [731.785]

24481 Earl, Amanda, and Danielle Sensier. *Masks* (5–7). Illus. Series: Traditions Around the World. 1994, Thomson Learning LB $24.26 (1-56847-226-9). 48pp. This multicultural introduction to masks discusses their origins and uses in religion, festivals, and the theater. (Rev: BL 2/1/95; SLJ 3/95) [391.43]

24482 Schwarz, Renée. *Making Masks* (4–6). Series: Kids Can Do It! 2002, Kids Can $12.95 (1-55074-929-3); paper $5.95 (1-55074-931-5). 40pp. A basic volume on making masks from a various of easily obtained materials. (Rev: BL 9/15/02; HBG 3/03; SLJ 12/02) [731.785]

Paper Crafts

24483 Araki, Chiyo. *Origami in the Classroom* (4–7). Illus. 1965, Tuttle vol. 1 $14.95 (0-8048-0452-4); vol. 2 $14.95 (0-8048-0453-2). In two volumes; each deals with paper crafts for two of the seasons.

24484 Balchin, Judy. *Papier Mâché* (4–7). Illus. Series: Step-by-Step. 2000, Heinemann LB $24.22 (1-57572-328-X). 32pp. Combines easy-to-follow projects with information on how papier-mâché has been used over the centuries, including applications in construction and furniture. (Rev: BL 10/15/00; HBG 10/01; SLJ 12/00) [745.54]

24485 Blanchette, Peg, and Terri Thibault. *Make Your Own Cool Cards: 40 Awesome Notes and Invitations!* (2–4). Series: Quick Starts for Kids! 2004, Ideals Publications paper $8.95 (1-885593-96-1). 64pp. Sixteen projects that use easy-to-obtain materials are presented in detail with clear illustrations. (Rev: BL 12/15/03)

24486 Bliss, Helen. *Paper* (3–6). Series: Craft Workshop. 1998, Crabtree LB $22.95 (0-86505-781-8); paper $10.95 (0-86505-791-5). 32pp. This book presents a history of paper as well as various paper-related activities such as making paper, masks, puppets, etc. (Rev: SLJ 9/98) [745]

24487 Borja, Robert, and Corinne Borja. *Making Chinese Papercuts* (4–7). Illus. by authors. 1980, Whitman LB $14.95 (0-8075-4948-7). A clear explanation of an ancient art with many examples and photographs.

24488 Boursin, Didier. *Origami Paper Airplanes* (4–7). Illus. 2001, Firefly LB $19.95 (1-55209-626-2); paper $9.95 (1-55209-616-5). 64pp. Paper airplane devotees will love the origami models offered here, which are categorized by difficulty of construction. (Rev: BCCB 12/01; BL 1/1–15/02; HBG 3/02; SLJ 12/01) [745.592]

24489 Carter, David A., and James Diaz. *The Elements of Pop-Up: A Pop-Up Book for Aspiring Paper Engineers* (3–8). Photos by Keith Sutter. Illus. by authors. 1999, Simon & Schuster $35.00 (0-689-82224-3). Instructions are given for constructing more than 50 pop-ups with working models of each. (Rev: BL 12/15/99; HBG 3/00; SLJ 2/00) [745.5]

24490 Carter, Tamsin. *Handmade Cards* (3–5). Illus. Series: Step-by-Step. 2002, Heinemann LB $24.22 (1-4034-0698-7). 32pp. This volume provides simple instructions, explained one step at a time, for creating and decorating greeting cards. (Rev: BL 12/15/02; HBG 3/03) [745.594]

24491 Check, Laura. *The Kids' Guide to Making Scrapbooks and Photo Albums! How to Collect, Design, Assemble, Decorate* (4–6). Illus. by Betsy Day. 2002, Williamson paper $12.95 (1-885593-59-7). 128pp. Check discusses the best ways to use images to tell stories as well as giving practical instructions for creating scrapbooks and albums. (Rev: SLJ 7/02) [745.593]

24492 Churchill, E. Richard. *Holiday Paper Projects* (3–6). Illus. by James Michaels. 1993, Sterling $14.95 (0-8069-8512-7). 128pp. Various paper crafts related to holidays are outlined with simple instructions that usually only involve cutting, folding, and pasting. (Rev: SLJ 12/93) [745]

24493 Diehn, Gwen. *Making Books That Fly, Fold, Wrap, Hide, Pop Up, Twist, and Turn: Books for Kids to Make* (4–8). Illus. 1998, Lark $19.95 (1-57990-023-2). Clear directions, diagrams, and many photographs guide youngsters in 18 projects to produce folded, wrapped, and pop-up books. (Rev: BL 7/98; SLJ 8/98) [736.98]

24494 Fiarotta, Phyllis, and Noel Fiarotta. *Paper-crafts Around the World* (4–6). Illus. 1996, Sterling $21.95 (0-8069-3990-7). 96pp. Paper crafts and projects from 31 countries are included with easy-to-follow instructions. (Rev: BL 7/96; SLJ 8/96) [745.54]

24495 Garza, Carmen Lomas. *Making Magic Windows: Creating Papel Picado / Cut-Paper Art* (3–7). 1999, Children's Book Pr. paper $9.95 (0-89239-159-6). 61pp. This bilingual book gives directions on making festive papel picado (cut paper) banners associated with the Southwest and Mexican Americans. (Rev: BL 5/1/99) [745.54]

24496 Grummer, Arnold E. *Paper by Kids* (5–7). Illus. 1990, Macmillan $12.95 (0-87518-191-0). 116pp. A clear, well-organized guide to papermaking.

24497 Henry, Sandi. *Cut-Paper Play! Dazzling Creations from Construction Paper* (K–5). Illus. by Norma Jean Jourdenais. Series: Kids Can! 1997, Williamson paper $12.95 (1-885593-05-8). 160pp. In this book, which indicates the relative difficulty of each activity, there are projects that include making a desktop robot, a frog, and a mosaic snowman. (Rev: SLJ 9/97) [745.5]

24498 Irvin, Christine M. *Paper Plate Mania* (K–2). Illus. Series: Craft Mania. 2002, Children's Book Pr. LB $22.00 (0-516-21675-9); paper $6.95 (0-516-27761-8). 32pp. Masks and sun catchers are among the many inventive uses for paper plates suggested in this book that emphasizes the importance of recycling. Also use *Paper Cup Mania* (2002). (Rev: SLJ 9/02) [745.54]

24499 Irvine, Joan. *How to Make Pop-Ups* (3–7). Illus. by Barbara Reid. 1988, Morrow paper $6.95 (0-688-07902-4). 96pp. Instructions on how to create three-dimensional wonders. (Rev: BL 4/15/88; SLJ 3/88)

24500 Irvine, Joan. *How to Make Super Pop-Ups* (4–7). Illus. 1992, Morrow $14.00 (0-688-10690-0); paper $6.95 (0-688-11521-7). 96pp. Lots of ideas and directions for making three-dimensional paper constructions with moving parts. (Rev: BL 1/15/93) [745]

24501 Johnson, Ginger. *Paper-Folding Fun! 50 Awesome Crafts to Weave, Twist and Curl* (3–5). Illus. Series: Kids Can. 2002, Williamson paper $12.95 (1-885593-67-8). 128pp. Step-by-step directions accompany each idea for making objects from paper, including jewelry, mobiles, and books. (Rev: BL 11/1/02) [745.54]

24502 Kelly, Emery J. *Paper Airplanes: Models to Build and Fly* (4–8). Illus. 1997, Lerner LB $23.93 (0-8225-2401-5). This is a practical manual on making and flying paper airplanes, with good coverage of the principles of aerodynamics. (Rev: BL 12/1/97; HBG 3/98; SLJ 2/98) [745.592]

24503 Lafosse, Michael G. *Making Origami Christmas Decorations Step by Step* (2–4). Illus. by author. Series: Kid's Guide to Origami. 2002, Rosen LB $21.25 (0-8239-5874-4). 24pp. Nine projects related to Christmas are suitable for beginning folders. (Rev: SLJ 10/02)

24504 Lafosse, Michael G. *Making Origami Masks Step by Step* (2–6). Illus. Series: A Kid's Guide to Origami. 2004, Rosen LB $21.25 (0-8239-6703-4). 24pp. Well-explained projects are suitable for different levels of expertise. Also use *Making Origami Puzzles Step by Step* and *Making Origami Science Experiments Step by Step* (both 2004). (Rev: SLJ 11/04) [745.592]

24505 Lafosse, Michael G. *Origami Activities* (4–6). Illus. Series: Asian Arts and Crafts for Creative Kids. 2004, Tuttle $9.95 (0-8048-3497-0). 64pp. Step-by-step instructions guide readers through 15 increasingly difficult projects. (Rev: SLJ 8/04) [736]

24506 Lewis, Amanda. *The Jumbo Book of Paper Crafts* (3–6). Illus. by Jane Kurisu. 2002, Kids Can paper $14.95 (1-55074-940-4). 160pp. Easy, illustrated techniques and instructions teach older children how to create a multitude of crafts with paper and cardboard. (Rev: BL 12/15/02; SLJ 12/02) [745]

24507 *Look What You Can Make with Paper Bags* (3–5). Ed. by Judy Burke. Illus. 1999, Boyds Mills paper $5.95 (1-56397-717-6). 48pp. Paper bags and other easily found materials are used in this series of creative craft projects, some of which require adult help. (Rev: BL 7/99; SLJ 5/99) [745.54]

24508 Newell, Keith. *Look and Make with Paper* (4–5). Photos by Steve Shott. Illus. by Michael Evans. Series: Look and Make. 2004, Sea-to-Sea LB $27.10 (1-932889-24-8). 32pp. Well-designed projects — such as paper sandals — use paper and glue and are presented with clear instructions and a photograph of the final product. (Rev: SLJ 4/05) [745.54]

24509 Nguyen, Duy. *Creepy Crawly Animal Origami* (4–8). Illus. 2003, Sterling $19.95 (0-8069-9012-0). 96pp. These challenging folded paper designs for 13 animals do require scissors and in some cases glue. (Rev: HBG 4/04; SLJ 9/03) [736]

24510 Nguyen, Duy. *Fantasy Origami* (5–7). Illus. by author. 2002, Sterling $19.95 (0-8069-8007-9).

96pp. These 16 origami designs, which are not for beginners, do call for the use of scissors and glue. (Rev: BL 1/1–15/02; SLJ 6/02) [736.982]

24511 Nguyen, Duy. *Jungle Animal Origami* (4–12). 2003, Sterling $19.95 (1-4027-0777-0). 96pp. Best suited for paper crafters with fairly advanced skills, this book by master artist Duy Nguyen offers instructions for creating a menagerie of origami animals. (Rev: BL 12/15/03; SLJ 3/04)

24512 Nguyen, Duy. *Under the Sea Origami* (5–7). Illus. 2005, Sterling $19.95 (1-4027-1541-2). 96pp. Sharks, an octopus, and a sea horse are among the marine animals featured in this origami collection. (Rev: SLJ 4/05) [736]

24513 *Paper* (3–6). Series: Let's Create! 2003, Gareth Stevens LB $22.60 (0-8368-3747-9). 32pp. An attractive introduction to paper crafts, including 12 projects and additional suggested resources. (Rev: SLJ 4/04) [745.54]

24514 *Papier-Mache* (3–4). Illus. Series: Let's Create! 2004, Gareth Stevens LB $16.95 (0-8368-4017-8). 32pp. Simple projects created by children may still require some adult help. Also use *Stones and "Stuff"* and *Metal* (both 2004). (Rev: BL 6/1–15/04; SLJ 11/04) [745.5]

24515 Powell, Michelle. *Printing* (4–7). Illus. Series: Step-by-Step. 2000, Heinemann LB $24.22 (1-57572-329-8). 32pp. Various easy-to-follow printing projects are presented along with material on printing methods from ancient Egypt onward. (Rev: BL 10/15/00; HBG 10/01) [761]

24516 Ross, Kathy, ed. *Look What You Can Make with Newspapers, Magazines, and Greeting Cards: Over 80 Pictured Crafts and Dozens of Other Ideas* (2–4). Photos by Hank Schneider. 2002, Boyds Mills paper $5.95 (1-56397-566-1). 48pp. Final products include dolls with clothes, boxes, banks, signs and cards, and mobiles; the illustrations enhance the written instructions. (Rev: SLJ 4/02) [745.54]

24517 Sarasas, Claude. *The ABC's of Origami* (4–6). Illus. 1964, Tuttle $14.95 (0-8048-0000-6). Directions on how to create 26 figures from an albatross to a zebra are given.

24518 Schmidt, Norman. *Incredible Paper Flying Machines* (5–8). Illus. 2001, Sterling $19.95 (1-895569-37-0). 96pp. Young model builders with some experience will enjoy these intricate models of historical aircraft that are glued and laminated. (Rev: HBG 10/02; SLJ 2/02) [745.592]

24519 Schwarz, Renée. *Papier-Mâché* (4–6). Illus. by author. Series: Kids Can! 2000, Kids Can $12.95 (1-55074-833-5); paper $5.95 (1-55074-727-4). 40pp. This work outlines 11 projects in papier-mâché with tips on getting the proper supplies, preparing the paste, and sanding and fixing mistakes. (Rev: HBG 10/00; SLJ 6/00) [745.5]

24520 Seix, Victoria. *Creating with Papier-Mâché* (3–6). Series: Crafts for All Seasons. 2000, Blackbirch LB $18.95 (1-56711-439-3). 32pp. Fifteen projects using either paper strips or paper pulp are outlined in this attractive craft book. (Rev: SLJ 2/01) [745.5]

24521 Siomades, Lorianne, ed. *Look What You Can Make With Boxes: Over 90 Pictured Crafts and Dozens of Other Ideas* (4–6). Photos by Hank Schneider. 1998, Boyds Mills paper $5.95 (1-56397-704-4). 48pp. Different kinds of boxes (cereal, greeting card, etc.) and simple materials, such as glue and paints, are used to create toys, games, decorations, and various useful objects in this easy-to-use craft manual. (Rev: SLJ 6/98) [745.5]

24522 Stevens, Clive. *Paperfolding* (4–7). Series: Step-by-Step. 2001, Heinemann LB $24.22 (1-57572-333-6). 32pp. Easy-to-find materials are used in a number of exciting paper folding projects, each of which is described in clear, detailed directions with step-by-step illustrations. (Rev: BL 8/1/01; HBG 10/01; SLJ 10/01) [745.5]

24523 Ungert, Ruth. *Easy Origami Animals* (1–4). 2003, Sterling paper $6.95 (1-4027-0189-6). 64pp. A step-by-step guide to creating simple origami animals. (Rev: SLJ 11/03) [736]

24524 Walter, F. Virginia. *Super Toys and Games from Paper* (4–6). Illus. 1993, Sterling $19.95 (1-895569-06-0). 104pp. Directions are given for almost 90 paper toys and games, such as newspaper golf clubs and cardboard-tube hammers. (Rev: BL 1/1/94; SLJ 12/93) [745.592]

24525 Watson, David. *Papermaking* (4–7). Series: Step-by-Step. 2000, Heinemann LB $24.22 (1-57572-327-1). 32pp. This book shows how you can use old paper to make new paper and create a number of wonderful art objects following simple step-by-step directions. (Rev: BL 10/15/00; HBG 10/01) [745.5]

24526 West, Robin. *Dinosaur Discoveries: How to Create Your Own Prehistoric World* (3–6). Illus. 1989, Carolrhoda $19.95 (0-87614-351-6). 72pp. Directions for creating models of dinosaurs using scissors, glue, and construction paper. (Rev: BL 11/15/89; SLJ 12/89) [745.54]

24527 Williams, Joy. *Paper Creations* (3–6). Illus. Series: Creative Kids. 2002, North Light paper $12.99 (1-58180-290-0). 64pp. Using everyday materials, the reader can learn to make projects including jewelry, gifts, and decorations. (Rev: SLJ 1/03)

Sewing and Needle Crafts

24528 Bial, Raymond. *With Needle and Thread: A Book About Quilts* (4–7). Illus. 1996, Houghton Mifflin $16.00 (0-395-73568-8). 48pp. An attractive introduction to quilts, their history, how they are made, and the people who sew them. (Rev: BCCB 2/96; BL 3/1/96; SLJ 6/96) [746.46]

24529 Bradberry, Sarah. *Kids Knit! Simple Steps to Nifty Projects* (4–8). Photos by Michael Hnatov. Illus. by Kim Coxey. 2004, Sterling $14.95 (0-8069-7733-7). 96pp. Simple, clear instructions and illustrations add to the value of this book full of appealing projects. (Rev: BL 12/15/04; SLJ 2/05)

24530 Clewer, Carolyn. *Kids Can Knit: Fun and Easy Projects for Small Knitters* (3–7). 2003, Bar-ron's paper $16.95 (0-7641-2718-7). 128pp. The reader gradually moves from simple techniques to more sophisticated projects. (Rev: BL 12/15/03; SLJ 3/04)

24531 Falick, Melanie. *Kids Knitting* (4–7). Illus. 1998, Workman $17.95 (1-885183-76-3). 128pp. Exceptionally clear pictures and text are used to present the basics of knitting for girls and boys, with instructions for such projects as backpacks, hats, scarves, and sweaters. (Rev: BL 4/1/98; SLJ 7/98) [746.43]

24532 Gibbons, Gail. *The Quilting Bee* (K–2). Illus. by author. 2004, HarperCollins $15.99 (0-688-16397-1). Adults and children participate in a quilting circle, from initial planning to displaying the final product; historical information is included as is a concept for an author and illustrator quilt. (Rev: SLJ 5/04) [746.46]

24533 Kinsler, Gwen Blakley, and Jackie Young. *Crocheting* (4–7). Series: Kids Can Do It! 2003, Kids Can $12.95 (1-55337-176-3); paper $5.95 (1-55337-177-1). 48pp. A simple introduction to crocheting with many easily followed diagrams and clear directions. (Rev: BL 3/15/03; HBG 10/03; SLJ 4/03) [745.5]

24534 Mahren, Sue. *Make Your Own Teddy Bears and Bear Clothes* (3–6). Illus. by Stan Jaskiel. Series: Quick Starts for Kids! 2001, Williamson paper $7.95 (1-885593-75-9). 64pp. Patterns for two teddy bears are followed by patterns for clothing that are clear and easy to follow using only scissors, needle, and thread. Also use *Kids' Easy Knitting Projects* and *Kids' Easy Quilting Projects* (both 2001). (Rev: SLJ 7/01) [745.592]

24535 Nicholas, Kristin, and John Gruen. *Kids' Embroidery: Projects for Kids of All Ages* (3–7). 2004, Stewart, Tabori & Chang $19.95 (1-58479-366-X). 144pp. Step-by-step instructions guide readers through 15 colorful embroidery projects. (Rev: BL 12/15/04)

24536 O'Reilly, Susie. *Knitting and Crochet* (3–5). Illus. Series: Arts and Crafts. 1994, Thomson Learning LB $21.40 (1-56847-221-8). 32pp. A good handicraft book that explains the basic stitches, gives directions for many projects, and encourages young knitters to create their own patterns. (Rev: SLJ 1/95) [745.5]

24537 Ronci, Kelli. *Kids Crochet: Projects for Kids of All Ages* (4–8). Photos by John Gruen. Illus. by Lena Corwin. 2005, Stewart, Tabori & Chang $19.95 (1-58479-413-5). 128pp. A poncho, a quilt, and a tool pouch are among the 15 crocheting projects presented, which are introduced by detailed coverage of techniques. (Rev: BL 5/15/04; SLJ 6/05) [745.5]

24538 Sadler, Judy Ann. *Corking* (4–8). Illus. Series: Kids Can! 1998, Kids Can paper $5.95 (1-55074-265-5). 32pp. Provides directions for a handmade knitting device that is used to create knit tubes or corks popular in toys and headbands. (Rev: BL 5/15/98) [746.4]

24539 Sadler, Judy Ann. *Embroidery* (4–8). Illus. by June Bradford. Series: Kids Can Do It! 2004, Kids

Can $12.95 (1-55337-616-1); paper $6.95 (1-55337-617-X). 40pp. In addition to a thorough introduction to embroidery and various stitches, Sadler provides nine projects that progress in difficulty. (Rev: SLJ 8/04) [746.44]

24540 Sadler, Judy Ann. *Knitting* (4–6). Series: Kids Can Do It! 2002, Kids Can $12.95 (1-55337-050-3); paper $5.95 (1-55337-051-1). 40pp. The basic stitches in knitting are described in text and color illustrations, followed by a series of easily accomplished knitting projects. (Rev: BL 9/15/02; HBG 3/03; SLJ 11/02) [746.43]

24541 Sadler, Judy Ann. *Making Fleece Crafts* (4–7). Illus. by June Bradford. 2000, Kids Can $12.95 (1-55074-847-5); paper $5.95 (1-55074-739-8). 40pp. Fifteen colorful and inviting projects using fleece including mittens, a scarf, and a jester's hat. (Rev: BL 9/15/00; SLJ 9/00) [745]

24542 Sadler, Judy Ann. *Simply Sewing* (4–8). Illus. by Jane Kurisu. Series: Kids Can Do It! 2004, Kids Can $12.95 (1-55337-659-5). 48pp. Detailed instructions for 12 projects — a makeup bag and a jeans skirt, for example — follow basic information on sewing by hand and by machine. (Rev: BL 12/15/04; SLJ 11/04)

24543 Sadler, Judy Ann, et al. *The Jumbo Book of Needlecrafts* (4–7). Illus. by Esperan a Melo, et al. 2005, Kids Can paper $16.95 (1-55337-793-1). 208pp. After advice on getting started, step-by-step directions guide readers through a range of needlecraft projects. (Rev: SLJ 5/05)

24544 Stoppleman, Monica, and Carol Crowe. *Fabric* (3–6). Series: Craft Workshop. 1998, Crabtree LB $22.95 (0-86505-779-6); paper $10.95 (0-86505-789-3). 32pp. A history of fabrics and related craft projects (some of which require adult supervision) make up this brief introduction to an interesting subject. (Rev: SLJ 9/98) [745]

24545 Storms, Biz. *All-American Quilts* (4–7). Illus. by June Bradford. Series: Kids Can Do It! 2003, Kids Can $12.95 (1-55337-539-6); paper $6.95 (1-55337-539-4). 40pp. Instructions are provided for making quilts with American themes — eagles, flags, and so forth. (Rev: BL 12/15/03) [746.46]

24546 Storms, Biz. *Quilting* (4–7). Illus. by June Bradford. Series: Kids Can Do It! 2001, Kids Can $12.95 (1-55074-967-6); paper $5.95 (1-55074-805-X). 40pp. Easy-to-follow, step-by-step instructions take kids through quilting projects of varying difficulty. (Rev: BL 11/1/01; HBG 3/02; SLJ 2/02) [746.46]

24547 Wenger, Jennifer, et al. *Teen Knitting Club: Chill Out and Knit Some Cool Stuff* (5–9). Illus. 2004, Artisan $17.95 (1-57965-244-1). 128pp. Children who already know how to know will derive the most benefit from this collection of 35 appealing projects. (Rev: BL 12/15/04; SLJ 2/05)

24548 Willing, Karen Bates, and Julie Bates Dock. *Fabric Fun for Kids: Step-by-Step Projects for Children (and Their Grown-ups)* (4–9). 1997, Now & Then LB $17.95 (0-9641820-4-1); paper $12.95 (0-9641820-5-X). 55pp. From simple sewing projects to more complex quilting work, this book gives

good step-by-step instructions, provides a rundown on necessary sewing tools and materials, and discusses methods for putting designs on fabrics. (Rev: SLJ 4/98) [746.46]

24549 Wilson, Sule Greg C. *African American Quilting: The Warmth of Tradition* (4–7). Illus. Series: Library of African American Arts and Culture. 1999, Rosen LB $31.95 (0-8239-1854-8). 64pp. This book traces African influences on textile patterns and techniques particularly as they have been applied to quilting by African Americans. (Rev: BL 2/15/00; SLJ 9/99) [746.46]

Toys and Dolls

24550 Churchill, E. Richard. *Paper Science Toys* (4–8). Illus. by James Michaels. 1990, Sterling $14.95 (0-8069-5834-0). 128pp. Forty-eight different toys made from easily obtainable materials. (Rev: BL 2/15/91) [745]

24551 Hall, Patricia. *The Real-for-Sure Story of Raggedy Ann* (PS–3). Illus. by Joni Gruelle Wannamaker. 2001, Pelican $14.95 (1-56554-763-2). A story about the origins of the doll, portraying the details of her clothes and the way the first dolls were made. (Rev: HBG 10/01; SLJ 11/01) [688.7]

24552 Kay, Helen. *The First Teddy Bear* (K–3). Illus. by Susan Detweiler. 1985, Stemmer $14.95 (0-88045-042-8). 40pp. A simple tale of the history of this well-loved stuffed animal. (Rev: BCCB 2/86; BL 11/15/85; SLJ 1/86)

24553 Markel, Michelle. *Cornhusk, Silk, and Wishbones: A Book of Dolls from Around the World* (3–6). Illus. 2000, Houghton Mifflin $15.00 (0-618-05487-1). 48pp. Photographs and double-page spreads present dolls from African, North American, South American, and Asian cultures using an alphabetical approach. (Rev: BL 10/1/00; HBG 3/01; SLJ 11/00) [688.7]

24554 Polacco, Patricia. *Betty Doll* (3–5). Illus. 2001, Penguin Putnam $16.99 (0-399-23638-4). 32pp. In this picture book for older children, Polacco tells the story of her mother's precious Betty Doll, which accompanied her mother on many journeys until her death, when the doll was passed on to her daughter. (Rev: BL 8/01; HBG 10/01; SLJ 4/01) [973.4]

24555 Sadler, Judy Ann. *Beanbag Buddies and Other Stuffed Toys* (4–7). Illus. by June Bradford. Series: Kids Can! 1999, Kids Can paper $5.95 (1-55074-590-5). 40pp. Using clear directions and many step-by-step illustrations, this book offers many ideas on how to create a variety of stuffed toys. (Rev: SLJ 10/99) [745]

24556 *The Ultimate LEGO Book* (K–3). Illus. 1999, DK $19.95 (0-7894-4691-X). 128pp. In addition to stunning photos of LEGO constructions, this account gives a history of the company, tells about model makers, and provides details on competitions open to youngsters. (Rev: BL 2/1/00) [688.1]

Woodworking

24557 Gibbons, Gail. *Tool Book* (K–3). Illus. by author. 1982, Holiday House LB $16.95 (0-8234-0444-7); paper $6.95 (0-8234-0694-6). 32pp. An introduction to various simple tools and their uses.

24558 Hendry, Linda, and Lisa Rebnord. *Making Picture Frames* (4–6). Photos by Frank Baldassarra. Illus. by Linda Hendry. Series: Kids Can! 1999, Kids Can paper $5.95 (1-55074-505-0). 40pp. This clearly illustrated book presents basic picture-frame construction plus variations for more appealing products. (Rev: SLJ 5/99) [684]

24559 Robertson, J. Craig, and Barbara Robertson. *The Kids' Building Workshop: 15 Woodworking Projects for Kids and Parents to Build Together* (3–7). Illus. 2004, Storey Kids $22.95 (1-58017-572-4); paper $12.95 (1-58017-488-4). 136pp. After discussing tools and techniques, 15 projects — a bird house, a stool, for example — are presented in order of increasing difficulty. (Rev: SLJ 2/05) [684]

24560 Walker, Lester. *Housebuilding for Children* (4–7). Illus. 1977, Overlook paper $16.95 (0-87951-332-2). 176pp. The construction of six different kinds of houses, including a tree house, is clearly described in text and pictures.

Hobbies

General and Miscellaneous

24561 Adkins, Jan. *The Art and Industry of Sandcastles* (4–6). Illus. 1982, Walker paper $9.95 (0-8027-7205-6). This is an illustrated guide to basic construction of sandcastles plus amazing background information.

24562 Blakey, Nancy. *Go Outside! Activities for Outdoor Adventures* (3–7). Photos by Dana Dean Doering. 2002, Tricycle paper $13.95 (1-58246-064-7). 144pp. Double-page spreads suggest outdoor activities for each of the seasons, some for learning and some for pure fun. (Rev: BL 4/15/02; SLJ 9/02) [796]

24563 Brent, Lynnette R. *At Play: Long Ago and Today* (2–4). Series: Times Change. 2003, Heinemann LB $24.22 (1-4034-4532-X). 32pp. A look at how various everyday activities have changed over the past century or so, with photographs illustrating "then" and "now." (Rev: SLJ 5/04) [790.1]

24564 Burgess, Ron. *Be a Clown! Techniques from a Real Clown* (K–3). Illus. by Heather Barberie. 2001, Williamson paper $7.95 (1-885593-57-0). 63pp. Aspiring clowns will appreciate this guide to clown costumes and makeup, actions and gags, and magic tricks, along with some historical information about traditional clowns and clowning. (Rev: SLJ 10/01) [791.3]

24565 Cook, Deanna F. *FamilyFun's Parties: 100 Party Plans for Birthdays, Holidays, and Every Day* (3–8). 1999, Hyperion $24.95 (0-7868-6454-0). 223pp. This spiral-bound book gives thorough details on planning and holding different kinds of holiday-related parties. Fifty children's birthday parties are outlined. (Rev: SLJ 9/99) [394.2]

24566 Cook, Nick. *Roller Coasters; or, I Had So Much Fun, I Almost Puked* (4–7). Illus. 1998, Carolrhoda LB $27.15 (1-57505-071-4). 56pp. This intriguing book describes the excitement of a roller-coaster ride and discusses the history, types, construction, and safety features of various roller coasters. (Rev: BCCB 6/98; BL 4/15/98; HBG 10/98) [791]

24567 Dunnewind, Stephanie. *Come to Tea: Fun Tea Party Themes, Recipes, Crafts, Games, Etiquette, and More* (3–6). Illus. by Capuchine Mazille. 2003, Sterling $19.95 (0-8069-7899-6). 80pp. Party themes, recipes, crafts, activities, and etiquette are all to be found in this colorful and practical volume. (Rev: HBG 10/03; SLJ 6/03) [641.5]

24568 Goodman, Michael. *Model Railroading* (5–8). Illus. Series: Hobby Guides. 1993, Crestwood LB $12.95 (0-89686-620-3). 48pp. As well as describing the basics of model railroading as a hobby, this account discusses clubs, displays, and organizations. (Rev: SLJ 2/94) [625.1]

24569 Goodman, Michael. *Radio Control Models* (5–8). Illus. Series: Hobby Guides. 1993, Crestwood LB $12.95 (0-89686-622-X). 48pp. Gives practical advice on getting started in this fascinating hobby, with good background information on radio control models plus coverage of equipment, competitions, and organizations. (Rev: SLJ 2/94) [621]

24570 Hunter, Dette. *38 Ways to Entertain Your Babysitter* (2–4). Illus. by Stephen MacEachern. 2003, Annick LB $19.95 (1-55037-795-7); paper $9.95 (1-55037-794-9). 48pp. A story about two siblings' efforts to keep their babysitter happy provides the framework for a collection of three dozen or so entertaining activities, each accompanied by easy-to-follow instructions. (Rev: SLJ 1/04) [793]

24571 Kiralfy, Bob. *The Most Excellent Book of How to Be a Cheerleader* (3–5). Series: Most Excellent Book Of. 1997, Millbrook LB $19.90 (0-7613-0617-X); paper $6.95 (0-7613-0631-5). 32pp. A step-by-step guide to cheerleading, with examples of moves and chants and tips on how to look the part. (Rev: BL 11/15/97; HBG 10/98; SLJ 3/98) [761.6]

24572 Mitchelson, Mitch. *The Most Excellent Book of How to Be a Juggler* (3–5). Series: Most Excellent Book Of. 1997, Millbrook LB $19.90 (0-7613-0618-8); paper $6.95 (0-7613-0632-3). 32pp. A step-by-step guide to juggling, with examples of techniques, routines, and tips for giving an effective performance. (Rev: BL 11/15/97; HBG 10/98) [790]

24573 Perkins, Catherine. *The Most Excellent Book of How to Be a Clown* (3–5). Illus. 1996, Millbrook LB $19.90 (0-7613-0486-X); paper $6.95 (0-7613-0499-1). 32pp. Hints on makeup and presentations plus suggestions for routines are given for aspiring clowns. (Rev: BL 6/1–15/96; SLJ 6/96) [791.3]

24574 Sinclair, Carla. *Braid Crazy: Simple Steps for Daring 'Dos* (3–8). Photos by Susan Sheridan. Illus. by Mark Frauenfelder. 2003, Chronicle $12.95 (0-8118-3602-9). Easy-to-follow instructions are provided for more than 20 hairstyles. (Rev: SLJ 4/03) [391.5]

24575 Stetson, Emily. *Knots to Know: 40 Hitches, Loops, Bends and Bindings* (3–6). Illus. by Marc Nadel and Sarah Rakitin. 2002, Williamson paper $7.95 (1-885593-70-8). 64pp. A simple guide to the types and uses of knots, with step-by-step instructions on how to tie them. (Rev: BL 8/02; SLJ 9/02) [623.88]

24576 Swain, Ruth Freeman. *Hairdo! What We Do and Did to Our Hair* (K–2). Illus. by Cat B. Smith. 2002, Holiday House $16.95 (0-8234-1522-8). 32pp. Entertaining facts about hair and hairstyles through the ages. (Rev: BL 12/15/02; HBG 3/03; SLJ 10/02) [391.5]

24577 Walker, Lester. *Block Building for Children: Making Buildings of the World with the Ultimate Construction Toy* (2–6). Illus. 1995, Overlook $22.95 (0-87951-609-7). 167pp. The 18 block-building projects in this book include a city of the future and the Emerald City of Oz. (Rev: SLJ 1/96) [621]

24578 Young, Robert. *Miniature Vehicles* (4–6). Illus. Series: Collectibles. 1993, Dillon LB $18.95 (0-87518-518-5). 71pp. A guide for young collectors of miniature vehicles that tells about current sources, how models are manufactured, and where famous collections can be found. (Rev: BL 10/1/93) [629.22]

Cooking

24579 *Addy's Cook Book: A Peek at Dining in the Past with Meals You Can Cook Today* (3–5). Illus. Series: American Girls Pastimes. 1994, Pleasant Co. paper $5.95 (1-56247-123-6). 44pp. This cookbook deals with foods prepared and served during the days of slavery in 19th-century America. (Rev: BCCB 2/95; BL 12/15/94; SLJ 4/95) [641.5]

24580 Amari, Suad. *Cooking the Lebanese Way*. Rev. ed. (5–10). Series: Easy Menu Ethnic Cookbooks. 2003, Lerner LB $25.26 (0-8225-4116-5). 72pp. Revised to include low-fat and vegetarian foods, this introduction to Lebanese cooking contains about 40 recipes, clearly explained and well-illustrated. (Rev: BL 9/15/02; HBG 3/03) [641.5]

24581 Bacon, Josephine. *Cooking the Israeli Way*. Rev. ed. (5–10). Series: Easy Menu Ethnic Cookbooks. 2002, Lerner LB $25.26 (0-8225-4112-2).

72pp. After a general introduction to Israel, this book discusses cooking terms and ingredients, and then gives a series of tantalizing recipes with clear instructions. (Rev: BL 7/02; HBG 10/02) [641]

24582 Bastyra, J., and C. Bradley. *Look and Make Cooking* (4–5). Photos by Howard Allman. Illus. by Michael Evans. Series: Look and Make. 2004, Sea-to-Sea LB $27.10 (1-932889-22-1). 32pp. Well-designed recipes are introduced by reminders about safety and the importance of gathering ingredients and equipment in advance. (Rev: SLJ 4/05)

24583 Bastyra, Judy. *Fun Food* (1–4). Photos by Michael Michaels and Steve Shott. Illus. by Mei Lim. Series: First Craft Books. 1998, Carolrhoda LB $12.95 (1-57505-204-0). 22pp. This book contains ten projects, each involving three simple steps, that result in such goodies as an ice-cream clown or a shortbread house. (Rev: SLJ 4/98) [745]

24584 Bisignano, Alphonse. *Cooking the Italian Way*. Rev. ed. (5–10). Series: Easy Menu Ethnic Cookbooks. 2001, Lerner $25.26 (0-8225-4113-0); paper $12.75 (0-8225-4161-0). 72pp. A revised edition that now includes vegetarian and low-fat recipes as well as an expanded introductory section on the country, the people, and the culture. (Rev: HBG 3/02; SLJ 9/01) [641]

24585 Bisignano, Alphonse. *Cooking the Italian Way* (5–8). Illus. 1982, Lerner LB $19.93 (0-8225-0906-7). 48pp. Fifteen recipes plus a description of the country, markets, and dinner tables.

24586 Blain, Diane. *The Boxcar Children Cookbook* (3–5). Illus. by L. Kate Deal and Eileen M. Neill. 1991, Whitman paper $9.95 (0-8075-0856-X). 96pp. Each of the simple recipes in this book is related to the Boxcar Children series. (Rev: BL 1/15/92; SLJ 11/91) [641]

24587 Buck-Murray, Marian. *The Mash and Smash Cookbook: Fun and Yummy Recipes Every Kid Can Make!* (3–6). Illus. 1997, Wiley paper $12.95 (0-471-17969-8). 128pp. A collection of recipes that are named to appeal to kids, with interesting sidebars containing background information about the ingredients. (Rev: BL 1/1–15/98; SLJ 2/98) [641.5]

24588 Bugni, Alice. *Moose Racks, Bear Tracks, and Other Alaska Kidsnacks: Cooking with Kids Has Never Been So Easy!* (K–5). Illus. by Shannon Cartwright. 1999, Sasquatch paper $8.95 (1-57061-214-5). This clever, fanciful book contains recipes and step-by-step instructions for the preparation of 25 easy-to-make snacks with enticing names. (Rev: SLJ 12/99) [641]

24589 Chung, Okwha, and Judy Monroe. *Cooking the Korean Way*. Rev. ed. (5–10). Illus. Series: Easy Menu Ethnic Cookbooks. 2003, Lerner LB $25.26 (0-8225-4115-7). 48pp. Tempting recipes and a brief look at where they come from. (Rev: BL 8/88; HBG 3/03; SLJ 9/88) [641.59519]

24590 Cook, Deanna F. *The Kids' Multicultural Cookbook: Food and Fun Around the World* (3–6). Illus. 1995, Williamson paper $12.95 (0-913589-91-8). 160pp. This collection of activities, recipes, and games includes material on various regions of the world. (Rev: BL 3/15/96; SLJ 2/96) [641.59]

24591 Cornell, Kari. *Holiday Cooking Around the World*. Rev. ed. (5–10). Illus. Series: Easy Menu Ethnic Cookbooks. 2002, Lerner LB $25.26 (0-8225-4128-9); paper $7.95 (0-8225-4159-9). 72pp. Beginning cooks will appreciate the clear instructions and varied options in this appealing book that includes cultural and social information. (Rev: BL 1/1–15/02; HBG 10/02; SLJ 5/02) [641.5]

24592 Coronado, Rosa. *Cooking the Mexican Way*. Rev. ed. (5–10). Series: Easy Menu Ethnic Cookbooks. 2002, Lerner LB $25.26 (0-8225-4117-3). 72pp. Recipes organized by type of meal are preceded by a section that covers the geography, culture, and festivals and by information on equipment, ingredients, and eating customs. Other titles in this series include *Cooking the East African Way* and *Cooking the Spanish Way* (both 2001). (Rev: HBG 3/02; SLJ 2/02) [641]

24593 Corwin, Judith Hoffman. *Cookie Fun* (4–6). Illus. by author. 1988, Simon & Schuster paper $5.95 (0-671-55019-5). 64pp. Simple recipes for delicious cookies in this reissued cookbook.

24594 Coyle, Rena. *My First Baking Book* (4–6). Illus. by Tedd Arnold. 1988, Workman paper $9.95 (0-89480-579-7). 144pp. Bialosky Bear offers several fun treats to make, with the emphasis on cooking safety. (Rev: BL 1/1/89; SLJ 1/89)

24595 Dahl, Roald, and Felicity Dahl. *Roald Dahl's Even More Revolting Recipes* (4–6). Illus. by Quentin Blake. 2001, Viking $17.99 (0-670-03515-7). 64pp. A follow-up to *Revolting Recipes* (1994), this volume includes 31 new recipes inspired by Dahl's books. (Rev: BL 2/1/02; HBG 3/02; SLJ 11/01) [641.5]

24596 D'Amico, Joan, and Karen Eich Drummond. *The Healthy Body Cookbook: Fun Activities and Delicious Recipes for Kids* (4–6). Illus. by Tina Cash-Walsh. 1999, Wiley paper $12.95 (0-471-18888-3). 192pp. The 56 recipes in this book are arranged according to the part of the body they benefit, e.g., heart, muscles, teeth, hair, nerves. (Rev: SLJ 2/99) [641]

24597 D'Amico, Joan, and Karen Eich Drummond. *The Science Chef Travels Around the World: Fun Food Experiments and Recipes for Kids* (4–8). Illus. 1996, Wiley paper $12.95 (0-471-11779-X). An entertaining combination of simple science experiments and international cooking, with recipes from 14 countries and activities that demonstrate scientific principles of various cooking and baking processes. (Rev: BL 2/1/96; SLJ 3/96) [641.5]

24598 D'Amico, Joan, and Karen Eich Drummond. *The United States Cookbook: Fabulous Foods and Fascinating Facts from All 50 States* (4–6). Illus. by Jeff Cline and Tina Cash-Walsh. 2000, Wiley paper $12.95 (0-471-35839-8). 186pp. This cookbook, which is divided into seven regions and then individual states, gives basic information about each state followed by tempting recipes and food and cooking tips. (Rev: BL 5/15/00; SLJ 5/00) [641]

24599 Davis, Robin. *The Star Wars Cookbook: Wookiee Cookies and Other Galactic Recipes* (3–5). Photos by Frankie Frankeny. 1998, Chronicle $14.95 (0-8118-2184-6). 60pp. Standard recipes, many using prepared foods, are recycled using *Star Wars* lingo in a spiral-bound cookbook. (Rev: SLJ 1/99) [641]

24600 *Desserts Around the World* (4–6). Illus. by Robert L. Wolfe and Diane Wolfe. Series: Easy Menu Ethnic Cookbooks. 1992, Lerner LB $19.93 (0-8225-0926-1). 56pp. This book gives recipes and background material on simple desserts as prepared in different countries and cultures. (Rev: BL 6/15/92) [641.8]

24601 Dooley, Norah. *Everybody Cooks Rice* (K–3). Illus. 1991, Carolrhoda LB $15.95 (0-87614-412-1); paper $6.95 (0-87614-591-8). 32pp. A story that shows the different ways Americans cook and eat rice. (Rev: BCCB 5/91; BL 4/15/91; SLJ 6/91) [641.6]

24602 Duden, Jane. *Vegetarianism for Teens* (4–7). Illus. Series: Nutrition and Fitness. 2001, Capstone LB $23.93 (0-7368-0712-8). 32pp. An overview of vegetarian diets that includes a checklist and tips on coping with people who discount the appeal of a meatless life. (Rev: BL 7/01; HBG 10/01; SLJ 7/01) [613.2]

24603 *Felicity's Cook Book: A Peek at Dining in the Past with Meals You Can Cook Today* (3–5). Illus. Series: American Girls Pastimes. 1994, Pleasant Co. paper $5.95 (1-56247-120-1). 44pp. This book, a mixture of history and recipes, re-creates meals that were current during the colonial period in American history. (Rev: BL 12/15/94) [641.5]

24604 Frankeny, Frankie, and Wesley Martin. *The Star Wars Cookbook II: Darth Malt and More Galactic Recipes* (3–5). Photos by Frankie Frankeny. 2000, Chronicle $15.95 (0-8118-2803-4). 62pp. A delightful cookbook with 29 recipes in five categories: breakfasts, snacks, main courses, desserts, and drinks. (Rev: SLJ 11/00) [641]

24605 Gardella, Tricia, comp. *Writers in the Kitchen: Children's Book Authors Share Memories of Their Favorite Recipes* (4–6). 1998, Boyds Mills paper $14.95 (1-56397-713-3). 247pp. One hundred and fifty authors and illustrators of children's books, including Paula Danziger and Jerry Spinelli, talk about food and share a favorite recipe. (Rev: SLJ 12/98) [641]

24606 Gillies, Judi, and Jennifer Glossop. *The Jumbo Vegetarian Cookbook* (4–8). Illus. 2002, Kids Can paper $14.95 (1-55074-977-3). 256pp. An introduction to the vegetarian lifestyle, including nutrition and recipes. (Rev: BCCB 7–8/02; BL 3/1/02; SLJ 7/02) [641.5]

24607 Gillies, Judi, and Jennifer Glossop. *The Kids Can Press Jumbo Cookbook* (5–8). Illus. 2000, Kids Can paper $14.95 (1-55074-621-9). 256pp. After a few cooking tips, this book provides recipes that range from the simple (scrambled eggs) to the difficult (crepes and carrot cake). (Rev: BL 5/1/00; SLJ 6/00) [641.8]

24608 Gioffre, Rosalba. *The Young Chef's French Cookbook* (4–7). Series: I'm the Chef! 2001, Crabtree LB $22.60 (0-7787-0282-0); paper $8.95 (0-7787-0296-0). 32pp. This oversize book uses double-page spreads to present 15 appetizing French recipes along with good background material, clear directions, and excellent illustrations. (Rev: BL 10/15/01) [641]

24609 Gioffre, Rosalba. *The Young Chef's Italian Cookbook* (4–7). Series: I'm the Chef! 2001, Crabtree LB $22.60 (0-7787-0279-0); paper $8.95 (0-7787-0293-6). 32pp. Along with good background material, clear instructions are presented for 15 Italian dishes in this well-illustrated, oversize book. (Rev: BL 10/15/01; SLJ 11/01) [641]

24610 Goodwin, Bob, and Candi Perez. *A Taste of Spain* (4–6). Illus. Series: Food Around the World. 1995, Thomson Learning LB $22.83 (1-56847-188-2). 48pp. Basic information is given about the history and culture of Spain, followed by material on Spanish food and a group of representative recipes. (Rev: SLJ 3/95) [641]

24611 Goss, Gary. *Blue Moon Soup: A Family Cookbook* (4–6). Illus. 1999, Little, Brown $16.95 (0-316-32991-6). 64pp. As well as eight to ten soup recipes for each of the seasons, this book gives related recipes for breads, salads, and snacks. (Rev: BL 11/1/99; HBG 3/00; SLJ 9/99) [641.8]

24612 Hargittai, Magdolna. *Cooking the Hungarian Way*. Rev. ed. (5–10). Series: Easy Menu Ethnic Cookbooks. 2002, Lerner LB $25.26 (0-8225-4132-7). 72pp. After an introduction to Hungary and its cuisine, there are about 40 clearly presented recipes from appetizers through desserts. (Rev: BL 9/15/02; HBG 3/03) [641.5]

24613 Hargittai, Magdolna. *Cooking the Hungarian Way* (5–7). Illus. 1986, Lerner LB $19.93 (0-8225-0916-4). 48pp. An Easy Menu Ethnic Cookbook, with information about Hungarian history and food. (Rev: BL 10/15/86)

24614 Harrison, Supenn, and Judy Monroe. *Cooking the Thai Way*. Rev. ed. (5–10). Series: Easy Menu Ethnic Cookbooks. 2002, Lerner LB $25.26 (0-8225-4124-6); paper $7.95 (0-8225-0608-4). 72pp. The country of Thailand is introduced followed by general information on its foods and several easy-to-follow recipes. (Rev: BL 9/15/02) [641.5]

24615 Harrison, Supenn, and Judy Monroe. *Cooking the Thai Way* (5–7). Illus. 1986, Lerner LB $19.93 (0-8225-0917-2). 48pp. Such recipes as Thai salads are included in this Easy Menu Ethnic Cookbook, along with history and information about Thai food. (Rev: BL 10/15/86)

24616 Hill, Barbara W. *Cooking the English Way*. Rev. ed. (5–10). Series: Easy Menu Ethnic Cookbooks. 2002, Lerner LB $25.26 (0-8225-4105-X). 72pp. The land and people of England are briefly introduced followed by material on their favorite dishes and easy-to-follow recipes. (Rev: BL 9/15/02) [641.5]

24617 Hill, Barbara W. *Cooking the English Way* (5–8). Illus. 1982, Lerner LB $19.93 (0-8225-0903-2). 48pp. Menus from breakfast through dinner are outlined plus national customs.

24618 Hill, Mary. *Let's Make Pizza* (PS–1). Series: In the Kitchen. 2002, Children's Book Pr. LB $14.50 (0-516-23959-7); paper $4.95 (0-516-24020-

X). 24pp. For beginning readers, this is a simple introduction to the ingredients of a pizza and the technique for making one. Also use *Let's Make Tacos* (2002). (Rev: SLJ 2/03)

24619 Hopkinson, Deborah. *Fannie in the Kitchen: The Whole Story from Soup to Nuts of How Fannie Farmer Invented Recipes with Precise Measurements* (K–3). Illus. by Nancy Carpenter. 2001, Simon & Schuster $16.00 (0-689-81965-X). 40pp. Fannie Farmer teaches a young girl to cook in this fictionalized account that is interspersed with excerpts from Farmer's cookbook. (Rev: BCCB 6/01; BL 5/15/01*; HB 5–6/01; HBG 10/01; SLJ 5/01*) [641.5]

24620 Hughes, Helga. *Cooking the Swiss Way* (5–8). Photos by Robert L. Wolfe and Diane Wolfe. Illus. Series: Easy Menu Ethnic Cookbooks. 1995, Lerner LB $19.93 (0-8225-0930-X). 47pp. After a general introduction to Switzerland, this book colorfully discusses its food and produce and gives a number of tempting recipes. (Rev: SLJ 7/95) [641]

24621 Ichord, Loretta Frances. *Skillet Bread, Sourdough, and Vinegar Pie: Cooking in Pioneer Days* (3–5). Illus. by Jan Davey Ellis. 2003, Millbrook LB $24.90 (0-7613-1864-X). 64pp. This fascinating overview of pioneer cuisine features a number of classic recipes as well as a look at unique food preparation challenges faced by early Americans. (Rev: HBG 10/03)

24622 Katzen, Mollie. *Honest Pretzels: And 64 Other Amazing Recipes for Cooks Ages 8 and Up* (4–6). Illus. 1999, Tricycle $19.95 (1-883672-88-0). 192pp. Here is a collection of 64 vegetarian recipes designed for older children. (Rev: BL 11/1/99; HBG 3/00; SLJ 9/99) [641.5]

24623 Katzen, Mollie, and Ann Henderson. *Pretend Soup and Other Real Recipes: A Cookbook for Preschoolers and Up* (PS–3). Illus. by Mollie Katzen. 1994, Tricycle $16.95 (1-883672-06-6). 95pp. Using pictures as well as text, 17 simple recipes are presented that are easy enough for youngsters to prepare with little supervision. (Rev: HB 7–8/94; SLJ 6/94*) [641]

24624 Kaufman, Cheryl Davidson. *Cooking the Caribbean Way*. Rev. ed. (5–10). Illus. Series: Easy Menu Ethnic Cookbooks. 1988, Lerner LB $25.26 (0-8225-4103-3). 48pp. A variety of dishes featuring the spices and fresh fruits that come from these islands. (Rev: BL 8/88; SLJ 9/88) [641.59729]

24625 *Kids' First Cookbook: Delicious-Nutritious Treats to Make Yourself!* (K–3). 1999, American Cancer Society $13.95 (0-944235-19-0). 88pp. A cookbook with 53 nutritionally sound recipes plus information on how to read a food label, kitchen safety, and a guide to the food pyramid. (Rev: SLJ 3/00) [641]

24626 *Kirsten's Cook Book: A Peek at Dining in the Past with Meals You Can Cook Today* (3–5). Illus. Series: American Girls Pastimes. 1994, Pleasant Co. paper $5.95 (1-56247-111-2). 44pp. Describes the food that pioneer Swedish families ate in the United States and gives 17 simple recipes. (Rev: BCCB 2/95; BL 12/15/94; SLJ 10/94) [641.5]

24627 Lagasse, Emeril. *Emeril's There's a Chef in My Family! Recipes to Get Everybody Cooking* (5–10). Photos by Quentin Bacon. Illus. by Charles Yuen. 2004, HarperCollins $22.99 (0-06-000439-8). 209pp. Seventy-six recipes are presented with clear instructions that focus on the enjoyment of cooking. (Rev: SLJ 7/04) [641.5]

24628 Lagasse, Emeril. *Emeril's There's a Chef in My Soup: Recipes for the Kid in Everyone* (5–8). Illus. by Charles Yuen. 2002, HarperCollins $22.99 (0-688-17706-9). 256pp. The famed TV chef presents a series of simple recipes for main dishes, pasta, desserts, breakfast and lunch items, and salads. (Rev: BL 5/1/02; HBG 10/02) [641.5]

24629 Lee, Frances. *The Young Chef's Chinese Cookbook* (4–7). Illus. Series: I'm the Chef! 2001, Crabtree LB $22.60 (0-7787-0280-4); paper $8.95 (0-7787-0294-4). 40pp. Fifteen child-friendly recipes for Chinese dishes are presented with step-by-step directions and photographs. (Rev: BL 10/15/01; SLJ 11/01) [641.5951]

24630 Locricchio, Matthew. *The Cooking of Greece* (5–10). Photos by Jack McConnell. Illus. Series: Superchef. 2004, Benchmark LB $20.95 (0-7614-1729-X). 80pp. Recipes follow an informative overview of regional cuisines in Greece and the ingredients commonly used. (Rev: SLJ 4/05)

24631 Locricchio, Matthew. *The Cooking of India* (4–8). Photos by Jack McConnell. Illus. Series: Superchef. 2004, Benchmark $20.95 (0-7614-1730-3). 80pp. Clear instructions guide readers through the steps involved in making dishes from various areas of India; fresh ingredients are recommended and safety is emphasized. Also use *The Cooking of Thailand* (2004). (Rev: SLJ 2/05) [641.5954]

24632 McCulloch, Julie. *The Caribbean* (3–6). Illus. Series: World of Recipes. 2001, Heinemann LB $24.22 (1-58810-153-3). 48pp. Recipes, arranged by difficulty, follow information on the region and typical food choices. (Rev: BL 8/01; HBG 10/01) [641.59]

24633 McCulloch, Julie. *China* (3–6). Illus. Series: World of Recipes. 2001, Heinemann LB $24.22 (1-58810-152-5). 48pp. Recipes, arranged by difficulty, follow information on China and the kinds of foods eaten there. (Rev: BL 8/01; HBG 10/01; SLJ 10/01) [641.5951]

24634 McCulloch, Julie. *India* (4–6). Illus. Series: A World of Recipes. 2001, Heinemann LB $24.22 (1-58810-085-5). 48pp. A discussion of the history and traditions of Indian food is accompanied by a selection of typical recipes, most of which require adult participation. Also use *Mexico*. (Rev: HBG 10/01; SLJ 12/01) [641.5954]

24635 McCulloch, Julie. *Japan* (4–6). Illus. by Nicholas Beresford-Davies. Series: A World of Recipes. 2001, Heinemann LB $24.22 (1-58810-087-1). 48pp. Step-by-step instructions clearly show how to make dishes that are typical of Japanese cuisine, accompanied by advice on handling chopsticks. Also use *China* (2001). (Rev: HBG 10/01; SLJ 10/01) [641.5952]

24636 McKenley, Yvonne. *A Taste of the Caribbean* (4–6). Illus. Series: Food Around the World. 1995, Thomson Learning LB $22.83 (1-56847-187-4). 48pp. Describes the food of the Caribbean islands, gives several recipes, and supplies basic background information on Caribbean history and culture. (Rev: SLJ 3/95) [641]

24637 MacLeod, Elizabeth. *Bake and Make Amazing Cakes* (4–6). Illus. by June Bradford. Series: Kids Can Do It! 2001, Kids Can $12.95 (1-55074-849-1); paper $5.95 (1-55074-848-3). 40pp. A collection of child-friendly cake recipes with easy-to-follow instructions. (Rev: SLJ 6/01) [641.8653]

24638 MacLeod, Elizabeth. *Bake and Make Amazing Cookies* (3–8). Illus. by June Bradford. Series: Kids Can Do It! 2004, Kids Can $12.95 (1-55337-631-5); paper $6.95 (1-55337-632-3). 40pp. Organized under headings such as "Holidays" and "Seasons," these are simple recipes for a wide variety of enticing cookies. (Rev: SLJ 2/05) [641.8]

24639 MacLeod, Elizabeth. *Bake It and Build It* (2–6). Illus. 1998, Kids Can paper $5.95 (1-55074-427-5). 40pp. This combination cooking and craft book shows how to make objects such as a cookie castle, an edible flower wreath, and cookie flowers out of various kinds of cookies, oatmeal, and different doughs. (Rev: BL 12/1/98; SLJ 1/99) [745.5]

24640 Madavan, Vijay. *Cooking the Indian Way* (5–8). Illus. 1985, Lerner LB $19.93 (0-8225-0911-3). 52pp. Cultural information is detailed plus both vegetarian and nonvegetarian recipes. (Rev: SLJ 9/85) [641.5954]

24641 Marchant, Kerena. *Hindu Cookbook* (3–5). Photos by Zul Mukhida. Series: Holiday Cookbooks from Around the World. 2001, Raintree LB $17.98 (0-7398-3264-6). 32pp. Marchant looks at three Hindu holidays (Holi, Divali, and Ganesh Chaturthi), describes how they are celebrated, and provides appropriate recipes, with appealing photographs. Also use *Chinese Cookbook* (2001). (Rev: SLJ 8/01) [641.5]

24642 Mayer, Marianna. *The Mother Goose Cookbook: Rhymes and Recipes for the Very Young* (1–3). Illus. by Carol Schwartz. 1998, Morrow $11.95 (0-688-15242-2). 40pp. Rather complex recipes for such dishes as pease porridge and plum pudding are accompanied by the traditional rhymes that inspired them. (Rev: BL 4/1/98; HBG 10/98; SLJ 4/98) [641.5]

24643 *Molly's Cook Book: A Peek at Dining in the Past with Meals You Can Cook Today* (3–5). Illus. Series: American Girls Pastimes. 1994, Pleasant Co. paper $5.95 (1-56247-117-1). 44pp. A look at life between the world wars is given in this cookbook with recipes that reflect those times. (Rev: BL 12/15/94) [641.5]

24644 Montgomery, Bertha Vining, and Constance Nabwire. *Cooking the West African Way*. Rev. ed. (5–10). Series: Easy Menu Ethnic Cookbooks. 2002, Lerner LB $25.26 (0-8225-4163-7). 72pp. An appealing introduction to West African cuisine, with information on the land, people, and culture, and several low-fat and vegetarian recipes. (Rev: HBG 10/02; SLJ 5/02) [641.5966]

24645 Munsen, Sylvia. *Cooking the Norwegian Way.* Rev. ed. (5–10). Series: Easy Menu Ethnic Cookbooks. 2002, Lerner LB $25.26 (0-8225-4118-1). 72pp. A revised edition of an earlier publication that gives information on the country and culture in addition to a selection of typical recipes. (Rev: BL 7/02; SLJ 9/02) [641.59]

24646 Nathan, Joan. *The Children's Jewish Holiday Kitchen: 70 Ways to Have Fun with Your Kids and Make Your Family's Celebrations Special* (4–6). Illus. 1995, Schocken $24.00 (0-8052-4130-2). 176pp. Seventy recipes arranged by holiday and by the degree of difficulty and need for supervision. (Rev: BL 10/15/95) [641.5]

24647 Nguyen, Chi, and Judy Monroe. *Cooking the Vietnamese Way* (5–10). Illus. Series: Easy Menu Ethnic Cookbooks. 1985, Lerner LB $25.26 (0-8225-4125-4). 48pp. The authors introduce the land and people of Vietnam before giving recipes for regional dishes. (Rev: BL 9/15/85; SLJ 9/85) [641]

24648 Nguyen, Chi, and Judy Monroe. *Cooking the Vietnamese Way* (5–8). Illus. 1985, Lerner LB $19.93 (0-8225-0914-8). 48pp. Information about the country is given plus recipes for native dishes and even how to eat with chopsticks. (Rev: SLJ 9/85)

24649 Ono, Kaoru. *Sushi for Kids: A Children's Introduction to Japan's Favorite Food* (2–5). Trans. from Japanese by Peter Howlett and Richard McNamera. Illus. by author. 2003, Tuttle $10.95 (0-8048-3346-X). 32pp. Atsushi visits a fish market and learns how sushi is prepared. (Rev: HBG 4/04; SLJ 10/03) [641.6]

24650 Osseo-Asare, Fran. *A Good Soup Attracts Chairs: A First African Cookbook for American Kids* (5–9). 1993, Pelican $18.95 (0-88289-816-7). A basic cookbook for youngsters that explores African cooking past and present and gives more than 35 recipes. (Rev: BL 10/15/93; SLJ 8/93) [641.5966]

24651 Parnell, Helga. *Cooking the German Way.* Rev. ed. (5–10). Illus. Series: Easy Menu Ethnic Cookbooks. 1988, Lerner LB $25.26 (0-8225-4107-6). 48pp. Includes such treats as Black Forest torte and apple cake. (Rev: BL 8/88) [641.5943]

24652 Parnell, Helga. *Cooking the South American Way.* Rev. ed. (5–10). Series: Easy Menu Ethnic Cookbooks. 2002, Lerner LB $25.26 (0-8225-4121-1). 72pp. The continent of South America is introduced followed by about 40 clearly presented recipes from several different countries. (Rev: BL 9/15/02; HBG 3/03) [641.5]

24653 Parnell, Helga. *Cooking the South American Way* (4–6). Illus. by Robert L. Wolfe and Diane Wolfe. 1992, Lerner LB $19.93 (0-8225-0925-3). 48pp. Great recipes and basic data about where the foods come from. (Rev: BL 6/15/92) [641]

24654 Plotkin, Gregory, and Rita Plotkin. *Cooking the Russian Way.* Rev. ed. (5–10). Illus. Series: Easy Menu Ethnic Cookbooks. 2002, Lerner LB $25.26 (0-8225-4120-3). 48pp. Included along with

history and information are such recipes as Russian honey spice cake. (Rev: BL 10/15/86) [641.5947]

24655 Plotkin, Gregory, and Rita Plotkin. *Cooking the Russian Way* (5–7). Illus. 1986, Lerner LB $19.93 (0-8225-0915-6). 48pp. Included along with history and information are such recipes as Russian honey spice cake, in this Easy Menu Ethnic Cookbook. (Rev: BL 10/15/86)

24656 Pratt, Dianne. *Hey Kids! You're Cookin' Now! A Global Awareness Cooking Adventure* (4–6). Illus. 1998, Harvest Hill $19.95 (1-886862-07-9). 160pp. Seventeen cooking projects, along with the necessary recipes and directions, are including in this handy volume dealing with such edibles as pizza and chocolate pudding and some non-edibles such as glue and play clay. (Rev: BL 12/15/98; SLJ 3/99) [641.5]

24657 Pulleyn, Micah, and Sarah Bracken. *Kids in the Kitchen: 100 Delicious, Fun and Healthy Recipes to Cook and Bake* (3–5). Illus. 1994, Sterling $24.95 (0-8069-0447-X). 112pp. Gives background information on food preparation for boys and girls plus lots of recipes, many of which require no cooking. (Rev: BL 7/94; SLJ 8/94) [641.5]

24658 Raabe, Emily. *An Easter Holiday Cookbook* (2–5). Series: Festive Foods for the Holidays. 2001, Rosen LB $19.50 (0-8239-5624-5). 24pp. Spring holidays and their foods are presented with large print and colorful illustrations. Also use *A Passover Holiday Cookbook* (2001). (Rev: SLJ 2/02) [641.568]

24659 Rotner, Shelley, and Julia P. Hellums. *Hold the Anchovies!* (K–2). Illus. 1996, Orchard LB $16.99 (0-531-08857-X). 32pp. The pizza, its ingredients, and methods of preparation are presented with a recipe for basic pizza dough. (Rev: BL 9/15/96; SLJ 10/96) [641.8]

24660 *Samantha's Cook Book: A Peek at Dining in the Past with Meals You Can Cook Today* (3–5). Illus. Series: American Girls Pastimes. 1994, Pleasant Co. paper $5.95 (1-56247-114-7). 44pp. Twentieth-century American history is reflected in a series of recipes for easily prepared meals. (Rev: BL 12/15/94; SLJ 10/94) [641]

24661 Sanger, Amy Wilson. *Yum Yum Dim Sum* (PS–K). Illus. by author. 2003, Tricycle $6.95 (1-58246-108-2). This appealing blend of rhyming text and mixed-media artwork introduces children to dim sum. (Rev: SLJ 1/04)

24662 Scherie, Strom. *Stuffin' Muffin: Muffin Pan Cooking for Kids* (4–6). Illus. by Dave Ferry. 1982, Young People's Pr. paper $18.95 (0-9606964-9-0). 100pp. A variety of foods without sugar or salt that can be made in muffin tins.

24663 Skrepcinski, Denice, et al. *Cody Coyote Cooks! A Southwest Cookbook for Kids* (4–6). Illus. 1996, Tricycle paper $14.95 (1-883672-37-6). 96pp. Recipes along with legends, history, and geographical facts highlight this book about cooking and eating in Texas, Arizona, and New Mexico. (Rev: BL 10/15/96; SLJ 10/96) [641]

24664 Townsend, Sue, and Caroline Young. *Indonesia* (5–8). Illus. Series: A World of Recipes. 2003, Heinemann LB $27.07 (1-4034-0976-5). 48pp.

After a discussion of Indonesian food and ingredients, clear directions, with illustrations, are given for recipes that are graded by ease of preparation. Also use *Russia* and *Vietnam* (both 2003). (Rev: HBG 4/04; SLJ 9/03)

24665 Townsend, Sue, and Caroline Young. *Russia* (5–8). Illus. Series: A World of Recipes. 2003, Heinemann LB $27.07 (1-4034-0981-1). 48pp. Graded from easy through difficult, recipes for various dishes are accompanied by well-thought-out instructions and useful photographs. (Rev: HBG 4/04; SLJ 9/03) [641.5]

24666 Townsend, Sue, and Caroline Young. *Vietnam* (5–8). Illus. Series: A World of Recipes. 2003, Heinemann LB $27.07 (1-4034-0980-3). 48pp. Graded from easy through difficult, recipes for various dishes are accompanied by well-thought-out instructions and useful photographs. (Rev: HBG 4/04; SLJ 9/03) [641.5]

24667 Van der Linde, Polly, and Tasha Van der Linde. *Around the World in Eighty Dishes* (3–7). Illus. by Horst Lemke. 1971, Scroll $12.95 (0-87592-007-1). 88pp. The compilers and testers of these recipes from many continents are two little girls, eight and ten years old.

24668 Vaughan, Jenny, and Penny Beauchamp. *Christmas Foods* (3–7). Series: A World of Recipes. 2004, Heinemann LB $30.00 (1-4034-4697-0). 48pp. Christmas dishes from around the world have straightforward directions and color photographs. (Rev: BL 6/1–15/04) [641.5]

24669 Vaughan, Jenny, and Penny Beauchamp. *Festival Foods* (3–7). Series: World of Recipes. 2004, Heinemann LB $30.00 (1-4034-4699-7). 48pp. The easy-to-follow recipes here focus on dishes for festive occasions worldwide. (Rev: BL 6/1–15/04) [745.594]

24670 Villios, Lynne W. *Cooking the Greek Way*. Rev. ed. (5–10). Illus. Series: Easy Menu Ethnic Cookbooks. 2003, Lerner LB $25.26 (0-8225-4131-9). 52pp. The young cook is introduced to the cuisine of Greece, with a chapter covering utensils and ingredient needs and a glossary of basic cooking terms. Recipes are varied and easy to prepare. (Rev: BL 7/02; SLJ 9/02) [641]

24671 Waldee, Lynne Marie. *Cooking the French Way* (5–10). Illus. 2002, Lerner LB $24.26 (0-8225-4106-8). 48pp. A nicely illustrated introduction to French recipes including breads and sauces. (Rev: HBG 3/02; SLJ 2/02) [641.5944]

24672 Walker, Barbara M. *The Little House Cookbook* (5–7). Illus. by Garth Williams. 1979, HarperCollins paper $9.99 (0-06-446090-8). 256pp. Frontier food, such as green pumpkin pie from the Little House books, served up in tasty, easily used recipes.

24673 Wallace, Paula S. *The World of Food* (2–4). Illus. Series: Life Around the World. 2003, Gareth Stevens LB $21.26 (0-8368-3660-X). 48pp. Explores the cuisine and specialty foods of 10 countries, including Brazil, Egypt, Germany, India, Japan, Mexico, Russia, and South Africa. (Rev: HBG 10/03; SLJ 10/03)

24674 Ward, Karen. *The Young Chef's Mexican Cookbook* (4–7). Illus. Series: I'm the Chef! 2001, Crabtree LB $22.60 (0-7787-0281-2); paper $8.95 (0-7787-0295-2). 40pp. This oversize book uses double-page spreads to present 15 appetizing Mexican recipes along with good background material, clear directions, and excellent illustrations. (Rev: BL 10/15/01) [641.587]

24675 Warner, Margaret Brink, and Ruth Ann Hayward. *What's Cooking? Favorite Recipes from Around the World* (5–8). Illus. 1981, Little, Brown $16.95 (0-316-35252-7). A collection of recipes from more than 30 countries contibuted by American teenagers who also supply information on their ethnic origins. [641.5]

24676 Warshaw, Hallie. *The Sleepover Cookbook* (4–8). Photos by Julie Brown. 2000, Sterling $19.95 (0-8069-4497-8). 126pp. Easy-to-prepare goodies for all kinds of sleepovers are outlined with color photographs on each spread. (Rev: HBG 10/00; SLJ 7/00) [641]

24677 Webb, Lois S. *Holidays of the World Cookbook for Students* (5–8). 1995, Oryx paper $30.95 (0-89774-884-0). 264pp. This excellent cookbook contains 388 recipes that represent holidays in 136 countries, including many from various regions of the United States. (Rev: SLJ 1/96) [641]

24678 Weston, Reiko. *Cooking the Japanese Way*. Rev. ed. (5–8). Illus. Series: Easy Menu Ethnic Cookbooks. 2002, Lerner LB $25.26 (0-8225-4114-9). 48pp. Directions for preparing traditional foods are given along with lists of terms, ingredients, and utensils. (Rev: HBG 3/02) [641.5952]

24679 White, Linda. *Cooking on a Stick: Campfire Recipes for Kids* (3–6). Illus. 1996, Gibbs Smith paper $8.95 (0-87905-727-0). 48pp. In addition to covering campfire cooking, this book discusses equipment and fire making. (Rev: BL 4/1/96) [641.5]

24680 Wilkes, Angela. *The Children's Quick and Easy Cookbook* (4–6). Illus. 1997, DK $16.95 (0-7894-2026-0). 96pp. Not nearly as "quick and easy" as the title would suggest, this book nevertheless contains some good recipes in an attractive format. (Rev: BL 12/15/97; HBG 3/98; SLJ 1/98) [641.5]

24681 Williamson, Sarah A. *Bake the Best-Ever Cookies!* (3–6). Illus. by Tom Ernst. Series: Quick Starts for Kids! 2001, Williamson paper $7.95 (1-885593-56-2). 64pp. Simple recipes follow basic information on equipment and ingredients and a number of frequently asked questions. (Rev: SLJ 11/01) [641.8654]

24682 Williamson, Sarah A., and Zachary Williamson. *Kids Cook! Fabulous Food for the Whole Family* (4–6). Illus. by Loretta Trezzo-Baren. 1992, Williamson paper $12.95 (0-913589-61-6). 157pp. Using recipes at three levels of difficulty, this book contains 153 recipes of foods that are fun to prepare. (Rev: SLJ 7/92) [641.5]

24683 Wishik, Cindy S. *Kids Dish It Up . . . Sugar-Free: A Versatile Teaching Tool for Beginning Cooks* (3–5). Illus. 1982, Peninsula paper $11.95 (0-

918146-22-4). 160pp. From soup to nuts with sugar-free recipes.

24684 Yu, Ling. *Cooking the Chinese Way*. Rev. ed. (5–10). Illus. Series: Easy Menu Ethnic Cookbooks. 1982, Lerner LB $25.26 (0-8225-4104-1). 48pp. From appetizers to desserts, with attractive illustrations. (Rev: HBG 3/02) [641.5]

24685 Zamojska-Hutchins, Danuta. *Cooking the Polish Way*. Rev. ed. (5–10). Illus. Series: Easy Menu Ethnic Cookbooks. 2002, Lerner LB $25.26 (0-8225-4119-X). 52pp. Simple Polish recipes include traditional dishes such as pierogi. Glossary of terms, plus listing of utensils and ingredients used. (Rev: BL 7/02; HBG 10/02) [641.5]

24686 Zanzarella, Marianne. *The Good Housekeeping Illustrated Children's Cookbook* (5–8). Illus. 1997, Morrow $17.95 (0-688-13375-4). A visually appealing cookbook containing a number of excellent recipes, some of which require adult supervision. (Rev: BL 12/15/97; HBG 3/98; SLJ 1/98) [641.5]

Gardening

24687 Björk, Christina. *Linnea's Windowsill Garden* (1–5). Trans. by Joan Sandin. Illus. by Lena Anderson. 1988, Farrar $13.00 (91-29-59064-7). 60pp. Linnea takes readers on a tour of her indoor garden. (Rev: BCCB 12/88; BL 1/15/89; SLJ 11/88) [635]

24688 Burns, Kate, and Dawn Apperley. *How Does Your Garden Grow?* (K–2). Illus. 1998, Levinson $10.95 (1-899607-51-X). In this interactive garden book, flowers and vegetables pop-up from seeds. (Rev: BL 1/1–15/99; SLJ 1/99) [635]

24689 Dietl, Ulla. *The Plant-and-Grow Project Book* (PS–3). Illus. 1994, Sterling $14.95 (0-8069-0456-9). 48pp. Contains a series of projects involving indoor gardening and growing such plants as cotton, corn, eggplant, and wheat. (Rev: BL 1/15/94) [635.9]

24690 Kite, L. Patricia. *Gardening Wizardry for Kids* (3–6). 1995, Barron's paper $14.95 (0-8120-1317-4). 220pp. A guide to windowsill and kitchen gardens, with informative explanations, projects and experiments. (Rev: BL 8/95) [635]

24691 Lerner, Carol. *My Backyard Garden* (4–6). Illus. 1998, Morrow $16.00 (0-688-14755-0). 48pp. Advice and inspiration are supplied in this book about planting and caring for a backyard vegetable garden. (Rev: BL 3/15/98; HBG 10/98; SLJ 4/98) [635]

24692 Lerner, Carol. *My Indoor Garden* (3–7). Illus. 1999, Morrow LB $15.93 (0-688-14754-2). 48pp. Pen-and-watercolor drawings are used to illustrate this guide to indoor gardening, the necessary tools, conditions, and the types of suitable plants. (Rev: BL 6/1–15/99; HB 7–8/99; HBG 10/99; SLJ 4/99) [635.9]

24693 Lovejoy, Sharon. *Roots, Shoots, Buckets and Boots: Gardening Together with Children* (1–4). Illus. by author. 1999, Workman $24.95 (0-7611-1765-2); paper $13.95 (0-7611-1056-9). 159pp. A fine how-to book on gardening with lore, tips, techniques, and ideas for adults and children to share including a list of the top 20 plans for kids. (Rev: SLJ 2/00) [635]

24694 Maass, Robert. *Garden* (1–3). Illus. 1998, Holt $15.95 (0-8050-5477-4). 32pp. Photographs of children gardening are used with a simple text to explain plants and their cultivation, including annuals, perennials, bulbs, planting, and composting. (Rev: BL 6/1–15/98; HBG 10/98; SLJ 4/98) [635]

24695 MacLeod, Elizabeth. *Grow It Again* (3–5). Illus. Series: Kids Can! 1999, Kids Can paper $5.95 (1-55074-558-1). 40pp. Using discarded parts of plants — carrot tops, avocado pits, and potato buds — this guide shows how to grow new vegetables and fruits and supplies a few tasty recipes and interesting projects. (Rev: BL 6/1–15/99; SLJ 6/99) [635]

24696 Maurer, Tracy Nelson. *Growing Flowers* (1–4). Series: Green Thumb Guides. 2000, Rourke LB $21.27 (1-55916-251-1). 24pp. A very simple gardening guide that includes material on what, where, and when to plant plus information on weeding, watering, and other gardening tips. Also use *Growing House Plants* and *Growing Vegetables* (both 2000). (Rev: SLJ 1/01) [635]

24697 Morris, Karyn. *The Kids Can Press Jumbo Book of Gardening* (3–6). Illus. 2000, Kids Can $14.95 (1-55074-690-1). 240pp. Some of the topics covered in this information-packed volume include fruit, vegetable, and flower gardens; native plants; gardens that attract wildlife; and group projects. (Rev: BL 7/00) [635]

24698 Nichol, Barbara. *One Small Garden* (3–6). Illus. by Barry Moser. 2001, Tundra $17.95 (0-88776-475-4). 56pp. A Toronto garden is the focus of this lyrical narrative describing plants, animals, and even the people who have enjoyed it. (Rev: BL 12/15/01; HBG 3/02; SLJ 12/01) [635]

24699 Rhoades, Diane. *Garden Crafts for Kids: 50 Great Reasons to Get Your Hands Dirty* (3–6). Illus. 1995, Sterling $21.95 (0-8069-0998-6). 144pp. A complete guide for the beginning gardener, from choosing the right spot, to selecting seeds and plants, preparing the soil, and growing healthy plants. (Rev: SLJ 8/95*) [635]

24700 Van Hage, Mary An. *Little Green Thumbs* (3–6). Photos by Lucy Tizard. Illus. by Bettina Paterson. 1996, Millbrook LB $21.40 (1-56294-270-0). 32pp. An activity book that offers 12 indoor and outdoor projects for each of the seasons, like building a dinosaur-theme terrarium or planting an orange tree. (Rev: SLJ 7/96) [635]

Magic

24701 Baker, James W. *Illusions Illustrated: A Professional Magic Show for Young Performers* (5–8). Illus. by Jeanette Swofford. 1994, Lerner paper $6.95 (0-8225-9512-5). 120pp. Directions on how to put on a magic show with 10 different tricks.

24702 Broekel, Ray, and Laurence B. White. *Hocus Pocus: Magic You Can Do* (4–6). Illus. by Mary Thelen. 1984, Whitman LB $13.95 (0-8075-3350-5). 48pp. Twenty simple tricks for beginners.

24703 Burgess, Ron. *Kids Make Magic: The Complete Guide to Becoming an Amazing Magician* (3–6). Illus. by Marie Ferrante-Doyle and Sarah Rakitin. Series: Kids Can! 2003, Williamson paper $12.95 (1-885593-87-2). 127pp. Step-by-step tips for aspiring magicians, from the tricks themselves to advice on setting up a magic show. Includes a detailed resource guide. (Rev: SLJ 3/04) [793.8]

24704 Clibbon, Meg. *Imagine You're a Wizard!* (K–4). Illus. by Lucy Clibbon. Series: Imagine This! 2003, Annick $19.95 (1-55037-793-0); paper $7.95 (1-55037-792-2). All about wizards and how to become one, with ideas for projects. (Rev: SLJ 3/04) [133.4]

24705 Cobb, Vicki. *Magic . . . Naturally! Science Entertainments and Amusements* (4–6). Illus. 1993, HarperCollins LB $16.89 (0-06-022475-4). 150pp. A group of experiments that demonstrate the magic found in many scientific phenomena. (Rev: BL 10/15/93; SLJ 10/93) [793.8]

24706 Colbert, David. *The Magical Worlds of Harry Potter: A Treasury of Myths, Legends, and Fascinating Facts* (5–9). Illus. 2001, Lumina $14.95 (0-9708442-0-4). 223pp. Information on more than 50 topics in Harry's universe — such as alchemy, Grindylows, and Voldemort — arranged in alphabetical order. (Rev: SLJ 2/02) [823]

24707 Friedhoffer, Robert. *Magic and Perception: The Art and Science of Fooling the Senses* (5–7). Illus. 1996, Watts LB $25.00 (0-531-11254-3). 109pp. Simple directions for magic tricks that involve altering perceptions. (Rev: BL 7/96; SLJ 9/96) [793.8]

24708 Gordon, Henry. *It's Magic* (4–6). Illus. 1989, Prometheus paper $13.00 (0-87975-545-8). 92pp. A treasury of simple magic tricks. (Rev: BL 12/1/89) [793.8]

24709 Jones, Richard. *That's Magic! 40 Foolproof Tricks to Delight, Amaze and Entertain* (5–8). Illus. 2001, New Holland $19.95 (1-85974-668-3). 112pp. Simple instructions and photographs teach the beginning magician a few tricks. (Rev: BL 1/1–15/02; SLJ 1/02) [793.8]

24710 Kilby, Janice Eaton, and Terry Taylor. *The Book of Wizard Magic: In Which the Apprentice Finds Marvelous Magic Tricks, Mystifying Illusions and Astonishing Tales* (3–6). Illus. by Lindy Burnett. 2003, Lark $19.95 (1-57990-345-2). 144pp. A 600-year-old wizard narrates this guide to performing more than 60 tricks and illusions. (Rev: HBG 4/04; SLJ 11/03) [793.8]

24711 McMaster, Shawn. *Magic Tricks: Absolutely Everything You Need to Know About Magic!* (3–6). Illus. by Mike Moran. 2000, Lowell House paper $9.95 (0-7373-0231-3). 119pp. As well as a number of tricks, this book gives a history of sleight-of-hand performances and spells out the skills required to become a magician. (Rev: SLJ 8/00) [793.8]

24712 McMaster, Shawn. *60 Super Simple Magic Tricks* (3–6). Illus. by Leo Abbett. 1996, Lowell House paper $6.95 (1-56565-384-X). 80pp. Simple instructions are used to describe clearly 60 magic tricks, with additional information on effective presentations and examples of magician's patter. (Rev: SLJ 2/97) [783.9]

24713 Presto, Fay. *Magic for Kids* (3–6). Illus. 1999, Kingfisher paper $10.95 (0-7534-5210-3). 72pp. Step-by-step instructions are given for 20 tricks sure to please the young amateur magician. (Rev: BL 11/15/99) [793.8]

24714 Rigney, Francis. *A Beginner's Book of Magic* (4–6). Illus. 1963, Devin $8.25 (0-8159-5103-5). This is a do-it-yourself book of tricks, magic, and stunts.

24715 Russell, Tom. *Magic Step-by-Step* (3–6). Illus. 1997, Sterling $17.95 (0-8069-9533-5). 80pp. Step-by-step instructions for such areas of magic as disappearing acts and tricks involving cards and coins. (Rev: SLJ 8/97) [793.8]

24716 Wenzel, Angela. *Do You See What I See? The Art of Illusion* (5–8). Trans. from German by Rosie Jackson. 2001, Prestel $14.95 (3-7913-2488-8). 29pp. Tricks with perspective and color, coded messages, and hidden images are all presented in this attractive volume that makes for excellent browsing. (Rev: HBG 3/02; SLJ 2/02) [152]

Model Making

24717 Bliss, Helen, and Ruth Thomson. *Models* (2–6). Series: Craft Workshop. 1998, Crabtree LB $22.95 (0-86505-778-8); paper $10.95 (0-86505-788-5). 32pp. A well-organized craft book that offers instruction on how to make miniature objects from various countries and cultures. (Rev: SLJ 10/98) [745]

24718 Harris, Jack C. *Plastic Model Kits* (5–8). Illus. Series: Hobby Guides. 1993, Crestwood LB $12.95 (0-89686-623-8). 48pp. The hobby of making plastic models from kits is introduced, with good background information for both the novice and the expert. (Rev: SLJ 2/94) [745]

24719 Schmidt, Norman. *Fabulous Paper Gliders* (5–10). 1998, Sterling $19.95 (1-895569-21-4). 96pp. This book can serve two purposes: as a guide to building 16 model gliders and as a history of how these motorless planes developed. (Rev: SLJ 6/98) [745]

24720 Simon, Seymour. *The Paper Airplane Book* (3–6). Illus. by Byron Barton. 1971, Puffin paper $5.99 (0-14-030925-X). Using how-to-make paper airplanes as the takeoff point, the author explains why planes fly and how changes in their construction can cause variations in flight.

Photography and Filmmaking

24721 Evans, Art. *First Photos: How Kids Can Take Great Pictures* (4–6). Illus. 1993, Photo Data Research paper $9.95 (0-9626508-7-0). 64pp. Focuses on disposable cameras and gives good tips on topics like composition, light, point of view, and camera handling. (Rev: BL 12/15/92; SLJ 9/93) [770]

24722 Friedman, Debra. *Picture This: Fun Photography and Crafts* (4–7). Series: Kids Can Do It! 2003, Kids Can $12.95 (1-55337-046-5); paper $5.95 (1-55337-047-3). 48pp. An easy-to-follow project book that combines photographs and crafts. (Rev: BL 3/15/03; HBG 10/03; SLJ 4/03) [770]

24723 Hilton, Jonathan, and Barrie Watts. *Photography* (4–6). Illus. Series: First Guide. 1994, Millbrook LB $23.90 (1-56294-398-7). 96pp. Basic photographic equipment is introduced, with techniques and tips on taking a variety of photos, from still lifes to portraits. (Rev: BL 12/15/94) [770]

24724 Lasky, Kathryn. *Think Like an Eagle: At Work with a Wildlife Photographer* (3–7). Illus. by Christopher G. Knight and Jack Swedberg. 1992, Little, Brown $15.95 (0-316-51519-1). 48pp. Following a wildlife photographer through the seasons and across the country. (Rev: BCCB 3/92; BL 6/1/92; SLJ 4/92) [778.9]

24725 Morgan, Terri, and Shmuel Thaler. *Photography: Take Your Best Shot* (5–8). Illus. Series: Media Workshop. 1991, Lerner LB $21.27 (0-8225-2302-7). 72pp. A comprehensive and well-put-together guide to photography that covers cameras, film, developing, composition, lighting, and special effects, as well as discussing career opportunities. (Rev: BL 10/1/91; SLJ 11/91) [771]

24726 Price, Susanna, and Tim Stephens. *Click! Fun with Photography* (4–8). 1997, Sterling $14.95 (0-8069-9541-6). A fine introduction to photography that covers both beginning and advanced subjects, including the operation of various cameras, exposure, lighting, different types of photography, and filters. (Rev: SLJ 8/97) [771]

24727 Shulman, Mark, and Hazlitt Korg. *Attack of the Killer Video Book: Tips and Tricks for Young Directors* (5–8). Illus. by Martha Newbigging. 2004, Annick $24.95 (1-55037-841-4); paper $12.95 (1-55037-840-6). 64pp. Practical advice on all aspects of movie making will be helpful for aspiring directors. (Rev: BL 5/15/04; SLJ 6/04) [778.59]

24728 Varriale, Jim. *Take a Look Around: Photography Activities for Young People* (5–8). Illus. 1999, Millbrook LB $24.90 (0-7613-1265-X). 32pp. Photographs taken by children in a summer camp photography class illustrate the importance of such elements as light and camera angles, framing, creating mood, and photographing action. (Rev: BL 3/15/00; HBG 3/00; SLJ 12/99) [770]

Stamp, Coin, and Other Types of Collecting

24729 Dobkin, Bonnie. *Collecting* (1–2). Illus. by Rick Hackney. Series: Rookie Readers. 1993, Children's Book Pr. LB $18.00 (0-516-02015-3). 32pp. For beginning readers, this rhyming story tells about the joys and problems of being a collector. (Rev: BL 3/1/94) [737]

24730 Dyson, Cindy. *Rare and Interesting Stamps* (5–8). Series: Costume, Tradition, and Culture: Reflecting on the Past. 1998, Chelsea $19.75 (0-7910-5171-4). The stories behind 25 rare and unusual stamps start with Britain's first one-penny stamp, which bore a portrait of Queen Victoria. (Rev: BL 3/15/99; HBG 10/99) [769.56]

24731 Hubley, Dan, and Mary Hubley. *Kids Collect: Amazing Collections for Fun, Crafts, and Science Fair Projects* (3–6). Illus. 2002, Bluefish Bay paper $13.95 (0-9707-2671-6). 176pp. Provides tips on the selection of an item to collect; the development of the collection itself through buying, trading, and selling; and using the collection as part of a science fair or other school project. (Rev: SLJ 3/03)

24732 Owens, Thomas S. *Collecting Baseball Cards: 21st Century Edition*. Rev. ed. (4–8). 2001, Millbrook LB $26.90 (0-7613-1708-2). 80pp. An entertaining introduction to collecting baseball cards, with information on the history of the industry, on how to determine the condition of cards, and how to use the Internet to buy and sell. (Rev: HBG 10/01; SLJ 7/01) [796]

24733 Owens, Thomas S. *Collecting Baseball Memorabilia* (4–6). Illus. 1996, Millbrook LB $23.40 (1-56294-579-3). 96pp. Ticket stubs, team schedules, autographs, and other related items are described, with hints for collectors on how to get them and how to organize and preserve a collection. (Rev: SLJ 6/96) [796.357]

24734 Owens, Thomas S. *Collecting Comic Books: A Young Person's Guide* (5–8). 1995, Millbrook LB $26.90 (1-56294-580-7). A beginner's guide to comic book collecting, with sections on kinds of collections, sources, and organizations. (Rev: BL 2/1/96; SLJ 1/96) [741.5]

24735 Owens, Thomas S. *Collecting Stock Car Racing Memorabilia* (4–8). Illus. 2001, Millbrook LB $26.90 (0-7613-1853-4). 80pp. NASCAR fans in particular will appreciate this practical and detailed guide to collecting, which includes extensive lists of useful addresses. (Rev: BL 12/15/01; HBG 3/02; SLJ 11/01) [796.72]

24736 Pellant, Chris. *Collecting Gems and Minerals: Hold the Treasures of the Earth in the Palm of Your Hand* (5–8). Illus. 1998, Sterling $14.95 (0-8069-9760-5). 80pp. After explaining how gems and minerals are formed, this book discusses necessary equipment for the hunter, where to look, how to identify specimens, and how to organize one's collection. (Rev: BL 6/1–15/98; SLJ 8/98) [553.8]

Jokes, Puzzles, Riddles, Word Games

Jokes and Riddles

24737 Adler, David A. *The Dinosaur Princess and Other Prehistoric Riddles* (2–6). Illus. 1988, Holiday House LB $14.95 (0-8234-0686-5). 64pp. An assortment of jokes and riddles and laughs with dinosaurs as the focus. (Rev: BL 5/1/88; SLJ 9/88)

24738 Becker, Helaine. *Boredom Blasters: Brain Bogglers, Awesome Activities, Cool Comics, Tasty Treats, and More . . .* (4–6). Illus. by Claudia D vila. 2004, Maple Tree $21.95 (1-897066-02-3); paper $9.95 (1-897066-03-1). 160pp. Cures for boredom include stories, jokes and riddles, tricks, games, and foods. (Rev: SLJ 1/05) [818]

24739 Bierhorst, John. *Lightning Inside You and Other Native American Riddles* (2–6). Illus. by Louise Brierley. 1992, Morrow $14.00 (0-688-09582-8). 104pp. Many subjects and difficulty levels are presented in this collection of 140 riddles from North, South, and Central America. (Rev: BCCB 7–8/92; BL 6/15/92; HB 9–10/92; SLJ 7/92) [398.6]

24740 Brewer, Paul. *You Must Be Joking!* (3–5). Illus. 2003, Cricket $15.95 (0-8126-2661-3). 128pp. More than 200 jokes are accompanied by tips for effective delivery. (Rev: BL 2/1/04; HBG 4/04; SLJ 2/04) [818]

24741 Brown, Marc. *Spooky Riddles* (1–4). Illus. by author. 1983, Random $7.99 (0-394-86093-4). 48pp. Simply read riddles involving ghosts, vampires, and so on.

24742 Burns, Diane L., and Andy Burns. *Home on the Range: Ranch-Style Riddles* (2–5). Illus. by Susan S. Burke. Series: You Must Be Joking! 1994, Lerner LB $14.60 (0-8225-2341-8). A collection of zany riddles about life on the range. (Rev: SLJ 8/94) [818]

24743 Charlip, Remy. *Arm in Arm: A Collection of Connections, Endless Tales, Reiterations, and Other Echolalia* (K–3). Illus. 1997, Tricycle $15.95 (1-883672-50-3). 48pp. Verbal and visual plays on

words are revealed through a series of riddles, jokes, and puzzles. (Rev: BL 9/1/97; HBG 3/98) [808]

24744 Christopher, Matt. *Baseball Jokes and Riddles* (2–4). Illus. 1996, Little, Brown paper $4.50 (0-316-14081-3). 48pp. Trivia and lots of jokes and riddles about baseball highlight this amusing collection. (Rev: BL 4/1/96; SLJ 6/96) [796.357]

24745 Cole, Joanna, and Stephanie Calmenson. *Why Did the Chicken Cross the Road? And Other Riddles Old and New* (2–4). Illus. by Alan Tiegreen. 1994, Morrow LB $14.93 (0-688-12203-5). 64pp. A lively collection of clever riddles arranged by broad subject or type. (Rev: BL 10/15/94; SLJ 9/94)

24746 Corwin, Judith Hoffman. *My First Riddles* (PS). Illus. 1998, HarperCollins $9.95 (0-694-01109-6). 24pp. A beginning riddle book that features nine simple riddles and many cheery illustrations. (Rev: BCCB 9/98; BL 6/1–15/98; HBG 10/98; SLJ 7/98)

24747 Eckstein, Joan, and Joyce Gleit. *The Best Joke Book for Kids Number 4* (3–6). Illus. by Joe Kohl. 1991, Avon paper $3.50 (0-380-76263-3). 64pp. There are riddles, knock-knocks, jokes, and tongue twisters in this book arranged by subjects. (Rev: BL 9/15/91) [793.73]

24748 Hall, Katy, and Lisa Eisenberg. *Dino Riddles* (K–2). Illus. by Nicole Rubel. 2002, Dial $13.99 (0-8037-2239-7). 40pp. A collection of easy-reading riddles for the dinosaur gang. (Rev: BCCB 3/02; HBG 10/02; SLJ 2/02) [793.735]

24749 Hall, Katy, and Lisa Eisenberg. *Piggy Riddles* (PS–2). Illus. by Renee Andriani. Series: Dial Easy-to-Read. 2004, Dial $14.99 (0-8037-2855-7). 40pp. The unifying theme throughout this brightly illustrated book of riddles is pigs. (Rev: BL 3/1/04; SLJ 7/04) [818]

24750 Hall, Katy, and Lisa Eisenberg. *Turkey Riddles* (1–3). Illus. by Kristin Sorra. 2002, Dial $13.99 (0-8037-2530-2). 40pp. A collection of silly, attractively illustrated riddles about turkeys, just right for Thanksgiving. (Rev: BL 9/1/02; HBG 3/03) [793.735]

24751 Helmer, Marilyn. *Critter Riddles* (1–3). Illus. by Eric Parker. Series: Kids Can Read. 2003, Kids Can \$14.95 (1-55337-445-2); paper \$3.95 (1-55337-411-8). 32pp. Animal-themed jokes and riddles teach vocabulary and wordplay. Also use the food-related *Yummy Riddles* (2003). (Rev: HBG 10/03; SLJ 5/03) [818]

24752 Helmer, Marilyn. *Yucky Riddles* (K–2). Illus. by Eric Parker. Series: Kids Can Read. 2003, Kids Can \$14.95 (1-55337-448-7); paper \$3.95 (1-55337-414-2). 32pp. Cartoon art accompanies jokes and riddles that feature both humor and suitable grossness. (Rev: BL 1/1–15/04; HBG 4/04) [818.54]

24753 Helmer, Marilyn, and Jane Kurisu. *Funtime Riddles* (2–3). Series: Kids Can Read. 2004, Kids Can \$14.95 (1-55337-579-3). 32pp. This collection of pun-filled riddles and jokes focuses on athletics and other leisure activities. (Rev: BL 6/1–15/04; SLJ 5/04) [818.5]

24754 Helmer, Marilyn, and Jane Kurisu. *Recess Riddles* (2–3). Series: Kids Can Read. 2004, Kids Can \$14.95 (1-55337-577-7). 32pp. Easy-to-read school-related riddles and jokes include many puns. (Rev: BL 6/1–15/04; SLJ 5/04) [818.5]

24755 Hills, Tad. *Knock, Knock! Who's There? My First Book of Knock-Knock Jokes* (PS–1). Illus. by author. 2000, Simon & Schuster \$6.99 (0-689-83413-6). Using flaps to conceal answers, this is an amusing collection of old and new knock-knock jokes. (Rev: SLJ 8/00) [818]

24756 Holub, Joan. *Geogra-fleas! Riddles All over the Map* (1–3). Illus. by Regan Dunnick. 2004, Whitman LB \$15.95 (0-8075-2818-8). Funny facts and riddles are presented by a little brown dog. (Rev: SLJ 11/04) [398.6]

24757 Jansen, John. *Class Act: Riddles for School* (3–5). Illus. by Susan S. Burke. Series: You Must Be Joking! 1995, Lerner paper \$3.95 (0-8225-9673-3). Riddles that take schools, students, and teachers as their subjects. Also use *Playing Possum: Riddles About Kangaroos, Koalas, and Other Marsupials* (1995). (Rev: SLJ 9/95)

24758 Joyce, Susan, comp. and ed. *ABC School Riddles* (2–5). Illus. by Freddie Levin. 2001, Peel \$13.95 (0-939217-54-6). This simple book presents one riddle for each letter of the alphabet. (Rev: HBG 10/01; SLJ 1/01)

24759 Keller, Charles. *Driving Me Crazy: Fun on Wheels Jokes* (2–6). Illus. by Lee Lorenz. 1989, Pippin \$13.95 (0-945912-05-6). A collection of jokes and riddles that deal with driving and vehicles. (Rev: BL 7/89) [398]

24760 Keller, Charles. *It's Raining Cats and Dogs: Cat and Dog Jokes* (2–6). Illus. by Robert Quackenbush. 1988, Pippin \$13.95 (0-945912-01-3). 40pp. Pleasing nonsense for young readers. Also use: *Colossal Fossils: Dinosaur Riddles* (1991, Simon & Schuster paper). (Rev: BCCB 11/88; BL 2/15/89; SLJ 2/89)

24761 Keller, Charles. *King Henry the Ape: Animal Jokes* (2–6). Illus. by Edward Frascino. 1990, Pippin LB \$13.95 (0-945912-08-0). 40pp. Animal guf-

faws sure to delight young readers. (Rev: BL 3/15/90; SLJ 4/90) [818]

24762 Keller, Charles. *The Planet of the Grapes: Show Biz Jokes and Riddles* (2–5). Illus. by Mischa Richter. 1992, Pippin \$13.95 (0-945912-17-X). All the performing arts are included in this collection of zany jokes. (Rev: SLJ 12/92) [808.7]

24763 Keller, Charles, ed. *Take Me to Your Liter: Science and Math Jokes* (3–6). Illus. by Gregory Filling. 1991, Pippin LB \$13.95 (0-945912-13-7). 40pp. Jokes and silly riddles about a serious subject. (Rev: BL 5/15/91; SLJ 7/91) [398.2]

24764 Leslie, Amanda. *Flappy Waggy Wiggly* (PS–K). Illus. 1999, Dutton \$12.99 (0-525-46182-5). 40pp. An interactive book in which answers to a series of animal riddles are found in pictures under the flaps. (Rev: BCCB 7–8/99; BL 8/99; HBG 10/99; SLJ 6/99)

24765 Lewis, J. Patrick. *Scien-Trickery: Riddles in Science* (1–4). Illus. by Frank Remkiewicz. 2004, Harcourt \$16.00 (0-15-216681-5). 32pp. Eighteen brain-teasing riddles feature colorful illustrations that provide hints and humor. (Rev: BL 2/15/04; SLJ 4/04) [811]

24766 Lupton, Hugh. *Riddle Me This! Riddles and Stories to Challenge Your Mind* (4–6). Illus. by Sophie Fatus. 2003, Barefoot \$19.99 (1-84148-169-6). 64pp. Riddles and riddle-related stories and poems, often with a humorous twist, are accompanied by folk-art illustrations. (Rev: BL 12/1/03; HBG 4/04; SLJ 4/04)

24767 Maestro, Giulio. *Riddle Roundup* (3–5). Illus. 1989, Houghton Mifflin paper \$6.95 (0-89919-537-7). 64pp. Puns, homonyms, and homographs for wordplay lovers. (Rev: BL 12/15/89; SLJ 2/90) [818]

24768 Maestro, Marco. *Geese Find the Missing Piece: School Time Riddle Rhymes* (1–2). Illus. by Giulio Maestro. Series: I Can Read. 1999, HarperCollins LB \$14.89 (0-06-026221-4). 48pp. An easy reader that contains 21 humorous riddles for new readers. (Rev: BL 10/1/99; HBG 3/00; SLJ 12/99)

24769 Martin, Jannelle. *ABC Math Riddles* (1–4). Illus. by Freddie Levin. 2003, Peel \$13.95 (0-939217-57-0). Colorfully illustrated riddles introduce key mathematical terms. (Rev: HBG 4/04; SLJ 2/04) [510]

24770 Marzollo, Jean. *I Spy: Gold Challenger!* (2–5). Illus. by Walter Wick. Series: I Spy. 1998, Scholastic \$12.95 (0-590-04296-3). 40pp. Objects are hidden in each photo in this puzzle book with appropriate riddles under each picture. (Rev: BL 1/1–15/99; HBG 3/99) [793.735]

24771 Marzollo, Jean. *I Spy Spooky Night* (2–5). Illus. by Walter Wick. 1996, Scholastic \$13.95 (0-590-48137-1). 40pp. Riddles give clues to objects hidden in accompanying pictures. (Rev: BL 9/15/96; SLJ 9/96*) [793.73]

24772 Most, Bernard. *Zoodles* (PS–2). Illus. 1992, Harcourt \$13.95 (0-15-299969-8). 32pp. An iguana who hogs all the food is a "piguana" in this riddle book that combines animal names. (Rev: BL 10/15/92; SLJ 1/93) [818]

24773 Peterson, Scott. *Plugged In: Electric Riddles* (3–5). Illus. by Susan S. Burke. Series: You Must Be Joking! 1995, Lerner paper $1.98 (0-8225-9700-4). Very funny jokes and riddles that involve appliances found around the house. (Rev: SLJ 9/95)

24774 Roop, Peter, and Connie Roop. *Holiday Howlers: Jokes for Punny Parties!* (1–3). Illus. by Brian Gable. Series: Make Me Laugh! 2003, Carolrhoda LB $19.93 (1-57505-645-3); paper $4.95 (1-57505-705-0). 32pp. Very corny jokes are tied to holidays and other important calendar dates, from Thanksgiving to Election Day. (Rev: HBG 4/04) [793]

24775 Rosenberg, Pam, comp. *Gross-Out Jokes* (2–4). Illus. by Patrick Girouard. Series: Laughing Matters. 2005, Child's World LB $22.79 (1-59296-280-7). 24pp. Tastelessness abounds in this collection illustrated with eye-catching cartoons. Also use *Historical Jokes* and *School Jokes* (2005). (Rev: SLJ 6/05)

24776 Rosenbloom, Joseph. *Biggest Riddle Book in the World* (3–6). Illus. by Joyce Behr. 1979, Sterling paper $7.95 (0-8069-8884-3). About 2,000 old and new riddles arranged under various subjects and amusingly illustrated.

24777 Rosenbloom, Joseph. *Giggle Fit: Silly Knock-Knocks* (PS–2). Illus. by Steve Harpster. 2001, Sterling $12.95 (0-8069-8015-X). 48pp. An A to Z of knock-knock nonsense answers of the "Olivia me alone" variety. (Rev: BL 12/15/01; HBG 3/02) [793.73]

24778 Rosenbloom, Joseph. *School Jokes* (2–4). Illus. by Steve Harpster. Series: Giggle Fit. 2003, Sterling $12.95 (0-4027-0440-2). 48pp. This entertaining title is loaded with knock-knock jokes, puns, joke dialogues, and riddles.

24779 Rosenbloom, Joseph. *Spooky Jokes* (2–4). Illus. by Steve Harpster. Series: Giggle Fit. 2003, Sterling $12.95 (1-4027-0439-9). 48pp. Age-appropriate jokes for the Halloween set. (Rev: HBG 10/03; SLJ 1/04) [818]

24780 Rosenbloom, Joseph. *The World's Best Sports Riddles and Jokes* (2–6). Illus. by Sanford Hoffman. 1988, Sterling paper $3.95 (0-8069-6846-6). 128pp. Young sports fans will enjoy these gaffaws. (Rev: BL 5/1/88)

24781 Rosenbloom, Joseph. *The Zaniest Riddle Book in the World* (3–6). Illus. by Sanford Hoffman. 1984, Sterling paper $4.95 (0-8069-6252-6). 128pp. A riddle book arranged by topics.

24782 Schultz, Sam. *Animal Antics: The Beast Jokes Ever!* (K–4). Illus. by Brian Gable. 2003, Carolrhoda LB $19.93 (1-57505-640-2); paper $4.95 (1-57505-702-6). 31pp. Animal-themed jokes and wordplay will entertain young readers. (Rev: SLJ 1/04) [972.91]

24783 Schultz, Sam. *Monster Mayhem: Jokes to Scare You Silly!* (1–3). Illus. by Brian Gable. Series: Make Me Laugh! 2003, Carolrhoda LB $19.93 (1-57505-642-9); paper $4.95 (1-57505-708-5). 32pp. Lots of silly jokes and riddles about monsters, with bright cartoon illustrations. (Rev: HBG 4/04) [793]

24784 Schwartz, Alvin. *Witcracks: Jokes and Jests from American Folklore* (3–6). Illus. by Glen Rounds. 1973, HarperCollins LB $14.89 (0-397-31475-2). 128pp. All sorts of humor associated with America's past, from old riddles to knock-knock jokes.

24785 Shields, Carol Diggory. *Sports* (PS–3). Illus. by Svjetlan Junakovic. Series: Animagicals. 2001, Handprint $9.95 (1-929766-28-9). 32pp. Rhyming riddles give clues about animals hidden under the flaps in this tall-format picture book. (Rev: BL 2/1/02; HBG 3/02; SLJ 2/02) [811]

24786 Sloat, Teri, and Robert Sloat. *Rib-Ticklers: A Book of Punny Animals* (2–4). Illus. 1995, Lothrop $15.00 (0-688-12519-0). 32pp. Using different animals as focal points, this book contains a choice collection of jokes, puns, and riddles. (Rev: BL 6/1–15/95; SLJ 7/95) [818]

24787 Steig, William. *C D B!* (3–6). Illus. by author. 1987, Simon & Schuster paper $3.95 (0-671-66689-4). 48pp. When each set of letters and/or numbers is repeated aloud and riddle buffs apply a bit of imagination, the amusing caption accompanying each cartoon becomes apparent. Also use: *C D C!* (1986, Farrar).

24788 Swanson, June. *Out to Dry: Riddles About Deserts* (2–5). Illus. by Susan S. Burke. Series: You Must Be Joking! 1994, Lerner LB $14.60 (0-8225-2343-4). A cornucopia of groaners dealing with deserts. More riddles can be found in *Summit Up: Riddles About Mountains* (1994). (Rev: SLJ 8/94) [818.5]

24789 Terban, Marvin. *Funny You Should Ask: How to Make Up Jokes and Riddles with Wordplay* (4–6). Illus. by John O'Brien. 1992, Houghton Mifflin paper $7.95 (0-395-58113-3). 64pp. How word manipulation works and how kids can become schoolyard hams. (Rev: BCCB 2/93; BL 10/1/92; SLJ 12/92) [808.7]

24790 Thaler, Mike. *Frankenstein's Pantyhose* (2–4). Illus. 1990, Avon paper $2.50 (0-380-75613-7). 92pp. This collection of jokes and riddles contains a special section of cigar jokes. (Rev: BL 3/15/90)

Puzzles

24791 Adshead, Paul. *Puzzle Island* (2–5). Illus. 1991, Child's Play $13.99 (0-85953-402-2); paper $7.99 (0-85953-403-0). 24pp. This puzzle book contains visual clues to decode a secret message and learn the identity of an extinct species. (Rev: BL 6/1/91) [793.73]

24792 Burnard, Damon. *I Spy in the Jungle* (PS–K). Illus. by Julia Cairns. 2001, Chronicle $6.95 (0-8118-2987-1). Die-cut circles give young readers a glimpse of the animal that is revealed when the page is turned. Also use *I Spy in the Ocean* (2001). (Rev: SLJ 11/01) [793.73]

24793 Burns, Marilyn. *The Book of Think (or How to Solve a Problem Twice Your Size)* (5–7). Illus. by Martha Weston. 1976, Little, Brown paper $14.99

(0-316-11743-9). A stimulating collection of puzzles to make children think; informally and entertainingly presented.

24794 Gardner, Martin. *Classic Brainteasers* (4–6). Illus. 1995, Sterling $14.95 (0-8069-1260-X). 96pp. An entertaining book of classic puzzles that involve math, science, and logic. (Rev: BL 5/1/95) [793.73]

24795 Garland, Michael. *The Great Easter Egg Hunt* (PS–2). Illus. Series: Look Again. 2005, Dutton $15.99 (0-525-47357-2). 32pp. Rhyming clues lead Tommy and readers to more than 200 objects hidden in the elaborate collage artwork. (Rev: BL 2/15/05; SLJ 2/05) [793.73]

24796 McMillan, Bruce. *Sense Suspense: A Guessing Game for the Five Senses* (PS–1). Illus. 1994, Scholastic $15.95 (0-590-47904-0). 32pp. A puzzle book that introduces the five senses and challenges youngsters to determine objects from close-up details. (Rev: BCCB 12/94; BL 12/1/94; SLJ 12/94*) [793.73]

24797 Marzollo, Jean. *I Spy: A Book of Picture Riddles* (K–4). Illus. 1992, Scholastic $13.95 (0-590-45087-5). 48pp. Readers are asked to search out certain items from collages or montages. (Rev: BCCB 2/92; BL 5/15/92; SLJ 4/92) [793.73]

24798 Marzollo, Jean. *I Spy: Extreme Challenger: A Book of Picture Riddles* (K–3). Photos by alter Wick. 2000, Scholastic $13.95 (0-439-19900-X). 40pp. This book contains 12 double-page picture puzzles with accompanying riddles. (Rev: BL 10/1/00; HBG 3/01; SLJ 12/00) [793.73]

24799 Marzollo, Jean. *I Spy Fantasy: A Book of Picture Riddles* (1–3). Illus. by Walter Wick. 1994, Scholastic $12.95 (0-590-46295-4). 40pp. In a series of photographic collages, children are challenged to find hidden objects. (Rev: BL 12/1/94; SLJ 10/94) [793.3]

24800 Marzollo, Jean. *I Spy Super Challenger! A Book of Picture Riddles* (PS–2). Illus. by Walter Wick. Series: I Spy. 1997, Scholastic $12.95 (0-590-34128-6). 32pp. This detailed picture puzzle book defies the reader to find a needle in the haystack, as well as other eye-dazzling problems. (Rev: BL 10/1/97; HBG 3/98; SLJ 9/97) [793.735]

24801 Marzollo, Jean. *I Spy Treasure Hunt: A Book of Picture Riddles* (K–3). Illus. by Walter Wick. Series: I Spy. 1999, Scholastic $12.95 (0-439-04244-5). 40pp. A series of picture puzzles in which children are asked to find hidden objects in the illustrations as well as solving the mystery of the pirate's hidden treasure. (Rev: BL 11/15/99; HBG 10/00; SLJ 1/00) [793.73]

24802 Marzollo, Jean. *I Spy Year-Round Challenger! A Book of Picture Riddles* (PS–2). Illus. by Walter Wick. 2001, Scholastic $13.95 (0-439-31634-0). 40pp. A book of double-page picture puzzles with holiday themes, one for each of the 12 months. (Rev: BL 2/1/02; HBG 10/02; SLJ 4/02) [793.73]

24803 Riedler, Isabella. *Tricky Puzzles for Clever Kids* (2–5). Illus. 2001, Sterling paper $5.95 (0-8069-6753-6). 128pp. A collection of challenging

visual puzzles illustrated in black and white. (Rev: BL 2/15/02) [793.73]

24804 Swinburne, Stephen R. *Guess Whose Shadow?* (PS–K). Illus. 1999, Boyds Mills $15.95 (1-56397-724-9). Shadows are introduced in a series of photographs and then readers are asked to identify objects by their shadows. (Rev: BCCB 4/99; BL 3/1/99; HBG 10/99; SLJ 4/99) [770]

24805 Townsend, Charles Barry. *The Curious Book of Mind-Boggling Teasers, Tricks, Puzzles and Games* (4–12). Illus. 2003, Sterling paper $12.95 (1-4027-0214-0). 286pp. Classic puzzles, games, and brain teasers are illustrated with Victorian-style drawings and helpful diagrams; solutions are at the back of the book. (Rev: SLJ 11/03)

24806 White, Graham. *Secrets of the Pyramids: A Maze Adventure* (3–6). Illus. 2002, National Geographic paper $8.95 (0-7922-6938-1). 32pp. Fans of mazes will enjoy helping 12-year-old Hemon look for his father in the pyramid, and will learn about ancient Egypt in the process. (Rev: SLJ 11/02) [793.7]

24807 Wick, Walter. *Can You See What I See? Cool Collections: Picture Puzzles to Search and Solve* (K–2). 2004, Scholastic $13.95 (0-439-61772-3). 40pp. In this colorful assortment of picture puzzles, Wick focuses on some of the diverse objects that people collect, including seashells, buttons, stuffed animals, and model cars. (Rev: BL 12/1/04; SLJ 10/04) [793.73]

24808 Wick, Walter. *Can You See What I See? Dream Machine: A Picture Adventure to Search and Solve* (PS–2). Photos by author. 2003, Scholastic $13.95 (0-439-39950-5). 35pp. A dozen picture puzzles each offer multiple challenges, including search-and-find quests, mazes, and matching games. (Rev: HBG 4/04; SLJ 11/03) [793.73]

24809 Wick, Walter. *Can You See What I See? Picture Puzzles to Search and Solve* (K–3). Illus. 2002, Scholastic $13.95 (0-429-16391-9). 40pp. A collection of clever picture puzzles that test the visual perception of young readers. (Rev: BL 4/15/02; HBG 10/02; SLJ 3/02) [792.73]

Word Games

24810 McCall, Francis, and Patricia Keeler. *A Huge Hog Is a Big Pig: A Rhyming Word Game* (K–3). Illus. 2002, HarperCollins LB $15.89 (0-06-029766-2). 32pp. "A wet hound is . . . a soggy doggy!" and other wondrous rhymes are accompanied by photographs of children from a mix of races and of the appropriate animals. (Rev: BL 12/15/01; HBG 10/02; SLJ 2/02)

24811 McMillan, Bruce, and Brett McMillan. *Puniddles* (2–4). Illus. 1982, Houghton Mifflin paper $6.95 (0-395-32076-3). Objects in photographs are used to illustrate word combinations.

24812 Most, Bernard. *Hippopotamus Hunt* (1–3). Illus. 1994, Harcourt $14.95 (0-15-234520-5). 32pp. Explores the pastime of finding words within words and, using *hippopotamus* as an example, comes up with 53 new words. (Rev: BL 9/1/94; SLJ 11/94)

24813 Rosenbloom, Joseph. *World's Toughest Tongue Twisters* (3–5). Illus. 1987, Sterling paper $4.95 (0-8069-6596-7). 128pp. More than 500 tongue twisters, alphabetically from A to Z.

24814 Schnur, Steven. *Autumn: An Alphabet Acrostic* (K–3). Illus. by Leslie Evans. 1997, Clarion $15.00 (0-395-77043-2). 32pp. An alphabet book that uses autumn and acrostic poems as a framework. (Rev: BL 9/1/97; HBG 3/98; SLJ 9/97) [793.73]

24815 Steig, William. *CDB!* Rev. ed. (PS–4). Illus. 2000, Simon & Schuster $16.00 (0-689-83160-9). 48pp. The great word-game book of 30 years ago is now reissued with color drawings. (Rev: BL 4/1/00; HBG 10/00) [793.734]

Mysteries, Monsters, Curiosities, and Trivia

24816 Allen, Eugenie. *The Best Ever Kids' Book of Lists* (4–8). Illus. 1991, Avon paper $2.95 (0-380-76357-5). 128pp. Brief lists of the biggest, smallest, strangest, ugliest, etc., with humorous drawings. (Rev: BL 12/15/91) [031.02]

24817 Allman, Toney. *Werewolves* (4–7). Series: Monsters. 2004, Gale/KidHaven LB $23.70 (0-7377-2620-2). 48pp. An examination of the origins of the werewolf, with references to and illustrations from movie and TV appearances by these monsters. (Rev: SLJ 4/05) [398]

24818 Asimov, Isaac. *Is There Life in Outer Space?* (3–5). Illus. Series: Isaac Asimov's 21st Century Library of the Universe. 2004, Gareth Stevens LB $24.67 (0-8368-3950-1). 32pp. A revised, well-illustrated edition of a previously published book, this offers thoughtful discussion of the possibility of alien life, with material on the development of life on Earth and on the recent views of Mars. (Rev: SLJ 3/05) [576.8]

24819 Aslan, Madalyn. *What's Your Sign? A Cosmic Guide for Young Astrologers* (5–9). Illus. by Jennifer Kalis. 2002, Grosset $12.99 (0-448-42693-5). A lively, spiral-bound guide to the 12 signs of the zodiac and the personality traits they represent, with information on the underlying mythology and lists of famous people born under each sign. (Rev: SLJ 9/02) [133.5]

24820 Becker, Helaine. *Are You Psychic? The Official Guide for Kids* (4–6). Illus. by Claudia D vila. 2005, Maple Tree $16.95 (1-897066-20-1); paper $9.95 (1-897066-21-X). 64pp. Telepathy, mind reading, and fortune telling are among the psychic abilities introduced in this breezy volume that includes activities. (Rev: SLJ 5/05) [001.9]

24821 Blackwood, Gary L. *Extraordinary Events and Oddball Occurrences* (4–7). Illus. Series: Secrets of the Unexplained. 1999, Marshall Cavendish LB $28.50 (0-7614-0748-0). 80pp. A book that covers such unusual occurrences as strange things falling from the sky, teleportation, and unexplained

appearances and disappearances. (Rev: BL 3/1/00; HBG 10/00) [001.9]

24822 Blackwood, Gary L. *Fateful Forebodings* (4–6). Series: Secrets of the Unexplained. 1998, Benchmark LB $19.95 (0-7614-0467-8). 80pp. This book covers the origins and practices of such forms of fortune telling as astrology, tarot-card reading, tea-leaf reading, and the I Ching. (Rev: HBG 10/99; SLJ 3/99) [133.3]

24823 Blackwood, Gary L. *Long-Ago Lives* (4–7). Illus. Series: Secrets of the Unexplained. 1999, Marshall Cavendish LB $19.95 (0-7614-0747-2). 80pp. A look at the subject of reincarnation. (Rev: BL 3/1/00; HBG 10/00) [133.9]

24824 Blackwood, Gary L. *Paranormal Powers* (4–6). Series: Secrets of the Unexplained. 1998, Benchmark LB $19.95 (0-7614-0468-6). 80pp. This book explores psychic abilities such as telepathy, clairvoyance, precognition, body magnetism, pain control, and spoon bending. (Rev: HBG 10/99; SLJ 3/99) [001.9]

24825 Campbell, Peter A. *Alien Encounters* (5–7). Illus. 2000, Millbrook LB $23.90 (0-7613-1402-4). 48pp. An overview of eight supposed encounters between humans and aliens. (Rev: BL 7/00; HBG 10/00; SLJ 4/00) [001.9]

24826 Cohen, Daniel. *Phone Call from a Ghost: Strange Tales from Modern America* (4–6). Illus. 1990, Pocket paper $3.50 (0-671-68242-3). 112pp. Stories about weird happenings to famous and average people. (Rev: BCCB 11/88; BL 6/1/88; SLJ 8/88)

24827 Crisp, Tony. *Super Minds: People with Amazing Mind Power* (4–7). Illus. by Mary Kuper. 1999, Element Books paper $4.95 (1-901881-03-2). 128pp. A survey of near-death experiences, feral children's case histories, and instances of strange mental powers. (Rev: SLJ 5/99) [001.9]

24828 Deem, James M. *How to Find a Ghost* (5–8). Illus. 1990, Avon paper $3.25 (0-380-70829-9). 144pp. An attempt to explain how to have a supernatural experience. (Rev: BCCB 11/88; BL 11/1/88; SLJ 11/88) [133.1]

24829 Delrio, Martin. *The Loch Ness Monster* (3–5). Series: Unsolved Mysteries. 2002, Rosen LB $25.25 (0-8239-3564-7). 48pp. Here is a rundown on the many sightings and stories surrounding the Lock Ness monster, including the expeditions that tried and failed to find the truth. (Rev: BL 10/15/02) [001.9]

24830 Donkin, Andrew. *Atlantis: The Lost City?* (2–4). Illus. Series: DK Readers. 2000, DK $12.95 (0-7894-6681-3). 48pp. The first part of this book discusses the legend of Atlantis; the second half tells of the search for this lost city at sites around the world. (Rev: BL 12/15/00; HBG 10/01) [001.94]

24831 Donkin, Andrew. *Bermuda Triangle* (2–4). Series: Eyewitness Reader. 2000, DK $12.95 (0-7894-5416-5); paper $3.95 (0-7894-5415-7). 48pp. An easily read study of the Bermuda Triangle that favors explanations leaning toward the supernatural — blaming UFOs or the lost continent of Atlantis. (Rev: HBG 10/00; SLJ 8/00) [001.9]

24832 Farman, John. *The Short and Bloody History of Ghosts* (4–6). Illus. by author. Series: Short and Bloody Histories. 2002, Lerner LB $19.93 (0-8225-0837-0); paper $5.95 (0-8225-0838-9). 96pp. Ghosts and other supernatural beings are the focus of this overview of sightings around the world today and in the past, with most of the events occurring in Britain. (Rev: HBG 3/03; SLJ 2/03)

24833 French, Jackie. *The Little Book of Big Questions* (3–6). Illus. by Martha Newbigging. 2000, Annick $19.95 (1-55037-655-1); paper $9.95 (1-55037-654-3). 127pp. Fifteen subject-oriented chapters cover such areas as the universe, animal intelligence, extraterrestrials, and mortality. (Rev: HBG 3/01; SLJ 11/00) [001.9]

24834 Gilman, Laura Anne. *Yeti, the Abominable Snowman* (3–5). Illus. Series: Unsolved Mysteries. 2002, Rosen LB $25.25 (0-8239-3565-5). 48pp. The author presents historical accounts of the elusive yeti of the Himalayas. (Rev: BL 10/15/02) [001.944]

24835 Gorman, Jacqueline Laks. *The Bermuda Triangle* (3–5). Illus. Series: X Science: An Imagination Library. 2002, Gareth Stevens LB $19.93 (0-8368-3196-9). 24pp. An introduction to the mysterious Bermuda Triangle, with discussion of theories, evidence, and research. Also use *Bigfoot* and *The Loch Ness Monster* (both 2002). (Rev: HBG 3/03; SLJ 2/03) [001.9]

24836 Herbst, Judith. *Hoaxes* (3–4). Illus. Series: The Unexplained. 2004, Lerner LB $26.60 (0-8225-1629-2). 48pp. Crop circles, fairy photographs, moon-men, and other famous and less-well-known hoaxes and publicity stunts are described. Also in this series is *Monsters* (2004). (Rev: SLJ 2/05) [001.9]

24837 Huang, Chungliang Al. *The Chinese Book of Animal Powers* (5–7). Illus. 1999, HarperCollins LB $16.89 (0-06-027729-7). 40pp. The 12 animals of the Chinese zodiac are introduced in double-page spreads, and the characteristics and powers of each

are outlined. (Rev: BCCB 12/99; BL 1/1–15/00; HBG 3/00) [133.5]

24838 Hubbard-Brown, Janet. *The Curse of the Hope Diamond* (4–7). Illus. 1991, Avon paper $2.99 (0-380-76222-6). 96pp. A mystery style is used to introduce historical information about this jewel and the bad luck it seems to carry. (Rev: BL 12/15/91) [736.23]

24839 Innes, Brian. *The Bermuda Triangle* (4–7). Illus. Series: Unsolved Mysteries. 1999, Raintree LB $30.40 (0-8172-5485-4). 48pp. The author explores many theories that have been proposed to explain disappearances off the southeast coast of the U.S. (Rev: BL 5/15/99; HBG 10/99) [001.94]

24840 Innes, Brian. *The Cosmic Joker* (4–7). Illus. Series: Unsolved Mysteries. 1999, Raintree LB $25.69 (0-8172-5487-0). 48pp. This book introduces Charles Fort, the Cosmic Joker, and the many strange facts and coincidences he has uncovered. (Rev: BL 5/15/99; HBG 10/99; SLJ 9/99) [001.94]

24841 Innes, Brian. *Giant Humanlike Beasts* (4–7). Series: Unsolved Mysteries. 1999, Raintree LB $30.40 (0-8172-5484-6). 48pp. This account explores stories about the Abominable Snowman, or yeti, and other sightings of primitive creatures, while questioning the possibility of living links with Neanderthals. (Rev: BL 5/15/99; HBG 10/99; SLJ 9/99) [001.9]

24842 Innes, Brian. *Millennium Prophecies* (5–8). Illus. 1999, Raintree LB $30.40 (0-8172-5486-2). All sorts of prophecies relating to the calendar and the millennium are explored in this attractive volume. (Rev: BL 5/15/99; HBG 10/99; SLJ 9/99) [001.7]

24843 Innes, Brian. *Mysterious Healing* (5–8). Illus. Series: Unsolved Mysteries. 1999, Raintree LB $25.69 (0-8172-5489-7). Hands-on healing, acupuncture, iridology, and auras are some of the subjects discussed in this volume. (Rev: BL 5/15/99; HBG 10/99; SLJ 9/99) [001.7]

24844 Jackson, Ellen. *The Book of Slime* (2–4). Illus. by Jan Davey Ellis. 1997, Millbrook LB $21.40 (0-7613-0042-2). 32pp. Describes various forms of slime in nature, including human mucus and saliva, along with their uses, slime jokes, and some recipes. (Rev: BL 3/15/97; SLJ 6/97) [001.9]

24845 Jenkins, Steve. *Duck's Breath and Mouse Pie: A Collection of Animal Superstitions* (2–4). Illus. 1994, Ticknor $14.95 (0-395-69688-7). 48pp. With breathtaking collages, 17 superstitions about animals and their origins are explored. (Rev: BL 10/1/94; SLJ 9/94) [398.24]

24846 Kallen, Stuart A. *Dreams* (4–8). Illus. Series: The Mystery Library. 2004, Gale/Lucent LB $27.45 (1-59018-288-X). 112pp. In this volume in the Mystery Library, Kallen examines topics including dream science, the interpretation of dreams, and telepathic dreaming. Also use *Ghosts, Possessions and Exorcisms,* and *Shamans* (all 2004). [154.6]

24847 Kallen, Stuart A. *Fortune-Telling* (4–8). Illus. Series: Mystery Library. 2004, Gale/Lucent LB $21.96 (1-59018-289-8). 112pp. This exploration of the history and mystery of fortune-telling separates fact from fiction. (Rev: BL 5/15/04) [133.3]

24848 Krull, Kathleen. *What Really Happened in Roswell? Just the Facts (Plus the Rumors) About UFOs and Aliens* (4–7). Illus. by Christopher Santoro. 2003, HarperCollins LB $16.89 (0-688-17249-0); paper $4.25 (0-688-17248-2). 54pp. Humorous drawings illustrate the story of the crash of a mysterious object in New Mexico in 1947 and the accusations of a government cover-up. (Rev: HBG 10/03; SLJ 10/03) [001.942]

24849 Landau, Elaine. *ESP* (4–6). Illus. Series: Mysteries of Science. 1996, Millbrook LB $20.90 (0-7613-0012-0). 48pp. The amazing phenomenon known as extrasensory perception is explored in an account that separates fact from fiction. (Rev: BL 10/15/96; SLJ 11/96) [133.8]

24850 Landau, Elaine. *Fortune Telling* (4–6). Illus. Series: Mysteries of Science. 1996, Millbrook LB $20.90 (0-7613-0013-9). 48pp. Various methods of future telling are covered, with material that debunks the claims of supposed clairvoyants. (Rev: BL 10/15/96; SLJ 11/96) [133.3]

24851 Landau, Elaine. *Near-Death Experiences* (4–6). Illus. Series: Mysteries of Science. 1995, Millbrook LB $20.90 (1-56294-543-2). 48pp. An objective account that surveys the evidence concerning the possible truth behind reported near-death experiences. (Rev: BL 12/15/95; SLJ 4/96) [133.9]

24852 Landau, Elaine. *UFOs* (4–6). Illus. Series: Mysteries of Science. 1995, Millbrook LB $20.90 (1-56294-542-4). 48pp. The controversy concerning UFO sightings is reported in an objective way, with many intriguing photographs. (Rev: BL 12/15/95; SLJ 4/96) [001.9]

24853 Larkspur, Penelope. *The Secret Life of Fairies* (3–5). Illus. 1999, Kids Can $14.95 (1-55074-547-6). 32pp. This account presents an inside look at fairy life including homes, dress, and food. (Rev: BL 11/1/99; HBG 3/00) [813.48]

24854 Lorenz, Albert, and Joy Schlen. *Buried Blueprints: Maps and Sketches of Lost Worlds and Mysterious Places* (3–8). Illus. by authors. 1999, Abrams $19.95 (0-8109-4110-4). Fact and fiction are mixed in this exploration of locales including the Seven Cities of Gold, Egyptian cities, Atlantis, and the Lost World created by Sir Arthur Conan Doyle. (Rev: BL 12/1/99; HBG 3/00; SLJ 2/00) [001.9]

24855 Miller, Raymond H. *Vampires* (4–7). Series: Monsters. 2004, Gale/KidHaven LB $23.70 (0-7377-2619-9). 48pp. An examination of the origins of the vampire, with references to and illustrations from movie and TV appearances by these monsters. (Rev: SLJ 4/05) [398]

24856 Myers, Janet Nuzum. *Strange Stuff: True Stories of Odd Places and Things* (5–8). Illus. 1999, Linnet LB $19.50 (0-208-02405-0). A collection of curiosities — items about zombies, quicksand, scorpions, poisonous snakes, black holes, Bigfoot, mermaids, voodoo, the Bermuda Triangle, and feral

children raised by wolves. (Rev: HBG 3/00; SLJ 7/99) [001.9]

24857 Nardo, Don. *Atlantis* (5–8). Illus. Series: The Mystery Library. 2004, Gale/Lucent LB $21.96 (1-59018-287-1). 112pp. The author examines whether the ancient story of the lost continent of Atlantis — as described by Plato — could be true. (Rev: SLJ 4/04) [001.94]

24858 Nardo, Don. *Extraterrestrial Life* (4–8). Illus. Series: Mystery Library. 2004, Gale/Lucent LB $21.96 (1-59018-320-7). 112pp. This overview of encounters with aliens and the search for life elsewhere separates fact from fiction. (Rev: BL 5/15/04) [579.8]

24859 Nardo, Don, and Bradley Steffens. *Medusa* (4–7). Series: Monsters. 2004, Gale/KidHaven LB $23.70 (0-7377-2617-2). 48pp. Describes the mythological personage, telling the story of Perseus killing Medusa, and showing her role in paintings, sculptures, movie stills, and computer games. Also use *Cyclops* (2004). (Rev: SLJ 4/05) [398.2]

24860 Nickell, Joe. *The Magic Detectives: Join Them in Solving Strange Mysteries* (3–7). Illus. 1989, Prometheus paper $12.00 (0-87975-547-4). 115pp. Each of the 30 brief chapters explores a mysterious phenomenon, such as Bigfoot. (Rev: BCCB 12/89; BL 12/1/89) [133]

24861 *The Nobel Book of Answers: The Dalai Lama, Mikhail Gorbachev, Shimon Peres, and Other Nobel Prize Winners Answer Some of Life's Most Intriguing Questions for Young People* (3–6). Ed. by Bettina Stiekel. 2003, Simon & Schuster $14.95 (0-689-86310-1). 272pp. Some of life's most intriguing questions are addressed — if not answered — in this collection of writings by 22 Nobel Price winners, including Bishop Desmond Tutu, mathematician Enrico Bombieri, and geneticist Richard J. Roberts. (Rev: BL 10/15/03; HBG 4/04; SLJ 11/03)

24862 *1001 Questions and Answers* (3–7). Illus. 1995, DK $16.95 (1-7894-0205-X). 64pp. More than 1,000 fascinating questions and amazing answers covering science and invention, history, the natural world, and recreation are detailed, with matching photographs. (Rev: BL 1/1–15/96) [031.02]

24863 O'Neill, Catherine. *Amazing Mysteries of the World* (3–8). Illus. 1983, National Geographic LB $12.50 (0-87044-502-2). 104pp. Stonehenge, Easter Island, and Bigfoot are three of the many mysteries explored.

24864 O'Neill, Terry, ed. *ESP* (5–8). Series: Fact or Fiction? 2003, Gale/Greenhaven LB $21.96 (0-7377-1066-7); paper $14.96 (0-7377-1065-9). 160pp. This objective survey of extrasensory perception presents opinions for and against its existence. (Rev: SLJ 7/03) [133.8]

24865 Oxlade, Chris. *The Mystery of Crop Circles* (4–6). Series: Can Science Solve? 1999, Heinemann LB $15.95 (1-57572-804-4). 32pp. This book examines the strange phenomenon known as crop circles, unusual circular patterns that appear in crop fields, and covers the various theories about them. (Rev: SLJ 8/99) [001.9]

24866 Oxlade, Chris. *The Mystery of the Bermuda Triangle* (4–6). Series: Can Science Solve? 1999, Heinemann LB $15.95 (1-57572-811-7). 32pp. A variety of natural explanations are examined in this dramatic presentation of material on the Bermuda Triangle. (Rev: SLJ 1/00) [001.9]

24867 Powell, Jillian. *Body Decoration* (4–8). Illus. Series: Traditions Around the World. 1995, Thomson Learning LB $24.26 (1-56847-276-5). 48pp. An interesting book that explains the uses of body decoration in history and discusses tattooing, face painting, and body piercing. (Rev: SLJ 7/95) [617]

24868 Reynolds, Helen. *Makeup and Body Decoration* (3–8). Illus. Series: A Fashionable History of Costume. 2003, Raintree LB $25.70 (1-4109-0028-2). 32pp. Chronicles the history of body decoration and makeup from the beginning of recorded history to the present. (Rev: HBG 10/03; SLJ 9/03) [391.6]

24869 *RIPLEY'S BELIEVE IT OR NOT!* (4–7). Illus. 2004, Ripley Entertainment $25.95 (1-893951-73-1). 256pp. Packed with fascinating trivia and fun for browsing, this appealing volume focuses on weird and amazing facts. (Rev: SLJ 2/05) [031.02]

24870 Roleff, Tamara L., ed. *Black Magic and Witches* (5–8). Series: Fact or Fiction? 2003, Gale LB $27.45 (0-7377-1318-6); paper $18.70 (0-7377-1319-4). 127pp. A good starting point for debate over witchcraft, with essays for and against witches, magic, and Harry Potter, and some history of persecution of witches. (Rev: SLJ 3/03) [133.43]

24871 Savage, Candace. *Wizards: An Amazing Journey Through the Last Great Age of Magic* (5–8). Illus. 2003, Greystone $17.95 (1-55054-943-X). 80pp. An appealing, oversize book full of information on witchcraft and wizardry in the late 17th century, when science and sorcery were not far apart. (Rev: BL 6/1–15/03) [133]

24872 Scalora, Suza. *The Fairies: Photographic Evidence of the Existence of Another World* (3–5). Illus. 1999, HarperCollins $19.95 (0-06-028234-7). 48pp. The author spent a year investigating the phenomenon of fairies and the results, including names, sightings, location, history, and photographs, are found in this intriguing book. (Rev: BL 11/1/99; HBG 3/00; SLJ 1/00) [001.9]

24873 Scott, Janine. *Cool Customs* (K–2). Series: Spyglass Books. 2002, Compass Point LB $18.60 (0-7565-0364-7). 24pp. A basic look, for beginning readers, at customs and traditions around the world. (Rev: SLJ 3/03) [394.2]

24874 Simon, Seymour. *Strange Mysteries from Around the World*. Rev. ed. (4–6). Illus. 1997, Morrow $16.00 (0-688-14636-8). 64pp. An updating of the 1980 title that describes nine unusual events, such as strange lights that periodically appear in the sky. (Rev: BL 2/15/97; SLJ 4/97) [001.9]

24875 Stirling, Janet. *UFOs* (3–5). Illus. Series: Unsolved Mysteries. 2002, Rosen LB $25.25 (0-8239-3566-3). 48pp. An account of UFO sightings over time, from early glimpses of Army blimps to the continuing flying saucer reports. (Rev: BL 10/15/02) [001.942]

24876 Tesar, Jenny. *America's Top 10 Curiosities* (3–7). Illus. Series: America's Top 10. 1997, Blackbirch LB $16.95 (1-56711-199-8). 24pp. Using double-page spreads, this book describes such phenomena as the Marfa Mystery Lights in Texas, the Flaming Fountain in South Dakota, and the Seattle Space Needle. (Rev: BL 1/1–15/98; HBG 3/98) [508.73]

24877 Thomas, Lyn. *What? What? What? Astounding, Weird, Wonderful and Just Unbelievable Facts* (3–5). Illus. by Dianne Eastman. 2003, Maple Tree $19.95 (1-894379-51-9); paper (1-894379-52-7). 128pp. This cleverly illustrated collection of trivia is loaded with facts and figures about a little bit of everything, from animals and human anatomy to haunted houses and inventions. (Rev: BL 6/1–15/03) [031.02]

24878 Tonge, Neil. *Unexplained: Mysterious Places* (5–8). Illus. Series: The Unexplained. 1998, Sterling $14.95 (0-8069-3863-3). Stonehenge and Easter Island are two of the unusual places described, followed by theories about their existence, ranging from scientific to the supernatural. (Rev: HBG 3/99; SLJ 10/98) [001.9]

24879 Walker, Paul R. *Bigfoot and Other Legendary Creatures* (4–6). Illus. by William Noonan. 1992, Harcourt $18.00 (0-15-207147-4). 56pp. Facts, legends, and seven original stories are included in this collection of material about several legendary creatures. (Rev: BL 2/15/92; SLJ 3/92) [001.9]

24880 Wallace, Holly. *The Mystery of Atlantis* (4–6). Series: Can Science Solve? 1999, Heinemann LB $15.95 (1-57572-803-6). 32pp. This account examines the efforts to prove the existence of the lost continent of Atlantis and looks at theories concerning its location and destruction. (Rev: SLJ 8/99) [001.9]

24881 Wallace, Holly. *The Mystery of the Abominable Snowman* (4–6). Series: Can Science Solve? 1999, Heinemann LB $15.95 (1-57572-810-9). 32pp. The possible existence of the abominable snowman is explored in this dramatic account with eye-catching illustrations. (Rev: SLJ 1/00) [001.9]

24882 Watkins, Graham. *Ghosts and Poltergeists* (3–5). Series: Unsolved Mysteries. 2002, Rosen LB $25.25 (0-8239-3563-9). 48pp. This book explores actual case histories of hauntings and poltergeist activity, as well as a look into the way a real ghost hunter works. (Rev: BL 10/15/02) [133.1]

24883 Watts, Claire, and Robert Nicholson. *Super Heroes* (3–6). Illus. Series: Info Adventure. 1995, Thomson Learning paper $6.00 (1-56847-316-8). 31pp. An introduction to many mythical and legendary heroes plus coverage on such modern marvels as Batman, James Bond, Tarzan, the Terminator, and Indiana Jones. (Rev: SLJ 12/95) [001.9]

24884 Wells, Robert E. *What's Older Than a Giant Tortoise?* (PS–3). Illus. 2004, Whitman LB $15.95 (0-8075-8831-8); paper $6.95 (0-8075-8832-6). 32pp. A giant tortoise takes young readers on a wide-ranging tour of items that are even older than he is; included are a giant sequoia tree, the pyramids of Egypt, and Mount Everest. (Rev: BL 10/15/04; SLJ 1/05) [500]

24885 Wood, Ted. *Ghosts of the Southwest: The Phantom Gunslinger and Other Real-Life Hauntings* (4–6). Illus. 1997, Walker LB $17.85 (0-8027-8483-6). 48pp. A trip through Arizona, New Mexico, Texas, and Oklahoma, with stops in locales where ghosts reside. (Rev: BL 3/1/97; SLJ 4/97) [133.1]

24886 Wood, Ted. *Ghosts of the West Coast: The Lost Souls of the Queen Mary and Other Real-Life Hauntings* (3–6). Illus. 1999, Walker LB $17.85 (0-8027-8669-3). 48pp. A chronicle of reported sightings of ghosts in California, Oregon, and Washington with information on who saw the phantoms, and when and where. (Rev: BCCB 7–8/99; BL 4/15/99; HBG 10/99; SLJ 6/99) [133.1]

24887 Yolen, Jane, and Heidi E. Y. Stemple. *Meet the Monsters* (K–2). Illus. by Patricia Ludlow. 1996, Walker LB $16.85 (0-8027-8442-9). A number of strange creatures — like zombies, vampires, mummies, and Medusa — are introduced in double-page spreads. (Rev: SLJ 11/96) [001.9]

Sports and Games

General and Miscellaneous

24888 Ajmera, Maya, and John D. Ivanko. *Come Out and Play* (PS–2). Series: It's a Kid's World. 2001, Charlesbridge LB $15.95 (1-57091-385-4); paper $6.95 (1-57091-386-2). Photographs and simple text show the differences and similarities in children's play around the world. (Rev: HBG 10/01; SLJ 8/01) [790]

24889 Ajmera, Maya K., and Michael Regan. *Let the Games Begin!* (3–5). Illus. 2000, Charlesbridge LB $16.95 (0-88106-067-4); paper $6.95 (0-88106-068-2). 32pp. This book examines the philosophy of sports and sportsmanship with double-page spreads on topics such as practice, teamwork, competition, and rules. (Rev: BL 4/1/00; HBG 10/00; SLJ 5/00) [796]

24890 Alexander, Kyle. *Pro Wrestling's Most Punishing Finishing Moves* (4–7). Series: Pro Wrestling Legends. 2000, Chelsea $19.75 (0-7910-5833-6). 64pp. This book describes the most effective finishing moves in the sport of wrestling and fighters who use them. (Rev: BL 3/1/01; HBG 3/01) [796.8]

24891 Alexander, Kyle. *The Women of Pro Wrestling* (4–7). Illus. Series: Pro Wrestling Legends. 2000, Chelsea $19.75 (0-7910-5839-5); paper $8.95 (0-7910-5840-9). 64pp. After introducing several famous women pro wrestlers, this account describes women's roles in this sport in and out of the ring. (Rev: BL 10/15/00; HBG 3/01) [796.812]

24892 Allison, Linda. *The Sierra Club Summer Book* (3–6). Illus. by author. 1989, Little, Brown paper $7.95 (0-316-03433-9). 160pp. All sorts of activities on how to spend a summer day in this updated activity book.

24893 Alter, Judith. *Rodeos: The Greatest Show on Dirt* (4–7). Illus. Series: First Books. 1996, Watts LB $22.00 (0-531-20245-3). 64pp. Includes a history of rodeos, standard events, rules, legendary performers, and women in rodeos. (Rev: SLJ 3/97) [791.8]

24894 Anderson, Dave. *The Story of Golf* (4–8). 1998, Morrow $16.00 (0-688-15796-3). A history of golf that highlights the careers of some of its great stars, plus material on the lure of the game, golf architecture, and caddies. (Rev: BL 5/15/98; HB 9–10/98; HBG 10/98; SLJ 7/98) [796.352]

24895 *The Baby's Game Book* (PS). Ed. by Isabel Wilner. Illus. by Sam Williams. 2000, Greenwillow $23.95 (0-688-15916-8). 48pp. Games like pat-a-cake and rub-a-dub-dub are included in this collection of games for babies and toddlers. (Rev: BL 5/15/00; HB 7–8/00; HBG 10/00; SLJ 5/00) [649]

24896 Barrett, Norman. *Hang Gliding* (3–5). Illus. 1988, Watts LB $20.00 (0-531-10350-1). 32pp. Basic techniques of this thrill-seeking sport. (Rev: BL 5/15/88; SLJ 11/88)

24897 Bellville, Cheryl Walsh. *Flying in a Hot Air Balloon* (3–5). Illus. 1993, Carolrhoda LB $22.60 (0-87614-750-3). 48pp. An introduction to hot-air ballooning past and present that uses a rally in Minnesota as a framework. (Rev: BCCB 3/94; BL 1/1/94; SLJ 2/94) [797.5]

24898 Bellville, Cheryl Walsh. *Rodeo* (1–3). Illus. by author. 1985, Lerner paper $5.95 (0-87614-492-X). 32pp. A brief introduction to rodeos, highlighted with color photos. (Rev: BL 4/1/85; HB 7–8/85; SLJ 4/85)

24899 Bizley, Kirk. *Inline Skating* (4–7). Series: Radical Sports. 1999, Heinemann LB $24.22 (1-57572-942-3). 32pp. As well as a history of inline skating, this book tells how to get started and gives information on equipment, techniques, terms, and safety. (Rev: SLJ 4/00) [796]

24900 Boardman, Bob. *Red Hot Peppers: The Skookum Book of Jump Rope Games, Rhymes, and Fancy Footwork* (3–6). Illus. by Diane Boardman. 1993, Sasquatch paper $8.95 (0-912365-74-9). 64pp. A collection of directions for jump-rope and other games, from simple to highly complex. (Rev: BL 7/93) [796.2]

24901 Brimner, Larry. *Bobsledding and the Luge* (2–4). Series: True Books. 1997, Children's Book

Pr. LB $22.00 (0-516-20436-X). 48pp. An introduction to the history, rules techniques, and people involved in these two hazardous winter sports. (Rev: BL 1/1–15/98; HBG 3/98; SLJ 2/98) [796]

24902 Brimner, Larry. *Rock Climbing* (4–6). Illus. 1997, Watts LB $22.50 (0-531-20269-0). 64pp. Equipment, techniques, and safety tips are covered in this basic introduction to rock climbing. (Rev: BL 6/1–15/97) [796.5]

24903 Bryant-Mole, Karen. *Games* (PS–3). Series: Picture This! 1997, Rigby $18.50 (1-57572-151-1). 24pp. Various games are introduced, with material on where they are played and the importance of healthy recreation. (Rev: BL 10/15/97) [790]

24904 Burgess, Ron. *Yo-Yo! Tips and Tricks from a Pro* (3–6). Illus. by author. 2001, Williamson paper $7.95 (1-885593-54-6). 64pp. Burgess shows simple and complex yo-yo techniques in easy-to-follow line drawings. (Rev: SLJ 1/02) [796.2]

24905 Chalmers, Aldie. *In-Line Skating* (3–6). Illus. Series: Fantastic Book Of. 1997, Millbrook LB $22.40 (0-7613-0623-4). 40pp. This introduction to inline skating covers equipment, safety gear, stretching exercises, drills, techniques, and tips for beginners. (Rev: HBG 3/98; SLJ 3/98) [796.9]

24906 Chambers, Veronica. *Double Dutch: A Celebration of Jump Rope, Rhyme, and Sisterhood* (4–8). Illus. 2002, Hyperion $18.99 (0-7868-0512-9). 72pp. An exuberant look at this brand of rope jumping, including its history and rhymes, with exciting photographs. (Rev: BCCB 10/02; BL 10/15/02; HBG 3/03; SLJ 12/02*) [796.2]

24907 Chapman, Garry. *Air* (3–5). Series: Extreme Sports. 2001, Chelsea LB $16.95 (0-7910-6609-6). 32pp. Sky diving, bungee jumping, sky surfing, and other aerial sports are covered in this attractively illustrated volume. (Rev: BL 10/15/01; HBG 3/02) [796]

24908 Chapman, Garry. *Mountains* (3–5). Series: Extreme Sports. 2001, Chelsea LB $16.95 (0-7910-6610-X). 32pp. Mountain climbing, adventure racing, mountain biking, and extreme hiking are highlighted in this book that also covers weather conditions, safety precautions, and competitions. (Rev: BL 10/15/01; HBG 3/02; SLJ 12/01) [796.5]

24909 Chapman, Garry. *Rivers* (3–5). Illus. Series: Extreme Sports. 2001, Chelsea LB $16.95 (0-7910-6608-8). 32pp. This account looks at "extreme" water sports (such as white-water kayaking and riverboarding), with information on required gear, terminology, and stunts, accompanied by photographs. (Rev: BL 10/15/01; HBG 3/02; SLJ 12/01) [797.1]

24910 Chapman, Garry. *Snow* (3–5). Series: Extreme Sports. 2001, Chelsea LB $16.95 (0-7910-6606-X). 32pp. A variety of snow sports such as skiing and sledding are presented, with descriptions of unique winter environments. (Rev: BL 10/15/01) [796.95]

24911 Chapman, Garry. *Streets* (3–5). Illus. Series: Extreme Sports. 2001, Chelsea LB $16.95 (0-7910-6612-6). 32pp. "Extreme" sports such as BMX riding, luge racing, and inline skating that can be practiced on the street are covered here, with infor-

mation on required gear, terminology, and stunts, accompanied by photographs. (Rev: BL 10/15/01; HBG 3/02) [796.2]

24912 Chester, Jonathan. *The Young Adventurer's Guide to Everest: From Avalanche to Zopkio* (5–8). Illus. 2002, Tricycle $15.95 (1-58246-069-8). 48pp. A book about Mount Everest and those who have climbed it, in an alphabetical format with photographs. (Rev: BL 5/15/02; HBG 10/02; SLJ 4/02) [796.52]

24913 Cole, Joanna, and Stephanie Calmenson. *The Eentsy, Weentsy Spider* (PS–1). Illus. by Alan Tiegreen. 1991, Morrow paper $6.95 (0-688-10805-9). 64pp. Thirty-eight rhymes that demonstrate the fun children have performing the actions. (Rev: BL 10/15/91; SLJ 10/91) [793.4]

24914 Cole, Joanna, and Stephanie Calmenson. *Fun on the Run: Travel Games and Songs* (3–6). Illus. by Alan Tiegreen. 1999, Morrow $17.00 (0-688-14660-0). 126pp. Good descriptions with detailed playing steps are given in this inventive book of games useful while traveling, particularly by car. (Rev: HBG 3/00; SLJ 10/99) [790]

24915 Cole, Joanna, and Stephanie Calmenson. *Pin the Tail on the Donkey and Other Party Games* (K–3). Illus. by Alan Tiegreen. 1993, Morrow LB $14.93 (0-688-11892-5). 48pp. A picture book with 20 simple party games. (Rev: BL 8/93) [793]

24916 Coleman, Lori. *Beginning Strength Training* (4–7). Photos by Jimmy Clarke. Series: Beginning Sports. 1998, Lerner LB $27.15 (0-8225-3511-4). 64pp. This abridged version of *Jeff Savage's Fundamental Strength Training* is a beginner's book on body development. (Rev: HBG 10/99; SLJ 2/99) [796]

24917 Cook, Nick. *Downhill In-Line Skating* (5–8). Series: Extreme Sports. 2000, Capstone LB $21.26 (0-7368-0482-X). 48pp. Downhill inline skating is introduced with material on its history, equipment, skills, and competitions. (Rev: HBG 10/00; SLJ 8/00) [796]

24918 Corbett, Doris, and John Cheffers, eds. *Unique Games and Sports Around the World: A Reference Guide* (4–9). Illus. 2001, Greenwood $67.95 (0-313-29778-9). 407pp. More than 300 games and sports are organized by continent and then by country, with details of the number of players, equipment, rules, and so forth, and indications of whether this is a suitable game for the classroom or playground. (Rev: SLJ 8/01) [790.1]

24919 Crisman, Ruth. *Racing the Iditarod Trail* (4–6). Illus. 1993, Macmillan LB $14.95 (0-87518-523-1). 72pp. The origins and history of the great Alaskan dog sledding race, the Iditarod. (Rev: SLJ 6/93) [979.8]

24920 Crossingham, John. *Cheerleading in Action* (4–7). Series: Sports in Action. 2003, Crabtree LB $15.96 (0-7787-0333-9); paper $6.26 (0-7787-0353-3). 32pp. This is a colorful, attractive introduction to cheerleading, the cheers, costumes, duties, and its importance in sports. (Rev: BL 11/15/03) [791]

24921 Crossingham, John. *In-Line Skating in Action* (4–7). Series: Sports in Action. 2002, Crabtree LB

$21.28 (0-7787-0328-2); paper $6.95 (0-7737-0348-7). 32pp. A fine introduction to this fast-growing sport with easy-to-follow descriptions of moves and techniques. (Rev: BL 1/1–15/03; SLJ 10/03) [796.9]

24922 Crossingham, John. *Lacrosse in Action* (4–7). Series: Sports in Action. 2002, Crabtree LB $21.28 (0-7787-0329-0); paper $6.95 (0-7737-0349-5). 32pp. A clear, concise introduction to lacrosse that discusses techniques, equipment, rules, and safety precautions. (Rev: BL 1/1–15/03) [796.34]

24923 Crossingham, John. *Wrestling in Action* (4–7). Series: Sports in Action. 2003, Crabtree LB $15.96 (0-7787-0336-3); paper $6.26 (0-7787-0356-8). 32pp. This introduction to wrestling describes basic moves, skills, and rules. (Rev: BL 11/15/03) [796.8]

24924 Crossingham, John, and Sarah Dann. *Volleyball in Action* (4–6). Series: Sports in Action. 1999, Crabtree LB $14.97 (0-7787-0164-6); paper $5.36 (0-7787-0176-X). 32pp. This well-organized account introduces volleyball and supplies information on techniques, equipment, rules, and safety considerations. (Rev: SLJ 6/00) [796.32]

24925 Crossingham, John, and Bobbie Kalman. *Skiing in Action* (3–5). Illus. Series: Sports in Action. 2004, Crabtree LB $16.95 (0-7787-0337-1); paper $6.26 (0-7787-0357-6). 32pp. For beginning skiers, this is an attractive and useful introduction to equipment, technique, and vocabulary. (Rev: BL 4/1/04; SLJ 6/05) [796.93]

24926 Curtis, Bruce, and Jay Morelli. *Beginning Golf* (5–8). Illus. 2000, Sterling $19.95 (0-8069-4970-8). 96pp. Beginning with an overview of golf, equipment, swing, full-play, and short game, and moving on to more complex topics, this fully illustrated volume is a fine introduction to golf. (Rev: BL 9/1/00; SLJ 1/01) [796.352]

24927 Davidson, Bob. *Hillary and Tenzing Climb Everest* (4–6). Illus. Series: Great 20th Century Expeditions. 1993, Dillon LB $13.95 (0-87518-534-7). 32pp. A description in text and photographs of many early attempts to conquer Everest, with emphasis on the successful 1953 expedition. (Rev: BL 9/15/93; SLJ 9/93) [796.5]

24928 Ditchfield, Christin. *Wrestling* (2–4). Illus. Series: True Books. 2000, Children's Book Pr. LB $21.50 (0-516-21611-2); paper $6.95 (0-516-27033-8). 48pp. This simple introduction to wrestling contains material on its history and how it is played and judged. (Rev: BL 9/15/00) [796.8]

24929 Dolan, Ellen M. *Susan Butcher and the Iditarod Trail* (5–7). Illus. 1993, Walker LB $15.85 (0-8027-8212-4). 112pp. This book gives the history of the Iditarod sled dog race and tells the story of Susan Butcher, who first entered the race in 1978. (Rev: BL 4/1/93; SLJ 4/93) [798.8]

24930 Donkin, Andrew. *Danger on the Mountain: Scaling the World's Highest Peaks* (2–4). Illus. Series: Dorling Kindersley Readers. 2001, DK $12.95 (0-7894-7386-0); paper $3.95 (0-7894-7385-2). 48pp. Donkin presents details of some famous expeditions as well as discussing the hazards involved and the way climbing equipment has

changed over the years. (Rev: HBG 10/01; SLJ 11/01) [796.52]

24931 Drake, Jane, and Ann Love. *The Kids Summer Games Book* (3–6). Illus. 1998, Kids Can paper $10.95 (1-55074-465-8). 176pp. This book includes a section on teams as well as ideas and rules for summer games, in and out of the water. (Rev: BL 5/15/98; SLJ 5/98) [796]

24932 Eckart, Edana. *I Can Bowl* (K–2). Series: Sports. 2002, Children's Book Pr. LB $14.50 (0-516-23972-4); paper $4.95 (0-516-24028-5). 24pp. This slim volume for beginning readers shows Emma bowling with her father and discusses equipment and safety. Also use *I Can Swim*, *I Can Play Soccer*, and *I Can Ride a Bike* (all 2002). (Rev: SLJ 9/02) [794.6]

24933 Erlbach, Arlene. *Sidewalk Games Around the World* (3–5). Illus. 1997, Millbrook LB $23.90 (0-7613-0008-2). 64pp. Informal sidewalk games from 26 countries are introduced, with material on the country and the games and their rules. (Rev: BL 5/1/97; SLJ 5/97) [796.1]

24934 Fine, John C. *Free Spirits in the Sky* (3–5). Illus. 1994, Atheneum $14.95 (0-689-31705-0). 32pp. With color photos on each page, this book gives a history of ballooning, tells how balloons fly, and explains the different types. (Rev: BL 1/15/94; SLJ 3/94) [797.5]

24935 Flowers, Sarah. *Sports in America* (5–8). Illus. Series: Overview. 1996, Lucent LB $27.45 (1-56006-178-2). An exploration of current controversies in the sports world such sa commercialism, huge salaries, endorsements, racism, sexism, steroids, and the conflict between education and sports in colleges. (Rev: BL 9/1/96) [306.5]

24936 Gay, Kathlyn. *They Don't Wash Their Socks! Sports Superstitions* (3–5). Illus. by John Kerschbaum. 1990, Walker LB $14.85 (0-8027-6917-9). 114pp. Superstitions from many sports are highlighted. (Rev: SLJ 6/90) [796]

24937 Gedatus, Gus. *In-Line Skating for Fitness* (4–7). Series: Nutrition and Fitness. 2001, Capstone LB $23.93 (0-7368-0707-1). 64pp. Inline skating is introduced with an emphasis on fitness benefits and the necessity of a healthy diet. (Rev: BL 9/15/01; HBG 10/01) [796]

24938 Gedatus, Gus. *Weight Training* (4–7). Illus. Series: Nutrition and Fitness. 2001, Capstone LB $23.95 (0-7368-0708-X). 32pp. Weight training equipment, proper form, and sample workouts are presented, as well as advice on diet and supplements. (Rev: BL 7/01; HBG 10/01) [613.7]

24939 Glenn, Jim, and Carey Denton. *The Treasury of Family Games: Hundreds of Fun Games for All Ages, Complete with Rules and Strategies* (5–10). Illus. 2003, Reader's Digest $29.95 (0-7621-0431-7). 256pp. Games of every kind are simply explained and illustrated in this compendium, with material on their rules and their history. (Rev: SLJ 6/04) [793]

24940 Gordon, John. *The Kids Book of Golf* (3–6). Illus. 2001, Kids Can $14.95 (1-55337-017-1); paper $7.95 (1-55074-617-0). 48pp. History, equipment, technique, rules, competitions, and humorous anecdotes are all included here, along with diagrams and full-color photographs showing children and famous golfers. (Rev: HBG 10/01; SLJ 7/01) [796.352]

24941 Grayson, Marion F. *Let's Do Fingerplays* (PS–2). Illus. by Nancy Weyl. 1962, Luce $14.95 (0-88331-003-1). Comprehensive collection of finger plays under such headings as "Things That Go," "Animal Antics," and "Holidays."

24942 Griffin, Margot. *The Sleepover Book* (2–7). Illus. by Jane Kurisu. 2001, Kids Can paper $14.95 (1-55074-522-0). 144pp. These sleepover activities range from making a music video, cooking midnight snacks, treasure hunts, games and crafts, and, of course, telling scary stories. (Rev: SLJ 6/01) [793.21]

24943 Gryski, Camilla. *Cat's Cradle, Owl's Eyes: A Book of String Games* (4–7). Illus. by Tom Sankey. 1984, Morrow LB $15.93 (0-688-03940-5); paper $6.95 (0-688-03941-3). 80pp. Explanations of 21 string figures, plus variations. [793.9]

24944 Gryski, Camilla. *Let's Play: Traditional Games of Childhood* (K–3). Illus. by Dusan Petricic. 1998, Kids Can $14.95 (1-55074-497-6). 47pp. A few of the games and activities that are described in this helpful manual are jacks, marbles, hopscotch, clapping games, and jump-rope rhymes. (Rev: HBG 10/98; SLJ 5/98) [790]

24945 Gryski, Camilla. *Many Stars and More String Games* (4–8). Illus. by Tom Sankey. 1985, Morrow paper $7.95 (0-688-05792-6). 80pp. Figures taken from a range of cultures to be mastered by agile fingers. (Rev: BL 12/15/85; SLJ 1/86) [793.9]

24946 Gryski, Camilla. *Super String Games* (4–6). Illus. by Tom Sankey. 1988, Morrow paper $6.95 (0-688-07684-X). 80pp. Advanced string games with harder-to-learn patterns. (Rev: BL 3/1/88; SLJ 8/88)

24947 Hall, Godfrey. *Games* (5–7). Illus. Series: Traditions Around the World. 1995, Thomson Learning LB $24.26 (1-56847-345-1). 48pp. An oversize book that covers, in text and large color pictures, various games played in different regions around the world. (Rev: BL 6/1–15/95; SLJ 9/95) [790.1]

24948 Harris, Jack C. *Adventure Gaming* (5–8). Illus. Series: Hobby Guides. 1993, Crestwood $13.95 (0-89686-621-1). 48pp. Clear, easy-to-read information is given, with coverage of all kinds of adventure games, including war and role-playing games and those that deal with magic and sorcery. (Rev: SLJ 2/94) [793.92]

24949 Hayhurst, Chris. *Wakeboarding! Throw a Tantrum* (4–8). Series: Extreme Sports. 2000, Rosen LB $26.50 (0-8239-3008-4). 64pp. This new water sport is described with material on the equipment needed and the necessary safety precautions. (Rev: BL 6/1–15/00; SLJ 8/00) [797.1]

24950 Herzog, Brad. *P Is for Putt* (3–6). Illus. by Bruce Langton. 2005, Sleeping Bear $16.95 (1-58536-252-2). 40pp. An alphabetical format is used to introduce various facts about the game of golf. (Rev: BL 5/1/05) [796.352]

24951 Hort, Lenny. *Treasure Hunts! Treasure Hunts! Treasure and Scavenger Hunts to Play with Friends and Family* (3–6). 2000, HarperCollins $15.95 (0-688-17245-8); paper $4.95 (0-688-17177-X). 80pp. This book supplies information for all sorts of treasure-hunting games with material on number of players, and where, when, and how to play. (Rev: BL 6/1–15/00; HBG 10/00; SLJ 11/00) [796.1]

24952 Howes, Chris. *Caving* (4–8). Series: Radical Sports. 2003, Heinemann LB $25.64 (1-58810-626-8). 32pp. Technique, safety, gear, and other vital aspects are covered in this introduction to the sport. (Rev: BL 2/15/03; HBG 3/03) [796.52]

24953 Hoyt-Goldsmith, Diane. *Lacrosse: The National Game of the Iroquois* (3–6). Illus. 1998, Holiday House $16.95 (0-8234-1360-8). 32pp. After an introduction to the Iroquois Confederacy, this book traces the history of lacrosse and its past and present roles in the life of the Iroquois. (Rev: BL 6/1–15/98; HBG 10/98; SLJ 6/98) [796.3]

24954 Hu, Evaleen. *A Big Ticket: Sports and Commercialism* (4–7). Illus. 1998, Lerner LB $28.75 (0-8225-3305-7). 96pp. This well-organized book explains the connections between sports and the media, including broadcast rights, endorsement contracts, pop culture, and the impact of television. (Rev: BL 7/98; HBG 10/98) [338.4]

24955 Hughes, Sarah. *Let's Jump Rope* (1–3). 2000, Children's Book Pr. LB $13.50 (0-516-23114-6); paper $4.95 (0-516-23039-5). 24pp. Colorful action photographs and a simple text are used to show the basics of rope jumping as described by young Christina. (Rev: SLJ 2/01) [796]

24956 Hughes, Sarah. *Let's Play Hopscotch* (1–3). 2000, Children's Book Pr. LB $13.50 (0-516-23112-X); paper $4.95 (0-516-23037-9). 24pp. Action photos and a simple text explain how to play hopscotch. (Rev: SLJ 2/01) [796.1]

24957 Hughes, Sarah. *Let's Play Jacks* (1–3). 2000, Children's Book Pr. LB $13.50 (0-516-23113-8); paper $4.95 (0-516-23038-7). 24pp. A little girl explains the rules of the game of jacks and how to play it. (Rev: SLJ 2/01) [790.1]

24958 Hull, Mary. *The Composite Guide to Golf* (5–7). Series: Composite Guide. 1998, Chelsea LB $18.65 (0-7910-4726-1). 64pp. An introduction to the game of golf and its history, along with highlights of the game's pioneers and current stars including Tiger Woods. (Rev: HBG 10/98; SLJ 9/98) [796.352]

24959 Hunter, Matt. *Pro Wrestling's Greatest Tag Teams* (4–7). Series: Pro Wrestling Legends. 2000, Chelsea $20.75 (0-7910-5835-2). 64pp. This title covers such tag teams as the Road Warriors, the Midnight Express, the Nasty Boys, Public Enemy, and Harlem Heat. (Rev: BL 10/15/00; HBG 3/01) [796.8]

24960 Hunter, Matt. *Ric Flair: The Story of the Wrestler They Call "The Natural Boy"* (4–7). Series: Pro Wrestling Legends. 2000, Chelsea $19.75 (0-7910-5825-5). 64pp. The story of the wrestler who has been at the top of his sport for most of the last three decades. (Rev: BL 10/15/00; HBG 3/01) [796.8]

24961 Jaffe, Elizabeth Dana. *Dominoes* (1–4). Illus. Series: Games Around the World. 2001, Compass Point LB $21.26 (0-7565-0132-6). 32pp. Variations of dominoes games are presented with instructions and diagrams, along with a section on using them to create a domino effect. (Rev: SLJ 10/01) [795.3]

24962 Jaffe, Elizabeth Dana. *Hopscotch* (3–5). Illus. Series: Games Around the World. 2001, Compass Point LB $21.26 (0-7565-0133-4). 32pp. All about the favorite game of hopscotch — its rules, variations, and history. Also use *Marbles* and *Jacks* (both 2001). (Rev: BL 12/1/01; SLJ 10/01) [796.2]

24963 Jaffe, Elizabeth Dana. *Juggling* (3–5). Series: Games Around the World. 2002, Compass Point LB $21.26 (0-7565-0191-1). 32pp. This work contains a history of juggling and describes equipment and basic techniques, using colorful illustrations. (Rev: BL 5/15/02; SLJ 7/02) [793.8]

24964 Jenkins, Steve. *The Top of the World: Climbing Mount Everest* (2–6). Illus. by author. 1999, Houghton Mifflin $16.00 (0-395-94218-7). After a history of climbing on Mount Everest, the author discusses necessary equipment, climbing routes, dangers, and the physical effects on climbers. (Rev: BCCB 4/99; HBG 10/99; SLJ 5/99) [796.5]

24965 Johnson, Neil. *Fire and Silk: Flying in a Hot Air Balloon* (K–3). Illus. 1991, Little, Brown $15.95 (0-316-46959-9). 32pp. The facts and feel of ballooning in a nonfiction book that reads like an adventure story. (Rev: BCCB 4/91; BL 5/1/91; HB 7–8/91; SLJ 7/91) [797.5]

24966 Kalman, Bobbie, and John Crossingham. *Extreme Climbing* (4–8). Series: Extreme Sports No Limits! 2004, Crabtree $22.60 (0-7787-1717-8). 32pp. Explores the full spectrum of climbing sports, looking at the specific challenges of each and offering readers valuable advice about equipment, climbing techniques, locations, and difficulty ratings, as well as profiles of notable climbers. (Rev: BL 9/1/04)

24967 Kalman, Bobbie, and John Crossingham. *Extreme Sports* (4–8). Series: Extreme Sports No Limits! 2004, Crabtree $22.60 (0-7787-1719-4). 32pp. All manner of extreme sports are covered in this overview. (Rev: BL 9/1/04)

24968 Kalman, Bobbie, and Sarah Dann. *Bowling in Action* (4–7). Series: Sports in Action. 2003, Crabtree LB $15.96 (0-7787-0335-5); paper $6.26 (0-7787-0355-X). 32pp. This well-illustrated introduction to bowling includes material on equipment, techniques, rules, and bowling alleys. (Rev: BL 11/15/03) [794.6]

24969 Kaminker, Laura. *In-Line Skating! Get Aggressive* (5–8). Series: Extreme Sports. 1999, Rosen LB $26.50 (0-8239-3012-2). 64pp. This book provides information for both beginning and advanced inline skaters and covers topics including equipment, history, techniques, and safety tips. (Rev: SLJ 4/00) [796]

24970 Kauchak, Therese. *Good Sports: Winning, Losing, and Everything in Between* (3–6). Illus. 1999, Pleasant Co. paper $8.95 (1-56247-747-1). 95pp. Upbeat advice for girls on how to participate effectively in sports, with material on preparation, team efforts, practice, cooperation, and good and bad behavior. (Rev: BCCB 12/99; BL 3/1/00; SLJ 11/99) [796]

24971 Kent, Deborah. *Athletes with Disabilities* (5–7). Illus. Series: Watts Library: Disabilities. 2003, Watts LB $24.00 (0-531-12019-8); paper $8.95 (0-531-16664-3). 64pp. Achievements of disabled athletes are accompanied by the history of such events as the Special Olympics and by information on new games, equipment, and techniques that widen horizons. (Rev: BL 10/15/03; SLJ 9/03) [371.9]

24972 King, Daniel. *Games: Learn to Play, Play to Win* (5–8). Illus. 2003, Kingfisher $16.95 (0-7534-5581-1). 64pp. An instructional introduction to 14 board and card games, including cribbage to chess, with appropriate historical background. (Rev: HBG 4/04; SLJ 5/04) [794]

24973 Klingel, Cynthia, and Robert B. Noyed. *In-Line Skating* (K–2). Series: Wonder Books. 2000, Child's World LB $21.36 (1-56766-816-X). 24pp. A page of large-print text faces a full-color photograph in this easy-to-read introduction to inline skating, the equipment involved, and safety measures necessary. (Rev: HBG 4/04; SLJ 3/01) [792.2]

24974 Klingel, Cynthia, and Robert B. Noyed. *Yo-Yo Tricks* (3–5). Series: Games Around the World. 2002, Compass Point LB $21.26 (0-7565-0193-8). 32pp. The development of the yo-yo is covered in this volume, along with colorful illustrations and diagrams that describe techniques and moves. (Rev: BL 5/15/02; SLJ 7/02) [796]

24975 Knotts, Bob. *Weightlifting* (2–4). Illus. Series: True Books. 2000, Children's Book Pr. LB $21.50 (0-516-21067-X); paper $6.95 (0-516-27032-X). 48pp. The sport of weightlifting is introduced in large-type text and many color photographs. (Rev: BL 9/15/00) [796.4]

24976 Kramer, S. A. *To the Top! Climbing the World's Highest Mountain* (2–4). Illus. by Thomas La Padula. 1993, Random paper $3.99 (0-679-83885-6). 47pp. An account of how Edmund Hillary and Tenzing Norgay conquered Mount Everest in 1953. (Rev: BCCB 6/93; SLJ 8/93) [796.5]

24977 Krause, Peter. *Fundamental Golf* (5–8). Photos by Andy King. Series: Fundamental Sports. 1995, Lerner LB $27.15 (0-8225-3454-1). 64pp. A clear introduction to golf that covers history, equipment, swings, rules, and courses. (Rev: SLJ 9/95) [796.352]

24978 Lehn, Barbara. *What Is an Athlete?* (PS–2). Illus. by Carol Krauss. 2002, Millbrook LB $21.90 (0-7613-2258-2). 32pp. An introduction of the concept of "athlete," presented in a friendly format for younger readers. (Rev: BL 12/15/02; HBG 3/03) [796]

24979 Manley, Claudia B. *Competitive Volleyball for Girls* (4–7). Illus. Series: Sportsgirl. 2001, Rosen LB $26.50 (0-8239-3404-7). 64pp. An introduction to the rules of volleyball, the training necessary, and the special opportunities for girls, with material on nutrition and the dangers of overtraining. (Rev: SLJ 3/02) [796.325]

24980 Marchon-Arnaud, Catherine. *A Gallery of Games* (5–7). Illus. by Marc Schwartz. Series: Young Artisan. 1994, Ticknor $12.95 (0-395-68379-3). 60pp. Historical information, clear directions, and rules of each game are supplied, but young novices might find some of these projects difficult. (Rev: BL 4/1/94; SLJ 3/94) [745]

24981 Masoff, Joy. *Everest: Reaching for the Sky* (2–4). Series: Scholastic History Readers. 2002, Scholastic paper $3.99 (0-439-26707-2). 48pp. For beginning readers, this is an appealing and informative account of Edmund Hillary and Tenzing Norgay's ascent in 1953. (Rev: SLJ 2/03) [796.5]

24982 Mason, Paul. *Skiing* (4–8). Illus. 2003, Heinemann LB $25.64 (1-58810-628-4). 32pp. Technique, safety, gear, and profiles of famous skiers are all covered in this introduction to the sport. (Rev: BL 2/15/03; HBG 3/03) [796.93]

24983 Mayo, Terry. *The Illustrated Rules of In-line Hockey* (3–5). Illus. by Ned Butterfield. Series: Illustrated Sports. 1996, Ideals paper $6.95 (1-57102-064-0). 32pp. An introduction to inline hockey, with a history of the sport, an explanation of the rules, a look at different positions and signals, and discussion of sportsmanship. (Rev: SLJ 8/96) [796.2]

24984 Miller, Thomas. *Taking Time Out: Recreation and Play* (5–8). Illus. Series: Our Human Family. 1995, Blackbirch LB $31.19 (1-56711-128-9). 80pp. Divided into five broad geographic areas, this account describes how people enjoy themselves at play in various cultures. (Rev: SLJ 1/96) [794]

24985 Moss, Marissa. *Dr. Amelia's Boredom Survival Guide: First Aid for Rainy Days, Boring Errands, Waiting Rooms, Whatever!* (3–5). Illus. by author. Series: Amelia. 1999, Pleasant Co. paper $5.95 (1-56247-794-3). A humorous collection of 51 activities to allay boredom: listing good and gross food, eye tricks, and making up jump-rope songs are just three examples. (Rev: SLJ 7/99) [796]

24986 Mott, Evelyn Clarke. *Balloon Ride* (K–3). Illus. 1991, Walker LB $14.85 (0-8027-8126-8). Megan takes her first trip in a hot-air balloon in this nonfiction account with photos by the author. (Rev: SLJ 10/91) [797.5]

24987 Nash, Bruce, and Allan Zullo. *The Greatest Sports Stories Never Told* (4–6). Illus. by John Gampert. 1993, Simon & Schuster paper $8.95 (0-671-75938-8). 96pp. From a variety of sports, this is a collection of 27 unusual but true stories. (Rev: BL 5/15/93; SLJ 6/93) [796]

24988 Nicholson, Lois. *The Composite Guide to Lacrosse* (4–8). Series: The Composite Guide. 1998, Chelsea LB $18.65 (0-7910-4719-9). 64pp. A fine guide to lacrosse, giving its history, how it is played today, and portraits of the game's greatest players. (Rev: HBG 3/99; SLJ 12/98) [796.34]

24989 Orozco, Jose-Luis. *Diez Deditos and Other Play Rhymes and Action Songs from Latin America* (PS–1). Illus. by Elisa Kleven. 1997, Dutton $18.99

(0-525-45736-4). 48pp. Thirty-four finger rhymes and songs in English and the original Spanish are included in this attractive collection. (Rev: BCCB 3/98; BL 1/1–15/98; HB 3–4/98; HBG 3/98) [782.42]

24990 Oxlade, Chris. *Rock Climbing* (4–8). Illus. Series: Extreme Sports. 2003, Lerner LB $22.60 (0-8225-1240-8). 32pp. An appealing introduction to the history, equipment, techniques, safety concerns, and challenges of this sport. (Rev: BL 3/1/04; HBG 4/04; SLJ 5/04) [790.52]

24991 Paros, Lawrence, and Ben Joshua Paros. *Smash Caps: The Official Milkcap Fun Book* (3–6). Illus. by Kuo W. Yang. 1995, Avon paper $7.99 (0-380-78459-9). 55pp. An introduction to POGS, a game originally from Hawaii, which is played with caps from different bottles. (Rev: SLJ 1/96) [796]

24992 Payan, Gregory. *Essential Snowmobiling for Teens* (5–9). Series: Outdoor Life. 2000, Children's Book Pr. LB $20.00 (0-516-23358-0); paper $6.95 (0-516-23358-3). 48pp. The invention of the snowmobile is covered plus material on license requirements, trail permits, equipment, clothing, safety, driving techniques, and maintenance. (Rev: SLJ 2/01) [796.94]

24993 Perry, Phyllis J. *Ballooning* (4–6). Illus. 1996, Watts LB $22.00 (0-531-20234-8). 63pp. Following a history of ballooning, this account describes the parts of balloons and provides race statistics. (Rev: BL 2/1/97; SLJ 2/97) [629.133]

24994 Perry, Phyllis J. *Soaring* (4–7). Illus. Series: First Books. 1997, Watts LB $22.00 (0-531-20258-5). 64pp. Covers the history of gliders, scientific principles — lift, thrust, and drag — and the sport of soaring and the equipment needed for it. (Rev: BL 7/97) [797.5]

24995 Peters, Craig. *Chants, Cheers, and Jumps* (5–8). Illus. Series: Let's Go Team. 2003, Mason Crest $19.95 (1-59084-535-8). 64pp. Readers will learn the difference between cheers and chants and how to do various jumps. Also use *Competitive Cheerleading* (2003). (Rev: BL 10/15/03; SLJ 9/03) [791.6]

24996 Peters, Craig. *Cheerleading Stars* (5–8). Series: Let's Go Team. 2003, Mason Crest LB $19.95 (1-59084-533-1). 64pp. This book highlights the careers and accomplishments of a select group of star cheerleaders. (Rev: BL 10/15/03; HBG 4/04) [791]

24997 Peters, Craig. *Techniques of Dance for Cheerleading* (5–8). Series: Let's Go Team. 2003, Mason Crest LB $19.95 (1-59084-531-5). 64pp. The importance of stretching and safety measures are emphasized in this volume that discusses choreography and the similarities and differences between cheerleading and dancing. (Rev: SLJ 9/03) [791.6]

24998 *Racing on the Tour de France: And Other Stories of Sports* (4–6). Illus. 1989, Zaner-Bloser $10.95 (0-88309-546-7). 63pp. A collection of sports articles reprinted from the past 20 years of the magazine Highlights for Children. (Rev: SLJ 3/90) [796]

24999 Roberts, Jeremy. *Rock and Ice Climbing! Top the Tower* (4–8). Illus. Series: Extreme Sports.

2000, Rosen LB $26.50 (0-8239-3009-2). 64pp. This book on climbing covers the dangers, different climbing styles, equipment, techniques, and venues, and profiles some young climbers. (Rev: BL 3/15/00; SLJ 8/00) [796.52]

25000 Roberts, Robin. *Sports for Life: How Athletes Have More Fun* (5–8). Illus. Series: Get in the Game! 2000, Millbrook LB $23.90 (0-7613-1407-5). 48pp. This account, mainly for girls, explains how to enjoy sports through applying discipline, patience, cooperation, health, and the sheer fun of competition. (Rev: BL 1/1–15/01; HBG 3/01) [796]

25001 Roberts, Robin. *Which Sport Is Right for You?* (5–8). Series: Get in the Game! 2001, Millbrook LB $23.90 (0-7613-2117-9). 48pp. Written with girls in mind, this short book explores how to choose a sport that is right for one's capabilities and interests. (Rev: BL 9/15/01; HBG 3/02; SLJ 1/02) [796]

25002 Roper, Ingrid. *Yo-Yos: Tricks to Amaze Your Friends* (3–6). 2001, HarperCollins $15.95 (0-688-14663-5); paper $7.95 (0-688-14665-1). 64pp. A guide to different kinds of yo-yos and yo-yo technique that starts with the basic and progresses to the more advanced. (Rev: BL 5/15/01; HBG 10/01; SLJ 8/01) [796.2]

25003 Ross, Dan. *Pro Wrestling's Greatest Wars* (4–7). Illus. Series: Pro Wrestling Legends. 2000, Chelsea $19.75 (0-7910-5837-9); paper $8.95 (0-7910-5838-7). 64pp. Some of the great feuds in wrestling history, such as Harlem Heat vs. the Nasty Boys, are described in this fast read. (Rev: BL 10/15/00; HBG 3/01) [796.812]

25004 Ross, Dan. *The Story of the Wrestler They Call "The Rock"* (4–7). Series: Pro Wrestling Legends. 2000, Chelsea $19.75 (0-7910-5831-X). 64pp. This is the story of the third-generation wrestler known as "The Rock." (Rev: BL 10/15/00; HBG 3/01) [796.8]

25005 Rowe, Julian. *Recreation* (4–7). Illus. Series: Science Encounters. 1997, Rigby paper $25.55 (1-57572-092-2). 32pp. Shows how science is used in theme park rides, backpacking and camping equipment, computer games, television, scuba diving, and hang gliding. (Rev: SLJ 10/97) [796]

25006 Rowe, Julian. *Sports* (4–7). Illus. Series: Science Encounters. 1997, Rigby paper $25.55 (1-57572-089-2). 32pp. Shows how science is used in such sports-related topics as the design of equipment, protective clothing, and sports medicine. (Rev: SLJ 10/97) [796]

25007 Ryan, Pat. *Rock Climbing* (4–7). Illus. Series: World of Sports. 2000, Smart Apple LB $16.95 (1-887068-57-0). 32pp. In addition to covering the origins and evolution of rock climbing, this book discusses the basics of the sport, equipment, and star athletes. (Rev: BL 9/15/00) [796.52]

25008 Savage, Jeff. *Top 10 Sports Bloopers and Who Made Them* (4–7). Illus. Series: Sports Top 10. 2000, Enslow LB $18.95 (0-7660-1271-9). 48pp. This collection of 10 famous sports mistakes also gives good background information on the perpetrators and the causes of the errors. (Rev: BL 9/15/00; HBG 10/00; SLJ 10/00) [796]

25009 Schwartz, Ellen. *I Love Yoga: A Guide for Kids and Teens* (5–12). Illus. by Ben Hodson. 2003, Tundra paper $9.95 (0-88776-598-X). 122pp. Illustrated instructions for 18 basic poses are accompanied by breathing and relaxation exercises, discussion of the benefits of yoga, and a description of the different types of yoga practiced around the world. (Rev: SLJ 12/03) [613.7]

25010 Seeberg, Tim. *Rock Climbing* (3–5). Illus. Series: Kids' Guides to the Outdoors. 2004, Child's World LB $27.07 (1-59296-033-2). 32pp. A useful guide for young people new to this sport, this book is loaded with tips about equipment and what to expect. [796.5]

25011 Shahan, Sherry. *Dashing Through the Snow: The Story of the Jr. Iditarod* (4–7). Illus. 1997, Millbrook $24.90 (0-7613-0208-5); paper $9.95 (0-7613-0143-7). 48pp. All aspects of the 150-mile Junior Iditarod are touched upon in this account, including how these young mushers communicate with their dogs. (Rev: BL 3/1/97; SLJ 4/97) [798]

25012 Sheely, Robert, and Louis Bourgeois. *Sports Lab: How Science Has Changed Sports* (4–7). Illus. Series: Science Lab. 1994, Silver Moon $14.95 (1-881889-49-1). 60pp. Traces the effect on sports of applying findings from such branches of science as aerodynamics, psychology, and medicine. (Rev: SLJ 9/94) [617.1]

25013 Sheinwold, Alfred. *101 Best Family Card Games* (5–12). Illus. 1993, Sterling paper $5.95 (0-8069-8635-2). A book filled with games enjoyed by many age groups. (Rev: BL 2/15/93) [795.4]

25014 Sherman, Josepha. *Barrel Racing* (4–6). Series: Rodeo. 2000, Heinemann LB $21.36 (1-57572-503-7). 32pp. Barrel racing training, skills, equipment, and schedules are covered here. Three other titles on rodeo events are *Bronc Riding, Bull Riding* and *Steer Wrestling* (all 2000). (Rev: BL 10/15/00; HBG 3/01; SLJ 8/00) [791.8]

25015 Sherman, Josepha. *Ropers and Riders* (4–6). Series: Rodeo. 2000, Heinemann LB $21.36 (1-57572-506-1). 32pp. A colorful book that features these stars of the rodeo, their skills, training, and lifestyles. (Rev: BL 10/15/00; HBG 3/01; SLJ 9/00) [791.8]

25016 Sherman, Josepha. *Welcome to the Rodeo!* (4–6). Illus. Series: Rodeo. 2000, Heinemann $14.95 (1-57572-508-8). 32pp. An introduction to rodeos with material on the various riding and roping competitions and on famous rodeo stars. (Rev: BL 10/15/00; HBG 3/01; SLJ 9/00) [791.8]

25017 Silas, Elizabeth, and Diane Goodney. *Yoga* (4–8). Illus. Series: Life Balance. 2003, Watts LB $19.50 (0-531-12258-1); paper $6.95 (0-531-15577-3). 80pp. Information on the spiritual and philosophical aspects of yoga follows chapters on basic yoga moves. (Rev: BL 10/15/03) [613.7]

25018 Skreslet, Laurie, and Elizabeth MacLeod. *To the Top of Everest* (5–9). Illus. 2001, Kids Can $16.95 (1-55074-721-5). 56pp. Skreslet relates his lifelong ambition to climb Everest and his actual experiences doing so, with many facts about the mountain and the dangers involved and stunning photographs of his adventure. (Rev: BCCB 10/01; BL 9/15/01; HBG 3/02; SLJ 9/01*) [796.52]

25019 Smith, Graham. *Karting* (4–8). Series: Radical Sports. 2002, Heinemann LB $25.64 (1-58810-624-1). 32pp. The sport of karting is introduced with discussion of equipment selection, basic skills, fitness and training, and safety. (Rev: BL 2/15/03; HBG 3/03) [796.7]

25020 Sobol, Donald J. *Encyclopedia Brown's Book of Wacky Sports* (3–6). Illus. by Ted Enik. 1984, Morrow $16.00 (0-688-03884-0). 112pp. A spin-off from the popular series, this is actually a book about wacky "happenings" in sports, covering a wide range of high school, college, and pro sports.

25021 Steiner, Andy. *Girl Power on the Playing Field: A Book About Girls, Their Goals, and Their Struggles* (5–10). Series: Girl Power. 2000, Lerner LB $30.35 (0-8225-2690-5). 96pp. This book explains women's roles in sports with good personal guidance for young girls on participation and goals. (Rev: HBG 10/00; SLJ 6/00) [796]

25022 Steiner, Andy. *A Sporting Chance: Sports and Gender* (4–8). Series: Sports Issues. 1995, Lerner LB $28.75 (0-8225-3300-6). An overview of the hurdles that female athletes have had to overcome and the persistent inequality between men and women in sports at all levels, from Little League to the pros. (Rev: BL 1/1–15/96; SLJ 1/96) [796]

25023 Sullivan, George. *Any Number Can Play: The Numbers Athletes Wear* (4–8). Illus. 2000, Millbrook LB $23.90 (0-7613-1557-8). 80pp. A fascinating glimpse at players' devotion to their assigned numbers, along with information on retired and banned numbers and who uses the number 13. (Rev: BL 12/15/00; HBG 3/01; SLJ 2/01) [796]

25024 Sullivan, George. *Don't Step on the Foul Line: Sports Superstitions* (4–8). Illus. 2000, Millbrook LB $23.90 (0-7613-1558-6). 80pp. This is an intriguing look at superstitions, customs, and traditions associated with many different sports. (Rev: BL 12/15/00; HBG 3/01; SLJ 2/01) [796.357]

25025 Takeda, Pete. *Climb! Your Guide to Bouldering, Sport Climbing, Trad Climbing, Ice Climbing, Alpinism, and More* (4–9). Illus. Series: Extreme Sports. 2002, National Geographic paper $8.95 (0-7922-6744-3). 64pp. An attractive guide to climbing of all types — sport, wall, ice, alpine, and so forth — and to the equipment, techniques, and dangers. (Rev: SLJ 1/03) [796.5223]

25026 Teitelbaum, Michael. *Great Moments in Women's Sports* (4–7). Series: Sports Greats. 2002, World Almanac LB $29.26 (0-8368-5349-0). 48pp. A timeline running from 1904 to 2001 provides a backdrop for information on athletes who participated in the Olympic Games and achieved other significant milestones. (Rev: SLJ 3/03) [796.082]

25027 Thomas, Keltic. *Blades, Boards and Scooters* (4–8). Illus. Series: Popular Mechanics for Kids Books. 2003, Maple Tree $21.95 (1-894379-45-4). 64pp. Practical information on equipment, maintenance, and safety are accompanied by discussion of the history, science, and culture of these sports. (Rev: BL 2/1/04) [796.2]

25028 U.S. Olympic Committee. *A Basic Guide to Decathlon* (4–8). Series: Olympic Guides. 2001, Gareth Stevens LB $22.60 (0-8368-2796-1). 152pp. This is an attractive introduction to the sport of decathlon, with information about equipment, training, and famous athletes. (Rev: HBG 10/01; SLJ 7/01) [796.42]

25029 Uschan, Michael V. *Golf* (4–8). Series: History of Sports. 2001, Lucent LB $27.45 (1-56006-744-6). 112pp. An absorbing exploration of the history of golf, with information on etiquette, famous players, tours, and famous courses, with many photographs and reproductions. (Rev: SLJ 7/01) [796.352]

25030 Valliant, Doris. *Going to College* (5–8). Series: Let's Go Team. 2003, Mason Crest LB $19.95 (1-59084-541-2). 64pp. This well-illustrated, breezy account describes the function of cheerleading in college sports activities. (Rev: BL 10/15/03; SLJ 1/04) [791]

25031 Valliant, Doris. *The History of Cheerleading* (5–8). Series: Let's Go Team. 2003, Mason Crest LB $19.95 (1-59084-534-X). 64pp. Using many illustrations, this slim volume describes the history and function of cheerleading at various levels in this country. (Rev: BL 10/15/03; HBG 4/04; SLJ 1/04) [791]

25032 Vecchione, Glen. *Sidewalk Games* (K–5). Illus. by Blanche Sims. 2003, Sterling $17.95 (1-4027-0289-2). 80pp. Tag and running games, jump rope, and ball games are all covered here, with clear instructions and bouncy illustrations. (Rev: BL 9/1/03; HBG 4/04) [796.14]

25033 Warshaw, Hallie, and Jake Miller. *Get Out! Outdoor Activities Kids Can Enjoy Anywhere (Except Indoors)* (3–6). Illus. 2001, Sterling $19.95 (0-8069-9091-0). 128pp. This well-designed, colorful volume suggests all kinds of games and activities kids can do outdoors, from crafts to community service. (Rev: BL 1/1–15/02; SLJ 4/02) [796]

25034 Warshaw, Hallie, and Mark Shulman. *Zany Rainy Days: Indoor Ideas for Active Kids* (2–5). Photos by Morten Kettel. Illus. 2001, Sterling $19.95 (0-8069-6623-8). 128pp. Games, crafts, projects, and recipes — from scavenger hunts and storytelling to making forts and dog biscuits — are presented in lively text with photographs and clear instructions, as well as icons that denote the difficulty of the undertaking and the length of time required. (Rev: SLJ 8/01) [793]

25035 Willard, Keith. *Ballooning* (4–7). Illus. Series: World of Sports. 2000, Smart Apple LB $16.95 (1-887068-51-1). 32pp. This brief introduction to ballooning mentions star balloonists, different kinds of ballooning, the origins of this sport, and how one becomes proficient at it. (Rev: BL 9/15/00) [797.5]

25036 Williamson, Susan. *Summer Fun! 60 Activities for a Kid-Perfect Summer* (2–6). Illus. by Michael Kline. Series: A Williamson Kids Can! Book. 1999, Williamson paper $12.95 (1-885593-33-3). 138pp. Sixty quiet activities — including making up riddles, learning sign language, and bug hunts — are presented with black-and-white cartoons. (Rev: SLJ 8/99) [796]

25037 Willker, Joshua D. G. *Everything You Need to Know About the Dangers of Sports Gambling* (5–10). Illus. Series: Need to Know Library. 2000, Rosen LB $25.25 (0-8239-3229-X). 64pp. This brief, well-written book surveys the world of gambling on sports, its legal and illegal aspects, and how it has ruined the careers of many fine athletes. (Rev: BL 1/1–15/01) [796]

25038 Wood, Ted. *Iditarod Dream: Dusty and His Sled Dogs Compete in Alaska's Jr. Iditarod* (2–5). Illus. 1996, Walker LB $17.85 (0-8027-8407-0). 48pp. Dusty, a 15-year-old Alaskan boy, prepares for and later enters the 158-mile Junior Iditarod. (Rev: BCCB 4/96; BL 3/15/96; SLJ 5/96) [798]

25039 Wulffson, Don L. *Toys! Amazing Stories Behind Some Great Inventions* (4–6). Illus. 2000, Holt $15.95 (0-8050-6196-7). 136pp. The story behind such toys as Mr. Potato Head, Slinky, Silly Putty, kites, checkers, and Parcheesi is told in 25 illustrated chapters each dealing with a different game or toy. (Rev: BCCB 6/00; BL 6/1–15/00; HBG 3/01; SLJ 9/00) [688.7]

25040 Young, Robert. *Sports Cards* (3–6). Illus. Series: Collectibles. 1993, Macmillan LB $13.95 (0-87518-519-3). 71pp. This book presents a history of trading cards and gives material both on their production and on how to collect them. (Rev: SLJ 8/93) [796]

25041 Zeigler, Heidi. *Hang Gliding* (4–8). Series: X-treme Outdoors. 2003, Children's Book Pr. LB $20.00 (0-516-24320-9); paper $6.95 (0-516-24382-9). 48pp. Dramatic color photographs accompany easily read information on the history of the sport, equipment needed, and major events. Also in this series is *Skysurfing* (2003). (Rev: BL 9/15/03; LMC 8–9/03; SLJ 7/03) [797]

Automobile Racing

25042 Benson, Michael. *Crashes and Collisions* (5–8). Series: Race Car Legends. 1997, Chelsea $18.65 (0-7910-4435-1). Multi-car pileups in car racing and the people who have survived them are the focus of this exciting volume. (Rev: HBG 3/98; SLJ 2/98) [629.228]

25043 Buckley, James, Jr. *Life in the Pits: Twenty Seconds That Make the Difference* (5–7). Series: The World of NASCAR. 2002, Tradition LB $24.21 (1-59187-008-9). 32pp. A look at the responsiblities of the pit crew, who work under incredible pressure; photographs convey the drama. (Rev: SLJ 6/03) [796.72]

25044 Deboard, Will. *Building a Stock Car: The Need for More Speed* (5–7). Series: The World of NASCAR. 2002, Tradition LB $24.21 (1-59187-000-3). 32pp. An inside look at what's involved in building a fast and stable race car. (Rev: SLJ 6/03) [629.228]

25045 Dooling, Michael. *The Great Horse-less Carriage Race* (2–4). Illus. 2002, Holiday House

$16.95 (0-8234-1640-2). 32pp. Car lovers will particularly appreciate this lively picture-book presentation of the country's first car race, which took place in Chicago in 1895, with competitors reaching the heady average speed of 7 mph. (Rev: BCCB 2/03; BL 11/15/02; HBG 3/03; SLJ 12/02) [796.72]

25046 Johnstone, Mike. *NASCAR* (5–8). Series: Need for Speed. 2002, Lerner LB $28.75 (0-8225-0389-1). 32pp. A look at the fast-growing sport of NASCAR auto racing, with detailed descriptions of the drivers, their cars, and the circuits. (Rev: BL 8/02; HBG 10/02; SLJ 7/02) [796.7]

25047 Kirkwood, Jon. *The Fantastic Book of Car Racing* (4–6). Illus. Series: Fantastic Book Of. 1997, Millbrook LB $22.40 (0-7613-0565-3). 39pp. A heavily illustrated book with foldout sections on the subject of car racing, its excitement, and its allure. (Rev: SLJ 8/97) [796.7]

25048 Parr, Danny. *Lowriders* (4–7). Illus. Series: Wild Rides! 2001, Capstone LB $21.26 (0-7368-0928-7). 32pp. This volume on "lowrider" cars discusses the types of vehicles that are popular, the history of this trend, and the competitions that are held. (Rev: BL 10/15/01; HBG 3/02) [628.28]

25049 Pitt, Matthew. *Drag Racer* (4–7). Illus. Series: Built for Speed. 2001, Children's Book Pr. LB $20.00 (0-516-23159-6); paper $6.95 (0-516-23262-2). 48pp. The cars, the driving techniques, the race regulations, and other information important to this activity are all covered in this attractive book. (Rev: BL 12/1/01) [796.72]

25050 Savage, Jeff. *Drag Racing* (4–8). Series: Action Events. 1996, Crestwood LB $14.95 (0-89686-890-7); paper $4.95 (0-382-39293-0). The thrill of drag racing is conveyed through many action photographs and a simple text. (Rev: SLJ 2/97) [796.7]

25051 Schaefer, A. R. *The Daytona 500* (4–7). Illus. Series: NASCAR Racing. 2004, Capstone LB $22.60 (0-7368-2423-5). 32pp. This slim volume celebrates one of America's most famous automobile racing venues and some of the illustrious drivers who achieved fame there. (Rev: BL 4/1/04) [790.72]

25052 Sullivan, George. *Burnin' Rubber: Behind the Scenes in Stock Car Racing* (4–6). 1998, Millbrook LB $21.90 (0-7613-1256-0). 48pp. A look at NASCAR racing, with interesting behind-the-scenes information on this uniquely American sport. (Rev: HBG 3/99; SLJ 1/99) [796.7]

Baseball

25053 Aylesworth, Thomas G. *The Kids' World Almanac of Baseball* (4–8). Illus. 1996, World Almanac $8.95 (0-88687-787-3). 288pp. An entertaining compendium of baseball facts. (Rev: BL 6/1/90) [796.357]

25054 Brown, Jonatha A. *Baseball* (1–3). Series: My Favorite Sport. 2005, Weekly Reader LB $19.33 (0-8368-4337-1). 24pp. For beginning readers, this is an introduction to the history and sport of baseball, defining key terms. (Rev: SLJ 5/05)

25055 Brundage, Buz. *Be a Better Hitter: Baseball Basics* (5–9). Illus. 2000, Sterling $17.95 (0-8069-2461-6). 96pp. Covers baseball hitting techniques including grip, stance, bunting, swing, contact, and follow-through. (Rev: BL 6/1–15/00; SLJ 9/00) [796.357]

25056 Buckley, James. *American League East* (4–6). Illus. Series: Behind the Plate. 2005, Child's World LB $18.95 (1-59296-359-5). 48pp. Essential information on the baseball teams in the American League East, in an exciting, fan-friendly format. (Rev: BL 4/1/05) [796.357]

25057 Buckley, James, Jr. *Play Ball! The Official Major League Baseball Guide for Young Players* (3–7). Illus. by Mike Eliason. 2002, DK $12.95 (0-7894-8509-5). 48pp. A colorful guide to the game of baseball, with tips from the pros, pointers on important skills, trivia, and more, including photographs of both boy and girl players. (Rev: BL 5/15/02; HBG 10/02; SLJ 7/02) [796.357]

25058 Christopher, Matt. *Great Moments in Baseball History* (3–5). 1996, Little, Brown paper $4.95 (0-316-14130-5). 104pp. Describes nine important baseball events, involving such luminaries as Babe Ruth and Reggie Jackson. (Rev: SLJ 5/96) [796.357]

25059 Clendening, John. *American League West* (4–6). Illus. Series: Behind the Plate. 2005, Child's World LB $18.95 (1-59296-360-9). 48pp. A photo-filled overview of this baseball division, with coverage of stars and stadiums. [796.357]

25060 Coleman, Janet Wyman, and Elizabeth V. Warren. *Baseball for Everyone: Stories from the Great Game* (4–6). 2003, Abrams $16.95 (0-8109-4580-0). 48pp. Based on an exhibition at the American Folk Art Museum, this attractively illustrated volume uses many interesting anecdotes in chronicling the history of baseball. (Rev: BL 9/1/03; HBG 4/04; SLJ 10/03) [796.357]

25061 Curlee, Lynn. *Ballpark: The Story of America's Baseball Fields* (4–6). Illus. 2005, Simon & Schuster $17.95 (0-689-86742-5). 48pp. All about baseball stadiums, both the loved and the not-so-loved, from the mid-1800s through today. (Rev: BL 3/15/05; SLJ 3/05) [796.357]

25062 Driscoll, Laura. *Negro Leagues: All-Black Baseball* (3–5). Illus. by Tracy Mitchell. Series: Smart About History. 2002, Grosset LB $14.89 (0-448-42821-0); paper $5.99 (0-448-42684-6). 32pp. Through Emily's report on her visit to the National Baseball Hall of Fame, readers learn about the history of the Negro Leagues and the famous African American players. (Rev: BL 9/1/02; HBG 3/03; SLJ 12/02) [796.35764]

25063 Dunnahoo, Terry, et al. *Baseball Hall of Fame* (4–6). Illus. Series: Halls of Fame. 1994, Macmillan LB $17.95 (0-89686-849-4). 48pp. In addition to providing a description of the Cooperstown, N.Y., museum, this book discusses the origins of the game, rules, and great players. (Rev: BL 9/1/94) [796.357]

25064 Fischer, David. *American League Central* (4–6). Illus. Series: Behind the Plate. 2005, Child's World LB $18.95 (1-59296-358-7). 48pp. A photo-filled overview of this baseball division, with coverage of stars and stadiums. [796.357]

25065 Fuerst, Jeffrey B. *The Kids' Baseball Workout: A Fun Way to Get in Shape and Improve Your Game* (5–8). Illus. by Anne Canevari Green. 2002, Millbrook LB $24.90 (0-7613-2307-4). 80pp. This book offers exercises, stretches, and skills that will help young baseball players improve their game. (Rev: BL 9/1/02; HBG 10/02; SLJ 7/02) [796.357]

25066 Gardner, Robert, and Dennis Shortelle. *The Forgotten Players: The Story of Black Baseball in America* (5–8). Illus. 1993, Walker LB $13.85 (0-8027-8249-3). 120pp. A discussion of the challenges that faced the players of the Negro Leagues. (Rev: BL 2/15/93; SLJ 4/93) [769.357]

25067 Gay, Douglas, and Kathlyn Gay. *The Not-So-Minor Leagues* (5–8). Illus. 1996, Millbrook LB $23.40 (1-56294-921-7). 96pp. The history, importance, and present status of the minor leagues in baseball. (Rev: BL 5/15/96; BR 11–12/96; SLJ 6/96) [796.357]

25068 Gibbons, Gail. *My Baseball Book* (PS–3). Illus. 2000, HarperCollins $5.95 (0-688-17137-0). An attractive introduction to baseball that describes the playing field, positions, equipment, and game plays. (Rev: BCCB 4/00; BL 5/1/00; HBG 10/00; SLJ 6/00) [796.357]

25069 Gigliotti, Jim. *National League West* (4–6). Illus. Series: Behind the Plate. 2005, Child's World LB $18.95 (1-59296-363-3). 48pp. A photo-filled overview of this baseball division, with coverage of stars and stadiums. [796.357]

25070 Grabowski, John. *The Boston Red Sox Baseball Team* (4–6). Series: Great Sports Teams. 2001, Enslow $18.95 (0-7660-1488-6). 48pp. This introduction to the Boston Red Sox gives lively information on the team's past, present, and future prospects. (Rev: BL 9/15/01; HBG 10/01) [796.357]

25071 Gutelle, Andrew. *Baseball's Best: Five True Stories* (2–4). Illus. by Cliff Spohn. 1990, Random paper $3.99 (0-394-80983-1). 48pp. Special moments in the careers of five famous players. (Rev: BCCB 6/90; BL 6/1/90) [796.357]

25072 Hanmer, Trudy J. *The All-American Girls Professional Baseball League* (5–8). Illus. Series: American Events. 1994, New Discovery LB $18.95 (0-02-742595-9). 96pp. As well as discussing the AAGPBL, this account describes women in baseball prior to the league and recent attempts to play at all levels from Little League to the majors. (Rev: SLJ 3/95) [796.357]

25073 Healy, Dennis. *The Illustrated Rules of Baseball* (3–5). Illus. Series: Illustrated Sports. 1995, Ideals paper $6.95 (1-57102-017-9). 32pp. The baseball diamond, playing positions, equipment, and rules are covered in this introduction to baseball. (Rev: BL 7/95; SLJ 5/95) [798.357]

25074 Isadora, Rachael. *Nick Plays Baseball* (2–4). Illus. 2001, Penguin Putnam $15.99 (0-399-23231-1). 32pp. Using a fictional story about Nick and his team as a framework, this oversize picture book gives information on batting, pitching, equipment, playing positions, and the rules of the game. (Rev: BCCB 2/01; BL 2/15/01; HBG 3/02) [796.357]

25075 Jensen, Julie. *Beginning Baseball* (3–5). Photos by Andy King. Series: Beginning Sports. 1995, Lerner LB $22.60 (0-8225-3505-X). 80pp. The fundamentals of baseball — like throwing, hitting, fielding, and baserunning — are presented, along with a history of the game. (Rev: SLJ 2/96) [796.357]

25076 Kasoff, Jerry. *Baseball Just for Kids: Skills, Strategies and Stories to Make You a Better Ballplayer* (3–7). Illus. 1996, Grand Slam paper $12.95 (0-9645826-7-8). 159pp. Baseball rules, techniques, tips, jokes, and trivia are included in this book that shows that the author loves the game. (Rev: SLJ 4/97) [796.357]

25077 Kellogg, David. *True Stories of Baseball's Hall of Famers* (4–8). Illus. 2000, Bluewood $8.95 (0-912517-41-7). 144pp. Using a chronological approach, this book profiles 60 Hall of Famers and tells why each is there. (Rev: BL 10/15/00) [796.357]

25078 Kennedy, Mike. *Baseball* (2–4). Series: True Books — Sports. 2002, Children's Book Pr. LB $23.50 (0-516-22334-8); paper $6.95 (0-516-29371-0). 48pp. Using large type and many color photographs, this is a simple introduction to baseball, its history, and how it is played. (Rev: BL 9/1/02; SLJ check) [796.357]

25079 Kisseloff, Jeff. *Who Is Baseball's Greatest Pitcher?* (5–7). Illus. 2003, Cricket $15.95 (0-8126-2685-0). 192pp. The author presents profiles of 33 pitchers, with relevant statistics, and challenges the reader to choose the best and justify this decision. (Rev: BL 7/03; HBG 10/03; SLJ 5/03) [796.359]

25080 Krasner, Steven. *Play Ball Like the Pros: Tips for Kids from 20 Big League Stars* (5–9). Illus. 2002, Peachtree paper $12.95 (1-56145-261-0). 160pp. Each chapter features a professional player talking about the position he plays and giving tips to the young athlete. (Rev: BL 5/1/02; SLJ 6/02) [796.357]

25081 Layden, Joe. *The Great American Baseball Strike* (5–8). Series: Headliners. 1995, Millbrook LB $25.90 (1-56294-930-6). A discussion of the issues that led to the 1995 baseball strike, with a review of the history of professional baseball and of the stormy relationship between the owners and players. (Rev: BL 11/15/95; SLJ 1/96) [796.357]

25082 Mackel, Kathy. *MadCat* (5–8). 2005, HarperCollins $15.99 (0-06-054869-X). 192pp. Madelyn Catherine (aka MadCat), catcher on her local girls' fast-pitch softball team, is at the center of this story about sports, team play, and family involvement. (Rev: BL 2/15/05; SLJ 3/05)

25083 Mackin, Bob. *Record-Breaking Baseball Trivia* (5–8). 2000, Douglas & McIntyre $6.95 (1-55054-757-7). 128pp. Questions, answers, and quizzes cover topics including baseball history, team play, World Series facts, and trivia from the plate and mound. (Rev: BL 9/15/00) [796.357]

25084 *My Baseball Book* (PS). Illus. 2002, DK $7.95 (0-7894-8508-7). 16pp. A preschooler's introduc-

tion to baseball, with descriptions of each position on the field and bright, colorful photographs of players in action. (Rev: BL 3/1/02) [796.357]

25085 Newman, Gerald. *Happy Birthday, Little League* (3–6). Illus. 1989, Watts LB $22.00 (0-531-10687-X). 64pp. A half-century tribute to Little League baseball, filled with impressive statistics. (Rev: BCCB 4/89; BL 4/1/89; SLJ 5/89)

25086 Nitz, Kristin Wolden. *Softball* (5–9). Series: Play-by-Play. 2000, Lerner paper $7.95 (0-8225-9875-2). 80pp. Good basic information about softball is given including history, rules, equipment, and positions. (Rev: SLJ 9/00) [796.357]

25087 Owens, Thomas S. *The Atlanta Braves Baseball Team* (4–6). Series: Great Sports Teams. 1998, Enslow LB $17.95 (0-7660-1021-X). 48pp. Provides a history of the Atlanta Braves and highlights their most famous players and exciting seasons. (Rev: BL 5/15/98; HBG 10/98) [796.357]

25088 Patrick, Jean L. S. *The Girl Who Struck Out Babe Ruth* (2–3). Illus. by Jeni Reeves. 2000, Lerner $21.27 (1-57505-397-7); paper $5.95 (1-57505-455-8). 48pp. In 1931, 17-year-old Jackie Mitchell, a pitcher in the minor leagues, played in an exhibition game in which she struck out Babe Ruth and Lou Gehrig. (Rev: BCCB 6/00; BL 4/15/00; HBG 10/00; SLJ 8/00) [796.357]

25089 Pietrusza, David. *The Baltimore Orioles Baseball Team* (4–6). Series: Great Sports Teams. 2000, Enslow LB $18.95 (0-7660-1283-2). 48pp. Covers the history of the Baltimore Orioles, the team's best players, and its performance today and tomorrow. (Rev: BL 5/15/00; HBG 10/00) [796.357]

25090 Pietrusza, David. *The Cleveland Indians Baseball Team* (4–6). Series: Great Sports Teams. 2001, Enslow $18.95 (0-7660-1491-6). 48pp. Using fast-paced writing and many photographs, Pietrusza supplies a good thumbnail sketch of the team, its famous players, and outstanding games. (Rev: BL 9/15/01; HBG 3/02) [796.357]

25091 Pietrusza, David. *The New York Yankees Baseball Team* (4–6). Illus. 1998, Enslow LB $17.95 (0-7660-1018-X). 48pp. A brief, well-illustrated account of the history of the Yankees, with emphasis on star players and important coaches. (Rev: BL 4/1/98; HBG 10/98) [796.357]

25092 Pietrusza, David. *The St. Louis Cardinals Baseball Team* (4–6). Series: Great Sports Teams. 2001, Enslow $18.95 (0-7660-1490-8). 48pp. An exciting introduction to the team with material on its history, key players, exciting seasons, and present status. (Rev: BL 9/15/01; HBG 3/02)

25093 Pietrusza, David. *The San Francisco Giants Baseball Team* (4–6). Series: Great Sports Teams. 2000, Enslow LB $18.95 (0-7660-1284-0). 48pp. Plenty of sports action is included in this introduction to the past, present, and future of the San Francisco Giants. (Rev: BL 5/15/00; HBG 10/00) [795.357]

25094 Preller, James. *McGwire and Sosa: A Season to Remember* (4–7). Illus. 1998, Simon & Schuster paper $5.99 (0-689-82871-3). 32pp. An oversize paperback that traces the baseball season that brought Sosa and McGwire to the nation's attention and made them sports heroes. (Rev: BL 1/1–15/99) [796.357]

25095 Shaughnessy, Dan. *The Legend of the Curse of the Bambino* (2–4). Illus. by C. F. Payne. 2005, Simon & Schuster $16.95 (0-689-87235-6). 32pp. A father tells his daughter about Babe Ruth and the "curse" that kept the Boston Red Sox from winning the World Series until 2004. (Rev: BL 3/15/05; SLJ 5/05) [796.357]

25096 Silbaugh, John. *National League Central* (4–6). Illus. Series: Behind the Plate. 2005, Child's World LB $18.95 (1-59296-361-7). 48pp. A photo-filled overview of this baseball division, with coverage of stars and stadiums. [796.357]

25097 Stewart, Wayne. *Baseball Bafflers* (4–7). Illus. 2000, Sterling paper $6.95 (0-8069-6561-4). 96pp. Using anecdotes, quotations, and statistics, this book describes some of baseball's most unusual plays and strategies. (Rev: BL 2/1/00) [796.357]

25098 Sublett, Anne. *The Illustrated Rules of Softball* (3–5). Illus. by Patrick Kelley. Series: Illustrated Sports. 1996, Ideals paper $6.95 (1-57102-063-2). 32pp. After a brief history of baseball, this account presents an explanation of rules and a look at various positions and signals, plus a glossary and discussion of sportsmanship. (Rev: SLJ 8/96) [796.357]

25099 Suen, Anastasia. *The Story of Baseball* (1–3). Illus. Series: Sports History. 2002, Rosen LB $16.00 (0-8239-6000-5). 24pp. A basic, easy-to-read introduction to the sport. (Rev: BL 5/15/02) [796.357]

25100 Sullivan, George. *Baseball's Boneheads, Bad Boys, and Just Plain Crazy Guys* (5–8). Illus. by Anne Canevari Green. 2003, Millbrook LB $23.90 (0-7613-2321-X); paper $8.95 (0-7613-1928-X). 64pp. An amusing collection of anecdotes that show the humor, superstitions, and general nuttiness of baseball players. (Rev: BL 7/03; HBG 10/03; SLJ 11/03) [790.357]

25101 Teitelbaum, Michael. *National League East* (4–6). Illus. Series: Behind the Plate. 2005, Child's World LB $18.95 (1-59296-362-5). 48pp. A photo-filled overview of this baseball division, with coverage of stars and stadiums. [796.357]

25102 Thomas, Keltie. *How Baseball Works* (3–6). Illus. by Greg Hall. 2004, Maple Tree $19.95 (1-894379-60-8); paper $9.95 (1-894379-61-6). 64pp. A detailed overview of baseball and its history and techniques, plus information on famous players. (Rev: BL 5/15/04; SLJ 11/04) [796]

25103 Tuttle, Dennis R. *Life in the Minor Leagues* (4–6). Illus. Series: Baseball Legends. 1999, Chelsea LB $16.95 (0-7910-5160-9). 64pp. An introduction to the minor leagues, how they developed, their organization, famous players, and daily life within the teams. (Rev: BL 8/99; HBG 10/99) [796.357]

25104 Weatherford, Carole Boston. *A Negro League Scrapbook* (2–4). Illus. 2005, Boyds Mills $19.95 (1-59078-091-4). 48pp. The colorful history of baseball's Negro Leagues is documented in an inter-esting scrapbook format. (Rev: BL 2/1/05; SLJ 3/05) [796.357]

25105 Will, Sandra. *Baseball for Fun!* (2–4). Illus. Series: Sports for Fun. 2003, Compass Point LB $21.26 (0-7565-0428-7). 48pp. Covering rules, necessary skills, and key figures, this is an attractive introduction for beginning readers. (Rev: SLJ 6/03) [796.357]

25106 Young, Robert. *A Personal Tour of Camden Yards* (4–7). Series: How It Was. 1999, Lerner LB $30.35 (0-8225-3578-5). 64pp. Designed to remind fans of famous old ballparks, this book visits Camden Yards, home of the Baltimore Orioles. The reader inspects the field, visits the old warehouse, and views the game from a skybox. (Rev: BL 6/1–15/99; HBG 10/99) [796.357]

Basketball

25107 Anderson, Dave. *The Story of Basketball* (4–8). Illus. 1997, Morrow $16.00 (0-688-14316-4). An updated introduction to basketball history, rules, players, and teams. (Rev: BL 1/1–15/98; HBG 3/98; SLJ 10/97) [796.32]

25108 Aretha, David. *The Detroit Pistons Basketball Team* (4–6). Series: Great Sports Teams. 2001, Enslow LB $18.95 (0-7660-1487-8). 48pp. In narrative and pictures, this volume highlights the history and achievements of the Detroit Pistons with material on their key players and important seasons, past and present. (Rev: BL 12/15/01; HBG 3/02) [796.323]

25109 Aretha, David. *The Seattle SuperSonics Basketball Team* (4–6). Illus. Series: Great Sports Teams. 1999, Enslow LB $18.95 (0-7660-1102-X). 48pp. A history of the Seattle SuperSonics is given, with information on famous players past and present and descriptions of important games. (Rev: BL 3/15/99; HBG 10/99) [796.323]

25110 Bennett, Frank. *The Illustrated Rules of Basketball* (3–5). Illus. 1994, Ideals paper $6.95 (1-57102-021-7). 32pp. Following the history of basketball, provides a detailed discussion of each rule. (Rev: BL 9/15/94; SLJ 11/94) [796.323]

25111 Brock, Ted. *Pacific Division: The Golden State Warriors, the Los Angeles Clippers, the Los Angeles Lakers, the Phoenix Suns, the Portland Trail Blazers, the Sacramento Kings, and the Seattle SuperSonics* (2–5). Illus. Series: Above the Rim: The NBA Library. 2004, Child's World LB $18.95 (1-59296-206-8). 48pp. The seven teams in basketball's Pacific Division are profiled here in an appealing format, with action photographs, statistical charts, and information on key players and seasons. [796.323]

25112 Burgan, Michael. *Great Moments in Basketball* (4–7). Series: Sports Greats. 2002, World Almanac LB $29.26 (0-8368-5345-8). 48pp. Great basketball achievements of the years from 1962 to 2002 are detailed here, with a timeline that starts in 1891 and comments from coaches and players. (Rev: SLJ 3/03) [796.3230973]

25113 Dixon, Tamecka, and Judith Cohen. *You Can Be a Woman Basketball Player* (3–6). Illus. 1999, Cascade Pass $13.95 (1-880599-40-6); paper $7.00 (1-880599-38-4). 40pp. As well as the story of Tamecka Dixon, a player on the Los Angeles Sparks, this book explains the fundamentals of basketball, its positions, and the duties of each team member. (Rev: BL 8/99; SLJ 9/99) [796.323]

25114 Dunnahoo, Terry, et al. *Basketball Hall of Fame* (4–6). Illus. Series: Halls of Fame. 1994, Macmillan LB $13.95 (0-89686-850-8). 48pp. As well as describing the functions of the Basketball Hall of Fame, this book explains how the sport evolved and tells about some of the great players. (Rev: BL 9/1/94; SLJ 8/94) [796.323]

25115 Dunning, Mark. *Basketball* (4–8). Series: Flowmotion. 2003, Sterling paper $9.95 (0-8069-9372-3). 96pp. Through a series of stop-action photographs, the sport of basketball is introduced in a logical step-by-step sequence. (Rev: BL 10/15/03) [796.323]

25116 Gibbons, Gail. *My Basketball Book* (K–2). Illus. 2000, HarperCollins $5.95 (0-688-17140-0). 24pp. This small-format paperback book contains the basics of basketball with coverage of equipment, positions, and rules. (Rev: BL 9/15/00; HBG 3/01; SLJ 11/00) [796.323]

25117 Gigliotti, Jim. *The Atlantic Division: The Boston Celtics, the Miami Heat, the New Jersey Nets, the New York Knicks, the Orlando Magic, the Philadelphia 76ers, and the Washington Wizards* (2–5). Series: Above the Rim. 2004, Child's World LB $27.07 (1-59296-192-4). The seven teams in basketball's Atlantic Division are profiled here in an appealing format, with action photographs, statistical charts, and information on key players and seasons. (Rev: BL 9/1/04) [796.323]

25118 Glenn, Mike. *Lessons in Success from the NBA's Top Players* (5–7). Illus. 1998, Visions 3000 paper $14.95 (0-9649795-5-1). 126pp. This noted sportsman tells about his career in the NBA while introducing each of the NBA teams and its strengths. (Rev: BL 7/98) [796.323]

25119 Kennedy, Mike. *Basketball* (3–5). Series: True Books — Sports. 2002, Children's Book Pr. LB $23.50 (0-516-22335-6); paper $6.95 (0-516-29372-9). 48pp. Covers the basic elements of basketball, its history, and superstars, with color photographs on each page plus large type and simple text. (Rev: BL 1/1–15/03) [796.323]

25120 Kramer, S. A. *Hoop Stars* (2–3). Illus. by Mitchell Heinze. 1995, Penguin Putnam paper $3.99 (0-448-40943-7). 48pp. Hakeem Olajuwon, Charles Barkley, Shaquille O'Neal, and David Robinson are the NBA stars briefly profiled in this beginning reader. (Rev: BL 1/1–15/96; SLJ 3/96) [796.323]

25121 Kuklin, Susan, and Sheryl Swoopes. *Hoops with Swoopes* (1–3). Illus. 2001, Hyperion $15.99 (0-7868-0551-X). 32pp. Basketball star Swoopes introduces the basics of the game in simple text and energetic illustrations. (Rev: BCCB 11/01; BL 6/1–15/01; HB 5–6/01; HBG 3/02; SLJ 8/01) [796.323]

25122 Lace, William W. *The Houston Rockets Basketball Team* (5–8). Series: Sports Greats. 1997, Enslow LB $18.95 (0-89490-792-1). A profile of the Houston Rockets, with sketches of the key players. (Rev: BL 10/15/97; HBG 3/98) [796.323]

25123 Lace, William W. *The Los Angeles Lakers Basketball Team* (4–6). Illus. Series: Great Sports Teams. 1998, Enslow LB $17.95 (0-7660-1020-1). 48pp. After a short introduction on Magic Johnson, this account focuses on the history of the team on which he played, with emphasis on their finest moments, their star players, and famous coaches. (Rev: BL 4/1/98; HBG 10/98) [796.323]

25124 Lannin, Joanne. *A History of Basketball for Girls and Women: From Bloomers to the Big Leagues* (5–9). Illus. Series: Sports Legacy. 2000, Lerner LB $31.95 (0-8225-3331-6); paper $15.95 (0-8225-9863-9). 144pp. From the creation of basketball in 1891 to today, this account describes women's roles. (Rev: BL 1/1–15/01; HBG 3/01; SLJ 2/01) [796.323]

25125 Morris, Greggory. *Basketball Basics* (4–6). Illus. by Tim Engelland. 1979, Prentice Hall $6.95 (0-13-072256-1). A player and coach explain four specific skills to young players.

25126 Owens, Thomas S. *Basketball Arenas* (5–8). Illus. Series: Sports Palaces. 2002, Millbrook LB $25.90 (0-7613-1766-X). 64pp. Lots of basketball lore and history are included in a visit to the Boston Garden, Chicago Stadium, and the old Madison Square Garden. (Rev: BL 6/1–15/02; HBG 10/02) [796.323]

25127 Owens, Thomas S. *The Chicago Bulls Basketball Team* (5–8). Illus. Series: Sports Greats. 1997, Enslow LB $18.95 (0-89490-793-X). A history of the Chicago Bulls, with emphasis on the stars who have made the team famous. (Rev: BL 10/15/97; HBG 3/98) [796.323]

25128 Parselle, Matt. *Basketball: Learn How to Be a Star Player* (3–5). Illus. by Mel Pickering. Series: Sports Club. 2000, Two-Can $9.95 (1-58728-000-0). 32pp. This basic book on basketball explains different kinds of passes and the rules of the game, as well as giving some history and profiles of a few important players. (Rev: SLJ 3/01) [796.323]

25129 Pietrusza, David. *The Phoenix Suns Basketball Team* (5–8). Series: Sports Greats. 1997, Enslow LB $18.95 (0-89490-795-6). An introduction to the Phoenix Suns, their great games, and their star players. (Rev: BL 10/15/97; HBG 3/98) [796.323]

25130 Preller, James. *NBA Game Day: An Inside Look a the NBA* (4–8). Illus. 1997, Scholastic paper $10.95 (0-590-76742-9). A photo-collage of a day in the life of the NBA, from morning workout to cleanup after the game, with pictures of prominent players at work and play. (Rev: BL 1/1–15/98; HBG 3/98) [796.323]

25131 Roberts, Robin. *Basketball Year: What It's Like to Be a Woman Pro* (4–6). Illus. Series: Get in the Game! 2000, Millbrook $21.90 (0-7613-1406-7). 48pp. This account follows women of the WNBA as they train, travel, play games, and try to lead normal lives. (Rev: BL 9/1/00; HBG 10/00; SLJ 8/00) [796.323]

25132 Rogers, Glenn. *The San Antonio Spurs Basketball Team* (5–8). Series: Sports Greats. 1997, Enslow LB $18.95 (0-89490-797-2). Profiles of important players and stories behind important games are included in this introduction to the San Antonio Spurs. (Rev: BL 10/15/97; HBG 3/98) [796.323]

25133 Rutledge, Rachel. *The Best of the Best in Basketball* (4–7). Illus. Series: Women in Sports. 1998, Millbrook LB $24.90 (0-7613-1301-X). 64pp. After a history of basketball, this account highlights women's role and covers today's most important female players. (Rev: BL 2/15/99; HBG 10/99; SLJ 3/99) [796.323]

25134 Schnakenberg, Robert E. *The Central Division: The Atlanta Hawks, the Chicago Bulls, the Cleveland Cavaliers, the Detroit Pistons, the Indiana Pacers, the Milwaukee Bucks, the New Orleans Hornets, and the Toronto Raptors* (2–5). Illus. Series: Above the Rim: The NBA Library. 2004, Child's World LB $27.07 (1-59296-204-1). 48pp. The eight teams in basketball's Central Division are profiled here in an appealing format, with action photographs, statistical charts, and information on key players and seasons. (Rev: BL 9/1/04) [796.32]

25135 Schulz, Randy. *The New York Knicks Basketball Team* (4–6). Series: Great Sports Teams. 2000, Enslow LB $18.95 (0-7660-1281-6). 48pp. The New York Nicks are profiled with material on the team's history, greatest players, and most exciting games. (Rev: BL 9/15/00; HBG 10/01) [796.323]

25136 Stewart, Mark. *The NBA Finals* (5–10). Series: Watts History of Sports. 2003, Watts LB $33.50 (0-531-11955-6). 95pp. National Basketball Association finals over more than half a century are detailed year by year, with ample information on the teams and the players. (Rev: SLJ 3/04) [797]

25137 Thomas, Keltie. *How Basketball Works* (5–8). Illus. 2005, Maple Tree $16.95 (1-897066-18-X); paper $6.95 (1-897066-19-8). 64pp. A lively overview of basketball's history, equipment, training, and skills, with interesting anecdotes and factoids. (Rev: BL 5/15/05) [796.323]

25138 Vancil, Mark. *NBA Basketball Offense Basics* (4–8). Illus. 1996, Sterling $16.95 (0-8069-4892-2). 96pp. Action photographs and lively text demonstrate such techniques as dribbling, passing, and shooting. (Rev: BL 9/1/96) [796.332]

25139 Walters, John. *Midwest Division: The Dallas Mavericks, the Denver Nuggets, the Houston Rockets, the Memphis Grizzlies, the Minnesota Timberwolves, the San Antonio Spurs, and the Utah Jazz* (2–5). Illus. Series: Above the Rim: The NBA Library. 2004, Child's World LB $18.95 (1-59296-205-X). 48pp. The seven teams in basketball's Midwest Division are profiled here in an appealing format, with action photographs, statistical charts, and information on key players and seasons. [796.323]

25140 Wilker, Josh. *The Harlem Globetrotters* (5–10). Series: African-American Achievers. 1996,

Chelsea LB $21.95 (0-7910-2585-3); paper $8.95 (0-7910-2586-1). This is a chronologically arranged history of the Harlem Globetrotters, the basketball team that has been entertaining crowds since 1927. (Rev: SLJ 3/97) [796.357]

Bicycles

25141 Bach, Julie. *Bicycling* (4–7). Illus. Series: World of Sports. 2000, Smart Apple LB $16.95 (1-887068-53-8). 32pp. A brief introduction to bicycling that gives material on the origins and evolution of the sport, equipment, and techniques, plus coverage of the sport's star athletes. (Rev: BL 9/15/00) [796.6]

25142 Bizley, Kirk. *Mountain Biking* (4–7). Series: Radical Sports. 1999, Heinemann LB $24.22 (1-57572-944-X). 32pp. Color photographs and a simple text introduce mountain biking, its history, equipment, skills, and safety concerns. (Rev: SLJ 5/00) [796.6]

25143 Brimner, Larry. *Mountain Biking* (5–7). Illus. 1997, Watts LB $22.00 (0-531-20243-7). 64pp. An attractive book that includes information on the history of mountain bikes, their construction, and how to choose, use, and maintain one. (Rev: BL 9/1/97; SLJ 8/97) [796.6]

25144 Cole, Steve. *Kids' Easy Bike Care: Tune-Ups, Tools and Quick Fixes* (5–9). Illus. by Sarah Rakitin. Series: Quick Starts for Kids! 2003, Williamson paper $8.95 (1-885593-86-4). 64pp. A detailed and accessible guide to the parts of a bicycle and their maintenance, bicycle safety, and preparing an emergency kit, with cartoon illustrations. (Rev: SLJ 12/03) [629.28]

25145 Crossingham, John. *Cycling in Action* (4–7). Illus. by Bonna Rouse. Series: Sports in Action. 2002, Crabtree LB $21.28 (0-7787-0118-2); paper $5.95 (0-7787-0124-7). 32pp. Photographs and drawings illustrate important concepts in this introduction to the sport of cycling that covers equipment and technique. (Rev: BL 9/1/02) [796.4]

25146 Deady, Kathleen W. *BMX Bikes* (4–7). Illus. Series: Wild Rides! 2001, Capstone LB $21.26 (0-7368-0925-2). 32pp. Bicycle motocross fans will enjoy the color photographs and concise text that explains the equipment and skills needed for BMX (bicycle motocross) racing. (Rev: BL 10/15/01; HBG 3/02) [629.22]

25147 Dick, Scott. *BMX* (4–8). Series: Radical Sports. 2002, Heinemann LB $25.64 (1-58810-623-3). 32pp. This introduction to bicycle motocross gives material on equipment, skills, training, and safety. (Rev: BL 2/15/03; HBG 3/03) [796.6]

25148 Ditchfield, Christin. *Cycling* (2–4). Illus. Series: True Books. 2000, Children's Book Pr. LB $21.50 (0-516-21061-0); paper $6.95 (0-516-27024-9). 48pp. A simply written introduction to the sport of cycling with material on competitions, equipment, and the history of the sport. (Rev: BL 9/15/00) [796.6]

25149 Englart, Mindi Rose. *Bikes* (3–5). Series: Made in the USA. 2002, Gale LB $21.54 (1-56711-486-5). 32pp. A behind-the-scenes look at how bicycles are made, starting with the raw materials and continuing through the finished product. (Rev: BL 9/15/02) [629]

25150 Erlbach, Arlene. *Bicycles* (3–5). Illus. Series: How It's Made. 1994, Lerner LB $19.93 (0-8225-2388-4); paper $6.95 (0-8225-9740-3). 48pp. The story of the bicycle is told, from its early design to the sleek machines of today. (Rev: BL 3/15/95) [629]

25151 Freeman, Gary. *Motocross* (4–8). Series: Radical Sports. 2002, Heinemann LB $25.64 (1-58810-627-6). 32pp. The sport of cross-country racing on motorcycles is introduced, with an emphasis on safety and skill development. (Rev: BL 2/15/03; HBG 3/03) [796.7]

25152 Gedatus, Gus. *Bicycling for Fitness* (4–7). Series: Nutrition and Fitness. 2001, Capstone LB $23.93 (0-7368-0705-5). 64pp. This book explains the benefits of bicycling in promoting good health and outlines a fitness plan, nutrition program, and delicious recipes. (Rev: BL 9/15/01; HBG 10/01) [796.6]

25153 Gibbons, Gail. *Bicycle Book* (K–4). Illus. 1995, Holiday House LB $16.95 (0-8234-1199-0). 32pp. A short book that covers such topics as the history of the bicycle, its types, care tips, and safety rules. (Rev: BL 12/1/95; SLJ 1/96) [629.227]

25154 Haduch, Bill. *Go Fly a Bike! The Ultimate Book About Bicycle Fun, Freedom, and Science* (4–8). Illus. by Chris Murphy. 2004, Dutton $16.99 (0-525-47024-7). 112pp. Packed with facts and cartoon illustrations, this comprehensive guide covers everything from the history of bicycling to practical tips for bike care and repair. (Rev: BL 2/1/04; SLJ 3/04) [796.6]

25155 Hayhurst, Chris. *Bicycle Stunt Riding!* (4–8). Series: Extreme Sports. 2000, Rosen LB $26.50 (0-8239-3011-4). 64pp. In this book, readers will learn about stunts like the vert and mega spin as well as finding out about the bikes and the safety equipment needed to start this sport. (Rev: BL 6/1–15/00) [629]

25156 Hayhurst, Chris. *Mountain Biking: Get on the Trail* (4–8). Illus. Series: Extreme Sports. 2000, Rosen LB $26.50 (0-8239-3013-0). 64pp. Stressing safety throughout, this book covers topics including the history of mountain biking, why mountain bikes are different than others, and riding techniques. (Rev: BL 3/15/00; SLJ 8/00) [796.6]

25157 Jensen, Julie. *Beginning Mountain Biking* (4–6). Photos by Andy King. Series: Beginning Sports. 1996, Lerner LB $21.27 (0-8225-3509-2). 63pp. A very simple, short account that introduces mountain biking to a young audience. (Rev: SLJ 2/97) [796.6]

25158 King, Andy. *Fundamental Mountain Biking* (5–9). Series: Fundamental Sports. 1996, Lerner LB $27.15 (0-8225-3459-2). This introduction to mountain biking discusses its history, equipment, maneu-

vers, competitions, tricks, safety reminders, and repair tips. (Rev: SLJ 2/97) [796.64]

25159 Maestro, Betsy, and Giulio Maestro. *Bike Trip* (2–4). Illus. 1992, HarperCollins $16.00 (0-06-022731-1). 32pp. Young Joshua tells a simple story of a bike trip he takes with his family from their rural home into town. (Rev: BL 1/1/92; SLJ 3/92) [796.6]

25160 Maurer, Tracy Nelson. *BMX Freestyle* (3–6). Series: Radsports. 2001, Rourke LB $27.93 (1-58952-102-1). 48pp. Safety is emphasized in this account of BMX history, equipment, and techniques. (Rev: SLJ 5/02) [796.62]

25161 Molzahn, Arlene Bourgeois. *Extreme Mountain Biking* (5–8). Series: Extreme Sports. 2000, Capstone LB $21.26 (0-7368-0483-8). 48pp. This introduction to mountain biking includes material on its history, equipment, safety concerns, skills, and competitions. (Rev: HBG 10/00; SLJ 8/00) [796.6]

25162 Otfinoski, Steven. *Pedaling Along: Bikes Then and Now* (1–3). Illus. Series: Here We Go! 1996, Benchmark LB $22.79 (0-7614-0402-3). 32pp. A copiously illustrated history of bicycles, from their invention to modern bikes. (Rev: SLJ 6/97) [629]

25163 Pinchuk, Amy. *The Best Book of Bikes* (4–7). Illus. 2003, Maple Tree $21.95 (1-894379-43-8); paper $12.95 (1-894379-44-6). 64pp. Diagrams, color photographs, and fascinating facts add to the appeal of the maintenance advice, racing strategies, and stunts provided. (Rev: BCCB 9/03; SLJ 9/03) [629.227]

25164 Raby, Philip, and Simon Nix. *Motorbikes* (5–8). Illus. Series: Need for Speed. 1999, Lerner LB $23.93 (0-8225-2486-4); paper $12.75 (0-8225-9854-X). 32pp. A variety of motorbikes are introduced including dirt, motorcross, and land speed bikes. (Rev: BL 1/1–15/00; HBG 3/00; SLJ 2/00) [629.227]

Bowling

25165 Nace, Don. *Bowling for Beginners: Simple Steps to Strikes and Spares* (5–10). Photos by Bruce Curtis. 2001, Sterling $19.95 (0-8069-4968-6). 96pp. Equipment, technique, scoring, competition play, and etiquette are all discussed here, with excellent diagrams and color photographs. (Rev: BL 6/1–15/01; SLJ 7/01) [794.6]

Camping and Backpacking

25166 Ching, Jacqueline. *Camping: Have Fun, Be Smart* (3–6). Series: Explore the Outdoors. 2000, Rosen LB $19.95 (0-8239-3173-0). 64pp. A basic introduction to camping that includes material on setting up a camp, gear and clothing, and different types of tents. (Rev: SLJ 1/01) [796.54]

25167 Drake, Jane, and Ann Love. *The Kids Campfire Book* (4–8). Illus. 1998, Kids Can paper $9.95 (1-55074-539-5). This manual describes how to select a location, build safe campfires, and later douse them, suggests fireside activities, including some science demonstrations, and offers safe cooking tips. (Rev: BL 3/15/98; HBG 9/98; SLJ 4/98) [796.54]

25168 Loy, Jessica. *Follow the Trail: A Young Person's Guide to the Great Outdoors* (2–6). Illus. 2003, Holt $18.95 (0-8050-6195-9). 48pp. This slim volume uses the story of a camping trip to convey information about identifying wildflowers and trees, building a campfire, and avoiding such perils as poison ivy, snakes, and bears. (Rev: BL 4/1/03; HBG 10/03; SLJ 6/03) [796.54]

25169 McManus, Patrick F. *Kid Camping from Aaaaiii! to Zip* (5–7). Illus. by Roy Doty. 1979, Avon paper $3.99 (0-380-71311-X). 128pp. A practical camping guide presented in an amusing way.

25170 Rhatigan, Joe. *The Kids' Guide to Nature Adventures: 80 Great Activities for Exploring the Outdoors* (3–7). 2003, Lark Books paper $17.95 (1-57990-373-8). 128pp. This beautifully illustrated guide is loaded with great ideas for having fun outdoors, including locations ranging from the family's backyard to America's large national parks. (Rev: BL 10/1/03; SLJ 1/04)

25171 Seeberg, Tim. *Camping* (3–5). Illus. Series: Kids' Guides to the Outdoors. 2004, Child's World LB $27.07 (1-59296-032-4). 32pp. For children with no experience of camping, the tips on safety, equipment, and advance planning provided here will be helpful. (Rev: BL 5/15/04) [796.54]

Chess

25172 Basman, Michael. *Chess for Kids* (4–8). Illus. 2001, DK paper $12.99 (0-7894-6540-X). 44pp. A guide to the game of chess that includes everything from the basic moves and important strategies to information on the game's origins and the roles the game has played in arenas ranging from literature to history. (Rev: BL 7/01; HBG 10/01) [794.1]

25173 Kidder, Harvey. *The Kids' Book of Chess* (4–8). Illus. by Kimberly Bulcken. 1990, Workman paper $15.95 (0-89480-767-6). 96pp. Using their origins in the Middle Ages as a focus, this book explains the role of each chess piece and the basics of the game. (Rev: SLJ 2/91) [794.1]

25174 Nottingham, Ted, et al. *Chess for Children* (4–6). Illus. 1994, Sterling $16.95 (0-8069-0452-6). 128pp. Three experts explain chess, the meaning and use of each piece, strategies, famous games, and the accomplishments of famous players. (Rev: BL 5/1/94) [794.1]

25175 Nottingham, Ted, and Bob Wade. *Winning Chess: Piece by Piece* (4–8). Illus. 1999, Sterling $17.95 (0-8069-9955-1). 128pp. This book is for chess players who already know the basics and are ready to improve their techniques. (Rev: BL 11/15/99) [794.1]

Fishing

25176 Fitzgerald, Ron. *Essential Fishing for Teens* (4–10). 2000, Children's Book Pr. LB $19.00 (0-516-23355-6); paper $6.95 (0-516-23555-9). 48pp. A thorough introduction to fishing that covers such topics as bait, boat, fly, and big-game fishing with material on equipment and the perfect fishing spot. (Rev: SLJ 3/01) [799.1]

25177 Morey, Shaun. *Incredible Fishing Stories for Kids* (3–6). Illus. 1993, Incredible Fishing Stories paper $11.95 (0-9633691-1-3). 96pp. These true stories tell how young anglers have made record catches. (Rev: BL 9/1/93)

25178 Schmidt, Gerald D. *Let's Go Fishing: A Book for Beginners* (4–7). Illus. by Brian W. Payne. 1990, Roberts Rinehart paper $11.95 (0-911797-84-X). 96pp. This practical guide to freshwater fishing includes material on tackle and kinds of fish. (Rev: BL 3/1/91; SLJ 5/91) [799.1]

25179 Seeberg, Tim. *Freshwater Fishing* (3–5). Illus. Series: Great Outdoors. 2004, Child's World LB $27.07 (1-59296-035-9). 32pp. A useful guide for young people planning their first fishing trip, this book is loaded with tips about equipment and what to expect. Also use *Fly-Fishing* (2004). (Rev: BL 5/15/04) [799.1]

25180 Solomon, Dane. *Fishing: Have Fun, Be Smart* (3–6). Illus. Series: Explore the Outdoors. 2000, Rosen $19.95 (0-8239-3168-4). This introduction to fishing includes material on fresh and salt water varieties and the equipment needed. (Rev: SLJ 1/01) [799.1]

Football

25181 Aretha, David. *The Notre Dame Fighting Irish Football Team* (4–6). Series: Great Sports Teams. 2001, Enslow LB $18.95 (0-7660-1486-X). 48pp. Fast-paced writing and many action photographs feature in this account of the Fighting Irish team, its most exciting seasons, star players, and present status. (Rev: BL 12/15/01; HBG 3/02) [796.48]

25182 Devaney, John. *Winners of the Heisman Trophy*. Rev. ed. (5–8). Illus. 1990, Walker LB $15.85 (0-8027-6907-1). A history of the award is given, with profiles of 15 past winners. (Rev: SLJ 6/90) [796.332]

25183 DiLorenzo, J. J. *The Miami Dolphins Football Team* (5–8). Series: Sports Greats. 1997, Enslow LB $18.95 (0-89490-796-4). A history of the Miami Dolphins that focuses on their brightest stars and best moments on the field. (Rev: BL 10/15/97; HBG 3/98) [796.48]

25184 Dunnahoo, Terry, et al. *Pro Football Hall of Fame* (4–6). Illus. Series: Halls of Fame. 1994, Macmillan LB $13.95 (0-89686-851-6). 48pp. The story of the Football Hall of Fame, its contents and history, plus many asides about the origins of American football and its star players. (Rev: BL 7/94; SLJ 8/94) [796.332]

25185 Gibbons, Gail. *My Football Book* (K–2). Illus. 2000, HarperCollins $5.95 (0-688-17139-7). 24pp. Equipment, the playing field, positions, and basic rules are covered in this small-format paperback introduction to football. (Rev: BL 9/15/00; HBG 3/01; SLJ 11/00) [796.332]

25186 Goin, Kenn. *Football for Fun!* (2–4). Illus. Series: Sports for Fun. 2003, Compass Point LB $21.26 (0-7565-0430-9). 48pp. Covering rules, necessary skills, and key figures, this is an attractive introduction for beginning readers. (Rev: SLJ 6/03) [796.332]

25187 Herzog, Brad. *T Is for Touchdown: A Football Alphabet* (3–5). Illus. by Mark Braught. 2004, Sleeping Bear $16.95 (1-58536-233-6). Football facts abound in this informative, alphabetical picture book, written in easy rhymes, that covers history, rules, teams and players, and famous plays. (Rev: SLJ 2/05)

25188 Kennedy, Mike. *Football* (3–5). Series: True Books — Sports. 2002, Children's Book Pr. LB $23.50 (0-516-22336-4); paper $6.95 (0-516-29373-7). 48pp. Large type and a simple text plus plenty of well-captioned color photographs are highlights of this basic introduction to football, its history, rules, and key players. (Rev: BL 1/1–15/03) [796.332]

25189 Kessler, Leonard. *Kick, Pass, and Run* (1–2). Illus. 1996, HarperCollins LB $15.89 (0-06-027105-1); paper $3.95 (0-06-444210-1). 64pp. An easily read reissue of a book that introduces football and its rules. (Rev: BL 11/15/96) [796.332]

25190 Lace, William W. *The Dallas Cowboys Football Team* (5–8). Illus. Series: Sports Greats. 1997, Enslow LB $18.95 (0-89490-791-3). Opening with the Dallas championship in 1973, this book traces the history of the team, with plenty of sports action. (Rev: BL 10/15/97; HBG 3/98) [796.48]

25191 Lace, William W. *The Pittsburgh Steelers Football Team* (4–6). Series: Great Sports Teams. 1999, Enslow LB $18.95 (0-7660-1099-6). 48pp. Using action photos and numerous quotes, this is a history of the Steelers and an account of their most famous moments. (Rev: BL 4/15/98; HBG 10/99) [796.332]

25192 Macnow, Glen. *The Denver Broncos Football Team* (4–6). Series: Great Sports Teams. 2001, Enslow $18.95 (0-7660-1489-4). 48pp. A simple account that gives information on the history of the team, its star players, and most exciting seasons. (Rev: BL 9/15/01; HBG 3/02) [796.332]

25193 Molzahn, Arlene Bourgeois. *The San Francisco 49ers Football Team* (4–6). Series: Great Sports Teams. 2000, Enslow LB $18.95 (0-7660-1280-8). 48pp. As well as giving a history of this great team, this short book describes the team's best players. (Rev: BL 9/15/00; HBG 10/01) [796.48]

25194 O'Shei, Tim. *The Chicago Bears Football Team* (4–6). Series: Great Sports Teams. 2001, Enslow LB $18.95 (0-7660-1285-9). 48pp. The history of the Chicago Bears is given in text and pictures with coverage of key seasons, important

players, and future outlook. (Rev: BL 12/15/01; HBG 3/02) [796.48]

25195 Patey, R. L. *The Illustrated Rules of Football* (3–5). Illus. by Eleanor Hoyt. Series: Illustrated Sports. 1995, Ideals paper $6.95 (1-57102-049-7). 32pp. Introduces football's basic plays and techniques, equipment, and the rules. (Rev: BL 10/15/95; SLJ 1/96) [796.332]

25196 Stewart, Mark. *Football: A History of the Gridiron Game* (4–6). Illus. 1998, Watts LB $32.00 (0-531-11493-7). 144pp. A history of football from rugbylike competitions in England to the big-business sport it is today. (Rev: BL 4/1/99; HBG 10/99) [796.332]

25197 Sullivan, George. *All About Football* (3–5). Illus. 1990, Penguin Putnam paper $9.99 (0-399-21907-2). 128pp. Numerous photos aid in the telling of the game's development, history, complexities, and notable personalities through the years. (Rev: BCCB 12/87; BL 2/1/88)

Gymnastics

25198 Bragg, Linda Wallenberg. *Fundamental Gymnastics* (3–6). Photos by Andy King. Illus. Series: Fundamental Sports. 1995, Lerner LB $22.60 (0-8225-3453-3). 80pp. A brief history of gymnastics is given, including six events for boys and four for girls and basic moves and workouts. (Rev: SLJ 3/96) [796.44]

25199 Ditchfield, Christin. *Gymnastics* (2–4). Illus. Series: True Books. 2000, Children's Book Pr. LB $21.50 (0-516-21063-7); paper $6.95 (0-516-27026-5). 48pp. A simple introduction to gymnastics that describes some of the events, their history, and the equipment. (Rev: BL 9/15/00) [796.44]

25200 Jackman, Joan. *Gymnastics* (3–6). Illus. Series: Superguides. 2000, DK $9.95 (0-7894-5430-0). 44pp. Excellent photos, fact boxes, and a good format are used to introduce gymnastics, with material on history, rules, and basic movements. (Rev: BL 6/1–15/00; HBG 10/00; SLJ 8/00) [796.44]

25201 Kalman, Bobbie, and John Crossingham. *Gymnastics in Action* (4–7). Series: Sports in Action. 2002, Crabtree LB $21.28 (0-7787-0330-4); paper $6.95 (0-7737-0350-9). 32pp. Various branches of gymnastics are introduced in text and pictures with coverage of techniques, equipment, and basic movements. (Rev: BL 1/1–15/03) [796.44]

25202 Kuklin, Susan. *Going to My Gymnastics Class* (4–6). Illus. 1991, Macmillan LB $13.95 (0-02-751236-3). 40pp. The experiences of preschoolers at gymnastics class. (Rev: BCCB 10/91; BL 8/91; SLJ 12/91) [796.44]

25203 Readhead, Lloyd. *Gymnastics* (3–6). Illus. Series: Fantastic Book Of. 1997, Millbrook LB $22.40 (0-7613-0622-6). 32pp. Covers gymnastics techniques, training, warm-up exercises, and equipment, with an eight-page foldout section on competitions. (Rev: BL 3/15/98; HBG 3/98) [796.44]

Horsemanship

25204 *A Basic Guide to Equestrian* (4–8). Illus. 2001, Gareth Stevens LB $22.60 (0-8368-2797-X). 150pp. An informative guide to Olympic equestrian competitions, edited by the U.S. Olympic Committee and including material on choosing and looking after a horse and learning to ride. (Rev: HBG 10/01; SLJ 7/01) [798.2]

25205 Binder, Sibylle Luise, and Gefion Wolf. *Riding for Beginners* (5–10). Trans. from German by Elisabeth E. Reinersmann. 1999, Sterling $21.95 (0-8069-6205-4). 144pp. A straightforward text, beautiful color photographs and illustrations, and an attractive layout present the English and Western styles of riding and give tips for the novice. (Rev: SLJ 8/99) [798.4]

25206 Bolt, Betty. *Jumping* (4–8). Series: Horse Library. 2001, Chelsea $19.75 (0-7910-6657-6). 64pp. Show jumping, eventing, and steeplechase riding are all covered in detail here. Also use *Western Riding*. (Rev: HBG 3/02; SLJ 3/02) [798.4]

25207 Davis, Caroline. *The Young Equestrian* (5–8). Illus. 2000, Firefly $29.95 (1-55209-495-2); paper $19.95 (1-55209-484-7). 128pp. With a generous use of color photographs, this account devotes chapters to riding aids and techniques, choosing schools and proper equipment, buying and caring for a horse, and competitions. (Rev: BL 2/15/01; SLJ 2/01) [798.2]

25208 Haas, Jessie. *Safe Horse, Safe Rider: A Young Rider's Guide to Responsible Horsekeeping* (4–7). Illus. 1994, Storey paper $16.95 (0-88266-700-9). 160pp. This guide to horsemanship stresses safety and covers such topics as understanding horse behavior. (Rev: BL 1/1/95) [636.1]

25209 Kimball, Cheryl. *Horse Showing for Kids* (4–8). Illus. 2004, Storey paper $16.95 (1-58017-501-5). 151pp. A comprehensive guide to showing horses, covering preparations for both horse and rider/handler, plus advice on safety, sportsmanship, and appropriate attire (for animals and humans). (Rev: SLJ 2/05) [798.2]

25210 Kirksmith, Tommie. *Ride Western Style: A Guide for Young Riders* (4–8). Illus. 1991, Howell Book House $16.95 (0-87605-895-0). 212pp. Background information and step-by-step instructions for young people interested in learning to ride Western style. (Rev: BL 4/1/92; SLJ 7/92) [798.2]

25211 Knotts, Bob. *Equestrian Events* (2–4). Illus. Series: True Books. 2000, Children's Book Pr. LB $21.50 (0-516-21062-9); paper $6.95 (0-516-27025-7). 48pp. Various horseback riding events are introduced with material on their history and how they are judged. (Rev: BL 9/15/00) [798.2]

25212 Ransford, Sandy. *First Riding Lessons* (3–7). Illus. 2002, Kingfisher $14.95 (0-7534-5454-8). 64pp. This no-nonsense book takes young horse fans through choosing a riding instructor, learning about different types of mounts, basic lessons and exercises, and a brief view of equine competitions. (Rev: BL 1/1–15/03; HBG 3/03; SLJ 12/02) [798.2]

25213 Shehata, Kat. *Seabiscuit vs. War Admiral: The Greatest Horse Race in History* (2–4). Illus. by Jo McElwee. 2003, Angel Bea $15.95 (0-9717843-1-0). The breathtaking 1938 match race between Seabiscuit and War Admiral springs to life in this richly illustrated book. (Rev: SLJ 10/03) [798.4]

25214 Winter, Ginny L. *The Riding Book* (K–3). Illus. by author. 1963, Astor-Honor $8.95 (0-8392-3031-1). An introductory account for the very young rider.

Ice Hockey

25215 Adelson, Bruce. *Hat Trick Trivia: Secrets, Statistics, and Little-Known Facts About Hockey* (4–7). Illus. 1998, Lerner LB $23.93 (0-8225-3315-5). 64pp. History, statistics, and trivia are combined in this lively discussion of hockey and its players. (Rev: BL 1/1–15/99) [796.962]

25216 Aretha, David. *The Montreal Canadiens Hockey Team* (4–6). Series: Great Sports Teams. 1998, Enslow LB $17.95 (0-7660-1022-8). 48pp. This book contains a history of the team and a rundown of their most valuable players and most exciting seasons. (Rev: BL 5/15/98; HBG 10/98) [796.48]

25217 Ayers, Tom. *The Illustrated Rules of Ice Hockey* (3–5). Illus. by Eleanor Hoyt. Series: Illustrated Sports. 1995, Ideals paper $6.95 (1-57102-048-9). 32pp. This book introduces the dimensions and parts of a hockey rink, the player's equipment, and basic rules of ice hockey. (Rev: BL 10/15/95; SLJ 1/96) [796.962]

25218 Brown, Jonatha A. *Hockey* (1–3). Series: My Favorite Sport. 2005, Weekly Reader LB $19.33 (0-8368-4340-1). 24pp. For beginning readers, this is an introduction to the history and sport of hockey, defining key terms. (Rev: SLJ 5/05)

25219 Carson, Paul, and Sean Rossiter. *Hockey the NHL Way: Tips from the Pros* (4–6). Illus. 2001, Sterling paper $9.95 (1-55054-864-6). 64pp. Excellent photographs accompany advice on skills and sportsmanship for young hockey fans from professional players and coaches. (Rev: BL 2/1/02) [796.962]

25220 Foley, Mike. *Fundamental Hockey* (4–8). Series: Fundamental Sports. 1996, Lerner LB $27.15 (0-8225-3456-8). The basics of ice hockey are introduced, accompanied by a brief history of the sport and an explanation of what the various players do. (Rev: SLJ 3/96) [796.962]

25221 Jensen, Julie, adapt. *Beginning Hockey* (4–8). Photos by Andy King. Series: Beginning Sports. 1996, Lerner LB $27.15 (0-8225-3506-8). 80pp. An introduction to hockey, its history, and the techniques and skills used by the players. (Rev: SLJ 3/96) [796.964]

25222 Kennedy, Mike. *Ice Hockey* (5–7). Series: Watts Library. 2003, Watts LB $24.00 (0-531-12273-5). 64pp. This overview explores the history of the sport, its rules, and styles of play, and provides information on some of the key players. (Rev: SLJ 2/04) [796.962]

25223 McFarlane, Brian. *Real Stories from the Rink* (5–8). Illus. by Steve Nease. 2002, Tundra paper $14.95 (0-88776-604-8). 96pp. Entertaining true stories give insight into ice hockey's history, rules, and players. (Rev: BL 2/15/03; SLJ 4/03) [796.962]

25224 Nicholson, Lorna Shultz. *Roughing* (5–8). 2005, Lorimer paper $5.50 (1-55028-858-X). 108pp. This story set in a hockey camp in Calgary, Alberta, features Josh, a boy with type 1 diabetes; Peter, a native Canadian; and Peter, a bully who plans to teach Peter a lesson. (Rev: BL 5/15/05)

25225 O'Shei, Tim. *The Detroit Red Wings Hockey Team* (4–6). Series: Great Sports Teams. 2000, Enslow LB $18.95 (0-7660-1282-4). 48pp. Profiles the Detroit Red Wings, their history, great moments from the past, and famous players. (Rev: BL 9/15/00; HBG 10/01) [796.962]

25226 Thomas, Keltie. *How Hockey Works* (4–7). Illus. 2002, Maple Tree $19.95 (1-894379-35-7); paper $9.95 (1-894379-36-5). 64pp. A volume focusing on the game of ice hockey that presents everything from important skills and equipment to common superstitions, with an appealing layout. (Rev: BL 9/1/02; SLJ 4/03) [796.962]

25227 Wilson, Stacy. *The Hockey Book for Girls* (4–7). Illus. 2000, Kids Can $12.95 (1-55074-860-2); paper $6.95 (1-55074-719-3). 40pp. This book, by the former captain of Canada's women's Olympic hockey team, introduces ice hockey's rules, positions, strategies, and training and includes interviews with star players. (Rev: BL 3/1/01; HBG 3/01; SLJ 12/00) [796.962]

Ice Skating

25228 Bray-Moffatt, Naia. *Ice Skating School* (K–3). Illus. 2004, DK $12.99 (0-7566-0267-X). 48pp. Young Lilly guides other children through the fundamentals of ice skating and later learns some advanced moves from a more experienced skater in this attractive volume. (Rev: BL 4/1/04; SLJ 7/04) [796.91]

25229 Brimner, Larry. *Speed Skating* (2–4). Illus. Series: True Books. 1997, Children's Book Pr. $22.00 (0-516-20451-3). 48pp. The story of speed skating: its history, equipment, techniques, and place in the Olympic Games. (Rev: BL 1/1–15/98; HBG 3/98; SLJ 2/98) [796.91]

25230 Cranston, Patty. *The Best on Ice: The World's Top Figure Skaters* (2–5). Illus. 1999, Kids Can paper $4.95 (1-55074-581-6). 32pp. This book on figure skating focuses on the careers of three young stars: Michelle Kwan, Todd Eldredge, and Tara Lipinski. (Rev: BL 10/15/99) [796.91]

25231 Helmer, Diana Star, and Thomas S. Owens. *The History of Figure Skating* (2–4). Series: Sports Throughout History. 2000, Rosen LB $17.26 (0-8239-5472-2). 24pp. This book gives a history of figure skating and information on equipment, along with biographical details on famous skaters. (Rev: SLJ 12/00) [796.91]

25232 Macnow, Glen. *The Philadelphia Flyers Hockey Team* (4–6). Series: Great Sports Teams. 2000, Enslow LB $18.95 (0-7660-1279-4). 48pp. With a generous number of color and black-and-white photos, this slim book traces the history of the Philadelphia Flyers, their star players, and their greatest successes. (Rev: BL 3/15/00; HBG 10/00) [796.964]

25233 Wilkes, Debbi. *The Figure Skating Book: A Young Person's Guide to Figure Skating* (4–8). Illus. 2000, Firefly LB $19.95 (1-55209-444-8); paper $12.95 (1-55209-445-6). 128pp. The author, an Olympic silver medalist, gives practical advice on figure skating from buying skates to simple and complicated skating techniques. (Rev: BL 7/00; SLJ 4/00) [796.9]

25234 Winter, Ginny L. *The Skating Book* (K–3). Illus. by author. 1963, Astor-Honor $8.95 (0-8392-3035-4). A beginning account for the young skater.

Indoor Games

25235 Bonner, Lori. *Putting on a Party: Adventure Parties for Kids* (3–6). Illus. by Fran Lee. 2004, Gibbs Smith paper $9.95 (1-58685-232-9). 63pp. Provides creative ideas for invitations, decorations, games and activities, and party foods with adventure themes — a polar expedition and a safari, for example. (Rev: SLJ 7/04) [793.2]

25236 Bruder, Mikyla. *The Star Wars Party Book: Recipes and Ideas for Galactic Occasions* (3–5). Photos by Frankie Frankeny. Illus. 2002, Chronicle $17.95 (0-8118-3491-3). 62pp. Six themed parties are suggested here, with recipes, crafts, games, and other activities. (Rev: SLJ 11/02) [642.4]

25237 Collis, Len. *Card Games for Children* (K–6). Illus. by Terry Carter and Bob George. 1989, Barron's paper $6.95 (0-8120-4290-5). 95pp. A collection of 41 card games with easily followed directions involving different numbers of players. (Rev: SLJ 3/90) [795.4]

25238 Erlbach, Arlene. *Video Games* (4–6). Illus. 1995, Lerner LB $19.93 (0-8225-2389-2). 48pp. An explanation of how video games came to be, how they are constructed, and how they work. (Rev: BL 8/95; SLJ 6/95) [794.8]

25239 Hetzer, Linda. *Rainy Days and Saturdays* (3–6). Illus. 1996, Workman paper $10.95 (1-56305-513-9). 227pp. About 150 activities are outlined on topics like sports, science, and cooking for youngsters confined indoors. (Rev: BL 6/1–15/96; SLJ 7/96) [793]

25240 Jones, Michelle. *The American Girls Party Book* (3–5). Illus. 1998, Pleasant Co. paper $7.95 (1-56247-677-7). 78pp. For each of the six American Girls, three thematic parties are outlined complete with games, crafts, and food recipes. (Rev: BL 1/1–15/99) [793.2]

25241 Kilby, Janice Eaton, and Terry Taylor. *Book of Wizard Parties: In Which the Wizard Shares the Secrets of Creating Enchanted Gatherings* (4–6). Illus. by Marla Baggetta. 2002, Sterling $19.95 (1-

57990-292-8). 144pp. Tips on how to throw the ultimate wizard-themed parties, including crafts, food, and magical motifs. (Rev: BL 8/02; HBG 10/02; SLJ 9/02) [793.2]

25242 Klingel, Cynthia, and Robert B. Noyed. *Card Tricks* (3–5). Series: Games Around the World. 2002, Compass Point LB $21.26 (0-7565-0190-3). 32pp. After background material on playing cards, this illustrated book highlights several baffling card tricks and shows how to perform them. (Rev: BL 5/15/02; SLJ 7/02) [795.4]

25243 Lankford, Mary D. *Dominoes Around the World* (3–5). Illus. 1998, Morrow $16.00 (0-688-14051-3). 40pp. After providing the history of dominoes, the author presents eight versions of the game as played in such places as Malta, Vietnam, and the United States. (Rev: BL 3/15/98; HBG 10/98; SLJ 4/98) [795.3]

25244 Piekart, Ferry. *Playing with Stuff: Outrageous Games with Ordinary Objects* (3–5). Trans. by Lorraine T. Miller. Illus. by Lars Deltrap. 2004, Kane/Miller paper $9.95 (1-929132-62-X). 48pp. In a large-format paperback, Piekart offers innovative ideas for having fun with readily available materials ranging from furniture and umbrellas to bottle caps and ice cubes. (Rev: BL 4/1/04; SLJ 6/04) [793]

Motor Bikes and Motorcycles

25245 Hendrickson, Steve. *Enduro Racing* (3–6). Series: Motorcycles. 2000, Capstone LB $21.26 (0-7368-0477-3). 48pp. A straightforward, heavily illustrated introduction to Enduro motorcycle racing with material on history, equipment, skills, and safety. (Rev: HBG 10/00; SLJ 10/00) [796.7]

25246 Maurer, Tracy Nelson. *ATV Riding* (4–6). Illus. Series: Radsports. 2002, Rourke LB $27.93 (1-58952-276-1). 48pp. A jargon- and action-filled introduction to a "radical" sport, with photographs and Web sites. (Rev: BL 2/15/03) [796.7]

25247 Stuart, Dee. *Motorcycles* (2–4). Series: Transportation and Communication. 2001, Enslow LB $18.95 (0-7660-1648-X). 48pp. Using simple language and many illustrations, this short book describes the history and present developments related to motorcycles and their uses. (Rev: BL 3/15/02; HBG 3/02) [7796.7]

25248 Youngblood, Ed. *Dirt Track Racing* (3–6). Series: Motorcycles. 2000, Capstone LB $21.26 (0-7368-0474-9). 48pp. Dirt track motorcycle racing is introduced, with material on its history, courses, skills required, and safety considerations. Also use *Hillclimbing* (2000). (Rev: HBG 10/00; SLJ 10/00) [796.7]

Olympic Games

25249 Anderson, Dave. *The Story of the Olympics.* Rev. ed. (4–9). 2000, HarperCollins $15.95 (0-688-16734-9). 168pp. This book on the Olympics is divided into two parts: the first gives historical highlights, the second profiles famous personalities and their trials and tribulations. (Rev: HBG 10/00; SLJ 6/00) [796.48]

25250 Brimner, Larry. *The Winter Olympics* (2–4). Illus. Series: True Books. 1997, Children's Book Pr. $22.00 (0-516-20456-4). 48pp. Describes the various sports in the Winter Olympics and gives a general history of the games and their goals and symbols. (Rev: BL 1/1–15/98; HBG 3/98; SLJ 2/98) [796.98]

25251 Fischer, David. *The Encyclopedia of the Summer Olympics* (4–8). Illus. Series: Watts Reference. 2003, Watts LB $36.00 (0-531-11886-X). 160pp. Events from archery to wrestling are organized in alphabetical order, with historical information from the first games to the forthcoming 2004 games, profiles of athletes, lists of gold medal winners, information on rules and equipment, and fast facts. (Rev: SLJ 12/03) [796.4]

25252 Gaff, Jackie. *Ancient Olympics* (3–6). Series: The Olympics. 2003, Heinemann LB $24.22 (1-4034-4676-8). 32pp. A concise look at the Ancient Olympics, with many illustrations and graphics, sidebars, and explanations of what the games involved as far back as 776 b.c. (Rev: SLJ 5/04) [796.48]

25253 Gifford, Clive. *Summer Olympics: The Definitive Guide to the World's Greatest Sports Celebration* (4–8). Illus. 2004, Kingfisher $12.95 (0-7534-5693-1). 80pp. An attractively illustrated overview of the history of the games with information on the individual sports, plus coverage of training, key athletes, important records, and so forth. (Rev: SLJ 8/04) [796.48]

25254 Knotts, Bob. *The Summer Olympics* (2–4). Illus. Series: True Books. 2000, Children's Book Pr. LB $21.50 (0-516-21064-5); paper $6.95 (0-516-27029-X). 48pp. This simple account gives a short history of the Olympic games, a rundown on the events, and an introduction to a few Olympic stars. (Rev: BL 8/00) [796.4809]

25255 Kristy, Davida. *Coubertin's Olympics: How the Games Began* (5–8). 1995, Lerner LB $31.95 (0-8225-3327-8). How the Olympic games began and information about Baron Pierre de Coubertin, their founder. (Rev: BL 8/95; SLJ 11/95) [338.4]

25256 Middleton, Haydn. *Ancient Olympic Games* (3–7). Series: Olympics. 1999, Heinemann LB $22.79 (1-57572-450-2). 32pp. This account describes the first Olympic Games, the nature of the events, and when and where they were held. (Rev: BL 4/15/00; SLJ 1/00) [796.49]

25257 Middleton, Haydn. *Crises at the Olympics* (3–7). Illus. Series: Olympics. 1999, Heinemann LB $22.79 (1-57572-452-9). 32pp. This account describes some of the scandals, controversies, and tragedies that have occurred at the Olympic Games including the 1972 terrorism attack in Munich and the current drug testing of athletes. (Rev: BL 12/15/99; SLJ 1/00) [796.48]

25258 Middleton, Haydn. *Great Olympic Moments* (3–7). Series: Olympics. 1999, Heinemann LB

$22.79 (1-57572-451-0). 32pp. Some of the great Olympic moments in modern times are retold in this exciting book. (Rev: BL 4/15/00) [796.49]

25259 Middleton, Haydn. *Modern Olympic Games* (3–7). Illus. 1999, Heinemann LB $22.79 (1-57572-453-7). 32pp. This account gives a history of the games from 1896 to the present with material on how new events are chosen and how the winter games came into being. (Rev: BL 12/15/99) [796.48]

25260 Middleton, Haydn. *Modern Olympics* (4–8). Series: The Olympics. 2003, Heinemann LB $16.95 (1-4034-4677-6). 32pp. A concise look at the modern games, with many illustrations, graphics, and sidebars, plus discussion of terrorism incidents, drug use, the choice of host cities, and the Paralympics. (Rev: SLJ 5/04) [796.48]

25261 *Olympism: A Basic Guide to the History, Ideals, and Sports of the Olympic Movement* (4–8). Illus. Series: Olympic Guides. 2001, Gareth Stevens LB $22.60 (0-8368-2800-3). 152pp. This is an attractive and authoritative overview of the Olympics' history and of the games' importance, edited by the U.S. Olympic Committee. (Rev: HBG 10/01; SLJ 7/01) [796.48]

25262 Ross, Stewart. *The Original Olympics* (4–7). Illus. Series: Ancient Greece. 2000, Bedrick $18.95 (0-87226-596-X). 48pp. Using a fictional narrative involving a day at the Olympic Games, this attractive book gives details on the types of events, the history of the games, and the roles of athletes in Greek life. (Rev: BL 1/1–15/01; HBG 10/00; SLJ 8/00) [796.48]

25263 Sandelson, Robert. *Ice Sports* (4–8). Illus. Series: Olympic Sports. 1992, Macmillan LB $13.95 (0-89686-667-X). 32pp. Discusses Winter Olympic events including bobsledding and ice hockey. (Rev: SLJ 4/92) [796.91]

25264 Woff, Richard. *The Ancient Greek Olympics* (4–6). Illus. 2000, Oxford $16.95 (0-19-521581-8). 32pp. A thoughtful, interesting account that supplies details on the origins, events, and athletes of the Olympics in ancient Greece. (Rev: BL 1/1–15/00; HBG 10/00; SLJ 5/00) [796.48]

Running and Jogging

25265 Griffis, Molly Levite. *The Great American Bunion Derby* (5–10). 2003, Eakin $15.95 (1-57168-801-3); paper $9.95 (1-57168-810-2). 87pp. The story of a poor part-Cherokee farm boy who joined a marathon run across the United States in the late 1920s and won the $25,000 top prize. (Rev: BL 1/1–15/04; HBG 4/04; SLJ 3/04) [796.42]

25266 Hughes, Morgan. *Track and Field: The Jumps: Instructional Guide to Track and Field* (4–8). Series: Compete Like a Champion. 2001, Rourke LB $27.93 (1-57103-290-8). 48pp. This book includes material on the long jump, the triple jump, the high jump, and the pole vault, along with training tips. Also use in the same series *Track and Field: Middle and Long Distance Runs* and *Track*

and Field: The Sprints (both 2001). (Rev: SLJ 3/01) [796.42]

25267 Manley, Claudia B. *Competitive Track and Field for Girls* (4–7). Illus. Series: Sportsgirl. 2001, Rosen LB $26.50 (0-8239-3408-X). 64pp. An introduction to the rules of track and field competitions, the training necessary, and the special opportunities for girls, with material on nutrition and the dangers of overtraining. (Rev: SLJ 3/02) [796.42]

25268 Savage, Jeff. *Running* (4–6). Illus. Series: Working Out. 1995, Silver Burdett LB $17.95 (0-89686-855-9); paper $7.95 (0-382-24948-8). 48pp. An introduction to running and its benefits, with information on how to begin, safety considerations, and a training schedule. (Rev: SLJ 10/95) [796.4]

Sailing and Boating

25269 Chan, Arlene. *Awakening the Dragon: The Dragon Boat Festival* (3–6). Illus. by Song Nan Zhang. 2004, Tundra $15.95 (0-88776-656-0). 24pp. Bright illustrations accompany this overview of the history and traditions associated with Chinese dragon boat races. (Rev: BL 8/04; SLJ 6/04) [394.2]

25270 Ditchfield, Christin. *Kayaking, Canoeing, Rowing, and Yachting* (2–4). Illus. Series: True Books. 2000, Children's Book Pr. LB $21.50 (0-516-21610-4); paper $6.95 (0-516-27027-3). 48pp. Introduces a range of water sports in a simple text with many color photos. (Rev: BL 9/15/00) [797.1]

25271 Hackler, Lew. *Boating with Cap'n Bob and Matey: An Encyclopedia for Kids of All Ages* (K–3). Illus. by Bobby Basnight. 1989, Seascape $12.95 (0-931595-03-7). 32pp. A guide for the very young on boating, which includes basic terms and useful tips. (Rev: SLJ 10/89) [796.125]

25272 Kalman, Bobbie. *A Canoe Trip* (2–4). Illus. 1995, Crabtree LB $19.96 (0-86505-619-6); paper $5.95 (0-86505-719-2). 32pp. Covers the parts of a canoe, safety considerations, and basic strokes. Also use *Summer Camp* (1994). (Rev: SLJ 7/95) [797.1]

25273 Revell, Phil. *Kayaking* (4–7). Series: Radical Sports. 1999, Heinemann LB $24.22 (1-57572-943-1). 32pp. A history of kayaks and kayaking is followed by material on basic skills, equipment, safety concerns, and competitions. (Rev: SLJ 5/00) [797.1]

25274 Thompson, Luke. *Essential Boating for Teens* (4–10). Series: Outdoor Life. 2000, Children's Book Pr. LB $19.00 (0-516-23352-1); paper $6.95 (0-516-23552-4). 48pp. Topics covered in this introduction to boats and boating include canoes and rowboats, powerboats, sailboats, maneuvering techniques, and safety tips. (Rev: SLJ 3/01) [797]

25275 Wilson, Rich. *Racing a Ghost Ship: The Incredible Journey of Great American II* (3–6). Illus. 1996, Walker LB $17.85 (0-8027-8417-8). 48pp. Photos, maps, and diagrams enliven this account of a voyage from San Francisco around the Cape Horn to Boston in 1993. (Rev: BL 10/1/96; SLJ 11/96) [910.4]

Self-Defense

25276 Atwood, Jane. *Capoeira: A Martial Art and a Cultural Tradition* (5–8). Series: The Library of African American Arts and Culture. 1999, Rosen LB $19.95 (0-8239-1859-9). Capoeira, a unique martial art developed by African slaves in Brazil, is described, along with its history and preparations for its debut in the 2004 Olympic games. (Rev: BR 9–10/99; SLJ 8/99) [796.8]

25277 Casey, Kevin K. *Judo* (4–6). Illus. by Jean Dixon. Series: Illustrated History of Martial Arts. 1994, Rourke LB $14.95 (0-86593-369-3). 32pp. How-to information on judo is given, plus a fascinating history of this martial art. Also use, from the same series, *Kung Fu* and *Tae Kwon Do* (both 1997). (Rev: SLJ 1/95) [796.8]

25278 Knotts, Bob. *Martial Arts* (2–4). Illus. Series: True Books. 2000, Children's Book Pr. LB $21.50 (0-516-21609-0); paper $6.95 (0-516-27028-1). 48pp. This simple sports book with large type and many color photos introduces karate and other martial arts with material on their history and how they are judged. (Rev: BL 9/15/00) [796.8]

25279 Leder, Jane M. *Karate* (3–5). Illus. 1992, Bancroft-Sage LB $14.95 (0-944280-34-X); paper $5.95 (0-944280-39-0). 47pp. Some topics covered are the history of karate, basic stances, kicks and punches, and different kinds of competitions. (Rev: SLJ 10/92) [796.8]

25280 Queen, J. Allen. *Learn Karate* (4–8). 1999, Sterling $17.95 (0-8069-8136-9). An excellent manual that covers the basics of karate — kicks, blocks, and stances — as well as stretches, meditation, safety, equipment, and sparring. (Rev: SLJ 5/99) [796.8]

25281 Rielly, Robin L. *Karate for Kids* (5–8). Illus. Series: The Martial Arts for Kids. 2004, Tuttle paper $11.95 (0-8048-3534-9). 48pp. After an overview of the history of karate, this appealing volume with clear illustrations looks at the moves, rules and etiquette, uniform and belts, and so forth. (Rev: BL 9/1/04; SLJ 2/05) [796.815]

25282 Scandiffio, Laura. *The Martial Arts Book* (3–5). Illus. by Nicolas Debon. 2003, Firefly $24.95 (1-55037-777-9); paper $9.95 (1-55037-776-0). 64pp. The focus of this overview is the origins and evolution of various martial arts, looking at the spiritual aspects and overall benefits. (Rev: BL 4/15/03) [796.8]

25283 Yates, Keith D., and Bryan Robbins. *Tae Kwon Do for Kids* (4–8). 1999, Sterling paper $5.95 (0-8069-1761-X). A step-by-step manual that introduces and describes Tae Kwon Do, a Korean form of self-defense, with material on stances, blocks, exercises, and important pressure points. (Rev: SLJ 6/99) [796.8]

Skateboarding

25284 Burke, L. M. *Skateboarding! Surf the Pavement* (5–8). Series: Extreme Sports. 1999, Rosen LB $26.50 (0-8239-3014-9). 64pp. This book supplies information for beginning and advanced skateboarders with coverage of history, techniques, equipment, and safety considerations. (Rev: SLJ 4/00) [796]

25285 Crossingham, John. *Skateboarding in Action* (4–7). Series: Sports in Action. 2002, Crabtree LB $21.28 (0-7787-0117-4); paper $5.95 (0-7787-0123-9). 32pp. A well-illustrated introduction to skateboarding with good material on equipment and injury prevention. (Rev: BL 9/1/02; SLJ 11/02) [795.2]

25286 Dieterich, Alice. *Tony Hawk and Andy MacDonald Ride* (2–3). Series: All Aboard Science Reader Station Stop. 2003, Penguin Putnam $13.89 (0-448-43231-5); paper $3.99 (0-448-43160-2). 48pp. Skateboarding stars Tony Hawk and Andy MacDonald share some of their boarding experiences with readers. (Rev: BL 10/15/03; HBG 4/04; SLJ 1/04)

25287 Freimuth, Jeri. *Extreme Skateboarding Moves* (4–7). Illus. Series: Behind the Moves. 2001, Capstone LB $21.26 (0-7368-0783-7). 32pp. Skateboard slang is just one appealing part of this account of proper equipment and technique, with safety tips and some tricks. (Rev: BL 6/1–15/01; HBG 10/01; SLJ 9/01) [796.22]

25288 Horsley, Andy. *Skateboarding* (4–7). Illus. Series: To the Limit. 2001, Raintree LB $25.69 (0-7398-3163-1). 32pp. A brief history of skateboarding is included here along with material on equipment, moves, and some advice on turning pro. (Rev: BL 6/1–15/01) [796.22]

25289 Loizos, Constance. *Skateboard! Your Guide to Street, Vert, Downhill, and More* (4–9). Illus. Series: Extreme Sports. 2002, National Geographic paper $8.95 (0-7922-8229-9). 64pp. An attractive guide to skateboarding equipment, technique, rules, etiquette, jargon, and safety. (Rev: SLJ 1/03) [796.22]

25290 Maurer, Tracy Nelson. *Skateboarding* (3–6). Series: Radsports. 2001, Rourke LB $27.93 (1-58952-104-8). 48pp. Safety is emphasized in this account of skateboarding's history, equipment, and techniques that includes "Pro Spotlights." (Rev: SLJ 5/02) [796.22]

25291 Powell, Ben. *Skateboarding* (4–8). Illus. Series: Flowmotion. 2003, Sterling paper $9.95 (0-8069-9374-X). 96pp. Clear instructions accompanied by photographs explain techniques and moves, with safety tips and a glossary. (Rev: BL 10/15/03) [796.2]

25292 Werner, Doug. *Skateboarder's Start-Up: A Beginner's Guide to Skateboarding* (4–8). 2000, Tracks paper $11.95 (1-884654-13-4). 144pp. Using a question-and-answer format, this introduction to skateboarding covers such subjects as equipment, history, and basic skating and technical tricks. (Rev: SLJ 12/00) [795.2]

Snowboarding

25293 Barr, Matt, and Chris Moran. *Snowboarding* (4–8). Illus. Series: Extreme Sports. 2003, Lerner LB $22.60 (0-8225-1242-4). 32pp. An appealing introduction to the history, equipment, techniques, safety concerns, and stars of this increasingly popular sport. (Rev: BL 3/1/04; HBG 4/04; SLJ 5/04) [790.9]

25294 Brimner, Larry. *Snowboarding* (4–6). Illus. Series: First Books. 1997, Watts LB $22.50 (0-531-20313-1). 64pp. Introduces the sport of snowboarding, its equipment, clothing, rules, techniques, and competitions. (Rev: BL 11/1/97; HBG 3/98; SLJ 2/98) [796.9]

25295 Brown, Gillian C. P. *Snowboarding* (5–8). Illus. Series: X-treme Outdoors. 2003, Children's Book Pr. LB $20.00 (0-516-24322-5); paper $6.95 (0-516-24383-7). 48pp. Equipment, technique, competition, and safety are covered here, as well as a history of this sport. (Rev: BL 4/15/03; SLJ 10/03) [796.9]

25296 Crossingham, John. *Snowboarding in Action* (4–7). Illus. by Bonna Rouse. Series: Sports in Action. 2002, Crabtree LB $21.28 (0-7787-0119-0); paper $5.95 (0-7787-0125-5). 32pp. Aspiring snowboarders will find much of interest here, including basic techniques. (Rev: BL 9/1/02; SLJ 11/02) [796.9]

25297 Fraser, Andy. *Snowboarding* (4–7). Series: Radical Sports. 1999, Heinemann LB $24.22 (1-57572-946-6). 32pp. This book covers the history of snowboarding, the equipment and clothing needed, techniques, terms, and how to get started. (Rev: SLJ 4/00) [796.9]

25298 Haycock, Kate. *Skiing* (4–8). Illus. Series: Olympic Sports. 1992, Macmillan LB $13.95 (0-89686-669-6). 32pp. The Winter Olympic events in skiing are discussed. (Rev: SLJ 4/92) [796.93]

25299 Hayhurst, Chris. *Snowboarding! Shred the Powder* (5–8). Series: Extreme Sports. 1999, Rosen LB $26.50 (0-8239-3010-6). 64pp. The book supplies both beginning and advanced information on this sport, including material on history, equipment, techniques, and safety considerations. (Rev: SLJ 4/00) [796.9]

25300 Herran, Joe, and Ron Thomas. *Snowboarding* (5–8). Illus. Series: Action Sports. 2003, Chelsea LB $18.95 (0-7910-7003-4). 32pp. Basic information on this sport's gear and performance is accompanied by biographical details about snowboarding champions. (Rev: BL 4/15/03; HBG 10/03) [796.9]

25301 Jensen, Julie, adapt. *Beginning Snowboarding* (4–8). Series: Beginning Sports. 1996, Lerner LB $27.15 (0-8225-3507-6). An introduction to snowboarding, with material on equipment, basic maneuvers, types of competition, and advanced stunts. (Rev: SLJ 3/96) [796.9]

25302 Lurie, John. *Fundamental Snowboarding* (4–8). Series: Fundamental Sports. 1996, Lerner LB $27.15 (0-8225-3457-6). With eye-catching photographs, the equipment and principles of snowboard-ing are covered, with material on basic and advanced maneuvers, skills, and stunts. (Rev: SLJ 3/96) [796.9]

Soccer

25303 Bizley, Kirk. *Soccer* (K–2). Series: You Can Do It! 1999, Heinemann LB $13.95 (1-57572-962-8). 24pp. Colorful photos and cartoons are used to cover basic topics about soccer: warm-up exercises, moves, playing areas, rules, and safety. (Rev: SLJ 1/00) [796.334]

25304 Blackall, Bernie. *Soccer* (4–8). Illus. by Vasja Koman. Series: Top Sport. 1999, Heinemann LB $21.36 (1-57572-840-0). 32pp. This introduction to soccer covers history, equipment, rules, skills, and a few male and female stars. (Rev: SLJ 12/99) [796.334]

25305 Blackstone, Margaret. *This Is Soccer* (PS–1). Illus. by John O'Brien. 1999, Holt $15.95 (0-8050-2801-3). 32pp. Using numerous illustrations, this book explains the game of soccer including equipment and moves. (Rev: BCCB 4/99; BL 4/15/99; HBG 10/99; SLJ 5/99) [796.334]

25306 Brown, Jonatha A. *Soccer* (1–3). Series: My Favorite Sport. 2005, Weekly Reader LB $19.33 (0-8368-4341-X). 24pp. For beginning readers, this is an introduction to the history and sport of soccer, defining key terms. (Rev: SLJ 5/05)

25307 Burleigh, Robert. *Goal* (K–3). Illus. by Stephen T. Johnson. 2001, Harcourt $16.00 (0-15-201789-5). 32pp. A picture book that explains, in a poetic manner, the important aspects of soccer. (Rev: BL 4/15/01; HBG 10/01; SLJ 4/01)

25308 Coleman, Lori. *Soccer* (5–9). Series: Play-by-Play. 2000, Lerner paper $7.95 (0-8225-9876-0). 64pp. A fine introduction to the rules, equipment, and tactics of soccer with historical coverage through 1999. (Rev: SLJ 9/00) [796.334]

25309 Fischer, George. *The Illustrated Laws of Soccer* (3–5). Illus. 1994, Ideals paper $6.95 (1-57102-020-9). 32pp. The history, equipment, field, and rules of soccer are given. (Rev: BL 9/15/94; SLJ 11/94) [796.334]

25310 Gibbons, Gail. *My Soccer Book* (PS–3). Illus. 2000, HarperCollins $5.95 (0-688-17138-9). This accessible guide describes the playing field, equipment, rules, and the method of scoring. (Rev: BCCB 4/00; BL 5/1/00; HBG 10/00; SLJ 6/00) [796.334]

25311 Gifford, Clive. *Soccer: The Ultimate Guide to the Beautiful Game* (5–8). Illus. 2002, Kingfisher $18.95 (0-7534-5416-5). 96pp. An attractive and comprehensive guide that covers history, rules, and tactics, with an emphasis on European teams and players. (Rev: BL 7/02; SLJ 7/02) [796.334]

25312 Goin, Kenn. *Soccer for Fun!* (2–4). Illus. Series: Sports for Fun. 2003, Compass Point LB $21.26 (0-7565-0431-7). 48pp. Covering rules, necessary skills, and key figures, this is an attractive introduction for beginning readers. (Rev: SLJ 6/03) [796.334]

25313 Helmer, Diana Star, and Thomas S. Owens. *The History of Soccer* (2–4). Series: Sports Throughout History. 2000, Rosen LB $17.26 (0-8239-5467-6). 24pp. In addition to a history of soccer, this book profiles some championship players. (Rev: SLJ 12/00) [796.334]

25314 Howard, Dale E. *Soccer Stars* (3–6). Illus. 1994, Children's Book Pr. LB $22.00 (0-516-08047-4). 48pp. As well as introducing key U.S. players, this account includes a glossary of soccer terms. (Rev: BL 9/1/94) [796.334]

25315 Kennedy, Mike. *Soccer* (3–5). Series: True Books — Sports. 2002, Children's Book Pr. LB $23.50 (0-516-22337-2); paper $6.95 (0-516-29374-5). 48pp. In addition to a short history of soccer, this account describes the different positions, moves, competitions, and famous players. (Rev: BL 1/1–15/03) [796.334]

25316 Klingel, Cynthia, and Robert B. Noyed. *Soccer* (K–2). Series: Wonder Books. 2000, Child's World LB $21.36 (1-56766-805-4). 24pp. A beginning reader that gives basic information about soccer, the main activities, equipment, and uniforms. (Rev: SLJ 3/01) [796.334]

25317 Lineker, Gary. *Soccer* (3–8). Series: Superguides. 2000, DK $9.95 (0-7894-5425-4). 44pp. Bright clear photographs and a straightforward text explain the fundamentals of soccer and give sound advice on improving one's game. (Rev: BL 6/1–15/00; HBG 10/00; SLJ 8/00) [796.334]

25318 Mackin, Bob. *Soccer the Winning Way: Play Like the Pros* (4–7). Illus. 2002, Douglas & McIntyre paper $10.95 (1-55054-825-5). 62pp. A guide to mastering crucial soccer skills, with photographs and words of wisdom from the pros. (Rev: BL 5/15/02) [796]

25319 Otten, Jack. *Soccer* (1–6). Series: Sports Training. 2002, Rosen LB $16.00 (0-8239-5972-4). 24pp. A brief and basic introduction to the sport that will be useful for reluctant readers and ESL students. (Rev: SLJ 3/02) [796.334]

25320 Owens, Thomas S., and Diana Star Helmer. *Soccer* (5–8). Series: Game Plan. 2000, Twenty-First Century LB $26.90 (0-7613-1400-8). 64pp. This introduction to soccer covers the different positions, game strategy, and memorable games and players of the past. (Rev: HBG 10/00; SLJ 7/00) [796.334]

25321 Page, Jason. *Soccer: Learn How to Be a Star Player* (3–5). Illus. by Mel Pickering. Series: Sports Club. 2000, Two-Can $9.95 (1-58728-001-9). 32pp. Soccer rules are explained along with some important plays and techniques, a little history, and profiles of important players. (Rev: SLJ 3/01) [796.334]

25322 Scott, Nina S. *The Thinking Kids Guide to Successful Soccer* (5–8). 1998, Millbrook LB $21.90 (0-7613-0324-3). An insider's look at strategies for kids playing soccer, including topics not frequently addressed such as dealing with inexperienced coaches, unfair calls from referees, not getting enough playing time, and pressures of competition. The author encourages kids to have a good

time and not to worry about making mistakes. (Rev: BL 5/15/99; HBG 9/99; SLJ 4/99) [796..334]

25323 Sherman, Josepha. *Competitive Soccer for Girls* (4–7). Series: Sportsgirl. 2001, Rosen LB $26.50 (0-8239-3405-5). 64pp. An introduction to the rules of soccer, the training necessary, and the special opportunities for girls, with material on nutrition and the dangers of overtraining. (Rev: SLJ 3/02) [796.334]

25324 Stewart, Mark. *The World Cup* (5–10). Series: The Watts History of Sports. 2003, Watts LB $33.50 (0-531-11957-2). 96pp. An overview of the international soccer championship that takes place every four years, this volume, which will be useful for reports, starts with the 1930 games and includes information on teams and players. (Rev: SLJ 3/04) [796.3]

25325 Suen, Anastasia. *The Story of Soccer* (1–3). Illus. Series: Sports History. 2002, Rosen LB $16.00 (0-8239-5998-8). 24pp. A basic, easy-to-read introduction to the sport. (Rev: BL 5/15/02; SLJ 3/02) [796.334]

25326 Venturini, Tisha Lea, and Judith Cohen. *You Can Be a Woman Soccer Player* (2–5). Illus. 2000, Cascade Pass $13.95 (1-880599-49-X); paper $7.00 (1-880599-48-1). 40pp. This is basically a biography of Venturini, a World Cup soccer player, plus tips on how to play the game and a brief history of the sport. (Rev: BL 10/1/00) [796.334]

25327 Wukovits, John. *The Composite Guide to Soccer* (4–8). 1998, Chelsea LB $18.65 (0-7910-4718-0). A basic guide to the history, rules, positions, and playing techniques of this sport, with material on its European popularity. (Rev: HBG 3/99; SLJ 12/98) [796.334]

Surfing

25328 Barker, Amanda. *Windsurfing* (4–7). Series: Radical Sports. 1999, Heinemann LB $24.22 (1-57572-948-2). 32pp. After a history of windsurfing, this book describes equipment, safety tips, and basic skills. (Rev: SLJ 5/00) [797.2]

25329 Chapman, Garry. *Surf* (3–5). Series: Extreme Sports. 2001, Chelsea LB $16.95 (0-7910-6611-8). 32pp. This book covers the history of surfing, safety in the surf, and the extreme sports that began as spin-offs of traditional surfing. (Rev: BL 10/15/01; HBG 3/02; SLJ 12/01) [797.2]

25330 Crossingham, John, and Niki Walker. *Swimming in Action* (4–7). Series: Sports in Action. 2002, Crabtree LB $21.28 (0-7787-0331-2); paper $6.95 (0-7737-0351-7). 32pp. Color photographs and many diagrams are used with a clear text to describe swimming basics, with tips on various strokes and safety. (Rev: BL 1/1–15/03; SLJ 10/03) [977.2]

25331 Maurer, Tracy Nelson. *Surfing* (4–6). Illus. Series: Radsports. 2002, Rourke LB $27.93 (1-58952-280-X). 48pp. A jargon- and action-filled introduction to a "radical" sport, with photographs and Web sites. (Rev: BL 2/15/03) [797.3]

25332 Vander Hook, Sue. *Scuba Diving* (4–7). Illus. Series: World of Sports. 2000, Smart Apple LB $16.95 (1-887068-59-7). 32pp. After a section on star scuba divers, this account describes the origins and evolution of the sport, its equipment, hazards, and techniques. (Rev: BL 9/15/00) [797.2]

25333 Voeller, Edward. *Extreme Surfing* (5–8). Series: Surfing. 2000, Capstone LB $21.26 (0-7368-0485-4). 48pp. An introduction to surfing that contains material on equipment, history, skills, safety considerations, and competitions. (Rev: HBG 10/00; SLJ 8/00) [797]

Swimming and Diving

25334 Bizley, Kirk. *Swimming* (K–2). Series: You Can Do It! 1999, Heinemann LB $13.95 (1-57572-963-6). 24pp. A beginners guide to swimming with material on topics including water wings, basic strokes, and safety rules. (Rev: SLJ 1/00) [797.2]

25335 Ditchfield, Christin. *Swimming and Diving* (2–4). Illus. Series: True Books. 2000, Children's Book Pr. LB $21.50 (0-516-21065-3); paper $6.95 (0-516-27030-3). 48pp. Large print and an informative text cover the sport of swimming, with material on the history of the sport, different strokes and dives, competitions, and famous swimmers. (Rev: BL 8/00) [797.2]

25336 Peterson, Sue H. *Swim with Me: A New Fun Approach to Learning to Swim* (PS–2). Illus. by Rama Von Baringer. 1999, Tricycle $12.95 (1-883672-94-5). 20pp. This book is intended for parents who are trying to prepare their children for swimming by showing how to teach floating, jumping in, gliding, proper breathing, and how to feel at home in the water. (Rev: SLJ 9/99) [797.2]

Tennis

25337 Blackall, Bernie. *Tennis* (4–8). Illus. by Vasja Koman. Series: Top Sport. 1999, Heinemann $21.36 (1-57572-842-7). 32pp. Double-page spreads present topics including the history of tennis, its equipment and rules, and important skills, plus a rundown on famous stars of the sport. (Rev: SLJ 12/99) [796.342]

25338 Crossingham, John. *Tennis in Action* (4–7). Series: Sports in Action. 2002, Crabtree LB $21.28 (0-7787-0116-6); paper $5.95 (0-7787-0122-0). 32pp. A fine introduction to tennis told through a concise text with easy-to-follow descriptions and material on equipment, rules, and techniques. (Rev: BL 9/1/02; SLJ 11/02) [796.342]

25339 Ditchfield, Christin. *Tennis* (1–3). Series: A True Book. 2003, Children's Pr. LB $23.50 (0-516-22589-8); paper $6.95 (0-516-26960-7). 48pp. Rules, scoring, and other basics of the game are outlined in simple text and photographs, plus profiles of some of the key players. (Rev: SLJ 6/03) [796.342]

25340 Gilbert, Nancy. *Wimbledon* (4–6). Illus. Series: Great Moments in Sports. 1991, Creative Ed. LB $21.30 (0-88682-319-6). 32pp. This brief history of the famous tennis tournament in England highlights some of the major players. (Rev: BL 1/1/92) [796.342]

25341 Kaiman, Bobbie, and Sarah Dann. *Badminton in Action* (4–7). Series: Sports in Action. 2003, Crabtree LB $15.96 (0-7787-0334-7); paper $6.26 (0-7787-0354-1). 32pp. This basic introduction to badminton includes material on racquets, courts, rules, and strategies. (Rev: BL 11/15/03) [796.34]

25342 Muskat, Carrie. *The Composite Guide to Tennis* (5–7). Series: Composite Guide. 1998, Chelsea LB $18.65 (0-7910-4728-8). 64pp. Past and present tennis stars are mentioned along with a general introduction to the game. (Rev: HBG 10/98; SLJ 9/98) [796.342]

25343 Rutledge, Rachel. *The Best of the Best in Tennis* (4–7). Illus. 1998, Millbrook LB $24.90 (0-7613-1303-6). 64pp. Using a lively text and many color photographs, this work gives a history of women in tennis and a rundown of today's most important female players. (Rev: BL 2/15/99; HBG 10/99; SLJ 3/99) [796.342]

25344 Tym, Wanda. *The Illustrated Rules of Tennis* (3–5). Illus. Series: Illustrated Sports. 1995, Ideals paper $6.95 (1-57102-016-0). 32pp. Such topics as equipment, the tennis court, scoring, and the rules are covered in this introduction to tennis. (Rev: BL 7/95; SLJ 6/95) [796.342]

Track and Field

25345 Crossingham, John, and Bobbie Kalman. *Track Events in Action* (3–5). Illus. by Bonna Rouse. Series: Sports in Action. 2004, Crabtree LB $16.95 (0-7787-0339-8); paper $6.26 (0-7787-0339-2). 32pp. For beginning sprinters, steeplechasers, and other track enthusiasts, this is an attractive and useful introduction to equipment, technique, and vocabulary. (Rev: SLJ 6/05) [796.42]

25346 Kalman, Bobbie. *Field Events in Action* (3–5). Illus. Series: Sports in Action. 2004, Crabtree LB $16.95 (0-7787-0340-1); paper $6.26 (0-7787-0360-6). 32pp. For beginning enthusiasts of high and long jumps, pole vault, javelin throwing, and other field events, this is an attractive and useful introduction to equipment, technique, and vocabulary. (Rev: SLJ 6/05) [796.42]

25347 Knotts, Bob. *Track and Field* (2–4). Illus. Series: True Books. 2000, Children's Book Pr. LB $21.50 (0-516-21066-1); paper $6.95 (0-516-27031-1). 48pp. Various track and field events are introduced in a simple text with material on their history and how they are judged. (Rev: BL 9/15/00) [796.42]

Author and Illustrator Index

Authors and illustrators are arranged alphabetically by last name, followed by book titles — which are also arranged alphabetically — and the text entry number. Book titles may refer to those that appear as a main entry or as an internal entry mentioned in the annotation. Fiction titles are indicated by (F) following the entry number.

Barringer, William. *Gregory and Alexander*, 1741(F)
Barron, Rex. *The Big Bug Ball*, 2416(F)
Showdown at the Food Pyramid, 3132(F)
Barron, T. A. *The Hero's Trail*, 19663
Tree Girl, 8015(F)
Where Is Grandpa? 5066(F)
Barroux. *Where's Mary's Hat?* 1742(F)
Barrow, Ann. *Big Blue*, 5391(F)
The Final Cut, 10543(F)
Full Court Fever, 10544(F)
Ghost Horse, 6904(F)
On the Line, 10545(F)
Barrow, Lloyd H. *Science Fair Projects Investigating Earthworms*, 20961
Barry, Frances. *Duckie's Ducklings*, 391(F)
Duckie's Rainbow, 277
Barry, Robert. *Mr. Willowby's Christmas Tree*, 5974(F)
Barsotti, Monica. *Why Are You Calling Me a Barbarian?* 15922
Bartek, Mary. *Funerals and Fly Fishing*, 8891(F)
Bartels, Alice L. *The Grandmother Doll*, 969(F)
Barter, James. *The Amazon*, 17197
The Nile, 16139
Renaissance Florence, 15972
A Renaissance Painter's Studio, 15012
Space Stations, 23645
The Yangtze, 16336
Barth, Linda. *Mohammed Reza Pahlavi*, 14859
Bartholomew, Alan. *Electric Mischief*, 23590
Bartholomew, Lois Thompson. *The White Dove*, 7111(F)
Bartlett, Alison. *Charlie's Checklist*, 2391(F)
Cock-a-Moo-Moo, 1964(F)
Oliver's Fruit Salad, 3765(F)
Oliver's Milk Shake, 4306(F)
Oliver's Vegetables, 4307(F)
Over in the Grasslands, 602(F)
Paddiwak and Cozy, 5351(F)
A Story for Hippo, 2661(F)
T. Rex, 15535
Ten Bright Eyes, 207(F)
Bartlett, Anne. *The Aboriginal Peoples of Australia*, 16557
Bartlett, Paula. *Chessie, the Travelin' Man*, 5434(F)
Bartlett, Susan. *Seal Island School*, 10323(F)
The Seal Island Seven, 7112(F)
Bartoletti, Susan C. *Growing Up in Coal Country*, 18122
Kids on Strike! 18123
Bartoletti, Susan Campbell. *A Coal Miner's Bride*, 9815(F)
The Flag Maker, 9516(F)
The Journal of Finn Reardon, a Newsie, 9816(F)
Nobody's Diggier Than a Dog, 5274(F)
Nobody's Nosier Than a Cat, 5275(F)
Barton, Byron. *Airplanes*, 23779
Airport, 5794(F)
Boats, 24145
Bones, Bones, Dinosaur Bones, 5276(F)
Building a House, 3133(F)
Dinosaurs, Dinosaurs, 15493
Gila Monsters Meet You at the Airport, 4467(F)
A Girl Called Al, 6997(F)
Good Morning, Chick, 11293
I Want to Be an Astronaut, 7113(F)

The Little Red Hen, 11161
Machines at Work, 24004
My Car, 5795(F)
The Paper Airplane Book, 24720
Roman Numerals, 23315
The Three Bears, 11162
Trains, 24116
Trucks, 24058
Wee Little Woman, 4232(F)
Barton, Harriett. *Books and Libraries*, 15081
Barton, Jill. *Clever Lollipop*, 8338(F)
Guess Who, Baby Duck! 2222(F)
It's Quacking Time! 5635(F)
Make the Team, Baby Duck! 2223(F)
Rattletrap Car, 4446(F)
Barton-Wood, Sara. *Bill Gates*, 14148
Queen Elizabeth II, 14789
Bartone, Elisa. *American Too*, 3134(F)
Peppe the Lamplighter, 4724(F)
Bartram, Simon. *Man on the Moon*, 4233(F)
Barwin, Gary. *The Magic Mustache*, 970(F)
Barwin, Steven. *Slam Dunk*, 10538(F)
Bascle, Brian. *The Adventures of Marco Polo*, 12444
Base, Graeme. *The Discovery of Dragons*, 10098(F)
The Eleventh Hour, 7114(F)
Jabberwocky, 12111
Jungle Drums, 1743(F)
Lewis Carroll's Jabberwocky, 12107
The Sign of the Seahorse, 971(F)
TruckDogs, 8016(F)
The Water Hole, 5277(F)
Bash, Barbara. *Desert Giant*, 22841
Dig, Wait, Listen, 5592(F)
Urban Roosts, 21767
What's Up, What's Down? 255
Baskin, Leonard. *Alberic the Wise*, 9332(F)
Ten Times Better, 513(F)
Baskin, Nora Raleigh. *Almost Home*, 9123(F)
Baskin-Salzberg, Anita. *Turtles*, 21160
Baskwill, Jane. *Somewhere*, 4523(F)
Basman, Michael. *Chess for Kids*, 25172
Basnight, Bobby. *Boating with Cap'n Bob and Matey*, 25271
Bass, Jules. *Herb, the Vegetarian Dragon*, 1744(F)
Bassede, Francine. *A Day with the Bellyflops*, 1745(F)
George's Store at the Shore, 392(F)
Bassett, Jeni. *The Biggest Pumpkin Ever*, 6220(F)
It's Groundhog Day! 5885(F)
Bassis, Volodymyr. *Ukraine*, 16802, 16803
Basso, Bill. *Night of the Living Gerbil*, 7837(F)
Bastedo, Jamie. *Tracking Triple Seven*, 7445(F)
Bastian, Lois Brunner. *Chipmunk Family*, 21646
Bastyra, J. *Look and Make Cooking*, 24582
Bastyra, Judy. *Fun Food*, 24583
Batchelor, Mary, ed. *Children's Prayers*, 19068
Bate, Lucy. *Little Rabbit's Loose Tooth*, 1746(F)
Bateman, Colin. *Running with the Reservoir Pups*, 8017(F)
Bateman, Noel. *Egyptian Stories*, 10918
Bateman, Teresa. *The Bully Blockers Club*, 5670(F)

Farm Flu, 972(F)
Fluffy, 1747(F)
Hamster Camp, 5067(F)
Harp O' Gold, 973(F)
Hunting the Daddyosaurus, 1748(F)
Leprechaun Gold, 974(F)
The Merbaby, 975(F)
A Plump and Perky Turkey, 6338(F)
The Princesses Have a Ball, 11121
Red, White, Blue and Uncle Who? 15102
The Ring of Truth, 10099(F)
Bates, Amy June. *The Next-Door Dogs*, 9061(F)
Bates, Cynthia. *Shooting Star*, 10539(F)
Bates, George. *Chicken Bedtime Is Really Early*, 762(F)
Bates, Ivan. *All By Myself*, 1749(F)
Big Truck and Little Truck, 1037(F)
Coconut Comes to School, 3216(F)
Do Like a Duck Does! 2231(F)
Grandma Elephant's in Charge, 21589
One Dark Night, 2958(F)
Bates, Katharine Lee. *America the Beautiful*, 15336, 15337
Bates, Matthew. *What Is Martin Luther King, Jr. Day?* 5860
Bateson-Hill, Margaret. *Chanda and the Mirror of Moonlight*, 11025
Lao Lao of Dragon Mountain, 976(F)
Shota and the Star Quilt, 3135(F)
Batt, Tanya. *The Fabrics of Fairytale*, 10773
The Princess and the White Bear King, 10643
Batt, Tanya Robyn. *A Child's Book of Faeries*, 10774
The Faerie's Gift, 10644
Batten, John D. *Celtic Fairy Tales*, 11206
English Fairy Tales, 11207
Indian Fairy Tales, 11034
Batten, Mary. *Aliens from Earth*, 20922
Anthropologist, 15623
Hey, Daddy! Animal Fathers and Their Babies, 21264
Who Has a Belly Button? 20273
The Winking, Blinking Sea, 22139
Battle-Lavert, Gwendolyn. *The Music in Derrick's Heart*, 3641(F)
Off to School, 5068(F)
Bauer, Brandy. *Brazil*, 17198
Iran, 16971
Bauer, Caroline Feller, ed. *Halloween*, 10041(F)
Rainy Day, 11693(F)
Bauer, Joan. *Stand Tall*, 7691(F)
Bauer, Louisa. *The Glass Mountain*, 11157
Bauer, Marion. *Clouds*, 4524
Bauer, Marion Dane. *Bear's Hiccups*, 6407(F)
Christmas in the Forest, 5975(F)
The Double-Digit Club, 10324(F)
An Early Winter, 9124(F)
Frog's Best Friend, 1750(F)
Ghost Eye, 8018(F)
If Frogs Made Weather, 11694(F)
If You Had a Nose Like an Elephant's Trunk, 977(F)
Land of the Buffalo Bones, 9630(F)
Love Song for a Baby, 11695(F)
My Mother Is Mine, 5861(F)
On My Honor, 6961(F)
Runt, 7446(F)
Snow, 23425
Toes, Ears, and Nose! 158(F)
Touch the Moon, 8019(F)
Turtle Dreams, 6408(F)

Carter, Noelle (jt. author). *The Nutcracker*, 11122
Carter, Ron. *The Youngest Drover*, 18129
Carter, Tamsin. *Handmade Cards*, 24490
Carter, Terry. *Card Games for Children*, 25237
Carter, Vince. *Vince Carter*, 14466
Cartlidge, Cherese. *Iran*, 16973
Cartlidge, Michelle. *Brave, Brave Mouse*, 2543(F)
Cartwright, Reg. *At the Edge of the Woods*, 421(F)
The Lot at the End of My Block, 5831(F)
The Three Golden Oranges, 11341
Cartwright, Shannon. *Alaska's Three Bears*, 5390(F)
Moose Racks, Bear Tracks, and Other Alaska Kidsnacks, 24588
Storm Run, 14687
Cartwright, Stephen. *Ted in a Red Bed*, 6496(F)
The Usborne Children's Songbook, 15345
Carus, Marianne, ed. *Fire and Wings*, 10516(F)
That's Ghosts for You, 8069(F)
Caruso, Sandra. *The Young Actor's Book of Improvisation*, 15422
Carwardine, Mark. *Killer Whale*, 22337
Cary, Alice. *Jean Craighead George*, 12996
Katherine Paterson, 13046
Casad, Mary Brooke. *Bluebonnet at the Marshall Train Depot*, 1902(F)
Casale, Paul. *Danger*, 7130(F)
Return of the Home Run Kid, 10565(F)
Surviving Jamestown, 9488(F)
Winners Take All, 10548(F)
Casanellas, Antonio. *Great Discoveries and Inventions That Advanced Industry and Technology*, 23725
Great Discoveries and Inventions That Helped Explore Earth and Space, 23659
Great Discoveries and Inventions That Improved Human Health, 20225
Casanova, Mary. *Cecile*, 9308(F)
Curse of a Winter Moon, 9309(F)
The Hunter, 10988
Moose Tracks, 7132(F)
One-Dog Canoe, 1903(F)
Caseley, Judith. *Bully*, 5684(F)
Field Day Friday, 5685(F)
On the Town, 3173(F)
Praying to A. L., 8911(F)
Priscilla Twice, 5088(F)
Sisters, 3696(F)
Witch Mama, 6193(F)
Caselli, Giovanni. *Greek Myths*, 11658
An Ice Age Hunter, 9221(F)
In Search of Knossos, 15651
In Search of Troy, 15652
In Search of Tutankhamun, 15777
Casey, Kevin K. *Judo*, 25277
Casey, Moe. *The Most Excellent Book of Dress Up*, 24396
Cash, Megan Montague. *What Makes the Seasons?* 4543(F)
Cash, Terry. *Bricks*, 23847
Cash-Walsh, Tina. *The Geography Book*, 15434
The Healthy Body Cookbook, 24596
The United States Cookbook, 24598
Casilla, Robert. *The Dream on Blanca's Wall / El sueño pegado en la pared de Blanca*, 11844
First Day in Grapes, 5748(F)

Jackie Robinson, 14418
Jalapeno Bagels, 4114(F)
The Legend of Mexicatl, 11578
Mama Had to Work on Christmas, 10068(F)
Midnight Forests, 14224
A Picture Book of Eleanor Roosevelt, 13948
A Picture Book of Jackie Robinson, 14419
A Picture Book of Jesse Owens, 14642
A Picture Book of John F. Kennedy, 13765
A Picture Book of Martin Luther King, Jr., 13274
A Picture Book of Rosa Parks, 13314
A Picture Book of Thurgood Marshall, 13305
The Pool Party, 9083(F)
Casparian, Marguerite. *Ada's Pal*, 5493(F)
Cassels, Jean. *Earthmates*, 12035
Fantastic Frogs, 21114
Lonesome George, the Giant Tortoise, 21168
Once I Knew a Spider, 5346(F)
Cassidy, Picot. *Italy*, 16759
Cassidy, Sean. *The Chicken Cat*, 2479(F)
Cassie, Brian. *The Butterfly Alphabet Book*, 22056
National Audubon Society First Field Guide, 21046, 22803
Say It Again, 20966
Shells, 22331
Castaldi, Elicia. *Miss Polly Has a Dolly*, 839(F)
Castaldo, Nancy F. *Oceans*, 22384
Rainforests, 23067
Winter Day Play! 24223
Castaldo, Nancy Fusco. *Rainy Day Play!* 24224
Castaneda, Omar S. *Abuela's Weave*, 4751(F)
Casterline, Linda. *Natural-born Killers*, 20226
Rare Animals, 21867
Castle, Caroline. *For Every Child*, 18846
Castle, Kate. *Ballet*, 15383
Caston, Javier Saez. *The Three Hedgehogs*, 5588(F)
Castro, Nick (jt. author). *What's Going on Down There?* 20587
Castro L., Antonio. *Pajaro Verde / The Green Bird*, 11528
Caswell, Maryanne. *Pioneer Girl*, 9176(F)
Catalano, Dominic. *Bernard Goes to School*, 2155(F)
Bernard Wants a Baby, 2156(F)
Bernard's Nap, 694(F)
Frog Went A-Courting, 15254
Hush! 834(F)
Mr. Basset Plays, 1904(F)
Santa and the Three Bears, 5999(F)
Sleeping Beauty, 10740
Catalano, Julie. *The Mexican Americans*, 19540
Catalanotto, Peter. *Daisy 1, 2, 3*, 406(F)
Dreamplace, 4902(F)
Dylan's Day Out, 1905(F)
Emily's Art, 3174(F)
Kitten Red, Yellow, Blue, 283(F)
Matthew A.B.C., 22(F)
Mother to Tigers, 13944
My House Has Stars, 740(F)
The Painter, 3697(F)
The Rolling Store, 4846(F)
We Wanted You, 4020(F)

Who Came Down That Road? 3386(F)
Catchpool, Michael. *Where There's a Bear, There's Trouble!* 1906(F)
Cates, Karin. *A Far-Fetched Story*, 4254(F)
The Secret Remedy Book, 3698(F)
Cathcart, Yvonne. *Robyn's Art Attack*, 6625(F)
Catlett, Elizabeth. *Lift Every Voice and Sing*, 15340
Cato, Sheila. *Addition*, 407(F)
Division, 408(F)
Measuring, 23344
Catran, Ken. *Voyage with Jason*, 11641
Catrow, David. *Cinderella Skeleton*, 10742(F)
Don't Take Your Snake for a Stroll, 3329(F)
The Fungus That Ate My School, 1117(F)
I Like Myself! 3136(F)
Little Pierre, 11555
Our Tree Named Steve, 4138(F)
Plantzilla, 4413(F)
Rotten Teeth, 4469(F)
Santa Claustrophobia, 6120(F)
Stand Tall, Molly Lou Melon, 5730(F)
Take Me out of the Bathtub and Other Silly Dilly Songs, 15363
That's Good! That's Bad! 4276(F)
That's Good! That's Bad! In the Grand Canyon, 4277(F)
We the Kids, 18908
Why Lapin's Ears Are Long and Other Tales from the Louisiana Bayou, 11513
Caudill, Rebecca. *A Certain Small Shepherd*, 10046(F)
Cauley, Lorinda Bryan. *The Trouble with Tyrannosaurus Rex*, 1907(F)
Caumartin, Francois. *Now You See Them, Now You Don't*, 1908(F)
Cavan, Seamus. *The Irish-American Experience*, 19541
W. E. B. Du Bois and Racial Relations, 13252
Cavanagh, Helen. *Panther Glade*, 7133(F)
Cave, Katherine. *Henry's Song*, 1909(F)
Cave, Kathryn. *One Child, One Seed*, 409
You've Got Dragons, 5089(F)
Cazet, Denys. *Annie, Bea, and Chi Chi Dolores*, 97(F)
Dancing, 3699(F)
Elvis the Rooster Almost Goes to Heaven, 6457(F)
A Fish in His Pocket, 1910(F)
Minnie and Moo, 6458(F), 6459(F), 6460(F)
Minnie and Moo and the Musk of Zorro, 6461(F)
Minnie and Moo and the Seven Wonders of the World, 8070(F)
Minnie and Moo and the Thanksgiving Tree, 6343(F)
Minnie and Moo Go Dancing, 6462(F)
Minnie and Moo Go to Paris, 6463(F)
Minnie and Moo Go to the Moon, 6464(F)
Minnie and Moo Meet Frankenswine, 6465(F)
Never Poke a Squid, 6194(F)
Night Lights, 652(F)
Nothing at All, 1911(F)
The Octopus, 6466(F)
Cecala, Frank. *What Makes You What You Are*, 20249

Denton, Terry. *Night Noises*, 5931(F)
  Storymaze 1, 8814(F)
Denzel, Justin. *Boy of the Painted Cave*,
  9224(F)
Depalma, Mary Newell. *The Strange Egg*,
  2000(F)
dePaola, Tomie. *Adelita*, 10665
  The Art Lesson, 5701(F)
  The Baby Sister, 3735(F)
  Big Anthony, 1097(F)
  Bill and Pete, 1098(F)
  Bill and Pete Go Down the Nile,
    2001(F)
  Bill and Pete to the Rescue, 2002(F)
  Bonjour, Mr. Satie, 2003(F)
  Charlie Needs a Cloak, 4552(F)
  Christopher, 14764
  The Cloud Book, 4553(F)
  The Clown of God, 6011(F)
  Country Angel Christmas, 6012(F)
  Days of the Blackbird, 11262(F)
  The Eagle and the Rainbow, 11583
  An Early American Christmas, 6013(F)
  Erandi's Braids, 4913(F)
  Fin M'Coul, 11178
  Four Friends in Autumn, 2004(F)
  Four Stories for Four Seasons, 2005(F)
  Francis, 14793
  Frida Kahlo, 12583
  Ghost Poems, 11946(F)
  Helga's Dowry, 4282(F)
  Here We All Are, 12974
  Hide-and-Seek All Week, 6514(F)
  The Holy Twins, 14731
  The Hunter and the Animals, 915(F)
  Jamie O'Rourke and the Big Potato,
    11179
  Jamie O'Rourke and the Pooka,
    1099(F)
  Kit and Kat, 6515(F)
  The Knight and the Dragon, 2006(F)
  The Lady of Guadalupe, 5872(F)
  The Legend of Old Befana, 6014(F)
  The Legend of the Bluebonnet, 11436
  The Legend of the Persian Carpet,
    11386
  The Legend of the Poinsettia, 11573
  Little Grunt and the Big Egg, 2007(F)
  Maggie and the Monster, 815(F)
  Mary, 19198
  Meet the Barkers, 2008(F)
  Merry Christmas, Strega Nona, 6015(F)
  Mice Squeak, We Speak, 5601(F)
  The Miracles of Jesus, 19199
  The Mysterious Giant of Barletta,
    11263
  A New Barker in the House, 2009(F)
  The Night Before Christmas, 12094(F)
  The Night of Las Posadas, 6016(F)
  Now One Foot, Now the Other, 5102(F)
  Oliver Button Is a Sissy, 5103(F)
  On My Way, 12975(F)
  Pancakes for Breakfast, 4283(F)
  The Parables of Jesus, 19200
  Pascual and the Kitchen Angels,
    4783(F)
  Patrick, 14860
  Petook, 6178(F)
  The Popcorn Book, 22704
  The Quicksand Book, 4554(F)
  The Quilt Story, 3345(F)
  Sing, Pierrot, Sing, 1100(F)
  Stagestruck, 5702(F)
  Strega Nona, 11264, 11265
  Strega Nona Meets Her Match, 1101(F)
  Strega Nona Takes a Vacation, 1102(F)
  T-Rex Is Missing! 2010(F)
  Things Will Never Be the Same, 12976

Tom, 3736(F)
Tomie dePaola's Book of Bible Stories,
  19201
*Tomie dePaola's Favorite Nursery
  Tales*, 10789
Tomie dePaola's Mother Goose, 875
Trouble in the Barkers' Class, 2011(F)
26 Fairmount Avenue, 12977
The Unicorn and the Moon, 1103(F)
The Vanishing Pumpkin, 6216(F)
*Watch Out for the Chicken Feet in Your
  Soup*, 3737(F)
What a Year! 12978
dePaola, Tomie, ed. *The Clown of God*,
  6011(F)
  *Tomie dePaola's Favorite Nursery
    Tales*, 10789
dePaola, Tomie, retel. *Fin M'Coul*, 11178
  The Legend of Old Befana, 6014(F)
  The Legend of the Bluebonnet, 11436
DePauw, Sandra A. *The Don't-Give-Up-
  Kid and Learning Differences*,
  5118(F)
de Pinna, Simon. *Electricity*, 23595
  Forces and Motion, 23536
  Sound, 23633
Derby, Kenneth. *The Top 10 Ways to
  Ruin the First Day of 5th Grade*,
  10147(F)
Derby, Sally. *Jacob and the Stranger*,
  8131(F)
  King Kenrick's Splinter, 4284(F)
  My Steps, 3209(F)
  Two Fools and a Horse, 8132(F)
De Regniers, Beatrice S. *David and
  Goliath*, 19202
  Little Sister and the Month Brothers,
    11291
  May I Bring a Friend? 4285(F)
  So Many Cats! 431(F)
De Regniers, Beatrice S., ed. *Sing a Song
  of Popcorn*, 11724(F)
DerKazarian, Susan. *You Have Head
  Lice!* 20120
deRosa, Dee. *Soccer Circus*, 7195(F)
DeRoy, Craig. *We Can Work it Out*,
  19817
deRubertis, Barbara. *A Collection for
  Kate*, 432(F)
  Count on Pablo, 433(F)
  Deena's Lucky Penny, 6516(F)
  Lulu's Lemonade, 434(F)
de Ruiz, Dana C. *La Causa*, 18720
Dervaux, Isabelle. *The Sky Is Always in
  the Sky*, 11812
DeSantis, Laura. *Come Home with Me*,
  3339(F)
de Sauza, James. *Brother Anansi and the
  Cattle Ranch / El Hermano Anansi y
  el Rancho de Ganada*, 11574
Deshpande, Chris. *Festival Crafts*, 24237
Desimini, Lisa. *All Year Round*, 4555(F)
  Doodle Dandies, 11821
  Dot the Fire Dog, 2012(F)
  Love Letters, 11683
  Moon Soup, 1104(F)
  Policeman Lou and Policewoman Sue,
    3210(F)
  The Snowflake Sisters, 6073(F)
  Sun and Moon, 1105(F)
  Touch the Poem, 11684
  Tulip Sees America, 3087(F)
Despain, Pleasant. *The Dancing Turtle*,
  11608
  Sweet Land of Story, 11511
  Tales of Cats, 10790
  Tales of Enchantment, 10791

Tales of Nonsense and Tomfoolery,
  10792
Tales of Tricksters, 10793
Tales of Wisdom and Justice, 10794
Tales to Frighten and Delight, 10795
Despain, Pleasant, retel. *Thirty-Three
  Multicultural Tales to Tell*, 10796
Desputeaux, Helene. *Baby Science*, 20550
  Munschworks 2, 4403(F)
de Trevino, Elizabeth. *I, Juan de Pareja*,
  9315(F)
Detweiler, Susan. *The First Teddy Bear*,
  24552
Detz, Joan. *You Mean I Have to Stand Up
  and Say Something?* 15181
Deuker, Carl. *High Heat*, 7748(F)
Devaney, John. *America Goes to War*,
  16044
  Bo Jackson, 14587
  Winners of the Heisman Trophy, 25182
Devard, Nancy. *The Mystery of the Miss-
  ing Dog*, 6613(F)
De Varennes, Monique. *The Sugar Child*,
  1106(F)
Deverell, Catherine. *Stradivari's Singing
  Violin*, 9316(F)
Devine, Monica. *Carry Me, Mama*,
  3211(F)
DeVita, James. *Blue*, 10460(F)
Devito, Anna. *If You Sailed on the
  Mayflower*, 17744
DeVito, Pam. *We'll Paint the Octopus
  Red*, 3551(F)
Devlin, Harry. *Cranberry Easter*, 6172(F)
  Old Black Witch! 1107(F)
Devlin, Harry (jt. author). *Cranberry
  Easter*, 6172(F)
  Old Black Witch! 1107(F)
Devlin, Wende. *Cranberry Easter*,
  6172(F)
  Old Black Witch! 1107(F)
Devon, Paddie. *The Grumpy Shepherd*,
  19203(F)
De Vos, Philip. *Carnival of the Animals*,
  12011
De Vries, Anke. *My Elephant Can Do
  Almost Anything*, 2013(F)
  Piggy's Birthday Dream, 2014(F)
deVries, Maggie. *How Sleep Found
  Tabitha*, 663(F)
Dewan, Ted. *Bing*, 2015(F), 2016(F)
Dewey, Ariane. *Antarctic Antics*, 12054
  The Chick and the Duckling, 2140(F)
  *Duck, Duck, Goose! (A Coyote's on the
    Loose!)*, 1753(F)
  Five Little Ducks, 558(F)
  Gregory, the Terrible Eater, 2759(F)
  Herman the Helper, 2354(F)
  How Chipmunk Got His Stripes, 11425
  The Littlest Wolf, 1827(F)
  Lizard's Guest, 2751(F)
  Lizard's Home, 2752(F)
  Mouse in Love, 2356(F)
  Mushroom in the Rain, 2828(F)
  One Duck, Another Duck, 554(F)
  Rockabye Crocodile, 1706(F)
  Rosa Raposa, 11343
  Safe, Warm, and Snug, 21258
  Turtle's Race with Beaver, 2862(F)
  Where Does the Sun Go at Night?
    1175(F)
Dewey, Ariane (jt. author). *Rockabye
  Crocodile*, 1706(F)
  Weird Friends, 21188
Dewey, Jennifer. *New Questions and
  Answers About Dinosaurs*, 15598
  The Secret Language of Snow, 23500
  The Song of the Sea Otter, 22280

Fleischner, Jennifer. *The Dred Scott Case*, 17879

I Was Born a Slave, 13264

Fleisher, Paul. *Ants*, 21909

Coral Reef, 22183

Gorillas, 21393

Ice Cream Treats, 22707

Oak Tree, 22806

Saguaro Cactus, 23029

Tide Pool, 22434

Fleishman, Seymour. *Gus Loves His Happy Home*, 1568(F)

Sometimes Things Change, 6531(F)

Fleming, Alice. *P. T. Barnum*, 12751

Fleming, Bill (jt. author). *Puppy Care and Critters, Too!* 22548

Fleming, Candace. *Boxes for Katje*, 4797(F)

Gator Gumbo, 8162(F)

The Hatmaker's Sign, 9525(F)

Lowji Discovers America, 7622(F)

Muncha! Muncha! Muncha! 4302(F)

Smile, Lily! 3759(F)

When Agnes Caws, 3061(F)

Fleming, Denise. *Alphabet Under Construction*, 44(F)

Barnyard Banter, 5366(F)

Buster, 5367(F)

Count! 448(F)

The Everything Book, 189(F)

In the Small, Small Pond, 4576(F)

In the Tall, Tall Grass, 5368(F)

Lunch, 2087(F)

Mama Cat Has Three Kittens, 2088(F)

Pumpkin Eye, 6202(F)

Time to Sleep, 2089(F)

Where Once There Was a Wood, 3245(F)

Fleming, Ian. *Chitty Chitty Bang Bang*, 8163(F)

Fleming, Robert. *Rescuing a Neighborhood*, 19671

Fleming, Virginia. *Be Good to Eddie Lee*, 5112(F)

Flera, Constance. *The Optical Illusion Book*, 23614

Fletcher, Brian. *Uncle Daddy*, 7766(F)

Fletcher, Corina (jt. author). *Ghoul School*, 1466(F)

Fletcher, Ralph. *Buried Alive*, 11746

The Circus Surprise, 3246(F)

Fig Pudding, 7767(F)

Flying Solo, 6990(F)

Grandpa Never Lies, 3760(F)

Have You Been to the Beach Lately? 11747

How Writers Work, 15186

Poetry Matters, 15187

Relatively Speaking, 11748

Tommy Trouble and the Magic Marble, 8947(F)

Twilight Comes Twice, 4577(F)

A Writing Kind of Day, 11749

Fletcher, Ralph J. *Hello, Harvest Moon*, 4578(F)

Spider Boy, 8948(F)

Fletcher, Susan. *Shadow Spinner*, 9266(F)

The Stuttgart Nanny Mafia, 8852(F)

Walk Across the Sea, 9847(F)

Flint, David. *China*, 16348

Egypt, 16922

Great Britain, 16713

Mexico, 17072

South Africa, 16231

The United Kingdom, 16714

Flintoft, Anthony. *My First Day at Nursery School*, 5704(F)

Floca, Brian. *Billy and the Rebel*, 9773(F)

The Frightful Story of Harry Walfish, 10354(F)

From Boys to Men, 19800

Let's Fly a Kite, 365(F)

Luck with Potatoes, 1270(F)

The Mayor of Central Park, 7986(F)

The Racecar Alphabet, 45(F)

Solomon Sneezes, 6888(F)

Sports! Sports! Sports! A Poetry Collection, 12244

Flood, Pansie Hart. *It's Test Day, Tiger Turcotte*, 7623(F)

Secret Holes, 7768(F)

Sylvia and Miz Lula Maye, 9980(F)

Flook, Helen. *The Middle School Survival Guide*, 19795

Florczak, Robert. *Birdsong*, 4700(F)

A Cowboy Christmas, 6161(F)

The Persian Cinderella, 10653

The Rainbow Bridge, 11500

Yikes!!! 1150(F)

Flores, Jessie J. *The Earth Science Book*, 22949

Florian, Douglas. *Autumnblings*, 12188

Bing Bang Boing, 12117

Bow Wow Meow Meow, 12015

In the Swim, 12016

Insectlopedia, 12017

Laugh-Eteria, 12118

Lizards, Frogs, and Polliwogs, 12018

Mammalabilia, 12019

Monster Motel, 1151(F)

Omnibeasts, 12020

On the Wing, 12021

A Pig Is Big, 340(F)

Summersaults, 12189(F)

Very Scary, 6217(F)

Winter Eyes, 12190

Zoo's Who, 12022

Flory, Verdon. *You Can Call Me Willy*, 5243(F)

Flowers, Pam. *Big-Enough Anna*, 22527

Flowers, Sarah. *Sports in America*, 24935

Floyd, Lucy. *A Place for Nicholas*, 6538(F)

Floyd, Madeleine. *Captain's Purr*, 2090(F)

Fluet, Connie. *A Day in the Life of a Nurse*, 19927

Flynn, Amy. *Doll Party*, 6391(F)

Flynn, Jean. *Annie Oakley*, 12854

Flynn, Kitson. *Carrot in My Pocket*, 3247(F)

Foa, Emma. *Edward Hopper*, 12576

Foa, Maryclare. *Odin's Family*, 11679

Songs Are Thoughts, 11873

Fogelin, Adrian. *Anna Casey's Place in the World*, 8853(F)

Crossing Jordan, 7624(F)

My Brother's Hero, 7769(F)

Foggo, Cheryl. *One Thing That's True*, 7770(F)

Foley, Erin. *Ecuador*, 17217

Foley, June. *Susanna Siegelbaum Gives Up Guys*, 10161(F)

Foley, Mike. *Fundamental Hockey*, 25220

Foley, Ronan. *World Health*, 20128

Follett, Ken. *The Power Twins*, 10466(F)

Foltz, Linda Lee. *Kids Helping Kids*, 19797

Fong, Ryan T. *Global Warning*, 7293(F)

Fontaine, Joel. *Long Ago in Oregon*, 11819(F)

Fontanel, Beatrice. *Monsters*, 21327

The Penguin, 21840

Fontenot, Mary Alice. *Clovis Crawfish and Echo Gecko*, 2091(F)

Fontes, Justine. *Abraham Lincoln*, 13780

Fontes, Justine Korman. *Signs of Spring*, 2092(F)

Fontes, Ron (jt. author). *Abraham Lincoln*, 13780

Foon, Dennis. *The Dirt Eaters*, 8164(F)

Foon, Stanley Wong Hoo. *The Dancing Dragon*, 5903(F)

Foran, Jill. *Dr. Seuss*, 12990

Search for the Northwest Passage, 17304

Forberg, Ati. *The Magic of the Glits*, 6955(F)

Samurai of Gold Hill, 9949(F)

Forbes, Anna. *Kids with AIDS*, 20129

When Someone You Know Has AIDS, 20130

Forbes, Esther. *Johnny Tremain*, 9526(F)

Ford, Barbara. *Saint Louis*, 18268

Walt Disney, 12562

Ford, Bernette. *Don't Hit Me!* 6539(F)

Ford, Bernette G. (jt. author). *Bright Eyes, Brown Skin*, 3322(F)

Ford, Carin T. *Abraham Lincoln*, 13781

The American Civil War, 18074

Andy Warhol, 12687

The Battle of Gettysburg and Lincoln's Gettysburg Address, 18075

Benjamin Franklin, 13477

Daring Women of the Civil War, 18076

Dr. Seuss, 12991

George Washington, 13859

Legends of American Dance and Choreography, 12473

Paul Revere, 13589

Slavery and the Underground Railroad, 18077

Thomas Jefferson, 13751

The Wright Brothers, 14265

Ford, Christine. *Snow!* 3248(F)

Ford, George. *Afro-Bets First Book About Africa*, 9230(F)

Bright Eyes, Brown Skin, 3322(F)

Hanging Out with Mom, 6413(F)

Jamal's Busy Day, 6621(F)

The Story of Ruby Bridges, 18209(F)

Wild, Wild Hair, 6562(F)

Ford, Juwanda G. *K Is for Kwanzaa*, 5875

Shop Talk, 6540(F)

Sunday Best, 6541(F)

Ford, M. Thomas. *Paula Abdul*, 12734

Ford, Miela. *Bear Play*, 5369(F)

Mom and Me, 5370(F)

My Day in the Garden, 3249(F)

On My Own, 2093(F)

What Color Was the Sky Today? 190(F)

Ford, Nick. *Jerusalem Under Muslim Rule in the Eleventh Century*, 16899

Ford, Pamela Baldwin. *Amazing World of Dinosaurs*, 15541

Wonders of the Desert, 23050

Ford, Roxanne (jt. author). *David Robinson*, 14532

Ford, Wayne. *Fast, Strong, and Striped*, 21320

Fordyce, Deborah. *Welcome to Afghanistan*, 16466

Foreman, Michael. *Cat in the Manger*, 6027(F)

Gentle Giant, 10718(F)

Hello World, 1152(F)

Jack's Fantastic Voyage, 1153(F)

Michael Foreman's Christmas Treasury, 19398

Michael Foreman's Mother Goose, 841

Michael Foreman's Playtime Rhymes, 866

Rock-A-Doodle-Do! 11127(F)

Saving Sinbad! 5371(F)

Howard, Arthur. *Bubba and Beau, Best Friends*, 4140(F)
Bubba and Beau Meet the Relatives, 4225(F)
Cosmo Zooms, 2249(F)
Hoodwinked, 1223(F)
The Hubbub Above, 5136(F)
Mr. Putter and Tabby Bake the Cake, 6126(F)
Mr. Putter and Tabby Catch the Cold, 6835(F)
Mr. Putter and Tabby Feed the Fish, 6836(F)
Mr. Putter and Tabby Fly the Plane, 6837(F)
Mr. Putter and Tabby Paint the Porch, 10278(F)
Mr. Putter and Tabby Pick the Pears, 6838(F)
Mr. Putter and Tabby Pour the Tea, 6839(F)
Mr. Putter and Tabby Stir the Soup, 6840(F)
Mr. Putter and Tabby Take the Train, 6841(F)
Mr. Putter and Tabby Toot the Horn, 6842(F)
Mr. Putter and Tabby Write the Book, 6843(F)
100th Day Worries, 425(F)
Serious Trouble, 4344(F)
Stop, Drop, and Roll, 5697(F)
Howard, Dale E. *Soccer Stars*, 25314
Howard, Elizabeth F. *Virgie Goes to School with Us Boys*, 5137(F)
What's in Aunt Mary's Room? 3836(F)
When Will Sarah Come? 3837(F)
Howard, Elizabeth Fitzgerald. *Flower Girl Butterflies*, 3838(F)
Howard, Ellen. *The Gate in the Wall*, 9398(F)
The Log Cabin Christmas, 6053(F)
The Log Cabin Church, 4838(F)
The Log Cabin Quilt, 4839(F)
Howard, Ginger. *William's House*, 9483(F)
Howard, Kim. *Bless Your Heart*, 3643(F)
The Chief's Blanket, 4756(F)
A Cloak for the Dreamer, 8953(F)
Percy to the Rescue, 2771(F)
Howard, Milly. *The Case of the Dog-napped Cat*, 7232(F)
Howard, Nancy S. *Jacob Lawrence*, 15025
William Sidney Mount, 12626
Howard, Paul. *Classic Poetry*, 11888
Full, Full, Full, of Love, 3711(F)
Grandma's Bears, 1636(F)
Howard, Pauline Rodriguez. *Family, Familia*, 3648(F)
Icy Watermelon / Sandia fria, 3770(F)
Remembering Grandma / Recordando a Abuela, 3629(F)
Uncle Chente's Picnic / El Picnic de Tio Chente, 5862(F)
Howard, Richard. *The Strength of the Hills*, 22670
Howarth, Sarah. *Colonial Places*, 17723
Howe, Deborah. *Bunnicula*, 10187(F)
Howe, James. *Bunnicula Strikes Again!* 10188(F)
Creepy-Crawly Birthday, 5938(F)
Dew Drop Dead, 7233(F)
Horace and Morris But Mostly Dolores, 2250(F)
Horace and Morris Join the Chorus / But What About Dolores? 2251(F)
The Hospital Book, 20263

Howie Monroe and the Doghouse of Doom, 10189(F)
I Wish I Were a Butterfly, 2252(F)
Invasion of the Mind Swappers from Asteroid 6! 8258(F)
Kaddish for Grandpa in Jesus' Name Amen, 3839(F)
The Misfits, 7015(F)
The New Nick Kramer or My Life as a Baby-Sitter, 10190(F)
Nighty-Nightmare, 10191(F)
Pinky and Rex and the Just-Right Pet, 7507(F)
Pinky and Rex and the New Baby, 6618(F)
Pinky and Rex Get Married, 6619(F)
Playing with Words, 13007
Return to Howliday Inn, 10192(F)
The Vampire Bunny, 6620(F)
When You Go to Kindergarten, 5719
Howe, James (jt. author). *Bunnicula*, 10187(F)
Howe, John. *Knights*, 15952
Howell, Kathleen C. *The Singing Green*, 12211
Howell, Theresa. *A Is for Airplane / A es para Avión*, 62(F)
Howell, Troy. *Favorite Greek Myths*, 11662
Favorite Norse Myths, 11678
Fox in a Trap, 7392(F)
The Maiden on the Moor, 11240
Mermaid Tales from Around the World, 10847
Sirens and Sea Monsters, 11664
Under Copp's Hill, 9811(F)
Howell, Will C. *I Call It Sky*, 4607(F)
Zoo Flakes ABC, 63
Howes, Chris. *Caving*, 24952
Howitt, Mary. *The Spider and the Fly*, 12034
Howland, Naomi. *ABCDrive!* 64(F)
Latkes, Latkes, Good to Eat, 6285(F)
The Matzah Man, 6286(F)
Howlett, Bud. *I'm New Here*, 5720(F)
Hoyt, Ard. *I'm a Manatee*, 8402(F)
One-Dog Canoe, 1903(F)
Hoyt, Beth Caldwell. *The Ultimate Girls' Guide to Science*, 20612
Hoyt, Eleanor. *The Illustrated Rules of Football*, 25195
The Illustrated Rules of Ice Hockey, 25217
Hoyt, Erich. *Meeting the Whales*, 22352
Whale Rescue, 22353
Hoyt-Goldsmith, Diane. *Apache Rodeo*, 17516
Arctic Hunter, 17309
Buffalo Days, 17517
Celebrating a Quinceañera, 19306
Celebrating Chinese New Year, 19307
Celebrating Hanukkah, 19455
Celebrating Kwanzaa, 19308
Celebrating Passover, 19456
Celebrating Ramadan, 19309
Day of the Dead, 7633(F)
Hoang Anh, 19579
Lacrosse, 24953
Las Posadas, 19403
Mardi Gras, 19310
Potlatch, 17518
Pueblo Storyteller, 17519
Three Kings Day, 19311
Hru, Dakari. *Joshua's Masai Mask*, 5138(F)
Tickle Tickle, 3840(F)
Hu, Evaleen. *A Big Ticket*, 24954
A Level Playing Field, 18877

Hu, Ying-Hwa. *Alicia's Happy Day*, 5960(F)
The Case of the Shrunken Allowance, 562(F)
Coming Home, 14383
Dance Y'All, 9937(F)
Jingle Dancer, 3537(F)
The Legend of Freedom Hill, 9621(F)
Make a Joyful Sound, 11997
Mei-Mei Loves the Morning, 5629(F)
Sam and the Lucky Money, 3176(F)
Singing for Dr. King, 6738(F)
Snow in Jerusalem, 4776(F)
We Are the Many, 13222
Zora Hurston and the Chinaberry Tree, 3957
Huang, Benrei. *Big Daddy, Frog Wrestler*, 1786(F)
Hunting the Daddyosaurus, 1748(F)
Let's Go Riding in Our Strollers, 3407(F)
Mrs. Sato's Hens, 517(F)
Sheep Don't Count Sheep, 645(F)
This Is the Earth That God Made, 19204
Twinkle, Twinkle, Little Star, 15276
Huang, Chunliang Al. *The Chinese Book of Animal Powers*, 24837
Huang, Shong-Yang. *Buddha in the Garden*, 9259(F)
Huang, Zhong-Yang. *The Dragon New Year*, 5863(F)
The Great Race, 10986
Hubbard, Coleen (jt. author). *Colorado Summer*, 7452(F)
Hubbard, Patricia. *My Crayons Talk*, 1224(F)
Trick or Treat Countdown, 6211(F)
Hubbard, Woodleigh. *Park Beat*, 4635(F)
Hubbard, Woodleigh Marx. *All That You Are*, 19676
Hubbard-Brown, Janet. *The Curse of the Hope Diamond*, 24838
The Secret of Roanoke Island, 17724
Hubbell, Patricia. *Black All Around!* 3320(F)
Black Earth, Gold Sun, 12202
Boo! Halloween Poems and Limericks, 6212
Bouncing Time, 5435(F)
City Kids, 11796
Earthmates, 12035
Hurray for Spring! 4608(F)
I Like Cats, 22502
Pots and Pans, 4345(F)
Sidewalk Trip, 3321(F)
Hubbell, Will. *Apples Here!* 22758
Hubble, Richard. *Ships*, 24158
Hubley, Dan. *Kids Collect*, 24731
Hubley, Mary (jt. author). *Kids Collect*, 24731
Huck, Charlotte. *The Black Bull of Norroway*, 11204
Toads and Diamonds, 11104
Hudson, Annabel. *Brown Bear Gets in Shape*, 6528(F)
Hudson, Cheryl W. *Bright Eyes, Brown Skin*, 3322(F)
Hold Christmas in Your Heart, 6054(F)
Hudson, Cheryl W. (jt. author). *How Sweet the Sound*, 15360
Hudson, Cheryl W. (jt. author). *In Praise of Our Fathers and Our Mothers*, 12481
Hudson, Cheryl Willis. *Hands Can*, 211(F)
Hudson, David L. *The Bill of Rights*, 18914

King, Wilma. *Children of the Emancipation*, 18092

King-Smith, Dick. *Animal Stories*, 8336(F)

Billy the Bird, 8337(F)

Clever Lollipop, 8338(F)

The Cuckoo Child, 7520(F)

The Golden Goose, 8339(F)

Harry's Mad, 7251(F)

Hogsel and Gruntel and Other Animal Stories, 8340(F)

The Invisible Dog, 7521(F)

Lady Lollipop, 8341(F)

Pigs Might Fly, 8342(F)

The Roundhill, 8343(F)

The School Mouse, 8344(F)

Titus Rules! 10199(F)

Kingman, Lee. *The Luck of the Miss L*, 7252(F)

Kingsbury, Robert. *Roberto Clemente*, 14368

Kinkade, Sheila. *Children of Slovakia*, 16628

Kinsey-Warnock, Natalie. *The Canada Geese Quilt*, 9003(F)

A Doctor Like Papa, 9886(F)

A Farm of Her Own, 3354(F)

The Fiddler of the Northern Lights, 1280(F)

From Dawn till Dusk, 4864(F)

Gifts from the Sea, 8859(F)

Lumber Camp Library, 8773(F)

Nora's Ark, 4865(F)

On a Starry Night, 1281(F)

The Summer of Stanley, 3075(F)

When Spring Comes, 4620(F)

Kinsler, Gwen Blakley. *Crocheting*, 24533

Kipling, Rudyard. *How the Camel Got His Hump*, 1282(F)

The Jungle Book, 7522(F), 7523(F)

Just So Stories, 7524(F), 7525(F)

Rikki-Tikki-Tavi, 1283(F), 8345(F)

Kiralfy, Bob. *The Most Excellent Book of How to Be a Cheerleader*, 24571

Kirby, Philippa. *Glorious Days, Dreadful Days*, 17829

Kirby, Susan E. *Ida Lou's Story*, 7828(F)

Kirk, Connie Ann. *The Mohawks of North America*, 17527

Sky Dancers, 4866(F)

Kirk, Daniel. *Block City*, 11930

Go! 15240

Hello, Hello! 21293

Jack and Jill, 859(F)

Lunchroom Lizard, 5725(F)

Moondogs, 1284(F)

My Truck Is Stuck! 2407(F)

Snow Family, 3880(F)

Kirk, Daniel F. *Dogs Rule!* 22535

Kirk, David. *Little Bird, Biddle Bird*, 5458(F)

Little Bunny, Biddle Bunny, 5459(F)

Little Miss Spider, 2332(F)

Little Miss Spider at Sunny Patch School, 2333(F)

Little Pig, Biddle Pig, 2334(F)

Miss Spider's ABC, 80(F)

Miss Spider's New Car, 2335(F)

Miss Spider's Tea Party, 2336(F)

Miss Spider's Wedding, 2337(F)

Kirk, Steve. *Bugs Before Time*, 15505

Kirkpatrick, Karey. *Disney's James and the Giant Peach*, 1285(F)

Kirkpatrick, Katherine. *Escape Across the Wide Sea*, 9199(F)

Redcoats and Petticoats, 9532(F)

The Voyage of the Continental, 9687(F)

Kirkpatrick, Patricia. *Maya Angelou*, 12938

Kirkpatrick, Rena K. *Look at Pond Life*, 23178

Kirksmith, Tommie. *Ride Western Style*, 25210

Kirkwood, Jon. *The Fantastic Book of Car Racing*, 25047

The Fantastic Cutaway Book of Giant Buildings, 23869

Kirsh, Florence (jt. author). *Fabulous Female Physicians*, 13996

Kirsh, Shannon. *Fabulous Female Physicians*, 13996

Kirtland, Mark. *Why Do We Do That?* 19728

Kirwan, Anna. *Victoria*, 9399(F)

Kiser, Kevin. *Buzzy Widget*, 4363(F)

Kisor, Henry (jt. author). *One TV Blasting and a Pig Outdoors*, 9121(F)

Kiss, Andrew. *When We Go Camping*, 3498(F)

Wild Babies, 21027

Kisseloff, Jeff. *Who Is Baseball's Greatest Pitcher?* 25079

Kitamura, Satoshi. *Comic Adventures of Boots*, 10200(F)

Fly with the Birds, 3223(F)

In the Attic, 1414(F)

Me and My Cat? 1286(F)

When Sheep Cannot Sleep, 484(F)

Kitano, Harry. *The Japanese Americans*, 19583

Kitchel, JoAnn E. *Bach's Goldberg Variations*, 4752(F)

The Farewell Symphony, 9310(F)

The Heroic Symphony, 4753(F)

Pictures at an Exhibition, 15229

Tales of the Shimmering Sky, 10836

Kitchen, Bert. *The Bremen Town Musicians and Other Animal Tales from Grimm*, 10724

The Frog, 21119

The Otter, 21363

The Rabbit, 21669

Kite, L. Patricia. *Cockroaches*, 21938

Dandelion Adventures, 22855

Gardening Wizardry for Kids, 24690

Insect, 21939

Maya Angelou, 12939

Kite, Patricia. *Down in the Sea*, 22203

Kittelsen, Theodor. *Norwegian Folk Tales*, 11327

Kittinger, Jo S. *Birds of North America*, 21710

Stories in Stone, 15558

Kittredge, Frances. *Neeluk*, 9448(F)

Kiuchi, Tatsuro. *The Seasons and Someone*, 4622(F)

Tsubu the Little Snail, 11065

Kjelgaard, James A. *Big Red*, 7526(F)

Kjelle, Marylou Morano. *Hilary Duff*, 12787

Katherine Paterson, 13047

Raymond Damadian and the Development of MRI, 14083

Klare, Roger. *Gregor Mendel*, 14196

Klass, Sheila S. *Kool Ada*, 9004(F)

Little Women Next Door, 9005(F)

A Shooting Star, 9887(F)

The Uncivil War, 9006(F)

Klassen, Heather. *I Don't Want to Go to Justin's House Anymore*, 5154(F)

Klausmeier, Robert. *Cowboy*, 17985

Klausner, Janet. *Sequoyah's Gift*, 13678

Klayman, Michael (jt. author). *Sharing Blessings*, 19465

Klein, Bill. *A Kids' Guide to Building Forts*, 24213

Klein, James. *Gold Rush! The Young Prospector's Guide to Striking It Rich*, 23231

Klein, Norma. *Mom, the Wolfman and Me*, 7829(F)

Klein, Robin. *The Sky in Silver Lace*, 7830(F)

Klein, Suzanna. *Womenfolk and Fairy Tales*, 10837

Klein, Tom. *Loon Magic for Kids*, 21711

Kleven, Elisa. *Abuela*, 1116(F)

The Dancing Deer and the Foolish Hunter, 1287(F)

Diez Deditos and Other Play Rhymes and Action Songs from Latin America, 24989

Fiestas, 15312

Our Big Home, 3271(F)

The Paper Princess, 1288(F)

The Paper Princess Finds Her Way, 1289(F)

Sun Bread, 2338(F)

The Whole Green World, 4614(F)

Kleven, Sandy. *The Right Touch*, 20591

Kline, Lisa Williams. *The Princesses of Atlantis*, 7027(F)

Kline, Michael. *Ancient Rome!* 15901

The Beast in You! 15632

Fizz, Bubble and Flash! 22889

Geology Rocks! 22920

Gizmos and Gadgets, 20663

Going West! 17967

In the Days of Dinosaurs, 11941

The Kids' Guide to First Aid, 20525

The Lewis and Clark Expedition, 17650

Little Hands Celebrate America! 24253

Real-World Math for Hands-On Fun! 23260

Science Play! 20664

Skyscrapers! 14944

Summer Fun! 25036

Vroom! Vroom! 24297

Who Really Discovered America? 15694

Kline, Nancy. *Elizabeth Blackwell*, 14044

Kline, Suzy. *Herbie Jones Moves On*, 8774(F)

Horrible Harry and the Ant Invasion, 4172(F)

Horrible Harry and the Dragon War, 5726(F)

Horrible Harry and the Holidaze, 10059(F)

Horrible Harry and the Locked Closet, 6644(F)

Horrible Harry and the Mud Gremlins, 6645(F)

Horrible Harry and the Purple People, 8346(F)

Horrible Harry at Halloween, 10378(F)

Horrible Harry Goes to Sea, 6646(F)

Horrible Harry Goes to the Moon, 5727(F)

Horrible Harry Moves Up to Third Grade, 10379(F)

Mary Marony and the Chocolate Surprise, 9007(F)

Molly Gets Mad, 10591(F)

Molly's in a Mess, 10201(F)

Orp Goes to the Hoop, 10202(F)

Song Lee and the "I Hate You" Notes, 10380(F)

Kling, Andrew A. *Rhode Island*, 17739

Klingel, Cynthia. *Card Tricks*, 25242

Chief Joseph, 13642

Coretta Scott King, 13268

Langstaff, John. *Frog Went A-Courtin'*, 15269
Langstaff, John (jt. author). *Making Music*, 15334
Sally Go Round the Moon, 15270
Langstaff, Nancy. *Sally Go Round the Moon*, 15270
Langton, Bruce. *P Is for Putt*, 24950
Langton, Jane. *The Fledgling*, 8365(F)
The Mysterious Circus, 8366(F)
The Queen's Necklace, 10692(F)
Salt, 11303
The Time Bike, 8367(F)
Lanino, Deborah. *Maria's Comet*, 4835(F)
Nina's Waltz, 3734(F)
Lankford, Mary D. *Birthdays Around the World*, 19336
Christmas Around the World, 19407
Dominoes Around the World, 25243
Lannin, Joanne. *A History of Basketball for Girls and Women*, 25124
Lanquetin, Anne-Sophie. *Ten Monkey Jamboree*, 537(F)
Lansky, Bruce. *Happy Birthday to Me!* 12081
Lansky, Bruce, ed. *A Bad Case of the Giggles*, 12129
Girls to the Rescue Book 2, 10821
Lansky, Bruce, ed. *Miles of Smiles*, 12130
Newfangled Fairy Tales, Book 1, 8368(F)
Lansky, Bruce, ed. *No More Homework! No More Tests! Kids' Favorite Funny School Poems*, 11813
Rolling in the Aisles, 12131
Lansky, Bruce, sel. *Girls to the Rescue*, 10820
Lansky, Vicki. *It's Not Your Fault, KoKo Bear*, 2374(F)
Lanteigne, Helen. *The Seven Chairs*, 4877(F)
Lanting, Frans. *Albatrosses of Midway Island*, 21707
Lanton, Sandy. *Lots of Latkes*, 6300(F)
Lantz, Francess. *Mom, There's a Pig in My Bed!* 7527(F)
Lantz, Francess Lin. *The Day Joanie Frankenhauser Became a Boy*, 7033(F)
Lantz, Paul. *The Matchlock Gun*, 9479(F)
La Padula, Thomas. *To the Top!* 24976
Tonka Big Book of Trucks, 5845
Tonka Trucks Night and Day, 24093
True-Life Treasure Hunts, 15654
La Pierre, Yvette. *Native American Rock Art*, 17531
Welcome to Josefina's World, 1824, 17986
Lararrigue, Jerome. *Freedom on the Menu*, 10032(F)
LaReau, Jenna. *Top Secret*, 15037
Larimer, Donna. *Mama, Daddy, Baby and Me*, 3777(F)
Larios, Julie. *Have You Ever Done That?* 3365(F)
Larios, Julie Hofstrand. *On the Stairs*, 2375(F)
Larios, Richard (jt. author). *La Causa*, 18720
Larkspur, Penelope. *The Secret Life of Fairies*, 24853
Laroche, Giles. *Bridges Are to Cross*, 23890
Down to the Sea in Ships, 11936
Who Sees the Lighthouse? 446(F)
LaRochelle, David. *The Bookstore Valentine*, 6721(F)

Laronde, Gary. *Juneteenth*, 19274(F)
Larrabee, Lisa. *Grandmother Five Baskets*, 11458(F)
Larrecq, John. *Broderick*, 2604(F)
A Green Christmas, 6068(F)
A Single Speckled Egg, 4371(F)
Larroche, Caroline. *Corot from A to Z*, 12544
Larsen, Anita. *Psychic Sleuths*, 18943
Larson, Bonni (jt. author). *Watakame's Journey*, 11582
Larson, Jean Russell. *The Fish Bride and Other Gypsy Tales*, 11090
Larson, Kirby. *Cody and Quinn, Sitting in a Tree*, 6659(F)
The Magic Kerchief, 1302(F)
Larson, Peter. *Bones Rock!* 15561
Larson, Timothy. *Anasazi*, 17532
Laser, Michael. *6–321*, 9015(F)
Lasker, Joe. *All Kinds of Families*, 19779
The Cobweb Christmas, 6003(F)
He's My Brother, 9149(F)
How Do I Feel? 7915(F)
Howie Helps Himself, 9134(F)
Nick Joins In, 5163(F)
Laskey, Elizabeth. *Sea Turtles*, 21172
Seahorses, 22240
Lasky, Kathryn. *Before I Was Your Mother*, 3896(F)
Born in the Breezes, 12463
A Brilliant Streak, 13111
Broken Song, 9340(F)
The Capture, 8369(F)
Days of the Dead, 17085
Dreams in the Golden Country, 9894(F)
Elizabeth I, 9400(F)
The Gates of the Wind, 1303(F)
Interrupted Journey, 21173
Jahanara, 9277(F)
The Journal of Augustus Pelletier, 17654
A Journey to the New World, 9489(F)
Love That Baby! 20553
Lucille Camps In, 3897(F)
The Man Who Made Time Travel, 14164
Marie Antoinette, 9341(F)
Marven of the Great North Woods, 3077(F)
Mary, Queen of Scots, 9342(F)
Mommy's Hands, 3898(F)
Monarchs, 22068
The Most Beautiful Roof in the World, 23100, 23101
The Night Journey, 9343(F)
Porkenstein, 6221(F)
Science Fair Bunnies, 2376(F)
Sugaring Time, 22722
Think Like an Eagle, 24724
A Time for Courage, 9895(F)
Tumble Bunnies, 2377(F)
A Voice of Her Own, 13123
Lass, Bonnie. *Who Took the Cookies from the Cookie Jar?* 2378(F)
Lassieur, Allison. *The Apsaalooke (Crow) Nation*, 17533
The Arapaho Tribe, 17534
Astronauts, 23696
The Blackfeet Nation, 17535
The Choctaw Nation, 17536
The Creek Nation, 17537
The Delaware People, 17538
Head Lice, 20162
The Hopi, 17539
The Inuit, 17315
The Moon, 20782
The Pequot Tribe, 17540
Scorpions, 22107

The Space Shuttle, 23697
The Sun, 20911
The Utes, 17541
Lassig, Jurgen. *Spiny*, 8370(F)
Latimer, Clay. *Muhammad Ali*, 14549
Latimer, Jonathan P. *Birds of Prey*, 21802
Bizarre Birds, 21713
Shorebirds, 21714
Lattimore, Deborah N. *Cinderhazel*, 6222(F)
The Flame of Peace, 9428(F)
Fool and the Phoenix, 9278(F)
Frida María, 7528(F)
Gittel's Hands, 1528(F)
I Wonder What's Under There? A Brief History of Underwear, 23909
The Lady with the Ship on Her Head, 4368(F)
Sasha's Matrioshka Dolls, 4784(F)
The Winged Cat, 9241(F)
Laubach, Christyna. *Raptor! A Kid's Guide to Birds of Prey*, 21803
Lauber, Patricia. *Be a Friend to Trees*, 22819
Fur, Feathers, and Flippers, 21003
Get Ready for Robots! 23963
How Dinosaurs Came to Be, 15562
Hurricanes, 23397
Lost Star, 12387
Purrfectly Purrfect, 8371(F)
Summer of Fire, 18356
The True-or-False Book of Dogs, 22536
The True-or-False Book of Horses, 22599
What You Never Knew About Fingers, Forks, and Chopsticks, 19729
What You Never Knew About Tubs, Toilets, and Showers, 15703
Who Came First? New Clues to Prehistoric Americans, 15704
Laufer, Peter. *Made in Mexico*, 17086
Laughlin, Rosemary. *John D. Rockefeller*, 14230
Laura, Huliska-Beit. *Poetry for Young People*, 12138
Laurabeatriz. *Tales of the Amazon*, 11616
Lauré, Jason, 16240
Bangladesh, 16500
Botswana, 16241
Namibia, 16242
Zambia, 16243
Zimbabwe, 16244
Lauré, Jason (jt. author). *Ghana*, 16274
Madagascar, 16223
Morocco, 16213
Nigeria, 16275
Portugal, 16877
Swaziland, 16224
Uganda, 16166
Lauren, Emily. *Connecticut*, 17741
Lauren, Jill. *Succeeding with LD*, 20298
Laurence, Daniel. *Captain and Matey Set Sail*, 6660(F)
Laurgaard, Rachel K. *Patty Reed's Doll*, 9690(F)
Lauter, Richard. *The War with Grandpa*, 7919(F)
Lauture, Denizé. *Running the Road to ABC*, 10386(F)
Lavallee, Barbara. *All You Need for a Snowman*, 3508(F)
The Gift, 4579(F)
Groucho's Eyebrows, 5303(F)
Mama, Do You Love Me? 3871(F)
This Place Is Crowded, 16422
This Place Is High, 23138
Uno, Dos, Tres, 522(F)

My Bones and Muscles, 20451
My Heart and Blood, 20332
My Stomach, 20351
One Giant Leap, 7327(F)
Purple Is Best, 6813(F)
Shoo, Crow! Shoo! 6814(F)
The Solar System, 20866
A Star in My Orange, 370
The Statue of Liberty, 18479
Ways to Go, 3469
Yahoo for You, 4007(F)
Rauth, Leslie. Maryland, 18649
Rauzon, Mark. Golden Eagles of Devil
  Mountain, 21810
Hummingbirds, 21736
Parrots, 21737
Vultures, 21738
Rauzon, Mark J. Parrots Around the
  World, 21739
Raven, Margot T. Angels in the Dust,
  9926(F)
Raven, Margot Theis. Circle Unbroken,
  4008(F)
Mercedes and the Chocolate Pilot,
  16081
Ravishankar, Anushka. Tiger on a Tree,
  4658(F)
Rawlings, Marjorie Kinnan. The Yearling,
  7567(F)
Rawlins, Carol B. The Colorado River,
  17420
The Orinoco River, 17268
Rawlins, Donna. Guess the Baby, 5712(F)
Tucking Mommy In, 727(F)
Ray, Deborah Kogan. The Barn Owls,
  5446(F)
The Flower Hunter, 14029
Hokusai, 12574
I Have a Sister, My Sister Is Deaf,
  5202(F)
Lily's Garden, 4009(F)
My Prairie Christmas, 6041(F)
Through Grandpa's Eyes, 3934(F)
Wagon Train, 9688(F)
Ray, Delia. Ghost Girl, 9927(F)
Ray, Jane. Adam and Eve and the Garden
  of Eden, 19244
The Bold Boy, 1121(F)
Ray, Kurt. Native Americans and the New
  American Government, 17580
New Roads, Canals, and Railroads in
  Early-19th-Century America, 17916
Typhoid Fever, 20182
Ray, Mary L. Basket Moon, 4966(F)
Mud, 4659(F)
Pumpkins, 1456(F)
Red Rubber Boot Day, 3470(F)
Ray, Mary Lyn. All Aboard! 1457(F)
Welcome, Brown Bird, 7568(F)
Raya-Norman, Faye. Wolf Songs, 767(F)
Rayevsky, Robert. Bernal and Florinda,
  11345
Joan of Arc, 14821
Squash It! A True and Ridiculous Tale,
  11346
Three Sacks of Truth, 11106
Two Fools and a Horse, 8132(F)
Under New York, 18441
Raymond, Victoria. Brown Cow, Green
  Grass, Yellow Mellow Sun, 4610(F)
Bumble Bee, 5300(F)
Rayner, Mary. Hobart, 8043(F)
Pigs Might Fly, 8342(F)
Rayner, Matthew. Cat, 22509
Dog, 22551
Hamster, 22484
Raynor, Maggie. Alan Apostrophe, 15130
Rayyan, Omar. Count Silvernose, 9337(F)

Hatching Magic, 8134(F)
King Midas, 11671
Moonsilver, 6524(F)
The Mountains of the Moon, 6525(F)
Ramadan, 5879
Rimonah of the Flashing Sword, 10924
The Ring of Truth, 10099(F)
The Sunset Gates, 6526(F)
Read, Andrew. Porpoises, 22215
Readhead, Lloyd. Gymnastics, 25203
Ready, Anna. Mississippi, 18650
Reasoner, Charles. Brave Bear and the
  Ghosts, 11437
Spider and His Son Find Wisdom,
  10933
Wanyana and Matchmaker Frog, 10934
Zimani's Drum, 10935
Rebman, Renee C. Euthanasia and the
  "Right to Die," 20011
Life on Ellis Island, 18480
Rebnord, Lisa (jt. author). Making Picture
  Frames, 24558
Recorvits, Helen. My Name Is Yoon,
  5208(F)
Where Heroes Hide, 10013(F)
Rector, Anne Elizabeth. Anne Elizabeth's
  Diary, 12650
Reczuch, Karen. The Dust Bowl, 4735(F)
Ghost Cat, 5258(F)
Just Like New, 4916(F)
Morning on the Lake, 4695(F)
Redbank, Tennant. Which Way, Wendy?
  4187(F)
Reddix, Valerie. Dragon Kite of the
  Autumn Moon, 4967(F)
Reddy, Michelle (jt. author). Dolphin
  Babies, 22220
Redenbaugh, Vicki Jo. Green Beans,
  4075(F)
Lots of Latkes, 6300(F)
Pug, Slug, and Doug the Thug, 2720(F)
When I'm Alone, 538(F)
Redfern, Martin. The Kingfisher Young
  People's Book of Planet Earth, 22939
The Kingfisher Young People's Book of
  Space, 20739
Rediger, Pat. Great African Americans in
  Business, 13223
Great African Americans in Civil
  Rights, 13224
Great African Americans in Entertain-
  ment, 12497
Great African Americans in Literature,
  12498
Great African Americans in Music,
  12499
Great African Americans in Sports,
  14316
Redmond, Jim. Landslides and Avalanch-
  es, 22940
Uniquely North Dakota, 18308
Redmond, Ronda (jt. author). Landslides
  and Avalanches, 22940
Redmond, Shirley-Raye. Grampa and the
  Ghost, 8521(F)
Redmond, Shirley Raye. Lewis and Clark,
  18002
Patriots in Petticoats, 13225
Tentacles! 22165
Reed, Gregory J. (jt. author). Dear Mrs.
  Parks, 18895
Reed, Jennifer. Earthquakes, 22970
Leonardo da Vinci, 12554
Reed, Jennifer Bond. The Saudi Royal
  Family, 17001
Reed, Lynn Rowe. The Halloween Show-
  down, 6246(F)
Punctuation Takes a Vacation, 1451(F)

Reed, Mike. The Bug in Teacher's Coffee,
  12116
A Chill in the Air, 12192
Even Firefighters Hug Their Moms,
  3399(F)
Oh No, Noah! 6624(F)
Shake Dem Halloween Bones, 6234(F)
A Tale of Two Dogs, 5465(F)
Reed, Nancy Amis. The Orphans of Nor-
  mandy, 16082
Reed-Jones, Carol. The Tree in the
  Ancient Forest, 22831
Reeder, Carolyn. Captain Kate, 9795(F)
Reedy, Jerry. Oklahoma, 18309
Reef, Catherine. Albert Einstein, 14115
Arlington National Cemetery, 18651
George Gershwin, 12710
Gettysburg, 18100
The Lincoln Memorial, 18481
Monticello, 18652
Mount Vernon, 18653
Ralph David Abernathy, 13230
The Supreme Court, 18841
This Our Dark Country, 16315
Washington, D.C., 18482
Reekie, Jocelyn. Tess, 9210(F)
Rees, Celia. The Soul Taker, 8522(F)
Witch Child, 9496(F)
Rees, Douglas. Grandy Thaxter's Helper,
  1458(F)
Rees, Mary. Spooky Poems, 11700
Rees, Rosemary. The Ancient Egyptians,
  15838
The Ancient Greeks, 15876
The Ancient Romans, 15923
The Aztecs, 17098
The Incas, 17269
Reeves, Diane L. Career Ideas for Kids
  Who Like Sports, 19902
Career Ideas for Kids Who Like
  Writing, 19901
Reeves, Diane Lindsey. Career Ideas for
  Kids Who Like Adventure, 19868
Career Ideas for Kids Who Like Com-
  puters, 19920
Career Ideas for Kids Who Like Math,
  19866
Career Ideas for Kids Who Like
  Science, 19982
Career Ideas for Kids Who Like
  Talking, 19867
Reeves, Jeni. The Girl Who Struck Out
  Babe Ruth, 25088
Pocahontas, 13666
Regan, Colm. People of the Islands,
  23016
Regan, Dana. Messy Bessey's Family
  Reunion, 6709(F)
Messy Bessey's Holidays, 6710(F)
Regan, Dian C. Daddies, 4010(F)
The Friendship of Milly and Tug,
  7897(F)
Princess Nevermore, 10496(F)
Regan, Laura. Mama Mama, 5522(F)
Spots, 492
Welcome to the Ice House, 17343
Welcome to the River of Grass, 18678
Regan, Michael (jt. author). Let the
  Games Begin! 24889
Reiach, Margaret Amy. The Life Cycle of
  a Wolf, 21553
Reich, Janet. Gus and the Green Thing,
  2671(F)
Reich, Susanna. Clara Schumann, 12896
Reichart, George. A Bag of Lucky Rice,
  9729(F)
Reiche, Dietlof. Freddy in Peril, 8523(F)
Ghost Ship, 7328(F)

1534

Sheindlin, Judy. *Judge Judy Sheindlin's You Can't Judge a Book by Its Cover*, 19712
Win or Lose by How You Choose! 19713
Sheinwold, Alfred. *101 Best Family Card Games*, 25013
Shelby, Anne. *Homeplace*, 3526(F)
The Someday House, 3527(F)
Shelby, Fay (jt. author). *Lost in Spillville*, 8138(F)
Sheldon, David. *Guess Who?* 6761(F)
Shell, Barry. *Great Canadian Scientists*, 14004
Shelley, John. *Bella Baxter Inn Trouble*, 7042(F)
Shelley, Rex. *Japan*, 16440
Shelly, Jeff. *A Plump and Perky Turkey*, 6338(F)
Shelowitz, Holly Anne. *Oh, Baby!* 20559
Shemie, Bonnie. *Building America*, 15034
Houses of Adobe, 17594
Houses of China, 16375
Houses of Snow, Skin and Bones, 17333
Mounds of Earth and Shell, 17595
Shemin, Margaretha. *The Little Riders*, 10020(F)
Shems, Ed. *Everyday Science*, 20668
Shenandoah, Joanne. *Skywoman*, 11486
Shepard, Aaron. *The Crystal Heart*, 11072
King o' the Cats, 11238
Lady White Snake, 11009
The Princess Mouse, 11338
The Sea King's Daughter, 11318
Shepard, Aaron, retel. *Savitri*, 11044
Shepard, Claudia. *Lake of the Big Snake*, 4936(F)
Shepard, E. H. *The Reluctant Dragon*, 10678(F)
The Wind in the Willows, 8194(F)
The World of Pooh, 8434(F)
Sheperd, Amanda. *Who Loves Me?* 741(F)
Shephard, Marie T. *Maria Montessori*, 14849
Shepherd, Donna Walsh. *The Aztecs*, 17103
New Zealand, 16595
Uranus, 20827
Shepherd, Jennifer. *Canada*, 17053
Shepherd, Rosalie M. *The Tuskegee Airmen Story*, 4833(F)
Women Who Fly, 23802
Shepperson, Rob. *Don't Know Much About Abraham Lincoln*, 13779
Don't Know Much About Thomas Jefferson, 13749
Sherburne, Andrew. *The Memoirs of Andrew Sherburne*, 13612
Sherkin-Langer, Ferne. *When Mommy Is Sick*, 4047(F)
Sherlock, Jean. *Forests and Jungles*, 21879
Sherlock, Patti. *Four of a Kind*, 7580(F)
Sherman, Allan. *Hello Muddah, Hello Faddah!* 15373
Sherman, Eileen B. *Independence Avenue*, 9935(F)
Sherman, Joanne. *Because It's My Body!* 19714
Sherman, Josepha. *Barrel Racing*, 25014
Bill Gates, 14152
Competitive Soccer for Girls, 25323
Deep Space Observation Satellites, 23705
The Ear, 20426
The History of the Internet, 23978

Jeff Bezos, 14042
Jerry Yang and David Filo, 14005
Magic Hoofbeats, 10861
Merlin's Kin, 10862
Rachel the Clever and Other Jewish Folktales, 11376
Ropers and Riders, 25015
Samuel de Champlain, 12344
Told Tales, 10863
The Upper Limbs, 20453
Welcome to the Rodeo! 25016
Your Travel Guide to Ancient Israel, 16959
Sherman, Pat. *The Sun's Daughter*, 11637
Sherman, Paul (jt. author). *Naked Mole-Rats*, 21340
Sherrow, Victoria. *Alexander Graham Bell*, 14037
Benjamin Franklin, 13488
Bill Clinton, 13725
The Exxon Valdez, 18573
Freedom of Worship, 18901
The Gecko, 21134
Hillary Rodham Clinton, 13907
The Hindenburg Disaster, 23827
Hurricane Andrew, 23410
Huskings, Quiltings, and Barn Raisings, 17759
The Iroquois Indians, 17596
Joseph McCarthy and the Cold War, 13554
Life During the Gold Rush, 18017
Life in a Medieval Monastery, 15965
The Maya Indians, 17139
The Oklahoma City Bombing, 19660
Pennsylvania, 17760
Phillis Wheatley, 13126
Plains Outbreak Tornadoes, 23411
Polio Epidemic, 20194
The Porcupine, 21369
San Francisco Earthquake, 1989, 18574
Sports Great Pete Sampras, 14626
Thomas Jefferson, 13758
Titanic, 24172
The Triangle Factory Fire, 18178
Uniquely South Carolina, 18657
Wilma Rudolph, 14650, 14651
The World Trade Center Bombing, 19661
Sherry, Clifford J. *Drugs and Eating Disorders*, 20045
Inhalants, 20046
Shetterly, Susan Hand. *Shelterwood*, 4679(F)
Shichtman, Sandra H. *Helen Keller*, 13933
Shields, Carol D. *Lunch Money and Other Poems About School*, 11900
Shields, Carol Diggory. *Almost Late to School and More School Poems*, 12161
Brain Juice, 11901, 20630
The Bugliest Bug, 2761(F)
Colors, 1522(F)
English, Fresh Squeezed! 15148
Food Fight! 1523(F)
Homes, 21308
Lucky Pennies and Hot Chocolate, 4048(F)
On the Go, 1524(F)
Sports, 24785
Shields, Charles J. *Belize*, 17140
Buffalo Bill Cody, 13453
Central America, 17141
George Lucas, 12839
John Cabot and the Rediscovery of North America, 12338

Roald Dahl, 12972
Saddam Hussein, 14818
Spike Lee, 12834
Vladimir Putin, 14864
Shiffman, Lena. *My First Book of Words*, 15149(F)
When I Lived with Bats, 21432
Shih, Bernadette L. *Ling Ling*, 2762(F)
Shimin, Symeon. *Onion John*, 9013(F)
Zeely, 8976(F)
Shimizu, Kiyashi. *Carnivorous Plants*, 22646
Shimmen, Andrea (jt. author). *Australia*, 16578
Shin, Sun Yung. *Cooper's Lesson*, 5226(F)
Shindler, Ramon. *Found Alphabet*, 136(F)
Shine, Andrea. *Count Your Way Through France*, 16666
Family Reunion, 11885
Loon Summer, 9068(F)
Stradivari's Singing Violin, 9316(F)
The Summer My Father Was Ten, 3152(F)
Shine, Deborah S., ed. *Make a Joyful Sound*, 11997
Shinjo, Shelly. *Ghosts for Breakfast*, 3557(F)
Shipe, Becky. *Breathe in, Breathe Out*, 20384
Think, Think, Think, 20367
Shipton, Paul. *The Mighty Skink*, 8599(F)
Shirley, David. *Alabama*, 18658
Gloria Estefan, 12795
North Carolina, 18659
Shirley, Jean (jt. author). *Frances Hodgson Burnett*, 12956
Robert Louis Stevenson, 13093
Shlichta, Joe. *Thirty-Three Multicultural Tales to Tell*, 10796
Shoemaker, Hurst H. (jt. author). *Fishes*, 22257
Shollar, Leah. *A Thread of Kindness*, 11377
Shone, Rob. *Professor Protein's Fitness, Health, Hygiene and Relaxation Tonic*, 20497
Shore, Nancy. *Spice Girls*, 12904
Short, Joan. *Platypus*, 21370
Whales, 22363
Shortall, Leonard. *The Bully of Barkham Street*, 7058(F)
Encyclopedia Brown, Boy Detective, 7366(F)
Mishmash, 7468(F)
Shortelle, Dennis (jt. author). *The Forgotten Players*, 25066
Shorto, Russell. *David Farragut and the Great Naval Blockade*, 13471
Jane Fonda, 12799
Shough, Carol Gandee. *All the Mamas*, 4049(F)
All the Papas, 4050(F)
Showers, Paul. *A Drop of Blood*, 20334
Hear Your Heart, 20335
How Many Teeth? 20474
The Listening Walk, 4051(F)
Look at Your Eyes, 20427
Sleep Is for Everyone, 20374
What Happens to a Hamburger? 20353
Your Skin and Mine, 20463
Shragg, Karen I. *A Solstice Tree for Jenny*, 5900(F)
Shragg, Karen I. (jt. author). *Nature's Yucky!* 21002
Shreeve, Elizabeth. *Hector Springs Loose*, 6880(F)
Shreve, Susan. *Blister*, 8877(F)

You Can't Smell a Flower with Your Ear! 20401

Smith, Norman F. *How to Do Successful Science Projects*, 20688

Smith, Patricia. *Janna and the Kings*, 4058(F)

Smith, Patricia C. (jt. author). *As Long As the Rivers Flow*, 13153

Smith, Patricia Clark. *Weetamoo*, 9460(F)

Smith, Patrick Clark (jt. author). *On the Trail of Elder Brother*, 11484

Smith, Pohla. *Superstars of Women's Figure Skating*, 14332

Smith, Robert K. *Chocolate Fever*, 10289(F)

Jelly Belly, 9080(F)

The War with Grandpa, 7919(F)

Smith, Roland. *African Elephants*, 21601

The Captain's Dog, 9738(F)

Cryptid Hunters, 7356(F)

Jaguar, 7357(F)

Vultures, 21746

Zach's Lie, 7920(F)

Smith, Rosie (jt. author). *Captain Pajamas*, 4499(F)

Smith, Sally J. *Dragon Soup*, 1632(F)

Smith, Sherwood. *Crown Duel*, 8608(F)

Wren's Quest, 8609(F)

Wren's War, 8610(F)

Smith, Stephen J. *Shy Vi*, 2411(F)

Smith, Stu. *Goldilocks and the Three Martians*, 1541(F)

Smith, Susan M. *The Booford Summer*, 7582(F)

Smith, Tammy. *Substitute Teacher Plans*, 5723(F)

Smith, Theresa. *Zzzng! Zzzng! Zzzng! A Yoruba Tale*, 10912

Smith, Trevor. *Earth's Changing Climate*, 23353

Smith, Wendy. *The Blood-and-Thunder Adventure on Hurricane Peak*, 8421(F)

Smith, Whitney. *Flag Lore of All Nations*, 15046

Smith, Will. *Just the Two of Us*, 4059(F)

Smith, William J. *Around My Room*, 12163

Laughing Time, 12164

Smith, William Jay, comp. *Up the Hill and Down*, 11915

Smith-Ary, Lynn. *A Present for Mrs. Kazinski*, 4188(F)

Smith-Baranzini, Marlene. *Brown Paper School USKids History*, 17430

Smith-Baranzini, Marlene (jt. author). *Book of the American Civil War*, 18071

US Kids History, 17706

Smith-Moore, J. J. *Honor the Flag*, 15043

Smolinski, Diane. *Battles of the French and Indian War*, 17764

Battles of the Spanish-American War, 18179

Soldiers of the French and Indian War, 17765

Soldiers of the Spanish-American War, 18180

Smolinski, Dick. *Bill Bowerman and Phil Knight*, 23906

Smothers, Ethel Footman. *Auntee Edna*, 4060(F)

The Hard-Times Jar, 5229(F)

Smucker, Barbara. *Runaway to Freedom*, 9605(F)

Smyth, Iain (jt. author). *Old MacDonald Had a Farm*, 15256

Smyth, Karen C. *Crystal*, 22366

Smythe, Anne. *Islands*, 4061(F)

Snedden, Robert. *Medical Ethics*, 20239

Technology in the Time of Ancient Rome, 15927

Sneed, Brad. *Aesop's Fables*, 11282

The Bravest of Us All, 3040(F)

Higgins Bend Song and Dance, 1366(F)

The Pumpkin Runner, 4717(F)

Sorry, 4086(F)

When Wishes Were Horses, 4216(F)

Sneed, Brad, retel. *Aesop's Fables*, 11282

Snell, Danny. *Bilby Moon*, 2794(F)

Snell, Gordon. *'Twas the Day After Christmas*, 12101

Snelling, Lauraine. *The Winner's Circle*, 7583(F)

Snelson, Karin. *Seattle*, 18575

Sneve, Virginia Driving Hawk. *The Apaches*, 17603

The Cherokees, 17604

The Cheyennes, 17605

The Hopis, 17606

The Iroquois, 17607

The Navajos, 17608

The Nez Perce, 17609

The Seminoles, 17610

The Sioux, 17611

The Trickster and the Troll, 8611(F)

Sneve, Virginia Driving Hawk, ed. *Dancing Teepees*, 12176(F)

Snicket, Lemony. *The Austere Academy*, 9420(F)

The Bad Beginning, 10290(F)

The Carnivorous Carnival, 10291(F)

The Ersatz Elevator, 7358(F)

The Hostile Hospital, 7359(F)

The Miserable Mill, 7360(F)

The Slippery Slope, 7361(F)

The Vile Village, 7362(F)

The Wide Window, 10292(F)

Snihura, Ulana. *I Miss Franklin P. Shuckles*, 4195(F)

Snodgrass, Mary Ellen. *Acid Rain*, 18815

Air Pollution, 18816

Solid Waste, 18800

Snow, Alan. *Here's What You Do When You Can't Find Your Shoe*, 12147

How Santa Really Works, 10078(F)

Stories from Hans Christian Andersen, 10635

The Truth About Cats, 2778(F)

Snow, Judith E. *How It Feels to Have a Gay or Lesbian Parent*, 19780

Snow, Pegeen. *Atlanta*, 18665

Snow, Scott. *West on the Wagon Train*, 9686(F)

Snyder, Carol. *God Must Like Cookies, Too*, 6325(F)

Snyder, Dianne. *The Boy of the Three-Year Nap*, 11062

Snyder, Joel. *Story of Dinosaurs*, 15530

Snyder, Zilpha Keatley. *The Ghosts of Rathburn Park*, 8612(F)

The Magic Nation Thing, 7057(F)

The Unseen, 8613(F)

So, Meilo. *The Beauty of the Beast*, 12048

A Bunny for All Seasons, 5599(F)

Central Heating, 11910

Gobble, Gobble, Slip, Slop, 11045

How to Cross a Pond, 12226

Hurry and the Monarch, 4575(F)

Moonbeams, Dumplings and Dragon Boats, 19368

The Tale of the Heaven Tree, 1251(F)

The White Swan Express, 3973(F)

So, Sungwan. *In a Chinese City*, 16377

Sobat, Vera. *Little Bear Brushes His Teeth*, 2373(F)

Sobel, June. *B Is for Bulldozer*, 139(F)

Sobel, Syl. *The U.S. Constitution and You*, 18922

Sobey, Ed. *Wrapper Rockets and Trombone Straws*, 20689

Sobol, Donald J. *Encyclopedia Brown and the Case of the Disgusting Sneakers*, 7363(F)

Encyclopedia Brown and the Case of the Jumping Frogs, 7364(F)

Encyclopedia Brown and the Case of the Mysterious Handprints, 7365(F)

Encyclopedia Brown, Boy Detective, 7366(F)

Encyclopedia Brown's Book of Wacky Sports, 25020

Sobol, Richard. *Adelina's Whales*, 22367

An Elephant in the Backyard, 21602

Socias, Marcel. *How Our Blood Circulates*, 20331

Soentpiet, Chris. *Dear Santa, Please Come to the 19th Floor*, 6165(F)

My Brother Martin, 13278

Saturdays and Teacakes, 7833(F)

Soentpiet, Chris K. *Coolies*, 5060(F)

Jin Woo, 3677(F)

The Last Dragon, 3439(F)

Molly Bannaky, 13892

Momma, Where Are You From? 4737(F)

More Than Anything Else, 4738(F)

Peacebound Trains, 9258(F)

A Sign, 19895

The Silence in the Mountains, 4019(F)

Silver Packages, 6127(F)

So Far from the Sea, 4745(F)

Something Beautiful, 3605(F)

Where Is Grandpa? 5066(F)

Sofer, Barbara. *Ilan Ramon*, 12454

Sogabe, Aki. *Aesop's Fox*, 11283

The Boy Who Drew Cats, 11052

The Hungriest Boy in the World, 1390(F)

Kogi's Mysterious Journey, 1426(F)

Oranges on Golden Mountain, 4950(F)

Sogabe, Aki, retel. *Aesop's Fox*, 11283

Sohi, Morteza E. *Look What I Did with a Leaf!* 24343

Look What I Did with a Shell! 24344

Soinale, Laura. *Sojourner Truth*, 13349

Sokol, Bill. *Time Cat*, 7965(F)

Solbert, Ronni. *Bronzeville Boys and Girls*, 11973(F)

The Pushcart War, 10230(F)

Solga, Kim. *Art Fun!* 24471

Craft Fun! 24345

Solheim, James. *It's Disgusting — and We Ate It! True Food Facts from Around the World — and Throughout History!* 22741

Sollers, Jim. *Little Tom Turkey*, 5293(F)

Solomon, Dane. *Fishing*, 25180

Solomon, Debra. *How Come Planet Earth?* 20640

Solomon, Heather. *Clever Beatrice*, 11566

Clever Beatrice and the Best Little Pony, 10881

Solomon, Heather M. *If I Were a Lion*, 3577(F)

Solway, Andrew. *Ancient Greece*, 15885

Ancient Rome, 15928

Classifying Insects, 21984

Rome, 15929

Soman, David. *The Aunt in Our House*, 3856(F)

The Leaving Morning, 3341(F)

One More Time, Mama, 3619(F)

Mabel Ran Away with the Toys, 4094(F)

Woods, Andrew. *Young Reggie Jackson,* 14391

Woods, Brenda. *The Red Rose Box,* 10034(F)

Woods, Geraldine. *Animal Experimentation and Testing,* 21040
The Navajo, 17635
The Oprah Winfrey Story, 12922

Woods, Geraldine (jt. author). *Bill Cosby,* 12780

Woods, Harold. *Bill Cosby,* 12780

Woods, Mae. *Charles Schulz,* 12672
Dr. Seuss, 12995
Insects of the Rain Forest, 23135
Laura Ingalls Wilder, 13144

Woods, Mary (jt. author). *Ancient Agriculture,* 15764
Ancient Machines from Wedges to Waterwheels, 15765

Woods, Mary B. *Ancient Communication,* 15115
Ancient Computing, 23286
Ancient Construction, 23891
Ancient Warfare, 24211

Woods, Mary B. (jt. author). *Ancient Medicine,* 15766
Ancient Transportation, 15767

Woods, Michael. *Ancient Agriculture,* 15764
Ancient Machines from Wedges to Waterwheels, 15765
Ancient Medicine, 15766
Ancient Transportation, 15767

Woods, Michael (jt. author). *Ancient Communication,* 15115
Ancient Computing, 23286
Ancient Construction, 23891
Ancient Warfare, 24211

Woods, Noah. *Tom Cat,* 3009(F)

Woods, Samuel. *Computer Animation,* 23998
The Pediatrician, 20246
Recycled Paper, 23775

Woods, Samuel G. *Chocolate,* 22750
Crayons, 23776
Guitars, 15335
Kids' Clothes from Start to Finish, 23929
Sneakers, 23930

Woods, Shirley. *Jack,* 7604(F)
Tooga, 7605(F)

Woodson, Jacqueline. *Hush,* 7953(F)
Locomotion, 12001
The Other Side, 4210(F)
Our Gracie Aunt, 5254(F)
Sweet, Sweet Memory, 5255(F)
Visiting Day, 4120(F)

Woodson, Marion. *My Brother's Keeper,* 7420(F)

Woodtor, Dee Parmer. *Big Meeting,* 4121(F)

Woodward, John. *What Lives in the Garden?* 21997

Woodward, Walter M. *Sam Houston,* 13525

Woodworth, Viki. *Daisy the Dancing Cow,* 3010(F)
Daisy the Firecow, 3011(F)

Woog, Adam. *The Beatles,* 12758
Bill Gates, 14153
A Cowboy in the Wild West, 18036
Killer Whales, 22372
New York, 17786
Suicide, 20324
A Sweatshop During the Industrial Revolution, 18198

Wool, David. *How Did We Find Out About Solar Power?* 23526
How Did We Find Out About Volcanoes? 22951

Wooldridge, Connie N. *Wicked Jack,* 11567

Wooldridge, Frosty. *Strike Three!* 10628(F)

Woolf, Alex. *Death and Disease,* 20222
Education, 15971
Osama Bin Laden, 14753

Woolfe, Angela. *Avril Crump and Her Amazing Clones,* 8710(F)

Worcester, Don. *Cowboy with a Camera, Erwin E. Smith,* 18037

Worland, Gayle. *The Computer,* 23999
The Radio, 24036

Wormell, Chris. *The Big Ugly Monster and the Little Stone Rabbit,* 1654(F)

Wormell, Christopher. *Puff-Puff, Chugga-Chugga,* 3012(F)
Teeth, Tales and Tentacles, 275(F)

Wormell, Mary. *Hilda Hen's Scary Night,* 3013(F)
Hilda Hen's Search, 3014(F)

Worms, Penny (jt. author). *Coping with Families,* 19783

Woronoff, Kristen. *Frida Kahlo,* 12589

Worth, Bonnie. *Oh Say Can You Say Dino-saur?* 15611

Worth, David. *Delaware,* 17787
The Great Empire of China and Marco Polo in World History, 15732
Mexican Immigrants, 19645
North Carolina, 17788
Ponce de Leon and the Age of Spanish Exploration in World History, 12449
Poverty, 19832
Robert Mugabe of Zimbabwe, 14851

Worth, Valerie. *Peacock and Other Poems,* 11965

Worthen, Bonnie (jt. author). *Period,* 20592

Worthen, Tom, ed. *Broken Hearts . . . Healing,* 11966

Wotjowycz, David. *Cock-a-doodle-doo! Barnyard Hullabaloo,* 1683(F)

Wray, Thomas (jt. author). *Home Is Where We Live,* 8967(F)

Wray, Ze. *101 Things to Do on the Internet,* 23987

Wrede, Patricia. *Dealing with Dragons,* 8711(F)

Wright, Beth. *Count Your Way Through Ireland,* 16721
Count Your Way Through Italy, 16770

Wright, Betty R. *Christina's Ghost,* 8712(F)
Crandalls' Castle, 8713(F)
The Dollhouse Murders, 7421(F)
The Ghost in Room 11, 8714(F)
A Ghost in the Family, 7422(F)
A Ghost in the House, 8715(F)
The Ghost of Popcorn Hill, 8716(F)
Haunted Summer, 8717(F)
The Moonlight Man, 8718(F)
Out of the Dark, 8719(F)
Pet Detectives, 3015(F)
Rosie and the Dance of the Dinosaurs, 9171(F)
The Summer of Mrs. MacGregor, 9118(F)
Too Many Secrets, 7423(F)
The Wish Master, 9119(F)

Wright, Betty Ren. *The Blizzard,* 5968(F)

Wright, Blanche Fisher. *Real Mother Goose,* 873

The Real Mother Goose Clock Book, 874

Wright, Cliff. *My Wishes for You,* 2133(F)
Santa's Ark, 6164(F)
When They Fight, 2963(F)

Wright, Courtni C. *Journey to Freedom,* 9619(F)
Jumping the Broom, 5056(F)

Wright, David. *Computers,* 24000

Wright, David K. *Arthur Ashe,* 14620
Brunei, 16545
Burma, 16546
John Lennon, 12836
Paul Robeson, 12881
The Story of Chevy Corvettes, 24109
The Story of Chevy Impalas, 24110
The Story of Ford Thunderbirds, 24111
The Story of Model T Fords, 24112
The Story of Porsches, 24113
The Story of Volkswagen Beetles, 24114
Vietnam, 16547
War in Vietnam, 16136

Wright, Joan Richards (jt. author). *Bugs,* 21960

Wright, Joseph P. (jt. author). *Math Games for Middle School,* 23305

Wright, Lynn F. *Flick,* 7606(F)

Wright, Lynne. *The Science of Noise,* 23642

Wright, Pamela (jt. author). *Bat Watching,* 21423
Butterfly Watching, 22054
Deer Watching, 21573
Eagle Watching, 21793
Sea Turtle Watching, 21159
Tide Pool Life Watching, 22429
Whale Watching, 22335

Wright, Rachel. *Paris 1789,* 16679

Wright, Susan K. *Dead Letters,* 7424(F)

Wright, Sydney. *Computer Fun Halloween,* 19436
Computer Fun Math, 23984

Wright-Frierson, Virginia. *First Grade Can Wait,* 5668(F)
An Island Scrapbook, 22444
A North American Rain Forest Scrapbook, 23136

Wroble, Lisa A. *Kids During the Great Depression,* 18199
Kids in Colonial Times, 17789
The New Deal and the Great Depression in American History, 18200

Wu, Dana Y. *Our Libraries,* 15100

Wu, Dana Ying-Hul. *The Chinese-American Experience,* 19646

Wu, Leslie. *Bijou, Bonbon and Beau,* 5003(F)
The Very Best Daddy of All, 3642(F)

Wu, Norbert. *Antarctic Ice,* 21041

Wu, Priscilla. *The Abacus Contest,* 9300(F)

Wukovits, John. *Annie Oakley,* 12859
The Composite Guide to Soccer, 25327

Wukovits, John F. *Butch Cassidy,* 13446
Colin Powell, 13586
George W. Bush, 13712
Jesse James, 13532
Life as a POW, 16114
Life of an American Soldier in Europe, 16115

Wulffson, Don L. *The Kid Who Invented the Trampoline,* 23777
Toys! Amazing Stories Behind Some Great Inventions, 25039

Wulfsohn, Gisèle. *A Child's Day in a South African City,* 16264

Title Index

This index contains both main entry and internal titles cited in the entries. References are to entry numbers, not page numbers. Fiction titles are indicated by (F) following the entry number.

1693

Subject/Grade Level Index

All entries are listed by subject and then according to grade level suitability (see the key at the foot of pages for grade level designations). Subjects are arranged alphabetically and subject heads may be subdivided into nonfiction (e.g., "Trucks") and fiction (e.g., "Trucks — Fiction"). References to entries are by entry number, not page number.

A

Aardema, Verna
PI: 12923, 1850
Aardvarks — Fiction
P: 1838, 1850
Aaron, Hank
PI: 14351 **I:** 14353 **IJ:** 14352
Abbott, Jim
PI: 14356 **IJ:** 14354–55
Abdul, Paula
I: 12734 **IJ:** 12735
Abdul-Jabbar, Kareem
I: 14453 **IJ:** 14452
Abenaki Indians — Folklore
I: 11421
Abernathy, David
IJ: 13230
Abilities
P: 19706
Abolitionists — Biography
PI: 13438 **I:** 13151, 13437, 13904
IJ: 13264, 13345, 13347, 13918
Abolitionists — Fiction
PI: 9677 **I:** 9675 **IJ:** 9591
Abominable snowman
See Big Foot; Yeti
I: 24881 **IJ:** 24841
Aborigines — Art
IJ: 14909
Aborigines (Australia)
I: 16558 **PI:** 16582 **IJ:** 16557, 16586, 16594
Aborigines (Australia) — Art
IJ: 14931
Aborigines (Australia) — Fiction
P: 4705, 4885 **I:** 9172
Aborigines (Australia) — Folklore
P: 11082
Abortion
IJ: 18839
Acadia — Fiction
I: 9472
Accidents
P: 20526 **I:** 20523, 20525, 20538
IJ: 20235, 20266, 20528
Accidents — Fiction
P: 3990 **I:** 8918, 9167 **IJ:** 7716

Acid rain
I: 18815
Acropolis (Greece)
IJ: 15880
Acting
IJ: 12278, 15420
Acting — Biography
IJ: 12495, 12754, 12767, 12769, 12773, 12775–76, 12782–83, 12810, 12829–30, 12837, 12841, 12847–48, 12861–62, 12864–65, 12876–77, 12881, 12888, 12892, 13429
Acting — Fiction
P: 5702 **PI:** 6487 **IJ:** 6960, 9374
Action rhymes
P: 876
Activism
IJ: 20240
Activism — Fiction
I: 7610
Actors — Biography
PI: 12874, 12901, 12917 **I:** 12850, 12885, 12915 **IJ:** 12823
Actors — Fiction
I: 9869 **IJ:** 8646
Actors and actresses — Biography
PI: 12787, 12880 **IJ:** 13608–9
Actresses — Biography
PI: 12755, 12768, 12800, 12811, 12814, 12818, 12838, 12845, 12879, 12890–91, 12899, 12911 **I:** 12799, 12801
Actresses — Fiction
I: 10369
Adams, Abigail
P: 13878 **PI:** 13876 **I:** 13875 **IJ:** 13874, 13877
Adams, Ansel
I: 12505
Adams, John
P: 13694 **PI:** 17814 **I:** 13693
IJ: 13690–92 **I:** 13697, 13699 **IJ:** 13696
Adams, John and Abigail
IJ: 13695 **I:** 13697, 13699 **IJ:** 13696
Adams, John Quincy
P: 13698 **I:** 13697, 13699 **IJ:** 13696
Adams, John Quincy — Fiction
PI: 4868 **I:** 9586
Adams, Samuel
P: 13401 **PI:** 13404 **IJ:** 13402–3
Addams, Jane
PI: 13879 **IJ:** 13880–83, 18266

Addictions
IJ: 20031, 20143
Addition
P: 600, 23259, 23273 **PI:** 23280
IJ: 23249
Adjectives
P: 15124
Adler, David A.
I: 12924
Adolescence
I: 19104 **IJ:** 20577
Adolescence — Fiction
I: 9027 **IJ:** 9141
Adolescence — Girls
IJ: 20582
Adoption
P: 3930, 3935, 19770 **IJ:** 19742, 19757–58, 19777
Adoption — Fiction
P: 2009, 2170, 2556, 2968, 3677, 3686, 3689, 3696, 3728, 3730, 3755, 3872, 3878, 3900, 3965, 3967, 3973, 3988, 4020, 4072, 4074, 4133, 4893, 5185, 5201, 5216, 6618, 6682 **PI:** 1829, 3685 **I:** 8839, 8863, 9168 **IJ:** 7588, 7758, 7853, 9016, 9723, 9832, 10602
Adventure and adventurers
IJ: 15430, 15720, 15723, 15727, 16880, 17641, 17666, 17668
Adventure and adventurers — Biography
IJ: 12294, 12311, 12326, 12334, 12338, 12353, 12357–58, 12372, 12377, 12387, 12392, 12409, 12415, 12421, 12432–33, 12438, 12443, 12450, 12459, 17661, 17667
Adventure and adventurers — Fiction
P: 3083 **I:** 7373, 7426 **IJ:** 6957, 6961, 6964, 6975–76, 6980, 6993, 7071, 7079, 7093, 7095, 7105, 7111, 7117, 7119, 7133, 7137, 7140, 7150–51, 7155, 7162, 7168, 7170, 7175, 7178, 7182, 7188, 7191, 7193, 7199, 7205, 7209, 7211, 7213, 7219, 7224–26, 7230, 7235–36, 7239, 7244, 7246–48, 7272, 7275, 7285, 7288, 7293–94, 7299, 7304, 7312, 7314–15, 7317, 7320, 7324–26, 7329, 7333, 7350, 7367–68, 7370–72, 7379, 7391, 7396, 7401, 7409, 7411, 7438, 7440, 7658, 7810, 7842, 7922, 7972, 8155, 8274, 8276, 8281, 8301, 8492, 8642, 8833, 9148, 9186, 9210, 9217, 9220, 9309, 9331, 9359, 9373, 9397, 9401–3,

P = Primary; PI = Primary-Intermediate; I = Intermediate; IJ = Intermediate-Junior High

Angels
I: 19141
Angels — Fiction
P: 787, 1547, 1566, 4481
PI: 1563, 8677, 8699 **I:** 8112
IJ: 8125, 9170
Angels — Poetry
P: 146, 11681
Anger
PI: 19681 **IJ:** 19701
Anger — Fiction
P: 2783, 5065, 5070, 5146, 5160, 5211, 5242
Angola
IJ: 16240
Anielewicz, Mordechai
IJ: 14745
Animal behavior
PI: 5587 **I:** 21251
Animal biology — Careers
P: 19975 **I:** 19963
Animal rescues — Fiction
IJ: 7225
Animal rights
P: 21019, 21037 **I:** 21028
Animal rights — Fiction
PI: 7454 **I:** 7517
Animal sounds — Fiction
P: 161, 2380
Animal stories — Fiction
P: 2749, 5499, 5605, 6718
PI: 7522 **I:** 7525, 7542
Animal welfare
IJ: 20965
Animals
P: 11, 271, 275, 3228, 5453, 17194, 20964, 20980, 20992, 21027, 21188, 21246, 21278, 23198 **PI:** 5586–87, 5899, 20970, 20986, 21038, 21209, 21367, 21954, 22458, 22472, 23044, 24409 **I:** 16520, 20923, 20950, 20959, 20975, 20991, 21229, 21327 **IJ:** 20944, 20951, 20989, 21009, 21030, 21036, 21039, 21333
Animals — Actors
I: 21021
Animals — Africa
P: 21034, 21225 **PI:** 21210, 21253–56 **I:** 21213, 21243
Animals — Africa — Fiction
P: 5596, 21225 **PI:** 21210, 21253–56 **I:** 21213, 21243
Animals — Anatomy
P: 20994, 21225 **PI:** 21210, 21253–56 **I:** 21213, 21243
Animals — Ark
P: 19188, 19195, 19222, 19251
Animals — Ark — Fiction
P: 2861 **PI:** 19215
Animals — Art
P: 14906 **PI:** 14948
IJ: 14975, 24428
Animals — Australia
P: 20958, 21624 **PI:** 16577, 22627
Animals — Babies
P: 5315, 5378, 5466, 5522, 5577, 5654, 21106, 21258, 21262–63, 21265, 21267, 21270, 21272–75, 21277, 21279, 21624, 22212, 22513, 22558, 22687 **PI:** 15597, 21266, 21268, 21276, 21721, 22147, 22593, 22626 **I:** 21269, 21271, 22280, 22366

Animals — Babies — Fiction
P: 2618, 5299
Animals — Bathing
P: 21187
Animals — Behavior
P: 3274, 5609, 5615, 20996, 21185–87, 21191–92, 21195, 21199, 21216, 21219, 21221–22, 21248, 21258, 21261, 21264 **PI:** 5586, 20940, 20998, 21002, 21209, 21232, 21242, 21314, 21654 **I:** 21004, 21213, 21230, 21249, 21339, 21454 **IJ:** 21196–97, 21200, 21205, 21208, 21224, 21241
Animals — Behavior — Fiction
P: 800, 5312, 5314, 5520
Animals — Bodies
PI: 21954
Animals — Bodies — Fiction
P: 912
Animals — California
I: 21011
Animals — Camouflage
P: 21248, 21280–81, 21283, 21286–87, 21716, 21980
PI: 21282, 21284–85
Animals — Camouflage — Fiction
P: 2911
Animals — Cannibalism
IJ: 21205
Animals — Care — Careers
IJ: 19851–52, 19855, 19863
Animals — Careers
I: 21021
Animals — Circuses
IJ: 21022
Animals — Classification
I: 15592, 21065, 22247
IJ: 20954, 21039
Animals — Coloration
P: 21007, 21247, 21283, 21291, 21293 **PI:** 21245, 21289–90
Animals — Colors
P: 21248, 21291, 21293
PI: 21245, 21289–90
Animals — Communication
P: 21288, 21291, 21293
PI: 21245, 21289–90
Animals — Crafts
I: 15592
Animals — Criminals and crime
I: 20990
Animals — Defenses
P: 9076, 21295–96
PI: 20940–41, 21297–98
I: 21294 **IJ:** 21204
Animals — Drawing and painting
PI: 24420 **I:** 24478
Animals — Emotions
I: 21206
Animals — Experimentation
IJ: 21040
Animals — Experiments and projects
I: 15592, 20695 **IJ:** 20967, 21208
Animals — Families
I: 21269
Animals — Feet
PI: 21252

Animals — Fiction
P: 101, 204, 226, 287–88, 448, 515, 538, 544, 549, 915, 1222, 1236, 1272, 1287, 1658, 1738, 1901, 2361, 3590, 4337, 4519, 4535, 4623, 4901, 5259, 5277, 5285, 5307, 5319, 5343, 5349, 5356, 5362, 5374, 5393, 5412, 5432, 5463, 5479, 5484, 5530, 5534, 5616, 5639, 5641–42, 5644, 5650, 6209, 6530, 6588, 7464, 7560, 7579, 7593
PI: 2699, 6123, 7437, 7524
I: 7519, 7529, 8336 **IJ:** 7018, 7523, 9158
Animals — Folklore
P: 10782, 10810, 10813, 10880, 10921, 11443
PI: 10770, 10861, 24845
I: 10874, 10897, 10902
IJ: 10857, 11423, 11430
Animals — Food
P: 21042, 21183, 21199
PI: 21220 **I:** 21251, 22624
IJ: 21204
Animals — General
See also Amphibians; Endangered animals; Endangered species; Fables; Farm life; Imaginary animals; Invertebrates; Marine animals; Pets; Prehistoric animals; Ranches and ranch life; Wildlife conservation; Zoos; as a subdivision under country or continent names; e.g., Africa — Animals; as individual animal species; or as part of a specific biome, e.g., Rain forests
P: 61, 494, 5341, 5387, 5578, 20953, 20957, 20960, 20966, 20969, 20974, 20978, 20984, 20993, 21024, 21029, 21189, 21216, 21319–20, 21328, 21335, 21371, 21385, 22622, 23037, 23203 **PI:** 20977, 21005, 21014, 21026, 21031, 21193, 21326, 21382, 23099, 23144, 23212 **I:** 20922, 20973, 20981, 21015–16, 21018, 21023, 21025, 21228, 21350, 21358
Animals — Grooming
P: 21240
Animals — Habitat
PI: 21654
Animals — Habitats
P: 18678, 20996, 21222, 21303–4, 21308, 21310
PI: 21035, 23030 **I:** 17138
IJ: 21003, 23114
Animals — Heads
PI: 21255
Animals — Hearing
P: 21211 **I:** 21182
Animals — Hibernation
P: 21300–1
Animals — Hibernation — Fiction
P: 5546
Animals — Homes
P: 5269, 21265, 21303, 21307, 21309, 21311 **PI:** 21305
IJ: 21003, 21302, 21306

Animals — Homes — Fiction
P: 6601
Animals — Intelligence
I: 21207
Animals — Jokes and riddles
P: 21308, 24772, 24785
PI: 24761, 24786
Animals — Life cycles
I: 21236
Animals — Locomotion
P: 5489, 21217, 21223, 21259
PI: 21260 **I:** 21214
Animals — Migration
P: 21201 **PI:** 21239 **I:** 21236
Animals — Migration — Fiction
P: 5375
Animals — Mothers
P: 5466
Animals — Mythology
PI: 11951
Animals — Names
PI: 20972
Animals — Noses
PI: 21254
Animals — Oddities
PI: 20940 **I:** 21327 **IJ:** 21362
Animals — Play
P: 21185, 21250
Animals — Poetry
P: 11789, 11891, 12004, 12006–8–12, 12020, 12022, 12028, 12033, 12037–38, 12045, 12062, 12136, 12171, 12224 **PI:** 12010, 12019, 12023, 12031, 12035, 12051
I: 12003, 12025, 12032, 12186
IJ: 11864, 12005
Animals — Poetry
P: 12009–12, 12020, 12022, 12028, 12033, 12037–38, 12045, 12062, 12136, 12171, 12224 **PI:** 12010, 12019, 12023, 12031, 12035, 12051
I: 12003, 12025, 12032, 12186
IJ: 11864, 12005
Animals — Poetry
P: 12011–12, 12020, 12022, 12028, 12033, 12037–38, 12045, 12062, 12136, 12171, 12224 **PI:** 12010, 12019, 12023, 12031, 12035, 12051
I: 12003, 12025, 12032, 12186
IJ: 11864, 12005
Animals — Poisonous
I: 20962 **IJ:** 20956
Animals — Predators
I: 21233
Animals — Puzzles
PI: 24791
Animals — Reproduction
P: 21312 **I:** 21271
Animals — Research
IJ: 21008
Animals — Riddles
P: 24764
Animals — Rights
IJ: 19582, 21040
Animals — Rights — Fiction
IJ: 7243
Animals — Senses
P: 21211, 21227 **I:** 21190, 21212
Animals — Shapes
P: 21248
Animals — Size
P: 5658

Addition; Concept books
— Addition
P: 488, 6224
Arizona
PI: 18691 **I:** 18697, 23046
IJ: 18685, 18689, 18705
Arizona Territory — Fiction
I: 10470
Arkansas
P: 18632 **PI:** 18615 **I:** 18639
IJ: 18589
Arkansas River
IJ: 23175
Arlington National Cemetery
I: 18651
Armadillos
PI: 21359 **I:** 21358, 21375,
21380
Armed forces
See also individual
branches, e.g., United
States Air Force
IJ: 15686, 24176, 24187
Armed forces — Biography
I: 14742
Armed forces — Fiction
P: 4065
Armed forces — Women
IJ: 18378
Armed forces (U.S.)
I: 19003
Armed forces (U.S.) —
Biography
IJ: 13581
Armenia
IJ: 16799, 16809
Armenia — Folklore
P: 11086 **PI:** 11096, 11390
Armenia — History
IJ: 14830
Armenia — Songs
P: 1175
Arms
IJ: 20453
Armstrong, Lance
P: 14654 **PI:** 14656–57
IJ: 14655, 14658
Armstrong, Louis
P: 12747 **PI:** 12745 **I:** 12744
IJ: 12746
Armstrong, Neil
P: 12315 **PI:** 12318 **I:** 12314
IJ: 12316–17
Army (U.S.)
IJ: 24197
Army (U.S.) — African
Americans
IJ: 19542
Army (U.S.) — Biography
IJ: 13195, 13551, 13574,
13584, 13586
Army (U.S.) — History
IJ: 16079
Army (U.S.) — Special Forces
IJ: 24184
Arner, Louise
I: 12319
Arnold, Benedict
I: 13413 **IJ:** 13411–12,
13414–15
Art
See also Art appreciation;
Artists; Drawing and
painting; Museums; and as
a subdivision under other
subjects, e.g., Animals —

Art; and names of
individuals, e.g., Van
Gogh, Vincent
P: 102, 1630, 14901, 14914,
14935, 14985, 14998, 19406
PI: 14917, 14936, 24466
I: 14959, 14965, 14974, 14993,
15011, 15020, 15665
IJ: 11762, 14909, 14920,
14940, 14947, 14952, 14979,
15000, 15002, 15004–5, 15009,
15014, 15018, 15021, 15026,
15902, 17956, 19196, 24453
Art — African American
IJ: 12002
Art — Biography
P: 12575, 12625, 12683
PI: 12507, 12509, 12529,
12531, 12578, 12583, 12606,
12629, 12632, 12654, 12687
I: 12488, 12545, 12650, 12673
IJ: 12470, 12480, 12511–12,
12523–25, 12527, 12532,
12536, 12538–39, 12543–44,
12548–50, 12552–53, 12560,
12562–63, 12566, 12568,
12570–71, 12576–77, 12579,
12584–86, 12592, 12594,
12597–98, 12605, 12608,
12611, 12616, 12626–27,
12636–37, 12639–43, 12645,
12649, 12651, 12657,
12659–60, 12663, 12667,
12680, 12685–86, 12690–91,
14925
Art — Careers
P: 19893 **IJ:** 19885
Art — Fiction
P: 934, 1373, 1426, 1559,
1720, 1988, 2366, 3154, 3174,
3591, 4712, 4750, 4823, 4826,
5004, 5217, 5759, 5770
PI: 2131, 9363 **I:** 9092, 9344
IJ: 7029, 7402, 7852, 9069,
9224, 9452, 9803
Art — Forgeries
I: 14963
Art — History
PI: 14930, 16333 **I:** 14969,
14982 **IJ:** 14933–34, 14945,
14960, 14973, 15012, 15026,
15858, 16673, 23774
Art — Inuit
I: 15008
Art — Islamic
IJ: 14905
Art — New York State
IJ: 18454
Art — Renaissance
P: 1370
Art — Supplies
P: 14935
Art appreciation
P: 7, 3568, 14900, 14906–7,
14913, 14915, 14926, 14929,
14961, 14968, 14972, 14990,
14992, 14998 **PI:** 14911,
14923–24, 14942, 14948,
14958, 14967, 14970, 14978,
14988, 14996–97, 24448
I: 12204, 14953, 14977, 14984,
14989 **IJ:** 12538, 12667,
14912, 14918, 14922,
14927–28, 14943, 14951,
14954–56, 14964, 14973,
14975–76, 14994
Art appreciation — Fiction
P: 2538, 14910

Arthritis
See also Rheumatoid
arthritis
PI: 20097
Arthritis — Fiction
IJ: 9162
Arthropods
I: 22133 **IJ:** 20971
Arthur, Chester A.
IJ: 13700
Arthur, King
PI: 11245 **IJ:** 11241, 11246
Arthur, King — Fiction
PI: 10070 **I:** 11221 **IJ:** 8114,
8443, 8729
Arthurdale (WV)
IJ: 18153
Artificial heart — Biography
I: 14172
Artificial insemination
PI: 20573
Artificial intelligence
IJ: 23952, 23983
Artificial limbs
P: 20070
Artists
P: 14991
Artists — Biography
P: 3809, 12526, 12559, 12588,
12638, 12647, 12675, 12682,
12682, 12689, 12993, 13059
PI: 3178, 12508, 12519–20,
12534, 12541, 12546–47,
12551, 12557, 12565, 12569,
12574, 12587, 12591, 12599,
12607, 12609, 12612–13,
12615, 12617, 12619, 12631,
12633, 12635, 12648, 12656,
12658, 12665–66, 12668,
12676–79, 12681, 12681,
12684, 12688, 12983, 13001,
13034, 15028 **I:** 12484, 12490,
12506, 12528, 12533, 12537,
12558, 12564, 12589–90,
12600–1, 12618, 12621, 12628,
12630, 12652, 12661–62,
12664, 12962, 13025, 14980
IJ: 12515, 12522, 12535,
12540, 12542, 12554, 12580,
12610, 12614, 12646, 12653,
12991
Artists — Fiction
P: 1604, 4818, 5042 **PI:** 9303
I: 9322, 9338, 10655 **IJ:** 9315
Arts — Careers
PI: 19886
Asante (African people)
IJ: 16276
Asch, Frank
P: 12941
Ashanti — Folklore
P: 10938 **I:** 10893
Ashe, Arthur
PI: 14618 **IJ:** 14617,
14619–20
Asia
See also specific countries,
e.g., China
IJ: 16323, 16331
Asia — Arts
IJ: 16330
Asia — Crafts
IJ: 16330
Asia — Folklore
P: 10971, 11066, 11073
PI: 10970, 10983 **I:** 10968

Asia — History
I: 15757 **IJ:** 16330, 16332
Asian Americans —
Biography
See also specific groups,
e.g., Chinese Americans
P: 13146 **IJ:** 12483, 13207,
14737
Asian Americans — Fiction
P: 3728, 4158 **IJ:** 9069
Asimov, Isaac
IJ: 12942–43
ASPCA
P: 21037
Aspen trees
PI: 22814
Assassinations
P: 13773 **PI:** 13765, 13783
I: 13776 **IJ:** 13782, 13786,
18931
Assault (race horse) —
Fiction
PI: 7562
Asteroids
P: 20853, 20868, 20874
I: 20849, 20858, 20862, 20865,
22933 **IJ:** 20860
Asthma
I: 20099, 20101, 20140, 20152,
20196 **IJ:** 20103, 20108,
20163, 20207, 20217
Asthma — Fiction
P: 5158, 5172 **IJ:** 9518
Astrology
IJ: 24819, 24837
Astronauts
P: 12466, 23782 **PI:** 23696
I: 23704 **IJ:** 23658, 23662,
23671, 23693
Astronauts — Biography
P: 12315, 12410 **PI:** 12318,
12411–12, 12425–26, 13498
I: 12314, 12324, 12397, 12413,
12423–24, 12457, 13496–97
IJ: 12308, 12316–17, 12323,
12428, 12437, 12454–56,
12462, 13495, 13499–500
Astronauts — Careers
PI: 19875 **IJ:** 19850
Astronauts — Fiction
P: 5758 **PI:** 7113
Astronomers — Biography
P: 14027 **IJ:** 14078
Astronomy
P: 20718, 20737–38, 20755,
20769, 20806, 20823, 20863,
20889, 20897, 20906
PI: 20710, 20724, 20731,
20741, 20754, 20759, 20785,
20824, 20853, 20884 **I:** 14198,
20711, 20717, 20720–21,
20723, 20727, 20730, 20739,
20744–45, 20749, 20825,
20856, 20890, 23650, 23689,
23702 **IJ:** 20709, 20713–14,
20716, 20719, 20722, 20726,
20734, 20748, 20751, 20753,
20883, 20891–92, 23705
Astronomy — Biography
I: 14077, 14146 **IJ:** 13980,
14076, 14145, 14171,
14233–34, 20725
Astronomy — Careers
PI: 19965 **I:** 19968

P = Primary; PI = Primary-Intermediate; I = Intermediate; IJ = Intermediate-Junior High

P = Primary; PI = Primary-Intermediate; I = Intermediate; IJ = Intermediate-Junior High

P = Primary; PI = Primary-Intermediate; I = Intermediate; IJ = Intermediate-Junior High

Blankets — Fiction
P: 3453, 19516 **I:** 19505
Blessings
See also Prayers
P: 19513, 19516 **I:** 19505
Blessings — Fiction
P: 3643
Blind
P: 6397 **PI:** 13928, 14210, 15107 **I:** 13899, 20094 **IJ:** 13226, 20058, 20074
Blind — Biography
P: 14051 **PI:** 14046, 14048, 14050 **IJ:** 13931, 14047, 14049
Blind — Fiction
P: 3934, 4548, 5115, 5212, 10954 **PI:** 9169 **I:** 6982, 7527, 7570, 8773, 9138, 9151, 9572 **IJ:** 7386, 7587–88, 9132
Blisters
I: 20466
Blizzard of 1888
IJ: 18169, 23386
Blizzard of 1888 — Fiction
IJ: 9852
Blizzards
P: 4642, 23392 **PI:** 18195 **I:** 23405
Blizzards — Fiction
P: 4594, 4650, 5968, 7177 **IJ:** 7288
Blood
P: 20333
Blood — Biography
I: 14094
Blood-sucking animals
I: 20999
Bloomer, Amelia — Fiction
P: 4771
Blue (color)
P: 281
Blue whales
IJ: 22362
Blues (music)
IJ: 15231, 15241
Blues (music) — Biography
PI: 12900 **IJ:** 12489
Blues (music) — Fiction
P: 2565, 5124
Blues (music) — Poetry
IJ: 11859
Bluford, Guion
I: 12324 **IJ:** 12323
Blume, Judy
PI: 12947–48
Bly, Nellie
PI: 13422, 13425–26 **I:** 13167, 13423 **IJ:** 13424, 13427
BMX
IJ: 25147
Boa constrictors
PI: 21147
Boa constrictors — Fiction
P: 2865
Board books
P: 187, 216, 312, 442, 1027, 1940, 2212, 3453
Board books — Fiction
P: 2906
Boars
PI: 21356
Boars — Fiction
P: 1706

Boat people (Vietnamese) — Fiction
I: 9296
Boats — Fiction
P: 7041, 21503 **I:** 21485, 21530
Boats and boating
See Dragon boat races; Sailing and boating; Ships and boats
Bobcats
P: 21481, 21503 **I:** 21485, 21530
Bobsledding
PI: 24901 **IJ:** 25263
Body decoration
IJ: 24867–68
Body language
PI: 19704
Bodybuilding
IJ: 24916
Bodyguards — Careers
IJ: 19845
Bogs
P: 23171
Bogs — Fiction
P: 4628
Boitano, Brian
IJ: 14554
Bolivia
PI: 17229 **IJ:** 17196, 17264
Bomb squads
PI: 19947
Bomb squads — Careers
IJ: 19861
Bonaparte, Napoleon
PI: 4753 **IJ:** 16736, 17862
Bonds
PI: 18718
Bonds, Barry
IJ: 14362
Bones
P: 20443 **I:** 20454, 20456
Bonetta, Sarah Forbes
IJ: 14756
Bonilla, Bobby
IJ: 14363–64
Bonney, William H.
IJ: 13421
Book making
PI: 15082 **IJ:** 24493
Book reports
I: 15200
Books — Fiction
P: 1045
Books and printing
P: 15084, 15087 **PI:** 15081, 15098 **I:** 12086 **IJ:** 15099
Books and printing — Biography
IJ: 14161
Books and printing — Fiction
P: 3163 **I:** 7721, 9357
Books and reading — Fiction
IJ: 10528
Books for beginning readers
P: 171, 432–33, 497, 4524, 4646, 5549, 5975, 6197, 6362, 6397, 6399, 6432, 6449, 6516, 6520, 6532, 6610, 6615, 6625, 6648, 6681, 6712, 6714, 6780, 6788, 6799, 6818, 6841, 6846, 6854, 6902–3, 6913, 11268, 11529, 12116, 12388, 12399, 12638, 13139, 13269, 13482–83, 13486, 13538,

13662, 13694, 13810–11, 13852, 13854, 13865, 13973, 13993, 14037, 14071, 14130, 14133, 14272, 14427, 14580, 14654, 14820, 14883, 15079, 15146, 15391, 15394, 15460, 15655, 15802, 15820, 16685, 16739, 16792, 17043, 17047, 17316, 17652, 17804, 17833, 18002, 18296, 18670, 19042, 19062, 19276, 19339, 19360–63, 19415, 19487, 19723, 19833–34, 19949, 20102, 20156, 20319, 20328, 20401, 20482–83, 20776, 20802, 20834, 20904–6, 20974, 20978, 20980, 21072, 21098, 21114, 21141, 21154, 21164, 21189, 21227, 21275, 21279, 21281, 21328–29, 21347, 21371, 21412, 21455, 21463–64, 21501, 21505, 21511, 21594, 21625, 21653, 21700, 21705, 21788, 21804, 21910, 21929–30, 21970, 21972, 22018, 22037, 22042, 22085, 22087, 22096, 22119, 22149, 22165, 22190, 22209, 22298, 22315, 22343, 22364, 22371, 22462–64, 22541, 22586, 22589, 22592, 22625, 22636, 22641, 22665, 22708, 22718, 22725, 22740, 22754, 22764, 22783, 22795, 22807–8, 22844, 22974–75, 22985, 23051, 23066, 23087, 23192, 23232, 23330, 23339, 23356, 23359, 23392, 23406, 23415, 23425, 23432, 23441, 23470, 23482, 23559, 23584, 23641, 23723, 23782–83, 23917, 23923, 23925, 24005, 24043, 24074, 24095, 24109, 24111–13, 24131, 24282, 24288, 24618, 24748, 24752, 24873, 25054, 25120, 25189, 25218, 25306, 25316, 25339 **PI:** 6478, 6519, 6552, 6751, 6800, 6880, 6927, 9807, 12381, 13324, 13356, 13506, 13935, 14656, 15507–8, 17476, 17937, 19497, 20637, 20690, 21491, 21495, 22584, 22736, 23837, 24172, 24831, 24981, 25071, 25105, 25186, 25312 **I:** 17417, 21111, 24019, 24050
Books for beginning readers — Biography
P: 13273, 13924, 14103, 14435 **PI:** 13276, 13949, 14630, 14695
Books for beginning readers — Fiction
P: 244, 435, 459, 511, 517, 536, 563, 575, 577, 1419, 1464, 2040–41, 2103, 2793, 3219, 3647, 4601, 5327, 5411, 5619, 5774, 5917, 5988, 6101, 6237, 6255, 6365, 6374, 6380–96, 6398, 6400–2, 6405–21, 6423–31, 6435–41, 6443–48, 6450–69, 6471–74, 6476–77, 6479–86, 6489, 6492, 6494–512, 6514–15, 6517–18, 6521–23, 6527–31, 6533–36, 6538–48, 6550, 6553–56, 6558, 6560–66, 6568, 6570–75, 6577–609, 6611–14, 6616–22,

6626–29, 6632–40, 6642–43, 6649–53, 6655–57, 6659–70, 6672, 6675, 6678–80, 6683–94, 6696–700, 6702, 6704–5, 6707, 6709–10, 6713, 6715–27, 6729–37, 6739–50, 6752–58, 6760–61, 6763, 6765–79, 6781–83, 6785–87, 6789–92, 6794–98, 6801–4, 6807–17, 6819, 6821–33, 6835, 6837–40, 6842–43, 6845, 6847–53, 6855–58, 6860–77, 6879, 6881–901, 6904–12, 6914–26, 6928–35, 6937–43, 6945–49, 6951–53, 7448, 7593, 7844, 8418, 8555, 9773, 10531, 23266, 23289, 24768, 24932 **PI:** 6475, 6487–88, 6490–91, 6493, 6524–26, 6549, 6551, 6557, 6559, 6567, 6569, 6623, 6630–31, 6641, 6644–47, 6654, 6658, 6671, 6673–74, 6676–77, 6701, 6703, 6706, 6708, 6711, 6728, 6759, 6762, 6784, 6820, 6834, 6836, 6950, 7374, 9543, 9688, 10425 **I:** 6996
Books for beginning readers — Poetry
P: 6433, 6878, 12033, 12123 **PI:** 11794
Books for beginning readers — Readers
P: 6434
Booksellers — Fiction
IJ: 9421
Boone, Daniel
PI: 12325, 12329 **I:** 12327, 12330–31, 18008 **IJ:** 12326, 12328
Boone, Daniel — Fiction
P: 4812
Boone, John William
IJ: 12762
Booth, Edwin and John Wilkes
IJ: 13428
Booth, John Wilkes
IJ: 13429, 18111
Borden, Lizzie
IJ: 18121
Boreal forests
PI: 23093
Boredom — Fiction
P: 2166
Borges, Jorge Luís
IJ: 12949
Borglum, Gutzon
I: 18259
Borneo — Animals
I: 16520
Bosch, Hieronymus
P: 1630
Bosnia
I: 16623–24 **IJ:** 14858, 16640
Bosnia — Fiction
P: 4741
Bosnia and Herzegovina
I: 16635
Bosnian Americans
I: 16624 **IJ:** 19627
Boston
PI: 24046 **I:** 18465
Boston — Fiction
P: 3180 **PI:** 8509, 9515 **I:** 9467, 9534, 9728, 9811
Boston (MA)
IJ: 17705, 24055

P = Primary; PI = Primary-Intermediate; I = Intermediate; IJ = Intermediate-Junior High

P = Primary; PI = Primary-Intermediate; I = Intermediate; IJ = Intermediate-Junior High

P = Primary; PI = Primary-Intermediate; I = Intermediate; IJ = Intermediate-Junior High

Corn
P: 22783, 22791 PI: 22778, 22792 I: 22779

Cornwall — Folklore
I: 11172

Cornwall (England) — Fiction
IJ: 9403

Corot, Jean Camille
IJ: 12544

Corrigan, Mairead
IJ: 16706

Cortes, Hernan
I: 12360

Corvette (automobile)
P: 24109

Cosby, Bill
I: 12777, 12779 IJ: 12778, 12780

Cosmetics — Biography
I: 14252 IJ: 14250

Cosmetics — History
IJ: 23907, 24868

Costa Rica
P: 17147 PI: 17116 I: 17146

Costa Rica — Folklore
P: 11591

Costa Rica — Holidays
PI: 17116

Costumes and costume making
PI: 24396 I: 24407
IJ: 24397, 24400, 24405

Costumes and costume making — Fiction
P: 6248

Costumes and costume making — History
I: 23908

Cotton
P: 23916, 23919

Cotton, Elizabeth
P: 5040

Cotton gin — Biography
P: 14257

Cottontail rabbits
P: 21650

Cougars
P: 21503, 21527 I: 21486, 21528

Cougars — Fiction
IJ: 7700

Counting
I: 23323

Counting books
P: 183, 212, 249, 260–62, 272, 275–76, 333, 380–81, 384–86, 388, 390–91, 393, 395, 399–404, 406–7, 409–10, 413–14, 417, 419–21, 424–30, 432–33, 435, 437, 439, 441–42, 444–47, 449, 451–52, 454, 456, 458–60, 465–67, 470, 472, 474–76, 478–83, 485, 491–99, 501–4, 506–8, 510–14, 516–20, 522–23, 525, 529, 531, 533–37, 539–40, 542–43, 545–48, 553, 555–57, 559–74, 576, 579–88, 590–91, 593–95, 597–603, 605–7, 610, 695, 745, 813, 884, 906, 1530, 1980, 4308, 5277, 5996, 6023, 6065, 6211, 6516, 6712, 21154, 22329, 23296
PI: 396, 16687, 16770–71, 16952, 17223 I: 16353, 16402, 16814, 16986

Counting books — Chinese
P: 487

Counting books — Fiction
P: 58, 143, 269, 382–83, 387, 389, 392, 394, 397–98, 405, 411–12, 415–16, 418, 422–23, 431, 438, 440, 443, 448, 450, 455, 457, 461, 463–64, 468, 471, 473, 477, 484, 486, 490, 500, 509, 515, 521, 524, 528, 538, 541, 544, 549, 554, 558, 575, 577, 589, 592, 596, 604, 608–9, 5804 PI: 532

Counting books — Poetry
P: 11750

Countries
PI: 15726

Country music — Biography
IJ: 12878

Courage
P: 19717

Courage — Fiction
P: 1893, 2018, 2621, 3042
I: 7410

Courtroom trials
IJ: 18825–26, 18831, 18834, 18838, 18840, 18843, 18926, 18958

Courts
I: 18824, 18828

Cousins — Fiction
I: 6973

Cousteau, Jacques
I: 12361–63

Cowboys
P: 13294 I: 18026, 18036–37, 18682 IJ: 17955, 18004, 18012, 18129

Cowboys — African Americans
IJ: 17948

Cowboys — Biography
P: 12869, 12886 PI: 13295
I: 13296 IJ: 12888

Cowboys — Cookbooks
IJ: 17960

Cowboys — Fiction
P: 1046, 1536, 3088, 3092–93, 3493, 4155, 4256, 4295, 6429, 10716 PI: 3074, 6161, 10303
I: 7287 IJ: 9018, 9635, 9722, 9724, 9735

Cowboys — Folklore
P: 11539

Cowboys — History
I: 17970 IJ: 17118, 18009, 18020

Cowgirls
IJ: 18011, 19879

Cowgirls — Fiction
P: 1046, 1206, 6883

Cows
See Cattle
P: 22665

Cows — Fiction
P: 1243, 2072, 2552, 5200, 5418, 5581, 5600, 5628

Cows — Folklore
P: 10925 PI: 11175

Coyotes
P: 21549 PI: 21564, 21566
I: 21563, 21567, 21571
IJ: 21560

Coyotes — Fiction
P: 2447, 5263 PI: 5429
I: 7595

Coyotes — Folklore
I: 11488, 11490

Crabs
P: 22198 PI: 22197, 22203
I: 22199, 22201–2

Crabs — Fiction
P: 3102

Crack (drug)
IJ: 20040

Crafts
See also specific crafts, e.g., Paper crafts
P: 4751, 17062, 24223–24, 24230, 24235, 24241, 24251, 24260, 24284, 24288, 24293–96, 24304, 24307–8, 24322–23, 24328, 24330–31, 24349, 24363, 24372, 24454, 24479, 24498 PI: 15318, 15795, 19282, 19288, 19388, 19413, 19434, 19437, 19440, 19468, 24215, 24222, 24225, 24231–32, 24244–47, 24249–50, 24252–53, 24258–59, 24261, 24266, 24269, 24285, 24297, 24306, 24310, 24313, 24315, 24317, 24320, 24327, 24329, 24332–33, 24337, 24345, 24347, 24351, 24356, 24360, 24362, 24366, 24376, 24378, 24380, 24387, 24391, 24396, 24447, 24472, 24480, 24497, 24516, 24536, 24570, 24639, 24717, 25034 I: 10836, 12931, 14987, 15404, 15574, 15773, 15930, 15941, 16055, 17426, 17584, 17686, 17738, 17939–40, 17972, 17984, 18162, 19426, 19467, 19479, 22780, 24214, 24216–17, 24221, 24229, 24233–34, 24236, 24238, 24240, 24242–43, 24248, 24254–56, 24262, 24264–65, 24267–68, 24270, 24272–74, 24278, 24281, 24287, 24291, 24298–302, 24309, 24312, 24314, 24316, 24318–19, 24324–26, 24334–36, 24338, 24342–44, 24346, 24353–54, 24358–59, 24361, 24365, 24367, 24375, 24388–89, 24482, 24490–92, 24499, 24501, 24506–7, 24517, 24519, 24521, 24524, 24526–27, 24534, 24562, 24720, 24942
IJ: 15749, 15800, 15859, 15905, 16537, 16566, 16847, 16856, 17073, 17083, 20663, 24212–13, 24218–20, 24226, 24237, 24239, 24257, 24263, 24271, 24275–77, 24280, 24292, 24303, 24340–41, 24352, 24355, 24357, 24369, 24371, 24374, 24377, 24381, 24383, 24392, 24394–95, 24416–17, 24483, 24487, 24496, 24500, 24522, 24541, 24546, 24980 All: 24286

Crafts — Bible
I: 24321

Crafts — Easter
I: 24243

Crafts — Food
P: 24583

Crafts — General
I: 24227

Crafts — Greece
IJ: 15852

Crafts — Historical
PI: 24368, 24370, 24373, 24379 IJ: 17771

Crafts — Middle Ages
I: 15947

Crafts — Rome
IJ: 15892

Crafts — Weaving
IJ: 24283

Crafts — Winter
P: 24282

Cranberries
PI: 22695

Crandall, Prudence
P: 13908

Crane, Stephen
IJ: 12968

Cranes — Fiction
P: 963, 10652 PI: 11048
I: 8908

Cranes — Poetry
P: 12060

Cranes (bird)
P: 21753 PI: 21742 I: 21690, 21757 IJ: 21693

Cranes (bird) — Fiction
I: 8433

Crayfish
P: 22200

Crayons
P: 23752 I: 23776

Crayons — Fiction
P: 1422, 6633

Crazy Horse — Fiction
PI: 9438

Crazy Horse, Chief
I: 13634, 13636 IJ: 13635

Creation
P: 1031, 19214

Creation — Fiction
P: 2465, 19117 PI: 19237

Creation — Folklore
P: 10856, 10929–30
PI: 10892, 11418, 19240, 19246 I: 10829 IJ: 10886

Creation — Mythology
IJ: 19137

Creation stories
P: 19190

Creative writing
PI: 15222

Credit cards
I: 18729

Cree Indians
I: 17049

Creek Indians
PI: 17537, 17582 I: 17569

Creek Indians — History
I: 17512

Creoles — Fiction
I: 7673

Crete — History
I: 15651

Creutzfeldt-Jakob disease
IJ: 20167

Crews, Donald
P: 3722

Crick, Francis
IJ: 13979

Crickets
I: 21953, 21976 IJ: 21964

Crickets — Fiction
P: 1890, 2252, 3073, 5989
I: 8588, 17959, 18925, 18927,

P = Primary; PI = Primary-Intermediate; I = Intermediate; IJ = Intermediate-Junior High

P = Primary; PI = Primary-Intermediate; I = Intermediate; IJ = Intermediate-Junior High

4925, 4966, 5002, 5054, 5119,
5214, 5553, 5608, 5929, 6295,
6442, 6653, 6924, 7507, 7897
PI: 3773, 3909, 4050, 7034,
7682, 7703, 7705, 7785, 7904,
8928, 10285, 12975, 16519,
18751 **I:** 7360, 7696, 7717,
7723, 7744, 7792, 7811, 7878,
7905, 7939, 9694, 9856, 9901,
10142, 10164, 10218, 10282,
10315, 17148 **IJ:** 7100, 7685,
7736, 7743, 7767, 7812, 7830,
7903, 7926, 7948, 8986, 9289,
10011, 16437

Family stories — Fiction
P: 643, 749, 969, 1120, 2133,
2310, 2548, 3138, 3248, 3253,
3465, 3526, 3614–15, 3619–20,
3623–25, 3627–28, 3631, 3633,
3635–37, 3640, 3645–46,
3649–54, 3657, 3664, 3667–68,
3672, 3683, 3686, 3690, 3693,
3695, 3699, 3702, 3710, 3715,
3717, 3719, 3721, 3723, 3725,
3727, 3733, 3735, 3737, 3740,
3742, 3747, 3750, 3753–55,
3762, 3764, 3771, 3775, 3778,
3780–81, 3784, 3787–90,
3793–95, 3799–800, 3808–10,
3812, 3814, 3816–17, 3820–21,
3827–29, 3836, 3839, 3841–43,
3847–49, 3851, 3856–59, 3862,
3870, 3874–76, 3878, 3881,
3884–85, 3892, 3895–99, 3910,
3913, 3916, 3919, 3923, 3925,
3928, 3932, 3934, 3936, 3938,
3943–44, 3949–50, 3954–56,
3958, 3964, 3966–67, 3972–73,
3975–76, 3979–80, 3986–88,
3998–99, 4003, 4006–7,
4009–10, 4013, 4016, 4018,
4020, 4022, 4025, 4027, 4037,
4040, 4042, 4046, 4049,
4051–53, 4056, 4060, 4064–65,
4068, 4071, 4077, 4081–82,
4085–88, 4090, 4092, 4098,
4101–3, 4107–10, 4112, 4115,
4117, 4120–21, 4123, 4127,
4130, 4134–35, 4137–38, 4254,
4272, 4465, 4520, 4549–50,
4723, 4825, 4863, 4968, 4978,
5000, 5006, 5146, 5164, 5185,
5334, 5661, 5684, 5736, 5867,
5926–27, 5943, 5951, 5992,
6118, 6312, 6401, 6440, 6506,
6615, 6666, 6693, 6830, 7695,
7729, 7741, 7818, 7833, 9068,
19768 **PI:** 3094, 3616, 3712,
3767, 3893, 4076, 4089, 4126,
4716, 5895, 5916, 6677, 7037,
7042, 7574, 7684, 7702, 7712,
7722, 7728, 7739, 7747, 7759,
7816–17, 7838–39, 7841, 7846,
7855–56, 7892, 7896, 7906–7,
7918, 7940, 9269, 9857, 9886,
9937, 9996, 10055, 10217
I: 6973, 7056, 7345, 7359,
7509, 7527, 7628, 7673,
7693–94, 7698, 7701, 7715,
7719, 7725–27, 7732, 7737,
7745–46, 7754–55, 7760, 7762,
7768, 7828, 7836, 7843, 7847,
7850–51, 7863, 7869, 7874,
7876, 7879, 7894–95, 7909,
7914, 7917, 7919, 7928,
7945–46, 8581, 8604, 8758,
8802, 8853, 8979, 8982, 9026,
9144, 9167, 9231, 9314, 9324,
9679, 9742, 9836–37, 9873,

9939, 9941, 9990, 10027,
10153 **IJ:** 7018, 7050, 7057,
7205, 7505, 7681, 7683, 7686,
7692, 7700, 7709, 7714, 7724,
7751, 7764–65, 7769, 7783,
7786–87, 7796, 7800, 7819,
7826, 7829, 7834–35, 7849,
7853–54, 7857, 7860, 7862,
7864, 7870, 7872, 7883,
7885–86, 7908, 7910–11, 7913,
7920, 7931, 7938, 7941,
7943–44, 7949, 7969, 8632,
8974, 9014, 9077, 9086, 9164,
9173, 9194, 9212, 9260, 9611,
9639, 9723, 9734–35, 9748,
9803, 9810, 9821, 9825, 9828,
9888, 9974, 10000, 10003,
10291, 10301, 10443, 10628

Famines
I: 22654
Famines — Fiction
IJ: 9715
Famines — Folklore
P: 11483
Fanning, Shawn
IJ: 14121
Fantasy
See also Fables; Folklore;
  Imaginary animals;
  Mythology; Science
  fiction; Supernatural; Tall
  tales; Time travel
P: 619, 633, 657, 659, 669,
674, 687–88, 700, 708, 759,
764, 767, 769, 777, 802, 818,
909, 931, 933–38, 940–44,
947–67, 969–70, 972–78,
980–83, 986, 988–92, 994–97,
999, 1001–3, 1005–8, 1010–13,
1015, 1017–19, 1022–26,
1026–30, 1033, 1035–38,
1040–42, 1044–45, 1047–49,
1051–53, 1055–60, 1062–66,
1068–79, 1081–82, 1084–87,
1089, 1093–95, 1097–119,
1121–33, 1135–39, 1141–49,
1151–56, 1158–72, 1174–79,
1181–87, 1189, 1191–93,
1196–201, 1204–6, 1208–11,
1214–19, 1221–31, 1233–39,
1242–44, 1246–47, 1249–61,
1263–71, 1273, 1275–83,
1285–88, 1290, 1292, 1294–96,
1299, 1302–16, 1318, 1320–21,
1323–26, 1330–32, 1334,
1336–41, 1343–53, 1355–63,
1365–68, 1370–72, 1374–80,
1382–85, 1387–91, 1393–98,
1400–1, 1403, 1406–12,
1414–18, 1420–22, 1424–25,
1427–28, 1430–31, 1434–35,
1437–38, 1440, 1442, 1444–53,
1457, 1459–64, 1467–68, 1472,
1475–79, 1481, 1483–85,
1487–89, 1491–505, 1508,
1511–24, 1526–35, 1537, 1540,
1544, 1548–50, 1552–54,
1556–59, 1561–62, 1565–77,
1579–83, 1585, 1587–92,
1594–95, 1598–603, 1605–10,
1613–16, 1618, 1620–26,
1628–29, 1631–36, 1638–44,
1646–49, 1651–53, 1655–59,
1661–63, 1665–66, 1792, 1813,
1877, 1903, 2564, 3013, 3334,
3352, 3576, 3733, 3943, 4251,
4427, 4505, 4677, 4712, 4876,
4895, 4938, 5850, 5871, 5910,

5970, 6005, 6032, 6066, 6313,
6533, 6544, 6548, 6582, 6600,
6635, 6714, 6716, 6901, 8176,
8184, 8243, 8380, 8434, 8635,
15468 **PI:** 25, 1000, 1021,
1025, 1039, 1043, 1096, 1157,
1173, 1180, 1297, 1329, 1333,
1369, 1413, 1423, 1436, 1439,
1454, 1456, 1466, 1471, 1482,
1510, 1525, 1538, 1542, 1551,
1563–64, 1578, 1584, 1593,
1627, 1645, 1650, 1660, 5994,
6016, 6092, 6524–26, 6800,
7524, 8002–3, 8006, 8021,
8030, 8043, 8047–48, 8053,
8068, 8078–79, 8081, 8084,
8122, 8131, 8135–36, 8142,
8147, 8153, 8168, 8175, 8178,
8188–89, 8195, 8200, 8203,
8211, 8235, 8245, 8247, 8259,
8266, 8290, 8310, 8312,
8316–17, 8338–42, 8344–47,
8351–52, 8355, 8357, 8359–61,
8366, 8368, 8370, 8378–79,
8404, 8413–14, 8422, 8430,
8437, 8439, 8441, 8445, 8468,
8487, 8497–99, 8502, 8509–11,
8519, 8534, 8541, 8549, 8554,
8557, 8601–2, 8606–7, 8615,
8618, 8633, 8640, 8644, 8662,
8669, 8675–76, 8683, 8694,
8696, 8699, 8701, 8716, 8721,
10044, 10070, 10151, 10246,
10708, 10768, 10791 **I:** 1637,
7289, 7525, 7581, 7710, 7727,
7965–66, 7971, 7973, 7977,
7979, 7985–86, 7988, 7990,
7992, 7994–96, 7998, 8005,
8010, 8016, 8020, 8026,
8034–35, 8039, 8044, 8052,
8054, 8058–59, 8061–62, 8075,
8085, 8087–88, 8095, 8100–1,
8105, 8108, 8112, 8121, 8133,
8144, 8148–49, 8163, 8166,
8169, 8171, 8174, 8187,
8192–93, 8201, 8205–10, 8228,
8231, 8238–39, 8241, 8248,
8258, 8262, 8271, 8277, 8297,
8299, 8305–6, 8309, 8313,
8319, 8322, 8328, 8337, 8350,
8353, 8358, 8367, 8371, 8373,
8385, 8397, 8401, 8403, 8405,
8415, 8419, 8421, 8425, 8431,
8433, 8446, 8448–51, 8454,
8456–59, 8474, 8478, 8480,
8485, 8501, 8504, 8514–15,
8517, 8524, 8531, 8535–39,
8551, 8558, 8566, 8572–73,
8585–89, 8597, 8599, 8603,
8616, 8622, 8625–28, 8637,
8639, 8645, 8654, 8659–61,
8666, 8671–74, 8678–79, 8681,
8686, 8688, 8695, 8702, 8708,
8710, 8712, 8717, 8725,
8731–33, 8736, 8742, 8814,
8823, 10052, 10263, 10488,
10516, 10755 **IJ:** 7052, 7398,
7406, 7537, 7956–57, 7959,
7961–64, 7967–68, 7970, 7972,
7974, 7978, 7982–83, 7987,
7993, 8000–1, 8007, 8009,
8014–16, 8017, 8019, 8022–25,
8029, 8031, 8033, 8037–38,
8042, 8045–46, 8049–50, 8055,
8057, 8060, 8063, 8065–67,
8071–73, 8080, 8082–83, 8086,
8089–93, 8098–99, 8102, 8110,
8113, 8117, 8134, 8138–40,
8143, 8145, 8150–52, 8154–55,

8157–59, 8165, 8172–73, 8177,
8180–83, 8185–86, 8190–91,
8194, 8198–99, 8213–16, 8220,
8222, 8225–26, 8236, 8240,
8246, 8249, 8251–55, 8260,
8265, 8269–70, 8273, 8275–76,
8278–79, 8281–84, 8286,
8288–89, 8291, 8293, 8295,
8298, 8300–4, 8307, 8311,
8315, 8318, 8321, 8324–26,
8329–30, 8343, 8348–49, 8356,
8363–65, 8369, 8372, 8374–77,
8383, 8389, 8393, 8395, 8398,
8406–12, 8416–17, 8426–28,
8435, 8440, 8442, 8447, 8453,
8460–61, 8464–65, 8467,
8469–70, 8473, 8475–76,
8481–84, 8489, 8492–93, 8495,
8505, 8507–8, 8512–13, 8516,
8526, 8529, 8542–44, 8546,
8552, 8556, 8560, 8562–63,
8567–69, 8582, 8593, 8600,
8608, 8612–14, 8617, 8619,
8624, 8642, 8647, 8649,
8651–52, 8656, 8663, 8670,
8680, 8693, 8700, 8703–4,
8709, 8711, 8722–24, 8726,
8730, 8734–35, 8813, 9075,
9105, 10529, 10616, 11260

Fantasy — Biography
IJ: 12472
Fantasy — Fiction
P: 932, 945, 979, 985, 1009,
1014, 1061, 1067, 1120, 1134,
1150, 1190, 1207, 1212,
1240–41, 1248, 1300, 1317,
1399, 1405, 1426, 1473–74,
1507, 1536, 1545, 1555, 1617,
1664, 2835, 4364, 5902, 6893,
8132, 8196–97, 8471, 8636,
8698, 10558 **PI:** 1441, 6488,
8094, 8107, 8333, 8402, 8444,
8486, 8496 **I:** 7989, 8011,
8036, 8056, 8219, 8244, 8400,
8576, 8598, 8604 **IJ:** 7017,
7021, 7960, 7969, 7975–76,
7984, 8004, 8008, 8027, 8064,
8097, 8103, 8111, 8116, 8141,
8146, 8156, 8164, 8167, 8170,
8242, 8256, 8280, 8285, 8287,
8296, 8314, 8331–32, 8334,
8382, 8384, 8388, 8429, 8462,
8466, 8490–91, 8503, 8530,
8545, 8547, 8553, 8561,
8609–11, 8631–32, 8643, 8650,
8655, 8657, 8665, 8706, 8720,
8819, 8824, 8833–34, 9128

Fantasy — Poetry
P: 1050, 1291, 1612
Fantasy — Short stories
PI: 8423
Farm animals
See also specific animals,
  e.g., Cattle
P: 22683
Farm animals — Fiction
P: 762, 812, 1227, 1642, 2253,
4559, 5322, 5611, 5652, 6611,
6767, 6915
Farm animals — Songs
P: 15284
Farm life
P: 15255, 22664, 22669,
22671–73, 22675, 22678
PI: 4886, 22662, 22682
I: 14070, 17973, 18434, 22670,
22684, 22689–90

P = Primary; PI = Primary-Intermediate; I = Intermediate; IJ = Intermediate-Junior High

P = Primary; PI = Primary-Intermediate; I = Intermediate; IJ = Intermediate-Junior High

P = Primary; PI = Primary-Intermediate; I = Intermediate; IJ = Intermediate-Junior High

P = Primary; PI = Primary-Intermediate; I = Intermediate; IJ = Intermediate-Junior High

P = Primary; PI = Primary-Intermediate; I = Intermediate; IJ = Intermediate-Junior High

P = Primary; PI = Primary-Intermediate; I = Intermediate; IJ = Intermediate-Junior High

P = Primary; PI = Primary-Intermediate; I = Intermediate; IJ = Intermediate-Junior High

P = Primary; PI = Primary-Intermediate; I = Intermediate; IJ = Intermediate-Junior High

P = Primary; PI = Primary-Intermediate; I = Intermediate; IJ = Intermediate-Junior High

Japan — Fiction
P: 957, 1390, 1426, 1596, 3751, 4725, 4827, 4842, 4852, 4928, 4976, 5790, 6128, 6378, 10652 **PI:** 1180, 3767, 4727, 4800 **I:** 8901, 9278, 10004, 10655, 10766 **IJ:** 8832, 9272–73, 9286–88, 9298, 9970
Japan — Folklore
P: 11050–55, 11057, 11059, 11061–62, 11065 **PI:** 4919, 11048, 11060, 11064 **I:** 11049, 11056, 11063 **IJ:** 11058
Japan — History
PI: 9292, 16038 **I:** 15697 **IJ:** 16326, 16415, 16418, 16433, 16435, 16439, 16442
Japan — Holidays
PI: 16430 **I:** 19328
Japan — Mythology
IJ: 11627
Japan — Poetry
P: 12067
Japanese Americans
P: 4032 **PI:** 19609, 19615 **I:** 19592, 19638 **IJ:** 16116, 18197, 19569, 19581, 19583
Japanese Americans — Biography
I: 12628, 13543, 14075 **IJ:** 12866, 13556
Japanese Americans — Fiction
P: 3606, 4722, 4933, 5017 **PI:** 4173, 4745, 5190, 7644, 10009, 10025, 10567 **I:** 7610, 10033 **IJ:** 9949, 9969, 10018, 10627
Japanese Americans — History
I: 16110 **IJ:** 18136, 18164
Japanese Americans — Holidays
I: 19328
Japanese Canadians — Fiction
IJ: 7674
Japanese language
I: 15062
Japanese language — Fiction
P: 1891
Jarvik, Robert
I: 14172
Jason (mythology)
IJ: 11641
Jataka stories
P: 11040 **PI:** 11033
Jay, John
I: 13533
Jazz
PI: 12745 **I:** 12721 **IJ:** 15241
Jazz — Biography
P: 12747, 12790 **I:** 12717, 12722, 12744 **IJ:** 12492, 12720
Jazz — Fiction
P: 1689, 3377, 3510, 3576, 3694, 4798, 4843, 4923, 4945, 5009, 5141 **PI:** 4747
Jealousy
P: 19809
Jealousy — Fiction
I: 10369
Jeeps
I: 24068

Jefferson, Thomas
P: 13747, 13753 **PI:** 13751, 13758–59 **I:** 13748, 13752, 13755, 18652 **IJ:** 13200, 13749–50, 13754, 13756–57, 17862, 17871, 18608, 18679
Jefferson, Thomas — Fiction
IJ: 9511
Jellyfish
P: 22185, 22190 **I:** 22189, 22193
Jemison, Mae
P: 12410 **PI:** 12411–12 **I:** 12413
Jemison, Mary
I: 17522
Jerusalem
I: 16955, 16957, 16964 **IJ:** 16899, 16901
Jerusalem — Biography
IJ: 14832
Jerusalem — Fiction
P: 4776
Jerusalem — History
I: 16954
Jerusalem — Poetry
I: 11967
Jesters — Fiction
P: 4974
Jesus
P: 19260
Jesus Christ
P: 6176, 19387 **PI:** 19238 **I:** 19199–200, 19216, 19396 **IJ:** 19218, 19230, 19265
Jesus Christ — Folklore
P: 11534 **PI:** 11316
Jeter, Derek
PI: 14394 **I:** 14392–93
Jewelry
IJ: 15653, 23912, 23921, 23926
Jewelry making
PI: 24347, 24406 **I:** 24399, 24403 **IJ:** 24394, 24398, 24401–2, 24404
Jewish Americans
P: 19597, 19642 **PI:** 19622 **I:** 19568 **IJ:** 19577, 19587, 19589, 19602, 19645
Jewish Americans — Biography
IJ: 13221
Jewish Americans — Fiction
P: 4959 **PI:** 3952, 9812 **IJ:** 7658, 9894, 9935
Jewish folklore
P: 11350, 11352, 11358, 11361–62, 11365–66, 11372, 11380–82, 11385 **PI:** 10928, 11349, 11351, 11354, 11356, 11363–64, 11368–70, 11377–78 **I:** 11360, 11367, 11371, 11373, 11376, 11384 **IJ:** 10858, 11379
Jewish holy days
See also specific holy days, e.g., Hanukkah
P: 6278, 6280, 6282–83, 6296–97, 15307, 19450, 19454, 19475 **PI:** 19440, 19451, 19456, 19460, 19462, 19466, 19470 **I:** 19439, 19441–42, 19445–47, 19455, 19457, 19464–65, 19476 **IJ:** 19438

Jewish holy days — Cookbooks
I: 24646
Jewish holy days — Crafts
PI: 19468 **I:** 19439, 19467
Jewish holy days — Fiction
P: 1615, 6273–74, 6277, 6279, 6281, 6287–92, 6295, 6298, 6310–11, 6314, 6316–17, 6320–22, 6324–25, 6328–29, 6333, 6337 **PI:** 9356 **I:** 10058
Jewish holy days — Poetry
P: 6308–9 **PI:** 12084
Jewish holy days — Short stories
IJ: 10077
Jewish New Year — Fiction
P: 6323
Jewish Theological Seminary
IJ: 18404
Jews — Biography
IJ: 13088, 13159, 13516, 14240, 14745
Jews — Cookbooks
I: 19447
Jews — Crafts
IJ: 15749
Jews — Fiction
P: 4022–23, 4776, 4894, 5005, 6107, 6335 **PI:** 4184, 4956, 6306, 7728, 8928, 9326, 9356, 9360, 10057 **I:** 7928, 8052, 9063, 9324, 9910, 9968, 10012, 10073 **IJ:** 7669, 7671, 7675, 7862, 7898, 9239, 9334, 9340, 9423, 9782, 9864, 9973, 9977, 10002, 10007, 10011, 10014, 10022, 10028–29
Jews — Folklore
P: 11353, 11383 **PI:** 11359, 11375 **I:** 11357
Jews — History
See also Holocaust; Immigration (U.S.); World War II
PI: 5055, 17926 **I:** 15761, 16037, 19193 **IJ:** 14798, 14873, 15749, 15749, 15753, 16005, 16010, 16012, 16039, 16047, 16049–50, 16054, 16062–63, 16074, 16085, 16108, 19082, 19101, 19174, 19471, 19577
Jews — History — Fiction
I: 10047
Jews — History — Poetry
I: 19453
Jews — Plays
I: 15424
Joan of Arc
P: 14820, 14826 **PI:** 14821 **IJ:** 14822, 14825
Joan of Arc, Saint
P: 14823 **I:** 14819, 14824
Jobs — Fiction
P: 3189, 3782
Jobs, Steve
PI: 14174 **IJ:** 14173, 14175
Jockeys — Biography
I: 14671–72 **IJ:** 14304
John J. Harvey (fireboat)
PI: 24159 **IJ:** 19125, 19154
John Paul II, Pope
I: 14827 **IJ:** 19125, 19154
Johnson, Andrew
IJ: 13760–61

Johnson, Brad
I: 14589
Johnson, Judy
IJ: 14395
Johnson, Lady Bird
P: 13923
Johnson, Lyndon B.
IJ: 13199, 13762–64
Johnson, Magic
IJ: 14489–90
Johnson, Mamie "Peanut"
IJ: 14396
Johnson, Walter
IJ: 14397
Johnston, Joseph E.
I: 13534
Johnstown Flood
IJ: 23389, 76, 222, 5508, 6040, 6082, 6284, 6570, 6794, 6948, 24741, 24743, 24746, 24748, 24751–55, 24764, 24768, 24772, 24774, 24777, 24783 **PI:** 6235, 11730, 24737, 24739–40, 24742, 24744–45, 24757, 24759–62, 24767, 24771, 24773, 24778–80, 24782, 24786, 24788, 24790 **I:** 15157–58, 24738, 24747, 24763, 24776, 24781, 24784, 24787, 24789
Jokes
PI: 24775, 76, 222, 5508, 6040, 6082, 6284, 6570, 6794, 6948, 24741, 24743, 24746, 24748, 24751–55, 24764, 24768, 24772, 24774, 24777, 24783 **PI:** 6235, 11730, 24737, 24739–40, 24742, 24744–45, 24757, 24759–62, 24767, 24771, 24773, 24778–80, 24782, 24786, 24788, 24790 **I:** 15157–58, 24738, 24747, 24763, 24776, 24781, 24784, 24787, 24789
Jokes and riddles
P: 28, 76, 222, 5508, 6040, 6082, 6284, 6570, 6794, 6948, 24741, 24743, 24746, 24748, 24751–55, 24764, 24768, 24772, 24774, 24777, 24783 **PI:** 6235, 11730, 24737, 24739–40, 24742, 24744–45, 24757, 24759–62, 24767, 24771, 24773, 24778–80, 24782, 24786, 24788, 24790 **I:** 15157–58, 24738, 24747, 24763, 24776, 24781, 24784, 24787, 24789
Jokes and riddles — Folklore
IJ: 10875
Jokes and riddles — Poetry
IJ: 11938
Jones, John Paul
P: 13538 **PI:** 13536 **I:** 13537 **IJ:** 13535, 13539
Jones, Marion
IJ: 14636
Jones, Quincy
IJ: 12719
Joplin, Scott
I: 12721–22 **IJ:** 12720
Jordan
IJ: 16978, 16993, 17006
Jordan, Barbara
I: 13265–66

P = Primary; PI = Primary-Intermediate; I = Intermediate; IJ = Intermediate-Junior High

P = Primary; PI = Primary-Intermediate; I = Intermediate; IJ = Intermediate-Junior High

P = Primary; PI = Primary-Intermediate; I = Intermediate; IJ = Intermediate-Junior High

P = Primary; PI = Primary-Intermediate; I = Intermediate; IJ = Intermediate-Junior High

P = Primary; PI = Primary-Intermediate; I = Intermediate; IJ = Intermediate-Junior High

P = Primary; PI = Primary-Intermediate; I = Intermediate; IJ = Intermediate-Junior High

N

Nature — Fiction
P: 696, 1287, 2286, 3151, 3260, 4039, 4179, 4520, 4533, 4546, 4564, 4572, 4584, 4599, 4602, 4614, 4634, 4645, 4667, 4670, 4679, 4684, 4695, 5306, 5368, 6531 IJ: 7025, 7559

Nature — Games
I: 24562

Nature — Photography
I: 24724

Nature — Poetry
P: 12024, 12067, 12182, 12193, 12208, 12214–16, 19506 PI: 12041, 12183, 12195–96, 12202, 12212, 12226 I: 12185–86, 12194, 12197, 12211, 12220, 12230

"The Nature Boy" — Wrestling
IJ: 24960

Nature study
P: 327, 4523, 4660, 4663, 21215 PI: 13062, 22444, 23170 I: 20650, 20923, 21025 IJ: 20929, 20988

Nature study — Biography
I: 14098, 14159 IJ: 14053, 14158, 14204

Nature study — Crafts
IJ: 24239

Nature study — Experiments and projects
I: 20641 IJ: 20926

Nature study — Fiction
P: 3204, 4571, 4580, 4586, 4643, 4669, 4683, 5631 PI: 4625

Navajo Indians
P: 17608 PI: 17447, 17571 I: 16089, 17585 IJ: 17474, 17509, 17584, 17635

Navajo Indians — Fiction
P: 1782, 4804, 4970, 4977 PI: 4756, 9033, 9446, 9463 I: 9450 IJ: 7655, 8067, 9435, 9464, 9785

Navajo Indians — Folklore
PI: 15010

Navel
P: 20556

Navy, Caryn
PI: 14210

Navy (U.S.)
IJ: 24199, 24203

Navy (U.S.) — Biography
IJ: 13535

Navy (U.S.) — History
IJ: 24152

Naylor, Phyllis Reynolds
IJ: 13043

Nazi Germany — Fiction
I: 9151 IJ: 9369–69

Nazis
See Germany — History; Holocaust; Nazi Germany; World War II

Nazis and Nazism — Fiction
IJ: 9368–69

Ndebele
IJ: 16256

Nebraska
I: 18306 IJ: 18302

Nebraska — Fiction
I: 7339 IJ: 8966, 9719, 9831

Needlecrafts
I: 24535 IJ: 24539

Needlecrafts — Fiction
P: 3233

Negro League baseball
PI: 25104 I: 25062
IJ: 14395, 14411, 25066

Negro League baseball — Biography
IJ: 14360, 14384, 14390, 14396, 14398

Negro League baseball — Fiction
P: 4845 I: 10573 IJ: 10601

Neighborhoods — Fiction
P: 1291, 5077

Nepal
I: 16492 IJ: 16457, 16483

Nepal — Fiction
PI: 9295 I: 9294

Neptune (planet)
PI: 20795, 20841 I: 20813, 20816 IJ: 20822, 20833

Nervous system
P: 20377 PI: 20378 I: 20359, 20363, 20369, 20376 IJ: 20360, 20364, 20366, 20370–71, 20375

Netherlands
P: 16792 PI: 16791 I: 16795 IJ: 16100, 16793

Netherlands — Crafts
PI: 16798

Netherlands — Fiction
P: 4714, 4797, 4816, 4934 I: 7544, 9304, 9322, 9365, 10020 IJ: 9313, 10014, 10028

Netherlands — Holidays
PI: 16798

Nevada
P: 18346 PI: 4981 I: 18327, 18357 IJ: 18364, 18372, 18374

Nevada — Fiction
I: 7518

New Amsterdam
PI: 17708 IJ: 13620

New Deal
IJ: 18131, 18153, 18200

New England
See also specific states, e.g., Massachusetts
IJ: 18445

New England — Fiction
P: 3160, 4819, 6013 PI: 9486, 10159 I: 7121 IJ: 8528

New England — History
IJ: 18400

New Hampshire
P: 18410 PI: 18420, 18449 I: 18396, 18459 IJ: 18463, 18491

New Hampshire — Fiction
P: 993 PI: 7053 I: 7791, 10039 IJ: 9551

New Hampshire — History
IJ: 17674, 17773

New Jersey
PI: 18421 I: 18426 IJ: 18385, 18468, 18492, 18494

New Jersey — Fiction
P: 3377 IJ: 7860, 10272

New Jersey — History
PI: 18499 IJ: 17770, 17772, 18407

New Kids on the Block (musical group)
IJ: 12849

New Mexico
PI: 17519, 18693 I: 17525, 18683, 18690 IJ: 18680, 18684, 18702

New Mexico — Biography
IJ: 12313

New Mexico — Fiction
P: 3424, 3634, 6131 I: 9741–42, 9873–74 IJ: 7607, 11503

New Mexico — Folklore
PI: 11528

New Mexico — History
I: 17930

New Orleans
PI: 18645

New Orleans — Fiction
IJ: 9563

New Orleans, Battle of
IJ: 17900

New Orleans, Louisiana — Fiction
P: 4917

New Stone Age
IJ: 15633

New Year's Day
P: 19289, 19364 I: 19371

New Year's Day — Fiction
PI: 5869

New York
I: 18399, 100, 18441, 18507 PI: 18195, 18464, 18479, 23880 I: 18376, 18401, 18444, 18471, 18500, 24039 IJ: 18403–4, 18455, 18462, 18486, 18497, 19671, 23871, 24041

New York — History
IJ: 17753, 100, 18441, 18507 PI: 18195, 18464, 18479, 23880 I: 18376, 18401, 18444, 18471, 18500, 24039 IJ: 18403–4, 18455, 18462, 18486, 18497, 19671, 23871, 24041

New York City
P: 36, 100, 18441, 18507 PI: 18195, 18464, 18479, 23880 I: 18376, 18401, 18444, 18471, 18500, 24039 IJ: 18403–4, 18455, 18462, 18486, 18497, 19671, 23871, 24041

New York City — Biography
IJ: 13624

New York City — Crafts
I: 18162, 1181, 1463, 1516, 1604, 2186, 2885, 3185, 3335, 3348, 3532, 3606, 3703, 4054, 4432, 4467, 4709, 4918, 4987, 5289, 5644, 6143, 7629 PI: 4724, 4768, 6998, 7950, 9812, 10083 I: 7639, 7928, 8588–89, 8764, 9102, 9517, 9584–85, 9868, 9906, 9910, 9943, 9953 IJ: 7561, 7835, 8191, 8934, 8949, 9015, 9846, 9880, 9888, 9890, 9894

New York City — Ecology and environment
I: 18791, 1181, 1463, 1516, 1604, 2186, 2885, 3185, 3335, 3348, 3532, 3606, 3703, 4054, 4432, 4467, 4709, 4918, 4987,

5289, 5644, 6143, 7629
PI: 4724, 4768, 6998, 7950, 9812, 10083 I: 7639, 7928, 8588–89, 8764, 9102, 9517, 9584–85, 9868, 9906, 9910, 9943, 9953 IJ: 7561, 7835, 8191, 8934, 8949, 9015, 9846, 9880, 9888, 9890, 9894

New York City — Fiction
P: 1116, 1181, 1463, 1516, 1604, 2186, 2885, 3185, 3335, 3348, 3532, 3606, 3703, 4054, 4432, 4467, 4709, 4918, 4987, 5289, 5644, 6143, 7629 PI: 4724, 4768, 6998, 7950, 9812, 10083 I: 7639, 7928, 8588–89, 8764, 9102, 9517, 9584–85, 9868, 9906, 9910, 9943, 9953 IJ: 7561, 7835, 8191, 8934, 8949, 9015, 9846, 9880, 9888, 9890, 9894

New York City — History
P: 4992 I: 9851, 17834 IJ: 13620, 18435, 19576

New York City — History — Fiction
P: 6105

New York City — Nature
I: 18791

New York City — Poetry
P: 11892

New York Knicks (basketball team)
I: 25135

New York State
PI: 18422, 18470, 18503 IJ: 18385, 18411, 18431, 18454, 18472, 18487, 18504

New York State — Fiction
PI: 6965 IJ: 8096, 8273, 8323, 9479, 9549, 9574, 9913

New York State — Folklore
P: 11515

New York State — History
P: 4966 I: 17727 IJ: 17786, 17917, 18384

New York Yankees (baseball team)
I: 25091

New Zealand
PI: 16569, 16593 I: 16564, 16598 IJ: 16565, 16573, 16595

New Zealand — Fiction
PI: 3054, 7278 I: 7280

New Zealand — Holidays
PI: 16569

Newbery Award
IJ: 12468

Newfoundland
I: 17039

Newfoundland — Fiction
IJ: 7209, 7236

Newspapers
P: 15188 I: 15185 IJ: 15168, 15191

Newspapers — Biography
P: 13917

Newspapers — Fiction
P: 2385, 3456 I: 9816, 9868, 10338 IJ: 10341

Newspapers — History
PI: 15067

Newton, Isaac
IJ: 14211–13

Newton, John
IJ: 13560

O

P = Primary; PI = Primary-Intermediate; I = Intermediate; IJ = Intermediate-Junior High

P = Primary; PI = Primary-Intermediate; I = Intermediate; IJ = Intermediate-Junior High

Phrenology — Fiction
IJ: 7244
Physical abuse — Fiction
IJ: 7774, 20086 PI: 20071
I: 20080, 20083 IJ: 14354,
20061, 20074–75, 20082,
20149
Physical disabilities
P: 20070, 20086 PI: 20071
I: 20080, 20083 IJ: 14354,
20061, 20074–75, 20082,
20149, 20086 PI: 20071
I: 20080, 20083 IJ: 14354,
20061, 20074–75, 20082,
20149
Physical disabilities —
Biography
P: 13930 PI: 13932, 13935
I: 13929, 13933–34
IJ: 13926–27, 14295, 14355
Physical disabilities — Fiction
P: 3747, 5134, 5251 PI: 5222
I: 9122 IJ: 7178, 7291, 7293,
8915, 8955, 9128, 9141, 9147,
9157, 9161, 9382, 9626, 9880,
9913
Physical disabilities — Sports
IJ: 14327
Physical fitness
P: 20481, 20505 PI: 20503
I: 20516 IJ: 20154, 20484,
20512
Physical geography
P: 23003–4, 23012 I: 23008
Physical geography — Fiction
P: 4551
Physical handicaps
P: 5078, 20064, 20092
PI: 14243, 14356
Physical handicaps — Fiction
P: 5076, 5084, 5119, 5130,
5163 PI: 4079, 8928, 9121,
9166 I: 7397, 9154, 9171
IJ: 9097
Physical problems — Fiction
IJ: 9133
Physics
PI: 23520 IJ: 23517, 23524
Physics — Biography
PI: 14109 I: 14116
IJ: 14073, 14112, 14145
Physics — Experiments and
projects
I: 23510, 23532, 23541
IJ: 23504, 23513–14
Physics — Water
I: 23429
Phytoplankton
IJ: 22144
Pianos — Fiction
P: 5210, 6166 I: 9171
Picasso, Pablo
P: 12638 PI: 12635, 12644
IJ: 12636–37, 12639–43,
12645
Picasso, Pablo — Fiction
P: 5516
Pickett, Bill
P: 12869 I: 12870
Picnics — Fiction
P: 2234, 3027, 6709
Picotte, Susan LaFlesche
I: 13658–59
Picts — Fiction
I: 8731

Picture books
See also Stories without
words
P: 295, 350, 1539, 1856, 1969,
2922, 4694
Picture books — Anthologies
P: 930
Picture books — Publishing
IJ: 15086
Picture frames — Crafts
I: 24558
Picture puzzles
P: 50, 4395, 5625, 24792,
24795–96, 24798–801, 24804,
24808–9 PI: 15458, 21044,
24770, 24797
Picture puzzles — Fiction
P: 3278, 5842
Pierce, Franklin
IJ: 13813
Pig farms
I: 22690
Pigeons
I: 21730
Pigeons — Fiction
IJ: 7551, 9084
Pigs
P: 21332, 21357, 22658,
22677, 22686 I: 22690
Pigs — Fiction
P: 47, 455, 1854, 1858, 2005,
2032, 2052, 2283, 2316–17,
2395, 2444, 2447, 2492–93,
2509, 2552, 2802, 2969, 3027,
4249, 4479, 5292, 5301, 5564,
6200, 6348, 6688 PI: 7437,
8342, 8694 I: 7527, 8239
IJ: 7956–57, 9920, 9976
Pigs — Folklore
P: 11171, 11190, 11213,
11237, 11533
Pike, Zebulon
I: 12441–42 IJ: 12440
Pilgrims (U.S.)
P: 19487 PI: 17744, 17778,
17780 I: 17644, 17693, 17707,
17779 IJ: 17638–39, 17690,
17692, 17721, 17755, 19478
Pilgrims (U.S.) — Fiction
P: 4858 IJ: 9489, 9497
Pill bugs
P: 21930 IJ: 22163
Pillbugs
PI: 21978
Pinatas — Fiction
P: 5919
Piñatas
P: 6008, 17062
Pinchot, Gifford
PI: 14224
Pinkerton, Allan
IJ: 13577–78
Pinkwater, Daniel
PI: 13055
Pioneer life (U.S.)
PI: 17878, 17944 IJ: 18032
Pioneer life (U.S.) — Fiction
IJ: 9630
Pipefishes
I: 22241
Pippen, Scottie
IJ: 14525–27
Piranhas
P: 22225 I: 22229, 22237
Pirates
P: 15706 PI: 15725 I: 15442,
15695, 15716

Pirates — Biography
PI: 12306 IJ: 12309, 12312,
12394
Pirates — Fiction
P: 1274, 1277, 1354, 2826,
3062–63, 3076, 4192, 4793,
6522 PI: 7003, 7055, 8414,
9486 I: 7176, 7181, 7279,
7346, 9494, 9569 IJ: 7104,
7180, 7211, 7322, 8274, 8311,
9179, 9500–2, 9571, 12279
Pirates — Folklore
I: 10878
Pirates — Women
I: 15442 IJ: 12309, 12312
Pitcher, Molly
I: 13947
Pittsburgh Steelers (football
team)
I: 25191
Pizza
P: 22725, 24618, 24659
I: 12141
Pizza — Fiction
P: 4480, 6545
Plagues — Fiction
IJ: 9382
Plagues — History
IJ: 15944
Plains Indians
I: 17554
Plains Indians — Folklore
P: 11442, 11444, 11446
I: 11447
Plains Indians — History
PI: 17511 I: 17498
Plains (U.S.)
See also Grasslands,
Prairies, and specific
states, e.g., Nebraska
IJ: 17941
Planes (physics)
P: 23616, 23623
Planetariums
P: 23657
Planets
See also specific planets,
e.g., Mars (planet)
P: 20791, 20802, 20806,
20823, 20834, 20861
PI: 20804, 20824, 20844–46,
20875 I: 20723, 20809,
20842–43 IJ: 20801, 20803,
20876
Planets — Exploration
IJ: 23655
Planets — Fiction
P: 1055
Plankton
IJ: 22144–45
Plantation life
P: 17895 I: 17899, 17905
Plantations (U.S.) — History
IJ: 17810
Plants
See also specific plants, e.g.,
Cactus
P: 4720, 22638, 22840, 22853,
22868–69, 22877, 23078,
23162–64, 23198
PI: 20940–41, 22842, 22848,
22852, 22854, 22862–63,
22880, 23044 I: 20922, 20950,
22843, 22851, 22858,
22870–71 IJ: 20944, 22635,
22637, 22645–46, 22788,
22845

Plants — Classification
IJ: 20954
Plants — Deserts
P: 23031
Plants — Experiments and
projects
P: 22866 PI: 22864 I: 22839,
22872 IJ: 22846
Plants — Fiction
P: 1006, 4413, 4690, 10656,
22692
Plants — Folklore
IJ: 11424, 22847
Plants — Life cycles
P: 22634, 22847
Plants — Oceans
I: 22859
Plants — Seashores
P: 22435
Plastics
P: 23756
Plate tectonics
IJ: 22928–29, 22944, 22944
Platypuses
P: 21321 PI: 21370
Play
P: 24888
Play — Fiction
P: 227, 3118, 3399, 3499, 3507
Play production
PI: 12251
Playgrounds — Fiction
P: 3109, 3461
Plays
See also Shakespeare,
William; Theaters
P: 12267 PI: 12252–53,
12264–65 I: 10046, 10074,
10369, 12254–55, 12268–70,
12281, 15421, 15424
IJ: 12257, 12276, 12282,
15426
Plays — American
IJ: 12263
Plays — Anthologies
I: 12271–72 IJ: 12260, 12273
Plays — Fiction
P: 4334
Plays — Folklore
PI: 12250
Plays — Multiculturalism
P: 12259
Plays — One-act
IJ: 12262
Plays — Radio
IJ: 15412
Plays — Scenes
IJ: 12275
Plays — Shakespeare
I: 12285 IJ: 12247–48,
12289–90, 12292
Playwrights — Biography
I: 13079 IJ: 13000
Pledge of Allegiance
P: 6913 PI: 17431, 18166
Plotkin, Mark
IJ: 14225
Plows
P: 22685
Plumbing — Careers
IJ: 19909
Pluto (planet)
PI: 20796, 20838, 20841,
20844 I: 20813 IJ: 20819
Plymouth Colony
PI: 17781 I: 17707

Pollock, Jackson
P: 12647 **PI:** 12648
IJ: 12649
Pollution
See also Ecology and
environment; Nuclear
waste
I: 17323, 18776, 18787, 18815
IJ: 18790, 18803, 18806,
18810, 18814, 18817, 20935,
23161
Pollution — Fiction
P: 4518, 4536, 4653, 4677
PI: 5521
Pollution, Air
I: 18816, 23476
Pollution, Marine
P: 18802
Pollution, Marine — Fiction
P: 971
Pollution, Water
P: 18808
Polo, Marco
I: 12444 **IJ:** 12443, 15732
Polynesia — Fiction
I: 9208 **IJ:** 7368
Polyphemus (mythology)
PI: 11648
Pompeii, Italy
I: 15903
Pompeii (Italy)
IJ: 15921
Pompeii (Italy) — Fiction
P: 9305
Ponce de Leon, Juan
I: 12446 **IJ:** 12445, 12447–49
Pond life
I: 23159
Ponds
P: 23156, 23174, 23178
PI: 23170 **I:** 23159
IJ: 23161, 23186
Ponds — Biography
I: 14199
Ponds — Fiction
P: 4576
Ponds — Plants
P: 23162
Ponds and pond life
I: 23179
Ponies
P: 22577–78 **PI:** 22594,
22611 **IJ:** 22579–80, 22582,
22612
Ponies — Fiction
P: 5579–80, 6584, 6739
Pony Express
PI: 17937
Pony Express — Fiction
PI: 4802 **IJ:** 9706
Pop art
IJ: 12480
Pop-up books
P: 5851, 15377, 24103
PI: 1466, 17424 **I:** 8335,
11122, 15960, 15964 **IJ:** 8025,
14932, 15836, 18498
Pop-up books — Fiction
P: 644, 4728 **PI:** 1039
Pop-ups — Construction
IJ: 24489
Popcorn
P: 22704, 22791
Popcorn — History
PI: 22720

Popcorn Park Zoo
I: 22630
Popes — Biography
I: 14827
Popes — Folklore
I: 11137
Poppies
P: 22860
Popular music
See specific types of music,
e.g., Rock music and
musicians
Population
I: 18821
Population problems
IJ: 18818, 18822
Porches — Fiction
P: 3280
Porcupines
I: 21369
Porcupines — Fiction
P: 2396
Porpoises
I: 22369 **IJ:** 22215
Porsche (automobile)
P: 24113
Portugal
IJ: 16877–78, 16880, 16883,
16891
Post-traumatic stress
disorder
IJ: 20299
Postage stamps — Dinosaurs
IJ: 15503
Postal Service (U.S.)
P: 13257, 18996, 19009
PI: 19018 **I:** 18997
Postal Service (U.S.) —
Fiction
P: 3502
Postal Service (U.S.) —
History
PI: 18998
Postal workers
P: 19836
Potassium
IJ: 22914–15
Potatoes
P: 22796
Potatoes — Fiction
P: 4997
Potatoes — Folklore
P: 11179
Potawatoni Indians
PI: 17503
Potlatch
IJ: 17518
Potter, Beatrix
P: 13059–61 **I:** 13058
Potter, Harry
I: 15205 **IJ:** 24706
Potters and pottery
PI: 14904, 17621, 24387
Pottery
IJ: 24392
Pottery — Biography
IJ: 12604
Pottery — Colonial Period
(U.S.)
I: 17709
Pottery — Fiction
IJ: 9284
Pottery — History
IJ: 15744
Potties
See Toilet training

P: 3167
Potties — Fiction
P: 3183, 3419, 3594
Poultry
P: 22702
Pout (fish)
PI: 22243
Poverty
P: 3500 **I:** 19053 **IJ:** 17117,
18856, 19814, 19832
Poverty — Biography
IJ: 13336
Poverty — Fiction
P: 3713, 4947, 4998, 5068,
5080, 5082, 5250 **PI:** 4908,
7841, 8967, 9039 **I:** 7710,
8982, 9034, 9868, 10045
IJ: 6971, 7665, 7733, 7776,
7835, 7870, 9262, 9388, 9392,
9815, 9919, 9923, 9933
Powell, Colin
PI: 13585 **I:** 13582–83
IJ: 13579–81, 13584, 13586
Powell, John Wesley
I: 12451, 18366 **IJ:** 12450
Powhatan Indians
IJ: 17465
Powhatan Indians —
Biography
PI: 13663 **IJ:** 13660
Powwows
PI: 17523 **I:** 17471, 17508
IJ: 17526
Powwows — Fiction
P: 3537 **I:** 9455
Prague — Fiction
P: 6277 **IJ:** 9334
Prairie dogs
P: 21667, 21670 **PI:** 21656
Prairies
See also Grasslands
P: 23196 **PI:** 23056, 23191,
23197, 23208–9, 23216
I: 23190, 23193, 23207
IJ: 18312, 23194, 23205
Prairies — Animals
P: 23192
Prairies — Fiction
PI: 6671 **I:** 9901
Prairies — Poetry
I: 12203
Prairies (U.S.)
I: 18252, 23214
Prairies (U.S.) — Fiction
PI: 9709
Prayers
See also Blessings
P: 19116, 19140, 19210,
19502, 19506–7, 19509, 19511,
19513–21 **PI:** 19501, 19504,
19512, 19522 **I:** 19500, 19503,
19505, 19510 **IJ:** 19068,
19139
Prayers — Fiction
P: 4119
Prayers — Jewish
P: 19508
Praying mantises
P: 21911 **I:** 21903
Pregnancy
P: 20557 **PI:** 20562
IJ: 20599
Pregnancy — Fiction
P: 3619, 3790, 3960, 20545
IJ: 7789, 7880, 9016
Pregnancy — Teenage
IJ: 20599

Prehistoric animals
See also Dinosaurs;
Mammoths
P: 15540, 15580 **PI:** 15511
I: 15494, 15533, 15609, 15642
Prehistoric animals — Fiction
P: 921
Prehistoric life
PI: 15518 **PI:** 15501 **I:** 15505,
15517, 15583 **IJ:** 15608,
15626, 15628, 15633, 15635,
15638, 15643–44, 15660–61,
17488
Prehistoric life — Fiction
IJ: 9222, 9224–25, 10109
Prehistoric peoples
PI: 15625 **I:** 15622, 15634
Prehistoric peoples — Art
I: 15630
Prehistoric peoples — Fiction
P: 4726, 4779, 6606 **PI:** 9221
I: 8034, 9223
Prejudice
See also Racism
P: 19052 **PI:** 19051, 19443
IJ: 15712, 18866, 18893,
19580
Prejudice — Fiction
P: 4167, 4875, 5186, 5240
PI: 7662, 8874, 9103 **I:** 7717,
8913, 9904 **IJ:** 6976, 7389,
7611, 7646, 7660, 7669, 7803,
9239, 9659, 9754, 9827, 9847,
9905, 9923, 9985, 10016
Prejudice — History
IJ: 18144
Prenatal development
P: 20548
Prepositions
PI: 15133
Preschool
P: 3110, 19697
Preschool — Fiction
P: 2155, 5672
Preserved bodies
IJ: 15717
Presidency (U.S.)
I: 19031
Presidents — Biography
P: 13777
Presidents' Day
P: 19356 **PI:** 19287
Presidents Day (U.S.)
PI: 19343
Presidents (Mexico) —
Biography
PI: 14828
Presidents (U.S.)
P: 13852, 19024, 19041
PI: 13228, 13703, 22460,
23784 **I:** 18991, 19015, 19019,
19029, 19031, 19035, 19043
IJ: 13161, 13214, 18205,
18994, 19012, 19027, 19036,
19038–39
Presidents (U.S.) —
Biographies
IJ: 13791
Presidents (U.S.) —
Biography
See also individual
presidents, e.g., Bush,
George W.
P: 13694, 13698, 13709,
13728, 13747, 13753, 13773,
13775, 13778, 13784–85,

Q

Quezada, Juan
PI: 14904
Quicksand — Fiction
P: 4554
Quilting
P: 24532
Quilts
P: 114 **PI:** 12200 **I:** 17940,
17996
Quilts — Fiction
P: 3345, 3744, 3785, 4080,
4791, 5967, 6480
Quilts and quilting
IJ: 24528, 24545–46,
24548–49
Quilts and quilting — Fiction
P: 1018, 5145
Quimby, Harriet
PI: 12452
**Quinceanera (coming-of-age
ritual)**
I: 19306
**Quinceanera (coming-of-age
ritual) — Fiction**
P: 5911
Quinn, Anthony
IJ: 12876
Quintanilla, Guadalupe
IJ: 13397
Quokka
PI: 21632
Quotations
IJ: 15215
Quotations — Anthologies
IJ: 15174

R

Rabbis — Fiction
P: 1111, 21653, 21669, 22464,
22466 **PI:** 22475, 22484
I: 21660, 21668, 22468
Rabbits
P: 21650, 21653, 21669,
22464, 22466 **PI:** 22475,
22484 **I:** 21660, 21668, 22468
Rabbits — Fiction
P: 418, 461, 780, 1612, 1746,
1821, 1853, 1855, 1897,
2343–44, 2536, 2651, 2804,
2858, 2976, 3038, 4302, 4415,
4558, 5442, 5459, 5558, 5599,
6169, 6174, 6177, 6419, 6891,
15361 **PI:** 8701 **I:** 10187,
10192 **IJ:** 8307, 8374, 8424
Rabbits — Folklore
P: 10889, 10939, 11040,
11255, 11529–30 **I:** 11524,
11620
Raccoons
P: 5653, 21316, 21330, 21354
I: 21336
Raccoons — Fiction
P: 4531, 5265, 5602, 5656,
5885 **PI:** 8081 **IJ:** 7465,
7541, 7559
Race relations
IJ: 18873
Race relations — Fiction
P: 3457 **I:** 9984
Racial prejudice
IJ: 18826
Racing cars
P: 24104 **IJ:** 24092

Racism
See also Prejudice
P: 19052, 19686 **PI:** 19051
IJ: 18893, 19534
Racism — Biography
PI: 14351
Racism — Fiction
P: 4921, 5223 **I:** 4872, 7652,
7717, 9950 **IJ:** 7016, 7620,
7631, 7678, 7831, 7953, 8216,
9232, 9368, 9849, 9866, 9914,
10594
Racism — History
IJ: 18144
Radio
PI: 24036
Radio — Fiction
IJ: 9965
Radio — History
PI: 24031 **I:** 24035
Radio control models
IJ: 24569
Radio operators — Fiction
PI: 9814
Radiology
IJ: 20245
Radium
IJ: 14080
Radium — Biography
IJ: 14079
Railroads and trains
P: 5797–98, 5841, 24116,
24119–20, 24128, 24130–31,
24133, 24135 **PI:** 24123,
24129, 24136 **IJ:** 24118,
24125
**Railroads and trains —
Fiction**
P: 1198, 1266, 1432, 1459,
3022, 3195, 3833, 4754, 4786,
4813, 5515, 5800, 5806, 5815,
5842, 5844, 5847, 5849, 5852,
5857, 6148, 6598, 6943, 24121
PI: 5060, 9629, 9718
IJ: 9642, 9655
**Railroads and trains —
History**
PI: 17916, 24115, 24134
I: 18030, 24117, 24140
IJ: 18035, 18168, 24122,
24124, 24126–27, 24132,
24137–39, 24141
Railroads and trains (model)
IJ: 24568
Rain
See also Monsoons
P: 23481 **I:** 23427 **IJ:** 23471
Rain — Fiction
P: 460, 1543, 2828, 3315,
3342, 3409, 3889, 4466, 4570,
4692, 4810
Rain — Folklore
P: 10887
Rain forests
See also Forests
P: 5045, 21094, 23071–72,
23083, 23087, 23111, 23115
PI: 119, 23067, 23073, 23077,
23094, 23100, 23102, 23104,
23117–19, 23122, 23124,
23129, 23131, 23135 **I:** 17282,
23025, 23063, 23069, 23076,
23081–82, 23091, 23097–98,
23112, 23121, 23133, 23136
IJ: 11616, 14225, 17275,
20942, 21729, 23061, 23068,
23079, 23092, 23101, 23103,

23107–8, 23110, 23113, 23128,
23134
Rain forests — Animals
P: 21001, 23083 **PI:** 23067
I: 23125 **IJ:** 23068, 23114
**Rain forests — Experiments
and projects**
I: 23081
Rain forests — Fiction
P: 2567, 4544, 5038, 11343,
23109 **PI:** 3079, 4567, 4759,
8003 **I:** 8433
Rain forests — Folklore
P: 11613
Rain forests — Poetry
PI: 12206
Rainbows
P: 23578 **PI:** 23451
Rainbows — Fiction
P: 1160
Raleigh, Sir Walter
I: 12453
**Rama (Hindu deity) —
Fiction**
IJ: 8242
Ramadan
P: 19096, 19346 **PI:** 5879,
19309
Ramayana — Folklore
P: 11075 **I:** 11026
Ramon, Ilan
IJ: 12454
Ramphele, Mamphela
IJ: 14865
**Ranches and ranch life —
Fiction**
I: 7518, 7577
Ranches and ranch life
P: 3396, 22700 **PI:** 22662
I: 13542, 22681
**Ranches and ranch life —
Fiction**
I: 8054 **IJ:** 9054, 9064
**Ranches and ranch life —
History**
IJ: 18009
Randolph, A. Philip
PI: 13327 **IJ:** 13328
Rap music
IJ: 15226
Rap music — Biography
IJ: 12832
Rap musicians — Biography
I: 12808
Rats
P: 21649 **PI:** 21662 **I:** 21648
IJ: 22473
Rats — Fiction
P: 1935, 2259, 10135 **I:** 7334,
8085, 8586 **IJ:** 8086, 8194,
8470
Rattlesnakes
P: 21139 **PI:** 21137
Rattlesnakes — Fiction
P: 11416
Rawlings, Marjorie Kinnan
I: 13064
Rays
IJ: 22231
Rays (fish)
I: 22320
Reading
P: 2781, 15095, 15097

Reading — Fiction
P: 1430, 2967, 3138, 3163,
3267, 3683, 4183, 4257, 4777,
6670, 6868 **I:** 7668, 10348
Reading — Poetry
P: 11790 **IJ:** 13202, 13816,
13818
***Reading Rainbow* (TV
program)**
PI: 15411 **IJ:** 13202, 13816,
13818
Reagan, Ronald
P: 13817 **IJ:** 13202, 13816,
13818
Rebus books
P: 1736, 6455
Rebus books — Fiction
P: 4408
Recipes
I: 24669
Reconstruction Period (U.S.)
IJ: 18141, 18183
**Reconstruction to World War
I (U.S.) — Fiction**
IJ: 9887
Reconstruction (U.S.)
PI: 18092 **IJ:** 18116,
18132–33
Reconstruction (U.S.)

IJ: 18150
Reconstruction (U.S.)
IJ: 18151
**Reconstruction (U.S.) —
Fiction**
IJ: 9930
Recreation
PI: 24563 **I:** 25033
IJ: 24212, 24906, 24984
Recreation — Careers
IJ: 19892
Rectangles
PI: 23292
Rector, Anne Elizabeth
I: 12650
Recycling
P: 527 **I:** 24278, 24299, 24342
IJ: 18796
Recycling — Paper
I: 23775
Red Cross
P: 18858 **IJ:** 13898, 18845
Red Cross — Biography
I: 13894 **IJ:** 13895
Red-eyed tree frogs
P: 21109
Red Sea
I: 22422
Reece, Gabrielle
IJ: 14686
Reese, Della
IJ: 12877
Reflection (physics)
I: 23569
Reform party (U.S.)
IJ: 18971
Reformation
IJ: 15977
Refugees
PI: 16458
Refugees — Fiction
P: 4862, 5194 **PI:** 9254
I: 9967 **IJ:** 9187, 9207, 9270,
10030
Reincarnation
IJ: 24823

P = Primary; PI = Primary-Intermediate; I = Intermediate; IJ = Intermediate-Junior High

P = Primary; PI = Primary-Intermediate; I = Intermediate; IJ = Intermediate-Junior High

P = Primary; PI = Primary-Intermediate; I = Intermediate; IJ = Intermediate-Junior High

Sea kraits
P: 22169
Sea lions
P: 22291 I: 22275
Sea mammals
I: 22153
Sea monsters — Fiction
PI: 6959
Sea otters
See also Otters; River otters
P: 22272 I: 22280, 22285
Sea snakes
P: 22169
Sea stars
I: 22261
Sea stories
P: 4796 I: 8212 IJ: 7140,
7219, 7236, 8276, 9237,
9401–2, 9562, 9571, 9573
Sea stories — Fiction
IJ: 9826
Sea swallows
I: 21718
Sea turtles
P: 21177 PI: 21163,
21165–66, 21174, 21181
I: 21161, 21173
Sea turtles — Fiction
P: 5266, 5554
Sea World (California)
PI: 22334
Seabirds
I: 21726
Seafaring — Biography
I: 13180 IJ: 13051
Seagulls
I: 21817
Seagulls — Fiction
P: 2712, 5323 I: 8373
Seals
P: 22277, 22287, 22292
I: 22273, 22275, 22278, 22282
Seals — Fiction
P: 4285, 4517, 5267, 5431
Sears Tower (Chicago)
I: 18264
Seas
See also Oceans
P: 22388 I: 22385, 22402
IJ: 15471, 22410
Seashells
P: 22329, 22332
Seashores
See also Beaches; Tidal
pools
P: 22427, 22432, 22440
PI: 22147, 22428, 22433,
22438–39, 22443–44 I: 22430,
22437, 23005 IJ: 22441,
22445, 23010
Seashores — Birds
I: 21714
Seashores — Fiction
P: 50, 254, 3262, 3597–98,
3638, 3738, 4547–48, 4573,
4691, 5105, 5323, 6722
PI: 3547
Seashores — Plants
P: 22435
Seasonings (food)
IJ: 22714
Seasons
See also Months; and
specific seasons, e.g.,
Autumn

P: 4543, 4588, 4660, 4697,
12221, 20762, 20769, 20904–5,
20913, 20916 PI: 6965,
12191, 20901, 22821, 23340
I: 20902–3, 20912 IJ: 20671,
22657
Seasons — Art
PI: 15031
Seasons — Crafts
I: 24312
Seasons — Fiction
P: 382, 2005, 3129, 3619,
3631, 3791, 4528–29, 4550,
4555, 4589–90, 4603, 4615,
4622, 4635, 4640, 4651, 4665,
4680, 4686, 4689, 4701
PI: 1650, 4609, 12178, 12187,
12192, 12219, 12233
PI: 12199–201, 12218, 12232
I: 12198, 12209, 12222, 12227
Seasons — Mythology
PI: 11637, 4609, 12178,
12187, 12192, 12219, 12233
PI: 12199–201, 12218, 12232
I: 12198, 12209, 12222, 12227
Seasons — Poetry
P: 4555, 4609, 12178, 12187,
12192, 12219, 12233
PI: 12199–201, 12218, 12232
I: 12198, 12209, 12222, 12227
Seattle
PI: 18575
**Seattle SuperSonics
(basketball team)**
I: 25109
Seau, Junior
I: 14606
Seaweed
P: 22173 IJ: 22175
Secord, Laura — Fiction
PI: 9555 I: 9589
**Secretary of State —
Biography**
I: 13405
**Secretary of State (U.S.) —
Biography**
IJ: 13406
Secrets — Fiction
P: 3285, 3433 PI: 10372
Security blankets — Fiction
P: 2317, 5094
Seeds
P: 22867, 22877, 22879, 22882
PI: 22880 I: 22876, 22878
IJ: 22875, 22881
Seeds — Fiction
P: 1294, 2908, 4539
Seeds — Folklore
P: 10992
Seeing Eye dogs
P: 22541
Segregation
PI: 18897 IJ: 18224
Segregation — Fiction
P: 4737, 5186 I: 7652
IJ: 7415, 7646
**Segregation (U.S.) —
Biography**
IJ: 13297, 13336
Segregation (U.S.) — Fiction
P: 4910, 4922 PI: 7613, 9979
Seismosaurus
PI: 15569
Selena (singer)
P: 12898 IJ: 12897
Seles, Monica
PI: 14628 IJ: 14627

Self-confidence — Fiction
IJ: 8891
Self-defense
IJ: 20524
Self-esteem
P: 20281
Self-esteem — Fiction
P: 1573, 1895, 2034, 2840,
2891, 2930, 3112, 3136, 3200,
3473, 3586, 5138, 5730, 8197
PI: 10424 IJ: 7031, 10216,
10629
Seminole Indians
PI: 17610 I: 17452
IJ: 13652, 17467
Seminole Indians — Fiction
P: 3415 PI: 9603 IJ: 7190
Seminole Indians — History
I: 13653 IJ: 17524
Seneca Indians — Folklore
IJ: 11466
Senegal
IJ: 16272, 16317
Senses
See also specific senses,
e.g., Smell
P: 20389, 20401, 20404–10,
20416–20, 20425, 20427,
20436, 24796 PI: 20400
I: 20398, 20411, 20415
IJ: 20414, 20435
Senses — Animal
I: 21212
**Senses — Experiments and
projects**
P: 20413 PI: 20395
Senses — Fiction
P: 4666
September 11, 2001
P: 18226 PI: 18392, 24159
I: 18227, 18231, 18234
IJ: 18212, 18221, 18455,
19649, 19653–55, 19657,
19849, 19872
**September 11, 2001 —
Biography**
PI: 13492
**September 11, 2001 —
Fiction**
P: 2700 IJ: 7225
Sequoia (tree)
PI: 22836
Sequoyah
P: 13679 PI: 13677
IJ: 13676, 13678
**Serengeti National Park
(Tanzania)**
I: 16188
Serengeti Plain
I: 21484
Serra, Junípero
IJ: 13398–99
Settlement houses
IJ: 18120
Seurat, Georges
I: 12673
Seuss, Dr.
See Dr. Seuss
Seventh-Day Adventists
IJ: 19086
Seward, William
IJ: 13611
Seward, William Henry
I: 13610
Sewing
IJ: 24542–43, 24548

Sex education
P: 20561, 20563, 20578,
20584–86, 20591 PI: 20572,
20575, 20580, 20588 I: 20581,
20595 IJ: 20016, 20571,
20574, 20577, 20587, 20589,
20596–97
Sex education — Fiction
I: 7509
Sex education — Girls
IJ: 19799
Sex roles — Fiction
I: 7033
Sextuplets
P: 20549
Sexual abuse
P: 19827, 20584–85
IJ: 19797, 20589
Sexual abuse — Fiction
IJ: 8969
Shabbat
P: 6296
Shabbat — Fiction
P: 6311, 6322, 6329
Shabbat (Jewish holy day)
P: 19461 PI: 19444
**Shabbat (Jewish holy day) —
Fiction**
P: 6324
Shackleton, Ernest
PI: 17319
Shackleton, Sir Ernest
PI: 17327 I: 12461
IJ: 12459–60, 17313
Shadows
P: 24804
Shadows — Fiction
P: 174, 254, 1595, 2858, 3454,
3951 PI: 8237
Shakers (religion)
I: 19074 IJ: 19075, 19079
Shakespeare, William
I: 11234, 12285, 13079, 15428
IJ: 12256, 13076–78,
13080–83, 14932, 15427
**Shakespeare, William —
Adaptations**
IJ: 12258, 12291
**Shakespeare, William —
Fiction**
P: 4867 IJ: 9372–73
**Shakespeare, William —
Plays**
P: 12287 PI: 12283 I: 12286
IJ: 12249, 12261, 12274,
12284, 12288
**Shakespeare, William —
Poetry**
P: 11899 IJ: 12274, 24331
Shanghai
IJ: 16381, 24331
Shapes
P: 370, 24331
**Shapes — Experiments and
projects**
See also Concept books —
Sizes and shapes
PI: 20658, 23257
Shapes — Fiction
P: 5380
Sharing — Fiction
P: 178, 533, 1876, 2633, 6947
Sharks
P: 15518, 22297–99, 22301,
22303–5, 22315, 22319, 22324,
22328 PI: 22306–7, 22316,

P = Primary; PI = Primary-Intermediate; I = Intermediate; IJ = Intermediate-Junior High

22318, 22322, 22326–27
I: 22302, 22308–14, 22317,
22320, 22323, 22325
IJ: 14074, 22300, 22321
Sharks — Fiction
I: 7192
Sharks — History
I: 15486
Sharmat, Marjorie Weinman
PI: 13084
Shaw, Anna Howard
P: 13962
Shawnee Indians
I: 17500, 17614
Shawnee Indians — Fiction
I: 7153
Shays' Rebellion
IJ: 17824
Sheba, Queen of
PI: 19213
Sheep
P: 22666, 22678, 22686
Sheep — Fiction
P: 484, 2462, 2726, 4804,
5480, 5565, 5957, 6877
IJ: 7589, 8409
Sheep — Poetry
P: 12171
Sheep farms
P: 22672, 22678
Sheepdogs — Fiction
P: 5392 **PI:** 7503
Shelley, Mary Wollstonecraft
IJ: 13085
Shells
P: 21311, 22332 **I:** 22330–31
Shells — Crafts
I: 24344
Shells — Fiction
P: 1239
Shepard, Alan
IJ: 12462
Shepherds — Fiction
P: 3372, 4552
Sheppard, Ella
PI: 3318
Sherburne, Andrew
IJ: 13612
Sheridan, Philip
I: 13613
Sherman, Roger
PI: 17814
Sherman, William T.
IJ: 13614
Shintoism
P: 19151
Ships and boats
See also Dragon boat races;
Sailing and boating; and
specific ships, e.g., *Titanic*
(ship)
P: 24142–43, 24145–46,
24150, 24155, 24161, 24164,
24169 **PI:** 6519, 23813, 24194
I: 24147, 24149, 24158, 24205
IJ: 16024, 16067, 17859,
24148, 24151–52
Ships and boats —
Cookbooks
IJ: 17877
Ships and boats —
Experiments and projects
PI: 20708
Ships and boats — Fiction
P: 983, 3102, 3450, 4368,
4435, 5816, 5819, 5827, 5836

PI: 3712, 4792, 5843, 7257
I: 9208, 9550 **IJ:** 7391, 9215
Ships and boats — Folklore
P: 11303, 11314
Ships and boats — History
PI: 18098, 24207 **I:** 18158,
24167, 24170 **IJ:** 17950,
24154, 24162–63, 24175,
24201
Ships and boats — Native
Americans
IJ: 17486
Ships and boats — Poetry
PI: 11936
Ships and boats— History
IJ: 24166
Shipwrecks
See also Titanic (ship)
P: 24174 **I:** 24157, 24165,
24182 **IJ:** 14759, 15675,
15758, 17486, 17950, 22419,
22450, 22453, 24152, 24154,
24162, 24166
Shipwrecks — Fiction
P: 4964, 5638, 6577 **PI:** 8662
I: 7426 **IJ:** 9205
Shoelaces — Fiction
P: 1167
Shoes
P: 2696, 23915 **PI:** 23906,
23931 **IJ:** 23910, 23922,
23932
Shoes — Fiction
P: 1633, 3145, 3237, 3326,
3479, 3985
Shoes — Folklore
P: 11129
Shoes — History
PI: 23918
Shoes — Poetry
P: 3595 **PI:** 11767
Shogun
IJ: 16435
Shona (African people)
IJ: 16263
Shopping
PI: 17348
Shopping — Fiction
P: 3431, 3448, 4347
Shopping — History
PI: 17348
Shopping malls
P: 18745
Short stories
P: 948, 6485, 10531, 11365
PI: 7524, 8640, 10072, 10151,
10520, 10524, 10684 **I:** 8039,
8212, 8336, 8350, 10069,
10117, 10517, 10521, 19591
IJ: 7017, 7021, 7212, 7310,
7497, 7648, 7664, 8069, 8619,
8630, 8821, 10452, 10518,
10522–23, 10526, 10528–29,
10532, 10575
Short stories — Fiction
PI: 8351, 10465 **I:** 9276
IJ: 7665, 8097, 8720, 9300,
10224, 10511, 10525, 10530
Shoshone Indians
PI: 17536 **IJ:** 17468
Shoshone Indians —
Biography
I: 13671–73
Shoshone Indians — Fiction
P: 3518
Shoshone Indians — Folklore
PI: 11489

Shreve, Henry Miller
IJ: 13615
Shrimp
P: 22198
Shrublands
IJ: 22993
Shyness
IJ: 19807
Shyness — Fiction
P: 2137, 3562, 4379, 5192,
6272, 6381, 9076 **PI:** 8919
I: 10564 **IJ:** 6954, 7004, 8971,
10583
Siamese cats — Fiction
P: 1874 **PI:** 1875
Siamese fighting fish
I: 22239
Siberia — Fiction
P: 5598
Sibling rivalry
P: 6412 **I:** 19762
Sibling rivalry — Fiction
P: 947, 1231, 1788, 2664,
3670, 3846, 3995, 4041, 4092
PI: 7816, 10270 **I:** 8856,
8875, 10255 **IJ:** 8348, 9155,
10574
Siblings
P: 20558
Siblings — Fiction
See also Twins
P: 1327, 1693, 2149, 2274,
2342, 2505, 3707, 3724, 3745,
3757, 3795, 3816, 3837, 3842,
3857, 3915, 3941, 4026, 4036,
4067, 4103, 4237, 5070, 6263,
6401, 7936 **PI:** 3909, 7747
I: 8907 **IJ:** 7842, 7886
Siblings — Folklore
P: 11004
Sickle cell anemia
IJ: 20133, 20136, 20202
Sickle cell disease
I: 20100
Siegel, Bugsy
IJ: 13616
Sight
P: 20404, 20406, 20417, 20428
I: 20094 **IJ:** 20432
Sign language
See also American Sign
Language
P: 829, 15103, 15109, 15114
PI: 15110, 15113 **I:** 15104–5,
15108 **IJ:** 20072
Sign language — Fiction
P: 23, 5188 **PI:** 5170
Signs and symbols
P: 15103, 15112, 15116
PI: 17820–21, 23784
I: 15102, 15104, 17351, 19044
Signs and symbols — Fiction
P: 3157
Sikhism
P: 19127 **I:** 16396, 19093
IJ: 19147
Silicon
IJ: 22906
Silk
PI: 23911
Silk — Fiction
P: 4834 **PI:** 4880
Silk Road
IJ: 15762
Silk route
IJ: 15718

Silk Route — Folklore
I: 10805
Silkworms
PI: 21979 **IJ:** 20995
Silva, Marina
IJ: 14871
Silver
IJ: 22914
Silverstein, Shel
P: 13086
Silverstone, Alicia
PI: 12899
Simmons, Philip
IJ: 12674
Simon, Seymour
I: 13087
Simple machines
See also Levers
P: 23616–17, 23623–28
PI: 23621–22
Simple machines —
Experiments and projects
PI: 23619 **I:** 23618
Simulation
IJ: 23764
Simulation (computers)
IJ: 23936
Simulators
IJ: 23722
Singapore
PI: 16472 **I:** 16449, 16456,
16535 **IJ:** 16450, 16501
Singer, Isaac Bashevis
IJ: 13088
Singers — Biography
P: 12740, 12898 **PI:** 12736,
12741, 12745, 12763, 12781,
12787, 12792, 12797, 12824,
12838, 12844 **I:** 12734, 12738,
12766, 12784, 12791, 12807,
12836, 12872–73
Singers and singing —
Biography
P: 12743 **PI:** 12880
I: 12714–15, 12742, 12798
IJ: 12491, 12493, 12496,
12735, 12764–65, 12770–71,
12774, 12785–86, 12793–96,
12815–16, 12822, 12825,
12827–28, 12831–32, 12837,
12877, 12881, 12889, 12897,
12910, 12918
Singers and singing — Fiction
P: 3929, 5040 **PI:** 3318
IJ: 6999, 7714, 7885
Singing games and songs
P: 15264, 15296
Single parents — Fiction
P: 3922 **IJ:** 7689
Sinkholes
IJ: 23225
Sioux Indians
P: 17611 **PI:** 13680 **I:** 13634,
13636, 13683–84, 17634
IJ: 13635, 13681, 17581
Sioux Indians — Fiction
IJ: 9637
Sioux Indians — Folklore
PI: 11437, 11445
Sister cities
IJ: 15436
Sisters — Fiction
P: 3670, 3709, 3749, 3953,
3991, 4185, 6412, 6432, 7897
PI: 4489, 9045 **I:** 7698, 7947
Sitting Bull — Fiction
IJ: 9437

P = Primary; PI = Primary-Intermediate; I = Intermediate; IJ = Intermediate-Junior High

Sitting Bull (Sioux chief)
PI: 13680, 13682 **I:** 13683–84
IJ: 13681
Six-Day War
IJ: 16896
Size
PI: 23346
Size — Fiction
P: 3624, 5191
Sizes and shapes
See Concept books — Sizes
and shapes
Skara Brae
IJ: 15644
Skateboarding
P: 25286 **I:** 24911, 25290
IJ: 25027, 25284–85,
25287–89, 25291–92, 20457
Skating
See specific types, e.g., Ice
skating
Skeletal system
IJ: 20453, 20457
Skeletons
P: 20441 **PI:** 20438 **I:** 20439,
20442, 20449, 20452, 20456
IJ: 20440, 20444
Skeletons — Fiction
P: 1500, 6389 **PI:** 4275
Skin
P: 20460, 20463, 20467
PI: 21238, 21253 **I:** 20464–66
Skin — Fiction
P: 3458
Skin injuries
I: 20464
Skin problems
I: 20465 **I:** 24910 **IJ:** 24982,
25298
Skipping
See Rope skipping
Skis and skiing
PI: 24925 **I:** 24910
IJ: 24982, 25298
Skis and skiing — Fiction
P: 1874
Skits
I: 12266
Skulls
PI: 113
Skunks
P: 21355 **PI:** 21383 **I:** 21372,
21379
Skunks — Fiction
P: 4482, 5664 **PI:** 5398
I: 10501
Sky — Fiction
P: 4540
Sky diving
I: 24907
Skyscrapers
P: 23865 **PI:** 23856, 23880
I: 14944, 23882, 23885, 23889
IJ: 23886
Skyscrapers — Fiction
P: 4866
Slater, Samuel
IJ: 17921
Slavery
See also African Americans;
Civil War (U.S.);
Emancipation
Proclamation
P: 13244, 13359, 17895
PI: 18092, 24579 **I:** 13341,
13971, 17899, 17905, 18063

IJ: 9607, 13259, 13343, 13345,
15696, 16294, 17689, 17810,
17860–61, 17879–81, 17888,
17906, 17911–12, 17914,
18773, 19566, 19570, 19572
Slavery — Biography
PI: 13097, 13239, 13249,
13331, 13438, 13892
I: 13250–51, 13311, 13349,
13366 **IJ:** 13232, 13264,
13347, 13352, 13560, 13918
Slavery — Fiction
P: 1400, 5050, 5056, 6254
PI: 4788, 9575, 9604–5, 9619,
9621, 10086 **I:** 9199, 9246,
9517, 9578, 9581, 9584, 9590,
9596, 9599, 9766, 9791, 9793
IJ: 7637, 8261, 8667, 9209,
9242, 9244, 9493, 9531, 9547,
9563, 9570, 9576, 9591, 9595,
9601, 9606, 9609, 9780, 9858,
17882
Slavery — Folklore
PI: 11543
Slavery — History
IJ: 15745, 15793
Slavery (U.S.)
P: 17909 **PI:** 13356, 18077
I: 17798, 17913, 18055, 18899
IJ: 11520, 17437, 17872–73,
17925, 18087, 18094, 18837,
18867, 18889, 19603, 19621
Slavery (U.S.) — Biography
P: 13346, 13354 **PI:** 13123,
13364 **I:** 13151, 13246, 13342,
13348, 13437 **IJ:** 13245,
13272, 13338, 13436
Slavery (U.S.) — Fiction
P: 4837, 4942, 4962, 5026–27,
9756 **PI:** 4883, 4927, 9503,
9603, 9616, 9620 **IJ:** 9536,
9556, 9598, 9610, 9789
Slavery (U.S.) — Folk songs
IJ: 15271
Slavery (U.S.) — History
PI: 17735 **IJ:** 17874
Sled dogs
See also Iditarod
P: 22527 **PI:** 22557 **I:** 24919
IJ: 24929
Sled dogs — Fiction
P: 5488 **PI:** 5290, 7600
I: 7625 **IJ:** 7314, 7931
Sled dogs — Racing
IJ: 25011
Sleds and sledding — Fiction
P: 6941
Sleep
P: 20374, 20508, 20539
I: 20540, 20542 **IJ:** 20541,
20544
Sleep — Fiction
P: 660, 683, 696, 1825, 2129,
2610, 3820, 4000, 4488, 4507
IJ: 8298
Sleep disorders
IJ: 20210
Sleeping sickness
IJ: 20181
Sleepovers
P: 19819 **I:** 24942
Sleepovers — Cookbooks
IJ: 24676
Sleepovers — Fiction
P: 4117, 6564
Slime
PI: 24844

Slocum, Joshua
I: 12463
Sloths
P: 21345 **I:** 21375
Slovakia
PI: 16628
Slovenia
IJ: 16638
Slugs
P: 22124–25 **IJ:** 21013
Smallpox
IJ: 20169
Smell (sense)
P: 20402, 20404, 20418
I: 20393, 20396, 20422, 20431
**Smell (sense) — Experiments
and projects**
I: 20396 **IJ:** 20686
Smell (sense) — Fiction
P: 5249
Smells — Fiction
P: 4362
Smiles
P: 19716
Smith, Bessie
PI: 12900
Smith, Emmitt
I: 14608 **IJ:** 14607, 14609
Smith, Jedediah
I: 12464
Smith, John
I: 12465
Smith, Sophia — Fiction
PI: 9963
Smith College — Fiction
PI: 9963
Smithsonian Institution
PI: 18393 **I:** 18995
Smits, Jimmy
PI: 12901
Smoking
IJ: 20025–26, 20028, 20039,
20042, 20052
Smoking — Fiction
PI: 8965
Smuggling
IJ: 18959
Smuggling — Fiction
IJ: 9998, 10305
Snails
P: 22121, 22124, 22127
PI: 22122 **I:** 22130, 22136
IJ: 21013
Snails — Fiction
P: 457, 1483, 2421, 5339
Snake charmers
PI: 16407
Snake River
IJ: 23165
Snakes
See also individual species,
e.g., Anacondas
P: 21064, 21139–41,
21151–52, 21154 **PI:** 21137,
21142, 21146, 21148, 21153,
21156 **I:** 21056, 21145, 21150,
21155, 21157 **IJ:** 21130,
21138, 21143–44, 21149,
22473
Snakes — Fiction
P: 596, 1283, 2361, 2865,
2890, 4230, 4325, 4437, 4582,
4936, 6456, 6905 **PI:** 5512,
10127
Snakes — Folklore
P: 11416

Sneakers
PI: 23906, 23931
Sneakers — Fiction
P: 4369
Sneakers (shoes)
I: 23930
Sneezing — Fiction
P: 1642
Snider, Duke
I: 14440
Snow
P: 12513, 23425 **PI:** 23466
I: 23428 **IJ:** 23500
Snow — Crafts
P: 24241
Snow — Fiction
P: 1047, 1211, 1300, 1517,
1572, 1599, 2316, 2344, 3090,
3169, 3221, 3261, 3316, 3460,
3528–29, 3565, 3601, 3608,
3621, 4574, 4616, 4618, 4654,
4827, 5152, 5755, 6737
Snow — Fiction
P: 3186, 3221, 3261, 3316,
3460, 3528–29, 3565, 3601,
3608, 3621, 4574, 4616, 4618,
4654, 4827, 5152, 5755, 6737
Snow — Fiction
P: 3197, 3221, 3261, 3316,
3460, 3528–29, 3565, 3601,
3608, 3621, 4574, 4616, 4618,
4654, 4827, 5152, 5755, 6737
Snow — Poetry
P: 4657 **PI:** 12232
Snow days — Fiction
P: 4438
Snow geese — Fiction
P: 5457
Snowboarding
I: 25294 **IJ:** 25027, 25293,
25295–97, 25299–302
Snowboarding — Fiction
I: 10552 **IJ:** 10542, 10568
Snowboards
I: 23767
Snowmen — Fiction
P: 911, 1020, 3508, 3880,
6062, 6831 **PI:** 6086
Snowmobiles
IJ: 24992
Snowplows
P: 24010, 24038
Snyder, Grace McCance
I: 18033
Soap
I: 24300
Soaring
IJ: 24994
Soccer
P: 24932, 25303, 25305–7,
25310, 25316, 25325
PI: 25312–13, 25319
I: 25309, 25314–15, 25321
IJ: 25304, 25308, 25311,
25317–18, 25320, 25322–24,
25327
Soccer — Biography
PI: 14668–69 **I:** 14340, 14667
IJ: 14321, 14684
Soccer — Fiction
P: 234, 1860, 2440, 3234,
6729, 6736 **PI:** 6728, 8354,
10537, 10579 **I:** 7195, 8776,
10556, 10569, 10585, 10590,
10599 **IJ:** 10580, 10583,
10604, 10614, 10621

P = Primary; PI = Primary-Intermediate; I = Intermediate; IJ = Intermediate-Junior High

P = Primary; PI = Primary-Intermediate; I = Intermediate; IJ = Intermediate-Junior High

P = Primary; PI = Primary-Intermediate; I = Intermediate; IJ = Intermediate-Junior High

P = Primary; PI = Primary-Intermediate; I = Intermediate; IJ = Intermediate-Junior High

Supernatural — Folklore
PI: 10791
Supernatural — Poetry
PI: 11700 I: 11880 IJ: 11881
Superstition — Fiction
IJ: 9070
Superstitions
PI: 11961, 24845
Superstitions — Fiction
P: 4280
Supply and demand (economics)
IJ: 18737
Supreme Court
IJ: 18823, 18844
Supreme Court (U.S.)
I: 18828, 18832 IJ: 18829,
18835, 18837, 18839, 18841,
18869
Supreme Court (U.S.) — Biography
P: 13307 PI: 13305–6, 13308,
13563 I: 13310, 13561–62,
13565 IJ: 13309, 13435,
13493, 13564
Supremes (musical group)
IJ: 12908
Surfboarding — Fiction
IJ: 7336
Surfing
I: 25329, 25331 IJ: 25328,
25333
Surfing — Fiction
P: 2604 I: 7585
Surgery — Fiction
P: 3294
Surrealism (art)
I: 14916
Survival
IJ: 14759, 14858, 17313
Survival — Fiction
I: 7147 IJ: 7119, 7137, 7170,
7199, 7226, 7235, 7320, 7387,
7389, 7401, 7810, 7929, 8642,
9237, 9434, 9583, 9779
Survival — Nature
I: 20927
Survival stories
PI: 17322
Survival stories — Fiction
I: 7118, 7154, 9561 IJ: 8922
IJ: 13621
Sushi
PI: 24649 IJ: 13621
Sutter, John
PI: 13622 IJ: 13621
Suzuki, Ichiro
I: 14444 IJ: 14445–46
Suzuki, Shinichi
IJ: 14874
Swahili — Folklore
P: 10889, 10925
Swallows — Fiction
P: 5556
Swamps
P: 22999 I: 22990
Swamps — Fiction
P: 6240, 21787 I: 21778,
21784
Swan Lake (ballet)
PI: 15398, 21787 I: 21778,
21784
Swans
P: 21785, 21787 I: 21778,
21784

Swans — Fiction
I: 8695
Swanson, Anne Barrett
PI: 14243
Swazi
IJ: 16249
Swaziland
PI: 16245 IJ: 16224
Sweden
P: 16874 I: 16839, 16872
IJ: 16840–41, 16846, 16848,
16870
Sweden — Fiction
P: 4731 PI: 10692 I: 10211
Sweden — Folklore
P: 11102
Sweden — Holidays
PI: 16868
Swedish Americans
PI: 24626 I: 19619 IJ: 19593
Swedish Americans — Fiction
P: 4975 PI: 9934 I: 9737
Swimming
P: 24932, 25334, 25336
PI: 25335 IJ: 25330
Swimming — Biography
PI: 14663, 14685 I: 14689
Swimming — Fiction
P: 1943, 2223, 3117, 3144,
5155, 5336 PI: 8342
Swindlers and swindling — Fiction
IJ: 7026
Switzerland
PI: 16633 I: 16619, 16626,
16629 IJ: 16636, 16641,
16644, 16648
Switzerland — Christmas
I: 19391
Switzerland — Cookbooks
IJ: 24620
Swoopes, Sheryl
P: 25121
Sydney (Australia)
I: 16596
Symbiosis
P: 21188 I: 20925 IJ: 20949
Symbols
See Signs and symbols
P: 15106 PI: 17352
Synagogues
P: 19170, 19181
Synagogues — Fiction
P: 6290
Synonyms
PI: 15127
Syphilis
IJ: 20117

T

T-ball — Fiction
P: 3046
Table manners
P: 2209
Table manners — History
PI: 19729
Tacos
P: 24618
Tadpoles
I: 21112

Tadpoles — Fiction
P: 5557
Tae Kwon Do
IJ: 25283
Tahiti
IJ: 16585
Taiga
I: 23064, 23089 IJ: 23095,
23126
Taino Indians — Folklore
P: 11592, 11598
Taiwan
IJ: 16461, 16474, 16512,
16549
Taiwan — Fiction
P: 4757, 4967 IJ: 9300
Taj Mahal
IJ: 16397
Tajikistan
IJ: 16832
Tall people — Fiction
IJ: 7691
Tall tales
P: 993, 1007, 1046, 1154,
1498, 1619, 4254, 4351, 10881,
11505, 11540, 11566
PI: 4349, 4458, 10154
I: 10156, 10210
Tall tales — Fiction
P: 4327, 6466
Tallchief, Maria
I: 12909
Tanks — History
IJ: 16068
Tanzania
IJ: 16165, 16207, 16211
Tanzania — Fiction
P: 2329, 4925, 5000–2, 5779
Tanzania — Folklore
P: 10947–48
Tap dancing
IJ: 15393
Tap dancing — Biography
P: 12882 IJ: 12894
Tap dancing — Fiction
P: 1007
Tap jazz
IJ: 15393
Tapeworms
I: 21006
Taproots
P: 22784
Tarantulas
P: 22118 IJ: 22109
Tarantulas — Fiction
P: 2863 I: 8894
Tarkenton, Fran
IJ: 14610
Taste
PI: 20412
Taste (sense)
P: 20419, 20433 I: 20393–94,
20399, 20423, 20431
Taste (sense) — Experiments and projects
I: 20399
Tattoos
IJ: 24867
Tattoos — Fiction
IJ: 10298
Taxes
PI: 18726
Taxes — United States
PI: 19002
Taxicabs — Fiction
P: 3404

Taylor, Marshall B.
PI: 13329–30
Taylor, Susie King
PI: 13331
Taylor, Zachary
PI: 13838 I: 13836 IJ: 13837
Tchaikovsky, Peter Ilyich
PI: 12732
Tchaikovsky, Peter Ilyich — Fiction
PI: 9883
Tea — Poetry
P: 11923
Teachers
P: 19842, 19857, 19860
Teachers — Biography
P: 13908 IJ: 13166
Teachers — Careers
P: 3241, 19874
Teachers — Fiction
P: 260, 1427, 3007, 5666–67,
5675, 5678, 5687, 5690, 5708,
5713, 5718, 5729 PI: 3835,
10387, 10582 I: 10367, 10383,
10453 IJ: 6978, 9719
Teamwork
P: 228
Teasing
PI: 19786
Technology
I: 23761 IJ: 23722, 23729,
23764, 23868, 24022
Technology — 1960s
IJ: 14908
Technology — careers
IJ: 19941
Technology — Fiction
P: 4391
Technology — History
IJ: 14933, 14945, 15785,
15927, 20603, 23774
Technology and engineering
P: 23760 I: 23759, 23766,
24024
Technology and engineering — History
PI: 15714 I: 23725
Tecumseh (Shawnee chief)
I: 13687
Tecumseh (Shawnee chief) — Fiction
IJ: 9731
Teddy bears — Fiction
P: 944, 984, 1293, 1470, 3403,
3584, 6752
Teddy bears — History
PI: 23734
Teddy bears — Manufacture
I: 23768
Teenagers — Civil rights
IJ: 18869
Teenagers — Violence
IJ: 18935, 18961, 18964–66
Teeth
P: 20462, 20468, 20471–74
PI: 20469 I: 20475
IJ: 20230, 20470
Teeth — Animals
PI: 21257
Teeth — Fiction
P: 1134, 1531, 1746, 2483,
3140, 3925, 4353, 4386, 5740,
6483, 6495, 6593, 6651, 6695,
6911 PI: 10122, 10416
Teeth — Folklore
P: 10776, 10779

Telecommunications
PI: 24017 I: 24020 IJ: 24016
Telephone
PI: 23753
Telephone — Biography
P: 14031 I: 14033–34
IJ: 14030
Telephones
P: 24005 PI: 24018
Telephones — Biography
IJ: 14035
Telescopes
PI: 20746 I: 20742
IJ: 20716, 20735, 20747
Telescopes — Fiction
P: 4468
Television
P: 15414, 24005 PI: 15411,
24028 I: 12749, 12777, 12850,
12922, 24025, 24033
IJ: 12778, 12780, 24023
Television — Biography
PI: 12893 I: 14022, 14123
IJ: 12914, 12919–20, 14122
Television — Careers
IJ: 19905
Television — Fiction
P: 1853, 2580, 3392
PI: 10130 IJ: 6960
Television — Programs
PI: 15406–7
Television — Special effects
IJ: 24030
Teller, Edward
IJ: 14244
Temper — Fiction
P: 5168
Temper tantrums — Fiction
P: 5109
Temperature — Experiments
   and projects
IJ: 23562
Ten Commandments (Bible)
P: 19255
Tenement housing
IJ: 18389
Tennessee
P: 18605, 18670 PI: 18613,
18624 I: 18588, 18661
IJ: 18590
Tennessee — Fiction
IJ: 9912
Tennessee River
IJ: 23169
Tennis
P: 25339 PI: 25344 I: 25340
IJ: 25337–38, 25342
Tennis — Biography
PI: 14618, 14622, 14625,
14628, 14630 I: 14293, 14330,
14623–24, 14634 IJ: 14283,
14615–17, 14619–21,
14626–27, 14629, 14631–33,
14704
Tennis — Fiction
IJ: 10533
Tennis — Women
IJ: 25343
Tennyson, Alfred Lord
IJ: 11687
Tepees
PI: 11452
Teresa, Mother
P: 14875, 14883 PI: 14876,
14878–79, 19168 I: 14880
IJ: 14877, 14881–82,
14884–85

Tereshkova, Valentina
P: 12466
Terezin (concentration camp)
IJ: 16085
Termites
P: 21920 I: 21990
Terrell, Mary Church
PI: 13334 I: 13335
IJ: 13332–33
Terriers
I: 22568
Terrorism
P: 18226 I: 18227, 18231,
19658 IJ: 16875, 16932,
16972, 16977, 18212, 18455,
18820, 19648, 19650–57,
19659, 19661, 24190
Terrorism — Biography
IJ: 13229, 14751–53
Terrorism — Fiction
IJ: 6957, 8647
Tesla, Nikola
IJ: 14245
Test tube babies
IJ: 20565, 20568
Texas
I: 18707 PI: 18692, 18699
I: 18683, 18696, 18709, 19591
IJ: 18681, 18687, 18700,
18706, 18711
Texas — Biography
PI: 13522 IJ: 13213, 13389,
13418, 13523, 13525, 13599
Texas — Fiction
P: 4729, 4780, 4822, 9638
PI: 1902, 10086 I: 7410,
8054, 9546, 9580, 9666, 9900,
9941 IJ: 7166, 7488, 7812,
9565–66, 9602, 9631, 9684,
9715, 9722, 9753, 9804
Texas — Folklore
P: 11436
Texas — History
PI: 13524, 17864 I: 14744,
17884, 17904, 17918, 17920
IJ: 13431, 17870, 17901,
17923, 18681, 18686, 18688,
18713, 22688
Textiles — Fiction
P: 4552
Thailand
P: 21602 I: 16453, 16463,
16521, 16536, 21586
IJ: 16470, 16527
Thailand — Cookbooks
IJ: 24614–15, 24631
Thailand — Fiction
P: 1296 I: 7859, 9268
IJ: 9267
Thailand — Folklore
P: 11069 IJ: 11071
Thailand — Holidays
PI: 16540
Thanksgiving
P: 6349, 6361, 19477, 19483,
19487 PI: 19283, 19481
I: 19485–86, 19488, 19490–91
Thanksgiving — Cookbooks
PI: 19480 I: 19486
Thanksgiving — Crafts
PI: 19481 I: 19479, 19486
Thanksgiving — Experiments
   and projects
PI: 19480
Thanksgiving — Fiction
P: 510, 4671, 6338–39,
6341–48, 6350–53, 6355–60,

6362–66, 10079 PI: 6340,
6354, 7284 I: 10039
Thanksgiving — History
PI: 19482, 19484
Thanksgiving — Poetry
PI: 12098
Thanksgiving — Riddles
P: 24750
Thanksgiving Day
P: 19492 IJ: 19478, 19489
Thanksgiving Day — Fiction
P: 3823, 4829
Thatcher, Margaret
IJ: 14886
Thaxter, Celia
P: 5012
Theater
IJ: 15423, 2072, 2462, 4255,
6339 IJ: 9374, 10223
Theater — Fiction
P: 1595, 2072, 2462, 4255,
6339 IJ: 9374, 10223
Theater — History
IJ: 15427
Theater games
IJ: 15420
Theaters
See also Actors and
   actresses; Plays
I: 15425 IJ: 15225
Therapy
IJ: 20276
Therese of Lisieux, Saint
P: 14887
Thesauruses
P: 15159 I: 15165
Theseus (mythology)
I: 11649
Thomas, Dave
PI: 13623
Thomas, Dylan
I: 13100
Thomas, Frank
I: 14447–48
Thomas, Isiah
IJ: 14540
Thomas, Thurman
IJ: 14611
Thompson, Jenny
I: 14689
Thoreau, Henry David
PI: 4632, 13102 I: 13101
Thoreau, Henry David —
   Fiction
IJ: 7068
Thorpe, Jim
P: 14652 IJ: 14653
Throat
I: 20203
Thumbsucking — Fiction
P: 5132
Thunderbird (automobile)
P: 24111
Thunderstorms
P: 23380 PI: 23414 I: 23395
Thunderstorms — Fiction
P: 1802, 3996
Tibet
P: 16339 I: 14775 IJ: 16485,
16494, 16499, 16502
Tibet — Biography
I: 14776 IJ: 14777
Tibet — Fiction
P: 4811 PI: 5018 IJ: 9299
Tibet — Folklore
P: 10967, 10980

Tic-tac-toe
P: 6902
Tidal pools
P: 22436 PI: 22429, 22431,
22434 I: 22442
Tidal waves
See also Tsunamis
I: 22425, 23419 IJ: 23420
Tidal waves — Fiction
P: 957 I: 8901
Tide pools
I: 22430
Tierra del Fuego
PI: 17244
Tigers
P: 21501, 21511, 21517,
21524, 21533, 21535
PI: 21495, 21516 I: 21500,
21502, 21507, 21520, 21525,
21532, 22628 IJ: 21490,
21518
Tigers — Fiction
P: 921, 924, 1181, 1730, 1969,
4658 I: 8932
Tigers — Folklore
I: 11076
Tigris River
IJ: 16912
Tikal (Guatemala)
IJ: 17132
Timbuktu — History
IJ: 16279
Time
IJ: 20606–7
Time — Poetry
P: 205 IJ: 11780
Time and clocks
P: 218, 236, 823, 2168, 23336,
23338–39, 23341 PI: 23333,
23337, 23340, 23342, 23346
I: 14164, 22948, 23343
Time and clocks —
   Experiments and projects
PI: 20644 I: 23332
Time and clocks — Fiction
P: 201, 219, 641, 2541, 2557,
3924 I: 10733
Time and clocks —
   Measurement
I: 23331
Time and clocks — Nursery
   rhymes
P: 874
Time capsules
I: 15724
Time travel
PI: 4989, 8578, 10070
I: 7999, 8129–30, 8201, 8217,
8241, 8477, 8518, 8524,
8532–33, 8572, 8575, 9767,
10488 IJ: 7203, 7960, 8007,
8028, 8037, 8092, 8134, 8138,
8152, 8204, 8214, 8216, 8218,
8221, 8261, 8314, 8392, 8408,
8412, 8436, 8489, 8579, 8605,
8684, 8687, 8703, 8706, 8709,
10276, 10436, 10440, 10472,
10502
Time travel — Fiction
P: 921, 1418, 1586, 6775, 9418
PI: 1509, 7572, 7997, 8574,
10071, 10508, 15512 I: 7342,
7965, 8010, 8034, 8105, 8160,
8224, 8367, 8527, 8573, 8577,
8591, 8604, 8628, 8638–39,
8731, 10470, 10489, 15054,
16653 IJ: 7388, 8013, 8116,

8213, 8417, 8482, 8658, 8700, 8825, 10037, 10461, 10483

Tipis
See Tepees
I: 17448

Titanic — Biography
I: 12321

Titanic (ship)
PI: 6519, 18181, 24153, 24172 **I:** 18184, 22455, 24149, 24158 **IJ:** 22446, 22454, 24144, 24160

Titanic (ship) — Fiction
P: 1080, 4734 **I:** 9830 **IJ:** 9841, 9957 **IJ:** 17469

Titian
P: 12675 **IJ:** 17469

Tlingit Indians
PI: 17629 **IJ:** 17469

Tlingit Indians — Folklore
I: 11498

Tlingit (people)
I: 18577

Toads
See Frogs and toads
I: 21108

Toasters
I: 23720

Tobacco
See Smoking

Tohono O'odham Indians — Poetry
PI: 15369

Toilet training
P: 3395, 3520, 3588, 20480

Toilet training — Fiction
P: 3183, 3250

Toilets
PI: 15703 **I:** 20346

Tokyo
P: 16441 **I:** 16417

Tokyo, Japan
I: 16428

Tolkien, J. R. R.
IJ: 13103

Tomatoes
P: 22748

Tongue twisters
P: 6859, 6869 **I:** 24813

Tonsillitis
I: 20203

Tools
P: 5809, 24557

Tooth decay
See also Teeth
I: 20475

Tooth fairies
P: 1001

Toothbrushes — Fiction
P: 1098

Toothbrushing — Fiction
P: 2878

Toothpaste
I: 23769

Toothpaste — Fiction
I: 10231

Torah
I: 11373

Torah scrolls
PI: 19136

Tornadoes
P: 23383, 23391, 23406 **PI:** 23376, 23381 **I:** 23355, 23377, 23394, 23396, 23403, 23409 **IJ:** 23372, 23374, 23398, 23404, 23411, 23416

Tornadoes — Fiction
P: 3040, 3043, 3067, 4001, 5130 **PI:** 6630 **I:** 7339, 8474

Toronto
I: 17051

Tortillas
P: 22733

Tortoises — Fiction
P: 4575, 5479

Torvalds, Linus
IJ: 14246

Touch
P: 20407, 20420 **PI:** 20412 **I:** 20394

Touch (sense)
I: 20392, 20424, 20431

Toulouse-Lautrec, Henri
PI: 12676

Tour guides — Careers
IJ: 19880

Touro Synagogue (RI)
IJ: 19101

Towels — Fiction
P: 3413

Tower of Babel (painting)
IJ: 14943

Towns — Deserts
P: 3263

Toxic wastes
IJ: 18817

Toy making
I: 24524 **IJ:** 23610, 24555

Toys
P: 23724, 24556 **PI:** 18181

Toys — Crafts
P: 24552 **IJ:** 24550

Toys — Experiments and projects
I: 20624

Toys — Fiction
P: 683, 987, 1034, 1143, 1193, 1202, 1232, 1234–35, 1240, 1289, 1322, 1356, 1392, 1415, 1486, 2487, 2715, 3118, 3296, 3372, 3401, 3446, 3545, 3585, 4234, 5169, 5915, 6125, 10639 **PI:** 8006, 8701 **I:** 8010, 8708 **IJ:** 8019, 8246

Toys — Folklore
PI: 11142

Toys — History
I: 17417, 25039

Track and field
PI: 25345–47 **IJ:** 25266–67

Track and field — Biography
P: 14642, 14646, 14650, 14705 **PI:** 14643 **I:** 14341, 14635, 14638, 14645, 14647, 14649, 14651 **IJ:** 14297, 14308, 14322, 14636–37, 14639, 14641, 14644, 14653, 14706

Track and field — Fiction
P: 5685

Track and field — Women
I: 14341

Track and field — Women — Biography
PI: 14648

Tractors
P: 22685, 24087

Tractors — Fiction
P: 5803

Trade
PI: 18743

Trade — History
IJ: 15719

Trade routes — History
IJ: 15718

Trail of Tears
PI: 17476, 17495 **I:** 17589

Trail of Tears — Fiction
IJ: 9439

Train wrecks — Fiction
P: 4786

Trains
See Railroads and trains
P: 5807, 5829, 15260

Trains — Fiction
P: 6791

Trains and railroads — Fiction
P: 1214

Transcontinental Railroad — History
I: 18030

Transplants
See Organ transplants

Transportation
See also specific types of transportation, e.g., Automobiles
P: 115, 3469, 5793, 5821, 24048, 24054, 24060 **PI:** 24040 **I:** 24047 **IJ:** 24051, 24053, 24055

Transportation — Careers
P: 19986

Transportation — Crafts
PI: 24297

Transportation — Fiction
P: 1980, 3172, 5796, 5798, 5839, 6521

Transportation — History
PI: 18193, 24042 **I:** 24050 **IJ:** 15767, 24044, 24056, 24108

Transportation — Poetry
P: 15240

Travel
PI: 16576 **I:** 15439

Travel — Fiction
P: 88, 2303, 3808 **IJ:** 7406

Travel — Folklore
PI: 11507

Travel — Poetry
I: 12165

Treason — Biography
IJ: 18925

Treasure hunts — Games
I: 24951

Tree frogs
P: 21091, 21094, 21109

Trees
P: 4583, 4656, 4888, 19285, 22768, 22802, 22807–8, 22811–12, 22823, 22828, 22830–32, 22834 **PI:** 22801, 22804, 22806, 22814, 22819, 22825–26, 22835–36 **I:** 22805, 22813, 22817, 22824, 22833 **IJ:** 17377, 22637, 22803, 22818, 22827, 22837

Trees — Experiments and projects
IJ: 22809

Trees — Fiction
P: 983, 1251, 1335, 1553, 2914, 3786, 4021, 4107, 4138, 4526, 4536, 4565–66, 4589, 4596, 4613, 4674, 4677, 4693, 4697, 4710, 5019 **IJ:** 9669

Trees — Folklore
P: 11534

Trees — Poetry
PI: 12073, 12195

Trevino, Lee
IJ: 14690

Trials
IJ: 18869

Trials — Fiction
IJ: 9823

Triangle Factory Fire
I: 18155

Triangle Shirtwaist Factory fire
IJ: 18176, 18178

Triangle Shirtwaist Factory fire — Fiction
I: 9899

Trinidad
PI: 17157

Trinidad — Holidays
PI: 17157, 4123

Triplets
PI: 19735, 4123

Triplets — Fiction
P: 3853, 4123

Trivia
PI: 24877 **I:** 24862 **IJ:** 24869

Trojan War
I: 15874 **IJ:** 11654

Trojan War (mythology)
PI: 15860

Trolls
P: 1005, 1309–10, 4895, 5984 **IJ:** 8649

Trolls — Folklore
P: 11326, 11330

Trompe l'Oeil
IJ: 14918

Tropical forests
See Rain forests
IJ: 23086

Trout
PI: 22226

Troy — History
I: 15874

Troy (Turkey)
IJ: 15652, 15887

Truck drivers
P: 19987

Truck drivers — Careers
P: 19988, 24094 **PI:** 19990

Trucks
P: 5820, 5825, 5828, 5845, 5848, 5855, 24038, 24049, 24057–60, 24063–64, 24066, 24070–71, 24073, 24088, 24093–94, 24103, 24106 **PI:** 24082, 24100, 24102, 24105 **IJ:** 24072

Trucks — Fiction
P: 913, 1037, 2407, 3022, 5799, 5824, 5833, 5850–51, 5853–54, 6796

Truman, Harry S.
PI: 13839, 13842 **I:** 13840 **IJ:** 13841, 13843

Trumpeters — Biography
I: 12843

Trumpets — Fiction
P: 5141 **I:** 8695

Truth — Fiction
P: 5177

Truth, Sojourner
P: 13346 **PI:** 13337, 13340, 13344 **I:** 13341–42, 13348–49

P = Primary; PI = Primary-Intermediate; I = Intermediate; IJ = Intermediate-Junior High

P = Primary; PI = Primary-Intermediate; I = Intermediate; IJ = Intermediate-Junior High

P = Primary; PI = Primary-Intermediate; I = Intermediate; IJ = Intermediate-Junior High

About the Authors

CATHERINE BARR is the coauthor of other volumes in the Best Books series (*Best Books for Middle School and Junior High Readers* and *Best Books for High School Readers*) and of *Popular Series Fiction for K–6 Readers, Popular Series Fiction for Middle School and Teen Readers*, and *High/Low Handbook: Best Books and Web Sites for Reluctant Teen Readers, 4th Edition.*

JOHN T. GILLESPIE, renowned authority in children's literature, is the author of more than 30 books on collection development. In addition to the previous editions of *Best Books for Children*, other volumes in this series are *Best Books for Middle School and Junior High Readers* and *Best Books for High School Readers*. He is also the author of the Middleplots, Juniorplots, Teenplots, and Seniorplots Book Talk Guides as well as *The Newbery Companion: Booktalk and Related Materials for Newbery Medal and Honor Books* and *The Children's and Young Adult Literature Handbook: A Research and Reference Guide.*